IN SIX VOLUMES, CAREFULLY REVISED AND CORRECTED

MATTHEW HENRY'S
COMMENTARY

ON THE WHOLE BIBLE

WHEREIN EACH CHAPTER IS SUMMED UP IN ITS CONTENTS: THE SACRED TEXT
INSERTED AT LARGE IN DISTINCT PARAGRAPHS; EACH PARAGRAPH
REDUCED TO ITS PROPER HEADS: THE SENSE GIVEN,
AND LARGELY ILLUSTRATED

WITH

PRACTICAL REMARKS AND OBSERVATIONS

VOL. IV.—ISAIAH TO MALACHI

Fleming H. Revell Company
Old Tappan, New Jersey

PREFACE.

THOSE books of scripture are all prophetical of which here, *in weakness, and in fear, and in much trembling,* we have endeavoured a methodical explication and a practical improvement. I call them *prophetical* because so they are for the main, though we have some histories (here and there brought in for the illustration of the prophecies) and a book of Lamentations. Our Saviour often puts *the Law and the Prophets* for all the Old Testament. The prophets, by waiving the ceremonial precepts, and not insisting on them, but only on the weightier matters of the law, plainly intimated the abolishing of that part of the law of Moses by the gospel; and by their many predictions of Christ, and the kingdom of his grace, they intimated the accomplishing and perfecting of that part of the law of Moses in the gospel. Thus the prophets were the *nexus*—*the connecting bond* between the law and the gospel, and are therefore fitly placed between them.

These books, being prophetical, are, as such, divine, and of heavenly origin and extraction. We have human laws, human histories, and human poems, as well as divine ones, but we can have no human prophecies. Wise and good men may make prudent conjectures concerning future events (*moral prognostications* we call them); but it is essential to true prophecy that it be of God. The learned Huetius[*] lays this down for one of his axioms, *Omnis prophetica facultas à Deo est*—*The prophetic talent is entirely from God;* and he proves it to be the sense both of Jews and heathen that it is God's prerogative to foresee things to come, and that whoever had such a power had it from God. And therefore the Jews reckon all prophecy to be given by the highest degree of inspiration, except that which was peculiar to Moses. When our Saviour asked the chief priests whether John's baptism were from heaven or of men, they durst not say *Of men,* because the people counted him a prophet, and, if so, then not of men. The Hebrew name for a prophet is נביא—*a speaker,* *preacher,* or *orator, a messenger,* or *interpreter,* that delivers God's messages to the children of men, as a herald to proclaim war or an ambassador to treat of peace. But then it must be remembered that he was formerly called ראה or חזה, that is, *a seer* (1 Sam. ix. 9); for prophets, with the eyes of their minds, first saw what they were to speak and then spoke what they had seen.

Prophecy, taken strictly, is the foretelling of things to come; and there were those to whom God gave this power, not only that it might be a sign for the confirming of the faith of the church concerning the doctrine preached when the things foretold should be fulfilled, but for warning, instruction, and comfort, in prospect of what they themselves might not live to see accomplished, but which should be fulfilled in its season: so predictions of things to come long after might be of present use.

The learned Dr. Grew[†] describes prophecy in this sense to be, "A declaration of the divine prescience, looking at any distance through a train of infinite causes, known and unknown to us, upon a sure and certain effect." Hence he infers, " That the being of prophecies supposes the non-being of contingents; for, though there are many things which seem to us to be contingents, yet, were they so indeed, there could have been no prophecy; and there can be no contingent seemingly so loose and independent but it is a link of some chain." And Huetius gives this reason why none but God can foretel things to come, Because every effect depends upon an infinite number of preceding causes, all which, in their order, must be known to him that foretels the effect, and therefore to God only, for he alone is omniscient. So Tully argues: *Qui teneat causas rerum futurarum, idem necesse est omnia teneat quæ futura sint; quod facere nemo nisi Deus potest*—*He who knows the causes of future events must necessarily know the events themselves; this is the prerogative of God alone*[‡]. And therefore we find that by *this* the God of Israel proves himself to be God, that by his prophets he foretold things to come, which came to pass according to the prediction, Isa. xlvi. 9, 10. And by *this* he disproves the pretensions of the Pagan deities, that they could not show the *things that were to come to pass hereafter,* Isa. xli. 23. Tertullian proves the divine authority of the scripture from the fulfilling of scripture-prophecies: *Idoneum, opinor, testimonium divinitatis, veritas divinationis*—*I conceive the accomplishment of prophecy to be a satisfactory attestation from God*§. And, besides the foretelling of things to come, the discovering of things secret by revelation from God is a branch of prophecy, as Ahijah's discovering Jeroboam's wife in disguise, and Elisha's telling Gehazi what passed between him and Naaman. But|| prophecy, in scripture language, is taken more largely for a declaration of such things to the children of men, either by word or

---

[*] Demonstrat. Evang. *pag.* 15.   [†] Cosmol. sacra, *lib.* 4. *cap.* 6.   [‡] Cicero de Divin. *lib* 1.
§ Apol. *cap.* 20.   Du Pin, Hist. of the Canon. *lib.* 1 *cap.* 2.

writing, as God has revealed to those that speak or write it, by vision, dream, or inspiration, guiding their minds, their tongues, and pens, by his Holy Spirit, and giving them not only ability, but authority, to declare such things in his name, and to preface what they say with, *Thus saith the Lord*. In this sense it is said, The prophecy of scripture *came not in old time by the will of man*, as other pious moral discourses might, *but holy men spoke* and wrote *as they were moved by the Holy Ghost*, 2 Pet. i. 20, 21. The same Holy Spirit that moved upon the face of the waters to produce the world moved upon the minds of the prophets to produce the Bible.

Now I think it is worthy to be observed that all nations, having had some sense of God and religion, have likewise had a notion of prophets and prophecy, have had a veneration for them, and a desire and expectation of acquaintance and communion with the gods they worshipped in that way. Witness their oracles, their augurs, and the many arts of divination they had in use among them in all the ages and all the countries of the world.

It is commonly urged as an argument against the atheists, to prove that there is a God, That all nations of the world acknowledged some god or other, some Being above them, to be worshipped and prayed to, to be trusted in and praised; the most ignorant and barbarous nations could not avoid the knowledge of it; the most learned and polite nations could not avoid the belief of it. And this is a sufficient proof of the general and unanimous consent of mankind to this truth, though far the greatest part of men made to themselves gods which yet were no gods. Now I think it may be urged with equal force against the Deists, for the proof of a divine revelation, that all nations of the world had, and had veneration for, that which they at least took to be a divine revelation, and could not live without it, though in this also they became *vain in their imaginations, and their foolish heart was darkened*. But, if there were not a true deity and a true prophecy, there would never have been pretended deities and counterfeit prophecies.

Lycurgus and Numa, those two great lawgivers of the Spartan and Roman commonwealths, brought their people to an observance of their laws by possessing them with a notion that they had them by divine revelation, and so making it a point of religion to observe them. And those that have been ever so little conversant with the Greek and Roman histories, as well as with the more ancient ones of Chaldea and Egypt, cannot but remember what a profound deference their princes and great commanders, and not their unthinking commonalty only, paid to the oracles and prophets, and the prognostications of their soothsayers, which, in all cases of importance, were consulted with abundance of gravity and solemnity, and how often the resolutions of councils and the motions of mighty armies turned upon them, though they appeared ever so groundless and farfetched.

There is a full account given by that learned philosopher and physician Caspar Peucer* of the many kinds of divination and prediction used among the Gentiles, by which they took on them to tell the fortune both of states and particular persons. They were all, he says, reduced by Plato to two heads: *Divinatio* Μαντικὴ), which was a kind of inspiration, or was thought to be so, the prophet or prophetess foretelling things to come by an internal *flatus* or fury; such was the oracle of Apollo at Delphos, and that of Jupiter Trophonius, which, with others like them, were famous for many ages, during the prevalency of the kingdom of darkness, but (as appears by some of the Pagan writers themselves) they were all silenced and struck dumb, when the gospel (that truly divine oracle) began to be preached to the nations. The other kind of divination was that which he calls Οἰωνιστικὴ, which was a prognostication by signs, according to rules of art, as by the flight of birds, the entrails of beasts, by stars or meteors, and abundance of ominous accidents, with which a foolish world was miserably imposed upon. A large account of this matter we have also in the late learned dissertations of Anton. Van Dale, to which I refer the reader†. But nothing of this kind made a greater noise in the Gentile world than the oracles of the Sibyls and their prophecies. Their name signifies *a divine counsel*: *Sibyllæ*, qu. *Siobulæ*, *Sios*, in the Æolic dialect, being put for *Theos*. Peucer says, "Almost every nation had its Sibyls, but those of Greece were most celebrated." They lived in several ages; the most ancient is said to be the *Sibylla Delphica*, who lived before the Trojan war, or about that time. The *Sibylla Erythrea* was the most noted; she lived about the time of Alexander the Great. But it is the *Sibylla Cumana* of whom the story goes that she presented herself, and nine books of oracles, to Tarquinius Superbus, which she offered to sell him at so vast a rate that he refused to purchase them, upon which she burnt three, and, upon his second refusal, three more, but made him give the same rate for the remaining three, which were deposited with great care in the Capitol. But, those being afterwards burnt accidentally with the Capitol, a collection was made of other Sibylline oracles, and those are they which Virgil refers to in his fourth Eclogue.‡ All the oracles of the Sibyls that are extant were put together, and published, in Holland, not many years ago, by Seryatius Gallæus, in Greek and Latin, with large and learned notes, together with all that could be met with of the metrical oracles that go under the names of Jupiter, Apollo, Serapis, and others, by Joannes Opsopæus.

The oracles of the Sibyls were appealed to by many of the fathers for the confirmation of the Christian religion. Justin Martyr§ appeals with a great deal of assurance, persuading the Greeks to give credit to that ancient Sibyl, whose works were extant all the world over; and to their testimony, and that of Hydaspis, he appeals concerning the general conflagration and the torments of hell. Clemens Alexandrinus‖ often quotes the Sibyls' verses with great respect; so does Lactantius ; ¶ St. Austin,** *De Civitate Dei*, has the famous acrostic at large, said to be one of the oracles of the *Sibylla Erythrea*, the first letters of the verses making Ἰησοὺς Χριστὸς Θεοῦ υἱὸς Σώτηρ— *Jesus Christ the Son of God the Saviour*. Divers passages they produce out of those oracles which

---

De Præcipuis Divinationum Generibus, *A.* 1591.   † De Verâ ac Falsâ Prophetiâ, *A.* 1696.
‡ Vid. Virg. Æneid. *lib.* 6.   § Ad Græcos Cohortat. *juxta finem*.   ‖ Apol. 2. *p.* mihi. 66. *l.*
¶ Quæst. et Respons. p. 436.   ** Aug. de Civ. Dei, *lib.* 18. *cap.* 23.

expressly foretel the coming of the Messiah, his being born of a virgin, his miracles, his sufferings, particularly his being buffeted, spit upon, crowned with thorns, having vinegar and gall given him to drink, &c. Whether these oracles were genuine and authentic or no has been much controverted among the learned. Baronius and the popish writers generally admit and applaud them, and build much upon them; so do some protestant writers; Isaac Vossius has written a great deal to support the reputation of them, and (as I find him quoted by Van Dale) will needs have it that they were formerly a part of the canon of scripture; and a learned prelate of our own nation, Bishop Montague, pleads largely, and with great assurance, for their authority, and is of opinion that some of them were divinely inspired. But many learned men look upon it to be a pious fraud, as they call it, concluding that those verses of the Sibyls which speak so very expressly of Christ and the future state were forged by some Christians and imposed upon the over-credulous. Huetius, * though of the Romish church, condemns both the ancient and more modern compositions of the Sibyls, and refers his reader, for the proof of their vanity, to the learned Blondel. Van Dale and Galiæus look upon them to be a forgery. And the truth is they speak so much more particularly and plainly concerning our Saviour and the future state than any of the prophets of the Old Testament do, that we must conclude St. Paul, who was the apostle of the Gentiles, guilty not only of a very great omission (that in all his preaching of the gospel to the Gentiles, and in all his epistles to the Gentile churches, he never so much as mentions the prophecies of the Sibyls, nor vouches their authority, as he does that of the Old-Testament prophets, in his preaching and writing to the Jews), but likewise of a very great mistake, in making it the particular advantage which the Jews had above the Gentiles that *to them were committed the oracles of God* (Rom. iii. 1, 2), and that they were the children of the prophets, while he speaks of the Gentiles as sitting in darkness and being afar off. We cannot conceive that heathen women, and those actuated by dæmons, should speak more clearly and fully of the Messiah than those holy men did who, we are sure, were moved by the Holy Ghost, nor that the Gentiles should be entrusted with larger and earlier discoveries of the great salvation than that people of whom, as concerning the flesh, Christ was to come. But enough, if not more than enough, of the pretenders to prophecy. It is a good remark which the learned Gallæus makes upon the great veneration which the Romans had for the oracles of the Sibyls, for which he quotes Dionysius Halicarnassæus, Οὐδὲν οὔτε Ῥωμαῖοι φυλάττουσιν, οὔτε ὅσιον κτῆμα οὔτε ἱερὸν, ὡς τὰ Σιβύλλεια θέσφατα—*The Romans preserve nothing with such sacred care, nor do they hold any thing in such high estimation, as the Sibylline oracles. Hi si pro vitreis suis thesauris adeò decertarunt, quid nos pro genuinis nostris, à Deo inspiratis ?—If they had such a value for these counterfeits, how precious should the true treasure of the divine oracles be to us !* Of these we come next to speak.

Prophecy, we are sure, was of equal date with the church; for *faith comes,* not by thinking and seeing, as philosophy does, but by hearing, *by hearing the word of God,* Rom. x. 17. In the antediluvian period Adam received divine revelation in the promise of the Seed of the woman, and no doubt communicated it in the name of the Lord, to his seed, and was prophet, as well as priest, to his numerous family. Enoch was a prophet, and foretold perhaps the deluge, certainly the last judgment, that of the great day. *Behold the Lord comes,* Jude 14. When men began, as a church, to *call upon the name of the Lord* (Gen. iv. 26), or to call themselves by his name, they were blessed with prophets, for the *prophecy came in old time* (2 Pet. i. 21); it is venerable for its antiquity. When God renewed his covenant of providence (and that a figure of the covenant of grace) with Noah and his sons, we soon after find Noah, as a prophet, foretelling, not only the servitude of Canaan, but God's enlarging Japhet by Christ, and his dwelling in the tents of Shem, Gen. ix. 26, 27. And when, upon the general revolt of mankind to idolatry (as, in the former period, upon the apostasy of Cain), God distinguished a church for himself by the call of Abraham, and by his covenant with him and his seed, he conferred upon him and the other patriarchs the spirit of prophecy; for, when he reproved kings for their sakes, he said, *Touch not my anointed,* who have received that unction from the Holy One, and *do my prophets no harm,* Ps. cv. 14, 15. And of Abraham he said expressly, *He is a prophet* (Gen. xx. 7); and it was with a prophetic eye, as a seer, that *Abraham saw Christ's day* (John viii. 56), saw it at so great a distance, and yet with so great an assurance triumphed in it. And Stephen seems to speak of the first settling of a correspondence between him and God, by which he was established to be a prophet, when he says, *The God of glory appeared to him* (Acts vii. 2), appeared in glory. Jacob, upon his death-bed, as a prophet, told his sons *what should befal them in the last days* (Gen. xlix. i. 10), and spoke very particularly concerning the Messiah.

Hitherto was the infancy of the church, and with it of prophecy; it was the dawning of that day; and that morning-light owed its rise to the Sun of righteousness, though he rose not till long after, but it shone more and more. During the bondage of Israel in Egypt, this, as other glories of the church, was eclipsed; but, as the church made a considerable and memorable advance in the deliverance of Israel out of Egypt and the forming of them into a people, so did the Spirit of prophecy in Moses, the illustrious instrument employed in that great service; and it was by that Spirit that he performed that service; so it is said, Hos. xii. 13, *By a prophet the Lord brought Israel out of Egypt, and by a prophet was he preserved* through the wilderness to Canaan, that is, by Moses as a prophet. It appears, by what God said to Aaron, that there were then other prophets among them, to whom God made known himself and his will in dreams and visions (Num. xii. 6), but to Moses he spoke in a peculiar manner, *mouth to mouth, even apparently, and not in dark speeches,* Num. xii. 8. Nay, such a plentiful effusion was there of the Spirit of prophecy at that time (because Moses was such a prophet as was to be a type of Christ the great prophet) that some of his Spirit was put upon seventy elders of Israel at once, *and they prophesied,* Num. xi. 25. What they

* Demonstrat. p. 748.

said was extraordinary, and not only under the direction of a prophetic inspiration, but under the constraint of a prophetic impulse, as appears by the case of Eldad and Medad.

When Moses, that great prophet, was laying down his office, he promised Israel that the *Lord God would raise them up a prophet of their brethren like unto him*, Deut. xviii. 15, 18. In these words, says the learned Bishop Stillingfleet * (though, in their full and complete sense, they relate to Christ, and to him they are more than once applied in the New Testament), there is included a promise of an order of prophets, which should succeed Moses in the Jewish church, and be the λόγια ζῶντα—*the living oracles* among them (Acts vii. 38), by which they might know the mind of God; for, in the next words, he lays down rules for the trial of prophets, whether what they said was of God or no, and it is observable that that promise comes in immediately upon an express prohibition of the Pagan rites of divination and the consulting of wizards and familiar spirits : "You shall not need to do that" (said Moses), "for, to your much better satisfaction, you shall have prophets divinely inspired, by whom you may know from God himself both what to do and what to expect." But as Jacob's dying prophecy concerning the sceptre in Judah, and the law-giver between his feet, did not begin to be remarkably fulfilled till David's time, most of the Judges being of other tribes, so Moses's promise of a succession of prophets began not to receive its accomplishment till Samuel's time, a little before the other promise began to emerge and operate ; and it was an introduction to the other, for it was by Samuel, as a prophet, that David was anointed king, which was an intimation that the prophetical office of our Redeemer should make way, both in the world and in the heart, for his kingly office; and therefore when he was asked, *Art thou a king?* (John xviii. 37) he answered, not evasively, but very pertinently, *I came to bear witness to the truth*, and so to rule as a king purely by the power of truth.

During the government of the Judges there was a pouring out of the Spirit, but more as a Spirit of skill and courage for war than as a Spirit of prophecy. Deborah is indeed called a *prophetess*, because of her extraordinary qualifications for judging Israel; but that is the only mention of prophecy, that I remember, in all the book of *Judges*. Extraordinary messages were sent by angels, as to Gideon and Manoah ; and it is expressly said that before the word of the Lord came to Samuel (1 Sam. iii. 1) it was *precious*, it was very scarce, there was *no open vision*. And it was therefore with more than ordinary solemnity that the word of the Lord came first to Samuel ; and by degrees notice and assurance were given to all Israel that *Samuel was established to be a prophet of the Lord*, 1 Sam. iii. 20. In Samuel's time, and by him, the schools of the prophets were erected, by which prophecy was dignified and provision made for a succession of prophets ; for it should seem that in those colleges, hopeful young men were bred up in devotion, in a constant attendance upon the instruction the prophets gave from God, and under a strict discipline, as candidates, or probationers, for prophecy, who were called *the sons of the prophets* ; and their religious exercises of prayer, conference, and psalmody especially, are called *prophesyings;* and their præfect, or president, is called *their father*, 1 Sam. x. 12. Out of these God ordinarily chose the prophets he sent ; yet not always : Amos was no prophet nor prophet's son (Amos vii. 14), had not his education in the schools of the prophets, and yet was commissioned to go on God's errands, and (which is observable) though he had not academical education himself, yet he seems to speak of it with great respect when he reckons it among the favours God had bestowed upon Israel that he *raised up of their sons for prophets and of their young men for Nazarites*, Amos ii. 11.

It is worth noting that when the glory of the priesthood was eclipsed by the iniquity of the house of Eli, the desolations of Shiloh, and the obscurity of the ark, there was then a more plentiful effusion of the Spirit of prophecy than had been before; a standing ministry of another kind was thereby erected, and a succession of it kept up. And thus afterwards, in the kingdom of the ten tribes, where there was no legal priesthood at all, yet there were prophets and prophets' sons ; in Ahab's time we meet with a hundred of them, whom Obadiah hid by *fifty in a cave*, 1 Kings xviii. 4. When the people of God, who desired to know his mind, were deprived of one way of instruction, God furnished them with another, and a less ceremonious one ; for he left not himself without witness, nor them without a guide. And when they had no temple or altar that they could attend upon with any safety or satisfaction they had private meetings at the prophets' houses, to which the devout faithful worshippers of God resorted (as we find the good Shunamite did, 2 Kings iv. 23), and where they kept their new-moons and their sabbaths, comfortably, and to their edification

David was himself a prophet; so St. Peter calls him (Acts ii. 30) ; and, though we read not of God's speaking to him by dreams and visions, yet we are sure that *the Spirit of the Lord spoke by him, and his word was in his tongue* (2 Sam. xxiii. 2), and he had those about him that were seers, that were his seers, as Gad and Iddo, that brought him messages from God, and wrote the history of his times. And now the productions of the Spirit of prophecy were translated into the service of the temple, not only in the model of the house which the Lord made David *understand in writing by his hand upon him* (1 Chron. xxviii. 19), but in the worship performed there ; for there we find Asaph, Heman, and Jeduthun, prophesying with harps and other musical instruments, according to the order of the king, not to foretel things to come, but to *give thanks* and to *praise the Lord* (1 Chron. xxv. 1—3) ; yet, in their psalms, they spoke much of Christ and his kingdom, and the glory to be revealed.

In the succeeding reigns, both of Judah and Israel, we frequently meet with prophets sent on particular errands to Rehoboam, Jeroboam, Asa, and other kings, who, it is probable, instructed the people in the things of God at other times, though it is not recorded. But, prophecy growing into contempt with many, God revived the honour of it, and put a new lustre upon it, in the power

* Orig. Sacr. B. 2. c. 4.

given to Elijah and Elisha to work miracles, and the great things that God did by them for the confirming of the people's faith in it, and the awakening of their regard to it, 2 Kings ii. 3; iv. 1, 38; .v. 22; vi. 1. In their time, and by their agency, it should seem, the schools of the prophets were revived, and we find sons of the prophets, fellows of those sacred colleges, employed in carrying messages to the great men, as to Ahab (1 Kings xx. 35), and to Jehu, 2 Kings ix. 1.

Hitherto, the prophets of the Lord delivered their messages by word of mouth, only we read of one writing which came from Elijah the prophet to Jehoram king of Israel, 2 Chron. xxi. 12. The histories of those times which are left us were compiled by prophets, under a divine direction; and, when the Old Testament is divided into the Law and the Prophets, the historical books are, for that reason, reckoned among the prophets. But, in the later times of the kingdoms of Judah and Israel, some of the prophets were divinely inspired to write their prophecies, or abstracts of them, and to leave them upon record, for the benefit of after-ages, that the children who should be born might praise the Lord for them, and, by comparing the event with the prediction, might have their faith confirmed. And, probably, those later prophets spoke more fully and plainly of the Messiah and his kingdom than their predecessors had done, and for that reason their prophecies were put in writing, not only for the encouragement of the pious Jews that looked for the consolation of Israel, but for the use of us Christians, upon whom the ends of the world have come, as David's psalms had been for the same reason, that the Old Testament and the New might mutually give light and lustre to each other. Many other faithful prophets there were at the same time, who spoke in God's name, who did not commit their prophecies to writing, but were of those whom God sent, rising up betimes and sending them, the contempt of whom, and of their messages, brought ruin without remedy upon that sottish people, that knew not the day of their visitation. In their captivity they had some prophets, some to *show them how long;* and though it was not by a prophet, like Moses, that they were brought out of Babylon, as they had been out of Egypt, but by Joshua the high priest first, and afterwards by Ezra the scribe, to show that God can do his work by ordinary means when he pleases, yet, soon after their return, the Spirit of prophecy was poured out plentifully, and continued (according to the Jews' computation) forty years in the second temple, but ceased in Malachi. Then (say the rabbin) *the Holy Spirit was taken from Israel,* and they had the benefit only of the *Bathkol—the daughter of a voice,* that is, a voice from heaven, which they look upon to be the lowest degree of divine revelation. Now herein they are witnesses against themselves for rejecting the true Messiah, for our Lord Jesus, and he only, was spoken to by a voice from heaven at his baptism, his transfiguration, and his entrance on his sufferings.

In John the Baptist prophecy revived, and therefore in him the gospel is said to begin, when the church had had no prophets for above 300 years. We have not only the *vox populi—the voice of the people* to prove John a prophet, for all the people counted him so, but *vox Dei—the voice of God* too; for Christ calls him a prophet, Matt. xi. 9, 10. He had an extraordinary commission from God to call people to repentance, was *filled with the Holy Ghost from his mother's womb,* and was therefore called the *prophet of the Highest,* because he *went before the face of the Lord, to prepare his way* (Luke i. 15, 16); and though he did no miracle, nor gave any sign or wonder, yet *this* proved him a true prophet, *that all he said of Christ was true,* John x. 41. Nay, and *this* proved him more than a prophet, than any of the other prophets, that whereas by other prophets Christ was discovered as at a great distance, by him he was discovered as already come, and he was enabled to say, *Behold the Lamb of God.* But after the ascension of our Lord Jesus there was a more plentiful effusion of the Spirit of prophecy than ever before; then was the promise fulfilled that God would *pour out his Spirit upon all flesh* (and not as hitherto upon the Jews only), and their *sons and their daughters should prophesy,* Acts ii. 16, &c. The gift of tongues was one new product of the Spirit of prophecy, and given for a particular reason, that, the Jewish pale being taken down, all nations might be brought into the church. These and other gifts of prophecy, being for a sign, have long since ceased and laid aside, and we have no encouragement to expect the revival of them; but, on the contrary, are directed to call the scriptures the *more sure word of prophecy,* more sure than voices from heaven; and to them we are directed to *take heed,* to search them, and to hold them fast, 2 Pet. i. 19. All God's spiritual Israel know that they are established to be the *oracles of God* (1 Sam. iii. 20), and if any add to, or take from, the book of that prophecy, they may read their doom in the close of it; God shall take blessings from them, and add curses to them, Rev. xxii. 18, 19.

Now concerning the prophets of the Old Testament, whose writings are before us, observe,

I. That they were all holy men. We are assured by the apostle that *the prophecy came in old time by holy men of God* (and *men of God* they were commonly called, because they were devoted to him), *who spoke as they were moved by the Holy Ghost.* They were men, *subject to like passions as we are* (so Elijah, one of the greatest of them, is said to have been, Jam. v. 17); but they were holy men, men that in the temper of their minds, and the tenour of their lives, were examples of serious piety. Though there were many pretenders, that, without warrant, said, *Thus saith the Lord,* when he sent them not, and some that prophesied in Christ's name, but he never knew them, and they indeed were workers of iniquity (Matt. vii. 22, 23), and though the cursing blaspheming lips of Balaam and Caiaphas, even when they actually designed mischief, were over-ruled to speak oracles, yet none were employed and commissioned to speak as prophets but those that had received the Spirit of grace and sanctification; for holiness becomes God's house. The Jewish doctors universally agree in this rule, That the Spirit of prophecy never rests upon any but a holy and wise man, and one whose passions are allayed, * or, as others express it, a humble man and a man of fortitude, that is, one that has power to keep his sensual animal part in due subjection to religion and right reason. And some of them† give this rule, That the Spirit of prophecy does not reside

---

* See Mr. Smith on Prophecy   † Gemara Schab. c. 2.

where there are either, on the one hand, grief and melancholy, or, on the other hand, laughter and lightness of behaviour, and impertinent idle talk: and it is commonly observed by them, both from the musical instruments used in the schools of the prophets in Samuel's time and from the instance of Elisha's calling for a minstrel (2 Kings iii. 15), that the divine presence does not reside with sadness, but with cheerfulness, and Elisha, they say, had not yet recovered himself from the sorrow he conceived at parting with Elijah. They have also a tradition (but I know no ground for it) that all the while Jacob mourned for Joseph, the Shechinah, or Holy Spirit, withdrew from him. Yet I believe that when David intimates that by his sin in the matter of Uriah he had lost the right Spirit, and the free Spirit, Ps. li. 10, 12 (which therefore he begs might be renewed in him and restored to him), it was not because he was under grief, but because he was under guilt. And therefore, in order to the return of that right and free Spirit, he prays that God would create in him a clean heart.

II. That they had all a full assurance in themselves of their divine mission ; and (though they could not always prevail to satisfy others) they were abundantly satisfied themselves that what they delivered as from God, and in his name, was indeed from him ; and with the same assurance did the apostles speak of the word of life, as that which they had heard, and seen, and looked on, and which their hands had handled, 1 John i. 1. Nathan spoke from himself when he encouraged David to build the temple, but afterwards knew he spoke from God when, in his name, he forbade him to do it. God had various ways of making known to his prophets the messages they were to deliver to his people ; it should seem, ordinarily, to have been by the ministry of angels. In the Apocalypse Christ is expressly said to have *signified by his angel to his servant John*, Rev. i. 1. It was sometimes done in a vision when the prophet was awake, sometimes in a dream when the prophet was asleep, and sometimes by a secret but strong impression upon the mind of the prophet. But Maimonides has laid down, as a maxim, That all prophecy makes itself known to the prophet that it is prophecy indeed ; that is, says another of the rabbin, By the vigour and liveliness of the perception whereby he apprehends the thing propounded (which Jeremiah intimates when he says, *The word of the Lord was as a fire in my bones*, Jer. xx. 9), and therefore they always spoke with great assurance, knowing they should be justified, Isa. l. 7.

III. That in their prophesying, both in receiving their message from God and in delivering it to the people, they always kept possession of their own souls. Dan. x. 8. Though sometimes their bodily strength was overpowered by the abundance of the revelations, and their eyes were dazzled with the visionary light, as in the instances of Daniel and John (Rev. i. 17), yet still their understanding remained with them, and the free exercise of their reason. This is excellently well expressed by a learned writer of our own:[*] "The prophetical Spirit, seating itself in the rational powers as well as in the imagination, did never alienate the mind, but inform and enlighten it ; and those that were actuated by it always maintained a clearness and consistency of reason, with strength and solidity of judgment. For" (says he afterwards[†]) "God did not make use of idiots or fools to reveal his will by, but such whose intellects were entire and perfect ; and he imprinted such a clear copy of his truth upon them as that it became their own sense, being digested fully into their understandings, so that they were able to deliver and represent it to others as truly as any can paint forth his own thoughts." God's messengers were speaking men, not speaking trumpets. The Fathers frequently took notice of this difference between the prophets of the Lord and the false prophets—that the pretenders to prophecy (who either were actuated by an evil spirit or were under the force of a heated imagination) underwent alienations of mind, and delivered what they had to say in the utmost agitation and disorder, as the Pythian prophetess, who delivered her infernal oracles with many antic gestures, tearing her hair and foaming at the mouth. And by this rule they condemned the Montanists, who pretended to prophecy, in the second century, that what they said was in a way of ecstasy, not like rational men, but like men in a frenzy. Chrysostom,[‡] having described the furious violent motions of the pretenders to prophecy, adds, Ὁ δὲ Προφήτης οὐχ οὕτως—*A true prophet does not do so. Sed mente sobrid, et constanti animi statu, et intelligens quæ profert, omnia pronunciat*—*He understands what he utters, and utters it soberly and calmly.* And Jerome, in his preface to his Commentaries upon Nahum, observes that it is called *the book of the vision of Nahum. Non enim loquitur ἐν ἐκστάσει, sed est liber intelligentis omnia quæ loquitur*—*For he speaks not in an ecstasy, but as one who understands every thing he says.* And again, § *Non ut amens loquitur propheta, nec in morem insanientium fœminarum dat sine mente sonum*—*The prophet speaks not as an insane person, nor, like women wrought into fury, does he utter sound without sense.*

IV. That they all aimed at one and the same thing, which was to bring people to repent of their sins and to return to God and to do their duty to him. This was the errand on which all God's messengers were sent, to beat down sin, and to revive and advance serious piety. The burden of every song was, *Turn you now every one from his evil way ; amend your ways and your doings, and execute judgment between a man and his neighbour*, Jer. vii. 3, 5. See Zech. vii. 8, 9 ; viii. 16. The scope and design of all their prophecies were to enforce the precepts and sanctions of the law of Moses, the moral law, which is of universal and perpetual obligation. Here is nothing of the ceremonial institutes, of the carnal ordinances that were imposed only *till the times of reformation*, Heb. ix. 10. Those were now waxing old and ready to vanish away ; but they make it their business to press the great and *weighty matters of the law, judgment, mercy, and truth*.

V. That they all bore witness to Jesus Christ and had an eye to him. God raising up the *horn of salvation for us, in the house of his servant David*, was consonant to, and in pursuance of, what *he spoke by the mouth of his holy prophets who have been since the world began*, Luke i. 69, 70. They

---

* Smith on Prophecy, p. 190.   † Pag. 266.   ‡ In 1 Cor. 12. 1.   § Prolog. in Habac.

prophesied of the grace that should come to us, and it was the Spirit of Christ in them, one and the same Spirit, that testified beforehand the *sufferings of Christ and the glory that should follow,* 1 Pet. i. 10, 11. Christ was then made known, and yet comparatively hid, in the predictions of the prophets, as before in the types of the ceremonial law. And the learned Huetius * observes it as really admirable that so many persons, in different ages, should conspire with one consent, as it were, to foretel, some one particular and others another, concerning Christ, all which had, at length, their full accomplishment in him. *Ab ipsis mundi incunabulis, per quatuor annorum millia, uno ore venturum Christum prædixerunt viri complures, in ejusque ortu, vitâ, virtutibus, rebus gestis, morte, ac totâ denique* Οἰκονομία *præmonstranda consenserunt—From the earliest period of time, for* 4000 *years, a great number of men have predicted the advent of Christ, and presented a harmonious statement of his birth, life, character, actions, and death, and of that economy which he came to establish.*

VI. That these prophets were generally hated and abused in their several generations by those that lived with them. Stephen challenges his judges to produce an instance to the contrary: *Which of the prophets have not your fathers persecuted ?* Yea, and, as it should seem, for this reason, because *they showed before of the coming of the Just One,* Acts vii. 52. Some there were that trembled at the word of God in their mouths, but by the most they were ridiculed and despised, and (as ministers are now by profane people) made a jest of (Hos. ix. 7); the prophet was the fool in the play. *Wherefore came this mad fellow unto thee ?* (2 Kings ix. 11) said one of the captains concerning one of the sons of the prophets ! The Gentiles never treated their false prophets so ill as the Jews did their true prophets, but, on the contrary, had them always in veneration. The Jews' mocking the messengers of the Lord, killing the prophets, and stoning those that were sent unto them, was as amazing unaccountable an instance of the enmity that is in the carnal mind against God as any that can be produced. And this makes their rejection of Christ's gospel the less strange, that the Spirit of prophecy, which, for many ages, was so much the glory of Israel, in every age met with so much opposition, and there were those that *always resisted the Holy Ghost* in the prophets, and *turned that glory into shame,* Acts vii. 51. But this was it that was the measure-filling sin of Israel, that brought upon them both their first destruction by the Chaldeans and their final ruin by the Romans, 2 Chron. xxxvi. 16.

VII. That though men slighted these prophets, God owned them and put honour upon them. As they were men of God, his immediate servants and his messengers, so he always showed himself *the Lord God of the holy prophets* (Rev. xxii. 6), stood by them and strengthened them, and by his Spirit they were full of power; and those that slighted them, when they had lost them, were made to know, to their confusion, that *a prophet had been among them.* What was said of one of the primitive fathers of the prophets was true of them all, *The Lord was with them, and did let none of their words fall to the ground,* 1 Sam. iii. 19. What they said by way of warning and encouragement, for the enforcing of their calls to repentance and reformation, was to be understood conditionally. When God spoke by them either, on the one hand, to build and to plant, or, on the other hand, to pluck up and pull down, the change of the people's way might produce a change of God's way (Jer. xviii. 7—10); such was Jonah's prophecy of Nineveh's ruin within forty days ; or God might sometimes be better than his word in granting a reprieve. But what they said by way of prediction of a particular matter, and as a sign, did always come to pass exactly as it was foretold ; yea, and the general predictions, sooner or later, took hold even of those that would fain have got clear of them (Zech. i. 6) ; for this is that which God glories in, that he *confirms the word of his servants* and *performs the counsel of his messengers,* Isa. xliv. 26.

In opening these prophecies I have endeavoured to give the genuine sense of them, as far as I could reach it, by consulting the best expositors, considering the scope and coherence, and comparing spiritual things with spiritual, the spiritual things of the Old Testament with those of the New, and especially by prayer to God for the guidance and direction of the Spirit of truth. But, after all, there are many things here *dark and hard to be understood,* concerning the certain meaning of which though I could not gain myself, much less expect to give my reader, full satisfaction, yet I have not, with the *unlearned* and *unstable, wrested them* to the destruction of any, 2 Pet. iii. 16. It is the prerogative of the *Lamb of God* to *take this book* and to *open* all *its seals.* I have likewise endeavoured to accommodate these prophecies to the use and service of those who desire to read the scripture, not only with understanding, but with pious affections, and to their edification in faith and holiness. And we shall find that whatever is *given by inspiration of God is profitable* (2 Tim. iii. 16), though not all alike profitable, not all alike easy or improvable ; but, when the mystery of God shall be finished, we shall see, what we are now bound to believe, that there is not one idle word in all the prophecies of this book. What God has said, as well as what he does, *we know not now, but we shall know hereafter.*

The pleasure I have had in studying and meditating upon those parts of these prophecies which are plain and practical, and especially those which are evangelical, has been an abundant balance to, and recompence for, the harder tasks we have met with in other parts that are more obscure. In many parts of this field the treasure must be dug for, as that in the mines ; but in other parts the surface is covered with rich and precious products, with corn, and flocks, of which we may say, as was said of Noah, These same have comforted us greatly concerning our work and the toil of our hands, and have made it very pleasant and delightful ; God grant it may be no less so to the readers !

And now let me desire the assistance of my friends, in setting up my Eben-Ezer here, in a thankful acknowledgment that hitherto the Lord has helped me. I desire to praise God that he has spared my life to finish the Old Testament, and has graciously given me some tokens of his

* Demonstrat. Evang. p. 737

presence with me in carrying this work, though the more I reflect upon myself the more unworthy I see myself of the honour of being thus employed, and the more need I see of Christ and his merit and grace. *Remember me, O my God! for good, and spare me according to the multitude of thy mercies.* The Lord forgive what is mine, and accept what is his own!

I purpose, if God continue my life and health, according to the measure of the grace given to me, and in a constant and entire dependence upon divine strength, to go through the New Testament in two volumes more. I intimated in my preface to the first volume that I had drawn up some expositions upon some parts of the New Testament; namely, The gospels of St. Matthew and St. John; but they are so large that, to make them bear some proportion to the rest, it is necessary that they be much contracted, so that I shall be obliged to write them all over again, and to make considerable alterations, and therefore I cannot expect they should be published but as these hitherto have been, if God permit, a volume every other year. I shall begin it now shortly, if the Lord will, and apply myself to it as closely as I can; and I earnestly desire the prayers of all that wish well to the undertaking that, if the Lord spare me to go on with it, I may be enabled to do it well, and so as that by it some may be led into the *riches of the full assurance of understanding in the mystery of God, even of the Father and of Christ,* Col. ii. 2. And, if it shall please God to remove me by death before it be finished, I trust I shall be able to say not only, Welcome his blessed will, but, Welcome that blessed world, in which, though now we *know but in part, and prophesy but in part, that knowledge which is perfect will come, and that which is partial will be done away* (1 Cor. xiii. 8—10, 12), in which all our mistakes will be rectified, all our doubts resolved, all our deficiencies made up, all our endeavours in preaching, catechising, and expounding, superseded and rendered useless, and all our prayers swallowed up in everlasting praises,—in which prophecy, now so much admired, shall fail, and tongues shall cease, and the knowledge we have now shall vanish away, as the light of the morning-star does when the sun has risen,—in which we shall no longer see through a glass darkly, but face to face. In a believing, comfortable, well-grounded, expectation of that true and perfect light, I desire to continue, living and dying; in a humble and diligent preparation for it let me spend my time, and in the full enjoyment of it Oh that I may spend a glorious eternity!

JULY 18, 1712.   M. H.

AN

EXPOSITION,

WITH PRACTICAL OBSERVATIONS,

OF THE BOOK OF THE PROPHET

ISAIAH.

PROPHET is a title that sounds very great to those that understand it, though, in the eye of the world, many of those that were dignified with it appeared very mean. A prophet is one that has a great intimacy with Heaven and a great interest there, and consequently a commanding authority upon earth. Prophecy is put for all divine revelation (2 Pet. i. 20, 21), because that was most commonly by dreams, voices, or visions, communicated to prophets first, and by them to the children of men, Num. xii. 6. Once indeed God himself spoke to all the thousands of Israel from the top of Mount Sinai; but the effect was so intolerably dreadful that they entreated God would for the future speak to them as he had done before, by men like themselves, *whose terror should not make them afraid, nor their hands be heavy upon them,* Job xxxiii. 7. God approved the motion *(they have well said,* says he, Deut. v. 27, 28), and the matter was then settled by consent of parties, that we must never expect to hear from God any more in that way, but by prophets, who received their instructions immediately from God, with a charge to deliver them to his church. Before the sacred canon of the Old Testament began to be written there were prophets, who were instead of Bibles to the church. Our Saviour seems to reckon Abel among the prophets, Matt. xxiii. 31. 35. Enoch was a prophet; and by him *that* was first in prediction which is to be last in execution—the judgment of the great day. Jude 14, *Behold, the Lord comes with his holy myriads.* Noah was a preacher of righteousness. God said of Abraham, He *is a prophet,* Gen. xx. 7. Jacob foretold things to come, Gen. xlix. 1. Nay, all the patriarchs are called *prophets.* Ps. cv. 15, *Do my prophets no harm.* Moses was, beyond all comparison, the most illustrious of all the Old-Testament prophets, for with him the Lord spoke *face to face,* Deut. xxxiv. 10. He was the first writing prophet, and by his hand the first foundations of holy writ were laid. Even those that were called to be his assistants in the government had the spirit of prophecy, such a plentiful effusion was there of that spirit at that time, Num. xi. 25. But after the death of Moses, for some ages, the Spirit of the Lord appeared and acted in the church of Israel more as a martial spirit than as a spirit of prophecy, and inspired men more for acting than speaking. I mean in the time of the judges. We find the Spirit of the Lord coming upon Othniel, Gideon, Samson, and others, for the service of their country, with their swords, not with their pens. Messages were then sent from heaven by angels, as to Gideon and Manoah, and to the people, Judges ii. 1. In all the book of Judges there is never once mention of a prophet, only Deborah is called a prophetess. Then the word of the Lord was precious; there was no open vision, 1 Sam. iii. 1. They had the law of Moses, recently written; let them study that. But in Samuel prophecy revived, and in him a famous epocha, or period, of the church began, a time of great light in a constant uninterrupted succession of prophets, till some time after the captivity, when the canon of the Old Testament was completed in Malachi, and then prophecy ceased for nearly 400 years, till the coming of the great prophet and his forerunner. Some prophets were divinely inspired to write the histories of the church. But they did not put their names to their writings; they only referred for proof to the authentic records of those times, which were known to be drawn up by prophets, as Gad, Iddo, &c. David and others were prophets, to write sacred songs for the use of the church. After them we often read of prophets sent on particular errands, and raised up for special public services, among whom the most famous were Elijah and Elisha in the kingdom of Israel. But none of these put their prophecies in writing, nor have we any remains of them but some fragments in the histories of their times; there was nothing of their own writing (that I remember) but one epistle of Elijah's, 2 Chron. xxi. 12.

But, towards the latter end of the kingdoms of Judah and Israel, it pleased God to direct his servants the prophets to write and publish some of their sermons, or abstracts of them. The dates of many of their prophecies are uncertain, but the earliest of them was in the days of Uzziah king of Judah, and Jeroboam the second, his contemporary, king of Israel, about 200 years before the captivity, and not long after Joash had slain Zechariah the son of Jehoiada in the courts of the temple. If they begin to murder the prophets, yet they shall not murder their prophecies; these shall remain as witnesses against them. Hosea was the first of the writing prophets; and Joel, Amos, and Obadiah, published their prophecies about the same time. Isaiah began some time after, and not long; but his prophecy is placed first, because it is the largest of them all, and has most in it of him to whom all the prophets bore witness; and indeed so much of Christ that he is justly styled the *Evangelical Prophet*, and, by some of the ancients, *a fifth Evangelist*. We shall have the general title of this book (*v.* 1) and therefore shall here only observe some things,

I. Concerning the prophet himself. He was (if we may believe the tradition of the Jews) of the royal family, his father being (they say) brother to king Uzziah. He was certainly much at court, especially in Hezekiah's time, as we find in his story, to which many think it is owing that his style is more curious and polite than that of some other of the prophets, and, in some places, exceedingly lofty and soaring. The Spirit of God sometimes served his own purpose by the particular genius of the prophet; for prophets were not speaking trumpets, *through* which the Spirit spoke, but speaking men, *by* whom the Spirit spoke, making use of their natural powers, in respect both of light and flame, and advancing them above themselves.

II. Concerning the prophecy. It is transcendently excellent and useful; it was so to the church of God then, serving for conviction of sin, direction in duty, and consolation in trouble. Two great distresses of the church are here referred to, and comfort prescribed in reference to them, that by Sennacherib's invasion, which happened in his own time, and that of the captivity in Babylon, which happened long after; and in the supports and encouragements laid up for each of these times of need we find abundance of the grace of the gospel. There are not so many quotations in the gospels out of any, perhaps not out of all, the prophecies of the Old Testament, as out of this; nor such express testimonies concerning Christ, witness that of his being born of a virgin (*ch.* vii.) and that of his sufferings, *ch.* liii. The beginning of this book abounds most with reproofs for sin and threatenings of judgment; the latter end of it is full of good words and comfortable words. This method the Spirit of Christ took formerly in the prophets and does still, first to convince and then to comfort; and those that would be blessed with the comforts must submit to the convictions. Doubtless Isaiah preached many sermons, and delivered many messages to the people, which are not written in this book, as Christ did; and probably these sermons were delivered more largely and fully than they are here related, but so much is left on record as Infinite Wisdom thought fit to convey to us *on whom the ends of the world have come ;* and these prophecies, as well as the histories of Christ, are written *that we might believe on the name of the Son of God, and that, believing, we might have life through his name ; for to us is the gospel here preached as well as unto those* that lived then, and more clearly. O that it may be mixed with faith!

CHAP. I.

The first verse of this chapter is intended for a title to the whole book, and it is probable that this was the first sermon that this prophet was appointed to publish and to affix in writing (as Calvin thinks the custom of the prophets was) to the door of the temple, as with us proclamations are fixed to public places, that all might read them (Hab. ii. 2), and those that would might take out authentic copies of them, the original being, after some time, laid up by the priests among the records of the temple. The sermon which is contained in this chapter has in it, I. A high charge exhibited, in God's name, against the Jewish church and nation, l. For their ingratitude, ver. 2, 3. 2. For their incorrigibleness, ver. 5. 3. For the universal corruption and degeneracy of the people. ver. 4, 6, 21, 22. 4. For the perversion of justice by their rulers, ver. 23. II. A sad complaint of the judgments of God, which they had brought upon themselves by their sins, and by which they were brought almost to utter ruin, ver. 7.—9. III. A just rejection of those shows and shadows of religion which they kept up among them, notwithstanding this general defection and apostasy, ver. 10—15. IV. An earnest call to repentance and reformation, setting before them life and death, life if they complied with the call and death if they did not, ver. 16—20. V. A threatening of ruin to those that would not be reformed, ver. 24, 28—31. VI. A promise of a happy reformation at last, and a return to their primitive purity and prosperity, ver. 25—27. And all this is to be applied by us, not only to the communities we are members of, in their public interests, but to the state of our own souls.

THE vision of Isaiah the son of Amoz, which he saw concerning

2

Judah and Jerusalem in the days of Uzziah, Jotham, Ahaz, *and* Hezekiah, kings of Judah.

Here is, I. The name of the prophet, *Isaiah*, or *Jesahiahu* (for so it is in the Hebrew), which, in the New Testament, is read *Esaias*. His name signifies *the salvation of the Lord*—a proper name for a prophet by whom God *gives knowledge of salvation to his people*, especially for this prophet, who prophesies so much of Jesus the Saviour and of the great salvation wrought out by him. He is said to be *the son of Amoz*, not Amos the prophet (the two names in the Hebrew differ more than in the English), but, as the Jews think, of Amoz the brother, or son, of Amaziah king of Judah, a tradition as uncertain as that rule which they give, That, where a prophet's father is named, he also was himself a prophet. The prophets' pupils and successors are indeed often called their *sons*, but we have few instances, if any, of their own sons being their successors.

II. The nature of the prophecy. It is a vision, being revealed to him in a vision, when he was *awake, and heard the words of God, and saw the visions of the Almighty* (as Balaam speaks, Num. xxiv. 4), though perhaps it was not so illustrious a vision at first as that afterwards, *ch.* vi. 1. The prophets were called *seers,* or seeing men, and therefore their prophecies are fitly called *visions.* It is what he saw with the eyes of his mind, and foresaw as clearly by divine revelation, was as well assured of it, as fully apprised of it, and as much affected with it, as if he had seen it with his bodily eyes. Note 1. God's prophets saw what they spoke of, knew what they said, and require our belief of nothing but what they themselves believed and were sure of, John vi. 69; 1 John i. 1. 2. They could not but speak what they saw, because they saw how much all about them were concerned in it, Acts iv. 20; 2 Cor. iv. 13.

III. The subject of the prophecy. It was what *he saw concerning Judah and Jerusalem,* the country of the two tribes, and that city which was their metropolis; and there is little in it relating to Ephraim, or the ten tribes, of whom there is so much in the prophecy of Hosea. Some chapters there are in this book which relate to Babylon, Egypt, Tyre, and some other neighbouring nations; but it takes its title from that which is the main substance of it, and is therefore said to be *concerning Judah and Jerusalem,* the other nations spoken of being such as the people of the Jews had concerns with. Isaiah brings to them in a special manner, 1. Instruction; for it is the privilege of Judah and Jerusalem that to them pertain the oracles of God. 2. Reproof and threatening; for if in Judah, where God is known, if in Salem, where his name is great, iniquity be found, they, sooner than any other, shall be reckoned with for it. 3. Comfort and encouragement in evil times; for the children of Zion shall be joyful in their king.

IV. The date of the prophecy. Isaiah prophesied *in the days of Uzziah, Jotham, Ahaz, and Hezekiah.* By this it appears, 1. That he prophesied long, especially if (as the Jews say) he was at last put to death by Manasseh, to a cruel death, being sawn asunder, to which some suppose the apostle refers, Heb. xi. 37. From the year that king Uzziah died (*ch.* vi. 1) to Hezekiah's sickness and recovery was forty-seven years; how much before, and after, he prophesied, is not certain; some reckon sixty, others eighty years in all. It was an honour to him, and a happiness to his country, that he was continued so long in his usefulness; and we must suppose both that he began young and that he held out to old age; for the prophets were not tied, as the priests were, to a cer-

tain age, for the beginning or ending of their ministration. 2. That he passed through variety of times. Jotham was a good king, and Hezekiah a better, and no doubt gave encouragement to and took advice from this prophet, were patrons to him, and he a privy-counsellor to them; but between them, and when Isaiah was in the prime of his time, the reign of Ahaz was very profane and wicked; then, no doubt, he was frowned upon at court, and, it is likely, forced to abscond. Good men and good ministers must expect bad times in this world, and prepare for them. Then religion was run down to such a degree that the *doors of the house of the Lord were shut up* and idolatrous *altars were erected in every corner of Jerusalem;* and Isaiah, with all his divine eloquence and messages immediately from God himself, could not help it. The best men, the best ministers, cannot do the good they would do in the world.

2 Hear, O heavens, and give ear, O earth: for the Lord hath spoken, I have nourished and brought up children, and they have rebelled against me. 3 The ox knoweth his owner, and the ass his master's crib: *but* Israel doth not know, my people doth not consider. 4 Ah sinful nation, a people laden with iniquity, a seed of evil doers, children that are corrupters: they have forsaken the Lord, they have provoked the Holy One of Israel unto anger, they are gone away backward. 5 Why should ye be stricken any more? Ye will revolt more and more: the whole head is sick, and the whole heart faint. 6 From the sole of the foot even unto the head *there is* no soundness in it; *but* wounds, and bruises, and putrefying sores: they have not been closed, neither bound up, neither mollified with ointment. 7 Your country *is* desolate, your cities *are* burned with fire: your land, strangers devour it in your presence, and *it is* desolate, as overthrown by strangers. 8 And the daughter of Zion is left as a cottage in a vineyard, as a lodge in a garden of cucumbers, as a besieged city. 9 Except the Lord of hosts had left unto us a very small remnant, we should have been as Sodom, *and* we should have been like unto Gomorrah.

We will hope to meet with a brighter and

3

more pleasant scene before we come to the end of this book ; but truly here, in the beginning of it, every thing looks very bad, very black, with Judah and Jerusalem. What is the wilderness of the world, if the church, the vineyard, has such a dismal aspect as this ?

I. The prophet, though he speaks in God's name, yet, despairing to gain audience with the children of his people, addresses himself to the heavens and the earth, and bespeaks their attention (*v.* 2) : *Hear, O heavens ! and give ear, O earth !* Sooner will the inanimate creatures hear, who observe the law and answer the end of their creation, than this stupid senseless people. Let the lights of heaven shame their darkness, and the fruitfulness of the earth their barrenness, and the strictness of each to its time their irregularity. Moses begins thus in Deut. xxxii. 1, to which the prophet here refers, intimating that now those times had come which Moses there foretold, Deut. xxxi. 29. Or this is an appeal to heaven and earth, to angels and then to the inhabitants of the upper and lower world. Let them *judge between God and his vineyard :* can either produce such an instance of ingratitude? Note, God will be justified when he speaks, and both heaven and earth shall declare his righteousness, Mic. vi. 1, 2 ; Ps. l. 6.

II. He charges them with base ingratitude, a crime of the highest nature. Call a man ungrateful, and you can call him no worse. Let heaven and earth hear and wonder at, 1. God's gracious dealings with such a peevish provoking people as they were : "I have nourished and brought them up as children ; they have been well fed and well taught" (Deut. xxxii. 6); "I have magnified and exalted them" (so some), "not only made them grow, but made them great—not only maintained them, but preferred them—not only trained them up, but raised them high." Note, We owe the continuance of our lives and comforts, and all our advancements, to God's fatherly care of us and kindness to us. 2. Their ill-natured conduct towards him, who was so tender of them : "*They have rebelled against me,*" or (as some read it) "they have revolted from me ; they have been deserters, nay traitors, against my crown and dignity." Note, All the instances of God's favour to us, as the God both of our nature and of our nurture, aggravate our treacherous departures from him and all our presumptuous oppositions to him—children, and yet rebels !

III. He attributes this to their ignorance and inconsideration (*v.* 3) : *The ox knows, but Israel does not.* Observe, 1. The sagacity of the ox and the ass, which are not only brute creatures, but of the dullest sort ; yet the ox has such a sense of duty as to know his owner and to serve him, to submit to his yoke and to draw in it ; the ass has such a sense of interest as to know his mas-

ter's crib, or manger, where he is fed, and to abide by it ; he will go to that of himself if he be turned loose. A fine pass man has come to when he is shamed even in knowledge and understanding by these silly animals, and is not only sent to school to them (Prov. vi. 6, 7), but set in a form below them (Jer. viii. 7), *taught more than the beasts of the earth* (Job xxxv. 11) and yet knowing less. 2. The sottishness and stupidity of Israel. God is their owner and proprietor. He made us, and his we are more than our cattle are ours ; he has provided well for us ; providence is our Master's crib : yet many that are called the people of God do not know and will not consider this, but ask, "*What is the Almighty, that we should serve him ?* He is not our owner ; and *what profit shall we have if we pray unto him ?* He has no crib for us to feed at." He had complained (*v.* 2) of the obstinacy of their wills : *They have rebelled against me.* Here he runs it up to its cause : "*Therefore* they have rebelled because they do not know, they do not consider." The understanding is darkened, and therefore the whole soul is alienated from the life of God, Eph. iv. 18. "*Israel does not know,* though their land is a land of light and knowledge ; *in Judah is God known,* yet, because they do not live up to what they know, it is in effect as if they did not know. They know ; but their knowledge does them no good, because they do not consider what they know ; they do not apply it to their case, nor their minds to it." Note, (1.) Even among those that profess themselves God's people, that have the advantages and lie under the engagements of his people, there are many that are very careless in the affairs of their souls. (2.) Inconsideration of what we do know is as great an enemy to us in religion as ignorance of what we should know. (3.) *Therefore* men revolt from God, and rebel against him, because they do not know and consider their obligations to God, in duty, gratitude, and interest.

IV. He laments the universal pravity and corruption of their church and kingdom. The disease of sin was epidemic, and all orders and degrees of men were infected with it : *Ah sinful nation ! v.* 4. The prophet bemoans those that would not bemoan themselves : Alas for them ! woe to them ! He speaks with a holy indignation at their degeneracy, and a dread of the consequences of it. See here,

1. How he aggravates their sin, and shows the malignity that there was in it, *v.* 4. (1.) The wickedness was universal. They were a sinful nation ; the generality of the people were vicious and profane. They were so in their national capacity. In the management of their public treaties abroad, and in the administration of public justice at home, they were corrupt. Note, It is ill with a people when sin becomes national. (2.) It

was very great and heinous in its nature. They were *laden with iniquity;* the guilt of it, and the curse incurred by that guilt, lay very heavily upon them. It was a heavy charge that was exhibited against them, and one which they could never clear themselves from; their wickedness was upon them as *a talent of lead,* Zech. v. 7, 8. Their sin, as it did easily beset them and they were prone to it, was a weight upon them, Heb. xii. 1. (3) They came of a bad stock, were a *seed of evil-doers.* Treachery ran in the blood; they had it by kind, which made the matter so much the worse, more provoking and less curable. They rose up in their fathers' stead, and trod in their fathers' steps, to *fill up the measure of their iniquity,* Num. xxxii. 14. They were a race and family of rebels. (4.) Those that were themselves debauched did what they could to debauch others. They were not only corrupt children, born tainted, but *children that were corrupters,* that propagated vice, and infected others with it—not only sinners, but tempters—not only actuated by Satan, but agents for him. If those that are called *children, God's children,* that are looked upon as belonging to his family, be wicked and vile, their example is of the most malignant influence. (5.) Their sin was a treacherous departure from God. They were deserters from their allegiance: " *They have forsaken the Lord,* to whom they had joined themselves; *they have gone away backward,* are alienated or separated from God, have turned the back upon him, deserted their colours, and quitted their service." When they were urged forward, they ran backward, *as a bullock unaccustomed to the yoke, as a backsliding heifer,* Hos. iv. 16. (6.) It was an impudent and daring defiance of him: *They have provoked the Holy One of Israel unto anger* wilfully and designedly; they knew what would anger him, and that they did. Note, The backslidings of those that have professed religion and relation to God are in a special manner provoking to him.

2. How he illustrates it by a comparison taken from a sick and diseased body, all overspread with leprosy, or, like Job's, with sore boils, *v.* 5, 6. (1.) The distemper has seized the vitals, and so threatens to be mortal. Diseases in the head and heart are most dangerous; now the head, the whole head, is sick—the heart, the whole heart, is faint. They had become corrupt in their judgment: the leprosy was in their head. They were utterly unclean; their affection to God and religion was cold and gone; the *things which remained were ready to die* away, Rev. iii. 2 (2.) It has overspread the whole body, and so becomes exceedingly noisome: *From the sole of the foot even to the head,* from the meanest peasant to the greatest peer, there is *no soundness,* no good principles, no religion (for that is

the health of the soul), nothing but *wounds and bruises,* guilt and corruption, the sad effects of Adam's fall, noisome to the holy God, painful to the sensible soul; they were so to David when he complained (Ps. xxxviii. 5), *My wounds stink, and are corrupt, because of my foolishness.* See Ps. xxxii. 3, 4. No attempts were made for reformation, or, if they were, they proved ineffectual: The wounds *have not been closed, nor bound up, nor mollified with ointment.* While sin remains unrepented of the wounds are unsearched, unwashed, the proud flesh in them not cut out, and while, consequently, it remains unpardoned, the wounds are not mollified or closed up, nor any thing done towards the healing of them and the preventing of their fatal consequences.

V. He sadly bewails the judgments of God which they had brought upon themselves by their sins, and their incorrigibleness under those judgments. 1. Their kingdom was almost ruined, *v.* 7. So miserable were they that both their towns and their lands were wasted, and yet so stupid that they needed to be told this, and to have it shown to them. " Look and see how it is; *your country is desolate;* the ground is not cultivated, for want of inhabitants, the villages being deserted, Judg. v. 7. And thus the fields and vineyards become like deserts, *all grown over with thorns,* Prov. xxiv. 31. *Your cities are burned with fire,* by the enemies that invade you" (fire and sword commonly go together); " as for the fruits of your land, which should be food for your families, *strangers devour them;* and, to your greater vexation, it is *before your eyes,* and you cannot prevent it; you starve while your enemies surfeit on that which should be your maintenance. The overthrow of your country is as the overthrow of strangers; it is used by the invaders, as one might expect it should be used by strangers." Jerusalem itself, which was as the daughter of Zion (the temple built on Zion was a mother, a nursing mother, to Jerusalem), or Zion itself, the holy mountain, which had been dear to God as a daughter, was now lost, deserted, and exposed *as a cottage in a vineyard,* which, when the vintage is over, nobody dwells in or takes any care of, and looks as mean and despicable as *a lodge,* or hut, *in a garden of cucumbers;* and every person is afraid of coming near it, and solicitous to remove his effects out of it, as if it were *a besieged city, v.* 8. And some think it is the calamitous state of the kingdom that is represented by a diseased body, *v.* 6. Probably this sermon was preached in the reign of Ahaz, when Judah was invaded by the kings of Syria and Israel, the Edomites and the Philistines, who slew many, and carried many away into captivity, 2 Chron. xxviii. 5, 17, 18. Note, National impiety and immorality bring national desolation. Canaan, the glory of all lands, Mount Zion, the joy of the whole earth, both became a reproach and a ruin; and sin made them so, that great mischief-maker. 2. Yet they were not at all reformed, and therefore God threatens to take another course with them (*v.* 5): " *Why should you be stricken any more*, with any expectation of doing you good by it, when you increase revolts as your rebukes are increased? *You will revolt more and more*, as you have done," as Ahaz particularly did, who, *in his distress, trespassed yet more against the Lord*, 2 Chron. xxviii. 22. Thus the physician, when he sees the patient's case desperate, troubles him no more with physic; and the father resolves to correct his child no more when, finding him hardened, he determines to disinherit him. Note, (1.) There are those who are made worse by the methods God takes to make them better; the more they are stricken the more they revolt; their corruptions, instead of being mortified, are irritated and exasperated by their afflictions, and their hearts more hardened. (2.) God sometimes, in a way of righteous judgment, ceases to correct those who have been long incorrigible, and whom therefore he designs to destroy. The reprobate silver shall be cast, not into the furnace, but to the dunghill, Jer. vi. 29, 30. See Ezek. xxiv. 13; Hos. iv. 14. He that is *filthy, let him be filthy still.*

VI. He comforts himself with the consideration of a remnant that should be the monuments of divine grace and mercy, notwithstanding this general corruption and desolation, *v.* 9. See here, 1. How near they were to an utter extirpation. They were almost like Sodom and Gomorrah in respect both of sin and ruin, had grown almost so bad that there could not have been found *ten righteous men among them*, and almost as miserable as if none had been left alive, but their country turned into a sulphureous lake. Divine Justice said, *Make them as Admah: set them as Zeboim:* but Mercy said, *How shall I do it?* Hos. xi. 8, 9. 2. What it was that saved them from it: *The Lord of hosts left unto them a very small remnant*, that were kept pure from the common apostasy and kept safe and alive from the common calamity. This is quoted by the apostle (Rom. ix. 27), and applied to those few of the Jewish nation who in his time embraced Christianity, when the body of the people rejected it, and in whom the promises made to the fathers were accomplished. Note, (1.) In the worst of times there is a remnant preserved from iniquity and reserved for mercy, as Noah and his family in the deluge, Lot and his in the destruction of Sodom. Divine grace triumphs in distinguishing by an act of sovereignty. (2.) This remnant is often a very small one in comparison with the vast numbers of revolting ruined sinners. Multitude is no mark of the true church. Christ's is a little

flock. (3.) It is God's work to sanctify and save some, when others are left to perish in their impurity. It is the work of his power as the Lord of hosts. Except he had left us that remnant, there would have been none left; the corrupters (*v.* 4) did what they could to debauch all, and the devourers (*v.* 7) to destroy all, and they would have prevailed if God himself had not interposed to secure to himself a remnant, who are bound to give him all the glory. (4.) It is good for a people that have been saved from utter ruin to look back and see how near they were to it, just upon the brink of it, to see how much they owed to a few good men that stood in the gap, and that that was owing to a good God, who left them these good men. *It is of the Lord's mercies that we are not consumed.*

10 Hear the word of the LORD, ye rulers of Sodom; give ear unto the law of our God, ye people of Gomorrah. 11 To what purpose *is* the multitude of your sacrifices unto me? saith the LORD: I am full of the burnt-offerings of rams, and the fat of fed beasts; and I delight not in the blood of bullocks, or of lambs, or of he-goats. 12 When ye come to appear before me, who hath required this at your hand, to tread my courts? 13 Bring no more vain oblations; incense is an abomination unto me; the new moons and sabbaths, the calling of assemblies, I cannot away with; *it is* iniquity, even the solemn meeting. 14 Your new moons and your appointed feasts my soul hateth: they are a trouble unto me; I am weary to bear *them*. 15 And when ye spread forth your hands, I will hide mine eyes from you: yea, when ye make many prayers, I will not hear: your hands are full of blood.

Here, I. God calls to them (but calls in vain) to hear his word, *v.* 10. 1. The title he gives them is very strange: *You rulers of Sodom*, and *people of Gomorrah*. This intimates what a righteous thing it would have been with God to make them like Sodom and Gomorrah in respect of ruin (*v.* 9), because they had made themselves like Sodom and Gomorrah in respect of sin. The men of Sodom were *wicked, and sinners before the Lord exceedingly* (Gen. xiii. 13), and so were the men of Judah. When the rulers were bad, no wonder the people were so. Vice overpowered virtue, for it had the rulers, the men of figure, on its side; and it out-polled it, for it had the people, the men of number, on its side. The streams being thus strong, no less a power than that of the Lord of hosts could secure a remnant, *v.* 9. The rulers are boldly attacked here by the prophet as rulers of Sodom; for he knew not how to give flattering titles. The tradition of the Jews is that for this he was impeached long after, and put to death, as having cursed the gods and *spoken evil of the ruler of his people.* 2. His demand upon them is very reasonable : " *Hear the word of the Lord,* and *give ear to the law of our God ;* attend to that which God has to say to you, and let his word be a law to you." The following declaration of dislike to their sacrifices would be a kind of new law to them, though really it was but an explication of the old law; but special regard is to be had to it, as is required to the like, Ps. l. 7, 8. " Hear this, and tremble ; hear it, and take warning."

II. He justly refuses to hear their prayers and accept their services, their sacrifices and burnt-offerings, the fat and blood of them (*v.* 11), their attendance in his courts (*v.* 12), their oblations, their incense, and their solemn assemblies (*v.* 13), their new moons and their appointed feasts (*v.* 14), their devoutest addresses (*v.* 15) ; they are all rejected, because their hands were full of blood. Now observe,

1. There are many who are strangers, nay, enemies, to the power of religion, and yet seem very zealous for the show and shadow and form of it. This sinful nation, this seed of evil-doers, these rulers of Sodom and people of Gomorrah, brought, not to the altars of false gods (they are not here charged with that), but to the altar of the God of Israel, sacrifices, a multitude of them, as many as the law required and rather more—not only peace-offerings, which they themselves had their share of, but burnt-offerings, which were wholly consumed to the honour of God ; nor did they bring the torn, and lame, and sick, but fed beasts, and the fat of them, the best of the kind. They did not send others to offer their sacrifices for them, but came themselves to appear before God. They observed the instituted *places* (not in high places or groves, but in God's own courts), and the instituted *time,* the new moons, and sabbaths, and appointed feasts, none of which they omitted. Nay, it should seem, they called extraordinary assemblies, and held solemn meetings for religious worship, besides those that God had appointed. Yet this was not all : they applied to God, not only with their ceremonial observances, but with the exercises of devotion. They prayed, prayed often, made many prayers, thinking they should be heard for their much speaking ; nay, they were fervent and importunate in prayer, they spread forth their hands as men in earnest. Now we should have thought these, and, no doubt, they thought themselves, a pious religious people ; and

yet they were far from being so, for (1.) Their hearts were empty of true devotion. They came to *appear* before God (*v.* 12), *to be seen* before him (so the margin reads it) ; they rested in the outside of the duties ; they looked no further than to be seen of men, and went no further than that which men see. (2.) Their hands were full of blood. They were guilty of murder, rapine, and oppression, under colour of law and justice. The people shed blood, and the rulers did not punish them for it ; the rulers shed blood, and the people were aiding and abetting, as the elders of Jezreel were to Jezebel in shedding Naboth's blood. Malice is heart-murder in the account of God ; he that hates his brother in his heart has, in effect, his hands full of blood.

2. When sinners are under the judgments of God they will more easily be brought to fly to their devotions than to forsake their sins and reform their lives. Their country was now desolate, and their cities were burnt (*v.* 7), which awakened them to bring their sacrifices and offerings to God more constantly than they had done, as if they would bribe God Almighty to remove the punishment and give them leave to go on in the sin. *When he slew them, then they sought him,* Ps. lxxviii. 34. *Lord, in trouble have they visited thee, ch.* xxvi. 16. Many that will readily part with their sacrifices will not be persuaded to part with their sins.

3. The most pompous and costly devotions of wicked people, without a thorough reformation of the heart and life, are so far from being acceptable to God that really they are an abomination to him. It is here shown in a great variety of expressions that *to obey is better than sacrifice ;* nay, that sacrifice, without obedience, is a jest, an affront and provocation to God. The comparative neglect which God here expresses of ceremonial observances was a tacit intimation of what they would come to at last, when they would all be done away by the death of Christ. What was now made little of would in due time be made nothing of. " *Sacrifice and offering,* and prayer made in the virtue of them, *thou wouldest not ; then said I, Lo, I come.*" Their sacrifices are here represented,

(1.) As fruitless and insignificant : *To what purpose is the multitude of your sacrifices? v* 11. They are *vain oblations, v.* 13. *In vain do they worship me,* Matt. xv. 9. Their attention to God's institutions was all lost labour, and served not to answer any good intention ; for, [1.] It was not looked upon as any act of duty or obedience to God : *Who has required these things at your hands? v.* 12. Not that God disowns his institutions, or refuses to stand by his own warrants ; but in what they did they had not an eye to him that required it, nor indeed did he require it of those whose hands were full of blood and who continued impenitent. [2.] It did not recommend them to God's favour. He delighted not in the blood of their sacrifices, for he did not look upon himself as honoured by it. [3.] It would not obtain any relief for them. They pray, but God will not hear, because they regard iniquity (Ps. lxvi. 18); he will not deliver them, for, though they make many prayers, none of them come from an upright heart. All their religious services turned to no account to them. Nay,

(2.) As odious and offensive. God did not only not accept them, but he did detest and abhor them. " They are *your* sacrifices, they are none of mine; I am full of them, even surfeited with them." He needed them not (Ps. l. 10), did not desire them, had had enough of them, and more than enough. Their coming into his courts he calls *treading them,* or trampling upon them; their very attendance on his ordinances was construed into a contempt of them. Their incense, though ever so fragrant, was an abomination to him, for it was burnt in hypocrisy and with an ill design. Their solemn assemblies he could not *away with,* could not see them with any patience, nor bear the affront they gave him. *The solemn meeting is iniquity ;* though the thing itself was not, yet, as they managed it, it became so. It is a *vexation* (so some read it), a provocation, to God, to have ordinances thus prostituted, not only by wicked people, but to wicked purposes: " *My soul hates them ; they are a trouble to me,* a burden, an incumbrance; I am perfectly sick of them, and *weary of bearing them.*" God is never weary of hearing the prayers of the upright, but soon weary of the costly sacrifices of the wicked. He hides his eyes from their prayers, as that which he has an aversion to and is angry at. All this is to show, [1.] That sin is very hateful to God, so hateful that it makes even men's prayers and their religious services hateful to him. [2.] That dissembled piety is double iniquity. Hypocrisy in religion is of all things most abominable to the God of heaven. Jerome applies the passage to the Jews in Christ's time, who pretended a great zeal for the law and the temple, but made themselves and all their services abominable to God by filling their hands with the blood of Christ and his apostles, and so filling up the measure of their iniquities.

16 Wash you, make you clean; put away the evil of your doings from before mine eyes; cease to do evil; 17 Learn to do well; seek judgment, relieve the oppressed, judge the fatherless, plead for the widow. 18 Come now, and let us reason together, saith the LORD: though your sins be as scarlet, they shall be as white as snow; though they be red like crimson, they shall be as wool. 19 If ye be willing and obedient, ye shall eat the good of the land: 20 But if ye refuse and rebel, ye shall be devoured with the sword: for the mouth of the LORD hath spoken *it.*

Though God had rejected their services as insufficient to atone for their sins while they persisted in them, yet he does not reject them as in a hopeless condition, but here calls upon them to forsake their sins, which hindered the acceptance of their services, and then all would be well. Let them not say that God picked quarrels with them; no, he proposes a method of reconciliation. Observe here,

I. A call to repentance and reformation : " If you would have your sacrifices accepted, and your prayers answered, you must begin your work at the right end : *Be converted to my law*" (so the Chaldee begins this exhortation), " make conscience of second-table duties, else expect not to be accepted in the acts of your devotion." As justice and charity will never atone for atheism and profaneness, so prayers and sacrifices will never atone for fraud and oppression; for righteousness towards men is as much a branch of pure religion as religion towards God is a branch of universal righteousness.

1. They must *cease to do evil,* must do no more wrong, shed no more innocent blood. This is the meaning of washing themselves and *making themselves clean, v,* 16. It is not only sorrowing for the sin they had committed, but breaking off the practice of it for the future, and mortifying all those vicious affections and dispositions which inclined them to it. Sin is defiling to the soul. Our business is to wash ourselves from it by repenting of it and turning from it to God. We must put away not only that evil of our doings which is before the eye of the world, by refraining from the gross acts of sin, but that which is before God's eyes, the roots and habits of sin, that are in our hearts; these must be crushed and mortified.

2. They must *learn to do well.* This was necessary to the completing of their repentance. Note, It is not enough that we cease to do evil, but we must learn to do well. (1.) We must be doing, not cease to do evil and then stand idle. (2.) We must be doing good, the good which the Lord our God requires and which will turn to a good account. (3.) We must do it well, in a right manner and for a right end; and, (4.) We must learn to do well; we must take pains to get the knowledge of our duty, be inquisitive concerning it, in care about it, and accustom ourselves to it, that we may readily turn our hands to our work and be-

come masters of this holy art of doing well. He urges them particularly to those instances of well-doing wherein they had been defective, to second-table duties : " *Seek judgment ;* enquire what is right, that you may do it ; be solicitous to be found in the way of your duty, and do not walk carelessly. Seek opportunities of doing good : *Relieve the oppressed,* those whom you yourselves have oppressed ; ease them of their burdens, *ch.* lviii. 6. You, that have power in your hands, use it for the relief of those whom others do oppress, for that is your business. Avenge those that suffer wrong, in a special manner concerning yourselves for the fatherless and the widow, whom, because they are weak and helpless, proud men trample upon and abuse ; do you appear for them at the bar, on the bench, as there is occasion. Speak for those that know not how to speak for themselves and that have not wherewithal to gratify you for your kindness." Note, We are truly honouring God when we are doing good in the world ; and acts of justice and charity are more pleasing to him than all burnt-offerings and sacrifices.

II. A demonstration, at the bar of right reason, of the equity of God's proceedings with them : " *Come now, and let us reason together* (*v.* 18) ; while your hands are full of blood I will have nothing to do with you, though you bring me a multitude of sacrifices ; but if you wash, and make yourselves clean, you are welcome to draw nigh to me ; come now, and let us talk the matter over." Note, Those, and those only, that break off their league with sin, shall be welcome into covenant and communion with God ; he says, *Come now,* who before forbade them his courts. See Jam. iv. 8. Or rather thus : There were those among them who looked upon themselves as affronted by the slights God put upon the multitude of their sacrifices, as *ch.* lviii. 3, *Wherefore have we fasted* (say they) *and thou seest not ?* They represented God as a hard Master, whom it was impossible to please. " Come," says God, " let us debate the matter fairly, and I doubt not but to make it out that *my ways are equal, but yours are unequal,*" Ezek. xviii. 25. Note, Religion has reason on its side ; there is all the reason in the world why we should do as God would have us do. The God of heaven condescends to reason the case with those that contradict him and find fault with his proceedings ; for *he will be justified when he speaks,* Ps. li. 4. The case needs only to be stated (as it is here very fairly) and it will determine itself. God shows here upon what terms they stood (as he does, Ezek. xviii. 21—24 ; xxxiii. 18, 19) and then leaves it to them to judge whether these terms are not fair and reasonable.

1. They could not in reason expect any more than that, if they repented and reformed, they should be restored to God's fa- ur,

notwithstanding their former provocations. " This you may expect," says God, and it is very kind ; who could have the face to desire it upon any other terms ? (1.) It is very little that is required, " only that you *be willing and obedient,* that you *consent to obey*" (so some' read it), " that you subject your wills to the will of God, acquiesce in that, and give up yourselves in all things to be ruled by him who is infinitely wise and good." Here is no penance imposed for their former stubbornness, nor the yoke made heavier or bound harder on their necks ; only, " Whereas hitherto you have been perverse and refractory, and would not comply with that which was for your own good, now be tractable, be governable." He does not say, " If you be *perfectly* obedient," but, " If you be *willingly* so ;" for, if there be a willing mind, it is accepted. (2) That is very great which is promised hereupon. [1] That all their sins should be pardoned to them, and should not be mentioned against them. " Though they be as red as scarlet and crimson, though you lie under the guilt of blood, yet, upon your repentance, even that shall be forgiven you, and you shall appear in the sight of God as white as snow." Note, The greatest sinners, if they truly repent, shall have their sins forgiven them, and so have their consciences pacified and purified. Though our sins have been as scarlet and crimson, a deep dye, a double dye, first in the wool of original corruption and afterwards in the many threads of actual transgression— though we have been often dipped, by our many backslidings, into sin, and though we have lain long soaking in it, as the cloth does in the scarlet dye, yet pardoning mercy will thoroughly discharge the stain, and, being by it purged as *with hyssop, we shall be clean,* Ps. li. 7. If we make ourselves clean by repentance and reformation (*v.* 16), God will make us white by a full remission. [2.] That they should have all the happiness and comfort they could desire. " Be but willing and obedient, and *you shall eat the good of the land,* the land of promise ; you shall have all the blessings of the new covenant, of the heavenly Canaan, all the good of that land." Those that go on in sin, though they dwell in a good land, cannot with any comfort eat the good of it ; guilt embitters all ; but, if sin be pardoned, creature-comforts become comforts indeed.

2. They could not in reason expect any other than that, if they continued obstinate in their disobedience, they should be abandoned to ruin, and the sentence of the law should be executed upon them ; what can be more just ? (*v.* 20) : " *If you refuse and rebel,* if you continue to rebel against the divine government and refuse the offers of divine grace, *you shall be devoured with the sword,* with the sword of your enemies, which shall be commissioned to destroy you

—with the sword of God's justice, his wrath, and vengeance, which shall be drawn against you; for this is that which *the mouth of the Lord has spoken*, and which he will make good, for the maintaining of his own honour." Note, Those that will not be governed by God's sceptre will certainly and justly be devoured by his sword.

"And now life and death, good and evil, are thus set before you. *Come, and let us reason together.* What have you to object against the equity of this, or against complying with God's terms?"

21 How is the faithful city become an harlot! It was full of judgment; righteousness lodged in it; but now murderers. 22 Thy silver is become dross, thy wine mixed with water: 23 Thy princes *are* rebellious, and companions of thieves: every one loveth gifts, and followeth after rewards: they judge not the fatherless, neither doth the cause of the widow come unto them. 24 Therefore saith the LORD, the LORD of hosts, the mighty One of Israel, Ah, I will ease me of mine adversaries, and avenge me of mine enemies: 25 And I will turn my hand upon thee, and purely purge away thy dross, and take away all thy tin: 26 And I will restore thy judges as at the first, and thy counsellors as at the beginning: afterward thou shalt be called, The city of righteousness, the faithful city. 27 Zion shall be redeemed with judgment, and her converts with righteousness. 28 And the destruction of the transgressors and of the sinners *shall be* together, and they that forsake the LORD shall be consumed. 29 For they shall be ashamed of the oaks which ye have desired, and ye shall be confounded for the gardens that ye have chosen. 30 For ye shall be as an oak whose leaf fadeth, and as a garden that hath no water. 31 And the strong shall be as tow, and the maker of it as a spark, and they shall both burn together, and none shall quench *them.*

Here, I. The woeful degeneracy of Judah and Jerusalem is sadly lamented. See, 1. What the royal city had been, a faithful city, faithful to God and the interests of his kingdom among men, faithful to the nation and its public interests. *It was full*

of judgment; justice was duly administered upon the thrones of judgment which were set there, the *thrones of the house of David,* Ps. cxxii. 5. Men were generally honest in their dealings, and abhorred to do an unjust thing. *Righteousness lodged in it,* was constantly resident in their palaces and in all their dwellings, not called in now and then to serve a turn, but at home there. Note, Neither holy cities nor royal ones, neither places where religion is professed nor places where government is administered, are faithful to their trust if religion do not dwell in them. 2. What it had now become. That beauteous virtuous spouse was now debauched, and become an adulteress; righteousness no longer dwelt in Jerusalem *(terras Astræa reliquit—Astrea left the earth):* even murderers were unpunished and lived undisturbed there; nay, the princes themselves were so cruel and oppressive that they had become no better than murderers; an innocent man might better guard himself against a troop of banditti or assassins than against a bench of such judges. Note, It is a great aggravation of the wickedness of any family or people that their ancestors were famed for virtue and probity; and commonly those that thus degenerate prove the most wicked of all men. *Corruptio optimi est pessima—That which was originally the best becomes when corrupted the worst,* Luke xi. 26; Eccl. iii. 16; See Jer. xxii. 15—17. The degeneracy of Jerusalem is illustrated, (1.) By similitudes (*v.* 22): *Thy silver has become dross.* This degeneracy of the magistrates, whose character is the reverse of that of their predecessors, is as great a reproach and injury to the kingdom as the debasing of their coin would be and the turning of their silver into dross. Righteous princes and righteous cities are as silver for the treasury, but unrighteous ones are as dross for the dunghill. *How has the gold become dim!* Lam. iv. 1. *Thy wine is mixed with water,* and so has become flat and sour. Some understand both these literally: the wine they sold was adulterated, it was half water; the money they paid was counterfeit, and so they cheated all they dealt with. But it is rather to be taken figuratively: justice was perverted by their princes, and religion and the word of God were sophisticated by their priests, and made to serve what turn they pleased. Dross may shine like silver, and the wine that is mixed with water may retain the colour of wine, but neither is worth any thing. Thus they retained a show and pretence of virtue and justice, but had no true sense of either. (2.) By some instances (*v.* 23): "Thy princes, that should keep others in their allegiance to God and subjection to his law, are themselves rebellious, and set God and his law at defiance. Those that should restrain thieves (proud and rich oppressors, those worst of robbers, and those that designedly cheat their creditors, who are no better), are themselves companions of thieves, connive at them, do as they do, and with greater security and success, because they are princes, and have power in their hands; they share with the thieves they protect in their unlawful gain (Ps. l. 18) and *cast in their lot among them,* Prov. i. 13, 14. [1.] The profit of their places is all their aim, to make the best hand they can of them, right or wrong. They love gifts, and follow after rewards; they set their hearts upon their salary, the fees and perquisites of their offices, and are greedy of them, and never think they can get enough; nay, they will do any thing, though ever so contrary to law and justice, for a gift in secret. Presents and gratuities will blind their eyes at any time, and make them pervert judgment. These they love and are eager in the pursuit of, Hos. iv. 18. [2.] The duty of their places is none of their care. They ought to protect those that are injured, and take cognizance of the appeals made to them; why else were they preferred? But *they judge not the fatherless,* take no care to guard the orphans, *nor does the cause of the widow come unto them,* because the poor widow has no bribe to give, with which to make way for her and to bring her cause on." Those will have a great deal to answer for who, when they should be the patrons of the oppressed, are their greatest oppressors.

II. A resolution is taken up to redress these grievances (v. 24): *Therefore saith the Lord, the Lord of hosts, the Mighty One of Israel*—who has power to make good what he says, who has hosts at command for the executing of his purposes, and whose power is engaged for his Israel—*Ah! I will ease me of my adversaries.* Observe,

1. Wicked people, especially wicked rulers that are cruel and oppressive, are God's enemies, his adversaries, and shall so be accounted and so dealt with. If the holy seed corrupt themselves, they are the foes of his own house.

2. They are a burden to the God of heaven, which is implied in his easing himself of them. The *Mighty One of Israel,* that can bear any thing, nay, that upholds all things, complains of his being *wearied with men's iniquities,* ch. xliii. 24. Amos ii. 13.

3. God will find out a time and a way to ease himself of this burden, by avenging himself on those that thus bear hard upon his patience. He here speaks as one triumphing in the foresight of it: *Ah! I will ease me.* He will ease the earth of the burden under which it *groans* (Rom. viii. 21, 22), will ease his own name of the reproaches with which it is loaded. He will be eased of his adversaries, by *taking vengeance on his enemies;* he will *spue them out of his mouth,* and so be eased of them, Rev. iii. 16. He speaks with pleasure of the *day of vengeance* being *in his heart,* ch. lxiii.

4. If God's professing people conform not to his image, as the Holy One of Israel (v. 4), they shall feel the weight of his hand as the Mighty One of Israel : his power, which was wont to be engaged for them, shall be armed against them. In two ways God will ease himself of this grievance :—

(1.) By reforming his church, and restoring good judges in the room of those corrupt ones. Though the church has a great deal of dross in it, yet it shall not be thrown away, but refined (v. 25): "*I will purely purge away thy dross.* I will amend what is amiss. Vice and profaneness shall be suppressed and put out of countenance, oppressors displaced and deprived of their power to do mischief." When things are ever so bad God can set them to rights, and bring about a complete reformation; when he begins he will make an end, will take away all the tin. Observe, [1.] The reformation of a people is God's own work, and, if ever it be done, it is he that brings it about: "*I will turn my hand upon thee;* I will do that for the reviving of religion which I did at first for the planting of it." He can do it easily, with the turn of his hand; but he does it effectually, for what opposition can stand before the arm of the Lord revealed? [2] He does it by blessing them with good magistrates and good ministers of state (v. 26): "*I will restore thy judges as at the first,* to put the laws in execution against evil-doers, *and thy counsellors,* to transact public affairs, *as at the beginning,*" either the same persons that had been turned out or others of the same character. [3.] He does it by restoring judgment and righteousness among them (v. 27), by planting in men's minds principles of justice and governing their lives by those principles. Men may do much by external restraints; but God does it effectually by the influences of *his Spirit,* as a *Spirit of judgment,* ch. iv. 4; xxviii. 6. See Ps. lxxxv. 10, 11. [4.] The reformation of a people will be the redemption of them and their converts, for sin is the worst captivity, the worst slavery, and the great and eternal redemption is that by which *Israel is redeemed from all his iniquities* (Ps. cxxx. 8), and the *blessed Redeemer* is he that *turns away ungodliness from Jacob* (Rom. xi. 26), and *saves his people from their sins,* Matt. i. 21. All the redeemed of the Lord shall be converts, and their conversion is their redemption: "*Her converts,* or *those that return of her* (so the margin), shall be redeemed with righteousness." God works deliverance for us by preparing us for it with judgment and righteousness. [5.] The reviving of a people's virtue is the restoring of their honour: *Afterwards thou shalt be called the city of righteousness, the faithful city;* that is, First, "Thou shalt *be so;*" the reforming of the magistracy is a good step towards the reforming of the city and the country too. Secondly, "Thou shalt have the *praise of* being so ;" and a greater praise there cannot be to any city than to *be called the city of righteousness*, and to retrieve the ancient honour which was lost when *the faithful city became a harlot, v.* 21.

(2.) By cutting off those that hate to be reformed, that they may not remain either as snares or as scandals to the faithful city. [1.] It is an utter ruin that is here threatened. They shall be destroyed and consumed, and not chastened and corrected only. The extirpation of them will be necessary to the redemption of Zion. [2.] It is a universal ruin, which will involve the transgressors and the sinners together, that is, the openly profane that have quite cast off all religion, and the hypocrites that live wicked lives under the cloak of a religious profession—they shall both be destroyed together, for they are both alike an abomination to God, both those that contradict religion and those that contradict themselves in their pretensions to it. *And those that forsake the Lord*, to whom they had formerly joined themselves, *shall be consumed*, as the water in the conduit-pipe is soon consumed when it is cut off from the fountain. [3.] It is an inevitable ruin; there is no escaping it. *First*, Their idols shall not be able to help them, *the oaks which they have desired, and the gardens which they have chosen;* that is, the images, the dunghill-gods, which they have worshipped in their groves and under the green trees, which they were fond of and wedded to, for which they forsook the true God, and which they worshipped privately in their own gardens even when idolatry was publicly discountenanced. " This was the practice of the transgressors and the sinners; but they shall be ashamed of it, not with a show of repentance, but of despair, *v.* 29. They shall have cause to be ashamed of their idols; for, after all the court they have made to them, they shall find no benefit by them; but the idols themselves *shall go into captivity,*" *ch.* xlvi. 1, 2. Note, Those that make creatures their confidence are but preparing confusion for themselves. " You were fond of the oaks and the gardens; but you yourselves shall be, 1. " *Like an oak without leaves*, withered and blasted, and stripped of all its ornaments." Justly do those wear no leaves that bear no fruit; as the fig-tree that Christ cursed. 2. " *Like a garden without water*, that is neither rained upon nor *watered with the foot* (Deut. xi. 10), that has no *fountain* (Cant. iv. 15), and consequently is parched, and all the fruits of it gone to decay." Thus shall those be that trust in idols, or in an *arm of flesh*, Jer. xvii. 5, 6. But those that trust in God never find him as a wilderness, or as waters that fail, Jer. ii. 31. *Secondly*, They shall not be able to help themselves (*v.* 31) : " *Even the strong man shall be as tow*, not only soon broken and pulled to pieces, but easily catching fire;

and *his work* (so the margin reads it), that by which he hopes to fortify and secure himself, shall be as a spark to his own tow, shall set him on fire, and he and his work shall burn together. His own counsels shall be his ruin; his own sin kindles the fire of God's wrath, which shall burn to the lowest hell, and none shall quench it." When the sinner has made himself as tow and stubble, and God makes himself to him as a consuming fire, what can prevent the utter ruin of the sinner?

Now all this is applicable, 1. To the blessed work of reformation which was wrought in Hezekiah's time after the abominable corruptions of the reign of Ahaz. Then good men came to be preferred, and the faces of the wicked were filled with shame. 2. To their return out of their captivity in Babylon, which had thoroughly cured them of idolatry. 3. To the gospel-kingdom and the pouring out of the Spirit, by which the New-Testament church should be made a new Jerusalem, a city of righteousness. 4. To the second coming of Christ, when he shall thoroughly purge his floor, his field, shall gather the wheat into his barn, into his garner, and burn the chaff, the tares, with unquenchable fire.

CHAP. II.

With this chapter begins a new sermon, which is continued in the two following chapters. The subject of this discourse is Judah and Jerusalem, ver. 1. In this chapter the prophet speaks, I. Of the glory of the Christians, Jerusalem, the gospel-church in the latter days, in the accession of many to it (ver. 2, 3), and the great peace it should introduce into the world (ver. 4), whence he infers the duty of the house of Jacob, ver. 5. II. Of the shame of the Jews, Jerusalem, as it then was, and as it would be after its rejection of the gospel and being rejected of God. 1. Their sin was their shame, ver. 6—9. 2. God by his judgments would humble them and put them to shame, ver. 10—17. 3. They should themselves be ashamed of their confidence in their idols and in an arm of flesh, ver. 18—22. And now which of these Jerusalems will we be the inhabitants of—that which is full of the knowledge of God, which will be our everlasting honour, or that which is full of horses and chariots, and silver and gold, and such idols, which will in the end be our shame?

THE word that Isaiah the son of Amoz saw concerning Judah and Jerusalem. 2 And it shall come to pass in the last days, *that* the mountain of the LORD's house shall be established in the top of the mountains, and shall be exalted above the hills; and all nations shall flow unto it. 3 And many people shall go and say, Come ye, and let us go up to the mountain of the LORD, to the house of the God of Jacob; and he will teach us of his ways, and we will walk in his paths: for out of Zion shall go forth the law, and the word of the LORD from Jerusalem. 4 And he shall judge among the nations, and shall rebuke many people : and they shall beat their swords

12

into ploughshares, and their spears into pruning-hooks : nation shall not lift up sword against nation, neither shall they learn war any more. 5 O house of Jacob, come ye, and let us walk in the light of the LORD.

The particular title of this sermon (*v.* 1) is the same with the general title of the book (*ch.* i. 1), only that what is there called the *vision* is here called *the word which Isaiah saw* (or the matter, or thing, which he saw), the truth of which he had as full an assurance of in his own mind as if he had seen it with his bodily eyes. Or this word was brought to him in a vision; something he saw when he received this message from God. John turned to *see the voice* that spoke with him. Rev. i. 12.

This sermon begins with the prophecy relating to the last days, the days of the Messiah, when his kingdom should be set up in the world, at the latter end of the Mosaic economy. In the last days of the earthly Jerusalem, just before the destruction of it, this heavenly Jerusalem should be erected, Heb. xii. 22 ; Gal. iv. 26. Note, Gospel times are the last days. For, 1. They were long in coming, were a great while waited for by the Old-Testament saints, and came at last. 2. We are not to look for any dispensation of divine grace but what we have in the gospel, Gal. i. 8, 9. 3. We are to look for the second coming of Jesus Christ at the end of time, as the Old-Testament saints did for his first coming ; *this is the last time,* 1 John ii. 18.

Now the prophet here foretels,

I. The setting up of the Christian church, and the planting of the Christian religion, in the world. Christianity shall then be the mountain of the Lord's house ; where that is professed God will grant his presence, receive his people's homage, and grant instruction and blessing, as he did of old in the temple on Mount Zion. The gospel church, incorporated by Christ's charter, shall then be the rendezvous of all the spiritual seed of Abraham. Now it is here promised, 1. That Christianity shall be openly preached and professed ; it shall be *prepared* (so the margin reads it) in the top of the mountains, in the view and hearing of all. Hence Christ's disciples are compared to a city on a hill, which *cannot be hid,* Matt. v. 14. They had many eyes upon them. Christ himself *spoke openly to the world,* John xviii. 20. What the apostles did was not *done in a corner,* Acts xxvi. 26. It was the lighting of a beacon, the setting up of a standard. Its being every where spoken *against* supposes that it was every where spoken *of.* 2. That it shall be firmly fixed and rooted ; it shall be established on the top of the everlasting mountains, built upon a *rock,* so that the *gates of hell shall not pre-*

vail against it, unless they could pluck up mountains by the roots. He that dwells safely is said to *dwell on high, ch.* xxxiii. 16. *The Lord has founded the gospel Zion.* 3. That it shall not only overcome all opposition, but overtop all competition ; it shall be *exalted above the hills.* This *wisdom of God in a mystery* shall outshine all the wisdom of this world, all its philosophy and all its politics. The spiritual worship which it shall introduce shall put down the idolatries of the heathen ; and all other institutions in religion shall appear mean and despicable in comparison with this. See Ps. lxviii. 16. *Why leap ye, ye high hills ? This is the hill which God desires to dwell in.*

II. The bringing of the Gentiles into it. 1. The nations shall be admitted into it, even the uncircumcised, who were forbidden to come into the courts of the temple at Jerusalem. The partition wall, which kept them out, kept them off, shall be taken down. 2. *All nations shall flow into it :* having liberty of access, they shall improve their liberty, and multitudes shall embrace the Christian faith. They shall flow into it, as streams of water, which denotes the abundance of converts that the gospel should make and their speed and cheerfulness in coming into the church. They shall not be forced into it, but shall naturally flow into it. *Thy people shall be willing,* all volunteers, Ps. cx. 3. To Christ shall the *gathering of the people be,* Gen. xlix. 10. See *ch.* lx. 4, 5.

III. The mutual assistance and encouragement which this confluence of converts shall give to one another. Their pious affections and resolutions shall be so intermixed that they shall come in in one full stream. As, when the Jews from all parts of the country went up thrice a year to worship at Jerusalem, they called on their friends in the road and excited them to go along with them, so shall many of the Gentiles court their relations, friends, and neighbours, to join with them in embracing the Christian religion (*v.* 3) : " *Come, and let us go up to the mountain of the Lord :* though it be up-hill and against heart, yet it is *the mountain of the Lord,* who will assist the ascent of our souls towards him." Note, Those that are entering into covenant and communion with God themselves should bring as many as they can along with them ; it becomes Christians to provoke one another to good works, and to further the communion of saints by inviting one another into it : not, " Do you *go up to the mountain of the Lord,* and pray for us, and we will stay at home ;" nor, " We will go, and do you do as you will ;" but, " *Come, and let us go,* let us go in concert, that we may strengthen one another's hands and support one another's reputation :" not, " We will consider of it, and advise about it, and go hereafter ;" but, *Come, and let us go forthwith.* See **Ps.**

cxxii. 1. Many shall say this. Those that have had it said to them shall say it to others. The gospel church is here called, not only *the mountain of the Lord*, but *the house of the God of Jacob ;* for in it God's covenant with Jacob and his praying seed is kept up and has its accomplishment; for to us now, as unto them, he never said, *Seek you me in vain, ch.* xlv. 19. Now see here, 1. What they promise themselves in going up to the *mountain of the Lord:* There *he will teach us of his ways.* Note, God's ways are to be learned in his church, in communion with his people, and in the use of instituted ordinances—the ways of duty which he requires us to walk in, the ways of grace in which he walks towards us. It is God that teaches his people, by his word and Spirit. It is worth while to take pains to go up to his holy mountain to be taught his ways, and those who are willing to take that pains shall never find it labour in vain. Then *shall we know if we follow on to know the Lord.* 2. What they *promise for themselves* and one another : " If he will *teach us his ways*, we will *walk in his paths ;* if he will let us know our duty, we will by his grace make conscience of doing it." Those who attend God's word with this humble resolution shall not be sent away without their lesson.

IV. The means by which this shall be brought about : *Out of Zion shall go forth the law*, the New-Testament law, the law of Christ, as of old the law of Moses from Mount Sinai, even *the word of the Lord from Jerusalem.* The gospel is a law, a law of faith ; it is the *word of the Lord ;* it *went forth from Zion*, where the temple was built, and from Jerusalem. Christ himself began in Galilee, Matt. iv. 23 ; Luke xxiii. 5. But, when he commissioned his apostles to preach the gospel to all nations, he appointed them to begin at Jerusalem, Luke xxiv. 47. See Rom. xv. 19. Though most of them had their home in Galilee, yet they must stay at Jerusalem, there to *receive the promise of the Spirit*, Acts i. 4. And in the temple on Mount Zion they preached the gospel, Acts v. 20. This honour was allowed to Jerusalem, even after Christ was crucified there, for the sake of what it had been. And it was by this gospel, which took rise from Jerusalem, that the gospel church was *established on the top of the mountains.* This was the rod of divine strength, that was *sent forth out of Zion*, Ps. cx. 2.

V. The erecting of the kingdom of the Redeemer in the world : *He shall judge among the nations.* He whose word goes forth out of Zion shall by that word not only subdue souls to himself, but rule in them, *v.* 4. He shall, in wisdom and justice, order and overrule the affairs of the world for the good of his church, and rebuke and restrain those that oppose his interest. By his Spirit working on men's consciences he

shall judge, and rebuke shall try men and check them ; his kingdom is spiritual, *and not of this world.*

VI. The great peace which should be the effect of the success of the gospel in the world (*v.* 4) : *They shall beat their swords into ploughshares ;* their instruments of war shall be converted into implements of husbandry ; as, on the contrary, when war is proclaimed, *ploughshares are beaten into swords*, Joel iii. 10. *Nation shall then not lift up sword against nation*, as now they do, *neither shall they learn war any more*, for they shall have no more occasion for it. This does not make all war absolutely unlawful among Christians, nor is it a prophecy that in the days of the Messiah there shall be no wars. The Jews urge this against Christians as an argument that Jesus is not the Messiah, because this promise is not fulfilled. But, 1. It was in part fulfilled in the peaceableness of the time in which Christ was born, when wars had in a great measure ceased, witness *the taxing*, Luke ii. 1. 2. The design and tendency of the gospel are to make peace and to slay all enmities. It has in it the most powerful obligations and inducements to peace ; so that one might reasonably have expected it should have this effect, and it would have had it if it had not been for those lusts of men from which come wars and fightings. 3. Jews and Gentiles were reconciled and brought together by the gospel, and there were no more such wars between them as there had been ; for they became *one sheep-fold under one shepherd.* See Eph. ii. 15. 4. The gospel of Christ, as far as it prevails, disposes men to be peaceable, softens men's spirits, and sweetens them ; and the love of Christ, shed abroad in the heart, constrains men to love one another. 5. The primitive Christians were famous for brotherly love ; their very adversaries took notice of it. 6. We have reason to hope that this promise shall yet have a more full accomplishment in the latter times of the Christian church, when the Spirit shall be poured out more plentifully from on high. Then there shall be on earth peace. *Who shall live when God doeth this ?* But do it he will in due time, for *he is not a man that he should lie.*

Lastly, Here is a practical inference drawn from all this (*v.* 5) : *O house of Jacob ! come you, and let us walk in the light of the Lord.* By the house of Jacob is meant either, 1. Israel according to the flesh. Let them be provoked by this *to a holy emulation*, Rom. xi. 14. " Seeing the Gentiles are thus ready and resolved for God, thus forward to go up to the house of the Lord, let us stir up ourselves to go too. Let it never be said that the sinners of the Gentiles were better friends to the holy mountain than the house of Jacob." Thus the zeal of some should provoke many. Or, 2. Spiritual Israel, all that are brought to the God of Jacob.

14

Shall there be such great knowledge in gospel times (v. 3) and such great peace (v. 4), and shall we share in these privileges? Come then, and let us live accordingly. Whatever others do, *come, O come !* let us *walk in the light of the Lord.* (1.) Let us walk circumspectly in the light of this knowledge. Will God teach us his ways? Will he show us his glory in the face of Christ? Let us then *walk as the children of the light and of the day*, Eph. v. 8; 1 Thess. v. 8; Rom. xiii. 12. (2.) Let us walk comfortably in the light of this peace. Shall there be no more war? Let us then go on our way rejoicing, and let this joy terminate in God, and be our strength, Neh. viii. 10. Thus shall we walk in the beams of the Sun of righteousness.

6 Therefore thou hast forsaken thy people the house of Jacob, because they be replenished from the east, and *are* soothsayers like the Philistines, and they please themselves in the children of strangers. 7 Their land also is full of silver and gold. neither *is there any* end of their treasures; their land is also full of horses, neither *is there any* end of their chariots : 8 Their land also is full of idols; they worship the work of their own hands, that which their own fingers have made : 9 And the mean man boweth down, and the great man humbleth himself : therefore forgive them not.

The calling in of the Gentiles was accompanied with the rejection of the Jews; it was their fall, and the *diminishing of them, that was the riches of the Gentiles ;* and the *casting off of them* was *the reconciling of the world* (Rom. xi. 12—15) ; and it should seem that these verses have reference to that, and are designed to justify God therein, and yet it is probable that they are primarily intended for the convincing and awakening of the men of that generation in which the prophet lived, it being usual with the prophets to speak of the things that then were, both in mercy and judgment, as types of the things that should be hereafter. Here is,

I. Israel's doom. This is set forth in two words, the first and the last of this paragraph; but they are two dreadful words, and which speak, 1. Their case sad, very sad (v. 6): *Therefore thou hast forsaken thy people.* Miserable is the condition of that people whom God has forsaken, and great certainly must the provocation be if he forsake those that have been his own people. This was the deplorable case of the Jewish church after they had rejected Christ. *Migremus hinc—Let us go hence.* Your *house is left unto*

you desolate, Matt. xxiii. 38. Whenever any sore calamity came upon the Jews thus far the Lord might be said to forsake them that he withdrew his help and succour from them, else they would not have fallen into the hands of their enemies. But God never leaves any till they first leave him. 2. Their case desperate, wholly desperate (*v.* 9) : *Therefore forgive them not.* This prophetical prayer amounts to a threatening that they should not be forgiven, and so some think it may be read : *And thou wilt not forgive them.* This refers not to particular persons (many of them repented and were pardoned), but to the body of that nation, against whom an irreversible doom was passed, that they should be wholly cut off and their church quite dismantled, never to be formed into such a body again, nor ever to have their old charter restored to them.

II. Israel's desert of this doom, and the reasons upon which it is grounded. In general, it is sin that brings destruction upon them; it is this, and nothing but this, that provokes God to forsake his people. The particular sins which the prophet specifies are such as abounded among them at that time, which he makes mention of for the conviction of those to whom he then preached, rather than that which afterwards proved the measure-filling sin, their crucifying Christ and persecuting his followers ; for the sins of every age contributed towards the making up of the dreadful account at last. And there was a partial and temporary rejection of them by the captivity in Babylon hastening on, which was a type of their final destruction by the Romans, and which the sins here mentioned brought upon them. Their sins were such as directly contradicted all God's kind and gracious designs concerning them.

1. God set them apart for himself, as a peculiar people, distinguished from, and dignified above, all other people (Num. xxiii. 9) ; but they were *replenished from the east* ; they *naturalized* foreigners, not *proselyted,* and encouraged them to settle among them, and mingled with them, Hos. vii. 8. Their country was peopled with Syrians and Chaldeans, Moabites and Ammonites, and other eastern nations, and with them they admitted the fashions and customs of those nations, and *pleased themselves in the children of strangers*, were fond of them, preferred their country before their own, and thought that the more they conformed to them the more polite and refined they were; thus did they profane their crown and their covenant. Note, Those are in danger of being estranged from God who please themselves with those who are strangers to him, for we soon learn the ways of those whose company we love.

2. God gave them his oracles, which they might ask counsel of, not only the scriptures and the seers, but the breast-plate of

15

judgment; but they slighted these, and became soothsayers like the Philistines, introduced their arts of divination, and hearkened to those who by the stars, or the clouds, or the flight of birds, or the entrails of beasts, or other magic superstitions, pretended to discover things secret or foretel things to come. The Philistines were noted for diviners, 1 Sam. vi. 2. Note, Those who slight true divinity are justly given up to lying divinations; and those will certainly be forsaken of God who thus forsake him and their own mercies for lying vanities.

3. God encouraged them to put their confidence in him, and assured them that he would be their wealth and strength; but, distrusting his power and promise, they made gold their hope, and furnished themselves with horses and chariots, and relied upon them for their safety, *v.* 7. God had expressly forbidden even their kings to multiply horses to themselves and *greatly to multiply silver and gold*, because he would have them to depend upon himself only; but they did not think their interest in God made them a match for their neighbours unless they had as full treasures of silver and gold, and as formidable hosts of chariots and horses, as they had. It is not having silver and gold, horses and chariots, that is a provocation to God, but, (1.) Desiring them insatiably, so that there is no end of the treasures, no end of the chariots, no bounds or limits set to the desire of them. Those shall never have enough in God (who alone is all-sufficient) that never know when they have enough of this world, which at the best is insufficient. (2.) Depending upon them, as if we could not be safe, and easy, and happy, without them, and could not but be so with them.

4. God himself was their God, the sole object of their worship, and he himself instituted ordinances of worship for them; but they slighted both him and his institutions, *v.* 8. Their land was full of idols; every city had its god (Jer. xi. 13); and, according to the goodness of their lands, they made goodly images, Hos. x. 1. Those that think one God too little will find two too many, and yet hundreds not sufficient; for those that love idols will multiply them; so sottish were they, and so wretchedly infatuated, that they *worshipped the work of their own hands*, as if that could be a god to them which was not only a creature, but *their* creature and that which their own fancies had devised and *their own fingers had made*. It was an aggravation of their idolatry that God had enriched them with silver and gold, and yet of that silver and gold they made idols; so it was, *Jeshurun waxed fat, and kicked*, see Hos. ii. 8.

5. God had advanced them, and put honour upon them; but they basely diminished and disparaged themselves (*v.* 9): The *mean man boweth down to his idol*, a thing below the meanest that has any spark of reason left. Sin is a disparagement to the poorest and those of the lowest rank. It becomes the mean man to bow down to his superiors, but it ill becomes him to *bow down to the stock of a tree, ch.* xliv. 19. Nor is it only the illiterate and poor-spirited that do this, but even the *great man* forgets his grandeur and humbles himself to worship idols, deifies men no better than himself, and consecrates stones so much baser than himself. Idolaters are said to *debase themselves even to hell, ch.* lvii. 9. What a shame is it that great men think the service of the true God below them and will not stoop to it, and yet will humble themselves to bow down to an idol! Some make this a threatening that the mean men shall be brought down, and the great men humbled, by the judgments of God, when they come with commission.

10 Enter into the rock, and hide thee in the dust, for fear of the LORD, and for the glory of his majesty. 11 The lofty looks of man shall be humbled, and the haughtiness of men shall be bowed down, and the LORD alone shall be exalted in that day. 12 For the day of the LORD of hosts *shall be* upon every *one that is* proud and lofty, and upon every *one that is* lifted up; and he shall be brought low: 13 And upon all the cedars of Lebanon, *that are* high and lifted up, and upon all the oaks of Bashan, 14 And upon all the high mountains, and upon all the hills *that are* lifted up, 15 And upon every high tower, and upon every fenced wall, 16 And upon all the ships of Tarshish, and upon all pleasant pictures. 17 And the loftiness of man shall be bowed down, and the haughtiness of men shall be made low: and the LORD alone shall be exalted in that day. 18 And the idols he shall utterly abolish. 19 And they shall go into the holes of the rocks, and into the caves of the earth, for fear of the LORD, and for the glory of his majesty, when he ariseth to shake terribly the earth. 20 In that day a man shall cast his idols of silver, and his idols of gold, which they made *each one* for himself to worship, to the moles and to the bats; 21 To go into the clefts of the rocks,

16

and into the tops of the ragged rocks, for fear of the LORD, and for the glory of his majesty, when he ariseth to shake terribly the earth. 22 Cease ye from man, whose breath *is* in his nostrils: for wherein is he to be accounted of?

The prophet here goes on to show what a desolation would be brought upon their land when God should have forsaken them. This may refer particularly to their destruction by the Chaldeans first, and afterwards by the Romans, or it may have a general respect to the method God takes to awaken and humble proud sinners, and to put them out of conceit with that which they delighted in and depended on more than God. We are here told that sooner or later God will find out a way,

I. To startle and awaken secure sinners, who cry peace to themselves, and bid defiance to God and his judgments (*v.* 10): "*Enter into the rock;* God will attack you with such terrible judgments, and strike you with such terrible apprehensions of them, that you shall be forced to *enter into the rock, and hide yourself in the dust, for fear of the Lord.* You shall lose all your courage, and tremble at the shaking of a leaf; your heart shall *fail you for fear* (Luke xxi. 26), and you shall *flee when none pursues,*" Prov. xxviii. 1. To the same purport, *v.* 19. *They shall go into the holes of the rocks, and into the caves of the earth,* the darkest the deepest places; they shall *call to the rocks and mountains to fall on them,* and rather crush them than not cover them, Hos. x. 8. It was so particularly at the destruction of Jerusalem by the Romans (Luke xxiii. 30) and of the persecuting pagan powers, Rev. vi. 16. And all *for fear of the Lord, and of the glory of his majesty,* looking upon him then to be a consuming fire and themselves as stubble before him, *when he arises to shake terribly the earth,* to *shake the wicked out of it* (Job xxxviii. 13), and to shake all those earthly props and supports with which they have buoyed themselves up, to shake them from under them. Note, 1. *With God is terrible majesty,* and the glory of it is such as sooner or later will oblige us all to flee before him. 2. Those that will not fear God and flee to him will be forced to fear him and flee from him to a refuge of lies. 3. It is folly for those that are pursued by the wrath of God to think to escape it, and to hide or shelter themselves from it. 4. The things of the earth are things that will be shaken; they are subject to concussions, and hastening towards a dissolution. 5. The shaking of the earth is, and will be, a terrible thing to those who set their affections wholly on things of the earth. 6. It will be in vain to think of finding refuge in the caves of the earth when the earth itself is shaken; there

will be no shelter then but in God and in things above.

II. To humble and abase proud sinners, that look big, and think highly of themselves, and scornfully of all about them (*v.* 11): *The lofty looks of man shall be humbled.* The eyes that aim high, the countenance in which the pride of the heart shows itself, shall be cast down in shame and despair. And the *haughtiness of men shall be bowed down,* their spirits shall be broken, and they shall be crest-fallen, and those things which they were proud of they shall be ashamed of. It is repeated (*v.* 17), *The loftiness of man shall be bowed down.* Note, Pride will, one way or other, have a fall. Men's haughtiness will be brought down, either by the grace of God convincing them of the evil of their pride, and clothing them with humility, or by the providence of God depriving them of all those things they were proud of and laying them low. Our Saviour often laid it down for a maxim that *he who exalts himself shall be abased;* he shall either abase himself in true repentance or God will abase him and pour contempt upon him. Now here we are told,

1. Why this shall be done: because the *Lord alone will be exalted.* Note, Proud men shall be vilified because the Lord alone will be magnified. It is for the honour of God's power to humble the proud; by this he proves himself to be God, and disproves Job's pretensions to rival with him, Job xl. 11—14. *Behold every one that is proud, and abase him; then will I also confess unto thee.* It is likewise for the honour of his justice. Proud men stand in competition with God, who is jealous for his own glory, and will not suffer men either to take to themselves or give to another that which is due to him only. They likewise stand in opposition to God; they resist him, and therefore he resists them; for he *will be exalted among the heathen* (Ps. xlvi. 10), and there is a day coming in which he alone will be exalted, when he shall have put *down all opposing rule, principality, and power,* 1 Cor. xv. 24.

2. How this shall be done: by humbling judgments, that shall mortify men, and bring them down (*v.* 12): *The day of the Lord of hosts,* the day of his wrath and judgment, *shall be upon every one that is proud.* He now laughs at their insolence because he sees that his day is coming, this day, which will be upon them ere they are aware, Ps. xxxvii. 13. This day of the Lord is here said to be upon *all the cedars of Lebanon, that are high and lifted up.* Jerome observes that the cedars are said to praise God (Ps. cxlviii. 9) and are *trees of the Lord* (Ps. civ. 16), *of his planting* (Isa. xli. 19), and yet here God's wrath fastens upon the cedars, which denotes (says he) that some of every rank of men, some great men, will be saved, and some perish. It is brought

in as an instance of the strength of God's voice that it *breaks the cedars* (Ps. xxix. 5), and here the day of the Lord is said to be *upon the cedars*, those of Lebanon, that were the straightest and stateliest,—upon the oaks, those of Bashan, that were the strongest and sturdiest,—upon the natural elevations and fortresses, *the high mountains and the hills that are lifted up* (*v.* 14), that overtop the valleys and seem to push the skies,—and upon the artificial fastnesses, *every high tower and every fenced wall, v.* 15. Understand these, (1.) As representing the proud people themselves, that are in their own apprehensions like the cedars and the oaks, firmly rooted, and not to be stirred by any storm, and looking on all around them as shrubs; these are the high mountains and the lofty hills that seem to fill the earth, that are gazed on by all, and think themselves immovable, but lie most obnoxious to God's thunderstrokes. *Feriuntque summos fulmina montes—The highest hills are most exposed to lightning.* And before the power of God's wrath these mountains are scattered and these hills bow and *melt like wax,* Hab. iii. 6; Ps. lxviii. 8. These vaunting men who are as high towers in which the noisy bells are hung, on which the thundering murdering cannon are planted—these fenced walls, that fortify themselves with their native hardiness, and intrench themselves in their fastnesses — shall be brought down. (2.) As particularizing the things they are proud of, in which they trust, and of which they make their boast. The day of the Lord shall be upon those very things in which they put their confidence as their strength and security; he will *take from them all their armour wherein they trusted.* Did the inhabitants of Lebanon glory in their cedars, and those of Bashan in their oaks, such as no country could equal? The day of the Lord should rend those cedars, those oaks, and the houses built of them. Did Jerusalem glory in the mountains that were round about it, as its impregnable fortifications, or in its walls and bulwarks? These should be levelled and laid low in the day of the Lord. Besides those things that were for their strength and safety they were proud, [1.] Of their trade abroad; but the day of the Lord shall be *upon all the ships of Tarshish;* they shall be broken as Jehoshaphat's were, shall founder at sea or be ship-wrecked in the harbour. Zebulun was a haven of ships, but should now no more rejoice in his going out. When God is bringing ruin upon a people he can sink all the branches of their revenue. [2.] Of their ornaments at home; but the day of the Lord shall be *upon all pleasant pictures,* the painting of their ships (so some understand it) or the curious pieces of painting they brought home in their ships from other countries, perhaps from Greece, which afterwards was

18

famous for painters. Upon *every thing that is beautiful to behold;* so some read it. Perhaps they were the pictures of their relations, and for that reason pleasant, or of their gods, which to the idolaters were delectable things; or they admired them for the fineness of their colours or strokes. There is no harm in making pictures, nor in adorning our rooms with them, provided they transgress not either the second or the seventh commandment. But to place our pictures among our pleasant things, to be fond of them and proud of them, to spend that upon them which should be laid out in charity, and to set our hearts upon them, as it ill becomes those who have so many substantial things to take pleasure in, so it tends to provoke God to strip us of all such vain ornaments.

III. To make idolaters ashamed of their idols, and of all the affection they have had for them and the respect they have paid to them (*v.* 18): *The idols he shall utterly abolish.* When the Lord alone shall be exalted (*v.* 17) he will not only pour contempt upon proud men, who like Pharaoh exalt themselves against him, but much more upon all pretended deities, who are rivals with him for divine honours. They shall be abolished, utterly abolished. Their friends shall desert them; their enemies shall destroy them; so that, one way or other, an utter riddance shall be made of them. See here, 1. The vanity of false gods; they cannot secure themselves, so far are they from being able to secure their worshippers. 2. The victory of the true God over them; for *great is the truth and will prevail.* Dagon fell before the ark, and Baal before the Lord God of Elijah. The gods of the heathen shall be famished (Zeph. ii. 11), and by degrees shall perish, Jer. x. 11. The rightful Sovereign will triumph over all pretenders. And, as God will abolish idols, so their worshippers shall abandon them, either from a gracious conviction of their vanity and falsehood (as Ephraim when he said, *What have I to do any more with idols?*) or from a late and sad experience of their inability to help them, and a woeful despair of relief by them, *v.* 20. When men are themselves frightened by the judgments of God into the holes of the rocks and the caves of the earth, and find that they do thus in vain shift for their own safety, they shall cast their idols, which they have made their gods and hoped to make their friends in the time of need, to the moles and to the bats, any where out of sight, that, being freed from the incumbrance of them, they may *go into the clefts of the rocks, for fear of the Lord, v.* 21. Note, (1.) Those that will not be reasoned out of their sins sooner or later shall be frightened out of them. (2.) God can make men sick of those idols that they have been most fond of, even the idols of silver and the idols of gold, the most precious. Covetous men make silver and gold their idols, money their god; but the time may come when they may feel it as much their burden as ever they made it their confidence, and may find themselves as much exposed by it as ever they hoped they should be guarded by it, when it tempts their enemy, sinks their ship, or retards their flight. There was a time when the mariners threw the wares, and even the *wheat, into the sea* (Jonah i. 5; Acts xxvii. 38), and the *Syrians cast away their garments for haste,* 2 Kings vii. 15. Or men may cast it away out of indignation at themselves for leaning upon such a broken reed. See Ezek. vii. 19. The idolaters here throw away their idols because they are ashamed of them and of their own folly in trusting to them, or because they are afraid of having them found in their possession when the judgments of God are abroad; as the thief throws away his stolen goods when he is searched for or pursued. (3.) The darkest holes, where the moles and the bats lodge, are the fittest places for idols, that have eyes and see not; and God can force men to cast their own idols there (*ch.* xxx. 22), when they are *ashamed of the oaks which they have desired,* ch. i. 29. *Moab shall be ashamed of Chemosh, as the house of Israel was ashamed of Bethel,* Jer. xlviii. 13. (4.) It is possible that sin may be both loathed and left and yet not truly repented of—loathed because surfeited on, left because there is no opportunity of committing it, yet not repented of out of any love to God, but only from a slavish fear of his wrath.

IV. To make those that have trusted in an arm of flesh ashamed of their confidence (*v.* 22): " *Cease from man.* The providences of God concerning you shall speak this aloud to you, and therefore take warning beforehand, that you may prevent the uneasiness and shame of a disappointment; and consider, 1. How weak man is: *His breath is in his nostrils,* puffed out every moment, soon gone for good and all." Man is a dying creature, and may die quickly; our nostrils, in which our breath is, are of the outward parts of the body; what is there is like one standing at the door, ready to depart; nay, the doors of the nostrils are always open, the breath in them may slip away ere we are aware, in a moment. Wherein then is man to be accounted of? Alas! no reckoning is to be made of him, for he is not what he seems to be, what he pretends to be, what we fancy him to be. Man is like vanity, nay, he is vanity, he is altogether vanity, he is less, he is lighter, than vanity, when weighed in the balances of the sanctuary. " 2. How wise therefore those are that cease from man;" it is our duty, it is our interest, to do so. " *Put not your trust in man,* nor make even the greatest and mightiest of men your confidence; cease to do so. Let not your eye be to the

power of man, for it is finite and limited, derived and depending; it is not from him that your judgment proceeds. Let not him be your fear, let not him be your hope; but look up to the power of God, to which all the powers of men are subject and subordinate; dread his wrath, secure his favour, take him for your help, and let your *hope be in the Lord your God.*"

CHAP. III.

The prophet, in this chapter, goes on to foretel the desolations that were coming upon Judah and Jerusalem for their sins, both that by the Babylonians and that which completed their ruin by the Romans, with some of the grounds of God's controversy with them. God threatens, I. To deprive them of all the supports both of their life and of their government, ver. 1—3. II. To leave them to fall into confusion and disorder, ver. 4, 5, 12. III. To deny them the blessing of magistracy, ver. 6—8. IV. To strip the daughters of Zion of their ornaments, ver. 17—24. V. To lay all waste by the sword of war, ver. 25, 26. The sins that provoked God to deal thus with them were, 1. Their defiance of God, ver. 8 2. Their impudence, ver. 9. 3. The abuse of power to oppression and tyranny, ver. 12—15. 4. The pride of the daughters of Zion, ver. 16. In the midst of the chapter the prophet is directed how to address particular persons. (1.) To assure good people that it should be well with them, notwithstanding those general calamities, ver. 10. (2.) To assure wicked people that, however God might, in judgment, remember mercy, yet it should go ill with them, ver. 11. O that the nations of the earth, at this day, would hearken to the rebukes and warnings which this chapter gives!

FOR, behold, the LORD, the LORD of hosts, doth take away from Jerusalem and from Judah the stay and the staff, the whole stay of bread, and the whole stay of water, 2 The mighty man, and the man of war, the judge, and the prophet, and the prudent, and the ancient, 3 The captain of fifty, and the honourable man, and the counsellor, and the cunning artificer, and the eloquent orator. 4 And I will give children *to be* their princes, and babes shall rule over them. 5 And the people shall be oppressed, every one by another, and every one by his neighbour: the child shall behave himself proudly against the ancient, and the base against the honourable. 6 When a man shall take hold of his brother of the house of his father, *saying,* Thou hast clothing, be thou our ruler, and *let* this ruin *be* under thy hand: 7 In that day shall he swear, saying, I will not be an healer; for in my house *is* neither bread nor clothing: make me not a ruler of the people. 8 For Jerusalem is ruined, and Judah is fallen: because their tongue and their doings *are* against the LORD, to provoke the eyes of his glory.

The prophet, in the close of the foregoing chapter, had given a necessary caution to all not to put confidence in man, or any creature; he had also given a general reason for that caution, taken from the frailty of human life and the vanity and weakness of human powers. Here he gives a particular reason for it—God was now about to ruin all their creature-confidences, so that they should meet with nothing but disappointments in all their expectations from them (*v.* 1): *The stay and the staff* shall be taken away, all their supports, of what kind soever, all the things they trusted to and looked for help and relief from. Their church and kingdom had now grown old and were going to decay, and they were (after the manner of aged men, Zech. viii. 4) leaning on a staff: now God threatens to take away their staff, and then they must fall of course, to take away the stays both of the city and of the country, of Jerusalem and of Judah, which are indeed stays to one another, and, if one fail, the other feels from it. He that does this is *the Lord, the Lord of hosts—Adon,* the Lord that is himself the stay or foundation; if that stay depart, all other stays certainly break under us, for he is the strength of them all. He that is the Lord, the ruler, that has authority to do it, and the Lord of hosts, that has ability to do it, he shall take away the stay and the staff. St. Jerome refers this to the sensible decay of the Jewish nation after they had crucified our Saviour, Rom. xi. 9, 10. I rather take it as a warning to all nations not to provoke God; for, if they make him their enemy, he can and will thus make them miserable. Let us view the particulars.

I. Was their plenty a support to them? It is so to any people; bread is the staff of life: but God can *take away the whole stay of bread and the whole stay of water;* and it is just with him to do so when fulness of bread becomes an iniquity (Ezek xvi. 49), and that which was given to be provision for the life is made provision for the lusts. He can take away the bread and the water by withholding the rain, Deut. xxviii. 23, 24 Or, if he allow them, he can take away the stay of bread and the stay of water by withholding his blessing, by which man lives, and not by bread only, and which is the staff of bread (Matt. iv. 4), and then the bread is not nourishing nor the water refreshing, Hag. i. 6. Christ is the bread of life and the water of life; if he be our stay, we shall find that this is a good part not to be taken away, John iv. 14; vi. 27.

II. Was their army a support to them— their generals, and commanders, and military men? These shall be taken away, either cut off by the sword or so discouraged with the defeats they meet with that they shall throw up their commissions and resolve to act no more; or they shall be disabled by sickness, or dispirited, so as to be unfit for business: *The mighty man, and the man of war,* and even the inferior officer, *the captain of fifty,* shall be removed. It bodes ill with a people when their valiant men

are lost. Let not the strong man therefore glory in his strength, nor any people trust too much to their mighty men; but let the strong *people glorify God* and *the city of the terrible nations fear him,* who can make them weak and despicable, *ch.* xxv. 3.

III. Were their ministers of state a support to them—their learned men, their politicians, their clergy, their wits and virtuoso? These also should be taken away—*the judges,* who were skilled in the laws, and expert in administering justice,—*the prophets,* whom they used to consult in difficult cases,—*the prudent,* who were celebrated as men of sense and sagacity above others and were assistants to the judges, *the diviners* (so the word is), those who used unlawful arts, who, though rotten stays, yet were stayed on (but it may be taken, as we read it, in a good sense),—*the ancients,* elders in age, in office,—*the honourable man,* the gravity of whose aspect commands reverence and whose age and experience make him fit to be a counsellor. Trade is one great support to a nation, even manufactures and handicraft trades; and therefore, when the whole stay is to be broken, *the cunning artificer* too shall be taken away; and the last is *the eloquent orator,* the man skilful of speech, who in some cases may do good service, though he be none of the prudent or the ancient, by putting the sense of others in good language. Moses cannot speak well, but Aaron can. God threatens to take these away, that is, 1. To disable them for the service of their country, *making the judges fools, taking away the speech of the trusty and the understanding of the aged,* Job xii. 17, &c. Every creature is that to us which God makes it to be; and we cannot be sure that those who have been serviceable to us shall always be so. 2. To put an end to their days; for the reason why princes are not to be trusted in is because their *breath goeth forth,* Ps cxlvi. 3, 4. Note, The removal of useful men by death, in the midst of their usefulness, is a very threatening symptom to any people.

IV. Was their government a support to them? It ought to have been so; it is the business of the sovereign to bear up the pillars of the land, Ps. lxxv. 3. But it is here threatened that this stay should fail them. When the mighty men and the prudent are removed *children shall be their princes*—children in age, who must be under tutors and governors, who will be clashing with one another and making a prey of the young king and his kingdom—children in understanding and disposition, childish men, such as are babes in knowledge, no more fit to rule than a child in the cradle. These shall rule over them, with all the folly, fickleness, and frowardness, of a child. And *woe unto thee, O land! when thy king* is such a one! Eccl. x. 16.

V. Was the union of the subjects among

themselves, their good order and the good understanding and correspondence that they kept with one another, a stay to them? Where this is the case a people may do the better for it, though their princes be not such as they should be; but it is here threatened that God would send an evil spirit among them too (as Judg. ix. 23), which would make them, 1. Injurious and unneighbourly one towards another (*v.* 5): "*The people shall be oppressed every one by his neighbour*, and their princes, being children, will take no care to restrain the oppressors or relieve the oppressed, nor is it to any purpose to appeal to them (which is a temptation to every man to be his own avenger), and therefore they bite and devour one another and will soon be consumed one of another. Then *homo homini lupus—man becomes a wolf to man; jusque datum sceleri—wickedness receives the stamp of law; nec hospes ab hospite tutus—the guest and the host are in danger from each other.* 2. Insolent and disorderly towards their superiors. It is as ill an omen to a people as can be when the rising generation among them are generally untractable, rude, and ungovernable, when *the child behaves himself proudly against the ancient*, whereas he should *rise up before the hoary head* and *honour the face of the old man*, Lev. xix. 32. When young people are conceited and pert, and behave scornfully towards their superiors, their conduct is not only a reproach to themselves, but of ill consequence to the public; it slackens the reins of government and weakens the hands that hold them. It is likewise ill with a people when persons of honour cannot support their authority, but are affronted by the base and beggarly, when judges are insulted and their powers set at defiance by the mob. Those have a great deal to answer for who do this.

VI. Is it some stay, some support, to hope that, though matters may be now ill-managed, yet others may be raised up, who may manage better? Yet this expectation also shall be frustrated, for the case shall be so desperate that no man of sense or substance will meddle with it.

1. The government shall go a begging, *v.* 6. Here, (1.) It is taken for granted that there is no way of redressing all these grievances, and bringing things into order again, but by good magistrates, who shall be invested with power by common consent, and shall exert that power for the good of the community. And it is probable that this was, in many places, the true origin of government; men found it necessary to unite in a subjection to one who was thought fit for such a trust, in order to the welfare and safety of them all, being aware that they must either be ruled or ruined. Here therefore is the original contract: "*Be thou our ruler*, and we will be subject to thee, and *let this ruin be under thy hand*, to be

repaired and restored, and then to be preserved and established, and the interests of it advanced, *ch.* lviii. 12. Take care to protect us by the sword of war from being injured from abroad, and by the sword of justice from being injurious one to another, and we will bear faith and true allegiance to thee." (2.) The case is represented as very deplorable, and things as having come to a sad pass; for, [1.] Children being their princes, every man will think himself fit to prescribe who shall be a magistrate, and will be for preferring his own relations; whereas, if the princes were as they should be, it would be left entirely to them to nominate the rulers, as it ought to be. [2.] Men will find themselves under a necessity even of forcing power into the hands of those that are thought to be fit for it: *A man shall take hold* by violence of one to make him a ruler, perceiving him ready to resist the motion: nay, he shall urge it upon his brother; whereas, commonly, men are not willing that their equals should be their superiors, witness the envy of Joseph's brethren. [3.] It will be looked upon as ground sufficient for the preferring of a man to be a ruler that he has clothing better than his neighbours—a very poor qualification to recommend a man to a place of trust in the government. It was a sign that the country was much impoverished when it was a rare thing to find a man that had good clothes, or that could afford to buy himself an alderman's gown or a judge's robes; and it was proof enough that the people were very unthinking when they had so much respect to a man in *gay clothing, with a gold ring* (Jam. ii. 2, 3), that, for the sake thereof, they would make him their ruler. It would have been some sense to have said, "Thou hast wisdom, integrity, experience; be thou our ruler." But it was a jest to say, *Thou hast clothing; be thou our ruler.* A *poor wise man*, though in vile raiment, *delivered a city*, Eccl. ix. 15. We may allude to this to show how desperate the case of fallen man was when our Lord Jesus was pleased to become our brother, and, though he was not courted, offered himself to be our ruler and Saviour, and to take this ruin under his hand.

2. Those who are thus pressed to come into office will swear themselves off, because, though they are taken to be men of some substance, yet they know themselves unable to bear the charges of the office and to answer the expectations of those that choose them (*v.* 7): *He shall swear* (shall lift up the hand, the ancient ceremony used in taking an oath) *I will not be a healer; make not me a ruler.* Note, Rulers must be healers, and good rulers will be so; they must study to unite their subjects, and not widen the differences that are among them. Those only are fit for government that are of a meek, quiet, healing, spirit. They must

also heal the wounds that are given to any of the interests of their people, by suitable applications. But why will he not be a ruler? Because *in my house is neither bread nor clothing.* (1.) If he said true, it was a sign that men's estates were sadly ruined when even those who made the best appearance really wanted necessaries—a common case, and a piteous one. Some who, having lived fashionably, are willing to put the best side outwards, are yet, if the truth were known, in great straits, and go with heavy hearts for want of bread and clothing. (2.) If he did not speak truth, it was a sign that men's consciences were sadly debauched, when, to avoid the expense of an office, they would load themselves with the guilt of perjury, and (which is the greatest madness in the world) would damn their souls to save their money, Matt. xvi. 26. (3.) However it was, it was a sign that the case of the nation was very bad when nobody was willing to accept a place in the government of it, as despairing to have either credit or profit by it, which are the two things aimed at in men's common ambition of preferment.

3. The reason why God brought things to this sad pass, even among his own people (which is given either by the prophet or by him that refused to be a ruler); it was not for want of good will to his country, but because he saw the case desperate and past relief, and it would be to no purpose to attempt it (*v.* 8): *Jerusalem is ruined* and *Judah is fallen;* and they may thank themselves. They have brought their destruction upon their own heads, for *their tongue and their doings ore against the Lord;* in word and action they broke the law of God and therein designed an affront to him; they wilfully intended to offend him, in contempt of his authority and defiance of his justice. Their tongue was against the Lord, for they contradicted his prophets; and their doings were no better, for they acted as they talked. It was an aggravation of their sin that God's eye was upon them, and that his glory was manifested among them; but they provoked him to his face, as if the more they knew of his glory the greater pride they took in slighting it, and turning it into shame. And this, this, is it for which Jerusalem is ruined. Note, The ruin both of persons and people is owing to their sins. If they did not provoke God, he would *do them no hurt,* Jer. xxv. 6.

9 The shew of their countenance doth witness against them; and they declare their sin as Sodom, they hide *it* not. Woe unto their soul! For they have rewarded evil unto themselves. 10 Say ye to the righteous, that *it shall be* well *with him:* for they shall eat the fruit of their doings. 11 Woe unto the wicked! *It shall be* ill *with him:* for the reward of his hands shall be given him. 12 *As for* my people, children *are* their oppressors, and women rule over them. O my people, they which lead thee cause *thee* to err, and destroy the way of thy paths. 13 The LORD standeth up to plead, and standeth to judge the people. 14 The LORD will enter into judgment with the ancients of his people, and the princes thereof: for ye have eaten up the vineyard; the spoil of the poor *is* in your houses. 15 What mean ye *that* ye beat my people to pieces, and grind the faces of the poor? saith the Lord GOD of hosts.

Here God proceeds in his controversy with his people. Observe,

I. The ground of his controversy. It was for sin that God contended with them; if they vex themselves, let them look a little further and they will see that they must *thank* themselves: *Woe unto their souls! For they have rewarded evil unto themselves. Alas for their souls!* (so it may be read, in a way of lamentation), *for they have procured evil to themselves, v.* 9. Note, The condition of sinners is woeful and very deplorable. Note also, It is the soul that is damaged and endangered by sin. Sinners may prosper in their outward estates, and yet at the same time there may be a woe to their souls. Note, further, Whatever evil befals sinners it is of their own procuring, Jer. ii. 19. That which is here charged upon them is, 1. That the shame which should have restrained them from their sins was quite thrown off and they had grown impudent, *v.* 9. This hardens men against repentance, and ripens them for ruin, as much as any thing: *The show of their countenance doth witness against them* that their minds are vain, and lewd, and malicious; their eyes declare plainly that they *cannot cease from sin,* 2 Pet. ii. 14. One may look them in the face and guess at the desperate wickedness that there is in their hearts: *They declare their sin as Sodom,* so impetuous, so imperious, are their lusts, and so impatient of the least check, and so perfectly are all the remaining sparks of virtue extinguished in them. The Sodomites declared their sin, not only by the exceeding greatness of it (Gen. xiii. 13), so that it cried to heaven (Gen. xviii. 20), but by their shameless owning of that which was most shameful (Gen. xix. 5); and thus Judah and Jerusalem did: they were so far from hiding it that they gloried in it, in the bold attempts they made upon virtue, and the victory they gained over their own con-

22

victions. They had a whore's forehead (Jer. iii. 3) and could not blush, Jer. vi. 15. Note, Those that have grown impudent in sin are ripe for ruin. Those that are past shame (we say) are past grace, and then past hope. 2. That their guides, who should direct them in the right way, put them out of the way (v. 12): "*Those who lead thee* (the princes, priests, and prophets) mislead thee; they *cause thee to err.*" Either they preached to them that which was false and corrupt, or, if they preached that which was true and good, they contradicted it by their practices, and the people would sooner follow a bad example than a good exhortation. Thus they *destroyed the way of their paths,* pulling down with one hand what they built up with the other. *Qui te beatificant—Those that call thee blessed* cause thee to err; so some read it. Their priests applauded them, as if nothing were amiss among them, cried *Peace, peace,* to them, as if they were in no danger; and thus they caused them to go on in their errors. 3. That their judges, who should have patronized and protected the oppressed, were themselves the greatest oppressors, v. 14, 15. The elders of the people, and the princes, who had learning and could not but know better things, who had great estates and were not under the temptation of necessity to encroach upon those about them, and who were men of honour and should have scorned to do a base thing, yet *they have eaten up the vineyard.* God's vineyard, which they were appointed to be the dressers and keepers of, they burnt (so the word signifies); they did as ill by it as its worst enemies could do, Ps. lxxx. 16. Or the vineyards of the poor they wrested out of their possession, as Jezebel did Naboth's, or devoured the fruits of them, fed their lusts with that which should have been the necessary food of indigent families; the spoil of the poor was hoarded up in their houses; when God came to search for stolen goods there he found it, and it was a witness against them. It was to be had, and they might have made restitution, but would not. God reasons with these great men (v. 15): "*What mean you, that you beat my people in pieces?* What cause have you for it? What good does it do you?" Or, "What hurt have they done you? Do you think you had power given you for such a purpose as this?" Note, There is nothing more unaccountable, and yet nothing which must more certainly be accounted for, than the injuries and abuses that are done to God's people by their persecutors and oppressors. "*You grind the faces of the poor;* you put them to as much pain and terror as if they were ground in a mill, and as certainly reduce them to dust by one act of oppression after another." Or, "Their faces are bruised and crushed with the blows you have given them; you have not only

ruined their estates, but have given them personal abuses." Our Lord Jesus was *smitten on the face,* Matt. xxvi. 67.

II. The management of this controversy. 1. God himself is the prosecutor (v. 13): *The Lord stands up to plead,* or he sets himself to debate the matter, and he *stands to judge the people,* to judge for those that were oppressed and abused; and he will *enter into judgment with the princes,* v. 14. Note, The greatest of men cannot exempt or secure themselves from the scrutiny and sentence of God's judgment, nor demur to the jurisdiction of the court of heaven. 2. The indictment is proved by the notorious evidence of the fact: "Look upon the oppressors, and the *show of their countenance witnesses against them* (v. 9); look upon the oppressed, and you see how their faces are battered and abused," v. 15. 3. The controversy is already begun in the change of the ministry. To punish those that had abused their power to bad purposes God sets those over them that had not sense to use their power to any good purposes: *Children are their oppressors, and women rule over them* (v. 12), men that have as weak judgments and strong passions as women and children: this was their sin, that their rulers were such, and it became a judgment upon them.

III. The distinction that shall be made between particular persons, in the prosecution of this controversy (v. 10, 11): *Say to the righteous, It shall be well with thee. Woe to the wicked; it shall be ill with him.* He had said (v. 9), they *have rewarded evil to themselves,* in proof of which he here shows that God will *render to every man according to his works.* Had they been righteous, it would have been well with them; but, if it be ill with them, it is because they are wicked and will be so. Thus God stated the matter to Cain, to convince him that he had no reason to be angry, Gen. iv. 7. Or it may be taken thus: God is threatening national judgments, which will ruin the public interests. Now, 1. Some good people might fear that they should be involved in that ruin, and therefore God bids the prophets comfort them against those fears: "Whatever becomes of the unrighteous nation, let *the righteous man* know that he shall not be lost in the crowd of sinners; the *Judge of all the earth will not slay the righteous with the wicked* (Gen. xviii. 25); no, assure him, in God's name, that it *shall be well with him.* The property of the trouble shall be altered to him, and he shall be *hidden in the day of the Lord's anger.* He shall have divine supports and comforts, which shall abound as afflictions abound, and so it shall be well with him." When the whole *stay of bread is taken away,* yet in the *day of famine the righteous shall be satisfied;* they *shall eat the fruit of their doings—* they shall have the testimony of their consciences for them that they kept themselves pure from the common iniquity, and there-fore the common calamity is not the same thing to them that it is to others; they brought no fuel to the flame, and therefore are not themselves fuel for it. 2. Some wicked people might hope that they should escape that ruin, and therefore God bids the prophets shake their vain hopes : *" Woe to the wicked ; it shall be ill with him, v.* 11. To him the judgments shall have a sting, and there shall be *wormwood and gall* in the *affliction and misery."* There is a woe to wicked people, and, though they may think to shelter themselves from public judgments, yet it shall be ill with them ; it will grow worse and worse with them if they repent not, and the worst of all will be at last; for *the reward of their hands shall be given them,* in the day when every man shall receive ac-cording to the things done in the body.

16 Moreover the LORD saith, Be-cause the daughters of Zion are haughty, and walk with stretched-forth necks and wanton eyes, walk-ing and mincing *as* they go, and making a tinkling with their feet: 17 Therefore the LORD will smite with a scab the crown of the head of the daughters of Zion, and the LORD will discover their secret parts. 18 In that day the LORD will take away the bravery of *their* tinkling orna-ments *about their feet,* and *their* cauls, and *their* round tires like the moon, 19 The chains, and the bracelets, and the mufflers, 20 The bonnets, and the ornaments of the legs, and the headbands, and the tablets, and the earrings; 21 The rings, and nose jewels, 22 The changeable suits of apparel, and the mantles, and the wimples, and the crisping pins, 23 The glasses, and the fine linen, and the hoods and the veils. 24 And it shall come to pass, *that* instead of sweet smell, there shall be stink; and instead of a girdle a rent; and instead of well-set hair baldness; and instead of a stomacher a girding of sackcloth; *and* burning instead of beauty. 25 Thy men shall fall by the sword, and thy mighty in the war. 26 And her gates shall lament and mourn ; and she *being* desolate shall sit upon the ground.

The prophet's business was to show all sorts of people what they had contributed to the national guilt and what share they must

expect in the national judgments that were coming. Here he reproves and warns the daughters of Zion, tells the ladies of their faults ; and Moses, in the law, having de-nounced God's wrath against *the tender and delicate woman* (the prophets being a com-ment upon the law, Deut. xxviii. 56), he here tells them how they shall smart by the calamities that are coming upon them. Observe,

I. The sin charged upon the daughters of Zion, *v.* 16. The prophet expressly vouches God's authority for what he said, lest it should be thought it was unbecoming in him to take notice of such things, and should be resented by the ladies : *The Lord saith it.* " Whether they will hear, or whether they will forbear, let them know that God takes notice of, and is much displeased with, the folly and vanity of proud women, and his law takes cognizance even of their dress." Two things they here stand indicted for— haughtiness and wantonness, directly con-trary to that *modesty, shamefacedness, and sobriety, with which women ought to adorn themselves,* 1 Tim. ii. 9. They discovered the disposition of their mind by their gait and gesture, and the lightness of their carriage. They are haughty, for they *walk with stretched-forth necks,* that they may seem tall, or, as thinking nobody good enough to speak to them or to receive a look or a smile from them. Their eyes are wan-ton, *deceiving* (so the word is): with their amorous glances they draw men into their snares. They affect a formal starched way of going, that people may look at them, and admire them, and know they have been at the dancing-school, and have learned the minuet-step. They go *mincing,* or nicely tripping, not willing to set so much as the sole of their foot to the ground, for tender-ness and delicacy. They make a *tinkling with their feet,* having, as some think, chains, or little bells, upon their shoes, that made a noise : they go *as if they were fettered* (so some read it), like a horse trammelled, that he may learn to pace. Thus Agag came delicately, 1 Sam. xv. 32. Such a nice affected mien is not only a force upon that which is natural, and ridiculous before men, men of sense ; but, as it is an evidence of a vain mind, it is offensive to God. And two things aggravated it here :—1. That these were the daughters of Zion, the holy mountain, who should have behaved with the gravity that becomes women professing godliness. 2. That it should seem, by the connexion, they were the wives and daugh-ters of the princes who spoiled and op-pressed the poor (*v.* 14, 15) that they might maintain this pride and luxury of their families.

II. The punishments threatened for this sin ; and they answer the sin as face answers to face in a glass, *v.* 17, 18. 1. They *walked with stretched-forth necks,* but God will *smite with a scab the crown of their head,* which shall lower their crests, and make them ashamed to show their heads, being obliged by it to cut off their hair. Note, Loathsome diseases are often sent as the just punishment of pride, and are sometimes the immediate effect of lewdness, the flesh and the body being consumed by it. 2. They cared not what they laid out in furnishing themselves with great variety of fine clothes; but God will reduce them to such poverty and distress that they shall not have clothes sufficient to cover their nakedness, but their uncomeliness shall be exposed through their rags. 3. They were extremely fond and proud of their ornaments; but God will strip them of those ornaments, when their houses shall be plundered, their treasures rifled, and they themselves led into captivity. The prophet here specifies many of the ornaments which they used as particularly as if he had been the keeper of their wardrobe or had attended them in their dressing-room. It is not at all material to enquire what sort of ornaments these respectively were and whether the translations rightly express the original words; perhaps 100 years hence the names of some of the ornaments that are now in use in our own land will be as little understood as some of those here mentioned now are. Fashions alter, and so do the names of them; and yet the mention of them is not in vain, but is designed to expose the folly of the daughters of Zion; for, (1.) Many of these things, we may suppose, were very odd and ridiculous, and, if they had not been in fashion, would have been hooted at. They were fitter to be toys for children to play with than ornaments for grown people to go to Mount Zion in. (2.) Those things that were decent and convenient, as *the linen, the hoods, and the veils,* needed not to be provided in such abundance and variety. It is necessary to have apparel and proper that all should have it according to their rank; but what occasion was there for so many changeable suits of apparel (*v.* 22), that they might not be seen two days together in the same suit? "They must have (as the " homily against excess of apparel speaks) " one gown for the day, another for the " night—one long, another short—one for " the working day, another for the holy-day " —one of this colour, another of that " colour—one of cloth, another of silk or " damask—one dress afore dinner, another " after—one of the Spanish fashion, another " Turkey, and never content with suffi- " cient." All this, as it is an evidence of pride and vain curiosity, so must needs spend a great deal in gratifying a base lust that ought to be laid out in works of piety and charity; and it is well if poor tenants be not racked, or poor creditors defrauded, to support it. (3.) The enumeration of

these things intimates what care they were in about them, how much their hearts were upon them, what an exact account they kept of them, how nice and critical they were about them, how insatiable their desire was of them, and how much of their comfort was bound up in them. A maid could forget none of these ornaments, though they were ever so many (Jer. ii. 32), but would report them as readily, and talk of them with as much pleasure, as if they had been things of the greatest moment. The prophet did not speak of these things as in themselves sinful (they might lawfully be had and used), but as things which they were proud of and should therefore be deprived of.

IV. They were very nice and curious about their clothes; but God would make those bodies of theirs, which they were at such expense to beautify and make easy, a reproach and burden to them (*v.* 24): *Instead of sweet smell* (those tablets, or boxes, of perfume, *houses of the soul* or *breath,* as they are called, *v.* 20, *margin) there shall be stink,* garments grown filthy with being long worn, or from some loathsome disease or plasters for the cure of it. *Instead of a* rich embroidered *girdle* used to make the clothes sit tight, there shall be *a rent,* a rending of the clothes for grief, or old rotten clothes rent into rags. *Instead of well-set hair,* curiously plaited and powdered, there shall be *baldness,* the hair being plucked off or shaven, as was usual in times of great affliction (*ch.* xv. 2; Jer. xvi. 6), or in great servitude, Ezek. xxix. 18. *Instead of a stomacher,* or a scarf or sash, there shall be *a girding of sackcloth,* in token of deep humiliation; *and burning instead of beauty.* Those that had a good complexion, and were proud of it, when they are carried into captivity shall be tanned and sun-burnt; and it is observed that the best faces are soonest injured by the weather. From all this let us learn, 1. Not to be nice and curious about our apparel, not to affect that which is gay and costly, nor to be proud of it. 2. Not to be secure in the enjoyment of any of the delights of sense, because we know not how soon we may be stripped of them, nor what straits we may be reduced to.

V. They designed by these ornaments to charm the gentlemen, and win their affections (Prov. vii. 16, 17), but there shall be none to be charmed by them (*v.* 25): *Thy men shall fall by the sword, and thy mighty in the war.* The *fire shall consume them,* and then the *maidens* shall *not be given in marriage:* as it is, Ps. lxxviii. 63. When the sword comes with commission the mighty commonly fall first by it, because they are most forward to venture. And, when Zion's guards are cut off, no marvel that Zion's gates *lament and mourn (v.* 26), the enemies having made themselves masters of them; and the city itself, being desolate, being emptied or swept, shall *sit upon the ground* like a disconsolate widow. If sin be harboured within the walls, lamentation and mourning are near the gates.

CHAP. IV.

In this chapter we have, I. A threatening of the paucity and scarceness of men (ver. 1), which might fitly enough have been added to the close of the foregoing chapter, to which it has a plain reference. II. A promise of the restoration of Jerusalem's peace and purity, righteousness and safety, in the days of the Messiah, ver. 2—6. Thus, in wrath, mercy is remembered, and gospel grace is a sovereign relief, in reference to the terrors of the law and the desolations made by sin.

AND in that day seven women shall take hold of one man, saying, We will eat our own bread, and wear our own apparel: only let us be called by thy name, to take away our reproach.

It was threatened (*ch.* iii. 25) that *the mighty men should fall by the sword in war,* and it was threatened as a punishment to the women that affected gaiety and a loose sort of conversation. Now here we have the effect and consequence of that great slaughter of men, 1. That though Providence has so wisely ordered that, *communibus annis*—*on an average of years,* there is nearly an equal number of males and females born into the world, yet, through the devastations made by war, there should scarcely be one man in seven left alive. As there are deaths attending the bringing forth of children, which are peculiar to the woman, who was first in the transgression, so, to balance that, there are deaths peculiar to men, those by the sword in the high places of the field, which perhaps devour more than child-bed does. Here it is foretold that such multitudes of men should be cut off that there should be *seven women to one man.* 2. That by reason of the scarcity of men, though marriage should be kept up for the raising of recruits and the preserving of the race of mankind upon earth, yet the usual method of it should be quite altered,—that, whereas men ordinarily make their court to the women, the women should now take hold of the men, foolishly fearing (as Lot's daughters did, when they saw the ruin of Sodom and perhaps thought it reached further than it did) that in a little time there would be none left (Gen. xix. 31),—that, whereas women naturally hate to come in sharers with others, seven should now, by consent, become the wives of one man,—and that whereas by the law the husband was obliged to provide food and raiment for his wife (Exod. xxi. 10), which with many would be the most powerful argument against multiplying wives, these women will be bound to support themselves; they will *eat bread of their own earning, and wear apparel of their own working,* and the man they court shall be at no expense upon them, only they desire to be called his wives, to *take away the reproach* of a single

26

life. They are willing to be wives upon any terms, though ever so unreasonable; and perhaps the rather because in these troublesome times it would be a kindness to them to have a husband for their protector. Paul, on the contrary, thinks the single state preferable in a time of distress, 1 Cor. vii. 26. It were well if this were not introduced here partly as a reflection upon the daughters of Zion, that, notwithstanding the humbling providences they were under (*ch.* iii. 18), they remained unhumbled, and, instead of repenting of their pride and vanity, when God was contending with them for them, all their care was to get husbands—that modesty, which is the greatest beauty of the fair sex, was forgotten, and with them the reproach of vice was nothing to the reproach of virginity, a sad symptom of the irrecoverable desolations of virtue.

2 In that day shall the branch of the LORD be beautiful and glorious, and the fruit of the earth *shall be* excellent and comely for them that are escaped of Israel. 3 And it shall come to pass, *that he that is* left in Zion, and *he that* remaineth in Jerusalem, shall be called holy, *even* every one that is written among the living in Jerusalem: 4 When the LORD shall have washed away the filth of the daughters of Zion, and shall have purged the blood of Jerusalem from the midst thereof by the spirit of judgment, and by the spirit of burning. 5 And the LORD will create upon every dwelling-place of mount Zion, and upon her assemblies, a cloud and smoke by day, and the shining of a flaming fire by night: for upon all the glory *shall be* a defence. 6 And there shall be a tabernacle for a shadow in the day time from the heat, and for a place of refuge, and for a covert from storm and from rain.

By the foregoing threatenings Jerusalem is brought into a very deplorable condition: every thing looks melancholy. But here the sun breaks out from behind the cloud. Many exceedingly great and precious promises we have in these verses, giving assurance of comfort which may be discerned through the troubles, and of happy days which shall come after them, and these certainly point at the kingdom of the Messiah, and the great redemption to be wrought out by him, under the figure and type of the restoration of Judah and Jerusalem by the reforming reign of Hezekiah after Ahaz and the return out of their captivity in Babylon; to both these events the passage may have some reference, but chiefly to Christ. It is here promised, as the issue of all these troubles,

I. That God will raise up a righteous branch, which shall produce fruits of righteousness (*v.* 2): *In that day*, that same day, at that very time, when Jerusalem shall be destroyed and the Jewish nation extirpated and dispersed, the kingdom of the Messiah shall be set up; and then shall be the reviving of the church, when every one shall fear the utter ruin of it.

1. Christ himself shall be exalted. He is the *branch of the Lord*, the man the branch; it is one of his prophetical names, *my servant the branch* (Zech. iii. 8; vi. 12), the *branch of righteousness* (Jer. xxiii. 5; xxxiii. 15), a *rod out of the stem of Jesse and a branch out of his roots* (*ch.* xi. 1), and this, as some think, is alluded to when he is called a *Nazarene*, Matt. ii. 23. Here he is called *the branch of the Lord*, because planted by his power and flourishing to his praise. The ancient Chaldee paraphrase here reads it, *The Christ, or Messiah, of the Lord.* He shall be the beauty, and glory, and joy. (1.) He shall himself be advanced to the joy set before him and the glory which he had with the Father before the world was. He that was a reproach of men, and whose visage was marred more than any man's, is now, in the upper world, beautiful and glorious, as the sun in his strength, admired and adored by angels. (2.) He shall be beautiful and glorious in the esteem of all believers, shall gain an interest in the world, and a name among men above every name. To those that believe he is precious, he is an honour (1 Pet. ii. 7), the *fairest of ten thousand* (Cant. v. 10), and altogether glorious. Let us rejoice that he is so, and let him be so to us.

2. His gospel shall be embraced. The success of the gospel is the fruit of the branch of·the Lord; all the graces and comforts of the gospel spring from Christ. But it is called *the fruit of the earth* because it sprang up in this world and was calculated for the present state. And Christ compares himself to a *grain of wheat*, that *falls into the ground and dies, and so brings forth much fruit*, John xii. 24. The success of the gospel is represented by *the earth's yielding her increase* (Ps. lxvii. 6), and the planting of the Christian church is God's *sowing it to himself in the earth*, Hos. ii. 23. We may understand it of both the persons and the things that are the products of the gospel: they shall be excellent and comely, shall appear very agreeable and be very acceptable to those that have escaped of Israel, to that remnant of the Jews which was saved from perishing with the rest in unbelief, Rom. xi. 5. Note, If Christ be precious to us, his gospel will be so and all its truths

and promises—his church will be so, and all that belong to it. These are the good fruit of the earth, in comparison with which all other things are but weeds. It will be a good evidence to us that we are of the chosen remnant, distinguished from the rest that are called *Israel*, and marked for salvation, if we are brought to see a transcendent beauty in Christ, and in holiness, and in the saints, the excellent ones of the earth. As a type of this blessed day, Jerusalem, after Sennacherib's invasion and after the captivity in Babylon, should again flourish as a branch, and be blessed with the fruits of the earth. Compare *ch.* xxxvii. 31, 32. *The remnant shall again take root downward and bear fruit upward.* And, if by the fruit of the earth here we understand the good things of this life, we may observe that these have peculiar sweetness in them to the chosen remnant, who, having a covenant-right to them, have the most comfortable use of them. If the branch of the Lord be beautiful and glorious in our eyes, even the fruit of the earth also will be excellent and comely, because then we may take it as the fruit of the promise, Ps. xxxvii. 16; 1 Tim. iv. 8.

II. That God will reserve to himself a holy seed, *v.* 3. When the generality of those that have a place and a name in Zion and in Jerusalem shall be cut off as withered branches, by their own unbelief, yet some shall be left. Some shall remain, some shall still cleave to the church, when its property is altered and it has become Christian; for God will not quite *cast off his people*, Rom. xi. 1. There is here and there one that is left. Now, 1. This is a remnant *according to the election of grace* (as the apostle speaks, Rom. xi. 5), such as are written among the living, marked in the counsel and fore-knowledge of God for life and salvation, *written to life* (so the word is), designed and determined for it unalterably; for "*what I have written I have written.*" Those that are kept alive in killing dying times were written for life in the book of divine Providence; and shall we not suppose those who are rescued from a greater death to be such as were *written in the Lamb's book of life?* Rev. xiii. 8. As many as were *ordained unto eternal life believed* to the salvation of the soul, Acts xiii. 48. Note, All that were *written among the living* shall be found among the living, every one; for of all that were given to Christ he will lose none. 2. It is a remnant *under the dominion of grace;* for every one that is *written among the living*, and is accordingly left, shall be called *holy*, shall be holy, and shall be accepted of God accordingly. Those only that are holy shall be left when the *Son of man shall gather out of his kingdom every thing that offends;* and all that are chosen to salvation are chosen to sanctification. See 2 Thess. ii. 13; Eph. i. 4.

III. That God will reform his church and

will rectify and amend whatever is amiss in it, *v.* 4. Then the remnant shall be *called holy, when the Lord shall have washed away their filth,* washed it from among them by cutting off the wicked persons, washed it from within them by purging out the wicked thing. They shall not be called so till they are in some measure made so. Gospel times are times of reformation (Heb. ix. 10), typified by the reformation in the days of Hezekiah and that after the captivity, to which this promise refers. Observe, 1. The places and persons to be reformed. Jerusalem, though the holy city, needed reformation ; and, being the holy city, the reformation of that would have a good influence upon the whole kingdom. The daughters of Zion also must be reformed, the women in a particular manner, whom he had reproved, *ch.* iii. 16. When they were decked in their ornaments they thought themselves wondrously clean ; but, being proud of them, the prophet calls them their *filth,* for no sin is more abominable to God than pride. Or by the daughters of Zion may be meant the country towns and villages, which were related to Jerusalem as the mother-city, and which needed reformation. 2. The reformation itself. The filth shall be washed away ; for wickedness is filthiness, particularly blood-shed, for which Jerusalem was infamous (2 Kings xxi. 16), and which defiles the land more than any other sin. Note, The reforming of a city is the cleansing of it. When vicious customs and fashions are suppressed, and the open practice of wickedness is restrained, the place is made clean and sweet which before was a dunghill; and this is not only for its credit and reputation among strangers, but for the comfort and health of the inhabitants themselves. 3. The author of the reformation : *The Lord shall do it.* Reformation-work is God's work ; if any thing be done to purpose in it, it is his doing. But how ? By the judgment of his providence the sinners were destroyed and consumed ; but it is by the Spirit of his grace that they are reformed and converted. This is work that is done, not by might, nor by power, but by the *Spirit of the Lord of hosts* (Zech. iv. 6), working both upon the sinners themselves that are to be reformed and upon magistrates, ministers, and others that are to be employed as instruments of reformation. The Spirit herein acts, (1.) As a spirit of judgment, enlightening the mind, convincing the conscience,—as a Spirit of wisdom, guiding us to deal prudently, (Isa. lii. 13),—as a discerning, distinguishing, Spirit, separating between the precious and the vile. (2.) As a Spirit of burning, quickening and invigorating the affections, and making men zealously affected in a good work. The Spirit works as fire, Matt. iii. 11. An ardent love to Christ and souls, and a flaming zeal

against sin, will carry men on with resolution in their endeavours to *turn away ungodliness from Jacob.* See Isa. xxxii. 15, 16.

IV. That God will protect his church, and all that belong to it (*v.* 5, 6); when they are purified and reformed they shall no longer lie exposed, but God will take a particular care of them. Those that are sanctified are well fortified ; for God will be to them a guide and a guard.

1. Their tabernacles shall be defended, *v.* 5.

(1.) This writ of protection refers to, [1.] Their dwelling-places, the tabernacles of their rest, their own houses, where they worship God, alone, and with their families. That blessing which is upon the *habitation of the just* shall be a protection to it, Prov. iii. 33. In the *tabernacles of the righteous* shall the *voice of rejoicing and salvation be,* Ps. cxviii. 15. Note, God takes particular cognizance and care of the dwelling-places of his people, of every one of them, the poorest cottage as well as the stateliest palace. When iniquity is *put far from the tabernacle* the Almighty shall be its defence, Job xxii. 23, 25. [2.] Their assemblies or tabernacles of meeting for religious worship. No mention is made of the temple, for the promise points at a time when not one stone of that shall be left upon another; but all the congregations of Christians, though but two or three met together in Christ's name, shall be taken under the special protection of heaven; they shall no more be scattered, no more disturbed, nor shall *any weapon formed against them prosper.* Note, we ought to reckon it a great mercy if we have liberty to worship God in public, free from the alarms of the sword of war or persecution.

(2.) This writ of protection is drawn up, [1.] In a similitude taken from the safety of the camp of Israel when they marched through the wilderness. God will give to the Christian church as real proofs, though not so sensible, of his care of them, as he then gave to Israel. The Lord will again *create a cloud and smoke by day,* to screen them from the scorching heat of the sun, and the *shining of a flaming fire by night,* to enlighten and warm the air, which in the night is cold and dark. See Exod. xiii. 21; Neh. ix. 19. This pillar of cloud and fire interposed between the Israelites and the Egyptians, Exod. xiv. 20. Note, Though miracles have ceased, yet God is the same to the New-Testament church that he was to Israel of old ; the very same yesterday, to-day, and for ever. [2.] In a similitude taken from the outside cover of rams' skins and badgers' skins that was upon the curtains of the tabernacle, as if every dwelling-place of Mount Zion and every assembly were as dear to God as that tabernacle was : *Upon all the glory shall be a defence,* to save it from wind and weather. Note, The church on earth has its glory. Gospel truths and ordinances, the scriptures and the ministry, are the church's glory; and upon all this glory there is a defence, and ever shall be, for the *gates of hell shall not prevail against the church.* If God himself be the glory in the midst of it, he will himself be a wall of fire round about it, impenetrable and impregnable. Grace in the soul is the glory of it, and those that have it are *kept by the power of God* as in a strong-hold, 1 Pet. i. 5.

2. Their tabernacle shall be a defence to them, *v.* 6. God's tabernacle was a pavilion to the saints (Ps. xxvii. 5); but, when that is taken down, they shall not want a covert: the divine power and goodness shall be a tabernacle to all the saints. God himself will be their hiding-place (Ps. xxxii. 7); they shall be at home in him, Ps. xci. 9. He will himself be to them as the *shadow of a great rock* (*ch.* xxxii. 2) and *his name a strong tower,* Prov. xviii. 10. He will be not only a shadow from the heat in the daytime, but a covert from storm and rain. Note, In this world we must expect change of weather and all the inconveniencies that attend it; we shall meet with storm and rain in this lower region, and at other times the heat of the day no less burdensome; but God is a refuge to his people in all weathers.

CHAP. V.

In this chapter the prophet, in God's name, shows the people of God their transgressions, even the house of Jacob their sins, and the judgments which were likely to be brought upon them for their sins, I. By a parable, under the similitude of an unfruitful vineyard, representing the great favours God had bestowed upon them, their disappointing his expectations from them, and the ruin they had thereby deserved, ver. 1—7. II. By an enumeration of the sins that did abound among them, with a threatening of punishments that should answer to the sins. 1. Covetousness, and greediness of worldly wealth, which shall be punished with famine, ver. 8—10. 2. Rioting, revelling, and drunkenness (ver. 11, 12, 22, 23), which shall be punished with captivity and all the miseries that attend it, ver. 13—17. 3. Presumption in sin, and defying the justice of God, ver. 18, 19. 4. Confounding the distinctions between virtue and vice, and so undermining the principles of religion, ver. 20. 5. Self-conceit, ver. 21. 6. Perverting justice, for which, and the other instances of reigning wickedness among them, a great and general desolation is threatened, which should lay all waste (ver. 24, 25), and which should be effected by a foreign invasion (ver. 26—30), referring perhaps to the havoc made not long after by Sennacherib's army.

NOW will I sing to my well-beloved a song of my beloved touching his vineyard. My well-beloved hath a vineyard in a very fruitful hill: 2 And he fenced it, and gathered out the stones thereof, and planted it with the choicest vine, and built a tower in the midst of it, and also made a wine-press therein: and he looked that it should bring forth grapes, and it brought forth wild grapes. 3 And now, O inhabitants of Jerusalem, and men of Judah, judge, I pray you, betwixt me and my vineyard. 4 What could have been done more to my vineyard,

that I have not done in it? Wherefore, when I looked that it should bring forth grapes, brought it forth wild grapes? 5 And now go to; I will tell you what I will do to my vineyard: I will take away the hedge thereof, and it shall be eaten up; *and* break down the wall thereof, and it shall be trodden down: 6 And I will lay it waste: it shall not be pruned, nor digged; but there shall come up briers and thorns: I will also command the clouds that they rain no rain upon it. 7 For the vineyard of the LORD of hosts *is* the house of Israel, and the men of Judah his pleasant plant: and he looked for judgment, but behold oppression; for righteousness, but behold a cry.

See what variety of methods the great God takes to awaken sinners to repentance, by convincing them of sin, and showing them their misery and danger by reason of it. To this purport he speaks sometimes in plain terms and sometimes in parables, sometimes in prose and sometimes in verse, as here. "We have tried to *reason with you* (*ch.* i. 18); now let us put your case into a poem, inscribed to the honour of my well beloved." God the Father dictates it to the honour of Christ his well beloved Son, whom he has constituted Lord of the vineyard. The prophet sings it to the honour of Christ too, for he is his well beloved. The Old-Testament prophets were friends of the bridegroom. Christ is God's beloved Son and our beloved Saviour. Whatever is said or sung of the church must be intended to his praise, even that which (like this) tends to our shame. This parable was put into a song that it might be the more moving and affecting, might be the more easily learned and exactly remembered, and the better transmitted to posterity; and it is an exposition of the song of Moses (Deut. xxxii.), showing that what he then foretold was now fulfilled. Jerome says, Christ the well-beloved did in effect sing this mournful song when he beheld Jerusalem *and wept over it* (Luke xix. 41), and had reference to it in the parable of the vineyard (Matt. xxi. 33, &c.), only here the fault was in the vines, there in the husbandmen. Here we have,

I. The great things which God had done for the Jewish church and nation. When all the rest of the world lay in common, not cultivated by divine revelation, that was his vineyard, they were his peculiar people. He acknowledged them as his own, set them apart for himself. The soil they were planted in was extraordinary; it was *a very fruitful hill, the horn of the son of oil:* so it

29

is in the margin. There was plenty, a cornucopia; and there was dainty: they did there eat the fat and drink the sweet, and so were furnished with abundance of good things to honour God with in sacrifices and free-will offerings. The advantages of our situation will be brought into the account another day. Observe further what God did for this vineyard. 1. He fenced it, took it under his special protection, kept it night and day under his own eye, lest any should hurt it, *ch.* xxvii. 2, 3. If they had not themselves thrown down their fence, no inroad could have been made upon them, Ps. cxxv. 2; cxxi. 4. 2. He gathered the stones out of it, that, as nothing from without might damage it, so nothing within might obstruct its fruitfulness. He proffered his grace to take away the stony heart. 3. He planted it with the choicest vine, set up a pure religion among them, gave them a most excellent law, instituted ordinances very proper for the keeping up of their acquaintance with God, Jer. ii. 21. 4. He built a tower in the midst of it, either for defence against violence or for the dressers of the vineyard to lodge in; or rather it was for the owner of the vineyard to sit in, to take a view of the vines (Cant. vii. 12)—a summer-house. The temple was this tower, about which the priests lodged, and where God promised to meet his people, and gave them the tokens of his presence among them and pleasure in them. 5. He made a wine-press therein, set up his altar, to which the sacrifices, as the fruits of the vineyard, should be brought.

II. The disappointment of his just expectations from them: *He looked that it should bring forth grapes,* and a great deal of reason he had for that expectation. Note, God expects vineyard-fruit from those that enjoy vineyard-privileges, not leaves only, as Mark xi. 13. A bare profession, though ever so green, will not serve: there must be more than buds and blossoms. Good purposes and good beginnings are good things, but not enough; there must be fruit, a good heart and a good life, vineyard fruit, thoughts and affections, words and actions, agreeable to the Spirit, which is the fatness of the vineyard (Gal. v. 22, 23), *answerable to the ordinances,* which are the dressings of the vineyard, acceptable to God, the Lord of the vineyard, and fruit according to the season. Such fruit as this God expects from us, grapes, the fruit of the vine, with which they honour God and man (Judg. ix. 13); and his expectations are neither high nor hard, but righteous and very reasonable. Yet see how his expectations are frustrated: *It brought forth wild grapes;* not only no fruit at all, but bad fruit, worse than none, grapes of Sodom, Deut. xxxii. 32. 1. Wild grapes are the fruits of the corrupt nature, fruit according to the crab-stock, not according to the engrafted branch,

30

from the root of bitterness, Heb. xii. 15. Where grace does not work corruption will. 2. Wild grapes are hypocritical performances in religion, that look like grapes, but are sour or bitter, and are so far from being pleasing to God that they are provoking, as theirs mentioned in *ch.* i. 11. Counterfeit graces are wild grapes.

III. An appeal to themselves whether upon the whole matter God must not be justified and they condemned, *v.* 3, 4. And now the case is plainly stated: *O inhabitants of Jerusalem, and men of Judah! judge, I pray you, betwixt me and my vineyard.* This implies that God was blamed about them. There was a controversy between them and him; but the equity was so plain on his side that he could venture to put the decision of the controversy to their own consciences. " Let any inhabitant of Jerusalem, any man of Judah, that has but the use of his reason and a common sense of equity and justice, speak his mind impartially in this matter." Here is a challenge to any man to show, 1. Any instance wherein God had been wanting to them: *What could have been done more to my vineyard, that I have not done in it?* He speaks of the external means of fruitfulness, and such as might be expected from the dresser of a vineyard, from whom it is not required that he should change the nature of the vine. *What ought to have been done more?* so it may be read. They had every thing requisite for instruction and direction in their duty, for quickening them to it and putting them in mind of it. No inducements were wanting to persuade them to it, but all arguments were used that were proper to work either upon hope or fear; and they had all the opportunities they could desire for the performance of their duty, the new moons, and the sabbaths, and solemn feasts; they had the scriptures, the lively oracles, a standing ministry in the priests and Levites, besides what was extraordinary in the prophets. No nation had statutes and judgments so righteous. 2. Nor could any tolerable excuse be offered for their walking thus contrary to God. " Wherefore, what reason can be given why it should bring forth wild grapes, when I looked for grapes?" Note, The wickedness of those that profess religion, and enjoy the means of grace, is the most unreasonable unaccountable thing in the world, and the whole blame of it must lie upon the sinners themselves. " *If thou scornest, thou alone shalt bear it,* and shalt not have a word to say for thyself in the judgment of the great day." God will prove his own ways equal and the sinner's ways unequal.

IV. Their doom read, and a righteous sentence passed upon them for their bad conduct towards God (*v.* 5, 6): " *And now go to,* since nothing can be offered in excuse of the crime or arrest of the judgment, *I will tell you what I am now determined to do to my vineyard.* I will be vexed and troubled with it no more ; since it will be good for nothing, it *shall* be good for nothing ; in short, it shall cease to be a vineyard, and be turned into a wilderness : the church of the Jews shall be unchurched ; their charter shall be taken away, and they shall become *lo-ammi—not my people.*" 1. " They shall no longer be distinguished as a peculiar people, but be laid in common : *I will take away the hedge thereof,* and then it will soon be eaten up and become as bare as other ground." They mingled with the nations and therefore were justly scattered among them. 2. " They shall no longer be protected as God's people, but left exposed. God will not only suffer the wall to go to decay, but he will break it down, will remove all their defences from them, and then they will become an easy prey to their enemies, who have long waited for an opportunity to do them a mischief, and will now tread them down and trample upon them." 3. " They shall no longer have the face of a vineyard, the form and shape of a church and commonwealth, but shall be levelled and laid waste." This was fulfilled when *Jerusalem for their sakes was ploughed as a field,* Mic. iii. 12. 4. " No more pains shall be taken with them by magistrates or ministers, the dressers and keepers of their vineyard ; it shall not be pruned nor digged, but every thing shall run wild, and nothing shall come up but briers and thorns, the products of sin and the curse," Gen. iii. 18. When errors and corruptions, vice and immorality, go without check or control, no testimony borne against them, no rebuke given them or restraint put upon them, the vineyard is unpruned, is not dressed, or ridded ; and then it will soon be like the vineyard of the man void of understanding, all grown over with thorns. 5. " That which completes its woe is that the dews of heaven shall be withheld ; he that has the key of the clouds will command them that they rain no rain upon it, and that alone is sufficient to turn it into a desert." Note, God, in a way of righteous judgment, denies his grace to those that have long received it in vain. The sum of all is that those who would not bring forth good fruit should bring forth none. The curse of barrenness is the punishment of the sin of barrenness, as Mark xi. 14. This had its partial accomplishment in the destruction of Jerusalem by the Chaldeans, its full accomplishment in the final rejection of the Jews, and has its frequent accomplishment in the departure of God's Spirit from those persons who have long resisted him and striven against him, and the removal of his gospel from those places that have been long a reproach to it, while it has been an honour to them. It is no loss to God to lay his vineyard waste ; for he can, when he please, turn a wilderness into a

fruitful field ; and, when he does thus dismantle a vineyard, it is but as he did by the garden of Eden, which, when man had by sin forfeited his place in it, was soon levelled with common soil.

V. The explanation of this parable, or a key to it (*v.* 7), where we are told, 1. What is meant by the vineyard (it is *the house of Israel,* the body of the people, incorporated in one church and commonwealth), and what by the vines, the pleasant plants, the plants of God's pleasure, which he had been pleased in and delighted in doing good to ; they are *the men of Judah ;* these he had dealt graciously with, and from them he expected suitable returns. 2. What is meant by the grapes that were expected and the wild grapes that were produced : *He looked for judgment and righteousness,* that the people should be honest in all their dealings and the magistrates should strictly administer justice. This might reasonably be expected among a people that had such excellent laws and rules of justice given them (Deut. iv. 8) ; but the fact was quite otherwise ; instead of judgment there was the cruelty of the oppressors, and instead of righteousness the cry of the oppressed. Every thing was carried by clamour and noise, and not by equity and according to the merits of the cause. It is sad with a people when wickedness has usurped the place of judgment, Eccl. iii. 16. It is very sad with a soul when instead of the grapes of humility, meekness, patience, love, and contempt of the world, which God looks for, there are the wild grapes of pride, passion, discontent, malice, and contempt of God—instead of the grapes of praying and praising, the wild grapes of cursing and swearing, which are a great offence to God. Some of the ancients apply this to the Jews in Christ's time, among whom God looked for righteousness (that is, that they should receive and embrace Christ), but behold a cry, that cry, *Crucify him, crucify him.*

8 Woe unto them that join house to house, *that* lay field to field, till *there be* no place, that they may be placed alone in the midst of the earth ! 9 In mine ears *said* the Lord of hosts, Of a truth many houses shall be desolate, *even* great and fair, without inhabitant. 10 Yea, ten acres of vineyard shall yield one bath, and the seed of an homer shall yield an ephah. 11 Woe unto them that rise up early in the morning, *that* they may follow strong drink ; that continue until night, *till* wine inflame them ! 12 And the harp, and the viol, the tabret, and pipe, and wine, are in their feasts : but they regard

31

not the work of the LORD, neither consider the operation of his hands. 13 Therefore my people are gone into captivity, because *they have* no knowledge : and their honourable men *are* famished, and their multitude dried up with thirst. 14 Therefore hell hath enlarged herself, and opened her mouth without measure: and their glory, and their multitude, and their pomp, and he that rejoiceth, shall descend into it. 15 And the mean man shall be brought down, and the mighty man shall be humbled, and the eyes of the lofty shall be humbled: 16 But the LORD of hosts shall be exalted in judgment, and God that is holy shall be sanctified in righteousness. 17 Then shall the lambs feed after their manner, and the waste places of the fat ones shall strangers eat.

The world and the flesh are the two great enemies that we are in danger of being overpowered by; yet we are in no danger if we do not ourselves yield to them. Eagerness of the world, and indulgence of the flesh, are the two sins against which the prophet, in God's name, here denounces woes. These were sins which then abounded among the men of Judah, some of the wild grapes they brought forth (*v.* 4), and for which God threatens to bring ruin upon them. They are sins which we have all need to stand upon our guard against and dread the consequences of.

I. Here is a woe to those who set their hearts upon the wealth of the world, and place their happiness in that, and increase it to themselves by indirect and unlawful means (*v.* 8), who *join house to house and lay field to field, till there be no place,* no room for any body to live by them. If they could succeed, they would be placed alone in the midst of the earth, would monopolize possessions and preferments, and engross all profits and employments to themselves. Not that it is a sin for those who have a house and a field, if they have wherewithal, to purchase another ; but

1. Their fault is, (1.) That they are inordinate in their desires to enrich themselves, and make it their whole care and business to raise an estate, as if they had nothing to mind, nothing to seek, nothing to do, in this world, but that. They never know when they have enough, but the more they have the more they would have ; and, like the *daughters of the horseleech,* they *cry, Give, give.* They cannot enjoy what they have, nor do good with it, but are constantly contriving

32

and studying to make it more. They must have variety of houses, a winter-house, and a summer-house, and if another man's house or field lie convenient to theirs, as Naboth's vineyard to Ahab's, they must have that too, or they cannot be easy. (2.) That they are herein careless of others, nay and injurious to them. They would live so as to let nobody live but themselves. So that their insatiable covetings may be gratified, they care not what becomes of all about them, what encroachments they make upon their neighbours' rights, what hardships they put upon those that they have power over or advantage against, nor what base and wicked arts they use to heap up treasure to themselves. They would swell so big as to fill all space, and yet are still unsatisfied (Eccl. v. 10), as Alexander, who, when he fancied he had conquered the world, wept because he had not another world to conquer. *Deficiente terrâ, non impletur avaritia* —*If the whole earth were monopolized, avarice would thirst for more.* What ! *will you be placed alone in the midst of the earth ?* (so some read it) ; will you be so foolish as to desire it, when we have so much need of the service of others and so much comfort in their society ? Will you be so foolish as to expect that the *earth shall be forsaken for us* (Job xviii. 4), when it is by multitudes that the earth is to be replenished ? *An propter vos solos tanta terra creata est ?*— *Was the wide world created merely for you ?* Lyra.

2. That which is threatened as the punishment of this sin is that neither the houses nor the fields they were thus greedy of should turn to any account, *v.* 9, 10. God whispered it to the prophet in his ear, as he speaks in a like case (*ch.* xxii. 14) : *It was revealed in my ears by the Lord of hosts* (as God told Samuel a thing *in his ear,* 1 Sam. ix. 15) ; he thought he heard it still sounding in his ears ; but he proclaimed it, as he ought, *upon the house-tops,* Matt. x. 27. (1) That the houses they were so fond of should be untenanted, should stand long empty, and so should yield them no rent, and go out of repair : *Many houses shall be desolate,* the people that should dwell in them, being cut off by sword, famine, or pestilence, or carried into captivity ; or trade being dead, and poverty coming upon the country like an armed man, those that had been housekeepers were forced to become lodgers, or shift for themselves elsewhere. Even great and fair houses, that would invite tenants, and (there being a scarcity of tenants) might be taken at low rates, shall stand empty without inhabitants. God created not the earth in vain ; he *formed it to be inhabited, ch.* xlv. 18. But men's projects are often frustrated, and what they frame answers not the intention. We have a saying, That fools build houses for wise men to live in ; but sometimes, as the event proves, they

are built for no man to live in. God has many ways to empty the most populous cities. (2.) That the fields they were so fond of should be unfruitful (*v.* 10) : *Ten acres of vineyard shall yield* only such a quantity of grapes as will make but *one bath* of wine (which was about eight gallons), *and the seed of a homer,* a bushel's sowing of ground, shall yield but an ephah, which was the tenth part of a homer ; so that through the barrenness of the ground, or the unseasonableness of the weather, they should not have more than a tenth part of their seed again. Note, Those that set their hearts upon the world will justly be disappointed in their expectations from it.

II. Here is a woe to those that dote upon the pleasures and delights of sense, *v.* 11, 12. Sensuality ruins men as certainly as worldliness and oppression. As Christ pronounced a woe against those that are rich, so also against those that laugh now and are full (Luke vi. 24, 25), and fare sumptuously, Luke xvi. 19. Observe,

1. Who the sinners are against whom this woe is denounced. (1.) They are such as are given to drink ; they make drinking their business, have their hearts upon it, and overcharge themselves with it. They rise early to follow strong drink, as husbandmen and tradesmen do to follow their employments; as if they were afraid of losing time from that which is the greatest misspending of time. Whereas commonly those that are drunken are drunken in the night, when they have despatched the business of the day, these neglect business, abandon it, and give up themselves to the service of the flesh ; for they sit at their cups all day, *and continue till night, till wine inflame them*—inflame their lusts (chambering and wantonness follow upon rioting and drunkenness)—inflame their passions ; for who but such have *contentions and wounds without cause?* Prov. xxiii. 29—35. They make a perfect trade of drinking ; nor do they seek the shelter of the night for this work of darkness, as men ashamed of it, but *count it a pleasure to riot in the day-time.* See 2 Pet. ii. 13. (2.) They are such as are given to mirth. They have their feasts, and they are so merrily disposed that they cannot dine or sup without music, musical instruments of all sorts, like David (Amos vi. 5), like Solomon (Eccl. ii. 8); *the harp and the viol, the tabret and pipe,* must accompany the wine, that every sense may be gratified to a nicety; they *take the timbrel and harp,* Job xxi. 12. The use of music is lawful in itself; but when it is excessive, when we set our hearts upon it, misspend time in it, so that it crowds our spiritual and divine pleasures and draws away the heart from God, then it turns into sin to us. (3.) They are such as never give their mind to any thing that is serious : *They regard not the work of the Lord;* they observe not his power, wisdom, and good-

ness, in those creatures which they abuse and subject to vanity, nor the bounty of his providence in giving them those good things which they make the food and fuel of their lusts. God's judgments have already seized them, and they are under the tokens of his displeasure, but they regard not; they consider not the hand of God in all these things; his hand is lifted up, but they will not see, because they will not disturb themselves in their pleasures nor think what God is doing with them.

2. What the judgments are which are denounced against them, and in part executed. It is here foretold, (1.) That they should be dislodged; the land should spue out these drunkards (*v.* 13): *My people* (so they called themselves, and were proud of it) have therefore *gone into captivity,* are as sure to go as if they were gone already, *because they have no knowledge :* how should they have knowledge when by their excessive drinking they make sots and fools of themselves ? They set up for wits ; but because they regard not God's controversy with them, nor take any care to make their peace with him, they may truly be said to have no knowledge; and the reason is because they will have none ; they are inconsiderate and wilful, and are therefore destroyed for lack of knowledge. (2.) That they should be impoverished, and come to want that which they had wasted and abused to excess : Even *their glory are men of famine,* subject to it and slain by it ; and *their multitude are dried up with thirst.* Both the great men and the common people are ready to perish for want of bread and water. This is the effect of the failure of the corn (*v.* 10), for *the king himself is served of the field,* Eccl. v. 9. And when the vintage fails the drunkards are called upon to weep, because *the new wine is cut off from their mouth* (Joel i. 5), and not so much because now they want it as because when they had it they abused it. It is just with God to make men want that for necessity which they have abused to excess. (3.) That multitudes should be cut off by famine and sword (*v.* 14) : *Therefore hell has enlarged herself.* Tophet, the common burying-place, proves too little ; so many are there to be buried that they shall be forced to enlarge it. The grave has opened her mouth without measure, *never saying, It is enough,* Prov. xxx. 15, 16. It may be understood of the place of the damned ; luxury and sensuality fill those regions of darkness and horror; there those are tormented who made a god of their belly, Luke xvi. 25 ; Phil. iii. 19. (4.) That they should be humbled and abased, and all their honours laid in the dust. This will be done effectually by death and the grave : *Their glory shall descend,* not only to the earth, but into it ; it shall not *descend after them* (Ps. xlix. 17), to stand

33

them in any stead on the other side death, but it shall die and be buried with them—poor glory, which will thus wither! Did they glory in their numbers? Their multitude shall go down to the pit, Ezek. xxxi. 18; xxxii. 32. Did they glory in the figure they made? Their pomp shall be at an end; their shouts with which they triumphed, and were attended. Did they glory in their mirth? Death will turn it into mourning; he that rejoices and revels, and never knows what it is to be serious, shall go thither where there are weeping and wailing. Thus the mean man and the mighty man meet together in the grave and under mortifying judgments. Let a man be ever so high, death will bring him low—ever so mean, death will bring him lower, in the prospect of which the eyes of the lofty should now be humbled, v. 15. It becomes those to look low that must shortly be laid low.

3. What the fruit of these judgments shall be.

(1.) God shall be glorified, v. 16. He that is the Lord of hosts, and the holy God, shall be exalted and sanctified in the judgment and righteousness of these dispensations. His justice must be owned in bringing those low that exalted themselves; and herein he is glorified, [1.] As a God of irresistible power. He will herein be exalted as the Lord of hosts, that is able to break the strongest, humble the proudest, and tame the most unruly. Power is not exalted but in judgment. It is the honour of God that, though he has a mighty arm, yet *judgment and justice are* always *the habitation of his throne,* Ps. lxxxix. 13, 14. [2.] As a God of unspotted purity. He that is holy, infinitely holy, shall be sanctified (that is, shall be owned and declared to be holy) in the righteous punishment of proud men. Note, When proud men are humbled the great God is honoured, and ought to be honoured by us.

(2.) Good people shall be relieved and succoured (v. 17): *Then shall the lambs feed after their manner;* the meek ones of the earth, who followed the Lamb, who were persecuted and put into fear by those proud oppressors, shall feed quietly, feed in the green pastures, and there shall be none to make them afraid. See Ezek. xxxiv. 14. When the enemies of the church are cut off then have the churches rest. *They shall feed at their pleasure;* so some read it. *Blessed are the meek, for they shall inherit the earth,* and delight themselves in abundant peace. *They shall feed according to their order or capacity* (so others read it), as they are able to hear the word, that bread of life.

(3.) The country shall be laid waste, and become a prey to the neighbours: The *waste places of the fat ones,* the possessions of those rich men that lived at their ease, shall be eaten by strangers that were nothing akin to them. In the captivity the

34

poor of the land were left for *vine-dressers and husbandmen* (2 Kings xxv. 12); these were the lambs that fed in the pastures of the fat ones, which were laid in common for strangers to eat. When the church of the Jews, those fat ones, was laid waste, their privileges were transferred to the Gentiles, who had been long strangers, and the lambs of Christ's flock were welcome to them.

18 Woe unto them that draw iniquity with cords of vanity, and sin as it were with a cart rope: 19 That say, Let him make speed, *and* hasten his work, that we may see *it :* and let the counsel of the Holy One of Israel draw nigh and come, that we may know *it!* 20 Woe unto them that call evil good, and good evil; that put darkness for light, and light for darkness; that put bitter for sweet, and sweet for bitter! 21 Woe unto *them that are* wise in their own eyes, and prudent in their own sight! 22 Woe unto *them that are* mighty to drink wine, and men of strength to mingle strong drink: 23 Which justify the wicked for reward, and take away the righteousness of the righteous from him! 24 Therefore as the fire devoureth the stubble, and the flame consumeth the chaff, *so* their root shall be as rottenness, and their blossom shall go up as dust : because they have cast away the law of the LORD of hosts, and despised the word of the Holy One of Israel. 25 Therefore is the anger of the LORD kindled against his people, and he hath stretched forth his hand against them, and hath smitten them : and the hills did tremble, and their carcases *were* torn in the midst of the streets. For all this his anger is not turned away, but his hand *is* stretched out still. 26 And he will lift up an ensign to the nations from far, and will hiss unto them from the end of the earth : and, behold, they shall come with speed swiftly : 27 None shall be weary nor stumble among them; none shall slumber nor sleep; neither shall the girdle of their loins be loosed, nor the latchet of their shoes be broken : 28 Whose arrows *are* sharp, and all their bows bent, their horses' hoofs shall be counted like

flint, and their wheels like a whirlwind: 29 Their roaring *shall be* like a lion, they shall roar like young lions : yea, they shall roar, and lay hold of the prey, and shall carry *it* away safe, and none shall deliver *it.* 30 And in that day they shall roar against them like the roaring of the sea : and if *one* look unto the land, behold darkness *and* sorrow, and the light is darkened in the heavens thereof.

Here are, I. Sins described which will bring judgments upon a people : and this perhaps is not only a charge drawn up against the men of Judah who lived at that time, and the particular articles of that charge, though it may relate primarily to them, but is rather intended for warning to all people, in all ages, to take heed of these sins, as destructive both to particular persons and to communities, and exposing men to God's wrath and his righteous judgments. Those are here said to be in a woeful condition,

1. Who are eagerly set upon sin, and violent in their sinful pursuits (*v.* 18), who *draw iniquity with cords of vanity*, who take as much pains to sin as the cattle do that draw in a team, who put themselves to the stretch for the gratifying of their inordinate appetites, and, to humour a base lust, offer violence to nature itself. They think themselves as sure of compassing their wicked project as if they were pulling it towards them with strong cart-ropes ; but they will find themselves disappointed, for they will prove cords of vanity, which will break when they come to any stress. For *the righteous Lord will cut in sunder the cords of the wicked*, Ps. cxxix. 4 ; Job iv. 8 ; Prov. xxii. 8. They are by long custom and confirmed habits so hardened in sin that they cannot get clear of it. Those that sin through infirmity are drawn away by sin ; those that sin presumptuously draw iniquity to them, in spite of the oppositions of Providence and the checks of conscience. Some by sin understand the punishment of sin : they pull God's judgments upon their own heads, as it were, with cart-ropes.

2. Who set the justice of God at defiance, and challenge the Almighty to do his worst (*v.* 19): *They say, Let him make speed, and hasten his work ;* this is the same language with that of the scoffers of the last days, who say, *Where is the promise of his coming?* and therefore it is that, like them, they *draw iniquity with cords of vanity*, are violent and daring in sin, and walk after their own lusts, 2 Pet. iii. 3, 4. (1.) They ridicule the prophets, and banter them. It is in scorn that they call God *the Holy One of Israel*, because the prophets used with great veneration to

call him so. (2.) They will not believe the revelation of God's wrath from heaven against their ungodliness and unrighteousness ; unless they see it executed, they will not know it, as if the curse were *brutum fulmen—a mere flash*, and all the threatenings of the word bugbears to frighten fools and children. (3.) If God should appear against them, as he has threatened, yet they think themselves able to make their part good with him, and provoke him to jealousy, as if they were stronger than he, 1 Cor. x. 22. " We have heard his word, but it is all talk ; let him hasten his work, we shall shift for ourselves well enough." Note, Those that wilfully persist in sin consider not the power of God's anger.

3. Who confound and overthrow the distinctions between moral good and evil, *who call evil good and good evil* (*v.* 20), who not only live in the omission of that which is good, but condemn it, argue against it, and, because they will not practise it themselves, run it down in others, and fasten invidious epithets upon it—not only do that which is evil, but justify it, and applaud it, and recommend it to others as safe and good. Note, (1.) Virtue and piety are good, for they are light and sweet, they are pleasant and right ; but sin and wickedness are evil : they are darkness, all the fruit of ignorance and mistake, and will be bitterness in the latter end. (2.) Those do a great deal of wrong to God, and religion, and conscience, to their own souls, and to the souls of others, who misrepresent these, and put false colours upon them—who call drunkenness good fellowship, and covetousness good husbandry, and, when they persecute the people of God, think they do him good service—and, on the other hand, who call seriousness illnature, and sober singularity ill-breeding, who say all manner of evil falsely concerning the ways of godliness, and do what they can to form in men's minds prejudices against them, and this in defiance of evidence as plain and convincing as that of sense, by which we distinguish, beyond contradiction, between light and darkness, and between that which to the taste is sweet and that which is bitter.

4. Who though they are guilty of such gross mistakes as these have a great opinion of their own judgments, and value themselves mightily upon their understanding (*v.* 21): They are *wise in their own eyes ;* they think themselves able to disprove and baffle the reproofs and convictions of God's word, and to evade and elude both the searches and the reaches of his judgments ; they think they can outwit Infinite Wisdom and countermine Providence itself. Or it may be taken more generally : God resists the proud, those particularly who are conceited of their own wisdom and lean to their own understanding ; such must become fools, that they may be truly wise, or else, at their end.

they shall appear to be fools before all the world.

5. Who glory in it as a great accomplishment that they are able to bear a great deal of strong liquor without being overcome by it (*v.* 22), *who are mighty to drink wine,* and use their strength and vigour, not in the service of their country, but in the service of their lusts. Let drunkards know from this scripture that, (1.) They ungratefully abuse their bodily strength, which God has given them for good purposes, and by degrees cannot but weaken it. (2.) It will not excuse them from the guilt of drunkenness that they can drink hard and yet keep their feet. (3.) Those who boast of their drinking down others glory in their shame. (4.) How light soever men make of their drunkenness, it is a sin which will certainly lay them open to the wrath and curse of God.

6. Who, as judges, pervert justice, and go counter to all the rules of equity, *v.* 23. This follows upon the former; they *drink and forget the law* (Prov. xxxi. 5), and *err through wine* (ch. xxviii. 7), and take bribes, that they may have wherewithal to maintain their luxury. They *justify the wicked for reward,* and find some pretence or other to clear him from his guilt and shelter him from punishment; and they condemn the innocent, and *take away their righteousness from them,* that is, overrule their pleas, deprive them of the means of clearing up their innocency, and give judgment against them. In causes between man and man, might and money would at any time prevail against right and justice; and he who was ever so plainly in the wrong would with a small bribe carry the cause and recover costs. In criminal causes, though the prisoner ever so plainly appeared to be guilty, yet for a reward they would acquit him; if he were innocent, yet if he did not fee them well, nay, if they were feed by the malicious prosecutor, or if they themselves had spleen against him, they would condemn him.

II. The judgments described, which these sins would bring upon them. Let not those expect to live easily who live thus wickedly; for the righteous God will take vengeance, *v.* 24—30. Here we may observe,

1. How complete this ruin will be, and how necessarily and unavoidably it will follow upon their sins. He had compared this people to a vine (*v.* 7), well fixed, and which, it was hoped, would be flourishing and fruitful; but the grace of God towards it was received in vain, and then the root became rottenness, being dried up from beneath, and the blossom would of course blow off as dust, as a light and worthless thing, Job xviii. 16. Sin weakens the strength, the root, of a people, so that they are easily rooted up; it defaces the beauty, the blossoms, of a people, and takes away the hopes of fruit. The sin of unfruit-

fulness is punished with the plague of unfruitfulness. Sinners make themselves as stubble and chaff, combustible matter, proper fuel to the fire of God's wrath, which then of course devours and consumes them, *as the fire devours the stubble,* and nobody can hinder it, or cares to hinder it. Chaff is consumed, unhelped and unpitied.

2. How just the ruin will be: *Because they have cast away the law of the Lord of hosts,* and would not have him to reign over them; and, as the law of Moses was rejected and thrown off, so *the word of the Holy One of Israel* by his servants the prophets, putting them in mind of his law and calling them to obedience, was despised and disregarded. God does not reject men for every transgression of his law and word; but, when his word is despised and his law cast away, what can they expect but that God should utterly abandon them?

3. Whence this ruin should come (*v.* 25): it is destruction from the Almighty. (1.) The justice of God appoints it; for that is *the anger of the Lord* which is *kindled against his people,* his necessary vindication of the honour of his holiness and authority. (2.) The power of God effects it: *He has stretched forth his hand against them.* That hand which had many a time been stretched out for them against their enemies is now stretched out against them at full length and in its full vigour; and *who knows the power of his anger?* Whether they are sensible of it or no, it is God that has smitten them, has blasted their vine and made it wither.

4. The consequences and continuance of this ruin. When God comes forth in wrath against a people the hills tremble, fear seizes even their great men, who are strong and high, the earth shakes under men and is ready to sink; and as this feels dreadful (what does more so than an earthquake?) so what sight can be more frightful than the carcases of men torn with dogs, or thrown *as dung* (so the margin reads it) *in the midst of the streets?* This intimates that great multitudes should be slain, not only soldiers in the field of battle, but the inhabitants of their cities put to the sword in cold blood, and that the survivors should neither have hands nor hearts to bury them. This is very dreadful, and yet such is the merit of sin that, *for all this, God's anger is not turned away;* that fire will burn as long as there remains any of the stubble and chaff to be fuel for it; *and his hand,* which he stretched forth against his people to smite them, because they do not by prayer take hold of it, nor by reformation submit themselves to it, *is stretched out still.*

5. The instruments that should be employed in bringing this ruin upon them: it should be done by the incursions of a foreign enemy, that should lay all waste. No particular enemy is named, and there-

fore we are to take it as a prediction of all the several judgments of this kind which God brought upon the Jews, Sennacherib's invasion soon after, and the destruction of Jerusalem by the Chaldeans first and at last by the Romans; and I think it is to be looked upon also as a threatening of the like desolation of those countries which harbour and countenance those sins mentioned in the foregoing verses; it is an exposition of those woes. When God designs the ruin of a provoking people,

(1.) He can send a great way off for instruments to be employed in effecting it; he can raise forces from afar, and summon them from the end of the earth to attend his service, *v.* 26. Those who know him not are made use of to fulfil his counsel, when, by reason of their distance, they can scarcely be supposed to have any ends of their own to serve. If God set up his standard, he can incline men's hearts to enlist themselves under it, though perhaps they know not why or wherefore. When the Lord of hosts is pleased to make a general muster of the forces he has at his command, he has a great army in an instant, Joel ii. 2, 11. He needs not sound a trumpet, nor beat a drum, to give them notice or to animate them; no, he does but hiss to them, or rather whistle to them, and that is enough; they hear that, and that puts courage into them. Note, God has all the creatures at his beck.

(2.) He can make them come into the service with incredible expedition: *Behold, they shall come with speed swiftly.* Note, [1.] Those who will do God's work must not loiter, must not linger, nor shall they when his time has come. [2.] Those who defy God's judgments will be ashamed of their insolence when it is too late; they said scornfully (*v.* 19), *Let him make speed, let him hasten his work*, and they shall find, to their terror and confusion, that he will; *in one hour has the judgment come.*

(3.) He can carry them on in the service with amazing forwardness and fury. This is described here in very elegant and lofty expressions, *v.* 27—30. [1.] Though their marches be very long, yet *none among them shall be weary;* so desirous shall they be to engage that they shall forget their weariness, and make no complaints of it. [2.] Though the way be rough, and perhaps embarrassed by the usual policies of war, yet none among them shall *stumble*, but all the difficulties in their way shall easily be got over. [3.] Though they be forced to keep constant watch, yet *none shall slumber nor sleep*, so intent shall they be upon their work, in prospect of having the plunder of the city for their pains. [4.] They shall not desire any rest or relaxation; they shall not put off their clothes, nor *loose the girdle of their loins*, but shall always have their belts on and swords by their sides. [5.] They shall not meet with the least hindrance to retard their march or

oblige them to halt; not a *latchet of their shoes shall be broken* which they must stay to mend, as Josh. ix. 13. [6.] Their arms and ammunition shall all be fixed, and in good posture; *their arrows sharp*, to wound deep, *and all their bows bent*, none unstrung, for they expect to be soon in action. [7.] Their horses and chariots of war shall all be fit for service; their horses so strong, so hardy, that *their hoofs shall be like flint*, far from being beaten, or made tender, by their long march; and the wheels of their chariots not broken, or battered, or out of repair, but swift *like a whirlwind*, turning round so strongly upon their axle-trees. [8.] All the soldiers shall be bold and daring (*v.* 29): *Their roaring*, or shouting, before a battle, *shall be like a lion*, who with his roaring animates himself, and terrifies all about him. Those who would not hear the voice of God speaking to them by his prophets, but stopped their ears against their charms, shall be made to hear the voice of their enemies roaring against them and shall not be able to turn a deaf ear to it. *They shall roar like the roaring of the sea* in a storm; it roars and threatens to swallow up, as the lion roars and threatens to tear in pieces. [9.] There shall not be the least prospect of relief or succour. The enemy shall come in like a flood, and there shall be none to lift up a standard against him. He shall seize the prey, and none shall deliver it, none shall be able to deliver it, nay, none shall so much as dare to attempt the deliverance of it, but shall give it up for lost. Let the distressed look which way they will, every thing appears dismal; for, if God frown upon us, how can any creature smile? *First*, Look round to the earth, to that land that used to be a land of light and the joy of the whole earth, and *behold darkness and sorrow*, all frightful, all mournful, nothing hopeful. *Secondly*, Look up to heaven, and there the light is darkened, where one would expect to have found it. If the light is darkened in the heavens, how great is that darkness! If God hide his face, no marvel the heavens hide theirs and appear gloomy, Job xxxiv. 29. It is our wisdom, by keeping a good conscience, to keep all clear between us and heaven, that we may have light from above even when clouds and darkness are round about us.

CHAP. VI.

Hitherto, it should seem, Isaiah had prophesied as a candidate, having only a virtual and tacit commission; but here we have him (if I may so speak) solemnly ordained and set apart to the prophetic office by a more express or explicit commission, as his work grew more upon his hands: or perhaps, having seen little success of his ministry, he began to think of giving it up; and therefore God saw fit to renew his commission here in this chapter, in such a manner as might excite and encourage his zeal and industry in the execution of it, though he seemed to labour in vain. In this chapter we have, I. A very awful vision which Isaiah saw of the glory of God (ver. 1—4), the terror it put him into (ver. 5), and the relief given him against that terror by an assurance of the pardon of his sins, ver. 6, 7. II. A very awful commission which Isaiah received to go as a prophet, in God's name (ver. 8), by his preaching to harden the impenitent in sin and ripen them for ruin (ver. 9—12), yet with a reservation of mercy for a remnant, ver. 13. And it was as to an evangelical prophet that these things were shown him and said to him.

IN the year that king Uzziah died I saw also the LORD sitting upon a throne, high and lifted up, and his train filled the temple. 2 Above it stood the seraphims: each one had six wings; with twain he covered his face, and with twain he covered his feet, and with twain he did fly. 3 And one cried unto another, and said, Holy, holy, holy, *is* the LORD of hosts: the whole earth *is* full of his glory. 4 And the posts of the door moved at the voice of him that cried, and the house was filled with smoke.

The vision which Isaiah saw when he was, as is said of Samuel, *established to be a prophet of the Lord* (1 Sam. iii. 20), was intended, 1. To confirm his faith, that he might himself be abundantly satisfied of the truth of those things which should afterwards be made known to him. Thus God opened the communications of himself to him; but such visions needed not to be afterwards repeated upon every revelation. Thus God appeared at first as a God of glory to Abraham (Acts vii. 2), and to Moses, Exod. iii. 2. Ezekiel's prophecies, and St. John's, begin with visions of the divine glory. 2. To work upon his affections, that he might be possessed with such a reverence of God as would both quicken him and fix him to his service. Those who are to teach others the knowledge of God ought to be well acquainted with him themselves.

The vision is dated, for the greater certainty of it. It was *in the year that king Uzziah died*, who had reigned, for the most part, as prosperously and well as any of the kings of Judah, and reigned very long, above fifty years. About the time that he died Isaiah saw this vision of God upon a throne; for when the breath of princes goes forth, and they return to their earth, this is our comfort, that *the Lord shall reign for ever*, Ps. cxlvi. 3, 4, 10. Israel's king dies, but Israel's God still lives. From the mortality of great and good men we should take occasion to look up with an eye of faith to the King eternal, immortal. King Uzziah died under a cloud, for he was shut up as a leper till the day of his death. As the lives of princes have their periods, so their glory is often eclipsed; but, as God is everliving, so his glory is everlasting. King Uzziah dies in an hospital, but the King of kings still sits upon his throne.

What the prophet here saw is revealed to us, that we, mixing faith with that revelation, may in it, as in a glass, behold the glory of the Lord; let us turn aside therefore, and see this great sight with humble reverence.

38

I. See God upon his throne, and that throne *high and lifted up*, not only above other thrones, as it transcends them, but over other thrones, as it rules and commands them. Isaiah saw not *Jehovah*—the essence of God (no man has seen that, or can see it), but *Adonai*—his dominion. He saw the Lord Jesus; so this vision is explained John xii. 41, that Isaiah now saw Christ's glory and spoke of him, which is an incontestable proof of the divinity of our Saviour. He it is who when, after his resurrection, he sat down on the right hand of God, did but sit down where he was before, John xvii. 5. See the rest of the Eternal Mind: Isaiah *saw the Lord sitting*, Ps. xxix. 10. See the sovereignty of the Eternal Monarch: he sits *upon a throne*—a throne of glory, before which we must worship,—a throne of government, under which we must be subject,—and a throne of grace, to which we may come boldly. This throne is high, and lifted up above all competition and contradiction.

II. See his temple, his church on earth, filled with the manifestations of his glory. His throne being erected at the door of the temple (as princes sat in judgment at the gates), *his train*, the skirts of his robes, *filled the temple*, the whole world (for it is all God's temple, and, as the heaven is his throne, so the earth is his footstool), or rather the church, which is filled, enriched, and beautified with the tokens of God's special presence.

III. See the bright and blessed attendants on his throne, in and by whom his glory is celebrated and his government served (v. 2): *Above the throne*, as it were hovering about it, or nigh to the throne, bowing before it, with an eye to it, *the seraphim stood*, the holy angels, who are called *seraphim—burners;* for he *makes his ministers a flaming fire*, Ps. civ. 4. They burn in love to God, and zeal for his glory and against sin, and he makes use of them as instruments of his wrath when he is a consuming fire to his enemies. Whether they were only two or four, or (as I rather think) an *innumerable company of angels*, that Isaiah saw, is uncertain; see Dan. vii. 10. Note, It is the glory of the angels that they are seraphim, have heat proportionable to their light, have abundance, not only of divine knowledge, but of holy love. Special notice is taken of their wings (and of no other part of their appearance), because of the use they made of them, which is designed for instruction to us. They had *each of them six wings*, not stretched upwards (as those whom Ezekiel saw, ch. i. 11), but, 1. Four were made use of for covering, as the wings of a fowl, sitting, are; with the two upper wings, next the head, they covered their faces, and with the two lowest wings they covered their feet, or lower parts. This bespeaks their great humility and reverence in their attendance upon God, for he is greatly feared in *the assembly of those saints*, Ps. lxxxix. 7. They not only cover their feet, those members of the body which are less honourable (1 Cor. xii. 23), but even their faces. Though angels' faces, doubtless, are much fairer than those of the children of men (Acts vi. 15), yet, in the presence of God, they cover them, because they cannot bear the dazzling lustre of the divine glory, and because, being conscious of an infinite distance from the divine perfection, they are ashamed to show their faces before the holy God, who *charges even his angels with folly* if they should offer to vie with him, Job iv. 18. If angels be thus reverent in their attendance on God, with what godly fear should we approach his throne! Else we do not the will of God as the angels do it. Yet Moses, when he went into the mount with God, took the veil from off his face. See 2 Cor. iii. 18. 2. Two were made use of for flight; when they are sent on God's errands they fly swiftly (Dan. ix. 21), more swiftly with their own wings than if they flew on the wings of the wind. This teaches us to do the work of God with cheerfulness and expedition. Do angels come upon the wing from heaven to earth, to minister for our good, and shall not we soar upon the wing from earth to heaven, to share with them in their glory? Luke xx. 36.

IV. Hear the anthem, or song of praise, which the angels sing to the honour of him that sits on the throne, *v.* 3. Observe,

1. How this song was sung. With zeal and fervency—*they cried* aloud; and with unanimity—*they cried one to another*, or one with another; they sang alternately, but in concert, and without the least jarring voice to interrupt the harmony.

2. What the song was; it is the same with that which is sung by the four living creatures, Rev. iv. 8. Note, Praising God always was, and will be to eternity, the work of heaven, and the constant employment of blessed spirits above, Ps. lxxxiv. 4. Note further, The church above is the same in its praises; there is no change of times or notes there. Two things the seraphim here give God the praise of:—

(1.) His infinite perfections in himself. Here is one of his most glorious titles praised: he is *the Lord of hosts*, of their hosts, of all hosts; and one of his most glorious attributes, his holiness, without which his being the Lord of hosts (or, as it is in the parallel place, Rev. iv. 8, *the Lord God Almighty*) could not be so much as it is the matter of our joy and praise; for power, without purity to guide it, would be a terror to mankind. None of all the divine attributes is so celebrated in scripture as this is. God's power was spoken twice (Ps. lxii. 11), but his holiness thrice, *Holy, holy, holy.* This bespeaks, [1.] The zeal and fervency of the angels in praising God; they even want words to express themselves, and therefore repeat the same again. [2.] The particular pleasure they take in contemplating the holiness of God; this is a subject they love to dwell upon, to harp upon, and are loth to leave. [3.] The superlative excellency of God's holiness, above that of the purest creatures. He is holy, thrice holy, infinitely holy, originally, perfectly, and eternally so. [4.] It may refer to the three persons in the Godhead, Holy Father, Holy Son, and Holy Spirit (for it follows, *v.* 8, *Who will go for us?*) or perhaps to that *which was, and is, and is to come;* for that title of God's honour is added to this song, Rev. iv. 8. Some make the angels here to applaud the equity of that sentence which God was now about to pronounce upon the Jewish nation. Herein he was, and is, and will be, holy; his ways are equal.

(2.) The manifestation of these to the children of men: *The earth is full of his glory*, of the glory of his power and purity; for he is holy in all his works, Ps. cxlv. 17. The Jews thought the glory of God should be confined to their land; but it is here intimated that in gospel times (which are pointed to in this chapter) the glory of God should fill all the earth, the glory of his holiness, which is indeed the glory of all his other attributes; this then *filled the temple* (*v.* 1), but, in the latter days, the earth shall be full of it.

V. Observe the marks and tokens of terror with which the temple was filled, upon this vision of the divine glory, *v.* 4. 1. The house was *shaken:* not only the door, but even *the posts of the door*, which were firmly fixed, *moved at the voice of him that cried*, at the voice of God, who called to judgment (Ps. l. 4), at the voice of the angel, who praised him. There are voices in heaven sufficient to drown all the noises of the many waters in this lower world, Ps. xciii. 3, 4. This violent concussion of the temple was an indication of God's wrath and displeasure against the people for their sins; it was an earnest of the destruction of it and the city by the Babylonians first, and afterwards by the Romans; and it was designed to strike an awe upon us. Shall walls and posts tremble before God, and shall not we tremble? 2. The house was *darkened;* it was *filled with smoke*, which was as a *cloud* spread upon *the face of his throne* (Job xxvi. 9); we cannot take a full view of it, nor order our speech concerning it, by reason of darkness. In the temple above there will be no smoke, but every thing will be seen clearly. There God dwells in light; here he *makes darkness his pavilion*, 2 Chron. vi. 1.

5 Then said I, Woe *is* me! for I am undone; because I *am* a man of unclean lips, and I dwell in the midst of a people of unclean lips: for mine

39

eyes have seen the King, the LORD of hosts. 6 Then flew one of the seraphims unto me, having a live coal in his hand, *which* he had taken with the tongs from off the altar : 7 And he laid *it* upon my mouth, and said, Lo, this hath touched thy lips; and thine iniquity is taken away, and thy sin purged. 8 Also I heard the voice of the LORD, saying, Whom shall I send, and who will go for us? Then said I, Here *am* I ; send me.

Our curiosity would lead us to enquire further concerning the seraphim, their songs, and their services; but here we leave them, and must attend to what passed between God and his prophet. *Secret things belong not to us,* the secret things of the world of angels, but things revealed to and by the prophets, which concern the administration of God's kingdom among men. Now here we have,

I. The consternation that the prophet was put into by the vision which he saw of the glory of God (*v.* 5): *Then said I, Woe is me!* I should have said, " Blessed art thou, who hast been thus highly favoured, highly honoured, and dignified, for a time, with the privilege of those glorious beings that *always behold the face of our Father.* Blessed were those eyes which saw the Lord sitting on his throne, and those ears which heard the angels' praises." And, one would think, he should have said, " Happy am I, for ever happy; nothing now shall trouble me, nothing make me blush or tremble;" but, on the contrary, he cries out, " *Woe is me! for I am undone.*· Alas for me ! I am a gone man; *I shall surely die* (Judges xiii. 22 ; vi. 22); I am silenced; I am struck dumb, struck dead." Thus Daniel, when he heard the words of the angel, *became dumb,* and there was *no strength, no breath, left in him,* Dan. x. 15, 17. Observe,

1. What the prophet reflected upon in himself which terrified him : " *I am undone* if God deal with me in strict justice, for I have made myself obnoxious to his displeasure, *because I am a man of unclean lips.*" Some think he refers particularly to some rash word he had spoken, or to his sinful silence in not reproving sin with the boldness and freedom that were necessary—a sin which God's ministers have too much cause to charge themselves with, and to blush at the remembrance of. But it may be taken more generally : *I am a sinner;* particularly, *I have offended in word;* and who is there that hath not? Jam. iii. 2. We all have reason to bewail it before the Lord, (1.) That we are of unclean lips ourselves; our lips are not consecrated to God; he has not had the *first-fruits of our lips* (Heb. xiii. 15), and therefore they are

40

counted common and unclean, *uncircumcised lips,* Exod. vi. 30. Nay, they have been polluted with sin. We have spoken the language of an unclean heart, that evil communication which corrupts good manners, and whereby many have been defiled. We are unworthy and unmeet to take God's name into our lips. With what a pure lip did the angels praise God!·" But," says the prophet, " I cannot praise him so, for *I am a man of unclean lips.*" The best men in the world have reason to be ashamed of themselves, and the best of their services, when they come into comparison with the holy angels. The angels had celebrated the purity and holiness of God; and therefore the prophet, when he reflects upon sin, calls it *uncleanness;* for the sinfulness of sin is its contrariety to the holy nature of God, and upon that account especially it should appear both hateful and frightful to us. The inpurity of our lips ought to be the grief of our souls, for by our words we shall be justified or condemned (2.) That we dwell among those who are so too. We have reason to lament not only that we ourselves are polluted, but that the nature and race of mankind are so; the disease is hereditary and epidemic, which is so far from lessening our guilt that it should rather increase our grief, especially considering that we have not done what we might have done for the cleansing of the pollution of other people's lips; nay, we have rather learned their way and spoken their language, as Joseph in Egypt learned the courtier's oath, Gen. xlii. 16. " *I dwell in the midst of a people* who by their impudent sinnings are pulling down desolating judgments upon the land, which I, who am a sinner too, may justly expect to be involved in."

2. What gave occasion for these sad reflections at this time : *My eyes have seen the King, the Lord of hosts.* He saw God's sovereignty to be incontestable—he is the King; and his power irresistible—he is the Lord of hosts. These are comfortable truths to God's people, and yet they ought to strike an awe upon us. Note, A believing sight of God's glorious majesty should affect us all with reverence and godly fear. We have reason to be abased in the sense of that infinite distance that there is between us and God, and our own sinfulness and vileness before him, and to be afraid of his displeasure. We are undone if there be not a Mediator between us and this holy God, 1 Sam. vi. 20. Isaiah was thus humbled, to prepare him for the honour he was now to be called to as a prophet. Note, Those are fittest to be employed for God who are low in their own eyes and are made deeply sensible of their own weakness and unworthiness.

II. The silencing of the prophet's fears by the good words, and comfortable words, with which the angel answered him, *v.* 6, 7·

One of the seraphim immediately flew to him, to purify him, and so to pacify him. Note, God has strong consolations ready for holy mourners. Those that humble themselves in penitential shame and fear shall soon be encouraged and exalted; those that are struck down with the visions of God's glory shall soon be raised up again with the visits of his grace; he that tears will heal. Note further, Angels are ministering spirits for the good of the saints, for their spiritual good. Here was one of the seraphim dismissed, for a time, from attending on the throne of God's glory, to be a messenger of his grace to a good man; and so well pleased was he with the office that he came flying to him. To our Lord Jesus himself, in his agony, there *appeared an angel from heaven, strengthening him,* Luke xxii. 43. Here is, 1. A comfortable sign given to the prophet of the purging away of his sin. The seraph *brought a live coal from the altar,* and touched his lips with it, not to hurt them, but to heal them—not to cauterize, but to cleanse them; for there were purifications by fire, as well as by water, and the filth of Jerusalem was purged by the *spirit of burning,* ch. iv. 4. The blessed Spirit works as fire, Matt. iii. 11. The seraph, being himself kindled with a divine fire, put life into the prophet, to make him also zealously affected; for the way to purge the lips from the uncleanness of sin is to fire the soul with the love of God. This live coal was taken from off the altar, either the altar of incense or that of burnt-offerings, for they had both of them fire burning on them continually. Nothing is powerful to cleanse and comfort the soul but what is taken from Christ's satisfaction and the intercession he ever lives to make in the virtue of that satisfaction. It must be a coal from his altar that must put life into us and be our peace; it will not be done with strange fire. 2. An explication of this sign: " *Lo, this has touched thy lips,* to assure thee of this, that *thy iniquity is taken away and thy sin purged.* The guilt of thy sin is removed by pardoning mercy, the guilt of thy tongue-sins. Thy corrupt disposition to sin is removed by renewing grace; and therefore nothing can hinder thee from being accepted with God as a worshipper, in concert with the holy angels, or from being employed for God as a messenger to the children of men." Those only who are thus purged from an evil conscience are prepared *to serve the living God,* Heb. ix. 14. The taking away of sin is necessary to our speaking with confidence and comfort either to God in prayer or from God in preaching; nor are any so fit to display to others the riches and power of gospel-grace as those who have themselves tasted the sweetness and felt the influence of that grace; and those shall have their sin taken away who complain of it as a burden and see themselves in danger of being undone by it.

III. The renewing of the prophet's mission, *v.* 8. Here is a communication between God and Isaiah about this matter. Those that would assist others in their correspondence with God must not themselves be strangers to it; for how can we expect that God should speak by us if we never heard him speaking to us, or that we should be accepted as the mouth of others to God if we never spoke to him heartily for ourselves? Observe here,

1 The counsel of God concerning Isaiah's mission. God is here brought in, after the manner of men, deliberating and advising with himself: *Whom shall I send? And who will go for us?* God needs not either to be counselled by others or to consult with himself; he knows what he will do; but thus he would show us that there is a counsel in his whole will, and teach us to consider our ways, and particularly that the sending forth of ministers is a work not to be done but upon mature deliberation. Observe, (1.) Who it is that is consulting. It is the Lord God in his glory, whom he saw upon the throne high and lifted up. It puts an honour upon the ministry that, when God would send a prophet to speak in his name, he appeared in all the glories of the upper world. Ministers are the ambassadors of the King of kings; how mean soever they are, he who sends them is great; it is God in three persons (Who will go for us? as Gen. i. 26, *Let us make man),* Father, Son, and Holy Ghost. They all concur, as in the creating, so in the redeeming and governing of man. Ministers are ordained in the same name into which all Christians are baptized. (2.) What the consultation is: *Whom shall I send? And who will go?* Some think this refers to the particular message of wrath against Israel, *v.* 9, 10. "Who will be willing to go on such a melancholy errand, on which they will go in the bitterness of their souls?" Ezek. iii. 14. But I rather take it more largely for all those messages which the prophet was entrusted to deliver, in God's name, to that people, in which that hardening work was by no means the primary intention, but a secondary effect of them, 2 Cor. ii. 16. *Whom shall I send?* intimating that the business was such as required a choice and well-accomplished messenger, Jer. xlix. 19. God now appeared, attended with holy angels, and yet asks, *Whom shall I send?* For he would send them a *prophet from among their brethren,* Heb. ii. 17. Note, [1.] It is the unspeakable favour of God to us that he is pleased to send us his mind by men like ourselves, whose terror shall not make us afraid, and who are themselves concerned in the messages they bring. Those who are workers together with God are sinners and sufferers together with us. [2.] It is a rare thing to find one who is fit to go for God, and to carry his messages to

the children of men : *Whom shall I send?* Who is sufficient? Such a degree of courage for God and concern for the souls of men as is necessary to make a man faithful, and withal such an insight into the mysteries of the kingdom of heaven as is necessary to make a man skilful, are seldom to be met with. Such an interpreter of the mind of God is one of a thousand, Job xxxiii. 23. [3.] None are allowed to go for God but those who are sent by him ; he will own none but those whom he appoints, Rom. x. 15. It is Christ's work to put men into the ministry, 1 Tim. i. 12.

2. The consent of Isaiah to it : *Then said I, Here am I; send me.* He was to go on a melancholy errand ; the office seemed to go a begging, and every body declined it, and yet Isaiah offered himself to the service. It is an honour to be singular in appearing for God, Judges v. 7. We must not say, " I would go if I thought I should have success ;" but, " I will go, and leave the success to God. Here am I; send me." Isaiah had been himself in a melancholy frame (*v.* 5), full of doubts and fears ; but now that he had the assurance of the pardon of his sin the clouds were blown over, and he was fit for service and forward to it. What he says denotes, (1.) His readiness : " Here am I, a volunteer, not pressed into the service." *Behold me :* so the word is. God says to us, *Behold me* (*ch.* lxv. 1), and, *Here I am* (*ch.* lviii. 9), even before we call; let us say so to him when he does call. (2.) His resolution : " *Here I am,* ready to encounter the greatest difficulties. *I have set my face as a flint.*" Compare this with *ch.* l. 4—7. (3.) His referring himself to God : " Send me whither thou wilt ; make what use thou pleasest of me. Send me, that is, Lord, give me commission and full instruction ; send me, and then, no doubt, thou wilt stand by me." It is a great comfort to those whom God sends that they go for God, and may therefore speak in his name, as having authority, and be assured that he will bear them out.

9 And he said, Go, and tell this people, Hear ye indeed, but understand not; and see ye indeed, but perceive not. 10 Make the heart of this people fat, and make their ears heavy, and shut their eyes ; lest they see with their eyes, and hear with their ears, and understand with their heart, and convert, and be healed. 11 Then said I, Lord, how long? And he answered, Until the cities be wasted without inhabitant, and the houses without man, and the land be utterly desolate, 12 And the LORD have removed men far away, and *there be* a great forsaking in the midst of

42

the land. 13 But yet in it *shall be* a tenth, and *it* shall return, and shall be eaten : as a teil-tree, and as an oak, whose substance *is* in them, when they cast *their leaves : so* the holy seed *shall be* the substance thereof.

God takes Isaiah at his word, and here sends him on a strange errand—to foretel the ruin of his people and even to ripen them for that ruin—to preach that which, by their abuse of it, would be to them a savour of death unto death. And this was to be a type and figure of the state of the Jewish church in the days of the Messiah, when they should obstinately reject the gospel, and should thereupon be rejected of God. These verses are quoted in part, or referred to, six times, in the New Testament, which intimates that in gospel times these spiritual judgments would be most frequently inflicted ; and though they make the least noise, and come not with observation, yet they are of all judgments the most dreadful. Isaiah is here given to understand these four things :—

1. That the generality of the people to whom he was sent would turn a deaf ear to his preaching, and wilfully shut their eyes against all the discoveries of the mind and will of God which he had to make to them (*v.* 9) : " *Go, and tell this people,* this foolish wretched people, tell them their own, tell them how stupid and sottish they are." Isaiah must preach to them, and they will *hear* him indeed, but that is all ; they will not heed him ; they will not *understand* him ; they will not take any pains, nor use that application of mind which is necessary to the understanding of him ; they are prejudiced against that which is the true intent and meaning of what he says, and therefore they will not understand him, or pretend they do not. They *see indeed* (for the vision is made plain on tables, so that he who runs may read it) ; *but they perceive not* their own concern in it ; it is to them as a tale that is told. Note, There are many who hear the sound of God's word, but do not feel the power of it.

2. That, forasmuch as they would not be made better by his ministry, they should be made worse by it ; those that were wilfully blind should be judicially blinded (*v.* 10) : " They will not understand or perceive thee, and therefore thou shalt be instrumental to *make their heart fat,* senseless, and sensual, and so to *make their ears* yet more *heavy,* and to *shut their eyes* the closer ; so that, at length, their recovery and repentance will become utterly impossible ; they shall no more *see with their eyes* the danger they are in, the ruin they are upon the brink of, nor the way of escape from it ; they shall no more *hear with their ears* the warnings and instructions that are given them, nor *understand with their heart* the things that belong

to their peace, so as to be converted from the error of their ways, and thus *be healed.*" Note, (1.) The conversion of sinners is the healing of them. (2.) A right understanding is necessary to conversion. (3.) God sometimes, in a way of righteous judgment, gives men up to blindness of mind and strong delusions, because they would not *receive the truth in the love of it,* 2 Thess. ii. 10—12. *He that is filthy let him be filthy still.* (4.) Even the word of God oftentimes proves a means of hardening sinners. The evangelical prophet himself makes the heart of this people fat, not only as he foretels it, passing this sentence upon them in God's name, and seals them under it, but as his preaching had a tendency to it, rocking some asleep in security (to whom it was a lovely song), and making others more outrageous, to whom it was such a reproach that they were not able to bear it. Some looked upon the word as a privilege, and their convictions were smothered by it (Jer. vii. 4); others looked upon it as a provocation, and their corruptions were exasperated by it.

3. That the consequence of this would be their *utter ruin, v.* 11, 12. The prophet had nothing to object against the justice of this sentence, nor does he refuse to go upon such an errand, but asks, " *Lord, how long?*" (an abrupt question) : " Shall it always be thus ? Must I and other prophets always labour in vain among them, and will things never be better ?" Or (as should seem by the answer) " Lord, what will it come to at last ? What will be in the end hereof ?" In answer to this he is told that it should issue in the final destruction of the Jewish church and nation. " When the word of God, especially the word of the gospel, has been thus abused by them, they shall be unchurched, and consequently undone. Their cities shall be uninhabited, and their country houses too; the land shall be untilled, *desolate with desolation* (as it is in the margin), the people who should replenish the houses and cultivate the ground being all cut off by sword, famine, or pestilence, and those who escape with their lives being removed far away into captivity, so that there shall be a great and general forsaking in the midst of the land; that populous country shall become desert, and that glory of all lands shall be abandoned." Note, Spiritual judgments often bring temporal judgments along with them upon persons and places. This was in part fulfilled in the destruction of Jerusalem by the Chaldeans, when the land, being left desolate, enjoyed her sabbaths seventy years ; but, the foregoing predictions being so expressly applied in the New Testament to the Jews in our Saviour's time, doubtless this points at the final destruction of that people by the Romans, in which it had a complete accomplishment, and the effects of it that people and that land remain under to this day.

4. That yet a remnant should be reserved to be the monuments of mercy, *v.* 13. There was a remnant reserved in the last destruction of the Jewish nation (Rom. xi 5, *At this present time there is a remnant) ;* for so it was written here : But *in it shall be a tenth,* a certain number, but a very small number in comparison with the multitude that shall perish in their unbelief. It is that which, under the law, was God's proportion; they shall be consecrated to God as the tithes were, and shall be for his service and honour. Concerning this tithe, this saved remnant, we are here told, (1.) That they shall return (*ch.* vi. 13 ; x. 21), shall return from sin to God and duty, shall return out of captivity to their own land. God will turn. them, and they shall be turned. (2.) That they shall be eaten, that is, shall be accepted of God as the tithe was, which was meat in God's house, Mal. iii. 10. The saving of this remnant shall be meat to the faith and hope of those that wish well to God's kingdom. (3.) That they shall be like a timber-tree in winter, which has life, though it has no leaves : *As a teil-tree and as an oak, whose substance is in them even when they cast their leaves,* so this remnant, though they may be stripped of their outward prosperity and share with others in common calamities, shall yet recover themselves, as a tree in the spring, and flourish again; though they fall, they shall not be utterly cast down. *There is hope of a tree, though it be cut down, that it will sprout again,* Job xiv. 7. (4.) That this distinguished remnant shall be the stay and support of the public interests. *The holy seed* in the soul is the substance of the man ; a principle of grace reigning in the heart will keep life there; he that is *born of God* has *his seed remaining in him,* 1 John iii. 9. So the holy seed in the land is the substance of the land, keeps it from being quite dissolved, *and bears up the pillars of it,* Ps. lxxv. 3. See *ch.* i. 9. Some read the foregoing clause with this, thus : *As the support at Shallecheth is in the elms and the oaks, so the holy seed is the substance thereof ;* as the trees that grow on either side of the causeway (the raised way, or terrace-walk, that leads from the king's palace to the temple (1 Kings x. 5), at the gate of Shallecheth, 1 Chron. xxvi. 16) support the causeway by keeping up the earth, which would otherwise be crumbling away, so the small residue of religious, serious, praying people, are the support of the state, and help to keep things together and save them from going to decay. Some make the holy seed to be Christ. The Jewish nation was *therefore* saved from utter ruin because *out of it, as concerning the flesh, Christ* was to come, Rom. ix. 5. *Destroy it not, for that blessing is in it* (*ch.* lxv. 8); and, when that blessing had come, it was soon destroyed. Now the consideration of this is designed for the

support of the prophet in his work. Though far the greater part should perish in their unbelief, yet to some his word should be a savour of life unto life. Ministers do not wholly lose their labour if they be but instrumental to save one poor soul.

CHAP. VII.

This chapter is an occasional sermon, in which the prophet sings both of mercy and judgment to those that did not perceive or understand either; he piped unto them, but they danced not, mourned unto them, but they wept not. Here is, I. The consternation that Ahaz was in upon an attempt of the confederate forces of Syria and Israel against Jerusalem, ver. 1, 2. II. The assurance which God, by the prophet, sent him for his encouragement, that the attempt should be defeated and Jerusalem should be preserved, ver. 3—9. III. The confirmation of this by a sign which God gave to Ahaz, when he refused to ask one, referring to Christ, and our redemption by him, ver. 10—16. IV. A threatening of the great desolation that God would bring upon Ahaz and his kingdom by the Assyrians, notwithstanding their escape from this present storm, because they went on still in their wickedness. ver. 17—25. And this is written both for our comfort and for our admonition.

AND it came to pass in the days of Ahaz the son of Jotham, the son of Uzziah, king of Judah, *that* Rezin the king of Syria, and Pekah the son of Remaliah, king of Israel, went up toward Jerusalem to war against it, but could not prevail against it. 2 And it was told the house of David, saying, Syria is confederate with Ephraim. And his heart was moved, and the heart of his people, as the trees of the wood are moved with the wind. 3 Then said the LORD unto Isaiah, Go forth now to meet Ahaz, thou, and Shear-jashub thy son, at the end of the conduit of the upper pool in the highway of the fuller's field; 4 And say unto him, Take heed, and be quiet; fear not, neither be fainthearted for the two tails of these smoking firebrands, for the fierce anger of Rezin with Syria, and of the son of Remaliah. 5 Because Syria, Ephraim, and the son of Remaliah, have taken evil counsel against thee, saying, 6 Let us go up against Judah, and vex it, and let us make a breach therein for us, and set a king in the midst of it, *even* the son of Tabeal: 7 Thus saith the Lord GOD, It shall not stand, neither shall it come to pass. 8 For the head of Syria *is* Damascus, and the head of Damascus *is* Rezin; and within threescore and five years shall Ephraim be broken, that it be not a people. 9 And the head of Ephraim *is* Samaria, and the head of Samaria *is* Remaliah's son. If ye will not believe, surely ye shall not be established.

44

The prophet Isaiah had his commission renewed in the year that king Uzziah died, *ch.* vi. 1. Jotham his son reigned, and reigned well, sixteen years. All that time, no doubt, Isaiah prophesied as he was commanded, and yet we have not in this book any of his prophecies dated in the reign of Jotham ; but this, which is put first, was in the days of Ahaz the son of Jotham. Many excellent useful sermons he preached which were not published and left upon record ; for, if all that was memorable had been written, *the world could not have contained the books,* John xxi 25. Perhaps in the reign of Ahaz, a wicked king, he had not opportunity to preach so much at court as in Jotham's time, and therefore then he wrote the more, for a testimony against them. Here is,

I. A very formidable design laid against Jerusalem by Rezin king of Syria and Pekah king of Israel, two neighbouring potentates, who had of late made descents upon Judah severally. At the end of the reign of Jotham, *the Lord began to send against Judah Rezin and Pekah,* 2 Kings xv. 37. But now, in the second or third year of the reign of Ahaz, encouraged by their former successes, they entered into an alliance against Judah. Because Ahaz, though he found the sword over his head, began his reign with idolatry, *God delivered him into the hand of the king of Syria and of the king of Israel* (2 Chron. xxviii. 5), and a great slaughter they made in his kingdom, *v.* 6, 7. Flushed with this victory, they went up towards Jerusalem, the royal city, to war against it, to besiege it, and make themselves masters of it; but it proved in the issue that they could not gain their point. Note, The sin of a land brings foreign invasions upon it and betrays the most advantageous posts and passes to the enemy; and God sometimes makes one wicked nation a scourge to another; but judgment, ordinarily, begins at the house of God.

II. The great distress that Ahaz and his court were in when they received advice of this design : *It was told the house of David* that Syria and Ephraim had signed a league against Judah, *v.* 2. This degenerate royal family is called the *house of David,* to put us in mind of that article of God's covenant with David (Ps. lxxxix. 30—33), *If his children forsake my law, I will chasten their transgression with the rod ; but my loving-kindness will I not utterly take away,* which is remarkably fulfilled in this chapter. News being brought that the two armies of Syria and Israel were joined, and had taken the field, the court, the city, and the country, were thrown into consternation : *The heart of Ahaz was moved with fear,* and then no wonder that *the heart of his people was so, as the trees of the wood are moved with the wind.* They were tossed and shaken, and put into a great disorder and confusion, were wavering and uncertain in their counsels, hurried hither and thither, and could not fix in any steady resolution. They yielded to the storm, and gave up all for gone, concluding it in vain to make any resistance. Now that which caused this fright was the sense of guilt and the weakness of their faith. They had made God their enemy, and knew not how to make him their friend, and therefore their fears tyrannised over them; while those whose consciences are kept *void of offence, and whose hearts are fixed, trusting in God, need not be afraid of evil tidings; though the earth be removed, yet will not they fear; but the wicked flee at the shaking of a leaf,* Lev. xxvi. 36.

III. The orders and directions given to Isaiah to go and encourage Ahaz in his distress; not for his own sake (he deserved to hear nothing from God but words of terror, which might add affliction to his grief), but because he was a son of David and king of Judah. God had kindness for him for his father's sake, who must not be forgotten, and for his people's sake, who must not be abandoned, but would be encouraged if Ahaz were. Observe,

1. God appointed the prophet to meet Ahaz, though he did not send to the prophet to speak with him, nor desire him to enquire of the Lord for him (v. 3): *Go to meet Ahaz.* Note, God is often found of those who seek him not, much more will he be found of those who seek him diligently. He speaks comfort to many who not only are not worthy of it, but do not so much as enquire after it.

2. He ordered him to take his little son with him, because he carried a sermon in his name, *Shear-jashub—A remnant shall return.* The prophets sometimes recorded what they preached in the significant names of their children (as Hos. i. 4, 6, 9); therefore Isaiah's children are said to be *for signs, ch.* viii. 18. This son was so called for the encouragement of those of God's people who were carried captive, assuring them that they should return, at least a remnant of them, which was more than they could pretend to merit: yet at this time God was better than his word; for he took care not only that a remnant should return, but the whole number of those whom the confederate forces of Syria and Israel had taken prisoners, 2 Chron. xxviii. 15.

3. He directed him where he should find Ahaz. He was to meet with him not in the temple, or the synagogue, or royal chapel, but *at the end of the conduit of the upper pool,* where he was, probably with many of his servants about him, contriving how to order the water-works, so as to secure them to the city, or deprive the enemy of the benefit of them (*ch.* xxii. 9—11; 2 Chron. xxxii. 3, 4), or giving some necessary directions for the fortifying of the city as well as they could; and perhaps finding every thing in a very bad posture of defence, the conduit out of repair, as well as other things gone to decay, his fears increased, and he was now in greater perplexity than ever; therefore, *Go, meet him there.* Note, God sometimes sends comforts to his people very seasonably, and, what time they are most afraid, encourages them to trust in him.

4. He put words in his mouth, else the prophet would not have known how to bring a message of good to such a bad man, a sinner in Zion, that ought to be afraid; but God intended it for the support of faithful Israelites.

(1.) The prophet must rebuke their fears, and advise them by no means to yield to them, but keep their temper, and preserve the possession of their own souls (v. 4): *Take heed, and be quiet.* Note, In order to comfort there is need of caution; that we may be quiet, it is necessary that we take heed and watch against those things that threaten to disquiet us. "Fear not with this amazement, this fear, that weakens, and has torment; neither *let thy heart be tender,* so as to melt and fail within thee; but pluck up thy spirits, have a good heart on it, and be courageous; let not fear betray the succours which reason and religion offer for thy support." Note, Those who expect God should help them must help themselves, Ps. xxvii. 14.

(2.) He must teach them to despise their enemies, not in pride, or security, or incogitancy (nothing more dangerous than so to despise an enemy), but in faith and dependence upon God. Ahaz's fear called them two powerful politic princes, for either of whom he was an unequal match, but, if united, he durst not look them in the face, nor make head against them. "No," says the prophet, "they are *two tails of smoking firebrands;* they are angry, they are fierce, they are furious, as firebrands, as fireballs; and they make one another worse by being in a confederacy, as sticks of fire put together burn the more violently. But they are only smoking firebrands: and where there is smoke there is some fire, but it may be not so much as was feared. Their threatenings will vanish into smoke. *Pharaoh king of Egypt is but a noise* (Jer. xlvi. 17), and Rezin king of Syria but a smoke; and such are all the enemies of God's church, *smoking flax,* that will soon be quenched. Nay, they are but *tails* of smoking firebrands, in a manner burnt out already; their force is spent; they have consumed themselves with the heat of their own anger; you may put your foot on them, and tread them out." The two kingdoms of Syria and Israel were now near expiring. Note, The more we have an eye to God as a consuming fire the less reason we shall have to fear men, though they are ever so furious, nay, we shall be able to despise them as smoking firebrands.

(3.) He must assure them that the present

45

design of these high allies (so they thought themselves) against Jerusalem should certainly be defeated and come to nothing, *v.* 5—7. [1.] That very thing which Ahaz thought most formidable is made the ground of their defeat—and that was the depth of their designs and the height of their hopes : " *Therefore* they shall be baffled and sent back with shame, *because they have taken evil counsel against thee,* which is an offence to God. These firebrands are a *smoke in his nose* (*ch.* lxv. 5), and therefore must be extinguished." *First,* They are very spiteful and malicious, and therefore they shall not prosper. Judah had done them no wrong ; they had no pretence to quarrel with Ahaz ; but, without any reason, they said, *Let us go up against Judah, and vex it.* Note, Those that are vexatious cannot expect to be prosperous ; those that love to do mischief cannot expect to do well. *Secondly,* They are very secure, and confident of success. They will vex Judah by going up against it ; yet that is not all : they do not doubt but to make a breach in the wall of Jerusalem wide enough for them to march their army in at ; or they count upon dissecting or dividing the kingdom into two parts, one for the king of Israel, the other for the king of Syria, who had agreed in one viceroy—*a king* to be *set in the midst of it, even the son of Tabeal,* some obscure person, it is uncertain whether a Syrian or an Israelite. So sure were they of gaining their point that they divided the prey before they had caught it. Note, Those that are most scornful are commonly least successful, for surely God scorns the scorners. [2.] God himself gives them his word that the attempt should not take effect (*v.* 7) : " *Thus saith the Lord God,* the sovereign Lord of all, who *brings the counsel of the heathen to nought* (Ps. xxxiii. 10), *It shall not stand, neither shall it come to pass ;* their measures shall all be broken, and they shall not be able to bring to pass their enterprise." Note, Whatever stands against God, or thinks to stand without him, cannot stand long. Man purposes, but God disposes ; and *who is he that saith and it cometh to pass if the Lord commands it not or countermands it ?* Lam. iii. 37. See Prov. xix. 21.

(4.) He must give them a prospect of the destruction of these enemies, at last, that were now such a terror to them. [1.] They should neither of them enlarge their dominions, nor push their conquests any further : *The head city of Syria is Damascus, and the head man of Damascus is Rezin ;* this he glories in, and this let him be content with, *v.* 8. *The head city of Ephraim* has long been *Samaria, and the head man in Samaria is* now Pekah *the son of Remaliah.* These shall be made to know their own ; their bounds are fixed, and they shall not pass them, to make themselves masters of the cities of Judah, much less to make

46

Jerusalem their prey. Note, As God has appointed men the bounds of their habitation (Acts xvii. 26), so he has appointed princes the bounds of their dominion, within which they ought to confine themselves, and not encroach upon their neighbours' rights. [2.] Ephraim, which perhaps was the more malicious and forward enemy of the two, should shortly be quite rooted out, and should be so far from seizing other people's lands that they should not be able to hold their own. Interpreters are much at a loss how to compute the sixty-five years within which *Ephraim shall cease to be a people ;* for the captivity of the ten tribes was but eleven years after this : and some make it a mistake of the transcriber, and think it should be read *within six and five years,* just eleven. But it is hard to allow that. Others make it to be sixty-five years from the time that the prophet Amos first foretold the ruin of the kingdom of the ten tribes ; and some late interpreters make it to look as far forward as the last desolation of that country by Esarhaddon, which was about sixty-five years after this ; then Ephraim was so broken that it was no more a people. Now it was the greatest folly in the world for those to be ruining their neighbours who were themselves marked for ruin, and so near to it. See what a prophet told them at this time, when they were triumphing over Judah, 2 Chron. xxviii. 10. *Are there not with you, even with you, sins against the Lord your God?*

(5.) He must urge them to mix faith with those assurances which he had given them (*v.* 9) : " *If you will not believe* what is said to you, *surely you shall not be established ;* your shaken and disordered state shall not be established, your unquiet unsettled spirit shall not ; though the things told you are very encouraging, yet they will not be so to you, unless you believe them, and be willing to take God's word." Note, The grace of faith is absolutely necessary to the quieting and composing of the mind in the midst of all the tosses of this present time, 2 Chron. xx. 20.

10 Moreover the Lord spake again unto Ahaz, saying, 11 Ask thee a sign of the Lord thy God ; ask it either in the depth, or in the height above. 12 But Ahaz said, I will not ask, neither will I tempt the Lord. 13 And he said, Hear ye now, O house of David ; *Is it* a small thing for you to weary men, but will ye weary my God also ? 14 Therefore the Lord himself shall give you a sign ; Behold, a virgin shall conceive, and bear a son, and shall call his name Immanuel. 15 Butter and

honey shall he eat, that he may know to refuse the evil, and choose the good. 16 For before the child shall know to refuse the evil, and choose the good, the land that thou abhorrest shall be forsaken of both her kings.

Here, I. God, by the prophet, makes a gracious offer to Ahaz, to confirm the foregoing predictions, and his faith in them, by such sign or miracle as he should choose (v. 10, 11): *Ask thee a sign of the Lord thy God.* See here the divine faithfulness and veracity. God tells us nothing but what he is able and ready to prove. See his wonderful condescension to the children of men, in that he is so *willing to show to the heirs of promise the immutability of his counsel,* Heb. vi. 17. He considers our frame, and that, living in a world of sense, we are apt to require sensible proofs, which therefore he has favoured us with in sacramental signs and seals. Ahaz was a bad man, yet God is called the Lord his God, because he was a child of Abraham and David, and of the covenants made with them. See how gracious God is even to the evil and unthankful; Ahaz is bidden to choose his sign, as Gideon about the fleece (Judg. vi. 37); let him ask for a sign in the air, or earth, or water, for God's power is the same in all.

II. Ahaz rudely refuses this gracious offer, and (which is not mannerly towards any superior) kicks at the courtesy, and puts a slight upon it (v. 12): *I will not ask.* The true reason why he would not ask for a sign was because, having a dependence upon the Assyrians, their forces, and their gods, for help, he would not thus far be beholden to the God of Israel, or lay himself under obligations to him. He would not ask a sign for the confirming of his faith because he resolved to persist in his unbelief, and would indulge his doubts and distrusts; yet he pretends a pious reason: *I will not tempt the Lord;* as if it would be a tempting of God to do that which God himself invited and directed him to do. Note, A secret disaffection to God is often disguised with the specious colours of respect to him; and those who are resolved that they will not trust God yet pretend that they will not tempt him.

III. The prophet reproves him and his court, him and the house of David, the whole royal family, for their contempt of prophecy, and the little value they had for divine revelation (v. 13): " *Is it a small thing for you to weary men* by your oppression and tyranny, with which you make yourselves burdensome and odious to all mankind? But *will you weary my God also* with the affronts you put upon him?" As the unjust judge that neither *feared God nor regarded man,* Luke xviii. 2. *You have wearied the Lord with your words,* Mal. ii. 17. Nothing is

more grievous to the God of heaven than to be distrusted. " *Will you weary my God?* Will you suppose him to be tired and unable to help you, or to be weary of doing you good? Whereas *the youths may faint and be weary,* you may have tired all your friends, *the Creator of the ends of the earth faints not, neither is weary.*" ch. xl. 28—31. Or thus: " In affronting the prophets, you think you put a slight only upon men like yourselves, and consider not that you affront God himself, whose messengers they are, and put a slight upon him, who will resent it accordingly." The prophet here calls God his God with a great deal of pleasure: Ahaz would not say, He is my God, though the prophet had invited him to say so (v. 11): *The Lord thy God;* but Isaiah will say, " He is mine." Note, Whatever others do, we must avouch the Lord for ours and abide by him.

IV. The prophet, in God's name, gives them a sign: " You will not ask a sign, but the unbelief of man shall not make the promise of God of no effect: *The Lord himself shall give you a sign* (v. 14), a double sign."

1. " A sign in general of his good-will to Israel and to the house of David. You may conclude that he has mercy in store for you, and that you are not forsaken of your God, how great soever your present distress and danger are; for of your nation, of your family, the Messiah is to be born, and you cannot be destroyed while that blessing is in you, which shall be introduced," (1.) " In a glorious manner; for, whereas you have been often told that he should be born among you, I am now further to tell you that he shall be born of a virgin, which will signify both the divine power and the divine purity with which he shall be brought into the world,—that he shall be an extraordinary person, for he shall not be born by ordinary generation,— and that he shall be a holy thing, not stained with the common pollutions of the human nature, therefore incontestably fit to have the throne of his father David given him." Now this, though it was to be accomplished above 500 years after, was a most encouraging sign to the house of David (and to them, under that title, this prophecy is directed, v. 13) and an assurance that God would not cast them off. Ephraim did indeed envy Judah (ch. xi. 13) and sought the ruin of that kingdom, but could not prevail; for the sceptre should never depart from Judah till the coming of Shiloh, Gen. xlix. 10. Those whom God designs for the great salvation may take that for a sign to them that they shall not be swallowed up by any trouble they may meet with in the way. (2.) The Messiah shall be introduced on a glorious errand, wrapped up in his glorious name: They *shall call his name Immanuel— God with us,* God in our nature, God at

peace with us, in covenant with us. This was fulfilled in their calling him *Jesus—a Saviour* (Matt. i. 21—25), for, if he had not been *Immanuel—God with us,* he could not have been *Jesus—a Saviour.* Now this was a further sign of God's favour to the house of David and the tribe of Judah; for he that intended to work this great salvation among them no doubt would work out for them all those other salvations which were to be the types and figures of this, and as it were preludes to this. "Here is a sign for you, not in the depth nor in the height, but in the prophecy, in the promise, in the covenant made with David, which you are no strangers to. The promised seed shall be Immanuel, *God with us ;* let that word comfort you (*ch.* viii. 10), that *God is with us,* and (*v.* 8) that your land is Immanuel's land. Let not *the heart of the house of David* be moved thus (*v.* 2), nor let Judah fear the setting up of the son of Tabeal (*v.* 6), for nothing can cut off the entail on the Son of David that shall be Immanuel." Note, The strongest consolations, in time of trouble, are those which are borrowed from Christ, our relation to him, our interest in him, and our expectations of him and from him. Of this child it is further foretold (*v.* 15) that though he shall not be born like other children, but of a virgin, yet he shall be really and truly man, and shall be nursed and brought up like other children : *Butter and honey shall he eat,* as other children do, particularly the children of that land which *flowed with milk and honey.* Though he be conceived by the power of the Holy Ghost, yet he shall not therefore be fed with angels' food, but, as it becomes him, shall be *in all things made like unto his brethren,* Heb. ii. 17. Nor shall he, though born thus by extraordinary generation, be a man immediately, but, as other children, shall advance gradually through the several states of infancy, childhood, and youth, to that of manhood, and, growing in wisdom and stature, shall at length wax strong in spirit, and come to maturity, so as to know how *to refuse the evil and choose the good.* See Luke ii. 40, 52. Note, Children are fed when they are little that they may be taught and instructed when they have grown up; they have their maintenance in order to their education.

2. Here is another sign in particular of the speedy destruction of these potent princes that were now a terror to Judah, *v.* 16. "Before *this* child (so it should be read), this child which I have now in my arms" (he means not Immanuel, but Shear-jashub his own son, whom he was ordered to take with him for a sign, *v.* 3), "before this *child shall know how to refuse the evil and choose the good"* (and those who saw what his present stature and forwardness were would easily conjecture how long that would be), "before this child be three or

48

four years older, *the land that thou abhorrest,* these confederate forces of Israelites and Syrians, which thou hast such an enmity to and standest in such dread of, *shall be forsaken of both their kings,* both Pekah and Rezin," who were in so close an alliance that they seemed as if they were the kings but of one kingdom. This was fully accomplished ; for, within two or three years after this, Hoshea conspired against Pekah, and slew him (2 Kings xv. 30), and, before that, the king of Assyria took Damascus, and slew Rezin, 2 Kings xvi. 9. Nay, there was a present event, which happened immediately, and which this child carried the prediction of in his name, which was a pledge and earnest of this further event. *Shear-jashub* signifies *The remnant shall return,* which doubtless points at the wonderful return of those 200,000 captives whom Pekah and Rezin had carried away, who were brought back, not by might or power, but by the Spirit of the Lord of hosts. Read the story, 2 Chron. xxviii. 8—15. The prophetical naming of this child having thus had its accomplishment, no doubt this, which was further added concerning him, should have its accomplishment likewise, that Syria and Israel should be deprived of both their kings. One mercy from God encourages us to hope for another, if it engages us to prepare for another.

17 The Lord shall bring upon thee, and upon thy people, and upon thy father's house, days that have not come, from the day that Ephraim departed from Judah ; *even* the king of Assyria. 18 And it shall come to pass in that day, *that* the Lord shall hiss for the fly that *is* in the uttermost part of the rivers of Egypt, and for the bee that *is* in the land of Assyria. 19 And they shall come, and shall rest all of them in the desolate valleys, and in the holes of the rocks, and upon all thorns, and upon all bushes. 20 In the same day shall the Lord shave with a razor that is hired, *namely,* by them beyond the river, by the king of Assyria, the head, and the hair of the feet : and it shall also consume the beard. 21 And it shall come to pass in that day, *that* a man shall nourish a young cow, and two sheep: 22 And it shall come to pass, for the abundance of milk *that* they shall give, he shall eat butter : for butter and honey shall every one eat that is left in the land. 23 And it shall come to pass in that

day, *that* every place shall be, where there were a thousand vines at a thousand silverlings, it shall *even* be for briers and thorns. 24 With arrows and with bows shall *men* come thither; because all the land shall become briers and thorns. 25 And *on* all hills that shall be digged with the mattock, there shall not come thither the fear of briers and thorns: but it shall be for the sending forth of oxen, and for the treading of lesser cattle.

After the comfortable promises made to Ahaz as a branch of the house of David, here follow terrible threatenings against him, as a degenerate branch of that house; for though the loving-kindness of God shall not be utterly taken away, for the sake of David and the covenant made with him, yet his iniquity shall be *chastened with the rod,* and his sin with stripes. Let those that will not mix faith with the promises of God expect to hear the alarms of his threatenings.

I. The judgment threatened is very great, *v.* 17. It is very great, for it is general; it shall be brought upon the prince himself (high as he is, he shall not be out of the reach of it), and upon the people, the whole body of the nation, and upon the royal family, *upon* all *thy father's house;* it shall be a judgment entailed on posterity, and shall go along with the royal blood. It is very great, for it shall be unprecedented—*days that have not come;* so dark, so gloomy, so melancholy, as never were the like since the revolt of the ten tribes, when Ephraim departed from Judah, which was indeed a sad time to the house of David. Note, The longer men continue in sin the sorer punishments they have reason to expect. It is the Lord that will bring these days upon them, for our times are in his hand, and who can resist or escape the judgments he brings?

II. The enemy that should be employed as the instrument of this judgment is the king of Assyria. Ahaz reposed great confidence in that prince for help against the confederate powers of Israel and Syria, and minded the less what God said to him by his prophet for his encouragement because he built much upon his interest in the king of Assyria, and had meanly promised to be his servant if he would send him some succours; he had also made him a present of gold and silver, for which he drained the treasures both of church and state, 2 Kings xvi. 7, 8. Now God threatens that that king of Assyria whom he made his stay instead of God should become a scourge to him. He was so speedily; for, when he *came to him, he distressed him, but strengthened him not* (2 Chron. xxviii. 20), the reed not only

broke under him, but ran into his hand, and pierced it, and thenceforward the kings of Assyria were, for a long time, grieving thorns to Judah, and gave them a great deal of trouble. Note, The creature that we make our hope commonly proves our hurt. The king of Assyria, not long after this, made himself master of the ten tribes, carried them captive, and laid their country waste, so as fully to answer the prediction here; and perhaps it may refer to that, as an explication of *v.* 8, where it is foretold that Ephraim shall be broken, that it shall not be a people; and it is easy to suppose that the prophet (at *v.* 17) turns his speech to the king of Israel, denouncing God's judgments against him for invading Judah. But the expositors universally understand it of Ahaz and his kingdom. Now observe, 1. Summons given to the invaders (*v.* 18): *The Lord shall whistle for the fly and the bee.* See *ch.* v. 26. Enemies that seem as contemptible as a fly or a bee, and are as easily crushed, shall yet, when God pleases, do his work as effectually as lions and young lions. Though they are as far distant from one another as the rivers of Egypt and the land of Assyria, yet they shall punctually meet to join in this work when God commands their attendance; for, when God has work to do, he will not be at a loss for instruments to do it with. 2. Possession taken by them, *v.* 19. It should seem as if the country were in no condition to make resistance. They find no difficulties in forcing their way, but *come and rest all of them in the desolate valleys,* which the inhabitants had deserted upon the first alarm, and left them a cheap and easy prey to the invaders. They shall come and rest in the low grounds like swarms of flies and bees, and shall render themselves impregnable by taking shelter in the holes of the rocks, as bees often do, and show themselves formidable by appearing openly upon all thorns and all bushes; so generally shall the land be overspread with them. These bees shall knit upon the thorns and bushes, and there rest undisturbed. 3. Great desolations made, and the country generally depopulated (*v.* 20): *The Lord shall shave the hair of the head, and beard, and feet;* he shall sweep all away, as the leper, when he was cleansed, *shaved off all his hair,* Lev. xiv. 8, 9. This is done with a razor which is hired, either which God has hired (as if he had none of his own; but what he hires, and whom he employs in any service for him, he will pay for. See Ezek. xxix. 18, 19), or which Ahaz has hired for his assistance. God will make that to be an instrument of his destruction which he hired into his service. Note, Many are beaten with that arm of flesh which they trusted to rather than to the arm of the Lord, and which they were at a great expense upon, when by faith and prayer they might have found cheap and

49

easy succour in God. 4. The consequences of this general depopulation. (1.) The flocks of cattle shall be all destroyed, so that a man who had herds and flocks in abundance shall be stripped of them all by the enemy, and shall with much ado save for his own use a young cow and two sheep—a poor stock (*v.* 21), yet he shall think himself happy in having any left. (2.) The few cattle that are left shall have such a large compass of ground to feed in that *they shall give abundance of milk*, and very good milk, such as shall produce butter enough, *v.* 22. There shall also be such want of men that the milk of one cow and two sheep shall serve a whole family, which used to keep abundance of servants and consume a great deal, but is now reduced. (3.) The breed of cattle shall be destroyed; so that those who used to eat flesh (as the Jews commonly did) shall be necessitated to confine themselves to butter and honey, for there shall be no flesh for them; and the country shall be so depopulated that there shall be butter and honey enough for the few that are left in it. (4.) Good land, that used to be let well, shall be all overrun with briers and thorns (*v.* 23); where there used to be a thousand vines planted, for which the tenants used to pay a thousand shekels, or pieces of silver, yearly rent, there shall be nothing now but briers and thorns, no profit either for landlord or tenant, all being laid waste by the army of the invaders. Note, God can soon turn a fruitful land into barrenness; and it is just with him to turn vines into briers if we, instead of bringing forth grapes to him, bring forth wild grapes, *ch.* v. 4. (5.) The implements of husbandry shall be turned into instruments of war, *v.* 24. The whole land having become briers and thorns, the grounds that men used to come to with sickles and pruning-hooks to gather in the fruits they shall now come to with arrows and bows, to hunt for wild beasts in the thickets, or to defend themselves from the robbers that lurk in the bushes, seeking for prey, or to kill the serpents and venomous beasts that are hid there. This denotes a very sad change of the face of that pleasant land. But what melancholy change is there which sin will not make with a people? (6.) Where briers and thorns were wont to be of use and to do good service, even in the hedges, for the defence of the enclosed grounds, they shall be plucked up, and all laid in common. There shall be briers and thorns in abundance where they should not be, but none where they should be, *v.* 25. *The hills that shall be digged with the mattock,* for special use, from which the cattle used to be kept off with the fear of briers and thorns, shall now be thrown open, the *hedges broken down for the boar out of the wood* to waste it, Ps. lxxx. 12, 13. It shall be left at large for oxen to run in and less cattle. See the

50

effect of sin and the curse; it has made the earth a forest of thorns and thistles, except as it is forced into some order by the constant care and labour of man. And see what folly it is to set our hearts upon possessions of lands, be they ever so fruitful, ever so pleasant; if they lie ever so little neglected and uncultivated, or if they be abused by a wasteful careless heir or tenant, or the country be laid waste by war, they will soon become frightful deserts. Heaven is a paradise not subject to such changes.

CHAPTER VIII.

This chapter, and the four next that follow it (to chap. xiii.) are all one continued discourse or sermon, the scope of which is to show the great destruction that should now shortly be brought upon the kingdom of Israel, and the great disturbance that should be given to the kingdom of Judah by the king of Assyria, and that both were for their sins; but rich provision is made of comfort for those that feared God in those dark times, referring especially to the days of the Messiah. In this chapter we have, I. A prophecy of the destruction of the confederate kingdoms of Syria and Israel by the king of Assyria, v. 1—4. II. Of the desolations that should be made by that proud victorious prince in the land of Israel and Judah, v. 5—8. III. Great encouragement given to the people of God in the midst of those distractions; they are assured, 1. That the enemies shall not gain their point against them, v. 9, 10. 2. That if they kept up the fear of God, and kept down the fear of man, they should find God their refuge (v. 11—14), and while others stumbled, and fell into despair, they should be enabled to wait on God, and should see themselves reserved for better times, v. 15—18. Lastly, He gives a necessary caution to all, at their peril, not to consult with familiar spirits, for they would thereby throw themselves into despair, but to keep close to the word of God, v. 19—22. And these counsels and these comforts will still be of use to us in time of trouble.

MOREOVER the LORD said unto me, Take thee a great roll, and write in it with a man's pen concerning Maher-shalal-hash-baz. 2 And I took unto me faithful witnesses to record, Uriah the priest, and Zechariah the son of Jeberechiah. 3 And I went unto the prophetess: and she conceived, and bare a son. Then said the LORD to me, Call his name Maher-shalal-hash-baz. 4 For before the child shall have knowledge to cry, My father, and my mother, the riches of Damascus and the spoil of Samaria shall be taken away before the king of Assyria. 5 The LORD spake also unto me again, saying, 6 Forasmuch as this people refuseth the waters of Shiloah that go softly, and rejoice in Rezin and Remaliah's son; 7 Now therefore, behold, the Lord bringeth up upon them the waters of the river, strong and many, *even* the king of Assyria, and all his glory: and he shall come up over all his channels, and go over all his banks: 8 And he shall pass through Judah; he shall overflow and go over, he shall reach *even* to the neck; and the stretching out of his wings shall fill the breadth of thy land, O Immanuel.

In these verses we have a prophecy of the successes of the king of Assyria against Damascus, Samaria, and Judah, that the two former should be laid waste by him, and the last greatly frightened. Here we have,

I. Orders given to the prophet to write this prophecy, and publish it to be seen and read of all men, and to leave it upon record, that when the thing came to pass they might know that God had sent him; for that was one end of prophecy, John xiv. 29. He must *take a great roll*, which would contain those five chapters fairly written in words at length; and he must write in it all that he had foretold concerning the king of Assyria's invading the country; he must *write it with a man's pen*, in the usual way and style of writing, so as that it might be legible and intelligible by all. See Hab. ii. 2, *Write the vision, and make it plain.* Those that speak and write of the things of God should avoid obscurity, and study to speak and write so as to be understood, 1 Cor. xiv. 19. Those that write for men should write with a man's pen, and not covet the pen or tongue of angels. And forasmuch as it is usual to put some short, but significant comprehensive title before books that are published, the prophet is directed to call his book *Maher-shalal-hash-baz—Make speed to the spoil, hasten to the prey*, intimating that the Assyrian army should come upon them with great speed and make great spoil. By this title the substance and meaning of the book would be enquired after by those that heard of it, and remembered by those that had read it or heard it read. It is sometimes a good help to memory to put much matter in few words, which serve as handles by which we take hold of more.

II. The care of the prophet to get this record well attested (*v.* 2): *I took unto me faithful witnesses to record;* he wrote the prophecy in their sight and presence, and made them subscribe their names to it, that they might be ready, if afterwards there should be occasion, to make oath of it, that the prophet had so long before foretold the descent which the Assyrians made upon that country. He names his witnesses for the greater certainty, that they might be appealed to by any. They were two in number (for *out of the mouth of two witnesses shall every word be established*); one was Uriah the priest; he is mentioned in the story of Ahaz, but for none of his good deeds, for he humoured Ahaz with an idolatrous altar (2 Kings xvi. 10, 11); however, at this time, no exception lay against him, being a faithful witness. See what full satisfaction the prophets took care to give to all persons concerned of the sincerity of their intentions, that we might know with a full assurance the *certainty of*

the things wherein we have been instructed, and that we have *not followed cunningly-devised fables.*

III. The making of the title of his book the name of his child, that it might be the more taken notice of and the more effectually perpetuated, *v.* 3. His wife (because the wife of a prophet) is called *the prophetess;* she *conceived and bore a son,* another son, who must carry a sermon in his name, as the former had done (*ch.* vii. 3), but with this difference, that spoke mercy, *Shear-jashub—The remnant shall return;* but, that being slighted, this speaks judgment, *Maher-shalal-hash-baz—In making speed to the spoil he shall hasten, or he has hastened, to the prey.* The prophecy is doubled, even in this one name, for the thing was certain. *I will hasten my word,* Jer. i. 12. Every time the child was called by his name, or any part of it, it would serve as a memorandum of the judgments approaching. Note, It is good for us often to put ourselves in mind of the changes and troubles we are liable to in this world, and which perhaps are at the door. When we look with pleasure on our children it should be with the allay of this thought, We know not what they are yet reserved for.

IV. The prophecy itself, which explains this mystical name.

1. That Syria and Israel, who were now in confederacy against Judah, should in a very little time become an easy prey to the king of Assyria and his victorious army (*v.* 4): *"Before the child,* now newly born and named, shall have *knowledge to cry, My father, and, My mother"* (which are usually some of the first things that children know and some of the first words that children speak), that is, "in about a year or two, *the riches of Damascus, and the spoil of Samaria,* those cities that are now so secure themselves and so formidable to their neighbours, *shall be taken away before the king of Assyria,* who shall plunder both city and country, and send the best effects of both into his own land, to enrich that, and as trophies of his victory." Note, Those that spoil others must expect to be themselves spoiled (*ch.* xxxiii. 1); for the Lord is righteous, and those that are troublesome shall be troubled.

2. That forasmuch as there were many in Judah that were secretly in the interests of Syria and Israel, and were disaffected to the house of David, God would chastise them also by the king of Assyria, who should create a great deal of vexation to Judah, as was foretold, *ch.* vii. 17. Observe, (1.) What was the sin of the discontented party in Judah (*v.* 6): *This people,* whom the prophet here speaks to, *refuse the waters of Shiloah that go softly,* despise their own country and the government of it, and love to run it down, because it does not make so great a figure and so great a noise, in the world, as some other kings and kingdoms

do. They refuse the comforts which God's prophets offer them from the word of God, speaking to them in a still small voice, and make nothing of them; but *they rejoice in Rezin and Remaliah's son,* who were the enemies of their country, and were now actually invading it; they cried them up as brave men, magnified their policies and strength, applauded their conduct, were well pleased with their successes, and were hearty well-wishers to their designs, and resolved to desert and go over to them. Such vipers does many a state foster in its bosom, that eat its bread, and yet adhere to its enemies, and are ready to quit its interests if they but seem to totter. (2.) The judgment which God would bring upon them for this sin. The same king of Assyria that should lay Ephraim and Syria waste should be a scourge and terror to those of their party in Judah, *v.* 7, 8. Because they *refuse the waters of Shiloah,* and will not accommodate themselves to the government God has set over them, but are uneasy under it, *therefore the Lord brings upon them the waters of the river, strong and many,* the river Euphrates. They slighted the land of Judah, because it had no river to boast of comparable to that; the river at Jerusalem was a very inconsiderable one. "Well," says God, "if you be such admirers of Euphrates, you shall have enough of it; the king of Assyria, whose country lies upon that river, shall come with his glory, with his great army, which you cry up as his glory, despising your own king because he cannot bring such an army as that into the field; God shall bring that army upon you." If we value men, if we over-value them, for their worldly wealth and power, it is just with God to make them thereby a scourge to us. It is used as an argument against magnifying rich men that *rich men oppress us,* Jam. ii. 3, 6. Let us be best pleased with the waters of Shiloah, that go softly, for rapid streams are dangerous. It is threatened that the Assyrian army should break in upon them like a deluge, or inundation of waters, bearing down all before it, should come up over all his channels, and overflow all his banks. It would be to no purpose to oppose or withstand them. Sennacherib and his army should pass through Judah, and meet with so little resistance that it should look more like a march through the country than a descent upon it. *He shall reach even to the neck,* that is, he shall advance so far as to lay siege to Jerusalem, the head of the kingdom, and nothing but that shall be kept out of his hands; for that was the holy city. Note, In the greatest deluge of trouble God can and will keep the head of his people above water, and so preserve their comforts and spiritual lives; the waters that come into their souls may reach to the neck (Ps. lxix. 1), but there shall their proud waves be stayed. And here is another comforta-

ble intimation that though the stretching out of the wings of the Assyrian, that bird of prey, though the right and left wing of his army, should fill the breadth of the land of Judah, yet still it was Immanuel's land. It is *thy land, O Immanuel!* It was to be Christ's land; for there he was to be born, and live, and preach, and work miracles. He was Zion's King, and therefore had a peculiar interest in and concern for that land. Note, The lands that Immanuel owns for his, as he does all those lands that own him, though they may be deluged, shall not be destroyed; *for, when the enemy shall come in like a flood,* Immanuel shall secure his own, and shall *lift up a standard against him, ch.* lix. 19.

9 Associate yourselves, O ye people, and ye shall be broken in pieces; and give ear, all ye of far countries: gird yourselves, and ye shall be broken in pieces; gird yourselves, and ye shall be broken in pieces. 10 Take counsel together, and it shall come to nought; speak the word, and it shall not stand: for God *is* with us. 11 For the LORD spake thus to me with a strong hand, and instructed me that I should not walk in the way of this people, saying, 12 Say ye not, A confederacy, to all *them to* whom this people shall say, A confederacy; neither fear ye their fear, nor be afraid. 13 Sanctify the LORD of hosts himself; and *let* him *be* your fear, and *let* him *be* your dread. 14 And he shall be for a sanctuary; but for a stone of stumbling and for a rock of offence to both the houses of Israel, for a gin and for a snare to the inhabitants of Jerusalem. 15 And many among them shall stumble, and fall, and be broken, and be snared, and be taken.

The prophet here returns to speak of the present distress that Ahaz and his court and kingdom were in upon account of the threatening confederacy of the ten tribes and the Syrians against them. And in these verses, I. He triumphs over the invading enemies, and, in effect, sets them at defiance, and bids them do their worst (*v.* 9, 10): "*O you people, you of far countries,* give ear to what the prophet says to you in God's name." 1. "We doubt not but you will now make your utmost efforts against Judah and Jerusalem. You *associate yourselves* in a strict alliance. You *gird yourselves,* and again you *gird yourselves;* you prepare for action; you address yourselves to it with resolution; you gird on your swords; you gird up your loins. You animate and encourage yourselves and one another with all the considerations you can think of: you *take counsel together*, call councils of war, and all heads are at work about the proper methods for making yourselves masters of the land of Judah. *You speak the word:* you come to resolutions concerning it, and are not always deliberating; you determine what to do, and are very confident of the success of it, that the matter will be accomplished with a word's speaking." Note, It is with a great deal of policy, resolution, and assurance, that the church's enemies carry on their designs against it; and abundance of pains they take to roll a stone that will certainly return upon them. 2. " This is to let you know that all your efforts will be ineffectual. You cannot, you shall not, gain your point, nor carry the day : *You shall be broken in pieces.* Though you associate yourselves, though you gird yourselves, though you proceed with all the policy and precaution imaginable, yet, I tell you again and again, all your projects shall be baffled, *you shall be broken in pieces.* Nay, not only shall your attempts be ruined, but your attempts shall be your ruin; you shall be broken by those designs you have formed against Jerusalem: *Your counsels shall come to nought:* for there is no wisdom nor counsel against the Lord. Your resolves will not be put in execution; they shall not stand. You speak the word, but *who is he that saith, and it cometh to pass, if the Lord commandeth it not?* What sets up itself against God, and his cause and counsel, cannot stand, but must inevitably fall. *For God is with us*" (this refers to the name of *Immanuel—God with us*) ; " the Messiah is to be born among us, and a people designed for such an honour cannot be given up to utter ruin. We have now the special presence of God with us in his temple, his oracles, his promises, and these are our defence. God is with us; he is on our side, to take our part and fight for us; and, *if God be for us, who can be against us?*" Thus does the daughter of Zion despise them.

II. He comforts and encourages the people of God with the same comforts and encouragements which he himself had received. The attempt made upon them was very formidable ; the house of David, the court and royal family, were at their wits' end (*ch.* vii. 2), and then no marvel if the people were in a consternation. Now,

1. The prophet tells us how he was himself taught of God not to give way to such amazing fears as the people were disturbed with, nor to run into the same measures with them (*v.* 11) : " *The Lord spoke to me with a strong hand not to walk in the way of this people*, not to say as they say nor do as they do, not to entertain the same frightful apprehensions of things nor to approve of their projects of making peace upon any terms, or calling in the help of the Assyrians." God instructed the prophet not to go down the stream. Note, (1.) There is a proneness in the best of men to be frightened at threatening clouds, especially when fears are epidemic. We are all too apt to walk in the way of the people we live among, though it be not a good way. (2.) Those whom God loves and owns he will instruct and enable to swim against the stream of common corruptions, particularly of common fears. He will find ways to teach his own people not to walk in the way of other people, but in a sober singularity. (3.) Corruption is sometimes so active in the hearts even of good men that they have need to be taught their duty with a strong hand, and it is God's prerogative to teach so, for he only can give an understanding and overpower the contradiction of unbelief and prejudice. He can teach the heart; and herein none teaches like him. (4.) Those that are to teach others have need to be themselves well instructed in their duty, and then they teach most powerfully when they teach experimentally. The word that comes from the heart is most likely to reach to the heart; and what we are ourselves by the grace of God instructed in we should, as we are able, teach others also.

2. Now what is it that he says to God's people ?

(1.) He cautions them against a sinful fear, *v.* 12. It seems it was the way of this people at this time, and fear is catching. He whose heart fails him makes his brethren's heart to fail, like his (Deut. xx. 8) ; therefore *Say you not, A confederacy, to all those to whom this people shall say, A confederacy:* that is, [1.] " Be not associated with them in the confederacies they are projecting and forecasting for. Do not join with those that, for the securing of themselves, are for making a league with the Assyrians, through unbelief, and distrust of God and their cause. Do not come into any such confederacy." Note, It concerns us, in time of trouble, to watch against all such fears as put us upon taking any indirect courses for our own security. [2.] " Be not afraid of the confederacies they frighten themselves and one another with. Do not distress yourselves with the apprehension of a confederacy upon every thing that stirs, nor, when any little thing is amiss, cry out presently, There is a plot, a plot. When they talk what dismal news there is, *Syria is joined with Ephraim*, what will become of us ? must we fight, or must we flee, or must we yield ? do not you fear their fear : *Be not afraid of the signs of heaven*, as the heathen are, Jer. x. 2. Be not afraid of evil tidings on earth, but let your hearts be fixed. Fear not that which they fear, nor be afraid as they are. Be not put into such a fright as causes trembling and shaking;" so the word signifies. Note, When the church's enemies have sinful confederacies on foot the church's friends should watch against the sinful fears of those confederacies.

(2.) He advises them to a gracious religious fear: *But sanctify the Lord of hosts himself, v.* 13. Note, The believing fear of God is a special preservative against the disquieting fear of man; see 1 Pet. iii. 14, 15, where this is quoted, and applied to suffering Christians. [1.] We must look upon God as the Lord of hosts, that has all power in his hand and all creatures at his beck. [2.] We must sanctify him accordingly, give him the glory due to that name, and behave towards him as those that believe him to be a holy God. [3.] We must make him our fear, the object of our fear, and make him our dread, keep up a reverence of his providence and stand in awe of his sovereignty, be afraid of his displeasure and silently acquiesce in all his disposals. Were we but duly affected with the greatness and glory of God, we should see the pomp of our enemies eclipsed and clouded, and all their power restrained and under check; see Neh. iv. 14. Those that are *afraid of the reproach of men forget the Lord their Maker, ch.* li. 12, 13. Compare Luke xii. 4, 5.

(3.) He assures them of a holy security and serenity of mind in so doing (*v.* 14): " *He shall be for a sanctuary;* make him your fear, and you shall find him your hope, your help, your defence, and your mighty deliverer. He will sanctify and preserve you. He will be for a sanctuary," [1.] To make you holy. He will be your sanctification;" so some read it. If we sanctify God by our praises, he will sanctify us by his grace. [2.] " To make you easy. He will be your sanctuary, to which you may flee for safety, and where you are privileged from all the arrests of fear; you shall find an inviolable refuge and security in him, and see yourselves out of the reach of danger. Those that truly fear God shall not need to fear any evil.

III. He threatens the ruin of the ungodly and unbelieving, both in Judah and Israel. They have no part nor lot in the foregoing comforts; that God who will be a sanctuary to those who trust in him will be a stone of stumbling, and a rock of offence, to those who *leave these waters of Shiloah, and rejoice in Rezin and Remaliah's son,* (*v.* 6), who make the creature their fear and their hope, *v.* 14, 15. The prophet foresees that the greatest part of both the houses of Israel would not *sanctify the Lord of hosts,* and to them he would be *for a gin and a snare;* he would be a terror to them, as he would be a support and stay to those that trusted in him. Instead of profiting by the word of God, they should be offended at it; and the providences of God, instead of leading them

to him, would drive them from him. What was a savour of life unto life to others would be a savour of death unto death to them. " So that *many among them shall stumble and fall;* they shall fall both into sin and into ruin; they shall fall by the sword, shall be taken prisoners, and go into captivity." Note, If the things of God be an offence to us, they will be an undoing to us. Some apply this to the unbelieving Jews, who rejected Christ, and to whom he became a stone of stumbling; for the apostle quotes this scripture with application to all those who persisted in their unbelief of the gospel of Christ (1 Pet. ii. 8); to them he is a rock of offence, because, being disobedient to the word, they stumble at it.

16 Bind up the testimony, seal the law among my disciples. 17 And I will wait upon the LORD, that hideth his face from the house of Jacob, and I will look for him. 18 Behold, I and the children whom the LORD hath given me *are* for signs and for wonders in Israel from the LORD of hosts, which dwelleth in mount Zion. 19 And when they shall say unto you, Seek unto them that have familiar spirits, and unto wizards that peep, and that mutter: should not a people seek unto their God? For the living to the dead? 20 To the law and to the testimony: if they speak not according to this word, *it is* because *there is* no light in them. 21 And they shall pass through it, hardly bestead and hungry: and it shall come to pass, that when they shall be hungry, they shall fret themselves, and curse their king and their God, and look upward. 22 And they shall look unto the earth; and behold trouble and darkness, dimness of anguish; and *they shall be* driven to darkness.

In these verses we have,

I. The unspeakable privilege which the people of God enjoy in having the oracles of God consigned over to them, and being entrusted with the sacred writings. That they may sanctify the Lord of hosts, may make him their fear and find him their sanctuary, *bind up the testimony, v.* 16. Note, It is a great instance of God's care of his church and love to it that he has lodged in it the invaluable treasure of divine revelation. 1. It is a *testimony* and a *law;* not only this prophecy is so, which must therefore be preserved safely for the comfort of God's people in the approaching times of trouble and distress, but the whole word of God is so; God has attested it, and he has enjoined it. As a testimony it directs our faith; as a law it directs our practice; and we ought both to subscribe to the truths of it and to submit to the precepts of it. 2. This testimony and this law are bound up and sealed, for we are not to add to them nor diminish from them; they are a letter from God to man, folded up and sealed, a proclamation under the broad seal. The binding up and sealing of the Old Testament signified that the full explication of many of the prophecies of it was reserved for the New-Testament times. Dan. xii. 4, *Seal the book till the time of the end;* but what was then bound up and sealed is now open and unsealed, and *revealed unto babes,* Matt. xi. 25. Yet with reference to the other world, and the future state, still the testimony is bound up and sealed, for we know but in part, and prophesy but in part. 3. They are lodged as a sacred deposit in the hands of the disciples of *the children of the prophets and the covenant,* Acts iii. 25. This is the good thing which is committed to them, and which they are charged with the custody of, 2 Tim. i. 13, 14. Those that had prophets for their tutors must still keep close to the written word.

II. The good use which we ought to make of this privilege. This we are taught, 1. By the prophet's own practice and resolutions, *v.* 17, 18. He embraced the law and the testimony, and he had the comfort of them, in the midst of the many discouragements he met with. Note, Those ministers can best recommend the word of God to others that have themselves found the satisfaction of relying upon it. Observe,

(1.) The discouragements which the prophet laboured under. He specifies two:— [1.] The frowns of God, not so much upon himself, but upon his people, whose interests lay very near his heart : " He *hides his face from the house of Jacob,* and seems at present to neglect them, and lay them under the tokens of his displeasure." The prophet was himself employed in revealing God's wrath against them, and yet grieved thus for it, as one that did not desire the woeful day. If the house of Jacob forsake the God of Jacob, let it not be thought strange that he hides his face from them. [2.] The contempt and reproaches of men, not only upon himself, but upon his disciples, among whom the law and the testimony were sealed : *I and the children whom the Lord has given me are for signs and wonders;* we are gazed at as monsters or outlandish people, pointed at as we go along the streets. Probably the prophetical names that were given to his children were ridiculed and bantered by the profane scoffers of the town. *I am as a wonder unto many,* Ps. lxxi. 7. God's people are the world's wonder (Zech. iii. 8) for their singularity, and because they run not

with them to the same excess of riot, 1 Pet. iv. 4. The prophet was herein a type of Christ; for this is quoted (Heb. ii. 13) to prove that believers are Christ's children : *Behold, I and the children whom God has given me.* Parents must look upon their children as God's gifts, his gracious gifts; Jacob did so, Gen. xxxiii. 5. Ministers must look upon their converts as their children, and be tender of them accordingly (1 Thess. ii. 7), and as the children whom God has given them; for, whatever good we are instrumental of to others, it is owing to the grace of God. Christ looks upon believers as his children, whom the Father gave him (John xvii. 6), and both he and they are for signs and wonders, spoken against (Luke ii. 34), every where spoken against, Acts xxviii. 22.

(2.) The encouragement he took in reference to these discouragements. [1.] He saw the hand of God in all that which was discouraging to him, and kept his eye upon that. Whatever trouble the house of Jacob is in, it comes from God's hiding his face; nay, whatever contempt was put upon him or his friends, it is from the Lord of hosts; he has bidden Shimei curse David, Job xix. 13; xxx. 11. [2.] He saw God dwelling in Mount Zion, manifesting himself to his people, and ready to hear their prayers and receive their homage. Though, for the present, he hide his face from the house of Jacob, yet they know where to find him and recover the sight of him; he dwells in Mount Zion. [3.] He therefore resolved to wait upon the Lord and to look for him; to attend his motions even while he hid his face, and to expect with a humble assurance his returns in a way of mercy. Those that wait upon God by faith and prayer may look for him with hope and joy. When we have not sensible comforts we must still keep up our observance of God and obedience to him, and then wait awhile; *at evening time it shall be light.*

2. By the counsel and advice which he gives to his disciples, among whom the law and the testimony were sealed, to whom were committed the lively oracles.

(1.) He supposes they would be tempted, in the day of their distress, to consult *those that had familiar spirits,* that dealt with the devil, asked his advice, and desired to be informed by him concerning things to come, that they might take their measures accordingly. Thus Saul, when he was in straits, made his application to the witch of Endor (1 Sam. xxviii. 7, 15), and Ahaziah to the god of Ekron, 2 Kings i. 2. These conjurors had strange fantastic gestures and tones : They *peeped and muttered;* they muffled their heads, that they could neither see nor be seen plainly, but peeped and were peeped at. Or both the words here used may refer to their voice and manner of speaking; they delivered what they had to say with a low, hollow, broken sound, scarcely articulate, and sometimes in a puling or mournful tone, like a crane, or a swallow, or a dove, *ch.* xxxviii. 14. They spoke not with that boldness and plainness which the prophets of the Lord spoke with, but as those who desire to amuse people rather than to instruct them; yet there were those who were so wretchedly sottish as to seek to them and to court others to do so, even the prophet's hearers, who knew better things, whom therefore the prophet warns not to say, *A confederacy* with such. There were express laws against this wickedness (Lev. xix. 31; xx. 27), and yet it was found in Israel, is found even in Christian nations; but let all that have any sense of religion show it, by startling at the thought of it. *Get thee behind me, Satan.* Dread the use of spells and charms, and consulting those that by hidden arts pretend to tell fortunes, cure diseases, or discover things lost; for this is a heinous crime, and, in effect, denies the God that is above.

(2.) He furnishes them with an answer to this temptation, puts words into their mouths. " If any go about thus to ensnare you, give them this reply : *Should not a people seek to their God?* What ! *for the living to the dead !*" [1.] " Tell them it is a principle of religion that a people ought to seek unto their God; now Jehovah is our God, and therefore to him we ought to seek, and to consult with him, and not with those that have familiar spirits. *All people will thus walk in the name of their God,* Mic. iv. 5. Those that made the hosts of heaven their gods *sought unto them,* Jer. viii. 2. Should not a people under guilt, and in trouble, seek to their God for pardon and peace ? Should not a people in doubt, in want, and in danger, seek to their God for direction, supply, and protection ? Since the Lord is our God, and we are his people, it is certainly our duty to seek him." [2.] " Tell them it is an instance of the greatest folly in the world to seek for living men to dead idols." What can be more absurd than to seek to lifeless images for life and living comforts, or to expect that our friends that are dead should do that for us, when we deify them and pray to them, which our living friends cannot do ? The *dead know not any thing,* nor is there with them *any device or working,* Eccl. ix. 5, 10. It is folly therefore for the living to make their court to them, with any expectation of relief from them. Necromancers consulted the dead, as the witch of Endor, and so proclaimed their own folly. We must live by the living, and not by the dead. What life or light can we look for from those that have no light or life themselves ?

(3.) He directs them to consult the oracles of God. If the prophets that were among them did not speak directly to every case, yet they had the written word, and to that

they must have recourse. Note, Those will never be drawn to consult wizards that know how to make a good use of their Bibles. Would we know how we may seek to our God, and come to the knowledge of his mind? *To the law and to the testimony.* There you will see what is good, and what the Lord requires of you. Make God's statutes your counsellors, and you will be counselled aright. Observe, [1.] What use we must make of the law and the testimony : we must *speak according to that word,* that is, we must make this our standard, conform to it, take advice from it, make our appeals to it, and in every thing be overruled and determined by it, consent to those wholesome healing words (1 Tim. vi. 3), and speak of the things of God in the words which the Holy Ghost teaches. It is not enough to say nothing against it, but we must speak according to it. [2.] Why we must make this use of the law and the testimony : because we shall be convicted of the greatest folly imaginable if we do not. Those that concur not with the word of God do thereby evince that *there is no light,* no morning light (so the word is) *in them;* they have no right sense of things; they do not understand themselves, nor the difference between good and evil, truth and falsehood. Note, Those that reject divine revelation have not so much as human understanding; nor do those rightly admit the oracles of reason who will not admit the oracles of God. Some read it as a threatening : " If they speak not according to this word, there shall be no light to them, no good, no comfort or relief; but they shall be driven to darkness and despair ;" as it follows here, *v.* 21, 22. What light had Saul when he consulted the witch ? 1 Sam. xxviii. 18, 20. Or what light can those expect that turn away from the Father of lights ?

(4.) He reads the doom of those that seek to familiar spirits and regard not God's law and testimony; there shall not only be no light to them, no comfort or prosperity, but they may expect all horror and misery, *v.* 21, 22. [1.] The trouble they feared shall come upon them : They shall *pass through* the land, or pass to and fro in the land, unfixed, unsettled, and driven from place to place by the threatening power of an invading enemy; they shall be *hardly bestead* whither to go for the necessary supports of life, either because the country would be so impoverished that there would be nothing to be had, or at least themselves and their friends so impoverished that there would be nothing to be had for them; so that those who used to be fed to the full shall be hungry. Note, Those that go away from God go out of the way of all good. [2.] They shall be very uneasy to themselves, by their discontent and impatience under their trouble. A good man may be in want, but then he quiets himself, and strives to make himself easy; but these people *when they shall be hungry shall fret themselves,* and when they have nothing to feed on their vexation shall prey upon their own spirits; for fretfulness is a sin that is its own punishment. [3.] They shall be very provoking to all about them, nay, to all above them; when they find all their measures broken, and themselves at their wits' end, they will forget all the rules of duty and decency, and will treasonably *curse their king* and blasphemously curse *their God,* and this more than *in their thought and in their bed-chamber,* Eccl. x. 20. They begin with cursing their king for managing the public affairs no better, as if the fault were his, when the best and wisest kings cannot secure success; but, when they have broken the bonds of their allegiance, no marvel if those of their religion do not hold them long: they next curse their God, curse him, and die; they quarrel with his providence, and reproach that, as if he had done them wrong. *The foolishness of man perverts his way,* and then *his heart frets against the Lord,* Prov. xix. 3. See what need we have to *keep our mouth as with a bridle* when our *heart is hot within us;* for the language of fretfulness is commonly very offensive. [4.] They shall abandon themselves to despair, and, which way soever they look, shall see no probability of relief. They shall look upward, but heaven shall frown upon them and look gloomy; and how can it be otherwise when they curse their God? They shall look to the earth, but what comfort can that yield to those with whom God is at war? There is nothing there but trouble, and darkness, and dimness of anguish, every thing threatening, and not one pleasant gleam, not one hopeful prospect; but they shall be driven to darkness by the violence of their own fears, which represent every thing about them black and frightful. This explains what he had said *v.* 20, that there shall be no light to them. Those that shut their eyes against the light of God's word will justly be abandoned to darkness, and left to wander endlessly, and the sparks of their own kindling will do them no kindness.

CHAP IX.

The prophet in this chapter (according to the directions given him, ch. iii. 10, 11) saith to the righteous, It shall be well with thee, but Woe to the wicked, it shall be ill with him. Here are, I. Gracious promises to those that adhere to the law and to the testimony; while those that seek to familiar spirits shall be driven into darkness and dimness, they shall see a great light, relief in the midst of their distresses, typical of gospel grace. 1. In the doctrine of the Messiah, ver. 1—3. 2. His victories, ver. 4, 5. 3. His government and dominion as Immanuel, ver. 6, 7. II. Dreadful threatenings against the people of Israel, who had revolted from and were enemies to the house of David, that they should be brought to utter ruin, that their pride should bring them down (ver. 8—10), that their neighbours should make a prey of them (ver. 11, 12), that, for their impenitence and hypocrisy, all their ornaments and supports should be cut off (ver. 13—17), and that by the wrath of God against them, and their wrath one against another, they should be brought to utter ruin, ver. 18—21. And this is typical of the final destruction of all the enemies of the Son of David and his kingdom.

NEVERTHELESS the dimness *shall* not *be* such as *was* in her

vexation, when at the first he lightly afflicted the land of Zebulun and the land of Naphtali, and afterward did more grievously afflict *her by* the way of the sea, beyond Jordan, in Galilee of the nations. 2 The people that walked in darkness have seen a great light: they that dwell in the land of the shadow of death, upon them hath the light shined. 3 Thou hast multiplied the nation, *and* not increased the joy: they joy before thee according to the joy in harvest, *and* as *men* rejoice when they divide the spoil. 4 For thou hast broken the yoke of his burden, and the staff of his shoulder, the rod of his oppressor, as in the day of Midian. 5 For every battle of the warrior *is* with confused noise, and garments rolled in blood; but *this* shall be with burning *and* fuel of fire. 6 For unto us a child is born, unto us a son is given: and the government shall be upon his shoulder: and his name shall be called Wonderful, Counsellor, The mighty God, The everlasting Father, The Prince of Peace. 7 Of the increase of *his* government and peace *there shall be* no end, upon the throne of David, and upon his kingdom, to order it, and to establish it with judgment and with justice from henceforth even for ever. The zeal of the LORD of hosts will perform this.

The first words of this chapter plainly refer to the close of the foregoing chapter, where every thing looked black and melancholy: *Behold, trouble, and darkness, and dimness*—very bad, yet not so bad but that *to the upright there shall arise light in the darkness* (Ps. cxii. 4) and *at evening time it shall be light,* Zech. xiv. 7. Nevertheless it *shall not be such dimness* (either not such for kind or not such for degree) as sometimes there has been. Note, In the worst of times God's people have a *nevertheless* to comfort themselves with, something to allay and balance their troubles; they are persecuted, but not forsaken (2 Cor. iv. 9), sorrowful yet always rejoicing, 2 Cor. vi. 10. And it is matter of comfort to us, when things are at the darkest, that he who *forms the light and creates the darkness* (ch. xlv. 7) has appointed to both their bounds and set the one over against the other, Gen. i. 4. He can say, "Hitherto the dimness shall go, so long it shall last, and no further, no longer."

I. Three things are here promised, and they all point ultimately at the grace of the gospel, which the saints then were to comfort themselves with the hopes of in every cloudy and dark day, as we now are to comfort ourselves in time of trouble with the hopes of Christ's second coming, though that be now, as his first coming then was, a thing at a great distance. The mercy likewise which God has in store for his church in the latter days may be a support to those that are mourning with her for her present calamities. We have here the promise,

1. Of a glorious light, which shall so qualify, and by degrees dispel, the dimness, that it shall not be as it sometimes has been : *Not such as was in her vexation ;* there shall not be such dark times as were formerly, *when at first he lightly afflicted the land of Zebulun and Naphtali* (which lay remote and most exposed to the inroads of the neighbouring enemies), *and afterwards he more grievously afflicted the land by the way of the sea and beyond Jordan* (v. 1), referring probably to those days when *God began to cut Israel short* and to *smite them in all their coasts*, 2 Kings x. 32. Note, God tries what less judgments will do with a people before he brings greater; but if a light affliction do not do its work with us, to humble and reform us, we must expect to be afflicted more grievously ; for when God judges he will overcome. Well, those were dark times with the land of Zebulun and Naphtali, and there was *dimness of anguish in Galilee of the Gentiles,* both in respect of ignorance (they did not speak according *to the law and the testimony,* and then there was *no light in them, ch.* viii. 20) and in respect of trouble, and the desperate posture of their outward affairs ; we have both together, 2 Chron. xv. 3, 5. *Israel has been without the true God and a teaching priest, and in those times there was no peace.* But the dimness threatened (*ch.* viii. 22) shall not prevail to such a degree ; for (*v.* 2) *the people that walked in darkness have seen a great light.* (1.) At this time when the prophet lived, there were many prophets in Judah and Israel, whose prophecies were a great light both for direction and comfort to the people of God, who adhered to the law and the testimony. Besides the written word, they had prophecy ; there were those that had shown them how long (Ps. lxxiv. 9), which was a great satisfaction to them, when in respect of their outward troubles they *sat in darkness, and dwelt in the land of the shadow of death.* (2.) This was to have its full accomplishment when our Lord Jesus began to appear as a prophet, and to preach the gospel in the land of Zebulun and Naphtali, and in Galilee of the Gentiles. And the Old-Testament prophets, as they

were witnesses to him, so they were types of him. When he came and dwelt in the borders of Zebulun and Naphtali, then this prophecy is said to have been fulfilled. Matt. iv. 13—16. Note, [1.] Those that want the gospel walk in darkness, and know not what they do nor whither they go ; and they dwell in the land of the shadow of death, in thick darkness, and in the utmost danger. [2.] When the gospel comes to any place, to any soul, light comes, a great light, a shining light, which will shine more and more. It should be welcome to us, as light is to those that sit in darkness, and we should readily entertain it, both because it is of such sovereign use to us and because it brings its own evidence with it. Truly this light is sweet.

2. Of a glorious increase, and a universal joy arising from it, (*v.* 3) *" Thou,* O God ! *hast multiplied the nation,* the Jewish nation which thou hast mercy in store for ; though it has been diminished by one sore judgment after another, yet now thou hast begun to multiply it again." The numbers of a nation are its strength and wealth if the numerous be industrious ; and it is God that increases nations, Job xii. 23. Yet it follows, " *Thou hast not increased the joy—* the carnal joy and mirth, and those things that are commonly the matter and occasion thereof. But, notwithstanding that, *they joy before thee ;* there is a great deal of serious spiritual joy among them, joy in the presence of God, with an eye to him." This is very applicable to the times of gospel light, spoken of *v.* 2. Then God multiplied the nation, the gospel Israel. "And to him" (so the Masorites read it) " thou hast magnified the joy, to every one that receives the light." The following words favour this reading : " *They joy before thee ;* they come before thee in holy ordinances with great joy ; their mirth is not like that of Israel under their vines and fig-trees (thou hast not increased that joy), but it is in the favour of God and in the tokens of his grace." Note, The gospel, when it comes in its light and power, brings joy along with it, and those who receive it aright do therein rejoice, yea, and will rejoice ; therefore the conversion of the nations is prophesied of by this (Ps. lxvii. 4), *Let the nations be glad, and sing for joy.* See Ps. xcvi. 11. (1.) It is holy joy : *They joy before thee ;* they rejoice in spirit (as Christ did, Luke x. 21), and that is before God. In the eye of the world they are always as sorrowful, and yet, in God's sight, *always rejoicing,* 2 Cor. vi. 10. (2.) It is great joy ; it is *according to the joy in harvest,* when those who sowed in tears, and have with long patience waited for the precious fruits of the earth, reap in joy ; and as in war men rejoice when, after a hazardous battle, *they divide the spoil.* The gospel brings with it plenty and victory ; but those that would have the joy of it

must expect to go through a hard work, as the husbandman before he has the joy of harvest, and a hard conflict, as the soldier before he has the joy of dividing the spoil; but the joy, when it comes, will be an abundant recompence for the toil. See Acts viii. 8, 39.

3. Of a glorious liberty and enlargement (*v.* 4, 5): "They shall rejoice before thee, and with good reason, *for thou hast broken the yoke of his burden,* and made him easy, for he shall no longer be in servitude; and thou hast broken *the staff of his shoulder and the rod of his oppressor,* that rod of the wicked which rested long on the lot of the righteous," as the Midianites' yoke was broken from off the neck of Israel by the agency of Gideon. If God makes former deliverances his patterns in working for us, we ought to make them our encouragements to hope in him and to seek to him, Ps. lxxxiii. 9. *Do unto them as to the Midianites.* What temporal deliverance this refers to is not clear, probably the preventing of Sennacherib from making himself master of Jerusalem, which was done, *as in the day of Midian,* by the immediate hand of God; and, whereas other battles were usually won with a great deal of noise and by the expense of much blood, this shall be done silently and without noise. *Under his glory God shall kindle a burning* (ch. x. 16); a *fire not blown shall consume him,* Job xx. 26. But doubtless it looks further, to the blessed fruits and effects of that great light which should visit those that sat in darkness; it would bring liberty along with it, *deliverance to the captives,* Luke iv. 18. (1.) The design of the gospel, and the grace of it, is to break the yoke of sin and Satan, to remove the burden of guilt and corruption, and to free us from the rod of those oppressors, that we might be brought into the glorious liberty of the children of God. Christ broke the yoke of the ceremonial law (Acts. xv. 10; Gal. v. 1), and delivered us *out of the hand of our enemies,* that we might *serve him without fear,* Luke i. 74, 75. (2.) This is done by the Spirit working like fire (Matt. iii. 11), not as the battle of the warrior is fought, with confused noise; no, the weapons of our warfare are not carnal; but it is done with the Spirit of judgment and the Spirit of burning, *ch.* iv. 4. It is done *as in the day of Midian,* by a work of God upon the hearts of men. Christ is our Gideon; it is his sword that doeth wonders.

II. But who, where, is he that shall undertake and accomplish these great things for the church? The prophet tells us (*v.* 6, 7) they shall be done by the Messiah, *Immanuel,* that son of a virgin whose birth he had foretold (*ch.* vii. 14), and now speaks of, in the prophetic style, as a thing already done: the *child is born,* not only because it was as certain, and he was as certain of it as if it had been done already, but because the church before his incarnation reaped great

benefit and advantage by his undertaking in virtue of that first promise concerning the *seed of the woman,* Gen. iii. 15. As he was the Lamb slain, so he was the child born, *from the foundation of the world,* Rev. xiii. 8. All the great things that God did for the Old-Testament church were done by him as the eternal Word, and for his sake as the Mediator. He was the Anointed, to whom God had respect (Ps. lxxxiv. 9), and it was for the Lord's sake, for the Lord Christ's sake, that God caused his face to shine upon his sanctuary, Dan. ix. 17. The Jewish nation, and particularly the house of David, were preserved many a time from imminent ruin only because that blessing was in them. What greater security therefore could be given to the church of God then that it should be preserved, and be the special care of the divine Providence, than this, that God had so great a mercy in reserve for it? The Chaldee paraphrast understands it of the man that shall endure for ever, even Christ. And it is an illustrious prophecy of him and of his kingdom, which doubtless those that waited for the consolation of Israel built much upon, often turned to, and read with pleasure.

1. See him in his humiliation. The same that is *the mighty God* is *a child born:* the ancient of days becomes an infant of a span long; the *everlasting Father* is a *Son given.* Such was his condescension in taking our nature upon him; thus did he humble and empty himself, to exalt and fill us. He is born into our world. *The Word was made flesh, and dwelt among us.* He is given, freely given, to be all that to us which our case, in our fallen state, calls for. God so loved the world that he gave him. He is born *to us,* he is given to us, us men, and not to the angels that sinned. It is spoken with an air of triumph, and the angel seems to refer to these words in the notice he gives to the shepherds of the Messiah's having come (Luke ii. 11), *Unto you is born, this day, a Saviour.* Note, Christ's being born and given to us is the great foundation of our hopes, and fountain of our joys, in times of greatest grief and fear.

2. See him in his exaltation. This child, this son, this Son of God, this Son of man, that is given to us, is in a capacity to do us a great deal of kindness; for he is invested with the highest honour and power, so that we cannot but be happy if he be our friend.

(1.) See the dignity he is advanced to, and the name he has above every name. He shall be called (and therefore we are sure he is and shall be) *Wonderful, Counsellor, &c.* His people shall know him and worship him by these names; and, as one that fully answers them, they shall submit to him and depend upon him. [1.] He is *wonderful, counsellor.* Justly is he called *wonderful,* for he is both God and man. His love is the wonder of angels and glorified saints; in his birth, life, death, resurrection, and ascension, he was wonderful. A constant series of wonders attended him, and, without controversy, great was the mystery of godliness concerning him. He is the *counsellor*, for he was intimately acquainted with the counsels of God from eternity, and he gives counsel to the children of men, in which he consults our welfare. It is by him that God has *given us counsel*, Ps. xvi. 7; Rev. iii. 18. He is the wisdom of the Father, and is made of God to us wisdom. Some join these together: He is the wonderful counsellor, a wonder or miracle of a counsellor; in this, as in other things, he has the pre-eminence; none teaches like him. [2.] He is *the mighty God—God, the mighty One*. As he has wisdom, so he has strength, to go through with his undertaking: he is able to save to the utmost; and such is the work of the Mediator that no less a power than that of the mighty God could accomplish it. [3.] He is *the everlasting Father*, or *the Father of eternity;* he is God, one with the Father, who is from everlasting to everlasting. His fatherly care of his people and tenderness towards them are everlasting. He is the author of everlasting life and happiness to them, and so is the Father of a blessed eternity to them. He is *the Father of the world to come* (so the LXX. read it), the father of the gospel-state, which is put in subjection to him, not to the angels, Heb. ii. 5. He was, from eternity, Father of the great work of redemption: his heart was upon it; it was the product of his wisdom as *the counsellor,* of his love as *the everlasting Father.* [4.] He is *the prince of peace.* As a King, he preserves the peace, commands peace, nay, he creates peace, in his kingdom. He is our peace, and it is his peace that both keeps the hearts of his people and rules in them. He is not only a peaceable prince, and his reign peaceable, but he is the author and giver of all good, all that peace which is the present and future bliss of his subjects.

(2.) See the dominion he is advanced to, and the throne he has above every throne (*v.* 6): *The government shall be upon his shoulder* —his only. He shall not only wear the badge of it upon his shoulder (the *key of the house of David, ch.* xxii. 22), but he shall bear the burden of it. The Father shall devolve it upon him, so that he shall have an incontestable right to govern; and he shall undertake it, so that no doubt can be made of his governing well, for he shall set his shoulder to it, and will never complain, as Moses did, of his being overcharged. *I am not able to bear all this people,* Num. xi. 11, 14. Glorious things are here spoken of Christ's government, *v.* 7. [1.] That it shall be an increasing government. It shall be multiplied; the bounds of his kingdom shall be more and more enlarged, and many shall be added to it daily. The lustre of it shall increase,
60

and it shall shine more and more brightly in the world. The monarchies of the earth were each less illustrious than the other, so that what began in gold ended in iron and clay, and every monarchy dwindled by degrees; but the kingdom of Christ is a growing kingdom, and will come to perfection at last. [2.] That it shall be a peaceable government, agreeable to his character as the prince of peace. He shall rule by love, shall rule in men's hearts; so that wherever his government is there shall be peace, and as his government increases the peace shall increase. The more we are subject to Christ the more easy and safe we are. [3.] That it shall be a rightful government. He that is the Son of David shall reign upon the throne of David and over his kingdom, which he is entitled to. *God shall give him the throne of his father David,* Luke i. 32, 33. The gospel church, in which Jew and Gentile are incorporated, is the holy hill of Zion, on which Christ reigns, Ps. ii. 6. [4.] That it shall be administered with prudence and equity, and so as to answer the great end of government, which is the establishment of the kingdom: *He shall order it, and settle it, with justice and judgment.* Every thing is, and shall be, well managed, in the kingdom of Christ, and none of his subjects shall ever have cause to complain. [5.] That it shall be an everlasting kingdom: *There shall be no end of the increase of his government* (it shall be still growing), no end of the increase of the peace of it, for the happiness of the subjects of this kingdom shall last to eternity and perhaps shall be progressive *in infinitum—for ever.* He shall reign *henceforth even for ever;* not only throughout all generations of time, but, even when the kingdom shall be delivered up to God even the Father, the glory both of the Redeemer and the redeemed shall continue eternally. [6.] That God himself has undertaken to bring all this about: " *The Lord of hosts,* who has all power in his hand and all creatures at his beck, *shall perform this,* shall preserve the throne of David till this prince of peace is settled in it; his *zeal* shall do it, his jealousy for his own honour, and the truth of his promise, and the good of his church." Note, The heart of God is much upon the advancement of the kingdom of Christ among men, which is very comfortable to all those that wish well to it; *the zeal of the Lord of hosts* will overcome all opposition.

8 The LORD sent a word into Jacob, and it hath lighted upon Israel. 9 And all the people shall know, *even* Ephraim and the inhabitants of Samaria, that say in the pride and stoutness of heart, 10 The bricks are fallen down, but we will build with hewn stones: the sycomores are cut down, but we will change *them into* cedars.

11 Therefore the LORD shall set up the adversaries of Rezin against him, and join his enemies together; 12 The Syrians before, and the Philistines behind; and they shall devour Israel with open mouth. For all this his anger is not turned away, but his hand *is* stretched out still. 13 For the people turneth not unto him that smiteth them, neither do they seek the LORD of hosts. 14 Therefore the LORD will cut off from Israel head and tail, branch and rush, in one day. 15 The ancient and honourable, he *is* the head; and the prophet that teacheth lies, he *is* the tail. 16 For the leaders of this people cause *them* to err; and *they that are* led of them *are* destroyed. 17 Therefore the LORD shall have no joy in their young men, neither shall have mercy on their fatherless and widows: for every one *is* an hypocrite and an evil doer, and every mouth speaketh folly. For all this his anger is not turned away, but his hand *is* stretched out still. 18 For wickedness burneth as the fire: it shall devour the briers and thorns, and shall kindle in the thickets of the forest, and they shall mount up *like* the lifting up of smoke. 19 Through the wrath of the LORD of hosts is the land darkened, and the people shall be as the fuel of the fire: no man shall spare his brother. 20 And he shall snatch on the right hand, and be hungry; and he shall eat on the left hand, and they shall not be satisfied: they shall eat every man the flesh of his own arm: 21 Manasseh, Ephraim; and Ephraim, Manasseh: *and* they together *shall be* against Judah. For all this his anger is not turned away, but his hand *is* stretched out still.

Here are terrible threatenings, which are directed primarily against Israel, the kingdom of the ten tribes, Ephraim and Samaria, the ruin of which is here foretold, with all the woeful confusions that were the prefaces to that ruin, all which came to pass within a few years after; but they look further, to all the enemies of the throne and kingdom of Christ the Son of David, and read the doom of all the nations that forget God, and will not have Christ to reign over them. Observe,

I. The preface to this prediction (*v.* 8):

The Lord sent a word into Jacob, sent it by his servants the prophets. He warns before he wounds. He sent notice what he would do, that they might meet him in the way of his judgments; but they would not take the hint, took no care to turn away his wrath, and so it lighted upon Israel; for no word of God shall fall to the ground. It fell upon them as a storm of rain and hail from on high, which they could not avoid: *It has lighted upon them,* that is, it is as sure to come as if come already, and all the people shall know by feeling it what they would not know by hearing of it. Those that are willingly ignorant of the wrath of God revealed from heaven against sin and sinners shall be made to know it.

II. The sins charged upon the people of Israel, which provoked God to bring these judgments upon them. 1. Their insolent defiance of the justice of God, thinking themselves a match for him: "They *say, in the pride and stoutness of their heart,* Let God himself do his worst; we will hold our own, and make our part good with him. If he ruin our houses, we will repair them, and make them stronger and finer than they were before. Our landlord shall not turn us out of doors, though we pay him no rent, but we will keep in possession. If the houses that were built of bricks be demolished in the war, we will rebuild them with hewn stones, that shall not so easily be thrown down. If the enemy cut down the sycamores, we will plant cedars in the room of them. We will make a hand of God's judgments, gain by them, and so outbrave them." Note, Those are ripening apace for ruin whose hearts are unhumbled under humbling providences; for God will walk contrary to those who thus walk contrary to him and provoke him to jealousy, as if they were stronger than he. 2. Their incorrigibleness under all the rebukes of Providence hitherto (*v.* 13): *The people turn not unto him that smiteth them* (they are not wrought upon to reform their lives, to forsake their sins, and to return to their duty), *neither do they seek the Lord of hosts:* either they are atheists, and have no religion, or idolaters, and seek to those gods that are the creatures of their own fancy and the works of their own hands. Note, That which God designs, in smiting us, is to turn us to himself and to set us a seeking him; and, if this point be not gained by less judgments, greater may be expected. God smites that he may not kill 3. Their general corruption of manners and abounding profaneness. (1.) Those that should have reformed them helped to debauch them (*v.* 16): *The leaders of this people* mislead them, and *cause them to err,* by conniving at their wickedness and countenancing wicked people, and by setting them bad examples; and then no wonder if those that are led of them be deceived and so destroyed. But it is ill with a people when their physicians are their worst disease. " *Those that bless this people,* or *call them blessed* (so the margin reads it), that flatter them, and soothe them in their wickedness, and cry *Peace, peace, to them,* cause them to err; and those *that are called blessed of them are swallowed up* ere they are aware. We have reason to be afraid of those that speak well of us when we do ill; see Prov. xxiv. 24; xxix. 5. (2.) Wickedness was universal, and all were infected with it (*v.* 17): *Every one is a hypocrite and an evil doer.* If there be any that are good, they do not, they dare not appear, for every mouth speaks folly and villany; every one is profane towards God (so the word properly signifies) and an evil doer towards man. These two commonly go together: those that fear not God regard not man; and then every mouth speaks folly, falsehood, and reproach, both against God and man; for *out of the abundance of the heart the mouth speaks.*

III. The judgments threatened against them for this wickedness of theirs; let them not think to go unpunished.

1. In general, hereby they exposed themselves to the wrath of God, which should both devour as fire and darken as smoke. (1.) It should devour as fire (*v.* 18): *Wickedness shall burn as the fire :* the displeasure of God, incurred by sin, shall consume the sinners, who have made themselves as briers and thorns before it, and as the thickets of the forest, combustible matter, which the wrath of the Lord of hosts, the mighty God, will go through and burn together. (2.) It should darken as smoke. The briers and thorns, when the fire consumes them, shall *mount up like the lifting up of smoke,* so that the whole land shall be darkened by it; they shall be in trouble, and see no way out (*v.* 19): *The people shall be as the fuel of the fire.* God's wrath fastens upon none but those that make themselves fuel for it, and then they mount up as the smoke of sacrifices, being made victims to divine justice.

2. God would arm the neighbouring powers against them, *v.* 11, 12. At this time the kingdom of Israel was in league with that of Syria against Judah; but the Assyrians, who were adversaries to the Syrians, when they had conquered them should invade Israel, and God would stir them up to do it, and join the enemies of Israel together in alliance against them, who yet had particular ends of their own to serve and were not aware of God's hand in their alliance. Note, When enemies are set up, and joined in confederacy against a people, God's hand must be acknowledged in it. Note further, Those that partake with each other in sin, as Syria and Israel in invading Judah, must expect to share in the punishment of sin. Nay, the Syrians themselves, whom they were now in league with, should be a scourge to them (for it is no unusual thing

for those to fall out that have been united in sin), they before and the Philistines behind, one attacking them in the front and the other flanking them or falling upon their rear; so that they should be surrounded with enemies on all sides, who should *devour them with open mouth, v.* 12. The Philistines were not now looked upon as formidable enemies, and the Syrians were looked upon as firm friends; and yet these shall devour Israel. When men's ways displease the Lord he makes even their friends to be at war with them.

3. God would take from the midst of them those they confided in and promised themselves help from, *v.* 14, 15. Because the people seek not God, those they seek to and depend upon shall stand them in no stead. *The Lord will cut off head and tail, branch and rush,* which is explained in the next verse. (1.) Their magistrates, who were honourable by birth and office and were the ancients of the people, these were *the head,* these were the branch which they promised themselves spirit and fruit from; but because these caused them to err they should be cut off, and their dignity and power should be no protection to them when the abuse of that dignity and power was the great provocation: and it was a judgment upon the people to have their princes cut off, though they were not such as they should have been. (2.) Their prophets, their false prophets, were *the tail* and the *rush,* the most despicable of all. A wicked minister is the worst of men. *Corruptio optimi est pessima—The best things become when corrupted the worst.* The blind led the blind, and so both fell into the ditch; and the blind leaders fell first and fell undermost.

4. That the desolation should be as general as the corruption had been, and none should escape it, *v.* 17. (1.) Not those that were the objects of complacency. None shall be spared for love: *The Lord shall have no joy in their young men,* that were in the flower of their youth; nor will he say, *Deal gently with the young men for my sake :* no, " Let them fall with the rest, and with them let the seed of the next generation perish." (2) Not those that were the objects of compassion. None shall be spared for pity: He *shall not have mercy on their fatherless and widows,* though he is, in a particular manner, the patron and protector of such. They had corrupted their way like all the rest; and, if the poverty and helplessness of their state was not an argument with them to keep them from sin, they could not expect it should be an argument with God to protect them from judgments.

5. That they should pull one another to pieces, that every one should help forward the common ruin, and they should be cannibals to themselves and one to another: *No man shall spare his brother,* if he come

in the way of his ambition or covetousness, or if he have any colour to be revenged on him; and how can they expect God should spare them when they show no compassion one to another? Men's passion and cruelty one against another provoke God to be angry with them all and are an evidence that he is so. Civil wars soon bring a kingdom to desolation. Such there were in Israel, when, *for the transgression of the land, many were the princes thereof,* Prov. xxviii. 2.

(1.) In these intestine broils, men *snatched on the right hand, and yet were hungry* still, and did eat the *flesh of their own arms,* preyed upon themselves for hunger or upon their nearest relations that were as their own flesh, *v.* 20. This bespeaks, [1.] Great famine and scarcity; when men had pulled all they could to them it was so little that they were still hungry, at least God did not bless it to them, so that *they eat and have not enough,* Hag. i. 6. [2.] Great rapine and plunder. *Jusque datum sceleri—iniquity is established by law.* The hedge of property, which is a hedge of protection to men's estates, shall be plucked up, and every man shall think all that his own which he can lay his hands on (*vivitur ex rapto, non hospes ab hospite tutus—they live on the spoil, and the rites of hospitality are all violated*); and yet, when men thus catch at that which is none of their own, they are not satisfied. Covetous desires are insatiable, and this curse is entailed on that which is ill got, that it will never do well.

(2) These intestine broils should be not only among particular persons and private families, but among the tribes (*v.* 21): *Manasseh shall devour Ephraim, and Ephraim Manasseh,* though they be combined against Judah. Those that could unite against Judah could not unite with one another; but that sinful confederacy of theirs against their neighbour *that dwelt securely by them* was justly punished by this separation of them one from another. Or Judah, having sinned like Manasseh and Ephraim, shall not only suffer with them, but suffer by them. Note, Mutual enmity and animosity among the tribes of God's Israel is a sin that ripens them for ruin, and a sad symptom of ruin hastening on apace. If Ephraim be against Manasseh, and Manasseh against Ephraim, and both against Judah, they will all soon become a very easy prey to the common enemy.

6. That, though they should be followed with all these judgments, yet God would not let fall his controversy with them. It is the heavy burden of this song (*v.* 12, 17, 21): *For all this his anger is not turned away, but his hand is stretched out still,* that is, (1.) They do nothing to turn away his anger; they do not repent and reform, do not humble themselves and pray, none stand in the gap, none answer God's calls nor comply

with the designs of his providences, but they are hardened and secure. (2.) His anger therefore continues to burn against them and *his hand is stretched out still.* The reason why the judgments of God are prolonged is because the point is not gained, sinners are not brought to repentance by them. *The people turn not to him that smites them,* and therefore he continues to smite them; for when God judges he will overcome, and the proudest stoutest sinner shall either bend or break.

CHAP. X.

The prophet, in this chapter, is dealing, I. With the proud oppressors of his people at home, that abused their power, to pervert justice, whom he would reckon with for their tyranny, ver. 1—4. II. With a threatening invader of his people from abroad, Sennacherib king of Assyria, concerning whom observe, 1. The commission given him to invade Judah, ver. 5, 6. 2. His pride and insolence in the execution of that commission, ver. 7—11, 13, 14. 3. A rebuke given to his haughtiness, and a threatening of his fall and ruin, when he had served the purposes for which God raised him up, ver. 12, 15—19. 4. A promise of grace to the people of God, to enable them to bear up under the affliction, and to get good by it, ver. 20—23. 5. Great encouragement given to them not to fear this threatening storm, but to hope that, though for the present all the country was put into a great consternation by it, yet it would end well, in the destruction of this formidable enemy, ver. 24—34. And this is intended to quiet the minds of good people in reference to all the threatening efforts of the wrath of the church's enemies. If God be for us, who can be against us? None to do us any harm.

WOE unto them that decree unrighteous decrees, and that write grievousness *which* they have prescribed; 2 To turn aside the needy from judgment, and to take away the right from the poor of my people, that widows may be their prey, and *that* they may rob the fatherless! 3 And what will ye do in the day of visitation, and in the desolation *which* shall come from far? To whom will ye flee for help? And where will ye leave your glory? 4 Without me they shall bow down under the prisoners, and they shall fall under the slain. For all this his anger is not turned away, but his hand *is* stretched out still.

Whether they were the princes and judges of Israel or Judah, or both, that the prophet denounced this woe against, is not certain: if those of Israel, these verses are to be joined with the close of the foregoing chapter, which is probable enough, because the burden of that prophecy (*for all this his anger is not turned away*) is repeated here (*v.* 4); if those of Judah, they then show what was the particular design with which God brought the Assyrian army upon them —to punish their magistrates for mal-administration, which they could not legally be called to account for. To them he speaks woes before he speaks comfort to God's own people. Here is,

I. The indictment drawn up against these oppressors, *v.* 1, 2. They are charged, 1.

With making wicked laws and edicts: They *decree unrighteous decrees*, contrary to natural equity and the law of God: and what mischief they *prescribe* those under them *write* it, enrol it, and put it into the formality of a law. " Woe to the superior powers that devise and decree these decrees ! they are not too high to be under the divine check. And woe to the inferior officers that draw them up, and enter them upon record —*the writers that write the grievousness,* they are not too mean to be within the divine cognizance. Principal and accessaries shall fall under the same woe." Note, It is bad to do hurt, but it is worse to do it with design and deliberation, to do wrong to many, and to involve many in the guilt of doing wrong. 2. With perverting justice in the execution of the laws that were made. No people had statutes and judgments so righteous as they had, and yet corrupt judges found ways to *turn aside the needy from judgment,* to hinder them from coming at their right and recovering what was their due, because they were needy and poor, and such as they could get nothing by nor expect any bribes from. 3. With enriching themselves by oppressing those that lay at their mercy, whom they ought to have protected. They make widows' houses and estates their prey, and they *rob the fatherless* of the little that is left them, because they have no friend to appear for them. Not to relieve them if they had wanted, not to right them if they were wronged, would have been crime enough in men that had wealth and power; but to rob them because on the side of the oppressors there was power, and the oppressed had no comforter (Eccl. iv. 1), was such a piece of barbarity as one would think none could ever be guilty of that had either the nature of a man or the name of an Israelite.

II. A challenge given them with all their pride and power to outface the judgments of God (*v.* 3): " *What will you do ?* To whom will you flee ?* You can trample upon the widows and fatherless ; but *what will you do when God riseth up ?"* Job xxxi. 14. Great men, who tyrannise over the poor, think they shall never be called to account for their tyranny, shall never hear of it again, or fare the worse for it ; but *shall not God visit for these things ?* Jer. v. 29. Will there not come a desolation upon those that have made others desolate ? Perhaps it may *come from far,* and therefore may be long in coming ; but it will come at last (reprieves are not pardons), and coming from far, from a quarter whence it was least expected, it will be the greater surprise and the more terrible. What will then become of these unrighteous judges ? Now they *see their help in the gate* (Job xxxi. 21); but to whom will they then flee for help ? Note, 1. There is a day of visitation coming, a day of enquiry and discovery, a searching day, which

will bring to light, to a true light, every man, and every man's work. 2. The day of visitation will be a day of desolation to all wicked people, when all their comforts and hopes will be lost and gone, and buried in ruin, and themselves left desolate. 3. Impenitent sinners will be utterly at a loss, and will not know what to do in the day of visitation and desolation. They cannot fly and hide themselves, cannot fight it out and defend themselves ; they have no refuge in which either to shelter themselves from the present evil *(to whom will you flee for help ?)* or to secure to themselves better times hereafter : " *Where will you leave your glory,* to find it again when the storm is over ?" The wealth they had got was their glory, and they had no place of safety in which to deposit that, but they should certainly see it flee away. If our souls be our glory, as they ought to be, and we make them our chief care, we know where to leave them, and into whose hands to commit them, even those of a faithful Creator. 4. It concerns us all seriously to consider what we shall do in the day of visitation, in a day of affliction, in the day of death and judgment, and to provide that we may do well.

III. Sentence passed upon them, by which they are doomed, some to imprisonment and captivity *(they shall bow down among the prisoners, or under them—those that were most highly elevated in sin shall be most heavily loaded and most deeply sunk in trouble), others to death : they shall fall first, and so shall fall under the rest of the slain. Those that had trampled upon the widows and fatherless shall themselves be trodden down, *v.* 4. " This it will come to," says God, " *without me,* that is, because you have deserted me and driven me away from you." Nothing but utter ruin can be expected by those that live without God in the world, that cast him behind their back, and so cast themselves out of his protection.

And yet, *for all this, his anger is not turned away,* which intimates not only that God will proceed in his controversy with them, but that they shall be in a continual dread of it ; they shall, to their unspeakable terror, see his hand still stretched out against them, and there shall remain nothing but *a fearful looking for of of judgment.*

5 O Assyrian, the rod of mine anger, and the staff in their hand is mine indignation. 6 I will send him against an hypocritical nation, and against the people of my wrath will I give him a charge, to take the spoil, and to take the prey, and to tread them down like the mire of the streets. 7 Howbeit he meaneth not so, neither doth his heart think so ; but *it is* in

his heart to destroy and cut off nations not a few. 8 For he saith, *Are* not my princes altogether kings? 9 *Is* not Calno as Carchemish? *Is* not Hamath as Arpad? *Is* not Samaria as Damascus? 10 As my hand hath found the kingdoms of the idols, and whose graven images did excel them of Jerusalem and of Samaria; 11 Shall I not, as I have done unto Samaria and her idols, so do to Jerusalem and her idols? 12 Wherefore it shall come to pass, *that* when the Lord hath performed his whole work upon mount Zion and on Jerusalem, I will punish the fruit of the stout heart of the king of Assyria, and the glory of his high looks. 13 For he saith, By the strength of my hand I have done *it*, and by my wisdom; for I am prudent: and I have removed the bounds of the people, and have robbed their treasures, and I have put down the inhabitants like a valiant *man.* 14 And my hand hath found as a nest the riches of the people: and as one gathereth eggs *that are* left, have I gathered all the earth; and there was none that moved the wing, or opened the mouth, or peeped. 15 Shall the axe boast itself against him that heweth therewith? *Or* shall the saw magnify itself against him that shaketh it? As if the rod should shake *itself* against them that lift it up, *or* as if the staff should lift up *itself, as if it were* no wood. 16 Therefore shall the Lord, the Lord of hosts, send among his fat ones leanness; and under his glory he shall kindle a burning like the burning of a fire. 17 And the light of Israel shall be for a fire, and his Holy One for a flame: and it shall burn and devour his thorns and his briers in one day; 18 And shall consume the glory of his forest, and of his fruitful field, both soul and body: and they shall be as when a standard-bearer fainteth. 19 And the rest of the trees of his forest shall be few, that a child may write them.

The destruction of the kingdom of Israel by Shalmaneser king of Assyria was fore-

told in the foregoing chapter, and it had its accomplishment in the sixth year of Hezekiah, 2 Kings xviii. 10. It was total and final, head and tail were all cut off. Now the correction of the kingdom of Judah by Sennacherib king of Assyria is foretold in this chapter; and this prediction was fulfilled in the fourteenth year of Hezekiah, when that potent prince, encouraged by the successes of his predecessor against the ten tribes, *came up against all the fenced cities of Judah and took them, and laid siege to Jerusalem* (2 Kings xviii. 13, 17), in consequence of which we may well suppose Hezekiah and his kingdom were greatly alarmed, though there was a good work of reformation lately begun among them: but it ended well, in the confusion of the Assyrians and the great encouragement of Hezekiah and his people in their return to God. Now let us see here,

I. How God, in his sovereignty, deputed the king of Assyria to be his servant, and made use of him as a mere tool to serve his own purposes with (*v.* 5, 6): "*O Assyrian!* I know this, that thou art *the rod of my anger:* and I will send thee to be a scourge to *the people of my wrath.*" Observe here, 1. How bad the character of the Jews was, though they appeared very good. They were *a hypocritical nation,* that made a profession of religion, and at this time particularly of reformation, but were not truly religious, not truly reformed, not so good as they pretended to be now that Hezekiah had brought goodness into fashion. When rulers are pious, and so religion is in reputation, it is common for nations to be hypocritical. They are *a profane nation;* so some read it. Hezekiah had in a great measure cured them of their idolatry, and now they ran into profaneness; nay, hypocrisy is profaneness: none profane the name of God so much as those who are called by that name and call upon it, and yet live in sin. Being a profane hypocritical nation, they are the people of God's wrath; they lie under his wrath, and are likely to be consumed by it. Note, Hypocritical nations are the people of God's wrath: nothing is more offensive to God than dissimulation in religion. See what a change sin made: those that had been God's chosen and hallowed people, above all people, had now become the *people of his wrath.* See Amos iii. 2. 2. How mean the character of the Assyrian was, though he appeared very great. He was but *the rod of God's anger,* an instrument God was pleased to make use of for the chastening of his people, that, being thus *chastened of the Lord, they might not be condemned with the world.* Note, The tyrants of the world are but the tools of Providence. Men are God's hand, his sword sometimes, to kill and slay (Ps. xvii. 13, 14), at other times his rod to correct. *The staff in their hand,* wherewith they smite his people, *is his indignation;* it is his wrath that puts the staff into their hand and enables them to deal blows at pleasure among such as thought themselves a match for them. Sometimes God makes an idolatrous nation, that serves him not at all, a scourge to a hypocritical nation, that serves him not in sincerity and truth. The Assyrian is called the *rod of God's anger* because he is employed by him. (1.) From him his power is derived : *I will send him ; I will give him a charge.* Note, All the power that wicked men have, though they often use it against God, they always receive from him. Pilate could have no power against Christ unless it were *given him from above,* John xix. 11. (2.) By him the exercise of that power is directed. The Assyrian is *to take the spoil and to take the prey,* not to shed any blood. We read not of any slain, but he is to plunder the country, rifle the houses, drive away the cattle, strip the people of all their wealth and ornaments, and *tread them down like the mire of the streets.* When God's professing people wallow in the mire of sin it is just with God to suffer their enemies to tread upon them like mire. But why must the Assyrian prevail thus against them ? Not that they might be ruined, but that they might be thoroughly reformed.

II. See how the king of Assyria, in his pride, magnified himself as his own master, and pretended to be absolute and above all control, to act purely according to his own will and for his own honour. *God ordained him for judgment,* even the *mighty God established him for correction* (Hab. i. 12), to be an instrument of bringing his people to repentance, *howbeit he means not so, nor does his heart think so, v. 7.*

1. He does not think that he is either God's servant or Israel's friend, either that he *can* do no more than God will let him or that he *shall* do no more than God will make to work for the good of his people. God designs to correct his people for, and so to cure them of, their hypocrisy, and bring them nearer to himself ; but was that Sennacherib's design? No, it was the furthest thing from his thoughts—*he means not so.* Note, (1.) The wise God often makes even the sinful passions and projects of men subservient to his own great and holy purposes. (2.) When God makes use of men as instruments in his hand to do his work it is very common for *him* to mean one thing and *them* to mean another, nay, for them to mean quite the contrary to what he intends. What Joseph's brethren designed for hurt God overruled for good, Gen. l. 20. See Mic. iv. 11, 12. Men have their ends and God has his, but we are sure *the counsel of the Lord shall stand.* But what is it the proud Assyrian aims at? The heart of kings is unsearchable, but God knew what was in his heart.

2. He designs nothing but *to destroy and to cut off nations not a few,* and to make himself master of them. [1.] He designs to gratify his own cruelty ; nothing will serve but to destroy and cut off. He hopes to regale himself with blood and slaughter ; that of particular persons will not suffice, he must cut off nations. It is below him to deal by retail ; he traffics in murders by wholesale. Nations, and those not a few, must have but one neck, which he will have the pleasure of cutting off. [2.] He designs to gratify his own covetousness and ambition, to set up for a universal monarch, *and to gather unto him all nations,* Hab. ii. 5. An insatiable desire of wealth and dominion is that which carries him on in this undertaking.

3. The prophet here brings him in vaunting and hectoring ; and by his general's letter to Hezekiah, written in his name, vainglory and arrogance seem to have entered very far into the spirit and genius of the man. His haughtiness and presumption are here described very largely, and his very language copied out, partly to represent him as ridiculous and partly to assure the people of God that he would be brought down ; for that maxim generally holds true, that pride goes before destruction. It also intimates that God takes notice, and keeps an account, of all men's proud and haughty words, with which they set heaven and earth at defiance. Those that speak *great swelling words of vanity* shall hear of them again.

(1.) He boasts of the great things he had done to other nations. [1.] He had made their kings his courtiers (v. 8) : " *My princes are altogether kings.* Those that are now my princes are such as have been kings." Or he means that he had raised his throne to such a degree that his servants, and those that were in command under him, were as great, and lived in as much pomp, as the kings of other countries. Or those that were absolute princes in their own dominions held their crowns under him, and did him homage. This was a vainglorious boast ; but how great is our God whom we serve, who is indeed King of kings, and whose subjects are made to him kings ! Rev. i. 6. [2.] He had made himself master of their cities. He names several (v. 9) that were all alike reduced by him. *Calno* soon yielded as *Carchemish* did, *Hamath* could not hold out any more than *Arpad,* and *Samaria* had become his as well as *Damascus.* To support his boasts he is obliged to bring the victories of his predecessor into the account ; for it was he that conquered Samaria, not Sennacherib. [3.] He had been too hard for their idols, their tutelar gods, *had found out the kingdoms of the idols* and found out ways to make them his own, v. 10. Their kingdoms took denomination from the idols they worshipped ; the Moabites are called *the people of Chemosh* (Jer. xlviii. 46), because they imagined their gods were their patrons and protectors ; and therefore Sennacherib vainly imagined that every conquest of a kingdom was the conquest of a god. [4.] He had enlarged his own dominions, and *removed the bounds of the people* (v. 13), enclosing many large territories within the limits of his own kingdom and shifting a great way further the ancient land-marks which his fathers had set ; he could not bear to be hemmed in so closely, but must have more room to thrive. By his *removing the border of the people* Mr. White understands his arbitrarily transplanting colonies from place to place, which was the constant practice of the Assyrians in all their conquests ; and this is a probable interpretation. [5.] He had enriched himself with their wealth, and brought it into his own exchequer : *I have robbed their treasures.* In this he said truly. Great conquerors are often no better than great robbers. [6.] He had mastered all the opposition he met with : " *I have put down the inhabitants as a valiant man.* Those that sat high, and thought they sat firmly, I have humbled and made to come down."

(2.) He boasts of the manner in which he had done them. [1.] That he had done all this by his own policy and power (v. 13): "*By the strength of my hand*, for I am valiant ; *and by my wisdom, for I am prudent ;*" not by the permission of Providence and the blessing of God. He knows not that it is God that makes him what he is, and puts the staff into his hand, but *sacrifices to his own net*, Hab. i. 16. "This wealth is all gotten by my might and the power of my hand," Deut. viii. 17. Downright atheism and profaneness, as well as pride and vanity, are at the bottom of men's attributing their prosperity and success thus to themselves and their own conduct, and raising their own character upon it. [2.] That he had done all this with a great deal of ease, and had made but a sport and diversion of it, as if he had been taking birds' nests (v. 14) : *My hand has found as a nest the riches of the people ;* and when he had found them there was no more difficulty in taking them than in rifling a nest, nor any more reluctance or regret within his own breast in destroying families and cities than in destroying crows'-nests; killing children was no more to him than killing birds. " *As one gathers the eggs that are left* in the nest by the dam, so easily have I gathered all the earth." Like Alexander, he thought he had conquered the world ; and whatever prey he seized there was none that *moved the wing, or opened the mouth, or peeped*, as birds do when their nests are rifled. They durst not make any opposition, no, nor any complaint ; such awe did they stand in of this mighty conqueror. They were so weak that they knew it was to no purpose to resist, and he was so arbitrary that they knew it was to no purpose to complain. Strange that ever men who were made to do good should take a pride and a pleasure in doing wrong, and doing mischief to all about them without control, and should

reckon that their glory which is their shame ! But *their* day will come to fall who thus make themselves *the terror of the mighty*, and much more of the feeble, *in the land of the living*.

(3.) He threatens what he will do to Jerusalem, which he was now about to lay siege to, v. 10, 11. He would master Jerusalem and her idols, as he had subdued other places and their idols, particularly Samaria. [1.] He blasphemously calls the God of Israel an *idol*, and sets him on a level with the false gods of other nations, as if none were the true God but Mithras, the sun, whom he worshipped. See how ignorant he was, and then we shall the less wonder that he was so proud. [2.] He prefers the graven images of other countries before those of Jerusalem and Samaria, when he might have known that the worshippers of the God of Israel were expressly forbidden to make any graven images, and if any did it must be by stealth, and therefore they could not be so rich and pompous as those of other nations. If he means the ark and the mercy-seat, he speaks like himself, very foolishly, and as one that judged by the sight of the eye, and might therefore be easily deceived in matters of spiritual concern. Those who make external pomp and splendour a mark of the true church go by the same rule. [3.] Because he had conquered Samaria, he concluded Jerusalem would fall of course : " *Shall not I do so to Jerusalem ?* can I not as easily, and may I not as justly ?" But it did not follow ; for Jerusalem adhered to her God, whereas Samaria had forsaken him.

III. See how God, in his justice, rebukes his pride and reads his doom. We have heard what the great king, the king of Assyria, says, and how big he talks. Let us now hear what the great God has to say by his servant the prophet, and we shall find that, wherein he deals proudly, God is above him.

1. He shows the vanity of his insolent and audacious boasts (v. 15) : *Shall the axe boast itself against him that hews therewith ? or shall the saw magnify itself against him that draws it ?* So absurd are the boasts of this proud man. " O what a dust do I make !" said the fly upon the cart-wheel in the fable. "What destruction do I make among the trees !" says the axe. Two ways the axe may be said to *boast itself against him that hews with it :*—(1.) By way of resistance and opposition. Sennacherib blasphemed God, insulted him, threatened to serve him as he had served the gods of the nations; now this was as if the axe should fly in the face of him that hews with it. The tool striving with the workman is no less absurd than the clay striving with the potter ; and as it is a thing not to be justified that men should fight against God with the wit, and wealth, and power, which he gives them, so it is a thing not to be suffered.

But if men will be thus proud and daring, and bid defiance to all that is just and sacred, let them expect that God will reckon with them; the more insolent they are the surer and sorer will their ruin be. (2.) By way of rivalship and competition. Shall the axe take to itself the praise of the work it is employed in? So senseless, so absurd was it for Sennacherib to say, *By the strength of my hand I have done it, and by my wisdom, v.* 13. It is as it the rod, when it is shaken, should boast that it guides the hand which shakes it; whereas, *when the staff is lifted up, is it not wood still?* so the last clause may be read. If it be an ensign of authority (as the nobles of the people carried staves, Num. xxi. 18), if it be an instrument of service, either to support a weak man or to correct a bad man, still it is wood, and can do nothing but as it is directed by him that uses it. The psalmist prays that God would make the nations to know that they *were but men* (Ps. ix. 20), the staff to know that it is but wood.

2. He foretels his fall and ruin.

(1.) That when God had done his work by him he would then do his work upon him, *v.* 12. For the comfort of the people of God in reference to Sennacherib's invasion, though it was a dismal time with them, let them know, [1.] That God designed to do good to Zion and Jerusalem by this providence. There is a work to be done upon them, which God intends, and which he will perform. Note, When God lets loose the enemies of his church and people, and suffers them for a time to prevail, it is in order to the performing of some great good work upon them; and, when that is done, then, and not till then, he will work deliverance for them. When God brings his people into trouble it is to try them (Dan. xi. 35), to bring sin to their remembrance and humble them for it, and to awaken them to a sense of their duty, to teach them to pray and to love and help one another; and *this must be the fruit, even the taking away of sin,* ch. xxvii. 9. When these points are, in some measure, gained by the affliction, it shall be removed, in mercy (Lev. xxvi. 41, 42), otherwise not; for, as the word, so the rod shall *accomplish that for which God sends it.* [2.] That when God had wrought this work of grace for his people he would work a work of wrath and vengeance upon their invaders: *I will punish the fruit of the stout heart of the king of Assyria.* His big words are here said to come from his stout heart, and they are the fruit of it; for *out of the abundance of the heart the mouth speaks.* Notice is taken too of the *glory of his high looks,* for a proud look is the indication of a proud spirit. The enemies of the church are commonly very high and haughty; but, sooner or later, God will reckon for their haughtiness. He glories in it as an incontestable proof of his power and sovereignty that he *looks upon proud men and abases them,* Job xl. 11, &c.

(2.) That, how threatening soever this attempt was upon Zion and Jerusalem, it should certainly be baffled, and broken, and come to nothing, and he should not be able to bring to pass his enterprise, *v.* 16, 19. Observe,

[1.] Who it is that undertakes his destruction, and will be the author of it; not Hezekiah, or his princes, or the militia of Judah and Jerusalem (what can they do against such a potent force?), but God himself will do it, as *the Lord of hosts,* and as *the light of Israel* First, We are sure he can do it, for he is *the Lord of hosts,* of all the hosts of heaven and earth. All the creatures are at his command; he makes what use he pleases of them and lays what restraints he pleases on them. He is the Lord of the hosts both of Judah and of Assyria, and can give the victory to which he pleases. Let us not fear the hosts of any enemy if we have the Lord of hosts for us. *Secondly,* We have reason to hope he will do it, for he is *the light of Israel, and his Holy One.* God is light; in him are perfect brightness, purity, and happiness. He is light, for he is the Holy One; his holiness is his glory. He is Israel's light, to direct and counsel his people, to favour and countenance them, and so to gladden and comfort them in the worst of times. He is their Holy One, for he is in covenant with them; his holiness is engaged and employed for them. God's holiness is the saints' comfort; they *give thanks at the remembrance* of it, and with a great deal of pleasure call him *their Holy One,* Hab. i. 12.

[2.] How this destruction is represented. It shall be, *First,* As a consumption of the body by a disease : *The Lord shall send leanness among his fatnesses,* or *his fat ones.* His numerous army, that was like a body covered with fatness, shall be diminished, and waste away, and become like a skeleton. *Secondly,* As a consumption of buildings, or trees and bushes, by fire : *Under his glory,* that very thing which he glories in, *he will kindle a burning, as the burning of a fire,* which shall lay his army in ruins as suddenly as a raging fire lays a stately house in ashes. Some make it an allusion to the fire kindled under the sacrifices; for proud sinners fall as sacrifices to divine justice. Observe, 1. How this fire shall be kindled, *v.* 17. The same God that is a rejoicing light to those that serve him faithfully will be a consuming fire to those that trifle with him or rebel against him. *The light of Israel shall be for a fire* to the Assyrians, as the same pillar of cloud was a light to the Israelites and a terror to the Egyptians in the Red Sea. What can oppose, what can extinguish, such a fire? 2. What desolation it shall make : *It shall burn and devour its thorns and briers,* his officers and soldiers, which are of little worth, and vexations to God's Israel, as thorns and briers, whose end is to be burned, and which are easily and quickly consumed by a devouring fire. "*Who would set the briers and thorns against me in battle?* They would be so far from stopping the fire that they would inflame it. *I would go through them and burn them together* (ch. xxvii. 4); they shall be devoured in one day, all cut off in an instant." When they cried not only Peace and safety, but Victory and triumph, then sudden destruction came; it came surprisingly, and was completed in a little time. "Even *the glory of his forest* (*v.* 18), the choice troops of his army, the veterans, the troops of the household, the bravest regiments he had, that he was most proud of and depended most upon, that he valued as men do their timber-trees (the glory of their forest) or their fruit-trees (the glory of their Carmel), shall be put as briers and thorns before the fire; they shall be consumed both soul and body, entirely consumed, not only a limb burned, but life taken away." Note, God is able to destroy both soul and body, and therefore we should fear him more than man, who can but kill the body. Great armies before him are but as great woods, which he can fell or fire when he pleases.

[3.] What would be the effect of this great slaughter. The prophet tells us, *First,* That the army would hereby be reduced to a very small number: *The rest of the trees of his forest shall be few;* very few shall escape the sword of the destroying angel, so few that there needs no artist, no mustermaster or secretary of war, to take an account of them, for even *a child may* soon reckon the numbers of them, and *write* the names of *them. Secondly,* That those few who re mained should be quite dispirited: *They shall be as when a standard-bearer fainteth.* When he either falls or flees, and his colours are taken by the enemy, this discourages the whole army, and puts them all into confusion. Upon the whole matter we must say, *Who is able to stand before this great and holy Lord God?*

20 And it shall come to pass in that day, *that* the remnant of Israel, and such as are escaped of the house of Jacob, shall no more again stay upon him that smote them; but shall stay upon the LORD, the Holy One of Israel, in truth. 21 The remnant shall return, *even* the remnant of Jacob, unto the mighty God. 22 For though thy people Israel be as the sand of the sea, *yet* a remnant of them shall return: the consumption decreed shall overflow with righteousness. 23 For the Lord GOD of hosts shall make a consumption, even determined, in the midst of all the land.

The prophet had said (*v.* 12) that *the Lord* would perform *his whole work upon Mount Zion and upon Jerusalem,* by Sennacherib's invading the land. Now here we are told what that work should be, a twofold work:—

I. The conversion of some, to whom this providence should be sanctified and yield the peaceable fruit of righteousness, though for the present it was not joyous, but grievous; these are but a remnant (*v.* 22), *the remnant of Israel* (*v.* 20), *the remnant of Jacob* (*v.* 21), but a very few in comparison with the vast numbers of the people of Israel, who were as the sand of the sea. Note, Converting work is wrought but on a remnant, who are distinguished from the rest and set apart for God. When we see how populous Israel is, how numerous the members of the visible church are, as the sand of the sea, and yet consider that of these a remnant only shall be saved, that of the many that are called there are but few chosen, we shall surely *strive to enter in at the strait gate* and fear lest we *seem to come short.* This remnant of Israel are said to be *such as had escaped of the house of Jacob,* such as escaped the corruptions of the house of Jacob, and kept their integrity in times of common apostasy; and that was a fair escape. And therefore they escape the desolations of that house, and shall be preserved in safety in times of common calamity; and that also will be a fair and narrow escape. Their *lives shall be given them for a prey,* Jer. xlv. 5. The *righteous scarcely are saved.* Now, 1. This remnant shall come off from all confidence in an arm of flesh, this providence shall cure them of that: "They *shall no more again stay upon him that smote them,* shall never depend upon the Assyrians, as they have done, for help against their other enemies, finding that they are themselves their worst enemies." *Ictus piscator sapit— sufferings teach caution.* "They have now learned by dear-bought experience the folly of leaning upon that staff as a stay to them which may perhaps prove a staff to beat them." It is part of the covenant of a returning people (Hos. xiv. 3), *Assyria shall not save us.* Note, By our afflictions we may learn not to make creatures our confidence. 2. They shall come home to God, to the mighty God (one of the names given to the Messiah, *ch.* ix. 6), to the Holy One of Israel: "*The remnant shall return* (that was signified by the name of the prophet's son, *Shear-jashub, ch.* vii. 3), *even the remnant of Jacob.* They shall return, after the raising of the siege of Jerusalem, not only to the quiet possession of their houses and lands, but to God and to their duty; they shall repent, and pray, and seek his face, and reform their lives." The remnant that escape are a returning remnant: they shall return to God, and shall stay upon him. Note, Those only may with comfort stay upon God that return to him; then may we have a humble confidence in God when we make conscience of our duty to him. They *shall stay upon the Holy One of Israel, in truth,* and not in pretence and profession only. This promise of the conversion and salvation of a remnant of Israel is applied by the apostle (Rom. ix. 27) to the remnant of the Jews which at the first preaching of the gospel received and entertained it, and sufficiently proves that it was no new thing for God to abandon to ruin a great many of the seed of Abraham and yet preserve his promise to Abraham in full force and virtue; for so it was now. The number of the children of Israel was *as the sand of the sea* (according to the promise, Gen. xxii. 17), and yet only a remnant shall be saved.

II. The consumption of others: *The Lord God of hosts shall make a consumption, v.* 23. This is not meant (as that *v.* 18) of the consumption of the Assyrian army, but of the consumption of the estates and families of many of the Jews by the Assyrian army. This is taken notice of to magnify the power and goodness of God in the escape of the distinguished remnant, and to let us know what shall become of those that will not return to God; they shall be wasted away by this consumption, this general decay *in the midst of the land.* Observe, 1. It is a consumption of God's own making; he is the author of it. The Lord God of hosts, whom none can resist, shall make this consumption. 2. It is *decreed.* It is not the product of a sudden resolve, but was before ordained. It is *determined,* not only that there shall be such a consumption, but it is *cut out* (so the word is); it is particularly appointed how far it shall extend and how long it shall continue, who shall be consumed by it and who not. 3. It is an overflowing consumption, that shall overspread the land, and, like a mighty torrent or inundation, bear down all before it. 4. Though it overflows, it is not at random, but in *righteousness,* which signifies both wisdom and equity. God will justly bring this consumption upon a provoking people, but he will wisely and graciously set bounds to it. *Hitherto it shall come, and no further.*

24 Therefore thus saith the Lord God of hosts, O my people that dwellest in Zion, be not afraid of the Assyrian: he shall smite thee with a rod, and shall lift up his staff against thee, after the manner of Egypt. 25 For yet a very little while, and the indignation shall cease, and mine anger in their destruction. 26 And the Lord of hosts shall stir up a scourge for him according to the slaughter of Midian at the rock of Oreb: and *as* his rod *was* upon the sea, so shall he lift it up after the manner of Egypt. 27 And

70

it shall come to pass in that day, *that* his burden shall be taken away from off thy shoulder, and his yoke from off thy neck, and the yoke shall be destroyed because of the anointing. 28 He is come to Aiath, he is passed to Migron; at Michmash he hath laid up his carriages: 29 They are gone over the passage: they have taken up their lodging at Geba; Ramah is afraid; Gibeah of Saul is fled. 30 Lift up thy voice, O daughter of Gallim: cause it to be heard unto Laish, O poor Anathoth. 31 Madmenah is removed; the inhabitants of Gebim gather themselves to flee. 32 As yet shall he remain at Nob that day: he shall shake his hand *against* the mount of the daughter of Zion, the hill of Jerusalem. 33 Behold, the Lord, the Lord of hosts, shall lop the bough with terror: and the high ones of stature *shall be* hewn down, and the haughty shall be humbled. 34 And he shall cut down the thickets of the forest with iron, and Lebanon shall fall by a mighty one.

The prophet, in his preaching, distinguishes between the precious and the vile; for God in his providence, even in the same providence, does so. He speaks terror, in Sennacherib's invasion, to the hypocrites, who were the *people of God's wrath, v.* 6. But here he speaks comfort to the sincere, who were the people of God's love. The judgment was sent for the sake of the former; the deliverance was wrought for the sake of the latter. Here we have,

I. An exhortation to God's people not to be frightened at this threatening calamity, nor to be put into any confusion or consternation by it. *Let the sinners in Zion be afraid* (ch. xxxiii. 14); but *O my people, that dwellest in Zion, be not afraid of the Assyrian, v.* 24. Note, It is against the mind and will of God that his people, whatever may happen, should give way to that fear which has torment and amazement. Those that dwell in Zion, where God dwells and where his people attend him, and are employed in his service, that are under the protection of the bulwarks that are *round about Zion* (Ps. xlviii. 13), need not be afraid of any enemy. Let their souls dwell at ease in God.

II. Considerations offered for the silencing of their fear.

1. The Assyrian shall do nothing against them but what God has appointed and determined. They are here told beforehand what he shall do, that it may be no surprise to them: *" He shall smite thee* by the divine

permission, but it shall be only *with a rod* to correct thee, not with a sword to wound and kill; nay, *he shall but lift up his staff against thee,* threaten thee, and frighten thee, and shake the rod at thee, *after the manner of Egypt,* as the Egyptians shook their staff against your fathers at the Red Sea, when they said, *We will pursue, we will overtake* (Exod. xv. 9), but could not reach to do them any hurt." Note, We should not be frightened at those enemies that can do no more than frighten us.

2. The storm shall soon blow over (*v.* 25): *Yet a very little while—a little, little while* (so the word is), *and the indignation shall cease, even my anger,* which is *the staff in their hand* (*v.* 5), so that when that ceases they are disarmed and disabled to do any further mischief. Note, God's anger against his people is but for a moment (Ps. xxx. 5), and when that ceases, and is turned away from us, we need not fear the fury of any man, for it is impotent passion.

3. The enemy that threatens them shall himself be reckoned with. God's anger against his people *shall cease in the destruction* of their enemies; when he turns away his wrath from Israel he shall turn it against the Assyrian; and the rod with which he corrected his people shall not only be laid aside, but thrown into the fire. He *lifted up his staff* against Zion, but God *shall stir up a scourge for him* (*v.* 26); he is a terror to God's people, but God will be a terror to him. The destroying angel shall be this scourge, which he can neither flee from nor contend with. The prophet, for the encouragement of God's people, quotes precedents, and puts them in mind of what God had done formerly against the enemies of his church, who were very strong and formidable, but were brought to ruin. The destruction of the Assyrian shall be, (1.) *According to the slaughter of Midian* (which was effected by an invisible power, but effected suddenly, and it was a total rout); and as, *at the rock of Oreb,* one of the princes of Midian, after the battle, was slain, so shall Sennacherib be in the temple of his god Nisroch, after the defeat of his forces, when he thinks the bitterness of death is past. Compare with this Ps. lxxxiii. 11, *Make their nobles like Oreb and like Zeeb;* and see how God's promises and his people's prayers agree. (2.) *As his rod was upon the sea,* the Red Sea, as Moses' rod was upon that, to divide it first for the escape of Israel and then to close it again for the destruction of their pursuers, so shall his rod now be *lifted up, after the manner of Egypt,* for the deliverance of Jerusalem and the destruction of the Assyrian. Note, It is good to observe a resemblance between God's latter and former appearances for his people, and against his and their enemies.

4. They shall be wholly delivered from the power of the Assyrian, and from the fear of it, *v.* 27. "They shall not only be eased

of the Assyrian army, which is now quartered upon them and which is a grievous yoke and burden to them, but they shall no more pay that tribute to the king of Assyria which before this invasion he exacted from them (2 Kings xviii. 14), shall be no longer at his service, nor lie at his mercy, as they have done; nor shall he ever again put the country under contribution." Some think it looks further, to the deliverance of the Jews out of their captivity in Babylon; and further yet, to the redemption of believers from the tyranny of sin and Satan. The yoke shall not only be taken away, but it *shall be destroyed.* The enemy shall no more recover his strength, to do the mischief he has done; and this *because of the anointing,* for their sakes who were partakers of the anointing. (1.) For Hezekiah's sake, who was the anointed of the Lord, who had been an active reformer, and was dear to God. (2.) For David's sake. This is particularly given as the reason why God would defend Jerusalem from Sennacherib (*ch.* xxxvii. 35), *For my own sake, and for my servant David's sake.* (3.) For his people Israel's sake, the good people among them that had received the unction of divine grace. (4.) For the sake of the Messiah, the Anointed of God, whom God had an eye to in all the deliverances of the Old-Testament church, and hath still an eye to in all the favours he shows to his people. It is for his sake that the yoke is broken, and that we are made free indeed.

III. A description both of the terror of the enemy and the terror with which many were struck by it, and the folly of both exposed, *v.* 28, to the end. Here observe,

1. How formidable the Assyrians were and how daring and threatening they affected to appear. Here is a particular description of the march of Sennacherib, what course he steered, what swift advances he made: *He has come to Aiath,* &c. "This and the other place he has made himself master of, and has met with no opposition." *At Michmash he has laid up his carriages,* as if he had no further occasion for his heavy artillery, so easily was every place he came to reduced; or the store-cities of Judah, which were fortified for that purpose, had now become his magazines. Some remarkable pass, and an important one, he had taken: *They have gone over the passage.*

2. How cowardly the men of Judah were, the degenerate seed of that lion's whelp. They were *afraid;* they *fled* upon the first alarm, and did not offer to make any head against the enemy. Their apostasy from God had dispirited them, so that one chased a thousand of them. Instead of a valiant shout, to animate one another, nothing was heard but lamentation, to discourage and weaken one another. And *poor Anathoth,* a priests' city, that should have been a pattern of courage, shrieks louder than any,

v. 30. With respect to those that *gathered themselves* together, it was not to fight, but to flee by consent, *v.* 31. This is designed either, (1.) To show how fast the news of the enemy's progress flew through the kingdom : *He has come to Aiath,* says one ; nay, says another, *He has passed to Migron,* &c. And yet, perhaps, it was not altogether so bad as common fame represented it. But we must watch against the fear, not only of evil things, but of evil tidings, which often make things worse than really they are, Ps. cxii. 7. Or, (2.) To show what imminent danger Jerusalem was in, when its enemies made so many bold advances towards it and its friends could not make one bold stand to defend it. Note, The more daring the church's enemies are, and the more dastardly those are that should appear for her, the more will God be exalted in his own strength, when, notwithstanding this, he works deliverance for her.

3. How impotent his attempt upon Jerusalem shall be : *He shall remain at Nob,* whence he may see Mount Zion, and there *he shall shake his hand* against it, *v.* 32. He shall threaten it, and that shall be all; it shall be safe, and shall set him at defiance. The daughter of Jerusalem, to be even with him, shall *shake her head* at him, *ch.* xxxvii. 22.

4. How fatal it would prove, in the issue, to himself. When he *shakes his hand at Jerusalem,* and is about to lay hands on it, then is God's time to appear against him; for Zion is the place of which God has said, *This is my rest for ever;* therefore those who threaten it affront God himself. Then *the Lord shall lop the bough with terror and cut down the thickets of the forest, v.* 33, 34. (1.) The pride of the enemy shall be humbled, the boughs that are lifted up on high shall be lopped off, the high and stately trees shall be hewn down; that is, the haughty shall be humbled. Those that lift up themselves in competition with God or opposition to him shall be abased. (2.) The power of the enemy shall be broken : *The thickets of the forest he shall cut down.* When the Assyrian soldiers were under their arms, and their spears erect, they looked like a forest, like Lebanon ; but, when in one night they all became as dead corpses, the pikes were laid on the ground, and Lebanon was of a sudden cut down *by a mighty one,* by the destroying angel, who in a little time slew so many thousands of them : and, if this shall be the exit of that proud invader, let not God's people be afraid of him. *Who art thou, that thou shouldst be afraid of a man that shall die ?*

CHAP. XI.

It is a very good transition in prophecy (whether it be so in rhetoric or no), and a very common one, to pass from the prediction of the temporal deliverances of the church to that of the great salvation, which in the fulness of time should be wrought out by Jesus Christ, of which the other were types and figures, to which all the prophets bore witness; and so the ancient Jews understood

them. For what else was it that raised so great an expectation of the Messiah at the time he came. Upon occasion of the prophecy of the deliverance of Jerusalem from Sennacherib, here comes in a prophecy concerning Messiah the Prince. I. His rise out of the house of David, ver. 1. II. His qualifications for his great undertaking, ver. 2, 3. III. The justice and equity of his government, ver. 3—5. IV. The peaceableness of his kingdom, ver. 6—9. V. The accession of the Gentiles to it (ver. 10), and with them the remnant of the Jews, that should be united with them in the Messiah's kingdom, ver. 11—16. And of all this God would now shortly give them a type, and some dark representation, in the excellent government of Hezekiah, the great peace which the nation should enjoy under him, after the ruin of Sennacherib's design, and the return of many of the ten tribes out of their dispersion to their brethren of the land of Judah, when they enjoyed that great tranquillity.

AND there shall come forth a rod out of the stem of Jesse, and a branch shall grow out of his roots : 2 And the spirit of the LORD shall rest upon him, the spirit of wisdom and understanding, the spirit of counsel and might, the spirit of knowledge and of the fear of the LORD ; 3 And shall make him of quick understanding in the fear of the LORD : and he shall not judge after the sight of his eyes, neither reprove after the hearing of his ears : 4 But with righteousness shall he judge the poor, and reprove with equity for the meek of the earth : and he shall smite the earth with the rod of his mouth, and with the breath of his lips shall he slay the wicked. 5 And righteousness shall be the girdle of his loins, and faithfulness the girdle of his reins. 6 The wolf also shall dwell with the lamb, and the leopard shall lie down with the kid; and the calf and the young lion and the fatling together ; and a little child shall lead them. 7 And the cow and the bear shall feed; their young ones shall lie down together : and the lion shall eat straw like the ox. 8 And the sucking child shall play on the hole of the asp, and the weaned child shall put his hand on the cockatrice' den. 9 They shall not hurt nor destroy in all my holy mountain : for the earth shall be full of the knowledge of the LORD, as the waters cover the sea.

The prophet had before, in this sermon, spoken of a child that should be born, a son that should be given, on whose shoulders the government should be, intending this for the comfort of the people of God in times of trouble, as dying Jacob, many ages before, had intended the prospect of Shiloh for the comfort of his seed in their affliction in Egypt. He had said (*ch.* x. 27) that *the yoke should be destroyed because of the anointing;* now here he tells us on whom that anointing should rest. He foretels,

I. That the Messiah should, in due time, arise out of the house of David, as that *branch* of the Lord which he had said (*ch.* iv. 2) should be excellent and glorious; the word is *Netzer,* which some think is referred to in Matt. ii. 23, where it is said to be spoken by the prophets of the Messiah that he *should be called a Nazarene.* Observe here, 1. Whence this branch should arise—from *Jesse.* He should be the son of David, with whom the covenant of royalty was made, and to whom it was promised with an oath that *of the fruit of his loins God would raise up Christ,* Acts ii. 30. David is often called *the son of Jesse,* and Christ is called so, because he was to be not only the Son of David, but David himself, Hos. iii. 5. 2. The meanness of his appearance. (1.) He is called a *rod,* and a *branch;* both the words here used signify a weak, small, tender product, a *twig* and a *sprig* (so some render them), such as is easily broken off. The enemies of God's church were just before compared to strong and stately boughs (*ch.* x. 33), which will not, without great labour, be hewn down, but Christ to a tender branch (*ch.* liii. 2); yet he shall be victorious over them. (2.) He is said to come out of Jesse rather than David, because Jesse lived and died in meanness and obscurity; his family was of small account (1 Sam. xviii. 18), and it was in a way of contempt and reproach that David was sometimes called the *son of Jesse,* 1 Sam xxii. 7. (3.) He comes forth out of the *stem,* or *stump,* of Jesse. When the royal family, that had been as a cedar, was cut down, and only the stump of it left, almost levelled with the ground and lost in the grass of the field (Dan. iv. 15), yet it shall sprout again (Job xiv. 7); nay, it *shall grow out of his roots,* which are quite buried in the earth, and, like the roots of flowers in the winter, have no stem appearing above ground. The house of David was reduced and brought very low at the time of Christ's birth, witness the obscurity and poverty of Joseph and Mary. The Messiah was thus to begin his estate of humiliation, for submitting to which he should be highly exalted, and would thus give early notice that his kingdom was not of this world. The Chaldee paraphrase reads this, *There shall come forth a King from the sons of Jesse, and the Messiah* (or Christ) *shall be anointed out of his sons' sons.*

II. That he should be every way qualified for that great work to which he was designed, that this tender branch should be so watered with the dews of heaven as to become a strong rod for a sceptre to rule, *v.* 2. 1. In general, *the Spirit of the Lord shall rest upon him.* The Holy Spirit, in all his gifts and graces, shall not only come, but rest

and abide upon him; he shall have the Spirit not by measure, but without measure, the fulness of the Godhead dwelling in him, Col. i. 19; ii. 9. He began his preaching with this (Luke iv. 18), *The Spirit of the Lord is upon me.* 2. In particular, the spirit of government, by which he should be every way fitted for that judgment which the Father has committed to him and *given him authority to execute* (John v. 22, 27), and not only so, but should be made the fountain and treasury of all grace to believers, that from his fulness they might all receive the Spirit of grace, as all the members of the body derive animal spirits from the head. (1.) He shall have *the spirit of wisdom and understanding, of counsel and knowledge;* he shall thoroughly understand the business he is to be employed in. *No man knows the Father but the Son,* Matt. xi. 27. What he is to make known to the children of men concerning God, and his mind and will, he shall be himself acquainted with and apprised of, John i. 18. He shall know how to administer the affairs of his spiritual kingdom in all the branches of it, so as effectually to answer the two great intentions of it, the glory of God and the welfare of the children of men. The terms of the covenant shall be settled by him, and ordinances instituted, in wisdom: treasures of wisdom shall be hid in him; he shall be our counsellor, and shall be made of God to us wisdom. (2.) *The spirit of courage,* or *might,* or fortitude. The undertaking was very great, abundance of difficulty must be broken through, and therefore it was necessary that he should be so endowed that he *might not fail or be discouraged, ch.* xlii. 4. He was famed for courage in his teaching the way of God in truth, and not caring for any man, Matt. xxii. 16. (3.) The spirit of religion, or *the fear of the Lord;* not only he shall himself have a reverent affection for his Father, as his servant (*ch.* xlii. 1), and he was heard in *that he feared* (Heb. v. 7), but he shall have a zeal for religion, and shall design the advancement of it in his whole undertaking. Our faith in Christ was never designed to supersede and jostle out, but to increase and support, our fear of the Lord.

III. That he should be accurate, and critical, and very exact in the administration of his government and the exercise of the power committed to him (*v.* 3): The Spirit wherewith he shall be clothed *shall make him of quick understanding in the fear of the Lord*—of an acute smell or scent (so the word is), for the apprehensions of the mind are often expressed by the sensations of the body. Note, 1. Those are must truly and valuably intelligent that are so in the fear of the Lord, in the business of religion, for that is both the foundation and top-stone of wisdom. 2. By this it will appear that we have the Spirit of God, if we have spiritual senses exercised, and are of *quick under-standing in the fear of the Lord.* Those have divine illumination that know their duty and know how to go about it. 3. *Therefore* Jesus Christ had the spirit without measure, that he might perfectly understand his undertaking; and he did so, as appears not only in the admirable answers he gave to all that questioned with him, which proved him to be of *quick understanding in the fear of the Lord,* but in the management of his whole undertaking. He has settled the great affair of religion so unexceptionably well (so as effectually to secure both God's honour and man's happiness) that, it must be owned, he thoroughly understood it.

IV. That he should be just and righteous in all the acts of his government, and there should appear in it as much equity as wisdom. He shall judge as he expresses it himself, and as he himself would be judged of, John vii. 24. 1. Not according to outward appearance (*v.* 3): *He shall not judge after the sight of his eyes,* with respect of persons (Job xxxiv. 19) and according to outward shows and appearances, nor *reprove after the hearing of his ears,* by common fame and report, and the representations of others, as men commonly do; nor does he judge of men by the fair words they speak, *calling him, Lord, Lord,* or their plausible actions before the eye of the world, which they do to be seen of men; but he will judge by the hidden man of the heart, and the inward principles men are governed by, of which he is an infallible witness. Christ will judge the secrets of men (Rom. ii. 16), will determine concerning them, not according to their own pretensions and appearances (that were to *judge after the sight of the eyes*), not according to the opinion others have of them (that were to judge after the hearing of the ears), but we are sure that *his judgment is according to truth.* 2. He will judge righteous judgment (*v.* 5): *Righteousness shall be the girdle of his loins.* He shall be righteous in the administration of his government, and his righteousness shall be his girdle; it shall constantly compass him and cleave to him, shall be his ornament and honour; he shall gird himself for every action, shall gird on his sword for war in righteousness; his righteousness shall be his strength, and shall make him expeditious in his undertakings, as a man with his loins girt. In conformity to Christ, his followers must have the girdle of truth (Eph. vi. 14) and it will be the stability of the times. Particularly, (1.) He shall in righteousness plead for the people that are poor and oppressed; he will be their protector (*v.* 4): *With righteousness shall he judge the poor;* he shall judge in favour and defence of those that have right on their side, though they are poor in the world, and because they are poor in spirit. It is the duty of princes to defend and deliver

the poor (Ps. lxxxii. 3, 4), and the honour of Christ that he is the poor man's King, Ps. lxxii 2, 4. He shall *debate with evenness for the meek of the earth,* or of the land; those that bear the injuries done them with meekness and patience are in a special manner entitled to the divine care and protection. *I, as a deaf man, heard not, for thou wilt hear,* Ps. xxxviii. 13, 14. Some read it, *He shall reprove or correct the meek of the earth with equity.* If his own people, the meek of the land, do amiss, he will *visit their transgression with the rod.* (2.) He shall in righteousness plead against his enemies that are proud and oppressors (*v.* 4): *But he shall smite the earth,* the man of the earth, that doth oppress (see Ps. x. 18), the men of the world, that *mind earthly things* only (Ps. xvii. 14); these he shall smite *with the rod of his mouth,* the word of his mouth, speaking terror and ruin to them; his threatenings shall take hold of them, and be executed upon them. *With the breath of his lips,* by the operation of his Spirit, according to his word, and working with and by it, *he shall slay the wicked.* He will do it easily, with a word's speaking, as he laid those flat who came to seize him, by saying *I am he,* John xviii. 6. Killing terrors shall arrest their consciences, killing judgments shall ruin them, their power, and all their interests; and in the other world everlasting tribulation will be recompensed to those that trouble his poor people. The apostle applies this to the destruction of the man of sin, whom he calls *that wicked one* (2 Thess. ii. 8) *whom the Lord will consume with the spirit of his mouth.* And the Chaldee here reads it, *He shall slay that wicked Romulus,* or Rome, as Mr. Hugh Broughton understands it.

V. That there should be great peace and tranquillity under his government; this is an explication of what was said in *ch.* ix. 6, that he should be the Prince of peace. Peace signifies two things:—

1. Unity or concord, which is intimated in these figurative promises, that even *the wolf shall dwell* peaceably *with the lamb;* men of the most fierce and furious dispositions, who used to bite and devour all about them, shall have their temper so strangely altered by the efficacy of the gospel and grace of Christ that they shall live in love even with the weakest and such as formerly they would have made an easy prey of. So far shall the sheep be from hurting one another, as sometimes they have done (Ezek. xxxiv. 20, 21), that even the wolves shall agree with them. Christ, who is our peace, came to slay all enmities and to settle lasting friendships among his followers, particularly between Jews and Gentiles: when multitudes of both, being converted to the faith of Christ, united in one sheep-fold, then the wolf and the lamb dwelt together; the wolf did not so much

as threaten the lamb, nor was the lamb afraid of the wolf. *The leopard shall* not only not tear the kid, but shall *lie down with her :* even *their young ones shall lie down together,* and shall be trained up in a blessed amity, in order to the perpetuating of it. *The lion* shall cease to be ravenous and *shall eat straw like the ox,* as some think all the beasts of prey did before the fall. *The asp* and *the cockatrice* shall cease to be venomous, so that parents shall let their children *play* with them and *put their hands* among them. A generation of vipers shall become a seed of saints, and the old complaint of *homo homini lupus—man is a wolf to man,* shall be at an end. Those that inhabit the holy mountain shall live as amicably as the creatures did that were with Noah in the ark, and it shall be a means of their preservation, for *they shall not hurt nor destroy* one another as they have done. Now, (1.) This is fulfilled in the wonderful effect of the gospel upon the minds of those that sincerely embrace it; it changes the nature, and makes those that trampled on the meek of the earth, not only meek like them, but affectionate towards them. When Paul, who had persecuted the saints, joined himself to them, then the *wolf dwelt with the lamb.* (2.) Some are willing to hope it shall yet have a further accomplishment in the latter days, when *swords shall be beaten into ploughshares.*

2. Safety or security. Christ, the great Shepherd, shall take such care of his flock that those who would hurt them shall not; they shall not only not destroy one another, but no enemy from without shall be permitted to give them any molestation. The property of troubles, and of death itself, shall be so altered that they shall not do any real hurt to, much less shall they be the destruction of, any that *have their conversation in the holy mountain,* 1 Pet. iii. 13. *Who, or what, can harm us, if we be followers of him that is good?* God's people shall be delivered, not only from evil, but from the fear of it. Even *the sucking child* shall without any terror *play upon the hole of the asp;* blessed Paul does so when he says, *Who shall separate us from the love of Christ?* and, *O death! where is thy sting?*

Lastly, Observe what shall be the effect, and what the cause, of this wonderful softening and sweetening of men's tempers by the grace of God. 1. The effect of it shall be tractableness, and a willingness to receive instruction : *A little child shall lead those* who formerly scorned to be controlled by the strongest man. Calvin understands it of their willing submission to the ministers of Christ, who are to instruct with meekness and not to use any coercive power, but to be as *little children,* Matt. xviii. 3. See 2 Cor. viii. 5. 2. The cause of it shall be the knowledge of God. The more there is of that the more there is of a disposition to

peace. They shall thus live in love, *for the earth shall be full of the knowledge of the Lord,* which shall extinguish men's heats and animosities. The better acquainted we are with the God of love the more shall we be changed into the same image and the better affected shall we be to all those that bear his image. The earth shall be as full of this knowledge as the channels of the sea are of water—so broad and extensive shall this knowledge be and so far shall it spread—so deep and substantial shall this knowledge be, and so long shall it last. There is much more of the knowledge of God to be got by the gospel of Christ than could be got by the law of Moses; and, whereas *then* in *Judah* only was God known, now *all shall know him,* Heb. viii. 11. But that is knowledge falsely so called which sows discord among men; the right knowledge of God settles peace.

10 And in that day there shall be a root of Jesse, which shall stand for an ensign of the people; to it shall the Gentiles seek : and his rest shall be glorious. 11 And it shall come to pass in that day, *that* the Lord shall set his hand again the second time to recover the remnant of his people, which shall be left, from Assyria, and from Egypt, and from Pathros, and from Cush, and from Elam, and from Shinar, and from Hamath, and from the islands of the sea. 12 And he shall set up an ensign for the nations, and shall assemble the outcasts of Israel, and gather together the dispersed of Judah from the four corners of the earth. 13 The envy also of Ephraim shall depart, and the adversaries of Judah shall be cut off : Ephraim shall not envy Judah, and Judah shall not vex Ephraim. 14 But they shall fly upon the shoulders of the Philistines toward the west; they shall spoil them of the east together : they shall lay their hand upon Edom and Moab; and the children of Ammon shall obey them. 15 And the Lord shall utterly destroy the tongue of the Egyptian sea; and with his mighty wind shall he shake his hand over the river, and shall smite it in the seven streams, and make *men* go over dry-shod. 16 And there shall be an highway for the remnant of his people, which shall be left,

from Assyria; like as it was to Israel in the day that he came up out of the land of Egypt.

We have here a further prophecy of the enlargement and advancement of the kingdom of the Messiah, under the type and figure of the flourishing condition of the kingdom of Judah in the latter end of Hezekiah's reign, after the defeat of Sennacherib.

I. This prediction was in part accomplished when the great things God did for Hezekiah and his people proved as an ensign, inviting the neighbouring nations to them *to enquire of the wonders done in the land*, on which errand the king of Babylon's ambassadors came. To them the Gentiles sought; and Jerusalem, the rest or habitation of the Jews, was then glorious, *v.* 10. Then many of the Israelites who belonged to the kingdom of the ten tribes, who upon the destruction of that kingdom by the king of Assyria were forced to flee for shelter into all the countries about and to some that lay very remote, even to the islands of the sea, were encouraged to return to their own country and put themselves under the protection and government of the king of Judah, the rather because it was an Assyrian army by which their country had been ruined and that was now routed. This is said to be a recovery of them *the second time* (*v.* 11), such an instance of the power and goodness of God, and such a reviving to them, as their first deliverance out of Egypt was. Then the *outcasts of Israel* should be gathered in, and brought home, and those of Judah too, who, upon the approach of the Assyrian army, shifted for their own safety. Then the old feud between Ephraim and Judah shall be forgotten, and they shall join against the Philistines and their other common enemies, *v.* 13, 14. Note, Those who have been sharers with each other in afflictions and mercies, dangers and deliverances, ought in consideration thereof to unite for their joint and mutual safety and protection; and it is likely to be well with the church when Ephraim and Judah are one against the Philistines. Then, whatever difficulties there may be in the way of the return of the dispersed, the Lord shall find out some way or other to remove them, as when he brought Israel out of Egypt he dried up the Red Sea and Jordan (*v.* 15) and led them to Canaan through the invincible embarrassments of a vast howling wilderness, *v.* 16. The like will he do this second time, or that which shall be equivalent. When God's time has come for the deliverance of his people mountains of opposition shall become plain before him. Let us not despair therefore when the interests of the church seem to be brought very low; God can soon turn gloomy days into glorious ones.

76

II. It had a further reference to the days of the Messiah and the accession of the Gentiles to his kingdom; for to these the apostle applies *v.* 10, of which the following verses are a continuation. Rom. xv. 12, *There shall be a root of Jesse; and he that shall rise to reign over the Gentiles, in him shall the Gentiles trust.* That is a key to this prophecy, which speaks of Christ as the root of Jesse, or *a branch out of his roots* (*v.* 1), *a root out of a dry ground*, ch. liii. 2. He is the *root of David* (Rev. v. 5), the *root and offspring of David* Rev. xxii. 16.

1. *He shall stand*, or be set up, *for an ensign of the people.* When he was crucified he was *lifted up from the earth*, that, as an ensign or beacon, he might *draw* the eyes and the hearts of *all men unto him*, John xii. 32. He is set up as an ensign in the preaching of the everlasting gospel, in which the ministers, as standard-bearers, display the banner of his love, to allure us to him (Cant. i. 4), the banner of his truth, under which we may enlist ourselves, to engage in a holy war against sin and Satan. Christ is the ensign to which *the children of God that were scattered abroad are gathered together* (John xi. 52), and in him they meet as the centre of their unity.

2. *To him shall the Gentiles seek.* We read of Greeks that did so (John xii. 21, *We would see Jesus)*, and upon that occasion Christ spoke of his being lifted up, to draw all men to him. The apostle, from the LXX. (or perhaps the LXX. from the apostle, in the editions after Christ) reads it (Rom. xv. 12), *In him shall the Gentiles trust;* they shall seek to him with a dependence on him.

3. *His rest shall be glorious.* Some understand this of the death of Christ (the triumphs of the cross made even that glorious), others of his ascension, when he sat down to rest at the right hand of God. Or rather it is meant of the gospel church, that Mount Zion of which Christ has said, *This is my rest*, and in which he resides. This, though despised by the world, having upon it the beauty of holiness, is truly glorious, a *glorious high throne*, Jer. xvii. 12.

4. Both Jews and Gentiles shall be gathered to him, *v.* 11. A remnant of both, a little remnant in comparison, which shall be recovered, as it were, with great difficulty and hazard. As formerly God delivered his people, and gathered them out of all the countries whither they were scattered (Ps. cvi. 47; Jer. xvi. 15, 16), so he will a second time, in another way, by the powerful working of the Spirit of grace with the word. He *shall set his hand* to do it; he shall exert his power, the *arm of the Lord shall be revealed* to do it. (1.) There shall be a remnant of the Jews gathered in: The *outcasts of Israel and the dispersed of Judah* (*v.* 12), many of whom, at the time of the bringing of them in to Christ, were *Jews of*

the dispersion, *the twelve tribes that were scattered abroad* (James i. 1; 1 Pet. i. 1), shall flock to Christ; and probably more of those scattered Jews were brought into the church, in proportion, than of those which remained in their own land. (2.) Many of *the nations,* the Gentiles, shall be brought in by the lifting up of the ensign. Jacob foretold concerning Shiloh that *to him should the gathering of the people be.* Those that were strangers and foreigners shall be made nigh. The Jews were jealous of Christ's going to the dispersed among the Gentiles and of his *teaching the Gentiles,* John vii. 35.

5. There shall be a happy accommodation between Judah and Ephraim, and both shall be safe from their adversaries and have dominion over them, *v.* 13, 14. The coalescence between Judah and Israel at that time was a type and figure of the uniting of Jews and Gentiles, who had been so long at variance in the gospel church. *The house of Judah shall walk with the house of Israel* (Jer. iii. 18) and become *one nation* (Ezek. xxxvii. 22); so the Jews and Gentiles are made of *twain one new man* (Eph. ii. 15), and, being at peace one with another, those that are adversaries to them both shall be cut off; for *they shall fly upon the shoulders of the Philistines,* as an eagle strikes at her prey, shall spoil those on the west side of them, and then they shall extend their conquests eastward over the Edomites, Moabites, and Ammonites. The gospel of Christ shall be successful in all parts, and some of all nations shall become obedient to the faith.

6. Every thing that might hinder the progress and success of the gospel shall be taken out of the way. As when God brought Israel out of Egypt he dried up the Red Sea and Jordan before them (*ch.* lxiii. 11, 12), and as afterwards when he brought up the Jews out of Babylon he *prepared them their way* (*ch.* lxii. 10), so when Jews and Gentiles are to be brought together into the gospel church all obstructions shall be removed (*v.* 15, 16), difficulties that seemed insuperable shall be strangely got over, *the blind shall be led by a way that they knew not.* See *ch.* xlii. 15, 16; xliii. 19, 20. Converts shall be brought in chariots and in litters, *ch.* lxvi. 20. Some think it is the further accession of multitudes to the church that is pointed at in that obscure prophecy of the drying up of the river Euphrates, that the way of the kings of the east may be prepared (Rev. xvi. 12), which seems to refer to this prophecy. Note, When God's time has come for the bringing of nations, or particular persons, home to himself, divine grace will be victorious over all opposition. At the presence of the Lord the sea shall flee and Jordan be driven back; and those who set their faces heavenward will find

there are not such difficulties in the way as they thought there were, for there is a highway thither, *ch.* xxxv. 8.

CHAP. XII.

The salvation promised in the foregoing chapter was compared to that of Israel "in the day that he came up out of the land of Egypt;" so that chapter ends. Now as Moses and the children of Israel then sang a song of praise to the glory of God (Exod. xv. 1) so shall the people of God do in that day when the root of Jesse shall stand for an ensign of the people and shall be the desire and joy of all nations. In that day, I. Every particular believer shall sing a song of praise for his own interest in that salvation (ver. 1, 3). " Thou shalt say, Lord, I will praise thee." Thanksgiving-work shall be closet-work. II. Many in concert shall join in praising God for the common benefit arising from this salvation (ver. 4—6): "You shall say, Praise you the Lord." Thanksgiving-work shall be congregation-work; and the praises of God shall be publicly sung in the congregations of the upright.

A ND in that day thou shalt say, O LORD, I will praise thee: though thou wast angry with me, thine anger is turned away, and thou comfortedst me. 2 Behold, God *is* my salvation; I will trust, and not be afraid: for the LORD JEHOVAH *is* my strength and *my* song; he also is become my salvation. 3 Therefore with joy shall ye draw water out of the wells of salvation.

This is the former part of the hymn of praise which is prepared for the use of the church, of the Jewish church when God would work great deliverances for them, and of the Christian church when the kingdom of the Messiah should be set up in the world in despite of the opposition of the powers of darkness: *In that day thou shalt say, O Lord! I will praise thee.* The scattered church, being united into one body, shall, as one man, with one mind and one mouth, thus praise God, who is one and his name one. *In that day,* when the Lord shall do these great things for thee, *thou shalt say, O Lord! I will praise thee.* That is,

I. " Thou shalt have cause to say so." The promise is sure, and the blessings contained in it are very rich, and, when they are bestowed, will furnish the church with abundant matter for rejoicing and therefore with abundant matter for thanksgiving. The Old-Testament prophecies of gospel times are often expressed by the joy and praise that shall then be excited; for the inestimable benefits we enjoy by Jesus Christ require the most elevated and enlarged thanksgivings.

II. " Thou shalt have a heart to say so." All God's other gifts to his people shall be crowned with this. He will give them grace to ascribe all the glory of them to him, and to speak of them upon all occasions with thankfulness to his praise. *Thou shalt say,* that is, thou oughtest to say so. *In that day,* when many are brought home to Jesus Christ and flock to him as doves to their windows, instead of envying the kind reception they find with Christ, as the Jews grudged the favour shown to the Gentiles, *thou shalt say, O Lord! I will praise thee.* Note, We ought to rejoice in, and give thanks for, the grace of God to others as well as to ourselves.

1. Believers are here taught to give thanks to God for the turning away of his displeasure from them and the return of his favour to them (*v.* 1): *O Lord! I will praise thee, though thou wast angry with me.* Note, Even God's frowns must not put us out of tune for praising him ; though he be angry with us, though he slay us, yet we must put our trust in him and give him thanks. God has often just cause to be angry with us, but we have never any reason to be angry with him, nor to speak otherwise than well of him ; even when he blames us we must praise him. *Thou wast angry with us,* but *thy anger is turned away.* Note, (1.) God is sometimes angry with his own people and the fruits of his anger do appear, and they ought to take notice of this, that they may humble themselves under his mighty hand. (2.) Though God may for a time be angry with his people, yet his anger shall at length be turned away ; it endures but for a moment, nor will he contend for ever. By Jesus Christ, the root of Jesse, God's anger against mankind was turned away ; for *he is our peace.* (3.) Those whom God is reconciled to he comforts ; even the turning away of his anger is a comfort to them ; yet that is not all : those that are *at peace with God* may *rejoice in hope of the glory of God,* Rom. v. 1, 2. Nay, God sometimes brings his people into a wilderness that there he may *speak comfortably to them,* Hosea ii. 14. (4.) The turning away of God's anger, and the return of his comforts to us, ought to be the matter of our joyful thankful praises.

2. They are taught to triumph in God and their interest in him (*v.* 2): " *Behold,* and wonder ; *God is my salvation ;* not only my Saviour, by whom I am saved, but my salvation, in whom I am safe. I depend upon him as my salvation, for I have found him to be so. He shall have the glory of all the salvations that have been wrought for me, and from him only will I expect the salvations I further need, and not from hills and mountains : and if God be my salvation, if he undertake my eternal salvation, *I will trust* in him to prepare me for it and preserve me to it. I will trust him with all my temporal concerns, not doubting but he will make all to work for my good. I will be confident, that is, I will be always easy in my own mind." Note, Those that have God for their salvation may enjoy themselves with a holy security and serenity of mind. Let faith in God as our salvation be effectual, (1.) To silence our fears. We must *trust, and not be afraid,* not be afraid that the God we trust in will fail us ; no, there is no danger of that ; not be afraid of any creature, though ever so formidable and threatening. Note, Faith in God is a sovereign remedy against disquieting tormenting fears. (2.) To support our hopes. Is the Lord Jehovah our

salvation? Then he will be our *strength and song.* We have work to do and temptations to resist, and we may depend upon him to enable us for both, to *strengthen us with all might by his Spirit in the inner man,* for he is our strength ; his grace is so, and that grace shall be sufficient for us. We have many troubles to undergo, and must expect griefs in a vale of tears ; and we may depend upon him to comfort us in all our tribulations, for he is our song ; he *giveth songs in the night.* If we make God our strength, and put our confidence in him, he will be our strength ; if we make him our song, and place our comfort in him, he will be our song. Many good Christians have God for their strength who have him not for their song ; they walk in darkness : but light is sown for them. And those that have God for their strength ought to make him their song, that is, to give him the glory of it (see Ps. lxviii. 35) and to take to themselves the comfort of it, for he will become their salvation. Observe the title here given to God : *Jah, Jehovah.* Jah is the contraction of Jehovah, and both signify his eternity and unchangeableness, which are a great comfort to those that depend upon him as their strength and their song. Some make Jah to signify the Son of God made man ; he is Jehovah, and in him we may glory as our strength, and song, and salvation.

3. They are aught to derive comfort to themselves from the love of God and all the tokens of that love (*v.* 3): " *Therefore,* because the Lord Jehovah is your strength and song and will be your salvation, *you shall draw water with joy.*" Note, The assurances God has given us of his love, and the experiences we have had of the benefit and comfort of his grace, should greatly encourage our faith in him and our expectations from him : " *Out of the wells of salvation* in God, who is the fountain of all good to his people, *you shall draw water with joy.* God's favour shall flow forth to you, and you shall have the comfort of it and make use of the blessed fruits of it." Note, (1.) God's promises revealed, ratified, and given out to us, in his ordinances, are wells of salvation ; wells of *the Saviour* (so some read it), for in them the Saviour and salvation are made known to us and made over to us. (2.) It is our duty by faith to draw water out of these wells, to take to ourselves the benefit and comfort that are treasured up for us in them, as those that acknowledge all our fresh springs to be there and all our fresh streams to be thence, Ps. lxxxvii. 7. (3.) Water is to be drawn out of the wells of salvation with a great deal of pleasure and satisfaction. It is the will of God that we should rejoice before him and rejoice in him (Deut. xxvi. 11), be joyful in his house of prayer (Isa. lvi. 7), and keep his feasts with gladness, Acts ii. 46.

4 And in that day shall ye say,

Praise the LORD, call upon his name, declare his doings among the people, make mention that his name is exalted. 5 Sing unto the LORD; for he hath done excellent things : this *is* known in all the earth. 6 Cry out and shout, thou inhabitant of Zion : for great *is* the Holy One of Israel in the midst of thee.

This is the second part of this evangelical song, and to the same purport with the former; there believers stir up themselves to praise God, here they invite and encourage one another to do it, and are contriving to spread his praise and draw in others to join with them in it. Observe,

I. Who are here called upon to praise God —*the inhabitants of Zion* and Jerusalem, whom God had in a particular manner protected from Sennacherib's violence, *v.* 6. Those that have received distinguishing favours from God ought to be most forward and zealous in praising him. The gospel church is Zion. Christ is Zion's King. Those that have a place and a name in the church should lay out themselves to diffuse the knowledge of Christ and to bring many to him. *Thou inhabitress of Zion ;* the word is feminine. Let the weaker sex be strong in the Lord, and out of their mouth praise shall be perfected.

II. How they must praise the Lord. 1. By prayer : *Call upon his name.* As giving thanks for former mercy is a decent way of begging further mercy, so begging further mercy is graciously accepted as a thankful acknowledgment of the mercies we have received. In calling upon God's name we give unto him some of the glory that is due to his name as our powerful and bountiful benefactor. 2. By preaching and writing. We must not only speak to God, but speak to others concerning him, not only call upon his name, but (as the margin reads it) *proclaim his name ;* let others know something more from us than they did before concerning God, and those things whereby he has made himself known. *Declare his doings,* his *counsels* (so some read it); the work of redemption is according to the counsel of his will, and in that and other wonderful works that he has done we must take notice of his *thoughts which are to us-ward,* Ps. xl. 5. Declare these *among the people,* among the heathen, that they may be brought into communion with Israel and the God of Israel. When the apostles preached the gospel to all nations, beginning at Jerusalem, then this scripture was fulfilled, that his doings should be declared among the people and that what he has done should be known in all the earth. 3. By a holy exultation and transport of joy : " *Cry out and shout,* welcome the gospel to yourselves and publish it to others with huzzas and loud acclamations,

as those that *shout for victory* (Exod. xxxii. 18) or for the coronation of a king," Num. xxiii. 21.

III. For what they must praise the Lord. 1. Because he has glorified himself. Remember it yourselves, and *make mention* of it to others, *that his name is exalted,* has become more illustrious and more conspicuous; in this every good man rejoices. 2. Because he has magnified his people : *He has done excellent things* for them, which make them look great and considerable. 3. Because he is, and will be, great among them : *Great is the Holy One,* for he is glorious in holiness ; *therefore* great, because holy. True goodness is true greatness. He is great as *the Holy One of Israel,* and *in the midst of them,* praised by them (Ps. lxxvi. 1), manifesting himself among them, and appearing gloriously in their behalf. It is the honour and happiness of Israel that the God who is in covenant with them, and in the midst of them, is infinitely great.

CHAP. XIII.

Hitherto the prophecies of this book related only to Judah and Israel, and Jerusalem especially ; but now the prophet begins to look abroad, and to read the doom of divers of the neighbouring states and kingdoms : for he that is King of saints is also King of nations, and rules in the affairs of the children of men as well as in those of his own children. But the nations to whom these prophecies do relate were all such as the people of God were in some way or other conversant and concerned with, such as had been kind or unkind to Israel, and accordingly God would deal with them, either in favour or in wrath ; for the Lord's portion is his people, and to them he has an eye in all the dispensations of his providence concerning those about them, Deut. xxxii. 8, 9. The threatenings we find here against Babylon, Moab, Damascus, Egypt, Tyre, &c., were intended for comfort to those in Israel that feared God, but were terrified and oppressed by those potent neighbours, and for alarm to those among them that were wicked. If God would thus severely reckon with those for their sins that knew him not, and made no profession of his name, how severe would he be with those that were called by his name and yet lived in rebellion against him ! And perhaps the directing of particular prophecies to the neighbouring nations might invite some of those nations to the reading of the Jews' Bible, and so they might be brought to their religion. This chapter, and that which follows, contain what God had to say to Babylon and Babylon's king, who were at present little known to Israel, but would in process of time become a greater enemy to them than any other had been, for which God would at last reckon with them. In this chapter we have, I. A general rendezvous of the forces that were to be employed against Babylon, ver. 1—5. II. The dreadfully bloody work that those forces should make in Babylon, ver. 6—18. III. The utter ruin and desolation of Babylon, which this should end in, ver. 19—22.

THE burden of Babylon, which Isaiah the son of Amoz did see. 2 Lift ye up a banner upon the high mountain, exalt the voice unto them, shake the hand, that they may go into the gates of the nobles. 3 I have commanded my sanctified ones, I have also called my mighty ones for mine anger, *even* them that rejoice in my highness. 4 The noise of a multitude in the mountains, like as of a great people ; a tumultuous noise of the kingdoms of nations gathered together : the LORD of hosts mustereth the host of the battle. 5 They come from a far country, from the end of heaven, *even* the LORD, and the weapons of his indignation, to destroy the whole land.

The general title of this book was, *The vision of Isaiah the son of Amoz, ch* i. 1. Here we have that which Isaiah saw, which was represented to his mind as clearly and fully as if he had seen it with his bodily eyes; but the particular inscription of this sermon is *the burden of Babylon.* 1. It is a burden, a lesson they were to learn (so some understand it), but they would be loth to learn it, and it would be a burden to their memories, or a load which should lie heavily upon them and under which they should sink. Those that will not make the word of God their rest (*ch.* xxviii. 12; *Jer.* vi. 16) shall find it made a burden to them. 2. It is the burden of Babylon or Babel, which at this time was a dependent upon the Assyrian monarchy (the metropolis of which was Nineveh), but soon after revolted from it and became a monarchy of itself, and a very potent one, in Nebuchadnezzar. This prophet afterwards foretold the captivity of the Jews in Babylon, *ch.* xxxix. 6. Here he foretels the reprisals God would make upon Babylon for the wrongs done to his people. In these verses a summons is given to those powerful and warlike nations whom God would make use of as the instruments of his wrath for the destruction of Babylon: he afterwards names them (*v.* 17) the *Medes*, who, in conjunction with the Persians, under the command of Darius and Cyrus, were the ruin of the Babylonian monarchy

I. The place doomed to destruction is Babylon; it is here called *the gates of the nobles* (*v.* 2), because of the abundance of noblemen's houses that were in it, stately ones and richly furnished, which would invite the enemy to come, in hopes of a rich booty. The gates of nobles were strong and well guarded, and yet they would be no fence against those who came with commission to execute God's judgments. Before his power and wrath palaces are no more than cottages. Nor is it only the gates of the nobles, but *the whole land*, that is doomed to destruction (*v.* 5); for, though the nobles were the leaders in persecuting and oppressing God's people, yet the whole land concurred with them in it.

II. The persons brought together to lay Babylon waste are here called, 1. God's *sanctified ones* (*v.* 3), designed for this service and set apart to it by the purpose and providence of God, disengaged from other projects, that they might wholly apply themselves to this, such as were qualified for that to which they were called, for what work God employs men in he does in some measure fit them for. It intimates likewise that in God's intention, though not in theirs, it was a holy war; they designed only the enlargement of their own empire, but God

80

designed the release of his people and a type of the destruction of the New-Testament Babylon. Cyrus, the person principally concerned, was justly called *a sanctified one*, for he was God's anointed (*ch.* xlv. 1) and a figure of him that was to come. It is a pity but all soldiers, especially those that fight the Lord's battles, should be in the strictest sense sanctified ones; and it is a wonder that those dare be profane ones who carry their lives in their hands. 2. They are called God's *mighty ones*, because they had their might from God and were now to use it for him. It is said of Cyrus that in this expedition *God held his right hand, ch.* xlv. 1. God's sanctified ones are his mighty ones. Those whom God calls he qualifies; and those whom he makes holy he makes strong in spirit. 3. They are said to rejoice in his highness, that is, to serve his glory and the purposes of it with great alacrity. Though Cyrus did not know God, nor actually design his honour in what he did, yet God used him as his servant (*ch.* xlv. 4, *I have surnamed thee* as my servant, though *thou hast not known me*), and he rejoiced in those successes by which God exalted his own name. 4. They are very numerous, *a multitude, a great people, kingdoms of nations* (*v.* 4), not rude and barbarous, but modelled and regular troops, such as are furnished out by well-ordered kingdoms. The great God has hosts at his command. 5. They are far-fetched: *They come from a far country, from the end of* heaven. The vast country of Assyria lay between Babylon and Persia. God can make those a scourge and ruin to his enemies that lie most remote from them and therefore are least dreaded.

III. The summons given them is effectual, their obedience ready, and they make a very formidable appearance: *A banner is lifted up upon the high mountain, v.* 2. God's standard is set up, a flag of defiance hung out against Babylon. It is erected on high, where all may see it; whoever will may come and enlist themselves under it, and they shall be taken immediately into God's pay. Those that beat up for volunteers must *exalt the voice* in making proclamation, to encourage soldiers to come in; they must *shake the hand*, to beckon those at a distance and to animate those that have enlisted themselves. And they shall not do this in vain; God has commanded and called those whom he designs to make use of (*v.* 3) and power goes along with his calls and commands, which cannot be resisted. He that makes men able to serve him can, when he pleases, make them willing too. It is the *Lord of hosts that musters the host of the battle, v.* 1. He raises them, brings them together, puts them in order, reviews them, has an exact account of them in his muster-roll, sees that they be all in their respective posts, and gives them their necessary orders Note, All the hosts of war are under the command of the Lord of hosts; and that which makes them truly formidable is that, when they come against Babylon, the Lord comes, and brings them with him as *the weapons of his indignation, v.* 5. Note, Great princes and armies are but tools in God's hand, weapons that he is pleased to make use of in doing his work, and it is his wrath that arms them and gives them success.

6 Howl ye; for the day of the Lord *is* at hand; it shall come as a destruction from the Almighty. 7 Therefore shall all hands be faint, and every man's heart shall melt: 8 And they shall be afraid: pangs and sorrows shall take hold of them; they shall be in pain as a woman that travaileth: they shall be amazed one at another; their faces *shall be as* flames. 9 Behold, the day of the Lord cometh, cruel both with wrath and fierce anger, to lay the land desolate: and he shall destroy the sinners thereof out of it. 10 For the stars of heaven and the constellations thereof shall not give their light: the sun shall be darkened in his going forth, and the moon shall not cause her light to shine. 11 And I will punish the world for *their* evil, and the wicked for their iniquity; and I will cause the arrogancy of the proud to cease, and will lay low the haughtiness of the terrible. 12 I will make a man more precious than fine gold; even a man than the golden wedge of Ophir. 13 Therefore I will shake the heavens, and the earth shall remove out of her place, in the wrath of the Lord of hosts, and in the day of his fierce anger. 14 And it shall be as the chased roe, and as a sheep that no man taketh up: they shall every man turn to his own people, and flee every one into his own land. 15 Every one that is found shall be thrust through; and every one that is joined *unto them* shall fall by the sword. 16 Their children also shall be dashed to pieces before their eyes; their houses shall be spoiled, and their wives ravished. 17 Behold, I will stir up the Medes against them, which shall not regard silver; and *as for* gold, they shall not delight in it. 18 *Their* bows also shall dash the young

men to pieces; and they shall have no pity on the fruit of the womb; their eye shall not spare children.

We have here a very elegant and lively description of the terrible confusion and desolation which should be made in Babylon by the descent which the Medes and Persians should make upon it. Those that were now secure and easy were bidden to *howl* and make sad lamentation; for,

I. God was about to appear in wrath against them, and it is a fearful thing to fall into his hands: *The day of the Lord is at hand* (v. 6), a little day of judgment, when God will act as a just avenger of his own and his people's injured cause. And there are those who will have reason to tremble when that day is at hand. *The day of the Lord cometh, v.* 9. Men have their day now, and they think to carry the day; but God laughs at them, for he sees that *his day is coming,* Ps. xxxvii. 13. Fury is not with God, and yet his day of reckoning with the Babylonians is said to be *cruel with wrath and fierce anger.* God will deal in severity with them for the severities they exercised upon God's people; with the froward, with the cruel, he will show himself froward, will show himself cruel, and give the blood-thirsty blood to drink.

II. Their hearts shall fail them, and they shall have neither courage nor comfort left; they shall not be able either to resist the judgment coming or to bear up under it, either to oppose the enemy or to support themselves, *v.* 7, 8. Those that in the day of their peace were *proud,* and *haughty,* and *terrible* (v. 11), shall, when trouble comes, be quite dispirited and at their wits' end: *All hands shall be faint,* and unable to hold a weapon, *and every man's heart shall melt,* so that they shall be ready to die for fear. The pangs of their fear shall be like those of a woman in hard labour, and *they shall be amazed one at another.* In frightening themselves, they shall frighten one another; they shall wonder to see those tremble that used to be bold and daring; or they shall be amazed looking one at another, as men at a loss, Gen. xlii. 1. *Their faces shall be as flames,* pale as flames, through fear (so some), or red as flames sometimes are, blushing at their own cowardice; or their faces shall be as faces scorched with the flame, or as theirs that labour in the fire, their *visage blacker than a coal,* or like *a bottle in the smoke,* Ps. cxix. 83.

III. All comfort and hope shall fail them (v. 10): *The stars of heaven shall not give their light,* but shall be clouded and overcast; *the sun shall be darkened in his going forth,* rising bright, but lost again, a certain sign of foul weather. They shall be as men in distress at sea, when neither sun nor stars appear, Acts xxvii. 20. It shall be as dreadful a time with them as it would be with the earth if all the heavenly luminaries were turned into darkness, a resemblance of the day of judgment, when the sun shall be turned into darkness. The heavens frowning thus is an indication of the displeasure of the God of heaven. When things look dark on earth, yet it is well enough if all be clear upwards ; but, if we have no comfort thence, wherewith shall we be comforted ?

IV. God will visit them *for their iniquity ;* and all this is intended *for the punishment* of sin, and particularly the sin of pride, *v.* 11. This puts wormwood and gall into the affliction and misery, 1. That sin must now have its punishment. Though Babylon be a little world, yet, being a wicked world, it shall not go unpunished. Sin brings desolation on the world of the ungodly ; and when the kingdoms of the earth are quarrelling with one another it is the fruit of God's controversy with them all. 2. That pride must now have its fall : *The haughtiness of the terrible* must now be *laid low,* particularly of Nebuchadnezzar and his son Belshazzar, who had, in their pride, trampled upon, and made themselves very terrible to, the people of God. *A man's pride will bring him low.*

V. There shall be so great a slaughter as will produce a scarcity of men (*v.* 12) : *I will make a man more precious than fine gold.* You could not have a man to be employed in any of the affairs of state, not a man to be enlisted in the army, not a man to match a daughter to, for the building up of a family, if you would give any money for one. The troops of the neighbouring nations would not be hired into the service of the king of Babylon, because they saw every thing go against him. Populous countries are soon depopulated by war. And God can soon make a kingdom that has been courted and admired to be dreaded and shunned by all, as a house that is falling, or a ship that is sinking.

VI. There shall be a universal confusion and consternation, such a confusion of their affairs that it shall be like the *shaking of the heavens* with dreadful thunders and the *removing of the earth* by no less dreadful earthquakes. All shall go to rack and ruin *in the day of the wrath of the Lord of hosts, v.* 13. And such a consternation shall seize their spirits that Babylon, which used to be like a roaring lion and a raging bear to all about her, shall become *as a chased roe and as a sheep that no man takes up, v.* 14. The army they shall bring into the field, consisting of troops of divers nations (as great armies usually do), shall be so dispirited by their own apprehensions and so dispersed by their enemies' sword that they shall *turn every man to his own people ;* each man shall shift for his own safety ; the *men of might shall not find their hands* (Ps. lxxvi. 5), but take to their heels.

VII. There shall be a general scene of blood and horror, as is usual where the sword devours. No wonder that every one makes the best of his way, since the conqueror gives no quarter, but puts all to the sword, and not those only that are found in arms, as is usual with us even in the most cruel slaughters (*v.* 15) : *Every one that is found alive shall be run through,* as soon as ever it appears that he is a Babylonian. Nay, because the sword devours one as well as another, *every one that is joined to them shall fall by the sword ;* those of other nations that come in to their assistance shall be cut off with them. It is dangerous being in bad company, and helping those whom God is about to destroy. Those particularly that join themselves to Babylon must expect to share in her plagues, Rev. xviii. 4. And, since the most sacred laws of nature, and of humanity itself, are silenced by the fury of war (though they cannot be cancelled), the conquerors shall, in the most barbarous brutish manner, *dash the children to pieces, and ravish the wives. Jusque datum sceleri—Wickedness shall have free course, v.* 16. They had thus dealt with God's people (Lam. v. 11), and now they shall be paid in their own coin, Rev. xiii. 10. It was particularly foretold (Ps. cxxxvii. 9) that the *little ones of Babylon should be dashed against the stones.* How cruel soever and unjust those were that did it, God was righteous who suffered it to be done, and to be done *before their eyes,* to their greater terror and vexation. It was just also that the houses which they had filled with the spoil of Israel should be spoiled and plundered. What is got by rapine is often lost in the same manner.

VIII. The enemy that God will send against them shall be inexorable, probably being by some provocation or other more than ordinarily exasperated against them ; or, in whatever way it may be brought about, God himself will *stir up the Medes* to use this severity with the Babylonians. He will not only serve his own purposes by their dispositions and designs, but will put it into their hearts to make this attempt upon Babylon, and suffer them to prosecute it with all this fury. God is not the author of sin, but he would not permit it if he did not know how to bring glory to himself out of it. These Medes, in conjunction with the Persians, shall make thorough work of it ; for, 1. They shall take no bribes, *v.* 17. All that men have they would give for their lives, but the Medes *shall not regard silver ;* it is blood they thirst for, not gold ; no man's riches shall with them be the ransom of his life. 2. They shall show no pity (*v.* 18), not to *the young men* that are in the prime of their time—they shall shoot them through with their bows, and then *dash them to pieces ;* not to the age of innocency—*they shall have no pity on the fruit of the womb, nor spare little children,* whose cries and frights one would think should make even marble eyes to weep, and hearts of adamant to relent. Pause a little here and wonder, (1.) That men should be thus cruel and inhuman, and so utterly divested of all compassion; and in it see how corrupt and degenerate the nature of man has become. (2.) That the God of infinite mercy should suffer it, nay, and should make it to be the execution of his justice, which shows that, though he is gracious, yet he is the God to whom vengeance belongs. (3.) That little infants, who have never been guilty of any actual sin, should be thus abused, which shows that there is an original guilt by which life is forfeited as soon as it is had.

19 And Babylon, the glory of kingdoms, the beauty of the Chaldees' excellency, shall be as when God overthrew Sodom and Gomorrah. 20 It shall never be inhabited, neither shall it be dwelt in from generation to generation: neither shall the Arabian pitch tent there; neither shall the shepherds make their fold there. 21 But wild beasts of the desert shall lie there; and their houses shall be full of doleful creatures; and owls shall dwell there, and satyrs shall dance there. 22 And the wild beasts of the islands shall cry in their desolate houses, and dragons in *their* pleasant palaces: and her time *is* near to come, and her days shall not be prolonged.

The great havoc and destruction which it was foretold should be made by the Medes and Persians in Babylon here end in the final destruction of it. 1. It is allowed that Babylon was a noble city. It was *the glory of kingdoms and the beauty of the Chaldees' excellency;* it was that *head of gold* (Dan. ii. 37, 38); it was called *the lady of kingdoms* (ch. xlvii. 5), *the praise of the whole earth* (Jer. li. 41), *like a pleasant roe* (so the word signifies); but it shall be as a *chased roe*, v. 14. The Chaldeans gloried in the beauty and wealth of this their metropolis. 2. It is foretold that it should be wholly destroyed, like Sodom and Gomorrah; not so miraculously, nor so suddenly, but as effectually, though gradually; and the destruction should come upon them as that upon Sodom, when they were secure, eating and drinking, Luke xvii. 28, 29. Babylon was taken when Belshazzar was in his revels; and, though Cyrus and Darius did not demolish it, yet by degrees it wasted away and in process of time it went all to ruin. It is foretold here (*v.* 20) *that it shall never be inhabited:* in Adrian's time nothing remained but the wall. And whereas it is

prophesied concerning Nineveh, that great city, that when it should be deserted and left desolate yet flocks should lie down in the midst of it, it is here said concerning Babylon that *the Arabians,* who were *shepherds, should not make their folds there;* the country about should be so barren that there would be no grazing there; no, not for sheep. Nay, it shall be the receptacle of *wild beasts,* that affect solitude; the houses of Babylon, where the sons and daughters of pleasure used to rendezvous, *shall be full of doleful creatures, owls and satyrs,* that are themselves frightened thither, as to a place proper for them, and by whom all others are frightened thence. Historians say that this was fulfilled in the letter. Benjamin Bar-Jona, in his Itinerary, speaking of Babel, has these words: " This is that Babel which was of old thirty miles in breadth; it is now laid waste. There are yet to be seen the ruins of a palace of Nebuchadnezzar, but the sons of men dare not enter in, for fear of serpents and scorpions, which possess the place." Let none be proud of their pompous palaces, for they know not but they may become worse than cottages; nor let any think that *their houses shall endure for ever* (Ps. xlix. 11), when perhaps nothing may remain but the ruins and reproaches of them. 3. It is intimated that this destruction should come shortly (*v.* 22): *Her time is near to come.* This prophecy of the destruction of Babylon was intended for the support and comfort of the people of God when they were captives there and grievously oppressed; and the accomplishment of the prophecy was nearly 200 years after the time when it was delivered; yet it followed soon after the time for which it was calculated. When the people of Israel were groaning under the heavy yoke of Babylonish tyranny, sitting down in tears by the rivers of Babylon and upbraided with the songs of Zion, when their insolent oppressors were most haughty and arrogant (*v.* 11), then let them know, for their comfort, that Babylon's time, her day to fall, is near to come, and the days of her prosperity shall not be prolonged, as they have been. When God begins with her he will make an end. Thus it is said of the destruction of the New-Testament Babylon, whereof the former was a type, *In one hour has her judgment come.*

CHAP. XIV.

In this chapter, I. More weight is added to the burden of Babylon, enough to sink it like a mill-stone; 1. It is Israel's cause that is to be pleaded in this quarrel with Babylon, ver. 1—3. 2. The king of Babylon, for the time being, shall be remarkably brought down and triumphed over, ver. 4—20. 3. The whole race of the Babylonians shall be cut off and extirpated, ver. 21—23. II. A confirmation of the prophecy of the destruction of Babylon, which was a thing at a distance, is here given in the prophecy of the destruction of the Assyrian army that invaded the land, which happened not long after, ver. 24—27. III. The success of Hezekiah against the Philistines is here foretold, and the advantages which his people would gain thereby, ver. 28—32.

FOR the LORD will have mercy on Jacob, and will yet choose Israel, and set them in their own land: and the strangers shall be joined with them, and they shall cleave to the house of Jacob. 2 And the people shall take them, and bring them to their place : and the house of Israel shall possess them in the land of the LORD for servants and handmaids : and they shall take them captives, whose captives they were ; and they shall rule over their oppressors. 3 And it shall come to pass in the day that the LORD shall give thee rest from thy sorrow, and from thy fear, and from the hard bondage wherein thou wast made to serve,—

This comes in here as the reason why Babylon must be overthrown and ruined, because God has mercy in store for his people, and therefore, 1. The injuries done to them must be reckoned for and revenged upon their persecutors. Mercy to Jacob will be wrath and ruin to Jacob's impenitent implacable adversaries, such as Babylon was. 2. The yoke of oppression which Babylon had long laid on their necks must be broken off, and they must be set at liberty ; and, in order to this, the destruction of Babylon is as necessary as the destruction of Egypt and Pharaoh was to their deliverance out of that house of bondage. The same prediction is a promise to God's people and a threatening to their enemies, as the same providence has a bright side towards Israel and a black or dark side towards the Egyptians. Observe,

I. The ground of these favours to Jacob and Israel—the kindness God had for them and the choice he had made of them (*v.* 1) : " The Lord will have mercy on Jacob, the seed of Jacob now captives in Babylon ; he will make it to appear that he has compassion on them and has mercy in store for them, and that he will not contend for ever with them, but *will yet choose them,* will yet again return to them ; though he has seemed for a time to refuse and reject them, he will show that they are his chosen people and that the election stands sure." However it may seem to us, God's mercy is not gone, nor does his promise fail, Ps. lxxvii. 8.

II. The particular favours he designed them. 1. He would bring them back to their native soil and air again : The *Lord will set them in their own land,* out of which they were driven. A settlement in the holy land, the land of promise, is a fruit of God's mercy, distinguishing mercy. 2. Many should be proselyted to their holy religion, and should return with them, induced to do so by the manifest tokens of God's favourable presence with them, the operations of God's grace in them, and his providence for them : *Strangers shall be joined with them,*

saying, *We will go with you, for we have heard that God is with you,* Zech. viii. 23. It adds much to the honour and strength of Israel when strangers are joined with them and there are added to the church many from without, Acts ii. 47. Let not the church's children be shy of strangers, but receive those whom God receives, and own those who cleave to the house of Jacob. 3. These proselytes should not only be a credit to their cause, but very helpful and serviceable to them in their return home : The *people* among whom they live *shall take them,* take care of them, take pity on them, and shall *bring them to their place*—as friends, loth to part with such good company—as servants, willing to do them all the good offices they could. God's people, wherever their lot is cast, should endeavour thus, by all the instances of an exemplary and winning conversation, to gain an interest in the affections of those about them, and recommend religion to their good opinion. This was fulfilled in the return of the captives from Babylon, when all that were about them, pursuant to Cyrus's proclamation, contributed to their removal (Ezra i. 4, 6), not as the Egyptians, because they were sick of them, but because they loved them. 4. They should have the benefit of their service when they had returned home, for many would of choice go with them in the meanest post, rather than not go with them : They *shall possess them in the land of the Lord for servants and handmaids ;* and as the laws of that land saved it from being the purgatory of servants, providing that they should not be oppressed, so the advantages of that land made it the paradise of those servants that had been strangers to the covenants of promise, for there was *one law to the stranger and to those that were born in the land.* Those whose lot is cast in the land of the Lord, a land of light, should take care that their servants and handmaids may share in the benefit of it, who will then find it better to be possessed in the Lord's land than possessors in any other. 5. They should triumph over their enemies, and those that would not be reconciled to them should be reduced and humbled by them : *They shall take those captives whose captives they were and shall rule over their oppressors,* righteously, but not revengefully. The Jews perhaps bought Babylonian prisoners out of the hands of the Medes and Persians and made slaves of them. Or this might have its accomplishment in their victories over their enemies in the times of the Maccabees. It is applicable to the success of the gospel (when those were brought into obedience to it who had made the greatest opposition to it, as Paul) and to the interest believers have in Christ's victories over their spiritual enemies, when he led captivity captive, to the power they gain over their own corruptions, and to the dominion the upright shall have in the morning, Ps. xlix. 14. 6. They should see a happy termination of all their grievances (*v.* 3): *The Lord shall give thee rest from thy sorrow and thy fear, and from thy hard bondage.* God himself undertakes to work a blessed change, (1.) In their state. They shall have rest from their bondage; the days of their affliction, though many, shall have an end; and the rod of the wicked, though it lie long, shall not always lie on their lot. (2.) In their spirit. They shall have rest from their sorrow and fear, sense of their present burdens and dread of worse. Sometimes fear puts the soul into a ferment as much as sorrow does, and those must needs feel themselves very easy to whom God has given rest from both. Those who are freed from the bondage of sin have a foundation laid for true rest from sorrow and fear.

4 That thou shalt take up this proverb against the king of Babylon, and say, How hath the oppressor ceased! the golden city ceased! 5 The LORD hath broken the staff of the wicked, *and* the sceptre of the rulers. 6 He who smote the people in wrath with a continual stroke, he that ruled the nations in anger, is persecuted, *and* none hindereth. 7 The whole earth is at rest, *and* is quiet: they break forth into singing. 8 Yea, the fir-trees rejoice at thee, *and* the cedars of Lebanon, *saying,* Since thou art laid down, no feller is come up against us. 9 Hell from beneath is moved for thee to meet *thee* at thy coming: it stirreth up the dead for thee, *even* all the chief ones of the earth; it hath raised up from their thrones all the kings of the nations. 10 All they shall speak and say unto thee, Art thou also become weak as we? Art thou become like unto us? 11 Thy pomp is brought down to the grave, *and* the noise of thy viols: the worm is spread under thee, and the worms cover thee. 12 How art thou fallen from heaven, O Lucifer, son of the morning! *How* art thou cut down to the ground, which didst weaken the nations! 13 For thou hast said in thine heart, I will ascend into heaven, I will exalt my throne above the stars of God: I will sit also upon the mount of the congregation, in the sides of the north: 14 I will ascend above the heights of the clouds; I will be like the Most High. 15 Yet

thou shalt be brought down to hell, to the sides of the pit. 16 They that see thee shall narrowly look upon thee, *and* consider thee, *saying, Is* this the man that made the earth to tremble, that did shake kingdoms; 17 *That* made the world as a wilderness, and destroyed the cities thereof; *that* opened not the house of his prisoners? 18 All the kings of the nations, *even* all of them, lie in glory, every one in his own house. 19 But thou art cast out of thy grave like an abominable branch, *and as* the raiment of those that are slain, thrust through with a sword, that go down to the stones of the pit; as a carcase trodden under feet. 20 Thou shalt not be joined with them in burial, because thou hast destroyed thy land, *and* slain thy people: the seed of evil doers shall never be renowned. 21 Prepare slaughter for his children for the iniquity of their fathers; that they do not rise, nor possess the land, nor fill the face of the world with cities. 22 For I will rise up against them, saith the LORD of hosts, and cut off from Babylon the name, and remnant, and son, and nephew, saith the LORD. 23 I will also make it a possession for the bittern, and pools of water: and I will sweep it with the besom of destruction, saith the LORD of hosts.

The kings of Babylon, successively, were the great enemies and oppressors of God's people, and therefore the destruction of Babylon, the fall of the king, and the ruin of his family, are here particularly taken notice of and triumphed in. In the day that God has given Israel rest they shall *take up this proverb against the king of Babylon.* We must not rejoice when our enemy falls, as ours; but when Babylon, the common enemy of God and his Israel, sinks, then *rejoice over her, thou heaven, and you holy apostles and prophets,* Rev. xviii. 20. The Babylonian monarchy bade fair to be an absolute, universal, and perpetual one, and, in these pretensions, vied with the Almighty; it is therefore very justly, not only brought down, but insulted over when it is down; and it is not only the last monarch, Belshazzar, who *was slain on that night* that Babylon was taken (Dan. v. 30), who is here triumphed over, but the whole monarchy, which sunk in him; not without special reference to Nebuchadnezzar, in whom that monarchy was at its height. Now here,

I. The fall of the king of Babylon is rejoiced in; and a most curious and elegant composition is here prepared, not to adorn his hearse or monument, but to expose his memory and fix a lasting brand of infamy upon it. It gives us an account of the life and death of this mighty monarch, how he *went down slain to the pit,* though he had been *the terror of the mighty in the land of the living,* Ezek. xxxii. 27. In this parable we may observe,

1. The prodigious height of wealth and power at which this monarch and monarchy arrived. Babylon was a *golden city, v.* 4 (it is a Chaldee word in the original, which intimates that she used to call herself so), so much did she abound in riches and excel all other cities, as gold does all other metals. She is *gold-thirsty,* or an exactness of gold (so some read it); for how do men get wealth to themselves but by squeezing it out of others? The New Jerusalem is the only truly golden city, Rev. xxi. 18, 21. The king of Babylon, having so much wealth in his dominions and the absolute command of it, by the help of that *ruled the nations (v.* 6), gave them law, read them their doom, and at his pleasure *weakened the nations (v.* 12), that they might not be able to make head against him. Such vast and victorious armies did he bring into the field, that, which way soever he looked, he *made the earth to tremble, and shook kingdoms (v.* 16); all his neighbours were afraid of him, and were forced to submit to him. No one man could do this by his own personal strength, but by the numbers he has at his beck. Great tyrants, by making some do what they will, make others suffer what they will. How piteous is the case of mankind, which thus seems to be in a combination against itself, and its own rights and liberties, which could not be ruined but by its own strength!

2. The wretched abuse of all this wealth and power, which the king of Babylon was guilty of, in two instances:—

(1.) Great oppression and cruelty. He is known by the name of the *oppressor (v.* 4); he has *the sceptre of the rulers (v.* 5), has the command of all the princes about him; but it is *the staff of the wicked,* a staff with which he supports himself in his wickedness and wickedly strikes all about him. *He smote the people,* not in justice, for their correction and reformation, but *in wrath (v.* 6), to gratify his own peevish resentments, and that *with a continual stroke,* pursued them with his forces, and gave them no respite, no breathing time, no cessation of arms. He ruled the nations, but he ruled them *in anger,* every thing he said and did was in a passion; so that he who had the government of all about him had no government of himself. He *made the world as a wilderness,* as if he had taken a pride in being the plague of his generation and a curse to mankind, *v.* 17. Great
86

princes usually glory in building cities, but he gloried in destroying them; see Ps. ix. 6. Two particular instances, worse than all the rest, are here given of his tyranny:—
[1.] That he was severe to his captives *(v.* 17): He *opened not the house of his prisoners;* he *did not let them loose homeward* (so the margin reads it); he kept them in close confinement, and never would suffer any to return to their own land. This refers especially to the people of the Jews, and it is that which fills up the measure of the king of Babylon's iniquity, that he had detained the people of God in captivity and would by no means release them; nay, and by profaning the vessels of God's temple at Jerusalem, did in effect say that they should never return to their former use, Dan. v. 3. For this he was quickly and justly turned out by one whose first act was to open the house of God's prisoners and send home the temple vessels. [2.] That he was oppressive to his own subjects *(v.* 20): *Thou hast destroyed thy land, and slain thy people;* and what did he get by that, when the wealth of the land and the multitude of the people are the strength and honour of the prince, who never rules so safely, so gloriously, as in the hearts and affections of the people? But tyrants sacrifice their interests to their lusts and passions; and God will reckon with them for their barbarous usage of those who are under their power, whom they think they may use as they please.

(2.) Great pride and haughtiness. Notice is here taken of his *pomp,* the extravagancy of his retinue, *v.* 11. He affected to appear in the utmost magnificence. But that was not the worst: it was the temper of his mind, and the elevation of that, that ripened him for ruin *(v.* 13, 14): *Thou hast said in thy heart,* like Lucifer, *I will ascend into heaven.* Here is the language of his vainglory, borrowed perhaps from that of the angels who fell, who not content with their first estate, the post assigned them, would vie with God, and become not only independent of him, but equal with him. Or perhaps it refers to the story of Nebuchadnezzar, who, when he would be more than a man, was justly turned into a brute, Dan. iv. 30. The king of Babylon here promises himself, [1.] That in pomp and power he shall surpass all his neighbours, and shall arrive at the very height of earthly glory and felicity, that he shall be as great and happy as this world can make him; that is the heaven of a carnal heart, and to that he hopes to ascend, and to be as far above those about him as the heaven is above the earth. Princes are the stars of God, which give some light to this dark world (Matt. xxiv. 29); but he will exalt his throne above them all. [2.] That he shall particularly insult over God's Mount Zion, which Belshazzar, in his last drunken frolic, seems to have had a particular spite against when he called for the vessels of the temple at Jerusalem, to profane them; see Dan. v. 2. In the same humour he here said, *I will sit upon the mount of the congregation* (it is the same word that is used for the holy *convocations*), *in the sides of the north;* so Mount Zion is said to be situated, Ps. xlviii. 2. Perhaps Belshazzar was projecting an expedition to Jerusalem, to triumph in the ruins of it, at the time when God cut him off. [3.] That he shall vie with the God of Israel, of whom he had indeed heard glorious things, that he had his residence *above the heights of the clouds.* " But thither," says he, " *will I ascend,* and be as great as he; I will be like him whom they call *the Most High.*" It is a gracious ambition to covet to be like the Most Holy, for he has said, *Be you holy, for I am holy;* but it is a sinful ambition to aim to be like the Most High, for he has said, *He that exalteth himself shall be abased,* and the devil drew our first parents in to eat forbidden fruit by promising them that they should be as gods. [4.] That he shall himself be deified after his death, as some of the first founders of the Assyrian monarchy were, and stars had even their names from them. " But," says he, " *I will exalt my throne above them* all." Such as this was his pride, which was the undoubted omen of his destruction.

3. The utter ruin that should be brought upon him. It is foretold, (1.) That his wealth and power should be broken, and a final period put to his pomp and pleasure. He has been long an oppressor, but he shall cease to be so, *v.* 4. Had he ceased to be so by true repentance and reformation, according to the advice Daniel gave to Nebuchadnezzar, it might have been a lengthening of his life and tranquillity. But those that will not cease to sin God will make to cease. " *The golden city,* which one would have thought might continue for ever, *has ceased;* there is an end of that Babylon. *The Lord,* the righteous God, *has broken the staff of that wicked prince,* broken it over his head, in token of the divesting him of his office. God has taken his power from him, and rendered him incapable of doing any more mischief: he has broken the sceptres; for even these are brittle things, soon broken and often justly." (2.) That he himself should be seized: *He is persecuted* (*v.* 6); violent hands are laid upon him, and none hinders. It is the common fate of tyrants, when they fall into the power of their enemies, to be deserted by their flatterers, whom they took for their friends. We read of another enemy like this, of whom it is foretold that *he shall come to his end and none shall help him,* Dan. xi. 45. Tiberius and Nero thus saw themselves abandoned. (3.) That he should be slain, and *go down to the congregation of the dead,* to be *free among them, as the slain that are no more remembered,* Ps. lxxxviii. 5. He shall be

weak as the dead are, and *like unto them, v.* 10. His *pomp is brought down to the grave* (*v.* 11), that is, it perishes with him; the pomp of his life shall not, as usual, end in a funeral pomp. True glory (that is, true grace) will go up with the soul to heaven, but vain pomp will go down with the body to the grave: there is an end of it. *The noise of his viols* is now heard no more. Death is a farewell to the pleasures, as well as to the pomps, of this world. This mighty prince, that used to lie on a bed of down, to tread upon rich carpets, and to have coverings and canopies exquisitely fine, now shall have the *worms spread under him and the worms covering him,* worms bred out of his own putrefied body, which, though he fancied himself a god, proved him to be made of the same mould with other men. When we are pampering and decking our bodies it is good to remember they will be worms'-meat shortly. (4.) That he should not have the honour of a burial, much less of a decent one and in the sepulchres of his ancestors. *The kings of the nations lie in glory* (*v.* 18), either their dead bodies themselves so embalmed as to be preserved from putrefaction, as of old among the Egyptians, or their effigies (as with us) erected over their graves. Thus, as if they would defy the ignominy of death, they lay in a poor faint sort of glory, *every one in his own house,* that is, his own burying-place (for the grave is the house appointed for all living), a sleeping-house, where the busy and troublesome will lie quiet and the troubled and weary lie at rest. But this king of Babylon is *cast out* and has no grave (*v.* 19); his dead body is thrown, like that of a beast, into the next ditch or upon the next dunghill, *like an abominable branch* of some noxious poisonous plant, which nobody will touch, or as the clothes of malefactors put to death and by the hand of justice *thrust through with a sword,* on whose dead bodies heaps of stones are raised, or they are thrown into some deep quarry among *the stones of the pit.* Nay, the king of Babylon's dead body shall be as the carcases of those who are slain in a battle, which are *trodden under feet* by the horses and soldiers and crushed to pieces. Thus he *shall not be joined with his ancestors in burial, v.* 20. To be denied decent burial is a disgrace, which, if it be inflicted for righteousness' sake (as Ps. lxxix. 2), may, as other similar reproaches, be rejoiced in (Matt. v. 12); it is the lot of the two witnesses, Rev. xi. 9. But if, as here, it be the just punishment of iniquity, it is an intimation that evil pursues impenitent sinners beyond death, greater evil than that, and that they shall *rise to everlasting shame and contempt.*

4. The many triumphs that should be in his fall.

(1.) Those whom he had been a great tyrant and terror to will be glad that they are rid of him, *v.* 7, 8. Now that he is gone *the whole earth is at rest and is quiet*, for he was the great disturber of the peace ; now they all *break forth into singing*, for *when the wicked perish there is shouting* (Prov. xi. 10); the fir-trees and cedars of Lebanon now think themselves safe ; there is no danger now of their being cut down, to make way for his vast armies or to furnish him with timber. The neighbouring princes and great men, who are compared to fir-trees and cedars (Zech. xi. 2), may now be easy, and out of fear of being dispossessed of their rights, for *the hammer of the whole earth is cut asunder and broken* (Jer. l. 23), the axe that *boasted itself against him that hewed with it, ch.* x. 15.

(2.) The congregation of the dead will bid him welcome to them, especially those whom he had barbarously hastened thither (*v.* 9, 10) : *" Hell from beneath is moved for thee, to meet thee at thy coming,* and to compliment thee upon thy arrival at their dark and dreadful regions." *The chief ones of the earth,* who when they were alive were kept in awe by him and durst not come near him, but rose from their thrones, to resign them to him, shall upbraid him with it when he comes into the state of the dead. They shall go forth to meet him, as they used to do when he made his public entry into cities he had become master of ; with such a parade shall he be introduced into those regions of horror, to make his disgrace and torment the more grievous to him. They shall scoffingly rise from their thrones and seats there, and ask him if he will please to sit down in them, as he used to do in their thrones on earth? The confusion that will then cover him they shall make a jest of : *" Hast thou also become weak as we? Who* would have thought it? It is what thou thyself didst not expect it would ever come to when thou wast in every thing too hard for us. Thou that didst rank thyself among the immortal gods, art thou come to take thy fate among us poor mortal men? Where is thy pomp now, and where thy mirth? *How hast thou fallen from heaven, O Lucifer! son of the morning! v.* 11, 12. The king of Babylon shone as brightly as the morning star, and fancied that whereever he came he brought day along with him; and has such an illustrious prince as this fallen, such a star become a clod of clay? Did ever any man fall from such a height of honour and power into such an abyss of shame and misery ?" This has been commonly alluded to (and it is a mere allusion) to illustrate the fall of the angels, who were as morning stars (Job xxxviii. 7), but *how have they fallen! How art thou cut down to the ground,* and levelled with it, that *didst weaken the nations!* God will reckon with those that invade the rights and disturb the peace of mankind, for he is King of nations as well as of saints. Now this recep-

tion of the king of Babylon into the regions of the dead, which is here described, surely is something more than a flight of fancy, and is designed to teach these solid truths :—[1.] That there is an invisible world, a world of spirits, to which the souls of men remove at death and in which they exist and act in a state of separation from the body. [2] That separate souls have acquaintance and converse with each other, though we have none with them : the parable of the rich man and Lazarus intimates this. [3.] That death and hell will be death and hell indeed to those that fall unsanctified from the height of this world's pomps and the fulness of its pleasures. *Son, remember,* Luke xvi. 25.

(3.) Spectators will stand amazed at his fall. When he shall be *brought down to hell, to the sides of the pit,* and be lodged there, *those that see him shall narrowly look upon him, and consider him* (*v.* 15, 16); they shall scarcely believe their own eyes. " Never was death so great a change to any man as it is to him. Is it possible that a man, who a few hours ago looked so great, so pleasant, and was so splendidly adorned and attended, should now look so ghastly, so despicable, and lie thus naked and neglected? *Is this the man that made the earth to tremble and shook kingdoms?* Who could have thought he should ever come to this?" Ps. lxxxii. 7.

5. Here is an inference drawn from all this (*v.* 20) : *The seed of evil-doers shall never be renowned.* The princes of the Babylonian monarchy were all a seed of evildoers, oppressors of the people of God, and therefore they had this infamy entailed upon them. *They shall not be renowned for ever* (so some read it) ; they may look big for a time, but all their pomp will only render their disgrace at last the more shameful. There is no credit in a sinful way.

II. The utter ruin of the royal family is here foretold, together with the desolation of The royal city.

1. The royal family is to be wholly extirpated. The Medes and Persians, that are to be employed in this destroying work, are ordered, when they have slain Belshazzar, to *prepare slaughter for his children* (*v.* 21) and not to spare them. The little ones of Babylon must be *dashed against the stones,* Ps. cxxxvii. 9. These orders sound very harshly; but, (1.) They must suffer *for the iniquity of their fathers,* which is often *visited upon the children,* to show how much God hates sin and is displeased at it, and to deter sinners from it, which is the end of punishment. Nebuchadnezzar had slain Zedekiah's sons (Jer. lii. 10), and, for that iniquity of his, his seed are paid in the same coin. (2.) They must be cut off now, that they *may not rise up to possess the land* and do as much mischief in their day as their fathers had done in theirs—that they may

not be as vexatious to the world by building cities for the support of their tyranny (which was Nimrod's policy, Gen. x. 10, 11) as their ancestors had been by destroying cities. Pharaoh oppressed Israel in Egypt by setting them to build cities, Exod. i. 11. The providence of God consults the welfare of nations more than we are aware of by cutting off some who, if they had lived, would have done mischief. Justly may the enemies cut off the children: *For I will rise up against them, saith the Lord of hosts* (v. 22), and if God reveal it as his mind that he will have it done, as none can hinder it, so none need scruple to further it. Babylon perhaps was proud of the numbers of her royal family, but God had determined to *cut off the name and remnant* of it, so that none should be left, to have both the sons and grandsons of the king slain; and yet we are sure he never did, nor ever will do, any wrong to any of his creatures.

2. The royal city is to be demolished and deserted, v. 23. It shall be a possession for solitary frightful birds, particularly *the bittern*, joined with the cormorant and the owl, *ch.* xxxiv. 11. And thus the utter destruction of the New-Testament Babylon is illustrated, Rev. xviii. 2. It *has become a cage of every unclean and hateful bird.* Babylon lay low, so that when it was deserted, and no care taken to drain the land, it soon became *pools of water*, standing noisome puddles, as unhealthful as they were unpleasant: and thus God *will sweep it with the besom of destruction.* When a people have nothing among them but dirt and filth, and will not be made clean with the besom of reformation, what can they expect but to be swept off the face of the earth with the besom of destruction?

24 The LORD of hosts hath sworn, saying, Surely as I have thought, so shall it come to pass; and as I have purposed, *so* shall it stand: 25 That I will break the Assyrian in my land, and upon my mountains tread him under foot: then shall his yoke depart from off them, and his burden depart from off their shoulders. 26 This *is* the purpose that is purposed upon the whole earth: and this *is* the hand that is stretched out upon all the nations. 27 For the LORD of hosts hath purposed, and who shall disannul it? And his hand *is* stretched out, and who shall turn it back? 28 In the year that king Ahaz died was this burden. 29 Rejoice not thou, whole Palestina, because the rod of him that smote thee is broken: for out of the ser-

pent's root shall come forth a cockatrice, and his fruit *shall be* a fiery flying serpent. 30 And the first-born of the poor shall feed, and the needy shall lie down in safety: and I will kill thy root with famine, and he shall slay thy remnant. 31 Howl, O gate; cry, O city; thou, whole Palestina, *art* dissolved: for there shall come from the north a smoke, and none *shall be* alone in his appointed times. 32 What shall *one* then answer the messengers of the nation? That the LORD hath founded Zion, and the poor of his people shall trust in it.

The destruction of Babylon and the Chaldean empire was a thing at a great distance; the empire had not risen to any considerable height when its fall was here foretold: it was almost 200 years from this prediction of Babylon's fall to the accomplishment of it. Now the people to whom Isaiah prophesied might ask, " What is this to us, or what shall we be the better for it, and what assurance shall we have of it?" To both questions he answers in these verses, by a prediction of the ruin both of the Assyrians and of the Philistines, the present enemies that infested them, which they should shortly be eye-witnesses of and have benefit by. These would be a present comfort to them, and a pledge of future deliverance, for the confirming of the faith of their posterity. God is to his people the same to day that he was yesterday and will be hereafter; and he will for ever be the same that he has been and is. Here is,

I. Assurance given of the destruction of the Assyrians (v. 25): *I will break the Assyrian in my land.* Sennacherib brought a very formidable army into the land of Judah, but there God broke it, broke all his regiments by the sword of a destroying angel. Note, Those who wrongfully invade God's land shall find that it is at their peril: and those who with unhallowed feet trample upon his holy mountains shall themselves there be trodden under foot. God undertakes to do this himself, his people having no might against the great company that came against them: " *I will break the Assyrian;* let me alone to do it who have angels, hosts of angels, at command." Now the breaking of the power of the Assyrian would be the breaking of the yoke from off the neck of God's people: *His burden shall depart from off their shoulders*, the burden of quartering that vast army and paying contribution; *therefore* the Assyrian must be broken, that Judah and Jerusalem may be eased. Let those that make themselves a yoke and a burden to God's people see what they are to expect. Now, 1. This prophecy is here ratified and confirmed by an oath (*v.* 24) : *The Lord of hosts hath sworn,* that he might show the immutability of his counsel, and that his people may have strong consolation, Heb. vi. 17, 18. What is here said of this particular intention is true of all God's purposes: *As I have thought, so shall it come to pass ;* for *he is in one mind, and who can turn him ?* Nor is he ever put upon new counsels, or obliged to take new measures, as men often are when things occur which they did not foresee. Let those who are *the called according to God's purpose* comfort themselves with this, that, *as God has purposed, so shall it stand,* and on that their stability depends. 2. The breaking of the Assyrian power is made a specimen of what God would do with all the powers of the nations that were engaged against him and his church (*v.* 26): *This is the purpose that is purposed upon the whole earth* (*the whole world,* so the LXX.), *all the inhabitants of the earth* (so the Chaldee), not only upon the Assyrian empire (which was then reckoned to be in a manner all the world, as afterwards the Roman empire was (Luke ii. 1) and with it many nations fell that had dependence upon it), but upon all those states and potentates that should at any time attack his land, his mountains. The fate of the Assyrian shall be theirs; they shall soon find that they meddle to their own hurt. Jerusalem, as it was to the Assyrians, will be *to all people a burdensome stone ; all that burden themselves with it shall infallibly be cut to pieces by it,* Zech. xii. 3, 6. The same hand of power and justice that is now to be stretched out against the Assyrian for invading the people of God shall be *stretched out upon all the nations* that do likewise. It is still true, and will ever be so, *Cursed is he that curses God's Israel,* Num. xxiv. 9. God will be an enemy to his people's enemies, Exod. xxiii. 22. 3. All the powers on earth are defied to change God's counsel (*v.* 27): " *The Lord of hosts has purposed* to break the Assyrian's yoke, and every rod of the wicked laid upon the lot of the righteous ; *and who shall disannul this purpose?* Who can persuade him to recal it, or find out a plea to evade it ? *His hand is stretched out* to execute this purpose ; *and who has power* enough *to turn it back* or to stay the course of his judgments ?"

II. Assurance is likewise given of the destruction of the Philistines and their power. This burden, this prophecy, that lay as a load upon them, to sink their state, came *in the year that king Ahaz died,* which was the first year of Hezekiah's reign, *v.* 28. When a good king came in the room of a bad one then this acceptable message was sent among them. When we reform, then, and not till then, we may look for good news from heaven. Now here we have, 1. A rebuke to the Philistines for triumphing in the death of king Uzziah. He had been as a serpent to them (*v.* 29), had bitten them, had smitten them, had brought them very low, 2 Chron. xxvi. 6. He *warred against the Philistines, broke down their walls, and built cities among them.* But when Uzziah died, or rather abdicated, it was told with joy in Gath and *published in the streets of Ashkelon.* It is inhuman thus to rejoice in our neighbour's fall. But let them not be secure ; for though when Uzziah was dead they made reprisals upon Ahaz, and took many of the cities of Judah (2 Chron. xxviii. 18), yet *out of the root* of Uzziah *should come a cockatrice,* a more formidable enemy than Uzziah was, even Hezekiah, the fruit of whose government should be to them *a fiery flying serpent,* for he should fall upon them with incredible swiftness and fury : we find he did so. 2 Kings xviii. 8, *He smote the Philistines even to Gaza.* Note, If God remove one useful instrument in the midst of his usefulness, he can, and will, raise up others to carry on and complete the same work that they were employed in and left unfinished. 2. A prophecy of the destruction of the Philistines by famine and war. (1.) By famine, *v.* 30. " When the people of God, whom the Philistines had wasted, and distressed, and impoverished, shall enjoy plenty again, and *the first-born of their poor shall feed* (the poorest among them shall have food convenient), then, as for the Philistines, God will kill *their root with famine.* That which was their strength, and with which they thought themselves established as the tree is by the root, shall be starved and dried up by degrees, as those die that die by famine ; and thus *he shall slay the remnant :* those that escape from one destruction are but reserved for another ; and, when there are but a few left, those few shall at length be cut off, for God will make a full end. (2.) By war. When *the needy* of God's people *shall lie down in safety,* not terrified with the alarms of war, but delighting in the songs of peace, then every gate and every city of the Philistines shall be howling and crying (*v.* 31), and there shall be a total dissolution of their state ; for from Judea, which lay north of the Philistines, *there shall come a smoke* (a vast army raising a great dust, a smoke that shall be the indication of a devouring fire at hand), *and none* of all that army *shall be alone in his appointed times ;* none shall straggle or be missing when they are to engage ; but they shall all be vigorous and unanimous in attacking the common enemy, when the time appointed for the doing of it comes. None of them shall decline the public service, as, in Deborah's time, Reuben abode among the sheepfolds and Asher on the sea-shore, Judg. v. 16, 17. When God has work to do he will wonderfully endow and dispose men for it.

III. The good use that should be made of all these events for the encouragement of the people of God (v. 32) : *What shall one then answer the messengers of the nations ?*

1. This implies, (1.) That the great things God does for his people are, and cannot but be, taken notice of by their neighbours; those among the heathen make remarks upon them, Ps. cxxvi. 2. (2.) That messengers will be sent to enquire concerning them. Jacob and Israel had long been a people distinguished from all others and dignified with uncommon favours; and therefore some for good-will, others for ill-will, and all for curiosity, are inquisitive concerning them. (3.) That it concerns us always to be ready to give a reason of the hope that we have in the providence of God, as well as in his grace, in answer to every one that asks it, *with meekness and fear,* 1 Pet. iii. 15. And we need go no further than the sacred truths of God's word for a reason; for God, in all he does, is fulfilling the scripture. (4.) The issue of God's dealings with his people shall be so clearly and manifestly glorious that any one, every one, shall be able to give an account of them to those that enquire concerning them. Now,

2. The answer which is to be given to the messengers of the nations is, (1.) That God is and will be a faithful friend to his church and people, and will secure and advance their interests. Tell them that *the Lord has founded Zion.* This gives an account both of the work itself that is done and of the reason of it. What is God doing in the world, and what is he designing in all the revolutions of states and kingdoms, in the ruin of some nations and the rise of others? He is, in all this, founding Zion; he is aiming at the advancement of his church's interests; and what he aims at he will accomplish. The messengers of the nations, when they sent to enquire concerning Hezekiah's successes against the Philistines, expected to learn by what politics, counsels, and arts of war he carried his point; but they are told that these successes were not owing to any thing of that nature, but to the care God took of his church and the interest he had in it. The Lord has founded Zion, and therefore the Philistines must fall. (2.) That his church has and will have a dependence upon him : *The poor of his people shall trust in it,* his poor people who have lately been brought very low, even the poorest of them ; they more than others, for they have nothing else to trust to, Zeph. iii. 12, 13. The *poor receive the gospel,* Matt. xi. 5. They shall trust to this, to this great truth, that the Lord has founded Zion ; on this they shall build their hopes, and not on an arm of flesh. This ought to give us abundant satisfaction as to public affairs, that however it may go with particular persons, parties, and interests, the church, having God himself for its founder and Christ the rock for its foundation, cannot but stand firm. *The poor of his people shall betake themselves to it* (so

some read it), shall join themselves to his church and embark in its interests; they shall concur with God in his designs to establish his people, and shall wind up all on the same plan, and make all their little concerns and projects bend to that. Those that take God's people for their people must be willing to take their lot with them and cast in their lot among them. Let the messengers of the nations know that the poor Israelites, who trust in God, having, like Zion, their foundation in the holy mountains (Ps. lxxxvii. 1), are like Zion, which *cannot be removed, but abides for ever* (Ps. cxxv. 1.), and therefore they will not fear what man can do unto them.

CHAP. XV.

This chapter, and that which follows it, are the burden of Moab—a prophecy of some great desolation that was coming upon that country, which bordered upon this land of Israel, and had often been injurious and vexatious to it, though the Moabites were descended from Lot, Abraham's kinsman and companion, and though the Israelites, by the appointment of God, had spared them when they might both easily and justly have cut them off with their neighbours. In this chapter we have, I. Great lamentation made by the Moabites, and by the prophet himself for them, ver. 1—5. II. The great calamities which should occasion that lamentation and justify it, ver. 6—9.

THE burden of Moab. Because in the night Ar of Moab is laid waste, *and* brought to silence; because in the night Kir of Moab is laid waste, *and* brought to silence; 2 He is gone to Bajith, and to Dibon, the high places, to weep: Moab shall howl over Nebo, and over Medeba: on all their heads *shall be* baldness, *and* every beard cut off. 3 In their streets they shall gird themselves with sackcloth : on the tops of their houses, and in their streets, every one shall howl, weeping abundantly. 4 And Heshbon shall cry, and Elealeh : their voice shall be heard *even* unto Jahaz : therefore the armed soldiers of Moab shall cry out ; his life shall be grievous unto him. 5 My heart shall cry out for Moab; his fugitives *shall flee* unto Zoar, an heifer of three years old: for by the mounting up of Luhith with weeping shall they go it up; for in the way of Horonaim they shall raise up a cry of destruction.

The country of Moab was of small extent, but very fruitful. It bordered upon the lot of Reuben on the other side Jordan and upon the Dead Sea. Naomi went to sojourn there when there was a famine in Canaan. This is the country which (it is here foretold) should be wasted and grievously harassed, not quite ruined, for we find another prophecy of its ruin (Jer. xlviii), which was accomplished by Nebuchadnezzar. This prophecy here was to be fulfilled *within*

91

three years (*ch.* xvi. 14), and therefore was fulfilled in the devastations made of that country by the army of the Assyrians, which for many years ravaged those parts, enriching themselves with spoil and plunder. It was done either by the army of Shalmaneser, about the time of the taking of Samaria, in the fourth year of Hezekiah (as is most probable), or by the army of Sennacherib, which, ten years after, invaded Judah. We cannot suppose that the prophet went among the Moabites to preach to them this sermon; but he delivered it to his own people, 1. To show them that, though judgment begins at the house of God, it shall not end there,—that there is a providence which governs the world and all the nations of it, —and that to the God of Israel the worshippers of false gods were accountable, and liable to his judgments. 2. To give them a proof of God's care of them and jealousy for them, and to convince them that God was an enemy to their enemies, for such the Moabites had often been. 3. That the accomplishment of this prophecy now shortly *(within three years)* might be a confirmation of the prophet's mission and of the truth of all his other prophecies, and might encourage the faithful to depend upon them.

Now concerning Moab it is here foretold, I. That their chief cities should be surprised and taken in a night by the enemy, probably because the inhabitants, as the men of Laish, indulged themselves in ease and luxury, and dwelt securely (*v.* 1): Therefore there shall be great grief, *because in the night Ar of Moab is laid waste and Kir of Moab*, the two principal cities of that kingdom. *In the night that they were taken,* or sacked, *Moab was cut off.* The seizing of them laid the whole country open, and made all the wealth of it an easy prey to the victorious army. Note, 1. Great changes and very dismal ones may be made in a very little time. Here are two cities lost in a night, though that is the time of quietness. Let us therefore lie down as those that know not what a night may bring forth. 2. As the country feeds the cities, so the cities protect the country, and neither can say to the other, *I have no need of thee.*

II. That the Moabites, being hereby put into the utmost consternation imaginable, should have recourse to their idols for relief, and pour out their tears before them (*v.* 2): *He* (that is, Moab, especially the king of Moab) *has gone up to Bajith* (or rather to the house or temple of Chemosh), *and Dibon,* the inhabitants of Dibon, *have gone up to the high places,* where they worshipped their idols, there to make their complaints. Note, It becomes a people in distress to seek to their God; and shall not we then thus *walk in the name of the Lord our God,* and call upon him in the time of trouble, before whom we shall not shed such useless profitless tears as they did before their gods?

III. That there should be the voice of universal grief all the country over. It is described here elegantly and very affectingly. Moab shall be a vale of tears—a little map of this world, *v.* 2. The Moabites shall lament the loss of Nebo and Medeba, two considerable cities, which, it is likely, were plundered and burnt. They shall tear their hair for grief to such a degree that *on all their heads shall be baldness, and they shall cut off their beards,* according to the customary expressions of mourning in those times and countries. When they go abroad they shall be so far from coveting to appear handsome that *in the streets they shall gird themselves with sackcloth* (*v.* 3), and perhaps being forced to use that poor clothing, the enemy having stripped them, and rifled their houses, and left them no other clothing. When they come home, instead of applying themselves to their business, they shall go up to *the tops of their houses* which were flat-roofed, and there they shall *weep abundantly,* nay, they shall *howl,* in crying to their gods. Those that *cry not to God with their hearts* do but *howl upon their beds,* Hos. vii. 14; Amos viii. 3. *They shall come down with weeping* (so the margin reads it); they shall come down from their high places and the tops of their houses weeping as much as they did when they went up. Prayer to the true God is heart's ease (1 Sam. i. 18), but prayers to false gods are not. Divers places are here named that should be full of lamentation (*v.* 4), and it is but a poor relief to have so many fellow-sufferers, fellow-mourners; to a public spirit it is rather an aggravation *socios habuisse doloris—to have associates in woe.*

IV. That the courage of their militia should fail them. Though they were bred soldiers, and were well armed, yet they *shall cry out* and shriek for fear, and every one of them shall have *his life become grievous to him,* though it is characteristic of a military life to delight in danger, *v.* 4. See how easily God can dispirit the stoutest of men, and deprive a nation of benefit by those whom it most depended upon for strength and defence. The Moabites shall generally be so overwhelmed with grief that life itself shall be a burden to them. God can easily make weary of life those that are fondest of it.

V. That the outcry for these calamities should propagate grief to all the adjacent parts, *v.* 5. 1. The prophet himself has very sensible impressions made upon his spirit by the prediction of it: "*My heart shall cry out for Moab;* though they are enemies to Israel, they are our fellow-creatures, of the same rank with us, and therefore it should grieve us to see them in such distress, the rather because we know not how soon it may be our own turn to drink of the same cup of trembling." Note, It becomes God's ministers to be of a tender spirit, not to desire the woeful day, but to be like their master, who wept over Jerusalem even when he gave her up to ruin, like their God, *who desires not the death of sinners.* 2. All the neighbouring cities shall echo to the lamentations of Moab. *The fugitives,* who are making the best of their way to shift for their own safety, shall carry the cry *to Zoar,* the city to which their ancestor Lot fled for shelter from Sodom's flames and which was spared for his sake. They shall make as great a noise with their cry *as a heifer of three years old* does when she goes *lowing* for her calf, as 1 Sam. vi. 12. They shall go up the hill of *Luhith* (as David went up the ascent of Mount Olivet, many a weary step and all in tears, 2 Sam. xv. 30), and *in the way of Horonaim* (a dual termination), the way that leads to the two Beth-horons, the upper and the nether, which we read of, Josh. xvi. 3, 5. Thither the cry shall be carried, there it shall be raised, even at that great distance : *A cry of destruction ;* that shall be the cry, like, "Fire, fire! we are all undone." Grief is catching, so is fear, and justly, for trouble is spreading and when it begins who knows where it will end?

6 For the waters of Nimrim shall be desolate : for the hay is withered away, the grass faileth, there is no green thing. 7 Therefore the abundance they have gotten, and that which they have laid up, shall they carry away to the brook of the willows. 8 For the cry is gone round about the borders of Moab ; the howling thereof unto Eglaim, and the howling thereof unto Beer-elim. 9 For the waters of Dimon shall be full of blood : for I will bring more upon Dimon, lions upon him that escapeth of Moab, and upon the remnant of the land.

Here the prophet further describes the woeful and piteous lamentations that should be heard throughout all the country of Moab when it should become a prey to the Assyrian army. "By this time *the cry has gone round about* all *the borders of Moab, v.* 8. Every corner of the country has received the alarm, and is in the utmost confusion upon it. It has reached to *Eglaim,* a city at one end of the country, and to *Beer-elim,* a city as far the other way. Where sin has been general, and all' flesh have corrupted their way, what can be expected but a general desolation? Two things are here spoken of as causes of this lamentation :—

I. *The waters of Nimrim are desolate (v.* 6), that is, the country is plundered and impoverished, and all the wealth and substance of it swept away by the victorious army. Famine is usually the sad effect of war. Look into the fields that were well watered, the fruitful meadows that yielded delightful

prospects and more delightful products, and there all is eaten up, or carried off by the enemy's foragers, and the remainder trodden to dirt by their horses. If an army encamp upon green fields, their greenness is soon gone. Look into the houses, and they are stripped too *(v. 7) : The abundance* of wealth that *they had gotten* with a great deal of art and industry, and *that which they had laid up* with a great deal of care and confidence, *shall they carry away to the brook of the willows.* Either the owners shall carry it thither to hide it or the enemies shall carry it thither to pack it up and send it home, by water perhaps, to their own country. Note, 1. Those that are eager to get abundance of this world, 'and solicitous to lay up what they have gotten, little consider what may become of it and in how short a time it may be all taken from them. Great abundance, by tempting the robbers, exposes the owners ; and those who depend upon it to protect them often find it does but betray them. 2. In times of distress great riches are often great burdens, and do but increase the owner's care or the enemies' strength. *Cantabit vacuus coram latrone viator—The penniless traveller will exult, when accosted by a robber, in having nothing about him.*

II. *The waters of Dimon are turned into blood (v.* 9), that is, the inhabitants of the country are slain in great numbers, so that the waters adjoining to the cities, whether rivers or pools, are discoloured with human gore, inhumanly shed like water. *Dimon* signifies *bloody ;* the place shall answer to its name. Perhaps it was that place in the country of Moab where the waters seemed to the *Moabites as blood* (2 Kings iii. 22, 23), which occasioned their overthrow. But now, says God, *I will bring more upon Dimon,* more blood than was shed, or thought to be seen, at that time. *I will bring additions upon Dimon* (so the word is), additional plagues ; I have yet more judgments in reserve for them. *For all this, God's anger is not turned away.* When he judges he will overcome ; and to the roll of curses shall be *added many like words,* Jer. xxxvi. 32. See here what is the *yet more evil* to be brought upon Dimon, upon Moab, which is now to be made a land of blood. Some flee, and make their escape, others sit still, and are overlooked, and are as a remnant of the land ; but upon both God *will bring lions,* beasts of prey (which are reckoned one of God's four judgments, Ezek. xiv. 21), and these shall glean up those that have escaped the sword of the enemy. Those that continue impenitent in sin, when they are preserved from one judgment, are but reserved for another.

CHAP. XVI.

This chapter continues and concludes the burden of Moab. In it, I. The prophet gives good counsel to the Moabites, to reform what was amiss among them, and particularly to be kind to God's people, as the likeliest way to prevent the judgments before threatened, ver. 1—5. II. Fearing they would not take this counsel (they were so proud), he goes on to foretel the lamentable devastation of their country, and the confusion they should be brought to, and this within three years, ver. 6—14.

SEND ye the lamb to the ruler of the land from Sela to the wilderness, unto the mount of the daughter of Zion. 2 For it shall be, *that,* as a wandering bird cast out of the nest, *so* the daughters of Moab shall be at the fords of Arnon. 3 Take counsel, execute judgment; make thy shadow as the night in the midst of the noon-day; hide the outcasts; bewray not him that wandereth. 4 Let mine outcasts dwell with thee, Moab; be thou a covert to them from the face of the spoiler: for the extortioner is at an end, the spoiler ceaseth, the oppressors are consumed out of the land. 5 And in mercy shall the throne be established: and he shall sit upon it in truth in the tabernacle of David, judging, and seeking judgment, and hastening righteousness.

God has made it to appear that he delights not in the ruin of sinners by telling them what they may do to prevent the ruin; so he does here to Moab.

I. He advises them to be just to the house of David, and to pay the tribute they had formerly covenanted to pay to the kings of his line (*v.* 1): *Send you the lamb to the ruler of the land.* David made the Moabites tributaries to him, 2 Sam. viii. 2. They *became his servants, and brought gifts.* Afterwards they paid their tribute to the kings of Israel (2 Kings iii. 4), and paid it in lambs. Now the prophet requires them to pay it to Hezekiah. Let it be raised and levied from all parts of the country, *from Selah,* a frontier city of Moab on the one side, *to the wilderness,* a boundary of the kingdom on the other side: and let it be sent, where it should be sent, *to the mount of the daughter of Zion,* the city of David. Some take it as an advice to send a lamb for a sacrifice to God, *the ruler of the earth* (so it may be read), the Lord of the whole earth, ruler of all lands, the land of Moab as well as the land of Israel. " Send it to the temple built on Mount Zion." And some think it is in this sense spoken ironically, upbraiding the Moabites with their folly in delaying to repent and make their peace with God. " Now you would be glad to send a lamb to Mount Zion, to make the God of Israel your friend; but it is too late: the decree has gone forth, the consumption is determined, and the *daughters of Moab* shall be cast out *as a wandering bird,"* v. 2. I rather take it as good advice seriously given, like that of Daniel to Nebuchadnezzar when he was reading him his

doom, Dan. iv. 27. *Break off thy sins by righteousness, if it may be a lengthening of thy tranquillity.* And it is applicable to the great gospel duty of submission to Christ, as the ruler of the land, and our ruler: " Send him the lamb, the best you have, yourselves a living sacrifice. When you come to God, the great ruler, come in the name of the Lamb, the Lamb of God. *For else it shall be"* (so we may read it) *" that, as a wandering bird cast out of the nest, so shall the daughters of Moab be.* If you will not pay your quit-rent, your just tribute to the king of Judah, you shall be turned out of your houses: *The daughters of Moab* (the country villages, or the women of your country) shall flutter about the *fords of Arnon,* attempting that way to make their escape to some other land, *like a wandering bird thrown out of the nest* half-fledged." Those that will not submit to Christ, nor be gathered under the shadow of his wings, shall be *as a bird that wanders from her nest,* that shall either be snatched up by the next bird of prey or shall wander endlessly in continual frights. Those that will not yield to the fear of God shall be made to yield to the fear of every thing else.

II. He advises them to be *kind to the seed of Israel* (*v.* 3): " Take counsel, call a convention, and consult among yourselves what is fit to be done in the present critical juncture; and you will find it your best way to execute judgment, to reverse all the unrighteous decrees you have made, by which you have put hardships upon the people of God, and, in token of your repentance for them, study now how to oblige them, and this shall be accepted of God more than all burnt-offering and sacrifice."

1. The prophet foresaw some storm coming upon the people of God, perhaps the good people of the ten tribes, or of the two and a half on the other side Jordan, whose country joined to that of Moab, and who, by the merciful providence of God, escaped the fury of the Assyrian army, had their lives given them for a prey, and were reserved for better times, but were put to the utmost extremity to shift for their own safety. The danger and trouble they were in were like the scorching heat at noon; the face of the spoiler was very fierce upon them and the oppressor and extortioner were ready to swallow them up after stripping them of what they had.

2. He bespeaks a shelter for them in the land of Moab, when their own land was made too hot for them. This judgment they must execute; thus wisely must they do for themselves, and thus kindly must they deal with the people of God. If they would themselves continue in their habitations, let them now open their doors to the distressed dispersed members of God's church, and be to them like a cool shade to those that *bear the burden and heat of the day.* Let them not discover those that absconded among them, nor de-

liver them up to the pursuers that made search for them: "*Betray not him that wandereth,* nor deliver him up" (as the Edomites did, Obad. 13, 14), "but *hide the outcasts.*" This was that good work by which Rahab's faith was justified, and proved to be sincere, Heb. xi. 31. "Nay, do not only hide them for a time, but, if there be occasion, let them be naturalized: *Let my outcasts dwell with thee, Moab* (v. 4); find a lodging for them and *be thou a covert to them.* Let them be taken under the protection of the government, though they are but poor, and likely to be a charge to thee." Note, (1.) It is often the lot even of those who are Israelites indeed to be outcasts, driven out of house and harbour by persecution or war, Heb. xi. 37. (2.) God owns them when men reject and disown them. They are *outcasts,* but they are *my outcasts.* The Lord knows those that are his wherever he finds them, even where no one else knows them. (3.) God will find a rest and shelter for his outcasts; for, though they are persecuted, they are not forsaken. He will himself be their dwelling-place if they have no other, and in him they shall be at home. (4.) God can, when he pleases, raise up friends for his people even among Moabites, when they can find none in all the land of Israel that can and dare shelter them. The earth often helps the woman, Rev. xii. 16. (5.) Those that expect to find favour when they are in trouble themselves must show favour to those that are in trouble; and what service is done to God's outcasts shall no doubt be recompensed one way or other.

3. He assures them of the mercy God had in store for his people. (1.) That they should not long need their kindness, or be troublesome to them: *For the extortioner is almost at an end* already, *and the spoiler ceases.* God's people shall not be long outcasts; they *shall have tribulation ten days* (Rev. ii. 10), and that is all. The spoiler would never cease spoiling if he might have his will; but God has him in a chain. *Hitherto he shall go, but no further.* (2.) That they should, ere long, be in a capacity to return their kindness (v. 5): "Though the throne of the ten tribes be sunk and overturned, yet *the throne of David shall be established in mercy,* by the mercy they receive from God and the mercy they show to others; and by the same methods may your throne be established if you please." It would engage great men to be kind to the people of God if they would but observe, as they easily might, how often such conduct brings the blessing of God upon kingdoms and families. "Make Hezekiah your friend, for you will find it your interest to do so upon the account both of the grace of God in him and the presence of God with him. He *shall sit upon the throne in truth,* and then he does indeed sit in honour and sit firmly. Then he shall sit

judging, and will then be a protector to those that have been a shelter to the people of God." And see in him the character of a good magistrate. [1.] He shall *seek judgment;* that is, he shall seek occasions of doing right to those that are wronged, and shall punish the injurious even before they are complained of: or he shall diligently search into every cause brought before him, that he may find where the right lies. [2.] He shall *hasten righteousness,* and not delay to do justice, nor keep those long waiting that make application to him for the redress of their grievances. Though he seeks judgment, and deliberates upon it, yet he does not, under pretence of deliberation, stay the progress of the streams of justice. Let the Moabites take example by this, and then assure themselves that their state shall be established.

6 We have heard of the pride of Moab; *he is* very proud: *even* of his haughtiness, and his pride, and his wrath: *but* his lies *shall* not *be* so. 7 Therefore shall Moab howl for Moab, every one shall howl: for the foundations of Kir-hareseth shall ye mourn; surely *they are* stricken. 8 For the fields of Heshbon languish, *and* the vine of Sibmah: the lords of the heathen have broken down the principal plants thereof, they are come *even* unto Jazer, they wandered *through* the wilderness: her branches are stretched out, they are gone over the sea. 9 Therefore I will bewail with the weeping of Jazer the vine of Sibmah: I will water thee with my tears, O Heshbon, and Elealeh: for the shouting for thy summer fruits and for thy harvest is fallen. 10 And gladness is taken away, and joy out of the plentiful field; and in the vineyards there shall be no singing, neither shall there be shouting: the treaders shall tread out no wine in *their* presses; I have made *their* vintage shouting to cease. 11 Wherefore my bowels shall sound like a harp for Moab, and mine inward parts for Kir-haresh. 12 And it shall come to pass, when it is seen that Moab is weary on the high place, that he shall come to his sanctuary to pray; but he shall not prevail. 13 This *is* the word that the LORD hath spoken concerning Moab since that time. 14 But now the LORD

hath spoken, saying, Within three years, as the years of a hireling, and the glory of Moab shall be contemned, with all that great multitude; and the remnant *shall be* very small *and* feeble.

Here we have, I. The sins with which Moab is charged, *v.* 6. The prophet seems to check himself for going about to give good counsel to the Moabites, concluding they would not take the advice he gave them. He told them their duty (whether they would hear or whether they would forbear), but despairs of working any good upon them; he would have healed them, but they would not be healed. Those that will not be counselled cannot be helped. Their sins were, 1. Pride. This is most insisted upon; for perhaps there are more precious souls ruined by pride than by any one lust whatsoever. The Moabites were notorious for this: *" We have heard* in both ears *of the pride of Moab;* it is what all their neighbours cry out shame upon them for. *He is very proud;* the body of the nation is so, forgetting the baseness of their origin and the brand of infamy fastened upon them by that law of God which forbade a Moabite to enter into the congregation of the Lord for ever, Deut. xxiii. 3. We have heard of *his haughtiness and his pride.* It is not the rash and rigid censure of one or two concerning them, but it is the character which all that know them will give of them. They are a proud people, and therefore they will not take good counsel when it is given them. They think themselves too wise to be advised; therefore they will not take example by Hezekiah to do justly and love mercy. They scorn to make him their pattern, for they think themselves able to teach him. They are proud, and therefore will not be subject to God himself nor regard the warnings he gives them. *The wicked, in the pride of his countenance, will not seek after God.* They are proud, and therefore will not entertain and protect God's outcasts; they scorn to have any thing to do with them." But this is not all :—2. " We have heard of *his wrath* too (for those that are very proud are commonly very passionate), particularly his wrath against the people of God, whom therefore he will rather persecute than protect. 3. It is with *his lies* that he gains the gratifications of his pride and his passion; *but his lies shall not be so;* he shall not compass his proud and angry projects as he hoped he should." Some read it, *His haughtiness, his pride, and his wrath, are greater than his strength.* " We know that, if we lay at his mercy, we should find no mercy with him, but he has not power equal to his malice. His pride draws down ruin upon him; for it is the preface to destruction, and he has not strength to ward it off."

96

II. The sorrows with which Moab is threatened (*v.* 7): *Therefore shall Moab howl for Moab.* All the inhabitants shall bitterly lament the ruin of their country. They shall complain one to another: *Every one shall howl* in despair, and not one shall either see any cause or have any heart to encourage his friend. Observe,

1. The causes of this sorrow. (1.) The destruction of their cities: *For the foundations of Kir-hareseth shall you mourn.* That great and strong city, which had held out against a mighty force (2 Kings iii. 25), should now be levelled with the ground, either burnt or broken down, and its foundations *stricken,* bruised and broken (so the word signifies); they shall howl when they see their splendid cities turned into ruinous heaps. (2.) The desolation of their country. Moab was famous for its fields and vineyards; but those shall all be laid waste by the invading army, *v.* 8, 10. See, [1.] What a fruitful pleasant country they had, as the garden of the Lord, Gen. xiii. 10. It was planted with choice and noble vines, with *principal plants,* which reached *even to Jazer,* a city in the tribe of Gad. The luxuriant branches of their vines *wandered,* and wound themselves along the ranges on which they were spread, even *through the wilderness* of Moab. There were vineyards there. Nay, they were *stretched out,* and went even to *the sea,* the Dead Sea: the best grapes grew in their hedge-rows. [2.] How merry and pleasant they had been in it. Many a time they had shouted *for their summer fruits, and for their harvest,* as the country people sometimes do with us when they have cut down all their corn. They had had *joy and gladness* in their fields and vineyards, *singing* and *shouting at the treading of their grapes.* Nothing is said of their praising God for their abundance, and giving him the glory of it. If they had made it the matter of their thanksgiving, they might still have had it the matter of their rejoicing; but they made it the food and fuel of their lusts; see therefore, [3.] How they should be stripped of all. *" The fields shall languish,* all the fruits of them being carried away or trodden down; they cannot now enrich their owners as they have done, and therefore they languish. The soldiers, called here *the lords of the heathen,* shall break down all the plants, though they were *principal plants,* the choicest that could be got. Now the shouting for the enjoyment of the summer fruits has fallen, and is turned into howling for the loss of them. The joy of harvest has ceased; there is no more singing, no more shouting, for the treading out of wine. They have not what they have had to rejoice in, nor have they a disposition to rejoice; the ruin of their country has marred their mirth." Note, *First,* God can easily change the note of those that are most addicted to mirth and pleasure, can soon turn their

laughter into mourning and their joy into heaviness. *Secondly,* Joy in God is, upon this account, far better than the joy of harvest, that it is what we cannot be robbed of, Ps. iv. 6, 7. Destroy the vines and the fig-trees, and you make all the mirth of a carnal heart to cease, Hos. ii. 11, 12. But a gracious soul can rejoice in the Lord as the God of its salvation even when the fig-tree does not blossom and there is no fruit in the vine, Hab. iii. 17, 18. In God therefore let us always rejoice with a holy triumph, and in other things let us always rejoice with a holy trembling, rejoice as though we rejoiced not.

2. The concurrence of the prophet with them in this sorrow: " *I will with weeping bewail Jazer, and the vine of Sibmah,* and look with a compassionate concern upon the desolations of such a pleasant country. *I will water thee with my tears, O Heshbon!* and mingle them with thy tears;" nay (*v.* 11), it appears to be an inward grief: *My bowels shall sound like a harp for Moab;* it should make such an impression upon him that he should feel an inward trembling, like that of the strings of a harp when it is played upon. It well becomes God's prophets to acquaint themselves with grief; the great prophet did so. The afflictions of the world, as well as those of the church, should be afflictions to us. See *ch.* xv. 5.

III. In the close of the chapter we have, 1. The insufficiency of the gods of Moab, the false gods, to help them, *v.* 12. " Moab shall be soon *weary of the high place.* He shall spend his spirits and strength in vain in praying to his idols; they cannot help him, and he shall be convinced that they cannot." It is seen that it is to no purpose to expect any relief from the high places on earth; it must come from above the hills. Men are generally so stupid that they will not believe, till they are made to see, the vanity of idols and of all creature-confidences, nor will come off from them till they are made weary of them. But, when he is weary of his high places, he will not go, as he should, to God's sanctuary, but to *his* sanctuary, to the temple of Chemosh, the principal idol of Moab (so it is generally understood); and he shall pray there to as little purpose, and as little to his own ease and satisfaction, as he did in his high places; for, whatever honours idolaters give to their idols, they do not thereby make them at all the better able to help them. Whether they are the *dii majorum gentium—gods of the higher order,* or *minorum —of the lower order,* they are alike the creatures of men's fancy and the work of men's hands. Perhaps it may be meant of their coming to God's sanctuary. When they found they could have no succours from their own high places some of them would come to the temple of God at Jerusalem, to pray there, but in vain; he will justly send

them back to *the gods whom they have served,* Judg. x. 14. 2. The sufficiency of the God of Israel, the only true God, to make good what he had spoken against them. (1.) The thing itself was long since determined (*v.* 13): *This is the word,* this is the thing, *that the Lord has spoken concerning Moab, since the time* that he began to be so proud, and insolent, and abusive to God's people. The country was long ago doomed to ruin ; this was enough to give an assurance of it that *it is the word which the Lord has spoken :* and, as he will never unsay what he has spoken, so all the power of hell and earth cannot gainsay it, or obstruct the execution of it. (2.) Now it was made known when it should be done. The time was before fixed in the counsel of God, but now it was revealed : *The Lord has spoken* that it shall be *within three years, v.* 14. *It is not for us to know,* or covet to know, *the times and the seasons,* any further than God has thought fit to make them known, and so far we may and must take notice of them. See how God makes known his mind by degrees; the light of divine revelation shone more and more, and so does the light of divine grace in the heart. Observe, [1.] The sentence passed upon Moab : *The glory of Moab shall be contemned,* that is, it shall be contemptible, when all those things they have gloried in shall come to nothing. Such is the glory of this world, so fading and uncertain, admired awhile, but soon slighted. Let that therefore which will soon be contemptible in the eyes of others be always contemptible in our eyes in comparison with the *far more exceeding weight of glory.* It was the glory of Moab that their country was very populous and their forces were courageous; but where is her glory when all that great multitude is in a manner swept away, some by one judgment and some by another, and the little remnant that is left shall be *very small and feeble,* not able to bear up under their own griefs, much less to make head against their enemies' insults ? Let not therefore the strong glory in their strength nor the many in their numbers. [2.] The time fixed for the execution of this sentence : *Within three years, as the years of a hireling,* that is, at the three years' end exactly, for a servant that is hired for a certain term keeps account to a day. Let Moab know that her ruin is very near, and prepare accordingly. Fair warning is given, and with it space to repent, which if they had improved, as Nineveh did, we have reason to think the judgments threatened would have been prevented.

CHAP. XVII.

Syria and Ephraim were confederate against Judah (ch. vii. 1, 2), and, they being so closely linked together in their counsels, this chapter, though it be entitled " the burden of Damascus" (which was the head city of Syria), reads the doom of Israel too. I. The destruction of the strong cities both of Syria and Israel is here foretold, ver. 1—5 and again ver. 9—11. II. In the midst of judgment mercy is remembered to Israel, and a gracious promise made that a remnant should be preserved from the calamities and should

97

get good by them, ver. 6—8. III. The overthrow of the Assyrian army before Jerusalem is pointed at ver. 12—14. In order of time this chapter should be placed next after ch. ix., for the destruction of Damascus, here foretold, happened in the reign of Ahaz, 2 Kings xvi. 9.

THE burden of Damascus. Behold, Damascus is taken away from *being* a city, and it shall be a ruinous heap. 2 The cities of Aroer *are* forsaken: they shall be for flocks, which shall lie down, and none shall make *them* afraid. 3 The fortress also shall cease from Ephraim, and the kingdom from Damascus, and the remnant of Syria: they shall be as the glory of the children of Israel, saith the LORD of hosts. 4 And in that day it shall come to pass, *that* the glory of Jacob shall be made thin, and the fatness of his flesh shall wax lean. 5 And it shall be as when the harvestman gathereth the corn, and reapeth the ears with his arm; and it shall be as he that gathereth ears in the valley of Rephaim.

We have here the burden of Damascus; the Chaldee paraphrase reads it, *The burden of the cup of the curse to drink to Damascus in;* and, the ten tribes being in alliance, they must expect to pledge Damascus in this cup of trembling that is to go round. 1. Damascus itself, the head city of Syria, must be destroyed; the houses, it is likely, will be burnt, at least the walls, and gates, and fortifications demolished, and the inhabitants carried away captive, so that for the present it is *taken away from being a city*, and is reduced not only to a village, but to *a ruinous heap, v.* 1. Such desolating work as this does sin make with cities. 2. The country towns are abandoned by their inhabitants, frightened or forced away by the invaders: *The cities of Aroer* (a province of Syria so called) *are forsaken (v.* 2); the conquered dare not dwell in them, and the conquerors have no occasion for them, nor did they seize them for want, but wantonness; so that the places which should be for men to live in are for *flocks to lie down in*, which they may do, and none will disturb nor dislodge them. Stately houses are converted into sheep-cotes. It is strange that great conquerors should pride themselves in being common enemies to mankind. But, how unrighteous soever they are, God is righteous in causing those cities to spue out their inhabitants, who by their wickedness had made themselves vile; it is better that *flocks should lie down there* than that they should harbour such as are in open rebellion against God and virtue. 3. The strongholds of Israel, the kingdom of the ten tribes, will be brought to ruin:

The fortress shall cease from Ephraim (v. 3), that in Samaria, and all the rest. They had joined with Syria in invading Judah very unnaturally; and now those that had been partakers in sin should be made partakers in ruin, and justly. When *the fortress shall cease from Ephraim*, by which Israel will be weakened, the kingdom will cease from Damascus, by which Syria will be ruined. The Syrians were the ring-leaders in that confederacy against Judah, and therefore they are punished first and sorest; and, because they boasted of their alliance with Israel, now that Israel is weakened they are upbraided with those boasts: " *The remnant of Syria shall be as the glory of the children of Israel:* those few that remain of the Syrians shall be in as mean and despicable a condition as the children of Israel are, and the glory of Israel shall be no relief or reputation to them." Sinful confederacies will be no strength, no stay, to the confederates, when God's judgments come upon them. See here what the glory of Jacob is when God contends with him, and what little reason Syria will have to be proud of resembling the glory of Jacob. (1.) It is wasted like a man in a consumption, *v.* 4. *The glory of Jacob* was their numbers, that they were as the sand of the sea for multitude; but this glory *shall be made thin*, when many are cut off, and few left. Then the *fatness of their flesh*, which was their pride and security, *shall wax lean*, and the body of the people shall become a perfect skeleton, nothing but skin and bones. Israel died of a lingering disease; the kingdom of the ten tribes wasted gradually; God was to them *as a moth*, Hos. v. 12. Such is all the glory of this world: it soon withers, and is made thin; but there is a far more exceeding and eternal weight of glory designed for the spiritual seed of Jacob, which is not subject to any such decay—fatness of God's house, which will not *wax lean*. (2.) It is all gathered and carried away by the Assyrian army, as the corn is carried out of the field by the husbandmen, *v.* 5. The corn is the glory of the fields (Ps. lxv. 13); but, when it is reaped and gone, where is the glory? The people had by their sins made themselves ripe for ruin, and their glory was as quickly, as easily, as justly, and as irresistibly, cut down and taken away, as the corn is out of the field by the husbandman. God's judgments are compared to the *thrusting in of the sickle when the harvest is ripe*, Rev. xiv. 15. And the victorious army, like the careful husbandmen in the valley of Rephaim, where the corn was extraordinary, would not, if they could help it, leave an ear behind, would lose nothing that they could lay their hands on.

6 Yet gleaning grapes shall be left in it, as the shaking of an olive

tree, two *or* three berries in the top of the uppermost bough, four *or* five in the outmost fruitful branches thereof, saith the LORD God of Israel. 7 At that day shall a man look to his Maker, and his eyes shall have respect to the Holy One of Israel. 8 And he shall not look to the altars, the work of his hands, neither shall respect *that* which his fingers have made, either the groves, or the images.

Mercy is here reserved, in a parenthesis, in the midst of judgment, for a remnant that should escape the common ruin of the kingdom of the ten tribes. Though the Assyrians took all the care they could that none should slip out of their net, yet the meek of the earth were hidden in the day of the Lord's anger, and had their lives given them for a prey and made comfortable to them by their retirement to the land of Judah, where they had the liberty of God's courts. 1. They shall be but a small remnant, a very few, who shall be marked for preservation (*v.* 6): *Gleaning grapes shall be left in it.* The body of the people were carried into captivity, but here and there one was left behind, perhaps one of two in a bed when the other was taken, Luke xvii. 34. The most desolating judgments in this world are short of the last judgment, which shall be universal and which none shall escape. In times of the greatest calamity some are kept safe, as in times of the greatest degeneracy some are kept pure. But the fewness of those that escape supposes the captivity of the far greatest part; those that are left are but like the poor remains of an olive tree when it has been carefully shaken by the owner; if there be *two or three berries in the top of the uppermost bough* (out of the reach of those that shook it), that is all. Such is the *remnant according to the election of grace*, very few in comparison with the multitudes that walk on in the broad way. 2. They shall be a sanctified remnant, *v.* 7, 8. These few that are preserved are such as, in the prospect of the judgment approaching, had repented of their sins and reformed their lives, and therefore were snatched thus as brands out of the burning, or such as having escaped, and becoming refugees in strange countries, were awakened, partly by a sense of the distinguishing mercy of their deliverance, and partly by the distresses they were still in, to return to God. (1.) They shall look up to their Creator, shall enquire, *Where is God my Maker, who giveth songs in the night,* in such a night of affliction as this? Job xxxv. 10, 11. They shall acknowledge his hand in all the events concerning them, merciful and afflictive, and shall submit to his hand. They shall give him the glory due to his

name, and be suitably affected with his providences. They shall expect relief and succour from him and depend upon him to help them. Their *eyes shall have respect* to him, *as the eyes of a servant to the hand of his master,* Ps. cxxiii. 2. Observe, It is our duty at all times to have respect to God, to have our eyes ever towards him, both as our Maker (the author of our being and the God of nature) and as the Holy One of Israel, a God in covenant with us and the God of grace; particularly, when we are in affliction, our eyes must be towards the Lord, to *pluck our feet out of the net* (Ps. xxv. 15); to bring us to this is the design of his providence as he is our Maker and the work of his grace as he is the Holy One of Israel. (2.) They shall look off from their idols, the creatures of their own fancy, shall no longer worship them, and seek to them, and expect relief from them. For God will be alone regarded, or he does not look upon himself as at all regarded. He that looks to his Maker must not *look to the altars, the work of his hands*, but disown them and cast them off, must not retain the least respect for *that which his fingers have made*, but break it to pieces, though it be his own workmanship—*the groves and the images;* the word signifies images made in honour of the sun and by which he was worshipped, the most ancient and most plausible idolatry, Deut. iv. 19; Job xxxi. 26. We have reason to account those happy afflictions which part between us and our sins, and by sensible convictions of the vanity of the world, that great idol, cool our affections to it and lower our expectations from it.

9 In that day shall his strong cities be as a forsaken bough, and an uppermost branch, which they left because of the children of Israel: and there shall be desolation. 10 Because thou hast forgotten the God of thy salvation, and hast not been mindful of the rock of thy strength, therefore shalt thou plant pleasant plants, and shalt set it with strange slips: 11 In the day shalt thou make thy plant to grow, and in the morning shalt thou make thy seed to flourish: *but* the harvest *shall be* a heap in the day of grief and of desperate sorrow.

Here the prophet returns to foretel the woeful desolations that should be made in the land of Israel by the army of the Assyrians. 1. That the cities should be deserted. Even the strong cities, which should have protected the country, shall not be able to protect themselves: They *shall be as a forsaken bough and an uppermost branch* of an old tree, which has gone to decay, is forsaken of its leaves, and appears on the top of the tree, bare, and dry, and dead; so shall their strong cities look when the inhabitants have deserted them and the victorious army of the enemy pillaged and defaced them, v. 9. They shall be as the cities (so it may be supplied) which the Canaanites left, the old inhabitants of the land, because of the children of Israel, when God brought them in with a high hand, to take possession of that good land, cities which they built not. As the Canaanites then fled before Israel, so Israel should now flee before the Assyrians. And herein the word of God was fulfilled, that, if they committed the same abominations, *the land* should *spue them out, as it spued out the nations that were before them* (Lev. xviii. 28), and that as, while they had God on their side, *one of them chased a thousand,* so, when they had made him their enemy, *a thousand* of them should *flee at the rebuke of one;* so that in the cities should be desolation, according to the threatenings in the law, Lev. xxvi. 31; Deut. xxviii. 52. 2. That the country should be laid waste, v. 10, 11. Observe here, (1.) The sin that had provoked God to bring so great a destruction upon that pleasant land. It was *for the iniquity of those that dwelt therein.* " It is *because thou hast forgotten the God of thy salvation* and all the great salvations he has wrought for thee, hast forgotten thy dependence upon him and obligations to him, and *hast not been mindful of the rock of thy strength,* not only who is himself a strong rock, but who has been thy strength many a time, or thou wouldst have been sunk and broken long since." Note, The God of our salvation is the rock of our strength; and our forgetfulness and unmindfulness of him are at the bottom of all sin. *Therefore* have we *perverted our way, because we have forgotten the Lord our God,* and so we undo ourselves. (2.) The destruction itself, aggravated by the great care they took to improve their land and to make it yet more pleasant. [1.] Look upon it at the time of the seedness, and it was all like a garden and a vineyard; that pleasant land was replenished with pleasant plants, the choicest of its own growth; nay, so nice and curious were the inhabitants that, not content with them, they sent to all the neighbouring countries for strange slips, the more valuable for being strange, uncommon, far-fetched, and dear-bought, though perhaps they had of their own not inferior to them. This was an instance of their pride and vanity, and (that ruining error) their affectation to be *like the nations. Wheat, and honey, and oil* were their staple commodities (Ezek. xxvii. 17); but, not content with these, they must have flowers and greens with strange names imported from other nations, and a great deal of care and pains must be taken by hot-beds to make these plants to grow; the soil must be forced, and they must be covered with glasses to

100

shelter them, and early in the morning the gardeners must be up to make the seed to flourish, that it may excel those of their neighbours. The ornaments of nature are not to be altogether slighted, but it is a folly to be over-fond of them, and to bestow more time, and cost, and pains about them than they deserve, as many do. But here this instance seems to be put in general for their great industry in cultivating their ground, and their expectations from it accordingly; they doubt not but their plants will grow and flourish. But, [2.] Look upon the same ground at the time of harvest, and it is all like a wilderness, a dismal melancholy place, even to the spectators, much more to the owners; for *the harvest shall be a heap,* all in confusion, *in the day of grief and of desperate sorrow.* The harvest used to be a time of joy, of singing and shouting (*ch.* xvi. 10); but this harvest the hungry eat up (Job v. 5), which makes it a day of grief, and the more because the plants were pleasant and costly (v. 10) and their expectations proportionably raised. The harvest had sometimes been a day of grief, if the crop was thin and the weather unseasonable; and yet in that case there was hope that the next would be better. But this shall be desperate sorrow, for they shall see not only this year's products carried off, but the property of the ground altered and their conquerors lords of it. The margin reads it, *The harvest shall be removed* (into the enemy's country or camp, Deut. xxviii. 33) *in the day of inheritance* (when thou thoughtest to inherit it), *and there shall be deadly sorrow.* This is a good reason why we should not lay up our treasure in those things which we may so quickly be despoiled of, but in that good part which shall never be taken away from us.

12 Woe to the multitude of many people, *which* make a noise like the noise of the seas ; and to the rushing of nations, *that* make a rushing like the rushing of mighty waters ! 13 The nations shall rush like the rushing of many waters : but *God* shall rebuke them, and they shall flee far off, and shall be chased as the chaff of the mountains before the wind, and like a rolling thing before the whirlwind. 14 And behold at evening tide trouble ; *and* before the morning he *is* not. This *is* the portion of them that spoil us, and the lot of them that rob us.

These verses read the doom of those that spoil and rob the people of God. If the Assyrians and Israelites invade and plunder Judah, if the Assyrian army take God's people captive and lay their country waste, let them know that ruin will be their lot and portion. They are here brought in, 1. Triumphing over the people of God. They relied upon their numbers. The Assyrian army was made up out of divers nations : it was *the multitude of many people* (v. 12), by which weight they hoped to carry the cause. They were very noisy, like the roaring of the seas ; they talked big, hectored, and threatened, to frighten God's people from resisting them, and all their allies from sending in to their aid. Sennacherib and Rabshakeh, in their speeches and letters, made a mighty noise to strike a terror upon Hezekiah and his people; the nations that followed them *made a rushing like the rushing of many waters*, and those mighty ones, that threaten to bear down all before them and carry away every thing that stands in their way. *The floods have lifted up their voice, have lifted up their waves ;* such is the tumult of the people, and the heathen, when they rage, Ps. ii. 1 ; xciii. 3. 2. Triumphed over by the judgments of God. They thought to carry their point by dint of noise; but woe to them (v. 12), for he *shall rebuke them*, that is, God shall, one whom they little think of, have no regard to, stand in no awe of ; he shall give them a check with an invisible hand, *and* then *they shall flee afar off.* Sennacherib, and Rabshakeh, and the remains of their forces, shall run away in a fright, and shall be chased by their own terrors, *as the chaff of the mountains* which stand bleak *before the wind, and like a rolling thing before the whirlwind,* like thistle-down (so the margin) ; they make themselves *as chaff before the wind* (Ps. xxxv. 5) and then *the angel of the Lord* (as it follows there), the same angel that slew many of them, shall chase the rest. God will make *them like a wheel,* or rolling thing, and then *persecute them with his tempest* and *make them afraid with his storm,* Ps. lxxxiii. 13, 15. Note, God can dispirit the enemies of his church when they are most courageous and confident, and dissipate them when they seem most closely consolidated. This shall be done suddenly (v. 14) : *At evening-tide* they are very troublesome, and threaten trouble to the people of God ; but *before the morning they are not.* At sleeping time they are cast into a deep sleep, Ps. lxxvi. 5, 6. It was in the night that the angel routed the Assyrian army. God can in a moment break the power of his church's enemies, even when it appears most formidable; and this is written for the encouragement of the people of God in all ages, when they find themselves an unequal match for their enemies ; for *this is the portion of those that spoil us,* they shall themselves be spoiled. God will plead his church's cause, and those that meddle do it to their own hurt.

CHAP. XVIII.

Whatever country it is that is meant here by " the land shadowing with wings," here is a woe denounced against it, for God has, upon his people's account, a quarrel with it. I. They threaten God's people, ver. 1, 2. II. All the neighbours are hereupon called to take notice what will be the issue, ver. 3. III. Though God seem unconcerned in the distress of his people for a time, he will at length appear against their enemies and will remarkably cut them off, ver. 4—6. IV. This shall redound very much to the glory of God, ver. 7.

WOE to the land shadowing with wings, which *is* beyond the rivers of Ethiopia : 2 That sendeth ambassadors by the sea, even in vessels of bulrushes upon the waters, *saying,* Go, ye swift messengers, to a nation scattered and peeled, to a people terrible from their beginning hitherto ; a nation meted out and trodden down, whose land the rivers have spoiled ! 3 All ye inhabitants of the world, and dwellers on the earth, see ye, when he lifteth up an ensign on the mountains ; and when he bloweth a trumpet, hear ye. 4 For so the LORD said unto me, I will take my rest, and I will consider in my dwelling place like a clear heat upon herbs, *and* like a cloud of dew in the heat of harvest. 5 For afore the harvest, when the bud is perfect, and the sour grape is ripening in the flower, he shall both cut off the sprigs with pruning-hooks, and take away *and* cut down the branches. 6 They shall be left together unto the fowls of the mountains, and to the beasts of the earth : and the fowls shall summer upon them, and all the beasts of the earth shall winter upon them. 7 In that time shall the present be brought unto the LORD of hosts of a people scattered and peeled, and from a people terrible from their beginning hitherto ; a nation meted out and trodden under foot, whose land the rivers have spoiled, to the place of the name of the LORD of hosts, the mount Zion.

Interpreters are very much at a loss where to find this land that lies beyond the rivers of Cush. Some take it to be Egypt, a maritime country, and full of rivers, and which courted Israel to depend upon them, but proved broken reeds ; but against this it is strongly objected that the next chapter is distinguished from this by the title of *the burden of Egypt.* Others take it to be Ethiopia, and read it, *which lies near,* or *about, the rivers of Ethiopia,* not that in Africa, which lay south of Egypt, but that which we call ·*Arabia,* which lay east of Canaan, which Tirhakah was now king of. He thought to protect the Jews, as it were, under *the shadow of his wings,* by giving a powerful diversion to the king of Assyria, when he made a descent upon his country, at the time that he was attacking Jerusalem, 2 Kings xix. 9. But though by his ambassadors he bade defiance to the king of Assyria, and encouraged the Jews to depend upon him, God by the prophet slights him, and will not go forth with him; he may take his own course, but God will take another course to protect Jerusalem, while he suffers the attempt of Tirhakah to miscarry and his Arabian army to be ruined; for the Assyrian army shall become a present or sacrifice to the Lord of hosts, and to the place of his name, by the hand of an angel, not by the hand of Tirhakah king of Ethiopia, v. 7. This is a very probable exposition of this chapter. But from a hint of Dr. Lightfoot's, in his Harmony of the Old Testament, I incline to understand this chapter as a prophecy against Assyria, and so a continuation of the prophecy in the last three verses of the foregoing chapter, with which therefore this should be joined. That was against the army of the Assyrians which rushed in upon Judah; this is against the land of Assyria itself, which lay beyond the rivers of Arabia, that is, the rivers Euphrates and Tigris, which bordered on *Arabia Deserta.* And in calling it *the land shadowing with wings* he seems to refer to what he himself had said of it (*ch.* viii. 8), that *the stretching out of his wings shall fill the breadth of thy land, O Immanuel!* The prophet might perhaps describe the Assyrians by such dark expressions, not naming them, for the same reason that St. Paul, in his prophecy, speaks of the Roman empire by a periphrasis: *He who now letteth,* 2 Thess. ii. 7. Here is,

I. The attempt made by this land (whatever it is) upon *a nation scattered and peeled, v.* 2. Swift messengers are sent by water to proclaim war against them, as a nation marked by Providence, and *meted out,* to be trodden under foot. Whether this refer to the Ethiopians waging war with the Assyrians, or the Assyrians with Judah, it teaches us, 1. That a people which have been terrible from their beginning, have made a figure and borne a mighty sway, may yet become scattered and peeled, and may be spoiled even by their own rivers, that should enrich both the husbandman and the merchant. Nations which have been formidable, and have kept all in awe about them, may by a concurrence of accidents become despicable and an easy prey to their insulting neighbours. 2. Princes and states that are ambitious of enlarging their territories will always have some pretence or other to quarrel with those whose countries they have a mind to. " It is a nation that has been terrible, and therefore we must be revenged on it; it is now a nation scattered and peeled, meted out and trodden down, and therefore it will be an easy prey

for us." Perhaps it was not brought so low as they represented it. God's people are trampled on as a nation scattered and peeled; but whoever think to swallow them up may find them still as terrible as they have been from their beginning; they are cast down, but not deserted, not destroyed.

II. The alarm sounded to the nations about, by which they are summoned to take notice of what God is about to do, *v.* 3. The Ethiopians and Assyrians have their counsels and designs, which they have laid deep, and promise themselves much from, and, in prosecution of them, send their ambassadors and messengers from place to place; but let us now enquire what the great God says to all this. 1. *He lifts up an ensign upon the mountains, and blows a trumpet,* by which he proclaims war against the enemies of his church, and calls in all her friends and well-wishers into her service, *v.* 3. He gives notice that he is about to do some great work, as *Lord of hosts.* 2. All the world is bidden to take notice of it; all the dwellers on earth must see the ensign and hear the trumpet, must observe the motions of the divine providence and attend the directions of the divine will. Let all enlist under God's banner, and be on his side, and hearken to the trumpet of his word, which gives not an uncertain sound.

III. The assurance God gives to his prophet, by him to be given to his people, that, though he might seem for a time to sit by as an unconcerned spectator, yet he would certainly and seasonably appear for the comfort of his people and the confusion of his and their enemies (*v.* 4): *So the Lord said unto me.* Men will have their saying, but God also will have his; and, as we may be sure his word shall stand, so he often whispers it in the ears of his servants the prophets. When he says, *I will take my rest,* it is not as if he were weary of governing the world, or as if he either needed or desired to retire from it and repose himself; but it intimates that the great God has a perfect, undisturbed, enjoyment of himself, in the midst of all the agitations and changes of this world (the Lord sits even upon the floods unshaken; the Eternal Mind is always easy), and, though he may sometimes seem to his people as if he took not wonted notice of what is done in this lower world (they are tempted to think he is *as one asleep,* or *as one astonished,* Ps. xliv. 23 ; Jer. xiv. 9), yet even then he knows very well what men are doing and what he himself will do.

1. He will take care of his people, and be a shelter to them. He will regard his *dwelling-place ;* his eye and his heart are, and shall be, upon it for good continually. Zion is his rest for ever, where he will dwell; and he will *look after it* (so some read it); he will lift up the light of his

countenance upon it, will consider over it what is to be done, and will be sure to do all for the best. He will adapt the comforts and refreshments he provides for his people to the exigencies of their case; and they will therefore be acceptable, because seasonable. (1.) Like a clear heat after rain (so the margin), which is very reviving and pleasant, and makes the herbs to flourish. (2.) Like a dew and *a cloud in the heat of harvest*, which are very welcome, the dew to the ground and the cloud to the labourers. Note, There is that in God which is a shelter and refreshment to his people in all weathers and arms them against the inconveniences of every change. Is the weather cool? There is that in his favour which will warm them. Is it hot? There is that in his favour which will cool them. Great men have their winter-house and their summer-house (Amos iii. 15); but those that are at home with God have both in him.

2. He will reckon with his and their enemies, *v.* 5, 6. When the Assyrian army promises itself a plentiful harvest in the taking of Jerusalem and the plundering of that rich city, when the bud of that project is perfect, before the harvest is gathered in, while the sour grape of their enmity to Hezekiah and his people is ripening in the flower and the design is just ready to be put in execution, God shall destroy that army as easily as the husbandman cuts off the sprigs of the vine with pruning hooks, or because the grape is sour and good for nothing, and will not be cured, *takes away and cuts down the branches.* This seems to point at the overthrow of the Assyrian army by a destroying angel, when the dead bodies of the soldiers were scattered like the branches and sprigs of a wild vine, which the husbandman has cut to pieces. *And they shall be left to the fowls of the mountains, and the beasts of the earth,* to prey upon, both winter and summer; for as God's people are protected all seasons of the year, both in cold and heat (*v.* 4), so their enemies are at all seasons exposed; birds and beasts of prey shall both summer and winter upon them, till they are quite ruined.

IV. The tribute of praise which should be brought to God from all this (*v.* 7): *In that time,* when this shall be accomplished, *shall the present be brought unto the Lord of hosts.* 1. Some understand this of the conversion of the Ethiopians to the faith of Christ in the latter days, of which we have the specimen and beginning in Philip's baptizing the Ethiopian eunuch, Acts viii. 27, &c. Those that were *a people scattered and peeled, meted out, and trodden down* (*v.* 2), shall be a present to the Lord: and, though they seem useless and worthless, they shall be an acceptable present to him who judges of men by the sincerity of their faith and love, not by the pomp and prosperity of their outward condition. *Therefore* the gospel was ministered to the Gentiles that *the offering up of the Gentiles might be acceptable,* Rom. xv. 16. It is prophesied (Ps. lxviii. 31) that *Ethiopia shall soon stretch out her hands unto God.* 2. Others understand it of the spoil of Sennacherib's army, out of which, as usual, presents were brought to *the Lord of hosts,* Num. xxxi. 50. It was the present of a people scattered and peeled. (1.) It was won from the Assyrians, who were now themselves reduced to such a condition as they scornfully described Judah to be in, *v.* 2. Those that unjustly trample upon others shall themselves be justly trampled upon. (2.) It was offered by the people of God, who were, in disdain, called *a people scattered and peeled.* God will put honour upon his people, though men put contempt upon them. *Lastly,* Observe, The present that is brought to the Lord of hosts must be brought *to the place of the name of the Lord of hosts;* what is offered to God must be offered in the way that he has appointed; we must be sure to attend him, and expect him to meet us, where he records his name.

CHAP. XIX.

As Assyria was a breaking rod to Judah, with which it was smitten, so Egypt was a broken reed, with which it was cheated; and therefore God had a quarrel with them both. We have before read the doom of the Assyrians; now here we have the burden of Egypt, a prophecy concerning that nation, I. That it should be greatly weakened and brought low, and should be as contemptible among the nations as now it was considerable, rendered so by a complication of judgments which God would bring upon them, ver. 1—17. II. That at length God's holy religion should be brought into Egypt, and set up there, in part by the Jews that should flee thither for refuge, but more fully by the preachers of the gospel of Christ, through whose ministry churches should be planted in Egypt in the days of the Messiah (ver. 18—25), which would abundantly balance all the calamities here threatened.

THE burden of Egypt. Behold, the LORD rideth upon a swift cloud, and shall come into Egypt: and the idols of Egypt shall be moved at his presence, and the heart of Egypt shall melt in the midst of it. 2 And I will set the Egyptians against the Egyptians: and they shall fight every one against his brother, and every one against his neighbour; city against city, *and* kingdom against kingdom. 3 And the spirit of Egypt shall fail in the midst thereof; and I will destroy the counsel thereof: and they shall seek to the idols, and to them that have familiar spirits, and to the wizards. 4 And the Egyptians will I give over into the hand of a cruel lord; and a fierce king shall rule over them, saith the Lord, the LORD of hosts. 5 And the waters shall fail from the sea, and the rivers shall be wasted and dried up. 6 And they shall turn the rivers far away; *and* the brooks of defence shall be emptied and dried up: the reeds and flags shall wither. 7 The paper reeds by the brooks, by the mouth of the brooks, and every thing sown by the brooks, shall wither, be driven away, and be no *more.* 8 The fishers also shall mourn, and all they that cast angle into the brooks shall lament, and they that spread nets upon the waters shall languish. 9 Moreover they that work in fine flax, and they that weave networks, shall be confounded. 10 And they shall be broken in the purposes thereof, all that make sluices *and* ponds for fish. 11 Surely the princes of Zoan *are* fools, the counsel of the wise counsellors of Pharaoh is become brutish: how say ye unto Pharaoh, I *am* the son of the wise, the son of ancient kings? 12 Where *are* they? Where *are* thy wise *men?* And let them tell thee now, and let them know what the Lord of hosts hath purposed upon Egypt. 13 The princes of Zoan are become fools, the princes of Noph are deceived; they have also seduced Egypt, *even they that are* the stay of the tribes thereof. 14 The Lord hath mingled a perverse spirit in the midst thereof: and they have caused Egypt to err in every work thereof, as a drunken *man* staggereth in his vomit. 15 Neither shall there be *any* work for Egypt, which the head or tail, branch or rush, may do. 16 In that day shall Egypt be like unto women: and it shall be afraid and fear because of the shaking of the hand of the Lord of hosts, which he shaketh over it. 17 And the land of Judah shall be a terror unto Egypt, every one that maketh mention thereof shall be afraid in himself, because of the counsel of the Lord of hosts, which he hath determined against it.

Though the land of Egypt had of old been a house of bondage to the people of God, where they had been ruled with rigour, yet among the unbelieving Jews there still remained much of the humour of their fathers, who said, *Let us make us a captain*

and return into Egypt. Upon all occasions they trusted to Egypt for help (*ch.* xxx. 2), and thither they fled, in disobedience to God's express command, when things were brought to the last extremity in their own country, Jer. xliii. 7. Rabshakeh upbraided Hezekiah with this, *ch.* xxxvi. 6. While they kept up an alliance with Egypt, and it was a powerful ally, they stood not in awe of the judgments of God; for against them they depended upon Egypt to protect them. Nor did they depend upon the power of God when at any time they were in distress; but Egypt was their confidence. To prevent all this mischief, Egypt must be mortified, and many ways God here tells them he will take to mortify them.

I. The gods of Egypt shall appear to them to be what they always really were, utterly unable to help them, *v.* 1. "*The Lord rides upon a cloud, a swift cloud, and shall come into Egypt.* As a judge goes in state to the bench to try and condemn the malefactors, or as a general takes the field with his troops to crush the rebels, so shall God come into Egypt with his judgments; and when he comes he will certainly overcome." In all this burden of Egypt here is no mention of any foreign enemy invading them; but God himself will come against them, and raise up the causes of their destruction from among themselves. He comes upon a cloud, above the reach of opposition or resistance. He comes apace upon a swift cloud; for their judgment lingers not when the time has come. He *rides upon the wings of the wind,* with a majesty far excelling the greatest pomp and splendour of earthly princes. He *makes the clouds his chariots,* Ps. xviii. 9; civ. 3. When he comes *the idols of Egypt shall be moved,* shall be removed at his presence, and perhaps be made to fall as Dagon did before the ark. Isis, Osiris, and Apis, those celebrated idols of Egypt, being found unable to relieve their worshippers, shall be disowned and rejected by them. Idolatry had got deeper rooting in Egypt than in any land besides, even the most absurd idolatries; and yet now the idols shall be moved and they shall be ashamed of them. When the Lord brought Israel out of Egypt he *executed judgments upon the gods of the Egyptians* (Num. xxxiii. 4); no marvel then if, when he comes, they begin to tremble. The Egyptians *shall seek to the idols,* when they are at their wits' end, and consult *the charmers and wizards* (*v.* 3); but all in vain; they see their ruin hastening on them notwithstanding.

II. The militia of Egypt, that had been famed for their valour, shall be quite dispirited and disheartened. No kingdom in the world was ever in a better method of keeping up a standing army than the Egyptians were; but now their heroes, that used to be celebrated for courage, shall be posted for cowards: *The heart of Egypt shall melt in the midst of it,* like wax before the fire (*v.*

1); *the spirit of Egypt shall fail, v.* 3.
They shall have no inclination, no resolution,
to stand up in defence of their country, their
liberty, and property; but shall tamely and
ingloriously yield all to the invader and oppressor. The Egyptians *shall be like women*
(*v.* 16); they shall be frightened and put
into confusion by the least alarm; even those
that dwell in the heart of the country, in the
midst of it, and therefore furthest from
danger, will be as full of frights as those
that are situate on the frontiers. Let not
the bold and brave be proud or secure, for
God can easily *cut off the spirit of princes*
(Ps. lxxvi. 12) and *take away their hearts,*
Job xii. 24.

III. The Egyptians shall be embroiled
in endless dissensions and quarrels among
themselves. There shall be no occasion to
bring a foreign force upon them to destroy
them; they shall destroy one another (*v.* 2):
I will set the Egyptians against the Egyptians.
As these divisions and animosities are their
sin, God is not the author of them, they
come from men's lusts; but God, as a
Judge, permits them for their punishment,
and by their destroying differences corrects
them for their sinful agreements. Instead
of helping one another, and acting each in
his place for the common good, *they shall
fight every one against his brother and neighbour,* whom he ought to love as himself—
*city against city, and kingdom against king-
dom.* Egypt was then divided into twelve
provinces, or dynasties; but Psammetichus,
the governor of one of them, by setting
them at variance with one another, at
length made himself master of them all.
A kingdom thus divided against itself
would soon be brought to desolation. *En
quo discordiá cives perduxit miseros!—Oh
the wretchedness brought upon a people by
their disagreements among themselves!* It is
brought to this by *a perverse spirit,* a spirit
of contradiction, which the Lord would
mingle, as an intoxicating draught made up
of several ingredients, for the Egyptians,
v. 14. One party shall be for a thing for
no other reason than because the other is
against it; that is a perverse spirit, which,
if it mingle with the public counsels, tends
directly to the ruin of the public interests.

IV. Their politics shall be all blasted,
and turned into foolishness. When God
will destroy the nation he will *destroy the
counsel thereof* (*v.* 3), by taking away wisdom
from the statesmen (Job xii. 20), or setting
them one against another (as Hushai and
Ahithophel), or by his providence breaking
their measures even when they seemed well
laid; so that the *princes of Zoan are fools:*
they make fools of one another, every one
betrays his own folly, and divine Providence
makes fools of them all, *v.* 11. Pharaoh
had his wise counsellors. Egypt was famous
for such. But their *counsel has all become
brutish;* they have lost all their forecast;

one would think they had become idiots,
and were bereaved of common sense. Let
no man glory then in his own wisdom, nor
depend upon that, nor upon the wisdom of
those about him; for he that gives understanding can when he please take it away.
And from those it is most likely to be
taken away that boast of their policy, as
Pharaoh's counsellors here did, and, to recommend themselves to places of public
trust, boast of their great understanding
("*I am the son of the wise,* of the God of
wisdom, of wisdom itself," says one; "my
father was an eminent privy-counsellor of
note in his day for wisdom"), or of the antiquity and dignity of their families: "I am,"
says another, "*the son of ancient kings.*"
The nobles of Egypt boasted much of their
antiquity, producing fabulous records of
their succession for above 10,000 years.
This humour prevailed much among them
about this time, as appears by Herodotus,
their common boast being that Egypt was
some thousands of years more ancient than
any other nation. "But *where are thy wise
men? v.* 12. Let them now show their
wisdom by foreseeing what ruin is coming
upon their nation, and preventing it, if they
can. Let them with all their skill *know
what the Lord of hosts has purposed upon
Egypt,* and arm themselves accordingly.
Nay, so far are they from doing this that they
themselves are, in effect, contriving the ruin
of Egypt, and hastening it on, *v.* 13. *The
princes of Noph* are not only deceived themselves, but they *have seduced Egypt,* by
putting their kings upon arbitrary proceedings" (by which both themselves and their
people were soon undone); "the governors
of Egypt, that are the stay and corner-
stones of the tribes thereof, are themselves
undermining it." It is sad with a people
when those that undertake for their safety
are helping forward their destruction, and
the physicians of the state are her worst
disease, when the things that belong to the
public peace are so far hidden from the eyes
of those that are entrusted with the public
counsels that in every thing they blunder
and take wrong measures; so here (*v.* 14):
*They have caused Egypt to err in every work
thereof.* Every step they took was a false
step. They always mistook either the end
or the means, and their counsels were all
unsteady and uncertain, like the staggerings
and stammerings of a drunken man in his
vomit, who knows not what he says nor
where he goes. See what reason we have
to pray for our privy-counsellors and ministers of state, who are the great supports and
blessings of the state if God give them a
spirit of wisdom, but quite the contrary if he
hide their heart from understanding.

V. The rod of government shall be turned
into the serpent of tyranny and oppression
(*v.* 4): "*The Egyptians will I give over into
the hand of a cruel lord,* not a foreigner, but

one of their own, one that shall rule over them by an hereditary right, but shall be a fierce king and rule them with rigour," either the twelve tyrants that succeeded Sethon, or rather Psammetichus that recovered the monarchy again; for he speaks of one cruel lord. Now the barbarous usage which the Egyptian task masters gave to God's Israel long ago was remembered against them and they were paid in their own coin by another Pharaoh. It is sad with a people when the powers that should be for edification are for destruction, and they are ruined by those by whom they should be ruled, when such as this is the manner of the king, as it is described (*in terrorem—in order to impress alarm*) 1 Sam. viii. 11.

VI. Egypt was famous for its river Nile, which was its wealth, and strength, and beauty, and was idolized by them. Now it is here threatened that *the waters shall fail from the sea* and the river shall be *wasted and dried up, v.* 5. Nature shall not herein favour them as she has done. Egypt was never watered with the rain of heaven (Zech. xiv. 18), and therefore the fruitfulness of their country depended wholly upon the overflowing of their river; if that therefore be dried up, their fruitful land will soon be turned into barrenness and their harvests cease: *Every thing sown by the brooks will wither* of course, will *be driven away, and be no more, v.* 7. If the paper-reeds by the brooks, at the very mouth of them, wither, much more the corn, which lies at a greater distance, but derives its moisture from them. Yet this is not all; the drying up of their rivers is the destruction, 1. Of their fortifications, for they are *brooks of defence* (*v.* 6), making the country difficult of access to an enemy. Deep rivers are the strongest lines, and most hardly forced. Pharaoh is said to be a *great dragon lying in the midst of his rivers,* and guarded by them, bidding defiance to all about him, Ezek. xxix. 3. But these *shall be emptied and dried up,* not by an enemy, as Sennacherib with the *sole of his foot dried up mighty rivers* (*ch.* xxxvii. 25), and as Cyrus, who took Babylon by drawing Euphrates into many streams, but by the providence of God, which sometimes *turns water-springs into dry ground,* Ps. cvii. 33. 2. It is the destruction of their fish, which in Egypt was much of their food, witness that base reflection which the children of Israel made (Num. xi. 5): *We remember the fish which we did eat in Egypt freely.* The drying up of the rivers will *kill the fish* (Ps. cv. 29), and will thereby ruin those who make it their business, (1) To catch fish, whether by angling or nets (*v.* 8); they shall *lament* and *languish,* for their trade is at an end. There is nothing which the children of this world do more heartily lament than the loss of that which they used to get money by. *Ploratur lachrymis amissa pecunia veris—Those are genuine tears which*

106

are shed over lost money. (2.) To keep fish, that it may be ready when it is called for. There were those that *made sluices and ponds for fish* (*v.* 10), but *they shall be broken in the purposes thereof;* their business will fail, either for want of water to fill their ponds or for want of fish to replenish their waters. God can find ways to deprive a country even of that which is its staple commodity. The Egyptians may themselves remember *the fish they have formerly eaten freely,* but now cannot have for money. And that which aggravates the loss of these advantages by the river is that it is their own doing (*v.* 6): *They shall turn the rivers far away.* Their kings and great men, to gratify their own fancy, will drain water from the main river to their own houses and grounds at a distance, preferring their private convenience before the public good, and so by degrees the force of the river is sensibly weakened. Thus many do themselves a greater prejudice at last than they think of, [1.] Who pretend to be wiser than nature, and to do better for themselves than nature has done. [2.] Who consult their own particular interest more than the common good. Such may gratify themselves, but surely they can never satisfy themselves, who to serve a turn contribute to a public calamity, which they themselves, in the long run, cannot avoid sharing in. Herodotus tells us that Pharaoh-Necho (who reigned not long after this), projecting to cut a free passage by water from Nilus into the Red Sea, employed a vast number of men to make a ditch or channel for that purpose, in which attempt he impaired the river, lost 120,000 of his people, and yet left the work unaccomplished.

VII. Egypt was famous for the linen manufacture; but that trade shall be ruined. Solomon's merchants traded with Egypt for linen-yarn, 1 Kings x. 28. Their country produced the best flax and the best hands to work it; but *those that work in fine flax shall be confounded* (*v.* 9), either for want of flax to work on or for want of a demand for that which they have worked or opportunity to export it. The decay of trade weakens and wastes a nation and by degrees brings it to ruin. The trade of Egypt must needs sink, for (*v.* 15) *there shall not be any work for Egypt* to be employed in; and where there is nothing to be done there is nothing to be got. There shall be a universal stop put to business, *no work which either head or tail, branch or rush, may do;* nothing for high or low, weak or strong, to do; *no hire,* Zech. viii. 10. Note, The flourishing of a kingdom depends much upon the industry of the people; and *then* things are likely to do well when all hands are at work, when the head and top-branch do not disdain to labour, and the labour of the tail and rush is not disdained. But when the learned professions are unemployed, the principal merchants have no stocks, and the handicraft tradesmen nothing to do, poverty comes upon a people *as one that travaileth* and *as an armed man.*

VIII. A general consternation shall seize the Egyptians; they *shall be afraid and fear* (*v.* 16), which will be both an evidence of a universal decay and a means and presage of utter ruin. Two things will put them into this fright:—1. What they hear from *the land of Judah; that shall be a terror to Egypt, v.* 17. When they hear of the desolations made in Judah by the army of Sennacherib, considering both the near neighbourhood and the strict alliance that was between them and Judah, they will conclude it must be their turn next to become a prey to that victorious army. When their neighbour's house was on fire they could not but see their own in danger; and therefore every one of the Egyptians that makes mention of Judah shall be afraid of himself, expecting the bitter cup shortly to be put into his hands. 2. What they see in their own land. They shall *fear* (*v.* 16) *because of the shaking of the hand of the Lord of hosts,* and (*v.* 17) *because of the counsel of the Lord of hosts,* which from the shaking of his hand they shall conclude *he has determined* against Egypt as well as Judah. For, if judgment begin at the house of God, where will it end? *If this be done in the green tree, what shall be done in the dry?* See here, (1.) How easily God can make those a terror to themselves that have been, not only secure, but a terror to all about them. It is but shaking his hand over them, or laying it upon some of their neighbours, and the stoutest hearts tremble immediately. (2.) How well it becomes us to fear before God when he does but shake his hand over us, and to humble ourselves under his mighty hand when it does but threaten us, especially when we see his counsel determined against us; for who can change his counsel?

18 In that day shall five cities in the land of Egypt speak the language of Canaan, and swear to the LORD of hosts; one shall be called, The city of destruction. 19 In that day shall there be an altar to the LORD in the midst of the land of Egypt, and a pillar at the border thereof to the LORD. 20 And it shall be for a sign and for a witness unto the LORD of hosts in the land of Egypt: for they shall cry unto the LORD because of the oppressors, and he shall send them a saviour, and a great one, and he shall deliver them. 21 And the LORD shall be known to Egypt, and the Egyptians shall know the LORD on that day, and shall do sacrifice and

oblation; yea, they shall vow a vow unto the LORD and perform *it.* 22 And the LORD shall smite Egypt: he shall smite and heal *it:* and they shall return *even* to the LORD, and he shall be entreated of them, and shall heal them. 23 In that day shall there be a highway out of Egypt to Assyria, and the Assyrian shall come into Egypt, and the Egyptian into Assyria, and the Egyptians shall serve with the Assyrians. 24 In that day shall Israel be the third with Egypt, and with Assyria, *even* a blessing in the midst of the land: 25 Whom the LORD of hosts shall bless, saying, Blessed *be* Egypt my people, and Assyria the work of my hands, and Israel mine inheritance.

Out of the thick and threatening clouds of the foregoing prophecy the sun of comfort here breaks forth, and it is the sun of righteousness. Still God has mercy in store for Egypt, and he will show it, not so much by reviving their trade and replenishing their river again as by bringing the true religion among them, calling them to, and accepting them in, the worship of the one only living and true God; and these blessings of grace were much more valuable than all the blessings of nature wherewith Egypt was enriched. We know not of any event in which this prophecy can be thought to have its full accomplishment short of the conversion of Egypt to the faith of Christ, by the preaching (as is supposed) of Mark the Evangelist, and the founding of many Christian churches there, which flourished for many ages. Many prophecies of this book point to the days of the Messiah; and why not this? It is no unusual thing to speak of gospel graces and ordinances in the language of the Old-Testament institutions. And, in these prophecies, those words, *in that day,* perhaps have not always a reference to what goes immediately before, but have a peculiar significancy pointing at that day which had been so long fixed, and so often spoken of, when the day-spring from on high should visit this dark world. Yet it is not improbable (which some conjecture) that this prophecy was in part fulfilled when those Jews who fled from their own country to take shelter in Egypt, when Sennacherib invaded their land, brought their religion along with them, and, being awakened to great seriousness by the troubles they were in, made an open and zealous profession of it there, and were instrumental to bring many of the Egyptians to embrace it, which was an earnest and specimen of the more plentiful harvest of souls that should be gathered in to God by the preaching of the gospel of Christ. Josephus indeed tells us that Onias the son of Onias the high priest, living an outlaw at Alexandria in Egypt, obtained leave of Ptolemy Philometer, then king, and Cleopatra his queen, to build a temple to the God of Israel, like that at Jerusalem, at Bubastis in Egypt, and pretended a warrant for doing it from this prophecy in Isaiah, that there shall be an *altar to the Lord in the land of Egypt;* and the service of God, Josephus affirms, continued in it about 333 years, when it was shut up by Paulinus soon after the destruction of Jerusalem by the Romans; see *Joseph. Antiq. l.* 13. *c.* 6, and *de Bell. Judaic. l.* 7. *c.* 30. But that temple was all along looked upon by the pious Jews as so great an irregularity, and an affront to the temple at Jerusalem, that we cannot suppose this prophecy to be fulfilled in it.

Observe how the conversion of Egypt is here described.

I. They shall *speak the language of Canaan*, the holy language, the scripture-language; they shall not only understand it, but use it (*v.* 18); they shall introduce that language among them, and converse freely with the people of God, and not, as they used to do, *by an interpreter*, Gen. xlii. 23. Note, Converting grace, by changing the heart, changes the language ; *for out of the abundance of the heart the mouth speaks. Five cities in Egypt* shall speak this language; so many Jews shall come to reside in Egypt, and they shall so multiply there, that they shall soon replenish five cities, one of which shall be the city of Heres, or of the sun, Heliopolis, where the sun was worshipped, the most infamous of all the cities of Egypt for idolatry; even there shall be a wonderful reformation, they shall speak the language of Canaan. Or it may be taken thus, as we render it— That for every five cities that shall embrace religion there shall be one (a sixth part of the cities of Egypt) that shall reject it, and that shall be called *a city of destruction*, because it refuses the methods of salvation.

II. They shall swear to the Lord of hosts, not only swear by him, giving him the honour of appealing to him, as all nations did to the gods they worshipped; but they shall by a solemn oath and vow devote themselves to his honour and bind themselves to his service. They shall swear to cleave to him with purpose of heart, and shall worship him, not occasionally, but constantly. They shall swear allegiance to him as their King, to Christ, to whom all judgment is committed.

III. They shall set up the public worship of God in their land (*v.* 19): *There shall be an altar to the Lord* in the *midst of the land of Egypt*, an altar on which *they shall do sacrifice and oblation* (*v.* 21); therefore it must be understood spiritually. Christ, the great altar, who sanctifies every gift, shall be owned there, and the gospel sacrifices of

108

prayer and praise shall be offered up ; for by the law of Moses there was to be no altar for sacrifice but that at Jerusalem. In Christ Jesus all distinction of nations is taken away; and a spiritual altar, a gospel church, in the midst of the land of Egypt, is as acceptable to God as one in the midst of the land of Israel; and spiritual sacrifices of faith and love, and a contrite heart, *please the Lord better than an ox or bullock.*

IV. There shall be a face of religion upon the nation, and an open profession made of it, discernible to all who come among them. Not only in the heart of the country, but even in *the borders* of it, *there shall be a pillar*, or pillars, inscribed, *To Jehovah*, to his honour, as before there had been such pillars set up in honour of false gods. As soon as a stranger entered upon the borders of Egypt he might perceive what God they worshipped. Those that serve God must not be ashamed to own him, but be forward to do any thing that may be for a sign and for a witness to the Lord of hosts. Even in the land of Egypt he had some faithful worshippers, who boasted of their relation to him and made his name their strong tower, or bulwark, on their borders, with which their coasts were fortified against all assailants.

V. Being in distress, they shall seek to God, and he shall be found of them; and this *shall be a sign and a witness for the Lord of hosts* that he is a *God hearing prayer* to *all flesh* that *come to him, v.* 20. See Ps. lxv. 2. When they cry to God by reason of their oppressors, the cruel lords that shall *rule over them* (*v.* 4), he *shall be entreated of them* (*v.* 22); whereas he had told his people Israel, who had made it their own choice to have such a king, that they should *cry to him by reason of their king*, and he *would not hear them*, 1 Sam. viii. 18.

VI. They shall have an interest in the great Redeemer. When they were under the oppression of cruel lords perhaps God sometimes raised them up mighty deliverers, as he did for Israel in the days of the judges ; and by them, though he had smitten the land, he healed it again; and, upon their return to God in a way of duty, he returned to them in a way of mercy, and repaired the breaches of their tottering state. For repenting Egyptians shall find the same favour with God that repenting Ninevites did. But all these deliverances wrought for them, as those for Israel, were but figures of gospel salvation. Doubtless Jesus Christ is *the Saviour and the great one* here spoken of, whom God will send the glad tidings of to the Egyptians, and by whom he will *deliver them out of the hands of their enemies*, that they may *serve him without fear*, Luke i. 74, 75. Jesus Christ delivered the Gentile nations from the service of dumb idols, and did himself both purchase and preach liberty to the captives.

VII. The knowledge of God shall prevail

among them, *v.* 21. 1. They shall have the means of knowledge. For many ages in *Judah only was God known,* for there only were the lively oracles found; but now *the Lord,* and his name and will, *shall be known to Egypt.* Perhaps this may in part refer to the translation of the Old Testament out of Hebrew into Greek by the LXX., which was done at Alexandria in Egypt, by the command of Ptolemy king of Egypt; and it was the first time that the scriptures were translated into any other language. By the help of this (the Grecian monarchy having introduced their language into that country) *the Lord was known to Egypt,* and a happy omen and means it was of his being further known. 2. They shall have grace to improve those means. It is promised not only that the Lord shall be known to Egypt, but that *the Egyptians shall know the Lord;* they shall receive and entertain the light granted to them, and shall submit themselves to the power of it. The Lord is known to our nation, and yet I fear there are many of our nation that do not know the Lord. But the promise of the new covenant is that *all shall know the Lord, from the least even to the greatest,* which promise is sure to all the seed. The effect of this knowledge of God is that *they shall vow a vow to the Lord and perform it.* For those do not know God aright who either are not willing to come under binding obligations to the Lord or do not make good those obligations.

VIII. They shall come into the communion of saints. Being joined to the Lord, they shall be added to the church, and be incorporated with all the saints. 1. All enmities shall be slain. Mortal feuds there had been between Egypt and Assyria; they often made war upon one another; but now *there shall be a highway between Egypt and Assyria* (*v.* 23), a happy correspondence settled between the two nations; they shall trade with one another, and every thing that passes between them shall be friendly. *The Egyptians shall serve* (shall worship the true God) *with the Assyrians;* and therefore the Assyrians shall come into Egypt and the Egyptians into Assyria. Note, It becomes those who have communion with the same God, through the same Mediator, to keep up an amicable correspondence with one another. The consideration of our meeting at the same throne of grace, and our serving with each other in the same business of religion, should put an end to all heats and animosities, and knit our hearts to each other in holy love. 2. The Gentile nations shall not only unite with each other in the gospel fold under Christ the great shepherd, but they shall all be united with the Jews. When Egypt and Assyria become partners in serving God *Israel* shall *make a third with* them (*v.* 24); they shall become a *three-fold cord, not easily broken.* The ceremonial law, which had long been the partition-wall between Jews and Gentiles, shall be taken down, and then they shall become *one sheep-fold under one shepherd.* Thus united, they shall be *a blessing in the midst of the land, whom the Lord of hosts shall bless, v.* 24, 25. (1.) Israel shall be a blessing to them all, because of *them, as concerning the flesh, Christ came,* and they were the natural branches of the good olive, to whom did originally pertain *its root and fatness,* and the Gentiles were but *grafted in among them,* Rom. xi. 17. Israel lay between Egypt and Assyria, and was a blessing to them both by bringing them to meet in that word of the Lord which went forth from Jerusalem, and that church which was first set up in the land of Israel. *Qui conveniunt in aliquo tertio inter se conveniunt —Those who meet in a third meet in each other.* Israel is that third in whom Egypt and Assyria agree, and is therefore a blessing; for those are real and great blessings to their generation who are instrumental to unite those that have been at variance. (2.) They shall all be a blessing to the world: so the Christian church is, made up of Jews and Gentiles; it is the beauty, riches, and support of the world. (3.) They shall all be blessed of the Lord. [1.] They shall all be owned by him as his. Though Egypt was formerly a house of bondage to the people of God, and Assyria an unjust invader of them, all this shall now be forgiven and forgotten, and they shall be as welcome to God as Israel. They are all alike his people whom he takes under his protection. They are formed by him, for they are the *work of his hands;* not only as *a* people, but as *his* people. They are formed for him; for they are his inheritance, precious in his eyes, and dear to him, and from whom he has his rent of honour out of this lower world. [2.] They shall be owned together by him as jointly his, his in concert; they shall all share in one and the same blessing. Note, Those that are united in the love and blessing of God ought, for that reason, to be united to each other in charity.

CHAP. XX.

This chapter is a prediction of the carrying away of multitudes both of the Egyptians and the Ethiopians into captivity by the king of Assyria. Here is, I. the sign by which this was foretold, which was the prophet's going for some time barefoot and almost naked, like a poor captive, ver. 1—2. II. The explication of that sign, with application to Egypt and Ethiopia, ver. 3—5. III. The good use which the people of God should make of this, which is never to trust in an arm of flesh, because thus it will deceive them, ver. 6.

IN the year that Tartan came unto Ashdod (when Sargon the king of Assyria sent him), and fought against Ashdod, and took it; 2 At the same time spake the LORD by Isaiah the son of Amos, saying, Go and loose the sackcloth from off thy loins, and put off thy shoe from thy foot. And he did so, walking naked and barefoot. 3 And the LORD said,

Like as my servant Isaiah hath walked naked and barefoot three years *for* a sign and wonder upon Egypt and upon Ethiopia ; 4 So shall the king of Assyria lead away the Egyptians prisoners, and the Ethiopians captives, young and old, naked and barefoot, even with *their* buttocks uncovered, to the shame of Egypt. 5 And they shall be afraid and ashamed of Ethiopia their expectation, and of Egypt their glory. 6 And the inhabitant of this isle shall say in that day, Behold, such *is* our expectation, whither we flee for help to be delivered from the king of Assyria : and how shall we escape ?

God here, as King of nations, brings a sore calamity upon Egypt and Ethiopia, but, as King of saints, brings good to his people out of it. Observe,

I. The date of this prophecy. It was in the year that Ashdod, a strong city of the Philistines (but which some think was lately recovered from them by Hezekiah, when he smote the Philistines even unto Gaza, 2 Kings xviii. 8), was besieged and taken by an army of the Assyrians. It is uncertain what year of Hezekiah that was, but the event was so remarkable that those who lived then could by that token fix the time to a year. He that was now king of Assyria is called *Sargon*, which some take to be the same with Sennacherib ; others think he was his immediate predecessor, and succeeded Shalmaneser. Tartan, who was general, or commander-in-chief, in this expedition, was one of Sennacherib's officers, sent by him to bid defiance to Hezekiah, in concurrence with Rabshakeh, 2 Kings xviii. 17.

II. The making of Isaiah a sign, by his unusual dress when he walked abroad. He had been a sign to his own people of the melancholy times that had come and were coming upon them, by the sackcloth which for some time he had worn, of which he had a gown made, which he girt about him. Some think he put himself into that habit of a mourner upon occasion of the captivity of the ten tribes. Others think sackcloth was what he commonly wore as a prophet, to show himself mortified to the world, and that he might learn to endure hardness ; soft clothing better becomes those that attend in king's palaces (Matt. xi. 8) than those that go on God's errands. Elijah wore hair-cloth (2 Kings i. 8), and John Baptist (Matt. iii. 4) and those that pretended to be prophets supported their pretension by wearing rough garments (Zech. xiii. 4) ; but Isaiah has orders given him to *loose his sackcloth from his loins*, not to exchange it for better clothing, but for none

at all—no upper garment, no mantle, cloak, or coat, but only that which was next to him, we may suppose his shirt, waistcoat, and drawers ; and he must *put off his shoes*, and go barefoot ; so that compared with the dress of others, and what he himself usually wore, he might be said to go *naked*. This was a great hardship upon the prophet ; it was a blemish to his reputation, and would expose him to contempt and ridicule ; the boys in the streets would hoot at him, and those who sought occasion against him would say, *The prophet is* indeed *a fool, and the spiritual man is mad,* Hosea ix. 7. It might likewise be a prejudice to his health ; he was in danger of catching a cold, which might throw him into a fever, and cost him his life ; but God bade him do it, that he might give a proof of his obedience to God in a most difficult command, and so shame the disobedience of his people to the most easy and reasonable precepts. When we are in the way of our duty we may trust God both with our credit and with our safety. The hearts of that people were strangely stupid, and would not be affected with what they only heard, but must be taught by signs, and therefore Isaiah must do this for their edification. If the dress was scandalous, yet the design was glorious, and what a prophet of the Lord needed not to be ashamed of.

III. The exposition of this sign, v. 3, 4. It was intended to signify that the Egyptians and the Ethiopians should be led away captive by the king of Assyria, thus stripped, or in rags, and very shabby clothing, as Isaiah was. God calls him his *servant Isaiah*, because in this matter particularly he had approved himself God's willing, faithful, obedient servant ; and for this very thing, which perhaps others laughed at him for, God gloried in him. To obey is better than sacrifice ; it pleases God and praises him more, and shall be more praised by him. Isaiah is said to have *walked naked and barefoot three years,* whenever in that time he appeared as a prophet. But some refer the three years, not to the sign, but to the thing signified : *He has walked naked and barefoot ;* there is a stop in the original · provided he did so once that was enough to give occasion to all about him to enquire what was the meaning of his doing so ; or, as some think, he did it three days, a day for a year ; and this for a three years' sign and wonder, for a sign of that which should be done three years afterwards or which should be three years in the doing. Three campaigns successively shall the Assyrian army make, in spoiling the Egyptians and Ethiopians, and carrying them away captive in this barbarous manner, not only the soldiers taken in the field of battle, but the inhabitants, young and old ; and it being a very piteous sight, and such as must needs move compassion in those that had the least degree of tenderness left them to see those

110

who had gone all their days well dressed now stripped, and scarcely having rags to cover their nakedness, that circumstance of their captivity is particularly taken notice of, and foretold, the more to affect those to whom this prophecy was delivered. It is particularly said to be *to the shame of Egypt* (*v.* 4), because the Egyptians were a proud people, and therefore when they did fall into disgrace it was the more shameful to them; and the higher they had lifted up themselves the lower was their fall, both in their own eyes and in the eyes of others.

IV. The use and appplication of this, *v.* 5, 6. 1. All that had any dependence upon, or correspondence with, Egypt and Ethiopia, should now be ashamed of them, and afraid of having any thing to do with them. Those countries that were in danger of being overrun by the Assyrians expected that Tirhakah, king of Ethiopia, with his numerous forces, would put a stop to the progress of their victorious arms, and be a barrier to his neighbours; and with yet more assurance they gloried that Egypt, a kingdom so famous for policy and prowess, would do their business, would oblige them to raise the siege of Ashdod and retire with precipitation. But, instead of this, by attempting to oppose the king of Assyria they did but expose themselves and make their country a prey to him. Hereupon all about them were ashamed that ever they promised themselves any advantage from two such weak and cowardly nations, and were more afraid now than ever they were of the growing greatness of the king of Assyria, before whom Egypt and Ethiopia proved but as briers and thorns put to stop a consuming fire, which do but make it burn the more strongly. Note, Those who make any creature their expectation and glory, and so put it in the place of God, will sooner or later be ashamed of it, and their disappointment in it will but increase their fear. See Ezek. xxix. 6, 7. 2. The Jews in particular should be convinced of their folly in resting upon such broken reeds, and should despair of any relief from them (*v.* 6): *The inhabitants of this isle* (the land of Judah, situated upon the sea, though not surrounded by it), of this country (so the margin); every one shall now have his eyes opened, and shall say, " *Behold, such is our expectation,* so vain, so foolish, and this is that which it will come to. We have fled for help to the Egyptians and Ethiopians, and have hoped by them to be delivered from the king of Assyria; but, now that they are broken thus, how shall we escape, that are not able to bring such armies into the field as they did?" Note, (1.) Those that confide in creatures will be disappointed, and will be made ashamed of their confidence; *for vain is the help of man, and in vain is salvation hoped for from the hills or the height and* *multitude of the mountains.* (2) Disappointment in creature confidences, instead of driving us to despair, as here *(how shall we escape?),* should drive us to God; for, if we flee to him for help, our expectation shall not be frustrated.

<h2 style="text-align:center">CHAP. XXI.</h2>

In this chapter we have a prophecy of sad times coming, and heavy burdens, I. Upon Babylon, here called " the desert of the sea," that it should be destroyed by the Medes and Persians with a terrible destruction, which yet God's people should have advantage by, ver. 1—10. II. Upon Dumah, or Idumea, ver. 11, 12. III. Upon Arabia, or Kedar, the desolation of which country was very near, ver. 13—17. These and other nations which the princes and people of Israel had so much to do with the prophets of Israel could not but have something to say to. Foreign affairs must be taken notice of as well as domestic ones, and news from abroad enquired after as well as news at home.

THE burden of the desert of the sea. As whirlwinds in the south pass through; *so* it cometh from the desert, from a terrible land. 2 A grievous vision is declared unto me; the treacherous dealer dealeth treacherously, and the spoiler spoileth. Go up, O Elam: besiege, O Media; all the sighing thereof have I made to cease. 3 Therefore are my loins filled with pain: pangs have taken hold upon me, as the pangs of a woman that travaileth: I was bowed down at the hearing *of it;* I was dismayed at the seeing *of it.* 4 My heart panted, fearfulness affrighted me: the night of my pleasure hath he turned into fear unto me. 5 Prepare the table, watch in the watchtower, eat, drink: arise, ye princes, *and* anoint the shield. 6 For thus hath the LORD said unto me, Go, set a watchman, let him declare what he seeth. 7 And he saw a chariot *with* a couple of horsemen, a chariot of asses, *and* a chariot of camels; and he hearkened diligently with much heed: 8 And he cried, A lion: My lord, I stand continually upon the watch-tower in the daytime, and I am set in my ward whole nights: 9 And, behold, here cometh a chariot of men, *with* a couple of horsemen. And he answered and said, Babylon is fallen, is fallen; and all the graven images of her gods he hath broken unto the ground. 10 O my threshing, and the corn of my floor: that which I have heard of the LORD of hosts, the God of Israel, have I declared unto you.

We had one burden of Babylon before (ch. xiii.); here we have another prediction of its fall. God saw fit thus to possess his people with the belief of this event by line upon line, because Babylon sometimes pretended to be a friend to them (as *ch.* xxxix. 1), and God would hereby warn them not to trust to that friendship, and sometimes was really an enemy to them, and God would hereby warn them not to be afraid of that enmity. Babylon is marked for ruin; and all that believe God's prophets can, through that glass, see it tottering, see it tumbling, even when with an eye of sense they see it flourishing and sitting as a queen. Babylon is here called the *desert* or *plain of the sea;* for it was a flat country, and full of lakes, or loughs (as they call them in Ireland), like little seas, and was abundantly watered with the many streams of the river Euphrates. Babylon did but lately begin to be famous, Nineveh having outshone it while the monarchy was in the Assyrian hands; but in a little time it became the lady of kingdoms; and, before it arrived at that pitch of eminency which it was at in Nebuchadnezzar's time, God by this prophet plainly foretold its fall, again and again, that his people might not be terrified at its rise, nor despair of relief in due time when they were its prisoners, Job v. 3; Ps. xxxvii. 35, 36. Some think it is here called a *desert* because, though it was now a populous city, it should in time be made a desert. And *therefore* the destruction of Babylon is so often prophesied of by this evangelical prophet, because it was typical of the destruction of the man of sin, the great enemy of the New-Testament church, which is foretold in the *Revelation* in many expressions borrowed from these prophecies, which therefore must be consulted and collated by those who would understand the prophecy of that book. Here is,

I. The powerful irruption and descent which the Medes and Persians should make upon Babylon (*v.* 1, 2): They will come *from the desert, from a terrible land.* The northern parts of Media and Persia, where their soldiers were mostly bred, was waste and mountainous, terrible to strangers that were to pass through it and producing soldiers that were very formidable. *Elam* (that is, Persia) is summoned to go up against Babylon, and, in conjunction with the forces of Media, to besiege it. When God has work of this kind to do he will find, though it be in a desert, in a terrible land, proper instruments to be employed in it. These forces come as *whirlwinds from the south,* so suddenly, so strongly, so terribly, such a mighty noise shall they make, and throw down every thing that stands in their way. As is usual in such a case, some deserters will go over to them: *The treacherous dealers will deal treacherously.* Historians tell us of Gadatas and Gobryas, two great officers of the king of Babylon, that went over to Cyrus, and,

being well acquainted with all the avenues of the city, led a party directly to the palace, where Belshazzar was slain. Thus with the help of the *treacherous dealers the spoilers spoiled.* Some read it thus: *There shall be a deceiver of that deceiver, Babylon, and a spoiler of that spoiler,* or, which comes all to one, *The treacherous dealer has found one that deals treacherously, and the spoiler one that spoils,* as it is expounded, *ch.* xxxiii. 1. The Persians shall pay the Babylonians in their own coin; those that by fraud and violence, cheating and plundering, unrighteous wars and deceitful treaties, have made a prey of their neighbours, shall meet with their match, and by the same methods shall themselves be made a prey of.

II. The different impressions made hereby upon those concerned in Babylon. 1. To the poor oppressed captives it would be welcome news; for they had been told long ago that Babylon's destroyer would be their deliverer, and therefore, "when they hear that Elam and Media are coming up to besiege Babylon, *all their sighing will be made to cease;* they shall no longer mingle their tears with Euphrates' streams, but resume their harps, and smile when they remember Zion, which, before, they wept at the thought of." For the sighing of the needy the God of pity will arise in due time (Ps. xii. 5); he will break the yoke from off their neck, will remove the rod of the wicked from off their lot, and so make their sighing to cease. 2. To the proud oppressors it would be a grievous vision (*v.* 2), particularly to the king of Babylon for the time being, and it should seem that he it is who is here brought in sadly lamenting his inevitable fate (*v.* 3, 4): *Therefore are my loins filled with pain; pangs have taken hold upon me, &c.,* which was literally fulfilled in Belshazzar, for that very night in which his city was taken, and himself slain, upon the sight of a hand writing mystic characters upon the wall *his countenance was changed and his thoughts troubled him, so that the joints of his loins were loosed and his knees smote one against another,* Dan. v. 6. And yet that was but the beginning of sorrows. Daniel's deciphering the writing could not but increase his terror, and the alarm which immediately followed of the executioners at the door would be the completing of it. And those words, *The night of my pleasure has he turned into fear to me,* plainly refer to that aggravating circumstance of Belshazzar's fall that he was slain on that night when he was in the height of his mirth and jollity, with his cups and concubines about him and a thousand of his lords revelling with him; that night of his pleasure, when he promised himself an undisturbed unallayed enjoyment of the most exquisite gratifications of sense, with a particular defiance of God and religion in the profanation of the temple vessels, was the night that was turned into all this fear. Let this give an effectual check to vain mirth and sensual pleasures, and forbid us ever to lay the reins on the neck of them—that we know not what heaviness the mirth may end in, nor how soon laughter may be turned into mourning; but this we know that for all these things God shall bring us into judgment; let us therefore mix trembling always with our joys.

III. A representation of the posture in which Babylon should be found when the enemy should surprise it—all in festival gaiety (*v.* 5): " Prepare the table with all manner of dainties. Set the guards; let them watch in the watch-tower while we eat and drink securely and make merry; and, if any alarm should be given, the princes shall arise and anoint the shield, and be in readiness to give the enemy a warm reception." Thus secure are they, and thus do they gird on the harness with as much joy as if they were putting it off.

IV. A description of the alarm which should be given to Babylon upon its being forced by Cyrus and Darius. The Lord, in vision, showed the prophet the watchman set in his watch-tower, near the palace, as is usual in times of danger; the king ordered those about him to post a sentinel in the most advantageous place for discovery, and, according to the duty of a watchman, let *him declare what he sees, v.* 6. We read of watchmen thus set to receive intelligence in the story of David (2 Sam. xviii. 24), and in the story of Jehu, 2 Kings ix. 17. This watchman here discovered a chariot with a couple of horsemen attending it, in which we may suppose the commander-in-chief to ride. He then saw another chariot drawn by asses or mules, which were much in use among the Persians, and a chariot drawn by camels, which were likewise much in use among the Medes; so that (as Grotius thinks) these two chariots signify the two nations combined against Babylon, or rather these chariots come to bring tidings to the palace; compare Jer. li. 31, 32. *One post shall run to meet another, and one messenger to meet another, to show the king of Babylon that his city is taken at one end* while he is revelling at the other end and knows nothing of the matter. This watchman, seeing these chariots at some distance, *hearkened diligently with much heed,* to receive the first tidings. And (*v.* 8) *he cried, A lion:* this word, coming out of a watchman's mouth, no doubt gave them a certain sound, and every body knew the meaning of it, though we do not know it now. It is likely that it was intended to raise attention: he that has an ear to hear, let him hear, as when a lion roars. Or *he cried as a lion,* very loud and in good earnest, the occasion being very urgent. And what has he to say? 1. He professes his constancy to the post assigned him: " *I stand, my lord, con-*

tinually upon the watch-tower, and have never discovered any thing material till just now; all seemed safe and quiet." Some make it to be a complaint of the people of God that they had long expected the downfal of Babylon, according to the prophecy, and it had not yet come; but withal a resolution to continue waiting; as Hab. ii. 1, *I will stand upon my watch, and set me upon the tower,* to see what will be the issue of the present providences. 2. He gives notice of the discoveries he had made (*v.* 9): *Here comes a chariot of men with a couple of horsemen,* a vision representing the enemy's entry into the city with all their force or the tidings brought to the royal palace of it.

V. A certain account is at length given of the overthrow of Babylon. He in the chariot *answered and said* (when he heard the watchman speak), *Babylon has fallen, has fallen;* or God answered thus to the prophet enquiring concerning the issue of these affairs: " It has now come to this, Babylon has surely and irrecoverably fallen. Babylon's business is done now. *All the graven images of her gods he has broken unto the ground.*" Babylon was the mother of harlots (that is, of idolatry), which was one of the grounds of God's quarrel with her; but her idols should now be so far from protecting her that some of them should be broken down to the ground, and others of them, that were worth carrying away, should go into captivity, and be a burden to the beasts that carried them, *ch.* xlvi. 1, 2.

VI. Notice is given to the people of God, who were then captives in Babylon, that this prophecy of the downfal of Babylon was particularly intended for their comfort and encouragement, and they might depend upon it that it should be accomplished in due season, *v.* 10. Observe,

1. The title the prophet gives them in God's name: *O my threshing, and the corn of my floor!* The prophet calls them *his,* because they were his countrymen, and such as he had a particular interest in and concern for; but he speaks it as from God, and directs his speech to those that were Israelites indeed, the faithful in the land. Note, (1.) The church is God's floor, in which the most valuable fruits and products of this earth are, as it were, gathered together and laid up. (2.) True believers are the corn of God's floor. Hypocrites are but as the chaff and straw, which take up a great deal of room, but are of small value, with which the wheat is now mixed, but from which it shall be shortly and for ever separated. (3.) The corn of God's floor must expect to be threshed by afflictions and persecutions. God's Israel of old was afflicted from her youth, often under the plougher's plough (Ps. cxxix. 3) and the thresher's flail. (4.) Even then God owns it for his threshing; it is his still; nay, **the**

threshing of it is by his appointment, and under his restraint and direction. The threshers could have no power against it *but what was given them from above.*

2. The assurance he gives them of the truth of what he had delivered to them, which therefore they might build their hopes upon : *That which I have heard of the Lord of hosts, the God of Israel*—that, and nothing else, that, and no fiction or fancy of my own—*have I declared unto you.* Note, In all events concerning the church, past, present, and to come, we must have an eye to God both as the Lord of hosts and as the God of Israel, who has power enough to do any thing for his church and grace enough to do every thing that is for her good, and to the words of his prophets, as words received from the Lord. As they dare not smother any thing which he has entrusted them to declare, so they dare not declare any thing as from him which he has not made known to them, 1 Cor. xi. 23.

11 The burden of Dumah. He calleth to me out of Seir, Watchman, what of the night? Watchman, what of the night? 12 The watchman said, The morning cometh, and also the night: if ye will inquire, inquire ye: return, come.

This prophecy concerning Dumah is very short, and withal dark and hard to be understood. Some think that Dumah is a part of Arabia, and that the inhabitants descended from Dumah the sixth son of Ishmael, as those of Kedar (*v.* 16, 17) from Ishmael's second son, Gen. xxv. 13, 14. Others, because Mount Seir is here mentioned, by Dumah understand Idumea, the country of the Edomites. Some of Israel's neighbours are certainly meant, and their distress is foretold, not only for warning to them to prepare them for it, but for warning to Israel not to depend upon them, or any of the nations about them, for relief in a time of danger, but upon God only. We must see all creature confidences failing us, and feel them breaking under us, that we may not lay more weight upon them than they will bear. But though the explication of this prophecy be difficult, because we have no history in which we find the accomplishment of it, yet the application will be easy. We have here,

1. A question put by an Edomite to the watchman. Some one or other *called out of Seir,* somebody that was more concerned for the public safety and welfare than the rest, who were generally careless and secure. As the man of Macedonia, in a vision, desired Paul to come over and help them (Acts xvi. 9), so this man of Mount Seir, in a vision, desired the prophet to inform and instruct them. He calls not many; it

is well there are any, that all are not alike unconcerned about the things that belong to the public peace. Some out of Seir ask advice of God's prophets, and are willing to be taught, when many of God's Israel heed nothing. The question is serious : *What of the night ?* It is put to a proper person, the *watchman,* whose office it is to answer such enquiries. He repeats the question, as one in care, as one in earnest, and desirous to have an answer. Note, (1.) God's prophets and ministers are appointed to be watchmen, and we are to look upon them as such. They are as watchmen in the city in a time of peace, to see that all be safe, to knock at every door by personal enquiries (" Is it locked ? Is the fire safe ?"), to direct those that are at a loss, and check those that are disorderly, Cant. iii. 3; v. 7. They are as watchmen in the camp in time of war, Ezek. xxxiii. 7. They are to take notice of the motions of the enemy and to give notice of them, to make discoveries and then give warning; and in this they must deny themselves. (2.) It is our duty to enquire of the watchmen, especially to ask again and again, *What of the night ?* for watchmen wake when others sleep. [1.] What time of the night ? After a long sleep in sin and security, is it not time to rise, high time to awake out of sleep ? Rom. xiii. 11. We have a great deal of work to do, a long journey to go; is it not time to be stirring ? "Watchman, what o'clock is it ? After a long dark night is there any hope of the day dawning ?" [2.] What tidings of the night ? *What from the night ?* (so some) ; " what vision has the prophet had to-night ? We are ready to receive it." Or, rather, " What occurs to night ? What weather is it ? What news ?" We must expect an alarm, and never be secure. The *day of the Lord will come as a thief in the night ;* we must prepare to receive the alarm, and resolve to keep our ground, and then take the first hint of danger, and to our arms presently, to our spiritual weapons.

2. The watchman's answer to this question. The watchman was neither asleep nor dumb though it was a man of Mount Seir that called to him, he was ready to give him an answer : *The morning comes.* He answers, (1.) By way of prediction : " There comes first a morning of light, and peace, and opportunity; you will enjoy one day of comfort more ; but afterwards comes a night of trouble and calamity." Note, In the course of God's providence it is usual that morning and night are counterchanged and succeed each other. Is it night ? Yet the morning comes, and the day-spring knows his place, Ps. xxx. 5. Is it day ? Yet the night comes also. If there be a morning of youth and health, there will come a night of sickness and old age ; if a morning of prosperity in the family, in the public, yet we must look for changes. But God usually gives a morn-

ing of opportunity before he sends a night of calamity, that his own people may be prepared for the storm and others left inexcusable. (2.) By way of excitement: *If you will enquire, enquire.* Note, It is our wisdom to improve the present morning in preparation for the night that is coming after it. " *Enquire, return, come.* Be inquisitive, be penitent, be willing and obedient." The manner of expression is very observable, for we are put to our choice what we will do : " *If you will enquire, enquire ;* if not, it is at your peril; you cannot say but you have a fair offer made you." We are also urged to be at a point : " If you will, say so, and do not stand pausing; what you will do do quickly, for it is no time to trifle." Those that return and come to God will find they have a great deal of work to do and but a little time to do it in, and therefore they have need to be busy.

13 The burden upon Arabia. In the forest in Arabia shall ye lodge, O ye travelling companies of Dedanim. 14 The inhabitants of the land of Tema brought water to him that was thirsty, they prevented with their bread him that fled. 15 For they fled from the swords, from the drawn sword, and from the bent bow, and from the grievousness of war. 16 For thus hath the LORD said unto me, Within a year, according to the years of a hireling, and all the glory of Kedar shall fail : 17 And the residue of the number of archers, the mighty men of the children of Kedar, shall be diminished : for the LORD God of Israel hath spoken *it.*

Arabia was a large country, that lay eastward and southward of the land of Canaan. Much of it was possessed by the posterity of Abraham. The *Dedanim,* here mentioned (*v.* 13), descended from Dedan, Abraham's son by Keturah ; the inhabitants of Tema and Kedar descended from Ishmael, Gen. xxv. 3, 13, 15. The Arabians generally lived in tents, and kept cattle, were a hardy people, inured to labour ; probably the Jews depended upon them as a sort of a wall between them and the more warlike eastern nations; and therefore, to alarm them, they shall hear *the burden of Arabia,* and see it sinking under its own burden.

I. A destroying army shall be brought upon them, with a sword, with *a drawn sword,* with *a bow* ready *bent,* and with all the *grievousness of war, v.* 15. It is probable that the king of Assyria, in some of the marches of his formidable and victorious

army, took Arabia in his way, and, meeting with little resistance, made an easy prey of them. The consideration of the grievousness of war should make us thankful for the blessings of peace.

II. The poor country people will hereby be forced to flee for shelter wherever they can find a place ; so that *the travelling companies of Dedanim,* which used to keep the high roads with their caravans, shall be obliged to quit them and *lodge in the forest in Arabia* (*v.* 13), and shall not have the wonted convenience of their own tents, poor and weather-beaten as they are.

III. They shall stand in need of refreshment, being ready to perish for want of it, in their flight from the invading army : " *O you inhabitants of the land of Tema !*" (who probably were next neighbours to the companies of Dedanim) " *bring you water*" (so the margin reads it) " *to him that is thirsty,* and *prevent with your bread those that flee,* for they are objects of your compassion ; they do not wander for wandering sake, nor are they reduced to straits by any extravagance of their own, but *they flee from the sword.*" Tema was a country where water was sometimes a scarce commodity (as we find, Job vi. 19), and we may conclude it would be in a particular manner acceptable to these poor distressed refugees. Let us learn hence, 1. To look for distress ourselves. We know not what straits we may be brought into before we die. Those that live in cities may be forced to lodge in forests ; and those may know the want of necessary food who now eat bread to the full. Our mountain stands not so strong but that it may be moved, rises not so high but that it may be scaled. These Arabians would the better bear these calamities because in their way of living they had used themselves to hardships. 2. To look with compassion upon those that are in distress, and with all cheerfulness to relieve them, not knowing how soon their case may be ours : " *Bring water to those that are thirsty,* and not only give bread to those that need and ask it, but prevent those with it that have need ; give it to them unasked." Those that do so shall find it remembered to their praise, as (according to our reading) it is here remembered to the praise of the land of Tema that they did bring water to the thirsty and relieved even those that were on the falling side.

IV. All that which is the glory of Kedar shall vanish away and fail. Did they glory in their numerous herds and flocks ? They shall all be driven away by the enemy. It seems they were famous above other nations for the use of the bow in battle ; but their archers, instead of foiling the enemy, shall fall themselves ; and *the residue of their number,* when they are reduced to a small number, *shall be diminished* (*v.* 17); their mighty able-bodied men, and men of spirit too, shall become very few ; for they, being most forward in the defence of their country, were most exposed, and fell first, either by the enemies' sword or into the enemies' hand. Note, Neither the skill of archers (though they be ever so good marksmen) nor the courage of mighty men can protect a people from the judgments of God, when they come with commission ; they rather expose the undertakers. That is poor glory which will thus quickly come to nothing.

V. All this shall be done in a little time : " *Within one year according to the years of a hireling* (within one year precisely reckoned) this judgment shall come upon Kedar." If this fixing of the time be of no great use to us now (because we find not either when the prophecy was delivered or when it was accomplished), yet it might be of great use to the Arabians then, to awaken them to repentance, that, like the men of Nineveh, they might prevent the judgment when they were thus told it was just at the door. Or, when it begins to be fulfilled, the business shall be done, be begun and ended in one year's time. God, when he please, can do a great work in a little time.

VI. It is all ratified by the truth of God (v. 16) : " *Thus hath the Lord said to me ;* you may take my word for it that it is his word ;" and we may be sure no word of his shall fall to the ground. And again (v. 17): *The Lord God of Israel hath spoken it,* as the God of Israel, in pursuance of his gracious designs concerning them ; and we may be sure *the strength of Israel will not lie.*

CHAP. XXII.

We have now come nearer home, for this chapter is " the burden of the valley of vision," Jerusalem ; other places had their burden for the sake of their being concerned in some way or other with Jerusalem, and were reckoned with either as spiteful enemies or deceitful friends to the people of God ; but now let Jerusalem hear her own doom. This chapter concerns, I. The city of Jerusalem itself and the neighbourhood depending upon it. Here is, 1. A prophecy of the grievous distress they should shortly be brought into by Sennacherib's invasion of the country and laying siege to the city, ver. 1—7. 2. A reproof given them for their misconduct in that distress, in two things :—(1.) Not having an eye to God in the use of the means of their preservation, ver. 8—11. (2.) Not humbling themselves under his mighty hand, ver. 12—14. II. The court of Hezekiah, and the officers of that court. 1. The displacing of Shebna, a bad man, and turning him out of the treasury, ver. 15—19, 25. 2. The preferring of Eliakim, who should do his country better service, to his place, ver. 20—24.

THE burden of the valley of vision. What aileth thee now, that thou art wholly gone up to the house-tops ? 2 Thou that art full of stirs, a tumultuous city, a joyous city : thy slain *men are* not slain with the sword, nor dead in battle. 3 All thy rulers are fled together, they are bound by the archers : all that are found in thee are bound together, *which* have fled from far. 4 Therefore said I, Look away from me ; I will weep bitterly, labour not to comfort me,

because of the spoiling of the daughter of my people. 5 For *it is* a day of trouble, and of treading down, and of perplexity by the Lord GOD of hosts in the valley of vision, breaking down the walls, and of crying to the mountains. 6 And Elam bare the quiver with chariots of men *and* horsemen, and Kir uncovered the shield. 7 And it shall come to pass, *that* thy choicest valleys shall be full of chariots, and the horsemen shall set themselves in array at the gate.

The title of this prophecy is very observable. It is *the burden of the valley of vision,* of Judah and Jerusalem ; so all agree. Fitly enough is Jerusalem called a valley, for the mountains were round about it, and the land of Judah abounded with fruitful valleys ; and by the judgments of God, though they had been as a towering mountain, they should be brought low, sunk and depressed, and become dark and dirty, as a valley. But most emphatically is it called a *valley of vision* because there God was known and his name was great, there the prophets were made acquainted with his mind by visions, and there the people saw the goings of their God and King in his sanctuary. Babylon, being a stranger to God, though rich and great, was called *the desert of the sea ;* but Jerusalem, being entrusted with his oracles, is *a valley of vision. Blessed are their eyes, for they see,* and they have seers by office among them. Where Bibles and ministers are there is a valley of vision, from which is expected fruit accordingly ; but here is a *burden of the valley of vision,* and a heavy burden it is. Note, Church privileges, if they be not improved, will not secure men from the judgments of God. *You only have I known of all the families of the earth : therefore will I punish you.* The valley of vision has a particular burden. *Thou Capernaum,* Matt. xi. 23. The higher any are lifted up in means and mercies the heavier will their doom be if they abuse them.

Now the *burden of the valley of vision* here is that which will not quite ruin it, but only frighten it ; for it refers not to the destruction of Jerusalem by Nebuchadnezzar, but to the attempt made upon it by Sennacherib, which we had the prophecy of, *ch.* x., and shall meet with the history of, *ch.* xxxvi. It is here again prophesied of, because the desolations of many of the neighbouring countries, which were foretold in the foregoing chapters, were to be brought to pass by the Assyrian army. Now let Jerusalem know that when the cup is going round it will be put into her hand ; and, although it will not be to her a fatal cup, yet it will be a cup of trembling. Here is foretold,

I. The consternation that the city should be

in upon the approach of Sennacherib's army. It used to be full of stirs, a city of great trade, people hurrying to and fro about their business, a tumultuous city, populous and noisy. Where there is great trade there is great tumult. It used to be a joyous revelling city. What with the busy part and what with the merry part of mankind, places of concourse are places of noise. " But what ails thee now, that the shops are quitted, and there is no more walking in the streets and exchange, *but thou hast wholly gone up to the house-tops* (v. 1), to bemoan thyself in silence and solitude, or to secure thyself from the enemy, or to look abroad and see if any succours come to thy relief, or which way the enemies' motions are." Let both men of business and sportsmen *rejoice as though they rejoiced not,* for something may happen quickly, which they little think of, that will be a damp to their mirth and a stop to their business, and send them to *watch as a sparrow alone upon the house-top,* Ps. cii. 7. But why is Jerusalem in such a fright? *Her slain men are not slain with the sword* (v. 2), but, 1. Slain with famine (so some); for Sennacherib's army having laid the country waste, and destroyed the fruits of the earth, provisions must needs be very scarce and dear in the city, which would be the death of many of the poorer sort of people, who would be constrained to feed on that which was unwholesome. 2. Slain with fear. They were put into this fright though they had not a man killed, but so disheartened themselves that they seemed as effectually stabbed with fear as if they had been run through with a sword.

II. The inglorious flight of the rulers of Judah, who fled from far, from all parts of the country, to Jerusalem (v. 3), fled together, as it were by consent, and were found in Jerusalem, having left their respective cities, which they should have taken care of, to be a prey to the Assyrian army, which, meeting with no opposition, when it *came up against all the defenced cities of Judah* easily *took them,* ch. xxxvi. 1. These rulers *were bound from the bow* (so the word is); they not only quitted their own cities like cowards, but, when they came to Jerusalem, were of no service there, but were as if their hands were tied from the use of the bow, by the extreme distraction and confusion they were in; they trembled, so that they could not draw a bow. See how easily God can dispirit men, and how certainly fear will dispirit them, when the tyranny of it is yielded to.

III. The great grief which this should occasion to all serious sensible people among them, which is represented by the prophet's laying the thing to heart himself; he lived to see it, and was resolved to share with the children of his people in their sorrows, v. 4, 5. He is not willing to proclaim his sorrow, and therefore bids those about him to look away from him; he will abandon himself to grief, and indulge himself in it, will weep secretly, but weep bitterly, and will have none go about to comfort him, for his grief is obstinate and he is pleased with his pain. But what is the occasion of his grief? A poor prophet had little to lose, and had been inured to hardship, when he walked naked and barefoot; but it is for *the spoiling of the daughter of his people.* Note, Public grievances should be our griefs. It is *a day of trouble, and of treading down, and of perplexity.* Our enemies trouble us and tread us down, and our friends are perplexed and know not what course to take to do us a kindness. The Lord God of hosts is now contending with the valley of vision; the enemies with their battering rams are breaking down the walls, and we are in vain crying to the mountains (to keep off the enemy, or to fall on us and cover us) or looking for help to come to us over the mountains, or appealing, as God does, to the mountains, to hear our controversy (Mic. vi. 1) and to judge between us and our injurious neighbours.

IV. The great numbers and strength of the enemy, that should invade their country and besiege their city, v. 6, 7. Elam (that is, the Persians) come with their quiver full of arrows, and with chariots of fighting men, and horsemen. Kir (that is, the Medes) muster up their arms, unsheath the sword, and uncover the shield, and get every thing ready for battle, every thing ready for the besieging of Jerusalem. Then the choice valleys about Jerusalem, that used to be clothed with flocks and covered over with corn, shall be full of chariots of war, and at the gate of the city *the horsemen shall set themselves in array,* to cut off all provisions from going in, and to force their way in. What a condition must the city be in that was beset on all sides with such an army!

8 And he discovered the covering of Judah, and thou didst look in that day to the armour of the house of the forest. 9 Ye have seen also the breaches of the city of David, that they are many: and ye gathered together the waters of the lower pool. 10 And ye have numbered the houses of Jerusalem, and the houses have ye broken down to fortify the wall. 11 Ye made also a ditch between the two walls for the water of the old pool: but ye have not looked unto the maker thereof, neither had respect unto him that fashioned it long ago. 12 And in that day did the Lord God of hosts call to weeping, and to mourning, and to baldness, and to girding with sackcloth: 13 And behold joy and gladness, slay-

ing oxen, and killing sheep, eating flesh, and drinking wine : let us eat and drink ; for to-morrow we shall die. 14 And it was revealed in mine ears by the LORD of hosts, Surely this iniquity shall not be purged from you till ye die, saith the Lord GOD of hosts.

What is meant by *the covering of Judah,* which in the beginning of this paragraph is said to be *discovered,* is not agreed. The fenced cities of Judah were a covering to the country; but these, being taken by the army of the Assyrians, ceased to be a shelter, so that the whole country lay exposed to be plundered. The weakness of Judah, its nakedness, and inability to keep itself, now appeared more than ever; and thus the covering of Judah was discovered. Its magazines and stores, which had been locked up, were now laid open for the public use. Dr. Lightfoot gives another sense of it, that by this distress into which Judah should be brought God would discover their covering (that is, uncloak their hypocrisy), would show all that was in their heart, as is said of Hezekiah upon another occasion, 2 Chron. xxxii. 31. Now they discovered both their carnal confidence (*v.* 9) and their carnal security, *v.* 13. Thus, by one means or other, *the iniquity of Ephraim will be discovered and the sin of Samaria,* Hos. vii. 1.

They were now in a great fright, and in this fright they manifested two things much amiss :—

I. A great contempt of God's goodness, and his power to help them. They made use of all the means they could think of for their own preservation; and it is not for doing this that they are blamed, but, in doing this, they did not acknowledge God Observe,

1. How careful they were to improve all advantages that might contribute to their safety. When Sennacherib had made himself master of all the defenced cities of Judah, and Jerusalem was left as a cottage in a vineyard, they thought it was time to look about them. A council was immediately called, a council of war ; and it was resolved to stand upon their defence, and not tamely to surrender. Pursuant to this resolve, they took all the prudent measures they could for their own security. We tempt God if, in times of danger, we do not the best we can for ourselves. (1.) They inspected the magazines and stores, to see if they were well stocked with arms and ammunition: *They looked to the armour of the house of the forest,* which Solomon built in Jerusalem for an armoury (1 Kings x. 17), and thence they delivered out what they had occasion for. It is the wisdom of princes, in time of peace, to provide for war, that they may not have arms to seek when they should use them, and per-

haps upon a sudden emergency. (2.) They viewed the fortifications, the *breaches of the city of David ;* they walked round the walls, and observed where they had gone to decay for want of seasonable repairs, or were broken by some former attempts made upon them. These breaches were many ; the more shame for the house of David that they suffered the city of David to lie neglected. They had probably often seen those breaches ; but now they saw them to consider what course to take about them. This good we should get by public distresses, we should be awakened by them to *repair our breaches,* and amend what is amiss. (3.) They made sure of water for the city, and did what they could to deprive the besiegers of it : *You gathered together the water of the lower pool,* of which there was probably no great store, and of which therefore they were the more concerned to be good husbands. See what a mercy it is that, as nothing is more necessary to the support of human life than water, so nothing is more cheap and common ; but it is bad indeed when that, as here, is a scarce commodity. (4.) They *numbered the houses of Jerusalem,* that every house might send in its quota of men for the public service, or contribute in money to it, which they raised by a poll, so much a head or so much a house. (5.) Because private property ought to give way to the public safety, those houses that stood in their way, when the wall was to be fortified, were broken down, which, in such a case of necessity, is no more an injury to the owner than blowing up houses in case of fire. (6.) They made a ditch between the outer and inner wall, for the greater security of the city ; and they contrived to draw the water of the old pool to it, that they might have plenty of water themselves and might deprive the besiegers of it ; for it seems that was the project, lest the Assyrian army *should come and find much water* (2 Chron. xxxii. 4) and so should be the better able to prolong the siege. If it be lawful to destroy the forage of a country, much more to divert the streams of its waters, for the straitening and starving of an enemy.

2. How regardless they were of God in all these preparations : *But you have not looked unto the Maker thereof* (that is, of Jerusalem, the city you are so solicitous for the defence of) and of all the advantages which nature has furnished it with for its defence—the *mountains round about it* (Ps. cxxv. 2), and the rivers, which were such as the inhabitants might turn which way soever they pleased for their convenience. Note, (1.) It is God that made his Jerusalem, and fashioned it long ago, in his counsels. The Jewish writers, upon this place, say, There were seven things which God made before the world (meaning which he had in his eye when he made the world): *the garden of Eden, the law, the just ones, Israel, the throne of glory, Jerusalem, and Messiah the Prince.*

The gospel church has God for its Maker. (2.) Whatever service we do, or endeavour to do, at any time, to God's Jerusalem, must be done with an eye to him as the Maker of it; and he takes it ill if it be done otherwise. It is here charged upon them that they did not look to God. [1.] They did not design his glory in what they did. They fortified Jerusalem because it was a rich city and their own houses were in it, not because it was the holy city and God's house was in it. In all our cares for the defence of the church we must look more at God's interest in it than at our own. [2.] They did not depend upon him for a blessing upon their endeavours, saw no need of it, and therefore sought not to him for it, but thought their own powers and policies sufficient for them. Of Hezekiah himself it is said that *he trusted in God* (2 Kings xviii. 5), and particularly upon this occasion (2 Chron. xxxii. 8); but there were those about him, it seems, who were great statesmen and soldiers, but had little religion in them. [3.] They did not give him thanks for the advantages they had, in fortifying their city, from *the waters of the old pool*, which were fashioned long ago, as Kishon is called *an ancient river*, Judg. v. 21. Whatever in nature is at any time serviceable to us, we must therein acknowledge the goodness of the God of nature, who, when he fashioned it long ago, fitted it to be so, and *according to whose ordinance it continues to this day*. Every creature is that to us which God makes it to be ; and therefore, whatever use it is of to us, we must *look at him that fashioned it*, bless him for it, and use it for him.

II. A great contempt of God's wrath and justice in contending with them, *v.* 12—14. Here observe,

1. What was God's design in bringing this calamity upon them : it was to humble them, bring them to repentance, and make them serious. In that day of trouble, and treading down, and perplexity, the Lord did thereby *call to weeping and mourning*, and all the expressions of sorrow, even *to baldness and girding with sackcloth ;* and all this to lament their sins (by which they had brought those judgments upon their land), to enforce their prayers (by which they might hope to avert the judgments that were breaking in), and to dispose themselves to a reformation of their lives by a holy seriousness and a tenderness of heart under the word of God. To this God called them by his prophets' explaining his providences, and by his providences awakening them to regard what his prophets said. Note, When God threatens us with his judgments he expects and requires that we humble ourselves under his mighty hand, that we tremble when the lion roars, and in a day of adversity consider.

2. How contrary they walked to this design of God (*v.* 13) : *Behold, joy and gladness*, mirth and feasting, all the gaiety and all the jollity imaginable. They were as secure and cheerful as they used to be, as if they had had no enemy in their borders or were in no danger of falling into his hands. When they had taken the necessary precautions for their security, then they set all deaths and dangers at defiance, and resolved to be merry, let come on them what would. Those that should have been among the mourners were among the *wine-bibbers, the riotous eaters of flesh ;* and observe what they said, *Let us eat and drink, for to-morrow we shall die.* This may refer either to the particular danger they were now in, and the fair warning which the prophet gave them of it, or to the general shortness and uncertainty of human life, and the nearness of death at all times. This was the language of the profane scoffers who *mocked the messengers of the Lord and misused his prophets.* (1.) They made a jest of dying. "The prophet tells us we must die shortly, perhaps to-morrow, and therefore we should mourn and repent to-day ; no, rather *let us eat and drink*, that we may be fattened for the slaughter, and may be in good heart to meet our doom; if we must have a short life, let it be a merry one." (2.) They ridiculed the doctrine of a future state on the other side death; for, if there were no such state, the apostle grants there would be something of reason in what they said, 1 Cor. xv. 32. If, when we die, there were an end of us, it were good to make ourselves as easy and merry as we could while we live; but, if *for all these things God shall bring us into judgment*, it is at our peril if we walk *in the way of our heart and the sight of our eyes*, Eccl. xi. 9. Note, A practical disbelief of another life after this is at the bottom of the carnal security and brutish sensuality which are the sin, and shame, and ruin of so great a part of mankind, as of the old world, who were *eating and drinking till the flood came.*

3. How much God was displeased at it. He signified his resentment of it to the prophet, *revealed it in his ears*, to be by him proclaimed upon the house-top: *Surely this iniquity shall not be purged from you till you die, v.* 14. It shall never be expiated with sacrifice and offering, any more than the iniquity of the house of Eli, 1 Sam. iii. 14. It is a sin against the remedy, a baffling of the utmost means of conviction and rendering them ineffectual; and therefore it is not likely they should ever repent of it or have it pardoned. The Chaldee reads it, *It shall not be forgiven you till you die the second death.* Those that walk contrary to God shall find that he will walk contrary to them; with the froward he will show himself froward

15 Thus saith the Lord God of hosts, Go, get thee unto this treasurer, *even* unto Shebna, which *is* over the house, *and say*, 16 What hast thou

here? and whom hast thou here, that thou hast hcwcd thec out a scpulchrc here, *as* he that heweth him out a sepulchre on high, *and* that graveth a habitation for himself in a rock? 17 Behold, the LORD will carry thee away with a mighty captivity, and will surely cover thee. 18 He will surely violently turn and toss thee *like* a ball into a large country: there shalt thou die, and there the chariots of thy glory *shall be* the shame of thy lord's house. 19 And I will drive thee from thy station, and from thy state shall he pull thee down. 20 And it shall come to pass in that day, that I will call my servant Eliakim the son of Hilkiah: 21 And I will clothe him with thy robe, and strengthen him with thy girdle, and I will commit thy government into his hand: and he shall be a father to the inhabitants of Jerusalem, and to the house of Judah. 22 And the key of the house of David will I lay upon his shoulder; so he shall open, and none shall shut; and he shall shut, and none shall open. 23 And I will fasten him *as* a nail in a sure place; and he shall be for a glorious throne to his father's house. 24 And they shall hang upon him all the glory of his father's house, the offspring and the issue, all vessels of small quantity, from the vessels of cups, even to all the vessels of flagons. 25 In that day, saith the LORD of hosts, shall the nail that is fastened in the sure place be removed, and be cut down, and fall; and the burden that *was* upon it shall be cut off: for the LORD hath spoken *it.*

We have here a prophecy concerning the displacing of Shebna, a great officer at court, and the preferring of Eliakim to the post of honour and trust that he was in. Such changes are common in the courts of princes; it is therefore strange that so much notice should be taken of it by the prophet here; but by the accomplishment of what was foretold concerning these particular persons God designed to confirm his word in the mouth of Isaiah concerning other and greater events; and it is likewise to show that, as God has burdens in store for those nations and kingdoms abroad that are open enemies to his church and people, so he has for those particular persons at home that are false friends to them and betray them. It is likewise a confirmation in general of the hand of divine Providence in all events of this kind, which to us seem contingent and to depend upon the wills and fancies of princes. *Promotion comes not from the east, nor from the west, nor from the south; but God is the Judge,* Ps. lxxv. 6, 7. It is probable that this prophecy was delivered at the same time with that in the former part of the chapter, and began to be fulfilled before Sennacherib's invasion; for now Shebna was *over the house,* but then Eliakim was (*ch.* xxxvi. 3); and Shebna, coming down gradually, was only scribe. Here is,

I. The prophecy of Shebna's disgrace. He is called *this treasurer,* being entrusted with the management of the revenue; and he is likewise said to be *over the house,* for such was his boundless ambition and covetousness that less than two places, and those two of the greatest importance at court, would not satisfy him. It is common for self-seeking men thus to grasp at more than they can manage, and so the business of their places is neglected, while the pomp and profit of them wholly engage the mind. It does not appear what were the particular instances of Shebna's mal-administration, for which Isaiah is here sent to prophesy against him; but the Jews say, "He kept up a traitorous correspondence with the king of Assyria, and was in treaty with him to deliver the city into his hands." However this was, it should seem that he was a foreigner (for we never read of the name of his father) and that he was an enemy to the true interests of Judah and Jerusalem: it is probable that he was first preferred by Ahaz. Hezekiah was himself an excellent prince; but the best masters cannot always be sure of good servants. We have need to pray for princes, that they may be wise and happy in the choice of those they trust. These were times of reformation, yet Shebna, a bad man, complied so far as to keep his places at court; and it is probable that many others did like him, for which reason Sennacherib is said to have been *sent against a hypocritical nation,* ch. x. 6. In this message to Shebna we have,

1. A reproof of his pride, vanity, and security (*v.* 16): "*What hast thou here, and whom hast thou here?* What a mighty noise and bustle dost thou make! What estate hast thou here, that thou wast born to? *Whom hast thou here,* what relations, that thou art allied to? Art thou not of mean and obscure original, *filius populi—a mere plebeian,* that comest we know not whence? What is the meaning of this then, that thou hast built thyself a fine house, *hast graved thyself a habitation?*" So very nice and curious was it that it seemed rather to be the work of an engraver than of a mason or carpenter; and it seemed engraven in a rock, so firmly was it founded and so impregnable

was it. "Nay, *thou hast hewed thee out a sepulchre,*" as if he designed that his pomp should survive his funeral. Though Jerusalem was not *the place of his fathers' sepulchres* (as Nehemiah called it with a great deal of tenderness, Neh. ii. 3), he designed it should be the place of his own, and therefore set up a monument for himself in his life-time, set it up on high. Those that make stately monuments for their pride forget that, how beautiful soever they appear outwardly, within *they are full of dead men's bones.* But it is a pity that the grave-stone should forget the grave.

2. A prophecy of his fall and the sullying of his glory. (1.) That he should now quickly be displaced and degraded (*v.* 19): *I will drive thee from thy station.* High places are slippery places; and those are justly deprived of their honour that are proud of it and puffed up with it, and deprived of their power that do hurt with it. God will do it, who shows himself to be God by *looking upon proud men and abasing them,* Job xl. 11, 12. To this *v.* 25 refers. "The nail that is *now fastened in the sure place* (that is, Shebna, who thinks himself immovably fixed in his office) *shall be removed, and cut down, and fall.* Those are mistaken who think any place in this world a sure place, or themselves as nails fastened in it; for there is nothing here but uncertainty. When the nail falls the burden that was upon it is cut off; when Shebna was disgraced all that had a dependence upon him fell into contempt too. Those that are in high places will have many hanging upon them as favourites whom they are proud of and trust to; but they are burdens upon them, and perhaps with their weight break the nail, and both fall together, and by deceiving ruin one another—the common fate of great men and their flatterers, who expect more from each other than either performs. (2.) That after a while he should not only be driven from his station, but driven from his country: *The Lord will carry thee away with the captivity of a mighty man, v.* 17, 18. Some think the Assyrians seized him, and took him away, because he had promised to assist them and did not, but appeared against them: or perhaps Hezekiah, finding out his treachery, banished him, and forbade him ever to return; or he himself, finding that he had become obnoxious to the people, withdrew into some other country, and there spent the rest of his days in meanness and obscurity. Grotius thinks he was stricken with a leprosy, which was a disease commonly supposed to come from the immediate hand of God's displeasure, particularly for the punishment of the proud, as in the case of Miriam and Uzziah; and by reason of this disease he was *tossed like a ball* out of Jerusalem. Those who, when they are in power, turn and toss others, will be justly turned and tossed themselves when their day shall come to fall. Many

who have thought themselves fastened like a nail may come to be tossed like a ball; for here have we *no continuing city.* Shebna thought his place too strait for him, he had no room to thrive; God will therefore send him *into a large country,* where he shall have room to wander, but never find the way back again; for *there he shall die,* and lay his bones there, and not in the sepulchre he had hewn out for himself. And *there the chariots* which had been the chariots of his glory, in which he had rattled about the streets of Jerusalem, and which he took into banishment with him, should but serve to upbraid him with his former grandeur, *to the shame of his lord's house,* of the court of Ahaz, who had advanced him.

II. The prophecy of Eliakim's advancement, *v.* 20, &c. He is God's servant, has approved himself faithfully so in other employments, and therefore God will call him to this high station. Those that are diligent in doing the duty of a low sphere stand fairest for preferment in God's books. Eliakim does not undermine Shebna, nor make an interest against him, nor does he intrude into his office; but God calls him to it: and what God calls us to we may expect he will own us in. It is here foretold, 1. That Eliakim should be put into Shebna's place of lord-chamberlain of the household, lord-treasurer, and prime-minister of state. The prophet must tell Shebna this, *v.* 21. "He shall have *thy robe,* the badge of honour, and *thy girdle,* the badge of power; for he shall have *thy government.*" To hear of it would be a great mortification to Shebna, much more to see it. Great men, especially if proud men, cannot endure their successors. God undertakes the doing of it, not only because he would put it into the heart of Hezekiah to do it, and his hand must be acknowledged guiding the hearts of princes in placing and displacing men (Prov. xxi. 1), but because the powers that are, subordinate as well as supreme, are ordained of God. It is God that clothes princes with their robes, and therefore we must submit ourselves to them for the Lord's sake and with an eye to him, 1 Pet. ii. 13. And, since it is he that *commits the government into their hand,* they must administer it according to his will, for his glory; they must judge for him by whom they judge and *decree justice,* Prov. viii. 15. And they may depend upon him to furnish them for what he calls them to, according to this promise: *I will clothe him;* and then it follows, *I will strengthen him.* Those that are called to places of trust and power should seek unto God for grace to enable them to do the duty of their places; for that ought to be their chief care. Eliakim's advancement is further described by the laying of the *key of the house of David upon his shoulders, v.* 22. Probably he carried a golden key upon his shoulder as a badge of his office, or had one embroidered upon his cloak or robe, to which this alludes. Being over the house, and having the key delivered to him, as the seals are to the lord-keeper, *he shall open and none shall shut, shut and none shall open.* He had access to *the house of the precious things, the silver, and the gold, and the spices;* and to the *house of the armour* and the *treasures* (*ch.* xxxix. 2), and disposed of the stores there as he thought fit for the public service. He put whom he pleased into the inferior offices and turned out whom he pleased. Our Lord Jesus describes his own power as Mediator by an allusion to this (Rev. iii. 7), that *he has the key of David,* wherewith he *opens and no man shuts,* he *shuts and no man opens.* His power in the kingdom of heaven, and in the ordering of all the affairs of that kingdom, is absolute, irresistible, and uncontrollable. 2. That he should be fixed and confirmed in that office. He shall have it for life, and not *durante bene placito— during pleasure* (*v.* 23): *I will fasten him as a nail in a sure place,* not to be removed or cut down. Thus lasting shall the honour be that comes from God to all those who use it for him. Our Lord Jesus is *as a nail in a sure place:* his kingdom cannot be shaken, and he himself is still the same. 3. That he should be a great blessing in his office; and it is this that crowns the favours here conferred upon him. God *makes his name great,* for he shall be a blessing, Gen. xii. 2. (1.) He shall be a blessing to his country (*v.* 21): *He shall be a father to the inhabitants of Jerusalem and to the house of Judah.* He shall take care not only of the affairs of the king's household, but of all the public interests in Jerusalem and Judah. Note, Rulers should be fathers to those that are under their government, to teach them with wisdom, rule them with love, and correct what is amiss with tenderness, to protect them and provide for them, and be solicitous about them as a man is for his own children and family. It is happy with a people when the court, the city, and the country, have no separate interests, but all centre in the same, so that the courtiers are true patriots, and whom the court blesses the country has reason to bless too; and when those who are fathers to Jerusalem, the royal city, are no less so to the house of Judah. (2.) He shall be a blessing to his family (*v.* 23, 24): *He shall be for a glorious throne to his father's house.* The consummate wisdom and virtue which recommended him to this great trust made him the honour of his family, which probably was very considerable before, but now became much more so. Children should aim to be a credit to their parents and relations. The honour men reflect upon their families by their piety and usefulness is more to be valued than that which they derive from their families by their names and titles. Eliakim being preferred, *all the glory of his father's house* was hung upon him; they all made their court to him, and his brethren's sheaves

122

bowed to his. Observe, The glory of this world gives a man no intrinsic worth or excellency; it is but hung upon him as an appurtenance, and it will soon drop from him. Eliakim was compared to *a nail in a sure place,* in pursuance of which comparison all the relations of his family (which, it is likely, were numerous, and that was the glory of it) are said to have a dependence upon him, as in a house the vessels that have handles to them are hung up upon nails and pins. It intimates likewise that he shall generously take care of them all, and bear the weight of that care: *All the vessels,* not only *the flagons,* but *the cups, the vessels of small quantity,* the meanest that belong to his family, shall be provided for by him. See what a burden those bring upon themselves that undertake great trusts; they little think how many and how much will hang upon them if they resolve to be faithful in the discharge of their trust. Our Lord Jesus, having the key of the house of David, is as a *nail in a sure place,* and all *the glory of his father's house hangs* upon him, is derived from him, and depends upon him; even the meanest that belong to his church are welcome to him, and he is able to bear the stress of them all. That soul cannot perish, nor that concern fall to the ground, though ever so weighty, that is by faith hung upon Christ.

CHAP. XXIII.

This chapter is concerning Tyre, an ancient wealthy city, situated upon the sea, and for many ages one of the most celebrated cities for trade and merchandise in those parts of the world. The lot of the tribe of Asher bordered upon it. See Joshua xix. 29, where it is called " the strong city Tyre." We seldom find it a dangerous enemy to Israel, but sometimes their faithful ally, as in the reigns of David and Solomon ; for trading cities maintain their grandeur, not by the conquest of their neighbours, but by commerce with them. In this chapter is foretold, I. The lamentable desolation of Tyre, which was performed by Nebuchadnezzar and the Chaldean army, about the time that they destroyed Jerusalem ; and a hard task they had of it, as appears Ezek. xxix. 18, wh ᵉ they are said to have " served a hard service against Tyre," and yet to have no wages, ver. 1—14. II. The restoration of Tyre after seventy years, and the return of the Tyrians out of their captivity to their trade again, ver. 15—18.

THE burden of Tyre. Howl, ye ships of Tarshish; for it is laid waste, so that there is no house, no entering in: from the land of Chittim it is revealed to them. 2 Be still, ye inhabitants of the isle; thou whom the merchants of Zidon, that pass over the sea, have replenished. 3 And by great waters the seed of Sihor, the harvest of the river, *is* her revenue; and she is a mart of nations. 4 Be thou ashamed, O Zidon: for the sea hath spoken, *even* the strength of the sea, saying, I travail not, nor bring forth children, neither do I nourish up young men, *nor* bring up virgins. 5 As at the report concerning Egypt, *so* shall they be sorely pained at the report of Tyre. 6 Pass ye over to Tarshish; howl, ye inhabitants of the isle. 7 *Is* this your joyous *city*, whose antiquity *is* of ancient days? Her own feet shall carry her afar off to sojourn. 8 Who hath taken this counsel against Tyre, the crowning *city*, whose merchants *are* princes, whose traffickers *are* the honourable of the earth? 9 The LORD of hosts hath purposed it, to stain the pride of all glory, *and* to bring into contempt all the honourable of the earth. 10 Pass through thy land as a river, O daughter of Tarshish: *there is* no more strength. 11 He stretched out his hand over the sea, he shook the kingdoms : the LORD hath given a commandment against the merchant *city*, to destroy the strong holds thereof. 12 And he said, Thou shalt no more rejoice, O thou oppressed virgin, daughter of Zidon : arise, pass over to Chittim; there also shalt thou have no rest. 13 Behold the land of the Chaldeans; this people was not, *till* the Assyrian founded it for them that dwell in the wilderness : they set up the towers thereof, they raised up the palaces thereof; *and* he brought it to ruin. 14 Howl, ye ships of Tarshish : for your strength is laid waste.

Tyre being a sea-port town, this prophecy of its overthrow fitly begins and ends with, *Howl, you ships of Tarshish;* for all its business, wealth, and honour, depended upon its shipping; if that be ruined, they will be all undone. Observe,

I. Tyre flourishing. This is taken notice of that her fall may appear the more dismal. 1. *The merchants of Zidon,* who traded at sea, had at first *replenished her, v.* 2. Zidon was the more ancient city, situated upon the same sea-coast, a few leagues more to the north, and Tyre was at first only a colony of that ; but the daughter had out-grown the mother, and become much more considerable. It may be a mortification to great cities to think how they were at first replenished. 2. Egypt had helped very much to raise her, *v.* 3. Sihor was the river of Egypt : by that river, and the ocean into which it ran, the Egyptians traded with Tyre ; and the harvest of that river was her revenue. The riches of the sea, and the gains by goods exported and imported, are as much the harvest to trading towns as that of hay and corn is to the country ; and sometimes *the harvest of the river* proves a better revenue than the harvest of the land. Or it may be meant of all the products of the Egyptian soil, which the men of Tyre traded in, and which were the harvest of the river Nile, owing themselves to the overflowing of that river. 3. She had become the mart of the nations, the great emporium of that part of the world. Some of every known nation might be found there, especially at certain times of the year, when there was a general rendezvous of merchants. This is enlarged upon by another prophet, Ezek. xxvii. 2, 3, &c. See how the hand of the diligent, by the blessing of God upon it, makes rich. Tyre became rich and great by industry, though she had no other ploughs going than those that plough the waters. 4. She was a *joyous city*, noted for mirth and jollity, *v.* 7. Those that were so disposed might find there all manner of sports and diversions, all the delights of the sons and daughters of men, balls, and plays, and operas, and every thing of that kind that a man had a fancy to. This made them secure and proud, and they despised the country people, who neither knew nor relished any joys of that nature. This also made them very loth to believe and consider what warnings God gave them by his servants ; they were too merry to mind them. Her *antiquity* likewise was *of ancient days,* and she was proud of that, and that helped to make her secure ; as if because she had been a city time out of mind, and her antiquity had been of ancient days, therefore she must continue a city time without end, and her continuance must be to the days of eternity. 5. She was a *crowning city* (*v.* 8), that crowned herself. Such were the power and pomp of her magistrates that they crown-ed those who had dependence on her and dealings with her. It is explained in the following words : *Her merchants are princes,* and live like princes for the ease and state they take ; and *her traffickers,* whatever country they go to, *are the honourable of the earth,* who are respected by all. How slightly soever some now speak of tradesmen, it seems formerly, and among the wisest nations, there were merchants, and traders, and men of business, that were the honourable of the earth.

II. Here is Tyre falling. It does not appear that she brought trouble upon herself by provoking her neighbours with her quarrels, but rather by tempting them with her wealth ; but, if it was this that induced Nebuchadnezzar to fall upon Tyre, he was disappointed ; for after it had stood out a siege of thirteen years, and could hold out no longer, the inhabitants got away by sea, with their families and goods, to other places where they had an interest, and left Nebuchadnezzar nothing but the bare city. See a history of Tyre in Sir Walter Raleigh's History of the World, *lib.* ii. *cap.* 7. *sect.* 3, 43. *pag.* 283, which will give much light to this prophecy and that in Ezekiel concerning Tyre.

1. See how the destruction of Tyre is here foretold. (1.) The haven shall be spoiled, or at least neglected. There shall be no convenient harbour for the reception of the ships of Tarshish, but all *laid waste* (*v.* 1), so that there shall be no house, no dock for the ships to ride in, no inns, or public houses for the seamen, no entering into the port. Perhaps it was choked with sand or blocked up by the enemy. Or, Tyre being destroyed and laid waste, the ships that used to come from Tarshish and Chittim into that port shall now no more enter in; for *it is revealed* or made known *to them*, they have received the dismal news, that Tyre is destroyed and laid waste; so that there is now no more business for them there. See how it is in this world; those that are spoiled by their enemies are commonly slighted by their old friends. (2.) The inhabitants are struck with astonishment. Tyre was an island. The inhabitants of it, who had made a mighty noise and bustle in the world, and revelled with loud huzzas, shall now be still and silent (*v.* 2); they shall sit down as mourners, so overwhelmed with grief that they shall not be able to express it. Their proud boasts of themselves, and defiances of their neighbours, shall be silenced. God can soon quiet those, and strike them dumb, that are the noisy busy people of the world. Be still; for God will do his work (Ps. xlvi. 10; Zech. ii. 13), and you cannot resist him. (3.) The neighbours are amazed, blush, and are in pain for them: *Zidon is ashamed* (*v.* 4), by whom Tyre was at first replenished; for the rolling waves of the sea brought to Zidon this news from Tyre; and there *the strength of the sea*, a high spring-tide, proclaimed saying, "*I travail not, nor bring forth children* now, as I have done. I do not now, as I used to do, bring ship-loads of young people to Tyre, to be bred up there in trade and business," which was the thing that had made Tyre so rich and populous. Or the sea, that used to be loaded with fleets of ships about Tyre, shall now be as desolate as a sorrowful widow that is bereaved of all her children, and has none about her to nourish and bring up. Egypt indeed was a much larger and more considerable kingdom than Tyre was; and yet Tyre had so large a correspondence, upon the account of trade, that all the nations about shall be as much in pain, upon the report of the ruin of that one city, as they would have been, and not long after were, upon the report of the ruin of all Egypt, *v.* 5. Or, as some read it, *When the report shall reach to the Egyptians they shall be sorely pained to hear it of Tyre*, both because of the loss of their trade with that city and because it was a threatening step towards their own ruin; when their neighbour's house was on fire their own was in danger.

124

(4.) The merchants, as many as could, should transmit their effects to other places, and abandon Tyre, where they had raised their estates, and thought they had made them sure (*v.* 6): "*You* that have long been *inhabitants of this isle*" (for it lay off in the sea about half a mile from the continent); "it is time to howl now, for you must pass over to Tarshish. The best course you can take is to make the best of your way to Tarshish, to the sea" (to Tartessus, a city in Spain; so some), "or to some other of your plantations." Those that think their mountain stands strong, and cannot be moved, will find that here they have no continuing city. *The mountains shall depart and the hills be removed.* (5.) Those that could not make their escape must expect no other than to be carried into captivity; for it was the way of conquerors, in those times, to take those they conquered to be bondmen in their own country, and send of their own to be freemen in theirs (*v.* 7): *Her own feet shall carry her afar off to sojourn;* they shall be hurried away on foot into captivity, and many a weary step they shall take towards their own misery. Those that have lived in the greatest pomp and splendour know not what hardships they may be reduced to before they die. (6.) Many of those that attempted to escape should be pursued and fall into the hands of the enemy. Tyre shall *pass through her land as a river* (*v.* 10), running down, one company after another, into the ocean or abyss of misery. Or, though they hasten away as a river, with the greatest swiftness, hoping to outrun the danger, yet *there is no more strength;* they are quickly tired, and cannot get forward, but fall an easy prey into the hands of the enemy. And, as Tyre has no more strength, so her sister Zidon has no more comfort (*v.* 12): "*Thou shalt no more rejoice, O oppressed virgin, daughter of Zidon,* that art now ready to be overpowered by the victorious Chaldeans! Thy turn is next; therefore *arise; pass over to Chittim;* flee to Greece, to Italy, any where to shift for thy own safety; yet *there also shalt thou have no rest;* thy enemies shall disturb thee, and thy own fears shall disquiet thee, where thou hopedst to find some repose." Note, We deceive ourselves if we promise ourselves rest any where in this world. Those that are uneasy in one place will be so in another; and, when God's judgments pursue sinners, they will overtake them.

2. But whence shall all this trouble come? (1.) God will be the author of it; it is a *destruction from the Almighty.* It will be asked (*v.* 8), "*Who has taken this counsel against Tyre?* Who has contrived it? Who has resolved it? Who can find in his heart to lay such a stately lovely city in ruins? And how is it possible that its ruin should be effected?" To this it will be answered, [1.] God has designed it, who is infinitely wise and just, and never did, nor ever will

do, any wrong to any of his creatures (v. 9). *The Lord of hosts*, that has all things at his disposal and gives not account of any of his matters, he *has purposed it.* It shall be done according to the counsel of his will; and that which he aims at herein is *to stain the pride of all glory*, to pollute it, profane it, and throw it to be trodden upon; *and to bring into contempt* and make despicable *all the honourable ones of the earth*, that they may not admire themselves and be admired by others as usual. God did not bring those calamities upon Tyre in a way of sovereignty, in an arbitrary and irresistible power; but he did it to punish the Tyrians for their pride. Many other sins, no doubt, reigned among them—idolatry, sensuality, and oppression; but the sin of pride is fastened upon as that which was the particular ground of God's controversy with Tyre; for he resists the proud. All the world observing and being surprised at the desolation of Tyre, we have here an exposition of it. God tells the world what he meant by it. *First,* He designed to convince men of the vanity and uncertainty of all earthly glory, to show them what a withering, fading, perishing thing it is even when it seems most substantial. It were well if men would be thoroughly taught this lesson, though it were at the expense of so great a destruction. Are men's learning and wealth, their pomp and power, their interest in, and influence upon, all about them, their glory? Are their stately houses, rich furniture, and splendid appearances, their glory? Look upon the ruins of Tyre, and see all this glory stained, and sullied, and buried in the dust. The honourable ones of heaven will be for ever such; but see the grandees of Tyre, some fled into banishment, others forced into captivity, and all impoverished, and you will conclude that the honourable of the earth, even the most honourable, know not how soon they may be brought into contempt. *Secondly,* He designed hereby to prevent their being proud of that glory, their being puffed up, and confident of the continuance of it. Let the ruin of Tyre be a warning to all places and persons to take heed of pride; for it proclaims to all the world that he who exalts himself shall be abased. [2.] God will do it, who has all power in his hand and can do it effectually (v. 11) : *He stretched out his hand over the sea.* He has done so many a time, witness the dividing of the Red Sea and the drowning of Pharaoh in it. He has often shaken the kingdoms that were most secure; and he has now given commandment concerning this merchant-city, to destroy the strongholds thereof. As its beauty shall not intercede for it, but that shall be stained, so its strength shall not protect it, but that shall be broken. If any think it strange that a city so well fortified, and that has so many powerful allies, should be so totally ruined, let them know that it is the Lord of hosts that has given a commandment to destroy the strongholds thereof : and who can gainsay his orders or hinder the execution of them ?

(2.) The Chaldeans shall be the instruments of it (v. 13) : *Behold the land of the Chaldeans;* how easily they and their land were destroyed by the Assyrians. Though their own hands *founded it, set up the towers* of Babylon, and *raised up its palaces,* yet the Assyrians brought it to ruin, whence the Tyrians might infer that as easily as the old Chaldeans were subdued by the Assyrians so easily shall Tyre be vanquished by those new Chaldeans. Babel was built by the Assyrians for *those that dwelt in the wilderness.* It may be rendered *for the ships* (the Assyrians founded it for ships and shipmen that traffic upon those vast rivers Tigris and Euphrates to the Persian and Indian seas), *for men of the desert,* for Babylon is called the *desert of the sea, ch.* xxi. 1. Thus Tyrus was built upon the sea for the like purpose. But the Assyrians (says Dr. Lightfoot) brought that to ruin, now lately, in Hezekiah's time, and so shall Tyre hereafter be brought to ruin by Nebuchadnezzar. If we looked more upon the falling and withering of others, we should not be so confident as we commonly are of the continuance of our own flourishing and standing.

15 And it shall come to pass in that day, that Tyre shall be forgotten seventy years, according to the days of one king : after the end of seventy years shall Tyre sing as a harlot. 16 Take a harp, go about the city, thou harlot that hast been forgotten; make sweet melody, sing many songs, that thou mayest be remembered. 17 And it shall come to pass after the end of seventy years, that the LORD will visit Tyre, and she shall turn to her hire, and shall commit fornication with all the kingdoms of the world upon the face of the earth. 18 And her merchandise and her hire shall be holiness to the LORD : it shall not be treasured nor laid up; for her merchandise shall be for them that dwell before the LORD, to eat sufficiently, and for durable clothing.

Here is, I. The time fixed for the continuance of the desolations of Tyre, which were not to be perpetual desolations : *Tyre shall be forgotten seventy years, v.* 15. So long it shall lie neglected and buried in obscurity. It was destroyed by Nebuchadnezzar much about the time that Jerusalem was, and lay as long as it did in its ruins. See the folly of that proud ambitious conqueror.

What the richer, what the stronger, was he for making himself master of Tyre, when all the inhabitants were driven out of it and he had none of his own subjects to spare for the replenishing and fortifying of it? It is surprising to see what pleasure men could take in destroying cities and making *their memorial perish with them,* Ps. ix. 6. He trampled on the pride of Tyre, and therein served God's purpose; but with greater pride, for which God soon after humbled him.

II. A prophecy of the restoration of Tyre to its glory again : *After the end of seventy years, according to the years of one king,* or one dynasty or family of kings, that of Nebuchadnezzar ; when that expired, the desolations of Tyre came to an end. And we may presume that Cyrus at the same time when he released the Jews, and encouraged them to rebuild Jerusalem, released the Tyrians also, and encouraged them to rebuild Tyre. Thus the prosperity and adversity of places, as well as persons, are *set the one over against the other,* that the most glorious cities may not be secure nor the most ruinous despair. It is foretold, 1. That God's providence shall again smile upon this ruined city (*v.* 17) : *The Lord will visit Tyre* in mercy ; for, though he contend, he will not contend for ever. It is not said, Her old acquaintance shall visit her, the colonies she has planted, and the trading cities she has had correspondence with (they have forgotten her); but, The Lord shall visit her by some unthought-of turn ; he shall cause his indignation towards her to cease, and then things will run of course in their former channel. 2. That she shall use her best endeavours to recover her trade again. She shall sing as a harlot, that has been some time under correction for her lewdness ; but, when she is set at liberty (so violent is the bent of corruption), she will use her old arts of temptation. The Tyrians having returned from their captivity, and those that remained recovering new spirits thereupon, they shall contrive how to force a trade, shall procure the best choice of goods, under-sell their neighbours, and be obliging to all customers ; as a harlot that has been forgotten, when she comes to be spoken of again, recommends herself to company by singing and playing, *takes a harp, goes about the city,* perhaps in the night, serenading, *makes sweet melody, and sings many songs.* These are innocent and allowable diversions, if soberly, and moderately, and modestly used ; but those that value themselves upon their virtue should not be over-fond of them, nor ambitious to excel in them, because, whatever they are now, anciently they were some of the baits with which harlots used to entice fools. Tyre shall now by degrees come to be the mart of nations again ; she shall *return to her hire,* to her traffic, *and shall commit fornication* (that is, she shall have dealings in trade, for the prophet carries on the similitude of a harlot)
126

with all the kingdoms of the world that she had formerly traded with in her prosperity. The love of worldly wealth is a spiritual whoredom, and therefore covetous people are called *adulterers and adulteresses* (James iv. 4), and covetousness is spiritual idolatry. 3. That, having recovered her trade again, she shall make a better use of it than she had done formerly; and this good she should get by her calamities (*v.* 18) : *Her merchandise, and her hire, shall be holiness to the Lord.* The trade of Tyre, and all the gains of her trade, shall be devoted to God and to his honour and employed in his service. It shall not be treasured and hoarded up, as formerly, to be the matter of their pride and the support of their carnal confidence ; but it shall be laid out in acts of piety and charity. What they can spare from the maintenance of themselves and their families *shall be for those that dwell before the Lord,* for the priests, the Lord's ministers, that attend in his temple at Jerusalem ; not to maintain them in pomp and grandeur, but that they and theirs may *eat sufficiently,* may have food convenient for them, with as little as may be of that care which would divert them from their ministration, and that they may have, not rich and fine clothing, but *durable clothing,* that which is strong and lasting, *clothing for old men* (so some read it), as if the priests, though they were young, must wear such plain grave clothing as old men used to wear. Now, (1.) This supposes that religion should be set up in New Tyre, that they should come to the knowledge of the true God and into communion with the Israel of God. Perhaps their being fellow-captives with the Jews in Babylon (who had prophets with them there) disposed them to join with them in their worship there, and turned them from idols, as it cured the Jews of their idolatry : and when they were released with them, and as they had reason to believe for their sakes, when they were settled again in Tyre, they would send gifts and offerings to the temple, and presents to the priests. We find men of Tyre then dwelling in the land of Judah, Neh. xiii. 16. Tyre and Sidon were better disposed to religion in Christ's time than the cities of Israel; for, if Christ had gone among them, *they would have repented,* Matt. xi. 21. And we meet with Christians at Tyre (Acts xxi. 3, 4), and, many years after, did Christianity flourish there. Some of the rabbin refer this prophecy of the conversion of Tyre to the days of the Messiah. (2.) It directs those that have estates to make use of them in the service of God and religion, and to reckon that best laid up which is so laid out. Both the merchandise of the tradesmen and the hire of the day-labourers shall be devoted to God. Both the merchandise (the employment we follow) and the hire (the gain of our employments) must *be holiness to the Lord,* alluding to the motto engraven on the frontlet of the high priest (Exod. xxxix. 30), and to the separation of the tithe under the law, Lev. xxvii. 30. See a promise like this referring to gospel times, Zech. xiv. 20, 21. We must first give up ourselves to be holiness to the Lord before what we do, or have, or get, can be so. When we abide with God in our particular callings, and do common actions after a godly sort—when we abound in works of piety and charity, are liberal in relieving the poor, and supporting the ministry, and encouraging the gospel—then our merchandise and our hire are holiness to the Lord, if we sincerely look at his glory in them. And our wealth need not be treasured and laid up on earth; for it is treasured and laid up in heaven, in *bags that wax not old,* Luke xii. 33.

CHAP. XXIV.

It is agreed that here begins a new sermon, which is continued to the end of chap. xxvii. And in it the prophet, according to the directions he had received, does, in many precious promises, " say to the righteous, It shall be well with them ;" and, in many dreadful threatenings, he says, " Woe to the wicked, it shall be ill with them" (ch. iii. 10, 11); and these are interwoven, that they may illustrate each other. This chapter is mostly threatening; and, as the judgments threatened are very sore and grievous ones, so the people threatened with those judgments are very many. It is not the burden of any particular city or kingdom, as those before, but the burden of the whole earth. The word indeed signifies only the land, because our own land is commonly to us as all the earth. But it is here explained by another word that is not so confined; it is the world (ver. 4); so that it must at least take in a whole neighbourhood of nations. 1. Some think (and very probably) that it is a prophecy of the great havoc that Sennacherib and his Assyrian army should now shortly make of many of the nations in that part of the world. 2. Others make it to point at the like devastations which, about 100 years afterwards, Nebuchadnezzar and his armies should make in the same countries, going from one kingdom to another, not only to conquer them, but to ruin them and lay them waste; for that was the method which those eastern nations took in their wars. The promises that are mixed with the threatenings are intended for the support and comfort of the people of God in those very calamitous times. And, since here are no particular nations named either by whom or on whom those desolations should be brought, I see not but it may refer to both those events. Nay, the scripture has many fulfillings, and we ought to give it its full latitude; and therefore I incline to think that the prophet, from those and the like instances which he had a particular eye to, designs here to represent in general the calamitous state of mankind, and the many miseries which human life is liable to, especially those that attend the wars of the nations. Surely the prophets were sent, not only to foretel particular events, but to form the minds of men to virtue and piety, and for that end their prophecies were written and preserved even for our learning, and therefore ought not to be looked upon as of private interpretation. Now since a thorough conviction of the vanity of the world, and its insufficiency to make us happy, will go far towards bringing us to God, and drawing out our affections towards another world, the prophet here shows what vexation of spirit we must expect to meet with in these things, that we may never take up our rest in them, nor promise ourselves satisfaction any where short of the enjoyment of God. In this chapter we have, I. A threatening of desolating judgments for sin (ver. 1—12), to which is added an assurance that in the midst of them good people should be comforted, ver. 13—15. II. A further threatening of the like desolations (ver. 16—22), to which is added an assurance that in the midst of all God should be glorified.

BEHOLD, the LORD maketh the earth empty, and maketh it waste, and turneth it upside down, and scattereth abroad the inhabitants thereof. 2 And it shall be, as with the people, so with the priest; as with the servant, so with his master; as with the maid, so with her mistress; as with the buyer, so with the seller; as with the lender, so with the borrower; as with the taker of usury, so with the giver of usury to him. 3 The land shall be utterly emptied, and utterly spoiled: for the LORD hath spoken this word. 4 The earth mourneth *and* fadeth away, the world languisheth *and* fadeth away, the haughty people of the earth do languish. 5 The earth also is defiled under the inhabitants thereof; because they have transgressed the laws, changed the ordinance, broken the everlasting covenant. 6 Therefore hath the curse devoured the earth, and they that dwell therein are desolate: therefore the inhabitants of the earth are burned, and few men left. 7 The new wine mourneth, the vine languisheth, all the merry-hearted do sigh. 8 The mirth of tabrets ceaseth, the noise of them that rejoice endeth, the joy of the harp ceaseth. 9 They shall not drink wine with a song; strong drink shall be bitter to them that drink it. 10 The city of confusion is broken down: every house is shut up, that no man may come in. 11 *There is* a crying for wine in the streets; all joy is darkened, the mirth of the land is gone. 12 In the city is left desolation, and the gate is smitten with destruction.

It is a very dark and melancholy scene that this prophecy presents to our view; turn our eyes which way we will, every thing looks dismal. The threatened desolations are here described in a great variety of expressions to the same purport, and all aggravating.

I. The earth is stripped of all its ornaments and looks as if it were taken off its basis; it is made *empty and waste* (v. 1), as if it were reduced to its first chaos, *Tohu* and *Bohu,* nothing but confusion and emptiness again (Gen. i. 2), *without form and void.* It is true earth sometimes signifies the *land,* and so the same word *eretz* is here translated (v. 3): *The land shall be utterly emptied and utterly spoiled;* but I see not why it should not there, as well as v. 1, be translated *the earth;* for mostly commonly, if not always, where it signifies some one particular land it has something joined to it, or at least not far from it, which does so appropriate it; as the land (or earth) of Egypt, or Canaan, or this land, or ours, or yours, or the like. It might indeed refer to some particular country, and an ambiguous word might be used to warrant such an application; for it is good to apply to ourselves, and our own lands, what the scripture says in general of the vanity and vexation of spirit that attend all things here below; but it should seem designed to speak what often happens to many countries, and will do while the world stands, and what may, we know not how soon, happen to our own, and what is the general character of all earthly things : they are empty of all solid comfort and satisfaction ; a little thing makes them waste. We often see numerous families, and plentiful estates, utterly emptied and utterly spoiled, by one judgment or other, or perhaps only by a gradual and insensible decay. Sin has turned the earth *upside down ;* the earth has become quite a different thing to man from what it was when God made it to be his habitation. Sin has also *scattered abroad the inhabitants thereof.* The rebellion at Babel was the occasion of the dispersion there. How many ways are there in which the inhabitants both of towns and of private houses are scattered abroad, so that near relations and old neighbours know nothing of one another! To the same purport is *v. 4 : The earth mourns, and fades away ;* it disappoints those that placed their happiness in it and raised their expectations high from it, and proves not what they promised themselves it would be. *The whole world languishes and fades away,* as hastening towards a dissolution. It is, at the best, like a flower, which withers in the hands of those that please themselves too much with it, and lay it in their bosoms. And, as the earth itself grows old, so those that dwell therein are desolate ; men carry crazy sickly bodies along with them, are often solitary, and confined by affliction, *v.* 6. When the earth languishes, and is not so fruitful as it used to be, then those that dwell therein, that make it their home, and rest, and portion, are desolate ; whereas those that by faith dwell in God can rejoice in him even when the fig-tree does not blossom. If we look abroad, and see in how many places pestilences and burning fevers rage, and what multitudes are swept away by them in a little time, so that sometimes the living scarcely suffice to bury the dead, perhaps we shall understand what the prophet means when he says, *The inhabitants of the earth are burned,* or consumed, some by one disease, others by another, and there are but *few men left,* in comparison. Note, The world we live in is a world of disappointment, a vale of tears, and a dying world ; and the children of men in it are but of few days, and full of trouble.

II. It is God that brings all these calamities upon the earth. *The Lord* that made the earth, and made it fruitful and beautiful, for the service and comfort of man, now *makes it empty and waste* (*v.* 1), for its Creator is and will be its Judge ; he has an incontestible right to pass sentence upon it and an irresistible power to execute that sentence. It is *the Lord* that *has spoken this*

128

word, and he will do the work (*v.* 3); it is his curse that has *devoured the earth* (*v.* 6), the general curse which sin brought upon *the ground for man's sake* (Gen. iii. 17), and all the particular curses which families and countries bring upon themselves by their enormous wickedness. See the power of God's curse, how it makes all empty and lays all waste ; those whom he curses are cursed indeed.

III. Persons of all ranks and conditions shall share in these calamities (*v.* 2) : *It shall be as with the people, so with the priest,* &c. This is true of many of the common calamities of human life ; all are subject to the same diseases of body, sorrows of mind, afflictions in relations, and the like. There is one event to those of very different stations ; time and chance happen to them all. It is in a special manner true of the destroying judgments which God sometimes brings upon sinful nations ; when he pleases he can make them universal, so that none shall escape them or be exempt from them ; whether men have little or much, they shall lose it all. Those of the meaner rank smart first by famine ; but those of the higher rank go first into captivity, while the poor of the land are left. It shall be all alike, 1. With high and low : *As with the people, so with the priest,* or prince. The dignity of magistrates and ministers, and the respect and reverence due to both, shall not secure them. *The faces of elders are not honoured,* Lam. v. 12. The priests had been as corrupt and wicked as the people ; and, if their character served not to restrain them from sin, how can they expect it should serve to secure them from judgments ? In both it is *like people, like priest,* Hosea iv. 8, 9. 2. With bond and free : *As with the servant, so with his master ; as with the maid, so with her mistress.* They have all corrupted their way, and therefore will all be made miserable when the earth is made waste. 3. With rich and poor. Those that have money beforehand, that are purchasing, and letting out money to interest, will fare no better than those that are so impoverished that they are forced to sell their estates and take up money at interest. There are judgments short of the great day of judgment in which rich and poor meet together. Let not those that are advanced in the world set their inferiors at too great a distance, because they know not how soon they may be set upon a level with them. *The rich man's wealth is his strong city* in his own conceit; but it does not always prove so.

IV. It is sin that brings these calamities upon the earth. The earth is made empty, and fades away, because it *is defiled under the inhabitants thereof* (*v.* 5) ; it is polluted by the sins of men, and therefore it is made desolate by the judgments of God. Such is the filthy nature of sin that it defiles the earth itself under the sinful inhabitants thereof, and it is rendered unpleasant in the eyes of God and good men. See Lev. xviii. 25, 27, 28. Blood, in particular, defiles the land, Num. xxxv. 33. The earth never spues out its inhabitants till they have first defiled it by their sins. Why, what have they done ? 1. They have transgressed the laws of their creation, not answered the ends of it. The bonds of the law of nature have been broken by them, and they have cast from them the cords of their obligations to the God of nature. 2. *They have changed the ordinances* of revealed religion, those of them that have had the benefit of that. *They have neglected the ordinances* (so some read it), and have made no conscience of observing them. They have passed over the laws, in the commission of sin, and have passed by the ordinance, in the omission of duty. 3. Herein they have *broken the everlasting covenant,* which is a perpetual bond and will be to those that keep it a perpetual blessing. It is God's wonderful condescension that he is pleased to deal with men in a covenant-way, to do them good, and thereby oblige them to do him service. Even those that had no benefit by God's covenant with Abraham had benefit by his covenant with Noah and his sons, which is called *an everlasting covenant,* his covenant with day and night; but they observe not the precepts of the sons of Noah, they acknowledge not God's goodness in the day and night, nor study to make him any grateful returns, and so break the everlasting covenant and defeat the gracious designs and intentions of it.

V. These judgments shall humble men's pride and mar their mirth. When the earth is made empty, 1. It is a great mortification to men's pride (*v.* 4): *The haughty people of the earth do languish;* for they have lost that which supported their pride, and for which they magnified themselves. As for those that have held their heads highest, God can make them hang the head. 2. It is a great damp to men's jollity. This is enlarged upon much (*v.* 7—9): *All the merry-hearted do sigh.* Such is the nature of carnal mirth, it is but *as the crackling of thorns under a pot,* Eccl. vii. 6. Great laughters commonly end in a sigh. Those that make the world their chief joy cannot rejoice evermore. When God sends his judgments into the earth he designs thereby to make those serious that were wholly addicted to their pleasures. *Let your laughter be turned into mourning.* When the earth is emptied the *noise of those that rejoice in it ends.* Carnal joy is a noisy thing; but the noise of it will soon be at an end, and the end of it is heaviness. Two things are made use of to excite and express vain mirth, and the jovial crew is here deprived of both :—
(1.) Drinking : *The new wine mourns;* it has grown sour for want of drinking ; for, how proper soever it may be for the heavy heart (Prov. xxxi. 6), it does not relish to them

as it does to the merry-hearted. *The vine languishes,* and gives little hopes of a vintage, and therefore *the merry-hearted do sigh;* for they know no other gladness than that of their corn, and wine, and oil increasing (Ps. iv. 7), and, if you *destroy their vines and their fig-trees, you make all their mirth to cease,* Hosea ii. 11, 12. *They shall not* now *drink wine with a song* and with huzzas, as they used to do, but rather drink it with a sigh ; nay, *Strong drink shall be bitter to those that drink it,* because they cannot but mingle their tears with it ; or, through sickness, they have lost the relish of it. God has many ways to embitter wine and strong drink to those that love them and have the highest gust of them : distemper of body, anguish of mind, the ruin of the estate or country, will make the strong drink bitter and all the delights of sense tasteless and insipid. (2.) Music : *The mirth of tabrets ceases, and the joy of the harp,* which used to be at their feasts, *ch.* v. 12. The captives in Babylon hang their harps on the willow trees. In short, *All joy is darkened ;* there is not a pleasant look to be seen, nor has any one power to force a smile ; all *the mirth of the land is gone* (*v.* 11); and, if it was that mirth which Solomon calls *madness,* there is no great loss of it.

VI. The cities will in a particular manner feel from these desolations of the country (*v.* 10): *The city of confusion is broken, is broken down* (so we read it) ; it lies exposed to invading powers, not only by the breaking down of its walls, but by the confusion that the inhabitants are in. *Every house is shut up,* perhaps by reason of the plague, which has burned or consumed the inhabitants, so that there are *few men left, v.* 6. Houses infected are usually shut up that no man may come in. Or they are shut up because they are deserted and uninhabited. *There is a crying for wine,* that is, for the spoiling of the vintage, so that there is likely to be no wine. *In the city,* in Jerusalem itself, that had been so much frequented, there shall be left nothing but *desolation ;* grass shall grow in the streets, and *the gate is smitten with destruction* (*v.* 12) ; all that used to pass and repass through the gate are smitten, and all the strength of the city is cut off. How soon can God make a city of order a city of confusion, and then it will soon be a city of desolation !

13 When thus it shall be in the midst of the land among the people, *there shall be* as the shaking of an olive-tree, *and* as the gleaning grapes when the vintage is done. 14 They shall lift up their voice, they shall sing for the majesty of the LORD, they shall cry aloud from the sea. 15 Wherefore glorify ye the LORD

in the fires, *even* the name of the LORD God of Israel in the isles of the sea.

Here is mercy remembered in the midst of wrath. In Judah and Jerusalem, and the neighbouring countries, when they are overrun by the enemy, Sennacherib or Nebuchadnezzar, there shall be a remnant preserved from the general ruin, and it shall be a devout and pious remnant. And this method God usually observes when his judgments are abroad; he does not make a full end, *ch.* vi. 13. Or we may take it thus: Though the greatest part of mankind have all their comfort ruined by the emptying of the earth, and the making of that desolate, yet there are some few who understand their interests better, who have laid up their treasure in heaven and not in things below, and therefore can keep up their comfort and joy in God even *when the earth mourns and fades away.* Observe,

I. The small number of this remnant, *v.* 13. When all goes to ruin *there shall be as the shaking of an olive-tree, and the gleaning grapes,* here and there one who shall escape the common calamity (as Noah and his family when the old world was drowned), that shall be able to sit down upon a heap of the ruins of all their creature comforts, and even then rejoice in the Lord (Hab. iii. 16—18), who, when all faces gather blackness, can lift up their heads with joy, Luke xxi. 26, 28. These few are dispersed, and at a distance from each other, like the gleanings of the olive-tree; and they are concealed, hid under the leaves. The Lord only knows those that are his; the world does not.

II. The great devotion of this remnant, which is the greater for their having so narrowly escaped this great destruction (*v.* 14): *They shall lift up their voice; they shall sing* 1. They shall sing for joy in their deliverance. When the mirth of carnal worldlings ceases the joy of the saints is as lively as ever; when the merry-hearted do sigh because the vine languishes the upright-hearted do sing because the covenant of grace, the fountain of their comforts and the foundation of their hopes, never fails. Those that rejoice in the Lord can rejoice in tribulation, and by faith may be in triumphs when all about them are in tears. 2. They shall sing to the glory and praise of God, shall sing not only for the mercy but *for the majesty of the Lord.* Their songs are awful and serious, and in their spiritual joys they have a reverend regard to the greatness of God, and keep at a humble distance when they attend him with their praises. The majesty of the Lord, which is matter of terror to wicked people, furnishes the saints with songs of praise. They shall sing for the magnificence, or transcendant excellency, of the Lord, shown both in his judgments and in his mercies; for we must sing, and sing unto him, of both, Ps. ci. 1. Those
130

who have made, or are making, their escape from the land (that being emptied and made desolate) to the sea and the isles of the sea, shall thence cry aloud; their dispersion shall help to spread the knowledge of God, and they shall make even remote shores to ring with his praises. It is much for the honour of God if those who fear him rejoice in him, and praise him, even in the most melancholy times.

III. Their holy zeal to excite others to the same devotion (*v.* 15); they encourage their fellow-sufferers to do likewise. 1. Those who are *in the fires,* in the furnace of affliction, those fires by which the *inhabitants of the earth are burned, v.* 6. Or in the valleys, the low, dark, dirty places. 2. Those who are *in the isles of the sea,* whither they are banished, or are forced to flee for shelter, and hide themselves remote from all their friends. They went *through fire and water* (Ps. lxvi. 12); yet in both let them glorify the Lord, and glorify him as the Lord God of Israel. Those who through grace can glory in tribulation ought to glorify God in tribulation, and give him thanks for their comforts, which abound as their afflictions do abound. We must in every fire, even the hottest, in every isle, even the remotest, keep up our good thoughts of God. When, though he slay us, yet we trust in him—when, though for his sake we are killed all the day long, yet none of these things move us—then we glorify the Lord in the fires. Thus the three children, and the martyrs that sang at the stake.

16 From the uttermost part of the earth have we heard songs, *even* glory to the righteous. But I said, My leanness, my leanness, woe unto me! The treacherous dealers have dealt treacherously; yea, the treacherous dealers have dealt very treacherously. 17 Fear, and the pit, and the snare, *are* upon thee, O inhabitant of the earth. 18 And it shall come to pass, *that* he who fleeth from the noise of the fear shall fall into the pit; and he that cometh up out of the midst of the pit shall be taken in the snare: for the windows from on high are open, and the foundations of the earth do shake. 19 The earth is utterly broken down, the earth is clean dissolved, the earth is moved exceedingly. 20 The earth shall reel to and fro like a drunkard, and shall be removed like a cottage; and the transgression thereof shall be heavy upon it; and it shall fall and not rise again. 21 And it shall

come to pass in that day, *that* the LORD shall punish the host of the high ones *that are* on high, and the kings of the earth upon the earth. 22 And they shall be gathered together, *as* prisoners are gathered in the pit, and shall be shut up in the prison, and after many days shall they be visited. 23 Then the moon shall be confounded, and the sun ashamed, when the LORD of hosts shall reign in mount Zion, and in Jerusalem, and before his ancients gloriously.

These verses, as those before, plainly speak,

I. Coi .fort to saints. They may be driven, by the common calamities of the places where they live, into *the uttermost parts of the earth*, or perhaps they are forced thither for their religion; but there they are singing, not sighing. Thence have we heard songs, and it is a comfort to us to hear them, to hear that good people carry their religion along with them even to the most distant regions, to hear that God visits them there and gives encouragement to hope that he will gather them thence, Deut. xxx. 4. And this is their song, *even glory to the righteous:* the word is singular, and may refer to *the righteous God*, who is just in all he has brought upon us. This is glorifying the Lord in the fires. Or the meaning may be, "These songs redound to the glory or beauty of the righteous that sing them." We do the greatest honour imaginable to ourselves when we employ ourselves in honouring and glorifying God. This may have reference to the sending of the gospel to the uttermost parts of the earth, as far off as this island of ours, in the days of the Messiah, the glad tidings of which are echoed back in songs heard thence, from churches planted there, even glory to the righteous God, agreeing with the angels' song, *Glory be to God in the highest*, and glory to all righteous men; for the work of redemption was ordained before the world for our glory.

II. Terror to sinners. The prophet, having comforted himself and others with the prospect of a saved remnant, returns to lament the miseries he saw breaking in like a mighty torrent upon the earth: "*But I said, My leanness! my leanness! woe unto me!* The very thought of it frets me, and makes me lean," *v.* 16. He foresees,

1. The prevalency of sin, that iniquity should abound (*v.* 16): *The treacherous dealers have dealt treacherously;* this is itself a judgment, and that which provokes God to bring other judgments. (1.) Men are false to one another; there is no faith in man, but a universal dishonesty. Truth, that sacred bond of society, has departed,

and there is nothing but treachery in men's dealings. See Jer. ix. 1, 2. (2.) They are all false to their God; as to him, and their covenant with him, the children of men are all treacherous dealers, and have dealt very treacherously with their God, in departing from their allegiance to him. This is the original, and this the aggravation, of the sin of the world; and, when men have been false to their God, how should they be true to any other?

2. The prevalency of wrath and judgment for that sin. (1.) The inhabitants of the earth will be pursued from time to time, from place to place, by one mischief or other (*v.* 17, 18): *Fear, and the pit, and the snare* (fear of the pit and the snare) are upon them wherever they are; for the sons of men know not what evil they may suddenly be snared in, Eccl. ix. 12. These three words seem to be chosen for the sake of an elegant paranomasia, or, as we now scornfully call it, a jingle of words: *Pachad, and Pachath, and Pach;* but the meaning is plain (*v.* 18), that *evil pursues sinners* (Prov. xiii. 21), that the curse shall overtake the disobedient (Deut. xxviii. 15), that those who are secure because they have escaped one judgment know not how soon another may arrest them. What this prophet threatens all the inhabitants of the earth with another makes part of the judgment of Moab, Jer. xlviii. 43, 44. But it is a common instance of the calamitous state of human life that when we seek to avoid one mischief we fall into a worse, and that the end of one trouble is often the beginning of another; so that we are least safe when we are most secure. (2.) The earth itself will be shaken to pieces. It will be literally so at last, when all *the works therein shall be burnt up;* and it is often figuratively so before that period. *The windows from on high are open* to pour down wrath, as in the universal deluge. *Upon the wicked God shall rain snares* (Ps. xi. 6); and, the fountains of the great deep being broken up, *the foundations of the earth do shake* of course, the frame of nature is unhinged, and all is in confusion. See how elegantly this is expressed (*v.* 19, 20): *The earth is utterly broken down; it is clean dissolved; it is moved exceedingly*, moved out of its place. *God shakes heaven and earth*, Hag. ii. 6. See the misery of those who lay up their treasure in the things of the earth and mind those things; they place their confidence in that which will shortly be *utterly broken down and dissolved. The earth shall reel to and fro like a drunkard;* so unsteady, so uncertain, are all the motions of these things. Worldly men dwell in it as in a palace, as in a castle, as in an impregnable tower; but *it shall be removed like a cottage*, so easily, so suddenly, and with so little loss to the great landlord. The pulling down of the earth will be but like the pulling down of *a*

cottage, which the country is willing to be rid of, because it does but harbour beggars; and therefore no care is taken to rebuild it: It *shall fall, and not rise again;* but there shall be new heavens and a new earth, in which shall dwell nothing but righteousness. But what is it that shakes the earth thus and sinks it? It is the transgression thereof that shall be heavy upon it. Note, Sin is a burden to the whole creation; it is a heavy burden, a burden under which it groans now and will sink at last. Sin is the ruin of states, and kingdoms, and families; they fall under the weight of that *talent of lead,* Zech. v 7, 8. (3.) God will have a particular controversy with the kings and great men of the earth (*v.* 21): *He will punish the host of the high ones.* Hosts of princes are no more before God than hosts of common men; what can a host of high ones do with their combined force when the Most High, the Lord of hosts, contends with them to abase their height, and scatter their hosts, and break all their confederacies? The high ones, that are on high, that are puffed up with their height and grandeur, that think themselves so high that they are out of the reach of any danger, God will visit upon them all their pride and cruelty, with which they have oppressed and injured their neighbours and subjects, and it shall now return upon their own heads. *The kings of the earth* shall now be reckoned with *upon the earth,* to show that verily there is a God that judges in the earth and will render to the proudest of kings according to the fruit of their doings. Let those that are trampled upon by the high ones of the earth comfort themselves with this, that though they cannot, dare not, must not, resist them, yet there is a God that will call them to an account, that will triumph over them upon their own dunghill: for the earth they are kings of is in the eye of God no better. This is general only. It is particularly foretold (*v.* 22) that they shall be *gathered together as prisoners,* convicted condemned prisoners, are *gathered in the pit,* or dungeon, and there they shall *be shut up* under close confinement. The kings and high ones, who took all possible liberty themselves, and took a pride and pleasure in shutting up others, shall now be themselves shut up. Let not the free man glory in his freedom, any more than the strong man in his strength, for he knows not what restraints he is reserved for. But *after many days they shall be visited,* either, [1.] They shall be visited in wrath; it is the same word, in another form, that is used (*v.* 21), *the Lord shall punish* them; they shall be reserved to the day of execution, as condemned prisoners are, and as fallen angels are *reserved in chains of darkness to the judgment of the great day,* Jude 6. Let this account for the delays of divine vengeance; sentence is not executed speedily, because execution-day has not yet come, and

perhaps will not come till after many days; but it is certain that the wicked is reserved for the day of destruction, and is therefore preserved in the mean time, but *shall be brought forth to the day of wrath,* Job xxi. 30. Let us therefore judge nothing before the time. [2.] They shall be visited in mercy, and be discharged from their imprisonment, and shall again obtain, if not their dignity, yet their liberty. Nebuchadnezzar, in his conquests, made many kings and princes his captives, and kept them in the dungeon in Babylon, and, among the rest, Jehoiachin king of Judah; but after many days, when Nebuchadnezzar's head was laid, his son visited them, and granted (as should seem) some reviving to them all in their bondage; for it is made an instance of his particular kindness to Jehoiachin that he *set his throne above the throne of the rest of the kings that were with him,* Jer. lii. 32. If we apply this to the general state of mankind, it imports a revolution of conditions; those that were high are punished, those that were punished are relieved, after many days, that none in this world may be secure though their condition be ever so prosperous, nor any despair though their condition be ever so deplorable.

3. Glory to God in all this, *v.* 23. When all this comes to pass, when the proud enemies of God's church are humbled and brought down, (1.) Then it shall appear, beyond contradiction, that the Lord reigns, which is always true, but not always alike evident. When the kings of the earth are punished for their tyranny and oppression, then it is proclaimed and proved to all the world that God is King of kings—King above them, by whom they are conquerable—King over them, to whom they are accountable—that he reigns as *Lord of hosts,* of all hosts, of their hosts,—that he reigns *in Mount Zion, and in Jerusalem,* in his church, for the honour and welfare of that, pursuant to the promises on which that is founded, reigns in his word and ordinances,—that he reigns *before his ancients,* before all his saints, especially before his ministers, the elders of his church, who have their eye upon all the out-goings of his power and providence, and, in all these events, observe his hand. God's ancients, the old disciples, the experienced Christians, that have often, when they have been perplexed, gone into the sanctuary of God in Zion and Jerusalem, and acquainted themselves with his manifestations of himself there, shall see more than others of God's dominion and sovereignty in these operations of his providence. (2.) Then it shall appear, beyond comparison, that he reigns *gloriously,* in such brightness and lustre that *the moon shall be confounded and the sun ashamed,* as the smaller lights are eclipsed and extinguished by the greater. Great men, who thought themselves to have as bright a lustre and as vast

a dominion as the sun and moon, shall be ashamed when God appears above them, much more when he appears against them. Then shall *their faces be filled with shame,* that they may seek God's name. The eastern nations worshipped the sun and moon; but, when God shall appear so gloriously for his people against his and their enemies, all these pretended deities shall be ashamed that ever they received the homage of their deluded worshippers. The glory of the Creator infinitely outshines the glory of the brightest creatures. In the great day, when the Judge of heaven and earth shall shine forth in his glory, *the sun shall* by his transcendent lustre *be turned into darkness and the moon into blood.*

CHAP. XXV.

After the threatenings of wrath in the foregoing chapter we have here, I. Thankful praises for what God had done, which the prophet, in the name of the church, offers up to God, and teaches us to offer the like, ver. 1—5. II. Precious promises of what God would yet further do for his church, especially in the grace of the gospel, ver. 6—8. III. The church's triumph in God over her enemies thereupon, ver. 9—12. This chapter looks as pleasantly upon the church as the former looked dreadfully upon the world.

O LORD, thou *art* my God; I will exalt thee, I will praise thy name; for thou hast done wonderful *things; thy* counsels of old *are* faithfulness *and* truth. 2 For thou hast made of a city an heap; *of* a defenced city a ruin: a palace of strangers to be no city; it shall never be built. 3 Therefore shall the strong people glorify thee, the city of the terrible nations shall fear thee. 4 For thou hast been a strength to the poor, a strength to the needy in his distress, a refuge from the storm, a shadow from the heat, when the blast of the terrible ones *is* as a storm *against* the wall. 5 Thou shalt bring down the noise of strangers, as the heat in a dry place; *even* the heat with the shadow of a cloud: the branch of the terrible ones shall be brought low.

It is said in the close of the foregoing chapter that the *Lord of hosts shall reign gloriously;* now, in compliance with this, the prophet here speaks of *the glorious majesty of his kingdom* (Ps. cxlv. 12), and gives him the glory of it; and, however this prophecy might have an accomplishment in the destruction of Babylon and the deliverance of the Jews out of their captivity there, it seems to look further, to the praises that should be offered up to God by the gospel church for Christ's victories over our spiritual enemies and the comforts he has provided for all believers. Here,

I. The prophet determines to praise God himself; for those that would stir up others should in the first place stir up themselves to praise God (*v.* 1): "*O Lord! thou art my God,* a God in covenant with me." When God is punishing *the kings of the earth upon the earth,* and making them to tremble before him, a poor prophet can go to him, and, with a humble boldness, say, O Lord! thou *art my God,* and therefore *I will exalt thee, I will praise thy name.* Those that have the Lord for their God are bound to praise him; for *therefore* he took us to be his people *that we might be unto him for a name and for a praise,* Jer. xiii. 11. In praising God we exalt him; not that we can make him higher than he is, but we must make him to appear to ourselves and others higher than he does. See Exod. xv. 2.

II. He pleases himself with the thought that others also shall be brought to praise God, *v.* 3. "*Therefore,* because of the *desolations thou hast made in the earth* by thy providence (Ps. xlvi. 8) and the just vengeance thou hast taken on thy and thy church's enemies, *therefore shall the strong people glorify thee* in concert, *and the city* (the metropolis) *of the terrible nations* (or the cities of such nations) *shall fear thee.*" This may be understood, 1. Of those people that have been strong and terrible against God. Those that have been enemies to God's kingdom, and have fought against the interests of it with a great deal of strength and terror, shall either be converted, and glorify God by joining with his people in his service, or at least convinced, so as to own themselves conquered. Those that have been the terror of the mighty shall be forced to tremble before the judgments of God and call in vain to rocks and mountains to hide them. Or, 2. Of those that shall be now made strong and terrible for God and by him, though before they were weak and trampled upon. God shall so visibly appear for and with those that fear him and glorify him that all shall acknowledge them a strong people and shall stand in awe of them. There was a time when *many of the people of the land became Jews, for the fear of the Jews fell upon them* (Esther viii. 17), and when those that knew their God were strong and did exploits (Dan. xi. 32), for which they glorified God.

III. He observes what is, and ought to be, the matter of this praise. We and others must exalt God and praise him; for, 1. He has done wonders, according to the counsel of his own will, *v.* 1. We exalt God by admiring what he has done as truly wonderful, wonderful proofs of his power beyond what any creature could perform, and wonderful proofs of his goodness beyond what such sinful creatures as we are could expect. These *wonderful things,* which are new and surprising to us, and altogether unthought of, are according to his *counsels of old,* devised by his wisdom and designed for his own glory and the comfort of his people. All the operations of providence are according to God's eternal counsels (and those faithfulness and truth itself), all consonant to his attributes, consistent with one another, and sure to be accomplished in their season. 2. He has in particular humbled the pride, and broken the power, of the mighty ones of the earth (*v.* 2): "*Thou hast made of a city,* of many a city, *a heap* of rubbish. Of many a defenced city, that thought itself well guarded by nature and art, and the multitude and courage of its militia, thou hast made a ruin." What created strength can hold out against Omnipotence? "Many a city so richly built that it might be called a *palace,* and so much frequented and visited by persons of the best rank from all parts that it might be called a *palace of strangers,* thou hast made to be no city; it is levelled with the ground, and not one stone left upon another, and it shall never be built again." This has been the case of many cities in divers parts of the world, and in our own nation particularly; cities that flourished once have gone to decay and are lost, and it is scarcely known (except by urns or coins digged up out of the earth) where they stood. How many of the cities of Israel have long since been heaps and ruins! God hereby teaches us that *here we have no continuing city* and must therefore seek one to come which will never be a ruin or go to decay. 3. He has seasonably relieved and succoured his necessitous and distressed people (*v.* 4): *Thou hast been a strength to the poor, a strength to the needy.* As God weakens the strong that are proud and secure, so he strengthens the weak that are humble and serious, and stay themselves upon him. Nay, he not only makes them strong, but he is himself their strength; for in him they strengthen themselves, and it is his favour that is the *strength of their hearts.* He is a *strength to the needy in his distress,* when he needs strength, and when his distress drives him to God. And, as he strengthens them against their inward decays, so he shelters them from outward assaults. He is *a refuge from the storm* of rain or hail, and *a shadow from the* scorching *heat* of the sun in summer. God is a sufficient protection to his people in all weathers, hot and cold, wet and dry. The armour of righteousness serves both *on the right hand* and *on the left,* 2 Cor. vi. 7. Whatever dangers or troubles God's people may be in, effectual care is taken that they shall sustain no real hurt or damage. When perils are most threatening and alarming God will then appear for the safety of his people: *When the blast of the terrible ones is as a storm against the wall,* which makes a great noise, but cannot overthrow the wall The enemies of God's poor are terrible ones; they do all they can to make themselves so to them. Their rage is like a blast of wind, loud, and blustering, and furious; but, like the wind, it is under a divine check; for God *holds the winds in his fist,* and God will be such a shelter to his people that they shall

be able to stand the shock, keep their ground, and maintain their integrity and peace. A storm beating on a ship tosses it, but that which beats on a wall never stirs it, Ps.lxxvi. 10; cxxxviii. 7.4. That he does and will shelter those that trust in him from the insolence of their proud oppressors (*v.* 5): *Thou shalt,* or thou dost, *bring down the noise of strangers;* thou shalt abate and still it, as *the heat in a dry place* is abated and moderated *by the shadow of a cloud* interposing. *The branch,* or rather the song or triumph, *of the terrible ones shall be brought low,* and they shall be made to change their note and lower their voice. Observe here, (1.) The oppressors of God's people are called *strangers;* for they forget that those they oppress are made of the same mould, of the same blood, with them. They are called *terrible ones;* for so they affect to be, rather than amiable ones: they would rather be feared than loved. (2.) Their insolence towards the people of God is noisy and hot, and that is all; it is but the noise of strangers, who think to carry their point by hectoring and bullying all that stand in their way, and talking big. *Pharaoh king of Egypt is but a noise,* Jer. xlvi. 17. It is like the heat of the sun scorching in the middle of the day; but where is it when the sun has set? (3) Their noise, and heat, and all their triumph, will be humbled and brought low, when their hopes are baffled and all their honours laid in the dust. The branches, even the top branches, of the terrible ones, will be broken off, and thrown to the dunghill. (4.) If the labourers in God's vineyard be at any time called to *bear the burden and heat of the day,* he will find some way or other to refresh them, as with the shadow of a cloud, that they may not be pressed above measure.

6 And in this mountain shall the LORD of hosts make unto all people a feast of fat things, a feast of wines on the lees, of fat things full of marrow, of wines on the lees well refined. 7 And he will destroy in this mountain the face of the covering cast over all people, and the veil that is spread over all nations. 8 He will swallow up death in victory; and the Lord GOD will wipe away tears from off all faces; and the rebuke of his people shall he take away from off all the earth: for the LORD hath spoken *it.*

If we suppose (as many do) that this refers to the great joy which there should be in Zion and Jerusalem when the army of the Assyrians was routed by an angel, or when the Jews were released out of their captivity in Babylon, or upon occasion of some other equally surprising deliverance, yet we cannot avoid making it to look further, to the grace of the gospel and the glory which is the crown and consummation of that grace ; for it is at our resurrection through Christ that the saying here written *shall be brought to pass ;* then, and not till then (if we may believe St. Paul), it shall have its full accomplishment : *Death is swallowed up in victory,* 1 Cor. xv. 54. This is a key to the rest of the promises here connected together. And so we have here a prophecy of the salvation and the grace brought unto us by Jesus Christ, into which *the prophets enquired and searched diligently,* 1 Pet. i 10.

I. That the grace of the gospel should be a royal feast for all people ; not like that of Ahasuerus, which was intended only to show the grandeur of the master of the feast (Esther i. 4) ; for this is intended to gratify the guests, and therefore, whereas all *there* was for show, all *here* is for substance. The preparations made in the gospel for the kind reception of penitents and supplicants with God are often in the New Testament set forth by the similitude of *a feast,* as Matt. xxii. 1. &c., which seems to be borrowed from this prophecy. 1. God himself is the Master of the feast, and we may be sure he prepares like himself, as becomes him to give, rather than as becomes us to receive. *The Lord of hosts* makes this feast. 2. The guests invited are *all people,* Gentiles as well as Jews. *Go preach the gospel to every creature.* There is enough for all, and whoever will may come, and partake freely, even those that are gathered out of the highways and the hedges. 3. The place is *Mount Zion.* Thence the preaching of the gospel takes rise : the preachers must begin at Jerusalem. The gospel church is the Jerusalem that is above; there this feast is made, and to it all the invited guests must go. 4. The provision is very rich, and every thing is of the best. It is a *feast,* which supposes abundance and variety; it is a continual feast to believers, it is their own fault if it be not. It is a *feast of fat things and full of marrow ;* so relishing, so nourishing, are the comforts of the gospel to all those that feast upon them and digest them. The returning prodigal was entertained with the fatted calf; and David has that pleasure in communion with God with which his soul is satisfied as with marrow and fatness. It is a feast *of wines on the lees,* the strongest-bodied wines, that have been kept long upon the lees, and then are well refined from them, so that they are clear and fine. There is that in the gospel which, like wine soberly used, makes glad the heart and raises the spirits, and is fit for those that are of a heavy heart, being under convictions of sin and mourning for it, that they may drink and forget their misery (for that is the proper use of wine—it is a cordial for those that need it, Prov. xxxi. 6, 7), may

be of good cheer, knowing that their sins are forgiven, and may be vigorous in their spiritual work and warfare, as a strong man refreshed with wine.

II. That the world should be freed from that darkness of ignorance and mistake in the mists of which it had been so long lost and buried (*v.* 7) : *He will destroy in this mountain the face of the covering* (the covering of the face) with which all people are covered (hood-winked or blind-folded) so that they cannot see their way nor go about their work, and by reason of which they wander endlessly. Their faces are covered as those of men condemned, or dead men. There is *a veil spread over all nations,* for they all sit in darkness ; and no marvel, when the Jews themselves, among whom *God was known,* had a *veil upon their hearts,* 2 Cor. iii. 15. But this veil the Lord will destroy, by the light of his gospel shining in the world, and the power of his Spirit opening men's eyes to receive it. He will raise those to spiritual life that have long been dead in trespasses and sins.

III. That death should be conquered, the power of it broken, and the property of it altered : *He will swallow up death in victory,* v. 8. 1. Christ will himself, in his resurrection, triumph over death, will break its bands, its bars, asunder, and cast away all its cords. The grave seemed to swallow him up, but really he swallowed it up. 2. The happiness of the saints shall be out of the reach of death, which puts a period to all the enjoyments of this world, embitters them, and stains the beauty of them. 3. Believers may triumph over death, and look upon it as a conquered enemy : *O death ! where is thy sting?* 4. When the dead bodies of the saints shall be raised at the great day, and their mortality swallowed up of life, then death will be for ever swallowed up of victory ; and it is the last enemy.

IV. That grief shall be banished, and there shall be perfect and endless joy : *The Lord God will wipe away tears from off all faces.* Those that mourn for sin shall be comforted and have their consciences pacified. In the covenant of grace there shall be that provided which is sufficient to counterbalance all the sorrows of this present time, to wipe away our tears, and to refresh us. Those particularly that suffer for Christ shall have consolations abounding as their afflictions do abound. But in the joys of heaven, and nowhere short of them, will fully be *brought to pass this saying,* as that before, for there it is that God shall *wipe away all tears,* Rev. vii. 17 ; xxi. 4. And *there shall be no more sorrow,* because *there shall be no more death.* The hope of this should now wipe away all excessive tears, all the weeping that hinders sowing.

V. That all the reproach cast upon religion and the serious professors of it shall be for ever rolled away : *The rebuke of his people*, which they have long lain under, the calumnies and misrepresentations by which they have been blackened, the insolence and cruelty with which their persecutors have trampled on them and trodden them down, *shall be taken away.* Their righteousness shall be brought forth as the light, in the view of all the world, who shall be convinced that they are not such as they have been invidiously characterized; and so their salvation from the injuries done them as such shall be wrought out. Sometimes in this world God does that for his people which *takes away their reproach from among men.* However, it will be done effectually at the great day; for the *Lord has spoken it*, who can, and will, make it good. Let us patiently bear sorrow and shame now, and improve both; for shortly both will be done away.

9 And it shall be said in that day, Lo, this *is* our God; we have waited for him, and he will save us: this *is* the LORD; we have waited for him, we will be glad and rejoice in his salvation. 10 For in this mountain shall the hand of the LORD rest, and Moab shall be trodden down under him, even as straw is trodden down for the dunghill. 11 And he shall spread forth his hands in the midst of them, as he that swimmeth spreadeth forth *his hands* to swim: and he shall bring down their pride together with the spoils of their hands. 12 And the fortress of the high fort of thy walls shall he bring down, lay low, *and* bring to the ground, *even* to the dust.

Here is, I. The welcome which the church shall give to these blessings promised in the foregoing verses (*v.* 9): *It shall be said in that day*, with a humble holy triumph and exultation, *Lo, this is our God; we have waited for him!* Thus will the deliverance of the church out of long and sore troubles be celebrated; thus will it be as life from the dead. With such transports of joy and praise will those entertain the glad tidings of the Redeemer who looked for him, and for redemption in Jerusalem by him; and with such a triumphant song as this will glorified saints *enter into the joy of their Lord.* 1. God himself must have the glory of all: " *Lo, this is our God, this is the Lord.* This which is done is his doing, and it is marvellous in our eyes. Herein he has done like himself, has magnified his own wisdom, power, and goodness. Herein he has done for us like our God, a God in covenant with us, and whom we serve." Note, Our triumphs must not terminate in

what God does for us and gives to us, but must pass through them to himself, who is the author and giver of them: *This is our God.* Have any of the nations of the earth such a God to trust to? No, *their rock is not as our rock. There is none like unto the God of Jeshurun.* 2. The longer it has been expected the more welcome it is. " This is he whom we have waited for, in dependence upon his word of promise, and a full assurance that he would come in the set time, in due time, and therefore we were willing to tarry his time; and now we find it is not in vain to wait for him, for the mercy comes at last, with an abundant recompence for the delay." 3. It is matter of joy unspeakable: " *We will be glad and rejoice in his salvation.* We that share in the benefits of it will concur in the joyful thanksgivings for it." 4. It is an encouragement to hope for the continuance and perfection of this salvation: *We have waited for him, and he will save us*, will carry on what he has begun; for *as for God*, our God, *his work is perfect.*

II. A prospect of further blessings for the securing and perpetuating of these. 1. The power of God shall be engaged for them and shall continue to take their part: *In this mountain shall the hand of the Lord rest, v.* 10. The church and people of God shall have continued proofs of God's presence with them and residence among them: his hand shall be continually over them, to protect and guard them, and continually stretched out to them, for their supply. Mount Zion is *his rest for ever;* here he will dwell. 2. The power of their enemies, which is engaged against them, shall be broken. *Moab* is here put for all the adversaries of God's people, that are vexatious to them; they *shall* all *be trodden down* or threshed (for *then* they beat out the corn by treading it) and shall be thrown out as *straw to the dunghill*, being good for nothing else. God having *caused his hand to rest upon this mountain*, it shall not be a hand that hangs down, or is folded up, feeble and inactive; but he shall *spread forth his hands, in the midst* of his people, *like one that swims*, which intimates that he will employ and exert his power for them vigorously,— that he will be doing for them on all sides, —that he will easily and effectually put by the opposition that is given to his gracious intentions for them, and thereby further and push forward his good work among them,—and that on their behalf he will be continually active, for so the swimmer is. It is foretold, particularly, what he shall do for them. (1.) He shall *bring down the pride* of their enemies (and Moab was notoriously guilty of pride, *ch.* xvi. 6) by one humbling judgment after another, stripping them of that which they are proud of. (2.) He shall bring down *the spoils of their hands*, shall take from them that which they have got by spoil and rapine. He shall bring down the arms of their hands, which are lifted up against God's Israel; he shall quite break their power, and disable them to do mischief. (3.) He shall ruin all their fortifications, *v.* 12. Moab has his walls, and his high forts, with which he hopes to secure himself, and from which he designs to annoy the people of God; but God shall *bring them all down, lay them low, bring them to the ground, to the dust ;* and so those who trusted to them will be left exposed. There is no fortress impregnable to Omnipotence, no fort so high but the arm of the Lord can overtop it and bring it down. This destruction of Moab is typical of Christ's victory over death (spoken of *v.* 8), his spoiling principalities and powers in his cross (Col. ii. 15), his pulling down Satan's strong-holds by the preaching of his gospel (2 Cor. x. 4), and his reigning till all his enemies be *made his footstool,* Ps. cx. 1.

CHAP. XXVI.

This chapter is a song of holy joy and praise, in which the great things God had engaged, in the foregoing chapter, to do for his people against his enemies and their enemies are celebrated : it is prepared to be sung when that prophecy should be accomplished ; for we must be forward to meet God with our thanksgivings when he is coming towards us with his mercies. Now the people of God are here taught, I. To triumph in the safety and holy security both of the church in general and of every particular member of it, under the divine protection, ver. 1—4. II. To triumph over all opposing powers, ver. 5, 6. III. To walk with God, and wait for him, in the worst and darkest times, ver. 7—9. IV. To lament the stupidity of those who regarded not the providence of God, either merciful or afflictive, ver. 10, 11. V. To encourage themselves, and one another, with hopes that God would still continue to do them good (ver. 12, 14), and engage themselves to continue in his service, ver. 13. VI. To recollect the kind providences of God towards them in their low and distressed condition, and their conduct under those providences, ver. 15—18. VII. To rejoice in hope of a glorious deliverance, which should be as a resurrection to them (ver. 19), and to retire in the expectation of it, ver. 20, 21. And this is written for the support and assistance of the faith and hope of God's people in all ages, even those upon whom the ends of the world have come.

IN that day shall this song be sung in the land of Judah; We have a strong city; salvation will *God* appoint *for* walls and bulwarks. 2 Open ye the gates, that the righteous nation which keepeth the truth may enter in. 3 Thou wilt keep *him* in perfect peace, *whose* mind *is* stayed *on thee :* because he trusteth in thee. 4 Trust ye in the LORD for ever : for in the LORD JEHOVAH *is* everlasting strength.

To the prophecies of gospel grace very fitly is a song annexed, in which we may give God the glory and take to ourselves the comfort of that grace : *In that day,* the gospel day, which the day of the victories and enlargements of the Old-Testament church was typical of (to some of which perhaps this has a primary reference), *in that day this song shall be sung ;* there shall be persons to sing it, and cause and hearts to sing it; it shall be sung *in the land of Judah,* which was a figure of the gospel church ; for the gospel covenant is said to

be made *with the house of Judah,* Heb. viii. 8. Glorious things are here said of the church of God.

I. That it is strongly fortified against those that are bad (*v.* 1): *We have a strong city.* It is a city incorporated by the charter of the everlasting covenant, fitted for the reception of all that are made free by that charter, for their employment and entertainment ; it is a strong city, as Jerusalem was, while it was a city compact together, and had God himself a wall of fire round about it, so strong that none would have believed that an enemy could ever *enter into the gates of Jerusalem,* Lam. iv. 12. The church is a strong city, for it has *walls and bulwarks,* or counterscarps, and those of God's own appointing ; for he has, in his promise, appointed salvation itself to be its defence. Those that are designed for salvation will find that to be their protection, 1 Pet. i. 4.

II. That it is richly replenished with those that are good, and they are instead of fortifications to it ; for the inhabitants of Jerusalem, if they are such as they should be, are its strength, Zech. xii. 5. The gates are here ordered to be opened, *that the righteous nation, which keeps the truth, may enter in, v.* 2. They had been banished and driven out by the iniquity of the former times, but now the laws that were made against them are repealed, and they have liberty to enter in again. Or, There is an act for a general naturalization of all the righteous, whatever nation they are of, encouraging them to come and settle in Jerusalem. When God has done great things for any place or people he expects that thus they should render according to the benefit done unto them ; they should be kind to his people, and take them under their protection and into their bosom. Note, 1. It is the character of righteous men that they keep the truths of God, a firm belief of which will have a commanding influence upon the regularity of the whole conversation. Good principles fixed in the head will produce good resolutions in the heart and good practices in the life. 2. It is the interest of states to countenance such, and court them among them, for they bring a blessing with them.

III. That all who belong to it are safe and easy, and have a holy security and serenity of mind in the assurance of God's favour. 1. This is here the matter of a promise (*v.* 3) : *Thou wilt keep him in peace, peace,* in *perfect peace,* inward peace, outward peace, peace with God, peace of conscience, peace at all times, under all events ; this peace shall *he* be put into, and kept in the possession of, *whose mind is stayed upon God, because it trusts in him.* It is the character of every good man that he trusts in God, puts himself under his guidance and government, and depends upon

137

him that it shall be greatly to his advantage to do so. Those that trust in God must have their minds stayed upon him, must trust him at all times, under all events, must firmly and faithfully adhere to him, with an entire satisfaction in him ; and such as do so God will keep in perpetual peace, and that peace shall keep them. When evil tidings are abroad *those* shall calmly expect the event, and not be disturbed by frightful apprehensions arising from them, whose hearts are *fixed, trusting in the Lord,* Ps. cxii. 7. 2. It is the matter of a precept (*v.* 4): " Let us make ourselves easy by *trusting in the Lord for ever ;* since God has promised peace to those that stay themselves upon him, let us not lose the benefit of that promise, but repose an entire confidence in him. Trust in him for ever, at all times, when you have nothing else to trust to ; trust in him for that peace, that portion, which will be for ever." Whatever we trust to the world for, it will be but for a moment : all we expect from it is confined within the limits of time. But what we trust in God for will last as long as we shall last. For in the *Lord Jehovah—Jah, Jehovah,* in him who was, and is, and is to come, there is a rock of ages, a firm and lasting foundation for faith and hope to build upon ; and the house built on that rock will stand in a storm. Those that trust in God shall not only find in him, but receive *from him, everlasting strength,* strength that will carry them to everlasting life, to that blessedness which is for ever ; and therefore let them trust in him for ever, and never cast away nor change their confidence.

5 For he bringeth down them that dwell on high ; the lofty city, he layeth it low ; he layeth it low, *even* to the ground ; he bringeth it *even* to the dust. 6 The foot shall tread it down, *even* the feet of the poor, *and* the steps of the needy. 7 The way of the just *is* uprightness : thou, most upright, dost weigh the path of the just. 8 Yea, in the way of thy judgments, O LORD, have we waited for thee ; the desire of *our* soul *is* to thy name, and to the remembrance of thee. 9 With my soul have I desired thee in the night ; yea, with my spirit within me will I seek thee early : for when thy judgments *are* in the earth, the inhabitants of the world will learn righteousness. 10 Let favour be showed to the wicked, *yet* will he not learn righteousness : in the land of uprightness will he deal unjustly, and will not behold the

138

majesty of the LORD. 11 LORD, *when* thy hand is lifted up, they will not see : *but* they shall see, and be ashamed for *their* envy at the people ; yea, the fire of thine enemies shall devour them.

Here the prophet further encourages us to trust in the Lord for ever, and to continue waiting on him ; for,

I. He will make humble souls that trust in him to triumph over their proud enemies, *v.* 5, 6. Those that exalt themselves shall be abased : For he *brings down those that dwell on high ;* and wherein they deal proudly he is, and will be, above them. Even the lofty city Babylon itself, or Nineveh, he lays it low, *ch.* xxv. 12. He can do it, be it ever so well fortified. He has often done it. He will do it, for he resists the proud. It is his glory to do it, for he proves himself to be God by *looking on the proud and abasing them,* Job xl. 12. But, on the contrary, those that humble themselves shall be exalted ; for *the feet of the poor* shall tread upon the lofty cities, *v.* 6. He does not say, Great armies shall tread them down ; but, When God will have it done, even the feet of the poor shall do it, Mal. iv. 3. *You shall tread down the wicked. Come, set your feet on the necks of these kings.* See Ps. cxlvii. 6 ; Rom. xvi. 20.

II. He takes cognizance of the way of his people and has delight in it (*v.* 7): *The way of the just is evenness* (so it may be read) : it is their endeavour and constant care to walk with God in an even steady course of obedience and holy conversation. *My foot stands in an even place,* goes in an even path, Ps. xxvi. 12. And it is their happiness that God makes their way plain and easy before them : *Thou, most upright, dost level* (or *make even*) *the path of the just,* by preventing or removing those things that would be stumbling-blocks to them, so that nothing shall offend them, Ps. cxix. 165. God *weighs* it (so we read it) ; he considers it, and will give them grace sufficient for them, to help them over all the difficulties they may meet with in their way. Thus with the upright God will show himself upright.

III. It is our duty, and will be our comfort, to wait for God, and to keep up holy desires towards him in the darkest and most discouraging times, *v.* 8, 9. This has always been the practice of God's people, even when God has frowned upon them, 1. To keep up a constant dependence upon him : " *In the way of thy judgments we* have still *waited for thee ;* when thou hast corrected us we have looked to no other hand than thine to relieve us," as the servant looks only *to the hand of his master, till he have mercy upon him,* Ps. cxxiii. 2. We cannot appeal from God's justice but to his mercy. If God's judgments continue long, if it be *a road of judgments* (so the word signifies), yet we must not be weary but continue waiting. 2. To send up holy desires towards him. Our troubles, how pressing soever, must never put us out of conceit with our religion, nor turn us away from God; but still *the desire of our soul must be to his name and to the remembrance of him ;* and in the night, the darkest longest night of affliction, *with our souls must we desire him.* (1.) Our great concern must be for God's name, and our earnest desire must be that his name may be glorified, whatever becomes of us and our names. This is that which we must wait for, and pray for. " *Father, glorify thy name,* and we are satisfied." (2.) Our great comfort must be in the remembrance of that name, of all that whereby God has made himself known. The remembrance of God must be our great support and pleasure; and, though sometimes we be unmindful of him, yet still our desire must be towards the remembrance of him and we must take pains with our own hearts to have him always in mind. (3.) Our desires towards God must be inward, fervent, and sincere. With our soul we must desire him, with our soul we must pant after him (Ps. xlii. 1), and with our spirits within us, with the innermost thought and the closest application of mind, we must seek him. We make nothing of our religion, whatever our profession be, if we do not make heart-work of it. (4.) Even in the darkest night of affliction our desires must be towards God, as our sun and shield; for, however God is pleased to deal with us, we must never think the worse of him, nor cool in our love to him. (5.) If our desires be indeed towards God, we must give evidence that they are so by seeking him, and seeking him early, as those that desire to find him, and dread the thoughts of missing him. Those that would seek God and find him must seek betimes, and seek him earnestly. Though we come ever so early, we shall find him ready to receive us.

IV. It is God's gracious design, in sending abroad his judgments, thereby to bring men to seek him and serve him : *When thy judgments are upon the earth,* laying all waste, then we have reason to expect that not only God's professing people, but even *the inhabitants of the world, will learn righteousness,* will have their mistakes rectified and their lives reformed, will be brought to acknowledge God's righteousness in punishing them, will repent of their own unrighteousness in offending God, and so be brought to walk in right paths. They will do this ; that is, judgments are designed to bring them to this, they have a natural tendency to produce this effect, and, though many continue obstinate, yet some even of the inhabitants of the world will profit by this discipline, and will learn righteousness : surely they will; they are strangely stupid if they do

not. Note, The intention of afflictions is to teach us righteousness; and blessed is the man whom God chastens, and thus teaches, Ps. xciv. 12. *Discite justitiam, moniti, et non temnere divos—Let this rebuke teach you to cultivate righteousness, and cease from despising the gods.*—Virgil.

V. Those are wicked indeed that will not be wrought upon by the favourable methods God takes to subdue and reform them; and it is necessary that God should deal with them in a severe way by his judgments, which shall prevail to humble those that would not otherwise be humbled. Observe,

1. How sinners walk contrary to God, and refuse to comply with the means used for their reformation and to answer the intentions of them, *v.* 10. (1.) *Favour is shown* to them. They receive many mercies from God; he causes his sun to shine and his rain to fall upon them, nay, he prospers them, and into their hands he brings plentifully; they escape many of the strokes of God's judgments, which others less wicked than they have been cut off by; in some particular instances they seem to be remarkably favoured above their neighbours, and the design of all this is that they may be won upon to love and serve that God who thus favours them; and yet it is all in vain : *they will not learn righteousness,* will not be led to repentance by the goodness of God, and therefore it is requisite that God should send his judgments into the earth, to reckon with men for abused mercies. (2.) They live *in a land of uprightness,* where religion is professed and is in reputation, where the word of God is preached, and where they have many good examples set them,—in a land of *evenness,* where there are not so many stumbling-blocks as in other places,— in a land of *correction,* where vice and profaneness are discountenanced and punished ; yet there they will *deal unjustly,* and go on frowardly in their evil ways. Those that do wickedly deal unjustly both with God and man, as well as with their own souls; and those that will not be reclaimed by the justice of the nation may expect the judgments of God upon them. Nor can those expect a place hereafter in the land of blessedness who now conform not to the laws and usages, nor improve the privileges and advantages, of the land of uprightness ; and why do they not ? It is because they *will not behold the majesty of the Lord,* will not believe, will not consider, what a God of terrible majesty he is whose laws and justice they persist in the contempt of. God's majesty appears in all the dispensations of his providence; but they regard it not, and therefore study not to answer the ends of those dispensations. Even when we receive of the mercy of the Lord we must still behold the *majesty of the Lord and his goodness.* (3.) God lifts up his hand to give them warning, that they may, by re-

pentance and prayer, make their peace with him; but they take no notice of it, are not aware that God is angry with them, or coming forth against them: *They will not see,* and none so blind as those who will not see, who shut their eyes against the clearest conviction of guilt and wrath, who ascribe that to chance, or common fate, which is manifestly a divine rebuke, who regard not the threatening symptoms of their own ruin, but cry Peace to themselves, when the righteous God is waging war with them.

2. How God will at length be too hard for them; for, when he judges, he will overcome: *They will not see, but they shall see,* shall be made to see, whether they will or no, that God is angry with them. Atheists, scorners, and the secure, will shortly feel what now they will not believe, that *it is a fearful thing to fall into the hands of the living God.* They will not see the evil of sin, and particularly the sin of hating and persecuting the people of God; but they shall see, by the tokens of God's displeasure against them for it and the deliverances in which God will plead his people's cause, that what is done against them he takes as done against himself and will reckon for it accordingly. They shall see that they have done God's people a great deal of wrong, and therefore shall be ashamed of their enmity and envy towards them, and their ill usage of such as deserved better treatment. Note, Those that bear ill-will to God's people have reason to be ashamed of it, so absurd and unreasonable is it; and, sooner or later, they shall be ashamed of it, and the remembrance of it shall fill them with confusion. Some read it, *They shall see and be confounded for the zeal of the people,* by the zeal God will show for his people; when they shall be made to know how jealous God is for the honour and welfare of his people they shall be confounded to think that they might have been of that people and would not. Their doom therefore is that, since they slighted the happiness of God's friends, *the fire of his enemies shall devour them,* that is, the fire which is prepared for his enemies and with which they shall be devoured, the fire designed for the devil and his angels. Note, Those that are enemies to God's people, and envy them, God looks upon as his enemies, and will deal with them accordingly.

12 Lord, thou wilt ordain peace for us: for thou also hast wrought all our works in us. 13 O Lord our God, *other* lords beside thee have had dominion over us: *but* by thee only will we make mention of thy name. 14 *They are* dead, they shall not live; *they are* deceased, they shall not rise: therefore hast thou visited and destroyed them, and made all

their memory to perish. 15 Thou hast increased the nation, O Lord, thou hast increased the nation: thou art glorified: thou hadst removed *it* far *unto* all the ends of the earth. 16 Lord, in trouble have they visited thee, they poured out a prayer *when* thy chastening *was* upon them. 17 Like as a woman with child, *that* draweth near the time of her delivery, is in pain, *and* crieth out in her pangs; so have we been in thy sight, O Lord. 18 We have been with child, we have been in pain, we have as it were brought forth wind; we have not wrought any deliverance in the earth; neither have the inhabitants of the world fallen. 19 Thy dead *men* shall live, *together with* my dead body shall they arise. Awake and sing, ye that dwell in dust: for thy dew *is as* the dew of herbs, and the earth shall cast out the dead.

The prophet in these verses looks back upon what God had done with them, both in mercy and judgment, and sings unto God of both, and then looks forward upon what he hoped God would do for them. Observe,

I. His reviews and reflections are mixed. When he looks back upon the state of the church he finds,

1. That God had in many instances been very gracious to them and had done great things for them. (1.) In general (*v.* 12): *Thou hast wrought all our works in us,* or *for* us. Whatever good work is done by us, it is owing to a good work wrought by the grace of God in us; it is he that puts good thoughts and affections into our hearts if at any time they be there, and that *works in us both to will and to do of his good pleasure. Acti, agimus—Being acted upon, we act.* And if any kindness be shown us, or any of our affairs be prosperous and successful, it is God that works it for us. Every creature, every business, that is in any way serviceable to our comfort, is made by him to be so; and sometimes he makes that to work for us which seemed to make against us. (2.) In particular (*v.* 15): " *Thou hast increased the nation, O Lord!* so that a little one has become a thousand (in Egypt they multiplied exceedingly, and afterwards in Canaan, so that they filled the land); and in this *thou art glorified,*" for the multitude of the people is the honour of the prince, and therein God was glorified as faithful to his covenant with Abraham, that he would make him a father of many nations. Note, God's nation is a growing nation, and it is

the glory of God that it is so. The increase of the church, that holy nation, is *therefore* to be rejoiced in because it is the increase of those that make it their business to glorify God in this world.

2. That yet he had laid them under his rebukes.

(1.) The neighbouring nations had sometimes oppressed them and tyrannised over them (*v.* 13): "*O Lord our God!* thou who hast the sole right to rule us, whose subjects and servants we are, to thee we complain (for whither else should we go with our complaints?) that *other lords besides thee have had dominion over us.*" Not only in the days of the Judges, but afterwards, God frequently sold them into the hand of their enemies, or rather, by their iniquities, they *sold themselves, ch.* lii. 3—5. When they had been careless in the service of God, God suffered their enemies to have dominion over them, that they might know the difference between his service *and the service of the kingdoms of the countries.* It may be understood as a confession of sin, their serving other gods, and subjecting themselves to the superstitious laws and customs of their neighbours, by which other lords (for they called their idols *baals, lords)* had dominion over them, besides God. But now they promise that it shall be so no more : " Henceforth *by thee only will we make mention of thy name;* we will worship thee only, and in that way only which thou hast instituted and appointed." The same may be our penitent reflection : *Other lords, besides God, have had dominion over us;* every lust has been our lord, and we have been led captive by it ; and it has been long enough, and too long, that we have thus wronged both God and ourselves. The same therefore must be our pious resolution, that henceforth we will make mention of God's name only and by him only, that we will keep close to God and to our duty and never desert it.

(2.) They had sometimes been carried into captivity before their enemies (*v.* 15): "The nation which at first thou didst increase, and make to take root, thou hast now diminished, and plucked up, and *removed to all the ends of the earth, driven out to the utmost parts of heaven,*" as is threatened, Deut. xxx. 4 ; xxviii. 64. But observe, Between the mention of the increasing of them and that of the removing of them it is said, *Thou art glorified;* for the judgments God inflicts upon his people for their sins are for his honour, as well as the mercies he bestows upon them in performance of his promise.

(3.) The prophet remembers that when they were thus oppressed and carried captive they cried unto God, which was a good evidence that they neither had quite forsaken him nor were quite forsaken of him, and that there were merciful intentions in the judgments they were under (*v.* 16): *Lord, in trouble have they visited thee.* This was usual with the people of Israel, as we find frequently in the story of the Judges. When *other lords had dominion over them* they *humbled themselves, and said, The Lord is righteous,* 2 Chron. xii. 6. See here, [1.] The need we have of afflictions. They are necessary to stir up prayer; when it is said, *In trouble have they visited thee,* it is implied that in their peace and prosperity they were strangers to God, kept at a distance from him, and seldom came near him, as if, when the world smiled upon them, they had no occasion for his favours. [2.] The benefit we often have by afflictions. They bring us to God, quicken us to our duty, and show us our dependence upon him. Those that before seldom looked at God now visit him ; they come frequently, they become friendly, and make their court to him. Before, prayer came drop by drop, but now they *pour out a prayer;* it comes now like water from a fountain, not like water from a still. They poured out *a secret speech;* so the margin. Praying is speaking to God, but it is a secret speech ; for it is the language of the heart, otherwise it is not praying. Afflictions bring us to secret prayer, in which we may be more free and particular in our addresses to him than we can be in public. In affliction those will seek God early who before sought him slowly, Hos. v. 15. It will make men fervent and fluent in prayer. "They poured out a prayer, as the drink-offerings were poured out, when thy chastening was upon them." But it is to be feared, when the chastening is off them, they will by degrees return to their former carelessness, as they had often done.

(4.) He complains that their struggles for their own liberty had been very painful and perilous, but that they had not been successful, *v.* 17, 18. [1.] They had the throes and pangs they dreaded: "We have been like a woman in labour, that cries out in her pangs; we have with a great deal of anxiety and toil endeavoured to help ourselves, and our troubles have been increased by those attempts;" as when Moses came to deliver Israel the tale of bricks was doubled. Their prayers were quickened by the acuteness of their pains, and became as strong and vehement as the cries of a woman in sore travail. *So have we been in thy sight, O Lord!* It was a comfort and satisfaction to them, in their distress, that God had his eye upon them, that all their miseries were in his sight ; he was no stranger to their pangs or their prayers. *Lord, all my desire is before thee, and my groaning is not hidden from thee,* Ps. xxxviii. 9. Whenever they came to *present themselves before the Lord* with their complaints and petitions they were in agonies like those of a woman in travail. [2.] They came short of the issue and success they desired and hoped for : "*We have been with child;* we have had great expectation of a speedy and happy deliverance, have been big with hopes, and, when we have been in pain, have comforted ourselves with this, that the joyful birth would make us forget *our misery*, John xvi. 21. But, alas! *we have as it were brought forth wind;* it has proved a false conception; our expectations have been frustrated, and our pains have been rather dying pains than travailing ones; we have had a miscarrying womb and dry breasts. All our efforts have proved abortive: *We have not wrought any deliverance in the earth*, for ourselves or for our friends and allies, but rather have made our own case and theirs worse; *neither have the inhabitants of the world*, whom we have been contesting with, *fallen* before us, either in their power or in their hopes; but they are still as high and arrogant as ever." Note, A righteous cause may be strenuously pleaded both by prayer and endeavour, both with God and man, and yet for a great while may be left under a cloud, and the point may not be gained.

II. His prospects and hopes are very pleasant. In general, " *Thou wilt ordain peace for us* (*v.* 12), that is, all that good which the necessity of our case calls for." What peace the church has, or hopes for, it is of God's ordaining; and we may comfort ourselves with this, that, what trouble soever may for a time be appointed to the people of God, peace will at length be ordained for them ; for the *end of those men is peace*. And, if God by his Spirit *work all our works in us*, he will ordain peace for us (for the work of righteousness shall be peace), and that is true and lasting peace, such as the world can neither give nor take away, which God ordains; for, to those that have it, it shall be unchangeable as the ordinances *of the day and of the night*. Moreover, from what God has done for us, we may encourage ourselves to hope that he will yet further do us good. "Thou hast heard the desire of the humble, and therefore wilt (Ps. x. 17); and, when this peace is ordained for us, then *by thee only will we make mention of thy name* (*v.* 13); we will give the glory of it to thee only, and not to any other, and we will depend upon thy grace only to enable us to do so." We cannot praise God's name but by his strength. Two things in particular the prophet here comforts the church with the prospect of:—

1. The amazing ruin of her enemies (*v.* 14): *They are dead*, those *other lords* that *have had dominion over us;* their power is irrecoverably broken; they are quite cut off and extinguished: and *they shall not live*, shall never be able to hold up the head any more. Being *deceased, they shall not rise*, but, like Haman, when they have begun to fall before the seed of the Jews they shall sink like a stone. Because they are sentenced to this final ruin, therefore, in pursuance of that sentence, God himself has visited them in wrath, as a righteous Judge, and has cut off both the men themselves *(he has destroyed them)* and *the remembrance of them:* they and

142

their names are buried together in the dust. He has *made all their memory to perish;* they are either forgotten or made mention of with detestation. Note, The cause that is maintained in opposition to God and his kingdom among men, though it may prosper awhile, will certainly sink at last, and all that adhere to it will perish with it. The Jewish doctors, comparing this with *v.* 19, infer that the resurrection of the dead belongs to the Jews only, and that those of other nations shall not rise. But we know better; we know that *all who are in their graves shall hear the voice of the Son of God*, and that this speaks of the final destruction of Christ's enemies, which is the second death. 2. The surprising resurrection of her friends, *v.* 19. Though the church rejoices not in the birth of the man-child, of which she travailed in pain, *but has as it were brought forth wind* (*v.* 18), yet the disappointment shall be balanced in a way equivalent: *Thy dead men shall live;* those who were thought to be dead, who had received a sentence of death within themselves, who were cast out as if they had been naturally dead, shall appear again in their former vigour. A spirit of life from God shall enter into the slain witnesses and they shall prophesy again, Rev. xi. 11. The *dry bones shall live*, and become an *exceedingly great army*, Ezek. xxxvii. 10. *Together with my dead body shall they arise.* If we believe the resurrection of the dead, of our dead bodies at the last day, as Job did, and the prophet here, that will facilitate our belief of the promised restoration of the church's lustre and strength in this world. When God's time shall have come, how low soever she may be brought, they shall arise, even Jerusalem, the city of God, but now lying like a dead body, a carcase to which the eagles are gathered together. God owns it still for his, so does the prophet; but it shall arise, shall be rebuilt, and flourish again. And therefore let the poor, desolate, melancholy remains of its inhabitants, that dwell as in dust, *awake and sing;* for they shall see Jerusalem, the *city of their solemnities, a quiet habitation again*, ch. xxxiii. 20. The dew of God's favour shall be to it as the evening dew to the herbs that were parched with the heat of the sun all day, shall revive and refresh them. And as the spring-dews, that water the earth, and make the herbs that lay buried in it to put forth and bud, so shall they flourish again, and *the earth shall cast out the dead*, as it casts the herbs out of their roots. The earth, in which they seemed to be lost, shall contribute to their revival. When the church and her interests are to be restored neither the dew of heaven nor the fatness of the earth shall be wanting to do their part towards the restoration. Now this (as Ezekiel's vision, which is a comment upon it) may be fitly accommodated, (1.) To the spiritual resurrection of those that were dead in sin, by the power of Christ's gospel and grace. So Dr. Lightfoot applies applies it, *Hor. Hebr. in Joh.* xii. 24. "The Gentiles shall live; with my body shall they arise; that is, they shall be called in after Christ's resurrection, shall rise with him, and sit with him in heavenly places; nay, they shall arise my body (says he); they shall become the mystical body of Christ, and shall arise as part of him." (2.) To the last resurrection, when dead saints shall live, and rise together with Christ's dead body; for he arose as the first-fruits, and believers shall arise by virtue of their union with him and their communion in his resurrection.

20 Come, my people, enter thou into thy chambers, and shut thy doors about thee: hide thyself as it were for a little moment, until the indignation be over-past. 21 For, behold, the LORD cometh out of his place to punish the inhabitants of the earth for their iniquity: the earth also shall disclose her blood, and shall no more cover her slain.

These two verses are supposed not to belong to the song which takes up the rest of the chapter, but to begin a new matter, and to be rather an introduction to the following chapter than the conclusion of this. Or whereas, in the foregoing song, the people of God had spoken to him, complaining of their grievances, here he returns an answer to their complaints, in which,

I. He invites them into their chambers (*v.* 20): "*Come, my people,* come to me, come with me" (he calls them nowhere but where he himself will accompany them); "let the storm that disperses others bring you nearer together. Come, and *enter into thy chambers;* stay not abroad, lest you be caught in the storm, as the Egyptians in the hail," Exod. ix. 21. 1. "Come into chambers of *distinction:* come into your own apartments, and continue not any longer mixed with the children of Babylon. *Come out from among them, and be you separate,*" 2 Cor. vi. 17; Rev. xviii. 4. If God has set apart those that are godly for himself, they ought to set themselves apart. 2. "Into chambers of *defence,* in which by the secrecy or the strength of them you may be safe in the worst of times." The attributes of God are the *secret of his tabernacle,* Ps. xxvii. 5. His name is a strong tower, into which we may run for shelter, Prov. xviii. 10. We must by faith find a way into these chambers, and there hide ourselves; that is, with a holy security and serenity of mind, we must put ourselves under the divine protection. Come, as Noah into the ark, for he *shut the doors about him.* When dangers are threatening it is good to retire, and lie hid, as Elijah did by the brook Cherith. 3. Into chambers of *devotion.* "Enter into thy closet,

and *shut thy door,* Matt. vi. 6. Be private with God: *Enter into thy chamber,* to examine thyself, and commune with thy own heart, to pray, and humble thyself before God." This work is to be done in times of distress and danger; and thus we hide ourselves, that is, we recommend ourselves to God to hide us, and he will hide us either under heaven or in heaven. Israel must keep within doors when the destroying angel is slaying the first-born of Egypt, else the blood on the door-posts will not secure them. So must Rahab and her family when Jericho is being destroyed. Those are most safe that are least seen. *Qui bene latuit, bene vixit*—He has lived well who has sought a proper degree of concealment.

II. He assures them that the trouble would be over in a very short time, that they should not long be in any fright or peril: "*Hide thyself for a moment,* the smallest part of time we can conceive, like an atom of matter; nay, if you can imagine one moment shorter than another, it is but for a *little* moment, and that with a *quasi* too, *as it were for a little moment,* less than you think of. When it is over it will seem as nothing to you; you will wonder how soon it is gone. You shall not need to lie long in confinement, long in concealment. The indignation will presently be over-past; that is, the indignation of the enemies against you, their persecuting power and rage, which force you to abscond. *When the wicked rise, a man is hid* This will soon be over; God will cut them off, will break their power, defeat their purposes, and find a way for your enlargement." When Athanasius was banished from Alexandria by an edict of Julian, and his friends greatly lamented it, he bade them be of good cheer. *Nubecula est quæ cito pertransibit—It is a little cloud, that will soon blow over. You shall have tribulation ten days;* that is all, Rev. ii. 10. This enables God's suffering people to call their afflictions light, that they are but for a moment.

III. He assures them that their enemies should be reckoned with for all the mischief they had done them by the sword, either of war or persecution, *v.* 21. The Lord will punish them for the blood they have shed. Here is, 1. The judgment set, and process issued out: *The Lord comes out of his place, to punish the inhabitants of the earth for their iniquity,* in giving such disturbance to all about them. There is a great deal of iniquity among the inhabitants of the earth; but though they all combine in it, though hand join in hand to carry it on, yet *it shall not go unpunished.* Besides the everlasting punishment into which the wicked shall go hereafter, there are often remarkable punishments of cruelty, oppression, and persecution, in this world. When men's indignation is over-past, and they have done their worst, let them then expect God's indignation, for he sees that his day is coming, Ps. xxxvii. 13.

God *comes out of his place to punish.* He shows himself in an extraordinary manner from heaven, the firmament of his power, from the sanctuary, the residence of his grace. He is *raised up out of his holy habitation,* where he seemed before to conceal himself; and now he will do something great, the product of his wise, just, and secret counsels, as a prince that goes to take the chair or take the field, Zech. ii. 13. Some observe that God's place is the mercy-seat; there he delights to be; when he punishes he comes out of his place, for he has no pleasure in the death of sinners. 2. The criminals convicted by the notorious evidence of the fact: *The earth shall disclose her blood;* the innocent blood, the blood of the saints and martyrs, which has been shed upon the earth like water, and has soaked into it, and been concealed and covered by it, shall now be brought to light, and brought to account; for God will make inquisition for it, and will give those that shed it blood to drink, for they are worthy. Secret murders, and other secret wickednesses, shall be discovered, sooner or later. And the slain which the earth has long covered she shall no longer cover, but they shall be produced as evidence against the murderers. The voice of Abel's blood cries from the earth, Gen. iv. 10, 11; Job xx. 27. Those sins which seemed to be buried in oblivion will be called to mind, and called over again, when the day of reckoning comes. Let God's people therefore wait awhile with patience, for behold the Judge stands before the door.

CHAP. XXVII.

In this chapter the prophet goes on to show, I. What great things God would do for his church and people, which should now shortly be accomplished in the deliverance of Jerusalem from Sennacherib and the destruction of the Assyrian army; but it is expressed generally, for the encouragement of the church in after ages, with reference to the power and prevalency of her enemies. 1. That proud oppressors should be reckoned with, ver. 1. 2. That care should be taken of the church, as of God's vineyard, ver. 2, 3. 3. That God would let fall his controversy with the people, upon their return to him, ver. 4, 5. 4. That he would greatly multiply and increase them, ver. 6. 5. That, as to their afflictions, the property of them should be altered (ver. 7), they should be mitigated and moderated (ver. 8), and sanctified, ver. 9. 6. That though the church might be laid waste, and made desolate, for a time (ver. 10, 11), yet it should be restored, and the scattered members should be gathered together again, ver. 12, 13. All this is applicable to the grace of the gospel, and God's promises to, and providences concerning, the Christian church, and such as belong to it.

IN that day the LORD with his sore and great and strong sword shall punish leviathan the piercing serpent, even leviathan that crooked serpent, and he shall slay the dragon that *is* in the sea. 2 In that day sing ye unto her, A vineyard of red wine. 3 I the LORD do keep it; I will water it every moment: lest *any* hurt it, I will keep it night and day. 4 Fury *is* not in me: who would set the briers *and* thorns against me in battle? I would go through them, I would burn them together. 5 Or let him take

144

hold of my strength, *that* he may make peace with me; *and* he shall make peace with me. 6 He shall cause them that come of Jacob to take root: Israel shall blossom and bud, and fill the face of the world with fruit.

The prophet is here singing of judgment and mercy,

I. Of judgment upon the enemies of God's church (*v.* 1), *tribulation to those that trouble it,* 2 Thess. i. 6. When the Lord *comes out of his place, to punish the inhabitants of the earth* (*ch.* xxvi. 21), he will be sure to punish *leviathan,* the *dragon that is in the sea,* every proud oppressing tyrant, that is the terror of the mighty, and, like the leviathan, is *so fierce that none dares stir him up,* and *his heart as hard as a stone,* and *when he raises up himself the mighty are afraid,* Job xli. 10, 24, 25. The church has many enemies, but commonly some one that is more formidable than the rest. So Sennacherib was in his day, and Nebuchadnezzar in his, and Antiochus in his; so Pharaoh had been formerly, and is called *leviathan* and *the dragon, ch.* li. 9; Ps. lxxiv. 13, 14; Ezek. xxix. 3. The New-Testament church has had its leviathans; we read of a great red dragon ready to devour it, Rev. xii. 3. Those malignant persecuting powers are here compared to the leviathan for bulk, and strength, and the mighty bustle they make in the world,—to dragons for their rage and fury, —to serpents, *piercing serpents,* penetrating in their counsels, quick in their motions, and which, if they once get in their head, will soon wind in their whole body,—*crossing like a bar* (so the margin), standing in the way of all their neighbours and obstructing them, —to *crooked serpents,* subtle and insinuating, but perverse and mischievous. Great and mighty princes, if they oppose the people of God, are in God's account as dragons and serpents, the plagues of mankind; and the Lord will punish them in due time. They are too big for men to deal with and call to an account, and therefore the great God will take the matter into his own hands. He has a *sore, and great, and strong sword,* wherewith to do execution upon them when the *measure of their iniquity is full* and their *day has come to fall.* It is emphatically expressed in the original: *The Lord with his sword, that cruel one, and that great one, and that strong one, shall punish* this unwieldy, this unruly criminal; and it shall be capital punishment: *He shall slay the dragon that is in the sea;* for the wages of his sin is death. This shall not only be a prevention of his doing further mischief, as the slaying of a wild beast, but a just punishment for the mischief he has done, as the putting of a traitor or rebel to death. God has a strong sword for the doing of this, variety of judgments sufficient to humble the proudest and break the most powerful of his enemies; and he will do it when the day of execution comes: *In that day* he will punish, his day which is coming, Ps. xxxvii. 13. This is applicable to the spiritual victories obtained by our Lord Jesus over the powers of darkness. He not only disarmed, spoiled, and cast out, the prince of this world, but with his strong sword, the virtue of his death and the preaching of his gospel, he does and will *destroy him that had the power of death, that is, the devil*, that great leviathan, that old serpent, the dragon. He shall be bound, that he may not deceive the nations, and that is a punishment to him (Rev. xx. 2, 3); and at length, for deceiving the nations, he shall be *cast into the lake of fire*, Rev. xx. 10.

II. Of mercy to the church. In that same day, when God is punishing the leviathan, let the church and all her friends be easy and cheerful; let those that attend her sing to her for her comfort, sing her asleep with these assurances; let it be sung in her assemblies,

1. That she is God's vineyard, and is under his particular care, *v.* 2, 3. She is, in God's eye, *a vineyard of red wine*. The world is as a fruitless worthless wilderness; but the church is enclosed as a vineyard, a peculiar place, and of value, that has great care taken of it and great pains taken with it, and from which precious fruits are gathered, wherewith they honour God and man. It is a vineyard of *red wine*, yielding the best and choicest grapes, intimating the reformation of the church, that it now brings forth good fruit unto God, whereas before it brought forth fruit to itself, or brought forth wild grapes, *ch.* v. 4. Now God takes care, (1.) Of the safety of this vineyard: *I the Lord do keep it*. He speaks this as glorying in it that he is, and has undertaken to be, the keeper of Israel. Those that bring forth fruit to God are and shall be always under his protection. He speaks this as assuring us that they shall be so: *I the Lord*, that can do every thing, but cannot lie nor deceive, *I do keep it; lest any hurt it, I will keep it night and day*. God's vineyard in this world lies much exposed to injury; there are many that would hurt it, would tread it down and lay it waste (Ps. lxxx. 13); but God will suffer no real hurt or damage to be done it, but what he will bring good out of. He will keep it constantly, night and day, and not without need, for the enemies are restless in their designs and attempts against it, and, both night and day, seek an opportunity to do it a mischief. God will keep it in the night of affliction and persecution, and in the day of peace and prosperity, the temptations of which are no less dangerous. God's people shall be preserved, not only from the *pestilence that walketh in darkness*, but from the *destruction that wasteth at noon-day*, Ps. xci. 6. This vineyard shall be well fenced. (2.) Of the

fruitfulness of this vineyard: *I will water it every moment*, and yet it shall not be over-watered. The still and silent dews of God's grace and blessing shall continually descend upon it, that it may bring forth much fruit. We need the constant and continual waterings of the divine grace; for, if that be at any time withdrawn, we wither, and come to nothing. God waters his vineyard by the ministry of the word by his servants the prophets, whose doctrine shall drop as the dew. Paul plants, and Apollos waters, but God gives the increase; for without him the watchman wakes and the husbandman waters in vain.

2. That, though sometimes he contends with his people, yet, upon their submission, he will be reconciled to them, *v.* 4, 5. *Fury is not in him* towards his vineyard; though he meets with many things in it that are offensive to him, yet he does not seek advantages against it, nor is extreme to mark what is amiss in it. It is true if he find in it briers and thorns instead of vines, and they be set in battle against him (as indeed that in the vineyard which is not for him is against him), he will tread them down and burn them; but otherwise, " If I am angry with my people, they know what course to take; let them humble themselves, and pray, and seek my face, and so *take hold of my strength* with a sincere desire to make their peace with me, and I will soon be reconciled to them, and all shall be well." God sees the sins of his people and is displeased with them; but, upon their repentance, he turns away his wrath. This may very well be construed as a summary of the doctrine of the gospel, with which the church is to be watered every moment. (1.) Here is a quarrel supposed between God and man; for here is a battle fought, and peace to be made. It is an old quarrel, ever since sin first entered. It is, on God's part, a righteous quarrel, but, on man's part, most unrighteous. (2.) Here is a gracious invitation given us to make up this quarrel, and to get these matters in variance accommodated: " Let him that is desirous to be at peace with God take hold of his strength, of his strong arm, which is lifted up against the sinner to strike him dead; and let him by supplication keep back the stroke. Let him wrestle with me, as Jacob did, resolving not to let me go without a blessing; and he shall be *Israel—a prince with God*." Pardoning mercy is called the power of our Lord; let him take hold of that. Christ is the *arm of the Lord, ch.* liii. 1. Christ *crucified is the power of God* (1 Cor. i. 24); let him by a lively faith take hold of him, as a man that is sinking catches hold of a bough, or cord, or plank, that is within his reach, or as the malefactor took hold of the horns of the altar, believing that there is no other name by which he can be saved, by which he can be reconciled. (3.) Here is a threefold cord of arguments

145

to persuade us to do this. [1.] Time and space are given us to do it in; for *fury is not in God;* he does not carry it towards us as great men carry it towards their inferiors, when the one is in a fault and the other in a fury. Men in a fury will not take time for consideration; it is, with them, but a word and a blow. Furious men are soon angry, and implacable when they are angry; a little thing provokes them, and no little thing will pacify them. But it is not so with God; he considers our frame, is slow to anger, does not stir up all his wrath, nor always chide. [2.] It is in vain to think of contesting with him. If we persist in our quarrel with him, and think to make our part good, it is but like setting briers and thorns before a consuming fire, which will be so far from giving check to the progress of it that they will but make it burn the more outrageously. We are not an equal match for Omnipotence. *Woe unto him* therefore *that strives with his Maker!* He knows not the power of his anger. [3.] This is the only way, and it is a sure way, to reconciliation: " Let him take this course to make peace with me, *and he shall make peace;* and thereby good, all good, shall come unto him." God is willing to be reconciled to us if we be but willing to be reconciled to him.

3. That the church of God in the world shall be a growing body, and come at length to be a great body (*v.* 6): *In times to come* (so some read it), *in after-times,* when these calamities are overpast, or in the days of the gospel, the latter days, *he shall cause Jacob to take root,* deeper root than ever yet; for the gospel church shall be more firmly fixed than ever the Jewish church was, and shall spread further. Or, *He shall cause those of Jacob* that come back out of their captivity, or (as we read it) *those that come of Jacob, to take root downward, and bear fruit upward,* ch. xxxvii. 31. They shall be established in a prosperous state, and then they shall *blossom and bud,* and give hopeful prospects of a great increase; and so it shall prove, for *they shall fill the face of the world with fruit.* Many shall be brought into the church, proselytes shall be numerous, some out of all the nations about that shall be to the God of Israel for a name and a praise; and the converts shall be fruitful in the fruits of righteousness. The preaching of the gospel *brought forth fruit in all the world* (Col. i. 6), fruit that remains, John xv. 16.

7 Hath he smitten him, as he smote those that smote him? *Or* is he slain according to the slaughter of them that are slain by him? 8 In measure, when it shooteth forth, thou wilt debate with it: he stayeth his rough wind in the day of the east-wind. 9

By this therefore shall the iniquity of Jacob be purged; and this *is* all the fruit to take away his sin; when he maketh all the stones of the altar as chalk-stones that are beaten in sunder, the groves and images shall not stand up. 10 Yet the defenced city *shall be* desolate, *and* the habitation forsaken, and left like a wilderness: there shall the calf feed, and there shall he lie down, and consume the branches thereof. 11 When the boughs thereof are withered, they shall be broken off: the women come, *and* set them on fire : for it *is* a people of no understanding : therefore he that made them will not have mercy on them, and he that formed them will show them no favour. 12 And it shall come to pass in that day, *that* the LORD shall beat off from the channel of the river unto the stream of Egypt, and ye shall be gathered one by one, O ye children of Israel. 13 And it shall come to pass in that day, *that* the great trumpet shall be blown, and they shall come which were ready to perish in the land of Assyria, and the outcasts in the land of Egypt, and shall worship the LORD in the holy mount at Jerusalem.

Here is the prophet again singing of mercy and judgment, not, as before, judgment to the enemies and mercy to the church, but judgment to the church and mercy mixed with that judgment.

I. Here is judgment threatened even to Jacob and Israel. *They shall blossom and bud* (*v.* 6), but, 1. They shall be *smitten* and *slain* (*v.* 7), some of them shall. If God find any thing amiss among them, he will lay them under the tokens of his displeasure for it. Judgment shall begin at the house of God, and those whom God has known of all the families of the earth he will punish in the first place. 2. Jerusalem, their *defenced city, shall be desolate, v.* 10, 11. " God having tried a variety of methods with them for their reformation, which, as to many, have proved ineffectual, he will for a time lay their country waste," which was accomplished when Jerusalem was destroyed by the Chaldeans; then that *habitation* was for a long time *forsaken.* If less judgments do not do the work, God will send greater; for *when he judges he will overcome.* Jerusalem had been a defenced city, not so much by art or nature as by grace and the divine protection; but, when God was provoked to withdraw, her defence departed from her, and then she was left like a wilderness. "And in the pleasant gardens of Jerusalem cattle shall feed, shall lie down there, and there shall be none to disturb them or drive them away; there they shall be *levant and couchant*, and they shall eat the tender branches of the fruit-trees," which perhaps further signifies that the people should become an easy prey to their enemies. "*When the boughs thereof are withered* as they grow upon the tree, being blasted by winds and frosts and not pruned, *they shall be broken off* for fuel, and *the women* and children shall *come and set them on fire*. There shall be a total destruction, for the very trees shall be destroyed." And this is a figure of the deplorable state of the vineyard (*v.* 2) when it *brought forth wild grapes* (*ch.* v. 2); and our Saviour seems to refer to this when he says of the branches of the vine which *abide not in him* that they are *cast forth and withered, and men gather them, and cast them into the fire, and they are burned* (John xv. 6), which was in a particular manner fulfilled in the unbelieving Jews. The similitude is explained in the following words, *It is a people of no understanding,* brutish and sottish, and destitute of the knowledge of God, and that have no relish or savour of divine things, like a withered branch that has no sap in it; and this is at the bottom of all those sins for which God left them desolate, their idolatry first and afterwards their infidelity. Wicked people, however in other things they may be wits and politicians, in their greatest concerns are of no understanding; and their ignorance, being wilful, shall not only not be their excuse, but it shall be the ground of their condemnation; for therefore *he that made them*, that gave them their being, *will not have mercy on them*, nor save them from the ruin they bring upon themselves; and *he that formed them* into a people, formed them for himself, to show forth his praise, seeing they do not answer the end of their formation, but hate to be reformed, to be new-formed, will reject them, and *show them no favour;* and then they are undone: for, if he that made us by his power do not make us happy in his favour, we had better never have been made. Sinners flatter themselves with hopes of impunity, at least that they shall not be dealt with so severely as their ministers tell them, because God is merciful and because he is their Maker. But here we see how weak and insufficient those pleas will be; for, if they be of no understanding, he that made them, though he made them, and hates nothing that he has made, and though he has mercy in store for those who so far understand their interests as to apply to him for it, yet on them he will have no mercy, and will show them no favour.

II. Here is a great deal of mercy mixed with this judgment; for there are good peo-

ple mixed with those that are corrupt and degenerate, *a remnant according to the election of grace*, on whom God will have mercy and to whom he will show favour: and these promises seem to point at all the calamities of the church, for which God would graciously provide these allays.

1. Though they shall be smitten and slain, yet not to that degree, and in that manner, in which their enemies shall be smitten and slain, *v.* 7. God has *smitten Jacob*, and he is slain. Many of those *that understand among the people shall fall by the sword and by flame many days*, Dan. xi. 33. But it shall not be as those are smitten and slain, (1.) Who smote him formerly, who were the rod of God's anger and the staff in his hand, which he made use of for the correction of his people, and to whose turn it shall come to be reckoned with even for that: the child is spared, but the rod is burnt. (2.) Who shall afterwards be slain by him, when he shall get the dominion, and repay them in their own coin, or slain for his sake in the pleading of his cause. God's people and God's enemies are here represented, [1.] As struggling with each other; so the seed of the woman and the seed of the serpent have been, are, and will be. In this contest there are slain on both sides. God makes use of wicked men, not only to smite, but to slay his people; for they are his sword, Ps. xvii. 13. But, when the cup of trembling comes to be put into their hand, it will be much worse with them than ever it was with God's people in their greatest straits. The seed of the woman has only his heel bruised, but the serpent has his head crushed and broken. Note, Though God's persecuted people may be great losers, and great sufferers, for a while, yet those that oppress them will prove to be greater losers and greater sufferers at last, here or hereafter; for God will render double to them, Rev. xviii. 6. [2.] As sharing together in the calamities of this present time. They are both smitten, both slain, and both by the hand of God; for there is *one event to the righteous and to the wicked*. But is Jacob smitten as his enemies are? No, by no means; to him the property is altered, and it becomes quite another thing. Note, However it may seem to us, there is really a vast difference between the afflictions and deaths of good people and the afflictions and deaths of wicked people.

2. Though God will debate with them, yet it shall be in measure, and the affliction shall be mitigated, moderated, and proportioned to their strength, not to their deserts, *v.* 8. He will deal out afflictions to them as the wise physician prescribes medicines to his patients, just such a quantity of each ingredient, or orders how much blood shall be taken when a vein is opened: thus God orders the troubles of his people, not *suffering them to be tempted above what they are able,*

1 Cor. x. 13. He measures out their afflictions by a little at a time, that they may not be pressed above measure; for he knows their frame, and corrects in judgment, and does not stir up all his wrath. When the affliction is shooting forth, when he is sending it out and giving it its commission, then he debates in measure, and not in extremity. He considers what we can bear when he begins to correct; and when he proceeds in his controversy, so that it is the *day of his eastwind*, which is not only blustering and noisy, but blasting and noxious, yet he stays his rough wind, checks it, and sets bounds to it, does not suffer it to blow so hard as was feared; when he is winnowing his corn, it is with a gentle gale, that shall only blow away the chaff, but not the good corn. God has the winds at his command, and every affliction under his check. *Hitherto it shall go, but no further.* Let us not despair when things are at the worst; be the winds ever so rough, ever so high, God can say unto them, *Peace, be still.*

3. Though God will afflict them, yet he will make their afflictions to work for the good of their souls, and correct them as the father does the child, to drive out the foolishness that is bound up in their hearts (*v. 9*): *By this therefore shall the iniquity of Jacob be purged.* This is the design of the affliction, to this it is adapted as a proper means, and, by the grace of God working with it, it shall have this blessed effect. It shall mortify the habits of sin; by this those defilements of the soul shall be purged away. It shall break them off from the practice of sin: *This is all the fruit*, this is it that God intends, this is all the harm it will do them, *to take away their sin*, than which they could not have a greater kindness done them, though it be at the expense of an affliction. Therefore, because the affliction is mitigated and moderated, and the rough wind stayed, therefore we may conclude that he designs their reformation, not their destruction; and, because he deals thus gently with us, we should therefore study to answer his ends in afflicting us. The particular sin which the affliction was intended to cure them of was the sin of idolatry, the sin which did most easily beset that people and to which they were strangely addicted. *Ephraim is joined to idols.* But by the captivity in Babylon they were not only weaned from this sin, but set against it. *Ephraim shall say, What have I to do any more with idols?* Jacob has his sin taken away, his beloved sin, *when he makes all the stones of the altar*, of his idolatrous altar, the stones of which were precious and sacred to him, *as chalkstones that are beaten asunder;* he not only has them in contempt, and values them no more than chalk-stones, but he conceives an indignation at them, and, in a holy revenge, beats them asunder as easily as chalk-stones are broken to pieces. *The groves and the*

images shall not stand before this penitent, but they shall be thrown down too, never to be set up again. This was according to the law for the demolishing and destroying of all the monuments of idolatry (Deut. vii. 5); and according to this promise, since the captivity in Babylon, no people in the world have such a rooted aversion to idols and idolatry as the people of the Jews. Note, The design of affliction is to separate between us and sin, especially that which has been *our own iniquity;* and then it appears that the affliction has done us good when we keep at a distance from the occasions of sin, and use all needful precaution that we may not only not relapse into it, but not so much as be tempted to it, Ps. cxix. 67.

4. Though Jerusalem shall be desolate and forsaken for a time, yet there will come a day when its scattered friends shall resort to it again out of all the countries whither they were dispersed (*v. 12, 13*); though the body of the nation is abandoned as a people of no understanding, yet those that are indeed children of Israel shall be gathered together again, as the sheep of the flock when the shepherds that scattered them are reckoned with, Ezek. xxxiv. 10—19. Now observe concerning these scattered Israelites, (1.) Whence they shall be fetched: *The Lord shall beat them off* as fruit from the tree, or beat them out as corn out of the ear. He shall find them out, and separate them from those among whom they dwelt, and with whom they seemed to be incorporated, *from the channel of the river* Euphrates northeast, *unto* Nile, *the stream of Egypt*, which lay south-west—those that were driven into the land of Assyria, and were captives there in the land of their enemies, where they were ready to perish for want of necessaries, and ready to despair of deliverance—and those that were *outcasts in the land of Egypt*, whither many of those that were left behind, after the captivity in Babylon, went, contrary to God's express command (Jer. xliii. 6, 7), and there lived as outcasts: God has mercy in store for them all, and will make it to appear that, though they are cast out, they are not cast off. (2.) In what manner they shall be brought back: *" You shall be gathered one by one*, not in multitudes, not in troops forcing your way; but silently, and as it were by stealth, dropping in, first one, and then another."* This intimates that the remnant that shall be saved consists but of few, and those saved with difficulty, and so as by fire, scarcely saved; they shall not come for company, but as God shall stir up every man's spirit. (3.) By what means they shall be gathered together: *The great trumpet shall be blown, and* then *they shall come.* Cyrus's proclamation of liberty to the captives is this great trumpet, which awakened the Jews that were asleep in their thraldom to bestir themselves; it was like the sounding of the jubilee-trumpet, which

published the year of release. This is applicable both to the preaching of the gospel, by which sinners are gathered in to the grace of God, such as were outcasts and ready to perish (those that were afar off are made nigh; the gospel proclaims the acceptable year of the Lord), and also to the archangel's trumpet at the last day, by which saints shall be gathered to the glory of God, that lay as outcasts in their graves. (4.) For what end they shall be gathered together: *To worship the Lord in the holy mount at Jerusalem.* When the captives rallied again, and returned to their own land, the chief thing they had their eye upon, and the first thing they applied themselves to, was the worship of God. The holy temple was in ruins, but they had the holy mount, *the place of the altar,* Gen. xiii. 4. Liberty to worship God is the most valuable and desirable liberty; and, after restraints and dispersions, a free access to his house should be more welcome to us than a free access to our own houses. Those that are gathered by the sounding of the gospel trumpet are brought in to worship God and added to the church; and the great trumpet of all will gather the saints together, *to serve God day and night in his temple.*

CHAP. XXVIII.

In this chapter, I. The Ephraimites are reproved and threatened for their pride and drunkenness, their security and sensuality, ver. 1—8. But, in the midst of this, here is a gracious promise of God's favour to the remnant of his people, ver. 5—6. II. They are likewise reproved and threatened for their dulness and stupidity, and unaptness to profit by the instructions which the prophets gave them in God's name, ver. 9—13. III. The rulers of Jerusalem are reproved and threatened for their insolent contempt of God's judgments, and setting them at defiance; and, after a gracious promise of Christ and his grace, they are made to know that the vain hopes of escaping the judgments of God with which they flattered themselves would certainly deceive them, ver. 14—22. IV. All this is confirmed by a comparison borrowed from the method which the husbandman takes with his ground and grain, according to which they must expect God would proceed with his people, whom he had lately called his threshing and the corn of his floor (ch. xxi. 10) ver. 23—29. This is written for our admonition, and is profitable for reproof and warning to us.

WOE to the crown of pride, to the drunkards of Ephraim, whose glorious beauty *is* a fading flower, which *are* on the head of the fat valleys of them that are overcome with wine! 2 Behold, the Lord hath a mighty and strong one, *which* as a tempest of hail *and* a destroying storm, as a flood of mighty waters overflowing, shall cast down to the earth with the hand. 3 The crown of pride, the drunkards of Ephraim, shall be trodden under feet: 4 And the glorious beauty, which *is* on the head of the fat valley, shall be a fading flower, *and* as the hasty fruit before the summer; which *when* he that looketh upon it seeth, while it is yet in his hand, he eateth it up. 5 In that day shall the LORD of hosts be

for a crown of glory, and for a diadem of beauty, unto the residue of his people, 6 And for a spirit of judgment to him that sitteth in judgment, and for strength to them that turn the battle to the gate. 7 But they also have erred through wine, and through strong drink are out of the way; the priest and the prophet have erred through strong drink, they are swallowed up of wine, they are out of the way through strong drink; they err in vision, they stumble *in* judgment. 8 For all tables are full of vomit *and* filthiness, *so that there is* no place *clean.*

Here, I. The prophet warns the kingdom of the ten tribes of the judgments that were coming upon them for their sins, which were soon after executed by the king of Assyria, who laid their country waste, and carried the people into captivity. Ephraim had his name from *fruitfulness,* their soil being very fertile and the products of it abundant and the best of the kind; they had a great many *fat valleys* (v 1, 4), and Samaria, which was situated on a hill, was, as it were, *on the head of the fat valleys.* Their country was rich and pleasant, and as the garden of the Lord: it was the glory of Canaan, as that was the glory of all lands; their harvest and vintage were the *glorious beauty* on the head of their valleys, which were covered over with corn and vines. Now observe,

1. What an ill use they made of their plenty. What God gave them to serve him with they perverted, and abused, by making it the food and fuel of their lusts. (1.) They were puffed up with pride by it. The goodness with which God crowned their years, which should have been to him a crown of praise, was to them a *crown of pride.* Those that are rich in the world are apt to be high-minded, 1 Tim. vi. 17. Their king, who wore the crown, was proud that he ruled over so rich a country; Samaria, their royal city, was notorious for pride. Perhaps it was usual at their festivals, or revels, to wear garlands made up of flowers and ears of corn, which they wore in honour of their fruitful country. Pride was a sin that generally prevailed among them, and therefore the prophet, in his name who resists the proud, boldly proclaims a *woe to the crown of pride.* If those who wear crowns be proud of them, let them not think to escape this woe. What men are proud of, be it ever so mean, is to them as a crown; he that is proud thinks himself as great as a king. But woe to those who thus exalt themselves, for they shall be abased; their pride is the preface to their destruction. (2.) They indulged themselves in sensuality.

Ephraim was notorious for drunkenness, and excess of riot; Samaria, the head of the fat valleys, was full of those that were *overcome with wine*, were *broken with it*, so the margin. See how foolishly drunkards act, and no marvel when, in the very commission of the sin, they make fools and brutes of themselves; they yield, [1.] To be conquered by the sin; it overcomes them, and *brings them into bondage* (2 Pet. ii. 19); they are led captive by it, and the captivity is the more shameful and inglorious because it is voluntary. Some of these wretched slaves have themselves owned that there is not a greater drudgery in the world than hard drinking. They are overcome not with the wine, but with the love of it. [2.] To be ruined by it. They are broken by wine. Their constitution is broken by it, and their health ruined. They are broken in their callings and estates, and their families are brought to ruin by it. Their peace with God is broken, and their souls are in danger of being eternally undone, and all this for the gratification of a base lust. Woe to these *drunkards of Ephraim!* Ministers must bring the general woes of the word home to particular places and persons. We must say, *Woe to drunkards;* their condition is a woeful condition, their brutish pleasures are to be pitied, and not envied; *they shall not inherit the kingdom of God* (1 Cor. vi. 10); the curse is in force against them, Deut. xxix. 19, 20. Nay, we must go further, and say, *Woe to the drunkards of such a place*, that they may hear and fear; nay, and, *Woe to this or that person*, if he be a drunkard. There is a particular woe to the drunkards of Ephraim, for they are of God's professing people, and it becomes them worse than any other; they know better, and therefore should give a better example. Some make the *crown of pride* to belong to the drunkards, and to mean the garlands with which those were crowned that got the victory in their wicked drinking matches and drank down the rest of the company. They were proud of their being mighty to drink wine; but woe to those who thus glory in their shame.

2. The justice of God in taking away their plenty from them, which they thus abused. Their *glorious beauty*, the plenty they were proud of, *is but a fading flower;* it is meat that perishes. The most substantial fruits, if God blast them and blow upon them, are but fading flowers, *v.* 1. God can easily *take away their corn in the season thereof* (Hos. ii. 9), and recover *locum vastatum—ground that has been alienated and has run to waste*, those goods of his which they prepared for Baal. God has an officer ready to make a seizure for him, has one at his beck, *a mighty and strong one*, who is able to do the business, even the king of Assyria, who *shall cast down to the earth with the hand*, shall easily and effectually, and with the turn of a hand, destroy all that

which they are proud of and pleased with, *v.* 2. He shall throw it down to the ground, to be broken to pieces with a strong hand, with a hand that they cannot oppose. Then *the crown of pride*, and *the drunkards of Ephraim, shall be trodden under foot* (*v.* 3); they shall lie exposed to contempt, and shall not be able to recover themselves. Drunkards, in their folly, are apt to talk proudly, and vaunt themselves most when they most shame themselves; but they thereby render themselves the more ridiculous. The beauty of their valleys, which they gloried in, will be, (1.) Like *a fading flower* (as before, *v.* 1); it will wither of itself, and has in itself the principles of its own corruption; it will perish in time by its own moth and rust. (2.) Like *the hasty fruit*, which, as soon as it is discovered, is plucked and eaten up; so the wealth of this world, besides that it is apt to decay of itself, is subject to be devoured by others as greedily as the first-ripe fruit, which is earnestly desired, Mic. vii. 1. *Thieves break through and steal.* The harvest which the worldling is proud of *the hungry eat up* (Job v. 5); no sooner do they see the prey but they catch at it, and swallow up all they can lay their hands on. It is likewise easily devoured, as that fruit which, being ripe before it has grown, is very small, and is soon eaten up; and there being little of it, and that of little worth, it is not reserved, but used immediately.

II. He next turns to the kingdom of Judah, whom he calls the *residue of his people* (*v.* 5), for they were but two tribes to the other ten.

1. He promises them God's favours, and that they shall be taken under his guidance and protection when the beauty of Ephraim shall be left exposed to be trodden down and eaten up, *v.* 5, 6. *In that day*, when the Assyrian army is laying Israel waste, and Judah might think that their neighbour's house being on fire their own was in danger, in that day of treading down and perplexity, then God will be to the residue of his people all they need and can desire; not only to the kingdom of Judah, but to those of Israel who had kept their integrity, and, as was probably the case with some, betook themselves to the land of Judah, to be sheltered by good king Hezekiah. When the Assyrian, that mighty one, was in Israel as *a tempest of hail*, noisy and battering, as *a destroying storm* bearing down all before it, especially at sea, and as *a flood of mighty waters overflowing* the country (*v.* 2), then *in that day will the Lord of hosts*, of all hosts, distinguish by peculiar favours his people who have distinguished themselves by a steady and singular adherence to him, and that which they most need he will himself be to them. This very much enhances the worth of the promises that God, covenanting to be to his people a God all-

sufficient, undertakes to be himself all that to them which they can desire. (1.) He will put all the credit and honour upon them which are requisite, not only to rescue them from contempt, but to gain them esteem and reputation. He will be to them *for a crown of glory and for a diadem of beauty.* Those that wore the crown of pride looked upon God's people with disdain, and trampled upon them, for they were the song of the drunkards of Ephraim; but God will so appear for them by his providence as to make it evident that they have his favour towards them, and that shall be to them a crown of glory; for what greater glory can any people have than for God to acknow-ledge them as his own? And he will so appear in them, by his grace, as to make it evident that they have his image renewed on them, and that shall be to them a diadem of beauty; for what greater beauty can any person have than the beauty of holiness? Note, Those that have God for their God have him for a crown of glory and a diadem of beauty; for they are made to him kings and priests. (2.) He will give them all the wisdom and grace necessary to the due dis-charge of the duty of their place. He will himself be *a spirit of judgment to those that sit in judgment;* the privy counsellors shall be guided by wisdom and discretion and the judges shall govern by justice and equity. It is a great mercy to any people when those that are called to places of power and public trust are qualified for their places, when those that sit in judgment have a spirit of judgment, a spirit of government. (3.) He will give them all the courage and boldness requisite to carry them resolutely through the difficulties and oppositions they are likely to meet with. He will be *for strength to those that turn the battle to the gate,* to the gates of the enemy whose cities they besiege, or to their own gates, when they sally out upon the enemies that besiege them. The strength of the soldiery depends as much upon God as the wisdom of the magistracy; and where God gives both these he is to that people a crown of glory. This may well be supposed to refer to Christ, and so the Chaldee para-phrast understands it: *In that day shall the Messiah be a crown of glory.* Simeon calls him the *glory of his people Israel;* and he is made of God to us wisdom, righteousness, and strength.

2. He complains of the corruptions that were found among them, and the many corrupt ones (*v.* 7): *But they also,* many of those of Judah, *have erred through wine.* There are drunkards of Jerusalem, as well as drunkards of Ephraim; and therefore the mercy of God is to be so much the more admired that he has not blasted the glory of Judah as he has done that of Ephraim. Sparing mercy lays us under peculiar obligations when it is thus distin-guishing. Ephraim's sins are found in

Judah, and yet not Ephraim's ruins. *They have erred through wine.* Their drinking to excess is itself a practical error; they think to raise their fancy by it, but they ruin their judgment, and so put a cheat upon themselves; they think to preserve their health by it and help digestion, but they spoil their constitution and hasten diseases and deaths. It is also the occasion of a great many errors in principle; their understanding is clouded and their con-science debauched by it; and therefore, to support themselves in it, they espouse cor-rupt notions, and form their minds in favour of their lusts. Probably some were drawn in to worship idols by their love of the wine and strong drink which there was plenty of at their idolatrous festivals; and so they erred through wine, as Israel, for love of the daughters of Moab, joined themselves to Baal-peor. Three things are here ob-served as aggravations of this sin :—(1.) That those were guilty of it whose business it was to warn others against it and to teach them better, and therefore who ought to have set a better example : *The priest and the prophet are swallowed up of wine;* their office is quite drowned and lost in it. The priests, as sacrificers, were obliged by a particular law to be temperate (Lev. x. 9), and, as rulers and magistrates, it was not for them to drink wine, Prov. xxxi. 4. The prophets were a kind of Nazarites (as ap-pears by Amos ii. 11), and, as reprovers by office, were concerned to keep at the utmost distance from the sins they reproved in others; yet there were many of them en-snared in this sin. What! a priest, a pro-phet, a minister, and yet drunk! *Tell it not in Gath.* Such a scandal are they to their coat. (2.) That the consequences of it were very pernicious, not only by the ill influence of their example, but the prophet, when he was drunk, *erred in vision;* the false prophets plainly discovered themselves to be so when they were in drink. The priest *stumbled in judgment and forgot the law* (Prov. xxxi. 5); he reeled and staggered as much in the operations of his mind as in the motions of his body. What wisdom or justice can be expected from those that sacrifice reason, and virtue, and conscience, and all that is valuable to such a base lust as the love of strong drink is? Happy art thou, O land! when *thy princes eat* and drink *for strength, and not for drunkenness,* Eccl. x. 17. (3.) That the disease was epidemic, and the generality of those that kept any thing of a table were infected with it : *All tables are full of vomit, v.* 8. See what an odious thing the sin of drunken-ness is, what an affront it is to human society; it is rude and ill-mannered enough to sicken the beholders, for the tables where they eat their meat are filthily stained with the marks of this sin, which the sinners declare as Sodom. Their tables are full of vomit, so that the victor, instead of being proud of his crown, ought rather to be ashamed of it. It bodes ill to any people when so sottish a sin as drunkenness has become national.

9 Whom shall he teach knowledge? And whom shall he make to understand doctrine? *Them that are* weaned from the milk, *and* drawn from the breasts. 10 For precept *must be* upon precept, precept upon precept, line upon line, line upon line; here a little, *and* there a little: 11 For with stammering lips and another tongue will he speak to this people. 12 To whom he said, This *is* the rest *wherewith* ye may cause the weary to rest; and this *is* the refreshing: yet they would not hear. 13 But the word of the LORD was unto them precept upon precept, precept upon precept; line upon line, line upon line; here a little, *and* there a little; that they might go, and fall backward, and be broken, and snared, and taken.

The prophet here complains of the wretched stupidity of this people, that they were unteachable and made no improvement of the means of grace which they possessed; they still continued as they were, their mistakes not rectified, their hearts not renewed, nor their lives reformed. Observe, I. What it was that their prophets and ministers designed and aimed at. It was to *teach* them *knowledge*, the knowledge of God and his will, and to *make them understand doctrine,* *v.* 9. This is God's way of dealing with men, to enlighten men's minds first with the knowledge of his truth, and thus to gain their affections, and bring their wills into a compliance with his laws; thus he enters in by the door, whereas the thief and the robber climb up another way. II. What method they took, in pursuance of this design. They left no means untried to do them good, but taught them as children are taught, little children that are beginning to learn, that are taken from the breast to the book (*v.* 9), for among the Jews it was common for mothers to nurse their children till they were three years old, and almost ready to go to school. And it is good to begin betimes with children, to teach them, as they are capable, the good knowledge of the Lord, and to instruct them even when they are but newly weaned from the milk. The prophets taught them as children are taught; for, 1. They were constant and industrious in teaching them. They took great pains with them, and
152

with great prudence, teaching them as they needed it and were able to bear it (*v.* 10): *Precept upon precept. It must be so,* or (as some read) *it has been so.* They have been taught, as children are taught to read, by *precept upon precept,* and taught to write by *line upon line, a little here* and *a little there,* a little of one thing and a little of another, that the variety of instructions might be pleasing and inviting,—a little at one time and a little at another, that they might not have their memories overcharged,—a little from one prophet and a little from another, that every one might be pleased with his friend and him whom he admired. Note, For our instruction in the things of God it is requisite that we have precept upon precept and line upon line, that one precept and line should be followed, and so enforced, by another; the precept of justice must be upon the precept of piety, and the precept of charity upon that of justice. Nay, it is necessary that the same precept and the same line should be often repeated and inculcated upon us, that we may the better understand them and the more easily recollect them when we have occasion for them. Teachers should accommodate themselves to the capacity of the learners, give them what they most need and can best bear, and a little at a time, Deut. vi. 6, 7. 2. They courted and persuaded them to learn, *v.* 12. God, by his prophets, said to them, " *This* way that we are directing you to, and directing you in, *is the rest,* the only rest, *wherewith you may cause the weary to rest; and this will be the refreshing* of your own souls, and will bring rest to your country from the wars and other calamities with which it has been long harassed." Note, God by his word calls us to nothing but what is really for our advantage; for the service of God is the only true rest for those that are weary of the service of sin and there is no refreshing but under the easy yoke of the Lord Jesus.

III. What little effect all this had upon the people. They were as unapt to learn as young children newly weaned from the milk, and it was as impossible to fasten any thing upon them (*v.* 9): nay, one would choose rather to teach a child of two years old than undertake to teach them; for they have not only (like such a child) no capacity to receive what is taught them, but they are prejudiced against it. As children, they have *need of milk,* and *cannot bear strong meat,* Heb. v. 12. 1. They *would not hear* (*v.* 12), no, not that which would be rest and refreshing to them. They had no mind to hear it. The word of God commanded their serious attention, but could not gain it; they were where it was preached, but they turned a deaf ear to it, or as it came in at one ear it went out at the other. 2. They would not heed. It was unto them *precept upon precept, and line upon line* (*v.* 13);

they went on in a road of external performances; they kept up the old custom of attending upon the prophet's preaching and it was continually sounding in their ears, but that was all; it made no impression upon them; they had the letter of the precept, but no experience of the power and spirit of it; it was continually beating upon them, but it beat nothing into them. Nay, 3. It should seem, they ridiculed the prophet's preaching, and bantered it. The word of the Lord was unto them *Tsau latsau, kau lakau;* in the original it is in rhyme; they made a song of the prophet's words, and sang it when they were merry over their wine. David was the song of the drunkards. It is great impiety, and a high affront to God, thus to make a jest of sacred things, to speak of that vainly which should make us serious.

IV. How severely God would reckon with them for this. 1 He would deprive them of the privilege of plain preaching, and speak to them *with stammering lips and another tongue, v.* 11. Those that will not understand what is plain and level to their capacity, but despise it as mean and trifling, are justly amused with that which is above them. Or God will send foreign armies among them, whose language they understand not, to lay their country waste. Those that will not hear the comfortable voice of God's word shall be made to hear the dreadful voice of his rod. Or these words may be taken as denoting God's gracious condescension to their capacity in his dealing with them; he lisped to them in their own language, as nurses do to their children, with stammering lips, to humour them; he changed his voice, tried first one way and then another; the apostle quotes it as a favour (1 Cor. xiv. 21), applying it to the gift of tongues, and complaining that yet for all this they would not hear. 2. He would bring utter ruin upon them. By their profane contempt of God and his word they are but hastening on their own ruin, and ripening themselves for it; it is *that they may go and fall backward,* may grow worse and worse, may depart further and further from God, and proceed from one sin to another, till they be quite *broken, and snared, and taken,* and ruined, *v.* 13. They have here a little and there a little of the word of God; they think it too much, and *say to the seers, See not;* but it proves too little to convert them, and will prove enough to condemn them. If it be not a *savour of life unto life,* it will be *a savour of death unto death.*

14 Wherefore hear the word of the Lord, ye scornful men, that rule this people which *is* in Jerusalem. 15 Because ye have said, We have made a covenant with death, and with hell are we at agreement; when the over-flowing scourge shall pass through, it shall not come unto us; for we have made lies our refuge, and under falsehood have we hid ourselves: 16 Therefore thus saith the Lord God, Behold, I lay in Zion for a foundation a stone, a tried stone, a precious corner-*stone*, a sure foundation: he that believeth shall not make haste. 17 Judgment also will I lay to the line, and righteousness to the plummet: and the hail shall sweep away the refuge of lies, and the waters shall overflow the hiding-place. 18 And your covenant with death shall be disannulled, and your agreement with hell shall not stand; when the overflowing scourge shall pass through, then ye shall be trodden down by it. 19 From the time that it goeth forth it shall take you: for morning by morning shall it pass over, by day and by night: and it shall be a vexation only *to* understand the report. 20 For the bed is shorter than that *a man* can stretch himself *on it:* and the covering narrower than that he can wrap himself *in it.* 21 For the Lord shall rise up as *in* mount Perazim, he shall be wroth as *in* the valley of Gibeon, that he may do his work, his strange work; and bring to pass his act, his strange act. 22 Now therefore be ye not mockers, lest your bands be made strong: for I have heard from the Lord God of hosts a consumption, even determined upon the whole earth.

The prophet, having reproved those that made a jest of the word of God, here goes on to reprove those that made a jest of the judgments of God, and set them at defiance; for he is a jealous God, and will not suffer either his ordinances or his providences to be brought into contempt. He addresses himself to *the scornful men who ruled in Jerusalem,* who were the magistrates of the city, *v.* 14. It is bad with a people when their thrones of judgment become the seats of the scornful, when rulers are scorners; but that the rulers of Jerusalem should be men of such a character, that they should make light of God's judgments and scorn to take notice of the tokens of his displeasure, is very sad. Who will be mourners in Zion if they are scorners? Observe,

I. How these scornful men lulled themselves asleep in carnal security, and even challenged God Almighty to do his worst (*v.*

15)· *You have said, We have made a covenant with death and the grave.* They thought themselves as sure of their lives, even when the most destroying judgments were abroad, as if they had made a bargain with death, upon a valuable consideration, not to come till they sent for him or not to take them away by any violence, but by old age. If we be at peace with God, and have made a covenant with him, we have in effect made a covenant with death that it shall come in the fittest time, that, whenever it comes, it shall be no terror to us, nor do us any real damage; death is ours if we be Christ's (1 Cor. iii. 22, 23): but to think of making death our friend, or being in league with it, while by sin we are making God our enemy and are at war with him, is the greatest absurdity that can be. It was a fond conceit which these scorners had, " *When the overflowing scourge shall pass through* our country, and others shall fall under it, yet *it shall not come to us,* not reach us, though it extend far, not bear us down, though it is an overflowing scourge." It is the greatest folly imaginable for impenitent sinners to think that either in this world or the other they shall fare better than their neighbours. But what is the ground of their confidence? Why, truly, *We have made lies our refuge.* Either, 1. Those things which the prophets told them would be lies and falsehood to them and would deceive, but which they themselves looked upon as substantial fences. The protection of their idols, the promises with which their false prophets soothed them, their policy, their wealth, their interest in the people; these they confided in, and not in God; nay, these they confided in against God. Or, 2. Those things which should be lies and falsehood to the enemy, who was *flagellum Dei*—*the scourge of God,* the overflowing scourge; they would secure themselves by imposing upon the enemy with their stratagems of war, or their feigned submissions in treaties of peace. The rest of the cities of Judah were taken because they made an obstinate defence; but the rulers of Jerusalem hope to succeed better. They think themselves greater politicians than those of the country towns; they will compliment the king of Assyria with a promise to surrender their city, or to become tributaries to him, with a purpose at the same time to shake off his yoke as soon as the danger is over, not caring though they be found liars to him, as the expression is, Deut. xxxiii. 29. Note, Those put a cheat upon themselves that think to gain their point by putting cheats upon those they deal with. Those that pursue their designs by trick and fraud, by mean and paltry shifts, may perhaps compass them, but cannot expect comfort in them. Honesty is the best policy. But such refuges as these are those driven to that depart from God, and throw themselves out of his protection.

II. How God, by the prophet, awakens them out of this sleep, and shows them the folly of their security.

1. He tells them upon what grounds they might be secure. He does not disturb their false confidences, till he has first shown them a firm bottom on which they may repose themselves (*v.* 16): *Behold, I lay in Zion for a foundation a stone.* This foundation is, (1.) The promises of God in general —his word, upon which he has caused his people to hope—his covenant with Abraham, that he would be a God to him and his; this is a foundation, a foundation of stone, firm and lasting, for faith to build upon; it is *a tried stone,* for all the saints have stayed themselves upon it and it never failed them. (2.) The promise of Christ in particular; for to him this is expressly applied in the New Testament, 1 Pet. ii. 6—8. He is that stone which has become *the head of the corner.* The great promise of the Messiah and his kingdom, which was to begin at Jerusalem, was sufficient to make God's people easy in the worst of times; for they knew well that till he came *the sceptre should not depart from Judah.* Zion shall continue while this foundation is yet to be laid there. " *Thus saith the Lord Jehovah,* for the comfort of those that dare not *make lies their refuge,* Behold, and look upon me as one that has undertaken to *lay in Zion a Stone.*" Jesus Christ is a foundation of God's laying. *This is the Lord's doing.* He is laid in Zion, in the church, in the holy hill. He is a tried stone, a trying stone (so some), a touch-stone, that shall distinguish between true and counterfeit. He is a precious stone, for such are the foundations of the New Jerusalem (Rev. xxi. 19), a corner-stone, in whom the sides of the building are united, the *head-stone of the corner.* And *he that believes* these promises, and rests upon them, *shall not make haste,* shall not run to and fro in a hurry, as men at their wits' end, shall not be shifting hither and thither for his own safety, nor be driven to his feet by any terrors, as the wicked man is said to be (Job xviii. 11), but with a fixed heart shall quietly wait the event, saying, *Welcome the will of God.* He *shall not make haste* in his expectations, so as to anticipate the time set in the divine counsels, but, though it tarry, will wait the appointed hour, knowing that *he that shall come will come, and will not tarry.* He that believes will not make more haste than good speed, but be satisfied that God's time is the best time, and wait with patience for it. The apostle from the LXX. explains this, 1 Pet. ii. 6. *He that believes on him shall not be confounded;* his expectations shall not be frustrated, but far out-done.

2. He tells them that upon the grounds which they now built on they could not be safe, but their confidences would certainly fail them (*v.* 17): *Judgment will I lay to the line, and righteousness to the plummet.* This denotes,

(1.) The building up of his church ; having laid the foundation (*v.* 16), he will raise the structure, as builders do, by line and plummet, Zech. iv. 10. Righteousness shall be the line and judgment the plummet. The church, being founded on Christ, shall be formed and reformed by the scripture, the standing rule of judgment and righteousness. *Judgment shall return unto righteousness,* Ps. xciv. 15. Or,

(2.) The punishing of the church's enemies, against whom he will proceed in strict justice, according to the threatenings of the law. He will give them their deserts, and bring upon them the judgments they have challenged, but in wisdom too, and by an exact rule, that the tares may not be plucked up with the wheat. And when God comes thus to execute judgment,

[1.] These scornful men will be made ashamed of the vain hopes with which they had deluded themselves. *First,* They designed to make lies their refuge ; but it will indeed prove a refuge of lies, which *the hail shall sweep away,* that tempest of hail spoken of *v.* 2. Those that make lies their refuge build upon the sand, and the building will fall when the storm comes, and bury the builder in the ruins of it. Those that make any thing their hiding place but Christ shall find that the waters will overflow it, as every shelter but the ark was over-topped and overthrown by the waters of the deluge. Such is the hope of the hypocrite ; this will come of all his confidences. *Secondly,* They boasted of a covenant with death, and an agreement with the grave ; but it shall be *disannulled,* as made without his consent who has the keys and sovereign command of hell and death. Those do but delude themselves that think by any wiles to evade the judgments of God. *Thirdly,* They fancied that when the overflowing scourge should pass through the land it should not come near them ; but the prophet tells them that then, when others were falling by the common calamity, they should not only share in it, but should be trodden down by it : " You shall be to it for a treading down ; it shall triumph over you as much as over any other, and you shall become its easy prey." They are further told (*v.* 19), 1. That it shall begin with them ; they shall be so far from escaping it that they shall be the first that shall fall by it : " *From the time it goes forth it shall take you,* as if it came on purpose to seize you." 2. That it shall pursue them closely : " *Morning by morning shall it pass over ;* as duly as the day returns you shall hear of some desolation or other made by it ; for divine justice will follow its blow ; you shall never be safe nor easy by day nor by night ; there shall be a pestilence walking in darkness and a destruction wasting at noonday." 3. That there shall be no avoiding it : " The understanding of the report of its approach shall not give you any opportunity

to make your escape, for there shall be no way of escape open ; but it shall be only a vexation, you shall see it coming, and not see how to help yourselves." Or, " The very report of it at a distance will be a terror to you ; what then will the thing itself be ?" Evil tidings are a terror and vexation to scorners, but he whose heart is fixed, *trusting in God, is not afraid of them ;* whereas, when the *overflowing scourge* comes, then all the comforts and confidences of scorners fail them, *v.* 20. (1.) That in which they thought to repose themselves reaches not to the length of their expectations : *The bed is shorter than that a man can stretch himself upon it,* so that he is forced to cramp and contract himself. (2.) That in which they thought to shelter themselves proves insufficient to answer the intention : *The covering is narrower than that a man can wrap himself in it.* Those that do not build upon Christ as their foundation, but rest in a righteousness of their own, will prove in the end thus to have deceived themselves ; they can never be easy, safe, nor warm ; the bed is too short, the covering is too narrow ; like our first parents' fig-leaves, the shame of their nakedness will still appear.

[2.] God will be glorified in the accomplishment of his counsels, *v.* 21. When God comes to contend with these scorners, *First, He will do his work, and bring to pass his act,* he will work for his own honour and glory, according to his own purpose ; the work shall appear to all that see it to be the work of God as the righteous Judge of the earth. *Secondly,* He will do it now against his people, as formerly he did it against their enemies, by which his justice will appear to be impartial ; he will now *rise up against Jerusalem as,* in David's time, against the Philistines *in Mount Perazim* (2 Sam. v. 20), and as, in Joshua's time, against the Canaanites *in the valley of Gibeon.* If those that profess themselves members of God's church by their pride and scornfulness make themselves like Philistines and Canaanites, they must expect to be dealt with as such. *Thirdly,* This will be *his strange work, his strange act,* his foreign deed. It is work that he is backward to : he rather delights in showing mercy, and *does not afflict willingly.* It is work that he is not used to as to his own people ; he protects and favours them. It is a strange work indeed if he *turn to be their enemy and fight against them,* ch. lxiii. 10. It is a work that all the neighbours will stand amazed at (Deut. xxix. 24), and therefore the ruins of Jerusalem are said to be *an astonishment,* Jer. xxv. 18.

Lastly, We have the use and application of all this (*v.* 22): " *Therefore be you not mockers ;* dare not to ridicule either the reproofs of God's word or the approaches of his judgments." *Mocking the messengers of the Lord* was Jerusalem's measure-filling sin. The consideration of the judgments of

God that are coming upon hypocritical professors should effectually silence mockers, and make them serious: "*Be you not mockers, lest your bands be made strong*, both the bands by which you are bound under the dominion of sin" (for there is little hope of the conversion of mockers) "and the bands by which you are bound over to the judgments of God." God has bands of justice strong enough to hold those that break all the bonds of his law asunder and cast away all his cords from them. Let not these mockers make light of divine threatenings, for the prophet (who is one of those with whom the secret of the Lord is) assures them that the Lord God of hosts has, in his hearing, *determined a consumption upon the whole earth;* and can they think to escape? or shall their unbelief invalidate the threatening?

23 Give ye ear, and hear my voice; hearken, and hear my speech. 24 Doth the ploughman plough all day to sow? Doth he open and break the clods of his ground? 25 When he hath made plain the face thereof, doth he not cast abroad the fitches, and scatter the cummin, and cast in the principal wheat and the appointed barley and the rie in their place? 26 For his God doth instruct him to discretion, *and* doth teach him. 27 For the fitches are not threshed with a threshing-instrument, neither is a cart-wheel turned about upon the cummin; but the fitches are beaten out with a staff; and the cummin with a rod. 28 Bread-*corn* is bruised; because he will not ever be threshing it, nor break *it with* the wheel of his cart, nor bruise it *with* his horsemen. 29 This also cometh forth from the Lord of hosts, *which* is wonderful in counsel, *and* excellent in working.

This parable, which (like many of our Saviour's parables) is borrowed from the husbandman's calling, is ushered in with a solemn preface demanding attention, *He that has ears to hear, let him hear,* hear and understand, *v.* 23.

I. The parable here is plain enough, that the husbandman applies himself to the business of his calling with a great deal of pains and prudence, *secundum artem—according to rule,* and, as his judgment directs him, observes a method and order in his work. 1. In his ploughing and sowing: *Does the ploughman plough all day to sow?* Yes, he does, and he *ploughs in hope* and *sows in hope,* 1 Cor. ix. 10. *Does he open and break the clods?* Yes, he does, that the land may be fit to receive the seed. And *when he has thus*

156

made plain the face thereof does he not sow his seed, seed suitable to the soil? For the husbandman knows what grain is fit for clayey ground and what for sandy ground, and, accordingly, he sows each in its place— *wheat in the principal place* (so the margin reads it), for it is the principal grain, and was a staple commodity of Canaan (Ezek. xxvii. 17), *and barley in the appointed place.* The wisdom and goodness of the God of nature are to be observed in this, that, to oblige his creatures with a grateful variety of productions, he has suited to them an agreeable variety of earths. 2. In his threshing, *v.* 27, 28. This also he proportions to the grain that is to be threshed out. *The fitches and the cummin,* being easily got out of their husk or ear, are only threshed with *a staff and a rod;* but *the bread-corn* requires more force, and therefore that must be bruised with *a threshing instrument,* a sledge shod with iron, that was drawn to and fro over it, to beat out the corn; and yet *he will not be ever threshing it,* nor any longer than is necessary to loosen the corn from the chaff; *he will not break it,* or crush it, into the ground *with the wheel of his cart, nor bruise it* to pieces *with his horsemen;* the grinding of it is reserved for another operation. Observe, by the way, what pains are to be taken, not only for the earning, but for the preparing of our necessary food; and yet, after all, it is *meat that perishes.* Shall we then grudge to labour much more for the *meat which endures to everlasting life? Bread-corn is bruised.* Christ was so; *it pleased the Lord to bruise him,* that he might be the bread of life to us. II. The interpretation of the parable is not so plain. Most interpreters make it a further answer to those who set the judgments of God at defiance: "Let them know that as the husbandman will not be always ploughing, but will at length sow his seed, so God will not be always threatening, but will at length execute his threatenings and bring upon sinners the judgments they have deserved; but in wisdom, and in proportion to their strength, not that they may be ruined, but that they may be reformed and brought to repentance by them." But I think we may give this parable a greater latitude in the exposition of it. 1. In general, that God who gives the husbandman this wisdom is, doubtless, himself infinitely wise. It is God that *instructs the husbandman to discretion,* as *his God, v.* 26. Husbandmen have need of discretion wherewith to order their affairs, and ought not to undertake that business unless they do in some measure understand it; and they should by observation and experience endeavour to improve themselves in the knowledge of it. Since *the king himself is served of the field,* the advancing of the art of husbandry is a common service to mankind more than the cultivating of most other arts. The skill of the husbandman is from God, as every good and perfect gift is.

This takes off somewhat of the weight and terror of the sentence passed on man for sin, that when God, in execution of it, sent man to till the ground, he taught him how to do it most to his advantage, otherwise, in the greatness of his folly, he might have been for ever *tilling the sand of the sea*, labouring to no purpose. It is he that gives men capacity for this business, an inclination to it, and a delight in it ; and if some were not by Providence cut out for it, and made to rejoice (as Issachar, that tribe of husbandmen) in their tents, notwithstanding the toil and fatigue of this business, we should soon want the supports of life. If some are more discreet and judicious in managing these or any other affairs than others are, God must be acknowledged in it ; and to him husbandmen must seek for direction in their business, for they, above other men, have an immediate dependence upon the divine Providence. As to the other instance of the husbandman's conduct in threshing his corn, it is said, *This also comes forth from the Lord of hosts, v.* 29. Even the plainest dictate of sense and reason must be acknowledged to *come forth from the Lord of hosts.* And, if it is from him that men do things wisely and discreetly, we must needs acknowledge him to be *wise in counsel and excellent in working.* God's working is according to his will ; he never acts against his own mind, as men often do, and there is a counsel in his whole will : he is *therefore* excellent in working, because he is wonderful in counsel. 2. God's church is his husbandry, 1 Cor. 3. 9. If Christ is the true vine, his Father is the husbandman (John xv. 1), and he is continually by his word and ordinances cultivating it. *Does the ploughman plough all day*, and *break the clods* of his ground, that it may receive the seed, and does not God by his ministers break up the fallow ground? Does not the ploughman, when the ground is fitted for the seed, cast in the seed in its proper soil ? He does so, and so the great God sows his word by the hand of his ministers (Matt. xiii. 19), who are to divide the word of truth and give every one his portion. Whatever the soil of the heart is, there is some seed or other in the word proper for it. And, as the word of God, so the rod of God is thus wisely made use of. Afflictions are God's threshing-instruments, designed to loosen us from the world, to separate between us and our chaff, and to prepare us for use. And, as to these, God will make use of them as there is occasion ; but he will proportion them to our strength ; they shall be no heavier than there is need. If the rod and the staff will answer the end, he will not make use of his cart-wheel and his horsemen. And where these are necessary, as for the bruising of the bread-corn (which will not otherwise be got clean from the straw), yet he will not be ever threshing it, will not always chide, but his anger shall

endure but for a moment ; nor will he *crush under his feet the prisoners of the earth.* And herein we must acknowledge him *wonderful in counsel and excellent in working.*

CHAP. XXIX

This woe to Ariel, which we have in this chapter, is the same with the "burden of the valley of vision" (ch. xxii. 1), and (it is very probable) points at the same event—the besieging of Jerusalem by the Assyrian army, which was cut off there by an angel ; yet it is applicable to the destruction of Jerusalem by the Chaldeans, and its last desolations by the Romans. Here is, I. The event itself foretold, that Jerusalem should be greatly distressed (ver. 1—4. 6), but that their enemies, who distressed them, should be baffled and defeated, ver. 5, 7, 8. II. A reproof to three sorts of sinners:—1. Those that were stupid, and regardless of the warnings which the prophet gave them, ver. 9—12. 2. Those that were formal and hypocritical in their religious performances, ver. 13, 14. 3. Those politicians that atheistically and profanely despised God's providence, and set up their own projects in competition with it, ver. 15, 16. III. Precious promises of grace and mercy to a distinguished remnant whom God would sanctify, and in whom he would be sanctified, when their enemies and persecutors should be cut off, ver. 17—24.

WOE to Ariel, to Ariel, the city *where* David dwelt! Add ye year to year ; let them kill sacrifices. 2 Yet I will distress Ariel, and there shall be heaviness and sorrow : and it shall be unto me as Ariel. 3 And I will camp against thee round about, and will lay siege against thee with a mount, and I will raise forts against thee. 4 And thou shalt be brought down, *and* shalt speak out of the ground, and thy speech shall be low out of the dust, and thy voice shall be, as of one that hath a familiar spirit, out of the ground, and thy speech shall whisper out of the dust. 5 Moreover the multitude of thy strangers shall be like small dust, and the multitude of the terrible ones *shall be* as chaff that passeth away : yea, it shall be at an instant suddenly. 6 Thou shalt be visited of the LORD of hosts with thunder, and with earthquake, and great noise, with storm and tempest, and the flame of devouring fire. 7 And the multitude of all the nations that fight against Ariel, even all that fight against her and her munition, and that distress her, shall be as a dream of a night-vision. 8 It shall even be as when a hungry *man* dreameth, and, behold, he eateth ; but he awaketh, and his soul is empty : or as when a thirsty man dreameth, and, behold, he drinketh ; but he awaketh, and, behold, *he is* faint, and his soul hath appetite : so shall the multitude of all the nations be, that fight against mount Zion.

That it is Jerusalem which is here called *Ariel* is agreed, for that was the city where

David dwelt; that part of it which was called *Zion* was in a particular manner the city of David, in which both the temple and the palace were. But why it is so called is very uncertain : probably the name and the reason were then well known. Cities, as well as persons, get surnames and nick-names. *Ariel* signifies *the lion of God*, or *the strong lion :* as the lion is king among beasts, so was Jerusalem among the cities, giving law to all about her; it was *the city of the great King* (Ps. xlviii. 1, 2); it was the head-city of Judah, who is called *a lion's whelp* (Gen. xlix. 9) and whose ensign was a lion; and he that is the lion of the tribe of Judah was the glory of it. Jerusalem was a terror sometimes to the neighbouring nations, and, while she was a righteous city, was bold as a lion. Some make *Ariel* to signify *the altar of burnt-offerings*, which devoured the beasts offered in sacrifice as the lion does his prey. Woe to that altar in the city where David dwelt; that was destroyed with the temple by the Chaldeans. I rather take it as a woe to Jerusalem, Jerusalem; it is repeated here, as it is Matt. xxiii. 37, that it might be the more awakening. Here is,

I. The distress of Jerusalem foretold. Though Jerusalem be a strong city, as a lion, though a holy city, as a lion of God, yet, if iniquity be found there, woe be to it. It was *the city where David dwelt ;* it was he that brought that to it which was its glory, and which made it a type of the gospel church, and his dwelling in it was typical of Christ's residence in his church. This is mentioned as an aggravation of Jerusalem's sin, that in it were set both the testimony of Israel and the *thrones of the house of David.* 1. Let Jerusalem know that her external performance of religious services will not serve as an exemption from the judgments of God (*v.* 1): "*Add year to year;* go on in the road of your annual feasts, let all your males appear there three times a year before the Lord, and none empty, according to the law and custom, and let them never miss any of these solemnities : *let them kill the sacrifices,* as they used to do; but, as long as their lives are unreformed and their hearts unhumbled, let them not think thus to pacify an offended God and to turn away his wrath." Note, Hypocrites may be found in a constant track of devout exercises, and treading around in them, and with these they may flatter themselves, but can never please God nor make their peace with him. 2. Let her know that God is coming forth against her in displeasure, that she shall be *visited of the Lord of hosts* (*v.* 6); her sins shall be enquired into and punished: God will reckon for them with terrible judgments, with the frightful alarms and rueful desolations of war, which shall be like *thunder and earthquakes, storms and tempests, and devouring fire,* especially upon the account of the *great noise.* When a foreign enemy was not

158

in the borders, but in the bowels of their country, roaring and ravaging, and laying all waste (especially such an army as that of the Assyrians, whose commanders being so very insolent, as appears by the conduct of Rabshakeh, the common soldiers, no doubt, were much more rude), they might see the Lord of those hosts visiting them with thunder and storm. Yet, this being here said to be *a great noise,* perhaps it is intimated that they shall be worse frightened than hurt. Particularly, (1.) Jerusalem shall be besieged, straitly besieged. He does not say, *I will destroy Ariel,* but *I will distress Ariel ;* and she is *therefore* brought into distress, that, being thereby awakened to repent and reform, she may not be brought to destruction. *I will* (*v.* 3) *encamp against thee round about.* It was the enemy's army that encamped against it; but God says that he will do it, for they are his hand, he does it by them. God had often and long, by a host of angels, encamped for them round about them for their protection and deliverance; but now he was *turned to be their enemy* and fought against them. The siege laid against them was of his laying, and the forts raised against them were of his raising. Note, When men fight against us we must, in them, see God contending with us. (2.) She shall be in grief to see the country laid waste and all the fenced cities of Judah in the enemies' hand: *There shall be heaviness and sorrow* (*v.* 2), *mourning and lamentation* — so these two words are sometimes rendered. Those that are most merry and jovial are commonly, when they come to be in distress, most overwhelmed with heaviness and sorrow; their laughter is then turned into mourning. "All Jerusalem *shall* then *be unto me as Ariel,* as the altar, with fire upon it and slain victims about it : so it was when Jerusalem was destroyed by the Chaldeans; and many, no doubt, were slain when it was besieged by the Assyrians. "The whole city shall be an altar, in which sinners, falling by the judgments that are abroad, shall be as victims to divine justice." Or thus :—" *There shall be heaviness and sorrow ;* they shall repent, and reform, and return to God, and then it shall be to me as Ariel. Jerusalem shall be like itself, shall become to me a Jerusalem again, a holy city," *ch.* i. 26. (3.) She shall be humbled, and mortified, and made submissive (*v.* 4): "*Thou shalt be brought down* from the height of arrogancy and insolence to which thou hast arrived : the proud looks and the proud language shall be brought down by one humbling providence after another." Those that despise God's judgments shall be humbled by them; for the proudest sinners shall either bend or break before him. They had talked big, had *lifted up the horn on high,* and had *spoken with a stiff neck* (Ps. lxxv. 5); but now *thou shalt speak out of the ground, out of the dust, as one that has a familiar spirit, whispering out of the dust.* This intimates, [1.] That they should be faint and feeble, not able to speak up, nor to say all they would say ; but as those who are sick, or whose spirits are ready to fail, their speech shall be low and interrupted. [2.] That they should be fearful, and in consternation, forced to speak low as being afraid lest their enemies should overhear them and take advantage against them. [3.] That they should be tame, and obliged to submit to the conquerors. When Hezekiah submitted to the king of Assyria, saying, *I have offended, that which thou puttest on me I will bear* (2 Kings xviii. 14), then his speech was low, out of the dust. God can make those to crouch that have been most daring, and quite dispirit them.

II. The destruction of Jerusalem's enemies is foretold, for the comfort of all that were her friends and well-wishers in this distress (*v.* 5, 7) : " *Thou shalt be brought down* (*v.* 4), *to speak out of the dust ;* so low thou shalt be reduced. *But*" (so it may be rendered) " *the multitude of thy strangers and thy terrible ones,* the numerous armies of the enemy, *shall* themselves *be like small dust,* not able to speak at all, or so much as whisper, but *as chaff that passes away.* Thou shalt be abased, but they shall be quite dispersed, smitten and slain after another manner (*ch.* xxvii. 7) ; they shall pass away, *yea it shall be in an instant, suddenly :* the enemy shall be surprised with the destruction, and you with the salvation." The army of the Assyrians was by an angel laid dead upon the spot, in an instant, suddenly. Such will be the destruction of the enemies of the gospel Jerusalem. *In one hour shall their judgment come,* Rev. xviii. 10. Again (*v.* 6), " *Thou shalt be visited,* or (as it used to be rendered) *She shall be visited with thunder and a great noise.* Thou shalt be put into a fright which thou shalt soon recover. But (*v.* 7) *the multitude of the nations that fight against her shall be as a dream of a night-vision ;* they and their prosperity and success shall soon vanish past recal." *The multitude of the nations that fight against Zion shall be as a hungry man who dreams that he eats,* but still is hungry ; that is, 1. Whereas they hoped to make a prey of Jerusalem, and to enrich themselves with the plunder of that opulent city, their hopes shall prove vain dreams, with which their fancies may please and sport themselves for a while, but they shall be disappointed. They fancied themselves masters of Jerusalem, but shall never be so. 2. They themselves, and all their pomp, and power, and prosperity, shall vanish like a dream when one awakes, shall be of as little value and as short continuance, Ps. lxxiii. 20. He shall *fly away as a dream,* Job xx. 8. The army of Sennacherib vanished and was gone quickly, though it had filled the country as a dream fills a man's head, especially as a dream of meat fills the head of

him that went to bed hungry. Many understand these verses as part of the threatening of wrath, when God comes to distress Jerusalem, and lay siege to her. (1.) The multitude of her friends, whom she relies upon for help shall do her no good ; for, though they are terrible ones, they shall be like the small dust, and shall pass away. (2.) The multitude of her enemies shall never think they can do her mischief enough ; but, when they have devoured her much, still they shall be but like a man who dreams he eats, hungry, and greedy to devour her more.

9 Stay yourselves, and wonder ; cry ye out, and cry : they are drunken, but not with wine ; they stagger, but not with strong drink. 10 For the LORD hath poured out upon you the spirit of deep sleep, and hath closed your eyes : the prophets and your rulers, the seers hath he covered. 11 And the vision of all is become unto you as the words of a book that is sealed, which *men* deliver to one that is learned, saying, Read this, I pray thee : and he saith, I cannot, for it *is* sealed : 12 And the book is delivered to him that is not learned, saying, Read this, I pray thee : and he saith, I am not learned. 13 Wherefore the LORD said, Forasmuch as this people draw near *me* with their mouth, and with their lips do honour me, but have removed their heart far from me, and their fear toward me is taught by the precept of men : 14 Therefore, behold, I will proceed to do a marvellous work amongst this people, *even* a marvellous work and a wonder : for the wisdom of their wise *men* shall perish, and the understanding of their prudent *men* shall be hid. 15 Woe unto them that seek deep to hide their counsel from the LORD, and their works are in the dark, and they say, Who seeth us, and who knoweth us ? 16 Surely your turning of things upside down shall be esteemed as the potter's clay : for shall the work say of him that made it, He made me not ? Or shall the thing framed say of him that framed it, He had no understanding ?

Here, I. The prophet stands amazed at

the stupidity of the greatest part of the Jewish nation. They had Levites, who taught *the good knowledge of the Lord* and had encouragement from Hezekiah in doing so, 2 Chron. xxx. 22. They had prophets, who brought them messages immediately from God, and signified to them what were the causes and what would be the effects of God's displeasure against them. Now, one would think, *surely this great nation,* that has all the advantages of divine revelation, is *a wise and understanding people,* Deut. iv. 6. But, alas! it was quite otherwise, *v.* 9. The prophet addresses himself to the sober thinking part of them, calling upon them to be affected with the general carelessness of their neighbours. It may be read, "They delay, they put off, their repentance, but wonder you that they should be so sottish. They sport themselves with their own deceivings; they riot and revel; but do you *cry out,* lament their folly, cry to God by prayer for them. The more insensible they are of the hand of God gone out against them the more do you lay to heart these things." Note, The security of sinners in their sinful ways is just matter of lamentation and wonder to all serious people, who should think themselves concerned to pray for those that do not pray for themselves. But what is the matter? What are we thus to wonder at? 1. We may well wonder that the generality of the people should be so sottish and brutish, and so infatuated, as if they were intoxicated: *They are drunken, but not with wine* (not with wine only, though with that they were often drunk), and they *erred through wine, ch.* xxviii. 7. They were drunk with the love of pleasures, with prejudices against religion, and with the corrupt principles they had imbibed. Like drunken men, they know not what they do or say, nor whither they go. They are not sensible of the divine rebukes they are under. *They have beaten me, and I felt it not,* says the drunkard, Prov. xxiii. 35. God speaks to them once, yea, twice; but, like men drunk, they perceive it not, they understand it not, but forget the law. *They stagger* in their counsels, are unstable and unsteady, and stumble at every thing that lies in their way. There is such a thing as spiritual drunkenness. 2. It is yet more strange that God himself should have *poured out upon them a spirit of deep sleep, and closed their eyes* (*v.* 10), that he who bids them awake and open their eyes should yet lay them to sleep and shut their eyes; but it is in a way of righteous judgment, to punish them for their *loving darkness rather than light,* their loving sleep. When God by his prophets called them they said, *Yet a little sleep, a little slumber;* and therefore he gave them up to strong delusions, and said, *Sleep on now.* This is applied to the unbelieving Jews, who rejected the gospel

of Christ, and were justly hardened in their infidelity, till wrath came upon them to the uttermost. Rom. xi. 8, *God has given them the spirit of slumber.* And we have reason to fear it is the woeful case of many who live in the midst of gospel light. 3 It is very sad that this should be the case with those who were their prophets, and rulers, and seers, that those who should have been their guides were themselves blindfolded; and it is easy to tell what the fatal consequences will be when the blind lead the blind. This was fulfilled when, in the latter days of the Jewish church, the chief priests, and the scribes, and the elders of the people, were the great opposers of Christ and his gospel, and brought themselves under a judicial infatuation. 4. The sad effect of this was that all the means of conviction, knowledge, and grace, which they enjoyed, were ineffectual, and did not answer the end (*v.* 11, 12): "*The vision of all the* prophets, true and false, *has become to you as the words of a book,* or letter, *that is sealed up;* you cannot discern the truth of the real visions and the falsehood of the pretended ones." Or, every vision particularly that this prophet had seen for them, and published to them, had become unintelligible; they had it among them, but were never the wiser for it, any more than a man (though a good scholar) is for a book delivered to him sealed up, and which he must not open the seals of. He sees it is a book, and that is all; he knows nothing of what is in it. So they knew that what Isaiah said was a vision and prophecy, but the meaning of it was hidden from them; it was only a sound of words to them, which they were not at all alarmed by, nor affected with; it answered not the intention, for it made no impression at all upon them. Neither the learned nor the unlearned were the better for all the messages God sent them by his servants the prophets, nor desired to be so. The ordinary sort of people excused themselves from regarding what the prophets said with their want of learning and a liberal education, as if they were not concerned to know and do the will of God because they were not bred scholars: *It is nothing to me, I am not learned.* Those of better rank pretended that the prophet had a peculiar way of speaking, which was obscure to them, and which, though they were men of letters, they had not been used to; and, *Si non vis intelligi, debes negligi—If you wish not to be understood, you deserve to be neglected.* Both these are groundless pretences; for God's prophets have been no unfaithful debtors either to the wise or to the unwise, Rom. i. 14. Or we may take it thus:—The book of prophecy was given to them sealed, so that they could not read it, as a just judgment upon them; because it had often been delivered to them unsealed, and they would not take pains to learn the language of it, and then made excuse for their not reading it because they were not learned. But observe, " The vision has become thus to you whose minds the god of this world has blinded; but it is not so in itself, it is not so to all; the same vision which to you is a *savour of death unto death* to others is and shall be a *savour of life unto life.*" Knowledge is easy to him that understands.

II. The prophet, in God's name, threatens those that were formal and hypocritical in their exercises of devotion, *v.* 13, 14. Observe here,

1. The sin that is here charged upon them—dissembling with God in their religious performances, *v.* 13. He that knows the heart, and cannot be imposed upon with shows and pretences, charges it upon them, whether their hearts condemn them for it or no. He that is greater than the heart, and knows all things, knows that though they *draw nigh to him with their mouth,* and *honour him with their lips,* yet they are not sincere worshippers. To worship God is to make our approaches to him, and to present our adorations of him; it is to draw nigh to him as those that have business with him, with an intention therein to honour him. This we are to do with our mouth and with our lips, in speaking of him and in speaking to him; we must *render to him the calves of our lips,* Hosea xiv. 2. And, if the heart be full of his love and fear, out of the abundance of that the mouth will speak. But there are many whose religion is lip-labour only. They say that which expresses an approach to God and an adoration of him, but it is only from the teeth outward. For, (1.) They do not apply their minds to the service. When they pretend to be speaking to God they are thinking of a thousand impertinences: *They have removed their hearts far from me,* that they might not be employed in prayer, nor come within reach of the word. When work was to be done for God, which required the heart, that was sent out of the way on purpose, with the fool's eyes, into the ends of the earth. (2.) They do not make the word of God the rule of their worship, nor his will their reason: *Their fear towards me is taught by the precept of men.* They worshipped the God of Israel, not according to his appointment, but their own inventions, the directions of their false prophets or their idolatrous kings, or the usages of the nations that were round about them. The tradition of the elders was of more value and validity with them than the laws which God commanded Moses. Or, if they did worship God in a way conformable to his institution in the days of Hezekiah, a great reformer, they had more an eye to the precept of the king than to God's command. This our Saviour applies to the Jews in his time, who were formal in their

devotions and wedded to their own inventions, and pronounces concerning them that in vain they did worship God, Matt. xv. 8, 9.

2. It is a spiritual judgment with which God threatens to punish them for their spiritual wickedness (*v.* 14): *I will proceed to do a marvellous work.* They did one strange thing; they removed all sincerity from their hearts Now God will go on and do another; he will remove all sagacity from their heads. *The wisdom of their wise men shall perish.* They played the hypocrite, and thought to put a cheat upon God, and now they are left to themselves to play the fool, and not only to put a cheat upon themselves, but to be easily cheated by all about them. Those that make religion no more than a pretence, to serve a turn, are out in their politics; and it is just with God to deprive those of their understanding who part with their uprightness. This was fulfilled in the wretched infatuation which the Jewish nation were manifestly under, after they had rejected the gospel of Christ; they removed their hearts far from God, and therefore God justly removed wisdom far from them, and hid from their eyes the things that belonged even to their temporal peace. This is a marvellous work; it is surprising, it is astonishing, that wise men should of a sudden lose their wisdom and be given up to strong delusions. Judgments on the mind, though least taken notice of, are to be most wondered at.

III. He shows the folly of those that thought to act separately and secretly from God, and were carrying on designs independent upon God and which they projected to conceal from his all-seeing eye. Here we have, 1. Their politics described (*v.* 15): *They seek deep to hide their counsel from the Lord,* that he may not know either what they do or what they design; they say, " Who sees us? No man, and therefore not God himself." The consultations they had about their own safety they kept to themselves, and never asked God's advice concerning them; nay, they knew they were displeasing to him, but thought they could conceal them from him; and, if he did not know them, he could not baffle and defeat them. See what foolish fruitless pains sinners take in their sinful ways; they seek deep, they sink deep, to hide their counsel from the Lord, who sits in heaven and laughs at them. Note, A practical disbelief of God's omniscience is at the bottom both of the carnal worships and of the carnal confidences of hypocrites; Ps. xciv. 7; Ezek. viii. 12; ix. 9. 2. The absurdity of their politics demonstrated (*v.* 16): " *Surely your turning of things upside down* thus, your various projects, turning your affairs this and that way to make them shape as you would have them—or rather your inverting the order of things, and thinking to make God's providence give attendance to your projects, and that God must know no more than you think fit, which is perfectly turning things upside down and beginning at the wrong end— *shall be esteemed as the potter's clay.* God will turn and manage you, and all your counsels, with as much ease and as absolute a power as the potter forms and fashions his clay. See how God despises, and therefore what little reason we have to dread, those contrivances of men that are carried on without God, particularly those against him. (1.) Those that think to hide their counsels from God do in effect deny him to be their Creator. It is as if the work should say of him that made it, " He made me not; I made myself." If God made us, he certainly knows us, as the Psalmist shows (Ps. cxxxix. 1, 13—16); so that those who say that he does not see them might as well say that he did not make them. Much of the wickedness of the wicked arises from this, they forget that God formed them, Deut. xxxii. 18. Or, (2.) Which comes to the same thing, they deny him to be a wise Creator: *The thing framed saith of him that framed it, He had no understanding ;* for if he had understanding to make us so curiously, especially to make us intelligent beings and to *put understanding into the inward part* (Job xxxviii. 36), no doubt he has understanding to know us and all we say and do. As those that quarrel with God, so those that think to conceal themselves from him, do in effect charge him with folly ; but *he that formed the eye, shall he not see ?* Ps. xciv. 9.

17 *Is* it not yet a very little while, and Lebanon shall be turned into a fruitful field, and the fruitful field shall be esteemed as a forest? 18 And in that day shall the deaf hear the words of the book, and the eyes of the blind shall see out of obscurity, and out of darkness. 19 The meek also shall increase *their* joy in the LORD, and the poor among men shall rejoice in the Holy One of Israel. 20 For the terrible one is brought to nought, and the scorner is consumed, and all that watch for iniquity are cut off: 21 That make a man an offender for a word, and lay a snare for him that reproveth in the gate, and turn aside the just for a thing of nought. 22 Therefore thus saith the LORD, who redeemed Abraham, concerning the house of Jacob, Jacob shall not now be ashamed, neither shall his face now wax pale. 23 But when he seeth

162

his children, the work of mine hands, in the midst of him, they shall sanctify my name, and sanctify the Holy One of Jacob, and shall fear the God of Israel. 24 They also that erred in spirit shall come to understanding, and they that murmured shall learn doctrine.

Those that thought to hide their counsels from the Lord were said to turn things upside down (*v.* 16), and they intended to do it unknown to God ; but God here tells them that he will turn things upside down his way ; and let us see whose word shall stand, his or theirs. They disbelieve Providence : " Wait awhile," says God, "and you shall be convinced by ocular demonstration that there is a God who governs the world, and that he governs it and orders all the changes that are in it for the good of his church." The wonderful revolution here foretold may refer primarily to the happy settlement of the affairs of Judah and Jerusalem after the defeat of Sennacherib's attempt, and the repose which good people then enjoyed, when they were delivered from the alarms of the sword both of war and persecution. But it may look further, to the rejection of the Jews at the first planting of the gospel (for their hypocrisy and infidelity were here foretold, *v.* 13) and the admission of the Gentiles into the church.

I. In general, it is a great and surprising change that is here foretold, *v.* 17. *Lebanon,* that was a forest, *shall be turned into a fruitful field ;* and Carmel, that was a fruitful field, shall become a forest. It is a counterchange. Note, Great changes, both for the better and for the worse, are often made in a very little while. It was a sign given them of the defeat of Sennacherib that the ground should be more than ordinarily fruitful (*ch.* xxxvii 30): *You shall eat this year such as grows of itself;* food for man shall be (as food for beasts is) the spontaneous product of the soil. Then Lebanon became a fruitful field, so fruitful that that which used to be reckoned a fruitful field in comparison with it was looked upon but as a forest. When a great harvest of souls was gathered in to Christ from among the Gentiles then the wilderness was turned into a fruitful field ; and the Jewish church, that had long been a fruitful field, became a desolate and deserted forest, *ch.* liv. 1.

II. In particular,
1. Those that were ignorant shall become intelligent, *v.* 18. Those that understood not this prophecy (but it was to them as a sealed book, *v.* 11) shall, when it is accomplished, understand it, and shall acknowledge, not only the hand of God in the event, but the voice of God in the prediction of it: *The deaf shall then hear the words of the book.* The fulfilling of prophecy is the best exposition of it. The poor Gentiles shall then have divine revelation brought among them ; and those

that sat in darkness shall see a great light, those that were blind shall see out of obscurity; for the gospel was sent to them to *open their eyes,* Acts xxvi. 18. Observe, In order to the making of men fruitful in good affections and actions, the course God's grace takes with them is to open their understandings and make them hear the words of God's book.

2. Those that were erroneous shall become orthodox (*v.* 24): *Those that erred in spirit,* that were under mistakes and misapprehensions concerning the words of the book and the meaning of them, shall come to understanding, to a right understanding of things; the Spirit of truth shall rectify their mistakes and lead them into all truth. This should encourage us to pray for *those that have erred and are deceived,* that God can, and often does, bring such to understanding. Those that murmured at the truths of God as hard sayings, and loved to pick quarrels with them, shall learn the true meaning of these doctrines, and then they will be better reconciled to them. Those that erred concerning the providence of God as to public affairs, and murmured at the disposals of it, when they shall see the issue of things shall better understand them and be aware of what God was designing in all, Hos. xiv. 9.

3. Those that were melancholy shall become cheerful and pleasant (*v.* 19): *The meek also shall increase their joy in the Lord.* Those who are poor in the world and poor in spirit, who, being in affliction, accommodate themselves to their affliction, are purely passive and not passionate, when they see God appearing for them, they shall *add,* or *repeat, joy in the Lord.* This intimates that even in their distress they kept up their joy in the Lord, but now they increased it. Note, Those who, when they are in trouble, can truly rejoice in God, shall soon have cause given them greatly to rejoice in him. When joy in the world is decreasing and fading joy in God is increasing and getting ground. This shining light shall shine more and more; for that which is aimed at is that *this joy may be full.* Even *the poor among men* may rejoice in the Holy One of Israel, and their poverty needs not deprive them of that joy, Hab. iii. 17, 18. And the meek, the humble, the patient, and dispassionate, shall grow in this joy. Note, The grace of meekness will contribute very much to the increase of our holy joy.

4. The enemies, that were formidable, shall become despicable. Sennacherib, that *terrible one,* and his great army, that put the country into such a consternation, shall be *brought to nought* (*v.* 20), shall be quite disabled to do any further mischief. The power of Satan, that terrible one indeed, shall be broken by the prevalency of Christ's gospel; and those that were subject to bondage through fear of him that had the

power of death shall be delivered, Heb. ii. 14, 15.

5. The persecutors, that were vexatious, shall be quieted, and so those they were troublesome to shall be quiet from the fear of them. To complete the repose of God's people, not only the terrible one from abroad shall be brought to nought, but the scorners at home too shall be consumed and cut off by Hezekiah's reformation. Those are a happy people, and likely to be so, who, when God gives them victory and success against their terrible enemies abroad, take care to suppress vice, and profaneness, and the spirit of persecution, those more dangerous enemies at home. Or, They shall be consumed and cut off by the judgments of God, shall be singled out to be made examples of. Or, They shall insensibly waste away, being put to confusion by the fulfilling of those predictions which they had made a jest of. Observe what had been the wickedness of these scorners, for which they should be cut off. They had been persecutors of God's people and prophets, probably of the prophet Isaiah particularly, and therefore he complains thus feelingly of them and of their subtle malice. Some as informers and persecutors, others as judges, did all they could to take away his life, or at least his liberty. And this is very applicable to the chief priests and Pharisees, who persecuted Christ and his apostles, and for that sin they and their nation of scorners were cut off and consumed. (1.) They ridiculed the prophets and the serious professors of religion; they despised them, and did their utmost to bring them into contempt; they were scorners, and sat in the seat of the scornful. (2.) They lay in wait for an occasion against them. By their spies they *watch for iniquity,* to see if they can lay hold of any thing that is said or done that may be called an iniquity. Or they themselves watch for an opportunity to do mischief, as Judas did to betray our Lord Jesus. (3.) They took advantage against them for the least slip of the tongue; and, if a thing were ever so little said amiss, it served them to ground an indictment upon. They *made a man,* though he were ever so wise and good a man, though he were a man of God, *an offender for a word,* a word mischosen or misplaced, when they could not but know that it was well meant, *v.* 21. They cavilled at every word that the prophets spoke to them by way of admonition, though ever so innocently spoken, and without any design to affront them. They put the worst construction upon what was said, and made it criminal by strained innuendoes. Those who consider how apt we all are to speak unadvisedly, and to mistake what we hear, will think it very unjust and unfair to *make a man an offender for a word.* (4.) They did all they could to bring those into trouble that dealt faithfully with them and told them of their faults. Those

that *reprove in the gates,* reprovers by office, that were bound by the duty of their place, as prophets, as judges, and magistrates, to show people their transgressions, they hated these, and laid snares for them, as the Pharisees' emissaries, who were sent to watch our Saviour that they might *entangle him in his talk* (Matt. xxii. 15), that they might have something to lay to his charge which might render him odious to the people or obnoxious to the government. *So persecuted they the prophets ;* and it is next to impossible for the most cautious to place their words so warily as to escape such snares. See how base wicked people are, who bear ill-will to those who, out of good-will to them, seek to save their souls from death; and see what need reprovers have both of courage to do their duty and of prudence to avoid the snare. (5.) They pervert judgment, and will never let an honest man carry an honest cause : *They turn aside the just for a thing of nought ;* they condemn him, or give the cause against him, upon no evidence, no colour or pretence whatsoever. They run a man down, and misrepresent him, by all the little arts and tricks they can devise, as they did our Saviour. We must not think it strange if we see the best of men thus treated ; *the disciple is not greater than his Master.* But wait awhile, and God will not only *bring forth their righteousness,* but cut off and consume these scorners.

6. Jacob, who was made to blush by the reproaches, and made to tremble by the threatenings, of his enemies, shall now be relieved both against his shame and against his fear, by the rolling away of those reproaches and the defeating of those threatenings (*v.* 22) : *Thus the Lord saith who redeemed Abraham,* that is, called him out of Ur of the Chaldees, and so rescued him from the idolatry of his fathers and plucked him as a *brand out of the fire.* He that redeemed Abraham out of his snares and troubles will redeem all that are by faith his genuine seed out of theirs. He that began his care of his church in the redemption of Abraham, when it and its Redeemer were in his loins, will not now cast off the care of it. Because the enemies of his people are so industrious both to blacken them and to frighten them, therefore he will appear for the house of Jacob, and they shall not be ashamed as they have been, but shall have wherewith to answer those that reproach them, nor shall *their faces now wax pale ;* but they shall gather courage, and look their enemies in the face without change of countenance, as those have reason to do who have the God of Abraham on their side.

7. Jacob, who thought his family would be extinct and the entail of religion quite cut off, shall have the satisfaction of seeing a numerous progeny devoted to God for a generation, *v.* 23. (1.) He shall see his children, multitudes of believers and praying people,

the spiritual seed of faithful Abraham and wrestling Jacob. Having his quiver full of these arrows, he *shall not be ashamed* (*v.* 22), but shall speak with his enemy in the gate, Ps. cxxvii. 5. Christ shall *not be ashamed* (*ch.* l. 7), for *he shall see his seed* (*ch.* liii. 10); he sees some, and foresees more, *in the midst of him,* flocking to the church, and residing there. (2.) His children are the work of God's hands ; being formed by him, they are formed for him, his *workmanship, created unto good works.* It is some comfort to parents to think that their children are God's creatures, the work of the hands of his providence. But it will be much more a comfort to them to see their children his new creatures, the work of the hands of his grace. (3.) He and his children shall sanctify the name of God as their God, as *the Holy One of Jacob,* and shall fear and worship the God of Israel. This is opposed to his being ashamed and waxing pale ; when he is delivered from his contempts and dangers he shall not magnify himself, but *sanctify the Holy One of Jacob.* If God make our condition easy, we must endeavour to make his name glorious. Parents and children are ornaments and comforts indeed to each other when they join in sanctifying the name of God. When parents give up their children, and children give up themselves, to God, to be *to him for a name and a praise,* then the forest will soon become a fruitful field.

CHAP. XXX.

The prophecy of this chapter seems to relate (as that in the foregoing chapter) to the approaching danger of Jerusalem and desolations of Judah by Sennacherib's invasion. Here is, I. A just reproof to those who, in that distress, trusted to the Egyptians for help, and were all in a hurry to fetch succours from Egypt, ver. 1—7. II. A terrible threatening against those who slighted the good advice which God by his prophets gave them for the repose of their minds in that distress, assuring them that whatever became of others the judgment would certainly overtake them, ver. 8—17. III. A gracious promise to those who trusted in God, that they should not only see through the trouble, but should see happy days after it, times of joy and reformation, plenty of the means of grace, and therewith plenty of outward good things and increasing joys and triumphs (ver. 18—26), and many of these promises are very applicable to gospel grace. IV. A prophecy of the total rout and ruin of the Assyrian army, which should be an occasion of great joy and an introduction to those happy times, ver. 27—33.

WOE to the rebellious children, saith the LORD, that take counsel, but not of me; and that cover with a covering, but not of my Spirit, that they may add sin to sin : 2 That walk to go down into Egypt, and have not asked at my mouth ; to strengthen themselves in the strength of Pharaoh, and to trust in the shadow of Egypt ! 3 Therefore shall the strength of Pharaoh be your shame, and the trust in the shadow of Egypt *your* confusion. 4 For his princes were at Zoan, and his ambassadors came to Hanes. 5 They were all ashamed of a people, *that* could not profit them, nor be a help nor profit, but a shame, and also a reproach. 6 The burden of the beasts of the south : into the land of trouble and anguish, from whence *come* the young and old lion, the viper and fiery flying serpent, they will carry their riches upon the shoulders of young asses, and their treasures upon the bunches of camels, to a people *that* shall not profit *them.* 7 For the Egyptians shall help in vain, and to no purpose : therefore have I cried concerning this, Their strength *is* to sit still.

It was often the fault and folly of the people of the Jews that, when they were insulted by their neighbours on one side, they sought for succour from their neighbours on the other side, instead of looking up to God and putting their confidence in him. Against the Israelites they sought to the Syrians, 2 Chron. xvi. 2, 3. Against the Syrians they sought to the Assyrians, 2 Kings xvi. 7. Against the Assyrians they here sought to the Egyptians, and Rabshakeh upbraided them with so doing, 2 Kings xviii. 21. Now observe here,

I. How this sin of theirs is described, and what there was in it that was provoking to God. When they saw themselves in danger and distress, 1. They would not consult God. They would do things of their own heads, and not advise with God, though they had a ready and certain way of doing it by Urim or prophets. They were so confident of the prudence of their own measures that they thought it needless to consult the oracle ; nay, they were not willing to put it to that issue : "They *take counsel* among themselves, and one from another; but they do not ask counsel, much less will they take counsel, of me. They *cover with a covering*" (they think to secure themselves with one shelter or other, which may serve to cover them from the violence of the storm), " *but not of my Spirit*" (not such as God by his Spirit, in the mouth of his prophets, directed them to), " and therefore it will prove too short a covering, and a refuge of lies." 2. They could not confide in God. They did not think it enough to have God on their side, nor were they at all solicitous to make him their friend, but they *strengthened themselves in the strength of Pharaoh ;* they thought him a powerful ally, and doubted not but to be able to cope with the Assyrian while they had him for them. *The shadow of Egypt* (and it was but a shadow) was the covering in which they wrapped themselves.

II. What was the evil of this sin. 1. It

bespoke them *rebellious children ;* and a woe is here denounced against them under that character, *v.* 1. They were, in profession, God's children ; but, not trusting in him, they were justly stigmatized as rebellious ; for, if we distrust God's providence, we do in effect withdraw ourselves from our allegiance. 2. They added sin to sin. It was sin that brought them into distress; and then, instead of repenting, they *trespassed yet more against the Lord,* 2 Chron. xxviii. 22. And those that had abused God's mercies to them, making them the fuel of their lusts, abused their afflictions too, making them an excuse for their distrust of God ; and so they make bad worse, and add sin to sin ; and those that do so, as they make their own chain heavy, so it is just with God to make their plagues wonderful. Now that which aggravated their sin was, (1.) That they took so much pains to secure the Egyptians for their allies : *They walk to go down to Egypt,* travel up and down to find an advantageous road thither ; but they *have not asked at my mouth,* never considered whether God would allow and approve of it or no. (2.) That they were at such a vast expense to do it, *v.* 6. They load *the beasts of the south* (horses fetched from Egypt, which lay south from Judea) with their riches, fancying, as it is common with people in a fright, that they were safer any where than where they were. Or they sent their riches thither as bribes to Pharaoh's courtiers, to engage them in their interests, or as pay for their army. God would have helped them *gratis ;* but, if they will have help from the Egyptians, they must pay dearly for it, and they seem willing to do so. The riches that are so spent will turn to a bad account. They carried their effects to Egypt through a land (so it may be read) of trouble and anguish, that vast howling wilderness which lay between Canaan and Egypt, *whence come the lion and fiery serpent,* Deut. viii. 15. They would venture through that dangerous wilderness, to bring what they had to Egypt. Or it may be meant of Egypt itself, which had been to Israel a house of bondage and therefore a land of trouble and anguish, and which abounded in ravenous and venomous creatures. See what dangers men run into that forsake God, and what dangers they will run into in pursuance of their carnal confidences and their expectations from the creature.

III. What would be the consequence of it. 1. The Egyptians would receive their ambassadors, would address them very respectfully, and be willing to treat with them (*v.* 4): *His princes were at Zoan,* at Pharaoh's court there, and had their audience of the king, who encouraged them to depend upon his friendship and the succours he would send them. But, 2. They would not answer their expectation : They *could not* profit them, v. 5. For God says, *They shall not profit them* (v. 6), and every creature is that to us (and no more) which he makes it to be. The forces they were to furnish them with could not be raised in time; or, when they were raised, they were not fit for service, and they would not venture any of their veteran troops in the expedition; or the march was so long that they could not come up when they had occasion for them; or the Egyptians would not be cordial to Israel, but would secretly incline to the Assyrians, upon some account or other: *The Egyptians shall help in vain, and to no purpose, v. 7.* They shall hinder and hurt, instead of helping. And therefore, 3. These people, that were now so fond of the Egyptians, would at length be ashamed of them, and of all their expectations from them and confidence in them (v. 3): "*The strength of Pharaoh, which was your pride, shall be your shame;* all your neighbours will upbraid you, and you will upbraid yourselves, with your folly in trusting to it. And the *shadow of Egypt,* that *land shadowing with wings* (ch. xviii. 1), which was your confidence, shall be your confusion; it will not only disappoint you, and be the matter of your shame, but it will weaken all your other supports, and be an occasion of mischief to you." God afterwards threatens the ruin of Egypt for this very thing, because they had dealt treacherously with Israel and *been a staff of a reed* to them, Ezek. xxix. 6, 7. The princes and ambassadors of Israel, who were so forward to court an alliance with them, when they come among them shall see so much of their weakness, or rather of their baseness, that *they shall all be ashamed of a people that could not be a help or profit to them,* but a *shame and reproach, v. 5.* Those that trust in God, in his power, providence, and promise, are never made ashamed of their hope; but those that put confidence in any creature will sooner or later find it a reproach to them. God is true, and may be trusted, but every man a liar, and must be suspected. The Creator is a rock of ages, the creature a broken reed. We cannot expect too little from man nor too much from God.

IV. The use and application of all this (v. 7): "*Therefore have I cried concerning this* matter, this project of theirs. I have published it, that all might take notice of it. I have pressed it as one in earnest. *Their strength is to sit still,* in a humble dependence upon God and his goodness and a quiet submission to his will, and not to wander about and put themselves to great trouble to seek help from this and the other creature." If we sit still in a day of distress, hoping and quietly waiting for the salvation of the Lord, and using only lawful regular methods for our own preservation, this will be the strength of our souls both for services and sufferings, and it will engage

166

divine strength for us. We weaken ourselves, and provoke God to withdraw from us, when we make flesh our arm, for then our hearts depart from the Lord. When we have tired ourselves by seeking for help from creatures we shall find it the best way of recruiting ourselves to repose in the Creator. *Here I am, let him do with me as he pleases.*

8 Now go, write it before them in a table, and note it in a book, that it may be for the time to come for ever and ever : 9 That this *is* a rebellious people, lying children, children *that* will not hear the law of the LORD : 10 Which say to the seers, See not ; and to the prophets, Prophesy not unto us right things, speak unto us smooth things, prophesy deceits : 11 Get you out of the way, turn aside out of the path, cause the Holy One of Israel to cease from before us. 12 Wherefore thus saith the Holy One of Israel, Because ye despise this word, and trust in oppression and perverseness, and stay thereon : 13 Therefore this iniquity shall be to you as a breach ready to fall, swelling out in a high wall, whose breaking cometh suddenly at an instant. 14 And he shall break it as the breaking of the potter's vessel that is broken in pieces ; he shall not spare ; so that there shall not be found in the bursting of it a sherd to take fire from the hearth, or to take water *withal* out of the pit. 15 For thus saith the Lord GOD, the Holy One of Israel ; In returning and rest shall ye be saved ; in quietness and in confidence shall be your strength : and ye would not. 16 But ye said, No ; for we will flee upon horses ; therefore shall ye flee : and, We will ride upon the swift ; therefore shall they that pursue you be swift. 17 One thousand *shall flee* at the rebuke of one ; at the rebuke of five shall ye flee : till ye be left as a beacon upon the top of a mountain, and as an ensign on a hill.

Here, I. The preface is very awful. The prophet must not only preach this, but he must write it (v. 8), *write it in a table,* to be hung up and exposed to public view ; he must carefully *note it,* not in loose papers which might be lost or torn, but *in a book,* to be pieserved for posterity, *in perpetuam rei memoriam — for a standing testimony* against this wicked generation; let it remain not only to the next succeeding ages, but for ever and ever, while the world stands; and so it shall, for the book of the scriptures no doubt, shall continue, and be read, to the end of time. Let it be written, 1. To shame the men of the present age, who would not hear and heed it when it was spoken. Let it be written, that it may not be lost; their children may profit by it, though they will not. 2. To justify God in the judgments he was about to bring upon them; people will be tempted to think he was too hard upon them, and over-severe, unless they know how very bad they were, how very provoking, and what fair means God tried with them before he brought it to this extremity. 3. For warning to others not to do as they did, lest they should fare as they fared. It is designed for admonition to those of the remotest place and age, even those *upon whom the ends of the world have come,* 1 Cor. x. 11. It may be of use for God's ministers not only to preach, but to write; for that which is written remains.

II. The character given of the profane and wicked Jews is very sad. He must, if he will draw them in their own colours, write this concerning them (and we are sure he does not bear false witness against them, nor make them worse than they were, for the judgment of God is according to truth), *That this is a rebellious people, v.* 9. The Jews were, for aught we know, the only professing people God had then in the world, and yet many of them were a rebellious people. 1. They rebelled against their own convictions and covenants: "They are *lying children,* that will not stand to what they say, that promise fair, but perform nothing;" when he took them into covenant with himself he said of them, *Surely they are my people, children that will not lie* (ch. lxiii. 8); but they proved otherwise. 2. They rebelled against the divine authority: "They are *children that will not hear the law of the Lord,* nor heed it, but will do as they have a mind, let God himself say what he will to the contrary."

III. The charge drawn up against them is very high and the sentence passed upon them very dreadful. Two things they here stand charged with, and their doom is read for both, a fearful doom :—

1. They forbade the prophets to speak to them in God's name, and to deal faithfully with them.

(1.) This their sin is described, *v.* 10, 11. They set themselves so violently against the prophets to hinder them from preaching, or at least from dealing plainly with them in their preaching, did so banter them and browbeat them, that they did in effect *say to the seers, See not.* They had the light, but they

loved darkness rather. It was their privilege that they had seers among them, but they did what they could to put out their eyes—that they had prophets among them, but they did what they could to stop their mouths; for they tormented them in their wicked ways, Rev. xi. 10. Those that silence good ministers, and discountenance good preaching, are justly counted, and called, *rebels against God.* See what it was in the prophets' preaching with which they found themselves aggrieved. [1.] The prophets told them of their faults, and warned them of their misery and danger by reason of sin, and they could not bear that. They must speak to them smooth things, must flatter them in their sins, and say that they did well, and there was no harm, no peril, in the course of life they lived in. Let a thing be ever so right and true, if it be not smooth, they will not hear it. But if it be agreeable to the good opinion they have of themselves, and will confirm them in that, though it be ever so false and ever so great a cheat upon them, they will have it prophesied to them. Those deserve to be deceived that desire to be so. [2.] The prophets stopped them in their sinful pursuits, and stood in their way like the angel in Balaam's road, with the sword of God's wrath drawn in their hand; so that they could not proceed without terror. And this they took as a great insult. When they went on frowardly in the way of their hearts they said to the prophets, " *Get you out of the way, turn aside out of the paths.* What do you do in our way? Cannot you let us alone to do as we please?" Those have their hearts fully set in them to do evil that bid their faithful monitors to stand out of their way. *Forbear, why shouldst thou be smitten?* 2 Chron. xxv. 16. [3.] The prophets were continually telling them of the Holy One of Israel, what an enemy he is to sin and how severely he will reckon with sinners; and this they could not endure to hear of. Both the thing itself and the expression of it were too serious for them; and therefore, if the prophets will speak to them, they will make it their bargain that they shall not call God *the Holy One of Israel;* for God's holiness is that attribute which wicked people most of all dread. Let us no more be troubled with that statepreface (as Mr. White calls it) to your impertinent harangues. Those have reason to fear perishing in their sins that cannot bear to be frightened out of them.

(2.) Now what is the doom passed upon them for this? We have it, *v.* 12, 13. Observe, [1.] Who it is that gives judgment upon them : *Thus saith the Holy One of Israel.* That title of God which they particularly excepted against the prophet makes use of. Faithful ministers will not be driven from using such expressions as are proper to awaken sinners, though they be displeasing. We must tell men that God is the *Holy One of Israel,* and so they shall find him, whether they will hear or whether they will forbear. [2.] What the ground of the judgment is: *Because they despise this word*—either, in general, every word that the prophets said to them, or this word in particular, which declares God to be *the Holy One of Israel :* " they despise this, and will neither make it their fear, to stand in awe of it, nor make it their hope, to put any confidence in it ; but, rather than they will be beholden to *the Holy One of Israel,* they will *trust in oppression and perverseness,* in the wealth they have got and the interest they have made by fraud and violence, or in the sinful methods they have taken for their own security, in contradiction to God and his will. On these they lean, and therefore it is just that they should fall." [3.] What the judgment is that is passed upon them : *" This iniquity shall be to you as a breach ready to fall.* This confidence of yours will be like a house built upon the sand, which will fall in the storm and bury the builder in the ruins of it. Your contempt of that word of God which you might build upon will make every thing else you trust to like a wall that bulges out, which, if any weight be laid upon it, comes down, nay, which often sinks with its own weight." The ruin they would hereby bring upon themselves should be, *First,* A surprising ruin : *The breaking shall come suddenly, at an instant,* when they do not expect it, which will make it the more frightful, and when they are not prepared or provided for it, which will make it the more fatal. *Secondly,* An utter ruin, universal and irreparable : " You and all your confidences shall be not only weak as the potter's clay (*ch.* xxix. 16), but *broken to pieces as the potter's vessel.* He that has the rod of iron shall break it (Ps. ii. 9) and he shall not spare, shall not have any regard to it, nor be in care to preserve or keep whole any part of it. But, when once it is broken so as to be unfit for use, let it be dashed, let it be crushed, all to pieces, so that there may not remain one *sherd* big enough *to take up* a little *fire or water*"—two things we have daily need of, and which poor people commonly fetch in a piece of a broken pitcher. They shall not only be as a *bowing wall* (Ps. lxii. 3), but as a broken mug or glass, which is good for nothing, nor can ever be made whole again.

2. They slighted the gracious directions God gave them, not only how to secure themselves and make themselves safe, but how to compose themselves and make themselves easy ; they would take their own way, *v.* 15—17. Observe here,

(1.) The method God put them into for salvation and strength. The God that knew them, and knew what was proper for them, and desired their welfare, gave them this prescription ; and it is recommended to us

all. [1.] Would we be saved from the evil of every calamity, guarded against the temptation of it and secured from the curse of it, which are the only evil things in it ? It must be *in returning and rest,* in returning to God and reposing in him as our rest. Let us return from our evil ways, into which we have gone aside, and rest and settle in the way of God and duty, and that is the way to be saved. " Return from this project of going down to Egypt, and rest satisfied in the will of God, and then you may trust him with your safety. *In returning* (in the thorough reformation of your hearts and lives) *and in rest* (in an entire submission of your souls to God and a complacency in him) *you shall be saved."* [2.] Would we be strengthened to do what is required of us and to bear what is laid upon us ? It must be *in quietness and in confidence ;* we must keep our spirits calm and sedate by a continual dependence upon God, and his power and goodness ; we must retire into ourselves with a holy quietness, suppressing all turbulent and tumultuous passions, and keeping the peace in our own minds. And we must rely upon God with a holy confidence that he can do what he will and will do what is best for his people. And this will be our strength ; it will inspire us with such a holy fortitude as will carry us with ease and courage through all the difficulties we may meet with.

(2.) The contempt they put upon this prescription ; they would not take God's counsel, though it was so much for their own good. And justly will those die of their disease that will not take God for their physician. We are certainly enemies to ourselves if we will not be subjects to him. They would not so much as try the method prescribed : " *But you said, No* (*v.* 16), we will not compose ourselves, for *we will flee upon horses* and *we will ride upon the swift ;* we will hurry hither and thither to fetch in foreign aids." They think themselves wiser than God, and that they know what is good for themselves better than he does. When Sennacherib took all the fenced cities of Judah, those rebellious children would not be persuaded to sit still and patiently to expect God's appearing for them, as he did wonderfully at last ; but they would shift for their own safety, and thereby they exposed themselves to so much the more danger.

(3.) The sentence passed upon them for this. Their sin shall be their punishment : " You will flee, and therefore *you shall flee ;* you will be upon the full speed, and therefore so shall those be that pursue you." The dogs are most apt to run barking after him that rides fast. The conquerors protected those that sat still, but pursued those that made their escape ; and so that very project by which they hoped to save themselves was justly their ruin and the most guilty suffered most. It is foretold, *v.* 17, [1.] That they should be easily cut off; they should be so dispirited with their own fears, increased by their flight, that one of the enemy should defeat a thousand of them, and five put an army to flight, which could never be *unless their Rock had sold them,* Deut. xxxii. 30. [2.] That they should be generally cut off, and only here and there one should escape alone in a solitary place, and be left for a spectacle too, *as a beacon upon the top of a mountain,* a warning to others to avoid the like sinful courses and carnal confidences.

18 And therefore will the LORD wait, that he may be gracious unto you, and therefore will he be exalted, that he may have mercy upon you: for the LORD *is* a God of judgment: blessed *are* all they that wait for him. 19 For the people shall dwell in Zion at Jerusalem: thou shalt weep no more: he will be very gracious unto thee at the voice of thy cry; when he shall hear it, he will answer thee. 20 And *though* the LORD give you the bread of adversity, and the water of affliction, yet shall not thy teachers be removed into a corner any more, but thine eyes shall see thy teachers. 21 And thine ears shall hear a word behind thee, saying, This *is* the way, walk ye in it, when ye turn to the right hand, and when ye turn to the left. 22 Ye shall defile also the covering of thy graven images of silver, and the ornament of thy molten images of gold: thou shalt cast them away as a menstruous cloth; thou shall say unto it, Get thee hence. 23 Then shall he give the rain of thy seed, that thou shalt sow the ground withal; and bread of the increase of the earth, and it shall be fat and plenteous: in that day shall thy cattle feed in large pastures. 24 The oxen likewise and the young asses that ear the ground shall eat clean provender, which hath been winnowed with the shovel and with the fan. 25 And there shall be upon every high mountain, and upon every high hill, rivers *and* streams of waters in the day of the great slaughter, when the towers fall. 26 Moreover the light of the moon shall be as the light of the sun, and the light of the sun shall be seven-fold, as the light of seven days, in the day that the LORD bindeth

up the breach of his people, and healeth the stroke of their wound.

The closing words of the foregoing paragraph (*You shall be left as a beacon upon a mountain*) some understand as a promise that a remnant of them should be reserved as monuments of mercy; and here the prophet tells them what good times should succeed these calamities. Or the first words in this paragraph may be read by way of antithesis, *Notwithstanding this, yet will the Lord wait that he may be gracious.* The prophet, having shown that those who made Egypt their confidence would be ashamed of it, here shows that those who sat still and made God alone their confidence would have the comfort of it. It is matter of comfort to the people of God, when the times are very bad, that *all will be well yet,* well with those that fear God, when we say to the wicked, *It shall be ill with you.*

I. God will be gracious to them and will have mercy on them. This is the foundation of all good. If we find favour with God, and he have mercy upon us, we shall have comfort according to the time that we have been afflicted.

1. The mercy in store for them is very affectingly expressed. (1.) "He will *wait to be gracious* (v. 18); he will wait till you return to him and seek his face, and then he will be ready to meet you with mercy. He will wait, that he may do it in the best and fittest time, when it will be most for his glory, when it will come to you with the most pleasing surprise. He will continually follow you with his favours, and not let slip any opportunity of being gracious to you." (2.) "He will stir up himself to deliver you, will be exalted, will be *raised up out of his holy habitation* (Zech. ii. 13), that he may appear for you in more than ordinary instances of power and goodness; *and thus he will be exalted,* that is, he will glorify his own name. This is what he aims at in having mercy on his people." (3.) *He will be very gracious* (v. 19), and this in answer to prayer, which makes his kindness doubly kind: "*He will be gracious to thee, at the voice of thy cry,* the cry of thy necessity, when that is most urgent—the cry of thy prayer, when that is most fervent. *When he shall hear it,* there needs no more; at the first word *he will answer thee,* and say, *Here I am.*" Herein he is very gracious indeed. In particular, [1.] Those who were disturbed in the possession of their estates shall again enjoy them quietly. When the danger is over *the people shall dwell in Zion, at Jerusalem,* as they used to do; they shall dwell safely, free from the fear of evil. [2.] Those who were all in tears shall have cause to rejoice, and shall weep no more; and those who dwell in Zion, the holy city, will find enough there to wipe away tears from their eyes.

2. This is grounded upon two great truths:

169

(1.) That *the Lord is a God of judgment;* he is both wise and just in all the disposals of his providence, true to his word and tender of his people. If he correct his children, it is *with judgment* (Jer. x. 24), with moderation and discretion, considering their frame. We think we may safely refer ourselves to a man of judgment; and shall we not commit our way to a God of judgment? (2.) That therefore all those are blessed who *wait for him,* who not only wait on him with their prayers, but wait for him with their hopes, who will not take any indirect course to extricate themselves out of their straits, or anticipate their deliverance, but patiently expect God's appearances for them in his own way and time. Because God is infinitely wise, those are truly happy who refer their cause to him.

II. They shall not again know the want of the means of grace, *v.* 20, 21. Here, 1. It is supposed that they might be brought into straits and troubles after this deliverance was wrought for them. It was promised (*v.* 19), that they should *weep no more* and that God would be *gracious to them;* and yet here it is taken for granted that God may give them the *bread of adversity and the water of affliction,* prisoners' fare (1 Kings xxii 27), coarse and sorry food, such as the poor use. When one trouble is over we know not how soon another may succeed; and we may have an interest in the favour of God, and such consolations as are sufficient to prohibit weeping, and yet may have bread of adversity given us to eat and water of affliction to drink. Let us therefore not judge of love or hatred by what is before us. 2. It is promised that their eyes should *see their teachers,* that is, that they should have faithful teachers among them, and should have hearts to regard them and not slight them as they had done; and then they might the better be reconciled to the bread of adversity and the water of affliction. It was a common saying among the old Puritans, *Brown bread and the gospel are good fare.* A famine of bread is not so great a judgment as a famine of the word of God, Amos viii. 11, 12. It seems that their teachers had been removed into corners (probably being forced to shift for their safety in the reign of Ahaz), but it shall be so no more. *Veritas non quærit angulos—Truth seeks no corners for concealment.* But the teachers of truth may sometimes be driven into corners for shelter; and it goes ill with the church when it is so, when the woman with her crown of twelve stars is forced to flee into the wilderness (Rev. xii. 6), when the prophets are *hidden by fifty in a cave,* 1 Kings xviii. 4. But God will find a time to call the teachers out of their corners again, and to replace them in their solemn assemblies, which shall *see their own teachers,* the *eyes of all the synagogue* being fastened on them, Luke iv. 20. And it will be the more pleasing be-

cause of the restraint they have been for some time under, as light out of darkness, as life from the dead. To all that love God and their own souls this return of faithful teachers out of their corners, especially with a promise that they *shall not be removed into corners any more,* is the most acceptable part of any deliverance, and has comfort enough in it to sweeten even the bread of adversity and the water of affliction. But this is not all: 3. It is promised that they shall have the benefit, not only of the public ministry, but of private and particular admonition and advice (*v.* 21): *" Thy ears shall hear a word behind thee,* calling after thee as a man calls after a traveller that he sees going out of his road."* Observe, (1.) Whence this word shall come—from *behind thee,* from some one whom thou dost not see, but who sees thee. *"Thy eyes see thy teachers;* but this is a teacher out of sight, it is thy own conscience, which shall now by the grace of God be awakened to do its office."* (2.) What the word shall be: *" This is the way, walk you in it.* When thou art doubting, conscience shall direct thee to the way of duty; when thou art dull and trifling, conscience shall quicken thee in that way."* As God has not left himself without witness, so he has not left us without guides to show us our way. (3.) The seasonableness of this word: It shall come *when you turn to the right hand or to the left.* We are very apt to miss our way; there are turnings on both hands, and those so tracked and seemingly straight that they may easily be mistaken for the right way. There are right-hand and left-hand errors, extremes on each side virtue; the tempter is busy courting us into the by-paths. It is happy then if by the particular counsels of a faithful minister or friend, or the checks of conscience and the strivings of God's Spirit, we be set right and prevented from going wrong. (4.) The success of this word: *"* It shall not only be spoken, but thy ears shall hear it; whereas God has formerly *spoken once, yea, twice,* and thou *hast not perceived it* (Job xxxiii. 14), now thou shalt listen attentively to these secret whispers, and hear them with an obedient ear."* If God gives us not only the word, but the hearing ear, not only the means of grace, but a heart to make a good use of those means, we have reason to say, He is very gracious to us, and reason to hope he has yet further mercy in store for us.

III. They shall be cured of their idolatry, shall fall out with their idols, and never be reconciled to them again, *v.* 22. The deliverance God shall work for them shall convince them that it is their interest, as well as duty, to serve him only; and they shall own that, as their trouble was brought upon them for their idolatries, so it was removed upon condition that they should not return to them. This is also the good effect of their seeing their teachers and hearing the word behind them; by this it shall appear that they are the better for the means of grace they enjoy—they shall break off from their best-beloved sin. Observe, 1. How foolishly mad they had formerly been upon their idols, in the day of their apostasy. Idolaters are said to be *mad upon their idols* (Jer. l. 38), doatingly fond of them. They had *graven images of silver*, and *molten images of gold*, and, though gold needs no painting, they had coverings and ornaments on these; they spared no cost in doing honour to their idols. 2. How wisely mad (if I may so speak) they now were at their idols, what a holy indignation they conceived against them in the day of their repentance. They not only degraded their images, but defaced them, not only defaced them, but defiled them; they not only spoiled the shape of them, but in a pious fury threw away the gold and silver they were made of, though otherwise valuable and convertible to a good use. They could not find in their hearts to make any vessel of honour of them. The rich clothes wherewith their images were dressed up they cast away as a filthy cloth which rendered those that touched it *unclean until the evening*, Lev. xv. 23. Note, To all true penitents sin has become very odious; they loathe it, and loathe themselves because of it; they cast it away to the dunghill, the fittest place for it, nay, to the cross, for they crucify the flesh; their cry against it is, *Crucify it, crucify it.* They say unto it, *Abi hinc in malam rem—Get thee hence.* They are resolved never to harbour it any more. They put as far from as they can all the occasions of sin and temptations to it, though they are as a right eye or a right hand, and protest against it as Ephraim did (Hos. xiv. 8), *What have I to do any more with idols?* Probably this was fulfilled in many particular persons, who, by the deliverance of Jerusalem from Sennacherib's army, were convinced of the folly of their idolatry and forsook it. It was fulfilled in the body of the Jewish nation at their return from their captivity in Babylon, for they abhorred idols ever after; and it is accomplished daily in the conversion of souls, by the power of divine grace, from spiritual idolatry to the fear and love of God. Those that join themselves to the Lord must abandon every sin, and say unto it, *Get thee hence.*

IV. God will then give them plenty of all good things. When he gives them their teachers, and they give him their hearts, so that they begin to seek the kingdom of God and the righteousness thereof, *then all other things shall be added to them*, Matt. vi. 33. And when the people are brought to praise God *then shall the earth yield her increase, and with it God, even our own God, shall bless us*, Ps. lxvii. 5, 6. So it follows here: "When you shall have abandoned your idols, *then shall God give the rain of your seed*," v.

23. When we return to God in a way of duty he will meet us with his favours. 1. God will give you rain of your seed, rain to water the seed you sow, just at the time that it calls for it, as much as it needs and no more. Observe, How man's industry and God's blessing concur to the good things we enjoy relating to the life that now is: *Thou shalt sow the ground*, that is thy part, and then *God will give the rain of thy seed*, that is his part. It is so in spiritual fruit; we must take pains with our hearts and then wait on God for his grace. 2. The increase of the earth shall be rich and good, and every thing the best of the kind; it shall be *fat and fat*, very fat and very good, *fat and plenteous* (so we read it), good and enough of it. Your land shall be Canaan indeed; it was remarkably so after the defeat of Sennacherib, by the special blessing of God, ch. xxxvii. 30. God would thus repair the losses they sustained by that devastation. 3. Not only the tillage, but the pasture-ground should be remarkably fruitful: *The cattle shall feed in large pastures;* those that are at grass shall have room enough, and the oxen and asses that are kept up for use, to ear the ground, which must be the better fed for their being worked, *shall eat clean provender.* The corn shall not be given them in the chaff as usual, to make it go the further, but they shall have good clean corn fit for man's use, being *winnowed with the fan.* The brute-creatures shall share in the abundance; it is fit they should, for they groan under the burden of the curse which man's sin has brought upon the earth. 4. Even the tops of the mountains, that used to be barren, shall be so well watered with the rain of heaven that there shall be *rivers and streams* there, and running down thence to the valleys (v. 25), and this *in the day of the great slaughter* that should be made by the angel in the camp of the Assyrians, *when the towers* and batteries they had erected for the carrying on of the siege of Jerusalem, the army being slain, *should fall* of course. It is probable that this was fulfilled in the letter of it, and that about the same time that that army was cut off there were extraordinary rains in mercy to the land.

V. The effect of all this should be extraordinary comfort and joy to the people of God, v. 26. Light shall increase; that is, knowledge shall increase (when the prophecies are accomplished they shall be fully understood) or rather triumph shall: the light of the joy that is sown for the righteous shall now come up with a great increase. *The light of the moon shall become as bright* and as strong as *that of the sun, and that of the sun* shall increase proportionably and be *as the light of seven days;* every one shall be much more cheerful and appear much more pleasant than usual. There shall be a high spring-tide of joy in Judah and Jerusalem, upon occasion of the ruin of the

Assyrian army, *when the Lord binds up the breach of his people,* not only saves them from being further wounded, but heals the wounds that have been given them by this invasion and makes up all their losses. The great distress they were reduced to, their despair of relief, and the suddenness of their deliverance, would much augment their joy. This is not unfitly applied by many to the light which the gospel brought into the world to those that sat in darkness, which as far exceeded the Old-Testament light as that of the sun does that of the moon, and which proclaims *healing to the broken-hearted, and the binding up of their wounds.*

27 Behold, the name of the LORD cometh from far, burning *with* his anger, and the burthen *thereof is* heavy: his lips are full of indignation, and his tongue as a devouring fire: 28 And his breath, as an over-flowing stream, shall reach to the midst of the neck, to sift the nations with the sieve of vanity: and *there shall be* a bridle in the jaws of the people, causing *them* to err. 29 Ye shall have a song, as in the night *when* a holy solemnity is kept; and gladness of heart, as when one goeth with a pipe to come into the mountain of the LORD, to the mighty One of Israel. 30 And the LORD shall cause his glorious voice to be heard, and shall show the lighting down of his arm, with the indignation of *his* anger, and *with* the flame of a devouring fire, *with* scattering, and tempest, and hailstones. 31 For through the voice of the LORD shall the Assyrian be beaten down, *which* smote with a rod. 32 And *in* every place where the grounded staff shall pass, which the LORD shall lay upon him, *it* shall be with tabrets and harps: and in battles of shaking will he fight with it. 33 For Tophet *is* ordained of old; yea, for the king it is prepared; he hath made *it* deep *and* large: the pile thereof *is* fire and much wood; the breath of the LORD, like a stream of brimstone, doth kindle it.

This terrible prediction of the ruin of the Assyrian army, though it is a threatening to them, is part of the promise to the Israel of God, that God would not only punish the Assyrians for the mischief they had done to the Israel of God, but would dis-
172

able and deter them from doing the like again; and this prediction, which would now shortly be accomplished, would ratify and confirm the foregoing promises, which should be accomplished in the latter days. Here is,

I. God Almighty angry, and coming forth in anger against the Assyrians. He is here introduced in all the power and all the terror of his wrath, *v.* 27. *The name of Jehovah,* which the Assyrians disdain and set at a distance from them, as if they were out of its reach and it could do them no harm, *behold, it comes from far.* A messenger in the name of the Lord comes from as far off as heaven itself. He is a messenger of wrath, *burning with his anger.* God's *lips are full of indignation* at the blasphemy of Rabshakeh, who compared the God of Israel with the gods of the heathen; *his tongue is as a devouring fire,* for he can speak his proud enemies to ruin; his very breath comes with as much force as an overflowing stream, and with it he shall slay the wicked, *ch.* xi. 4. He does not stifle or smother his resentments, as men do theirs when they are either causeless or impotent; but he *shall cause his glorious voice to be heard* when he proclaims war with an enemy that sets him at defiance, *v.* 30. He shall display *the indignation of his anger,* anger in the highest degree; it shall be as *the flame of a devouring fire,* which carries and consumes all before it, with *lightning* or dissipation, and with *tempest and hailstones,* all which are the formidable phenomena of nature, and therefore expressive of the terror of the Almighty God of nature.

II. The execution done by this anger of the Lord. Men are often angry when they can only threaten and talk big; but when God causes his glorious voice to be heard that shall not be all: he will *show the lighting down of his arm* too, *v.* 30. The operations of his providence shall accomplish the menaces of his word. Those that *would not see the lifting up of his arm* (*ch.* xxvi. 11) shall feel the lighting down of it, and find, to their cost, that the burden thereof is heavy (*v.* 27), so heavy that they cannot bear it, nor bear up against it, but must unavoidably sink and be crushed under it. *Who knows the power of his anger* or imagines what an offended God can do? Five things are here prepared for the execution :—1. Here is *an overflowing stream,* that *shall reach to the midst of the neck,* shall quite overwhelm the whole body of the army, and Sennacherib only, the head of it, shall keep above water and escape this stroke, while yet he is reserved for another in the house of Nisroch his god. The Assyrian army had been to Judah *as an overflowing stream, reaching even to the neck* (*ch.* viii. 7, 8), and now the breath of God's wrath will be so to it. 2. Here is *a sieve of vanity,* with which God would sift those nations of which the

Assyrian army was composed, *v.* 28. The great God can sift nations, for they are all before him as the small dust of the balance; he will sift them, not to gather out of them any that should be preserved, but so as to shake them one against another, put them into great consternation, and shake them all away at last; for it is a sieve of vanity (which retains nothing) that they are shaken with, and they are found all chaff. 3. Here is *a bridle,* which God has in their jaws, to curb and restrain them from doing the mischief they would do, and to force and constrain them to serve his purposes against their own will, *ch.* x. 7. God particularly says of Sennacherib (*ch.* xxxvii. 29) that he will put a hook in his nose and a bridle in his lips. It is a *bridle causing them to err,* forcing them to such methods as will certainly be destructive to themselves and their interest and in which they will be infatuated. God with a word guides his people into the right way (*v.* 21), but with a bridle he turns his enemies headlong upon their own ruin. 4. Here is *a rod* and *a staff,* even *the voice of the Lord,* his word giving orders concerning it, with which *the Assyrian shall be beaten down, v.* 31. The Assyrian had been himself a rod in God's hand for the chastising of his people, and had smitten them, *ch.* x. 5. That was a transient rod; but against the Assyrian shall go forth *a grounded staff,* that shall give a steady blow, shall stick close to him and strike home, so as to leave an impression upon him. It is a staff with a foundation, founded upon the enemies' deserts and God's determinate counsel. It is a consumption determined (*ch.* x. 23), and therefore there is no escaping it, no getting out of the reach of it; it shall pass in every place where an Assyrian is found, and the Lord shall *lay it upon him,* and cause it to rest, *v.* 32. Such is the woeful case of those that persist in enmity to God: *the wrath of God abides on them.* 5. Here is *Tophet ordained* and *prepared* for them, *v.* 33. The valley of the son of Hinnom, adjoining to Jerusalem, was called *Tophet.* In that valley, it is supposed, many of the Assyrian regiments lay encamped, and were there slain by the destroying angel; or there the bodies of those that were so slain were burned. Hezekiah had *lately, and from yesterday* (so the word is) *ordained it ;* that is, say some, he had cleared it of the images that were set up in it, to which they there burnt their children, and so prepared it to be a receptacle for the dead bodies of their enemies, *for the king of Assyria* (that is, for his army) *it is prepared,* and there is fuel enough ready to burn them all; and they shall be consumed as suddenly and effectually as if the fire were kept burning by a continual stream of brimstone, for such the breath of the Lord, his word and his wrath, will be to it. Now as the prophet, in the foregoing promises, slides insensibly into

the promises of gospel graces and comforts, so here, in the threatening of the ruin of Sennacherib's army, he points at the final and everlasting destruction of all impenitent sinners. Our Saviour calls the future misery of the damned *Gehenna,* in allusion to the valley of Hinnom, which gives some countenance to the applying of this to that misery, as also that in the Apocalypse it is so often called the *lake that burns with fire and brimstone.* This is said to be prepared of old for the devil and his angels, for the greatest of sinners, the proudest, and that think themselves not accountable to any for what they say and do; even for kings it is prepared. It is *deep and large,* sufficient to receive the world of the ungodly; the *pile thereof is fire and much wood.* God's wrath is the fire, and sinners make themselves fuel to it; and *the breath of the Lord* (the power of his anger) *kindles it,* and will keep it ever burning. See *ch.* lxvi. 24. Wherefore *stand in awe and sin not.*

III. The great joy which this should occasion to the people of God. The Assyrian's fall is Jerusalem's triumph (*v.* 29): *You shall have a song as in the night,* a psalm of praise such as those sing who *by night stand in the house of the Lord,* and sing to his glory who *gives songs in the night.* It shall not be a song of vain mirth, but a sacred song, such as was sung when a holy solemnity was kept in a grave and religious manner. Our joy in the fall of the church's enemies must be a holy joy, *gladness of heart, as when one goes, with a pipe* (such as the sons of the prophets used when they prophesied, 1 Sam. x. 5), *to the mountain of the Lord,* there to celebrate the praises of *the Mighty One of Israel.* Nay, in every place where the divine vengeance shall pursue the Assyrians they shall not only fall unlamented, but all their neighbours shall attend their fall *with tabrets and harps,* pleased to see how God, *in battles of shaking,* such as shake them out of the world, fights with them (*v.* 32); for *when the wicked perish there is shouting;* and it is with a particular satisfaction that wise and good men see the ruin of those who, like the Assyrians, have insolently bidden defiance to God and trampled upon all mankind.

CHAP. XXXI.

This chapter is an abridgment of the foregoing chapter; the heads of it are much the same. Here is, 1. A woe to those who, when the Assyrian army invaded them, trusted to the Egyptians, and not to God, for succour, ver. 1—3. II. Assurance given of the care God would take of Jerusalem in that time of danger and distress, ver. 4, 5. III. A call to repentance and reformation, ver. 6, 7. IV. A prediction of the fall of the Assyrian army, and the fright which the Assyrian king should thereby be put into, ver. 8, 9.

WOE to them that go down to Egypt for help; and stay on horses, and trust in chariots, because *they are* many; and in horsemen, because they are very strong; but they look not unto the Holy One of

Israel, neither seek the LORD! 2 Yet he also *is* wise, and will bring evil, and will not call back his words: but will arise against the house of the evil doers, and against the help of them that work iniquity. 3 Now the Egyptians *are* men, and not God; and their horses flesh, and not spirit. When the LORD shall stretch out his hand, both he that helpeth shall fall, and he that is holpen shall fall down, and they all shall fail together. 4 For thus hath the LORD spoken unto me, Like as the lion and the young lion roaring on his prey, when a multitude of shepherds is called forth against him, *he* will not be afraid of their voice, nor abase himself for the noise of them: so shall the LORD of hosts come down to fight for mount Zion, and for the hill thereof. 5 As birds flying, so will the LORD of hosts defend Jerusalem; defending also he will deliver *it; and* passing over he will preserve *it*.

This is the last of four chapters together that begin with woe; and they are all woes to the sinners that were found among the professing people of God, to the *drunkards of Ephraim* (ch. xxviii 1), to *Ariel* (ch. xxix. 1), to the *rebellious children* (ch. xxx. 1), and here to *those that go down to Egypt for help;* for men's relation to the church will not secure them from divine woes if they live in contempt of divine laws. Observe,

I. What the sin was that is here reproved, *v.* 1. 1. Idolizing the Egyptians, and making court to them, as if happy were the people that had the Egyptians for their friends and allies. They *go down to Egypt for help* in every exigence, as if the worshippers of false gods had a better interest in heaven and were more likely to have success on earth than the servants of the living and true God. That which invited them to Egypt was that the Egyptians had many chariots to accommodate them with, and horses and horsemen that were strong; and, if they could get a good body of forces thence into their service, they would think themselves able to deal with the king of Assyria and his numerous army. Their kings were forbidden to multiply horses and chariots, and were told of the folly of trusting to them (Ps. xx. 7); but they think themselves wiser than their Bible. 2. Slighting the God of Israel: *They look not to the Holy One of Israel*, as if he were not worth taking notice of in this distress. They advise not with him, seek not his favour, nor are in any care to make him their friend.

II. The gross absurdity and folly of this sin. 1. They neglected one whom, if they would not hope in him, they had reason to fear. They do not seek the Lord, nor make their application to him, *yet he also is wise, v.* 2. They are solicitous to get the Egyptians into an alliance with them, because they have the reputation of a politic people; and is not God wise too? and would not infinite wisdom, engaged on their side, stand them in more stead than all the policies of Egypt? They are at the pains of going down to Egypt, a tedious journey, when they might have had better advice, and better help, by looking up to heaven, and would not. But, if they will not court God's wisdom to act for them, they shall find it act against them. He is wise, too wise for them to outwit, and he will bring evil upon those who thus affront him. He will not call back his words as men do (because they are fickle and foolish), but he *will arise against the house of the evil-doers*, this cabal of them that go down to Egypt; God will appear to their confusion, according to the word that he has spoken, and will oppose the help they think to bring in from the workers of iniquity. Some think the Egyptians made it one condition of their coming into an alliance with them that they should worship the gods of Egypt, and they consented to it, and therefore they are both called *evil-doers* and *workers of iniquity.* 2. They trusted to those who were unable to help them and would soon appear to be so, *v.* 3. Let them know that *the Egyptians*, whom they depend so much upon, *are men and not God.* As it is good for men to *know themselves to be but men* (Ps. ix. 20), so it is good for us to consider that those we love and trust to are but men. They therefore can do nothing without God, nothing against him, nothing in comparison with him. They are men, and therefore fickle and foolish, mutable and mortal, here to day and gone to morrow; they are men, and therefore let us not make gods of them, by making them our hope and confidence, and expecting that in them which is to be found in God only; they are not God, they cannot do that for us which God can do, and will, if we trust in him. Let us not then neglect him, to seek to them; let us not forsake the rock of ages for broken reeds, nor the fountain of living waters for broken cisterns. The Egyptians indeed have horses that are very strong; but *they are flesh, and not spirit*, and therefore, strong as they are, they may be wearied with a long march, and become unserviceable, or be wounded and slain in battle, and leave their riders to be ridden over. Every one knows this, that the Egyptians are not God and their horses are not spirit; but those that seek to them for help do not consider it, else they would not put such confidence in them. Sinners may be convicted of folly by the plainest and most self-evident truths,

174

which they cannot deny, but will not believe. 3. They would certainly be ruined with the Egyptians they trusted in, *v. 3. When the Lord does but stretch out his hand* how easily, how effectually, will he make them ashamed of their confidence in Egypt, and the Egyptians ashamed of the encouragement they gave them to trust in them; for *he that helps and he that is helped shall fall together*, and their mutual alliance shall prove their joint ruin. The Egyptians were shortly to be reckoned with, as appears by the *burden of Egypt* (*ch.* xix), and then those who fled to them for shelter and succour should fall with them; for there is no escaping the judgments of God. *Evil pursues sinners*, and it is just with God to make that creature a scourge to us which we make an idol of. 4. They took God's work out of his hands. They pretended a great deal of care to preserve Jerusalem, in advising to an alliance with Egypt; and, when others would not fall in with their measures, they pleaded self preservation, and went to Egypt themselves. Now the prophet here tells them that Jerusalem should be preserved without aid from Egypt and that those who tarried there should be safe when those who fled to Egypt should be ruined. Jerusalem was under God's protection, and therefore there was no occasion to put it under the protection of Egypt. But a practical distrust of God's all-sufficiency is at the bottom of all our sinful departures from him to the creature. The prophet tells them he had it from God's own mouth: *Thus hath the Lord spoken to me.* They might depend upon it, (1.) That God would appear against Jerusalem's enemies with the boldness of a *lion over his prey, v. 4.* When the lion comes out to seize his prey *a multitude of shepherds come out against him;* for it becomes neighbours to help one another when persons or goods are in danger. These shepherds dare not come near the lion; all they can do is to make a *noise*, and with that they think to frighten him off. But does he regard it? *No: he will not be afraid of their voice*, nor abase himself so far as to be in the least moved by it either to quit his prey or to make any more haste than otherwise he would do in seizing it. *Thus will the Lord of hosts come down to fight for Mount Zion*, with such an unshaken undaunted resolution not to be moved by any opposition; and he will as easily and irresistibly destroy the Assyrian army as a lion tears a lamb in pieces. Whoever appear against God, they are but like a multitude of poor simple shepherds shouting at a lion, who scorns to take notice of them or so much as to alter his pace for them. Surely those that have such a protector need not go to Egypt for help. (2.) That God would appear for Jerusalem's friends with the tenderness of a bird over her young, *v. 5.* God was ready to *gather Jerusalem, as a hen gathers her brood under her wings* (Matt. xxiii. 37); but those that trusted to the Egyptians would not be gathered. *As birds flying* to their nests with all possible speed, when they see them attacked, and fluttering about their nests with all possible concern, hovering over their young ones to protect them and drive away the assailants, with such compassion and affection *will the Lord of hosts defend Jerusalem.* As an eagle stirs up her young when they are in danger, *takes them and bears them on her wings*, so the Lord led Israel out of Egypt (Deut. xxxii. 11, 12); and he has now the same tender concern for them that he had then, so that they need not flee into Egypt again for shelter. *Defending, he will deliver it;* he will so defend it as to secure the continuance of its safety, not defend it for a while and abandon it at last, but defend it so that it shall not fall into the enemies' hand. *I will defend this city to save it*, ch. xxxvii 35. *Passing over he will preserve it;* the word for passing over is used in this sense only here and Exod. xii. 12, 23, 27, concerning the destroying angel's passing over the houses of the Israelites when he slew all the first-born of the Egyptians, to which story this passage refers. The Assyrian army was to be routed by a destroying angel, who should pass over Jerusalem, though that deserved to be destroyed, and draw his sword only against the besiegers. They shall be slain by the pestilence, but none of the besieged shall take the infection. Thus he will again pass over the houses of his people and secure them.

6 Turn ye unto *him from* whom the children of Israel have deeply revolted. 7 For in that day every man shall cast away his idols of silver, and his idols of gold, which your own hands have made unto you *for* a sin. 8 Then shall the Assyrian fall with the sword, not of a mighty man; and the sword, not of a mean man, shall devour him: but he shall flee from the sword, and his young men shall be discomfited. 9 And he shall pass over to his strong hold for fear, and his princes shall be afraid of the ensign, saith the LORD, whose fire *is* in Zion, and his furnace in Jerusalem.

This explains the foregoing promise of the deliverance of Jerusalem; she shall be fitted for deliverance, and then it shall be wrought for her; for in that method God delivers.

I. Jerusalem shall be reformed, and so she shall be delivered from her enemies within her walls, *v.* 6, 7. Here is, 1. A gracious call to repentance. This was the Lord's voice crying in the city, the voice of the rod, the voice of the sword, and the voice of the prophets interpreting the judgment: " *Turn you,* O turn you now, from *your evil ways, unto God,* return to your allegiance to him *from whom the children of Israel have deeply revolted,* from whom you, *O children of Israel!* have revolted." He reminds them of their birth and parentage, that they were *children of Israel,* and therefore under the highest obligations imaginable to the God of Israel, as an aggravation of their revolt from him and as an encouragement to them to return to him. " They have been backsliding children, yet children ; therefore let them return, and their backslidings shall be healed. They have deeply revolted, with great address as they supposed (*the revolters are profound,* Hos. v. 2) ; but the issue will prove that they have revolted dangerously. The stain of their sins has gone deeply into their nature, not to be easily got out, like the blackness of the Ethiopian. *They have deeply corrupted themselves* (Hos. ix. 9) ; they have sunk deep into misery, and cannot easily recover themselves ; therefore you have need to hasten your return to God." 2. A gracious promise of the good success of this call (*v. 7*) : *In that day every man shall cast away his idols,* in obedience to Hezekiah's orders, which, till they were alarmed by the Assyrian invasion, many refused to do. That is a happy fright which frightens us from our sins. (1.) It shall be a general reformation : every man shall cast away his own idols, shall begin with them before he undertakes to demolish other people's idols, which there will be no need of when every man reforms himself. (2.) It shall be a thorough reformation ; for they shall part with their idolatry, their beloved sin, with their *idols of silver and gold,* their idols that they are most fond of. Many make an idol of their silver and gold, and by the love of that idol are drawn to revolt from God ; but those that turn to God cast that away out of their hearts and will be ready to part with it when God calls. (3.) It shall be a reformation upon a right principle, a principle of piety, not of politics. They shall cast away their idols, because they have been unto them *for a sin,* an occasion of sin ; therefore they will have nothing to do with them, though they had been the work of their *own hands,* and upon that account they had a particular fondness for them. Sin is the work of our own hands, but in working it we have been working our own ruin, and therefore we must cast it away ; and those are strangely wedded to it who will not be prevailed upon to cast it away when they see that otherwise they themselves will be castaways. Some make this to be only a prediction that those who trust in idols, when they find they stand them in no stead, will cast them away in indignation. But it agrees so exactly with *ch.* xxx. 22 that I rather

take it as a promise of a sincere reformation.

II. Jerusalem's besiegers shall be routed, and so she shall be delivered from the enemies about her walls. The former makes way for this. If a people return to God, they may leave it to him to plead their cause against their enemies. When they have cast away their idols, *then shall the Assyrian fall, v.* 8, 9. 1. The army of the Assyrians shall be laid dead upon the spot *by the sword, not of a mighty man, nor of a mean man,* not of any man at all, either Israelite or Egyptian, not forcibly by the sword of a mighty man nor surreptitiously by the sword of a mean man, but by the sword of an angel, who strikes more strongly than a mighty man and yet more secretly than a mean man, by the sword of the Lord, and his power and wrath in the hand of the angel. Thus the young men of the army shall melt, and be discomfited, and become tributaries to death. When God has work to do against the enemies of his church we expect it must be done by mighty men and mean men, officers and common soldiers ; whereas God can, if he pleases, do it without either. *He* needs not armies of men who has legions of angels at command, Matt. xxvi. 53. 2. The king of Assyria shall flee for the same, shall flee from that invisible sword, hoping to get out of the reach of it ; and he shall make the best of his way to his own dominions, shall pass over to some strong-hold of his own, for fear lest the Jews should pursue him now that his army was routed. Sennacherib had been very confident that he should make himself master of Jerusalem, and in the most insolent manner had set both God and Hezekiah at defiance ; yet now he is made to tremble for fear of both. God can strike a terror into the proudest of men, and make the stoutest heart to tremble. See Job xviii. 11 ; xx. 24. *His princes* that accompany him *shall be afraid of the ensign,* shall be in a continual fright at the remembrance of the ensign in the air, which perhaps the destroying angel displayed before he gave the fatal blow. Or they shall be afraid of every ensign they see, suspecting it is a party of the Jews pursuing them. The banner that God displays for the encouragement of his people (Ps. lx. 4) will be a terror to his and their enemies. Thus he *cuts off the spirit of princes and is terrible to the kings of the earth.* But who will do this ? It is *the Lord, whose fire is in Zion and his furnace in Jerusalem.* (1.) Whose residence is there, and who there keeps house, as a man does where his fire and his oven are. It is the city of the great King, and let not the Assyrians think to turn him out of the possession of his own house. (2.) Who is there a consuming fire to all his enemies, and will make them as a fiery oven in the day of his wrath, Ps. xxi. 9. He is himself *a wall of fire round about Jerusalem,* so that whoever assaults her does so at his peril, Zech. ii. 5; Rev. xi. 5. (3.) Who has his altar there, on which the holy fire is continually kept burning and sacrifices are daily offered to his honour, and with which he is well pleased; and therefore he will defend this city, especially having an eye to the great sacrifice which was there also to be offered, of which all the sacrifices were types. If we keep up the fire of holy love and devotion in our hearts and houses, we may depend upon God to be a protection to us and them.

CHAP. XXXII.

This chapter seems to be such a prophecy of the reign of Hezekiah as amounts to an abridgment of the history of it, and this with an eye to the kingdom of the Messiah, whose government was typified by the thrones of the house of David, for which reason he is so often called "the Son of David." Here is, I. A prophecy of that good work of reformation with which he should begin his reign, and the happy influence it should have upon the people, who had been wretchedly corrupted and debauched in the reign of his predecessor, ver. 1—8. II. A prophecy of the great disturbance that would be given to the kingdom in the middle of his reign by the Assyrian invasion, ver. 9—14. III. A promise of better times afterwards, towards the latter end of his reign, in respect both of piety and peace (ver. 15—20), which promise may be supposed to look as far forward as the days of the Messiah.

BEHOLD, a king shall reign in righteousness, and princes shall rule in judgment. 2 And a man shall be as a hiding-place from the wind, and a covert from the tempest; as rivers of water in a dry place, as the shadow of a great rock in a weary land. 3 And the eyes of them that see shall not be dim, and the ears of them that hear shall hearken. 4 The heart also of the rash shall understand knowledge, and the tongue of the stammerers shall be ready to speak plainly. 5 The vile person shall be no more called liberal, nor the churl said *to be* bountiful. 6 For the vile person will speak villany, and his heart will work iniquity, to practise hypocrisy, and to utter error against the LORD, to make empty the soul of the hungry, and he will cause the drink of the thirsty to fail. 7 The instruments also of the churl *are* evil: he deviseth wicked devices to destroy the poor with lying words, even when the needy speaketh right. 8 But the liberal deviseth liberal things; and by liberal things shall he stand.

We have here the description of a flourishing kingdom. "Blessed art thou, O land! when it is thus with thee, when kings, princes, and people, are in their places such as they should be." It may be taken as a directory both to magistrates and subjects, what both ought to do, or as a panegyric to

Hezekiah, who ruled well and saw something of the happy effects of his good government, and it was designed to make the people sensible how happy they were under his administration and how careful they should be to improve the advantages of it, and withal to direct them to look for the kingdom of Christ, and the times of reformation which that kingdom should introduce. It is here promised and prescribed, for the comfort of the church,

I. That magistrates should do their duty in their places, and the powers answer the great ends for which they were ordained of God, v. 1, 2. 1. There shall be a king and princes that shall reign and rule; for it cannot go well when there is no king in Israel. The princes must have a king, a monarch over them as supreme, in whom they may unite; and the king must have princes under him as officers, by whom he may act, 1 Pet. ii. 13, 14. They both shall know their place and fill it up. The king shall reign, and yet, without any diminution to his just prerogative, the princes shall rule in a lower sphere, and all for the public good. 2. They shall use their power according to law, and not against it. They shall reign in righteousness and in judgment, with wisdom and equity, protecting the good and punishing the bad; and those kings and princes Christ owns as reigning by him who decree justice, Prov. viii. 15. Such a King, such a Prince, Christ himself is; he reigns by rule, and *in righteousness will he judge the world*, ch. ix. 7; xi. 4. 3. Thus they shall be great blessings to the people (v. 2): *A man*, that man, that king that reigns in righteousness, *shall be as a hiding-place*. When princes are as they should be people are as they would be. (1.) They are sheltered and protected from many mischiefs. This good magistrate is a covert to the subject from the tempest of injury and violence; he *defends the poor and fatherless*, that they be not made a prey of by the mighty. Whither should oppressed innocency flee, when blasted by reproach or borne down by violence, but to the magistrate as its hiding-place? To him it appeals, and by him it is righted. (2.) They are refreshed and comforted with many blessings. This good magistrate gives such countenance to those that are poor and in distress, and such encouragement to every thing that is praiseworthy, that he is *as rivers of water in a dry place*, cooling and cherishing the earth and making it fruitful, and *as the shadow of a great rock*, under which a poor traveller may shelter himself from the scorching heat of the sun *in a weary land*. It is a great reviving to a good man, who makes conscience of doing his duty, in the midst of contempt and contradiction, at length to be backed, and favoured, and smiled upon in it by a good magistrate. All this, and much more, the man Christ Jesus is to all the

177

willing faithful subjects of his kingdom. When the greatest evils befal us, not only the wind, but the tempest, when storms of guilt and wrath beset us and beat upon us, they drive us to Christ, and in him we are not only safe, but satisfied that we are so; in him we find rivers of water for those that hunger and thirst after righteousness, all the refreshment and comfort that a needy soul can desire, and the shadow, not of a tree, which sun or rain may beat through, but of a rock, of a great rock, which reaches a great way for the shelter of the traveller. Some observe here that as the covert, and the hiding-place, and the rock, do themselves receive the battering of the wind and storm, to save those from it that take shelter in them, so Christ bore the storm himself to keep it off from us.

II. That subjects should do their duty in their places.

1. They shall be willing to be taught, and to understand things aright. They shall lay aside their prejudices against their rulers and teachers, and submit to the light and power of truth, v. 3. When this blessed work of reformation is set on foot, and men do their parts towards it, God will not be wanting to do his: Then *the eyes of those that see*, of the prophets, the seers, *shall not be dim;* but God will bless them with visions, to be by them communicated to the people; and those that read the word written shall no longer have a veil upon their hearts, but shall see things clearly. Then *the ears of those that hear* the word preached *shall hearken* diligently and readily receive what they hear, and not be so dull of hearing as they have been. This shall be done by the grace of God, especially gospel-grace; for *the hearing ear, and the seeing eye, the Lord has made*, has new-made, even both of them.

2. There shall be a wonderful change wrought in them by that which is taught them, v. 4. (1.) They shall have a clear head, and be able to discern things that differ, and distinguish concerning them. *The heart of those that were* hasty and *rash*, and could not take time to digest and consider things, shall now be cured of their precipitation, and *shall understand knowledge;* for the Spirit of God will open their understanding. This blessed work Christ wrought in his disciples after his resurrection (Luke xxiv. 45), as a specimen of what he would do for all his people, in giving them an understanding, 1 John v. 20. The pious designs of good princes are likely to take effect when their subjects allow themselves liberty to consider, and to think, so freely as to take things right. (2.) They shall have a ready utterance: *The tongue of the stammerers*, that used to blunder whenever they spoke of the things of God, *shall now be ready to speak plainly*, as those that understand what they speak of, that believe,

and therefore speak. There shall be a great increase of such clear, distinct, and methodical knowledge in the things of God, that those from whom one would not have expected it shall speak intelligently of these things, very much to the honour of God and the edification of others. Their hearts being full of this good matter, their tongues shall be *as the pen of a ready writer*, Ps. xlv. 1.

3. The differences between good and evil, virtue and vice, shall be kept up, and no more confounded by those who put darkness for light and light for darkness (v. 5): *The vile shall no more be called liberal.*

(1.) Bad men shall no more be preferred by the prince. When a king reigns in justice he will not put those in places of honour and power that are ill-natured, and of base and sordid spirits, and care not what injury or mischief they do so they may but compass their own ends. Such are *vile* persons (as Antiochus is called, Dan. xi. 21); when they are advanced they are called *liberal* and *bountiful;* they are called *benefactors* (Luke xxii. 25): but it shall not always be thus; when the world grows wiser men shall be preferred according to their merit, and honour (which was never thought seemly for a fool, Prov. xxvi. 1) shall no longer be thrown away upon such.

(2.) Bad men shall be no more had in reputation among the people, nor vice disguised with the colours of virtue. It shall no more be said to Nabal, *Thou art Nadib* (so the words are); such a covetous muckworm as Nabal was, a fool but for his money, shall not be complimented with the title of a gentleman or a prince; nor shall they call a *churl*, that minds none but himself, does no good with what he has, but is an unprofitable burden of the earth, *My lord;* or, rather, they shall not say of him, *He is rich;* for so the word signifies. Those only are to be reckoned rich that are rich in good works; not those that have abundance, but those that use it well. In short, it is well with a people when men are generally valued by their virtue, and usefulness, and beneficence to mankind, and not by their wealth or titles of honour. Whether this was fulfilled in the reign of Hezekiah, and how far it refers to the kingdom of Christ (in which we are sure men are judged of by what they are, not by what they have, nor is any man's character mistaken), we will not say; but it prescribes an excellent rule both to prince and people, to respect men according to their personal merit. To enforce this rule, here is a description both of the vile person and of the liberal; and by it we shall see such a vast difference between them that we must quite forget ourselves if we pay that respect to the vile person and the churl which is due only to the liberal.

[1.] A vile person and a churl will do mischief, and the more if he be preferred and have power in his hand; his honours will make him worse and not better, *v.* 6, 7. See the character of these base ill-conditioned men. *First,* They are always plotting some unjust thing or other, designing ill either to particular persons or to the public, and contriving how to bring it about; and so many silly piques they have to gratify, and mean revenges, that there appears not in them the least spark of generosity. Their hearts will be still working some iniquity or other. Observe, There is the work of the heart, as well as the work of the hands. As thoughts are words to God, so designs are works in his account. See what pains sinners take in sin. They labour at it; their hearts are intent upon it, and with a great deal of art and application they *work iniquity.* They *devise wicked devices* with all the subtlety of the old serpent and a great deal of deliberation, which makes the sin exceedingly sinful; and the more there is of plot and management in a sin the more there is of Satan in it. *Secondly,* They carry on their plots by trick and dissimulation. When they are meditating iniquity, they *practise hypocrisy,* feign themselves just men, Luke xx. 20. The most abominable mischiefs shall be disguised with the most plausible pretences of devotion to God, regard to man, and concern for some common good. Those are the vilest of men that intend the worst mischiefs when they speak fair. *Thirdly,* They *speak villany.* When they are in a passion you will see what they are by the base ill language they give to those about them, which no way becomes men of rank and honour; or, in giving verdict or judgment, they villanously put false colours upon things, to pervert justice. *Fourthly,* They affront God, who is a righteous God and loves righteousness: They *utter error against the Lord,* and therein they practise profaneness; for so the word which we translate *hypocrisy* signifies. They give an unjust sentence, and then profanely make use of the name of God for the ratification of it; as if, because the *judgment is God's* (Deut. i. 17), therefore their false and unjust judgment was his. This is *uttering error against the Lord,* under pretence of uttering truth and justice for him; and nothing can be more impudently done against God than to use his name to patronise wickedness. *Fifthly,* They abuse mankind, those particularly whom they are bound to protect and relieve. 1. Instead of supplying the wants of the poor, they impoverish them, they *make empty the souls of the hungry;* either taking away the food they have, or, which is almost equivalent, denying the supply which they want and which they have to give. And they *cause the drink of the thirsty to fail;* they cut off the relief they used to have, though they need it as much as ever. Those are vile persons indeed that rob the spital. 2. Instead of righting the poor, when they appeal to their judgment, they contrive to destroy the poor, to ruin them in their courts of judicature with lying words in favour of the rich, to whom they are plainly partial; yea, though the needy speak right, though the evidence be ever so full for them to make out the equity of their cause, it is the bribe that governs them, not the right. *Sixthly,* These churls and vile persons have always bad instruments about them, that are ready to serve their villanous purposes: *All their servants are wicked.* There is no design so palpably unjust but there may be found those that would be employed as tools to put it in execution. *The instruments of the churl are evil,* and one cannot expect otherwise; but this is our comfort, that they can do no more mischief than God permits them.

[2.] One that is truly liberal, and deserves the honour of being called so, makes it his business to do good to every body according as his sphere is, *v.* 8. Observe, *First,* The care he takes, and the contrivances he has, to do good. He *devises liberal things.* As much as the churl or niggard projects how to save and lay up what he has for himself only, so much the good charitable man projects how to use and lay out what he has in the best manner for the good of others. Charity must be directed by wisdom, and liberal things done prudently and with device, that the good intention of them may be answered, that it may not be charity misplaced. The liberal man, when he has done all the liberal things that are in his own power, devises liberal things for others to do according to their power, and puts them upon doing them. *Secondly,* the comfort he takes, and the advantage he has, in doing good: *By liberal things he shall stand,* or be established. The providence of God will reward him for his liberality with a settled prosperity and an established reputation. The grace of God will give him abundance of satisfaction and confirmed peace in his own bosom. What disquiets others shall not disturb him; his heart is fixed. This is the recompence of charity, Ps. cxii. 5, 6. Some read it, *The prince, or honourable man, will take honourable courses; and by such honourable or ingenuous courses he shall stand or be established.* It is well with a land when the honourable of it are indeed men of honour and scorn to do a base thing, when its king is thus the son of nobles.

9 Rise up, ye women that are at ease; hear my voice, ye careless daughters; give ear unto my speech. 10 Many days and years shall ye be troubled, ye careless women: for the vintage shall fail, the gathering shall not come. 11 Tremble, ye women that are at ease; be troubled, ye careless ones: strip you, and make you

bare, and gird *sackcloth* upon *your* loins. 12 They shall lament for the teats, for the pleasant fields, for the fruitful vine. 13 Upon the land of my people shall come up thorns *and* briers; yea, upon all the houses of joy *in* the joyous city: 14 Because the palaces shall be forsaken; the multitude of the city shall be left; the forts and towers shall be for dens for ever, a joy of wild asses, a pasture of flocks; 15 Until the Spirit be poured upon us from on high, and the wilderness be a fruitful field, and the fruitful field be counted for a forest. 16 Then judgment shall dwell in the wilderness, and righteousness remain in the fruitful field. 17 And the work of righteousness shall be peace; and the effect of righteousness quietness and assurance for ever. 18 And my people shall dwell in a peaceable habitation, and in sure dwellings, and in quiet resting-places; 19 When it shall hail, coming down on the forest; and the city shall be low in a low place. 20 Blessed *are* ye that sow beside all waters, that send forth *thither* the feet of the ox and the ass.

In these verses we have God rising up to judgment against the vile persons, to punish them for their villany; but at length returning in mercy to the liberal, to reward them for their liberality.

I. When there was so great a corruption of manners, and so much provocation given to the holy God, bad times might well be expected, and here is a warning given of such times coming. The alarm is sounded to the *women that were at ease* (*v.* 9) and the *careless daughters,* to feed whose pride, vanity, and luxury, their husbands and fathers were tempted to starve the poor. Let them hear what the prophet has to say to them in God's name: "*Rise up, and hear* with reverence and attention."

1. Let them know that God was about to bring wasting desolating judgments upon the land in which they *lived in pleasure and were wanton.* This seems to refer primarily to the desolations made by Sennacherib's army when he seized all the fenced cities of Judah: but then those words, *many days and years,* must be rendered (as the margin reads them) *days above a year,* that is, something above a year shall this havock be in the making: so long it was from the first entrance of that army into the land of Judah to the overthrow of it. But it is applicable

180

to the wretched disappointment which those will certainly meet with, first or last, that set their hearts upon the world and place their happiness in it: *You shall be troubled, you careless women.* It will not secure us from trouble to cast away care when we are at ease; nay, to those who affect to live carelessly even little troubles will be great vexations and press hard upon them. They were careless and at ease because they had money enough and mirth enough; but the prophet here tells them, (1.) That the country whence they had their rents and dainties should shortly be laid waste: "*The vintage shall fail;* and then what will you do for wine to make merry with? *The gathering* of fruit *shall not come,* for there shall be none to be gathered, and you will find the want of them, *v.* 10. You will want *the teats,* the good milk from the cows, *the pleasant fields* and their productions;" the useful fields that are serviceable to human life are the pleasant ones. "You will want the fruitful vine, and the grapes it used to yield you." The abuse of plenty is justly punished with scarcity; and those deserve to be deprived of the supports of life who make them the food and fuel of lust and prepare them for Baal. (2.) That the cities too, the cities of Judah, where they lived at ease, spent their rents, and made themselves merry with their dainties, should be laid waste (*v.* 13, 14): *Briers and thorns,* the fruits of sin and the curse, *shall come up,* not only *upon the land of my people,* which shall lie uncultivated, but upon *all the houses of joy*— the play-houses, the gaming-houses, the taverns—*in the joyous cities.* When a foreign army was ravaging the country the houses of joy, no doubt, became houses of mourning; then the palaces, or noblemen's houses, were forsaken by their owners, who perhaps fled to Egypt for refuge; the multitude of the city were left by their leaders to shift for themselves. Then the stately houses *shall be for dens for ever,* which had been as forts and towers for strength and magnificence. They shall be abandoned; the owners shall never return to them; every body shall look upon them to be like Jericho, an anathema; so that, even when peace returns, they shall not be rebuilt, but shall be thrown to the waste: *A joy of wild asses and a pasture of flocks.* Thus is many a house brought to ruin by sin. *Jam seges est ubi Troja fuit—Corn grows on the site of Troy.*

2. In the foresight of this let them *tremble* and *be troubled, strip themselves, and gird sackcloth upon their loins, v.* 11. This intimates not only that when the calamity comes they shall thus be made to tremble and be forced to strip themselves, that then God's judgments would strip them and make them bare, but, (1.) That the best prevention of the trouble would be to repent and humble themselves for their sin, and lie in the dust

before God in true remorse and godly sorrow, which would be the lengthening out of their tranquillity. This is meeting God in the way of his judgments, and saving a correction by correcting our own mistakes. Those only shall break that will not bend. (2.) That the best preparation for the trouble would be to deny themselves and live a life of mortification, and to sit loose to all the delights of sense. Those that have already by a holy contempt of this world stripped themselves can easily bear to be stripped when trouble and death come.

II. While there was still a remnant that kept their integrity they had reason to hope for good times at length and such times the prophet here gives them a pleasant prospect of. Such times they saw in the latter end of the reign of Hezekiah; but the prophecy may well be supposed to look further, to the days of the Messiah, who is *King of righteousness* and *King of peace,* and to whom all the prophets bear witness. Now observe,

1. How those blessed times shall be introduced—by the *pouring out of the Spirit from on high* (v. 15), which speaks not only of the good-will of God towards us, but the good work of God in us; for then, and not till then, there will be good times, when God by his grace gives men good hearts; and therefore God's *giving his Holy Spirit to those that ask him* is in effect his giving them all good things, as appears by comparing Luke xi. 13 with Matt. vii. 11. This is the great thing that God's people comfort themselves with the hopes of, that *the Spirit shall be poured out upon them,* that there shall be a more plentiful effusion of the Spirit of grace than formerly, according as the necessity of the church, in its desolate estate, calls for. This comes from on high, and therefore they look up to their Father in heaven for it. When God designs favours for his church he pours out his Spirit, both to prepare his people to receive his favours and to qualify and give success to those whom he designs to employ as instruments of his favour; for their endeavours to repair the desolations of the church are all fruitless *until the Spirit be poured out upon them,* and then the work is done suddenly. The kingdom of the Messiah was brought in, and set up, by the pouring out of the Spirit (Acts ii.), and so it is still kept up, and will be to the end.

2. What a wonderfully happy change shall then be made. That which was *a wilderness,* dry and barren, *shall become a fruitful field,* and that which we now reckon *a fruitful field,* in comparison with what it shall be then, *shall be counted for a forest. Then shall the earth yield her increase.* It is promised that in the days of the Messiah the *fruit of the earth shall shake like Lebanon,* Ps. lxxii. 16. Some apply this to the admission of the Gentiles into the gospel church (which made the wilderness a fruitful field),

and the rejection and exclusion of the Jews, which made that a forest which had been a fruitful field. On the Gentiles was poured out a spirit of life, but on the Jews a spirit of slumber. See what is the evidence and effect of the pouring out of the Spirit upon any soul; it is thereby made fruitful, and has its fruit unto holiness. Three things go to make these times happy :—

(1) Judgment and righteousness, *v.* 16. When the Spirit is poured out upon a land, *then judgment shall dwell in the wilderness* and turn it into a fruitful field, and *righteousness shall remain in the fruitful field* and make it yet more fruitful. Ministers shall expound the law and magistrates execute it, and both so judiciously and faithfully that by both the bad shall be made good and the good made better. Among all sorts of people, the poor and low and unlearned, that are neglected as the wilderness, and the rich and great and learned, that are valued as the fruitful field, there shall be right thoughts of things, good principles commanding, and conscience made of good and evil, sin and duty. Or in all parts of the land, both champaign and enclosed, country and city, the ruder parts and those that are more cultivated and refined, justice shall be duly administered. The law of Christ introduces a judgment or rule by which we must be governed, and the gospel of Christ a righteousness by which we must be saved; and, wherever the Spirit is poured out, both these dwell and remain as an everlasting righteousness.

(2.) Peace and quietness, *v.* 17, 18. The peace here promised is of two kinds :—

[1.] Inward peace, *v.* 17. This follows upon the indwelling of righteousness, *v.* 16. Those in whom that work is wrought shall experience this blessed product of it. It is itself peace, and the effect of it is *quietness and assurance for ever,* that is, a holy serenity and security of mind, by which the soul enjoys itself and enjoys its God, and it is not in the power of this world to disturb it in those enjoyments. Note, Peace, and quietness, and everlasting assurance may be expected, and shall be found, in the way and work of righteousness. True satisfaction is to be had only in true religion, and there it is to be had without fail. Those are the quiet and peaceable lives that are spent *in all godliness and honesty,* 1 Tim. ii. 2. *First,* Even *the work of righteousness shall be peace.* In the doing of our duty we shall find abundance of true pleasure, a present great reward of obedience in obedience. Though the work of righteousness may be toilsome and costly, and expose us to contempt, yet it is peace, such peace as is sufficient to bear our charges. *Secondly, The effect of righteousness shall be quietness and assurance,* not only to the end of time, of our time, and in the end, but to the endless ages of eternity. Real holiness is real happiness now and shall

181

be perfect happiness, that is, perfect holiness, for ever.

[2.] Outward peace, *v.* 18. It is a great mercy when those who by the grace of God have quiet and peaceable spirits are by the providence of God made to *dwell in quiet and peaceable habitations,* not disturbed in their houses or solemn assemblies. When the terror of Sennacherib's invasion was over, the people, no doubt, were more sensible than ever of the mercy of a quiet habitation, not disturbed with the alarms of war. Let every family study to keep itself quiet from strifes and jars within, not two against three and three against two in the house, and then put itself under God's protection to dwell safely, and to be *quiet from the fear of evil* without. Jerusalem shall be a peaceable habitation; compare *ch.* xxxiii. 20. Even *when it shall hail,* and there shall be a violent battering storm *coming down on the forest* that lies bleak, then shall Jerusalem be *a quiet resting-place, for the city shall be low in a low place,* under the wind, not exposed (as those cities are that stand high) to the fury of the storm, but sheltered by the *mountains that are round about Jerusalem,* Ps. cxxv. 2. The *high forts and towers are brought down* (*v.* 14), but the city that lies low shall be a quiet resting-place. Those are most safe, and may dwell most at ease, that are humble, and are willing to dwell low, *v.* 19. Those that would dwell in a peaceable habitation must be willing to dwell low, and in a low place. Some think here is an allusion to the preservation of the land of Goshen from the plague of hail, which made great destruction in the land of Egypt.

(3.) Plenty and abundance. There shall be such good crops gathered in every where, and every year, that the husbandmen shall be commended, and thought happy, who *sow beside all waters* (*v.* 20), who sow all the grounds that are fit for seedness, who *cast their bread,* or bread-corn, *upon the waters,* Eccl. xi. 1. God will give the increase, but then the husbandman must be industrious, and mind his business, and sow beside all waters; and, if he do this, the corn shall come up so thick and rank that he shall turn in his cattle, even the ox and the ass, to eat the tops of it and keep it under. This is applicable, [1.] To the preaching of the word. Some think it points at the ministry of the apostles, who, as husbandmen, went forth to sow their seed (Matt. xiii. 3); they sowed beside all waters; they preached the gospel wherever they came. Waters signify people, and they preached to multitudes. Wherever they found men's hearts softened, and moistened, and disposed to receive the word, they cast in the good seed. And whereas, by the law of Moses, the Jews were forbidden to *plough with an ox and an ass together* (Deut. xxii. 10), which intimated that Jews and Gentiles should not intermix, now that distinction

182

shall be taken away, and both the ox and the ass, both Jews and Gentiles, shall be employed in, and enjoy the benefit of, the gospel husbandry. [2.] To works of charity When God sends these happy times blessed are those that improve them in doing good with what they have, that sow beside all waters, that embrace all opportunities of relieving the necessitous; for in due season they shall reap.

CHAP. XXXIII.

This chapter relates to the same events as the foregoing chapter, the distress of Judah and Jerusalem by Sennacherib's invasion and their deliverance out of that distress by the destruction of the Assyrian army. These are intermixed in the prophecy, in the way of a Pindaric. Observe, I. The great distress that Judah and Jerusalem should then be brought into, ver. 7—9. II. The particular frights which the sinners in Zion should then be in, ver. 13, 14. III. The prayers of good people to God in this distress, v. 2. IV. The holy security which they should enjoy in the midst of this trouble, ver. 15, 16. V. The destruction of the army of the Assyrians (ver. 1—3), in which God would be greatly glorified, ver. 5, 10—12. VI. The enriching of the Jews with the spoil of the Assyrian camp, ver. 4, 23, 24. VII. The happy settlement of Jerusalem, and the Jewish state, upon this. Religion shall be uppermost (ver. 6), and their civil state shall flourish, ver. 17—22. This was soon fulfilled, but is written for our learning.

WOE to thee that spoilest, and thou *wast* not spoiled; and dealest treacherously, and they dealt not treacherously with thee ! When thou shalt cease to spoil, thou shalt be spoiled; *and* when thou shalt make an end to deal treacherously, they shall deal treacherously with thee. 2 O LORD, be gracious unto us; we have waited for thee: be thou their arm every morning, our salvation also in the time of trouble. 3 At the noise of the tumult the people fled; at the lifting up of thyself the nations were scattered. 4 And your spoil shall be gathered *like* the gathering of the caterpillar: as the running to and fro of locusts shall he run upon them. 5 The LORD is exalted; for he dwelleth on high: he hath filled Zion with judgment and righteousness. 6 And wisdom and knowledge shall be the stability of thy times, *and* strength of salvation: the fear of the LORD *is* his treasure. 7 Behold, their valiant ones shall cry without: the ambassadors of peace shall weep bitterly. 8 The highways lie waste, the wayfaring man ceaseth; he hath broken the covenant, he hath despised the cities, he regardeth no man. 9 The earth mourneth *and* languisheth: Lebanon is ashamed *and* hewn down: Sharon is like a wilderness; and Bashan and Carmel shake off *their fruits.* 10 Now will

I rise, saith the LORD; now will I be exalted; now will I lift up myself. 11 Ye shall conceive chaff, ye shall bring forth stubble: your breath, *as* fire, shall devour you. 12 And the people shall be *as* the burnings of lime: *as* thorns cut up shall they be burned in the fire.

Here we have,

I. The proud and false Assyrian justly reckoned with for all his fraud and violence, and laid under a woe, *v.* 1. Observe, 1. The sin which the enemy had been guilty of. He had spoiled the people of God, and made a prey of them, and herein had broken his treaty of peace with them, and dealt treacherously. Truth and mercy are two such sacred things, and have so much of God in them, that those cannot but be under the wrath of God that make conscience of neither, but are perfectly lost to both, that care not what mischief they do, what spoil they make, what dissimulations they are guilty of, nor what solemn engagements they violate, to compass their own wicked designs. Bloody and deceitful men are the worst of men. 2. The aggravation of this sin. He spoiled those that had never done him any injury and that he had no pretence to quarrel with, and dealt treacherously with those that had always dealt faithfully with him. Note, The less provocation we have from men to a wrong thing the more provocation we give to God by doing it. 3. The punishment he should fall under for this sin. He that spoiled the cities of Judah shall have his own army destroyed by an angel and his camp plundered by those whom he had made a prey of. The Chaldeans shall deal treacherously with the Assyrians and revolt from them. Two of Sennacherib's own sons shall deal treacherously with him and basely murder him at his devotions. Note, The righteous God often pays sinners in their own coin. *He that leads into captivity shall go into captivity*, Rev. xiii. 10; xviii. 6. 4. The time when he shall be thus dealt with. When he shall *make an end to spoil, and to deal treacherously*, not by repentance and reformation, which might prevent his ruin (Dan. iv. 27), but when he shall have done his worst, when he shall have gone as far as God would permit him to go, to the utmost of his tether, then the cup of trembling shall be put into his hand. When he shall have arrived at his full stature in impiety, shall have filled up the measure of his iniquity, then all shall be called over again. When he has done God will begin, for his day is coming.

II. The praying people of God earnest at the throne of grace for mercy for the land now in its distress (*v.* 2): "*O Lord! be merciful to us.* Men are cruel; be thou gracious. We have deserved thy wrath, but

we entreat thy favour; and, if we may find thee propitious to us, we are happy; the trouble we are in cannot hurt us, shall not ruin us. It is in vain to expect relief from creatures; we have no confidence in the Egyptians, but *we have waited for thee* only, resolving to submit to thee, whatever the issue of the trouble be, and hoping that it shall be a comfortable issue." Those that by faith humbly wait for God shall certainly find him gracious to them. They prayed, 1. For those that were employed in military services for them: "*Be thou their arm every morning.* Hezekiah, and all his princes, and all the men of war, need continual supplies of strength and courage from thee; supply their need therefore, and be to them a God all-sufficient. Every morning, when they go forth upon the business of the day, and perhaps have new work to do and new difficulties to encounter, let them be afresh animated and invigorated, and, *as the day, so let the strength be.*" In our spiritual warfare our own hands are not sufficient for us, nor can we bring any thing to pass unless God not only strengthen our arms (Gen. xlix. 24), but be himself our arm; so entirely do we depend upon him as our arm every morning, so constantly do we depend upon his power, as well as his compassions, which are new every morning, Lam. iii. 23. If God leaves us to ourselves any morning, we are undone; we must therefore every morning commit ourselves to him, and go forth in his strength to do the work of the day in its day. 2. For the body of the people: "*Be thou our salvation also in the time of trouble,* ours who sit still, and do not venture into the high places of the field." They depend upon God not only as their Saviour, to work deliverance for them, but as their salvation itself; for, whatever becomes of their secular interests, they will reckon themselves safe and saved if they have him for their God. If he undertake to be their Saviour, he will be their salvation; for *as for God his work is perfect.* Some read it thus: "*Thou who wast their arm every morning,* who wast the continual strength and help of our fathers before us, *be thou our salvation also in time of trouble.* Help us as thou helpedst them; *they looked unto thee and were lightened* (Ps. xxxiv. 5); let us then not walk in darkness."

III. The Assyrian army ruined and their camp made a rich but cheap and easy prey to Judah and Jerusalem. No sooner is the prayer made (*v.* 2) than it is answered (*v.* 3), nay, it is outdone. They prayed that God would save them from their enemies; but he did more than that; he gave them victory over their enemies and abundant cause to triumph; for, 1. The strength of the Assyrian camp was broken (*v.* 3) when the destroying angel slew so many thousands of them: *At the noise of the tumult,* of the shrieks of the dying men (who, we may suppose, did not die silently), the rest of *the people fled,* and shifted every one for his own safety. When God did thus lift up himself the several nations, or clans, of which the army was composed, were scattered. It was time to stir when such an unprecedented plague broke out among them. When God arises his enemies are scattered, Ps. lxviii. 1. 2. The spoil of the Assyrian camp is seized, by way of reprisal, for all the desolations of the defenced cities of Judah (*v.* 4): *Your spoil shall be gathered* by the inhabitants of Jerusalem, *like the gathering of the caterpillar,* and *as the running to and fro of locusts,* that is, the spoilers shall as easily and as quickly make themselves masters of the riches of the Assyrians as a host of caterpillars, or locusts, make a field, or a tree, bare. Thus *the wealth of the sinner is laid up for the just* and Israel is enriched with the spoil of the Egyptians. Some make the Assyrians to be the caterpillars and locusts, which, when they are killed, are gathered together in heaps, as the frogs of Egypt, and are run upon and trodden to dirt.

IV. God and his Israel glorified and exalted hereby. When the spoil of the enemy is thus gathered, 1. God will have the praise of it (*v.* 5): *The Lord is exalted.* It is his honour thus to abase proud men, and hide them in the dust, together; thus he magnifies his own name, and his people give him the glory of it, as Israel when the Egyptians were drowned, Exod. xv. 1, 2, &c. He is exalted as one that dwells on high, out of the reach of their blasphemies, and that has an over-ruling power over them, and wherein they deal proudly delights to show himself above them—that does what he will, and they cannot resist him. 2. His people will have the blessing of it. When God lifts up himself to scatter the nations that are in confederacy against Jerusalem (*v.* 3) then, as a preparative for that, or as the fruit and product of it, *he has filled Zion with judgment and righteousness,* not only with a sense of justice, but with a zeal for it and a universal care that it be duly administered. It shall again be called, *The city of righteousness, ch.* i. 26. In this the grace of God is exalted, as much as his providence was in the destruction of the Assyrian army. We may conclude God has mercy in store for a people when he fills them with judgment and righteousness, when all sorts of people, and all their actions and affairs, are governed by them, and they are so full of them that no other considerations can crowd in to sway them against these. Hezekiah and his people are encouraged (*v.* 6) with an assurance that God would stand by them in their distress. Here is, (1.) A gracious promise of God for them to stay themselves upon: *Wisdom and knowledge shall be the stability of thy times, and strength of salvation.* Here is a desirable end proposed, and that is *the stability of our times,* that things

184

be not disturbed and unhinged at home, and the *strength of salvation,* deliverance from, and success against, enemies abroad. The salvation that God ordains for his people has strength in it; it is a horn of salvation. And here are the way and means for obtaining this end—*wisdom and knowledge,* not only piety, but prudence. That is it which, by the blessing of God, will be the *stability of our times and the strength of salvation,* that wisdom which is first pure, then peaceable, and which sacrifices private interests to a public good; such prudence as this will establish truth and peace, and fortify the bulwarks in defence of them. (2.) A pious maxim of state for Hezekiah and his people to govern themselves by: *The fear of the Lord is his treasure.* It is God's treasure in the world, from which he receives his tribute; or, rather, it is the prince's treasure. A good prince accounts it so (that wisdom is better than gold) and he shall find it so. Note, True religion is the true treasure of any prince or people; it denominates them rich. Those places that have plenty of Bibles, and ministers, and serious good people, are really rich; and it contributes to that which makes a nation rich in this world. It is therefore the interest of a people to support religion among them and to take heed of every thing that threatens to hinder it.

V. The great distress that Jerusalem was brought into described, that those who believed the prophet might know beforehand what troubles were coming and might provide accordingly, and that when the foregoing promise of their deliverance should have its accomplishment the remembrance of the extremity of their case might help to magnify God in it and make them the more thankful, *v.* 7—9. It is here foretold, 1. That the enemy would be very insolent and abusive and there would be no dealing with him, either by treaties of peace (*for he has broken the covenant* without any hesitation, as if it were below him to be a servant to his word), or by the preparations of war, for *he has despised the cities;* he scorns to take notice either of their appeals to justice or of their petitions for mercy. He makes himself master of them so easily (though they are called *fenced cities*), and meets with so little resistance, that he despises them, and has no relentings when he puts all to the sword; for he regards no man, has no pity or concern, no, not for those that he is under particular obligations to. He neither fears God nor regards man, but is haughty and imperious to every one. There are those that take a pride in trampling upon all mankind, and have neither veneration for the honourable nor compassion for the miserable. 2. That therefore he would not be brought to any terms of reconciliation: *The valiant ones of Jerusalem,* being unable to make their parts good with him, must be contentedly run down with noise and insolence, which will make them cry without, because they cannot serve their country as they might have done against a fair adversary. *The ambassadors* sent by Hezekiah to treat *of peace*, finding him so haughty and unmanageable, *shall weep bitterly* for vexation at the disappointment they had met with in their negociations; they shall weep like children, as despairing to find out any expedient to pacify him. 3. That the country should be made quite desolate for a time by his army. (1.) No man durst travel the roads; so that a stop was put to trade and commerce, and (which was worse) no man could safely go up to Jerusalem, to keep the solemn feasts: *The highways lie waste.* While the fields lie waste, trodden like the highways, the highways lie waste, untrodden like the fields, for *the traveller ceases.* (2.) No man had any profit from the grounds, *v.* 9. The earth used to rejoice in its own productions for the service of God's Israel, but now the enemies of Israel eat them up, or tread them down: it *mourns and languishes;* the country looks melancholy and the country people have misery in their countenances, wanting necessary food for themselves and their families; the wonted joy of harvest is turned into lamentation, so withering and uncertain are all worldly joys. The desolation is universal. That part of the country which belonged to the ten tribes was already laid waste: "*Lebanon* famed for cedars, *Sharon* for roses, *Bashan* for cattle, *Carmel* for corn, all very fruitful, have now become like wildernesses, *are ashamed* to be called by their old names, they are so unlike what they were. They *shake off their fruits* before their time into the hand of the spoiler, which used to be gathered seasonably by the hand of the owner."

VI. God appearing, at length, in his glory against this proud invader, *v.* 10—12. When things are brought thus to the last extremity, 1. God will magnify himself. He had seemed to sit by as an unconcerned spectator: "But *now will I arise, saith the Lord;* now will I appear and act, and therein I will be not only evidenced, but exalted." He will not only demonstrate that there is a God that judges in the earth, but that he is God over all, and higher than the highest. "Now *will I lift up myself,* will prepare for action, will act vigorously, and will be glorified in it." God's time to appear for his people is when their affairs are reduced to the lowest ebb, *when their strength is gone and there is none shut up nor left,* Deut. xxxii. 36. When all other helpers fail, then is God's time to help. 2. He will bring down the Assyrian: "You, O Assyrians! are big with hopes that you shall have all the wealth of Jerusalem for your own, and are in pain till it be so; but all your hopes shall come to nothing: *You*

shall conceive chaff, and bring forth stubble, which is not only worthless and good for nothing, but combustible and proper fuel for the fire, which it cannot escape, when *your* own *breath as fire shall devour you,* that is, the breath of God's wrath, provoked against you by the breath of your sins— your malignant breath, the threatenings and slaughter you breathe out against the people of God, this shall devour you, and your blasphemous breath against God and his name." God would make their own tongues to fall upon them, and their own breath to blow the fire that should consume them; and then no wonder that the people are *as the burnings of lime* in a lime-kiln, all on fire together, and *as thorns cut up,* which are dried and withered, and therefore easily take fire and are soon burnt up. Such was the destruction of the Assyrian army; it was like the burning up of thorns, which can well be spared, or the burning of lime, which makes it good for something. The burning of that army enlightened the world with the knowledge of God's power and made his name shine brightly.

13 Hear, ye *that are* far off, what I have done; and, ye *that are* near, acknowledge my might. 14 The sinners in Zion are afraid; fearfulness hath surprised the hypocrites. Who among us shall dwell with the devouring fire? Who among us shall dwell with everlasting burnings? 15 He that walketh righteously, and speaketh uprightly; he that despiseth the gain of oppressions, that shaketh his hands from holding of bribes, that stoppeth his ears from hearing of blood, and shutteth his eyes from seeing evil; 16 He shall dwell on high: his place of defence *shall be* the munitions of rocks: bread shall be given him; his waters *shall be* sure. 17 Thine eyes shall see the king in his beauty: they shall behold the land that is very far off. 18 Thine heart shall meditate terror. Where *is* the scribe? Where *is* the receiver? Where *is* he that counted the towers? 19 Thou shalt not see a fierce people, a people of deeper speech than thou canst perceive; of a stammering tongue, *that thou canst* not understand. 20 Look upon Zion, the city of our solemnities: thine eyes shall see Jerusalem a quiet habitation, a tabernacle *that* shall not be taken down; not one of the stakes

185

thereof shall ever be removed, neither shall any of the cords thereof be broken. 21 But there the glorious LORD *will be* unto us a place of broad rivers *and* streams; wherein shall go no galley with oars, neither shall gallant ship pass thereby. 22 For the LORD *is* our judge, the LORD *is* our lawgiver, the LORD *is* our king; he will save us. 23 Thy tacklings are loosed; they could not well strengthen their mast, they could not spread the sail: then is the prey of a great spoil divided; the lame take the prey. 24 And the inhabitant shall not say, I am sick: the people that dwell therein *shall be* forgiven *their* iniquity.

Here is a preface that commands attention; and it is fit that all should attend, both near and afar off, to what God says and does (*v.* 13): *Hear, you that are afar off,* whether in place or time. Let distant regions and future ages hear what God has done. They do so; they will do so from the scripture, with as much assurance as those that were near, the neighbouring nations and those that lived at that time. But whoever hears what God has done, whether near or afar off, let them acknowledge his might, that it is irresistible, and that he can do every thing. Those are very stupid who hear what God has done and yet will not acknowledge his might. Now what is it that God has done which we must take notice of, and in which we must acknowledge his might?

I. He has struck a terror upon the sinners in Zion (*v.* 14): *Fearfulness has surprised the hypocrites.* There are sinners in Zion, hypocrites, that enjoy Zion's privileges and concur in Zion's services, but their hearts are not right in the sight of God; they keep up secret haunts of sin under the cloak of a visible profession, which convicts them of hypocrisy. Sinners in Zion will have a great deal to answer for above other sinners; and their place in Zion will be so far from being their security that it will aggravate both their sin and their punishment. Now those sinners in Zion, though always subject to secret frights and terrors, were struck with a more than ordinary consternation from the convictions of their own consciences. 1. When they saw the Assyrian army besieging Jerusalem, and ready to set fire to it and lay it in ashes, and burn the wasps in the nest. Finding they could not make their escape to Egypt, as some had done, and distrusting the promises God had made by his prophets that he would deliver them, they were at their wits' end, and ran about like men distracted, crying, " *Who among us shall dwell with devouring fire?* Let us therefore abandon

the city, and shift for ourselves elsewhere; one had as good live in everlasting burnings as live here." *Who will stand up for us against this devouring fire?* so some read it. See here how the sinners in Zion are affected when the judgments of God are abroad; while they were only threatened they slighted them and made nothing of them; but, when they come to be executed, they run into the other extreme, then they magnify them, and make the worst of them; they call them *devouring fire* and *everlasting burnings,* and despair of relief and succour. Those that rebel against the commands of the word cannot take the comforts of it in a time of need. Or, rather, 2. When they saw the Assyrian army destroyed; for the destruction of that is the fire spoken of immediately before, *v.* 11, 12. When the sinners in Zion saw what dreadful execution the wrath of God made they were in a great fright, being conscious to themselves that they had provoked this God by their secretly worshipping other gods; and therefore they cry out, *Who among us shall dwell with this devouring fire,* before which so vast an army is as thorns? *Who among us shall dwell with* these *everlasting burnings,* which have made the Assyrians *as the burnings of lime? v.* 12. Thus they said, or should have said. Note, God's judgments upon the enemies of Zion should strike a terror upon the sinners in Zion, nay, David himself trembles at them, Ps. cxix. 120. God himself is this devouring fire, Heb. xii. 29. Who is able to stand before him? 1 Sam. vi. 20. His wrath will burn those everlastingly that have made themselves fuel for it. It is a fire that shall never be quenched, nor will ever go out of itself; for it is the wrath of an everlasting God preying upon the conscience of an immortal soul. Nor can the most daring sinners bear up against it, so as to bear either the execution of it or the fearful expectation of it. Let this awaken us all to flee from the wrath to come, by fleeing to Christ as our refuge.

II. He has graciously provided for the security of his people that trust in him: *Hear this, and acknowledge his* power in making those that *walk righteously,* and *speak uprightly,* to *dwell on high, v.* 15, 16. We have here,

1. The good man's character, which he preserves even in times of common iniquity, in divers instances. (1.) He walks righteously. In the whole course of his conversation he acts by rules of equity, and makes conscience of rendering to all their due, to God his due, as well as to men theirs. His walk is righteousness itself; he would not for a world wilfully do an unjust thing. (2.) He speaks uprightly, *uprightnesses* (so the word is); he speaks what is true and right, and with an honest intention. He cannot think one thing and speak another, nor look one way and row another His word is to

him as sacred as his oath, and is not yea and nay. (3.) He is so far from coveting ill-gotten gain that he despises it. He thinks it a mean and sordid thing, and unbecoming a man of honour, to enrich himself by any hardship put upon his neighbour. He scorns to do a wrong thing, nay, to do a severe thing, though he might get by it. He does not over-value gain itself, and therefore easily abhors the gain that is not honestly come by. (4.) If he have a bribe at any time thrust into his hand, to pervert justice, *he shakes his hands from holding* it, with the utmost detestation, taking it as an affront to have it offered him. (5.) *He stops his ears from hearing* any thing that tends to cruelty or bloodshed, or any suggestions stirring him up to revenge, Job xxxi. 31. He turns a deaf ear to those that delight in war and entice him to *cast in his lot among them,* Prov. i. 14, 16. (6.) He *shuts his eyes from seeing evil.* He has such an abhorrence of sin that he cannot bear to see others commit it, and does himself watch against all the occasions of it. Those that would preserve the purity of their souls must keep a strict guard upon the senses of their bodies, must stop their ears to temptations, and turn away their eyes from beholding vanity.

2. The good man's comfort, which he may preserve even in times of common calamity, v. 16. (1.) He shall be safe; he shall escape the devouring fire and the everlasting burnings; he shall have access to, and communion with, that God who is a devouring fire, but shall be to him a rejoicing light. And, as to present troubles, *he shall dwell on high,* out of the reach of them, nay, out of the hearing of the noise of them; he shall not be really harmed by them, nay, he shall not be greatly frightened at them: *The floods of great waters shall not come nigh him;* or, if they should attack him, *his place of defence shall be the munitions of rocks,* strong and impregnable, fortified by nature as well as art. The divine power will keep him safe, and his faith in that power will keep him easy. God, the rock of ages, will be his high tower. (2.) He shall be supplied; he shall want nothing that is necessary for him: *Bread shall be given him,* even when the siege is straitest and provisions are cut off; and *his waters shall be sure,* that is, he shall be sure of the continuance of them, so that he shall not drink his water by measure and with astonishment. Those that fear the Lord shall not want any thing that is good for them.

III. He will protect Jerusalem, and deliver it out of the hands of the invaders. This storm that threatened them should blow over, and they should enjoy a prosperous state again. Many instances are here given of this prosperity.

1. Hezekiah shall put off his sackcloth and all the sadness of his countenance, and shall appear publicly in his beauty, in his royal robes and with a pleasing aspect (v. 17), to the great joy of all his loving subjects. Those that walk uprightly shall not only have bread given them, and their water sure, but they shall with an eye of faith see the King of kings in his beauty, the beauty of holiness, and that beauty shall be upon them.

2. The siege being raised, by which they were kept close within the walls of Jerusalem, they shall now be at liberty to go abroad upon business or pleasure without danger of falling into the enemies' hand: *They shall behold the land that is very far off;* they shall visit the utmost corners of the nation, and take a prospect of the adjacent countries, which will be the more pleasant after so long a confinement. Thus believers behold the heavenly Canaan, that land that is very far off, and comfort themselves with the prospect of it in evil times.

3. The remembrance of the fright they were in shall add to the pleasure of their deliverance (v. 18): *Thy heart shall meditate terror,* meditate it with pleasure when it is over. Thou shalt think thou still hearest the alarm in thy ears, when all the cry was, "Arm, arm, arm! every man to his post. *Where is the scribe* or secretary of war? Let him appear to draw up the muster-roll. *Where is the receiver* and pay-master of the army? Let him see what he has in bank, to defray the charge of a defence. *Where is he that counted the towers?* Let him bring in the account of them, that care may be taken to put a competent number of men in each." Or these words may be taken as Jerusalem's triumph over the vanquished army of the Assyrians, and the rather because the apostle alludes to them in his triumphs over the learning of this world, when it was baffled by the gospel of Christ, 1 Cor. i. 20. The virgin, the daughter of Zion, despises all their military preparations. Where is the scribe or muster-master of the Assyrian army? Where is their weigher (or treasurer), and where are their engineers that counted the towers? They are all either dead or fled. There is an end of them.

4. They shall no more be terrified with the sight of the Assyrians, who were a fierce people naturally, and were particularly fierce against the people of the Jews, and were of a strange language, that could understand neither their petitions nor their complaints, and therefore had a pretence for being deaf to them, nor could themselves be understood: "They are *of a deeper speech than thou canst perceive,* which will make them the more formidable, v. 19. Thy eyes shall no more see them thus fierce, but their countenances changed when they shall all become dead corpses."

5. They shall no more be under apprehensions of the danger of Jerusalem—Zion, and the temple there (v. 20): "*Look upon Zion, the city of our solemnities,* the city where our solemn sacred feasts are kept, where we

used to meet to worship God in religious assemblies." The good people among them, in the time of their distress, were most in pain for Zion upon this account, that it was the city of their solemnities, that the conquerors would burn their temple and they should not have that to keep their solemn feasts in any more. In times of public danger our concern should be most about our religion, and the cities of our solemnities should be dearer to us than either our strong cities or our store-cities. It is with an eye to this that God will work deliverance for Jerusalem, because it is the city of religious solemnities: let those be conscientiously kept up, as the glory of a people, and we may depend upon God to create a defence upon that glory. Two things are here promised to Jerusalem:—(1.) A well-grounded security. It shall be *a quiet habitation* for the people of God; they shall not be molested and disturbed, as they have been, by the alarms of the sword either of war or persecution, *ch.* xxix. 20. It shall be a quiet habitation, as it is the city of our solemnities. It is desirable to be quiet in our own houses, but much more so to be quiet in God's house and have none to make us afraid there. Thus it shall be with Jerusalem; and *thy eyes shall see it*, which will be a great satisfaction to a good man, Ps. cxxviii. 5, 6. *"Thou shalt see the good of Jerusalem, and peace upon Israel;* thou shalt live to see it and share in it." (2.) An unmoved stability. Jerusalem, the city of our solemnities, is indeed but *a tabernacle*, in comparison with the New Jerusalem. The present manifestations of the divine glory and grace are nothing in comparison with those that are reserved for the future state. But it is such a tabernacle as *shall not be taken down.* After this trouble is over Jerusalem shall long enjoy a confirmed peace; and her sacred privileges, which are the stakes and cords of her tabernacle, shall not be removed from her, nor any disturbance given to the course and circle of her religious services. God's church on earth is a tabernacle, which, though it may be shifted from one place to another, shall not be taken down while the world stands; for in every age Christ will have a seed to serve him. The promises of the covenant are its stakes, which shall never be removed, and the ordinances and institutions of the gospel are its cords, which shall never be broken. They are things which cannot be shaken, though heaven and earth be, but shall remain.

6. God himself will be their protector and Saviour, *v.* 21, 22. This is the principal ground of their confidence: "He that is himself *the glorious Lord* will display his glory for us and be a glory to us, such as shall eclipse the rival-glory of the enemy. God, in being a gracious Lord, is a glorious Lord; for his goodness is his glory. God will be the Saviour of Jerusalem and her glorious

Lord, (1.) As a guard against their adversaries abroad. He will be *a place of broad rivers and streams.* Jerusalem had no considerable river running by it, as most great cities have, nothing but the brook Kidron, and so wanted one of the best natural fortifications, as well as one of the greatest advantages for trade and commerce, and upon this account their enemies despised them and doubted not but to make an easy prey of them; but the presence and power of God are sufficient at any time to make up to us the deficiencies of the creature and of its strength and beauty. We have all in God, all we need or can desire. Many external advantages Jerusalem has not which other places have, but in God there is more than an equivalent. But, if there be broad rivers and streams about Jerusalem, may not these yield an easy access to the fleet of an invader? No; these are rivers and streams *in which shall go no galley with oars*, no man of war or gallant ship. If God himself be the river, it must needs be inaccessible to the enemy; they can neither find nor force their way by it. (2.) As a guide to their affairs at home: *" For the Lord is our Judge,* to whom we are accountable, to whose judgment we refer ourselves, by whose judgment we abide, and who therefore (we hope) will judge for us. *He is our lawgiver;* his word is a law to us, and to him every thought within us is brought into obedience. *He is our King,* to whom we pay homage and tribute, and an inviolable allegiance, and therefore *he will save us."* For, as protection draws allegiance, so allegiance may expect protection, and shall have it with God. By faith we take Christ for our prince and Saviour, and as such depend upon him and devote ourselves to him. Observe with what an air of triumph, and with what an emphasis laid upon the glorious name of God, they comfort themselves with this: *Jehovah is our Judge, Jehovah is our Lawgiver, Jehovah is our King, who, being self-existent, is self-sufficient, and all-sufficient to us.*

7. The enemies shall be quite infatuated, and all their powers and projects broken, like a ship at sea in stress of weather, that cannot ride out the storm, but having her tackle torn, her masts split, and nothing wherewith to repair them, is given up for a wreck, *v.* 23. *The tacklings* of the Assyrian *are loosed;* they are like a ship whose tacklings are loosed, or forsaken by the ship's crew, when they give it over for lost, finding that they cannot strengthen the mast, but it will come down. They thought themselves sure of Jerusalem; but when they were just entering the port as it were, and thought all was their own, they were quite becalmed, and *could not spread their sail*, but lay wind-bound till God poured the fury of his wrath upon them. The enemies of God's church are often disarmed and unrigged when they think they have almost gained their point.

8. The wealth of their camp shall be a rich booty for the Jews : *Then is the prey of a great spoil divided.* When the greater part were slain the rest fled in confusion, and with such precipitation that (like the Syrians) they *left their tents as they were,* so that all the treasure in them fell into the hands of the besieged ; and even *the lame take the prey.* Those that tarried at home did divide the spoil. It was so easy to come at that not only the strong man might make himself master of it, but even the lame man, whose hands were lame, that he could not fight, and his feet, that he could not pursue. As the victory shall cost them no peril, so the prey shall cost them no toil. And there was such abundance of it that when those who were forward, and came first, had carried off as much as they would, even the lame, who came late, found sufficient. Thus God brought good out of evil, and not only delivered Jerusalem, but enriched it, and abundantly recompensed the losses they had sustained. Thus comfortably and well do the frights and distresses of the people of God often end.

9. Both sickness and sin shall be taken away; and then sickness is taken away in mercy when this is all the fruit of it, and the recovery from it, even the taking away of sin. (1.) *The inhabitant shall not say, I am sick. As the lame shall take the prey,* so shall the sick, notwithstanding their weakness, make a shift to get to the abandoned camp and seize something for themselves; or there shall be such a universal transport of joy upon this occasion that even the sick shall, for the present, forget their sickness and the sorrows of it, and join with the public in its rejoicings; the deliverance of their city shall be their cure. Or it intimates that, whereas infectious diseases are commonly the effect of long sieges, it shall not be so with Jerusalem, but the inhabitants of it with their victory and peace shall have health also, and there shall be no complaining upon the account of sickness within their gates. Or those that are sick shall bear their sickness without complaining as long as they see it goes well with Jerusalem. Our sense of private grievances should be drowned in our thanksgivings for public mercies. (2.) *The people that dwell therein shall be forgiven their iniquity,* not only the body of the nation forgiven their national guilt in the removing of the national judgment, but particular persons, that dwell therein, shall repent, and reform, and have their sins pardoned. And this is promised as that which is at the bottom of all other favours; he will do so and so for them, *for he will be merciful to their unrighteousness,* Heb. viii. 12. Sin is the sickness of the soul. When God pardons the sin he heals the disease; and, when the diseases of sin are healed by pardoning mercy, the sting of bodily sickness is taken out and the cause of it removed;

so that either the inhabitant shall not be sick or at least shall not say, *I am sick.* If iniquity be taken away, we have little reason to complain of outward affliction. *Son, be of good cheer ; thy sins are forgiven thee.*

CHAP. XXXIV.

In this chapter we have the fatal doom of all the nations that are enemies to God's church and people, though Edom only is mentioned, because of the old enmity of Esau to Jacob, which was typical, as much as that more ancient enmity of Cain to Abel, and flowed from the original enmity of the serpent to the seed of the woman. It is probable that this prophecy had its accomplishment in the great desolations made by the Assyrian army first, or rather by Nebuchadnezzar's army some time after, among those nations that were neighbours to Israel and had been in some way or other injurious to them. That mighty conqueror took a pride in shedding blood, and laying countries waste, and therein, quite beyond his design, he was fulfilling what God here threatened against his and his people's enemies. But we have reason to think it is intended as a denunciation of the wrath of God against all those who fight against the interests of his kingdom among men, that it has its frequent accomplishment in the havoc made by the wars of the nations and other desolating judgments, and will have its full accomplishment in the final dissolution of all things at the day of judgment and perdition of ungodly men.   Here is, I. A demand of universal attention, ver. 1. II. A direful scene of blood and confusion presented, ver. 2—7. III. The reason given for these judgments, ver. 8. IV. The continuance of this desolation, the country being made like the lake of Sodom (ver. 9, 10), and the cities abandoned to wild beasts and melancholy fowls, ver. 11. —15. V. The solemn ratification of all this, ver. 16, 17. Let us hear, and fear.

COME near, ye nations, to hear; and hearken, ye people : let the earth hear, and all that is therein; the world, and all things that come forth of it. 2 For the indignation of the LORD *is* upon all nations, and *his* fury upon all their armies : he hath utterly destroyed them, he hath delivered them to the slaughter. 3 Their slain also shall be cast out, and their stink shall come up out of their carcases, and the mountains shall be melted with their blood. 4 And all the host of heaven shall be dissolved, and the heavens shall be rolled together as a scroll : and all their host shall fall down, as the leaf falleth off from the vine, and as a falling *fig* from the fig-tree. 5 For my sword shall be bathed in heaven : behold, it shall come down upon Idumea, and upon the people of my curse, to judgment. 6 The sword of the LORD is filled with blood, it is made fat with fatness, *and* with the blood of lambs and goats, with the fat of the kidneys of rams : for the LORD hath a sacrifice in Bozrah, and a great slaughter in the land of Idumea. 7 And the unicorns shall come down with them, and the bullocks with the bulls ; and their land shall be soaked with blood, and their dust made fat with fatness. 8 For *it is* the day of the LORD's vengeance, *and* the year of recompences for the controversy of Zion.

Here we have a prophecy, as elsewhere we have a history, of the wars of the Lord, which we are sure are all both righteous and successful. This world, as it is his creature, he does good to; but as it is in the interest of Satan, who is called *the god of this world*, he fights against it.

I. Here is the trumpet sounded and the war proclaimed, *v.* 1. All nations must hear and hearken, not only because what God is about to do is well worthy their remark (as *ch.* xxxiii. 13), but because they are all concerned in it; it is with them that God has a quarrel; it is against them that God is coming forth in wrath. Let them all take notice that the great God is angry with them; his indignation is upon all nations, and therefore let all nations come near to hear. *The trumpet is blown in the city* (Amos iii. 6), *and the watchmen on the walls cry, Hearken to the sound of the trumpet*, Jer. vi. 17. *Let the earth hear, and the fulness thereof, for it is the Lord's* (Ps. xxiv. 1) and ought to hearken to its Maker and Master. The world must hear, and *all things that come forth of it*, the children of men, that are of the earth earthy, come out of it, and must return to it; or the inanimate products of the earth are called to, as more likely to hearken than sinners, whose hearts are hardened against the calls of God. *Hear, O you mountains! the Lord's controversy*, Micah vi. 2. It is so just a controversy that all the world may be safely appealed to concerning the equity of it.

II. Here is the manifesto published, setting forth,

1. Whom he makes war against (*v.* 2): *The indignation of the Lord is upon all nations;* they are all in confederacy against God and religion, all in the interests of the devil, and therefore he is angry with them all, even with all the nations that forget him. He has long *suffered all nations to walk in their own ways* (Acts xiv. 16), but now he will no longer keep silence. As they have all had the benefit of his patience, so they must all expect now to feel his resentments. *His fury is* in a special manner *upon all their armies*, (1.) Because with them they have done mischief to the people of God; those are they that have made bloody work with them, and therefore they must be sure to have blood given them to drink. (2.) Because with them they hope to make their part good against the justice and power of God; they trust to them as their defence, and therefore on them, in the first place, God's fury will come. Armies before God's fury are but as dry stubble before a consuming fire, though ever so numerous and courageous.

2. Whom he makes war for, and what are the grounds and reasons of the war
190

(*v.* 8): *It is the day of the Lord's vengeance,* and he it is *to whom vengeance belongs,* and who is never *unrighteous in taking vengeance,* Rom. iii. 5. As there is a day of the Lord's patience, so there will be a day of his vengeance; for, though he bear long, he will not bear always. It is *the year of recompences for the controversy of Zion.* Zion is the holy city, the city of our solemnities, a type and figure of the church of God in the world. Zion has a just quarrel with her neighbours for the wrongs they have done her, for all their treacherous and barbarous usage of her, profaning her holy things, laying waste her palaces, and slaying her sons. She has left it to God to plead her cause, and he will do so when the time, even the set time, to favour Zion shall have come; then he will recompense to her persecutors and oppressors all the mischiefs they have done her. The controversy will be decided, that Zion has been wronged, and therein Zion's God has been himself abused. Judgment will be given upon this decision, and execution done. Note, There is a time prefixed in the divine counsels for the deliverance of the church and the destruction of her enemies, a year of the redeemed, which will come, *a year of recompences for the controversy of Zion;* and we must patiently wait till then, and *judge nothing before the time.*

III. Here are the operations of the war, and the methods of it, settled, with an infallible assurance of success. 1. The sword of the Lord is *bathed in heaven;* this is all the preparation here made for the war, *v.* 5. It may probably allude to some custom they had then of bathing their swords in some liquor or other, to harden them or brighten them; it is the same with the furbishing of it, that it may glitter, Ezek. xxi. 9—11. God's sword is bathed in heaven, in his counsel and decree, in his justice and power, and then there is no standing before it. 2. *It shall come down.* What he has determined shall without fail be put in execution. It shall come down from heaven, and the higher the place is, whence it comes, the heavier will it fall. It will come down *upon Idumea, the people of God's curse,* the people that lie under his curse and are by it doomed to destruction. Miserable, for ever miserable, are those that have by their sins made themselves the people of God's curse; for the sword of the Lord will infallibly attend the curse of the Lord and execute the sentences of it; and those whom he curses are cursed indeed. It shall come down *to judgment,* to execute judgment upon sinners. Note, God's sword of war is always a sword of justice. It is observed of him out of whose mouth goeth the sharp sword that *in righteousness he doth judge and make war,* Rev. xix. 11, 15. 3. The nations and their armies shall be given up to the sword (*v.* 2): *God has delivered them to the slaughter,* and then they cannot deliver themselves, nor can all the friends they have deliver them from it. Those only are slain whom God delivers to the slaughter, for the keys of death are in his hand; and, in delivering them to the slaughter, he has *utterly destroyed* them; their destruction is as sure, when God has doomed them to it, as if they were destroyed already, utterly destroyed. God has, in effect, delivered all the cruel enemies of his church to the slaughter by that word (Rev. xiii. 10), *He that kills with the sword must be killed by the sword,* for the Lord is righteous. 4. Pursuant to the sentence, a terrible slaughter shall be made among them (*v.* 6): *The sword of the Lord,* when it comes down with commission, does vast execution; it *is filled,* satiated, surfeited, *with blood,* the blood of the slain, and *made fat with their fatness.* When the day of God's abused mercy and patience is over the sword of his justice gives no quarter, spares none. Men have by sin lost the honour of the human nature and made themselves like the beasts that perish; they are therefore justly denied the compassion and respect that are owing to the human nature and killed as beasts, and no more is made of slaying an army of men than of butchering a flock of lambs or goats and feeding on the fat of the kidneys of rams. Nay, the sword of the Lord shall not only dispatch the lambs and goats, the infantry of their armies, the poor common soldiers, but (*v.* 7) *the unicorns* too *shall* be made to *come down with them, and the bullocks with the bulls,* though they are ever so proud, and strong, and fierce (*the great men, and the mighty men, and the chief captains* Rev. vi. 15), the sword of the Lord will make as easy a prey of as of the lambs and the goats. The greatest of men are nothing before the wrath of the great God. See what bloody work will be made: *The land shall be soaked with blood,* as with the rain that comes often upon it and in great abundance; *and their dust,* their dry and barren land, shall be *made fat with the fatness of* men slain in their full strength, as with manure. Nay even *the mountains,* which are hard and rocky, *shall be melted with their blood, v.* 3. These expressions are hyperbolical (as St. John's vision of *blood to the horse-bridles,* Rev. xiv. 20), and are made use of because they sound very dreadful to sense (it makes us even shiver to think of such abundance of human gore), and are therefore proper to express the terror of God's wrath, which is dreadful beyond conception and expression. See what work sin and wrath make even in this world, and think how much more terrible the wrath to come is, which will bring down the unicorns themselves to the bars of the pit. 5. This great slaughter will be a great sacrifice to the justice of God (*v.* 6): *The Lord has a sacrifice in Bozrah;* there it is that the great Redeemer has his *garments dyed with*

blood, ch. lxiii. 1. Sacrifices were intended for the honour of God, to make it appear that he hates sin and demands satisfaction for it, and that nothing but blood will make atonement; and for these ends the slaughter is made, that in it *the wrath of God may be revealed from heaven against all the ungodliness and unrighteousness of men,* especially their ungodly unrighteous enmity to his people, which was the sin that the Edomites were notoriously guilty of. In great sacrifices abundance of beasts were killed, hecatombs offered, and their blood poured out before the altar; and so will it be in this day of the Lord's vengeance. And thus would the whole earth have been soaked with the blood of sinners if Jesus Christ, the great propitiation, had not shed his blood for us; but those who reject him, and will not make a covenant with God by that sacrifice, will themselves fall as victims to divine wrath. Damned sinners are everlasting sacrifices, Mark ix. 48, 49. Those that sacrifice not (which is the character of the ungodly, Eccl. ix. 2) must be sacrificed. 6. These slain shall be detestable to mankind, and shall be as much their loathing as ever they were their terror (*v.* 3): *They shall be cast out,* and none shall pay them the respect of a decent burial; but *their stink shall come up out of their carcases,* that all people by the odious smell, as well as by the ghastly sight, may be made to conceive an indignation against sin and a dread of the wrath of God. They lie unburied, that they may remain monuments of divine justice. 7. The effect and consequence of this slaughter shall be universal confusion and desolation, as if the whole frame of nature were dissolved and melted down (*v.* 4): *All the host of heaven shall pine and waste away* (so the word is); the sun shall be darkened, and the moon look black, or be turned into blood; *the heavens* themselves *shall be rolled together as a scroll* of parchment when we have done with it, and lay it by, or as when it is shrivelled up by the heat of the fire. The stars shall fall as the leaves in autumn; all the beauty, joy, and comfort, of the vanquished nation shall be lost and done away, magistracy and government shall be abolished, and all dominion and rule, but that of the sword of war, shall fall. Conquerors, in those times, affected to lay waste the countries they conquered; and such a complete desolation is here described by such figurative expressions as will yet have a literal and full accomplishment in the dissolution of all things at the end of time, of which last day of judgment the judgments which God does now sometimes remarkably execute on sinful nations are figures, earnests, and forerunners; and by these we should be awakened to think of that, for which reason these expressions are used here and Rev. vi. 12, 13. But they are used without a metaphor, 2 Pet. iii. 10, where we are told that *the heavens shall pass away with a great noise and the earth shall be burnt up.*

9 And the streams thereof shall be turned into pitch, and the dust thereof into brimstone, and the land thereof shall become burning pitch. 10 It shall not be quenched night nor day; the smoke thereof shall go up for ever: from generation to generation it shall lie waste; none shall pass through it for ever and ever. 11 But the cormorant and the bittern shall possess it; the owl also and the raven shall dwell in it: and he shall stretch out upon it the line of confusion, and the stones of emptiness. 12 They shall call the nobles thereof to the kingdom, but none *shall be* there, and all her princes shall be nothing. 13 And thorns shall come up in her palaces, nettles and brambles in the fortresses thereof: and it shall be a habitation of dragons, *and* a court for owls. 14 The wild beasts of the desert shall also meet with the wild beasts of the island, and the satyr shall cry to his fellow; the screech-owl also shall rest there, and find for herself a place of rest. 15 There shall the great owl make her nest, and lay, and hatch, and gather under her shadow: there shall the vultures also be gathered, every one with her mate. 16 Seek ye out of the book of the LORD, and read: no one of these shall fail, none shall want her mate: for my mouth it hath commanded, and his spirit it hath gathered them. 17 And he hath cast the lot for them, and his hand hath divided it unto them by line: they shall possess it for ever, from generation to generation shall they dwell therein.

This prophecy looks very black, but surely it looks so further than upon Edom and Bozrah. 1. It describes the melancholy changes that are often made by the divine Providence, in countries, cities, palaces, and families. Places that have flourished and been much frequented strangely go to decay. We know not where to find the places where many great towns, celebrated in history, once stood. Fruitful countries, in process of time, are turned into barrenness, and pompous populous cities into ruinous heaps. Old decayed castles look frightful, and their ruins are almost as much dreaded as ever their garrisons were. 2. It describes the

destroying judgments which are the effects of God's wrath and the just punishment of those that are enemies to his people, which God will inflict when *the year of the redeemed has come,* and *the year of recompences for the controversy of Zion.* Those that aim to ruin the church can never do that, but will infallibly ruin themselves. 3. It describes the final desolation of this wicked world, which is *reserved unto fire at the day of judgment,* 2 Pet. iii. 7. The earth itself, when it, and all the works that are therein, shall be burnt up, will (for aught I know) be turned into a hell to all those that set their affections only on earthly things. However, this prophecy shows us what will be the lot of the *generation of God's curse.*

I. The country shall become like the lake of Sodom, *v.* 9, 10. *The streams thereof,* that both watered the land and pleased and refreshed the inhabitants, *shall* now *be turned into pitch,* shall be congealed, shall look black, and shall move slowly, or not at all. *Their floods to lazy streams of pitch shall turn;* so Sir R. Blackmore. *The dust thereof shall be turned into brimstone;* so combustible has sin made their land that it shall take fire at the first spark of God's wrath struck upon it; and, when it has taken fire, it shall become burning pitch; the fire shall be universal, not a house, or town, on fire, but a whole country; and it shall not be in the power of any to suppress or extinguish it. It shall burn continually, burn perpetually, and *shall not be quenched night nor day.* The torment of those in hell, or that have a hell within them in their own consciences, is without interruption; the *smoke of this fire goes up for ever.* As long as there are provoking sinners on earth, *from one generation to another,* an increase of sinful men, to *augment the fierce anger of the Lord* (Num. xxxii. 14), there will be a righteous God in heaven to punish them for it. And as long as a people keep up a succession of sinners God will have a succession of plagues for them; nor will any that fall under the wrath of God be ever able to recover themselves. It will be found, how light soever men make of it, that it is a *fearful thing to fall into the hands of the living God.* If the land be doomed to destruction, none shall pass through it, but travellers will choose rather to go a great way about than come within the smell of it.

II. The cities shall become like old decayed houses, which, being deserted by the owners, look very frightful, being commonly possessed by beasts of prey or birds of ill omen. See how dismally the palaces of the enemy look; the description is peculiarly elegant and fine. 1. God shall mark them for ruin and destruction. *He shall stretch out upon Bozrah the line of confusion with the stones* or plummets *of emptiness, v.* 11. This intimates the equity of the sentence passed upon it; it is given according to the rules of justice and the exact agreeableness of the execution with the sentence; the destruction is not wrought at random, but by line and level. The confusion and emptiness that shall overspread the face of the whole country shall be like that of the whole earth when it was *Tohu and Bohu* (the very words here used)—*without form and void.* Gen. i. 2. Sin will soon turn a paradise into a chaos, and sully the beauty of the whole creation. When there is confusion there will soon be emptiness; but both are appointed by the governor of the world, and in exact proportions. 2. Their great men shall be all cut off, and none of them shall dare to appear (*v.* 12): *They shall call the nobles of the kingdom* to take care of the arduous affairs which lie before them, but none shall be there to take this ruin under their hand, and all her princes, having the sad tidings brought them, shall be nothing, shall be at their wits' end, and not be able to stand them in stead, to shelter them from destruction.

III. Even the houses of state, and those of strength, shall become as wildernesses (*v.* 13); not only grass shall grow, but *thorns shall come up, in her palaces, nettles and brambles in the fortresses thereof,* and there shall be none to cut them up or tread them down. We sometimes see ruined buildings thus overgrown with rubbish. It intimates that the place shall not only be uninhabited and unfrequented where a full court used to be kept, but that it shall be under the curse of God; for thorns and thistles were the production of the curse, Gen. iii 18.

IV. They shall become the residence and rendezvous of fearful frightful beasts and birds, which usually frequent such melancholy places, because there they may be undisturbed, and, when they are frightened thither, they help to frighten men thence. This circumstance of the desolation, being apt to strike a horror upon the mind, is much enlarged upon here, *v.* 11. *The cormorant shall possess it,* or the pelican, which affects to be solitary (Ps. cii. 6); and *the bittern,* which makes a hideous noise, *the owl,* a melancholy bird, *the raven,* a bird of prey, invited by the dead carcases, shall dwell there (*with all the ill-boding monsters of the air,* Sir *R. B.*), all the unclean birds, which were not for the service of man, *v.* 13. *It shall be a habitation for dragons,* which are poisonous and hurtful.

And in their lofty rooms of state,
 Where cringing sycophants did wait,
Dragons shall hiss and hungry wolves shall howl:
 In courts before by mighty lords possess'd
 The serpent shall erect his speckled crest,
 Or fold his circling spires to rest.
Sir R. Blackmore.

That which was a court for princes shall now be a court for owls or ostriches, *v.* 14. *The wild beasts of the desert,* the dry and sandy country, shall meet, as it were by appointment, with the wild beasts of the island, the wet marshy country, and shall regale themselves with such a perfect desolation as they shall find there.

Leopards, and all the rav'ning brotherhoods
That range the plains, or lurk in woods,
Each other shall invite to come,
And make this wilder place their home.
Fierce beasts of every frightful shape and size
Shall settle here their bloody colonies.
Sir R. Blackmore.

The satyr shall cry to his fellow to go with him to this desert place, or, being there, they shall please themselves that they have found such an agreeable habitation. There shall *the screech-owl rest,* a night-bird and an ominous one. *The great owl shall there make her nest (v.* 15) *and lay and hatch;* the breed of them shall be kept up to provide heirs for this desolate place. *The vultures,* which feast on carcases, *shall be gathered there, every one with his mate.* Now observe, 1. How the places which men have deserted, and keep at a distance from, are proper receptacles for other animals, which the providence of God takes care of, and will not neglect. 2. Whom those resemble that are morose, unsociable, and unconversable, and affect a melancholy retirement; they are like these solitary creatures that take delight in desolations. 3. What a dismal change sin makes; it turns a fruitful land into barrenness, a frequented city into a wilderness.

V. Here is an assurance given of the full accomplishment of this prediction, even to the most minute circumstance of it (*v.* 16, 17): " *Seek you out of the book of the Lord and read.* When this destruction comes compare the event with the prediction, and you will find it to answer exactly." Note, The book of the prophets is the book of the Lord, and we ought to consult it and converse with it as of divine origin and authority. We must not only read it, but seek out of it, search into it, turn first to one text and then to another and compare them together. Abundance of useful knowledge might thus be extracted, by a diligent search, out of the scriptures, which cannot be got by a superficial reading of them. When you have read the prediction out of the book of the Lord then observe, 1. That according to what you have read so you see; *not one of these shall fail,* either beast or fowl: and, it being foretold that they shall possess it *from generation to generation,* in order to that, that the species may be propagated, *none shall want her mate;* these marks of desolation shall be fruitful, and multiply, and replenish the land. 2. That God's mouth having commanded this direful muster *his Spirit shall gather them,* as the creatures by instinct were gathered to Adam to be named and to Noah to be housed. What God's word has appointed his Spirit will effect and bring about, for no word of

God shall fall to the ground. The word of God's promise shall in like manner be accomplished by the operations of the Spirit. 3. That there is an exact order and proportion observed in the accomplishment of this threatening : *He has cast the lot* for these birds and beasts, so that each one shall know his place as readily as if it were marked by line. See the like, Joel ii. 7, 8, *They shall not break their ranks, neither shall one thrust another.* The soothsayers among the heathen foretold events by the flight of birds, as if the fate of men depended on them. But here we find that the flight of birds is under the direction of the God of Israel : *he has cast the lot for them.* 4. That the desolation shall be perpetual : *They shall possess it for ever.* God's Jerusalem may be laid in ruins; but Jerusalem of old recovered itself out of its ruins, till it gave place to the gospel Jerusalem, which may be brought low, but shall be rebuilt, and shall continue till it give place to the heavenly Jerusalem. But the enemies of the church shall be for ever desolate, shall be punished with an everlasting destruction.

CHAP. XXXV.

As after a prediction of God's judgments upon the world (ch. xxiv.) follows a promise of great mercy to be had in store for his church (chap. xxv.), so here after a black and dreadful scene of confusion in the foregoing chapter we have, in this, a bright and pleasant one, which, though it foretel the flourishing estate of Hezekiah's kingdom in the latter part of his reign, yet surely looks as far beyond that as the prophecy in the foregoing chapter does beyond the destruction of the Edomites ; both were typical, and it concerns us most to look at those things which they were typical of, the kingdom of Christ and the kingdom of heaven. When the world, which lies in wickedness, shall be laid in ruins, and the Jewish church, which persisted in infidelity, shall become a desolation, then the gospel church shall be set up and made to flourish. I. The Gentiles shall be brought into it, ver. 1, 2, 7. II. The wellwishers to it, who were weak and timorous, shall be encouraged, ver. 3, 4. III. Miracles shall be wrought both on the souls and on the bodies of men, ver. 5, 6. IV. The gospel church shall be conducted in the way of holiness, ver. 8, 9. V. It shall be brought at last to endless joys, ver. 10. Thus do we find more of Christ and heaven in this chapter than one would have expected in the Old Testament.

THE wilderness and the solitary place shall be glad for them; and the desert shall rejoice, and blossom as the rose. 2 It shall blossom abundantly, and rejoice even with joy and singing : the glory of Lebanon shall be given unto it, the excellency of Carmel and Sharon, they shall see the glory of the Lord, *and* the excellency of our God. 3 Strengthen ye the weak hands, and confirm the feeble knees. 4 Say to them *that are* of a fearful heart, Be strong, fear not : behold, your God will come *with* vengeance, *even* God *with* a recompence ; he will come and save you.

In these verses we have,

I. The desert land blooming. In the foregoing chapter we had a populous and fruitful country turned into a horrid wilderness ; here we have, in lieu of that, a wil-

194

derness turned into a good land. When the land of Judah was freed from the Assyrian army, those parts of the country that had been made as a wilderness by the ravages and outrages they committed began to recover themselves, and to look pleasantly again, and to blossom as the rose. When the Gentile nations, that had been long as a wilderness, bringing forth no fruit to God, received the gospel, joy came with it to them, Ps. lxvii. 3, 4 ; xcvi. 11, 12. When Christ was preached in Samaria there was *great joy in that city* (Acts viii. 8) ; those that sat in darkness saw a great and joyful light, and then they blossomed, that is, gave hopes of abundance of fruit ; for that was it which the preachers of the gospel aimed at (John xv. 16), to *go and bring forth fruit*, Rom. i. 13 ; Col. i. 6. Though blossoms are not fruit, and often miscarry and come to nothing, yet they are in order to fruit. Converting grace makes the soul that was *a wilderness to rejoice with joy and singing*, and to *blossom abundantly*. This flourishing desert shall have all *the glory of Lebanon* given to it, which consisted in the strength and stateliness of its cedars, together with *the excellency of Carmel and Sharon*, which consisted in corn and cattle. Whatever is valuable in any institution is brought into the gospel. All the beauty of the Jewish church was admitted into the Christian church, and appeared in its perfection, as the apostle shows at large in his epistle to the Hebrews. Whatever was excellent and desirable in the Mosaic economy is translated into the evangelical institutes.

II. The glory of God shining forth : *They shall see the glory of the Lord.* God will manifest himself more than ever in his grace and love to mankind (for that is his glory and excellency), and he shall give them eyes to see it, and hearts to be duly affected with it. This is that which will make the desert blossom. The more we see by faith of the glory of the Lord and the excellency of our God the more joyful and the more fruitful shall we be.

III. The feeble and faint-hearted encouraged, *v.* 3, 4. God's prophets and ministers are in a special manner charged, by virtue of their office, to *strengthen the weak hands*, to comfort those who could not yet recover the fright they had been put into by the Assyrian army with an assurance that God would now return in mercy to them. This is the design of the gospel, 1. To strengthen those that are weak and to confirm them—the weak hands, which are unable either to work or fight, and can hardly be lifted up in prayer, and the feeble knees, which are unable either to stand or walk and unfit for the race set before us. The gospel furnishes us with strengthening considerations, and shows us where strength is laid up for us. Among true Christians there are many that have weak hands and feeble knees, that are yet but babes in Christ; but it is our duty to strengthen our brethren (Luke xxii. 32), not only to bear with the weak, but to do what we can to confirm them, Rom. xv. 1; 1 Thess. v. 14. It is our duty also to strengthen ourselves, to lift up *the hands which hang down* (Heb. xii. 12), improving the strength God has given us, and exerting it. 2. To animate those that are timorous and discouraged: *Say to those that are of a fearful heart,* because of their own weakness and the strength of their enemies, that are *hasty* (so the word is), that are for betaking themselves to flight upon the first alarm, and giving up the cause, that say, in their haste, "We are cut off and undone" (Ps. xxxi. 22), there is enough in the gospel to silence these fears; it says to them, and let them say it to themselves and one to another, *Be strong, fear not* Fear is weakening; the more we strive against it the stronger we are both for doing and suffering; and, for our encouragement to strive, he that says to us, *Be strong* has laid help for us upon one that is mighty.

IV. Assurance given of the approach of a Saviour: "*Your God will come with vengeance.* God will appear for you against your enemies, will recompense both their injuries and your losses." The Messiah will come, in the fulness of time, to take vengeance on the powers of darkness, to spoil them, and make a show of them openly, to recompense those that mourn in Zion with abundant comforts. *He will come and save us.* With the hopes of this the Old-Testament saints strengthened their weak hands. He will come again at the end of time, will come in flaming fire, to recompense tribulation to those who have troubled his people, and, to those who were troubled, rest, such a rest as will be not only a final period to, but a full reward of, all their troubles, 2 Thess. i. 6, 7. Those whose *hearts tremble for the ark of God,* and who are under a concern for his church in the world, may silence their fears with this, God will take the work into his own hands. Your God will come, who pleads your cause and owns your interest, even God himself, who is God alone.

5 Then the eyes of the blind shall be opened, and the ears of the deaf shall be unstopped. 6. Then shall the lame *man* leap as a hart, and the tongue of the dumb sing : for in the wilderness shall waters break out, and streams in the desert. 7 And the parched ground shall become a pool, and the thirsty land springs of water : in the habitation of dragons, where each lay, *shall be* grass with reeds and rushes. 8 And a highway shall be there, and a way, and it shall

be called The way of holiness ; the unclean shall not pass over it; but it *shall be* for those : the wayfaring men, though fools, shall not err *therein.* 9 No lion shall be there, nor *any* ravenous beast shall go up thereon, it shall not be found there; but the redeemed shall walk *there :* 10 And the ransomed of the LORD shall return, and come to Zion with songs and everlasting joy upon their heads : they shall obtain joy and gladness, and sorrow and sighing shall flee away.

"*Then,* when your God shall come, even Christ, to set up his kingdom in the world, to which all the prophets bore witness, especially towards the conclusion of their prophecies of the temporal deliverances of the church, and this evangelical prophet especially—then look for great things."

I. Wonders shall be wrought in the kingdoms both of nature and grace, wonders of mercy wrought upon the children of men, sufficient to evince that it is no less than a God that comes to us. 1. Wonders shall be wrought on men's bodies (*v.* 5, 6): *The eyes of the blind shall be opened ;* this was often done by our Lord Jesus when he was here upon earth, with a word's speaking, and one he gave sight to that was *born* blind, Matt. ix. 27; xii. 22; xx. 30; John ix. 6. By his power the ears of the deaf also were unstopped, with one word, *Ephphatha—Be opened,* Mark vii. 34. Many that were lame had the use of their limbs restored so perfectly that they could not only go, but *leap,* and with so much joy to them that they could not forbear leaping for joy, as that impotent man, Acts iii. 8. The dumb also were enabled to speak, and then no marvel that they were disposed to sing for joy, Matt. ix. 32, 33. These miracles Christ wrought to prove that he was sent of God (John iii. 2), nay, working them by his own power and in his own name, he proved that he was God, the same who at first made man's mouth, the hearing ear, and the seeing eye. When he would prove to John's disciples his divine mission he did it by miracles of this kind, in which this scripture was fulfilled. 2. Wonders, greater wonders, shall be wrought on men's souls. By the word and Spirit of Christ those that were spiritually blind were enlightened (Acts xxvi. 18), those that were deaf to the calls of God were made to hear them readily, as Lydia, whose heart *the Lord opened,* so *that she attended,* Acts xvi. 14. Those that were impotent to every thing that is good by divine grace are made, not only able for it, but active in it, and run the way of God's commandments. Those also that were dumb, and knew not how to speak of God or to God, having their understandings opened to know him, shall thereby have their lips opened to show forth his praise. The tongue of the dumb shall sing for joy, the joy of God's salvation. Praise shall be perfected out of the mouth of babes and sucklings.

II. The Spirit shall be poured out from on high. There shall be *waters and streams*, rivers of living water; when our Saviour spoke of these as the fulfilling of the scripture, and most probably of this scripture, the evangelist tells us, *He spoke of the Spirit* (John vii. 38, 39), as does also this prophet (*ch.* xxxii. 15); so here (*v.* 6), *in the wilderness*, where one would least expect it, *shall waters break out.* This was fulfilled when the *Holy Ghost fell upon the Gentiles* that *heard the word* (Acts x. 44); then were the fountains of life opened, whence streams flowed, that watered the earth abundantly. These waters are said to *break out*, which denotes a pleasing surprise to the Gentile world, such as brought them, as it were, into a new world. The blessed effect of this shall be that the *parched ground shall become a pool, v.* 7. Those that laboured and were heavily laden, under the burden of guilt, and were scorched with the sense of divine wrath, found rest, and refreshment, and abundant comforts in the gospel. In *the thirsty land,* where no water was, no ordinances (Ps. lxiii. 1), there shall be *springs of water*, a gospel ministry, and by that the administration of all gospel ordinances in their purity and plenty, which are *the river that makes glad the city of our God*, Ps. xlvi. 4. *In the habitation of dragons*, who chose to dwell in the parched scorched ground (*ch.* xxxiv. 9, 13), these waters shall flow, and dispossess them, so that, *where each lay shall be grass with reeds and rushes*, great plenty of useful productions. Thus it was when Christian churches were planted, and flourished greatly, in the cities of the Gentiles, which, for many ages, had been habitations of dragons, or devils rather, as Babylon (Rev. xviii. 2); when the property of the idols' temples was altered, and they were converted to the service of Christianity, then the habitations of dragons became fruitful fields.

III. The way of religion and godliness shall be laid open: it is here called *the way of holiness* (*v.* 8), the way both of holy worship and a holy conversation. Holiness is the rectitude of the human nature and will, in conformity to the divine nature and will. The way of holiness is that course of religious duties in which men ought to walk and press forward, with an eye to the glory of God and their own felicity in the enjoyment of him. "When our God shall come to save us he shall chalk out to us this way by his gospel, so as it had never been before described." 1. It shall be an appointed way; not a way of sufferance, but *a high-way*, a way into which we are directed by a divine authority and in which we are pro-

196

tected by a divine warrant. It is the King's highway, the King of kings' highway, in which, though we may be waylaid, we cannot be stopped. The *way of holiness* is the way of God's commandments; it is (as highways usually are) the *good old way*, Jer. vi. 16. 2. It shall be an appropriated way, the way in which God will bring his own chosen to himself, but *the unclean shall not pass over it*, either to defile it or to disturb those that walk in it. It is a way by itself, distinguished from the way of the world, for it is a way of separation from, and nonconformity to, this world. *It shall be for those* whom the Lord has *set apart for himself* (Ps. iv. 3), shall be reserved for them: *The redeemed shall walk there*, and the satisfaction they take in these *ways of pleasantness* shall be out of the reach of molestation from an evil world. *The unclean shall not pass over it*, for it shall be a fair way; those that walk in it are the *undefiled in the way*, who *escape the pollution that is in the world.* 3. It shall be a straight way: *The wayfaring men*, who choose to travel in it, *though fools*, of weak capacity in other things, shall have such plain directions from the word and Spirit of God in this way that they *shall not err therein;* not that they shall be infallible even in their own conduct, or that they shall in nothing mistake, but they shall not be guilty of any fatal misconduct, shall not so miss their way but that they shall recover it again, and get well to their journey's end. Those that are in the narrow way, though some may fall into one path and others into another, not all equally right, but all meeting at last in the same end, shall yet never fall into the broad way again; the Spirit of truth shall lead them into all truth that is necessary for them. Note, The way to heaven is a plain way, and easy to hit. *God has chosen the foolish things of the world*, and made them wise to salvation. *Knowledge is easy to him that understands.* 4. It shall be a safe way: *No lion shall be there, nor any ravenous beast* (*v.* 9), none *to hurt or destroy.* Those that keep close to this way keep out of the reach of Satan the roaring lion, that wicked one touches them not. Those that walk in the way of holiness may proceed with a holy security and serenity of mind, knowing that nothing can do them any real hurt; they shall be quiet from the fear of evil. It was in Hezekiah's days, some time after the captivity of the ten tribes, that God, being displeased with the colonies settled there, *sent lions among them*, 2 Kings xvii. 25. But Judah keeps her integrity, and therefore *no lions shall be there.* Those that walk in the *way of holiness* must separate themselves from the unclean and the ravenous, must *save themselves from an untoward generation;* hoping that they themselves are of the redeemed, let them walk *with the redeemed* who *shall walk there.*

IV. The end of this way shall be everlasting joy, *v.* 10. This precious promise of peace now will end shortly in endless joys and rest for the soul. Here is good news for the citizens of Zion, rest to the weary: *The ransomed of the Lord*, who therefore ought to follow him wherever he goes (Rev. xiv. 4), *shall return and come to Zion*, 1. To serve and worship God in the church militant: they shall deliver themselves out of Babylon (Zech. ii. 7), shall *ask the way to Zion* (Jer. l. 5), and shall *find the way* ch. lii. 12. God will open to them a door of *(escape out of their captivity*, and it shall be 'an effectual door, though there be many adversaries. They shall join themselves to the gospel church, that *city of the living God*, Heb. xii. 22. They shall come with songs of joy and praise for their deliverance out of Babylon, where they wept upon every *remembrance of Zion*, Ps. cxxxvii. 1. Those that by faith are made citizens of the gospel Zion may *go on their way rejoicing* (Acts viii. 39); they shall sing in the ways of the Lord, and be still praising him. They rejoice in Christ Jesus, and the sorrows and sighs of their convictions are made to flee away by the power of divine consolations. Those that mourn shall be blessed, for they shall be comforted. 2. To see and enjoy God in the church triumphant; those that walk in *the way of holiness*, under the guidance of their Redeemer, shall come to Zion at last, to the heavenly Zion, shall come in a body, shall all be presented together, *faultless, at the coming of Christ's glory with exceeding joy* (Jude 24; Rev. vii 17); they shall come with songs. When God's people returned out of Babylon to Zion they came *weeping* (Jer. l. 4); but they shall come to heaven singing a new song, which no man can learn, Rev. xiv. 3. When they shall *enter into the joy of their Lord* it shall be what the joys of this world never could be, *everlasting joy*, without mixture, interruption, or period. It shall not only fill their hearts, to their own perfect and perpetual satisfaction, but it shall be *upon their heads*, as an ornament of grace and a crown of glory, as a garland worn in token of victory. Their joy shall be visible, and no longer a secret thing, as it is here in this world; it shall be proclaimed, to the glory of God and their mutual encouragement. They shall then obtain the joy and gladness which they could never expect on this side heaven; *and sorrow and sighing shall flee away* for ever, as the shadows of the night before the rising sun. Thus these prophecies, which relate to the Assyrian invasion, conclude, for the support of the people of God under that calamity, and to direct their joy, in their deliverance from it, to something higher. Our joyful hopes and prospects of eternal life should swallow up both all the sorrows and all the joys of this present time.

CHAP. XXXVI.

The prophet Isaiah is, in this and the three following chapters, an historian; for the scripture history, as well as the scripture prophecy, is given by inspiration of God, and was dictated to holy men. Many of the prophecies of the foregoing chapters had their accomplishment in Sennacherib's invading Judah and besieging Jerusalem, and the miraculous defeat he met with there; and therefore the story of this is here inserted, both for the explication and for the confirmation of the prophecy. The key of prophecy is to be found in history; and here, that we might have the readier entrance, it is, as it were, hung at the door. The exact fulfilling of this prophecy might serve to confirm the faith of God's people in the other prophecies, the accomplishment of which was at a greater distance. Whether this story was taken from the book of the Kings and added here, or whether it was first written by Isaiah here and hence taken into the book of Kings, is not material. But the story is the same almost verbatim; and it was so memorable an event that it was well worthy to be twice recorded, 2 Kings xviii. and xix., and here, and an abridgment of it likewise, 2 Chron. xxxii. We shall be but short in our observations upon this story here, having largely explained it there. In this chapter we have, I. The descent which the king of Assyria made upon Judah, and his success against all the defenced cities, ver. 1. II. The conference he desired to have with Hezekiah, and the managers on both sides, ver. 2, 3. III. Rabshakeh's railing blasphemous speech, with which he designed to frighten Hezekiah into a submission, and persuade him to surrender at discretion, ver. 4–10. IV. His appeal to the people, and his attempt to persuade them to desert Hezekiah, and so force him to surrender, ver. 11–20. V. The report of this made to Hezekiah by his agents, ver. 21, 22.

NOW it came to pass in the fourteenth year of king Hezekiah, *that* Sennacherib king of Assyria came up against all the defenced cities of Judah, and took them. 2 And the king of Assyria sent Rabshakeh from Lachish to Jerusalem unto king Hezekiah with a great army. And he stood by the conduit of the upper pool in the highway of the fuller's field. 3 Then came forth unto him Eliakim, Hilkiah's son, which was over the house, and Shebna the scribe, and Joah, Asaph's son, the recorder. 4 And Rabshakeh said unto them, Say ye now to Hezekiah, Thus saith the great king, the king of Assyria, What confidence *is* this wherein thou trustest? 5 I say, *sayest thou,* (but *they are but* vain words) *I have* counsel and strength for war: now on whom dost thou trust, that thou rebellest against me? 6 Lo, thou trustest in the staff of this broken reed, on Egypt; whereon if a man lean, it will go into his hand, and pierce it: so *is* Pharaoh king of Egypt to all that trust in him. 7 But if thou say to me, We trust in the LORD our God: *is it* not he whose high places and whose altars Hezekiah hath taken away, and said to Judah and to Jerusalem, Ye shall worship before this altar? 8 Now therefore give pledges, I pray thee, to my master the king of Assyria, and I will give thee two thousand horses, if thou be able on thy part to set riders upon them. 9 How then wilt thou turn away the face of one captain of the least of my master's servants, and put thy trust on Egypt for chariots and for horsemen? 10 And am I now come up without the LORD against this land to destroy it? The LORD said unto me, Go up against this land and destroy it.

We shall here only observe some practical lessons. 1. A people may be in the way of their duty and yet meet with trouble and distress. Hezekiah was reforming, and his people were in some measure reformed; and yet their country is at that time invaded and a great part of it laid waste. Perhaps they began to grow remiss and cool in the work of reformation, were doing it by halves, and ready to sit down short of a thorough reformation; and then God visited them with this judgment, to put life into them and that good cause. We must not wonder if, when we are doing well, God sends afflictions to quicken us to do better, to do our best, and to press forward towards perfection. 2. That we must never be secure of the continuance of our peace in this world, nor think our mountain stands so strong that it cannot be moved. Hezekiah was not only a pious king, but prudent, both in his administration at home and in his treaties abroad. His affairs were in a good posture, and he seemed particularly to be upon good terms with the king of Assyria, for he had lately made his peace with him by a rich present (2 Kings xviii. 14), and yet that perfidious prince pours an army into his country all of a sudden and lays it waste. It is good for us therefore always to keep up an expectation of trouble, that, when it comes, it may be no surprise to us, and then it will be the less a terror. 3. God sometimes permits the enemies of his people, even those that are most impious and treacherous, to prevail far against them. The king of Assyria took all, or most, of the defenced cities of Judah, and then the country would of course be an easy prey to him. Wickedness may prosper awhile, but cannot prosper always. 4. Proud men love to talk big, to boast of what they are, and have, and have done, nay and of what they will do, to insult over others, and set all mankind at defiance, though thereby they render themselves ridiculous to all wise men and obnoxious to the wrath of that God who resists the proud. But thus they think to make themselves feared, though they make themselves hated, and to carry their point by *great swelling words* of vanity, Jude 16. 5. The enemies of God's people endeavour to conquer them by frightening them, especially by frightening them from their confidence in God.

198

Thus Rabshakeh here, with noise and banter, runs down Hezekiah as utterly unable to cope with his master, or in the least to make head against him. It concerns us therefore, that we may keep our ground against the enemies of our souls, to keep up our spirits by keeping up our hope in God. 6. It is acknowledged, on all hands, that those who forsake God's service forfeit his protection. If that had been true which Rabshakeh alleged, that Hezekiah had thrown down God's altars, he might justly infer that he could not with any assurance trust in him for succour and relief, *v.* 7, We may say thus to presuming sinners, who say that they trust in the Lord and in his mercy. Is not this he whose commandments they have lived in the contempt of, whose name they have dishonoured, and whose ordinances they have slighted? How then can they expect to find favour with him? 7. It is an easy thing, and very common, for those that persecute the church and people of God to pretend a commission from him for so doing. Rabshakeh could say, *Have I now come up without the Lord?* when really he had come up *against* the Lord, *ch.* xxxvii. 28. Those that kill the servants of the Lord think they do him service and say, *Let the Lord be glorified.* But, sooner or later, they will be made to know their error to their cost, to their confusion.

11 Then said Eliakim and Shebna and Joah unto Rabshakeh, Speak, I pray thee, unto thy servants in the Syrian language; for we understand *it :* and speak not to us in the Jews' language, in the ears of the people that *are* on the wall. 12 But Rabshakeh said, Hath my master sent me to thy master and to thee to speak these words? *Hath he* not *sent me* to the men that sit upon the wall, that they may eat their own dung, and drink their own piss with you? 13 Then Rabshakeh stood, and cried with a loud voice in the Jews' language, and said, Hear ye the words of the great king, the king of Assyria. 14 Thus saith the king, Let not Hezekiah deceive you : for he shall not be able to deliver you. 15 Neither let Hezekiah make you trust in the LORD, saying, The LORD will surely deliver us: this city shall not be delivered into the hand of the king of Assyria. 16 Hearken not to Hezekiah : for thus saith the king of Assyria, Make *an agreement* with me *by* a present, and come out to me : and eat ye every

one of his vine, and every one of his fig-tree, and drink ye every one the waters of his own cistern; 17 Until I come and take you away to a land like your own land, a land of corn and wine, a land of bread and vineyards. 18 *Beware* lest Hezekiah persuade you, saying, The Lord will deliver us. Hath any of the gods of the nations delivered his land out of the hand of the king of Assyria? 19 Where *are* the gods of Hamath and Arphad? where *are* the gods of Sepharvaim? and have they delivered Samaria out of my hand? 20 Who *are they* among all the gods of these lands, that have delivered their land out of my hand, that the Lord should deliver Jerusalem out of my hand? 21 But they held their peace, and answered him not a word: for the king's commandment was, saying, Answer him not. 22 Then came Eliakim, the son of Hilkiah, that *was* over the household, and Shebna the scribe, and Joah, the son of Asaph, the recorder, to Hezekiah with *their* clothes rent, and told him the words of Rabshakeh.

We may hence learn these lessons:—1. That, while princes and counsellors have public matters under debate, it is not fair to appeal to the people. It was a reasonable motion which Hezekiah's plenipotentiaries made, that this parley should be held in a language which the people did not understand (*v.* 11), because reasons of state are secret things and ought to be kept secret, the vulgar being incompetent judges of them. It is therefore an unfair practice, and not doing as men would be done by, to incense subjects against their rulers by base insinuations. 2. Proud and haughty scorners, the fairer they are spoken to, commonly speak the fouler. Nothing could be said more mildly and respectfully than that which Hezekiah's agents said to Rabshakeh. Besides that the thing itself was just which they desired, they called themselves his *servants*, they petitioned for it: *Speak, we pray thee;* but this made him the more spiteful and imperious. To give rough answers to those who give us soft answers is one way of rendering evil for good; and those are wicked indeed, and it is to be feared incurable, with whom that which usually turns away wrath does but make bad worse. 3. When Satan would tempt men from trusting in God, and cleaving to him, he does so by insinuating that in yielding to him they may

better their condition; but it is a false suggestion, and grossly absurd, and therefore to be rejected with the utmost abhorrence. When the world and the flesh say to us, " *Make an agreement* with us *and come out to us*, submit to our dominion and come into our interests, and *you shall eat every one of his own vine*," they do but deceive us, promising liberty when they would lead us into the basest captivity and slavery. One might as well take Rabshakeh's word as theirs for kind usage and fair quarter; therefore, *when they speak fair, believe them not.* Let them say what they will, there is no land like the land of promise, the holy land. 4. Nothing can be more absurd in itself, nor a greater affront to the true and living God, than to compare him with the gods of the heathen; as if he could do no more for the protection of his worshippers than they can for the protection of theirs, and as if the God of Israel could as easily be mastered as the gods of Hamath and Arphad, whereas they are vanity and a lie. They are nothing; he is the great *I AM:* they are the creatures of men's fancy and the works of men's hands; he is the Creator of all things. 5. Presumptuous sinners are ready to think that, because they have been too hard for their fellow-creatures, they are therefore a match for their Creator. This and the other nation they have subdued, and therefore the Lord himself shall not deliver Jerusalem out of their hand. But, though the potsherds may strive with the potsherds of the earth, let them not strive with the potter. 6. It is sometimes prudent not to *answer a fool according to his folly.* Hezekiah's command was, " *Answer him not ;* it will but provoke him to rail and blaspheme yet more and more; leave it to God to stop his mouth, for you cannot." They had reason enough on their side, but it would be hard to speak it to such an unreasonable adversary without a mixture of passion ; and, if they should fall a railing like him, Rabshakeh would be much too hard for them at that weapon. 7. It becomes the people of God to lay to heart the dishonour done to God by the blasphemies of wicked men, though they do not think it prudent to reply to those blasphemies. Though they *answered him not a word*, yet they rent their clothes, in a holy zeal for the glory of God's name and a holy indignation at the contempt put upon it. They tore their garments when they heard blasphemy, as taking no pleasure in their own ornaments when God's honour suffered.

CHAP. XXXVII.

In this chapter we have a further repetition of the story which we had before in the book of Kings concerning Sennacherib. In the foregoing chapter we had him conquering and threatening to conquer. In this chapter we have him falling, and at last fallen, in answer to prayer, and in fulfilment of many of the prophecies which we have met with in the foregoing chapters. Here we have, 1. Hezekiah's pious reception of Rabshakeh's impious discourse, ver. 1. II. The gracious message he sent to Isaiah to desire his prayers, ver. 2—5. III. The encouraging answer which Isaiah sent to him from God, assuring him that God would plead his cause against the king of Assyria, ver. 6, 7. IV. An abusive letter which the king of Assyria sent to Hezekiah, to the same purport with Rabshakeh's speech, ver. 8—13. V. Hezekiah's humble prayer to God upon the receipt of this letter, ver. 14—20. VI. The further full answer which God sent him by Isaiah, promising him that his affairs should shortly take a happy turn, that the storm should blow over and every thing should appear bright and serene, ver. 21—35. VII. The immediate accomplishment of this prophecy in the ruin of his army (ver. 36) and the murder of himself, ver. 37, 38. All this was largely opened, 2 Kings xix.

AND it came to pass, when king Hezekiah heard *it*, that he rent his clothes, and covered himself with sackcloth, and went into the house of the Lord. 2 And he sent Eliakim, who *was* over the household, and Shebna the scribe, and the elders of the priests covered with sackcloth, unto Isaiah the prophet the son of Amoz. 3 And they said unto him, Thus saith Hezekiah, This day *is* a day of trouble, and of rebuke, and of blasphemy: for the children are come to the birth, and *there is* not strength to bring forth. 4 It may be the Lord thy God will hear the words of Rabshakeh, whom the king of Assyria his master hath sent to reproach the living God, and will reprove the words which the Lord thy God hath heard: wherefore lift up *thy* prayer for the remnant that is left. 5 So the servants of king Hezekiah came to Isaiah. 6 And Isaiah said unto them, Thus shall ye say unto your master, Thus saith the Lord, Be not afraid of the words that thou hast heard, wherewith the servants of the king of Assyria have blasphemed me. 7 Behold, I will send a blast upon him, and he shall hear a rumour, and return to his own land; and I will cause him to fall by the sword in his own land.

We may observe here, 1. That the best way to baffle the malicious designs of our enemies against us is to be driven by them to God and to our duty and so to fetch meat out of the eater. Rabshakeh intended to frighten Hekekiah from the Lord, but it proves that he frightens him to the Lord. The wind, instead of forcing the traveller's coat from him, makes him wrap it the closer about him. The more Rabshakeh reproaches God the more Hezekiah studies to honour him, by rending his clothes for the dishonour done to him and attending in his sanctuary to know his mind. 2. That it well becomes great men to desire the prayers of good men and good ministers. Hezekiah sent messengers, and honourable ones, those of the first rank, to Isaiah, to desire his prayers, remembering how much his pro-

phecies of late had plainly looked towards the events of the present day, in dependence upon which, it is probable, he doubted not but that the issue would be comfortable, yet he would have it to be so in answer to prayer : *This is a day of trouble*, therefore let it be a day of prayer. 3. When we are most at a plunge we should be most earnest in prayer : Now that the *children are brought to the birth*, but *there is not strength to bring forth*, now let prayer come, and help at a dead lift. When pains are most strong let prayers be most lively ; and, when we meet with the greatest difficulties, then is a time to stir up not ourselves only, but others also, to take hold on God. Prayer is the midwife of mercy, that helps to bring it forth. 4. It is an encouragement to pray though we have but some hopes of mercy (*v.* 4) : *It may be the Lord thy God will hear ; who knows but he will return and repent?* The *it may be* of the prospect of the haven of blessings should quicken us with double diligence to ply the oar of prayer. 5. When there is a remnant left, and but a remnant, it concerns us to lift up a prayer for that remnant, *v.* 4. The prayer that reaches heaven must be lifted up by a strong faith, earnest desires, and a direct intention to the glory of God, all which should be quickened when we come to the last stake. 6. Those that have made God their enemy we have no reason to be afraid of, for they are marked for ruin ; and, though they may hiss, they cannot hurt. Rabshakeh has blasphemed God, and therefore let not Hezekiah be afraid of him, *v.* 6. He has made God a party to the cause by his invectives, and therefore judgment will certainly be given against him. God will certainly plead his own cause. 7. Sinners' fears are but prefaces to their falls. He shall *hear the rumour* of the slaughter of his army, which shall oblige him to retire to his own land, and there he shall be slain, *v.* 7. The terrors that pursue him shall bring him at last to the *king of terrors*, Job xviii. 11, 14. The curses that come upon sinners shall overtake them.

8 So Rabshakeh returned, and found the king of Assyria warring against Libnah : for he had heard that he was departed from Lachish. 9 And he heard say concerning Tirhakah king of Ethiopia, He is come forth to make war with thee. And when he heard *it*, he sent messengers to Hezekiah, saying, 10 Thus shall ye speak to Hezekiah king of Judah, saying, Let not thy God, in whom thou trustest, deceive thee, saying, Jerusalem shall not be given into the hand of the king of Assyria. 11 Behold, thou hast heard what the kings

of Assyria have done to all lands by destroying them utterly; and shalt thou be delivered? 12 Have the gods of the nations delivered them which my fathers have destroyed, *as* Gozan, and Haran, and Rezeph, and the children of Eden which *were* in Telassar? 13 Where *is* the king of Hamath, and the king of Arphad, and the king of the city of Sepharvaim, Hena, and Ivah? 14 And Hezekiah received the letter from the hand of the messengers, and read it: and Hezekiah went up unto the house of the LORD, and spread it before the LORD. 15 And Hezekiah prayed unto the LORD, saying, 16 O LORD of hosts, God of Israel, that dwellest *between* the cherubims, thou *art* the God, *even* thou alone, of all the kingdoms of the earth: thou hast made heaven and earth. 17 Incline thine ear, O LORD, and hear; open thine eyes, O LORD, and see: and hear all the words of Sennacherib, which hath sent to reproach the living God. 18 Of a truth, LORD, the kings of Assyria have laid waste all the nations, and their countries, 19 And have cast their gods into the fire, for they *were* no gods, but the work of men's hands, wood and stone: therefore they have destroyed them. 20 Now therefore, O LORD our God, save us from his hand, that all the kingdoms of the earth may know that thou *art* the LORD, *even* thou only.

We may observe here, 1. That, if God give us inward satisfaction in his promise, this may confirm us in our silently bearing reproaches. God answered Hezekiah, but it does not appear that he, after deliberation, sent any answer to Rabshakeh; but, God having taken the work into his own hands, he quietly left the matter with him. So *Rabshakeh returned* to the king his master for fresh instructions. 2. Those that delight in war shall have enough of it. Sennacherib, without provocation given to him or warning given by him, went forth to war against Judah; and now with as little ceremony the king of Ethiopia goes forth to war against him, v. 9. Those that are quarrelsome may expect to be quarrelled with; and God sometimes checks the rage of his enemies by giving it a powerful diversion. 3. It is bad to talk proudly and profanely, but it is worse to write so, for this argues more deliberation and design, and what is written

spreads further, lasts longer, and does the more mischief. Atheism and irreligion, written, will certainly be reckoned for another day. 4. Great successes often harden sinners' hearts in their sinful ways and make them the more daring. Because the kings of Assyria have destroyed all lands (though, in fact, they were but a few that fell within their reach), therefore they doubt not but to destroy God's land; because the gods of the nations were unable to help they conclude the God of Israel is so; because the idolatrous kings of Hamath and Arphad became an easy prey to them therefore the religious reforming king of Judah must needs be so too. Thus is this proud man ripened for ruin by the sunshine of prosperity. 5. Liberty of access to the throne of grace, and liberty of speech there, are the unspeakable privilege of the Lord's people at all times, especially in times of distress and danger. Hezekiah took Sennacherib's letter, and spread it before the Lord, not designing to make any complaints against him but those grounded upon his own handwriting. Let the thing speak itself; here it is in black and white: *Open thy eyes, O Lord! and see.* God allows his praying people to be humbly free with him, to utter all their words, as Jephthah did, before him, to spread the letter, whether of a friend or an enemy, before him, and leave the contents, the concern of it, with him. 6. The great and fundamental principles of our religion, applied by faith and improved in prayer, will be of sovereign use to us in our particular exigencies and distresses, whatever they are; to them therefore we must have recourse, and abide by them; so Hezekiah did here. He encouraged himself with this, that the God of Israel is *the Lord of hosts,* of all hosts, of the hosts of Israel, to animate them, of the hosts of their enemies, to dispirit and restrain them,—that he is God *alone,* and there is none that can stand in competition with him,—that he is the *God of all the kingdoms of the earth,* and disposes of them all as he pleases; for he made heaven and earth, and therefore both can do any thing and does every thing. 7. When we are afraid of men that are great destroyers we may with humble boldness appeal to God as the great Saviour. They have indeed destroyed the nations, who had thrown themselves out of the protection of the true God by worshipping false gods, but the Lord, the God alone, is our God, our King, our lawgiver, and he will save us, who is *the Saviour of those that believe.* 8. We have enough to take hold of, in our wrestling with God by prayer, if we can but plead that his glory is interested in our case, that his name will be profaned if we are run down and glorified if we are relieved. Thence therefore will our most prevailing pleas be drawn: " Do it for thy glory's sake."

21 Then Isaiah the son of Amoz sent unto Hezekiah, saying, Thus saith the LORD GOD of Israel, Whereas thou hast prayed to me against Sennacherib king of Assyria: 22 This *is* the word which the LORD hath spoken concerning him; The virgin, the daughter of Zion, hath despised thee, *and* laughed thee to scorn; the daughter of Jerusalem hath shaken her head at thee. 23 Whom hast thou reproached and blasphemed? and against whom hast thou exalted *thy* voice, and lifted up thine eyes on high? *Even* against the Holy One of Israel. 24 By thy servants hast thou reproached the LORD, and hast said, By the multitude of my chariots am I come up to the height of the mountains, to the sides of Lebanon; and I will cut down the tall cedars thereof, *and* the choice fir-trees thereof: and I will enter into the height of his border, *and* the forest of his Carmel. 25 I have digged, and drunk water; and with the sole of my feet have I dried up all the rivers of the besieged places. 26 Hast thou not heard long ago, *how* I have done it; *and* of ancient times, that I have formed it? Now have I brought it to pass, that thou shouldest be to lay waste defenced cities *into* ruinous heaps. 27 Therefore their inhabitants *were* of small power, they were dismayed and confounded: they were *as* the grass of the field, and *as* the green herb, *as* the grass on the house-tops, and *as corn* blasted before it be grown up. 28 But I know thy abode, and thy going out, and thy coming in, and thy rage against me. 29 Because thy rage against me, and thy tumult, is come up into mine ears, therefore will I put my hook in thy nose, and my bridle in thy lips, and I will turn thee back by the way by which thou camest. 30 And this *shall be* a sign unto thee, Ye shall eat *this* year such as groweth of itself; and the second year that which springeth of the same: and in the third year sow ye, and reap, and plant vineyards, and eat the fruit

202

thereof. 31 And the remnant that is escaped of the house of Judah shall again take root downward, and bear fruit upward: 32 For out of Jerusalem shall go forth a remnant, and they that escape out of mount Zion: the zeal of the LORD of hosts shall do this. 33 Therefore thus saith the LORD concerning the king of Assyria, He shall not come into this city, nor shoot an arrow there, nor come before it with shields, nor cast a bank against it. 34 By the way that he came, by the same shall he return, and shall not come into this city, saith the LORD. 35 For I will defend this city to save it for mine own sake, and for my servant David's sake. 36 Then the angel of the LORD went forth, and smote in the camp of the Assyrians a hundred and fourscore and five thousand: and when they arose early in the morning, behold, they *were* all dead corpses. 37 So Sennacherib king of Assyria departed, and went and returned, and dwelt at Nineveh. 38 And it came to pass, as he was worshipping in the house of Nisroch his god, that Adrammelech and Sharezer his sons smote him with the sword; and they escaped into the land of Armenia: and Esar-haddon his son reigned in his stead.

We may here observe, 1. That those who receive messages of terror from men with patience, and send messages of faith to God by prayer, may expect messages of grace and peace from God for their comfort, even when they are most cast down. Isaiah sent a long answer to Hezekiah's prayer in God's name, sent it in writing (for it was too long to be sent by word of mouth), and sent it by way of return to his prayer, relation being thereunto had: " *Whereas thou hast prayed to me,* know, for thy comfort, that thy prayer is heard." Isaiah might have referred him to the prophecies he had delivered (particularly that *ch.* x.) and bid him pick out an answer from thence; but, that he might have abundant consolation, a message is sent him on purpose. The correspondence between earth and heaven is never let fall on God's side. 2. Those who magnify themselves, especially who magnify themselves against God and his people, do really vilify themselves, and make themselves contemptible, in the eyes of all wise men: " *The virgin, the daughter of Zion, has despised*

Sennacherib, and all his impotent malice and menaces; she knows that, while she preserves her integrity, she is sure of the divine protection, and that though the enemy may bark he cannot bite. All his threats are a jest; it is all but *brutum fulmen—a mere flash.*" 3. Those who abuse the people of God affront God himself; and he takes what is said and done against them as said and done against himself: " *Whom hast thou reproached?* Even *the Holy One of Israel,* whom thou hast *therefore* reproached because he is a Holy One." And it aggravated the indignity Sennacherib did to God that he not only reproached him himself, but set his servants on to do the same: *By thy servants,* the abjects, *thou hast reproached me.* 4. Those who boast of themselves and their own achievements reflect upon God and his providence: " *Thou hast said, I have digged, and drunk water;* I have done mighty feats, and will do more; and wilt not own that *I have done it,*" *v.* 24—26. The most active men are no more than God makes them, and God makes them no more than of old he designed to make them: " *What I have formed of ancient times, in* an eternal counsel, *now have I brought to pass*" (for God does all according to the counsel of his will), " *that thou shouldst be to lay waste defenced cities;* it is therefore intolerable arrogance to make it thy own doing." 5. All the malice, and all the motions and projects, of the church's enemies, are under the cognizance and check of the church's God. Sennacherib was active and quick, here, and there, and every where, but God knew his going out and coming in, and had always an eye upon him, *v.* 28. And that was not all; he had a hand upon him too, a strict hand, a strong hand, *a hook in his nose and a bridle in his lips,* with which, though he was very headstrong and unruly, he could and would *turn him back by the way which he came, v.* 29. *Hitherto he shall come and no further.* God had signed Sennacherib's commission against Judah (*ch.* x. 6); here he supersedes it. He has frightened them, but he must not hurt them, and therefore is discharged from going any further; nay, his commitment is here signed, by which he is clapped up, to answer for what he had done beyond his commission. 6. God is his people's bountiful benefactor, as well as their powerful protector, both a sun and a shield to those that trust in him. Jerusalem shall be defended (*v.* 35), the besiegers shall not come into it, no, nor come before it with any regular attack, but they shall be routed before they begin the siege, *v.* 33. But this is not all; God will return in mercy to his people, and will do them good. Their land shall be more than ordinarily fruitful, so that their losses shall be abundantly repaired; they shall not feel any of the ill effects either of the enemies' wasting the

country or of their own being taken off from husbandry. But the earth, as at first, shall bring forth of itself, and they shall live and live plentifully upon its spontaneous productions. The blessing of the Lord can, when he pleases, make rich without the hand of the diligent. And let them not think that the desolations of their country would excuse them from observing the sabbatical year, which happened (as it should seem) the year after, and when they were not to plough or sow; no, though they had not now their usual stock beforehand for that year, yet they must religiously observe it, and depend upon God to provide for them. God must be trusted in the way of duty. 7. There is no standing before the judgments of God when they come with commission. (1.) The greatest numbers cannot stand before them: one angel shall, in one night, lay a vast army of men dead upon the spot, when God commissions him so to do, *v.* 36. Here are 185,000 brave soldiers in an instant turned into so many dead corpses. Many think the 76th Psalm was penned upon occasion of this defeat, where, from *the spoiling of the stout-hearted,* and sending them to sleep their long sleep (*v.* 5), it is inferred that God is *more glorious and excellent than the mountains of prey* (*v.* 4), and that *he, even he, is to be feared, v.* 7. Angels are employed, more than we are aware of, as ministers of God's justice, to punish the pride and break the power of wicked men. (2.) The greatest men cannot stand before them: *The great king, the king of Assyria,* looks very little when he is forced to return, not only with shame, because he cannot accomplish what he had projected with so much assurance, but with terror and fear, lest the angel that had destroyed his army should destroy him; yet he is made to look less when his own sons, who should have guarded him, sacrificed him to his idol, whose protection he sought, *v.* 37, 38. God can quickly stop their breath who *breathe out threatenings and slaughter* against his people, and will do it when they have filled up the measure of their iniquity; and *the Lord is known by* these *judgments which he executes,* known to be a God that resists the proud. Many prophecies were fulfilled in this providence, which should encourage us, as far as they look further, and are designed as common and general assurances of the safety of the church and of all that trust in God, to depend upon God for the accomplishment of them. He that has delivered does and will deliver. Lord, forgive our enemies; but, *so let all thy enemies perish, O Lord!*

CHAP. XXXVIII.

This chapter proceeds in the history of Hezekiah. Here is, I. His sickness, and the sentence of death he received within himself, ver. 1. II. His prayer in his sickness, ver. 2, 3. III. The answer of peace which God gave to that prayer, assuring him that he should recover, that he should live fifteen years yet, that Jerusalem should be delivered from the king of Assyria, and that, for a sign to confirm his faith herein, the sun should go back ten degrees, ver. 4—8. And this we read and opened before, 2 Kings xx. 1, &c. But, IV. Here is Hezekiah's thanksgiving for his recovery, which we had not before, ver. 9—20. To which are added the means used (ver. 21), and the end the good man aimed at in desiring to recover, ver. 22. This is a chapter which will entertain the thoughts, direct the devotions, and encourage the faith and hopes of those that are confined by bodily distempers; it visits those that are visited with sickness.

IN those days was Hezekiah sick unto death. And Isaiah the prophet the son of Amoz came unto him, and said unto him, Thus saith the LORD, Set thine house in order: for thou shalt die, and not live. 2 Then Hezekiah turned his face toward the wall, and prayed unto the LORD, 3 And said, Remember now, O LORD, I beseech thee, how I have walked before thee in truth and with a perfect heart, and have done *that which is* good in thy sight. And Hezekiah wept sore. 4 Then came the word of the LORD to Isaiah, saying, 5 Go, and say to Hezekiah, Thus saith the LORD, the God of David thy father, I have heard thy prayer, I have seen thy tears: behold, I will add unto thy days fifteen years. 6 And I will deliver thee and this city out of the hand of the king of Assyria: and I will defend this city. 7 And this *shall be* a sign unto thee from the LORD, that the LORD will do this thing that he hath spoken; 8 Behold, I will bring again the shadow of the degrees, which is gone down in the sun-dial of Ahaz, ten degrees backward. So the sun returned ten degrees, by which degrees it was gone down.

We may hence observe, among others, these good lessons:—1. That neither men's greatness nor their goodness will exempt them from the arrests of sickness and death. Hezekiah, a mighty potentate on earth and a mighty favourite of Heaven, is struck with a disease, which, without a miracle, will certainly be mortal; and this in the midst of his days, his comforts, and usefulness. *Lord, behold, he whom thou lovest is sick.* It should seem, this sickness seized him when he was in the midst of his triumphs over the ruined army of the Assyrians, to teach us always to rejoice with trembling. 2. It concerns us to prepare when we see death approaching: " *Set thy house in order,* and thy heart especially; put both thy affections and thy affairs into the best posture thou canst, that, when thy Lord comes, thou mayest be found of him in peace with God, with thy own conscience, and with all men,

204

and mayest have nothing else to do but to die." Our being ready for death will make it come never the sooner, but much the easier: and those that are fit to die are most fit to live. 3. Is any afflicted with sickness? *Let him pray,* James v. 13. Prayer is a salve for every sore, personal or public. When Hezekiah was distressed by his enemies he prayed; now that he was sick he prayed. Whither should the child go, when any thing ails him, but to his Father? Afflictions are sent to bring us to our Bibles and to our knees. When Hezekiah was in health he *went up to the house of the Lord* to pray, for that was then the house of prayer. When he was sick in bed *he turned his face towards the wall,* probably towards the temple, which was a type of Christ, to whom we must look by faith in every prayer. 4. The testimony of our consciences for us that by the grace of God we have lived a good life, and have walked closely and humbly with God, will be a great support and comfort to us when we come to look death in the face. And though we may not depend upon it as our righteousness, by which to be justified before God, yet we may humbly plead it as an evidence of our interest in the righteousness of the Mediator. Hezekiah does not demand a reward from God for his good services, but modestly begs that God would remember, not how he had reformed the kingdom, taken away the high places, cleansed the temple, and revived neglected ordinances, but, which was *better than all burnt-offerings and sacrifices,* how he had approved himself to God with a single eye and an honest heart, not only in these eminent performances, but in an even regular course of holy living: *I have walked before thee in truth* and sincerity, *and with a perfect,* that is, an upright, *heart;* for uprightness is our gospel perfection. 5. God has a gracious ear open to the prayers of his afflicted people. The same prophet that was sent to Hezekiah with warning to prepare for death is sent to him with a promise that he shall not only recover, but be restored to a confirmed state of health and live fifteen years yet. As Jerusalem was distressed, so Hezekiah was diseased, that God might have the glory of the deliverance of both, and that prayer too might have the honour of being instrumental in the deliverance. When we pray in our sickness, though God send not to us such an answer as he here sent to Hezekiah, yet, if by his Spirit he bids us be of good cheer, assures us that our sins are forgiven us, that his grace shall be sufficient for us, and that, whether we live or die, we shall be his, we have no reason to say that we pray in vain. God answers us if he *strengthens us with strength in our souls,* though not with bodily strength, Ps. cxxxviii. 3. 6. A good man cannot take much comfort in his own health and prosperity unless withal he see the welfare and prosperity of the church of God. Therefore God, knowing what lay near Hezekiah's heart, promised him not only that he should live, but that he should *see the good of Jerusalem all the days of his life* (Ps. cxxviii. 5), otherwise he cannot live comfortably. Jerusalem, which is now delivered, shall still be defended from the Assyrians, who perhaps threatened to rally again and renew the attack. Thus does God graciously provide to make Hezekiah upon all accounts easy. 7. God is *willing to show to the heirs of promise the immutability of his counsel,* that they may have an unshaken faith in it, and therewith a strong consolation. God had given Hezekiah repeated assurances of his favour; and yet, as if all were thought too little, that he might expect from him uncommon favours, a sign is given him, an uncommon sign. None that we know of having had an absolute promise of living a certain number of years to come, as Hezekiah had, God thought fit to confirm this unprecedented favour with a miracle. The sign was the going back of the shadow upon the sun-dial. The sun is a faithful measurer of time, and *rejoices as a strong man to run a race;* but he that set that clock a going can set it back when he pleases, and make it to return; for the Father of all lights is the director of them.

9 The writing of Hezekiah king of Judah, when he had been sick, and was recovered of his sickness: 10 I said in the cutting off of my days, I shall go to the gates of the grave: I am deprived of the residue of my years. 11 I said, I shall not see the LORD, *even* the LORD, in the land of the living: I shall behold man no more with the inhabitants of the world. 12 Mine age is departed, and is removed from me as a shepherd's tent: I have cut off like a weaver my life: he will cut me off with pining sickness: from day *even* to night wilt thou make an end of me. 13 I reckoned till morning, *that,* as a lion, so will he break all my bones: from day *even* to night wilt thou make an end of me. 14 Like a crane *or* a swallow, so did I chatter: I did mourn as a dove: mine eyes fail *with looking* upward: O LORD, I am oppressed; undertake for me. 15 What shall I say? He hath both spoken unto me, and himself hath done *it:* I shall go softly all my years in the bitterness of my soul. 16 O LORD, by these *things*

men live, and in all these *things is* the life of my spirit: so wilt thou recover me, and make me to live. 17 Behold, for peace I had great bitterness: but thou hast, in love to my soul, *delivered it* from the pit of corruption: for thou hast cast all my sins behind thy back. 18 For the grave cannot praise thee, death can *not* celebrate thee: they that go down into the pit cannot hope for thy truth. 19 The living, the living, he shall praise thee, as I *do* this day: the father to the children shall make known thy truth. 20 The LORD *was ready* to save me: therefore we will sing my songs to the stringed instruments all the days of our life in the house of the LORD. 21 For Isaiah had said, Let them take a lump of figs, and lay *it* for a plaster upon the boil, and he shall recover. 22 Hezekiah also had said, What *is* the sign that I shall go up to the house of the LORD?

We have here Hezekiah's thanksgiving-song, which he penned, by divine direction, after his recovery. He might have taken some of the psalms of his father David, and made use of them for his purpose; he might have found many very pertinent ones. He appointed *the Levites to praise the Lord with the words of David,* 2 Chron. xxix. 30. But the occasion here was extraordinary, and, his heart being full of devout affections, he would not confine himself to the compositions he had, though of divine inspiration, but would offer up his affections in his own words, which is most natural and genuine. He put this thanksgiving in writing, that he might review it himself afterwards, for the reviving of the good impressions made upon him by the providence, and that it might be recommended to others also for their use upon the like occasion. Note, There are writings which it is proper for us to draw up after we have been sick and have recovered. It is good to write a memorial of the affliction, and of the frame of our hearts under it, —to keep a record of the thoughts we had of things when we were sick, the affections that were then working in us,—to write a memorial of the mercies of a sick bed, and of our release from it, that they may never be forgotten,—to write a thanksgiving to God, write a sure covenant with him, and seal it,—to give it under our hands that we will never return again to folly. It is an excellent writing which Hezekiah here left, upon his recovery; and yet we find (2 Chron xxxii. 25) that *he rendered not again accord-*

205

ing to the benefit done to him. The impressions, one would think, should never have worn off, and yet, it seems, they did. Thanksgiving is good, but thanksliving is better. Now in this writing he preserves upon record,

I. The deplorable condition he was in when his disease prevailed, and his despair of recovery, *v.* 10—13.

1. He tells us what his thoughts were of himself when he was at the worst; and these he keeps in remembrance, (1.) As blaming himself for his despondency, and that he gave up himself for gone; whereas while there is life there is hope, and room for our prayer and God's mercy. Though it is good to consider sickness as a summons to the grave, so as thereby to be quickened in our preparations for another world, yet we ought not to make the worst of our case, nor to think that every sick man must needs be a dead man presently. He that brings low can raise up. Or, (2.) As reminding himself of the apprehensions he had of death approaching, that he might always know and consider his own frailty and mortality, and that, though he had a reprieve for fifteen years, it was but a reprieve, and the fatal stroke he had now such a dread of would certainly come at last. Or, (3.) As magnifying the power of God in restoring him when his case was desperate, and his goodness in being so much better to him than his own fears. Thus David sometimes, when he was delivered out of trouble, reflected upon the black and melancholy conclusions he had made upon his own case when he was in trouble, and what he had then *said in his haste,* as Ps. xxxi. 22 ; lxxvii. 7—9.

2. Let us see what Hezekiah's thoughts of himself were.

(1.) He reckoned that the number of his months was cut off in the midst. He was now about thirty-nine or forty years of age, and when he had a fair prospect of many years and happy ones, very happy, very many, before him. This distemper that suddenly seized him he concluded would be the *cutting off of his days,* that he should now be *deprived of the residue of his years,* which in a course of nature he might have lived (not which he could command as a debt due to him, but which he had reason to expect, considering the strength of his constitution), and with them he should be deprived not only of the comforts of life, but of all the opportunities he had of serving God and his generation. To the same purport (*v.* 12), "My age has *departed* and gone, and is removed from me as a shepherd's tent, out of which I am forcibly dislodged by the pulling of it down in an instant." Our present residence is but like that of a shepherd in his tent, a poor, mean, and cold lodging, where we are upon duty, and with a trust committed to our charge, as the shepherd has, of which we must give an account, and which will easily be taken down by the drawing of one pin or

206

two. But observe, It is not the final period of our age, but only the removal of it to another world, where the tents of Kedar that are taken down, coarse, black, and weather-beaten, shall be set up again in the New Jerusalem, *comely as the curtains of Solomon.* He adds another similitude : *I have cut off, like a weaver, my life.* Not that he did by any act of his own cut off the thread of his life ; but, being told that he must needs die, he was forced to cut off all his designs and projects, his *purposes were broken off,* even the *thoughts of his heart,* as Job's were, *ch.* xvii. 11. Our days are compared to the weaver's shuttle (Job vii. 6), passing and repassing very swiftly, every throw leaving a thread behind it ; and, when they are finished, the thread is cut off, and the piece taken out of the loom, and shown to our Master, to be judged of whether it be well woven or no, that we may *receive according to the things done in the body.* But as the weaver, when he has cut off his threads, has done his work, and the toil is over, so a good man, when his life is cut off, his cares and fatigues are cut off with it, and he rests from his labours. "But did I say, *I have cut off my life ?* No, my times are not in my own hand ; they are in God's hand, and it is he that *will cut me off from the thrum* (so the margin reads it) ; he has appointed what shall be the length of the piece, and, when it comes to that length, he will cut it off."

(2.) He reckoned that he should go to the gates of the grave—to the grave, the gates of which are always open ; for it is still crying, Give, give. The grave is here put not only for the sepulchre of his fathers, in which his body would be deposited with a great deal of pomp and magnificence (for he was buried in the chief of the sepulchres of the kings, and all *Judah did him honour at his death,* 2 Chron. xxxii. 33), which yet he himself took no care of, nor gave any order about, when he was sick ; but for the state of the dead, that is, the *sheol,* the *hades,* the invisible world, to which he saw his soul going.

(3.) He reckoned that he was deprived of all the opportunities he might have had of worshipping God and doing good in the world (*v.* 11): "*I said,*" [1.] "*I shall not see the Lord,* as he manifests himself in his temple, in his oracles and ordinances, *even the Lord* here *in the land of the living.*" He hopes to see him on the other side death, but he despairs of seeing him any more on this side death, as he had seen him in the sanctuary, Ps. lxiii. 2. He shall no more see (that is, serve) the Lord in the land of the living, the land of conflict between his kingdom and the kingdom of Satan, this seat of war. He dwells much upon this : *I shall no more see the Lord, even the Lord ;* for a good man wishes not to live for any other end than that he may serve God and have communion with him. [2.] "*I shall see man no more.*"

He shall see his subjects no more, whom he may protect and administer justice to, shall see no more objects of charity, whom he may relieve, shall see his friends no more, who were often sharpened by his countenance, as iron is by iron. Death puts an end to conversation, and removes our acquaintance into darkness, Ps. lxxxviii. 18.

(4.) He reckoned that the agonies of death would be very sharp and severe: "*He will cut me off with pining sickness,* which will waste me, and wear me off, quickly." The distemper increased so fast, without intermission or remission, either day or night, morning or evening, that he concluded it would soon come to a crisis and make an end of him—that God, whose servants all diseases are, would by them, *as a lion, break all his bones* with grinding pain, *v.* 13. He thought that next morning was the utmost he could expect to live in such pain and misery; when he had outlived the first day's illness the second day he repeated his fears, and concluded that this must needs be his last night: *From day even to night wilt thou make an end of me.* When we are sick we are very apt to be thus calculating our time, and, after all, we are still at uncertainty. It should be more our care how we shall get safely to another world than how long we are likely to live in this world.

II. The complaints he made in this condition (*v.* 14): "*Like a crane, or swallow, so did I chatter;* I made a noise as those birds do when they were frightened." See what a change sickness makes in a little time; he that, but the other day, spoke with so much freedom and majesty, now, through the extremity of pain or deficiency of spirits, *chatters like a crane or a swallow.* Some think he refers to his praying in his affliction; it was so broken and interrupted with groanings which could not be uttered that it was more like the chattering of a crane or a swallow than what it used to be. Such mean thoughts had he of his own prayers, which yet were acceptable to God, and successful. He *mourned like a dove,* sadly, but silently and patiently. He had found God so ready to answer his prayers at other times that he could not but look upwards, in expectation of some relief now, but in vain: his *eyes failed,* and he saw no hopeful symptom, nor felt any abatement of his distemper; and therefore he prays, "*I am oppressed,* quite overpowered and ready to sink; *Lord, undertake for me;* bail me out of the hands of the serjeant that has arrested me; *be surety for thy servant for good,* Ps. cxix. 122. Come between me and the gates of the grave, to which I am ready to be hurried." When we recover from sickness, the divine pity does, as it were, beg a day for us, and undertakes we shall be forthcoming another time and answer the debt in full. And, when we receive the sentence of death within ourselves, we are undone if the divine grace do not undertake for us to carry us through the valley of the shadow of death, and to preserve us blameless to the heavenly kingdom on the other side of it—if Christ do not undertake for us, to bring us off in judgment, and present us to his Father, and to do all that for us which we need, and cannot do for ourselves. *I am oppressed, ease me* (so some read it); for, when we are agitated by a sense of guilt and the fear of wrath, nothing will make us easy but Christ's undertaking for us.

III. The grateful acknowledgment he makes of God's goodness to him in his recovery. He begins this part of the writing as one at a stand how to express himself (*v.* 15): "*What shall I say?* Why should I say so much by way of complaint when this is enough to silence all my complaints—*He has spoken unto me;* he has sent his prophet to tell me that I shall recover and live fifteen years yet; *and he himself has done it:* it is as sure to be done as if it were done already. What God has spoken he will himself do, for no word of his shall fall to the ground." God having spoken it, he is sure of it (*v.* 16): "*Thou wilt restore me, and make me to live;* not only restore me from this illness, but make me to live through the years assigned me." And, having this hope,

1. He promises himself always to retain the impressions of his affliction (*v.* 15): "*I will go softly all my years in the bitterness of my soul,* as one in sorrow for my sinful distrusts and murmurings under my affliction, as one in care to make suitable returns for God's favour to me and to make it appear that I have got good by the providences I have been under. *I will go softly,* gravely and considerately, and with thought and deliberation, not as many, who, when they have recovered, live as carelessly and as much at large as ever." Or, "I will go pleasantly" (so some understand it); "when God has delivered me I will walk cheerfully with him in all holy conversation, as having tasted that he is gracious." Or, "I will go softly," that is, "mournfully, in the bitterness of my soul for my sins." Or, "I will go softly, even *after the bitterness of my soul*" (so it may be read); "when the trouble is over I will endeavour to retain the impression of it, and to have the same thoughts of things that I had then."

2. He will encourage himself and others with the experiences he had had of the goodness of God (*v.* 16): "*By these things* which thou hast done for me *they live,* the kingdom lives" (for the life of such a king was the life of the kingdom); "all that hear of it shall live and be comforted; by the same power and goodness that have restored me all men have their souls held in life, and they ought to acknowledge it. *In all these things is the life of my spirit,* my spiritual life, that is supported and maintained by what God has done for the preservation of

my natural life." The more we taste of the loving-kindness of God in every providence the more will our hearts be enlarged to love him and live to him, and that will be the life of our spirit. Thus our souls live, and they shall praise him.

3. He magnifies the mercy of his recovery, on several accounts.

(1.) That he was raised up from great extremity (*v.* 17) : *Behold, for peace I had great bitterness.* When, upon the defeat of Sennacherib, he expected nothing but an uninterrupted peace to himself and his government, he was suddenly seized with sickness, which embittered all his comforts to him, and went to such a height that it seemed to be the bitterness of death itself— *bitterness, bitterness,* nothing but gall and wormwood. This was his condition when God sent him seasonable relief.

(2.) That it came from the love of God, from love to his soul. Some are spared and reprieved in wrath, that they may be reserved for some greater judgment when they have filled up the measure of their iniquities ; but temporal mercies are sweet indeed to us when we can taste the love of God in them. *He delivered me because he delighted in me* (Ps. xviii. 19) ; and the word here signifies a very affectionate love : *Thou hast loved my soul from the pit of corruption ;* so it runs in the original. God's love is sufficient to bring a soul from the pit of corruption. This is applicable to our redemption by Christ ; it was in love to our souls, our poor perishing souls, that he delivered them from the bottomless pit, snatched them as brands out of everlasting burnings. *In his love and in his pity he redeemed us.* And the preservation of our bodies, as well as the provision made for them, is doubly comfortable when it is in love to our souls— when God repairs the house because he has a kindness for the inhabitant.

(3.) That it was the effect of the pardon of sin : *" For thou hast cast all my sins behind thy back,* and thereby hast *delivered my soul from the pit of corruption,* in love to it." Note, [1.] When God pardons sin he casts it behind his back, as not designing to look upon it with an eye of justice and jealousy. He remembers it no more, to visit for it. The pardon does not make the sin not to have been, or not to have been sin, but not to be punished as it deserves. When we cast our sins behind our back, and take no care to repent of them, God sets them before his face, and is ready to reckon for them ; but when we set them before our face in true repentance, as David did when his sin was ever before him, God casts them behind his back. [2.] When God pardons sins he pardons all, casts them all behind his back, though they have been as scarlet and crimson. [3.] The pardoning of the sin is the delivering of the soul from the pit of corruption. [4.] It is pleasant indeed to think

of our recoveries from sickness when we see them flowing from the remission of sin ; then the cause is removed, and then it is in love to the soul.

(4.) That it was the lengthening out of his opportunity to glorify God in this world, which he made the business, and pleasure, and end of life. [1.] If this sickness had been his death, it would have put a period to that course of service for the glory of God and the good of the church which he was now pursuing, *v.* 18. Heaven indeed praises God, and the souls of the faithful, when at death they remove thither, do that work of heaven as the angels, and with the angels, there ; but what is this world the better for that ? What does that contribute to the support and advancement of God's kingdom among men in this state of struggle ? *The grave cannot praise God,* nor the dead bodies that lie there. *Death cannot celebrate him,* cannot proclaim his perfections and favours, to invite others into his service. *Those who go down to the pit,* being no longer in a state of probation, nor living by faith in his promises, cannot give him honour by hoping for his truth. Those that lie rotting in the grave, as they are not capable of receiving any further mercy from God, so neither are they capable of offering any more praises to him, till they shall be raised at the last day, and then they shall both receive and give glory. [2.] Having recovered from it, he resolves not only to proceed, but to abound, in praising and serving God (*v.* 19) : *The living, the living, he shall praise thee.* They may do it ; they have an opportunity of praising God, and that is the main thing that makes life valuable and desirable to a good man. Hezekiah was *therefore* glad to live, not that he might continue to enjoy his royal dignity and the honour and pleasure of his late successes, but that he might continue to praise God. The living must praise God ; they live in vain if they do not. Those that have been dying and yet are living, whose life is from the dead, are in a special manner obliged to praise God, as being most sensibly affected with his goodness. Hezekiah, for his part, having recovered from this sickness, will make it his business to praise God : *" I do it this day ;* let others do it in like manner." Those that give good exhortations should set good examples, and do themselves what they expect from others. *" For my part,"* says Hezekiah, *" the Lord was ready to save me ;* he not only did save me, but he was ready to do it just then when I was in the greatest extremity ; his help came in seasonably ; he showed himself willing and forward to save me *The Lord was to save me,* was at hand to do it, saved me at the first word ; and therefore," *First,* " I will publish and proclaim his praises. I and my family, I and my friends, I and my people, will have a concert of praise to his glory : *We will sing my songs to the stringed instruments,* that others may attend to them, and be affected with them, when they are in the most devout and serious frame in the house of the Lord." It is for the honour of God, and the edification of his church, that special mercies should be acknowledged in public praises, especially mercies to public persons, Ps. cxvi. 18, 19. *Secondly,* " I will proceed and persevere in his praises." We should do so all the days of our life, because every day of our life is itself a fresh mercy and brings many fresh mercies along with it ; and, as renewed mercies call for renewed praises, so former eminent mercies call for repeated praises. It is by the mercy of God that we live, and therefore, as long as we live, we must continue to praise him, while we have breath, nay, while we have being. *Thirdly,* " I will propagate and perpetuate his praises." We should not only praise him all the days of our life, but *the father to the children should make known his truth,* that the ages to come may give God the glory of his truth by trusting to it. It is the duty of parents to possess their children with a confidence in the truth of God, which will go far towards keeping them close to the ways of God. Hezekiah, doubtless, did this himself, and yet Manasseh his son walked not in his steps. Parents may give their children many good things, good instructions, good examples, good books, but they cannot give them grace.

IV. In the last two verses of this chapter we have two passages relating to this story which were omitted in the narrative of it here, but which we had 2 Kings xx., and therefore shall here only observe two lessons from them :—1. That God's promises are intended not to supersede, but to quicken and encourage, the use of means. Hezekiah is sure to recover, and yet he must *take a lump of figs and lay it on the boil, v.* 21. We do not trust God, but tempt him, if, when we pray to him for help, we do not second our prayers with our endeavours. We must not put physicians, or physic, in the place of God, but make use of them in subordination to God and to his providence ; help thyself and God will help thee. 2. That the chief end we should aim at, in desiring life and health, is that we may glorify God, and do good, and improve ourselves in knowledge, and grace, and meetness for heaven. Hezekiah, when he meant, *What is the sign that I shall recover?* asked, *What is the sign that I shall go up to the house of the Lord,* there to honour God, to keep up acquaintance and communion with him, and to encourage others to serve him? *v.* 22. It is taken for granted that if God would restore him to health he would immediately go up to the temple with his thank-offerings. There Christ found the impotent man whom he had healed, John v. 14. The exercises of religion are so much the business and de-

light of a good man that to be restrained from them is the greatest grievance of his afflictions, and to be restored to them is the greatest comfort of his deliverances. *Let my soul live, and it shall praise thee.*

CHAP. XXXIX.

The story of this chapter likewise we had before, 2 Kings xx. 12, &c. It is here repeated, not only as a very memorable and improvable passage, but because it concludes with a prophecy of the captivity in Babylon ; and as the former part of the prophecy of this book frequently referred to Sennacherib's invasion and the defeat of that, to which therefore the history of that was very fitly subjoined, so the latter part of this book speaks much of the Jews' captivity in Babylon and their deliverance out of that, to which therefore the first prediction of it, with the occasion thereof, is very fitly prefixed. We have here, I. The pride and folly of Hezekiah, in showing his treasures to the king of Babylon's ambassadors that were sent to congratulate him on his recovery, ver. 1, 2. II. Isaiah's examination of him concerning it, in God's name, and his confession of it, ver. 3, 4. III. The sentence passed upon him for it, that all his treasures should, in process of time, be carried to Babylon, ver. 5—7. IV. Hezekiah's penitent and patient submission to this sentence, ver. 8.

AT that time Merodach-baladan, the son of Baladan, king of Babylon, sent letters and a present to Hezekiah : for he had heard that he had been sick, and was recovered. 2 And Hezekiah was glad of them, and showed them the house of his precious things, the silver, and the gold, and the spices, and the precious ointment, and all the house of his armour, and all that was found in his treasures : there was nothing in his house, nor in all his dominion, that Hezekiah showed them not. 3 Then came Isaiah the prophet unto king Hezekiah, and said unto him, What said these men? and from whence came they unto thee? And Hezekiah said, They are come from a far country unto me, *even* from Babylon. 4 Then said he, What have they seen in thine house? And Hezekiah answered, All that *is* in mine house have they seen : there is nothing among my treasures that I have not showed them.

Hence we may learn these lessons :—1. That humanity and common civility teach us to rejoice with our friends and neighbours when they rejoice, and to congratulate them on their deliverances, and particularly their recoveries from sickness. The king of Babylon, having heard that Hezekiah had been sick, and had recovered, sent to compliment him upon the occasion. If Christians be unneighbourly, heathens will shame them. 2. It becomes us to give honour to those whom our God puts honour upon. The sun was the Babylonians' god ; and when they understood that it was with a respect to Hezekiah that the sun, to their great surprise, went back ten degrees, on such a day, they thought themselves obliged to do Hezekiah all the honour they could. Will all people thus walk in the name of their God, and shall not we? 3. Those that do not value good men for their goodness may yet be brought to pay them great respect by other inducements, and for the sake of their secular interests. The king of Babylon made his court to Hezekiah, not because he was pious, but because he was prosperous, as the Philistines coveted an alliance with Isaac because they saw the Lord was with him, Gen. xxvi. 28. The king of Babylon was an enemy to the king of Assyria, and therefore was fond of Hezekiah, because the Assyrians were so much weakened by the power of his God. 4. It is a hard matter to keep the spirit low in the midst of great advancements. Hezekiah is an instance of it: he was a wise and good man, but, when one miracle after another was wrought in his favour, he found it hard to keep his heart from being lifted up, nay, a little thing then drew him into the snare of pride. Blessed Paul himself needed a thorn in the flesh, to keep him from being *lifted up with the abundance of revelations.* 5. We have need to watch over our own spirits when we are showing our friends our possessions, what we have done and what we have got, that we be not' proud of them, as if our might or our merit had purchased and procured us this wealth. When we look upon our enjoyments, and have occasion to speak of them, it must be with humble acknowledgments of our own unworthiness and thankful acknowledgments of God's goodness, with a just value for the achievements of others and with an expectation of losses and changes, not dreaming that our mountain stands so strong but that it may soon be moved. 6. It is a great weakness for good men to value themselves much upon the civil respects that are paid them (yea, though there be something particular and uncommon in them) by the children of this world, and to be fond of their acquaintance. What a poor thing was it for Hezekiah, whom God had so dignified, to be thus over proud of the respect paid him by a heathen prince as if that added any thing to him! We ought to return the courtesies of such with interest, but not to be proud of them. 7. We must expect to be called to an account for the workings of our pride, though they are secret, and in such instances as we thought there was no harm in; and therefore we ought to call ourselves to an account for them; and when we have had company with us that have paid us respect, and been pleased with their entertainment, and commended every thing, we ought to be jealous over ourselves with a godly jealousy lest our hearts have been lifted up. As far as we see cause to suspect that this sly and subtle sin of pride has insinuated itself into our breasts, and mingled itself with our conversation, let us be ashamed of it, and, as Hezekiah here,

210

ingenuously confess it and take shame to ourselves for it.

5 Then said Isaiah to Hezekiah, Hear the word of the Lord of hosts: 6 Behold, the days come, that all that *is* in thine house, and *that* which thy fathers have laid up in store until this day, shall be carried to Babylon: nothing shall be left, saith the Lord. 7 And of thy sons that shall issue from thee, which thou shalt beget, shall they take away; and they shall be eunuchs in the palace of the king of Babylon. 8 Then said Hezekiah to Isaiah, Good *is* the word of the Lord which thou hast spoken. He said moreover, For there shall be peace and truth in my days.

Hence let us observe, 1. That, if God love us, he will humble us, and will find some way or other to pull down our spirits when they are lifted up above measure. A mortifying message is sent to Hezekiah, that he might be humbled for the pride of his heart, and be convinced of the folly of it; for though God may suffer his people to fall into sin, as he did Hezekiah here, to *prove him, that he might know all that was in his heart,* yet he will not suffer them to lie still in it. 2. It is just with God to take that from us which we make the matter of our pride, and on which we build a carnal confidence. When David was proud of the numbers of his people God took a course to make them fewer; and when Hezekiah boasts of his treasures, and looks upon them with too great a complacency, he is told that he acts like the foolish traveller who shows his money and gold to one that proves a thief and is thereby tempted to rob him. 3. If we could but see things that will be, we should be ashamed of our thoughts of things that are. If Hezekiah had known that the seed and successors of this king of Babylon would hereafter be the ruin of his family and kingdom, he would not have complimented his ambassadors as he did; and, when the prophet told him that it would be so, we may well imagine how he was vexed at himself for what he had done. We cannot certainly foresee what will be, but are told, in general, *All is vanity,* and therefore it is vanity for us to take complacency and put confidence in any thing that goes under that character. 4. Those that are fond of an acquaintance or alliance with irreligious men will first or last have enough of it, and will have cause to repent it. Hezekiah thought himself very happy in the friendship of Babylon, though it was the mother of harlots and idolatries; but Babylon, who now courted Jerusalem, in process of time conquered her and carried her captive. Leagues with sinners, and leagues with sin too, will end thus ; it is therefore our wisdom to keep at a distance from them. 5. Those that truly repent of their sins will take it well to be reproved for them and will be willing to be told of their faults. Hezekiah reckoned *that* word of the Lord good which discovered sin to him, and made him sensible that he had done amiss, which before he was not aware of. The language of true penitents is, *Let the righteous smite me ; it shall be a kindness ;* and the law is *therefore* good, because, being spiritual, in it sin appears sin, and exceedingly sinful. 6. True penitents will quietly submit, not only to the reproofs of the word, but to the rebukes of Providence for their sins. When Hezekiah was told of the punishment of his iniquity he said, *Good is the word of the Lord,* not only the mitigation of the sentence, but the sentence itself; he has nothing to object against the equity of it, but says Amen to the threatening. Those that see the evil of sin, and what it deserves, will justify God in all that is brought upon them for it, and own that he punishes them less than their iniquities deserve. 7. Though we must not be regardless of those that come after us, yet we must reckon ourselves well done by if there be *peace and truth in our days,* and better than we had reason to expect. If a storm be coming, we must reckon it a favour to get into the harbour before it comes, and be gathered to the grave in peace ; yet we can never be secure of this, but must prepare for changes in our own time, that we may stand complete in all the will of God, and bid it welcome whatever it is.

CHAP. XL.

At this chapter begins the latter part of the prophecy of this book, which is not only divided from the former by the historical chapters that come between, but seems to be distinguished from it in the scope and style of it. In the former part the name of the prophet was frequently prefixed to the particular sermons, besides the general title (as ch. ii. 1 ; vii. 3 ; xiii. 1) ; but this is all one continued discourse, and the prophet not so much as once named. That consisted of many burdens, many woes ; this consists of many blessings. There the distress which the people of God were in by the Assyrian, and their deliverance out of that, were chiefly prophesied of ; but that is here spoken of as a thing past (ch. lii. 4) ; and the captivity in Babylon, and their deliverance out of that, which were much greater events, of more extensive and abiding concern, are here largely foretold. Before God sent his people into captivity he furnished them with precious promises for their support and comfort in their trouble ; and we may well imagine of what great use to them the glorious, gracious, light of this prophecy was, in that cloudy and dark day, and how much it helped to dry up their tears by the rivers of Babylon. But it looks further yet, and to greater things ; much of Christ and gospel grace we meet with in the foregoing part of this book, but in this latter part we shall find much more ; and, as if it were designed for a prophetic summary of the New Testament, it begins with that which begins the gospels, " The voice of one crying in the wilderness" (ch. xl. 3), and concludes with that which concludes the book of the Revelation, " The new heavens and the new earth," ch. lxvi. 22. Even Mr. White acknowledges that, as all the mercies of God to the Jewish nation bore some resemblance to those glorious things performed by our Saviour for man's redemption, so they are by the Spirit of God expressed in such terms as show plainly that while the prophet is speaking of the redemption of the Jews he had in his thoughts a more glorious deliverance. And we need not look for any further accomplishment of these prophecies yet to come ; for if Jesus be he, and his kingdom be it, that should come, we are to look for no other, but the carrying on and completing of the same blessed work which was begun in the first preaching and planting of Christianity in the world.

In this chapter we have, I. Orders given to preach and publish the glad tidings of redemption, ver. 1, 2. II. These glad tidings introduced by a voice in the wilderness, which gives assurance that all obstructions shall be removed (ver. 3—5); and that, though all

creatures fail and fade, the word of God shall be established and accomplished, ver. 6—8. III. A joyful prospect given to the people of God of the happiness which this redemption should bring along with it, ver. 9—11. IV. The sovereignty and power of that God magnified who undertakes to work out this redemption, ver. 12—17. V. Idols therefore triumphed over and idolaters upbraided with their folly, ver. 18—26. VI. A reproof given to the people of God for their fears and despondencies, and enough said, in a few words, to silence those fears, ver. 27—31. And we, through patience and comfort of this scripture, may have hope.

COMFORT ye, comfort ye my people, saith your God. 2 Speak ye comfortably to Jerusalem, and cry unto her, that her warfare is accomplished, that her iniquity is pardoned : for she hath received of the Lord's hand double for all her sins.

We have here the commission and instructions given, not to this prophet only, but, with him, to all the Lord's prophets, nay, and to all Christ's ministers, to proclaim comfort to God's people. 1. This did not only warrant, but enjoin, this prophet himself to encourage the good people who lived in his own time, who could not but have very melancholy apprehensions of things when they saw Judah and Jerusalem by their daring impieties ripening apace for ruin, and God in his providence hastening ruin upon them. Let them be sure that, notwithstanding all this, God had mercy in store for them. 2. It was especially a direction to the prophets that should live in the time of the captivity, when Jerusalem was in ruins ; they must encourage the captives to hope for enlargement in due time. 3. Gospel ministers, being employed by the blessed Spirit as comforters, and as helpers of the joy of Christians, are here put in mind of their business. Here we have,

I. Comfortable words directed to God's people in general, *v.* 1. The prophets have instructions from their God (for he is the *Lord God of the holy prophets,* Rev. xxii. 6) to comfort the people of God ; and the charge is doubled, *Comfort you, comfort you*—not because the prophets are unwilling to do it (no, it is the most pleasant part of their work), but because sometimes the souls of God's people refuse to be comforted, and their comforters must repeat things again and again, ere they can fasten any thing upon them. Observe here, 1. There are a people in the world that are God's people. 2. It is the will of God that his people should be a comforted people, even in the worst of times. 3. It is the work and business of ministers to do what they can for the comfort of God's people. 4. Words of conviction, such as we had in the former part of this book, must be followed with words of comfort, such as we have here ; for he that has torn will heal us.

II. Comfortable words directed to Jerusalem in particular : " *Speak to the heart of Jerusalem* (*v.* 2) ; speak that which will revive her heart, and be a cordial to her and

to all that belong to her and wish her well.
Do not whisper it, but *cry unto her :* cry
aloud, to show saints their comforts as well
as to show sinners their transgressions;
make her hear it :" 1. " That the days of
her trouble are numbered and finished :
Her warfare is accomplished, the set time of
her servitude; the campaign is now at an
end, and she shall retire into quarters of refreshment." Human life is a warfare (Job
vii. 1); the Christian life much more. But
the struggle will not last always; the
warfare will be accomplished, and then the
good soldiers shall not only enter into rest,
but be sure of their pay. 2. "That the cause
of her trouble is removed, and, when that is
taken away, the effect will cease. Tell her
that *her iniquity is pardoned,* God is reconciled to her, and she shall no longer be
treated as one guilty before him." Nothing
can be spoken more comfortably than this,
*Son, be of good cheer ; thy sins are forgiven
thee.* Troubles are *then* removed in love
when sin is pardoned. 3. " That the end
of her trouble is answered : *She has received
of the Lord double for* the cure of *all her sins,*
sufficient, and more than sufficient, to separate between her and her idols," the worship
of which was the great sin for which God
had a controversy with them, and from which
he designed to reclaim them by their captivity in Babylon : and it had that effect upon
them ; it begat in them a rooted antipathy to
idolatry, and was physic doubly strong for
the purging out of that iniquity. Or it may
be taken as the language of the divine compassion : *His soul was grieved for the misery
of Israel* (Judges x. 16), and, like a tender
father, *since he spoke against them he earnestly
remembered them* (Jer. xxxi. 20), and was
ready to say that he had given them too
much correction. They, being very penitent, acknowledged that God had *punished
them less than their iniquities deserved ;* but
he, being very pitiful, owned, in a manner,
that he had punished them more than they
deserved. True penitents have indeed, in
Christ and his sufferings, *received of the
Lord's hand double for all their sins ;* for the
satisfaction Christ made by his death was of
such an infinite value that it was more than
double to the demerits of sin ; *for God spared
not his own Son.*

3 The voice of him that crieth in
the wilderness, Prepare ye the way
of the Lord, make straight in the
desert a highway for our God. 4
Every valley shall be exalted, and
every mountain and hill shall be
made low : and the crooked shall be
made straight, and the rough places
plain : 5 And the glory of the Lord
shall be revealed, and all flesh shall
see *it* together : for the mouth of the

212

Lord hath spoken *it.* 6 The voice
said, Cry. And he said, What shall
I cry? All flesh *is* grass, and all the
goodliness thereof *is* as the flower of
the field : 7 The grass withereth, the
flower fadeth : because the Spirit of
the Lord bloweth upon it : surely
the people *is* grass. 8 The grass
withereth, the flower fadeth : but the
word of our God shall stand for ever.

The time to favour Zion, yea, the set time,
having come, the people of God must be
prepared, by repentance and faith, for the
favours designed them ; and, in order to
call them to both these, we have here *the
voice of one crying in the wilderness,* which
may be applied to those prophets who were
with the captives in their wilderness-state,
and who, when they saw the day of their
deliverance dawn, called earnestly upon them
to prepare for it, and assured them that all
the difficulties which stood in the way of
their deliverance should be got over. It is
a good sign that mercy is preparing for us if
we find God's grace preparing us for it, Ps.
x. 17. But it *must* be applied to John the
Baptist ; for, though God was the speaker,
he was *the voice of one crying in the wilderness,* and his business was to *prepare the
way of the Lord,* to dispose men's minds for
the reception and entertainment of the gospel
of Christ. The way of the Lord is prepared,
I. By repentance for sin ; that was it
which John Baptist preached to all Judah
and Jerusalem (Matt. iii. 2, 5), and thereby
made ready a people prepared for the Lord,
Luke i. 17.

1. The alarm is given ; let all take notice
of it at their peril ; God is coming in a way
of mercy, and we must prepare for him, *v.*
3—5. If we apply it to their captivity, it
may be taken as a promise that, whatever
difficulties lie in their way, when they return they shall be removed. This voice in
the wilderness (divine power going along
with it) sets pioneers on work to level the
roads. But it may be taken as a call to
duty, and it is the same duty that we are
called to, in preparation for Christ's entrance
into our souls. (1.) We must get into such
a frame of spirit as will dispose us to receive
Christ and his gospel : " *Prepare you the
way of the Lord;* prepare yourselves for him,
and let all that be suppressed which would
be an obstruction to his entrance Make
room for Christ : *Make straight a highway
for him.*" If he prepare the end for us, we
ought surely to prepare the way for him.
Prepare for the Saviour ; *lift up your heads,
O you gates!* Ps. xxiv. 7, 9. Prepare for
the salvation, the great salvation, and other
minor deliverances. Let us get to be fit for
them, and then God will work them out.
Let us not stand in our own light, nor put a
bar in our own door, but find, or make, a

highway for him, even in that which was desert ground. This is that for which he waits to be gracious. (2.) We must get our hearts levelled by divine grace. Those that are hindered from comfort in Christ by their dejections and despondencies are the valleys that must be exalted. Those that are hindered from comfort in Christ by a proud conceit of their own merit and worth are the mountains and hills that must be made low. Those that have entertained prejudices against the word and ways of God, that are untractable, and disposed to thwart and contradict even that which is plain and easy because it agrees not with their corrupt inclinations and secular interests, are the crooked that must be made straight and the rough places that must be made plain. Let but the gospel of Christ have a fair hearing, and it cannot fail of acceptance. This prepares the way of the Lord; and thus God will by his grace prepare his own way in all the vessels of mercy, whose hearts he opens as he did Lydia's.

2. When this is done *the glory of the Lord shall be revealed, v.* 5. (1.) When the captives are prepared for deliverance Cyrus shall proclaim it, and those shall have the benefit of it, and those only, whose hearts the Lord shall stir up with courage and resolution to break through the discouragements that lay in their way, and to make nothing of the hills, and valleys, and all the rough places. (2.) When John Baptist has for some time preached repentance, mortification, and reformation, and so made ready a people prepared for the Lord (Luke i. 17), then the Messiah himself shall be revealed in his glory, working miracles, which John did not, and by his grace, which is his glory, binding up and healing with consolations those whom John had wounded with convictions. And this revelation of divine glory shall be *a light to lighten the Gentiles. All flesh shall see it together,* and not the Jews only; they shall see and admire it, see it and bid it welcome; as the return out of captivity was taken notice of by the neighbouring nations, Ps. cxxvi. 2. And it shall be the accomplishment of the word of God, not one *iota* or tittle of which shall fall to the ground : *The mouth of the Lord has spoken it,* and therefore the hand of the Lord will effect it.

II. By confidence in the word of the Lord, and not in any creature. *The mouth of the Lord having spoken it,* the voice has this further to cry (he that has ears to hear let him hear it), *The word of our God shall stand for ever, v.* 8.

1. By this accomplishment of the prophecies and promises of salvation, and the performance of them to the utmost in due time, it appears that the word of the Lord is sure and what may be safely relied on. *Then* we are prepared for deliverance when we depend entirely upon the word of God, build our hopes on that, with an assurance that it will not make us ashamed : in a dependence upon this word we must be brought to own that *all flesh is grass,* withering and fading. (1.) The power of man, when it does appear against the deliverance, is not to be feared; for it shall be as grass before the word of the Lord : it shall wither and be trodden down. The insulting Babylonians, who promise themselves that the desolations of Jerusalem shall be perpetual, are but as grass which the Spirit of the Lord blows upon, makes nothing of, but blasts all its glory; for the word of the Lord, which promises their deliverance, shall stand for ever, and it is not in the power of their enemies to hinder the execution of it. (2.) The power of man, when it would appear for the deliverance, is not to be trusted to; for it is but as grass in comparison with the word of the Lord, which is the only firm foundation for us to build our hope upon. When God is about to work salvation for his people he will take them off from depending upon creatures, and looking for it from hills and mountains. They shall fail them, and their expectations from them shall be frustrated : *The Spirit of the Lord shall blow upon them ;* for God will have no creature to be a rival with him for the hope and confidence of his people; and, as it is his word only that shall stand for ever, so in that word only our faith must stand. When we are brought to this, then, and not till then, we are fit for mercy.

2. The word of our God, that glory of the Lord which is now to be revealed, the gospel, and that grace which is brought with it to us and wrought by it in us, shall stand for ever ; and this is the satisfaction of all believers, when they find all their creature-comforts withering and fading like grass. Thus the apostle applies it to *the word which by the gospel is preached unto us, and which lives and abides for ever as the incorruptible seed by which we are born again,* 1 Pet. i. 23—25. To prepare the way of the Lord we must be convinced, (1.) Of the vanity of the creature, that all flesh is grass, weak and withering. We ourselves are so, and therefore cannot save ourselves ; all our friends are so, and therefore are unable to save us. All the beauty of the creature, which might render it amiable, is but as the flower of grass, soon blasted, and therefore cannot recommend us to God and to his acceptance. We are dying creatures; all our comforts in this world are dying comforts, and therefore cannot be the felicity of our immortal souls. We must look further for a salvation, look further for a portion. (2.) Of the validity of the promise of God. We must be convinced that the word of the Lord can do that for us which all flesh cannot—that, forasmuch as it stands for ever, it will furnish us with a happiness that will run parallel with the duration of our souls, which must live for ever; for the things that are not seen, but must be believed, are eternal.

9 O Zion, that bringest good tidings, get thee up into the high mountain; O Jerusalem, that bringest good tidings, lift up thy voice with strength; lift *it* up, be not afraid; say unto the cities of Judah, Behold your God! 10 Behold, the Lord GOD will come with strong *hand*, and his arm shall rule for him: behold, his reward *is* with him, and his work before him. 11 He shall feed his flock like a shepherd: he shall gather the lambs with his arm, and carry *them* in his bosom, *and* shall gently lead those that are with young.

It was promised (*v.* 5) *that the glory of the Lord shall be revealed;* that is it with the hopes of which God's people must be comforted. Now here we are told,

I. How it shall be revealed, *v.* 9. 1. It shall be revealed to Zion and Jerusalem; notice shall be given of it to the remnant that are left in Zion and Jerusalem, the poor of the land, who were vine-dressers and husbandmen; it shall be told them that their brethren shall return to them. This shall be told also to the captives who belonged to Zion and Jerusalem, and retained their affection for them. Zion is said to *dwell with the daughter of Babylon* (Zech. ii. 7); and there she receives notice of Cyrus's gracious proclamation; and so the margin reads it, *O thou that tellest good tidings to Zion, &c.*, meaning the persons who were employed in publishing that proclamation; let them do it with a good will, let them make the country ring of it, and let them tell it to the sons of Zion in their own language, *saying to them, Behold your God.* 2. It shall be published by Zion and Jerusalem (so the text reads it); those that remain there, or that have already returned, when they find the deliverance proceeding towards perfection, let them proclaim it in the most public places, whence they may be best heard by all the cities of Judah; let them proclaim it as loudly as they can: let them *lift up their voice with strength*, and not be afraid of overstraining themselves; let them not be afraid lest the enemy should hear it and quarrel with them, or lest it should not prove true, or not such good tidings as at first it appeared; let them say to the cities of Judah, and all the inhabitants of the country, *Behold your God.* When God is going on with the salvation of his people, let them industriously spread the news among their friends, let them tell them that it is God that has done it; whoever were the instruments, God was the author; it is *their* God, a God in covenant with them, and he does it as theirs, and they will reap the benefit and comfort of it. " Behold him, take
214

notice of his hand in it, and look above second causes; behold, the God you have long looked for has come at last (*ch.* xxv. 9): *This is our God, we have waited for him.*" This may refer to the invitation which was sent forth from Jerusalem to the cities of Judah, as soon as they had set up an altar, immediately upon their return out of captivity, to come and join with them in their sacrifices, Ezra iii. 2—4. " When the worship of God is set up again, send notice of it to all your brethren, that they may share with you in the comfort of it." But this was to have its full accomplishment in the apostles' public and undaunted preaching of the gospel to all nations, beginning at Jerusalem. The voice crying in the wilderness gave notice that he was coming; but now notice is given that he has come. *Behold the Lamb of God;* take a full view of your Redeemer. Behold your King, behold your God.

II. What that glory is which shall be revealed. " Your God will come, will show himself,"

1. " With the power and greatness of a prince (*v.* 10): *He will come with strong hand,* too strong to be obstructed, though it may be opposed. His strong hand sha l subdue his people to himself, and shall re. strain and conquer his and their enemies. He will come who is strong enough to break through all the difficulties that lie in his way." Our Lord Jesus was full of power, a mighty Saviour. Some read it, *He will come against the mighty one,* and overpower him, overcome him. Satan is the strong man armed; but our Lord Jesus is stronger than he, and he shall make it to appear that he is so, for, (1.) He shall reign in defiance of all opposition: *His arm shall rule,* shall overrule *for him,* for the fulfilling of his counsels, to his own glory; for he is his own end. (2.) He shall recompense to all according to their works, as a righteous Judge: *His reward is with him;* he brings along with him, as a returning prince, punishments for the rebels and preferments for his loyal subjects. (3.) He shall proceed and accomplish his purpose: *His work is before him,* that is, he knows perfectly well what he has to do, which way to go about it, and how to compass it. *He himself knows what he will do.*

2. " With the pity and tenderness of a shepherd," *v.* 11. God is the *Shepherd of Israel* (Ps. lxxx. 1); Christ is the good Shepherd, John x. 11. The same that rules with the strong hand of a prince leads and feeds with the kind hand of a shepherd. (1.) He takes care of all his flock, the little flock: *He shall feed his flock like a shepherd.* His word is food for his flock to feed on; his ordinances are fields for them to feed in; his ministers are under-shepherds that are appointed to attend them. (2.) He takes particular care of those that most need his care,

the lambs that are weak, and cannot help themselves, and are unaccustomed to hardship, and *those that are with young,* that are therefore heavy, and, if any harm be done them, are in danger of casting their young. He particularly takes care for a succession, that it may not fail or be cut off. The good Shepherd has a tender care for children that are towardly and hopeful, for young converts, that are setting out in the way to heaven, for weak believers, and those that are of a sorrowful spirit. These are the lambs of his flock, that shall be sure to want nothing that their case requires. [1.] He will gather them in the arms of his power; his strength shall be made *perfect in their weakness,* 2 Cor. xii. 9. He will gather them in when they wander, gather them up when they fall, gather them together when they are dispersed, and gather them home to himself at last; and all this with his own arm, out of which none shall be able to pluck them, John x. 28. [2.] He will carry them in the bosom of his love and cherish them there. When they tire or are weary, are sick and faint, when they meet with foul ways, he will carry them on, and take care they be not left behind. [3.] He will gently lead them. By his word he requires no more service, and by his providence he inflicts no more trouble, than he will fit them for; for he considers their frame.

12 Who hath measured the waters in the hollow of his hand, and meted out heaven with a span, and comprehended the dust of the earth in a measure, and weighed the mountains in scales, and the hills in a balance? 13 Who hath directed the Spirit of the Lord, or *being* his counsellor hath taught him? 14 With whom took he counsel, and *who* instructed him, and taught him in the path of judgment, and taught him knowledge, and showed to him the way of understanding? 15 Behold, the nations *are* as a drop of a bucket, and are counted as the small dust of the balance: behold, he taketh up the isles as a very little thing. 16 And Lebanon *is* not sufficient to burn, nor the beasts thereof sufficient for a burnt-offering. 17 All nations before him *are* as nothing; and they are counted to him less than nothing, and vanity.

The scope of these verses is to show what a great and glorious being the Lord Jehovah is, who is Israel's God and Saviour. It comes in here, 1. To encourage his people that were captives in Babylon to hope in him, and to depend upon him for deliver-

ance, though they were ever so weak and their oppressors ever so strong. 2. To engage them to cleave to him, and not to turn aside after other gods; for there are none to be compared with him. 3. To possess all those who receive the glad tidings of redemption by Christ with a holy awe and reverence of God. Though it was said (*v.* 9), *Behold your God,* and (*v.* 11) *He shall feed his flock like a shepherd,* yet these condescensions of his grace must not be thought of with any diminution to the transcendencies of his glory. Let us see how great our God is, and fear before him; for,

I. His power is unlimited, and what no creature can compare with, much less contend with, *v.* 12. 1. He has a vast reach. View the celestial globe, and you are astonished at the extent of it; but the great God *metes the heavens with a span;* to him they are but a hand-breadth, so large-handed is he. View the terraqueous globe, and he has the command of that too. All the waters in the world he can *measure in the hollow of his hand,* where we can hold but a little water; and the dry land he easily manages, for he *comprehends the dust of the earth in a measure,* or with his three fingers; it is no more to him than a *pugil,* or that which we take up between our thumb and two fingers. 2. He has a vast strength, and can as easily move mountains and hills as the tradesman heaves his goods into the scales and out of them again; he poises them with his hand as exactly as if he weighed them in a pair of balances. This may refer to the work of creation, when the heavens were stretched out as exactly as that which is spanned, and the earth and waters were put together in just proportions, as if they had been measured, and the mountains made of such a weight as to serve for ballast to the globe, and no more. Or it may refer to the work of providence (which is a continued creation) and the consistency of all the creatures with each other.

II. His wisdom is unsearchable, and what no creature can give either information or direction to, *v.* 13, 14. As none can do what God has done and does, so none can assist him in the doing of it or suggest any thing to him which he thought not of. When the Lord by his Spirit made the world (Job xxvi. 13) there was none that directed his Spirit, or gave him any advice, either what to do or how to do it. Nor does he need any counsellor to direct him in the government of the world, nor is there any with whom he consults, as the wisest kings do with those that *know law and judgment,* Esther i. 13. God needs not to be told what is done, for he knows it perfectly; nor needs he be advised concerning what is to be done, for he knows both the right end and the proper means. This is much insisted upon here, because the poor captives had no politicians among them to manage their concerns at court or to put them in a way of gaining their liberty. "No matter," says the prophet; "you have a God to act for you, who needs not the assistance of statesmen." In the great work of our redemption by Christ matters were concerted *before the world was,* when there was none to *teach God in the path of judgment,* 1 Cor. ii. 7.

III. The nations of the world are nothing in comparison of him, *v.* 15, 17. Take them all together, all the great and mighty nations of the earth, kings the most pompous, kingdoms the most populous, both the most wealthy; take the isles, the multitude of them, the isles of the Gentiles: *Before him,* when they stand in competition with him or in opposition to him, they are *as a drop of the bucket* compared with the vast ocean, or *the small dust of the balance* (which does not serve to turn it, and therefore is not regarded, it is so small) in comparison with all the dust of the earth. *He takes them up,* and throws them away from him, *as a very little thing,* not worth speaking of. They are all in his eye *as nothing,* as if they had no being at all; for they add nothing to his perfection and all-sufficiency. *They are counted by him,* and are to be counted by us in comparison of him, *less than nothing, and vanity.* When he pleases, he can as easily bring them all into nothing as at first he brought them out of nothing. When God has work to do he values not either the assistance or the resistance of any creature. They are all *vanity;* the word that is used for the chaos (Gen. i. 2), to which they will at last be reduced. Let this beget in us high thoughts of God and low thoughts of this world, and engage us to make God, and not man, both our fear and our hope. This magnifies God's love to the world, that, though it is of such small account and value with him, yet, for the redemption of it, he *gave his only-begotten Son,* John iii. 16.

IV. The services of the church can make no addition to him nor do they bear any proportion to his infinite perfections (*v.* 16): *Lebanon is not sufficient to burn;* not the wood of it, to be for the fuel of the altar, though it be so well stocked with cedars; not the beasts of it, to be for sacrifices, though it be so well stocked with cattle, *v.* 16. Whatever we honour God with, it falls infinitely short of the merit of his perfection; for he is exalted *far above all blessing and praise,* all burnt-offerings and sacrifices.

18 To whom then will ye liken God? Or what likeness will ye compare unto him? 19 The workman melteth a graven image, and the goldsmith spreadeth it over with gold, and casteth silver chains. 20 He that *is* so impoverished that he hath no oblation, chooseth a tree *that* will not rot; he seeketh unto him a cun-

216

ning workman to prepare a graven image, *that* shall not be moved. 21 Have ye not known? Have ye not heard? Hath it not been told you from the beginning? Have ye not understood from the foundations of the earth? 22 *It is* he that sitteth upon the circle of the earth, and the inhabitants thereof *are* as grasshoppers; that stretcheth out the heavens as a curtain, and spreadeth them out as a tent to dwell in: 23 That bringeth the princes to nothing; he maketh the judges of the earth as vanity. 24 Yea, they shall not be planted; yea, they shall not be sown: yea, their stock shall not take root in the earth: and he shall also blow upon them, and they shall wither, and the whirlwind shall take them away as stubble. 25 To whom then will ye liken me, or shall I be equal? saith the Holy One. 26 Lift up your eyes on high, and behold who hath created these *things,* that bringeth out their host by number: he calleth them all by names by the greatness of his might, for that *he is* strong in power; not one faileth.

The prophet here reproves those, 1. Who represented God by creatures, and so changed his truth into a lie and his glory into shame, who made images and then said that they resembled God, and paid their homage to them accordingly. 2. Who put creatures in the place of God, who feared them more than God, as if they were a match for him, or loved them more than God, as if they were fit to be rivals with him. Twice the challenge is here made, *To whom will you liken God?* v. 18, and again v. 25. The Holy One himself says, *To whom will you liken me?* This shows the folly and absurdity, (1.) Of corporal idolatry, making visible images of him who is invisible, imagining the image to be animated by the deity, and the deity to be presentiated by the image, which, as it was an instance of the corruption of the human nature, so it was an intolerable injury to the honour of the divine nature. (2.) Of spiritual idolatry, making creatures equal with God in our affections. Proud people make themselves equal with God; covetous people make their money equal with God; and whatever we esteem or love, fear or hope in, more than God, that creature we equal with God, which is the highest affront imaginable to him who is *God over all.* Now, to show the absurdity of this,

I. The prophet describes idols as despicable things, and worthy of the greatest contempt (v. 19, 20): "Look upon the better sort of them, which rich people set up, and worship; they are made of some base metal, cast into what shape the founder pleases, and that is gilded, or overlaid with plates of gold, that it may pass for a golden image. It is a creature; for the workman made it; *therefore it is not God,* Hos. viii. 6. It depended upon his will whether it should be a god at all, and of what shape it should be. It is a cheat; for it is gold on the outside, but within it is lead or copper, in this indeed representing the deities, that they were not what they seemed to be, and deceived their admirers. How despicable then are the worst sort of them—the poor men's gods! *He that is so impoverished* that he has scarcely a sacrifice to offer to his god when he has made him will yet not be without an enshrined deity of his own; and, though he cannot procure one of brass or stone, he will have a wooden one rather than none, and for that purpose *chooses a tree that will not soon rot,* and of that he will have his graven image made. Both agree to have their image well fastened, that they may not be robbed of it. The better sort have silver chains to fix theirs with; and, though it be but a wooden image, care is taken that it *shall not be moved."* Let us pause a little and see, 1. How these idolaters shame themselves, and what a reproach they put upon their own reason, in dreaming that gods of their own making (*Nehushtans,* pieces of brass or logs of wood) should be able to do them any kindness. Thus vain were they in their imaginations; and how was their foolish heart darkened! 2. See how these idolaters shame us, who worship the only living and true God. They spared no cost upon their idols; we grudge that as waste which is spent in the service of our God. They took care that their idols should not be moved; we wilfully provoke our God to depart from us.

II. He describes God as infinitely great, and worthy of the highest veneration; so that between him and idols, whatever competition there may be, there is no comparison. To prove the greatness of God he appeals,

1. To what they had *heard of him by the hearing of the ear,* and the consent of all ages and nations concerning him (v. 21): "*Have you not known* by the very light of nature? *Has it not been told you by your fathers* and teachers, according to the constant tradition received from their ancestors and predecessors, even from the beginning?" (Those notices of God are as ancient as the world.) "*Have you not understood* it as always acknowledged *from the foundation of the earth,* that God is a great God, and a great King above all gods?" It has been a truth universally admitted that there is an infinite Being who is the fountain of all

being. This is understood not only ever since the beginning of the world, but from and by the origin of the universe. It is founded upon the foundation of the earth. The invisible things of God are *clearly seen from the creation of the world,* Rom. i. 20. Thou mayest not only ask thy father, and he shall tell thee this, and thy elders (Deut. xxxii. 7); but *ask those that go by the way* (Job xxi. 29), ask the first man you meet, and he will say the same. Some read it, *Will you not know? Will you not hear?* For those that are ignorant of this are willingly ignorant; the light shines in their faces, but they shut their eyes against it. Now that which is here said of God is, (1.) That he has the command of all the creatures. The heaven and the earth themselves are under his management: *He sits upon the circle,* or globe, *of the earth, v.* 22. He that has the special residence of his glory in the upper world maintains a dominion over this lower world, gives law to it, and directs all the motions of it to his own glory. He sits undisturbed upon the earth, and so establishes it. He is still stretching out the heavens, his power and providence keep them still stretched out, and will do so till the day comes that they shall be rolled together like a scroll. He spreads them out as easily as we draw a curtain to and fro, opening these curtains in the morning and drawing them close again at night. And the heaven is to this earth *as a tent to dwell in;* it is a canopy drawn over our heads, *et quod tegit omnia cœlum—and it encircles all.*—Ovid. See Ps. civ. 2. (2.) That the children of men, even the greatest and mightiest, are as nothing before him. The numerous inhabitants of this earth are in his eye as grasshoppers in ours, so little and inconsiderable, of such small value, of such little use, and so easily crushed. Proud men's lifting up themselves is but like the grasshopper's leap; in an instant they must stoop down to the earth again. If the spies thought themselves grasshoppers before the sons of Anak (Num. xiii. 33), what are we before the great God? Grasshoppers live but awhile, and live carelessly, not like the ant; so do the most of men. (3.) That those who appear and act against him, how formidable soever they may be to their fellow-creatures, will certainly be humbled and brought down by the mighty hand of God, v. 23, 24. Princes and judges, who have great authority, and abuse it to the support of oppression and injustice, make nothing of those about them; *as for all their enemies they puff* at them (Ps. x. 5; xii. 5); but, when the great God takes them to task, he brings them to nothing; he humbles them, and tames them, and makes them as vanity, little regarded, neither feared nor loved. He makes them utterly unable to stand before his judgments, which shall either, [1.] Prevent their settlement in their authority: *They* shall not be planted ; *they shall not be sown ;* and those are the two ways of propagating plants, either by seed or slips. Nay, if they should gain a little interest, and so be planted or sown, yet *their stock shall not take root in the earth,* they shall not continue long in power. Eliphaz saw the foolish taking root, but *suddenly cursed their habitation.* And then how soon is the fig-tree withered away ! Or, [2.] He will blast them when they think they are settled. He does but *blow upon them,* and then *they shall wither,* and come to nothing, and *the whirlwind shall take them away as stubble.* For God's wrath, though it seem at first to blow slightly upon them, will soon become a mighty whirlwind. When God judges he will overcome. Those that will not bow before him cannot stand before him.

2. He appeals to what *their eyes saw of him* (v. 26) : *" Lift up your eyes on high ;* be not always poring on this earth" *(O curvæ in terras animæ et cœlestium inanes !—Degenerate minds, that can bend so towards the the earth, having nothing celestial in them !),* " but sometimes look up" *(Os homini sublime dedit, cœlumque tueri jussit—Heaven gave to man an erect countenance, and bade him gaze on the stars) ;* " behold the glorious lights of heaven, consider who has created them. They neither made nor marshalled themselves ; doubtless, therefore, there is a God that gave them their being, power, and motion." What we see of the creature should lead us to the Creator. The idolaters, when they lifted up their eyes and beheld the hosts of heaven, being wholly immerged in sense, looked no further, but worshipped them, Deut. iv. 19 ; Job xxxi. 26. Therefore the prophet here directs us to make use of our reason as well as our senses, and to consider who created them, and to pay our homage to him. Give him the glory of his sovereignty over them—He *brings out their host by number,* as a general draws out the squadrons and battalions of his army ; of the knowledge he has of them—*He calls them all by names,* proper names, according as their place and influence are (Ps. cxlvii. 4) ; and of the use he makes of them ; when he calls them out to any service, so obsequious are they that, *by the greatness of his might, not one of them fails,* but, as when *the stars in their courses fought against Sisera,* every one does that to which he is appointed. To make these creatures therefore rivals with God, which are such ready servants to him, is an injury to them as well as an affront to him.

27 Why sayest thou, O Jacob, and speakest, O Israel, My way is hid from the LORD, and my judgment is passed over from my God? 28 Hast thou not known? hast thou not heard, *that* the everlasting God, the LORD, the Creator

218

of the ends of the earth, fainteth not, neither is weary? *There is* no searching of his understanding. 29 He giveth power to the faint ; and to *them that have* no might, he increaseth strength. 30 Even the youths shall faint and be weary, and the young men shall utterly fall : 31 But they that wait upon the LORD shall renew *their* strength ; they shall mount up with wings as eagles ; they shall run, and not be weary ; *and* they shall walk, and not faint.

Here, I. The prophet reproves the people of God, who are now supposed to be captives in Babylon for their unbelief and distrust of God, and the dejections and despondencies of their spirit under their affliction (v. 27) : *" Why sayest thou, O Jacob !* to thyself and to those about thee, *My way is hidden from the Lord ?* Why dost thou make hard and melancholy conclusions concerning thyself and thy present case, as if the latter were desperate ?" 1. The titles he here gives them were enough to shame them out of their distrusts : *O Jacob ! O Israel !* Let them remember whence they took these names—from one who had found God faithful to him and kind in all his straits ; and why they bore these names—as God's professing people, a people in covenant with him. 2. The way of reproving them is by reasoning with them : "Why? Consider whether thou hast any ground to say so." Many of our foolish frets and foolish fears would vanish before a strict enquiry into the causes of them. 3. That which they are reproved for is an ill-natured, ill-favoured, word they spoke of God, as if he had cast them off. There seems to be an emphasis laid upon their saying it : Why *sayest* thou and *speakest* thou ? It is bad to have evil thoughts rise in our mind, but it is worse to put an imprimatur—a sanction to them, and turn them into evil words. David reflects with regret upon what he said in his haste, when he was in distress. 4. The ill word they said was a word of despair concerning their present calamitous condition. They were ready to conclude, (1.) That God would not heed them : *" My way is hidden from the Lord ;* he takes no notice of our straits, nor concerns himself any more in our concernments. There are such difficulties in our case that even divine wisdom and power will be nonplussed." A man *whose way is hidden* is one whom *God has hedged in,* Job iii. 23. (2.) That God could not help them : *" My judgment is passed over from my God ;* my case is past relief, so far past it that God himself cannot redress the grievances of it. *Our bones are dried."* Ezek. xxxvii. 11.

II. He reminds them of that which, if duly considered, was sufficient to silence all those fears and distrusts. For their conviction, as before for the conviction of idolaters (*v.* 21), he appeals to what they had known and what they had heard. Jacob and Israel were a knowing people, or might have been, and their knowledge came by hearing; for Wisdom cried in their chief places of concourse. Now, among other things, they had heard that *God had spoken once, twice,* yea, many a time they had *heard it, That power belongs unto God* (Ps. lxii. 11), That is,

1. He is himself an almighty God. He must needs be so, for he is *the everlasting God, even Jehovah.* He was from eternity; he will be to eternity; and therefore with him there is no deficiency, no decay. He has his being of himself, and therefore all his perfections must needs be boundless. He is without beginning of days or end of life, and therefore with him there is no change. He is also *the Creator of the ends of the earth,* that is, of the whole earth and all that is in it from end to end. He therefore is the rightful owner and ruler of all, and must be concluded to have an absolute power over all and an all-sufficiency to help his people in their greatest straits. Doubtless he is still as able to save his church as he was at first to make the world. (1.) He has wisdom to contrive the salvation, and that wisdom is never at a loss: *There is no searching out of his understanding,* so as to countermine the counsels of it and defeat its intentions; no, nor so as to determine what he will do, for he has ways by himself, ways in the sea. None can say, "Thus far God's wisdom can go, and no further;" for, when we know not what to do, he knows. (2.) He has power to bring about the salvation, and that power is never exhausted: *He faints not, nor is weary;* he upholds the whole creation, and governs all the creatures, and is neither tired nor toiled; and therefore, no doubt, he has power to relieve his church, when it is brought ever so low, without weakness or weariness.

2. He gives strength and power to his people, and helps them by enabling them to help themselves. He that is the strong God is the strength of Israel. (1.) He can help the weak, *v.* 29. Many a time *he gives power to the faint,* to those that are ready to faint away; and *to those that have no might he* not only gives, but *increases strength,* as there is more and more occasion for it. Many out of bodily weakness are wonderfully recovered, and made strong, by the providence of God: and many that are feeble in spirit, timorous and faint-hearted, unfit for services and sufferings, are yet strengthened by the grace of God *with all might in the inward man.* To those who are sensible of their weakness, and ready to acknowledge they have no might, God does in a special manner increase strength; for, *when we are weak* in ourselves, *then are we strong in the Lord.* (2.) He will help the willing, will help those who, in a humble dependence

upon him, help themselves, and will do well for those who do their best, *v.* 30, 31. Those who trust to their own sufficiency, and are so confident of it that they neither exert themselves to the utmost nor seek unto God for his grace, are *the youths* and *the young men,* who are strong, but are apt to think themselves stronger than they are. And they *shall faint and be weary,* yea, they *shall utterly fail* in their services, in their conflicts, and under their burdens; they shall soon be made to see the folly of trusting to themselves. *But those that wait on the Lord,* who make conscience of their duty to him, and by faith rely upon him and commit themselves to his guidance, shall find that God will not fail them. [1.] They shall have grace sufficient for them: They *shall renew their strength* as their work is renewed, as there is new occasion; they shall be anointed, and their lamps supplied, with fresh oil. God will be their *arm every morning, ch.* xxxiii. 2. If at any time they have been foiled and weakened they shall recover themselves, and so renew their strength. Heb. *They shall change their strength,* as their work is changed—doing work, suffering work; they shall have strength to labour, strength to wrestle, strength to resist, strength to bear. As the day so shall the strength be. [2.] They shall use this grace for the best purposes. Being strengthened, *First,* They shall soar upward, upward towards God: *They shall mount up with wings like eagles,* so strongly, so swiftly, so high and heaven-ward. In the strength of divine grace, their souls shall ascend above the world, and even enter into the holiest. Pious and devout affections are the eagles' wings on which gracious souls mount up, Ps. xxv. 1. *Secondly,* They shall press forward, forward towards heaven. They shall walk, they shall run, the way of God's commandments, cheerfully and with alacrity (they *shall not be weary*), constantly and with perseverance (they *shall not faint*); and therefore in due season they shall reap. Let Jacob and Israel therefore, in their greatest distresses, continue waiting upon God, and not despair of timely and effectual relief and succour from him.

CHAP. XLI.

This chapter, as the former, is intended both for the conviction of idolaters and for the consolation of all God's faithful worshippers; for the Spirit is sent, and ministers are employed by him, both to convince and to comfort. And however this might be primarily intended for the conviction of Babylonians, and the comfort of Israelites, or for the conviction of those in Israel that were addicted to idolatry, as multitudes were, and the comfort of those that kept their integrity, doubtless it was intended both for admonition and encouragement to us, admonition to keep ourselves from idols and encouragement to trust in God. Here, I. God by the prophet shows the folly of those that worshipped idols, especially that thought their idols able to contest with him and control him, ver. 1—9. II. He encourages his faithful ones to trust in him, with an assurance that he would take their part against their enemies, make them victorious over them, and bring about a happy change of their affairs, ver. 10—20. III. He challenges the idols, that were rivals with him for men's adoration, to vie with him either for knowledge or power, either to show things to come or to do good or evil, ver. 21—29. So that the chapter may be summed up in those words of Elijah, "If Jehovah be God, then follow him; but, if Baal be God, then follow him;" and in the people's acknowledgment, upon the issue of the trial, " Jehovah he is the God, Jehovah he is the God."

KEEP silence before me, O islands; and let the people renew *their* strength : let them come near ; then let them speak : let us come near together to judgment. 2 Who raised up the righteous *man* from the east, called him to his foot, gave the nations before him, and made *him* rule over kings? He gave *them* as the dust to his sword, *and* as driven stubble to his bow. 3 He pursued them, *and* passed safely ; *even* by the way *that* he had not gone with his feet. 4 Who hath wrought and done *it*, calling the generations from the beginning? I the LORD, the first, and with the last ; I *am* he. 5 The isles saw *it*, and feared ; the ends of the earth were afraid, drew near, and came. 6 They helped every one his neighbour ; and *every one* said to his brother, Be of good courage. 7 So the carpenter encouraged the goldsmith, *and* he that smootheth *with* the hammer him that smote the anvil, saying, It *is* ready for the soldering : and he fastened it with nails, *that* it should not be moved. 8 But thou, Israel, *art* my servant, Jacob whom I have chosen, the seed of Abraham my friend. 9 *Thou* whom I have taken from the ends of the earth, and called thee from the chief men thereof, and said unto thee, Thou *art* my servant ; I have chosen thee, and not cast thee away.

That particular instance of God's care for his people Israel in raising up Cyrus to be their deliverer is here insisted upon as a great proof both of his sovereignty above all idols and of his power to protect his people. Here is,

I. A general challenge to the worshippers and admirers of idols to make good their pretensions, in competition with God and opposition to him, *v.* 1. It is renewed (*v.* 21) : *Produce your cause.* The court is set, summonses are sent to the islands that lay most remote, but not out of God's jurisdiction, for he is the *Creator and possessor of the ends of the earth*, to make their appearance and give their attendance. Silence (as usual) is proclaimed while the cause is in trying : " *Keep silence before me*, and judge nothing before the time ;" while the cause is in trying between the kingdom of God and the kingdom of Satan it becomes all people silently to expect the issue, not to object

220

against God's proceedings, but to be confident that he will carry the day. The defenders of idolatry are called to say what they can in defence of it : " *Let them renew their strength*, in opposition to God, and see whether it be equal to the strength which those renew that wait upon him (*ch.* xl. 31); let them try their utmost efforts, whether by force of arms or force of argument. *Let them come near ;* they shall not complain that God's *dread makes them afraid* (Job xiii. 21), so that they cannot say what they have to say, in vindication and honour of their idols ; no, *let them speak* freely : *Let us come near together to judgment.*" Note, 1. The cause of God and his kingdom is not afraid of a fair trial ; if the case be but fairly stated, it will be surely carried in favour of religion. 2. The enemies of God's church and his holy religion may safely be challenged to say and do their worst for the support of their unrighteous cause. He that *sits in heaven laughs at them*, and the *daughter of Zion despises them ;* for *great is the truth and will prevail.*

II. He particularly challenges the idols to do that for their worshippers, and against his, which he had done and would do for his worshippers, and against theirs. Different senses are given of *v.* 2, concerning *the righteous man raised up from the east ;* and, since we cannot determine which is the true, we will make use of each as good.

1. That which is to be proved is, (1.) That *the Lord is God* alone, *the first and with the last* (*v.* 4), that he is infinite, eternal, and unchangeable, that he governed the world from the beginning, and will to the end of time. He has reigned of old, and will reign for ever ; the counsels of his kingdom were from eternity, and the continuance of it will be to eternity. (2.) That *Israel* is *his servant* (*v.* 8), whom he owns, and protects, and employs, and in whom he is and will be glorified. As there is a God in heaven, so there is a church on earth that is his particular care. Elijah prays (1 Kings xviii. 36), *Let it be known that thou art God, and that I am thy servant.* Now,

2. To prove this he shows,

(1.) That it was he who called Abraham, the father of this despised nation, out of an idolatrous country, and by many instances of his favour *made his name great*, Gen. xii. 2. He is *the righteous man whom God raised up from the east.* Of him the Chaldee paraphrast expressly understands it : *Who brought Abraham publicly from the east ?* To maintain the honour of the people of Israel, it was very proper to show what a figure this great ancestor of theirs made in his day ; and *v.* 8 seems to be the explication of it, where God calls Israel the *seed of Abraham my friend ;* and (*v.* 4) he *calls the generations* (namely, the generations of Israel) *from the beginning.* Also, to put contempt upon idolatry, and particularly the Chaldean idolatry, it was proper to show how Abraham was called from serving other gods (Josh. xxiv. 2, 3, &c.), so that an early testimony was borne against that idolatry which boasted so much of its antiquity. Also, to encourage the captives in Babylon to hope that God would find a way for their return to their own land, it was proper to remind them how at first he brought their father Abraham out of the same country into this land, to give it to him for an inheritance, Gen. xv. 7. Now observe what is here said concerning him. [1.] That he was a *righteous man*, or *righteousness*, a *man of righteousness*, that *believed God, and it was counted to him for righteousness;* and so he became the father of all those who by faith in Christ are made the *righteousness of God through him*, Rom. iv. 3, 11 ; 2 Cor. v. 21. He was a great example of righteousness in his day, and *taught his household to do judgment and justice*, Gen. xviii. 19. [2.] That God *raised him up from the east*, from Ur first and afterwards from Haran, which lay east from Canaan. God would not let him settle in either of those places, but did by him as the eagle by her young, when she stirs up her nest: he raised him out of iniquity and made him pious, out of obscurity and made him famous. [3.] He *called him to his foot*, to follow him with an implicit faith ; for he *went out, not knowing whither he went*, but whom he followed, Heb. xi. 8. Those whom God effectually calls he calls to his foot, to be subject to him, to attend him, and *follow the Lamb whithersoever he goes;* and we must all either come to his foot or be made his footstool. [4.] *He gave nations before him*, the nations of Canaan, which he promised to make him master of, and thus far gave him an interest in that the Hittites acknowledged him a mighty prince among them, Gen. xxiii. 6. He *made him rule over* those *kings* whom he conquered for the rescue of his brother Lot, Gen. xiv. And when God *gave them as dust to his sword, and as driven stubble to his bow* (that is, made them an easy prey to his catechised servants), *he* then *pursued them, and passed safely*, or in peace, under the divine protection, though it was in a way he was altogether unacquainted with; and so considerable was this victory that Melchizedec himself appeared to celebrate it. Now who did this but the great Jehovah ? Can any of the gods of the heathen do so ?

(2.) That it is he who will, ere long, raise up Cyrus from the east. It is spoken of according to the language of prophecy as a thing past, because as sure to be done in its season as if it were already done. *God will raise him up in righteousness* (so it may be read, ch. xlv. 13), *will call him to his foot*, make what use of him he pleases, and make him victorious over the nations that oppose his coming to the crown, and give him success in all his wars ; and he shall be a type of

Christ, who is righteousness itself, the Lord our righteousness, whom God will, in the fulness of time, raise up and make victorious over the powers of darkness ; so that he shall spoil them and make a show of them openly.

III. He exposes the folly of idolaters, who, notwithstanding the convincing proofs which the God of Israel had given of his being God alone, obstinately persisted in their idolatry, nay, were so much the more hardened in it (*v.* 5) : *The isles of the Gentiles saw this*, not only what God did for Abraham himself, but what he did for his seed, for his sake, how he brought them out of Egypt, and made them *rule over kings*, and *they feared*, Exod. xv. 14—16. They were afraid, and, according to the summons (*v.* 1), they *drew near, and came ;* they could not avoid taking notice of what God did for Abraham and his seed ; but, instead of helping to reason one another out of their sottish idolatries, they helped to confirm one another in them, *v.* 6, 7. 1. They looked upon it as a dangerous design upon their religion, which they were jealous for the honour of, and were resolved, right or wrong, to adhere to, and therefore were alarmed to appear vigorously for the support of it, as the Ephesians for their Diana. When God, by his wonderful appearances on the behalf of his people, went about to wrest their idols from them, they held them so much the faster, and said one to another, " *Be of good courage;* let us unanimously agree to keep up the reputation of our gods. Though Dagon fall before the ark, he shall be set up again in his place." One tradesman encourages another to come into a confederacy for the keeping up of the noble craft of god-making. Thus men's convictions often exasperate their corruptions, and they are made worse both by the word and the works of God, which should make them better. 2. They looked upon it as a dangerous design upon themselves. They thought themselves in danger from the growing greatness both of Abraham that was a convert from idolatry, and of the people of Israel that were separatists from it ; and therefore they not only had recourse to their old gods for protection, but made *new* ones, Deut. xxxii. 17. *So the carpenter*, having done his part to the timber-work, *encouraged the goldsmith* to do his part in gilding or overlaying it ; and, when it came into the goldsmith's hand, *he that smooths with the hammer*, that polishes it, or beats it thin, quickened *him that smote the anvil*, bade him be expeditious, and told him it was *ready for the soldering*, which perhaps was the last operation about it, and then it is *fastened with nails*, and you have a god of it presently. Do sinners thus animate and quicken one another in the ways of sin ? And shall not the servants of the living God both stir up one another to, and strengthen one another in, his service ? Some read all this ironically, and by way of permission : *Let* them help every one his neighbour; let the carpenter encourage the goldsmith: but all in vain; idols shall fall for all this.

IV. He encourages his own people to trust in him (v. 8, 9): " But thou, Israel, art my servant. They know me not, but thou knowest me, and knowest better than to join with such ignorant besotted people as these" (for it is intended for a warning to the people of God not to *walk in the way of the heathen*); " they put themselves under the protection of these impotent deities, but thou art under my protection. *Those that make them are like unto them, and so is every one that trusts in them; but thou, O Israel! art the servant of a better Master.*" Observe what is suggested here for the encouragement of God's people when they are threatened and insulted over. 1. They are God's servants, and he will not see them abused, especially for what they do in his service: *Thou art my servant* (v. 8), and (v. 9) " *I have said unto thee, Thou art my servant;* and I will not go back from my word." 2. He has *chosen* them to be a peculiar people to himself. They were not forced upon him, but of his own good-will he set them apart. 3. They were the seed of Abraham his friend. It was the honour of Abraham that he was *called the friend of God* (James ii. 23), whom God covenanted and conversed with as a friend, and the *man of his counsel;* and *this honour have all the saints,* John xv. 15. And for the father's sake the people of Israel were beloved. God was pleased to look upon them as the posterity of an old friend of his, and therefore to be kind to them; for the covenant of friendship was made with Abraham and his seed. 4. He had sometimes, when they had been scattered among the heathen, fetched them from the ends of the earth and taken them out of the hands of the chief ones thereof, and therefore he would not now abandon them. Abraham their father was fetched from a place at a great distance, and they in his loins; and those who had been thus far-fetched and dear-bought he could not easily part with. 5. He had not yet cast them away, though they had often provoked him, and therefore he would not now abandon them. What God has done for his people, and what he has further engaged to do, should encourage them to trust in him at all times.

10 Fear thou not; for I *am* with thee: be not dismayed; for I *am* thy God: I will strengthen thee; yea, I will help thee; yea, I will uphold thee with the right hand of my righteousness. 11 Behold, all they that were incensed against thee shall be ashamed and confounded : they shall be as nothing; and they that strive with thee shall perish. 12 Thou

shalt seek them, and shalt not find them, *even* them that contended with thee : they that war against thee shall be as nothing, and as a thing of nought. 13 For I the LORD thy God will hold thy right hand, saying unto thee, Fear not ; I will help thee. 14 Fear not, thou worm Jacob, *and* ye men of Israel; I will help thee, saith the LORD, and thy Redeemer, the Holy One of Israel. 15 Behold, I will make thee a new sharp threshing instrument having teeth : thou shalt thresh the mountains, and beat *them* small, and shalt make the hills as chaff. 16 Thou shalt fan them, and the wind shall carry them away, and the whirlwind shall scatter them : and thou shalt rejoice in the LORD, *and* shalt glory in the Holy One of Israel. 17 *When* the poor and needy seek water, and *there is* none, *and* their tongue faileth for thirst, I the LORD will hear them, *I* the God of Israel will not forsake them. 18 I will open rivers in high places, and fountains in the midst of the valleys : I will make the wilderness a pool of water, and the dry land springs of water. 19 I will plant in the wilderness the cedar, the shittah-tree, and the myrtle, and the oil-tree; I will set in the desert the fir-tree, *and* the pine, and the box-tree together : 20 That they may see, and know, and consider, and understand together, that the hand of the LORD hath done this, and the Holy One of Israel hath created it.

The scope of these verses is to silence the fears, and encourage the faith, of the servants of God in their distresses. Perhaps it is intended, in the first place, for the support of God's Israel, in captivity ; but all that faithfully serve God *through patience and comfort of this scripture may have hope.* And it is addressed to Israel as a single person, that it might the more easily and readily be accommodated and applied by every Israelite indeed to himself. That is a word of caution, counsel, and comfort, which is so often repeated, *Fear thou not;* and again (v. 13), *Fear not;* and (v. 14), " *Fear not, thou worm Jacob;* fear not the threatenings of the enemy, doubt not the promises of thy God; fear not that thou shalt perish in thy affliction or that the promise of thy deliverance shall fail." It is against the mind of God that his people should be a timorous people. For the suppressing of fear he assures them,

I. That they may depend upon his presence with them as their God, and a God all-sufficient for them in the worst of times. Observe with what tenderness God speaks, and how willing he is to let the heirs of promise know the immutability of his counsel, and how desirous to make them easy: " *Fear thou not, for I am with thee,* not only within call, but present with thee; *be not dismayed* at the power of those that are against thee, for *I am thy God,* and engaged for thee. Art thou weak? *I will strengthen thee.* Art thou destitute of friends? *I will help thee* in the time of need. Art thou ready to sink, ready to fall? *I will uphold thee with the right hand of my righteousness,* that right hand which is full of righteousness, in dispensing rewards and punishments," Ps. xlviii. 10. And again (*v.* 13) it is promised, 1. That God will strengthen their hands, that is, will help them: " *I will hold thy right hand,* go hand in hand with thee" (so some); he will take us by the hand as our guide, to lead us in our way, will help us up when we are fallen or prevent our falls; when we are weak he will hold us up—wavering, he will fix us—trembling, he will encourage us, and so *hold us by the right hand,* Ps. lxxiii. 23. 2. That he will silence their fears: *Saying unto thee, Fear not.* He has said it again and again in his word, and has there provided sovereign antidotes against fear: but he will go further; he will by his Spirit say it to their hearts, and make them to hear it, and so will help them.

II. That though their enemies be now very formidable, insolent, and severe, yet the day is coming when God will reckon with them and they shall triumph over them. There are those that are incensed against God's people, that *strive with them* (*v.* 11), that war against them (*v.* 12), that hate them, that seek their ruin, and are continually picking quarrels with them. But let not God's people be incensed at them, nor strive with them, nor render evil for evil; but wait God's time, and believe, 1. That they shall be convinced of the folly, at least, if not of the sin of striving with God's people; and, finding it to no purpose, *they shall be ashamed and confounded,* which might bring them to repentance, but will rather fill them with rage. 2. That they shall be quite ruined and undone (*v.* 11): *They shall be as nothing* before the justice and power of God. When God comes to deal with his proud enemies he makes nothing of them. Or they shall be brought to nothing, shall be as if they had never been. This is repeated (*v.* 12): They *shall be as nothing and as a thing of nought,* or as that which is gone and has failed. Those that were formidable shall become despicable; those that fancied they could do any

thing shall be able to bring nothing to pass; those that made a figure in the world, and a mighty noise, shall become mere ciphers and be buried in silence. They shall perish, not only be nothing, but be miserable: *Thou shalt seek them,* shalt enquire what has become of them, that they do not appear as usual, but thou *shalt not find them,* as David, Ps. xxxvii. 36. *I sought him, but he could not be found.*

III. That they themselves should become a terror to those who were now a terror to them, and victory should turn on their side, *v.* 14—16. See here, 1. How Jacob and Israel are reduced and brought very low. It is the *worm Jacob,* so little, so weak, and so defenceless, despised and trampled on by every body, forced to creep even into the earth for safety; and we must not wonder that Jacob has become a worm, when even Jacob's King calls himself *a worm and no man,* Ps. xxii. 6. God's people are sometimes as worms, in their humble thoughts of themselves and their enemies' haughty thoughts of them—worms, but not vipers, as their enemies are, not of the serpent's seed. God regards Jacob's low estate, and says, " *Fear not, thou worm Jacob;* fear not that thou shalt be crushed; and *you men of Israel*" (you few men, so some read it, *you dead men,* so others) " do not give up yourselves for gone notwithstanding." Note, The grace of God will silence fears even when there seems to be the greatest cause for them. *Perplexed but not in despair.* 2. How Jacob and Israel are advanced from this low estate, and made as formidable as ever they have been despicable. But *by whom shall Jacob arise, for he is small?* We are here told: *I will help thee, saith the Lord;* and it is the honour of God to help the weak. He will help them, for he is their Redeemer, who is wont to redeem them, who has undertaken to do it. Christ is the Redeemer, from him is our help found. He will help them, for he is the *Holy One of Israel,* worshipped among them in the beauty of holiness and engaged by promise to them. The Lord will help them by enabling them to help themselves and making Jacob to become *a threshing instrument.* Observe, He is but an instrument, a tool in God's hand, that he is pleased to make use of; and he is an instrument of God's making and is no more than God makes him. But, if God make him a threshing instrument, he will make use of him, and therefore will make him fit for use, *new* and *sharp,* and *having teeth,* or sharp spikes; and then, by divine direction and strength, *thou shalt thresh the mountains,* the highest, and strongest, and most stubborn of thy enemies: thou shalt not only beat them, but *beat them small;* they shall not be as corn threshed out, which is valuable, and is carefully preserved (such God's people are when they are under the flail, ch. xxi. 10 : *O my threshing ! yet the corn of my floor,* that shall not be lost) ; but these are made *as chaff,* which is good for nothing, and which the husbandman is glad to get rid of. He pursues the metaphor, *v.* 16. Having threshed them, *thou shalt winnow them, and the wind shall scatter them.* This perhaps had its accomplishment, in part, in the victories of the Jews over their enemies in the times of the Maccabees ; but it seems in general designed to read the final doom of all the implacable enemies of the church of God, and to have its accomplishment likewise in the triumphs of the cross of Christ, the gospel of Christ, and all the faithful followers of Christ, over the powers of darkness, which, first or last, shall all be dissipated, and in Christ all believers shall be more than conquerors, and *he that overcomes shall have power over the nations,* Rev. ii. 26.

IV. That, hereupon, they shall have abundance of comfort in God, and God shall have abundance of honour from them : *Thou shalt rejoice in the Lord, v.* 16. When we are freed from that which hindered our joy, and are blessed with that which is the matter of it, we ought to remember that God is our exceeding joy and in him all our joys must terminate. When we rejoice over our enemies we must rejoice in the Lord, for to him alone we owe our liberties and victories. " Thou shalt also *glory in the Holy One of Israel,* in thy interest in him and relation to him, and what he has done for thee." And, if thus we make God our praise and glory, we become to him for a praise and a glory.

V. That they shall have seasonable and suitable supplies of every thing that is proper for them in the time of need ; and, if there be occasion, God will again do for them as he did for Israel in their march from Egypt to Canaan, *v.* 17—19. When the captives, either in Babylon or in their return thence, are in distress for want of water or shelter, God will take care of them, and, one way or other, make their journey, even through a wilderness, comfortable to them. But doubtless this promise has more than such a private interpretation. Their return out of Babylon was typical of our redemption by Christ ; and so the contents of these promises, 1. Were provided by the gospel of Christ. That glorious discovery of his love has given full assurance to all those who hear this joyful sound that God has provided inestimable comforts for them, sufficient for the supply of all their wants, the balancing of all their griefs, and the answering of all their prayers. 2. They are applied by the grace and Spirit of Christ to all believers, that they may have strong consolation in their way and a complete happiness in their end. Our way to heaven lies through the wilderness of this world. Now, (1.) It is here supposed that the

people of God, in their passage through this world, are often in straits : *The poor and needy seek water, and there is none ; the poor in spirit hunger and thirst after righteousness.* The soul of man, finding itself empty and necessitous, seeks for satisfaction somewhere, but soon despairs of finding it in the world, that has nothing in it to make it easy : creatures are *broken cisterns, that can hold no water ;* so that *their tongue fails for thirst,* they are weary of seeking that satisfaction in the world which is not to be had in it. Their sorrow makes them thirsty ; so does their toil. (**2.**) It is here promised that, one way or other, all their grievances shall be redressed and they shall be made easy. [1.] God himself will be nigh unto them in all that which they call upon him for. Let all the praying people of God take notice of this, and take comfort of it ; he has said, " *I the Lord will hear them,* will answer them ; *I, the God of Israel, will not forsake them ;* I will be with them, as I have always been, in their distresses." While we are in the wilderness of this world this promise is to us what the pillar of cloud and fire was to Israel, an assurance of God's gracious presence. [2.] They shall have a constant supply of fresh water, as Israel had in the wilderness, even where one would least expect it (*v.* 18): *I will open rivers in high places,* rivers of grace, rivers of pleasure, *rivers of living water,* which he spoke of the Spirit (John vii. 38, 39), that Spirit which should be poured out upon the Gentiles, who had been as high places, dry and barren, and lifted up in their own conceit above the necessity of that gift. And there shall be *fountains in the midst of the valleys,* the valleys of Baca (Ps. lxxxiv. 6), that are sandy and wearisome ; or among the Jews, who had been as fruitful valleys in comparison with the Gentile mountains. The preaching of the gospel to the world turned that wilderness into a pool of water, yielding fruit to the owner of it and relief to the travellers through it. [3.] They shall have a pleasant shade to screen them from the scorching heat of the sun, as Israel when they pitched at Elim, where they had not only wells of water, but palm-trees (Exod. xv. 27): " *I will plant in the wilderness the cedar, v.* 19. I will turn the wilderness into an orchard or garden, such as used to be planted with these pleasant trees, so that they shall pass through the wilderness with as much ease and delight as a man walks in his grove. These trees shall be to them what the pillar of cloud was to Israel in the wilderness, a shelter from the heat." Christ and his grace are so to believers, *as the shadow of a great rock,* ch. xxxii. 2. When God sets up his church in the Gentile wilderness there shall be as great a change made by it in men's characters as if thorns and briers were turned into cedars, and fir-trees, and myrtles ; and by this a blessed change is described, *ch.* lv. 13. [4.] They shall see and acknowledge the hand of God, his power and his favour, in this, *v.* 20. God will do these strange and surprising things on purpose to awaken them to a conviction and consideration of his hand in all: *That they may see* this wonderful change, *and knowing* that it is above the ordinary course and power of nature may consider that therefore it comes from a superior power, and, comparing notes upon it, *may understand together*, and concur in the acknowledgment of it, *that the hand of the Lord*, that mighty hand of his which is stretched out for his people and stretched out to them, *has done this*, and *the Holy One of Israel has created it*, made it anew, made it out of nothing, made it for the comfort of his people. Note, God does great things for his people, that he may be taken notice of.

21 Produce your cause, saith the Lord; bring forth your strong reasons, saith the King of Jacob. 22 Let them bring *them* forth, and show us what shall happen: let them show the former things, what they *be*, that we may consider them, and know the latter end of them; or declare us things for to come. 23 Show the things that are to come hereafter, that we may know that ye *are* gods: yea, do good, or do evil, that we may be dismayed, and behold *it* together. 24 Behold, ye *are* of nothing, and your work of nought: an abomination *is he* that chooseth you. 25 I have raised up *one* from the north, and he shall come: from the rising of the sun shall he call upon my name: and he shall come upon princes as *upon* mortar, and as the potter treadeth clay. 26 Who hath declared from the beginning, that we may know? and beforetime, that we may say, *He is* righteous? yea, *there is* none that showeth, yea, *there is* none that declareth, yea, *there is* none that heareth your words. 27 The first *shall say* to Zion, Behold, behold them: and I will give to Jerusalem one that bringeth good tidings. 28 For I beheld, and *there was* no man; even among them, and *there was* no counsellor, that, when I asked of them, could answer a word. 29 Behold, they *are* all vanity; their works *are* nothing: their molten images *are* wind and confusion.

The Lord, by the prophet, here repeats the challenge to idolaters to make out the pretensions of their idols: " *Produce your cause* (*v.* 21) and make your best of it; *bring forth the strongest reasons* you have to prove that your idols are gods, and worthy of your adoration." Note, There needs no more to show the absurdity of sin than to produce the reasons that are given in defence of it, for they carry with them their own confutation.

I. The idols are here challenged to bring proofs of their knowledge and power. Let us see what they can inform us of, and what they can do. Understanding and active power are the accomplishments of a man. Whoever pretends to be a god must have these in perfection; and have the idols made it to appear that they have? No;

1. "They can tell us nothing that we did not know before, so ignorant are they. We challenge them to inform us," (1.) "What has been formerly: *Let them show the former things*, and raise them out of the oblivion in which they were buried" (God inspired Moses to write such a history of the creation as the gods of the heathen could never have dictated to any of their enthusiasts); or "let the defenders of idols tell us what mighty achievements they can boast of as performed by their gods in former times. What did they ever do that was worth taking notice of? Let them specify any thing, and it shall be considered, its due weight shall be given it, and it shall be compared with the latter end of it; and if, in the issue, it prove to be as great as it pretended to be, they shall have the credit of it." (2.) "We challenge them to tell us what shall happen, to declare to us *things to come* (*v.* 22), and again (*v.* 23), *show the things that are to come hereafter.* Give this evidence of your omniscience, that nothing can be hidden from you, and of your sovereignty and dominion. Make it to appear that you have the doing of all, by letting us know beforehand what you design to do. Do this kindness to the world; let them know what is to come, that they may provide accordingly. Do this, and we will own that you are gods above us, and gods to us, and worthy of our adorations." No creature can foretel things to come, otherwise than by divine information, with any certainty.

2. "They can do nothing that we cannot do ourselves, so impotent are they." He challenges them to do either *good or evil*, good to their friends or evil to their enemies: "Let them do, if they can, any thing extraordinary, that people will admire and be affected with. Let them either bless or curse, with power. Let us see them either inflict such plagues as God brought on Egypt or bestow such blessings as God bestowed on Israel. Let them do some great thing, and we shall be amazed when we see it, and frightened into a veneration of them, as many have been into a veneration of the true God." That which is charged upon

these idols, and let them disprove it if they can, is that *they are of nothing, v.* 24. Their claims have no foundation at all, nor is there any ground or reason in the least for men's paying them the respect they do; there is nothing in them worthy our regard. "They are less than nothing, worse than nothing;" so some read it. "*The work they do is of nought,* and so is the ado that is made about them. There is no pretence or colour for it; it is all a jest; it is all a sham put upon the world; and therefore *he that chooses you,* and so gives you your deity, and" (as some read it) "*that delights in* you, *is an abomination* to God and all wise and good men. He that *chooses you chooses an abomination;*" so some take it. A servant is at liberty to choose his master, but a man is not at liberty to choose his God. He that chooses any other than the true God chooses an abomination; his choosing it makes it so.

II. God here produces proofs that he is the true God, and that there is none besides him. Let him produce his strong reasons.

1. He has an irresistible power. This he will shortly make to appear in the raising up of Cyrus and making him a type of Christ (*v.* 25): *He will raise him up from the north* and *from the rising of the sun.* Cyrus by his father was a Mede, by his mother a Persian; and his army consisted of Medes, whose country lay north, and Persians, whose country lay east, from Babylon. God will raise him up to great power, and he shall come against Babylon with ends of his own to serve. But, (1.) *He shall proclaim God's name;* so it may be read. He shall publish the honour of the God of Israel; so he did remarkably when, in his proclamation for the release of the Jews out of their captivity, he acknowledged that the Lord God of Israel was the Lord God of heaven, and *the God:* and he might be said to call on his name when he encouraged the building of his temple, and very probably did himself call upon him and pray to him, Ezra i. 2, 3. (2.) All opposition shall fall before him: *He shall come upon the princes of Babylon,* and all others that stood in his way, *as mortar,* and trample upon them *as the potter treads clay,* to serve his own purposes with it. Christ, as man, was raised up from the north, for Nazareth lay in the northern parts of Canaan; as the angel of the covenant, he ascends from the east. He maintained the honour of heaven *(he shall call upon my name),* and broke the powers of hell, came upon the prince of darkness as mortar and trod him down.

2. He has an infallible foresight. He would not only do this, but he did now, by his prophet, foretel it. Now the false gods not only could not do it, but they could not foresee it. (1.) He challenges them to produce any of their pretended deities, or their diviners, that had given notice of this, or could (*v.* 26): "*Who has declared from the*
226

beginning any thing of this kind, or has told it before-time? Tell us if there be any that you know of, for we know not any; if there be any, *we will say, He is righteous,* he is true, his cause is just, his claims are proved, and he is in the right in demanding to be worshipped." This agrees with *v.* 22, 23. (2.) He challenges to himself the sole honour of doing it and foretelling it (*v.* 27): *I am the first* (so it may be read) *that will say to Zion, Behold, behold them,* that will let the people of Israel know their deliverers are at hand (for there were those who understood by books, God's books, the approach of the time, Dan. ix. 2), and I am he that *will give to Jerusalem one that brings good tidings,* these good tidings of their enlargement. This is applicable to the work of redemption, in which the Lord showed himself much more than in the release of the Jews out of Babylon: he it was that contrived our salvation, and he brought it about, and he has given to us the glad tidings of reconciliation.

III. Judgment is here given upon this trial. 1. None of all the idols had foretold, or could foresee, this work of wonder. Other nations besides the Jews were released out of captivity in Babylon by Cyrus, or at least were greatly concerned in the revolution of the monarchy and the transferring of it to the Persians; and yet none of them had any intelligence given them of it beforehand, by any of their gods or prophets: "*There is none that shows* (*v.* 26), *none that declares,* none that gives the least intimation of it; *there is none* of the nations *that hears your words,* that can pretend to have heard from their gods such words as you, O Israelites! have heard from your God, by your prophets," Ps. cxlvii. 20. None of all the gods of the nations have shown their worshippers the way of salvation, which God will show by the Messiah. The good tidings which the Lord will send in the gospel is a mystery hidden from ages and generations, Rom. xvi. 25, 26. 2. None of those who pleaded for them could produce any instance of their knowledge or power that had in it any colour of proof that they were gods. All their advocates were struck dumb with this challenge (*v.* 28): "*I beheld, and there was no man* that could give evidence for them, even among those that were their most zealous admirers; *and there was no counsellor,* none that could offer any thing for the support of their cause. Even among the idols themselves there was none fit to give counsel in the most trivial matters, and yet there were those that asked counsel of them in the most important and difficult affairs. When I asked them what they had to say for themselves they stood mute; the case was so plain against them that there was *none who could answer a word.*" Judgment must therefore be given against the defendant upon *Nihil dicit—He is mute.* He has nothing to say for himself. *He was speechless,* Matt. xxii. 12. 3. Sentence is therefore given according to the charge exhibited against them (*v.* 24): "*Behold, they are all vanity* (*v.* 29); they are a lie and a cheat; they are not in themselves what they pretend to be, nor will their worshippers find that in them which they promise themselves. *Their works are nothing,* of no force, of no worth; their enemies need fear no hurt from them; their worshippers can hope for no good from them. *Their molten images,* and indeed all their images, *are wind and confusion,* vanity and vexation; those that worship them will be deceived in them, and will reflect upon their own folly with the greatest bitterness. Therefore, *dearly beloved, flee from idolatry,*" 1 Cor. x. 14.

CHAP. XLII.

The prophet seems here to launch out yet further into the prophecy of the Messiah and his kingdom under the type of Cyrus; and, having the great work of man's salvation by him yet more in view, he almost forgets the occasion that led him into it and drops the return out of Babylon; for indeed the prospect of this would be a greater comfort and support to the believing pious Jews, in their captivity, than the hope of that. And (as Mr. Gataker well observes) in this and similar prophecies of Christ, that are couched in types, as of David and Solomon, some passages agree to the type and not to the truth, others to the truth and not to the type, and many to the type in one sense and the truth in another. Here is, I. A prophecy of the Messiah's coming with meekness, and yet with power, to do the Redeemer's work, ver. 1—4. II. His commission opened, which he received from the Father, ver. 5—9. III. The joy and rejoicing with which the glad tidings of this should be received, ver. 10—12. IV. The wonderful success of the gospel, for the overthrow of the devil's kingdom, ver. 13—17. V. The rejection and ruin of the Jews for their unbelief, ver. 18—25.

BEHOLD my servant, whom I uphold; mine elect, *in whom* my soul delighteth; I have put my spirit upon him: he shall bring forth judgment to the Gentiles. 2 He shall not cry, nor lift up, nor cause his voice to be heard in the street. 3 A bruised reed shall he not break, and the smoking flax shall he not quench: he shall bring forth judgment unto truth. 4 He shall not fail nor be discouraged, till he have set judgment in the earth: and the isles shall wait for his law.

We are sure that these verses are to be understood of Christ, for the evangelist tells us expressly that in this prophecy was fulfilled, Matt. xii. 17—21. *Behold* with an eye of faith, behold and observe, behold and admire, *my servant, whom I uphold.* Let the Old-Testament saints behold and expect him; let the New-Testament saints behold and remember him. Now what must we behold and consider concerning him?

I. The Father's concern for him and relation to him, the confidence he put and the complacency he took in him. This put an honour upon him, and made him remarkable, above any other circumstance, *v.* 1. 1. God owns him as one employed for him:

He is *my servant.* Though he was a Son, yet, as a Mediator, he *took upon him the form of a servant,* learned obedience to the will of God and practised it, and laid out himself to advance the interests of God's kingdom, and so he was God's servant. 2. As one chosen by him: He is *my elect.* He did not thrust himself into the service, but was called of God, and pitched upon as the fittest person for it. Infinite Wisdom made the choice and then avowed it. 3. As one he put a confidence in: He is *my servant on whom I lean;* so some read it. The Father put a confidence in him that he would go through with his undertaking, and, in that confidence, brought many sons to glory. It was a great trust which the Father reposed in the Son, but he knew him to be *par negotio—equal to it,* both able and faithful. 4. As one whom he took care of: He is *my servant whom I uphold;* so we read it. The Father bore him up, and bore him out, in his undertaking: both were included in his upholding him; he stood by him and strengthened him. 5. As one whom he took an entire complacency in: *My elect, in whom my soul delights.* His delight was in him from eternity, when he was *by him as one brought up with him,* Prov. viii. 30. He had a particular satisfaction in his undertaking: he declared himself *well pleased in him* (Matt. iii. 17; xvii. 5), and *therefore* loved him, because he laid down his life for the sheep. Let our souls delight in Christ, rely on him, and rejoice in him; and thus let us be united to him, and then, for his sake, the Father will be well pleased with us.

II. The qualification of him for his office: *I have put my Spirit upon him,* to enable him to go through his undertaking, *ch.* lxi. i. The Spirit did not only come, but rest, upon him (*ch.* xi. 2), not by measure, as on others of God's servants, but without measure. Those whom God employs as his servants; as he will uphold them and be well pleased with them, so he will put his Spirit upon them.

III. The work to which he is appointed; it is to *bring forth judgment to the Gentiles,* that is, in infinite wisdom, holiness, and equity, to set up a religion in the world under the bonds of which the Gentiles should come and the blessings of which they should enjoy. The judgments of the Lord, which had been hidden from the Gentiles (Ps. cxlvii. 20), he came to bring forth to the Gentiles, for he was *to be a light to lighten them.*

IV. The mildness and tenderness with which he should pursue this undertaking, *v.* 2, 3. He shall carry it on, 1. In silence, and without noise: *He shall not strive nor cry.* It shall not be proclaimed, *Lo, here, is Christ,* or *Lo, he is there;* as when great princes ride in progress or make a public entry. He shall have no trumpet sounded before him, nor any noisy retinue to follow him. The opposition he meets with he shall not strive against, but patiently *endure the contradiction of sinners against himself.* His kingdom is spiritual, and therefore its weapons are not carnal, nor is its appearance pompous; it comes not with observation. 2. Gently, and without rigour. Those that are wicked he will be patient with; when he has begun to crush them, so that they are as bruised reeds, he will give them space to repent and not immediately break them; though they are very offensive, as smoking flax (*ch.* lxv. 5), yet he will bear with them, as he did with Jerusalem. Those that are weak he will be tender of; those that have but a little life, a little heat, that are weak as a reed, oppressed with doubts and fears, *as a bruised reed,* that are as *smoking flax,* as the wick of a candle newly lighted, which is ready to go out again, he will not despise them, will not plead against them with his great power, nor lay upon them more work or more suffering than they can bear, which would break and quench them, but will graciously consider their frame. More is implied than is expressed. *He will not break the bruised reed,* but will strengthen it, that it may become as a cedar in the courts of our God. *He will not quench the smoking flax,* but blow it up into a flame. Note, Jesus Christ is very tender towards those that have true grace, though they are but weak in it, and accepts the willingness of the spirit, pardoning and passing by the weakness of the flesh.

V. The courage and constancy with which he should persevere in this undertaking, so as to carry his point at last (*v.* 4): *He shall not fail nor be discouraged.* Though he meets with hard service and much opposition, and foresees how ungrateful the world will be, yet he goes on with his part of the work, till he is able to say, *It is finished;* and he enables his apostles and ministers to go on with theirs too, and not to fail nor be discouraged, till they also have finished their testimony. And thus he accomplishes what he undertook. 1. *He brings forth judgment unto truth.* By a long course of miracles, and his resurrection at last, he shall fully evince the truth of his doctrine and the divine origin and authority of that holy religion which he came to establish. 2. He *sets judgment in the earth.* He erects his government in the world, a church for himself among men, reforms the world, and by the power of his gospel and grace fixes such principles in the minds of men as tend to make them wise and just. 3. *The isles* of the Gentiles *wait for his law,* wait for his gospel, that is, bid it welcome as if it had been a thing they had long waited for. They shall become his disciples, shall sit at his feet, and be ready to receive the law from his mouth. *What wilt thou have us to do?*

5 Thus saith God the LORD, he that created the heavens, and stretch-

228

ed them out; he that spread forth the earth, and that which cometh out of it; he that giveth breath unto the people upon it, and spirit to them that walk therein: 6 I the LORD have called thee in righteousness, and will hold thine hand, and will keep thee, and give thee for a covenant of the people, for a light of the Gentiles; 7 To open the blind eyes, to bring out the prisoners from the prison, *and* them that sit in darkness out of the prison-house. 8 I *am* the LORD: that *is* my name: and my glory will I not give to another, neither my praise to graven images. 9 Behold, the former things are come to pass, and new things do I declare: before they spring forth I tell you of them. 10 Sing unto the LORD a new song, *and* his praise from the end of the earth, ye that go down to the sea, and all that is therein; the isles, and the inhabitants thereof. 11 Let the wilderness and the cities thereof lift up *their voice,* the villages *that* Kedar doth inhabit: let the inhabitants of the rock sing, let them shout from the top of the mountains. 12 Let them give glory unto the LORD, and declare his praise in the islands.

Here is, I. The covenant God made with and the commission he gave to the Messiah, *v.* 5—7, which are an exposition of *v.* 1, *Behold my servant, whom I uphold.*

1. The royal titles by which the great God here makes himself known, and distinguishes himself from all pretenders, speak very much his glory (*v.* 5): *Thus saith God the Lord.* And who art thou, Lord? Why, he is the fountain of all being and therefore the fountain of all power. He is the fountain of being, 1. In the upper world; *he created the heavens and stretched them out* (*ch.* xl. 22), and keeps the vast expanse still upon the stretch. 2. In the lower world; for *he spread forth the earth,* and made it a capacious habitation, *and that which comes out of it* is produced by his power. 3. In the world of mankind: *He gives breath to the people upon it,* not only air to breathe in, but the breath of life itself and organs to breathe with; nay, he gives *spirit,* the powers and faculties of a rational soul, to those that walk therein. Now this is prefixed to God's covenant with the Messiah, and the commission given him, not only to show that he has authority to make such a covenant and give such a commission, and had power sufficient to bear him out, but

that the design of the work of redemption was to maintain the honour of the Creator, and to restore man to the allegiance he owes to God as his Maker.

2. The assurances which he gives to the Messiah of his presence with him in all he did pursuant to his undertaking speak much encouragement to him, *v.* 6. (1.) God owns that the Messiah did not take the honour of being Mediator to himself, but was called of God, that he was no intruder, no usurper, but was fairly brought to it (Heb. v. 4): *I have called thee in righteousness.* God not only did him no wrong in calling him to this hard service, he having voluntarily offered himself to it, but did himself right in providing for his own honour and performing the word which he had spoken. (2.) He promises to stand by him and strengthen him in it, to hold his hand, not only to his work, but in it, to hold his hand, that it might not shake, that it might not fail, and so to keep him. When an angel was sent from heaven to strengthen him in his agonies, and the Father himself was with him, then this promise was fulfilled. Note, Those whom God calls he will own and help, and will hold their hands.

3. The great intentions of this commission speak abundance of comfort to the children of men. He was given *for a covenant of the people,* for a mediator, or guarantee, of the covenant of grace, which is all summed up in him. God, in giving us Christ, has with him freely given us all the blessings of the new covenant. Two glorious blessings Christ, in his gospel, brings with him to the Gentile word—light and liberty. (1.) He is given *for a light to the Gentiles,* not only to reveal to them what they were concerned to know, and which otherwise they could not have known, but to open the blind eyes, that they might know it. By his Spirit in the word he presents the object; by his Spirit in the heart he prepares the organ. When the gospel came light came, a great light, to those that sat in darkness, Matt. iv. 16; John iii. 19. And St. Paul was sent to the Gentiles *to open their eyes,* Acts xxvi. 18. Christ is the light of the world. (2.) He is sent to proclaim liberty to the captives, as Cyrus did, *to bring out the prisoners;* not only to open the prison-doors, and give them leave to go out, which was all that Cyrus could do, but to bring them out, to induce and enable them to make use of their liberty, which none did but those whose spirits God stirred up. This Christ does by his grace.

II. The ratification and confirmation of this grant. That we may be assured of the validity of it consider, 1. The authority of him that makes the promise (*v.* 8): *I am the Lord, Jehovah, that is my name,* and that was the name by which he made himself known when he began to perform the promise made to the patriarchs; whereas, be-

fore, he manifested himself by the name of God Almighty, Exod. vi. 3. If he is the Lord that gives being and birth to all things, he will give being and birth to this promise. If his name be *Jehovah,* which speaks him God alone, we may be sure his name is *jealous,* and he *will not give his glory to another,* whoever it is that stands in competition with him, especially not to *graven images.* He will send the Messiah to open men's eyes, that so he may turn them from the service of dumb idols to serve the living God, because, though he has long winked at the times of ignorance, he will now maintain his prerogative, and will not give his glory to graven images. He will perform his word because he will not lose the honour of being true to it, nor be ever charged with falsehood by the worshippers of false gods. He will deliver his people from under the power of idolaters because it looks as if he had given his praise to graven images when he gives up his own worshippers to be worshippers of images. 2. The accomplishment of the promises he had formerly made concerning his church, which are proofs of the truth of his word and the kindness he bears to his people (*v.* 9): "*Behold, the former things have come to pass;* hitherto the Lord has helped his church, has supported her under former burdens, relieved her in former straits; and this in performance of the promises made to the fathers. *There has not failed one word,* 1 Kings viii. 56. *And* now *new things do I declare.* Now I will make new promises, which shall as certainly be fulfilled in their season as old ones were; now I will bestow new favours, such as have not been conferred formerly. Old-Testament blessings you have had abundantly; now I declare New-Testament blessings, not a fruitful country and dominion over your neighbours, but *spiritual blessings in heavenly things. Before they spring forth* in the preaching of the gospel *I tell you of them,* under the type and figure of the former things." Note, The receipt of former mercies may encourage us to hope for further mercies; for God is constant in his care for his people, and his compassions are still new.

III. The song of joy and praise which should be sung hereupon to the glory of God (*v.* 10): *Sing unto the Lord a new song,* a New-Testament song. The giving of Christ for *a light to the Gentiles* (*v.* 6) was a new thing, and very surprising. The apostle speaks of it as a mystery which, in other ages, was not made known, as it is now revealed, *that the Gentiles should be fellow-heirs,* Eph. iii. 5, 6. Now, this being the new thing which God declares, the newness of the song which is to be sung on this occasion is this, that whereas, before, the songs of the Lord were very much confined to the temple at Jerusalem (David's psalm were in the language of the Jews only, and sung by them and in their own country only; for, when they were in a strange land, they hung their harps on the willow-trees and could not sing the Lord's song, as we find, Ps. cxxxvii. 2—4), now the songs of holy joy and praise shall be sung all the world over. The Gentile nations shall share equally with the Jews in New-Testament blessings, and therefore shall join in New-Testament praises and acts of worship. There shall be churches set up in Gentile nations and they shall sing a new song. The conversion of the Gentiles is often fore-told under this notion, as appears, Rom. xv. 9—11. It is here promised that the praises of God's grace shall be sung with joy and thankfulness, 1. By those that live in *the end of the earth,* in countries that lie most remote from Jerusalem. *From the utter-most parts of the earth have we heard songs,* ch. xxiv. 16. This was fulfilled when Chris-tianity was planted in our land. 2. By mari-ners and merchants, and those that *go down to the sea,* that do business in great waters, and suck the riches of the sea, and so make themselves masters of the fulness thereof and all that is therein, with which they shall praise God, and justly, for it is his, Ps. xxiv. 1; xcv. 5. The Jews traded little at sea; if therefore God's praises be sung by those that go down to the sea, it must be by Gentiles. Sea-faring men are called upon to praise God, Ps. cvii. 23. 3. By *the islands and the inhabitants thereof, v.* 10, and again, *v.* 12. Let them *declare his praise in the islands,* the isles of the Gen-tiles, probably referring to the islands of Greece. 4. *By the wilderness and the cities thereof, and the villages of Kedar.* These lay east from Jerusalem, as the islands lay west, so that the gospel songs should be sung from the rising of the sun to the going down of the same. The whole Gentile world had been like an island, cut off from communication with God's church, and like a wilderness, uncultivated and bringing forth no fruit to God; but now the islands and the wilderness shall praise God. 5. By *the inhabitants of the rock,* and those that dwell *on the tops of the mountains,* not only the Gentiles, but the poorest and meanest and most despicable, those that dwell in cottages, as well as those that inhabit cities and villages. The rude and most barbarous, as the mountaineers commonly are, shall be civilized by the gospel. Or by the inhabi-tants of the rock may be meant the inhabi-tants of that part of Arabia which is called *Petræa—the rocky.* Perhaps the neigh-bouring countries shared in the joy of the Israelites when they returned out of Baby-lon and some of them came and joined with them in their praises; but we find not that it was to any such degree as might fully answer this illustrious prophecy, and must conclude that it reaches further, and was fulfilled in that which many other prophe-

230

cies of the joy of the nations are said in the New-Testament to be fulfilled in, the con-version of the Gentiles to the faith of Christ. When they are brought into the church they are brought to give glory to the Lord; then they are to him for a name and a praise, and they make it their business to praise him. He is glorified in them and by them.

13 The LORD shall go forth as a mighty man, he shall stir up jealousy like a man of war: he shall cry, yea, roar; he shall prevail against his enemies. 14 I have long time holden my peace; I have been still, *and* re-frained myself: *now* will I cry like a travailing woman; I will destroy and devour at once. 15 I will make waste mountains and hills, and dry up all their herbs; and I will make the rivers islands, and I will dry up the pools. 16 And I will bring the blind by a way *that* they knew not; I will lead them in paths *that* they have not known: I will make dark-ness light before them, and crooked things straight. These things will I do unto them, and not forsake them. 17 They shall be turned back, they shall be greatly ashamed, that trust in graven images, that say to the molten images, Ye *are* our gods.

It comes all to one whether we make these verses (as some do) the song itself that is to be sung by the Gentile world or a pro-phecy of what God will do to make way for the singing of that song, that evangelical new song. I. He will appear in his power and glory more than ever. So he did in the preaching of his gospel, in the divine power and energy which went along with it, and in the won-derful success it had in the *pulling down of Satan's strongholds,* v. 13, 14. *He had long held his peace, and been still, and refrained himself, while he winked at the times of the ignorance of the Gentile world* (Acts xvii. 30), and *suffered all nations to walk in their own ways* (Acts xiv. 16); but now *he shall go forth as a mighty man, as a man of war,* to attack the devil's kingdom and give it a fatal blow. The going forth of the gospel is thus represented, Rev. vi. 2. Christ, in it, went forth conquering and to conquer. The ministry of the apostles is called their *warfare;* and they were the soldiers of Jesus Christ. *He shall stir up jealousy,* shall appear more jealous than ever for the glory of his own name and against idolatry. 1. *He shall cry,* in the preaching of his word, *cry like a travailing woman;* for the ministers of Christ preached as men in earnest, and that travailed in birth again till they saw Christ formed in the souls of the people, Gal. iv. 19. *He shall cry, yea, roar,* in the gospel woes, which are more terrible than the roaring of a lion, and which must be preached along with gospel blessings to awaken a sleeping world. 2. He shall conquer by the power of his Spirit : *He shall prevail against his enemies,* shall prevail to make them friends, Col. i. 21. Those that contradict and blaspheme his gospel, he shall prevail to put them to silence and shame. He will destroy and devour at once all the oppositions of the powers of darkness. Satan shall fall as lightning from heaven, and he that had the power of death shall be destroyed. As a type and figure of this, to make way for the redemption of the Jews out of Babylon, God will humble the pride, and break the power, of their oppressors, and *will at once destroy and devour* the Babylonian monarchy. In accomplishing this destruction of Babylon by the Persian army under the command of Cyrus, *he will make waste mountains and hills,* level the country, and *dry up all their herbs.* The army, as usual, shall either carry off the forage or destroy it, and by laying bridges of boats over rivers shall turn them into islands, and so drain the fens and low grounds, to make way for the march of their army, that the pools shall be dried up. Thus, when the gospel shall be preached, it shall have a free course, and that which hinders the progress of it shall be taken out of the way.

II. He will manifest his favour and grace towards those whose spirits he had stirred up to follow him, as Ezra i. 5. Those who ask the way to Zion he will show the way, and lead in it, *v.* 16. Those who by nature were blind, and those who, being under convictions of sin and wrath are quite at a loss and know not what to do with themselves, God will *lead by a way that they knew not,* will show them the way to life and happiness by Jesus Christ, who is the way, and will conduct and carry them on in that way, which before they were strangers to. Thus, in the conversion of Paul, he was struck blind first, and then God revealed his Son in him, and made the scales to fall from his eyes. They are weak in knowledge, and the truths of God at first seem unintelligible; but God will *make darkness light before them,* and knowledge shall be easy to them. They are weak in duty, the commands of God seem impracticable, and insuperable difficulties are in the way of their obedience; but God will make *crooked things straight;* their way shall be plain, and the yoke easy. Those whom God brings into the right way he will guide in it. As a type of this, he will lead the Jews, when they return out of captivity, in a ready road to their own land again, and nothing shall occur to perplex or embarrass them in

their journey. These are great things, and kind things, very great and very kind; but lest any should say, "They are too great, too kind, to be expected from God by such an undeserving people as that of the Jews, such an undeserving world as that of the Gentiles," he adds, *These things will I do unto them,* take my word for it I will, and *I will not forsake them ;* he that begins to show this great mercy will go on to do them good.

III. He will particularly put those to confusion who adhere to idols notwithstanding the attempts made by the preaching of the gospel to turn them from idols (*v.* 17): *They shall be turned back, and greatly ashamed, that trust in graven images.* The Babylonians shall when they see how the Jews, who despise their images, are owned and delivered by the God they worship without images, and the Gentiles when they see how idolatry falls before the preaching of the gospel, is scattered like darkness before the light of the sun, and melts like snow before its heat. They shall be ashamed that ever they said to these molten images, *You are our gods ;* for how can those help their worshippers who cannot help themselves, nor save themselves from falling into contempt? In times of reformation, when many turn from iniquity, and sin, being generally deserted, becomes unfashionable, it may be hoped that those who will not otherwise be reclaimed will be wrought upon by that consideration to be ashamed of it.

18 Hear, ye deaf; and look, ye blind, that ye may see. 19 Who *is* blind, but my servant? Or deaf, as my messenger *that* I sent? Who *is* blind as *he that is* perfect, and blind as the LORD's servant? 20 Seeing many things, but thou observest not ; opening the ears, but he heareth not. 21 The LORD is well pleased for his righteousness' sake ; he will magnify the law, and make *it* honourable. 22 But this *is* a people robbed and spoiled ; *they are* all of them snared in holes, and they are hid in prison-houses : they are for a prey, and none delivereth ; for a spoil, and none saith, Restore. 23 Who among you will give ear to this? *Who* will hearken and hear for the time to come? 24 Who gave Jacob for a spoil, and Israel to the robbers? Did not the LORD, he against whom we have sinned? For they would not walk in his ways, neither were they obedient unto his law. 25 Therefore he hath poured upon him the fury of

his anger, and the strength of battle: and it hath set him on fire round about, yet he knew not ; and it burned him, yet he laid *it* not to heart.

The prophet, having spoken by way of comfort and encouragement to the believing Jews who waited for the consolation of Israel, here turns to those among them who were unbelieving, for their conviction and humiliation. Among those who were in captivity in Babylon there were some who were as the evil figs in Jeremiah's vision, who were sent thither *for their hurt, to be removed into all the kingdoms of the earth, for a reproach and a proverb*, Jer. xxiv. 9. In them there was a type of the Jews who rejected Christ and were rejected by him, and then fell more than ever under the curse, when those who believed were inheriting the blessing; for they were broken, and ruined, and remain dispersed unto this day. Observe,

I. The call that is given to this people (*v.* 18): "*Hear, you deaf,* and attend to the joyful sound, *and look you blind, that you may see* the joyful light." There is no absurdity in this command, nor is it unbecoming the wisdom and goodness of God to call us to do that good which yet of ourselves we are not sufficient for ; for those have natural powers which they may employ so as to do better than they do, and may have supernatural grace if it be not their own fault, who yet labour under a moral impotency to that which is good. This call to the deaf to hear and the blind to see is like the command given to the man that had the withered hand to stretch it forth; though he could not do this, because it was withered, yet, if he had not attempted to do it, he would not have been healed, and his being healed thereupon was owing, not to his act, but to the divine power.

II. The character that is given of them (*v.* 19, 20): *Who is blind, but my servant, or deaf as my messenger?* The people of the Jews were in profession God's servants, and their priests and elders his messengers (Mal. ii. 7); but they were deaf and blind. The verse before may be understood as spoken to the Gentile idolaters, whom he calls *deaf* and *blind*, because they worshipped gods that were so. " But," says he, " no wonder you are deaf and blind when my own people are as bad as you, and many of them as much set upon idolatry."

1. He complains of their sottishness—they are blind ; and of their stubbornness—they are deaf. They were even worse than the Gentiles themselves. *Corruptio optimi est pessima—What is best becomes, when corrupted, the worst.* " Who is so wilfully, so scandalously, blind and deaf as my servant and my messenger, as Jacob who is my servant *ch.* xli. 8), and as their prophets and teachers who are my messengers? Who

232

is blind as he that in profession and pretension is perfect, that should come nearer to perfection than other people, their priests and prophets? The one prophesies falsely, and the other bears rule by their means; and who so blind as those that will not see when they have the light shining in their faces?" Note, (1.) It is a common thing, but a very sad thing, for those that in profession are God's servants and messengers to be themselves blind and deaf in spiritual things, ignorant, erroneous, and very careless. (2.) Blindness and deafness in spiritual things are worse in those that profess themselves to be God's servants and messengers than in others. It is in them the greater sin and shame, the greater dishonour to God, and to themselves a greater damnation.

2. The prophet goes on (*v.* 20) to describe the blindness and obstinacy of the Jewish nation, just as our Saviour describes it in his time (Matt. xiii. 14, 15): *Seeing many things, but thou observest not.* Multitudes are ruined for want of observing that which they cannot but see ; they perish, not through ignorance, but mere carelessness. The Jews in our Saviour's time saw many proofs of his divine mission, but they did not observe them; they seemed to open their ears to him, but they did not hear, that is, they did not heed, did not understand, or believe, or obey, and then it was all one as if they had not heard.

III. The care God will take of the honour of his own name, notwithstanding their blindness and deafness, especially of his word, which he has magnified above all his name. *Shall the unbelief and obstinacy of men make the promise of God of no effect? God forbid*, Rom. iii. 3, 4. No, though they are blind and deaf, God will be no loser in his glory (*v.* 21): *The Lord is well pleased for his righteousness' sake;* not well pleased with their sin, but well pleased in the manifestation of his own righteousness, in rejecting them for rejecting the great salvation. He speaks as one well pleased, *ch.* i. 24 : *Ah! I will ease me of my adversaries;* and Ezek. v. 13, *I will be comforted.* The scripture was fulfilled in the casting off of the Jews as well as in the calling in of the Gentiles, and therein the Lord will be well pleased. *He will magnify the law* (divine revelation in all the parts of it) *and will make it honourable.* The law is truly honourable, and the things of it are great things; and, if men will not magnify it by their obedience to it, God will magnify it himself by punishing them for their disobedience. He will magnify the law by accomplishing what is written in it, will magnify its authority, its efficacy, its equity. He will do it at last, when all men shall be judged by the law of liberty, James ii. 12. He is doing it every day. What is it that God is doing in the world, but magnifying the law and making it honourable ? IV. The calamities God will bring upon the Jewish nation for their wilful blindness and deafness, v. 22. They are *robbed and spoiled.* Those that were impenitent and unreformed in Babylon were sentenced to perpetual captivity. It was for their sins that they were spoiled of all their possessions, not only in their own land, but in the land of their enemies. They were some of them *snared in holes,* and others *hidden in prison-houses.* They cannot help themselves, for they are snared. Their friends cannot help them, for they are hidden; and their enemies have forgotten them in their prisons. They, and all they have, are for a prey and for a spoil; and there is none that delivers either by force or ransom, nor any that dares say to the proud oppressors, *Restore.* There they lie, and there they are likely to lie. This had its full accomplishment in the final destruction of the Jewish nation by the Romans, which God brought upon them for rejecting the gospel of Christ.

V. The counsel given them in order to their relief; for, though their case be sad, it is not desperate.

1. The generality of them are deaf; they will not hearken to the voice of God's word. He will therefore try his rod, and see *who among them will give ear to that, v.* 23. We must not despair concerning those who have been long reasoned with in vain; some of them may, at length, give ear and hearken. If one method do not take effect, another may, and sinners shall be left inexcusable. Observe, (1.) We may all of us, if we will, hear the voice of God, and we are called and invited to hear it. (2.) It is worth while to enquire who they are that perceive God speaking to them and are willing to hear him. (3.) Of the many that hear the voice of God there are very few that hearken to it or heed it, that hear it with attention and application. (4.) In hearing the word we must have an eye to the time to come. We must hear for hereafter, for what may occur between us and the grave; we must especially hear for eternity. We must hear the word with another world in our eye.

2. The counsel is, (1.) To acknowledge the hand of God in their afflictions, and, whoever were the instruments, to have an eye to him as the principal agent (v. 24): "*Who gave Jacob and Israel,* that people that used to have such an interest in heaven and such a dominion on earth, who gave them *for a spoil to the robbers,* as they are now to the Babylonians and to the Romans? *Did not the Lord?* You know he did; consider it then, and hear his voice in these judgments." (2.) To acknowledge that they had provoked God thus to abandon them, and had brought all these calamities upon themselves. [1.] These punishments were first inflicted on them for their disobedience to the laws of God: It is he *against whom we have sinned;* the prophet puts himself into the number of the sinners, as Dan. ix.

7, 8. "*We have sinned;* we have all brought fuel to the fire; and there are those among us that have wilfully refused to walk in his ways. Jacob and Israel would never have been given up to the robbers if they had not by their iniquities sold themselves. *Therefore* it is, because they have violated the commands of the law, that God has brought upon them the curses of the law; he has not dropped, but *poured upon him the fury of his anger and the strength of battle,* all the desolations of war, which have *set him on fire round about;* for God surrounds the wicked with his judgments, as he does the righteous with his favours. See the power of God's anger; there is no resisting it, no escaping it. See the mischief that sin makes; it provokes God to anger against a people, and so kindles a universal conflagration, sets all on fire. [2.] These judgments were continued upon them for their senselessness and incorrigibleness under the rod of God. The fire of God's wrath kindled upon him, and *he knew it not,* was not aware of it, took no notice of the judgments, at least not of the hand of God in them. Nay, *it burned him,* and, though he could not then but know it and feel it, yet he *laid it not to heart,* was not awakened by the fiery rebukes he was under nor at all affected with them. Those who are not humbled by less judgments must expect greater; for when God judges he will overcome.

CHAP. XLIII.

The contents of this chapter are much the same with those of the foregoing chapter, looking at the release of the Jews out of their captivity, but looking through that, and beyond that, to the great work of man's redemption by Jesus Christ, and the grace of the gospel, which through him believers partake of. Here are, I. Precious promises made to God's people in their affliction, of his presence with them, for their support under it, and their deliverance out of it, ver. 1—7. II. A challenge to idols to vie with the omniscience and omnipotence of God, ver. 8—13. III. Encouragement given to the people of God to hope for their deliverance out of Babylon, from the consideration of what God did for their fathers when he brought them out of Egypt, ver. 14—21. IV. A method taken to prepare the people for their deliverance, by putting them in mind of their sins, by which they had provoked God to send them into captivity and continue them there, that they might repent and seek to God for pardoning mercy, ver. 22—28.

BUT now thus saith the LORD that created thee, O Jacob, and he that formed thee, O Israel, Fear not: for I have redeemed thee, I have called *thee* by thy name; thou *art* mine. 2 When thou passest through the waters, I *will be* with thee; and through the rivers, they shall not overflow thee: when thou walkest through the fire, thou shalt not be burnt; neither shall the flame kindle upon thee. 3 For I *am* the LORD thy God, the Holy one of Israel, thy Saviour: I gave Egypt *for* thy ransom, Ethiopia and Seba for thee. 4 Since thou wast precious in my sight, thou hast been honourable, and I

233

have loved thee : therefore will I give men for thee, and people for thy life. 5 Fear not: for I *am* with thee : I will bring thy seed from the east, and gather thee from the west ;　6 I will say to the north, Give up ; and to the south, Keep not back : bring my sons from far, and my daughters from the ends of the earth ;　7 *Even* every one that is called by my name : for I have created him for my glory, I have formed him; yea, I have made him.

This chapter has a plain connexion with the close of the foregoing chapter, but a very surprising one. It was there said that Jacob and Israel would not walk in God's ways, and that when he corrected them for their disobedience they were stubborn and laid it not to heart ; and now one would think it should have followed that God would utterly abandon and destroy them ; but no, the next words are, *But now, fear not, O Jacob! O Israel! I have redeemed thee, and thou art mine.* Though many among them were untractable and incorrigible, yet God would continue his love and care for his people, and the body of that nation should still be reserved for mercy. God's goodness takes occasion from man's badness to appear so much the more illustrious. *Where sin abounded, grace did much more abound* (Rom. v. 20), and mercy *rejoices against judgment,* as having prevailed and carried the day, Jam. ii. 13. Now the sun, breaking out thus of a sudden from behind a thick and dark cloud, shines the brighter, and with a pleasing surprise. The expressions of God's favour and good-will to his people here are very high, and speak abundance of comfort to all the spiritual seed of upright Jacob and praying Israel; for *to us is this gospel preached as well as unto those* that were captives in Babylon, Heb. iv. 2. Here we have,

I. The grounds of God's care and concern for his people and the interests of his church and kingdom among men. Jacob and Israel, though in a sinful miserable condition, shall be looked after; for, 1. They are God's *workmanship, created by him unto good works,* Eph. ii. 10. He has created them and formed them, not only given them a being, but this being, formed them into a people, constituted their government, and incorporated them by the charter of his covenant. The new creature, wherever it is, is of God's forming, and *he will not forsake the work of his own hands.* 2. They are the people of his purchase : he has redeemed them. Out of the land of Egypt he first redeemed them, and out of many another bondage, *in his love, and in his pity* (ch. lxiii. 9) ; much more will he take care of those who are redeemed with the blood of his Son. 3. They are his peculiar people, whom he has distinguished

234

from others, and set apart for himself: he has called them by name, as those he has a particular intimacy with and concern for, and they are his, are appropriated to him and he has a special interest in them.　4. He is their God in covenant (*v.* 3) : *I am the Lord thy God,* worshipped by thee and engaged by promise to thee, *the Holy One of Israel,* the God of Israel ; for the true God is a holy one, and holiness becomes his house. And upon all these accounts he might justly say, *Fear not* (*v.* 1), and again *v.* 5, *Fear not.* Those that have God for them need not fear who or what can be against them.

II. The former instances of this care. 1. God had purchased them dearly : *I gave Egypt for thy ransom;* for Egypt was quite laid waste by one plague after another, all their first-born were slain and all their men of war drowned ; and all this to force a way for Israel's deliverance from them. Egypt shall be sacrificed rather than Israel shall continue in slavery, when the time has come for their release. The Ethiopians had invaded them in Asa's time ; but they shall be destroyed rather than Israel shall be disturbed. And if this was reckoned so great a thing, to give Egypt for their ransom, what reason have we to admire God's love to us in giving his own Son to be a *ransom for us!* 1 John iv. 10. What are Ethiopia and Seba, all their lives and all their treasures, compared with the blood of Christ ?　2. He had prized them accordingly, and they were very dear to him (*v.* 4) : *Since thou hast been precious in my sight thou hast been honourable.* Note, True believers are precious in God's sight ; they are his jewels, his peculiar treasure (Exod. xix. 5) ; he loves them, his delight is in them, above any people. His church is his vineyard. And this makes God's people truly honourable, and their name great ; for men are really what they are in God's eye. When the forces of Sennacherib, that they might be diverted from falling upon Israel, were directed by Providence to fall upon Egypt, Ethiopia, and Seba, then God gave those countries for Israel, and showed how precious his people were in his sight. So some understand it.

III. The further instances God would yet give them of his care and kindness. 1. He would be present with them in their greatest difficulties and dangers (*v.* 2) : " *When thou passest* through the waters and the rivers, through the fire and the flame, *I will be with thee,* and that shall be thy security ; when dangers are very imminent and threatening, thou shalt be delivered out of them." Did they, in their journey, pass through deep waters? They should not perish in them : " *The rivers shall not overflow thee.* Should they by their persecutors be cast into a fiery furnace, for their constant adherence to their God, yet then the flame should not kindle upon them, which was fulfilled in the letter in the wonderful preservation of the three children, Dan. iii. Though they went through fire and water, which would be to them as the *valley of the shadow of death*, yet, while they had God with them, they need fear no evil, they should be borne up, and *brought out into a wealthy place*, Ps. lxvi. 12. 2. He would still, when there was occasion, make all the interests of the children of men give way to the interests of his own children : " *I will give men for thee*, great men, mighty men, and men of war, *and people* (men by whole-sale) *for thy life.* Nations shall be sacrificed to thy welfare." All shall be cut off rather than God's Israel shall, so precious are they in his sight. The affairs of the world shall all be ordered and directed so as to be most for the good of the church, 2 Chron. xvi. 9. 3. Those of them that were scattered and dispersed in other nations should all be gathered in and share in the blessings of the public, *v.* 5—7. Some of the seed of Israel were dispersed into all countries, east, west, north, and south, or into all the parts of the country of Babylon ; but those whose spirits God stirred up to go to Jerusalem should be fetched in from all parts ; divine grace should reach those that lay most remote, and at the greatest distance from each other ; and, when the time should come, nothing should prevent their coming together to return in a body, in answer to that prayer (Ps. cvi. 47), *Gather us from among the heathen*, and in performance of that promise (Deut. xxx. 4), *If any of thine be driven to the utmost parts of heaven, thence will the Lord thy God gather thee*, which we find pleaded on behalf of the children of the captivity, Neh. i. 9. But who are the seed of Israel that shall be thus carefully gathered in ? He tells us (*v.* 7) they are such as God has marked for mercy ; for, (1.) They are called by his name ; they make profession of religion, and are distinguished from the rest of the world by their covenant-relation to God and denomination from him. (2.) They are created for his glory ; the spirit of Israelites is created in them, and they are formed according to the will of God, and these shall be gathered in. Note, Those only are fit to be called by the name of God that are created by his grace for his glory ; and those whom God has created and called shall be gathered in now to Christ as their head and hereafter to heaven as their home. *He shall gather in his elect from the four winds.* This promise points at the gathering in of the dispersed of the Gentiles, and the strangers scattered, by the gospel of Christ, who died to *gather together in one* the children of God that were scattered abroad ; for the promise was to all that were afar off, even as many as the Lord our God shall call and create. God is with the church, and therefore let her not fear ; none that belong to her shall be lost.

8 Bring forth the blind people that have eyes, and the deaf that have ears. 9 Let all the nations be gathered together, and let the people be assembled : who among them can declare this, and show us former things ? Let them bring forth their witnesses, that they may be justified : or let them hear, and say, *It is* truth. 10 Ye *are* my witnesses, saith the LORD, and my servant whom I have chosen : that ye may know and believe me, and understand that I *am* he : before me there was no God formed, neither shall there be after me. 11 I, *even* I, *am* the LORD ; and beside me *there is* no saviour. 12 I have declared, and have saved, and I have showed, when *there was* no strange *god* among you : therefore ye *are* my witnesses, saith the LORD, that I *am* God. 13 Yea, before the day *was*, I *am* he ; and *there is* none that can deliver out of my hand : I will work, and who shall let it ?

God here challenges the worshippers of idols to produce such proofs of the divinity of their false gods as even this very instance (to go no further) of the redemption of the Jews out of Babylon furnished the people of Israel with, to prove that their God is the true and living God, and he only.

I. The patrons of idolatry are here called to appear, and say what they have to say in defence of their idols, *v.* 8, 9. Their gods have *eyes and see not, ears and hear not*, and those that make them and trust in them are like unto them ; so David had said (Ps. cxv. 8), to which the prophet seems here to refer when he calls idolaters *blind people that have eyes, and deaf people that have ears.* They have the shape, capacities, and faculties, of men ; but they are, in effect, destitute of reason and common sense, or they would never worship gods of their own making. " *Let all the nations therefore be gathered together*, let them help one another, and with a combined force plead the cause of their dunghill gods ; and, if they have nothing to say in their own justification, let them hear what the God of Israel has to say for their conviction and confutation."

II. God's witnesses are subpœnaed, or summoned to appear, and give in evidence for him (*v.* 10) : " *You, O Israelites!* all you that are *called by my name*, you *are all my witnesses, and* so is *my servant whom I have chosen.*" It was Christ himself that was so described (*ch.* xlii. 1), *My servant and my elect.* Observe,

1. All the prophets that testified to Christ, and Christ himself, the great prophet, are here appealed to as God's witnesses. (1.)

God's people are witnesses for him, and can attest, upon their own knowledge and experience, concerning the power of his grace, the sweetness of his comforts, the tenderness of his providence, and the truth of his promise. They will be forward to witness for him that he is gracious and that no word of his has fallen to the ground. (2.) His prophets are in a particular manner witnesses for him, with whom his secret is, and who know more of him than others do. But the Messiah especially is given to be a witness for him to the people; having lain in his bosom from eternity, he has declared him. Now,

2. Let us see what the point is which these witnesses are called to prove (*v.* 12): *You are my witnesses, saith the Lord, that I am God.* Note, Those who do themselves acknowledge that the Lord is God should be ready to testify what they know of him to others, that they also may be brought to the acknowledgment of it. *I believed, therefore have I spoken.* Particularly, " Since you cannot but know, and believe, and understand, you must be ready to bear record, (1.) That I am he, the only true God, that I am a being self-existent and self-sufficient; I am he whom you are to fear, and worship, and trust in. Nay (*v.* 13), *before the day was* (before the first day of time, before the creation of the light, and, consequently, from eternity) *I am he.*" The idols were but of yesterday, *new gods that came newly up* (Deut. xxxii. 17); but the God of Israel was from everlasting. (2.) That *there was no God formed before me, nor shall be after me.* The idols were gods formed (*dii facti—made gods,* or rather *fictitii—fictitious) : by nature they were no gods,* Gal. iv. 8. But God had a being from eternity, yea, and a religion in this world before there were either idols or idolaters (truth is more ancient than error); and he will have a being to eternity, and will be worshipped and glorified when idols are famished and abolished and idolatry shall be no more. True religion will keep its ground, and survive all opposition and competition. *Great is the truth, and will prevail.* (3.) That *I, even I, am the Lord,* the great Jehovah, who is, and was, and is to come ; and *besides me there is no Saviour, v.* 11. See what it is that the great God glories in, not so much that he is the only ruler as that he is the only Saviour ; for he *delights to do good:* he is the *Saviour of all men,* 1 Tim. iv. 10.

3. Let us see what the proofs are which are produced for the confirmation of this point. It appears,

(1.) That the Lord is God, by two proofs : [1.] He has an infinite and infallible knowledge, as is evident from *the predictions of his word* (*v.* 12): *I have declared and I have shown* that which has without fail come to pass ; nay, I never declared nor showed any thing but it has been accomplished. *I showed*

236

when there was no strange god among you, that is, when you pretended not to consult any oracles but mine, nor to have any prophets but mine." It is said, when they came out of Egypt, that *the Lord alone did lead him, and there was no strange god with him.* [2.] He has an infinite and irresistible power, as is evident from the performances of his providence. He pleads not only, I have *shown,* but, I have *saved,* not only foretold what none else could foresee, but done what none else could do ; for (*v.* 13), " *None can deliver out of my hand* those whom I will punish ; not only no man can, but none of all the gods of the heathen can protect." It is therefore a *fearful thing to fall into the hands of the living God,* because there is no getting out of them again. " I will work what I have designed, both in mercy and judgment, and who shall either oppose or retard it ?"

(2.) That the gods of the heathen, who are rivals with him, are not only inferior to him, but no gods at all, which is proved (*v* 9) by a challenge : *Who among them can declare this* that I now declare? Who can foretel things to come? Nay, which of them can *show us former things?* ch. xli. 22. They cannot so much as inspire an historian, much less a prophet. They are challenged to join issue upon this : *Let them bring forth their witnesses,* to prove their omniscience and omnipotence. And, [1.] If they do prove them, they shall be justified, the idols in demanding homage and the idolaters in paying it. [2.] If they do not prove them, *let them say, It is truth ;* let them own the true God, and receive the truth concerning him, that he is God alone. The cause of God is not afraid to stand a fair trial ; but it may reasonably be expected that those who cannot justify themselves in their irreligion should submit to the power of the truth and true religion.

14 Thus saith the LORD, your Redeemer, the Holy One of Israel; For your sake I have sent to Babylon, and have brought down all their nobles, and the Chaldeans, whose cry *is* in the ships. 15 I *am* the LORD, your Holy One, the creator of Israel, your King. 16 Thus saith the LORD, which maketh a way in the sea, and a path in the mighty waters; 17 Which bringeth forth the chariot and horse, the army and the power; they shall lie down together, they shall not rise : they are extinct, they are quenched as tow. 18 Remember ye not the former things, neither consider the things of old. 19 Behold, I will do a new thing ; now it shall spring forth ;

shall ye not know it? I will even make a way in the wilderness, *and* rivers in the desert. 20 The beast of the field shall honour me, the dragons and the owls: because I give waters in the wilderness, *and* rivers in the desert, to give drink to my people, my chosen. 21 This people have I formed for myself; they shall show forth my praise.

To so low an ebb were the faith and hope of God's people in Babylon brought that there needed line upon line to assure them that they should be released out of their captivity; and therefore, that they might have strong consolation, the assurances of it are often repeated, and here very expressly and encouragingly.

I. God here takes to himself such titles of his honour as were very encouraging to them. He is *the Lord their Redeemer*, not only he will redeem them, but will take it upon him as his office and make it his business to do so. If he be their God, he will be all that to them which they need, and therefore, when they are in bondage, he will be their Redeemer. He is the *Holy One of Israel* (*v.* 14), and again (*v.* 15), *their Holy One*, and therefore will make good every word he has spoken to them. He is *the Creator of Israel*, that made them a people out of nothing (for that is creation), nay, worse than nothing; and he is their *King*, that owns them as his people and presides among them.

II. He assures them he will find out a way to break the power of their oppressors that held them captives and filled up the measure of their own iniquity by their resolution never to let them go, *ch.* xiv. 17. God will take care to send a victorious prince and army to Babylon, that shall *bring down all their nobles*, and lay their honour in the dust, and all their people too, even *the Chaldeans, whose cry is in the ships* (for seamen are apt to be noisy), or whose cry is *to the ships*, as their refuge when the city is taken, that they may escape by the benefit of their great river. Note, The destruction of Babylon must make way for the enlargement of God's people. And in the prediction of the fall of the New-Testament Babylon we meet with the cries and lamentations of the sailors, Rev. xviii. 17, 18. And observe, It is for Israel's sake that Babylon is ruined, to make way for their deliverance.

III. He reminds them of the great things he did for their fathers when he brought them out of the land of Egypt; for so it may be read (*v.* 16, 17): " *Thus saith the Lord, who did make a way in the sea*, the Red Sea, and did *bring forth* Pharaoh's *chariot and horse*, that they might lie down together in the bottom of the sea, and never rise, but be extinct. He that did this can,

if he please, make a way for you in the sea when you return out of Babylon, and will do so rather than leave you there." Note, For the encouragement of our faith and hope, it is good for us often to remember what God has done formerly for his people against his and their enemies. Think particularly what he did at the Red Sea, how he made it, 1. A road to his people, a straight way, a near way, nay, a refuge to them, into which they fled and were safe, the waters being a wall unto them. 2. A grave to his enemies. The chariot and horse were drawn out by him who is Lord of all hosts, on purpose that they might fall together; howbeit, *they meant not so*, Mic. iv. 11, 12.

IV. He promises to do yet greater things for them than he had done in the days of old; so that they should not have reason to ask, in a way of complaint, as Gideon did, *Where are all the wonders that our fathers told us of?* for they should see them repeated, nay, they should see them outdone (*v.* 18): " *Remember not the former things*, from them to take occasion, as some do, to undervalue the present things, as if *the former days were better than these:* no, you may, if you will, comparatively forget them, and yet know enough by the events of your own day to convince you that the Lord is God alone; for, *behold, the Lord will do a new thing*, no way inferior, both for the wonder and the worth of the mercy, to the things of old!" The best exposition of this is, Jer. xvi. 14, 15; xxiii. 7, 8. *It shall no more be said, The Lord liveth that brought up the children of Israel out of the land of Egypt:* that is an old thing, the remembrance of which will be in a manner lost in the new thing, in the new proof that the Lord liveth, for he *brought up the children of Israel out of the land of the north*. Though former mercies must not be forgotten, fresh mercies must in a special manner be improved. *Now it springs forth*, as it were a surprise upon you; you are like those that dream. *Shall you not know it?* And will you not own God's hand in it?

V. He promises not only to deliver them out of Babylon, but to conduct them safely and comfortably to their own land (*v.* 19, 20): *I will make a way in the wilderness and rivers in the desert:* for, it seems, the way from Babylon to Canaan, as well as from Egypt, lay through a desert land, which, while the returning captives passed through, God would provide for them, that their camp should be both well victualled and under a good conduct. The same power that made a *way in the sea* (*v.* 16) can make a *way in the wilderness*, and will force its passage through the greatest difficulties. And he that made dry land in the waters can produce waters in the dryest land, in such abundance as not only to *give drink to his people, his chosen*, but to the *beasts of the field*, also *the dragons and the ostriches*, who are therefore said to honour God for it; it is such a sensible refreshment, and yields them so much satisfaction, that, if they were capable of doing it, they would praise God for it, and shame man, who is made capable of praising his benefactor and does not. Now, 1. This looks back to what God did for Israel when he led them through the wilderness from Egypt to Canaan, and fetched water out of a rock to follow them; what God did for them formerly he would do again, for he is still the same. And, though we do not find that the miracle was repeated in their return out of Babylon, yet the mercy was, in the common course of Providence, for which it became them to be no less thankful to God. 2. It looks forward, not only to all the instances of God's care of the Jewish church in the latter ages of it, between their return from Babylon and the coming of Christ, but to the grace of the gospel, especially as it is manifested to the Gentile world, by which a way is opened in the wilderness and rivers in the desert; the world, which lay like a desert, in ignorance and unfruitfulness, was blessed with divine direction and divine comforts, and, in order to both, with a plentiful effusion of the Spirit. The sinners of the Gentiles, who had been as the beasts of the field, running wild, fierce as the dragons, stupid as the owls or ostriches, shall be brought to honour God for the extent of his grace to his chosen among them.

VI. He traces up all these promised blessings to their great original, the purposes and designs of his own glory (v. 21): *This people have I formed for myself*, and therefore I do all this for them, that they may *show forth my praise*. Note, 1. The church is of God's forming, and so are all the living members of it. The new heavens, the new earth, the new man, are the work of God's hand, and are no more, no better, than he makes them; they are fashioned according to his will. 2. He forms it for himself. He that is the first cause is the highest end both of the first and of the new creation. *The Lord has made all things for himself*, his Israel especially, to be to him for *a people, and for a name, and for a praise;* and no otherwise can they be for him, or serviceable to him, than as his grace is glorified in them, Jer. xiii. 11; Eph. i. 6, 12, 14. 3. It is therefore our duty to show forth his praise, not only with our lips, but in our lives, by giving up ourselves to his service. As he formed us, so he feeds us, and keeps us, and leads us, and all for himself; for every instance therefore of his goodness we must praise him, else we answer not the end of the beings and blessings we have.

22 But thou hast not called upon me, O Jacob; but thou hast been weary of me, O Israel. 23 Thou hast not brought me the small cattle

238

of thy burnt-offerings; neither hast thou honoured me with thy sacrifices. I have not caused thee to serve with an offering, nor wearied thee with incense. 24 Thou hast bought me no sweet cane with money, neither hast thou filled me with the fat of thy sacrifices: but thou hast made me to serve with thy sins, thou hast wearied me with thine iniquities. 25 I, *even* I, *am* he that blotteth out thy transgressions for mine own sake, and will not remember thy sins. 26 Put me in remembrance: let us plead together: declare thou, that thou mayest be justified. 27 Thy first father hath sinned, and thy teachers have transgressed against me. 28 Therefore I have profaned the princes of the sanctuary, and have given Jacob to the curse, and Israel to reproaches.

This charge (and a high charge it is which is here exhibited against Jacob and Israel, God's professing people) comes in here, 1. To clear God's justice in bringing them into captivity, and to vindicate that. Were they not in covenant with him? Had they not his sanctuary among them? *Why then did the Lord deal thus with his land?* Deut. xxix. 24. Here is a good reason given: they had neglected God and had cast him off, and therefore he justly rejected them and gave them to the curse (v. 28); and they must be brought to own this before they are prepared for deliverance; and they did so, Dan. ix. 5; Neh. ix. 33. 2. To advance God's mercy in their deliverance and to make that appear more glorious. Many things are before observed to magnify the power of God in it; but this magnifies his goodness, that he should do such great and kind things for a people that had been so very provoking to him and were now suffering the just punishment of their iniquity. The pardoning of their sin was as great an instance of God's power (for so Moses reckons it, Num. xiv. 17, &c.) as the breaking of the yoke of their captivity. Now observe here,

I. What the sins are which they are here charged with.

1. Omissions of the good which God had commanded; and this part of the charge is here much insisted upon. Observe how it comes in with a *but;* compare v. 21, where God tells them what favours he had bestowed upon them and what his just expectations were from them. He had formed them for himself, intending they should show forth his praise. But they had not done so; they had frustrated God's expectations from them, and made very ill returns to him for his

favours. For, (1.) They had cast off prayer : *Thou hast not called upon me, O Jacob !* Jacob was a man famous for prayer (Hosea xii. 4) ; his seed bore his name, but did not tread in his steps, and therefore are justly upbraided with it. God takes it ill when children degenerate from the virtue and devotion of their pious ancestors. To boast of the name of Jacob, and yet live without prayer, is to mock God and deceive ourselves. If Jacob does not call upon God, who will? (2.) They had grown weary of their religion : "Thou art Israel, the seed not only of a praying but of a prevailing father, that was a prince with God ; and yet, not valuing his experiences any more than his example, *thou hast been weary of me.*" They had been in relation to God, employed in his service and in communion with him ; but they began to snuff at it, and to say, *Behold, what a weariness is it !* Note, Those who neglect to call upon God do in effect tell him they are weary of him and have a mind to change their Master. (3.) They grudged the expense of their devotion, and were niggardly and penurious in it. They were for a cheap religion ; and in those acts of devotion that were costly they desired to be excused. They had *not brought*, no, not their *small cattle*, the lambs and kids, which God required for *burnt-offerings* (v. 23), much less did they bring their greater cattle, pretending they could not spare them, they must have them for the maintenance of their families. So little sense had they of the greatness of God and their obligations to him that they could not find in their hearts to part with a lamb out of their flock for his honour, though he called for it and would graciously have accepted it. *Sweet cane*, or *calamus*, was used for the holy oil, incense, and perfume ; but they were not willing to be at the charge of that, v. 24. What they had must serve, though it was old and good for nothing ; they would not buy fresh. Perhaps it was usual for devout pious persons to bring free-will incense as well as other free-will offerings ; but they were not so generous, nor did they fill the altar of God, nor moisten it abundantly, as they should have done, *with the fat of their sacrifices ;* what sacrifices they did bring were of the lean and refuse of their cattle, that had no fat in them to regale the altar with. (4.) What sacrifices they did offer they did not honour God with them, and so they were, in effect, as no sacrifices (v. 23) : *Neither hast thou honoured me with thy sacrifices.* Some of them offered their sacrifices to false gods ; others, who offered them to the true God, were either careless in the manner of offering them or hypocritical in their intentions, so that they might be truly said not to honour God with them, but rather to dishonour him. (5.) That which aggravated their neglect of sacrificing was that, as God had appointed it, it was no burdensome thing ; it was not a service

that they had any reason at all to complain of : "*I have not caused thee to serve with an offering ;* I have not made it a task and drudgery to you, whatever you, through the corruption of your natures, have made it yourselves. I have *not wearied thee with incense.*" None of God's commandments are grievous, no, not those concerning sacrifice and incense. They were not more costly than might be afforded by those that lived in such a plentiful country, nor did their attendance on them require any more time than they could well spare. But that which especially forbade them to call it *a wearisome service* was that they were required to be cheerful and pleasant, and to rejoice before God in all their approaches to him, Deut. xii. 12. They had many feasts and good days, but only one day in all the year in which they were to afflict their souls. The ordinances of the ceremonial law, though, in comparison with Christ's easy yoke, they are spoken of as heavy (Acts xv. 10), yet, in comparison with the service that idolaters did to their false gods, they were light, and not to be called *services* nor found fault with as wearisome. God did not require them to sacrifice their children, as Moloch did.

2. Commissions of the evil which God had forbidden ; and omissions commonly make way for commissions : *Thou hast made me to serve with thy sins.* When we make God's gifts the food and fuel of our lusts, and his providence the patron of our wicked projects, especially when we encourage ourselves to continue in sin because grace has abounded, then we make God to serve with our sins. Or it may denote what a grief and burden sin is to God ; it not only wearies men and makes the creation groan, but it *wearies my God also* (ch. vii. 13) and makes the Creator complain that he is *grieved* (Ps. xcv. 10), that he is *broken* (Ezek. vi. 9), that he is pressed with sinners *as a cart is pressed that is full of sheaves* (Amos ii. 13), and to cry out, *Ah! I will ease me of my adversaries*, ch. i. 24. The antithesis is observable : God had not made them to serve with their sacrifices, but they had. made him to serve with their sins. The master had not tired the servants with his commands, but they had tired him with their disobedience. Those are wicked servants indeed that behave so ill to so good a Master. God is tender of our comfort, but we are careless of his honour. Let *this* engage us to keep close to our duty, that it is easy and reasonable, and no disparagement to us, nor too hard for us.

II. What were the aggravations of their sin, v. 27. 1. That they were children of disobedience ; for their *first father* (that is, their forefathers) *had sinned ;* and they had not only sinned in their loins, but sinned like them. Ezra confesses this : *Since the days of our fathers have we been in a great trespass, ch.* ix. 7. But their forefathers are called their *first father* to put us in mind of the apostasy and rebellion of our first father Adam, to which corrupt fountain we must trace up the streams of all our transgressions. 2. That they were scholars of disobedience too ; for *their teachers had transgressed against God*, were guilty of gross scandalous sins, and the people, no doubt, would learn to do as they did. It is ill with a people when their leaders cause them to err, and their teachers, who should reform them, corrupt them.

III. What were the tokens of God's displeasure against them for their sins, *v.* 23. He brought ruin both upon church and state. 1. The honour of their church was laid in the dust and trampled on : *I have profaned the princes of the sanctuary*, that is, the priests and Levites who presided with great dignity and power in the temple-service ; they profaned themselves, and made themselves vile, by their enormities, and then God profaned them and made them vile, by their calamities and the contempt they fell into, Mal. ii. 9. 2. The honour of their state was ruined likewise : " *I have given Jacob to the curse*, that is, to be cursed, and hated, and abused by all their neighbours, *and Israel to reproach*,to be insulted, ridiculed, and triumphed over by their enemies." They reproached them perhaps for that in them that was good ; they *mocked at their sabbaths* (Lam. i. 7) ; but God gave them up to reproach, to correct them for what was amiss. Note, The dishonour which men at any time do us should humble us for the dishonour we have done to God ; and we must bear it patiently because we suffer it justly, and must acknowledge that to us belongs confusion.

IV. What were the riches of God's mercy towards them notwithstanding (*v.* 25) : *I, even I, am he who* notwithstanding all this *blotteth out thy transgressions.*

1. This gracious declaration of God's readiness to pardon sin comes in very strangely. The charge ran very high : *Thou hast wearied me with thy iniquities, v.* 24. Now one would think it should follow : " *I, even I, am he* that will destroy thee, and burden myself no longer with care about thee." No, *I, even I, am he that will forgive thee ;* as if the great God would teach us that forgiving injuries is the best way to make ourselves easy and to keep ourselves from being wearied with them. This comes in here to encourage them to repent, because there is forgiveness with God, and to show the freeness of divine mercy ; where sin has been exceedingly sinful grace appears exceedingly gracious. Apply this, (1.) To the forgiving of the sins of Israel as a people, in their national capacity. When God stopped the course of threatening judgments, and saved them from utter ruin, even then when he had them under severe rebukes,

then he might be said to *blot out their transgressions.* Though he corrected them, he was reconciled to them again, and did not cut them off from being a people. This he did many a time, till they rejected Christ and his gospel, which was a sin against the remedy, and then he would forgive them no more as a nation, but utterly destroyed them. (2.) To the forgiving of the sins of every particular believing penitent—*transgressions and sins*, infirmities though ever so numerous, backslidings though ever so heinous. Observe here, [1.] How the pardon is expressed ; he will *blot them out*, as a cloud is blotted out by the beams of the sun (*ch.* xliv. 22), as a debt is blotted out not to appear against the debtor (the book is crossed as if the debt were paid, because it is pardoned upon the payment which the surety has made), or as a sentence is blotted out when it is reversed, as the curse was blotted out with the waters of jealousy, which made it of no effect to the innocent, Num. v. 23. He *will not remember* the sin, which intimates not only that he will remit the punishment of what is past, but that it shall be no diminution to his love for the future. When God forgives he forgets. [2.] What is the ground and reason of the pardon. It is not for the sake of any thing in us, but for his own sake, for his mercies'-sake, his promise-sake, and especially for his Son's sake, and that he may himself be glorified in it. [3.] How God glories in it : *I, even I, am he.* He glories in it as his prerogative. None can forgive sin but God only, and he will do it ; it is his settled resolution. He will do it willingly and with delight ; it is his pleasure ; it is his honour ; so he is pleased to reckon it.

2. Those words (*v.* 26), *Put me in remembrance,* may be understood either (1.) As a rebuke to a proud Pharisee, that stands upon his own justification before God, and expects to find favour for his merits and not to be beholden to free grace : " If you have any thing to say in your own justification, any thing to offer for the sake of which you should be pardoned, and not for my sake, put me in remembrance of it. I will give you leave to plead your own cause with me ; declare what your merits are, that you may be justified by them :" but those who are thus challenged will be speechless. Or, (2.) As a direction and encouragement to a penitent publican. Is God thus ready to pardon sin, and, when he pardons it, will he remember it no more ? Let us then put him in remembrance, mention before him those sins which he has forgiven ; for they must be ever before us, to humble us, though they are pardoned, Ps. li. 3. Put him in remembrance of the promises he has made to penitents, and the satisfaction his Son has made for them. Plead these with him in wrestling for pardon, and declare these things, in order that thou mayest be justified freely by his

grace. This is the only way, and it is a sure way, to peace. *Only acknowledge thy transgression.*

CHAP. XLIV.

God, by the prophet, goes on in this chapter, as before, I. To encourage his people with the assurance of great blessings he had in store for them at their return out of captivity, and those typical of much greater which the gospel church, his spiritual Israel, should partake of in the days of the Messiah; and hereby he proves himself to be God alone against all pretenders, ver. 1—8. II. To expose the sottishness and amazing folly of idol-makers and idol-worshippers, ver. 9—20. III. To ratify and confirm the assurances he had given to his people of those great blessings, and to raise their joyful and believing expectations of them, ver. 21—28.

YET now hear, O Jacob my servant; and Israel, whom I have chosen: 2 Thus saith the LORD that made thee, and formed thee from the womb, *which* will help thee; Fear not, O Jacob, my servant; and thou, Jesurun, whom I have chosen. 3 For I will pour water upon him that is thirsty, and floods upon the dry ground: I will pour my Spirit upon thy seed, and my blessing upon thine offspring: 4 And they shall spring up *as* among the grass, as willows by the water-courses. 5 One shall say, I *am* the LORD's; and another shall call *himself* by the name of Jacob; and another shall subscribe *with* his hand unto the LORD, and surname *himself* by the name of Israel. 6 Thus saith the LORD the King of Israel, and his Redeemer the LORD of hosts; I *am* the first, and I *am* the last; and beside me *there is* no God. 7 And who, as I, shall call, and shall declare it, and set it in order for me, since I appointed the ancient people? And the things that are coming, and shall come, let them show unto them. 8 Fear ye not, neither be afraid: have not I told thee from that time, and have declared *it?* Ye *are* even my witnesses. Is there a God beside me? Yea, *there is* no God; I know not *any.*

Two great truths are abundantly made out in these verses:—

I. That the people of God are a happy people, especially upon account of the covenant that is between them and God. The people of Israel were so as a figure of the gospel Israel. Three things complete their happiness:—

1. The covenant-relations wherein they stand to God, *v.* 1, 2. Israel is here called *Jeshurun—the upright one;* for those only, like Nathanael, are Israelites indeed, in whom is no guile, and those only shall have

the everlasting benefit of these promises. Jacob and Israel had been represented, in the close of the foregoing chapter, as very provoking and obnoxious to God's wrath, and already given to the curse and to reproaches; but, as if God's bowels yearned towards him and his repentings were kindled together, mercy steps in with a *non-obstante—notwithstanding,* to all these quarrels : " *Yet now hear, O Jacob my servant!* thou and I will be friends again for all this." God had said (*ch.* xliii. 25), *I am he that blotteth out thy transgression,* which is the only thing that creates this distance; and when that is taken away the streams of mercy run again in their former channel. The pardon of sin is the inlet of all the other blessings of the covenant. So and so I will do for them, says God (Heb. viii. 12), *for I will be merciful to their unrighteousness.* Therefore *hear, O Jacob!* hear these comfortable words; therefore *fear not, O Jacob!* fear not thy sins, for they are pardoned; fear not thy troubles, for by the pardon of sin the property of them too is altered. Now the relations wherein they stand to him are very encouraging. (1.) They are his *servants;* and those that serve him he will own and stand by and see that they be not wronged. (2.) They are his *chosen,* and he will abide by his choice; he knows those that are his, and those whom he has chosen he takes under special protection. (3.) They are his creatures. He *made them,* and brought them into being; he *formed them,* and cast them into shape; he began betimes with them, for he *formed them from the womb;* and therefore he will help them over their difficulties and help them in their services.

2. The covenant-blessings which he has secured to them and theirs, *v.* 3, 4. (1.) Those that are sensible of their spiritual wants, and the insufficiency of the creature to supply them, shall have abundant satisfaction in God: *I will pour water upon him that is thirsty,* that thirsts after righteousness; he shall be filled. Water shall be poured out to those who truly desire spiritual blessings above all the delights of sense. (2.) Those that are barren as the dry ground shall be watered with the grace of God, with floods of that grace, and God will himself give the increase. If the ground be ever so dry, God has floods of grace to water it with. (3.) The water God will pour out is *his Spirit* (John vii. 39), which God will pour out without measure upon the seed, that is, Christ (Gal. iii. 16), and by measure upon all the seed of the faithful, upon all the praying wrestling seed of Jacob, Luke xi. 13. This is the great New-Testament promise, that God, having sent his servant Christ, and upheld him, will send his Spirit to uphold us. (4.) This gift of the Holy Ghost is the great blessing God had reserved the plentiful effusion of for the latter days: *I will pour my Spirit,* that is,

my blessing ; for where God gives his Spirit he will give all other blessings. (5.) This is reserved for the seed and offspring of the church; for so the covenant of grace runs: *I will be a God to thee and to thy seed.* To all who are thus made to partake of the privileges of adoption God will give the spirit of adoption. (6.) Hereby there shall be a great increase of the church. Thus it shall be spread to distant places. Thus it shall be propagated and perpetuated to after-times: *They shall spring up* and grow as fast *as willows by the watercourses,* and in every thing that is virtuous and praiseworthy shall be eminent and excel all about them, as the willows overtop the grass among which they grow, *v.* 4. Note, It is a great happiness to the church, and a great pleasure to good men, to see the rising generation hopeful and promising. And it will be so if God pour his Spirit upon them, that blessing, that blessing of blessings.

3. The consent they cheerfully give to their part of the covenant, *v.* 5. When the Jews returned out of captivity they renewed their covenant with God (Jer. l. 5), particularly that they would have no more to do with idols, Hos. xiv. 2, 3, 8. Backsliders must thus repent and do their first works. Many of those that were without did at that time join themselves to them, invited by that glorious appearance of God for them, Zech. viii. 23; Esth. viii. 17. And they say, *We are the Lord's* and *call themselves by the name of Jacob;* for there was one law, one covenant, *for the stranger and for those that were born in the land.* And doubtless it looks further yet, to the conversion of the Gentiles, and the multitudes of them who, upon the effusion of the Spirit, after Christ's ascension, should be *joined to the Lord* and *added to the church.* These converts are *one and another,* very many, of different ranks and nations, and all welcome to God, Col. iii. 11. When one does it another shall by his example be invited to do it, and then another; thus the zeal of one may provoke many. (1.) They shall resign themselves to God: not one in the name of the rest, but every one for himself shall say, " *I am the Lord's ;* he has an incontestable right to rule me, and I submit to him, to all his commands, to all his disposals. I am, and will be, his only, his wholly, his for ever, will be for his interests, will be for his praise; living and dying I will be his." (2.) They shall incorporate themselves with the people of God, *call themselves by the name of Jacob,* forgetting their own people and their fathers' house, and desirous to wear the character and livery of God's family. They shall love all God's people, shall associate with them, give them the right hand of fellowship, espouse their cause, seek the good of the church in general and of all the particular members of it, and be willing to take their lot with them in all conditions. (3.) They

242

shall do this very solemnly. Some of them shall *subscribe with their hand unto the Lord,* as, for the confirming of a bargain, a man sets his hand to it, and delivers it as his act and deed. The more express we are in our covenanting with God the better, Exod. xxiv. 7; Josh. xxiv. 26, 27; Neh. ix. 38. Fast bind, fast find.

II. That, as the Israel of God are a happy people, so the God of Israel is a great God, and he is God alone. This also, as the former, speaks abundant satisfaction to all that trust in him, *v.* 6—8. Observe here, to God's glory and our comfort, 1. That the God we trust in is a God of incontestable sovereignty and irresistible power. He is *the Lord,* Jehovah, self-existent and self-sufficient; and he is *the Lord of hosts,* of all the hosts of heaven and earth, of angels and men. 2. That he stands in relation to, and has a particular concern for, his church. He is *the King of Israel and his Redeemer ; therefore* his Redeemer because his King; and those that take God for their King shall have him for their Redeemer. When God would assert himself God alone he proclaims himself Israel's God, that his people may be encouraged both to adhere to him and to triumph in him. 3. That he is eternal—*the first and the last.* He is God from everlasting, before the worlds were, and will be so to everlasting, when the world shall be no more. If there were not a God to create, nothing would ever have been; and, if there were not a God to uphold, all would soon come to nothing again. He is all in all, is the first cause, from whom are all things, and the last end, to and for whom are all things (Rom. xi. 36), the *Alpha and the Omega,* Rev. i. 11. 4. That he is God alone (*v.* 6): *Besides me there is no God. Is there a God besides me ? v.* 8. We will appeal to the greatest scholars. Did they ever in all their reading meet with any other? To those that have had the largest acquaintance with the world. Did they ever meet with any other? There are *gods many* (1 Cor. viii. 5, 6), *called gods,* and counterfeit gods: but is there any besides our God that is infinite and eternal, any besides him that is the creator of the world and the protector and benefactor of the whole creation, any besides him that can do that for their worshippers which he can and will do for his? " *You are my witnesses.* I have been a nonsuch to you. You have tried other gods; have you found any of them all-sufficient to you, or any of them like me? *Yea, there is no god,"* *no rock* (so the word is), none besides Jehovah that can be a rock for a foundation to build on, a rock for shelter to flee to. God is the rock, and *their rock is not as ours,* Deut. xxxii. 4, 31. *I know not any ;* as if he had said, " I never met with any that offered to stand in competition with me, or that durst bring their pretensions to a fair trial; if I did know of any that could befriend you better than I can, I would recommend you to them; but I know not any." There is no God besides Jehovah. He is infinite, and therefore there can be no other; he is all-sufficient, and therefore there needs no other. This is designed for the confirming of the hopes of God's people in the promise of their deliverance out of Babylon, and, in order to that, for the curing of them of their idolatry; when the affliction had done its work it should be removed. They are reminded of the first and great article of their creed, that *the Lord their God is one Lord,* Deut. vi. 4. And therefore, (1.) They needed not to hope in any other god. Those on whom the sun shines need neither moon nor stars, nor the light of their own fire. (2.) They needed not to fear any other god. Their own God was more able to do them good than all the false and counterfeit gods of their enemies were to do them hurt. 5. That none besides could foretel these things to come, which God now by his prophet gave notice of to the world, above 200 years before they came to pass (*v.* 7): "*Who, as I, shall call,* shall call Cyrus to Babylon, shall call Israel out of Babylon? Is there any but God that can call effectually, and has every creature, every heart, at his beck? Who *shall declare it,* how it shall be, and by whom, as I do?" Nay, God goes further; he not only sees it in order, as having the foreknowledge of it, but *sets it in order,* as having the sole management and direction of it. Can any other pretend to this? He has always set things in order according to the counsel of his own will, ever *since he appointed the ancient people,* the people of Israel, who could give a truer and fuller account of the antiquities of their own nation than any other kingdom in the world could give of theirs. Ever since he appointed that people to be his peculiar people his providence was particularly conversant about them, and he told them beforehand the events that should occur respecting them—their bondage in Egypt, their deliverance from it, and their settlement in Canaan. All was set in order in the divine predictions as well as in the divine purposes. Could any other have done so? Would any other have been so far concerned for them? He challenges the pretenders to show the things that shall come hereafter: "Let them, if they can, tell us the name of the man that shall destroy Babylon and deliver Israel? Nay, if they cannot pretend to tell us *the things that shall come* hereafter, let them tell us the things that *are coming,* that are nigh at hand and at the door. Let them tell us what shall come to pass to-morrow; but they cannot do that; fear them not therefore, nor be afraid of them. What harm can they do you? What hindrance can they give to your deliverance, when I have told thee it shall be accomplished in its **season,**

and I have solemnly declared it?" Note, Those who have the word of God's promise to depend upon need not be afraid of any adverse powers or policies whatsoever.

9 They that make a graven image *are* all of them vanity; and their delectable things shall not profit; and they *are* their own witnesses; they see not, nor know; that they may be ashamed. 10 Who hath formed a god, or molten a graven image *that* is profitable for nothing? 11 Behold, all his fellows shall be ashamed: and the workmen, they *are* of men: let them all be gathered together, let them stand up; *yet* they shall fear, *and* they shall be ashamed together. 12 The smith with the tongs both worketh in the coals, and fashioneth it with hammers, and worketh it with the strength of his arms: yea, he is hungry, and his strength faileth: he drinketh no water, and is faint. 13 The carpenter stretcheth out *his* rule; he marketh it out with a line; he fitteth it with planes, and he marketh it out with the compass, and maketh it after the figure of a man, according to the beauty of a man; that it may remain in the house. 14 He heweth him down cedars, and taketh the cypress and the oak, which he strengtheneth for himself among the trees of the forest: he planteth an ash, and the rain doth nourish *it.* 15 Then shall it be for a man to burn: for he will take thereof, and warm himself; yea, he kindleth *it,* and baketh bread; yea, he maketh a god, and worshippeth *it;* he maketh it a graven image, and falleth down thereto. 16 He burneth part thereof in the fire; with part thereof he eateth flesh; he roasteth roast, and is satisfied: yea, he warmeth *himself,* and saith, Aha, I am warm, I have seen the fire: 17 And the residue thereof he marketh a god, *even* his graven image: he falleth down unto it, and worshippeth *it,* and prayeth unto it, and saith, Deliver me; for thou *art* my god. 18 They have not known nor understood: for he hath shut their eyes, that they cannot see; *and* their hearts, that they cannot under-

stand. 19 And none considereth in his heart, neither *is there* knowledge nor understanding to say, I have burned part of it in the fire; yea, also I have baked bread upon the coals thereof; I have roasted flesh, and eaten *it:* and shall I make the residue thereof an abomination? Shall I fall down to the stock of a tree? 20 He feedeth on ashes: a deceived heart hath turned him aside, that he cannot deliver his soul, nor say, *Is there* not a lie in my right hand?

Often before, God, by the prophet, had mentioned the folly and strange sottishness of idolaters; but here he enlarges upon that head, and very fully and particularly exposes them to contempt and ridicule. This discourse is intended, 1. To arm the people of Israel against the strong temptation they would be in to worship idols when they were captives in Babylon, in compliance with the custom of the country (they being far from the city of their own solemnities) and to humour those who were now their lords and masters. 2. To cure them of their inclination to idolatry, which was the sin that did most easily beset them and to reform them from which they were sent into Babylon. As the rod of God is of use to enforce the word, so the word of God is of use to explain the rod, that the voice of both together may be heard and answered. 3. To furnish them with something to say to their Chaldean task-masters. When they insulted over them, when they asked, *Where is your God?* they might hence ask them, *What are your gods?* 4. To take off their fear of the gods of their enemies, and to encourage their hope in their own God that he would certainly appear against those who set up such scandalous competitors as these with him for the throne.

Now here, for the conviction of idolaters, we have,

I. A challenge given to them to clear themselves, if they can, from the imputation of the most shameful folly and senselessness imaginable, v. 9—11. They set their wits on work to contrive, and their hands on work to frame, graven images, and they call them *their delectable things:* extremely fond they are of them, and mighty things they expect from them. Note, Through the corruption of men's nature, those things that should be detestable to them are desirable and delectable; but those are far gone in a distemper to whom that which is the food and fuel of it is most agreeable. Now, 1. We tell them that those that do so are all vanity; they deceive themselves and one another, and put a great cheat upon those for whom they make these images. 2. We tell them that *their delectable things shall not profit*

244

them, nor make them any return for the pleasure they take in them; they can neither supply them with good nor protect them from evil. The *graven images* are *profitable for nothing* at all, nor will they ever get any thing by the devoirs they pay to them. 3. We appeal to themselves whether it be not a silly sottish thing to expect any good from gods of their own making: *They are their own witnesses,* witnesses against themselves, if they would but give their own consciences leave to deal faithfully with them, that they are blind and ignorant in doing thus. *They see not nor know,* and let them own it, *that they may be ashamed.* If men would but be true to their own convictions, ordinarily we might be sure of their conversion, particularly idolaters; for *who has formed a god?* Who but a madman, or one out of his wits, would think of forming a god, of making that which, if he make it a god, he must suppose to be his maker? 4. We challenge them to plead their own cause with any confidence or assurance. If any one has the front to say that he has formed a god, when all his fellows come together to declare what each of them has done towards the making of this god, they will all be ashamed of the cheat they have put upon themselves, and laugh in their sleeves at those whom they have imposed upon; for *the workmen that* formed this god *are of men,* weak and impotent, and therefore cannot possibly make a being that shall be omnipotent, nor can they without blushing pretend to do so. *Let them all be gathered together,* as Demetrius and the craftsmen were, to support their sinking trade; *let them stand up* to plead their own cause, and make the best they can of it, with hand joined in hand; *yet they shall fear* to undertake it when it comes to the setting to, as conscious to themselves of the weakness and badness of their cause, *and they shall be ashamed* of it, not only when they appear singly, but when by appearing together they hope to keep one another in countenance. Note, Idolatry and impiety are things which men may justly both tremble and blush to appear in the defence of.

II. A particular narrative of the whole proceeding in making a god; and there needs no more to expose it than to describe it and tell the story of it.

1. The persons employed about it are handicraft tradesmen, the meanest of them, the very same that you would employ in making the common utensils of your husbandry, a cart or a plough. You must have a *smith,* a blacksmith, who *with the tongs works in the coals;* and it is hard work, for he *works with the strength of his arms,* till *he is hungry* and his strength fails, so eager is he, and so hasty are those who set him at the work to get it despatched. He cannot allow himself time to eat or drink, for *he drinks no water, and* therefore *is faint,* v. 12.

Perhaps it was a piece of superstition among them for the workman not to eat or drink while he was making a god. The plates with which the smith was to cover the image, or whatever iron-work was to be done about it, *he fashioned with hammers,* and made it all very exact, according to the model given him. Then comes *the carpenter,* and he takes as much care and pains about the timber-work, v. 13. He brings his box of tools, for he has occasion for them all : *He stretches out his rule* upon the piece of wood, *marks it with a line,* where it must be sawed or cut off; *he fits it,* or polishes it, *with planes,* the greater first and then the less; *he marks out with the compasses* what must be the size and shape of it; and it is just what he pleases.

2. The form in which it is made is that of a man, a poor, weak, dying creature; but it is the noblest form and figure that he is acquainted with, and, being his own, he has a peculiar fondness for it and is willing to put all the reputation he can upon it. He makes it *according to the beauty of a man,* in comely proportion, with those limbs and lineaments that are the beauty of a man, but are altogether unfit to represent the beauty of the Lord. God put a great honour upon man when, in respect of the powers and faculties of his soul, he made him after the image of God; but man does a great dishonour to God when he makes him, in respect of bodily parts and members, after the image of man. Nor will it at all atone for the affront so far to compliment his god as to take the fairest of the children of men for his original whence to take his copy, and to give him all the beauty of a man that he can think of; for all the *beauty of the body of a man,* when pretended to be put upon him who is an infinite Spirit, is a deformity and diminution to him. And, when the goodly piece is finished, it must *remain in the house,* in the temple or shrine prepared for it, or perhaps in the dwelling house if it be one of the *lares* or *penates—the household gods.*

3. The matter of which it is mostly made is sorry stuff to make a god of; it is the stock of a tree.

(1) The tree itself was fetched out *of the forest,* where it grew among other trees, of no more virtue or value than its neighbours. It was a *cedar,* it may be, or a *cypress,* or an *oak,* v. 14. Perhaps he had an eye upon it some time before for this use, and *strengthened it for himself,* used some art or other to make it stronger and better-grown than other trees were. Or, as some read it, *which hath strengthened or lifted up itself among the trees of the forest,* the tallest and strongest he can pick out. Or, it may be, it pleases his fancy better to take *an ash,* which is of a quicker growth, and which was of his own planting for this use, and which has been nourished with rain from

heaven. See what a fallacy he puts upon himself, in making that his refuge which was of his own planting, and which he not only gave the form to, but prepared the matter for; and what an affront he puts upon the God of heaven in setting up that as a rival with him which was nourished by his rain, that rain which falls upon the just and unjust.

(2) The boughs of this tree were good for nothing but for fuel; to that use were they put, and so were the chips that were cut off from it in the working of it; they are *for a man to burn,* v. 15, 16. To show that that tree has no innate virtue in it for its own protection, it is as capable of being burnt as any other tree; and, to show that he who chose it had no more antecedent value for it than for any other tree, he makes no difficulty of throwing part of it into the fire as common rubbish, asking no question for conscience' sake. [1.] It serves him for his parlour-fire : *He will take thereof and warm himself* (v. 15), and he finds the comfort of it, and is so far from having any regret in his mind for it that he saith, *Aha! I am warm; I have seen the fire;* and certainly that part of the tree which served him for fuel, the use for which God and nature designed it, does him a much greater kindness and yields him more satisfaction than ever that will which he makes a god of. [2.] It serves him for his kitchen-fire : *He eats flesh* with it, that is, he dresses the flesh with it which he is to eat; he *roasteth roast, and is satisfied* that he has not done amiss to put it to this use. Nay, [3.] It serves him to heat the oven with, in which we use that fuel which is of least value : *He kindles it and bakes bread* with the heat of it, and none charges him with doing wrong.

(3.) Yet, after all, the stock or body of the tree shall serve to make a god of, when it might as well have served to make a bench, as one of themselves, even a poet of their own, upbraids them, *Horat. Sat.* i. 8 :

Olim truncus eram ficulnus, inutile lignum,
Quum faber, incertus scamnum faceretne Priapum,
Maluit esse deum ; deus inde ego——

> In days of yore our godship stood
> A very worthless log of wood,
> The joiner, doubting or to shape us
> Into a stool or a Priapus,
> At length resolved, for reasons wise,
> Into a god to bid me rise.   Francis.

And another of them threatens the idol to whom he had committed the custody of his woods that, if he did not preserve them to be fuel for his fire, he should himself be made use of for that purpose :

Furaces moneo manus repellas,
Et silvam domini focis reserves,
Si defecerit hæc, et ipse lignum es.

Drive the plunderers away, and preserve the wood for thy master's hearth, or thou thyself shalt be converted into fuel.—Martial.

When the besotted idolater has thus served the meanest purposes with part of his tree, and the rest has had time to season (he makes that a god in his imagination while that is in the doing, *and worships it)* : He *makes it a graven image, and falls down thereto* (*v.* 15), that is (*v.* 17), *The residue thereof he makes a god, even his graven image,* according to his fancy and intention; he *falls down to it, and worships it,* gives divine honours to it, prostrates himself before it in the most humble reverent posture, as a servant, as a suppliant; *he prays to it,* as having a dependence upon it, and great expectations from it; *he saith, Deliver me, for thou art my god.* There where he pays his homage and allegiance he justly looks for protection and deliverance. What a strange infatuation is this, to expect help from gods that cannot help themselves! But it is this praying to them that makes them gods, not what the smith or the carpenter did to them. What we place our confidence in for deliverance that we make a god of.

Qui fingit sacros, auro vel marmore, vultus
Non facit ille deos ; qui rogat, ille facit.

He who supplicates the figure, whether it be of gold or of marble, makes it a god, and not he who merely constructs it.—MARTIAL.

III. Here is judgment given upon this whole matter, *v.* 18—20. In short, it is the effect and evidence of the greatest stupidity and sottishness that one could ever imagine rational beings to be guilty of, and shows that man has become worse than the beasts that perish ; for they act according to the dictates of sense, but man acts not according to the dictates of reason (*v.* 18) : *They have not known nor understood* common sense ; men that act rationally in other things in this act most absurdly. Though they have some knowledge and understanding, yet they are strangers to, nay, they are rebels against the great law of consideration (*v.* 12) : *None considers in his heart,* nor has so much application of mind as to reason thus with himself, which one would think he might easily do, though there were none to reason with him : " *I have burnt part of this tree in the fire,* for baking and roasting; *and* now *shall I make the residue thereof an abomination ?* (that is, *an idol,* for that is an abomination to God and all wise and good men) ; "shall I ungratefully choose to do, or presumptuously dare to do, what the Lord hates ? shall I be such a fool as to fall down to the stock of a tree—a senseless, lifeless, helpless thing ? shall I so far disparage myself, and make myself like that I bow down to ?" A growing tree may be a beautiful stately thing, but the stock of a tree has lost its glory, and he has lost his that gives glory to it. Upon the whole, the sad character given of these idolaters is, 1. That they put a cheat upon themselves (*v.* 20) : *They feed on ashes ;* they feed themselves with hopes of advantage by worshipping these idols, but

246

they will be disappointed as much as a man that would expect nourishment by feeding on ashes. Feeding on ashes is an evidence of a depraved appetite and a distempered body ; and it is a sign that the soul is overpowered by very bad habits when men, in their worship, go no further than the sight of their eyes will carry them. They are wretchedly deluded, and it is their own fault : *A deceived heart* of their own, more than the deceiving tongue of others, *has turned them aside* from the faith and worship of the living God to dumb idols. They are *drawn away of their own lusts and enticed.* The apostasy of sinners from God is owing entirely to themselves and to the evil heart of unbelief that is in their own bosom. A revolting and rebellious heart is a deceived heart. 2. That they wilfully persist in their self-delusion and will not be undeceived. There is none of them that can be persuaded so far to suspect himself as to say, *Is there not a lie in my right hand?* and so to think of delivering his soul. Note, (1.) Idolaters have a lie in their right hand ; for an idol is a lie, is not what it pretends, performs not what it promises, and it is a *teacher of lies,* Hab. ii. 18. (2.) It highly concerns those that are secure in an evil way seriously to consider whether there be not a lie in their right hand. Is not that a lie which with complacency we hold fast as our chief good? Are our hearts set upon the wealth of the world and the pleasures of sense? They will certainly prove a lie in our right hand. And is not that a lie which with confidence we hold fast by, as the ground on which we build our hopes for heaven? If we trust to our external professions and performances, as if those would save us, we deceive ourselves with a lie in our right hand, with a house built on the sand. (3.) Self-suspicion is the first step towards self-deliverance. We cannot be faithful to ourselves unless we are jealous of ourselves. He that would deliver his soul must begin with putting this question to his own conscience, *Is there not a lie in my right hand?* (4.) Those that are given up to believe in a lie are under the power of strong delusions, which it is hard to get clear of, 2 Thes. ii. 11.

21 Remember these, O Jacob and Israel ; for thou *art* my servant : I have formed thee ; thou *art* my servant : O Israel, thou shalt not be forgotten of me. 22 I have blotted out, as a thick cloud, thy transgressions, and, as a cloud, thy sins : return unto me ; for I have redeemed thee. 23 Sing, O ye heavens ; for the LORD hath done *it :* shout, ye lower parts of the earth : break forth into singing, ye mountains, O forest, and every tree therein : for the LORD

hath redeemed Jacob, and glorified himself in Israel. 24 Thus saith the LORD, thy redeemer, and he that formed thee from the womb, I *am* the LORD that maketh all *things;* that stretcheth forth the heavens alone ; that spreadeth abroad the earth by myself; 25 That frustrateth the tokens of the liars, and maketh diviners mad ; that turneth wise *men* backward, and maketh their knowledge foolish ; 26 That confirmeth the word of his servant, and performeth the counsel of his messengers ; that saith to Jerusalem, Thou shalt be inhabited ; and to the cities of Judah, Ye shall be built, and I will raise up the decayed places thereof: 27 That saith to the deep, Be dry, and I will dry up thy rivers : 28 That saith of Cyrus, *He is* my shepherd, and shall perform all my pleasure : even saying to Jerusalem, Thou shalt be built ; and to the temple, Thy foundation shall be laid.

In these verses we have,

I. The duty which Jacob and Israel, now in captivity, were called to, that they might be qualified and prepared for the deliverance designed them. Our first care must be to get good by our afflictions, and then we may hope to get out of them. The duty is expressed in two words : *Remember* and *return,* as in the counsel to Ephesus, Rev. ii. 4, 5. 1. " *Remember these, O Jacob !* Remember what thou hast been told of the folly of idolatry, and let the convictions thou art now under be ready to thee whenever thou art tempted to that sin. Remember that *thou art my servant,* and therefore must not serve other masters." 2. *Return unto me, v.* 22. It is the great concern of those who have backslidden from God to hasten their return to him ; and this is that which he calls them to when they are in affliction, and when he is returning to them in a way of mercy.

II. The favours which Jacob and Israel, now in captivity, were assured of ; and what is here promised to them upon their remembering and returning to God is in a spiritual sense promised to all that in like manner return to God. It is a very comfortable word, for more is implied in it than is expressed (*v.* 21) : " *O Israel ! thou shalt not be forgotten of me,* though for the present thou seemest to be so." When we begin to remember God he will begin to remember us ; nay, it is he that remembers us first. Now observe here,

1. The grounds upon which God's favour-

able intentions to his people were built and on which they might build their expectations from him. He will deliver them out of captivity ; for, (1.) They are his servants, and therefore he has a just quarrel with those that detain them. *Let my people go, that they may serve me.* The servants of the King of kings are under special protection. (2.) He formed them into a people, formed them *from the womb, v.* 24. From the first beginning of their increase into a nation they were under his particular care and government, more than any other people ; their national constitution was of his framing, and his covenant with them was the charter by which they were incorporated. They are his, and he will save them. (3.) He has redeemed them formerly, has many a time redeemed them out of great distress, and he is still the same, in the same relation to them, has the same concern for them. " Therefore *return unto me, for I have redeemed thee, v.* 22. Whither wilt thou go, but to me ?" Having redeemed them, as well as formed them, he has acquired a further title to them and propriety in them, which is a good reason why they should dutifully return to him and why he will graciously return to them. The *Lord has redeemed Jacob ;* he is about to do it (*v* 23); he has determined to do it ; for he is the Lord their Redeemer, *v.* 24. Note, The work of redemption which God has by his Son wrought for us encourages us to hope for all promised blessings from him. He that has redeemed us at so vast an expense will not lose his purchase. (4.) He has *glorified himself in them* (*v.* 23), and therefore will do so still, John xii. 28. It is matter of comfort to us to see God's glory interested in the deliverances of the church ; for *therefore* he will certainly redeem Jacob, because thus he will glorify himself. And *this* assures us that he will perfect the redemption of his saints by Jesus Christ, because there is a day set when he will be glorified and admired in them all. (5.) He has pardoned their sins, which were the cause of their calamity and the only obstruction to their deliverance, *v.* 22. *Therefore* he will break the yoke of captivity from off their necks, because he has *blotted out, as a thick cloud, their transgressions.* Note, [1.] Our transgressions and our sins are as a cloud, a thick cloud ; they interpose between heaven and earth, and for a time suspend and intercept the correspondence between the upper and lower world (sin *separates between us and God,* ch. lix. 2) ; they threaten a storm, a deluge of wrath, as thick clouds do, which God will rain upon sinners, Ps. xi. 6. [2.] When God pardons sin he blots out this cloud, this thick cloud, so that the intercourse with heaven is laid open again. God looks down upon the soul with favour ; the soul looks up to him with pleasure. The cloud is scattered by the influence of the

Sun of righteousness. It is only through Christ that sin is pardoned. When sin is pardoned, like a cloud that is scattered, it appears no more, it is quite gone. The *iniquity of Jacob shall be sought for, and not found,* Jer l. 20. And the comforts that flow into the soul when sin is pardoned are like the *clear shining after clouds and rain.*

2. The universal joy which the deliverance of God's people should bring along with it (*v.* 23): *Sing, O you heavens !* This intimates, (1.) That the whole creation shall have cause for joy and rejoicing in the redemption of God's people; to that it is owing that it subsists (that it is rescued from the curse which the sin of man brought upon the ground) and that it is again put into a capacity of answering the ends of its being, and is assured that though now it groans, being burdened, it shall at last be delivered from the bondage of corruption. The greatest establishment of the world is the kingdom of God in it, Ps. xcvi. 11—13; xcviii. 7—9. (2.) That the angels shall rejoice in it, and the inhabitants of the upper world. The heavens shall sing, for the Lord has done it. And there is joy in heaven when God and man are reconciled (Luke xv. 7), joy when Babylon falls, Rev. xviii. 20. (3.) That those who lay at the greatest distance, even the inhabitants of the Gentile world, should join in these praises, as sharing in these joys. The *lower parts of the earth,* the forest and the trees there, shall bring in the tribute of thanksgiving for the redemption of Israel.

3. The encouragement we have to hope that though great difficulties, and such as have been thought insuperable, lie in the way of the church's deliverance, yet, when the time for it shall come, they shall all be got over with ease; for *thus saith Israel's Redeemer, I am the Lord that maketh all things,* did make them at first and am still making them; for providence is a continued creation. All being, power, life, motion, and perfection, are from God. He *stretches forth the heavens alone,* has no help nor needs any; and the earth too he *spreads abroad by himself,* and by his own power. Man was not by him when he did it (Job xxxviii. 4), nor did any creature advise or assist; only his own eternal wisdom and Word was by him then as *one brought up with him,* Prov. viii. 30. His stretching out the heavens by himself denotes the boundless extent of his power. The strongest man, if he has to stretch a thing out, must get somebody or other to lend a hand; but God stretched out the vast expanse, and keeps it still upon the stretch, himself, by his own power. Let not Israel be discouraged then; nothing is too hard for him to do that made the world, Ps. cxxiv. 8. And, having made all things, he can make what use he pleases of all, and has it in his power to serve his own purposes by them.

248

4. The confusion which this would put upon the oracles of Babylon, by the confutation it would give them, *v.* 25. God, by delivering his people out of Babylon, would *frustrate the tokens of the liars,* of all the lying prophets, that said the Babylonian monarchy had many ages yet to live, and pretended to ground their predictions upon some token, some sign or other, which, according to the rules of their art, foreboded its prosperity. How mad will these conjurors grow with vexation when they see that their skill fails them, and that the contrary happens to that which they so coveted and were so confident of. Nor would it only baffle their pretended prophets, but their celebrated politicians too : He *turns the wise men backward.* Finding they cannot go on with their projects, they are forced to quit them; and so he makes the judges fools, *and makes their knowledge foolish.* Those that are made acquainted with Christ see all the knowledge they had before to be foolishness in comparison with the knowledge of him. And those that are adversaries to him will find all their counsels, like Ahithophel's, turned into foolishness, and themselves *taken in their own craftiness,* 1 Cor. iii. 19.

5. The confirmation which this would give to the oracles of God, which the Jews had distrusted and their enemies despised : God *confirms the word of his servant* (*v.* 26) ; he confirms it by accomplishing it in its season ; and *performs the counsel of the messengers* whom he hath many a time sent to his people, to tell them what great blessings he had in store for them. Note, The exact fulfilling of the prophecies of scripture is a confirmation of the truth of the whole book and an incontestable evidence of its divine origin and authority.

6. The particular favours God designed for his people, that were now in captivity, *v.* 26—28. These were foretold long before they went into captivity, that they might see reason to expect a correction, but no reason to fear a final destruction. (1.) It is here supposed that Jerusalem, and the cities of Judah, should for a time lie in ruins, dispeopled and uninhabited ; but it is promised that they shall be rebuilt and repeopled. When Isaiah lived, Jerusalem and the cities of Judah were full of inhabitants ; but they will be emptied, burnt, and destroyed. It was then hard to believe that concerning such strong and populous cities. But the justice of God will do that ; and, when that is done, it will be hard to believe that ever they will recover themselves again, and yet the zeal of the Lord of hosts will do that too. God has said to Jerusalem, *Thou shalt be inhabited ;* for, while the world stands, God will have a church in it, and therefore he will raise up those who *shall say to Jerusalem, Thou shalt be built ;* for, if it be not built, it cannot be inhabited, Ps. lxix. 35, 36. When God's

time shall have come for the building up of his church, let him alone to find both houses for his people (for they shall not lie exposed) and people for his houses, for they shall not stand empty. The cities of Judah too shall again be built. The Assyrian army under Sennacherib only took them, and then, upon the defeat of that army, they returned undamaged to the right owners; but the Chaldean army demolished them, and by carrying away the inhabitants left them to go to decay of themselves; for, if less judgments prevail not to humble and reform men, God will send greater. Yet these desolations shall not be perpetual. God will *raise up the* wastes and *decayed places thereof;* for he will not contend for ever. The city of strangers, when it is ruined, shall never be built (*ch.* xxv. 2), but the city of God's own children is but discontinued for a time. (2.) It is here supposed that the temple too should be destroyed, and lie for a time razed to the foundations; but it is promised that the foundation of it shall again be laid, and no doubt built upon. As the desolation of the sanctuary was to all the pious Jews the most mournful part of the destruction, so the restoration and re-establishment of it would be the most joyful part of the deliverance. What joy can they have in the rebuilding of Jerusalem if the temple there be not rebuilt? for it is that which makes it a holy city and truly beautiful. This therefore was the chief thing that the Jews had at heart and had in view in their return; therefore they would go back to Jerusalem, to *build the house of the Lord God of Israel there,* Ezra i. 3. (3.) It is here supposed that very great difficulties would lie in the way of this deliverance, which it would be impossible for them to wade through; but it is promised that by a divine power they shall all be removed (*v.* 27): *God saith to the deep, Be dry;* so he did when he brought Israel out of Egypt, and so he will again when he brings them out of Babylon, if there be occasion. *Who art thou, O great mountain?* Dost thou stand in the way? Before Zerubbabel, the commander-in-chief of the returning captives, *thou shalt become a plain,* Zech. iv. 7. So, *Who art thou, O great deep?* Dost thou retard their passage and think to block it up? Thou shalt be dry, and thy rivers that supply thee shall be dried up. When Cyrus took Babylon by draining the river Euphrates into many channels, and so making it passable for his army, this was fulfilled. Note, Whatever obstructions lie in the way of Israel's redemption, God can remove them with a word's speaking. (4.) It is here supposed that none of the Jews themselves would be able by might and power to force their way out of Babylon; but it is promised that God will raise up a stranger from afar off, that shall fairly open the way for them, and now at length he names the very man, many

scores of years before he was born or thought of (*v.* 28): *That saith of Cyrus, He is my shepherd.* Israel is his people, and the sheep of his pasture. These sheep are now in the midst of wolves, in the hands of the thief and robber; they are impounded for trespass. Now Cyrus shall be his shepherd, employed by him to release these sheep, and to take care of their return to their own green pastures again. "In this *he shall perform all my pleasure,* shall bring about what is purposed by me and will be highly pleasing to me." Note, [1.] The most contingent things are certain to the divine prescience. He knew who was the person, and what was his name, that should be the deliverer of his people, and, when he pleased, he could let his church know it, that, when they heard of such a name beginning to be talked of in the world, they might *lift up their heads with joy, knowing that their redemption drew nigh.* [2.] It is the greatest honour of the greatest men to be employed for God as instruments of his favour to his people. It was more the praise of Cyrus to be God's shepherd than to be emperor of Persia. [3.] God makes what use he pleases of men, of mighty men, of those that act with the greatest freedom; and, when they think to do as they please, he can overrule them, and make them do as he pleases. Nay, in those very things wherein they are serving themselves, and look no further than that, God is serving his own purposes by them and making them to perform all his pleasure. Rich princes shall do what poor prophets have foretold.

CHAP. XLV.

Cyrus was nominated, in the foregoing chapter, to be God's shepherd; more is said to him and more of him in this chapter, not only because he was to be instrumental in the release of the Jews out of their captivity, but because he was to be therein a type of the great Redeemer, and that release was to be typical of the great redemption from sin and death; for that was the salvation of which all the prophets witnessed. We have here, I. The great things which God would do for Cyrus, that he might be put into a capacity to release God's people, ver. 1—4. II. The proof God would hereby give of his eternal power and godhead, and his universal, incontestable, sovereignty, ver. 5—7. III. A prayer for the hastening of this deliverance, ver. 8. IV. A check to the unbelieving Jews, who quarrelled with God for the lengthening out of their captivity, ver. 9, 10. V. Encouragement given to the believing Jews, who trusted in God and continued instant in prayer, assuring them that God would in due time accomplish this work by the hand of Cyrus, ver. 11—15. VI. A challenge given to the worshippers of idols and their doom read, and satisfaction given to the worshippers of the true God and their comfort secured, with an eye to the Mediator, who is made of God to us both righteousness and sanctification, ver. 16—25. And here, as in many other parts of this prophecy, there is much of Christ and of gospel grace.

THUS saith the LORD to his anointed, to Cyrus, whose right hand I have holden, to subdue nations before him; and I will loose the loins of kings, to open before him the two-leaved gates; and the gates shall not be shut; 2 I will go before thee, and make the crooked places straight: I will break in pieces the gates of brass, and cut in sunder the bars of iron: 3 And I will give thee the treasures of darkness, and hidden riches of secret places, that thou mayest know that I, the LORD, which call *thee* by thy name, *am* the God of Israel. 4 For Jacob my servant's sake, and Israel mine elect, I have even called thee by thy name: I have surnamed thee, though thou hast not known me.

Cyrus was a Mede, descended (as some say) from Astyages king of Media. The pagan writers are not agreed in their accounts of his origin. Some tell us that in his infancy he was an outcast, left exposed, and was saved from perishing by a herdsman's wife. However, it is agreed that, being a man of an active genius, he soon made himself very considerable, especially when Crœsus king of Lydia made a descent upon his country, which he not only repulsed, but revenged, prosecuting the advantages he had gained against Crœsus with such vigour that in a little time he took Sardis and made himself master of the rich kingdom of Lydia and the many provinces that then belonged to it. This made him very great (for Crœsus was rich to a proverb) and enabled him to pursue his victories in many countries ; but it was nearly ten years afterwards that, in conjunction with his uncle Darius and with the forces of Persia, he made this famous attack upon Babylon, which is here foretold, and which we have the history of Dan. v. Babylon had now grown exorbitantly rich and strong. It was forty-five miles in compass (some say more): the walls were thirty-two feet thick and 100 cubits high. Some say, They were so thick that six chariots might drive abreast upon them ; others say, They were fifty cubits thick and 200 high. Cyrus seems to have had a great ambition to make himself master of this place, and to have projected it long ; and at last he performed it. Now here, 210 years before it came to pass, we are told,

I. What great things God would do for him. that he might put it into his power to release his people. In order to this he shall be a mighty conqueror and a wealthy monarch, and nations shall become tributaries to him and help him both with men and money. Now that which God here promised to do for Cyrus he could have done for Zerubbabel, or some of the Jews themselves ; but the wealth and power of this world God has seldom seen fit to entrust his own people with much of, so many are the snares and temptations that attend them; but if there has been occasion, for the good of the church, to make use of them, God has been pleased rather to put them into the hands of others, to be employed for

them, than to venture them in their own hands. Cyrus is here called God's *anointed*, because he was both designed and qualified for this great service by the counsel of God, and was to be herein a type of the Messiah. God engages to hold his right hand, not only to strengthen and sustain him, but to direct his motions and intentions, as Elisha put his hands upon the king's hands when he was to shoot his arrow against Syria, 2 Kings xiii. 16. Being under such direction,

1. He shall extend his conquests very far and shall make nothing of the opposition that will be given him. Babylon is too strong a place for a young hero to begin with ; and therefore, that he may be able to deal with that, great additions shall be made to his strength by other conquests. (1. Populous kingdoms shall yield to him. God will *subdue nations before him;* when he is in the full career of his successes he shall make nothing of a nation's being born to him at once : yet it is not he that subdues them ; it is God that subdues them for him ; the battle is his, and therefore his is the victory. (2.) Potent kings shall fall before him : *I will loose the loins of kings,* either the girdle of their loins (divesting them of their power and dignity) or the strength of their loins, and then it was literally fulfilled in Belshazzar, for, when he was terrified by the handwriting on the wall, *the joints of his loins were loosed,* Dan. v. 6. (3.) Great cities shall surrender themselves into his hands, without giving him or themselves any trouble. God will incline the keepers of the city to *open before him the two-leaved gates,* not treacherously nor timorously, but from a full conviction that it is to no purpose to contend with him; and therefore the gates shall not be shut to keep him out as an enemy, but thrown open to admit him as a friend. (4.) The longest and most dangerous marches shall be made easy and ready to him : *I will go before thee,* to clear the way, and to conduct thee in it, and then the *crooked places* shall be made *straight;* or, as some read it, the hilly places shall be levelled and made even. Those will find a ready road that have God going before them. (5.) No opposition shall stand before him. He that gives him his commission *will break in pieces the gates of brass* that are shut against him, *and cut asunder the bars of iron* wherewith they are fastened. This was fulfilled in the letter, if that be true which Herodotus reports, that the city of Babylon had 100 gates all of brass, with posts and hooks of the same metal.

2. He shall replenish his coffers very much (*v.* 3) : *I will give thee the treasures of darkness,* treasures of gold and silver, that have been long kept close under lock and key and had not seen the light of many years, or had been buried under ground by the inhabitants, in their fright, upon the taking of the city. The riches of many

nations had been brought to Babylon, and Cyrus seized all together. *The hidden riches of secret places,* which belonged either to the crown or to private persons, shall all be a prey to Cyrus. Thus God, designing him to do a piece of service to his church, paid him richly for it beforehand; and Cyrus very honestly owned God's goodness to him, and, in consideration of that, released the captives. Ezra i. 2, *God has given me all the kingdoms of the earth* and thereby has obliged *me to build him a house at Jerusalem.*

II. We are here told what God designed in doing all this for Cyrus. What Cyrus aimed at in undertaking his wars we may easily guess; but what God aimed at in giving him such wonderful success in his wars we are here told.

1. It was that the God of Israel might be glorified: " *That thou mayest know* by all this *that I the Lord am the God of Israel ;* for I have *called thee by thy name* long before thou wast born.*" When Cyrus should have this prophecy of Isaiah shown to him, and should there find his own name and his own achievements particularly described so long before, he should thereby be brought to acknowledge that the God of Israel was the Lord, Jehovah, the only living and true God, and that he continued to own his Israel though now in captivity. It is well when thus men's prosperity brings them to the knowledge of God, for too often it makes them forget him.

2. It was that the Israel of God might be released, *v.* 4. Cyrus knew not God as the God of Israel. Having been trained up in the worship of idols, the true God was to him an unknown God. But, though he knew not God, God not only knew him when he came into being, but foreknew him, and bespoke him for his shepherd. He called him by his name, *Cyrus,* nay, which was yet a greater honour, he surnamed him and called him his *anointed.* And why did God do all this for Cyrus? Not for his own sake, be it known to him; whether he was a man of virtue or no is questioned. Xenophon indeed, when he would describe the heroic virtues of an excellent prince, made use of Cyrus's name, and many of the particulars of his story, in his Cyropædia; but other historians represent him as haughty, cruel, and bloodthirsty. The reason why God preferred him was *for Jacob his servant's sake.* Note, (1.) In all the revolutions of states and kingdoms, the sudden falls of the great and strong, and the surprising advancements of the weak and obscure, God is designing the good of his church. (2.) It is therefore the wisdom of those to whom God has given wealth and power to use them for his glory, by showing kindness to his people. Cyrus is preferred that Israel may be released. He shall have a kingdom, only that God's people may have their liberty; for

their kingdom is not of this world, it is yet to come. In all this Cyrus was a type of Christ, who was made victorious over principalities and powers, and entrusted with unsearchable riches, for the use and benefit of God's servants, his elect. *When he ascended on high hé led captivity captive,* took those captives that had taken others captives, and *opened the prison to those that were bound.*

5 I *am* the Lord, and *there is* none else, *there is* no God beside me : I girded thee, though thou hast not known me : 6 That they may know from the rising of the sun, and from the west, that *there is* none beside me. I *am* the Lord, and *there is* none else. 7 I form the light, and create darkness : I make peace, and create evil : I the Lord do all these *things.* 8 Drop down, ye heavens, from above, and let the skies pour down righteousness : let the earth open, and let them bring forth salvation, and let righteousness spring up together; I the Lord have created it. 9 Woe unto him that striveth with his Maker ! *Let* the potsherd *strive* with the potsherds of the earth. Shall the clay say to him that fashioneth it, What makest thou ? or thy work, He hath no hands ? 10 Woe unto him that saith unto *his* father, What begettest thou ? or to the woman, What hast thou brought forth ?

God here asserts his sole and sovereign dominion, as that which he designed to prove and manifest to the world in all the great things he did for Cyrus and by him. Observe,

I. How this doctrine is here laid down concerning the sovereignty of the great Jehovah, in two things :—1. That he is God alone, and there is no God besides him. This is here inculcated as a fundamental truth, which, if it were firmly believed, would abolish idolatry out of the world. With what an awful, commanding, air of majesty and authority, bidding defiance, as it were, to all pretenders, does the great God here proclaim it to the world : *I am the Lord, I the Lord, Jehovah,* and *there is none else, there is no God besides me,* no other self-existent, self-sufficient, being, none infinite and eternal. And again (*v.* 6), *There is none besides me ;* all that are set up in competition with me are counterfeits; they are all vanity and a lie, for *I am the Lord, and there is none else.* This is here said to Cyrus, not only to cure him of the sin of his ancestors, which was the worshipping of idols, but to prevent his falling into the sin of some of his predecessors in victory and universal monarchy, which was the setting up of themselves for gods and being idolized, to which some attribute much of the origin of idolatry. Let Cyrus, when he becomes thus rich and great, remember that still he is but a man, and there is no God but one. 2. That he is Lord of all, and there is nothing done without him (*v.* 7): *I form the light*, which is grateful and pleasing, and *I create darkness*, which is grievous and unpleasing. *I make peace* (put here for all good) and *I create evil*, not the evil of sin (God is not the author of that), but the evil of punishment. *I the Lord* order, and direct, and *do all these things*. Observe, (1.) The very different events that befal the children of men. Light and darkness are opposite to each other, and yet, in the course of providence, they are sometimes intermixed, like the morning and evening twilights, *neither day nor night*, Zech. xiv. 6. There is a mixture of joys and sorrows in the same cup, allays to each other. Sometimes they are counterchanged, as noonday light and midnight darkness. In the revolution of every day each takes its turn, and there are short transitions from the one to the other, witness Job's case. (2.) The self-same cause of both, and that is he that is the first Cause of all: *I the Lord*, the fountain of all being, am the fountain of all power. He who formed the natural light (Gen. i. 3) still forms the providential light. He who at first made peace among the jarring seeds and principles of nature makes peace in the affairs of men. He who allowed the natural darkness, which was a mere privation, creates the providential darkness; for concerning troubles and afflictions he gives positive orders. Note, The wise God has the ordering and disposing of all our comforts, and all our crosses, in this world.

II. How this doctrine is here proved and published. 1. It is proved by that which God did for Cyrus: " *There is no God besides me*, for (*v.* 5) *I girded thee, though thou hast not known me*. It was not thy own idol, which thou didst know and worship, that girded thee for this expedition, that gave thee authority and ability for it. No, it was I that girded thee, I whom thou didst not know, nor seek to." By *this* it appears that the God of Israel is the only true God, that he manages and makes what use he pleases even of those that are strangers to him and pay their homage to other gods. 2. It is published to all the world by the word of God, by his providence, and by the testimony of the suffering Jews in Babylon, that all may know from the east and from the west, sunrise and sun-set, that the Lord is God and there is none else. The wonderful deliver-

ance of the Isr.el of God proclaimed to all the world that *there is none like unto the God of Jeshurun, that rides on the heavens for their help.*

III. How this doctrine is here improved and applied. 1. For the comfort of those that earnestly longed, and yet quietly waited, for the redemption of Israel (*v.* 8): *Drop down, you heavens, from above.* Some take this as the saints' prayer for the deliverance. I rather take it as God's precept concerning it; for he is said to *command deliverances*, Ps. xliv. 4. Now the precept is directed to heaven and earth, and all the hosts of both, as royal precepts commonly run—*To all officers, civil and military.* All the creatures shall be made in their places to contribute to the carrying on of this great work, when God will have it done. If men will not be aiding and assisting, God will produce it without them, as he does the dews of heaven and the grass of the earth, which *tarry not for man, nor wait for the sons of men*, Mic. v. 7. Observe, (1.) The method of this great deliverance that is to be wrought for Israel. *Righteousness* must first be wrought in them; they must be brought to repent of their sins, to renounce their idolatries, to return to God, and reform their lives, and then the salvation shall be wrought for them, and not till then. We must not expect salvation without righteousness, for they spring up together and together the Lord hath created them; what he has joined together, let not us therefore put asunder. See Ps. lxxxv. 9—11. Christ died to save us from our sins, not in our sins, and is made redemption to us by being made to us righteousness and sanctification. (2.) The means of this great deliverance. Rather than it shall fail, when the set time for it shall come, the *heavens shall drop down righteousness, and the earth shall open to bring forth salvation*, and both concur to the reformation, and so to the restoration, of God's Israel. It is from heaven, from above the skies, that righteousness drops down, for every grace and good gift is from above; nay, since the more plentiful effusion of the Spirit it is now *poured* down, and, if our hearts be open to receive it, the product will be the fruits of righteousness and the great salvation.

2. For reproof to those of the church's enemies that opposed this salvation, or those of her friends that despaired of it (*v.* 9): *Woe unto him that strives with his Maker!* God is the Maker of all things, and therefore our Maker, which is a reason why we should always submit to him and never contend with him. (1.) Let not the proud oppressors, in the elevation of their spirits, oppose God's designs concerning the deliverance of his people, nor think to detain them any longer when the time shall come for their release. Woe to the insulting Baby-

lonians that set God at defiance, as Pharaoh did, and will not let his people go! (2.) Let not the poor oppressed, in the dejection of their spirits, murmur and quarrel with God for the prolonging of their captivity, as if he dealt unjustly or unkindly with them, or think to force their way out before God's time shall come. Note, Those will find themselves in a woeful condition that strive with their Maker; for none ever hardened his heart against God and prospered. Sinful man is indeed a quarrelsome creature; but *let the potsherds strive with the potsherds of the earth.* Men are but earthen pots, nay, they are broken potsherds, and are made so very much by their mutual contentions. They are dashed in pieces one against another; and, if they are disposed to strive, let them strive with one another, let them meddle with their match; but let them not dare to contend with him that is infinitely above them, which is as senseless and absurd as, [1.] For the clay to find fault with the potter: *Shall the clay say to him that forms it, " What makest thou?* Why dost thou make me of this shape and not that?"* Nay, it is as if the clay should be in such a heat and passion with the potter as to tell him that *he has no hands,* or that he works as awkwardly as if he had none. " Shall the clay pretend to be wiser than the potter and therefore to advise him, or mightier than the potter and therefore to control him?" He that gave us being, that gave us this being, may design concerning us, and dispose of us, as he pleases; and it is impudent presumption for us to prescribe to him. Shall we impeach God's wisdom, or question his power, who are ourselves so curiously, so wonderfully, made? Shall we say, *He has no hands,* whose hands made us and in whose hands we are? The doctrine of God's sovereignty has enough in it to silence all our discontents and objections against the methods of his providence and grace, Rom. ix. 20, 21. [2.] It is as unnatural as for the child to find fault with the parents, to say to the father, *What begettest thou?* or to the mother, " What hast thou brought forth?* Why was I not begotten and born an angel, exempt from the infirmities of human nature and the calamities of human life?" Must not those who are children of men expect to share in the common lot and to fare as others fare? If God is our Father, where is the honour we owe to him by submitting to his will?

11 Thus saith the LORD, the Holy One of Israel, and his Maker, Ask me of things to come concerning my sons, and concerning the work of my hands command ye me. **12** I have made the earth, and created man upon it: I, *even* my hands, have stretched out the heavens, and all

their host have I commanded. **13** I have raised him up in righteousness, and I will direct all his ways: he shall build my city, and he shall let go my captives, not for price nor reward, saith the LORD of hosts. **14** Thus saith the LORD, The labour of Egypt, and merchandise of Ethiopia and of the Sabeans, men of stature, shall come over unto thee, and they shall be thine: they shall come after thee; in chains they shall come over, and they shall fall down unto thee, they shall make supplication unto thee, *saying,* Surely God *is* in thee; and *there is* none else, *there is* no god. **15** Verily thou *art* a God that hidest thyself, O God of Israel, the Saviour. **16** They shall be ashamed, and also confounded, all of them: they shall go to confusion together *that are* makers of idols. **17** *But* Israel shall be saved in the LORD with an everlasting salvation: ye shall not be ashamed nor confounded world without end. **18** For thus saith the LORD that created the heavens; God himself that formed the earth and made it; he hath established it, he created it not in vain, he formed it to be inhabited: I *am* the LORD; and *there is* none else. **19** I have not spoken in secret, in a dark place of the earth: I said not unto the seed of Jacob, Seek ye me in vain: I the LORD speak righteousness, I declare things that are right.

The people of God in captivity, who reconciled themselves to the will of God in their affliction and were content to wait his time for their deliverance, are here assured that they should not wait in vain.

I. They are invited to enquire concerning the issue of their troubles, *v.* 11. *The Holy One of Israel, and his Maker,* though he does not allow them to strive with him, yet encourages them, 1. To consult his word: *"Ask of me things to come;* have recourse to the prophets and their prophecies, and see what they say concerning these things. Ask the watchmen, What of the night? Ask them, How long?" Things to come, as far as they are revealed, belong to us and to our children, and we must not be strangers to them. 2. To seek unto him by prayer: " *Concerning my sons and concerning the work of my hands,* which as becomes them submit to the will of their Father, the will of their potter, *com-*

mand you me, not by way of prescription, but by way of petition. Be earnest in your requests, and confident in your expectations, as far as both are guided by and grounded upon the promise." We may not strive with our Maker by passionate complaints, but we may wrestle with him by faithful and fervent prayer. *My sons, and the work of my hands, commend to me* (so some read it), bring them to me and leave them with me. See the power of prayer, and its prevalency with God : *Thou shalt cry, and he shall say, Here I am ; what would you that I should do unto you?* Some read it with an interrogation, as carrying on the reproof (v. 9, 10) : *Do you question me concerning things to come?* and am I bound to give you an account? *And concerning my children, even concerning the work of my hands, will you command me,* or prescribe to me? Dare you do so? *Shall any teach God knowledge,* or give law to him? Those that complain of God do in effect assume an authority over him.

II. They are encouraged to depend upon the power of God when they are brought very low and are utterly incapable of helping themselves, v. 12. Their *help stands in the name of the Lord, who made heaven and earth,* which he mentions here, not only for his own glory, but for their comfort. The heavens and earth shall contribute, if he please, to the deliverance of the church (v. 8), for he created both, and therefore has both at command. 1. He *made the earth, and created man upon it,* for it was intended to be a habitation for man, Ps. cxv. 16. He has therefore not only authority, but wisdom and power sufficient to govern man here on this earth and to make what use he pleases of him. 2. His *hands have stretched out the heavens, and all their hosts he commanded* into being at first, and therefore still governs all their motions and influences. It is good news to God's Israel that their God is the creator and governor of the world.

III. They are particularly told what God would do for them, that they might know what to depend upon ; and this shall lead them to expect a more glorious Redeemer and redemption, of whom, and of which, Cyrus and their deliverance by him were types and figures.

1. Liberty shall be proclaimed to them, v. 13. Cyrus is the man that shall proclaim it; and, in order hereunto, God will put power into his hands : *I have raised him up in righteousness,* that is, in pursuance and performance of my promises and to plead my people's just but injured cause. He will give him success in all his enterprises, particularly that against Babylon : *I will direct all his ways;* and then it follows that he will prosper him, for those must needs speed well that are under a divine direction. God will make plain the way of those whom he designs to employ for him. Two things Cyrus must do for God :—(1.) Jerusalem is God's

254

city, but it is now in ruins, and he must rebuild it, that is, he must give orders for the rebuilding of it, and give wherewithal to do it. (2.) Israel is God's people, but they are now captives, and he must release them freely and generously, not demanding any ransom, nor compounding with them for price or reward. And Christ is anointed to do that for poor captive souls which Cyrus was to do for the captive Jews, to proclaim the *opening of the prison to those that were bound* (ch. lxi. 1), enlargement from a worse bondage than that in Babylon.

2. Provision shall be made for them. They went out poor, and unable to bear the expenses of their return and re-establishment ; and therefore it is promised that the labour of Egypt and other nations should come over to them and be theirs, v. 14. Cyrus, having conquered those countries, out of their spoils provided for the returning Jews; and he ordered his subjects to furnish them with necessaries (Ezra i. 4), so that they did not go out empty from Babylon any more than from Egypt. Those that are redeemed by Christ shall be not only provided for, but enriched. Those whose spirits God stirs up to go to the heavenly Zion may depend upon him to bear their charges. The world is theirs as far as is good for them.

3. Proselytes shall be brought over to them : *Men of stature shall come after thee in chains; they shall fall down to thee, saying, Surely God is in thee.* This was in part fulfilled when many of the people of the land became Jews (Esther viii. 17), *and said, We will go with you,* humbly begging leave to do so, *for we have heard that God is with you,* Zech. viii. 23. The restoration would be a means of the conviction of many and the conversion of some. Perhaps many of the Chaldeans who were now themselves conquered by Cyrus, when they saw the Jews going back in triumph, came and begged pardon for the affronts and abuses they had given them, owned that God was among them and that he was God alone, and therefore desired to join themselves to them. But this promise was to have its full accomplishment in the gospel church,—when the Gentiles shall become obedient by word and deed to the faith of Christ (Rom. xv. 18), as willing captives to the church (Ps. cx. 3), glad to wear her chains,—when an infidel, beholding the public worship of Christians, shall own himself convinced that *God is with them of a truth* (1 Cor. xiv. 24, 25) and shall assay to join himself to them, —and when those that had been *of the synagogue of Satan shall come and worship before the church's feet,* and be made to know *that God has loved thee* (Rev. iii. 9), and the *kings of the earth and the nations shall bring their glory into the gospel Jerusalem,* Rev. xxi. 24. Note, It is good to be with those, though it be in chains, that have God with them.

IV. They are taught to trust God further

than they can see him. The prophet puts this word into their mouths, and goes before them in saying it (*v.* 15): *Verily, thou art a God that hidest thyself.* 1. God hid himself when he brought them into the trouble, *hid himself and was wroth,* ch. lvii. 17. Note, Though God be his people's God and Saviour, yet sometimes, when they provoke him, he hides himself from them in displeasure, suspends his favours, and lays them under his frowns: but let them *wait upon the Lord that hides his face, ch.* viii. 17. 2. He hid himself when he was bringing them out of the trouble. Note, When God is acting as Israel's God and Saviour commonly *his way is in the sea,* Ps. lxxvii. 19. The salvation of the church is carried on in a mysterious way, by the Spirit of the Lord of hosts working on men's spirits (Zech. iv. 6), by weak and unlikely instruments, small and accidental occurrences, and not wrought till the last extremity; but this is our comfort, though God hide himself, we are sure he is *the God of Israel,* the *Saviour.* See Job xxxv. 14.

V. They are instructed to triumph over idolaters and all the worshippers of other gods (*v.* 16): *Those who are makers of idols,* not only who frame them, but who make gods of them by praying to them, *shall be ashamed and confounded,* when they shall be convinced of their mistakes and shall be forced to acknowledge that the God of Israel is the only true God, and when they shall be disappointed in their expectations from their idols, under whose protection they had put themselves. They shall go to confusion when they shall find that they can neither excuse the sin nor escape the punishment of it, Ps. xcvii. 7. It is not here and there one more timorous than the rest that shall thus shrink, and give up the cause, but *all of them;* nay, though they appear in a body, though hand join in hand, and they do all they can to keep one another in countenance, yet *they shall go to confusion together.* Bind them in bundles, to burn them.

VI. They are assured that those who trust in God shall never be made ashamed of their confidence in him, *v.* 17. Now that God was about to deliver them out of Babylon he directed them by his prophet, 1. To look up to him as the author of their *salvation: Israel shall be saved in the Lord.* Not only their salvation shall be wrought out by his power, but it shall be treasured up for them in his grace and promise, and so secured to them. They shall be saved in him; for his name shall be their strong tower, into which they shall run, and in which they shall be safe. 2. To look beyond this temporal deliverance to that which is spiritual and has reference to another world, to think of that salvation by the Messiah which is an everlasting salvation, the salvation of the soul, a rescue from everlasting misery and a restoration to everlasting bliss. " Give diligence

to make that sure, for it may be made sure, so sure that *you shall not be ashamed nor confounded world without end.* You shall not only be delivered from the *everlasting shame and contempt* which will be the portion of idolaters (Dan. xii. 2), but you shall have everlasting honour and glory." [1.] There is a world without end ; and it will be well or ill with us according as it will be with us in that world. [2.] Those who are saved with the everlasting salvation shall never be ashamed of what they did or suffered in the hopes of it ; for it will so far outdo their expectations as to be a more abundant reimbursement. The returning captives owned that to them did *belong confusion of face* (Dan. ix. 7, 8) ; yet God tells them that they shall not be confounded, but shall have assurance for ever. Those who are confounded as penitents for their own sin shall not be confounded as believers in God's promise and power.

VII. They are engaged for ever to cleave to God, and never to desert him, never to distrust him. What had been often inculcated before is here again repeated, for the encouragement of his people to continue faithful to him, and to hope that he would be so to them: *I am the Lord, and there is none else.* That the Lord we serve and trust in is God alone appears by the two great lights, that of nature and that of revelation.

1. It appears by the light of nature ; for he made the world, and therefore may justly demand its homage (*v.* 18): " *Thus saith the Lord, that created the heavens and formed the earth, I am the Lord,* the sovereign Lord of all, *and there is none else.*" The gods of the heathen did not do this, nay, they did not pretend to do it. He here mentions the creation of the heavens, but enlarges more upon that of the earth, because that is the part of the creation which we have the nearest view of and are most conversant with. It is here observed, (1.) That he formed it. It is not a rude and indigested chaos, but cast into the most proper shape and size by Infinite Wisdom. (2.) That he fixed it. When he had made it he established it, *founded it on the seas* (Ps. xxiv. 2), *hung it on nothing* (Job xxvi. 7) as at first he made it of nothing, and yet made it substantial and hung it fast, *ponderibus librata suis— poised by its own weight.* (3.) That he fitted it for use, and for the service of man, to whom he designed to give it. *He created it not in vain,* merely to be a proof of his power ; but *he formed it to be inhabited* by the children of men, and for that end he drew the waters off from it, with which it was at first covered, and made the *dry land appear,* Ps. civ. 6. 7. Be it observed here, to the honour of God's wisdom, that he made nothing in vain, but intended every thing for some end and fitted it to answer the intention. If any man prove to have been made in vain, it is his own fault. It should also be observed, to the

honour of God's goodness and his favour to man, that he reckoned that not made in vain which serves for his use and benefit, to be a habitation and maintenance for him.

2. It appears by the light of revelation. As the works of God abundantly prove that he is God alone, so does his word, and the discovery he has made of himself and of his mind and will by it. His oracles far exceed those of the Pagan deities, as well as his operations, *v.* 19. The preference is here placed in three things :—All that God has said is plain, satisfactory, and just. (1.) In the manner of the delivery of it it is plain and open : *I have not spoken in secret, in a dark place of the earth.* The Pagan deities delivered their oracles out of dens and caverns, with a low and hollow voice, and in ambiguous expressions ; those that had familiar spirits whispered and muttered (*ch.* viii. 19) ; but God delivered his law from the top of Mount Sinai before all the thousands of Israel, in distinct, audible, and intelligible sounds. Wisdom *cries in the chief places of concourse,* Prov. i. 20, 21 ; viii. 1—3. The vision is written, and made plain, so that he who runs may read it ; if it be obscure to any, they may thank themselves. Christ pleaded in his own defence what God says here, *In secret have I said nothing,* John xviii. 20. (2.) In the use and benefit of it it was highly satisfactory : *I said not unto the seed of Jacob,* who consulted these oracles and governed themselves by them, *Seek you me in vain,* as the false gods did to their worshippers, who sought *for the living to the dead, ch.* viii. 19. This includes all the gracious answers that God gave both to those who consulted him (his word is to them a faithful guide) and to those that prayed to him. The seed of Jacob are a praying people ; it is the *generation of those that seek him,* Ps. xxiv. 6. And, as he has in his word invited them to seek him, so he never denied their believing prayers nor disappointed their believing expectations. He said not to them, to any of them, *Seek you me in vain;* for, if he did not think fit to give them the particular thing they prayed for, yet he gave them such a sufficiency of grace and such comfort and satisfaction of soul as were equivalent. What we say of winter is true of prayer, It never rots in the skies. God not only gives a gracious answer to those that diligently seek him, but will be their bountiful rewarder. (3.) In the matter of it it was incontestably just, and there was no iniquity in it : *I the Lord speak righteousness, I declare things that are right,* and consonant to the eternal rules and reasons of good and evil. The heathen deities dictated those things to their worshippers which were the reproach of human nature and tended to the extirpation of virtue; but God speaks righteousness, dictates that which is right in itself and tends to make men righteous ; and therefore he is God, and there is none else.

256

20 Assemble yourselves and come ; draw near together, ye *that are* escaped of the nations : they have no knowledge that set up the wood of their graven image, and pray unto a god *that* cannot save. 21 Tell ye, and bring *them* near ; yea, let them take counsel together : Who hath declared this from ancient time? *Who* hath told it from that time? *Have* not I the LORD? And *there is* no God else beside me ; a just God and a Saviour ; *there is* none beside me. 22 Look unto me, and be ye saved, all the ends of the earth : for I *am* God, and *there is* none else. 23 I have sworn by myself, the word is gone out of my mouth *in* righteousness, and shall not return, That unto me every knee shall bow, every tongue shall swear. 24 Surely, shall one say, In the LORD have I righteousness and strength : *even* to him shall *men* come ; and all that are incensed against him shall be ashamed. 25 In the LORD shall all the seed of Israel be justified, and shall glory.

What is here said is intended, as before,

I. For the conviction of idolaters, to show them their folly in worshipping gods that cannot help them, and neglecting a God that can. Let all *that have escaped of the nations,* not only the people of the Jews, but those of other nations that were by Cyrus released out of captivity in Babylon, let them come, and hear what is to be said against the worshipping of idols, that they may be cured of it as well as the Jews, that Babylon, which had of old been the womb of idolatry, might now become the grave of it. Let the refugees assemble themselves and come together; God has something to say to them for their own good, and it is this, that idolatry is a foolish sottish thing, upon two accounts :—

1. It is setting up a refuge of lies for themselves : *They set up the wood of their graven image;* for that is the *substratum.* Though they overlay it with gold, deck it with ornaments, and make a god of it, yet still it is but wood. They *pray to a god that cannot save;* for he cannot hear, he cannot help, he can do nothing. How do those disparage themselves who give honour to that as a god which cannot, as a god, give good to them! How do those deceive themselves who pray for relief to that which is in no capacity at all to relieve them! Certainly those have no knowledge, or are brutish in their knowledge, who take so much pains, and do so much penance, in seeking the favour of a god that has no power.

2. It is setting up a rival with God, the only living and true God (*v.* 21) : "Summon them all; tell them that the great cause shall again be tried, though once adjudged, between God and Baal. *Bring them near, and let them take counsel together* what to say in defence of themselves and their idols. It shall, as before, be put upon this issue: let them show when any of their gods did with any certainty foretel future events, as the God of Israel has done, and it shall be acknowledged that they have some colour for their pretensions. But none of them ever did; their prophets were lying prophets; but *I the Lord have told it from that time,* long before it came to pass; therefore you must own *there is no other God besides me.*" (1.) None besides is fit to rule. He is *a just God,* and rules in justice, and will execute justice for those that are oppressed. (2.) None besides is able to help. As he is a just God, so he is *the Saviour,* who can save without the assistance of any, but without whom none can save. Those therefore have no sense of truth and falsehood, good and evil, no, nor of their own interest, that set up any in competition with him.

II. For the comfort and encouragement of all God's faithful worshippers, whoever they are, *v.* 22. Those that worship idols pray to gods that cannot save; but the God of Israel says it to all the ends of the earth, to his people, though they are scattered into the utmost corners of the world and seem to be lost and forgotten in their dispersion, "Let them but *look to me* by faith and prayer, look above instruments and second causes, look off from all pretenders, and look up to me, and they shall *be saved.*" It seems to refer further to the conversion of the Gentiles that live in the ends of the earth, the most distant nations, when the standard of the gospel is set up. *To it shall the Gentiles seek.* When Christ is lifted up from the earth, as the brazen serpent upon the pole, he shall draw the eyes of all men to him. They shall all be invited to look unto him, as the stung Israelites did to the brazen serpent; and so strong is the eye of faith that by divine grace it will reach the Saviour and fetch in salvation by him even from the ends of the earth; for *he is God, and there is none else.* Two things are here promised, for the abundant satisfaction of all that by faith look to the Saviour :—

1. That the glory of the God they serve shall be greatly advanced; and this will be good news to all the Lord's people, that, how much soever they and their names are depressed, God will be exalted, *v.* 23. This is confirmed by an oath, that we might have strong consolation : *I have sworn by myself* (and God can swear by no greater, Heb. vi. 13); *the word has gone out of my mouth,* and shall neither be recalled nor return empty; it has gone forth *in righteousness,* for it is the most reasonable equitable thing

in the world that he who made all should be Lord of all, that, since all beings are derived from him, they should all be devoted to him. He has said it, and it shall be made good, *I will be exalted,* Ps. xlvi. 10. He has assured us, (1.) That he will be universally submitted to, that the kingdoms of the world shall become his kingdom. They shall do him homage—*Unto me every knee shall bow ;* and they shall bind themselves by an oath of allegiance to him—*Unto me every tongue shall swear.* This is applied to the dominion of our Lord Jesus, Rom. xiv. 10, 11. *We shall all stand before the judgment-seat of Christ* and give account to him, for it is written, As I live, saith the Lord, *every knee shall bow to me and every tongue shall confess to God ;* and it seems to be referred to, Ps. ii. 9, 10. If the heart be brought into obedience to Christ, and made willing in the day of his power, the knee will bow to him in humble adorations and addresses, and in cheerful obedience to his commands, submission to his disposals, and compliance with his will in both ; and the tongue will swear to him, will lay a bond upon the soul to engage it for ever to him; for he that bears an honest mind never startles at assurances. (2) That he will be universally sought unto, and application shall be made to him from all parts of the world : *Unto him shall men of distant countries come,* to implore his favour. *Unto thee shall all flesh come* with their request, Ps. lxv. 2. And, when Christ was *lifted up from the earth, he drew all men to him.* (3.) That it will be to no purpose to make opposition to him. *All that are incensed against him,* that rage at his bonds and cords—the nations that are angry because he has taken to himself his great power and has reigned, that have been incensed at the strictness of his laws, the success of his gospel, and the spiritual nature of his kingdom—they *shall be ashamed ;* some shall be brought to a penitential shame for it, others to a remediless ruin. One way or other, sooner or later, all that are uneasy at Christ's government and victories will be made ashamed of their folly and obstinacy. Blessed be God for the assurance here given us that, whatever becomes of us and our interests, the Lord will reign for ever !

2. That the welfare of the souls they are concerned for shall be effectually secured : *Surely shall one say,* and another shall learn by his example to say the same, so that all the seed of Israel, according to the Spirit, shall say, and stand to it, (1.) That God has a sufficiency for them and that in Christ there is enough to supply all their needs: *In the Lord is all righteousness and strength* (so the margin reads it); he is himself righteous and strong. He can do every thing, and yet will do nothing but what is unquestionably just and equitable. He has also wherewithal to supply the needs of those that seek to him and depend upon him, upon

the equity of his providence and the treasures of his grace; nay, we may say, not only "*He* has it," but, "In him *we* have it," because he has said that he will be to us a God. In the Lord the captive Jews had righteousness (that is, grace both to sanctify their afflictions to them and to qualify them for deliverance) and strength for their support and escape. In the Lord Jesus we have righteousness to recommend us to the good-will of God towards us, and strength to begin and carry on the good work of God in us. He is the fountain of both, and on him we must depend for both, must *go forth in his strength, and make mention of his righteousness*, Ps. lxxi. 16. (2.) That they shall have an abundant bliss and satisfaction in this. [1.] The people of the Jews shall in the Lord be justified before men and openly glory in their God. The oppressors reproached them, loaded them with calumny, and boasted even of a right to oppress them, as abandoned by their God; but, when God shall work out their deliverance, that shall be their justification from these hard censures, and therefore they shall glory in it. [2.] All true Christians, that depend upon Christ for strength and righteousness, in him shall be justified and shall glory in that. Observe, *First*, All believers are the seed of Israel, an upright praying seed. *Secondly*, The great privilege they enjoy by Jesus Christ is that in him, and for his sake, they are justified before God, Christ being made of God to them righteousness. All that are justified will own it is in Christ that they are justified, nor could they be justified by any other; and those who are justified shall be glorified. And therefore, *Thirdly*, The great duty believers owe to Christ is to glory in him, and to make their boast of him. *Therefore* he is made all in all to us, that *whoso glories may glory in the Lord;* and let us comply with this intention.

CHAP. XLVI.

God, by the prophet here, designing shortly to deliver them out of their captivity, prepares them for that deliverance by possessing them with a detestation of idols and with a believing confidence in God, even their own God. I. Let them not be afraid of the idols of Babylon, as if they could in any way obstruct their deliverance, for they should be defaced (ver. 1, 2); but let them trust in that God who had often delivered them to do it still, to do it now, ver. 3, 4. II. Let them not think to make idols of their own, images of the God of Israel, by them to worship him, as the Babylonians worship their gods, ver. 5—7. Let them not be so sottish (ver. 8), but have an eye to God in his word, not in an image; let them depend upon that, and upon the promises and predictions of it, and God's power to accomplish them all, ver. 9—11. And let them know that the unbelief of man shall not make the word of God of no effect, ver. 12, 13.

BEL boweth down, Nebo stoopeth, their idols were upon the beasts, and upon the cattle: your carriages *were* heavy loaden; *they are* a burden to the weary *beast*. 2 They stoop, they bow down together; they could not deliver the burden, but themselves are gone into captivity. 3 Hearken unto me, O house of Ja-

258

cob, and all the remnant of the house of Israel, which are borne *by me* from the belly, which are carried from the womb: 4 And *even* to *your* old age I *am* he; and *even* to hoar hairs will I carry *you:* I have made, and I will bear; even I will carry, and will deliver *you.*

We are here told,

I. That the false gods will certainly fail their worshippers when they have most need of them, *v.* 1, 2. Bel and Nebo were two celebrated idols of Babylon. Some make Bel to be a contraction of Baal; others rather think not, but that it was Belus, one of their first kings, who after his death was deified. As Bel was a deified prince, so (some think) Nebo was a deified prophet, for so Nebo signifies; so that Bel and Nebo were their Jupiter and their Mercury or Apollo. Barnabas and Paul passed at Lystra for Jupiter and Mercury. The names of these idols were taken into the names of their princes, Bel into Belshazzar's, Nebo into Nebuchadnezzar's and Nebuzaradan's, &c. These gods they had long worshipped, and in their revels praised them for their successes (as appears, Dan. v. 4); and they insulted over Israel as if Bel and Nebo were too hard for Jehovah and could detain them in captivity in defiance of their God. Now, that this might be no discouragement to the poor captives, God here tells them what shall become of these idols, which they threaten them with. When Cyrus takes Babylon, down go the idols. It was usual then with conquerors to destroy the gods of the places and people they conquered, and to put the gods of their own nation in the room of them, *ch.* xxxvii. 19. Cyrus will do so; and then Bel and Nebo, that were set up on high, and looked great, bold, and erect, shall *stoop and bow down* at the feet of the soldiers that plunder their temples. And because there is a great deal of gold and silver upon them, which was intended to adorn them, but serves to expose them, they carry them away with the rest of the spoil. The carriers' horses, or mules, are laden with them and their other idols, to be sent among other lumber (for so it seems they accounted them rather than treasure) into Persia. So far are they from being able to support their worshippers that they are themselves a heavy load in the waggons, and *a burden to the weary beast.* The idols cannot help one another (*v.* 2): *They stoop, they bow down together.* They are all alike, tottering things, and their day has come to fall. Their worshippers cannot help them: *They could not deliver the burden* out of the enemy's hand, *but themselves* (both the idols and the idolaters) *have gone into captivity.* Let not therefore God's people be afraid of either. When God's ark was taken prisoner by the

Philistines it proved a burden, not to the beasts, but to the conquerors, who were forced to return it; but, when Bel and Nebo have gone into captivity, their worshippers may even give their good word with them: they will never recover themselves.

II. That the true God will never fail his worshippers: "You hear what has become of Bel and Nebo, now *hearken to me, O house of Jacob! v.* 3, 4. Am I such a god as these? No; though you are brought low, and the house of Israel is but a remnant, your God has been, is, and ever will be, your powerful and faithful protector."

1. Let God's Israel do him the justice to own that he has hitherto been kind to them, careful of them, tender over them, and has all along done well for them. Let them own, (1.) That he bore them at first: *I have made.* Out of what womb came they, but that of his mercy, and grace, and promise? He formed them into a people and gave them their constitution. Every good man is what God makes him. (2.) That he bore them up all along: You have been *borne by me from the belly,* and *carried from the womb.* God began betimes to do them good, as soon as ever they were formed into a nation, nay, when as yet they were very few, and strangers. God took them under a special protection, and *suffered no man to do them wrong,* Ps. cv. 12—14. In the infancy of their state, when they were not only foolish and helpless, as children, but froward and peevish, God carried them in the arms of his power and love, bore them *as upon eagles' wings,* Exod. xix. 4; Deut. xxxii. 11. Moses had not patience *to carry them as the nursing father does the sucking child* (Num. xi. 12), but God bore them, and *bore their manners,* Acts xiii. 18. And as God began early to do them good (when *Israel was a child, then I loved him),* so he had constantly continued to do them good: he had carried them from the womb to this day. And we may all witness for God that he has been thus gracious to us. We have been borne by him from the belly, from the womb, else we should have died from the womb and given up the ghost when we came out of the belly. We have been the constant care of his kind providence, carried in the arms of his power and in the bosom of his love and pity. The new man is so; all that in us which is born of God is borne up by him, else it would soon fail. Our spiritual life is sustained by his grace as necessarily and constantly as our natural life by his providence. The saints have acknowledged that God has carried them from the womb, and have encouraged themselves with the consideration of it in their greatest straits, Ps. xxii. 9, 10; lxxi. 5, 6, 17.

2. He will then do them the kindness to promise that he will never leave them. He that was their first will be their last; he that was the author will be the finisher of

their well-being (*v.* 4): "You have been *borne by me from the belly,* nursed when you were children; and *even to your old age I am he,* when, by reason of your decays and infirmities, you will need help as much as in your infancy." Israel were now growing old, so was their covenant by which they were incorporated, Heb. viii. 13. *Gray hairs were here and there upon them,* Hos. vii 9. And they had hastened their old age, and the calamities of it, by their irregularities. But God will not cast them off now, will not fail them when their strength fails; he is still their God, will still carry them in the same everlasting arms that were laid under them in Moses's time, Deut. xxxiii. 27. He has made them and owns his interest in them, and therefore he will bear them, will bear with their infirmities, and bear them up under their afflictions: "*Even I will carry and will deliver* them; I will now bear them upon eagles' wings out of Babylon, as in their infancy I bore them out of Egypt." This promise to aged Israel is applicable to every aged Israelite. God has graciously engaged to support and comfort his faithful servants, even in their old age: "*Even to your old age,* when you grow unfit for business, when you are compassed with infirmities, and perhaps your relations begin to grow weary of you, yet *I am he*—he that I am, he that I have been— the very same by whom you have been borne from the belly and carried from the womb. You change, but I am the same. I am he that I have promised to be, he that you have found me, and he that you would have me to be. *I will carry you, I will bear,* will bear you up and bear you out, and will carry you on in your way and carry you home at last."

5 To whom will ye liken me, and make *me* equal, and compare me, that we may be like? 6 They lavish gold out of the bag, and weigh silver in the balance, *and* hire a goldsmith; and he maketh it a god: they fall down, yea, they worship. 7 They bear him upon the shoulder, they carry him, and set him in his place, and he standeth; from his place shall he not remove: yea, *one* shall cry unto him, yet can he not answer, nor save him out of his trouble. 8 Remember this, and show yourselves men: bring *it* again to mind, O ye transgressors. 9 Remember the former things of old: for I *am* God, and *there is* none else; *I am* God, and *there is* none like me, 10 Declaring the end from the beginning, and from ancient times *the things* that are not *yet* done, saying, My counsel shall

stand, and I will do all my pleasure :
11 Calling a ravenous bird from the east, the man that executeth my counsel from a far country : yea, I have spoken *it*, I will also bring it to pass ; I have purposed *it*, I will also do it.
12 Hearken unto me, ye stout-hearted, that *are* far from righteousness : 13 I bring near my righteousness ; it shall not be far off, and my salvation shall not tarry : and I will place salvation in Zion for Israel my glory.

The deliverance of Israel by the destruction of Babylon (the general subject of all these chapters) is here insisted upon, and again promised, for the conviction both of idolaters who set up as rivals with God, and of oppressors who were enemies to the people of God.

I. For the conviction of those who made and worshipped idols, especially those of Israel who did so, who would have images of their God, as the Babylonians had of theirs,

1. He challenges them either to frame an image that should be thought a resemblance of him or to set up any being that should stand in competition with him (*v.* 5) : *To whom will you liken me?* It is absurd to think of representing an infinite and eternal Spirit by the figure of any creature whatsoever. It is to change his truth into a lie and to turn his glory into shame. None ever saw any similitude of him, nor can see his face and live. *To whom then can we liken God?* ch. xl. 18, 25. It is likewise absurd to think of making any creature equal with the Creator, who is infinitely above the noblest creatures, yea, or to make any comparison between the creature and the Creator, since between infinite and finite there is no proportion.

2. He exposes the folly of those who made idols and then prayed to them, *v.* 6, 7. (1.) They were at great charge upon their idols and spared no cost to fit them for their purpose : *They lavish gold out of the bag ;* no little will serve, and they do not care how much goes, though they pinch their families and weaken their estates by it. How does the profuseness of idolaters shame the niggardliness of many who call themselves God's servants but are for a religion that will cost them nothing! Some *lavish gold out of the bag* to make an idol of it in the house, while others *hoard up gold in the bag* to make an idol of it in the heart ; for *covetousness is idolatry*, as dangerous, though not as scandalous, as the other. *They weigh silver in the balance*, either to be the matter of their idol (for even those that were most sottish had so much sense as to think that God should be served with the best they had, the best they could possibly afford; those that represented him by a calf made it
260

a golden one) or to pay the workmen's wages. The service of sin often proves very expensive. (2.) They were in great care about their idols and took no little pains about them (*v.* 7) : *They bear him upon their own shoulders*, and do not hire porters to do it ; they *carry him, and set him in his place*, more like a dead corpse than a living God. They set him on a pedestal, *and he stands*. They take a great deal of pains to fasten him, and *from his place he shall not remove*, that they may know where to find him, though at the same time they know he can neither move a hand nor stir a step to do them any kindness. (3.) After all, they paid great respect to their idols, though they were but the works of their own hands and the creatures of their own fancies. When the goldsmith has made it that which they please to call a god *they fall down, yea, they worship it.* If they magnified themselves too much in pretending to make a god, as if they would atone for that, they vilified themselves as much in prostrating themselves to a god that they knew the original of. And, if they were deceived by the custom of their country in making such gods as these, they did no less deceive themselves when they cried unto them, though they knew they could not answer them, could not understand what they said to them, nor so much as reply Yea, or No, much less could they *save them out of their trouble.* Now shall any that have some knowledge of, and interest in, the true and living God, thus make fools of themselves ?

3. He puts it to themselves, and their own reason, let that judge in the case (*v.* 8) : *" Remember this*, that has been often told you, what senseless helpless things idols are, *and show yourselves men*—men and not brutes, men and not babes. Act with reason ; act with resolution ; act for your own interest. Do a wise thing ; do a brave thing ; and scorn to disparage your own judgment as you do when you worship idols."* Note, Sinners would become saints if they would but show themselves men, if they would but support the dignity of their nature and use aright its powers and capacities. " Many things you have been reminded of ; *bring them again to mind*, recal them into your memories, and revolve them there. *O! you transgressors, consider your ways ; remember whence you have fallen, and repent*, and so recover yourselves."*

4. He again produces incontestable proofs that he is God, that he and none besides is so (*v.* 9) : *I am God, and there is none else*, none besides me ; *I am God, and there is none like me.* This is that which we have need to be reminded of again and again ; for proof of it he refers, (1.) To the sacred history : *" Remember the former things of old*, what the God of Israel did for his people in their beginnings, whether he did not that for them which no one else could, and which the false gods did not, nor could do, for

their worshippers. Remember those things, and you will own that *I am God and there is none else.*" This is a good reason why we should give glory to him as a nonsuch, and why we should not give that glory to any other which is due to him alone, Exod. xv. 11. (2.) To the sacred prophecy. He is God alone, for it is he only that *declares the end from the beginning,* v. 10. From the beginning of time he declared the end of time, the end of all things. Enoch prophesied, *Behold, the Lord comes.* From the beginning of a nation he declares what the end of it will be. He told Israel what should befal them in *the latter days,* what *their end should be,* and wished they were so wise as to consider it, Deut. xxxii. 20, 29. From the beginning of an event he declares what the end of it will be. *Known unto God are all his works,* and, when he pleases, he makes them known. Further than prophecy guides us it is impossible for us to *find out the work that God makes from the beginning to the end,* Eccl. iii. 11. He *declares from ancient times the things that are not yet done.* Many scripture prophecies which were delivered long ago are not yet accomplished; but the accomplishment of some in the mean time is an earnest of the accomplishment of the rest in due time. By this it appears that he is *God, and none else;* it is he, and none besides, that can say, and make his words good, " *My counsel shall stand,* and all the powers of hell and earth cannot control or disannul it nor all their policies correct or countermine it." As God's operations are all according to his counsels, so his counsels shall all be fulfilled in his operations, and none of his measures shall be broken, none of his designs shall miscarry. This yields abundant satisfaction to those who have bound up all their comforts in God's counsels, that his counsel shall undoubtedly stand; and, if we are brought to this, that whatever pleases God pleases us, nothing can contribute more to make us easy than to be assured of this, that *God will do all his pleasure,* Ps. cxxxv. 6. The accomplishment of this particular prophecy, which relates to the elevation of Cyrus and his agency in the deliverance of God's people out of their captivity, is mentioned for the confirmation of this truth, that the Lord is God and there is none else; and this is a thing which shall shortly come to pass, v. 11. God by his counsel *calls a ravenous bird from the east,* a bird of prey, *Cyrus,* who (they say) had a nose like the beak of a hawk or eagle, to which some think this alludes, or (as others say) to the eagle which was his standard, as it was afterwards that of the Romans, to which there is supposed to be a reference, Matt. xxiv. 28. Cyrus came from the east at God's call: for God is Lord of hosts and of those that have hosts at command. And, if God give him a call, he will give him success. He is the man that shall *execute God's*

counsel, though he comes *from a far country* and knows nothing of the matter. Note, Even those that know not, and mind not, God's revealed will, are made use of to fulfil the counsels of his secret will, which shall all be punctually accomplished in their season by what hand he pleases. That which is here added, to ratify this particular prediction, may abundantly show to the heirs of promise the immutability of his counsel : " *I have spoken it* by my servants the prophets, and what I have spoken is just the same with what *I have purposed.*" For, though God has many things in his purposes which are not in his prophecies, he has nothing in his prophecies but what are in his purposes. And he *will do it,* for he will never change his mind ; he *will bring it to pass,* for it is not in the power of any creature to control him. Observe with what majesty he says it, as one having authority : *I have spoken it, I will also bring it to pass.* Dictum, factum—no sooner said than done. *I have purposed it,* and he does not say, " I will take care it shall be done," but, " *I will do it.*" Heaven and earth shall pass away sooner than one tittle of the word of God.

II. For the conviction of those that daringly opposed the counsels of God assurance is here given not only that they shall be accomplished, but that they shall be accomplished very shortly, v. 12, 13.

1. This is addressed to the *stout-hearted,* that is, either, (1.) The proud and obstinate Babylonians, *that are far from righteousness,* far from doing justice or showing mercy to those they have power over, that say they will never let the oppressed go free, but will still detain them in spite of their petitions or God's predictions, that are far from any thing of clemency or compassion to the miserable. Or, (2.) The unhumbled Jews, that have been long under the hammer, long in the furnace, but are not broken, are not melted, that, like the unbelieving murmuring Israelites in the wilderness, think themselves far from God's righteousness (that is, from the performance of his promise, and his appearing to judge for them), and by their distrusts set themselves at a yet further distance from it, and keep good things from themselves, as their fathers, who could not enter into the land of promise because of unbelief. This is applicable to the Jewish nation when they rejected the gospel of Christ ; though they *followed after the law of righteousness,* they *attained not to righteousness, because they sought it not by faith,* Rom. ix. 31, 32. They perished far from righteousness ; and it was because they were *stout-hearted,* Rom. x. 3.

2. Now to them God says that, whatever they think, the one in presumption, the other in despair, (1.) Salvation shall be certainly wrought for God's people. If men will not do them justice, God will, and his righteousness shall effect that for them which men's

righteousness would not reach to. He *will place salvation in Zion,* that is, he will make Jerusalem a place of safety and defence to all those who will plant themselves there; thence shall salvation go forth *for Israel his glory.* God glories in his Israel; and he will be glorified in the salvation he designs to work out for them; it shall redound greatly to his honour. This salvation shall be in Zion; for thence the gospel shall take rise (*ch.* ii. 3), thither the Redeemer comes (*ch.* lix. 20, Rom. xi. 26), and it is Zion's King that has salvation, Zech. ix. 9. (2.) It shall be very shortly wrought. This is especially insisted on with those who thought it at a distance: *" I bring near my righteousness,* nearer than you think of; perhaps it is nearest of all when your straits are greatest and your enemies most injurious; it shall not be far off when there is occasion for it, Ps. lxxxv. 9. *Behold, the Judge stands before the door.* My salvation shall not tarry any longer than till it is ripe and you are ready for it; and therefore, *though it tarry, wait for it;* wait patiently, for *he that shall come will come, and will not tarry."*

CHAP. XLVII.

Infinite Wisdom could have ordered things so that Israel might have been released and yet Babylon unhurt; but if they will harden their hearts, and will not let the people go, they must thank themselves that their ruin is made to pave the way to Israel's release. That ruin is here, in this chapter, largely foretold, not to gratify a spirit of revenge in the people of God, who had been used barbarously by them, but to encourage their faith and hope concerning their own deliverance, and to be a type of the downfal of that great enemy of the New-Testament church which, in the Revelation, goes under the name of " Babylon." In this chapter we have, I. The greatness of the ruin threatened, that Babylon should be brought down to the dust, and made completely miserable, should fall from the height of prosperity into the depth of adversity, ver. 1—5. II. The sins that provoked God to bring this ruin upon them. 1. Their cruelty to the people of God, ver. 6. 2. Their pride and carnal security, ver. 7—9. 3. Their confidence in themselves and contempt of God, ver. 10. 4. Their use of magic arts and their dependence upon enchantments and sorceries, which should be so far from standing them in any stead that they should but hasten their ruin, ver. 11—15.

COME down, and sit in the dust, O virgin daughter of Babylon, sit on the ground: *there is* no throne, O daughter of the Chaldeans: for thou shalt no more be called tender and delicate. 2 Take the millstones, and grind meal: uncover thy locks, make bare the leg, uncover the thigh, pass over the rivers. 3 Thy nakedness shall be uncovered, yea, thy shame shall be seen: I will take vengeance, and I will not meet *thee as* a man. 4 *As for* our redeemer, the LORD of hosts *is* his name, the Holy One of Israel. 5 Sit thou silent, and get thee into darkness, O daughter of the Chaldeans: for thou shalt no more be called, The lady of kingdoms. 6 I was wroth with my people, I have polluted mine inheritance, and given them into thine hand: thou

didst show them no mercy; upon the ancient hast thou very heavily laid thy yoke.

In these verses God by the prophet sends a messenger even to Babylon, like that of Jonah to Nineveh: "The time is at hand when Babylon shall be destroyed." Fair warning is thus given her, that she may by repentance prevent the ruin and there may be a lengthening of her tranquillity. We may observe here,

I. God's controversy with Babylon. We will begin with that, for there all the calamity begins; she has made God her enemy, and then who can befriend her: Let her know that the righteous Judge, to whom vengeance belongs, has said (*v.* 3), *I will take vengeance.* She has provoked God, and shall be reckoned with for it when the measure of her iniquities is full. Woe to those on whom God comes to take vengeance; for who knows the power of his anger and what a fearful thing it is to fall into his hands? Were it a man like ourselves who would be revenged on us, we might hope to be a match for him, either to make our escape from him or to make our part good with him. But he says, *"I will not meet thee as a man,* not with the compassions of a man, but I will be to thee as a lion, and a *young lion"* (Hos. v. 14); or, rather, not with the strength of a man, which is easily resisted, but with the power of a God, which cannot be resisted. Not with the justice of a man, which may be bribed, or biassed, or mollified by a foolish pity, but with the justice of a God, which is strict and severe, and can never be evaded. As in pardoning the penitent, so in punishing the impenitent, he is *God and not man,* Hos. xi. 9.

II. The particular ground of this controversy. We are sure that there is cause for it, and it is a just cause; it is the *vengeance of his temple* (Jer. l. 28); it is for *violence done to Zion,* Jer. li. 35. God will plead his people's cause against them. It is acknowledged (*v.* 6) that God had, in wrath, delivered his people into the hands of the Babylonians, had made use of them for the correction of his children, and had by their means *polluted his inheritance,* had left his peculiar people exposed to suffer in common with the rest of the nations, had suffered the heathen, who should have been kept at a distance, to *come into his sanctuary* and *defile his temple,* Ps. lxxix. 1. Herein God was righteous; but the Babylonians carried the matter too far, and, when they had them in their hands (triumphing to see a people that had been so much in reputation for wisdom, holiness, and honour, brought thus low), with a base and servile spirit they trampled upon them, *and showed them no mercy,* no, not the common instances of humanity which the miserable are entitled to purely by their misery. They used them barbarously, and with an air of contempt, nay, and of complacency in their calamities. They were brought under the yoke; but, as if that were not enough, they *laid the yoke on very heavily*, adding affliction to the afflicted. Nay, they laid it *on the ancient*—the elders in years, who were past their labour, and must sink under a yoke which those in their youthful strength would easily bear—the elders in office, those that had been judges and magistrates, and persons of the first rank. They took a pride in putting these to the meanest hardest drudgery. Jeremiah laments this, that the *faces of elders were not honoured*, Lam. v. 12. Nothing brings a surer or a sorer ruin upon any people than cruelty, especially to God's Israel.

III. The terror of this controversy. She has reason to tremble when she is told who it is that has this quarrel with her (*v.* 4): " *As for our Redeemer*, our *Goël*, that undertakes to plead our cause as the avenger of our blood, he has two names which speak not only comfort to us, but terror to our adversaries." 1. " He is *the Lord of hosts*, that has all the creatures at his command, and therefore has *all power both in heaven and in earth*." Woe to those against whom the Lord fights, for the whole creation is at war with them. 2. " He is the *Holy One of Israel*, a God in covenant with us, who has his residence among us, and will faithfully perform all the promises he has made to us." God's power and holiness are engaged against Babylon and for Zion. This may fitly be applied to Christ, our great Redeemer. He is both Lord of hosts and the Holy One of Israel.

IV. The consequences of it to Babylon. She is called a *virgin*, because so she thought herself, though she was the mother of harlots. She was beautiful as a virgin, and courted by all about her; she had been called *tender and delicate* (*v.* 1), and *the lady of kingdoms* (*v.* 5); but now the case is altered. 1. Her honour is gone, and she must bid farewell to all her dignity. She that had sat at the upper end of the world, sat in state and sat at ease, must now *come down and sit in the dust*, as very mean and a deep mourner, must *sit on the ground*, for she shall be so emptied and impoverished that she shall not have a seat left her to sit upon. 2. Her power is gone, and she must bid farewell to all her dominion. She shall rule no more as she has done, nor give law as she has done to her neighbours: *There is no throne, none for thee, O daughter of the Chaldeans!* Note, Those that abuse their honour or power provoke God to deprive them of it, and to make them *come down and sit in the dust.* 3. Her ease and pleasure are gone: " She shall *no more be called tender and delicate* as she has been, for she shall not only be deprived of all those things with which she pampered herself, but shall

be put to hard service and made to feel both want and pain, which will be more than doubly grievous to her who formerly *would not venture to set* so much as *the sole of her foot to the ground for tenderness and for delicacy,*" Deut. xxviii. 56. It is our wisdom not to use ourselves to be tender and delicate, because we know not how hardly others may use us before we die nor what straits we may be reduced to. 4. Her liberty is gone, and she is brought into a state of servitude and as sore a bondage as she in her prosperity had brought others to. Even the great men of Babylon must now receive the same law from the conquerors that they used to give to the conquered : " *Take the mill-stones and grind meal* (*v.* 2), set to work, to hard labour" (like beating hemp in Bridewell), " which will make thee sweat so that thou must throw off all thy head-dresses, and *uncover thy locks.*" When they were driven from one place to another, at the capricious humours of their masters, they must be forced to wade up to the middle through the waters, to *make bare the leg* and *uncover the thigh*, that they might *pass over the rivers*, which would be a great mortification to those that used to ride in state. But let them not complain, for just thus they had formerly used their captives; and *with what measure they* then *meted* it is now *measured to them again.* Let those that have power use it with temper and moderation, considering that the spoke which is uppermost will be under. 5. All her glory, and all her glorying, are gone. Instead of glory, she has ignominy (*v.* 3): *Thy nakedness shall be uncovered and thy shame shall be seen*, according to the base and barbarous usage they commonly gave their captives, to whom, for covetousness of their clothes, they did not leave rags sufficient to cover their nakedness, so void were they of the modesty as well as of the pity due to the human nature. Instead of glorying she *sits silently, and gets into darkness* (*v.* 5), ashamed to show her face, for she has quite lost her credit and *shall no more be called the lady of kingdoms.* Note, God can make those sit silently that used to make the greatest noise in the world, and send those into darkness that used to make the greatest figure. Let him that glories, therefore, glory in a God that changes not, and not in any worldly wealth, pleasure, or honour, which are subject to change.

7 And thou saidst, I shall be a lady for ever : *so* that thou didst not lay these *things* to thy heart, neither didst remember the latter end of it. 8 Therefore hear now this, *thou that art* given to pleasures, that dwellest carelessly, that sayest in thine heart, I *am*, and none else beside me ; I shall not sit *as* a widow, neither shall

I know the loss of children : 9 But these two *things* shall come to thee in a moment in one day, the loss of children, and widowhood : they shall come upon thee in their perfection for the multitude of thy sorceries, *and* for the great abundance of thine enchantments. 10 For thou hast trusted in thy wickedness : thou hast said, None seeth me. Thy wisdom and thy knowledge, it hath perverted thee ; and thou hast said in thine heart, I *am*, and none else beside me. 11 Therefore sh'all evil come upon thee ; thou shalt not know from whence it riseth : and mischief shall fall upon thee ; thou shalt not be able to put it off : and desolation shall come upon thee suddenly, *which* thou shalt not know. 12 Stand now with thine enchantments, and with the multitude of thy sorceries, wherein thou hast laboured from thy youth ; if so be thou shalt be able to profit, if so be thou mayest prevail. 13 Thou art wearied in the multitude of thy counsels. Let now the astrologers, the stargazers, the monthly prognosticators, stand up, and save thee from *these things* that shall come upon thee. 14 Behold, they shall be as stubble ; the fire shall burn them ; they shall not deliver themselves from the power of the flame : *there shall* not *be* a coal to warm at, *nor* fire to sit before it. 15 Thus shall they be unto thee with whom thou hast laboured, *even* thy merchants, from thy youth : they shall wander every one to his quarter ; none shall save thee.

Babylon, now doomed to ruin, is here justly upbraided with her pride, luxury, and security, in the day of her prosperity, and the confidence she had in her own wisdom and forecast, and particularly in the prognostications and counsels of the astrologers. These things are mentioned both to justify God in bringing these judgments upon her and to mortify her, and put her to so much the greater shame, under these judgments ; for, when God comes forth to take vengeance, glory belongs to him, but confusion to the sinner.

I. The Babylonians are here upbraided with their pride and haughtiness, and the great conceit they had of themselves, because of their wealth and power, and the

264

vast extent of their dominion ; it was the language both of the government and of the body of the people : *Thou sayest in thy heart* (and God, who searches all hearts, can tell men what they say there, though they never speak it out) *I am, and none else besides me, v.* 8 and 10. The repetition of this part of the charge intimates that they said it often, and that it was very offensive to God. It is the very word that God has often said concerning himself, *I am, and none else besides me*, denoting his self-existence, his infinite and incomparable perfections, and his sole supremacy. All this Babylon pretends to ; and no wonder if she that assumed a power to make what gods and goddesses she pleased for the people to worship made herself one among the rest. It is presumption to say of any creature, " It is, and there is not its like, there is none besides it " (for creatures stand very nearly upon a level with one another) ; but it is insufferable arrogance for any to say so of themselves, and an evidence of their self-ignorance.

II. They are upbraided with their luxury and love of ease (*v.* 8) : " *Thou that art given to pleasures*, art a slave to them, art in them as in thy element, and, that thou mayest enjoy them without disturbance or interruption, *dwellest carelessly* and layest nothing to heart." Great wealth and plenty are great temptations to sensuality, and, where there is fulness of bread, there is commonly abundance of idleness. But if those that are given to pleasures, and dwell carelessly, would but hear this, that *for all these things God will bring them into judgment*, it would be a damp to their mirth, an allay to their pleasure, and would find them something to be in care about.

III. They are upbraided with their carnal security and their vain confidence of the perpetuity of their pomps and pleasures. This is much insisted on here. Observe,

1. The cause of their security. They thought themselves safe and out of danger, not because they were ignorant of the uncertainty of all earthly enjoyments and the inevitable fate that attends states and kingdoms as well as particular persons, but *because they did not lay this to heart*, did not apply it to themselves, nor give it a due consideration. They lulled themselves asleep in ease and pleasure, and dreamt of nothing else but that *to-morrow should be as this day, and much more abundant*. They did not *remember the latter end of it*—the latter end of their prosperity, that it is a fading flower, and will wither—the latter end of their iniquity, that it will be bitterness, that the day will come when their injustice and oppression must be reckoned for and punished. *She did not remember her latter end* (so some read it) ; she forgot that her day would come to fall and what would be in the end hereof. It was the ruin of Jerusalem (Lam.

i. 9) that *she remembered not her last end, therefore she came down wonderfully;* and it was Babylon's ruin too. The children of men are easy, and think themselves safe, in their sinful ways, only because they never think of death, and judgment, and their future state.

2. The ground of their security. They trusted in their wickedness and in their wisdom, *v.* 10. (1.) Their power and wealth, which they had gotten by fraud and oppression, were their confidence: *Thou hast trusted in thy wickedness,* as Doeg, Ps. lii. 7. Many have so debauched their own consciences, and have got to such a pitch of daring wickedness, that they stick at nothing; and this they trust to to carry them through those difficulties which embarrass men who make conscience of what they say and do. They doubt not but they shall be too hard for all their enemies, because they dare lie, and kill, and forswear themselves, and do any thing for their interest. Thus they trust in their wickedness to secure them, which is the only thing that will ruin them. (2.) Their policy and craft, which they called their *wisdom,* were their confidence. They thought they could outwit all mankind, and therefore might set all their enemies at defiance. But their *wisdom and knowledge perverted them,* and turned them out of the way, made them forget themselves, and the preparation necessary to be made for hereafter.

3. The expressions of their security. Three things this proud and haughty monarchy said, in her security:—(1.) *"I shall be a lady for ever,"* v. 7. She looked upon the patent of her honour to be not merely during the pleasure of the sovereign Lord, the fountain of honour, or during her own good behaviour, but to be perpetual to the present generation and their heirs and successors for ever. She was not only proud that she was a lady, but confident that she should be a lady for ever. Thus the New-Testament Babylon says, *I sit as a queen, and shall see no sorrow,* Rev. xviii. 7. Those ladies mistake themselves, and consider not their latter end, who think they shall be ladies for ever; for death will shortly lay their honour with them in the dust. Saints will be saints for ever, but lords and ladies will not be so for ever. (2.) *"I shall not sit as a widow,"* in solitude and sorrow, shall never lose the power and wealth I am thus wedded to; the monarchy shall never want a monarch to espouse and protect it, and be a husband to the state; *nor shall I know the loss of children,"* v. 8. She was as confident of the continuance of the numbers of her people as of the dignity of her prince, and had no fear of being either deposed or depopulated. Those that are in the height of prosperity are apt to fancy themselves out of the reach of adverse fate. (3.) *" No one sees me* when I do amiss, and therefore there will be none to call me to an account," *v.* 10. It is common for sinners to promise themselves impunity, because they promise themselves secrecy, in their wicked ways. They trust to their wicked arts and designs to stand them in stead, because they think they have carried them on so plausibly that none can discern the wickedness and deceit of them.

4. The punishment of their security. It shall be their ruin; and it will be, (1.) A complete ruin, the ruin of all their comforts and confidences: *" These two things shall come upon thee* (the very two things that thou didst set at defiance), *loss of children and widowhood, v.* 9. Both thy princes and thy people shall be cut off, so that thou shalt be no more a government, no more a nation." Note, God often brings upon secure sinners those very mischiefs which they least feared and thought themselves in least danger of. *" They shall come upon thee in their perfection,* with all their aggravating circumstances and without any thing to allay or mitigate them." Afflictions to God's children are not afflictions in perfection. Widowhood is not to them a calamity in perfection, for they have this to comfort themselves with, that their Maker is their husband; loss of children is not, for he is better to them than ten sons. But on his enemies they come in perfection. Widowhood and loss of children are either of them great griefs, but both together great indeed. Naomi thinks she may well be called *Marah* when she is *left both of her sons and of her husband* (Ruth i. 5); and yet on her these evils did not come in perfection, for she had two daughters-in-law left, that were comforts to her. But on Babylon they come in perfection; she has no comfort remaining. (2.) It will be a sudden and surprising ruin. The evil shall come *in one day,* nay, *in a moment,* which will make it much the more terrible, especially to those that were so very secure. *" Evil shall come upon thee (v.* 11) and thou shalt have neither time nor way to provide against it, or to prepare for it; for *thou shalt not know whence it rises,* and therefore shalt not know where to stand upon thy guard." *Thou shalt not know the morning thereof;* so the Hebrew phrase is. We know just when and where the day will break and the sun rise, but we know not what the day, when it comes, will bring forth, nor when or where trouble will arise; perhaps the storm may come from that point of the compass which we little thought of. Babylon pretended to great wisdom and knowledge (*v.* 10), but with all her knowledge she cannot foresee, nor with all her wisdom prevent, the ruin threatened: *" Desolation shall come upon thee suddenly,* as a thief in the night, *which thou shalt not know,* that is, which thou little thoughtest of." Fair warning was indeed given them, by

Isaiah and other prophets of the Lord, of this desolation; but they slighted that notice, and would give no credit to it, and therefore justly is it so ordered that they should have no other notice of it, but that partly through their own security, and partly through the swiftness and subtlety of the enemy, when it came it should be a perfect surprise to them. Those that slight the warnings of the written word, let them not expect any other premonitions. (3.) It will be an irresistible ruin, and such as they will have no fence against : "*Mischief shall come upon thee* so suddenly that thou shalt have no time to turn thee in, so strongly that thou shalt not be able to make head against it and to put it off and save thyself." There is no opposing the judgments of God when they come with commission. Babylon herself, with all her wealth, and power, and multitude, is not able to put off the mischief that comes.

IV. They are upbraided with their divinations, their magical and astrological arts and sciences, which the Chaldeans, above any other nation, were notorious for, and from them other nations borrowed all their learning of that kind.

1. This is here spoken of as one of their provoking sins, which would bring the judgments of God upon them, *v.* 9. "These evils shall come upon thee to punish thee *for the multitude of thy sorceries, and the great abundance of thy enchantments.*" Witchcraft is a sin in its own nature exceedingly heinous; it is giving that honour to the devil which is due to God only, making God's enemy our guide and the father of lies our oracle. In Babylon it was a national sin, and had the protection and countenance of the government; conjurors, for aught that appears, were their privy counsellors and prime ministers of state. And shall not God visit for these things ? Observe what a multitude, what a great abundance, of sorceries and enchantments there were among them. Such a bewitching sin this was that when it was once admitted it spread like wildfire, and they never knew any end of it; the deceived and the deceivers both increased strangely.

2. It is here spoken of as one of their vain confidences, which they relied much upon, but should be deceived in, for it would not serve so much as to give them notice of the judgments coming, much less to guard against them. (1.) They are here upbraided with the mighty pains they had taken about their sorceries and enchantments : Thou hast *laboured in them from thy youth, v.* 12. They trained up their young men in these studies, and those that applied themselves to them were indefatigable in their labours about them—reading books, making observations, trying experiments. Well, let them stand up now with their enchantments, and *try* their skill in the critical

266

moment. Let them make a stand, if they can, in opposition to the invading enemy; let them stand to offer their service to their country; but to what purpose ? "*Thou art wearied in the multitude of thy counsels* of this kind (*v.* 13); thou hast advised with them all, but hast received no satisfaction from them ; the different schemes they have erected, and the different judgments they have given, have but increased thy perplexity and tired thee out." In the multitude of such counsellors there is no safety. (2.) They are upbraided with the variety they had of such kinds of people among them, *v.* 13. They had their *astrologers*, or viewers of the heavens, that did not consider them, as David, to behold the wisdom and power of God in them; but, under pretence of foretelling future events by them, they viewed the heavens and forgot him that made them and set *their dominion on the earth* (Job xxxviii. 33), and has himself dominion over them, for he rides on the heavens. They had their *star-gazers*, who by the motions of the stars, their conjunctions and oppositions, read the doom of states and kingdoms. They had their *monthly prognosticators*, their almanac-makers, that told what weather it should be or what news they should have each month. The great stock they had of these was what they valued themselves much upon ; but they were all cheats, and their art was a sham. I confess I see not how the judicial astrology which some now pretend to, by the rules of which they undertake to prophecy concerning things to come, can be distinguished from that of the Chaldeans, nor therefore how it can escape the censure and contempt which this text lays that under; yet I fear there are some who study their almanacs, and regard them and their prognostications, more than their Bibles and the prophecies there. (3.) They are upbraided with the utter inability and insufficiency of all these pretenders to do them any kindness in the day of their distress. Let them see whether with the help of their enchantments they can prevail against their enemies, or profit themselves, inspirit their own forces or dispirit those that come against them, *v.* 12. Let them see what service those can do them who make a trade of divination : "*Let them stand up*, and either by their power save thee from these evils that are coming upon thee or by their foresight make such a discovery of them beforehand that thou mayest by needful precautions save thyself ;" as Elisha, by notifying to the king of Israel the motions of the Syrian army, enabled him to *save himself, not once nor twice,* 2 Kings vi. 10. This baffling of the diviners was literally fulfilled when, the night that Babylon was taken and Belshazzar slain, all his astrologers, soothsayers, and wise men, were quite nonplussed with the handwriting on the wall that pronounced the fatal sentence, Dan. v. 8. (4.) They are upbraided with the fall of the wise men themselves in the common ruin, *v.* 14. Those are unlikely to stand their friends in any stead who cannot secure themselves; they are as stubble at the best, worthless and useless, and *they shall be as stubble* before a consuming fire. The Persians, to make room for their own wise men, will cut off those of Babylon; that *fire shall burn them,* and *they shall not deliver themselves from the power of the flame.* Those can expect no other than to be devoured who by their sins make themselves fuel to a devouring fire. When God kindles a fire among them it *shall not be a coal to warm at,* and *a fire to sit before,* but a coal to burn them. Or, rather, it denotes that they shall be utterly consumed by the judgments of God, burnt quite to ashes, and there shall not remain one live coal to do any body any service; for *when God judges he will overcome.* (5.) They are upbraided with their merchants, and those they dealt with (*v.* 15), such as they dealt with from their youth, either, [1.] In a way of consultation. These astrologers, that dealt in the black art, they always loved to be dealing with, and they were in effect their merchants; fortune-telling was one of the best trades in Babylon, and those that followed that trade probably lived as splendidly and got as much money as the richest merchants; yet, when some of them were devoured, others fled their country, *every one to his quarter,* and there was none to save Babylon. Miserable comforters are they all. Or, [2.] In a way of commerce. As their astrologers, with whom they had laboured, failed them, so did their merchants; they took care to secure their own effects, and then valued not what became of Babylon. They *wandered every one to his own quarter;* each man shifted for his own safety, but none would offer to lend a helping hand, no, not to a city by which they had got so much money. Every one was for himself, but few for his friends. The New-Testament Babylon is lamented by the merchants that were made rich by her, but they very prudently stand afar off to lament her (Rev. xviii. 15), not willing to attempt any thing for her succour. Happy are those who by faith and prayer deal with one that will be a *very present help in time of trouble !*

CHAP. XLVIII.

God, having in the foregoing chapter reckoned with the Babylonians, and shown them their sins and the desolation that was coming upon them for their sins, to show that he hates sin wherever he finds it and will not connive at it in his own people, comes, in this chapter, to show the house of Jacob their sins, but, withal, the mercy God had in store for them notwithstanding; and he therefore sets their sins in order before them, that by their repentance and reformation they might be prepared for that mercy. I. He charges them with hypocrisy in that which is good and obstinacy in that which is evil, especially in their idolatry, notwithstanding the many convincing proofs God had given them that he is God alone, ver. 1—8. II. He assures them that their deliverance would be wrought purely for the sake of God's own name and not for any merit of theirs, ver. 9—11. III. He encourages them to depend purely upon God's power and promise for this

deliverance, ver. 12—15. IV. He shows them that, as it was by their own sin that they brought themselves into captivity, so it would be only by the grace of God that they would obtain the necessary preparatives for their enlargement, ver. 16—19. V. He proclaims their release, yet with a proviso that the wicked shall have no benefit by it, ver. 20—22.

HEAR ye this, O house of Jacob, which are called by the name of Israel, and are come forth out of the waters of Judah, which swear by the name of the LORD, and make mention of the God of Israel, *but* not in truth, nor in righteousness. 2 For they call themselves of the holy city, and stay themselves upon the God of Israel; the LORD of hosts *is* his name. 3 I have declared the former things from the beginning; and they went forth out of my mouth, and I showed them; I did *them* suddenly, and they came to pass. 4 Because I knew that thou *art* obstinate, and thy neck *is* an iron sinew, and thy brow brass; 5 I have even from the beginning declared *it* to thee; before it came to pass I showed *it* thee: lest thou shouldest say, Mine idol hath done them, and my graven image, and my molten image, hath commanded them. 6 Thou hast heard, see all this; and will not ye declare *it* ? I have showed thee new things from this time, even hidden things, and thou didst not know them. 7 They are created now, and not from the beginning; even before the day when thou heardest them not; lest thou shouldest say, Behold, I knew them. 8 Yea, thou heardest not; yea, thou knewest not; yea, from that time *that* thine ear was not opened: for I knew that thou wouldest deal very treacherously, and wast called a transgressor from the womb.

We may observe here,

I. The hypocritical profession which many of the Jews made of religion and relation to God. To those who made such a profession the prophet is here ordered to address himself, for their conviction and humiliation, that they might own God's justice in what he had brought upon them. Now observe here,

1. How high their profession of religion soared, what a fair show they made in the flesh and how far they went towards heaven, what a good livery they wore and what a good face they put upon a very bad heart. (1.) They were the *house of Jacob;* they had a place and a name in the visible

church. *Jacob have I loved.* Jacob is God's chosen; and they are not only retainers to his family, but descendants from him. (2.) They were *called by the name of Israel*, an honourable name; they were of that people to whom pertained both the giving of the law and the promises. *Israel* signifies *a prince with God;* and they prided themselves in being of that princely race. (3.) *They came forth out of the waters of Judah*, and thence were called *Jews;* they were of the royal tribe, the tribe of which Shiloh was to come, the tribe that adhered to God when the rest revolted. (4.) They *swore by the name of the Lord*, and thereby owned him to be the true God, and their God, and gave glory to him as the righteous Judge of all. They *swore to the name of the Lord* (so it may be read); they took an oath of allegiance to him as their King and joined themselves to him in covenant. (5.) They *made mention of the God of Israel* in their prayers and praises; they often spoke of him, observed his memorials, and pretended to be very mindful of him. (6.) They *called themselves of the holy city*, and, when they were captives in Babylon, purely from a principle of honour, and jealousy for their native country, they valued themselves upon their interest in it. Many, who are themselves unholy, are proud of their relation to the church, the holy city. (7.) They *stayed themselves upon the God of Israel*, and boasted of his promises and his covenant with them; they *leaned on the Lord*, Mic. iii. 11. And, if they were asked concerning their God, they could say, " *The Lord of hosts is his name*, the Lord of all;" happy are we therefore, and very great, who have relation to him!

2. How low their profession of religion sunk, notwithstanding all this. It was all in vain; for it was all a jest; it was *not in truth and righteousness.* Their hearts were not true nor right in these professions. Note, All our religious professions avail nothing further than they are made in truth and righteousness. If we be not sincere in them, we do but *take the name of the Lord our God in vain.*

II. The means God used, and the method he took, to keep them close to himself, and to prevent their turning aside to idolatry. The many excellent laws he gave them, with their sanctions, and the hedges about them, it seems, would not serve to restrain them from that sin which did most easily beset them, and therefore to those God added remarkable prophecies, and remarkable providences in pursuance of those prophecies, which were all designed to convince them that their God was the only true God and that it was therefore both their duty and interest to adhere to him. 1. He both dignified and favoured them with remarkable prophecies (v. 3) : *I have declared the former things from the beginning.* Nothing material happened to their nation from its original

which was not prophesied of before—their bondage in Egypt, their deliverance thence, the situation of their tribes in Canaan, &c. All these things *went forth out of God's mouth and he showed them.* Herein they were honoured above any nation, and even their curiosity was gratified. Their prophecies were such as they could rely upon, and such as concerned themselves and their own nation; and they were all verified by the accomplishment of them. *I did them suddenly,* when they were least expected by themselves or others, and therefore could not be foreseen by any but a divine prescience. *I did them and they came to pass;* for what God does he does effectually. The very calamities they were now groaning under in Babylon God did from the beginning declare to them by Moses, as the certain consequences of their apostasy from God, Lev. xxvi. 31, &c.; Deut. xxviii. 36, &c; xxix. 28. He also declared to them their return to God, and to their own land again, Deut. xxx. 4, &c.; Lev. xxvi. 44, 45. Thus he showed them how he would deal with them long before it came to pass. Let them compare their present state together with the deliverance they had now in prospect with what was written in the law, and they would find the scripture exactly fulfilled. 2. He both dignified and favoured them with remarkable providences (v. 6): *I have shown thee new things from this time.* Besides the general view given from the beginning of God's proceedings with them, he showed them new things by the prophets of their own day, and created them. They were *hidden things*, which they could not otherwise know, as the prophecy concerning Cyrus and the exact time of their release out of Babylon. These things God *created now, v. 7.* Their restoration was in effect their creation, and they had a promise of it not from the beginning, but of late; for to prevent their apostasy from God, or to recover them, prophecy was kept up among them. Yet it was told them when they could not come to the knowledge of it in any other way than by divine revelation. " Consider," says God, " how much soever it is talked of now among you and expected, it was told you by the prophets, when it was the furthest thing from your thoughts, when you had not heard it, when you had not known it, nor had any reason to expect it, and when your ear was not opened concerning it (v. 7, 8), when the thing seemed utterly impossible, and you would scarcely have given any one the hearing who should have told you of it." God had shown them hidden things which were out of the reach of their knowledge, and done for them great things, out of the reach of their power: " Now," says he (v. 6), " *thou hast heard; see all this.* Thou hast heard the prophecy; see the accomplishment of it, and observe whether the word and works of God do not exactly agree; *and will you not declare it,* that as you have heard so you have seen? Will you not own that the Lord is the true God, the only true God, that he has the knowledge and power which no creature has and which none of the gods of the nations can pretend to? Will you not own that your God has been a good God to you? Declare this to his honour, and your own shame, who have dealt so deceitfully with him and preferred others before him."

III. The reasons why God would take this method with them.

1. Because he would anticipate their boastings of themselves and their idols. (1.) God by his prophets told them beforehand of their deliverance, lest they should attribute the accomplishment of it to their idols. Thus he saw it necessary to secure the glory of it to himself, which otherwise would have been given by some of them to their graven images: " I spoke of it," says God, " *lest thou shouldst say, My idol has done it or has commanded it to be done," v. 5.* There were those that would be apt to say so, and so would be confirmed in their idolatry by that which was intended to cure them of it. But they would now be for ever precluded from saying this; for, if the idols had done it, the prophets of the idols would have foretold it; but, the prophets of the Lord having foretold it, it was no doubt the power of the Lord that effected it. (2.) God foretold it by his prophets, lest they should assume the foresight of it to themselves. Those that were not so profane as to have ascribed the thing itself to an idol were yet so proud as to have pretended that by their own sagacity they foresaw it, if God had not been beforehand with them and spoken first: *Lest thou shouldst say, Behold, I knew them, v. 7.* Thus vain men, who would be thought wise, commonly undervalue a thing which is really great and surprising with this suggestion, that it was no more than they expected and they knew it would come to this. To anticipate this, and that this boasting might for ever be excluded, God told them of it before the day, when as yet they dreamed not of it. God has said and done enough to prevent men's boastings of themselves, and that *no flesh may glory in his presence,* and, if it have not the intended effect, it will aggravate the sin and ruin of the proud; and, sooner or later, *every mouth shall be stopped, and all flesh shall become silent before God.*

2. Because he would leave them inexcusable in their obstinacy. *Therefore* he took this pains with them, because he knew they were obstinate, *v. 4.* He knew they were so obstinate and perverse that, if he had not supported the doctrine of providence by prophecy, they would have had the impudence to deny it, and would have said that their idol had done that which God did. He knew very well, (1.) How

wilful they would be, and how fully bent they would be upon that which is evil : *I knew that thou wast hard;* so the word is. There were prophecies as well as precepts which God gave them because of the hardness of their hearts : " *Thy neck is an iron sinew,* unapt to yield and submit to the yoke of God's commandments, unapt to turn and look back upon his dealings with thee or look up to his displeasure against thee; not flexible to the will of God, nor pliable to his intentions, nor manageable by his word or providence. *Thy brow is brass;* thou art impudent and canst not blush, insolent and wilt not fear or give back, but wilt thrust on in the way of thy heart." God uses means to bring sinners to comply with him, though he knows they are obstinate. (2.) How deceitful they would be and how insincere in that which is good, *v. 8.* God sent his prophets to them, but they did not hear, they would not know, and it was no more than was expected, considering what they had been. Thou *wast called,* and not miscalled, *a transgressor from the womb.* Ever since they were first formed into a people they were prone to idolatry; they brought with them out of Egypt a strange addictedness to that sin; and they were murmurers as soon as ever they began their march to Canaan. They were justly upbraided with it then, Deut. ix. 7, 24. Therefore *I knew that thou wouldst deal very treacherously.* God foresaw their apostasy, and gave this reason for it, that he had always found them false and fickle, Deut. xxxi. 16, 27, 29. This is applicable to particular persons. We are all born children of disobedience; we were called *transgressors from the womb,* and therefore it is easy to foresee that we shall deal treacherously, very treacherously. Where original sin is actual sin will follow of course. God knows it, and yet deals not with us according to our deserts.

9 For my name's sake will I defer mine anger, and for my praise will I refrain for thee, that I cut thee not off. 10 Behold, I have refined thee, but not with silver; I have chosen thee in the furnace of affliction. 11 For mine own sake, *even* for mine own sake, will I do *it :* for how should *my name* be polluted? And I will not give my glory unto another. 12 Hearken unto me, O Jacob and Israel, my called; I *am* he; I *am* the first, I also *am* the last. 13 Mine hand also hath laid the foundation of the earth, and my right hand hath spanned the heavens: *when* I call unto them, they stand up together. 14 All ye, assemble yourselves,

and hear; which among them hath declared these *things?* The LORD hath loved him: he will do his pleasure on Babylon, and his arm *shall be on* the Chaldeans. 15 I, *even* I, have spoken; yea, I have called him: I have brought him, and he shall make his way prosperous.

The deliverance of God's people out of their captivity in Babylon was a thing upon many accounts so improbable that there was need of line upon line for the encouragement of the faith and hope of God's people concerning it. Two things were discouraging to them—their own unworthiness that God should do it for them and the many difficulties in the thing itself; now, in these verses, both these discouragements are removed, for here is,

I. A reason why God would do it for them, though they were unworthy; not for their sake, be it known to them, but *for his name's sake, for his own sake, v.* 9—11. 1. It is true they had been very provoking, and God had been justly angry with them. Their captivity was the punishment of their iniquity; and if, when he had them in Babylon, he had left them to pine away and perish there, and made the desolations of their country perpetual, he would only have dealt with them according to their sins, and it was what such a sinful people might expect from an angry God. "But," says God, "*I will defer my anger*" (or, rather, *stifle and suppress it*); "I will make it appear that I am slow to wrath, and will refrain from thee, not pour upon thee what I justly might, that I should cut thee off from being a people." And why will God thus stay his hand? *For my name's sake;* because this people was called by his name, and made profession of his name, and, if they were cut off, the enemies would blaspheme his name. It is for my praise; because it would redound to the honour of his mercy to spare and reprieve them, and, if he continued them to be to him a people, they might be to him for a name and a praise. 2. It is true they were very corrupt and ill-disposed, but God would himself refine them, and make them fit for the mercy he intended for them: "*I have refined thee,* that thou mightest be made a vessel of honour." Though he does not find them meet for his favour, he will make them so. And this accounts for his bringing them into the trouble, and continuing them in it so long as he did. It was not to cut them off, but to do them good. It was to refine them, *but not as silver,* or *with silver,* not so thoroughly as men refine their silver, which they continue in the furnace till all the dross is separated from it; if God should take that course with them, they would be always in the furnace, for they are all dross, and,

as such, might justly be put away (Ps. cxix. 119) as reprobate silver, Jer. vi. 30. He therefore takes them as they are, refined in part only, and not thoroughly. "*I have chosen thee in the furnace of affliction,* that is, I have made thee a choice one by the good which the affliction has done thee, and then designed thee for great things." Many have been brought home to God as chosen vessels and a good work of grace has been begun in them in the furnace of affliction. Affliction is no bar to God's choice, but subservient to his purpose. 3. It is true they could not pretend to merit at God's hand so great a favour as their deliverance out of Babylon, which would put such an honour upon them and bring them so much joy; therefore, says God, *For my own sake, even for my own sake, will I do it, v.* 11. See how the emphasis is laid upon that; for it is a reason that cannot fail, and therefore the resolution grounded upon it cannot fall to the ground. God will do it, not because he owes them such a favour, but to save the honour of his own name, that that may not be polluted by the insolent triumphs of the heathen, who, in triumphing over Israel, thought they triumphed over the God of Israel and imagined their gods too hard for him. This was plainly the language of Belshazzar's revels, when he profaned the holy vessels of God's temple at the same time that he praised his idols (Dan. v. 2, 4), and of the Babylonians' demand (Ps. cxxxvii. 3), *Sing us one of the songs of Zion.* God will therefore deliver his people, because he will not suffer his glory to be thus given to another. Moses pleaded this often with God: Lord, *what will the Egyptians say?* Note, God is jealous for the honour of his own name, and will not suffer the wrath of man to proceed any further than he will make it turn to his praise. And it is matter of comfort to God's people that, whatever becomes of them, God will secure his own honour; and, as far as is necessary to that, God will work deliverance for them.

II. Here is a proof that God could do it for them, though they were unable to help themselves and the thing seemed altogether impracticable. Let Jacob and Israel hearken to this, and believe it, and take the comfort of it. They are God's called, *called according to his purpose,* called by him out of Egypt (Hos. xi. 1) and now out of Babylon, a people whom with a distinguishing favour he calls by name, and to whom he calls. They are his called, for they are called to him, called by his name, and called his; and therefore he will look after them, and they may be assured that, as he will deliver them for his own sake, so he will deliver them by his own strength. They need not fear then, for, 1. He is God alone, and the eternal God (*v.* 12): "*I am he* who can do what I will and will do what is best, he whom none can compare with, much less contend with. *I am the first; I also am the last.*" Who can be too quick for him that is the first, or anticipate him? Who can be too hard for him that is the last, and will keep the field against all opposers, and will reign till they are all made his footstool? What room then is left to doubt of their deliverance when *he* undertakes it whose designs cannot but be well laid, for he is the first, and well executed, for he is the last. As for this God, his work is perfect. 2. He is the God that made the world, and he that did that can do any thing, *v.* 13. Look we down? We see the earth firm under us, and feel it so; it was his hand that *laid the foundation* of it. Look we up? We see the heavens spread out as a canopy over our heads, and it was his hand that spread them, that *spanned* them, that stretched them out, and did it by an exact measure, as the workman sometimes metes out his work by spans. This intimates that God has a vast reach and can compass designs of the greatest extent. *If the palm of his right hand* (so the margin reads it) has gone so far as to stretch out the heavens, what will he do with his outstretched arm? Yet this is not all: he has not only made the heavens and the earth, and therefore he in whom our hope and help is is omnipotent (Ps. cxxiv. 8), but he has the command of all the hosts of both; when he calls them into his service, to go on his errands, they stand up together, they come at the call, they answer to their names: "Here we are; what wilt thou have us to do?" They stand up, not only in reverence to their Creator, but in a readiness to execute his orders: *They stand up together,* unanimously concurring, and helping one another in the service of their Maker. If God therefore will deliver his people, he cannot be at a loss for instruments to be employed in effecting their deliverance. 3. He has already foretold it, and, having infinite knowledge, so that he foresaw it, no doubt he has almighty power to effect it: "*All you* of the house of Jacob, *assemble yourselves, and hear* this for your comfort, *Which among them,* among the gods of the heathen, or their wise men, *has declared these things,* or could declare them?" *v.* 14. They had no foresight of them at all, but those who consulted them were very confident that Babylon should be a lady for ever and Israel a perpetual slave; and their oracles did not give them the least hint to the contrary, to undeceive them; whereas God by his prophets had given notice to the Jews, long before, of their captivity and the destruction of Jerusalem, as he had now likewise given them notice of their release (*v.* 15): *I, even I, have spoken;* and he would not have spoken it if he could not have made it good: none could out-see him, and therefore we may be sure that none could outdo him. 4. The person is pitched

upon who is to be employed in this service, and the measures are concerted in the divine counsels, which are unalterable. Cyrus is the man who must do it; and it tends much to strengthen our assurance that a thing shall be done when we are particularly informed how and by whom. It is not left at uncertainty who shall do it, but the matter is fixed. (1.) It is one whom God is well pleased in, upon this account, because he is designed for this service: *The Lord has loved him* (*v.* 14); he has done him this favour, this honour, to make him an instrument in the redemption of his people and therein a type of the great Redeemer, God's beloved Son, *in whom he was well pleased.* Those God does a great kindness to, and has a great kindness for, whom he makes serviceable to his church. (2.) It is one to whom God will give authority and commission: *I have called him,* have given him a sufficient warrant, and therefore will bear him out. (3.) It is one whom God will by a series of providences lead to this service: "*I have brought him from a far country,* brought him to engage against Babylon, brought him step by step, quite beyond his own intentions." Whom God calls he will bring, will *cause them to come* (so the word is), to come at the call. (4.) It is one whom God will own and give success to. Cyrus will *do God's pleasure on Babylon,* that which it is his pleasure should be done and which he will be pleased with the doing of, though Cyrus has ends of his own to serve and has no regard either to the will of God or to his favour in the doing of it. *His arm* (Cyrus's army, and in it God's arm) *shall* come, and *be upon the Chaldeans,* to bring them down (*v.* 14); for, if God call him and bring him, he will certainly *make his way prosperous, v.* 15. *Then* we may hope to prosper in our way when we follow a divine call and guidance.

16 Come ye near unto me, hear ye this; I have not spoken in secret from the beginning; from the time that it was, there *am* I: and now the Lord God, and his Spirit, hath sent me. 17 Thus saith the Lord, thy Redeemer, the Holy One of Israel; I *am* the Lord thy God which teacheth thee to profit, which leadeth thee by the way *that* thou shouldest go. 18 O that thou hadst hearkened to my commandments! then had thy peace been as a river, and thy righteousness as the waves of the sea: 19 Thy seed also had been as the sand, and the offspring of thy bowels like the gravel thereof; his name should not have been cut off nor destroyed from before me. 20 Go ye

forth of Babylon, flee ye from the Chaldeans, with a voice of singing declare ye, tell this, utter it *even* to the end of the earth; say ye, The LORD hath redeemed his servant Jacob. 21 And they thirsted not *when* he led them through the deserts: he caused the waters to flow out of the rock for them: he clave the rock also, and the waters gushed out. 22 *There is* no peace, saith the LORD, unto the wicked.

Here, as before, Jacob and Israel are summoned to hearken to the prophet speaking in God's name, or rather to God speaking in and by the prophet, and that as a type of the great prophet by whom God has in these last days spoken unto us, and that is sufficient: *Come near* therefore, *and hear this.* Note, Those that would hear and understand what God says must come near, and approach to him; let them come as near as they can. Let those that have hearkened to the tempter now come near, and hear this, that they may be confirmed in their resolutions to serve God. Those that draw nigh to God may depend upon this, that his secret shall be with them. Here,

I. God refers them to what he had both said to them and done for them formerly, which if they would reflect upon, they might thence fetch great encouragement to trust in God at this time. 1. He had always spoken plainly to them *from the beginning*, by Moses and all the prophets: *I have not spoken in secret*, but publicly, from the top of Mount Sinai, and in the chief places of concourse, the solemn assemblies of their tribes; he did not deliver his oracles obscurely and ambiguously, but so that they might be understood, Hab. ii. 2. 2. He had always acted wonderfully for them: " *From the time* that they were first formed into a people *there am I*, there have I been resident among them and presiding in their affairs (he sent them prophets, raised them up judges, and frequently appeared for them), and therefore there I will be still." He that has been with his people hitherto will be to the end.

II. The prophet himself, as a type of the great prophet, asserts his own commission to deliver this message: *Now the Lord God* (the same that spoke from the beginning and did not speak in secret) *has by his Spirit sent me, v.* 16. The Spirit of God is here spoken of as a person distinct from the Father and the Son, and having a divine authority to send prophets. Note, Whom God sends the Spirit sends. Those whom God commissions for any service the Spirit in some measure qualifies for it; and those may speak boldly, and must be heard obediently, whom God and his Spirit send. As that which the prophet says to the same

272

purport with this (*ch.* lxi. 1) is applied to Christ (Luke iv. 21), so may this be; the Lord God sent him, and he had the Spirit without measure.

III. God by the prophet sends them a gracious message for their support and comfort under their affliction. The preface to this message is both awful and encouraging (*v.* 17): *Thus saith Jehovah,* the eternal God, *thy Redeemer*, that has often been so, that has engaged to be so, and will be faithful to the engagement, for he is *the Holy One*, that cannot deceive, *the Holy One of Israel*, that will not deceive them. The same words that introduce the law, and give authority to that, introduce the promise, and give validity to that: " *I am the Lord thy God,* whom thou mayest depend upon as in relation to thee and in covenant with thee."

1. Here is the good work which God undertakes to fulfil in them. He that is their Redeemer, in order to that, will be, (1.) Their instructor: " *I am thy God that teaches thee to profit,* that is, teaches thee such things as are profitable for thee, things that belong to thy peace." By *this* God shows himself to be a God in covenant with us, by his *teaching us* (Heb. viii. 10, 11); and none teaches like him, for he gives an understanding. Whom God redeems he teaches; whom he designs to deliver out of their afflictions he first teaches to profit by their afflictions, makes them partakers of his holiness, for that is the *profit for which he chastens us,* Heb. xii. 10. (2.) Their guide: *He leads them* to the way and *in the way by which they should go.* He not only enlightens their eyes, but directs their steps. By his grace he leads them in the way of duty, by his providence he leads them in the way of deliverance. Happy are those that are under such a guidance!

2. Here is the good-will which God declares he had for them by his good wishes concerning them, *v.* 18, 19. He had indeed brought them into captivity, but it was owing to themselves, nor did he afflict them willingly. (1.) As when he gave them his law he earnestly wished they might be obedient (*O that there were such a heart in them!* Deut. v. 29. *O that they were wise!* Deut. xxxii. 29), so, when he had punished them for the breach of his law, he wished they had been obedient: *O that thou hadst hearkened to my commandments! v.* 18. *O that my people had hearkened unto me!* Ps. lxxxi. 13. This confirms what God had said and sworn, that he has *no pleasure in the death of sinners.* (2.) He assures them that, if they had been obedient, that would not only have prevented their captivity, but would have advanced and perpetuated their prosperity. He had abundance of good things ready to bestow upon them if their sins had not *turned them away, ch.* lix. 1, 2. [1.] They should have been carried on in a constant

uninterrupted stream of prosperity : " *Thy peace should have been as a river ;* thou shouldst have enjoyed a series of mercies, one continually following another, as the waters of a river, which always last." *Labitur, et labetur in omne volubilis ævum—It flows, and will for ever flow ;* not like the waters of a land-flood, which are soon gone. [2.] Their virtue and honour, and the justice of their cause, should in all cases have borne down opposition by their own strength, *as the waves of the sea.* Such should their righteousness have been that nothing should have stood before it ; whereas, now they had been disobedient, the current of their prosperity was interrupted, and their righteousness overpowered. [3.] The rising generation should have been very numerous and very prosperous ; whereas they were now very few, as appears by the small number of the returning captives (Ezra ii. 64), not so many as of one tribe when they came out of Egypt. They should have been *numberless as the sand,* according to the promise (Gen. xxii. 17), which they had forfeited the benefit of : " *The offspring of thy bowels* would have been innumerable, *like the gravel of the sea,* if thy righteousness had been irresistible and unconquerable as the waves of the sea." [4.] The honour of Israel should still have been unstained, untouched : *His name should not have been cut off,* as now it is in the land of Israel, which is either desolate or inhabited by strangers ; nor should it have *been destroyed from before God.* We cannot reckon the name either of a family or of a kingdom destroyed till it is destroyed from before God, till it ceases to be a name in his holy place. Now God tells them thus what he would have done for them if they had persevered in their obedience, *First,* That they might be the more humbled for their sins, by which they had forfeited such rich mercies. Note, *This* should engage us (I might say, enrage us) against sin, that it has not only deprived us of the good things we have enjoyed, but prevented the good things God had in store for us. It will make the misery of the disobedient the more intolerable to think how happy they might have been. *Secondly,* That his mercy might appear the more illustrious in working deliverance for them, though they had forfeited it and rendered themselves unworthy of it. Nothing but a prerogative of mercy would have saved them.

3. Here is assurance given of the great work which God designed to work for them, even their salvation out of their captivity, when he had accomplished his work in them.

(1.) Here is a commission granted them to leave Babylon. God proclaimed, long before Cyrus did, that whoever would might return to his own land (*v.* 20) : " You have a full discharge sent you : *Go you forth out of Babylon ;* the prison-doors are thrown open, and the trumpet sounds, proclaiming a release." Perhaps with this word, as a means, the Spirit of the Lord stirred up the spirits of those that did take the benefit of Cyrus's proclamation (Ezra i. 5) : *Flee you from the Chaldeans,* not with an ignominious stolen flight, as Jacob fled from Laban, but with a holy disdain, as scorning to stay any longer among them ; flee you, not silently and sorrowfully, but with a voice, with a voice of singing, as they fled of old out of Egypt, Exod. xv. 1.

(2.) Here is the news of this sent to all parts : " Let it be declared ; let it be told ; let it be uttered ; make it to be heard by the most remote, by the most remiss ; send the tidings of it by word of mouth ; send it by writing, from city to city, from kingdom to kingdom, even to the utmost regions, *to the ends of the earth.*" This was a figure of the publishing of the gospel to all the world ; but that brings glad tidings which all the world is concerned in, this only that which it is fit all should take notice of, that they may be invited by it to forsake their idols and come into the service of the God of Israel. Let them all know then, [1.] That those whom God owns for his are such as he has dearly bought and paid for : *The Lord has redeemed his servant Jacob ;* he has done it formerly, when he brought them out of Egypt, and now he is about to do it again. Jacob was God's servant, and therefore he redeemed him ; for what had other masters to do with God's servants ? Israel is God's son, therefore Pharaoh must let him go. God redeemed Jacob, and therefore it was fit that he should be his servant (Ps. cxvi. 16) ; the bonds God had loosed tied them the faster to him. He that redeemed us has an unquestionable right to us. [2.] That those whom God designs to bring home to himself he will take care of, that they want not for the necessary expenses of their journey. When he brought them out of Egypt, and *led them through the deserts,* they *thirsted not* (*v.* 21), for in all their removals the water out of the rock followed them ; thence *he caused the waters to flow,* and, since rock-water is the clearest and finest, God *clave the rock, and the waters gushed out ;* for he can fetch in necessary supplies for his people in a way that they think the least likely. This refers to what he did for them when he brought them out of Egypt ; when all this was literally true. But it should now be in effect done again, in their return out of Babylon, so well provided for should they and theirs be in their return. God does his work as effectually by marvellous providences as by miracles, though perhaps they are not so much taken notice of. This is applicable to those treasures of grace laid up for us in Jesus Christ, from which all good flows to us as the water did to Israel out of the rock, for that rock is Christ.

(3.) Here is a caveat put in against the wicked who go on still in their trespasses.

Let not them think to have any benefit among God's people. Though in show and profession they herd themselves among them, let them not expect to come in sharers; no (*v.* 22), though God's thoughts concerning the body of that people were thoughts of peace, yet to those among them that were *wicked* and hated to be reformed *there is no peace*, no peace with God or their own consciences, no real good, wha.ever is pretended to. What have those to do with peace who are enemies to God? Their false prophets cried Peace to those to whom it did not belong; but God tells them that there shall be no peace, nor any thing like it, to the wicked. The quarrel sinners have commenced with God, if not taken up in time by repentance, will be an everlasting quarrel.

CHAP. XLIX.

Glorious things had been spoken in the previous chapters concerning the deliverance of the Jews out of Babylon; but lest any should think, when it was accomplished, that it looked much greater and brighter in the prophecy than in the performance, and that the return of about 40,000 Jews in a poor condition out of Babylon to Jerusalem was not an event sufficiently answering to the height and grandeur of the expressions used in the prophecy, he here comes to show that the prophecy had a further intention, and was to have its full accomplishment in a redemption that should as far outdo these expressions as the other seemed to come short of them, even the redemption of the world by Jesus Christ, of whom not only Cyrus, who was God's servant in working the Jews' deliverance, but Isaiah too, who was God's servant in foretelling it, was a type. In this chapter we have, I. The designation of Christ, under the type of Isaiah, to his office as Mediator, ver. 1 —3. II. The assurance given him of the success of his undertaking among the Gentiles, ver. 4—8. III. The redemption that should be wrought by him, and the progress of that redemption, ver. 9— 12. IV. The encouragement given hence to the afflicted church, ver. 13—17. V. The addition of many to it, and the setting up of a church among the Gentiles, ver. 18—23. VI. A ratification of the prophecy of the Jews' release out of Babylon, which was to be the figure and type of all these blessings, ver. 24—26. If this chapter be rightly understood, we shall see ourselves to be more concerned in the prophecies relating to the Jews' deliverance out of Babylon than we thought we were.

L ISTEN, O isles, unto me; and hearken, ye people, from far; The LORD hath called me from the womb; from the bowels of my mother hath he made mention of my name. 2 And he hath made my mouth like a sharp sword; in the shadow of his hand hath he hid me, and made me a polished shaft; in his quiver hath he hid me; 3 And said unto me, Thou *art* my servant, O Israel, in whom I will be glorified. 4 Then I said, I have laboured in vain, I have spent my strength for nought, and in vain : *yet* surely my judgment *is* with the LORD, and my work with my God. 5 And now, saith the LORD that formed me from the womb *to be* his servant, to bring Jacob again to him, Though Israel be not gathered, yet shall I be glorious in the eyes of the LORD, and my God shall be my strength. 6 And he said, It is a light thing that thou shouldest be my

servant to raise up the tribes of Jacob, and to restore the preserved of Israel : I will also give thee for a light to the Gentiles, that thou mayest be my salvation unto the end of the earth.

Here, I. An auditory is summoned together and attention demanded. The sermon in the foregoing chapter was directed to the house of Jacob and the people of Israel, *v.* 1, 12. But this is directed to the isles (that is, the Gentiles, for they are called *the isles of the Gentiles*, Gen. x. 5) and to the *people from far*, that were *strangers to the commonwealth of Israel*, and afar off. Let these listen (*v.* 1) as to a thing at a distance, which yet they are to hear with desire and attention. Note, 1. The tidings of a Redeemer are sent to the Gentiles, and to those that lie most remote; and they are concerned to listen to them. 2. The Gentiles listened to the gospel when the Jews were deaf to it.

II. The great author and publisher of the redemption produces his authority from heaven for the work he had undertaken. 1. God had appointed him and set him apart for it : *The Lord has called me from the womb* to this office and *made mention of my name*, nominated me to be the Saviour. By an angel he called him *Jesus—a Saviour*, who *should save his people from their sins*, Matt. i. 21. Nay, from the womb of the divine counsels, before all worlds, he was called to this service, and help was laid upon him; and he came at the call, for he said, *Lo, I come*, with an eye to what was written of him *in the volume of the book*. This was said of some of the prophets, as types of him, Jer. i. 5. Paul was separated to the apostleship from his mother's womb, Gal i. 15. 2. God had fitted and qualified him for the service to which he designed him. He *made his mouth like a sharp sword*, and *made him* like *a polished shaft*, or a bright arrow, furnished him with every thing necessary to fight God's battles against the powers of darkness, to conquer Satan, and bring back God's revolted subjects to their allegiance, by his word : that is the *two-edged sword* (Heb. iv. 12) which comes out of his mouth, Rev. xix. 15. The convictions of the word are the arrows that shall be sharp in the hearts of sinners, Ps. xlv. 5. 3. God had preferred him to the service for which he had reserved him : *He has hidden me in the shadow of his hand* and in his quiver, which denotes, (1.) Concealment. The gospel of Christ, and the calling in of the Gentiles by it, were long hidden from ages and generations, hidden in God (Eph. iii. 5, Rom. xvi. 25), hidden in the shadow of the ceremonial law and the Old-Testament types. (2) Protection. The house of David was the particular care of the divine Providence, because that blessing was in it.

Christ in his infancy was sheltered from the rage of Herod. 4. God had owned him, had said unto him, " *Thou art my servant,* whom I have employed and will prosper; thou art Israel, in effect, *the prince with God,* that hast wrestled and prevailed; and in thee I will be glorified." The people of God are *Israel,* and they are all gathered together, and summed up, as it were, in Christ, the great representative of all Israel, as the high priest who had the names of all the tribes on his breastplate; and in him God is and will be glorified; so he said by a voice from heaven, John xii. 27, 28. Some read the words in two clauses: *Thou art my servant* (so Christ is, *ch.* xlii. 1); *it is Israel in whom I will be glorified by thee;* it is the spiritual Israel, the elect, in the salvation of whom by Jesus Christ God will be glorified, and his free grace for ever admired.

III. He is assured of the good success of his undertaking; for whom God calls he will prosper. And as to this,

1. He objects the discouragement he had met with at his first setting out (*v.* 4): " Then I said, with a sad heart, *I have laboured in vain;* those that were ignorant, and careless, and strangers to God, are so still: *I have called, and they have refused; I have stretched out my hands to a gainsaying people.*" This was Isaiah's complaint, but it was no more than he was told to expect, *ch.* vi. 9. The same was a temptation to Jeremiah to resolve he would labour no more, Jer. xx. 9. It is the complaint of many a faithful minister, that has not loitered, but laboured, not spared, but spent, his strength, and himself with it, and yet, as to many, it is all in vain and for nought; they will not be prevailed with to repent and believe. But here it seems to point at the obstinacy of the Jews, among whom Christ went in person preaching the gospel of the kingdom, laboured and spent his strength, and yet the rulers and the body of the nation rejected him and his doctrine; so very few were brought in, when one would think none should have stood out, that he might well say, " *I have laboured in vain,* preached so many sermons, wrought so many miracles, in vain." Let not the ministers think it strange that they are slighted when the Master himself was.

2. He comforts himself under this discouragement with this consideration, that it was the cause of God in which he was engaged and the call of God that engaged him in it: *Yet surely my judgment is with the Lord,* who is the Judge of all, *and my work with my God,* whose servant I am. His comfort is, and it may be the comfort of all faithful ministers, when they see little success of their labours, (1.) That, however it be, it is a righteous cause that they are pleading. They are with God, and for God; they are on his side, and workers together with him. They like not their judgment, the rule they go by, nor their work,

the business they are employed in, ever the worse for this. The unbelief of men gives them no cause to suspect the truth of their doctrine, Rom. iii. 3. (2.) That their management of this cause, and their prosecution of this work, were known to God, and they could appeal to him concerning their sincerity, and that it was not through any neglect of theirs that they laboured in vain. *He knows the way that I take; my judgment is with the Lord,* to determine whether I have not delivered my soul and left the blood of those that perish on their own heads." (3.) Though the labour be in vain as to those that are laboured with, yet not as to the labourer himself, if he be faithful: his judgment is with the Lord, who will justify him and bear him out, though men condemn him and run him down; and his work (the reward of his work) is with his God, who will take care he shall be no loser, no, not by his lost labour. (4.) Though the judgment be not yet brought forth unto victory, nor the work to perfection, yet both are with the Lord, to carry them on and give them success, according to his purpose, in his own way and time.

3. He receives from God a further answer to this objection, *v.* 5, 6. He knew very well that God had set him on work, had *formed him from the womb to be his servant,* had not only called him so early to it (*v.* 1), but begun so early to fit him for it and dispose him to it. Those whom God designs to employ as his servants he is fashioning and preparing to be so long before, when perhaps neither themselves nor others are aware of it. It is he that forms the spirit of man within him. Christ was to be *his servant, to bring Jacob again to him,* that had treacherously departed from him. The seed of Jacob therefore, according to the flesh, must first be dealt with, and means used to bring them back. Christ, and the word of salvation by him, are sent to them first; nay, Christ comes in person to them only, *to the lost sheep of the house of Israel.* But what if Jacob will not be brought back to God and Israel will not be gathered? So it proved; but this is a satisfaction in that case, (1.) Christ will be glorious in the eyes of the Lord; and those are truly glorious that are so in God's eyes. Though few of the Jewish nation were converted by Christ's preaching and miracles, and many of them loaded him with ignominy and disgrace, yet God put honour upon him, and made him glorious, at his baptism, and in his transfiguration, spoke to him from heaven, sent angels to minister to him, made even his shameful death glorious by the many prodigies that attended it, much more his resurrection. In his sufferings God was his strength, so that though he met with all the discouragement imaginable, by the contempts of a people whom he had done so much to oblige, yet he *did not fail nor was*

discouraged. An angel was sent from heaven to *strengthen* him, Luke xxii. 43. Faithful ministers, though they see not the fruit of their labours, shall yet be accepted of God, and in that they shall be truly glorious, for his favour is our honour; and they shall be assisted to proceed and persevere in their labours notwithstanding. This weakens their hands, but their God will be their strength. (2.) The gospel shall be glorious in the eyes of the world; though it be not so in the eyes of the Jews, yet it shall be entertained by the nations, *v.* 6. The Messiah seemed as if he had been primarily designed to *bring Jacob back, v.* 5. But he is here told that it is comparatively but a small matter; a higher orb of honour than that, and a larger sphere of usefulness, are designed him: *" It is a light thing that thou shouldst be my servant, to raise up the tribes of Jacob* to the dignity and dominion they expect by the Messiah, and to *restore the preserved of Israel,* and make them a flourishing church and state as formerly"* (nay, considering what a little handful of people they are, it would be but a small matter, in comparison, for the Messiah to be the Saviour of them only); *"and therefore I will give thee for a light to the Gentiles* (many great and mighty nations by the gospel of Christ shall be brought to the knowledge and worship of the true God), *that thou mayest be my salvation,* the author of that salvation which I have designed for lost man, and this *to the end of the earth,* to nations at the greatest distance." Hence Simeon learned to call Christ *a light to lighten the Gentiles* (Luke ii. 32), and St. Paul's exposition of this text is what we ought to abide by, and it serves for a key to the context, Acts xiii. 47. *Therefore,* says he, we turn to the Gentiles, to preach the gospel to them, *because so has the Lord commanded us, saying, I have set thee to be a light to the Gentiles.* In this the Redeemer was truly glorious, though Israel was not gathered; the setting up of his kingdom in the Gentile world was more his honour than if he had raised up all the tribes of Jacob. This promise is in part fulfilled already, and will have a further accomplishment, if that time be yet to come which the apostle speaks of, when the fulness of the Gentiles shall be brought in. Observe, God calls it his salvation, which some think intimates how well pleased he was with it, how he gloried in it, and (if I may so say) how much his heart was upon it. They further observe that Christ is given for a light to all those to whom he is given for salvation. It is in darkness that men perish. Christ enlightens men's eyes, and so makes them holy and happy.

7 Thus saith the LORD, the Redeemer of Israel, *and* his Holy One, to him whom man despiseth, to him whom the nation abhorreth, to a servant of rulers, Kings shall see and

276

arise, princes also shall worship, because of the LORD that is faithful, *and* the Holy One of Israel, and he shall choose thee. ⸱ 8 Thus saith the LORD, In an acceptable time have I heard thee, and in a day of salvation have I helped thee : and I will preserve thee, and give thee for a covenant of the people, to establish the earth, to cause to inherit the desolate heritages ; 9 That thou mayest say to the prisoners, Go forth; to them that *are* in darkness, Show yourselves.⸱ They shall feed in the ways, and their pastures *shall be* in all high places. 10 They shall not hunger nor thirst; neither shall the heat nor sun smite them : for he that hath mercy on them shall lead them, even by the springs of water shall he guide them. 11 And I will make all my mountains a way, and my highways shall be exalted. 12 Behold, these shall come from far : and, lo, these from the north and from the west; and these from the land of Sinim.

In these verses we have,

I. The humiliation and exaltation of the Messiah (*v.* 7) : *The Lord, the Redeemer of Israel, and Israel's Holy One,* who had always taken care of the Jewish church and wrought out for them those deliverances that were typical of the great salvation, speaks here to him, who was the undertaker of that salvation. And, 1. He takes notice of his humiliation, the instances of which were uncommon, nay, unparalleled. He was one *whom man despised.* He is *despised and rejected of men, ch.* liii. 3. To be despised by so mean a creature (man, who is himself a worm) bespeaks the lowest and most contemptible condition imaginable. Man, whom he came to save and to put honour upon, yet despised him and put contempt upon him ; so wretchedly ungrateful were his persecutors. The ignominy he underwent was not the least of his sufferings. They not only made him despicable, but odious. He was *one whom the nation abhorred ;* they treated him as the worst of men, and cried out, *Crucify him, crucify him.* The nation did it, the Gentiles as well as Jews, and the Jews herein worse than Gentiles ; for his cross was *to the one a stumbling-block* and *to the other foolishness.* He was *a servant of rulers ;* he was trampled upon, abused, scourged, and crucified as a slave. Pilate boasted of his power over him, John xix. 10. This he submitted to for our salvation. 2. He promises him his exaltation. Honour was done him even in the depth of his humiliation. Herod the king stood in awe of him, saying, *It is John the Baptist ;* noblemen, rulers, centurions came and kneeled to him. But this was more fully accomplished when kings received his gospel, and submitted to his yoke, and joined in the worship of him, and called themselves the vassals of Christ. Not that Christ values the rich more than the poor (they stand upon a level with him), but it is for the honour of his kingdom among men when the great ones of the earth appear for him and do homage to him. This shall be the accomplishment of God's promise, and he will give him the heathen for his inheritance, and *therefore* it shall be done, *because of the Lord who is faithful* and true to his promise; and this shall be an evidence that Christ had a commission for what he did, and that God had chosen him, and would own the choice he had made.

II. The blessings he has in store for all those to whom he is made salvation.

1. God will own and stand by him in his undertaking (*v.* 8): *In an acceptable time have I heard thee,* that is, I will hear thee. Christ, *in the days of his flesh, offered up strong cries, and was heard,* Heb. v. 7. He knew that the *Father heard him always* (John xi. 42), heard him for himself (for, though the cup might not pass from him, yet he was enabled to drink it), heard him for all that are his, and therefore he interceded for them as one having authority. *Father, I will,* John xvii. 24. All our happiness results from the Son's interest in the Father and the prevalency of his intercession, that he always heard him; and this makes the gospel time an acceptable time, welcome to us, because we are accepted of God, both reconciled and recommended to him, that God hears the Redeemer for us, Heb. vii. 25. Nor will he hear him only, but help him to go through with his undertaking. The Father was always with him at his right hand, and did not leave him when his disciples did. Violent attacks were made upon our Lord Jesus by the powers of darkness, when it was their hour, to drive him off from his undertakings, but God promises to preserve him and enable him to persevere in it; on that *one stone were seven eyes,* Zech. iii. 9. God would preserve him, would preserve his interest, his kingdom among men, though fought against on all sides. Christ is preserved while Christianity is.

2. God will authorize him to apply to his church the benefits of the redemption he is to work out. God's preserving and helping him was to make the day of his gospel a day of salvation. And so the apostle understands it: *Behold, now is the day of salvation,* now the word of reconciliation by Christ is preached, 2 Cor. vi. 2.

(1.) He shall be guarantee of the treaty of peace between God and man : I will *give thee for a covenant of the people.* This we

had before (*ch.* xlii. 6), and it is here repeated as faithful, and well worthy of all acceptation and observation. He is given for a covenant, that is, for a pledge of all the blessings of the covenant. It was in him that God was *reconciling the world to himself ;* and he that *spared not his own Son* will deny us nothing. He is given for a covenant, not only as he is the Mediator of the covenant, the blessed *days-man who has laid his hand upon us both,* but as he is all in all in the covenant. All the duty of the covenant is summed up in our being his ; and all the privilege and happiness of the covenant are summed up in his being ours.

(2.) He shall repair the decays of the church and build it upon a rock. He shall *establish the earth,* or rather the *land,* the land of Judea, a type of the church. He shall *cause the desolate heritages to be inherited ;* so the cities of Judah were after the return out of captivity, and so the church, which in the last and degenerate ages of the Jewish nation had been as a country laid waste, but was again replenished by the fruits of the preaching of the gospel.

(3.) He shall free the souls of men from the bondage of guilt and corruption and bring them into the glorious liberty of God's children. He shall *say to the prisoners* that were bound over to the justice of God, and bound under the power of Satan, *Go forth, v.* 9. Pardoning mercy is a release from the curse of the law, and renewing grace is a release from the dominion of sin. Both are from Christ, and are branches of the great salvation. It is he that says, *Go forth ;* it is the Son that makes us free, and then we are free indeed. He saith *to those that are in darkness, Show yourselves ;* " not only *see,* but *be seen,* to the glory of God and your own comfort." When he discharged the lepers from their confinement, he said, *Go show yourselves to the priest.* When we see the light, let our light shine.

(4.) He shall provide for the comfortable passage of those whom he sets at liberty to the place of their rest and happy settlement, *v.* 9—11. These verses refer to the provision made for the Jews' return out of their captivity, who were taken under the particular care of the divine Providence, as favourites of Heaven, and now so in a special manner ; but they are applicable to that guidance of divine grace which all God's spiritual Israel are under, from their release out of bondage to their settlement in the heavenly Canaan. [1.] They shall have their charges borne and shall be fed at free cost with food convenient : *They shall feed in the ways,* as sheep ; for now, as formerly, God *leads Joseph like a flock.* When God pleases even highway ground shall be good ground for the sheep of his pasture to feed in. Their pastures shall be not only in the valleys, but *in all high places,* which are commonly dry and barren. Wherever God brings his people he will take care they shall want nothing that is good for them, Ps. xxxiv. 10. And so well shall they be provided for that they shall not hunger nor thirst, for what they need they shall have seasonably, before their need of it comes to an extremity. [2.] They shall be sheltered and protected from every thing that would incommode them : *Neither shall the heat nor sun smite them, for* God causes *his flock to rest at noon,* Cant. i. 7. No evil thing shall befal those that put themselves under a divine protection ; they shall be enabled to *bear the burden and heat of the day.* [3.] They shall be under God's gracious guidance : *He that has mercy on them,* in bringing them out of their captivity, *shall lead them,* as he did their fathers in the wilderness, by a pillar of cloud and fire. *Even by springs of water,* which will be ready to them in their march, *shall he guide them.* God will furnish them with suitable and seasonable comforts, not like the pools of rainwater in the valley of Baca, but like the water out of the rock which followed Israel. Those who are under a divine guidance, and follow that closely, while they do so, may, upon good grounds, hope for divine comforts and cordials. The world leads its followers by broken cisterns, or brooks that fail in summer ; but God leads those that are his by springs of water. And those whom God guides shall find a ready road and all obstacles removed (*v.* 11) : *I will make all my mountains a way.* He that in times past made the sea a way, now with as much ease will make the mountains a way, though they seemed impassable. The highway, or causeway, shall be raised, to make it both the plainer and the fairer. Note, The ways in which God leads his people he himself will be the overseer of, and will take care that they be well mended and kept in repair, as of old the ways that led to the cities of refuge. The levelling of the roads from Babylon, as it was foretold (*ch.* xl. 2, 3), was applied to gospel work, and so may this be. Though there be difficulties in the way to heaven, which we cannot by our own strength get over, yet the grace of God shall be sufficient to help us over them and to make even the mountains a way, *ch.* xxxv. 8.

(5) He shall bring them all together from all parts, that they may return in a body, that they may encourage one another and be the more taken notice of. They were dispersed into several parts of the country of Babylon, as their enemies pleased, to prevent any combination among themselves. But, when God's time shall come to bring them home together, one spirit shall animate them all, all that lie at the greatest distance from each other, and those also that had taken shelter in other countries shall meet them in the land of Judah, *v.* 12. Here shall a party *come from far,* some *from the north,* some *from the west,* some *from the land of Sinim,*
278

which probably is some province of Babylon not elsewhere named in scripture, but some make it to be a country belonging to one of the chief cities of Egypt, called *Sin,* of which we read, Ezek. xxx. 15, 16. Now this promise was to have a further accomplishment in the great confluence of converts to the gospel church, and its full accomplishment when God's chosen shall come from the east and from the west to sit down with the patriarchs in the kingdom of God, Matt. viii. 11.

13 Sing, O heavens ; and be joyful, O earth ; and break forth into singing, O mountains : for the LORD hath comforted his people, and will have mercy upon his afflicted. 14 But Zion said, The LORD hath forsaken me, and my Lord hath forgotten me. 15 Can a woman forget her sucking child, that she should not have compassion on the son of her womb ? Yea, they may forget, yet will I not forget thee. 16 Behold, I have graven thee upon the palms of *my* hands ; thy walls *are* continually before me. 17 Thy children shall make haste ; thy destroyers and they that made thee waste shall go forth of thee.

The scope of these verses is to show that the return of the people of God out of their captivity, and the eternal redemption to be wrought out by Christ (of which that was a type), would be great occasions of joy to the church and great proofs of the tender care God has of the church.

I. Nothing can furnish us with better matter for songs of praise and thanksgiving, *v.* 13. Let the whole creation join with us in songs of joy, for it shares with us in the benefits of the redemption, and all they can contribute to this sacred melody is little enough in return for such inestimable favours, Ps. xcvi. 11. Let there be joy in heaven, and let the angels of God celebrate the praises of the great Redeemer ; let the earth and the. mountains, particularly the great ones of the earth, *be joyful,* and *break forth into singing, for the earnest expectation of the creature* that *waits for the glorious liberty of the children of God* (Rom. viii. 19, 21) shall now be *abundantly answered.* God's people are the blessings and ornaments of the world, and therefore let there be universal joy, for *God has comforted his people* that were in sorrow and *he will have mercy upon the afflicted* because of his compassion, upon *his* afflicted because of his covenant.

II. Nothing can furnish us with more convincing arguments to prove the most tender and affectionate concern God has for his church, and her interests and comforts.

1. The troubles of the church have given some occasion to question God's care and

concern for it, *v.* 14. *Zion,* in distress, *said,* The Lord *has forsaken me,* and looks after me no more ; *my Lord has forgotten me,* and *will* look after me no more. See how deplorable the case of God's people may be sometimes, such that they may seem to be forsaken and forgotten of their God ; and at such a time their temptations may be alarmingly violent. Infidels, in their presumption, say *God has forsaken the earth* (Ezek. viii. 12), and has *forgotten their sins,* Ps. x. 11. Weak believers, in their despondency, are ready to say, " God has forsaken his church and forgotten the sorrows of his people." But we have no more reason to question his promise and grace than we have to question his providence and justice. He is as sure a rewarder as he is a revenger. Away therefore with these distrusts and jealousies, which are the bane of friendship.

2. The triumphs of the church, after her troubles, will in due time put the matter out of question.

(1.) What God will do for Zion we are told, *v.* 17. [1.] Her friends, who had deserted her, shall be gathered to her, and shall contribute their utmost to her assistance and comfort : *Thy children shall make haste.* Converts to the faith of Christ are the children of the church ; they shall join themselves to her with great readiness and cheerfulness, and flock into the communion of saints, as doves to their windows. " *Thy builders shall make haste*" (so some read it), " who shall build up thy houses, thy walls, especially thy temple ; they shall do it with expedition." Church work is usually slow work ; but, when God's time shall come, it shall be done suddenly. [2.] Her enemies, who had threatened and assaulted her, shall be forced to withdraw from her : *Thy destroyers, and those who made thee waste,* who had made themselves masters of the country and ravaged it, *shall go forth of thee.* By Christ the prince of this world, the great destroyer, is cast out, is dispossessed, has his power broken and his attempts quite baffled.

(2.) Now by this it will appear that Zion's suggestions were altogether groundless, that God has not forsaken her, nor forgotten her, nor ever will. Be assured, [1.] That God has a tender affection for his church and people, *v.* 15. In answer to Zion's fears, God speaks as one concerned for his own glory (he takes himself to be reflected upon if Zion say, *The Lord has forsaken me,* and he will clear himself), as one concerned also for his people's comfort ; he would not have them droop, and be discouraged, and give way to any uneasy thoughts. " You think that I have forgotten you. *Can a woman forget her sucking child ?*" *First,* It is not likely that she should. A woman, whose honour it is to be of the tender sex as well as the fair one, cannot but have compassion for a child, which, being both harmless and helpless, is a proper object of compassion.

A mother, especially, cannot but be concerned for her own child ; for it is her own, a piece of herself, and very lately one with her. A nursing mother, most of all, cannot but be tender of her sucking child ; her own breasts will soon put her in mind of it if she should forget it. But, *Secondly,* It is possible that she may forget. A woman may perhaps be so unhappy as not to be able to remember her sucking child (she may be sick, and dying, and going to the land of forgetfulness), or she may be so unnatural as not to have *compassion on the son of her womb,* as those who, to conceal their shame, are the death of their children as soon as they are their life, Lam. iv. 10 ; Deut. xxviii. 57. But, says God, *I will not forget thee.* Note, God's compassions to his people infinitely exceed those of the tenderest parents towards their children. What are the affections of nature to those of the God of nature ! [2.] That he has a constant care of his church and people (*v.* 16) : *I have engraven thee upon the palms of my hands.* This does not allude to the foolish art of palmistry, which imagines every man's fate to be engraved in the palms of his hands and to be legible in the lines there, but to the custom of those who tie a string upon their hands or fingers to put them in mind of things which they are afraid they shall forget, or to the wearing of signet or locketrings in remembrance of some dear friend. His setting them thus as a seal upon his arm denotes his setting them as a seal upon his heart, and his being ever mindful of them and their interests, Cant. viii. 6. If we *bind God's law as a sign upon our hand* (Deut. vi. 8, 11, 18), he will engrave our interests as a sign on his hand, and will look upon that and remember the covenant. He adds, " *Thy walls shall be continually before me :* thy ruined walls, though no pleasing spectacle, shall be in my thoughts of compassion." Do Zion's friends *favour her dust ?* Ps. cii. 14. So does her God. Or, " The plan and model of thy walls, that are to be rebuilt, is before me, and they shall certainly be built according to it." Or, " Thy walls (that is, thy safety) are my continual care ; so are the watchmen on thy walls." Some apply his engraving his church on the palms of his hands to the wounds in Christ's hands when he was crucified ; he will look on the marks of them, and remember those for whom he suffered and died.

18 Lift up thine eyes round about, and behold : all these gather themselves together, *and* come to thee. *As* I live, saith the LORD, thou shalt surely clothe thee with them all, as with an ornament, and bind them *on thee,* as a bride *doeth.* 19 For thy waste and thy desolate places, and the land of thy destruction, shall even

now be too narrow by reason of the inhabitants, and they that swallowed thee up shall be far away. 20 The children which thou shalt have, after thou hast lost the other, shall say again in thine ears, The place *is* too strait for me: give place to me that I may dwell. 21 Then shalt thou say in thine heart, Who hath begotten me these, seeing I have lost my children, and am desolate, a captive, and removing to and fro? and who hath brought up these? Behold, I was left alone; these, where *had* they *been?* 22 Thus saith the Lord God, Behold, I will lift up mine hand to the Gentiles, and set up my standard to the people: and they shall bring thy sons in *their* arms, and thy daughters shall be carried upon *their* shoulders. 23 And kings shall be thy nursing fathers, and their queens thy nursing mothers: they shall bow down to thee with *their* face toward the earth, and lick up the dust of thy feet; and thou shalt know that I *am* the Lord: for they shall not be ashamed that wait for me.

Two things are here promised, which were to be in part accomplished in the reviving of the Jewish church after its return out of captivity, but more fully in the planting of the Christian church by the preaching of the gospel of Christ; and we may take the comfort of these promises.

I. That the church shall be replenished with great numbers added to it. It was promised (*v.* 17) that *her children should make haste;* that promise is here enlarged upon, and is made very encouraging. It is promised,

1. That multitudes shall flock to the church from all parts. *Look round, and see how they gather themselves to thee* (*v.* 18), by a local accession to the Jewish church. They come to Jerusalem from all the adjacent countries, for that was then the centre of their unity; but, under the gospel, it is by a spiritual accession to the mystical body of Christ in faith and love. Those that *come to Jesus as the Mediator of the new covenant* do thereby *come to the Mount Zion, the church of the first-born,* Heb. xii. 22, 23. *Lift up thy eyes, and behold* how *the fields are white unto the harvest,* John iv. 35. Note, It is matter of joy to the church to see a multitude of converts to Christ.

2. That such as are added to the church shall not be a burden and blemish to her, but her strength and ornament. This part

280

of the promise is confirmed with an oath: *As I live, saith the Lord, thou shalt surely clothe thyself with them all.* The addition of such numbers to the church shall complete her clothing; and, when all that were chosen are effectually called, then the bride, the Lamb's wife, shall have made herself ready, shall be quite dressed, Rev. xix. 7. They shall make her to appear comely and considerable; and she shall therefore bind them on with as much care and complacency as a bride does her ornaments. When those that are added to the church are serious, and holy, and exemplary in their conversation, they are an ornament to it.

3. That thus the country which was waste and desolate, and *without inhabitant* (*ch.* v. 9; vi. 11), shall be again peopled, nay, it shall be over-peopled (*v.* 19): " *Thy waste and thy desolate places,* that have long lain so, *and the land of thy destruction,* that land of thine which was destroyed with thee and which nobody cared for dwelling in, shall now be so full of people that there shall be no room for the inhabitants." Here is a blessing poured out till there be not *room enough to receive it,* Mal. iii. 10. Not that they shall be crowded by their enemies, or straitened for room, as Abraham and Lot were, because of the Canaanite in the land. " No, *those that swallow thee up,* and took possession of thy land when thy possession of it was discontinued, *shall be far away.* Thy people shall be numerous, and there shall be no stranger, no enemy, among them." Thus the *kingdom of God among men,* which had been impoverished and almost depopulated, partly by the corruptions of the Jewish church and partly by the abominations of the Gentile world, was again peopled and enriched by the setting up of the Christian church, and by its graces and glories.

4. That the new converts shall strangely increase and multiply. Jerusalem, after she has lost abundance of her children by the sword, famine, and captivity, shall have a new family growing up instead of them, children which she *shall have after she has lost the other* (*v.* 20), as Seth, who was *appointed another seed instead of Abel,* and Job's children, which God blessed him with instead of those that were killed in the ruins of the house. God will repair his church's losses and secure to himself a seed to serve him in it. It is promised to the Jews, after their return, that *Jerusalem shall be full of boys and girls playing in the streets,* Zech. viii. 5. The church, after it has lost the Jews, who will be cut off by their own infidelity, shall have abundance of children still, more than she had when the Jews belonged to her. See Gal. iv. 27. They shall be so numerous that, (1.) The children shall complain for want of room; they shall say (and it is a good hearing), " Our numbers increase so fast that *the place is too*

strait for us;" as the sons of the prophets complained, 2 Kings vi. 1. But, strait as the place is, still more shall desire to be admitted, and the church shall gladly admit them, and the inconvenient straitness of the place shall be no hindrance to either; for it will be found, whatever we think, that even when the *poor and the maimed, the halt and the blind*, are brought in, *yet still there is room*, room enough for those that are in and room for more, Luke xiv. 21, 22. (2.) The mother shall stand amazed at the increase of her family, *v.* 21. She shall say, *Who has begotten me these?* and, *Who has brought up these?* They come to her with all the duty, affection, and submission of children; and yet she never bore any pain for them, nor took any pains with them, but has them ready reared to her hand. This gives her a pleasing surprise, and she cannot but be astonished at it, considering what her condition had been very lately and very long. The Jewish nation had left her children; they were cut off. She had been desolate, without ark, and altar, and temple-service, those tokens of God's espousals to them; nay, she had been a captive, and continually removing to and fro, in an unsettled condition, and not likely to bring up children either for God or herself. She was left alone in obscurity (*this is Zion whom no man seeks after*), left in all the solitude and sorrow of a widowed state. How then came she to be thus replenished? See here, [1.] That the church is not perpetually visible, but there are times when it is desolate, and left alone, and made few in number. [2.] That yet on the other hand its desolations shall not be perpetual, nor will it be found too hard for God to repair them, and out of stones to raise up children unto Abraham. [3.] That sometimes this is done in a very surprising way, as when a nation is born at once, *ch.* lxvi. 8.

5. That this shall be done with the help of the Gentiles, *v.* 22. The Jews were cast off, among whom it was expected that the church should be built up; but God will *sow it to himself in the earth,* and will thence reap a plentiful crop, Hos. ii. 23. Observe, (1.) How the Gentiles shall be called in. God will *lift up his hand to them,* to invite or beckon them, having all the day stretched it out in vain to the Jews, *ch.* lxv. 2. Or it denotes the exerting of an almighty power, that of his Spirit and grace, to compel them to come in, to make them willing. And he will *set up his standard to them,* the preaching of the everlasting gospel, to which they shall gather, and under which they shall enlist themselves. (2.) How they shall come: *They shall bring thy sons in their arms.* They shall assist the sons of Zion, which are found among them, in their return to their own country, and shall forward them with as much tenderness as ever

any parent carried a child that was weak and helpless. God can raise up friends for returning Israelites even among Gentiles. *The earth helped the woman,* Rev. xii. 16. Or, "When they come themselves, they shall bring their children, and make them thy children;" compare *ch.* lx. 4. "Dost thou ask, *Who has begotten and brought up these?* Know that they were begotten and brought up among the Gentiles, but they are now brought into thy family." Let all that are concerned about young converts, and young beginners in religion, learn hence to deal very tenderly and carefully with them, as Christ does with the lambs which he *gathers with his arms and carries in his bosom.*

II. That the church shall have a great and prevailing interest in the nations, *v.* 22, 23. 1. Some of the princes of the nations shall become patrons and protectors to the church: *Kings shall be thy nursing fathers,* to carry thy sons in their arms (as Moses, Num. xi. 12); and, because women are the most proper nurses, *their queens shall be thy nursing mothers.* This promise was in part fulfilled to the Jews, after their return out of captivity. Several of the kings of Persia were very tender of their interests, countenanced and encouraged them, as Cyrus, Darius, and Artaxerxes; Esther the queen was a nursing mother to the Jews that remained in their captivity, putting her life in her hand to snatch the child out of the flames. The Christian church, after a long captivity, was happy in some such kings and queens as Constantine and his mother Helena, and afterwards Theodosius, and others, who nursed the church with all possible care and tenderness. Whenever the sceptre of government is put into the hands of religious princes, then this promise is fulfilled. The church in this world is in an infant state, and it is in the power of princes and magistrates to do it a great deal of service; it is happy when they do so, when their power is a praise to those that do well. 2. Others of them, who stand it out against the church's interests, will be forced to yield and to repent of their opposition: *They shall bow down to thee and lick the dust.* The promise to the church of Philadelphia seems to be borrowed from this (Rev. iii. 9): *I will make those of the synagogue of Satan to come and worship before thy feet.* Or it may be meant of the willing subjection which kings and kingdoms shall pay to Christ the church's King, as he manifests himself in the church (Ps. lxxii. 11): *All kings shall fall down before him.* And by all this it shall be made to appear, (1.) That God is the Lord, the sovereign Lord of all, against whom there is no standing out nor rising up. (2.) That those who wait for him, in a dependence upon his promise and a resignation to his will, shall not be made ashamed of their hope; for the vision of peace is for an appointed time, and at the end *it shall speak and shall not lie.*

24 Shall the prey be taken from the mighty, or the lawful captive delivered? 25 But thus saith the LORD, Even the captives of the mighty shall be taken away, and the prey of the terrible shall be delivered: for I will contend with him that contendeth with thee, and I will save thy children. 26 And I will feed them that oppress thee with their own flesh; and they shall be drunken with their own blood, as with sweet wine: and all flesh shall know that I the LORD *am* thy Saviour and thy Redeemer, the Mighty One of Jacob.

Here is, I. An objection started against the promise of the Jews' release out of their captivity in Babylon, suggesting that it was a thing not to be expected; for (*v.* 24) they were a prey in the hand of the mighty, of such as were then the greatest potentates on earth, and therefore it was not likely they should be rescued by force. Yet that was not all: they were lawful captives; by the law of God, having offended, they were justly delivered into captivity; and by the law of nations, being taken in war, they were justly detained in captivity till they should be ransomed or exchanged. Now this is spoken either, 1. By the enemies, as justifying themselves in their refusal to let them go. They plead both might and right. Proud men think all their own that they can lay their hands on and their title good if they have but the longest sword. Or, 2. By their friends, either in a way of distrust, despairing of the deliverance ("for who is able to deal with those that detain us, either by force of arms or a treaty of peace?"), or in a way of thankfulness, admiring the deliverance. "Who would have thought that ever the prey should be *taken from the mighty?* Yet it is done." This is applicable to our redemption by Christ. As to Satan, we were a prey in the hand of the mighty, and yet delivered even from him that had the power of death, by him that had the power of life. As to the justice of God, we were lawful captives, and yet delivered by a price of inestimable value.

II. This objection answered by an express promise, and a further promise; for God's promises being all yea, and amen, they may well serve to corroborate one another. 1. Here is an express promise with a *non-obstante—notwithstanding* to the strength of the enemy (*v.* 25): "*Even the captives of the mighty*, though they are mighty, shall be taken away, and it is to no purpose for them to oppose it; *and the prey of the terrible*, though they are terrible, shall be delivered;

and, as they cannot with all their strength outforce, so they cannot with all their impudence outface, the deliverance, and the counsels of God concerning it." *The Lord saith thus,* who, having all power and all hearts in his hands is able to make his words good. 2. Here is a further promise, showing how, and in what way, God will bring about the deliverance. He will bring judgments upon the oppressors, and so will work salvation for the oppressed: "*I will contend with him that contends with thee*, will plead thy cause against those that justify themselves in oppressing thee; whoever it be, though but a single person, that contends with thee, he shall know that it is at his peril, and thus *I will save thy children.*" The captives shall be delivered by *leading captivity captive*, that is, sending those into captivity that had held God's people captive, Rev. xiii. 10. Nay, they shall have blood for blood (*v.* 26): "*I will feed those that oppress thee with their own flesh*, and *they shall be drunken with their own blood.* The proud Babylonians shall become not only an easy, but an acceptable, prey to one another. God will send a dividing spirit among them, and their ruin, which was begun by a foreign invasion, shall be completed by their intestine divisions. They shall *bite and devour one another*, till they are *consumed one of another.* They shall greedily and with delight prey upon those that are their own flesh and blood." God can make the oppressors of his church to be their own tormentors and their own destroyers. The New-Testament Babylon, having made herself drunk with the blood of the saints, shall have *blood given her to drink, for she is worthy.* See how cruel men sometimes are to themselves and to one another: indeed those who are so to others are so to themselves, for God's justice and men's revenge will mete to them what they have measured to others. They not only thirst after blood, but drink it so greedily that they are drunken with it, and with as much pleasure as if it were sweet wine. If God had not more mercy on sinners than they would have one upon another were their passions let loose, the world would be soon an *Aceldama*, nay, a desolation.

III. See what will be the effect of Babylon's ruin: *All flesh shall know that I the Lord am thy Saviour.* God will make it to appear, to the conviction of all the world, that, though Israel seem lost and cast off, they have a Redeemer, and, though they are made a prey to the mighty, Jacob has a mighty One, who is able to deal with all his enemies. God intends, by the deliverances of his church, both to notify and to magnify his own name.

CHAP. L.

In this chapter, I. Those to whom God sends are justly charged with bringing all the troubles they were in upon themselves, by their own wilfulness and obstinacy, it being made to appear that God was able and ready to help them if they had been fit for deliverance, ver. 1—3. II. He by whom God sends produces his commission (ver. 4), alleges his own readiness to submit to all the services and sufferings he was called to in the execution of it (ver. 5, 6), and assures himself that God, who sent him, would stand by him and bear him out against all opposition, ver. 7—9. III. The message that is sent is life and death, good and evil, the blessing and the curse, comfort to desponding saints and terror to presuming sinners, ver. 10, 11. Now all this seems to have a double reference, 1. To the unbelieving Jews in Babylon, who quarrelled with God for his dealings with them, and to the prophet Isaiah, who, though dead long before the captivity, yet, prophesying so plainly and fully of it, saw fit to produce his credentials, to justify what he had said. 2. To the unbelieving Jews in our Saviour's time, whose own fault it was that they were rejected, Christ having preached much to them, and suffered much from them, and being herein borne up by a divine power. The "contents" of this chapter, in our Bibles, give this sense of it, very concisely, thus :—" Christ shows that the dereliction of the Jews is not to be imputed to him, by his ability to save, by his obedience in that work, and by his confidence in divine assistance." The prophet concludes with an exhortation to trust in God and not in ourselves.

T HUS saith the LORD, Where *is* the bill of your mother's divorcement, whom I have put away? Or which of my creditors *is it* to whom I have sold you? Behold, for your iniquities have ye sold yourselves, and for your transgressions is your mother put away. 2 Wherefore, when I came, *was there* no man? When I called, *was there* none to answer? Is my hand shortened at all, that it cannot redeem? Or have I no power to deliver? Behold, at my rebuke I dry up the sea, I make the rivers a wilderness: their fish stinketh, because *there is* no water, and dieth for thirst. 3 I clothe the heavens with blackness, and I make sackcloth their covering.

Those who have professed to be the people of God, and yet seem to be dealt severely with, are apt to complain of God, and to lay the fault upon him, as if he had been hard with them. But, in answer to their murmurings, we have here,

I. A challenge given them to prove, or produce any evidence, that the quarrel began on God's side, *v.* 1. They could not say that he had done them any wrong or had acted arbitrarily. 1. He had been a husband to them ; and husbands were then allowed a power to put away their wives upon any little disgust: if their wives found not favour in their eyes, they made nothing of giving them a bill of divorce, Deut. xxiv. 1 ; Matt. xix. 7. But they could not say that God had dealt so with them. It is true they were now separated from him, and had abode many days without ephod, altar, or sacrifice ; but whose fault was that? They could not say that God had given their mother a bill of divorce ; let them produce it if they can, for a bill of divorce was given into the hand of her that was divorced. 2. He had been a father to them ; and fathers had then a power to sell their children for slaves to their creditors, in satisfaction for the debts they were not otherwise able to pay. Now it is true the Jews were sold to the Baby-

lonians then, and afterwards to the Romans ; but did God sell them for payment of his debts? No, he was not indebted to any of those to whom they were sold, or, if he had sold them, he *did not increase his wealth by their price*, Ps. xliv. 12. When God chastens his children, it is neither for his pleasure (Heb. xii. 10) nor for his profit. All that are saved are saved by a prerogative of grace, but those that perish are cut off by an act of divine holiness and justice, not of absolute sovereignty.

II. A charge exhibited against them, showing them that they were themselves the authors of their own ruin : " *Behold, for your iniquities*, for the pleasure of them and the gratification of your own base lusts, *you have sold yourselves, for your iniquities you are sold :* not as children are sold by their parents, to pay their debts, but as malefactors are sold by the judges, to punish them for their crimes. You sold yourselves to work wickedness, and therefore God justly sold you into the hands of your enemies, 2 Chron. xii. 5, 8. It is for your transgressions that your mother is put away, for her whoredoms and adulteries," which were always allowed to be a just cause of divorce. The Jews were sent into Babylon for their idolatry, a sin which broke the marriage covenant, and were at last rejected for crucifying the Lord of glory ; these were the iniquities for which they were sold and put away.

III. The confirmation of this challenge and this charge. 1. It is plain that it was owing to themselves that they were cast off ; for God came and offered them his favour, offered them his helping hand, either to prevent their trouble or to deliver them out of it, but they slighted him and all the tenders of his grace. " Do you lay it upon me ?" (says God) ; " tell me, then, wherefore, *when I came, was there no man* to meet me, *when I called, was there none to answer me ?*" *v.* 2. God came to them by his servants the prophets, demanding the fruits of his vineyard (Matt. xxi. 34) ; he sent them his messengers, *rising up betimes and sending them* (Jer. xxxv. 15) ; he called to them to leave their sins, and so prevent their own ruin : but *was there* no man, or next to none, that had any regard to the warnings which the prophets gave them, none that answered the calls of God, or complied with the messages he sent them ; and this was it for which they were sold and put away. Because they *mocked the messengers of the Lord*, therefore *God brought upon them the king of the Chaldeans*, 2 Chron. xxxvi. 16, 17. Last of all *he sent unto them his Son.* He *came to his own*, but *his own received him not :* he called them to himself, but there were none that answered ; he would have gathered Jerusalem's children together, but they would not ; they knew not, because they would not know, the things that belonged to their peace, nor the day of their visitation, and for that transgression it was that they were put away and their house was left desolate, Matt. xxi. 41 ; xxiii. 37, 38 ; Luke xix. 41, 42. When God calls men to happiness, and they will not answer, they are justly left to be miserable. 2. It is plain that it was not owing to a want of power in God, for he is almighty, and could have recovered them from so great a death ; nor was it owing to a want of power in Christ, for he is *able to save to the uttermost.* The unbelieving Jews in Babylon thought they were not delivered because their God was not able to deliver them ; and those in Christ's time were ready to ask, in scorn, *Can this man save us?* For *himself he cannot save.* "But" (says God) "*is my hand shortened at all,* or is it weakened?" Can any limits be set to Omnipotence? Cannot he redeem who is the great Redeemer? Has he no *power to deliver* whose all power is? To put to silence, and for ever to put to shame, their doubts concerning his power, he here gives unquestionable proofs of it. (1.) He can, when he pleases, *dry up the seas,* and make the rivers a wilderness. He did so for Israel when he redeemed them out of Egypt, and he can do so again for their redemption out of Babylon. It is done at his *rebuke,* as easily as with a word's speaking. He can so dry up the rivers as to leave the fish to die for want of water, and to putrefy. When God *turned the waters of Egypt into blood* he *slew the fish,* Ps. cv. 29. The expression our Saviour sometimes used concerning the power of faith, that it will *remove mountains and plant sycamores in the sea,* is not unlike this ; if their faith could do that, no doubt their faith would save them, and therefore they were inexcusable if they perished in unbelief. (2.) He can, when he pleases, eclipse the lights of heaven, *clothe them with blackness, and make sackcloth their covering* (*v.* 3) by thick and dark clouds interposing, which he balances, Job xxxvi. 32; xxxvii. 16.

4 The Lord God hath given me the tongue of the learned, that I should know how to speak a word in season to *him that is* weary : he wakeneth morning by morning, he wakeneth mine ear to hear as the learned. 5 The Lord God hath opened mine ear, and I was not rebellious, neither turned away back. 6 I gave my back to the smiters, and my cheeks to them that plucked off the hair : I hid not my face from shame and spitting. 7 For the Lord God will help me ; therefore shall I not be confounded : therefore have I set my face like a flint, and I know

that I shall not be ashamed. 8 *He is* near that justifieth me; who will contend with me ? Let us stand together : who *is* mine adversary? Let him come near to me. 9 Behold the Lord God will help me ; who *is* he *that* shall condemn me ? Lo, they all shall wax old as a garment ; the moth shall eat them up.

Our Lord Jesus, having proved himself able to save here shows himself as willing as he is able. We suppose the prophet Isaiah to say something of himself in these verses, engaging and encouraging himself to go on in his work as a prophet, notwithstanding the many hardships he met with, not doubting but that God would stand by him and strengthen him ; but, like David, he speaks of himself as a type of Christ, who is here prophesied of and promised to be the Saviour.

I. As an acceptable preacher. Isaiah, as a prophet, was qualified for the work to which he was called, so were the rest of God's prophets, and others whom he employed as his messengers ; but Christ was anointed with the Spirit above his fellows. To make the man of God perfect, he has, 1. *The tongue of the learned,* to know how to give instruction, *how to speak a word in season to him that is weary, v.* 4. God, who made man's mouth, gave Moses the tongue of the learned, to speak for the terror and conviction of Pharaoh, Exod. iv. 11, 12. He gave to Christ the tongue of the learned, to speak a word in season for the comfort of those that are weary and heavily laden under the burden of sin, Matt. xi. 28. *Grace was poured into his lips,* and they are said to *drop sweet-smelling myrrh.* See what is the best learning of a minister, to know how to comfort troubled consciences, and to speak pertinently, properly, and plainly, to the various cases of poor souls. An ability to do this is God's gift, and it is one of the best gifts, which we should covet earnestly. Let us repose ourselves in the many comfortable words which Christ has spoken to the weary. 2. The ear of the learned, to receive instruction. Prophets have as much need of this as of the tongue of the learned ; for they must deliver what they are taught and no other, must hear the word from God's mouth diligently and attentively, that they may speak it exactly, Ezek. iii. 17. Christ himself received that he might give. None must undertake to be teachers who have not first been learners. Christ's apostles were first disciples, *scribes instructed unto the kingdom of heaven,* Matt. xiii. 52. Nor is it enough to hear, but we must *hear as the learned,* hear and understand, hear and remember, hear as those that would learn by what we hear. Those that would ¦ ear as the learned must be awake, **and** wakeful; for we are naturally drowsy and sleepy, and unapt to hear at all, or we hear by the halves, hear and do not heed. Our ears need to be wakened; we need to have something said to rouse us, to awaken us out of our spiritual slumbers, that we may hear as for our lives. We need to be awakened *morning by morning*, as duly as the day returns, to be awakened to do the work of the day in its day. Our case calls for continual fresh supplies of divine grace, to free us from the dulness we contract daily. The morning, when our spirits are most lively, is a proper time for communion with God; then we are in the best frame both to speak to him *(my voice shalt thou hear in the morning)* and to hear from him. The people came *early in the morning* to hear Christ in the temple (Luke xxi. 38), for, it seems, his were morning lectures. And it is God that wakens us morning by morning. If we do any thing to purpose in his service, it is he who, as our Master, calls us up; and we should doze perpetually if he did not waken us morning by morning.

II. As a patient sufferer, *v.* 5, 6. One would think that he who was commissioned and qualified to speak comfort to the weary should meet with no difficulty in his work, but universal acceptance. It is however quite otherwise; he has both hard work to do and hard usage to undergo; and here he tells us with what undaunted constancy he went through with it. We have no reason to question but that the prophet Isaiah went on resolutely in the work to which God had called him, though we read not of his undergoing any such hardships as are here supposed; but we are sure that the prediction was abundantly verified in Jesus Christ: and here we have, 1. His patient obedience in his doing work. "The Lord God has not only wakened my ear to hear what he says, but has opened my ear to receive it, and comply with it" (Ps. xl. 6, 7, *My ear hast thou opened; then said I, Lo, I come); for* when he adds, *I was not rebellious, neither turned away back,* more is implied than expressed—that he was willing, that though he foresaw a great deal of difficulty and discouragement, though he was to take pains and give constant attendance as a servant, though he was to empty himself of that which was very great and humble himself to that which was very mean, yet he did not fly off, did not fail, nor was discouraged. He continued very free and forward to his work even when he came to the hardest part of it. Note, As a good understanding in the truths of God, so a good will to the work and service of God, is from the grace of God. 2. His obedient patience in his suffering work. I call it obedient patience because he was patient with an eye to his Father's will, thus pleading with himself, *This commandment have I received of my Father,* and thus submitting to God,

Not as I will, but as thou wilt. In this submission he resigned himself, (1.) To be scourged: *I gave my back to the smiters;* and that not only by submitting to the indignity when he was smitten, but by permitting it (or admitting it rather) among the other instances of pain and shame which he would voluntarily undergo for us. (2.) To be buffeted: *I gave my cheeks to those that* not only smote them, but *plucked off the hair* of the beard, which was a greater degree both of pain and of ignominy. (3.) To be spit upon: *I hid not my face from shame and spitting.* He could have hidden his face from it, could have avoided it, but he would not, because he was made a reproach of men, and thus he would answer to the type of Job, that man of sorrows, of whom it is said that they *smote him on the cheek reproachfully* (Job xvi. 10) and *spared not to spit in his face* (Job xxx. 10), which was an expression not only of contempt, but of abhorrence and indignation. All this Christ underwent for us, and voluntarily, to convince us of his willingness to save us.

III. As a courageous champion, *v.* 7—9. The Redeemer is as famous for his boldness as for his humility and patience, and, though he yields, yet he is more than a conqueror. Observe, 1. The dependence he has upon God. What was the prophet Isaiah's support was the support of Christ himself (*v.* 7): *The Lord God will help me;* and again, *v.* 9. Those whom God employs he will assist, and will take care they want not any help that they or their work call for. God, having laid help upon his Son for us, gave help to him, and his hand was all along *with the man of his right hand.* Nor will he only assist him in his work, but accept of him (*v.* 8): *He is near that justifieth me.* Isaiah, no doubt, was falsely accused and loaded with reproach and calumny, as other prophets were; but he despised the reproach, knowing that God would roll it away and bring forth his righteousness as the light, perhaps in this world (Ps. xxxvii. 6), at furthest in the great 'day, when there will be a resurrection of names as well as bodies, and the righteous shall shine forth as the morning sun. And so it was verified in Christ; by his resurrection he was proved to be not the man that he was represented, not a blasphemer, not a deceiver, not an enemy to Cæsar. The judge that condemned him owned he found no fault in him; the centurion, or sheriff, that had charge of his execution, declared him a righteous man: so near was he that justified him. But it was true of him in a further and more peculiar sense: the Father justified him when he accepted the satisfaction he made for the sin of man, and constituted him *the Lord our righteousness,* who was made sin for us. He was *justified in the Spirit,* 1 Tim. iii. 16. He was near who did it; for his resurrection, by which he was justified, soon followed his condemnation and crucifixion. He was straightway glorified, John xiii. 32. 2. The confidence he thereupon has of success in his undertaking: "If God will help me, if he will justify me, will stand by me and bear me out, *I shall not be confounded*, as those are that come short of the end they aimed at and the satisfaction they promised themselves: *I know that I shall not be ashamed*." Though his enemies did all they could to put him to shame, yet he kept his ground, he kept his countenance, and was not ashamed of the work he had undertaken. Note, Work for God is work that we should not be ashamed of; and hope in God is hope that we shall not be ashamed of. Those that trust in God for help shall not be disappointed; they know whom they have trusted, and therefore know they shall not be ashamed. 3. The defiance which in this confidence he bids to all opposers and opposition: God will help me, and *therefore have I set my face like a flint.*" The prophet did so; he was bold in reproving sin, in warning sinners (Ezek. iii. 8, 9), and in asserting the truth of his predictions. Christ did so; he went on in his work, as Mediator, with unshaken constancy and undaunted resolution; he did not fail nor was discouraged; and here he challenges all his opposers, (1.) To enter the lists with him: *Who will contend with me*, either in law or by the sword? *Let us stand together* as combatants, or as the plaintiff and defendant. *Who is my adversary?* Who is *the master of my cause?* so the word is. "Who will pretend to enter an action against me? Let him appear, and *come near to me*, for I will not abscond." Many offered to dispute with Christ, but he put them to silence. The prophet speaks this in the name of all faithful ministers; those who keep close to the pure word of God, in delivering their message, need not fear contradiction; the scriptures will bear them out, whoever contends with them. *Great is the truth and will prevail.* Christ speaks this in the name of all believers, speaks it as their champion. Who dares be an enemy to those whom he is a friend to, or contend with those for whom he is an advocate? Thus St. Paul applies it (Rom. viii. 33): *Who shall lay any thing to the charge of God's elect?* (2.) He challenges them to prove any crime upon him (v. 9): *Who is he that shall condemn me?* The prophet perhaps was condemned to die; Christ we are sure was; and yet both could say, *Who is he that shall condemn?* For there is no condemnation to those whom God justifies. There were those that did condemn them, but what became of them? *They all shall wax old as a garment.* The righteous cause of Christ and his prophets shall outlive all opposition. The *moth shall eat them up* silently and insensibly; a little thing will serve to destroy them. But the roaring lion himself shall not prevail

286

against God's witnesses. All believers are enabled to make this challenge, *Who is he that shall condemn? It is Christ that died.*

10 Who *is* among you that feareth the LORD, that obeyeth the voice of his servant, that walketh *in* darkness, and hath no light? Let him trust in the name of the LORD, and stay upon his God. 11 Behold, all ye that kindle a fire, that compass *yourselves* about with sparks: walk in the light of your fire, and in the sparks *that* ye have kindled. This shall ye have of mine hand; ye shall lie down in sorrow.

The prophet, having the tongue of the learned given him, that he might give to every one his portion, here makes use of it, rightly dividing the word of truth. It is the summary of the gospel. *He that believes shall be saved* (he that trusts in the name of the Lord shall be comforted, though for a while he walk in darkness and have no light), but *he that believes not shall be damned;* though for a while he walk in the light of his own fire, yet he shall lie down in sorrow.

I. Comfort is here spoken to disconsolate saints, and they are encouraged to trust in God's grace, *v.* 10. Here observe, 1. What is always the character of a child of God. He is one that fears the Lord with a filial fear, that stands in awe of his majesty and is afraid of incurring his displeasure. This is a grace that usually appears most in good people when they walk in darkness, when other graces appear not. They then *tremble at his word* (ch. lxvi. 2) and are *afraid of his judgments*, Ps. cxix. 120. He is one that obeys the voice of God's servant, is willing to be ruled by the Lord Jesus, as God's servant in the great work of man's redemption, one that yields a sincere obedience to the law of Christ and cheerfully comes up to the terms of his covenant. Those that truly fear God will obey the voice of Christ. 2. What is sometimes the case of a child of God. It is supposed that though he has in his heart the fear of God, and faith in Christ, yet for a time he walks in darkness and has no light, is disquieted and has little or no comfort. Who is there that does so? This intimates that it is a case which sometimes happens among the professors of religion, yet not very often; but, whenever it happens, God takes notice of it. It is no new thing for the children and heirs of light sometimes to walk in darkness, and for a time not to have any glimpse or gleam of light. This is not meant so much of the comforts of this life (those that fear God, when they have ever so great an abundance of them, do not walk in them as their light) as of their spiritual comforts, which relate to their souls. They walk in darkness when their evidences for heaven are clouded, their joy in God is interrupted, the testimony of the Spirit is suspended, and the light of God's countenance is eclipsed. Pensive Christians are apt to be melancholy, and those who fear always are apt to fear too much. 3. What is likely to be an effectual cure in this sad case. He that is thus in the dark, (1.) *Let him trust in the name of the Lord,* in the goodness of his nature, and that which he has made known of himself, his wisdom, power, and goodness. *The name of the Lord is a strong tower,* let him run into that. Let him depend upon it that if he walk before God, which a man may do though he walk in the dark, he shall find God all-sufficient to him. (2.) Let him *stay himself upon his God,* his in covenant; let him keep hold of his covenant-relation to God, and call God *his God,* as Christ on the cross, *My God, My God.* Let him stay himself upon the promises of the covenant, and build his hopes on them. When a child of God is ready to sink he will find enough in God to stay himself upon. Let him trust in Christ, for God's *name is in him* (Exod. xxiii. 21), trust in that name of his, *The Lord our righteousness,* and stay himself upon God as his God, in and through a Mediator.

II. Conviction is here spoken to presuming sinners, and they are warned not to trust in themselves, *v.* 11. Observe, 1. The description given of them. They *kindle a fire,* and *walk in the light of that fire.* They depend upon their own righteousness, offer all their sacrifices, and burn all their incense, with that fire (as Nadab and Abihu) and not with the fire from heaven. In their hope of acceptance with God they have no regard to the righteousness of Christ. They refresh and please themselves with a conceit of their own merit and sufficiency, and warm themselves with that. It is both light and heat to them. They *compass themselves about with sparks of their own kindling.* As they trust in their own righteousness, and not in the righteousness of Christ, so they place their happiness in their worldly possessions and enjoyments, and not in the favour of God. Creature-comforts are as sparks, short-lived and soon gone; yet the children of this world, while they last, warm themselves by them, and walk with pride and pleasure in the light of them. 2. The doom passed upon them. They are ironically told to *walk in the light of their own fire.* "Make your best of it, while it lasts. But what will be in the end thereof, what will it come to at last? This shall you have of my hand (says Christ, for to him the judgment is committed), *you shall lie down in sorrow,* shall go to bed in the dark." See Job xviii. 5, 6. *His candle shall be put out with him.* Those that make the world their comfort, and their own righteousness their confidence, will certainly meet with a fatal disappointment, which will be bitterness in the end. A

godly man's way may be melancholy, but his end shall be peace and everlasting light. A wicked man's way may be pleasant, but his end and endless abode will be utter darkness.

CHAP. LI.

This chapter is designed for the comfort and encouragement of those that fear God and keep his commandments, even when they walk in darkness and have no light. Whether it was intended primarily for the support of the captives in Babylon is not certain, probably it was; but comforts thus generally expressed ought not to be so confined. Whenever the church of God is in distress her friends and well-wishers may comfort themselves and one another with these words, I. That God, who raised his church at first out of nothing, will take care that it shall not perish, ver. 1—3. II. That the righteousness and salvation he designs for his church are sure and near, very near and very sure, ver. 4—6. III. That the persecutors of the church are weak and dying creatures, ver. 7, 8. IV. That the same power which did wonders for the church formerly is now engaged and employed for her protection and deliverance, ver. 9—11. V. That God himself, the Maker of the world, had undertaken both to deliver his people out of their distress and to comfort them under it, and sent his prophet to assure them of it, ver. 12—16. VI. That, deplorable as the condition of the church now was (ver. 17—20), to the same woeful circumstances her persecutors and oppressors should shortly be reduced, and worse, ver. 21—23. The first three paragraphs of this chapter begin with, " Hearken unto me," and they are God's people that are all along called to hearken; for even when comforts are spoken to them sometimes they " hearken not, through anguish of spirit" (Exod. vi. 9); therefore they are again and again called to hearken, ver. 1, 4, 7. The two other paragraphs of this chapter begin with " Awake, awake;" in the former (ver. 9) God's people call upon him to awake and help them; in the latter (ver. 17) God calls upon them to awake and help themselves.

H EARKEN to me, ye that follow after righteousness, ye that seek the Lord: look unto the rock *whence* ye are hewn, and to the hole of the pit *whence* ye are digged. 2 Look unto Abraham your father, and unto Sarah *that* bare you: for I called him alone, and blessed him, and increased him. 3 For the Lord shall comfort Zion: he will comfort all her waste places; and he will make her wilderness like Eden, and her desert like the garden of the Lord; joy and gladness shall be found therein, thanksgiving, and the voice of melody.

Observe, 1. How the people of God are here described, to whom the word of this consolation is sent and who are called upon to hearken to it, *v.* 1. They are such as *follow after righteousness,* such as are very desirous and solicitous both to be justified and to be sanctified, are pressing hard after this, to have the favour of God restored to them and the image of God renewed on them. These are those *that seek the Lord,* for it is only in the way of righteousness that we can seek him with any hope of finding him. 2. How they are here directed to look back to their original, and the smallness of their beginning: " *Look unto the rock whence you were hewn*" (the idolatrous family in Ur of the Chaldees, out of which Abraham was taken, the generation of slaves which the heads and fathers of their tribes were in Egypt); " look unto *the hole of the pit out of which you were digged,* as clay, when God formed you into a people." Note, It is good for those that are privileged by a new birth to consider what they were by their first birth, how they were *conceived in iniquity and shapen in sin.* That which is *born of the flesh is flesh.* How hard was that rock out of which we were hewn, unapt to receive impressions, and how miserable *the hole of that pit out of which we were digged!* The consideration of this should fill us with low thoughts of ourselves and high thoughts of divine grace. Those that are now advanced would do well to remember how low they began (v. 2) : " *Look unto Abraham your father,* the father of all the faithful, of all that follow after the righteousness of faith as he did (Rom. iv. 11), *and unto Sarah that bore you,* and whose daughters you all are as long as you do well. Think how Abraham was *called alone,* and yet was *blessed* and *multiplied;* and let that encourage you to depend upon the promise of God even when a sentence of death seems to be upon all the means that lead to the performance of it. Particularly let it encourage the captives in Babylon, though they are reduced to a small number, and few of them left, to hope that yet they shall increase so as to replenish their own land again." When Jacob is very small, yet he is not so small as Abraham was, who yet became father of many nations. " Look unto Abraham, and see what he got by trusting in the promise of God, and take example by him to follow God with an implicit faith." 3. How they are here assured that their present seedness of tears should at length end in a harvest of joys, v. 3. The church of God on earth, even the gospel Zion, has sometimes had her deserts and waste places, many parts of the church, through either corruption or persecution, made like a wilderness, unfruitful to God or uncomfortable to the inhabitants ; but God will find out a time and way to *comfort Zion,* not only by speaking comfortably to her, but by acting graciously for her. God has comforts in store even for the *waste places* of his church, for those parts of it that seem not regarded or valued. (1.) He will make them fruitful, and so give them cause to rejoice ; her wildernesses shall put on a new face, and look pleasant as Eden, and abound in all good fruits, *as the garden of the Lord.* Note, It is the greatest comfort of the church to be made serviceable to the glory of God, and to be as his garden in which he delights. (2.) He will make them cheerful, and so give them hearts to rejoice. With the *fruits of righteousness, joy and gladness shall be found therein;* for the more holiness men have, and the more good they do, the more gladness they have. And where there is gladness, to their satisfaction, it is fit that there should be thanksgiving, to God's honour ; for whatever is the matter of our rejoicing ought to be the matter of our thanksgiving ; and the returns of God's favour ought to be celebrated with the voice of melody, which will be the more melodious when God gives *songs in the night,* songs in the desert.

288

4 Hearken unto me, my people ; and give ear unto me, O my nation : for a law shall proceed from me, and I will make my judgment to rest for a light of the people. 5 My righteousness *is* near ; my salvation is gone forth, and mine arms shall judge the people ; the isles shall wait upon me, and on mine arm shall they trust. 6 Lift up your eyes to the heavens, and look upon the earth beneath : for the heavens shall vanish away like smoke, and the earth shall wax old like a garment, and they that dwell therein shall die in like manner : but my salvation shall be for ever, and my righteousness shall not be abolished. 7 Hearken unto me, ye that know righteousness, the people in whose heart *is* my law ; fear ye not the reproach of men, neither be ye afraid of their revilings. 8 For the moth shall eat them up like a garment, and the worm shall eat them like wool : but my righteousness shall be for ever, and my salvation from generation to generation.

Both these proclamations, as I may call them, end alike with an assurance of the perpetuity of God's righteousness and his salvation ; and therefore we put them together, both being designed for the comfort of God's people. Observe,

I. Who they are to whom this comfort belongs : " *My people,* and *my nation,* that I have set apart for myself, that own me and are owned by me." Those are God's people and his nation who are subject to him as their King and their God, pay allegiance to him, and put themselves under his protection accordingly. They are a people who *know righteousness,* who not only have the means of knowledge, and to whom righteousness is made known, but who improve those means, and are able to form a right judgment of truth and falsehood, good and evil. And, as they have good heads, so they have good hearts, for they have the law of God in them, written and ruling there. Those God owns for his people *in whose hearts his law is.* Even those who know righteousness, and have the law of God in their hearts, may yet be in great distress and sorrow, and loaded with reproach and contempt ; but their God will comfort them with the righteousness they know and the law they have in their hearts.

II. What the comfort is that belongs to God's people. 1. That the gospel of Christ shall be preached and published to the world : *A law shall proceed from me,* an evangelical law, the law of Christ, the law of faith, *ch.* ii. 3. This law is his judgment; for it is that law of liberty by which the world shall be governed and judged. This shall not only go forth, but shall continue and rest, it shall take firm footing and deep root in the world. It shall rest, not only for the benefit of the Jews, who had the first notice of it, but *for a light of the people* of other nations. It is this law, this judgment, that we are required to hearken and give ear to, at our peril; for how shall we escape if we neglect it and turn a deaf ear to it? When a law proceeds from God, *he that has ears to hear, let him hear.* 2. That this law and judgment shall bring with them right-eousness and salvation, shall open a ready way to the children of men, that they may be justified and saved, *v.* 5. These are called *God's righteousness* and *his* salvation, be-cause of his contriving and bringing them about. The former is a righteousness which he will accept for us and accept us for, and a righteousness which he will work in us and graciously accept of. The latter is the *salvation of the Lord,* for it arises from him and terminates in him. Observe, There is no salvation without righteousness; and, wherever there is the *righteousness of God,* there shall be his salvation. All those, and those only, that are justified and sanctified shall be glorified. 3. That this righteous-ness and salvation shall very shortly appear: *My righteousness is near.* It is near in time; behold, all things are now ready. It is near in place, not far to seek, but the word is nigh us, and Christ in the word, righteousness in the word, Rom. x. 8. *My salvation has gone forth.* The decree has gone forth con-cerning it; it shall as certainly be introduced as if it had gone forth already, and the time for it is at hand. 4. That this evangelical righteousness and salvation shall not be con-fined to the Jewish nation, but shall be extended to the Gentiles: *My arms shall judge the people.* Those that will not yield to the judgments of God's mouth shall be crushed by the judgments of his hand. Some shall thus be judged by the gospel, for *for judgment Christ came into this world;* but others, and those of *the isles, shall wait upon him,* and bid his gospel, and the com-mands as well as the comforts of it, welcome. It was a comfort to God's people, to his nation, that multitudes should be added to them, and the increase of their number should be the increase of their strength and beauty. It is added, *And on my arm shall they trust,* that *arm of the Lord* which is re-vealed in Christ, *ch.* liii. 1. Observe, God's arm shall judge the people that are impeni-tent, and yet on his arm shall others trust and be saved by it; for it is to us as we make it, a savour of life or of death. 5. That this righteousness and salvation *shall be for ever,* and shall never be abolished, *v.* 8. It is an everlasting righteousness that the Messiah brings in (Dan. ix. 24), an eternal redemp-

tion that he is the author of, Heb. v. 9. As it shall spread through all the nations of the earth, so it shall last through all the ages of the world. We must never expect any other way of salvation, any other covenant of peace or rule of righteousness, than what we have in the gospel, and what we have there shall continue to the end, Matt. xxviii. 20. It is for ever; for the consequences of it shall be to eternity, and by this law of liberty men's everlasting state will be determined. This perpetuity of the gospel and the blessed things it brings in is illustrated by the fading and perishing of this world and all things in it. Look up to the visible heavens above, which have continued hitherto, and seem likely to continue, but they shall *vanish like smoke* that soon spends itself and disap-pears; they shall be rolled like a scroll, and their lights shall fall like leaves in autumn. Look down to the earth beneath; that abides too for a short *ever* (Eccl. i. 4), but it shall *wax old like a garment* that will be the worse for wearing; *and those that dwell therein,* all the inhabitants of the earth, even those that seem to have the best settlement in it, *shall die in like manner:* the soul shall, as to this world, vanish like smoke, and the body be thrown by like a garment waxen old. They shall be easily crushed (Job iv. 19), and no loss of them. But when *heaven and earth pass away,* when all flesh and the glory of it wither as grass, the *word of the Lord endures for ever,* and *not one iota or tittle of that shall fall to the ground.* Those whose happiness is bound up in Christ's righteous-ness and salvation will have the comfort of it when time and days shall be no more.

III. What use they are to make of this comfort. If God's righteousness and salva-tion are near to them, then let them *not fear the reproach of men,* of mortal miserable men, nor be *afraid of their revilings* or spiteful taunts, theirs who bid you sing them the songs of Zion, or who ask you, in scorn, *Where is now your God?* Let not those who embrace the gospel righteousness be afraid of those who will call them *Beelzebub,* and will say all manner of evil against them falsely. Let them not be afraid of them; let them not be disturbed by these oppro-brious speeches, nor made uneasy by them, as if they would be the ruin of their reputa-tion and honour and they must for ever lie under the load of them. Let them not be afraid of their executing their menaces, nor be deterred thereby from their duty, nor frightened into any sinful compliances, nor driven to take any indirect courses for their own safety. Those can bear but little for Christ that cannot bear a hard word for him. Let us not fear the reproach of men; for, 1. They will be quickly silenced (*v.* 8): The *moth shall eat them up like a garment, ch.* l. 9. *The worm shall eat them like wool,* or woollen cloth. If we have the approbation of a living God, we may despise the censure of dying men; the matter is not great what those say of us who must shortly be food for worms Or it intimates the judgments of God with which they shall be visited, with which they shall be consumed, for their malice against the people of God; they shall be slowly and silently, but effectually destroyed, when God shall come to reckon with them *for all their hard speeches,* Jude 14, 15. 2. The cause we suffer for cannot be run down. The falsehood of their reproaches will be detected, but truth shall triumph, and the righteousness of religion's injured cause shall be for ever plain. Clouds darken the sun, but give no obstruction to his progress.

9 Awake, awake, put on strength, O arm of the LORD; awake, as in the ancient days, in the generations of old. *Art* thou not it that hath cut Rahab, *and* wounded the dragon? 10 *Art* thou not it which hath dried the sea, the waters of the great deep; that hath made the depths of the sea a way for the ransomed to pass over? 11 Therefore the redeemed of the LORD shall return, and come with singing unto Zion; and everlasting joy *shall be* upon their head: they shall obtain gladness and joy; *and* sorrow and mourning shall flee away. 12 I, *even* I, *am* he that comforteth you: who *art* thou, that thou shouldest be afraid of a man *that* shall die, and of the son of man *which* shall be made *as* grass; 13 And forgettest the LORD thy maker, that hath stretched forth the heavens, and laid the foundations of the earth; and hast feared continually every day because of the fury of the oppressor, as if he were ready to destroy? And where *is* the fury of the oppressor? 14 The captive exile hasteneth that he may be loosed, and that he should not die in the pit, nor that his bread should fail. 15 But I *am* the LORD thy God, that divided the sea, whose waves roared: the LORD of hosts *is* his name. 16 And I have put my words in thy mouth, and I have covered thee in the shadow of mine hand, that I may plant the heavens, and lay the foundations of the earth, and say unto Zion, Thou *art* my people.

In these verses we have,

I. A prayer that God would, in his providence, appear and act for the deliverance of his people and the mortification of his

and their enemies. *Awake, awake! put on strength, O arm of the Lord! v.* 9. The arm of the Lord is Christ, or it is put for God himself, as Ps. xliv. 23. *Awake! why sleepest thou?* He that keeps Israel neither slumbers nor sleeps; but, when we pray that he would awake, we mean that he would make it to appear that he watches over his people and is always awake to do them good. The arm of the Lord is said to awake when the power of God exerts itself with more than ordinary vigour on his people's behalf. When a hand or arm is benumbed we say, It is asleep; when it is stretched forth for action, It awakes. God needs not to be reminded nor excited by us, but he gives us leave thus to be humbly earnest with him for such appearances of his power as will be for his own praise. *"Put on strength,"* that is, "put forth strength: appear in thy strength, as we appear in the clothes we put on," Ps. xxi. 13. The church sees her case bad, her enemies many and mighty, her friends few and feeble; and therefore she depends purely upon the strength of God's arm for her relief. *"Awake, as in the ancient days,"* that is, " do for us now as thou didst for our fathers formerly, repeat *the wonders they told us of,"* Judg. vi. 13.

II. The pleas to enforce this prayer. 1. They plead precedents, the experiences of their ancestors, and the great things God had done for them. " Let the arm of the Lord be made bare on our behalf; for it has done great things formerly in defence of the same cause, and we are sure it is neither shortened nor weakened. It did wonders against the Egyptians, who enslaved and oppressed God's son, his first-born; it *cut Rahab* to pieces with one direful plague after another, *and wounded* Pharaoh, *the dragon,* the Leviathan (as he is called, Ps. lxxiv. 13, 14); it gave him his death's wound. It did wonders for Israel. *It dried up the sea,* even *the waters of the great deep,* as far as was requisite to open *a way* through the sea *for the ransomed to pass over," v.* 10. God is never at a loss for a way to accomplish his purposes concerning his people, but will either find one or make one. Past experiences, as they are great supports to faith and hope, so they are good pleas in prayer. *Thou hast; wilt thou not?* Ps. lxxxv. 1—6. 2. They plead promises (*v.* 11): *And the redeemed of the Lord shall return,* that is (as it may be supplied), *thou hast said, They shall,* referring to ch. xxxv. 10, where we find this promise, that *the redeemed of the Lord,* when they are released out of their captivity in Babylon, *shall come with singing unto Zion.* Sinners, when they are brought out of the slavery of sin into the glorious liberty of God's children, may come singing, as a bird got loose out of the cage. The souls of believers, when they are delivered out of the prison of the body, come to the heavenly Zion with singing. Then this promise will have its full accomplishment, and we may plead it in the mean time. He that designs such joy for us at last will he not work such deliverances for us in the mean time as our case requires? When the saints come to heaven they *enter into the joy of their Lord :* it crowns their heads with immortal honour; it fills their hearts with complete satisfaction. *They shall obtain* that *joy and gladness* which they could never obtain in this vale of tears. In this world of changes it is a short step from joy to sorrow, but in that world *sorrow and mourning shall flee away*, never to return or come in view again.

III. The answer immediately given to this prayer (*v.* 12) : *I, even I, am he that comforteth you.* They prayed for the operations of his power; he answers them with the consolations of his grace, which may well be accepted as an equivalent. If God do not wound the dragon, and dry the sea, as formerly, yet, if he comfort us in soul under our afflictions, we have no reason to complain. If God do not answer immediately *with the saving strength of his right hand,* we must be thankful if he answer us, as an angel himself was answered (Zech. i. 13), *with good words and comfortable words.* See how God resolves to comfort his people : *I, even I,* will do it. He had ordered his ministers to do it (*ch.* xl. 1); but, because they cannot reach the heart, he takes the work into his own hands : *I, even I,* will do it. See how he glories in it; he takes it among the titles of his honour to be *the God that comforts those that are cast down ;* he delights in being so. Those whom God comforts are comforted indeed; nay, his undertaking to comfort them is comfort enough to them.

1. He comforts those that were in fear; and fear has torment, which calls for comfort. The fear of man has a snare in it which we have need of comfort to preserve us from. He comforts the timorous by chiding them, and that is no improper way of comforting either others or ourselves : *Why art thou cast down, and why disquieted? v.* 12, 13. God, who comforts his people, would not have them disquiet themselves with amazing perplexing fears of the reproach of men (*v.* 7), or of their growing threatening power and greatness, or of any mischief they may intend against us or our people. Observe,

(1.) The absurdity of those fears. It is a disparagement to us to give way to them : *Who art thou, that thou shouldst be afraid?* In the original, the pronoun is feminine, *Who art thou, O woman!* unworthy the name of a man? Such a weak and womanish thing it is to give way to perplexing fears. [1.] It is absurd to be in such dread of a dying man. What! *afraid of a man that shall die*, shall certainly and shortly die, *of the son of man who shall be made as grass,* shall wither and be trodden down or eaten up? The greatest men, and the most for-

midable, that are *the terror of the mighty in the land of the living*, are *but men* (Ps. ix. 20) and shall *die like men* (Ps. lxxxii. 7), are but grass sprung out of the earth, cleaving to it, and retiring again into it. Note, We ought to look upon every man as a man that shall die. Those we admire, and love, and trust to, are men that shall die; let us not therefore delight too much in them nor depend too much upon them. Those we fear we must look upon as frail and mortal, and consider what a foolish thing it is for the servants of the living God to be afraid of dying men, that are here to-day and gone to-morrow. [2.] It is absurd to *fear continually every day* (*v.* 13), to put ourselves upon a constant rack, so as never to be easy, nor to have any enjoyment of ourselves. Now and then a danger may be imminent and threatening, and it may be prudent to fear it; but to be always in a toss, jealous of dangers at every step, and to tremble at the shaking of every leaf, is to make ourselves all our lifetime *subject to bondage* (Heb. ii. 15), and to bring upon ourselves that sore judgment which is threatened, Deut. xxviii. 66, 67. *Thou shalt fear, day and night.* [3.] It is absurd to fear beyond what there is cause : " Thou art *afraid of the fury of the oppressor.* It is true, there is an oppressor, and he is furious, and he designs, it may be, when he has an opportunity, to do thee a mischief, and it will be thy wisdom therefore to stand upon thy guard; but thou art afraid of him, *as if he were ready to destroy,* as if he were just now going to cut thy throat, and as if there were no possibility of preventing it." A timorous spirit is thus apt to make the worst of every thing, and to apprehend the danger greater and nearer than really it is. Sometimes God is pleased at once to show us the folly of so doing : " *Where is the fury of the oppressor?* It is gone in an instant, and the danger is over ere thou art aware." His heart is turned, or his hands are tied. *Pharaoh king of Egypt is but a noise,* and the king of Babylon no more. What has become of all the furious oppressors of God's Israel, that hectored them, and threatened them, and were a terror to them? they passed away, and, lo, they were not; and so shall these.

(2.) The impiety of those fears : " Thou art *afraid of a man that shall die, and forgettest the Lord thy Maker,* who is also the Maker of all the world, who *has stretched forth the heavens and laid the foundations of the earth,* and therefore has all the hosts and all the powers of both at his command and disposal." Note, Our inordinate fear of man is a tacit forgetfulness of God. When we disquiet ourselves with the fear of man we forget that there is a God above him, and that the greatest of men have no power but what is given them from above; we forget the providence of God, by which he orders and overrules all events according to the counsel of his own will; we forget the promises he has made to protect his people, and the experiences we have had of his care concerning us, and his seasonable interposition for our relief many a time, when we thought the oppressor ready to destroy; we forget our Jehovah-jirehs, monuments of mercy in the mount of the Lord. Did we remember to make God our fear and our dread, we should not be so much afraid as we are of the frowns of men, *ch.* viii. 12, 13. Happy is the man that fears God always, Prov. xxviii. 14; Luke xii. 4, 5.

2. He comforts those that were in bonds, *v.* 14, 15. See here, (1.) What they do for themselves: *The captive exile hastens that he may be loosed* and may return to his own country, from which he is banished; his care is *that he may not die in the pit* (not die a prisoner, through the inconveniencies of his confinement), and that *his bread should not fail*, either the bread he should have to keep him alive in prison or that which should bear his charges home; his stock is low, and therefore he hastens to be loosed. Now some understand this as his fault. He is distrustfully impatient of delays, cannot wait God's time, but thinks he is undone and must die in the pit if he be not released immediately. Others take it to be his praise, that when the doors are thrown open he does not linger, but applies himself with all diligence to procure his discharge. And then it follows, *But I am the Lord thy God,* which intimates, (2.) What God will do for them, even that which they cannot do for themselves. God has all power in his hand to help the captive exiles; for he has *divided the sea,* when the roaring of its waves was more frightful than any of the impotent menaces of proud oppressors. He has *stilled* or *quieted the sea,* so some think it should be read, Ps. lxv. 7; lxxxix. 9. This is not only a proof of what God can do, but a resemblance of what he has done, and will do, for his people; he will find out a way to still the threatening storm, and bring them safely into the harbour. *The Lord of hosts is his name,* his name for ever, the name by which his people have long known him. And, as he is able to help them, so he is willing and engaged to do it; for he is *thy God,* O captive-exile! thine in covenant. This is a check to the desponding captives. Let them not conclude that they must either be loosed immediately or die in the pit; for he that is the Lord of hosts can relieve them when they are brought ever so low. It is also an encouragement to the diligent captives, who, when liberty is proclaimed, are willing to lose no time; let them know that the Lord is their God, and, while they thus strive to help themselves, they may be sure he will help them.

3. He comforts all his people who depended upon what the prophets said to them in the name of the Lord, and built their

hopes upon it. When the deliverances which the prophets spoke of either did not come so soon as they looked for them or did not come up to the height of their expectation they began to be cast down in their own eyes; but, as to this, they are encouraged (*v.* 16) by what God says to his prophet, not to this only, but to all his prophets, nor to this, or them, principally, but to Christ, the great prophet. It is a great satisfaction to those to whom the message is sent to hear the God of truth and power say to his messenger, as he does here, *I have put my words in thy mouth, that* by them *I may plant the heavens.* God undertook to comfort his people (*v.* 12); but still he does it by his prophets, by his gospel; and, that he may do it by these, he here tells us, (1.) That his word in them is very true. He owns what they have said to be what he had directed and enjoined them to say: " *I have put my words in thy mouth,* and therefore he that receives thee and them receives me." This is a great stay to our faith, that Christ's doctrine was not his, but his that sent him, and that the words of the prophets and apostles were God's words, which he put into their mouths. God's Spirit not only revealed to them the things themselves they spoke of, but dictated to them the words they should speak (2 Pet. i. 21; 1 Cor. ii. 13); so that these are the true sayings of God, of a God that cannot lie. (2.) That it is very safe: I have *covered thee in the shadow of my hand* (as before, *ch.* xlix. 2), which speaks the special protection not only of the prophets, but of their prophecies, not only of Christ, but of Christianity, of the gospel of Christ; it is not only the faithful word of God which the prophets deliver to us, but it shall be carefully preserved till it have its accomplishment for the use of the church, notwithstanding the restless endeavours of the powers of darkness to extinguish this light. They shall *prophesy again* (Rev. x. 11), though not in their persons, yet in their writings, which God has always *covered in the shadow of his hand,* preserved by a special providence, else they would have been lost ere this. (3.) That this word, when it comes to be accomplished, will be very great and will not fall short of the pomp and grandeur of the prophecy: " *I have put my words in thy mouth,* not that by the performance of them I may plant a nation, or found a city, but *that I may plant the heavens and lay the foundations of the earth,* may do that for my people which will be a new creation." This must look as far forward as to the great work done by the gospel of Christ and the setting up of his holy religion in the world. As God by Christ made the world at first (Heb. i. 2), and by him formed the Old-Testament church (Zech. vi. 12), so by him, and the words put into his mouth, he will set up, [1.] A new world, will again plant the heavens and found the earth. Sin having put the whole creation into disorder, Christ's taking away the sin of the world put all into order again. *Old things have passed away, all things have become new;* things in heaven and things on earth are reconciled, and so put into a new posture, Col. i. 20. Through him, according to the promise, *we look for new heavens and a new earth* (2 Pet. iii. 13), and to this the prophets bear witness. [2.] He will set up a new church, a New-Testament church: *He will say unto Zion, Thou art my people.* The gospel church is called *Zion* (Heb xii. 22) and *Jerusalem* (Gal. iv. 26); and, when the Gentiles are brought into it, it shall be said unto them, *You are my people.* When God works great deliverances for his church, and especially when he shall complete the salvation of it in the great day, he will thereby own that poor despised handful to be his people, whom he has chosen and loved.

17 Awake, awake, stand up, O Jerusalem, which hast drunk at the hand of the LORD the cup of his fury; thou hast drunken the dregs of the cup of trembling, *and* wrung *them* out. 18 *There is* none to guide her among all the sons *whom* she hath brought forth; neither *is there any* that taketh her by the hand of all the sons *that* she hath brought up. 19 These two *things* are come unto thee; (Who shall be sorry for thee?) desolation, and destruction, and the famine, and the sword: by whom shall I comfort thee? 20 Thy sons have fainted, they lie at the head of all the streets, as a wild bull in a net: they are full of the fury of the LORD, the rebuke of thy God. 21 Therefore hear now this, thou afflicted, and drunken, but not with wine: 22 Thus saith thy Lord the LORD, and thy God *that* pleadeth the cause of his people, Behold, I have taken out of thine hand the cup of trembling, *even* the dregs of the cup of my fury; thou shalt no more drink it again: 23 But I will put it into the hand of them that afflict thee; which have said to thy soul, Bow down, that we may go over: and thou hast laid thy body as the ground, and as the street, to them that went over.

God, having awoke for the comfort of his people, here calls upon them to awake, as afterwards, *ch.* lii. 1. It is a call to awake not so much out of the sleep of sin (though that also is necessary in order to their being ready for deliverance) as out of the stupor of despair. When the inhabitants of Jerusalem were in captivity they, as well as those who remained upon the spot, were so overwhelmed with the sense of their troubles that they had no heart or spirit to mind any thing that tended to their comfort or relief; they were as the disciples in the garden, *sleeping for sorrow* (Luke xxii. 45), and therefore, when the deliverance came, they are said to have been *like those that dream*, Ps. cxxvi. 1. Nay, it is a call to awake, not only from sleep, but from death, like that to the dry bones to live, Ezek. xxxvii. 9. "Awake, and look about thee, that thou mayest see the day of thy deliverance dawn, and mayest be ready to bid it welcome. Recover thy senses; sink not under thy load, but stand up, and bestir thyself for thy own help." This may be applied to the Jerusalem that was in the apostle's time, which is said to have been *in bondage with her children* (Gal. iv. 25), and to have been under the power of *a spirit of slumber* (Rom. xi. 8); they are called to awake, and mind the things that belonged to their everlasting peace, and then the cup of trembling should be taken out of their hands, peace should be spoken to them, and they should triumph over Satan, who had blinded their eyes and lulled them asleep. Now,

I. It is owned that Jerusalem had long been in a very deplorable condition, and sunk into the depths of misery.

1. She had lain under the tokens of God's displeasure. He had put into her hand *the cup of his fury*, that is, her share of his displeasure. The dispensations of his providence concerning her had been such that she had reason to think he was angry with her. She had provoked him to anger most bitterly, and was made to taste the bitter fruits of it. The cup of God's fury is, and will be, a *cup of trembling* to all those that have it put into their hands: damned sinners will find it so to eternity. It is said (Ps. lxxv. 8) that *the dregs of the cup*, the loathsome sediments in the bottom of it, *all the wicked of the earth shall wring them out, and drink them;* but here Jerusalem, having made herself as the wicked of the earth, is compelled to wring them out and drink them; for wherever there has been a cup of fornication, as there had been in Jerusalem's hand when she was idolatrous, sooner or later there will be a cup of fury, a cup of trembling. Therefore *stand in awe and sin not.*

2. Those that should have helped her in her distress failed her, and were either unable or unwilling to help her, as might have been expected, *v.* 18. She is intoxicated with the cup of God's fury, and, being so, staggers, and is very unsteady in her counsels and attempts. She knows not what she says or does, much less knows she what to say or do; and, in this unhappy condition, *of all the sons that she has brought forth* and

brought up, that she has borne and educated (and there were many famous ones, for of Zion it was said *that this and that man were born there,* Ps. lxxxvii. 5), *there is none to guide her,* none to take her by the hand to keep her either from falling or from shaming herself, to lend either a hand to help her out of her trouble or a tongue to comfort her under it. Think it not strange if wise and good men are disappointed in their children, and have not that succour from them which they expected, but those that were arrows in their hand prove arrows in their heart, when Jerusalem herself has none of all her sons, prince, priest, nor prophet, that has such a sense either of duty or gratitude as to help her when she has most need of help. Thus they complain; Ps. lxxiv. 9. There is *none to tell us how long.* Now that which aggravated this disappointment was, (1) That her trouble was very great, and yet there was none to pity or help her: *These two things have come unto thee* (v. 19), to complete thy desolation and destruction, even *the famine and the sword,* two sore judgments, and very terrible. Or the two things were the *desolation and destruction* by which the city was wasted and the famine and sword by which the citizens perished. Or the two things were the trouble itself (made up of desolation, destruction, famine, and sword) and her being helpless, forlorn, and comfortless, under it. "Two sad things indeed, to be in this woeful case, and to have none to pity thee, to sympathize with thee in thy griefs, or to help to bear the burden of thy cares, to have none to comfort thee, by suggesting that to thee which might help to alleviate thy grief or doing that for thee which might help to redress thy grievances." Or these two things that had come upon Jerusalem are the same with the two things that were afterwards to come upon Babylon (*ch.* xlvii. 9), *loss of children and widowhood* —piteous case, and yet, "when thou hast brought it upon thyself by thy own sin and folly, *who shall be sorry for thee?*—a case that calls for comfort, and yet, when thou art froward under thy trouble, frettest, and makest thyself uneasy, *by whom shall I comfort thee?'* Those that will not be counselled cannot be helped. (2.) That those who should have been her comforters were their own tormentors (v. 20): *They have fainted,* as quite dispirited and driven to despair; they have no patience in which to keep possession of their own souls and the enjoyment of themselves, nor any confidence in God's promise, by which to keep possession of the comfort of that. They throw themselves upon the ground, in vexation at their troubles, and there *they lie at the head of all the streets,* complaining to all that pass by (Lam. i. 12), pining away for want of necessary food; there they lie like *a wild bull in a net,* fretting and raging, struggling and pulling, to help themselves,

but entangling themselves so much the more, and making their condition the worse by their own passions and discontents. Those that are of a meek and quiet spirit are, under affliction, like a dove in a net, mourning indeed, but silent and patient. Those that are of a froward peevish spirit are like a like a wild bull in a net, uneasy to themselves, vexatious to their friends, and provoking to their God: *They are full of the fury of the Lord, the rebuke of our God.* God is angry with them, and contends with them, and they are full of that only, and take no notice of his wise and gracious designs in afflicting them, never enquire wherefore he contends with them, and therefore nothing appears in them but anger at God and quarrelling with him. They are displeased at God for the dispensations of his providence concerning them, and so they do but make bad worse. This had long been Jerusalem's woeful case, and God took cognizance of it. But,

II. It is promised that Jerusalem's troubles shall at length come to an end, and be transferred to her persecutors (v. 21): *Nevertheless hear this, thou afflicted.* It is often the lot of God's church to be afflicted, and God has always something to say to her then which she will do well to hearken to. "Thou art *drunken, not* as formerly *with wine,* not with the intoxicating cup of Babylon's whoredoms and idolatries, but with the cup of affliction. Know then, for thy comfort," 1. " That the Lord Jehovah is thy Lord and thy God, for all this." It is expressed emphatically (v. 22): " *Thus saith thy Lord, the Lord, and thy God*—the Lord, who is able to help thee, and has wherewithal to relieve thee,—*thy* Lord, who has an incontestable right to thee, and will not alienate it,—thy God, in covenant with thee, and who has undertaken to make thee happy." Whatever the distresses of God's people may be, he will not disown his relation to them, nor have they lost their interest in him and in his promise. 2. " That he is the God *who pleads the cause of his people,* as their patron and protector, who takes what is done against them as done against himself." The cause of God's people, and of that holy religion which they profess, is a righteous cause, otherwise the righteous God would not appear for it; yet it may for a time be run down, and seem as if it were lost. But God will plead it, either by convincing the consciences or confounding the mischievous projects of those that fight against it. He will plead it by clearing up the equity and excellency of it to the world and by giving success to those that act in defence of it. It is his own cause; he has espoused it, and therefore will plead it with jealousy. 3. That they should shortly take leave of their troubles and bid a final farewell to them: "*I will take out of thy hand the cup of trembling,* that bitter cup; it shall pass from thee." Throwing away the cup of trembling will not do, nor saying, " We will not, we cannot, drink it;" but, if we patiently submit, he that put it into our hands will himself take it out of our hands. Nay, it is promised, " *Thou shalt no more drink it again.* God has let fall his controversy with thee, and will not revive the judgment." 4. That their persecutors and oppressors should be made to drink of the same bitter cup of which they had drunk so deeply, *v.* 23. See here, (1.) How insolently they had abused and trampled upon the people of God: *They have said to thy soul,* to thee, to thy life, *Bow down, that we may go over.* Nay, they have said it to thy conscience, taking a pride and pleasure in forcing thee to worship idols. Herein the New-Testament Babylon treads in the steps of that old oppressor, tyrannizing over men's consciences, giving law to them, putting them upon the rack, and compelling them to sinful compliances. Those that set up an infallible head and judge, requiring an implicit faith in his dictates and obedience to his commands, do in effect say to men's souls, *Bow down, that we may go over,* and they say it with delight. (2.) How meanly the people of God (having by their sin lost much of their courage and sense of honour) truckled to them : *Thou hast laid thy body as the ground.* Observe. The oppressors required souls to be subjected to them, that every man should believe and worship just as they would have them. But all they could gain by their threats and violence was that people laid their bodies on the ground ; they brought them to an external and hypocritical conformity, but conscience cannot be forced, nor is it mentioned to their praise that they yielded thus far. But observe, (3.) How justly God will reckon with those who have carried it so imperiously towards his people: *The cup of trembling shall be put into their hand.* Babylon's case shall be as bad as ever Jerusalem's was. Daniel's persecutors shall be thrown into Daniel's den ; let them see how they like it. And the Lord is known by these judgments which he executes.

CHAP. LII.

The greater part of this chapter is on the same subject with the chapter before, concerning the deliverance of the Jews out of Babylon, which yet is applicable to the great salvation Christ has wrought out for us ; but the last three verses are on the same subject with the following chapter, concerning the person of our Redeemer, his humiliation and exaltation. Observe, I. The encouragement that is given to the Jews in captivity to hope that God would deliver them in his own way and time, ver. 1—6. II. The great joy and rejoicing that shall be both with ministers and people upon that occasion, ver. 7—10. III. The call given to those that remained in captivity to shift for their own enlargement when liberty was proclaimed, ver. 11, 12. IV. A short idea given here of the Messiah, which is enlarged upon in the next chapter, ver. 13—15.

AWAKE, awake ; put on thy strength, O Zion ; put on thy beautiful garments, O Jerusalem, the ho y city : for henceforth there shall no more come into thee the uncircumcised and the unclean. 2 Shake thyself from the dust ; arise, *and* sit down, O Jerusalem : loose thyself from the bands of thy neck, O captive daughter of Zion. 3 For thus saith the LORD, Ye have sold yourselves for nought ; and ye shall be redeemed without money. 4 For thus saith the Lord GOD, My people went down aforetime into Egypt to sojourn there ; and the Assyrian oppressed them without cause. 5 Now therefore, what have I here, saith the LORD, that my people is taken away for nought? They that rule over them make them to howl, saith the LORD ; and my name continually every day *is* blasphemed. 6 Therefore my people shall know my name: therefore *they shall know* in that day that I *am* he that doth speak : behold, *it is* I.

Here, I. God's people are stirred up to appear vigorous for their own deliverance, *v.* 1, 2. They had desired that God would *awake* and *put on his strength, ch.* li. 9. Here he calls upon them to *awake* and *put on their strength,* to bestir themselves; let them awake from their despondency, and pluck up their spirits, encourage themselves and one another with the hope that all will be well yet, and no longer succumb and sink under their burden. Let them awake from their distrust, look above them, look about them, look into the promises, look into the providences of God that were working for them, and let them raise their expectations of great things from God. Let them awake from their dullness, sluggishness, and incogitancy, and raise up their endeavours, not to take any irregular courses for their own relief, contrary to the law of nations concerning captives, but to use all likely means to recommend themselves to the favour of the conqueror and make an interest with him. God here gives them an assurance, 1. That they should be reformed by their captivity : *There shall no more come into thee the uncircumcised and the unclean* (*v.* 1); their idolatrous customs should be no more introduced, or at least not harboured ; for when by the marriage of strange wives, in Ezra's time and Nehemiah's, the unclean crept in, they were soon by the vigilance and zeal of the magistrates expelled again, and care was taken that Jerusalem should be a holy city. Thus the gospel Jerusalem is purified by the blood of Christ and the grace of God, and made indeed a holy city. 2. That they should be relieved and rescued out of their captivity, that the bands of their necks should be loosed, that they should not now be any longer oppressed, nay, that they should not be any more invaded, as they had been : *There shall no more come against thee* (so it may be read) *the uncircumcised and the un-*

clean. The heathen shall not again enter into God's sanctuary and profane his temple, Ps. lxxix. 1. This must be understood with a condition. If they keep close to God, and keep in with him, God will keep off, will keep out the enemy; but, if they again corrupt themselves, Antiochus will profane their temple and the Romans will destroy it. However, for some time they shall have peace. And to this happy change, now approaching, they are here called to accommodate themselves. (1.) Let them prepare for joy : " *Put on thy beautiful garments,* no longer to appear in mourning weeds and the habit of thy widowhood. Put on a new face, a smiling countenance, now that a new and pleasant scene begins to open." The beautiful garments were laid up then, when the harps were hung on the willow trees; but, now there is occasion for both, let both be resumed together. "Put on thy strength, and, in order to that, put on thy beautiful garments, in token of triumph and rejoicing." Note, *The joy of the Lord will be our strength* (Neh. viii. 10), and our beautiful garments will serve for armour of proof against the darts of temptation and trouble. And observe, Jerusalem must put on her beautiful garments when she becomes a holy city, for the beauty of holiness is the most amiable beauty, and the more holy we are the more cause we have to rejoice. (2.) Let them prepare for liberty: " *Shake thyself from the dust* in which thou hast lain, and into which thy proud oppressors have trodden thee (*ch.* li.23), or into which thou hast in thy extreme sorrow rolled thyself." *Arise, and set up;* so it may be read. " O Jerusalem! prepare to get clear of all the marks of servitude thou hast been under and to shift thy quarters : *Loose thyself from the bands of thy neck;* be inspired with generous principles and resolutions to assert thy own liberty." The gospel proclaims liberty to those who were bound with fears and makes it their duty to take hold of their liberty. Let those who have been weary and heavily laden under the burden of sin, finding relief in Christ, shake themselves from the dust of their doubts and fears and loose themselves from those bands ; for, *if the Son make them free, they shall be free indeed.*

II. God stirs up himself to appear jealous for the deliverance of his people. He here pleads their cause with himself, and even stirs up himself to come and save them, for his reasons of mercy are fetched from himself. Several things he here considers.

1. That the Chaldeans who oppressed them never acknowledged God in the power they gained over his people, any more than Sennacherib did, who, when God made use of him as an instrument for the correction and reformation of his people, meant not so, *ch.* x. 6, 7. " *You have sold yourselves for nought ;* you got nothing by it, nor did I," *v.* 3. (God considers that when they by sin had sold themselves he himself, who had

the prior, nay, the sole, title to them, *did not increase his wealth by their price,* Ps. xliv. 12. They did not so much as pay their debts to him with it; the Babylonians gave him no thanks for them, but rather reproached and blasphemed his name upon that account.) " And therefore they, having so long had you for nothing, shall at last restore you for nothing : *You shall be redeemed without price,*" as was promised, *ch.* xlv. 13. Those that give nothing must expect to get nothing ; however, God is a debtor to no man.

2. That they had been often before in similar distress, had often smarted for a time under the tyranny of their task-masters, and therefore it was a pity that they should now be left always in the hand of these oppressors (*v.* 4) : " *My people went down into Egypt,* in an amicable way to settle there; but they enslaved them, and ruled them with rigour." And then they were delivered, notwithstanding the pride, and power, and policies of Pharaoh. And why may we not think God will deliver his people now ? At other times *the Assyrian oppressed* the people of God *without cause,* as when the ten tribes were carried away captive by the king of Assyria ; soon afterwards Sennacherib, another Assyrian, with a destroying army oppressed and made himself master of all the defenced cities of Judah. The Babylonians might not unfitly be called *Assyrians,* their monarchy being a branch of the Assyrians ; and they now oppressed them without cause. Though God was righteous in delivering them into their hands, they were unrighteous in using them as they did, and could not pretend a dominion over them as their subjects, as Pharaoh might when they were settled in Goshen, a part of his kingdom. When we suffer by the hands of wicked and unreasonable men it is some comfort to be able to say that as to them it is without cause, that we have not given them any provocation, Ps. vii. 3—5, &c.

3. That God's glory suffered by the injuries that were done to his people (*v.* 5): *What have I here,* what do I get by it, *that my people are taken away for nought ?* God is not worshipped as he used to be in Jerusalem, his altar there is gone and his temple in ruins ; but if, in lieu of that, he were more and better worshipped in Babylon, either by the captives or by the natives, it were another matter—God might be looked upon as in some respects a gainer in his honour by it; but, alas! it is not so. (1.) The captives are so dispirited that they cannot praise him; instead of this they are continually howling, which grieves him and moves his pity : *Those that rule over them make them to howl,* as the Egyptians of old made them to sigh, Exod. ii. 23. So the Babylonians now, using them more hardly, extorted from them louder complaints and made them to howl. This gives us no pleasing idea of the temper the

captives were now in; their complaints were not so rational and pious as they should have been, but brutish rather; they *howled*, Hos. vii. 14. However God heard them, and came down to deliver them, as he did out of Egypt, Exod. iii. 7, 8. (2.) The natives are so insolent that they will not praise him, but, instead of that, they are continually blaspheming, which affronts him and moves his anger. They boasted that they were too hard for God because they were too hard for his people, and set him at defiance, as unable to deliver them, and thus his *name continually every day was blasphemed among them*. When they praised their own idols they *lifted up themselves against the Lord of heaven*, Dan. v. 23. " Now," says God, " this is not to be suffered. I will go down to deliver them; for what honour, what rent, what tribute of praise have I from the world, when my people, who should be to me for a name and a praise, are to me for a reproach? For their oppressors will neither praise God themselves nor let them do it." The apostle quotes this with application to the wicked lives of the Jews, by which God was dishonoured among the Gentiles then, as much as now he was by their sufferings, Rom. ii. 23, 24.

4. That his glory would be greatly manifested by their deliverance (*v.* 6): " *Therefore*, because my name is thus blasphemed, I will arise, and *my people shall know my name*, my name Jehovah." By this name he had made himself known in delivering them out of Egypt, Exod. vi. 3. God will do something to vindicate his own honour, something for his great name; and his people, who have almost lost the knowledge of it, shall know it to their comfort and shall find it their strong tower. They shall know that God's providence governs the world, and all the affairs of it, that it is he who speaks deliverance for them by the word of his power, that it is he only, who at first spoke and it was done. They shall know that God's word, which Israel is blessed with above other nations, shall without fail have its accomplishment in due season, that it is he who speaks by the prophet; it is he, and they do not speak of themselves; for not one iota or tittle of what they say shall fall to the ground.

7 How beautiful upon the mountains are the feet of him that bringeth good tidings, that publisheth peace; that bringeth good tidings of good, that publisheth salvation; that saith unto Zion, Thy God reigneth! 8 Thy watchmen shall lift up the voice; with the voice together shall they sing: for they shall see eye to eye, when the LORD shall bring again Zion. 9 Break forth into joy, sing together,

ye waste places of Jerusalem: for the LORD hath comforted his people, he hath redeemed Jerusalem. 10 The LORD hath made bare his holy arm in the eyes of all the nations; and all the ends of the earth shall see the salvation of our God. 11 Depart ye, depart ye, go ye out from thence, touch no unclean *thing*; go ye out of the midst of her; be ye clean, that bear the vessels of the LORD. 12 For ye shall not go out with haste, nor go by flight: for the LORD will go before you; and the God of Israel *will be* your rereward.

The removal of the Jews from Babylon to their own land again is here spoken of both as a mercy and as a duty; and the application of *v.* 7 to the preaching of the gospel (by the apostle, Rom. x. 15) plainly intimates that that deliverance was a type and figure of the redemption of mankind by Jesus Christ, to which what is here said of their redemption out of Babylon ought to be accommodated.

I. It is here spoken of as a great blessing, which ought to be welcomed with abundance of joy and thankfulness. 1. Those that bring the tidings of their release shall be very acceptable (*v.* 7): *How beautiful upon the mountains*, the mountains round about Jerusalem, over which these messengers are seen coming at a distance, *how beautiful are their feet*, when it is known what tidings they bring!" It is not meant so much of the common posts, or the messengers sent express by the government to disperse the proclamation, but rather of some of the Jews themselves, who, being at the fountain-head of intelligence, had early notice of it, and immediately went themselves, or sent their own messengers, to all parts, to disperse the news, and even to Jerusalem itself, to tell the few who remained there that their brethren would be with them shortly; for it is published not merely as matter of news, but as a proof that Zion's God reigns, for in that language it is published: they say unto Zion, *Thy God reigns*. Those who bring the tidings of peace and salvation, that Cyrus has given orders for the release of the Jews, tidings which were so long expected by those that waited for the consolation of Israel, those *good tidings* (so the original reads it, without the tautology of our translation, *good tidings of good*), put this construction upon it, *O Zion! thy God reigns*. Note, When bad news is abroad this is good news, and when good news is abroad this is the best news, that Zion's God reigns, that God is Zion's God, in covenant with her, and as such he reigns, Ps. cxlvi. 10; Zech. ix. 9. *The Lord has founded Zion, ch.* xiv. 32. All events have their rise in the disposals of the kingdom of his providence and their tendency to the advancement of the kingdom of his grace. This must be applied to the preaching of the gospel, which is a proclamation of peace and salvation; it is gospel indeed, good news, glad tidings, tidings of victory over our spiritual enemies and liberty from our spiritual bondage. The good news is that the Lord Jesus reigns and all power is given to him. Christ himself brought these tidings first (Luke iv. 18, Heb. ii. 3), and of him the text speaks: *How beautiful are his feet!* his feet that were nailed to the cross, how beautiful upon Mount Calvary! his feet when he came *leaping upon the mountains* (Cant. ii. 8), how beautiful were they to those who knew his voice and knew it to be the voice of their beloved! His ministers proclaim these good tidings; they ought to keep their feet clean from the pollutions of the world, and then they ought to be beautiful in the eyes of those to whom they are sent, who sit at their feet, or rather at Christ's in them, to hear his word. They must be *esteemed in love* for *their work's sake* (1 Thess. v. 13), for their message sake, which is well worthy of all acceptation. 2. Those to whom the tidings are brought shall be put thereby into a transport of joy. (1.) Zion's watchmen shall then rejoice because they are surprisingly illuminated, *v.* 8. The watchmen on Jerusalem's walls shall lead the chorus in this triumph. Who they were we are told, *ch.* lxii. 6. They were such as God set on the walls of Jerusalem, to make mention of his name, and to continue instant in prayer to him, till he again *made Jerusalem a praise in the earth.* These watchmen stand upon their watch-tower, waiting for an answer to their prayers (Hab. ii. 1); and therefore when the good news comes they have it first, and the longer they have continued and the more importunate they have been in praying for it the more will they be elevated when it comes: They shall *lift up the voice, with the voice together shall they sing* in concert, to invite others to join with them in their praises. And that which above all things will transport them with pleasure is that *they shall see eye to eye,* that is, face to face. Whereas God had been a God hiding himself, and they could scarcely discern any thing of his favour through the dark cloud of their afflictions, now that the cloud is scattered they shall plainly see it. They shall see *Zion's king eye to eye;* so it was fulfilled when the Word was made flesh and dwelt among us, and there were those that *saw his glory* (John i. 14) *and looked upon it,* 1 John i. 1. They shall see an exact agreement and correspondence between the prophecy and the event, the promise and the performance; they shall see how they look one upon another eye to eye, and be satisfied that the same God spoke the one and did the other. When the Lord shall bring again Zion out of her captivity the

prophets shall thence receive and give fuller discoveries than ever of God's good-will to his people. Applying this also, as the foregoing verse, to gospel times, it is a promise of the pouring out of the Spirit upon gospel ministers, as a spirit of wisdom and revelation, to lead them into all truth, so that they shall see eye to eye, shall see God's grace more clearly than the Old-Testament saints could see it: and they shall herein be unanimous; in these great things concerning the common salvation they shall concur in their sentiments as well as their songs. Nay, St. Paul seems to allude to this when he makes it the privilege of our future state that *we shall see face to face.* (2.) Zion's waste places shall then rejoice because they shall be surprisingly comforted (*v.* 9): *Break forth into joy, sing together, you waste places of Jerusalem;* that is, all parts of Jerusalem, for it was all in ruins, and even those parts that seemed to lie most desolate shall share in the joy; and they, having little expected it, shall break forth into joy, as men that dream. Ps. cxxvi. 1, 2. Let them sing together. Note, Those that share in mercies ought to join in praises. Here is matter for joy and praise. [1.] God's people will have the comfort of this salvation; and what is the matter of our rejoicing ought to be the matter of our thanksgiving. *He has redeemed Jerusalem* (the inhabitants of Jerusalem that were sold into the hands of their enemies) and thereby he has *comforted his people* that were in sorrow. The redemption of Jerusalem is the joy of all God's people, whose character it is that they look for that redemption, Luke ii. 38. [2.] God will have the glory of it, *v.* 10. He *has made bare his holy arm* (manifested and displayed his power) *in the eyes of all the nations.* God's arm is a holy arm, stretched out in purity and justice, in defence of holiness and in pursuance of his promise. [3.] All the world will have the benefit of it. In the great salvation wrought out by our Lord Jesus the *arm of the Lord was revealed and all the ends of the earth were made to see the great salvation,* not as spectators of it only, as they saw the deliverance of the Jews out of Babylon, but as sharers in it; some of all nations, the most remote, shall partake of the benefits of the redemption. This is applied to our salvation by Christ. Luke iii. 6, *All flesh shall see the salvation of God,* that *great salvation.*

II. It is here spoken of as a great business, which ought to be managed with abundance of care and circumspection. When the liberty is proclaimed, 1. Let the people of God hasten out of Babylon with all convenient speed; though they are ever so well settled there, let them not think of taking root in Babylon, but *Depart, depart* (*v.* 11), *go out from the midst of her;* not only those that are in the borders, but those that are in the midst, in the heart of the country, let them be gone. Babylon is no place for Israelites. As soon as they have leave to go, let them lose no time. With this word God stirred up the spirits of those that were moved to go up, Ezra i. 5. And it is a call to all those who are yet in the bondage of sin and Satan to make use of the liberty which Christ has proclaimed to them. And, if the Son *make them free, they shall be free indeed.* 2. Let them take heed of carrying away with them any of the pollutions of Babylon: *Touch no unclean thing.* Now that God makes bare his holy arm for you, *be you holy as he is, and keep yourselves from every wicked thing.* When they came out of Egypt they brought with them the idolatrous customs of Egypt (Ezek. xxiii. 3), which were their ruin; let them take heed of doing so now that they come out of Babylon. Note, When we are receiving any special mercy from God we ought more carefully than ever to watch against all impurity. But especially let those be *clean* who *bear the vessels of the Lord,* that is, the priests, who had the charge of the vessels of the sanctuary (when they were restored by a particular grant) to carry them to Jerusalem, Ezra i. 7; viii. 24, &c. Let them not only avoid touching any unclean thing, but be very careful to *cleanse themselves according to the purification of the sanctuary.* Christians are made to our God spiritual priests, Rev. i. 6. They are to bear the vessels of the Lord, are entrusted to keep the ordinances of God pure and entire; it is a good thing that is committed to them, and they ought to be clean, to wash their hands in innocency and so to compass God's altars and carry his vessels, and keep themselves pure. 3. Let them depend upon the presence of God with them and his protection in their removal (*v.* 12): *You shall not go out with haste.* They were to go with a diligent haste, not to lose time nor linger as Lot in Sodom, but they were not to go with a diffident distrustful haste, as if they were afraid of being pursued (as when they came out of Egypt) or of having the orders for their release recalled and countermanded: no, they shall find that, as for God, his work is perfect, and therefore they need not make more haste than good speed. Cyrus shall give them an honourable discharge, and they shall have an honourable return, and not steal away; *for the Lord will go before them* as their general and commander-in-chief, *and the God of Israel will be their rearward,* or he that will gather up those that are left behind. God will both lead their van and bring up their rear; he will secure them from enemies that either meet them or follow them, for with his favour will he compass them. The pillar of cloud and fire, when they came out of Egypt, sometimes went behind them, to secure their rear (Exod. xiv. 19), and God's presence with them would now be that to them which that pillar was a visible token of. Those that are in the way of their duty are under God's special protection; and he that believes this will not make haste.

13 Behold, my servant shall deal prudently, he shall be exalted and extolled, and be very high. 14 As many were astonished at thee; his visage was so marred more than any man, and his form more than the sons of men: 15 So shall he sprinkle many nations; the kings shall shut their mouths at him: for *that* which had not been told them shall they see; and *that* which they had not heard shall they consider.

Here, as in other places, for the confirming of the faith of God's people and the encouraging of their hope in the promises of temporal deliverances, the prophet passes from them to speak of the great salvation which should in the fulness of time be wrought out by the Messiah. As the prophecy of Christ's incarnation was intended for the ratification of the promise of their deliverance from the Assyrian army, so this of Christ's death and resurrection is to confirm the promise of their return out of Babylon; for both these salvations were typical of the great redemption and the prophecies of them had a reference to that. This prophecy, which begins here and is continued to the end of the next chapter, points as plainly as can be at Jesus Christ; the ancient Jews understood it of the Messiah, though the modern Jews take a great deal of pains to pervert it, and some of ours (no friends therein to the Christian religion) will have it understood of Jeremiah; but Philip, who hence preached Christ to the eunuch, has put it past dispute that *of him speaks the prophet this,* of him and of no other man, Acts viii. 34, 35. Here,

I. God owns Christ to be both commissioned and qualified for his undertaking. 1. He is appointed to it. "He is *my servant,*" whom I employ and therefore will uphold." In his undertaking he does his Father's will, seeks his Father's honour, and serves the interests of his Father's kingdom. 2. He is qualified for it. He *shall deal prudently,* for the *spirit of wisdom and understanding shall rest upon him,* ch. xi. 2. The word is used concerning David when he *behaved himself wisely,* 1 Sam. xviii. 14. Christ is wisdom itself, and, in the contriving and carrying on the work of our redemption, there appeared much of *the wisdom of God in a mystery,* 1 Cor. ii. 7. Christ, when he was here upon earth, dealt very prudently, to the admiration of all.

II. He gives a short prospect both of his humiliation and his exaltation. See here, 1. How he humbled himself: *Many were astonished at him,* as they were at David when by reason of his sorrows and troubles he became a *wonder unto many*, Ps. lxxi. 7. Many wondered to see what base usage he met with, how inveterate people were against him, how inhuman, and what indignities were done him: *His visage was marred more than any man's* when he was buffeted, smitten on the cheek, and crowned with thorns, and *hid not his face from shame and spitting. His face was foul with weeping*, for he was *a man of sorrows;* he that really was *fairer than the children of men* had his face spoiled with the abuses that were done him. Never was man used so barbarously; his form, when he took upon him *the form of a servant,* was more mean and abject than that of any of the sons of men. Those that saw him said, " Surely never man looked so miserably, *a worm and no man,"* Ps. xxii. 6. The *nation abhorred him* (ch. xlix. 7), treated him as the *off-scouring of all things. Never was sorrow like unto his sorrow.* 2. How highly God exalted him, and exalted him because he humbled himself. Three words are used for this (v. 13): *He shall be exalted and extolled and be very high.* God shall exalt him, men shall extol him, and with both he shall be very high, higher than the highest, higher than the heavens. He shall prosper in his work, and succeed in it, and that shall raise him very high. (1.) Many nations shall be the better for him, for *he shall sprinkle them*, and not the Jews only ; the blood of sprinkling shall be applied to their consciences, to purify them. He suffered, and died, and so sprinkled many nations; for in his death there was *a fountain opened*, Zech. xiii. 1. He shall sprinkle many nations by his heavenly doctrine, which shall drop as the rain and distil as the dew. Moses's did so only on one nation (Deut. xxxii. 2), but Christ's on many nations. He shall do it by baptism, which is the washing of the body with pure water, Heb. x. 22. So that this promise had its accomplishment when Christ sent his apostles to disciple all nations, by baptizing or sprinkling them. (2.) The great ones of the nation shall show him respect : *Kings shall shut their mouths at him*, that is, they shall not open their mouths against him, as they have done, to contradict and blaspheme his sacred oracles; nay, they shall acquiesce in, and be well pleased with, the methods he takes of setting up his kingdom in the world; they shall with great humility and reverence receive his oracles and laws, as those who, when they heard Job's wisdom, *after his speech spoke not again*, Job xxix. 9, 22. *Kings shall see and arise*, ch. xlix. 7. (3.) The mystery which was kept secret from the beginning of the world shall by him be *made known to all nations for the obedience of faith*, as the apostle speaks, Rom. xvi 25, 26. *That which had not been told them shall they see ;* the gospel brings to light things new and unheard of, which will awaken the attention and engage the reverence of kings and kingdoms. This

is applied to the preaching of the gospel in the Gentile world, Rom. xv. 21. These words are there quoted according to the Septuagint translation : *To whom he was not spoken of they shall see, and those that have not heard shall understand.* As the things revealed had long been kept secret, so the persons to whom they were revealed had long been kept in the dark; but now they shall see and consider the glory of God shining in the face of Christ, which before they had not been told of—*they had not heard.* That shall be discovered to them by the gospel of Christ which could never be told them by all the learning of their philosophers, or the art of their diviners, or any of their pagan oracles. Much had been said in the Old Testament concerning the Messiah ; much had been told them, and they had heard it. But, as the queen of Sheba found concerning Solomon, what they shall see in him, when he comes, shall far exceed what had been told them. Christ disappointed the expectations of those who looked for a Messiah according to their fancies, as the carnal Jews, but outdid theirs who looked for such a Messiah as was promised. According to their faith, nay, and beyond it, it was to them.

CHAP. LIII

The two great things which the Spirit of Christ in the Old-Testament prophets testified beforehand were the sufferings of Christ and the glory that should follow, 1 Pet. i. 11. And that which Christ himself, when he expounded Moses and all the prophets, showed to be the drift and scope of them all was that Christ ought to suffer and then to enter into his glory, Luke xxiv. 26, 27. But nowhere in all the Old-Testament are these two so plainly and fully prophesied of as here in this chapter, out of which divers passages are quoted with application to Christ in the New-Testament. This chapter is so replenished with the unsearchable riches of Christ that it may be called rather the gospel of the evangelist Isaiah than the prophecy of the prophet Isaiah. We may observe here, I. The reproach of Christ's sufferings—the meanness of his appearance, the greatness of his grief, and the prejudices which many conceived in consequence against his doctrine, ver. 1—3. II. The rolling away of this reproach, and the stamping of immortal honour upon his sufferings, notwithstanding the disgrace and ignominy of them, by four considerations ;—1. That therein he did his Father's will, ver. 4, 6, 10. 2. That thereby he made atonement for the sin of man (ver. 4—6, 8, 11, 12), for it was not for any sin of his own that he suffered, ver. 9. 3. That he bore his sufferings with an invincible and exemplary patience, ver. 7. 4. That he should prosper in his undertaking, and his sufferings should end in his immortal honour, ver. 10—12. By mixing faith with the prophecy of this chapter we may improve our acquaintance with Jesus Christ and him crucified, with Jesus Christ and him glorified, dying for our sins and rising again for our justification.

WHO hath believed our report? And to whom is the arm of the LORD revealed ? 2 For he shall grow up before him as a tender plant, and as a root out of a dry ground : he hath no form nor comeliness ; and when we shall see him, *there is* no beauty that we should desire him. 3 He is despised and rejected of men; a man of sorrows, and acquainted with grief : and we hid as it were *our* faces from him ; he was despised, and we esteemed him not.

The prophet, in the close of the former chapter, had foreseen and foretold the kind reception which the gospel of Christ should find among the Gentiles, that nations and their kings should bid it welcome, that those who had not seen him should believe in him; and though they had not any prophecies among them of gospel grace, which might raise their expectations, and dispose them to entertain it, yet upon the first notice of it they should give it its due weight and consideration. Now here he foretels, with wonder, the unbelief of the Jews, notwithstanding the previous notices they had of the coming of the Messiah in the Old Testament and the opportunity they had of being personally acquainted with him Observe here,

I. The contempt they put upon the gospel of Christ, *v.* 1. The unbelief of the Jews in our Saviour's time is expressly said to be the fulfilling of this word, John xii. 38. And it is applied likewise to the little success which the apostles' preaching met with among Jews and Gentiles, Rom. x. 16. Note, 1. Of the many that hear the report of the gospel there are few, very few, that believe it. It is reported openly and publicly, not whispered in a corner, or confined to the schools, but proclaimed to all; and it is so faithful a saying, and so well worthy of all acceptation, that one would think it should be universally received and believed. But it is quite otherwise; few believed the prophets who spoke before of Christ; when he came himself none of the rulers nor of the Pharisees followed him, and but here and there one of the common people; and, when the apostles carried this report all the world over, some in every place believed, but comparatively very few. To this day, of the many that profess to believe this report, there are few that cordially embrace it and submit to the power of it. 2. *Therefore* people believe not the report of the gospel, because *the arm of the Lord is not revealed* to them; they do not discern, nor will be brought to acknowledge, that divine power which goes along with the word. The *arm of the Lord is made bare* (as was said, *ch.* lii. 10) in the miracles that were wrought to confirm Christ's doctrine, in the wonderful success of it, and its energy upon the conscience; though it is a still voice, it is a strong one; but they do not perceive this, nor do they experience in themselves that working of the Spirit which makes the word effectual. They believe not the gospel because, by rebelling against the light they had, they had forfeited the grace of God, which therefore he justly denied them and withheld from them, and for want of that they believed not. 3. This is a thing we ought to be much affected with; it is to be wondered at, and greatly lamented, and ministers may go to God and complain of it to him, as the prophet here. What a pity is it that such rich grace should be received in vain, that precious souls should perish at the pool's side, because they will not step in and be healed!

II. The contempt they put upon the person of Christ because of the meanness of his appearance, *v.* 2, 3. This seems to come in as a reason why they rejected his doctrine, because they were prejudiced against his person. When he was on earth many that heard him preach, and could not but approve of what they heard, would not give it any regard or entertainment, because it came from one that made so small a figure and had no external advantages to recommend him. Observe here,

1. The low condition he submitted to, and how he abased and emptied himself. The entry he made into the world, and the character he wore in it, were no way agreeable to the ideas which the Jews had formed of the Messiah and their expectations concerning him, but quite the reverse. (1.) It was expected that his extraction would be very great and noble. He was to be the Son of David, of a family that had *a name like to the names of the great men that were in the earth,* 2 Sam. vii. 9. But he sprang out of this royal and illustrious family when it was reduced and sunk, and Joseph, that son of David, who was his supposed father, was but a poor carpenter, perhaps a ship-carpenter, for most of his relations were fishermen. This is here meant by his being *a root out of a dry ground,* his being born of a mean and despicable family, in the north, in Galilee, of a family out of which, like a dry and desert ground, nothing green, nothing great, was expected, in a country of such small repute that it was thought no good thing could come out of it. His mother, being a virgin, was as dry ground, yet from her *he* sprang who is not only fruit, but root. The seed on the stony ground had no root; but, though Christ grew out of a dry ground, he is both *the root and the offspring of David,* the root of the good olive. (2.) It was expected that he should make a public entry, and come in pomp and with observation; but, instead of that, he grew up before God, not before men. God had his eye upon him, but men regarded him not: *He grew up as a tender plant,* silently and insensibly, and without any noise, as the corn, that tender plant, grows up, *we know not how,* Mark iv. 27. Christ rose as a tender plant, which, one would have thought, might easily be crushed, or might be nipped in one frosty night. The gospel of Christ, in its beginning, was as a grain of mustard-seed, so inconsiderable did it seem, Matt. xiii. 31, 32. (3.) It was expected that he should have some uncommon beauty in his face and person, which should charm the eye, attract the heart, and raise the expectations of all that saw him. But there was nothing of this kind in him; not that he was in the least deformed or misshapen, but *he had no form nor comeliness,* nothing extraordinary, which one might have thought to meet with in the countenance of an in-

carnate deity. Those who saw him could not see that there was any beauty in him *that they should desire him, nothing in him more than in another beloved,* Cant. v. 9. Moses, when he was born, was exceedingly fair, to such a degree that it was looked upon as a happy presage, Acts vii. 20; Heb. xi. 23. David, when he was anointed, was *of a beautiful countenance, and goodly to look to,* 1 Sam. xvi. 12 But our Lord Jesus had nothing of that to recommend him. Or it may refer not so much to his person as to the manner of his appearing in the world, which had nothing in it of sensible glory. His gospel is preached, *not with the enticing words of man's wisdom,* but with all plainness, agreeable to the subject. (4.) It was expected that he should live a pleasant life, and have a full enjoyment of all the delights of the sons and daughters of men, which would have invited all sorts to him; but, on the contrary, he was *a man of sorrows and acquainted with grief.* It was not only his last scene that was tragical, but his whole life was so, not only mean, but miserable,

———— but one continued chain
Of labour, sorrow, and consuming pain.
SIR R. BLACKMORE.

Thus, being *made sin for us,* he underwent the sentence sin had subjected us to, that we should *eat in sorrow all the days of our life* (Gen. iii. 17), and thereby relaxed much of the rigour and extremity of the sentence as to us. His condition was, upon many accounts, sorrowful. He was unsettled, had not where to lay his head, lived upon alms, was opposed and menaced, and *endured the contradiction of sinners against himself.* His spirit was tender, and he admitted the impressions of sorrow. We never read that he laughed, but often that he wept. Lentulus, in his epistle to the Roman senate concerning Jesus, says, *" He was never seen to laugh ;"* and so worn and macerated was he with continual grief that when he was but a little above thirty years of age he was taken to be nearly fifty, John viii. 57. Grief was his intimate acquaintance; for he acquainted himself with the grievances of others, and sympathized with them, and he never set his own at a distance; for in his transfiguration he talked of his own decease, and in his triumph he wept over Jerusalem. Let us look unto him and mourn.

2. The low opinion that men had of him, upon this account. Being generally apt to judge of persons and things by the sight of the eye, and according to outward appearance, they saw no beauty in him that they should desire him. There was a great deal of true beauty in him, the beauty of holiness and the beauty of goodness, enough to render him *the desire of all nations ;* but the far greater part of those among whom he lived, and conversed, saw none of this beauty, for it was spiritually discerned. Carnal hearts see no excellency in the Lord Jesus,

302

nothing that should induce them to desire an acquaintance with him or interest in him. Nay, he is not only not desired, but *he is despised and rejected,* abandoned and abhorred, a reproach of men, an abject, one that men were shy of keeping company with and had not any esteem for, a worm and no man. He was despised as a mean man, rejected as a bad man. He was the stone which the builders refused; they would not have him to reign over them. Men, who should have had so much reason as to understand things better, so much tenderness as not to trample upon a man in misery—men whom he came to seek and save rejected him : *" We hid as it were our faces from him,* looked another way, and his sufferings were as nothing to us; though *never sorrow was like unto his sorrow.* Nay, we not only behaved as having no concern for him, but as loathing him, and having him in detestation." It may be read, *He hid as it were his face from us,* concealed the glory of his majesty, and drew a veil over it, and therefore *he was despised and we esteemed him not,* because we could not see through that veil. Christ having undertaken to make satisfaction to the justice of God for the injury man had done him in his honour by sin (and God cannot be injured except in his honour), he did it not only by divesting himself of the glories due to an incarnate deity, but by submitting himself to the disgraces due to the worst of men and malefactors ; and thus by vilifying himself he glorified his Father : but this is a good reason why we should esteem him highly, and study to do him honour ; let *him* be received by us whom men rejected.

4 Surely he hath borne our griefs, and carried our sorrows : yet we did esteem him stricken, smitten of God, and afflicted. 5 But he *was* wounded for our transgressions, *he was* bruised for our iniquities : the chastisement of our peace *was* upon him ; and with his stripes we are healed. 6 All we like sheep have gone astray; we have turned every one to his own way; and the LORD hath laid on him the iniquity of us all. 7 He was oppressed, and he was afflicted, yet he opened not his mouth : he is brought as a lamb to the slaughter, and as a sheep before her shearers is dumb, so he openeth not his mouth. 8 He was taken from prison and from judgment: and who shall declare his generation? For he was cut off out of the land of the living : for the transgression of my people was he stricken.

9 And he made his grave with the wicked, and with the rich in his death; because he had done no violence, neither *was any* deceit in his mouth.

In these verses we have,

I. A further account of the sufferings of Christ. Much was said before, but more is said here, of the very low condition to which he abased and humbled himself, to which he became obedient even to the death of the cross. 1. He had griefs and sorrows; being acquainted with them, he kept up the acquaintance, and did not grow shy, no, not of such melancholy acquaintance. Were griefs and sorrows allotted him? He bore them, and blamed not his lot; he carried them, and did neither shrink from them, nor sink under them. The load was heavy and the way long, and yet he did not tire, but persevered to the end, till he said, *It is finished.* 2. He had blows and bruises; he was *stricken, smitten, and afflicted.* His sorrows bruised him; he felt pain and smart from them; they touched him in the most tender part, especially when God was dishonoured, and when he forsook him upon the cross. All along he was smitten with the tongue, when he was cavilled at and contradicted, put under the worst of characters, and had all manner of evil said against him. At last he was smitten with the hand, with blow after blow. 3. He had wounds and stripes. He was scourged, not under the merciful restriction of the Jewish law, which allowed not above forty stripes to be given to the worst of malefactors, but according to the usage of the Romans. And his scourging, doubtless, was the more severe because Pilate intended it as an equivalent for his crucifixion, and yet it proved a preface to it. He was wounded in his hands, and feet, and side. Though it was so ordered that not a bone of him should be broken, yet he had scarcely in any part a whole skin (how fond soever we are to sleep in one, even when we are called out to suffer for him), but from the crown of his head, which was crowned with thorns, to the soles of his feet, which were nailed to the cross, nothing appeared but wounds and bruises. 4. He was wronged and abused (v. 7): *He was oppressed,* injuriously treated and hardly dealt with. That was laid to his charge which he was perfectly innocent of, that laid upon him which he did not deserve, and in both he was oppressed and injured. *He was afflicted* both in mind and body; being oppressed, he laid it to heart, and, though he was patient, was not stupid under it, but mingled his tears with those of the oppressed, that have no comforter, because *on the side of the oppressors there is power*, Eccl. iv. 1. Oppression is a sore affliction; it has made many a wise man mad (Eccl. vii. 7); but our Lord Jesus, though, when he was oppressed, he was afflicted, kept possession

of his own soul. 5. He was judged and imprisoned, as is implied in his being *taken from prison and judgment, v.* 8. God having made him sin for us, he was proceeded against as a malefactor; he was apprehended and taken into custody, and made a prisoner; he was judged, accused, tried, and condemned, according to the usual forms of law: God filed a process against him, judged him in pursuance of that process, and confined him in the prison of the grave, at the door of which a stone was rolled and sealed. 6. He was *cut off* by an untimely death *from the land of the living*, though he lived a most useful life, did so many good works, and they were all such that one would be apt to think it was for some of them that they stoned him. He was stricken to the death, to the grave which he made *with the wicked* (for he was crucified between two thieves, as if he had been the worst of the three) and yet *with the rich*, for he was buried in a sepulchre that belonged to Joseph, an honourable counsellor. Though he died with the wicked, and according to the common course of dealing with criminals should have been buried with them in the place where he was crucified, yet God here foretold, and Providence so ordered it, that he should make his grave with the innocent, with the rich, as a mark of distinction put between him and those that really deserved to die, even in his sufferings.

II. A full account of the meaning of his sufferings. It was a very great mystery that so excellent a person should suffer such hard things; and it is natural to ask with amazement, "How came it about? What evil had he done?" His enemies indeed looked upon him as suffering justly for his crimes; and, though they could lay nothing to his charge, they *esteemed him stricken, smitten of God, and afflicted, v.* 4. Because they hated him, and persecuted him, they thought that God did, that he was his enemy and fought against him; and therefore they were the more enraged against him, saying, *God has forsaken him; persecute and take him,* Ps. lxxi. 11. Those that are justly smitten are smitten of God, for by him princes decree justice; and so they looked upon him to be smitten, justly put to death as a blasphemer, a deceiver, and an enemy to Cæsar. Those that saw him hanging on the cross enquired not into the merits of his cause, but took it for granted that he was guilty of every thing laid to his charge and that therefore vengeance suffered him not to live. Thus Job's friends esteemed him smitten of God, because there was something uncommon in his sufferings. It is true he was *smitten of God, v.* 10 (or, as some read it, *he was God's smitten and afflicted*, the Son of God, though smitten and afflicted), but not in the sense in which they meant it; for, though he suffered all these things,

1. He never did any thing in the least to

deserve this hard usage. Whereas he was charged with perverting the nation, and sowing sedition, it was utterly false; he had *done no violence*, but went about doing good. And, whereas he was called *that deceiver*, he never deserved that character; for *there was no deceit in his mouth* (v. 9), to which the apostle refers, 1 Pet. ii. 22. *He did no sin, neither was guile found in his mouth.* He never offended either in word or deed, nor could any of his enemies take up that challenge of his, *Which of you convinceth me of sin?* The judge that condemned him owned he found no fault in him, and the centurion that executed him professed that certainly he was a righteous man.

2. He conducted himself under his sufferings so as to make it appear that he did not suffer as an evil-doer; for, though he was *oppressed and afflicted*, yet he *opened not his mouth* (v. 7), no, not so much as to plead his own innocency, but freely offered himself to suffer and die for us, and objected nothing against it. This takes away the scandal of the cross, that he voluntarily submitted to it, for great and holy ends. By his wisdom he could have evaded the sentence, and by his power have resisted the execution; but *thus it was written, and thus it behoved him to suffer. This commandment he received from his Father*, and therefore he was led *as a lamb to the slaughter*, without any difficulty or reluctance (he is the *Lamb of God*); and as a *sheep is dumb before the shearers*, nay, before the butchers, so he *opened not his mouth*, which denotes not only his exemplary patience under affliction (Ps. xxxix. 9), and his meekness under reproach (Ps. xxxviii. 13), but his cheerful compliance with his Father's will. *Not my will, but thine be done. Lo, I come.* By this will we are sanctified, his making his own soul, his own life, an offering for our sin.

3. It was for our good, and in our stead, that Jesus Christ suffered. This is asserted here plainly and fully, and in a very great variety of emphatical expressions.

(1.) It is certain that we are all guilty before God. We have all sinned, and have come short of the glory of God (v. 6): *All we like sheep have gone astray*, one as well as another. The whole race of mankind lies under the stain of original corruption, and every particular person stands charged with many actual transgressions. We have all gone astray from God our rightful owner, alienated ourselves from him, from the ends he designed us to move towards and the way he appointed us to move in. We have gone astray like sheep, which are apt to wander, and are unapt, when they have gone astray, to find the way home again. That is our true character; we are bent to backslide from God, but altogether unable of ourselves to return to him. This is mentioned not only as our infelicity (that we go astray from the green pastures and expose our-

selves to the beasts of prey), but as our iniquity. We affiont God in going astray from him, for we turn aside every one to his own way, and thereby set up ourselves, and our own will, in competition with God and his will, which is the malignity of sin. Instead of walking obediently in God's way, we have turned wilfully and stubbornly to our own way, the way of our own heart, the way that our own corrupt appetites and passions lead us to. We have set up for ourselves, to be our own masters, our own carvers, to do what we will and have what we will. Some think it intimates our own evil way, in distinction from the evil way of others. Sinners have their own iniquity, their beloved sin, which does most easily beset them, their own evil way, that they are particularly fond of and bless themselves in.

(2.) Our sins are our sorrows and our griefs (v. 4), or, as it may be read, *our sicknesses and our wounds :* the LXX. read it, *our sins ;* and so the apostle, 1 Pet. ii. 24. Our original corruptions are the sickness and disease of the soul, an habitual indisposition; our actual transgressions are the wounds of the soul, which put conscience to pain, if it be not seared and senseless. Or our sins are called our *griefs and sorrows* because all our griefs and sorrows are owing to our sins and our sins deserve all our griefs and sorrows, even those that are most extreme and everlasting.

(3.) Our Lord Jesus was appointed and did undertake to make satisfaction for our sins and so to save us from the penal consequences of them. [1.] He was appointed to do it, by the will of his Father; for *the Lord has laid on him the iniquity of us all.* God chose him to be the Saviour of poor sinners, and would have him to save them in this way, by bearing their sins and the punishment of them; not the *idem*—*the same* that we should have suffered, but the *tantundem*—that which was more than equivalent for the maintaining of the honour of the holiness and justice of God in the government of the world. Observe here, *First*, In what way we are saved from the ruin to which by sin we had become liable—by laying our sins on Christ, as the sins of the offerer were laid upon the sacrifice and those of all Israel upon the head of the scape-goat. Our sins were *made to meet upon him* (so the margin reads it); the sins of all that he was to save, from every place and every age, met upon him, and he was met with for them. They were made to fall upon him (so some read it) as those rushed upon him that came with swords and staves to take him. The laying of our sins upon Christ implies the taking of them off from us; we shall not fall under the curse of the law if we submit to the grace of the gospel. They were laid upon Christ when he was *made sin* (that is, a sin-offering) *for us*, and redeemed us from the curse of the law by *being made a curse for us ;* thus he put himself into a capacity to make those easy that come to him heavily laden under the burden of sin. See Ps. xl. 6—12. *Secondly*, By whom this was appointed. It was the Lord that laid our iniquities on Christ; he contrived this way of reconciliation and salvation, and he accepted of the vicarious satisfaction Christ was to make. Christ was delivered to death *by the determinate counsel and foreknowledge of God.* None but God had power to lay our sins upon Christ, both because the sin was committed against him and to him the satisfaction was to be made, and because Christ, on whom the iniquity was to be laid, was his own Son, the Son of his love, and his holy child Jesus, who himself knew no sin. *Thirdly*, For whom this atonement was to be made. It was *the iniquity of us all* that was laid on Christ; for in Christ there is a sufficiency of merit for the salvation of all, and a serious offer made of that salvation to all, which excludes none that do not exclude themselves. It intimates that this is the one only way of salvation. All that are justified are justified by having their sins laid on Jesus Christ, and, though they were ever so many, he is able to bear the weight of them all. [2.] He undertook to do it. God laid upon him our iniquity; but did he consent to it? Yes, he did; for some think that the true reading of the next words (*v.* 7) is, *It was exacted, and he answered;* divine justice demanded satisfaction for our sins, and he engaged to make the satisfaction. He became our surety, not as originally bound with us, but as bail to the action : "Upon me be the curse, my Father." And therefore, when he was seized, he stipulated with those into whose hands he surrendered himself that that should be his disciples' discharge : *If you seek me, let these go their way*, John xviii. 8. By his own voluntary undertaking he made himself responsible for our debt, and it is well for us that he was responsible. Thus *he restored that which he took not away.*

(4.) Having undertaken our debt, he underwent the penalty. Solomon says : *He that is surety for a stranger shall smart for it.* Christ, being surety for us, did smart for it. [1.] *He bore our griefs and carried our sorrows, v.* 4. He not only submitted to the common infirmities of human nature, and the common calamities of human life, which sin had introduced, but he underwent the extremities of grief, when he said, *My soul is exceedingly sorrowful.* He made the sorrows of this present time heavy to himself, that he might make them light and easy for us. Sin is the wormwood and the gall in the affliction and the misery. Christ bore our sins, and so *bore our griefs*, bore them off us, that we should never be pressed above measure. This is quoted (Matt. viii. 17) with application to the compassion Christ had for the sick that came to him to be cured and the power he put forth to cure them.

[2.] He did this by suffering for our sins (*v.* 5) : *He was wounded for our transgressions*, to make atonement for them and to purchase for us the pardon of them. Our sins were the thorns in his head, the nails in his hands and feet, the spear in his side. Wounds and bruises were the consequences of sin, what we deserved and what we had brought upon ourselves, *ch.* i. 6. That these wounds and bruises, though they are painful, may not be mortal, *Christ was wounded for our transgressions*, was tormented or pained (the word is used for the pains of a woman in travail) for our revolts and rebellions. *He was bruised*, or crushed, *for our iniquities;* they were the procuring cause of his death. To the same purport is *v.* 8, *for the transgression of my people was he smitten, the stroke* was *upon him* that should have been upon us; and so some read it, *He was cut off for the iniquity of my people, unto whom the stroke* belonged, or *was due*. He *was delivered* to death *for our offences,* Rom. iv. 25. Hence it is said to be *according to the scriptures*, according to this scripture, that Christ *died for our sins,* 1 Cor. xv. 3. Some read this, *by the transgressions of my people;* that is, by the wicked hands of the Jews, who were, in profession, God's people, he was stricken, was crucified and slain, Acts ii. 23. But, doubtless, we are to take it in the former sense, which is abundantly confirmed by the angel's prediction of the Messiah's undertaking, solemnly delivered to Daniel, that he shall *finish transgression, make an end of sin, and make reconciliation for iniquity,* Dan. ix. 24.

(5.) The consequence of this to us is our peace and healing, *v.* 5. [1.] Hereby we have peace : *The chastisement of our peace was upon him;* he, by submitting to these chastisements, slew the enmity, and settled an amity, between God and man; he *made peace by the blood of his cross.* Whereas by sin we had become odious to God's holiness and obnoxious to his justice, through Christ God is reconciled to us, and not only forgives our sins and saves us from ruin, but takes us into friendship and fellowship with himself, and thereby *peace* (that is, all good) *comes unto us,* Col. i. 20. *He is our peace,* Eph. ii. 14. Christ was in pain that we might be at ease ; he gave satisfaction to the justice of God that we might have satisfaction in our own minds, might be of good cheer, knowing that through him our sins are forgiven us. [2.] Hereby we have healing ; for *by his stripes we are healed.* Sin is not only a crime, for which we were condemned to die and which Christ purchased for us the pardon of, but it is a disease, which tends directly to the death of our souls and which Christ provided for the cure of. By his stripes (that is, the sufferings he underwent) he purchased for us the Spirit and grace of God to mortify our corruptions, which are the distempers of our souls, and to put our souls in a good state of health, that they may be fit to serve God and prepared to enjoy him. And by the doctrine of Christ's cross, and the powerful arguments it furnishes us with against sin, the dominion of sin is broken in us and we are fortified against that which feeds the disease.

(6.) The consequence of this to Christ was his resurrection and advancement to perpetual honour. This makes the offence of the cross perfectly to cease; he yielded himself to die as a sacrifice, as a lamb, and, to make it evident that the sacrifice he offered of himself was accepted, we are told here, *v.* 8, [1.] That he was discharged: *He was taken from prison and from judgment;* whereas he was imprisoned in the grave under a judicial process, lay there under an arrest for our debt, and judgment seemed to be given against him, he was by an express order from heaven taken out of the prison of the grave, an angel was sent on purpose to roll away the stone and set him at liberty, by which the judgment given against him was reversed and taken off; this redounds not only to his honour, but to our comfort; for, being *delivered for our offences,* he was *raised again for our justification.* That discharge of the bail amounted to a release of the debt. [2.] That he was preferred · *Who shall declare his generation?* his *age,* or *continuance* (so the word signifies), the time of his life? He rose *to die no more; death had no more dominion over him.* He that *was dead is alive,* and *lives for evermore;* and who can describe that immortality to which he rose, or number the years and ages of it? And he is advanced to this eternal life because for the transgression of his people he became obedient to death. We may take it as denoting the time of his usefulness, as David is said to *serve his generation,* and so to answer the end of living. Who can declare how great a blessing Christ by his death and resurrection will be to the world? Some by *his generation* understand his spiritual seed: Who can count the vast numbers of converts that shall by the gospel be begotten to him, like the dew of the morning?

When thus exalted he shall live to see
A numberless believing progeny
Of his adopted sons; the godlike race
Exceed the stars that heav'n's high arches
    grace.   Sir R. BLACKMORE.

Of this generation of his let us pray, as Moses did for Israel, *The Lord God of our fathers make them a thousand times so many more as they are, and bless them as he has promised them,* Deut. i. 11.

10 Yet it pleased the LORD to bruise him; he hath put *him* to grief: when thou shalt make his soul an offering for sin, he shall see *his* seed, he shall prolong *his* days, and the pleasure of the LORD shall prosper in his

306

hand. 11 He shall see of the travail of his soul, *and* shall be satisfied: by his knowledge shall my righteous servant justify many; for he shall bear their iniquities. 12 Therefore will I divide him *a portion* with the great, and he shall divide the spoil with the strong; because he hath poured out his soul unto death: and he was numbered with the transgressors; and he bare the sin of many, and made intercession for the transgressors.

In the foregoing verses the prophet had testified very particularly of the sufferings of Christ, yet mixing some hints of the happy issue of them; here he again mentions his sufferings, but largely foretels the glory that should follow. We may observe, in these verses,

I. The services and sufferings of Christ's state of humiliation. Come, and see how he loved us, see what he did for us.

1. He submitted to the frowns of Heaven (*v.* 10): *Yet it pleased the Lord to bruise him, to put him to* pain, or torment, or *grief.* The scripture nowhere says that Christ in his sufferings underwent the wrath of God; but it says here, (1.) That the Lord bruised him, not only permitted men to bruise him, but awakened his own sword against him, Zech. xiii. 7. They esteemed him smitten of God for some very great sin of his own (*v.* 4); now it was true that he was smitten of God, but it was for our sin; the Lord bruised him, for he *did not spare him, but delivered him up for us all,* Rom. viii. 32. He it was that put the bitter cup into his hand, and obliged him to drink it (John xviii. 11), having laid upon him our iniquity. He it was that made him sin and a curse for us, and turned to ashes all his burnt-offering, in token of the acceptance of it, Ps. xx. 3. (2.) That he bruised him so as to put him to grief. Christ accommodated himself to this dispensation, and received the impressions of grief from his Father's delivering him up; and he was troubled to such a degree that it put him into an agony, and he began to be amazed and very heavy. (3.) It pleased the Lord to do this. He determined to do it; it was the result of an eternal counsel; and he delighted in it, as it was an effectual method for the salvation of man and the securing and advancing of the honour of God.

2. He substituted himself in the room of sinners, as a sacrifice. He *made his soul an offering for sin;* he himself explains this (Matt. xx. 28), that *he came to give his life a ransom for many.* When men brought bulls and goats as sacrifices for sin they made them offerings, for they had an interest in them, God having put them under the feet

of man. But Christ made himself an offering; it was his own act and deed. We could not put him in our stead, but he put himself, and said, *Father, into thy hands I commit my spirit,* in a higher sense than David said, or could say it. " Father, *I commit my soul to thee,* I deposit it in thy hands, as the life of a sacrifice and the price of pardons." Thus he shall bear the iniquities of the many that he designed to justify (*v.* 11), shall take away the sin of the world by taking it upon himself, John i. 29. This is mentioned again (*v.* 12): *He bore the sin of many,* who, if they had borne it themselves, would have been sunk by it to the lowest hell. See how this is dwelt upon; for, whenever we think of the sufferings of Christ, we must see him in them bearing our sin.

3. He subjected himself to that which to us is the wages of sin (*v.* 12): *He has poured out his soul unto death,* poured it out as water, so little account did he make of it, when the laying of it down was the appointed means of our redemption and salvation. He *loved not his life unto the death,* and his followers, the martyrs, did likewise, Rev. xii. 11. Or, rather, he poured it out as a drink-offering, to make his sacrifice complete, poured it out as wine, that his blood might be drink indeed, as his flesh is meat indeed to all believers. There was not only a colliquation of his body in his sufferings (Ps. xxii. 14, *I am poured out like water),* but a surrender of his spirit; he poured out that, even unto death, though he is the Lord of life.

4. He suffered himself to be ranked with sinners, and yet offered himself to be an intercessor for sinners, *v.* 12. (1.) It was a great aggravation of his sufferings that he was *numbered with transgressors,* that he was not only condemned as a malefactor, but executed in company with two notorious malefactors, and he in the midst, as if he had been the worst of the three, in which circumstance of his suffering, the evangelist tells us, this prophecy was fulfilled, Mark xv. 27, 28. Nay, the vilest malefactor of all, Barabbas, who was a traitor, a thief, and a murderer, was put in election with him for the favour of the people, and carried it; for they would not have Jesus released, but Barabbas. In his whole life he was numbered among the transgressors; for he was called and accounted a sabbath-breaker, a drunkard, and a friend to publicans and sinners. (2.) It was a great commendation of his sufferings, and redounded very much to his honour, that in his sufferings he *made intercession for the transgressors,* for those that reviled and crucified him; for he prayed, *Father, forgive them,* thereby showing, not only that he forgave them, but that he was now doing that upon which their forgiveness, and the forgiveness of all other transgressors, were to be founded. That prayer was the language of his blood, crying, not for vengeance, but for mercy, and therein it speaks better things than that of Abel, even for those who with wicked hands shed it.

II. The graces and glories of his state of exaltation; and the graces he confers on us are not the least of the glories conferred on him. These are secured to him by the covenant of redemption, which these verses give us some idea of. He promises to make his soul an offering for sin, consents that the Father shall deliver him up, and undertakes to bear the sin of many, in consideration of which the Father promises to glorify him, not only with the glory he had, as God, before the world was (John xvii. 5), but with the glories of the Mediator.

1. He shall have the glory of an everlasting Father. Under this title he was *brought into the world* (*ch.* ix. 6), and he shall not fail to answer the title when he goes out of the world. This was the promise made to Abraham (who herein was a type of Christ), that he should be *the father of many nations* and so be *the heir of the world,* Rom. iv. 13, 17. As he was the root of the Jewish church, and the covenant was made with him and his seed, so is Christ of the universal church and with him and his spiritual seed is the covenant of grace made, which is grounded upon and grafted in the covenant of redemption, which here we have some of the glorious promises of. It is promised,

(1.) That the Redeemer shall have a seed to serve him and to bear up his name, Ps. xxii. 30. True believers are the seed of Christ; the Father gave them to him to be so, John xvii. 6. He died to purchase and purify them to himself, fell to the ground as a corn of wheat, that he might *bring forth much fruit,* John xii. 24. The word, that incorruptible seed, of which they are born again, is his word; the Spirit, the great author of their regeneration, is his Spirit; and it is his image that is impressed upon them.

(2.) That he shall live to see his seed. Christ's children have a living Father, and because he lives they shall live also, for he is their life. Though he died, he rose again, and left not his children orphans, but took effectual care to secure to them the spirit, the blessing, and the inheritance of sons. He shall see a great increase of them; the word is plural, *He shall see his seeds,* multitudes of them, so many that they cannot be numbered.

(3.) That he shall himself continue to take care of the affairs of this numerous family: *He shall prolong his days.* Many, when they see their seed, their seed's seed, wish to depart in peace; but Christ will not commit the care of his family to any other, no, he shall himself live long, and *of the increase of his government and peace there shall be no end,* for he ever lives. Some refer it to believers: *He shall see a seed that shall prolong its days,* agreeing with Ps. lxxxix. 29, 36, *His seed shall endure for ever.* While the world stands Christ will have a church in it, which he himself will be the life of.

(4.) That his great undertaking shall be successful and shall answer expectation: *The pleasure of the Lord shall prosper in his hand.* God's purposes shall take effect, and not one iota or tittle of them shall fail. Note, [1.] The work of man's redemption is in the hands of the Lord Jesus, and it is in good hands. It is well for us that it is in his, for our own hands are not sufficient for us, but he is able to save to the uttermost. It is in his hands who upholds all things. [2.] It is the good pleasure of the Lord, which denotes not only his counsel concerning it, but his complacency in it; and *therefore* God loved him, and was well pleased in him, because he undertook to lay down his life for the sheep. [3.] It has prospered hitherto, and shall prosper, whatever obstructions or difficulties have been, or may be, in the way of it. Whatever is undertaken according to God's pleasure shall prosper, *ch.* xlvi. 10. Cyrus, a type of Christ, shall perform all God's pleasure (*ch.* xliv. 28), and therefore, no doubt, Christ shall. Christ was so perfectly well qualified for his undertaking, and prosecuted it with so much vigour, and it was from first to last so well devised, that it could not fail to prosper, to the honour of his Father and the salvation of all his seed.

(5.) That he shall himself have abundant satisfaction in it (*v.* 11): *He shall see of the travail of his soul, and shall be satisfied.* He shall see it beforehand (so it may be understood); he shall with the prospect of his sufferings have a prospect of the fruit, and he shall be satisfied with the bargain. He shall see it when it is accomplished in the conversion and salvation of poor sinners. Note, [1.] Our Lord Jesus was in travail of soul for our redemption and salvation, in great pain, but with longing desire to be delivered, and all the pains and throes he underwent were in order to it and hastened it on. [2.] Christ does and will see the blessed fruit of the travail of his soul in the founding and building up of his church and the eternal salvation of all that were given him. He will not come short of his end in any part of his work, but will himself see that he has not laboured in vain. [3.] The salvation of souls is a great satisfaction to the Lord Jesus. He will reckon all his pains well bestowed, and himself abundantly recompensed, if the many sons be by him brought through grace to glory. Let him have this, and he has enough. God will be glorified, penitent believers will be justified, and then Christ will be satisfied. Thus, in conformity to Christ, it should be a satisfaction to us if we can do any thing to serve the interests of God's kingdom in the world. Let it always be our meat and drink, as it was Christ's, to do God's will.

2. He shall have the glory of bringing in an everlasting righteousness; for so it was

foretold concerning him, Dan. ix. 24. And here, to the same purport, *By his knowledge* (the knowledge of him, and faith in him) *shall my righteous servant justify many;* for he shall bear the sins of many, and so lay a foundation for our justification from sin. Note, (1.) The great privilege that flows to us from the death of Christ is justification from sin, our being acquitted from that guilt which alone can ruin us, and accepted into God's favour, which alone can make us happy. (2.) Christ, who purchased our justification for us, applies it to us, by his intercession made for us, his gospel preached to us, and his Spirit witnessing in us. The Son of man had power even on earth to forgive sin. (3.) There are many whom Christ justifies, not all (multitudes perish in their sins), yet many, even as many as he gave his life a ransom for, as many as the Lord our God shall call. He shall justify not here and there one that is eminent and remarkable, but those of the many, the despised multitude. (4.) It is by faith that we are justified, by our consent to Christ and the covenant of grace; in this way we are saved, because thus God is most glorified, free grace most advanced, self most abased, and our happiness most effectually secured. (5.) Faith is the knowledge of Christ, and without knowledge there can be no true faith. Christ's way of gaining the will and affections is by enlightening the understanding and bringing that unfeignedly to assent to divine truths. (6.) That knowledge of Christ, and that faith in him, by which we are justified, have reference to him both as a servant to God and as a surety for us. [1.] As one that is employed for God to pursue his designs and secure and advance the interests of his glory. "He is my righteous servant, and as such justifies men." God has authorized and appointed him to do it; it is according to God's will and for his honour that he does it. He is himself righteous, and of his righteousness have all we received. He that is himself righteous (for he could not have made atonement for our sin if he had had any sin of his own to answer for) is *made of God to us righteousness, the Lord our righteousness.* [2.] As one that has undertaken for us. We must know him, and believe in him, as one that bore our iniquities—saved us from sinking under the load by taking it upon himself.

3. He shall have the glory of obtaining an incontestable victory and universal dominion, *v.* 12. Because he has done all these good services, *therefore will I divide him a portion with the great,* and, according to the will of the Father, *he shall divide the spoil with the strong,* as a great general, when he has driven the enemy out of the field, takes the plunder of it for himself and his army, which is both an unquestionable evidence of the victory and a recompense for all the toils and perils of the battle. Note, (1.) God the Father has

engaged to reward the services and sufferings of Christ with great glory : " I will set him among the great, highly exalt him, and give him a name above every name." Great riches are also assigned to him : *He shall divide the spoil,* shall have abundance of graces and comforts to bestow upon all his faithful soldiers. (2.) Christ comes at his glory by conquest. He has set upon the strong man armed, dispossessed him, and divided the spoil. He has vanquished principalities and powers, sin and Satan, death and hell, the world and the flesh ; these are the strong that he has disarmed and taken the spoil of. (3.) Much of the glory with which Christ is recompensed, and the spoil which he has divided, consists in the vast multitudes of willing, faithful, loyal subjects, that shall be brought in to him ; for so some read it : *I will give many to him, and he shall obtain many for a spoil.* God will *give him the heathen for his inheritance and the uttermost parts of the earth for his possession,* Ps. ii. 8. *His dominion shall be from sea to sea.* Many shall be wrought upon by the grace of God to give up themselves to him to be ruled, and taught, and saved by him, and hereby he shall reckon himself honoured, and enriched, and abundantly recompensed for all he did and all he suffered. (4.) What God designed for the Redeemer he shall certainly gain the possession of : " I will divide it to him," and immediately it follows, *He shall divide it,* notwithstanding the opposition that is given to him ; for, as Christ finished the work that was given him to do, so God completed the recompence that was promised him for it ; for he is both able and faithful. (5.) The spoil which God divided to Christ he divides (it is the same word), he distributes, among his followers ; for, when he *led captivity captive,* he received gifts for men, that he might give gifts to men ; for as he has told us (Acts xx. 35) he did himself reckon it more blessed and honourable to give than to receive. Christ conquered for us, and through him we are more than conquerors. He has divided the spoils, the fruits of his conquest, to all that are his : let us therefore cast in our lot among them.

CHAP. LIV.

The death of Christ is the life of the church and of all that truly belong to it ; and therefore very fitly, after the prophet had foretold the sufferings of Christ, he foretels the flourishing of the church, which is a part of his glory, and that exaltation of him which was the reward of his humiliation : it was promised him that he should see his seed, and this chapter is an explication of that promise. It may easily be granted that it has a primary reference to the welfare and prosperity of the Jewish church after their return out of Babylon, which (as other things that happened to them) was typical of the glorious liberty of the children of God, which through Christ we are brought into ; yet it cannot be denied but that it has a further and principal reference to the gospel church, into which the Gentiles were to be admitted. And the first words being understood by the apostle Paul of the New-Testament Jerusalem (Gal. iv. 26, 27) may serve as a key to the whole chapter and that which follows. It is here promised concerning the Christian church, I. That, though the beginnings of it were small, it should be greatly enlarged by the accession of many to it among the Gentiles, who had been wholly destitute of church privileges, ver. 1—5. II. That though sometimes God might seem to withdraw from her, and suspend the tokens of his favour, he would return in mercy and would not return to contend with them any more, ver. 6—10. III. That, though for a while she was in sorrow and under oppres-

sion, she should at length be advanced to greater honour and splendour than ever, ver. 11, 12. IV. That knowledge, righteousness, and peace, should flourish and prevail, ver. 13, 14. V. That all attempts against the church should be baffled, and she should be secured from the malice of her enemies, ver. 14—17.

SING, O barren, thou *that* didst not bear ; break forth into singing, and cry aloud, thou *that* didst not travail with child : for more *are* the children of the desolate than the children of the married wife, saith the LORD. 2 Enlarge the place of thy tent, and let them stretch forth the curtains of thine habitations : spare not, lengthen thy cords, and strengthen thy stakes ; 3 For thou shalt break forth on the right hand and on the left ; and thy seed shall inherit the Gentiles, and make the desolate cities to be inhabited. 4 Fear not ; for thou shalt not be ashamed : neither be thou confounded ; for thou shalt not be put to shame : for thou shalt forget the shame of thy youth, and shalt not remember the reproach of thy widowhood any more. 5 For thy Maker *is* thine husband ; the LORD of hosts *is* his name ; and thy Redeemer the Holy One of Israel ; the God of the whole earth shall he be called.

If we apply this to the state of the Jews after their return out of captivity, it is a prophecy of the increase of their nation after they were settled in their own land. Jerusalem had been in the condition of a wife written childless, or a desolate solitary widow ; but now it is promised that the city should be replenished and the country peopled again, that not only the ruins of Jerusalem should be repaired, but the suburbs of it extended on all sides and a great many buildings erected upon new foundations,— that those estates which had for many years been wrongfully held by the Babylonian Gentiles should now return to the right owners. God will again be a husband to them, and the reproach of their captivity, and the small number to which they were then reduced, shall be forgotten. And it is to be observed that, by virtue of the ancient promise made to Abraham of the increase of his seed, when they were restored to God's favour they multiplied greatly. Those that first came out of Babylon were but 42,000 (Ezra ii. 64), about a fifteenth part of their number when they came out of Egypt ; many came dropping to them afterwards, but we may suppose that to be the greatest number that ever came in a body ; and yet above 500 years after, a little before their destruction by the Romans, a calculation was made by the number of the paschal lambs, and the lowest computation by that rule (allowing only ten to a lamb, whereas they might be twenty) made the nation to be nearly three millions. Josephus says, seven and twenty hundred thousand and odd, *De Bell. Jud. lib. 7. cap.* 17. But we must apply it to the church of God in general ; I mean the kingdom of God among men, God's city in the world, the children of God incorporated. Now observe,

I. The low and languishing state of religion in the world for a long time before Christianity was brought in. It was like one *barren, that did not bear,* or travail with child, was like one desolate, that had lost husband and children ; the church lay in a little compass, and brought forth little fruit. The Jews were indeed by profession married to God, but few proselytes were added to them, the rising generations were unpromising, and serious godliness manifestly lost ground among them. The Gentiles had less religion among them than the Jews ; their proselytes were in a dispersion ; and the children of God, like the children of a broken, reduced family, were *scattered abroad* (John xi. 52), did not appear nor make any figure.

II. Its recovery from this low condition by the preaching of the gospel and the planting of the Christian church.

1. Multitudes were converted from idols to the living God. Those were the church's children that were born again, were partakers of a new and divine nature, by the word. *More were the children of the desolate than of the married wife ;* there were more good people found in the Gentile church (when that was set up) that had long been afar off, and without God in the world, than ever were found in the Jewish church. God's sealed ones out of the tribes of Israel are numbered (Rev. vii. 4), and they were but a remnant compared with the thousands of Israel ; but those of other nations were so many, and crowded in so thickly, and lay so much scattered in all parts, that no man could number them, *v.* 9. Sometimes more of the power of religion is found in those places and families that have made little show of it, and have enjoyed but little of the means of grace, than in others that have distinguished themselves by a flourishing profession ; and then more are the children of the desolate, more the fruits of their righteousness, than those of the married wife ; so the last shall be first. Now this is spoken of as matter of great rejoicing to the church, which is called upon to break forth into singing upon this account. The increase of the church is the joy of all its friends and strengthens their hands. The longer the church has lain desolate the greater will the transports of its joy be when it begins to recover the ground it has lost and to gain more. Even in heaven, among the angels of God, there is an uncommon joy for a sinner that repents, much more for a nation that does so. If the barren fig-tree at length

310

bring forth fruit, it is well ; it shall rejoice, and others with it.

2. The bounds of the church were extended much further than ever before, *v.* 2, 3. (1.) It is here supposed that the present state of the church is a tabernacle state ; it dwells in tents, like the heirs of promise of old (Heb. xi. 9) ; its dwelling is mean and movable, and of no strength against a storm. The city, the continuing city, is reserved for hereafter. A tent is soon taken down and shifted, so the candlestick of church privileges is soon *removed out of its place* (Rev. ii. 5), and, when God pleases, it is as soon fixed elsewhere. (2.) Though it be a tabernacle state, it is sometimes very remarkably a growing state ; and, if this family increase, no matter though it be in a tent. Thus it was in the first preaching of the gospel ; it was the business of the apostles to disciple all nations, to stretch forth the curtains of the church's habitation, to preach the gospel where Christ had not yet been named (Rom. xv. 20), to leaven with the gospel those towns and countries that had hitherto been strangers to it, and so to lengthen the cords of this tabernacle, that more might be enclosed, which would make it necessary to strengthen the stakes proportionably, that they might bear the weight of the enlarged curtains. The more numerous the church grows the more cautious she must be to fortify herself against errors and corruptions, and to support her seven pillars, Prov. ix. 1. (3.) It was a proof of divine power going along with the gospel that in all places it *grew and prevailed mightily,* Acts xix. 20. It broke forth, as the breaking forth of waters—*on the right hand and on the left,* that is, on all hands. The gospel spread itself into all parts of the world ; there were eastern and western churches. The church's seed inherited the Gentiles, and the cities that had been desolate (that is, destitute of the knowledge and worship of the true God) came to be inhabited, that is, to have religion set up in them and the name of Christ professed.

3. This was the comfort and honour of the church (*v.* 4) : "*Fear not, for thou shalt not be ashamed,* as formerly, of the straitness of thy borders, and the fewness of thy children, which thy enemies upbraided thee with, but shalt *forget the reproach of thy youth,* because there shall be no more ground for that reproach." It was the reproach of the Christian religion, in its youth, that none of the rulers or princes of this world embraced it and that it was entertained and professed by a despicable handful of men ; but, after awhile, nations were discipled, the empire became Christian, and then this *reproach of its youth was forgotten.*

4. This was owing to the relation in which God stood to his church, as her husband (*v.* 5) : *Thy Maker is thy husband.* Believers are said to be married to Christ, that they

may *bring forth fruit unto God* (Rom. vii. 4); so the church is married to him, that she may bear and bring up a holy seed to God, that shall be accounted to him for a generation. Jesus Christ is the church's Maker, by whom she is formed into a people—her Redeemer, by whom she is brought out of captivity, the bondage of sin, the worst of slaveries. This is he that espoused her to himself; and, (1.) He is *the Lord of hosts*, who has an irresistible power, an absolute sovereignty, and a universal dominion! Kings who are lords of some hosts, find there are others who are lords of other hosts, as many and mighty as theirs; but God is the Lord of all hosts. (2.) He is *the Holy One of Israel*, the same that presided in the affairs of the Old-Testament church and was the Mediator of the covenant made with it. The promises made to the New-Testament Israel are as rich and sure as those made to the Old-Testament Israel; for he that is our Redeemer is the Holy One of Israel. (3.) He is and shall be called *the Lord of the whole earth*, as God, and as Mediator, for he is the heir of all things; but *then* he shall be called so, when the ends of the earth shall be made to see his salvation, when all the earth shall call him their God and have an interest in him. Long he had been called, in a peculiar manner, *the God of Israel;* but now, the partition wall between Jew and Gentile being taken down, he shall be called *the God of the whole earth* even where he has been, as at Athens itself, an *unknown God.*

6 For the Lord hath called thee as a woman forsaken and grieved in spirit, and a wife of youth, when thou wast refused, saith thy God. 7 For a small moment have I forsaken thee; but with great mercies will I gather thee. 8 In a little wrath I hid my face from thee for a moment; but with everlasting kindness will I have mercy on thee, saith the Lord thy Redeemer. 9 For this *is as* the waters of Noah unto me : for *as* I have sworn that the waters of Noah should no more go over the earth; so have I sworn that I would not be wroth with thee, nor rebuke thee. 10 For the mountains shall depart, and the hills be removed; but my kindness shall not depart from thee, neither shall the covenant of my peace be removed, saith the Lord that hath mercy on thee.

The seasonable succour and relief which God sent to his captives in Babylon, when they had a discharge from their bondage there, are here foretold, as a type and figure of all those consolations of God which are treasured up for the church in general and all believers in particular, in the covenant of grace.

I. Look back to former troubles, and in comparison with them God's favours to his people appear very comfortable, *v.* 6—8. Observe, 1. How sorrowful the church's condition had been. She had been as a woman forsaken, whose husband was dead, or had fallen out with her, though she was *a wife of youth*, upon which account she is grieved in spirit, takes it very ill, frets, and grows melancholy upon it; or she had been as one refused and rejected, and therefore full of discontent. Note, Even those that are espoused to God may yet seem to be refused and forsaken, and may be grieved in spirit under the apprehensions of being so. Those that shall never be forsaken and left in despair may yet for a time be perplexed and in distress. The similitude is explained (*v.* 7, 8) : *For a small moment have I forsaken thee. In a little wrath I hid my face from thee.* When God continues his people long in trouble he seems to forsake them; so their enemies construe it (Ps. lxxi. 11); so they themselves misinterpret it, *ch.* xlix. 14. When they are comfortless under their troubles, because their prayers and expectations are not answered, God hides his face from them, as if he regarded them not nor designed them any kindness. God owns that he had done this; for he keeps an account of the afflictions of his people, and, though he never turned his face against them (as against the wicked, Ps. xxxiv. 16), he remembers how often he turned his back upon them. This arose indeed from his displeasure. It was in wrath that he forsook them and hid his face from them (*ch.* lvii. 17); yet it was but in a little wrath : not·that God's wrath ever is a little thing, or to be made light of (*Who knows the power of his anger?*), but little in comparison with what they had deserved, and what others justly suffer, on whom the full vials of his wrath are poured out. He did not stir up all his wrath. But God's people, though they be sensible of ever so small a degree of God's displeasure, cannot but be grieved in spirit because of it. As for the continuance of it, it was but *for a moment*, a *small* moment; for God does not keep his anger against his people for ever; no, it is soon over. As he is slow to anger, so he is swift to show mercy. The afflictions of God's people, as they are light, so they are but for a moment, a cloud that presently blows over. 2. How sweet the returns of mercy would be to them when God should come and comfort them according to the time that he had afflicted them. God called them into covenant with himself when they were forsaken and grieved; he called them out of their afflictions when they were most pressing, *v.* 6. God's anger endures for a moment, but he will gather his people when they think themselves neglected, will gather them out of their dispersions, that they may return in a body to their own land,—will gather them into his arms, to protect them, embrace them, and bear them up,—and will gather them at last to himself, *will gather the wheat into the barn.* He will have mercy on them. This supposes the turning away of his anger and the admitting of them again into his favour. God's gathering his people takes rise from his mercy, not any merit of theirs; and it is with *great mercies* (*v.* 7), *with everlasting kindness, v.* 8. The wrath is little, but the mercies are great; the wrath is for a moment, but the kindness everlasting. See how one is set over against the other, that we may neither despond under our afflictions nor despair of relief.

II. Look forward to future dangers, and in defiance of them God's favours to his people appear very constant, and his kindness everlasting; for it is formed into a covenant, here called a *covenant of peace,* because it is founded in reconciliation and is inclusive of all good. Now,

1. This is as firm as the covenant of providence. It is *as the waters of Noah,* that is, as that promise which was made concerning the deluge that there should never be the like again to disturb the course of summer and winter, seed-time and harvest, *v.* 9. God then contended with the world in great wrath, and for a full year, and yet at length returned in mercy, everlasting mercy; for he gave his word, which was as inviolable as his oath, that Noah's flood should never return, that he would never drown the world again; see Gen. viii. 21, 22; ix. 11. And God has ever since kept his word, though the world has been very provoking; and he will keep it to the end; for the world that now is is reserved unto fire. And thus inviolable is the covenant of grace: *I have sworn that I would not be wroth with thee,* as I have been, *and rebuke thee,* as I have done. He will not be so angry with them as to cast them off and break his covenant with them (Ps. lxxxix. 34), nor rebuke them as he has rebuked the heathen, to destroy them, and *put out their name for ever and ever,* Ps. ix. 5.

2. It is more firm than the strongest parts of the visible creation (*v.* 10): The *mountains shall depart,* which are called *everlasting mountains,* and *the hills be removed,* though they are called *perpetual hills,* Hab. iii. 6. Sooner shall they remove than God's covenant with his people be broken. Mountains have sometimes been shaken by earthquakes, and removed; but the promises of God were never broken by the shock of any event. The day will come when all *the mountains shall depart* and all *the hills be removed,* not only the tops of them covered, as they were by the waters of Noah, but the roots of them torn up; for the earth and all the

works that are therein shall be burned up; but then the covenant of peace between God and believers shall continue in the everlasting bliss of all those who are the children of that covenant. Mountains and hills signify great men, men of bulk and figure. Do these mountains seem to support the skies (as Atlas) and bear them up? They shall depart and be removed. Creature-confidences shall fail us. *In vain is salvation hoped for from those hills and mountains.* But the firmament is firm, and answers to its name, when those who seem to prop it are gone. When our friends fail us our God does not, nor does his kindness depart? Do these mountains threaten, and seem to top the skies, and bid defiance to them, as Pelion and Ossa? Do the kings of the earth, and the rulers, set themselves against the Lord? They shall depart and be removed. Great mountains, that stand in the way of the salvation of the church, shall be *made plain* (Zech. iv. 7); but God's kindness shall never depart from his people, for whom he loves he loves to the end; nor shall the covenant of his peace ever be removed, for he is the Lord that has mercy on his people. *Therefore* the covenant is immovable and inviolable, because it is built not on our merit, which is a mutable uncertain thing, but on God's mercy, which is from everlasting to everlasting.

11 O thou afflicted, tossed with tempest, *and* not comforted, behold, I will lay thy stones with fair colours, and lay thy foundations with sapphires. 12 And I will make thy windows of agates, and thy gates of carbuncles, and all thy borders of pleasant stones. 13 And all thy children *shall be* taught of the Lord; and great *shall be* the peace of thy children. 14 In righteousness shalt thou be established: thou shalt be far from oppression; for thou shalt not fear: and from terror; for it shall not come near thee. 15 Behold, they shall surely gather together, *but* not by me: whosoever shall gather together against thee shall fall for thy sake. 16 Behold, I have created the smith that bloweth the coals in the fire, and that bringeth forth an instrument for his work; and I have created the waster to destroy. 17 No weapon that is formed against thee shall prosper; and every tongue *that* shall rise against thee in judgment thou shalt condemn. This *is* the heritage of the servants of the Lord, and their righteousness *is* of me, saith the Lord.

Very precious promises are here made to the church in her low condition, that God would not only continue his love to his people under their troubles as before, but that he would restore them to their former prosperity, nay, that he would raise them to greater prosperity than any they had yet enjoyed. In the foregoing chapter we had the humiliation and exaltation of Christ; here we have the humiliation and exaltation of the church; for, if we suffer with him, we shall reign with him. Observe,

I. The distressed state the church is here reduced to by the providence of God (*v.* 11): " *O thou afflicted,* poor, and indigent society, that art *tossed with tempests,* like a ship driven from her anchors by a storm and hurried into the ocean, where she is ready to be swallowed up by the waves, and in this condition *not comforted* by any compassionate friend that will sympathize with thee, or suggest to thee any encouraging considerations (Eccl. iv. 1), not comforted by any allay to thy trouble, or prospect of deliverance out of it." This was the condition of the Jews in Babylon, and afterwards, for a time, under Antiochus. It is often the condition of Christian churches and of particular believers; without are fightings, within are fears; they are like the disciples in a storm, ready to perish; and where is their faith?

II. The glorious state the church is here advanced to by the promise of God. God takes notice of the afflicted distressed state of his church, and comforts her, when she is most disconsolate and has no other comforter. Let the people of God, when they are afflicted and tossed, think they hear God speaking comfortably to them by these words, taking notice of their griefs and fears, what afflictions they are under, what distresses they are in, and what comforts their case calls for. When they bemoan themselves, God bemoans them, and speaks to them with pity: *O thou afflicted, tossed with tempests, and not comforted;* for in all their afflictions he is afflicted. But this is not all; he engages to raise her up out of her affliction, and encourages her with the assurance of the great things he would do for her, both for her prosperity and for the securing of that prosperity to her.

1. Whereas now she lay in disgrace, God promises that which would be her beauty and honour, which would make her easy to herself and amiable in the eyes of others.

(1.) This is here promised by a similitude taken from a city, and it is an apt similitude, for the church is the city of the living God, the heavenly Jerusalem. Whereas now Jerusalem lay in ruins, a heap of rubbish, it shall be not only rebuilt, but beautified, and appear more splendid than ever; the stones shall be laid not only firm, but fine, laid with fair colours; they shall be *glistering stones,* 1 Chron. xxix. 2. The foundations

shall be laid or garnished with *sapphires,* the most precious of the precious stones here mentioned; for Christ (the church's foundation), and the foundation of the apostles and prophets, are precious above any thing else. The windows of this house, city, or temple, shall be made of *agates,* the gates of *carbuncles,* and all the *borders* (the walls that enclose the courts, or the boundaries by which her limits are marked, the mere-stones) shall be *of pleasant stones, v.* 12. Never was this literally true; but it intimates, [1.] That, God having graciously undertaken to build his church, we may expect that to be done for it, that to be wrought in it, which is very great and uncommon. [2.] That the glory of the New-Testament church shall far exceed that of the Jewish church, not in external pomp and splendour, but in those gifts and graces of the Spirit which are infinitely more valuable, that wisdom which is *more precious than rubies* (Prov. iii. 15), than the precious onyx and the sapphire, and which the *topaz of Ethiopia cannot equal,* Job xxviii. 16, 19. [3.] That the wealth of this world, and those things of it that are accounted most precious, shall be despised by all the true living members of the church, as having no value, no glory, in comparison with that which far excels. That which the children of this world lay up among their treasures, and too often in their hearts, the children of God make pavements of, and put under their feet, the fittest place of it.

(2.) It is here promised in the particular instances of those things that shall be the beauty and honour of the church, which are knowledge, holiness, and love, the very image of God, in which man was created, renewed, and restored. And these are the sapphires and carbuncles, the precious and pleasant stones, with which the gospel temple shall be enriched and beautified, and these wrought by the power and efficacy of those doctrines which the apostle compares to gold, silver, and precious stones, that are to be *built upon the foundation,* 1 Cor. iii. 12. Then the church is all glorious, [1.] When it is full of the knowledge of God, and that is promised here (*v.* 13): *All thy children shall be taught of the Lord.* The church's children, being born of God, shall be taught of God; being his children by adoption, he will take care of their education. It was promised (*v.* 1) that the church's children should be many; but lest we should think that being many, as sometimes it happens in numerous families, they will be neglected, and not have instruction given them so carefully as if they were but few, God here takes that work into his own hand: *They shall all be taught of the Lord;* and none teaches like him. *First,* It is a promise of the means of instruction and those means authorized by a divine institution: *They shall all be taught of God,* that is, they shall be taught by those whom God shall appoint and whose labours shall be under his direction and blessing. He will ordain the methods of instruction, and by his word and ordinances will diffuse a much greater light than the Old-Testament church had. Care shall be taken for the teaching of the church's children, that knowledge may be transmitted from generation to generation, and that all may be enriched with it, from the least even to the greatest. *Secondly,* It is a promise of the Spirit of illumination. Our Saviour quotes it with application to gospel grace, and makes it to have its accomplishment in all those that were brought to believe in him (John vi. 45): *It is written in the prophets, They shall be all taught of God,* whence he infers that those, and those only, come to him by faith that have heard and learned of the Father, that are *taught by him as the truth is in Jesus,* Eph. iv. 21. There shall be a plentiful effusion of the Spirit of grace upon Christians, to *teach them all things,* John xiv. 26. [2.] When the members of it live in love and unity among themselves: *Great shall be the peace of thy children.* Peace may be taken here for all good. As where no knowledge of God is no good can be expected, so those that are taught of God to know him are in a fair way to prosper for both worlds. *Great peace have those that* know and *love God's law,* Ps. cxix. 165. But it is often put for love and unity; and so we may take it. All that are taught of God are taught to *love one another* (1 Thess. iv. 9) and that will keep peace among the church's children and prevent their falling out by the way. [3.] When holiness reigns; for that above any thing is the beauty of the church (*v.* 14): *In righteousness shalt thou be established.* The reformation of manners, the restoration of purity, the due administration of public justice, and the prevailing of honesty and fair dealing among men, are the strength and stability of any church or state. The kingdom of God, set up by the gospel of Christ, is not meat and drink, but this righteousness and peace, holiness and love.

2. Whereas now she lay in danger, God promises that which would be her protection and security.

(1.) God engages here that though, in the day of her distress, without were fightings and within were fears, now she shall be safe from both. [1.] There shall be no fears within (*v.* 14): "*Thou shalt be far from oppression.*" Those that have oppressed thee shall be removed, those that would oppress thee shall be restrained, and therefore thou shalt not fear, but mayest look upon it as a thing at a great distance, that thou art now in no danger of. Thou shalt be far from terror, not only from evil, but from the fear of evil, for it shall not come near thee so as to do thee any hurt or to put thee in any fright." Note, Those are far from terror that are far from oppression; for it is as great a terror as can fall on a peo-

314

ple to have the rod of government turned into the serpent of oppression, because against this there is no fence, nor is there any flight from it. [2.] There shall be no fightings without. Though attempts should be made upon them to insult them, to invade their country, or besiege their towns, they should all be in vain, and none of them succeed, *v.* 15. It is granted, "*They shall surely gather together against thee;* thou must expect it." The confederate force of hell and earth will be renewing their assaults. As long as there is a devil in hell, and a persecutor out of it, God's people must expect frequent alarms; but, *First,* God will not own them, will not give them either commission or countenance; they gather together, hand joins in hand, but it is *not by me.* God gave them no such order as he did to Sennacherib, *to take the spoil, and to take the prey, ch.* x. 6. And therefore, *Secondly,* Their attempt will end in their own ruin: "*Whosoever shall gather together against thee,* be they ever so many and ever so mighty, they shall not only be baffled, but they *shall fall for thy sake,* or they shall fall before thee, which shall be the just punishment of their enmity to thee." God will make them to fall for the sake of the love he bears to his church and the care he has of it, in answer to the prayers made by his people, and in pursuance of the promises made to them. "They shall fall, that thou mayest stand," Ps. xxvii. 2.

(2.) That we may with the greatest assurance depend upon God for the safety of his church, we have here, [1.] The power of God over the church's enemies asserted, *v.* 16. The truth is they have *no power but what is given them from above,* and he that gave them their power can limit and restrain them. *Hitherto they shall go, and no further. First,* They cannot carry on their design without arms and weapons of war; and the smith that makes those weapons is God's creature, and he gave him his skill to work in iron and brass (Exod. xxxi. 3, 4) and particularly to make proper instruments for warlike purposes. It is melancholy to think, as if men did not die fast enough of themselves, how ingenious and industrious they are to make instruments of death and to find out ways and means to kill one another. *The smith blows the coals in the fire,* to make his iron malleable, to soften it first, that it may be hardened into steel, and so *he may bring forth an instrument proper for the work of those that seek to destroy.* It is the iron age that is the age of war. But *God has created the smith,* and therefore can tie his hands, so that the project of the enemy shall miscarry (as many a project has done) for want of arms and ammunition. Or the smith that forges the weapons is perhaps put here for the council of war that forms the design, blows the coals of contention, and brings forth the plan of the war; these can do no more than God will let them.

Secondly, They cannot carry it on without men, they must have soldiers, and it is *God that created the waster to destroy.* Military men value themselves upon their great offices and splendid titles, and even the common soldiers call themselves *gentlemen ;* but God calls them *wasters made to destroy,* for wasting and destruction are their business. They think their own ingenuity, labour, and experience, made them soldiers ; but it was God that created them, and gave them strength and spirit for that hazardous employment ; and therefore he not only can restrain them, but will serve his own purposes and designs by them. [2.] The promise of God concerning the church's safety solemnly laid down, as *the heritage of the servants of the Lord* (v. 17), as that which they may depend upon and be confident of, that God will protect them from their adversaries both in camps and courts. *First,* From their field-adversaries, that think to destroy them by force and violence, and dint of sword : " *No weapon that is formed against thee* (though ever so artfully formed by the smith that blows the coals, *v.* 16, though ever so skilfully managed by the waster that seeks to destroy) *shall prosper ;* it shall not prove strong enough to do any harm to the people of God ; it shall miss its mark, shall fall out of the hand or perhaps recoil in the face of him that uses it against thee." It is the happiness of the church that *no weapon formed against it shall prosper* long, and therefore the folly of its enemies will at length be made manifest to all, for they are but preparing instruments of ruin for themselves. *Secondly,* From their law-adversaries, that think to run them down under colour of right and justice. When the weapons of war do not prosper there are tongues that rise in judgment. Both are included in the gates of hell, that seek to destroy the church ; for they had their courts of justice, as well as their magazines and military stores, in their gates. The tongues that rise in judgment against the church are such as either demand a dominion over it, as if God's children were their lawful captives, pretending an authority to oppress their consciences, or they are such as misrepresent them, and falsely accuse them, and by slanders and calumnies endeavour to make them odious to the people and obnoxious to the government. This the enemies of the Jews did, to incense the kings of Persia against them, Ezra iv. 12 ; Esth. iii. 8. " But these insulting threatening tongues thou shalt condemn ; thou shalt have wherewith to answer their insolent demands, and to put to silence their malicious reflections. Thou shalt do it *by well-doing* (1 Pet. ii. 15), by doing that which will make thee manifest in the consciences even of thy adversaries, that thou art not what thou art represented to be. *Thou shalt condemn them,* that is, God shall condemn them for thee. *He shall bring forth thy right-*

eousness as the light, Ps. xxxvii. 6. Thou shalt condemn them as Noah condemned the old world that reproached him, by building the ark, and so saving his house, in contempt of their contempts." The day is coming when God will reckon with wicked men for all their hard speeches which they have spoken against him, Jude 15.

The last words refer not only to this promise, but to all that go before : *This is the heritage of the servants of the Lord.* God's servants are his sons, for he has provided an inheritance for them, rich, sure, and indefeasible. God's promises are their *heritage for ever* (Ps. cxix. 111) ; *and their righteousness is of me, saith the Lord.* God will clear up the righteousness of their cause before men. It is with him, for he knows it ; it is with him, for he will plead it. Or their reward for their righteousness, and for all that which they have suffered unrighteously, is of God, that God who judges in the earth, and with whom *verily there is a reward for the righteous.* Or their righteousness itself, all that in them which is good and right, is of God, who works it in them ; it is of Christ who is made righteousness to them. In those for whom God designs a heritage hereafter he will work righteousness now.

CHAP. LV.

As we had much of Christ in the 53rd chapter, and much of the church of Christ in the 54th chapter, so in this chapter we have much of the covenant of grace made with us in Christ. The " sure mercies of David," which are promised here (ver. 3), are applied by the apostle to the benefits which flow to us from the resurrection of Christ (Acts xiii. 34), which may serve as a key to this chapter ; not but that it was intended for the comfort of the people of God that lived then, especially of the captives in Babylon, and others of the dispersed of Israel ; but unto us was this gospel preached as well as unto them, and much more clearly and fully in the New Testament. Here is, I. A free and gracious invitation to all to come and take the benefit of gospel grace, ver. 1. II. Pressing arguments to enforce this invitation, ver. 2—4. III. A promise of the success of this invitation among the Gentiles, ver. 5. IV. An exhortation to repentance and reformation, with great encouragement given to hope for pardon thereupon, ver. 6—9. V. The ratification of all this, with the certain efficacy of the word of God, ver. 10, 11. And a particular instance of the accomplishment of it in the return of the Jews out of their captivity, which was intended for a sign of the accomplishment of all these other promises.

HO, every one that thirsteth, come ye to the waters, and he that hath no money ; come ye, buy, and eat ; yea, come, buy wine and milk without money and without price. 2 Wherefore do ye spend money for *that which is* not bread ? and your labour for *that which* satisfieth not ? Hearken diligently unto me, and eat ye *that which is* good, and let your soul delight itself in fatness. 3 Incline your ear, and come unto me : hear, and your soul shall live ; and I will make an everlasting covenant with you, *even* the sure mercies of David. 4 Behold, I have given him *for* a witness to the people, a leader and commander to the people. 5

Behold, thou shalt call a nation *that* thou knowest not, and nations *that* knew not thee shall run unto thee because of the LORD thy God, and for the Holy One of Israel; for he hath glorified thee.

Here, I. We are all invited to come and take the benefit of that provision which the grace of God has made for poor souls in the new covenant, of that which is the *heritage of the servants of the Lord* (*ch.* liv. 17), and not only their heritage hereafter, but their cup now, *v.* 1. Observe,

1. Who are invited: *Ho, every one.* Not the Jews only, to whom first the word of salvation was sent, but the Gentiles, the poor and the maimed, the halt and the blind, are called to this marriage supper, whoever can be picked up out of the highways and the hedges. It intimates that in Christ there is enough for all and enough for each, that ministers are to make a general offer of life and salvation to all, that in gospel times the invitation should be more largely made than it had been and should be sent to the Gentiles, and that the gospel covenant excludes none that do not exclude themselves. The invitation is published with an *Oyez*—*Ho*, take notice of it. *He that has ears to hear let him hear.*

2. What is the qualification required in those that shall be welcome—they must thirst. All shall be welcome to gospel grace upon those terms only that gospel grace be welcome to them. Those that are satisfied with the world and its enjoyments for a portion, and seek not for a happiness in the favour of God,—those that depend upon the merit of their own works for a righteousness, and see no need they have of Christ and his righteousness,—these do not thirst; they have no sense of their need, are in no pain or uneasiness about their souls, and therefore will not condescend so far as to be beholden to Christ. But those that thirst are invited to the waters, as those that labour, and are heavy-laden, are invited to Christ for rest. Note, Where God gives grace he first gives a thirsting after it; and, where he has given a thirsting after it, he will give it, Ps. lxxxi. 10.

3. Whither they are invited: *Come you to the waters.* Come to the water-side, to the ports, and quays, and wharfs, on the navigable rivers, into which goods are imported; thither come and buy, for that is the market-place of foreign commodities; and to us they would have been for ever foreign if Christ had not brought in an everlasting righteousness. Come to Christ; for he is the fountain opened; he is the rock smitten. Come to holy ordinances, to those streams that make glad the city of our God; come to them, and though they may seem to you plain and common things, like waters, yet to those who believe in Christ the things

signified will be as wine and milk, abundantly refreshing. Come to the healing waters; come to the living waters. Whoever will, let him come, and *partake of the waters of life*, Rev. xxii. 17. Our Saviour referred to it, John vii. 37. *If any man thirst, let him come to me and drink.*

4. What they are invited to do. (1.) *Come, and buy.* Never did any tradesman court customers that he hoped to get by as Christ courts us to that which we only are to be the gainers by. " Come and buy, and we can assure you you shall have a good bargain, which you will never repent of nor lose by. Come and buy; make it your own by an application of the grace of the gospel to yourselves; make it your own upon Christ's terms, nay, your own upon any terms, and stand not hesitating about the terms, nor deliberating whether you shall agree to them." (2.) " *Come, and eat ;* make it still more your own, as that which we eat is more our own than that which we only buy." We must buy the truth, not that we may lay it by to be looked at, but that we may feed and feast upon it, and that the spiritual life may be nourished and strengthened by it. We must buy necessary provisions for our souls, be willing to part with any thing, though ever so dear to us, so that we may but have Christ and his graces and comforts. We must part with sin, because it is an opposition to Christ, part with all opinion of our own righteousness, as standing in competition with Christ, and part with life itself, and its most necessary supports, rather than quit our interest in Christ. And, when we have bought what we need, let us not deny ourselves the comfortable use of it, but enjoy it, and eat the labour of our hands: *Buy, and eat.*

5. What is the provision they are invited to: " *Come, and buy wine and milk*, which will not only quench the thirst" (fair water would do that), " but nourish the body, and revive the spirits." The world comes short of our expectations. We promise ourselves, at least, water in it, but we are disappointed of that, as *the troops of Tema*, Job vi. 19. But Christ outdoes our expectations. We come to the waters, and would be glad of them, but we find there wine and milk, which were the staple commodities of the tribe of Judah, and which the Shiloh of that tribe is furnished with to entertain the *gathering of the people to him*, Gen. xlix. 10, 12. *His eyes shall be red with wine and his teeth white with milk.* We must come to Christ, to have milk for babes, to nourish and cherish those that are but lately born again ; and with him strong men shall find that which will be a cordial to them : they shall have wine to make glad their hearts. We must part with our puddle-water, nay, with our poison, that we may procure this wine and milk.

6. The free communication of this provision : *Buy it without money, and without price.*

A strange way of buying, not only without ready money (that is common enough), but without any money, or the promise of any; yet it seems not so strange to those who have observed Christ's counsel to Laodicea, that was wretchedly poor, to *come and buy,* Rev. iii. 17, 18. Our buying without money intimates, (1.) That the gifts offered us are invaluable and such as no price can be set upon. Wisdom is that which cannot be gotten for gold. (2.) That he who offers them has no need of us, nor of any returns we can make him. He makes us these proposals, not because he has occasion to sell, but because he has a disposition to give. (3.) That the things offered are already bought and paid for. Christ purchased them at the full value, with price, not with money, but with *his own blood,* 1 Pet. i. 19. (4.) That we shall be welcome to the benefits of the promise, though we are utterly unworthy of them, and cannot make a tender of any thing that looks like a valuable consideration. We ourselves are not of any value, nor is any thing we have or can do, and we must own it, that, if Christ and heaven be ours, we may see ourselves for ever indebted to free grace.

II. We are earnestly pressed and persuaded (and O that we would be prevailed with!) to accept this invitation, and make this good bargain for ourselves.

1. That which we are persuaded to is to hearken to God and to his proposals: "*Hearken diligently unto me, v.* 2. Not only give me the hearing, but approve of what I say, and apply it to yourselves (*v.* 3): *Incline your ear,* as you do to that which you find yourselves concerned in and pleased with; bow the ear, and let the proud heart stoop to the humbling methods of the gospel; bend the ear this way, that you may hear with attention and remark; hear, *and come unto me;* not only come and treat with me, but comply with me, come up to my terms;" accept God's offers as very advantageous; answer his demands as very fit and reasonable.

2. The arguments used to persuade us to this are taken,

(1.) From the unspeakable wrong we do to ourselves if we neglect and refuse this invitation: "*Wherefore do you spend money for that which is not bread,* which will not yield you, no, not beggar's food, dry bread, when with me you may have wine and milk without money? *Wherefore do you spend your labour* and toil *for that which* will not be so much as dry bread to you, for it *satisfies not?*" See here, [1.] The vanity of the things of this world. They are not bread, not proper food for a soul; they afford no suitable nourishment or refreshment. Bread is the staff of the natural life, but it affords no support at all to the spiritual life. All the wealth and pleasure in the world will not make one meal's meat for a soul. Eternal truth and eternal good are the only food

for a rational and immortal soul, the life of which consists in reconciliation and conformity to God, and in union and communion with him, which the things of the world will not at all befriend. *They satisfy not;* they yield not any solid comfort and content to the soul, nor enable it to say, "Now I have what I would have." Nay, they do not satisfy even the appetites of the body. The more men have the more they would have, Eccl. i. 8. Haman was unsatisfied in the midst of his abundance. They flatter, but they do not fill; they please for a while, like the dream of a hungry man, who awakes and his soul is empty. They soon surfeit, but they never satisfy; they cloy a man, but do not content him, or make him truly easy. It is all vanity and vexation. [2.] The folly of the children of this world. They spend their money and labour for these uncertain unsatisfying things. Rich people live by their money, poor people by their labour; but both mistake their truest interest, while the one is trading, the other toiling, for the world, both promising themselves satisfaction and happiness in it, but both miserably disappointed. God vouchsafes compassionately to reason with them: "Wherefore do you thus act against your own interest? Why do you suffer yourselves to be thus imposed upon?" Let us reason thus with ourselves, and let the result of these reasonings be a holy resolution not to *labour for the meat that perishes, but for that which endures to everlasting life,* John vi. 27. Let all the disappointments we meet with in the world help to drive us to Christ, and lead us to seek for satisfaction in him only. This is the way to make that sure which will be made sure.

(2.) From the unspeakable kindness we do to ourselves if we accept this invitation and comply with it. [1.] Hereby we secure to ourselves present pleasure and satisfaction: "If you hearken to Christ, you *eat that which is good,* which is both wholesome and pleasant, good in itself and good for you." God's good word and promise, a good conscience, and the comforts of God's good Spirit, are a continual feast to those that hearken diligently and obediently to Christ. Their souls shall *delight themselves in fatness,* that is, in the richest and most grateful delights. Here the invitation is not, "Come, and *buy,*" lest that should discourage, but, "Come, and *eat;* come and entertain yourselves with that which will be abundantly pleasing; eat, O friends!" It is sad to think that men should need to be courted thus to their own bliss. [2.] Hereby we secure to ourselves lasting happiness: "*Hear, and your soul shall live;* you shall not only be saved from perishing eternally, but you shall be eternally blessed:" for less than that cannot be the life of an immortal soul. The words of Christ are spirit and life, life to spirits (John vi 33, 63), the words of this life, Acts v. 20. On what easy terms is happiness offered to us! It is but "Hear, and you shall live." [3.] The great God graciously secures all this to us: "Come to me, *and I will make an everlasting covenant with you,* will put myself into covenant-relations and under covenant-engagements to you, and thereby settle upon you *the sure mercies of David.*" Note, *First,* If we come to God to serve him, he will covenant with us to do us good and make us happy; such are his condescension to us and concern for us. *Secondly,* God's covenant with us is an everlasting covenant—its contrivance from everlasting, its continuance to everlasting. *Thirdly,* The benefits of this covenant are mercies suited to our case, who, being miserable, are the proper objects of mercy. They come from God's mercy, and are ordered every way in kindness to us. *Fourthly,* They are the mercies of David, such mercies as God promised to David (Ps. lxxxix. 28, 29, &c.), which are called *the mercies of David his servant,* and are appealed to by Solomon, 2 Chron. vi. 42. It shall be a covenant as sure as that with David, Jer. xxxiii. 25, 26. The covenant of royalty was a figure of the covenant of grace, 2 Sam. xxiii. 5. Or, rather, by David here we are to understand the Messiah. Covenant-mercies are all *his* mercies; they are purchased by him; they are promised in him; they are treasured up in his hand, and out of his hand they are dispensed to us. He is the Mediator and trustee of the covenant; to him this is applied, Acts xiii. 34. They are the τὰ ὅσια (the word used there, and by the LXX. here) — *the holy things* of David, for they are confirmed by the holiness of God (Ps. lxxxix. 35) and are intended to advance holiness among men. *Fifthly,* They are sure mercies. The covenant, being well-ordered in all things, is sure. It is sure in the general proposal of it; God is real and sincere, serious and in earnest, in the offer of these mercies. It is sure in the particular application of it to believers; God's gifts and callings are without repentance. They are the mercies of David, and therefore sure, for in Christ the promises are all yea and amen.

III. Jesus Christ is promised for the making good of all the other promises which we are here invited to accept of, *v.* 4. He is that David whose sure mercies all the blessings and benefits of the covenant are. "And God has *given him* in his purpose and promise, has constituted and appointed him, and in the fulness of time will as surely send him as if he had already come, to be all that to us which is necessary to our having the benefit of these preparations." He has given him freely; for what more free than a gift? There was nothing in us to merit such a favour, but Christ is the gift of God. We want one, 1. To attest the truth of the promises which we are invited to take the benefit of; and Christ is given *for a witness*

318

that God is willing to receive us into his favour upon gospel terms, to confirm the promises made unto the fathers, that we may venture our souls upon those promises with entire satisfaction. Christ is a faithful witness, we may take his word—a competent witness, for he lay in the bosom of the Father from eternity, and was perfectly apprised of the whole matter. Christ, as a prophet, testifies the will of God to the world; and to believe is to receive his testimony. 2. To assist us in closing with the invitation, and coming up to the terms of it. We know not how to find the way to the waters where we are to be supplied, but Christ is given to be *a leader.* We know not what to do that we may be qualified for it, and become sharers in it, but he is given for *a commander,* to show us what to do and enable us to do it. Much difficulty and opposition lie in our way to Christ; we have spiritual enemies to grapple with, but, to animate us for the conflict, we have a good captain, like Joshua, a leader and commander to tread our enemies under our feet and to put us in possession of the land of promise. Christ is a commander by his precept and a leader by his example; our business is to obey him and follow him.

IV. The Master of the feast being fixed, it is next to be furnished with guests, for the provision shall not be lost, nor made in vain, *v.* 5. 1. The Gentiles shall be called to this feast, shall be invited out of the highways and the hedges: " *Thou shalt call a nation that thou knowest not,* that is, that was not formerly called and owned as thy nation, that thou didst not send prophets to as to Israel, the people whom God knew above all the families of the earth." The Gentiles shall now be favoured as they never were before; their knowing God is said to be rather their *being known of God,* Gal. iv. 9. 2. They shall come at the call: *Nations that knew not thee shall run unto thee;* those that had long been afar off from Christ shall be made nigh; those that had been running from him shall run to him, with the greatest speed and alacrity imaginable. There shall be a concourse of believing Gentiles to Christ, who, being lifted up from the earth, will draw all men to him. Now see the reason, (1.) Why the Gentiles will thus flock to Christ; it is *because of the Lord his God,* because he is the Son of God, and is declared to be so with power, because they now see his God is one with whom they have to do, and there is no coming to him as their God but by making an interest in his Son. Those that are brought to be acquainted with God, and understand how the concern lies between them and him, cannot but run to Jesus Christ, who is the only Mediator between God and man, and there is no coming to God but by him. (2.) Why God will bring them to him; it is because he is the Holy One of Israel, true to his promises, and he has promised to glorify him by giving him the heathen for his inheritance. When Greeks began to enquire after Christ he said, *The hour has come that the Son of man should be glorified,* John xii. 22, 23. And his being glorified in his resurrection and ascension was the great argument by which multitudes were wrought upon to run to him.

6 Seek ye the LORD while he may be found, call ye upon him while he is near: 7 Let the wicked forsake his way, and the unrighteous man his thoughts : and let him return unto the LORD, and he will have mercy upon him ; and to our God, for he will abundantly pardon. 8 For my thoughts *are* not your thoughts, neither *are* your ways my ways, saith the LORD. 9 For *as* the heavens are higher than the earth, so are my ways higher than your ways, and my thoughts than your thoughts. 10 For as the rain cometh down, and the snow from heaven, and returneth not thither, but watereth the earth, and maketh it bring forth and bud, that it may give seed to the sower, and bread to the eater : 11 So shall my word be that goeth forth out of my mouth : it shall not return unto me void, but it shall accomplish that which I please, and it shall prosper *in the thing* whereto I sent it. 12 For ye shall go out with joy, and be led forth with peace : the mountains and the hills shall break forth before you into singing, and all the trees of the field shall clap *their* hands. 13 Instead of the thorn shall come up the fir-tree, and instead of the brier shall come up the myrtle-tree : and it shall be to the LORD for a name, for an everlasting sign *that* shall not be cut off.

We have here a further account of that covenant of grace which is made with us in Jesus Christ, both what is required and what is promised in the covenant, and of those considerations that are sufficient abundantly to confirm our believing compliance with and reliance on that covenant. This gracious discovery of God's good-will to the children of men is not to be confined either to the Jew or to the Gentile, to the Old Testament or to the New, much less to the captives in Babylon. No, both the precepts and the promises are here given to all, to *every one that thirsts after happiness, v.* 1. And who does not ? Hear this, and live.

I. Here is a gracious offer made of par-

don, and peace, and all happiness, to poor sinners, upon gospel terms, *v.* 6, 7.

1. Let them pray, and their prayers shall be heard and answered (*v.* 6) : " *Seek the Lord while he may be found.* Seek him whom you have left by revolting from your allegiance to him and whom you have lost by provoking him to withdraw his favour from you. *Call upon him* now *while he is near,* and within call." Observe here,

(1.) The duties required. [1.] " Seek the Lord. Seek to him, and enquire of him, as your oracle. *Ask the law at his mouth. What wilt thou have me to do ?* Seek for him, and enquire after him, as your portion and happiness ; seek to be reconciled to him and acquainted with him, and to be happy in his favour. Be sorry that you have lost him ; be solicitous to find him ; take the appointed method of finding him, making use of Christ as your way, the Spirit as your guide, and the word as your rule." [2.] " Call upon him. Pray to him, to be reconciled, and, being reconciled, pray to him for every thing else you have need of."

(2.) The motives made use of to press these duties upon us : *While he may be found* —*while he is near.* [1.] It is implied that now God is near and will be found, so that it shall not be in vain to seek him and to call upon him. Now his patience is waiting on us, his word is calling to us, and his Spirit striving with us. Let us now improve our advantages and opportunities ; for now is the accepted time. But, [2.] There is a day coming when he will be afar off, and will not be found, when the day of his patience is over, and his Spirit will strive no more. There may come such a time in this life, when the heart is incurably hardened ; it is certain that at death and judgment the door will be *shut,* Luke xvi. 26 ; xiii. 25, 26. Mercy is now offered, but then judgment without mercy will take place.

2. Let them repent and reform, and their sins shall be pardoned, *v.* 7. Here is a call to the unconverted, to *the wicked and the unrighteous*—to the wicked, who live in known gross sins, to the unrighteous, who live in the neglect of plain duties : to them is the word of this salvation sent, and all possible assurance given that penitent sinners shall find God a pardoning God. Observe here,

(1.) What it is to repent. There are two things involved in repentance :—[1.] It is to turn from sin ; it is to forsake it. It is to leave it, and to leave it with loathing and abhorrence, never to return to it again. The wicked must *forsake his way,* his evil way, as we would forsake a false way that will never bring us to the happiness we aim at, and a dangerous way, that leads to destruction. Let him not take one step more in that way. Nay, there must be not only a change of the way, but a change of the mind ; the unrighteous must *forsake his thoughts.* Repentance, if it be true, strikes at the root,

319

and washes the heart from wickedness. We must alter our judgments concerning persons and things, dislodge the corrupt imaginations and quit the vain pretences under which an unsanctified heart shelters itself. Note, It is not enough to break off from evil practices, but we must enter a caveat against evil thoughts. Yet this is not all: [2.] To repent is to *return to the Lord ;* to return to him as our God, our sovereign Lord, against whom we have rebelled, and to whom we are concerned to reconcile ourselves; it is to return to the Lord as the fountain of life and living waters, which we had forsaken for broken cisterns.

(2.) What encouragement we have thus to repent. If we do so, [1.] God *will have mercy.* He will not deal with us as our sins have deserved, but will have compassion on us. Misery is the object of mercy. Now both the consequences of sin, by which we have become truly miserable (Ezek. xvi. 5, 6), and the nature of repentance, by which we are made sensible of our misery and are brought to bemoan ourselves (Jer. xxxi. 18), both these make us objects of pity, and with God there are tender mercies. [2.] *He will abundantly pardon. He will multiply to pardon* (so the word is), as we have multiplied to offend. Though our sins have been very great and very many, and though we have often backslidden and are still prone to offend, yet God will repeat his pardon, and welcome even backsliding children that return to him in sincerity.

II. Here are encouragements given us to accept this offer and to venture our souls upon it. For, look which way we will, we find enough to confirm us in our belief of its validity and value.

1. If we look up to heaven, we find God's counsels there high and transcendent, his thoughts and ways infinitely above ours, *v.* 8, 9. The wicked are urged to forsake their evil ways and thoughts (*v.* 7) and to return to God, that is, to bring their ways and thoughts to concur and comply with his; "for" (says he) "my thoughts and ways are not as yours. Yours are conversant only about things beneath; they are of the earth earthy : but mine are above, *as the heaven is high above the earth ;* and, if you would approve yourselves true penitents, yours must be so too, and your affections must be set on things above." Or, rather, it is to be understood as an encouragement to us to depend upon God's promise to pardon sin, upon repentance. Sinners may be ready to fear that God will not be reconciled to them, because they could not find in their hearts to be reconciled to one who should have so basely and so frequently offended them. "But" (says God) "my thoughts in this matter are not as yours, but as far above them as heaven is above the earth." They are so in other things. Men's sentiments concerning sin, and Christ, and holiness, concerning this world and the other, are vastly different from God's ; but in nothing more than in the matter of reconciliation. We think God apt to take offence and backward to forgive—that, if he forgives once, he will not forgive a second time. Peter thought it a great deal to *forgive seven times* (Matt. xviii. 21), and a hundred pence go far with us ; but God meets returning sinners with pardoning mercy ; he forgives freely, and as he gives : it is without upbraiding. We forgive and cannot forget ; but, when God forgives sin, he remembers it no more. Thus God invites sinners to return to him, by possessing them with good thoughts of him, as Jer. xxxi. 20.

2. If we look down to this earth, we find God's word there powerful and effectual, and answering all its great intentions, *v.* 10, 11. Observe here, (1.) The efficacy of God's word in the kingdom of nature. He saith to the snow, Be thou on the earth ; he appoints when it shall come, to what degree, and how long it shall lie there ; he saith so *to the small rain and the great rain of his strength,* Job xxxvii. 6. And according to his order they come down from heaven, and do *whatsoever he commands them upon the face of the world, whether it be for correction, or for his land, or for mercy, v.* 12, 13. It returns not *re infectâ—without having accomplished its end,* but waters the earth, which he is therefore said to do *from his chambers,* Ps. civ. 13. And the watering of the earth is in order to its fruitfulness. Thus he makes it to *bring forth and bud,* for the products of the earth depend upon the dews of heaven ; and thus it gives not only *bread to the eater,* present maintenance to the owner and his family, but *seed* likewise *to the sower,* that he may have food for another year. The husbandman must be a sower as well as an eater, else he will soon see the end of what he has. (2.) The efficacy of his word in the kingdom of providence and grace, which is as certain as the former : " *So shall my word be,* as powerful in the mouth of prophets as it is in the hand of providence ; *it shall not return unto me void,* as unable to effect what it was sent for, or meeting with an insuperable opposition ; no, *it shall accomplish that which I please"* (for it is the declaration of his will, according to the counsel of which he works all things) *" and it shall prosper in the thing for which I sent it."* This assures us, [1.] That the promises of God shall all have their full accomplishment in due time, and not one iota or tittle of them shall fail, 1 Kings viii. 56. These promises of mercy and grace shall have as real an effect upon the souls of believers, for their sanctification and comfort, as ever the rain had upon the earth, to make it fruitful. [2.] That according to the different errands on which the word is sent it will have its different effects. If it be not a savour of life unto life, it will be a savour

of death unto death; if it do not convince the conscience and soften the heart, it will sear the conscience and harden the heart; if it do not ripen for heaven, it will ripen for hell. See *ch.* vi. 9. One way or other, it will take effect. [3.] That Christ's coming into the world, as the dew from heaven (Hos. xiv. 5), will not be in vain. For, if Israel be not gathered, he will be glorious in the conversion of the Gentiles; to them therefore the tenders of grace must be made when the Jews refuse them, that the wedding may be furnished with guests and the gospel not return void.

3. If we take a special view of the church, we shall find what great things God has done, and will do, for it (*v.* 12, 13): *You shall go out with joy, and be led forth with peace.* This refers, (1.) To the deliverance and return of the Jews out of Babylon. They shall go out of their captivity, and be led forth towards their own land again. God will go before them as surely, though not as sensibly, as before their fathers in the pillar of cloud and fire. They shall go out, not with trembling, but with triumph, not with any regret to part with Babylon, or any fear of being fetched back, but *with joy* and *peace*. Their journey home over the mountains shall be pleasant, and they shall have the good-will and good wishes of all the countries they pass through. *The hills* and their inhabitants *shall,* as in a transport of joy, *break forth into singing;* and, if the people should altogether hold their peace, even *the trees of the field* would attend them with their applauses and acclamations. And, when they come to their own land, it shall be ready to bid them welcome; for, whereas they expected to find it all overgrown with briers and thorns, it shall be set with *fir-trees and myrtle-trees:* for, though it lay desolate, yet it *enjoyed its sabbaths* (Lev. xxvi. 34), which, when they were over, like the land after the sabbatical year, it was the better for. And this shall redound much to the honour of God and be to him *for a name.* But, (2.) Without doubt it looks further. This shall be *for an everlasting sign,* that is, [1.] The redemption of the Jews out of Babylon shall be a ratification of those promises that relate to gospel times. The accomplishment of the predictions relating to that great deliverance would be a pledge and earnest of the performance of all the other promises; for thereby it shall appear that *he is faithful who has promised.* [2.] It shall be a representation of the blessings promised and a type and figure of them. *First,* Gospel grace will set those at liberty that were in bondage to sin and Satan. They *shall go out and be led forth.* Christ shall make them free, and then they shall be free indeed. *Secondly,* It will fill those with joy that were melancholy. Ps. xiv. 7, *Jacob shall rejoice, and Israel shall be glad.* The earth and the inferior part of the creation shall

share in the joy of this salvation, Ps. xcvi. 11, 12. *Thirdly,* It will make a great change in men's characters. Those that were as thorns and briers, good for nothing but the fire, nay, hurtful and vexatious, shall become graceful and useful as the fir-tree and the myrtle-tree. Thorns and briers came in with sin and were the fruits of the curse, Gen. iii. 18. The raising of pleasant trees in the room of them signifies the removal of the curse of the law and the introduction of gospel blessings. The church's enemies were as thorns and briers; but, instead of them, God will raise up friends to be her protection and ornament. Or it may denote the world's growing better; instead of a generation of thorns and briers, there shall come up a generation of fir-trees and myrtles; the children shall be wiser and better than the parents. And, *fourthly,* in all this God shall be glorified. It shall be to him for a name, by which he will be made known and praised, and by it the people of God shall be encouraged. It shall be for an everlasting sign of God's favour to them, assuring them that, though it may for a time be clouded, it shall never *be cut off.* The covenant of grace is an everlasting covenant; for the present blessings of it are signs of everlasting ones.

CHAP. LVI.

After the exceedingly great and precious promises of gospel grace, typified by temporal deliverances, which we had in the foregoing chapter, we have here, I. A solemn charge given to us all to make conscience of our duty, as we hope to have the benefit of those promises, ver. 1, 2. II. Great encouragement given to strangers that were willing to come under the bonds of the covenant, assuring them of the blessings of the covenant, ver. 3—8. III. A high charge drawn up against the watchmen of Israel, that were careless and unfaithful in the discharge of their duty (ver. 9—12), which seems to be the beginning of a new sermon, by way of reproof and threatening, which is continued in the following chapters. And the word of God was intended for conviction, as well as for comfort and instruction in righteousness.

THUS saith the LORD, Keep ye judgment, and do justice: for my salvation *is* near to come, and my righteousness to be revealed. 2 Blessed *is* the man *that* doeth this, and the son of man *that* layeth hold on it; that keepeth the sabbath from polluting it, and keepeth his hand from doing any evil.

The scope of these verses is to show that when God is coming towards us in a way of mercy we must go forth to meet him in a way of duty.

I. God here tells us what are his intentions of mercy to us (*v.* 1): *My salvation is near to come*—the great salvation wrought out by Jesus Christ (for that was the salvation of which the *prophets enquired and searched diligently,* 1 Pet. i. 10), typified by the salvation of the Jews from Sennacherib or out of Babylon. Observe, 1. The gospel salvation is the salvation of the Lord. It was contrived and brought about by him; he glories in it as his. 2. In that salvation God's righteousness is revealed, which is so much the beauty of the gospel that St. Paul makes this the ground of his glorying in it. (Rom. i. 17), *because therein is the righteousness of God revealed from faith to faith.* The law revealed that righteousness of God by which all sinners stand condemned, but the gospel reveals that by which all believers stand acquitted. 3. The Old-Testament saints saw this salvation coming, and drawing near to them, long before it came; and they had notice by the prophets of its approach. As Daniel understood by Jeremiah's books the approach of the redemption out of Babylon, at the end of seventy years, so others understood by Daniel's books the approach of our redemption by Christ at the end of seventy weeks of years.

II. He tells us what are his expectations of duty from us, in consideration thereof. Say not, " We see the salvation near, and therefore we may live as we list, for there is no danger now of missing it or coming short of it;" that is turning the grace of God into wantonness. But, on the contrary, when the salvation is near double your guard against sin. Note, The fuller assurances God gives us of the performance of his promises the stronger obligations he lays us under to obedience. The salvation here spoken of has now come; yet, there being still a further salvation in view, the apostle presses duty upon us Christians with the same argument. Rom. xiii. 11, *Now is our salvation nearer than when we believed.* That which is here required to qualify and prepare us for the approaching salvation is,

1. That we be honest and just in all our dealings: *Keep you judgment and do justice.* Walk by rule, and make conscience of what you say and do, that you do no wrong to any. Render to all their dues exactly, and, in exacting what is due to you, keep up a court of equity in your own bosom, to moderate the rigours of the law. Be ruled by that golden rule, " Do as you would be done by." Magistrates must administer justice wisely and faithfully. This is required to evidence the sincerity of our faith and repentance, and to open the way of mercy. *Repent for the kingdom of heaven is at hand.* God is true to us; let us be so to one another.

2. That we religiously observe the sabbath day, *v.* 2. We are not just if we rob God of his time. Sabbath-sanctification is here put for all the duties of the first table, the fruits of our love to God, as justice and judgment are put for all those of the second table, the fruits of our love to our neighbour. Observe, (1.) The duty required, which is to *keep the sabbath*, to keep it as a talent we are to trade with, as a treasure we are entrusted with. " Keep it holy; keep it safe; keep it with care and caution; keep it from polluting it. Allow neither yourselves nor others either to violate the holy rest or omit the holy work of that day." If this be intended primarily for the Jews in Babylon, it was fit that they should be particularly

322

put in mind of this, because when, by reason of their distance from the temple, they could not observe the other institutions of their law, yet they might distinguish themselves from the heathen by putting a difference between God's day and other days. But it being required more generally of man, and *the son of man*, it intimates that sabbath-sanctification should be a duty in gospel times, when the bounds of the church should be enlarged and other rites and ceremonies abolished. Observe, Those that would keep the sabbath from polluting it must put on resolution, must not only do this, but lay hold on it, for sabbath time is precious, but is very apt to slip away if we take not great care; and therefore we must lay hold on it and keep our hold, must do it and persevere in it. (2.) The encouragement we have to do this duty: *Blessed is he that doeth it.* The way to have the blessing of God upon our employments all the week is to make conscience, and make a business, of sabbath-sanctification; and in doing so we shall be the better qualified to do judgment and justice. The more godliness the more honesty, 1 Tim. ii. 2.

3. That we have nothing to do with sin: *Blessed is the man* that *keeps his hand from doing evil*, any wrong to his neighbour, in body, goods, or good name—or, more generally, any thing that is displeasing to God and hurtful to his own soul. Note, The best evidence of our having kept the sabbath well will be a care to keep a good conscience all the week. By this it will appear that we have been in the mount with God if our faces shine in a holy conversation before men.

3 Neither let the son of the stranger, that hath joined himself to the LORD, speak, saying, The LORD hath utterly separated me from his people: neither let the eunuch say, Behold, I *am* a dry tree. 4 For thus saith the LORD unto the eunuchs that keep my sabbaths, and choose *the things* that please me, and take hold of my covenant; 5 Even unto them will I give in mine house and within my walls a place and a name better than of sons and of daughters: I will give them an everlasting name, that shall not be cut off. 6 Also the sons of the stranger, that join themselves to the LORD, to serve him, and to love the name of the LORD, to be his servants, every one that keepeth the sabbath from polluting it, and taketh hold of my covenant; 7 Even them will I bring to my holy mountain, and make them joyful in my house of prayer: **their**

burnt-offerings and their sacrifices *shall be* accepted upon mine altar; for mine house shall be called a house of prayer for all people. 8 The LORD God which gathereth the outcasts of Israel saith, Yet will I gather *others* to him, beside those that are gathered unto him.

The prophet is here, in God's name, encouraging those that were hearty in joining themselves to God and yet laboured under great discouragements. 1. Some were discouraged because they were not of the seed of Abraham. They had *joined themselves to the Lord*, had bound their souls with a bond to be his for ever (this is the root and life of religion, to break off from the world and the flesh, and devote ourselves entirely to the service and honour of God); but they questioned whether God would accept them, because they were of *the sons of the stranger*, v. 3. They were Gentiles, strangers to the commonwealth of Israel and aliens from the covenants of promise, and therefore feared they had no part nor lot in the matter. They said, " *The Lord has utterly separated me from his people*, and will not own me as one of them, nor admit me to their privileges." It was often said that there should be *one law for the stranger and for him that was born in the land* (Exod. xii. 49), and yet they came to this melancholy conclusion. Note, Unbelief often suggests things to the discouragement of good people which are directly contrary to what God himself has said, things which he has expressly guarded against. Let not the *sons of the stranger* therefore say thus, for they have no reason to say it. Note, Ministers must have answers ready for the disquieting fears and jealousies of weak Christians, which, how unreasonable soever, they must take notice of. 2. Others were discouraged because they were not fathers in Israel. The eunuch said, *Behold, I am a dry tree.* So he looked upon himself, and it was his grief; so others looked upon him, and it was his reproach. He was thought to be of no use because he had no children, nor was ever likely to have any. This was then the more grievous because eunuchs were not admitted to be priests (Lev. xxi. 20), nor to *enter into the congregation* (Deut. xxiii. 1), and because the promise of a numerous posterity was the particular blessing of Israel and the more valuable because from among them the Messiah was to come. Yet God would not have the eunuchs to make the worst of their case, nor to think that they should be excluded from the gospel church, and from being spiritual priests, because they were shut out from the congregation of Israel and the Levitical priesthood; no, as the taking down of the partition wall, contained in ordinances, admitted the Gentiles, so it let in likewise those that had been

kept out by ceremonial pollutions. Yet, by the reply here given to this suggestion, it should seem the chief thing which the eunuch laments in his case is his being written childless.

Now suitable encouragements are given to each of these.

I. To those who have no children of their own, who, though they had the honour to be the children of the church and the covenant themselves, yet had none to whom they might transmit that honour, none to receive the sign of circumcision and the privileges secured by that sign. Now observe,

1. What a good character they have, though they lie under this ignominy and affliction ; and those only are entitled to the following comforts who in some measure answer to these characters. (1.) They *keep God's sabbaths* as he has appointed them to be kept. In the primitive times, if a Christian were asked, " Hast thou kept holy the Lord's day?" He would readily answer, " I am a Christian, and dare not do otherwise." (2.) In their whole conversation they *choose those things that please God.* They do that which is good; they do it with a sincere design to please God in it ; they do it of choice, and with delight. If sometimes, through infirmity, they come short in doing that which pleases God, yet they choose it, they endeavour after it, and aim at it. Note, Whatever is God's pleasure should without dispute be our choice. (3.) They *take hold of his covenant*, and that is a thing that pleases God as much as any thing. The covenant of grace is proposed and proffered to us in the gospel; to take hold of it is to consent to it, to accept the offer and come up to the terms, deliberately and sincerely to take God to be to us a God and to give up ourselves to him to be to him a people. Taking hold of the covenant denotes an entire and resolute consent to it, taking hold as those that are afraid of coming short, catching at it as a good bargain, and as those that are resolved never to let it go, for it is our life : and we take hold of it as a criminal took hold of the horns of the altar to which he fled for refuge.

2. What a great deal of comfort they may have if they answer to this character, though they are not built up into families (v. 5): *Unto them will I give a better place and name.* It is supposed that there is a place and a name, which we have from sons and daughters, that is valuable and desirable. It is a pleasing notion we have that we live in our children when we are dead. But there is a better place, and a better name, which those have that are in covenant with God, and it is sufficient to counterbalance the want of the former. A place and a name denote rest and reputation ; a place to live comfortably in themselves, and a name to live creditably with among their neighbours; they shall be happy, and may be easy both

at home and abroad. Though they have not children to be the music of their house, or arrows in their quiver, to keep them in countenance when they speak with their enemies in the gate, yet they shall have a place and a name more than equivalent. For, (1.) God will give it to them, will give it to them by promise; he will himself be both their habitation and their glory, their place and their name. (2.) He will give it to them in his house, and within his walls; there they shall have a place, shall be planted so as to take root (Ps. xcii. 13), shall *dwell all the days of their life*, Ps. xxvii. 4. They shall be at home in communion with God, as Anna, that *departed not from the temple night nor day.* There they shall have a name. A name for good things with God and good people is a name *better than that of sons and daughters.* Our relation to God, our interest in Christ, our title to the blessings of the covenant, and our hopes of eternal life, are things that give us in God's house a blessed place and a blessed name. (3.) It shall be *an everlasting name, that shall never* be extinct, shall never *be cut off:* like the place and name of angels, who *therefore* marry not, because they die not. Spiritual blessings are unspeakably better than those of sons and daughters; for children are a certain care and may prove the greatest grief and shame of a man's life, but the blessings we partake of in God's house are a sure and constant joy and honour, comforts which cannot be embittered.

II. To those that are themselves the children of strangers.

1. It is here promised that they shall now be welcome to the church, *v.* 6, 7. When God's Israel come out of Babylon, let them bring as many of their neighbours along with them as they can persuade to come, and God will find room enough for them all in his house. And here (as before) we may observe,

(1.) Upon what terms they shall be welcome. Let them know that God's Israel, when they come out of Babylon, will not be plagued, as they were when they came out of Egypt, with a mixed multitude, that went with them, but were not cordially for them; no, the sons of the strangers shall have a place and a name in God's house provided, [1.] That they forsake other gods, all rivals and pretenders whatsoever, and *join themselves to the Lord*, so as to become *one spirit*, 1 Cor. vi. 17. [2.] That they join themselves to him as subjects to their prince and soldiers to their general, by an oath of fidelity and obedience, *to serve him*, not occasionally, as one would serve a turn, but to be constantly his servants, entirely subject to his command, and devoted to his interest. [3.] That they join themselves to him as friends to his honour and the interests of his kingdom in the world, *to love the name of the Lord*, to be well pleased with all the discoveries he has made of himself and all

324

the memorials they make of him. Observe, Serving him and loving him go together; for those that love him truly will serve him faithfully, and that obedience is most acceptable to him, as well as most pleasant to us, which flows from a principle of love, for then *his commandments are not grievous*, 1 John v. 3. [4.] That they keep the sabbath from polluting it; for the stranger that is within thy gates is particularly required to do that. [5.] That they take hold of the covenant, that is, that they come under the bonds of it, and put in for the benefits of it.

(2.) To what privileges they shall be welcome, *v.* 7. Three things are here promised them, in their coming to God:—[1.] Assistance: "*I will bring them to my holy mountain*, not only bid them welcome when they come, but incline them to come, will show them the way, and lead them in it." David himself prays that God by his light and truth would bring them to his *holy hill*, Ps. xliii. 3. And the sons of the stranger shall be under the same guidance. The church is God's holy hill, on which he hath set his King, and, in bringing them to Zion Hill, he brings them to be subjects to Zion's King, as well as worshippers in Zion's holy temple. [2.] Acceptance: "*Their burnt-offerings and their sacrifices shall be accepted on my altar*, and be never the less acceptable for being theirs, though they are sons of the stranger." The prayers and praises (those spiritual sacrifices) of devout Gentiles shall be as pleasing to God as those of the pious Jews, and no difference shall be made between them; for, though they are Gentiles by birth, yet through grace they shall be looked upon as the believing seed of faithful Abraham and the praying seed of wrestling Jacob, for in Christ Jesus there is neither Greek nor Jew, circumcision nor uncircumcision. [3.] Comfort. They shall not only be accepted, but they themselves shall have the pleasure of it: *I will make them joyful in my house of prayer.* They shall have grace, not only to serve God, but to serve him cheerfully and with gladness, and that shall make the service the more acceptable to him; for, when we sing in the ways of the Lord, then great is the glory of our God. They shall go away and *eat their bread with joy*, because God *now accepts their works*, Eccl. ix. 7. Nay, though they came mourning to the house of prayer, they shall go away rejoicing, for they shall there find such ease, by casting their cares and burdens upon God, and referring themselves to him, that, like Hannah, they shall go away and their countenance shall be no more sad. Many a sorrowful spirit has been made joyful in the house of prayer.

2. It is here promised that multitudes of the Gentiles shall come to the church, not only that the few who come dropping in shall be made welcome, but that great numbers shall come in, and the door be thrown open

to them : *My house shall be called a house of prayer for all people.* The temple was then God's house, and to that Christ applies these words (Matt. xxi. 13), but with an eye to it as a type of the gospel church, Heb. ix. 8, 9. For Christ calls it *his house*, Heb. iii. 6. Now concerning this house it is promised, (1.) That it shall not be a house of sacrifice, but a house of prayer. The religious meetings of God's people shall be meetings for prayer, in which they shall join together, as a token of their united faith and mutual love. (2.) That it shall be a house of prayer, not for the people of the Jews only, but for all people. This was fulfilled when Peter was made, not only to perceive it himself, but to tell it to the world, that *in every nation he that fears God and works righteousness is accepted of him*, Acts x. 35. It had been declared again and again that *the stranger that comes nigh shall be put to death*, but Gentiles shall now be looked upon no longer as strangers and foreigners, Eph. ii. 19. And it appears by Solomon's prayer, at the dedication of the temple, both that it was primarily intended for a house of prayer and that strangers should be welcome to it, 1 Kings viii. 30, 41, 43. And it is intimated here (*v.* 8) that when the Gentiles are called in they shall be incorporated into one body with the Jews, that (as Christ says, John x. 16) there may be *one fold and one Shepherd;* for, [1] God will *gather the outcasts of Israel.* Many of the Jews that had by their unbelief cast themselves out shall by faith be brought in again, *a remnant according to the election of grace*, Rom. xi. 5. Christ came to the *lost sheep of the house of Israel* (Matt. xv. 24), to *gather their outcasts* (Ps. cxlvii. 2), to *restore their preserved* (*ch.* xlix. 6), and *to be their glory*, Luke ii. 32. [2.] He will gather others also to him, besides his own outcasts that are gathered to him. Or, though some of the Gentiles have come over now and then into the church, that shall not serve (as some may think) to answer the extent of these promises; no, there are still more and more to be brought in : *" I will gather others to him besides these ;* these are but the first-fruits in comparison with the harvest that shall be gathered for Christ in the nations of the earth, when the fulness of the Gentiles shall come in." Note, The church is a growing body : when some are gathered to it we may still hope there shall be more, till the mystical body be completed. *Other sheep I have.*

9 All ye beasts of the field, come to devour, *yea*, all ye beasts in the forest. 10 His watchmen *are* blind : they are all ignorant, they *are* all dumb dogs, they cannot bark ; sleeping, lying down, loving to slumber. 11 Yea, *they are* greedy dogs *which* can never have enough, and they *are*

shepherds *that* cannot understand : they all look to their own way, every one for his gain, from his quarter. 12 Come ye, *say they*, I will fetch wine, and we will fill ourselves with strong drink ; and to-morrow shall be as this day, *and* much more abundant.

From words of comfort the prophet here, by a very sudden change of his style, passes to words of reproof and conviction, and goes on in that strain, for the most part, in the three following chapters ; and therefore some here begin a new sermon. He had assured the people that in due time God would deliver them out of captivity, which was designed for the comfort of those that should live when God would do this. Now here he shows what their sins and provocations were, for which God would send them into captivity, and this was designed for the conviction of those that lived in his own time, nearly a hundred years before the captivity, who were now filling up the measure of the nation's sin, and to justify God in what he brought upon them. God will lay them waste by the fierceness of their enemies, for the falseness of their friends.

I. Desolating judgments are here summoned, *v.* 9. The sheep of God's pasture are now to be made the sheep of his slaughter, to fall as victims to his justice, and therefore *the beasts of the field and the forest* are called to come and devour. They are beasts of prey, and do it from their own ravenous disposition ; but God permits them to do it, nay, he employs them as his servants in doing it, the ministers of his justice, though they mean not so, neither does their heart think so. If this refers primarily to the descent made upon them by the Babylonians, and their devouring them, yet it may look further, to the destruction of Jerusalem and the Jewish nation by the Romans, after these outcasts of them (mentioned *v.* 8) were gathered in to the Christian church. The Roman armies came upon them as beasts of the forest to devour them, and they quite *took away their place and nation.* Note, When God has bloody work to do he has beasts of prey within call, to be employed in doing it.

II. The reason of these judgments is here given. The shepherds, who should have been the watchmen of the flock, to discover the approaches of the beasts of prey, to keep them off, and protect the sheep, were treacherous and careless, minded not their business, nor made any conscience of the trust reposed in them, and so the sheep became an easy prey to the wild beasts. Now this may refer to the false prophets that lived in Isaiah's, Jeremiah's, and Ezekiel's time (who flattered the people in their wicked ways, and told them they should have peace though

325

they went on) and to the priests that bore rule by their means. Or it may refer to the wicked princes, the sons of Josiah, that *did evil in the sight of the Lord,* and other wicked magistrates under them, who betrayed their trust, were vicious and profane, and, instead of making up the breach at which the judgments of God were breaking in upon them, made it wider, and augmented the fierce anger of the Lord instead of doing any thing to turn it away. They should have kept judgment and justice (*v.* 1), but they abandoned both, Jer. v. 1. Or it may refer to those who were the nation's watchmen in our Saviour's time, the chief priests and the scribes, who should have discerned the signs of the times and have given notice to the people of the approach of the Messiah, but who, instead of that, opposed him, and did all they could to keep people from coming to the knowledge of him and to prejudice them against him. It is a very sad character that is here given of these watchmen. *Woe unto thee, O land!* when thy guides are such. 1. They had no sense or knowledge of their business. They were wretchedly ignorant of their work, and very unfit to teach, being so ill-taught themselves: *His watchmen are blind,* and therefore utterly unfit to be watchmen. If the seers see not, who shall see for us? *If the light that is in us be darkness, how great is that darkness!* Christ describes the Pharisees to be *blind leaders of the blind,* Matt. xv. 14. The beasts of the field come to devour, and the watchmen are blind, and are not aware of them. *They are all ignorant* (*v.* 10), *shepherds that cannot understand* (*v.* 11), that know not what is to be done about the sheep, nor can *feed them with understanding,* Jer. iii. 15. 2. What little knowledge they had they made no use of it; no one was the better for it. As they were blind watchmen, that could not discern the danger, so they were *dumb dogs,* that would not give warning of it. And why are the dogs set to guard the sheep if they cannot bark to waken the shepherd and frighten the wolf? Such were these; those that had the charge of souls never reproved men for their faults, nor told them what would be in the end thereof, never gave them notice of the judgments of God that were breaking in upon them. They barked at God's prophets, and bit them too, and worried the sheep, but made no opposition to the wolf or thief. 3. They were very lazy, and would take no pains. They loved their ease, and hated business, were always *sleeping, lying down* and *loving to slumber.* They were not overcome and overpowered by sleep, as the disciples, through grief and fatigue, but they lay down on purpose to invite sleep, and said, *Soul, take thy ease. Yet a little sleep.* It is bad with a people when their shepherds slumber (Nah. iii. 18), and it is well for God's people that their shepherd, the keeper of Israel, neither slumbers nor sleeps. 4.

They were very covetous and eager after the world—*greedy dogs that can never have enough.* If they had ever so much, they would think it too little. They so love silver as never to be satisfied with silver, Eccl. v. 10. All their enquiry is what they shall get, not what they shall do. Let them have the wages, and they care not whether the work be done or no; they feed not the flock, but fleece it. They are every one looking to his *own way,* minding his own private interests, and have no regard at all to the public welfare. It was St. Paul's complaint of the watchmen in his time (Phil. ii. 21), *All seek their own, not the things that are Jesus Christ's.* Every one is for propagating his own opinion, advancing his own party, raising his own family, and having every thing to his own mind, while the common concerns of the public are wretchedly neglected and postponed. They look *every one to his gain from his quarter,* from his end or part of the work. They are for gain from every quarter (*Rem, rem, quocunque modo rem—Money, money, by fair means or by foul we must have money*), but especially from their own quarter, where they will be sure to take care that they lose nothing, nor miss any thing that is to be got. If any one put not into their mouths they not only will do him no service, but they *prepare war against him,* Mic. iii. 5. 5. They were perfect epicures, given to their pleasures, never so much in their element as in their drunken revels (*v.* 12): *Come* (say they), *I will fetch wine* (they have that at command; their cellars are better furnished than their closets) *and we will fill ourselves,* or be drunk, *with strong drink.* They were often drunk, not overseen (as we say) or overtaken in drink, but designedly. The watchmen did thus invite and encourage one another to drink to excess, or they courted the people to sit and drink with them, and so confirmed those in their wicked ways, and hardened their hearts, whom they should have reproved. How could they think it any harm to be drunk when the watchmen themselves joined with them and led them to it! 6. They were very secure and confident of the continuance of their prosperity and ease; they said, *"To-morrow shall be as this day and much more abundant;* we shall have as much to spend upon our lusts to-morrow as we have to-day."* They had no thought at all of their own frailty and mortality, though they were shortening their days and hastening their deaths by their excesses. They had no dread of the judgments of God, though they were daily provoking him and making themselves liable to his wrath and curse. They never considered the uncertainty of all the delights and enjoyments of sense, how they perish in the using and pass away with the lusts of them. They resolved to continue in this wicked course, whatever their consciences said to the contrary, to be as merry to-morrow as they are to-day. *But boast* *not thyself of to-morrow* when perhaps *this night thy soul shall be required of thee.*

CHAP. LVII.

The prophet, in this chapter, makes his observations, I. Upon the deaths of good men, comforting those that were taken away in their integrity and reproving those that did not make a due improvement of such providences, ver. 1, 2. II. Upon the gross idolatries and spiritual whoredoms which the Jews were guilty of, and the destroying judgments they were thereby bringing upon themselves, ver. 3—12. III. Upon the gracious returns of God to his people to put an end to their captivity and re-establish their prosperity, ver. 13—21.

THE righteous perisheth, and no man layeth *it* to heart: and merciful men *are* taken away, none considering that the righteous is taken away from the evil *to come.* 2 He shall enter into peace : they shall rest in their beds, *each one* walking *in* his uprightness.

The prophet, in the close of the foregoing chapter, had condemned the watchmen for their ignorance and sottishness; here he shows the general stupidity and senselessness of the people likewise. No wonder they were inconsiderate when their watchmen were so, who should have awakened them to consideration. We may observe here,

I. The providence of God removing good men apace out of this world. *The righteous,* as to this world, *perish;* they are gone and their place knows them no more. Piety exempts none from the arrests of death, nay, in persecuting times, the most righteous are most exposed to the violences of bloody men. The first that died died a martyr. Righteousness delivers from the sting of death, but not from the stroke of it. They are said to *perish* because they are utterly removed from us, and to express the great loss which this world sustains by the removal of them, not that their death is their undoing, but it often proves an undoing to the places where they lived and were useful. Nay, even *merciful men are taken away,* those good men that are distinguished from the righteous, for whom *some would even dare to die,* Rom. v. 7. Those are often removed that could be worst spared; the fruitful trees are cut down by death and the barren left still to cumber the ground. Merciful men are often taken away by the hands of men's malice. Many good works they have done, and for some of them they are stoned. Before the captivity in Babylon perhaps there was a more than ordinary mortality of good men, so that there were scarcely any left, Jer. v. 1. The godly ceased, and the faithful failed, Ps. xii. 1.

II. The careless world slighting these providences, and disregarding them : *No man lays it to heart, none considers it.* There are very few that lament it as a public loss, very few that take notice of it as a public warning. The death of good men is a thing to be laid to heart and considered more than common deaths. Serious enquiries ought to be made, wherefore God contends with us, what good lessons are to be learned by such

providences, what we may do to help to make up the breach and to fill up the room of those that are removed. God is justly displeased when such events are not laid to heart, when the voice of the rod is not heard nor the intentions of it answered, much more when it is rejoiced in, as the slaying of the witnesses is, Rev. xi. 10. Some of God's choicest blessings to mankind, being thus easily parted with, are really undervalued; and it is an evidence of very great incogitancy. Little children, when they are little, least lament the death of their parents, because they know not what a loss it is to them.

III. The happiness of the righteous in their removal.

1. They *are taken away from the evil to come,* then when it is just coming, (1.) In compassion to them, that they may not *see the evil* (2 Kings xxii. 20), nor share in it, nor be in temptation by it. When the deluge is coming they are called into the ark, and have a hiding-place and rest in heaven when there was none for them under heaven. (2.) In wrath to the world, to punish them for all the injuries they have done to the righteous and merciful ones; those are taken away that stood in the gap to turn away the judgments of God, and then what can be expected but a deluge of them? It is a sign that God intends war when he calls home his ambassadors.

2. They go to be easy out of the reach of that evil. The righteous man, who while he lived walked in his uprightness, when he dies *enters into peace* and *rests in his bed.* Note, (1.) Death is gain, and rest, and bliss, to those only who walked in their uprightness, and who, when they die, can appeal to God concerning it, as Hezekiah (2 Kings xx. 3). *Now, Lord, remember it.* (2.) Those that practised uprightness, and persevered in it to the end, shall find it well with them when they die. Their souls then enter into peace, into the world of peace, where peace is in perfection and where there is no trouble. *Enter thou into the joy of thy Lord.* Their bodies rest in their beds. Note, The grave is a bed of rest to all the Lord's people ; there they rest from all their labours, Rev. xiv. 13. And the more weary they were the more welcome will that rest be to them, Job iii. 17. This bed is made in the darkness, but that makes it the more quiet ; it is a bed out of which they shall rise refreshed in the morning of the resurrection.

3 But draw near hither, ye sons of the sorceress, the seed of the adulterer and the whore. 4 Against whom do ye sport yourselves? Against whom make ye a wide mouth, *and* draw out the tongue? *Are* ye not children of transgression, a seed of falsehood, 5 Inflaming yourselves with idols under every green tree,

slaying the children in the valleys under the clifts of the rocks? 6 Among the smooth *stones* of the stream *is* thy portion; they, they *are* thy lot: even to them hast thou poured a drink-offering, thou hast offered a meat-offering. Should I receive comfort in these? 7 Upon a lofty and high mountain hast thou set thy bed: even thither wentest thou up to offer sacrifice. 8 Behind the doors also and the posts hast thou set up thy remembrance: for thou hast discovered *thyself to another* than me, and art gone up; thou hast enlarged thy bed, and made thee *a covenant* with them; thou lovedst their bed where thou sawest *it*. 9 And thou wentest to the king with ointment, and didst increase thy perfumes, and didst send thy messengers far off, and didst debase *thyself even* unto hell. 10 Thou art wearied in the greatness of thy way; *yet* saidst thou not, There is no hope: thou hast found the life of thine hand; therefore thou wast not grieved. 11 And of whom hast thou been afraid or feared, that thou hast lied, and hast not remembered me, nor laid *it* to thy heart? Have not I held my peace even of old, and thou fearest me not? 12 I will declare thy righteousness, and thy works; for they shall not profit thee.

We have here a high charge, but a just one no doubt, drawn up against that wicked generation out of which God's righteous ones were removed, because the world was not worthy of them. Observe,

I. The general character here given of them, or the name and title by which they stand indicted, *v.* 3. They are told to draw near and hear the charge, are set to the bar, and arraigned there as *sons of the sorceress,* or of a witch, *the seed of an adulterer and a whore,* that is, they were such themselves, they were strongly inclined to be such, and their ancestors were such before them. Sin is sorcery and adultery, for it is departing from God and dealing with the devil. They were *children of disobedience.* "Come," says the prophet, " draw near hither, and I will read you your doom; to the righteous death will bring peace and rest, but not to you; you are *children of transgression* and *a seed of falsehood* (*v.* 4), that have it by kind, and have it woven into your very nature, to backslide from God and to deal treacherously with him," *ch.* xlviii. 8.

328

II. The particular crimes laid to their charge.

1. Scoffing at God and his word. They were a generation of scorners (*v.* 4): *"Against whom do you sport yourselves?* You think it is only against the poor prophets, whom you trample upon as contemptible men, but really it is against God himself, who sends them, and whose message they deliver." Mocking the messengers of the Lord was Jerusalem's measure-filling sin, for what was done to them God took as done to himself. When they were reproved for their sins, and threatened with the judgments of God, they ridiculed the word of God with the rudest and most indecent gestures and expressions of disdain. They sported themselves, and made themselves merry, with that which should have made them serious, and under which they should have humbled themselves. They made wry mouths at the prophets, and drew out the tongue, contrary to all the laws of good breeding; nor did they treat God's prophets with the common civility with which they would have treated a gentleman's servant that had been sent to them on an errand. Note, Those who mock at God, and bid defiance to his judgments, had best consider who it is towards whom they conduct themselves so insolently.

2. Idolatry. This was that sin which the people of the Jews were most notoriously guilty of before the captivity; but that affliction cured them of it. In Isaiah's time it abounded, witness the abominable idolatries of Ahaz (which some think are particularly referred to here) and of Manasseh. (1.) They were dotingly fond of their idols, were inflamed with them, as those that burn in unlawful unnatural lusts, Rom. i. 27. They were *mad upon their idols,* Jer. l. 38. They inflamed themselves with them by their violent passions in the worship of them, as those of Baal's prophets that *leaped upon the altar, and cut themselves,* 1 Kings xviii. 26, 28. Note, Vile corruptions, the more they are gratified the more they are inflamed. They worshipped their idols *under every green tree,* in the open air, and in the shade; yet that did not cool the heat of their impetuous lusts, but rather the charming beauty of the green trees made them the more fond of their idols which they worshipped there. Thus that in nature which is pleasing, instead of drawing them to the God of nature, drew them from him. The flame of their zeal in the worship of false gods may shame us for our coldness and indifference in the worship of the true God. They strove to inflame themselves, but we distract and deaden ourselves. (2.) They were barbarous and unnaturally cruel in the worship of their idols. They slew their children, and offered them in sacrifice to their idols, not only in the valley of the son of Hinnom, the headquarters of that monstrous idolatry, but in other valleys, in imitation of that, and *under*

the cliffs of the rock, in dark and solitary places, the fittest for such works of darkness. (3.) They were abundant and insatiable in their idolatries. They never thought they could have idols enough, nor could spend enough upon them and do enough in their service. The Syrians had once a notion of the God of Israel that he was a God of the hills, but not a *God of the valleys* (1 Kings xx. 28); but these idolaters, to make sure work, had both. [1.] They had gods of the valleys, which they worshipped in the low places by the water side (*v.* 6): *Among the smooth stones of the valley,* or brook, *is thy portion.* If they saw a smooth carved stone, though set up but for a way-mark or a mere-stone, they were ready to worship it, as the papists do crosses. Or in stony valleys they set up their gods, which they called their *portion,* and took for their lot, as God's people take him for their lot and portion. But these gods of stone would really be no better a portion for them, no better a lot, than the smooth stones of the stream near which they were set up, for sometimes they worshipped their rivers. "*They, they, are the lot* which thou trustest to and art pleased with, but thou shalt be put off with it for thy lot, and miserable will thy case be." See the folly of sinners, who take the smooth stones of the stream for their portion, when they might have the precious stones of God's Jerusalem, and the high priest's ephod, to portion themselves with. Having taken these idols for their lot and portion, they stick at no charge in doing honour to them: "*To them hast thou poured a drink-offering, and offered a meat-offering,* as if they had given thee thy meat and drink." They loved their idols better than their children, for their own tables must be robbed to replenish the altars of their idols. Have we taken the true God for our portion? Is he, even he, our lot? Let us then serve him with our meat and drink, not, as they did, by depriving ourselves of the use of them, but by eating and drinking to his glory. Here, in a parenthesis, comes in an expression of God's just resentment of this wickedness of theirs: *Should I receive comfort in these*—in such a a people as this? Can those expect that God will take any pleasure in them, or accept their devotions at his altar, who thus serve Baal with the gifts of his providence? God takes comfort in his people, while they are faithful to him; but what comfort can he take in them when those that should be his witnesses against the idolatries of the world do themselves fall in with them? *Should I have compassion on these?* (so some), or *should I repent me concerning these?* so others. "How can they expect that I should spare them, and either adjourn or abate their punishment, when they are so very provoking? *Shall I not visit for these things?*" Jer. v. 7, 9. [2.] They had gods of the hills too (*v.* 7): "*Upon a lofty and high mountain*

(as if thou wouldst vie with the high and lofty One himself, *v.* 15) *hast thou set thy bed,* thy idol, thy idol's temple and altar, the bed of thy uncleanness, where thou committest spiritual whoredom, with all the wantonness of an idolatrous fancy, and in direct violation of the covenant of thy God. *Thither wentest thou up* readily enough, though it was up-hill, *to offer sacrifice.*" Some think this bespeaks the impudence they arrived at in their idolatries; at first they had some sense of shame, when they worshipped their idols in the valleys, in obscure places; but they soon conquered that, and came to do it upon the lofty high mountains. They were not ashamed, neither could they blush. [3.] As if these were not enough, they had household-gods too, their *lares* and *penates. Behind the doors and the posts* (*v.* 8), where the law of God should be written for a memorandum to them of their duty, they set up the remembrance of their idols, not so much to keep up their own remembrance of them (they were so fond of them that they could not forget them), but to show to others how mindful they were of them, and to put their children in mind of them, and possess them betimes with a veneration for these dunghill deities. [4.] As they were insatiable in their idolatries, so they were inseparable from them. They were hardened in their wickedness; they worshipped their idols openly and in public view, as being neither ashamed of the sin nor afraid of the punishment; they went as publicly, and in as great crowds, to the idol-temples, as ever they had gone to God's house. This was like an impudent harlot, *discovering themselves to another than God,* making profession of another than the true religion. They took a pride in making proselytes to their idolatries, and not only went up themselves to their high places, but *enlarged their bed,* that is, their idol-temples, and (as the margin reads the following words) *thou hewedst it for thyself larger than theirs,* than theirs from whom thou copiedst it, and tookest the platform of it, as Ahaz of his altar from that which he saw at Damascus, 2 Kings xvi. 10. And being thus involved over head and ears, as it were, in their idolatries, there is no parting them from them. Ephraim is now joined to idols both in love and league. *First,* In league: "*Thou hast made a covenant with them,* with the idols, with the idol-worshippers, to live and die together." This was a complete renunciation of their covenant with God and an avowed resolution to persist in their apostasy from him. *Secondly,* In love: "*Thou lovedst their bed,* that is, the temple of an idol, wherever thou sawest it." Justly therefore were they given up to their own hearts' lusts.

3. Another sin charged upon them is their trusting in and seeking to foreign aids and succours, and contracting a communion with the Gentile powers (*v.* 9): *Thou wentest to*

the king, which some understand of the idol they worshipped, particularly *Moloch*, which signifies *a king*. " Thou didst every thing to ingratiate thyself with those idols, didst offer incense and sweet ointments at their altars." Or it may be meant of the king of Assyria, whom Ahaz made his court to, or of the king of Babylon, whose ambassadors Hezekiah caressed, or of other kings of the nations whose idolatrous usages they admired and were desirous to learn and imitate, and for that end went and sent to cultivate an acquaintance and correspondence with them, that they might be like them and strengthen themselves by an alliance with them. See here, (1.) What an expense they were at in forming and procuring this grand alliance. They went *with ointments and perfumes*, either bestowed upon themselves, to beautify their own faces and so make themselves considerable and worthy the friendship of the greatest king, or to be presented to those whose favour they were ambitious of, because a man's gift makes room for him and brings him before great men. " When the first present of rich perfumes was thought too little, thou didst increase them ;" and thus many seek the ruler's favour, forgetting that, after all, every man's judgment proceeds from the Lord. So fond were they of those heathen princes that they not only went themselves, in all their airs, to those that were near them, but sent messengers to those that were afar of, *ch.* xviii. 2. (2.) How much they hereby disparaged themselves and laid the honour of their crown and nation in the dust: *Thou didst debase thyself even unto hell.* They did so by their idolatries. It is a dishonour to the children of men, who are endued with the powers of reason, to worship that as their god which is the creature of their own fancy and the work of their own hands, to bow down to the stock of a tree. It is much more a dishonour to the children of God, who are blessed with the privilege of divine revelation, to forsake such a God as they know theirs to be for a thing of nought, their own mercies for lying vanities. They likewise debased themselves by truckling to their heathen neighbours, and depending upon them, when they had a God to go to who is all-sufficient and in covenant with them. How did those shame themselves to the highest degree, and sink themselves to the lowest, that forsook the fountain of life for broken cisterns and the rock of ages for broken reeds ! Note, Sinners disparage and debase themselves ; the service of sin is an ignominious slavery ; and those who thus debase themselves to hell will justly have their portion there.

III. The aggravations of their sin. 1. They had been tired with disappointments in their wicked courses, and yet they would not be convinced of the folly of them (*v.* 10) : " *Thou art wearied in the greatness of thy way ;* thou hast undertaken a mighty task, to find

330

out true satisfaction and happiness in that which is vanity and a lie." Those that set up idols, instead of God, for the object of their worship, and princes, instead of God, for the object of their hope and confidence, and think thus to better themselves and make themselves easy, go a great way about, and will never come to their journey's end : *Thou art wearied in the multitude*, or *multiplicity, of thy ways* (so some read it) : those that forsake the only right way wander endlessly in a thousand by-paths, and lose themselves in the many inventions which they have sought out. They weary themselves with fresh chases and fierce ones, but never gain their point, like the Sodomites, that *wearied themselves to find the door* (Gen. xix. 11) and could not find it at last. The pleasures of sin will soon surfeit, but never satisfy ; a man may quickly tire himself in the pursuit of them, but can never repose himself in the enjoyment of them. They found this by experience. The idols they had often worshipped never did them any kindness ; the kings they courted distressed them, and helped them not ; and yet they were so wretchedly besotted that they could not say, " *There is no hope ;* it is in vain any longer to expect that satisfaction in creature-confidences, and in the worship of idols, which we have so often looked for, and never met with." Note, Despair of happiness in the creature, and of satisfaction in the service of sin, is the first step towards a well-grounded hope of happiness in God and a well-fixed resolution to keep to his service ; and those are inexcusable who have had sensible convictions of the vanity of the creature, and yet will not be brought to say, " There is no hope to be happy short of the Creator." 2. Though they were convinced that the way they were in was a sinful way, yet, because they had found some present sensual pleasure and worldly profit by it, they could not persuade themselves to be sorry for it : " *Thou hast found the life of thy hand*" (or *the living of it) ;* thou boastest how fortune smiles upon thee, and therefore thou art not grieved, any more than Ephraim when he said (Hos. xii. 8), *I have become rich ; I have found out substance.*" Note, Prosperity in sin is a great bar to conversion from sin. Those that live at ease in their sinful pleasures, and raise estates by their sinful projects, are tempted to think God favours them, and therefore they have nothing to repent of. Some read it ironically, or by way of question : " Thou hast found the life of thy hand, hast found true satisfaction and happiness, no doubt thou hast ; hast thou not ? And therefore thou art so far from being grieved that thou blessest thyself in thy own evil way ; but review thy gains once more, and come to a balance of profit and loss, and then say, What fruit hast thou of those things whereof thou art ashamed and for which *God shall bring thee into judgment ?*"

Rom vi. 21. 3. They had dealt very unworthily with God by their sin; for, (1.) It should seem they pretended that the reason why they left God was because he was too terrible a majesty for them to deal with; they must have gods that they could be more free and familiar with. " But," says God, " *of whom hast thou been afraid or feared, that thou hast lied,* that thou hast dealt falsely and treacherously with me, and dissembled in thy covenants with me and prayers to me? What did I ever do to frighten thee from me? What occasion have I given thee to think hardly of me, that thou hast gone to seek a kinder master?" (2.) However, it is certain that they had no true reverence of God nor any serious regard to him. So that question is commonly understood, " *Of whom hast thou been afraid, or feared?* Of none; for thou hast not feared me whom thou shouldst fear; for thou hast lied to me." Those that dissemble with God make it to appear they stand in no awe of him. " Thou *hast not remembered me,* neither what I have said nor what I have done, neither the promises nor the threatenings, nor the performances of either; thou hast *not laid them to thy heart,* as thou wouldst have done if thou hadst feared me." Note, Those who lay not the word of God and his providences to their hearts do thereby show that they have not the fear of God before their eyes. And multitudes are ruined by fearlessness, forgetfulness, and mere carelessness; they do not aright nor to good purpose fear any thing, remember any thing, nor lay any thing to heart. Nay, (3.) They were hardened in their sin by the patience and forbearance of God. " *Have not I held my peace of old,* and for a long time? These things thou hast done and I kept silence. And therefore, as it follows here, thou fearest me not;" as if because God had spared long he would never punish, Eccl. viii. 11. Because he kept silence the sinner thought him altogether such a one as himself, and stood in no awe of him.

IV. Here is God's resolution to call them to an account, though he had long borne with them (v. 12): " *I will declare* (like that, Ps. l. 21, *But I will reprove thee*), *I will declare thy righteousness,* which thou makest thy boast of, and let the world see, and thyself too, to thy confusion, that it is all a sham, all a cheat, it is not what it pretends to be. When thy righteousness comes to be examined it will be found that it was unrighteousness, and that there was no sincerity in all thy pretensions. I will declare *thy works,* what they have been and what the gain thou pretendest to have gotten by them, and it will appear that at long-run *they shall not profit thee,* nor turn to any account." Note, Sinful works, as they are works of darkness, and there is no reason nor righteousness in them, so they are unfruitful works and there is nothing got by them; and, however they

look now, it will be made to appear so another day. Sin profits not, nay, it ruins and destroys.

13 When thou criest, let thy companies deliver thee; but the wind shall carry them all away; vanity shall take *them:* but he that putteth his trust in me shall possess the land, and shall inherit my holy mountain; 14 And shall say, Cast ye up, cast ye up, prepare the way, take up the stumbling block out of the way of my people. 15 For thus saith the high and lofty One that inhabiteth eternity, whose name *is* Holy; I dwell in the high and holy *place,* with him also *that is* of a contrite and humble spirit, to revive the spirit of the humble, and to revive the heart of the contrite ones. 16 For I will not contend for ever, neither will I be always wroth: for the spirit should fail before me, and the souls *which* I have made.

Here, I. God shows how insufficient idols and creatures were to relieve and succour those that worshipped them and confided in them (v. 13): " *When thou criest* in thy distress and anguish, lamentest thy misery and callest for help, *let thy companies deliver thee,* thy idol-gods which thou hast heaped to thyself companies of, the troops of the confederate forces which thou hast relied so much upon, let them deliver thee if they can; expect no other relief than what they can give." Thus God said to Israel, when in their trouble they called upon him (Judg. x. 14), Go, *and cry to the gods which you have chosen, let them deliver you.* But in vain is salvation hoped for from them: *The wind shall carry them all away,* the wind of God's wrath, that breath of his mouth which shall slay the wicked; they have made themselves as chaff, and therefore the wind will of course hurry them away. Vanity they are, and *vanity shall take them* away, to vanity they shall be reduced, and vanity shall be their recompence. Both the idols and their worshippers shall come to nothing.

II. He shows that there was a sufficiency, an all-sufficiency, in him for the comfort and deliverance of all those that put their confidence in him and made their application to him. Their safety and satisfaction appear the more comfortable because their hopes are crowned with fruition, when those that seek to other helpers have their hopes frustrated: " *He that puts his trust in me,* and in me only, he shall be happy, both for soul and body, for this world and the other."

1. Observe, in general, (1.) Those that trust in God's providence take the best course to secure their secular interests. They *shall possess the land,* as much of it as

is good for them, and what they have they shall have it from a good hand and hold it by a good title. Ps. xxxvii. 3, *They shall dwell in the land, and verily they shall be fed.* (2.) Those that trust in God's grace take the best course to secure their sacred interests. They *shall inherit my holy mountain.* They shall enjoy the privileges of the church on earth, and be brought at length to the joys of heaven; and no wind shall carry them away.

2. More particularly,

(1.) The captives, that trust in God, shall be released (*v.* 14): *They shall say* (that is, the messengers of his word, and all the ministers of his providence, in that great event shall say), *Cast you up, cast you up, prepare the way.* When God's time shall have come for their deliverance the way of bringing it about shall be made plain and easy, obstacles shall be removed, difficulties that seemed insuperable shall be speedily got over, and all things shall concur both to accelerate and facilitate their return. See *ch.* xl. 3, 4. This refers to the provision which the gospel, and the grace of it, have made for our ready passage through this world to a better. The way of religion is now cast up; it is a highway; ministers' business is to direct people in it, and to help them over the discouragements they meet with, that nothing may offend them.

(2.) The contrite, that trust in God, shall be *revived, v.* 15. Those that trusted to idols and creatures for help went with their *ointments and perfumes* (*v.* 9); but here God shows that those who may expect help from him are such as are destitute of, and set themselves at a distance from, the gaieties of the world and the delights of sense. God's glory appears here very bright, [1.] In his greatness and majesty: He is *the high and lofty One that inhabits eternity.* Let this inspire us with very high and honourable thoughts of the God with whom we have to do, *First,* That his being and perfections are exalted infinitely above every creature, not only above what they have themselves, but above what they can conceive concerning him, *far above all* their *blessing and praise,* Neh. ix. 5. *He is the high and lofty One,* and there is no creature like him, nor any to be compared with him. The language likewise intimates his sovereign dominion over all and the incontestable right he has to give both law and judgment to all. He is *higher than the highest* (Eccl v. 8), than the *highest heavens,* Ps. cxiii. 4. *Secondly,* That with him there is neither beginning of days nor end of life, nor change of time; he is both immortal and immutable. He only *has immortality,* 1 Tim. vi. 16. He has it of himself, and he has it constantly; he inhabits it, and cannot be dispossessed of it. We must shortly remove into eternity, but God always inhabits it. *Thirdly,* That there is an infinite rectitude in his nature, and an exact conformity with himself and a steady

design of his own glory in all that he does; and this appears in every thing by which he has made himself known, for his name is *holy,* and all that desire to be acquainted with him must know him as a holy God. *Fourthly,* That the peculiar residence and manifestation of his glory are in the mansions of light and bliss above: " *I dwell in the high and holy place,* and will have all the world to know it." Whoever have any business with God must direct to him as their Father in heaven, for there he dwells. These great things are here said of God to inspire us with a holy reverence of him, to encourage our confidence in him, and to magnify his compassion and condescension to us, that though he is thus high yet he has respect unto the lowly; he that rides on the heavens by his name JAH stoops to concern himself for poor *widows* and *fatherless,* Ps. lxviii. 4, 5. [2.] In his grace and mercy. He has a tender pity for the humble and contrite, for those that are so in respect of their state. If they be his people, he will not overlook them though they are poor and low in the world, and despised and trampled upon by men; but he here refers to the temper of their mind; he will have a tender regard to those who, being in affliction, accommodate themselves to their affliction, and bring their mind to their condition, be it ever so low and ever so sad and sorely broken—those that are truly penitent for sin, who mourn in secret for it, and have a dread of the wrath of God, which they have made themselves obnoxious to, and are submissive under all his rebukes. Now, *First,* With these God will dwell. He will visit them graciously, will converse familiarly with them by his word and Spirit, as a man does with those of his own family; he will be always nigh to them and present with them. He that dwells in the highest heavens dwells in the lowest hearts and inhabits sincerity as surely as he inhabits eternity. In these he delights. *Secondly,* He will revive their heart and spirit, will speak that to them, and work that in them by the word and Spirit of his grace, which will be reviving to them, as a cordial to one that is ready to faint. He will give them reviving joys and hopes sufficient to counterbalance all the griefs and fears that break their spirits. He dwells with them, and his presence is reviving.

(3.) Those with whom he contends, if they trust in him, shall be relieved, and received into favour, *v.* 16. He will *revive the heart of the contrite ones,* for he will not contend for ever. Nothing makes a soul contrite so much as God's contending, and therefore nothing revives it so much as his ceasing his controversy. Here is, [1.] A gracious promise. It is not promised that he will never be angry with his people, for their sins are displeasing to him, or that he will never contend with them, for they must expect the rod ; but he *will not contend for ever*, nor be always wroth. As he is not soon angry, so he is not long angry. He will not always chide. Though he contend with them by convictions of sin, he will not contend for ever; but, instead of the spirit of bondage, they shall receive the Spirit of adoption. He has torn, but he will heal. Though he contend with them by the rebukes of providence, yet the correction shall not last always, shall not last long, shall last no longer than there is need (1 Pet. i. 6), no longer than they can bear, no longer than till it has done its work. Though their whole life be calamitous, yet their end will be peace, and so will their eternity be. [2.] A very compassionate consideration, upon which this promise is grounded : " If I should contend for ever, *the spirit would fail before me, even the souls which I have made.*" Note, First, God is the Father of spirits, Heb. xii. 9. Those with whom he will not always contend are the souls that he has made, that he gave being to by creation and a new being to by regeneration. *Secondly*, Though the Lord is for the body, yet he concerns himself chiefly for the souls of his people, that the spirit do not fail, and its graces and comforts. *Thirdly*, When troubles last long, the spirit even of good men is apt to fail. They are tempted to entertain hard thoughts of God, to think it in vain to serve him ; they are ready to put comfort away from them, and to despair of relief, and then the spirit fails. *Fourthly*, It is in consideration of this that God will not contend for ever ; for he will not forsake the work of his own hands nor defeat the purchase of his Son's blood. The reason is taken not from our merit, but from our weakness and infirmity ; for *he remembers that we are flesh* (Ps. lxxviii. 39) and that flesh is weak.

17 For the iniquity of his covetousness was I wroth, and smote him : I hid me, and was wroth, and he went on frowardly in the way of his heart. 18 I have seen his ways, and will heal him : I will lead him also, and restore comforts unto him and to his mourners. 19 I create the fruit of the lips ; Peace, peace, to *him that is* far off, and to *him that is* near, saith the Lord ; and I will heal him. 20 But the wicked *are* like the troubled sea, when it cannot rest, whose waters cast up mire and dirt. 21 *There is* no peace, saith my God, to the wicked.

The body of the people of Israel, in this account of God's dealings with them, is spoken of as a particular person (*v.* 17, 18), but divided into two sorts, differently dealt with—some who were sons of peace, to whom peace is spoken (*v.* 19), and others who were

not, who have nothing to do with peace, *v.* 20, 21. Observe here,

I. The just rebukes which that people were brought under for their sin : *For the iniquity of his covetousness I was wroth, and smote him.* Covetousness was a sin that abounded very much among that people. Jer. vi. 13, *From the least to the greatest of them, every one is given to covetousness.* Those that did not worship images were yet carried away by this spiritual idolatry : for such is covetousness; it is making money the god, Col. iii. 5. No marvel that the people were covetous when their watchmen themselves were notoriously so, *ch.* lvi. 11. Yet, covetous as they were, in the service of their idols they were prodigal, *v.* 6. And it is hard to say whether their profuseness in that or their covetousness in every thing else was more provoking. But for this iniquity, among others, God was angry with them, and brought one judgment after another upon them, and their destruction at last by the Chaldeans. 1. God was wroth. He resented it, took it very ill that a people who were devoted to himself, and portioned in himself, should be so entirely given up to the world and choose that for their portion. Note, Covetousness is an iniquity that is very displeasing to the God of heaven. It is a heart-sin, but he sees it, and *therefore* hates it, and looks upon it with jealousy, because it sets up a rival with him in the soul. It is a sin which men *bless themselves in* (Ps. xlix. 18) and in which their neighbours *bless them* (Ps. x. 3) ; but God abhors it. 2. He smote him, reproved him for it by his prophets, corrected him by his providence, punished him in those very things he so doted upon and was covetous of. Note, Sinners shall be made to feel from the anger of God. Those whom he is wroth with he smites ; and covetousness particularly lays men under the tokens of God's displeasure. Those that set their hearts upon the wealth of this world are disappointed of it or it is embittered to them ; it is either clogged with a cross or turned into a curse. 3. God hid himself from him when he was under these rebukes, and continued wroth with him. When we are under the rod, if God manifest himself to us, we may bear it the better ; but if he both smite us and hide himself from us, send us no prophets, speak to us no comfortable word, show us no token for good, if he *tear and go away* (Hos. v. 14), we are very miserable.

II. Their obstinacy and incorrigibleness under these rebukes : *He went on frowardly in the way of his heart*, in his evil way. He was not sensible of the displeasure of God that he was under. He felt the smart of the rod, but had no regard at all to the hand ; the more he was crossed in his worldly pursuits the more eager he was in them. He either would not see his error or if he saw it would not amend it. Covetousness was the way of his heart; it was what he was in-clined to and intent upon, and he would not be reclaimed, but *in his distress he trespassed yet more*, 2 Chron. xxviii. 22. See the strength of the corruption of men's hearts, and the sinfulness of sin, which will take its course in despite of God himself and all the flames of his wrath. See also how insuffi-cient afflictions of themselves are to reform men, unless God's grace work with them.

III. God's wonderful return in mercy to them, notwithstanding the obstinacy of the generality of them.

1. The greater part of them went on fro-wardly, but there were some among them that were mourners for the obstinacy of the rest; and with an eye to them, or rather for his own name's sake, God determines not to contend for ever with them. *With the fro-ward* God may justly *show himself froward* (Ps. xviii. 26), and *walk contrary* to those that *walk contrary* to him, Lev. xxvi. 24. When this sinner here went on frowardly in the way of his heart, one would think it should have followed, " I have seen his ways and will destroy him, will abandon him, will never have any thing more to do with him." But such are the riches of divine mercy and grace, and so do they rejoice against judg-ment, that it follows, *I have seen his ways and will heal him.* See how God's goodness takes occasion from man's badness to ap-pear so much the more illustrious; and where sin has abounded grace much more abounds. God's reasons of mercy are fetched from within himself, for in us there appears nothing but what is provoking: " I have seen his ways, and yet I will heal him for my own name's sake." God knew how bad the people were, and yet would not cast them off. But observe the method. God will first give him grace, and then, and not till then, give him peace: " I have seen his way, that he will never turn to me of him-self, and therefore I will turn him." Those whom God has mercy in store for he has grace in readiness for, to prepare and qualify them for that mercy which they were run-ning from as fast as they could. (1.) God will heal him of his corrupt and vicious dis-position, will cure him of his covetousness, though it be ever so deeply rooted in him and his heart have been long exercised to covetous practices. There is no spiritual disease so inveterate, but almighty grace can conquer it. (2.) God *will lead him also ;* not only amend what was amiss in him, that he may cease to do evil, but direct him into the way of duty, that he may learn to do well. He goes on frowardly, as Saul, yet breathing out threatenings and slaughter, but God will lead him into a better mind, a better path. And then, (3.) He will restore those comforts to him which he had forfeited and lost, and for the return of which he had thus prepared him. There was a wonderful reformation wrought upon the captives in

334

Babylon, and then a wonderful redemption wrought for them, which brought comfort to them, to their mourners, to those among them that mourned for their own sins, the sins of their people, and the desolations of the sanctuary. To those mourners the mercy would be most comfortable, and to them God had an eye in working it out. Blessed are those that mourn, for to them comfort be-longs, and they shall have it.

2. Now, as when that people went into captivity some of them were good figs, very good, others of them bad figs, very bad, and accordingly their captivity was to them for their good or for *their hurt* (Jer. xxiv. 8, 9), so, when they came out of captivity, still some of them were good, others bad, and the deliverance was to them accordingly.

(1.) To those among them that were good their return out of captivity was peace, such peace as was a type and earnest of the peace which should be preached by Jesus Christ (*v.* 19): *I create the fruit of the lips, peace.* [1.] God designed to give them matter for praise and thanksgiving, for that is the *fruit of the lips* (Heb. xiii. 15), the *calves of the lips*, Hos. xiv. 2. *I create this.* Creation is out of nothing, and this is surely out of worse than nothing, when God creates mat-ter of praise for those that went on frowardly in the way of their heart. [2.] In order to this, peace shall be published : *Peace, peace* (perfect peace, all kinds of peace) *to him that is afar off* from the general rendezvous, or from the head-quarters, as well as *to him that is near.* Peace with God ; though he has contended with them, he will be recon-ciled and will let fall his controversy. Peace of conscience, a holy security and serenity of mind, after the many reproaches of con-science and agitations of spirit they had been under in their captivity. Thus God creates the fruit of the lips, fresh matter for thanks-giving ; for, when he speaks peace to us, we must speak praises to him. This peace is itself of God's creating. He, and he only, can work it ; it is the fruit of the lips, of his lips—he commands it, of the minister's lips —he speaks it by them, *ch.* xl. 1. It is the fruit of preaching lips and praying lips ; it is the fruit of Christ's lips, whose lips drop as a honeycomb ; for to him this is applied, Eph. ii. 17 : *He came and preached peace to you who were afar off*, you Gentiles as well as to the Jews, who were nigh—to after-ages, who were afar off in time, as well as to those of the present age.

(2.) To those among them that were wicked, though they might return with the rest, their return was no peace, *v.* 20. The wicked, wherever he is, in Babylon or in Jerusalem, carries about with him the prin-ciple of his own uneasiness, and is like the troubled sea. God healed those to whom he spoke peace (*v.* 19) : *I will heal them ;* all shall be well again and set to rights ; but the wicked would not be healed by the grace of God and therefore shall not be healed by his comforts. They are always like the sea in a storm, for they carry about with them, [1.] Unmortified corruptions. They are not cured and conquered, and their ungoverned lusts and passions make them like the troubled sea when it cannot rest, vexatious to all about them and therefore uneasy to themselves, noisy and dangerous. When the intemperate heats of the spirit break out in scurrilous and abusive language, then the troubled sea casts forth mire and dirt. [2.] Unpacified consciences. They are under a frightful apprehension of guilt and wrath, that they cannot enjoy themselves; when they seem settled they are in disquietude, when they seem merry they are in heaviness; like Cain, who always dwelt in the land of shaking. The terrors of conscience disturb all their enjoyments, and cast forth such mire and dirt as make them a burden to themselves. Though this does not appear (it may be) at present, yet it is a certain truth, what this prophet had said before (*ch.* xlviii. 22), and here repeats (*v.* 21), *There is no peace to the wicked*, no reconciliation to God (nor can they be upon good terms with him, while they go on still in their trespasses), no quietness or satisfaction in their own mind, no real good, no peace in death, because no hope. *My God hath said it*, and all the world cannot unsay it, That there is no peace to those that allow themselves in any sin. What have they to do with peace?

CHAP. LVIII.

The prophet, in this chapter, has his commission and charge renewed to reprove the sinners in Zion, particularly the hypocrites, to show them their transgressions, ver. 1. It is intended for admonition and warning to all hypocrites, and is not to be confined to those of any one age. Some refer it primarily to those at that time when Isaiah prophesied; see chap. xxxiii. 14; xxix. 13. Others to the captives in Babylon, the wicked among them, to whom the prophet had declared there was no peace, ch. lvii. 21. Against the terror of that word they thought to shelter themselves with their external performances, particularly their fastings, which they kept up in Babylon, and for some time after their return to their own land, Zech. vii. 3, &c. The prophet therefore here shows them that their devotions would not entitle them to peace while their conversations were not at all of a piece with them. Others think it is principally intended against the hypocrisy of the Jews, especially the Pharisees before and in our Saviour's time: they boasted of their fastings, but Christ (as the prophet here) showed them their transgressions (Matt. xxiii.), much the same with those they are here charged with. Observe, I. The plausible profession of religion which they made, ver. 2. II. The boasts they made of that profession, and the blame they laid upon God for taking no more notice of it, ver. 3. III. The sins they are charged with, which spoiled the acceptableness of their fasts, ver. 4, 5. IV. Instructions given them how to keep fasts aright, ver. 6, 7. V. Precious promises made to those who do so keep fasts, ver. 8—12. VI. The like precious promises made to those that sanctify sabbaths aright, ver. 13, 14.

CRY aloud, spare not, lift up thy voice like a trumpet, and show my people their transgression, and the house of Jacob their sins. 2 Yet they seek me daily, and delight to know my ways, as a nation that did righteousness, and forsook not the ordinance of their God: they ask of me the ordinances of justice; they take delight in approaching to God.

When our Lord Jesus promised to send the Comforter he added, *When he shall come he shall convince* (John xvi. 7, 8); for conviction must prepare for comfort, and must also separate between the precious and the vile, and mark out those to whom comfort does not belong. God had appointed this prophet to comfort his people (*ch.* xl. 1); here he appoints him to convince them, and show them their sins.

I. He must tell them how very bad they really were, *v.* 1. 1. He must deal faithfully and plainly with them. "Though they are called *the people of God* and *the house of Jacob*, though they wear an honourable title and character, by which they are interested in many glorious privileges, yet do not flatter them, but show them their transgressions and their sins, be particular in telling them their faults, what sins are committed among them, which they do not know of, nay, what sins are committed by them which they do not acknowledge to be sins; though in some things they are reformed, let them know that in other things they are still as bad as ever. Show them their transgressions and their sins, that is, all their transgressions in their sins, their sins and all the aggravations of them," Lev. xvi. 21. Note, (1.) God sees sin in his people, in the house of Jacob, and is displeased with it. (2.) They are often unapt and unwilling to see their own sins, and need to have them shown them, and to be told, *Thus and thus thou hast done.* 2. He must be vehement and in good earnest herein, must *cry aloud, and not spare*, not spare them (not touch them with his reproofs as if he were afraid of hurting them, but search the wound to the bottom, lay it bare to the bone), not spare himself or his own pains, but cry as loud as he can; though he spend his strength and waste his spirits, though he get their ill-will by it and get himself into an ill name, yet he must not spare. He must lift up his voice like a trumpet, to make those hear of their faults that were apt to be deaf when admonition was addressed to them. He must give his reproofs in the most powerful and pressing manner possible, as one who desired to be heeded. The trumpet does not give an uncertain sound, but, though loud and shrill, is intelligible; so must his alarms be, giving them warning of the fatal consequences of sin, Ezek. xxxiii. 3.

II. He must acknowledge how very good they seemed to be, notwithstanding (*v.* 2): *Yet they seek me daily.* When the prophet went about to show them their transgressions they pleaded that they could see no transgressions which they were guilty of; for they were diligent and constant in attending on God's worship—and what more would he have of them? Now,

1. He owns the matter of fact to be true As far as hypocrites do that which is good,

they shall not be denied the praise of it; let them make their best of it. It is owned that they have a form of godliness. (1.) They go to church, and observe their hours of prayer: *They seek me daily;* they are very constant in their devotions and never omit them nor suffer any thing to put them by. (2.) They love to hear good preaching: *They delight to know my ways,* as Herod, who heard John gladly, and the stony ground, that received the seed of the word with joy; it is to them *as a lovely song,* Ezek. xxxiii. 32. (3.) They seem to take a great pleasure in the exercises of religion and to be in their element when they are at their devotions: *They delight in approaching to God,* not for his sake to whom they approach, but for the sake of some pleasing circumstance, the company, or the festival. (4.) They are inquisitive concerning their duty and seem desirous only to know it, making no question but that then they should do it: *They ask of me the ordinances of justice,* the rules of piety in the worship of God, the rules of equity in their dealings with men, both which are ordinances of justice. (5.) They appear to the eye of the world as if they made conscience of doing their duty: *They are as a nation that did righteousness and forsook not the ordinances of their God;* others took them for such, and they themselves pretended to be such. Nothing lay open to view that was a contradiction to their profession, but they seemed to be such as they should be. Note, Men may go a great way towards heaven and yet come short; nay, may go to hell with a good reputation. But, 2. He intimates that this was so far from being a cover or excuse for their sin that really it was an aggravation of it: "Show them their sins which they go on in notwithstanding their knowledge of good and evil, sin and duty, and the convictions of their consciences concerning them."

3 Wherefore have we fasted, *say they,* and thou seest not? *Wherefore* have we afflicted our soul, and thou takest no knowledge? Behold, in the day of your fast ye find pleasure, and exact all your labours. 4 Behold, ye fast for strife and debate, and to smite with the fist of wickedness: ye shall not fast as *ye do this* day, to make your voice to be heard on high. 5 Is it such a fast that I have chosen? A day for a man to afflict his soul? *Is it* to bow down his head as a bulrush, and to spread sackcloth and ashes *under him?* Wilt thou call this a fast, and an acceptable day to the LORD? 6 *Is* not this the fast that I have chosen? To loose the bands of wickedness, to undo the heavy bur-
336

dens, and to let the oppressed go free, and that ye break every yoke? 7 *Is* it not to deal thy bread to the hungry, and that thou bring the poor that are cast out to thy house? when thou seest the naked, that thou cover him; and that thou hide not thyself from thine own flesh?

Here we have, I. The displeasure which these hypocrites conceived against God for not accepting the services which they themselves had a mighty opinion of (v. 3): *Wherefore have we fasted, say they, and thou seest not?* Thus they went in the way of Cain, who was angry at God, and resented it as a gross affront that his offering was not accepted. Having gone about to put a cheat upon God by their external services, here they go about to pick a quarrel with God for not being pleased with their services, as if he had not done fairly or justly by them. Observe, 1. How they boast of themselves, and magnify their own performances: "*We have fasted, and afflicted our souls;* we have not only sought God daily (v. 2), but have kept some certain times of more solemn devotion." Some think this refers to the yearly fast (which was called *the day of atonement),* others to their arbitrary occasional fasts. Note, It is common for unhumbled hearts to be proud of their professions of humiliation, as the Pharisee (Luke xviii. 12), *I fast twice in the week.* 2. What they expected from their performances. They thought God should take great notice of them, and own himself a debtor to them for their services. Note, It is a common thing for hypocrites, while they perform the external services of religion, to promise themselves that acceptance with God which he has promised only to the sincere; as if they must be accepted of course, or for a compliment. 3. How heinously they take it that God had not put some particular marks of his favour upon them, that he had not immediately delivered them out of their troubles and advanced them to honour and prosperity. They charge God with injustice and partiality, and seem resolved to throw up their religion, and justify themselves in doing so with this, that they had found no *profit in praying* to God, Job xxi. 14, 15; Mal. iii. 14. Note, Reigning hypocrisy often breaks out in daring impiety and an open contempt and reproach of God and religion for that which the hypocrisy itself must bear all the blame of. Sinners reflect upon religion as a hard and melancholy service, and one which there is nothing to be got by, when really it is owing to themselves that it seems so to them, because they are not sincere in it.

II. The true reason assigned why God did not accept their fastings, nor answer the prayers they made on their fast-days; it was because they did not fast aright—*to*

God, even to him, Zech. vii. 5. They fasted indeed, but they persisted in their sins, and did not, as the Ninevites, turn every one from his evil way; but *in the day of their fast,* and notwithstanding the professed humiliations and covenants of that day, they went on to *find pleasure,* that is, to do whatsoever seemed right in their own eyes, lawful or unlawful, *quicquid libet, licet—making their inclinations their law;* though they seemed to afflict their souls, they still gratified their lusts as much as ever. 1. They were as covetous and unmerciful as ever: " *You exact all your labours* from your servants, and will neither release them according to the law nor relax the rigour of their servitude." This was their fault before the captivity, Jer. xxxiv. 8, 9. It was no less their fault after their captivity, notwithstanding all their solemn fasts, Neh. v. 5. " *You exact all your dues,* your *debts*" (so some read it); you are as rigorous and severe in extorting what you demand from those that are poor as ever you were, though it was at the close of the yearly fast that the release was proclaimed." 2. They were contentious and spiteful (*v.* 4): *Behold, you fast for strife and debate.* When they proclaimed a fast to deprecate God's judgments, they pretended to search for those sins which provoked God to threaten them with his judgments, and under that pretence perhaps particular persons were falsely accused, as Naboth in the day of Jezebel's fast, 1 Kings xxi. 12. Or the contending parties among them upon those occasions were bitter and severe in their reflections one upon another, one side crying out, " It is owing to you," and the other, " It is owing to you, that our deliverance is not wrought." Thus, instead of judging themselves, which is the proper work of a fast-day, they condemned one another. They *fasted for strife,* with emulation which should make the most plausible appearance on a fast-day and humour the matter best. Nor was it only tongue-quarrels that were fomented in the times of their fasting, but they came to blows too: *You smite with the fist of wickedness.* The cruel task-masters beat their servants, and the creditors their insolvent debtors, whom they delivered to the tormentors; they abused poor innocents *with wicked hands.* Now while they thus *continued in sin,* in those very sins which were directly contrary to the intention of a fasting day, (1.) God would not allow them the use of such solemnities: " *You shall not fast* at all if you fast *as you do this day, causing your voice to be heard on high,* in the heat of your clamours one against another, or in your devotions, which you perform so as to make them to be taken notice of for ostentation. *Bring me no more* of these empty, noisy, *vain oblations,*" ch. i. 13. Note, Those are justly forbidden the honour of a profession of religion that will not submit to the power of it. (2.) He would

not accept of them in the use of them : " *You shall not fast,* that is, it shall not be looked upon as a fast, nor shall the voice of your prayers on those days be heard on high in heaven." Note, Those that fast and pray, and yet go on in their wicked ways, do but mock God and deceive themselves.

III. Plain instructions given concerning the true nature of a religious fast.

1. In general, a fast is intended, (1.) For the honouring and pleasing of God. It must be such a performance as he has chosen (*v.* 5); it must be *an acceptable day to the Lord,* in the duties of which we must study to approve ourselves to him and obtain his favour, else it is not a fast, else there is nothing done to any purpose. (2.) For the humbling and abasing of ourselves. A fast is *a day to afflict the soul;* if it do not express a genuine sorrow for sin, and do not promote a real mortification of sin, it is not a fast; the law of the day of atonement was that on that day they should *afflict their souls,* Lev. xvi. 29. That must be done on a fast-day which is a real affliction to the soul, as far as it is yet unregenerate and unsanctified, though a real pleasure and advantage to the soul as far as it is itself.

2. It concerns us therefore to enquire, on a fast-day, what it is that will be acceptable to God, and afflictive to our corrupt nature, and tending to its mortification.

(1.) We are here told negatively what is not the fast that God has chosen, and which does not amount to the afflicting of the soul. [1.] It is not enough to look demure, to put on a grave and melancholy aspect, to bow down the head like a bulrush that is withered and broken: as the hypocrites, that were *of a sad countenance, and disfigured their faces, that they might appear unto men to fast,* Matt. vi. 16. Hanging down the head did indeed well enough become the publican, whose heart was truly humbled and broken for sin, and who therefore, in token of that, *would not so much as lift up his eyes to heaven* (Luke xviii. 13) ; but when it was only mimicked, as here, it was justly ridiculed : it is but *hanging down the head like a bulrush,* which nobody regards or takes any notice of. As the hypocrite's humiliations are but like the hanging down of a bulrush, so his elevations in his hopes are but like the *flourishing of a bulrush* (Job viii. 11, 12), which, *while it is yet in its greenness, withers before any other herb.* [2.] It is not enough to do penance, to mortify the body a little, while the body of sin is untouched. It is not enough for a man *to spread sackcloth and ashes under him,* which may indeed give him some uneasiness for the present, but will soon be forgotten when he returns to *stretch himself upon his beds of ivory,* Amos vi. 4. *Wilt thou call this a fast?* No, it is but the shadow and carcase of a fast. *Wilt thou call this an acceptable day to the Lord?* No, it is so far from being so that the hypocrisy of it is an abomination to him. Note, The shows of religion, though they show ever so fair in the eye of the world, will not be accepted of God without the substance of it.

(2.) We are here told positively what is the fast that God has chosen, what that is which will recommend a fast-day to the divine acceptance, and what is indeed afflicting the soul, that is, crushing and subduing the corrupt nature. It *is not afflicting the soul for a day* (as some read it, *v.* 5) that will serve; no, it must be the business of our whole lives. It is here required, [1.] That we be just to those with whom we have dealt hardly. The fast that God has chosen consists in reforming our lives and undoing what we have done amiss (*v.* 6): *To loose the bands of wickedness*, the bands which we have wickedly tied, and by which others are bound out from their right or bound down under severe usage. Those which perhaps were at first bands of justice, tying men to pay a due debt, become, when the debt is exacted with rigour from those whom Providence has reduced and emptied, *bands of wickedness*, and they must be loosed, or they will bring us into bonds of guilt much more terrible. It is *to undo the heavy burden* laid on the back of the poor servant, under which he is ready to sink. It is *to let the oppressed go free* from the oppression which makes his life bitter to him. "Let the prisoner for debt that has nothing to pay be discharged, let the vexatious action be quashed, let the servant that is forcibly detained beyond the time of his servitude be released, and thus *break every yoke;* not only let go those that are wrongfully kept under the yoke, but break the yoke of slavery itself, that it may not serve again another time nor any be made again to serve under it." [2.] That we be charitable to those that stand in need of charity, *v.* 7. The particulars in the former verse *may* be taken as acts of charity, that we not only release those whom we have unjustly oppressed—that is justice, but that we contribute to the rescue and ransom of those that are oppressed by others, to the release of captives and the payment of the debts of the poor; but those in this verse are *plainly* acts of charity. This then is the fast that God has chosen. *First*, To provide food for those that want it. This is put first, as the most necessary, and which the poor can but a little while live without. It is *to break thy bread to the hungry.* Observe, "It must be *thy* bread, that which is honestly got (not that which thou hast robbed others of), the bread which thou thyself hast occasion for, the bread of thy allowance." We must deny ourselves, that we may have to give to him that needeth. "Thy bread which thou hast spared from thyself and thy family, on the fast-day, if that, or the value of it, be not given to the poor, it is the miser's fast, which he makes

338

a hand of; it is fasting for the world, not for God. This is the true fast, to break thy bread to the hungry, not only to give them that which is already broken meat, but to break bread on purpose for them, to give them loaves and not to put them off with scraps." *Secondly*, To provide lodging for those that want it: It is *to take care of the poor that are cast out*, that are forced from their dwelling, turned out of house and harbour, *are cast out as rebels* (so some critics render it), that are attainted, and whom therefore it is highly penal to protect. "If they suffer unjustly, make no difficulty of sheltering them; do not only find out quarters for them and pay for their lodging elsewhere, but, which is a greater act of kindness, bring them to thy own house, make them thy own guests. Be not forgetful to entertain strangers: for though thou mayest not, as some have done, thereby entertain angels, thou mayest entertain Christ himself, who will recompense it in the resurrection of the just. *I was a stranger and you took me in.*" *Thirdly*, To provide clothing for those that want it: "*When thou seest the naked, that thou cover him*, both to shelter him from the injuries of the weather and to enable him to appear decently among his neighbours; give him clothes to come to church in, and in these and other instances *hide not thyself from thy own flesh.*" Some understand it more strictly of a man's own kindred and relations: "If those of thy own house and family fall into decay, thou art *worse than an infidel* if thou dost not *provide* for them," 1 Tim. v. 8. Others understand it more generally; all that partake of the human nature are to be looked upon as our own flesh, for have we not all one Father? And for this reason we must not hide ourselves from them, not contrive to be out of the way when a poor petitioner enquires for us, not look another way when a moving object of charity and compassion presents itself; let us remember that they are flesh of our flesh and therefore we ought to sympathize with them, and in doing good to them we really do good to our own flesh and spirit too in the issue; for thus *we lay up for ourselves a good foundation*, a good bond, *for the time to come.*

8 Then shall thy light break forth as the morning, and thine health shall spring forth speedily: and thy righteousness shall go before thee; the glory of the LORD shall be thy rereward. 9 Then shalt thou call, and the LORD shall answer; thou shalt cry, and he shall say, Here I *am.* If thou take away from the midst of thee the yoke, the putting forth of the finger, and speaking vanity; 10 And *if* thou draw out thy soul to the hun-

gry, and satisfy the afflicted soul; then shall thy light rise in obscurity, and thy darkness *be* as the noon-day: 11 And the LORD shall guide thee continually, and satisfy thy soul in drought, and make fat thy bones: and thou shalt be like a watered garden, and like a spring of water, whose waters fail not. 12 And *they that shall be* of thee shall build the old waste places: thou shalt raise up the foundations of many generations; and thou shalt be called, The repairer of the breach, the restorer of paths to dwell in.

Here are precious promises for those to feast freely and cheerfully upon by faith who keep the fast that God has chosen; let them know that God will make it up to them. Here is,

I. A further account of the duty to be done in order to our interest in these promises (*v.* 9, 10); and here, as before, it is required that we both do justly and love mercy, that we cease to do evil and learn to do well. 1. We must abstain from all acts of violence and fraud. "Those must be *taken away from the midst of thee*, from the midst of *thy person*, out of *thy heart*" (so some); "thou must not only refrain from the practice of injury, but mortify in thee all inclination and disposition towards it." Or *from the midst of thy people.* Those in authority must not only not be oppressive themselves, but must do all they can to prevent and restrain oppression in all within their jurisdiction. They must not only *break the yoke* (*v.* 6), but take away the yoke, that those who have been oppressed may never be re-enslaved (as they were Jer. xxxiv. 10, 11); they must likewise *forbear threatening* (Eph. vi. 9) and take away the *putting forth of the finger*, which seems to have been then, as sometimes with us, a sign of displeasure and the indication of a purpose to correct. Let not the finger be put forth to point at those that are poor and in misery, and so to expose them to contempt; such expressions of contumely as are provoking, and the products of ill-nature, ought to be banished from all societies. And let them not *speak vanity*, flattery or fraud, to one another, but let all conversation be governed by sincerity. Perhaps that dissimulation which is the bane of friendship is meant by the putting forth of the finger (as Prov. vi. 13 by *teaching with the finger*), or it is putting forth the finger with the ring on it, which was the badge of authority, and which therefore they produced when they spoke iniquity, that is, gave unrighteous sentences. 2. We must abound in all acts of charity and beneficence. We must not only give alms accord-

ing as the necessities of the poor require, but, (1.) We must give freely and cheerfully, and from a principle of charity. We must *draw out our soul to the hungry* (*v.* 10), not only draw out the money and reach forth the hand, but do this from the heart, heartily, and without grudging, from a principle of compassion and with a tender affection to such as we see to be in misery. Let the heart go along with the gift; for God loves a cheerful giver, and so does a poor man too. When our Lord Jesus healed and fed the multitude it was as having compassion on them. (2.) We must give plentifully and largely, so as not to tantalize, but to *satisfy, the afflicted soul:* "Do not only feed the hungry, but gratify the desire of the afflicted, and, if it lies in your power, make them easy." What are we born for, and what have we our abilities of body, mind, and estate for, but to do all the good we can in this world with them? And the poor we always have with us.

II. Here is a full account of the blessings and benefits which attend the performance of this duty. If a person, a family, a people, be thus disposed to every thing that is good, let them know for their comfort that they shall find God their bountiful rewarder and what they lay out in works of charity shall be abundantly made up to them. 1. God will surprise them with the return of mercy after great affliction, which shall be as welcome as the light of the morning after a long and dark night (*v.* 8): "*Then shall thy light break forth as the morning* and (*v.* 10) *thy light shall rise in obscurity.* Though thou hast been long buried alive thou shalt recover thy eminency; though long overwhelmed with grief, thou shalt again look pleasant as the dawning day." Those that are cheerful in doing good God will make cheerful in enjoying good; and this also is a special *gift of God*, Eccl. ii. 24. Those that have shown mercy shall find mercy. Job, who in his prosperity had done a great deal of good, had friends raised up for him by the Lord when he was reduced, who helped him with their substance, so that his light rose in obscurity. "Not only thy light, which is sweet, but thy health too, or the healing of the wounds thou hast long complained of, shall spring forth speedily; all thy grievances shall be redressed, and thou shalt renew thy youth and recover thy vigour." Those that have helped others out of trouble will obtain help of God when it is their turn. 2. God will put honour upon them. Good works shall be recompensed with a good name; this is included in that *light which rises out of obscurity.* Though a man's extraction be mean, his family obscure, and he has no external advantages to gain him honour, yet, if he do good in his place, that will procure him respect and veneration, and his darkness shall by this means become *as the noon-day*, that is, he shall become

339

very eminent and shine brightly in his generation. See here what is the surest way for a man to make himself illustrious; let him study to do good. He that would be the greatest of all, and best-beloved, let him by humility and industry make himself a servant of all. *" Thy righteousness shall* then *go before thee,* that is, it shall introduce thee into the esteem of many, and make thee an interest. *Thy righteousness shall answer for thee* (as Jacob says, Gen. xxx. 33), that is, it shall silence reproaches, nay, it shall bespeak thee more praises than thy humility can be pleased with." He that has *given to the poor, his righteousness* (that is, the honour of it) *endures for ever,* Ps. cxii. 9. 3. They shall always be safe under the divine protection: *" Thy righteousness shall go before* thee as thy vanguard, to secure thee from enemies that charge thee in the front, and *the glory of the Lord shall be thy rearward,* the gathering host, to bring up those of thee that are weary and are left behind, and to secure thee from the enemies, that, like Amalek, fall upon thy rear." Observe, How good people are safe on all sides. Let them look which way they will, behind them or before them; let them look backward or forward; they see themselves safe, and find themselves easy and quiet from the fear of evil. And observe what it is that is their defence; it is their righteousness, and the glory of the Lord, that is, as some suppose, Christ; for it is by him that we are justified, and God is glorified. He it is that goes before us, and is the captain of our salvation, as he is the Lord our righteousness; he it is that is our rearward, on whom alone we can depend for safety when our sins pursue us and are ready to take hold on us. Or, " God himself in his providence and grace shall both go before thee as thy guide to conduct thee, and attend thee as thy rearward to protect thee, and this shall be the reward of thy righteousness and so shall be for the glory of the Lord as the rewarder of it." 4. God will be always nigh unto them, to hear their prayers, *v.* 9. As, on the one hand, he that shuts his ears to the cry of the poor shall himself cry and God will not hear him; so, on the other hand, he that is liberal to the poor, his prayers shall come up with his alms for a memorial before God, as Cornelius's did (Acts x. 4): *" Then shalt thou call,* on thy fast-days, which ought to be days of prayer, *and the Lord shall answer,* shall give thee the things thou callest to him for; *thou shalt cry* when thou art in any distress or sudden fright, *and he shall say, Here I am."* This is a very condescending expression of God's readiness to hear prayer. When God calls to us by his word it becomes us to say, *Here we are; what saith our Lord unto his servants?* But that God should say to us, *Behold me, here I am,* is strange. When we cry to him, as if he were at a distance, he will let us know that he is

near, even at our right hand, nearer than we thought he was. *It is I, be not afraid* When danger is near our protector is nearer, *a very present help.* " Here I am, ready to give you what you want, and do for you what you desire; what have you to say to me ?" God is attentive to the prayers of the upright, Ps. cxxx. 2. No sooner do they call to him than he answers, *Ready, ready.* Wherever they are praying, God says, " Here I am hearing; I am *in the midst of you."* He is *nigh unto them in all things,* Deut. iv. 7. 5. God will direct them in all difficult and doubtful cases (*v.* 11): *The Lord shall guide thee continually.* While we are here, in the wilderness of this world, we have need of continual direction from heaven; for, if at any time we be left to ourselves, we shall certainly miss our way; and therefore it is to those who are good in God's sight that he gives the wisdom which in all cases is profitable to direct, and he will be to them *instead of eyes,* Eccl. ii. 26. His providence will make their way plain to them, both what is their duty and what will be most for their comfort. 6. God will give them abundance of satisfaction in their own minds. As the world is a wilderness in respect of wanderings, so that they need to be guided continually, so also is it in respect of wants, which makes it necessary that they should have continual supplies, as Israel in the wilderness had not only the pillar of cloud to guide them continually, but manna and water out of the rock to satisfy their souls in drought, *in a dry and thirsty land where no water is,* Ps. lxiii. 1. To a good man God gives not only wisdom and knowledge, but joy; he is satisfied in himself with the testimony of his conscience and the assurances of God's favour. " These will *satisfy thy soul,* will put gladness into thy heart, even *in the drought* of affliction; *these will make fat thy bones,* and fill them with marrow, will give thee that pleasure which will be a support to thee as the bones to the body, that joy of the Lord which will be thy strength. *He shall give thy bones rest"* (so some read it), " rest from the pain and sickness which they have laboured under and been chastened with ;" so it agrees with that promise made to the merciful. The Lord will *make all his bed in his sickness,* Ps. xli. 3. " *Thou shalt be like a watered garden,* so flourishing and fruitful in graces and comforts, *and like a spring of water,* like a garden that has a spring of water in it, *whose waters fail not* either in droughts or in frosts." The principle of holy love in those that are good shall be a *well of living water,* John iv. 14. As a spring of water, though it is continually sending forth its streams, is yet always full, so the charitable man abounds in good as he abounds in doing good and is never the poorer for his liberality. He that waters shall himself be watered. 7. They and their families shall be public blessings. It is a good reward to those that are fruitful and useful to be rendered more so, and especially to have those who descend from them to be so too. This is here promised (*v.* 12): "Those that now are of thee, thy princes, and nobles, and great men, shall have such authority and influence as they never had;" or, "*Those that* hereafter *shall be of thee*, thy posterity, shall be serviceable to their generation, as thou art to thine." It completes the satisfaction of a good man, as to this world, to think that those that come after him shall be doing good when he is gone. 1. They shall re-edify cities that have been long in ruins, *shall build the old waste places*, which had lain so long desolate that the rebuilding of them was quite despaired of. This was fulfilled when the captives, after their return, repaired the cities of Judah, and dwelt in them, and many of those in Israel too, which had lain waste ever since the carrying away of the ten tribes. 2. They shall carry on and finish that good work which was begun long before, and shall be helped over the obstructions which had retarded the progress of it : *They shall raise up* to the top that building *the foundation of* which was laid long since and has been for *many generations* in the rearing. This was fulfilled when the building of the temple was revived after it had stood still for many years, Ezra v. 2. Or, "They shall raise up foundations which shall continue for many generations yet to come;" they shall do that good which shall be of lasting consequence. 3. They shall have the blessing and praise of all about them : "*Thou shalt be called* (and it shall be to thy honour) *the repairer of the breach*, the breach made by the enemy in the wall of a besieged city, which whoso has the courage and dexterity to make up, or make good, gains great applause." Happy are those who make up the breach at which virtue is running out and judgments are breaking in. "Thou shalt be *the restorer of paths*, safe and quiet paths, not only to travel in, but *to dwell in*, so safe and quiet that people shall make no difficulty of building their houses by the road-side." The sum is that, if they keep such fasts as God as chosen, he will settle them again in their former peace and prosperity, and there shall be none to make them afraid. See Zech. vii. 5, 9; viii. 3—5. It teaches us that those who do justly and love mercy shall have the comfort thereof in this world.

13 If thou turn away thy foot from the sabbath, *from* doing thy pleasure on my holy day; and call the sabbath a delight, the holy of the LORD, honourable ; and shalt honour him, not doing thine own ways, nor finding thine own pleasure, nor speaking *thine own* words : 14 Then shalt thou

delight thyself in the LORD; and I will cause thee to ride upon the high places of the earth, and feed thee with the heritage of Jacob thy father : for the mouth of the LORD hath spoken *it*.

Great stress was always laid upon the due observance of the sabbath day, and it was particularly required from the Jews when they were captives in Babylon, because by keeping that day, in honour of the Creator, they distinguished themselves from the worshippers of the gods that have not made the heavens and the earth. See *ch.* lvi. 1, 2, where keeping the sabbath is joined, as here, with *keeping judgment* and *doing justice.* Some, indeed, understand this of the day of atonement, which they think is the fast spoken of in the former part of the chapter, and which is called a *sabbath of rest*, Lev. xxiii. 32. But, as the fasts before spoken of seem to be those that were occasional, so this sabbath is doubtless the weekly sabbath, that great sign between God and his professing people—his appointing it a sign of his favour to them and their observing it a sign of their obedience to him. Now observe here,

I. How the sabbath is to be sanctified (*v.* 13); and, there remaining still a sabbatism for the people of God, this law of the sabbath is still binding to us on our Lord's day.

1. Nothing must be done that puts contempt upon the sabbath day, or looks like having mean thoughts of it, when God has so highly dignified it. We must *turn away our foot from the sabbath*, from trampling upon it, as profane atheistical people do, from travelling on that day (so some); we must turn away our foot *from doing our pleasure on that holy day*, that is, from living at large, and taking a liberty to do what we please on sabbath days, without the control and restraint of conscience, or from indulging ourselves in the pleasures of sense, in which the modern Jews wickedly place the sanctification of the sabbath, though it is as great a profanation of it as any thing. On sabbath days we must not walk in *our own ways* (that is, not follow our callings), not *find our own pleasure* (that is, not follow our sports and recreations) ; nay, we must not *speak our own words*, words that concern either our callings or our pleasures ; we must not allow ourselves a liberty of speech on that day as on other days, for we must then mind God's ways, make religion the business of the day ; we must choose the things that please him ; and speak his words, speak of divine things as we sit in the house and walk by the way. In all we say and do we must put a difference between this day and other days.

2. Every thing must be done that puts an honour on the day and is expressive of our high thoughts of it. We must call it *a delight*, not a *task and a burden ;* we must delight ourselves in it, in the restraints it lays

upon us and the services it obliges us to. We must be in our element when we are worshipping God, and in communion with him. *How amiable are thy tabernacles, O Lord of hosts!* We must not only count it a delight, but call it so, must openly profess the complacency we take in the day and the duties of it. We must call it so to God, in thanksgiving for it and earnest desire of his grace to enable us to do the work of the day in its day, because we delight in it. We must call it so to others, to invite them to come and share in the pleasure of it; and we must call it so to ourselves, that we may not entertain the least thought of wishing the sabbath gone that we may sell corn. We must call it *the Lord's holy day, and honourable.* We must call it *holy,* separated from common use and devoted to God and to his service, must call it *the holy of the Lord,* the day which he has sanctified to himself. Even in Old-Testament times the sabbath was called *the Lord's day,* and therefore it is fitly called so still, and for a further reason, because it is the *Lord Christ's day,* Rev. i. 10. It is holy because it is the Lord's day, and upon both accounts it is honourable. It is a beauty of holiness that is upon it; it is ancient, and its antiquity is its honour; and we must make it appear that we look upon it as honourable by honouring God on that day. We put honour upon the day when we give honour to him that instituted it, and to whose honour it is dedicated.

II. What the reward is of sabbath-sanctification, *v.* 14. If we thus *remember the sabbath day to keep it holy,*

1. We shall have the comfort of it; the work will be its own wages. *If we call the sabbath a delight, then shall we delight ourselves in the Lord;* he will more and more manifest himself to us as the delightful subject of our thoughts and meditations and the delightful object of our best affections. Note, The more pleasure we take in serving God the more pleasure we shall find in it. If we go about duty with cheerfulness, we shall go from it with satisfaction and shall have reason to say, "It is good to be here, good to draw near to God."

2. We shall have the honour of it: *I will cause thee to ride upon the high places of the earth,* which denotes not only a great security (as that, *ch.* xxxiii. 16, *He shall dwell on high),* but great dignity and advancement. "Thou shalt ride in state, shalt appear conspicuous, and the eyes of all thy neighbours shall be upon thee." It was said of Israel, when God led them triumphantly out of Egypt, that *he made them to ride on the high places of the earth,* Deut. xxxii. 12, 13. Those that honour God and his sabbath he will thus honour. If God by his grace enable us to live above the world, and so to manage it as not only not to be hindered by it, but to be furthered and carried on by it in our journey towards heaven, then

342

he makes us *to ride on the high places of the earth.*

3. We shall have the profit of it: I will *feed thee with the heritage of Jacob thy father,* that is, with all the blessings of the covenant and all the precious products of Canaan (which was a type of heaven), for these were the heritage of Jacob. Observe, The heritage of believers is what they shall not only be portioned with hereafter, but fed with now, fed with the hopes of it, and not flattered, fed with the earnests and foretastes of it; and those that are so fed have reason to say that they are well fed. In order that we may depend upon it, it is added, *" The mouth of the Lord has spoken it;* you may take God's word for it, for he cannot lie nor deceive; what his mouth has spoken his hand will give, his hand will do, and not one iota or tittle of his good promise shall fall to the ground." *Blessed, therefore,* thrice blessed, *is he that doeth this, and lays hold on it, that keeps the sabbath from polluting it.*

CHAP. LIX.

In this chapter we have sin appearing exceedingly sinful, and grace appearing exceedingly gracious; and, as what is here said of the sinner's sin (ver. 7, 8) is applied to the general corruption of mankind (Rom. iii. 15), so what is here said of a Redeemer (ver. 20) is applied to Christ, Rom. xi. 26. I. It is here charged upon this people that they had themselves stopped the current of God's favours to them, and the particular sins are specified which kept good things from them, ver. 1—8. II. It is here charged upon them that they had themselves procured the judgments of God upon them, and they are told both what the judgments were which they had brought upon their own heads (ver. 9—11) and what the sins were which provoked God to send those judgments, ver. 12—15. III. It is here promised that, notwithstanding this, God would work deliverance for them, purely for his own name's sake (ver. 16—19), and would reserve mercy in store for them and entail it upon them, ver. 20, 21.

BEHOLD, the LORD's hand is not shortened, that it cannot save; neither his ear heavy, that it cannot hear: 2 But your iniquities have separated between you and your God, and your sins have hid *his* face from you, that he will not hear. 3 For your hands are defiled with blood, and your fingers with iniquity; your lips have spoken lies, your tongue hath muttered perverseness. 4 None calleth for justice, nor *any* pleadeth for truth: they trust in vanity, and speak lies; they conceive mischief, and bring forth iniquity. 5 They hatch cockatrice' eggs, and weave the spider's web: he that eateth of their eggs dieth, and that which is crushed breaketh out into a viper. 6 Their webs shall not become garments, neither shall they cover themselves with their works: their works *are* works of iniquity, and the act of violence *is* in their hands. 7 Their feet run to evil, and they make haste to shed innocent blood: their thoughts *are* thoughts of iniquity; wasting and destruction *are* in their paths. 8 The way of peace they know not; and *there is* no judgment in their goings: they have made them crooked paths: whosoever goeth therein shall not know peace.

The prophet here rectifies the mistake of those who had been quarrelling with God because they had not the deliverances wrought for them which they had been often fasting and praying for, *ch.* lviii. 3. Now here he shows,

I. That it was not owing to God. They had no reason to lay the fault upon him that they were not saved out of the hands of their enemies; for, 1. He was still as able to help as ever: *His hand is not shortened,* his power is not at all lessened, straitened, or abridged. Whether we consider the extent of his power or the efficacy of it, God can reach as far as ever and with as strong a hand as ever. Note, The church's salvation comes from the hand of God, and that has not waxed weak nor is it at all shortened. *Has the Lord's hand waxed short?* (says God to Moses, Num. xi. 23). No, it has not; he will not have it thought so. Neither length of time nor strength of enemies, no, nor weakness of instruments, can shorten or straiten the power of God, with which it is all one to save by many or by few. 2. He was still as ready and willing to help as ever in answer to prayer: *His ear is not heavy, that it cannot hear.* Though he has many prayers to hear and answer, and though he has been long hearing prayer, yet he is still as ready to hear prayer as ever. The prayer of the upright is as much his delight as ever it was, and the promises which are pleaded and put in suit in prayer are still yea and amen, inviolably sure. More is implied than is expressed; not only his ear is not heavy, but he is quick of hearing. *Even before they call he answers, ch.* lxv. 24. If your prayers be not answered, and the salvation we wait for be not wrought for us, it is not because God is weary of hearing prayer, but because we are weary of praying, not because his ear is heavy when we speak to him, but because our ears are heavy when he speaks to us.

II. That it was owing to themselves; they stood in their own light and put a bar in their own door. God was coming towards them in ways of mercy and they hindered him. *Your iniquities have kept good things from you,* Jer. v. 25.

1. See what mischief sin does. (1.) It hinders God's mercies from coming down upon us; it is a partition wall that separates between us and God. Notwithstanding the infinite distance that is between God and man by nature, there was a correspondence settled between them, till sin set them at variance, justly provoked God against man

and unjustly alienated man from God; thus it *separates between them and God.* "He is your God, yours in profession, and therefore there is so much the more malignity and mischievousness in sin, which separates between you and him." Sin *hides his face from us* (which denotes great displeasure, Deut. xxxi. 17); it provokes him in anger to withdraw his gracious presence, to suspend the tokens of his favour and the instances of his help; he hides his face, as refusing to be seen or spoken with. See here sin in its colours, sin exceedingly sinful, withdrawing the creature from his allegiance to his Creator; and see sin in its consequences, sin exceedingly hurtful, separating us from God, and so separating us not only *from all good,* but *to all evil* (Deut. xxix. 21), which is the very quintessence of the curse. (2.) It hinders our prayers from coming up unto God; it provokes him to hide his face, that he will not hear, as he has said, *ch.* i. 15. If we *regard iniquity in our heart,* if we indulge it and allow ourselves in it, God *will not hear our prayers,* Ps. lxvi. 18. We cannot expect that he should countenance us while we go on to affront him.

2. Now, to justify God in hiding his face from them, and proceeding in his controversy with them, the prophet shows very largely, in the following verses, how many and great their iniquities were, according to the charge given him (*ch.* lviii. 1), *to show God's people their transgressions;* and it is a black bill of indictment that is here drawn up against them, consisting of many particulars, any one of which was enough to separate between them and a just and a holy God. Let us endeavour to reduce these articles of impeachment to proper heads.

(1.) We must begin with their thoughts, for there all sin begins, and thence it takes its rise: *Their thoughts are thoughts of iniquity, v.* 7. Their imaginations are so, only evil continually. Their projects and designs are so; they are continually contriving some mischief or other, and how to compass the gratification of some base lust (*v.* 4): *They conceive mischief* in their fancy, purpose, counsel, and resolution (thus the embryo receives its shape and life), and then they *bring forth iniquity,* put it in execution when it is ripened for it. Though it is in pain perhaps that the iniquity is brought forth, through the oppositions of Providence and the checks of their own consciences, yet, when they have compassed their wicked purpose, they look upon it with as much pride and pleasure as if it were a *man-child born into the world;* thus, *when lust has conceived, it bringeth forth sin,* Jam. i. 15. This is called (*v.* 5) *hatching the cockatrice' egg and weaving the spider's web.* See how the thoughts and contrivances of wicked men are employed, and about what they set their wits on work. [1.] At the best it is about that which is foolish and frivolous. Their

343

thoughts are vain, like weaving the spider's web, which the poor silly animal takes a great deal of pains about, and, when all is done, it is a weak insignificant thing, a reproach to the place where it is, and which the besom sweeps away in an instant: such are the thoughts which worldly men entertain themselves with, building castles in the air, and pleasing themselves with imaginary satisfaction, like the *spider*, which *takes hold with her hands* very finely (Prov. xxx. 28), but cannot keep her hold. [2.] Too often it is about that which is malicious and spiteful. They hatch the eggs of the cockatrice or adder, which are poisonous and produce venomous creatures ; such are the thoughts of the wicked who delight in doing mischief. *He that eats of their eggs* (that is, has any dealings with them) *dies* (that is, he is in danger of having some mischief or other done him), *and that which is crushed* in order to be eaten of, or which begins to be hatched and you promise yourself some useful fowl from it, *breaks out into a viper*, which you meddle with at your peril. Happy are those that have least to do with such men. Even the spider's web which they wove was woven with a spiteful design to catch flies in and make a prey of them ; for, rather than not be doing mischief, they will play at small game.

(2.) Out of this abundance of wickedness in the heart their mouth speaks, and yet it does not always speak out the wickedness that is within, but, for the more effectually compassing the mischievous design, it is dissembled and covered *with much fair speech* (v. 3) : *Your lips have spoken lies ;* and again (v. 4), *They speak lies*, pretending kindness where they intend the greatest mischief ; or by slanders and false accusations they blasted the credit and reputation of those they had a spite to and so did them a real mischief unseen, and perhaps by suborning witnesses against them took from them their estates and lives ; for a false tongue is sharp arrows, and coals of juniper, and every thing that is mischievous. *Your tongue has muttered perverseness.* When they could not, for shame, speak their malice against their neighbours aloud, or durst not, for fear of being disproved and put to confusion, they muttered it secretly. Backbiters are called *whisperers.*

(3.) Their actions were all of a piece with their thoughts and words. They were guilty of shedding innocent blood, a crime of the most heinous nature : *Your hands are defiled with blood* (v. 3) ; for blood is defiling ; it leaves an indelible stain of guilt upon the conscience, which nothing but the blood of Christ can cleanse it from. Nor was this a case of surprise, or one that occurred when there was something of a force put upon them ; but (v. 7) *their feet ran to this evil*, naturally and eagerly, and, hurried on by the *impetus* of their malice and revenge, *they made haste to shed innocent blood*, as if they were afraid of losing an opportunity to do a

344

barbarous thing, Prov. i. 16 ; Jer. xxii. 17. *Wasting and destruction are in their paths.* Wherever they go they carry mischief along with them, and the tendency of their way is to lay waste and destroy, nor do they care what havoc they make. Nor do they only thirst after blood, but with other iniquities are their *fingers defiled* (v. 3) ; they wrong people in their estates and make every thing their own that they can lay their hands on. *They trust in vanity* (v. 4) ; they depend upon their arts of cozenage to enrich themselves with, which will prove vanity to them, and their deceiving others will but deceive themselves. *Their works*, which they take so much pains about and have their hearts so much upon, *are* all *works of iniquity ;* their whole business is one continued course of oppressions and vexations, *and the act of violence is in their hands*, according to the arts of violence that are in their heads and the thoughts of violence in their hearts.

(4.) No methods are taken to redress these grievances and reform these abuses (v 4) : *None calls for justice*, none complains of the violation of the sacred laws of justice, nor seeks to right those that suffer wrong or to get the laws put in execution against vice and profaneness, and those lewd practices which are the shame, and threaten to be the bane, of the nation. Note, When justice is not done there is blame to be laid not only upon the magistrates that should administer justice, but upon the people that should call for it. Private persons ought to contribute to the public good by discovering secret wickedness, and giving those an opportunity to punish it that have the power of doing so in their hands ; but it is ill with a state when princes rule ill and the people love to have it so. Truth is opposed, and there is not any that *pleads for it*, not any that has the conscience and courage to appear in defence of an honest cause, and confront a prosperous fraud and wrong. *The way of peace* is as little regarded as the way of truth ; they *know it not*, that is, they never study the things that make for peace, no care is taken to prevent or punish the breaches of the peace and to accommodate matters in difference among neighbours ; they are utter strangers to every thing that looks quiet and peaceable, and affect that which is blustering and turbulent. *There is no judgment in their goings;* they have not any sense of justice in their dealings ; it is a thing they make no account of at all, but can easily break through all its fences if they stand in the way of their malicious covetous designs.

(5.) In all this they act foolishly, very foolishly, and as much against their interest as against reason and equity. Those that practise iniquity *trust in vanity*, which will certainly deceive them, v. 4. *Their webs*, which they weave with so much art and industry, *shall not become garments, neither shall they cover themselves,* either for shelter or for ornament, *with their works, v.* 6. They may do hurt to others with their projects, but can never do any real service or kindness to themselves by them. There is nothing to be got by sin, and so it will appear when profit and loss come to be compared. Those paths of iniquity are *crooked paths* (*v.* 8), which will perplex them, but will never bring them to their journey's end ; whoever go therein, though they say that they shall have peace notwithstanding they go on, deceive themselves; for they shall not know peace, as appears by the following verses.

9 Therefore is judgment far from us, neither doth justice overtake us : we wait for light, but behold obscurity ; for brightness, *but* we walk in darkness. 10 We grope for the wall like the blind, and we grope as if *we had* no eyes : we stumble at noon-day as in the night; *we are* in desolate places as dead *men.* 11 We roar all like bears, and mourn sore like doves : we look for judgment, but *there is* none; for salvation, *but* it is far off from us. 12 For our transgressions are multiplied before thee, and our sins testify against us : for our transgressions *are* with us; and *as for* our iniquities, we know them ; 13 In transgressing and lying against the Lord, and departing away from our God, speaking oppression and revolt, conceiving and uttering from the heart words of falsehood. 14 And judgment is turned away backward, and justice standeth afar off : for truth is fallen in the street, and equity cannot enter. 15 Yea, truth faileth ; and he *that* departeth from evil maketh himself a prey : and the Lord saw *it,* and it displeased him that *there was* no judgment.

The scope of this paragraph is the same with that of the last, to show that sin is the great mischief-maker ; as it is that which keeps good things from us, so it is that which brings evil things upon us. But as *there* it is spoken by the prophet, in God's name, to the people, for their conviction and humiliation, and that God might be justified when he speaks and clear when he judges, so *here* it seems to be spoken by the people to God, as an acknowledgment of that which was there told them and an expression of their humble submission and subscription to the justice and equity of God's proceedings against them. Their uncircumcised hearts here seem to be humbled in some measure,

and they are brought to confess (the confession is at least extorted from them) that God had justly walked contrary to them, because they had walked contrary to him.

I. They acknowledge that God had contended with them and had walked contrary to them. Their case was very deplorable, *v.* 9—11. 1. They were in distress, trampled upon and oppressed by their enemies, unjustly dealt with, and ruled with rigour ; and God did not appear for them, to plead their just and injured cause : *" Judgment is far from us, neither does justice overtake us, v.* 9. Though, as to our persecutors, we are sure that we have right on our side, and they are the wrong-doers, yet we are not relieved, we are not righted. We have not done justice to one another, and therefore God suffers our enemies to deal thus unjustly with us, and we are as far as ever from being restored to our right and recovering our property again. Oppression is near us, and judgment is far from us. Our enemies are far from giving our case its due consideration, but still hurry us on with the violence of their oppressions, and justice does not overtake us, to rescue us out of their hands." 2. Herein their expectations were sadly disappointed, which made their case the more sad : *" We wait for light* as those that wait for the morning, *but behold obscurity ;* we cannot discern the least dawning of the day of our deliverance. *We look for judgment, but there is none* (*v.* 11); neither God nor man appears for our succour ; we look for salvation, because God (we think) has promised it, and we have prayed for it with fasting ; we look for it as for brightness, but it is far off from us, as far off as ever for aught we can perceive, and still *we walk in darkness;* and the higher our expectations have been raised the sorer is the disappointment." 3. They were quite at a loss what to do to help themselves and were at their wits' end (*v.* 10) : *" We grope for the wall like the blind ;* we see no way open for our relief, nor know which way to expect it, or what to do in order to it." If we shut our eyes against the light of divine truth, it is just with God to hide from our eyes the things that belong to our peace ; and, if we use not our eyes as we should, it is just with him to let us be as if we had no eyes. Those that will not see their duty shall not see their interest. Those whom God has given up to a judicial blindness are strangely infatuated ; they stumble at noon-day as in the night ; they see not either those dangers, or those advantages, which all about them see. *Quos Deus vult perdere, eos dementat—God infatuates those whom he means to destroy.* Those that love darkness rather than light shall have their doom accordingly. 4. They sunk into despair and were quite overwhelmed with grief, the marks of which appeared in every man's countenance ; they grew melancholy upon it, shunned conversation, and affected solitude : *We are in desolate places as dead men.* The state of the Jews in Babylon is represented by *dead and dry bones* (Ezek. xxxvii. 12) and the explanation of the comparison there (*v.* 11) explains this text: *Our hope is lost; we are cut off for our parts.* In this despair the sorrow and anguish of some were loud and noisy : *We roar like bears;* the sorrow of others was silent, and preyed more upon their spirits : " *We mourn sore like doves,* like doves of the valleys ; we mourn both *for our iniquities* (Ezek. vii. 16) and for our calamities." Thus they owned that *the hand of the Lord had gone out against them.*

II. They acknowledge that they had provoked God thus to contend with them, that he had done right, for they had done wickedly, *v.* 12—15. 1. They owned that they had sinned, and that to this day they were in a great trespass, as Ezra speaks (Ezra x. 10): " *Our transgressions are with us;* the guilt of them is upon us, the power of them prevails among us, we are not yet reformed, nor have we parted with our sins, though they have done us so much mischief. Nay, *our transgressions are multiplied;* they are more numerous and more heinous than they have been formerly. Look which way we will, we cannot look off them ; all places, all orders and degrees of men, are infected. The sense of our transgression is with us, as David said, *My sin is ever before me;* it is too plain to be denied or concealed, too bad to be excused or palliated. God is a witness to them : *They are multiplied before thee,* in thy sight, under thy eye. We are witnesses against ourselves : *As for our iniquities, we know them,* though we may have foolishly endeavoured to cover them. Nay, they themselves are witnesses : *Our sins* stare us in the face and *testify against us,* so many have they been and so deeply aggravated." 2. They owned the great evil and malignity of sin, of their sin ; it is *transgressing and lying against the Lord, v.* 13. The sins of those that profess themselves God's people, and bear his name, are upon *this* account worse than the sins of others, that in transgressing they *lie against the Lord,* they falsely accuse him, they misrepresent and belie him, as if he had dealt hardly and unfairly with them ; or they perfidiously break covenant with him and falsify their most sacred and solemn engagements to him, which is *lying against him : it is departing away from our God,* to whom we are bound as our God and to whom we ought to cleave with purpose of heart ; from him we have departed, as the rebellious subject from his allegiance to his rightful prince, and the adulterous wife from the guide of her youth and the covenant of her God. 3. They owned that there was a general decay of moral honesty ; and it is not strange that those who were false to their God were unfaithful to one another. They *spoke oppression,* declared openly for that,

though it was a revolt from their God and a revolt from truth, by the sacred bonds of which we should always be tied and held fast. They *conceived and uttered words of falsehood.* Many an ill thing is conceived in the mind, yet is prudently stifled there, and not suffered to go any further ; but these sinners were so impudent, so daring, that whatever wickedness they conceived, they gave it an *imprimatur—a sanction,* and made no difficulty of publishing it. To think an ill thing is bad, but to say it is much worse. Many a word of falsehood is uttered in haste, for want of consideration ; but these were conceived and uttered, were uttered deliberately and of malice prepense. They were words of falsehood, and yet they are said to be uttered *from the heart,* because, though they differed from the real sentiments of the heart and therefore were words of falsehood, yet they agreed with the malice and wickedness of the heart, and were the natural language of that ; it was a *double heart,* Ps. xii. 2. Those who by the grace of God kept themselves free from these enormous crimes yet put themselves into the confession of sin, because members of that nation which was generally thus corrupted. 4. They owned that that was not done which might have been done to reform the land and to amend what was amiss, *v.* 14. " *Judgment,* that should go forward, and bear down the opposition that is made to it, that should run in its course like a river, like a mighty stream, *is turned away backward,* a contrary course. The administration of justice has become but a cover to the greatest injustice. Judgment, that should check the proceedings of fraud and violence, is driven back, and so they go on triumphantly. *Justice stands afar off,* even from our courts of judicature, which are so crowded with the patrons of oppression that *equity cannot enter,* cannot have admission into the court, cannot be heard, or at least will not be heeded. Equity enters not into the unrighteous decrees which they decree, *ch.* x. 1. *Truth is fallen in the street,* and there she may lie to be trampled upon by every foot of pride, and she has never a friend that will lend a hand to help her up ; *yea, truth fails* in common conversation, and in dealings between man and man, so that one knows not whom to believe nor whom to trust." 5. They owned that there was a prevailing enmity in men's minds to those that were good : *He that does evil goes unpunished,* but *he that departs from evil makes himself a prey* to those beasts of prey that were before described. It is crime enough with them for a man not to do as they do, and they treat *him* as an enemy who will not partake with them in their wickedness. *He that departs from evil is accounted mad;* so the margin reads. Sober singularity is branded as folly, and he is thought next door to a madman who swims against the stream that runs so strongly. 6. They owned that all this could not but be very displeasing to the God of heaven. The evil was done in his sight. They knew very well, though they were not willing to acknowledge it, that the Lord saw it; though it was done secretly, and gilded over with specious pretences, yet it could not be concealed from his all-seeing eye. All the wickedness that is in the world is naked and open before the eyes of God; and, as he is of quicker eyes than not to see iniquity, so he is of purer eyes than to behold it with the least approbation or allowance. *He saw it, and it displeased him,* though it was among his own professing people that he saw it. It was evil in his eyes; he saw the sinfulness of all this sin, and that which was most offensive to him was *that there was no judgment,* no reformation; had he seen any signs of repentance, though the sin displeased him, he would soon have been reconciled to the sinners upon their returning from their evil way. *Then* the sin of a nation becomes national, and brings public judgments, when it is not restrained by public justice.

16 And he saw that *there was* no man, and wondered that *there was* no intercessor: therefore his arm brought salvation unto him; and his righteousness, it sustained him. 17 For he put on righteousness as a breast-plate, and a helmet of salvation upon his head; and he put on the garments of vengeance *for* clothing, and was clad with zeal as a cloak. 18 According to *their* deeds, accordingly he will repay, fury to his adversaries, recompence to his enemies; to the islands he will repay recompence. 19 So shall they fear the name of the LORD from the west, and his glory from the rising of the sun. When the enemy shall come in like a flood, the Spirit of the LORD shall lift up a standard against him. 20 And the Redeemer shall come to Zion, and unto them that turn from transgression in Jacob, saith the LORD. 21 As for me, this *is* my covenant with them, saith the LORD; My Spirit that *is* upon thee, and my words which I have put in thy mouth, shall not depart out of thy mouth, nor out of the mouth of thy seed, nor out of the mouth of thy seed's seed, saith the LORD, from henceforth and for ever.

How sin abounded we have read, to our great amazement, in the former part of the chapter; how grace does much more abound we read in these verses. And, as sin took occasion from the commandment to become more exceedingly sinful, so grace took occasion from the transgression of the commandment to appear more exceedingly gracious. Observe,

I. Why God wrought salvation for this provoking people, notwithstanding their provocations. It was purely for his own name's sake; because there was nothing in them either to bring it about, or to induce him to bring it about for them, no merit to deserve it, no might to effect it, he would do it himself, would be exalted in his own strength, for his own glory.

1. He took notice of their weakness and wickedness: *He saw that there was no man* that would do any thing for the support of the bleeding cause of religion and virtue among them, not a man that would execute judgment (Jer. v. 1), that would bestir himself in a work of reformation; those that complained of the badness of the times had not zeal and courage enough to appear and act against it; there was a universal corruption of manners, and nothing done to stem the tide; most were wicked, and those that were not so were yet weak, and durst not attempt any thing in opposition to the wickedness of the wicked. *There was no intercessor,* either none to intercede with God, to stand in the gap by prayer to turn away his wrath (it would have pleased him to be thus met, and he wondered that he was not), or, rather, none to interpose for the support of justice and truth, which were trampled upon and run down (*v.* 14), no advocate to speak a good word for those who were made a prey of because they kept their integrity, *v.* 15. They complained that God did not appear for them (*ch.* lviii. 3); but God with much more reason complains that they did nothing for themselves, intimating how ready he would have been to do them good if he had found among them the least motion towards a reformation.

2. He engaged his own strength and righteousness for them. They shall be saved, notwithstanding all this; and, (1.) Because they have no strength of their own, nor any active men that will set to it in good earnest to redress the grievances either of their iniquities or of their calamities, therefore *his own arm shall bring salvation to him,* to his people, or to him whom he would raise up to be the deliverer, Christ, the power of God and arm of the Lord, that man of his right hand whom he made strong for himself. The work of reformation (that is the first and principal article of the salvation) shall be wrought by the immediate influences of the divine grace on men's consciences. Since magistrates and societies for reformation fail of doing their part, one will not do justice nor the other call for it, God will let them know that he can do it without them when his time shall come thus to prepare his peo-

ple for mercy, and then the work of deliverance shall be wrought by the immediate operations of the divine Providence on men's affections and affairs. When God stirred up the spirit of Cyrus, and brought his people out of Babylon, *not by might, nor by power, but by the Spirit of the Lord of hosts,* then his own arm, which is never shortened, brought salvation. (2.) Because they have no righteousness of their own to merit these favours, and to which God might have an eye in working for them, therefore *his* own *righteousness sustained him* and bore him out in it. Divine justice, which by their sins they had armed against them, through grace appears for them. Though they can expect no favour as due to them, yet he will be just to himself, to his own purpose and promise, and covenant with his people : he will, in righteousness, punish the enemies of his people; see Deut. ix. 5. *Not for thy righteousness, but for the wickedness of these nations* they are driven out. In our redemption by Christ, since we had no righteousness of our own to produce, on which God might proceed in favour to us, he brought in a righteousness by the merit and mediation of his own Son (it is called *the righteousness which is of God by faith,* Phil. iii. 9), and this righteousness sustained him, and bore him out in all his favours to us, notwithstanding our provocations. *He put on righteousness as a breast-plate,* securing his own honour, as a breast-plate does the vitals, in all his proceedings, by the justice and equity of them ; and then he put *a helmet of salvation upon his head ;* so sure is he to effect the salvation he intends that he takes salvation itself for his helmet, which therefore must needs be impenetrable, and in which he appears very illustrious, formidable in the eyes of his enemies and amiable in the eyes of his friends. When righteousness is his coat of arms, salvation is his crest. In allusion to this, among the pieces of a Christian's armour we find *the breast-plate of righteousness,* and for a helmet *the hope of salvation* (Eph. vi. 14—17 ; 1 Thess. v. 8), and it is called *the armour of God,* because he wore it first and so fitted it for us. (3.) Because they have no spirit or zeal to do any thing for themselves, God will *put on the garments of vengeance for clothing, and clothe himself with zeal as a cloak ;* he will make his justice upon the enemies of his church and people, and his jealousy for his own glory and the honour of religion and virtue among men, to appear evident and conspicuous in the eye of the world; and in these he will show himself great, as a man shows himself in his rich attire or in the distinguishing habit of his office. If men be not zealous against sin, God will, and will take vengeance on it for all the injury it has done to his honour and his people's welfare ; and this was the business of Christ in the world, to take away sin and be revenged on it.

348

II. What the salvation is that shall be wrought out by the righteousness and strength of God himself.

1. There shall be a present temporal salvation wrought out for the Jews in Babylon, or elsewhere in distress and captivity. This is promised (*v.* 18, 19) as a type of something further. When God's time shall come he will do his own work, though those fail that should forward it. It is here promised, (1.) That God will reckon with his enemies and will render to them according to their deeds, to the enemies of his people abroad, that have oppressed them, to the enemies of justice and truth at home, that have oppressed them, for they also are God's enemies ; and, when the day of vengeance shall have come, he will deal with both as they have deserved, *according to retribution* (so the word is), the law of retributions (Rev. xiii. 10), or *according to former retributions ;* as he has rendered to his enemies formerly, accordingly he will now repay, *fury to his adversaries, recompence to his enemies ;* his fury shall not exceed the rules of justice, as men's fury commonly does. Even *to the islands,* that lie most remote, if they have appeared against him, *he will repay recompence ;* for *his hand shall find out all his enemies* (Ps. xxi. 8), and his arrows reach them. Though God's people have behaved so ill that they do not deserve to be delivered, yet his enemies behave so much worse that they do deserve to be destroyed. (2.) That, whatever attempts the enemies of God's people may afterwards make upon them to disturb their peace, they shall be baffled and brought to nought : *When the enemy shall come in like a flood,* like a high spring-tide, or a land-flood, which threaten to bear down all before them without control, then *the Spirit of the Lord* by some secret undiscerned power *shall lift up a standard against him,* and so (as the margin reads it) *put him to flight.* He that has delivered will still deliver. When God's people are weak and helpless, and have no standard to lift up against the invading power, God will *give a banner to those that fear him* (Ps. lx. 4), will by his Spirit lift up a standard, which will draw multitudes together to appear on the church's behalf. Some read it, *He shall come* (the name of the Lord, and his glory, before foreseen of the Messiah promised) *like a straight river, the Spirit of the Lord lifting him up for an ensign.* Christ by the preaching of his gospel shall cover the earth with the knowledge of God as with the waters of a flood, the *Spirit of the Lord* setting up Christ as a *standard* to the *Gentiles, ch.* xi. 10. (3.) That all this should redound to the glory of God and the advancement of religion in the world (*v.* 19) : *So shall they fear the name of the Lord and his glory* in all nations that lie eastward or westward. The deliverance of the Jews out of captivity, and the destruction brought on their oppressors, would awaken multitudes to enquire

concerning the God of Israel, and induce them to serve and worship him and enlist themselves under the standard which the Spirit of the Lord shall lift up. God's appearances for his church shall occasion the accession of many to it. This had its full accomplishment in gospel times, when many came *from the east and west,* to fill up the places of *the children of the kingdom* that were *cast out,* when there were set up eastern and western churches, Matt. viii. 11.

2. There shall be a more glorious salvation wrought out by the Messiah in the fulness of time, which salvation all the prophets, upon all occasions, had in view. We have here the two great promises relating to that salvation :—

(1.) That the Son of God shall come to us to be our Redeemer (*v.* 20): *Thy Redeemer shall come ;* it is applied to Christ, Rom. xi. 26. *There shall come the deliverer.* The coming of Christ as the Redeemer is the summary of all the promises both of the Old and New Testament, and this was the redemption in Jerusalem which the believing Jews looked for, Luke ii. 38. Christ is our *Goël,* our next kinsman, that redeems both the person and the estate of the poor debtor. Observe, [1.] The place where this Redeemer shall appear: He *shall come to Zion,* for there, on that holy hill, the Lord would set him up as his King, Ps. ii. 6. In Zion the chief corner-stone was to be laid, 1 Pet. ii. 6. He came to his temple there, Mal. iii. 1. There salvation was to be placed (*ch.* xlvi. 13), for thence the law was to go forth, *ch.* ii. 3. Zion was a type of the gospel church, for which the Redeemer acts in all his appearances: *The Redeemer shall come for the sake of Zion ;* so the LXX. read it. [2.] The persons that shall have the comfort of the Redeemer's coming, that shall then lift up their heads, knowing that their redemption draws nigh. He shall come *to those that turn from ungodliness in Jacob,* to those that are in Jacob, to the praying seed of Jacob, in answer to their prayers; yet not to all that are in Jacob, that are within the pale of the visible church, but to those only that turn from transgression, that repent, and reform, and forsake those sins which Christ came to redeem them from. The sinners in Zion will fare never the better for the Redeemer's coming to Zion if they go on still in their trespasses.

(2.) That the Spirit of God shall come to us to be our sanctifier, *v.* 21. In the Redeemer there was a new covenant made with us a covenant of promises; and this is the great and comprehensive promise of that covenant, that God will give and continue his word and Spirit to his church and people throughout all generations. God's giving the *Spirit to those that ask him* includes the giving of them all *good things,* Luke xi. 13; Matt. vii. 11. This covenant is here said to *be made with them,* that is, with those that turn

from transgression; for those that cease to do evil shall be taught to do well. But the promise is made to a single person—*My Spirit that is upon thee,* being directed either, [1.] To Christ as the head of the church, who received that he might give. The Spirit promised to the church was first upon him, and from his head that precious ointment descended to the skirts of his garments; and the word of the gospel was first put into his mouth ; for *it began to be spoken by the Lord.* And all believers are his seed, in whom he prolongs his days, *ch.* liii. 10. Or, [2.] To the church; and so it is a promise of the continuance and perpetuity of the church in the world to the end of time, parallel to those promises that the throne and seed of Christ shall endure for ever, Ps. lxxxix. 29, 36 ; xxii. 30. Observe, *First,* How the church shall be kept up, in a succession, as the world of mankind is kept up, by the seed and the seed's seed. As one generation passes away another generation shall come. *Instead of the fathers shall be the children. Secondly,* How long it shall be kept up— *henceforth and for ever,* always, even *unto the end of the world ;* for, the world being left to stand for the sake of the church, we may be sure that as long as it does stand Christ will have a church in it, though not always visible. *Thirdly,* By what means it shall be kept up; by the constant residence of the word and Spirit in it. 1. The Spirit that was upon Christ shall always continue in the hearts of the faithful; there shall be some in every age on whom he shall work, and in whom he shall dwell, and thus the Comforter shall abide with the church for ever, John xiv. 16. 2. The word of Christ shall always continue in the mouths of the faithful; there shall be some in every age who, *believing with the heart* unto righteousness, shall *with the tongue make confession unto salvation.* The word shall never depart out of the mouth of the church; for there shall still be a seed to speak Christ's holy language and profess his holy religion. Observe, The Spirit and the word go together, and by them the church is kept up. For the word in the mouths of our ministers, nay, the word in our own mouths, will not profit us, unless the Spirit work with the word, and give us an understanding. But the Spirit does his work by the word and in concurrence with it; and whatever is pretended to be a dictate of the Spirit must be tried by the scriptures. On these foundations the church is built, stands firmly, and shall stand for ever, Christ himself being the chief corner-stone.

CHAP. LX.

This whole chapter is all to the same purport, all in the same strain ; it is a part of God's covenant with his church, which is spoken of in the last verse of the foregoing chapter, and the blessings here promised are the fruits of the word and Spirit there promised. The long continuance of the church, even unto the utmost ages of time, was there promised, and here the large extent of the church, even unto the utmost regions of the earth ; and both these tend to the honour of the Redeemer. It is here promised, I. That the church shall be enlightened and shone upon, ver. 1, 2. II. That it shal be enlarged and great additions made to it, to join in the service of God, ver. 3—8. III. That the new converts shall be greatly serviceable to the church and to the interests of it, ver. 9—13. IV. That the church shall be in great honour and reputation among men, ver. 14—16. V. That it shall enjoy a profound peace and tranquillity, ver. 17, 18. VI. That, the members of it being all righteous, the glory and joy of it shall be everlasting, ver. 19—22. Now this has some reference to the peaceable and prosperous condition which the Jews were sometimes in after their return out of captivity into their own land; but it certainly looks further, and was to have its full accomplishment in the kingdom of the Messiah, the enlargement of that kingdom by the bringing in of the Gentiles into it, and the spiritual blessings in heavenly things by Christ Jesus with which it should be enriched, and all these earnests of eternal joy and glory.

ARISE, shine; for thy light is come, and the glory of the LORD is risen upon thee. 2 For, behold, the darkness shall cover the earth, and gross darkness the people: but the LORD shall arise upon thee, and his glory shall be seen upon thee. 3 And the Gentiles shall come to thy light, and kings to the brightness of thy rising. 4 Lift up thine eyes round about, and see: all they gather themselves together, they come to thee: thy sons shall come from far, and thy daughters shall be nursed at *thy* side. 5 Then thou shalt see, and flow together, and thine heart shall fear, and be enlarged; because the abundance of the sea shall be converted unto thee, the forces of the Gentiles shall come unto thee. 6 The multitude of camels shall cover thee, the dromedaries of Midian and Ephah; all they from Sheba shall come: they shall bring gold and incense; and they shall show forth the praises of the LORD. 7 All the flocks of Kedar shall be gathered together unto thee, the rams of Nebaioth shall minister unto thee: they shall come up with acceptance on mine altar, and I will glorify the house of my glory. 8 Who *are* these *that* fly as a cloud, and as the doves to their windows?

It is here promised that the gospel temple shall be very lightsome and very large.

I. It shall be very lightsome: *Thy light has come.* When the Jews returned out of captivity they had *light and gladness, and joy and honour;* they then were made to *know the Lord* and to *rejoice in his great goodness;* and upon both accounts their light came. When the Redeemer came to Zion he brought light with him, he himself came to be a light. Now observe, 1. What this light is, and whence it springs: *The Lord shall arise upon thee* (v. 2), *the glory of the Lord* (v. 1) *shall be seen upon thee.* God is the father and fountain of lights, and it is in his light that we shall see light. As

far as we have the knowledge of God in us, and the favour of God towards us, our light has come. When God appears to us, and we have the comfort of his favour, then *the glory of the Lord rises upon us* as the morning light; when he appears for us, and we have the credit of his favour, when he shows us some token for good and proclaims his favour to us, then his glory is seen upon us, as it was upon Israel in the *pillar of cloud and fire.* When Christ arose as the sun of righteousness, and in him *the day-spring from on high visited us,* then *the glory of the Lord was* seen upon us, the glory *as of the first-begotten of the Father.* 2. What a foil there shall be to this light: *Darkness shall cover the earth;* but, though it be gross darkness, darkness that might be felt, like that of Egypt, that shall overspread the people, yet the church, like Goshen, shall have light at the same time. When the case of the nations that have not the gospel shall be very melancholy, those *dark corners of the earth* being *full of the habitations of cruelty* to poor souls, the state of the church shall be very pleasant. 3. What is the duty which the rising of this light calls for: " *Arise, shine;* not only receive this light, and" (as the margin reads it) " *be enlightened by it,* but reflect this light; *arise and shine* with rays borrowed from it." The children of light ought to shine as lights in the world. If God's glory be seen upon us to our honour, we ought not only with our lips, but in our lives, to return the praise of it *to his honour,* Matt. v. 16; Phil. ii. 15.

II. It shall be very large. When the Jews were settled again in their own land, after their captivity, many of the people of the land joined themselves to them; but it does not appear that there ever was any such numerous accession to them as would answer the fulness of this prophecy; and therefore we must conclude that this looks further, to the bringing of the Gentiles into the gospel church, not their flocking to one particular place, though under that type it is here described. There is no place now that is the centre of the church's unity; but the promise respects their flocking to Christ, and coming by faith, and hope, and holy love, into that society which is incorporated by the charter of his gospel, and of the unity of which he only is the centre—that family which is named from him, Eph. iii. 15. The gospel church is expressly called *Zion* and *Jerusalem,* and under that notion all believers are said to *come* to it (Heb. xii. 22, *You have come unto Mount Zion, to the city of the living God, the heavenly Jerusalem),* which serves for a key to this prophecy, Eph. ii. 19. Observe,

1. What shall invite such multitudes to the church: " They shall *come to thy light and to the brightness of thy rising, v.* 3. They shall be allured to join themselves to thee," (1.) " By the light that shines upon

thee," the light of the glorious gospel, which the churches hold forth, in consequence of which they are called *golden candlesticks*. This light which discovers so much of God and his good will to man, by which life and immortality are brought to light, this shall invite all the serious well-affected part of mankind to come and join themselves to the church, that they may have the benefit of this light to inform them concerning truth and duty. (2.) " By the light with which thou shinest." The purity and love of the primitive Christians, their heavenly-mindedness, contempt of the world, and patient sufferings, were the brightness of the church's rising, which drew many into it. The beauty of holiness was the powerful attractive by which Christ had a willing people brought to him in *the day of his power*, Ps. cx. 3.

2. What multitudes shall come to the church. Great numbers *shall come, Gentiles* (or *nations) of those that are saved*, as it is expressed with allusion to this, Rev. xxi. 24. *Nations* shall be *discipled* (Matt. xxviii. 19), and even kings, men of figure, power, and influence, shall be *added to the church.* They come from all parts (*v.* 4) : *Lift up thy eyes round about, and see* them coming, *devout men out of every nation under heaven,* Acts ii. 5. See how *white the fields are already to the harvest,* John iv. 35. See them coming in a body, as one man, and with one consent : They *gather themselves together,* that they may strengthen one another's hands, and encourage one another. *Come, and let us go, ch.* ii. 3. " They come from the remotest parts : *They come to thee from far,* having *heard the report* of thee, as the queen of Sheba, or *seen thy star in the east,* as the wise men, and they will not be discouraged by the length of the journey from coming to thee. There shall come some of both sexes. Sons and daughters shall come in the most dutiful manner, as thy sons and thy daughters, resolved to be of thy family, to submit to the laws of thy family and put themselves under the tuition of it. They shall come *to be nursed at thy side,* to have their education with thee from their cradle." The church's children must be nursed at her side, not sent out to be nursed among strangers ; there, where alone the unadulterated milk of the word is to be had, must the church's new-born babes be nursed, *that they may grow thereby,* 1 Pet. ii. 1, 2. Those that would enjoy the dignities and privileges of Christ's family must submit to the discipline of it.

3. What they shall bring with them and what advantage shall accrue to the church by their accession to it. Those that are brought into the church by the grace of God will be sure to bring all they are worth in with them, which with themselves they will devote to the honour and service of God and do good with in their places. (1.) The merchants shall write *holiness to the Lord* upon

their merchandise and their hire, as *ch.* xxiii. 18. " *The abundance of the sea,* either the wealth that is fetched out of the sea (the fish, the pearls) or that which is imported by sea, *shall* all *be converted to thee* and to thy use." The wealth of the rich merchants shall be laid out in works of piety and charity. (2.) The mighty men of the nations shall employ their might in the service of the church : " *The forces,* or troops, *of the Gentiles shall come unto thee,* to guard thy coasts, strengthen thy interests, and, if occasion be, to fight thy battles." The forces of the Gentiles had often been against the church, but now they shall be for it ; for as God, when he pleases, can, and, when we please him, will, make even *our enemies to be at peace with us* (Prov. xvi. 7), so, when Christ overcomes the strong man armed, he divides his spoils, and makes that to serve his interests which had been used against them, Luke xi. 22. (3.) The wealth imported by land-carriage, as well as that by sea, shall be made use of in the service of God and the church (*v.* 6): *The camels and dromedaries that bring gold and incense* (gold to make the golden altar of and incense and sweet perfumes to burn upon it), *those of Midian and Sheba,* shall bring the richest commodities of their country, not to trade with, but to honour God with, and not in small quantities, but camel-loads of them. This was in part fulfilled when the *wise men of the east* (perhaps some of the countries here mentioned), drawn by the brightness of the star, came to Christ, and presented to him treasures of *gold, frankincense, and myrrh,* Matt. ii. 11. (4.) Great numbers of sacrifices shall be brought to God's altar, acceptable sacrifices, and, though brought by Gentiles, they shall find acceptance, *v.* 7. *Kedar* was famous for flocks, and probably the fattest rams were those of *Nebaioth;* these shall come up with acceptance on God's altar. God must be served and honoured with what we have, according as he has blessed us, and with the best we have. This was fulfilled when by the decree of Darius the governors beyond the rivers (perhaps of some of these countries) were ordered to furnish the temple at Jerusalem *with bullocks, rams, and lambs, for the burnt-offering of the God of heaven,* Ezra vi. 9. It had a further accomplishment, and we trust will have, in the bringing in of the fulness of the Gentiles to the church, which is called the *sacrificing* or *offering up of the Gentiles* unto God, Rom. xv. 16. The flocks and rams are precious souls ; for they are said to minister to the church, and to come up as living sacrifices, presenting themselves to God by a *reasonable service* on *his altar,* Rom. xii. 1.

4. How God shall be honoured by the increase of the church and the accession of such numbers to it. (1.) They shall intend the honour of God's name in it. When they bring their gold and incense it shall not be to show the riches of their country, nor to

gain applause to themselves for piety and devotion, but to *show forth the praises of the Lord, v.* 6. Our greatest services and gifts to the church are not acceptable further than we have an eye to the glory of God in them. And this must be our business in our attendance on public ordinances, to *give unto the Lord the glory due to his name ;* for *therefore,* as these here, we are called out of darkness into light, that we should *show forth the praises of him that called us,* 1 Pet. ii. 9. (2.) God will advance the honour of his own name by it ; so he has said (*v.* 7) : *I will glorify the house of my glory.* The church is the house of God's glory, where he manifests his glory to his people and receives that homage by which they do honour to him. And it is for the glory of this house, and of him that keeps house there, both that the Gentiles shall bring their offerings to it and that they shall be accepted therein.

5. How the church shall herself be affected with this increase of her numbers, *v.* 5. (1.) She shall be in a transport of joy upon this account : " *Thou shalt see* and *flow together*" (or flow to and fro), " as in a pleasing agitation about it, surprised at it, but extremely glad of it." (2.) There shall be a mixture of fear with this joy : " *Thy heart shall fear,* doubting whether it be lawful to *go in to the uncircumcised* and *eat with them.*" Peter was so impressed with this fear that he needed a vision and voice from heaven to help him over it, Acts x. 28. But, (3.) " When this fear is conquered thy heart shall be enlarged in holy love, so enlarged that thou shalt have room in it for all the Gentile converts ; thou shalt not have such a narrow soul as thou hast had nor affections so confined within the Jewish pale." When God intends the beauty and prosperity of his church he gives this largeness of heart and an extensive charity. (4.) These converts flocking to the church shall be greatly admired (*v.* 8) : *Who are these that fly as a cloud?* Observe, [1.] How the conversion of souls is here described. It is flying to Christ and to his church, for thither we are directed ; it is flying like a cloud, though in great multitudes, so as to overspread the heavens, yet with great unanimity, all as one cloud. They shall come with speed, as a cloud flying on the wings of the wind, and come openly, and in the view of all, *their* very *enemies beholding them* (Rev. xi. 12), and yet not able to hinder them. They shall *fly as doves to their windows,* in great flights, many together ; they fly on the wings of the harmless dove, which flies low, denoting their innocency and humility. They fly to Christ, to the church, to the word and ordinances, as doves, by instinct, to their own windows, to their own home ; thither they fly for refuge and shelter when they are pursued by the birds of prey, and thither they fly for rest when they have been wandering and are weary, as Noah's dove to the ark.

352

[2.] How the conversion of souls is here admired. It is spoken of with wonder and pleasure : *Who are these?* We have reason to wonder that so many flock to Christ : when we see them all together we shall wonder whence they all came. And we have reason to admire with pleasure and affection those that do flock to him : *Who are these?* How excellent, how amiable are they ! What a pleasant sight is it to see poor souls hastening to Christ, with a full resolution to abide with him !

9 Surely the isles shall wait for me, and the ships of Tarshish first, to bring thy sons from far, their silver and their gold with them, unto the name of the LORD thy God, and to the Holy One of Israel, because he hath glorified thee. 10 And the sons of strangers shall build up thy walls, and their kings shall minister unto thee : for in my wrath I smote thee, but in my favour have I had mercy on thee. 11 Therefore thy gates shall be open continually ; they shall not be shut day nor night ; that *men* may bring unto thee the forces of the Gentiles, and *that* their kings *may be* brought. 12 For the nation and kingdom that will not serve thee shall perish ; yea, *those* nations shall be utterly wasted. 13 The glory of Lebanon shall come unto thee, the fir-tree, the pine-tree, and the box together, to beautify the place of my sanctuary ; and I will make the place of my feet glorious. 14 The sons also of them that afflicted thee shall come bending unto thee ; and all they that despised thee shall bow themselves down at the soles of thy feet ; and they shall call thee, The city of the LORD, the Zion of the Holy One of Israel.

The promises made to the church in the foregoing verses are here repeated, ratified, and enlarged upon, designed still for the comfort and encouragement of the Jews after their return out of captivity, but certainly looking further, to the enlargement and advancement of the gospel church and the abundance of spiritual blessings with which it shall be enriched.

I. God will be very gracious and propitious to them. We must begin with that promise, because thence all the rest take rise. The sanctuary that was desolate begins to be repaired when God *causes his face to shine upon it,* Dan. ix. 17. All the favour that the people of God find with men is owing to the light of God's countenance and his favour to them (*v.* 10): " All shall now make court to thee, *for in my wrath I smote thee,* while thou wast in captivity" (and the sufferings of the church, especially by its corruptions, decays, and divisions, against which these promises will be its relief, are sad tokens of God's displeasure), " but now *in my favour have I had mercy on thee,* and therefore have all this mercy in store for thee."

II. Many shall be brought into the church, even from far countries (*v.* 9): *Surely the isles shall wait for me,* shall welcome the gospel, and shall attend God with their praises for it and their ready subjection to it. *The ships of Tarshish,* transport-ships, shall lie ready to carry members from far distant regions to the church, or (which is equivalent) to carry the ministers of the church to remote parts, to preach the gospel and to bring in souls to join themselves to the Lord. Observe, 1. Who are brought— *thy sons,* that is, such as are designed to be so, those *children of God that are scattered abroad,* John xi. 52. 2. What they shall bring with them. They live at such a distance that they cannot bring their flocks and their rams; but, like those who lived remote from Jerusalem (who, when they came up to worship at the feast, because they could not bring their tithes in kind, turned them into money), they shall *bring their silver and gold with them.* Note, When we give up ourselves to God we must with ourselves give up all we have to him. If we honour him with our spirits, we shall honour him with our substance. 3. To whom they shall devote and dedicate themselves and all they are worth—*to the name of the Lord thy God,* to God as the Lord of all and the church's God and King, even to the *Holy One of Israel* (whom Israel worships as a Holy One, in the beauty of holiness), *because he has glorified thee.* Note, The honour God puts upon his church and people should not only engage us to honour them, but invite us to join ourselves to them. *We will go with you, for God is with you,* Zech. viii. 23.

III. Those that come into the church shall be welcome; for so spacious is the holy city that though, *Lord, it is done as thou hast commanded, yet still there is room.* " *Therefore thy gates shall be open continually* (*v.* 11), not only because thou hast no reason to fear thy enemies, but because thou hast reason to expect thy friends." It is usual with us to leave our doors open, or leave some one ready to open them, all night, if we look for a child or a guest to come in late. Note, Christ is always ready to entertain those that come to him, is never out of the way, nor can they ever come unseasonably; the gate of mercy is always open, night and day, or shall soon be opened to those that knock. Ministers, the door-keepers, must be always ready to admit those that offer themselves to the Lord. God not only keeps a good house in his church, but he keeps open house, that at any time, by the preaching of the word, *in season and out of season, the forces of the Gentiles,* and the kings or commanders of those forces, *may be brought* into the church. *Lift up your heads, O you gates!* and let such welcome guests as these come in.

IV. All that are about the church shall be made in some way or other serviceable to it. Though dominion is far from being founded in men's grace, it is founded in God's; and he that made the inferior creatures useful to man will make the nations of men useful to the church. The earth helped the woman. *All things are for your sakes.* So here (*v.* 10), " Even *the sons of strangers,* that have neither knowledge of thee nor kindness for thee, that have always been *aliens to the commonwealth of Israel,* even they *shall build up thy wall, and their kings shall* in that and other things *minister unto thee* and not think it any disparagement to them to do so." This was fulfilled when the king of Persia, and the governors of the provinces by his order, were aiding and assisting Nehemiah in building the wall about Jerusalem. Rather than Jerusalem's walls shall lie still in ruins, the *sons of the stranger* shall be raised up to build them. Even those that do not belong to the church may be a protection to it. And the greatest of men should not think it below them to minister to the church, but rejoice that they are in a capacity, and have a heart, to do it any service. Nay, it is the duty of all to do what they can in their places to advance the interests of God's kingdom among men; it is at their peril if they do not; for (*v.* 12), *The nation and kingdom that will not serve thee shall perish :* not that they must perish by the sword or by human anathemas, or as if this gave any countenance to the using of external force for the propagating of the gospel, or as if men might be compelled by penalties and punishments to come into the church; by no means. But those who will not by faith submit to Jesus Christ, the King of the church, and serve him, shall perish eternally, Ps. ii. 12. Those that will not be subject to Christ's golden sceptre, to the government of his word and Spirit, that will not be brought under, or kept in, by the discipline of his family, shall be broken in pieces by his iron rod. *Bring them forth and slay them before me,* Luke xix. 27. Nations of such shall be utterly and eternally wasted, when Christ shall come to take vengeance on those that obey *not his gospel,* 2 Thess. i. 8.

V. There shall be abundance of beauty added to the ordinances of divine worship (*v.* 13): *The glory of Lebanon,* the strong and stately cedars that grow there, *shall come unto thee,* as of old to Solomon, when he built the temple (2 Chron. ii. 16), and with them shall be brought other timber, proper

353

for the carved work thereof, which the enemy had broken down, Ps. lxxiv. 5, 6. The temple, the *place of God's sanctuary*, shall be not only rebuilt, but beautified. It is the *place of his feet*, where he rests and resides, Ezek. xliii. 7. The ark is called his *footstool*, because it was under the mercy-seat, Ps. cxxxii. 7. This he will make glorious in the eyes of his people and of all their neighbours. *The glory of the latter house*, to which this refers, though in many instances inferior, was yet really *greater than the glory of the former*, because Christ came to that temple, Mal. iii. 1. It was likewise *adorned with goodly stones and gifts* (Luke xxi. 5), to which this promise may have some reference; yet so slightly did Christ speak of them there that we must suppose it to have its full accomplishment in the beauties of holiness, and the graces and comforts of the Spirit, with which gospel ordinances are adorned and enriched.

VI. The church shall appear truly great and honourable, *v.* 14. The people of the Jews, after their return out of captivity, by degrees became more considerable, and made a better figure than one would have expected, after they had been so much reduced, and than any of the other nations recovered that had been in like manner humbled by the Chaldeans. It is probable that many of those who had oppressed them in Babylon, when they were themselves driven out by the Persians, made their court to the Jews for shelter and supply and were willing to scrape acquaintance with them. This prophecy is further fulfilled when those that have been enemies to the church are wrought upon by the grace of God to see their error, and come, and join themselves to it: " *The sons of those that afflicted thee*, if not they themselves, yet their children, shall crouch to thee, shall beg pardon for their folly and beg an interest in thy favour and admission into thy family," 1 Sam. ii. 36. A promise like this is made to the church of Philadelphia, Rev. iii. 9. And it is intended to be, 1. A mortification to the proud oppressors of the church, that have afflicted her, and despised her, and taken a pleasure in doing so; they shall be brought down; their spirits shall be broken, and their condition shall be so mean and miserable that they shall be glad to be obliged to those whom they have most studied to disoblige. Note, Sooner or later God will pour contempt upon those that put contempt upon his people. 2. An exaltation to the poor oppressed ones of the church; and this is the honour that shall be done to them, they shall have an opportunity of doing good to those who have done evil to them and saving those alive who have afflicted and despised them. It is a pleasure to a good man, and he accounts it an honour, to show mercy to those with whom he has found no mercy. Yet this is not all. " They shall not only become suppliants to thee for their own interest, but they shall give honour to thee : *They shall call thee, The city of the Lord;* they shall at length be convinced that thou art a favourite of heaven, and the particular care of the divine providence." That city is truly great and honourable, it is strong, it is rich, it is safe, it is beautiful, it is the most desirable place that can be to live in, which is *the city of the Lord*, which he owns, in which he dwells, in which religion is uppermost. Such a one is Zion; it is the place which God has chosen to put his name there; it is *the Zion of the Holy One of Israel;* therefore, we may be sure, it is a holy city, else the Holy One of Israel would never be called the patron of it.

15 Whereas thou hast been forsaken and hated, so that no man went through *thee*, I will make thee an eternal excellency, a joy of many generations. 16 Thou shalt also suck the milk of the Gentiles, and shalt suck the breast of kings : and thou shalt know that I the LORD *am* thy Saviour and thy Redeemer, the Mighty One of Jacob. 17 For brass I will bring gold, and for iron I will bring silver, and for wood brass, and for stones iron : I will also make thy officers peace, and thine exactors righteousness. 18 Violence shall no more be heard in thy land, wasting nor destruction within thy borders ; but thou shalt call thy walls Salvation, and thy gates Praise. 19 The sun shall be no more thy light by day ; neither for brightness shall the moon give light unto thee : but the LORD shall be unto thee an everlasting light, and thy God thy glory. 20 Thy sun shall no more go down ; neither shall thy moon withdraw itself : for the LORD shall be thine everlasting light, and the days of thy mourning shall be ended. 21 Thy people also *shall be* all righteous : they shall inherit the land for ever, the branch of my planting, the work of my hands, that I may be glorified. 22 A little one shall become a thousand, and a small one a strong nation : I the LORD will hasten it in his time.

The happy and glorious state of the church is here further foretold, referring principally and ultimately to the Christian church and the spiritual peace of that, but under the type of that little gleam of outward peace which the Jews sometimes enjoyed after their return out of captivity. This is here spoken of,

I. As compared with what it had been. *This* made her peace and honour the more pleasant, that her condition had been much otherwise.

1. She had been despised, but now she should be honoured, *v.* 15, 16. Jerusalem had been forsaken and hated, abandoned by her friends, abhorred by her enemies; no man went through that desolate city, but declined it as a rueful spectacle; it was an *astonishment and a hissing.* But now it shall be made an eternal excellency, being reformed from idolatry and having recovered the tokens of God's favour, and it shall be *the joy* of good people for *many generations.* Yet considering how short Jerusalem's excellency was, and how short it came of the vast compass of this promise, we must look for the full accomplishment of it in the perpetual excellencies of the gospel church, far exceeding those of the Old-Testament church, and the glorious privileges and advantages of the Christian religion, which are indeed the joy of many generations. Two things are here spoken of as her excellency and joy, in opposition to her having been forsaken and hated:—(1.) She shall find herself countenanced by her neighbours. The nations, and their kings, that are brought to embrace Christianity, shall lay themselves out for the good of the church, and maintain its interests with the tenderness and affection that the nurse shows to the child at her breast (*v.* 16): "*Thou shalt suck the milk of the Gentiles,* not suck their blood (that is not the spirit of the gospel); thou *shalt suck the breast of kings,* who shall be to thee as nursing fathers." (2.) She shall find herself countenanced by her God: "*Thou shalt know that I the Lord am thy Saviour and thy Redeemer,* shalt know it by experience; for such a salvation, such a redemption, shall be wrought out for thee as plainly discovers itself to be the work of the Lord, the work of a mighty one, for it is a great salvation, of the *Mighty One of Jacob,* for it secures the welfare of all those that are Israelites indeed." They before knew the Lord to be their God; now they know him to be their Saviour, their Redeemer. Their Holy One now appears their Mighty One.

2. She had been impoverished, but now she shall be enriched, and every thing shall be changed for the better with her, *v.* 17. When those who were raised out of the dust are set among princes, instead of brass money in their purses they have gold, and instead of iron vessels in their houses they have silver ones, and other improvements agreeable: so much shall the spiritual glory of the New-Testament church exceed the external pomp and splendour of the Jewish economy, which had no glory in comparison with that which quite excels it, 2 Cor. iii. 10. When we had baptism in the room of circumcision, the Lord's supper in the room of the passover, and a gospel ministry in the room of a Levitical priesthood, we had gold instead of brass. Sin turned gold into brass when Rehoboam made brazen shields instead of the golden ones he had pawned; but God's favour, when that returns, will turn brass again into gold.

3. She had been oppressed by her own princes, which was sadly complained of, not only as her sin, but as her misery (*ch.* lix. 14); but now all the grievances of that kind shall be redressed (*v.* 17): "*I will make thy officers peace;* men of peace shall be made officers, and shall be indeed justices, not patrons of injustice, and justices of peace, not instruments of trouble and vexation. They shall *be peace,* that is, they shall sincerely seek thy welfare and by their means thou shalt enjoy good " They shall be *peace,* for they shall be righteousness; and *then* the peace is as a river, when the righteousness is as the waves of the sea. Even *exactors,* whose business it is to demand the public tribute, though they be exact, must not be exacting, but must be just to the subject as well as to the prince, and, according to the instructions John Baptist gave to the publicans must *exact no more than is appointed them,* Luke iii. 13.

4. She had been insulted by her neighbours, invaded, spoiled, and plundered; but now it shall be so no more (*v.* 18): "*Violence shall no more be heard in thy land;* neither the threats and triumphs of those that do violence nor the outcries and complaints of those that suffer violence shall again be heard, but every man shall peaceably enjoy his own. There shall be no *wasting nor destruction,* either of persons or possessions, any where *within thy borders;* but *thy walls shall be called salvation* (they shall be safe, and means of safety to thee) *and thy gates shall be praise,* praise to thee (every one shall commend thee for the good condition they are kept in), and praise to thy God, *who strengthens the bars of thy gates,*" Ps. cxlvii. 13. When God's salvation is upon the walls it is fit that his praises should be in the gates, the places of concourse.

II. As completed in what it shall be. It should seem that in the close of this chapter we are directed to look further yet, as far forward as to the glory and happiness of heaven, under the type and figure of the flourishing state of the church on earth, which yet was never such as to come any thing near to what is here foretold; and several of the images and expressions here made use of we find in the description of the *new Jerusalem,* Rev. xxi. 23; xxii. 5. As the prophets sometimes insensibly pass from the blessings of the Jewish church to the spiritual blessings of the Christian church, which are eternal, so sometimes they rise from the church militant to the church triumphant, where, and where only, all the promised peace, and joy, and honour will be in perfection. 1. God shall be all in all in the happiness here promised; so he is always to true believers (*v.* 19): *The sun and the moon shall be no more thy light.* God's people, when they enjoy his favour, and walk in the light of his countenance, make little account of sun and moon, and the other lights of this world, but could walk comfortably in the light of the Lord though they should withdraw their shining. In heaven there shall be no occasion for sun or moon, for it is the inheritance of the saints in light, such light as will swallow up the light of the sun as easily as the sun does that of a candle. " Idolaters worshipped the sun and moon (which some have thought the most ancient and plausible idolatry); but these *shall be no more thy light,* shall no more be idolized, but the Lord shall be to thee a constant light, both day and night, in the night of adversity as well as in the day of prosperity." Those that make God their only light shall have him their all-sufficient light, their *sun and shield.* *Thy God shall be thy glory.* Note, God is the glory of those whose God he is and will be so to eternity. It is their glory that they have him for their God, and they glory in it; it is to them instead of beauty. God's people are, upon *this* account, an honourable people, that they have an interest in God as theirs in covenant. 2. The happiness here promised shall know no change, period, or allay (*v.* 20): " *Thy sun shall no more go down,* but it shall be eternal day, eternal sunshine, with thee; that shall not be thy sun which is sometimes eclipsed, often clouded, and, though it shine ever so bright, ever so warm, will certainly set and leave thee in the dark, in the cold, in a few hours; but *he* shall be a sun, a fountain of light to thee, who is himself the *Father of all lights,* with whom there is *no variableness,* nor *shadow of turning,*" James i 17. We read of the sun's standing still once, and not hasting to go down for the space of a day, and it was a glorious day, never was the like; but what was that to the day that shall never have a night? Or, if it had, it should be a light night; for *neither shall thy moon withdraw itself:* it shall never wane, shall never change, but be always at the full. The comforts and joys that are in heaven, the glories provided for the soul, as the light of the sun, and those prepared for the glorified body too, as the light of the moon, shall never know the least cessation or interruption; how should they when *the Lord shall* himself *be thy everlasting light*— a light which never wastes nor can ever be extinguished? *And the days of thy mourning shall be ended,* so as never to return; for *all tears shall be wiped away,* and the fountains of them, sin and affliction, dried up, so that *sorrow and sighing shall flee away* for ever. 3. Those that are entitled to this happiness, being duly prepared and qualified for

it, shall never be put out of the possession of it (*v.* 21): *Thy people,* that shall inhabit this New Jerusalem, *shall all be righteous,* all justified by the righteousness of the Messiah, all sanctified by his Spirit; all that people, that Jerusalem, must be righteous, must have that *holiness without which no man shall see the Lord.* They are all righteous, for we know that *the unrighteous shall not inherit the kingdom of God.* There are no people on earth that are all righteous; there is a mixture of some bad in the best societies on this side heaven; but there are no mixtures there. They shall be *all righteous,* that is, they shall be entirely righteous; as there shall be none corrupt among them, so there shall be no corruption in them; the *spirits of just men* shall there be *made perfect.* And they shall be *all the righteous* together who shall replenish the New Jerusalem; it is called the *congregation of the righteous,* Ps. i. 5. And, because they are *all righteous,* therefore *they shall inherit the land for ever,* for nothing but sin can turn them out of it. The perfection of the saints' holiness secures the perpetuity of their happiness. 4. The glory of the church shall redound to the honour of the church's God: " They shall appear to be the *branch of my planting, the work of my hands,* and I will own them as such." It was by the grace of God that they were designed to this happiness; they are *the branch of his planting,* or of his plantations; he broke them off from the wild olive and grafted them into the good olive, transplanted them out of the field, when they were as tender branches, into his nursery, that, being now planted in his *garden on earth,* they might shortly be removed to his *paradise in heaven.* It was by his grace likewise that they were prepared and fitted for this happiness; they *are the work of his hands* (Eph. ii. 10), are *wrought to the self-same thing,* 2 Cor. v. 5. It is a work of time, and, when it shall be finished, will appear a work of wonder; and God will be glorified, who began it, and carried it on; for the Lord Jesus will then be *admired in all those that believe.* God will glorify himself in glorifying his chosen. 5. They will appear the more glorious, and God will be the more glorified in them, if we compare what they are with what they were, the happiness they have arrived at with the smallness of their beginnings (*v.* 22): "*A little one shall become a thousand and a small one a strong nation.* The captives that returned out of Babylon strangely multiplied, and became a strong nation. The Christian church was a little one, a very small one at first—the number of their names was once but 120; yet it became a thousand. The stone cut out of the mountain without hands swelled so as to fill the earth. The triumphant church, and every glorified saint, will be a thousand out of a little one, a strong nation out of a small one. The grace and peace of the saints were at first like a *grain of mustard-seed,* but they increase and multiply, and make a little one to become a thousand, the weak to be as David. When they come to heaven, and look back upon the smallness of their beginning, they will wonder how they got thither. And so wonderful is all this promise that it needed the ratification with which it is closed: *I the Lord will hasten it in his time*—all that is here said relating to the Jewish and Christian church, to the militant and triumphant church, and to every particular believer. (1.) It may seem too difficult to be brought about, and therefore may be despaired of; but the God of almighty power has undertaken it: "*I the Lord will do it,* who can do it, and who have determined to do it." It will be done by him whose power is irresistible and his purposes unalterable. (2.) It may seem to be delayed and put off so long that we are out of hopes of it; but, as the Lord will do it, so he will *hasten it,* will do it with all convenient speed; though much time may pass before it is done, no time shall be lost; he will *hasten it in its time,* in the proper time, in the season wherein it will be beautiful; he will do it in the time appointed by his wisdom, though not in the time prescribed by our folly. And this is really hastening it; for, though it seem to tarry, it does not tarry if it come in God's time, for we are sure that that is the best time, which he that believes will patiently wait for.

CHAP. LXI.

In this chapter, I. We are sure to find the grace of Christ, published by himself to a lost world in the everlasting gospel, under the type and figure of Isaiah's province, which was to foretel the deliverance of the Jews out of Babylon, ver. 1–3. II. We think we find the glories of the church of Christ, its spiritual glories, described under the type and figure of the Jews' prosperity after their return out of their captivity. 1. It is promised that the decays of the church shall be repaired, ver. 4. 2. That those from without shall be made serviceable to the church, ver. 5. 3. That the church shall be a royal priesthood, maintained by the riches of the Gentiles, ver. 6. 4. That she shall have honour and joy in lieu of all her shame and sorrow, ver. 7. 5. That her affairs shall prosper, ver. 8. 6. That posterity shall enjoy these blessings, ver. 9. 7. That righteousness and salvation shall be the eternal matter of the church's rejoicing and thanksgiving, ver. 10, 11. If the Jewish church was ever thus blessed, much more shall the Christian church be so, and all that belong to it.

THE Spirit of the Lord GOD *is* upon me; because the LORD hath anointed me to preach good tidings unto the meek; he hath sent me to bind up the broken-hearted, to proclaim liberty to the captives, and the opening of the prison to *them that are* bound; 2 To proclaim the acceptable year of the LORD, and the day of vengeance of our God; to comfort all that mourn; 3 To appoint unto them that mourn in Zion, to give unto them beauty for ashes, the oil of joy for mourning, the garment of praise for the spirit of heaviness; that they might be called trees of righteousness, the planting of the LORD, that he might be glorified.

He that is the best expositor of scripture has no doubt given us the best exposition of these verses, even our Lord Jesus himself, who read this in the synagogue at Nazareth (perhaps it was the lesson for the day) and applied it entirely to himself, saying, *This day is this scripture fulfilled in your ears* (Luke iv. 17, 18, 21); and the gracious words which proceeded out of his mouth, in the opening of this text, were admired by all that heard them. As Isaiah was authorized and directed to proclaim liberty to the Jews in Babylon, so was Christ, God's messenger, to publish a more joyful jubilee to a lost world. And here we are told,

I. How he was fitted and qualified for this work: *The Spirit of the Lord God is upon me, v.* 1. The prophets had the Spirit of God moving them at times, both instructing them what to say and exciting them to say it. Christ had the Spirit always resting on him without measure; but to the same intent that the prophets had, as a Spirit of counsel and a Spirit of courage, *ch.* xi. 1—3. When he entered upon the execution of his prophetical office the Spirit, as a dove, *descended upon him,* Matt. iii. 16. This Spirit which was upon him he communicated to those whom he sent to proclaim the same glad tidings, saying to them, when he gave them their commission, *Receive you the Holy Ghost,* thereby ratifying it.

II. How he was appointed and ordained to it: *The Spirit of God is upon me, because the Lord God has anointed me.* What service God called him to he furnished him for; *therefore* he gave him his Spirit, because he had by a sacred and solemn unction set him apart to this great office, as kings and priests were of old destined to their offices by anointing. Hence the Redeemer was called the *Messiah,* the *Christ,* because he was *anointed with the oil of gladness above his fellows. He has sent me;* our Lord Jesus did not go unsent; he had a commission from him that is the fountain of power; *the Father sent him* and *gave him commandment.* This is a great satisfaction to us, that, whatever Christ said, he had a warrant from heaven for; his doctrine was not his, but his that sent him.

III. What the work was to which he was appointed and ordained.

1. He was to be a preacher, was to execute the office of a prophet. So well pleased was he with the good-will God showed towards men through him that he would himself be the preacher of it, that an honour might thereby be put upon the ministry of the gospel and the faith of the saints might be confirmed and encouraged. He must preach *good tidings* (so *gospel* signifies) *to the meek,* to the penitent, and humble, and poor in spirit; to them the tidings of a Redeemer

357

will be indeed good tidings, pure gospel, *faithful sayings, and worthy of all acceptation.* The poor are commonly best disposed to receive the gospel (Jam. ii. 5), and it is likely to profit us when it is received with meekness, as it ought to be; to such Christ preached good tidings when he said, *Blessed are the meek.*

2. He was to be a healer. He was sent to *bind up the broken-hearted,* as pained limbs are rolled to give them ease, as broken bones and bleeding wounds are bound up, that they may knit and close again. Those whose hearts are broken for sin, who are truly humbled under the sense of guilt and dread of wrath, are furnished in the gospel of Christ with that which will make them easy and silence their fears. Those only who have experienced the pains of a penitential contrition may expect the pleasure of divine cordials and consolations.

3. He was to be a deliverer. He was sent as a prophet to preach, as a priest to heal, and as a king to issue out proclamations and those of two kinds:—(1.) Proclamations of peace to his friends: He shall *proclaim liberty to the captives* (as Cyrus did to the Jews in captivity) and the *opening of the prison to those that were bound.* Whereas, by the guilt of sin, we are bound over to the justice of God, are his lawful captives, sold for sin till payment be made of that great debt, Christ lets us know that he has made satisfaction to divine justice for that debt, that his satisfaction is accepted, and if we will plead that, and depend upon it, and make over ourselves and all we have to him, in a grateful sense of the kindness he has done us, we may by faith sue out our pardon and take the comfort of it; there is, and shall be, *no condemnation to us.* And whereas, by the dominion of sin in us, we are bound under the power of Satan, sold under sin, Christ lets us know that he has conquered Satan, has *destroyed him that had the power of death and his works,* and provided for us grace sufficient to enable us to shake off the yoke of sin and to loose ourselves from *those bands of our neck. The Son* is ready by his Spirit to *make us free;* and then we shall be *free indeed,* not only discharged from the miseries of captivity, but advanced to all the immunities and dignities of citizens. This is the gospel proclamation, and it is like the blowing of the jubilee-trumpet, which proclaimed the great year of release (Lev. xxv. 9, 40), in allusion to which it is here called *the acceptable year of the Lord,* the time of our acceptance with God, which is the origin of our liberties; or it is called the *year of the Lord* because it publishes his free grace, to his own glory, and an *acceptable year* because it brings glad tidings to us, and what cannot but be very acceptable to those who know their capacities and necessities of their own souls. (2.) Proclamations of war against

his enemies. Christ proclaims *the day of vengeance of our God,* the vengeance he takes, [1.] On sin and Satan, death and hell, and all the powers of darkness, that were to be destroyed in order to our deliverance; these Christ triumphed over in his cross, having spoiled and weakened them, shamed them, and *made a show of them openly,* therein taking vengeance on them for all the injury they had done both to God and man, Col. ii. 15. [2.] On those of the children of men that stand it out against those fair offers. They shall not only be left, as they deserve, in their captivity, but be dealt with as enemies; we have the gospel summed up, Mark xvi. 16, where that part of it, *He that believes shall be saved,* proclaims *the acceptable year of the Lord* to those that will accept of it; but the other part, *He that believes not shall be damned,* proclaims *the day of vengeance of our God,* that vengeance which he will take on those that *obey not the gospel of Jesus Christ,* 2 Thess. i. 8.

4. He was to be a comforter, and so he is as preacher, healer, and deliverer; he is sent to *comfort all who mourn,* and who, mourning, seek to him, and not to the world, for comfort. Christ not only provides comfort for them, and proclaims it, but he applies it to them; he does by his Spirit comfort them. There is enough in him to *comfort all who mourn,* whatever their sore or sorrow is; but this comfort is sure to those who *mourn in Zion,* who sorrow *after a godly sort,* according to God, for his residence is in Zion,—who *mourn because of Zion's* calamities and desolations, and mingle their tears by a holy sympathy with those of all God's suffering people, though they themselves are not in trouble; such tears God has *a bottle* for (Ps. lvi. 8), such mourners he has comfort in store for. As *blessings out of Zion* are spiritual blessings, so *mourners in Zion* are holy mourners, such as carry their sorrows to the throne of grace (for in Zion was the mercy-seat) and pour them out as Hannah did before the Lord. To such as these Christ has appointed by his gospel, and will give by his Spirit (*v.* 3), those consolations which will not only support them under their sorrows, but turn them into songs of praise. He will give them, (1.) *Beauty for ashes.* Whereas they lay in ashes, as was usual in times of great mourning, they shall not only be raised out of their dust, but made to look pleasant. Note, The holy cheerfulness of Christians is their beauty and a great ornament to their profession. Here is an elegant *paronomasia* in the original: He will give them *pheer—beauty,* for *epher—ashes;* he will turn their sorrow into joy as quickly and as easily as you can transpose a letter; for he speaks, and it is done. (2.) *The oil of joy,* which *makes the face to shine,* instead of *mourning,* which *disfigures the countenance* and makes

it unlovely. This *oil of joy* the saints have from that *oil of gladness* with which Christ himself was *anointed above his fellows,* Heb. i. 9. (3.) *The garments of praise,* such beautiful garments as were worn on thanksgiving-days, instead of the *spirit of heaviness, dimness,* or *contraction*—open joys for secret mournings. The *spirit of heaviness* they keep to themselves (Zion's mourners *weep in secret);* but the joy they are recompensed with they are clothed with as with a garment in the eye of others. Observe, Where God gives the oil of joy he gives the garment of praise. Those comforts which come from God dispose the heart to, and enlarge the heart in, thanksgivings to God. Whatever we have the joy of God must have the praise and glory of.

5. He was to be a planter; for the church is God's husbandry. *Therefore* he will do all this for his people, will cure their wounds, release them out of bondage, and comfort them in their sorrows, *that they may be called trees of righteousness, the planting of the Lord,* that they may be such and be acknowledged to be such, that they may be ornaments to God's vineyard and may be *fruitful in the fruits of righteousness,* as the branches of *God's planting,* ch. lx. 21. All that Christ does for us is to make us God's people, and some way serviceable to him as living trees, *planted in the house of the Lord,* and *flourishing in the courts of our God;* and all this *that he may be glorified*—that we may be brought to glorify him by a sincere devotion and an exemplary conversation (for *herein is our Father glorified, that we bring forth much fruit),* that others also may take occasion from God's favour shining on his people, and his grace shining in them, to praise him, and that he may be for ever *glorified in his saints.*

4 And they shall build the old wastes, they shall raise up the former desolations, and they shall repair the waste cities, the desolations of many generations. 5 And strangers shall stand and feed your flocks, and the sons of the alien *shall be* your ploughmen and your vine-dressers. 6 But ye shall be named the priests of the LORD: *men* shall call you the ministers of our God: ye shall eat the riches of the Gentiles, and in their glory shall ye boast yourselves. 7 For your shame *ye shall have* double; and *for* confusion they shall rejoice in their portion: therefore in their land they shall possess the double: everlasting joy shall be unto them. 8 For I the LORD love judgment, I hate robbery for burnt-offering; and

I will direct their work in truth, and I will make an everlasting covenant with them. 9 And their seed shall be known among the Gentiles, and their offspring among the people: all that see them shall acknowledge them, that they *are* the seed *which* the LORD hath blessed.

Promises are here made to the Jews now returned out of captivity, and settled again in their own land, which are to be extended to the gospel church, and all believers, who through grace are delivered out of spiritual thraldom; for they are capable of being spiritually applied.

I. It is promised that their houses shall be rebuilt (*v.* 4), that their cities shall be raised out of the ruins in which they had long lain, and be fitted up for their use again: *They shall build the old wastes;* the *old wastes* shall be built, the *waste cities shall be repaired,* the *former desolations,* even *the desolations of many generations,* which it was feared would never be repaired, shall be *raised up.* The setting up of Christianity in the world repaired the decays of natural religion and raised up those desolations both of piety and honesty which had been for many generations the reproach of mankind. An unsanctified soul is like a city that is broken down and has no walls, like a house in ruins; but by the power of Christ's gospel and grace it is repaired, it is put in order again, and fitted to be a habitation of God through the Spirit. And *they* shall do this, those that are released out of captivity; for we are brought out of the house of bondage that we may serve God, both in building up ourselves to his glory and in helping to build up his church on earth.

II. Those that were so lately servants themselves, working for their oppressors and lying at their mercy, shall now have servants to do their work for them and be at their command, not of their brethren (they are all the Lord's freemen), but of *the strangers, and the sons of the alien,* who shall *keep their sheep, till their ground,* and *dress their gardens,* the ancient employments of Abel, Cain, and Adam: *Strangers shall feed your flocks, v.* 5. When, by the grace of God, we attain to a holy indifference as to all the affairs of this world, *buying as though we possessed not*— when, though our hands are employed about them, our hearts are not entangled with them, but reserved entire for God and his service—then *the sons of the alien are our ploughmen and vine-dressers.*

III. They shall not only be released out of their captivity, but highly preferred and honourably employed (*v.* 6): "While the strangers are *keeping your flocks,* you shall be keeping *the charge of the sanctuary;* instead of being slaves to your task-masters, *you shall be named the priests of the Lord,* a high and holy calling." Priests were princes' peers, and in Hebrew were called by the same name. You *shall be the ministers of our God*, as the Levites were. Note, Those whom God sets at liberty he sets to work; he *delivers them out of the hands of their enemies* that they may *serve him*, Luke i. 74, 75; Ps. cxvi. 16. But his service is perfect freedom, nay, it is the greatest honour. When God brought Israel out of Egypt he took them to be to him a *kingdom of priests*, Exod. xix. 6. And the gospel church is a *royal priesthood*, 1 Pet. ii. 9. All believers are made to our God kings and priests; and they ought to conduct themselves as such in their devotions and in their whole conversation, with *holiness to the Lord* written upon their foreheads, that men may *call them the priests of the Lord*.

IV. The wealth and honour of the Gentile converts shall redound to the benefit and credit of the church, *v.* 6. *The Gentiles* shall be brought into the church. Those that were strangers shall become *fellow-citizens with the saints;* and with themselves they shall bring all they have, to be devoted to the glory of God and used in his service; and the priests, the Lord's ministers, shall have the advantage of it. It will be a great strengthening and quickening, as well as a comfort and encouragement, to all good Christians, to see the Gentiles serving the interests of God's kingdom. 1. They shall *eat the riches of the Gentiles*, not which they have themselves seized by violence, but which are fairly and honourably presented to them, as *gifts brought to the altar*, which the priests and their families lived comfortably upon. It is not said, "You shall *hoard the riches of the Gentiles*, and treasure them," but, "You shall *eat them;*" for there is nothing better in riches than to use them and to do good with them. 2. They shall *boast themselves in their glory*. Whatever was the honour of the Gentile converts before their conversion—their nobility, estates, learning, virtue, or places of trust and power—it shall all turn to the reputation of the church to which they have joined themselves; and whatever is their glory after their conversion—their holy zeal and strictness of conversation, their usefulness, their patient suffering, and all the displays of that blessed change which divine grace has made in them—shall be very much for the glory of God and therefore all good men shall glory in it.

V. They shall have abundance of comfort and satisfaction in their own bosoms, *v.* 7. The Jews no doubt were thus privileged after their return; they were in a new world, and now knew how to value their liberty and property, the pleasures of which were continually fresh and blooming. Much more do all those rejoice whom Christ has brought into the glorious liberty of God's children, especially when the privileges of their adoption shall be completed in the resurrection of the

body. 1. *They shall rejoice in their portion;* they shall not only have their own again, but (which is a further gift of God) they shall have the comfort of it, and a heart to rejoice in it, Eccl. ii. 13. Though the houses of the returned Jews, as well as their temple, be much inferior to what they were before the captivity, yet they shall be well pleased with them and thankful for them. It is a portion *in their land*, their own land, the holy land, Immanuel's land, and therefore they shall rejoice in it, having so lately known what it was to be *strangers in a strange land*. Those that have God and heaven for their portion have reason to say that they have a worthy portion and to rejoice in it. 2. *Everlasting joy shall be unto them*, that is, a joyful state of their people, which shall last long, much longer than the captivity had lasted. Yet that joy of the Jewish nation was so much allayed, so often interrupted, and so soon brought to an end, that we must look for the accomplishment of this promise in the spiritual joy which believers have in God and the eternal joy they hope for in heaven. 3. This shall be a double recompence to them, and more than double, for all the reproach and vexation they have lain under in the land of their captivity: "*For your shame you shall have double* honour, and *in your land* you *shall possess double* wealth, to what you lost; the blessing of God upon it, and the comfort you shall have in it, shall make an abundant reparation for all the damages you have received. You shall be owned not only as *God's sons*, but as his *first-born* (Exod. iv. 22), and therefore entitled to a double portion." As the miseries of their captivity were so great that in them they are said to have received *double for all their sins* (ch. xl. 2), so the joys of their return shall be so great that in them they shall receive *double for all their shame*. The former is applicable to the fulness of Christ's satisfaction, in which God received *double for all our sins;* the latter to the fulness of heaven's joys, in which we shall receive more than *double for all our services* and sufferings. Job's case illustrates this: when God *turned again his captivity*, he gave him *twice as much as he had before.*

VI. God will be their faithful guide and a God in covenant with them (*v.* 8): *I will direct their work in truth*. God by his providence will order their affairs for the best, according to the word of his truth. He will guide them in the ways of true prosperity, by the rules of true policy. He will by his grace direct the works of good people in the right way, the true way that leads to happiness; he will direct them to be done in sincerity and then they are pleasing to him. God *desires truth in the inward parts;* and, if we do our works in truth, he will *make an everlasting covenant with us;* for to those that *walk before him* and *are upright* he will certainly be a *God all-sufficient*. Now, as a reason both of this and of the foregoing promise, that God will recompense to them *double for their shame*, those words come in, in the former part of the verse, *I the Lord love judgment.* He loves that judgment should be done among men, both between magistrates and subjects and between neighbour and neighbour, and therefore he hates all injustice ; and, when wrongs are done to his people by their oppressors and persecutors, he is displeased with them, not only because they are done to his people, but because they are wrongs, and against the eternal rules of equity. If men do not do justice, he loves to do judgment himself in giving redress to those that suffer wrong and punishing those that do wrong. God pleads his people's injured cause, not only because he is jealous for them, but because he is jealous for justice. To illustrate this, it is added that he *hates robbery for burnt-offering.* He hates injustice even in his own people, who honour him with what they have in their burnt-offerings, much more does he hate it when it is against his own people ; if he hates robbery when it is for burnt-offerings to himself, much more when it is for burnt-offerings to idols, and when not only his people are robbed of their estates, but he is robbed of his offerings. It is a truth much to the honour of God that ritual services will never atone for the violation of moral precepts, nor will it justify any man's robbery to say, "It was for burnt-offerings," or *Corban—It is a gift.* Behold, *to obey is better than sacrifice,* to *do justly and love mercy* better than *thousands of rams ;* nay, that robbery is most of all hateful to God which is covered with this pretence, for it makes the righteous God to be the patron of unrighteousness. Some make this a reason of the rejection of the Jews upon the bringing in of the Gentiles (*v.* 6), because they were so corrupt in their morals, and, while they tithed mint and cummin, made nothing of *judgment and mercy* (Matt. xxiii. 23), whereas *God loves judgment* and insists upon that, and he hates both *robbery for burnt offerings* and *burnt-offerings for robbery* too, as that of the Pharisees, who made long prayers that they might the more plausibly devour widows' houses. Others read these words thus : *I hate rapine by iniquity,* that is, the spoil which the enemies of God's people had unjustly made of them ; God hated this, and therefore would reckon with them for it.

VII. God will entail a blessing upon their posterity after them (*v.* 9) : *Their seed* (the children of those persons themselves that are now the blessed of the Lord, or their successors in profession, the church's seed) shall be *accounted to the Lord for a generation,* Ps. xxii. 30. 1. They shall signalize themselves and make their neighbours to take notice of them : *They shall be known among the Gentiles,* shall distinguish themselves by

the gravity, seriousness, humility, and cheerfulness of their conversation, especially by that brotherly love by which all men shall know them to be Christ's disciples. And, they thus distinguishing themselves, God shall dignify them, by making them the blessings of their age and instruments of his glory, and by giving them remarkable tokens of his favour, which shall make them eminent and gain them respect from all about them. Let the children of godly parents live in such a manner that they may be known to be such, that all who observe them may see in them the fruits of a good education, and an answer to the prayers that were put up for them ; and then they may expect that God will make them known, by the fulfilling of that promise to them, that *the generation of the upright shall be blessed.* 2. God shall have the glory of this, for every one shall attribute it to the blessing of God ; all that see them shall see so much of the grace of God in them, and his favour towards them, that they shall *acknowledge them to be the seed which the Lord has blessed* and doth bless, for it includes both. See what it is to be blessed of God. Whatever good appears in any it must be taken notice of as the fruit of God's blessing and he must be glorified in it.

10 I will greatly rejoice in the LORD, my soul shall be joyful in my God ; for he hath clothed me with the garments of salvation, he hath covered me with the robe of righteousness, as a bridegroom decketh *himself* with ornaments, and as a bride adorneth *herself* with her jewels. 11 For as the earth bringeth forth her bud, and as the garden causeth the things that are sown in it to spring forth ; so the Lord GOD will cause righteousness and praise to spring forth before all the nations.

Some make this the song of joy and praise to be sung by the prophet in the name of Jerusalem, congratulating her on the happy change of her circumstances in the accomplishment of the foregoing promises ; others make it to be spoken by Christ in the name of the New-Testament church triumphing in gospel grace. We may take in both, the former as a type of the latter. We are here taught to rejoice with holy joy, to God's honour, 1. In the beginning of this good work, the clothing of the church *with righteousness and salvation, v.* 10. Upon this account *I will greatly rejoice in the Lord.* Those that rejoice in God have cause to rejoice greatly, and we need not fear running into an extreme in the greatness of our joy when we make God the gladness of our joy. The first gospel song begins like this, *My soul doth magnify the Lord, and my spirit hath rejoiced in God my Saviour,* Luke i. 46, 47. There is just matter for this joy, and all the reason in the world why it should terminate in God; for salvation and righteousness are wrought out and brought in, and the church is clothed with them. The salvation God wrought for the Jews, and that righteousness of his in which he appeared for them, and that reformation which appeared among them, made them look as glorious in the eyes of all wise men as if they had been clothed in robes of state or nuptial garments. Christ has clothed his church with an eternal salvation (and that is truly great) by clothing it with the righteousness both of justification and sanctification. The *clean linen is the righteousness of saints,* Rev. xix. 8. Observe how these two are put together; those, and those only, shall be clothed with the garments of salvation hereafter that are covered with the robe of righteousness now: and those garments are rich and splendid clothing, like the priestly garments (for so the word signifies) with which the *bridegroom decks himself.* The brightness of the sun itself is compared to them. Ps. xix. 5, *He is as a bridegroom* coming out of his chamber, completely dressed. Such is the beauty of God's grace in those that are clothed with the robe of righteousness, that by the righteousness of Christ are recommended to God's favour and by the sanctification of the Spirit have God's image renewed upon them; they are decked as a bride to be espoused to God, and taken into covenant with him; they are decked as a priest to be employed for God, and taken into communion with him. 2. In the progress and continuance of this good work, *v.* 11. It is not like a day of triumph, which is glorious for the present, but is soon over. No; the righteousness and salvation with which the church is clothed are durable clothing; so they are said to be, *ch.* xxiii. 18. The church, when she is pleasing herself with the righteousness and salvation that Jesus Christ has clothed her with, rejoices to think that these inestimable blessings shall both spring for future ages and spread to distant regions. (1.) They shall spring forth for ages to come, as the fruits of the earth which are produced every year, from generation to generation. *As the earth,* even that which lies common, *brings forth her bud,* the tender grass at the return of the year, and as *the garden* enclosed *causes the things that are sown in it to spring forth* in their season, so duly, so constantly, so powerfully, and with such advantage to mankind *will the Lord God cause righteousness and praise to spring forth,* by virtue of the covenant of grace, as, in the former case, by virtue of the covenant of providence. See what the promised blessings are—*righteousness and praise* (for those that are clothed with righteousness *show forth the praises* of him that clothed them); these shall spring

362

forth under the influence of the dew of divine grace. Though it may sometimes be winter with the church, when those blessings seem to wither and do not appear, yet the root of them is fixed, a spring-time will come, when through the reviving beams of the approaching Sun of righteousness they shall flourish again. (2.) They shall spread far, and *spring forth before all the nations;* the great salvation shall be published and proclaimed to all the world and the ends of the earth shall see it.

CHAP. LXII.

The business of prophets was both to preach and pray. In this chapter, I. The prophet determines to apply closely and constantly to this business, ver. 1. II. God appoints him and others of his prophets to continue to do so, for the encouragement of his people during the delays of their deliverance, ver. 6, 7. III. The promises are here repeated and ratified of the great things God would do for his church, for the Jews after their return out of captivity and for the Christian church when it shall be set up in the world. 1. The church shall be made honourable in the eyes of the world, ver. 2. 2. It shall appear to be very dear to God, precious and honourable in his sight, ver. 3—5. 3. It shall enjoy great plenty, ver. 8, 9. 4. It shall be released out of captivity and grow up again into a considerable nation, particularly owned and favoured by heaven, ver. 10—12.

FOR Zion's sake will I not hold my peace, and for Jerusalem's sake I will not rest, until the righteousness thereof go forth as brightness, and the salvation thereof as a lamp *that* burneth. 2 And the Gentiles shall see thy righteousness, and all kings thy glory: and thou shalt be called by a new name, which the mouth of the LORD 'shall name. 3 Thou shalt also be a crown of glory in the hand of the LORD, and a royal diadem in the hand of thy God. 4 Thou shalt no more be termed Forsaken; neither shall thy land any more be termed Desolate: but thou shalt be called Hephzi-bah, and thy land Beulah: for the LORD delighteth in thee, and thy land shall be married. 5 For *as* a young man marrieth a virgin, *so* shall thy sons marry thee: and *as* the bridegroom rejoiceth over the bride, *so* shall thy God rejoice over thee.

The prophet here tells us,

I. What he will do for the church. A prophet, as he is a seer, so he is a spokesman. This prophet resolves to perform that office faithfully, *v.* 1. He *will not hold his peace;* he *will not rest;* he will mind his business, will take pains, and never desire to take his ease; and herein he was a type of Christ, who was indefatigable in executing the office of a prophet and made it his meat and drink till he had finished his work. Observe here, 1. What the prophet's resolution is: *He will not hold his peace.* He will continue instant in preaching, will not only faithfully deliver, but frequently repeat, the messages he has *received from the Lord.* If people receive not the precepts and promises at first, he will inculcate them and give them line upon line. And he will continue instant in prayer; he will never hold his peace at the throne of grace till he has prevailed with God for the mercies promised; he will *give himself to prayer and to the ministry of the word*, as Christ's ministers must (Acts vi. 4), who must labour frequently in both and never be weary of this well-doing. The business of ministers is to speak from God to his people and to God for his people; and in neither of these must they be silent. 2. What is the principle of this resolution—*for Zion's sake, and for Jerusalem's*, not for the sake of any private interest of his own, but for the church's sake, because he has an affection and concern for Zion, and it lies near his heart. Whatever becomes of his own house and family, he desires to *see the good of Jerusalem* and resolves to seek it all the days of his life, Ps. cxxii. 8, 9; cxxviii. 5. It is God's Zion and his Jerusalem, and it is *therefore* dear to him, because it is so to God and because God's glory is interested in its prosperity. 3. How long he resolves to continue this importunity—till the promise of the church's righteousness and salvation, given in the foregoing chapter, be accomplished. Isaiah will not himself live to see the release of the captives out of Babylon, much less the bringing in of the gospel, in which *grace reigns through righteousness unto life* and salvation; yet he will *not hold his peace till* these be accomplished, even the utmost of them, because his prophecies will continue speaking of these things, and there shall in every age be a remnant that shall continue to pray for them, as successors to him, till the promises be performed, and so the prayers answered that were grounded upon them. Then the church's *righteousness* and *salvation* will *go forth as brightness*, and *as a lamp that burns*, so plainly that it will carry its own evidence along with it. It will bring honour and comfort to the church, which will hereupon both look pleasant and appear illustrious; and it will bring instruction and direction to the world, a light not only to the eyes but to the feet, and to *the paths* of those who before *sat in darkness and in the shadow of death*.

II. What God will do for the church. The prophet can but pray and preach, but God will confirm the word and answer the prayers. 1. The church shall be greatly admired. When that righteousness which is her salvation, her praise, and her glory, shall be *brought forth*, the *Gentiles shall see* it. The tidings of it shall be carried to the Gentiles, and a tender of it made to them; they may so see this righteousness as to share in it if it be not their own fault. " Even kings shall see and be in love with the *glory of thy righteousness*" (*v.* 2), shall overlook the glory of their own courts and kingdoms, and look at, and look after, the spiritual glory of the church as that which excels. 2. She shall be truly admirable. Great names make men considerable in the world, and great respect is paid them thereupon; now it is agreed that *honor est in honorante*—honour derives its value from the dignity of him who confers it. God is the fountain of honour and from him the church's honour comes: " *Thou shalt be called by a new name*, a pleasant name, such as thou wast never called by before, no, not in the day of thy greatest prosperity, and the reverse of that which thou wast called by in the day of thy affliction; thou shalt have a new character, be advanced to a new dignity, and those about thee shall have new thoughts of thee." This seems to be alluded to in that promise (Rev. ii. 17) of the *white stone and in the stone a new name*, and that (Rev. iii. 12) of the *name of the city of my God* and my *new name*. It is a name *which the mouth of the Lord shall name*, who, we are sure, miscalls nothing, and who will oblige others to call her by the name he has given her; for his judgment is according to truth and all shall concur with it sooner or later. Two names God shall give her:—(1.) He shall call her his crown (*v.* 3): *Thou shalt be a crown of glory in the hand of the Lord*, not on his head (as adding any real honour or power to him, as crowns do to those that are crowned with them), but in his hand. He is pleased to account them, and show them forth, as a glory and beauty to him. When he took them to be his people it was that they might be *unto him for a name, and for a praise, and for a glory* (Jer xiii. 11): " *Thou shalt be a crown of glory* and a *royal diadem*, through the hand, the good hand, of thy God upon thee; he shall make thee so, for he shall be *to thee a crown of glory*, ch. xxviii. 5. Thou shalt be so *in his hand*, that is, under his protection; he that shall put glory upon thee shall *create a defence upon all that glory*, so that the flowers of thy crown shall never wither nor shall its jewels be lost." (2.) He shall call her his spouse, *v.* 4, 5. This is a yet greater honour, especially considering what a forlorn condition she had been in. [1.] Her case had been very melancholy. She was called *forsaken* and her land *desolate* during the captivity, like a woman reproachfully divorced or left a disconsolate widow. Such was the state of religion in the world before the preaching of the gospel—it was in a manner forsaken and desolate, a thing that no man looked after nor had any real concern for. [2.] It should now be very pleasant, for God would return in mercy to her. Instead of those two names of reproach, she shall be called by two honourable names. *First,* She shall be called *Hephzi-bah*, which signifies, *My delight is in her ;* it was the name of Hezekiah's queen, Manasseh's mother (2 Kings xxi. 1), a proper name for a wife,

who ought to be her husband's delight, Prov.
v. 19. And here it is the church's Maker
that is her husband : *The Lord delights in
thee.* God by his grace has wrought that
in his church which makes her his delight,
she being refined, and reformed, and brought
home to him; and then by his providence
he does that for her which makes it appear
that she is his delight and that he delights
to do her good. *Secondly,* She shall be
called *Beulah,* which signifies *married,* whereas she had been desolate, a condition opposed
to that of the *married wife, ch.* liv. 1. " *Thy
land shall be married,* that is, it shall become
fruitful again, and be replenished." Though
she has long been barren, she shall again be
peopled, shall again be made to keep house
and to be a joyful mother of children, Ps.
cxiii. 9. *She shall be married,* for, 1. Her
sons shall heartily espouse the land of their
nativity and its interests, which they had for
a long time neglected, as despairing ever to
have any comfortable enjoyment of it : *Thy
sons shall marry thee,* that is, they shall live
with thee and take delight in thee. When
they were in Babylon, they seemed to have
espoused that land, for they were appointed
to settle, and to seek the peace of it, Jer. xxix.
5—7. But now they shall again marry their
own land, *as a young man marries a virgin*
that he takes great delight in, is extremely
fond of, and is likely to have many children
by. It bodes well to a land when its own
natives and inhabitants are pleased with it,
prefer it before other lands, when its princes
marry their country and resolve to take their
lot with it. 2. *Her God* (which is much better)
shall *betroth her to himself in righteousness,*
Hosea ii. 19, 20. He will take pleasure in
his church : *As the bridegroom rejoices over
the bride,* is pleased with his relation to her
and her affection to him, *so shall thy God
rejoice over thee :* he shall rest in his love to
thee (Zeph. iii. 17) ; *he shall take pleasure*
in thee (Ps. cxlvii. 11), and shall *delight to
do thee good with his whole heart and his
whole soul,* Jer. xxxii. 41. This is very applicable to the love Christ has for his church
and the complacency he takes in it, which
appears so brightly in Solomon's Song, and
which will be complete in heaven.

6 I have set watchmen upon thy
walls, O Jerusalem, *which* shall never
hold their peace day nor night : ye
that make mention of the LORD, keep
not silence, 7 And give him no rest,
till he establish, and till he make Jerusalem a praise in the earth. 8 The
LORD hath sworn by his right hand,
and by the arm of his strength, Surely
I will no more give thy corn *to be* meat
for thine enemies ; and the sons of
the stranger shall not drink thy wine,
for the which thou hast laboured : 9
364

But they that have gathered it shall
eat it, and praise the LORD ; and they
that have brought it together shall
drink it in the courts of my holiness.

Two things are here promised to Jerusalem :—
I. Plenty of the means of grace—abundance of good preaching and good praying
(*v.* 6, 7), and this shows the method God
takes when he designs mercy for a people ;
he first brings them to their duty and pours
out a spirit of prayer upon them, and then
brings salvation to them. Provision is made,
1. That ministers may do their duty as
watchmen. It is here spoken of as a token
for good, as a step towards further mercy
and an earnest of it, that, in order to what
he designed for them, he would set *watchmen on their walls who should never hold their
peace.* Note, (1.) Ministers are watchmen
on the church's walls, for it is as a city besieged, whose concern it is to have sentinels
on the walls, to take notice and give notice
of the motions of the enemy. It is necessary that, as watchmen, they be wakeful,
and faithful, and willing to endure hardness.
(2.) They are concerned to stand upon their
guard day and night ; they must never be
off their watch as long as those for whose
souls they watch are not out of danger. (3.)
They must never hold their peace ; they
must take all opportunities to give warning
to sinners, in season, out of season, and must
never betray the cause of Christ by a treacherous or cowardly silence. They must
never hold their peace at the throne of grace ;
they must *pray, and not faint,* as Moses
lifted up his hands and kept them steady,
till Israel had obtained the victory over
Amalek, Exod. xvii. 10, 12.
2. That people may do their duty. As
those that make mention of the Lord, let
not them keep silence neither, let not them
think it enough that their watchmen pray
for them, but let them pray for themselves ;
all will be little enough to meet the approaching mercy with due solemnity. Note,
(1.) It is the character of God's professing
people that they make mention of the
Lord, and continue to do so even in bad
times, when the land is termed *forsaken*
and *desolate.* They are *the Lord's remem-
brancers* (so the margin reads it) ; they remember the Lord themselves and put one
another in mind of him. (2.) God's professing people must be a praying people, must
be public-spirited in prayer, must wrestle
with God in prayer, and continue to do so :
" *Keep not silence ;* never grow remiss in
the duty nor weary of it." *Give him no rest*—
alluding to an importunate beggar, to the
widow that with her continual coming
wearied the judge into a compliance. God
said to *Moses, Let me alone* (Exod. xxxii. 10),
and Jacob to Christ, *I will not let thee go
except thou bless me,* Gen. xxxii. 26. (3.)

God is so far from being displeased with our pressing importunity, as men commonly are, that he invites and encourages it; he bids us to cry after him; he is not like those disciples who discouraged a petitioner, Matt. xv. 23. He bids us make pressing applications at the throne of grace, and *give him no rest*, Luke xi. 5, 8 He suffers himself not only to be reasoned with, but to be wrestled with. (4.) The public welfare or prosperity of God's Jerusalem is that which we should be most importunate for at the throne of grace; we should pray for the good of the church. [1.] That it may be safe, that he would *establish* it, that the interests of the church may be firm, may be settled for the present and secured to posterity. [2.] That it may be great, may be *a praise in the earth*, that it may be praised, and God may be praised for it. When gospel truths are cleared and vindicated, when gospel ordinances are duly administered in their purity and power, when the church becomes eminent for holiness and love, then Jerusalem is a praise in the earth, then it is in reputation. (5.) We must persevere in our prayers for mercy to the church till the mercy come; we must do as the prophet's servant did, go yet seven times, till the promising cloud appear, 1 Kings xviii. 44. (6.) It is a good sign that God is coming towards a people in ways of mercy when he pours out a spirit of prayer upon them and stirs them up to be fervent and constant in their intercessions.

II. Plenty of all other good things, *v.* 8. This follows upon the former; when the people praise God, when *all the people praise him, then shall the earth yield her increase* (Ps. lxvii. 5, 6), and outward prosperity, crowning its piety, shall help to make Jerusalem a praise in the earth. Observe,

1. The great distress they had been in, and the losses they had sustained. Their corn had been meat for their enemies, which they hoped would be meat for themselves and their families. Here was a double grievance, that they themselves wanted that which was necessary to the support of life and were in danger of perishing for want of it, and that their enemies were strengthened by it, had their camp victualled with it, and so were the better able to do them a mischief. God is said to give their corn to their enemies, because he not only permitted it, but ordered it, to be the just punishment both of their abuse of plenty and of their symbolizing with strangers, *ch.* i. 7. The wine which they had laboured for, and which in their affliction they needed for the relief of those among them that were of a heavy heart, strangers drank it, to gratify their lusts with; this sore judgment was threatened for their sins, Lev. xxvi. 16; Deut. xxviii. 33. See how uncertain our creature-comforts are, and how much it is our wisdom to labour for that meat which we can never be robbed of.

2. The great fulness and satisfaction they should now be restored to (*v.* 9): *Those that have gathered it shall eat it, and praise the Lord.* See here, (1.) God's mercy in giving plenty, and peace to enjoy it,—that the earth yields her increase, that there are hands to be employed in gathering it in, and that they are not taken off by plague and sickness, or otherwise employed in war,—that strangers and enemies do not come and gather it for themselves, or take it from us when we have gathered it,—that we eat the labour of our hands and the bread is not eaten out of our mouths,—and especially that we have opportunity and a heart to honour God with it, and that his courts are open to us and we are not restrained from attending on him in them. (2.) Our duty in the enjoyment of this mercy. We must gather what God gives, with care and industry; we must eat it freely and cheerfully, not bury the gifts of God's bounty, but make use of them. We must, when we have eaten and are full, *bless the Lord*, and give him thanks for his bounty to us; and we must serve him with our abundance, use it in works of piety and charity, eat it and *drink it in the courts of his holiness*, where the altar, the priest, and the poor must all have their share. The greatest comfort that a good man has in his meat and drink is that it furnishes him with a meat-offering and a drink-offering for the Lord his God (Joel ii. 14); the greatest comfort that he has in an estate is that it gives him an opportunity of honouring God and doing good. This wine is to be *drunk in the courts of God's holiness*, and therefore moderately and with sobriety, as before the Lord.

3. The solemn ratification of this promise: *The Lord has sworn by his right hand, and by the arm of his strength*, that he will do this for his people. God confirms it by an oath, that his people, who trust in him and his word, may have *strong consolation*, Heb. vi. 17, 18. And, since he can swear by no greater, he swears by himself, sometimes by his being *(As I live*, Ezek. xxxiii. 11), sometimes by his holiness (Ps. lxxxix. 35), here by his power, his right hand (which was lifted up in swearing, Deut. xxxii. 40), and his arm of power; for it is a great satisfaction to those who build their hopes on God's promise to be sure that *what he has promised he is able to perform*, Rom. iv. 21. To assure us of this he has sworn by his strength, pawning the reputation of his omnipotence upon it; if he do not do it, let it be said, *It was because he could not*, which the Egyptians shall never say (Num. xiv. 16) nor any other. It is the comfort of God's people that his power is engaged for them, his right hand, where the Mediator sits.

10 Go through, go through the gates; prepare ye the way of the people; cast up, cast up the highway; gather out the stones; lift up a stand-

ard for the people. 11 Behold, the LORD hath proclaimed unto the end of the world, Say ye to the daughter of Zion, Behold, thy salvation cometh ; behold, his reward *is* with him, and his work before him. 12 And they shall call them, The holy people, The redeemed of the LORD: and thou shalt be called, Sought out, A city not forsaken.

This, as many like passages before, refers to the deliverance of the Jews out of Babylon, and, under the type and figure of that, to the great redemption wrought out by Jesus Christ, and the proclaiming of gospel grace and liberty through him. 1. Way shall be made for this salvation ; all difficulties shall be removed, and whatever might obstruct it shall be taken out of the way, *v.* 10. The gates of Babylon shall be thrown open, that they may with freedom go through them ; the way from Babylon to the land of Israel shall be prepared ; causeways shall be made and cast up through wet and miry places, and the stones gathered out from places rough and rocky ; in the convenient places appointed for their rendezvous standards shall be set up for their direction and encouragement, that they may embody for their greater safety. Thus John Baptist was sent to *prepare the way of the Lord,* Matt. iii. 3. And, before Christ by his graces and comforts comes to any for salvation, preparation is made for him by repentance, which is called the *preparation of the gospel of peace,* Eph. vi. 15. Here the way is levelled by it, there the feet are shod with it, which comes all to one, for both are in order to a journey. 2. Notice shall be given of this salvation, *v.* 11, 12. It shall be proclaimed to the captives that they are set at liberty and may go if they please ; it shall be proclaimed to their neighbours, to all about them, *to the end of the world,* that God has pleaded Zion's just, injured, and despised cause. Let it be said to Zion, for her comfort, *Behold, thy salvation comes* (that is, thy Saviour, who brings salvation) ; he will bring such a work, such a reward, in this salvation, as shall be admired by all, a reward of comfort and peace with him ; but a work of humiliation and reformation before him, to prepare his people for that recompence of their sufferings ; and then, with reference to each, it follows, they shall be called, *The holy people,* and the *redeemed of the Lord. The work before him,* which shall be wrought in and upon them, shall denominate them a holy people, cured of their inclination to idolatry and consecrated to God only ; and the *reward with him,* the deliverance wrought for them, shall denominate them the *redeemed of the Lord,* so redeemed as none but God could redeem them, and redeemed to be his, their bonds loosed, that they might be his servants.

Jerusalem shall then be called, *Sought out, a city not forsaken.* She had been forsaken for many years ; there were neither traders nor worshippers that enquired the way to Jerusalem as formerly, when it was frequented by both. But now God will again make her considerable. She shall be sought out, visited, resorted to, and court made to her, as much as ever. When Jerusalem is called a *holy city,* then it is called *sought out;* for holiness puts an honour and beauty upon any place or person, which draws respect, and makes them to be admired, beloved, and enquired after. But this being proclaimed to the end of the world must have a reference to the gospel of Christ, which was to be preached to every creature; and it intimates, (1.) The glory of Christ. It is published immediately to the church, but is thence echoed to every nation : *Behold, thy salvation cometh.* Christ is not only the Saviour, but the salvation itself ; for the happiness of believers is not only from him, but in him, *ch.* xii. 2. His salvation consists both in the work and in the reward which he brings with him; for those that are his shall neither be idle nor lose their labour. (2.) The beauty of the church. Christians shall be called *saints* (1 Cor. i. 2), *the holy people,* for they are chosen and called to salvation through sanctification. They shall be called *the redeemed of the Lord;* to him they owe their liberty, and therefore to him they owe their service, and they shall not be ashamed to own both. None are to be *called the redeemed of the Lord* but those that are the *holy people;* the people of God's purchase are a holy nation. And they shall be called, *Sought out.* God shall seek them out, and find them, wherever they are dispersed, eclipsed, or lost in a crowd ; men shall seek them out, that they may join themselves to them, and not forsake them. It is good to associate with *the holy people,* that we may learn their ways, and with *the redeemed of the Lord,* that we may share in the blessings of the redemption.

CHAP. LXIII.

In this chapter we have, I. God coming towards his people in ways of mercy and deliverance, and this is to be joined to the close of the foregoing chapter, where it was said to Zion, " Behold, thy salvation comes ;" for here it is shown how it comes, ver. 1—6. II. God's people meeting him with their devotions, and addressing themselves to him with suitable affections ; and this part of the chapter is carried on to the close of the next. In this we have, 1. A thankful acknowledgment of the great favours God had bestowed upon them, ver. 7. 2. The magnifying of these favours, from the consideration of God's relation to them (ver. 8), his compassionate concern for them (ver. 9), their unworthiness (ver. 10), and the occasion which it gave both him and them to call to mind former mercies, ver. 11—14. 3. A very humble and earnest prayer to God to appear for them in their present distress, pleading God's mercy (ver. 15), their relation to him (ver. 16), their desire towards him (ver. 17), and the insolence of their enemies, ver. 18, 19. So that, upon the whole, we learn to embrace God's promises with an active faith, and then to improve them, and make use of them, both in prayers and praises.

WHO *is* this that cometh from Edom, with dyed garments from Bozrah ? this *that is* glorious in his apparel, travelling in the greatness of his strength? I that speak in righteousness, mighty to save. 2 Wherefore *art thou* red in thine apparel, and thy garments like him that treadeth in the wine-fat? 3 I have trodden the wine-press alone; and of the people *there was* none with me: for I will tread them in mine anger, and trample them in my fury; and their blood shall be sprinkled upon my garments, and I will stain all my raiment. 4 For the day of vengeance *is* in mine heart, and the year of my redeemed is come. 5 And I looked, and *there was* none to help; and I wondered that *there was* none to uphold: therefore mine own arm brought salvation unto me; and my fury, it upheld me. 6 And I will tread down the people in mine anger, and make them drunk in my fury, and I will bring down their strength to the earth.

It is a glorious victory that is here enquired into first and then accounted for. 1. It is a victory obtained by the providence of God over the enemies of Israel; over the Babylonians (say some), whom Cyrus conquered and God by him, and they will have the prophet to make the first discovery of him in his triumphant return when he is in the country of Edom: but this can by no means be admitted, because the country of Babylon is always spoken of as the land of the north, whereas Edom lay south from Jerusalem, so that the conqueror would not return through that country; the victory therefore is obtained over the Edomites themselves, who had triumphed in the destruction of Jerusalem by the Chaldeans (Ps. cxxxvii. 7) and cut off those who, making their way as far as they could from the enemy, escaped to the Edomites (Obad. 12, 13), and were therefore reckoned with when Babylon was; for no doubt that prophecy was accomplished, though we do not meet in history with the accomplishment of it (Jer. xlix. 13), *Bozrah shall become a desolation.* Yet this victory over Edom is put as an instance or specimen of the like victories obtained over other nations that had been enemies to Israel. This over the Edomites is named for the sake of the old enmity of Esau against Jacob (Gen. xxvii. 41) and perhaps with an allusion to David's glorious triumphs over the Edomites, by which it should seem, more than by any other of his victories, he *got himself a name*, Ps. lx., title, 2 Sam. viii. 13, 14. But this is not all: 2. It is a victory obtained by the grace of God in Christ over our spiritual enemies. We find the garments dipped in blood adorning him whose name is called *The Word of God*, Rev. xix. 13. And who that is we know

very well; for it is through him that we are more than conquerors over those principalities and powers which on the cross he spoiled and triumphed over.

In this representation of the victory we have,

I. An admiring question put to the conqueror, *v.* 1, 2. It is put by the church, or by the prophet in the name of the church. He sees a mighty hero returning in triumph from a bloody engagement, and makes bold to ask him two questions:—1. Who he is. He observes him to come from the country of Edom, to come in such apparel as was glorious to a soldier, not embroidered or laced, but besmeared with blood and dirt. He observes that he does not come as one either frightened or fatigued, but that he *travels in the greatness of his strength*, altogether unbroken.

Triumphant and victorious he appears,
And honour in his looks and habit wears.
How strong he treads! how stately doth he go!
Pompous and solemn is his pace,
And full of majesty, as is his face;
Who is this mighty hero—who?—Mr. NORRIS.

The question, *Who is this?* perhaps means the same with that which Joshua put to the same person when he appeared to him with his sword drawn (Josh v. 13): *Art thou for us or for our adversaries?* Or, rather, the same with that which Israel put in a way of adoration (Exod. xv. 11): *Who is a God like unto thee?* 2. The other question is, "*Wherefore art thou red in thy apparel?* What hard service hast thou been engaged in, that thou carriest with thee these marks of toil and danger?" Is it possible that one who has such majesty and terror in his countenance should be employed in the mean and servile work of *treading the wine-press?* Surely it is not. That which is really the glory of the Redeemer seems, *primâ facie—at first*, a disparagement to him, as it would be to a mighty prince to do the work of the wine-dressers and husbandmen; for he *took upon him the form of a servant*, and carried with him the marks of servitude.

II. An admirable answer returned by him. 1. He tells who he is: *I that speak in righteousness, mighty to save.* He is the Saviour. God was Israel's Saviour out of the hand of their oppressors; the Lord Jesus is ours; his name, *Jesus*, signifies a *Saviour*, for he *saves his people from their sins.* In the salvation wrought he will have us to take notice, (1.) Of the truth of his promise, which is therein performed: He speaks *in righteousness*, and will therefore make good every word that he has spoken with which he will have us to compare what he does, that, setting the word and the work the one over against the other, what he does may ratify what he has said and what he has said may justify what he does. (2.) Of the efficacy of his power, which is therein exerted:

He is *mighty to save*, able to bring about the promised redemption, whatever difficulties and oppositions may lie in the way of it.

'Tis I who to my promise faithful stand,
I, who the powers of death, hell, and the grave,
Have foil'd with this all-conquering hand,
I, who most ready am, and mighty too, to save.
　　　　　　　　　　　　Mr. NORRIS.

2. He tells how he came to appear in this hue (*v.* 3): *I have trodden the wine-press alone.* Being compared to one that treads in the wine-fat, such is his condescension, in the midst of his triumphs, that he does not scorn the comparison, but admits it and carries it on. He does indeed *tread the wine-press*, but it is *the great wine-press of the wrath of God* (Rev. xiv. 19), in which we sinners deserved to be cast; but Christ was pleased to cast our enemies into it, and to *destroy him that had the power of death*, that he might deliver us. And of this the bloody work which God sometimes made among the enemies of the Jews, and which is here foretold, was a type and figure. Observe the account the conqueror gives of his victory.

(1.) He gains the victory purely by his own strength : *I have trodden the wine-press alone, v.* 3. When God delivered his people and destroyed their enemies, if he made use of instruments, he did not need them. But among his people, for whom the salvation was to be wrought, no assistance offered itself ; they were weak and helpless, and had no ability to do any thing for their own relief ; they were desponding and listless, and had no heart to do any thing ; they were not disposed to give the least stroke or struggle for liberty, neither the captives themselves nor any of their friends for them (*v* 5) : "*I looked, and there was none to help*, as one would have expected, nothing of a bold active spirit appeared among them ; nay, there was not only none to lead, but, which was more strange, *there was none to uphold*, none that would come in as a second, that had the courage to join with Cyrus against their oppressors ; *therefore my arm brought* about *the salvation; not by created might or power, but by the Spirit of the Lord of hosts, my own arm.*" Note, God can help when all other helpers fail ; nay, that is his time to help, and therefore for that very reason he will put forth his own power so much the more gloriously. But this is most fully applicable to Christ's victories over our spiritual enemies, which he obtained by a single combat. He trod the wine-press of his Father's wrath alone, and triumphed over principalities and powers *in himself*, Col. ii. 15. *Of the people there was none with him;* for, when he entered the lists with the powers of darkness, *all his disciples forsook him and fled.* There was *none to help*, none that could, none that durst ; and he might well wonder that among the children of men, whose concern it was, there was not only *none to uphold*, but that

368

there were so many to oppose and hinder it if they could.

(2.) He undertakes the war purely out of his own zeal. It is *in his anger*, it is *in his fury*, that he *treads down* his enemies (*v.* 3), and that *fury upholds him* and carries him on in this enterprise, *v.* 5. God wrought salvation for the oppressed Jews purely because he was very angry with the oppressing Babylonians, angry at their idolatries and sorceries, their pride and cruelty, and the injuries they did to his people, and, as they increased their abominations and grew more insolent and outrageous, his anger increased to fury. Our Lord Jesus wrought out our redemption in a holy zeal for the honour of his Father and the happiness of mankind, and a holy indignation at the daring attempts Satan had made upon both ; this zeal and indignation upheld him throughout his whole undertaking. Two branches there were of this zeal that animated him :—[1.] He had a zeal against his and his people's enemies : *The day of vengeance is in my heart* (*v.* 4), the day fixed in the eternal counsels for taking vengeance on them ; this was written in his heart, so that he could not forget it, could not let it slip ; his heart was full of it, and it lay as a charge, as a weight, upon him, which made him push on this holy war with so much vigour. Note, There is a day fixed for divine vengeance, which may be long deferred, but will come at last ; and we may be content to wait for it, for the Redeemer himself does so, though his heart is upon it. [2] He had a zeal for his people, and for all that he designed to make sharers in the intended salvation : "*The year of my redeemed has come*, the year appointed for their redemption." There was a year fixed for the deliverance of Israel out of Egypt, and God kept time to a day (Exod. xii. 41); so there was for their release out of Babylon (Dan. ix. 2) ; so there was for Christ's coming to destroy the works of the devil ; so there is for all the deliverances of the church, and the deliverer has an eye to it. Observe, *First*, With what pleasure he speaks of his people ; they are his *redeemed;* they are his own, dear to him. Though their redemption is not yet wrought out, yet he calls them *his redeemed*, because it shall as surely be done as if it were done already. *Secondly*, With what pleasure he speaks of his people's redemption ; how glad he is that *the time has come*, though he is likely to meet with a sharp encounter. "Now that the year of my redeemed has come, *Lo, I come;* delay shall be no longer. *Now will I arise*, saith the Lord. *Now thou shalt see what I will do to Pharaoh.*" Note, The promised salvation must be patiently waited for till the time appointed comes ; yet we must attend the promises with our prayers. Does Christ say, *Surely I come quickly;* let our hearts reply, *Even so come;* let the *year of the redeemed* come.

(3.) He will obtain a complete victory over them all. [1.] Much is already done; for he now appears *red in his apparel;* such abundance of blood is shed that the conqueror's garments are all stained with it. This was predicted, long before, by dying Jacob, concerning *Shiloh* (that is, *Christ)*, that he should *wash his garments in wine and his clothes in the blood of grapes,* which perhaps this alludes to, Gen. xlix. 11.

With ornamental drops bedeck'd I stood,
And wrote my vict'ry with my en'my's blood.
Mr. NORRIS.

In the destruction of the antichristian powers we meet with abundance of blood shed (Rev. xiv. 20, xix. 13), which yet, according to the dialect of prophecy, may be understood spiritually, and doubtless so may this here. [2.] More shall yet be done (*v.* 6): *I will tread down the people* that yet stand it out against me, *in my anger;* for the victorious Redeemer, when the *year of the redeemed shall have come,* will go on *conquering and to conquer,* Rev. vi. 2. When he begins he will also make an end. Observe how he will complete his victories over the enemies of his church. *First,* He will infatuate them; he will make them drunk, so that there shall be neither sense nor steadiness in their counsels; they shall drink of the cup of his fury, and that shall intoxicate them: or he will make them *drunk with their own blood,* Rev. xvii. 6. Let those that make themselves drunk with the cup of riot (and then they are in their fury) repent and reform, lest God make them drunk with the *cup of trembling,* the cup of his fury. *Secondly,* He will enfeeble them; he will *bring down their strength,* and so bring them down *to the earth;* for what strength can hold out against Omnipotence?

7 I will mention the loving-kindnesses of the LORD, *and* the praises of the LORD, according to all that the LORD hath bestowed on us, and the great goodness toward the house of Israel, which he hath bestowed on them according to his mercies, and according to the multitude of his loving-kindnesses. 8 For he said, Surely they *are* my people, children *that* will not lie: so he was their Saviour. 9 In all their affliction he was afflicted, and the angel of his presence saved them: in his love and in his pity he redeemed them; and he bare them, and carried them all the days of old. 10 But they rebelled, and vexed his holy Spirit: therefore he was turned to be their enemy, *and* he fought against them. 11 Then he remembered the days of

old, Moses, *and* his people, *saying,* Where *is* he that brought them up out of the sea with the shepherd of his flock? Where *is* he that put his holy Spirit within him? 12 That led *them* by the right hand of Moses with his glorious arm, dividing the water before them, to make himself an everlasting name? 13 That led them through the deep, as a horse in the wilderness, *that* they should not stumble? 14 As a beast goeth down into the valley, the Spirit of the LORD caused him to rest: so didst thou lead thy people, to make thyself a glorious name.

The prophet is here, in the name of the church, taking a review, and making a thankful recognition, of God's dealings with his church all along, ever since he founded it, before he comes, in the latter end of this chapter and in the next, as a watchman upon the walls, earnestly to pray to God for his compassion towards her in her present deplorable state; and it was usual for God's people, in their prayers, thus to look back.

I. Here is a general acknowledgment of God's goodness to them all along, *v.* 7. It was said, in general, of God's prophets and people (*ch.* lxii. 6) that they *made mention of the Lord;* now here we are told what it is in God that they do especially delight to make mention of, and that is his goodness, which the prophet here so makes mention of as if he thought he could never say enough of it. He mentions the *kindness of God* (which never appeared so evident, so eminent, as in his love to mankind in *sending his Son* to save us, Tit. iii. 4), his loving-kindness, kindness that shows itself in every thing that is endearing; nay, so plenteous are the springs, and so various the streams, of divine mercy, that he speaks of it in the plural number— *his loving-kindnesses;* for, if we would count the fruits of his loving-kindness, they are *more in number than the sand.* With his loving-kindnesses he mentions his *praises,* that is, the thankful acknowledgments which the saints make of his loving-kindness, and the angels too. It must be mentioned, to God's honour, what a tribute of praise is paid to him by all his creatures in consideration of his loving-kindness. See how copiously he speaks, 1. Of the goodness that is from God, the gifts of his loving-kindness—*all that the Lord has bestowed* on us in particular, relating to life and godliness, in our personal and family capacity. Let every man speak for himself, speak as he has found, and he must own that he has had a great deal bestowed upon him by the divine bounty. But we must also mention the favours bestowed upon his church, his *great* goodness towards the house of Israel, which he has bestowed on them. Note, We must bless God for the mercies enjoyed by others as well as for those enjoyed by ourselves, and reckon that bestowed on ourselves which is bestowed on *the house of Israel.* 2. Of the goodness that is in God. God does good because he is good; what he bestowed upon us must be traced up to the original; it is *according to his mercies* (not according to our merits) and *according to the multitude of his loving-kindnesses,* which can never be spent. Thus we should magnify God's goodness, and speak honourably of it, not only when we plead it (as David, Ps. li. 1), but when we praise it.

II. Here is particular notice taken of the steps of God's mercy to Israel ever since it was formed into a nation.

1. The expectations God had concerning them that they would conduct themselves well, *v.* 8. When he brought them out of Egypt and took them into covenant with himself he said, " *Surely they are my people,* I take them as such, and am willing to hope they will approve themselves so, *children that will not lie,*" that will not *dissemble with God* in their covenantings with him, nor treacherously depart from him by breaking their covenant and starting aside like a broken bow. They said, more than once, *All that the Lord shall say unto us we will do and will be obedient;* and thereupon he took them to be his peculiar people, saying, *Surely they will not lie.* God deals fairly and faithfully with them, and therefore expects they should deal so with him. They are *children of the covenant* (Acts iii. 25), children of those that clave unto the Lord, and therefore it may be hoped that they will tread in the steps of their fathers' constancy. Note, God's people are *children that will not lie;* for those that will are not his children but the devil's.

2. The favour he showed them with an eye to these expectations: *So he was their Saviour* out of the bondage of Egypt and all the calamities of their wilderness-state, and many a time since he had been their Saviour. See particularly (*v.* 9) what he did for them as their Saviour. (1.) The principle that moved him to work salvation for them; it was *in his love and in his pity,* out of mere compassion to them and a tender affection for them, not because he either needed them or could be benefited by them. This is strangely expressed here: *In all their affliction he was afflicted;* not that the Eternal Mind was capable of grieving or God's infinite blessedness of suffering the least damage or diminution (God cannot be afflicted); but thus he is pleased to show forth the love and concern he has for his people in their affliction; thus far he sympathizes with them, that he takes what injury is done to them as done to himself and will reckon for it accordingly. Their cries move him

370

(Exod. iii. 7), and he appears for them as vigorously as if he were pained in their pain. *Saul, Saul, why persecutest thou me?* This is matter of great comfort to God's people in their affliction that God is so far from *afflicting willingly* (Lam. iii. 33) that, if they humble themselves under his hand, he is *afflicted in their affliction,* as the tender parents are in the severe operations which the case of a sick child calls for. There is another reading of these words in the original: *In all their affliction there was no affliction;* though they were in great affliction, yet the property of it was so altered by the grace of God sanctifying it to them for their good, the rigour of it was so mitigated and it was so allayed and balanced with mercies, they were so wonderfully supported and comforted under it, and it proved so short, and ended so well, that it was in effect no affliction. The troubles of the saints are not that to them which they are to others; they are not afflictions, but medicines; saints are enabled to call them *light,* and *but for a moment,* and, with an eye to heaven as all in all, to make nothing of them. (2.) The person employed in their salvation —*the angel of his face,* or presence. Some understand it of a created angel. The highest angel in heaven, even the angel of his presence, that attends next the throne of his glory, is not thought too great, too good, to be sent on this errand. Thus the little ones' angels are said to be those that *always behold the face of our Father,* Matt. xviii. 10. But this is rather to be understood of Jesus Christ, the eternal Word, that angel of whom God spoke to Moses (Exod. xxiii. 20, 21), whose *voice Israel was to obey.* He is called *Jehovah,* Exod. xiii. 21; xiv. 21, 24. He is the angel of the covenant, God's messenger to the world, Mal. iii. 1. He is the *angel of God's face,* for he is the *express image of his person;* and the glory of God shines in the face of Christ. He that was to work out the eternal salvation, as an earnest of that, wrought out the temporal salvations that were typical of it. (3.) The progress and perseverance of this favour. He not only redeemed them out of their bondage, but *he bore them and carried them all the days of old;* they were weak, but he supported them by his power, sustained them by his bounty; when they were burdened, and ready to sink, he bore them up; in the wars they made upon the nations he stood by them and bore them out; though they were peevish, he bore with them and suffered their manners, Acts xiii. 18. He carried them as the nursing father does the child, though they would have tired any arms but his; he carried them as the eagle her young upon her wings, Deut. xxxii. 11. And it was a long time that he was *troubled with them* (if we may so speak): it was *all the days of old;* his care of them was not at an end even when they had grown up and were settled in Canaan. All this was *in his love and pity, ex mero motu—of his mere good-will;* he loved them because he would love them, as he says, Deut. vii. 7, 8.

3. Their disingenuous conduct towards him, and the trouble they thereby brought upon themselves (*v.* 10): *But they rebelled.* Things looked very hopeful and promising; one would have thought that they should have continued dutiful children to God, and then there was no doubt but he would have continued a gracious Father to them; but here is a sad change on both sides, and *on them be the breach.* (1.) They revolted from their allegiance to God and took up arms against him: *They rebelled, and vexed his Holy Spirit* with their unbelief and murmuring, besides the iniquity of the golden calf; and this had been their way and manner ever since. Though he was ready to say of them, *They will not lie,* though he had done so much for them, *borne them and carried them,* yet they thus ill requited him, like *foolish people and unwise,* Deut. xxxii. 6. This grieved him, Ps. xcv. 10. The ungrateful rebellions of God's children against him are a vexation to his Holy Spirit. (2.) Thereupon he justly withdrew his protection, and not only so, but made war upon them, as a prince justly does upon the rebels. He who had been so much their friend was *turned to be their enemy and fought against them,* by one judgment after another, both in the wilderness and after their settlement in Canaan. See the malignity and mischievousness of sin; it makes God an enemy even to those for whom he has done the part of a good friend, and makes him angry who was all love and pity. See the folly of sinners; they wilfully lose him for a friend who is the most desirable friend, and make him their enemy who is the most formidable enemy. This refers especially to those calamities that were of late brought upon them by their captivity in Babylon for their idolatries and other sins. That which is both the original and the great aggravation of their troubles was that God was *turned to be their enemy.*

4. A particular reflection made, on this occasion, upon what God did for them when he first formed them into a people: *Then he remembered the days of old, v.* 11.

(1.) This may be understood either of the people or of God. [1.] We may understand it of the people. Israel then (spoken of as a single person) *remembered the days of old,* looked into their Bibles, read the story of God's bringing their fathers out of Egypt, considered it more closely than ever they did before, and reasoned upon it, as Gideon did (Judg. vi. 13), *Where are all the wonders that our fathers told us of?* " *Where is he that brought them up* out of Egypt? Is he not as able to bring us up out of Babylon? *Where is the Lord God of Elijah? Where is the Lord God of our fathers?*" This they consider as an inducement and an encou-

ragement to them to repent and return to him; their fathers were a provoking people and yet found him a pardoning God; and why may not they find him so if they return to him? They also use it as a plea with God in prayer for the turning again of their captivity, like that *ch.* li. 9, 10. Note, When the present days are dark and cloudy it is good to *remember the days of old,* to recollect our own and others' experiences of the divine power and goodness and make use of them, to look back upon *the years of the right hand of the Most High* (Ps. lxxvii. 5, 10), and remember that he is *God, and changes not.* [2.] We may understand it of God; he put himself in mind of the days of old, of his covenant with Abraham (Lev. xxvi. 42); he said, *Where is he that brought Israel up out of the sea?* stirring up himself to come and save them with this consideration, " Why should not I appear for them now as I did for their fathers, who were as undeserving, as ill-deserving, as they are?" See how far off divine mercy will go, how far back it will look, to find out a reason for doing good to his people, when no present considerations appear but what make against them. Nay, it makes that a reason for relieving them which might have been used as a reason for abandoning them. He might have said, " I have delivered them formerly, but they have again brought trouble upon themselves (Prov. xix. 19); therefore *I will deliver them no more,*" Judg. x. 13. But no; mercy rejoices against judgment, and turns the argument the other way: " I have formerly delivered them and therefore will now."

(2.) Which way soever we take it, whether the people plead it with God or God with himself, let us view the particulars, and they agree very much with the confession and prayer which the children of the captivity made upon a solemn fast-day (Neh. ix. 5. &c.), which may serve as a comment on these verses which call to mind *Moses and his people,* that is, what God did by Moses for his people, especially in bringing them through the Red Sea, for that is it that is here most insisted on; for it was a work which he much gloried in and which his people therefore may in a particular manner encourage themselves with the remembrance of. [1.] God *led them by the right hand of Moses* (*v.* 12) and the wonder-working rod in his hand. Ps. lxxvii. 20, *Thou leddest thy people like a flock by the hand of Moses.* It was not Moses that led them, any more than it was Moses that fed them (John vi. 32), but God by Moses; for it was he that qualified Moses for, called him to, assisted and prospered him in that great undertaking. Moses is here called *the shepherd of his flock;* God was the owner of the flock and the chief shepherd of Israel (Ps. lxxx. 1); but Moses was a shepherd under him, and he was inured to labour and patience, and so fitted for this pastoral care, by his being trained up to *keep the flock of his father Jethro.* Herein he was a type of Christ the good shepherd, that *lays down his life for the sheep,* which was more than Moses did for Israel, though he did a great deal for them. [2.] He *put his holy Spirit within him; the Spirit of God was among them,* and not only his providence, but his grace, did work for them. Neh. ix. 20, *Thou gavest thy good Spirit to instruct them.* The Spirit of wisdom and courage, as well as the Spirit of prophecy, was put into Moses, to qualify him for that service among them to which he was called; and some of his spirit was put upon the seventy elders, Num. xi. 17. This was a great blessing to Israel, that they had among them not only inspired writings, but inspired men. [3] He carried them safely through the Red Sea, and thereby saved them out of the hands of Pharaoh. *First, He divided the water before them* (v. 12), so that it gave them not only passage, but protection, not only opened them a lane, but erected them a wall on either side. *Secondly, He led them through the deep as a horse in the wilderness,* or *in the plain* (v. 13); they and their wives and children, with all their baggage, went as easily and readily through the bottom of the sea (though we may suppose it muddy or stony, or both) as a horse goes along upon even ground; so that they did not stumble, though it was an untrodden path, which neither they nor any one else ever went before. If God make us a way, he will make it plain and level; the road he opens to his people he will lead them in. *Thirdly,* To complete the mercy, he *brought them up out of the sea,* v. 11. Though the ascent, it is likely, was very steep, dirty, slippery, and unconquerable (at least by the women and children, and the men, considering how they were loaded, Exod. xii. 34, and how fatigued), yet God by his power brought them up from the depths of the earth; and it was a kind of resurrection to them; it was as *life from the dead.* [4.] He brought them safely to a place of rest: *As a beast goes down into the valley,* carefully and gradually, so *the Spirit of the Lord caused him to rest.* Many a time in their march through the wilderness they had resting-places provided for them by the direction of the Spirit of the Lord in Moses, v. 11. And at length they were made to rest finally in Canaan, and the Spirit of the Lord gave them that rest according to the promise. It is by the Spirit of the Lord that God's Israel are caused to return to God and repose in him as their rest. [5.] All this he did for them by his own power, for his own praise. *First,* It was by his own power, as the God of nature, that has all the powers of nature at his command; he did it with his glorious arm, *the arm of his gallantry,* or *bravery :* so the word signifies. It was not Moses's rod, but God's glorious arm, that did it. *Secondly,* It was for his own praise, to *make himself an everlasting name* (v. 12), *a glorious name* (v.

372

14), that he might be glorified, everlastingly glorified, upon this account. This is that which God is doing in the world with his glorious arm, he is making to himself a glorious name, and it shall last to endless ages, when the most celebrated names of the great ones of the earth shall be written in the dust.

15 Look down from heaven, and behold from the habitation of thy holiness and of thy glory: where *is* thy zeal and thy strength, the sounding of thy bowels and of thy mercies toward me? Are they restrained? 16 Doubtless thou *art* our father, though Abraham be ignorant of us, and Israel acknowledge us not: thou, O LORD, *art* our father, our Redeemer; thy name *is* from everlasting. 17 O LORD, why hast thou made us to err from thy ways, *and* hardened our heart from thy fear? Return for thy servants' sake, the tribes of thine inheritance. 18 The people of thy holiness have possessed *it* but a little while: our adversaries have trodden down thy sanctuary. 19 We are *thine :* thou never barest rule over them; they were not called by thy name.

The foregoing praises were intended as an introduction to this prayer, which is continued to the end of the next chapter, and it is an affectionate, importunate, pleading prayer. It is calculated for the time of the captivity. As they had promises, so they had prayers, prepared for them against that time of need, that they might take with them words in turning to the Lord, and say unto him what he himself taught them to say, in which they might the better hope to prevail, the words being of God's own inditing. Some good interpreters think this prayer looks further, and that it expresses the complaints of the Jews under their last and final rejection from God and destruction by the Romans; for there is one passage in it (*ch.* lxiv. 4) which is applied to the grace of the gospel by the apostle (1 Cor. ii. 9), that grace for the rejecting of which they were rejected. In these verses we may observe,

I. The petitions they put up to God. 1. That he would take cognizance of their case and of the desires of their souls towards him: *Look down from heaven, and behold, v.* 15. They knew very well that God sees all, but they prayed that he would regard them, would condescend to favour them, would look upon them with an eye of compassion and concern, as he looked upon the affliction of his people in Egypt when he was about to appear for their deliverance. In begging that he would only look down upon them and behold them they did in effect appeal to his justice against their enemies, and pray for judgment against them (as Jehoshaphat, 2 Chron. xx. 11, 12, *Behold, how they reward us. Wilt thou not judge them?*), implicitly confiding in his mercy and wisdom as to the way in which he will relieve them (Ps. xxv. 18, *Look upon my affliction and my pain): Look down from the habitation of thy holiness and of thy glory.* God's holiness is his glory. Heaven is his habitation, the throne of his glory, where he most manifests his glory, and whence he is said to look down upon this earth, Ps. xxxiii. 14. His holiness is in a special manner celebrated there by the blessed angels (*ch.* vi. 3 ; Rev. iv. 8); there his holy ones attend him, and are continually about him; so that it is the *habitation of his holiness.* It is an encouragement to all his praying people, who desire to be holy as he is holy, that he *dwells in a holy place.* 2. That he would take a course for their relief (*v.* 17) : "*Return ;* change thy way towards us, and proceed not in thy controversy with us; return in mercy, and let us have not only a gracious look towards us, but thy gracious presence with us." God's people dread nothing more than his departures from them and desire nothing more than his returns to them.

II. The complaints they made to God. Two things they complained of :—1. That they were given up to themselves, and God's grace did not recover them, *v.* 17. It is a strange expostulation, "*Why hast thou made us to err from thy ways,* that is, many among us, the generality of us; and this complaint we have all of us some cause to make that *thou hast hardened our heart from thy fear.* Some make it to be the language of those among them that were impious and profane ; when the prophets reproved them for the *error of their ways,* their *hardness of heart,* and *contempt of God's word and commandments,* they with a daring impudence charged their sin upon God, made him the author of it, and asked *why doth he then find fault?* Note, Those are wicked indeed that lay the blame of their wickedness upon God. But I rather take it to be the language of those among them that lamented the unbelief and impenitence of their people, not accusing God of being the author of their wickedness, but complaining of it to him. They owned that they had *erred from God's ways,* that their *hearts* had been *hardened from his fear,* that they had not received the impressions which the fear of God ought to make upon them and this was the cause of all their errors from his ways ; or *from his fear* may mean from the true worship of God, and that is a hard heart indeed which is alienated from the service of a God so incontestably great and good. Now this they complain of, as their great misery and burden, that God had for their sins left them to this, had permitted them to *err from his ways* and had

justly withheld his grace, so that their *hearts were hardened from his fear.* When they ask, *Why hast thou done this?* it is not as charging him with wrong, but lamenting it as a sore judgment. God had *caused them to err and hardened their hearts,* not only by withdrawing his Spirit from them, because they had grieved, and vexed, and quenched him (*v.* 10), but by a judicial sentence upon them (*Go, make the heart of this people fat, ch.* vi. 9, 10) and by his providences concerning them, which had proved sad occasions for their departure from him. David complains of his banishment, because in it he was in effect bidden to *go and serve other gods,* 1 Sam. xxvi. 19. Their troubles had alienated many of them from God, and prejudiced them against his service ; and, because the *rod of the wicked had lain long on their lot,* they were ready to *put forth their hand unto iniquity* (Ps. cxxv. 3), and this was the thing they complained most of; their afflictions were their temptations, and to many of them invincible ones. Note, Convinced consciences complain most of spiritual judgments and dread that most in an affliction which draws them from God and duty. 2. That they were given up to their enemies, and God's providence did not rescue and relieve them (*v.* 18) : *Our adversaries have trodden down thy sanctuary.* As it was a grief to them that in their captivity the generality of them had lost their affection to God's worship, and had their hearts hardened from it by their affliction, so it was a further grief that they were deprived of their opportunities of worshipping God in solemn assemblies. They complained not so much of the adversaries treading down their houses and cities as of their treading down God's sanctuary, because thereby God was immediately affronted, and they were robbed of the comforts they valued most and took most pleasure in.

III. The pleas they urged with God for mercy and deliverance. 1. They pleaded the tender compassion God used to show to his people and his ability and readiness to appear for them, *v.* 15. The most prevailing arguments in prayer are those that are taken *from God himself;* such these are. *Where is thy zeal and thy strength?* God has a zeal for his own glory, and for the comfort of his people; his name is *Jealous ;* and he is a jealous God ; and he has strength proportionable to secure his own glory and the interest of his people, in despite of all opposition. Now where are these ? Have they not formerly appeared? Why do they not appear now ? It cannot be that divine zeal, which is infinitely wise and just, should be cooled, that divine strength, which is infinite, should be weakened. Nay, his people had experienced not only *his zeal and his strength, but the sounding of his bowels,* or rather the yearning of them, such a degree of compassion to them as in men causes a commotion and agitation within them, as Hos. xi. 8, *My* heart is turned within me, my repentings are kindled together; and Jer. xxxi. 20, *My bowels are troubled* (or sound) *for him.* "Thus God used to be affected towards his people, and to express a *multitude of mercies towards them;* but where are they now? *Are they restrained?* Ps. lxxvii. 9. Has God, who so often remembered to be gracious, now forgotten to be so? *Has he in anger shut up his tender mercies?* It can never be." Note, We may ground good expectations of further mercy upon our experiences of former mercy. 2. They pleaded God's relation to them as their Father (v. 16): "Thy tender mercies are not restrained, for they are the tender mercies of a father, who, though he may be for a time displeased with his child, will yet, through the force of natural affection, soon be reconciled. *Doubtless thou art our Father,* and therefore thy bowels will yearn towards us." Such good thoughts of God as these we should always keep up in our hearts. *However it be, yet God is good;* for he is our Father. They own themselves fatherless if he be not their Father, and so cast themselves upon him with whom *the fatherless findeth mercy,* Hos. xiv. 3. It was the honour of their nation that *they had Abraham to their father* (Matt. iii. 9), who was the friend of God, and Israel, who was a prince with God; but what the better were they for that unless they had God himself for their Father? "Abraham and Israel cannot help us; they have not the power that God has; they are dead long since, and are *ignorant of us, and acknowledge us not;* they know not what our case is, nor what our wants are, and therefore know not which way to do us a kindness. If Abraham and Israel were alive with us, they would intercede for us and advise us; but they have gone to the other world, and we know not that they have any communication at all with this world, and therefore are not capable of doing us any kindness any further than that we have the honour of being called their children." When the father is dead *his sons come to honour and he knows it not,* Job xiv. 21. "But *thou, O Lord! art our Father still* (the fathers of our flesh may call themselves *ever-loving;* but they are not *ever-living;* it is God only that is the immortal Father, that always knows us, and is never at a distance from us), and therefore *our Redeemer from everlasting is thy name,* the name by which we will know and own thee. It is the name by which from of old thou hast been known; thy people have always looked upon thee as the God to whom they might appeal to redress their grievances and plead their cause. Nay" (according to the sense some give of this place), "though Abraham and Israel not only cannot, but would not, help us, thou wilt. They have not the pity thou hast. We are so degenerate and corrupt that Abraham and Israel would not own us for their children, yet we fly to thee as our Father. Abraham cast out his son Ishmael; Jacob disin-

374

herited his son Reuben and cursed Simeon and Levi; but our heavenly Father, in pardoning sin, is *God, and not man,*" Hos. xi. 9. 3. They pleaded God's interest in them, that he was their Lord, their owner and proprietor: "We are thy servants; what service we can do thou art entitled to, and therefore we ought not to serve strange kings and strange gods: *Return for thy servants' sake.*" As a father finds himself obliged by natural affection to relieve and protect his child, so a master thinks himself obliged in honour to rescue and protect his servant: "*We are thine* by the strongest engagements, as well as the highest endearments. Thou hast borne rule over us; therefore, Lord, assert thy own interest, maintain thy own right; for *we are called by thy name,* and therefore whither shall we go but to thee, to be righted and protected? *We are thine, save us* (Ps. cxix. 94), thy own, acknowledge us. We are the *tribes of thy inheritance,* not only thy servants, but thy tenants; we are thine, not only to do work for thee, but to pay rent to thee. The tribes of Israel are God's inheritance, whence issue the little praise and worship that he receives from this lower world; and wilt thou suffer thy own servants and tenants to be thus abused?" 4. They pleaded that they had had but a short enjoyment of the land of promise and the privileges of the sanctuary (v. 18): *The people of thy holiness have possessed it but a little while.* From Abraham to David were but fourteen generations, and from David to the captivity but fourteen more (Matt. i. 17), and that was but a little while in comparison with what might have been expected from the promise of the *land of Canaan for an everlasting possession* (Gen. xvii. 8) and from the power that was put forth to bring them into that land and settle them in it. "Though we are *the people of thy holiness,* distinguished from other people and consecrated to thee, yet we are soon dislodged." But this they might thank themselves for; they were, in profession, the *people of God's holiness,* but it was their wickedness that turned them out of the possession of that land. 5. They pleaded that those who had and kept possession of their land were such as were strangers to God, such as he had no service or honour from: "*Thou never didst bear rule over them,* nor did they ever yield thee any obedience; they *were not called by thy name,* but professed relation to other gods and were the worshippers of them. Will God suffer those that do not stand in any relation to him to trample upon those that do?" Some give another reading of this: "*We have become as those over whom thou didst never bear rule and who were never called by thy name;* we are rejected and abandoned, despised and trampled upon, as if we never had been in thy service nor had thy name called upon us." Thus the shield of *Saul was vilely cast away, as though he had not been anointed with oil.* But the covenant that seems to be forgotten shall be remembered again.

CHAP. LXIV.

This chapter goes on with that pathetic pleading prayer which the church offered up to God in the latter part of the foregoing chapter. They had argued from their covenant-relation to God and his interest and concern in them; now here, I. They pray that God would appear in some remarkable and surprising manner for them against his and their enemies, ver. 1, 2. II. They plead what God had formerly done, and was always ready to do, for his people, ver. 3—5. III. They confess themselves to be sinful and unworthy of God's favour, and that they had deserved the judgments they were now under, ver. 6, 7. IV. They refer themselves to the mercy of God as a Father, and submit themselves to his sovereignty, ver. 8. V. They represent the very deplorable condition they were in, and earnestly pray for the pardon of sin and the turning away of God's anger, ver. 9—12. And this was not only intended for the use of the captive Jews, but may serve for direction to the church in other times of distress, what to ask of God and how to plead with him. Are God's people at any time in affliction, in great affliction? Let them pray, let them thus pray.

OH that thou wouldest rend the heavens, that thou wouldest come down, that the mountains might flow down at thy presence, 2 As *when* the melting fire burneth, the fire causeth the waters to boil, to make thy name known to thine adversaries, *that* the nations may tremble at thy presence! 3 When thou didst terrible things *which* we looked not for, thou camest down, the mountains flowed down at thy presence. 4 For since the beginning of the world *men* have not heard, nor perceived by the ear, neither hath the eye seen, O God, beside thee, *what* he hath prepared for him that waiteth for him. 5 Thou meetest him that rejoiceth and worketh righteousness, *those that* remember thee in thy ways: behold, thou art wroth; for we have sinned: in those is continuance, and we shall be saved.

Here, I. The petition is that God would appear wonderfully for them now, *v.* 1, 2. Their case was represented in the close of the foregoing chapter as very sad and very hard, and in this case it was time to cry, "Help, Lord; O that God would manifest his zeal and his strength!" They had prayed (*ch.* lxiii. 15) that God would *look down from heaven;* here they pray that he would come down to deliver them, as he had said, Exod. iii. 8. 1. They desire that God would in his providence manifest himself both to them and for them. When God works some extraordinary deliverance for his people he is said to *shine forth,* to show himself strong; so, here, they pray that he would *rend the heavens and come down,* as when he delivered David he is said to *bow the heavens, and come down* (Ps. xviii. 9), to display his power, and justice, and goodness, in an extraordinary

manner, so that all may take notice of them and acknowledge them. This God's people desire and pray for, that they themselves having the satisfaction of seeing him though his way be in the sea, others may be made to see him when his way is in the clouds. This is applicable to the second coming of Christ, when *the Lord himself shall descend from heaven with a shout. Come, Lord Jesus, come quickly.* 2. They desire that he would vanquish all opposition and that it might be made to give way before him: *That the mountains might flow down at thy presence,* that the fire of thy wrath may burn so fiercely against thy enemies as even to dissolve the rockiest mountains and melt them down before it, as metal in the furnace, which is made liquid and cast into what shape the operator pleases; so *the melting fire burns, v.* 2. Let things be put into a ferment, in order to a glorious revolution in favour of the church: *As the fire causes the waters to boil.* There is an allusion here, some think, to the *volcanoes,* or burning mountains, which sometimes send forth such sulphureous streams as make the adjacent rivers and seas to boil, which, perhaps, are left as sensible intimations of the power of God's wrath and warning-pieces of the final conflagration. 3. They desire that this may tend very much to the glory and honour of God, *may make his name known,* not only to his friends (they knew it before, and trusted in his power), but to his adversaries likewise, that they may know it and *tremble at his presence,* and may say, with the men of Bethshemesh, *Who is able to stand before this holy Lord God? Who knows the power of his anger?* Note, Sooner or later God will make his name known to his adversaries and force those to *tremble at his presence* that would not come and worship in his presence. God's name, if it be not a stronghold for us, into which we may run and be safe, will be a strong-hold against us, out of the reach of which we cannot run and be safe. The day will come when nations shall be made to tremble at the presence of God, though they be ever so numerous and strong.

II. The plea is that God had appeared wonderfully for his people formerly; and *thou hast,* therefore *thou wilt,* is good arguing at the throne of grace, Ps. x. 17.

1. They plead what he had done for his people Israel in particular when he brought them out of Egypt, *v.* 3. He then *did terrible things* in the plagues of Egypt, *which they looked not for:* they despaired of deliverance, so far were they from any thought of being delivered with such a high hand and outstretched arm. Then he came down upon Mount Sinai in such terror as made that and the adjacent mountains to *flow down at his presence,* to *skip like rams* (Ps. cxiv. 4), to tremble, so that they were scattered and the perpetual hills were made to bow, Hab.

iii. 6. In the many great salvations God wrought for that people he did *terrible things which they looked not for,* made great men, that seemed as stately and strong as mountains, to fall before him, and great opposition to give way. See Judg. v. 4, 5; Ps. lxviii. 7, 8. Some refer this to the defeat of Sennacherib's powerful army, which was as surprising an instance of the divine power as the melting down of rocks and mountains would be.

2. They plead what God had been used to do, and had declared his gracious purpose to do, for his people in general. The provision he has made for the safety and happiness of his people, even of all those that seek him, and serve him, and trust in him, is very rich and very ready, so that they need not fear being either disappointed of it, for it is sure, or disappointed in it, for it is sufficient.

(1.) It is very rich, *v.* 4. Men have not heard nor seen what God has *prepared for those that wait for him.* Observe the character of God's people; they are such as wait for him in the way of duty, wait for the salvation he has promised and designed for them. Observe where the happiness of this people is bound up; it is *what God has prepared for them,* what he has designed for them in his counsel and is in his providence and grace preparing for them and preparing them for, what he has *done* or *will* do, so it may be read. Some of the Jewish doctors have understood this of the blessings reserved for the days of the Messiah, and to them the apostle applies these words; and others extend them to the glories of the world to come. It is all that goodness which God has *laid up for those that fear him, and wrought for those that trust in him,* Ps. xxxi. 19. Of this it is here said that *since the beginning of the world,* in the most prying and inquisitive ages of it, men have not, either by hearing or seeing, the two learning senses, come to the full knowledge of it. None have seen, nor heard, nor can understand, but God himself, what the provision is that is made for the present and future felicity of holy souls. For, [1.] Much of it was concealed in former ages; they knew it not, because the *unsearchable riches of Christ* were *hidden in God,* were *hidden from the wise and prudent;* but in latter ages they were revealed by the gospel; so the apostle applies this (1 Cor. ii. 9), for it follows (*v.* 10), *But God has revealed them unto us by his Spirit;* compare Rom. xvi. 25, 26, with Eph. iii. 9. That which men had not heard *since the beginning of the world* they should hear before the end of it, and at the end of it should see, when the veil shall be rent to introduce the glory that is yet to be revealed. God himself knew what he had in store for believers, but none knew besides him. [2.] It cannot be fully comprehended by the human understanding, no,

not when it is revealed; it is spiritual, and refined from those ideas which our minds are most apt to receive in this world of sense; it is very great, and will far outdo the utmost of our expectations. Even the present peace of believers, much more their future bliss, is such as surpasses all conception and expression, Phil. iv. 7. None can comprehend it but God himself, whose understanding is infinite. Some give another reading of these words, referring the transcendency, not so much to the work itself as to the author of it: *Neither has the eye seen a god besides thee, who doth so* (or has done or can do so) *for him that waits for him.* We must infer from God's works of wondrous grace, as well as from his works of wondrous power, from the kind things, as well as from the great things, he does, that there is *no god like him,* nor any among the sons of men mighty to be compared with him.

(2.) It is very ready (*v.* 5): " *Thou meetest him that rejoices and works righteousness,* meetest him with that good which thou hast prepared for him (*v.* 4), and dost not forget *those that remember thee in thy ways.*" See here what communion there is between a gracious God and a gracious soul. [1.] What God expects from us, in order to our having communion with him. *First,* We must make conscience of doing our duty in every thing, we must *work righteousness,* must do that which is good and which the Lord our God requires of us, and must do it well. *Secondly,* We must be cheerful in doing our duty, we must *rejoice and work righteousness,* must delight ourselves in God and in his law, must be cheerful in his service and sing at our work. God loves a cheerful giver, a cheerful worshipper. We must *serve the Lord with gladness. Thirdly,* We must conform ourselves to all the methods of his providence concerning us and be suitably affected with them, must *remember him in his ways,* in all the ways wherein he walks, whether he walks towards us or walks contrary to us. We must mind him and make mention of him with thanksgiving when his ways are ways of mercy (*in a day of prosperity be joyful),* with patience and submission when he contends with us. *In the way of thy judgments we have waited for thee;* for *in a day of adversity* we must *consider.* [2.] We are here told what we may expect from God if we thus attend him in the way of duty: *Thou meetest him.* This intimates the friendship, fellowship, and familiarity to which God admits his people; he meets them, to converse with them, to manifest himself to them, and to receive their addresses, Exod. xx. 24; xxix. 43. It likewise intimates his freeness and forwardness in doing them good; he will *anticipate them with the blessings of his goodness,* will *rejoice to do good* to those that *rejoice in working righteousness,* and wait to be gracious to those that *wait for him.* He meets his penitent people with a pardon, as the father of the prodigal met his returning son, Luke xv. 20. He meets his praying people with an answer of peace, while they are yet speaking, *ch.* lxv. 24.

3. They plead the unchangeableness of God's favour and the stability of his promise, notwithstanding the sins of his people and his displeasure against them for their sins: "*Behold, thou hast* many a time *been wroth with us because we have sinned*, and we have been under the tokens of thy wrath; *but in those*, those ways of thine, the ways of mercy in which we have *remembered thee, in those is continuance*," or "*in those thou art ever*" (his mercy endures for ever), "*and therefore we shall* at last *be saved*, though thou art wroth, and we have sinned." This agrees with the tenour of God's covenant, that, if we *forsake the law*, he will *visit our transgression with a rod*, but *his lovingkindness* he *will not utterly take away, his covenant he will not break* (Ps. lxxxix. 30, &c.), and by this his people have been many a time saved from ruin when they were just upon the brink of it; see Ps. lxxviii. 38. And by this continuance of the covenant we hope to be saved, for its being an everlasting covenant is all our salvation. Though God has been angry with us for our sins, and justly, yet his anger has endured but for a moment and has been soon over; but *in his favour is life*, because *in it is continuance;* in the ways of his favour he proceeds and perseveres, and on that we depend for our salvation, see *ch.* liv. 7, 8. It is well for us that our hopes of salvation are built not upon any merit or sufficiency of our own (for in that there is no certainty, even Adam in innocency did not abide), but upon God's mercies and promises, for *in those*, we are sure, *is continuance.*

6 But we are all as an unclean *thing*, and all our righteousnesses *are* as filthy rags; and we all do fade as a leaf; and our iniquities, like the wind, have taken us away. 7 And *there is* none that calleth upon thy name, that stirreth up himself to take hold of thee: for thou hast hid thy face from us, and hast consumed us, because of our iniquities. 8 But now, O Lord, thou *art* our father; we *are* the clay, and thou our potter; and we all *are* the work of thy hand. 9 Be not wroth very sore, O Lord, neither remember iniquity for ever: behold, see, we beseech thee, we *are* all thy people. 10 Thy holy cities are a wilderness, Zion is a wilderness, Jerusalem a desolation. 11 Our holy and our beautiful house, where our fathers praised thee, is burned up with fire: and all our pleasant things are laid waste. 12 Wilt thou refrain thyself for these *things*, O Lord? Wilt thou hold thy peace, and afflict us very sore?

As we have the Lamentations of Jeremiah, so here we have the Lamentations of Isaiah; the subject of both is the same—the destruction of Jerusalem by the Chaldeans and the sin of Israel that brought that destruction—only with this difference, Isaiah sees it at a distance and laments it by the Spirit of prophecy, Jeremiah saw it accomplished. In these verses,

I. The people of God in their affliction confess and bewail their sins, thereby justifying God in their afflictions, owning themselves unworthy of his mercy, and thereby both improving their troubles and preparing for deliverance. Now that they were under divine rebukes for sin they had nothing to trust to but the mere mercy of God and the continuance of that; for among themselves there is none to help, none to uphold, none to stand in the gap and make intercession, for they are all polluted with sin and therefore unworthy to intercede, all careless and remiss in duty and therefore unable and unfit to intercede.

1. There was a general corruption of manners among them (*v.* 6): *We are all as an unclean thing*, or as an unclean *person*, as one overspread with a leprosy, who was to be shut out of the camp. The body of the people were like one under a ceremonial pollution, who was not admitted into the courts of the tabernacle, or like one labouring under some loathsome disease, from the crown of the head to the sole of the foot *nothing but wounds and bruises*, *ch.* i. 6. We have all by sin become not only obnoxious to God's justice, but odious to his holiness; for sin is that *abominable thing which the Lord hates*, and cannot endure to look upon. *Even all our righteousnesses are as filthy rags.* (1.) "The best of our persons are so; we are all so corrupt and polluted that even those among us who pass for righteous men, in comparison with what our fathers were who *rejoiced and wrought righteousness* (*v.* 5), are but as filthy rags, fit to be cast to the dunghill. *The best of them is as a brier.*" (2.) "The best of our performances are so. There is not only a general corruption of manners, but a general defection in the exercises of devotion too; those which pass for the *sacrifices of righteousness*, when they come to be enquired into, are *the torn, and the lame, and the sick*, and therefore are provoking to God, as nauseous as filthy rags." Our performances, though they be ever so plausible, if we depend upon them as our righteousness and think to merit by them at God's hand, are as filthy rags—rags,

and will not cover us—filthy rags, and will but defile us. True penitents cast away their idols as filthy rags (*ch.* xxx. 22), odious in their sight; here they acknowledge even their righteousness to be so in God's sight if he should deal with them in strict justice. Our best duties are so defective, and so far short of the rule, that they are as rags, and so full of sin and corruption cleaving to them that they are as filthy rags. When we would do good evil is present with us; and the iniquity of our holy things would be our ruin if we were under the law.

2. There was a general coldness of devotion among them, *v.* 7. The measure was filled by the abounding iniquity of the people, and nothing was done to empty it. (1.) Prayer was in a manner neglected : " *There is none that calls on thy name,* none that seeks to thee for grace to reform us and take away sin, or for mercy to relieve us and take away the judgments which our sins have brought upon us." *Therefore* people are so bad, because they do not pray ; compare Ps. xiv. 3, 4, *They have altogether become filthy, for they call not upon the Lord.* It bodes ill to a people when prayer is restrained among them. (2.) It was very negligently performed. If there was here and there one that called on God's name, it was with a great deal of indifferency : *There is none that stirs up himself to take hold of God.* Note, [1.] To pray is to *take hold of God,* by faith to take hold of the promises and the declarations God has made of his good-will to us and to plead them with him, —to take hold of him as of one who is about to depart from us, earnestly begging of him not to leave us, or of one that has departed, soliciting his return,—to take hold of him as he that wrestles takes hold of him he wrestles with ; for the seed of Jacob wrestle with him and so prevail. But when we *take hold of God* it is as the boatman with his hook takes hold on the shore, as if he would pull the shore to him, but really it is to pull himself to the shore ; so we pray, not to bring God to our mind, but to bring ourselves to his. [2.] Those that would take hold of God in prayer so as to prevail with him must stir up themselves to do it ; all that is within us must be employed in the duty (and all little enough), our thoughts fixed and our affections flaming. In order hereunto all that is within us must be engaged and summoned into the service ; we must *stir up the gift that is in us* by an actual consideration of the importance of the work that is before us and a close application of mind to it ; but how can we expect that God should come to us in ways of mercy when there are none that do this, when those that profess to be intercessors are mere triflers ?

II. They acknowledge their afflictions to be the fruit and product of their own sins and God's wrath. 1. They brought their

troubles upon themselves by their own folly: " *We are all as an unclean thing, and* therefore *we do all fade away as a leaf* (*v.* 6), we not only wither and lose our beauty, but we fall and drop off" (so the word signifies) " as leaves in autumn ; our profession of religion withers, and we grow dry and sapless ; our prosperity withers and comes to nothing ; we fall to the ground, as despicable and contemptible ; and then *our iniquities like the wind have taken us away* and hurried us into captivity, as the winds in autumn blow off, and then blow away, the faded withered leaves," Ps. i. 3, 4. Sinners are blasted, and then carried away, by the malignant and violent wind of their own iniquity ; it withers them and then ruins them. 2. God brought their troubles upon them by his wrath (*v.* 7): *Thou hast hidden thy face from us ;* hast been displeased with us and refused to afford us any succour. When they made themselves *as an unclean thing* no wonder that God turned his face away from them, as loathing them. Yet this was not all : *Thou hast consumed us because of our iniquities.* This is the same complaint with that (Ps. xc. 7, 8), *We are consumed by thy anger ;* thou hast *melted us,* so the word is. God had put them in the furnace, not to consume them as dross, but to melt them as gold, that they might be refined and new-cast.

III. They claim relation to God as their God, and humbly plead it with him, and in consideration of it cheerfully refer themselves to him (*v.* 8) : " *But now, O Lord ! thou art our Father :* though we have conducted ourselves very undutifully and ungratefully towards thee, yet still we have owned thee as our Father ; and, though thou hast corrected us, yet thou hast not cast us off. Foolish and careless as we are, poor and despised and trampled upon as we are by our enemies, yet still *thou art our Father ;* to thee therefore we return in our repentance, as the prodigal arose and came to his father ; to thee we address ourselves by prayer ; from whom should we expect relief and succour but from our Father ? It is the wrath of a Father that we are under, who will be reconciled and not *keep his anger for ever.*" God is their Father, 1. By creation ; he gave them their being, formed them into a people, shaped them as he pleased : " *We are the clay and thou our potter,* therefore we will not quarrel with thee, however thou art pleased to deal with us, Jer. xviii. 6. Nay, therefore we will hope that thou wilt deal well with us, that thou who madest us wilt new-make us, new-form us, though we have unmade and deformed ourselves : *We are all as an unclean thing,* but *we are all the work of thy hands,* therefore do away our uncleanness, that we may be fit for thy use, the use we were made for. We are the *work of thy hands,* therefore *forsake us not,*" Ps. cxxxviii. 8. 2. By covenant ; this is pleaded *(v. 9):* "*Behold, see, we beseech thee, we are all thy people,* all the people thou hast in the world, that make open profession of thy name. We are called *thy people,* our neighbours look upon us as such, and therefore what we suffer reflects upon thee, and the relief that our case requires is expected from thee. *We are thy people;* and *should not a people seek unto their God? ch.* viii. 19. *We are thine; save us,*" Ps. cxix. 94. Note, When we are under providential rebukes from God it is good to keep fast hold of our covenant-relation to him.

IV. They are importunate with God for the turning away of his anger and the pardoning of their sins (*v.* 9): "*Be not wroth very sore, O Lord!* though we have deserved that thou shouldst, *neither remember iniquity for ever* against us." They do not expressly pray for the removal of the judgment they were under; as to that, they refer themselves to God. But, 1. They pray that God would be reconciled to them, and then they can be easy whether the affliction be continued or removed: "*Be not wroth to extremity,* but let thy anger be mitigated by the clemency and compassion of a father." They do not say, *Lord, rebuke us not,* for that may be necessary, but *Not in thy anger, not in thy hot displeasure.* It is but *in a little wrath* that God hides his face. 2. They pray that they may not be dealt with according to the desert of their sin: *Neither remember iniquity for ever.* Such is the evil of sin that it deserves to be remembered for ever; and this is that which they deprecate, that consequence of sin, which is for ever. Those make it to appear that they are truly humbled under the hand of God who are more afraid of the terror of God's wrath, and the fatal consequences of their own sin, than of any judgment whatsoever, looking upon these as the sting of death.

V. They lodge in the court of heaven a very melancholy representation, or memorial, of the lamentable condition they were in and the ruins they were groaning under. 1. Their own houses were in ruins, *v.* 10. The cities of Judah were destroyed by the Chaldeans and the inhabitants of them were carried away, so that there was none to repair them or take any notice of them, which would in a few years make them look like perfect deserts: *Thy holy cities are a wilderness.* The cities of Judah are called *holy cities,* for the people were unto God a kingdom of priests. The cities had synagogues in them, in which God was served; and therefore they lamented the ruins of them, and insisted upon this in pleading with God for them, not so much that they were stately cities, rich or ancient ones, but that they were holy cities, cities in which God's name was known, professed, and called upon. "These cities are a wilderness; the beauty of them is sullied; they are neither inhabited nor visited, as formerly. *They have burnt up*

all the synagogues of God in the land," Ps. lxxiv. 8. Nor was it only the smaller cities that were thus left as a wilderness unfrequented, but even "*Zion is a wilderness;* the city of David itself lies in ruins; Jerusalem, that was *beautiful for situation* and *the joy of the whole earth,* is now deformed, and has become the scorn and scandal of the whole earth; that noble city is a desolation, a heap of rubbish." See what devastations sin brings upon a people; and an external profession of sanctity will be no fence against them; *holy cities,* if they become wicked cities, will be soonest of all turned into a wilderness, Amos iii. 2. 2. God's house was in ruins, *v.* 11. This they lament most of all, that *the temple was burnt with fire;* but, as soon as it was built, they were told what their sin would bring it to. 2 Chron. vii. 21, *This house, which is high, shall be an astonishment.* Observe how pathetically they bewail the ruins of the temple. (1.) It was *their holy and beautiful house;* it was a most sumptuous building, but the holiness of it was in their eye the greatest beauty of it, and consequently the profanation of it was the saddest part of its desolation and that which grieved them most, that the sacred services which used to be performed there were discontinued. (2.) It was the place *where their fathers praised God* with their sacrifices and songs; what a pity is it that that should lie in ashes which had been for so many ages the glory of their nation! It aggravated their present disuse of the songs of Zion that their fathers had so often praised God with them. They interest God in the cause when they plead that it was the house where *he had been praised,* and put him in mind too of his covenant with their fathers by taking notice of their fathers' praising him. (3.) With it *all their pleasant things were laid waste,* all their desires and delights, all those things which were employed by them in the service of God, which they had a great delight in; not only the furniture of the temple, the altars and table, but especially the sabbaths and new moons, and all their religious feasts, which they used to keep with gladness, their ministers and solemn assemblies, these were all a desolation. Note, God's people reckon their sacred things their most delectable things; rob them of holy ordinances and the means of grace, and you *lay waste all their pleasant things.* What have they more? Observe here how God and his people have their interest twisted and interchanged; when they speak of the cities for their own habitation they call them *thy holy cities,* for to God they were dedicated; when they speak of the temple wherein God dwelt they call it *our beautiful* house and its furniture *our pleasant things,* for they had heartily espoused it and all the interests of it. If thus we interest God in all our concerns by devoting them to his service, and interest ourselves in all his concerns by laying them near our hearts, we may with satisfaction leave both with him, for he will perfect both.

VI. They conclude with an affectionate expostulation, humbly arguing with God concerning their present desolations (*v.* 12): " *Wilt thou refrain thyself for these things?* Or, *Canst thou contain thyself at these things?* Canst thou see thy temple ruined and not resent it, not revenge it? Has the jealous God forgotten to be jealous? Ps. lxxiv. 22, *Arise, O God! plead thy own cause.* Lord, thou art insulted, thou art blasphemed ; and *wilt thou hold thy peace* and take no notice of it? Shall the highest affronts that can be done to Heaven pass unrebuked ?" When we are abused we hold our peace, because vengeance does not belong to us, and because we have a God to refer our cause to. When God is injured in his honour it may justly be expected that he should speak in the vindication of it ; his people prescribe not to him what he shall say, but their prayer is (as here) Ps. lxxxiii. 1, *Keep not thou silence, O God!* and Ps. cix. 1, " *Hold not thy peace, O God of my praise!* Speak for the conviction of thy enemies, speak for the comfort and relief of thy people ; for *wilt thou afflict us very grievously,* or *afflict us for ever ?*" It is a sore affliction to good people to see God's sanctuary laid waste and nothing done towards the raising of it out of its ruins. But God has said that he *will not contend for ever,* and therefore his people may depend upon it that their afflictions shall be neither to extremity nor to eternity, but *light* and *for a moment.*

CHAP. LXV.

We are now drawing towards the conclusion of this evangelical prophecy, the last two chapters of which direct us to look as far forward as the new heavens and the new earth, the new world which the gospel dispensation should bring in, and the separation that should by it be made between the precious and the vile. " For judgment" (says Christ) " have I come into this world." And why should it seem absurd that the prophet here should speak of that to which all the prophets bore witness? 1 Pet. i. 10, 11. The rejection of the Jews, and the calling in of the Gentiles, are often mentioned in the New Testament as that which was foreseen and foretold by the prophets, Acts x. 43; xiii. 40; Rom. xvi. 26. In this chapter we have, I. The anticipating of the Gentiles with the gospel call, ver. 1. II. The rejection of the Jews for their obstinacy and unbelief, ver. 2–7. III. The saving of a remnant of them by bringing them into the gospel church, ver. 8–10. IV. The judgments of God that should pursue the rejected Jews, ver. 11–16. V. The blessings reserved for the Christian church, which should be its joy and glory, ver. 17–25. But these things are here prophesied of under the type and figure of the difference God would make between some and others of the Jews after their return out of captivity, between those that feared God and those that did not, with reproofs of the sins then found among them and promises of the blessings then in reserve for them.

I AM sought of *them that* asked not for me ; I am found of *them that* sought me not : I said, Behold me, behold me, unto a nation *that* was not called by my name. 2 I have spread out my hands all the day unto a rebellious people, which walketh in a way *that was* not good, after their own thoughts ; 3 A people that provoketh me to anger continually to my

face ; that sacrificeth in gardens, and burneth incense upon altars of brick ; 4 Which remain among the graves, and lodge in the monuments, which eat swine's flesh, and broth of abominable *things is in* their vessels ; 5 Which say, Stand by thyself, come not near to me ; for I am holier than thou. These *are* a smoke in my nose, a fire that burneth all the day. 6 Behold, *it is* written before me : I will not keep silence, but will recompense, even recompense into their bosom, 7 Your iniquities, and the iniquities of your fathers together, saith the LORD, which have burned incense upon the mountains, and blasphemed me upon the hills : therefore will I measure their former work into their bosom.

The apostle Paul (an expositor we may depend upon) has given us the true sense of these verses, and told us what was the event they pointed at and were fulfilled in, namely, the calling in of the Gentiles and the rejection of the Jews, by the preaching of the gospel, Rom. x. 20, 21. And he observes that herein *Esaias is very bold,* not only in foretelling a thing so improbable ever to be brought about, but in foretelling it to the Jews, who would take it as a gross affront to their nation, and therein Moses's words would be made good (Deut. xxxii. 21), *I will provoke you to jealousy by those that are no people.*

I. It is here foretold that the Gentiles, who had been afar off, should be made nigh, *v.* 1. Paul reads it thus : *I was found of those that sought me not ; I was made manifest to those that asked not for me.* Observe what a wonderful and blessed change was made with them and how they were surprised into it. 1. Those who had long been without God in the world shall now be set a seeking him ; those who had not said, *Where is God my maker?* shall now begin to enquire after him. Neither they nor their fathers had called upon his name, but either lived without prayer or prayed to stocks and stones, the work of men's hands. But now they shall *be baptized and call on the name of the Lord,* Acts ii. 21. With what pleasure does the great God here speak of his being sought unto, and how does he glory in it, especially by those who in time past had not asked for him ! For there is joy in heaven over great sinners who repent. 2. God shall anticipate their prayers with his blessings : *I am found of those that sought me not.* This happy acquaintance and correspondence between God and the Gentile world began on his side ; they came to know God because they were *known of him* (Gal. iv. 9), to seek

God and find him because they were first sought and found of him. Though in after-communion God is found of those that seek him (Prov. viii. 17), yet in the first conversion he is found of those that seek him not; for *therefore we love him because he first loved us.* The design of the bounty of common providence to them was *that they might seek the Lord, if haply they might feel after him and find him,* Acts xvii. 27. But they sought him not; still he was to them *an unknown God,* and yet God was found of them. 3. God gave the advantages of a divine revelation to those who had never made a profession of religion : *I said, Behold me, behold me* (gave them a sight of me and invited them to take the comfort and benefit of it) to those who *were not called by my name,* as the Jews for many ages had been. When the apostles went about from place to place, preaching the gospel, this was the substance of what they preached : *"Behold God, behold him,* turn towards him, fix the eyes of your minds upon him, acquaint yourselves with him, admire him, adore him ; look off from your idols that you have made, and look upon the living God who made you." Christ in them said, *Behold me, behold me* with an eye of faith ; *look unto me, and be you saved.* And this was said to those that had long been *lo-ammi,* and *lo-ruhamah* (Hos. i. 8, 9), *not a people,* and that *had not obtained mercy,* Rom. ix. 25, 26.

II. It is here foretold that the Jews, who had long been a people near to God, should be cast off and set at a distance, *v.* 2. The apostle applies this to the Jews in his time, as a seed of evil-doers. Rom. x. 21, *But to Israel he saith, All day long I have stretched forth my hands unto a disobedient and gainsaying people.* Here observe,

1. How the Jews were courted to the divine grace. God himself, by his prophets, by his Son, by his apostles, *stretched forth his hands to them,* as Wisdom did, Prov. i. 24. God *spread out his hands to them,* as one reasoning and expostulating with them, not only beckoned to them with the finger, but *spread out his hands,* as being ready to embrace and entertain them, reaching forth the tokens of his favour to them, and importuning them to accept them. When Christ was crucified his hands were *spread out and stretched forth,* as if he were preparing to receive returning sinners into his bosom ; and this *all the day,* all the gospel-day. He waited to be gracious, and was not weary of waiting ; even those that came in at the eleventh hour of the day were not rejected.

2. How they contemned the invitation ; it was given to a rebellious and gainsaying people ; they were invited to the wedding-supper, and would not come, but *rejected the counsel of God against themselves.* Now here we have,

(1.) The bad character of this people. The world shall see that it was not for no-

thing that they were rejected of God ; no, it was for their whoredoms that they were put away.

[1.] Their character in general was such as one would not expect of those who had been so much the favourites of Heaven. *First,* They were very wilful. Right or wrong they would do as they had a mind. " They generally *walk* on *in a way that is not good,* not the right way, not a safe way, for they *walk after their own thought,* their own devices and desires." If our guide be our own thoughts, our way is not likely to be good ; for *every imagination of the thought of our hearts is only evil.* God had told them his thoughts, what his mind and will were, but they would walk *after their own thoughts,* would do what they thought best. *Secondly,* They were very provoking. This was God's complaint of them all along—they grieved him, they *vexed his Holy Spirit,* as if they would contrive how to make him their enemy : They *provoke me to anger continually to my face.* They cared not what affront they gave to God, though it were in his sight and presence, in a downright contempt of his authority and defiance of his justice ; and this *continually :* it had been their way and manner ever since they were a people, witness the *day of temptation in the wilderness.*

[2.] The prophet speaks more particularly of *their iniquities and the iniquities of their fathers,* as the ground of God's casting them off, *v.* 7. Now he gives instances of both.

First, The most provoking iniquity of their fathers was idolatry ; this, the prophet tells them, was provoking God to his face ; and it is an iniquity which, as appears by the second commandment, God often *visits upon the children.* This was the sin that brought them into captivity, and, though the captivity pretty well cured them of it, yet, when the final ruin of that nation came, that was again brought into the account against them ; for in the day when God visits he will visit that, Exod. xxxii. 34. Perhaps there were many, long after the captivity, who, though they did not worship other gods, were yet guilty of the disorders here mentioned ; for they married strange wives. 1. They forsook God's temple, and *sacrificed in gardens or groves,* that they might have the satisfaction of doing it in their own way, for they liked not God's institutions. 2. They forsook God's altar, and *burnt incense upon bricks,* altars of their own contriving (they burnt incense according to their own inventions, which were of no more value, in comparison with God's institution, than an altar of bricks in comparison with the golden altar which God appointed them to burn incense on), or *upon tiles* (so some read it), such as they covered their flat-roofed houses with, and on them sometimes they burnt incense to their idols, as appears, 2 Kings xxiii. 12, where we read of altars *on the top of the upper chamber of Ahaz,* and Jer. xix. 13, of their burning incense to the host of heaven upon the roofs of their houses. 3. "They used necromancy, or consulting with the dead, and, in order to that, they *remained among the graves*, and *lodged in the monuments*," to seek for the living to the dead (*ch.* viii. 19), as the witch of Endor. Or they used to consult the evil spirits that haunted the sepulchres. 4. They violated the laws of God about their meat, and broke through the distinction between clean and unclean before it was taken away by the gospel. They *ate swine's flesh*. Some indeed chose rather to die than to eat swine's flesh, as Eleazar and the seven brethren in the story of the Maccabees; but it is probable that many ate of it, especially when it came to be a condition of life. In our Saviour's time we read of a vast herd of swine among them, which gives us cause to suspect that there were many then who made so little conscience of the law as to eat swine's flesh, for which they were justly punished in the destruction of the swine. *And the broth*, or pieces, of other forbidden meats, called here *abominable things*, was *in their vessels*, and was made use of for food. The forbidden meat is called *an abomination*, and those that meddle with it are said to *make themselves abominable*, Lev. xi. 42, 43. Those that durst not eat the meat yet made bold with the broth, because they would come as near as might be to that which was forbidden, to show how they coveted the forbidden fruit. Perhaps this is here put figuratively for all forbidden pleasures and profits which are obtained by sin, that *abominable thing which the Lord hates;* they loved to be dallying with it, to be tasting of its broth. But those who thus take a pride in venturing upon the borders of sin, and the brink of it, are in danger of falling into the depths of it. But, *Secondly,* The most provoking iniquity of the Jews in our Saviour's time was their pride and hypocrisy, that sin of the scribes and Pharisees against which Christ denounced so many woes, *v.* 5. They say, "*Stand by thyself,* keep off" (*get thee to thine*, so the original is); "keep to thy own companions, but *come not near to me*, lest thou pollute me; *touch me not;* I will not allow thee any familiarity with me, *for I am holier than thou*, and therefore thou art not good enough to converse with me; *I am not as other men are, nor even as this publican.*" This they were ready to say to every one they met with, so that, in saying, *I am holier than thou*, they thought themselves holier than any, not only very good, as good as they should be, as good as they needed to be, but better than any of their neighbours. *These are a smoke in my nose* (says God), such a smoke as comes not from a quick fire, which soon becomes glowing and pleasant, but from a fire of wet wood, which *burns all the day,* and is nothing but smoke. Note, Nothing in men is more odious and offensive

382

to God than a proud conceit of themselves and contempt of others; for commonly those are most unholy of all that think themselves holier than any.

(2.) The controversy God had with them for this. The proof against them is plain: *Behold, it is written before me, v.* 6. It is written, to be remembered against them in time to come; for they may not perhaps be immediately reckoned with. The sins of sinners, and particularly the vainglorious boasts and scorns of hypocrites, are *laid up in store* with God, Deut. xxxii. 34. And what is written shall be read and proceeded upon: "*I will not keep silence* always, though I may keep silence long." They shall not think him altogether such a one as themselves, as sometimes they have done; but *he will recompense, even recompense into their bosom.* Those basely abuse religion, that honourable and sacred thing, who make their profession of it the matter of their pride, and the jealous God will reckon with them for it; the profession they boast of shall but serve to aggravate their condemnation. [1.] The *iniquity of their fathers* shall come against them; not but that their own sin deserved whatever judgments God brought upon them, and much heavier; and this they owned, Ezra ix. 13. But God would not have wrought so great a desolation upon them if he had not therein had an eye to the sins of their fathers. Therefore in the last destruction of Jerusalem God is said to bring upon them the blood of the Old-Testament martyrs, even that of *Abel*, Matt. xxiii. 35. God will reckon with them, not only for their fathers' idols, but for their *high places*, their *burning incense upon the mountains and the hills*, though perhaps it was to the true God only. This was blaspheming or reproaching God; it was a reflection upon the choice he had made of the place where he would record his name, and the promise he had made that there he would meet them and bless them. [2.] Their own with that shall bring ruin upon them: *Your iniquities and the iniquities of your fathers* together, the one aggravating the other, constitute the former work, which, though it may seem to be overlooked and forgotten, shall be *measured into their bosom.* God will render into the bosom, not only of his open enemies (Ps. lxxix. 12), but of his false and treacherous friends, *the reproach wherewith they have reproached him.*

8 Thus saith the LORD, As the new wine is found in the cluster, and *one* saith, Destroy it not; for a blessing *is* in it: so will I do for my servants' sakes, that I may not destroy them all. 9 And I will bring forth a seed out of Jacob, and out of Judah an inheritor of my mountains: and mine elect shall inherit it, and my servants shall dwell there. 10 And

Sharon shall be a fold of flocks, and the valley of Achor a place for the herds to lie down in, for my people that have sought me.

This is expounded by St. *Paul*, Rom. xi. 1—5, where, when, upon occasion of the rejection of the Jews, it is asked, *Hath God then cast away his people?* he answers, No; for *at this time there is a remnant according to the election of grace.* This prophecy has reference to that distinguished remnant. When that hypocritical nation is to be destroyed God will separate and secure to himself some from among them; some of the Jews shall be brought to embrace the Christian faith, shall be added to the church, and so be saved. And our Saviour has told us that *for the sake of these elect* the days of the destruction of the Jews should be shortened, and a stop put to the desolation, which otherwise would have proceeded to such a degree that *no flesh should be saved,* Matt. xxiv. 22. Now,

I. This is illustrated here by a comparison, *v.* 8. When a vine is so blasted and withered that there seems to be no sap nor life in it, and therefore the dresser of the vineyard is inclined to pluck it up or cut it down, yet, if ever so little of the juice of the grape, fit to make new wine, be found, though but in one cluster, a stander-by interposes, and says, *Destroy it not, for a blessing is in it;* there is life in the root, and hope that yet it may become good for something. Good men are blessings to the places where they live; and sometimes God spares whole cities and nations for the sake of a few such in them. How ambitious should we be of this honour, not only to be distinguished from others, but serviceable to others!

II. Here is a description of those that shall make up this saved saving remnant. 1. They are such as serve God. It is *for my servants' sake* (*v.* 8), and they are *my servants* that *shall dwell there, v.* 9. God's faithful servants, however they are looked upon, are the best friends their country has; and those who serve him do therein *serve their generation.* 2. They are such as seek God, make it the end of their lives to glorify God and the business of their lives to call upon him. It is *for my people that have sought me.* Those that seek God shall find him, and shall find him their bountiful rewarder.

III. Here is an account of the mercy God has in store for them. The remnant that shall return out of captivity shall have a happy settlement again in their own land, and that by an hereditary right, as *a seed out of Jacob,* in whom the family is kept up and the entail preserved, and from whom, as from the seed sown, shall spring a numerous increase; and these typify the remnant of Jacob that shall be incorporated into the gospel church by faith. 1. They shall have

a good portion for themselves. They shall inherit *my mountains,* the holy mountains on which Jerusalem and the temple were built, or the mountains of Canaan, *the land of promise,* typifying the covenant of grace, which all God's servants, his elect, both inhabit and inherit; they make it their refuge, their rest and residence, so they dwell in it, are at home in it; and they have taken it to be their heritage for ever, and it shall be to them an inheritance incorruptible. God's chosen, the spiritual seed of praying Jacob, shall be the inheritors of his mountains of bliss and joy, and shall be carried safely to them through the vale of tears. 2. They shall have a green pasture for their flocks, *v.* 10. *Sharon and the valley of Achor* shall again be as well replenished as ever they were with cattle. Sharon lay westward, near Joppa; Achor lay eastward, near Jordan. It is therefore intimated that they shall recover the possession of the whole land, that they shall have wherewith to stock it all, and that they shall peaceably enjoy it and there shall be none to disturb them nor make them afraid. Gospel-ordinances are the fields and valleys where the sheep of Christ *shall go in and out and find pasture* (John x. 9), and where they are *made to lie down* (Ps. xxiii. 2), as Israel's herds in *the valley of Achor,* Hos. ii. 15.

11 But ye *are* they that forsake the LORD, that forget my holy mountain, that prepare a table for that troop, and that furnish the drink-offering unto that number. 12 Therefore will I number you to the sword, and ye shall all bow down to the slaughter: because when I called, ye did not answer; when I spake, ye did not hear; but did evil before mine eyes, and did choose *that* wherein I delighted not. 13 Therefore thus saith the Lord GOD, Behold, my servants shall eat, but ye shall be hungry: behold, my servants shall drink, but ye shall be thirsty: behold, my servants shall rejoice, but ye shall be ashamed: 14 Behold, my servants shall sing for joy of heart, but ye shall cry for sorrow of heart, and shall howl for vexation of spirit. 15 And ye shall leave your name for a curse unto my chosen: for the Lord GOD shall slay thee, and call his servants by another name: 16 That he who blesseth himself in the earth shall bless himself in the God of truth; and he that sweareth in the earth shall swear by the God of truth; because the former

troubles are forgotten, and because they are hid from mine eyes.

Here the different states of the godly and wicked, of the Jews that believed and of those that still persisted in unbelief, are set the one over-against the other, as life and death, good and evil, the blessing and the curse.

I. Here is the fearful doom of those that persisted in their idolatry after the deliverance out of Babylon, and in infidelity after the preaching of the gospel of Christ. Observe,

1. What the doom is that is here threatened: "*I will number you to the sword* as sheep for the slaughter, and there shall be no escaping, no standing out; *you shall all bow down to it,*" *v.* 12. God's judgments come, (1.) Regularly, and are executed according to the commission. Those fall by the sword that are numbered or counted out to it, and none besides. Though the sword seems to devour promiscuously *one as well as another,* yet it is made to know its number and shall not exceed. (2.) Irresistibly. The strongest and most stout-hearted sinners shall be forced to bow before them; for none ever hardened their hearts against God and prospered.

2. What the sins are that number them to the sword. (1.) Idolatry was the ancient sin (*v.* 11): "*You are those* who, instead of seeking me and serving me as my people, *forsake the Lord,* disown him, and cast him off to embrace other gods, who *forget my holy mountain* (the privileges it confers and the obligations it lays you under) to burn incense upon the mountains of your idols (*v.* 7), and have deserted the one only living and true God." They *prepared a table for that troop of* deities which the heathen worship and *poured out drink-offerings to that* numberless number of them; for those that thought one God too little ever thought scores and hundreds sufficient, but were still adding to the number of them, till they had as many gods as cities and their altars were as thick \as *heaps in the furrows of the field,* Hos. xii. 11. Some take *Gad* and *Meni,* which we translate *a troop* and *a number,* to be the proper names of two of their idols, answering to Jupiter and Mercury. Whatever they were, their worshippers spared no cost to do them honour; they prepared a table for them, and filled out mixed wine for drink-offerings to them; they would pinch their families rather than stint their devotions, which should shame the worshippers of the true God out of their niggardliness. (2.) Infidelity was the sin of the later Jews (*v.* 12): *When I called, you did not answer,* which refers to the same that *v.* 2 did *(I have stretched out my hands to a rebellious people),* and that is applied to those who rejected the gospel. Our Lord Jesus himself called (he *stood and cried,* John vii. 37), but they did not hear, they would not answer; they were not convinced

by his reasonings nor moved by his expostulations; both the fair warnings he gave them of death and ruin and the fair offers he made them of life and happiness were slighted and made no impression upon them. Yet this was not all: *You did evil before my eyes,* not by surprise, or through inadvertency, but with deliberation: *You did choose that wherein I delighted not;* he means that which he utterly detested and abhorred. It is not strange that those who will not be persuaded to choose that which is good persist in their choice and pursuit of that which is evil. See the malignity of sin; it is evil in God's eyes, highly offensive to him, and yet it is committed before his eyes, in his sight and presence, and in contempt of him; it is likewise a contradiction to the will of God; it is doing that, of choice, which we know will displease him.

II. The aggravation of this doom, from the consideration of the happy state of those that were brought to repentance and faith.

1. The blessedness of those that serve God, and the woeful condition of those that rebel against him, are here set the one over-against the other, that they may serve as a foil to each other, *v.* 13—16. (1.) God's servants may well think themselves happy, and for ever indebted to that free grace which made them so, when they see how miserable some of their neighbours are for want of that grace, who are hardened, and likely to perish for ever in unbelief, and what a narrow escape they had of being among them. See *ch.* lxvi. 24. (2.) It will add to the grief of those that perish to see the happiness of God's servants (whom they had hated, and vilified, and looked upon with the utmost disdain), and especially to think that they might have shared in their bliss if it had not been their own fault. It made the torment of the rich man in hell the more grievous that he *saw Abraham afar off and Lazarus in his bosom,* Luke xvi. 23. See Luke xiii. 28. Sometimes the providence of God makes such a difference as this between good and bad in this world, and the prosperity of the righteous becomes a grievous eye-sore and vexation of heart to the wicked (Ps. cxii. 10), and it will certainly be so in the great day. *We fools counted his life madness and his end without honour; but now how is he numbered with the saints and his lot is among the chosen.* Now,

2. The difference of their states lies in two things :—

(1.) In point of comfort and satisfaction. [1.] God's servants shall eat and drink; they shall have the bread of life to feed, to feast upon, continually, shall be abundantly replenished with the goodness of his house, and shall want nothing that is good for them. Heaven's happiness will be to them an everlasting feast; they shall be filled with that which now they hunger and thirst after. But those who set their hearts upon the world, and place their happiness in that, shall be hungry and thirsty, always empty, always craving; for it is not bread; it surfeits, but it satisfies not. In communion with God, and dependence upon him, there is full satisfaction; but in sinful pursuits there is nothing but disappointment. [2.] God's servants *shall rejoice* and sing for joy of heart. They have constant cause for joy, and there is nothing that may be an occasion of grief to them but they have an allay sufficient for it; and, as far as faith is in act and exercise, they have a heart to rejoice, and their joy is their strength. They shall rejoice in their hope, because it shall not make them ashamed. Heaven will be a world of everlasting joy to all that are now sowing in tears. But, on the other hand, those that forsake the Lord shut themselves out from all true joy, for *they shall be ashamed* of their vain confidence in themselves, and their own righteousness, and the hopes they had built thereon. When the expectations of bliss wherewith they had flattered themselves are frustrated, O what confusion will fill their faces! Then shall they *cry for sorrow of heart, and howl for vexation of spirit,* perhaps in this world, when their laughter shall be turned into mourning and their joy into heaviness, and certainly in that world where the torment will be endless, easeless, and remediless—nothing but weeping, and wailing, and gnashing of teeth, to eternity. Let these two be compared, *Now he is comforted* and *thou art tormented,* and which of the two will we choose to take our lot with?

(2.) In point of honour and reputation, *v.* 15, 16. *The memory of the just is,* and shall be, *blessed, but the name of the wicked shall rot.* [1.] The name of the idolaters and unbelievers shall be left *for a curse,* shall be loaded with ignominy and made for ever infamous. It shall be used in giving bad characters—*Thou art as cruel as a Jew;* and in imprecation—*God make thee as miserable as a Jew.* It shall be *for a curse to God's chosen,* that is, for a warning to them; they shall be afraid of falling under the curse upon the Jewish nation, of perishing after the *same example of unbelief.* The curse of those whom God rejects should make his chosen stand in awe. *The Lord God shall slay thee;* he shall quite extirpate the Jews and cut them off from being a people; they shall no longer live as a nation, nor ever be incorporated again. [2.] The name of God's chosen shall become a blessing: *He shall call his servants by another name.* The children of the covenant shall no longer be called *Jews,* but *Christians;* and to them, under that name, all the promises and privileges of the new covenant shall be secured. This other name shall be an honourable name; it shall not be confined to one nation, but with it men shall *bless themselves in the earth,* all the world over. God shall have servants out of all nations who shall all be

dignified with this new name. They shall bless themselves *in the God of truth.* First, They shall give honour to God both in their prayers and in their solemn oaths, in their addresses for his favour as their felicity and their appeals to his justice as their Judge. This is a part of the homage we owe to God; we must bless ourselves in him, that is, we must reckon that we have enough to make us happy, that we ,need no more, and can desire no more, if we have him for our God. It is of great consequence what we bless ourselves in, what we most please ourselves with and value ourselves by our interest in. Worldly people bless themselves in the abundance they have of this world's goods (Ps. xlix. 18; Luke xii. 19); but God's servants bless themselves in him, as a God all-sufficient for them. He is their crown of glory and diadem of beauty, their strength and portion. By him also *they shall swear,* and not by any creature or any false god. To his judgment they shall refer their cause, from whom every man's judgment doth proceed. *Secondly,* They shall give honour to him as *the God of truth, the God of the Amen* (so the word is); some understand it of Christ who is himself the *Amen,* the *faithful witness* (Rev. iii. 14), and in whom all the promises are *yea and amen,* 2 Cor. i. 20. In him we must bless ourselves, and by him we must swear unto the Lord and covenant with him. He that is *blessed in the earth* (so some read it) *shall be blessed in the true God,* for Christ is *the true God and eternal life,* 1 John v. 20. And it was promised of old that *in him all the families of the earth should be blessed,* Gen. xii. 3. Some read it, *He shall bless himself in the God of the faithful people,* in God as the God of all believers, desiring no more than to share in the blessings wherewith they are blessed, to be dealt with as he deals with them. *Thirdly,* They shall give him honour as the author of this blessed change which they have the experience of; they shall think themselves happy in having him for their God who has made them to forget their former troubles, the remembrance of them being swallowed up in their present comforts: *Because they are hidden from God's eyes,* that is, they are quite taken away; for, if there were any remainder of their troubles, God would be sure to have his eye upon it, in compassion to them and concern for them. They shall no longer feel them; for God will no longer see them. He is pleased to speak as if he would make himself easy by making them easy; and therefore they shall with a great deal of satisfaction bless themselves in him.

17 For, behold, I create new heavens and a new earth: and the former shall not be remembered, nor come into mind. 18 But be ye glad and rejoice for ever *in that* which I create:

for, behold, I create Jerusalem a rejoicing, and her people a joy. 19 And I will rejoice in Jerusalem, and joy in my people : and the voice of weeping shall be no more heard in her, nor the voice of crying. 20 There shall be no more thence an infant of days, nor an old man that hath not filled his days : for the child shall die a hundred years old; but the sinner *being* a hundred years old shall be accursed. 21 And they shall build houses, and inhabit *them ;* and they shall plant vineyards, and eat the fruit of them. 22 They shall not build, and another inhabit ; they shall not plant, and another eat : for as the days of a tree *are* the days of my people, and mine elect shall long enjoy the work of their hands. 23 They shall not labour in vain, nor bring forth for trouble ; for they *are* the seed of the blessed of the LORD, and their offspring with them. 24 And it shall come to pass, that before they call, I will answer ; and while they are yet speaking, I will hear. 25 The wolf and the lamb shall feed together, and the lion shall eat straw like the bullock : and dust *shall be* the serpent's meat. They shall not hurt nor destroy in all my holy mountain, saith the LORD.

If these promises were in part fulfilled when the Jews, after their return out of captivity, were settled in peace in their own land and brought as it were into a new world, yet they were to have their full accomplishment in the gospel church, militant first and at length triumphant. *The Jerusalem that is from above is free and is the mother of us all.* In the graces and comforts which believers have in and from Christ we are to look for this new heaven and new earth. It is in the gospel that *old things have passed away and all things have become new,* and by it that those who are in Christ are *new creatures,* 2 Cor. v. 17. It was a mighty and happy change that was described *v.* 16, that *the former troubles were forgotten ;* but here it rises much higher : even the *former world* shall be *forgotten* and *shall no more come into mind.* Those that were converted to the Christian faith were so transported with the comforts of it that all the comforts they were before acquainted with became as nothing to them ; not only their foregoing griefs, but their foregoing joys, were lost and swallowed up in this. The glorified saints will there-
386

fore have forgotten this world, because they will be entirely taken up with the other : *For, behold, I create new heavens and a new earth.* See how inexhaustible the divine power is ; the same God that created one heaven and earth can create another. See how entire the happiness of the saints is ; it shall be all of a piece ; with the new heavens God will create them (if they have occasion for it to make them happy) a new earth too. *The world is yours* if you be Christ's, 1 Cor. iii. 22. When God is reconciled to us, which gives us a new heaven, the creatures too are reconciled to us, which gives us a new earth. The future glory of the saints will be so entirely different from what they ever knew before that it may well be called *new heavens and a new earth,* 2 Pet. iii. 13. *Behold, I make all things new,* Rev. xxi. 5.

I. There shall be new joys. For, 1. All the church's friends, and all that belong to her, shall rejoice (*v.* 18) : You shall *be glad and rejoice for ever in that which I create.* The new things which God creates in and by his gospel are and shall be matter of everlasting joy to all believers. *My servants shall rejoice* (*v.* 13), at last they shall, though now they mourn. *Enter thou into the joy of thy Lord.* 2. The church shall be the matter of their joy, so pleasant, so prosperous, shall her condition be : *I create Jerusalem a rejoicing and her people a joy.* The church shall not only rejoice but be rejoiced in. Those that have sorrowed with the church shall rejoice with her. 3. The prosperity of the church shall be a rejoicing to God himself, who has pleasure in the prosperity of his servants (*v.* 19) : *I will rejoice in Jerusalem's joy,* and will *joy in my people ;* for in *all their affliction he was afflicted.* God will not only rejoice in the church's well-doing, but will himself *rejoice to do her good* and *rest in his love* to her, Zeph. iii. 17. What God rejoices in it becomes us to rejoice in. 4. There shall be no allay of this joy, nor any alteration of this happy condition of the church : *The voice of weeping shall be no more heard in her.* If this relate to any state of the church in this life, it means no more than that the former occasions of grief shall not return, but God's people shall long enjoy an uninterrupted tranquillity. But in heaven it shall have a full accomplishment, in respect both of the perfection and the perpetuity of the promised joy; there *all tears shall be wiped away.*

II. There shall be new life, *v.* 20. Untimely deaths by the sword or sickness shall be no more known as they have been, and by this means there shall be *no more the voice of crying, v.* 19. When there shall be *no more death* there shall be *no more sorrow,* Rev. xxi. 4. As death has reigned by sin, so life shall reign by righteousness, Rom v. 14, 21. 1. Believers through Christ shall be satisfied with life, though it be ever so short on earth. If an infant end its days quickly, yet it shall not be reckoned to die untimely; for the shorter its life is the longer will its rest be. Though *death reign over those that have not sinned after the similitude of Adam's trangression,* yet they, dying in the arms of Christ, the second Adam, and belonging to his kingdom, are not to be called *infants of days,* but even the child shall be reckoned to *die a hundred years old,* for he shall rise again at full age, shall rise to eternal life. Some understand it of children who in their childhood are so eminent for wisdom and grace, and by death nipped in the blossom, that they may be said to die a hundred years old. And, as for old men, it is promised that *they shall fill their days* with the *fruits of righteousness,* which they shall *still bring forth in old age, to show that the Lord is upright,* and then it is a good old age. An old man who is wise, and good, and useful, may truly be said to have *filled his days.* Old men who have their hearts upon the world have never filled their days, never have enough of this world, but would still continue longer in it. But that man dies old, and *satur dierum—full of days,* who, with Simeon, having seen God's salvation, desires now to depart in peace. 2. Unbelievers shall be unsatisfied and unhappy in life, though it be ever so long. The sinner, though he live to be *a hundred years old, shall be accursed.* His living so long shall be no token to him of the divine favour and blessing, nor shall it be any shelter to him from the divine wrath and curse. The sentence he lies under will certainly be executed, and his long life is but a long reprieve; nay, it is itself a curse to him, for the longer he lives the more wrath he treasures up against the day of wrath and the more sins he will have to answer for. So that the matter is not great whether our lives on earth be long or short, but whether we live the lives of saints or the lives of sinners.

III. There shall be a new enjoyment of the comforts of life. Whereas before it was very uncertain and precarious, their enemies *inhabited the houses* which *they built* and *ate the fruit* of the trees which *they planted,* now it shall be otherwise; they shall *build houses and inhabit them,* shall *plant vineyards* and *eat the fruit of them, v.* 21, 22. This intimates that the labour of their hands shall be blessed and be made to prosper; they shall gain what they aimed at, and what they have gained shall be preserved and secured to them; they shall enjoy it comfortably, and nothing shall embitter it to them, and they shall live to enjoy it long. Strangers shall not break in upon them, to expel them, and plant themselves in their room, as sometimes they have done: *My elect shall wear out, or long enjoy, the work of their hands;* it is honestly got, and it will wear well; it is *the work of their hands,* which they themselves have laboured for, and it is most comfortable to enjoy that, and not to eat the *bread*

of idleness, or *bread of deceit.* If we have a heart to enjoy it, that is the gift of God's grace (Eccl. iii. 13); and, if we live to enjoy it long, it is the gift of God's providence, for that is here promised: *As the days of a tree are the days of my people;* as the *days of an oak (ch.* vi. 13), *whose substance is in it, though it cast its leaves;* though it be stripped every winter, it recovers itself again, and lasts many ages; as the days *of the tree of life;* so the LXX. Christ is to them the tree of life, and in him believers enjoy all those spiritual comforts which are typified by the abundance of temporal blessings here promised; and it shall not be in the power of their enemies to deprive them of these blessings or disturb them in the enjoyment of them.

IV. There shall be a new generation rising up in their stead to inherit and enjoy these blessings (*v.* 23): *They shall not labour in vain,* for they shall not only enjoy the work of their hands themselves, but they shall leave it with satisfaction to those that shall come after them, and not with such a melancholy prospect as Solomon did, Eccl. ii. 18, 19. They shall not beget and *bring forth* children *for trouble; for they are* themselves *the seed of the blessed of the Lord,* and there is a blessing entailed upon them by descent from their ancestors which *their offspring with them* shall partake of, and shall be, as well as they, *the seed of the blessed of the Lord.* They shall not bring forth for trouble; for, 1. God will make their children that rise up comforts to them; they shall have the joy of seeing them *walk in the truth.* 2. He will make the times that come after comfortable to their children. As they shall be good, so it shall be well with them; they shall not be brought forth to days of trouble; nor shall it ever be said, *Blessed is the womb that bore not.* In the gospel church Christ's name shall be borne up by a succession. *A seed shall serve him* (Ps. xxii. 30), *the seed of the blessed of the Lord.*

V. There shall be a good correspondence between them and their God (*v.* 24): *Even before they call, I will answer.* God will anticipate their prayers with the blessings of his goodness. David did but say, *I will confess,* and *God forgave,* Ps. xxxii. 5. The father of the prodigal met him in his return. *While they are yet speaking,* before they have finished their prayer, I will give them the thing they pray for, or the assurances and earnests of it. These are high expressions of God's readiness to hear prayer; and this appears much more in the grace of the gospel than it did under the law; we owe the comfort of it to the mediation of Christ as our advocate with the Father and are obliged in gratitude to give a ready ear to God's calls.

VI. There shall be a good correspondence between them and their neighbours (*v.* 25):

The wolf and the lamb shall feed together, as they did in Noah's ark. God's people, though they are as sheep in the midst of wolves, shall be safe and unhurt; for God will not so much break the power and tie the hands of their enemies as formerly, but he will turn their hearts, will alter their dispositions by his grace. When Paul, who had been a persecutor of the disciples (and who, being of the tribe of Benjamin, ravened *as a wolf*, Gen. xlix. 27) joined himself to them and became one of them, then *the wolf and the lamb fed together.* So also when the enmity between Jews and Gentiles was slain, all hostilities ceased, and they fed together as one sheepfold under Christ the great Shepherd, John x. 16. The enemies of the church ceased to do the mischief they had done, and its members ceased to be so quarrelsome with and injurious to one another as they had been, so that there was none either from without or from within to hurt or destroy, none to disturb it, much less to ruin it, *in all the holy mountain;* as was promised, ch. xi. 9. For, 1. Men shall be changed: *The lion* shall no more be a beast of prey, as perhaps he never would have been if sin had not entered, but *shall eat straw like the bullock*, shall *know his owner*, and *his master's crib*, as *the ox* does. When those that lived by spoil and rapine, and coveted to enrich themselves, right or wrong, are brought by the grace of God to accommodate themselves to their condition, to live by honest labour, and to be content with such things as they have—when those that stole steal no more, but work with their hands the thing that is good—then this is fulfilled, that *the lion shall eat straw like the bullock.* 2. Satan shall be chained, the dragon bound; for *dust shall be the serpent's meat again.* That great enemy, when he has been let loose, has glutted and regaled himself with the precious blood of saints, who by his instigation have been persecuted, and with the precious souls of sinners, who by his instigation have become persecutors and have ruined themselves for ever; but now he shall be confined to dust, according to the sentence, *On thy belly shalt thou go, and dust shalt thou eat,* Gen. iii. 14. All the enemies of God's church, that are subtle and venomous as serpents, shall be conquered and subdued, and be made to lick the dust. Christ shall reign as Zion's King till all the enemies of his kingdom be made his footstool, and theirs too. In the holy mountain above, and there only, shall this promise have its full accomplishment, that there shall be none to hurt nor destroy.

CHAP. LXVI.

The scope of this chapter is much the same as that of the foregoing chapter and many expressions of it are the same; it therefore looks the same way, to the different state of the good and bad among the Jews at their return out of captivity, but that typifying the rejection of the Jews in the days of the Messiah, the conversion of the Gentiles, and the setting up of the gospel-kingdom in the world. The first verse of this chapter is applied by Stephen to the dismantling of the temple by the planting of the Christian church (Acts vii. 49, 50), which may serve as a key to the whole chapter. We have here, I. The contempt God puts upon cere-

monial services in comparison with moral duties, and an intimation therein of his purpose shortly to put an end to the temple, and sacrifice and reject those that adhered to them, ver. 1—4. II. The salvation God will in due time work for his people out of the hands of their oppressors (ver. 5), speaking terror to the persecutors (ver. 6) and comfort to the persecuted, a speedy and complete deliverance (ver. 7—9), a joyful settlement (ver. 10, 11), the accession of the Gentiles to them, and abundance of satisfaction therein, ver. 12—14. III. The terrible vengeance which God will bring upon the enemies of his church and people, ver. 15—18. IV. The happy establishment of the church upon large and sure foundations, its constant attendance on God and triumph over its enemies, ver. 19—24. And we may well expect that this evangelical prophet, here, in the close of his prophecy, should (as he does) look as far forward as to the latter days, to the last day, to the days of eternity.

THUS saith the LORD, The heaven *is* my throne, and the earth *is* my footstool: where *is* the house that ye build unto me? and where *is* the place of my rest? 2 For all those *things* hath mine hand made, and all those *things* have been, saith the LORD: but to this *man* will I look, *even* to *him that is* poor and of a contrite spirit, and trembleth at my word. 3 He that killeth an ox *is as if* he slew a man; he that sacrificeth a lamb, *as if* he cut off a dog's neck; he that offereth an oblation, *as if he offered* swine's blood; he that burneth incense, *as if* he blessed an idol. Yea, they have chosen their own ways, and their soul delighteth in their abominations. 4 I also will choose their delusions, and will bring their fears upon them; because when I called, none did answer; when I spake, they did not hear: but they did evil before mine eyes, and chose *that* in which I delighted not.

Here, I. The temple is slighted in comparison with a gracious soul, *v.* 1, 2. The Jews in the prophet's time, and afterwards in Christ's time, gloried much in the temple and promised themselves great things from it; to humble them therefore, and to shake their vain confidence, both the prophets and Christ foretold the ruin of the temple, that God would leave it and then it would soon be desolate. After it was destroyed by the Chaldeans it soon recovered itself and the ceremonial services were revived with it; but by the Romans it was made a perpetual desolation, and the ceremonial law was abolished with it. That the world might be prepared for this, they were often told, as here, of what little account the temple was with God. 1. That he did not need it. Heaven is the throne of his glory and government; there he sits, infinitely exalted in the highest dignity and dominion, above all blessing and praise. The earth is his footstool, on which he stands, overruling all the affairs of it according to his will. If God has so bright a throne, so large a footstool, *where then is the house they can build* unto God, that can be the residence of his glory, or *where is the place of his rest?* What satisfaction can the Eternal Mind take in a house made with men's hands? What occasion has he, as we have, for a house to repose himself in, who *faints not neither is weary*, who neither slumbers nor sleeps? Or, if he had occasion, he *would not tell us* (Ps. 1 12), for *all these things hath his hand made*, heaven and all its courts, earth and all its borders, and all the hosts of both. All *these things have been*, have had their beginning, by the power of God, who was happy from eternity before they were, and therefore could not be benefited by them. *All these things are* (so some read it); they still continue, upheld by the same power that made them; so that *our goodness extends not to him.* If he required a house for himself to dwell in, he would have made one himself when he made the world; and, if he had made one, it would have continued to this day, as other creatures do, according to his ordinance; so that he had no need of a temple made with hands. 2. That he would not heed it as he would a humble, penitent, gracious heart. He has a heaven and earth of his own making, and a temple of man's making; but he overlooks them all, that he may look with favour to him that is poor in spirit, humble and serious, self-abasing and self-denying, whose heart is truly contrite for sin, penitent for it, and in pain to get it pardoned, and who *trembles at God's word*, not as Felix did, with a transient qualm that was over when the sermon was done, but with an habitual awe of God's majesty and purity and an habitual dread of his justice and wrath. Such a heart is a living temple for God; he dwells there, and it is the place of his rest; it is like heaven and earth, his throne and his footstool.

II. Sacrifices are slighted when they come from ungracious hands. *The sacrifice of the wicked* is not only unacceptable, but it *is an abomination to the Lord* (Prov. xv. 8); this is largely shown here, *v.* 3, 4. Observe, 1. How detestable their sacrifices were to God. The carnal Jews, after their return out of captivity, though they relapsed not to idolatry, grew very careless and loose in the service of God; they brought the *torn, and the lame, and the sick* for *sacrifice* (Mal. i. 8, 13), and this made their services abominable to God; they had no regard to their sacrifices, and therefore how could they think God would have any regard to them? The unbelieving Jews, after the gospel was preached and in it notice given of the offering up of the great sacrifice, which put an end to all the ceremonial services, continued to offer sacrifices, as if the law of Moses had been still in force and could *make the comers thereunto perfect :* this was an abomination. *He that kills an ox* for his own table is welcome to do it; but he that now kills it, that thus kills it, for God's altar, *is as if he slew a man ;* it is as

great an offence to God as murder itself ; he that does it does in effect set aside Christ's sacrifice, *treads under foot the blood of the covenant*, and makes himself accessory to the guilt of *the body and blood of the Lord*, setting up what Christ died to abolish. *He that sacrifices a lamb*, if it be a corrupt thing, and not the male in his flock, the best he has, if he think to put God off with any thing, he affronts him, instead of pleasing him ; it is *as if he cut off a dog's neck*, a creature in the eye of the law so vile that, whereas an ass might be redeemed, the price of a dog was never to be brought into the treasury, Deut. xxiii. 18. *He that offers an oblation*, a meat offering or drink-offering, is as if he thought to make atonement with *swine's blood*, a creature that must not be eaten nor touched, the *broth of it* was abominable (*ch.* lxv. 4), much more the blood of it. *He that burns incense to God*, and so puts contempt upon the incense of Christ's intercession, is *as if he blessed an idol ;* it was as great an affront to God as if they had paid their devotions to a false god. Hypocrisy and profaneness are as provoking as idolatry. 2. What their wickedness was which made their sacrifices thus detestable. It was *because they had chosen their own ways*, the ways of their own wicked hearts, and not only their hands did but *their souls delighted in their abominations.* They were vicious and immoral in their conversations, chose the way of sin rather than the way of God's commandments, and took pleasure in that which was provoking to God ; this made their sacrifices so offensive to God, *ch.* i. 11—15. Those that pretend to honour God by a profession of religion, and yet live wicked lives, put an affront upon him, as if he were the patron of sin. And that which was an aggravation of their wickedness was that they persisted in it, notwithstanding the frequent calls given them to repent and reform ; they turned a deaf ear to all the warnings of divine justice and all the offers of divine grace: *When I called, none did answer*, as before, *ch.* lxv. 12. And the same follows here that did there : *They did evil before my eyes.* Being deaf to what he said, they cared not what he saw, but *chose that in which* they knew *he delighted not.* How could those expect to please him in their devotions who took no care to please him in their conversations, but, on the contrary, designed to provoke him ? 3. The doom passed upon them for this. They *chose their own ways*, therefore, says God, I also will *choose their delusions. They have made their choice* (as Mr. Gataker paraphrases it), *and now I will make mine ; they have taken what course they pleased with me, and I will take what course I please with them.* I will choose their *illusions*, or *mockeries* (so some); as they have mocked God and dishonoured him by their wickedness, so God will give them up to their enemies, to be trampled upon and insulted by them. Or they shall be deceived by those vain confidences with which they have deceived themselves. God will make their sin their punishment; they shall be beaten with their own rod and hurried into ruin by their own delusions. God will *bring their fears upon them*, that is, will bring upon them that which shall be a great terror to them, or that which they themselves have been afraid of and thought to escape by sinful shifts. Unbelieving hearts, and unpurified unpacified consciences, need no more to make them miserable than to have their own fears brought upon them.

5 Hear the word of the LORD, ye that tremble at his word ; your brethren that hated you, that cast you out for my name's sake, said, Let the LORD be glorified : but he shall appear to your joy, and they shall be ashamed. 6 A voice of noise from the city, a voice from the temple, a voice of the LORD that rendereth recompence to his enemies. 7 Before she travailed, she brought forth; before her pain came, she was delivered of a man child. 8 Who hath heard such a thing? Who hath seen such things? Shall the earth be made to bring forth in one day? *Or* shall a nation be born at once? For as soon as Zion travailed, she brought forth her children. 9 Shall I bring to the birth, and not cause to bring forth? saith the LORD: shall I cause to bring forth, and shut *the womb?* saith thy God. 10 Rejoice ye with Jerusalem, and be glad with her, all ye that love her: rejoice for joy with her, all ye that mourn for her: 11 That ye may suck, and be satisfied with the breasts of her consolations; that ye may milk out, and be delighted with the abundance of her glory. 12 For thus saith the LORD, Behold, I will extend peace to her like a river, and the glory of the Gentiles like a flowing stream: then shall ye suck, ye shall be borne upon *her* sides, and be dandled upon *her* knees. 13 As one whom his mother comforteth, so will I comfort you ; and ye shall be comforted in Jerusalem. 14 And when ye see *this*, your heart shall rejoice, and your bones shall flourish like a herb: and the hand of the LORD shall be known toward his ser-

vants, and *his* indignation toward his enemies.

The prophet, having denounced God's judgments against a hypocritical nation, that made a jest of God's word and would not answer him when he called to them, here turns his speech to those that *trembled at his word*, to comfort and encourage them; they shall not be involved in the judgments that are coming upon their unbelieving nation. Ministers must distinguish thus, that, when they speak terror to the wicked, they may not *make the hearts of the righteous sad. Bone Christiane, hoc nihil ad te—Good Christian, this is nothing to thee.* The prophet, having assured those that tremble at God's word of a gracious look from him (*v.* 2), here brings them a gracious message from him. The word of God has comforts in store for those that by true humiliation for sin are prepared to receive them. There were those (*v.* 4) who, when *God spoke, would not hear ;* but, if some will not, others will. If the heart *tremble at the word*, the ear will be open to it. Now what is here said to them?

I. Let them know that God will plead their just but injured cause against their persecutors (*v.* 5): *Your brethren that hated you said, Let the Lord be glorified. But he shall appear to your joy.* This perhaps might have reference to the case of some of the Jews at their return out of captivity; but nothing like it appears in the history, and therefore it is rather to be referred to the first preachers and professors of the gospel among the Jews, to whose case it is very applicable. Observe, 1. How the faithful servants of God were persecuted : *Their brethren hated them.* The apostles were Jews by birth, and yet even in the cities of the Gentiles the Jews they met with there were their most bitter and implacable enemies and *stirred up the Gentiles* against them. The spouse complains (Cant. i. 6) that her *mother's children were angry with her.* Pilate upbraided our Lord Jesus with this, *Thy own nation have delivered thee unto me,* John xviii. 35. Their brethren, who should have loved them and encouraged them for their work's sake hated them, and cast them out of their synagogues, excommunicated them as if they had been the greatest blemishes, when they were really the greatest blessings, of their church and nation. This was a fruit of the old enmity in the *seed of the serpent* against the *seed of the woman.* Those that hated Christ hated his disciples, because they supported his kingdom and interest (John xv. 18), and they *cast them out for his name's sake,* because they were called by his name, and called upon his name, and laid out themselves to advance his name. Note, It is no new thing for church censures to be misapplied, and for her artillery, which was intended for her defence, to be turned against her best friends, by the treachery of

her governors. And those that did this *said,
Let the Lord be glorified;* they pretended
conscience and a zeal for the honour of God
and the church in it, and did it with all the
formalities of devotion. Our Saviour explains this, and seems to have reference to
it, John xvi. 2. *They shall put you out of
their synagogues,* and *whosoever kills you will
think that he does God service. In nomine
Domini incipit omne malum—In the name of
the Lord commences evil of every kind.* Or
we may understand it as spoken in defiance
of God : " You say God will be glorified
in your deliverance; *let him be glorified
then ; let him make speed and hasten his work*
(ch. v. 19) ; *let him deliver him, seeing he delighted in him.*" Some take it to be the
language of the profane Jews in captivity,
bantering their brethren that hoped for deliverance, and ridiculing the expectations
they often comforted themselves with, that
God would shortly be glorified in it. They
thus did what they could to *shame the counsel of the poor,* Ps. xiv. 6. 2. How they
were encouraged under these persecutions :
" Let your faith and patience hold out yet a
little while ; your enemies hate you and oppress you, your brethren hate you and cast
you out, but your Father in heaven loves
you, and will appear for you when no one
else will or dare. His providence shall order
things so as shall be for comfort to you ; he
shall appear *for your joy* and for the confusion of those that abuse you and trample on
you ; they *shall be ashamed* of their enmity
to you." This was fulfilled when, upon the
signals given of Jerusalem's approaching
ruin, the *Jews' hearts failed them for fear ;*
but the disciples of Christ, whom they had
hated and persecuted, *lifted up their heads
with joy, knowing that their redemption drew
nigh,* Luke xxi. 26, 28. Though God seem to
hide himself, he will in due time show himself.

II. Let them know that God's appearances
for them will be such as will make a great
noise in the world (v. 6) : There shall be a
voice of noise from the city, from the temple.
Some make it the joyful and triumphant
voice of the church's friends, others the
frightful lamenting voice of her enemies,
surprised in the city, and fleeing in vain to
the temple for shelter. These voices do but
echo to the *voice of the Lord,* who is now
rendering a *recompence to his enemies ;* and
those that will not hear him speaking this
terror shall hear them returning the alarms
of it in doleful shrieks. We may well think
what a confused noise there was in the city
and temple when Jerusalem, after a long
siege, was at last taken by the Romans.
Some think this prophecy was fulfilled in
the prodigies that went before that destruction of Jerusalem, related by Josephus in
his History of the Wars of the Jews (*lib.* 7.
cap. 31), that the temple-doors flew open
suddenly of their own accord, and the priests
heard a noise of motion or shifting in the

most holy place, and presently a voice,
saying, *Let us depart hence.* And, some
time after, one Jesus Bar-Annas went up
and down the city, at the feast of tabernacles,
continually crying, *A voice from the east, a
voice from the west, a voice from the four
winds, a voice against Jerusalem and the
temple, a voice against all this people.*

III. Let them know that God will set up
a church for himself in the world, which
shall be abundantly replenished in a little
time (v. 7) : *Before she travailed she brought
forth.* This is to be applied in the type to
the deliverance of the Jews out of their captivity in Babylon, which was brought about
very easily and silently, without any pain
or struggle, such as was when they were
brought out of Egypt; that was done *by
might and power* (Deut. iv. 34), but this *by
the Spirit of the Lord of hosts,* Zech. iv. 6.
The man-child of the deliverance is rejoiced
in, and yet the mother was never in labour
for it ; *before her pain came she was delivered.*
This is altogether surprising, uncommon,
and without precedent, unless in the story
which the Egyptian midwives told of the
Hebrew women (Exod. i. 19), that *they were
lively and were delivered ere the midwives
came in unto them.* But *shall the earth be
made to bring forth her fruits in one day?*
No, it is the work of some weeks in the
spring to *renew the face of the earth* and
cover it with its products. Some read this
to the same purport with the next clause,
Shall a land be brought forth in one day, or
shall a nation be born at once? Is it to be
imagined that a woman at one birth should
bring children sufficient to people a country
and that they should in an instant grow up
to maturity? No; something like this was
done in the creation; but God has since
rested from all such works, and leaves
second causes to produce their effects gradually. *Nihil facit per saltum—He does
nothing abruptly.* Yet, in this case, *as soon
as Zion travailed she brought forth.* Cyrus's
proclamation was no sooner issued out than
the captives were formed into a body and
were ready to make the best of their way to
their own land. And the reason is given
(v. 9), because *it is the Lord's doing ; he*
undertakes it whose work is perfect. If he
bring to the birth in preparing his people for
deliverance, he will *cause to bring forth* in the
accomplishment of the deliverance. When
every thing is ripe and ready for their release,
and the number of their months is accomplished, so that *the children are brought to the
birth,* shall not I then *give strength to bring
forth,* but leave mother and babe to perish
together in the most miserable case ? How
will this agree with the divine pity ? Shall I
begin a work and not go through with it ?
How will that agree with the divine power and
perfection? *Am I he that causes to bring forth*
(so the following clause may be read) *and shall
I restrain her?* Does God cause mankind, and

all the species of living creatures, to propagate, and *replenish the earth*, and *will he restrain Zion?* Will he not make her fruitful in a blessed offspring to replenish the church? Or, *Am I he that begat, and should I restrain from bringing forth?* Did God beget the deliverance in his purpose and promise, and will he not bring it forth in the accomplishment and performance of it? But this was a figure of the setting up of the Christian church in the world, and the replenishing of that family with children which was to be named from Jesus Christ. When the Spirit was poured out, and the gospel went forth from Zion, multitudes were converted in a little time and with little pains compared with the vast product. The apostles, even before they travailed, brought forth, and the children born to Christ were so numerous, and so suddenly and easily produced, that they were rather like the dew from the morning's womb than like the son from the mother's womb, Ps. cx. 3. The success of the gospel was astonishing; that light, like the morning, strangely diffused itself till it took hold even of *the ends of the earth.* Cities and nations were born at once to Christ. The same day that the Spirit was poured out there were 3000 souls added to the church. And, when this glorious work was once begun, it was carried on wonderfully, beyond what could be imagined, *so mightily grew the word of God and prevailed.* He that brought to the birth in conviction of sin caused to bring forth in a thorough conversion to God.

IV. Let them know that their present sorrows shall shortly be turned into abundant joys, *v.* 10, 11. Observe, 1. How the church's friends are described; they are such as *love her, and mourn* with her and *for her.* Note, All that love God love Jerusalem; they love the church of God, and lay its interest very near their heart. They admire the beauty of the church, take pleasure in communion with it, and heartily espouse its cause. And those that have a sincere affection for the church have a cordial sympathy with her in all the cares and sorrows of her militant state. They mourn for her; all her grievances are their griefs; if Jerusalem be in distress, their harps are hung on the willow-trees. 2. How they are encouraged: *Rejoice with her,* and again and again *I say, Rejoice.* This intimates that Jerusalem shall have cause to rejoice; the days of her mourning shall be at an end, and she shall be comforted according to the time that she has been afflicted. It is the will of God that all her friends should join with her in her joys, for they shall share with her in those blessings that will be the matter of her joy. If *we suffer with Christ* and sorrow with his church, *we shall reign with him* and rejoice with her. We are here called, (1.) To bear our part in the church's praises: "Come, *rejoice with her, rejoice for joy with her,* rejoice greatly,

392

rejoice and know why you rejoice, rejoice on the days appointed for public thanksgiving. You that mourned for her in her sorrows cannot but from the same principle rejoice with her in her joys." (2.) To take our part in the church's comforts. We must *suck and be satisfied with the breasts of her consolations.* The word of God, the covenant of grace (especially the promises of that covenant), the ordinances of God, and all the opportunities of attending on him and conversing with him, are the breasts, which the church calls and counts the *breasts of her consolations,* where her comforts are laid up, and whence by faith and prayer they are drawn. With her therefore we must suck from these breasts, by an application of the promises of God to ourselves and a diligent attendance on his ordinances; and with the consolations which are drawn hence we must be satisfied, and not be dissatisfied though we have ever so little of earthly comforts. It is the glory of the church that she has the Lord for her God, that to her *pertain the adoption and the service of God;* and with the abundance *of* this *glory* we must be *delighted.* We must take more pleasure in our relation to God and communion with him than in all the delights of the sons and daughters of men. Whatever is the glory of the church must be *our glory and joy,* particularly her purity, unity, and increase.

V. Let them know that he who gives them this call to rejoice will give them cause to do so and hearts to do so, *v.* 12—14.

1. He will give them cause to do so. For, (1.) They shall enjoy a long uninterrupted course of prosperity: *I will extend,* or am extending, *peace to her* (that is, all good to her) *like a river* that runs in a constant stream, still increasing till it be swallowed up in the ocean. The gospel brings with it, wherever it is received in its power, such peace as this, which shall go on *like a river,* supplying souls with all good and making them fruitful, as a river does the lands it passes through, such a *river of peace* as the springs of the world's comforts cannot send forth and the dams of the world's troubles cannot stop nor drive back nor its sands rack up, such a river of peace as will carry us to the ocean of boundless and endless bliss. (2.) There shall be large and advantageous additions made to them: *The glory of the Gentiles* shall come to them *like a flowing stream.* Gentile converts shall come pouring into the church, and swell the river of her peace and prosperity; for they shall *bring their glory* with them; their wealth and honour, their power and interest, shall all be devoted to the service of God and employed for the good of the church: " *Then shall you suck* from the breasts of her consolations. When you see such crowding for a share in those comforts you shall be the more solicitous and the more vigorous to secure your share, not for fear of having the less for others coming in to

partake of Christ" (there is no danger of that; he has enough for all and enough for each), "but *their zeal* shall *provoke you to a holy jealousy*." It is well when it does so, Rom. xi. 14; 2 Cor. ix. 2. (3.) God shall be glorified in all, and that ought to be more the matter of our joy than any thing else (v. 14): *The hand of the Lord shall be known towards his servants,* the protecting supporting hand of his almighty power, the supplying enriching hand of his inexhaustible goodness; the benefit which his servants have by both these *shall be known* to his glory as well as theirs. And, to make this the more illustrious, he will at the same time make known *his indignation towards his enemies.* God's mercy and justice shall both be manifested and for ever magnified.

2. God will not only give them cause to rejoice, but will speak comfort to them, will speak it *to their hearts;* and it is he only that can do that, and make it fasten there. See what he will do for the comfort of all the sons of Zion. (1.) Their country shall be their tender nurse: You shall be *carried on her sides,* under her arms, as little children are, and shall be *dandled upon her knees,* as darlings are, especially when they are weary and out of humour, and must be got to sleep. Those that are joined to the church must be treated thus affectionately. The great Shepherd *gathers the lambs in his arms and carries them in his bosom,* and so must the undershepherds, that they may not be discouraged. Proselytes should be favourites. (2) God will himself be their powerful comforter: *As one whom his mother comforts,* when he is sick or sore, or upon any account in sorrow, *so will I comfort you;* not only with the rational arguments which a prudent father uses, but with the tender affections and compassions of a loving mother, that bemoans her afflicted child when it has fallen and hurt itself, that she may quiet it and make it easy, or endeavours to pacify it after she has chidden it and fallen out with it (Jer. xxxi. 20): *Since I spoke against him, my bowels are troubled for him;* he is a dear son, he is a pleasant child. Thus the mother comforts. Thus *you shall be comforted in Jerusalem,* in the favours bestowed on the church, which you shall partake of, and in the thanksgivings offered by the church, which you shall concur with. (3.) They shall feel the blessed effects of this comfort in their own souls (v. 13): *When you see this,* what a happy state the church is restored to, not only your tongues and your countenances, but *your hearts shall rejoice.* This was fulfilled in the wonderful satisfaction which Christ's disciples had in the success of their ministry. Christ, with an eye to that, tells them (John xvi. 22), *Your heart shall rejoice and your joy no man taketh from you.* Then *your bones,* that were dried and withered (the marrow of them quite exhausted), shall recover a youthful strength

and vigour and *shall flourish like a herb.* Divine comforts reach the inward man; *they are marrow* and moistening to the bones, Prov. iii. 8. The bones are the strength of the body; those shall be made to flourish with these comforts. *The joy of the Lord* will be *your strength,* Neh. viii. 10.

15 For, behold, the LORD will come with fire, and with his chariots like a whirlwind, to render his anger with fury, and his rebuke with flames of fire. 16 For by fire and by his sword will the LORD plead with all flesh: and the slain of the LORD shall be many. 17 They that sanctify themselves, and purify themselves in the gardens behind one *tree* in the midst, eating swine's flesh, and the abomination, and the mouse, shall be consumed together, saith the LORD. 18 For I *know* their works and their thoughts: it shall come, that I will gather all nations and tongues; and they shall come, and see my glory. 19 And I will set a sign among them, and I will send those that escape of them unto the nations, *to* Tarshish, Pul, and Lud, that draw the bow, *to* Tubal, and Javan, *to* the isles afar off, that have not heard my fame, neither have seen my glory; and they shall declare my glory among the Gentiles. 20 And they shall bring all your brethren *for* an offering unto the LORD out of all nations, upon horses, and in chariots, and in litters, and upon mules, and upon swift beasts, to my holy mountain Jerusalem, saith the LORD, as the children of Israel bring an offering in a clean vessel into the house of the LORD. 21 And I will also take of them for priests *and* for Levites, saith the LORD. 22 For as the new heavens and the new earth, which I will make, shall remain before me, saith the LORD, so shall your seed and your name remain. 23 And it shall come to pass, *that* from one new moon to another, and from one sabbath to another, shall all flesh come to worship before me, saith the LORD. 24 And they shall go forth, and look upon the carcases of the men that have transgressed against me: for their worm shall not die, neither shall their fire

be quenched; and they shall be an abhorring unto all flesh.

These verses, like the pillar of cloud and fire, have a dark side towards the enemies of God's kingdom and all that are rebels against his crown, and a bright side towards his faithful loyal subjects. Probably they refer to the Jews in captivity in Babylon, of whom some are said to have been sent thither for their hurt, and with them God here threatens to proceed in his controversy; they hated to be reformed, and therefore should be ruined by the calamity (Jer. xxiv. 9); others were sent thither for their good, and they should have the trouble sanctified to them, should in due time get well through it and see many a good day after it. Many of the expressions here used are accommodated to that glorious dispensation; but doubtless the prophecy looks further, to the judgment for which Christ did come once, and will come again, into this world, and to the distinction which his word in both makes *between the precious and the vile.*

I. Christ will appear to the confusion and terror of all those that stand it out against him. Sometimes he will appear in temporal judgments. The Jews that persisted in infidelity were cut off *by fire* and *by his sword.* The ruin was very extensive; *the Lord* then *pleaded with all flesh;* and, it being his sword with which they are cut off, they are called *his slain,* sacrificed to his justice, and they *shall be many.* In the great day the wrath of God will be his fire and sword, with which he will cut off and consume all the impenitent; and his word, when it takes hold of sinners' consciences, burns like fire, and is sharper *than any two-edged sword.* Idolaters will especially be contended with in the day of wrath, *v* 17. Perhaps some of those who returned out of Babylon retained such instances of idolatry and superstition as are here mentioned, had their *idols in their gardens* (not daring to set them up publicly in the high places) and there *purified themselves* (as the worshippers of the true God used to do) when they went about their idolatrous rites, *one after another,* or, as we read it, *behind one tree in the midst,* behind *Ahad* or *Ehad,* some idol that they worshipped by that name and in honour of which they *ate swine's flesh* (which was expressly forbidden by the law of God), *and other abominations,* as *the mouse,* or some other like animal. But the prophecy may refer to all those judgments which the wrath of God, according to the word of God, will bring upon provoking sinners, that live in contempt of God and are devoted to the world and the flesh: They *shall be consumed together.* From the happiness of heaven we find expressly excluded all *idolaters, and whosoever worketh abomination,* Rev. xxi. 27; xxii. 15. In the day of vengeance secret wickedness will be brought to light and

brought to the account; for (*v.* 18), *I know their works and their thoughts.* God knows both what men do and from what principle and with what design they do it; and therefore is fit to judge the world, because he can *judge the secrets of men,* Rom. ii. 16.

II. He will appear to the comfort and joy of all that are faithful to him in the setting up of his kingdom in this world, the kingdom of grace, the earnest and first-fruits of the kingdom of glory. The time shall come that he will *gather all nations and tongues to himself,* that they may *come and see his glory* as it shines in the face of Jesus Christ, *v.* 18. This was fulfilled when all nations were to be discipled and the gift of tongues was bestowed in order thereunto. The church had hitherto been confined to one nation and in one tongue only God was worshipped; but in the days of the Messiah the partition-wall should be taken down, and those that had been strangers to God should be brought acquainted with him and should *see his glory* in the gospel, as the Jews had seen it *in the sanctuary.* As to this, it is here promised,

1. That some of the Jewish nation should, by the grace of God, be distinguished from the rest, and marked for salvation: I will not only set up a *gathering ensign* among them, to which the Gentiles shall seek (as is promised, *ch.* xi. 12), but there shall be those among them on whom *I will set a differencing sign;* for so the word signifies. Though they are a corrupt degenerate nation, yet God will set apart a remnant of them, that shall be devoted to him and employed for him, and a mark shall be set upon them, with such certainty will God own them, Ezek. ix. 4. The *servants of God* shall be *sealed in their foreheads,* Rev. vii. 3. The Lord knows those that are his. Christ's sheep are marked.

2. That those who are themselves distinguished thus by the grace of God shall be commissioned to invite others to come and take the benefit of that grace. Those that escape the power of those prejudices by which the generality of that nation is kept in unbelief shall be *sent to the nations* to carry the gospel among them, and preach it to every creature. Note, Those who themselves have escaped the wrath to come should do all they can to snatch others also as brands out of the burning. God chooses to send those on his errands that can deliver their message feelingly and experimentally, and warn people of their danger by sin as those who have themselves narrowly escaped the danger. (1.) They shall be sent *to the nations,* several of which are here named, Tarshish, and Pul, and Lud, &c. It is uncertain, nor are interpreters agreed, what countries are here intended. *Tarshish* signifies in general *the sea,* yet some take it for Tarsus in Cilicia. *Pul* is mentioned sometimes as the name of one of the kings of Assyria; perhaps some part of that country

might likewise bear that name. *Lud* is supposed to be Lydia, a warlike nation, famed for archers : the Lydians are said to *handle* and *bend the bow*, Jer. xlvi. 9. *Tubal*, some think, is Italy or Spain ; and *Javan* most agree to be Greece, the Iones ; and the *isles of the Gentiles*, that were peopled by the posterity of Japhet (Gen. x. 5), probably are here meant by the *isles afar off, that have not heard my name, neither have seen my glory.* In Judah only was God known, and there only his name was great for many ages. Other countries sat in darkness, heard not the joyful sound, saw not the joyful light. This deplorable state of theirs seems to be spoken of here with compassion ; for it is a pity that any of the children of men should be at such a distance from their Maker as not to hear his name and see his glory. In consideration of this, (2.) Those that are sent to the nations shall go upon God's errand, to *declare his glory among the Gentiles.* The Jews that shall be dispersed among the nations shall declare the glory of God's providence concerning their nation all along, by which many shall be invited to join with them, as also by the appearances of God's glory among them in his ordinances. Some out of all languages of the nations shall *take hold of the skirt of him that is a Jew*, entreating him to take notice of them, to admit them into his company, and to stay a little while for them, till they are ready, " for *we will go with you, having heard that God is with you*," Zech. viii. 23. Thus the glory of God was in part declared among the Gentiles ; but more clearly and fully by the apostles and early preachers of the gospel, who were sent into all the world, even to the isles afar off, to publish the glorious gospel of the blessed God. They *went forth and preached every where, the Lord working with them*, Mark xvi. 20.

3. That many converts shall hereby be made, *v.* 20.

(1.) *They shall bring all your brethren* (for proselytes ought to be owned and embraced as brethren) *for an offering unto the Lord*. God's glory shall not be in vain declared to them, but they shall be both invited and directed to join themselves to the Lord. Those that are sent to them shall succeed so well in their negociation that thereupon there shall be as great flocking to Jerusalem as used to be at the time of a solemn feast, when all the males from all parts of the country were to attend there, and not to appear empty. Observe, [1.] The conveniences that they shall be furnished with for their coming. Some shall come *upon horses*, because they came from far and the journey was too long to travel on foot, as the Jews usually did to their feasts. Persons of quality shall come *in chariots*, and the aged, and sickly, and little children, shall be brought *in litters* or covered waggons, and the young men *on mules and swift beasts*. This intimates their zeal and for-

wardness to come. They ~~are~~ trouble nor charge to get t~~o~~ Those that cannot ride on hor~~ses~~ come in litters ; and in such haste be, and so impatient of delay, that t~~hey~~ can shall ride upon mules and swift These expressions are figurative, and various means of conveyance are heape~~d~~ to intimate (says the learned Mr. Gatak~~er~~ the abundant provision of all those graciou~~s~~ helps requisite for the bringing of God's elect home to Christ. All shall be welcome, and nothing shall be wanting for their assistance and encouragement. [2.] The character under which they shall be brought. They shall come, not as formerly they used to come to Jerusalem, to be offerers, but to be themselves *an offering unto the Lord*, which must be understood spiritually, of their being presented to God as *living sacrifices*, Rom. xii. 1. The apostle explains this, and perhaps refers to it, Rom. xv. 16, where he speaks of his *ministering the gospel to the Gentiles*, that the *offering up*, or *sacrificing, of the Gentiles might be acceptable.* They shall offer themselves, and those who are the instruments of their conversion shall offer them, as the spoils which they have taken for Christ and which are devoted to his service and honour. They shall be brought *as the children of Israel bring an offering in a clean vessel*, with great care that they be holy, purified from sin, and sanctified to God. It is said of the converted Gentiles (Acts xv. 9) that *their hearts were purified by faith*. Whatever was brought to God was brought in a clean vessel, a vessel appropriated to religious uses. God will be served and honoured in the way that he has appointed, in the ordinances of his own institution, which are the proper vehicles for these spiritual offerings. When the soul is offered up to God the body must be a clean vessel for it, possessed *in sanctification and honour, and not in the lusts of uncleanness* (1 Thess. iv. 4, 5) ; and converts to Christ are not only *purged from an evil conscience*, but have their *bodies also washed with pure water*, Heb. x. 22. Now,

(2.) This may refer, [1.] To the Jews, devout men, and proselytes out of every nation under heaven, that flocked together to Jerusalem, expecting the kingdom of the Messiah to appear, Acts ii. 5, 6, 10. They came from all parts to the holy *mountain of Jerusalem*, as an *offering to the Lord*, and there many of them were brought to the faith of Christ by the gift of tongues poured out on the apostles. Methinks there is some correspondence between that history and this prophecy. The eunuch some time after came to worship at Jerusalem in his chariot and took home with him the knowledge of Christ and his holy religion. [2.] To the Gentiles, some of all nations, that should be converted to Christ, and so added to his church, which, though a spiritual accession, often in prophecy represented by a local notion. The apostle says of all true Christians that they *have come to Mount Zion, and the heavenly Jerusalem* (Heb. xii. 22), which explains this passage, and shows that the meaning of all this parade is only that they shall be brought into the church by the grace of God, and in the use of the means of that grace, as carefully, safely, and comfortably, as if they were carried in chariots and litters. Thus God shall *persuade Japhet* and he shall *dwell in the tents of Shem,* Gen. ix. 27.

4. That a gospel ministry shall be set up in the church, it being thus enlarged by the addition of such a multitude of members to it (*v.* 21): *I will take of them* (of the proselytes, of the Gentile converts) *for priests and for Levites,* to minister in holy things and to preside in their religious assemblies, which is very necessary for doctrine, worship, and discipline. Hitherto the priests and Levites were all taken from among the Jews and were all of one tribe; but in gospel times God will take of the converted Gentiles to minister to him in holy things, to teach the people, to bless them in the name of the Lord, to be the stewards of the mysteries of God as the priests and Levites were under the law, to be pastors and teachers (or bishops), to *give themselves to the word and prayer,* and deacons to *serve tables,* and, as the Levites, to take care of the *outward business of the house of God,* Phil. i. 1; Acts vi. 2—4. The apostles were all Jews, and so were the seventy disciples; the great apostle of the Gentiles was himself *a Hebrew of the Hebrews;* but, when churches were planted among the Gentiles, they had ministers settled who were *of themselves, elders in every church* (Acts xiv. 23, Tit. i. 5), which made the ministry to spread the more easily, and to be the more familiar, and, if not the more venerable, yet the more acceptable; gospel grace, it might be hoped, would cure people of those corruptions which kept a prophet from having *honour in his own country.* God says, *I will take,* not *all of them,* though they are all in a spiritual sense made to our God kings and priests, but *of them,* some of them. It is God's work originally to choose ministers by qualifying them for and inclining them to the service, as well as to make ministers by giving them their commission. *I will take them,* that is, I will admit them, though Gentiles, and will accept of them and their ministrations. This is a great honour and advantage to the Gentile church, as it was to the Jewish church that God *raised up of their sons for prophets* and *their young men for Nazarites,* Amos ii. 11.

5. That the church and ministry, being thus settled, shall continue and be kept up in a succession from one generation to another, *v.* 22. The change that will be made by the setting up of the kingdom of the Messiah is here described to be, (1.) A very great and universal change; it shall be a new

world, *the new heavens and the new earth* promised before, *ch.* lxv. 17. *Old things have passed away,* behold *all things have become new* (2 Cor. v. 17), the old covenant of peculiarity is set aside, and a new covenant, a covenant of grace, established, Heb. viii. 13. We are now to serve *in newness of the spirit,* and *not in the oldness of the letter,* Rom. vii. 6. New commandments are given relating both to heaven and earth, and new promises relating to both, and both together make a New Testament; so that they are new heavens and a new earth that God will create, and these a preparative for the new heavens and new earth designed at the end of time, 2 Pet. iii. 13. (2.) A change of God's own making; he will create the new heavens and the new earth. The change was made by him that had authority to make new ordinances, as well as power to make new worlds. (3.) It will be an abiding lasting change, a change never to be changed, a new world that will be always new, and never wax old, as that does which is ready to vanish away: *It shall remain before me* unalterable; for the gospel dispensation is to continue to the end of time and not to be succeeded by any other. The kingdom of Christ is a *kingdom that cannot be moved;* the laws and privileges of it are *things that cannot be shaken,* but shall *for ever remain,* Heb. xii. 27, 28. It shall *therefore* remain, because it is before God; it is under his eye, and care, and special protection. (4.) It will be maintained in a seed that shall serve Christ: *Your seed,* and in them *your name, shall remain*—a seed of ministers, a seed of Christians; as one generation of both passes away, another generation shall come; and thus the name of Christ, with that of Christians, shall continue on earth while the earth remains, and his throne as the days of heaven. The gates of hell, though they fight against the church, shall not *prevail,* nor *wear out the saints of the Most High.*

6. That the public worship of God in religious assemblies shall be carefully and constantly attended upon by all that are thus brought *as an offering to the Lord, v.* 23. This is described in expressions suited to the Old-Testament dispensation, to show that though the ceremonial law should be abolished, and the temple service should come to an end, yet God should be still as regularly, constantly, and acceptably worshipped as ever. Heretofore only Jews went up to appear before God, and they were bound to attend only three times a year, and the males only; but now all flesh, Gentiles as well as Jews, women as well as men, shall *come and worship before God,* in his presence, though not in his temple at Jerusalem, but in religious assemblies dispersed all the world over, which shall be to them as the tabernacle of meeting was to the Jews. God will in them record his name, and, though but two or three come together, he will be among them,

will meet them, and bless them. And they shall have the benefit of these holy convocations frequently, every new moon and every sabbath, not, as formerly, at the three annual feasts only. There is no necessity of one certain place, as the temple was of old. Christ is our temple, in whom by faith all believers meet, and now that the church is so far extended it is impossible that all should meet at one place; but it is fit that there should be a certain time appointed, that the service may be done certainly and frequently, and a token thereby given of the spiritual communion which all Christian assemblies have with each other by faith, hope, and holy love. The *new moons* and the *sabbaths* are mentioned because, under the law, though the yearly feasts were to be celebrated at Jerusalem, yet the new moons and the sabbaths were religiously observed all the country over, in the *schools of the prophets* first and afterwards *in the synagogues* (2 Kings iv. 23, Amos viii. 5, Acts xv. 21), according to the model of which Christian assemblies seem to be formed. Where the Lord's day is weekly sanctified, and the Lord's supper monthly celebrated, and both are duly attended on, there this promise is fulfilled, there the Christian new moons and sabbaths are observed. See, here, (1.) That God is to be worshipped in solemn assemblies, and that it is the duty of all, as they have opportunity, to wait upon God in those assemblies: *All flesh must come;* though flesh, weak, corrupt, and sinful, let them come that the flesh may be mortified. (2.) In worshipping God we present ourselves before him, and are in a special manner in his presence. (3.) For doing this there ought to be stated times, and are so; and we must see that it is our interest as well as our duty constantly and conscientiously to observe these times.

7. That their thankful sense of God's distinguishing favour to them should be very much increased by the consideration of the fearful doom and destruction of those that persist and perish in their infidelity and impiety, *v.* 24. Those that have been worshipping the Lord of hosts, and rejoicing before him in the goodness of his house, shall, in order to affect themselves the more with their own happiness, take a view of the misery of the wicked. Observe, (1.) Who they are whose misery is here described. They are men that have *transgressed against God,* not only broken his laws, but broken covenant with him, and thought themselves able to contend with him. It may be meant

especially of the unbelieving Jews that rejected the gospel of Christ. (2.) What their misery is. It is here represented by the frightful spectacle of a field of battle, covered with the *carcases* of the slain, that lie rotting above ground, full of *worms* crawling about them and feeding on them; and, if you go to burn them, they are so scattered, and it is such a noisome piece of work to get them together, that it would be endless, and the *fire would never be quenched;* so that they are an *abhorring to all flesh,* nobody cares to come near them. Now this is sometimes accomplished in temporal judgments, and perhaps never nearer the letter than in the destruction of Jerusalem and the Jewish nation by the Romans, in which destruction it is computed that above two millions, first and last, were cut off by the sword, besides what perished by famine and pestilence. It may refer likewise to the spiritual judgments that came upon the unbelieving Jews, which St. Paul looks upon, and shows us, Rom. xi. 8, &c. They became dead in sins, twice dead. The church of the Jews was a *carcase* of a church; all its members were putrid carcases; *their worm died not,* their own consciences made them continually uneasy, and the fire of their rage against the gospel was not quenched, which was their punishment as well as their sin; and they became, more than ever any nation under the sun, an *abhorring to all flesh.* But our Saviour applies it to the everlasting misery and torment of impenitent sinners in the future state, where their *worm dies not, and their fire is not quenched* (Mark ix. 44); for the soul, whose conscience is its constant tormentor, is immortal, and God, whose wrath is its constant terror, is eternal. (3.) What notice shall be taken of it. Those that worship God shall *go forth and look upon them,* to affect their own hearts with the love of their Redeemer, when they see what misery they are redeemed from. As it will aggravate the miseries of the damned to see others in the kingdom of heaven and *themselves thrust out* (Luke xiii. 28), so it will illustrate the joys and glories of the blessed to see what becomes of those that died in their transgression, and it will elevate their praises to think that they were themselves as brands plucked out of that burning. To the honour of that free grace which thus distinguished them let the redeemed of the Lord with all humility, and not without a holy trembling, sing their triumphant songs.

EXPOSITION,

WITH PRACTICAL OBSERVATIONS,

OF THE BOOK OF THE PROPHET

JEREMIAH.

THE Prophecies of the Old Testament, as the Epistles of the New, are placed rather according to their bulk than their seniority—the longest first, not the oldest. There were several prophets, and writing ones, that were contemporaries with Isaiah, as Micah, or a little before him, as Hosea, and Joel, and Amos, or soon after him, as Habakkuk and Nahum are supposed to have been; and yet the prophecy of Jeremiah, who began many years after Isaiah finished, is placed next to his, because there is so much in it. Where we meet with most of God's word, there let the preference be given; and yet those of less gifts are not to be despised nor excluded. Nothing now occurs to be observed further concerning prophecy in general; but concerning this prophet Jeremiah we may observe, I. That he was betimes a prophet; he began young, and therefore could say, from his own experience, that it is good first, not the oldest. There were several prophets, both of service and of affliction, Lam. iii. 27. Jerome observes that Isaiah, who had more years over his head, had his tongue touched with a coal of fire, to purge away his iniquity (*ch.* vi. 7), but that when God touched Jeremiah's mouth, who was yet but young, nothing was said of the purging of his iniquity (*ch.* i. 9), because, by reason of his tender years, he had not so much sin to answer for. II. That he continued long a prophet, some reckon fifty years, others above forty. He began in the thirteenth year of Josiah, when things went well under that good king, but he continued through all the wicked reigns that followed; for when we set out for the service of God, though the wind may then be fair and favourable, we know not how soon it may turn and be tempestuous. III. That he was a reproving prophet, was sent in God's name to tell Jacob or their sins and to warn them of the judgments of God that were coming upon them; and the critics observe that therefore his style or manner of speaking is more plain and rough, and less polite, than that of Isaiah and some others of the prophets. Those that are sent to discover sin ought to lay aside the enticing words of man's wisdom. Plain-dealing is best when we are dealing with sinners to bring them to repentance. IV. That he was a weeping prophet; so he is commonly called, not only because he penned the Lamentations, but because he was all along a mournful spectator of the sins of his people and of the desolating judgments that were coming upon them. And for this reason, perhaps, those who imagined our Saviour to be one of the prophets thought him of any of them to be most like to Jeremiah (Matt. xvi. 14), because he was *a man of sorrows and acquainted with grief.* V. That he was a suffering prophet. He was persecuted by his own people more than any of them, as we shall find in the story of this book; for he lived and preached just before the Jews' destruction by the Chaldeans, when their character seems to have been the same as it was just before their destruction by the Romans, when they *killed the Lord Jesus, and persecuted* his *disciples, pleased not God, and were contrary to all men, for wrath had come upon them to the uttermost,* 1 Thess. ii. 15, 16. The last account we have of him in his history is that the remaining Jews forced him to go down with them into Egypt; whereas the current tradition is, among Jews and Christians, that he suffered martyrdom. Hottinger, out of Elmakin, an Arabic historian, relates that, continuing to prophesy in Egypt against the Egyptians and other nations, he was stoned to death; and that long after, when Alexander entered Egypt, he took up the bones of Jeremiah where they were buried in obscurity, and carried them to Alexandria, and buried them there. The prophecies of this book which we have in the first nineteen chapters seem to be the heads of the sermons he preached in a way of general reproof for sin and denunciation of judgment; afterwards they are more particular and occasional, and mixed with the history of his day, but not placed in due order of time. With the threatenings are intermixed many gracious promises of mercy to the penitent, of the deliverance of the Jews out of their captivity, and some that have a plain reference to the kingdom of the Messiah. Among the Apocryphal writings an epistle is extant said to be written by Jeremiah to the captives in Babylon, warning them against the worship of idols, by exposing the vanity of idols and the folly of idolaters. It is in Baruch, *ch.* vi. But it is supposed not to be authentic; nor has it, I think, any thing like the life and spirit of Jeremiah's writings. It is also related concerning Jeremiah (2 Mac. ii. 4) that, when Jerusalem was destroyed by the Chaldeans, he, by

398

direction from God, took the ark and the altar of incense, and, carrying them to Mount Nebo lodged them in a hollow cave there and stopped the door; but some that followed him, and thought that they had marked the place, could not find it. He blamed them for seeking it, telling them that the place should be unknown till the time that God should gather his people together again. But I know not what credit is to be given to that story, though it is there said to be found in the records. We cannot but be concerned, in the reading of Jeremiah's prophecies, to find that they were so little regarded by the men of that generation; but let us make use of that as a reason why we should regard them the more; for they are written for our learning too, and for warning to us and to our land.

CHAP. I.

In this chapter we have, I. The general inscription or title of this book, with the time of the continuance of Jeremiah's public ministry, ver. 1—3. II. The call of Jeremiah to the prophetic office, his modest objection against it answered, and an ample commission given him for the execution of it, ver. 4—10. III. The visions of an almond-rod and a seething-pot, signifying the approaching ruin of Judah and Jerusalem by the Chaldeans, ver. 11—16. IV. Encouragement given to the prophet to go on undauntedly in his work, in an assurance of God's presence with him, ver. 17—19. Thus is he set to work by one that will be sure to bear him out.

THE words of Jeremiah the son of Hilkiah, of the priests that *were* in Anathoth in the land of Benjamin: 2 To whom the word of the LORD came in the days of Josiah the son of Amon king of Judah, in the thirteenth year of his reign. 3 It came also in the days of Jehoiakim the son of Josiah king of Judah, unto the end of the eleventh year of Zedekiah the son of Josiah king of Judah, unto the carrying away of Jerusalem captive in the fifth month.

We have here as much as it was thought fit we should know of the genealogy of this prophet and the chronology of this prophecy. 1. We are told what family the prophet was of. He was *the son of Hilkiah*, not that Hilkiah, it is supposed, who was high priest in Josiah's time (for then he would have been called so, and not, as here, one *of the priests that were in Anathoth*), but another of the same name. Jeremiah signifies one *raised up by the Lord*. It is said of Christ that he is a prophet whom the Lord our God *raised up unto us*, Deut. xviii. 15, 18. He was *of the priests*, and, as a priest, was authorized and appointed to teach the people; but to that authority and appointment God added the extraordinary commission of a prophet. Ezekiel also was a priest. Thus God would support the honour of the priesthood at a time when, by their sins and God's judgments upon them, it was sadly eclipsed. He was of the priests in Anathoth, a city of priests, which lay about three miles from Jerusalem. Abiathar had his country house there, 1 Kings ii. 26. 2. We have the general date of his prophecies, the knowledge of which is requisite to the understanding of them. (1.) He began to prophesy in the thirteenth year of Josiah's reign, *v.* 2. Josiah, in the twelfth year of his reign, began a work of reformation, applied himself with all sincerity to purge Judah and Jerusalem

from the *high places, and the groves, and the images*, 2 Chron. xxxiv. 3. And very seasonably then was this young prophet raised up to assist and encourage the young king in that good work. Then *the word of the Lord* came to him, not only a charge and commission to him to prophesy, but a revelation of the things themselves which he was to deliver. As it is an encouragement to ministers to be countenanced and protected by such pious magistrates as Josiah was, so it is a great help to magistrates, in any good work of reformation, to be advised and animated, and to have a great deal of their work done for them, by such faithful zealous ministers as Jeremiah was. Now, one would have expected when these two joined forces, such a prince, and such a prophet (as in a like case, Ezra v. 1, 2), and both young, such a complete reformation would be brought about and settled as would prevent the ruin of the church and state; but it proved quite otherwise. In the eighteenth year of Josiah we find there were a great many of the relics of idolatry that were not purged out; for what can the best princes and prophets do to prevent the ruin of a people that hate to be reformed? And therefore, though it was a time of reformation, Jeremiah continued to foretel the destroying judgments that were coming upon them; for there is no symptom more threatening to any people than fruitless attempts of reformation. Josiah and Jeremiah would have healed them, but they would not be healed. (2.) He continued to prophesy through the reigns of Jehoiakim and Zedekiah, each of whom reigned eleven years. He prophesied *to the carrying away of Jerusalem captive (v. 3)*, that great event which he had so often prophesied of. He continued to prophesy after that, *ch.* xl. 1. But the computation here is made to end with that because it was the accomplishment of many of his predictions; and from the thirteenth year of Josiah to the captivity was just forty years. Dr. Lightfoot observes that as Moses was so long with the people, a teacher in the wilderness, till they entered into their own land, Jeremiah was so long in their own land a teacher, before they went into the wilderness of the heathen: and he thinks that *therefore* a special mark is set upon the last forty years of the iniquity of Judah, which Ezekiel bore forty days, a day for a year, because during all that time they had Jeremiah prophesying among them, which was a great aggravation of their impenitency. God, in this prophet, suffered their manners, their ill manners, forty years, and at length swore in his wrath that they should not continue in his rest.

4 Then the word of the LORD came unto me, saying, 5 Before I formed thee in the belly I knew thee; and before thou camest forth out of the womb I sanctified thee, *and* I ordained thee a prophet unto the nations. 6 Then said I, Ah, Lord GOD! behold, I cannot speak: for I *am* a child. 7 But the LORD said unto me, Say not, I *am* a child: for thou shalt go to all that I shall send thee, and whatsoever I command thee thou shalt speak. 8 Be not afraid of their faces: for I *am* with thee to deliver thee, saith the LORD. 9 Then the LORD put forth his hand, and touched my mouth. And the LORD said unto me, Behold, I have put my words in thy mouth. 10 See, I have this day set thee over the nations and over the kingdoms, to root out, and to pull down, and to destroy, and to throw down, to build, and to plant.

Here is, I. Jeremiah's early designation to the work and office of a prophet, which God gives him notice of as a reason for his early application to that business (*v.* 4, 5): *The word of the Lord came to him*, with a satisfying assurance to himself that it was the word of the Lord and not a delusion; and God told him, 1. That he had *ordained him a prophet to the nations*, or *against the nations*, the nation of the Jews in the first place, who are now *reckoned among the nations* because they had learned their works and mingled with them in their idolatries, for otherwise they would not have been numbered with them, Num. xxiii. 9. Yet he was given to be a prophet, not to the Jews only, but to the neighbouring nations, to whom he was to *send yokes* (ch. xxvii. 2, 3) and whom he must make to *drink of the cup* of the Lord's anger, ch. xxv. 17. He is still in his writings a prophet to the nations (to our nation among the rest), to tell them what the national judgments are which may be expected for national sins. It would be well for the nations would they take Jeremiah for their prophet and attend to the warnings he gives them. 2. That before he was born, even in his eternal counsel, he had designed him to be so. Let him know that he who gave him his commission is the same that gave him his being, that *formed him in the belly* and brought him *forth out of the womb*, that therefore he was his rightful owner and might employ him and make

use of him as he pleased, and that this commission was given him in pursuance of the purpose God had purposed in himself concerning him, before he was born: "*I knew thee, and I sanctified thee*," that is, "I determined that thou shouldst be a prophet and set thee apart for the office." Thus St. Paul says of himself that God had *separated him from his mother's womb* to be a Christian and an apostle, Gal. i. 15. Observe, (1.) The great Creator knows what use to make of every man before he makes him. He has *made all for himself*, and of the same lumps of clay designs *a vessel of honour or dishonour*, as he pleases, Rom. ix. 21. (2.) What God has designed men for he will call them to; for his purposes cannot be frustrated. Known unto God are all his own works beforehand, and his knowledge is infallible and his purpose unchangeable. (3.) There is a particular purpose and providence of God conversant about his prophets and ministers; they are by special counsel designed for their work, and what they are designed for they are fitted for: I that *knew thee, sanctified thee*. God destines them to it, and forms them for it, when he first forms the spirit of man within him. *Propheta nascitur, non fit—Original endowment, not education, makes a prophet.*

II. His modestly declining this honourable employment, *v.* 6. Though God had predestinated him to it, yet it was news to him, and a mighty surprise, to hear that he should be *a prophet to the nations.* We know not what God intends us for, but he knows. One would have thought he would catch at it as a piece of preferment, for so it was; but he objects against it, as a work for which he is unqualified: "*Ah, Lord God! behold, I cannot speak* to great men and multitudes, as prophets must; I cannot speak finely nor fluently, cannot word things well, as a message from God should be worded; I cannot speak with any authority, nor can expect to be heeded, *for I am a child* and my youth will be despised." Note, It becomes us, when we have any service to do for God, to be afraid lest we mismanage it, and lest it suffer through our weakness and unfitness for it; it becomes us likewise to have low thoughts of ourselves and to be diffident of our own sufficiency. Those that are young should consider that they are so, should be afraid, as Elihu was, and not venture beyond their length.

III. The assurance God graciously gave him that he would stand by him and carry him on in his work.

1. Let him not object that he is a child; he shall be a prophet for all that (*v.* 7): "*Say not* any more, *I am a child.* It is true thou art; but," (1.) "Thou hast God's precept, and let not thy being young hinder thee from obeying it. Go to all *to whom I shall send thee and speak whatsoever I command thee.*" Note, Though a sense of our

own weakness and insufficiency should make us go humbly about our work, yet it should not make us draw back from it when God calls us to it. God was angry with Moses even for his modest excuses, Exod. iv. 14. (2.) "Thou hast God's presence, and let not thy being young discourage thee from depending upon it. Though thou art a child, thou shalt be *enabled to go to all to whom I shall send thee*, though they are ever so great and ever so many. And *whatsoever I command thee* thou shalt have judgment, memory, and language, wherewith to speak it as it should be spoken." Samuel delivered a message from God to Eli, when he was a little child. Note, God can, when he pleases, make children prophets, and *ordain strength out of the mouth of babes and sucklings.*

2. Let him not object that he shall meet with many enemies and much opposition; God will be his protector (*v.* 8): "*Be not afraid of their faces;* though they look big, and so think to outface thee and put thee out of countenance, yet *be not afraid to speak to them;* no, not to speak that to them which is most unpleasing. Thou speakest in the name of the King of kings, and by authority from him, and with that thou mayest *face them down.* Though they look angry, be not afraid of their displeasure nor disturbed with apprehensions of the consequences of it." Those that have messages to deliver from God must not be *afraid of the face of man,* Ezek. iii. 9. "And thou hast cause both to be bold and easy; for *I am with thee,* not only to assist thee in thy work, but to deliver thee out of the hands of the persecutors; and, *if God be for thee, who can be against thee?*" If God do not deliver his ministers from trouble, it is to the same effect if he support them under their trouble. Mr. Gataker well observes here, That earthly princes are not wont to go along with their ambassadors; but God goes along with those whom he sends, and is, by his powerful protection, at all times and in all places present with them; and with this they ought to animate themselves, Acts xviii. 10.

3. Let him not object that he cannot speak as becomes him—God will enable him to speak.

(1.) To speak intelligently, and as one that had acquaintance with God, *v.* 9. He having now a vision of the divine glory, the Lord *put forth his hand,* and by a sensible sign conferred upon him so much of the gift of the tongue as was necessary for him: *He touched his mouth,* and with that touch *opened his lips,* that his mouth should show forth God's praise, with that touch sweetly conveyed *his words into his mouth,* to be ready to him upon all occasions, so that he could never want words who was thus furnished by him that *made man's mouth.* God not only put knowledge into his head, but *words into his mouth;* for there are *words which the Holy Ghost teaches,* 1 Cor. ii. 13. It is fit God's message should be delivered in his

own words, that it may be delivered accurately. Ezek. iii. 4, *Speak with my words.* And those that faithfully do so shall not want instructions as the case requires; God will give them a mouth and wisdom *in that same hour,* Matt. x. 19.

(2.) To speak powerfully, and as one that had authority from God, *v.* 10. It is a strange commission that is here given him: *See, I have this day set thee over the nations and over the kingdoms.* This sounds very great, and yet Jeremiah is a poor despicable priest still; he is not set over the kingdoms as a prince to rule them by the sword, but as a prophet by the power of the word of God. Those that would hence prove the pope's supremacy over kings, and his authority to depose them and dispose of their kingdoms at his pleasure, must prove that he has the same extraordinary spirit of prophecy that Jeremiah had, else how can he have the power that Jeremiah had by virtue of that spirit? And yet the power that Jeremiah had (who, notwithstanding his power, lived in meanness and contempt, and under oppression) would not content these proud men. Jeremiah was *set over the nations,* the Jewish nation in the first place, and other nations, some great ones besides, against whom he prophesied; he was set over them, not to demand tribute from them nor to enrich himself with their spoils, but to *root out, and pull down, and destroy,* and yet withal *to build and plant.* [1.] He must attempt to reform the nations, to *root out, and pull down, and destroy* idolatry and other wickednesses among them, to extirpate those vicious habits and customs which had long taken root, to *throw down* the kingdom of sin, that religion and virtue might be *planted* and *built* among them. And, to the introducing and establishing of that which is good, it is necessary that that which is evil be removed. [2.] He must tell them that it would be well or ill with them according as they were, or were not, reformed. He must set before them *life and death, good and evil,* according to God's declaration of the method he takes with kingdoms and nations, *ch.* xviii. 7—10. He must assure those who persisted in their wickedness that they should be *rooted out and destroyed,* and those who repented that they should be *built and planted.* He was authorized to read the doom of nations, and God would *ratify it* and *fulfil it* (Isa. xliv. 26), would do it according to his word, and therefore is said to do it *by* his word. It is thus expressed partly to show how sure the word of prophecy is—it will as certainly be accomplished as if it were done already, and partly to put an honour upon the prophetic office and make it look truly great, that others may not despise the prophets nor they disparage themselves. And yet more honourable does the gospel ministry look, in that declarative power Christ gave his apostles to remit and *retain sin* (John xx. 23), *to bind and loose,* Matt. xviii. 18.

11 Moreover, the word of the LORD came unto me, saying, Jeremiah, what seest thou? And I said, I see a rod of an almond-tree. 12 Then said the LORD unto me, Thou hast well seen: for I will hasten my word to perform it. 13 And the word of the LORD came unto me the second time, saying, What seest thou? And I said, I see a seething-pot; and the face thereof *is* towards the north. 14 Then the LORD said unto me, Out of the north an evil shall break forth upon all the inhabitants of the land. 15 For, lo, I will call all the families of the kingdoms of the north, saith the LORD; and they shall come, and they shall set every one his throne at the entering of the gates of Jerusalem, and against all the walls thereof round about, and against all the cities of Judah. 16 And I will utter my judgments against them touching all their wickedness, who have forsaken me, and have burned incense unto other gods, and worshipped the works of their own hands. 17 Thou therefore gird up thy loins, and arise, and speak unto them all that I command thee: be not dismayed at their faces, lest I confound thee before them. 18 For, behold, I have made thee this day a defenced city, and an iron pillar, and brasen walls against the whole land, against the kings of Judah, against the princes thereof, against the priests thereof, and against the people of the land. 19 And they shall fight against thee; but they shall not prevail against thee; for I *am* with thee, saith the LORD, to deliver thee.

Here, I. God gives Jeremiah, in vision, a view of the principal errand he was to go upon, which was to foretel the destruction of Judah and Jerusalem by the Chaldeans, for their sins, especially their idolatry. This was at first represented to him in a way proper to make an impression upon him, that he might have it upon his heart in all his dealings with this people.

1. He intimates to him that the people were ripening apace for ruin and that ruin was hastening apace towards them. God, having answered his objection, that he was a child, goes on to initiate him in the prophetical learning and language; and, having

promised to enable him to speak intelligibly to the people, he here teaches him to understand what God says to him; for prophets must have eyes in their heads as well as tongues, must be seers as well as speakers. He therefore asks him, *"Jeremiah, what seest thou?* Look about thee, and observe now." And he was soon aware of what was presented to him: *"I see a rod,* denoting affliction and chastisement, a correcting rod hanging over us; and it is a *rod of an almond-tree,* which is one of the forwardest trees in the spring, is in the bud and blossom quickly, when other trees are scarcely broken out;" it flourishes, says Pliny, in the month of January, and by March has ripe fruits; hence it is called in the Hebrew, *Shakedh,* the *hasty tree.* Whether this rod that Jeremiah saw had already budded, as some think, or whether it was stripped and dry, as others think, and yet Jeremiah knew it to be of an almond-tree, as Aaron's rod was, is uncertain; but God explained it in the next words (*v.* 12): *Thou hast well seen.* God commended him that he was so observant, and so quick of apprehension, as to be aware, though it was the first vision he ever saw, that it was a *rod of an almond-tree,* that his mind was so composed as to be able to distinguish. Prophets have need of good eyes; and those that see well shall be commended, and not those only that speak well. *"Thou hast seen a hasty tree,* which signifies that *I will hasten my word to perform it."* Jeremiah shall prophesy that which he himself shall live to see accomplished. We have the explication of this, Ezek. vii. 10, 11, *" The rod hath blossomed, pride hath budded, violence has risen up into a rod of wickedness.* The measure of Jerusalem's iniquity fills very fast; and, as if their destruction slumbered too long, they waken it, they hasten it, and I will hasten to perform what I have spoken against them."

2. He intimates to him whence the intended ruin should arise. Jeremiah is a second time asked: *What seest thou?* and he sees *a seething-pot* upon the fire (*v.* 13), representing Jerusalem and Judah in great commotion, like boiling water, by reason of the descent which the Chaldean army made upon them; made *like a fiery oven* (Ps. xxi. 9), all in a heat, wasting away as boiling water does and sensibly evaporating and growing less and less, ready to boil over, to be thrown out of their own city and land, as out of the pan into the fire, from bad to worse. Some think that those scoffers referred to this who said (Ezek. xi. 3), *This city is the cauldron, and we are the flesh.* Now the mouth or face of the furnace or hearth, over which this pot boiled, was *towards the north,* for thence the fire and the fuel were to come that must *make the pot boil thus.* So the vision is explained (*v.* 14): *Out of the north an evil shall break forth,* or *shall be opened.* It had been long designed by the

justice of God, and long deserved by the sin of the people, and yet hitherto the divine patience had restrained it, and held it in, as it were; the enemies had intended it, and God had checked them; but now all restraints shall be taken off, and the *evil shall break forth;* the direful scene shall open, and the enemy shall come in like a flood. It shall be a universal calamity; it shall come *upon all the inhabitants of the land,* from the highest to the lowest, for they have all corrupted their way. Look for this storm to arise *out of the north, whence fair weather usually comes,* Job xxxvii. 22. When there was friendship between Hezekiah and the king of Babylon they promised themselves many advantages *out of the north;* but it proved quite otherwise: *out of the north* their trouble arose. Thence sometimes the fiercest tempests come whence we expected fair weather. This is further explained *v.* 15, where we may observe, (1.) The raising of the army that shall invade Judah and lay it waste: *I will call all the families of the kingdoms of the north, saith the Lord.* All the northern crowns shall unite under Nebuchadnezzar, and join with him in this expedition. They lie dispersed, but God, who has all men's hearts in his hand, will bring them together; they lie at a distance from Judah, but God, who directs all men's steps, will call them, and they shall come, though they be ever so far off. God's summons shall be obeyed; those whom he calls shall come. When he has work to do of any kind he will find instruments to do it, though he send to the utmost parts of the earth for them. And, that the armies brought into the field may be sufficiently numerous and strong, he will call not only the *kingdoms of the north, but all the families* of those kingdoms, into the service; not one able-bodied man shall be left behind. (2.) The advance of this army. The commanders of the troops of the several nations shall take their post in carrying on the siege of Jerusalem and the other cities of Judah. They shall set *every one his throne,* or seat. When a city is besieged we say, The enemy sits down before it. They shall encamp some at the *entering of the gates, others against the walls round about,* to cut off both the going out of the mouths and the coming in of the meat, and so to starve them.

3. He tells him plainly what was the procuring cause of all these judgments; it was the *sin of Jerusalem* and of the *cities of Judah* (*v.* 16): *I will pass sentence upon them* (so it may be read) or *give judgment against them* (this sentence, this judgment) *because of all their wickedness;* it is this that plucks up the flood-gates and lets in this inundation of calamities. They *have forsaken God* and revolted from their allegiance to him, and have *burnt incense to other gods,* new gods, strange gods, and all false gods, pretenders, usurpers, the creatures of their own

fancy, and *they have worshipped the works of their own hands.* Jeremiah was young, had looked but little abroad into the world, and perhaps did not know, nor could have believed, what abominable idolatries the children of his people were guilty of; but God tells him, that he might know what to level his reproofs against and what to ground his threatenings upon, and that he might himself be satisfied in the equity of the sentence which in God's name he was to pass upon them.

II. God excites and encourages Jeremiah to apply himself with all diligence and seriousness to his business. A great trust is committed to him. He is sent in God's name as a herald at arms, to proclaim war against his rebellious subjects; for God is pleased to give warning of his judgments beforehand, that sinners may be awakened to meet him by repentance, and so *turn away his wrath,* and that, if they do not, they may be left inexcusable. With this trust Jeremiah has a charge given him (*v.* 17): "*Thou, therefore, gird up thy loins;* free thyself from all those things that would unfit thee for or hinder thee in this service; buckle to it with readiness and resolution, and be not entangled with doubts about it. He must be quick: *Arise,* and lose no time. He must be busy: *Arise, and speak unto them* in season, out of season. He must be bold: *Be not dismayed at their faces,* as before, *v.* 8. In a word, he must be faithful; it is required of ambassadors that they be so.

1. In two things he must be faithful:—(1.) He must speak all that he is charged with: *Speak all that I command thee.* He must forget nothing as minute, or foreign, or not worth mentioning; every word of God is weighty. He must conceal nothing for fear of offending; he must alter nothing under pretence of making it more fashionable or more palatable, but, without addition or diminution, *declare the whole counsel of God.* (2.) He must speak to all that he is charged against; he must not whisper it in a corner to a few particular friends that will take it well, but he must appear *against the kings of Judah,* if they be wicked kings, and bear his testimony against the sins even *of the princes thereof;* for the greatest of men are not exempt from the judgments either of God's hand or of his mouth. Nay, he must not spare *the priests thereof;* though he himself was a priest, and was concerned to maintain the dignity of his order, yet he must not therefore flatter them in their sins. He must appear against the *people of the land,* though they were his own people, as far as they were against the Lord.

2. Two reasons are here given why he should do thus:—(1.) Because he had reason to fear the wrath of God if he should be false: "*Be not dismayed at their faces,* so as to desert thy office, or shrink from the duty of it, *lest I confound and dismay thee before them,* lest I give thee up to thy faint-

heartedness." Those that consult their own credit, ease, and safety, more than their work and duty, are justly left of God to themselves, and to bring upon themselves the shame of their own cowardliness. Nay, *lest I reckon with thee for thy faint-heartedness, and break thee to pieces;* so some read it. Therefore this prophet says (*ch.* xvii. 17), Lord, *be not thou a terror to me.* Note, The fear of God is the best antidote against the fear of man. Let us always be afraid of offending God, who after he has killed has power to cast into hell, and then we shall be in little danger of fearing the faces of men that can but kill the body, Luke xii. 4, 5. See Neh. iv. 14. It is better to have all the men in the world our enemies than God our enemy. (2.) Because he had no reason to fear the wrath of men if he were faithful; for the God whom he served would protect him, and bear him out, so that they should neither sink his spirits nor drive him off from his work, should neither stop his mouth nor take away his life, till he had finished his testimony, *v.* 18. This young stripling of a prophet is made by the power of God as an impregnable city, fortified with iron pillars and surrounded with walls of brass; he sallies out upon the enemy in reproofs and threatenings, and *keeps them in awe.* They set upon him on every side; the kings and princes batter him with their power, the priests thunder against him with their church-censures, and *the people of the land* shoot their arrows at him, even slanderous and bitter words; but he shall keep his ground and make his part good with them; he shall still be a curb upon them (*v.* 19): *They shall fight against thee, but they shall not prevail to destroy thee, for I am with thee to deliver thee* out of their hands; nor shall they prevail to defeat the word that God sends them by Jeremiah, nor to deliver themselves; it shall take hold of them, for God is against them to destroy them. Note, Those who are sure that they have God with them (as he is if they be with him) need not, ought not, to be afraid, whoever is against them.

CHAP. II.

It is probable that this chapter was Jeremiah's first sermon after his ordination; and a most lively pathetic sermon it is as any we have in all the books of the prophets. Let him not say, "I cannot speak, for I am a child;" for, God having touched his mouth and put his words into it, none can speak better. The scope of the chapter is to show God's people their transgressions, even the house of Jacob their sins; it is all by way of reproof and conviction, that they might be brought to repent of their sins and so prevent the ruin that was coming upon them. The charge drawn up against them is very high, the aggravations are black, the arguments used for their conviction very close and pressing, and the expostulations very pungent and affecting. The sin which they are most particularly charged with here is idolatry, forsaking the true God, their own God, for other false gods. Now they are told, I. That this was ungrateful to God, who had been so kind to them, ver. 1—8. II. That it was without precedent, that a nation should change their god, ver. 9—13. III. That hereby they had disparaged and ruined themselves, ver. 14—19. IV. That they had broken their covenants and degenerated from their good beginnings, ver. 20, 21. V. That their wickedness was too plain to be concealed and too bad to be excused, ver. 22, 23, 35. VI. That they persisted wilfully and obstinately in it, and were irreclaimable and indefatigable in their idolatries, ver. 24, 25, 33, 36. VII. That they shamed themselves by their idolatry and should shortly be made ashamed of it when they should find their idols

404

unable to help them, ver. 26—29, 37. VIII. That they had not been convinced and reformed by the rebukes of Providence they had been under, ver. 30. IX. That they had put a great contempt upon God, ver. 31, 32. X. That with their idolatries they had mixed the most unnatural murders, shedding the blood of the poor innocents, ver. 34. Those hearts were hard indeed that were untouched and unhumbled when their sins were thus set in order before them. O that by meditating on this chapter we might be brought to repent of our spiritual idolatries, giving that place in our souls to the world and the flesh which should have been reserved for God only!

MOREOVER the word of the Lord came to me, saying, 2 Go and cry in the ears of Jerusalem, saying, Thus saith the Lord; I remember thee, the kindness of thy youth, the love of thine espousals, when thou wentest after me in the wilderness, in a land *that was* not sown. 3 Israel *was* holiness unto the Lord, *and* the first-fruits of his increase: all that devour him shall offend; evil shall come upon them, saith the Lord. 4 Hear ye the word of the Lord, O house of Jacob, and all the families of the house of Israel: 5 Thus saith the Lord, What iniquity have your fathers found in me, that they are gone far from me, and have walked after vanity, and are become vain? 6 Neither said they, Where *is* the Lord that brought us up out of the land of Egypt, that led us through the wilderness, through a land of deserts and of pits, through a land of drought, and of the shadow of death, through a land that no man passed through, and where no man dwelt? 7 And I brought you into a plentiful country, to eat the fruit thereof and the goodness thereof; but when ye entered, ye defiled my land, and made mine heritage an abomination. 8 The priests said not, Where *is* the Lord? And they that handle the law knew me not: the pastors also transgressed against me, and the prophets prophesied by Baal, and walked after *things that* do not profit.

Here is, I. A command given to Jeremiah to go and carry a message from God to the inhabitants of Jerusalem. He was charged in general (*ch.* i. 17) to go and *speak to them;* here he is particularly charged to go and speak *this* to them. Note, It is good for ministers by faith and prayer to take out a fresh commission when they address themselves solemnly to any part of their work. Let a minister carefully compare what he has to deliver with the word of God, and see that it agrees with it, that he may be able to say, not only, *The Lord sent me,* but, He sent me to *speak this.* He must go from Ana-thoth, where he lived in a pleasant retire-ment, spending his time (it is likely) among a few friends and in the study of the law, and must make his appearance at Jerusalem, that noisy tumultuous city, and *cry in their ears,* as a man in earnest and that would be heard : " Cry aloud, that all may hear, and none may plead ignorance. Go close to them, and *cry in the ears* of those that have stopped their ears."

II. The message he was commanded to deliver. He must upbraid them with their horrid ingratitude in forsaking a God who had been of old so kind to them, that this might either make them ashamed and bring them to repentance, or might justify God in turning his hand against them.

1. God here puts them in mind of the favours he had of old bestowed upon them, when they were first formed into a people (*v.* 2): "*I remember for thy sake,* and I would have thee to remember it, and improve the remembrance of it for thy good; I cannot forget *the kindness of thy youth and the love of thy espousals.*"

(1.) This may be understood of the kind-ness they had for God; it was not such in-deed as they had any reason to boast of, or to plead with God for favour to be shown them (for many of them were very unkind and provoking, and, when they did return and enquire early after God, they did but flatter him), yet God is pleased to mention it, and plead it with them; for, though it was but little love that they showed him, he took it kindly. When *they believed the Lord and his servant Moses,* when they *sang God's praise at the Red Sea,* when at the foot of Mount Sinai they promised, *All that the Lord shall say unto us we will do and will be obedient,* then was the *kindness of their youth and the love of their espousals.* When they seemed so forward for God he said, *Surely they are my people,* and will be faithful to me, *children that will not lie.* Note, Those that begin well and promise fair, but do not perform and persevere, will justly be up-braided with their hopeful and promising beginnings. God remembers the *kindness of our youth and the love of our espousals,* the zeal we then seemed to have for him and the affection wherewith we made our covenants with him, the buds and blossoms that never came to perfection ; and it is good for us to remember them, that we may remember whence we have fallen, and return to our first love, Rev. ii. 4, 5 ; Gal. iv. 15. In two things appeared the *kindness of their youth :* —[1.] That they followed the direction of the pillar of cloud and fire in the wilderness; and though sometimes they spoke of return-ing into Egypt, or pushing forward into Canaan, yet they did neither, but for forty years together *went after God in the wilder-ness,* and trusted him to provide for them, though it was *a land that was not sown.*

This God took kindly, and took notice of it to their praise long after, that, though much was amiss among them, yet they never for-sook the guidance they were under. Thus, though Christ often chid his disciples, yet he commended them, at parting, for con-tinuing with him, Luke xxii. 28. It must be the strong affection of the youth, and the espousals, that will carry us on to follow God in a wilderness, with an implicit faith and an entire resignation ; and it is a pity that those who have so followed him should ever leave him. [2.] That they entertained divine institutions, set up the tabernacle among them, and attended the service of it. Israel *was then holiness to the Lord ;* they joined themselves to him in covenant as a peculiar people. Thus they began in the spirit, and God puts them in mind of it, that they might be ashamed of ending *in the flesh.*

(2.) Or it may be understood of God's kindness to them; of that he afterwards speaks largely. *When Israel was a child, then I loved him,* Hos. xi. 1. He then espoused that people to himself with all the affection with which a *young man marries a virgin* (Isaiah lxii. 5), for the time was *a time of love,* Ezek. xvi. 8. [1.] God appro-priated them to himself. Though they were a sinful people, yet, by virtue of the cove-nant made with them and the church set up among them, they were *holiness to the Lord,* dedicated to his honour and taken under his special tuition ; they were the *first fruits of his increase,* the first constituted church he had in the world ; they were the first-fruits, but the full harvest was to be gathered from among the Gentiles. The *first-fruits of the increase* were God's part of it, were offered to him, and he was honoured with them ; so were the people of the Jews; what little tri-bute, rent, and homage, God had from the world, he had it chiefly from them ; and it was their honour to be thus set apart for God. This honour have all the saints ; they are the *first-fruits of his creatures,* Jam. i. 18. [2.] Having espoused them, he espoused their cause, and became an *enemy to their enemies,* Exod. xxiii. 22. Being the *first-fruits of his increase, all that devoured him* (so it should be read) *did offend ;* they tres-passed, they contracted guilt, and evil befel them, as those were reckoned *offenders* that *devoured the first-fruits,* or any thing else that was *holy to the Lord,* that embezzled them, or converted them to their own use, Lev. v. 15. Whoever offered any injury to the people of God did so at their peril ; their God was ready to avenge their quarrel, and said to the proudest of kings, *Touch not my anointed,* Ps. cv. 14, 15 ; Exod. xvii. 14. He had in a special manner a controversy with those that attempted to debauch them and draw them off from being *holiness to the Lord ;* witness his *quarrel with the Midianites about the matter of Peor,* Num. xxv. 17, 18.

[3.] He *brought them out of Egypt* with a high hand and great terror (Deut. iv. 34), and yet with a kind hand and great tenderness led them through a vast howling wilderness (*v.* 6), *a land of deserts and pits,* or of *graves, terram sepulchralem—a sepulchral land,* where there was ground, not to feed them, but to bury them, where there was no good to be expected, for it was a *land of drought,* but all manner of evil to be feared, for it was *the shadow of death.* In that darksome valley they walked forty years; but *God was with them; his rod,* in Moses's hand, *and his staff, comforted them,* and even there God *prepared a table for them* (Ps. xxiii. 4, 5), gave them bread out of the clouds and drink out of the rocks. It was a land abandoned by all mankind, as yielding neither road nor rest. It was no thoroughfare, for *no man passed through it*—no settlement, for *no man dwelt there.* For God will teach his people to tread untrodden paths, to dwell alone, and to be singular. The difficulties of the journey are thus insisted on, to magnify the power and goodness of God in bringing them, through all, safely to their journey's end at last. All God's spiritual Israel must own their obligations to him for a safe conduct through the wilderness of this world, no less dangerous to the soul than that was to the body. [4.] At length he settled them in Canaan (*v.* 7): *I brought you into a plentiful country,* which would be the more acceptable after they had been for so many years in *a land of drought.* They did *eat the fruit thereof* and the *goodness thereof,* and were allowed so to do. I brought you *into a land of Carmel* (so the word is); Carmel was a place of extraordinary fruitfulness, and Canaan was as one great fruitful field, Deut. viii. 7. [5.] God gave them the means of knowledge and grace, and communion with him; this is implied, *v.* 8. They had priests that *handled the law,* read it, and expounded it to them; that was part of their business, Deut. xxxiii. 8. They had pastors, to guide them and take care of their affairs, magistrates and judges; they had prophets to consult God for them and to make known his mind to them.

2. He upbraids them with their horrid ingratitude, and the ill returns they had made him for these favours; let them all come and answer to this charge (*v.* 4); it is exhibited in the name of God against *all the families of the house of* Israel, for they can none of them plead, *Not guilty.* (1.) He challenges them to produce any instance of his being unjust and unkind to them. Though he had conferred favours upon them in some things, yet, if in other things he had dealt hardly with them, they would not have been altogether without excuse. He therefore puts it fairly to them to show cause for their deserting him (*v.* 5): "*What iniquity have your fathers found in me,* or you either? Have you, upon trial, found God a hard

master? Have his commands put any hardship upon you or obliged you to any thing unfit, unfair, or unbecoming you? Have his promises put any cheats upon you, or raised your expectations of things which you were afterwards disappointed of? You that have renounced your covenant with God, can you say that it was a hard bargain and that which you could not live upon? You that have forsaken the ordinances of God, can you say that it was because they were a wearisome service, or work that there was nothing to be got by? No; the disappointments you have met with were owing to yourselves, not to God. The yoke of his commandments is easy, and in the *keeping of them there is great reward.*" Note, Those that forsake God cannot say that he has ever given them any provocation to do so: for this we may safely appeal to the consciences of sinners; the slothful servant that offered such a plea as this had it overruled *out of his own mouth,* Luke xix. 22. Though he afflicts us, we cannot say that there is iniquity in him; he does us no wrong. The ways of the Lord are undoubtedly equal; all the iniquity is in our ways. (2.) He charges them with being very unjust and unkind to him notwithstanding. [1.] They had quitted his service: "*They have gone from me,* nay, they have gone *far from me.*" They studied how to estrange themselves from God and their duty, and got as far as they could out of the reach of his commandments and their own convictions. Those that have deserted religion commonly set themselves at a greater distance from it, and in a greater opposition to it, than those that never knew it. [2.] They had quitted it for the service of idols, which was so much the greater reproach to God and his service; they went from him, not to better themselves, but to cheat themselves: *They have walked after vanity,* that is, idolatry; for an idol is a vain thing; it is *nothing in the world,* 1 Cor. viii. 4; Deut. xxxii. 21; Jer. xiv. 22. Idolatrous worships are vanities, Acts xiv. 15. Idolaters are vain, for those that make idols *are like unto them* (Ps. cxv. 8), as much stocks and stones as the images they worship, and good for as little. [3.] They had with idolatry introduced all manner of wickedness. When they entered into the good land which God gave them they defiled it (*v.* 7), by defiling themselves and disfitting themselves for the service of God. It was God's land; they were but tenants at will, sojourners in it, Lev. xxv. 23. It was his heritage, for it was a holy land, Immanuel's land; but they *made it an abomination,* even to God himself, who was wroth, and greatly abhorred Israel. [4.] Having forsaken God, though they soon found that they had changed for the worse, yet they had no thoughts of returning to him again, nor took any steps towards it. Neither the people nor the priests made any enquiry after him, took any thought about their duty to him, nor expressed any desire to recover his favour. *First,* The people said not, *Where is the Lord? v.* 6. Though they were trained up in an observance of him as their God, and had been often told that he *brought them out of the land of Egypt,* to be a people peculiar to himself, yet they never asked after him nor desired the *knowledge of his ways. Secondly,* The priests said not, *Where is the Lord? v.* 8. Those whose office it was to attend immediately upon him were in no concern to acquaint themselves with him, or approve themselves to him. Those who should have instructed the people in the knowledge of God took no care to get the knowledge of him themselves. The scribes, who *handled the law,* did not know God nor his will, could not expound the scriptures at all, or not aright. The pastors, who should have kept the flock from transgressing, were themselves ringleaders in transgression: *They have transgressed against me.* The pretenders to prophecy prophesied by Baal, in his name, to his honour, being backed and supported by the wicked kings to confront the Lord's prophets. Baal's prophets joined with Baal's priests, and walked after the *things which do not profit,* that is, after the idols which can be no way helpful to their worshippers. See how the best characters are usurped, and the best offices liable to corruption; and wonder not at the sin and ruin of a people when the *blind* are *leaders of the blind.*

9 Wherefore I will yet plead with you, saith the LORD, and with your children's children will I plead. 10 For pass over the isles of Chittim, and see; and send unto Kedar, and consider diligently, and see if there be such a thing. 11 Hath a nation changed *their* gods, which *are* yet no gods? But my people have changed their glory for *that which* doth not profit. 12 Be astonished, O ye heavens, at this, and be horribly afraid, be ye very desolate, saith the LORD. 13 For my people have committed two evils; they have forsaken me the fountain of living waters, *and* hewed them out cisterns, broken cisterns, that can hold no water.

The prophet, having shown their base ingratitude in forsaking God, here shows their unparalleled fickleness and folly (*v.* 9): *I will yet plead with you.* Note, Before God punishes sinners he pleads with them, to bring them to repentance. Note, further, When much has been said of the evil of sin, still there is more to be said; when one article of the charge is made good, there is another to be urged; when we have said a great deal,

still *we have yet to speak on God's behalf,* Job xxxvi. 2. Those that deal with sinners, for their conviction, must urge a variety of arguments and follow their blow. God had before pleaded with their fathers, and asked why they *walked after vanity* and became vain, *v.* 5. Now he pleads with those who persisted in that *vain conversation received by tradition from their fathers,* and *with their children's children,* that is, with all that in every age tread in their steps. Let those that forsake God know that he is willing to argue the case fairly with them, that he may be *justified when he speaks.* He pleads that with us which we should plead with ourselves.

I. He shows that they acted contrary to the usage of all nations. Their neighbours were more firm and faithful to their false gods than they were to the true God. They were ambitious of being *like the nations,* and yet in this they were unlike them. He challenges them to produce an instance of any nation that had *changed their gods (v.* 10, 11) or were apt to change them. Let them survey either the old records or the present state of the isles of Chittim, Greece, and the European islands, the countries that were more polite and learned, and of Kedar, that lay south-east (as the other north-west from them), which were more rude and barbarous; and they should not find an instance of a nation that had *changed their gods,* though they had never done them any kindness, nor could do, for *they were no gods.* Such a veneration had they for their gods, so good an opinion of them, and such a respect for the choice their fathers had made, that though they were gods of wood and stone they would not change them for gods of silver and gold, no, not for the living and true God. *Shall we praise them for this? We praise them not.* But it may well be urged, to the reproach of Israel, that they, who were the only people that had no cause to change their God, were yet the only people that had changed him. Note, Men are with difficulty brought off from that religion which they have been brought up in, though ever so absurd and grossly false. The zeal and constancy of idolaters should shame Christians out of their coldness and inconstancy.

II. He shows that they acted contrary to the dictates of common sense, in that they not only changed (it may sometimes be our duty and wisdom to do so), but that they changed for the worse, and made a bad bargain for themselves. 1. They parted from a God who was their glory, who made them truly glorious and every way put honour upon them, one whom they might with a humble confidence glory in as theirs, who is himself a glorious God and the glory of those whose God he is; he was particularly the glory of his people Israel, for his glory had often appeared on their tabernacle. 2. They closed with gods that could do them no good, gods that *do not profit* their worshippers.

Idolaters change God's glory into shame (Rom. i. 23) and so they do their own; in dishonouring him, they disgrace and disparage themselves, and are enemies to their own interest. Note, Whatever those turn to who forsake God, it will never do them any good; it will flatter them and please them, but it *cannot profit them.* Heaven itself is here called upon to stand amazed at the sin and folly of these apostates from God (*v.* 12, 13): *Be astonished, O you heavens! at this.* The earth is so universally corrupt that it will take no notice of it; but let the heavens and heavenly bodies be astonished at it. Let the sun blush to see such ingratitude and be afraid to shine upon such ungrateful wretches. Those that forsook God worshipped *the host of heaven,* the sun, moon, and stars; but these, instead of being pleased with the adorations that were paid to them, *were astonished and horribly afraid;* and would rather have been *very desolate, utterly exhausted* (as the word is) and deprived of their light, than that it should have given occasion to any to worship them. Some refer it to the *angels of heaven;* if they rejoice at the return of souls to God, we may suppose that they are astonished and horribly afraid at the revolt of souls from him. The meaning is that the conduct of this people towards God was, (1.) Such as we may well be astonished and wonder at, that ever men, who pretend to reason, should do a thing so very absurd. (2.) Such as we ought to have a holy indignation at as impious, and a high affront to our Maker, whose honour every good man is jealous for. (3.) Such as we may tremble to think of the consequences of. What will be in the end hereof? Be horribly afraid to think of the wrath and curse which will be the portion of those who thus throw themselves out of God's grace and favour. Now what is it that is to be thought of with all this horror? It is this: "*My people,* whom I have taught and should have ruled, *have committed two* great evils, ingratitude and folly; they have acted contrary both to their duty and to their interest." [1.] They have *affronted their God,* by turning their back upon him, as if he were not worthy their notice: "*They have forsaken me, the fountain of living waters,* in whom they have an abundant and constant supply of all the comfort and relief they stand in need of, and have it freely." God is their *fountain of life,* Ps. xxxvi. 9. There is in him an all-sufficiency of grace and strength; all our springs are in him and our streams from him; to forsake him is, in effect, to deny this. He has been to us a bountiful benefactor, a *fountain of living waters,* over-flowing, ever-flowing, in the gifts of his favour; to forsake him is to refuse to acknowledge his kindness and to withhold that tribute of love and praise which his kindness calls for. [2.] They have cheated themselves. They forsook *their own mercies,* but it was for

lying vanities. They took a great deal of pains to *hew themselves out cisterns,* to dig pits or pools in the earth or rock which they would carry water to, or which should receive the rain; but they proved *broken cisterns,* false at the bottom, so that they could *hold no water.* When they came to quench their thirst there they found nothing but mud and mire, and the filthy sediments of a standing lake. Such idols were to their worshippers, and such a change did those experience who turned from God to them. If we make an idol of any creature—wealth, or pleasure, or honour,—if we place our happiness in it, and promise ourselves the comfort and satisfaction in it which are to be had in God only,—if we make it our joy and love, our hope and confidence, we shall find it a cistern, which we take a great deal of pains to hew out and fill, and at the best it will hold but a little water, and that dead and flat, and soon corrupting and becoming nauseous. Nay, it is a broken cistern, that cracks and cleaves in hot weather, so that the water is lost when we have most need of it, Job vi. 15. Let us therefore with purpose of heart cleave to the Lord only, for whither else *shall we go?* He has *the words of eternal life.*

14 *Is* Israel a servant? *Is* he a home-born *slave?* Why is he spoiled? 15 The young lions roared upon him, *and* yelled, and they made his land waste: his cities are burned without inhabitant. 16 Also the children of Noph and Tahapanes have broken the crown of thy head. 17 Hast thou not procured this unto thyself, in that thou hast forsaken the LORD thy God, when he led thee by the way? 18 And now what hast thou to do in the way of Egypt, to drink the waters of Sihor? Or what hast thou to do in the way of Assyria, to drink the waters of the river? 19 Thine own wickedness shall correct thee, and thy backslidings shall reprove thee: know therefore and see that *it is* an evil *thing* and bitter, that thou hast forsaken the LORD thy God, and that my fear *is* not in thee, saith the Lord GOD of hosts.

The prophet, further to evince the folly of their forsaking God, shows them what mischiefs they had already brought upon themselves by so doing; it had already cost them dear, for to this were owing all the calamities their country was now groaning under, which were but an earnest of more and greater if they repented not. See how they smarted for their folly.

I. Their neighbours, who were their professed enemies, prevailed against them, and this was owing to their sin. 1. They were enslaved and lost their liberty (*v.* 14): *Is Israel a servant?* No; *Israel is my son, my first-born,* Exod. iv. 22. They are children; they are heirs. Nay, their extraction is noble; they are the seed of Abraham, God's friend, and of Jacob his chosen. *Is he a home-born slave?* No; he is not the *son of the bond-woman,* but of the free. They were designed for dominion, not for servitude. Every thing in their constitution carried about it the marks of freedom and honour. *Why then is he spoiled* of his liberty? Why is he used as a servant, as a *home-born slave?* Why does he *make himself a slave* to his lusts, to his idols, to that which does not profit? *v.* 11. What a thing is this, that such a birthright should be sold for a mess of pottage, such a crown profaned and laid in the dust! Why is he made a slave to the oppressor? God provided that a Hebrew servant should be free the seventh year, and that their slaves should be *of the heathen,* not *of their brethren,* Lev. xxv. 44, 46. But, not-withstanding this, the princes made slaves of their subjects, and masters made slaves of their servants (*ch.* xxxiv. 11), and so made their country mean and miserable, which God had made happy and honourable. The neighbouring princes and powers broke in upon them, and made some of them slaves even in their own country, and perhaps sold others for slaves into foreign countries. And how came they thus to lose their liberties? For *their iniquities they sold themselves,* Isa. l. 1. We may apply this spiritually. Is the soul of man a *servant? Is it a home-born slave?* No, it is not. Why then is it spoiled? It is because it has sold its own liberty and enslaved itself to divers lusts and passions, which is a lamentation, and should be for a lamentation. 2. They were impoverished and had lost their wealth. God brought them into a plentiful country (*v.* 7), but all their neighbours made a prey of it (*v.* 15): *Young lions roar aloud over him and yell;* they are a continual terror to him. Some-times one potent enemy, and sometimes another, and sometimes many in confederacy, fall upon him, and triumph over him. They carry off the fruits of his land, and make that *waste,* and *burn his cities,* when first they have plundered them, so that they remain *without inhabitant,* either because there are no houses to dwell in or because those that should dwell in them are carried into cap-tivity. 3. They were abused, and insulted over, and beaten by every body (*v.* 16): " Even *the children of Noph and Tahapanes,* despicable people, not famed for military courage nor strength, *have broken the crown of thy head,* or fed upon it. In all their struggles with thee they have been too hard for thee, and thou hast always come off with a broken head. The principal part of thy country, that which lay next Jerusalem, has

been and is a prey to them." How calamitous the condition of Judah had been of late in the reign of Manasseh we find, 2 Chron. xxxiii. 11, and perhaps it had not now much recovered itself. 4. All this was owing to their sin (*v.* 17): *Hast thou not procured this unto thyself?* By their sinful confederacies with the nations, and especially their con-formity to them in their idolatrous customs and usages, they had made themselves very mean and contemptible, as all those do that have made a profession of religion and after-wards throw it off. Nothing now appeared of that which, by their constitution, made them both honourable and formidable, and therefore nobody either respected them or feared them. But this was not all; they had provoked God to give them up into the hands of their enemies, and to make them a scourge to them and give them success against them; and "thus thou hast *procured it to thyself, in that thou hast forsaken the Lord thy God,* re-volted from thy allegiance to him and so thrown thyself out of his protection; for pro-tection and allegiance go together." What-ever trouble we are in at any time we may thank ourselves for it; for we bring it upon our own head by our forsaking God: " *Thou hast forsaken thy God at the time that he was leading thee by the way*" (so it should be read); " then when he was leading thee on to a happy peace and settlement, and thou wast within a step of it, then thou forsookest him, and so didst put a bar in thy own door."

II. Their neighbours, that were their pre-tended friends, deceived them, distressed them, and helped them not, and this also was owing to their sin. 1. They did in vain seek to Egypt and Assyria for help (*v.* 18): " *What hast thou to do in the way of Egypt?* When thou art under apprehen-sions of danger thou art running to Egypt for help, Isa. xxx. 1, 2; xxxi. 1. Thou art for *drinking the waters of Sihor,*" that is, *Nilus.* " Thou reliest upon their multitude, and refreshest thyself with the fair promises they make thee. At other times thou art *in the way of Assyria,* sending or going with all speed to fetch recruits thence, and think-est to satisfy thyself with the *waters of the river Euphrates;* what *hast thou to do* there? What wilt thou get by applying to them? They shall *help in vain,* shall be broken reeds to thee, and what thou thoughtest would be to thee as a river will be but a broken cis-tern." 2. This also was because of their sin. The judgment shall unavoidably come upon them which their sin has deserved; and then to what purpose is it to call in help against it? *v.* 19. " *Thy own wickedness shall correct thee,* and then it is impossible for them to save thee; *know and see* therefore, upon the whole matter, *that it is an evil thing that thou hast forsaken God,* for it is that which makes thy enemies enemies indeed, and thy friends friends in vain." Observe here, (1.) The nature of sin; it is *forsaking the Lord* as our God; it is the soul's alienation from him and aversion to him. Cleaving to sin is leaving God. (2.) The cause of sin; it is because *his fear is not in us.* It is for want of a good principle in us, particularly for want of the fear of God; this is at the bottom of our apostasy from him; men forsake their duty to God because they stand in no awe of him nor have any dread of his displeasure. (3.) The malignity of sin; it is *an evil thing and a bitter.* Sin is an evil thing, only evil, an evil that has no good in it, an evil that is the root and cause of all other evil; it is evil indeed, for it is not only the greatest contrariety to the divine nature, but the greatest corruption of the human nature. It is *bitter;* a state of sin is the *gall of bitterness*, and every sinful way will be *bitterness in the latter end;* the wages of it is death, and death is bitter. (4.) The fatal consequences of sin; as it is in itself evil and bitter, so it has a direct tendency to make us miserable: *" Thy own wickedness shall correct thee, and thy backslidings shall reprove thee,* not only destroy and ruin thee hereafter, but correct and reprove thee now; they will certainly bring trouble upon thee; the punishment will so inevitably follow the sin that the sin shall itself be said to punish thee. Nay, the punishment, in its kind and circumstances, shall so directly answer to the sin, that thou mayest read the sin in the punishment; and the justice of the punishment shall be so plain that thou shalt not have a word to say for thyself; thy own wickedness shall convince thee and stop thy mouth for ever and thou shalt be forced to own that *the Lord is righteous."* (5.) The use and application of all this: *" Know therefore,* and see it, and repent of thy sin, that so the iniquity which is thy correction may not be thy ruin."

20 For of old time I have broken thy yoke, *and* burst thy bands; and thou saidst, I will not transgress; when upon every high hill and under every green tree thou wanderest, playing the harlot. 21 Yet I had planted thee a noble vine, wholly a right seed: how then art thou turned into the degenerate plant of a strange vine unto me? 22 For though thou wash thee with nitre, and take thee much soap, *yet* thine iniquity is marked before me, saith the Lord GOD. 23 How canst thou say, I am not polluted, I have not gone after Baalim? See thy way in the valley, know what thou hast done: *thou art* a swift dromedary traversing her ways; 24 A wild ass used to the wilderness, *that* snuffeth up the wind at her pleasure; in her

410

occasion who can turn her away? All they that seek her will not weary themselves; in her month they shall find her. 25 Withhold thy foot from being unshod, and thy throat from thirst: but thou saidst, There is no hope: no; for I have loved strangers, and after them will I go. 26 As the thief is ashamed when he is found, so is the house of Israel ashamed; they, their kings, their princes, and their priests, and their prophets, 27 Saying to a stock, Thou *art* my father; and to a stone, Thou hast brought me forth: for they have turned *their* back unto me, and not *their* face: but in the time of their trouble they will say, Arise, and save us. 28 But where *are* thy gods that thou hast made thee? Let them arise, if they can save thee in the time of thy trouble: for *according to* the number of thy cities are thy gods, O Judah.

In these verses the prophet goes on with his charge against this backsliding people. Observe here,

I. The sin itself that he charges them with —idolatry, that great provocation which they were so notoriously guilty of. 1. They frequented the places of idol-worship (*v.* 20): *" Upon every high hill and under every green tree,* in the high places and the groves, such as the heathen had a foolish fondness and veneration for, *thou wanderest,* first to one and then to another, like one unsettled, and still uneasy and unsatisfied; but in all *playing the harlot,"* worshipping false gods, which is spiritual whoredom, and was commonly accompanied with corporal whoredom too. Note, Those that leave God wander endlessly, and a vagrant lust is insatiable. 2. They made images for themselves, and gave divine honour to them (*v.* 26, 27); not only the common people, but even the kings and princes, who should have restrained the people from doing ill, and the priests and prophets, who should have taught them to do well, were themselves so wretchedly sottish and stupid, and under the power of such a strong delusion, as to *say to a stock,* "*Thou art my father* (that is, Thou art my god, the author of my being, to whom I owe duty and on whom I have a dependence)," and *to a stone,* to an idol made of stone, *" Thou hast* begotten me, or *brought me forth;* therefore protect me, provide for me, and bring me up." What greater affront could men put upon God, who is our Father that has made us? It was a downright disowning of their obligations to him. What greater affront could men put upon themselves and their own reason than to acknowledge that which is in itself absurd and impossible, and, by making stocks and stones their parents, to make themselves no better than stocks and stones? When these were first made the objects of worship they were supposed to be animated by some celestial power or spirit; but by degrees the thought of this was lost, and so vain did idolaters become *in their imagination*, even the princes and priests themselves, that the very idol, though made of wood and stone, was supposed to be their father, and adored accordingly. 3. They multiplied these dunghill deities endlessly (v. 28): *According to the number of thy cities are thy gods, O Judah!* When they had forsaken that God who is one, and all-sufficient for all, (1.) They were not satisfied with any gods they had, but still desired more, that idolatry being in this respect of the same nature with covetousness, which is spiritual idolatry (for the more men have the more they would have), which is a plain evidence that what men make an idol of they find to be insufficient and unsatisfying, and that it cannot *make the comers thereunto perfect.* (2.) They could not agree in the same god. Having left the centre of unity, they fell into endless discord; one city fancied one deity and another another, and each was anxious to have one of its own to be near them and to take special care of them. Thus did they in vain seek that in many gods which is to be found in one God only.

II. The proof of this. No witnesses need be called; it is proved by the notorious evidence of the facts. 1. They went about to deny it, and were ready to plead, *Not guilty.* They pretended that they would acquit themselves from this guilt, they *washed themselves with nitre*, and *took much soap*, offered many things in excuse and extenuation of it, v. 22. They pretended that they did not worship these as gods, but as demons, and mediators between the immortal God and mortal men, or that it was not divine honour that they gave them, but civil respect; thus they sought to evade the convictions of God's word and to screen themselves from the dread of his wrath. Nay, some of them had the impudence to deny the thing itself; they said, *I am not polluted, I have not gone after Baalim,* v. 23. Because it was done secretly, and industriously concealed (Ezek. viii. 12), they thought it could never be proved upon them, and they had impudence enough to deny it. In this, as in other things, their way was like that of *the adulterous woman, that says, I have done no wickedness*, Prov. xxx. 20. 2. Notwithstanding all their evasions, they are convicted of it and found guilty: "*How canst thou* deny the fact, and *say, I have not gone after Baalim?* How canst thou deny the fault, and say, *I am not polluted?*" The prophet speaks with wonder at their impudence: "How canst thou put on a face to say so, when it is certain?" (1.) "God's omniscience is a witness against thee: *Thy*

iniquity is marked before me, saith the Lord God; it is laid up and hidden, to be produced against thee in the day of judgment, *sealed up among his treasures,*" Deut. xxxii. 34; Job xxi. 19; Hos. xiii. 12. "It is *imprinted deeply* and *stained* before me;" so some read it. "Though thou endeavour to wash it out, as murderers to get the stain of the blood of the person slain out of their clothes, yet it will never be got out." God's eye is upon it, and we are sure that his judgment is according to truth. (2.) "Thy own conscience is a witness against thee. *See thy way in the valley*" (they had worshipped idols, not only on the high hills, but in the valleys, Isa. lvii. 5, 6), in the *valley over-against Beth-peor* (so some), where they worshipped Baal-peor (Deut. xxxiv. 6, Num. xxv. 3), as if the prophet looked as far back as the *iniquity of Peor;* but, if it mean any particular valley, surely it is the *valley of the son of Hinnom*, for that was the place where they sacrificed their children to Moloch and which therefore witnessed against them more than any other: "look into that valley, and thou canst not but *know what thou hast done.*"

III. The aggravations of this sin with which they are charged, which made it exceedingly sinful.

1. God had done great things for them, and yet they revolted from him and rebelled against him (v. 20): *Of old time I have broken thy yoke and burst thy bonds;* this refers to the bringing of them out of the *land of Egypt* and the *house of bondage*, which they would not remember (v. 6), but God did; for, when he told them that they should have no other gods before him, he prefixed this as a reason: *I am the Lord thy God that brought thee out of the land of Egypt!* These bonds of theirs which God had loosed should have bound them for ever to him; but they had ungratefully broken the bonds of duty to that God who had broken the bonds of their slavery.

2. They had promised fair, but had not made good their promise: "*Thou saidst, I will not transgress;* then, when the mercy of thy deliverance was fresh, thou wast so sensible of it that thou wast willing to lay thyself under the most sacred ties to continue faithful to thy God and never to forsake him." Then they said, *Nay, but we will serve the Lord,* Josh. xxiv. 21. How often have we said that we *would not transgress*, we would not offend any more, and yet we have *started aside, like a deceitful bow*, and repeated and multiplied our transgressions!

3. They had wretchedly degenerated from what they were when God first formed them into a people (v. 21). *I had planted thee a noble vine.* The constitution of their government both in church and state was excellent, their laws were righteous, and all the ordinances instructive and very significant; and a generation of good men there was among them when they first settled in Ca-

naan. *Israel served the Lord,* and kept close to him *all the days of Joshua, and the elders that out-lived Joshua,* Josh. xxiv. 31. They were then *wholly a right seed,* likely to replenish the vineyard they were planted in with choice vines. But it proved otherwise ; the very next generation *knew not the Lord, nor the works which he had done* (Judg. ii 10), and so they were worse and worse till they became *the degenerate plants of a strange vine.* They were now the reverse of what they were at first. Their constitution was quite broken, and there was nothing in them of that good which one might have expected from a people so happily formed, nothing of the purity and piety of their ancestors. *Their vine is as the vine of Sodom,* Deut. xxxii. 32. This may fitly be applied to the nature of man ; it was planted by its great author *a noble vine,* a *right seed* (God made man upright) ; but it is so universally corrupt that it has become the *degenerate plant of a strange vine,* that *bears gall and wormwood,* and it is so to God, it is highly distasteful and offensive to him.

4 They were violent and eager in the pursuit of their idolatries, doted on their idols, and were fond of new ones, and they would not be restrained from them either by the word of God or by his providence, so strong was the *impetus* with which they were carried out after this sin. They are here compared to a *swift dromedary traversing her ways,* a female of that species of creatures hunting about for a male (*v.* 23), and, to the same purport, *a wild ass used to the wilderness* (*v.* 24), not tamed by labour, and therefore very wanton, *snuffing up the wind at her pleasure* when she comes near the he-ass, and on such an *occasion who can turn her away?* Who can hinder her from that which she lusts after ? *Those that seek her* then *will not weary themselves for her,* for they know it is to no purpose ; but will have a little patience till she is big with young, till that month comes which is the last of *the months that she fulfils* (Job xxxix. 2), when she is heavy and unwieldy, and then *they shall find her,* and she cannot out-run them. Note, (1.) Eager lust is a brutish thing, and those that will not be turned away from the gratifying and indulging of it by reason, and conscience, and honour, are to be reckoned as brute-beasts and no better, such as were born, and still are, *like the wild ass's colt ;* let them not be looked upon as rational creatures. (2.) Idolatry is strangely intoxicating, and those that are addicted to it will with great difficulty be cured of it. That lust is as headstrong as any. (3.) There are some so violently set upon the prosecution of their lusts that it is to no purpose to attempt to give check to them : those that do so weary themselves in vain. *Ephraim is joined to idols ; let him alone.* (4.) The time will come when the most fierce will be tamed and the most wanton will be manageable ; when dis-

tress and anguish come upon them, then their ears will be open to discipline, that is the month in which you may find them, Ps. cxli. 5, 6.

5. They were obstinate in their sin, and, as they could not be restrained, so they would not be reformed, *v.* 25. Here is, (1.) Fair warning given them of the ruin that this wicked course of life would certainly bring them to at last, with a caution therefore not to persist in it, but to break off from it. He would certainly bring them into a miserable captivity, when their feet should be unshod, and they should be forced to travel barefoot, and when they would be denied fair water by their oppressors, so that their throat should be dried with thirst ; this will be in the end hereof. Those that affect strange gods, and strange ways of worship, will justly be made prisoners to a strange king in a strange land. "Take up in time therefore ; thy running after thy idols will run the *shoes off thy feet,* and thy panting after them will bring thy throat to thirst ; withhold therefore thy foot from these violent pursuits, and thy throat from these violent desires." One would think that it should effectually check us in the career of sin to consider what it will bring us to at last. (2.) Their rejecting this fair warning. They said to those that would have persuaded them to repent and reform, " *There is no hope ; no,* never expect to work upon us, or prevail with us to cast away our idols, for *we have loved strangers, and after them we will go ;* we are resolved we will, and therefore trouble not yourselves nor us any more with your admonitions ; it is to no purpose. There is no hope that we should ever break the corrupt habit and disposition we have got, and therefore we may as well yield to it as go about to get the mastery of it." Note, Their case is very miserable who have brought themselves to such a pass that their corruptions triumph over their convictions ; they know they should reform, but own they cannot, and therefore resolve they will not. But, as we must not despair of the mercy of God, but believe that sufficient for the pardon of our sins, though ever so heinous, if we repent and sue for that mercy ; so neither must we despair of the grace of God, but believe that able to subdue our corruptions, though ever so strong, if we pray for and improve that grace. A man must never say *There is no hope,* as long as he is on this side hell.

6. They had shamed themselves by their sin, in putting confidence in that which would certainly deceive them in the day of their distress, and putting him away that would have helped them, *v.* 26—28. *As the thief is ashamed* when, notwithstanding all his arts and tricks to conceal his theft, he is found, and brought to punishment, *so are the house of Israel ashamed,* not with a penitent shame for the sin they had been guilty of, but with a penal shame for the

disappointment they met with in that sin. They will be ashamed when they find, (1.) That they are forced to cry to the God whom they had put contempt upon. In their prosperity they had turned the back to God and not the face; they had slighted him, acted as if they had forgotten him, or did what they could to forget him, would not look towards him, but looked another way; they went from him as fast and as far as they could; but in the time of their trouble they will find no satisfaction but in applying to him; then *they will say, Arise, and save us.* Their fathers had many a time taken this shame to themselves (Judg. iii. 9, iv. 3, x. 10), yet they would not be persuaded to cleave to God, that they might come to him in their trouble with the more confidence. (2.) That they have no relief from the gods they have made their court to. They will be ashamed when they perceive that the gods they have made cannot serve them, and that the God who made them will not serve them. To bring them to this shame, if so be they might hereby be brought to repentance, they are here sent *to the gods whom they served,* Judg. x. 14. They cried to God, *Arise, and save us.* God says of the idols, *" Let them arise, and save thee,* for thou hast no reason to expect that I should. Let them arise, if they can, from the places where they are fixed; let them try whether they can save thee: but thou wilt be ashamed when thou findest that they can do thee no good, for, though thou hadst a god for every city, yet *thy cities are burnt without inhabitant,"* *v.* 15. Thus it is the folly of sinners to please themselves with that which will certainly be their grief, and pride themselves in that which will certainly be their shame.

29 Wherefore will ye plead with me? Ye all have transgressed against me, saith the LORD. 30 In vain have I smitten your children; they received no correction: your own sword hath devoured your prophets, like a destroying lion. 31 O generation, see ye the word of the LORD. Have I been a wilderness unto Israel? a land of darkness? Wherefore say my people, We are lords; we will come no more unto thee? 32 Can a maid forget her ornaments, *or* a bride her attire? Yet my people have forgotten me days without number. 33 Why trimmest thou thy way to seek love? Therefore hast thou also taught the wicked ones thy ways. 34 Also in thy skirts is found the blood of the souls of the poor innocents: I have not found it by secret search, but upon all these. 35 Yet thou sayest, Because I am innocent, surely his anger shall turn from me. Behold, I will plead with thee, because thou sayest, I have not sinned. 36 Why gaddest thou about so much to change thy way? Thou also shalt be ashamed of Egypt, as thou wast ashamed of Assyria. 37 Yea, thou shalt go forth from him, and thine hands upon thine head: for the LORD hath rejected thy confidences, and thou shalt not prosper in them.

The prophet here goes on in the same strain, aiming to bring a sinful people to repentance, that their destruction might be prevented.

I. He avers the truth of the charge. It was evident beyond contradiction; it was the greatest absurdity imaginable in them to think of denying it (*v.* 29): *" Wherefore will you plead with me,* and put me upon the proof of it, or wherefore will you go about to plead any thing in excuse of the crime or to obtain a mitigation of the sentence? Your plea will certainly be overruled, and judgment given against you: you know *you have all transgressed,* one as well as another; why then do you *quarrel with me* for contending with you?"

II. He heightens it from the consideration both of their incorrigibleness and of their ingratitude. 1. They had not been wrought upon by the judgments of God which they had been under (*v.* 30): *In vain have I smitten your children,* that is, the children or people of Judah. They had been under divine rebukes of many kinds. God therein designed to bring them to repentance; but it was *in vain.* They did not answer God's end in afflicting them; their consciences were not awakened, nor their hearts softened and humbled, nor were they driven to seek unto God; *they received no instruction* by the *correction,* were not made the better by it; and it is a great loss thus to lose an affliction. They *did not receive,* they did not submit to, or comply with, the correction, but their hearts fretted against the Lord, and so they were *smitten in vain.* Even *the children,* the *young people,* among them (so it may be taken), were *smitten in vain:* they were so soon prejudiced against repentance that they were as untractable as the old ones that had been long *accustomed to do evil.* 2. They had not been wrought upon by the word of God which he had sent them in the mouth of his servants the prophets; nay, they had killed the messengers for the sake of the message: *" Your own sword has devoured your prophets like a destroying lion;* you have put them to death for their faithfulness with as much rage and fury, and with as much greediness and pleasure, as a lion devours his prey. Their prophets, who were their greatest blessings, were treated by them as if they had been the plagues of their generation, and this was their measure-filling sin, 2 Chron. xxxvi. 16. They *killed their own prophets*, 1 Thess. ii. 15. 3. They had not been wrought upon by the favours God had bestowed upon them (*v.* 31): " *O generation !*" (he does not call them, as he might, *O faithless* and *perverse* generation ! *O generation of vipers !* but speaks gently, O you men of this generation !) " *see the word of the Lord*, do not only hear it, but consider it diligently, apply your minds closely to it." As we are bidden to *hear the rod* (Micah vi. 9), for that has its voice, so we are bidden to *see the word*, for that has its visions, its views. It intimates that what is here said is plain and undeniable ; you may see it to be very evident; it is written as with a sun-beam, so that he that runs may read it : *Have I been a wilderness to Israel, a land of darkness.* Note, None of those who have had any dealings with God ever had reason to complain of him as *a wilderness* or a *land of darkness.* He has blessed us with the fruits of the earth, and therefore we cannot say that he has been a wilderness to us, a dry and barren land, that (as Mr. Gataker expresses it) he has held us to *hard meat*, as cattle fed upon the common. No ; his sheep have been led into green pastures. He has also blessed us with the lights of heaven, and has not withheld them, so that we cannot say, He has been to us a land of darkness. He has caused his sun to shine, as well as his rain to fall, upon the evil and unthankful. Or the meaning is, in general, that the service of God has not been to any either an unpleasant or an unprofitable service. God sometimes has led his people *through a wilderness* and a *land of darkness*, but he himself was then to them all that which they needed ; he so fed them with manna, and led them by a pillar of fire, that it was to them a fruitful field and a land of light. The world is, to those who make it their home and their portion, a wilderness and a land of darkness, vanity and vexation of spirit; but those that dwell in God have the *lines fallen to them in pleasant places.* 4. Instead of being wrought upon by these, they had grown intolerably insolent and imperious. They say, *We are lords : we will come no more unto thee.* Now that they had become a potent kingdom, or thought themselves such, they set up for themselves, and shook off their dependence upon God. This is the language of presumptuous sinners, and it is not only very impious and profane, but very unreasonable and foolish. (1.) It is absurd for us who are subjects to say, *We are lords* (that is, *rulers*) and we will come no more to *God* to receive commands from him ; for, as he is King of old, so he is King for ever, and we can never pretend to be from under his authority. (2.) It is absurd for us who are

414

beggars to say, *We are lords*, that is, We are rich, and we will come no more to God, to receive favours from him, as if we could live without him and need not be beholden to him. God justly takes it ill when those to whom he has been a bountiful benefactor care not either for hearing from him or speaking to him.

III. He lays the blame of all their wickedness upon their forgetting God (*v.* 32) : *They have forgotten me ;* they have industriously banished the thoughts of God out of their minds, jostled those thoughts out with thoughts of their idols, and avoided all those things that would put them in mind of God. 1. Though they were his own people, in covenant with him and professing relation to him, and had the tokens of his presence in the midst of them and of his favour to them, yet they forgot him. 2. They had long neglected him, *days without number*, time out of mind, as we say. They had not for a great while entertained any serious thoughts of him ; so that they seem quite to have forgotten him, and resolved never to remember him again. How many days of our lives have passed without suitable remembrance of God ! Who can number those empty days ? 3. They had not had such a regard and affection to him as young ladies generally have to their fine clothes : *Can a maid forget her ornaments or a bride her attire ?* No ; their hearts are upon them ; they value them so much, and themselves upon them, that they are ever and anon thinking and speaking of them. When they are to appear in public they do not forget any of *their ornaments*, but put every one in its place, as they are described, Isa. iii. 18, &c. And *yet my people have forgotten me.* It is sad that any should be more in love with their fine clothes than with their God, and should rather leave their religion behind them, or part with that, than leave any of their ornaments behind them, or part with them. Is not God our ornament ? Is he not *a crown of glory* and a *diadem of beauty* to his people ? Did we look upon him to be so, and upon our religion as an *ornament of grace to our head* and *chains about our neck* (Prov. i. 9), we should be as mindful of them as ever any maid was of her ornaments, or a bride of her attire, we should be as careful to preserve them and as fond to appear in them.

IV. He shows them what a bad influence their sins had had upon others. The sins of God's professing people harden and encourage those about them in their evil ways, especially when they appear forward and ringleaders in sin (*v.* 33) : *Why trimmest thou thy way to seek love ?* There is an allusion here to the practice of lewd women who strive to recommend themselves by their ogling looks and gay dress, as Jezebel, who *painted her face and tired her head.* Thus had they courted their neighbours into sinful confederacies with them and communion in their idolatries, and had *taught the wicked ones their ways,* their ways of mixing God's institutions with their idolatrous customs and usages, which was a great profanation of that which was sacred and made the ways of their idolatry worse than that of others. Those have a great deal to answer for who, by their fellowship with the unfruitful works of darkness, make wicked ones more wicked than otherwise they would be.

V. He charges them with the guilt of murder added to the guilt of their idolatry (*v.* 34): *Also in thy skirts is found the blood of the souls,* the life-blood *of the poor innocents,* which cried to heaven, and for which God was now *making inquisition.* The reference is to the children that were offered in sacrifice to Moloch; or it may be taken more generally for all the *innocent blood* which Manasseh shed, and with which he had *filled Jerusalem* (2 Kings xxi. 16), the *righteous blood,* especially the blood of the prophets and others that witnessed against their impieties. This blood was found *not by secret search,* not *by digging* (so the word is), but *upon all these;* it was above ground. This intimates that the guilt of this kind which they had contracted was certain and evident, not doubtful or which would bear a dispute; and that it was avowed and barefaced, and which they had not so much sense either of shame or fear as to endeavour to conceal, which was a great aggravation of it.

VI. He overrules their plea of, *Not guilty.* Though this matter be so plain, yet thou sayest, *Because I am innocent, surely his anger shall turn from me;* and again, *Thou sayest, I have not sinned* (*v.* 35); therefore *I will plead with thee,* and will convince thee of thy mistake. Because they deny the charge, and stand upon their own justification, therefore God will join issue with them and plead with them, both by his word and by his rod. Those shall be made to know how much they deceive themselves, 1. Who say that they have not offended God, that they are innocent, though they have been guilty of the grossest enormities. 2. Who expect that God will be reconciled to them though they do not repent and reform. They own that they had been under the tokens of God's anger, but they think that it was causeless, and that they by pleading innocency had proved it to be so, and therefore they conclude that God will immediately let fall his action and *his anger shall be turned from them.* This is very provoking, and God will plead with them, and convince them that his anger is just, for they have sinned, and he will never cease his controversy till they, instead of justifying themselves thus, humble, and judge, and condemn themselves.

VII. He upbraids them with the shameful disappointments they met with, in making creatures their confidence, while they made

God their enemy, *v.* 36, 37. It was a piece of spiritual idolatry they were often guilty of that they trusted in *an arm of flesh* and their hearts therein *departed from the Lord.* Now here he shows them the folly of it. 1. They were restless, and unsatisfied in the choice of their confidences: " *Why gaddest thou about so much to change thy way?* Doubtless it is because thou meetest not with that in those thou didst confide in which thou promisedst thyself." Those that make God their hope, and walk in a continual dependence upon him, need not *gad about to change their way:* for their souls may return to him, and repose in him, as their rest: but those that trust in creatures will be perpetually uneasy, like Noah's dove, that found no rest for the sole of her foot. Every thing they trust to fails them, and then they think to change for the better, but they will be still disappointed. They first trusted to Assyria, and, when that proved a broken reed, they depended upon Egypt, and that proved no better. Creatures being vanity, they will be vexation of spirit to all those that put their confidence in them; they *gad about, seeking rest* and finding none. 2. They were quite disappointed in the confidences they made choice of; so the prophet tells them they should be: *Thou shalt be ashamed of Egypt,* which thou now trustest in, as formerly *thou wast of Assyria, who distressed them and helped them not,* 2 Chron. xxviii. 20. The Jews were a peculiar people in their profession of religion, and for that reason none of the neighbouring nations cared for them, nor could heartily love them; and yet the Jews were still courting them, and confiding in them, and were well enough served when deceived by them. See what will come of it (*v.* 37): *Thou shalt go forth from him,* thy ambassadors or envoys shall return from Egypt *re infectâ—disappointed,* and therefore *with their hands upon their heads,* lamenting the desperate condition of their people. Or, *Thou shalt go forth hence,* that is, into captivity in a strange land, *with thy hands upon thy head,* holding it because it aches *(ubi dolor ibi digitus— where the pain is the finger will be applied),* or as people ashamed, for Tamar, in the height of her confusion, *laid her hand on her head,* 2 Sam. xiii. 19. "And Egypt, that thou reliest on, shall not be able to prevent it nor to rescue thee out of captivity." Those that will not lay their hand on their heart in godly sorrow, which works life, shall be made to lay their hand on their head in the sorrow of the world, which works death. And no wonder that Egypt cannot help them, when God will not. If the Lord do not help thee, whence should I? The Egyptians are broken reeds, for *the Lord has rejected thy confidences;* he will not make use of them for thy relief, will neither so far honour them, nor so far give countenance to thy confidence in them, as to appoint them to be the instruments of any good to thee, and therefore *thou shalt not prosper in them ;* they shall not stand thee in any stead nor give thee any satisfaction. As *there is no counsel or wisdom* that can prevail against the Lord, so there is none that can prevail without him. Some read it, *The Lord has rejected thee for thy confidences;* because thou hast dealt so unfaithfully with him as to trust in his creatures, nay, in his enemies when thou shouldst have trusted in him only, he has abandoned thee to that destruction from which thou thoughtest thus to shelter thyself; and then thou *canst not prosper,* for none ever either hardened himself against God or estranged himself from God and prospered.

CHAP. III.

The foregoing chapter was wholly taken up with reproofs and threatenings against the people of God, for their apostasies from him ; but in this chapter gracious invitations and encouragements are given them to return and repent, notwithstanding the multitude and greatness of their provocations, which are here specified, to magnify the mercy of God, and to show that as sin abounded grace did much more abound. Here, I. It is further shown how bad they had been and how well they deserved to be quite abandoned, and yet how ready God was to receive them into his favour upon their repentance, ver. 1—5. II. The impenitence of Judah, and their persisting in sin, are aggravated from the judgments of God upon Israel, which they should have taken warning by, ver. 6—11. III. Great encouragements are given to these backsliders to return and repent, and promises made of great mercy which God had in store for them, and which he would prepare them for by bringing them home to himself, ver. 12—19. IV. The charge renewed against them for their apostasy from God, and the invitation repeated to return and repent, to which are here added the words that are put in their mouth, which they should make use of in their return to God, ver. 20—25.

THEY say, If a man put away his wife, and she go from him, and become another man's, shall he return unto her again? Shall not that land be greatly polluted? But thou hast played the harlot with many lovers; yet return again to me, saith the LORD. 2 Lift up thine eyes unto the high places, and see where thou hast not been lien with. In the ways hast thou sat for them, as the Arabian in the wilderness; and thou hast polluted the land with thy whoredoms and with thy wickedness. 3 Therefore the showers have been withholden, and there hath been no latter rain ; and thou hadst a whore's forehead, thou refusedst to be ashamed. 4 Wilt thou not from this time cry unto me, My Father, thou *art* the guide of my youth? 5 Will he reserve *his anger* for ever? Will he keep *it* to the end? Behold, thou hast spoken and done evil things as thou couldest.

These verses some make to belong to the sermon in the foregoing chapter, and they open a door of hope to those who receive the conviction of the reproofs we had there; God wounds that he may heal. Now observe here,

I. How basely this people had forsaken God and gone a whoring from him. The charge runs very high here. 1. They had multiplied their idols and their idolatries. To have admitted one strange God among them would have been bad enough, but they were insatiable in their lustings after false worships: *Thou hast played the harlot with many lovers, v.* 1. She had become a common prostitute to idols; not a foolish deity was set up in all the neighbourhood but the Jews would have it quickly. Where was a high place in the country but they had had an idol in it? *v.* 2. Note, In repentance it is good to make sorrowful reflections upon the particular acts of sin we have been guilty of, and the several places and companies where it has been committed, that we may give glory to God and take shame to ourselves by a particular confession of it. 2. They had sought opportunity for their idolatries, and had sent about to enquire for new gods : *In the* high-*ways hast thou sat for them,* as Tamar when she put on the disguise of *a harlot* (Gen. xxxviii. 14), and as the *foolish woman,* that sits to *call passengers, who go right on their way,* Prov. ix. 14, 15. *As the Arabian in the wilderness*—the *Arabian huckster* (so some), that courts customers, or waits for the merchants to get a good bargain and forestal the market—or the *Arabian thief* (so others), that watches for his prey ; so had they waited either to court new gods to come among them (the newer the better, and the more fond they were of them) or to court others to join with them in their idolatries. They were not only sinners, but Satans, not only traitors themselves, but tempters to others. 3. They had grown very impudent in sin. They not only polluted themselves, but *their land, with their whoredoms and with their wickedness (v.* 2) ; for it was universal and unpunished, and so became a national sin. And yet (*v.* 3), " *Thou hadst a whore's forehead,* a brazen face of thy own. *Thou refusedst to be ashamed ;* thou didst enough to shame thee for ever, and yet wouldst not take shame to thyself." Blushing is the colour of virtue, or at least a relic of it ; but those that are past shame (we say) are past hope. Those that have an adulterer's heart, if they indulge that, will come at length to have a whore's forehead, void of all shame and modesty. 4. They abounded in all manner of sin. They polluted the land not only with *their whoredoms* (that is, their idolatries), but with *their wickedness,* or malice (*v.* 2), sins against the second table : for how can we think that those will be true to their neighbour that are false to their God ? " Nay (*v.* 5), *thou hast spoken and done evil things as thou couldst,* and wouldst have spoken and done worse if thou hadst known how ; thy will was to do it, but thou lackedst opportunity." Note, Those are wicked indeed that sin to the utmost of their power, that never refuse to comply with a temptation because they should not, but because they cannot.

II. How gently God had corrected them for their sins. Instead of raining fire and brimstone upon them, because, like Sodom, they had *avowed their sin* and had gone after strange gods as Sodom after strange flesh, he only *withheld the showers from them*, and that only one part of the year: *There has been no latter rain*, which might serve as an intimation to them of their continual dependence upon God; when they had the former rain, that was no security to them for the latter, but they must still look up to God. But it had not this effect.

III. How justly God might have abandoned them utterly, and refused ever to receive them again, though they should return; this would have been but according to the known rule of divorces, *v.* 1. *They say* (it is an adjudged case, nay, it is a case in which the law is very express, and it is what every body knows and speaks of, Deut. xxiv. 4), that if a woman be once put away for whoredom, and be joined to *another man*, her first husband shall never, upon any pretence whatsoever, take her again to be his wife; such playing fast and loose with the marriage-bond would be a horrid profanation of that ordinance and would *greatly pollute that land.* Observe, What the law says in this case—*They say*, that is, every one will say, and subscribe to the equity of the law in it; for every man finds something in himself that forbids him to entertain one that is *another man's.* And in like manner they had reason to expect that God would refuse ever to take them to be his people again, who had not only been joined to one strange god, but had *played the harlot with many lovers.* If we had to do with a man like ourselves, after such provocations as we have been guilty of, he would be implacable, and we might have despaired of his being reconciled to us.

IV. How graciously he not only invites them, but directs them, to return to him.

1. He encourages them to hope that they shall find favour with him, upon their repentance : " Though thou hast been bad, *yet return again to me*," *v.* 1. This implies a promise that he will receive them : " Return, and thou shalt be welcome." God has not tied himself by the laws which he made for us, nor has he the peevish resentment that men have; he will be more kind to Israel, for the sake of his covenant with them, than ever any injured husband was to an adulterous wife; for in receiving penitents, as much as in any thing, he is *God and not man.*

2. He therefore kindly expects that they will repent and return to him, and he directs them what to say to him (*v.* 4): " *Wilt thou not from this time cry unto me ?* Wilt not thou, who hast been in such relation to me, and on whom I have laid such obligations,

wilt not thou cry to me ? Though thou hast gone a whoring from me, yet, when thou findest the folly of it, surely thou wilt think of returning to me, now at least, now at last, in this thy day. Wilt thou not *at this time*, nay, wilt thou not *from this time* and forward, *cry unto me ?* Whatever thou hast said or done hitherto, wilt thou not *from this time* apply to me ? *From this time* of conviction and correction, now that thou hast been made to see thy sins (*v.* 2) and to smart for them (*v.* 3), wilt thou not now forsake them and return to me, saying, *I will go and return to my first husband, for then it was better with me than now ?*" Hos. ii. 7. Or " *from this time* that thou hast had so kind an invitation to return, and assurance that thou shalt be well received : will not this grace of God overcome thee ? Now that pardon is proclaimed wilt thou not come in and take the benefit of it ? Surely thou wilt."

(1.) He expects that they will claim relation to God, as theirs : *Wilt thou not cry unto me, My Father, thou art the guide of my youth ?* [1.] They will surely come towards him as a father, to beg his pardon for their undutiful behaviour to him *(Father, I have sinned)* and will hope to find in him the tender compassions of a father towards a returning prodigal. They will come to him as a father, to whom they will make their complaints, and in whom they will put their confidence for relief and succour. They will now own him as their father, and themselves fatherless without him; and therefore, hoping to find mercy with him (as those penitents, Hos. xiv. 3), [2.] They will come to him as *the guide of their youth*, that is, as their husband, for so that relation is described, Mal. ii. 14. " Though thou hast gone after many lovers, surely thou wilt at length remember the love of thy espousals, and return to the *husband of thy youth.*" Or it may be taken more generally : " As *my Father*, thou *art the guide of my youth.*" Youth needs a guide. In our return to God we must thankfully remember that he *was the guide of our youth* in the way of comfort; and we must faithfully covenant that he shall be our guide henceforward in the way of duty, and that we will follow his guidance, and give up ourselves entirely to it, that in all doubtful cases we will be determined by our religion.

(2.) He expects that they will appeal to the mercy of God and crave the benefit of that mercy (*v.* 5), that they will reason thus with themselves for their encouragement to return to him : " *Will he reserve his anger for ever ?* Surely he will not, for he has proclaimed his name *gracious and merciful.*" Repenting sinners may encourage themselves with this, that, though God chide, he will not always chide, though he be angry, he will not keep his anger to the end, but, *though he cause grief, he will have compassion*, and may thus plead for reconciliation. Some understand this as describing their hypocrisy, and the impudence of it: "Though thou hast *a whore's forehead* (v. 3) and art still *doing evil as thou canst* (v. 5), yet art thou not ever and anon *crying to me, My Father?*" Even when they were most addicted to idols they pretended a regard to God and his service and kept up the forms of godliness and devotion. It is a shameful thing for men thus to call God father, and yet to do the *works of the devil* (as the Jews, John viii. 44), to call him the *guide of their youth,* and yet give up themselves to *walk after the flesh,* and to flatter themselves with the expectation that *his anger shall have an end,* while they are continually *treasuring up to themselves wrath against the day of wrath.*

6 The LORD said also unto me in the days of Josiah the king, Hast thou seen *that* which backsliding Israel hath done? She is gone up upon every high mountain, and under every green tree, and there hath played the harlot. 7 And I said after she had done all these *things,* Turn thou unto me. But she returned not. And her treacherous sister Judah saw *it.* 8 And I saw, when for all the causes whereby backsliding Israel committed adultery I had put her away, and given her a bill of divorce; yet her treacherous sister Judah feared not, but went and played the harlot also. 9 And it came to pass through the lightness of her whoredom, that she defiled the land, and committed adultery with stones and with stocks. 10 And yet for all this her treacherous sister Judah hath not turned unto me with her whole heart, but feignedly, saith the LORD. 11 And the LORD said unto me, The backsliding Israel hath justified herself more than treacherous Judah.

The date of this sermon must be observed, in order to the right understanding of it; it was *in the days of Josiah,* who set on foot a blessed work of reformation, in which he was hearty, but the people were not sincere in their compliance with it; to reprove them for that, and warn them of the consequences of their hypocrisy, is the scope of that which God here said to the prophet, and which he *delivered to them.* The case of the two kingdoms of Israel and Judah is here compared, the *ten tribes* that revolted from the throne of David and the temple of Jerusalem and the *two tribes* that adhered to both. The distinct history of those two kingdoms we have in the two books of the Kings, and here
418

we have an abstract of both, as far as relates to this matter.

I. Here is a short account of Israel, the ten tribes. Perhaps the prophet had been just reading the history of that kingdom when God came to him, and said, *Hast thou seen what backsliding Israel has done? v. 6.* For he could not see it otherwise than in history, they having been carried into captivity long before he was born. But what we read in the histories of scripture should instruct us and affect us, as if we ourselves had been eye-witnesses of it. She is called *backsliding Israel* because that kingdom was first founded in an apostasy from the divine institutions, both in church and state. Now he had seen concerning them, 1. That they were wretchedly addicted to idolatry. They had *played the harlot upon every high mountain and under every green tree* (v. 6), that is, they had worshipped other gods in their high places and groves; and no marvel, when from the first they had worshipped God by the images of the *golden calves* at Dan and Bethel. The way of idolatry is down-hill: those that are in love with images, and will have them, soon become in love with other gods, and will have them too; for how should those stick at the breach of the first commandment who make no conscience of the second? 2. That God by his prophets had invited and encouraged them to repent and reform (v. 7): "*After she had done all these things,* for which she might justly have been abandoned, yet *I* said unto her, *Turn thou unto me* and I will receive thee.*" Though they had forsaken both the house of David and the house of Aaron, who both had their authority *jure divino—from God,* without dispute, yet God sent his prophets among them, to call them *to return to him,* to the worship of him only, not insisting so much as one would have expected upon their return to the house of David, but pressing their return to the house of Aaron. We read not that Elijah, that great reformer, ever mentioned their return to the house of David, while he was anxious for their return to the faithful service of the true God according as they had it among them. It is serious piety that God stands upon more than even his own rituals. 3. That, notwithstanding this, they had persisted in their idolatries: *But she returned not,* and God *saw it ;* he took notice of it, and was much displeased with it, v. 7, 8. Note, God keeps account, whether we do or no, how often he has called to us to turn to him and we have refused. 4. That he had therefore cast them off, and given them up into the hands of their enemies (v. 8): *When I saw* (so it may be read) *that for all the actions wherein she had committed adultery I must dismiss her, I gave her a bill of divorce.* God divorced them when he threw them out of his protection and left them an easy prey to any that would lay hands on them, when he scattered all their synagogues and the schools of the prophets and excluded them from laying any further claim to the covenant made with their fathers. Note, Those will justly be divorced from God that join themselves to such as are rivals with him. For proof of this go and see what God did to Israel.

II. Let us now see what was the case of Judah, the kingdom of the two tribes. She is called *treacherous sister Judah*, a sister because descended from the same common stock, Abraham and Jacob; but, as Israel had the character of a *backslider*, so Judah is called *treacherous*, because, though she professed to keep close to God when Israel had backslidden (she adhered to the kings and priests that were of God's own appointing, and did not withdraw from her allegiance, so that it was expected she should deal faithfully), yet she proved treacherous, and false, and unfaithful to her professions and promises. Note, The treachery of those who pretend to cleave to God will be reckoned for, as well as the apostasy of those who openly revolt from him. Judah saw what Israel did, and what came of it, and should have taken warning. Israel's captivity was intended for Judah's admonition; but it had not the designed effect. Judah feared not, but thought herself safe because she had Levites to be her priests and sons of David to be her kings. Note, It is an evidence of great stupidity and security when we are not awakened to a holy fear by the judgments of God upon others. It is here charged on Judah, 1. That when they had a wicked king that debauched them they heartily concurred with him in his debaucheries. Judah was forward enough to *play the harlot*, to worship any idol that was introduced among them and to join in any idolatrous usage; so that *through the lightness* (or, as some read it, the *vileness* and *baseness*) *of her whoredom*, or (as the margin reads it) by the fame and *report* of her whoredom, her *notorious* whoredom, for which she had become infamous, she *defiled the land*, and made it an abomination to God; for she *committed adultery with stones and stocks*, with the basest idols, those made of *wood and stone*. In the reigns of Manasseh and Amon, when they were disposed to idolatry, the people were so too, and all the country was corrupted with it, and none feared the ruin which Israel by this means had brought upon themselves. 2. That when they had a good king, that reformed them, they did not heartily concur with him in the reformation. This was the present case. God tried whether they would be good in a good reign, but the evil disposition was still the same : *They returned not to me with their whole heart, but feignedly, v.* 10. Josiah went further in destroying idolatry than the best of his predecessors had done, and for his own part he *turned to* the Lord with all his heart and with all his soul ; so it is said of him, 2 Kings xxiii. 25. The people were forced to an external compliance with him, and joined with him in keeping a very solemn passover and in renewing their covenants with God (2 Chron. xxxiv. 32, xxxv. 17); but they were not sincere in it, nor were their *hearts right with God.* For this reason God at that very time said, *I will remove Judah out of my sight, as I removed Israel* (2 Kings xxiii. 27), because Judah was not removed from their sin by the sight of Israel's removal from their land. Hypocritical and ineffectual reformations bode ill to a people. We deceive ourselves if we think to deceive God by a feigned return to him. I know no religion without sincerity.

III. The case of these sister kingdoms is compared, and judgment given upon the comparison, that of the two Judah was the worse (v. 11) : *Israel has justified herself more than Judah*, that is, she is not so bad as Judah is. This comparative justification will stand Israel in little stead ; what will it avail us to say, *We are not so bad as others*, when yet we are not really good ourselves ? But it will serve as an aggravation of the sin of Judah, which was in two respects worse than that of Israel :—1. More was expected from Judah than from Israel ; so that Judah dealt treacherously, they vilified a more sacred profession, and falsified a more solemn promise, than Israel did. 2. Judah might have taken warning by the ruin of Israel for their idolatry, and would not. God's judgments upon others, if they be not means of our reformation, will help to aggravate our destruction. The prophet Ezekiel (*ch.* xxiii. 11) makes the same comparison between Jerusalem and Samaria that this prophet here makes between Judah and Israel, nay, and (Ezek. xvi. 48) between Jerusalem and Sodom, and Jerusalem is made the worst of the three.

12 Go, and proclaim these words toward the north, and say, Return, thou backsliding Israel, saith the LORD ; *and* I will not cause mine anger to fall upon you : for I am merciful, saith the LORD, *and* I will not keep *anger* for ever. 13 Only acknowledge thine iniquity, that thou hast transgressed against the LORD thy God, and hast scattered thy ways to the strangers under every green tree, and ye have not obeyed my voice, saith the LORD. 14 Turn, O backsliding children, saith the LORD; for I am married unto you : and I will take you one of a city, and two of a family, and I will bring you to Zion : 15 And I will give you pastors

according to mine heart, which shall feed you with knowledge and understanding. 16 And it shall come to pass, when ye be multiplied and increased in the land, in those days, saith the LORD, they shall say no more, The ark of the covenant of the LORD: neither shall it come to mind: neither shall they remember it; neither shall they visit *it;* neither shall *that* be done any more. 17 At that time they shall call Jerusalem the throne of the LORD; and all the nations shall be gathered unto it, to the name of the LORD, to Jerusalem: neither shall they walk any more after the imagination of their evil heart. 18 In those days the house of Judah shall walk with the house of Israel, and they shall come together out of the land of the north to the land that I have given for an inheritance unto your fathers. 19 But I said, How shall I put thee among the children, and give thee a pleasant land, a goodly heritage of the hosts of nations? And I said, Thou shalt call me, My father; and shalt not turn away from me.

Here is a great deal of gospel in these verses, both that which was always gospel, God's readiness to pardon sin and to receive and entertain returning repenting sinners, and those blessings which were in a special manner reserved for gospel times, the forming and founding of the gospel church by bringing into it the *children of God that were scattered abroad,* the superseding of the ceremonial law, and the uniting of Jews and Gentiles, typified by the uniting of Israel and Judah in their return out of captivity. The prophet is directed to *proclaim these words towards the north,* for they are a call to backsliding Israel, the ten tribes that were carried captive into Assyria, which lay north from Jerusalem. That way he must look, to show that God had not forgotten them, though their brethren had, and to upbraid the men of Judah with their obstinacy in refusing to answer the calls given them. One might as well call to those who lay many hundred miles off in the land of the north; they would as soon hear as these unbelieving and disobedient people; *backsliding Israel* will sooner accept of mercy, and have the benefit of it, than *treacherous Judah.* And perhaps the proclaiming of these words towards the north looks as far forward as the *preaching of repentance and remission of sins unto all nations, beginning at Jerusalem,* Luke xxiv. 47. A call to Israel in the land of the north is a call to others in

that land, even as many as belong to the election of grace. When it was suspected that Christ would *go to the dispersed* Jews among the Gentiles, it was concluded that he would *teach the Gentiles,* John vii. 35. So here.

I. Here is an invitation given to *backsliding Israel,* and in them to the backsliding Gentiles, to *return unto God,* the God from whom they had revolted (*v.* 12): *Return, thou backsliding Israel.* And again (*v.* 14): "*Turn, O backsliding children!* repent of your backslidings, return to your allegiance, come back to that good way which you have missed and out of which you have turned aside." Pursuant to this invitation, 1. They are encouraged to return. "*Repent, and be converted, and your sins shall be blotted out,* Acts iii. 19. You have incurred God's displeasure, but return to me, and *I will not cause my anger to fall upon you.*" God's anger is ready to fall upon sinners, as a lion falls on his prey, and there is none to deliver, as a mountain of lead falling on them, to sink them past recovery into the lowest hell. But if they repent it shall be turned away, Isa. xii. 1. *I will not keep my anger for ever,* but will be reconciled, *for I am merciful.* We that are sinful were for ever undone if God were not merciful; but the goodness of his nature encourages us to hope that, if we by repentance undo what we have done against him, he will by a pardon unsay what he has said against us. 2. They are directed how to return (*v.* 13): "*Only acknowledge thy iniquity,* own thyself in a fault and thereby take shame to thyself and give glory to God." *I will not keep my anger for ever* (that is a previous promise); you shall be delivered from that anger of God which is everlasting, from the wrath to come; but upon what terms? Very easy and reasonable ones. *Only acknowledge thy sins. If we confess our sins, he is faithful and just to forgive them.* This will aggravate the condemnation of sinners, that the terms of pardon and peace were brought so low, and yet they would not come up to them. *If the prophet had told thee to do some great thing wouldst thou not have done it?* How much more when he says, Only acknowledge thy iniquity? 2 Kings v. 13. In confessing sin, (1.) We must own the corruption of our nature: *Acknowledge thy iniquity,* the perverseness and irregularity of thy nature. (2.) We must own our actual sins: "*That thou hast transgressed against the Lord thy God,* hast affronted him and offended him." (3.) We must own the multitude of our transgressions: "*That thou hast scattered thy ways to the strangers,* run hither and thither in pursuit of thy idols, *under every green tree.* Wherever thou hast rambled thou hast left behind thee the marks of thy folly. (4.) We must aggravate our sin from the disobedience that there is in it to the divine law. The sinfulness of sin is the worst thing in it : "*You have not obeyed my voice ;* acknowledge that, and let that humble you more than any thing else."

II. Here are precious promises made to. these backsliding children, if they do return, which were in part fulfilled in the return of the Jews out of their captivity, many that belonged to the ten tribes having perhaps joined themselves to those of the two tribes, in the prospect of their deliverance, and returning with them ; but the prophecy is to have its full accomplishment in the gospel church, and the gathering together of *the children of God that were scattered abroad* to that : "Return, for, though you are backsliders, yet you are children ; nay, though a treacherous wife, yet a wife, for *I am married to you* (*v.* 14) and will not disown the relation. Thus God remembers his covenant with their fathers, that marriage covenant, and in consideration of that he *remembers their land*, Lev. xxvi. 42.

1. He promises to gather them together from all places whither they are dispersed and scattered abroad, John xi. 52, *I will take you, one of a city, and two of a family*, or clan ; *and I will bring you to Zion, v.* 14. All those that by repentance return to their duty shall return to their former comfort. Observe, (1.) God will graciously receive those that return to him, nay, it is he that by his distinguishing grace takes them out from among the rest that persist in their backslidings ; if he had left them, they would have been undone. (2.) Of the many that have backslidden from God there are but few, very few in comparison, that return to him, like the gleanings of the vintage— *one of a city and two of a country ;* Christ's flock is a little flock, and *few there are that find the strait gate.* (3.) Of those few, though dispersed, yet not one shall be lost. Though there be but *one in a city,* God will find out that one ; he shall not be overlooked in a crowd, but shall be brought safely to Zion, safely to heaven. The scattered Jews shall be brought to Jerusalem, and those of the ten tribes shall be as welcome there as those of the two. God's chosen, scattered all the world over, shall be brought to *the gospel church,* that Mount Zion, the heavenly Jerusalem, that holy hill on which Christ reigns.

2. He promises to set those over them that shall be every way blessings to them (*v.* 15) : *I will give you pastors after my heart,* alluding to the character given of David when God pitched upon him to be king. 1 Sam. xiii. 14, *The Lord hath sought him a man after his own heart.* Observe, (1.) When a church is gathered it must be governed. "*I will bring them to Zion,* not to live as they list, but to be under discipline, not as wild beasts, that range at pleasure, but as sheep that are under the direction of a shepherd. *I will give them pastors,* that is, both magistrates and ministers ; both are God's ordinance for the support of his kingdom.

(2.) It is well with a people when their pastors are *after God's own heart,* such as they should be, such as we would have them be, who shall make his will their rule in all their administrations, and such as endeavour in some measure to conform to his example, who rule for him, and, as they are capable, rule like him. (3.) Those are pastors after God's own heart who make it their business to feed the flock, not to *feed themselves and fleece the flocks,* but to do all they can for the good of those that are under their charge, who *feed them with wisdom and understanding* (that is, wisely and understandingly), as David fed them, in the *integrity of his heart* and by the *skilfulness of his hand,* Ps. lxxviii. 72. Those who are not only pastors, but teachers, must feed them with the word of God, which is wisdom and understanding, which is able to make us wise to salvation.

3. He promises that there shall be no more occasion for the *ark of the covenant,* which had been so much the glory of the tabernacle first and afterwards of the temple, and was the token of God's presence with them ; that shall be set aside, and there shall be no more enquiry after, nor enquiring of, it (*v.* 16) : *When you shall be multiplied and increased in the land,* when the kingdom of the Messiah shall be set up, which by the accession of the Gentiles will bring in to the church a vast increase (and the days of the Messiah the Jewish masters themselves acknowledge to be here intended), then *they shall say no more, The ark of the covenant of the Lord,* they shall have it no more among them to value, or value themselves upon, because they shall have a pure spiritual way of worship set up, in which there shall be no occasion for any of those external ordinances ; with the *ark of the covenant* the whole ceremonial law shall be set aside, and all the institutions of it, for Christ, the truth of all those types, exhibited to us in the word and sacraments of the New Testament, will be to us instead of all. It is very likely (whatever the Jews suggest to the contrary) that *the ark of the covenant* was in the second temple, being restored by Cyrus with the other *vessels of the house of the Lord,* Ezra i. 7. But in the gospel temple Christ *is the ark ;* he is the propitiatory, or mercy-seat ; and it is the spiritual presence of God in his ordinances that we are now to expect. Many expressions are here used concerning the setting aside of the ark, that it shall not *come to mind,* that they *shall not remember it,* that they shall *not visit it,* that none of these things shall be *any more done ;* for the *true worshippers shall worship the Father in spirit and in truth,* John iv. 24. But this variety of expressions is used to show that the ceremonies of the law of Moses should be totally and finally abolished, never to be used any more, but that it would be with difficulty that those who had been so long wedded to them should be weaned from them ;

421

and that they would not quite let them go till their holy city and holy house should both be levelled with the ground.

4. He promises that the gospel church, here called *Jerusalem*, shall become eminent and conspicuous, *v.* 17. Two things shall make it famous:—(1.) God's special residence and dominion in it. It shall be called, *The throne of the Lord*—the throne of *his glory*, for that shines forth in the church—the throne of *his government*, for that also is erected there; there he rules his willing people by his word and Spirit, and brings every thought into obedience to himself. As the gospel got ground this *throne of the Lord* was set up even where *Satan's seat* had been. It is especially the throne of *his grace;* for those that by faith come to this Jerusalem come to *God the judge of all*, and to *Jesus the mediator of the new covenant,* Heb. xii. 22—24. (2.) The accession of the Gentiles to it. *All the nations shall be* discipled, and so *gathered* to the church, and shall become subjects to that *throne of the Lord* which is there set up, and devoted to the honour of that *name of the Lord* which is there both manifested and called upon.

5. He promises that there shall be a wonderful reformation wrought in those that are gathered to the church : *They shall not walk any more after the imagination of their evil hearts.* They shall not live as they list, but live by rules, not do according to their own corrupt appetites, but according to the will of God. See what leads in sin—*the imagination of our own evil hearts;* and what sin is—it is *walking after* that imagination, being governed by fancy and humour; and what converting grace does—it takes us off from walking after *our own inventions* and brings us to be governed by religion and right reason.

6. That Judah and Israel shall be happily united in one body, *v.* 18. They were so in their return out of captivity and their settlement again in Canaan : *The house of Judah shall walk with the house of Israel,* as being perfectly agreed, and become *one stick in the hand of the Lord,* as Ezekiel also foretold, *ch.* xxxvii. 16, 17. Both Assyria and Chaldea fell into the hands of Cyrus, and his proclamation extended to all the Jews in all his dominions. And therefore we have reason to think that many of *the house of Israel* came with those of Judah out of *the land of the north;* though at first there returned but 42,000 (whom we have an account of, Ezra ii.) yet Josephus says (*Antiq. lib.* 11. *cap.* 4) that some few years after, under Darius, Zerubbabel went and fetched up above 4,000,000 of souls, *to the land that was given for an inheritance to their fathers.* And we never read of such animosities and enmities between Israel and Judah as had been formerly. This happy coalescence between Israel and Judah in Canaan was a type of the uniting of Jews and Gentiles in the gospel church, when, all enmities being slain,

they should become one *sheepfold under one shepherd.*

III. Here is some difficulty started, that lies in the way of all this mercy; but an expedient is found to get over it.

1. God asks, *How shall I* do this for thee ? Not as if God showed favour with reluctancy, as he punishes with a *How shall I give thee up ?* Hos. xi 8, 9. No, though he is slow to anger, he is swift to show mercy But it intimates that we are utterly unworthy of his favours, that we have no reason to expect them, that there is nothing in us to deserve them, that we can lay no claim to them, and that he contrives how to do it in such a way as may save the honour of his justice and holiness in the government of the world. *Means* must be *devised that his banished be not for ever expelled from him,* 2 Sam. xiv. 14. How shall I do it? (1.) Even backsliders, if they return and repent, shall be *put among the children;* and who could ever have expected that? *Behold what manner of love is this!* 1 John iii. 1. How should we who are so mean and weak, so worthless and unworthy, and so provoking, ever be *put among the children.* (2.) To those whom God puts among the children he will *give the pleasant land,* the land of Canaan, that glory of all lands, *that goodly heritage of the hosts of nations,* which nations and their hosts wish for and prefer to their own country, or which the hosts of the nations have now got possession of. It was a type of heaven, where there are *pleasures for evermore.* Now who could expect a place in that *pleasant land* that has so often *despised it* (Ps. cvi. 24) and is so unworthy of it and unfit for it? Is this the manner of men ?

2. He does himself return answer to this question : *But I said, Thou shalt call me, My Father.* God does himself answer all the objections that are taken from our unworthiness, or they would never be got over. (1.) That he may put returning penitents *among the children,* he will give them the *Spirit of adoption,* teaching them *to cry, Abba, Father,* Gal. iv. 6. " *Thou shalt call me, My Father ;* thou shalt return to me, and resign thyself to me as a father, and that shall recommend thee to my favour." (2.) That he may *give them the pleasant land,* he will *put his fear in their hearts,* that they may never *turn from him,* but may persevere to the end.

20 Surely *as* a wife treacherously departeth from her husband, so have ye dealt treacherously with me, O house of Israel, saith the LORD. 21 A voice was heard upon the high places, weeping *and* supplications of the children of Israel : for they have perverted their way, *and* they have forgotten the LORD their God. 22 Return, ye backsliding children, *and*

I will heal your backslidings. Behold, we come unto thee; for thou *art* the LORD our God. 23 Truly in vain *is salvation hoped for* from the hills, *and from* the multitude of mountains: truly in the LORD our God *is* the salvation of Israel. 24 For shame hath devoured the labour of our fathers from our youth; their flocks and their herds, their sons and their daughters. 25 We lie down in our shame, and our confusion covereth us: for we have sinned against the LORD our God, we and our fathers, from our youth even unto this day, and have not obeyed the voice of the LORD our God.

Here is, I. The charge God exhibits against Israel for their treacherous departures from him, *v.* 20. As an adulterous wife elopes from her husband, so have they gone a whoring from God. They were joined to God by a marriage-covenant, but they broke that covenant, they *dealt treacherously* with God, who had always dealt kindly and faithfully with them. Treacherous dealing with men like ourselves is bad enough, but to deal treacherously with God is to deal treasonably.

II. Their conviction and confession of the truth of this charge, *v.* 21. When God reproved them for their apostasy, there were some among them, even such as God would take and *bring to Zion,* whose *voice was heard upon the high places weeping and praying,* humbling themselves before the God of their fathers, lamenting their calamities, and their sins, the procuring cause of them; for this is that which they lament, for this they bemoan themselves, that *they have perverted their way and forgotten the Lord their God.* Note, 1. Sin is the perverting of our way, it is turning aside to crooked ways and *perverting that which is right.* 2. Forgetting the Lord our God is at the bottom of all sin. If men would remember God, his eye upon them and their obligation to him, they would not transgress as they do. 3. By sin we embarrass ourselves, and bring ourselves into trouble, for that also is the perverting of our way, Lam. iii. 9. 4. Prayers and tears well become those whose consciences tell them that they have *perverted their way and forgotten their God.* When the *foolishness of man perverts his way his heart* is apt to *fret against the Lord* (Prov. xix. 3), whereas it should be melted and poured out before him.

III. The invitation God gives them to return to him (*v.* 22): *Return, you backsliding children.* He calls them *children* in tenderness and compassion to them, foolish and froward as children, yet *his sons,* whom though he corrects he will not disinherit;

for, though they are *refractory children* (so some render it), yet they are *children.* God bears with such children, and so must parents. When they are convinced of sin (*v.* 21), and humbled for that, then they are prepared and then they are *invited* to *return,* as Christ invites those to him that are *weary* and *heavy-laden.* The promise to those that return is, "*I will heal your backslidings;* I will comfort you under the grief you are in for your backslidings, deliver you out of the troubles you have brought yourselves into by your backslidings, and cure you of your refractoriness and tendency to backslide." God will *heal our backslidings* by his pardoning mercy, his quieting peace, and his renewing grace.

IV. The ready consent they give to this invitation, and their cheerful compliance with it: *Behold, we come unto thee.* This is an echo to God's call; as a voice returned from broken walls, so this from broken hearts. God says, *Return;* they answer, *Behold, we come.* It is an immediate speedy answer, without delay, not, "We will come hereafter," but, "We do come now; we need not take time to consider of it;" not, "We come towards thee," but, "We come to thee, we will make a thorough turn of it." Observe how unanimous they are: *We come,* one and all. 1. They come devoting themselves to God as theirs: "*Thou art the Lord our God;* we take thee to be ours, we give up ourselves to thee to be thine; whither shall we go but to thee? It is our sin and folly that we have gone from thee" It is very comfortable, in our returns to God after our backslidings, to look up to him as ours in covenant. 2. They come disclaiming all expectations of relief and succour but from God only: "*In vain is salvation hoped for from the hills and from the multitude of the mountains;* we now see our folly in relying upon creature-confidences, and will never so deceive ourselves any more." They worshipped their idols upon hills and mountains (*v.* 6), and they had a multitude of idols upon their mountains, which they had sought unto and put a confidence in; but now they will have no more to do with them. In vain do we look for any thing that is good from them, while from God we may look for every thing that is good, even salvation itself. Therefore, 3. They come depending upon God only as their God: *In the Lord our God is the salvation of Israel.* He is *the Lord,* and he only can save; he can save when all other succours and saviours fail; and he is *our God,* and will in his own way and time work salvation for us. It is very applicable to the great salvation from sin, which Jesus Christ wrought out for us; that is the *salvation of the Lord,* his *great salvation.* 4. They come justifying God in their troubles and judging themselves for their sins, *v.* 24, 25. (1.) They impute all the calamities they had been under to their idols, which had not only

423

done them no good, but had done them abundance of mischief, all the mischief that had been done them : *Shame* (the idol, that shameful thing) *has devoured the labour of our fathers.* Note, [1.] True penitents have learned to call sin *shame;* even the beloved sin which has been as an idol to them, which they have been most pleased with and proud of, even that they shall call a scandalous thing, shall put contempt upon it and be ashamed of it. [2.] True penitents have learned to call sin death and ruin, and to charge upon it all the mischiefs they suffer : " It has *devoured* all those good things which our fathers *laboured for* and left to us ; we have found *from our youth* that our idolatry has been the destruction of our prosperity." Children often throw away upon their lusts that which their fathers took a great deal of pains for ; and it is well if at length they are brought (as these here) to see the folly of it, and to call those vices their shame which have wasted their estates and *devoured the labour of their fathers.* Of the labour of their fathers, which their idols had devoured, they mention particularly *their flocks and their herds, their sons and their daughters. First,* Their idolatries had provoked God to bring these desolating judgments upon them, which had ruined their country and families, and made their estates a prey and their children captives to the conquering enemy. They had *procured these things to themselves.* Or, rather, *Secondly,* These had been sacrificed to their idols, had been *separated unto that shame* (Hos. ix. 10), and they had devoured them without mercy ; they did *eat the fat of their sacrifices* (Deut. xxxii. 38), even their human sacrifices. (2.) They take to themselves the shame of their sin and folly (*v.* 25) : " *We lie down in our shame,* being unable to bear up under it ; *our confusion covers us,* that is, both our penal and our penitential shame. Sin has laid us under such rebukes of God's providence, and such reproaches of our own consciences, as surround us and fill us with shame. For *we have sinned,* and shame came in with sin and still attends upon it. We are sinners by descent ; guilt and corruption are entailed upon us : *We and our fathers have sinned.* We were sinners betimes ; we began early in a course of sin : We have sinned *from our youth;* we have continued in sin, have sinned *even unto this day,* though often called to repent and forsake our sins. That which is the malignity of sin, the worst thing in it, is the affront we have put upon God by it : *We have not obeyed the voice of the Lord our God,* forbidding us to sin and commanding us, when we have sinned, to repent." Now all this seems to be the language of the penitents of *the house of Israel* (*v.* 20), of the ten tribes, either of those that were in captivity or those of them that remained in their own land. And the prophet takes notice of their repentance to

424

provoke the men of Judah to a holy emulation. David used it as an argument with the elders of Judah that it would be a shame for those that were *his bone and his flesh* to be *the last in bringing the king back,* when the men of Israel appeared forward in it, 2 Sam. xix. 11, 12. So the prophet excites Judah to repent because Israel did : and well it were if the zeal of others less likely would provoke us to strive to get before them and go beyond them in that which is good.

CHAP. IV.

It should seem that the first two verses of this chapter might better have been joined to the close of the foregoing chapter, for they are directed to Israel, the ten tribes, by way of reply to their compliance with God's call, directing and encouraging them to hold their resolution, ver. 1, 2. The rest of the chapter concerns Judah and Jerusalem. I. They are called to repent and reform, ver. 3, 4. II. They are warned of the advance of Nebuchadnezzar and his forces against them, and are told that it is for their sins, from which they are again exhorted to wash themselves, ver. 5—18. III. To affect them the more with the greatness of the desolation that was coming, the prophet does himself bitterly lament it, and sympathize with his people in the calamities it brought upon them, and the plunge it brought them to, representing it as a reduction of the world to its first chaos, ver. 19—31.

IF thou wilt return, O Israel, saith the Lord, return unto me : and if thou wilt put away thine abominations out of my sight, then shalt thou not remove. 2 And thou shalt swear, The Lord liveth, in truth, in judgment, and in righteousness ; and the nations shall bless themselves in him, and in him shall they glory.

When God called to backsliding Israel to return (*ch.* iii. 22) they immediately answered, *Lord, we return;* now God here takes notice of their answer, and, by way of reply to it,

I. He directs them how to pursue their good resolutions : " Dost thou say, *I will return?*" 1. " Then thou must *return unto me;* make a thorough work of it. Do not only turn from thy idolatries, but return to the instituted worship of the God of Israel." Or, " Thou must return speedily and not delay (as Isa. xxi. 12, *If you will enquire, enquire you);* if you will return unto me, return you : do not talk of it, but do it." 2. Thou must utterly abandon all sin, and not retain any of the relics of idolatry : *Put away thy abominations out of my sight,*" that is, out of all places (for every place is under the eye of God), especially out of the temple, the house which he had in a particular manner his eye upon, to see that it was kept clean. It intimates that their idolatries were not only obvious, but offensive, to the eye of God. They were abominations which he could not endure the sight of ; therefore they must be *put away out of his sight,* because they were a provocation to the pure eyes of God's glory. Sin must be put away out of the heart, else it is not put away out of God's sight, for the heart and all that is in it lie open before his eye. 3. They must not return to sin again ; so some understand that, *Thou shalt not remove,* reading it, *Thou* shalt not, or *must not, wander. " If thou wilt put away thy abominations, and wilt not wander* after them again, as thou hast done, all shall be well." 4. They must give unto God the glory due unto his name (*v.* 2): " *Thou shalt swear, The Lord liveth.* His existence shall be with thee the most sacred fact, than which nothing can be more sure, and his judgment the supreme court to which thou shalt appeal, than which nothing can be more awful." Swearing is an act of religious worship, in which we are to give honour to God three ways :—(1.) We must swear by the true God only, and not by creatures, or any false gods,—by the God that liveth, not by the gods that are deaf and dumb and dead,—by him only, and not *by the Lord and by Malcham,* as Zeph. i. 5. (2.) We must swear that only which is true, *in truth and in righteousness,* not daring to assert that which is false, or which we do not know to be true, nor to assert that as certain which is doubtful, nor to promise that which we mean not to perform, nor to violate the promise we have made. To say that which is untrue, or to do that which is unrighteous, is bad, but to back either with an oath is much worse. (3.) We must do it solemnly, swear *in judgment,* that is, when judicially called to it, and not in common conversation. Rash swearing is as great a profanation of God's name as solemn swearing is an honour to it. See Deut. x. 20; Matt. v. 34, 37.

II. He encourages them to keep in this good mind and adhere to their resolutions. If the scattered Israelites will thus return tc God, 1. They shall be blessed themselves; for to that sense the first words may be read : " *If thou wilt return to me,* then *thou shalt return,* that is, thou shalt be brought back out of thy captivity into thy own land again, as was of old promised," Deut. iv. 29 ; xxx. 2. Or, "Then *thou shalt rest in me,* shalt return to me as thy rest, even while thou art in the land of thy captivity." 2. They shall be blessings to others ; for their returning to God again will be a means of others turning to him who never knew him. If thou wilt own the living Lord, thou wilt thereby influence the nations among whom thou art to bless themselves in him, to place their happiness in his favour and to think themselves happy in being brought to the fear of him. See Isa. lxv. 16. They shall bless themselves *in the God of truth,* and not in false gods, shall do themselves the honour, and give themselves the satisfaction, to join themselves to him ; and then *in him shall they glory ;* they shall make him their glory, and shall please, nay, shall pride, themselves in the blessed change they have made. Those that part with their sins to return to God, however they scrupled at the bargain at first, *when they go away, then they boast.*

3 For thus saith the LORD to the

men of Judah and Jerusalem, Break up your fallow ground, and sow not among thorns. 4 Circumcise yourselves to the LORD, and take away the foreskins of your heart, ye men of Judah and inhabitants of Jerusalem : lest my fury come forth like fire, and burn that none can quench *it,* because of the evil of your doings.

The prophet here turns his speech, in God's name, to the men of the place where he lived. We have heard what words he proclaimed *towards the north* (*ch.* iii. 12), for the comfort of those that were now in captivity and were humbled under the hand of God ; let us now see what he says to the *men of Judah and Jerusalem,* who were now in prosperity, for their conviction and awakening. In these two verses he exhorts them to repentance and reformation, as the only way left them to prevent the desolating judgments that were ready to break in upon them. Observe,

I. The duties required of them, which they are concerned to do.

1. They must do by their hearts as they do by their ground that they expect any good of ; they must plough it up (*v.* 3): " *Break up your fallow-ground. Plough to yourselves a ploughing* (or *plough up your plough land),* that you *sow not among thorns,* that you may not labour in vain, for your own safety and welfare, as those do that sow good seed among thorns, and as you have been doing a great while. Put yourselves into a frame fit to receive mercy from God, and put away all that which keeps it from you, and then you may expect to receive mercy and to prosper in your endeavours to help yourselves." Note, (1.) An unconvinced unhumbled heart is like fallow-ground, ground untilled, unoccupied. It is ground capable of improvement ; it is our ground, let out to us, and we must be accountable for it ; but it is fallow ; it is unfenced and lies common ; it is unfruitful and of no advantage to the owner, and (which is principally intended) it is overgrown with thorns and weeds, which are the natural product of the corrupt heart ; and, if it be not renewed with grace, rain and sunshine are lost upon it, Heb. vi. 7, 8. (2.) We are concerned to get this fallow-ground ploughed up. We must search into our own hearts, let the word of God divide (as the plough does) *between the joints and the marrow,* Heb. iv. 12. We must *rend our hearts,* Joel ii. 13. We must pluck up by the roots those corruptions which, as thorns, choke both our endeavours and our expectations, Hos. x. 12.

2. They must do that to their souls which was done to their bodies when they were taken into covenant with God (*v.* 4) : " *Circumcise yourselves to the Lord, and take away the foreskin of your heart.* Mortify the flesh

and the lusts of it. Pare off that *superfluity of naughtiness* which hinders your *receiving with meekness the engrafted word*, Jam. i. 21. Boast not of, and rest not in, the circumcision of the body, for that is but a sign, and will not serve without the thing signified. It is a dedicating sign. Do that in sincerity which was done in profession by your circumcision; devote and consecrate yourselves unto the Lord, to be to him a peculiar people. Circumcision is an *obligation to keep the law*: lay yourselves afresh under that obligation. It is a *seal of the righteousness of faith*: lay hold then of that righteousness, and so *circumcise yourselves to the Lord.*"

II. The danger they are threatened with, which they are concerned to avoid. Repent and reform, *lest my fury come forth like fire*, which it is now ready to do, as that fire which came forth from the Lord and consumed the sacrifices, and which was always kept burning upon the altar and none might quench it; such is God's wrath against impenitent sinners, *because of the evil of their doings.* Note, 1. That which is to be dreaded by us more than any thing else is the wrath of God; for that is the spring and bitterness of all present miseries and will be the quintessence and perfection of everlasting misery. 2. It is the *evil of our doings* that kindles the fire of God's wrath against us. 3. The consideration of the imminent danger we are in of falling and perishing under this wrath should awaken us with all possible care to *sanctify ourselves to God's glory* and to see to it that we be *sanctified by his grace.*

5 Declare ye in Judah, and publish in Jerusalem; and say, Blow ye the trumpet in the land: cry, gather together, and say, Assemble yourselves, and let us go into the defenced cities. 6 Set up the standard toward Zion: retire, stay not: for I will bring evil from the north, and a great destruction. 7 The lion is come up from his thicket, and the destroyer of the Gentiles is on his way; he is gone forth from his place to make thy land desolate; *and* thy cities shall be laid waste, without an inhabitant. 8 For this gird you with sackcloth, lament and howl: for the fierce anger of the LORD is not turned back from us. 9 And it shall come to pass at that day, saith the LORD, *that* the heart of the king shall perish, and the heart of the princes; and the priests shall be astonished, and the prophets shall wonder. 10 Then said I, Ah, Lord GOD! surely thou hast greatly deceived this people and Jerusalem,

saying, Ye shall have peace; whereas the sword reacheth unto the soul. 11 At that time shall it be said to this people and to Jerusalem, A dry wind of the high places in the wilderness toward the daughter of my people, not to fan, nor to cleanse, 12 *Even* a full wind from those *places* shall come unto me: now also will I give sentence against them. 13 Behold, he shall come up as clouds, and his chariots *shall be* as a whirlwind: his horses are swifter than eagles. Woe unto us! for we are spoiled. 14 O Jerusalem, wash thine heart from wickedness, that thou mayest be saved. How long shall thy vain thoughts lodge within thee? 15 For a voice declareth from Dan, and publisheth affliction from mount Ephraim. 16 Make ye mention to the nations; behold, publish against Jerusalem, *that* watchers come from a far country, and give out their voice against the cities of Judah. 17 As keepers of a field, are they against her round about; because she hath been rebellious against me, saith the LORD. 18 Thy way and thy doings have procured these *things* unto thee; this *is* thy wickedness, because it is bitter, because it reacheth unto thine heart.

God's usual method is to warn before he wounds. In these verses, accordingly, God gives notice to the Jews of the general desolation that would shortly be brought upon them by a foreign invasion. This must be declared and published in all the cities of Judah and streets of Jerusalem, that all might hear and fear, and by this loud alarm be either brought to repentance or left inexcusable. The prediction of this calamity is here given very largely, and in lively expressions, which one would think should have awakened and affected the most stupid. Observe,

I. The war proclaimed, and general notice given of the advance of the enemy. It is published now, some years before, by the prophet; but, since this will be slighted, it shall be published after another manner when the judgment is actually breaking in, *v.* 5, 6. The *trumpet* must be *blown*, the *standard* must be *set up*, a summons must be issued out to the people to *gather together* and to draw *towards Zion*, either to guard it or expecting to be guarded by it. There must be a general rendezvous. The militia must be raised and all the forces mustered.

Those that are able men, and fit for service, must *go into the defenced cities*, to garrison them; those that are weak, and would lessen their provisions, but not increase their strength, must *retire*, and *not stay*.

II. An express arrived with intelligence of the approach of the king of Babylon and his army. It is an evil that God will *bring from the north* (as he had said, ch. i. 15), *even a great destruction*, beyond all that had yet come upon the nation of the Jews. The enemy is here compared, 1. To *a lion* that *comes up from his thicket*, when he is hungry, to seek his prey, v. 7. The helpless beasts are so terrified with his roaring (as some report) that they cannot flee from him, and so become an easy prey to him. Nebuchadnezzar is this roaring tearing lion, *the destroyer of the nations*, that has laid many countries waste, and now is *on his way* in full speed towards the land of Judah. The *destroyer of the Gentiles* shall be the *destroyer of the Jews* too, when they have by their idolatry made themselves like the Gentiles. " He has *gone forth from his place*, from Babylon, or the place of the rendezvous of his army, on purpose against *this land;* that is the prey he has now his eye upon, not to plunder it only, but to make it desolate, and herein he shall succeed to such a degree that the cities shall be *laid waste, without inhabitants*, shall be *overgrown with grass* as a field; so some read it. 2. To a *drying* blasting *wind* (v. 11), a parching scorching wind, which spoils the fruits of the earth and withers them, not a wind which brings rain, but such as comes *out of the north*, which *drives away rain* (Prov. xxv. 23), but brings something worse instead of it; such shall this evil out of the north be to this people, a *black* freezing wind, which they can neither fence against nor flee from, but, wherever they go, it shall surround and pursue them; and they cannot see it before it comes, but, when it comes, they shall feel it. It is a *wind of the high places in the wilderness*, or *plain*, that beats upon the tops of the hills or that carries all before it in the plain, where there is no shelter, but the ground is all champaign. It shall come in its full force *towards the daughters of my people*, that have been brought up so tenderly and delicately that they could not endure to have the wind blow upon them. Now this fierce wind shall come against them, *not to fan, nor cleanse* them, not such a gentle wind as is used in winnowing corn, but a *full wind* (v. 12), a strong and violent wind, blowing full upon them. This shall come *to me*, or rather *for me;* it shall come with commission from God and shall accomplish that for which he sends it; for this, as other *stormy winds, fulfils his word*. 3. To clouds and whirlwinds for swiftness, v. 13. The Chaldean army shall *come up as clouds* driven with the wind, so thick shall they stand, so fast shall they march, and it shall be to no purpose to offer

to stop them or to make head against them, any more than to arrest a cloud or give check to a whirlwind. The horses are *swifter than eagles* when they fly upon their prey; it is in vain to think either of opposing them or of outrunning them. 4. To watchers and the keepers of a field, v. 15—17. *The voice declares from Dan*, a city which lay furthest north of all the cities of Canaan, and therefore received the first tidings of this *evil from the north* and hastened it to Mount Ephraim, that part of the land of Israel which lay next to Judea; they received the news of the affliction and transmitted it to Jerusalem. Ill news flies apace; and an impenitent people, that hates to be reformed, can expect no other than ill news. Now, what is the news? " *Tell the nations*, those mixed nations that now inhabit the cities of the ten tribes, mention it to them, that they may provide for their own safety; but publish it *against Jerusalem*, that is the place aimed at, the game shot at, let them know that *watchers have come from a far country*, that is, soldiers, that will watch all opportunities to do mischief." Private soldiers we call *private sentinels*, or *watchmen*. " They are coming in full career, and *give out their voice against the cities of Judah;* they design to invest them, to make themselves masters of them, and to attack them with loud shouts, as sure of victory. As *keepers of a field* surround it, to keep all out from it, so shall they surround the cities of Judah, to keep all in them, till they be constrained to surrender at discretion; they are *against her round about, compassing her in on every side*." See Luke xix. 43. As formerly the good angels, *those watchers* and *holy ones*, were like *keepers of a field* to Jerusalem, watching about it, that nothing might go in to its prejudice, so now their enemies were as watchers and keepers of a field, surrounding it that nothing might go in to its relief and succour.

III. The lamentable cause of this judgment. How is it that Judah and Jerusalem come to be thus abandoned to ruin? See how it came to this. 1. They sinned against God; it was all owing to themselves: *She has been rebellious against me, saith the Lord*, v. 17. Their enemies surrounded them as keepers of a field, because they had taken up arms against their rightful Lord and sovereign, and were to be seized as rebels. The Chaldeans were breaking in upon them, and it was sin that opened the gap at which they entered: *Thy way and thy doings have procured these things unto thee* (v. 18), thy evil way and thy doings that have not been good. It was not a false step or two that did them this mischief, but their way and course of living were bad. Note, Sin is the procuring cause of all our troubles. Those that go on in sin while they are endeavouring to ward off mischiefs with one hand are at the same time pulling them upon their own heads with the other. 2. God was angry with them for their sin. It is the *fierce anger of the Lord* that makes the army of the Chaldeans thus fierce, thus furious; that is kindled against us, and is *not turned back from us,* v. 8. Note, In men's anger against us, and the violence of that, we must see and own God's anger and the power of that. If that were turned back from us, our enemies could not come forward against us. 3. In his just and holy anger he condemned them to this dreadful punishment: *Now also will I give sentence against them,* v. 12. The execution was done, not in a heat, but in pursuance of a sentence solemnly passed, according to equity, and upon mature deliberation. Some read it, *Now will I do execution upon them,* according to the doom formerly passed; and *we are sure that the judgment of God is according to truth,* and the execution of that judgment.

IV. The lamentable effects of this judgment, upon the first alarm given of it. 1. The people that should fight shall quite despair and shall not have a heart to make the least stand against the enemy (*v.* 8): *"For this gird yourself with sackcloth, lament and howl,"* that is, "you will do so. When the cry is made through the kingdom, *Arm, arm!* all will be seized with a consternation, and all put into confusion. Instead of girding on the sword, they will gird on the sackcloth; instead of animating one another to a vigorous resistance, they will *lament and howl,* and so dishearten one another. While the enemy is yet at a distance they will give up all for gone, and cry, *Woe unto us! for we are spoiled,* v. 13. We are all undone, the spoilers will certainly carry the day, and it is in vain to make head against them." Judah and Jerusalem had been famed for valiant men; but see what is the effect of sin: by depriving men of their confidence towards God, it deprives them of their courage towards men. 2. Their great men, who should contrive for the public safety, shall be at their wits' end (*v.* 9): *At that day the heart of the king shall perish,* both his wisdom and his courage. Despairing of success, he shall have no spirit to do any thing, and, if he had, he will not know what to do. His princes and privy-counsellors, who should animate and advise him, shall be as much at a loss and as much in despair as he. See how easily, how effectually, God can bring ruin upon a people that are doomed to it, merely by dispiriting them, *taking away the heart of the chief* of them (Job xii. 20, 24), *cutting off the spirit of princes,* Ps. lxxvi. 12. The business of the priests was to encourage the people in the time of war; they were to say to the people, *Fear not, and let not your hearts faint,* Deut. xx. 2, 3. They were to blow the trumpets, for an assurance to them that in the day of battle they should be *remembered before the Lord their God,* Num. x. 9. But now *the priests* themselves *shall be astonished,* and shall have no heart

themselves to do their office, and therefore shall not be likely to put spirit into the people. *The prophets* too, the false prophets, who had cried *peace* to them, shall be put into the greatest amazement imaginable, seeing their own guilty blood ready to be shed by that sword which they had often told the people there was no danger of. Note, God's judgments come with the greatest terror upon those that have been most secure. Our Saviour foretels that at the last destruction of Jerusalem *men's hearts* should *fail them for fear,* Luke xxi. 26. And it is common for those who have cheated and flattered people into a carnal security not only to fail them, but to discourage them, when the trouble comes.

V. The prophet's complaint of the people's being deceived, *v.* 10. It is expressed strangely, as we read it: *Ah! Lord God, surely thou hast greatly deceived this people, saying, You shall have peace.* We are sure that God deceives none. *Let no man say, when he is tempted* or deluded, that God has tempted or deluded him. But, 1. The people deceived themselves with the promises that God had made in general of his favour to that nation, and the many peculiar privileges with which they were dignified, building upon them, though they took no care to perform the conditions on which the accomplishment of those promises and the continuance of those privileges did depend; and they had no regard to the threatenings which in the law were set over-against those promises. Thus they cheated themselves and then wickedly complained that God had cheated them. 2. The false prophets deceived them with promises of peace, which they made in God's name, *ch.* xxiii. 17; xxvii. 9. If God had sent them, he had indeed greatly deceived the people, but he had not. It was the people's fault that they gave them credit; and here also they deceived themselves. 3. God had permitted the false prophets to deceive, and the people to be deceived by them, giving both up to *strong delusions,* to punish them *for not receiving the truth in the love of it.* Herein the Lord was righteous; but the prophet complains of it as the sorest judgment of all, for by this means they had been hardened in their sins. 4. It may be read with an interrogation, *"Hast thou indeed thus deceived this people?"* It is plain that they are greatly deceived, for they expect *peace,* whereas *the sword reaches unto the soul;* that is, it is a killing sword, abundance of lives are lost, and more likely to be." Now, was it God that deceived them? No, he had often given them warning of judgments in general and of this in particular; but their own prophets deceive them, and cry peace to those to whom the God of heaven does not speak peace. It is a pitiable thing, and that which every good man greatly laments, to see people flattered into their own ruin, and promising themselves peace when war is at the door; and this we should complain of to God, who alone can prevent such a fatal delusion.

VI. The prophet's endeavour to undeceive them. When the prophets they loved and caressed dealt falsely with them, he whom they hated and persecuted dealt faithfully. 1. He shows them their wound. They were loth to see it, very loth to have it searched into; but, if they will allow themselves the liberty of a free thought, they might discover their punishment in their sin (*v.* 18): " *This is thy wickedness, because it is bitter.* Now thou seest that it is a bitter thing to depart from God, and will certainly be *bitterness in the latter end, ch.* ii. 19. It produces bitter effects, and grief that *reaches unto the heart,* touches to the quick, and in the most tender part; the sword *reaches to the soul,*" *v.* 10. God can make trouble reach the heart even of those that would lay nothing to heart. " And by this thou mayest see *what is thy wickedness,* that it is a bitter thing, a *root of bitterness, that bears gall and wormwood,* and that it has *reached to the heart;* it is the corruption of the soul, of the *imagination of the thought of the heart.*" If the heart were not polluted with sin, it would not be disturbed and disquieted as it is with trouble. 2. He shows them the cure, *v.* 14. " Since *thy wickedness reaches to the heart,* there the application must be made. *O Jerusalem! wash thy heart from wickedness, that thou mayest be saved.*" By Jerusalem he means each one of the inhabitants of Jerusalem; for every man has a heart of his own to take care of, and it is personal reformation that must help the public. Every one must return from *his own evil way,* and, in order to that, cleanse *his own evil heart.* "And let *the heart of the city* too be purified, not the suburbs only, the outskirts of it." The vitals of a state must be amended by the reformation of those that have the commanding influence upon it. Note, (1.) Reformation is absolutely necessary to salvation. There is no other way of preventing judgments, or turning them away when we are threatened with them, but taking away the sin by which we have procured them to ourselves. (2.) No reformation is saving but that which reaches the heart. There is heart-wickedness that is defiling to the soul, from which we must wash ourselves. By repentance and faith we must wash our hearts from the guilt we have contracted by spiritual wickedness, by those sins which begin and end in the heart and go no further; and by mortification and watchfulness we must suppress and prevent this heart-wickedness for the future. The tree must be made good, else the fruit will not. Jerusalem was all overspread with the leprosy of sin. Now as the physicians agree with respect to the body when afflicted with leprosy that external applications will do no good, unless physic be taken inwardly to carry off the humours that lurk there and to change the mass of the blood, so it is with the soul, so it is with the state: there will be no effectual reformation of the manners without a reformation of the mind; the mistakes there must be rectified, the corruptions there must be mortified, and the evil dispositions there changed. "Though thou art Jerusalem, called a *holy city,* that will not save thee, unless thou *wash thy heart from wickedness.*" In the latter part of the verse he reasons with them: *How long shall thy vain thoughts lodge within thee?* He complains here, [1.] Of the delays of their reformation : " *How long* shall that filthy heart of thine continue unwashed? When shall it once be?" Note, The God of heaven thinks the time long that his room is usurped, and his interest opposed, in our souls, *ch.* xiii. 27. [2.] Of the root of their corruption, the *vain thoughts that lodged within them* and defiled their hearts, from which they must wash their hearts. *Thoughts of iniquity* or *mischief,* these are the evil thoughts that are the spawn of the evil *heart,* from which all other wickedness is produced, Matt. xv. 19. These are our own, the conceptions of our own lusts (Jam. i. 15), and they are most dangerous when they lodge within us, when they are admitted and entertained as guests, and are suffered to continue. Some read it *thoughts of affliction,* such thoughts as will bring nothing but affliction and misery. Some by the vain thoughts here understand all those frivolous pleas and excuses with which they turned off the reproofs and calls of the word and rendered them ineffectual, and bolstered themselves up in their wickedness. *Wash thy heart from wickedness,* and think not to say, *We are not polluted* (ch. ii. 23), or, " We are Jerusalem; *we have Abraham to our father,*" Matt. iii. 8, 9.

19 My bowels, my bowels! I am pained at my very heart; my heart maketh a noise in me; I cannot hold my peace, because thou hast heard, O my soul, the sound of the trumpet, the alarm of war. 20 Destruction upon destruction is cried; for the whole land is spoiled: suddenly are my tents spoiled, *and* my curtains in a moment. 21 How long shall I see the standard, *and* hear the sound of the trumpet? 22 For my people *is* foolish, they have not known me; they *are* sottish children, and they have none understanding: they *are* wise to do evil, but to do good they have no knowledge. 23 I beheld the earth, and, lo, *it was* without form, and void; and the heavens, and they *had* no light. 24 I beheld the moun-

tains, and, lo, they trembled, and all the hills moved lightly. 25 I beheld, and, lo, *there was* no man, and all the birds of the heavens were fled. 26 I beheld, and, lo, the fruitful place *was* a wilderness, and all the cities thereof were broken down at the presence of the Lord, *and* by his fierce anger. 27 For thus hath the Lord said, The whole land shall be desolate; yet will I not make a full end. 28 For this shall the earth mourn, and the heavens above be black: because I have spoken *it*, I have purposed *it*, and will not repent, neither will I turn back from it. 29 The whole city shall flee for the noise of the horsemen and bowmen; they shall go into thickets, and climb up upon the rocks: every city *shall be* forsaken, and not a man dwell therein. 30 And *when* thou *art* spoiled, what wilt thou do? Though thou clothest thyself with crimson, though thou deckest thee with ornaments of gold, though thou rentest thy face with painting, in vain shalt thou make thyself fair; *thy* lovers will despise thee, they will seek thy life. 31 For I have heard a voice as of a woman in travail, *and* the anguish as of her that bringeth forth her first child, the voice of the daughter of Zion, *that* bewaileth herself, *that* spreadeth her hands, *saying*, Woe *is* me now! for my soul is wearied because of murderers.

The prophet is here in an agony, and cries out like one upon the rack of pain with some acute distemper, or as a woman in travail. The expressions are very pathetic and moving, enough to melt a heart of stone into compassion: *My bowels! my bowels! I am pained at my very heart;* and yet well, and in health himself, and nothing ails him. Note, A good man, in such a bad world as this is, cannot but be a *man of sorrows. My heart makes a noise in me*, through the tumult of my spirits, and *I cannot hold my peace.* Note, The grievance and the grief sometimes may be such that the most prudent patient man cannot forbear complaining.

Now, what is the matter? What is it that puts this good man into such agitation? It is not for himself, or any affliction in his family that he grieves thus; but it is purely upon the public account, it is his people's case that he lays to heart thus.

I. They are very sinful and will not be reformed, *v.* 22. These are the words of God himself, for so the prophet chose to give

430

this character of the people, rather than in his own words, or as from himself: *My people are foolish.* God calls them his people, though they are foolish. They have cast him off, but he has not cast them off, Rom. xi. 1. "They are *my people*, whom I have been in covenant with, and still have mercy in store for. They are *foolish*, for *they have not known me.*" Note, Those are foolish indeed that have not known God, especially that call themselves his people, and have the advantages of coming into acquaintance with him, and yet have not known him. They are *sottish children*, stupid and senseless, and have *no understanding.* They cannot distinguish between truth and falsehood, good and evil; they cannot discern the mind of God either in his word or in his providence; they do not understand what their true interest is, nor on which side it lies. They are *wise to do evil*, to plot mischief against the quiet in the land, wise to contrive the gratification of their lusts, and then to conceal and palliate them. But *to do good they have no knowledge*, no contrivance, no application of mind; they know not how to make a good use either of the ordinances or of the providences of God, nor how to bring about any design for the good of their country. Contrary to this should be our character. Rom. xvi. 19, *I would have you wise unto that which is good, and simple concerning evil.*

II. They are very miserable, and cannot be relieved.

1. He cries out, *Because thou hast heard, O my soul! the sound of the trumpet*, and *seen the standard*, both giving *the alarm of war, v.* 19, 21. He does not say, *Thou hast heard*, O my *ear!* but, O my *soul!* because the event was yet future, and it is by the spirit of prophecy that he sees it and receives the impression of it. His *soul* heard it from the words of God, and therefore he was as well assured of it, and as much affected with it, as if he had heard it with his bodily ears. He expresses this deep concern, (1.) To show that, though he foretold this calamity, yet he was far from *desiring the woeful day;* for a woeful day it would be to him. It becomes us to tremble at the thoughts of the misery that sinners are running themselves into, though we have good hopes, through grace, that we ourselves are *delivered from the wrath to come.* (2.) To awaken them to a holy fear, and so to a care to prevent so great a judgment by a true and timely repentance. Note, Those that would affect others with the word of God should evidence that they are themselves affected with it. Now,

2. Let us see what there is in the destruction here foreseen and foretold that is so very affecting.

(1.) It is a swift and *sudden* destruction; it comes upon Judah and Jerusalem ere they are aware, and pours in so fast upon them that they have not the least breathing time.

They have no time to recollect their thoughts, much less to recruit or recover their strength: *Destruction upon destruction is cried* (*v.* 20), *breach upon breach,* one sad calamity, like Job's messengers, treading upon the heels of another. The death of Josiah breaks the ice, and plucks up the flood-gates; within three months after that his son and successor Jehoahaz is deposed by the king of Egypt; within two or three years after Nebuchadnezzar besieged Jerusalem and took it, and thenceforward he was continually making descents upon the land of Judah with his armies during the reigns of Jehoiakim, Jeconiah, and Zedekiah, till about nineteen years after he completed their ruin in the destruction of Jerusalem: but *suddenly were their tents spoiled and their curtains in a moment.* Though the cities held out for some time, the country was laid waste at the very first. The shepherds and all that lived in tents were plundered immediately; they and their effects fell into the enemies' hands; therefore we find the Rechabites, who dwelt in tents, upon the first coming of the army of the Chaldees into the land retiring to Jerusalem, Jer. xxxv. 11. The inhabitants of the villages soon ceased: *Suddenly were the tents spoiled.* The plain men that dwelt in tents were first made a prey of.

(2.) This dreadful war continued a great while, not in the borders, but in the bowels of the country; for the people were very obstinate, and would not submit to the king of Babylon, but took all opportunities to rebel against him, which did but lengthen out the calamity; they might as well have yielded at first as at last. This is complained of (*v.* 21): *How long shall I see the standard?* Shall the sword devour for ever? Good men are none of those that *delight in war,* for they know not how to fish in troubled waters; they are *for peace* (Ps. cxx. 7), and will heartily say *Amen* to that prayer, "Give peace in our time, O Lord!" *O thou sword of the Lord! when wilt thou be quiet?*

(3.) The desolations made by it in the land were general and universal: *The whole land is spoiled,* or plundered (*v.* 20); so it was at first, and at length it became a perfect chaos. It was such a desolation as amounted in a manner to a dissolution; not only the superstructure, but even the foundations, were all *out of course.* The prophet in vision saw the extent and extremity of this destruction, and he here gives a most lively description of it, which one would think might have made those uneasy in their sins who dwelt in a land doomed to such a ruin, which might yet have been prevented by their repentance. [1.] The earth is *without form, and void* (*v.* 23), as it was Gen. i. 2. It is *Tohu* and *Bohu,* the words there used, as far as the land of Judea goes. It is *confusion* and *emptiness,* stripped of all its beauty, void of all its wealth, and, compared with

what it was, every thing out of place and out of shape. To a worse chaos than this will the earth be reduced at the end of time, when it, *and all the works that are therein, shall be burnt up.* [2.] The *heavens* too are *without light,* as the earth is without fruits. This alludes to the *darkness* that was *upon the face of the deep* (Gen. i. 2), and represents God's displeasure against them, as the eclipse of the sun did at our Saviour's death. It was not only the earth that failed them, but heaven also frowned upon them; and with their trouble they had darkness, for they could not see through their troubles. The smoke of their houses and cities which the enemy burnt, and the dust which their army raised in its march, even darkened the sun, so that *the heavens had no light.* Or it may be taken figuratively: *The earth* (that is, the common people) was impoverished and in confusion; and the *heavens* (that is, the princes and rulers) *had no light,* no wisdom in themselves, nor were any comfort to the people, nor a guide to them. Comp. Matt. xxiv. 29. [3.] The *mountains trembled, and the hills moved lightly, v.* 24. So formidable were the appearances of God against his people, as in the days of old they had been for them, that *the mountains skipped like rams and the little hills like lambs,* Ps. cxiv. 4. The *everlasting mountains* seemed to be *scattered,* Hab. iii. 6. The mountains on which they had worshipped their idols, the mountains over which they had looked for succours, all trembled, as if they had been conscious of the people's guilt. The mountains, those among them that seemed to be highest and strongest, and of the firmest resolution, trembled at the approach of the Chaldean army. The hills moved lightly, as being eased of the burden of a *sinful nation,* Isa. i. 24. [4.] Not the earth only, but the air, was dispeopled, and left uninhabited (*v.* 25): *I beheld* the cities, the countries that used to be populous, *and, lo, there was no man* to be seen; all the inhabitants were either killed, or fled, or taken captives, such a ruining depopulating thing is sin: nay, even *the birds of the heavens,* that used to fly about and *sing among the branches,* had now *fled* away, and were no more to be seen or heard. The *land of Judah* had now become like the *lake of Sodom,* over which (they say) no bird flies; see Deut. xxix. 23. The enemies shall make such havoc of the country that they shall not so much as leave a bird alive in it. [5.] Both the ground and the houses shall be laid waste (*v.* 26): *Lo, the fruitful place was a wilderness,* being deserted by the inhabitants that should cultivate it, and then soon overgrown with thorns and briers, or being trodden down by the destroying army of the enemy. The *cities* also and their gates and walls are *broken down* and levelled with the ground. Those that look no further than second causes impute it to the policy and fury of the invaders;

but the prophet, who looks to the first cause, says that it is *at the presence of the Lord,* at *his face* (that is, the anger of his countenance), even *by his fierce anger,* that this was done. Even angry men cannot do us any real hurt, unless God be angry with us. If our *ways please him,* all is well. [6.] The meaning of all this is that the nation shall be entirely ruined, and every part of it shall share in the destruction; neither town nor country shall escape. *First,* Not the country, for *the whole land shall be desolate,* corn land and pasture land, both common and enclosed, it shall all be laid waste (*v.* 27); the conquerors will have occasion for it all. *Secondly,* Not the men, for (*v.* 29) *the whole city shall flee,* all the inhabitants of the town shall quit their habitations by consent, *for fear of the horsemen and bowmen.* Rather than lie exposed to their fury, they shall *go into the thickets,* where they are in danger of being torn by briers, nay, to be torn in pieces by wild beasts; and they shall *climb up upon the rocks,* where their lodging will be hard and cold, and the precipice dangerous. Let us not be over-fond of our houses and cities; for the time may come when rocks and thickets may be preferable, and chosen rather. This shall be the common case, for *every city shall be forsaken,* and *not a man* shall be left that dares *dwell therein.* Both government and trade shall be at an end, and all civil societies and incorporations dissolved. It is a very dismal idea which this gives of the approaching desolation; but in the midst of all these threatenings comes in one comfortable word (*v.* 27): *Yet will not I make a full end*—not a total consumption, for God will reserve a remnant to himself, that shall be hidden in the day of the Lord's anger—not a final consumption, for Jerusalem shall again be built and the land inhabited. This comes in here, in the midst of the threatenings, for the comfort of those that *trembled at God's word;* and it intimates to us the changeableness of God's providence; as it breaks down, so it raises up again; every end of our comforts is not a full end, however we may be ready to think it so. It also intimates the unchangeableness of God's covenant, which stands so firmly, that, though he may correct his people very severely, yet he will not *cast them off, ch.* xxx. 11.

(4.) Their case was helpless and without remedy. [1.] God would not help them; so he tells them plainly, *v.* 28. And, if the Lord do not help them, who can? This is that which makes their case deplorable. " *For this the earth mourns and the heavens above are black* (there are no prospects but what are very dismal), *because I have spoken it;* I have given the word which shall not be called back; *I have purposed it* (it is a consumption decreed, determined) *and I will not repent,* not change this way, but proceed in it, and will not *turn back from it.*" They

would not repent and turn back from the way of their sins (*ch.* ii. 25), and therefore God will not repent and turn back from the way of his judgments. [2.] They could not help themselves, *v.* 30, 31. When the thing appeared at a distance they flattered themselves with hopes that, though God should not appear for them as he had done for Hezekiah against the Assyrian army, yet they should find some means or other to secure themselves and give check to the forces of the enemy. But the prophet tells them that, when it comes to the setting to, they will be quite at a loss: " *When thou art spoiled, what wilt thou do?* What course wilt thou take? Sit down now, and consider this in time." He assures them that, whatever were now their contrivances and confidences, *First,* They will then be despised by their allies whom they depended upon for assistance. He had often compared the sin of Jerusalem to whoredom, not only her idolatry, but her trust in creatures, in the neighbouring powers. Now here he compares her to a harlot abandoned by all the lewd ones that used to make court to her. She is supposed to do all she can to keep up her interest in their affections. She does what she can to make herself appear considerable among the nations, and a valuable ally. She compliments them by her ambassadors to the highest degree, to engage them to stand by her now in her distress. She *clothes herself with crimson,* as if she were rich, and *decks herself with ornaments of gold,* as if her treasuries were still as full as ever they had been. She *rents her face with painting,* puts the best colours she can upon her present distresses and does her utmost to palliate and extenuate her losses, sets a good face upon them. But this painting, though it beautifies the face for the present, really rends it; the frequent use of paint spoils the skin, cracks it, and makes it rough; so the case which by false colours has been made to appear better than really it was, when truth comes to light, will look so much the worse. " And, after all, *in vain shalt thou make thyself fair;* all thy neighbours are sensible how low thou art brought; the Chaldeans will strip thee of thy crimson and ornaments, and then thy confederates will not only slight thee and refuse to give thee any succour, but they will join with those that *seek thy life,* that they may come in for a share in the prey of so rich a country." Here seems to be an allusion to the story of Jezebel, who thought, by making herself look fair and fine, to outface her doom, but in vain, 2 Kings ix. 30, 33. See what creatures prove when we confide in them, how treacherous they are; instead of saving the life, they seek the life; they often change, so that they will sooner do us an ill turn than any service. And see to how little purpose it is for those that have by sin deformed themselves in God's eyes to think by any arts they can use to beautify themselves in the eye of the world. *Secondly,* They will then be themselves in despair; they will find their troubles to be like the pains of a woman in travail, which she cannot escape: *I have heard the voice of the daughter of Zion,* her groans echoing to the triumphant shouts of the Chaldean army, which he heard, *v.* 15. It is like the *voice of a woman in travail,* whose pain is exquisite, and the fruit of sin and the curse too (Gen. iii. 16), and extorts lamentable outcries, especially of a *woman in travail of her first child,* who, having never known before what that pain is, is the more terrified by it. Troubles are most grievous to those that have not been used to them. Zion, in this distress, since her neighbours refuse to pity her, *bewails herself,* fetching *deep sighs* (so the word signifies), and she *spreads her hands,* either wringing them for grief or reaching them forth for succour. All the cry is, *Woe is me now!* (now that the decree has gone forth against her and is past recal), for *my soul is wearied because of murderers.* The Chaldean soldiers put all to the sword that gave them any opposition, so that the land was full of murders. Zion was weary of hearing tragical stories from all parts of the country, and cried out, *Woe is me!* It was well if their sufferings put them in mind of their sins, the murders committed upon them of the murders committed by them; for God was now making inquisition for the *innocent blood* shed in Jerusalem, *which the Lord would not pardon,* 2 Kings xxiv. 4. Note, As sin will find out the sinner, so sorrow will, sooner or later, find out the secure.

CHAP. V.

Reproofs for sin and threatenings of judgment are intermixed in this chapter, and are set the one over against the other: judgments are threatened, that the reproofs of sin might be the more effectual to bring them to repentance; sin is discovered, that God might be justified in the judgments threatened. I. The sins they are charged with are very great:—Injustice (ver. 1), hypocrisy in religion (ver. 2), incorrigibleness (ver. 3), the corruption and debauchery of both poor and rich (ver. 4, 5), idolatry and adultery (ver. 7, 8), treacherous departures from God (ver. 11), an impudent defiance of him (ver. 12, 13), and, that which is at the bottom of all this, want of the fear of God, notwithstanding the frequent calls given them to fear him, ver. 20—24. In the close of the chapter they are charged with violence and oppression (ver. 26—28), and a combination of those to debauch the nation who should have been active to reform it, ver. 30, 31. II. The judgments they are threatened with are very terrible. In general, they shall be reckoned with, ver. 9, 29. A foreign enemy shall be brought in upon them (ver. 15—17), shall set guards upon them (ver. 6), shall destroy their fortifications (ver. 10), shall carry them away into captivity (ver. 19), and keep all good things from them, v. 25. Herein the words of God's prophets shall be fulfilled, v. 14. But, III. Here is an intimation twice given that God would in the midst of wrath remember mercy, and not utterly destroy them, ver. 10, 18. This was the scope and purport of Jeremiah's preaching in the latter end of Josiah's reign and the beginning of Jehoiakim's; but the success of it did not answer expectation.

RUN ye to and fro through the streets of Jerusalem, and see now, and know, and seek in the broad places thereof, if ye can find a man, if there be *any* that executeth judgment, that seeketh the truth; and I will pardon it. 2 And though they say, The LORD liveth; surely

they swear falsely. 3 O LORD, *are* not thine eyes upon the truth? Thou hast stricken them, but they have not grieved; thou hast consumed them, *but* they have refused to receive correction: they have made their faces harder than a rock; they have refused to return. 4 Therefore I said, Surely these *are* poor; they are foolish: for they know not the way of the LORD, *nor* the judgment of their God. 5 I will get me unto the great men, and will speak unto them; for they have known the way of the LORD, *and* the judgment of their God: but these have altogether broken the yoke, *and* burst the bonds. 6 Wherefore a lion out of the forest shall slay them, *and* a wolf of the evenings shall spoil them, a leopard shall watch over their cities: every one that goeth out thence shall be torn in pieces: because their transgressions are many, *and* their backslidings are increased. 7 How shall I pardon thee for this? Thy children have forsaken me, and sworn by *them that are* no gods: when I had fed them to the full, they then committed adultery, and assembled themselves by troops in the harlots' houses. 8 They were *as* fed horses in the morning: every one neighed after his neighbour's wife. 9 Shall I not visit for these *things?* saith the LORD: and shall not my soul be avenged on such a nation as this?

Here is, I. A challenge to produce any one right honest man, or at least any considerable number of such, in Jerusalem, *v.* 1. Jerusalem had become like the old world, in which *all flesh had corrupted their way.* There were some perhaps who flattered themselves with hopes that there were yet many good men in Jerusalem, who would stand in the gap to turn away the wrath of God; and there might be others who boasted of its being the holy city and thought that this would save it. But God bids them search the town, and intimates that they should scarcely find a man in it who executed judgment and made conscience of what he said and did: " Look in *the streets,* where they make their appearance and converse together, and in *the broad places,* where they keep their markets; *see if you can find a man, a magistrate* (so some), *that executes judgment,* and administers justice impartially, that will put the laws in execution against vice and profaneness." When the faithful thus cease and fail it is time to cry, *Woe is me!* (Mic. vii. 1, 2), high time to cry, *Help, Lord,* Ps. xii. 1. " If there be here and there a man that is truly conscientious, and does at least *speak the truth,* yet you shall not find him *in the streets and broad places;* he dares not appear publicly, lest he should be abused and run down. *Truth has fallen in the street* (Isa. lix. 14), and is forced to *seek for corners.*" So pleasing would it be to God to find any such that for their sake he would pardon the city; if there were but ten righteous men in Sodom, if but one of a thousand, of ten thousand, in Jerusalem, it should be spared. See how ready God is to forgive, how swift to show mercy. But it might be said, " What do you make of those in Jerusalem that continue to make profession of religion and relation to God? Are not they men for whose sakes Jerusalem may be spared?" No, for they are not sincere in their profession (*v.* 2): *They say, The Lord liveth,* and will swear by his name only, but they *swear falsely,* that is, 1. They are not sincere in the profession they make of respect to God, but are false to him; they *honour him with their lips, but their hearts are far from him.* 2. Though they appeal to God only, they make no conscience of calling him to witness to a lie. Though they do not swear by idols, they forswear themselves, which is no less an affront to God, as the God of truth, than the other is as the only true God.

II. A complaint which the prophet makes to God of the obstinacy and wilfulness of these people. God had appealed to their eyes (*v.* 1); but here the prophet appeals to his eyes (*v.* 3): " *Are not thy eyes upon the truth?* Dost thou not see every man's true character? And is not this the truth of their character, that *they have made their faces harder than a rock?*" Or, " *Behold, thou desirest truth in the inward part;* but where is it to be found among the men of this generation? For though they say, *The Lord liveth,* yet they never regard him; *thou hast stricken them* with one affliction after another, *but they have not grieved* for the affliction, they have been as stocks and stones under it, much less have they grieved for the sin by which they have brought it upon themselves. *Thou* hast gone further yet, *hast consumed them,* hast corrected them yet more severely; *but they have refused to receive correction,* to accommodate themselves to thy design in correcting them and to answer to it. They would not receive instruction by the correction. They have set themselves to outface the divine sentence and to outbrave the execution of it, for *they have made their faces harder than a rock;* they cannot change countenance, neither blush for shame nor look pale for fear, cannot be beaten back from the pursuit of their lusts, whatever check is given them;

for, though often called to it, *they have refused to return,* and would go forward, right or wrong, as *the horse into the battle.*"

III. The trial made both of rich and poor, and the bad character given of both.

1. The poor were ignorant, and therefore they were wicked. He found many that *refused to return,* for whom he was willing to make the best excuse their case would bear, and it was this (*v.* 4): " *Surely, these are poor, they are foolish.* They never had the advantage of a good education, nor have they wherewithal to help themselves now with the means of instruction. They are forced to work hard for their living, and have no time nor capacity for reading or hearing, so that *they know not the way of the Lord, nor the judgments of their God;* they understand neither the way in which God by his precept will have them to walk towards him nor the way in which he by his providence is walking towards them." Note, (1.) Prevailing ignorance is the lamentable cause of abounding impiety and iniquity. What can one expect but works of darkness from brutish sottish people that know nothing of God and religion, but choose to *sit in darkness?* (2.) This is commonly a reigning sin among poor people. There are the devil's poor as well as God's, who, notwithstanding their poverty, might *know the way of the Lord,* so as to walk in it and do their duty, without being booklearned; but they are willingly ignorant, and therefore their ignorance will not be their excuse.

2. The rich were insolent and haughty, and therefore they were wicked (*v.* 5): " *I will get me to the great men,* and see if I can find them more pliable to the word and providence of God. I will *speak to them,* preach at court, in hopes to make some impression upon men of polite literature. But all in vain; *for,* though *they know the way of the Lord and the judgment of their God,* yet they are too stiff to stoop to his government: *These have altogether broken the yoke and burst the bonds.* They know their Master's will, but are resolved to have their own will, to *walk in the way of their heart and in the sight of their eyes.* They think themselves too goodly to be controlled, too big to be corrected, even by the sovereign Lord of all himself. They are for breaking even *his bands asunder,* Ps. ii. 3. The poor are weak, the rich are wilful, and so neither do their duty."

IV. Some particular sins specified, which they were most notoriously guilty of, and which cried most loudly to heaven for vengeance. *Their transgressions* indeed *were many,* of many kinds and often repeated, *and their backslidings were increased;* they added to the number of them and grew more and more impudent in them, *v.* 6. But two sins especially were justly to be looked upon as unpardonable crimes:—1. Their spiritual whoredom, giving that honour to idols which is due to God only. " *Thy children have forsaken me,* to whom they were born and dedicated and under whom they have been brought up, *and* they *have sworn by those that are no gods,* have made their appeal to them as if they had been omniscient and their proper judges." This is here put for all acts of religious worship due to God only, but with which they had honoured their idols. *They have sworn to them* (so it may be read), have joined themselves to them and covenanted with them. Those that forsake God make a bad change for those that are no gods. 2. Their corporal whoredom. Because they had forsaken God and served idols, he gave them up to vile affections; and those that dishonoured him were left to dishonour themselves and their own families. They *committed adultery* most scandalously, without sense of shame or fear of punishment, for they *assembled themselves by troops in the harlots' houses* and did not blush to be seen by one another in the most scandalous places. So impudent and violent was their lust, so impatient of check, and so eager to be gratified, that they became perfect beasts (*v.* 8); like high-fed horses, they *neighed every one after his neighbour's wife, v.* 8. Unbridled lusts make men *like natural brute beasts,* such monstrous odious things are they. And that which aggravated their sin was that it was the abuse of God's favours to them : *When they were fed to the full,* then their lusts grew thus furious. Fulness of bread was fuel to the fire of Sodom's lusts. *Sine Cerere et Baccho friget Venus—Luxurious living feeds the flame of lust.* Fasting would help to tame the unruly evil that is so *full of deadly poison,* and bring the body into subjection.

V. A threatening of God's wrath against them for their wickedness and the universal debauchery of their land.

1. The particular judgment that is threatened, *v.* 6. A foreign enemy shall break in upon them, get dominion over them, and shall lay all waste : their country shall be as if it were overrun and perfectly mastered by wild beasts. This enemy shall be, (1.) Like *a lion of the forest,* so strong, so furious, so irresistible; and he *shall slay them.* (2.) Like *a wolf of the evening,* which comes out at night, when he is hungry, to seek his prey, and is very fierce and ravenous : and the noise both of the lions' roaring and of the wolves' howling is very hideous. (3.) Like *a leopard,* which is very swift and very cruel, and withal careful not to miss his prey. The army of the enemy shall *watch over their cities* so strictly as to put the inhabitants to this sad dilemma—if they stay in, they are starved; if they stir out, they are stabbed : *Every one that goeth out thence shall be torn in pieces,* which intimates that in many places the enemy gave no quarter. And all this bloody work is owing to the *multitude*

of their transgressions. It is sin that makes the great slaughter.

2. An appeal to themselves concerning the equity of it (*v.* 9) : " *Shall I not visit for these things ?* Can you yourselves think that the God whose name is *Jealous* will let such idolatries go unpunished, or that a God of infinite purity will connive at such abominable uncleanness ?" These are things that must be reckoned for, else the honour of God's government cannot be maintained, nor his laws saved from contempt ; but sinners will be tempted to think him *altogether such a one as themselves,* contrary to that conviction of their own consciences concerning the judgment of God which is necessary to be supported, That *those who* do *such things are worthy of death,* Rom. i. 32. Observe, When God punishes sin, he is said to *visit* for it, or enquire into it; for he weighs the cause before he passes sentence. Sinners have reason to expect punishment upon the account of God's holiness, to which sin is highly offensive, as well as upon the account of his justice, to which it renders us obnoxious; this is intimated in that, *Shall not my soul be avenged on such a nation as this ?* It is not only the word of God, but his soul, that takes vengeance. And he has national judgments wherewith to take vengeance for national sins. *Such nations as this* was cannot long go unpunished. *How shall I pardon thee for this ? v.* 7. Not but that those who have been guilty of these sins have found mercy with God, as to their eternal state (Manasseh himself did, though so much accessory to the iniquity of these times) ; but nations, *as such,* being rewardable and punishable only in this life, it would not be for the glory of God to let a nation so very wicked as this pass without some manifest tokens of his displeasure.

10 Go ye up upon her walls, and destroy ; but make not a full end : take away her battlements ; for they *are* not the LORD's. 11 For the house of Israel and the house of Judah have dealt very treacherously against me, saith the LORD. 12 They have belied the LORD, and said, *It is* not he; neither shall evil come upon us; neither shall we see sword nor famine : 13 And the prophets shall become wind, and the word *is* not in them : thus shall it be done unto them. 14 Wherefore thus saith the LORD God of hosts, Because ye speak this word, behold, I will make my words in thy mouth fire, and this people wood, and it shall devour them. 15 Lo, I will bring a nation upon you from far, O house of Israel, saith the LORD :

it *is* a mighty nation, it *is* an ancient nation, a nation whose language thou knowest not, neither understandest what they say. 16 Their quiver *is* as an open sepulchre, they *are* all mighty men. 17 And they shall eat up thine harvest, and thy bread, *which* thy sons and thy daughters should eat: they shall eat up thy flocks and thine herds: they shall eat up thy vines and thy fig-trees: they shall impoverish thy fenced cities, wherein thou trustedst, with the sword. 18 Nevertheless in those days, saith the Lord, I will not make a full end with you. 19 And it shall come to pass, when ye shall say, Wherefore doeth the Lord our God all these *things* unto us ? then shalt thou answer them, Like as ye have forsaken me, and served strange gods in your land, so shall ye serve strangers in a land *that is* not your's.

We may observe in these verses, as before,

I. The sin of this people, upon which the commission signed against them is grounded. God disowns them and dooms them to destruction, *v.* 10. But *is there not a cause?* Yes; for, 1. They have deserted the law of God (*v.* 11): *The house of Israel and the house of Judah,* though at variance with one another, yet both agreed to *deal very treacherously against God.* They forsook the worship of him, and therein violated their covenants with him; they revolted from him, and played the hypocrite with him. 2. They have defied the judgments of God and given the lie to his threatenings in the mouth of his prophets, *v.* 12, 13. They were often told that evil would certainly come upon them; they must expect some desolating judgment, *sword or famine;* but they were secure, and said, *We shall have peace, though we go on.* For, (1.) They did not fear what God is. They belied him, and confronted the dictates even of natural light concerning him; for they said, " *It is not he,* that is, he is not such a one as we have been made to believe he is; he does not see, or not regard, or will not require it; and therefore *no evil shall come upon us.*" Multitudes are ruined by being made to believe that God will not be so strict with them as his word says he will; nay, by this artifice Satan undid us all: *You shall not surely die.* So here: *Neither shall we see sword nor famine.* Vain hopes of impunity are the deceitful support of all impiety. (2.) They did not fear what God said. The prophets gave them fair warning, but they turned it off with a jest: "They do but talk so, because it is their trade; they are words of course, and words are but wind. It is not the word of the

436

Lord that is in them; it is only the language of their melancholy fancy or their ill-will to their country, because they are not preferred." Note, Impenitent sinners are not willing to own any thing to be the word of God that makes against them, that tends either to part them from, or disquiet them in, their sins. They threaten the prophets: " *They shall become wind,* shall pass away unregarded, and *thus shall it be done unto them;* what they threaten against us we will inflict upon them. Do they frighten us with famine? Let them be *fed with the bread of affliction.*" So Micaiah was, 1 Kings xxii. 27. " Do they tell us of the sword? Let them perish by the sword," *ch.* ii. 30. Thus their mocking and misusing God's messengers filled the measure of their iniquity.

II. The punishment of this people for their sin. 1. The threatenings they laughed at shall be executed (*v.* 14): *Because you speak this word* of contempt concerning the prophets, and the word in their mouths, therefore God will put honour upon them and their words, for not one iota or tittle of them shall *fall to the ground,* 1 Sam. iii. 19. Here God turns to the prophet Jeremiah, who had been thus bantered, and perhaps had been a little uneasy at it: *Behold, I will make my words in thy mouth fire.* God owns them for his words, though men denied them, and will as surely make them to take effect as the fire consumes combustible matter that is in its way. *The word shall be fire and the people wood.* Sinners by sin make themselves fuel to that wrath of God which is *revealed from heaven against all ungodliness and unrighteousness of men* in the scripture. The word of God will certainly be too hard for those that contend with it. Those shall break who will not bow before it. 2. The enemy they thought themselves in no danger of shall be brought upon them. God gives them their commission (*v.* 10): " *Go you up upon her walls,* mount them, trample upon them, tread them down. Walls of stone, before the divine commission, shall be but mud walls. Having made yourselves masters of the walls, you may *destroy* at pleasure. You may *take away her battlements,* and leave the fenced fortified cities to lie open; for her battlements *are not the Lord's;* he does not own them and therefore will not protect and fortify them." They were not erected in his fear, nor with a dependence upon him; the people have trusted to them more than to God, and therefore they are not his. When the city is filled with sin God will not patronise the fortifications of it, and then they are paper walls. What can defend us when he who is our defence, and the defender of all our defences, has *departed from us?* Num. xiv. 9. What is not of God cannot stand, not stand long, nor stand us in any stead. What dreadful work these invaders should make is here described (*v.* 15): *Lo, I will bring a nation upon you, O house of Israel!* Note, God has all nations at his command, does what he pleases with them and makes what use he pleases of them. And sometimes he is pleased to make the nations of the earth, the heathen nations, a scourge to the house of Israel, when that has become a *hypocritical nation.* This nation of the Chaldeans is here said to be a remote nation; it is *brought upon them from afar,* and therefore will make the greater spoil and the longer stay, that the soldiers may pay themselves well for so long a march. "It is a nation that thou hast had no commerce with, by reason of their distance, and therefore canst not expect to find favour with." God can bring trouble upon us from places and causes very remote. It is a *mighty nation,* that there is no making head against, an *ancient nation,* that value themselves upon their antiquity and will therefore be the more haughty and imperious. It is *a nation whose language thou knowest not;* they spoke the Syriac tongue, which the Jews at that time were not acquainted with, as appears, 2 Kings xviii. 26. The difference of language would make it the more difficult to treat with them of peace. Compare this with the threatening, Deut. xxviii. 49, which it seems to have a reference to, for the law and the prophets exactly agree. They are well armed: *Their quiver is as an open sepulchre;* their arrows shall fly so thick, hit so sure, and wound so deep, that they shall be reckoned to breathe nothing but death and slaughter: they are able-bodied, all effective, *mighty men, v.* 16. And, when they have made themselves masters of the country, they shall devour all before them, and reckon all their own that they can lay their hands on, *v.* 17. (1.) They shall strip the country, shall not only sustain, but surfeit, their soldiers with the rich products of this fruitful land. "They shall not store up (then it might possibly be retrieved), but *eat up thy harvest* in the field *and thy bread* in the house, *which thy sons and thy daughters should eat.*" Note, What we have we have for our families, and it is a comfort to see our sons and daughters eating that which we have taken care and pains for. But it is a grievous vexation to see it devoured by strangers and enemies, to see their camps victualled with our stores, while those that are dear to us are perishing for want of it: this also is according to the curse of the law, Deut. xxviii. 33. "*They shall eat up thy flocks and herds,* out of which thou hast taken sacrifices for thy idols; they shall not leave thee the fruit of *thy vines and fig-trees.*" (2.) They shall starve the towns: "They *shall impoverish thy fenced cities*" (and what fence is there against poverty, when it comes like an armed man?), "those cities *wherein thou trustedst* to be a protection to the country." Note, It is just with God to impoverish that which we make our confidence. They shall

impoverish them *with the sword,* cutting off all provisions from coming to them and intercepting trade and commerce, which will impoverish even fenced cities.

III. An intimation of the tender compassion God has yet for them. The enemy is commissioned to destroy and lay waste, but must not *make a full end, v.* 10. Though they make a great slaughter, yet some must be left to live; though they make a great spoil, yet something must be left to live upon, for God has said it (*v.* 18) with a *non obstante*—a *nevertheless* to the present desolation: "Even *in those days,* dismal as they are, *I will not make a full end with you;*" and, if God will not, the enemy shall not. God has mercy in store for this people, and therefore will set bounds to this desolating judgment. *Hitherto it shall come, and no further.*

IV. The justification of God in these proceedings against them. As he will appear to be gracious in not making a full end with them, so he will appear to be righteous in coming so near it, and will have it acknowledged that he has done them no wrong, *v.* 19. Observe, 1. A reason demanded, insolently demanded, by the people for these judgments. They *will say, "Wherefore doth the Lord our God do all this unto us?* What provocation have we given him, or what quarrel has he with us?" As if against such a sinful nation there did not appear cause enough of action. Note, Unhumbled hearts are ready to charge God with injustice in their afflictions, and pretend they have to seek for the cause of them when it is written in the forehead of them. But, 2. Here is a reason immediately assigned. The prophet is instructed what answer to give them; for God *will be justified when he speaks,* though he speaks with ever so much terror. He must tell them that God does this against them for what they have done against him, and that they may, if they please, read their sin in their punishment. Do not they know very well that they have *forsaken God,* and therefore can they think it strange if he has forsaken them? Have they forgotten how often they *served strange gods in their own land,* that good land, in the abundance of the fruits of which they ought to have served God with gladness of heart? and therefore is it not just with God to make them *serve strangers* in a strange land, where they can call nothing their own, as he has threatened to do? Deut. xxviii. 47, 48. Those that are fond of strangers, to strangers let them go.

20 Declare this in the house of Jacob, and publish it in Judah, saying,

21 Hear now this, O foolish people, and without understanding; which have eyes, and see not; which have ears, and hear not: 22 Fear ye not me? saith the LORD: will ye not tremble at my presence, which have

placed the sand *for* the bound of the sea by a perpetual decree, that it cannot pass it: and though the waves thereof toss themselves, yet can they not prevail; though they roar, yet can they not pass over it? 23 But this people hath a revolting and a rebellious heart; they are revolted and gone. 24 Neither say they in their heart, Let us now fear the LORD our God, that giveth rain, both the former and the latter, in his season: he reserveth unto us the appointed weeks of the harvest.

The prophet, having reproved them for sin and threatened the judgments of God against them, is here sent to them again upon another errand, which he must *publish in Judah;* the purport of it is to persuade them to fear God, which would be an effectual principle of their reformation, as the want of that fear had been at the bottom of their apostasy.

I. He complains of the shameful stupidity of this people, and their bent to backslide from God, speaking as if he knew not what course to take with them. For,

1. Their understandings were darkened and unapt to admit the rays of the divine light : They are a *foolish people and without understanding;* they apprehend not the mind of God, though ever so plainly declared to them by the written word, by his prophets, and by his providence (*v.* 21): *They have eyes, but they see not, ears, but they hear not,* like the idols which they made and worshipped, Ps. cxv. 5, 6, 8. One would have thought that they took notice of things, but really they did not; they had intellectual faculties and capacities, but they did not employ and improve them as they ought. Herein they disappointed the expectations of all their neighbours, who, observing what excellent means of knowledge they had, concluded, *Surely they are a wise and an understanding people* (Deut. iv. 6), and yet really they are a *foolish people and without understanding.* Note, We cannot judge of men by the advantages and opportunities they enjoy : there are those that sit in darkness in a land of light, that live in sin even in a holy land, that are bad in the best places. 2. Their wills were stubborn and unapt to submit to the rules of the divine law (*v.* 23): *This people has a revolting and a rebellious heart;* and no wonder when they were *foolish and without understanding,* Ps. lxxxii. 5. Nay, it is the corrupt bias of the will that bribes and besots the understanding : none so blind as those that will not see. The character of this people is the true character of all people by nature, till the grace of God has wrought a change. We

438

are *foolish*, slow of understanding, and apt to mistake and forget; yet that is not the worst. We have *a revolting and a rebellious heart*, a carnal mind, that is enmity against God and is not in subjection to his law, not only revolting from him by a rooted aversion to that which is good, but rebellious against him by a strong inclination to that which is evil. Observe, The revolting heart is a rebellious one : those that withdraw from their allegiance to God do not stop there, but by siding in with sin and Satan take up arms against him. *They have revolted and gone.* The revolting heart will produce a revolting life. *They are gone,* and they *will go* (so it may be read) ; now *nothing will be restrained from them,* Gen. xi. 6.

II. He ascribed this to the want of the fear of God. When he observes them to be without understanding he asks, " *Fear you not me, saith the Lord, and will you not tremble at my presence? v.* 22. If you would but keep up an awe of God, you would be more observant of what he says to you; and, did you but understand your own interest better, you would be more under the commanding rule of God's fear." When he observes that *they have revolted and gone* he adds this, as the root and cause of their apostasy (*v.* 24), *Neither say they in their hearts, Let us now fear the Lord our God.* Therefore so many bad thoughts come into their mind, and hurry them to that which is evil, because they will not admit and entertain good thoughts, and particularly not this good thought, *Let us now fear the Lord our God.* It is true it is God's work to put his fear into our hearts; but it is our work to stir up ourselves to fear him, and to fasten upon those considerations which are proper to affect us with a holy awe of him; and it is because we do not do this that our hearts are so destitute of his fear as they are, and so apt to revolt and rebel.

III. He suggests some of those things which are proper to possess us with a holy fear of God.

1. We must fear the Lord and his greatness, *v.* 22. Upon this account he demands our fear : *Shall we not tremble at his presence,* and be afraid of affronting him, or trifling with him, who in the kingdom of nature and providence gives such incontestable proofs of his almighty power and sovereign dominion? Here is one instance given of very many that might be given : he keeps the sea within compass. Though the tides flow with a mighty strength twice every day, and if they should flow on awhile would drown the world, though in a storm the billows rise high and dash to the shore with incredible force and fury, yet they are under check, they return, they retire, and no harm is done. *This is the Lord's doing,* and, if it were not common, it would be *marvellous in our eyes.* He has *placed the sand for the bound of the sea,* not only for a *meer-stone,*

to mark out how far it may come and where it must stop, but as a *mound*, or fence, to put a stop to it. A wall of sand shall be as effectual as a wall of brass to check the flowing waves, when God is pleased to make it so; nay, that is chosen rather, to teach us that a *soft answer*, like the soft sand, *turns away wrath*, and quiets a foaming rage, when *grievous words*, like hard rocks, do but exasperate, and make *the waters cast forth* so much the more *mire and dirt*. This bound is placed *by a perpetual decree*, by an ordinance *of antiquity* (so some read it), and then it sends us as far back as to the creation of the world, when God divided between the sea and the dry land, and fixed marches between them, Gen. i. 9, 10 (which is elegantly described, Ps. civ. 6, &c., and Job xxxviii. 8, &c.), or to the period of Noah's flood, when God promised that he would never drown the world again, Gen. ix. 11. An ordinance of *perpetuity*—so our translation takes it. It is a *perpetual decree;* it has had its effect all along to this day and shall still continue till day and night come to an end. This *perpetual decree* the waters of the sea *cannot pass over* nor break through. *Though the waves thereof toss themselves,* as the *troubled sea* does *when it cannot rest,* yet *can they not prevail; though they roar* and rage as if they were vexed at the check given them, *yet can they not pass over.* Now this is a good reason why we should fear God; for, (1.) By this we see that he is a God of almighty power and universal sovereignty, and therefore to be feared and had in reverence. (2.) This shows us how easily he could drown the world again and how much we continually lie at his mercy, and therefore we should be afraid of making him our enemy. (3.) Even the unruly waves of the sea observe his decree and retreat at his check, and shall not we then? Why are our hearts revolting and rebellious, when the sea neither revolts nor rebels?

2. We must fear the Lord and his goodness, Hos. iii. 5. The instances of this, as of the former, are fetched from God's common providence, *v.* 24. We must *fear the Lord our God,* that is, we must worship him, and give him glory, and be always in care to keep ourselves in his love, because he is continually doing us good : he gives us both *the former and the latter rain,* the former a little after seed-time, the latter a little before harvest, and both *in their season;* and by this means *he reserves to us the appointed weeks of harvest.* Harvest is reckoned by weeks, because in a few weeks enough is gathered to serve for sustenance the year round. The weeks of the harvest are appointed us by the promise of God, that *seed-time and harvest shall not fail.* And in performance of that promise they are reserved to us by the divine providence, otherwise we should come short of them. In harvest mercies therefore God is to be acknowledged, his power, and goodness, and

faithfulness, for they all come from him. And it is a good reason why we should fear him, that we may keep ourselves in his love, because we have such a necessary dependence upon him. The fruitful seasons were witnesses for God, even to the heathen world, sufficient to leave them inexcusable in their contempt of him (Acts xiv. 17) ; and yet the Jews, who had the written word to explain their testimony by, were not wrought upon to fear the Lord, though it appears how much it is our interest to do so.

25 Your iniquities have turned away these *things,* and your sins have withholden good *things* from you. 26 For among my people are found wicked *men :* they lay wait, as he that setteth snares; they set a trap, they catch men. 27 As a cage is full of birds, so *are* their houses full of deceit : therefore they are become great, and waxen rich. 28 They are waxen fat, they shine : yea, they overpass the deeds of the wicked : they judge not the cause, the cause of the fatherless, yet they prosper; and the right of the needy do they not judge. 29 Shall I not visit for these *things?* saith the LORD : shall not my soul be avenged on such a nation as this? 30 A wonderful and horrible thing is committed in the land; 31 The prophets prophesy falsely, and the priests bear rule by their means; and my people love *to have it* so : and what will ye do in the end thereof?

Here, I. The prophet shows them what mischief their sins had done them : They *have turned away these things* (v. 25), the *former and the latter rain,* which they used to have *in due season* (v. 24), but which had of late been withheld (*ch.* iii. 3), by reason of which the appointed weeks of harvest had sometimes disappointed them. " It is *your sin* that *has withholden good from you,* when God was ready to bestow it upon you." Note, It is sin that stops the current of God's favours to us, and deprives us of the blessings we used to receive. It is that which makes the heavens as brass and the earth as iron.

II. He shows them how great their sins were, how heinous and provoking. When they had forsaken the worship of the true God, even moral honesty was lost among them : *Among my people are found wicked men* (v. 26), some of the worst of men, and so much the worse they were for being found among God's people. 1. They were spiteful and malicious. Such are properly *wicked men,* men that delight in doing mischief. They were *found* (that is, caught) in the very act of their wickedness. As hunters or fowlers lay snares for their game, so did they *lie in wait to catch men*, and made a sport of it, and took as much pleasure in it as if they had been entrapping beasts or birds. They contrived ways of doing mischief to good people (whom they hated for their goodness), especially to those that faithfully reproved them (Isa. xxix. 21), or to those that stood in the way of their preferment or whom they supposed to have affronted them or done them a diskindness, or to those whose estates they coveted; so Jezebel ensnared Naboth for his vineyard. Nay, they did mischief for mischief sake. 2. They were false and treacherous (*v.* 27): "*As a cage*, or coop, is *full of birds*, and of food for them to fatten them for the table, so are *their houses full of deceit*, of wealth obtained by fraudulent practices or of arts and methods of defrauding. All the business of their families is done with deceit; whoever deals with them, they will cheat him if they can, which is easily done by those who make no conscience of what they say and do. Herein *they overpass the deeds of the wicked, v.* 28. Those that act by deceit, with a colour of law and justice, do more mischief perhaps than those wicked men (*v.* 26) that carry all before them by open force and violence; or they are worse than the heathen themselves, yea, the worst of them. And (would you think it?) they prosper in these wicked courses and therefore their hearts are hardened in them. They are greedy of the world, because they find it flows in upon them, and they stick not at any wickedness in pursuit of it, because they find that it is so far from hindering their prosperity that it furthers it: *They have become great* in the world; *they have waxen rich*, and thrive upon it. They have wherewithal to make provision for the flesh to fulfil all the lusts of it, to which they are very indulgent, so that *they have waxen fat* with living at ease and bathing themselves in all the delights of sense. They are sleek and smooth: *They shine;* they look fair and gay; every body admires them. And they *pass by matters of evil* (so some read the following words); they escape the evils which one would expect their sins should bring upon them; *they are not in trouble as other men*, much less as we might expect bad men," Ps. lxxiii. 5, &c. 3. When they had grown great, and had got power in their hands, they did not do that good with it which they ought to have done: *They judge not the cause, the cause of the fatherless, and the right of the needy.* The fatherless are often needy, always need assistance and advice, and advantage is taken of their helpless condition to do them an injury. Who should succour them then but the great and rich? What have men wealth for but to do good with it? But these would take no cognizance of any such distressed cases: they

had not so much sense of justice, or compassion for the injured ; or, if they did concern themselves in the cause, it was not to do right, but to protect those that did wrong. And *yet they prosper* still; *God layeth not folly to them.* Certainly then the things of this world are not the best things, for oftentimes the worst men have the most of them; yet we are not to think that, because they prosper, God allows of their practices. No; *though sentence against* their *evil works be not executed speedily*, it will be executed. 4. There was a general corruption of all orders and degrees of men among them (*v.* 30, 31): *A wonderful and horrible thing is committed in the land.* The degeneracy of such a people, so privileged and advanced, was a wonderful thing, and to be viewed with amazement. How could they ever break through so many obligations? It was a horrible thing, a thing to be detested and the consequences of it dreaded. To frighten ourselves from sin, let us call it a horrible thing. What was the matter? In short, this : (1.) The leaders misled the people : *The prophets prophesy falsely*, counterfeit a commission from heaven when they are factors for hell. Religion is never more dangerously attacked than under colour and pretence of divine revelation. But why did not the priests, who had power in their hands for that purpose, restrain these false prophets? Alas! instead of doing that they made use of them as the tools of their ambition and tyranny : *The priests bear rule by their means;* they supported themselves in their grandeur and wealth, their laziness and luxury, their impositions and oppressions, by the help of the false prophets and their interest in the people. Thus they were in a combination against every thing that was good, and strengthened one another's hands in evil. (2.) The people were well enough pleased to be so misled : " They are *my people*," says God, " and should have stood up for me, and borne their testimony against the wickedness of their priests and prophets ; but they *love to have it so.*" If the priests and prophets will let them alone in their sins, they will give them no disturbance in theirs. They love to be ridden with a loose rein, and like those rulers very well that will not restrain their lusts and those teachers that will not reprove them.

III. He shows them how fatal the consequences of this would certainly be. Let them consider,

1. What the reckoning would be for their wickedness (*v.* 29): *Shall not I visit for these things?* as before, *v.* 9. Sometimes mercy rejoices against judgment: *How shall I give thee up, Ephraim?* Here, judgment is reasoning against mercy: *Shall I not visit?* We are sure that Infinite Wisdom knows how to accommodate the matter between them. The manner of expression is very emphatic, and denotes, (1.) The certainty

and necessity of God's judgments: *Shall not my soul be avenged?* Yes, without doubt, vengeance will come, it must come, if the sinner repent not. (2.) The justice and equity of God's judgments; he appeals to the sinner's own conscience, Do not those deserve to be punished that have been guilty of such abominations? Shall he not be avenged on *such a nation,* such a wicked provoking nation as this?

2. What the direct tendency of their wickedness was: *What will you do in the end thereof?* That is, (1.) "What a pitch of wickedness will you come to at last! *What will you do?* What will you not do that is base and wicked? What will this grow to? You will certainly grow worse and worse, till you have filled up the measure of your iniquity." (2.) "What a pit of destruction will you come to at last! When things are brought to such a pass as this, as nothing can be expected from you but a deluge of sin, so nothing can be expected from God but a deluge of wrath; and what will you do when that shall come?" Note, Those that walk in bad ways would do well to consider the tendency of them both to greater sin and utter ruin. An end will come; the end of a wicked life will come, when it will be all called over again, and without doubt will be bitterness in the latter end.

CHAP. VI.

In this chapter, as before, we have, I. A prophecy of the invading of the land of Judah and the besieging of Jerusalem by the Chaldean army (ver. 1—6), with the spoils they should make of the country (ver. 9) and the terror which all should be seized with on that occasion, ver. 22—26. II. An account of those sins of Judah and Jerusalem which provoked God to bring this desolating judgment upon them. Their oppression (ver. 7), their contempt of the word of God (ver. 10—12), their worldliness (ver. 13), the treachery of their prophets (ver. 14), their impudence in sin (ver. 15), their obstinacy against reproofs (ver. 18, 19), which made their sacrifices unacceptable to him (ver. 20), and for which he gave them up to ruin (ver. 21), but tried them first (ver. 27) and then rejected them as irreclaimable, ver. 28—30. III. Good counsel given them in the midst of all this, but in vain, ver. 8, 16, 17.

O YE children of Benjamin, gather yourselves to flee out of the midst of Jerusalem, and blow the trumpet in Tekoa, and set up a sign of fire in Beth-haccerem: for evil appeareth out of the north, and great destruction. 2 I have likened the daughter of Zion to a comely and delicate *woman.* 3 The shepherds with their flocks shall come unto her; they shall pitch *their* tents against her round about; they shall feed every one in his place. 4 Prepare ye war against her; arise, and let us go up at noon. Woe unto us! for the day goeth away, for the shadows of the evening are stretched out. 5 Arise, and let us go by night, and let us destroy her palaces. 6 For thus hath the LORD of hosts said, Hew ye

down trees, and cast a mount against Jerusalem: this *is* the city to be visited; she *is* wholly oppression in the midst of her. 7 As a fountain casteth out her waters, so she casteth out her wickedness: violence and spoil is heard in her; before me continually *is* grief and wounds. 8 Be thou instructed, O Jerusalem, lest my soul depart from thee; lest I make thee desolate, a land not inhabited.

Here is, I. Judgment threatened against Judah and Jerusalem. The city and the country were at this time secure and under no apprehension of danger; they saw no cloud gathering, but every thing looked safe and serene: but the prophet tells them that they shall shortly be invaded by a foreign power, an army shall be brought against them *from the north,* which shall lay all waste, and shall cause not only a general consternation, but a general desolation. It is here foretold,

1. That the alarm of this should be loud and terrible. This is represented, v. 1. The children of Benjamin, in which tribe part of Jerusalem lay, are here called to shift for their own safety in the country; for the city (to which it was first thought advisable for them to flee, *ch.* iv. 5, 6) would soon be made too hot for them, and they would find it the wisest course to flee out of the midst of it. It is common, in public frights, for people to think any place safer than that in which they are; and therefore those in the city are for shifting into the country, in hopes there to escape out of danger, and those in the country are for shifting into the city, in hopes there to make head against the danger; but it is all in vain when evil pursues sinners with commission. They are told to send the alarm into the country, and to do what they can for their own safety: *Blow the trumpet in Tekoa,* a city which lay twelve miles north from Jerusalem. Let them be stirred up to stand upon their guard: *Set up a sign of fire* (that is, kindle the beacons) *in Beth-haccerem,* the *house of the vineyard,* which lay on a hill between Jerusalem and Tekoa. Prepare to make a vigorous resistance, *for the evil appears out of the north.* This may be taken ironically: "Betake yourselves to the best methods you can think of for your own preservation, but all shall be in vain; for, when you have done your best, it will be a great destruction, for it is in vain to contend with God's judgments."

2. That the attempt upon them should be bold and formidable, and such as they should be a very unequal match for. (1.) See what *the daughter of Zion* is, on whom the assault is made. She is compared *to a comely and delicate woman* (v. 2), bred up in every thing that is nice and soft, that will not set

so much as the *sole of her foot to the ground for tenderness and delicacy* (Deut. xxviii. 56), nor suffer the wind to blow upon her; and, not being accustomed to hardship, she will be the less able either to resist the enemy (for those that make war must *endure hardness*) or to bear the destruction with that patience which is necessary to make it tolerable. The more we indulge ourselves in the pleasures of this life the more we disfit ourselves for the troubles of this life. (2.) See what the daughter of Babylon is, by whom the assault is made. The generals and their armies are compared to *shepherds* and *their flocks* (v. 3), in such numbers and in such order did they come, the soldiers following their leaders as the sheep their shepherds. The daughter of *Zion dwelt at home* (so some read it), expecting to be courted with love, but was invaded with fury. This comparing of the enemies to shepherds inclines me to embrace another reading, which some give of v. 2, *The daughter of Zion is like a comely pasture-ground and a delicate land,* which invite the shepherds to bring their flocks thither to graze; and as the shepherds easily make themselves masters of an open field, which (as was then usual in some parts) lies common, owned by none, *pitch their tents* in it, and their flocks quickly eat it bare, so shall the Chaldean army easily break in upon the land of Judah, force for themselves a free quarter where they please, and in a little time devour all. For the further illustration of this he shows, [1.] How God shall commission them to make this destruction even of the holy land and the holy city, which were his own possession. It is he that says (v. 4), *Prepare you war against her;* for he is the *Lord of hosts,* that has all hosts at his command, and he has said (v. 6), *Hew you down trees, and cast a mount against Jerusalem,* in order to the attacking of it. The Chaldeans have great power against Judah and Jerusalem, and yet they have no power but what is *given them from above.* God has marked out Jerusalem for destruction. He has said, "*This is the city to be visited,* visited in wrath, visited by the divine justice, and this is the time of her visitation." The day is coming when those that are careless and secure in sinful ways will certainly be visited. [2.] How they shall animate themselves and one another to execute that commission. God's counsels being against Jerusalem, which cannot be altered or disannulled, the councils of war which the enemies held are made to agree with his counsels. God having said, *Prepare war against her,* their determinations are made subservient to his; and, notwithstanding the distance of place and the many difficulties that lay in the way, it is soon resolved, *nemine contradicente—unanimously. Arise, and let us go.* Note, It is good to see how the counsel and decree of God are pursued and executed in the de-

vices and designs of men, even theirs that know him not, Isa. x. 6, 7. In this campaign, *First,* They resolve to be very expeditious. They have no sooner resolved upon it than they address themselves to it; it shall never be said that they left any thing to be done towards it to-morrow which they could do to-day: *Arise, let us go up at noon,* though it be in the heat of the day; nay (v. 5), *Arise, let us go up by night,* though it be in the dark. Nothing shall hinder them; they are resolved to *lose no time.* They are described as men in care to make despatch (v. 4): "*Woe unto us, for the day goes away,* and we are not going on with our work; *the shadows of the evening are stretched out,* and we sit still, and let slip the opportunity." O that we were thus eager in our spiritual work and warfare, thus afraid of losing time, or any opportunity, in taking the *kingdom of heaven by violence!* It is folly to trifle when we have an eternal salvation to work out, and the enemies of that salvation to fight against. *Secondly,* They confidently expect to be very successful: "*Let us go up,* and let us destroy her palaces and make ourselves masters of the wealth that is in them." It was not that they might fulfil God's counsels, but that they might fill their own treasures, that they were thus eager; yet God thereby served his own purposes.

II. The cause of this judgment assigned. It is all for their wickedness; they have brought it upon themselves; they must bear it, for they must bear the blame of it. They are thus oppressed because they have been oppressors; they have dealt hardly with one another, each in his turn, as they have had power and advantage, and now the enemy shall come and deal hardly with them all. This sin of oppression, and violence, and wrong-doing, is here charged upon them, 1. As a national sin (v. 6): *Therefore* this city *is to be visited,* it is time to make inquisition, for *she is wholly oppression in the midst of her.* All orders and degrees of men, from the prince on the throne to the meanest master of a shop, were oppressive to those that were under them. Look which way you might, there were causes for complaints of this kind. 2. As a sin that had become in a manner natural to them (v. 7): She *casts out wickedness,* in all the instances of malice and mischievousness, *as a fountain casts out her waters,* so plentifully and constantly, the streams bitter and poisonous, like the fountain. The waters out of the fountain will not be restrained, but will find or force their way, nor will they be checked by laws or conscience in their violent proceedings. This is fitly applied to the corrupt heart of man in his natural state; it *casts out wickedness,* one evil imagination or other, as a fountain *casts out her waters,* naturally and easily; it is always flowing, and yet always full. 3. As that which had become a constant practice with them · *Vio-*

lence and spoil are heard in her. The cry of it had come up before God as that of Sodom: *Before me continually are grief and wounds* —the complaint of those that find themselves aggrieved, being unjustly wounded in their bodies or spirits, in their estates or reputation. Note, He that is the common Parent of mankind regards and resents, and sooner or later will revenge, the mischiefs and wrongs that men do to one another.

III. The counsel given them how to prevent this judgment. Fair warning is given now upon the whole matter : " *Be thou instructed, O Jerusalem! v.* 8. Receive the instruction given them both by the law of God and by his prophets; be wise at length for thyself." They knew very well what they had been instructed to do; nothing remained but to do it, for till then they could not be said to be instructed. The reason for this counsel is taken from the inevitable ruin they ran upon if they refused to comply with the instructions given them: *Lest my soul depart,* or *be disjoined, from thee.* This intimates what a tender affection and concern God had had for them; his very soul had been joined to them, and nothing but sin could disjoin it. Note, 1. The God of mercy is loth to depart even from a provoking people, and is earnest with them by true repentance and reformation to prevent things coming to that extremity. 2. Their case is very miserable from whom God's soul is disjoined; it intimates the loss not only of their outward blessings, but of those comforts and favours which are the more immediate and peculiar tokens of his love and presence. Compare this with that dreadful word (Heb. x. 38), *If any man draw back, my soul shall have no pleasure in him.* 3. Those whom God forsakes are certainly undone; when God's soul departs from Jerusalem she soon becomes desolate and uninhabited, Matt. xxiii. 38.

9 Thus saith the LORD of hosts, They shall thoroughly glean the remnant of Israel as a vine: turn back thine hand as a grape-gatherer into the baskets. 10 To whom shall I speak, and give warning, that they may hear ? Behold, their ear *is* uncircumcised, and they cannot hearken: behold, the word of the LORD is unto them a reproach ; they have no delight in it. 11 Therefore I am full of the fury of the LORD ; I am weary with holding in: I will pour it out upon the children abroad, and upon the assembly of young men together : for even the husband with the wife shall be taken, the aged with *him that is* full of days. 12 And their houses shall be turned unto others, *with their*

fields and wives together : for I will stretch out my hand upon the inhabitants of the land, saith the LORD. 13 For from the least of them even unto the greatest of them every one *is* given to covetousness ; and from the prophet even unto the priest, every one dealeth falsely. 14 They have healed also the hurt *of the daughter* of my people slightly, saying, Peace, peace ; when *there is* no peace. 15 Were they ashamed when they had committed abomination ? Nay, they were not at all ashamed, neither could they blush : therefore they shall fall among them that fall : at the time *that* I visit them they shall be cast down, saith the LORD. 16 Thus saith the LORD, Stand ye in the ways, and see, and ask for the old paths, where *is* the good way, and walk therein, and ye shall find rest for your souls. But they said, We will not walk *therein.* 17 Also I set watchmen over you, *saying,* Hearken to the sound of the trumpet. But they said, We will not hearken.

The heads of this paragraph are the very same with those of the last ; for precept must be upon precept and line upon line.

I. The ruin of Judah and Jerusalem is here threatened. We had before the haste which the Chaldean army made to the war (*v.* 4, 5) ; now here we have the havoc made by the war. How lamentable are the desolations here described ! The enemy shall so long quarter among them, and be so insatiable in their thirst after blood and treasure, that they shall seize all they can meet with, and what escapes them at one time shall fall into their hands another (*v.* 9): *They shall thoroughly glean the remnant of Israel as ɩ vine;* as the *grape gatherer,* who is resolved to leave none behind, still *turns back his hand into the baskets,* to put more in, till he has gathered all, so shall they be picked up by the enemy, though dispersed, though hid, and none of them shall escape their eye and hand. Perhaps the people, being *given to covetousness* (*v.* 13), had not observed that law of God which forbade them to *glean all their grapes* (Lev. xix. 10), and now they themselves shall be in like manner *thoroughly gleaned* and shall either fall by the sword or go into captivity. This is explained *v.* 11, 12, where God's *fury* and his *hand* are said to be *poured out* and *stretched out,* in the fury and by the hand of the Chaldeans; for even wicked men are often made use of as God's hand (Ps. xvii. 14), and in their anger we may see God angry. Now see on whom the fury is poured out in full vials—*upon the children abroad,* or *in the streets,* where they are playing (Zech. viii. 5) or whither they run out innocently to look about them : the sword of the merciless Chaldeans shall not spare them, *ch.* ix. 21. The children perish in the calamity which the fathers' sins have procured. The execution shall likewise reach *the assembly of young men,* their merry meetings, their clubs which they keep up to strengthen one another's hands in wickedness; they shall be *cut off together.* Nor shall those only fall into the enemies' hands who meet for lewdness (*ch.* v. 7), but *even the husband with the wife shall be taken,* these two in bed together, and neither left, but both taken prisoners. And, as they have no compassion for the weak but fair sex, so they have none for the decrepit but venerable age : *The old with the full of days,* whose deaths can contribute no more to their safety than their lives to their service, who are not in a capacity to do them either good or harm, shall be either cut off or carried off. *Their houses shall then be turned to others* (*v.* 12); the conquerors shall dwell in their habitations, use their goods, and live upon their stores ; their *fields and wives* shall fall *together* into their hands, as was threatened, Deut. xxviii. 30, &c. For God *stretches out his hand upon the inhabitants of the land,* and none can go out of the reach of it. Now as to this denunciation of God's wrath, 1. The prophet justifies himself in preaching thus terribly, for herein he dealt faithfully (*v.* 11) : *" I am full of the fury of the Lord,* full of the thoughts and apprehensions of it, and am carried out with a powerful impulse, by the spirit of prophecy, to speak of it thus vehemently." He took no delight in threatening, nor was it any pleasure to him with such sermons as these to make those about him uneasy ; but he could not contain himself; he was *weary with holding in ;* he suppressed it as long as he could, as long as he durst, but he was so *full of power by the Spirit of the Lord of hosts* that he must speak, whether they will hear or whether they will forbear. Note, When ministers preach the terrors of the Lord according to the scripture we have no reason to be displeased at them ; for they are but messengers, and must deliver their message, pleasing or unpleasing. 2. He condemns the false prophets who preached plausibly, for therein they flattered people and dealt unfaithfully (*v.* 13, 14) : *The priest and the prophet,* who should be their watchmen and monitors, have *dealt falsely,* have not been true to their trust nor told the people their faults and the danger they were in; they should have been their physicians, but they murdered their patients by letting them have their will, by giving them every thing they had a mind to, and flattering them into an opinion that they were in no danger (*v.* 14) : They have *healed*

the hurt of the daughter of my people slightly, or *according to the cure of some slight hurt,* skinning over the wound and never searching it to the bottom, applying lenitives only, when there was need of corrosives, soothing people in their sins, and giving them opiates to make them easy for the present, while the disease was preying upon the vitals. They said, *" Peace, peace*—all shall be well" (if there were some thinking people among them, who were awake, and apprehensive of danger, they soon stopped their mouths with their priestly and prophetical authority, boldly averring that neither church nor state was in any danger), when *there is no peace,* because they went on in their idolatries and daring impieties. Note, Those are to be reckoned our false friends (that is, our worst and most dangerous enemies) who flatter us in a sinful way

II. The sin of Judah and Jerusalem, which provoked God to bring this ruin upon them and justified him in it, is here declared. 1. They would by no means bear to be told of their faults, nor of the danger they were in. God bids the prophet give them warning of the judgment coming (*v.* 9); "but," says he, " *to whom shall I speak and give warning ?* I cannot find out any that will so much as give me a patient hearing. I may give warning long enough, but there is nobody that will take warning. I cannot speak *that they may hear,* cannot speak to any purpose, or with any hope of success ; for *their ear is uncircumcised,* it is carnal and fleshly, indisposed to receive the voice of God, so that *they cannot hearken.* They have, as it were, a thick skin grown over the organs of hearing, so that divine things might to as much purpose be spoken to a stone as to them. Nay, they are not only deaf to it, but prejudiced against it; therefore they cannot hear, because they are resolved that they will not : The *word of the Lord is unto them a reproach ;* both the reproofs and the threatenings of the word are so ;" they reckoned themselves wronged and affronted by both, and resented the prophet's plain-dealing with them as they would the most causeless slander and calumny. This was *kicking against the pricks* (Acts ix. 5), as the lawyers against the word of Christ. Luke xi. 45, *Thus saying, thou reproachest us also.* Note, Those reproofs that are counted reproaches, and hated as such, will certainly be turned into the heaviest woes. When it is here said, *They have no delight in the word,* more is implied than is expressed ; " they have an antipathy to it ; their hearts rise at it; it exasperates them, and enrages their corruptions, and they are ready to fly in the face and pull out the eyes of their reprovers." And how can those expect that the word of the Lord should speak any comfort to them who have no delight in it, but would rather be any where than within hearing of it ? 2. They were inordinately set upon the world, and wholly carried away by the love of it (*v.* 13) : " *From the least of them even to the greatest,* old and young, rich and poor, high and low, those of all ranks, professions, and employments, *every one is given to covetousness,* greedy of filthy lucre, all for what they can get, *per fas per nefas—right or wrong;*" and this made them oppressive and violent (*v.* 6, 7), for of those evils, as well as others, the love of money is the bitter root. Nay, and this hardened their hearts against the word of God and his prophets. It was the covetous Pharisees that derided Christ, Luke xvi. 14. 3. They had become impudent in sin and were past shame. After such a high charge of flagrant crimes proved upon them, it was very proper to ask (*v.* 15), *Were they ashamed when they had committed* all these *abominations,* which are such a reproach to their reason and religion? Did they blush at the conviction, and acknowledge that confusion of face belonged to them? If so, there is some hope of them yet. But, alas! there did not appear so much as this colour of virtue among them; their hearts were so hardened that *they were not at all ashamed, neither could they blush,* they had so brazened their faces. They even gloried in their wickedness, and openly confronted the convictions which should have humbled them and brought them to repentance. They resolved to face it out against God himself and not to own their guilt. Some refer this to the priests and prophets, who had healed the people slightly and told them that they should have peace, and yet were not ashamed of their treachery and falsehood, no, not when the event disproved them and gave them the lie. Those that are shameless are graceless and their case is hopeless. But those that will not submit to a penitential shame, nor take that to themselves as their due, shall not escape an utter ruin ; for so it follows : *Therefore they shall fall among those that fall;* they shall have their portion with those that are quite undone ; and, when God visits the nation in wrath, they shall be sure to be cast down and be made to tremble, because they would not blush. Note, Those that sin and cannot blush for it are in an evil case now, and it will be worse with them shortly. At first they hardened themselves and would not blush, afterwards they were so hardened that they could not. *Quod unum habebant in malis bonum perdunt, peccandi verecundiam—They have lost the only good property which once blended itself with many bad ones, that is, shame for having done amiss.*—Senec. De Vit. Beat.

III. They are put in mind of the good counsel which had been often given them, but in vain. They had a great deal said to them to little purpose,

1. By way of advice concerning their duty, *v.* 16. God had been used to say to them,

Stand in the ways and see. That is, (1.) He would have them to consider, not to proceed rashly, but to do as travellers in the road, who are in care to find the right way which will bring them to their journey's end, and therefore pause and enquire for it. If they have any reason to think that they have missed their way, they are not easy till they have obtained satisfaction. O that men would be thus *wise for their souls,* and would ponder the path of their feet, as those that believe lawful and unlawful are of no less consequence to us than the right way and the wrong are to a traveller! (2.) He would have them to consult antiquity, the observations and experiences of those that went before them : " *Ask for the old paths,* enquire *of the former age* (Job viii. 8), *ask thy father, thy elders* (Deut. xxxii. 7), and thou wilt find that the way of godliness and righteousness has always been the way which God has owned and blessed and in which men have prospered. Ask for the *old paths,* the paths prescribed by the law of God, the written word, that true standard of antiquity. Ask for the paths that the patriarchs travelled in before you, Abraham, and Isaac, and Jacob ; and, as you hope to inherit the promises made to them, tread in their steps. *Ask for the old paths, Where is the good way ?*" We must not be guided merely by antiquity, as if the plea of prescription and long usage were alone sufficient to justify our path. No ; there is an *old way which wicked men have trodden,* Job xxii. 15. But, when we ask for the old paths, it is only in order to find out the *good way,* the highway of the upright. Note, The way of religion and godliness is a good old way, the way that all the saints in all ages have walked in. (3.) He would have them to resolve to act according to the result of these enquiries : " When you have found out which is the good way, *walk therein,* practise accordingly, keep closely to that way, proceed, and persevere in it." Some make this counsel to be given them with reference to the struggles that were between the true and false prophets, between those that said they should have peace and those that told them trouble was at the door ; they pretended they knew not which to believe : " *Stand in the way,*" says God, " and see, and enquire, which of these two agrees with the written word and the usual methods of God's providence, which of these directs you to the good way, and do accordingly." (4.) He assures them that, if they do thus, it will secure the welfare and satisfaction of their own souls : " *Walk in the good old way and* you will find that your walking in that way will be easy and pleasant ; you will enjoy both your God and yourselves, and the way will lead you to true rest. Though it cost you some pains to walk in that way, you will find an abundant recompence at your journey's end." (5.) He laments that this good counsel, which was so rational in itself and so proper for them, could not find acceptance : *" But they said, We will not walk therein,* not only we will not be at the pains to enquire *which is the good way,* the *good old way;* but when it is told us, and we have nothing to say to the contrary but that it is the right way, yet we will not deny ourselves and our humours so far as to *walk in it."* Thus multitudes are ruined for ever by downright wilfulness.

2. By way of admonition concerning their danger. Because they would not be ruled by fair reasoning, God takes another method with them ; by less judgments he threatens greater, and sends his prophets to give them this explication of them, and to frighten them with an apprehension of the danger they were in (*v.* 17): *Also I set watchmen over you.* God's ministers are watchmen, and it is a great mercy to have them set over us in the Lord. Now observe here, (1.) The fair warning given by these watchmen. This was the burden of their song ; they cried again and again, *Hearken to the sound of the trumpet.* God, in his providence, sounds the trumpet (Zech. ix. 14) ; the watchmen hear it themselves and are affected with it (Jer. iv. 19), and they are to call upon others to hearken to it too, to hear the Lord's controversy, to observe the voice of Providence, to improve it, and answer the intentions of it. (2.) This fair warning slighted : *" But they said, We will not hearken;* we will not hear, we will not heed, we will not believe ; the prophets may as well save themselves and us the trouble." The reason why sinners perish is because they *do not hearken to the sound of the trumpet;* and the reason why they do not is because they will not; and they have no reason to give why they will not but because they will not, that is, they are herein most unreasonable. One may more easily deal with ten men's reasons than one man's will.

18 Therefore hear, ye nations, and know, O congregation, what *is* among them. 19 Hear, O earth: behold, I will bring evil upon this people, *even* the fruit of their thoughts, because they have not hearkened unto my words, nor to my law, but rejected it. 20 To what purpose cometh there to me incense from Sheba, and the sweet cane from a far country ? your burnt-offerings *are* not acceptable, nor your sacrifices sweet unto me. 21 Therefore thus saith the LORD, Behold, I will lay stumbling-blocks before this people, and the fathers and the sons together shall fall upon them; the neighbour and his friend shall perish. 22 Thus

saith the LORD, Behold, a people cometh from the north country, and a great nation shall be raised from the sides of the earth. 23 They shall lay hold on bow and spear ; they *are* cruel, and have no mercy ; their voice roareth like the sea ; and they ride upon horses, set in array as men for war against thee, O daughter of Zion. 24 We have heard the fame thereof: our hands wax feeble : anguish hath taken hold of us, *and* pain, as of a woman in travail. 25 Go not forth into the field, nor walk by the way; for the sword of the enemy *and* fear *is* on every side. 26 O daughter of my people, gird *thee* with sackcloth, and wallow thyself in ashes : make thee mourning, *as for* an only son, most bitter lamentation: for the spoiler shall suddenly come upon us. 27 I have set thee *for* a tower *and* a fortress among my people, that thou mayest know and try their way. 28 They *are* all grievous revolters, walking with slanders : *they are* brass and iron; they *are* all corrupters. 29 The bellows are burned, the lead is consumed of the fire ; the founder melteth in vain : for the wicked are not plucked away. 30 Reprobate silver shall *men* call them, because the LORD hath rejected them.

Here, I. God appeals to all the neighbours, nay, to the whole world, concerning the equity of his proceedings against Judah and Jerusalem (*v.* 18, 19): *" Hear, you nations, and know* particularly, *O congregation* of the mighty, the great men of the nations, that take cognizance of the affairs of the states about you and make remarks upon them. Observe now what is doing among those of Judah and Jerusalem ; you hear of the desolations brought upon them, the earth rings of it, trembles under it; you all wonder that *I* should *bring evil upon this people,* that are in covenant with me, that profess relation to me, that have worshipped me, and been highly favoured by me ; you are ready to ask, *Wherefore has the Lord done thus to this land?* Deut. xxix. 24. Know then," 1. " That it is the natural product of their devices. The evil brought upon them is *the fruit of their thought.* They thought to strengthen themselves by their alliance with foreigners, and by that very thing they weakened and diminished themselves, they betrayed and exposed themselves." 2. " That it is the just punishment of their disobedience and rebellion. God does but execute upon them the curse of the law for their violation of its commands. It is because *they have not hearkened to my words nor to my law*, nor regarded a word I have said to them, but rejected it all. They would never have been ruined thus by the judgments of God's hand if they had not refused to be ruled by the judgments of his mouth: therefore you cannot say that they have any wrong done them."

II. God rejects their plea, by which they insisted upon their external services as sufficient to atone for all their sins. Alas! it is a frivolous plea (*v.* 20): "*To what purpose come there to me incense and sweet cane*, to be burnt for a perfume on the golden altar, though it was the best of the kind, and far-fetched? What care I for *your burnt-offerings* and *your sacrifices?*" They not only cannot profit God (no sacrifice does, Ps. l. 9), but they do not please him, for none does this but the sacrifice of the upright; that of the wicked is an *abomination to him*. Sacrifice and incense were appointed to excite their repentance, and to direct them to a Mediator, and assist their faith in him. Where this good use was made of them they were acceptable, God had respect to them and to those that offered them. But when they were offered with an opinion that thereby they made God their debtor, and purchased a license to go on in sin, they were so far from being pleasing to God that they were a provocation to him.

III. He foretels the desolation that was now coming upon them. 1. God designs their ruin because they hate to be reformed (*v.* 21): *I will lay stumbling-blocks before this people*, occasions of falling not into sin, but into trouble. Those whom God has marked for destruction he perplexes and embarrasses in their counsels, and obstructs and retards all the methods they take for their own safety. The parties of the enemy, which they met with wherever they went, were stumbling-blocks to them; in every corner they stumbled upon them and were dashed to pieces by them: *The fathers and the sons together shall fall upon them;* neither the fathers with their wisdom, nor the sons with their strength and courage, shall escape them, or get over them. The sons that sinned with their fathers fall with them. Even the *neighbour and his friend shall perish* and not be able to help either themselves or one another. 2. He will make use of the Chaldeans as instruments of it; for whatever work God has to do he will find out proper instruments for the doing of it. This is a people fetched *from the north, from the sides of the earth*. Babylon itself lay a great way off northward; and some of the countries that were subject to the king of Babylon, out of which his army was levied, lay much further. These must be employed in this service, *v.* 22, 23.

For, (1.) It is a people very numerous, *a great nation*, which will make their invasion the more formidable. (2.) It is a warlike people. *They lay hold on bow and spear*, and at this time know how to use them, for they are used to them. *They ride upon horses*, and therefore they march the more swiftly, and in battle press the harder. No nation had yet brought into the field a better cavalry than the Chaldeans. (3.) It is a barbarous people. They *are cruel and have no mercy*, being greedy of prey and flushed with victory. They take a pride in frightening all about them; their voice *roars like the sea*. And, (4.) They have a particular design upon Judah and Jerusalem, in hopes greatly to enrich themselves with the spoil of that famous country. They are *set in array against thee, O daughter of Zion!* The sins of God's professing people make them an easy prey to those that are God's enemies as well as theirs.

IV. He describes the very great consternation which Judah and Jerusalem should be in upon the approach of this formidable enemy, *v.* 24—26. 1. They own themselves in a fright, upon the first intelligence brought them of the approach of the enemy: "When *we have but heard the fame thereof our hands wax feeble*, and we have no heart to make any resistance; *anguish has taken hold of us*, and we are immediately in an extremity of pain, like that of *a woman in travail*." Note, Sense of guilt quite dispirits men, upon the approach of any threatening trouble. What can those hope to do for themselves who have made God their enemy? 2. They confine themselves by consent to their houses, not daring to show their heads abroad; for, though they could not but expect that the sword of the enemy would at last find them out there, yet they would rather die tamely and meanly there than run any venture, either by fight or flight, to help themselves. Thus they say one to another, "*Go not forth into the field*, no, not to fetch in your provision thence, *nor walk by the way;* dare not to go to church or market, it is at your peril if you do, for the *sword of the enemy*, and the fear of it, are *on every side;* the highways are unoccupied, as in Jael's time," Judg. v. 6. Let this remind us, when we travel the roads in safety and there is none to make us afraid, to bless God for our share in the public tranquillity. 3. The prophet calls upon them sadly to lament the desolations that were coming upon them. He was himself the lamenting prophet, and called upon his people to join with him in his lamentations: "*O daughter of my people*, hear thy God calling thee to weeping and mourning, and answer his call: do not only put on sackcloth for a day, but gird it on for thy constant wear; do not only put ashes on thy head, but *wallow thyself in ashes;* put thyself into close mourning, and use all the tokens of bitter lamentation, not forced and for show only, but with the greatest sincerity, as parents *mourn for an only son*, and think themselves comfortless because they are childless. Thus do thou lament for *the spoiler that suddenly comes upon us.* Though he has not come yet, he is *coming*, the decree has *gone forth:* let us therefore meet the execution of it with a suitable sadness " As saints may rejoice in hope of God's mercies, though they see them only in the promise, so sinners must mourn for fear of God's judgments, though they see them only in the threatenings.

V. He constitutes the prophet a judge over this people that now stand upon their trial : as *ch.* i. 10, *I have set thee over the nations ;* so here, *I have set thee for a tower*, or as a sentinel, or a watchman, upon a tower, *among my people*, as an inspector of their actions, *that thou mayest know, and try their way, v.* 27. Not that God needed any to inform him concerning them ; on the contrary, the prophet knew little of them in comparison but by the spirit of prophecy. But thus God appeals to the prophet himself, and his own observation concerning their character, that he might be fully satisfied in the equity of God's proceedings against them and with the more assurance give them warning of the judgments coming. God set him for a tower, conspicuous to all and attacked by many, but made him a *fortress*, a *strong tower*, gave him courage to stem the tide and bear the shock of their displeasure. Those that will be faithful reprovers have need to be firm as fortresses. Now in trying their way he will find two things :—1. That they are wretchedly debauched (*v.* 28) : *They are all grievous revolters, revolters of revolters* (so the word is), the worst of revolters, as a *servant of servants* is the meanest servant. They have a revolting heart, have deeply revolted, and revolt more and more. They seemed to start fair, but they revolt and start back. They *walk with slanders;* they make nothing of belying and backbiting one another, nay, they make a perfect trade of it; it is their constant course, and they govern themselves by the slanders they hear, hating those that they hear ill-spoken of, though ever so unjustly. They are *brass and iron*, base metals, and there is nothing in them that is valuable. They were as silver and gold, but they have degenerated. Nay, as *they are all revolters*, so *they are all corrupters*, not only debauched themselves, but industrious to debauch others, to corrupt them as they themselves are corrupt; nay, to make them seven times more the children of hell than themselves. It is often so ; sinners soon become tempters. 2. That they would never be reclaimed and reformed ; it was in vain to think of reforming them, for various methods had been tried with them, and all to no purpose, *v.* 29, 30. He compares them to ore that was supposed to have some good

metal in it, and was therefore put into the furnace by the refiner, who used all his art, and took abundance of pains, about it, but it proved all dross, nothing of any value could be extracted out of it. God by his prophets and by his providences had used the most proper means to refine this people and to purify them from their wickedness ; but it was all in vain. By the continual preaching of the word, and a series of afflictions, they had been kept in a constant fire, but all to no purpose. *The bellows* have been still kept so near the fire, to blow it, that they *are burnt* with the heat of it, or they are quite worn out with long use and thrown into the fire as good for nothing. The prophets have preached their throats sore with crying aloud against the sins of Israel, and yet they are not convinced and humbled. The *lead*, which was then used in refining silver, as quicksilver is now, *is consumed of the fire*, and has not done its work. *The founder melts in vain;* his labour is lost, *for the wicked are not plucked away*, no care is taken to separate between the precious and the vile, to purge out the old leaven, to cast out of communion those who, being corrupt themselves, are in danger of infecting others. Or, *Their wickednesses are not removed* (so some read it) ; they are still as bad as ever, and nothing will prevail to part between them and their sins. They will not be brought off from their idolatries and immoralities by all they have heard, and all they have felt, of the wrath of God against them; and therefore that doom is passed upon them (*v.* 30) : *Reprobate silver shall they be called*, useless and worthless ; they glitter as if they had some silver in them, but there is nothing of real virtue or goodness to be found among them ; and for this reason *the Lord has rejected them.* He will no more own them as his people, nor look for any good from them ; he will *take them away like dross* (Ps. cxix. 119), and prepare a consuming fire for those that would not be purified by a refining fire. By this it appears, (1.) That God has *no pleasure in the death* and ruin of sinners, for he tries all ways and methods with them to prevent their destruction and qualify them for salvation. Both his ordinances and his providences have a tendency this way, to part between them and their sins; and yet with many it is all lost labour. *We have piped unto you, and you have not danced; we have mourned unto you, and you have not wept.* Therefore, (2.) God will be justified in the death of sinners and all the blame will lie upon themselves. He did not reject them till he had used all proper means to reform them; did not cast them off so long as there was any hope of them, nor abandon them as dross till it appeared that they were *reprobate silver*.

CHAP. VII.

The prophet having in God's name reproved the people for their sins, and given them warning of the judgments of God that were coming upon them, in this chapter prosecutes the same intention for their humiliation and awakening. I. He shows them the invalidity of the plea they so much relied on, that they had the temple of God among them and constantly attended the service of it, and endeavours to take them off from their confidence in their external privileges and performances, ver. 1—11. II. He reminds them of the desolations of Shiloh, and foretels that such should be the desolations of Jerusalem, ver. 12—16. III. He represents to the prophet their abominable idolatries, for which he was thus incensed against them, ver. 17—20. IV. He sets before the people that fundamental maxim of religion that " to obey is better than sacrifice" (1 Sam. xv. 22), and that God would not accept the sacrifices of those that obstinately persisted in disobedience, ver. 21—28. V. He threatens to lay the land utterly waste for their idolatry and impiety, and to multiply their slain as they had multiplied their sin, ver. 29—34.

THE word that came to Jeremiah from the LORD, saying, 2 Stand in the gate of the LORD's house, and proclaim there this word, and say, Hear the word of the LORD, all *ye of* Judah, that enter in at these gates to worship the LORD. 3 Thus saith the LORD of hosts, the God of Israel, Amend your ways and your doings, and I will cause you to dwell in this place. 4 Trust ye not in lying words, saying, The temple of the LORD, the temple of the LORD, the temple of the LORD, *are* these. 5 For if ye throughly amend your ways and your doings; if ye throughly execute judgment between a man and his neighbour; 6 *If* ye oppress not the stranger, the fatherless, and the widow, and shed not innocent blood in this place, neither walk after other gods to your hurt: 7 Then will I cause you to dwell in this place, in the land that I gave to your fathers, for ever and ever. 8 Behold, ye trust in lying words, that cannot profit. 9 Will ye steal, murder, and commit adultery, and swear falsely, and burn incense unto Baal, and walk after other gods, whom ye know not; 10 And come and stand before me in this house, which is called by my name, and say, We are delivered to do all these abominations? 11 Is this house, which is called by my name, become a den of robbers in your eyes? behold, even I have seen *it*, saith the LORD. 12 But go ye now unto my place which *was* in Shiloh, where I set my name at the first, and see what I did to it for the wickedness of my people Israel. 13 And now, because ye have done all these works, saith the LORD, and I spake unto you, rising up early and speaking, but ye heard not; and I called you, but ye

answered not; 14 Therefore will I do unto *this* house, which is called by my name, wherein ye trust, and unto the place which I gave to you and to your fathers, as I have done to Shiloh. 15 And I will cast you out of my sight, as I have cast out all your brethren, *even* the whole seed of Ephraim.

These verses begin another sermon, which is continued in this and the two following chapters, much to the same effect with those before, to reason them to repentance. Observe,

I. The orders given to the prophet to preach this sermon; for he had not only a general commission, but particular directions and instructions for every message he delivered. This was *a word* that *came to him from the Lord, v.* 1. We are not told when this sermon was to be preached; but are told, 1. Where it must be preached—*in the gate of the Lord's house,* through which they entered into the outer court, or the *court of the people.* It would affront the priests, and expose the prophet to their rage, to have such a message as this delivered within their precincts; but the prophet must not fear the face of man, he cannot be faithful to his God if he do. 2. To whom it must be preached —to the men of *Judah, that enter in at these gates to worship the Lord;* probably it was at one of the three feasts, when all the males from all parts of the country were to appear before the Lord in the courts of his house, and not to *appear empty:* then he had many together to preach to, and that was the most seasonable time to admonish them not to trust to their privileges. Note, (1.) Even those that profess religion have need to be preached to as well as those that are without. (2.) It is desirable to have opportunity of preaching to many together. Wisdom chooses to cry *in the chief place of concourse,* and, as Jeremiah here, *in the opening of the gates,* the temple-gates. (3.) When we are going to worship God we have need to be admonished to *worship him in the spirit,* and *to have no confidence in the flesh,* Phil. iii. 3.

II. The contents and scope of the sermon itself. It is delivered in the name of *the Lord of hosts, the God of Israel,* who commands the world, but covenants with his people. As creatures we are bound to regard the *Lord of hosts,* as Christians *the God of Israel:* what he said to them he says to us, and it is much the same with that which John Baptist said to those whom he baptized (Matt. iii. 8, 9), *Bring forth fruits meet for repentance: and think not to say within yourselves, We have Abraham to our father.* The prophet here tells them,

1. What were the true words of God, which they might trust to. In short, they might depend upon it that if they would re-

pent and reform their lives, and return to God in a way of duty, he would restore and confirm their peace, would redress their grievances, and return to them in a way of mercy (v. 3): *Amend your ways and your doings.* This implies that there had been much amiss in their ways and doings, many faults and errors. But it is a great instance of the favour of God to them that he gives them liberty to amend, shows them where and how they must amend, and promises to accept them upon their amendment: "*I will cause you to dwell* quietly and peaceably *in this place,* and a stop shall be put to that which threatens your expulsion." Reformation is the only way, and a sure way, to prevent ruin. He explains himself (v. 5—7), and tells them particularly, (1.) What the amendment was which he expected from them. They must *thoroughly amend;* in *making good,* they must *make good their ways and doings;* they must reform with resolution, and it must be a universal, constant, persevering reformation—not partial, but entire—not hypocritical, but sincere —not wavering, but constant. They must make the tree good, and so make the fruit good, must amend their hearts and thoughts, and so amend their ways and doings. In particular, [1.] They must be honest and just in all their dealings. Those that had power in their hands must *thoroughly execute judgment between a man and his neighbour,* without partiality, and according as the merits of the cause appeared. They must not either in judgment or in contract *oppress the stranger, the fatherless, or the widow,* nor countenance or protect those that did oppress, nor refuse to do them justice when they sought for it. They must *not shed innocent blood,* and with it defile *this place* and the land wherein they dwelt. [2.] They must keep closely to the worship of the true God only: "*Neither walk after other gods;* do not hanker after them, nor hearken to those that would draw you into communion with idolaters; for it is, and will be, *to your own hurt.* Be not only so just to your God, but so wise for yourselves, as not to throw away your adorations upon those who are not able to help you, and thereby provoke him who is able to destroy you." Well, this is all that God insists upon.

(2.) He tells them what the establishment is which, upon this amendment, they may expect from him (v. 7): "Set about such a work of reformation as this with all speed, go through with it, and abide by it; *and I will cause you to dwell in this place,* this temple; it shall continue your place of resort and refuge, the place of your comfortable meeting with God and one another; and you shall dwell *in the land that I gave to your fathers for ever and ever,* and shall never be turned out either from God's house or from your own." It is promised that they shall still enjoy their civil and sacred privileges, that they shall have a comfortable enjoyment

of them : *I will cause you to dwell here;* and those dwell at ease to whom God gives a settlement. They shall enjoy it by covenant, by virtue of the grant made of it to their fathers, not by providence, but by promise. They shall continue in the enjoyment of it without eviction or molestation ; they shall not be disturbed, much less dispossessed, *for ever and ever;* nothing but sin could throw them out. An everlasting inheritance in the heavenly Canaan is hereby secured to all that live in godliness and honesty. And the vulgar Latin reads a further privilege here, v. 3, 7. *Habitabo vobiscum—I will dwell with you in this place;* and we should find Canaan itself but an uncomfortable place to dwell in if God did not dwell with us there.

2. What were the lying words of their own hearts, which they must not trust to. He cautions them against this self-deceit (v. 4): "*Trust not in lying words.* You are told in what way, and upon what terms, you may be easy, safe, and happy; now do not flatter yourselves with an opinion that you may be so on any other terms, or in any other way." Yet he charges them with this self-deceit arising from vanity (v. 8): "*Behold,* it is plain that *you* do *trust in lying words,* notwithstanding what is said to you; you trust in *words that cannot profit;* you rely upon a plea that will stand you in no stead." Those that slight the words of truth, which would profit them, take shelter in words of falsehood, which cannot profit them. Now these lying words were, "*The temple of the Lord, the temple of the Lord, the temple of the Lord are these.*" These buildings, the courts, the holy place, and the holy of holies, are the *temple of the Lord,* built by his appointment, to his glory; here he resides, here he is worshipped, here we meet three times a year to pay our homage to him as our King in his palace." This they thought was security enough to them to keep God and his favours from leaving them, God and his judgments from breaking in upon them. When the prophets told them how sinful they were, and how miserable they were likely to be, still they appealed to the temple : "How can we be either so or so, as long as we have that holy happy place among us?" The prophet repeats it because they repeated it upon all occasions. It was the cant of the times; it was in their mouths upon all occasions. If they heard an awakening sermon, if any startling piece of news was brought to them, they lulled themselves asleep again with this, "We cannot but do well, for we have *the temple of the Lord among us.*" Note, The privileges of a *form of godliness* are often the pride and confidence of those that are strangers and enemies to the power of it. It is common for those that are furthest from God to boast themselves most of their being near to the church. They are *haughty because of the holy mountain* (Zeph.

iii. 11), as if God's mercy were so tied to them that they might defy his justice. Now to convince them what a frivolous plea this was, and what little stead it would stand them in,

(1.) He shows them the gross absurdity of it in itself. If they knew any thing either of the *temple of the Lord* or of the *Lord of the temple,* they must think that to plead that, either in excuse of their sin against God or in arrest of God's judgment against them, was the most ridiculous unreasonable thing that could be. [1.] God is a holy God; but this plea made him the patron of sin, of the worst of sins, which even the light of nature condemns, v. 9, 10. "What," says he, " *will you steal, murder, and commit adultery,* be guilty of the vilest immoralities, and which the common interest, as well as the common sense, of mankind witness against? *Will you swear falsely,* a crime which all nations (who with the belief of a God have had a veneration for an oath) have always had a horror of ? Will *you burn incense to Baal,* a dunghill-deity, that sets up as a rival with the great Jehovah, and, not content with that, *will you walk after other gods* too, *whom you know not,* and by all these crimes put a daring affront upon God, both as *the Lord of hosts* and as the *God of Israel ?* Will you exchange a God of whose power and goodness you have had such a long experience for gods of whose ability and willingness to help you you know nothing ? And, when you have thus done the worst you can against God, will you brazen your faces so far as to come and *stand before him in this house which is called by his name* and in which his name is called upon —stand before him as servants waiting his commands, as suppliants expecting his favour ? Will you act in open rebellion against him, and yet herd among his subjects, among the best of them ? By this, it should seem, you think that either he does not discover or does not dislike your wicked practices, to imagine either of which is to put the highest indignity possible upon him. It is as if you should say, *We are delivered to do all these abominations.*" If they had not the front to say this, *totidem verbis—in so many words,* yet their actions spoke it aloud. They could not but own that God, even their own God, had many a time delivered them, and been a present help to them, when otherwise they must have perished. He, in delivering them, designed to reduce them to himself, and by his goodness to lead them to repentance; but they resolved to persist in their abominations notwithstanding. As soon as they were delivered (as of old in the days of the Judges) they *did evil again in the sight of the Lord,* which was in effect to say, in direct contradiction to the true intent and meaning of the providences which had affected them, that God had delivered them in order to put them again into a capacity of rebelling against him, by sacrificing the more profusely to

their idols. Note, Those who continue in sin because grace has abounded, or that grace may abound, do in effect make Christ the minister of sin. Some take it thus: " You present yourselves before God with your sacrifices and sin-offerings, and then say, *We are delivered,* we are discharged from our guilt, now it shall do us no hurt ; when all this is but to blind the world, and stop the mouth of conscience, that you may, the more easily to yourselves and the more plausibly before others, *do all these abominations.*" [2.] His temple was a holy place; but this plea made it a protection to the most unholy persons: "*Has this house, which is called by my name* and is a standing sign of God's kingdom, set up among men in opposition to the kingdom of sin and Satan— *has this become a den of robbers in your eyes?* Do you think it was built to be not only a rendezvous of, but a refuge and shelter to, the vilest of malefactors ?" No ; though the horns of the altar were a sanctuary to him that slew a man unawares, yet they were not so to a wilful murderer, nor to one that did aught presumptuously, Exod. xxi. 14 ; 1 Kings ii. 29. Those that think to excuse themselves in unchristian practices with the Christian name, and sin the more boldly and securely because there is a sin-offering provided, do, in effect, make God's house of prayer a den of thieves, as the priests in Christ's time, Matt. xxi. 13. But could they thus impose upon God ? No : *Behold, I have seen it, saith the Lord,* have seen the real iniquity through the counterfeit and dissembled piety. Note, Though men may deceive one another with the appearances of devotion, yet they cannot deceive God.

(2.) He shows them the insufficiency of this plea adjudged long since in the case of Shiloh. [1.] It is certain that Shiloh was ruined, though it had God's sanctuary in it, when by its wickedness it profaned that sanctuary (v. 12): *Go you now to my place which was in Shiloh.* It is probable that the ruins of that once flourishing city were yet remaining ; they might, at least, read the history of it, which ought to affect them as if they saw the place. There God *set his name at the first,* there the tabernacle was set up when Israel first took possession of Canaan (Josh. xviii. 1), and thither the tribes went up ; but those that attended the service of the tabernacle there corrupted both themselves and others, and from them arose the *wickedness of his people Israel ;* that fountain was poisoned, and sent forth malignant streams ; and what came of it ? Go, *see what God did to it !* Was it protected by its having the tabernacle in it ? No ; God *forsook* it (Ps. lxxviii. 60), sent his ark into captivity, cut off the house of Eli that presided there ; and it is very probable that the city was quite destroyed, for we never read any more of it but as a monument of divine vengeance upon holy places when they harbour wicked people. Note, God's judgments upon others, who have really revolted from God while they have kept up a profession of nearness to him, should be a warning to us not to *trust in lying words.* It is good to consult precedents, and make use of them. *Remember Lot's wife;* remember Shiloh and the seven churches of Asia; and know that the ark and candlestick are moveable things, Rev. ii. 5; Matt. xxi. 43. [2.] It is as certain that Shiloh's fate will be Jerusalem's doom if a speedy and sincere repentance prevent it not. *First,* Jerusalem was now as sinful as ever Shiloh was; that is proved by the unerring testimony of God himself against them (*v.* 13): " *You have done all these works,* you cannot deny it:" and they continued obstinate in their sin; that is proved by the testimony of God's messengers, by whom he *spoke to them* to return and repent, *rising up early and speaking,* as one in care, as one in earnest, as one who would lose no time in dealing with them, nay, who would take the fittest opportunity for speaking to them early *in the morning,* when, if ever, they were sober, and had their thoughts free and clear; but it was all in vain. God spoke, but they *heard not,* they heeded not, they never minded; he *called them,* but they *answered not;* they would not come at his call. Note, What God has spoken to us greatly aggravates what we have done against him. *Secondly,* Jerusalem shall shortly be as miserable as ever Shiloh was: *Therefore I will do unto this house as I did to Shiloh,* ruin it, and lay it waste, *v.* 14. Those that tread in the steps of the wickedness of those that went before them must expect to fall by the like judgments, for all these things *happened to them for ensamples.* The temple at Jerusalem, though ever so strongly built, if wickedness was found in it, would be as unable to keep its ground and as easily conquered as even the tabernacle in Shiloh was, when God's day of vengeance had come. " This house" (says God) " is *called by my name,* and therefore you may think that I should protect it; it is the house *in which you trust,* and you think that it will protect you; this land is *the place,* this city *the place, which I gave to you and your fathers,* and therefore you are secure of the continuance of it, and think that nothing can turn you out of it; but the men of Shiloh thus flattered themselves and did but deceive themselves." He quotes another precedent (*v.* 15), the ruin of the kingdom of the ten tribes, who were the seed of Abraham, and had the covenant of circumcision, and possessed the land which God gave to them and their fathers, and yet their idolatries threw them out and extirpated them: " And can you think but that the same evil courses will be as fatal to you?" Doubtless they will be so; for God is uniform and of a piece with himself in his judicial proceedings. It is a rule of justice, *ut parium par*

452

sit ratio—*that in similar cases the same judgment should proceed* " You have corrupted *yourselves as your brethren* the *seed of Ephraim* did, and have become their brethren in iniquity, and therefore I will *cast you out of my sight, as I have cast them.*" The interpretation here given of the judgment makes it a terrible one indeed; the casting of them out of their land signified God's casting them out of his sight, as if he would never look upon them, never look after them, more. Wherever we are cast, it is well enough, if we be kept in the love of God; but, if we are thrown out of his favour, our case is miserable though we dwell in our own land. This threatening, that God would make this house like Shiloh, we shall meet with again, and find Jeremiah indicted for it, *ch.* xxvi. 6.

16 Therefore pray not thou for this people, neither lift up cry nor prayer for them, neither make intercession to me: for I will not hear thee. 17 Seest thou not what they do in the cities of Judah, and in the streets of Jerusalem? 18 The children gather wood, and the fathers kindle the fire, and the women knead *their* dough, to make cakes to the queen of heaven, and to pour out drink-offerings unto other gods, that they may provoke me to anger. 19 Do they provoke me to anger? saith the LORD: *do they* not *provoke* themselves to the confusion of their own faces? 20 Therefore thus saith the Lord GOD; Behold, mine anger and my fury shall be poured out upon this place, upon man, and upon beast, and upon the trees of the field, and upon the fruit of the ground; and it shall burn, and shall not be quenched.

God had shown them, in the foregoing verses, that the temple and the service of it, of which they boasted and in which they trusted, should not avail to prevent the judgment threatened. But there was another thing which might stand them in some stead, and which yet they had no value for, and that was the prophet's intercession for them; his prayers would do them more good than their own pleas: now here that support is taken from them; and their case is sad indeed who have lost their interest in the prayers of God's ministers and people.

I. God here forbids the prophet to pray for them (*v.* 16): " The decree has gone forth, their ruin is resolved on, therefore *pray not thou for this people,* that is, pray not for the preventing of this judgment threatened; they have *sinned unto death,* and therefore pray not for their life, but for the life of their souls," 1 John v. 16. See here,

1. That God's prophets are praying men; Jeremiah foretold the destruction of Judah and Jerusalem, and yet prayed for their preservation, not knowing that the decree was absolute; and it is the will of God that we *pray for the peace of Jerusalem.* Even when we threaten sinners with damnation we must pray for their salvation, that they may *turn and live.* Jeremiah was hated, and persecuted, and reproached, by the children of his people, and yet he prayed for them; for it becomes us to render good for evil. 2. That God's praying prophets have a great interest in heaven, how little soever they have on earth. When God has determined to destroy this people, he bespeaks the prophet not to pray for them, because he would not have his prayers to lie (as prophets' prayers seldom did) unanswered. God said to Moses, *Let me alone,* Exod. xxii. 10. 3. It is an ill omen to a people when God restrains the spirits of his ministers and people from praying for them, and gives them to see their case so desperate that they have no heart to speak a good word for them. 4. Those that will not regard good ministers' preaching cannot expect any benefit by their praying. If you will not hear us when we speak from God to you, God will not hear us when we speak to him for you.

II. He gives him a reason for this prohibition. Praying breath is too precious a thing to be lost and thrown away upon a people hardened in sin and marked for ruin.

1. They are resolved to persist in their rebellion against God, and will not be turned back by the prophet's preaching. For this he appeals to the prophet himself, and his own inspection and observation (*v.* 17): *Seest thou not what they do* openly and publicly, without either shame or fear, *in the cities of Judah and in the streets of Jerusalem?* This intimates both that the sin was evident and could not be denied and that the sinners were impudent and would not be reclaimed; they committed their wickedness even in the prophet's presence and under his eye; he saw what they did, and yet they did it, which was an affront to his office, and to him whose officer he was, and bade defiance to both. Now observe,

(1.) What the sin is with which they are here charged—it is idolatry, *v.* 18. Their idolatrous respects are paid to the *queen of heaven,* the moon, either in an image or in the original, or both. They worshipped it probably under the name of *Ashtaroth,* or some other of their goddesses, being in love with the brightness in which they saw the moon walk, and thinking themselves indebted to her for her benign influences or fearing her malignant ones, Job xxxi. 26. The worshipping of the moon was much in use among the heathen nations, *ch.* xliv. 17, 19. Some read it the *frame* or *workmanship of heaven.* The whole celestial globe with all its ornaments and powers was the object of their adoration. They *worshipped the host of heaven,* Acts vii. 42. The homage they should have paid to their Prince they paid to the statues that beautified the frontispiece of his palace; they worshipped the creatures instead of him that made them, the servants instead of him that commands them, and the gifts instead of him that gave them. *With the queen of heaven* they worshipped *other gods,* images of things not only in *heaven above, but in earth beneath, and in the waters under the earth;* for those that forsake the true God wander endlessly after false ones. To these deities of their own making they offer *cakes* for meat-offerings, and *pour out drink-offerings,* as if they had their meat and drink from them and were obliged to make to them their acknowledgments: and see how busy they are, and how every hand is employed in the service of these idols, according as they used to be employed in their domestic services. *The children* were sent to *gather wood; the fathers kindled the fire* to heat the oven, being of the poorer sort that could not afford to keep servants to do it, yet they would rather do it themselves than it should be undone; *the women kneaded the dough* with their own hands, for perhaps, though they had servants to do it, they took a pride in showing their zeal for their idols by doing it themselves. Let us be instructed, even by this bad example, in the service of our God. [1.] Let us *honour him with our substance,* as those that have our subsistence from him, and eat and drink to the glory of him from whom we have our meat and drink. [2.] Let us not decline the hardest services, nor disdain to stoop to the meanest, by which God may be honoured; for none shall *kindle a fire on God's altar for nought.* Let us think it an honour to be employed in any work for God. [3.] Let us bring up our children in the acts of devotion; let them, as they are capable, be employed in doing something towards the keeping up of religious exercises.

(2.) What is the direct tendency of this sin: "It is *that they may provoke me to anger;* they cannot design any thing else in it. But (*v.* 19) *do they provoke me to anger?* Is it because I am hard to be pleased, or easily provoked? Or am I to bear the blame of the resentment? No; it is their own doing; they may thank themselves, and they alone shall bear it." *Is it against God that they provoke him to wrath?* Is he the worse for it? Does it do him any real damage? No; is it *not against themselves,* to the *confusion of their own faces?* It is malice against God, but it is impotent malice; it cannot hurt him: nay, it is foolish malice; it will hurt themselves. They show their spite against God, but they do the spite to themselves. Canst thou think any other than that a people, thus desperately set upon their own ruin, should be abandoned?

2. God is resolved to proceed in his judg-

ments against them, and will not be turned back by the prophet's prayers (v. 20): *Thus saith the Lord God,* and what he saith he will not unsay, nor can all the world gainsay it; hear it therefore, and tremble. *"Behold, my anger and my fury shall be poured out upon this place,* as the flood of waters was upon the old world or the shower of fire and brimstone upon Sodom; since they will anger me, let them see what will come of it." They shall soon find, (1.) That there is no escaping this deluge of fire, either by flying from it or fencing against it; it shall be poured out on *this place,* though it be a holy place, the Lord's house. It shall reach both *man and beast,* like the plagues of Egypt, and, like some of them, shall destroy the *trees of the field and the fruit of the ground,* which they had designed and *prepared for Baal,* and of which they had made *cakes to the queen of heaven.* (2.) There is no extinguishing it: *It shall burn and shall not be quenched;* prayers and tears shall then avail nothing. When *his wrath is kindled but a little,* much more when it is kindled to such a degree, there shall be no quenching it. God's wrath is that fire unquenchable which eternity itself will not see the period of. *Depart, you cursed, into everlasting fire.*

21 Thus saith the LORD of hosts, the God of Israel; Put your burnt-offerings unto your sacrifices, and eat flesh. 22 For I spake not unto your fathers, nor commanded them in the day that I brought them out of the land of Egypt, concerning burnt offerings or sacrifices: 23 But this thing commanded I them, saying, Obey my voice, and I will be your God, and ye shall be my people: and walk ye in all the ways that I have commanded you, that it may be well unto you. 24 But they hearkened not, nor inclined their ear, but walked in the counsels *and* in the imagination of their evil heart, and went backward, and not forward. 25 Since the day that your fathers came forth out of the land of Egypt unto this day I have even sent unto you all my servants the prophets, daily rising up early and sending *them:* 26 Yet they hearkened not unto me, nor inclined their ear, but hardened their neck: they did worse than their fathers. 27 Therefore thou shalt speak all these words unto them; but they will not hearken to thee: thou shalt also call unto them; but they will not answer thee. 28 But thou shalt say

unto them, This *is* a nation that obeyeth not the voice of the LORD their God, nor receiveth correction: truth is perished, and is cut off from their mouth.

God, having shown the people that the temple would not protect them while they polluted it with their wickedness, here shows them that their sacrifices would not atone for them, nor be accepted, while they went on in disobedience. See with what contempt he here speaks of their ceremonial service (v. 21). *" Put your burnt-offerings to your sacrifices;* go on in them as long as you please; add one sort of sacrifice to another; turn your *burnt-offerings* (which were to be wholly burnt to the honour of God) into *peace-offerings"* (which the offerer himself had a considerable share of), *"* that you may *eat flesh,* for that is all the good you are likely to have from your sacrifices, a good meal's meat or two; but expect not any other benefit by them while you live at this loose rate. *Keep your sacrifices to yourselves"* (so some understand it); *"* let them be served up at your own table, for they are no way acceptable at God's altars." For the opening of this,

I. He shows them that obedience was the only thing he required of them, v. 22, 23. He appeals to the original contract, by which they were first formed into a people, when they were brought out of Egypt. God made them a *kingdom of priests* to himself, not that he might be regaled with their sacrifices, as the devils, whom the heathen worshipped, which are represented as eating with pleasure the fat of their sacrifices and drinking the wine of their drink-offerings, Deut. xxxii. 38. No: *Will God eat the flesh of bulls?* Ps. l. 13. *I spoke not to your fathers concerning burnt-offerings or sacrifices,* not of them *at first.* The precepts of the moral law were given before the ceremonial institutions; and those came afterwards, as trials of their obedience and assistances to their repentance and faith. The Levitical law begins thus: *If any man of you will bring an offering,* he must do so and so (Lev. i. 2, ii. 1), as if it were intended rather to regulate sacrifice than to require it. But that which God commanded, which he bound them to by his supreme authority and which he insisted upon as the condition of the covenant, was, *Obey my voice;* see Exod. xv. 26, where this was the statute and the ordinance by which God proved them: *Hearken diligently to the voice of the Lord thy God.* The condition of their being God's peculiar people was this (Exod. xix. 5), *If you will obey my voice indeed.* "Make conscience of the duties of natural religion, observe positive institutions from a principle of obedience, and then *I will be your God and you shall be my people,"* which is the greatest honour, happiness, and satisfaction, that any of the children of men are capable of. "Let your conversation be regular, and in every thing study to comply with the will and word of God ; *walk* within the bounds that I have set you, and *in all the ways that I have commanded you,* and then you may assure yourselves that *it shall be well with you.*" The demand here is very reasonable, that we should be directed by Infinite Wisdom to that which is fit, that he that made us should command us, and that he should give us law who gives us our being and all the supports of it ; and the promise is very encouraging : Let God's will be your rule and his favour shall be your felicity.

II. He shows them that disobedience was the only thing for which he had a quarrel with them. *He would not reprove them for their sacrifices,* for the omission of them ; they had been *continually before him* (Ps. l. 8) ; with them they hoped to bribe God, and purchase a license to go on in sin. That therefore which God had all along laid to their charge was breaking his commandments in the course of their conversation, while they observed them, in some instances, in the course of their devotion, *v.* 24, 25, &c. 1. They set up their own will in competition with the will of God : *They hearkened not to God* and to his law ; they never heeded that ; it was to them as if it had never been given or were of no force ; they *inclined not their ear* to attend to it, much less their hearts to comply with it. But they would have their own way, would do as they chose, and not as they were bidden. *Their own counsels* were their guide, and not the dictates of divine wisdom ; that shall be lawful and good with them which they think so, though the word of God says quite contrary. *The imagination of their evil heart,* the appetites and passions of it, shall be a law to them, and they will walk in the way of it, and in the sight of their eyes. 2. If they began well, yet they did not· proceed, but soon flew off. They *went backward,* when they talked of making a captain, and returning to Egypt again, and would not go forward under God's conduct. They promised fair : *All that the Lord shall say unto us we will do ;* and, if they would but have kept in that good mind, all would have been well ; but, instead of going on in the way of duty, they drew back into the way of sin, and were worse than ever. 3. When God sent to them by word of mouth to put them in mind of the written word, which was the business of the prophets, it was all one ; still they were disobedient. God had servants of his among them in every age, *since they came out of Egypt unto this day,* some or other to tell them of their faults and put them in mind of their duty, whom he *rose up early to send* (as before, *v.* 13), as men rise up early to call servants to their work ; but they were as deaf to the prophets as they were to the law (*v.* 26) : *Yet they hearkened not, nor in-*

clined their ear. This had been their way and manner all along ; they were of the same stubborn refractory disposition with those that went before them ; it had all along been the genius of the nation, and an evil genius it was, that continually haunted them till it ruined them at last. 4. Their practice and character·were still the same. They are worse, and not better, *than their fathers.* (1.) Jeremiah can himself witness against them that they were disobedient, or he shall soon find it so (*v.* 27) : "*Thou shalt speak all these words to them,* shalt particularly charge them with disobedience and obstinacy. But even that will not work upon them : *They will not hearken to thee,* nor heed thee. Thou shalt go, and *call to them* with all the plainness and earnestness imaginable, but *they will not answer thee ;* they will either give thee no answer at all or not an obedient answer ; they will not come at thy call." (2.) He must therefore own that they deserved the character of a disobedient people, that were ripe for destruction, and must go to them and tell them so to their faces (*v.* 28) : "*Say unto them, This is a nation that obeys not the voice of the Lord their God.* They are notorious for their obstinacy ; they sacrifice to the Lord as their God, but they will not be ruled by him as their God ; they will not receive either the instruction of his word or the correction of his rod ; they will not be reclaimed or reformed by either. *Truth has perished* among them ; they cannot receive it ; they will not submit to it nor be governed by it. They will not speak truth ; there is no believing a word they say, for it is *cut off from their mouth,* and lying comes in the room of it. They are false both to God and man."

29 Cut off thine hair, *O Jerusalem,* and cast *it* away, and take up a lamentation on high places ; for the Lord hath rejected and forsaken the generation of his wrath. 30 For the children of Judah have done evil in my sight, saith the Lord : they have set their abominations in the house which is called by my name, to pollute it. 31 And they have built the high places of Tophet, which *is* in the valley of the son of Hinnom, to burn their sons and their daughters in the fire ; which I commanded *them* not, neither came it into my heart. 32 Therefore, behold, the days come, saith the Lord, that it shall no more be called Tophet, nor the valley of the son of Hinnom, but the valley of slaughter ; for they shall bury in Tophet, till there be no place. 33 And the carcases of this people shall be meat for the fowls of the heaven,

and for the beasts of the earth; and none shall fray *them* away. 34 Then will I cause to cease from the cities of Judah, and from the streets of Jerusalem, the voice of mirth, and the voice of gladness, the voice of the bridegroom, and the voice of the bride: for the land shall be desolate.

Here is, I. A loud call to weeping and mourning. Jerusalem, that had been a joyous city, the joy of the whole earth, must now *take up a lamentation on high places* (v. 29), the high places where they had served their idols; there must they now bemoan their misery. In token both of sorrow and slavery, Jerusalem must now *cut off her hair and cast it away;* the word is peculiar to the hair of the Nazarites, which was the badge and token of their dedication to God, and it is called *their crown.* Jerusalem had been a city which was a Nazarite to God, but now must *cut off her hair,* must be profaned, degraded, and separated from God, as she had been separated to him. It is time for those that have lost their holiness to lay aside their joy.

II. Just cause given for this great lamentation.

1. The sin of Jerusalem appears here very heinous, nowhere worse, or more exceedingly sinful (v. 30): "*The children of Judah*" (God's professing people, that *came forth out of the waters of Judah,* Isa. xlviii. 1) "*have done evil in my sight,* under my eye, in my presence; they have affronted me to my face, which very much aggravates the affront:" or, "They have done that which they know to be *evil in my sight,* and in the highest degree offensive to me." Idolatry was the sin which was above all other sins evil in God's sight. Now here are two things charged upon them in their idolatry, which were very provoking:—(1.) That they were very impudent in it towards God and set him at defiance : *They have set their abominations* (their abominable idols and the altars erected to them) *in the house that is called by my name,* in the very courts of the temple, *to pollute it* (Manasseh did so, 2 Kings xxi. 7, xxiii. 12), as if they thought God would connive at it, or cared not though he was ever so much displeased with it, or as if they would reconcile heaven and hell, God and Baal. The heart is the place which God has chosen to *put his name there;* if sin have the innermost and uppermost place there, we pollute the temple of the Lord, and therefore he resents nothing more than *setting up idols in the heart,* Ezek. xiv. 4. (2.) That they were very barbarous in it towards their own children, v. 31. They have particularly *built the high places of Tophet,* where the image of Moloch was set up, *in the valley of the son of Hinnom,* adjoining to Jerusalem; and there they *burnt their sons and their daugh-*

ters *in the fire,* burnt them alive, killed them, and killed them in the most cruel manner imaginable, to honour or appease those idols that were devils and not gods. This was surely the greatest instance that ever was of the power of Satan in the children of disobedience, and of the degeneracy and corruption of the human nature. One would willingly hope that there were not many instances of such a barbarous idolatry; but it is amazing that there should be any, that men could be so perfectly void of natural affection as to do a thing so inhuman as to burn little innocent children, and their own too, that they should be so perfectly void of natural religion as to think it lawful to do this, nay, to think it acceptable. Surely it was in a way of righteous judgment, because they had changed the glory of God into the similitude of a beast, that God gave them up to such vile affections that changed them into worse than beasts. God says of this that it was *what he commanded them not, neither came it into his heart,* which is not meant of his not commanding them thus to worship Moloch (this he had expressly *forbidden* them), but he had never commanded that his worshippers should be at such an expense, nor put such a force upon their natural affection, in honouring him; it never came into his heart to have children offered to him, yet they had forsaken his service for the service of such gods as, by commanding this, showed themselves to be indeed enemies to mankind.

2. The destruction of Jerusalem appears here very terrible. That speaks misery enough in general (v. 29), *The Lord hath rejected and forsaken the generation of his wrath.* Sin makes those the generation of God's wrath that had been the generation of his love. And God will reject and quite forsake those who have thus by their impenitence made themselves *vessels of wrath fitted to destruction.* He will disown them for his. "Verily, I say unto you, I know you not." And he will give them up to the terrors of their own guilt, and leave them in those hands. (1.) Death shall triumph over them, v. 32, 33. Sin reigns unto death; for that is the wages of it, the end of those things. *Tophet,* the valley adjoining to Jerusalem, *shall be called the valley of slaughter,* for there multitudes shall be slain, when, in their sallies out of the city and their attempts to escape, they shall fall into the hands of the besiegers. Or it shall be called *the valley of slaughtered ones,* because thither the corpses of those that are slain shall be brought to be buried, all other burying places being full; and there they shall bury *until there be no more place* to make a grave. This intimates the multitude of those that shall die by the sword, pestilence, and famine. Death shall ride on prosperously, with dreadful pomp and power, *conquering and to conquer. The slain of the Lord shall be many.* This valley of Tophet was a place where the citizens of

Jerusalem walked to take the air; but it shall now be spoiled for that use, for it shall be so full of graves that there shall be no walking there, because of the danger of contracting a ceremonial pollution by the touch of a grave. There it was that they sacrificed some of their children, and dedicated others to Moloch, and there they should fall as victims to divine justice. Tophet had formerly been the burying place, or burning place, of the dead bodies of the besiegers, when the Assyrian army was routed by an angel; and for this it was *ordained of old,* Isa. xxx. 33. But they having forgotten this mercy, and made it the place of their sin, God will now turn it into a burying place for the besieged. In allusion to this valley, hell is in the New Testament called *Gehenna—the valley of Hinnom,* for there were buried both the invading Assyrians and the revolting Jews; so hell is a receptacle after death both for infidels and hypocrites, the open enemies of God's church and its treacherous friends; it is *the congregation of the dead;* it is prepared for the *generation of God's wrath.* But so great shall that slaughter be that even the spacious valley of Tophet shall not be able to contain the slain; and at length there shall not be enough left alive to bury the dead, so that *the carcases of the people shall be meat* for the birds and beasts of prey, that shall feed upon them like carrion, and none shall have the concern or courage to frighten them away, as Rizpah did from the dead bodies of Saul's sons, 2 Sam. xxi. 10. This was according to the threatening in the law, and a branch of the curse, Deut. xxviii. 26, *Thy carcase shall be meat to the fowls and beasts, and no man shall drive them away.* Thus do the law and the prophets agree, and the execution with both. The decent burying of the dead is a piece of humanity, in remembrance of what the dead body has been —the tabernacle of a reasonable soul. Nay, it is a piece of divinity, in expectation of what the dead body shall be at the resurrection. The want of it has sometimes been an instance of the rage of men against God's witnesses, Rev. xi. 9. Here it is threatened as an instance of the wrath of God against his enemies, and is an intimation that *evil pursues sinners* even after death. (2.) Joy shall depart from them (v. 34): Then will I cause to cease the voice of mirth. God had called by his prophets, and by less judgments, *to weeping and mourning;* but they walked contrary to him, and would hear of nothing but joy and gladness, Isa. xxii. 12, 13. And what came of it? Now God *called to lamentation* (v. 29), and he made his call effectual, leaving them neither cause nor heart for joy and gladness. Those that will not weep shall weep; those that will not by the grace of God be cured of their vain mirth shall by the justice of God be deprived of all mirth; for *when God judges he*

will overcome. It is threatened here that there shall be nothing to rejoice in. There shall be none of the joy of weddings; no mirth, for there shall be no marriages. The comforts of life shall be abandoned, and all care to keep up mankind upon earth cast off; there shall be none of *the voice of the bridegroom and* the *bride,* no music, no nuptial songs. Nor shall there be any more of the joy of harvest, *for the land shall be desolate,* uncultivated and unimproved. Both *the cities of Judah and the streets of Jerusalem* shall look thus melancholy; and when they thus look about them, and see no cause to rejoice, no marvel if they retire into themselves and find no heart to rejoice. Note, God can soon mar the mirth of the most jovial, and make it to cease, which is a reason why we should always rejoice with trembling, be merry and wise.

CHAP. VIII.

The prophet proceeds, in this chapter, both to magnify and to justify the destruction that God was bringing upon this people, to show how grievous it would be and yet how righteous. I. He represents the judgments coming as so very terrible that death should appear so as most to be dreaded and yet should be desired, ver. 1—3. II. He aggravates the wretched stupidity and wilfulness of this people as that which brought this ruin upon them, ver. 4—12. III. He describes the great confusion and consternation that the whole land should be in upon the alarm of it, ver. 13—17. IV. The prophet is himself deeply affected with it and lays it very much to heart, ver. 18—22.

AT that time, saith the LORD, they shall bring out the bones of the kings of Judah, and the bones of his princes, and the bones of the priests, and the bones of the prophets, and the bones of the inhabitants of Jerusalem, out of their graves: 2 And they shall spread them before the sun, and the moon, and all the host of heaven, whom they have loved, and whom they have served, and after whom they have walked, and whom they have sought, and whom they have worshipped: they shall not be gathered, nor be buried; they shall be for dung upon the face of the earth. 3 And death shall be chosen rather than life by all the residue of them that remain of this evil family, which remain in all the places whither I have driven them, saith the LORD of hosts.

These verses might fitly have been joined to the close of the foregoing chapter, as giving a further description of the dreadful desolation which the army of the Chaldeans should make in the land. It shall strangely alter the property of death itself, and for the worse too.

I. Death shall not now be, as it always used to be—the repose of the dead. When Job makes his court to the grave it is in hope of this, that *there he shall rest with* kings and counsellors of the earth: but now the ashes of the dead, even of *kings* and *princes,* shall be disturbed, and their *bones scattered at the grave's mouth,* Ps. cxli. 7. It was threatened in the close of the former chapter that the slain should be unburied; that might be through neglect, and was not so strange; but here we find the graves of those that were buried industriously and maliciously opened by the victorious enemy, who either for covetousness, hoping to find treasure in the graves, or for spite to the nation and in a rage against it, *brought out the bones of the kings of Judah and the princes.* The dignity of their sepulchres could not secure them, nay, did the more expose them to be rifled; but it was base and barbarous thus to trample upon royal dust. We will hope that the bones of good Josiah were not disturbed, because he piously protected the bones of the man of God when he burnt the bones of the idolatrous priests, 2 Kings xxiii. 18. The bones of the priests and prophets too were digged up and thrown about. Some think the false prophets and the idol-priests, God putting this mark of ignominy upon them: but, if they were God's prophets and his priests, it is what the Psalmist complains of as the fruit of the outrage of the enemies, Ps. lxxix. 1, 2. Nay, those of the spiteful Chaldeans that could not reach to violate the sepulchres of princes and priests would rather play at small game than sit out, and therefore pulled the bones of the ordinary *inhabitants of Jerusalem out of their graves.* The barbarous nations were sometimes guilty of these absurd and inhuman triumphs over those they had conquered, and God permitted it here, for a mark of his displeasure against the generation of his wrath, and for terror to those that survived. The bones, being dug out of the graves, were spread abroad upon the face of the earth in contempt, and to make the reproach the more spreading and lasting. They spread them to be dried that they might carry them about in triumph, or might make fuel of them, or make some superstitious use of them. *They shall be spread before the sun* (for they shall not be ashamed openly to avow the fact at noon day) and before *the moon and* stars, even *all the host of heaven,* whom they have made idols of, *v.* 2. From the mention of the *sun, moon, and stars,* which should be the unconcerned spectators of this tragedy, the prophet takes occasion to show how they had idolized them, and paid those respects to them which they should have paid to God only, that it might be observed how little they got by worshipping the creature, for the creatures they worshipped when they were in distress saw it, but regarded it not, nor gave them any relief, but were rather pleased to see those abused in being vilified by whom they had been abused in being deified. See how their

respects to their idols are enumerated, to show how we ought to behave towards our God. 1. They *loved* them. As amiable beings and bountiful benefactors they esteemed them and delighted in them, and therefore did all that follows. 2. They *served* them, did all they could in honour of them, and thought nothing too much; they conformed to all the laws of their superstition, without disputing. 3. They *walked after* them, strove to imitate and resemble them, according to the characters and accounts of them they had received, which gave rise and countenance to much of the abominable wickedness of the heathen. 4. They *sought* them, consulted them as oracles, appealed to them as judges, implored their favour, and prayed to them as their benefactors. 5. They *worshipped* them, gave them divine honour, as having a sovereign dominion over them. Before these lights of heaven, which they had courted, shall their dead bodies be cast, and left to putrefy, and to be *as dung upon the face of the earth:* and the sun's shining upon them will but make them the more noisome and offensive. Whatever we make a god of but the true God only, it will stand us in no stead on the other side death and the grave, not for the body, much less for the soul.

II. Death shall now be what it never used to be—the choice of the living, not because there appears in it any thing delightsome; on the contrary, death never appeared in more horrid frightful shapes than now, when they cannot promise themselves either a comfortable death or a human burial; and yet every thing in this world shall become so irksome, and all the prospects so black and dismal, that *death shall be chosen rather than life* (*v.* 3), not in a believing hope of happiness in the other life, but in an utter despair of any ease in this life. The nation is now reduced to a *family,* so small is *the residue of those that remain* in it; and it is an *evil family,* still as bad as ever, their hearts unhumbled and their lusts unmortified. These *remain* alive (and that is all) in the many *places whither they were driven* by the judgments of God, some prisoners in the country of their enemies, others beggars in their neighbour's country, and others fugitives and vagabonds there and in their own country. And, though those that died died very miserably, yet those that survived and were thus driven out should live yet more miserably, so that they should *choose death rather than life,* and wish a thousand times that they had fallen with those that fell by the sword. Let this cure us of the inordinate love of life, that the case may be such that it may become a burden and terror, and we may be strongly tempted to *choose strangling* and death rather.

4 Moreover thou shalt say unto them, Thus saith the LORD; Shall

they fall, and not arise? shall he turn away, and not return? 5 Why *then* is this people of Jerusalem slidden back by a perpetual backsliding? they hold fast deceit, they refuse to return. 6 I hearkened and heard, *but* they spake not aright: no man repented him of his wickedness, saying, What have I done? every one turned to his course, as the horse rusheth into the battle. 7 Yea, the stork in the heaven knoweth her appointed times; and the turtle and the crane and the swallow observe the time of their coming; but my people know not the judgment of the Lord. 8 How do ye say, We *are* wise, and the law of the Lord *is* with us? Lo, certainly in vain made he *it;* the pen of the scribes *is* in vain. 9 The wise *men* are ashamed, they are dismayed and taken: lo, they have rejected the word of the Lord; and what wisdom *is* in them? 10 Therefore will I give their wives unto others, *and* their fields to them that shall inherit *them:* for every one from the least even unto the greatest is given to covetousness, from the prophet even unto the priest every one dealeth falsely. 11 For they have healed the hurt of the daughter of my people slightly, saying, Peace, peace; when *there is* no peace. 12 Were they ashamed when they had committed abomination? nay, they were not at all ashamed, neither could they blush: therefore shall they fall among them that fall: in the time of their visitation they shall be cast down, saith the Lord.

The prophet here is instructed to set before this people the folly of their impenitence, which was it that brought this ruin upon them. They are here represented as the most stupid senseless people in the world, that would not be made wise by all the methods that Infinite Wisdom took to bring them to themselves and their right mind, and so to prevent the ruin that was coming upon them.

I. They would not attend to the dictates of reason. They would not act in the affairs of their souls with the same common prudence with which they acted in other things. Sinners would become saints if they would but show themselves men, and religion would soon rule them if right reason might. Ob-

serve it here. *Come, and let us reason together, saith the Lord* (v. 4, 5): *Shall men fall and not arise?* If men happen to fall to the ground, to fall into the dirt, will they not get up again as fast as they can? They are not such fools as to lie still when they are down. Shall *a man turn aside* out of the right way? Yes, the most careful traveller may miss his way; but then, as soon as he is aware of it, *will he not return?* Yes, certainly he will, with all speed, and will thank him that showed him his mistake. Thus men do in other things. *Why then has this people of Jerusalem slidden back by a perpetual backsliding?* Why do not they, when they have fallen into sin, hasten to get up again by repentance? Why do not they, when they see they have missed their way, correct their error and reform? No man in his wits will go on in a way that he knows will never bring him to his journey's end; *why then has this people slidden back by a perpetual backsliding?* See the nature of sin—it is a *backsliding,* it is going back from the right way, not only into a by-path, but into a contrary path, back from the way that leads to life to that which leads to utter destruction. And this backsliding, if almighty grace do not interpose to prevent it, will be a perpetual backsliding. The sinner not only wanders endlessly, but proceeds end-ways towards ruin. The same subtlety of the tempter that brings men to sin holds them fast in it, and they contribute to their own captivity: *They hold fast deceit.* Sin is a great cheat, and they *hold it fast;* they love it dearly, and resolve to stick to it, and baffle all the methods God takes to separate between them and their sins. The excuses they make for their sins are deceits, and so are all their hopes of impunity; yet they hold fast these, and will not be undeceived, and therefore they *refuse to return.* Note, There is some deceit or other which those hold fast that go on wilfully in sinful ways, some *lie in their right hand,* by which they keep hold of their sins.

II. They would not attend to the dictates of conscience, which is our reason reflecting upon ourselves and our own actions, v. 6. Observe, 1. What expectations there were from them, that they would bethink themselves: *I hearkened and heard.* The prophet listened to see what effect his preaching had upon them; God himself listened, as one that desires not the death of sinners, that would have been glad to hear any thing that promised repentance, that would certainly have heard it if there had been any thing said of that tendency, and would soon have answered it with comfort, as he did David when he said, *I will confess,* Ps. xxxii. 5. God *looks upon men* when they have done amiss (Job xxxiii. 27), to see what they will do next; he *hearkens and hears.* 2. How these expectations were disappointed: *They spoke not aright,* as I thought they would have done. They did not only not *do right,* but not so much as *speak right;* God could not get a good word from them, nothing on which to ground any favour to them or hopes concerning them. There was *none of them* that *spoke aright,* none that *repented him of his wickedness.* Those that have sinned, then, and then only, speak aright when they speak of repenting ; and it is sad when those that have made so much work for repentance do not say a word of repenting. Not only did God not find any repenting of the national wickedness, which might have helped to empty the measure of public guilt, but none repented of that particular wickedness which he knew himself guilty of. (1.) They did not so much as take the first step towards repentance ; they did not so much as say, *What have I done?* There was no motion towards it, not the least sign or token of it. Note, True repentance begins in a serious and impartial enquiry into ourselves, *what we have done,* arising from a conviction that we have done amiss. (2.) They were so far from repenting of their sins that they went on resolutely in their sins : *Every one turned to his course,* his wicked course, that course of sin which he had chosen and accustomed himself to, *as the horse rushes into the battle,* eager upon action, and scorning to be curbed. How the horse rushes into the battle is elegantly described, Job xxxix. 21, &c. *He mocks at fear and is not affrighted.* Thus the daring sinner laughs at the threatenings of the word as bugbears, and runs violently upon the instruments of death and slaughter, and nothing will be restrained from him.

III. They would not attend to the dictates of providence, nor understand the voice of God in them, *v.* 7. 1. It is an instance of their sottishness that, though they are God's people, and therefore should readily understand his mind upon every intimation of it, yet they *know not the judgment of the Lord;* they apprehend not the meaning either of a mercy or an affliction, not how to accommodate themselves to either, nor to answer God's intention in either. They know not how to improve the seasons of grace that God affords them when he sends them his prophets, nor how to make use of the rebukes they are under when *his voice cries in the city.* They *discern not the signs of the times* (Matt. xvi. 3), nor are aware how God is dealing with them. They know not that way of duty which God had prescribed them, though it be written both in their hearts and in their books. 2. It is an aggravation of their sottishness that there is so much sagacity in the inferior creatures. *The stork in the heaven knows her appointed times* of coming and continuing ; so do other season-birds, *the turtle, the crane, and the swallow.* These by a natural instinct change their quarters, as the temper of the air alters ; they come when the spring comes, and go, we know not whither, when

460

the winter approaches, probably into warmer climates, as some birds come with winter and go when that is over.

IV. They would not attend to the dictates of the written word. They say, *We are wise;* but *how* can they say so ? *v.* 8. With what face can they pretend to any thing of wisdom, when they do not understand themselves so well as the brute-creatures ? Why, truly, they think they are wise because *the law of the Lord is with them,* the book of the law and the interpreters of it ; and their neighbours, for the same reason, conclude they are wise, Deut. iv. 6. But their pretensions are groundless for all this : *Lo, certainly in vain made he it;* surely never any people had Bibles to so little purpose as they have. They might as well have been without the law, unless they had made a better use of it. God has indeed made it able to make men wise to salvation, but as to them it is made so in vain, for they are never the wiser for it : *The pen of the scribes,* of those that first wrote the law and of those that now write expositions of it, *is in vain.* Both the favour of their God and the labour of their scribes are lost upon them ; they receive the grace of God therein in vain. Note, There are many that enjoy abundance of the means of grace, that have great plenty of Bibles and ministers, but they have them in vain ; they do not answer the end of their having them. But it might be said, They have some wise men among them, to whom the law and the pen of the scribes are not in vain. To this it is answered (*v.* 9) : *The wise men are ashamed,* that is, they have reason to be so, that they have not made a better use of their wisdom, and lived more up to it. *They are confounded and taken;* all their wisdom has not served to keep them from those courses that tend to their ruin. They are taken in the same snares that others of their neighbours, who have not pretended to so much wisdom, are taken in, and filled with the same confusion. Those that have more knowledge than others, and yet do no better than others for their own souls, have reason to be ashamed. They talk of their wisdom, but, *Lo, they have rejected the word of the Lord;* they would not be governed by it, would not follow its direction, would not do what they knew ; *and* then *what wisdom is in them?* None to any purpose ; none that will be found to their praise at the great day, how much soever it is found to their pride now. The pretenders to wisdom, who said, " *We are wise and the law of the Lord is with us,*" were the priests and the false prophets ; with them the prophet here deals plainly. 1. He threatens the judgments of God against them. Their families and estates shall be ruined (*v.* 10) : *Their wives shall be given to others,* when they are taken captives, *and their fields* shall be taken from them by their victorious enemy and shall be given *to those that shall inherit them,* not only strip them for once, but take possession of them as their own and acquire a property in them, which they shall transmit to their posterity. And (*v.* 12), notwithstanding all their pretensions to wisdom and sanctity, *they shall fall among those that fall;* for, *if the blind lead the blind, both shall fall together into the ditch. In the time of their visitation,* when the wickedness of the land comes to be enquired into, it will be found that they have contributed to it more than any, and therefore *they shall be* sure to be *cast down* and cast out. 2. He gives a reason for these judgments (*v.* 10—12), even the same account of their badness which we meet with before (*ch.* vi. 13—15), where it was opened at large. (1.) They were greedy of the wealth of this world, which is bad enough in any, but worst in prophets and priests, who should be best acquainted with another world and therefore should be most dead to this. But these, *from the least to the greatest,* were *given to covetousness.* The *priests teach for hire* and the *prophets divine for money,* Mic. iii. 11. (2.) They made no conscience of speaking truth, no, not when they spoke as priests and prophets : *Every one deals falsely,* looks one way and rows another. There is no such thing as sincerity among them. (3.) They flattered people in their sins, and so flattered them into destruction. They pretended to be the physicians of the state, but knew not how to apply proper remedies to its growing maladies; they *healed them slightly,* killed the patient with palliative cures, silencing their fears and complaints with, " *Peace, peace,* all is well, and there is no danger," when the God of heaven was proceeding in his controversy with them, so that there could be no peace to them. (4.) When it was made to appear how basely they prevaricated *they* were not at all ashamed of it, but rather gloried in it, (*v.* 12) : *They could not blush,* so perfectly lost were they to all sense of virtue and honour. When they were convicted of the grossest forgeries they would justify what they had done, and laugh at those whom they had imposed upon. Such as these were ripe for ruin.

13 I will surely consume them, saith the Lord : *there shall be* no grapes on the vine, nor figs on the fig-tree, and the leaf shall fade ; and *the things that* I have given them shall pass away from them. 14 Why do we sit still ? Assemble yourselves, and let us enter into the defenced cities, and let us be silent there : for the Lord our God hath put us to silence, and given us water of gall to drink, because we have sinned against

the Lord. 15 We looked for peace, but no good *came ; and* for a time of health, and behold trouble ! 16 The snorting of his horses was heard from Dan : the whole land trembled at the sound of the neighing of his strong ones ; for they are come, and have devoured the land, and all that is in it ; the city, and those that dwell therein. 17 For, behold, I will send serpents, cockatrices, among you, which *will* not *be* charmed, and they shall bite you, saith the Lord. 18. *When* I would comfort myself against sorrow, my heart *is* faint in me. 19 Behold the voice of the cry of the daughter of my people because of them that dwell in a far country : *Is* not the Lord in Zion ? *Is* not her king in her ? Why have they provoked me to anger with their graven images, *and* with strange vanities ? 20 The harvest is past, the summer is ended, and we are not saved. 21 For the hurt of the daughter of my people am I hurt ; I am black ; astonishment hath taken hold on me. 22 *Is there* no balm in Gilead ? *Is there* no physician there ? Why then is not the health of the daughter of my people recovered ?

In these verses we have,

I. God threatening the destruction of a sinful people. He has borne long with them, but they are still more and more provoking, and therefore now their ruin is resolved on : *I will surely consume them* (*v.* 13), *consuming I will consume them,* not only surely, but utterly, consume them, will follow them with one judgment after another, till they are quite consumed ; it is a *consumption determined,* Isa. x. 23. 1. They shall be quite stripped of all their comforts (*v.* 13) : *There shall be no grapes on the vine.* Some understand this as intimating their sin ; God came looking for grapes from this vineyard, seeking fruit upon this fig-tree, but he *found none* (as Isa. v. 2, Luke xiii. 6) ; nay, they had not so much as leaves, Matt. xxi. 19. But it is rather to be understood of God's judgments upon them, and may be meant literally—The enemy shall seize the fruits of the earth, shall pluck the grapes and figs for themselves and beat down the very leaves with them ; or, rather, figuratively—They shall be deprived of all their comforts and shall have nothing left them wherewith to *make glad their hearts.* It is expounded in the last clause : *The things that I have given them shall pass away from*

461

them. Note, God's gifts are upon condition, and revocable upon non-performance of the condition. Mercies abused are forfeited, and it is just with God to take the forfeiture. 2. They shall be set upon by all manner of grievances, and surrounded with calamities (v 17) : *I will send serpents among you,* the Chaldean army, fiery serpents, flying serpents, cockatrices; these shall bite them with their venomous teeth, give them wounds that shall be mortal; and they *shall not be charmed,* as some serpents used to be, with music. These are serpents of another nature, that are not so wrought upon; or they are as *the deaf adder, that stops her ear, and will not hear the voice of the charmer.* The enemies are so intent upon making slaughter that it will be to no purpose to accost them gently, or offer any thing to pacify them, or mollify them, or to bring them to a better temper. No peace with God, therefore none with them.

II. The people sinking into despair under the pressure of those calamities. Those that were void of fear (when the trouble was at a distance) and set it at defiance, are void of hope now that it breaks in upon them, and have no heart either to make head against it or to bear up under it, *v.* 14. They cannot think themselves safe in the open villages : *Why do we sit still here? Let us assemble, and go in a body into the defenced cities.* Though they could expect no other than to be surely cut off there at last, yet not so soon as in the country, and therefore, " *Let us go, and be silent there;* let us attempt nothing, nor so much as make a complaint; for to what purpose?" It is not a submissive, but a sullen silence, that they here condemn themselves to. Those that are most jovial in their prosperity commonly despond most, and are most melancholy, in trouble. Now observe what it is that sinks them.

1. They are sensible that God is angry with them : " *The Lord our God has put us to silence,* has struck us with astonishment, and *given us water of gall to drink,* which is both bitter and stupifying, or intoxicating. Ps. lx. 3, *Thou hast made us to drink the wine of astonishment.* We had better sit still than rise up and fall; better say nothing than say nothing to the purpose. To what purpose is it to contend with our fate when God himself has become our enemy and fights against us? *Because we have sinned against the Lord,* therefore we are brought to this plunge." This may be taken as the language, (1.) Of their indignation. They seem to quarrel with God as if he had dealt hardly with them in putting them to silence, not permitting them to speak for themselves, and then telling them that it was because they had sinned against him. Thus men's foolishness *perverts their way, and* then *their hearts fret against the Lord.* Or rather, (2.) Of their convictions. At length they

begin to see the hand of God lifted up against them, and stretched out in the calamities under which they are now groaning, and to own that they have provoked him to contend with them. Note, Sooner or later God will bring the most obstinate to acknowledge both his providence and his justice in all the troubles they are brought into, to see and say both that it is his hand and that he is righteous.

2. They are sensible that the enemy is likely to be too hard for them, *v.* 16. They are soon apprehensive that it is to no purpose to make head against such a mighty force ; they and their people are quite dispirited ; and, when the courage of a nation is gone, their numbers will stand them in little stead. *The snorting of the horses was heard from Dan,* that is, the report of the formidable strength of their cavalry was soon carried all the nation over and every body *trembled at the sound of the neighing of his steeds;* for *they have come,* and there is no opposing them ; they *have devoured the land and all that is in the city;* both town and country are laid waste before them, not only the wealth, but the inhabitants, of both, *those that dwell therein.* Note, When God appears against us, every thing else that is against us appears very formidable; whereas, if he be for us, every thing appears very despicable, Rom. viii. 31.

3. They are disappointed in their expectations of deliverance out of their troubles, as they had been surprised when their troubles came upon them; and this double disappointment very much aggravated their calamity. (1.) The trouble came when they little expected it (*v.* 15) : *We looked for peace,* the continuance of our peace, *but no good came,* no good news from abroad ; we looked *for a time of health* and prosperity to our nation, but, *behold, trouble,* the alarms of war ; for, as it follows (*v.* 16), *the noise of the* enemies' *horses was heard from Dan.* Their false prophets had cried *Peace, peace,* to them, which made it the more terrible when the scene of war opened on a sudden. This complaint will occur again, *ch.* xiv. 19. (2.) The deliverance did not come when they had long expected it (*v.* 20) : *The harvest is past, the summer is ended;* that is, there is a great deal of time gone. Harvest and summer are parts of the year, and when they are gone the year draws towards a conclusion ; so the meaning is, " One year passes after another, one campaign after another, and yet our affairs are in as bad a posture as ever they were ; no relief comes, nor is any thing done towards it : *We are not saved.*" Nay, there is a great deal of opportunity lost, the season of action is over and slipped, the summer and harvest are gone, and a cold and melancholy winter succeeds. Note, The salvation of God's church and people often goes on very slowly, and God keeps his people long in the ex-

pectation of it, for wise and holy ends. Nay, they stand in their own light, and put a bar in their own door, and are not saved because they are not ready for salvation.

4. They are deceived in those things which were their confidence and which they thought would have secured their peace to them (v. 19): *The daughter of my people* cries, cries aloud, *because of those that dwell in a far country*, because of the foreign enemy that invades them, that comes from a far country to take possession of ours; this occasions the cry; and what is the cry? It is this: *Is not the Lord in Zion? Is not her king in her?* These were the two things that they had all along buoyed up themselves with and depended upon, (1.) That they had among them the temple of God, and the tokens of his special presence with them. The common cant was, " *Is not the Lord in Zion?* What danger then need we fear?" And they held by this when the trouble was breaking in upon them. " Surely we shall do well enough, for have we not God among us?" But, when it grew to an extremity, it was an aggravation of their misery that they had thus flattered themselves. (2.) That they had the throne of the house of David. As they had a temple, so they had a monarchy, *jure divino—by divine right: Is not Zion's king in her?* And will not Zion's God protect Zion's king and his kingdom? Surely he will; but why does he not? " What" (say they) " has Zion neither a God nor a king to stand by her and help her, that she is thus run down and likely to be ruined?" This outcry of theirs reflects upon God, as if his power and promise were broken or weakened; and therefore he returns an answer to it immediately: *Why have they provoked me to anger with their graven images?* They quarrel with God as if he had dealt unkindly by them in forsaking them, whereas they by their idolatry had driven him from them; they have withdrawn from their allegiance to him, and so have thrown themselves out of his protection. They *fret themselves, and curse their king and their God* (Isa. viii. 21), when it is their own sin that *separates between them and God* (Isa. lix. 2); they *feared not the Lord*, and then *what can a king do for them?* Hos. x. 3.

III. We have here the prophet himself bewailing the calamity and ruin of his people; for there were more of the lamentations of Jeremiah than those we find in the book that bears that title. Observe here, 1. How great his griefs were. He was an eyewitness of the desolations of his country, and saw those things which by the spirit of prophecy he had foreseen. In the foresight, much more in the sight, of them, he cries out, " *My heart is faint in me*, I sink, I die away at the consideration of it, v. 18. *When I would comfort myself against my sorrow*, I do but labour in vain; nay, every attempt to alleviate the grief does but aggravate it."

It is our wisdom and duty, under mournful events, to do what we can to *comfort ourselves against our sorrow*, by suggesting to ourselves such considerations as are proper to allay the grief and balance the grievance. But sometimes the sorrow is such that the more it is repressed the more strongly it recoils. This may sometimes be the case of very good men, as of the prophet here, whose soul refused to be comforted and fainted at the cordial, Ps. lxxvii. 2, 3. He tells us (v. 21) what was the matter: " It is *for the hurt of the daughter of my people* that I am thus hurt; it is for their sin, and the miseries they have brought upon themselves by it; it is for this that *I am black*, that I look black, that I go in black as mourners do, and that *astonishment has taken hold on me*, so that I know not what to do nor which way to turn." Note, The miseries of our country ought to be very much the grief of our souls. A gracious spirit will be a public spirit, a tender spirit, a mourning spirit. It becomes us to lament the miseries of our fellow-creatures, much more to lay to heart the calamities of our country, and especially of the church of God, to *grieve for the affliction of Joseph*. Jeremiah had prophesied the destruction of Jerusalem, and, though the truth of his prophecy was questioned, yet he did not rejoice in the proof of the truth of it by the accomplishment of it, preferring the welfare of his country before his own reputation. If Jerusalem had repented and been spared, he would have been far from fretting as Jonah did. Jeremiah had many enemies in Judah and Jerusalem, that hated, and reproached, and persecuted him; and in the judgments brought upon them God reckoned with them for it and pleaded his prophet's cause; yet he was far from rejoicing in it, so truly did he forgive his enemies and desire that God would forgive them. 2. How small his hopes were (v. 22): " *Is there no balm in Gilead*—no medicine proper for a sick and dying kingdom? *Is there no physician there*—no skilful faithful hand to apply the medicine?" He looks upon the case to be deplorable and past relief. There is no balm in Gilead that can cure the disease of sin, no physician there that can restore the health of a nation quite overrun by such a foreign army as that of the Chaldeans. The desolations made are irreparable, and the disease has presently come to such a height that there is no checking it. Or this verse may be understood as laying all the blame of the incurableness of their disease upon themselves; and so the question must be answered affirmatively: *Is there no balm in Gilead—no physician there?* Yes, certainly there is; God is able to help and heal them, there is a sufficiency in him to redress all their grievances. Gilead was a place in their own land, not far off. They had among themselves God's law and his prophets, with the help of which they might have been brought to repentance, and their ruin might have been prevented. They had princes and priests, whose business it was to reform the nation and redress their grievances. What could have been done more than had been done for their recovery? *Why then was not* their health restored? Certainly it was not owing to God, but to themselves; it was not for want of balm and a physician, but because they would not admit the application nor submit to the methods of cure. The physician and physic were both ready, but the patient was wilful and irregular, would not be tied to rules, but must be humoured. Note, If sinners die of their wounds, their blood is upon their own heads. The blood of Christ is balm in Gilead, his Spirit is the physician there, both sufficient, all-sufficient, so that they might have been healed, but would not.

CHAP. IX.

In this chapter the prophet goes on faithfully to reprove sin and to threaten God's judgments for it, and yet bitterly to lament both, as one that neither rejoiced at iniquity nor was glad at calamities. I. He here expresses his great grief for the miseries of Judah and Jerusalem, and his detestation of their sins, which brought those miseries upon them, ver. 1—11. II. He justifies God in the greatness of the destruction brought upon them, ver. 9—16. III. He calls upon others to bewail the woeful case of Judah and Jerusalem, ver. 17—22. IV. He shows them the folly and vanity of trusting in their own strength or wisdom, or the privileges of their circumcision, or any thing but God only, ver. 23—26.

OH that my head were waters, and mine eyes a fountain of tears, that I might weep day and night for the slain of the daughter of my people! 2 Oh that I had in the wilderness a lodging-place of wayfaring men; that I might leave my people, and go from them! for they *be* all adulterers, an assembly of treacherous men. 3 And they bend their tongues *like* their bow *for* lies: but they are not valiant for the truth upon the earth; for they proceed from evil to evil, and they know not me, saith the LORD. 4 Take ye heed every one of his neighbour, and trust ye not in any brother: for every brother will utterly supplant, and every neighbour will walk with slanders. 5 And they will deceive every one his neighbour, and will not speak the truth: they have taught their tongue to speak lies, *and* weary themselves to commit iniquity. 6 Thine habitation *is* in the midst of deceit; through deceit they refuse to know me, saith the LORD. 7 Therefore thus saith the LORD of hosts, Behold, I will melt them, and try them; for how shall I do for the daughter of my people? 8 Their tongue *is as* an arrow shot out; it speaketh deceit: *one* speaketh peaceably to his neighbour with his mouth, but in heart he layeth his wait. 9 Shall I not visit them for these *things?* saith the LORD: shall not my soul be avenged on such a nation as this? 10 For the mountains will I take up a weeping and wailing, and for the habitations of the wilderness a lamentation, because they are burned up, so that none can pass through *them;* neither can *men* hear the voice of the cattle; both the fowl of the heavens and the beast are fled; they are gone. 11 And I will make Jerusalem heaps, *and* a den of dragons; and I will make the cities of Judah desolate, without an inhabitant.

The prophet, being commissioned both to foretel the destruction coming upon Judah and Jerusalem and to point out the sin for which that destruction was brought upon them, here, as elsewhere, speaks of both very feelingly: what he said of both came from the heart, and therefore one would have thought it would reach to the heart.

I. He abandons himself to sorrow in consideration of the calamitous condition of his people, which he sadly laments, as one that preferred Jerusalem before his chief joy and her grievances before his chief sorrows.

1. He laments the slaughter of the persons, the blood shed and the lives lost (*v.* 1): "*O that my head were waters,* quite melted and dissolved with grief, that so *my eyes* might be *fountains of tears,* weeping abundantly, continually, and without intermission, still sending forth fresh floods of tears as there still occur fresh occasions for them!" The same word in Hebrew signifies both *the eye* and *a fountain,* as if in this land of sorrows our eyes were designed rather for weeping than seeing. Jeremiah wept much, and yet wished he could weep more, that he might affect a stupid people and rouse them to a due sense of the hand of God gone out against them. Note, It becomes us, while we are here in this vale of tears, to conform to the temper of the climate and to sow in tears. *Blessed are those that mourn, for they shall be comforted* hereafter; but let them expect that while they are here the *clouds will still return after the rain.* While we find our hearts such fountains of sin, it is fit that our eyes should be fountains of tears. But Jeremiah's grief is upon the public account: he would *weep day and night,* not so much for the death of his own near relations, but *for the slain of the daughter of his people,* the multitudes of his countrymen that fell by the sword of war. Note, When we hear of the numbers of the slain in great battles and sieges we ought to be

much affected with the intelligence, and not to make a light matter of it; yea, though they be not of the daughter of our people, for, whatever people they are of, they are of the same human nature with us, and there are so many precious lives lost, as dear to them as ours to us, and so many precious souls gone into eternity.

2. He laments the desolations of the country. This he brings in (*v.* 10), for impassioned mourners are not often very methodical in their discourses : " Not only for the towns and cities, but *for the mountains, will I take up a weeping and wailing*" (not barren mountains, but the fruitful hills with which Judea abounded), and for *the habitations of the wilderness*, or rather *the pastures of the plain*, that used to be *clothed with flocks* or *covered over with corn*, and a goodly sight it was; but now *they are burnt up* by the Chaldean army (which, according to the custom of war, destroyed the forage and carried off all the cattle), so that no one dares to pass through them, for fear of meeting with some parties of the enemy, no one cares to pass through them, every thing looks so melancholy and frightful, no one has any business to pass through them, for they *hear not the voice of the cattle* there as usual, the bleating of the sheep and the lowing of the oxen, that grateful music to the owners; nay, *both the fowl of the heavens* and the *beasts have fled*, either frightened away by the rude noises and terrible fires which the enemies make, or forced away because there is no subsistence for them. Note, God has many ways of turning *a fruitful land into barrenness for the wickedness of those that dwell therein;* and the havoc war makes in a country cannot but be for a lamentation to all tender spirits, for it is a tragedy which destroys the stage it is acted on.

II. He abandons himself to solitude, in consideration of the scandalous character and conduct of his people. Though he dwells in Judah where God is known, in Salem where his tabernacle is, yet he is ready to cry out, *Woe is me that I sojourn in Mesech !* Ps. cxx. 5. While all his neighbours are fleeing to the defenced cities, and Jerusalem especially, in dread of the enemies' rage (*ch.* iv. 5, 6), he is contriving to retire into some desert, in detestation of his people's sin (*v.* 2) : " O *that I had in the wilderness a lodging-place of wayfaring men*, such a lonely cottage to dwell in as they have in the deserts of Arabia, which are uninhabited, for travellers to repose themselves in, *that I might leave my people and go from them !*" Not only because of the ill usage they gave him (he would rather venture himself among the wild beasts of the desert than among such treacherous barbarous people), but principally because his *righteous soul was vexed from day to day*, as Lot's was in Sodom, with the *wickedness of their conversation*, 2 Pet. ii. 7, 8. This does not imply any intention or resolution that he

had thus to retire. God had cut him out work among them, which he must not quit for his own ease. We must not *go out of the world*, bad as it is, before our time. If he could not reform them, he could bear a testimony against them; if he could not do good to many, yet he might to some. But it intimates the temptation he was in to leave them, involves a threatening that they should be deprived of his ministry, and especially expresses the holy indignation he had against their abominable wickedness, which continued notwithstanding all the pains he had taken with them to reclaim them. It made him even weary of his life to see them dishonouring God as they did and destroying themselves. Time was when the place which God had chosen to put his name there was the desire and delight of good men. David, in a wilderness, longed to be again in the courts of God's house ; but now Jeremiah, in the courts of God's house (for there he was when he said this), wishes himself in a wilderness. Those have made themselves very miserable that have made God's people and ministers weary of them and willing to get from them. Now, to justify his willingness to leave them, he shows,

1. What he himself had observed among them.

(1.) He would not think of leaving them because they were poor and in distress, but because they were wicked. [1.] They were filthy : *They are all adulterers*, that is, the generality of them are, *ch.* v. 8. They all either practised this sin or connived at those that did. Lewdness and uncleanness constituted that crying sin of Sodom at which righteous Lot was vexed in soul, and it is a sin that renders men loathsome in the eyes of God and all good men ; it makes men an abomination. [2.] They were false. This is the sin that is most enlarged upon here. Those that had been unfaithful to their God were so to one another, and it was a part of their punishment as well as their sin, for even those that love to cheat, yet hate to be cheated. *First*, Go into their solemn meetings for the exercises of religion, for the administration of justice, or for commerce—to church, to court, or to the exchange—and they are *an assembly of treacherous men;* they are so by consent, they strengthen one another's hands in doing any thing that is perfidious. There they will cheat deliberately and industriously, with design, with a malicious design, for (*v.* 3) *they bend their tongues, like their bow, for lies*, with a great deal of craft ; their tongues are fitted for lying, as a bow that is bent is for shooting, and are as constantly used for that purpose. Their tongue turns as naturally to a lie as the bow to the string. *But they are not valiant for the truth upon the earth.* Their tongues are like a bow strung, with which they might do good service if they would use the art and resolution which they are so much masters of in the cause of truth; but they will not do so. They appear not in defence of the truths of God, which were delivered to them by the prophets; but even those that could not deny them to be truths were content to see them run down. In the administration of justice they have not courage to stand by an honest cause that has truth on its side, if greatness and power be on the other side. Those that will be faithful to the truth must be valiant for it, and not be daunted by the opposition given to it, nor fear the face of man. *They are not valiant for the truth in the land,* the land which has truth for the glory of it. Truth has fallen in the land, and they dare not lend a hand to help it up, Isa. lix. 14, 15. We must answer, another day, not only for our enmity in opposing truth, but for our cowardice in defending it. *Secondly,* Go into their families, and you will find they will cheat their own brethren *(every brother will utterly supplant);* they will trip up one another's heels if they can, for they lie at the catch to seek all advantages against those they hope to make a hand of. Jacob had his name from *supplanting;* it is the word here used; they followed him in his name, but not in his true character, *without guile.* So very false are they that you cannot *trust in a brother,* but must stand as much upon your guard as if you were dealing with a stranger, with a Canaanite that has *balances of deceit in his hand.* Things have come to an ill pass indeed when a man cannot put confidence in his own brother. *Thirdly,* Go into company and observe both their commerce and their conversation, and you will find there is nothing of sincerity or common honesty among them. *Nec hospes ab hospite tutus—The host and the guest are in danger from each other.* The best advice a wise man can give you is *to take heed every one of his neighbour,* nay, of his *friend* (so some read it), of him whom he has befriended and who pretends friendship to him. No man thinks himself bound to be either grateful or sincere. Take them in their conversation and *every neighbour will walk with slander;* they care not what ill they say one of another, though ever so false; that way that the slander goes they will go; they will *walk with* it. They will walk about from house to house too, carrying slanders along with them, all the ill-natured stories they can pick up or invent to make mischief. Take them in their trading and bargaining, and *they will deceive every one his neighbour,* will say any thing, though they know it to be false, for their own advantage. Nay, they will lie for lying sake, to keep their tongues in use to it, for *they will not speak the truth,* but will tell a deliberate lie and laugh at it when they have done.

(2.) That which aggravates the sin of this false and lying generation is, [1.] That they are ingenious to sin: *They have taught their tongue to speak lies,* implying that through

the reluctances of natural conscience they found it difficult to bring themselves to it. Their tongue would have spoken truth, but they *taught it to speak lies,* and by degrees have made themselves masters of the art of lying, and have got such a habit of it that use has made it a second nature to them. They learnt it when they were young (for *the wicked are estranged from the womb, speaking lies,* Ps. lviii. 3), and now they have grown dexterous at it. [2.] That they are industrious to sin: *They weary themselves to commit iniquity;* they put a force upon their consciences to bring themselves to it; they tire out their convictions by offering them continual violence, and they take a great deal of pains, till they have even spent themselves in bringing about their malicious designs. They are wearied with their sinful pursuits and yet not weary of them. The service of sin is a perfect drudgery; men run themselves out of breath in it, and put themselves to a great deal of toil to damn their own souls. [3.] That they grow worse and worse (*v.* 3): *They proceed from evil to evil,* from one sin to another, from one degree of sin to another. They began with less sins. *Nemo repente fit turpissimus—No one reaches the height of vice at once.* They began with equivocating and bantering, but at last came to downright lying. And they are now proceeding to greater sins yet, for *they know not me, saith the Lord;* and where men have no knowledge of God, or no consideration of what they have known of him, what good can be expected from them? Men's ignorance of God is the cause of all their ill conduct one towards another.

2. The prophet shows what God had informed him of their wickedness, and what he had determined against them.

(1.) God had marked their sin. He could tell the prophet (and he speaks of it with compassion) what sort of people they were that he had to deal with. *I know thy works, and where thou dwellest,* Rev. ii. 13. So here (*v.* 6): "*Thy habitation is in the midst of deceit,* all about thee are addicted to it; therefore stand upon thy guard." If *all men are liars,* it concerns us to *beware of men,* and to be *wise as serpents.* They are deceitful men; therefore there is little hope of thy doing any good among them; for, make things ever so plain, they have some trick or other wherewith to shuffle off their convictions. This charge is enlarged upon, *v.* 8. Their tongue was a *bow bent* (*v.* 3), plotting and preparing mischief; here it is *an arrow shot out,* putting in execution what they had projected. It is as a *slaying arrow* (so some readings of the original have it); their tongue has been to many an instrument of death. They *speak peaceably to their neighbours,* against whom they are at the same time *lying in wait;* as Joab kissed Abner when he was about to kill him, and Cain, that he might not be suspected of any ill design, *talked with his brother,* freely and familiarly. Note, Fair words, when they are not attended with good intentions, are despicable, but, when they are intended as a cloak and cover for wicked intentions, they are abominable. While they did all this injury to one another they put a great contempt upon God : " Not only they *know not me,* but (*v.* 6) *through deceit,* through the delusions of the false prophets, *they refuse to know me;* they are so cheated into a good opinion of their own ways, the ways of their own heart, that they desire not the knowledge of my ways." Or, " They are so wedded to this sinful course which they are in, and so bewitched with that, and its gains, that they will by no means admit the *knowledge of God,* because that would be a check upon them in their sins." This is the ruin of sinners : they might be taught the good knowledge of the Lord and they will not learn it ; and where no knowledge of God is, what good can be expected ? Hos. iv. 1.

(2.) He had marked them for ruin, *v.* 7, 9, 11. Those that will not know God as their lawgiver shall be made to know him as their judge. God determines here to bring his judgments upon them, for the refining of some and the ruining of the rest. [1.] Some shall be refined (*v.* 7) : " Because they are thus corrupt, *behold, I will melt them and try them,* will bring them into trouble and see what that will do towards bringing them to repentance, whether the furnace of affliction will purify them from their dross, and whether, when they are melted, they will be new-cast in a better mould." He will make trial of less afflictions before he brings upon them utter destruction ; for he *desires not the death of sinners.* They shall not be *rejected as reprobate silver* till *the founder has melted in vain, ch.* vi. 29, 30. *For how shall I do for the daughter of my people?* He speaks as one consulting with himself what to do with them that might be for the best, and as one that could not find in his heart to cast them off and give them up to ruin till he had first tried all means likely to bring them to repentance. Or, " *How else shall I do for them?* They have grown so very corrupt that there is no other way with them but to put them into the furnace; what other course can I take with them? Isa. v. 4, 5. It is *the daughter of my people,* and I must do something to vindicate my own honour, which will be reflected upon if I connive at their wickedness. I must do something to reduce and reform them." A parent corrects his own children because they are his own. Note, When God afflicts his people, it is with a gracious design to mollify and reform them ; it is but when need is and when he knows it is the best method he can use. [2.] The rest shall be ruined (*v.* 9): *Shall I not visit for these things?* Fraud and falsehood are sins which God hates and which he will reckon for. " *Shall not my soul be avenged on such a nation as*

this, that is so universally corrupt, and, by its impudence in sin, even dares and defies divine vengeance? The sentence is passed, the decree has gone forth (*v.* 11): *I will make Jerusalem heaps* of rubbish, and lay it in such ruins that it shall be fit for nothing but to be *a den of dragons ;* and *the cities of Judah* shall be *a desolation.*" God makes them so, for he gives the enemy warrant and power to do it: but why is the holy city made a heap? The answer is ready, Because it has become an unholy one?

12 Who *is* the wise man, that may understand this? And *who is he* to whom the mouth of the Lord hath spoken, that he may declare it, for what the land perisheth *and* is burned up like a wilderness, that none passeth through? 13 And the Lord saith, Because they have forsaken my law which I set before them, and have not obeyed my voice, neither walked therein ; 14 But have walked after the imagination of their own heart, and after Baalim, which their fathers taught them : 15 Therefore thus saith the Lord of hosts, the God of Israel ; Behold, I will feed them, *even* this people, with wormwood, and give them water of gall to drink. 16 I will scatter them also among the heathen, whom neither they nor their fathers have known : and I will send a sword after them, till I have consumed them. 17 Thus saith the Lord of hosts, Consider ye, and call for the mourning women, that they may come ; and send for cunning *women,* that they may come : 18 And let them make haste, and take up a wailing for us, that our eyes may run down with tears, and our eye-lids gush out with waters. 19 For a voice of wailing is heard out of Zion, How are we spoiled! we are greatly confounded, because we have forsaken the land, because our dwellings have cast *us* out. 20 Yet hear the word of the Lord, O ye women, and let your ear receive the word of his mouth, and teach your daughters wailing, and every one her neighbour lamentation. 21 For death is come up into our windows, *and* is entered into our palaces, to cut off the children from without, *and* the young men from the streets. 22 Speak, Thus saith the Lord, Even the

carcases of men shall fall as dung upon the open field, and as the handful after the harvestman, and none shall gather *them*.

Two things the prophet designs, in these verses, with reference to the approaching destruction of Judah and Jerusalem :—1. To convince people of the justice of God in it, that they had by sin brought it upon themselves and that therefore they had no reason to quarrel with God, who did them no wrong at all, but a great deal of reason to fall out with their sins, which did them all this mischief. 2. To affect people with the greatness of the desolation that was coming, and the miserable effects of it, that by a terrible prospect of it they might be awakened to repentance and reformation, which was the only way to prevent it, or, at least, mitigate their own share in it. This being designed,

1. He calls for the thinking men, by them to show people the equity of God's proceedings, though they seemed harsh and severe (v. 12) : " *Who*, where, *is the wise man*, or the prophet, *to whom the mouth of the Lord hath spoken?* You boast of your wisdom, and of the prophets you have among you ; produce me any one that has but the free use of human reason or any acquaintance with divine revelation, and he will soon understand this himself, and it will be so clear to him that he will be ready to declare it to others, that there is a just ground of God's controversy with this people." Do these wise men enquire, *For what does the land perish?* What is the matter, that such a change is made with this land? It used to be a land that God cared for, and he had his eyes upon it for good (Deut. xi. 12), but it is now a land that he has forsaken and that his face is against. It used to flourish as the garden of the Lord and to be replenished with inhabitants ; but now it is burnt up like a wilderness, that *none passeth through* it, much less cares to settle in it. It was supposed, long ago, that it would be asked, when it came to this, *Wherefore has the Lord done thus unto this land? What means the heat of this great anger?* (Deut. xxix. 24), to which question God here gives a full answer, before which all flesh must be silent. He produces out of the record,

1. The indictment preferred and proved against them, upon which they had been found guilty, v. 13, 14. It is charged upon them, and it cannot be denied, (1.) That they have revolted from their allegiance to their rightful Sovereign. *Therefore* God has *forsaken their land*, and justly, because they have *forsaken his law*, which he had so plainly, so fully, so frequently *set before them*, and had not observed his orders, not *obeyed his voice*, nor *walked in* the ways that he had appointed. Here their wickedness began, in the omission of their duty to their God and a con-

tempt of his authority. But it did not end here. It is further charged upon them, (2.) That they have entered themselves into the service of pretenders and usurpers, have not only withdrawn themselves from their obedience to their prince, but have taken up arms against him. For, [1.] They have acted according to the dictates of their own lusts, have set up their own will, the wills of the flesh, and the carnal mind, in competition with, and contradiction to the will of God : *They have walked after the imagination of their own hearts ;* they would do as they pleased, whatever God and conscience said to the contrary. [2.] They have worshipped the creatures of their own fancy, the work of their own hands, according to the tradition received from their fathers : *They have walked after Baalim :* the word is plural ; they had many Baals, Baal-peor and Baal-berith, the Baal of this place and the Baal of the other place ; for they had *lords many*, which *their fathers taught them* to worship, but which the God of their fathers had again and again forbidden. This was it for which *the land perished*. The King of kings never makes war thus upon his own subjects but when they treacherously depart from him and rebel against him, and it has become necessary by this means to chastise their rebellion and reduce them to their allegiance ; and they themselves shall at length acknowledge that he is just in all that is brought upon them.

2. The judgment given upon this indictment, the sentence upon the convicted rebels, which must now be executed, for it was righteous and nothing could be done in arrest of it : *The Lord of hosts, the God of Israel, hath said it* (v. 15, 16), and who can reverse it? (1.) That all their comforts at home shall be poisoned and embittered to them : *I will feed this people with wormwood* (or rather with *wolf's-bane*, for it signifies a herb that is not wholesome, as wormwood is though it be bitter, but some herb that is both nauseous and noxious), *and* I will *give them water of gall* (or *juice of hemlock* or some other herb that is poisonous) *to drink*. Every thing about them, till it comes to their very meat and drink, shall be a terror and torment to them. God will *curse their blessings*, Mal. ii. 2. (2.) That their dispersion abroad shall be their destruction (v. 16) : *I will scatter them among the heathen*. They were corrupted and debauched by their intimacy with the heathen, with whom they *mingled* and *learned their works ;* and now they shall lose themselves, where they lost their virtue, *among the heathen ;* they had violated the laws of that truth which is the bond and cement of society and commerce, and addicted themselves to deceit and lying, and therefore are justly crumbled to dust and *scattered among the heathen*. They set up gods which *neither they nor their fathers had known*, strange gods, new gods (Deut.

xxxii. 17); and now God will put them among neighbours whom *neither they nor their fathers have known,* whom they can claim no acquaintance with, and therefore can expect no favour from. And yet, though they are scattered so as that they will not know where to find one another, God will know where to find them all out (Ps. xxi 8) with that evil which still pursues impenitent sinners : *I will send a sword after them,* some killing judgment or other, *till I have consumed them ;* for when God judges he will overcome, when he pursues he will overtake. And now we see for what the land perishes ; all this desolation is the desert of their deeds and the performance of God's words.

II. He calls for the mourning women, and engages them, with the arts they practise to affect people and move their passions, to lament these sad calamities that had come or were coming upon them, that the nation might be alarmed to prepare for them : *The Lord of hosts* himself says, Call *for the mourning women, that they may come, v.* 17. The scope of this is to show how very woeful and lamentable the condition of this people was likely to be. 1. Here is work for the counterfeit mourners : *Send for the cunning women,* that know how to compose mournful ditties, or at least to sing them in mournful tunes and accents, and therefore are made use of at funerals to supply the want of true mourners. Let these *take up a wailing* for us, *v.* 18. The deaths and funerals were so many that people wept for them till they *had no more power to weep,* as those, 1 Sam. xxx. 4. Let those therefore do it now whose trade it is. Or, rather, it intimates the extreme sottishness and stupidity of the people, that laid not to heart the judgments they were under, nor, even when there was so much blood shed, could find in their hearts to shed a tear. *They cry not when God binds them,* Job xxxvi. 13. God sent his mourning prophets to them, to call them to weeping and mourning, but his word in their mouths did not work upon their faith ; rather therefore than they shall go laughing to their ruin, let the mourning women come, and try to work upon their fancy, *that their eyes may* at length *run down with tears, and their eyelids gush out with waters.* First or last, sinners must be weepers. 2. Here is work for the real mourners. (1.) There is that which is a lamentation. The present scene is very tragical (*v.* 19) : *A voice of wailing is heard out of Zion.* Some make this to be the song of the mourning women : it is rather an echo to it, returned by those whose affections were moved by their wailings. In Zion the voice of joy and praise used to be heard, while the people kept closely to God. But sin has altered the note ; it is now the *voice of lamentation.* It should seem to be the voice of those who fled from all parts of the country to the castle of Zion

for protection. Instead of rejoicing that they had got safely thither, they lamented that they were forced to seek for shelter there : " *How are we spoiled !* How are we stripped of all our possessions ! *We are greatly confounded,* ashamed of ourselves and our poverty ;" for that is it that they complain of, that is it that they blush at the thoughts of, rather than of their sin : *We are confounded* because *we have forsaken the land* (forced so to do by the enemy), not because we *have* forsaken the Lord, being drawn aside of *our own lust and enticed—because our dwellings have cast us out,* not because our God has cast us off. Thus unhumbled hearts lament their calamity, but not their iniquity, the procuring cause of it. (2.) There is more still to come which shall be for a lamentation. Things are bad, but they are likely to be worse. Those whose land has *spued them out* (as it did their predecessors the Canaanites, and justly, because they trod in their steps, Lev. xviii. 28) complain that they are driven into the city, but, after a while, those of the city, and they with them, shall be forced thence too : *Yet hear the word of the Lord ;* he has something more to say to you (*v.* 20) ; let *the women* hear it, whose tender spirits are apt to receive the impressions of grief and fear, for the men will not heed it, will not give it a patient hearing. The prophets will be glad to preach to a congregation of women that *tremble at God's word. Let your ear receive the word of God's mouth,* and bid it welcome, though it be a word of terror. Let the women *teach their daughters wailing ;* this intimates that the trouble shall last long, grief shall be entailed upon the generation to come. Young people are apt to love mirth, and expect mirth, and are disposed to be gay and airy ; but let the elder women teach the younger to be serious, tell them what a vale of tears they must expect to find this world, and train them up among the mourners in Zion, Tit. ii. 4, 5. Let *every one teach her neighbour lamentation ;* this intimates that the trouble shall spread far, shall go from house to house. People shall not need to sympathize with their friends ; they shall all have cause enough to mourn for themselves. Note, Those that are themselves affected with the terrors of the Lord should endeavour to affect others with them. The judgment here threatened is made to look terrible. [1.] Multitudes shall be slain, *v.* 21. Death shall ride in triumph, and there shall be no escaping his arrests when he comes with commission, neither within doors nor without. Not within doors, for let the doors be shut ever so fast, let them be ever so firmly locked and bolted, *death comes up into our windows,* like a thief in the night ; it steals upon us ere we are aware. Nor does it thus boldly attack the cottages only, but it has *entered into our palaces,* the palaces of our princes and great men, though ever so stately, ever so strongly built and guarded. Note,

No palaces can keep out death. Nor are those more safe that are abroad; death *cuts off* even *the children from without and the young men from the streets.* The children who might have been spared by the enemy in pity, because they had never been hurtful to them, and the young men who might have been spared in policy, because capable of being serviceable to them, shall fall together by the sword. It is usual now, even in the severest military executions, to put none to the sword but those that are found in arms; but then even the boys and girls playing in the streets were sacrificed to the fury of the conqueror. [2.] Those that are slain shall be left unburied (*v.* 22): *Speak, Thus saith the Lord* (for the confirmation and aggravation of what was before said), *Even the carcases of men shall fall as dung,* neglected, and left to be offensive to the smell, as dung is. Common humanity obliges the survivors to bury the dead, even for their own sake; but here such numbers shall be slain, and those so dispersed all the country over, that it shall be an endless thing to bury them all, nor shall there be hands enough to do it, nor shall the conquerors permit it, and those that should do it shall be overwhelmed with grief, so that they shall have no heart to do it. The dead bodies even of the fairest and strongest, when they have lain awhile, become as dung, such vile bodies have we. And here such multitudes shall fall that their bodies shall lie as thick as heaps of dung *in the furrows of the field,* and no more notice shall be taken of them than of the *handfuls* which *the harvestman* drops for the gleaners, for *none shall gather them,* but they shall remain in sight, monuments of divine vengeance, that the eye of the impenitent survivors may affect their heart. *Slay them not,* bury them not, *lest my people forget,* Ps. lix. 11.

23 Thus saith the LORD, Let not the wise *man* glory in his wisdom, neither let the mighty *man* glory in his might, let not the rich *man* glory in his riches: 24 But let him that glorieth glory in this, that he understandeth and knoweth me, that I *am* the LORD which exercise loving-kindness, judgment, and righteousness, in the earth: for in these *things* I delight, saith the LORD. 25 Behold, the days come, saith the LORD, that I will punish all *them which are* circumcised with the uncircumcised; 26 Egypt, and Judah, and Edom, and the children of Ammon, and Moab, and all *that are* in the utmost corners, that dwell in the wilderness: for all *these* nations *are* uncircumcised, and

470

all the house of Israel *are* uncircumcised in the heart.

The prophet had been endeavouring to possess this people with a holy fear of God and his judgments, to convince them both of sin and wrath; but still they had recourse to some sorry subterfuge or other, under which to shelter themselves from the conviction and with which to excuse themselves in their obstinacy and carelessness. He therefore sets himself here to drive them from these refuges of lies and to show them the insufficiency of them.

I. When they were told how inevitable the judgment would be they pleaded the defence of their politics and powers, which, with the help of their wealth and treasure, they thought made their city impregnable. In answer to this he shows them the folly of trusting to and boasting of all these stays, while they have not a God in covenant to stay themselves upon, *v.* 23, 24. Here he shows, 1. What we may not depend upon in a day of distress: *Let not the wise man glory in his wisdom* as if with the help of that he could outwit or countermine the enemy, or in the greatest extremity find out some evasion or other; for a man's wisdom may fail him when he needs it most, and he may be taken in his own craftiness. Ahithophel was befooled, and counsellors are often *led away spoiled.* But, if a man's policies fail him, yet surely he may gain his point by might and dint of courage. No: *Let not the strong man glory in his strength,* for the battle is not always to the strong. David the stripling proves too hard for Goliath the giant. All human force is nothing without God, worse than nothing against him. But may not the *rich man's wealth* be *his strong city?* (money answers all things) No: *Let not the rich man glory in his riches,* for they may prove so far from sheltering him that they may expose him and make him the fairer mark. Let not the people boast of the *wise men, and mighty men, and rich men* that they have among them, as if they could make their part good against the Chaldeans because they have wise men to advise concerning the war, mighty men to fight their battles, and rich men to bear the charges of the war. Let not particular persons think to escape the common calamity by their wisdom, might, or money; for all these will prove but *vain things for safety.* 2. He shows what we may depend upon in a day of distress. (1.) Our only comfort in trouble will be that we have done our duty. Those that *refused to know God* (*v.* 6) will boast in vain of their wisdom and wealth; but those that *know God,* intelligently, that *understand* aright *that he is the Lord,* that have not only right apprehensions concerning his nature, and attributes, and relations to man, but receive and retain the impressions of them, may *glory in this,* it will be their rejoicing in the day of evil. (2.) Our only confidence in trouble will be that, having through grace in some measure done our duty, we shall find God a God all-sufficient to us. We may *glory in this*, that, wherever we are, we have an acquaintance with and an interest in a God that *exercises lovingkindness, and judgment, and righteousness in the earth*, that is not only just to all his creatures and will do no wrong to any of them, but kind to all his children and will protect them and provide for them. *For in these things I delight.* God delights to show kindness and to execute judgment himself, and is pleased with those who herein are *followers of him as dear children*. Those that have such knowledge of the glory of God as to be changed into the same image, and to partake of his holiness, find it to be their perfection and glory; and the God they thus faithfully conform to they may cheerfully confide in, in their greatest straits. But the prophet intimates that the generality of this people took no care about this. Their wisdom, and might, and riches, were their joy and hope, which would end in grief and despair. But those few among them that had the knowledge of God might please themselves with it, and boast themselves of it; it would stand them in better stead than *thousands of gold and silver*.

II. When they were told how provoking their sins were to God they vainly pleaded the covenant of their circumcision. They were undoubtedly the people of God; as they had the temple of the Lord in their city, so they had the mark of his children in their flesh. " It is true the Chaldean army has laid such and such nations waste, because they were uncircumcised, and therefore not under the protection of the divine providence, as we are." To this the prophet answers, That the days of visitation were now at hand, in which God would punish all wicked people, without making any distinction between the circumcised and uncircumcised, *v.* 25, 26. They had by sin profaned the crown of their peculiarity, and lived in common with the uncircumcised nations, and so had forfeited the benefit of that peculiarity and must expect to fare never the better for it. God will *punish the circumcised with the uncircumcised*. As the ignorance of the uncircumcised shall not excuse their wickedness, so neither shall the privileges of the circumcised excuse theirs, but they shall be punished together. Note, The Judge of all the earth is impartial, and none shall fare the better at his bar for any external advantages, but he will render to every man, circumcised or uncircumcised, according to his works. The condemnation of impenitent sinners that are baptized will be as sure as, nay, and more severe than, that of impenitent sinners that are unbaptized. It would affect one to find here Judah industriously put between Egypt and Edom, as standing upon a level with them and under the same

doom, *v.* 26. These nations were forbidden a share in the Jews' privileges (Deut. xxiii. 3) ; but the Jews are here told that they shall share in their punishments. Those *in the utmost corners, that dwell in the wilderness*, are supposed to be the Kedarenes and those of the kingdoms of Hazor, as appears by comparing *ch.* xlix. 28—32. Some think they are so called because they dwelt as it were in a corner of the world, others because they had *the hair of their head polled into corners*. However that was, they were of those nations that were uncircumcised in flesh, and the Jews are ranked with them and are as near to ruin for their sins as they; for *all the house of Israel are uncircumcised in the heart :* they have the sign, but not the thing signified, *ch.* iv. 4. They are heathens in their hearts, strangers to God, and enemies in their minds by wicked works. Their hearts are disposed to idols, as the hearts of the uncircumcised Gentiles are. Note, The seals of the covenant, though they dignify us, and lay us under obligations, will not save us, unless the temper of our minds and the tenour of our lives agree with the covenant. That only is circumcision, and that baptism, which is *of the heart*, Rom. ii. 28, 29.

CHAP. X.

We may conjecture that the prophecy of this chapter was delivered after the first captivity, in the time of Jeconiah or Jehoiachin, when many were carried away to Babylon ; for it has a double reference :—I. To those that were carried away into the land of the Chaldeans, a country notorious above any other for idolatry and superstition ; and they are here cautioned against the infection of the place, not to learn the way of the heathen (ver. 1, 2), for their astrology and idolatry are both foolish things (ver. 3—5), and the worshippers of idols brutish, ver. 8, 9. So it will appear in the day of their visitation, ver. 14, 15. They are likewise exhorted to adhere firmly to the God of Israel, for there is none like him, ver. 6, 7. He is the true God, lives for ever, and has the government of the world (ver. 10—13), and his people are happy in him, ver. 16. II. To those that yet remained in their own land. They are cautioned against security, and told to expect distress (ver. 17, 18) and that by a foreign enemy, which God would bring upon them for their sin, ver. 20—22. This calamity the prophet laments (ver. 19) and prays for the mitigation of it, ver. 23—25.

HEAR ye the word which the LORD speaketh unto you, O house of Israel: 2 Thus saith the LORD, Learn not the way of the heathen, and be not dismayed at the signs of heaven; for the heathen are dismayed at them. 3 For the customs of the people *are* vain: for *one* cutteth a tree out of the forest, the work of the hands of the workman, with the ax. 4 They deck it with silver and with gold; they fasten it with nails and with hammers, that it move not. 5 They *are* upright as the palm-tree, but speak not: they must needs be borne, because they cannot go. Be not afraid of them; for they cannot do evil, neither also *is it* in them to do good. 6 Forasmuch as *there is* none like unto thee, O LORD; thou *art* great, and thy name *is* great in might. 7 Who would not fear thee, O King of nations? for to thee doth it appertain: forasmuch as among all the wise *men* of the nations, and in all their kingdoms, *there is* none like unto thee. 8 But they are altogether brutish and foolish: the stock *is* a doctrine of vanities. 9 Silver spread into plates is brought from Tarshish, and gold from Uphaz, the work of the workman, and of the hands of the founder: blue and purple *is* their clothing: they *are* all the work of cunning *men.* 10 But the LORD *is* the true God, he *is* the living God, and an everlasting King: at his wrath the earth shall tremble, and the nations shall not be able to abide his indignation. 11 Thus shall ye say unto them, The gods that have not made the heavens and the earth, *even* they shall perish from the earth, and from under these heavens. 12 He hath made the earth by his power, he hath established the world by his wisdom, and hath stretched out the heavens by his discretion. 13 When he uttereth his voice, *there is* a multitude of waters in the heavens, and he causeth the vapours to ascend from the ends of the earth; he maketh lightnings with rain, and bringeth forth the wind out of his treasures. 14 Every man is brutish in *his* knowledge: every founder is confounded by the graven image: for his molten image *is* falsehood, and *there is* no breath in them. 15 They *are* vanity, *and* the work of errors: in the time of their visitation they shall perish. 16 The portion of Jacob *is* not like them: for he *is* the former of all *things;* and Israel *is* the rod of his inheritance: The LORD of hosts *is* his name.

The prophet Isaiah, when he prophesied of the captivity in Babylon, added warnings against idolatry and largely exposed the sottishness of idolaters, not only because the temptations in Babylon would be in danger of drawing the Jews there to idolatry, but because the afflictions in Babylon were designed to cure them of their idolatry. Thus the prophet Jeremiah here arms people against the idolatrous usages and customs

472

of the heathen, not only for the use of those that had gone to Babylon, but of those also that staid behind, that being convinced and reclaimed, by the word of God, the rod might be prevented; and it is *written for our learning.* Observe here,

I. A solemn charge given to the people of God not to conform themselves to the ways and customs of the heathen. Let the house of Israel hear and receive this word from the God of Israel: *" Learn not the way of the heathen,* do not approve of it, no, nor think indifferently concerning it, much less imitate it or accustom yourselves to it. Let not any of their customs steal in among you (as they are apt to do insensibly) nor mingle themselves with your religion." Note, It ill becomes those that are taught of God to *learn the way of the heathen,* and to think of worshipping the true God with such rites and ceremonies as they used in the worship of their false gods. See Deut. xii. 29—31. It was the way of the heathen to worship the host of heaven, the sun, moon, and stars; to them they gave divine honours, and from them they expected divine favours, and therefore, according as *the signs of heaven* were, whether they were auspicious or ominous, they thought themselves countenanced or discountenanced by their deities, which made them observe those signs, the eclipses of the sun and moon, the conjunctions and oppositions of the planets, and all the unusual phenomena of the celestial globe, with a great deal of anxiety and trembling. Business was stopped if any thing occurred that was thought to bode ill; if it did but thunder on their left hand, they were almost as if they had been thunderstruck. Now God would not have his people to be *dismayed at the signs of heaven,* to reverence the stars as deities, nor to frighten themselves with any prognostications grounded upon them. Let them fear the God of heaven, and keep up a reverence of his providence, and then they need not be *dismayed at the signs of heaven,* for the *stars in their courses* fight not against any that are at peace with God. The heathen are dismayed at these signs, for they know no better; but let not the *house of Israel,* that are taught of God, be so.

II. Divers good reasons given to enforce this charge.

1. The way of the heathen is very ridiculous and absurd, and is condemned even by the dictates of right reason, *v.* 3. The statutes and ordinances of the heathen are vanity itself; they cannot stand the test of a rational disquisition. This is again and again insisted upon here, as it was by Isaiah. The Chaldeans valued themselves upon their wisdom, in which they thought that they excelled all their neighbours; but the prophet here shows that they, and all others that worshipped idols and expected help and relief from them, were brutish and sottish, and had not common sense. (1.) Consider

what the idol is that is worshipped. It was a *tree cut out of the forest* originally. It was fitted up by *the hands of the workman*, squared, and sawed, and worked into shape; see Isa. xliv. 12, &c. But, after all, it was but the stock of a tree, fitter to make a gate-post of than any thing else. But, to hide the wood, *they deck it with silver and gold*, they gild or lacker it, or they deck it with gold and silver lace, or cloth of tissue. *They fasten it* to its place, which they themselves have assigned it, *with nails and hammers*, that it fall not, nor be thrown down, nor stolen away, *v.* 4. The image is made straight enough, and it cannot be denied but that the workman did his part, for it *is upright as the palm-tree* (*v.* 5); it looks stately, and stands up as if it were going to speak to you, but it *cannot speak;* it is a poor dumb creature; nor can it take one step towards your relief. If there be any occasion for it to shift its place, it must be carried in procession, for it *cannot go.* Very fitly does the admonition come in here, "*Be not afraid of them*, any more than of the signs of heaven; be not afraid of incurring their displeasure, for *they can do no evil;* be not afraid of forfeiting their favour, for *neither is it in them to do good.* If you think to mend the matter by mending the materials of which the idol is made, you deceive yourselves. Idols of gold and silver are as unworthy to be worshipped as wooden gods. *The stock is a doctrine of vanities, v.* 8. It teaches lies, teaches lies concerning God. It is *an instruction of vanities: it is wood.*" It is probable that the idols of gold and silver had wood underneath for the substratum, and then *silver spread into plates is brought from Tarshish*, imported from beyond sea, *and gold from Uphaz*, or *Phaz*, which is sometimes rendered the *fine* or *pure gold*, Ps. xxi. 3. A great deal of art is used, and pains taken, about it. They are not such ordinary mechanics that are employed about these as about the wooden gods, *v.* 3. These are cunning men; it is *the work of the workman;* the graver must do his part when it has passed through *the hands of the founder.* Those were but decked here and there with silver and gold; these are silver and gold all over. And, that these gods might be reverenced as kings, *blue and purple are their clothing*, the colour of royal robes (*v.* 9), which amuses ignorant worshippers, but makes the matter no better. For what is the idol when it is made and when they have made the best they can of it? He tells us (*v.* 14): *They are falsehood;* they are not what they pretend to be, but a great cheat put upon the world. They are worshipped as the gods that give us breath and life and sense, whereas they are lifeless senseless things themselves, and *there is no breath in them;* there is *no spirit in them* (so the word is); they are not animated, or inhabited, as they are supposed to be, by any *divine spirit*

or *numen*—divinity. They are so far from being gods that they have not so much as the spirit of a beast that goes downward. *They are vanity, and the work of errors, v.* 15. Enquire into the use of them and you will find they are vanity; they are good for nothing; no help is to be expected from them nor any confidence put in them. They are a *deceitful work, works of illusions*, or *mere mockeries;* so some read the following clause. They *delude* those that put their trust in them, make fools of them, or, rather, they make fools of themselves. Enquire into the rise of them and you will find they are *the work of errors*, grounded upon the grossest mistakes that ever men who pretended to reason were guilty of. They are the creatures of a deluded fancy; and the errors by which they were produced they propagate among their worshippers. (2.) Infer hence what the idolaters are that worship these idols (*v.* 8): *They are altogether brutish and foolish.* Those that make them are like unto them, senseless and stupid, and there is no spirit in them—no use of reason, else they would never believe in such gods —no sense of honour, else they would never stoop to them, *v.* 14. *Every man* that makes or worships idols has become *brutish in his knowledge*, that is, brutish for want of knowledge, or brutish in that very thing which one would think they should be fully acquainted with; compare Jude 10, *What they know naturally*, what they cannot but know by the light of nature, *in those things as brute beasts they corrupt themselves.* Though in the works of creation they cannot but see the eternal power and godhead of the Creator, yet they have become *vain in their imaginations, not liking to retain God in their knowledge.* See Rom. i. 21, 28. Nay, whereas they thought it a piece of wisdom thus to multiply gods, it really was the greatest folly they could be guilty of. *The world by wisdom knew not God*, 1 Cor. i. 21; Rom. i. 22. *Every founder is* himself *confounded by the graven image;* when he has made it by a mistake he is more and more confirmed in his mistake by it; he is bewildered, bewitched, and cannot disentangle himself from the snare; or it is what he will one time or other be ashamed of.

2. The God of Israel is the one only living and true God, and those that have him for their God need not make their application to any other; nay, to set up any other in competition with him is the greatest affront and injury that can be done him. Let the house of Israel cleave to the God of Israel and serve and worship him only, for,

(1.) He is a n ı-such. Whatever men may set in compe tion with him, there is none to be compare with him. The prophet turns from speaki g with the utmost disdain of the idols of the heathen (as well he might) to speak wit ı the most profound and awful reverence of the God of Israel (*v.* 6,

7): " *Forasmuch as there is none like unto thee, O Lord!* none of all the heroes which the heathen have deified and make such ado about," the dead men of whom they made dead images, and whom they worshipped. " Some were deified and adored for their wisdom ; but, *among all the wise men of the nations,* the greatest philosophers or states-men, as Apollo or Hermes, *there is none like thee.* Others were deified and adored for their dominion; but, *in all their royalty*" (so it may be read), " among all their kings, as Saturn and Jupiter, *there is none like unto thee.*" What is the glory of a man that in-vented a useful art or founded a flourish-ing kingdom (and these were grounds suffi-cient among the heathen to entitle a man to an apotheosis) compared with the glory of him that is the Creator of the world and that *forms the spirit of man within him?* What is the glory of the greatest prince or poten-tate, compared with the glory of him whose *kingdom rules over all?* He acknowledges (v. 6), *O Lord! thou art great,* infinite and immense, and *thy name is great in might ;* thou hast all power, and art known to have it. Men's name is often beyond their might; they are thought to be greater than they are ; but God's *name is great,* and no greater than he really is. And therefore *who would not fear thee, O King of nations?* Who would not choose to worship such a God as this, that can do every thing, rather than such dead idols as the heathen worship, that can do nothing ? Who would not be afraid of offending or forsaking a God whose name is so *great in might ?* Which of all the na-tions, if they understood their interests aright, *would not fear him* who is the *King of nations ?* Note, It is not only the house of Israel that is bound to worship the great Jehovah as the *God of Israel,* the *King of saints* (Rev. xv. 3, 4), but all the families of the earth are bound to worship him as *King of nations ;* for *to him it appertains,* to him it suits and agrees. Note, There is an ad-mirable decency and congruity in the wor-shipping of God only. It is fit that he who is God alone should alone be served, that he who is Lord of all should be served by all, that he who is great should be greatly feared and greatly praised.

(2.) His verity is as evident as the idol's vanity, v. 10. They are the work of men's hands, and therefore nothing is more plain than that it is a jest to worship them, if that may be called a jest which is so great an indignity to him that made us : *But the Lord is the true God,* the God of truth; he is God in truth. *God Jehovah is truth ;* he is not a counterfeit and pretender, as they are, but is really what he has revealed him-self to be ; he is one we may depend upon, in whom and by whom we cannot be de-ceived. [1.] Look upon him as he is in himself, and he is *the living God.* He is life itself, has life in himself, and is the

474

fountain of life to all the creatures. The gods of the heathen are dead things, worth-less and useless, but ours is a living God, and hath immortality. [2.] Look upon him with relation to his creatures, he is a *King,* and absolute monarch, over them all, is their owner and ruler, has an incontestable right both to command them and dispose of them. As a king, he protects the creatures, pro-vides for their welfare, and preserves peace among them. He is *an everlasting king.* The counsels of his kingdom were from ever-lasting and the continuance of it will be to everlasting. He is a *King of eternity.* The idols whom they call their kings are but of yesterday, and will soon be abolished ; and the kings of the earth, that set them up to be worshipped, will themselves be in the dust shortly; but *the Lord shall reign for ever, thy God, O Zion! unto all generations.*

(3.) None knows the power of his anger. Let us stand in awe, and not dare to provoke him by giving that glory to another which is due to him alone ; for *at his wrath the earth shall tremble,* even the strongest and stoutest of the kings of the earth ; nay, the earth, firmly as it is fixed, when he pleases is made to quake and the rocks to tremble, Ps. civ. 32 ; Hab. iii. 6, 10. Though the nations should join together to contend with him, and unite their force, yet they would be found utterly unable not only to resist, but even *to abide his indignation.* Not only can they not make head against it, for it would overcome them, but they cannot bear up under it, for it would overload them, Ps. lxxvi. 7, 8 ; Nah. i. 6.

(4.) He is the God of nature, the foun-tain of all being ; and all the powers of nature are at his command and disposal, v. 12, 13. The God we worship is he that made the heavens and the earth, and has a sovereign dominion over both ; so that his *invisible things* are manifested and proved in the *things that are seen.* [1.] If we look back, we find that the whole world owed its origin to him as its first cause. It was a common saying even among the Greeks— *He that sets up to be another god ought first to make another world.* While the heathen worship gods that they made, we worship the God that made us and all things. *First, The earth* is a body of vast bulk, has valuable treasures in its bowels and more valuable fruit on its surface. It and them he has *made by his power ;* and it is by no less than an infinite power that it *hangs upon nothing,* as it does (Job xxvi. 7)—*ponderibus librata suis*—poised *by its own weight. Secondly, The world,* the habitable part of the earth, is admirably fitted for the use and service of man, and *he hath established it* so *by his wisdom,* so that it continues serviceable in constant changes and yet a continual stabi-lity from one generation to another. There-fore both the earth and the world are his, Ps. xxiv. 1. *Thirdly, The heavens* are wonderfully *stretched out* to an incredible extent, and it is *by his discretion* that they are so, and that the motions of the heavenly bodies are directed for the benefit of this lower world. These *declare his glory* (Ps. xix. 1), and oblige us to declare it, and not give that glory to the heavens which is due to him that made them. [2.] If we look up, we see his providence to be a continued creation (*v.* 13): *When he uttereth his voice* (gives the word of command) *there is a multitude of waters in the heavens*, which are poured out on the earth, whether for judgment or mercy, as he intends them. When he utters his voice in the thunder, immediately there follow thunder-showers, in which there are a multitude of waters; and those come with *a noise*, as the margin reads it; and we read of the *noise of abundance of rain*, 1 Kings xviii. 41. Nay, there are wonders done daily in the kingdom of nature without noise: *He causes the vapours to ascend from the ends of the earth,* from all parts of the earth, even the most remote, and chiefly those that lie next the sea. All the earth pays the tribute of vapours, because all the earth receives the blessing of rain. And thus the moisture in the universe, like the money in a kingdom and the blood in the body, is continually circulating for the good of the whole. Those vapours produce wonders, for of them are formed *lightnings for the rain*, and *the winds* which God from time to time *brings forth out of his treasures*, as there is occasion for them, directing them all in such measure and for such use as he thinks fit, as payments are made out of the treasury. All the meteors are so ready to serve God's purposes that he seems to have treasures of them, that cannot be exhausted and may at any time be drawn from, Ps. cxxxv. 7. God glories in the treasures he has of these, Job xxxviii. 22, 23. This God can do; but which of the idols of the heathen can do the like? Note, There is no sort of weather but what furnishes us with a proof and instance of the wisdom and power of the great Creator.

(5.) This God is Israel's God in covenant, and the felicity of every Israelite indeed. Therefore let the house of Israel cleave to him, and not forsake him to embrace idols; for, if they do, they certainly change for the worse, for (*v.* 16) *the portion of Jacob is not like them;* their rock is not as our rock (Deut. xxxii. 31), nor ours like their molehills. Note, [1.] Those that have the Lord for their God have a full and complete happiness in him. The *God of Jacob* is the *portion of Jacob;* he is his all, and in him he has enough and needs no more in this world nor the other. In him we have a worthy portion, Ps. xvi. 5. [2.] If we have entire satisfaction and complacency in God as our portion, he will have a gracious delight in us as his people, whom he owns as *the rod of his inheritance,* his possession and

treasure, with whom he dwells and by whom he is served and honoured. [3.] It is the unspeakable comfort of all the Lord's people that he who is their God is *the former of all things,* and therefore is able to do all that for them, and give all that to them, which they stand in need of. Their *help stands in his name who made heaven and earth.* And he is the *Lord of hosts,* of all the hosts in heaven and earth, has them all at his command, and will command them into the service of his people when there is occasion. This is the name by which they know him, which they first give him the glory of and then take to themselves the comfort of. [4.] Herein God's people are happy above all other people, happy indeed, *bona si sua norint—did they but know their blessedness.* The gods which the heathen pride, and please, and so portion themselves in, are vanity and a lie; but *the portion of Jacob is not like them.*

3. The prophet, having thus compared the gods of the heathen with the God of Israel (between whom there is no comparison), reads the doom, the certain doom, of all those pretenders, and directs the Jews, in God's name, to read it to the worshippers of idols, though they were their lords and masters (*v.* 11): *Thus shall ye say unto them* (and the God you serve will bear you out in saying it), *The gods which have not made the heavens and the earth* (and therefore are no gods, but usurpers of the honour due to him only who did make heaven and earth) *shall perish,* perish of course, because they are vanity—perish by his righteous sentence, because they are rivals with him. As gods they shall perish *from off the earth* (even all those things *on earth beneath* which they make gods of) *and from under these heavens,* even all those things in the firmament of heaven, under the highest heavens, which are deified, according to the distribution in the second commandment. These words in the original are not in the Hebrew, like all the rest, but in the Chaldee dialect, that the Jews in captivity might have this ready to say to the Chaldeans in their own language when they tempted them to idolatry: "Do you press us to worship your gods? We will never do that; for," (1.) "They are counterfeit deities; they are no gods, for they *have not made the heavens and the earth,* and therefore are not entitled to our homage, nor are we indebted to them either for the products of the earth or the influences of heaven, as we are to the God of Israel." The primitive Christians would say, when they were urged to worship such a god, *Let him make a world and he shall be my god.* While we have him to worship who made heaven and earth, it is very absurd to worship any other. (2.) "They are condemned deities. They *shall perish;* the time shall come when they shall be no more respected as they are now,

but shall be buried in oblivion, and they and their worshippers shall sink together. The earth shall no longer bear them ; the heavens shall no longer cover them; but both shall abandon them." It is repeated (*v.* 15), *In the time of their visitation* they shall perish. When God comes to reckon with idolaters he will make them weary of their idols, and glad to be rid of them. They shall *cast them to the moles and to the bats,* Isa. ii. 20. Whatever runs against God and religion will be run down at last.

17 Gather up thy wares out of the land, O inhabitant of the fortress. 18 For thus saith the LORD, Behold, I will sling out the inhabitants of the land at this once, and will distress them, that they may find *it so.* 19 Woe is me for my hurt! my wound is grievous : but I said, Truly this *is* a grief, and I must bear it. 20 My tabernacle is spoiled, and all my cords are broken : my children are gone forth of me, and they *are* not : *there is* none to stretch forth my tent any more, and to set up my curtains. 21 For the pastors are become brutish, and have not sought the LORD : therefore they shall not prosper, and all their flocks shall be scattered. 22 Behold, the noise of the bruit is come, and a great commotion out of the north country, to make the cities of Judah desolate, *and* a den of dragons. 23 O LORD, I know that the way of man *is* not in himself : *it is* not in man that walketh to direct his steps. 24 O LORD, correct me, but with judgment ; not in thine anger, lest thou bring me to nothing. 25 Pour out thy fury upon the heathen that know thee not, and upon the families that call not on thy name : for they have eaten up Jacob, and devoured him, and consumed him, and have made his habitation desolate.

In these verses,

I. The prophet threatens, in God's name, the approaching ruin of Judah and Jerusalem, *v.* 17, 18. The Jews that continued in their own land, after some were carried into captivity, were very secure ; they thought themselves *inhabitants of a fortress;* their country was their strong hold, and, in their own conceit, impregnable ; but they are here told to think of leaving it : they must prepare to go after their brethren, and pack up their effects in expectation of it : " *Gather up thy wares out of the land;* contract your

affairs, and bring them into as small a compass as you can. *Arise, depart, this is not your rest,* Mic. ii. 10. Let not what you have lie scattered, for the Chaldeans will be upon you again, to be the executioners of the sentence God has passed upon you (*v.* 18) : " *Behold, I will sling out the inhabitants of the land at this once ;* they have hitherto dropped out, by a few at a time, but one captivity more shall make a thorough riddance, and they shall be slung out as a stone out of a sling, so easily, so thoroughly, shall they be cast out ; nothing of them shall remain. They shall be thrown out with violence, and driven to a place at a great distance off, in a little time." See this comparison used to signify an utter destruction, 1 Sam. xxv. 29. *Yet once more* God will shake their land, and *shake the wicked out of it,* Heb. xii. 26. He adds, *And I will distress them, that they may find it so.* He will not only throw them out hence (that he may do and yet they may be easy elsewhere) ; but, whithersoever they go, trouble shall follow them ; they shall be continually perplexed and straitened, and at a loss within themselves : and who or what can make those easy whom God *will distress,* whom he will distress *that they may find it so,* that they may feel that which they would not believe ? They were often told of the weight of God's wrath and their utter inability to make head against it, or bear up under it. They were told that their sin would be their ruin, and they would not regard nor credit what was told them ; but now *they shall find it so ;* and *therefore* God will pursue them with his judgments, *that they may find it so,* and be forced to acknowledge it. Note, Sooner or later sinners will find it just as the word of God has represented things to them, and no better, and that the threatenings were not bugbears.

II. He brings in the people sadly lamenting their calamities (*v.* 19) : *Woe is me for my hurt !* Some make this the prophet's own lamentation, not for himself, but for the calamities and desolations of his country. He mourned for those that would not be persuaded to mourn for themselves ; and, since there were none that had so much sense as to join with them, he weeps in secret, and cries out, *Woe is me !* In mournful times it becomes us to be of a mournful spirit. But it may be taken as the language of the people, considered as a body, and therefore speaking as a single person. The prophet puts into their mouths the words they *should* say ; whether they would say them or no, they should have cause to say them. Some among them would thus bemoan themselves, and all of them, at last, would be forced to do it. 1. They lament that the affliction is very great, and it is very hard to them to bear it, the more hard because they had not been used to trouble and now did not expect it : " *Woe is me for my hurt,* not for what I fear, but for what I feel;" for they are not, as some are, worse frightened than hurt. Nor is it a slight hurt, but *a wound*, a wound that is *grievous*, very painful, and very threatening. 2. That there is no remedy but patience. They cannot help themselves, but must sit still, and abide it: *But I said*, when I was about to complain of my wound, To what purpose is it to complain? *This is a grief, and I must bear it* as well as I can. This is the language rather of a sullen than of a gracious submission, of a patience per force, not a patience by principle. When I am in affliction I should say, "This is an evil, and I will bear it, because it is the will of God that I should, because his wisdom has appointed this for me and his grace will make it work for good to me." This is *receiving evil* at the hand of God, Job ii. 10. But to say, "This is an evil, *and I must bear it*, because I cannot help it," is but a brutal patience, and argues a want of those good thoughts of God which we should always have, even under our afflictions, saying, not only, God can and will do what he pleases, but, *Let him do what he pleases.* 3. That the country was quite ruined and wasted (*v.* 20): *My tabernacle is spoiled.* Jerusalem, though a strong city, now proves as weak and moveable as a tabernacle: their government is dissolved, and their state has fallen to pieces, like a tabernacle or tent, when it is taken down, and *all its cords*, that should keep it together, are *broken.* Or by the tabernacle here may be meant the temple, the sanctuary, which at first was but a tabernacle, and is now called so, as then it was sometimes called a temple. Their church is ruined, and all the supports of it fail. It was a general destruction of church and state, city and country, and there were none to repair these desolations. "*My children have gone forth of me;* some have fled, others are slain, others carried into captivity, so that as to me *they are not;* I am likely to be an outcast, and to perish for want of shelter; for *there is none to stretch forth my tent any more*, none of my children that used to do it for me, *none to set up my curtains*, none to do me any service." *Jerusalem has none to guide her of all her sons*, Isa. li. 18. 4. That the rulers took no care, nor any proper measures, for the redress of their grievances and the re-establishing of their ruined state (*v.* 21): *The pastors have become brutish.* When the tents, the shepherds' tents, were spoiled (*v.* 20), it concerned the shepherds to look after them; but they were foolish shepherds. Their kings and princes had no regard at all for the public welfare, seemed to have no sense of the desolations of the land, but were quite besotted and infatuated. The priests, the pastors of God's tabernacle, did a great deal towards the ruin of religion, but nothing towards the repair of it. They are *brutish* indeed, for *they have not sought the Lord;* they have neither made their peace with him

nor their prayer to him; they had no eye to him and his providence, in their management of affairs; they neither acknowledged the judgment, nor expected the deliverance, to come from his hand. Note, Those are brutish people that do not seek the Lord, that live without prayer, and live without God in the world. Every man is either a saint or a brute. But it is sad indeed with a people when their pastors, that should *feed them with knowledge and understanding*, are themselves thus brutish. And what comes of it? *Therefore they shall not prosper;* none of their attempts for the public safety shall succeed. Note, Those cannot expect to prosper who do not by faith and prayer take God along with them in all their ways. And, when the pastors are brutish, what else can be expected but that *all their flocks* should be *scattered?* For, *if the blind lead the blind, both will fall into the ditch.* The ruin of a people is often owing to the brutishness of their pastors. 5. That the report of the enemy's approach was very dreadful (*v.* 22): *The noise of the bruit has come*, of the report which at first was but whispered and bruited abroad, as wanting confirmation. It now proves too true: *A great commotion* arises *out of the north country*, which threatens to make all *the cities of Judah desolate and a den of dragons;* for they must all expect to be sacrificed to the avarice and fury of the Chaldean army. And what else can that place expect but to be made a den of dragons which has by sin made itself a den of thieves?

III. He turns to God, and addresses himself to him, finding it to little purpose to speak to the people. It is some comfort to poor ministers that, if men will not hear them, God will; and to him they have liberty of access at all times. Let them close their preaching with prayer, as the prophet, and then they shall have no reason to say that they have laboured in vain.

1. The prophet here acknowledges the sovereignty and dominion of the divine Providence, that by it, and not by their own will and wisdom, the affairs both of nations and particular persons are directed and determined, *v.* 23. This is an article of our faith which it is very proper for us to make confession of at the throne of grace when we are complaining of an affliction or suing for a mercy: "*O Lord, I know*, and believe, *that the way of man is not in himself;* Nebuchadnezzar did not come of himself against our land, but by the direction of a divine Providence." We cannot of ourselves do any thing for our own relief, unless God work with us and command deliverance for us; for *it is not in man that walketh to direct his steps*, though he seem in his walking to be perfectly at liberty and to choose his own way. Those that had promised themselves a long enjoyment of their estates and possessions were made to know, by sad experience, when they were thrown out by the

Chaldeans, that *the way of man is not in himself;* the designs which men lay deep, and think well-formed, are dashed to pieces in a moment. We must all apply this to ourselves, and mix faith with it, that we are not at our own disposal, but under a divine direction; the event is often overruled so as to be quite contrary to our intention and expectation. We are not masters of our own way, nor can we think that every thing should be according to our mind; we must therefore refer ourselves to God and acquiesce in his will. Some think that the prophet here mentions this with a design to make this comfortable use of it, that, the way of the Chaldean army being not in themselves, they can do no more than God permits them; he can set bounds to these proud waves, and say, *Hitherto they shall come, and no further.* And a quieting consideration it is that the most formidable enemies have *no power against us but what is given them from above.*

2. He deprecates the divine wrath, that it might not fall upon God's Israel, *v.* 24. He speaks not for himself only, but on the behalf of his people: *O Lord, correct me, but with judgment* (in measure and with moderation, and in wisdom, no more than is necessary for the driving out of the foolishness that is bound up in our hearts), *not in thy anger* (how severe soever the correction be, let it come from thy love, and be designed for our good and made to work for good), not to *bring us to nothing,* but to bring us home to thyself. Let it not be according to the desert of our sins, but according to the designs of thy grace. Note, (1.) We cannot pray in faith that we may never be corrected, while we are conscious to ourselves that we need correction and deserve it, and know that as many as God loves he chastens. (2.) The great thing we should dread in affliction is the wrath of God. Say not, Lord, *do not correct* me, but, Lord, do not correct me *in anger;* for that will infuse wormwood and gall into the affliction and misery that will *bring us to nothing.* We may bear the smart of his rod, but we cannot bear the weight of his wrath.

3. He imprecates the divine wrath against the oppressors and persecutors of Israel (*v.* 25): *Pour out thy fury upon the heathen that know thee not.* This prayer does not come from a spirit of malice or revenge, nor is it intended to prescribe to God whom he should execute his judgments upon, or in what order; but, (1.) It is an appeal to his justice. As if he had said, " Lord, we are a provoking people; but are there not other nations that are more so? And shall we only be punished? We are thy children, and may expect a fatherly correction; but they are thy enemies, and against them we have reason to think thy indignation should be, not against us." This is God's usual method. The *cup put into the hands* of God's people is *full of mixtures,* mixtures of mercy; but

478

the *dregs of the cup* are reserved for *the wicked of the earth,* let them *wring them out,* Ps. lxxv. 8. (2.) It is a prediction of God's judgments upon all the impenitent enemies of his church and kingdom. If *judgment begin* thus *at the house of God,* what shall be *the end of those that obey not his gospel?* 1 Pet. iv. 17. See how the heathen are described, on whom God's fury shall be poured out. [1] They are strangers to God, and are content to be so. They *know him not,* nor desire to know him. They are families that live without prayer, that have nothing of religion among them; they *call not on God's name.* Those that restrain prayer prove that they know not God; for those that know him will seek to him and entreat his favour. [2.] They are persecutors of the people of God and are resolved to be so. *They have eaten up Jacob* with as much greediness as those that are hungry eat their necessary food; nay, with more, for they never know when they have enough; they have *devoured him, and consumed him, and made his habitation desolate,* that is, the land in which he lives, or the temple of God, which is his habitation among them. Note, What the heathen, in their rage and malice, do against the people of God, though therein he makes use of them as the instruments of his correction, yet he will, for that, make them the objects of his indignation. This prayer is taken from Ps. lxxix. 6, 7.

CHAP. XI.

In this chapter, I. God by the prophet puts the people in mind of the covenant he had made with their fathers, and how much he had insisted upon it, as the condition of the covenant, that they should be obedient to him, ver. 1—7. II. He charges it upon them that they, in succession to their fathers, and in confederacy among themselves, had obstinately refused to obey him, ver. 8—10. III. He threatens to punish them with utter ruin for their disobedience, especially for their idolatry (ver. 11, 13), and tells them that their idols should not save them (ver. 12), that their prophets should not pray for them (ver. 14); he also justifies his proceedings herein, they having brought all this mischief upon themselves by their own folly and wilfulness, ver. 15—17. IV. Here is an account of a conspiracy formed against Jeremiah by his fellow-citizens, the men of Anathoth; God's discovery of it to him (ver. 18, 19), his prayer against them (ver. 20), and a prediction of God's judgments upon them for it, ver. 21—23.

THE word that came to Jeremiah from the LORD, saying, 2 Hear ye the words of this covenant, and speak unto the men of Judah, and to the inhabitants of Jerusalem; 3 And say thou unto them, Thus saith the LORD God of Israel; Cursed *be* the man that obeyeth not the words of this covenant, 4 Which I commanded your fathers in the day *that* I brought them forth out of the land of Egypt, from the iron furnace, saying, Obey my voice, and do them, according to all which I command you: so shall ye be my people, and I will be your God: 5 That I may perform the oath which I have sworn unto your fathers, to give them a land flowing with milk and honey, as *it is* this day. Then answered I, and said, So be it, O LORD. 6 Then the LORD said unto me, Proclaim all these words in the cities of Judah, and in the streets of Jerusalem, saying, Hear ye the words of this covenant, and do them. 7 For I earnestly protested unto your fathers in the day *that* I brought them up out of the land of Egypt, *even* unto this day, rising early and protesting, saying, Obey my voice. 8 Yet they obeyed not, nor inclined their ear, but walked every one in the imagination of their evil heart : therefore I will bring upon them all the words of this covenant, which I commanded *them* to do ; but they did *them* not. 9 And the LORD said unto me, A conspiracy is found among the men of Judah, and among the inhabitants of Jerusalem. 10 They are turned back to the iniquities of their forefathers, which refused to hear my words ; and they went after other gods to serve them : the house of Israel and the house of Judah have broken my covenant which I made with their fathers.

The prophet here, as prosecutor in God's name, draws up an indictment against the Jews for wilful disobedience to the commands of their rightful Sovereign. For the more solemn management of this charge,

I. He produces the commission he had to draw up the charge against them. He did not take pleasure in accusing the children of his people, but God commanded him to *speak it to the men of Judah, v.* 1, 2. In the original it is plural : *Speak you this.* For what he said to Jeremiah was the same that he gave in charge to all his servants the prophets. They none of them said any other than what Moses, in the law, had said ; to that therefore they must refer themselves, and direct the people : *" Hear the words of this covenant ;* turn to your Bibles, be judged by them." Jeremiah must now proclaim this in the cities *of Judah and the streets of Jerusalem,* that all may hear, for all are concerned. All the words of reproof and conviction which the prophets spoke were grounded upon the *words of the covenant,* and agreed with that ; and therefore *" hear these words,* and understand by them upon what terms you stood with God at first ; and then, by comparing yourselves with the covenant, you will soon be aware upon what terms you now stand with him."

II. He opens the charter upon which their state was founded and by which they held their privileges. They had forgotten the tenour of it, and lived as if they thought that the grant was absolute and that they might do what they pleased and yet have what God had promised, or as if they thought that the keeping up of the ceremonial observances was all that God required of them. He therefore shows them, with all possible plainness, that the thing God insisted upon was *obedience,* which was *better than sacrifice.* He said, *Obey my voice, v.* 4 and again *v.* 7. " Own God for your Master ; give up yourselves to him as his subjects and servants ; attend to all the declarations of his mind and will, and make conscience of complying with them. *Do my commandments,* not only in some things, but *according to all which I command you ;* make conscience of moral duties especially, and rest not in those that are merely ritual ; hear the words of the covenant, and do them." 1. This was the original contract between God and them, when he first formed them into a people. It was what he *commanded their fathers* when he first *brought them forth out of the land of Egypt, v.* 4 and again *v.*7. He never intended to take them under his guidance and protection upon any other terms. This was what he required from them in gratitude for the great things he did for them when he brought them *from the iron furnace.* He redeemed them out of the service of the Egyptians, which was perfect slavery, that he might take them into his own service, which is perfect freedom, Luke i. 74, 75. 2. This was not only laid before them then, but it was with the greatest importunity imaginable pressed upon them, *v.* 7. God not only commanded it, but *earnestly protested it to their fathers,* when he brought them into covenant with himself. Moses inculcated it again and again, by precept upon precept and line upon line. 3. This was made the condition of the relation between them and God, which was so much their honour and privilege : *" So shall you be my people and I will be your God ;* I will own you for mine, and you may call upon me as yours ;" this intimates that, if they refused to obey, they could no longer claim the benefit of the relation 4. It was upon these terms that the land of Canaan was given them for a possession : *Obey my voice, that I may perform the oath sworn to your fathers, to give them a land flowing with milk and honey, v.* 5. God was ready to fulfil the promise, but then they must fulfil the condition ; if not, the promise is void, and it is just with God to turn them out of possession. Being brought in upon their good behaviour, they had no wrong done them if they were turned out upon their ill behaviour. Obedience was the rent reserved by the lease, with a power to re-enter for non-payment. 5. This obedience was not only made a condition of the blessing, but was required under the penalty of a curse. This is mentioned first here (*v.* 3), that they might, if possible, be awakened by the terrors of the Lord : *Cursed be the man,* though it were but a single person, *that obeys not the words of this covenant,* much more when it is the body of the nation that rebels. There are curses of the covenant as well as blessings: and Moses set before them not only *life and good,* but *death and evil* (Deut. xxx. 15), so that they had fair warning given them of the fatal consequences of disobedience. 6. Lest this covenant should be forgotten, and, because out of mind, should be thought out of date, God had from time to time called to them to remember it, and by his servants the prophets had made a continual claim of this rent, so that they could not plead, in excuse of their non-payment, that it had never been demanded ; *from the day when he brought them out of Egypt to this day* (and that was nearly 1000 years) he had been, in one way or other, *at sundry times and in divers manners,* protesting to them the necessity of obedience. God keeps an account how long we have enjoyed the means of grace and how powerful those means have been, how often we have been not only spoken to, but protested to, concerning our duty. 7. This covenant was consented to (*v.* 5): *Then answered I, and said, So be it, O Lord!* These are the words of the prophet, expressing either, (1.) His own consent to the covenant for himself, and his desire to have the benefit of it. God promised Canaan to the obedient : " Lord," says he, " I take thee at thy word, I will be obedient ; let me have my inheritance in the land of promise, of which Canaan is a type." Or, (2.) His good will, and good wish, that his people might have the benefit of it. " *Amen :* Lord, let them still be kept in possession of this good land, and not turned out of it ; make good the promise to them." Or, (3.) His people's consent to the covenant : " *Then answered I,* in the name of the people, *So be it.*" Taking it in this sense, it refers to the declared consent which the people gave to the covenant, not only to the precepts of it when they said, *All that the Lord shall say unto us we will do and will be obedient,* but to the penalties when they said *Amen* to all the curses upon Mount Ebal. The more solemnly we have engaged ourselves to God the more reason we have to hope that the engagement will be perpetual ; and yet here it did not prove so.

III. He charges them with breach of covenant, such a breach as amounted to a forfeiture of their charter, *v.* 8. God had said again and again, by his law and by his prophets, " Obey my voice, do as you are bidden, and all shall be well ;" *yet they obeyed not :* and, because they were resolved not to submit their souls to God's commandments, they would not so much as incline their ears to them, but got as far as they could out of call : *They walked every one in the imagination*

480

of their evil heart, followed their own inventions ; every man did as his fancy and humour led him, right or wrong, lawful or unlawful, both in their devotions and in their conversations ; see *ch.* vii. 24. What then could they expect, but to fall under the curse of the covenant, since they would not comply with the commands and conditions of it? *Therefore I will bring upon them all the words of this covenant,* that is, all the threatenings contained in it, because *they did not what they were commanded.* Note, The words of the covenant shall not fall to the ground. If we do not by our obedience qualify ourselves for the blessings of it, we shall by our disobedience bring ourselves under the curses of it. That which aggravated their defection from God, and rebellion against him, was that it was general, and as it were *by consent, v.* 9, 10. Jeremiah himself saw that many lived in open disobedience to God, but the Lord told him that the matter was worse than he thought of : *A conspiracy is found among them,* by him whose eye is upon the hidden works of darkness. There is a combination against God and religion, a dangerous design formed to overthrow God's government and bring in the pretenders, the counterfeit deities. This intimates that they were wilful and deliberate in wickedness (they rebelled against God, not through incogitancy, but presumptuously, and with a high hand),—that they were subtle and ingenious in wickedness, and carried on their plot against religion with a great deal of art and contrivance,—that they were linked together in the design, and, as is usual among conspirators, engaged to stand by one another in it and to live and die together ; they were resolved to go through with it. A cursed conspiracy ! O that there were not the like in our day ! Observe, 1. What the conspiracy was. They designed to overthrow divine revelation, and set that aside, and persuade people not to hear, not to heed, the words of God. They did all they could to derogate from the authority of the scriptures and to lessen the value of them ; they designed to draw people *after other gods to serve them,* to consult them as their oracles and make court to them as their benefactors. Human reason shall be their god, a light within their god, an infallible judge their god, saints and angels their gods, the god of this or the other nation shall be theirs ; thus, under several disguises, they are in the same confederacy *against the Lord and against his anointed.* 2. Who were in the conspiracy. One would have expected to find some foreigners ringleaders in it ; but no, (1.) *The inhabitants of Jerusalem* are in conspiracy with *the men of Judah ;* city and country agree in this, however they may differ in other things. (2.) Those of this generation seem to be in conspiracy with those of the foregoing generation, to carry on the war from age to age against religion : *They are turned back to the iniquities of their forefathers,* and have risen up in their stead, *a seed of evil-doers,* an *increase of sinful men,* Num. xxxii. 14. In Josiah's time there had been a reformation, but after his death the people returned to the idolatries which then they had renounced. (3.) Judah and Israel, the kingdom of the ten tribes and that of the two, that were often at daggers-drawing one with another, were yet *in a conspiracy* to *break the covenant God had made with their fathers,* even with the heads of all the twelve tribes. The house of Israel began the revolt, but the house of Judah soon came into the conspiracy. Now what else could be expected but that God should take severe methods, both for the chastising of these conspirators and the crushing of this conspiracy; for none ever hardened his heart thus against God and prospered? He that rolls this stone will find it return upon him.

11 Therefore thus saith the LORD, Behold, I will bring evil upon them, which they shall not be able to escape ; and though they shall cry unto me, I will not hearken unto them. 12 Then shall the cities of Judah and inhabitants of Jerusalem go, and cry unto the gods unto whom they offer incense : but they shall not save them at all in the time of their trouble. 13 For *according to* the number of thy cities were thy gods, O Judah ; and *according to* the number of the streets of Jerusalem have ye set up altars to *that* shameful thing, *even* altars to burn incense unto Baal. 14 Therefore pray not thou for this people, neither lift up a cry or prayer for them : for I will not hear *them* in the time that they cry unto me for their trouble. 15 What hath my beloved to do in mine house, *seeing* she hath wrought lewdness with many, and the holy flesh is passed from thee? when thou doest evil, then thou rejoicest. 16 The LORD called thy name, A green olive-tree, fair, *and* of goodly fruit : with the noise of a great tumult he hath kindled fire upon it, and the branches of it are broken. 17 For the LORD of hosts, that planted thee, hath pronounced evil against thee, for the evil of the house of Israel and of the house of Judah, which they have done against themselves to provoke me to anger in offering incense unto Baal.

This paragraph, which contains so much of God's wrath, might very well be expected to follow upon that which goes next before, which contained so much of his people's sin. When God found so much evil among them we cannot think it strange if it follows, *Therefore I will bring evil upon them* (v. 11), the evil of punishment for the evil of sin ; and there is no remedy, no relief : the decree has gone forth and the sentence will be executed.

I. They cannot help themselves, but will be found too weak to contest with God's judgments ; it is *evil which they shall not be able to escape,* or to *go forth out of,* by any evasion whatsoever. Note, Those that will not submit to God's government shall not be able to escape his wrath. There is no fleeing from his justice, no avoiding his cognizance. Evil pursues sinners and entangles them in snares out of which they cannot extricate themselves.

II. Their God will not help them; his providence shall no way favour them : *Though they shall cry unto me, I will not hearken unto them.* In their affliction they will seek the God whom before they slighted, and cry to him whom before they would not vouchsafe to speak to. But how can they expect to speed? For he has plainly told us that he that *turns away his ears from hearing the law,* as they did, for they *inclined not their ear* (v. 8), even his prayer shall be an abomination to him, as the word of the Lord was now to them a reproach.

III. Their idols shall not help them, v. 12. They shall *go, and cry to the gods to whom they* now *offer incense,* and put them in mind of the costly services wherewith they had honoured them, expecting they should now have relief from them, but in vain. They shall be sent to the *gods whom they served* (Judg. x. 14 ; Deut. xxxii. 37, 38), and what the better? *They shall not save them at all,* shall do nothing towards their salvation, nor give them any prospect of it ; they shall not afford them the least comfort, nor relief, nor mitigation of their trouble. It is God only that is a friend at need, *a present* powerful *help in time of trouble.* The idols cannot help themselves; how then should they help their worshippers? Those that make idols of the world and the flesh will in vain have recourse to them in a day of distress. If the idols could have done any real kindness to their worshippers, they would have done it for this people, who had renounced the true God to embrace them, had multiplied them *according to the number of their cities* (v. 13), nay, in Jerusalem, *according to the number of their streets.* Suspecting both their sufficiency and their readiness to help them, they must have many, lest a few would not serve; they must have them dispersed in every corner, lest they should be out of the way when they had occasion for them. In *Je-*

rusalem, the city which God had chosen to put his name there, publicly in the streets of Jerusalem, in every street, they had *altars to that shameful thing,* that *shame,* even to Baal, which they ought to have been ashamed of, with which they did reproach the Lord and bring confusion upon themselves. But now in their distress their many gods, and many altars, should stand them in no stead. Note, Those that will not be ashamed of their commission of sin as a wicked thing will be ashamed of their expectations from sin as a fruitless thing.

IV. Jeremiah's prayers shall not help them, *v.* 14. What God had said to him before (*ch.* vii. 16) he here says again, *Pray not thou for this people.* This is not designed for a command to the prophet, so much as for a threatening to the people, that they should have no benefit by the prayers of their friends for them. God would give no encouragement to the prophets to pray for them, would not stir up the spirit of prayer, but cast a damp upon it, would put it into their hearts to pray, not for the body of the people, but for the remnant among them, to pray for their eternal salvation, not for their deliverance from the temporal judgments that were coming upon them; and what other prayers were put up for them should not be heard. Those are in a sad case indeed that are cut off from the benefit of prayer. *" I will not hear them when they cry,* and therefore do not thou pray for them."* Note, Those that have so far thrown themselves out of God's favour that he will not hear their prayers cannot expect benefit by the prayers of others for them.

V. The profession they make of religion shall stand them in no stead, *v.* 15. They were originally God's *beloved,* his spouse, he was married to them by the covenant of peculiarity; even the unbelieving Jews are said to be *beloved for the fathers' sake,* Rom. xi. 28. As such they had a place *in God's house;* they were admitted to worship in the courts of his temple; they partook of God's altar; they ate of the flesh of their peace-offerings, here called the *holy flesh,* which God had the honour of and they had the comfort of. This they gloried in, and trusted to. What harm could come to those who were God's beloved, who were under the protection of his house? Even when they *did evil* yet *they rejoiced* and gloried in this, made a mighty noise of this. And *when their evil was* (so the margin reads it), when trouble came upon them, *they rejoiced in this,* and made this their confidence; but their confidence would deceive them, for God has rejected it, they themselves having forfeited the privileges they so much boasted of. They have *wrought lewdness with many,* have been guilty of spiritual whoredom, have worshipped many idols; and therefore, 1. God's temple will *yield them no protection;* it is fit that the adulteress, especially when

she has so often repeated her whoredoms and has grown so impudent in them and irreclaimable, should be *put away,* and turned out of doors : *" What has my beloved to do in my house?* She is a scandal to it, and therefore it shall no longer be a shelter to her."* 2. God's altar will yield them no satisfaction, nor can they expect any comfort from that : *" The holy flesh has passed from thee,* that is, an end will soon be put to thy sacrifices, when the temple shall be laid in ruins; and where then will the holy flesh be, that thou art so proud of?"* A holy heart will be a comfort to us when the holy flesh has passed from us; an inward principle of grace will make up the want of the outward means of grace. But woe unto us if the departure of the holy flesh be accompanied with the departure of the Holy Spirit.

VI. God's former favours to them shall stand them in no stead, *v.* 16, 17. Their remembrance of them shall be no comfort to them under their troubles, and God's remembrance of them shall be no argument for their relief. 1. It is true God had done great things for them; that people had been favourites above any people under the sun; they had been the darlings of heaven. God had *called Israel's name a green olive-tree,* and had made them so, for he miscalls nothing; he had *planted* them (*v.* 17), had formed them into a people, with all the advantages they could have to make them a fruitful and flourishing people, so good was their law and so good was their land. One would think no other than that a people so planted, so watered, so cultivated, should be, as the olive-tree is, ever green, in respect both of piety and prosperity, Ps. lii. 8. God called them *fair and of goodly fruit,* both good for food and pleasant to the eye, both amiable and serviceable to God and man, for with the greenness and fatness of the olive both are honoured, Judg. ix. 9. 2. It is as true that they have done evil things against God. He had planted them a green olive, a good olive, but they had degenerated into a *wild olive,* Rom. xi. 17. Both *the house of Israel* and the *house of Judah* had *done evil,* had *provoked God to anger in burning incense unto Baal,* setting up other mediators between them and the supreme God besides the promised Messiah; nay, setting up other gods in competition with the true and living God, for they had *gods many,* as well as *lords many.* 3. When they have conducted themselves so ill they can expect no other than that, notwithstanding what good he has done to them and designed for them, he should now bring upon them the evil he has *pronounced against them.* He that made them will not save them. He that planted this green olive-tree, and expected fruit from it, finding it barren and grown wild, *has kindled fire upon it,* to burn it as it stands; for, being without fruit, it is *twice dead, plucked up by the roots* (Jude 12), it is *cut down and cast into the fire*, the fittest place for trees that cumber the ground, Matt. iii. 10. The *branches of it*, the *high and lofty boughs* (so the word signifies), are *broken*, are *broken down*, both princes and priests cut off. And thus it proves that the evil done against God, to *provoke him to anger*, is really done *against themselves;* they *wrong their own souls;* God is out of their reach, but they ruin themselves. See *ch.* vii. 19. Note, Every sin against God is a sin against ourselves, and so it will be found sooner or later.

18 And the LORD hath given me knowledge *of it*, and I know *it :* then thou showedst me their doings. 19 But I *was* like a lamb *or* an ox *that* is brought to the slaughter; and I knew not that they had devised devices against me, *saying,* Let us destroy the tree with the fruit thereof, and let us cut him off from the land of the living, that his name may be no more remembered. 20 But, O LORD of hosts, that judgest righteously, that triest the reins and the heart, let me see thy vengeance on them : for unto thee have I revealed my cause. 21 Therefore thus saith the LORD of the men of Anathoth, that seek thy life, saying, Prophesy not in the name of the LORD, that thou die not by our hand : 22 Therefore thus saith the LORD of hosts, Behold, I will punish them : the young men shall die by the sword; their sons and their daughters shall die by famine : 23 And there shall be no remnant of them : for I will bring evil upon the men of Anathoth, *even* the year of their visitation.

The prophet Jeremiah has much in his writings concerning himself, much more than Isaiah had, the times he lived in being very troublesome. Here we have (as it should seem) the beginning of his sorrows, which arose from the people of his own city, Anathoth, a priest's city, and yet a malignant one. Observe here,

I. Their plot against him, *v.* 19. They *devised devices against him*, laid their heads together to contrive how they might be in the most plausible and effectual manner the death of him. Malice is ingenious in its devices, as well as industrious in its prosecutions. They said concerning Jeremiah, *Let us destroy the tree with the fruit thereof*—a proverbial expression, meaning, "Let us utterly destroy him root and branch. Let us

destroy both the father and the family" (as, when Naboth was put to death for treason, his sons were put to death with him), or rather "both the prophet and the prophecy ; let us kill the one and defeat the other. *Let us cut him off from the land of the living*, as a false prophet, and load him with ignominy and disgrace, *that his name may be no more remembered* with respect. Let us sink his reputation, and so spoil the credit of his predictions." This was their plot; and, 1. It was a cruel one ; but so cruel have the persecutors of God's prophets been. They *hunt for* no less than *the precious life*, and very precious the lives are that they hunt for. But, (2.) It was a baffled one. They thought to put an end to his days, but he survived most of his enemies; they thought to blast his memory, but it lives to this day, and will be blessed while time lasts.

II. The information which God gave him of this conspiracy against him. He knew nothing of it himself, so artfully had they concealed it; he came to Anathoth, meaning no harm to them and therefore fearing no harm from them, *like a lamb or an ox*, that thinks he is driven as usual to the field, *when he is brought to the slaughter ;* so little did poor Jeremiah dream of the design his citizens that hated him had upon him. None of his friends could, and none of his enemies would, give him any notice of his danger, that he might shift for his own safety, as Paul's sister's son gave him intelligence of the Jews that were lying in wait for him. There is but a step between Jeremiah and death ; but then *the Lord gave him knowledge of it*, by dream or vision, or impression upon his spirit, that he might save himself, as the king of Israel did upon the notice Elisha gave him, 2 Kings vi. 10. Thus he came to *know it*. God *showed him their doings;* and such were their devices that the discovering of them was the defeating of them. If God had not let him know his own danger, it would have been improved by unreasonable men against the reputation of his predictions, that he who foretold the ruin of his country could not foresee his own peril and avoid it. See what care God takes of his prophets : He *suffers no man to do them wrong ;* all the rage of their enemies cannot prevail to take them off till they have finished their testimony. God knows all the secret designs of his and his people's enemies, and can, when he pleases, make them know. *A bird of the air shall carry the voice.*

III. His appeal to God hereupon, *v.* 20. His eye is to God as *the Lord of hosts, that judges righteously*. It is matter of comfort to us, when men deal unjustly with us, that we have a God to go to who does and will plead the cause of injured innocency and appear against the injurious. God's justice, which is a terror to the wicked, is a comfort to the godly. His eye is towards him as the God that *tries the reins and the heart*, that perfectly sees what is in man, what are his thoughts and intents. He knew the integrity that was in Jeremiah's heart, and that he was not the man they represented him to be. He knew the wickedness that was in their hearts, though ever so cunningly concealed and disguised. Now, 1. Jeremiah prays judgment against them : *" Let me see thy vengeance on them,* that is, do justice between me and them in such a way as thou pleasest " Some think there was something of human frailty in this prayer; at least Christ has taught us another lesson, both by precept and by pattern, which is to pray for our persecutors. Others think it comes from a pure zeal for the glory of God and a pious and prophetic indignation against men that were by profession priests, the Lord's ministers, and yet were so desperately wicked as to fly out against one that did them no harm, merely for the service he did to God. This petition was a prediction that he should see God's vengeance on them. 2. He refers his cause entirely to the judgment of God : *" Unto thee have I revealed my cause;* to thee I have committed it, not desiring nor expecting to interest any other in it." Note, It is our comfort, when we are wronged, that we have a God to commit our cause to, and our duty to commit it to him, with a resolution to acquiesce in his definitive sentence, to subscribe, and not prescribe, to him.

IV. Judgment given against his persecutors, *the men of Anathoth.* It was to no purpose for him to appeal to the courts at Jerusalem, he could not have justice done him there : the priests there would stand by the priests at Anathoth, and rather second them than discountenance them; but God will *therefore* take cognizance of the cause himself, and we are sure that *his judgment is according to truth.* Here is, 1. Their crime recited, on which the sentence is grounded, *v.* 21. They sought the prophet's life, for they forbad him to prophesy upon pain of death; they were resolved either to silence him or to slay him. The provocation he gave them was his prophesying *in the name of the Lord* without license from those that were the governors of the city which he was a member of, and not prophesying such smooth things as they always bespoke. Their forbidding him to prophesy was in effect seeking his life, for it was seeking to defeat the end and business of his life and to rob him of the comfort of it. It is as bad to God's faithful ministers to have their mouth stopped as to have their breath stopped. But especially when it was resolved that if he did prophesy, as certainly he would notwithstanding their inhibition, he should *die by their hand;* they would be accusers, judges, executioners, and all. It used to be said that *a prophet could not perish but at Jerusalem,* for there the great council sat; but so bitter were the men of Anathoth against Jeremiah that they would undertake to

be the death of him themselves. A prophet then shall find not only no honour, but no favour, in his own country. 2. The sentence passed upon them for this crime, *v.* 22, 23. God says, *I will punish them;* let me alone to deal with them. *I will visit* this *upon them;* so the word is. God will enquire into it and reckon for it. Two of God's four sore judgments shall serve to ruin their town :—*The sword* shall devour their *young men,* though they were young priests, not men of war (their character shall not be their protection), and *famine* shall destroy the children, *sons and daughters,* that tarry at home, which is a more grievous death than that by the sword, Lam. iv. 9. The destruction shall be final (*v.* 23) : *There shall be no remnant of them left,* none to be the seed of another generation. They sought Jeremiah's life, and therefore they shall die ; they would destroy him *root and branch,* that *his name* might be *no more remembered,* and therefore *there shall be no remnant of them;* and herein the Lord is righteous. Thus *evil is brought upon them, even the year of their visitation,* and that is evil enough, a recompence according to their deserts. Then shall Jeremiah *see his desire upon his enemies.* Note, Their condition is sad who have the prayers of good ministers and good people against them.

CHAP. XII.

In this chapter we have, I. The prophet's humble complaint to God of the success that wicked people had in their wicked practices (ver. 1, 2) and his appeal to God concerning his own integrity (ver. 3), with a prayer that God would, for the sake of the public, bring the wickedness of the wicked to an end, ver. 3, 4. II. God's rebuke to the prophet for his uneasiness at his present trc̄...es, bidding him prepare for greater, ver. 5, 6. III. A sad lamentation of the present deplorable state of the Israel of God, ver. 7—13. IV. An intimation of mercy to God's people, in a denunciation of wrath against their neighbours that helped forward their affliction, that they should be plucked out; but with a promise that if they would at last join themselves with the people of God they should come in sharers with them in their privileges, ver. 14—17.

R IGHTEOUS *art* thou, O LORD, when I plead with thee : yet let me talk with thee of *thy* judgments : Wherefore doth the way of the wicked prosper ? *wherefore* are all they happy that deal very treacherously? 2 Thou hast planted them, yea, they have taken root : they grow, yea, they bring forth fruit : thou *art* near in their mouth, and far from their reins. 3 But thou, O LORD, knowest me : thou hast seen me, and tried mine heart toward thee: pull them out like sheep for the slaughter, and prepare them for the day of slaughter. 4 How long shall the land mourn, and the herbs of every field wither, for the wickedness of them that dwell therein ? the beasts are consumed, and the birds; because they said, He shall not see our last end. 5 If thou hast run with the footmen, and they have wearied thee, then how canst thou contend with horses? and *if* in the land of peace, *wherein* thou trustedst, *they wearied thee,* then how wilt thou do in the swelling of Jordan? 6 For even thy brethren, and the house of thy father, even they have dealt treacherously with thee; yea, they have called a multitude after thee: believe them not, though they speak fair words unto thee.

The prophet doubts not but it would be of use to others to know what had passed between God and his soul, what temptations he had been assaulted with and how he had got over them; and therefore he here tells us,

I. What liberty he humbly took, and was graciously allowed him, to reason with God concerning his judgments, *v.* 1. He is about to *plead* with God, not to quarrel with him, or find fault with his proceedings, but to enquire into the meaning of them, that he might more and more see reason to be satisfied in them, and might have wherewith to answer both his own and others' objections against them. The works of the Lord, and the reasons of them, are *sought out* even *of those that have pleasure therein,* Ps. cxi. 2. We may not *strive with our Maker,* but we may reason with him. The prophet lays down a truth of unquestionable certainty, which he resolves to abide by in managing this argument: *Righteous art thou, O Lord! when I plead with thee.* Thus he arms himself against the temptation wherewith he was assaulted, to envy the prosperity of the wicked, before he entered into a parley with it. Note, When we are most in the dark concerning the meaning of God's dispensations we must still resolve to keep up right thoughts of God, and must be confident of this, that he never did, nor ever will do, the least wrong to any of his creatures; even when his *judgments are* unsearchable as *a great deep,* and altogether unaccountable, yet *his righteousness* is as conspicuous and immoveable as *the great mountains,* Ps. xxxvi. 6. Though sometimes *clouds and darkness are round about him,* yet *justice and judgment are* always *the habitation of his throne,* Ps. xcvii. 2. When we find it hard to understand particular providences we must have recourse to general truths as our first principles, and abide by them; however dark the providence may be, *the Lord is righteous;* see Ps. lxxiii. 1. And we must acknowledge it to him, as the prophet here, even when we *plead with him,* as those that have no thoughts of contending, but of learning, being fully assured that he will be *justified when he speaks.* Note How-

ever we may see cause for our own information to plead with God, yet it becomes us to own that, whatever he says or does, he is in the right.

II. What it was in the dispensations of divine Providence that he stumbled at and that he thought would bear a debate. It was that which has been a temptation to many wise and good men, and such a one as they have with difficulty got over. They see the designs and projects of wicked people successful: *The way of the wicked prospers;* they compass their malicious designs and gain their point. They see their affairs and concerns in a good posture: *They are happy,* happy as the world can make them, though *they deal* treacherously, *very treacherously,* both with God and man. Hypocrites are chiefly meant (as appears, *v.* 2), who dissemble in their good professions, and depart from their good beginnings and good promises, and in both they deal treacherously, very treacherously. It has been said that men cannot expect to prosper who are unjust and dishonest in their dealings; but these deal treacherously, and yet *they are happy.* The prophet shows (*v.* 2) both their prosperity and their abuse of their prosperity. 1. God had been very indulgent to them and they were got beforehand in the world: " They are planted in a good land, a land flowing with milk and honey, and *thou hast planted them!* nay, thou didst cast out the heathen to plant them," Ps. xliv. 2 ; lxxx. 8. Many a tree is planted that yet never grows nor comes to any thing ; but *they have taken root;* their prosperity seems to be confirmed and settled. They take root in the earth, for there they fix themselves, and thence they draw the sap of all their satisfaction. Many trees however take root which yet never come on ; but these *grow, yea, they bring forth fruit;* their families are built up, they live high, and spend at a great rate ; and all this was owing to the benignity of the divine Providence, which smiled upon them, Ps. lxxiii. 7. 2. Thus God had favoured them, though they had dealt treacherously with him : *Thou art near in their mouth and far from their reins.* This was no uncharitable censure, for he spoke by the Spirit of prophecy, without which it is not safe to charge men with hypocrisy whose appearances are plausible. Observe, (1.) Though they cared not for thinking of God, nor had any sincere affection to him, yet they could easily persuade themselves to speak of him frequently and with an air of seriousness. Piety from the teeth outward is no difficult thing. Many speak the language of Israel that are not Israelites indeed. (2.) Though they had on all occasions the name of God ready in their mouth, and accustomed themselves to those forms of speech that savoured of piety, yet they could not persuade themselves to keep up the fear of God in their hearts. The form of godliness should engage us to keep up the power of it; but with them it did not do so.

III. What comfort he had in appealing to God concerning his own integrity (*v.* 3) : *But thou, O Lord! knowest me.* Probably the wicked men he complains of were forward to reproach and censure him (*ch.* xviii. 18), in reference to which this was his comfort, that God was a witness of his integrity. God knew he was not such a one as they were (who had God *near in their mouths, but far from their reins*), nor such a one as they took him to be, and represented him, a deceiver and a false prophet; those that thus abused him did not know him, 1 Cor. ii. 8. " *But thou, O Lord! knowest me*, though they think me not worth their notice." 1. Observe what the matter is concerning which he appeals to God: Thou knowest *my heart towards thee.* Note, We are as our hearts are, and our hearts are good or bad according as they are, or are not, towards God; and this is that therefore concerning which we should examine ourselves, that we may approve ourselves to God. 2. The cognizance to which he appeals: " *Thou knowest me* better than I know myself, not by hearsay or report, for *thou hast seen me*, not with a transient glance, but thou hast *tried my heart.* God's knowledge of us is as clear and exact and certain as if he had made the most strict scrutiny. Note, The God with whom we have to do perfectly knows how our hearts are towards him. He knows both the guile of the hypocrite and the sincerity of the upright.

IV. He prays that God would turn his hand against these wicked people, and not suffer them to prosper always, though they had prospered long : " Let some judgment come to *pull them out* of this fat pasture *as sheep for the slaughter*, that it may appear their long prosperity was but like the feeding of lambs in a large place, to *prepare them for the day of slaughter*," Hos. iv. 16. God suffered them to prosper that by their pride and luxury they might fill up the measure of their iniquity and so be ripened for destruction; and therefore he thinks it a piece of necessary justice that they should fall into mischief themselves, because they had done so much mischief to others, that they should be pulled out of their land, because they had brought ruin upon the land, and the longer they continued in it the more hurt they did, as the plagues of their generation (*v.* 4) : " *How long shall the land mourn* (as it does under the judgments of God inflicted upon it) *for the wickedness of those that dwell therein?* Lord, shall those prosper themselves that ruin all about them?" 1. See here what the judgment was which the land was now groaning under : *The herbs of every field wither* (the grass is burnt up and all the products of the earth fail), and then it follows of course, the beasts are consumed, and

the birds, 1 Kings xviii. 5. This was the effect of a long drought, or want of rain, which happened, as it should seem, at the latter end of Josiah's reign and the beginning of Jehoiakim's; it is mentioned *ch.* iii. 3, viii. 13, ix. 10, 12, and more fully afterwards, *ch.* xiv. If they would have been brought to repentance by this less judgment, the greater would have been prevented. Now why was it that this *fruitful land* was *turned into barrenness*, but *for the wickedness of those that dwelt therein?* Ps. cvii. 34. Therefore the prophet prays that these wicked people might *die for their own sin*, and that the whole nation might not suffer for it. 2. See here what was the language of their wickedness : *They said*, He *shall not see our last end*, either, (1.) God himself shall not. Atheism is the root of hypocrisy. God is *far from their reins*, though *near in their mouth*, because they say, How *doth God know?* Ps. lxxiii. 11; Job xxii. 13. He knows not what way we take nor what it will end in. Or, (2.) Jeremiah *shall not see our last end ;* whatever he pretends, when he asks us what shall be in the end hereof he cannot himself foresee it. They look upon him as a false prophet. Or, " whatever it is, he shall not live to see it, for we will be the death of him," *ch.* xi. 21. Note, [1.] Men's setting their latter end at a great distance, or looking upon it as uncertain, is at the bottom of all their wickedness, Lam. i. 9. [2.] The whole creation groans under the burden of the sin of man, Rom. viii. 22. It is for this that *the earth mourns* (so it may be read); *cursed is the ground for thy sake.*

V. He acquaints us with the answer God gave to those complaints of his, *v.* 5, 6. We often find the prophets admonished, whose business it was to admonish others, as Isa. viii. 11. Ministers have lessons to learn as well as lessons to teach, and must themselves hear God's voice and preach to themselves. Jeremiah complained much of the wickedness of the men of Anathoth, and that, notwithstanding that, they prospered. Now this seems to be an answer to that complaint. 1. It is allowed that he had cause to complain (*v.* 6) : " *Thy brethren*, the priests of Anathoth, who are of *the house of thy father*, who ought to have protected thee and pretended to do so, *even they have dealt treacherously with thee*, have been false to thee, and, under colour of friendship, have designedly done thee all the mischief they could ; they *have called a multitude after thee*, raised the mob upon thee, and incensed the common people against thee, to whom they have endeavoured, by all arts possible, to render thee despicable or odious, while at the same time they pretended that they had no design to persecute thee nor to deprive thee of thy liberty. They are indeed such as thou canst *not believe, though they speak fair words to thee.* They seem to be thy friends, but are really thy enemies." Note, God's faithful servants must not think it at all strange if their foes be *those of their own house* (Matt. x. 36), and if those they expect kindness from prove such as they can put no confidence in, Mic. vii. 5. 2. Yet he is told that he carried the matter too far. (1.) He laid the unkindness of his countrymen too much to heart. *They wearied* him, because it was *in a land of peace wherein he trusted, v.* 5. It was very grievous to him to be thus hated and abused by his own kindred. He was disturbed in his mind by it; his spirit was sunk and overwhelmed with it, so that he was in great agitation and distress about it. Nay, he was discouraged in his work by it, began to be weary of prophesying, and to think of giving it up. (2.) He did not consider that this was but the beginning of his sorrow, and that he had sorer trials yet before him; and, whereas he should endeavour by a patient bearing of this trouble to prepare himself for greater, by his uneasiness under this he did but unfit himself for what further lay before him : *If thou hast run with the footmen and they have wearied thee,* and run thee quite out of breath, *then how wilt thou contend with horses ?* If the injuries done him by the men of Anathoth made such an impression upon him, what would he do when the princes and chief priests at Jerusalem should set upon him with their power, as they did afterwards? *ch.* xx. 2; xxxii. 2. If he was so soon tired *in a land of peace,* where there was little noise or peril, *what would he do in the swellings of Jordan,* when that overflows all its banks and frightens even lions out of their thickets? *ch.* xlix. 19. Note, [1.] While we are in this world we must expect troubles and difficulties. Our life is a race, a warfare ; we are in danger of being run down. [2.] God's usual method being to begin with smaller trials, it is our wisdom to expect greater than any we have yet met with. We may be called out to *contend with horsemen,* and the sons of Anak may perhaps be reserved for the last encounter. [3.] It highly concerns us to prepare for such trials and to consider what we should do in them. How shall we preserve our integrity and peace when we come to *the swellings of Jordan ?* [4.] In order to our preparation for further and greater trials, we are concerned to approve ourselves well in present smaller trials, to keep up our spirits, keep hold of the promise, keep in our way, with our eye upon the prize, so run that we may obtain it. Some good interpreters understand this as spoken to the people, who were very secure and fearless of the threatened judgments. If they have been so humbled and impoverished by smaller calamities, so wasted by the Assyrians,—if the Ammonites and Moabites, who were their brethren, and with whom they were in league, proved false to them (as undoubtedly they would),—then

how would they be able to deal with such a powerful adversary as the Chaldeans would be ? How would they bear up their head against that invasion which should come like *the swelling of Jordan ?*

7 I have forsaken mine house, I have left mine heritage ; I have given the dearly beloved of my soul into the hand of her enemies. 8 Mine heritage is unto me as a lion in the forest ; it crieth out against me : therefore have I hated it. 9 Mine heritage *is* unto me *as* a speckled bird, the birds round about *are* against her ; come ye, assemble all the beasts of the field, come to devour. 10 Many pastors have destroyed my vineyard, they have trodden my portion under foot, they have made my pleasant portion a desolate wilderness. 11 They have made it desolate, *and being* desolate it mourneth unto me ; the whole land is made desolate, because no man layeth *it* to heart. 12 The spoilers are come upon all high places through the wilderness : for the sword of the LORD shall devour from the *one* end of the land even to the *other* end of the land : no flesh shall have peace. 13 They have sown wheat, but shall reap thorns : they have put themselves to pain, *but* shall not profit : and they shall be ashamed of your revenues because of the fierce anger of the LORD.

The people of the Jews are here marked for ruin.

I. God is here brought in falling out with them and leaving them desolate ; and they could never have been undone if they had not provoked God to desert them. It is a terrible word that God here says (*v.* 7) : *I have forsaken my house*—the temple, which had been his palace ; they had polluted it, and so forced him out of it : *I have left my heritage,* and will look after it no more. His people that he has taken such delight in and care of, are now thrown out of his protection. They had been *the dearly beloved of his soul,* precious in his sight and honourable above any people, which is mentioned to aggravate their sin in returning him hatred for his love and their misery in throwing themselves out of the favour of one that had such a kindness for them, and to justify God in his dealings with them. He sought not occasion against them, but, if they would have conducted themselves with any tolerable propriety, he would have made the best of them, for they were *the beloved of his soul;* but they had conducted themselves so that they had provoked him to *give them into the hand of their enemies,* to leave them unguarded, an easy prey to those that bore them ill-will. But what was the quarrel God had with a people that had been so long dear to him? Why, truly, they had degenerated. 1. They had become like *beasts of prey,* which nobody loves, but every body avoids and gets as far off from as he can (*v.* 8): *My heritage is unto me as a lion in the forest.* Their sins cry to heaven for vengeance as loud as a lion roars. Nay, they *cry out against God* in the threatenings and slaughter which they breathe against his prophets that speak to them in his name; and what is said and done against them God takes as said and done against himself. They blaspheme his name, oppose his authority, and bid defiance to his justice, and so *cry out against him as a lion in the forest.* Those that were the *sheep of God's pasture* had become barbarous and ravenous, and as ungovernable as lions in the forest; *therefore he hated them;* for what delight could the God of love take in a people that had now become as roaring lions and raging beasts, fit to be taken and shot at, as a vexation and torment to all about them? 2. They had become like *birds of prey,* and therefore also unworthy a place in God's house, where neither beasts nor birds of prey were admitted to be offered in sacrifice (*v.* 9): *My heritage is unto me as a bird with talons* (so some read it, and so the margin); they are continually pulling and pecking at one another; they have by their unnatural contentions made their country a cock-pit. Or *as a speckled bird,* dyed, or sprinkled, or bedewed with the blood of her prey. The shedding of innocent blood was Jerusalem's measure-filling sin, and hastened their ruin, not only as it provoked God against them, but as it provoked their neighbours likewise; for those that have *their hand against every man* shall have *every man's hand against them* (Gen. xvi. 12), and so it follows here: *The birds round about are against her.* Some make her a *speckled, pied,* or *motley bird,* upon the account of their mixing the superstitious customs and usages of the heathen with divine institutions in the worship of God; they were fond of a party-coloured religion, and thought it made them fine, when really it made them odious. God's turtle-dove is no speckled bird.

II. The enemies are here brought in falling upon them and laying them desolate. And some think it is upon this account that they are compared to a speckled bird, because fowls usually make a noise about a bird of an odd unusual colour. God's people are, among the children of this world, as *men wondered at,* as a *speckled bird;* but this people had by their own folly made themselves so; and the beasts and birds are called

488

and commissioned to prey upon them. Let *all the birds round* be *against her,* for God has forsaken her, and with them let *all the beasts of the field come to devour.* Those that have made a prey of others shall themselves be preyed upon. It did not lessen the sin of the nations, but very much increased the misery of Judah and Jerusalem, that the desolation brought upon them was by order from heaven. The birds and beasts are perhaps called to feast upon the bodies of the slain, as in St. John's vision, Rev. xix. 17, 18. The utter desolation of the land by the Chaldean army is here spoken of as a thing done, so sure, so near, was it. God speaks of it as a thing which he had appointed to be done, and yet which he had no pleasure in, any more than in the death of other sinners.

1. See with what a tender affection he speaks of this land, notwithstanding the sinfulness of it, in remembrance of his covenant, and the tribute of honour and glory he had formerly had from it: It is *my vineyard, my portion, my pleasant portion, v.* 10. Note, God has a kindness and concern for his church, though there be much amiss in it; and his correcting it will every way consist with his complacency in it.

2. See with what a tender compassion he speaks of the desolations of this land : *Many pastors* (the Chaldean generals that made themselves masters of the country and ate it up with their armies as easily as the Arabian shepherds with their flocks eat up the fruits of a piece of ground that lies common) *have destroyed my vineyard,* without any consideration had either of the value of it or of my interest in it ; they have with the greatest insolence and indignation *trodden it under foot,* and that which was a pleasant land they have made a *desolate wilderness.* The destruction was universal: *The whole land is made desolate, v.* 11. It is made so by the sword of war : *The spoilers,* the Chaldean soldiers, *have come through the plain upon all high places;* they have made themselves masters of all the natural fastnesses and artificial fortresses, *v.* 12. *The sword devours from one end of the land to the other;* all places lie exposed, and the numerous army of the invaders disperse themselves into every corner of that fruitful country, so that *no flesh shall have peace,* none shall be exempt from the calamity nor be able to enjoy any tranquillity. When all flesh have corrupted their way, no flesh shall have peace; those only have peace that walk after the Spirit.

3. See whence all this misery comes. (1.) It comes from the displeasure of God. It is *the sword of the Lord* that *devours, v.* 12. While God's people keep close to him the sword of their protectors and deliverers is the sword of the Lord, witness that of Gideon; but when they have forsaken him, so that he has become their enemy and fights against them, then the sword of their in-

vaders and destroyers becomes the *sword of the Lord;* witness this of the Chaldeans. It is *because of the fierce anger of the Lord* (*v.* 13); it was this that kindled this fire among them and made their enemies so furious. And *who may stand before him when he is angry?* (2.) It is their sin that has made God their enemy, particularly their incorrigibleness under former rebukes (*v.* 11): The land *mourns unto me;* the country that lies desolate does, as it were, pour out its complaint before God and humble itself under his hand; but the inhabitants are so senseless and stupid that *none of them lays it to heart;* they do not mourn to God, but are unaffected with his displeasure, while the very ground they go upon shames them. Note, When God's hand is lifted up, and men will not see, it shall be laid on, and they shall be made to feel, Isa. xxvi. 11.

4. See how unable they should be to guard against it (*v.* 13): "*They have sown wheat,* that is, they have taken a great deal of pains for their own security and promised themselves great matters from their endeavours, but it is all in vain; *they shall reap thorns,* that is, that which shall prove very grievous and vexatious to them. Instead of helping themselves, they shall but make themselves more uneasy. *They have put themselves to pain,* both with their labour and with their expectations, *but it shall not profit;* they shall not prevail to extricate themselves out of the difficulties into which they have plunged themselves. *They shall be ashamed of your revenues,* ashamed that they have depended so much upon their preparations for war and particularly upon their ability to bear the charges of it." Money constitutes the sinews of war; they thought they had enough of that, but shall be ashamed of it; for their silver and gold shall not profit them in the day of the Lord's anger.

14 Thus saith the LORD against all mine evil neighbours, that touch the inheritance which I have caused my people Israel to inherit; Behold, I will pluck them out of their land, and pluck out the house of Judah from among them. 15 And it shall come to pass, after that I have plucked them out I will return, and have compassion on them, and will bring them again, every man to his heritage, and every man to his land. 16 And it shall come to pass, if they will diligently learn the ways of my people, to swear by my name, The LORD liveth; as they taught my people to swear by Baal; then shall they be built in the midst of my people. 17 But if they will not obey, I will ut-

terly pluck up and destroy that nation, saith the LORD.

The prophets sometimes, in God's name, delivered messages both of judgment and mercy to the nations that bordered on the land of Israel: but here is a message to all those in general who had in their turns been one way or other injurious to God's people, had either oppressed them or triumphed in their being oppressed. Observe,

I. What the quarrel was that God had with them. They were *his evil neighbours* (*v.* 14), evil neighbours to his church, and what they did against it he took as done against himself, and therefore called them *his evil neighbours,* that should have been neighbourly to Israel, but were quite otherwise. Note, It is often the lot of good people to live among bad neighbours, that are unkind and provoking to them; and it is bad indeed when they are all so. These evil neighbours were the Moabites, Ammonites, Syrians, Edomites, Egyptians, that had been evil neighbours to Israel in helping to debauch them and draw them from God (therefore God calls them his evil neighbours), and now they helped to make them desolate, and joined with the Chaldeans against them. It is just with God to make those the instruments of trouble to us whom we have made instruments of sin. That which God lays to their charge is: They have *meddled with the inheritance which I have caused my people Israel to inherit;* they unjustly seized that which was none of their own: nay, they sacrilegiously turned that to their own use which was given to God's peculiar people. He that said, *Touch not my anointed,* said also, "*Touch not their inheritance;* it is at your peril if you do." Not only the persons but the estates of God's people are under his protection.

II. What course he would take with them. 1. He would break the power they had got over his people, and force them to make restitution: *I will pluck out the house of Judah from among them.* This would be a great favour to God's people, who had either been taken captive by them, or, when they fled to them for shelter, had been detained and made prisoners; but it would be a great mortification to their enemies, who would be like a lion disappointed of his prey. The house of Judah either cannot or will not make any bold struggles towards their own liberty; but God will with a gracious violence pluck them out, will by his Spirit compel them to come out and by his power compel their task-masters to let them go, as he plucked Israel out of Egypt. 2. He would bring upon them the same calamities that they had been instrumental to bring upon his people: *I will pluck them out of their land.* Judgment began at the house of God, but it did not end there. Nebuchadnezzar, when he had wasted the land of Israel, turned his hand against their evil neighbours and was a scourge to them.

III. What mercy God had in store for such of them as would join themselves to him and become his people, *v.* 15, 16. They had drawn in God's backsliding people to join with them in the service of idols. If now they would be drawn by a returning people to join with them in the service of the true and living God, they should not only have their enmity to the people of God forgiven them, but the distance which they had been kept at before should be removed, and they should be received to stand upon the same level with the Israel of God. This had its accomplishment in part when, after the return out of captivity, many of the people of the lands that had been evil neighbours to Israel became Jews; and it was to have its full accomplishment in the conversion of the Gentiles to the faith of Christ. Let not Israel, though injured by them, be implacable towards them, for God is not: *After that I have plucked them out,* in justice for their sins and in jealousy for the honour of Israel, *I will return,* will change my way, *and have compassion on them.* Though, being heathen, they can lay no claim to the mercies of the covenant, yet they shall have benefit by the compassions of the Creator, who will notwithstanding look upon them as the work of his hands. Note, God's controversies with his creatures, though they cannot be disputed, may be accommodated. Those who (as these) have been not only strangers, but *enemies in their minds by wicked works,* may be *reconciled,* Col. i. 21. Observe here,

1. What were the terms on which God would show favour to them. It is always provided *that they will diligently learn the ways of my people,* that is, in general, the ways that they walk in when they conduct themselves as *my people* (not the crooked ways into which they have turned aside), the ways which my people are directed to take. Note, (1) There are good ways that are peculiarly *the ways of God's people,* which, however they may differ in the choice of their paths, they are all agreed to walk in. The ways of holiness and heavenly-mindedness, of love and peaceableness, the ways of prayer and sabbath-sanctification, and diligent attendance on instituted ordinances—these, and the like, are *the ways of God's people.* (2.) Those that would have their lot with God's people, and their last end like theirs, must learn their ways and walk in them, must observe the rule they walk by and conform to that rule, must notice the steps they take by that rule and go forth by those footsteps. By an intimate conversation with God's people they must learn to do as they do. (3.) It is impossible to learn the ways of God's people as they should be learnt, without a great deal of care and pains. We must diligently observe these ways and diligently oblige ourselves to walk in them, must look diligently (Heb. xii. 15), and

490

work diligently, Luke xiii. 24. In particular, they must learn to give honour to God's name by making all their solemn appeals to him. They must learn to say, *The Lord liveth* (to own him, to adore him, and to abide by his judgment), *as they taught my people to swear by Baal.* It was bad enough that they did themselves swear by Baal, worse that they taught others, and worst of all that they taught God's own people, who had been better taught; and yet, if they will at length reform, they shall be accepted. Observe, [1.] We must not despair of the conversion of the worst; no, not of those who have been instrumental to pervert and debauch others; even they may be brought to repentance, and, if they be, shall find mercy. [2.] Those whom we have been industrious to draw to that which is evil, when God opens their eyes and ours, we should be as industrious to follow in that which is good. It will be a holy revenge upon ourselves to become pupils to those in the way of duty to whom we have been tutors in the way of sin. [3.] The conversion of the deceived may prove a happy occasion of the conversion even of the deceivers. Thus those who fall together into the ditch are sometimes plucked together out of it.

2. What should be the tokens and fruits of this favour when they return to God and God to them. (1.) They shall be restored to and re-established in their own land (*v.* 15): *I will bring them again every man to his heritage.* The same hand that plucked them up shall plant them again. (2.) They shall become entitled to the spiritual privileges of God's Israel: "If they will be towardly, and *learn the ways of my people,* will conform to the rules and confine themselves to the restraints of my family, *then shall they be built in the midst of my people.* They shall not only be brought among them, to have a name and a place in the house of the Lord, where there was a court for the Gentiles, but they shall be built among them; they shall unite with them; the former enmities shall be slain; they shall be both edified and settled among them. See Isa. lvi 5—7. Note, Those that diligently learn the ways of God's people shall enjoy the privileges and comforts of his people.

IV. What should become of those that were still wedded to their own evil ways, yea, though many of those about them turned to the Lord (*v.* 17): *If they will not obey,* if any of them continue to stand it out, *I will utterly pluck up and destroy that nation,* that family, that particular person, *saith the Lord.* Those that will not be ruled by the grace of God shall be ruined by the justice of God. And, if disobedient nations shall be destroyed, much more disobedient churches from whom better things are expected.

CHAP. XIII.

Still the prophet is attempting to awaken this secure and stubborn people to repentance, by the consideration of the judgments of God that were coming upon them. He is to tell them, I. By the sign of a girdle spoiled that their pride should be stained, ver. 1—11. II. By the sign of bottles filled with wine that their counsels should be blasted, ver. 12—14. III. In consideration hereof he is to call them to repent and humble themselves, ver. 15—21. IV. He is to convince them that it is for their obstinacy and incorrigibleness that the judgments of God are so prolonged and brought to extremity, ver. 22—27.

THUS saith the LORD unto me, Go and get thee a linen girdle, and put it upon thy loins, and put it not in water. 2 So I got a girdle according to the word of the LORD, and put *it* on my loins. 3 And the word of the LORD came unto me the second time, saying, 4 Take the girdle that thou hast got, which *is* upon thy loins, and arise, go to Euphrates, and hide it there in a hole of the rock. 5 So I went, and hid it by Euphrates, as the LORD commanded me. 6 And it came to pass after many days, that the LORD said unto me, Arise, go to Euphrates, and take the girdle from thence, which I commanded thee to hide there. 7 Then I went to Euphrates, and digged, and took the girdle from the place where I had hid it: and behold, the girdle was marred, it was profitable for nothing. 8 Then the word of the LORD came unto me, saying, 9 Thus saith the LORD, After this manner will I mar the pride of Judah, and the great pride of Jerusalem. 10 This evil people, which refuse to hear my words, which walk in the imagination of their heart, and walk after other gods, to serve them, and to worship them, shall even be as this girdle, which is good for nothing. 11 For as the girdle cleaveth to the loins of a man, so have I caused to cleave unto me the whole house of Israel and the whole house of Judah, saith the LORD; that they might be unto me for a people, and for a name, and for a praise, and for a glory: but they would not hear.

Here is, I. A sign, the marring of a girdle, which the prophet had worn for some time, by hiding it in a hole of a rock near the river Euphrates. It was usual with the prophets to teach by signs, that a stupid unthinking people might be brought to consider, and believe, and be affected with what was thus set before them. 1. He was to wear a linen girdle for some time, *v.* 1, 2. Some think he wore it under his clothes, because it was linen, and it is said to *cleave to his loins, v.* 11. It should rather seem to be worn upon his clothes, for it was worn for a name and a praise, and probably was a fine sash, such as officers wear and such as are commonly worn at this day in the eastern nations. He must *not put it in water*, but wear it as it was, that it might be the stronger, and less likely to rot: linen wastes almost as much with washing as with wearing. Being not wet, it was the more stiff and less apt to bend, yet he must make a shift to wear it. Probably it was very fine linen which will wear long without washing. The prophet, like John Baptist, was none of those that wore soft clothing, and therefore it would be the more strange to see him with a linen girdle on, who probably used to wear a leathern one. 2. After he had worn this linen girdle for some time, he must go, and *hide it in a hole of a rock* (*v.* 4) by the water's side, where, when the water was high, it would be wet, and when it fell would grow dry again, and by that means would soon rot, sooner than if it were always wet or always dry. 3. After many days, he must look for it, and he should find it quite spoiled, gone all to rags and good for nothing, *v.* 7. It has been of old a question among interpreters whether this was really done, so as to be seen and observed by the people, or only in a dream or vision, so as to go no further than the prophet's own mind. It seems hard to imagine that the prophet should be sent on two such long journeys as to the river Euphrates, each of which would take him up some weeks' time, when he could so ill be spared at home. For this reason most incline to think the journey, at least, was only in vision, like that of Ezekiel, from the captivity in Chaldea to Jerusalem (Ezek. viii. 3) and thence back to Chaldea (*ch.* xi. 24); and the explanation of this sign is given only to the prophet himself (*v.* 8), not to the people, the sign not being public. But there being, it is probable, at that time, great conveniences of travelling between Jerusalem and Babylon, and some part of Euphrates being not so far off but that it was made the utmost border of the land of promise (Josh. i. 4), I see no inconvenience in supposing the prophet to have made two journeys thither; for it is expressly said, *He did as the Lord commanded him;* and thus gave a signal proof of his obsequiousness to his God, to shame the stubbornness of a disobedient people: the toil of his journey would be very proper to signify both the pains they took to corrupt themselves with their idolatries and the sad fatigue of their captivity; and Euphrates being the river of Babylon, which was to be the place of their bondage, was a material circumstance in this sign.

II. The thing signified by this sign. The prophet was willing to be at any cost and pains to affect this people with the word of the Lord. Ministers must spend, and be spent, for the good of souls. We have the explanation of this sign, *v.* 9—11.

1. The people of Israel had been to God as this girdle in two respects:—(1.) He had taken them into covenant and communion with himself: *As the girdle cleaves* very closely *to the loins of a man* and surrounds him, *so have I caused to cleave to me the houses of Israel and Judah.* They were a people near to God (Ps. cxlviii. 14); they were his own, a peculiar people to him, a kingdom of priests that had access to him above other nations. He *caused them to cleave* to him by the law he gave them, the prophets he sent among them, and the favours which in his providence he showed them. He required their stated attendance in the courts of his house, and the frequent ratification of their covenant with him by sacrifices. Thus they were made so to cleave to him that one would think they could never have been parted. (2.) He had herein designed his own honour. When he took them to be *to him for a people,* it was that they might be to him *for a name, and for a praise, and for a glory,* as a girdle is an ornament to a man, and particularly the *curious girdle of the ephod* was to the high-priest *for glory and for beauty.* Note, Those whom God takes to be to him for a people he intends to be to him for a praise. [1.] It is their duty to honour him, by observing his institutions and aiming therein at his glory, and thus adorning their profession. [2.] It is their happiness that he reckons himself honoured in them and by them. He is pleased with them, and glories in his relation to them, while they behave themselves as becomes his people. He was pleased to take it among the titles of his honour to be *the God of Israel,* even a *God to Israel,* 1 Chron. xvii. 24. In vain do we pretend to be to God for a people if we be not to him for a praise.

2. They had by their idolatries and other iniquities loosed themselves from him, thrown themselves at a distance, robbed him of the honour they owed him, buried themselves in the earth, and foreign earth too, mingled among the nations, and were so spoiled and corrupted that they were *good for nothing:* they could no more be to God, as they were designed, *for a name and a praise,* for they would not hear either their duty to do it or their privilege to value it : *They refused to hear the words of God,* by which they might have been kept still cleaving closely to him. *They walked in the imagination of their heart,* wherever their fancy led them; and denied themselves no gratification they had a mind to, particularly in their worship. They would not *cleave to God,* but *walked after other gods, to serve them,* and *to worship them:* they doted upon the gods of the heathen nations that lay towards Euphrates, so that they were quite spoiled for the service of their own God, and were *as this girdle,* this rotten girdle, a disgrace to their profession and not an ornament. A thousand pities it was that such a girdle should be so spoiled, that such a people should so wretchedly degenerate.

3. God would by his judgments separate them from him, send them into captivity, deface all their beauty and ruin their excellency, so that they should be like a fine girdle gone to rags, a worthless, useless, despicable people God will after this manner *mar the pride of Judah, and the great pride of Jerusalem.* He would strip them of all that which was the matter of their pride, of which they boasted and in which they trusted; it should not only be sullied and stained, but quite destroyed, like this linen girdle. Observe, He speaks of *the pride of Judah* (the country people were proud of their holy land, their good land), but of *the great pride of Jerusalem;* there the temple was, and the royal palace, and therefore those citizens were more proud than the inhabitants of other cities. God takes notice of the degrees of men's pride, the pride of some and the great pride of others; and he will mar it, he will stain it. Pride will have a fall, for God resists the proud. He will either mar the pride that is in us (that is, mortify it by his grace, make us ashamed of it, and, like Hezekiah, humble us for the pride of our hearts, the great pride, and cure us of it, great as it is ; and this marring of the pride will be the making of the soul; happy for us if by humbling providences our hearts be humbled) or else he will mar the thing we are proud of. Parts, gifts, learning, power, external privileges, if we are proud of these, it is just with God to blast them ; even the temple, when it became Jerusalem's pride, was marred and laid in ashes. It is the honour of God to *look upon every one that is proud and abase him.*

12 Therefore thou shalt speak unto them this word ; Thus saith the LORD God of Israel, Every bottle shall be filled with wine : and they shall say unto thee, Do we not certainly know that every bottle shall be filled with wine ? 13 Then shalt thou say unto them, Thus saith the LORD, Behold, I will fill all the inhabitants of this land, even the kings that sit upon David's throne, and the priests, and the prophets, and all the inhabitants of Jerusalem, with drunkenness. 14 And I will dash them one against another, even the fathers and the sons together, saith the LORD : I will not pity, nor spare, nor have mercy, but destroy them. 15 Hear ye, and give ear ; be not proud : for the LORD hath spoken. 16 Give glory to the LORD your God, before he cause darkness, and before your feet stumble upon the dark mountains, and, while

ye look for light, he turn it into the shadow of death, *and* make *it* gross darkness. 17 But if ye will not hear it, my soul shall weep in secret places for *your* pride; and mine eye shall weep sore, and run down with tears, because the LORD's flock is carried away captive. 18 Say unto the king and to the queen, Humble yourselves, sit down: for your principalities shall come down, *even* the crown of your glory. 19 The cities of the south shall be shut up, and none shall open *them:* Judah shall be carried away captive all of it, it shall be wholly carried away captive. 20 Lift up your eyes, and behold them that come from the north: where *is* the flock *that* was given thee, thy beautiful flock? 21 What wilt thou say when he shall punish thee? for thou hast taught them *to be* captains, *and* as chief over thee: shall not sorrows take thee, as a woman in travail?

Here is, I. A judgment threatened against this people that would quite intoxicate them. This doom is pronounced against them in a figure, to make it the more taken notice of and the more affecting (*v.* 12): *Thus saith the Lord God of Israel, every bottle shall be filled with wine;* that is, those that by their sins have made themselves *vessels of wrath fitted to destruction* shall be filled with the wrath of God as a bottle is with wine; and, as every vessel of mercy prepared for glory shall be filled with mercy and glory, so they shall *be full of the fury of the Lord* (Isa. li. 20); and they shall be brittle as bottles; and, like old bottles into which new wine is put, they shall burst and be broken to pieces, Matt. ix. 17. Or, They shall have their heads as full of wine as bottles are; for so it is explained, *v.* 13, *They shall be filled with drunkenness;* compare Isa. li. 17. It is probable that this was a common proverb among them, applied in various ways; but they, not being aware of the prophet's meaning in it, ridiculed him for it: " *Do we not certainly know* that *every bottle shall be filled with wine?* What strange thing is there in that? Tell us something that we did not know before." Perhaps they were thus touchy with the prophet because they apprehended this to be a reflection upon them for their drunkenness, and probably it was in part so intended. They *loved flagons of wine,* Hos. iii. 1. They made their king *sick with bottles of wine,* Hos. vii. 5. Their watchmen were all *for wine,* Isa. lvi. 12. They loved their false prophets *that prophesied to them of wine* (Mic. ii. 11), that bade them be merry, for

that they should never want their bottle to make them so. " Well," says the prophet, "you shall have your *bottles full of wine,* but not such wine as you desire." They suspected that he had some mystical meaning in it which prophesied no good concerning them, but evil; and he owns that so he had. What he meant was this,

1. That they should be as giddy as men in drink. A drunken man is fitly compared to a bottle or cask full of wine; for, when the wine is in, the wit, and wisdom, and virtue, and all that is good for any thing, are out. Now God threatens (*v.* 13) that they shall all be *filled with drunkenness;* they shall be full of confusion in their counsels, shall falter in all their talk and stagger in all their motions; they shall not know what they say or do, much less what they should say or do. They shall be sick of all their enjoyments and throw them up as drunken men do, Job xx. 15. They shall fall into a slumber, and be utterly unable to help themselves, and, like men that have drunk away their reason, shall lie at the mercy and expose themselves to the contempt of all about them. And this shall be the condition not of some among them (if any had been sober, they might have helped the rest), but *even the kings that sit upon the throne of David,* that should have been like their father David, who was *wise as an angel of God,* shall be thus intoxicated. Their priests and prophets too, their false prophets, that pretended to guide them, were as indulgent of their lusts, and therefore were justly as much deprived of their senses, as any other. Nay, *all the inhabitants* both *of the land* and *of Jerusalem* were as far gone as they. Whom God will destroy he infatuates.

2. That, being giddy, they should run upon one another. The cup of the wine of the Lord's fury shall throw them not only into a lethargy, so that they shall not be able to help themselves or one another, but into a perfect phrenzy, so that they shall do mischief to themselves and one another (*v.* 14): *I will dash a man against his brother.* Not only their drunken follies, but their drunken frays, shall help to ruin them. Drunken men are often quarrelsome, and upon that account they have *woe and sorrow* (Prov. xxiii. 29, 30); so their sin is their punishment; it was so here. God sent an evil spirit into families and neighbourhoods (as Judg. ix. 23), which made them jealous of, and spiteful towards, one another; so that *the fathers and sons* went *together* by the ears, and were ready to pull one another to pieces, which made them all an easy prey to the common enemy. This decree against them having gone forth, God says, *I will not pity, nor spare, nor have mercy, but destroy them;* for they *will not pity, nor spare, nor have mercy,* but destroy one another; see Hab. ii. 15, 16.

II. Here is good counsel given, which,

if taken, would prevent this desolation. It is, in short, to *humble themselves under the mighty hand of God.* If they will *hearken and give ear,* this is that which God has to say to them, *Be not proud, v.* 15. This was one of the sins for which God had a controversy with them (*v.* 9); let them mortify and forsake this sin, and God will let fall his controversy. "*Be not proud;* when God speaks to you by his prophets do not think yourselves too good to be taught; be not scornful, be not wilful, let not your hearts rise against the word, nor slight the messengers that bring it to you. When God is coming forth against you in his providence (and by them he speaks) be not secure when he threatens, be not impatient when he strikes, for pride is at the bottom of both." It is the great God that has spoken, whose authority is incontestable, whose power is irresistible; therefore to what he says, and *be not proud,* as you have been. They must not be proud, for,

1. They must advance God, and study how to do him honour: " *Give glory to the Lord your God,* and not to your idols, not to other gods. Give him glory by confessing your sins, owning yourselves guilty before him, and accepting the punishment of your iniquity, *v.* 16. Give him glory by a sincere repentance and reformation." Then, and not till then, we begin to live as we should, and to some good purpose, when we begin to *give glory to the Lord our God,* to make his honour our chief end and to seek it accordingly. " *Do this quickly,* while your space to repent is continued to you; *before he cause darkness,* before he bring his judgments upon you, which you will see no way of escaping." Note, Darkness will be the portion of those that will not repent to *give glory to God.* When those that by the fourth vial were scorched with heat *repented not, to give glory to God,* the next vial filled them with *darkness,* Rev. xvi. 9, 10. The aggravation of the darkness here threatened is, (1.) That their attempts to escape shall hasten their ruin: *Their feet shall stumble* when they are making all the haste they can over *the dark mountains,* and they shall fall, and be unable to get up again. Note, Those that think to out-run the judgments of God will find their road impassable; let them make the best of their way, they can make nothing of it, the judgments that pursue them will overtake them; their way is dark and slippery, Ps. xxxv. 6. And therefore, before it comes to that extremity, it is our wisdom to give glory to him, and so make our peace with him, to fly to his mercy, and then there will be no occasion to fly from his justice. (2.) That their hopes of a better state of things will be disappointed: *While you look for light,* for comfort and relief, he will *turn it into the shadow of death,* which is very dismal and terrible, and make it *gross darkness,* like that of Egypt, when Pharaoh continued

494

to harden his heart, which was darkness that might be felt. The expectation of impenitent sinners perishes when they die and think to have it satisfied.

2. They must abase themselves, and take shame to themselves; the prerogative of the king and queen will not exempt them from this (*v.* 18): " *Say to the king and queen,* that, great as they are, they must *humble themselves* by true repentance, and so give both glory to God and a good example to their subjects." Note, Those that are exalted above others in the world must humble themselves before God, who is higher than the highest, and to whom kings and queens are accountable. They must *humble themselves,* and *sit down*—sit down, and consider what is coming—sit down in the dust, and lament themselves. Let them humble themselves, for God will otherwise take an effectual course to humble them: " *Your principalities shall come down,* the honour and power on which you value yourselves and in which you confide, *even the crown of your glory,* your *goodly or glorious crown:* when you are led away captives, where will your principality and all the badges of it be then?" Blessed be God there is a crown of glory, which those shall inherit who do humble themselves, that shall never *come down.*

III. This counsel is enforced by some arguments if they continue proud and unhumbled.

1. It will be the prophet's unspeakable grief (*v.* 17): " *If you will not hear it,* will not submit to the word, but continue refractory, not only my eye, but *my soul shall weep in secret places.*" Note, The obstinacy of people, in refusing to hear the word of God, will be heart-breaking to their poor ministers, who know something of the terrors of the Lord and the worth of souls, and are so far from desiring that they tremble at the thoughts of the death of sinners. His grief for it was undissembled (his *soul wept*) and void of affection, for he chose to weep *in secret places,* where no eye saw him but his who is all eye. He would mingle his tears not only with his public preaching, but with his private devotions. Nay, thoughts of their case would make him melancholy, and he would become a perfect recluse. It would grieve him, (1.) To see their sins unrepented of: " *My soul shall weep for your pride,* your haughtiness, and stubbornness, and vain confidence." Note, The sins of others should be matter of sorrow to us. We must mourn for that which we cannot mend, and mourn the more for it because we cannot mend it. (2.) To see their calamity past redress and remedy: " *My eyes shall weep sorely,* not so much because my relations, friends, and neighbours are in distress, but *because the Lord's flock,* his people and the sheep of his pasture, *are carried away captive.*" That

should always grieve us most by which God's honour suffers and the interest of his kingdom is weakened.

2. It will be their own inevitable ruin, *v.* 19—21. (1.) The land shall be laid waste : *The cities of the south shall be shut up.* The cities of Judah lay in the southern part of the land of Canaan ; these shall be straitly besieged by the enemy, so that there shall be no going in and out, or they shall be deserted by the inhabitants, that there shall be none to go in and out. Some understand it of the cities of Egypt, which was south from Judah ; the places there whence they expected succours shall fail them, and they shall find no access to them. (2.) The inhabitants shall be hurried away into a foreign country, there to live in slavery : *Judah shall be carried away captive.* Some were already carried off, which they hoped might serve to answer the prediction, and that the residue should still be left ; but no : *It shall be carried away all of it.* God will make a full end with them : *It shall be wholly carried away.* So it was in the last captivity under Zedekiah, because they repented not. (3.) The enemy was now at hand that should do this (*v.* 20): "*Lift up your eyes.* I see upon their march, and you may if you will *behold, those that come from the north,* from the land of the Chaldeans ; see how fast they advance, how fierce they appear." Upon this he addresses himself to the king, or rather (because the pronouns are feminine) to the city or state. [1.] " What will you do now with the people who are committed to your charge, and whom you ought to protect ? *Where is the flock that was given thee, thy beautiful flock?* Whither canst thou take them now for shelter ? How can they escape these ravening wolves ?" Magistrates must look upon themselves as shepherds, and those that are under their charge as their flock, which they are entrusted with the care of and must give an account of ; they must take delight in them as their beautiful flock, and consider what to do for their safety in times of public danger. Masters of families, who neglect their children and suffer them to perish for want of a good education, and ministers who neglect their people, should think they hear God putting this question to them : *Where is the flock that was given thee* to feed, *that beauteous flock?* It is starved ; it is left exposed to the beasts of prey. What account wilt thou give of them when the chief shepherd shall appear ? [2.] " What have you to object against the equity of God's proceedings ? *What wilt thou say when he shall visit upon thee* the former days? *v.* 21. Thou canst say nothing, but that *God is just in all that is brought upon thee.*" Those that flatter themselves with hopes of impunity, what will they say ? What confusion will cover their faces when they shall find themselves deceived and that God punishes them ! [3.] " What thoughts

will you now have of your own folly, in giving the Chaldeans such power over you, by seeking to them for assistance, and joining in league with them ? Thus *thou hast taught them against thyself to be captains* and *to become the head.*" Hezekiah began when he showed his treasures to the ambassadors of the king of Babylon, tempting him thereby to come and plunder him. Those who, having a God to trust to, court foreign alliances and confide in them, do but make rods for themselves and teach their neighbours how to become their masters. [4.] " How will you bear the trouble that is at the door ? *Shall not sorrows take thee as a woman in travail?* Sorrows which thou canst not escape nor put off, extremity of sorrows ; and in these respects more grievous than those of a woman in travail that they were not expected before, and that there is no man-child to be born, the joy of which shall make them afterwards to be forgotten."

22 And if thou say in thine heart, Wherefore come these things upon me ? For the greatness of thine iniquity are thy skirts discovered, *and* thy heels made bare. 23 Can the Ethiopian change his skin, or the leopard his spots ? *then* may ye also do good, that are accustomed to do evil. 24 Therefore will I scatter them as the stubble that passeth away by the wind of the wilderness. 25 This *is* thy lot, the portion of thy measures from me, saith the LORD ; because thou hast forgotten me, and trusted in falsehood. 26 Therefore will I discover thy skirts upon thy face, that thy shame may appear. 27 I have seen thine adulteries, and thy neighings, the lewdness of thy whoredom, *and* thine abominations on the hills in the fields. Woe unto thee, O Jerusalem ! wilt thou not be made clean ? when *shall it* once *be ?*

Here is, I. Ruin threatened as before, that the Jews shall go into captivity, and fall under all the miseries of beggary and bondage, shall be stripped of their clothes, *their skirts discovered* for want of upper garments to cover them, and their *heels made bare* for want of shoes, *v.* 22. Thus they used to deal with prisoners taken in war, when they drove them into captivity, *naked and barefoot,* Isa. xx. 4. Being thus carried off into a strange country, they shall be scattered there, *as the stubble that is blown away by the wind of the wilderness,* and nobody is concerned to bring it together again, *v.* 24. If the stubble escape the fire, it shall be carried away by the wind. If one judgment do not do the work, another shall, with those that by sin have made themseves as stubble. They shall be stripped of all their ornaments, and exposed to shame, as harlots that are carted, *v.* 26. They made their pride appear, but God will *make their shame appear;* so that those who have doted on them shall be ashamed of them.

II. An enquiry made by the people into the cause of this ruin, *v.* 22. Thou wilt *say in thy heart* (and God knows how to give a proper answer to what men say in their hearts, though they do not speak it out; *Jesus, knowing their thoughts,* replied to *them,* Matt. ix. 4), *Wherefore came these things upon me?* The question is supposed to come into the heart, 1. Of a sinner quarrelling with God and refusing to receive correction. They could not see that they had done any thing which might justly provoke God to be thus angry with them. They durst not speak it out; but in their hearts they thus charged God with unrighteousness, as if he had *laid upon them more than was meet.* They seek for the cause of their calamities, when, if they had not been wilfully blind, they might easily have seen it. Or, 2. Of a sinner returning to God. If there come but a penitent thought into the heart at any time (saying, *What have I done?* (*ch.* viii. 6) wherefore am I in affliction? why doth God contend with me?) God takes notice of it, and is ready by his Spirit to impress the conviction, that, sin being discovered, it may be repented of.

III. An answer to this enquiry. God will be justified when he speaks and will oblige us to justify him, and therefore will set the sin of sinners in order before them. Do they ask, *Wherefore come these things upon us?* Let them know it is all owing to themselves. 1. It is for the greatness of their iniquities, *v.* 22. God does not take advantage against them for small faults; no, the sins for which he now punishes them are of the first rate, very heinous in their own nature and highly aggravated—for *the multitude of thy iniquity* (so it may be read), sins of every kind and often repeated and relapsed into. Some think we are more in danger from the multitude of our smaller sins than from the heinousness of our greater sins; of both we may say, *Who can understand his errors?* 2. It is for their obstinacy in sin, their being so long accustomed to it that there was little hope left of their being reclaimed from it (*v.* 23): *Can the Ethiopian change his skin,* that is by nature black, or the *leopard his spots,* that are even woven into the skin? Dirt contracted may be washed off, but we cannot alter the natural colour of a hair (Matt. v. 36), much less of the skin; and so impossible is it, morally impossible, to reclaim and reform these people. (1.) They had been long *accustomed to do evil.* They were taught to do evil; they had been educated and brought up in sin; they had served

an apprenticeship to it, and had all their days made a trade of it. It was so much their constant practice that it had become a second nature to them. (2.) Their prophets therefore despaired of ever bringing them to do good. This was what they aimed at; they persuaded them to cease to do evil and learn to do well, but could not prevail. They had so long been used to do evil that it was next to impossible for them to repent, and amend, and begin to do good. Note, Custom in sin is a very great hindrance to conversion from sin. The disease that is inveterate is generally thought incurable. Those that have been long accustomed to sin have shaken off the restraints of fear and shame; their consciences are seared; the habits of sin are confirmed; it pleads prescription; and it is just with God to give those up to their own hearts' lusts that have long refused to give up themselves to his grace. Sin is the blackness of the soul, the deformity of it; it is its spot, the discolouring of it; it is natural to us, we were shapen in it, so that we cannot get clear of it by any power of our own. But there is an almighty grace that is able to change the Ethiopian's skin, and that grace shall not be wanting to those who in a sense of their need of it seek it earnestly and improve it faithfully.

3. It is for their treacherous departures from the God of truth and dependence on lying vanities (*v.* 25): *" This is thy lot,* to be scattered and driven away; this is *the portion of thy measures from me,* the punishment assigned thee as by line and measure; this shall be thy share of the miseries of this world; expect it, and think not to escape it: it is *because thou hast forgotten me,* the favours I have bestowed upon thee and the obligations thou art under to me; thou hast no sense, no remembrance, of these." Forgetfulness of God is at the bottom of all sin, as the remembrance of our Creator betimes is the happy and hopeful beginning of a holy life. " Having *forgotten me, thou hast trusted in falsehood,* in idols, in an arm of flesh, in Egypt and Assyria, in the self-flatteries of a deceitful heart." Whatever those trust to that forsake God, they will find it a *broken reed, a broken cistern.*

4. It is for their idolatry, their spiritual whoredom, that sin which is of all sins most provoking to the *jealous God.* They are exposed to a shameful calamity (*v.* 26) because they have been guilty of a shameful iniquity and yet are shameless in it (*v.* 27): *"I have seen thy adulteries* (thy inordinate fancy for strange gods, which thou hast been impatient for the gratification of, and hast even *neighed* after it), even the *lewdness of thy whoredoms,* thy impudence and insatiableness in them, thy eager worshipping of idols *on the hills in the fields,* upon the high places. This is that for which a *woe* is denounced against thee, *O Jerusalem!* nay, and many woes.

IV. Here is an affectionate expostulation

with them, in the close, upon the whole matter. Though it was adjudged next to impossible for them to be brought to do good (v. 23), yet while there is life there is hope, and therefore still he reasons with them to bring them to repentance, v. 27. 1. He reasons with them concerning the thing itself : *Wilt thou not be made clean?* Note, It is the great concern of those who are polluted by sin to be made clean by repentance, and faith, and a universal reformation. The reason why sinners are not made clean is because they will not be made clean ; and herein they act most unreasonably : " *Wilt thou not be made clean?* Surely thou wilt at length be persuaded to *wash thee, and make thee clean,* and so be wise for thyself.'' 2. Concerning the time of it : *When shall it once be?* Note, It is an instance of the wonderful grace of God that he desires the repentance and conversion of sinners, and thinks the time long till they are brought to relent ; but it is an instance of the wonderful folly of sinners that they put that off from time to time which is of such absolute necessity that, if it be not done some time, they are certainly undone for ever. They do not say that they will never be cleansed, but not yet ; they will defer it to a more convenient season, but cannot tell us when it shall once be.

CHAP. XIV.

This chapter was penned upon occasion of a great drought, for want of rain. This judgment began in the latter end of Josiah's reign, but, as it should seem, continued in the beginning of Jehoiakim's : for less judgments are sent to give warning of greater coming, if not prevented by repentance. This calamity was mentioned several times before, but here, in this chapter, more fully. Here is, I. A melancholy description of it, ver. 1—6. II. A prayer to God to put an end to this calamity and to return in mercy to their land, ver. 7—9. III. A severe threatening that God would proceed in his controversy, because they proceeded in their iniquity, ver. 10—12. IV. The prophet's excusing the people, by laying the blame on their false prophets ; and the doom passed both on the deceivers and the deceived, ver. 13—16. V. Directions given to the prophet, instead of interceding for them, to lament them ; but his continuing notwithstanding to intercede for them, ver. 17—22.

THE word of the LORD that came to Jeremiah concerning the dearth. 2 Judah mourneth, and the gates thereof languish ; they are black unto the ground ; and the cry of Jerusalem is gone up. 3 And their nobles have sent their little ones to the waters : they came to the pits, *and* found no water ; they returned with their vessels empty ; they were ashamed and confounded, and covered their heads. 4 Because the ground is chapt, for there was no rain in the earth, the ploughmen were ashamed, they covered their heads. 5 Yea, the hind also calved in the field, and forsook *it*, because there was no grass. 6 And the wild asses did stand in the high places, they snuffed up the wind like dragons ; their eyes did fail,

because *there was* no grass. 7 O LORD, though our iniquities testify against us, do thou *it* for thy name's sake : for our backslidings are many ; we have sinned against thee. 8 O the hope of Israel, the Saviour thereof in time of trouble, why shouldest thou be as a stranger in the land, and as a wayfaring man *that* turneth aside to tarry for a night? 9 Why shouldest thou be as a man astonied, as a mighty man *that* cannot save? yet thou, O LORD, *art* in the midst of us, and we are called by thy name ; leave us not.

The first verse is the title of the whole chapter : it does indeed all *concern the dearth,* but much of it consists of the prophet's prayers concerning it ; yet these are not unfitly said to be, *The word of the Lord which came to him* concerning it, for every acceptable prayer is that which God puts into our hearts ; nothing is our word that comes to him but what is first his word that comes from him. In these verses we have, I. The language of nature lamenting the calamity. When the heavens were as brass, and distilled no dews, the earth was as iron, and produced no fruits ; and then the grief and confusion were universal. 1. The people of the land were all in tears. Destroy their vines and their fig-trees and you cause all their mirth to cease, Hos. ii. 11, 12. All their joy fails with the joy of harvest, with that of their corn and wine. *Judah mourns* (v. 2), not for the sin, but for the trouble— for the withholding of the rain, not for the withdrawing of God's favour. *The gates thereof,* all that go in and out at their gates, *languish,* look pale, and grow feeble, for want of the necessary supports of life and for fear of the further fatal consequences of this judgment. *The gates,* through which supplies of corn formerly used to be brought into their cities, now look melancholy, when, instead of that, the inhabitants are departing through them to seek for bread in other countries. Even those that sit in the gates languish ; *they are black unto the ground,* they go in black as mourners and sit on the ground, as the poor beggars at the gates are *black in the face* for want of food, *blacker than a coal,* Lam. iv. 8. Famine is represented by a black horse, Rev. vi. 5. They fall to the ground through weakness, not being able to go along the streets. *The cry of Jerusalem has gone up ;* that is, of the citizens (for the city is *served by the field),* or of people from all parts of the country met at Jerusalem to pray for rain ; so some. But I fear it was rather the cry of their trouble, and the cry of their sin, than the cry of their prayer. 2. The great men of the land felt from this judgment (v. 3): *The nobles sent their little ones to the water,* perhaps their own children, having been forced to part with their servants because they had not wherewithal to keep them, and being willing to train up their children, when they were little, to labour, especially in a case of necessity, as this was. We find Ahab and Obadiah, the king and the lord chamberlain of his household, in their own persons, seeking for water in such a time of distress as this was, 1 Kings xviii. 5, 6. Or, rather, *their meaner ones*, their servants and inferior officers; these they sent to seek for water, which there is no living without; but there was none to be found: They *returned with their vessels empty;* the springs were dried up when there was no rain to feed them; and then *they* (their masters that sent them) *were ashamed and confounded* at the disappointment. They would not be ashamed of their sins, nor confounded at the sense of them, but were unhumbled under the reproofs of the word, thinking their wealth and dignity set them above repentance; but God took a course to make them ashamed of that which they were so proud of, when they found that even on this side hell their nobility would not purchase them a drop of water to cool their tongue. Let our reading the account of this calamity make us thankful for the mercy of water, that we may not by the feeling of the calamity be taught to value it. What is most needful is most plentiful. 3. The husbandmen felt most sensibly and immediately from it (*v.* 4): *The ploughmen were ashamed*, for the ground was so parched and hard that it would not admit the plough even when it was so *chapt* and cleft that it seemed as if it did not need the plough. They were ashamed to be idle, for there was nothing to be done, and therefore nothing to be expected. The *sluggard, that will not plough by reason of cold*, is not ashamed of his own folly; but the diligent husbandman, that cannot plough by reason of heat, is ashamed of his own affliction. See what an immediate dependence husbandmen have upon the divine Providence, which therefore they should always have an eye to, for they cannot plough nor sow in hope unless God *water their furrows*, Ps. lxv. 10. 4. The case even of the wild beasts was very pitiable, *v.* 5, 6. Man's sin brings those judgments upon the earth which make even the inferior creatures groan: and the prophet takes notice of this as a plea with God for mercy. Judah and Jerusalem have sinned, but the hinds and the wild asses, what have they done? The hinds are pleasant creatures, lovely and loving, and particularly tender of their young; and yet such is the extremity of the case that, contrary to the instinct of their nature, they leave their young, even when they are newly calved and most need them, to seek for grass elsewhere; and, if they can find none, they *abandon* them, because not able to suckle them. It grieved not the hind so much that she had

498

no grass for herself as that she had none for her young, which will shame those who spend that upon their lusts which they should preserve for their families. The hind, when she has brought forth her young, is said to have *cast forth her sorrows* (Job xxxix. 3), and yet she continues her cares; but, as it follows there, she soon sees the good effect of them, for *her young ones* in a little while *grow up*, and trouble her no more, *v.* 4. But here the great trouble of all is that she has nothing for them. Nay, one would be sorry even for the *wild asses* (though they are creatures that none have any great affection for); for, though the *barren land* is made *their dwelling* at the best (Job xxxix. 5, 6), yet even that is now made too hot for them, so hot that they cannot breathe in it, but they get to the *highest places* they can reach, where the air is coolest, and *snuff up the wind like dragons*, like those creatures which, being very hot, are continually panting for breath. *Their eyes fail*, and so does their strength, *because there is no grass* to support them. The tame ass, that serves her owner, is welcome to *his crib* (Isa. i. 3) and has her keeping for her labour, when the *wild ass*, that *scorns the crying of the driver*, is forced to *live upon air*, and is well enough served for not serving. He that *will not labour, let him not eat.*

II. Here is the language of grace, lamenting the iniquity, and complaining to God of the calamity. The people are not forward to pray, but the prophet here prays for them, and so excites them to pray for themselves, and puts words into their mouths, which they may make use of, in hopes to speed, *v.* 7 —9. In this prayer, 1. Sin is humbly confessed. When we come to pray for the preventing or removing of any judgment we must always acknowledge that we deserve it and a thousand times worse. We cannot hope by extenuating the crime to obtain a mitigation of the punishment, but must acknowledge that our *iniquities testify against us*. Our sins are witnesses against us, and true penitents see them to be such. They testify, for they are plain and evident; we cannot deny the charge. They testify against us, for our conviction, which tends to our present shame and confusion, and our future condemnation. They disprove and overthrow all our pleas for ourselves; and so not only accuse us, but answer against us. If we boast of our own excellencies, and trust to our own righteousness, our iniquities testify against us, and prove us perverse. If we quarrel with God as dealing unjustly or unkindly with us in afflicting us, our iniquities testify against us that we do him wrong; "for *our backslidings are many* and our revolts are great, whereby *we have sinned against thee*— too numerous to be concealed, for they are many, too heinous to be excused, for they are against thee." 2. Mercy is earnestly begged: "*Though our iniquities testify against us*, and against the granting of the favour which the necessity of our case calls for, yet *do thou it.*" They do not say particularly what they would have done; but, as becomes penitents and beggars, they refer the matter to God: "Do with us as thou thinkest fit," Judg. x. 15. Not, *Do thou it* in this way or at this time, but, "*Do thou it for thy name's sake:* do that which will be most for the glory of thy name." Note, Our best pleas in prayer are those that are fetched from the glory of God's own name. "Lord, do it, that thy mercy may be magnified, thy promise fulfilled, and thy interest in the world kept up; we have nothing to plead in ourselves, but every thing in thee." There is another petition in this prayer, and it is a very modest one (*v.* 9): "*Leave us not*, withdraw not thy favour and presence." Note, We should dread and deprecate God's departure from us more than the removal of any or all our creature-comforts. 3. Their relation to God, their interest in him, and their expectations from him grounded thereupon, are most pathetically pleaded with him, *v.* 8, 9. (1.) They look upon him as one they have reason to think should deliver them when they are in distress, yea, though their iniquities testify against them; for in him mercy has often rejoiced against judgment. The prophet, like Moses of old, is willing to make the best he can of the case of his people, and therefore, though he must own that they have sinned many a great sin (Exod. xxxii. 31), yet he pleads, *Thou art the hope of Israel.* God has encouraged his people to hope in him; in calling himself so often the *God of Israel*, the *rock of Israel*, and the *Holy One of Israel*, he has made himself the *hope of Israel*. He has given Israel his word to hope in, and caused them to hope in it; and there are those yet in Israel that make God alone their hope, and expect he will be *their Saviour in time of trouble*, and they look not for salvation in any other: "Thou hast many a time been such, in the time of their extremity." Note, Since God is his people's all-sufficient Saviour, they ought to hope in him in their greatest straits; and, since he is their only Saviour, they ought to hope in him alone. They plead likewise, "*Thou art in the midst of us;* we have the special tokens of thy presence with us, thy temple, thy ark, thy oracles, and *we are called by thy name*, the *Israel* of God; and therefore we have reason to hope thou wilt not leave us; *we are thine, save us.* Thy name is called upon us, and therefore what evils we are under reflect dishonour upon thee, as if thou wert not able to relieve thy own." The prophet had often told the people that their profession of religion would not protect them from the judgments of God; yet here he pleads it with God, as Moses, Exod. xxxii. 11. Even this may go far as to temporal punishments with a God of mercy. *Valeat quantùm valere*

potest—Let the plea avail as far as is proper. (2.) It therefore grieves them to think that he does not appear for their deliverance; and, though they do not charge it upon him as unrighteous, they humbly plead it with him why he should be gracious, for the glory of his own name. For otherwise he will seem, [1.] Unconcerned for his own people: *What will the Egyptians say?* They will say, "Israel's hope and Saviour does not mind them; he has become *as a stranger in the land*, that does not at all interest himself in its interests; his temple, which he called *his rest for ever*, is no more so, but he is in it *as a wayfaring man, that turns aside to tarry but for a night* in an inn, which he never enquires into the affairs of, nor is in any care about." Though God never is, yet he sometimes seems to be, as if he cared not what became of his church: Christ slept when his disciples were in a storm. [2.] Incapable of giving them any relief: The enemies once said, Because the Lord *was not able to bring* his people to Canaan, he let them *perish in the wilderness* (Num. xiv. 16); so now they will say, "Either his wisdom or his power fails him; either he is *as a man astonished* (who, though he has the reason of a man, yet, being astonished, is quite at a loss and at his wits' end) or as a *mighty man* who is overpowered by such as are more mighty, and therefore *cannot save:* though mighty, yet a man, and therefore having his power limited." Either of these would be a most insufferable reproach to the divine perfections; and therefore, why has the God that we are sure *is in the midst of us* become *as a stranger?* Why does the almighty God seem as if he were no more than a mighty man, who, when he is astonished, though he would, yet cannot save? It becomes us in prayer to show ourselves concerned more for God's glory than for our own comfort. Lord, *what wilt thou do unto thy great name?*

10 Thus saith the Lord unto this people, Thus have they loved to wander, they have not refrained their feet, therefore the Lord doth not accept them; he will now remember their iniquity, and visit their sins. 11 Then said the Lord unto me, Pray not for this people for *their* good. 12 When they fast, I will not hear their cry; and when they offer burnt-offering and an oblation, I will not accept them: but I will consume them by the sword, and by the famine, and by the pestilence. 13 Then said I, Ah, Lord God! behold, the prophets say unto them, Ye shall not see the sword, neither shall ye have

famine; but I will give you assured peace in this place. 14 Then the LORD said unto me, The prophets prophesy lies in my name: I sent them not, neither have I commanded them, neither spake unto them: they prophesy unto you a false vision and divination, and a thing of nought, and the deceit of their heart. 15 Therefore thus saith the LORD concerning the prophets that prophesy in my name, and I sent them not, yet they say, Sword and famine shall not be in this land; By sword and famine shall those prophets be consumed. 16 And the people to whom they prophesy shall be cast out in the streets of Jerusalem because of the famine and the sword; and they shall have none to bury them, them, their wives, nor their sons, nor their daughters: for I will pour their wickedness upon them.

The dispute between God and his prophet, in this chapter, seems to be like that between the owner and the dresser of the vineyard concerning the barren fig-tree, Luke xiii. 7. The justice of the owner condemns it to be cut down; the clemency of the dresser intercedes for a reprieve. Jeremiah had been earnest with God, in prayer, to return in mercy to this people. Now here,

I. God overrules the plea which he had offered in their favour, and shows him that it would not hold. In answer to it thus he says concerning *this people, v.* 10. He does not say, concerning *my people,* for he disowns them, because they had broken covenant with him. It is true they were *called by his name,* and had the tokens of his presence among them; but they had sinned, and provoked God to withdraw. This the prophet had owned, and had hoped to obtain mercy for them, notwithstanding this, through intercession and sacrifice; therefore God here tells him, 1. That they were not duly qualified for a pardon. The prophet had owned that *their backslidings were many;* and, though they were so, yet there was hope for them if they returned. But *this people* show no disposition at all to return; they have wandered, and *they have loved to wander;* their backslidings have been their choice and their pleasure, which should have been their shame and pain, and therefore they will be their ruin. They cannot expect God should take up his rest with them when they take such delight in going astray from him after their idols. It is not through necessity or inadvertency that they wander, but they love to wander. Sinners are wanderers from God; their wanderings forfeit God's favour, but it is their

loving to wander that quite cuts them off from it. They were told what their wanderings would come to, that one sin would hurry them on to another, and all to ruin; and yet they have not taken warning and *refrained their feet.* So far were they from returning to their God that neither his prophets nor his judgments could prevail upon them to give themselves the least check in a sinful pursuit. This is that for which God is now reckoning with them. When he denies them rain from heaven he is *remembering their iniquity* and *visiting their sin;* that is it for which their *fruitful land* is thus *turned into barrenness.* 2. That they had no reason to expect that the God they had rejected should accept them; no, not though they betook themselves to fasting and prayer and put themselves to the expense of burnt-offerings and sacrifice: *The Lord doth not accept them, v.* 10. *He takes no pleasure in them* (so the word is); for what pleasure can the holy God take in those that take pleasure in his rivals, in any service, in any society, rather than his? *"When they fast* (v. 12), which is a proper expression of repentance and reformation,—*when they offer a burnt offering and an oblation,* which was designed to be an expression of faith in a Mediator,—though their prayers be thus enforced, and offered up in those vehicles that used to be acceptable, yet, because they do not proceed from humble, penitent, and renewed hearts, but still they *love to wander,* therefore *I will not hear their cry,* be it ever so loud; *nor will I accept them,* neither their persons nor their performances." It had been long since declared, *The sacrifice of the wicked is an abomination to the Lord;* and those only are *accepted* that *do well,* Gen. iv. 7. 3. That they had forfeited all benefit by the prophet's prayers for them because they had not regarded his preaching to them. This is the meaning of that repeated prohibition given to the prophet (v. 11): *Pray not thou for this people for their good,* as before, ch. vii. 16; xi. 14. This did not forbid him thus to express his *good-will* to them (Moses continued to intercede for Israel after God had said, *Let me alone,* Exod. xxxii. 10), but it forbade them to expect any good effect from it as long as they *turned away their ear from hearing the law.* Thus was the doom of the impenitent ratified, as that of Saul's rejection was by that word to Samuel, *When wilt thou cease to mourn for Saul?* It therefore follows (v. 12), *I will consume them,* not only by this famine, but by the further sore judgments of sword and pestilence; for God has many arrows in his quiver, and those that will not be convinced and reclaimed by one shall be consumed by another.

II. The prophet offers another plea in excuse for the people's obstinacy, and it is but an excuse, but he was willing to say whatever their case would bear; it is this, That the prophets, who pretended a commission from heaven, imposed upon them, and flattered them with assurances of peace though they went on in their sinful way, *v.* 13. He speaks of it with lamentation : " *Ah !* Lord God, the poor people seem willing to take notice of what comes in thy name, and there are those who in thy name tell them that they *shall not see the sword nor famine;* and they say it as from thee, with all the gravity and confidence of prophets : *I will* continue you *in this place,* and will *give you assured peace* here, peace of truth. I tell them the contrary; but I am one against many, and every one is apt to credit that which makes for them; therefore, Lord, pity and spare them, for *their leaders cause them to err.*" This excuse would have been of some weight if they had not had warning given them, before, of false prophets, and rules by which to distinguish them; so that if they were deceived it was entirely their own fault. But this teaches us, as far as we can with truth, to make the best of bad, and judge as charitably of others as their case will bear.

III. God not only overrules this plea, but condemns both the blind leaders and the blind followers to fall together into the ditch. 1. God disowns the flatteries (*v.* 14) : *They prophesy lies in my name.* They had no commission from God to prophesy at all : *I neither sent them, nor commanded them, nor spoke unto them.* They never were employed to go on any errand at all from God; he never made himself known to them, much less by them to the people; never any word of the Lord came to them, no call, no warrant, no instruction, much less did he send them on this errand, to rock them asleep in security. No; men may flatter themselves, and Satan may flatter them, but God never does. It is *a false vision, and a thing of nought.* Note, What is false and groundless is vain and worthless. The vision that is not true, be it ever so pleasing, is good for nothing; it is the *deceit of their heart,* a spider's web spun out of their own bowels, and in it they think to shelter themselves, but it will be swept away in a moment and prove a great cheat. Those that oppose their own thoughts to God's word (God indeed says so, but they think otherwise) walk in the *deceit of their heart,* and it will be their ruin. 2. He passes sentence upon the flatterers, *v.* 15. As for the prophets, who put this abuse upon the people by telling them they shall have peace, and this affront upon God by telling them so in God's name, let them know that they shall have no peace themselves. They shall fall first by those very judgments which they have flattered others with the hopes of an exemption from. They undertook to warrant people that *sword and famine* should *not be in the land;* but it shall soon appear how little their warrants are good for, when they themselves shall be cut off by sword

and famine. How should they secure others or foretel peace to them when they cannot secure themselves, nor have such a foresight of their own calamities as to get out of the way of them? Note, The sorest punishments await those who promise sinners impunity in their sinful ways. 3. He lays the flattered under the same doom : The *people to whom they prophesy lies,* and who willingly suffer themselves to be thus imposed upon, *shall die by sword and famine, v.* 16. Note, The unbelief of the deceived, with all the falsehood of the deceivers, shall not make the divine threatenings of no effect; sword and famine will come, whatever they say to the contrary; and those will be least safe that are most secure. Impenitent sinners will not escape the damnation of hell by saying that they can never believe there is such a thing, but will feel what they will not fear. It is threatened that this people shall not only fall by *sword and famine,* but that they shall be as it were hanged up in chains, as monuments of that divine justice which they set at defiance; their bodies shall be *cast out,* even *in the streets of Jerusalem,* which of all places, one would think, should be kept clear from such nuisances : there they shall lie unburied; their nearest relations, who should do them that last office of love, being so poor that they cannot afford it, or so weakened with hunger that they are not able to attend it, or so overwhelmed with grief that they have no heart to it, or so destitute of natural affection that they will not pay them so much respect. Thus will God *pour their wickedness upon them,* that is, the punishment of their wickedness; the full vials of God's wrath shall be poured upon them, to which they have made themselves obnoxious. Note, When sinners are overwhelmed with trouble they must in it see their own wickedness poured upon them. This refers to the wickedness both of the false prophets and of the people; the blind lead the blind, and both fall together into the ditch, where they will be miserable comforters one to another.

17 Therefore thou shalt say this word unto them; Let mine eyes run down with tears night and day, and let them not cease : for the virgin daughter of my people is broken with a great breach, with a very grievous blow. 18 If I go forth into the field, then behold the slain with the sword! and if I enter into the city, then behold them that are sick with famine ! yea, both the prophet and the priest go about into a land that they know not. 19 Hast thou utterly rejected Judah? hath thy soul loathed Zion ? why hast thou smitten us, and *there*

is no healing for us? we looked for peace, and *there is* no good; and for the time of healing, and behold trouble! 20 We acknowledge, O LORD, our wickedness, *and* the iniquity of our fathers: for we have sinned against thee. · 21 Do not abhor *us,* for thy name's sake, do not disgrace the throne of thy glory: remember, break not thy covenant with us. 22 Are there *any* among the vanities of the Gentiles that can cause rain? or can the heavens give showers? *art* not thou he, O LORD our God? therefore we will wait upon thee: for thou hast made all these *things.*

The present deplorable state of Judah and Jerusalem is here made the matter of the prophet's lamentation (*v.* 17, 18) and the occasion of his prayer and intercession for them (*v.* 19), and I am willing to hope that the latter, as well as the former, was by divine direction, and that these words (*v.* 17), *Thus shalt thou say unto them* (or *concerning them,* or *in their hearing*), refer to the intercession, as well as to the lamentation, and then it amounts to a revocation of the directions given to the prophet not to pray for them, *v.* 11. However, it is plain, by the prayers we find in these verses, that the prophet did not understand it as a prohibition, but only as a discouragement, like that 1 John v. 16, *I do not say he shall pray for that.* Here,

I. The prophet stands weeping over the ruins of his country; God directs him to do so, that, showing himself affected, he might, if possible, affect them with the foresight of the calamities that were coming upon them. Jeremiah must say it not only to himself, but to them too: *Let my eyes run down with tears, v.* 17. Thus he must signify to them that he certainly foresaw *the sword* coming, and another sort of famine, more grievous even than this which they were now groaning under; this was in the country for want of rain, that would be in the city through the straitness of the siege. The prophet speaks as if he already saw the miseries attending the descent which the Chaldeans made upon them: *The virgin daughter of my people,* that is as dear to me as a daughter to her father, *is broken with a great breach, with a very grievous blow,* much greater and more grievous than any she has yet sustained; for (*v.* 18) *in the field* multitudes lie dead that were *slain by the sword,* and in the city multitudes lie dying for want of food. Doleful spectacles! " *The prophets and the priests,* the false prophets that flattered them with their lies and the wicked priests that persecuted the true prophets,

502

are now expelled their country, and *go about* either as prisoners and captives, whithersoever their conquerors lead them, or as fugitives and vagabonds, wherever they can find shelter and relief, *in a land that they know not.*" Some understand this of the true prophets, Ezekiel and Daniel, that were carried to Babylon with the rest. The prophet's eyes must run down *with tears day and night,* in prospect of this, that the people might be convinced, not only that this woeful day would infallibly come, and would be a very woeful day indeed, but that he was far from desiring it, and would as gladly have brought them messages of peace as their false prophets, if he might have had warrant from heaven to do it. Note, Because God, though he inflicts death on sinners, yet delights not in it, it becomes his ministers, though in his name they pronounce the death of sinners, yet sadly to lament it.

II. He stands up to make intercession for them; for who knows but God will yet return and repent? While there is life there is hope, and room for prayer. And, though there were many among them who neither prayed themselves nor valued the prophet's prayers, yet there were some who were better affected, would join with him in his devotions, and set the seal of their *Amen* to them.

1. He humbly expostulates with God concerning the present deplorableness of their case, *v.* 19. It was very sad, for, (1.) Their expectations from their God failed them; they thought he had avouched Judah to be his, but now, it seems, he has *utterly rejected* it, and cast it off, will not own any relation to it nor concern for it. They thought Zion was the beloved of his soul, was his rest for ever; but now *his soul* even *loathes Zion,* loathes even the services there performed, for the sake of the sins there committed. (2.) Then no marvel that all their other expectations failed them: *They were smitten,* and their wounds were multiplied, but there was *no healing* for them; they *looked for peace,* because after a storm there usually comes a calm and fair weather after a long fit of wet; but *there was no good,* things went still worse and worse. They looked for a *healing time,* but could not gain so much as a *breathing time.* " *Behold, trouble* at the door, by which we hoped peace would enter. And is it so then? *Hast thou* indeed *rejected Judah?* Justly thou mightest. *Hath thy soul loathed Zion?* We deserve it should. But wilt thou not at length in wrath remember mercy?"

2. He makes a penitent confession of sin, speaking that language which they all should have spoken, though but few did (*v.* 20): " *We acknowledge our wickedness,* the abounding wickedness of our land *and the iniquity of our fathers,* which we have imitated, and therefore justly smart for. *We know, we*

acknowledge, that *we have sinned against thee,* and therefore thou art just in all that is brought upon upon us ; but, because we confess our sins, we hope to find thee faithful and just in forgiving our sins."

3. He deprecates God's displeasure, and by faith appeals to his honour and promise, *v.* 21. His petition is, " *Do not abhor us ; though thou afflict us, do not abhor us ; though thy hand be turned against* us, let not thy heart be so, nor let thy mind be alienated from us." They own God might justly abhor them, they had rendered themselves odious in his eyes ; yet, when they pray, *Do not abhor us,* they mean, " Receive us into favour again. *Let not thy soul loathe Zion, v.* 19. Let not our incense be an abomination." They appeal, (1.) To the honour of God, the honour of his scriptures, by which he has made himself known—his *word,* which he has *magnified above all his name :* " *Do not abhor us, for thy name's sake,* that name of thine by which we are called and which we call upon." The honour of his sanctuary is pleaded : " Lord, do not abhor us, for that will *disgrace the throne of thy glory*" (the temple, which is called *a glorious high throne from the beginning,* ch. xvii. 12) ; let not that which has been the *joy of the whole earth* be made a *hissing* and an *astonishment.* We deserve to have disgrace put upon us, but let it not be so as to reflect upon thyself ; let not the desolations of the temple give occasion to the heathen to reproach him that used to be worshipped there, as if he could not, or would not, protect it, or as if the gods of the Chaldeans had been too hard for him. Note, Good men lay the credit of religion, and its profession in the world, nearer their hearts than any private interest or concern of their own ; and those are powerful pleas in prayer which are fetched thence and great supports to faith. We may be sure that God will not *disgrace the throne of his glory* on earth ; nor will he eclipse the glory of his throne by one providence without soon making it shine forth, and more brightly than before, by another. God will be no loser in his honour at the long-run. (2) To the promise of God ; of this they are humbly bold to put him in mind : *Remember thy covenant with us, and break not* that covenant. Not that they had any distrust of his fidelity, or that they thought he needed to be put in mind of his promise to them, but what he had said he would plead with himself they take the liberty to plead with him. *Then will I remember my covenant,* Lev. xxvi. 42.

4. He professes a dependence upon God for the mercy of rain, which they were now in want of, *v.* 22. If they have forfeited their interest in him as their God in covenant, yet they will not let go their hold on him as the God of nature. (1.) They will never make application to the idols of the heathen, for that would be foolish and fruit-

less : *Are there any among the vanities of the Gentiles that can cause rain ?* No ; in a time of great drought in Israel, Baal, though all Israel presented their prayers to him in the days of Ahab, could not relieve them ; it was that God only who *answered by fire* that could answer *by water* too. (2.) They will not terminate their regards in second causes, nor expect supply from nature only : *Can the heavens give showers ?* No, not without orders from the God of heaven ; for it is he that has the key of the clouds, that *opens the bottles of heaven* and *waters the earth from his chambers.* But, (3.) All their expectation therefore is from him and their confidence in him : " *Art not thou he, O Lord our God !* from whom we may expect succour and to whom we must apply ? Art thou not he that *causest rain* and *givest showers ?* For *thou hast made all these things ;* thou gavest them being, and therefore thou givest them law and hast them all at thy command ; thou madest that moisture in nature which is in a constant circulation to serve the intentions of Providence, and thou directest it, and makest what use thou pleasest of it ; *therefore we will wait upon thee,* and upon thee only ; we will *ask of the Lord rain,* Zech. x. 1. We will trust in him to give it to us in due time, and be willing to tarry his time ; it is fit that we should, and it will not be in vain to do so." Note, The sovereignty of God should engage, and his all-sufficiency encourage, our attendance on him and our expectations from him at all times.

CHAP. XV.

When we left the prophet, in the close of the foregoing chapter, so pathetically pouring out his prayers before God, we had reason to hope that in this chapter we should find God reconciled to the land and the prophet brought into a quiet composed frame ; but, to our great surprise, we find it much otherwise as to both. I. Notwithstanding the prophet's prayers, God here ratifies the sentence given against the people, and abandons them to ruin, turning a deaf ear to all the intercessions made for them, ver. 1—9. II. The prophet himself, notwithstanding the satisfaction he had in communion with God, still finds himself uneasy and out of temper. 1. He complains to God of his continual struggle with his persecutors, ver. 10. 2. God assures him that he shall be taken under special protection, though there was a general desolation coming upon the land, ver. 11—14. 3. He appeals to God concerning his sincerity in the discharge of his prophetic office and thinks it hard that he should not have more of the comfort of it, ver. 15—18. 4. Fresh security is given him that, upon condition he continue faithful, God will continue his care of him and his favour to him, ver. 19—21. And thus, at length, we hope he regained the possession of his own soul.

THEN said the LORD unto me, Though Moses and Samuel stood before me, *yet* my mind *could* not *be* toward this people : cast *them* out of my sight, and let them go forth.

2 And it shall come to pass, if they say unto thee, Whither shall we go forth ? then thou shalt tell them, Thus saith the LORD ; Such as *are* for death, to death ; and such as *are* for the sword, to the sword ; and such as *are* for the famine, to the famine ; and such as *are* for the captivity, to

the captivity. 3 And I will appoint over them four kinds, saith the LORD: the sword to slay, and the dogs to tear, and the fowls of the heaven, and the beasts of the earth, to devour and destroy. 4 And I will cause them to be removed into all kingdoms of the earth, because of Manasseh the son of Hezekiah king of Judah, for *that* which he did in Jerusalem. 5 For who shall have pity upon thee, O Jerusalem? or who shall bemoan thee? or who shall go aside to ask how thou doest? 6 Thou hast forsaken me, saith the LORD, thou art gone backward: therefore will I stretch out my hand against thee, and destroy thee; I am weary with repenting. 7 And I will fan them with a fan in the gates of the land; I will bereave *them* of children, I will destroy my people, *since* they return not from their ways. 8 Their widows are increased to me above the sand of the seas: I have brought upon them against the mother of the young men a spoiler at noon-day: I have caused *him* to fall upon it suddenly, and terrors upon the city. 9 She that hath borne seven languisheth: she hath given up the ghost; her sun is gone down while *it was* yet day: she hath been ashamed and confounded: and the residue of them will I deliver to the sword before their enemies, saith the LORD.

We scarcely find any where more pathetic expressions of divine wrath against a provoking people than we have here in these verses. The prophet had prayed earnestly for them, and found some among them to join with him; and yet not so much as a reprieve was gained, nor the least mitigation of the judgment; but this answer is given to the prophet's prayers, that the decree had gone forth, was irreversible, and would shortly be executed. Observe here,

I. What the sin was upon which this severe sentence was grounded. 1. It is in remembrance of a former iniquity; it is because of Manasseh, for that which he did in Jerusalem, *v.* 4. What that was we are told, and that it was for it that Jerusalem was destroyed, 2 Kings xxiv. 3, 4. It was for his idolatry, and *the innocent blood which he shed, which the Lord would not pardon.* He is called *the son of Hezekiah* because his relation to so good a father was a great aggravation of his sin, so far was it from

504

being an excuse of it. The greatest part of a generation was worn off since Manasseh's time, yet his sin is brought into the account; as in Jerusalem's last ruin God brought upon it all *the righteous blood shed on the earth,* to show how heavy the guilt of blood will light and lie somewhere, sooner or later, and that reprieves are not pardons. 2. It is in consideration of their present impenitence. See how their sin is described (*v.* 6): " *Thou hast forsaken me,* my service and thy duty to me; *thou hast gone backward* into the ways of contradiction, art become the reverse of what thou shouldst have been and of what God by his law would have led thee forward to." See how the impenitence is described (*v.* 7): *They return not from their ways,* the ways of their own hearts, into the ways of God's commandments again. There is mercy for those who have turned aside if they will return; but what favour can those expect that persist in their apostasy?

II. What the sentence is. It is such as denotes no less than an utter ruin.

1. God himself abandons and abhors them: *My mind cannot be towards them.* How can it be thought that the holy God should have any remaining complacency in those that have such a rooted antipathy to him? It is not in a passion, but with a just and holy indignation, that he says, " *Cast them out of my sight,* as that which is in the highest degree odious and offensive, and *let them go forth,* for I will be troubled with them no more."

2. He will not admit any intercession to be made for them (*v.* 1): " *Though Moses and Samuel stood before me,* by prayer or sacrifice to reconcile me to them, yet I could not be prevailed with to admit them into favour." Moses and Samuel were two as great favourites of Heaven as ever were the blessings of this earth, and were particularly famed for the success of their mediation between God and his offending people; many a time they would have been destroyed if Moses had not stood before him in the breach; and to Samuel's prayers they owed their lives (1 Sam. xii. 19); yet even their intercessions should not prevail, no, not though they were now in a state of perfection, much less Jeremiah's, who was now *a man subject to like passions* as others. The putting of this as a case, *Though they should stand before me,* supposes that they do not, and is an intimation that saints in heaven are not intercessors for saints on earth. It is the prerogative of the Eternal Word to be the only Mediator in *the other world,* whatever Moses, and Samuel, and others were in this.

3. He condemns them all to one destroying judgment or other. When God casts them out of his presence, *whither shall they go forth? v.* 2. Certainly nowhere to be safe or easy, but to be met by one judgment while they are pursued by another, till they

find themselves surrounded with mischiefs on all hands, so that they cannot escape : *Such as are for death to death.* By death here is meant the pestilence (Rev. vi. 8), for it is death without visible means. *Such as are for death to death,* or *for the sword to the sword;* every man shall perish in that way that God has appointed : the law that appoints the malefactor's death determines what death he shall die. Or, He that is by his own choice for this judgment, let him take it, or for that, let him take it, but by the one or the other they shall all fall and none shall escape. It is a choice like that which David was put to, and was thereby put into a *great strait,* 2 Sam. xxiv. 14. *Captivity* is mentioned last, some think, because the sorest judgment of all, it being both a complication and continuance of miseries. That of *the sword* is again repeated (*v.* 3), and is made the first of another four frightful set of destroyers, which God will *appoint over them,* as officers over the soldiers, to do what they please with them. As those that escape *the sword* shall be cut off by pestilence, famine, or captivity, so those that fall by the sword shall be cut off by divine vengeance, which pursues sinners on the other side death ; there shall be *dogs to tear* in the city and *fowls of the air* and *wild beasts* in the field to devour. And, if there be any that think to outrun justice, they shall be made the most public monuments of it : *They shall be removed into all kingdoms of the earth* (*v.* 4), like Cain, who, that he might be made a spectacle of horror to all, became *a fugitive and a vagabond* in the earth.

4. They shall fall without being relieved. Who can do any thing to help them ? for (1.) God, even their own God (so he had been) appears against them : *I will stretch out my hand against thee,* which denotes a deliberate determined stroke, which will reach far and wound deeply. *I am weary with repenting* (*v.* 6) ; it is a strange expression ; they had behaved so provokingly, especially by their treacherous professions of repentance, that they had put even infinite patience itself to the stretch. God had often turned away his wrath when it was ready to break forth against them ; but now he will grant no more reprieves. Miserable is the case of those who have sinned so long against God's mercy that at length they have sinned it away. (2.) Their own country expels them, and is ready to *spue them out,* as it had done the Canaanites that were before them ; for so it was threatened (Lev. xviii. 28) : *I will fan them with a fan in the gates of the land,* in their own gates, through which they shall be scattered, or *into the gates of the earth,* into the cities of all the nations about them, *v.* 7. (3.) Their own children, that should assist them when they speak with the enemy in the gate, shall be cut off from them : *I will bereave them of children,* so that they

shall have little hopes that the next generation will retrieve their affairs, for *I will destroy my people ;* and, when the inhabitants are slain, the land will soon be desolate. This melancholy article is enlarged upon, *v.* 8, 9, where we have, [1.] The destroyer brought upon them. When God has bloody work to do he will find out bloody instruments to do it with. Nebuchadnezzar is here called *a spoiler at noon-day,* not a thief in the night, that is afraid of being discovered, but one that without fear shall break through and destroy all the fences of rights and properties, and this in the face of the sun and in defiance of its light : *I have brought against the mother a young man, a spoiler* (so some read it); for Nebuchadnezzar, when he first invaded Judah, was but a *young man,* in the first year of his reign. We read it, *I have brought upon them,* even *against the mother of the young men, a spoiler,* that is, against Jerusalem, a mother city, that had a very numerous family of young men : or that invasion was in a particular manner terrible to those mothers who had many sons fit for war, who must now hazard their lives in the high places of the field, and, being an unequal match for the enemy, would be likely to fall there, to the inexpressible grief of their poor mothers, who had nursed them up with a great deal of tenderness. The same God that brought the spoiler upon them *caused him to fall upon it,* that is, upon the spoil delivered to him, *suddenly* and by surprise ; and then *terrors came upon the city.* The original is very abrupt—*the city and terrors.* O *the city!* what a consternation will it then be in ! O *the terrors* that shall then seize it ! Then the city and terrors shall be brought together, that seemed at a distance from each other. *I will cause to fall suddenly upon her* (upon Jerusalem) *a watcher and terrors ;* so Mr. Gataker reads it, for the word is used for a watcher (Dan. iv. 13, 23), and the Chaldean soldiers were called watchers, *ch.* iv. xvi. [2.] The destruction made by this destroyer. A dreadful slaughter is here described. *First,* The wives are deprived of their husbands : *Their widows are increased above the sand of the seas,* so numerous have they now grown. It was promised that the men of Israel (for those only were numbered) should be *as the sand of the sea for multitude ;* but now *they* shall be all cut off, and their widows shall be so. But observe, God says, *They are increased to me.* Though the husbands were cut off by the sword of his justice, their poor widows were gathered in the arms of his mercy, who has taken it among the titles of his honour to be *the God of the widows.* Widows are said to be *taken into the number,* the number of those whom God has a particular compassion and concern for. *Secondly,* The parents are deprived of their children : *She that has borne seven* sons, whom she expected to be the support and joy of her age, now *languishes,* when she has seen them all cut off by the sword in one day, who had been many years her burden and care. *She that had many children has waxed feeble,* 1 Sam. ii. 5. See what uncertain comforts children are; and let us therefore rejoice in them *as though we rejoiced not.* When the children are slain the mother *gives up the ghost,* for her life was bound up in theirs : *Her sun has gone down while it was yet day;* she is bereaved of all her comforts just when she thought herself in the midst of the enjoyment of them. She is now *ashamed and confounded* to think how proud she was of her sons, how fond of them, and how much she promised herself from them. Some understand, by this languishing mother, Jerusalem lamenting the death of her inhabitants as passionately as ever poor mother bewailed her children. Many are cut off already, *and the residue of them,* who have yet escaped, and, as was hoped, were reserved to be the seed of another generation, even these *will I deliver to the sword before their enemies* (as the condemned malefactor is delivered to the sheriff to be executed), *saith the Lord,* the Judge of heaven and earth, who, we are sure, herein judges according to truth, though the judgment seem severe.

5. They shall fall without being pitied (*v.* 5): " *For who shall have pity on thee, O Jerusalem ?* When thy God has *cast thee out of his sight,* and his compassions fail and are shut up from thee, neither thy enemies nor thy friends shall have any compassion for thee. They shall have no sympathy with thee ; they shall not *bemoan thee* nor be sorry for thee ; they shall have no concern for thee, shall not go a step out of their way to *ask how thou dost.*" For, (1.) Their friends, who were expected to do these friendly offices, were all involved with them in the calamities, and had enough to do to bemoan themselves. (2.) It was plain to all their neighbours that they had brought all this misery upon themselves by their obstinacy in sin, and that they might easily have prevented it by repentance and reformation, which they were often in vain called to; and therefore *who can pity them ? O Israel! thou hast destroyed thyself.* Those will perish for ever unpitied that might have been saved upon such easy terms and would not. (3.) God will thus complete their misery. He will set their acquaintance, as he did Job's, at a distance from them; and his hand, his righteous hand, is to be acknowledged in all the unkindnesses of our friends, as well as in all the injuries done us by our foes.

10 Woe is me, my mother, that thou hast borne me a man of strife and a man of contention to the whole earth ! I have neither lent on usury, nor men have lent to me on usury;

yet every one of them doth curse me. 11 The Lord said, Verily it shall be well with thy remnant ; verily I will cause the enemy to entreat thee *well* in the time of evil and in the time of affliction. 12 Shall iron break the northern iron and the steel ? 13 Thy substance and thy treasures will I give to the spoil without price, and *that* for all thy sins, even in all thy borders. 14 And I will make *thee* to pass with thine enemies into a land *which* thou knowest not : for a fire is kindled in mine anger, *which* shall burn upon you.

Jeremiah has now returned from his public work and retired into his closet; what passed between him and his God there we have an account of in these and the following verses, which he published afterwards, to affect the people with the weight and importance of his messages to them. Here is,

I. The complaint which the prophet makes to God of the many discouragements he met with in his work, *v.* 10.

1. He met with a great deal of contradiction and opposition. He was a *man of strife and contention to the whole land* (so it might be read, rather than to *the whole earth,* for his business lay only in that land); both city and country quarrelled with him, and set themselves against him, and said and did all they could to thwart him. He was a peaceable man, gave no provocation to any, nor was apt to resent the provocations given him, and yet *a man of strife,* not a man striving, but a man striven with ; he was for peace, but, when he spoke, they were for war. And, whatever they pretended, that which was the real cause of their quarrels with him was his faithfulness to God and to their souls. He showed them their sins that were working their ruin, and put them into a way to prevent that ruin, which was the greatest kindness he could do them; and yet this was it for which they were incensed against him and looked upon him as their enemy. Even the prince of peace himself was thus a man of strife, a sign spoken against, continually *enduring the contradiction of sinners against himself.* And the gospel of peace brings division, even to fire and sword, Matt. x. 34, 35 ; Luke xii. 49, 51. Now this made Jeremiah very uneasy, even to a degree of impatience. He cried out, *Woe is me, my mother, that thou hast borne me,* as if it were his mother's fault that she bore him, and he had better never have been born than be born to such an uncomfortable life ; nay, he is angry that she had *borne him a man of strife,* as if he had been fatally determined to this by the stars that were in the ascendant at his birth. If

he had any meaning of this kind, doubtless it was very much his infirmity; we rather hope it was intended for no more than a pathetic lamentation of his own case. Note, (1.) Even those who are most quiet and peaceable, if they serve God faithfully, are often made men of strife. We can but *follow peace;* we have the making only of one side of the bargain, and therefore can but, *as much as in us lies, live peaceably.* (2.) It is very uncomfortable to those who are of a peaceable disposition to live among those who are continually picking quarrels with them. (3.) Yet, if we cannot live so peaceably as we desire with our neighbours, we must not be so disturbed at it as thereby to lose the repose of our own minds and put ourselves upon the fret.

2. He met with a great deal of contempt, contumely, and reproach. They every one of them cursed him; they branded him as a turbulent factious man, as an incendiary and a sower of discord and sedition. They ought to have blessed him, and to have blessed God for him; but they had arrived at such a pitch of enmity against God and his word that for his sake they cursed his messenger, spoke ill of him, wished ill to him, did all they could to make him odious. They all did so; he had scarcely one friend in Judah or Jerusalem that would give him a good word. Note, It is often the lot of the best of men to have the worst of characters ascribed to them. *So persecuted they the prophets.* But one would be apt to suspect that surely Jeremiah had given them some provocation, else he could not have lost himself thus: no, not the least: *I have neither lent* money *nor borrowed* money, have been neither creditor nor debtor; for so general is the signification of the words here. (1.) It is implied here that those who deal much in the business of this world are often involved thereby in strife and contention; *meum et tuum—mine and thine* are the great make-bates; lenders and borrowers sue and are sued, and great dealers often get a great deal of ill-will. (2.) It was an instance of Jeremiah's great prudence, and it is written for our learning, that, being called to be a prophet, he *entangled not himself in the affairs of this life,* but kept clear from them, that he might apply the more closely to the business of his profession and might not give the least shadow of suspicion that he aimed at secular advantages in it nor any occasion to his neighbours to contend with him. He *put out* no money, for he was no usurer, nor indeed had he any money to lend: he *took up* no money, for he was no purchaser, no merchant, no spendthrift. He was perfectly dead to this world and the things of it: a very little served to keep him, and we find (*ch.* xvi. 2) that he had neither wife nor children to keep. And yet, (3.) Though he behaved thus discreetly, and so as one would think should have

gained him universal esteem, yet he lay under a general odium, through the iniquity of the times. Blessed be God, bad as things are with us, they are not so bad but that there are those with whom virtue has its praise; yet let not those who behave most prudently think it strange if they have not the respect and esteem they deserve. *Marvel not, my brethren, if the world hate you.*

II. The answer which God gave to this complaint. Though there was in it a mixture of passion and infirmity, yet God graciously took cognizance of it, because it was *for his sake* that the prophet suffered reproach. In this answer, 1. God assures him that he should weather the storm and be made easy at last, *v.* 11. Though his neighbours quarrelled with him for what he did in the discharge of his office, yet God accepted him and promised to stand by him. It is in the original expressed in the form of an oath: "*If I* take not care of thee, let me never be counted faithful; *verily it shall go well with thy remnant,* with the remainder of thy life" (for so the word signifies); "the residue of thy days shall be more comfortable to thee than those hitherto have been." *Thy end shall be good;* so the Chaldee reads it. Note, It is a great and sufficient support to the people of God that, how troublesome soever their way may be, it shall be well with them in their latter end, Ps. xxxvii. 37. They have still a *remnant,* a *residue,* something behind and left in reserve, which will be sufficient to counterbalance all their grievances, and the hope of it may serve to make them easy. It should seem that Jeremiah, besides the vexation that his people gave him, was uneasy at the apprehension he had of sharing largely in the public judgments which he foresaw coming; and, though he mentioned not this, God replied to his thought of it, as to Moses, Exod. iv. 19. Jeremiah thought, "If my friends are thus abusive to me, what will my enemies be?" And God had thought fit to awaken in him an expectation of this kind, *ch.* xii. 5. But here he quiets his mind with this promise: "*Verily I will cause the enemy to entreat thee well in the time of evil,* when all about thee shall be laid waste." Note, God has all men's hearts in his hand, and can turn those to favour his servants whom they were most afraid of. And the prophets of the Lord have often met with fairer and better treatment among open enemies than among those that call themselves his people. When we see trouble coming, and it looks very threatening, let us not despair, but hope in God, because it may prove better than we expect. This promise was accomplished when Nebuchadnezzar, having taken the city, charged the captain of the guard to be kind to Jeremiah, and let him have every thing he had a mind to, *ch.* xxxix. 11, 12. The following words, *Shall iron break the northern iron, and the steel,* or *brass?* (*v.* 12), being compared with the promise of God made to Jeremiah (*ch.* i. 18), that he would make him an *iron pillar* and *brazen walls*, seem intended for his comfort. They were continually clashing with him, and were rough and hard as iron; but Jeremiah, being armed with power and courage from on high, is as northern iron, which is naturally stronger, and as steel, which is hardened by art; and therefore they shall not prevail against him; compare this with Ezek. ii. 6; iii. 8, 9. He might the better bear their quarrelling with him when he was sure of the victory. 2. God assures him that his enemies and persecutors should be lost in the storm, should be ruined at last, and that therein the word of God in his mouth should be accomplished and he proved a true prophet, *v.* 13, 14. God here turns his speech from the prophet to the people. To them also *v.* 12 may be applied: *Shall iron break the northern iron, and the steel?* Shall their courage and strength, and the most hardy and vigorous of their efforts, be able to contest either with the counsel of God or with the army of the Chaldeans, which are as inflexible, as invincible, as the northern iron and steel. Let them therefore hear their doom: *Thy substance and thy treasure will I give to the spoil,* and that *without price;* the spoilers shall have it *gratis;* it shall be to them a cheap and easy prey. Observe, The prophet was poor; he neither lent nor borrowed; he had nothing to lose, neither *substance* nor *treasure,* and therefore the enemy will treat him well, *Cantabit vacuus coram latrone viator—The traveller that has no property about him will congratulate himself when accosted by a robber.* But the people that had great estates in money and land would be slain for what they had, or the enemy, finding they had much, would use them hardly, to make them confess more. And it is their own iniquity that herein corrects them: It is *for all thy sins, even in all thy borders.* All parts of the country, even those which lay most remote, had contributed to the national guilt, and all shall now be brought to account. Let not one tribe lay the blame upon another, but each take shame to itself: It is for *all thy sins in all thy borders.* Thus shall they stay at home till they see their estates ruined, and then they shall be carried into captivity, to spend the sad remains of a miserable life in slavery: *" I will make thee to pass with thy enemies,* who shall lead thee in triumph *into a land that thou knowest not,* and therefore canst expect to find no comfort in it." All this is the fruit of God's wrath: " It is *a fire kindled in my anger, which shall burn upon you,* and, if not extinguished in time, will burn eternally."

15 O Lord, thou knowest: remember me, and visit me, and revenge me of my persecutors; take me not away in

508

thy long-suffering: know that for thy sake I have suffered rebuke. 16 Thy words were found, and I did eat them; and thy word was unto me the joy and rejoicing of mine heart: for I am called by thy name, O Lord God of hosts. 17 I sat not in the assembly of the mockers, nor rejoiced; I sat alone, because of thy hand: for thou hast filled me with indignation. 18 Why is my pain perpetual, and my wound incurable, *which* refuseth to be healed? wilt thou be altogether unto me as a liar, *and as* waters *that* fail? 19 Therefore thus saith the Lord, If thou return, then will I bring thee again, *and* thou shalt stand before me: and if thou take forth the precious from the vile, thou shalt be as my mouth: let them return unto thee; but return not thou unto them. 20 And I will make thee unto this people a fenced brazen wall: and they shall fight against thee, but they shall not prevail against thee: for I *am* with thee to save thee and to deliver thee, saith the Lord. 21 And I will deliver thee out of the hand of the wicked, and I will redeem thee out of the hand of the terrible.

Here, as before, we have,

I. The prophet's humble address to God, containing a representation both of his integrity and of the hardships he underwent notwithstanding. It is matter of comfort to us that, whatever ails us, we have a God to go to, before whom we may spread our case and to whose omniscience we may appeal, as the prophet here, " O Lord! thou knowest; thou knowest my sincerity, which men are resolved they will not acknowledge; thou knowest my distress, which men disdain to take notice of." Observe here,

1. What it is that the prophet prays for, *v.* 15. (1.) That God would consider his case and be mindful of him: " O Lord! remember me; think upon me for good." (2.) That God would communicate strength and comfort to him: " *Visit me;* not only remember me, but let me know that thou rememberest me, that thou art nigh unto me." (3.) That he would appear for him against those that did him wrong: *Revenge me of my persecutors,* or rather, *Vindicate me from my persecutors;* give judgment against them, and let that judgment be executed so far as is necessary for my vindication and to compel them to acknowledge that they have done me wrong. Further than this **a** good man will not desire that God should

avenge him. Let something be done to convince the world that (whatever blasphemers say to the contrary) Jeremiah is a righteous man and the God whom he serves is a righteous God. (4.) That he would yet spare him and continue him in the land of the living : " *Take me not away* by a sudden stroke, but *in thy long-suffering* lengthen out my days." The best men will own themselves so obnoxious to God's wrath that they are indebted to his patience for the continuance of their lives. Or, " While thou exercisest long-suffering towards my persecutors, let not them prevail to take me away." Though in a passion he complained of his birth (*v.* 10), yet he desires here that his death might not be hastened ; for life is sweet to nature, and the life of a useful man is so to grace. *I pray not that thou shouldst take them out of the world.*

2. What it is that he pleads with God for mercy and relief against his enemies, persecutors, and slanderers.

(1.) That God's honour was interested in this case: *Know,* and make it known, *that for thy sake I have suffered rebuke.* Those that lay themselves open to reproach by their own fault and folly have great reason to bear it patiently, but no reason to expect that God should appear for them. But if it is for doing well that we suffer ill, and for righteousness' sake that we have all manner of evil said against us, we may hope that God will vindicate our honour with his own. To the same purport (*v.* 16), *I am called by thy name, O Lord of hosts!* It was for that reason that his enemies hated him, and therefore for that reason he promised himself that God would own him and stand by him.

(2.) That the word of God, which he was employed to preach to others, he had experienced the power and pleasure of in his own soul, and therefore had the graces of the Spirit to qualify him for the divine favour, as well as his gifts. We find some rejected of God who yet could say, *Lord, we have prophesied in thy name.* But Jeremiah could say more (*v.* 16): " *Thy words were found,* found *by me*" (he searched the scripture, diligently studied the law, and found that in it which was reviving to him: if we seek we shall find), "found *for me*" (the words which he was to deliver to others were laid ready to his hand, were brought to him by inspiration), " *and I did* not only taste them, but *eat them,* received them entirely, conversed with them intimately ; they were welcome to me, as food to one that is hungry ; I entertained them, digested them, turned them *in succum et sanguinem—into blood and spirits,* and was myself delivered into the mould of those truths which I was to deliver to others." The prophet was told to *eat the roll,* Ezek. ii. 8 ; Rev. x. 9. *1 did eat it*—that is, as it follows, it *was to me the joy and rejoicing of my heart,* nothing could be more agreeable. Understand it, [1.] Of the message itself

which he was to deliver. Though he was to foretel the ruin of his country, which was dear to him, and in the ruin of which he could not but have a deep share, yet all natural affections were swallowed up in zeal for God's glory, and even these messages of wrath, being divine messages, were a satisfaction to him. He also rejoiced, at first, in hope that the people would take warning and prevent the judgment. Or, [2.] Of the commission he received to deliver this message. Though the work he was called to was not attended with any secular advantages, but, on the contrary, exposed him to contempt and persecution, yet, because it put him in a way to serve God and do good, he took pleasure in it, was glad to be so employed, and it was his *meat and drink to do the will of him that sent him,* John iv. 34. Or, [3.] Of the promise God gave him that he would assist and own him in his work (*ch.* i. 8); he was satisfied in that, and depended upon it, and therefore hoped it should not fail him.

(3.) That he had applied himself to the duty of his office with all possible gravity, seriousness, and self-denial, though he had had of late but little satisfaction in it, *v.* 17. [1.] It was his comfort that he had given up himself wholly to the business of his office and had done nothing inconsistent with it, nothing either to divert himself from it or disfit himself for it. He kept no unsuitable company, denied himself the use even of lawful recreations, abstained from every thing that looked like levity, lest thereby he should make himself mean and less regarded. He *sat alone,* spent a great deal of time in his closet, *because of the hand* of the Lord that was strong upon him to carry him on his work, Ezek. iii. 14. " *For thou hast filled me with indignation,* with such messages of wrath against this people as have made me always pensive." Note, It will be a comfort to God's ministers, when men despise them, if they have the testimony of their consciences for them that they have not by any vain foolish behaviour made themselves despicable, that they have been dead not only to the wealth of the world, as this prophet was (*v.* 10), but to the pleasures of it too, as here. But, [2.] It is his complaint that he had had but little pleasure in his work. It was at first the rejoicing of his heart, but of late it had made him melancholy, so that he had no heart to *sit in the meeting of those that make merry.* He cared not for company, for indeed no company cared for him. He *sat alone,* fretting at the people's obstinacy and the little success of his labours among them. This filled him with a holy *indignation.* Note, It is the folly and infirmity of some good people that they lose much of the pleasantness of their religion by the fretfulness and uneasiness of their natural temper, which they humour and indulge, instead of mortifying it.

(4.) He throws himself upon God's pity

and promise in a very passionate expostulation (*v.* 18): " *Why is my pain perpetual,* and nothing done to ease it? Why are the wounds which my enemies are continually giving both to my peace and to my reputation incurable, and nothing done to retrieve either my comfort or my credit? I once little thought that I should be thus neglected; will the God that has promised me his presence *be to me as a liar,* the God on whom I depend be to me *as waters that fail?"* We are willing to make the best we can of it, and to take it as an appeal, [1.] To the mercy of God: " I know he will not let the pain of his servant be perpetual, but he will ease it, will not let his wound be incurable, but he will heal it; and therefore I will not despair." [2.] To his faithfulness: " *Wilt thou be to me as a liar?* No; I know thou wilt not. God is not a man that he should lie. The fountain of life will never be to his people as *waters that fail."*

II. God's gracious answer to this address, *v.* 19—21. Though the prophet betrayed much human frailty in his address, yet God vouchsafed to answer him with good words and comfortable words; for he knows our frame. Observe,

1. What God here requires of him as the condition of the further favours he designed him. Jeremiah had done and suffered much for God, yet God is no debtor to him, but he is still upon his good behaviour. God will own him. But, (1.) He must recover his temper, and be reconciled to his work, and friends with it again, and not quarrel with it any more as he had done. He must *return,* must shake off these distrustful discontented thoughts and passions, and not give way to them, must regain the peaceable possession and enjoyment of himself, and resolve to be easy. Note, When we have stepped aside into any disagreeable frame or way our care must be to return and compose ourselves into a right temper of mind again; and *then* we may expect God will help us, if thus we endeavour to help ourselves. (2.) He must resolve to be faithful in his work, for he could not expect the divine protection any longer than he did approve himself so. Though there was no cause at all to charge Jeremiah with unfaithfulness, and God knew his heart to be sincere, yet God saw fit to give him this caution. Those that do their duty must not take it ill to be told their duty. In two things he must be faithful:—[1.] He must distinguish between some and others of those he preached to: Thou must *take forth the precious from the vile.* The righteous are the precious be they ever so mean and poor; the wicked are the vile be they ever so rich and great. In our congregations these are mixed, wheat and chaff in the same floor; we cannot distinguish them by name, but we must by character, and must give to each a portion, speaking comfort to precious saints and

510

terror to vile sinners, neither *making the heart of the righteous sad* nor *strengthening the hands of the wicked* (Ezek. xiii. 22), but *rightly dividing the word of truth.* Ministers must take those whom they see to be precious into their bosoms, and not *sit alone* as Jeremiah did, but keep up conversation with those they may do good to and get good by. [2.] He must closely adhere to his instructions, and not in the least vary from them: *Let them return to thee, but return not thou to them,* that is, he must do the utmost he can, in his preaching, to bring people up to the mind of God; he must tell them they must, at their peril, comply with that. Those that had flown off from him, that did not like the terms upon which God's favour was offered to them, " *Let them return to thee,* and, upon second thoughts, come up to the terms and strike the bargain; but do not thou *return to them,* do not compliment them, nor comply with them, nor think to make the matter easier to them than the word of God has made it." Men's hearts and lives must come up to God's law and comply with that, for God's law will never come down to them nor comply with them.

2. What God here promises to him upon the performance of these conditions. If he approve himself well, (1.) God will tranquillize his mind and pacify the present tumult of his spirits: *If thou return, I will bring thee again,* will *restore thy soul,* as Ps. xxiii. 3. The best and strongest saints, if at any time they have gone aside out of the right way, and are determined to return, need the grace of God to bring them again. (2.) God will employ him in his service as a prophet, whose work, even in those bad times, had comfort and honour enough in it to be its own wages : " *Thou shalt stand before me,* to receive instructions from me, as a servant from his master; and *thou shalt be as my mouth* to deliver my messages to the people, as an ambassador is the mouth of the prince that sends him." Note, Faithful ministers are God's mouth to us; they are so to look upon themselves, and to speak God's mind and *as becomes the oracles of God;* and we are so to look upon them, and to hear God speaking to us by them. Observe, If thou keep close to thy instructions, *thou shalt be as my mouth,* not otherwise; so far, and no further, God will stand by ministers, as they go by the written word. " *Thou shalt be as my mouth,* that is, what thou sayest shall be made good, as if I myself had said it." See Isa. xliv. 26; 1 Sam. iii. 19. (3.) He shall have strength and courage to face the many difficulties he meets with in his work, and his spirit shall not fail again as now it does (*v.* 20): " *I will make thee unto this people as a fenced brazen wall,* which the storm batters and beats violently upon, but cannot shake. *Return not thou to them* by any sinful compliances, and then trust thy God to arm thee by his grace

with holy resolutions. Be not cowardly, and God will make thee daring." He had complained that he was made a *man of strife.* Expect to be so (says God); they will *fight against thee,* they will sti'l continue their opposition, *but they shall not prevail against thee* to drive thee off from thy work nor to cut thee off from the land of the living." (4.) He shall have God for his protector and mighty deliverer: *I am with thee to save thee.* Those that have God with them have a Saviour with them who has wisdom and strength enough to deal with the most formidable enemy; and those that are with God, and faithful to him, he will deliver (*v.* 21) either from trouble or through it. They may perhaps fall *into the hand of the wicked,* and they may appear terrible to them, but God will rescue them *out of their hands.* They shall not be able to kill them till they have finished their testimony; they shall not prevent their happiness. God will so deliver them as to *preserve them to his heavenly kingdom* (2 Tim. iv. 18), and that is deliverance enough. There are many things that appear very frightful that yet do not prove at all hurtful to a good man.

CHAP. XVI.

In this chapter, I. The greatness of the calamity that was coming upon the Jewish nation is illustrated by prohibitions given to the prophet neither to set up a house of his own (ver. 1—4) nor to go into the house of mourning (ver. 5—7) nor into the house of feasting, ver. 8, 9. II. God is justified in these severe proceedings against them by an account of their great wickedness, ver. 10—13. III. An intimation is given of mercy in reserve, ver. 14, 15. IV. Some hopes are given that the punishment of the sin should prove the reformation of the sinners, and that they should return to God at length in a way of duty, and so be qualified for his returns to them in a way of favour, ver. 16—21.

THE word of the LORD came also unto me, saying, 2 Thou shalt not take thee a wife, neither shalt thou have sons nor daughters in this place. 3 For thus saith the LORD concerning the sons and concerning the daughters that are born in this place, and concerning their mothers that bare them, and concerning their fathers that begat them in this land; 4 They shall die of grievous deaths; they shall not be lamented; neither shall they be buried; *but* they shall be as dung upon the face of the earth: and they shall be consumed by the sword, and by famine; and their carcases shall be meat for the fowls of heaven, and for the beasts of the earth. 5 For thus saith the LORD, Enter not into the house of mourning, neither go to lament nor bemoan them: for I have taken away my peace from this people, saith the LORD, *even* lovingkindness and mercies. 6 Both the great and the small shall die in this land: they shall not be buried, neither shall *men* lament for them, nor cut themselves, nor make themselves bald for them: 7 Neither shall *men* tear *themselves* for them in mourning, to comfort them for the dead; neither shall *men* give them the cup of consolation to drink for their father or for their mother. 8 Thou shalt not also go into the house of feasting, to sit with them to eat and to drink. 9 For thus saith the LORD of hosts, the God of Israel; Behold, I will cause to cease out of this place in your eyes, and in your days, the voice of mirth, and the voice of gladness, the voice of the bridegroom, and the voice of the bride.

The prophet is here for a sign to the people. They would not regard what he said; let it be tried whether they will regard what he *does.* In general, he must conduct himself so, in every thing, as became one that expected to see his country in ruins very shortly. This he foretold, but few regarded the prediction; therefore he is to show that he is himself fully satisfied in the truth of it. Others go on in their usual course, but he, in the prospect of these sad times, is forbidden and therefore forbears marriage, mourning for the dead, and mirth. Note, Those that would convince others of and affect them with the word of God must make it appear, even in the most self-denying instances, that they do believe it themselves and are affected with it. If we would rouse others out of their security, and persuade them to sit loose to the world, we must ourselves be mortified to present things and show that we expect the dissolution of them.

I. Jeremiah must not marry, nor think of having a family and being a housekeeper (*v.* 2): *Thou shalt not take thee a wife,* nor think of *having sons and daughters in this place,* not in the land of Judah, not in Jerusalem, not in Anathoth. The Jews, more than any people, valued themselves on their early marriages and their numerous offspring. But Jeremiah must live a bachelor, not so much in honour of virginity as in diminution of it. By this it appears that it was advisable and seasonable only in calamitous times and times of *present distress,* 1 Cor. vii. 26. That it is so is a part of the calamity. There may be a time when it will be said, *Blessed is the womb that bears not,* Luke xxiii. 29. When we see such times at hand it is wisdom for all, especially for prophets, to keep themselves as much as may be from being *entangled with the affairs of this life* and encumbered with that which, the dearer it is to them, the more it will be the matter of their care, and fear, and grief, at such a time. The reason here given is because the *fathers* and *mothers, the sons and the daughters, shall die of grievous deaths, v.* 3, 4. As for those that have wives and children, 1. They will have such a clog upon them that they cannot flee from those deaths. A single man may make his escape and shift for his own safety, when he that has a wife and children can neither find means to convey them with him nor find in his heart to go and leave them behind him. 2. They will be in continual terror for fear of those deaths; and the more they have to lose by them the greater will the terror and consternation be when death appears every where in its triumphant pomp and power. 3. The death of every child, and the aggravating circumstances of it, will be a new death to the parent. Better have no children than have them brought forth and bred up *for the murderer* (Hos. ix. 13, 14), than see them live and die in misery. Death is grievous, but some deaths are more grievous than others, both to those that die and to their relations that survive them; hence we read of *so great a death,* 2 Cor. i. 10. Two things are used a little to palliate and alleviate the terror of death as to this world, and to sugar the bitter pill—bewailing the dead and burying them; but, to make those deaths grievous indeed, these are denied: *They shall not be lamented,* but shall be carried off, as if all the world were weary of them; nay, they *shall not be buried,* but left exposed, as if they were designed to be monuments of justice. *They shall be as dung upon the face of the earth,* not only despicable, but detestable, as if they were good for nothing but to manure the ground; being *consumed,* some *by the sword* and some *by famine, their carcases shall be meat for the fowls of heaven and the beasts of the earth.* Will not any one say, " Better be without children than live to see them come to this ?" What reason have we to say, *All is vanity and vexation of spirit,* when those creatures that we expect to be our greatest comforts may prove not only our heaviest cares, but our sorest crosses !

II. Jeremiah must not go to the house of mourning upon occasion of the death of any of his neighbours or relations (*v.* 5): *Enter thou not into the house of mourning.* It was usual to condole with those whose relations were dead, to *bemoan them,* to *cut themselves,* and *make themselves bald,* which, it seems, was commonly practised as an expression of mourning, though forbidden by the law, Deut. xiv. 1. Nay, sometimes, in a passion of grief, they did *tear themselves for them* (*v.* 6, 7), partly in honour of the deceased, thus signifying that they thought there was a great loss of them, and partly in compassion to the surviving relations, to whom the burden will be made the lighter by their having sharers with them in their grief. They used to mourn with them, and so *to comfort them*

for the dead, as Job's friends with him and the Jews with Martha and Mary; and it was a friendly office to *give them a cup of consolation to drink,* to provide cordials for them and press them earnestly to drink of them for the support of their spirits, give wine to those that are of heavy heart *for their father* or *mother,* that it may be some comfort to them to find that, though they have lost their parents, yet they have some friends left that have a concern for them. Thus the usage stood, and it was a laudable usage. It is a good work to others, as well as of good use to ourselves, to *go to the house of mourning.* It seems, the prophet Jeremiah had been wont to abound in good offices of this kind, and it well became his character both as a pious man and as a prophet; and one would think it should have made him better beloved among his people than it should seem he was. But now God bids him not lament the death of his friends as usual, for, 1. His sorrow for the destruction of his country in general must swallow up his sorrow for particular deaths. His tears must now be turned into another channel; and there is occasion enough for them all. 2. He had little reason to lament those who died now just before the judgments entered which he saw at the door, but rather to think those happy who were seasonably *taken away from the evil to come.* 3. This was to be a type of what was coming, when there should be such universal confusion that all neighbourly friendly offices should be neglected. Men shall be in deaths so often, and even dying daily, that they shall have no time, no room, no heart, for the ceremonies that used to attend death. The sorrows shall be so ponderous as not to admit relief, and every one so full of grief for his own troubles that he shall have no thought of his neighbours. All shall be mourners then, and no comforters; every one will find it enough to bear his own burden; for (*v.* 5), " *I have taken away my peace from this people,* put a full period to their prosperity, deprived them of health, and wealth, and quiet, and friends, and every thing wherewith they might comfort themselves and one another." Whatever peace we enjoy, it is God's peace; it is his gift, and, *if he give quietness, who then can make trouble?* But, if we make not a good use of his peace, he can and will take it away; and where are we then ? Job xxxiv. 29. " I will take away my peace, *even my loving-kindness and mercies ;*" these shall be shut up and restrained, which are the fresh springs from which all their fresh streams flow, and then farewell all good. Note, Those have cut themselves off from all true peace that have thrown themselves out of the favour of God. All is gone when God takes away from us his lovingkindness and his mercies. Then it follows (*v.* 6), *Both the great and the small shall die,* even *in this land,* the land of Canaan, that used to be called the *land of the living*. God's favour is our life; take away that, and *we die, we perish, we all perish*.

III. Jeremiah must not go to the house of mirth, any more than to the house of mourning, *v*. 8. It had been his custom, and it was innocent enough, when any of his friends made entertainments at their houses and invited him to them, to *go and sit with them*, not merely to drink, but *to eat and to drink*, soberly and cheerfully. But now he must not take that liberty, 1. Because it was unseasonable, and inconsistent with the providences of God in reference to that land and nation. God called aloud to *weeping, and mourning, and fasting;* he was coming forth against them in his judgments; and it was time for them to *humble themselves;* and it well became the prophet who gave them the warning to give them an example of taking the warning, and complying with it, and so to make it appear that he did himself believe it. Ministers ought to be examples of self-denial and mortification, and to show themselves affected with those terrors of the Lord with which they desire to affect others. And it becomes all the sons of Zion to sympathize with her in her afflictions, and not to be merry when she is perplexed, Amos vi. 6. 2. Because he must thus show the people what sad times were coming upon them. His friends wondered that he would not meet them, as he used to do, in the house of feasting. But he lets them know it was to intimate to them that all their feasting would be at an end shortly (*v*. 9): "*I will cause to cease the voice of mirth*. You shall have nothing to feast on, nothing to rejoice in, but be surrounded with calamities that shall mar your mirth and cast a damp upon it." God can find ways to tame the most jovial. "This shall be done *in this place*, in Jerusalem, that used to be the *joyous city* and thought her joys were all secure to her. It shall be done *in your eyes*, in your sight, to be a vexation to you, who now look so haughty and so merry. It shall be done *in your days;* you yourselves shall live to see it." The voice of praise they had made to cease by their iniquities and idolatries, and therefore justly God made to cease among them *the voice of mirth and gladness*. The voice of God's prophets was not heard, was not heeded, among them, and therefore no longer shall *the voice of the bridegroom and of the bride*, of the songs that used to grace the nuptials, be heard among them. See *ch*. vii. 34.

10 And it shall come to pass, when thou shalt show this people all these words, and they shall say unto thee, Wherefore hath the LORD pronounced all this great evil against us? or what *is* our iniquity? or what *is* our sin that we have committed against the LORD our God? 11 Then shalt thou say unto them, Because your fathers have forsaken me, saith the LORD, and have walked after other gods, and have served them, and have worshipped them, and have forsaken me, and have not kept my law; 12 And ye have done worse than your fathers; (for behold, ye walk every one after the imagination of his evil heart, that they may not hearken unto me:) 13 Therefore will I cast you out of this land into a land that ye know not, *neither* ye nor your fathers; and there shall ye serve other gods day and night; where I will not show you favour.

Here is, 1. An enquiry made into the reasons why God would bring those judgments upon them (*v*. 10): *When thou shalt show this people all these words*, the words of this curse, they will say unto thee, *Wherefore has the Lord pronounced all this great evil against us?* One would hope that there were some among them that asked this question with a humble penitent heart, desiring to know what was the sin for which God contended with them, that they might cast it away and prevent the judgment: "Show us the Jonah that raises the storm and we will throw it overboard." But it seems here to be the language of those who quarrelled at the word of God, and challenged him to show what they had done which might deserve so severe a punishment: "*What is our iniquity? Or what is our sin?* What crime have we ever been guilty of, proportionable to such a sentence?" Instead of humbling and condemning themselves, they stand upon their own justification and insinuate that God did them wrong in pronouncing this evil against them, that he *laid upon them more than was right*, and that they had reason to *enter into judgment with God*, Job xxxiv. 23. Note, It is amazing to see how hardly sinners are brought to justify God and judge themselves when they are in trouble, and to own the iniquity and the sin that have procured them the trouble. 2. A plain and full answer given to this enquiry. Do they ask the prophet why, and for what reason, God is thus angry with them? He shall not stop their mouths by telling them that they may be sure there is a sufficient reason, the righteous God is never *angry without cause*, without good cause; but he must tell them particularly what is the cause, that they may be convinced and humbled, or at least that God may be justified. Let them know then, (1) That God visited upon them the iniquities of their fathers (*v*. 11): *Your fathers have forsaken me, and have not kept my law*. They shook

513

off divine institutions and grew weary of them (they thought them too plain, too mean), and then they *walked after other gods*, whose worship was more gay and pompous; and, being fond of variety and novelty, they *served them and worshipped them;* and this was the sin which God had said, in the second commandment, he would *visit upon their children*, who kept up these idolatrous usages, because they received them *by tradition from their fathers*, 1 Pet. i. 18. (2.) That God reckoned with them for their own iniquities (*v.* 12): " You have made your fathers' sin your own, and have become obnoxious to the punishment which in their days was deferred, for *you have done worse than your fathers*." If they had made a good use of their fathers' reprieve, and had been led by the patience of God to repentance, they would have fared the better for it and the judgment would have been prevented, the reprieve turned into a national pardon; but, making an ill use of it, and being hardened by it in their sins, they fared the worse for it, and, the reprieve having expired, an addition was made to the sentence and it was executed with the more severity. They were more impudent and obstinate in sin than their fathers, *walked every one after the imagination of his own heart*, made that their guide and rule and were resolved to follow that, on purpose *that they might not hearken to God* and his prophets. They designedly suffered their own lusts and passions to be noisy, that they might drown the voice of their consciences. No wonder then that God has taken up this resolution concerning them (*v.* 13): " *I will cast you out of this land*, this land of light, this valley of vision. Since you will not hearken to me, you shall not hear me; you shall be hurried away, not into a neighbouring country which you have formerly had some acquaintance and correspondence with, but into a far country, *a land that you know not, neither you nor your fathers*, in which you have no interest, nor can expect to meet with any comfortable society, to be an allay to your misery." Justly were those banished into a strange land who doted upon strange gods, which neither they nor their fathers knew, Deut. xxxii. 17. Two things would make their case there very miserable, and both of them relate to the soul, the better part; the greatest calamities of their captivity were those which affected that and debarred that from its bliss. [1.] " It is the happiness of the soul to be employed in the service of God; but *there shall you serve other gods day and night;* that is, you shall be in continual temptation to serve them and perhaps compelled to do it by your cruel task-masters; and, when you are forced to worship idols, you will be as sick of such worship as ever you were fond of it when it was forbidden you by your godly kings." See how God often makes men's sin their punishment, and *fills the backslider in heart*

514

with his own ways. " You shall have no public worship at all but the worship of idols, and then you will think with regret how you slighted the worship of the true God." [2.] " It is the happiness of the soul to have some tokens of the lovingkindness of God, but you shall go to a strange land, *where I will not show you favour.*" If they had had God's favour, that would have made even the land of their captivity a pleasant land; but, if they lie under his wrath, the yoke of their oppression will be intolerable to them.

14 Therefore, behold, the days come, saith the LORD, that it shall no more be said, The LORD liveth, that brought up the children of Israel out of the land of Egypt; 15 But, The LORD liveth, that brought up the children of Israel from the land of the north, and from all the lands whither he had driven them: and I will bring them again into their land that I gave unto their fathers. 16 Behold, I will send for many fishers, saith the LORD, and they shall fish them; and after will I send for many hunters, and they shall hunt them from every mountain, and from every hill, and out of the holes of the rocks. 17 For mine eyes *are* upon all their ways: they are not hid from my face, neither is their iniquity hid from mine eyes. 18 And first I will recompense their iniquity and their sin double; because they have defiled my land, they have filled mine inheritance with the carcases of their detestable and abominable things. 19 O LORD, my strength, and my fortress, and my refuge in the day of affliction, the Gentiles shall come unto thee from the ends of the earth, and shall say, Surely our fathers have inherited lies, vanity, and *things* wherein *there is* no profit. 20 Shall a man make gods unto himself, and they *are* no gods? 21 Therefore behold, I will this once cause them to know, I will cause them to know mine hand and my might; and they shall know that my name *is* The LORD.

There is a mixture of mercy and judgment in these verses, and it is hard to know to which to apply some of the passages here —they are so interwoven, and some seem to look as far forward as the times of the gospel.

I. God will certainly execute judgment upon them for their idolatries. Let them expect it, for the decree has gone forth. 1. God sees all their sins, though they commit them ever so secretly and palliate them ever so artfully (v. 17): *My eyes are upon all their ways.* They have not their eye upon God, have no regard to him, stand in no awe of him; but he has his eye upon them; neither they nor their sins are *hidden from his face, from his eyes.* Note, None of the sins of sinners either can be concealed from God or shall be overlooked by him, Prov. v. 21; Job xxxiv. 21; Ps. xc. 8. 2. God is highly displeased, particularly at their idolatries, v. 18. As his omniscience convicts them, so his justice condemns them: *I will recompense their iniquity and their sin double,* not double to what it deserves, but double to what they expect and to what I have done formerly. Or I will recompense it *abundantly;* they shall now pay for their long reprieve and the divine patience they have abused. The sin for which God has a controversy with them is their having *defiled God's land* with their idolatries, and not only alienated that which he was entitled to as his inheritance, but polluted that which he dwelt in with delight as his inheritance, and made it offensive to him *with the carcases of their detestable things,* the gods themselves which they worshipped, the images of which, though they were of gold and silver, were as loathsome to God as the putrid carcases of men or beasts are to us. Idols are *carcases of detestable things.* God hates them, and so should we. Or he might refer to the sacrifices which they offered to these idols, with which *the land was filled;* for they had high places in all the coasts and corners of it. This was the sin which, above any other, incensed God against them. 3. He will find out and raise up instruments of his wrath, that shall *cast them out of their land,* according to the sentence passed upon them (v. 16): *I will send for many fishers and many hunters*—the Chaldean army, that shall have many ways of ensnaring and destroying them, by fraud as fishers, by force as hunters. They shall find them out wherever they are, and shall chase and closely pursue them, to their ruin. They shall discover them wherever they are hid, in *hills* or *mountains,* or *holes of the rocks,* and shall drive them out. God has various ways of prosecuting a people with his judgments that avoid the convictions of his word. He has men at command fit for his purpose; he has them within call, and can send for them when he pleases. 4. Their bondage in Babylon shall be sorer and much more grievous than that in Egypt, their task-masters more cruel, and their lives made more bitter. This is implied in the promise (v. 14, 15), that their deliverance out of Babylon shall be more illustrious in itself, and more welcome to them, than that out of Egypt. Their slavery in Egypt came upon them gradually and almost insensibly; that

in Babylon came upon them at once and with all the aggravating circumstances of terror. In Egypt they had a Goshen of their own, but none such in Babylon. In Egypt they were used as servants that were useful, in Babylon as captives that had been hateful. 5. They shall be warned, and God shall be glorified, by these judgments brought upon them. These judgments have a voice, and speak aloud, (1.) Instruction to them. When God chastens them he teaches them. By this rod God expostulates with them (v. 20): *"Shall a man make gods to himself?* Will any man be so perfectly void of all reason and consideration as to think that a god of his own making can stand him in any stead? Will you ever again be such fools as you have been, to make to yourselves gods which are no gods, when you have a God whom you may call your own, who made you, and is himself the true and living God?"* (2.) Honour to God; for he will be known by the judgments which he executes. He will first recompense their iniquity (v. 18), and then he will *this once* (v. 21)—this once for all, not by many interruptions of their peace, but this one desolation and destruction of it. *"For this once,* and no more, *I will cause them to know my hand,* the length and weight of my punishing hand, how far it can reach and how deeply it can wound. *And they shall know that my name is Jehovah,* a God with whom there is no contending, who gives being to threatenings and puts life into them as well as promises."

II. Yet he has mercy in store for them, intimations of which come in here for the encouragement of the prophet himself and of those few among them that tremble at God's word. It was said, with an air of severity (v. 13), that God would banish them into a strange land; but, that thereby they might not be driven to despair, there follow immediately words of comfort.

1. *The days will come,* the joyful days, when the same hand that dispersed them shall gather them again, v. 14, 15. They are cast out, but they are not cast off, they are not cast away. They shall be *brought up from the land of the north,* the land of their captivity, where they are held with a strong hand, *and from all the lands whither they are driven,* and where they seemed to be lost and buried in the crowd; nay, *I will bring them again into their own land,* and settle them there. As the foregoing threatenings agreed with what was written in the law, so does this promise. *Yet will I not cast them away,* Lev. xxvi. 44. *Thence will the Lord thy God gather thee,* Deut. xxx. 4. And the following words (v. 16) may be understood as a promise; God will send for fishers and hunters, the Medes and Persians, that shall find them out in the countries where they are scattered, and send them back to their own land; or Zerubbabel, and others of their own nation, who should fish

them out and hunt after them, to persuade them to return ; or whatever instruments the Spirit of God made use of to *stir up their spirits to go up,* which at first they were backward to do. They began to nestle in Babylon ; but, *as an eagle stirs up her nest and flutters over her young,* so God did by them, Zech. ii. 7.

2. Their deliverance out of Babylon should, upon some accounts, be more illustrious and memorable than their deliverance out of Egypt was. Both were the Lord's doing and marvellous in their eyes ; both were proofs that the Lord liveth and were to be kept in everlasting remembrance, to his honour, as the living God ; but the fresh mercy shall be so surprising, so welcome, that it shall even abolish the memory of the former. Not but that new mercies should put us in mind of old ones, and give us occasion to renew our thanksgivings for them ; yet because we are tempted to think that the former days were better than these, and to ask, *Where are all the wonders that our fathers told us of?* as if God's *arm* had *waxed short,* and to cry up the age of miracles above the later ages, when mercies are wrought in a way of common providence, therefore we are allowed here comparatively to forget the bringing of Israel out of Egypt as a deliverance outdone by that out of Babylon. That was done *by might and power,* this *by the Spirit of the Lord of hosts,* Zech. iv. 6. In this there was more of pardoning mercy (the most glorious branch of divine mercy) than in that ; for their captivity in Babylon had more in it of the punishment of sin than their bondage in Egypt ; and therefore that which comforts Zion in her deliverance out of Babylon is this, that *her iniquity is pardoned,* Isa. xl. 2. Note, God glorifies himself, and we must glorify him, in those mercies that have no miracles in them, as well as in those that have. And, though the favours of God to our fathers must not be forgotten, yet those to ourselves in our own day we must especially give thanks for.

3. Their deliverance out of captivity shall be accompanied with a blessed reformation, and they shall return effectually cured of their inclination to idolatry, which will complete their deliverance and make it a mercy indeed. They had defiled their own land with their *detestable things, v.* 18. But, when they have smarted for so doing, they shall come and humble themselves before God, *v.* 19—21. (1.) They shall be brought to acknowledge that their God only is God indeed, for he is a God in need—"*My strength* to support and comfort me, *my fortress* to protect and shelter me, *and my refuge* to whom I may flee *in the day of affliction.*" Note, Need drives many to God who had set themselves at a distance from him. Those that slighted him in the day of their prosperity will be glad to flee to him in the day of

516

their affliction. (2.) They shall be quickened to return to him by the conversion of the Gentiles : *The Gentiles shall come to thee from the ends of the earth ;* and therefore shall not we come ? Or, "The Jews, who had by their idolatries made themselves as Gentiles (so I rather understand it), *shall come to thee* by repentance and reformation, shall return to their duty and allegiance, even *from the ends of the earth,* from all the countries whither they were driven. The prophet comforts himself with the hope of this, and in a transport of joy returns to God the notice he had given him of it : "*O Lord! my strength and my fortress,* I am now easy, since thou hast given me a prospect of multitudes that shall *come to thee from the ends of the earth,* both of Jewish converts and of Gentile proselytes." Note, Those that are brought to God themselves cannot but rejoice greatly to see others coming to him, coming back to him. (3.) They shall acknowledge the folly of their ancestors, which it becomes them to do, when they were smarting for the sins of their ancestors : "*Surely our fathers have inherited,* not the satisfaction they promised themselves and their children, but *lies, vanity, and things wherein there is no profit.* We are now sensible that our fathers were cheated in their idolatrous worship ; it did not prove what it promised, and therefore what have we to do any more with it ?" Note, It were well if the disappointment which some have met with in the service of sin, and the pernicious consequences of it to them, might prevail to deter others from treading in their steps. (4.) They shall reason themselves out of their idolatry ; and that reformation is likely to be sincere and durable which results from a rational conviction of the gross absurdity there is in sin. They shall argue thus with themselves (and it is well argued), *Should a man* be such a fool, so perfectly void of the reason of a man, as to *make gods to himself,* the creatures of his own fancy, the work of his own hands, when they are really *no gods? v.* 20. Can a man be so besotted, so perfectly lost to human understanding, as to expect any divine blessing or favour from that which pretends to no divinity but what it first received from him ? (5.) They shall herein give honour to God, and make it to appear that they know both his hand in his providence and his name in his word, and that they are brought to know his name by what they are made to know of his hand, *v.* 21. *This once,* now at length, they shall be made to know that which they would not be brought to know by all the pains the prophets took with them. Note, So stupid are we that nothing less than the mighty hand of divine grace, known experimentally, can make us know rightly the name of God as it is revealed to us.

4. Their deliverance out of captivity shall be a type and figure of the great salvation to

be wrought out by the Messiah, who shall *gather together in one the children of God that were scattered abroad.* And this is that which so far outshines the deliverance out of Egypt as even to eclipse the lustre of it, and make it even to be forgotten. To this some apply that of the *many fishers* and *hunters,* the preachers of the gospel, who were *fishers of men,* to enclose souls with the gospel net, to find them out *in every mountain* and *hill,* and secure them for Christ. Then the Gentiles came to God, some *from the ends of the earth,* and turned to the worship of him from the service of dumb idols.

CHAP. XVII.

In this chapter, I. God convicts the Jews of the sin of idolatry by the notorious evidence of the fact, and condemns them to captivity for it, ver. 1—4. II. He shows them the folly of all their carnal confidences, which should stand them in no stead when God's time came to contend with them, and that this was one of the sins upon which his controversy with them was grounded, ver. 5 —11. III. The prophet makes his appeal and address to God upon occasion of the malice of his enemies against him, committing himself to the divine protection, and begging of God to appear for him, ver. 12—18. IV. God, by the prophet, warns the people to keep holy the sabbath day, assuring them that, if they did, it should be the lengthening out of their tranquillity, but that, if not, God would by some desolating judgment assert the honour of his sabbaths, ver. 19—27.

THE sin of Judah *is* written with a pen of iron, *and* with the point of a diamond : *it is* graven upon the table of their heart, and upon the horns of your altars ; 2 Whilst their children remember their altars and their groves by the green trees upon the high hills. 3 O my mountain in the field, I will give thy substance *and* all thy treasures to the spoil, *and* thy high places for sin, throughout all thy borders. 4 And thou, even thyself, shalt discontinue from thine heritage that I gave thee ; and I will cause thee to serve thine enemies in the land which thou knowest not : for ye have kindled a fire in mine anger, *which* shall burn for ever.

The people had asked (ch. xvi. 10), *What is our iniquity, and what is our sin?* as if they could not be charged with any thing worth speaking of, for which God should enter into judgment with them ; their challenge was answered there, but here we have a further reply to it, in which,

I. The indictment is fully proved upon the prisoners, both the fact and the fault; their sin is too plain to be denied and too bad to be excused, and they have nothing to plead either in extenuation of the crime or in arrest and mitigation of the judgment. 1. They cannot plead *Not guilty,* for their sins are upon record in the book of God's omniscience and their own conscience ; nay, and they are obvious to the eye and observation of the world, *v.* 1, 2. They are *written* before God in the most legible and indelible characters, and *sealed among his treasures,*

never to be forgotten, Deut. xxxii. 34. They are written there with *a pen of iron and with the point of a diamond;* what is so written will not be worn out by time, but is, as Job speaks, *graven in the rock for ever.* Note, The sin of sinners is never forgotten till it is forgiven. It is ever before God, till by repentance it comes to be ever before us. *It is graven upon the table of their heart;* their own consciences witness against them, and are instead of a thousand witnesses. What is *graven on the heart,* though it may be covered and closed up for a time, yet, being graven, it cannot be erased, but will be produced in evidence when the books shall be opened. Nay, we need not appeal to the tables of the heart, perhaps they will not own the convictions of their consciences. We need go no further, for proof of the charge, than *the horns of their altars,* on which the blood of their idolatrous sacrifices was sprinkled, and perhaps the names of the idols to whose honour they were erected were inscribed. Their neighbours will witness against them, and all the creatures they have abused by using them in the service of their lusts. To complete the evidence, their own children shall be witnesses against them; they will tell truth when their fathers dissemble and prevaricate; they *remember the altars and the groves* to which their parents took them when they were little, *v.* 2. It appears that they were full of them, and acquainted with them betimes, they talked of them so frequently, so familiarly, and with so much delight. 2. They cannot plead that they repent, or are brought to a better mind. No, as the guilt of their sin is undeniable, so their inclination to sin is invincible and incurable. In this sense many understand *v.* 1, 2. Their sin is deeply *engraven* as with *a pen of iron in the tables of their hearts.* They have a rooted affection to it; it is woven into their very nature; their sin is dear to them, as that is dear to us of which we say, It is *engraven on our hearts.* The bias of their minds is still as strong as ever towards their idols, and they are not wrought upon either by the word or rod of God to forget them and abate their affection to them. It is written *upon the horns of their altars,* for they have given up their names to their idols and resolve to abide by what they have done; they have bound themselves, as with cords, to the horns of their altars. And *v.* 2 may be read fully to this sense : *As they remember their children, so remember they their altars and their groves;* they are as fond of them and take as much pleasure in them as men do in their own children, and are as loth to part with them; they will live and die with their idols, and can no more forget them than *a woman* can *forget her sucking child.*

II. The indictment being thus fully proved, the judgment is affirmed and the sentence ratified, *v.* 3, 4. Forasmuch as they are thus wedded to their sins, and will not part with them, 1. They shall be made to part with their treasures, and those shall be given into the hands of strangers. Jerusalem is God's *mountain in the field;* it was built on a hill in the midst of a plain. *All the treasures* of that wealthy city will God *give to the spoil.* Or, *My mountains with the fields, thy wealth and all thy treasures will I expose to spoil;* both the products of the country and the stores of the city shall be seized by the Chaldeans. Justly are men stripped of that which they have served their idols with and have made the food and fuel of their lusts. *My mountain* (so the whole land was, Ps. lxxviii. 54, Deut. xi. 11) you have turned into *your high places for sin,* have worshipped your idols upon *the high hills* (*v.* 2), and now they shall be *given for a spoil in all your borders.* What we make for a sin God will make for a spoil; for what comfort can we expect in that wherewith God is dishonoured? 2. They shall be made to part with their inheritance, with their real estates, as well as personal, and shall be carried captives into a strange land (*v.* 4) : *Thou, even thyself* (or *thou thyself and those that are in thee,* all the inhabitants), *shall discontinue from thy heritage that I gave thee.* God owns that it was their heritage, and that he gave it to them ; they had an unquestionable title to it, which was an aggravation of their folly in throwing themselves out of the possession of it. It is *through thyself* (so some read it), through thy own default, that thou art disseised. *Thou shalt discontinue,* or *intermit,* the occupation of thy land. The law appointed them to *let their land rest* (it is the word here used) one year in seven, Exod. xxiii. 11. They did not observe that law, and now God would compel them to *let it rest* (the land shall *enjoy her sabbaths,* Lev. xxvi. 34); and yet it shall be no rest to them ; they shall *serve their enemies in a land they know not.* Observe, (1.) Sin works a discontinuance of our comforts and deprives us of the enjoyment of that which God has given us. Yet, (2.) A discontinuance of the possession is not a defeasance of the right, but it is intimated that upon their repentance they shall recover possession again. For the present, *you have kindled a fire in my anger,* which burns so fiercely that it seems as if it would burn *for ever;* and so it will unless you repent, for it is the anger of an everlasting God fastening upon immortal souls, and *who knows the power of that anger ?*

5 Thus saith the Lord ; Cursed *be* the man that trusteth in man, and maketh flesh his arm, and whose heart departeth from the Lord. 6 For he shall be like the heath in the desert, and shall not see when good cometh ; but shall inhabit the parched places in the wilderness, *in* a salt land, and

not inhabited. 7 Blessed *is* the man that trusteth in the Lord, and whose hope the Lord is. 8 For he shall be as a tree planted by the waters, and *that* spreadeth out her roots by the river, and shall not see when heat cometh, but her leaf shall be green ; and shall not be careful in the year of drought, neither shall cease from yielding fruit. 9 The heart *is* deceitful above all *things,* and desperately wicked : Who can know it ? 10 I the Lord search the heart, *I* try the reins, even to give every man according to his ways, *and* according to the fruit of his doings. 11 *As* the partridge sitteth *on eggs,* and hatcheth *them* not ; *so* he that getteth riches, and not by right, shall leave them in the midst of his days, and at his end shall be a fool.

It is excellent doctrine that is preached in these verses, and of general concern and use to us all, and it does not appear to have any particular reference to the present state of Judah and Jerusalem. The prophet's sermons were not all prophetical, but some of them practical ; yet this discourse, which probably we have here only the heads of, would be of singular use to them by way of caution not to misplace their confidence in the day of their distress. Let us all learn what we are taught here,

I. Concerning the disappointment and vexation those will certainly meet with who depend upon creatures for success and relief when they are in trouble (*v.* 5, 6) : *Cursed be the man that trusts in man.* God pronounces him cursed for the affront he thereby puts upon him. Or, *Cursed* (that is, miserable) *is the man* that does so, for he leans upon a broken reed, which will not only fail him, but will *run into his hand and pierce it.* Observe, 1. The sin here condemned ; it is *trusting in man,* putting that confidence in the wisdom and power, the kindness and faithfulness, of men, which should be placed in those attributes of God only, making our applications to men as principal agents, whereas they are but instruments in the hand of Providence. It is *making flesh the arm* we stay upon, the arm we work with and with which we hope to work our point, the arm under which we shelter ourselves and on which we depend for protection. God is his people's *arm,* Isa. xxxiii. 2. We must not think to make any creature to be that to us which God has undertaken to be. Man is called *flesh,* to show the folly of those that make him their confidence ; he is flesh, weak and feeble as flesh without bones or sinews, that has no strength at all in it; he is inactive as flesh without spirit, which is a dead thing; he is mortal and dying as flesh, which soon putrefies and corrupts, and is continually wasting. Nay, he is false and sinful, and has lost his integrity; so his being flesh signifies, Gen. vi. 3. 2. The great malignity there is in this sin; it is the *departure of the evil heart of unbelief from the living God.* Those that trust in man perhaps draw nigh to God with their mouth and honour him with their lips, they call him their hope and say that they trust in him, but really *their heart departs from him;* they distrust him, despise him, and decline a correspondence with him. Cleaving to the cistern is leaving the fountain, and is resented accordingly. 3. The fatal consequences of this sin. He that puts a confidence in man puts a cheat upon himself; for (*v.* 6) *he shall be like the heath in the desert,* a sorry shrub, the product of barren ground, sapless, useless, and worthless; his comforts shall all fail him and his hopes be blasted; he shall wither, be dejected in himself and trampled on by all about him. *When good comes he shall not see* it, he shall not share in it; when the times mend they shall not mend with him, but he shall *inhabit the parched places in the wilderness;* his expectation shall be continually frustrated; when others have a harvest he shall have none. Those that trust to their own righteousness and strength, and think they can do well enough without the merit and grace of Christ, thus *make flesh their arm,* and their souls cannot prosper in graces or comforts; they can neither produce the fruits of acceptable services to God nor reap the fruits of saving blessings from him; they *dwell in a dry land.*

II. Concerning the abundant satisfaction which those have, and will have, who make God their confidence, who live by faith in his providence and promise, who refer themselves to him and his guidance at all times and repose themselves in him and his love in the most unquiet times, *v.* 7, 8. Observe, 1. The duty required of us—to *trust in the Lord,* to do our duty to him and then depend upon him to bear us out in doing it—when creatures and second causes either deceive or threaten us, either are false to us or fierce against us, to commit ourselves to God as all-sufficient both to fill up the place of those who fail us and to protect us from those who set upon us. It is to *make the Lord our hope,* his favour the good we hope for and his power the strength we hope in. 2. The comfort that attends the doing of this duty. He that does so shall be *as a tree planted by the waters,* a choice tree, about which great care has been taken to set it in the best soil, so far from being like *the heath in the wilderness;* he shall be like a tree that *spreads out its roots,* and thereby is firmly fixed, spreads them out *by the rivers,* whence it draws abundance of sap, which denotes

both the establishment and the comfort which those have who make God their hope; they are easy, they are pleasant, and enjoy a continual security and serenity of mind. A tree thus planted, thus watered, shall *not see when heat comes,* shall not sustain any damage from the most scorching heats of summer; it is so well moistened from its roots that it shall be sufficiently guarded against drought. Those that make God their hope, (1.) They shall flourish in credit and comfort, like a tree that is *always green,* whose leaf does not wither; they shall be cheerful to themselves and beautiful in the eyes of others. Those who thus give honour to God by giving him credit God will put honour upon, and make them the ornament and delight of the places where they live, as green trees are. (2.) They shall be fixed in an inward peace and satisfaction: They *shall not be careful in a year of drought,* when there is want of rain; for, as the tree has *seed in itself,* so it has *its moisture.* Those who make God their hope have enough in him to make up the want of all creature-comforts. We need not be solicitous about the breaking of a cistern as long as we have the fountain. (3.) They shall be fruitful in holiness, and in all good works. Those who trust in God, and by faith derive strength and grace from him, *shall not cease from yielding fruit;* they shall still be enabled to do that which will redound to the glory of God, the benefit of others, and their own account.

III. Concerning the sinfulness of man's heart, and the divine inspection it is always under, *v.* 9, 10. It is folly to trust in man, for he is not only frail, but false and deceitful. We are apt to think that we trust in God, and are entitled to the blessings here promised to those who do so. But this is a thing about which our own hearts deceive us as much as any thing. We think that we trust in God when really we do not, as appears by this, that our hopes and fears rise or fall according as second causes smile or frown.

1. It is true in general. (1.) There is that wickedness in our hearts which we ourselves are not aware of and do not suspect to be there; nay, it is a common mistake among the children of men to think themselves, their own hearts at least, a great deal better than they really are. *The heart,* the conscience of man, in his corrupt and fallen state, *is deceitful above all things.* It is subtle and false; it is apt to *supplant* (so the word properly signifies); it is that from which Jacob had his name, a *supplanter.* It calls evil good and good evil, puts false colours upon things, and cries peace to those to whom peace does not belong. When men say in their hearts (that is, suffer their hearts to whisper to them) that there is no God, or he does not see, or he will not require, or they shall have peace though they go on; in these, and a thousand similar suggestions,

the heart is deceitful. It cheats men into their own ruin; and this will be the aggravation of it, that they are self-deceivers, self-destroyers. Herein the heart is *desperately wicked;* it is deadly, it is desperate. The case is bad indeed, and in a manner deplorable and past relief, if the conscience which should rectify the errors of the other faculties is itself a mother of falsehood and a ringleader in the delusion. What will become of a man if that in him which should be *the candle of the Lord* give a false light, if God's deputy in the soul, that is entrusted to support his interests, betrays them? Such is the deceitfulness of the heart that we may truly say, *Who can know it?* Who can describe how bad the heart is? We cannot know our own hearts, not what they will do in an hour of temptation (Hezekiah did not, Peter did not), not what corrupt dispositions there are in them, nor in how many things they have turned aside; who can understand his errors? Much less can we know the hearts of others, or have any dependence upon them. But, (2.) Whatever wickedness there is in the heart God sees it, and knows it, is perfectly acquainted with it and apprised of it: *I the Lord search the heart.* This is true of all that is in the heart, all the thoughts of it, the quickest, and those that are most carelessly overlooked by ourselves —all the intents of it, the closest, and those that are most artfully disguised, and industriously concealed from others. Men may be imposed upon, but God cannot. He not only searches the heart with a piercing eye, but he tries the reins, to pass a judgment upon what he discovers, to give every thing its true character and due weight. He tries it, as the gold is tried whether it be standard or no, as the prisoner is tried whether he be guilty or no. And this judgment which he makes of the heart is in order to his passing judgment upon the man; it is *to give to every man according to his ways* (according to the desert and the tendency of them, life to those that walked in the ways of life, and death to those that persisted in *the paths of the destroyer) and according to the fruit of his doings,* the effect and influence his doings have had upon others, or according to what is settled by the word of God to be the fruit of men's doings, blessings to the obedient and curses to the disobedient. Note, *Therefore* God is *Judge himself,* and he alone, because he, and none besides, knows the hearts of the children of men.

2. It is true especially of all the deceitfulness and wickedness of the heart, all its corrupt devices, desires, and designs. God observes and discerns them; and (which is more than any man can do) he judges of the overt act by the heart. Note, God knows more evil of us than we do of ourselves, which is a good reason why we should not flatter ourselves, but always stand in awe of the judgment of God.

IV. Concerning the curse that attends wealth unjustly gotten. Fraud and violence had been reigning crying sins in Judah and Jerusalem; now the prophet would have those who had been guilty of these sins, and were now stripped of all they had, to read their sin in their punishment (*v.* 11): *He that gets riches and not by right,* though he may make them his hope, shall never have joy of them. Observe, It is possible that those who use unlawful means to get wealth may succeed therein and prosper for a time; and it is a temptation to many to defraud and oppress their neighbours when there is money to be got by it. He who has got *treasures* by *vanity* and a *lying tongue* may hug himself in his success, and say, *I am rich;* nay, and I am innocent too (Hos. xii. 8), but *he shall leave them in the midst of his days;* they shall be taken from him, or he from them; God shall cut him off with some surprising stroke then when he says, *Soul, take thy ease, thou hast goods laid up for many years,* Luke xii. 19, 20. He shall leave them to he knows not whom, and shall not be able to take any of his riches away with him. It intimates what a great vexation it is to a worldly man at death that he must leave his riches behind him; and justly may it be a terror to those who got them unjustly, for, though the wealth will not follow them to another world, the guilt will, and the torment of an everlasting, *Son, remember,* Luke xvi. 25. Thus, *at his end, he shall be a fool,* a Nabal, whose wealth did him no good, which he had so sordidly hoarded, when *his heart* became *dead as a stone.* He was a fool all along; sometimes perhaps his own conscience told him so, but *at his end* he will appear to be so. Those are fools indeed who are fools in *their latter end;* and such multitudes will prove who were applauded as *wise men,* that did *well for themselves,* Ps. xlix. 13, 18. Those that get grace will be wise *in the latter end,* will have the comfort of it in death and the benefit of it to eternity (Prov. xix. 20); but those that place their happiness in the wealth of the world, and, right or wrong, *will be rich,* will rue the folly of it when it is too late to rectify the fatal mistake. This is like *the partridge that sits on eggs and hatches them not,* but they are broken (as Job xxxix. 15), or stolen (as Isa. x. 14), or they become addle: some sort of fowl there was, well known among the Jews, whose case this commonly was. The rich man takes a great deal of pains to get an estate together, and sits brooding upon it, but never has any comfort nor satisfaction in it; his projects to enrich himself by sinful courses miscarry and come to nothing. Let us therefore be wise in time—what we get to get it honestly, and what we have to use it charitably, that we may lay up in store a good foundation and be wise for eternity.

12 A glorious high throne from the

beginning *is* the place of our sanctuary. 13 O LORD, the hope of Israel, all that forsake thee shall be ashamed, *and* they that depart from me shall be written in the earth, because they have forsaken the LORD, the fountain of living waters. 14 Heal me, O LORD, and I shall be healed; save me, and I shall be saved: for thou *art* my praise. 15 Behold, they say unto me, Where *is* the word of the LORD? let it come now. 16 As for me, I have not hastened from *being* a pastor to follow thee: neither have I desired the woeful day; thou knowest: that which came out of my lips was *right* before thee. 17 Be not a terror unto me: thou *art* my hope in the day of evil. 18 Let them be confounded that persecute me, but let not me be confounded: let them be dismayed, but let not me be dismayed: bring upon them the day of evil, and destroy them with double destruction.

Here, as often before, we have the prophet retired for private meditation, and *alone with God.* Those ministers that would have comfort in their work must be much so. In his converse here with God and his own heart he takes the liberty which devout souls sometimes use in their soliloquies, to pass from one thing to another, without tying themselves too strictly to the laws of method and coherence.

I. He acknowledges the great favour of God to his people in setting up a revealed religion among them, and dignifying them with divine institutions (*v.* 12): *A glorious high throne from the beginning is the place of our sanctuary.* The temple at Jerusalem, where God manifested his special presence, where the lively oracles were lodged, where the people paid their homage to their Sovereign, and whither they fled for refuge in distress, was the *place of their sanctuary.* That was a *glorious high throne.* It was a throne of holiness, which made it truly glorious; it was God's throne, which made it truly high. Jerusalem is called *the city of the great King,* not only Israel's King, but the King of the whole earth, so that it might justly be deemed the metropolis, or royal city, of the world. It was *from the beginning* so, from the first projecting of it by David and building of it by Solomon, 2 Chron. ii. 9. It was the honour of Israel that God set up such a glorious throne among them. *As the glorious and high throne* (that is, heaven) *is the place of our sanctuary;* so some read it. Note, All good men have a high value and veneration for the ordi-

nances of God, and reckon the place of the sanctuary a glorious high throne. Jeremiah here mentions this either as a plea with God for mercy to their land, in honour of the *throne of his glory* (*ch.* xiv. 21), or as an aggravation of the sin of his people in forsaking God though his throne was among them, and so profaning his crown and the place of his sanctuary.

II. He acknowledges the righteousness of God in abandoning those to ruin that forsook him and revolted from their allegiance to him, *v.* 13. He speaks it to God, as subscribing both to the certainty and to the equity of it: *O Lord! the hope of* those in Israel that adhere to thee, *all that forsake thee shall be ashamed.* They must of necessity be so, for they forsake thee for lying vanities, which will deceive them and make them ashamed. They will be ashamed, for they shame themselves. They will justly be put to shame, for they have forsaken him who alone can keep them in countenance when troubles come. *Let them be ashamed* (so some read it); and so it is a pious imprecation of the wrath of God upon them, or a petition for his grace, to make them penitently ashamed. *" Those that depart from me,* from the word of God which I have preached, do in effect depart from God;" as those that return to God are said to return to the prophet, *ch.* xv. 19. *Those that depart from thee* (so some read it) *shall be written in the earth.* They shall soon be blotted out, as that is which is written in the dust. They shall be trampled upon and exposed to contempt. They belong to the earth, and shall be numbered among earthly people, who lay up their treasure on earth and whose names are not *written in heaven.* And they deserve to be thus written with the fools in Israel, that their folly may be made manifest unto all, because they have *forsaken the Lord, the fountain of living waters* (that is, spring waters), and that for broken cisterns. Note, God is to all that are his a *fountain of living waters.* There is a fulness of comfort in him, an over-flowing ever-flowing fulness, like that of a fountain; it is always fresh, and clear, and clean, like spring water, while the pleasures of sin are puddle-waters. They are free to it; it is not a *fountain sealed.* They deserve therefore to be condemned, as Adam, to *red earth,* to which by the corruption of their nature they are allied, because they have forsaken the *garden of the Lord,* which is so well watered. Those that depart from God are *written in the earth.*

III. He prays to God for healing saving mercy for himself. " If the case of those that depart from God be so miserable, let me always draw nigh to him (Ps. lxxiii. 27, 28), and, in order to that, Lord, *heal me,* and *save me, v.* 14. Heal my backslidings, my bent to backslide, and save me from being carried away by the strength of the stream to forsake thee." He was wounded in spirit with grief upon many accounts. "Lord, *heal me* with thy comforts, and make me easy." He was continually exposed to the malice of unreasonable men. "Lord, *save me* from them, and let me not fall into their wicked hands. *Heal me*, that is, sanctify me by thy grace; *save me*, that is, bring me to thy glory." All that shall be saved hereafter are sanctified now; unless the disease of sin be purged out the soul cannot live. To enforce this petition he pleads, 1. The firm belief he had of God's power: *Heal thou me, and then I shall be healed;* the cure will certainly be wrought if thou undertake it; it will be a thorough cure and not a palliative one. Those that come to God to be healed ought to be abundantly satisfied in the all-sufficiency of their physician. *Save me*, and *then I shall* certainly *be saved*, be my dangers and enemies ever so threatening. If God hold us up, we shall live; if he protect us, we shall be safe. 2. The sincere regard he had to God's glory: "*For thou art my praise*, and for that reason I desire to be healed and saved, *that I may live and praise thee*, Ps. cxix. 175. Thou art he whom I praise, and the praise due to thee I never gave to another. Thou art he whom I glory in, and boast of, for on thee do I depend. Thou art he that furnishes me with continual matter for praise, and I have given thee the praise of the favours already bestowed upon me. *Thou shalt be my praise*" (so some read it); "heal me, and save me, and thou shalt have the glory of it. *My praise shall be continually of thee*," Ps. lxxi. 6; lxxix. 13.

IV. He complains of the infidelity and daring impiety of the people to whom he preached. It greatly troubled him, and he shows before God this trouble, as the servant that had slights put upon him by the guests he was sent to invite *came and showed his Lord these things*. He had faithfully delivered God's message to them; and what answer has he to return to him that sent him? *Behold, they say unto me, Where is the word of the Lord? Let it come now, v.* 15; Isa. v. 19. They bantered the prophet, and made a jest of that which he delivered with the greatest seriousness. 1. They denied the truth of what he said: "If that be the *word of the Lord* which thou speakest to us, *where is it?* Why is it not fulfilled?" Thus the patience of God was impudently abused as a ground to question his veracity. 2. They defied the terror of what he said. "Let God Almighty do his worst; let all he has said come to pass; we shall do well enough; the lion is not so fierce as he is painted," Amos v. 18. "Lord, to what purpose is it to speak to men that will neither believe nor fear?"

V. He appeals to God concerning his faithful discharge of the duty to which he was called, *v.* 16. The people did all they could to make him weary of his work, to

exasperate him and make him uneasy, and to tempt him to prevaricate and alter his message for fear of displeasing them; but, "Lord," says he, "*thou knowest* I have not yielded to them." 1. He continued constant to his work. His office, instead of being his credit and protection, exposed him to reproach, contempt, and injury. "Yet," says he, "*I have not hastened from being a pastor after thee;* I have not left my work, nor sued for a discharge or a *quietus*." Prophets were pastors to the people, to feed them with the good word of God; but they were to be *pastors after God*, and all ministers must be so, *according to his heart* (ch. iii. 15), to follow him and the directions and instructions he gives. Such a pastor Jeremiah was; and, though he met with as much difficulty and discouragement as ever any man did, yet he did not fly off as Jonah did, nor desire to be excused from going any more on God's errands. Note, Those that are employed for God, though their success answer not their expectations, must not therefore throw up their commission, but continue to follow God, though the storm be in their faces. 2. He kept up his affection to the people. Though they were very abusive to him, he was compassionate to them: *I have not desired the woeful day.* The day of the accomplishment of his prophecies would be a woeful day indeed to Jerusalem, and therefore he deprecated it, and wished it might never come, though, as to himself, it would be the avenging of him upon his persecutors and the proving of him a true prophet (which they had questioned, *v.* 15), and upon those accounts he might be tempted to desire it. Note, God does not, and therefore ministers must not, desire the death of sinners, but rather that they may turn and live. Though we warn of the woeful day, we must not wish for it, but rather weep because of it, as Jeremiah did. 3. He kept closely to his instructions. Though he might have curried favour with the people, or at least have avoided their displeasure, if he had not been so sharp in his reproofs and severe in his threatenings, yet he would deliver his message faithfully; and that he had done so was a comfort to him. "Lord, *thou knowest that that which came out of my lips was right before thee;* it exactly agreed with what I received from thee, and therefore thou art reflected upon in their quarrelling with me." Note, If what we say and do be right before God, we may easily despise the reproaches and censures of men. *It is a small thing to be judged of their judgment.*

VI. He humbly begs of God that he would own him, and protect him, and carry him on cheerfully in that work to which God had so plainly called him and to which he had so sincerely devoted himself. Two things he here desires:—1. That he might have comfort in serving the God that sent him (*v.* 17) : *Be not thou a terror to me.* Surely more is implied than is expressed. "Be thou a comfort to me, and let thy favour rejoice my heart and encourage me, when my enemies do all they can to terrify me and either to drive me from my work or to make me drive on heavily in it." Note, The best have that in them which might justly make God a terror to them, as he was for some time to Job (*ch.* vi. 4), to Asaph (Ps. lxxvii. 3), to Heman, Ps. lxxxviii. 15. And this is that which good men, *knowing the terrors of the Lord,* dread and deprecate more than any thing; nay, whatever frightful accidents may befal them, or how formidable soever their enemies may appear to them, they can do well enough so long as God is not a terror to them. He pleads, "*Thou art my hope;* and then nothing else is my fear, no, not *in the day of evil,* when it is most threatening, most pressing. My dependence is upon thee; and therefore *be not a terror to me.*" Note, Those that by faith make God their confidence shall have him for their comfort in the worst of times, if it be not their own fault : if we make him our trust, we shall not find him our terror. 2. That he might have courage in dealing with the people to whom he was sent, *v.* 18. Those persecuted him who should have entertained and encouraged him. "Lord," says he, "*let them be confounded* (let them be overpowered by the convictions of the word and made ashamed of their obstinacy, or else let the judgments threatened be at length executed upon them), *but let not me be confounded,* let not me be terrified by their menaces, so as to betray my trust." Note, God's ministers have work to do which they need not be either ashamed or afraid to go on in, but they do need to be helped by the divine grace *to go on in it* without shame or fear. Jeremiah had not desired the woeful day upon his country in general; but as to his persecutors, in a just and holy indignation at their malice, he prays, *Bring upon them the day of evil,* in hope that the bringing of it upon them might prevent the bringing of it upon the country; if they were taken away, the people would be better; "therefore *destroy them with a double destruction;* let them be utterly destroyed, root and branch, and let the prospect of that destruction be their present confusion." This the prophet prays, not at all that he might be avenged, nor so much that he might be eased, but that *the Lord* may be *known by the judgments which he executes.*

19 Thus said the LORD unto me; Go and stand in the gate of the children of the people, whereby the kings of Judah come in, and by the which they go out, and in all the gates of Jerusalem; 20 And say unto them, Hear ye the word of the LORD, ye kings of Judah, and all Judah, and all the inhabitants of Jerusalem, that enter in by these gates : 21 Thus saith the LORD; Take heed to yourselves, and bear no burden on the sabbath-day, nor bring *it* in by the gates of Jerusalem; 22 Neither carry forth a burden out of your houses on the sabbath-day, neither do ye any work, but hallow ye the sabbath-day, as I commanded your fathers. 23 But they obeyed not, neither inclined their ear, but made their neck stiff, that they might not hear, nor receive instruction. 24 And it shall come to pass, if ye diligently hearken unto me, saith the LORD, to bring in no burden through the gates of this city on the sabbath-day, but hallow the sabbath-day, to do no work therein; 25 Then shall there enter into the gates of this city kings and princes sitting upon the throne of David, riding in chariots and on horses, they, and their princes, the men of Judah, and the inhabitants of Jerusalem : and this city shall remain for ever. 26 And they shall come from the cities of Judah, and from the places about Jerusalem, and from the land of Benjamin, and from the plain, and from the mountains, and from the south, bringing burnt-offerings, and sacrifices, and meat-offerings, and incense, and bringing sacrifices of praise, unto the house of the LORD. 27 But if ye will not hearken unto me to hallow the sabbath-day, and not to bear a burden, even entering in at the gates of Jerusalem on the sabbath-day; then will I kindle a fire in the gates thereof, and it shall devour the palaces of Jerusalem, and it shall not be quenched.

These verses are a sermon concerning sabbath-sanctification. It is a word which the prophet *received from the Lord,* and was ordered to deliver in the most solemn and public manner to the people; for they were sent not only to reprove sin, and to press obedience, in general, but they must descend to particulars. This message concerning the sabbath was probably sent in the days of Josiah, for the furtherance of that work of reformation which he set on foot; for the promises here (*v.* 25, 26) are such as I think we scarcely find when things come nearer to the extremity. This message

must be proclaimed in all the places of concourse, and therefore in *the gates*, not only
because through them people were continually passing and repassing, but because
in them they kept their courts and laid up
their stores. It must be proclaimed (as the
king or queen is usually proclaimed) at the
court-gate first, the gate *by which the kings
of Judah come in and go out, v.* 19. Let
them be told their duty first, particularly
this duty; for, if sabbaths be not sanctified
as they should be, *the rulers of Judah are to
be contended with* (so they were, Neh. xiii.
17), for they are certainly wanting in their
duty. He must also preach it *in all the
gates of Jerusalem.* It is a matter of great
and general concern; therefore let all take
notice of it. Let the *kings of Judah* hear the
word of the Lord (for, high as they are, he
is above them), *and all the inhabitants of
Jerusalem*, for, mean as they are, he takes
notice of them, and of what they say and do
on sabbath days. Observe,

I. How the sabbath is to be sanctified,
and what is the law concerning it, *v.* 21, 22.
1. They must rest from their worldly employment on the sabbath day, must do no
servile work. They must *bear no burden*
into the city nor out of it, into their houses
nor out of them; husbandmen's burdens of
corn must not be carried in, nor manure
carried out; nor must tradesmen's burdens
of wares or merchandises be imported or exported. There must not a loaded horse, or
cart, or waggon, be seen on the sabbath
day either in the streets or in the roads; the
porters must not ply on that day, nor must
the servants be suffered to fetch in provisions
or fuel. It is a day of rest, and must not be
made a day of labour, unless in case of necessity. 2. They must apply themselves to
that which is the proper work and business
of the day: "*Hallow you the sabbath*, that
is, consecrate it to the honour of God and
spend it in his service and worship." It is
in order to this that worldly business must
be laid aside, that we may be entire for, and
intent upon, that work, which requires and
deserves the whole man. 3. They must
herein be very circumspect: "*Take heed to
yourselves*, watch against every thing that
borders upon the profanation of the sabbath."
Where God is jealous we must be cautious.
"*Take heed to yourselves*, for it is at your
peril if you rob God of that part of your
time which he has reserved to himself."
Take heed to your souls (so the word is); in
order to the right sanctifying of sabbaths,
we must look well to the frame of our spirits
and have a watchful eye upon all the motions of the inward man. Let not the soul
be burdened with the cares of this world on
sabbath days, but let that be employed, even
all that is within us, in the work of the day.
And, 4. He refers them to the law, the
statute in this case made and provided:
"This is no new imposition upon you, but

is what *I commanded your fathers; it is an*
ancient law; it was an article of the original
contract; nay, it was a command to the
patriarchs."

II. How the sabbath had been profaned
(*v.* 23): "Your fathers were required to
keep holy the sabbath day, *but they obeyed
not; they hardened their necks* against this
as well as other commands that were given
them." This is mentioned to show that
there needed a reformation in this matter,
and that God had a just controversy with
them for the long transgression of this law
which they had been guilty of. They hardened their necks against this command, that
they might not hear and receive instruction
concerning other commands. Where sabbaths are neglected all religion sensibly goes
to decay.

III. What blessings God had in store for
them if they would make conscience of sabbath-sanctification. Though their fathers
had been guilty of the profanation of the
sabbath they should not only not smart for
it, but their city and nation should recover
its ancient glory, if they would keep sabbaths better, *v.* 24—26. Let them take care
to *hallow the sabbath* and *do no work therein;* and then, 1. The court shall flourish.
Kings in succession, or the many branches of
the royal family at the same time, all as great
as kings, with the other *princes* that *sit upon
the thrones* of judgment, *the thrones of the
house of David* (Ps. cxxii. 5), shall ride in
great pomp *through the gates of Jerusalem*,
some in chariots and some on horses,
attended with a numerous retinue of the
men of Judah. Note, The honour of the
government is the joy of the kingdom; and
the support of religion would contribute
greatly to both. 2. The city shall flourish.
Let there be a face of religion kept up in
Jerusalem, by sabbath-sanctification, that it
may answer to its title, *the holy city*, and then
it *shall remain for ever, shall for ever be inhabited* (so the word may be rendered); it
shall not be destroyed and dispeopled, as it
is threatened to be. Whatever supports religion tends to establish the civil interests of
a land. 3. The country shall flourish: *The
cities of Judah and the land of Benjamin* shall
be replenished with vast numbers of inhabitants, and those abounding in plenty
and living in peace, which will appear by
the multitude and value of their offerings,
which they shall present to God. By this
the flourishing of a country may be judged
of, What does it do for the honour of God?
Those that starve their religion either are
poor or are in a fair way to be so. 4. The
church shall flourish: *Meat-offerings, and
incense, and sacrifices of praise*, shall be
brought *to the house of the Lord*, for the
maintenance of the service of that house
and the servants that attend it. God's insti-
tutions shall be conscientiously observed; no sacrifice nor incense shall be offered to

idols, nor alienated from God, but every thing shall go in the right channel. They shall have both occasion and hearts to bring sacrifices of praise to God. This is made an instance of their prosperity. Then a people truly flourish when religion flourishes among them. And this is the effect of sabbath-sanctification; when that branch of religion is kept up other instances of it are kept up likewise; but, when that is lost, devotion is lost either in superstition or in profaneness. It is a true observation, which some have made, that the streams of all religion run either deep or shallow according as the banks of the sabbath are kept up or neglected.

IV. What judgments they must expect would come upon them if they persisted in the profanation of the sabbath (v. 27): "*If you will not hearken to me* in this matter, to keep the gates shut on sabbath days, so that there may be no unnecessary *entering in*, or going out, on that day—if you will break through the enclosure of the divine law, and lay that day in common with other days—know that God will *kindle a fire in the gates* of your city," intimating that it shall be kindled by an enemy besieging the city and assaulting the gates, who shall take this course to force an entrance. Justly shall those gates be fired that are not used as they ought to be to shut out sin and to keep people in to an attendance on their duty. This fire shall devour even *the palaces of Jerusalem*, where the princes and nobles dwelt, who did not use their power and interest as they ought to have done to keep up the honour of God's sabbaths; but *it shall not be quenched* until it has laid the whole city in ruins. This was fulfilled by the army of the Chaldeans, *ch.* lii. 13. The profanation of the sabbath is a sin for which God has often contended with a people by fire.

CHAP. XVIII.

In this chapter we have, I. A general declaration of God's ways in dealing with nations and kingdoms, that he can easily do what he will with them, as easily as the potter can with the clay (ver. 1—6), but that he certainly will do what is just and fair with them. If he threaten their ruin, yet upon their repentance he will return in mercy to them, and, when he is coming towards them in mercy, nothing but their sin will stop the progress of his favours, ver. 7—10. II. A particular demonstration of the folly of the men of Judah and Jerusalem in departing from their God to idols, and so bringing ruin upon themselves notwithstanding the fair warnings given them and God's kind intentions towards them, ver. 11—17. III. The prophet's complaint to God of the base ingratitude and unreasonable malice of his enemies, persecutors, and slanderers, and his prayers against them, ver. 18—23.

THE word which came to Jeremiah from the LORD, saying, 2 Arise, and go down to the potter's house, and there I will cause thee to hear my words. 3 Then I went down to the potter's house, and, behold he wrought a work on the wheels. 4 And the vessel that he made of clay was marred in the hand of the potter: so he made it again another vessel, as seemed good to the potter to make *it*.

5 Then the word of the LORD came to me, saying, 6 O house of Israel, cannot I do with you as this potter? saith the LORD. Behold, as the clay *is* in the potter's hand, so *are* ye in mine hand, O house of Israel. 7 *At what* instant I shall speak concerning a nation, and concerning a kingdom, to pluck up, and to pull down, and to destroy *it;* 8 If that nation, against whom I have pronounced, turn from their evil, I will repent of the evil that I thought to do unto them. 9 And *at what* instant I shall speak concerning a nation, and concerning a kingdom, to build and to plant *it;* 10 If it do evil in my sight, that it obey not my voice, then I will repent of the good, wherewith I said I would benefit them.

The prophet is here sent to *the potter's house* (he knew where to find it), not to preach a sermon as before to the gates of Jerusalem, but to prepare a sermon, or rather to receive it ready prepared. Those needed not to study their sermons that had them, as he had this, by immediate inspiration. "*Go to the potter's house*, and observe how he manages his work, and there *I will cause thee*, by silent whispers, *to hear my words*. There thou shalt receive a message, to be delivered to the people." Note, Those that would know God's mind must observe his appointments, and attend where they may hear his words. The prophet was never *disobedient to the heavenly vision*, and therefore went to the potter's house (v. 3) and took notice how he *wrought his work upon the wheels*, just as he pleased, with a great deal of ease, and in a little time. And (v. 4) when a lump of clay that he designed to form into one shape either proved too stiff, or had a stone in it, or some way or other came to be *marred in his hand*, he presently turned it into another shape; if it will not serve for a vessel of honour, it will serve for a vessel of dishonour, just *as seems good to the potter*. It is probable that Jeremiah knew well enough how the potter wrought his work, and how easily he threw it into what form he pleased; but he must go and observe it *now*, that, having the idea of it fresh in his mind, he might the more readily and distinctly apprehend that truth which God designed thereby to represent to him, and might the more intelligently explain it to the people. God *used similitudes by his servants the prophets* (Hos. xii. 10), and it was requisite that they should themselves understand the similitudes they used. Ministers will make a good use of their converse with the business and affairs of this life if they learn thereby to speak more plainly and familiarly

525

to people about the things of God, and to expound scripture comparisons. For they ought to make all their knowledge some way or other serviceable to their profession.

Now let us see what the message is which Jeremiah receives, and is entrusted with the delivery of, at the potter's house. While he looks carefully upon the potter's work, God darts into his mind these two great truths, which he must preach to *the house of Israel :—*

I. That God has both an incontestable authority and an irresistible ability to form and fashion kingdoms and nations as he pleases, so as to serve his own purposes: *" Cannot I do with you as this potter, saith the Lord? v.* 6. Have not I as absolute a power over you in respect both of might and of right?" Nay, God has a clearer title to a dominion over us than the potter has over the clay ; for the potter only gives it its form, whereas we have both matter and form from God. *As the clay is in the potter's hand* to be moulded and shaped as he pleases, *so are you in my hand.* This intimates, 1. That God has an incontestable sovereignty over us, is not debtor to us, may dispose of us as he thinks fit, and is not accountable to us, and that it would be as absurd for us to dispute this as for the clay to quarrel with the potter. 2. That it is a very easy thing with God to make what use he pleases of us and what changes he pleases with us, and that we cannot resist him. One turn of the hand, one turn of the wheel, quite alters the shape of the clay, makes it a vessel, unmakes it, new-makes it. Thus are our times in God's hand, and not in our own, and it is in vain for us to strive with him. It is spoken here of nations ; the most politic, the most potent, are what God is pleased to make them, and no other. See this explained by Job (*ch.* xii. 23), *He increaseth the nations and destroyeth them ; he enlargeth the nations and straiteneth them again.* See Ps. cvii. 33, &c., and compare Job xxxiv. 29. *All nations before God are as the drop of the bucket,* soon wiped away, *or the small dust of the balance,* soon blown away (Isa. xl. 15), and therefore, no doubt, as easily managed as the clay by the potter. 3. That God will not be a loser by any in his glory, at long run, but, if he be not glorified by them, he will be glorified upon them. If the potter's vessel be marred for one use, it shall serve for another ; those that will not be monuments of mercy shall be monuments of justice. *The Lord has made all things for himself, yea, even the wicked for the day of evil,* Prov. xvi. 4. God formed us out of the clay (Job xxxiii. 6), nay, and we are still as clay in his hands (Isa. lxiv. 8) ; and has not he the same power over us that the potter has over the clay? (Rom. ix. 21), and are not we bound to submit, as the clay to the potter's wisdom and will ? Isa. xxix. 15, 16 ; xlv. 9.

526

II. That, in the exercise of this authority and ability, he always goes by fixed rules of equity and goodness. He dispenses favours indeed in a way of sovereignty, but never punishes by arbitrary power. *High is his right hand,* yet he rules not with a *high hand,* but, as it follows there, *Justice and judgment are the habitation of his throne,* Ps. lxxxix. 13, 14. God asserts his despotic power, and tells us what he might do, but at the same time assures us that he will act as a righteous and merciful Judge. 1. When God is coming against us in ways of judgment we may be sure that it is for our sins, which shall appear by this, that national repentance will stop the progress of the judgments (*v.* 7, 8) : *If God speak concerning a nation to pluck up* its fences that secure it, and so lay it open, its fruit-trees that adorn and enrich it, and so leave it desolate—to pull down its fortifications, that the enemy may have liberty to enter in, its habitations, that the inhabitants may be under a necessity of going out, and so *destroy it* as either a vineyard or a city is destroyed—in this case, if *that nation* take the alarm, repent of their sins and reform their lives, turn every one from his evil way and return to God, God will graciously accept them, will not proceed in his controversy, will return in mercy to them, and, though he cannot change his mind, he will change his way, so that it may be said, He *repents him of the evil he said he would do to them.* Thus often in the time of the Judges, when the oppressed people were penitent people, still God raised them up saviours ; and, when they turned to God, their affairs immediately took a new turn. It was Nineveh's case, and we wish it had oftener been Jerusalem's ; see 2 Chron. vii. 14. It is an undoubted truth that a sincere conversion from the evil of sin will be an effectual prevention of the evil of punishment ; and God can as easily raise up a penitent people from their ruins as the potter can make anew the vessel of clay when it was *marred in his hand.* 2. When God is coming towards us in ways of mercy, if any stop be given to the progress of that mercy, it is nothing but sin that gives it (*v.* 9, 10) : *If God speak concerning a nation to build and to plant it,* to advance and establish all the true interests of it, it is *his husbandry* and *his building* (1 Cor. iii. 9), and, if he speak in favour of it, it is done, it is increased, it is enriched, it is enlarged, its trade flourishes, its government is settled in good hands, and all its affairs prosper and its enterprises succeed. But if this nation, which God is thus loading with benefits, *do evil in his sight* and *obey not his voice,*—if it lose its virtue, and become debauched and profane,—if religion grow into contempt, and vice get to be fashionable, and so be kept in countenance and reputation, and there be a general decay of serious godliness among them,—then God will turn his hand against them, will pluck up what he was planting, and pull down what he was building (*ch.* xlv. 4); the good work that was in the doing shall stand still and be let fall, and what favours were further designed shall be withheld; and this is called his *repenting of the good wherewith he said he would benefit them*, as he changed his purpose concerning Eli's house (1 Sam. ii. 30) and hurried Israel back into the wilderness when he had brought them within sight of Canaan. Note, Sin is the great mischief-maker between God and a people; it forfeits the benefit of his promises and spoils the success of their prayers. It defeats his kind intentions concerning them (Hos. vii. 1) and baffles their pleasing expectations from him. It ruins their comforts, prolongs their grievances, brings them into straits, and retards their deliverances, Isa. lix. 1, 2.

11 Now therefore go to, speak to the men of Judah, and to the inhabitants of Jerusalem, saying, Thus saith the LORD; Behold, I frame evil against you, and devise a device against you: return ye now every one from his evil way, and make your ways and your doings good. 12 And they said, There is no hope: but we will walk after our own devices, and we will every one do the imagination of his evil heart. 13 Therefore thus saith the LORD; Ask ye now among the heathen, who hath heard such things: the virgin of Israel hath done a very horrible thing. 14 Will *a man* leave the snow of Lebanon *which cometh* from the rock of the field? *or* shall the cold flowing waters that come from another place be forsaken? 15 Because my people hath forgotten me, they have burned incense to vanity, and they have caused them to stumble in their ways *from* the ancient paths, to walk in paths, *in* a way not cast up; 16 To make their land desolate, *and* a perpetual hissing; every one that passeth thereby shall be astonished, and wag his head. 17 I will scatter them as with an east wind before the enemy; I will show them the back, and not the face, in the day of their calamity.

These verses seem to be the application of the general truths laid down in the foregoing part of the chapter to the nation of the Jews and their present state.

I. God was now speaking concerning them *to pluck up,* and *to pull down,* and *to destroy :*

for it is that part of the rule of judgment that their case agrees with (*v.* 11): "*Go, and tell* them" (saith God), "*Behold, I frame evil against you and devise a device against you.* Providence in all its operations is plainly working towards your ruin. Look upon your conduct towards God, and you cannot but see that you deserve it; look upon his dealings with you, and you cannot but see that he designs it." He frames evil, as the potter frames the vessel, so as to answer the end.

II. He invites them by repentance and reformation to meet him in the way of his judgments and so to prevent his further proceedings against them : "*Return you now every one from his evil ways,* that so (according to the rule before laid down) God may turn from the evil he had purposed to do unto you, and that providence which seemed to be framed like a vessel on the wheel against you shall immediately be thrown into a new shape, and the issue shall be in favour of you." Note, The warnings of God's word, and the threatenings of his providence, should be improved by us as strong inducements to us to reform our lives, in which it is not enough to *turn from our evil ways,* but we must *make our ways and our doings good,* conformable to the rule, to the law.

III. He foresees their obstinacy, and their perverse refusal to comply with this invitation, though it tended so much to their own benefit (*v.* 12): *They said, "There is no hope.* If we must not be delivered unless we return from our evil ways, we may even despair of ever being delivered, for we are resolved that *we will walk after our own devices.* It is to no purpose for the prophets to say any more to us, to use any more arguments, or to press the matter any further; we will have our way, whatever it cost us; *we will do every one the imagination of his* own *evil heart,* and will not be under the restraint of the divine law." Note, That which ruins sinners is affecting to live as they list. They call it liberty to live at large; whereas for a man to be a slave to his lusts is the worst of slaveries. See how strangely some men's hearts are hardened by the deceitfulness of sin that they will not so much as promise amendment; nay, they set the judgments of God at defiance : "We will go on with *our own devices,* and let God go on with his; and we will venture the issue."

IV. He upbraids them with the monstrous folly of their obstinacy, and their hating to be reformed. Surely never were people guilty of such an absurdity, never any that pretended to reason acted so unreasonably (*v.* 13): *Ask you among the heathen,* even those that had not the benefit of divine revelation, no oracles, no prophets, as Judah and Jerusalem had, yet, even among them, *who hath heard such a thing?* The Ninevites, when thus warned, turned from their evil ways. Some of the worst of men, when they are told of their faults, especially when they begin to smart for them, will at least promise reformation and say that they will endeavour to mend. But *the virgin of Israel* bids defiance to repentance, is resolved to go on frowardly, whatever conscience and Providence say to the contrary, and thus *has done a horrible thing.* She should have preserved herself pure and chaste for God, who had espoused her to himself; but she has alienated herself from him, and refuses to return to him. Note, It is *a horrible thing*, enough to make one tremble to think of it, that those who have made their condition sad by sinning should make it desperate by refusing to reform. Wilful impenitence is the grossest self-murder; and that is *a horrible thing*, which we should abhor the thought of.

V. He shows their folly in two things:—

1. In the nature of the sin itself that they were guilty of. They forsook God for idols, which was the most horrible thing that could be, for they put a most dangerous cheat upon themselves (*v.* 14, 15): *Will a* thirsty traveller *leave the snow*, which, being melted, runs down from the mountains *of Lebanon*, and, passing over *the rock of the field*, flows in clear, clean, crystal streams? Will he leave these, pass these by, and think to better himself with some dirty puddle-water? *Or shall the cold flowing waters that come from any other place be forsaken* in the heat of summer? No; when men are parched with heat and drought, and meet with cooling refreshing streams, they will make use of them, and not turn their backs upon them. The margin reads it, "*Will a man* that is travelling the road *leave my fields*, which are plain and level, *for a rock*, which is rough and hard, *or for the snow of Lebanon*, which, lying in great drifts, makes the road impassable? *Or shall the running waters be forsaken for the strange cold waters?* No; in these things men know when they are well off, and will keep so; they will not leave a certainty for an uncertainty. But *my people have forgotten me* (*v.* 15), have quitted *a fountain of living waters for broken cisterns. They have burnt incense to* idols, that are as vain as *vanity* itself, that are not what they pretend to be nor can perform what is expected from them." They had not the common wit of travellers, but even their leaders caused them to err, and they were content to be misled. (1.) They left *the ancient paths*, which were appointed by the divine law, which had been walked in by all the saints, which were therefore the right way to their journey's end, a safe way, and, being welltracked, were both easy to hit and easy to walk in. But, when they were advised to keep to the good old way, they positively said that they would not, *ch.* vi. 16. (2.) They chose by-paths; they walked *in a way not cast up*, not in the highway, the King's highway, in which they might travel safely, and which would certainly lead them to their right end, but in a dirty way, a rough way,

528

a way in which they could not but *stumble;* such was the way of idolatry (such is the way of all iniquity—it is a false way, it is a way full of stumbling-blocks) and yet this way they chose to walk in and lead others in.

2. In the mischievous consequences of it. Though the thing itself were bad, they might have had some excuse for it if they could have promised themselves any good out of it. But the direct tendency of it was *to make their land desolate, and,* consequently, themselves miserable (for so the inhabitants must needs be if their country be laid waste), and both themselves and their land *a perpetual hissing.* Those deserve to be hissed that have fair warning given them and will not take it. *Every one that passes by* their land shall make his remarks upon it, and *shall be astonished, and wag his head,* some wondering, others commiserating, others triumphing in the desolations of a country that had been *the glory of all lands.* They shall wag their heads in derision, upbraiding them with their folly in forsaking God and their duty, and so pulling this misery upon their own heads. Note, Those that revolt from God will justly be made the scorn of all about them, and, having reproached the Lord, will themselves be a reproach. *Their land* being made *desolate*, in pursuance of their destruction, it is threatened (*v.* 17), *I will scatter them as with an east wind*, which is fierce and violent; by it they shall be hurried to and fro *before the enemy*, and find no way open to escape. They shall not only flee before the enemy (that they might do and yet make an orderly retreat), but they shall be scattered, some one way and some another. That which completes their misery is, *I will show them the back, and not the face, in the day of their calamity.* Our calamities may be easily borne if God look towards us, and smile upon us, when we are under them, if he countenance us and show us favour; but if he turn *the back* upon us, if he show himself displeased, if he be deaf to our prayers and refuse us his help, if he forsake us, leave us to ourselves, and stand at a distance from us, we are quite undone. *If he hide his face, who then can behold him?* Job xxxiv. 29. Herein God would deal with them as they had dealt with him (*ch.* ii. 27), *They have turned their back unto me, and not their face.* It is a righteous thing with God to show himself strange to those in the day of their trouble who have shown themselves rude and undutiful to him in their prosperity. This will have its full accomplishment in that day when God will say to those who, though they have been professors of piety, were yet workers of iniquity, *Depart from me, I know you not*, nay, *I never knew you.*

18 Then said they, Come, and let us devise devices against Jeremiah; for the law shall not perish from the priest, nor counsel from the wise, nor

the word from the prophet. Come, and let us smite him with the tongue, and let us not give heed to any of his words. 19 Give heed to me, O Lord, and hearken to the voice of them that contend with me. 20 Shall evil be recompensed for good? for they have digged a pit for my soul. Remember that I stood before thee to speak good for them, *and* to turn away thy wrath from them. 21 Therefore deliver up their children to the famine, and pour out their *blood* by the force of the sword; and let their wives be bereaved of their children, and *be* widows; and let their men be put to death; *let* their young men *be* slain by the sword in battle. 22 Let a cry be heard from their houses, when thou shalt bring a troop suddenly upon them: for they have digged a pit to take me, and hid snares for my feet. 23 Yet, Lord, thou knowest all their counsel against me to slay *me*: forgive not their iniquity, neither blot out their sin from thy sight, but let them be overthrown before thee; deal *thus* with them in the time of thine anger.

The prophet here, as sometimes before, brings in his own affairs, but very much for instruction to us.

I. See here what are the common methods of the persecutors. We may see this in Jeremiah's enemies, *v.* 18.

1. They laid their heads together to consult what they should do against him, both to be revenged on him for what he had said and to stop his mouth for the future: *They said, Come and let us devise devices against Jeremiah.* The enemies of God's people and ministers have been often very crafty themselves, and confederate with one another, to do them mischief. What they cannot act to the prejudice of religion separately they will try to do in concert. *The wicked plots against the just.* Caiaphas, and the chief priests and elders, did so against our blessed Saviour himself. The opposition which the gates of hell give to the kingdom of heaven is carried on with a great deal of cursed policy. God had said (*v.* 11), *I devise a device against you;* and now, as if they resolved to be quits with him and to outwit Infinite Wisdom itself, they resolve to *devise devices against* God's prophet, not only against his person, but against the word he delivered to them, which they thought by their subtle management to defeat. O the prodigious madness of those that hope to disannul God's counsel!

2. Herein they pretended a mighty zeal

for the church, which, they suggested, was in danger if Jeremiah was tolerated to preach as he did: "*Come,*" say they, "let us silence and crush him, *for the law shall not perish from the priest; the law of truth is in their mouths* (Mal. ii. 6) and there we will seek it; the administration of ordinances according to the law is in their hands, and neither the one nor the other shall be wrested from them. *Counsel shall not perish from the wise;* the administration of public affairs shall always be lodged with the privy-counsellors and ministers of state, to whom it belongs; *nor* shall *the word* perish *from the prophets*"—they mean those of their own choosing, who prophesied to them smooth things, and flattered them with visions of peace. Two things they insinuated :—(1.) That Jeremiah could not be himself a true prophet, but was a pretender and a usurper, because he neither was commissioned by the priests nor concurred with the other prophets, whose authority therefore will be despised if he be suffered to go on. "If Jeremiah be regarded as an oracle, farewell the reputation of our priests, our wise men, and prophets; but *that* must be supported, which is reason enough why he must be suppressed." (2.) That the matter of his prophecies could not be from God, because it reflected sometimes upon the prophets and priests; he had charged them with being the ringleaders of all the mischief (*ch.* v. 31), and deceiving the people (*ch.* xiv. 14); he had foretold that their *heart should perish,* and *be astonished* (*ch.* iv. 9), that *the wise men should be dismayed* (*ch.* viii. 9, 10), that the priests and prophets should be intoxicated, *ch.* xiii. 13. Now this galled them more than any thing else. Presuming upon the promise of God's presence with their priests and prophets, they could not believe that he would ever leave them. The guides of the church must needs be infallible, and therefore he who foretold their being infatuated must be condemned as a false prophet. Thus, under colour of zeal for the church, have its best friends been run down.

3. They agreed to do all they could to blast his reputation: "*Come, let us smite him with the tongue,* put him into an ill name, fasten a bad character upon him, represent him to some as despicable and fit to be slighted, to others as dangerous and fit to be prosecuted, to all as odious and not fit to be tolerated." This was their device, *fortiter calumniari, aliquid adhærebit—to throw the vilest calumnies at him, in hopes that some would adhere to him,* to dress him up in bearskins, otherwise they could not bait him. Those who projected this, it is likely, were men of figure, whose tongue was no small slander, whose representations, though ever so false, would be credited both by princes and people, to make him obnoxious to the justice of the one and the fury of the other. The scourge of such tongues will give not

only smart lashes, but deep wounds; it is a great mercy therefore to be *hidden from it,* Job v. 21.

4. To set others an example, they resolved that they would not themselves regard any thing he said, though it appeared ever so weighty and ever so well confirmed as a message from God: *Let us not give heed to any of his words ;* for, right or wrong, they will look upon them to be *his words,* and not the words of God. What good can be done with those who hear the word of God with a resolution not to heed it or believe it? Nay,

5. That they may effectually silence him, they resolve to be the death of him (*v.* 23): *All their counsel against me* is *to slay me.* They *hunt for the precious life ;* and a precious life indeed it was that they hunted for. Long was this Jerusalem's wretched character, *Thou that killedst* many of *the prophets,* and wouldst have killed them all.

II. See here what is the common relief of the persecuted. This we may see in the course that Jeremiah took when he met with this hard usage. He immediately applied to his God by prayer, and so gave himself ease.

1. He referred himself and his cause to God's cognizance, *v.* 19. They would not regard a word he said, would not admit his complaints, nor take any notice of his grievances; but, *Lord* (says he), *do thou give heed to me.* It is matter of comfort to faithful ministers that, if men will not give heed to their preaching, yet God will give heed to their praying. He appeals to God as an impartial Judge, that will hear both sides, as every judge ought to do. Do not only *give heed to me,* but *hearken to the voice of those that contend with me ;* hear what they have to say against me and for themselves, and then make it to appear that thou *sittest in the throne, judging right.* Hear the voice of my contenders, how noisy and clamorous they are, how false and malicious all they say is, and let them be *judged out of their own mouth ; cause their own tongues to fall upon them.*

2. He complains of their base ingratitude to him (*v.* 20): " *Shall evil be recompensed for good,* and shall it go unpunished? Wilt not thou recompense me good for that evil?" 2 Sam. xvi. 12. To render good for good is human, evil for evil is brutish, good for evil is Christian, but evil for good is devilish ; it is so very absurd and wicked a thing that we cannot think but God will avenge it. See how great the evil was that they did against him : *They have dug a pit for my soul ;* they aimed to take away his life (no less would satisfy them), and that not in a generous way, by an open assault, against which he might have an opportunity of defending himself, but in a base, cowardly, clandestine way : *they dug pits for* him, which there was no fence against, Ps. cxix. 85. But see how great the good was which he had done for them : *Remember that I stood before thee to speak good for them ;* he had been an inter-

530

cessor with God for them, had used his interest in heaven on their behalf, which was the greatest kindness they could expect from one of his character. *He is a prophet and he shall pray for thee,* Gen. xx. 7. Moses often did this for Israel, and yet they quarrelled with him, and sometimes *spoke of stoning him.* He did them this kindness when they were in imminent danger of destruction and most needed it. They had themselves provoked God's wrath against them, and it was ready to break in upon them, but he stood in the gap (as Moses, Ps. cvi. 23) *and turned away* that *wrath.* Now, (1.) This was very base in them. Call a man ungrateful and you can call him no worse. But it was not strange that those who had forgotten their God did not know their best friends. (2.) It was very grievous to him, as the like was to David. Ps. xxxv. 13 ; cix. 4, *For my love they are my adversaries.* Thus disingenuously do sinners deal with the great intercessor, crucifying him afresh, and speaking against him on earth, while his blood is speaking for them in heaven. See John x. 32. But, (3.) It was a comfort to the prophet that, when they were so spiteful against him, he had the testimony of his conscience for him that he had done his duty to them; and the same will be our rejoicing in such a day of evil. *The blood-thirsty hate the upright, but the just seek his soul,* Prov. xxix. 10.

3. He imprecates the judgments of God upon them, not from a revengeful disposition, but in a prophetical indignation against their horrid wickedness, *v.* 21—23. He prays, (1.) That their families might be starved for want of bread : " *Deliver up their children to the famine,* to the famine in the country for want of rain, and that in the city through the straitness of the siege. Thus let this iniquity of the fathers be visited upon the children." (2.) That they might be cut off *by the sword* of war, which, whatever it was in the enemy's hand, would be, in God's hand, a sword of justice : " *Pour them out* (so the word is) *by the hands of the sword ;* let their blood be shed as profusely as water, that their wives may be left childless *and widows,* their husbands being taken away by *death"* (some think that the prophet refers to *pestilence) ; let their young men,* that are the strength of this generation and the hope of the next, *be slain by the sword in battle.* (3.) That the terrors and desolations of war might seize them suddenly and by surprise, that thus their punishment might answer to their sin (*v.* 22) : " *Let a cry be heard from their houses,* loud shrieks, *when thou shalt bring a troop* of the Chaldeans *suddenly upon them,* to seize them and all they have, to make them prisoners and their estates a prey ;" for thus they would have done by Jeremiah ; they aimed to ruin him at once ere he was aware : " *They have dug a pit* for *me,* as for a wild beast, *and* have *hid snares for* me, as for some ravenous noxious fowl. Note,

Those that think to ensnare others will justly be themselves ensnared in an evil time. (4.) That they might be dealt with according to the desert of this sin, which was without excuse : " *Forgive not their iniquity, neither blot out their sin from thy sight; that is,* let them not escape the just punishment of it ; let them lie under all the miseries of those whose sins are unpardoned." (5.) That God's wrath against them might be their ruin : *Let them be overthrown before thee.* This intimates that justice was in pursuit of them, that they endeavoured to make their escape from it, but in vain; they shall be made to stumble in their flight, and being overthrown they will certainly be overtaken." And then, Lord, *in the time of thy anger,* do to them (he does not say what he would have done to them, but) do to them as thou thinkest fit, as thou usest to do with those whom thou art angry with—*deal thus with them.* Now this is not written for our imitation. Jeremiah was a prophet, and by the impulse of the spirit of prophecy, in the foresight of the ruin certainly coming upon his persecutors, might pray such prayers as we may not; and, if we think by this example to justify ourselves in such imprecations, we *know not what manner of spirit we are of :* our Master has taught us, by his precept and pattern, to *bless those that curse us and pray for those that despitefully use us.* Yet it is written for our instruction, and is of use to teach us, [1.] That those who have forfeited the benefit of the prayers of God's prophets for them may justly expect to have their prayers against them. [2.] That persecution is a sin that fills the measure of a people's iniquity very fast, and will bring as sure and sore a destruction upon them as any thing. [3.] Those who will not be won upon by the kindness of God and his prophets will certainly at length feel the just resentments of both.

CHAP. XIX.

The same melancholy theme is the subject of this chapter that was of those foregoing—the approaching ruin of Judah and Jerusalem for their sins. This Jeremiah had often foretold ; here he has particularly full orders to foretel it again. I. He must set their sins in order before them, as he had often done, especially their idolatry, ver. 4, 5. II. He must describe the particular judgments which were now coming apace upon them for these sins, ver. 6—9. III. He must do this in the valley of Tophet, with great solemnity, and for some particular reasons, ver. 2, 3. IV. He must summon a company of the elders together to be witnesses of this, ver. 1. V. He must confirm this, and endeavour to affect his hearers with it, by a sign, which was the breaking of an earthen bottle, signifying that they should be dashed to pieces like a potter's vessel, ver. 10—13. VI. When he had done this in the valley of Tophet he ratified it in the court of the temple, ver. 14, 15. Thus were all likely means tried to awaken this stupid senseless people to repentance, that their ruin might be prevented ; but all in vain.

THUS saith the LORD, Go and get a potter's earthen bottle, and *take* of the ancients of the people, and of the ancients of the priests ; 2 And go forth unto the valley of the son of Hinnom, which *is* by the entry of the east gate, and proclaim there the words that I shall tell thee, 3 And say,

Hear ye the word of the LORD, O kings of Judah, and inhabitants of Jerusalem ; Thus saith the LORD of hosts, the God of Israel ; Behold, I will bring evil upon this place, the which whosoever heareth, his ears shall tingle. 4 Because they have forsaken me and have estranged this place, and have burnt incense in it unto other gods, whom neither they nor their fathers have known, nor the kings of Judah, and have filled this place with the blood of innocents ; 5 They have built also the high places of Baal, to burn their sons with fire *for* burnt-offerings unto Baal, which I commanded not, nor spake *it,* neither came *it* into my mind : 6 Therefore, behold, the days come, saith the LORD, that this place shall no more be called Tophet, nor The valley of the son of Hinnom, but The valley of slaughter. 7 And I will make void the counsel of Judah and Jerusalem in this place ; and I will cause them to fall by the sword before their enemies, and by the hands of them that seek their lives : and their carcases will I give to be meat for the fowls of the heaven, and for the beasts of the earth. 8 And I will make this city desolate, and a hissing ; every one that passeth thereby shall be astonished and hiss, because of all the plagues thereof. 9 And I will cause them to eat the flesh of their sons and the flesh of their daughters, and they shall eat every one the flesh of his friend in the siege and straitness, wherewith their enemies, and they that seek their lives, shall straiten them.

The corruption of man having made it necessary that *precept* should be *upon precept, and line upon line* (so unapt are we to receive, and so very apt to let slip, the things of God), the grace of God has provided that there shall be, accordingly, *precept upon precept, and line upon line,* that those who are irreclaimable may be inexcusable. For this reason the prophet is here sent with a message to the same purport with what he had often delivered, but with some circumstances that might make it the more taken notice of, a thing which ministers should study, for a little circumstance may sometimes be a great advantage, and those that would win souls must be wise.

I. He must take of the elders and chief

men, both in church and state, to be his auditors and witnesses to what he said—*the ancients of the people and the ancients of the priests*, the most eminent men both in the magistracy and in the ministry, that they might be *faithful witnesses to record*, as those Isa. viii. 2. It is strange that these great men should be at the beck of a poor prophet, and obey his summons to attend him out of the city, they knew not whither and they knew not why. But, though the generality of the elders were disaffected to him, yet it is likely that there were some few among them who looked upon him as a prophet of the Lord, and would pay this respect to the heavenly vision. Note, Persons of rank and figure have an opportunity of honouring God by a diligent attendance on the ministry of the word and other divine institutions; and they ought to think it an honour, and no disparagement to themselves, yea, though the circumstances be mean and despicable. It is certain that the greatest of men is less than the least of the ordinances of God.

II. He must *go to the valley of the son of Hinnom*, and deliver this message there; for *the word of the Lord* is not bound to any one place; as good a sermon may be preached in the valley of Tophet as in the gate of the temple. Christ preached on a mountain and out of a ship. This valley lay partly on the south side of Jerusalem, but the prophet's way to it was *by the entry on the east gate—the sun-gate* (v. 2), so some render it, and suppose it to look not towards the sunrising, but the noon sun—*the potter's gate*, so some. This sermon must be preached in that place, in *the valley of the son of Hinnom*, 1. Because there they had been guilty of the vilest of their idolatries, the sacrificing of their children to Moloch, a horrid piece of impiety, which the sight of the place might serve to remind them of and upbraid them with. 2. Because there they should feel the sorest of their calamities; there the greatest slaughter should be made among them; and, it being the common sink of the city, let them look upon it and see what a miserable spectacle this magnificent city would be when it should be all like the valley of Tophet. God bids him go thither, *and proclaim there the words that I shall tell thee*, when thou comest thither; whereby it appears (as Mr. Gataker well observes) that God's messages were frequently not revealed to the prophets before the very instant of time wherein they were to deliver them.

III. He must give general notice of a general ruin now shortly coming upon Judah and Jerusalem, *v*. 3. He must, as those that make proclamation, begin with an *Oyes: Hear you the word of the Lord*, though it be a terrible word, for you may thank yourselves if it be so. Both rulers and ruled must attend to it, at their peril; the *kings of Judah*, the king and his sons, the king and his princes and privy-counsellors, must hear

the word of the King of kings, for, high as they are, he is above them. The *inhabitants of Jerusalem* also must hear what God has to say to them. Both princes and people have contributed to the national guilt and must concur in the national repentance, or they will both share in the national ruin. Let them all know that *the Lord of hosts*, who is therefore able to do what he threatens, though he is *the God of Israel*, nay, because he is so, will therefore punish them in the first place for their iniquities (Amos iii. 2): *He will bring evil upon this place* (upon *Judah and Jerusalem)* so surprising, and so dreadful, that *whosoever hears* it, *his ears shall tingle;* whosoever hears the prediction of it, hears the report and representation of it, it shall make such an impression of terror upon him that he shall still think he hears it sounding in his ears and shall not be able to get it out of his mind. The ruin of Eli's house is thus described (1 Sam. iii. 11), and of Jerusalem, 2 Kings xxi. 12.

IV. He must plainly tell them what their sins were for which God had this controversy with them, *v*. 4, 5. They are charged with apostasy from God *(They have forsaken me)* and abuse of the privileges of the visible church, with which they had been dignified —*They have estranged this place*. Jerusalem (the holy city), the temple (the holy house), which was designed for the honour of God and the support of his kingdom among men, they had alienated from those purposes, and (as some render the word) *they had strangely abused*. They had so polluted both with their wickedness that God had disowned both, and abandoned them to ruin. He charges them with an affection for and the adoration of false *gods*, such as *neither they nor their fathers have known*, such as never had recommended themselves to their belief and esteem by any acts of power or goodness done for them or their ancestors, as that God had abundantly done whom they forsook; yet they took them at a venture for their gods; nay, being fond of change and novelty, they liked them the better for their being upstarts, and new fashions in religion were as grateful to their fancies as in other things. They also stand charged with murder, wilful murder, from malice prepense: *They have filled this place with the blood of innocents*. It was Manasseh's sin (2 Kings xxiv. 4), *which the Lord would not pardon*. Nay, as if idolatry and murder, committed separately, were not bad enough and affront enough to God and man, they have put them together, have consolidated them into one complicated crime, that of burning their children in the fire to Baal (*v*. 5), which was the most insolent defiance to all the laws both of natural and revealed religion that ever mankind was guilty of; and by it they openly declared that they loved their new gods better than ever they loved the true God, though they were such cruel task-masters that they required human sacrifices (inhuman I should call them), which the Lord Jehovah, whose all lives and souls are, never demanded from his worshippers; he never *spoke* of such a thing, nor *came it into his mind.* See *ch.* vii. 31.

V. He must endeavour to affect them with the greatness of the desolation that was coming upon them. He must tell them (as he had done before, *ch.* vii. 32) that this *valley of the son of Hinnom* shall acquire a new name, *the valley of slaughter* (*v.* 6), for (*v.* 7) multitudes shall *fall* there *by the sword,* when either they sally out upon the besiegers and are repulsed or attempt to make their escape and are seized: *They* shall *fall before their enemies,* who not only endeavour to make themselves masters of their houses and estates, but have such an implacable enmity to them that they *seek their lives;* they thirst after their blood, and, when they are dead, will not allow a cartel for the burying of the slain, but *their carcases* shall *be meat for the fowls of the heaven and beasts of the earth.* What a dismal place will the valley of Tophet be then! And as for those that remain within the city, and will not capitulate with the besiegers, they shall perish for want of food, when first they have eaten *the flesh of their sons and daughters,* and dearest *friends,* through the *straitness wherewith their enemies shall straiten them, v.* 9. This was threatened in the law as an instance of the extremity to which the judgments of God should reduce them (Lev. xxvi. 29, Deut. xxviii. 53) and was accomplished, Lam. iv. 10. And, *lastly,* the whole *city* shall be *desolate,* the houses laid in ashes, the inhabitants slain or taken prisoners; there shall be no resort to it, nor any thing in it but what looks rueful and horrid; so that *every one that passes by shall be astonished* (*v.* 8), as he had said before, *ch.* xviii. 16. That place which holiness had made *the joy of the whole earth* sin had made the reproach and shame of the whole earth.

VI. He must assure them that all their attempts to prevent and avoid this ruin, so long as they continued impenitent and unreformed, would be fruitless and vain (*v.* 7): *I will make void the counsel of Judah and Jerusalem* (of the princes and senators of Judah and Jerusalem) *in this place,* in the royal palace, which lay on the south side of the city, not far from the place where the prophet now stood. Note, There is no fleeing from God's justice but by fleeing to his mercy. Those that will not make good God's counsel, by humbling themselves under his mighty hand, shall find that God will make void their counsel and blast their projects, which they think ever so well concerted for their own preservation. There is *no counsel* or strength *against the Lord.*

10 Then shalt thou break the bottle in the sight of the men that go with thee, 11 And shalt say unto them,

Thus saith the Lord of hosts; Even so will I break this people and this city, as *one* breaketh a potter's vessel, that cannot be made whole again: and they shall bury *them* in Tophet, till *there be* no place to bury. 12 Thus will I do unto this place, saith the Lord, and to the inhabitants thereof, and *even* make this city as Tophet: 13 And the houses of Jerusalem, and the houses of the kings of Judah, shall be defiled as the place of Tophet, because of all the houses upon whose roofs they have burnt incense unto all the host of heaven, and have poured out drink-offerings unto other gods. 14 Then came Jeremiah from Tophet, whither the Lord had sent him to prophesy; and he stood in the court of the Lord's house; and said to all the people, 15 Thus saith the Lord of hosts, the God of Israel; Behold, I will bring upon this city and upon all her towns all the evil that I have pronounced against it, because they have hardened their necks, that they might not hear my words.

The message of wrath delivered in the foregoing verses is here enforced, that it might gain credit, two ways:—

I. By a visible sign. The prophet was to take along with him an *earthen bottle* (*v.* 1), and, when he had delivered his message, he was to *break the bottle* to pieces (*v.* 10), and the same that were auditors of the sermon must be spectators of the sign. He had compared this people, in the chapter before, to the potter's clay, which is easily marred in the making. But some might say, "It is past that with us; we have been made and hardened long since." "And what though you be," says he, "the potter's vessel is as soon broken in the hand of any man as the vessel while it is soft clay is marred in the potter's hand, and its case is, in this respect, much worse, that the vessel while it is soft clay, though it be marred, may be moulded again, but, after it is hardened, when it is broken it can never be pieced again." Perhaps what they see will affect them more than what they only hear talk of; that is the intention of sacramental signs, and teaching by symbols was anciently used. In the explication of this sign he must inculcate what he had before said, with a further reference to the place where this was done, in the valley of Tophet. 1. As the bottle was easily, irresistibly, and irrecoverably broken, so shall *Judah and Jerusalem* be broken by the Chaldean army, *v.* 11. They depended much upon the firmness of their constitution, and the fixedness of their courage, which they thought hardened them like a vessel of brass; but the prophet shows that all that did but harden them like a vessel of earth, which, though hard, is brittle and sooner broken than that which is not so hard. Though they were made vessels of honour, still they were vessels of earth, and so they shall be made to know if they dishonour God and themselves, and serve not the purposes for which they were made. It is God himself, who made them, that resolves to unmake them: *I will break this people and this city*, dash them in pieces like *a potter's vessel;* the doom of the heathen (Ps. ii. 9, Rev. ii. 27), but now Jerusalem's doom, Isa. xxx. 14. *A potter's vessel*, when once broken, *cannot be made whole again, cannot be cured,* so the word is. The ruin of Jerusalem shall be an utter ruin; no hand can repair it but his that broke it; and if they return to him, though he has torn, he will heal. 2. This was done in Tophet, to signify two things: —(1.) That Tophet should be the receptacle of the slain: *They shall bury in Tophet, for want of room to bury elsewhere* (so some read it), and, if they had had conveniences any where else, they would not have buried there, where all the filth of the city was carried. Or, as we read it, *They shall bury in Tophet till there be no place to bury* any more there; they shall jostle for room to lay their dead, and a very little room will then serve those who, while they lived, *laid house to house and field to field.* Those that would be *placed alone in the midst of the earth* while they were above ground, and obliged all about them to keep their distance, must lie with the multitude when they are underground, for there are innumerable before them. (2.) That Tophet should be a resemblance of the whole city (*v.* 12): *I will make this city as Tophet.* As they had filled the valley of Tophet with the slain which they sacrificed to their idols, so God will fill the whole city with the slain that shall fall as sacrifices to the justice of God. We read (2 Kings xxiii. 10) of Josiah's defiling Tophet, because it had been abused to idolatry, which he did (as should seem, *v.* 14) by *filling it with the bones of men;* and, whatever it was before, thenceforward it was looked upon as a detestable place. Dead carcases, and other filth of the city, were carried thither, and a fire was continually kept there for the burning of it. This was the posture of that valley when Jeremiah was sent thither to prophesy; and so execrable a place was it looked upon to be that, in the language of our Saviour's time, hell was called, in allusion to it, *Gehenna, the valley of Hinnom.* "Now" (says God) "since that blessed reformation, when Tophet was defiled, did not proceed as it ought to have done, nor prove a thorough reformation, but though the idols in Tophet were abolished and made odious those in Jerusalem remained, therefore will I do with the

city as Josiah did by Tophet, fill it with the bodies of men, and make it a heap of rubbish." Even *the houses of Jerusalem, and those of the kings of Judah,* the royal palaces not excepted, *shall be defiled as the place of Tophet* (*v.* 13), and for the same reason, because of the idolatries that have been committed there; since they will not defile them by a reformation, God will defile them by a destruction, *because* upon the *roofs of their houses they have burnt incense unto the host of heaven.* The flat roofs of their houses were sometimes used by devout people as convenient places for prayer (Acts x. 9), and by idolaters they were used as high places, on which they sacrificed to strange gods, especially to *the host of heaven,* the sun, moon, and stars, that there they might be so much nearer to them and have a clearer and fuller view of them. We read of those that *worshipped the host of heaven upon the house-tops* (Zeph. i. 5), and of *altars on the top of the upper chamber of Ahaz,* 2 Kings xxiii. 12. This sin upon the house-tops brought a curse into the house, which consumed it, and made it a dunghill like Tophet.

II. By a solemn recognition and ratification of what he had said *in the court of the Lord's house, v.* 14, 15. The prophet returned from Tophet to the temple, which stood upon the hill over that valley, and there confirmed, and probably repeated, what he had said in the valley of Tophet, for the benefit of those who had not heard it; what he had said he would stand to. Here, as often before, he both assures them of judgments coming upon them and assigns the cause of them, which was their sin. Both these are here put together in a little compass, with a reference to all that had gone before. 1. The accomplishment of the prophecies is here the judgment threatened. The people flattered themselves with a conceit that God would be better than his word, that the threatening was but to frighten them and keep them in awe a little; but the prophet tells them that they deceive themselves if they think so: *For thus saith the Lord of hosts,* who is able to make his words good, *I will bring upon this city, and upon all her towns,* all the smaller cities that belong to Jerusalem the metropolis, *all the evil that I have pronounced against it.* Note, Whatever men may think to the contrary, the executions of Providence will fully answer the predictions of the word, and God will appear as terrible against sin and sinners as the scripture makes him; nor shall the unbelief of men make either his promises or his threatenings of no effect or of less effect than they were thought to be of. 2. The contempt of the prophecies is here the sin charged upon them, as the procuring cause of this judgment. It is *because they have hardened their necks,* and would not bow and bend them to the yoke of God's commands, would *not hear my words,* that is, would not heed them and yield obedience to them. Note, The obstinacy of sinners in their sinful ways is altogether their own fault; if their necks are hardened, it is their own act and deed, they have hardened them; if they are deaf to the word of God, it is because they have stopped their own ears. We have need therefore to pray that God, by his grace, would deliver us *from hardness of heart and contempt of his word and commandments.*

CHAP. XX.

Such plain dealing as Jeremiah used in the foregoing chapter, one might easily foresee, if it did not convince and humble men, would provoke and exasperate them; and so it did; for here we find, I. Jeremiah persecuted by Pashur for preaching that sermon, ver. 1, 2. II. Pashur threatened for so doing, and the word which Jeremiah had preached confirmed, ver. 3—6. III. Jeremiah complaining to God concerning it, and the other instances of hard measure that he had since he began to be a prophet, and the grievous temptations he had struggled with (ver. 7—10), encouraging himself in God, lodging his appeal with him, not doubting but that he shall yet praise him, by which it appears that he had much grace (ver. 11—13), and yet peevishly cursing the day of his birth (ver. 14—18), by which it appears that he had sad remainders of corruption in him too, and was a man subject to like passions as we are.

NOW Pashur the son of Immer the priest, who *was* also chief governor in the house of the LORD, heard that Jeremiah prophesied these things. 2 Then Pashur smote Jeremiah the prophet, and put him in the stocks that *were* in the high gate of Benjamin, which *was* by the house of the LORD. 3 And it came to pass on the morrow, that Pashur brought forth Jeremiah out of the stocks. Then said Jeremiah unto him, The LORD hath not called thy name Pashur, but Magor-missabib. 4 For thus saith the LORD, Behold, I will make thee a terror to thyself, and to all thy friends: and they shall fall by the sword of their enemies, and thine eyes shall behold *it :* and I will give all Judah into the hand of the king of Babylon, and he shall carry them captive into Babylon, and shall slay them with the sword. 5 Moreover I will deliver all the strength of this city, and all the labours thereof, and all the precious things thereof, and all the treasures of the kings of Judah will I give into the hand of their enemies, which shall spoil them, and take them, and carry them to Babylon. 6 And thou, Pashur, and all that dwell in thine house shall go into captivity: and thou shalt come to Babylon, and there thou shalt die, and shalt be buried there, thou, and all thy friends, to whom thou hast prophesied lies.

Here is, I. Pashur's unjust displeasure against Jeremiah, and the fruits of that dis-

pleasure, *v.* 1, 2. This Pashur was a priest, and therefore, one would think, should have protected Jeremiah, who was of his own order, a priest too, and the more because he was a prophet of the Lord, whose interests the priests, his ministers, ought to consult. But this priest was a persecutor of him whom he should have patronized. He was *the son of Immer ;* that is, he was of the sixteenth course of the priests, of which Immer, when these courses were first settled by David, was father (1 Chron. xxiv. 14), as Zechariah was of the order of Abiah, Luke i. 5. Thus this Pashur is distinguished from another of the same name mentioned *ch.* xxi. 1, who was of the fifth course. This Pashur was *chief governor in the temple ;* perhaps he was only so *pro tempore—for a short period,* the course he was head of being now in waiting, or he was suffragan to the high priest, or perhaps captain of the temple or of the guards about it. Acts iv. 1. This was Jeremiah's great enemy. The greatest malignity to God's prophets was found among those that professed sanctity and concern for God and the church. We cannot suppose that Pashur was one of those ancients of the priests that went with Jeremiah to the valley of Tophet to hear him prophesy, unless it were with a malicious design to take advantage against him; but, when he came into the courts of the Lord's house, it is probable that he was himself a witness of what he said, and so it may be read (*v.* 1), *He heard Jeremiah prophesying these things.* As we read it, the information was brought to him by others, whose examinations he took: *He heard that Jeremiah prophesied these things,* and could not bear it, especially that he should dare to preach in the courts of the Lord's house, where he was *chief governor,* without his leave. When power in the church is abused, it is the most dangerous power that can be employed against it. Being incensed at Jeremiah, 1. He *smote* him, struck him with his hand or staff of authority. Perhaps it was a blow intended only to disgrace him, like that which the high priest ordered to be given to Paul (Acts xxiii. 2), he struck him on the mouth, and bade him hold his prating. Or perhaps he gave him many blows intended to hurt him; he beat him severely, as a malefactor. It is charged upon the husbandmen (Matt. xxi. 35) that they beat the servants. The method of proceeding here was illegal; the high priest, and the rest of the priests, ought to have been consulted, Jeremiah's credentials examined, and the matter enquired into, whether he had an authority to say what he said. But these rules of justice are set aside and despised, as mere formalities; right or wrong, Jeremiah must be run down. The enemies of piety would never suffer themselves to be bound by the laws of equity. 2. He *put him in the stocks.* Some make it only a place of confinement; he imprisoned him. It rather seems to be an instrument of closer restraint, and intended to put him both to pain and shame. Some think it was a pillory for his neck and arms; others (as we) a pair of stocks for his legs: whatever engine it was, he continued in it all night, and in a public place too, *in the high gate of Benjamin, which was* in, or *by, the house of the Lord,* probably a gate through which they passed between the city and the temple. Pashur intended thus to chastise him, that he might deter him from prophesying; and thus to expose him to contempt and render him odious, that he might not be regarded if he did prophesy. Thus have the best men met with the worst treatment from this ungracious ungrateful world; and the greatest blessings of their age have been counted as the *off-scouring of all things.* Would it not raise a pious indignation to see such a man as Pashur upon the bench and such a man as Jeremiah in the stocks? It is well that there is another life after this, when persons and things will appear with another face.

II. God's just displeasure against Pashur, and the tokens of it. *On the morrow Pashur gave* Jeremiah his discharge, *brought him out of the stocks* (v. 3); it is probable that he continued him there, in little-ease, as long as was usual to continue any in that punishment. And now Jeremiah has a message from God to him. We do not find that, when Pashur put Jeremiah in the stocks, the latter gave him any check for what he did; he appears to have quietly and silently submitted to the abuse; *when he suffered, he threatened not.* But, when he brought him out of the stocks, then God put a word into the prophet's mouth, which would awaken his conscience, if he had any. For, when the prophet of the Lord was bound, *the word of the Lord was not.* What can we think Pashur aimed at in smiting and abusing Jeremiah? Whatever it is, we shall see by what God says to him that he is disappointed.

1. Did he aim to establish himself, and make himself easy, by silencing one that told him of his faults and would be likely to lessen his reputation with the people? He shall not gain this point; for, (1.) Though the prophet should be silent, his own conscience shall fly in his face and make him always uneasy. To confirm this he shall have a name given him, *Magor-missabib—Terror round about,* or *Fear on every side.* God himself shall give him this name, whose calling him so will make him so. It seems to be a proverbial expression, bespeaking a man not only in distress but in despair, not only in danger on every side (that a man may be and yet by faith may be in no terror, as David, Ps. iii. 6, xxvii. 3), but in fear on every side, and that a man may be when there appears no danger. *The wicked flee when no man pursues,* are in *great fear where no fear is.* This shall be Pashur's case (v. 4): " *Behold, I will make thee a terror to thyself;* that is,

thou shalt be subject to continual frights, and thy own fancy and imagination shall create thee a constant uneasiness." Note, God can make the most daring sinner a terror to himself, and will find out a way to frighten those that frighten his people from doing their duty. And those that will not hear of their faults from God's prophets, that are reprovers in the gate, shall be made to hear of them from conscience, which is a reprover in their own bosoms that will not be daunted nor silenced. And miserable is the man that is thus made a terror to himself. Yet this is not all; some are very much a terror to themselves, but they conceal it and seem to others to be pleasant; but, " *I will make thee a terror to all thy friends;* thou shalt, upon all occasions, express thyself with so much horror and amazement that all thy friends shall be afraid of conversing with thee and shall choose to stand aloof from thy torment." Persons in deep melancholy and distraction are a terror to themselves and all about them, which is a good reason why we should be very thankful, so long as God continues to us the use of our reason and the peace of our consciences. (2.) His friends, whom he put a confidence in and perhaps studied to oblige in what he did against Jeremiah, shall all fail him. God does not presently strike him dead for what he did against Jeremiah, but lets him live miserably, like Cain in the *land of shaking,* in such a continual consternation that wherever he goes he shall be a monument of divine justice; and, when it is asked, " What makes this man in such a continual terror?" it shall be answered, " It is God's hand upon him for putting Jeremiah in the stocks." His friends, who should encourage him, shall all be cut off; they shall *fall by the sword of the enemy,* and *his eyes shall behold it,* which dreadful sight shall increase his terror. (3.) He shall find, in the issue, that his terror is not causeless, but that divine vengeance is waiting for him (v. 6); he and his family shall *go into captivity,* even *to Babylon;* he shall neither die before the evil comes, as Josiah, nor live to survive it, as some did, but he shall die a captive, and shall in effect be buried in his chains, he *and all his friends.* Thus far is the doom of Pashur. Let persecutors read it, and tremble; tremble to repentance before they be made to tremble to their ruin.

2. Did he aim to keep the people easy, to prevent the destruction that Jeremiah prophesied of, and by sinking his reputation to make his words fall to the ground? It is probable that he did; for it appears by v. 6 that he did himself set up for a prophet, and told the people that they should have peace. He *prophesied lies to them;* and because Jeremiah's prophecy contradicted his, and tended to awaken those whom he endeavoured to rock asleep in their sins, therefore he set himself against him. But could he gain his

point? No; Jeremiah stands to what he has said against Judah and Jerusalem, and God by his mouth repeats it. Men get nothing by silencing those who reprove and warn them, for the word will have its course; so it had here. (1.) The country shall be ruined (v. 4): *I will give all Judah into the hand of the king of Babylon.* It had long been God's own land, but he will now transfer his title to it to Nebuchadnezzar, he shall be master of the country and dispose of the inhabitants some to the sword and some to captivity, as he pleases, but none shall escape him. (2.) The city shall be ruined too, v. 5. The king of Babylon shall spoil that, and carry all that is valuable in it to Babylon. [1.] He shall seize their magazines and military stores (here called *the strength of this city*) and turn them against them. These they trusted to as their strength; but what stead could they stand them in when they had thrown themselves out of God's protection, and when he who was indeed their strength had departed from them? [2.] He shall carry off all their stock in trade, their wares and merchandises, here called *their labours*, because it was what they laboured about and got by their labour. [3.] He shall plunder their fine houses, and take away their rich furniture, here called their *precious things*, because they valued them and set their hearts so much upon them. Happy are those who have secured to themselves precious things in God's precious promises, which are out of the reach of soldiers. [4.] He shall rifle the exchequer, and take away the jewels of the crown and *all the treasures of the kings of Judah.* This was that instance of the calamity which was first of all threatened to Hezekiah long ago as his punishment for showing his treasures to the king of Babylon's ambassadors, Isa. xxxix. 6. The treasury, they thought, was their defence; but that betrayed them, and became an easy prey to the enemy.

7 O LORD, thou hast deceived me, and I was deceived: thou art stronger than I, and hast prevailed: I am in derision daily, every one mocketh me. 8 For since I spake, I cried out, I cried violence and spoil; because the word of the LORD was made a reproach unto me, and a derision, daily. 9 Then I said, I will not make mention of him, nor speak any more in his name. But *his word* was in mine heart as a burning fire shut up in my bones, and I was weary with forbearing, and I could not *stay.* 10 For I heard the defaming of many, fear on every side. Report, *say they*, and we will report it. All my familiars watched for my halting, *saying*, Per-

adventure he will be enticed, and we shall prevail against him, and we shall take our revenge on him. 11 But the LORD *is* with me as a mighty terrible one: therefore my persecutors shall stumble, and they shall not prevail: they shall be greatly ashamed; for they shall not prosper: *their* everlasting confusion shall never be forgotten. 12 But, O LORD of hosts, that triest the righteous, *and* seest the reins and the heart, let me see thy vengeance on them: for unto thee have I opened my cause. 13 Sing unto the LORD, praise ye the LORD: for he hath delivered the soul of the poor from the hand of evil doers.

Pashur's doom was to be a *terror to himself;* Jeremiah, even now, in this hour of temptation, is far from being so; and yet it cannot be denied but that he is here, through the infirmity of the flesh, strangely agitated within himself. Good men are but men at the best. God is not extreme to mark what they say and do amiss, and therefore we must not be so, but make the best of it. In these verses it appears that, upon occasion of the great indignation and injury that Pashur did to Jeremiah, there was a struggle in his breast between his graces and his corruptions. His discourse with himself and with his God, upon this occasion, was somewhat perplexed; let us try to methodize it.

I. Here is a sad representation of the wrong that was done him and the affronts that were put upon him; and this representation, no doubt, was according to truth, and deserves no blame, but was very justly and very fitly made to him that sent him, and no doubt would bear him out. He complains,

1. That he was ridiculed and laughed at; they made a jest of every thing he said and did; and this cannot but be a great grievance to an ingenuous mind (v. 7, 8): *I am in derision; I am mocked.* They played upon him, and made themselves and one another merry with him, as if he had been a fool, good for nothing but to make sport. Thus he was continually: *I was in derision daily.* Thus he was universally: *Every one mocks me;* the greatest so far forget their own gravity, and the meanest so far forget mine. Thus our Lord Jesus, on the cross, was reviled both by priests and people; and the revilings of each had their peculiar aggravation. And what was it that thus exposed him to contempt and scorn? It was nothing but his faithful and zealous discharge of the duty of his office, v. 8. They could find nothing for which to deride him but his preaching; it was *the word of the Lord* that *was made a reproach.* That for which they should have honoured and re-

spected him—that he was entrusted to deliver the *word of the Lord* to them was the very thing for which they reproached and reviled him. He never preached a sermon, but, though he kept as closely as possible to his instructions, they found something or other in it for which to banter and abuse him. Note, It is sad to think that, though divine revelation be one of the greatest blessings and honours that ever was bestowed upon the world, yet it has been turned very much to the reproach of the most zealous preachers and believers of it. Two things they derided him for :—(1.) The manner of his preaching : *Since he spoke, he cried out.* He had always been a lively affectionate preacher, and since he began to speak in God's name he always spoke as a man in earnest ; he *cried aloud and did not spare,* spared neither himself nor those to whom he preached ; and this was enough for those to laugh at who hated to be serious. It is common for those that are unaffected with, and disaffected to, the things of God themselves, to ridicule those that are much affected with them. Lively preachers are the scorn of careless unbelieving hearers. (2.) The matter of his preaching : He *cried violence and spoil.* He reproved them for the violence and spoil which they were guilty of towards one another ; and he prophesied of the violence and spoil which should be brought upon them as the punishment of that sin ; for the former they ridiculed him as over-precise, for the latter as over-credulous ; in both he was provoking to them, and therefore they resolved to run him down. This was bad enough, yet he complains further.

2. That he was plotted against and his ruin contrived ; he was not only ridiculed as a weak man, but reproached and misrepresented as a bad man and dangerous to the government. This he laments as his grievance, *v.* 10. Being laughed at, though it touches a man in point of honour, is yet a thing that may be easily laughed at again ; for, as it has been well observed, it is no shame to be laughed at, but to deserve to be so. But there were those that acted a more spiteful part, and with more sublety. (1.) They spoke ill of him behind his back, when he had no opportunity of clearing himself, and were industrious to spread false reports concerning him : *I heard,* at second hand, *the defaming of many, fear on every side (of many Magor-missabibs,* so some read it), of many such men as Pashur was, and who may therefore expect his doom. Or this was the matter of their defamation ; they represented Jeremiah as a man that instilled fears and jealousies on every side into the minds of the people, and so made them uneasy under the government, and disposed them to a rebellion. Or he perceived them to be so malicious against him that he could not but be *afraid on every side ;* wherever he was he had reason to fear informers ; so that they made him almost a *Magor-missabib.* These words are found

in the original, *verbatim,* the same, Ps. xxxi. 13, *I have heard the slander* or *defaming of many, fear on every side.* Jeremiah, in his complaint, chooses to make use of the same words that David had made use of before him, that it might be a comfort to him to think that other good men had suffered similar abuses before him, and to teach us to make use of David's psalms with application to ourselves, as there is occasion. Whatever we have to say, we may thence take with us words. See how Jeremiah's enemies contrived the matter : *Report, say they, and we will report it.* They resolve to cast an odium upon him, and this is the method they take : " Let some very bad thing be said of him, which may render him obnoxious to the government, and, though it be ever so false, we will second it, and spread it, and add to it." (For the reproaches of good men lose nothing by the carriage.) " Do you that frame a story plausibly, or you that can pretend to some acquaintance with him, report it once, and we will all report it from you, in all companies that we come into. Do you say it, and we will swear it ; do you set it a going, and we will follow it." And thus both are eqally guilty, those that raise and those that propagate the false report. The receiver is as bad as the thief. (2.) They flattered him to his face, that they might get something from him on which to ground an accusation, as the spies that came to Christ feigning themselves to be just men, Luke xx. 20 ; xi. 53, 54. His familiars, that he conversed freely with and put a confidence in, *watched for his halting,* observed what he said, which they could by any strained *innuendo* put a bad construction upon, and carried it to his enemies. His case was very sad when those betrayed him whom he took to be his friends. They said among themselves, " If we accost him kindly, and insinuate ourselves into his acquaintance, per-adventure he will be enticed to own that he is in confederacy with the enemy and a pensioner to the king of Babylon, or we shall wheedle him to speak some treasonable words ; and then *we shall prevail against him,* and *take our revenge on him* for telling us of our faults and threatening us with the judgments of God." Note, Neither the innocence of the dove, no, nor the prudence of the serpent to help it, can secure men from unjust censure and false accusation.

II. Here is an account of the temptation he was in under this affliction ; his *feet were almost gone,* as the psalmist's, Ps. lxxiii. 2. And this is that which is most to be dreaded in affliction, being driven by it to sin, Neh. vi. 13. 1. He was tempted to quarrel with God for making him a prophet. This he begins with (*v.* 7) : *O Lord ! thou hast deceived me, and I was deceived.* This, as we read it, sounds very harshly. God's servants have been always ready to own that he is a faithful Master and never cheated them; and therefore this is the language of Jeremiah's folly and corruption. If, when God called him to be a prophet and told him he would *set him over the kingdoms* (ch. i. 10) and *make him a defenced city,* he flattered himself with an expectation of having universal respect paid to him as a messenger from heaven, and living safe and easy, and afterwards it proved otherwise, he must not say that God had deceived him; but that he had deceived himself; for he knew how the prophets before him had been persecuted, and had no reason to expect better treatment. Nay, God had expressly told him that all the *princes, priests, and people of the land would fight against him* (ch. i. 18, 19), which he had forgotten, else he would not have laid the blame on God thus. Christ thus told his disciples what opposition they should meet with, *that they might not be offended,* John xvi. 1, 2. But the words may very well be read thus : *Thou hast persuaded me, and I was persuaded;* it is the same word that was used, Gen. ix. 27, margin, *God shall persuade Japhet.* And Prov. xxv. 15, *By much forbearance is a prince persuaded.* And Hos. ii. 14, *I will allure her.* And this agrees best with what follows : " *Thou wast stronger than I,* didst over-persuade me with argument ; nay, didst overpower me, by the influence of thy Spirit upon me, and *thou hast prevailed.*" Jeremiah was very backward to undertake the prophetic office ; he pleaded that he was under age and unfit for the service ; but God overruled his pleas, and told him that *he must go,* ch. i. 6, 7. " Now, Lord," says he, " since thou hast put this office upon me, why dost thou not stand by me in it? Had I thrust myself upon it, I might justly have been in derision ; but why am I so when thou didst thrust me into it?" It was Jeremiah's infirmity to complain thus of God as putting a hardship upon him in calling him to be a prophet, which he would not have done had he considered the lasting honour thereby done him, sufficient to counterbalance the present contempt he was under. Note. As long as we see ourselves in the way of God and duty it is weakness and folly, when we meet with difficulties and discouragements in it, to wish we had never set out in it. 2. He was tempted to quit his work and give it over, partly because he himself met with so much hardship in it and partly because those to whom he was sent, instead of being edified and made better, were exasperated and made worse (v. 9) : " *Then I said,* Since by prophesying in the name of the Lord I gain nothing to him or myself but dishonour and disgrace, *I will not make mention of him* as my author for any thing I say, nor *speak any more in his name;* since my enemies do all they can to silence me, I will even silence myself, and speak no more, for I may as well speak to the stones as to them." Note, It

is a strong temptation to poor ministers to resolve that they will preach no more when they see their preaching slighted and wholly ineffectual. But let people dread putting their ministers into this temptation. Let not their labour be in vain with us, lest we provoke them to say that they will take no more pains with us, and provoke God to say, They shall take no more. Yet let not ministers hearken to this temptation, but go on in their duty, notwithstanding their discouragements, for this is the more thankworthy ; and, *though Israel be not gathered,* yet they *shall be glorious.*

III. Here is an account of his faithful adherence to his work and cheerful dependence on his God notwithstanding.

1. He found the grace of God mighty in him to keep him to his business, notwithstanding the temptation he was in to throw it up : " *I said,* in my haste, *I will speak no more in his name;* what I have in my heart to deliver I will stifle and suppress. But I soon found it was *in my heart as a burning fire shut up in my bones,* which glowed inwardly, and must have vent ; it was impossible to smother it ; I was like a man in a burning fever, uneasy and in a continual agitation ; while *I kept silence from good my heart was hot within me,* it was *pain and grief to me,* and I must speak, that I might be refreshed ;" Ps. xxxix. 2, 3 ; Job xxxii. 20. *While I kept silence, my bones waxed old,* Ps. xxxii. 3. See the power of the spirit of prophecy in those that were actuated by it ; and thus will a holy zeal for God even eat men up, and make them forget themselves. *I believed, therefore have I spoken.* Jeremiah was soon weary with forbearing to preach, and could not contain himself ; nothing puts faithful ministers to pain so much as being silenced, nor to terror so much as silencing themselves. Their convictions will soon triumph over temptations of that kind ; for *woe is unto me if I preach not the gospel,* whatever it cost me, 1 Cor. ix. 16. And it is really a mercy to have the word of God thus mighty in us to overpower our corruptions.

2. He was assured of God's presence with him, which would be sufficient to baffle all the attempts of his enemies against him (v. 11) : "They say, *We shall prevail against him;* the day will undoubtedly be our own. But I am sure that *they shall not prevail, they shall not prosper.* I can safely set them all at defiance, for *the Lord is with me,* is on my side, to take my part against them (Rom. viii. 31), to protect me from all their malicious designs upon me. He is with me to support me and bear me up under the burden which now presses me down. He is with me to make the word I preach answer the end he designs, though not the end I desire. He is with me as a mighty terrible one, to strike a terror upon them, and so to overcome them." Note, Even that in God which is terrible is really comfortable to his

servants that trust in him, for it shall be turned against those that seek to terrify his people. God's being a mighty God bespeaks him a terrible God to all those that take up arms against him or any one that, like Jeremiah, was commissioned by him. How terrible will the wrath of God be to those that think to daunt all about them and will themselves be daunted by nothing! The most formidable enemies that act against us appear despicable when we see the Lord for us as a *mighty terrible one,* Neh. iv. 14. Jeremiah speaks now with a good assurance: " If *the Lord be with me, my persecutors shall stumble,* so that, when they pursue me, they shall not overtake me (Ps. xxvii. 2), and then *they shall be greatly ashamed* of their impotent malice and fruitless attempts. Nay, *their everlasting confusion* and infamy *shall never be forgotten;* they shall not forget it themselves, but it shall be to them a constant and lasting vexation, whenever they think of it; others shall not forget it, but it shall leave upon them an indelible reproach."

3. He appeals to God against them as a righteous Judge, and prays judgment upon his cause, *v.* 12. He looks upon God as the God that *tries the righteous,* takes cognizance of them, and of every cause that they are interested in. He does not judge in favour of them with partiality, but *tries them,* and finding that they have right on their side, and that their persecutors wrong them and are injurious to them, he gives sentence for them. He that tries the righteous tries the unrighteous too, and he is very well qualified to do both; for he *sees the reins and the heart,* he certainly knows men's thoughts and affections, their aims and intentions, and therefore can pass an unerring judgment on their words and actions. Now this is the God, (1.) To whom the prophet here refers himself, and in whose court he lodges his appeal: *Unto thee have I opened my cause.* Not but that God perfectly knew his cause, and all the merits of it, without his opening; but the cause we commit to God we must spread before him. He knows it, but he will know it from us, and allows us to be particular in the opening of it, not to affect him, but to affect ourselves. Note, It will be an ease to our spirits, when we are oppressed and burdened, to open our cause to God and pour out our complaints before him. (2.) By whom he expects to be righted: *" Let me see thy vengeance on them,* such vengeance as thou thinkest fit to take for their conviction and my vindication, the vengeance thou usest to take on persecutors." Note, Whatever injuries are done us, we must not study to avenge ourselves, but must leave it to that God to do it *to whom vengeance belongs,* and who hath said, *I will repay.*

4. He greatly rejoices and praises God, in a full confidence that God would appear for his deliverance, *v.* 13. So full is he of

the comfort of God's presence with him, the divine protection he is under, and the divine promise he has to depend upon, that in a transport of joy he stirs up himself and others to give God the glory of it: *Sing unto the Lord, praise you the Lord* Here appears a great change with him since he began this discourse; the clouds are blown over, his complaints all silenced and turned into thanksgivings. He has now an entire confidence in that God whom (*v.* 7) he was distrusting; he stirs up himself to praise that name which (*v.* 9) he was resolving no more to make mention of. It was the lively exercise of faith that made this happy change, that turned his sighs into songs and his tremblings into triumphs. It is proper to express our hope in God by our praising him, and our praising God by our singing to him. That which is the matter of the praise is, *He hath delivered the soul of the poor from the hand of the evil-doers;* he means especially himself, his own poor soul. "He hath delivered me formerly when I was in distress, and now of late out of the hand of Pashur, and he will continue to deliver me, 2 Cor. i. 10. He will deliver my soul from the sin that I am in danger of falling into when I am thus persecuted. He hath *delivered me from the hand of evil-doers,* so that they have not gained their point, nor had their will." Note, Those that are faithful in well-doing need not fear those that are spiteful in evil-doing, for they have a God to trust to who has well-doers under the hand of his protection and evil-doers under the hand of his restraint.

14 Cursed *be* the day wherein I was born: let not the day wherein my mother bare me be blessed. 15 Cursed *be* the man who brought tidings to my father, saying, A man child is born unto thee; making him very glad. 16 And let that man be as the cities which the LORD overthrew, and repented not: and let him hear the cry in the morning, and the shouting at noon tide; 17 Because he slew me not from the womb; or that my mother might have been my grave, and her womb *to be* always great *with me.* 18 Wherefore came I forth out of the womb to see labour and sorrow, that my days should be consumed with shame?

What is the meaning of this? Does there *proceed out of the same mouth blessing and cursing?* Could he that said so cheerfully (*v.* 13), *Sing unto the Lord, praise you the Lord,* say so passionately (*v.* 14), *Cursed be the day wherein I was born?* How shall we reconcile these? What we have in these verses the prophet records, I suppose, to his own shame, as he had recorded that in the foregoing verses to God's glory. It seems to be a relation of the ferment he had been in while he was in the stocks, out of which by faith and hope he had recovered himself, rather than a new temptation which he afterwards fell into, and it should come in like that of David (Ps. xxxi. 22), *I said in my haste, I am cut off:* this is also implied, Ps. lxxvii. 7. When grace has got the victory it is good to remember the struggles of corruption, that we may be ashamed of ourselves and our own folly, may admire the goodness of God in not taking us at our word, and may be warned by it to double our guard upon our spirits another time. See here how strong the temptation was which the prophet, by divine assistance, got the victory over, and how far he yielded to it, that we may not despair if we through the weakness of the flesh be at any time thus tempted. Let us see here,

I. What the prophet's language was in this temptation. 1. He fastened a brand of infamy upon his birth-day, as Job did in a heat (*ch.* iii. 1): " *Cursed be the day wherein I was born.* It was an ill day to me (*v.* 14), because it was the beginning of sorrows, and an inlet to all this misery." It is a wish that he had never been born. Judas in hell has reason to wish so (Matt. xxvi. 24), but no man on earth has reason to wish so, because he knows not but he may yet become a vessel of mercy, much less has any good man reason to wish so. Whereas some keep their birth-day, at the return of the year, with gladness, he will look upon his birthday as a melancholy day, and will solemnize it with sorrow, and will have it looked upon as an ominous day. 2. He wished ill to the messenger that brought his father the news of his birth, *v.* 15. It made his father very glad to hear that he had a child born (perhaps it was his first-born), especially that it was a man-child, for then, being of the family of the priests, he might live to have the honour of serving God's altar; and yet he is ready to curse the man that brought him the tidings, when perhaps the father to whom they were brought gave him a gratuity for it. Here Mr. Gataker well observes, "That parents are often much rejoiced at the birth of their children when, if they did but foresee what misery they are born to, they would rather lament over them than rejoice in them." He is very free and very fierce in the curses he pronounces upon the messenger of his birth (*v.* 16): " *Let him be as the cities of Sodom and Gomorrah, which the Lord utterly overthrew, and repented not,* did not in the least mitigate or alleviate their misery. *Let him hear the cry* of the invading besieging enemy *in the morning,* as soon as he is stirring; then let him take the alarm, and by noon let him hear their *shouting* for victory. And thus let him live in constant terror.' 3. He is angry that the fate of the

Hebrews' children in Egypt was not his, that he was not *slain from the womb,* that his first breath was not his last, and that he was not strangled as soon as he came into the world, *v.* 17. He wishes the messenger of his birth had been better employed and had been his murderer; nay, that his mother of whom he was born had been, to her great misery, always with child of him, and so the womb in which he was conceived would have served, without more ado, as a grave for him to be buried in. Job intimates a near alliance and resemblance between the womb and the grave, Job i. 21. *Naked came I out of my mother's womb, and naked shall I return thither.* 4. He thinks his present calamities sufficient to justify these passionate wishes (*v.* 18): " *Wherefore came I forth out of the womb,* where I lay hid, was not seen, was not hated, where I lay safely and knew no evil, to see all this *labour and sorrow,* nay to have my *days consumed with shame,* to be continually vexed and abused, to have my life not only spent in trouble, but wasted and worn away by trouble?"

II. What use we may make of this. It is not recorded for our imitation, and yet we may learn good lessons from it. 1. See the vanity of human life and the vexation of spirit that attends it. If there were not another life after this, we should be tempted many a time to wish that we had never known this; for our few days here are full of trouble. 2. See the folly and absurdity of sinful passion, how unreasonably it talks when it is suffered to ramble. What nonsense is it to curse a day—to curse a messenger for the sake of his message! What a brutish barbarous thing for a child to wish his own mother had never been delivered of him! See Isa. xlv. 10. We can easily see the folly of it in others, and should take warning thence to suppress all such intemperate heats and passions in ourselves, to stifle them at first and not to suffer these evil spirits to speak. When the heart is hot, let the tongue be bridled, Ps. xxxix. 1, 2. 3. See the weakness even of good men, who are but men at the best. See how much those who think they stand are concerned to take heed lest they fall, and to pray daily, Father in heaven, *lead us not into temptation!*

CHAP. XXI.

It is plain that the prophecies of this book are not placed here in the same order in which they were preached; for there are chapters after this which concern Jehoahaz, Jehoiakim, and Jeconiah, who all reigned before Zedekiah, in whose reign the prophecy of this chapter bears date. Here is, I. The message which Zedekiah sent to the prophet, to desire him to enquire of the Lord for them, ver. 1, 2. II. The answer which Jeremiah, in God's name, sent to that message, in which, 1. He foretels the certain and inevitable ruin of the city, and the fruitlessness of their attempts for its preservation, ver. 3–7. 2. He advises the people to make the best of bad, by going over to the king of Babylon, ver. 8–10. 3. He advises the king and his family to repent and reform (ver. 11, 12), and not to trust to the strength of their city and grow secure, ver. 13, 14.

THE word which came unto Jeremiah from the Lord, when king Zedekiah sent unto him Pashur the son of Melchiah, and Zephaniah the son of Maaseiah the priest, saying, 2 Enquire, I pray thee, of the LORD for us; for Nebuchadrezzar king of Babylon maketh war against us; if so be that the LORD will deal with us according to all his wondrous works, that he may go up from us. 3 Then said Jeremiah unto them, Thus shall ye say to Zedekiah: 4 Thus saith the LORD God of Israel; Behold, I will turn back the weapons of war that *are* in your hands, wherewith ye fight against the king of Babylon, and *against* the Chaldeans, which besiege you without the walls, and I will assemble them into the midst of this city. 5 And I myself will fight against you with an outstretched hand and with a strong arm, even in anger, and in fury, and in great wrath. 6 And I will smite the inhabitants of this city, both man and beast: they shall die of a great pestilence. 7 And afterward, saith the LORD, I will deliver Zedekiah king of Judah, and his servants, and the people, and such as are left in this city from the pestilence, from the sword, and from the famine, into the hand of Nebuchadrezzar king of Babylon, and into the hand of their enemies, and into the hand of those that seek their life: and he shall smite them with the edge of the sword; he shall not spare them, neither have pity, nor have mercy.

Here is, I. A very humble decent message which king Zedekiah, when he was in distress, sent to Jeremiah the prophet. It is indeed charged upon this Zedekiah that he *humbled not himself before Jeremiah the prophet, speaking from the mouth of the Lord* (2 Chron. xxxvi. 12); he did not always humble himself as he did sometimes; he never humbled himself till necessity forced him to it; he humbled himself so far as to desire the prophet's assistance, but not so far as to take his advice, or to be ruled by him. Observe,

1. The distress which king Zedekiah was now in: *Nebuchadnezzar made war upon him*, not only invaded the land, but besieged the city, and had now actually invested it. Note, Those that put the evil day far from them will be the more terrified when it comes upon them; and those who before slighted God's ministers may then perhaps be glad to court an acquaintance with them.

2. The messengers he sent—*Pashur and*

Zephaniah, one belonging to the fifth course of the priests, the other to the twenty-fourth, 1 Chron. xxiv. 9, 18. It was well that he sent, and that he sent persons of rank; but it would have been better if he had desired a personal conference with the prophet, which no doubt he might easily have had if he would so far have humbled himself. Perhaps these priests were no better than the rest, and yet, when they were commanded by the king, they must carry a respectful message to the prophet, which was both a mortification to them and an honour to Jeremiah. He had rashly said (*ch.* xx. 18), *My days are consumed with shame;* and yet here we find that he lived to see better days than those were when he made that complaint; now he appears in reputation. Note, It is folly to say, when things are bad with us, "They will always be so." It is possible that those who are despised may come to be respected; and it is promised that those who *honour God he will honour,* and that those who have *afflicted his people shall bow to them,* Isa. lx. 14.

3. The message itself: *Enquire, I pray thee, of the Lord for us, v.* 2. Now that the Chaldean army had got into their borders, into their bowels, they were at length convinced that Jeremiah was a true prophet, though loth to own it and brought too late to it. Under this conviction they desire him to stand their friend with God, believing him to have that interest in heaven which none of their other prophets had, who had flattered them with hopes of peace. They now employ Jeremiah, (1.) To consult the mind of God for them: "*Enquire of the Lord for us;* ask him what course we shall take in our present strait, for the measures we have hitherto taken are all broken." Note, Those that will not take the direction of God's grace how to get clear of their sins would yet be glad of the directions of his providence how to get clear of their troubles. (2.) To seek the favour of God for them (so some read it): "*Entreat the Lord for us;* be an intercessor for us with God." Note, Those that slight the prayers of God's people and ministers when they are in prosperity may perhaps be glad of an interest in them when they come to be in distress. *Give us of your oil.* The benefit they promise themselves is, *It may be the Lord will deal with us* now *according to the wondrous works he wrought for our fathers,* that the enemy may raise the siege and *go up from us.* Observe, [1.] All their care is to get rid of their trouble, not to make their peace with God and be reconciled to him—"That our enemy may *go up from us,*" not, "That our God may return to us." Thus Pharaoh (Exod. x. 17): *Entreat the Lord that he may take away this death.* [2.] All their hope is that God had done wondrous works formerly in the deliverance of Jerusalem when Sennacherib besieged it, at the prayer of Isaiah (so we

are told, 2 Chron. xxxii. 20, 21), and who can tell but he may destroy these besiegers (as he did those) at the prayer of Jeremiah? But they did not consider how different the character of Zedekiah and his people was from that of Hezekiah and his people : those were days of general reformation and piety, these of general corruption and apostasy. Jerusalem is now the reverse of what it was then. Note, It is folly to think that God should do for us while we hold fast our iniquity as he did for those that held fast their integrity.

II. A very startling cutting reply which God, by the prophet, sent to that message. If Jeremiah had been to have answered the message of himself we have reason to think that he would have returned a comfortable answer, in hope that their sending such a message was an indication of some good purposes in them, which he would be glad to make the best of, for he did not desire the woeful day. But God knows their hearts better than Jeremiah does, and sends them an answer which has scarcely one word of comfort in it. He sends it to them in the name of *the Lord God of Israel* (v. 3), to intimate to them that though God allowed himself to be called the *God of Israel*, and had done great things for Israel formerly, and had still great things in store for Israel, pursuant to his covenants with them, yet this should stand the present generation in no stead, who were Israelites in name only, and not in deed, any more than God's dealings with them should cut off his relation to Israel as their God. It is here foretold,

1. That God will render all their endeavours for their own security fruitless and ineffectual (v. 4) : "I will be so far from teaching your hands to war, and putting an edge upon your swords, that I will *turn back the weapons of war that are in your hand*, when you sally out upon the besiegers to beat them off, so that they shall not give the stroke you design ; nay, they shall recoil into your own faces, and be turned upon yourselves." Nothing can make for those who have God against them.

2. That the besiegers shall in a little time make themselves masters of Jerusalem, and of all its wealth and strength : *I will assemble those in the midst of this city* who are now surrounding it. Note, If that place which should have been a centre of devotion be made a centre of wickedness, it is not strange if God make it a rendezvous of destroyers.

3. That God himself will be their enemy ; and then I know not who can befriend them, no, not Jeremiah himself (v. 5) : "I will be so far from protecting you, as I have done formerly in a like case, that *I myself will fight against you.*" Note, Those who rebel against God may justly expect that he will make war upon them, and that, (1.) With the power of a God who is irresistibly victo-

rious : *I will fight against you with an outstretched hand*, which will reach far, and *with a strong arm*, which will strike home and wound deeply. (2.) With the displeasure of a God who is indisputably righteous. It is not a correction in love, but an execution *in anger, in fury, and in great wrath ;* it is upon a sentence sworn in wrath, against which there will lie no exception, and it will soon be found what a fearful thing it is to fall into the hands of the living God.

4. That those who, for their own safety, decline sallying out upon the besiegers, and so avoid their sword, shall yet not escape the sword of God's justice (v. 6) : *I will smite those that abide in the city* (so it may be read), *both man and beast*, both the beasts that are for food and those that are for service in war, foot and horse *; they shall die of a great pestilence*, which shall rage within the walls, while the enemies are encamped about them. Though Jerusalem's gates and walls may for a time keep out the Chaldeans, they cannot keep out God's judgments. His arrows of pestilence can reach those that think themselves safe from other arrows.

5. That the king himself, and all the people that escape the *sword, famine*, and *pestilence*, shall fall *into the hands* of the Chaldeans, who shall cut them off in cold blood (v. 7) : They *shall not spare them*, nor *have pity* on them. Let not those expect to find mercy with men who have forfeited God's compassions, and shut themselves out from his mercy. Thus had the decree gone forth ; and then to what purpose was it for Jeremiah to *enquire of the Lord for them?*

8 And unto this people thou shalt say, Thus saith the LORD ; Behold, I set before you the way of life, and the way of death. 9 He that abideth in this city shall die by the sword, and by the famine, and by the pestilence : but he that goeth out, and falleth to the Chaldeans that besiege you, he shall live, and his life shall be unto him for a prey. 10 For I have set my face against this city for evil, and not for good, saith the LORD : it shall be given into the hand of the king of Babylon, and he shall burn it with fire. 11 And touching the house of the king of Judah, *say*, Hear ye the word of the LORD ; 12 O house of David, thus saith the LORD ; Execute judgment in the morning, and deliver *him that is* spoiled out of the hand of the oppressor, lest my fury go out like fire, and burn that none can quench *it*, because of the evil of your doings. 13 Behold, I

am against thee, O inhabitant of the valley, *and* rock of the plain, saith the LORD; which say, Who shall come down against us? or who shall enter into our habitations? 14 But I will punish you according to the fruit of your doings, saith the LORD: and I will kindle a fire in the forest thereof, and it shall devour all things round about it.

By the civil message which the king sent to Jeremiah it appeared that both he and the people began to have a respect for him, which it would have been Jeremiah's policy to make some advantage of for himself; but the reply which God obliges him to make is enough to crush the little respect they begin to have for him, and to exasperate them against him more than ever. Not only the predictions in the foregoing verses, but the prescriptions in these, were provoking; for here,

I. He advises the people to surrender and desert to the Chaldeans, as the only means left them to save their lives, *v.* 8—10. This counsel was very displeasing to those who were flattered by their false prophets into a desperate resolution to hold out to the last extremity, trusting to the strength of their walls and the courage of their soldiery to keep out the enemy, or to their foreign aids to raise the siege. The prophet assures them, " *The city shall be given into the hand of the king of Babylon,* and he shall not only plunder it, but *burn it with fire,* for God himself hath *set his face against this city for evil and not for good,* to lay it waste and not to protect it, *for evil* which shall have no good mixed with it, no mitigation or merciful allay; and therefore, if you would make the best of bad, you must beg quarter of the Chaldeans, and surrender prisoners of war." In vain did Rabshakeh persuade the Jews to do this while they had God for them (Isa. xxxvi. 16), but it was the best course they could take now that God was against them. Both the law and the prophets had often set before them life and death in another sense —life if they obey the voice of God, death if they persist in disobedience, Deut. xxx. 19. But they had slighted that life which would have made them truly happy, to upbraid them with which the prophet here uses the same expression (*v.* 8): *Behold, I set before you the way of life and the way of death,* which denotes not, as that, a fair proposal, but a melancholy dilemma, advising them of two evils to choose the less; and that less evil, a shameful and wretched captivity, is all the life now left for them to propose to themselves. *He that abides in the city,* and trusts to that to secure him, shall certainly die either by *the sword* without the walls or *famine* or *pestilence* within. But he that can so far bring down his spirit, and quit his

vain hopes, as to go out, and fall *to the Chaldeans, his life shall be given him for a prey;* he shall save his life, but with much difficulty and hazard, as a prey is taken from the mighty. It is an expression like that, *He shall be saved, yet so as by fire.* He shall escape but very narrowly, or he shall have such surprising joy and satisfaction in escaping with his life from such a universal destruction as shall equal theirs that divide the spoil. They thought to make a prey of the camp of the Chaldeans, as their ancestors did that of the Assyrians (Isa. xxxiii. 23), but they will be sadly disappointed; if by yielding at discretion they can but save their lives, that is all the prey they must promise themselves. Now one would think this advice from a prophet, in God's name, should have gained some credit with them and been universally followed; but, for aught that appears, there were few or none that took it; so wretchedly were their hearts hardened, to their destruction.

II. He advises the king and princes to reform, and make conscience of the duty of their place. Because it was the king that sent the message to him, in the reply there shall be a particular word for *the house of the king,* not to compliment or court them (that was no part of the prophet's business, no, not when they did him the honour to send to him), but to give them wholesome counsel (*v.* 11, 12): " *Execute judgment in the morning;* do it carefully and diligently. Those magistrates that would fill up their place with duty had need rise betimes. Do it quickly, and do not delay to do justice upon appeals made to you, and tire out poor petitioners as you have done. Do not lie in your beds in a morning to sleep away the debauch of the night before, nor spend the morning in pampering the body (as those princes, Eccl. x. 16), but spend it in the despatch of business. You would be delivered out of the hand of those that distress you, and expect that therein God should do you justice; see then that you do justice to those that apply to you, and *deliver them out of the hand of their oppressors, lest my fury go out like fire* against you in a particular manner, and you fare worst who think to escape best, *because of the evil of your doings."* Now, 1. This intimates that it was their neglect to do their duty that brought all this desolation upon the people. It was the *evil of their doings* that kindled the fire of God's wrath. Thus plainly does he deal even with the *house of the king;* for those that would have the benefit of a prophet's prayers must thankfully take a prophet's reproofs. 2. This directs them to take the right method for a national reformation. The princes must begin, and set a good example, and then the people will be invited to reform. They must use their power for the punishment of wrong, and then the people will be obliged to reform. He reminds them that they are *the house of David,* and therefore should tread in his steps, who executed judgment and justice to his people. 3. This gives them some encouragement to hope that there may yet be a lengthening of their tranquillity, Dan. iv. 27. If any thing will recover their state from the brink of ruin, this will.

III. He shows them the vanity of all their hopes so long as they continued unreformed, *v.* 13, 14. Jerusalem is an *inhabitant of the valley,* guarded with mountains on all sides, which were their natural fortifications, making it difficult for an army to approach them. It is a *rock of the plain,* which made it difficult for an enemy to undermine them. These advantages of their situation they trusted to more than to the power and promise of God; and, thinking their city by these means to be impregnable, they set the judgments of God at defiance, saying, " *Who shall come down against us?* None of our neighbours dare make a descent upon us, or, if they do, *who shall enter into our habitations?*" They had some colour for this confidence; for it appears to have been the sense of all their neighbours that no enemy could force his way into Jerusalem, Lam. iv. 12. But those are least safe that are most secure. God soon shows the vanity of that challenge, *Who shall come down against us?* when he says (*v.* 13), *Behold, I am against thee.* They had indeed by their wickedness driven God out of their city when he would have tarried with them as a friend; but they could not by their bulwarks keep them out of their city when he came against them as an enemy. If God be for us, who can be against us? But, if he be against us, who can be for us, to stand us in any stead? Nay, he comes against them not as an enemy that may lawfully and with some hope of success be resisted, but as a judge that cannot be resisted; for he says (*v.* 14), *I will punish you,* by due course of law, *according to the fruit of your doings,* that is, according to the merit of them and the direct tendency of them. That shall be brought upon you which is the natural product of sin. Nay, he will not only come with the anger of an enemy and the justice of a judge, but with the force of a consuming fire, which has no compassion, as a judge sometimes has, nor spares any thing combustible that comes in its way. Jerusalem has become a forest, in which God will *kindle a fire* that shall consume all before it; for our God is himself *a consuming fire;* and *who is able to stand in his sight* when once he is angry?

CHAP. XXII.

Upon occasion of the message sent in the foregoing chapter to the house of the king, we have here recorded some sermons which Jeremiah preached at court, in some preceding reigns, that it might appear they had had fair warning long before that fatal sentence was pronounced upon them, and were put in a way to prevent it. Here is, I. A message sent to the royal family, as it should seem in the reign of Jehoiakim, relating partly to Jehoahaz, who was carried away captive into Egypt, and partly to Jehoiakim, who succeeded him and was now upon the throne. The king and princes are exhorted to execute judgment, and are assured that, if they did so, the royal family should flourish, but otherwise it

should be ruined, ver. 1—9. Jehoahaz, called here Shallum, is lamented, ver. 10—12. Jehoiakim is reproved and threatened, ver. 13—19. II. Another message sent them in the reign of Jehoiachin (alias, Jeconiah) the son of Jehoiakim. He is charged with an obstinate refusal to hear, and is threatened with destruction, and it is foretold that in him Solomon's house should fail, ver. 20—30.

THUS saith the LORD; Go down to the house of the king of Judah, and speak there this word, 2 And say, Hear the word of the LORD, O king of Judah, that sittest upon the throne of David, thou, and thy servants, and thy people that enter in by these gates: 3 Thus saith the LORD; Execute ye judgment and righteousness, and deliver the spoiled out of the hand of the oppressor: and do no wrong, do no violence to the stranger, the fatherless, nor the widow, neither shed innocent blood in this place. 4 For if ye do this thing indeed, then shall there enter in by the gates of this house kings sitting upon the throne of David, riding in chariots and on horses, he, and his servants, and his people. 5 But if ye will not hear these words, I swear by myself, saith the LORD, that this house shall become a desolation. 6 For thus saith the LORD unto the king's house of Judah; Thou *art* Gilead unto me, *and* the head of Lebanon: *yet* surely I will make thee a wilderness, *and* cities *which* are not inhabited. 7 And I will prepare destroyers against thee, every one with his weapons: and they shall cut down thy choice cedars, and cast *them* into the fire. 8 And many nations shall pass by this city, and they shall say every man to his neighbour, Wherefore hath the LORD done thus unto this great city? 9 Then they shall answer, Because they have forsaken the covenant of the LORD their God, and worshipped other gods, and served them.

Here we have,

I. Orders given to Jeremiah to go and preach before the king. In the foregoing chapter we are told that Zedekiah sent messengers to the prophet, but here the prophet is bidden to go, in his own proper person, *to the house of the king,* and demand his attention to the word of the King of kings (*v.* 2): *Hear the word of the Lord, O king of Judah!* Subjects must own that where the word of the king is there is power over them, but kings must own that where the word of the Lord is there is power over them.

The *king of Judah* is here spoken to as *sitting upon the throne of David*, who was a man after God's own heart, as holding his dignity and power by the covenant made with David; let him therefore conform to his example, that he may have the benefit of the promises made to him. With the king his *servants* are spoken to, because a good government depends upon a good ministry as well as a good king.

II. Instructions given him what to preach.

1. He must tell them what was their duty, what was the good which the Lord their God required of them, *v.* 3. They must take care, (1.) That they do all the good they can with the power they have. They must do justice in defence of those that were injured, and must *deliver the spoiled out of the hand of their oppressors.* This was the duty of their place, Ps. lxxxii. 3. Herein they must be ministers of God for good. (2.) That they do no hurt with it, *no wrong, no violence.* That is the greatest wrong and violence which is done under colour of law and justice, and by those whose business it is to punish and protect from wrong and violence. They must *do no wrong to the stranger, fatherless, and widow;* for these God does in a particular manner patronise and take under his tuition, Exod. xxii. 21, 22.

2. He must assure them that the faithful discharge of their duty would advance and secure their prosperity, *v.* 4. There shall then be a succession of kings, an uninterrupted succession, *upon the throne of David* and of his line, these enjoying a perfect tranquillity, and living in great state and dignity, *riding in chariots and on horses,* as before, *ch.* xvii. 25. Note, the most effectual way to preserve the dignity of the government is to do the duty of it.

3. He must likewise assure them that the iniquity of their family, if they persisted in it, would be the ruin of their family, though it was a royal family (*v.* 5): *If you will not hear,* will not obey, *this house shall become a desolation,* the palace of the kings of Judah shall fare no better than other habitations in Jerusalem. Sin has often been the ruin of royal palaces, though ever so stately, ever so strong. This sentence is ratified by an oath: *I swear by myself* (and God can swear by no greater, Heb. vi. 13) that this house shall be laid in ruins. Note, Sin will be the ruin of the houses of princes as well as of mean men.

4. He must show how fatal their wickedness would be to their kingdom as well as to themselves, to Jerusalem especially, the royal city, *v.* 6—9. (1.) It is confessed that Judah and Jerusalem had been valuable in God's eyes and considerable in their own: *Thou art Gilead unto me and the head of Lebanon.* Their lot was cast in a place that was rich and pleasant as Gilead; Zion was a stronghold, as stately as Lebanon: this they trusted to as their security. But, (2.) This shall not protect them; the country that is now fruitful

546

as Gilead shall be made *a wilderness.* The cities that are now strong as Lebanon shall be cities *not inhabited;* and, when the country is laid waste, the cities must be dispeopled. See how easily God's judgments can ruin a nation, and how certainly sin will do it. When this desolating work is to be done, [1.] There shall be those that shall do it effectually (*v.* 7): *I will prepare destroyers against thee;* I will *sanctify* them" (so the word is); " I will appoint them to this service and use them in it." Note, When destruction is designed destroyers are prepared, and perhaps are in the preparing, and things are working towards the designed destruction, and are getting ready for it, long before. And who can contend with destroyers of God's preparing? They shall destroy cities as easily as men fell trees in a forest: *They shall cut down thy choice cedars;* and yet, when they are down, shall value them no more than thorns and briers; they shall *cast them into the fire,* for their choicest cedars have become rotten ones and good for nothing else. [2.] There shall be those who shall be ready to justify God in the doing of it (*v.* 8, 9); persons of *many nations,* when they *pass by* the ruins of *this city* in their travels, will ask, *"Wherefore hath the Lord done thus unto this city?* How came so strong a city to be overpowered? so rich a city to be impoverished? so populous a city to be depopulated? so holy a city to be profaned? and a city that had been so dear to God to be abandoned by him?"* The reason is so obvious that it shall be ready in every man's mouth. Ask those *that go by the way,* Job xxi. 29. Ask the next man you meet, and he will tell you it was because they changed their gods, which other nations never used to do. They forsook *the covenant* of Jehovah their own God, revolted from their allegiance to him and from the duty which their covenant with him bound them to, and they *worshipped other gods and served them,* in contempt of him; and therefore he gave them up to this destruction. Note, God never casts any off until they first cast him off. *" Go,"* says God to the prophet, " and preach this to the royal family."

10 Weep ye not for the dead, neither bemoan him: *but* weep sore for him that goeth away: for he shall return no more, nor see his native country. 11 For thus saith the LORD touching Shallum the son of Josiah king of Judah, which reigned instead of Josiah his father, which went forth out of this place; He shall not return thither any more: 12 But he shall die in the place whither they have led him captive, and shall see this land no more. 13 Woe unto him that buildeth his house by unrighteous-

ness, and his chambers by wrong; *that* useth his neighbour's service without wages, and giveth him not for his work; 14 That saith, I will build me 'a wide house and large chambers, and cutteth him out windows; and *it is* ceiled with cedar, and painted with vermilion. 15 Shalt thou reign, because thou closest *thyself* in cedar? did not thy father eat and drink, and do judgment and justice, *and* then *it was* well with him? 16 He judged the cause of the poor and needy; then *it was* well *with him: was* not this to know me? saith the LORD. 17 But thine eyes and thine heart *are* not but for thy covetousness, and for to shed innocent blood, and for oppression, and for violence, to do *it*. 18 Therefore thus saith the LORD concerning Jehoiakim the son of Josiah king of Judah; They shall not lament for him, *saying*, Ah my brother! or, Ah sister! they shall not lament for him, *saying*, Ah lord! or, Ah his glory! 19 He shall be buried with the burial of an ass, drawn and cast forth beyond the gates of Jerusalem.

Kings, though they are gods to us, are men to God, and shall *die like men;* so it appears in these verses, where we have a sentence of death passed upon two kings who reigned successively in Jerusalem, two brothers, and both the ungracious sons of a very pious father.

I. Here is the doom of Shallum, who doubtless is the same with Jehoahaz; for he is that son of Josiah king of Judah who reigned *in the stead of Josiah his father* (v. 11), which Jehoahaz did by the act of the people, who made him king though he was not the eldest son, 2 Kings xxiii. 30; 2 Chron. xxxvi. 1. Among the sons of Josiah (1 Chron. iii. 15) there is one Shallum mentioned, and not Jehoahaz. Perhaps the people preferred him before his elder brother because they thought him a more active daring young man, and fitter to rule; but God soon showed them the folly of their injustice, and that it could not prosper, for within three months the king of Egypt came upon him, deposed him, and carried him away prisoner into Egypt, as God had threatened, Deut. xxviii. 68. It does not appear that any of the people were taken into captivity with him. We have the story 2 Kings xxiii. 34; 2 Chron. xxxvi. 4. Now here, 1. The people are directed to lament him rather than his father Josiah: " *Weep not for the dead*, weep not any more for Josiah." Jeremiah had been himself a true

mourner for him, and had stirred up the people to mourn for him (2 Chron. xxxv. 25): yet now he will have them go out of mourning for him, though it was but three months after his death, and to turn their tears into another channel. They must weep sorely for Jehoahaz, who had gone into Egypt; not that there was any great loss of him to the public, as there was of his father, but that his case was much more deplorable. Josiah went to the grave in peace and honour, was prevented from seeing the evil to come in this world and removed to see the good to come in the other world; and therefore, *Weep not for him*, but for his unhappy son, who is likely to live and die in disgrace and misery, a wretched captive. Note, Dying saints may be justly envied, while living sinners are justly pitied. And so dismal perhaps the prospect of the times may be that tears even for a Josiah, even for a Jesus, must be restrained, that they may be reserved for *ourselves and for our children*, Luke xxiii. 28. 2. The reason given is because he shall never return out of captivity, as he and his people expected, but shall die there. They were loth to believe this, therefore it is repeated here again and again, He shall *return no more*, v. 10. He shall never have the pleasure of seeing *his native country*, but shall have the continual grief of hearing of the desolations of it. He has gone *forth out of this place*, and shall *never return*, v. 11. *He shall die in the place whither they have led him captive*, v. 12. This came of his forsaking the good example of his father, and usurping the right of his elder brother. In Ezekiel's lamentation for the princes of Israel this Jehoahaz is represented as a young lion, that soon learned to *catch the prey*, but was taken, and brought in chains to Egypt, and was long expected to return, but in vain. See Ezek. xix. 3—5.

II. Here is the doom of Jehoiakim, who succeeded him. Whether he had any better right to the crown than Shallum we know not; for, though he was older than his predecessor, there seems to be another son of Josiah, older than he, called *Johanan*, 1 Chron. iii. 15. But this we know he ruled no better, and fared no better at last. Here we have,

1. His sins faithfully reproved. It is not fit for a private person to say to a king, *Thou art wicked;* but a prophet, who has a message from God, betrays his trust if he does not deliver it, be it ever so unpleasing, even to kings themselves. Jehoiakim is not here charged with idolatry, and probably he had not yet put Urijah the prophet to death (as we find afterwards he did, ch. xxvi. 22, 23), for then he would have been told of it here; but the crimes for which he is here reproved are, (1.) Pride, and affectation of pomp and splendour; as if all the business of a king were to look great, and to do good were to be the least of his care. He must build him-

self a stately palace, a *wide house*, and *large chambers, v.* 14. He must have *windows cut out* after the newest fashion, perhaps like sash-windows with us. The rooms must be *ceiled with cedar*, the richest sort of wood. His house must be as well roofed and wainscoted as the temple itself, or else it will not please him, 1 Kings vi. 15, 16. Nay, it must exceed that, for it must be painted with *minium*, or *vermilion*, which dyes red, or, as some read it, with *indigo*, which dyes blue. No doubt it is lawful for princes and great men to build, and beautify, and furnish their houses so as is agreeable to their dignity; but he that knows what is in man knew that Jehoiakim did this in the pride of his heart, which makes that to be sinful, exceedingly sinful, which is in itself lawful. Those therefore that are enlarging their houses, and making them more sumptuous, have need to look well to the frame of their own spirits in the doing of it, and carefully to watch against all the workings of vain-glory. But that which was particularly amiss in Jehoiakim's case was that he did this when he could not but perceive, both by the word of God and by his providence, that divine judgments were breaking in upon him. He reigned his first three years by the permission and allowance of the king of Egypt, and all the rest by the permission and allowance of the king of Babylon; and yet he that was no better than a viceroy will covet to vie with the greatest monarchs in building and furniture. Observe how peremptory he is in this resolution: " *I will build myself a wide house;* I am resolved *I will*, whoever advises me to the contrary." Note, It is the common folly of those that are sinking in their estates to covet to make a fair show. Many have unhumbled hearts under humbling providences, and look most haughty when God is bringing them down. This is striving with our Maker. (2.) Carnal security and confidence in his wealth, depending upon the continuance of his prosperity, as if his mountain now stood so strong that it could never be moved. He thought he must reign without any disturbance or interruption because he had *enclosed himself in cedar* (*v.* 15), as if that were too fine to be assaulted and too strong to be broken through, and as if God himself could not, for pity, give up such a stately house as that to be burned. Thus when Christ spoke of the destruction of the temple his disciples came to him, to show him what a magnificent structure it was, Matt. xxiii. 38; xxiv. 1. Note, Those wretchedly deceive themselves who think their present prosperity is a lasting security, and dream of reigning because they are *enclosed in cedar*. It is but in his own conceit that *the rich man's wealth is his strong city.* (3.) Some think he is here charged with sacrilege, and robbing the house of God to beautify and adorn his own house. He *cuts him out my windows* (so it is in the margin), which

some understand as if he had taken windows out of the temple to put into his own palace and then *painted them* (as it follows) *with vermilion*, that it might not be discovered, but might look of a piece with his own buildings. Note, Those cheat themselves, and ruin themselves at last, who think to enrich themselves by robbing God and his house; and, however they may disguise it, God discovers it. (4.) He is here charged with extortion and oppression, violence and injustice. He *built his house by unrighteousness*, with money unjustly got and materials which were not honestly come by, and perhaps upon ground obtained as Ahab obtained Naboth's vineyard. And, because he went beyond what he could afford, he defrauded his workmen of their wages, which is one of the sins that *cries in the ears of the Lord of hosts*, Jam. v. 4. God takes notice of the wrong done by the greatest of men to their poor servants and labourers, and will repay those, in justice, that will not in justice pay those whom they employ, but *use their neighbour's service without wages*. Observe, The greatest of men must look upon the meanest as their neighbours, and be just to them accordingly, and love them as themselves. Jehoiakim was oppressive, not only in his buildings, but in the administration of his government. He did not do justice, made no conscience of shedding innocent blood, when it was to serve the purposes of his ambition, avarice, and revenge. He was all for *oppression* and *violence*, not to threaten it only, but to do it; and, when he was set upon any act of injustice, nothing should stop him, but he would go through with it. And that which was at the bottom of all was covetousness, that love of *money which is the root of all evil. Thy eyes and thy heart are not but for covetousness;* they were for that, and nothing else. Observe, In covetousness the heart walks after the eyes: it is therefore called *the lust of the eye*, 1 John ii. 16; Job xxxi. 7. It is *setting the eyes upon that which is not*, Prov. xxiii. 5. The eyes and the heart are then for covetousness when the aims and affections are wholly set upon the wealth of this world; and, where they are so, the temptation is strong to murder, oppression, and all manner of violence and villany. (5.) That which aggravated all his sins was that he was the son of a good father, who had left him a good example, if he would but have followed it (*v.* 15, 16): *Did not thy father eat and drink?* When Jehoiakim enlarged and enlightened his house it is probable that he spoke scornfully of his father for contenting himself with such a mean and inconvenient dwelling, below the grandeur of a sovereign prince, and ridiculed him as one that had a dull fancy, a low spirit, and could not find in his heart to lay out his money, nor cared for what was fashionable; that should not serve him which served his father: but God, by the prophet, tells him that his father, though he had not the spirit of building, was a man of an excellent spirit, a better man than he, and did better for himself and his family. Those children that despise their parents' old fashions commonly come short of their real excellences. Jeremiah tells him, [1.] That he was directed to do his duty by his father's practice: He *did judgment and justice;* he never did wrong to any of his subjects, never oppressed them, nor put any hardship upon them, but was careful to preserve all their just rights and properties. Nay, he not only did not abuse his power for the support of wrong, but he used it for the maintaining of right. He *judged the cause of the poor and needy,* was ready to hear the cause of the meanest of his subjects and do them justice. Note, The care of magistrates must be, not to support their grandeur and take their ease, but to do good, not only not to oppress the poor themselves, but to defend those that are oppressed. [2.] That he was encouraged to do his duty by his father's prosperity. *First,* God accepted him : " *Was not this to know me, saith the Lord?* Did he not hereby make it to appear that he rightly knew his God, and worshipped him, and consequently was known and owned of him?" Note, The right knowledge of God consists in doing our duty, particularly that which is the duty of our place and station in the world. *Secondly,* He himself had the comfort of it: *Did he not eat and drink* soberly and cheerfully, so as to fit himself for his business, *for strength and not for drunkenness?* Eccl. x. 17. He did *eat, and drink, and do judgment;* he did not (as perhaps Jehoiakim and his princes did) *drink, and forget the law, and pervert the judgment of the afflicted,* Prov. xxxi. 5. He did *eat and drink;* that is, God blessed him with great plenty, and he had the comfortable enjoyment of it himself and gave handsome entertainments to his friends, was very hospitable and very charitable. It was Jehoiakim's pride that he had built a fine house, but Josiah's true praise that he kept a good house. Many times those have least in them of true generosity that have the greatest affection for pomp and grandeur ; for, to support the extravagant expense of that, hospitality, bounty to the poor, yea, and justice itself, will be pinched. It is better to live with Josiah in an old-fashioned house, and do good, than live with Jehoiakim in a stately house, and leave debts unpaid. Josiah did *justice and judgment,* and then *it was well with him, v.* 15, and it is repeated again, *v.* 16. He lived very comfortably ; his own subjects, and all his neighbours, respected him ; and whatever he put his hand to prospered. Note, While we do well we may expect it will be well with us. This Jehoiakim knew, that his father found the way of duty to be the way of comfort, and yet he would not tread in his steps. Note, It should engage us to keep up religion in our day that our godly parents

kept it up in theirs and recommended it to us from their own experience of the benefit of it. They told us that they had found the promises which godliness has of the *life that now is* made good to them, and that religion and piety are friendly to outward prosperity. So that we are inexcusable if we turn aside from that good way.

2. Here we have Jehoiakim's doom faithfully read, *v.* 18, 19. We may suppose that it was in the utmost peril of his own life that Jeremiah here foretold the shameful death of Jehoiakim ; but *thus saith the Lord concerning* him, and therefore thus saith he. (1.) He shall die unlamented ; he shall make himself so odious by his oppression and cruelty that all about him shall be glad to part with him, and none shall do him the honour of dropping one tear for him, whereas his father, who *did judgment and justice,* was universally lamented ; and it is promised to Zedekiah that he should be lamented at his death, for he conducted himself better than Jehoiakim had done, *ch.* xxxiv. 5. His relations shall not *lament him,* no, not with the common expressions of grief used at the funeral of the meanest, where they cried, *Ah, my brother!* or, *Ah, sister!* His subjects shall not lament him, nor cry out, as they used to do at the graves of their princes, *Ah, lord!* or, *Ah his glory!* It is sad for any to live so that, when they die, none will be sorry to part with them. Nay, (2.) He shall lie unburied. This is worse than the former. Even those that have no tears to grace the funerals of the dead with would willingly have them buried out of their sight ; but Jehoiakim shall be *buried with the burial of an ass,* that is, he shall have no burial at all, but his dead body shall be cast into a ditch or upon a dunghill ; it shall be *drawn,* or dragged, ignominiously, and *cast forth beyond the gates of Jerusalem.* It is said, in the story of Jehoiakim (2 Chron. xxxvi. 6), that Nebuchadnezzar *bound him in fetters, to carry him to Babylon,* and (Ezek. xix. 9) that he was *brought in chains to the king of Babylon.* But it is probable that he died a prisoner, before he was carried away to Babylon as was intended ; perhaps he died for grief, or, in the pride of his heart, hastened his own end, and, for that reason, was denied a decent burial, as self-murderers usually are with us. Josephus says that Nebuchadnezzar slew him at Jerusalem, and left his body thus exposed, somewhere at a great distance from the *gates of Jerusalem.* And it is said (2 Kings xxiv. 6) *he slept with his fathers.* When he built himself a stately house, no doubt he designed himself a stately sepulchre ; but see how he was disappointed. Note, Those that are lifted up with great pride are commonly reserved for some great disgrace in life or death.

20 Go up to Lebanon, and cry ; and lift up thy voice in Bashan, and

cry from the passages: for all thy lovers are destroyed. 21 I spake unto thee in thy prosperity; *but* thou saidst, I will not hear. This *hath been* thy manner from thy youth, that thou obeyest not my voice. 22 The wind shall eat up all thy pastors, and thy lovers shall go into captivity: surely then shalt thou be ashamed and confounded for all thy wickedness. 23 O inhabitant of Lebanon, that makest thy nest in the cedars, how gracious shalt thou be when pangs come upon thee, the pain as of a woman in travail! 24 *As* I live, saith the LORD, though Coniah the son of Jehoiakim king of Judah were the signet upon my right hand, yet would I pluck thee thence; 25 And I will give thee into the hand of them that seek thy life, and into the hand *of them* whose face thou fearest, even into the hand of Nebuchadrezzar king of Babylon, and into the hand of the Chaldeans. 26 And I will cast thee out, and thy mother that bare thee, into another country, where ye were not born; and there shall ye die. 27 But to the land whereunto they desire to return, thither shall they not return. 28 *Is* this man Coniah a despised broken idol? *is he* a vessel wherein *is* no pleasure? wherefore are they cast out, he and his seed, and are cast into a land which they know not? 29 O earth, earth, earth, hear the word of the LORD. 30 Thus saith the LORD, Write ye this man childless, a man *that* shall not prosper in his days: for no man of his seed shall prosper, sitting upon the throne of David, and ruling any more in Judah.

This prophecy seems to have been calculated for the ungracious inglorious reign of Jeconiah, or Jehoiachin, the son of Jehoiakim, who succeeded him in the government, reigned but three months, and was then carried captive to Babylon, where he lived many years, *ch.* lii. 31. We have, in these verses, a prophecy, I. Of the desolations of the kingdom, which were now hastening on apace, *v.* 20—23. Jerusalem and Judah are here spoken to, or the Jewish state as a single person, and we have it here under a threefold character:—1. Very haughty in a day of peace and safety (*v.* 21): "*I spoke unto thee in thy*

prosperity, spoke by my servants the prophets, reproofs, admonitions, counsels, *but thou saidst, I will not hear*, I will not heed, *thou obeyedst not my voice*, and wast resolved that thou wouldst not, and hadst the front to tell me so." It is common for those that live at ease to live in contempt of the word of God. *Jeshurun waxed fat, and kicked.* This is so much the worse that they had it by kind: *This has been thy manner from thy youth.* They were called *transgressors from the womb*, Isa xlviii. 8. 2. Very timorous upon the alarms of trouble (*v.* 20): "When thou seest *all thy lovers destroyed*, when thou findest thy idols unable to help thee and thy foreign alliances failing thee, thou wilt then go up to Lebanon, and cry, as one undone and giving up all for lost, cry with a bitter cry; thou wilt cry, *Help, help, or we are lost;* thou wilt *lift up thy voice* in fearful shrieks upon *Lebanon* and *Bashan*, two high hills, in hope to be heard thence by the advantage of the rising ground. Thou wilt *cry from the passages*, from the roads, where thou wilt ever and anon be in distress." Thou wilt cry from *Abarim* (so some read it, as a proper name), a famous mountain in the border of Moab. "Thou wilt cry, as those that are in great consternation use to do, to all about thee; but in vain, for (*v.* 22) *the wind shall eat up all thy pastors*, or *rulers*, that should protect and lead thee, and provide for thy safety; they shall be blasted, and withered, and brought to nothing, as buds and blossoms are by a bleak or freezing wind; they shall be devoured suddenly, insensibly, and irresistibly, as fruits by the wind. *Thy lovers*, that thou dependest upon and hast an affection for, shall *go into captivity*, and shall be so far from saving thee that they shall not be able to save themselves." 3. Very tame under the heavy and lasting pressures of trouble: "When there appears no relief from any of thy confederates, and thy own priests are at a loss, *then shalt thou be ashamed and confounded for all thy wickedness*," *v.* 22. Note, Many will never be ashamed of their sins till they are brought by them to the last extremity; and it is well if we get this good by our straits to be brought by them to confusion for our sins. The Jewish state is here called *an inhabitant of Lebanon*, because that famous forest was within their border (*v.* 23), and all their country was wealthy, and well-guarded as with Lebanon's natural fastnesses; but so proud and haughty were they that they are said to *make their nest in the cedars*, where they thought themselves out of the reach of all danger, and whence they looked with contempt upon all about them. "But, *how gracious wilt thou be when pangs come upon thee!* Then thou wilt humble thyself before God and promise amendment. When thou art overthrown in stony places thou wilt be glad to *hear those words* which in thy prosperity *thou wouldst not hear*, Ps.

cxli. 6. Then thou wilt endeavour to make thyself acceptable with that God whom, before, thou madest light of." Note, Many have their pangs of piety who, when the pangs are over, show that they have no true piety. Some give another sense of it: "What will all thy pomp, and state, and wealth avail thee? What will become of it all, or what comfort shalt thou have of it, when thou shalt be in these distresses? No more than *a woman in travail*, full of pains and fears, can take comfort in her ornaments while she is in that condition." So Mr. Gataker. Note, Those that are proud of their worldly advantages would do well to consider how they will look when pangs come upon them, and how they will then have lost all their beauty.

II. Here is a prophecy of the disgrace of the king; his name was *Jeconiah*, but he is here once and again called *Coniah*, in contempt. The prophet shortens or nicks his name, and gives him, as we say, a nickname, perhaps to denote that he should be despoiled of his dignity, that his reign should be shortened, and the number of his months cut off in the midst. Two instances of dishonour are here put upon him :—

1. He shall be carried away *into captivity* and shall spend and end his days in bondage. He was born to a crown, but it should quickly fall from his head, and he should exchange it for fetters. Observe the steps of this judgment. (1.) God will abandon him, *v.* 24. The God of truth says it, and confirms it with an oath : " *Though he were the signet upon my right hand* (his predecessors have been so, and he might have been so if he had conducted himself well, but he being degenerated) *I will pluck him thence.*" The godly kings of Judah had been as signets on God's right hand, near and dear to him; he had gloried in them, and made use of them as instruments of his government, as the prince does of his signet-ring, or sign manual ; but Coniah has made himself utterly unworthy of the honour, and therefore the privilege of his birth shall be no security to him ; notwithstanding that, he shall be thrown off. Answerable to this threatening against Jeconiah is God's promise to Zerubbabel, when he made him his people's guide in their return out of captivity (Hag. ii. 23) : *I will take thee, O Zerubbabel! my servant, and make thee as a signet.* Those that think themselves as signets on God's right hand must not be secure, but fear lest they be plucked thence. (2.) The king of Babylon shall seize him. *Those* know not what enemies and mischiefs they lie exposed to who have thrown themselves out of God's protection, *v.* 25. The Chaldeans are here said to be such as had a spite to *Coniah ;* they *sought his life ;* no less than that, they thought, would satisfy their rage ; they were such as he had a dread of (they are those *whose face thou fearest*) which would make

it the more terrible to him to fall into their hands, especially when it was God himself that gave *him into their hands*. And, if God deliver him to them, who can deliver him from them? (3.) He and his family shall be carried to Babylon, where they shall wear out many tedious years of their lives in a miserable captivity—*he and his mother* (*v.* 26), *he and his seed* (*v.* 28), that is, he and all the royal family (for he had no children of his own when he went into captivity), or he and the children in his loins ; they shall all be cast out to another country, to a strange country, *a country where they were not born*, nor such a country as that where they were born, *a land which they know not*, in which they have no acquaintance with whom to converse or from whom to expect any kindness. Thither they shall be carried, from a land where they were entitled to dominion, into a land where they shall be compelled to servitude. But have they no hopes of seeing their own country again? No : *To the land whereunto they desire to return, thither shall they not return, v.* 27. They conducted themselves ill in it when they were in it, and therefore they shall never see it more. Jehoahaz was carried to Egypt, the land of the south, Jeconiah to Babylon, the land of the north, both far remote, the quite contrary way, and must never expect to meet again, nor either of them to breathe their native air again. Those that had abused the dominion they had over others were justly brought thus under the dominion of others. Those that had indulged and gratified their sinful desires, by their oppression, luxury, and cruelty, were justly denied the gratification of their innocent desire to see their own native country again. We may observe something very emphatic in that part of this threatening (*v.* 26), *In the country where you were not born, there shall you die.* As there is a *time to be born* and a *time to die*, so there is a place to be born in and a place to die in. We know where we were born, but where we shall die we know not; it is enough that our God knows. Let it be our care that we die in Christ, and then it will be well with us, wherever we die, though it should be in a far country. (4.) This shall render him very mean and despicable in the eyes of all his neighbours. They shall be ready to say (*v.* 26), "*Is this Coniah a despised broken idol?* Yes, certainly he is, and much debased from what he was." [1.] Time was when he was dignified, nay, when he was almost deified. The people who had seen his father lately deposed were ready to adore him when they saw him upon the throne, but now *he is a despised broken idol,* which, when it was whole, was worshipped, but, when it is rotten and broken, is thrown by and despised, and nobody regards it, or remembers what it has been. Note, What is idolized will, first or last, be despised and broken ; what is unjustly honoured will be justly contemned, and rivals with God will be the scorn of man. Whatever we idolize we shall be disappointed in and then shall despise. [2.] Time was when he was delighted in; but now he is *a vessel in which is no pleasure*, or to which there is no desire, either because grown out of fashion or because cracked or dirtied, and so rendered unserviceable. Those whom God has no pleasure in will, some time or other, be so mortified that men will have no pleasure in them.

2. He shall leave no posterity to inherit his honour. The prediction of this is ushered in with a solemn preface (*v.* 29): *O earth, earth, earth! hear the word of the Lord.* Let all the inhabitants of the world take notice of these judgments of God upon a nation and a family that had been near and dear to him, and thence infer that God is impartial in the administration of justice. Or it is an appeal to the earth itself on which we tread, since those that dwell on earth are so deaf and careless, like that (Isa. i. 2), *Hear, O heavens! and give ear, O earth!* God's word, however slighted, will be heard ; the earth itself will be made to hear it, and yield to it, when it, and all the works that are therein, shall be burnt up. Or it is a call to men that *mind earthly things*, that are swallowed up in those things and are inordinate in the pursuit of them; such have need to be called upon again and again, and a third time, to *hear the word of the Lord.* Or it is a call to men considered as mortal, of the earth, and hastening to the earth again. We all are so ; earth we are, *dust we are*, and, in consideration of that, are concerned to hear and regard *the word of the Lord*, that, though we are earth, we may be found among those whose names are written in heaven. Now that which is here to be taken notice of is that Jeconiah is *written childless* (*v.* 30), that is, as it follows, *No man of his seed shall prosper, sitting upon the throne of David.* In him the line of David was extinct as a royal line. Some think that he had children born in Babylon because mention is made of his seed being cast out there (*v.* 28) and that they died before him. We read in the genealogy (1 Chron. iii. 17) of seven sons of Jeconiah Assir (that is, Jeconiah the captive) of whom Salathiel is the first. Some think that they were only his adopted sons, and that when it is said (Matt. i. 12), *Jeconiah begat Salathiel*, no more is meant than that he bequeathed to him what claims and pretensions he had to the government, the rather because Salathiel is called the *son of Neri* of *the house of Nathan*, Luke iii. 27, 31. Whether he had children begotten, or only adopted, thus far he was childless that none of his seed ruled as kings in Judah. He was the *Augustulus* of that empire, in whom it determined. Whoever

552

are childless, it is God that writes them so; and those who take no care to do good in their days cannot expect to prosper in their days.

CHAP. XXIII.

In this chapter the prophet, in God's name, is dealing his reproofs and threatenings, I. Among the careless princes, or pastors of the people (ver. 1, 2), yet promising to take care of the flock, which they had been wanting in their duty to, ver. 3—8. II. Among the wicked prophets and priests, whose bad character is here given at large in divers instances, especially their imposing upon the people with their pretended inspirations, at which the prophet is astonished, and for which they must expect to be punished, ver. 9—32. III. Among the profane people, who ridiculed God's prophets and bantered them, ver. 33—40. When all have thus corrupted their way they must all expect to be told faithfully of it.

WOE be unto the pastors that destroy and scatter the sheep of my pasture! saith the Lord. 2 Therefore thus saith the Lord God of Israel against the pastors that feed my people; Ye have scattered my flock, and driven them away, and have not visited them: behold, I will visit upon you the evil of your doings, saith the Lord. 3 And I will gather the remnant of my flock out of all countries whither I have driven them, and will bring them again to their folds ; and they shall be fruitful and increase. 4 And I will set up shepherds over them which shall feed them: and they shall fear no more, nor be dismayed, neither shall they be lacking, saith the Lord. 5 Behold, the days come, saith the Lord, that I will raise unto David a righteous Branch, and a king shall reign and prosper, and shall execute judgment and justice in the earth. 6 In his days Judah shall be saved, and Israel shall dwell safely: and this *is* his name whereby he shall be called, THE LORD OUR RIGHTEOUSNESS. 7 Therefore, behold, the days come, saith the Lord, that they shall no more say, The Lord liveth, which brought up the children of Israel out of the land of Egypt; 8 But, The Lord liveth, which brought up and which led the seed of the house of Israel out of the north country, and from all countries whither I had driven them ; and they shall dwell in their own land.

I. Here is a word of terror to the negligent shepherds. The day is at hand when God will reckon with them concerning the trust and charge committed to them : *Woe be to the pastors* (to the *rulers*, both in church and state) who should be to those they are set over as pastors to lead them, feed them, protect them, and take care of them. They are not owners of the sheep. God here calls them *the sheep of my pasture*, whom I am interested in, and have provided good pasture for. Woe be to those therefore who are commanded to feed God's people, and pretend to do it, but who, instead of that, *scatter the flock*, and *drive them away* by their violence and oppression, and *have not visited them*, nor taken any care for their welfare, nor concerned themselves at all to do them good. In not visiting them, and doing their duty to them, they did in effect scatter them and drive them away. The beasts of prey scattered them, and the shepherds are in the fault, who should have kept them together. *Woe be to them* when God will visit upon them the evil of their doings and deal with them as they deserve. They would not visit the flock in a way of duty, and therefore God will visit them in a way of vengeance.

II. Here is a word of comfort to the neglected sheep. Though the under-shepherds take no care of them, no pains with them, but betray them, the chief Shepherd will look after them. *When my father and my mother forsake me, then the Lord taketh me up.* Though the interests of God's church in the world are neglected by those who should take care of them, and postponed to their own private secular interests, yet they shall not therefore sink. God will perform his promise, though those he employs do not perform their duty.

1. The dispersed Jews shall at length return to their own land, and be happily settled there under a good government, *v.* 3, 4. Though there be but a remnant of God's flock left, a little remnant, that has narrowly escaped destruction, he will gather that remnant, will find them out wherever they are and find out ways and means to bring them back out of all countries *whither he had driven them*. It was the justice of God, for the sin of their shepherds, that dispersed them; but the mercy of God shall gather in the sheep, when the shepherds that betrayed them are cut off. *They shall be brought* to their former habitations, as sheep to their folds, and there *they shall be fruitful, and increase* in numbers. And, though their former shepherds took no care of them, it does not therefore follow that they shall have no more. If some have abused a sacred office, that is no good reason why it should be abolished. "They destroyed the sheep, but I will set shepherds over them who shall make it their business to feed them." Formerly they were continually exposed and disturbed with some alarm or other; but now *they shall fear no more, nor be dismayed;* they shall be in no danger from without, in no fright from within. Formerly some or other of them were ever and anon picked up by the beasts

of prey; but now *none of them shall be lacking,* none of them missing. Though the times may have been long bad with the church, it does not follow that they will be ever so. Such pastors as Zerubbabel and Nehemiah, though they lived not in the pomp that Jehoiakim and Jeconiah did, nor made such a figure, were as great blessings to the people as the others were plagues to them. The church's peace is not bound up in the pomp of her rulers.

2. Messiah the Prince, that great and good Shepherd of the sheep, shall in the latter days be raised up to bless his church, and to be *the glory of his people Israel, v.* 5, 6. The house of David seemed to be quite sunk and ruined by that threatening against Jeconiah (*ch.* xxii. 30), that none of his seed should ever *sit upon the throne of David*. But here is a promise which effectually secures the honour of the covenant made with David notwithstanding; for by it the house will be raised out of its ruins to a greater lustre than ever, and shine brighter far than it did in Solomon himself. We have not so many prophecies of Christ in this book as we had in that of the prophet Isaiah; but here we have one, and a very illustrious one; of him doubtless the prophet here speaks, of him, and of no other man. The first words intimate that it would be long ere this promise should have its accomplishment: *The days come,* but they are not yet. *I shall see him, but not now.* But all the rest intimate that the accomplishment of it will be glorious. (1.) Christ is here spoken of as a *branch from David,* the man *the branch* (Zech. iii. 8), his appearance mean, his beginnings small, like those of a bud or sprout, and his rise seemingly out of the earth, but growing to be green, to be great, to be loaded with fruits. A branch from David's family, when it seemed to be a *root in a dry ground,* buried, and not likely to revive. Christ is the *root and offspring of David,* Rev. xxii. 16. In him doth the *horn of David bud,* Ps. cxxxii. 17, 18. He is a branch of God's raising up; he sanctified him, and sent him into the world, gave him his commission and qualifications. He is *a righteous branch,* for he is righteous himself, and through him many, even all that are his, are made righteous. As an advocate, he is *Jesus Christ the righteous.* (2.) He is here spoken of as his church's King. This branch shall be raised as high as the throne of his father David, and there *he shall reign and prosper,* not as the kings that now were of the house of David, who went backward in all their affairs. No; he shall set up a kingdom in the world that shall be victorious over all opposition. In the chariot of the everlasting gospel he shall go forth, he shall go on *conquering and to conquer.* If God raise him up, he will prosper him, for he will own the work of his own hands; what is *the good pleasure of the Lord* shall *prosper*

in the hands of those to whom it is committed. He shall prosper; for *he shall execute judgment and justice in the earth,* all the world over, Ps. xcvi. 13. The present kings of the house of David were unjust and oppressive, and therefore it is no wonder that they did not prosper. But Christ shall, by his gospel, break the usurped power of Satan, institute a perfect rule of holy living, and, as far as it prevails, make all the world righteous. The effect of this shall be a holy security and serenity of mind in all his faithful loyal subjects. *In his days,* under his dominion, *Judah shall be saved and Israel shall dwell safely;* that is, all the spiritual seed of believing Abraham and praying Jacob shall be protected from the curse of heaven and the malice of hell, shall be privileged from the arrests of God's law and delivered from the attempts of Satan's power, shall be saved from sin, the guilt and dominion of it, and then shall *dwell safely,* and be quiet from the fear of all evil. See Luke i. 74, 75. Those that shall be saved hereafter from the wrath to come may dwell safely now; for, *if God be for us, who can be against us?* In the days of Christ's government in the soul, when he is uppermost there, the soul *dwells at ease.* (3.) He is here spoken of as *The Lord our righteousness.* Observe, [1.] Who and what he is. As God, he is *Jehovah,* the incommunicable name of God, denoting his eternity and self-existence. As Mediator, he is *our righteousness.* By making satisfaction to the justice of God for the sin of man, he has brought in an everlasting righteousness, and so made it over to us in the covenant of grace that, upon our believing consent to that covenant, it becomes ours. His being *Jehovah our righteousness* implies that he is so our righteousness as no creature could be. He is a sovereign, all-sufficient, eternal righteousness. All our righteousness has its being from him, and by him it subsists, and we are made *the righteousness of God in him.* [2.] The profession and declaration of this: *This is the name whereby he shall be called,* not only he shall be so, but he shall be known to be so. God shall call him by this name, for he shall appoint him to be *our righteousness.* By this name Israel shall call him, every true believer shall call him, and call upon him. That is our righteousness by which, as an allowed plea, we are justified before God, acquitted from guilt, and accepted into favour; and nothing else have we to plead but this, " Christ has died, yea, rather has risen again;" and we have taken him for our Lord.

3. This great salvation, which will come to the Jews in the latter days of their state, after their return out of Babylon, shall be so illustrious as far to outshine the deliverance of Israel out of Egypt (*v.* 7, 8): *They shall no more say, The Lord liveth that brought up Israel out of Egypt; but, The Lord liveth*

that brought them up out of the north. This we had before, *ch.* xvi. 14, 15. But here it seems to point more plainly than it did there to the days of the Messiah, and to compare not so much the two deliverances themselves (giving the preference to the latter) as the two states to which the church by degrees grew after those deliverances. Observe the proportion: Just 480 years after they had come out of Egypt Solomon's temple was built (1 Kings vi. 1); and at that time that nation, which was so wonderfully brought up out of Egypt, had gradually arrived to its height, to its zenith. Just 490 years (70 weeks) after they came out of Babylon Messiah the Prince set up the gospel temple, which was the greatest glory of that nation that was so wonderfully brought out of Babylon; see Dan. ix. 24, 25. Now the spiritual glory of the second part of that nation, especially as transferred to the gospel church, is much more admirable and illustrious than all the temporal glory of the first part of it in the days of Solomon; for that was no glory compared with the glory which excelleth.

9 Mine heart within me is broken, because of the prophets; all my bones shake; I am like a drunken man, and like a man whom wine hath overcome, because of the Lord, and because of the words of his holiness. 10 For the land is full of adulterers; for because of swearing the land mourneth; the pleasant places of the wilderness are dried up, and their course is evil, and their force *is* not right. 11 For both prophet and priest are profane; yea, in my house have I found their wickedness, saith the Lord. 12 Wherefore their way shall be unto them as slippery *ways* in the darkness: they shall be driven on, and fall therein: for I will bring evil upon them, *even* the year of their visitation, saith the Lord. 13 And I have seen folly in the prophets of Samaria; they prophesied in Baal, and caused my people Israel to err. 14 I have seen also in the prophets of Jerusalem a horrible thing: they commit adultery, and walk in lies: they strengthen also the hands of evil doers, that none doth return from his wickedness: they are all of them unto me as Sodom, and the inhabitants thereof as Gomorrah. 15 Therefore thus saith the Lord of hosts concerning the prophets; Behold, I will feed them

with wormwood, and make them drink the water of gall: for from the prophets of Jerusalem is profaneness gone forth into all the land. 16 Thus saith the LORD of hosts, Hearken not unto the words of the prophets that prophesy unto you : they make you vain : they speak a vision of their own heart, *and* not out of the mouth of the LORD. 17 They say still unto them that despise me, The LORD hath said, Ye shall have peace; and they say unto every one that walketh after the imagination of his own heart, No evil shall come upon you. 18 For who hath stood in the counsel of the LORD, and hath perceived and heard his word? who hath marked his word, and heard *it ?* 19 Behold, a whirlwind of the LORD is gone forth in fury, even a grievous whirlwind : it shall fall grievously upon the head of the wicked. 20 The anger of the LORD shall not return, until he have executed, and till he have performed the thoughts of his heart: in the latter days ye shall consider it perfectly. 21 I have not sent these prophets, yet they ran : I have not spoken to them, yet they prophesied. 22 But if they had stood in my counsel, and had caused my people to hear my words, then they should have turned them from their evil way, and from the evil of their doings. 23 *Am* I a God at hand, saith the LORD, and not a God afar off? 24 Can any hide himself in secret places that I shall not see him? saith the LORD. Do not I fill heaven and earth? saith the LORD. 25 I have heard what the prophets said, that prophesy lies in my name, saying, I have dreamed, I have dreamed. 26 How long shall *this* be in the heart of the prophets that prophesy lies? yea, *they are* prophets of the deceit of their own heart; 27 Which think to cause my people to forget my name by their dreams which they tell every man to his neighbour, as their fathers have forgotten my name for Baal. 28 The prophet that hath a dream, let him tell a dream; and he that hath my word, let him speak my

word faithfully. What *is* the chaff to the wheat? saith the LORD. 29 *Is* not my word like as a fire? saith the LORD; and like a hammer *that* breaketh the rock in pieces? 30 Therefore, behold, I *am* against the prophets, saith the LORD, that steal my words every one from his neighbour. 31 Behold, I *am* against the prophets, saith the LORD, that use their tongues, and say, He saith. 32 Behold, I *am* against them that prophesy false dreams, saith the LORD, and do tell them, and cause my people to err by their lies, and by their lightness ; yet I sent them not, nor commanded them : therefore they shall not profit this people at all, saith the LORD.

Here is a long lesson for the false prophets. As none were more bitter and spiteful against God's true prophets than they, so there were none on whom the true prophets were more severe, and justly. The prophet had complained to God of those false prophets (*ch.* xiv. 13), and had often foretold that they should be involved in the common ruin; but here they have woes of their own.

I. He expresses the deep concern that he was under upon this account, and what a trouble it was to him to see men who pretended to a divine commission and inspiration ruining themselves, and the people among whom they dwelt, by their falsehood and treachery (*v.* 9): *My heart within me is broken ; I am like a drunken man.* His head was in confusion with wonder and astonishment; his heart was under oppression with grief and vexation. Jeremiah was a man that laid things much to heart, and what was any way threatening to his country made a deep impression upon his spirits. He is here in trouble, 1. *Because of the prophets* and their sin, the false doctrine they preached, the wicked lives they lived; especially it filled him with horror to hear them making use of God's name and pretending to have their instructions from him. Never was the Lord so abused, and *the words of his holiness*, as by these men. Note, The dishonour done to God's name, and the profanation of his holy word, are the greatest grief imaginable to a gracious soul. 2. " *Because of the Lord,* and his judgments, which by this means are brought in upon us like a deluge." He trembled to think of the ruin and desolation which were coming *from the face of the Lord* (so the word is) *and from the face of the word of his holiness,* which will be inflicted by the power of God's wrath, according to the threatenings of his word, confirmed by *his holiness.* Note, Even those that have God for them cannot but tremble to think of the misery of those that have God against them.

II. He laments the abounding abominable wickedness of the land and the present tokens of God's displeasure they were under for it (*v.* 10): *The land is full of adulterers;* it is full both of spiritual and corporal whoredom. They go a whoring from God, and, having cast off the fear of him, no marvel that they abandon themselves to all manner of lewdness; and, having dishonoured themselves and their own bodies, they dishonour God and his name by rash and false swearing, *because of which the land mourns.* Both perjury and common swearing are sins for which a land must mourn in true repentance or it will be made to mourn under the judgments of God. Their land mourned now under the judgment of famine; the *pleasant places,* or rather *the pastures,* or (as some read it) *the habitations of the wilderness,* are dried up for want of rain, and yet we see no signs of repentance. They answer not the end of the correction. The tenour and tendency of men's conversations are sinful, *their course continues evil,* as bad as ever, and they will not be diverted from it. They have a great deal of resolution, but it is turned the wrong way; they are *zealously affected,* but not *in a good thing: Their force is not right;* their *heart is fully set in them to do evil,* and they are not valiant for the truth, have not courage enough to break off their evil courses, though they see God thus contending with them.

III. He charges it all upon the prophets and priests, especially the prophets. They are *both profane* (*v.* 11); the priests profane the ordinances of God they pretend to administer; the prophets profane the word of God they pretend to deliver; their converse and all their conversation are profane, and then it is not strange that the people are so debauched. They both *play the hypocrite* (so some read it); under sacred pretensions they carry on the vilest designs; yea, not only in their own houses, and the bad houses they frequent, but *in my house have I found their wickedness;* in the temple, where the priests ministered, where the prophets prophesied, there were they guilty both of idolatry and immorality. See a woeful instance in Hophni and Phinehas, 1 Sam. ii. 22. God searches his house, and what wickedness is there he will find it out; and the nearer it is to him the more offensive it is. Two things e charged upon them:—1. That they taught people to sin by their examples. He compares them with the prophets of Samaria, the head city of the kingdom of the ten tribes, which had been long since laid waste. It was the folly of the prophets of Samaria that *they prophesied in Baal,* in Baal's name; so Ahab's prophets did, and so *they caused my people Israel to err,* to forsake the service of the true God and to worship Baal, *v.* 13. Now the prophets of Jerusalem did not do

556

so; they prophesied in the name of the true God, and valued themselves upon that, that they were not like the prophets of Samaria, who prophesied in Baal; but what the better, when they debauched the nation as much by their immoralities as the other had done by their idolatries? It is a horrible thing in the prophets of Jerusalem that they make use of the name of the holy God, and yet wallow in all manner of impurity; they make nothing of committing adultery. They make use of the name of the God of truth, and yet *walk in lies;* they not only prophesy lies, but in their common conversation one cannot believe a word they say. It is all either jest and banter or fraud and design. Thus they encourage sinners to go on in their wicked ways; for every one will say, "Surely we may do as the prophets do; who can expect that we should be better than our teachers?" By this means it is that none returns from his wickedness; but they all say that they shall have *peace,* though they go on, for their prophets tell them so. By this means Judah and Jerusalem have become *as Sodom and Gomorrah,* that were wicked, *and sinners before the Lord exceedingly;* and God looked upon them accordingly as fit for nothing but to be destroyed, as they were, with fire and brimstone. 2. That they encouraged people in sin by their false prophecies. They made themselves believe that there was no harm, no danger in sin, and practised accordingly; and then no marvel that they made others believe so too (*v.* 16): *They speak a vision of their own heart;* it is the product of their own invention, and agrees with their own inclination, but it is *not out of the mouth of the Lord;* he never dictated it to them, nor did it agree either with the law of Moses or with what God has spoken by other prophets. They tell sinners that it shall be well with them though they persist in their sins, *v.* 17. See here who those are that they encourage —those that *despise God,* that slight his authority, and have low and mean thoughts of his institutions, and those that *walk after the imagination of their own heart,* that are worshippers of idols and slaves to their own lusts; those that are devoted to their pleasures put contempt upon their God. Yet see how these prophets caressed and flattered them: they should have been still saying, There is no peace to those that go on in their evil ways—*Those that despise God shall be lightly esteemed*—Woe, and a thousand woes, to them; but they still said, *You shall have peace; no evil shall come upon you.* And, which was worst of all, they told them, *God has said so,* so making him to patronise sin, and to contradict himself. Note, Those that are resolved to go on in their evil ways will justly be given up to believe the strong delusions of those who tell them that they shall have peace though they go on.

IV. God disowns all that these false prophets said to sooth people up in their sins (*v.* 21): *I have not sent these prophets;* they never had any mission from God. They were not only not sent by him on this errand, but they were never sent by him on any errand; he never had employed them in any service or business for him; and, as to this matter, whereas they pretended to have instructions from him to assure this people of peace, he declares that he never gave them any such instructions. Yet they were very forward—*they ran;* they were very bold—*they prophesied* without any of that difficulty with which the true prophets sometimes struggled. They said to sinners, *You shall have peace.* But (*v.* 18): *" Who hath stood in the counsel of the Lord?"* Who of you has, that are so confident of this? You deliver this message with a great deal of assurance; but have you consulted God about it? No; you never considered whether it be agreeable to the discoveries God has made of himself, whether it will consist with the honour of his holiness and justice, to let sinners go unpunished. You have not *perceived and heard his word,* nor *marked* that; you have not compared this with the scripture; if you had taken notice of that, and of the constant tenour of it, you would never have delivered such a message." The prophets themselves must try the spirits by the touchstone of the law and of the testimony, as well as those to whom they prophesy; but which of those did so that prophesied of peace? That they did not *stand in God's counsel* nor *hear his word* is proved afterwards, *v.* 22. *If they had stood in my counsel,* as they pretend, 1. They would have made the scriptures their standard: *They would have caused my people to hear my words,* and would have conscientiously kept closely to them. But, not speaking according to that rule, it is a plain evidence that there is no light in them. 2. They would have made the conversion of souls their business, and would have aimed at that in all their preaching. They would have done all they could to *turn people from their evil way* in general and from all the particular *evil of their doings.* They would have encouraged and assisted the reformation of manners, would have made this their scope in all their preaching, to part between men and their sins; but it appeared that this was a thing they never aimed at, but, on the contrary, to encourage sinners in their sins. 3. They would have had some seals of their ministry. This sense our translation gives it: *If they had stood in my counsel,* and the words they had preached had been *my words,* then they should *have turned them from their evil way;* a divine power should have gone along with the word for the conviction of sinners. God will bless his own institutions. Yet this is no certain rule; Jeremiah himself, though God sent him, prevailed with but few to *turn from their evil way.*

V. God threatens to punish these prophets for their wickedness. They promised the people *peace;* and to show them the folly of that God tells them that they should have no peace themselves. They were very unfit to warrant the people, and pass their word to them that no evil shall come upon them, when all evil is coming upon themselves and they are not aware of it, *v.* 12. Because the prophets and priests are profane, *therefore their ways shall be unto them as slippery ways in the darkness.* Those that undertake to lead others, because they mislead them, and know they do so, shall themselves have no comfort in their way. 1. They pretend to show others the way, but they shall themselves be in the dark, or in a mist; their light or sight shall fail, so that they shall not be able to look before them, shall have no forecast for themselves. 2. They pretend to give assurances to others, but they themselves shall find no firm footing: *Their ways shall be to them as slippery ways,* in which they shall not go with any steadiness, safety, or satisfaction. 3. They pretend to make the people easy with their flatteries, but they shall themselves be uneasy: *They shall be driven,* forced forward as captives, or making their escape as those that are pursued, and *they shall fall in the way* by which they hoped to escape, and so fall into the enemies' hands. 4. They pretend to prevent the evil that threatens others, but God will *bring evil upon them, even the year of their visitation,* the time fixed for calling them to an account; such a time is fixed concerning all that do not judge themselves, and it will be an evil time. *The year of visitation* is the year of recompences. It is further threatened (*v.* 15), *I will feed them with wormwood,* or poison, with that which is not only nauseous, but noxious, and *make them drink waters of gall,* or (as some read it) *juice of hemlock;* see *ch.* ix. 15. Justly is the cup of trembling put into their hand first, for *from the prophets of Jerusalem,* who should have been patterns of piety and every thing that is praiseworthy, even *from them has profaneness gone forth into all the lands.* Nothing more effectually debauches a nation than the debauchery of ministers.

VI. The people are here warned not to give any credit to these false prophets; for, though they flattered them with hopes of impunity, the judgments of God would certainly break out against them, unless they repented (*v.* 16): " Take notice of what God says, and *hearken not to the words of these prophets;* for you will find, in the issue, that God's word shall stand, and not theirs. God's word will make you serious, but *they make you vain,* feed you with vain hopes, which will fail you at last. They tell you, *No evil shall come upon you;* but hear what God says (*v.* 19), *Behold, a whirlwind of the Lord has gone forth in fury.* They tell you, All shall be calm and serene; but God tells you, There is a storm coming, a *whirlwind of the Lord,* of his sending, and therefore there is no standing before it. It is a whirlwind raised by divine wrath; it has *gone forth in fury*, a wind that is brought forth out of the treasures of divine vengeance; and therefore it is a *grievous whirlwind*, and shall light heavily, with rain and hail, *upon the head of the wicked*, which they cannot avoid nor find any shelter from." It shall *fall upon the wicked* prophets themselves who deceived the people, and the wicked people who suffered themselves to be deceived. A *horrible tempest* shall be *the portion of their cup*, Ps. xi. 6. This sentence is bound on as irreversible (*v.* 20): *The anger of the Lord shall not return*, for the decree has gone forth. God will not alter his mind, nor suffer his anger to be turned away, *till he have executed* the sentence and *performed the thoughts of his heart*. God's whirlwind, when it comes *down from heaven, returns not thither, but accomplishes that for which he sent it*, Isa. lv. 11. This they will not consider now; but *in the latter days you shall consider it perfectly*, consider it *with understanding* (so the word is) or *with consideration*. Note, Those that will not fear the threatenings shall feel the execution of them, and will then perfectly understand what they will not now admit the evidence of, what a *fearful thing it is to fall into the hands of* a just and jealous God. Those that will not consider in time will be made to consider when it is too late. *Son, remember.*

VII. Several things are here offered to the consideration of these false prophets for their conviction, that, if possible, they might be brought to recant their error and acknowledge the cheat they had put upon God's people.

1. Let them consider that though they may impose upon men God is too wise to be imposed upon. Men cannot see through their fallacies, but God can and does. Here,

(1.) God asserts his own omnipresence and omniscience in general, *v.* 23, 24. When they told the people that no evil should befal them though they went on in their evil ways they went upon atheistical principles, that the Lord doth not see their sin, that he cannot judge through the dark cloud, that he will not require it; and therefore they must be taught the first principles of their religion, and confronted with the most incontestable self-evident truths. [1.] That though God's throne is prepared in the heavens, and this earth seems to be at a distance from him, yet he is a God here in this lower world, which seems to be afar off, as well as in the upper world, which seems to be at hand, *v.* 23. The eye of God is the same on earth that it is in heaven. Here it *runs to and fro* as well as there (2 Chron. xvi. 9); and what is in the minds of men, whose spirits are veiled in flesh, is as clearly seen by him as what is in the mind of angels, those unveiled spirits above that surround his throne. The power of God is the same

on earth among its inhabitants that it is in heaven among its armies. With us nearness and distance make a great difference both in our observations and in our operations, but it is not so with God; to him darkness and light, at hand and afar off, are both alike. [2.] That, how ingenious and industrious soever men are to disguise themselves and their own characters and counsels, they cannot possibly be concealed from God's all-seeing eye (*v.* 24): " *Can any hide himself in the secret places* of the earth, *that I shall not see him?* Can any hide his projects and intentions in the secret places of the heart, that I shall not see them?" No arts of concealment can hide men from the eye of God, nor deceive his judgment of them. [3.] That he is every where present; he does not only rule heaven and earth, and uphold both by his universal providence, but he *fills heaven and earth* by his essential presence, Ps. cxxxix. 7, 8, &c. No place can either include him or exclude him.

(2.) He applies this to these prophets, who had a notable art of disguising themselves (*v.* 25, 26): *I have heard what the prophets said that prophesy lies in my name.* They thought that he was so wholly taken up with the other world that he had no leisure to take cognizance of what passed in this. But God will make them know that he knows all their impostures, all the shams they have put upon the world, under colour of divine revelation. What they intended to humour the people with they pretended to have had from God in a dream, when there was no such thing. This they could not discover. If a man tell me that he dreamed so and so, I cannot contradict him; he knows I cannot. But God discovered the fraud. Perhaps the false prophets whispered what they had to say in the ears of such as were their confidants, saying, So and so *I have dreamed;* but God overheard them. The heart-searching eye of God traced them in all the methods they took to deceive the people, and he cries out, *How long?* Shall I always bear with them? *Is it in the hearts of those prophets* (so some read it) *to be ever prophesying lies and prophesying the deceits of their own hearts?* Will they never see what an affront they put upon God, what an abuse they put upon the people, and what judgments they are preparing for themselves?

2. Let them consider that their palming upon people counterfeit revelations, and fathering their own fancies upon divine inspiration, was the ready way to bring all religion into contempt and make men turn atheists and infidels; and this was the thing they really intended, though they frequently made mention of the name of God, and prefaced all they said with, *Thus saith the Lord.* Yet, says God, *They think to cause my people to forget my name by their dreams.* They designed to draw people off from the wor-

ship of God, from all regard to God's laws and ordinances and the true prophets, as their fathers *forgot God's name for Baal.* Note, The great thing Satan aims at is to make people forget God, and all that whereby he has made himself known; and he has many subtle methods to bring them to this. Sometimes he does it by setting up false gods (bring men in love with Baal, and they soon forget the name of God), sometimes by misrepresenting the true God, as if he were altogether such a one as ourselves. Pretences to new revelation may prove as dangerous to religion as the denying of all revelation; and false prophets in God's name may perhaps do more mischief to the power of godliness than false prophets in Baal's name, as being less guarded against.

3. Let them consider what a vast difference there was between their prophecies and those that were delivered by the true prophets of the Lord (*v.* 28): *The prophet that has a dream,* which was the way of inspiration that the false prophets most pretended to, if he has a dream, *let him tell it as a dream;* so Mr. Gataker reads it. "Let him lay no more stress upon it than men do upon their dreams, nor expect any more regard to be had to it. Let them not say that it is from God, nor call their foolish dreams divine oracles. But let the true prophet, that *has my word, speak my word faithfully,* speak it *as a truth*" (so some read it) : "let him keep closely to his instructions, and you will soon perceive a vast difference between the dreams that the false prophets tell and the divine dictates which the true prophets deliver. He that pretends to have a message from God, whether by dream or voice, let him declare it, and it will easily appear which is of God and which is not. Those that have spiritual senses exercised will be able to distinguish; for *what is the chaff to the wheat?* The promises of peace which these prophets make to you are no more to be compared to God's promises than chaff to wheat." Men's fancies are light, and vain, and worthless, as the chaff *which the wind drives away.* But the word of God has substance in it; it is of value, is food for the soul, the bread of life. Wheat was the staple commodity of Canaan, that valley of vision, Deut. viii. 8; Ezek. xxvii. 17. There is as much difference between the vain fancies of men and the pure word of God as between the chaff and the wheat. It follows (*v.* 29), *Is not my word like a fire, saith the Lord?* Is their word so? Has it the power and efficacy that the word of God has? No; nothing like it; there is no more comparison than between painted fire and real fire. Theirs is like an *ignis fatuus*—a *deceiving meteor,* leading men into by-paths and dangerous precipices. Note, The word of God is like fire. The law was a fiery law (Deut. xxxiii. 2), and of the gospel Christ says, *I have come to send fire on the earth,* Luke xii. 49. Fire has different

effects, according as the matter is on which it works; it hardens clay, but softens wax; it consumes the dross, but purifies the gold. So the word of God is to some *a savour of life unto life, to others of death unto death.* God appeals here to the consciences of those to whom the word was sent : "*Is not my word like fire?* Has it not been so to you? Zech. i. 6. Speak as you have found." It is compared likewise to a *hammer breaking the rock in pieces.* The unhumbled heart of man is like a rock; if it will not be melted by the word of God as the fire, it will be broken to pieces by it as the hammer. Whatever opposition is given to the word, it will be borne down and broken to pieces.

4. Let them consider that while they went on in this course God was against them. Three times they are told this, *v.* 30, 31, 32. *Behold, I am against the prophets.* They pretended to be for God, and made use of his name, but were really against him; he looks upon them as they were really, and is against them. How can they be long safe, or at all easy, that have a God of almighty power against them? While these prophets were promising peace to the people God was proclaiming war against them. They stand indicted here, (1.) For robbery : *They steal my word every one from his neighbour.* Some understand it of that word of God which the good prophets preached; they stole their sermons, their expressions, and mingled them with their own, as hucksters mingle bad wares with some that are good, to make them vendible. Those that were strangers to the spirit of the true prophets mimicked their language, picked up some good sayings of theirs, and delivered them to the people as if they had been their own, but with an ill grace; they were not of a piece with the rest of their discourses. *The legs of the lame are not equal, so is a parable in the mouth of fools,* Prov. xxvi. 7. Others understand it of the word of God as it was received and entertained by some of the people; they stole it out of their hearts, as the wicked one in the parable is said to steal the good seed of the word, Matt. xiii. 19. By their insinuations they diminished the authority, and so weakened the efficacy, of the word of God upon the minds of those that seemed to be under convictions by it. (2.) They stand indicted for counterfeiting the broad seal. *Therefore* God is against them (*v.* 31), because they *use their tongues* at their pleasure in their discourses to the people; they say what they themselves think fit, and then father it upon God, pretend they had it from him, and say, He saith it. Some read it, *They smooth their tongues;* they are very complaisant to the people, and say nothing but what is pleasing and plausible; they never reprove them nor threaten them, but *their words are smoother than butter.* Thus they ingratiate themselves with them, and

get money by them; and they have the impudence and impiety to make God the patron of their lies; they say, "He saith so." What greater indignity can be done to the God of truth than to lay the brats of the father of lies at his door? (3.) They stand indicted as common cheats (*v.* 32): *I am against them*, for they *prophesy false dreams*, pretending that to be a divine inspiration which is but an invention of their own. This is a horrid fraud; nor will it excuse them to say, *Caveat emptor—Let the buyer take care of himself*, and *Si populus vult decipi, decipiatur—If people will be deceived, let them*. No; it is the people's fault that they err, that they take things upon trust, and do not try the spirits; but it is much more the prophets' fault that they cause God's people *to err by their lies and by their lightness*, by the flatteries of their preaching soothing them up in their sins, and by the looseness and lewdness of their conversation encouraging them to persist in them. [1.] God disowns their having any commission from him: *I sent them not, nor commanded them;* they are not God's messengers, nor is what they say his message. [2.] He therefore justly denies his blessing with them: *Therefore they shall not profit this people at all.* All the profit they aim at is to make them easy; but they shall not so much as do that, for God's providences will at the same time be making them uneasy. They *do not profit this people* (so some read it); and more is implied than is expressed; they not only do them no good, but do them a great deal of hurt. Note, Those that corrupt the word of God, while they pretend to preach it, are so far from edifying the church that they do it the greatest mischief imaginable.

33 And when this people, or the prophet, or a priest, shall ask thee, saying, What *is* the burden of the LORD? thou shalt then say unto them, What burden? I will even forsake you, saith the LORD. 34 And *as for* the prophet, and the priest, and the people, that shall say, The burden of the LORD, I will even punish that man and his house. 35 Thus shall ye say every one to his neighbour, and every one to his brother, What hath the LORD answered? and, What hath the LORD spoken? 36 And the burden of the LORD shall ye mention no more: for every man's word shall be his burden; for ye have perverted the words of the living God, of the LORD of hosts our God. 37 Thus shalt thou say to the prophet, What hath the LORD answered thee? and, What hath the LORD

spoken? 38 But since ye say, The burden of the LORD; therefore thus saith the LORD; Because ye say this word, The burden of the LORD, and I have sent unto you, saying, Ye shall not say, The burden of the LORD; 39 Therefore, behold, I, even I, will utterly forget you, and I will forsake you, and the city that I gave you and your fathers, *and cast you* out of my presence: 40 And I will bring an everlasting reproach upon you, and a perpetual shame, which shall not be forgotten.

The profaneness of the people, with that of the priests and prophets, is here reproved in a particular instance, which may seem of small moment in comparison of their greater crimes; but profaneness in common discourse, and the debauching of the language of a nation, being a notorious evidence of the prevalency of wickedness in it, we are not to think it strange that this matter was so largely and warmly insisted upon here. Observe,

I. The sin here charged upon them is bantering God's prophets and the dialect they used, and jesting with sacred things. They asked, *What is the burden of the Lord? v.* 33 and *v.* 34. They say, *The burden of the Lord, v.* 38. This was the word that gave great offence to God, that, whenever they spoke of *the word of the Lord*, they called it, in scorn and derision, *the burden of the Lord.* Now, 1. This was a word that the prophets much used, and used it seriously, to show what a weight the word of God was upon their spirits, of what importance it was, and how pressingly it should come upon those that heard it. The words of the false prophets had nothing ponderous in them, but God's words had; those were as chaff, these as wheat. Now the profane scoffers took this word, and made a jest and a byword of it; they made people merry with it, that so, when the prophets used it, they might not make people serious with it. Note, It has been the artifice of Satan, in all ages, to obstruct the efficacy of sacred things by turning them into matter of sport and ridicule; the mocking of God's messengers was the baffling of his messages. 2. Perhaps this word was caught at and reproached by the scoffers as an improper word, newly-coined by the prophets, and not used in that sense by any classic author. It was only in this and the last age that the *word of the Lord* was called the *burden of the Lord*, and it could not be found in their lexicons to have that signification. But if men take a liberty, as we see they do, to form new phrases which they think more expressive and significant in other parts of learning, why not in divinity? But especially we must observe it as a rule that the Spirit of God is not tied to our rules of speaking. 3. Some think that because when the *word of the Lord* is called a *burden* it signifies some word of reproof and threatening, which would lay a load upon the hearers (yet I know not whether that observation will always hold), therefore in using this word *the burden of the Lord* in a canting way they reflected upon God as always bearing hard upon them, always teazing them, always frightening them, and so making the word of God a perpetual uneasiness to them. They make the word of God a burden to themselves, and then quarrel with the ministers for making it a burden to them. Thus the scoffers of the latter days, while they slight heaven and salvation, reproach faithful ministers for preaching hell and damnation. Upon the whole we may observe that, how light soever men may make of it, the great God takes notice of, and is much displeased with, those who burlesque sacred things, and who, that they may make a jest of scripture truths and laws, put jests upon scripture language. In such wit as this I am sure there is no wisdom, and so it will appear at last. *Be you not mockers, lest your bands be made strong.* Those that were here guilty of this sin were some of the false prophets, who perhaps came to steal the word of God from the true prophets, some of the priests, who perhaps came to seek occasions against them on which to ground an information, and some of the people, who had learned of the profane priests and prophets to play with the things of God. The people would not have affronted the prophet and his God thus if the priests and the prophets, those ringleaders of mischief, had not shown them the way.

II. When they are reproved for this profane way of speaking they are directed how to express themselves more decently. We do not find that the prophets are directed to make no more use of this word; we find it used long after this (Zech. ix. 1; Mal. i. 1; Nah. i. 1; Hab. i. 1); and we do not find it once used in this sense by Jeremiah either before or after. It is true indeed that in many cases it is advisable to make no use of such words and things as some have made a bad use of, and it may be prudent to avoid such phrases as, though innocent enough, are in danger of being perverted and made stumbling-blocks. But here God will have the prophet keep to his rule (*ch.* xv. 19), *Let them return unto thee, but return not thou unto them.* Do not thou leave off using this word, but let them leave off abusing it. You *shall not mention the burden of the Lord any more in this profane careless manner* (*v.* 36), for it is *perverting the words of the living God* and making a bad use of them, which is an impious dangerous thing; for, consider, he is *the Lord of hosts our God.* Note, If we will but look upon God as we ought to do in his greatness and goodness, and be but duly

sensible of our relation and obligation to him, it may be hoped that we shall not dare to affront him by making a jest of his words. It is an impudent thing to abuse him that is the *living God*, the *Lord of hosts*, and *our God.* How then must they express themselves? He tells them (*v.* 37): *Thus shalt thou say to the prophet*, when thou art enquiring of him, *What hath the Lord answered thee? And what hath the Lord spoken?* And they must say thus when they enquire of *their neighbours, v.* 35. Note, We must always speak of the things of God reverently and seriously, and as becomes the oracles of God. It is a commendable practice to enquire after the mind of God, to enquire of our brethren what they have heard, to enquire of our prophets what they have to say from God; but then, to show that we enquire for a right end, we must do it after a right manner. Ministers may learn here, when they reprove people for what they say and do amiss, to teach them how to say and do better.

III. Because they would not leave off this bad way of speaking, though they were admonished of it, God threatens them here with utter ruin. They would still say, *The burden of the Lord*, though God had sent to them to forbid them, *v.* 38. What little regard have those to the divine authority that will not be persuaded by it to leave an idle word! But see what will come of it. 1. Those shall be severely reckoned with that thus *pervert the words of God*, that put a wrong construction on them and make a bad use of them; and it shall be made to appear that it is a great provocation to God to mock his messengers: *I will even punish that man and his house;* whether he be prophet or priest, or one of the common people, it shall be visited upon him, *v.* 34. Perverting God's word, and ridiculing the preachers of it, are sins that bring ruining judgments upon families and entail a curse upon a house. Another threatening we have *v.* 36: *Every man's word shall be his own burden;* that is, the guilt of this sin shall be so heavy upon him as to sink him into the pit of destruction. God *shall make their own tongue to fall upon them*, Ps. lxiv. 8. God will give them enough of their jest, so that *the burden of the Lord* they shall have no heart to mention any more; it will be too heavy to make a jest of. They are as *the madman that casts firebrands, arrows, and death*, while they pretend to be *in sport.* 2. The words of God, though thus perverted, shall be accomplished. Do they ask, *What is the burden of the Lord?* Let the prophet ask them, *What burden* do you mean? Is it this: *I will even forsake you? v.* 33. This is the burden that shall be laid and bound upon them (*v.* 39, 40): " *Behold I, even I, will utterly forget you, and I will forsake you.* I will leave you, and have no thoughts of returning to you." Those are miserable indeed that are forsaken and forgotten of God; and men's bantering God's judgments will not baffle them. Jerusalem was the city God had taken to himself as a holy city, and then *given to them and their fathers;* but that shall now be forsaken and forgotten. God had taken them to be a people near to him; but they shall now be *cast out of his presence.* They had been great and honourable among the nations; but now God will bring upon them an *everlasting reproach* and a *perpetual shame.* Both their sin and their punishment shall be their lasting disgrace. It is here upon record, to their infamy, and will remain so to the world's end. Note, God's word will be magnified and made honourable when those that mock at it shall be vilified and made contemptible. *Those that despise me shall be lightly esteemed.*

CHAP. XXIV.

In the close of the foregoing chapter we had a general prediction of the utter ruin of Jerusalem, that it should be forsaken and forgotten, which, whatever effect it had upon others, we have reason to think made the prophet himself very melancholy. Now, in this chapter, God encourages him, by showing him that, though the desolation seemed to be universal, yet all were not equally involved in it, but God knew how to distinguish, how to separate, between the precious and the vile. Some had gone into captivity already with Jeconiah; over them Jeremiah lamented, but God tells him that it should turn to their good. Others yet remained hardened in their sins, against whom Jeremiah had a just indignation; but those, God tells him, should go into captivity, and it should prove to their hurt. To inform the prophet of this, and affect him with it, here is, I. A vision of two baskets of figs, one very good and the other very bad, ver. 1—3. II. The explication of this vision, applying the good figs to those that were already sent into captivity for their good (ver. 4—7), the bad figs to those that should hereafter be sent into captivity for their hurt, ver. 8—10.

THE Lord showed me, and, behold, two baskets of figs *were* set before the temple of the Lord, after that Nebuchadrezzar king of Babylon had carried away captive Jeconiah the son of Jehoiakim king of Judah, and the princes of Judah, with the carpenters and smiths, from Jerusalem, and had brought them to Babylon. 2 One basket *had* very good figs, *even* like the figs *that are* first ripe: and the other basket *had* very naughty figs, which could not be eaten, they were so bad. 3 Then said the Lord unto me, What seest thou, Jeremiah? And I said, Figs; the good figs, very good; and the evil, very evil, that cannot be eaten, they are so evil. 4 Again the word of the Lord came unto me, saying, 5 Thus saith the Lord, the God of Israel; Like these good figs, so will I acknowledge them that are carried away captive of Judah, whom I have sent out of this place into the land of the Chaldeans for *their* good. 6 For I will set mine eyes upon them for good,

and I will bring them again to this land: and I will build them, and not pull *them* down; and I will plant them and not pluck *them* up. 7 And I will give them a heart to know me, that I *am* the Lord: and they shall be my people, and I will be their God: for they shall return unto me with their whole heart. 8 And as the evil figs, which cannot be eaten, they are so evil; surely thus saith the Lord, So will I give Zedekiah the king of Judah, and his princes, and the residue of Jerusalem, that remain in this land, and them that dwell in the land of Egypt: 9 And I will deliver them to be removed into all the kingdoms of the earth for *their* hurt, *to be* a reproach and a proverb, a taunt and a curse, in all places whither I shall drive them. 10 And I will send the sword, the famine, and the pestilence, among them, till they be consumed from off the land that I gave unto them and to their fathers.

This short chapter helps us to put a very comfortable construction upon a great many long ones, by showing us that the same providence which to some is a *savour of death unto death* may by the grace and blessing of God be made to others a *savour of life unto life;* and that, though God's people share with others in the same calamity, yet it is not the same to them that it is to others, but is designed for their good and shall issue in their good; to them it is a correcting rod in the hand of a tender Father, while to others it is an avenging sword in the hand of a righteous Judge. Observe,

I. The date of this sermon. It was after, a little after, Jeconiah's captivity, *v.* 1. Jeconiah was himself a *despised broken vessel,* but with him were carried away some very valuable persons, Ezekiel for one (Ezek. i. 12); many of the *princes of Judah* then went into captivity, Daniel and his fellows were carried off a little before; of the people only *the carpenters and the smiths* were forced away, either because the Chaldeans needed some ingenious men of those trades (they had a great plenty of astrologers and star-gazers, but a great scarcity of smiths and carpenters) or because the Jews would severely feel the loss of them, and would, for want of them, be unable to fortify their cities and furnish themselves with weapons of war. Now, it should seem, there were many good people carried away in that captivity, which the pious prophet laid much to heart, while there were those that triumphed in it, and insulted over those to whose lot it fell to go into captivity. Note, We must not conclude concerning the first and greatest sufferers that they were the worst and greatest sinners; for perhaps it may appear quite otherwise, as it did here.

II. The vision by which this distinction of the captives was represented to the prophet's mind. He saw *two baskets of figs, set before the temple*, there ready to be offered as firstfruits to the honour of God. Perhaps the priests, being remiss in their duty, were not ready to receive them and dispose of them according to the law, and therefore Jeremiah sees them standing *before the temple.* But that which was the significancy of the vision was that the figs in one basket were extraordinarily good, those in the other basket extremely bad. The children of men are all as the fruits of the fig-tree, capable of being made serviceable to God and man (Judg. ix. 11); but some are as good figs, than which nothing is more pleasant, others as damaged rotten figs, than which nothing is more nauseous. What creature viler than a wicked man, and what more valuable than a godly man! The good figs were like those that are first ripe, which are most acceptable (Mic. vii. 1) and most prized when newly come into season. The bad figs are such as could *not be eaten, they were so evil;* they could not answer the end of their creation, were neither pleasant nor good for food; and what then were they good for? If God has no honour from men, nor their generation any service, they are even like the bad figs, that cannot be eaten, that will not answer any good purpose. *If the salt have lost its savour, it is thenceforth* fit for nothing but *the dunghill.* Of the persons that are presented to the Lord at the door of his tabernacle, some are sincere, and they are very good; others dissemble with God, and they are very bad. Sinners are the worst of men, hypocrites the worst of sinners. *Corruptio optimi est pessima—That which is best becomes, when corrupted, the worst.*

III. The exposition and application of this vision. God intended by it to raise the dejected spirit of those that had gone into captivity, by assuring them of a happy return, and to humble and awaken the proud and secure spirits of those who continued yet in Jerusalem, by assuring them of a miserable captivity.

1. Here is the moral of the good figs, that were very good, the first ripe. These represented the pious captives, that seemed first ripe for ruin, for they went first into captivity, but should prove first ripe for mercy, and their captivity should help to ripen them; these are pleasing to God, as good figs are to us, and shall be carefully preserved for use. Now observe here,

(1.) Those that were already carried into captivity were the good figs that God would own. This shows, [1.] That we cannot determine of God's love or hatred *by all that is before us.* When God's judgments are abroad those are not always the worst that are first seized by them. [2.] That early suffering sometimes proves for the best to us. The sooner the child is corrected the better effect the correction is likely to have. Those that went first into captivity were as the son whom the *father loves, and chastens betimes,* chastens while there is hope; and it did well. But those that staid behind were like a child long *left to himself,* who, when afterwards corrected, is stubborn, and made worse by it, Lam. iii. 27.

(2.) God owns their captivity to be his doing. Whoever were the instruments of it, he ordered and directed it (*v.* 5): *I have sent them out of this place into the land of the Chaldeans.* It is God that puts his gold into the furnace, to be tried; his hand is, in a special manner, to be eyed in the afflictions of good people. The judge orders the malefactor into the hand of an executioner, but the father corrects the child with his own hand.

(3.) Even this disgraceful uncomfortable captivity God intended for their benefit; and we are sure that his intentions are never frustrated: *I have sent them into the land of the Chaldeans for their good.* It seemed to be every way for their hurt, not only as it was the ruin of their estates, honours, and liberties, separated them from their relations and friends, and put them under the power of their enemies and oppressors, but as it sunk their spirits, discouraged their faith, deprived them of the benefit of God's oracles and ordinances, and exposed them to temptations; and yet it was designed for their good, and proved so, in the issue, as to many of them. *Out of the eater came forth meat.* By their afflictions they were convinced of sin, humbled under the hand of God, weaned from the world, made serious, taught to pray, and turned from their iniquity; particularly they were cured of their inclination to idolatry; and thus it was *good for them that they were afflicted,* Ps. cxix. 67, 71.

(4.) God promises them that he will own them in their captivity. Though they seem abandoned, they shall be acknowledged; the scornful relations they left behind will scarcely own them, or their kindred to them, but God says, *I will acknowledge them.* Note, *The Lord knows those that are his,* and will own them in all conditions; nakedness and sword shall not separate them from his love.

(5.) God assures them of his protection in their trouble, and a glorious deliverance out of it in due time, *v.* 6. Being sent into captivity *for their good,* they shall not be lost there; but it shall be with them as it is with gold which the refiner puts into the furnace. [1.] He has his eye upon it while it is there, and it is a careful eye, to see that it sustain no damage: *" I will set my eyes upon them for good,* to order every thing for the best, that all the circumstances of the affliction may concur to the answering of the great intention of it." [2.] He will be sure to take it out of the furnace again as soon as the work designed upon it is done : *I will bring them again to this land.* They were sent abroad for improvement awhile, under a severe discipline ; but they shall be fetched back, when they have gone through their trial there, to their Father's house. [3.] He will fashion his gold when he has refined it, will make it a vessel of honour fit for his use ; so, when God has brought them back from their trial, he *will build them* and make them a habitation for himself, will *plant them* and make them a vineyard for himself. Their captivity was to square the rough stones and make them fit for his building, to prune up the young trees and make them fit for his planting.

(6.) He engages to prepare them for these temporal mercies which he designed for them by bestowing spiritual mercies upon them, *v. 7.* It is this that will make their captivity be for their good ; this shall be both the improvement of their affliction and their qualification for deliverance. When our troubles are sanctified to us, then we may be sure that they will end well. Now that which is promised is, [1.] That they should be better acquainted with God ; they should learn more of God by his providences in Babylon than they had learned by all his oracles and ordinances in Jerusalem, thanks to divine grace, for, if that had not wrought mightily upon them in Babylon, they would for ever have forgotten God. It is here promised, *I will give them,* not so much a head to know me, but *a heart to know me,* for the right knowledge of God consists not in notion and speculation, but in the convictions of the practical judgment directing and governing the will and affections. *A good understanding have all those that do his commandments,* Ps. cxi. 10. Where God gives a sincere desire and inclination to know him he will give that knowledge. It is God himself that gives a heart to know him, else we should perish for ever in our ignorance. [2.] That they should be entirely converted to God, to his will as their rule, his service as their business, and his glory as their end : *They shall return to me with their whole heart.* God himself undertakes for them that they shall ; and, if he turn us, we shall be turned. This follows upon the former ; for those that have a heart to know God aright will not only turn to him, but turn with their whole heart ; for those that are either obstinate in their rebellion, or hypocritical in their religion, may truly be said to be ignorant of God. [3.] That thus they should be again taken into covenant with God, as much to their comfort as ever : *They shall be my people, and I will be their God.* God will own them, as formerly, for his people, in the discoveries of himself to them, in his accept-

ance of their services, and in his gracious appearances on their behalf ; and they shall have liberty to own him for their God in their prayers to him and their expectations from him. Note, Those that have backslidden from God, if they do in sincerity return to him, are admitted as freely as any to all the privileges and comforts of the everlasting covenant, which is herein well-ordered, that every transgression in the covenant does not throw us out of covenant, and that afflictions are not only consistent with, but flowing from, covenant-love.

2. Here is the moral of the bad figs. *Zedekiah and his princes* and partizans *yet remain in the land,* proud and secure enough, Ezek. xi. 3. Many had fled into Egypt for shelter, and they thought they had shifted well for themselves and their own safety, and boasted that though therein they had gone contrary to the command of God yet they had acted prudently for themselves. Now as to both these, that looked so scornfully upon those that had gone into captivity, it is here threatened, (1.) That, whereas those who were already carried away were settled in one country, where they had the comfort of one another's society, though in captivity, these should be dispersed *and removed into all the kingdoms of the earth,* where they should have no joy one of another. (2.) That, whereas those were carried captives for their good, these should be removed into all countries *for their hurt.* Their afflictions should be so far from humbling them that they should harden them, not bring them nearer to God, but set them at a greater distance from him. (3.) That, whereas those should have the honour of being owned of God in their troubles, these should have the shame of being abandoned by all mankind : *In all places whither I shall drive them they shall be a reproach and a proverb.* " Such a one is as false and proud as a Jew"—" Such a one is as poor and miserable as a Jew." All their neighbours shall make a jest of them, and of the calamities brought upon them. (4.) That, whereas those should *return to their own land,* these should be *consumed from that land,* never to see it more, and it shall be of no avail to them to plead that it was the land God gave to their fathers, for they had it from God, and he gave it to them upon condition of their obedience. (5.) That, whereas those were reserved for better times, these were reserved for worse ; wherever they are removed *the sword, and famine, and pestilence,* shall be sent after them, shall soon overtake them, and, coming with commission so to do, shall overcome them. God has variety of judgments wherewith to prosecute those that fly from justice ; and those that have escaped one may expect another, till they are brought to repent and reform.

Doubtless this prophecy had its accomplishment in the men of that *generation :*

yet, because we read not of any such remarkable difference between those of Jeconiah's captivity and those of Zedekiah's, it
is probable that this has a typical reference
to the last destruction of the Jews by the
Romans, in which those of them that believed were taken care of, but those that
continued obstinate in unbelief were driven
into all countries for *a taunt and a curse,* and
so they remain to this day.

CHAP. XXV.

The prophecy of this chapter bears date some time before those
prophecies in the chapters next foregoing, for they are not placed
in the exact order of time in which they were delivered. This is
dated in the first year of Nebuchadrezzar, that remarkable year
when the sword of the Lord began to be drawn and furbished.
Here is, I. A review of the prophecies that had been delivered to
Judah and Jerusalem for many years past, by Jeremiah himself
and other prophets, with the little regard given to them and the
little success of them, ver. 1—7. II. A very express threatening
of the destruction of Judah and Jerusalem, by the king of Babylon, for their contempt of God, and their continuance in sin (ver.
8—11), to which is annexed a promise of their deliverance out of
their captivity in Babylon, after 70 years, ver. 12—14. III. A prediction of the devastation of divers other nations about, by Nebuchadrezzar, represented by a "cup of fury" put into their hands
(ver. 15—28), by a sword sent among them (ver. 29—33), and a desolation made among the shepherds and their flocks and pastures
(ver. 34—38); so that we have here judgment beginning at the
house of God, but not ending there.

THE word that came to Jeremiah
concerning all the people of
Judah in the fourth year of Jehoiakim
the son of Josiah king of Judah, that
was the first year of Nebuchadrezzar
king of Babylon; 2 The which Jeremiah the prophet spake unto all the
people of Judah, and to all the inhabitants of Jerusalem, saying, 3 From
the thirteenth year of Josiah the son
of Amon king of Judah, even unto
this day, that *is* the three and twentieth year, the word of the Lord
hath come unto me, and I have
spoken unto you, rising early and
speaking; but ye have not hearkened.
4 And the Lord hath sent unto you all
his servants the prophets, rising early
and sending *them;* but ye have not
hearkened, nor inclined your ear to
hear. 5 They said, Turn ye again
now every one from his evil way, and
from the evil of your doings, and
dwell in the land that the Lord hath
given unto you and to your fathers for
ever and ever: 6 And go not after
other gods to serve them, and to worship them, and provoke me not to
anger with the works of your hands;
and I will do you no hurt. 7 Yet
ye have not hearkened unto me, saith
the Lord; that ye might provoke me
to anger with the works of your hands
to your own hurt.

We have here a message from God con-

cerning all the people of Judah (*v.* 1), which
Jeremiah delivered, in his name, unto all
the people of Judah, *v.* 2. Note, That which
is of universal concern ought to be of universal cognizance. It is fit that the word
which concerns all the people, as the word
of God does, the word of the gospel particularly, should be divulged to all in general,
and, as far as may be, addressed to each in
particular. Jeremiah had been sent to the
house of the king (*ch.* xxii. 1), and he took
courage to deliver his message there; here
he is sent to *all the people,* and he takes the
pains to deliver his message to them, probably when they had all come up to Jerusalem to worship at one of the solemn feasts;
then he had them together, and it was to
be hoped then, if ever, they would be well
disposed to hear counsel and receive instruction.

This prophecy is dated in the fourth year
of Jehoiakim and the first of Nebuchadrezzar. It was in the latter end of Jehoiakim's third year that Nebuchadrezzar began
to reign by himself alone (having reigned
some time before in conjunction with his
father), as appears, Dan. i. 1. But Jehoiakim's fourth year was begun before
Nebuchadrezzar's first was completed. Now
that that active, daring, martial prince began
to set up for the world's master, God, by his
prophet, gives notice that he is his servant,
and intimates what work he intends to employ him in, that his growing greatness,
which was so formidable to the nations,
might not be construed as any reflection
upon the power and providence of God in
the government of the world. Nebuchadrezzar should not bid so fair for universal
monarchy (I should have said universal
tyranny) but that God had purposes of his
own to serve by him, in the execution of
which the world shall see the meaning of
God's permitting and ordering a thing that
seemed such a reflection on his sovereignty
and goodness.

Now in this message we may observe the
great pains that had been taken with the
people to bring them to repentance, which
they are here put in mind of, as an aggravation of their sin and a justification of God
in his proceedings against them.

I. Jeremiah, for his part, had been a constant preacher among them twenty-three
years; he began in the thirteenth year of
Josiah, who reigned thirty-one years, so that
he prophesied about eighteen or nineteen
years in his reign, then in the reign of Jehoahaz, and now four years of Jehoiakim's
reign. Note, God keeps an account, whether
we do or no, how long we have enjoyed the
means of grace; and the longer we have
enjoyed them the heavier will our account
be if we have not improved them. *These
three years* (these three and twenty years,
have I come seeking fruit on this fig-tree.
All this while, 1. God had been constant in

sending messages to them, as there was occasion for them: "From that time *to this very day the word of the Lord has come unto me,* for your use." Though they had the substance of the warning sent them already in the books of Moses, yet, because those were not duly regarded and applied, God sent to enforce them and make them more particular, that they might be without excuse. Thus God's Spirit was striving with them, as with the old world, Gen. vi. 3. 2. Jeremiah had been faithful and industrious in delivering those messages. He could appeal to themselves, as well as to God and his own conscience, concerning this: *I have spoken to you, rising early and speaking.* He had declared to them *the whole counsel of God;* he had taken a great deal of care and pains to discharge his trust in such a manner as might be most likely to win and work upon them. What men are solicitous about and intent upon they rise up early to prosecute. It intimates that his head was so full of thoughts about it, and his heart so intent upon doing good, that it broke his sleep, and made him get up betimes to project which way he might take that would be most likely to do them good. He rose early, both because he would lose no time and because he would lay hold on and improve the best time to work upon them, when, if ever, they were sober and sedate. Christ came *early in the morning* to preach in the temple, and the people as early to hear him, Luke xxi. 38. Morning lectures have their advantages. *My voice shalt thou hear in the morning.*

II. Besides him, God had sent them other prophets, on the same errand, *v.* 4. Of the writing prophets Micah, Nahum, and Habakkuk, were a little before him, and Zephaniah contemporary with him. But, besides those, there were many other of God's *servants the prophets* who preached awakening sermons, which were never published. And here God himself is said to *rise early* and *send them,* intimating how much his heart also was upon it, that this people should *turn and live,* and not *go on and die,* Ezek. xxxiii. 11.

III. All the messages sent them were to the purpose, and much to the same purport, *v.* 5, 6. 1. They all told them of their faults, *their evil way,* and the *evil of their doings.* Those were not of God's sending who flattered them as if there were nothing amiss among them. 2. They all reproved them particularly for their idolatry, as a sin that was in a special manner provoking to God, their *going after other gods, to serve them and to worship them,* gods that were *the work of their own hands.* 3. They all called on them to repent of their sins and to reform their lives. This was the burden of every song, *Turn you now every one from his evil way.* Note, Personal and particular reformation must be insisted on as necessary to a national deliverance: *every one* must

turn from his own *evil way.* The street will not be clean unless every one sweep before his own door. 4. They all assured them that, if they did so, it would certainly be the *lengthening out of their tranquillity.* The mercies they enjoyed should be continued to them: "*You shall dwell in the land,* dwell at ease, dwell in peace, in this good land, *which the Lord has given you and your fathers.* Nothing but sin will turn you out of it, and that shall not if you turn from it." The judgments they feared should be prevented: *Provoke me not, and I will do you no hurt.* Note, We should never receive from God the evil of punishment if we did not provoke him by the evil of sin. God deals fairly with us, never corrects his children without cause, nor causes grief to us unless we give offence to him.

IV. Yet all was to no purpose. They were not wrought upon to take the right and only method to turn away the wrath of God. Jeremiah was a very lively affectionate preacher, yet *they hearkened not* to him, *v.* 3. The other prophets dealt faithfully with them, but neither did they *hearken to them,* nor *incline their ear, v.* 4. That very particular sin which they were told, of all others, was most offensive to God, and made them obnoxious to his justice, they wilfully persisted in: You *provoke me with the works of your hands to your own hurt.* Note, What is a provocation to God will prove, in the end, hurt to ourselves, and we must bear the blame of it. *O Israel! thou hast destroyed thyself.*

8 Therefore thus saith the LORD of hosts; Because ye have not heard my words, 9 Behold, I will send and take all the families of the north, saith the LORD, and Nebuchadrezzar the king of Babylon, my servant, and will bring them against this land, and against the inhabitants thereof, and against all these nations round about, and will utterly destroy them, and make them an astonishment, and a hissing, and perpetual desolations. 10 Moreover I will take from them the voice of mirth, and the voice of gladness, the voice of the bridegroom, and the voice of the bride, the sound of the millstones, and the light of the candle. 11 And this whole land shall be a desolation, *and* an astonishment; and these nations shall serve the king of Babylon seventy years. 12 And it shall come to pass, when seventy years are accomplished, *that* I will punish the king of Babylon, and that nation, saith the LORD, for their

iniquity, and the land of the Chaldeans, and will make it perpetual desolations. 13 And I will bring upon that land all my words which I have pronounced against it, *even* all that is written in this book, which Jeremiah hath prophesied against all the nations. 14 For many nations and great kings shall serve themselves of them also: and I will recompense them according to their deeds, and according to the works of their own hands.

Here is the sentence grounded upon the foregoing charge: "*Because you have not heard my words,* I must take another course with you," *v.* 8. Note, When men will not regard the judgments of God's mouth they may expect to feel the judgments of his hands, to hear the rod, since they would not hear the word; for the sinner must either be parted from his sin or perish in it. Wrath comes without remedy against those only that sin without repentance. It is not so much men's turning aside that ruins them as their not returning.

I. The ruin of the land of Judah by the king of Babylon's armies is here decreed, *v.* 9. God sent to them *his servants the prophets,* and they were not heeded, and therefore God will send for *his servant the king of Babylon,* whom they cannot mock, and despise, and persecute, as they did his servants the prophets. Note, The messengers of God's wrath will be sent against those that would not receive the messengers of his mercy. One way or other God will be heeded, and will make men know that *he is the Lord.* Nebuchadrezzar, though a stranger to the true God, the God of Israel, nay, an enemy to him and afterwards a rival with him, was yet, in the descent he made upon this country, *God's servant,* accomplished his purpose, was employed by him, and was an instrument in his hand for the correction of his people. He was really serving God's designs when he thought he was serving his own ends. Justly therefore does God here call himself *The Lord of hosts* (*v.* 8), for here is an instance of his sovereign dominion, not only over the inhabitants, but over the armies of this earth, of which he makes what use he pleases. He has them all at his command. The most potent and absolute monarchs are his servants. Nebuchadrezzar, who is an instrument of his wrath, is as truly his servant as Cyrus, who is an instrument of his mercy. The land of Judah being to be made desolate, God here musters his army that is to make it so, gathers it together, takes *all the families of the north,* if there be occasion for them, leads them on as their commander-in-chief, *brings them against this land,* gives

them success, not only against Judah and Jerusalem, but against *all the nations round about,* that there might be no dependence upon them as allies or assistants against that threatening force. The utter destruction of this and all the neighbouring lands is here described, *v.* 9—11. It shall be total: *The whole land shall be a desolation,* not only desolate, but a desolation itself; both city and country shall be laid waste, and all the wealth of both be made a prey of. It shall be lasting, even *perpetual desolations;* they shall continue so long in ruins, and after long waiting there shall appear so little prospect of relief, that every one shall call it perpetual. This desolation shall be the ruin of their credit among their neighbours; it shall bury their honour in the dust, shall *make them an astonishment and a hissing;* every one will be amazed at them, and hiss them off the stage of action with just disgrace for deserting a God who would have been their protection for impostors who would certainly be their destruction. It will likewise be the ruin of all their comfort among themselves; it shall be a final period of all their joy: *I will take from them the voice of mirth,* hang their harps on the willow-trees, and put them out of tune for songs. *I will take from them the voice of mirth;* they shall neither have cause for it nor hearts for it. They would not hear the voice of God's word and therefore the voice of mirth shall no more be heard among them. They shall be deprived of food: *The sound of the mill-stones shall not be heard;* for, when the enemy has seized their stores, the sound of the grinding must needs be low, Eccl. xii. 4. An end shall be put to all business; there shall not be seen *the light of a candle,* for there shall be no work to be done worth candle-light. And, *lastly,* they shall be deprived of their liberty: *Those nations shall serve the king of Babylon seventy years.* The fixing of the time during which the captivity should last would be of great use, not only for the confirmation of the prophecy, when the event (which in this particular could by no human sagacity be foreseen) should exactly answer the prediction, but for the comfort of the people of God in their calamity and the encouragement of faith and prayer. Daniel, who was himself a prophet, had an eye to it, Dan. ix. 2. Nay, God himself had an eye to it (2 Chron. xxxvi. 22); for *therefore* he *stirred up the spirit of Cyrus,* that the word spoken by the mouth of Jeremiah might be accomplished. *Known unto God are all his works from the beginning of the world,* which appears by this, that, when he has thought fit, some of them have been made known to his servants the prophets and by them to his church.

II. The ruin of Babylon, at last, is here likewise foretold, as it had been, long before, by Isaiah, *v.* 12—14. The destroyers must themselves be destroyed, and the rod thrown into the fire, when the correcting work is done with it. This shall be done when *seventy years are accomplished;* for the destruction of Babylon must make way for the deliverance of the captives. It is a great doubt when these *seventy years* commence; some date them from the captivity in the fourth year of Jehoiakim and first of Nebuchadrezzar, others from the captivity of Jehoiachin eight years after. I rather incline to the former, because then these nations began *to serve the king of Babylon,* and because usually God has taken the earliest time from which to reckon the accomplishment of a promise of mercy, as will appear in computing the 400 years' servitude in Egypt. And, if so, eighteen or nineteen years of the seventy had run out before Jerusalem and the temple were quite destroyed in the eleventh year of Zedekiah. However that be, when the time, the set time, to favour Zion, has come, the king of Babylon must be visited, and all the instances of his tyranny reckoned for; then that nation shall be punished *for their iniquity,* as the other nations have been punished for theirs. That land must then be a *perpetual desolation,* such as they had made other lands; for the *Judge of all the earth* will both *do right* and *avenge wrong,* as King of nations and King of saints. Let proud conquerors and oppressors be moderate in the use of their power and success, for it will come at last to their own turn to suffer; their day will come to fall. In this destruction of Babylon, which was to be brought about by the Medes and Persians, reference shall be had, 1. To what God had said: *I will bring upon that land all my words;* for all the wealth and honour of Babylon shall be sacrificed to the truth of the divine predictions, and all its power broken, rather than one iota or tittle of God's word shall fall to the ground. The same Jeremiah that prophesied the destruction of other nations by the Chaldeans foretold also the destruction of the Chaldeans themselves; and this must be brought upon them, *v.* 13. It is with reference to this very event that God says, I will *confirm the word of my servant,* and *perform the counsel of my messengers,* Isa. xliv. 26. 2. To what they had done (*v.* 14): *I will recompense them according to their deeds,* by which they transgressed the law of God, even then when they were made to serve his purposes. They had made many nations to serve them, and trampled upon them with the greatest insolence imaginable; but now that the measure of their iniquity is full *many nations and great kings,* that are in alliance with and come in to the assistance of Cyrus king of Persia, shall *serve themselves of them* also, shall make themselves masters of their country, enrich themselves with their spoils, and make them the footstool by which to mount the throne of universal monarchy. They shall make use of them for servants and

soldiers. *He that leads into captivity shall go into captivity.*

15 For thus saith the LORD God of Israel unto me; Take the wine cup of this fury at my hand, and cause all the nations, to whom I send thee, to drink it. 16 And they shall drink, and be moved, and be mad, because of the sword that I will send among them. 17 Then took I the cup at the LORD's hand, and made all the nations to drink, unto whom the LORD had sent me: 18 *To wit,* Jerusalem, and the cities of Judah, and the kings thereof, and the princes thereof, to make them a desolation, an astonishment, a hissing, and a curse; as *it is* this day; 19 Pharaoh king of Egypt, and his servants, and his princes, and all his people; 20 And all the mingled people, and all the kings of the land of Uz, and all the kings of the land of the Philistines, and Ashkelon, and Azzah, and Ekron, and the remnant of Ashdod, 21 Edom, and Moab, and the children of Ammon, 22 And all the kings of Tyrus, and all the kings of Zidon, and the kings of the isles which *are* beyond the sea, 23 Dedan, and Tema, and Buz, and all *that are* in the utmost corners, 24 And all the kings of Arabia, and all the kings of the mingled people that dwell in the desert, 25 And all the kings of Zimri, and all the kings of Elam, and all the kings of the Medes, 26 And all the kings of the north, far and near, one with another, and all the kingdoms of the world, which *are* upon the face of the earth: and the king of Sheshach shall drink after them. 27 Therefore thou shalt say unto them, Thus saith the LORD of hosts, the God of Israel; Drink ye, and be drunken, and spue, and fall, and rise no more, because of the sword which I will send among you. 28 And it shall be, if they refuse to take the cup at thine hand to drink, then shalt thou say unto them, Thus saith the LORD of hosts; Ye shall certainly drink. 29 For, lo, I begin to bring evil on the city which is called by my name, and should ye

be utterly unpunished? Ye shall not be unpunished: for I will call for a sword upon all the inhabitants of the earth, saith the LORD of hosts.

Under the similitude of a cup going round, which all the company must drink of, is here represented the universal desolation that was now coming upon that part of the world which Nebuchadrezzar, who just now began to reign and act, was to be the instrument of, and which should at length recoil upon his own country. The cup in the vision is to be a sword in the accomplishment of it: so it is explained, *v.* 16. It is *the sword that I will send among them*, the sword of war, that should be irresistibly strong and implacably cruel.

I. As to the circumstances of this judgment, observe,

1. Whence this destroying sword should come—*from the hand of God*. It is the sword *of the Lord* (ch. xlvii. 6), *bathed in heaven*, Isa. xxxiv. 5. Wicked men are made use of as his sword, Ps. xvii. 13. It is *the wine-cup of his fury*. It is the just anger of God that sends this judgment. The nations have provoked him by their sins, and they must fall under the tokens of his wrath. These are compared to some intoxicating liquor, which they shall be forced to drink of, as, formerly, condemned malefactors were sometimes executed by being compelled to drink poison. The wicked are said to *drink the wrath of the Almighty*, Job xxi. 20; Rev. xiv. 10. Their share of troubles in his world is represented by the dregs of a cup of red wine full of mixture, Ps. lxxv. 8. See Ps. xi. 6. The wrath of God in this world is but as a cup, in comparison of the full streams of it in the other world.

2. By whose hand it should be sent to them—by the hand of Jeremiah as the judge *set over the nations* (ch. i. 10), to pass his sentence upon them, and by the hand of Nebuchadrezzar as the executioner. What a much greater figure then does the poor prophet make than what the potent prince makes, if we look upon their relation to God, though in the eye of the world it was the reverse of it! Jeremiah must *take the cup at God's hand*, and compel the nations *to drink it*. He foretels no hurt to them but what God appoints him to foretel; and what is foretold by a divine authority will certainly be fulfilled by a divine power.

3. On whom it should be sent—on all the nations within the verge of Israel's acquaintance and the lines of their communication. Jeremiah took the cup, and *made all the nations to drink of it*, that is, he prophesied concerning each of the nations here mentioned that they should share in this great desolation that was coming. *Jerusalem and the cities of Judah* are put first (*v.* 18); for *judgment begins at the house of God* (1 Pet. iv. 17), at the sanctuary, Ezek. ix. 6. Whe-

ther Nebuchadrezzar had his eye principally upon Jerusalem and Judah in this expedition or no does not appear; probably he had; for it was as considerable as any of the nations here mentioned. However God had his eye principally to them. And this part of the prophecy was already begun to be accomplished; this is denoted by that melancholy parenthesis (*as it is this day*), for in the fourth year of Jehoiakim things had come into a very bad posture, and all the foundations were out of course. *Pharaoh king of Egypt* comes next, because the Jews trusted to that broken reed (*v.* 19); the remains of them fled to Egypt, and there Jeremiah particularly foretold the destruction of that country, ch. xliii. 10, 11. All the other nations that bordered upon Canaan must pledge Jerusalem in this bitter cup, this cup of trembling. The *mingled people*, the Arabians (so some), some rovers of divers nations that lived by rapine (so others); *the kings of the land of Uz*, joined to the country of the Edomites. The Philistines had been vexatious to Israel, but now their cities and their lords become a prey to this mighty conqueror. Edom, Moab, Ammon, Tyre, and Zidon, are places well known to border upon Israel; the *Isles beyond*, or *beside, the sea*, are supposed to be those parts of Phœnicia and Syria that lay upon the coast of the Mediterranean Sea. Dedan and the other countries mentioned (*v.* 23, 24) seem to have lain upon the confines of Idumea and Arabia the desert. Those of Elam are the Persians, with whom the Medes are joined, now looked upon as inconsiderable and yet afterwards able to make reprisals upon Babylon for themselves and all their neighbours. The *kings of the north*, that lay nearer to Babylon, and others that lay at some distance, will be sure to be seized on and made a prey of by the victorious sword of Nebuchadrezzar. Nay, he shall push on his victories with such incredible fury and success that all the kingdoms of the world that were then and there known should become sacrifices to his ambition. Thus Alexander is said to have conquered *the world*, and the Roman empire is called *the world*, Luke ii. 1. Or it may be taken as reading the doom of *all the kingdoms* of the earth; one time or other, they shall feel the dreadful effects of war. The world has been, and will be, a great cockpit, while men's lusts war as they do *in their members*, Jam. iv. 1. But, that the conquerors may see their fate with the conquered, it concludes, *The king of Sheshach shall drink after them*, that is, the king of Babylon himself, who has given his neighbours all this trouble and vexation, shall at length have it return upon his own head. That by Sheshach is meant Babylon is plain from ch. li. 41; but whether it was another name of the same city or the name of another city of the same kingdom is uncertain. Babylon's ruin was foretold, *v.* 12, 13. Upon this prophecy of its being the author of the ruin of so many nations it is very fitly repeated here again.

4. What should be the effect of it. The desolations which the sword should make in all these kingdoms are represented by the consequences of excessive drinking (*v.* 16): *They shall drink, and be moved, and be mad. They shall be drunken, and spue, and fall and rise no more, v.* 27. Now this may serve, (1.) To make us loathe the sin of drunkenness, that the consequences of it are made use of to set forth a most woeful and miserable condition. Drunkenness deprives men, for the present, of the use of their reason, makes them mad. It takes from them likewise that which, next to reason, is the most valuable blessing, and that is health; it makes them sick, and endangers the bones and the life. Men in drink often *fall and rise no more;* it is a sin that is its own punishment. How wretchedly are those intoxicated and besotted that suffer themselves at any time to be intoxicated, especially to be by the frequent commission of the sin besotted with wine or strong drink! (2.) To make us dread the judgments of war. When God sends the sword upon a nation, with warrant to make it desolate, it soon becomes like a drunken man, filled with confusion at the alarms of war, put into a hurry; its counsellors *mad,* and at their wits' end, staggering in all the measures they take, all the motions they make, sick at heart with continual vexation, *vomiting up the riches* they have greedily *swallowed down* (Job xx. 15),*falling* down before the enemy, and as unable to get up again, or do any thing to help themselves, as a man *dead drunk is,* Hab. ii. 16.

5. The undoubted certainty of it, with the reason given for it, *v.* 28, 29. They will *refuse to take the cup at thy hand;* not only they will be loth that the judgment should come, but they will be loth to believe that ever it will come; they will not give credit to the prediction of so despicable a man as Jeremiah. But he must tell them that it is *the word of the Lord of hosts,* he hath said it; and it is in vain for them to struggle with Omnipotence: *You shall certainly drink.* And he must give them this reason, It is a time of visitation, it is a reckoning day, and Jerusalem has been called to an account already: *I begin to bring evil on the city that is called by my name;* its relation to me will not exempt it from punishment, and *should you be utterly unpunished?* No; *If this be done in the green tree, what shall be done in the dry?* If those who have some good in them smart so severely for the evil that is found in them, can those expect to escape who have worse evils, and no good, found among them? If Jerusalem be punished for learning idolatry of the nations, shall not the nations be punished, of whom they

learned it? No doubt they shall: *I will call for a sword upon all the inhabitants of the earth,* for they have helped to debauch the inhabitants of Jerusalem.

II. Upon this whole matter we may observe, 1. That there is a God that judges in the earth, to whom all the nations of the earth are accountable, and by whose judgment they must abide. 2. That God can easily bring to ruin the greatest nations, the most numerous and powerful, and such as have been most secure. 3. That those who have been vexatious and mischievous to the people of God will be reckoned with for it at last. Many of these nations had in their turns given disturbance to Israel, but now comes destruction on them. The year of the redeemer will come, even the *year of recompenses* for the controversy of Zion. 4. That the *burden of the word of the Lord* will at last become the burden of his judgments. Isaiah had prophesied long since against most of these nations (*ch.* xiii. &c.) and now at length all his prophecies will have their complete fulfilling. 5. That those who are ambitious of power and dominion commonly become the troublers of the earth and the plagues of their generation. Nebuchadrezzar was so proud of his might that he had no sense of right. These are the men that turn the world upside down, and yet expect to be admired and adored. Alexander thought himself a great prince when others thought him no better than a great pirate. 6. That the greatest pomp and power in this world are of very uncertain continuance. Before Nebuchadrezzar's greater force kings themselves must yield and become captives.

30 Therefore prophesy thou against them all these words, and say unto them, The LORD shall roar from on high, and utter his voice from his holy habitation; he shall mightily roar upon his habitation; he shall give a shout, as they that tread *the grapes,* against all the inhabitants of the earth. 31 A noise shall come *even* to the ends of the earth; for the LORD hath a controversy with the nations, he will plead with all flesh; he will give them *that are* wicked to the sword, saith the LORD. 32 Thus saith the LORD of hosts, Behold, evil shall go forth from nation to nation, and a great whirlwind shall be raised up from the coasts of the earth. 33 And the slain of the LORD shall be at that day from *one* end of the earth even unto the *other* end of the earth: they shall not be lamented, neither gathered, nor buried; they shall be

dung upon the ground. 34 Howl, ye shepherds, and cry; and wallow youselves *in the ashes,* ye principal of the flock: for the days of your slaughter and of your dispersions are accomplished; and ye shall fall like a pleasant vessel. 35 And the shepherds shall have no way to flee, nor the principal of the flock to escape. 36 A voice of the cry of the shepherds, and a howling of the principal of the flock, *shall be heard:* for the Lord hath spoiled their pasture. 37 And the peaceable habitations are cut down because of the fierce anger of the Lord. 38 He hath forsaken his covert, as the lion: for their land is desolate because of the fierceness of the oppressor, and because of his fierce anger.

We have, in these verses, a further description of those terrible desolations which the king of Babylon with his armies should make in all the countries and nations round about Jerusalem. In Jerusalem God had erected his temple; there were his oracles and ordinances, which the neighbouring nations should have attended to and might have received benefit by; thither they should have applied for the knowledge of God and their duty, and then they might have had reason to bless God for their neighbourhood to Jerusalem; but they, instead of that, taking all opportunities either to debauch or to disturb that holy city, when God came to reckon with Jerusalem because it learned so much of the *way of the nations,* he reckoned with the nations because they learned so little of the way of Jerusalem.

They will soon be aware of Nebuchadrezzar's making war upon them; but the prophet is here directed to tell them that it is God himself that makes war upon them, a God with whom there is no contending. 1. The war is here proclaimed (*v.* 30): *The Lord shall roar from on high:* not *from Mount Zion and Jerusalem* (as Joel iii. 16, Amos i. 2), but from *heaven,* from *his holy habitation* there; for now Jerusalem is one of the places against which he roars. *He shall mightily roar upon his habitation* on earth from that above. He has been long silent, and seemed not to take notice of the wickedness of the nations; the times of this ignorance God winked at; but now *he shall give a shout,* as the assailants in battle do, *against all the inhabitants of the earth,* to whom it shall be a shout of terror, and yet a shout of joy in heaven, as theirs that *tread the grapes;* for, when God is reckoning with the proud enemies of his kingdom among men, there is a *great voice of much people*

heard in heaven, saying, Hallelujah, Rev. xix. 1. He *roars as a lion* (Amos iii. 4, 8), as a lion that has *forsaken his covert* (*v.* 38), and is going abroad to seek his prey, upon which he roars, that he may the more easily seize it. 2. The manifesto is here published, showing the causes and reasons why God proclaims this war (*v.* 31): *The Lord has a controversy with the nations;* he has just cause to contend with them, and he will take this way of pleading with them. His quarrel with them is, in one word, for their wickedness, their contempt of him, and his authority over them and kindness to them. *He will give those that are wicked to the sword.* They have provoked God to anger, and thence comes all this destruction; it is *because of the fierce anger of the Lord* (*v.* 37 and again *v.* 38), the *fierceness of the oppressor,* or (as it might better be read) *the fierceness of the oppressing sword* (for the word is feminine) is *because of his fierce anger;* and we are sure that he is never angry without cause; but *who knows the power of his anger?* 3. The alarm is here given and taken: *A noise will come even to the ends of the earth,* so loud shall it roar, so far shall it reach, *v.* 31. The alarm is not given by sound of trumpet, or beat of drum, but by a *whirlwind, a great whirlwind, storm,* or *tempest,* which shall be *raised up from the coasts,* the remote coasts *of the earth, v.* 32. The Chaldean army shall be like a hurricane raised in the north, but thence carried on with incredible fierceness and swiftness, bearing down all before it. It is like the whirlwind out of which God answered Job, which was exceedingly terrible, Job xxxvii. 1; xxxviii. 1. And, when the wrath of God thus roars like a lion from heaven, no marvel if it be echoed with shrieks from earth; for who can choose but tremble when God thus speaks in displeasure? See Hosea xi. 10. Now the shepherds shall *howl and cry,* the kings, and princes, and the great ones of the earth, the *principal of the flock.* They used to be the most courageous and secure, but now their hearts shall fail them; *they shall wallow themselves in the ashes, v.* 34. Seeing themselves utterly unable to make head against the enemy, and seeing their country, which they have the charge of and a concern for, inevitably ruined, they shall abandon themselves to sorrow. There shall be *a voice of the cry of the shepherds,* and a *howling of the principal of the flock shall be heard, v.* 36. Those are great calamities indeed that strike such a terror upon the great men, and put them into this consternation. *The Lord hath spoiled their pasture,* in which they fed their flock, and out of which they fed themselves; the spoiling of that makes them cry-out thus. Perhaps, carrying on the metaphor of a lion roaring, it alludes to the great fright that shepherds are in when they hear a roaring lion coming towards their flocks, and find they have *no way to flee* (*v.* 35) for their own safety, neither can the *principal of their flock escape.* The enemy will be so numerous, so furious, so sedulous, and the extent of their armies so vast, that it will be impossible to avoid falling into their hands. Note, As we cannot out-face, so we cannot out-run, the judgments of God This is that for which the shepherds *howl and cry.* 4. The progress of this war is here described (*v.* 32) : *Behold, evil shall go forth from nation to nation* ; as the cup goes round, every nation shall have its share and take its turn, because one does not take warning by the calamities of another to repent and reform. Nay, as if this were to be a little representation of the last and general judgment, it shall reach *from one end of the earth even unto the other end of the earth, v.* 33. The day of vengeance is in his heart, and now *his hand shall find out all his enemies,* wherever they are, Ps. xxi. 8. Note, When our neighbour's house is on fire it is time to be concerned for our own. When one nation is a seat of war every neighbouring nation should hear, and fear, and make its peace with God. 5. The dismal consequences of this war are here foretold : *The days of slaughter and dispersions are accomplished,* that is, they are fully come (*v.* 34), the time fixed in the divine counsel for the slaughter of some and the dispersion of the rest, which will make the nations completely desolate. Multitudes shall fall by the sword of the merciless Chaldeans, so that *the slain of the Lord* shall be every where found : they are slain by commission from him, and are sacrificed to his justice. The slain for sin are the *slain of the Lord.* To complete the misery of their slaughter, *they shall not be lamented* in particular, so general shall the matter of lamentation be. Nay, they shall not *be gathered* up, nor *buried,* for they shall have no friends left to bury them, and the enemies shall not have so much humanity in them as to do it ; and then they shall be *as dung upon the earth,* so vile and noisome : and it is well if, as dung manures the earth and makes it fruitful, so these horrid spectacles, which lie as monuments of divine justice, might be a means to awaken the inhabitants of the earth to *learn righteousness.* The effect of this war will be the *desolation of the whole land* that is the seat of it (*v.* 38), one land after another. But here are two expressions more that seem to make the case in a particular manner piteous. (1.) *You shall fall like a pleasant vessel, v.* 34. The most desirable persons among them, who most valued themselves and were most valued, who were looked upon as *vessels of honour,* shall fall by the sword. You shall fall as a Venice glass or a China dish, which is soon broken all to pieces. Even the tender and delicate shall share in the common calamity ; the sword devours one as well as another. (2) Even *the peaceable habitations*

572

are cut down. Those that used to be quiet, and not molested, the habitations in which you have long dwelt in peace, shall now be no longer such, but *cut down* by the war. Or, Those who used to be quiet, and not molesting any of their neighbours, those who lived in peace, easily, and gave no provocation to any, even those shall not escape. This is one of the direful effects of war, that even those who were most harmless and inoffensive suffer hard things. Blessed be God, there is a *peaceable habitation* above for all the sons of peace, which is out of the reach of fire and sword.

CHAP. XXVI.

As in the history of the Acts of the Apostles that of their preaching and that of their suffering are interwoven, so it is in the account we have of the prophet Jeremiah ; witness this chapter, where we are told, I. How faithfully he preached, ver. 1—6. II. How gracefully he was persecuted for so doing by the priests and the prophets, ver. 7—11. III. How bravely he stood to his doctrine, in the face of his persecutors, ver. 12—15. IV. How wonderfully he was protected and delivered by the prudence of the princes and elders, ver. 16—19. Though Urijah, another prophet, was about the same time put to death by Jehoiakim (ver. 20—23), yet Jeremiah met with those that sheltered him, ver. 24.

IN the beginning of the reign of Jehoiakim the son of Josiah king of Judah came this word from the LORD, saying, 2 Thus saith the LORD ; Stand in the court of the LORD's house, and speak unto all the cities of Judah, which come to worship in the LORD's house, all the words that I command thee to speak unto them ; diminish not a word : 3 If so be they will hearken, and turn every man from his evil way, that I may repent me of the evil, which I purpose to do unto them because of the evil of their doings. 4 And thou shalt say unto them, Thus saith the LORD ; If ye will not hearken to me, to walk in my law, which I have set before you, 5 To hearken to the words of my servants the prophets, whom I sent unto you, both rising up early, and sending *them,* but ye have not hearkened ; 6 Then will I make this house like Shiloh, and will make this city a curse to all the nations of the earth.

We have here the sermon that Jeremiah preached, which gave such offence that he was in danger of losing his life for it. It is here left upon record, as it were, by way of appeal to the judgment of impartial men in all ages, whether Jeremiah was worthy to die for delivering such a message as this from God, and whether his persecutors were not very wicked and unreasonable men.

I. God directed him where to preach this sermon, and when, and to what auditory, *v.* 2. Let not any censure Jeremiah as indiscreet in the choice of place and time, nor say that he might have delivered his message more privately, in a corner, among his friends that he could confide in, and that he deserved to smart for not acting more cautiously; for God gave him orders to preach *in the court of the Lord's house*, which was within the peculiar jurisdiction of his sworn enemies the priests, and who would therefore take themselves to be in a particular manner affronted. He must preach this, as it should seem, at the time of one of the most solemn festivals, when persons had come from all the *cities of Judah* to *worship in the Lord's house.* These worshippers, we may suppose, had a great veneration for their priests, would credit the character they gave of men, and be exasperated against those whom they defamed, and would, consequently, side with them and strengthen their hands against Jeremiah. But none of these things must move him or daunt him; in the face of all this danger he must preach this sermon, which, if it were not convincing, would be very provoking. And because the prophet might be in some temptation to palliate the matter, and make it better to his hearers than God had made it to him, to exchange an offensive expression for one more plausible, therefore God charges him particularly *not to diminish a word*, but to speak all the things, nay, *all the words*, that he had commanded him. Note, God's ambassadors must keep closely to their instructions, and not in the least vary from them, either to please men or to save themselves from harm. They must neither *add* nor *diminish*, Deut. iv. 2.

II. God directed him what to preach, and it is that which could not give offence to any but such as were resolved to go on still in their trespasses. 1. He must assure them that if they would *repent of their sins*, and turn from them, though they were in imminent danger of ruin and desolating judgments were just at the door, yet a stop should be put to them, and God would proceed no further in his controversy with them, *v.* 3. This was the main thing God intended in sending him to them, to try if they would return from their sins, that so God might turn from his anger and turn away the judgments that threatened them, which he was not only willing, but very desirous to do, as soon as he could do it without prejudice to the honour of his justice and holiness. See how God *waits to be gracious*, waits till we are duly qualified, till we are fit for him to be gracious to, and in the mean time tries a variety of methods to bring us to be so. 2. He must, on the other hand, assure them that if they continued obstinate to all the calls God gave them, and would persist in their disobedience, it would certainly end in the ruin of their city and temple, *v.* 4—6. (1.) That which God re-

quired of them was that they should be observant of what he had said to them, both by the written word and by his ministers, that they should *walk in all his law which he set before them*, the law of Moses and the ordinances and commandments of it, and that they should *hearken to the words of his servants the prophets*, who pressed nothing upon them but what was agreeable to the law of Moses, which was *set before them* as a touchstone to try the spirits by; and by this they were distinguished from the false prophets, who drew them from the law, instead of drawing them to it. The law was what God himself set before them. The prophets were his own servants, and were immediately sent by him to them, and sent with a great deal of care and concern, *rising early to send them*, lest they should come too late, when their prejudices had got possession and become invincible. They had hitherto been deaf both to the law and to the prophets: *You have not hearkened.* All he expects now is that at length they should heed what he said, and make his word their rule—a reasonable demand. (2.) That which is threatened in case of refusal is that this city, and the temple in it, shall fare as their predecessors did, Shiloh and the tabernacle there, for a like refusal to walk in God's law and hearken to his prophets, then when the present dispensation of prophecy just began in Samuel. Now could a sentence be expressed more unexceptionably? Is it not a rule of justice *ut parium par sit ratio—that those whose cases are the same be dealt with alike?* If Jerusalem be like Shiloh in respect of sin, why should it not be like Shiloh in respect of punishment? Can any other be expected? This was not the first time he had given them warning to this effect; see *ch.* vii. 12—14. When the temple, which was the glory of Jerusalem, was destroyed, the city was thereby *made a curse*; for the temple was that which made it a blessing. *If the salt lose* that *savour, it is thenceforth good for nothing.* It shall be *a curse*, that is, it shall be the pattern of a curse; if a man would curse any city, he would say, *God make it like Jerusalem!* Note, Those that will not be subject to the commands of God make themselves subject to the curse of God.

7 So the priests and the prophets and all the people heard Jeremiah speaking these words in the house of the Lord. 8 Now it came to pass, when Jeremiah had made an end of speaking all that the Lord had commanded *him* to speak unto all the people, that the priests and the prophets and all the people took him, saying, Thou shalt surely die. 9 Why hast thou prophesied in the

573

name of the LORD, saying, This house shall be like Shiloh, and this city shall be desolate without an inhabitant? And all the people were gathered against Jeremiah in the house of the LORD. 10 When the princes of Judah heard these things, then they came up from the king's house unto the house of the LORD, and sat down in the entry of the new gate of the LORD's *house.* 11 Then spake the priests and the prophets unto the princes and to all the people, saying, This man *is* worthy to die; for he hath prophesied against this city, as ye have heard with your ears. 12 Then spake Jeremiah unto all the princes and to all the people, saying, The LORD sent me to prophesy against this house and against this city all the words that ye have heard. 13 Therefore now amend your ways and your doings, and obey the voice of the LORD your God; and the LORD will repent him of the evil that he hath pronounced against you. 14 As for me, behold, I *am* in your hand: do with me as seemeth good and meet unto you. 15 But know ye for certain, that if ye put me to death, ye shall surely bring innocent blood upon yourselves, and upon this city, and upon the inhabitants thereof: for of a truth the LORD hath sent me unto you to speak all these words in your ears.

One would have hoped that such a sermon as that in the foregoing verses, so plain and practical, so rational and pathetic, and delivered in God's name, would work upon even this people, especially meeting them now at their devotions, and would prevail with them to repent and reform; but, instead of awakening their convictions, it did but exasperate their corruptions, as appears by this account of the effect of it.

I. Jeremiah is charged with it as a crime that he had preached such a sermon, and is apprehended for it as a criminal. The *priests,* and *false prophets,* and *people, heard him speak these words,* v. 7. They had patience, it seems, to hear him out, did not disturb him when he was preaching, nor give him any interruption till he had *made an end of speaking all that the Lord commanded him to speak,* v. 8. So far they dealt more fairly with him than some of the persecutors of God's ministers have done; they let him say all he had to say, and yet perhaps with a bad design, in hopes to have something worse

574

yet to lay to his charge; but, having no worse, this shall suffice to ground an indictment upon: He hath said, *This house shall be like Shiloh,* v. 9. See how unfair they are in representing his words. He had said, in God's name, *If you will not hearken to me, then will I make this house like Shiloh;* but they leave out God's hand in the desolation (*I will make* it so) and their own hand in it in not hearkening to the voice of God, and charge it upon him that he *blasphemed this holy place,* the crime charged both on our Lord Jesus and on Stephen: He said, *This house shall be like Shiloh.* Well might he complain, as David does (Ps. lvi. 5), *Every day they wrest my words;* and we must not think it strange if we, and what we say and do, be thus misrepresented. When the accusation was so weakly grounded, no marvel that the sentence passed upon it was unjust: *Thou shalt surely die.* What he had said agreed with what God had said when he took possession of the temple (1 Kings ix. 6—8), *If you shall at all turn from following after me, then this house shall be* abandoned; and yet he is condemned to die for saying it. It is not out of any concern for the honour of the temple that they appear thus warm, but because they were resolved not to part with their sins, in which they flatter themselves with a conceit that the *temple of the Lord* will protect them; therefore, right or wrong, *Thou shalt surely die.* This outcry of the priests and prophets raised the mob, and *all the people were gathered together against Jeremiah* in a popular tumult, ready to pull him to pieces, were *gathered about him* (so some read it); they flocked together, some crying one thing and some another. *The people* that were at first present were hot against him (*v.* 8), but their clamours drew more together, only to see what the matter was.

II. He is arraigned and indicted for it before the highest court of judicature they had. Here, 1. The *princes of Judah* were his judges, *v.* 10. Those that filled the thrones of judgment, *the thrones of the house of David,* the elders of Israel, they, hearing of this tumult in the temple, *came up from the king's house,* where they usually sat near the court, *to the house of the Lord,* to enquire into this matter, and to see that nothing was done disorderly. They *sat down in the entry of the new gate of the Lord's house,* and held a court, as it were, by a special commission of *Oyer and Terminer.* 2. The *priests and prophets* were his prosecutors and accusers, and were violently set against him. They appealed to *the princes,* and to *all the people,* to the court and the jury, whether *this man* were not *worthy to die,* v. 11. The corrupt priests and counterfeit prophets have always been the most bitter enemies of the prophets of the Lord; they had ends of their own to serve, which they thought such preaching as this would be **an obstruc-**

tion to. When Jeremiah prophesied in the house of the king concerning the fall of the royal family (*ch.* xxii. 1, &c.), the court, though very corrupt, bore it patiently, and we do not find that they persecuted him for it; but when he comes into the *house of the Lord*, and touches the copyhold of the priests, and contradicts the lies and flatteries of the false prophets, then he is adjudged *worthy to die.* For the prophets *prophesied falsely*, and the *priests bore rule by their means*, ch. v. 31. Observe, When Jeremiah is indicted before the princes the stress of his accusation is laid upon what he said concerning the city, because they thought the princes would be most concerned about that. But concerning the words spoken they appeal to the people, " *You have heard* what he hath said; let it be given in evidence."

III. Jeremiah makes his defence before the princes and the people. He does not go about to deny the words, nor to diminish aught from them; what he has said he will stand to, though it cost him his life; he owns that he had prophesied against *this house* and *this city*, but, 1. He asserts that he did this by good authority, not maliciously nor seditiously, not out of any ill-will to his country nor any disaffection to the government in church or state, but, *The Lord sent me* to prophesy thus: so he begins his apology (*v.* 12), and so he concludes it, for this is that which he resolves to abide by as sufficient to bear him out (*v.* 15): *Of a truth the Lord hath sent me unto you, to speak all these words.* As long as ministers keep closely to the instructions they have from heaven they need not fear the opposition they may meet with from hell or earth. He pleads that he is but a messenger, and, if he faithfully deliver his message, he must bear no blame; but he is a messenger from the Lord, to whom they were accountable as well as he, and therefore might demand regard. If he speak but what God appointed him to speak, he is under the divine protection, and whatever affront they offer to the ambassador will be resented by the Prince that sent him. 2. He shows them that he did it with a good design, and that it was their fault if they did not make a good use of it. It was said, not by way of fatal sentence, but of fair warning; if they would take the warning, they might prevent the execution of the sentence, *v.* 13. Shall I take it ill of a man that tells me of my danger, while I have an opportunity of avoiding it, and not rather return him thanks for it, as the greatest kindness he could do me? " *I have* indeed (says Jeremiah) prophesied *against this city;* but, *if you will now amend your ways and your doings*, the threatened ruin shall be prevented, which was the thing I aimed at in giving you the warning." Those are very unjust who complain of ministers for preaching hell and damnation, when it is only to keep them from that place of torment and to

bring them to heaven and salvation. 3. He therefore warns them of their danger if they proceed against him (*v.* 14): " *As for me*, the matter is not great what becomes of me; *behold, I am in your hand;* you know I am; I neither have any power, nor can make any interest, to oppose you, nor is it so much my concern to save my own life: *do with me as seems meet unto you;* if I be led to the slaughter, it shall be as a lamb." Note, It becomes God's ministers, that are warm in preaching, to be calm in suffering and to behave submissively to the powers that are over them, though they be persecuting powers. But, for themselves, he tells them that it is at their peril if they put him to death: *You shall surely bring innocent blood upon yourselves, v.* 15. They might think that killing the prophet would help to defeat the prophecy, but they would prove wretchedly deceived; it would but add to their guilt and aggravate their ruin. Their own consciences could not but tell them that, if Jeremiah was (as certainly he was) sent of God to bring them this message, it was at their utmost peril if they treated him for it as a malefactor. Those that persecute God's ministers hurt not them so much as themselves.

16 Then said the princes and all the people unto the priests and to the prophets; This man *is* not worthy to die: for he hath spoken to us in the name of the LORD our God. 17 Then rose up certain of the elders of the land, and spake to all the assembly of the people, saying, 18 Micah the Morasthite prophesied in the days of Hezekiah king of Judah, and spake to all the people of Judah, saying, Thus saith the LORD of hosts; Zion shall be ploughed *like* a field, and Jerusalem shall become heaps, and the mountain of the house as the high places of a forest. 19 Did Hezekiah king of Judah and all Judah put him at all to death? did he not fear the LORD, and besought the LORD, and the LORD repented him of the evil which he had pronounced against them? Thus might we procure great evil against our souls. 20 And there was also a man that prophesied in the name of the LORD, Urijah the son of Shemaiah of Kirjath-jearim, who prophesied against this city and against this land according to all the words of Jeremiah: 21 And when Jehoiakim the king, with all his mighty men, and all the princes, heard his words, the king sought to put him to death:

but when Urijah heard it, he was afraid, and fled, and went into Egypt; 22 And Jehoiakim the king sent men into Egypt, *namely,* Elnathan the son of Achbor, and *certain* men with him into Egypt. 23 And they fetched forth Urijah out of Egypt, and brought him unto Jehoiakim the king; who slew him with the sword, and cast his dead body into the graves of the common people. 24 Nevertheless the hand of Ahikam the son of Shaphan was with Jeremiah, that they should not give him into the hand of the people to put him to death.

Here is, I. The acquitting of Jeremiah from the charge exhibited against him. He had indeed spoken the words as they were laid in the indictment, but they are not looked upon to be seditious or treasonable, ill-intended or of any bad tendency, and therefore the court and country agree to find him not guilty. The priests and prophets, notwithstanding his rational plea for himself, continued to demand judgment against him; but the princes, and all the people, are clear in it that *this man is not worthy to die* (*v.* 16); for (say they) *he hath spoken to us,* not of himself, but *in the name of the Lord our God.* And are they willing to own that he did indeed speak to them *in the name of the Lord* and that that Lord is their God? Why then did they not amend their ways and doings, and take the method he prescribed to prevent the ruin of their country? If they say, His prophecy is *from heaven,* it may justly be asked, *Why did you not then believe him?* Matt. xxi. 25. Note, It is a pity that those who are so far convinced of the divine original of gospel preaching as to protect it from the malice of others do not submit to the power and influence of it themselves.

II. A precedent quoted to justify them in acquitting Jeremiah. Some of the *elders of the land,* either the princes before mentioned or the more intelligent men of the people, stood up, and put the assembly in mind of a former case, as is usual with us in giving judgment; for the wisdom of our predecessors is a direction to us. The case referred to is that of Micah. We have extant the book of his prophecy among the minor prophets. 1. Was it thought strange that Jeremiah prophesied against this city and the temple? Micah did so before him, even in the reign of Hezekiah, that reign of reformation, *v.* 18. Micah said it as publicly as Jeremiah had now spoken to the same purport, *Zion shall be ploughed like a field,* the building shall be all destroyed, so that nothing shall hinder but it may be ploughed; *Jerusalem shall become heaps* of ruins, and

the mountain *of the house* on which the temple is built shall be *as the high places of the forest,* overrun with briers and thorns. That prophet not only spoke this, but wrote it, and left it on record; we find it, Mic. iii. 12. By this it appears that a man may be, as Micah was, a true prophet of the Lord, and yet may prophesy the destruction of Zion and Jerusalem. When we threaten secure sinners with the taking away of the Spirit of God and the kingdom of God from them, and declining churches with the removal of the candlestick, we say no more than what has been said many a time, and what we have warrant from the word of God to say. 2. Was it thought fit by the princes to justify Jeremiah in what he had done? It was what Hezekiah did before them in a like case. Did Hezekiah, and the people of Judah (that is, the representatives of the people, the commons in parliament), did they complain of Micah the prophet? Did they impeach him, or make an act to silence him and put him to death? No; on the contrary, they took the warning he gave them. Hezekiah, that renowned prince, of blessed memory, set a good example before his successors, for he *feared the Lord* (*v.* 19), as Noah, who, being *warned of God of things not seen as yet,* was *moved with fear.* Micah's preaching drove him to his knees; he *besought the Lord* to turn away the judgment threatened and to be reconciled to them, and he found it was not in vain to do so, for *the Lord repented him of the evil* and returned in mercy to them; he sent an angel, who routed the army of the Assyrians, that threatened to plough *Zion like a field.* Hezekiah got good by the preaching, and then you may be sure he would do no harm to the preacher. These elders conclude that it would be of dangerous consequence to the state if they should gratify the importunity of the priests and prophets in putting Jeremiah to death: *Thus might we procure great evil against our souls.* Note, It is good to deter ourselves from sin with the consideration of the mischief we shall certainly do to ourselves by it and the irreparable damage it will be to our own souls.

III. Here is an instance of another prophet that was put to death by Jehoiakim for prophesying as Jeremiah had done, *v.* 20, &c. Some make this to be urged by the prosecutors, as a case that favoured the prosecution, a modern case, in which speaking such words as Jeremiah had spoken was adjudged treason. Others think that the elders, who were advocates for Jeremiah, alleged this to show that thus they might *procure great evil against their souls,* for it would be adding sin to sin. Jehoiakim, the present king, had slain one prophet already; let them not fill up the measure by slaying another. Hezekiah, who protected Micah, prospered; but did Jehoiakim prosper who slew Urijah? No; they all saw the contrary. As good examples, and the good consequences of them, should encourage us in that which is good, so the examples of bad men, and the bad consequences of them, should deter us from that which is evil. But some good interpreters take this narrative from the historian that penned the book, Jeremiah himself, or Baruch, who, to make Jeremiah's deliverance by means of the princes the more wonderful, takes notice of this that happened about the same time; for both were in the reign of Jehoiakim, and this *in the beginning of his reign, v.* 1. Observe, 1. Urijah's prophecy. It was *against this city, and this land, according to all the words of Jeremiah.* The prophets of the Lord agreed in their testimony, and one would have thought that out of the mouth of so many witnesses the word would be regarded. 2. The prosecution of him for it, *v.* 21. Jehoiakim and his courtiers were exasperated against him, and *sought to put him to death;* in this wicked design the king himself was principally concerned. 3. His absconding thereupon: *When he heard* that the king had become his enemy, and sought his life, *he was afraid, and fled, and went into Egypt.* This was certainly his fault, and an effect of the weakness of his faith, and it sped accordingly. He distrusted God, and his power to protect him and bear him out; he was too much under the power of that *fear of man* which *brings a snare.* It looked as if he durst not stand to what he had said or was ashamed of his Master. It was especially unbecoming him to flee *into Egypt,* and so in effect to abandon the land of Israel and to throw himself quite out of the way of being useful. Note, There are many that have much grace, but they have little courage, that are very honest, but withal very timorous. 4. His execution notwithstanding. Jehoiakim's malice, one would think, might have contented itself with his banishment, and it might suffice to have driven him out of the country; but those are *bloodthirsty* that *hate the upright,* Prov. xxix. 10. It was the life, that precious life, that he hunted after, and nothing else would satisfy him. So implacable is his revenge that he sends a party of soldiers into Egypt, some hundreds of miles, and they bring him back by force of arms. It would not sufficiently gratify him to have him slain in Egypt, but he must feed his eyes with the bloody spectacle. They *brought him to Jehoiakim,* and he *slew him with the sword,* for aught I know with his own hands. Yet neither did this satisfy his insatiable malice, but he loads the dead body of the good man with infamy, would not allow it the decent respects usually and justly paid to the remains of men of distinction, but cast it into *the graves of the common people,* as if he had not been a prophet of the Lord; thus was the *shield of Saul vilely cast away, as though he had not been anointed with oil.* Thus Jehoiakim

hoped both to ruin his reputation with the people, that no heed might be given to his predictions, and to deter others from prophesying in like manner; but in vain; Jeremiah says the same. There is no contending with the word of God. Herod thought he had gained his point when he had cut off John Baptist's head, but found himself deceived when, soon after, he heard of Jesus Christ, and said, in a fright, *This is John the Baptist.*

IV. Here is Jeremiah's deliverance. Though Urijah was lately put to death, and persecutors, when they have tasted the blood of saints, are apt to thirst after more (as Herod, Acts xii. 2, 3), yet God wonderfully preserved Jeremiah, though he did not flee, as Urijah did, but stood his ground. Ordinary ministers may use ordinary means, provided they be lawful ones, for their own preservation; but those that had an extraordinary mission might expect an extraordinary protection. God raised up a friend for Jeremiah, whose hand was with him; he took him by the hand in a friendly way, encouraged him, assisted him, appeared for him. It was *Ahikam the son of Shaphan,* one that was a minister of state in Josiah's time; we read of him, 2 Kings xxii. 12. Some think Gedaliah was the son of this Ahikam. He had a great interest, it should seem, among the princes, and he used it in favour of Jeremiah, to prevent the further designs of the priests and prophets against him, who would have had him turned over *into the hand of the people,* not those people (*v.* 16) that had adjudged him innocent, but the rude and insolent mob, whom they could persuade by their cursed insinuations not only to cry, *Crucify him, crucify him,* but to *stone him to death* in a popular tumult; for perhaps Jehoiakim had been so reproached by his own conscience for slaying Urijah that they despaired of making him the tool of their malice. Note, God can, when he pleases, raise up great men to patronise good men; and it is an encouragement to us to trust him in the way of duty that he has all men's hearts in his hands.

CHAP. XXVII.

Jeremiah the prophet, since he cannot persuade people to submit to God's precept, and so to prevent the destruction of their country by the king of Babylon, is here persuading them to submit to God's providence, by yielding tamely to the king of Babylon, and becoming tributaries to him, which was the wisest course they could now take, and would be a mitigation of the calamity, and prevent the laying of their country waste by fire and sword; the sacrificing of their liberties would be the saving of their lives. I. He gives this counsel, in God's name, to the kings of the neighbouring nations, that they might make the best of bad, assuring them that there was no remedy, but they must serve the king of Babylon; and yet in time there should be relief, for his dominion should last but 70 years, ver. 1—11. II. He gives this counsel to Zedekiah king of Judah particularly (ver. 12—15) and to the priests and people, assuring them that the king of Babylon should still proceed against them till things were brought to the last extremity, and a patient submission would be the only way to mitigate the calamity and make it easy, ver. 16—22. Thus the prophet, if they would but have hearkened to him, would have directed them in the paths of true policy as well as of true piety.

I N the beginning of the reign of Jehoiakim the son of Josiah king of Judah came this word unto Jeremiah from the LORD, saying, 2 Thus saith the LORD to me; Make thee bonds and yokes, and put them upon thy neck, 3 And send them to the king of Edom, and to the king of Moab, and to the king of the Ammonites, and to the king of Tyrus, and to the king of Zidon, by the hand of the messengers which come to Jerusalem unto Zedekiah king of Judah; 4 And command them to say unto their masters, Thus saith the LORD of hosts, the God of Israel; Thus shall ye say unto your masters; 5 I have made the earth, the man and the beast that *are* upon the ground, by my great power and by my out-stretched arm, and have given it unto whom it seemed meet unto me. 6 And now have I given all these lands into the hand of Nebuchadnezzar the king of Babylon, my servant; and the beasts of the field have I given him also to serve him. 7 And all nations shall serve him, and his son, and his son's son, until the very time of his land come: and then many nations and great kings shall serve themselves of him. 8 And it shall come to pass, *that* the nation and kingdom which will not serve the same Nebuchadnezzar the king of Babylon, and that will not put their neck under the yoke of the king of Babylon, that nation will I punish, saith the LORD, with the sword, and with the famine, and with the pestilence, until I have consumed them by his hand. 9 Therefore hearken not ye to your prophets, nor to your diviners, nor to your dreamers, nor to your enchanters, nor to your sorcerers, which speak unto you, saying, Ye shall not serve the king of Babylon: 10 For they prophesy a lie unto you, to remove you far from your land; and that I should drive you out, and ye should perish. 11 But the nations that bring their neck under the yoke of the king of Babylon, and serve him, those will I let remain still in their own land, saith the LORD; and they shall till it, and dwell therein.

Some difficulty occurs in the date of this prophecy. This word is said to come to

Jeremiah *in the beginning of the reign of Jehoiakim* (v. 1), and yet the messengers, to whom he is to deliver the badges of servitude, are said (v. 3) to come to *Zedekiah king of Judah*, who reigned not till eleven years after the beginning of Jehoiakim's reign. Some make it an error of the copy, and think that it should be read (v. 1), *In the beginning of the reign of Zedekiah*, for which some negligent scribe, having his eye on the title of the foregoing chapter, wrote *Jehoiakim*. And, if one would admit a mistake any where, it should be here, for Zedekiah is mentioned again (v. 12), and the next prophecy is dated the same year, and said to be in the *beginning of the reign of Zedekiah, ch.* xxviii. 1. Dr. Lightfoot solves it thus: In the beginning of Jehoiakim's reign Jeremiah is to make these bonds and yokes, and to put them upon his own neck, in token of Judah's subjection to the king of Babylon, which began at that time; but he is to send them to the neighbouring kings afterwards in the reign of Zedekiah, of whose succession to Jehoiakim, and the ambassadors sent to him, mention is made by way of prediction.

I. Jeremiah is to prepare a sign of the general reduction of all these countries into subjection to the king of Babylon (v. 2): *Make thee bonds and yokes*, yokes with bonds to fasten them, that the beast may not slip his neck out of the yoke. Into these the prophet must put his own neck to make them taken notice of as a prophetic representation; for every one would enquire, What is the meaning of Jeremiah's yokes? We find him with one on, *ch.* xxviii. 10. Hereby he intimated that he advised them to nothing but what he was resolved to do himself; for he was not one of those that *bind heavy burdens* on others, which they themselves will not *touch with one of their fingers*. Ministers must thus lay themselves under the weight and obligation of what they preach to others.

II. He is to send this, with a sermon annexed to it, to all the neighbouring princes; those are mentioned (v. 3) that lay next to the land of Canaan. It should seem, there was a treaty of alliance on foot between the king of Judah and all those other kings. Jerusalem was the place appointed for the treaty. Thither they all sent their plenipotentiaries; and it was agreed that they should bind themselves in a league offensive and defensive, to stand by one another, in opposition to the growing threatening greatness of the king of Babylon, and to reduce his exorbitant power. They had great confidence in their strength thus united, and were ready to call themselves the high allies; but, when the envoys were returning to their respective masters with the ratification of this treaty, Jeremiah gives each of them a yoke to carry to his master, to signify to him that he must either by consent or by compulsion become a servant to the king of Babylon, let him choose which he will. In the sermon upon this sign, 1. God asserts his own indisputable right to dispose of kingdoms as he pleases, *v.* 5. He is the Creator of all things ; he *made the earth* at first, established it, and it abides : it is still the same, though *one generation passes away and another comes.* He still by a continued creation produces *man and beast upon the ground,* and it is by his *great power* and *outstretched arm.* His arm has infinite strength, though it be stretched out. Upon this account he may give and convey a property and dominion to whomsoever he pleases. As he hath graciously *given the earth to the children of men* in general (Ps. cxv. 16), so he gives to each his share of it, be it more or less. Note, Whatever any have of the good things of this world, it is what God sees fit to give them ; we ourselves should therefore be content, though we have ever so little, and not envy any their share, though they have ever so much. 2. He publishes a grant of all these countries to Nebuchadnezzar. Know all men by these presents. *Sciant præsentes et futuri—Let those of the present and those of the future age know.* "This is to certify to all whom it may concern that I have *given all these lands,* with all the wealth of them, into *the hands of the king of Babylon ;* even the beasts *of the field,* whether tame or wild, *have I given to him,* parks and pastures ; they are all his own." Nebuchadnezzar was a proud wicked man, an idolater ; and yet God, in his providence, gives him this large dominion, these vast possessions. Note, The things of·this world are not the best things, for God often gives the largest share of them to bad men, that are rivals with him and rebels against him. He was a wicked man, and yet what he had he had by divine grant. Note, Dominion is not founded in grace. Those that have not any colourable title to eternal happiness may yet have a justifiable title to their temporal good things. Nebuchadnezzar is a very bad man, and yet God calls him his servant, because he employed him as an instrument of his providence for the chastising of the nations, and particularly his own people ; and for his service therein he thus liberally repaid him. Those whom God makes use of shall not lose by him ; much more will he be found the bountiful rewarder of all those that designedly and sincerely serve him. 3. He assures them that they should all be unavoidably brought under the dominion of the king of Babylon for a time (*v.* 7) : *All nations,* all these nations and many others, *shall serve him, and his son, and his son's son.* His son was Evil-merodach, and his son's son Belshazzar, in whom his kingdom ceased : then the time of reckoning with his land came, when the tables were turned, and *many nations and great kings,* incorporated into the empire of the Medes and Persians, *served themselves of him,* as before, *ch.* xxv.

14. Thus Adonibezek was trampled upon himself, as he had trampled on other kings. 4. He threatens those with military execution that stood out and would not submit to the king of Babylon (*v.* 8) : That nation that will not *put their neck under his yoke* I will *punish with sword and famine,* with one judgment after another, till it is *consumed by his hand.* Nebuchadnezzar was very unjust and barbarous in invading the rights and liberties of his neighbours thus, and forcing them into a subjection to him ; yet God had just and holy ends in permitting him to do so, to punish these nations for their idolatry and gross immoralities. Those that would not serve the God that made them were justly made to serve their enemies that sought to ruin them. 5. He shows them the vanity of all the hopes they fed themselves with, that they should preserve their liberties, *v.* 9, 10. These nations had their prophets too, that pretended to foretel future events by the stars, or by dreams, or enchantments ; and they, to please their patrons, and because they would themselves have it so, flattered them with assurances that they *should not serve the king of Babylon.* Thus they designed to animate them to a vigorous resistance ; and, though they had no ground for it, they hoped hereby to do them service. But he tells them that it would prove to their destruction ; for by resisting they would provoke the conqueror to deal severely with them, to *remove them,* and *drive them out* into a miserable captivity, in which they should all be lost and buried in oblivion. Particular prophecies against these nations that bordered on Israel severally, the ruin of which is here foretold in the general, we shall meet with, *ch.* xlviii. and xlix., and Ezek. xxv., which had the same accomplishment with this here. Note, *When God judges he will overcome.* 6. He puts them in a fair way to prevent their destruction by a quiet and easy submission, *v.* 11. The nations that will be content to *serve the king of Babylon,* and pay him tribute for seventy years (ten apprenticeships), *those will I let remain still in their own land.* Those that will bend shall not break. Perhaps the dominion of the king of Babylon may bear no harder upon them than that of their own kings had done. It is often more a point of honour than true wisdom to prefer liberty before life. It is not mentioned to the disgrace of Issachar that because he saw·rest was *good,* and the *land pleasant,* that he might peaceably enjoy it, he bowed *his shoulder to bear,* and *became a servant to tribute* (Gen. xlix. 14, 15), as these are here advised to do : *Serve the king of Babylon and you shall till the land* and *dwell therein.* Some would condemn this as the evidence of a mean spirit, but the prophet recommends it as that of a meek spirit, which yields to necessity, and by a quiet submission to the hardest turns of Providence makes the best of bad : it is

better to do so than by struggling to make it worse.

Many might have prevented destroying providences by humbling themselves under humbling providences. It is better to take up a lighter cross in our way than to pull a heavier on our own head.

12 I spake also to Zedekiah king of Judah according to all these words, saying, Bring your necks under the yoke of the king of Babylon, and serve him and his people, and live. 13 Why will ye die, thou and thy people, by the sword, by the famine, and by the pestilence, as the LORD hath spoken against the nation that will not serve the king of Babylon? 14 Therefore hearken not unto the words of the prophets that speak unto you, saying, Ye shall not serve the king of Babylon: for they prophesy a lie unto you. 15 For I have not sent them, saith the LORD, yet they prophesy a lie in my name; that I might drive you out, and that ye might perish, ye, and the prophets that prophesy unto you. 16 Also I spake to the priests and to all this people, saying, Thus saith the LORD; Hearken not to the words of your prophets that prophesy unto you, saying, Behold, the vessels of the LORD's house shall now shortly be brought again from Babylon: for they prophesy a lie unto you. 17 Hearken not unto them; serve the king of Babylon, and live: wherefore should this city be laid waste? 18 But if they *be* prophets, and if the word of the LORD be with them, let them now make intercession to the LORD of hosts, that the vessels which are left in the house of the LORD, and *in* the house of the king of Judah, and at Jerusalem, go not to Babylon. 19 For thus saith the LORD of hosts concerning the pillars, and concerning the sea, and concerning the bases, and concerning the residue of the vessels that remain in this city, 20 Which Nebuchadnezzar king of Babylon took not, when he carried away captive Jeconiah the son of Jehoiakim king of Judah from Jerusalem to Babylon, and all the nobles of Judah and Jerusalem; 21 Yea, thus saith the LORD of hosts, the God of Israel, concerning the vessels that remain *in* the house of the LORD, and *in* the house of the king of Judah and of Jerusalem; 22 They shall be carried to Babylon, and there shall they be until the day that I visit them, saith the LORD; then will I bring them up, and restore them to this place.

What was said to all the nations is here with a particular tenderness applied to the nation of the Jews, for whom Jeremiah was sensibly concerned. The case at present stood thus: Judah and Jerusalem had often contested with the king of Babylon, and still were worsted; many both of their valuable persons and their valuable goods were carried to Babylon already, and some of the *vessels of the Lord's house* particularly. Now how this struggle would issue was the question. They had those among them at Jerusalem who pretended to be prophets, who bade them hold out and they should, in a little time, be too hard for the king of Babylon and recover all that they had lost. Now Jeremiah is sent to bid them yield and knock under, for that, instead of recovering what they had lost, they should otherwise lose all that remained; and to press them to this is the scope of these verses.

I. Jeremiah humbly addresses the king of Judah, to persuade him to surrender to the king of Babylon. His act would be the people's and would determine them, and therefore he speaks to him as to them all (*v* 12): *Bring your necks under the yoke of the king of Babylon and live.* Is it their wisdom to submit to the heavy iron yoke of a cruel tyrant, that they may secure the lives of their bodies? And is it not much more our wisdom to submit to the sweet and easy yoke of our rightful Lord and Master Jesus Christ, that we may secure the lives of our souls? Bring down your spirits to repentance and faith, and that is the way to bring up your spirits to heaven and glory. And with much more cogency and compassion may we expostulate with perishing souls than Jeremiah here expostulates with a perishing people: "*Why will you die by the sword and the famine*—miserable deaths, which you inevitably run yourselves upon, under pretence of avoiding miserable lives?" What God had spoken, in general, of all those that would not submit to the king of Babylon, he would have them to apply to themselves and be afraid of. It were well if sinners would, in like manner, be afraid of the destruction threatened against all those that will not have *Christ to reign over them,* and reason thus with themselves, "*Why should we die the second death, which is a thousand times worse than that by sword and famine,* when we might submit and live?"

II. He addresses himself likewise to the priests and the people (*v.* 16), to persuade them to *serve the king of Babylon,* that they might *live,* and might prevent the desolation of the city (*v.* 17): "*Wherefore should it be laid waste,* as certainly it will be if you stand it out?" The priests had been Jeremiah's enemies, and had sought his life to destroy it, yet he approves himself their friend, and seeks their lives, to preserve and secure them, which is an example to us to render *good for evil.* When the *blood-thirsty hate the upright,* yet *the just seek his soul,* and the welfare of it, Prov. xxix. 10. The matter was far gone here; they were upon the brink of ruin, which they would not have been brought to if they would have taken Jeremiah's counsel; yet he continues his friendly admonitions to them, to save the last stake and manage that wisely, and now at length in this their day to understand the *things that belong to their peace,* when they had but one day to turn them in.

III. In both these addresses he warns them against giving credit to the false prophets that rocked them asleep in their security, because they saw that they loved to slumber: "*Hearken not to the words of the prophets* (*v.* 14), *your prophets, v.* 16. They are not God's prophets; he never sent them; they do not serve him, nor seek to please him; they are yours, for they say what you would have them say, and aim at nothing but to please you." Two things their prophets flattered them into the belief of:—1. That the power which the king of Babylon had gained over them should now shortly be broken. They said (*v.* 14), "*You shall not serve the king of Babylon;* you need not submit voluntarily, for you shall not be compelled to submit." This they prophesied *in the name of the Lord* (*v.* 15), as if God had sent them to the people on this errand, in kindness to them, that they might not disparage themselves by an inglorious surrender. But it was a lie. They said that God sent them; but that was false; he disowns it: *I have not sent them, saith the Lord.* They said that they should never be brought into subjection to the king of Babylon; but that was false too, the event proved it so. They said that to hold out to the last would be the way to secure themselves and their city; but that was false, for it would certainly end in their being driven out and perishing. So that it was all a lie, from first to last; and the prophets that deceived the people with these lies did, in the issue, but deceive themselves; the blind leaders and the blind followers fell together into the ditch: That *you might perish, you, and the prophets that prophesy unto you,* who will be so far from warranting your security that they cannot secure themselves. Note, Those that encou-

rage sinners to go on in their sinful ways will in the end perish with them.   2. They prophesied that the vessels of the temple, which the king of Babylon had already carried away, should now shortly be brought back (*v.* 16); this they fed the priests with the hopes of, knowing how acceptable it would be to them, who loved the *gold of the temple* better than the *temple that sanctified the gold.* These vessels were taken away when Jeconiah was carried captive into Babylon, *v.* 20. We have the story, and it is a melancholy one, 2 Kings xxiv. 13, 15; 2 Chron. xxxvi. 10. All the *goodly vessels* (that is, all the *vessels of gold* that were in *the house of the Lord*), with all the treasures, were taken as prey, and brought to Babylon. This was grievous to them above any thing; for the temple was their pride and confidence, and the stripping of that was too plain an indication of that which the true prophet told them, that their *God had departed from them.* Their false prophets therefore had no other way to make them easy than by telling them that the king of Babylon should be forced to restore them in a little while. Now here, (1.) Jeremiah bids them think of preserving the vessels that remained by their prayers, rather than of bringing back those that were gone by their prophecies (*v.* 18): *If they be prophets,* as they pretend, and if *the word of the Lord be with them*—if they have any intercourse with heaven and any interest there, let them improve it for the stopping of the progress of the judgment; let them step into the gap, and stand with their censer *between the living and the dead,* between that which is carried away and that which remains, that *the plague may be stayed; let them make intercession with the Lord of hosts,* that the vessels which are left go not after the rest. [1.] Instead of prophesying, let them pray. Note, Prophets must be praying men; by being much in prayer they must make it to appear that they keep up a correspondence with heaven. We cannot think that those do, as prophets, ever hear thence, who do not frequently by prayer send thither. By praying for the safety and prosperity of the sanctuary they must make it to appear that, as becomes prophets, they are of a public spirit; and by the success of their prayers it will appear that God favours them. [2.] Instead of being concerned for the retrieving of what they had lost, they must bestir themselves for the securing of what was left, and take it as a great favour if they can gain that point. When God's judgments are abroad we must not seek great things, but be thankful for a little. (2.) He assures them that even this point should not be gained, but the brazen vessels should go after the golden ones, *v.* 19, 22. Nebuchadnezzar had found so good a booty once that he would be sure to come again and take all he could find, not only in *the house of the Lord,* but in the *king's house.* They shall all be carried to Babylon in triumph, and *there shall they be.* But he concludes with a gracious promise that the time should come when they should all be returned : *Until the day that I visit them in mercy,* according to appointment, and *then I will bring* those vessels *up again, and restore them to this place,* to their place. Surely they were under the protection of a special Providence, else they would have been melted down and put to some other use ; but there was to be a second temple, for which they were to be reserved. We read particularly of the return of them, Ezra i. 8. Note, Though the return of the church's prosperity do not come in our time, we must not therefore despair of it, for it will come in God's time. Though those who said, *The vessels of the Lord's house* shall *shortly* be brought again, prophesied a lie (*v.* 16), yet he that said, They shall *at length* be brought again, prophesied the truth. We are apt to set our clock before God's dial, and then to quarrel because they do not agree ; but the Lord is a God of judgment, and it is fit that we should wait for him.

CHAP. XXVIII.

In the foregoing chapter Jeremiah had charged those prophets with lies who foretold the speedy breaking of the yoke of the king of Babylon and the speedy return of the vessels of the sanctuary ; now here we have his contest with a particular prophet upon those heads. I. Hananiah, a pretender to prophecy, in contradiction to Jeremiah, foretold the sinking of Nebuchadnezzar's power and the return both of the persons and of the vessels that were carried away (ver. 1—4), and, as a sign of this, he broke the yoke from the neck of Jeremiah, ver. 10, 11. II. Jeremiah wished his words might prove true, but appealed to the event whether they were so or no, not doubting but that would disprove them, ver. 5—9. III. The doom both of the deceived and the deceiver is here read. The people that were deceived should have their yoke of wood turned into a yoke of iron (ver. 12—14), and the prophet that was the deceiver should be shortly cut off by death, and he was so, accordingly, within two months, ver. 15—17.

AND it came to pass the same year, in the beginning of the reign of Zedekiah king of Judah, in the fourth year, *and* in the fifth month, *that* Hananiah the son of Azur the prophet, which *was* of Gibeon, spake unto me in the house of the LORD, in the presence of the priests, and of all the people, saying, 2 Thus speaketh the LORD of hosts, the God of Israel, saying, I have broken the yoke of the king of Babylon. 3 Within two full years will I bring again into this place all the vessels of the LORD's house, that Nebuchadnezzar king of Babylon took away from this place, and carried them to Babylon : 4 And I will bring again to this place Jeconiah the son of Jehoiakim king of Judah, with all the captives of Judah, that went into Babylon, saith the LORD: for I will break the yoke of the king of Babylon. 5 Then the

prophet Jeremiah said unto the prophet Hananiah in the presence of the priests, and in the presence of all the people that stood in the house of the LORD, 6 Even the prophet Jeremiah said, Amen: the LORD do so: the LORD perform thy words which thou hast prophesied, to bring again the vessels of the LORD's house, and all that is carried away captive, from Babylon into this place. 7 Nevertheless hear thou now this word that I speak in thine ears, and in the ears of all the people ; 8 The prophets that have been before me and before thee of old prophesied both against many countries, and against great kingdoms, of war, and of evil, and of pestilence. 9 The prophet which prophesieth of peace, when the word of the prophet shall come to pass, *then* shall the prophet be known, that the LORD hath truly sent him.

This struggle between a true prophet and a false one is said here to have happened *in the beginning of the reign of Zedekiah,* and yet *in the fourth year,* for the first four years of his reign might well be called *the beginning,* or former part, of it, because during those years he reigned under the dominion of the king of Babylon and as a tributary to him ; whereas the rest of his reign, which might well be called the *latter part* of it, in distinction from that *former part,* he reigned in rebellion against the king of Babylon. In this fourth year of his reign he went in person to Babylon (as we find, *ch.* li. 59), and it is probable that this gave the people some hope that his negociation in person would put a good end to the war, in which hope the false prophets encouraged them, this Hananiah particularly, who was of Gibeon, a priests' city, and therefore probably himself a priest, as well as Jeremiah. Now here we have,

I. The prediction which Hananiah delivered publicly, solemnly, *in the house of the Lord,* and in the name of the Lord, in an august assembly, *in the presence of the priests and of all the people,* who probably were expecting to have some message from heaven. In delivering this prophecy, he faced Jeremiah, he spoke it to him (*v.* 1), designing to confront and contradict him, as much as to say, " Jeremiah, thou liest." Now this prediction is that the king of Babylon's power, at least his power over Judah and Jerusalem, should be speedily broken, that *within two full years* the vessels of the temple should be brought back, and Jeremiah, and all the captives that were carried away with him, should return ; whereas Jeremiah had foretold that the yoke of the king of Babylon should be bound on yet faster, and that the vessels and captives should not return for 70 years, *v.* 2—4. Now, upon the reading of this sham prophecy, and comparing it with the messages that God sent by the true prophets, we may observe what a vast difference there is between them. Here is nothing of the spirit and life, the majesty of style and sublimity of expression, that appear in the discourses of God's prophets, nothing of that divine flame and *flatus.* But that which is especially wanting here is an air of piety; he speaks with a great deal of confidence of the return of their prosperity, but here is not a word of good counsel given them to repent, and reform, and return to God, to pray, and seek his face, that they may be prepared for the favours God had in reserve for them. He promises them temporal mercies, in God's name, but makes no mention of those spiritual mercies which God always promised should go along with them, as *ch.* xxiv. 7, *I will give them a heart to know me.* By all this it appears that, whatever he pretended, he had only the *spirit of the world*, not the *Spirit of God* (1 Cor. ii. 12), that he aimed to please, not to profit.

II. Jeremiah's reply to this pretended prophecy. 1. He heartily wishes it might prove true. Such an affection has he for his country, and so truly desirous is he of the welfare of it, that he would be content to lie under the imputation of a false prophet, so that their ruin might be prevented. He said, *Amen; the Lord do so; the Lord perform thy words, v.* 5, 6. This was not the first time that Jeremiah had prayed for his people, though he had prophesied against them, and deprecated the judgments which yet he certainly knew would come; as Christ prayed, *Father, if it be possible, let this cup pass from me,* when yet he knew it must not pass from him. Though, as a faithful prophet, he foresaw and foretold the destruction of Jerusalem, yet, as a faithful Israelite, he prayed earnestly for the preservation of it, in obedience to that command, *Pray for the peace of Jerusalem.* Though the will of God's purpose is the rule of prophecy and patience, the will of his precept is the rule of prayer and practice. God himself, though he has determined, does not desire, the death of sinners, but would *have all men to be saved.* Jeremiah often interceded for his people, *ch.* xviii. 20. The false prophets thought to ingratiate themselves with the people by promising them peace; now the prophet shows that he bore them as great a good-will as their prophets did, whom they were so fond of; and, though he had no warrant from God to promise them peace, yet he earnestly desired it and prayed for it. How strangely were those besotted who caressed those who did them the greatest wrong imaginable by flattering them, and persecuted him who did them the greatest service imaginable by interceding for them! See *ch.* xxvii. 18. 2.

He appeals to the event, to prove it false, *v.* 7—9. The false prophets reflected upon Jeremiah, as Ahab upon Micaiah, because he never *prophesied good concerning them, but evil.* Now he pleads that this had been the purport of the prophecies that other prophets had delivered, so that it ought not to be looked upon as a strange thing, or as rendering his mission doubtful; for prophets of old prophesied against *many countries and great kingdoms,* so bold were they in delivering the messages which God sent by them, and so far from fearing men, or seeking to please them, as Hananiah did. They made no difficulty, any more than Jeremiah did, of threatening war, famine, and pestilence, and what they said was regarded as coming from God; why then should Jeremiah be run down as *a pestilent fellow, and a sower of sedition,* when he preached no otherwise than God's prophets had always done before him? Other prophets had foretold destruction, and sometimes the destruction did not come, which yet did not disprove their divine mission, as in the case of Jonah; for God is gracious, and ready to turn away his wrath from those that turn away from their sins. But the prophet that *prophesied of peace* and prosperity, especially as Hananiah did, absolutely and unconditionally, without adding that necessary proviso, that they do not by wilful sin put a bar in their own door and stop the current of God's favours, will be proved a true prophet only by the accomplishment of his prediction; if it come to pass, then it shall be known that *the Lord has sent him,* but, if not, he will appear to be a cheat and an impostor.

10 Then Hananiah the prophet took the yoke from off the prophet Jeremiah's neck, and brake it. 11 And Hananiah spake in the presence of all the people, saying, Thus saith the LORD; Even so will I break the yoke of Nebuchadnezzar king of Babylon from the neck of all nations within the space of two full years. And the prophet Jeremiah went his way. 12 Then the word of the LORD came unto Jeremiah *the prophet,* after that Hananiah the prophet had broken the yoke from off the neck of the prophet Jeremiah, saying, 13 Go and tell Hananiah, saying, Thus saith the LORD; Thou hast broken the yokes of wood; but thou shalt make for them yokes of iron. 14 For thus saith the LORD of hosts, the God of Israel; I have put a yoke of iron upon the neck of all these nations, that they may serve Nebuchadnezzar king of Babylon;

and they shall serve him: and I have given him the beasts of the field also. 15 Then said the prophet Jeremiah unto Hananiah the prophet, Hear now, Hananiah; The LORD hath not sent thee; but thou makest this people to trust in a lie. 16 Therefore thus saith the LORD; Behold, I will cast thee from off the face of the earth: this year thou shalt die, because thou hast taught rebellion against the LORD. 17 So Hananiah the prophet died the same year in the seventh month.

We have here an instance,

I. Of the insolence of the false prophet. To complete the affront he designed Jeremiah, *he took the yoke from off his neck* which he carried as a memorial of what he had prophesied concerning the enslaving of the nations to Nebuchadnezzar, and he broke it, that he might give a sign of the accomplishment of this prophecy, as Jeremiah had given of his, and might seem to have conquered him, and to have defeated the intention of his prophecy. See how the lying spirit, in the mouth of this false prophet, mimics the language of the Spirit of truth: *Thus saith the Lord, So will I break the yoke of the king of Babylon*, not only from the neck of this nation, but *from the neck of all nations, within two full years.* Whether by the force of a heated imagination Hananiah had persuaded himself to believe this, or whether he knew it to be false, and only persuaded them to believe it, does not appear; but it is plain that he speaks with abundance of assurance. It is no new thing for lies to be fathered upon the God of truth.

II. Of the patience of the true prophet. Jeremiah quietly *went his way*, and *when he was reviled he reviled not again*, and would not contend with one that was in the height of his fury and in the midst of the priests and people that were violently set against him. The reason why he went his way was not because he had nothing to answer, but because he was willing to stay till God was pleased to furnish him with a direct and immediate answer, which as yet he had not received. He expected that God would send a special message to Hananiah, and he would say nothing till he had received that. *I, as a deaf man, heard not, for thou wilt hear*, and *thou shalt answer, Lord, for me.* It may sometimes be our wisdom rather to retreat than to contend. *Currenti cede furori—Give place unto wrath.*

III. Of the justice of God in giving judgment between Jeremiah and his adversary. Jeremiah went his way, as a man *in whose mouth there was no rebuke*, but God soon put a word into his mouth; for he will appear for those who silently commit their cause to him. 1. The word of God, in the mouth of Jeremiah, is ratified and confirmed. Let not Jeremiah himself distrust the truth of what he had delivered in God's name because it met with such a daring opposition and contradiction. If what we have spoken be the truth of God, we must not unsay it because men gainsay it; for *great is the truth and will prevail.* It will stand, therefore let us stand to it, and not fear that men's unbelief or blasphemy will make it of no effect. Hananiah has broken the *yokes of wood*, but Jeremiah must make for them *yokes of iron*, which cannot be broken (*v.* 13), for (says God) " *I have put a yoke of iron upon the neck of all these nations*, which shall lie heavier, and bind harder, upon them (*v.* 14), *that they may serve the king of Babylon*, and not be able to shake off the yoke however they may struggle, for they shall serve him whether they will or no;" and who is he that can contend with God's counsel? What was said before is repeated again: *I have given him the beasts of the field also*, as if there were something significant in that. Men had by their wickedness made themselves *like the beasts that perish*, and therefore deserved to be ruled by an arbitrary power, as beasts are ruled, and such a power Nebuchadnezzar ruled with; for *whom he would he slew and whom he would he kept alive.* 2. Hananiah is sentenced to die for contradicting it, and Jeremiah, when he has received commission from God, boldly tells him so to his face, though before he received that commission he went away and said nothing. (1.) The crimes of which Hananiah stands convicted are cheating the people and affronting God: *Thou makest this people to trust in a lie*, encouraging them to hope that they shall have peace, which will make their destruction the more terrible to them when it comes; yet this was not the worst: *Thou hast taught rebellion against the Lord;* thou hast taught them to despise all the good counsel given them in God's name by the true prophets, and hast rendered it ineffectual. Those have a great deal to answer for who, by telling sinners that they shall have peace though they go on, harden their hearts in a contempt of the reproofs and admonitions of the word, and the means and methods God takes to bring them to repentance. (2.) The judgment given against him is, " *I will cast thee off from the face of the earth*, as unworthy to live upon it; thou shalt be buried in it. *This year thou shalt die*, and die as a rebel against the Lord, to whom death will come with a sting and a curse." This sentence was executed, *v.* 17. Hananiah died the same year, within two months; for his prophecy is dated the fifth month (*v.* 1) and his death the seventh. Good men may perhaps be suddenly taken off by death in the midst of their days, and in mercy to them, as Josiah was; but this being foretold as the punishment of his sin, and coming to pass accordingly, it may safely be construed as a testimony from Heaven against him and a confirmation of Jeremiah's mission. And, if the people's hearts had not been wretchedly hardened by the deceitfulness of sin, it would have prevented their being further hardened by the deceitfulness of their prophets.

CHAP. XXIX.

The contest between Jeremiah and the false prophets was carried on before by preaching, here by writing; there we had sermon against sermon, here we have letter against letter, for some of the false prophets are now carried away into captivity in Babylon, while Jeremiah remains in his own country. Now here is, I. A letter which Jeremiah wrote to the captives in Babylon, against their prophets that they had there (ver. 1—3), in which letter, 1. He endeavours to reconcile them to their captivity, to be easy under it and to make the best of it, ver. 4—7. 2 He cautions them not to give any credit to their false prophets, who fed them with hopes of a speedy release, ver. 8, 9. 3. He assures them that God would restore them in mercy to their own land again, at the end of 70 years, ver. 10—14. 4. He foretels the destruction of those who yet continued, and that they should be persecuted with one judgment after another, and sent at last into captivity, ver. 15—19. 5. He prophesies the destruction of two of their false prophets that they had in Babylon, that both soothed them up in their sins and set them bad examples (ver. 20—23), and this is the purport of Jeremiah's letter. II. Here is a letter which Shemaiah, a false prophet in Babylon, wrote to the priests at Jerusalem, to stir them up to persecute Jeremiah (ver. 24—29), and a denunciation of God's wrath against him for writing such a letter, ver. 30—32. Such struggles as these have there always been between the seed of the woman and the seed of the serpent.

N OW these *are* the words of the letter that Jeremiah the prophet sent from Jerusalem unto the residue of the elders which were carried away captives, and to the priests, and to the prophets, and to all the people whom Nebuchadnezzar had carried away captive from Jerusalem to Babylon; 2 (After that Jeconiah the king, and the queen, and the eunuchs, the princes of Judah and Jerusalem, and the carpenters, and the smiths, were departed from Jerusalem;) 3 By the hand of Elasah the son of Shaphan, and Gemariah the son of Hilkiah, (whom Zedekiah king of Judah sent unto Babylon to Nebuchadnezzar king of Babylon,) saying, 4 Thus saith the LORD of hosts, the God of Israel, unto all that are carried away captives, whom I have caused to be carried away from Jerusalem unto Babylon; 5 Build ye houses, and dwell *in them;* and plant gardens, and eat the fruit of them; 6 Take ye wives, and beget sons and daughters; and take wives for your sons, and give your daughters to husbands, that they may bear sons and daughters; that ye may be increased there, and not diminished. 7 And seek the peace of the city whither I have caused you to be carried away captives, and pray unto the LORD for it: for in the peace thereof shall ye have peace.

We are here told,

I. That Jeremiah wrote to the captives in Babylon, in the name of the Lord. Jeconiah had surrendered himself a prisoner, with the queen his mother, the chamberlains of his household, called here the *eunuchs,* and many of *the princes of Judah and Jerusalem,* who were at that time the most active men; *the carpenters and smiths* likewise, being demanded, were yielded up, that those who remained might not have any proper hands to fortify their city or furnish themselves with weapons of war. By this tame submission it was hoped that Nebuchadnezzar would be pacified. *Satis est prostrasse leoni—It suffices the lion to have laid his antagonist prostrate;* but the imperious conqueror grows upon their concessions, like Benhadad upon Ahab's, 1 Kings xx. 5, 6. And, not content with this, when these had *departed from Jerusalem* he comes again, and fetches away more of *the elders, the priests, the prophets, and the people* (v. 1), such as he thought fit, or such as his soldiers could lay hands on, and carries them to Babylon. The case of these captives was very melancholy, the rather because they, being thus distinguished from the rest of their brethren who continued in their own land, looked as if they were greater sinners than all men who dwelt at Jerusalem. Jeremiah therefore writes a letter to them, to comfort them, assuring them that they had no reason either to despair of succour themselves or to envy their brethren that were left behind. Note, 1. The word of God written is as truly given by *inspiration of God* as his word spoken was; and this was the proper way of spreading the knowledge of God's will among his *children scattered abroad.* 2. We may serve God and do good by writing to our friends at a distance pious letters of seasonable comforts and wholesome counsels. Those whom we cannot speak to we may write to; that which is written remains. This letter of Jeremiah's was sent to the captives in Babylon by the hands of the ambassadors whom king Zedekiah sent to Nebuchadnezzar, probably to pay him his tribute and renew his submission to him, or to treat of peace with him, in which treaty the captives might perhaps hope that they should be included, *v.* 3. By such messengers Jeremiah chose to send this message, to put an honour upon it, because it was a message from God, or perhaps because there was no settled way of sending letters to Babylon, but as such an occasion as this offered, and then it made the condition of the captives there the more melancholy, that they could rarely hear from their friends and relations they had left behind, which is some reviving and satisfaction to those that are separated from one another.

II. We are here told what he wrote. A copy of the letter at large follows here to *v* 24. In these verses,

1. He assures them that he wrote in the name of the *Lord of hosts, the God of Israel,* who indited the letter; Jeremiah was but the scribe or amanuensis. It would be comfortable to them, in their captivity, to hear that God is *the Lord of hosts,* of all hosts, and is therefore able to help and deliver them; and that he is the *God of Israel* still, a God in covenant with his people, though he contend with them, and their enemies for the present are too hard for them. This would likewise be an admonition to them to stand upon their guard against all temptations to the idolatry of Babylon, because the *God of Israel,* the God whom they served, is *Lord of hosts.* God's sending to them in this letter might be an encouragement to them in their captivity, as it was an evidence that he had not cast them off, had not abandoned them and disinherited them, though he was displeased with them and corrected them; for, if the Lord had been pleased to kill them, he would not have written to them.

2. God by him owns the hand he had in their captivity: *I have caused you to be carried away, v.* 4 and again, *v.* 7. All the force of the king of Babylon could not have done it if God had not ordered it; nor could he have any power against them but what was given him from above. If God caused them to be carried captives, they might be sure that he neither did them any wrong nor meant them any hurt. Note, It will help very much to reconcile us to our troubles, and to make us patient under them, to consider that they are what God has appointed us to. *I opened not my mouth, because thou didst it.*

3. He bids them think of nothing but settling there; and therefore let them resolve to make the best of it (*v.* 5, 6): *Build yourselves houses and dwell in them,* &c. By all this it is intimated to them, (1.) That they must not feed themselves with hopes of a speedy return out of their captivity, for that would keep them still unsettled and consequently uneasy; they would apply themselves to no business, take no comfort, but be always tiring themselves and provoking their conquerors with the expectations of relief; and their disappointment at last would sink them into despair and make their condition much more miserable than otherwise it would be. Let them therefore reckon upon a continuance there, and accommodate themselves to it as well as they can. Let them *build,* and *plant,* and *marry,* and dispose of their children there as if they were at home in their own land. Let them take a pleasure in seeing their families built up and multiplied; for, though they must expect themselves to die in captivity, yet their children may live to see better days. If they live in the fear of God, what should hinder them but they may live comfortably in Babylon? They cannot but *weep* sometimes *when they remember Zion.*

But let not weeping hinder sowing; let them not *sorrow as those that have no hope,* no joy; for they have both. Note, In all conditions of life it is our wisdom and duty to make the best of that which is, and not to throw away the comfort of what we may have because we have not all we would have. We have a natural affection for our native country; it strangely draws our minds; but it is with a *nescio qua dulcedine—we can give no good account of the sweet attraction;* and therefore, if Providence remove us to some other country, we must resolve to live easy there, to bring our mind to our condition when our condition is not in every thing to our mind. If the *earth be the Lord's,* then, wherever a child of God goes, he does not go off his Father's ground. *Patria est ubicunque bene est—That place is our country in which we are well off.* If things be not as they have been, instead of fretting at that, we must live in hopes that they will be better than they are. *Non si male nunc, et olim sic erit—Though we suffer now we shall not always.* (2.) That they must not disquiet themselves with fears of intolerable hardships in their captivity. They might be ready to suggest (as persons in trouble are always apt to make the worst of things) that it would be in vain to build houses, for their lords and masters would not suffer them to dwell in them when they had built them, nor to eat the fruit of the vineyards they planted. "Never fear," says God; "if you live peaceably with them, you shall find them civil to you." Meek and quiet people, that work and mind their own business, have often found much better treatment, even with strangers and enemies, than they expected; and God has made his people to be *pitied of those that carry them captives* (Ps. cvi. 46), and a pity it is but that those who have built houses should dwell in them. Nay,

4. He directs them to seek the good of the country where they were captives (*v.* 7), to pray for it, to endeavour to promote it. This forbids them to attempt any thing against the public peace while they were subjects to the king of Babylon. Though he was a heathen, an idolater, an oppressor, and an enemy to God and his church, yet, while he gave them protection, they must pay him allegiance, and live *quiet and peaceable lives* under him, *in all godliness and honesty,* not plotting to shake off his yoke, but patiently leaving it to God in due time to work deliverance for them. Nay, they must pray to God for the peace of the places where they were, that they might oblige them to continue their kindness to them and disprove the character that had been given their nation, that they were *hurtful to kings and provinces,* and *moved sedition,* Ezra iv. 15. Both the wisdom of the serpent and the innocency of the dove required them to be true to the government they lived under: *For in the peace thereof you shall have peace;*

should the country be embroiled in war, they would have the greatest share in the calamitous effects of it. Thus the primitive Christians, according to the temper of their holy religion, prayed for the powers that were, though they were persecuting powers. And, if they were to pray for and seek the peace of the land of their captivity, much more reason have we to pray for the welfare of the land of our nativity, where we are a free people under a good government, *that in the peace thereof* we and ours *may have peace.* Every passenger is concerned in the safety of the ship.

8 For thus saith the LORD of hosts, the God of Israel; Let not your prophets and your diviners, that *be* in the midst of you, deceive you, neither hearken to your dreams which ye cause to be dreamed. 9 For they prophesy falsely unto you in my name: I have not sent them, saith the LORD. 10 For thus saith the LORD, that after seventy years be accomplished at Babylon I will visit you, and perform my good word toward you, in causing you to return to this place. 11 For I know the thoughts that I think toward you, saith the LORD, thoughts of peace, and not of evil, to give you an expected end. 12 Then shall ye call upon me, and ye shall go and pray unto me, and I will hearken unto you. 13 And ye shall seek me, and find *me*, when ye shall search for me with all your heart. 14 And I will be found of you, saith the LORD: and I will turn away your captivity, and I will gather you from all the nations, and from all the places whither I have driven you, saith the LORD; and I will bring you again into the place whence I caused you to be carried away captive.

To make the people quiet and easy in their captivity,

I. God takes them off from building upon the false foundation which their pretended prophets laid, *v.* 8, 9. They told them that their captivity should be short, and therefore that they must not think of taking root in Babylon, but be upon the wing to go back : " Now herein *they deceive you,*" says God ; " they *prophesy a lie to you,* though they prophesy *in my name.* But *let them not deceive you,* suffer not yourselves to be deluded by them." As long as we have the word of truth to try the spirits by it is our own fault if we be deceived ; for by it we may be undeceived. *Hearken not to your dreams,*

which you cause to be dreamed. He means either the dreams or fancies which the people pleased themselves with, and with which they filled their own heads (by thinking and speaking of nothing else but a speedy enlargement when they were awake they caused themselves to dream of it when they were asleep, and then took that for a good omen, and with it strengthened themselves in their vain expectations), or the dreams which the prophets dreamed and grounded their prophecies upon. God tells the people, *They are your dreams,* because they pleased them, were the dreams that they desired and wished for. They *caused them to be dreamed ;* for they hearkened to them, and encouraged the prophets to put such deceits upon them, desiring them to prophesy nothing but *smooth things,* Isa. xxx. 10. They were dreams of their own bespeaking. False prophets would not flatter people in their sins, but that they love to be flattered, and speak smoothly to their prophets that their prophets may speak smoothly to them.

II. He gives them a good foundation to build their hopes upon. We would not persuade people to pull down the house they have built upon the sand, but that there is a rock ready for them to rebuild upon. God here promises them that, though they should not return quickly, they should return at length, *after seventy years be accomplished.* By this it appears that the seventy years of the captivity are not to be reckoned from the last captivity, but the first. Note, Though the deliverance of the church do not come in our time, it is sufficient that it will come in God's time, and we are sure that that is the best time. The promise is that God will visit them in mercy; though he had long seemed to be strange to them, he will come among them, and appear for them, and put honour upon them, as great men do upon their inferiors by coming to visit them. He will put an end to *their captivity,* and *turn away* all the calamities of it. Though they are dispersed, some in one country and some in another, he will *gather them from all the places whither they are driven,* will set up a standard for them all to resort to, and incorporate them again in one body. And though they are at a great distance they shall be brought again to their own land, *to the place whence* they were *carried captive, v.* 14. Now, 1. This shall be the performance of God's promise to them (*v.* 10): *1 will perform my good word towards you.* Let not the failing of those predictions which are delivered as from God lessen the reputation of those that really are from him. That which is indeed God's word is a *good word,* and therefore it will be made good, and not one iota or tittle of it shall fall to the ground. *Hath he said, and shall he not do it ?* This will make their return out of captivity very comfortable, that it will be the performance of God's good word to them, the product of a gracious promise. 2. This shall be in pursuance of God's purposes concerning them (*v.* 11): *I know the thoughts that I think towards you.* Known unto God are all his works, for known unto him are all his thoughts (Acts xv. 18) and his works agree exactly with his thoughts; he does all *according to the counsel of his will.* We often do not know our own thoughts, nor know our own mind, but God is never at any uncertainty within himself. We are sometimes ready to fear that God's designs concerning us are all against us; but he knows the contrary concerning his own people, that they are *thoughts of good and not of evil;* even that which seems evil is designed for good. His thoughts are all working towards the expected end, which he will give in due time. The end they expect will come, though perhaps not when they expect it. Let them have patience till the fruit is ripe, and then they shall have it. He will give them *an end, and expectation,* so it is in the original. (1) He will give them to see *the end* (the comfortable termination) of their trouble; though it last long, it shall not last always. The *time to favour Zion,* yea, the *set time, will come.* When things are at the worst they will begin to mend; and he will give them to see the glorious perfection of their deliverance; for, as for God, his work is perfect. He that in the beginning finished the *heavens and the earth,* and all the *hosts* of both, will finish all the blessings of both to his people. When he begins in ways of mercy he will *make an end.* God does nothing by halves. (2.) He will give them to see the *expectation,* that *end* which they desire and hope for, and have been long waiting for. He will give them, not the expectations of their fears, nor the expectations of their fancies, but the expectations of their faith, the end which he has promised and which will turn for the best to them. 3. This shall be in answer to their prayers and supplications to God, *v.* 12—14. (1.) God will stir them up to pray: *Then shall you call upon me,* and *you shall go, and pray unto me.* Note, When God is about to give his people the expected good he pours out a spirit of prayer, and it is a good sign that he is coming towards them. Then, when you see the *expected end* approaching, *then you shall call upon me.* Note, Promises are given, not to supersede, but to quicken and encourage prayer: and when deliverance is coming we must by prayer go forth to meet it. When Daniel understood that the 70 years were near expiring, then he *set his face* with more fervency than ever *to seek the Lord,* Dan. ix. 2, 3. (2.) He will then stir up himself to come and save them (Ps. lxxx. 2): *I will hearken unto you,* and *I will be found of you.* God has said it, and we may depend upon it, *Seek and you shall find.* We have a general rule laid down (*v.* 13): *You shall find me when you shall search for*

me with all your heart. In seeking God we must search for him, accomplish a diligent search, search for directions in seeking him and encouragements to our faith and hope. We must continue seeking, and take pains in seeking, as those that search; and this we must do with our heart (that is, in sincerity and uprightness), and with our whole heart (that is, with vigour and fervency, putting forth *all that is within us* in prayer), and those who thus *seek God* shall *find him,* and shall find him their bountiful rewarder, Heb. xi. 6. He never said to such, *Seek you me in vain.*

15 Because ye have said, The Lord hath raised us up prophets in Babylon; 16 *Know* that thus saith the Lord of the king that sitteth upon the throne of David, and of all the people that dwelleth in this city, *and* of your brethren that are not gone forth with you into captivity; 17 Thus saith the Lord of hosts; Behold, I will send upon them the sword, the famine, and the pestilence, and will make them like vile figs, that cannot be eaten, they are so evil. 18 And I will persecute them with the sword, with the famine, and with the pestilence, and will deliver them to be removed to all the kingdoms of the earth, to be a curse, and an astonishment, and a hissing, and a reproach, among all the nations whither I have driven them: 19 Because they have not hearkened to my words, saith the Lord, which I sent unto them by my servants the prophets, rising up early and sending *them;* but ye would not hear, saith the Lord. 20 Hear ye therefore the word of the Lord, all ye of the captivity, whom I have sent from Jerusalem to Babylon: 21 Thus saith the Lord of hosts, the God of Israel, of Ahab the son of Kolaiah, and of Zedekiah the son of Maaseiah, which prophesy a lie unto you in my name; Behold, I will deliver them into the hand of Nebuchadrezzar king of Babylon; and he shall slay them before your eyes; 22 And of them shall be taken up a curse by all the captivity of Judah which *are* in Babylon, saying, The Lord make thee like Zedekiah and like Ahab, whom the king of Babylon roasted in the fire; 23 Because they

have committed villany in Israel, and have committed adultery with their neighbours' wives, and have spoken lying words in my name, which I have not commanded them; even I know, and *am* a witness, saith the LORD.

Jeremiah, having given great encouragement to those among the captives whom he knew to be serious and well-affected, assuring them that God had very kind and favourable intentions concerning them, here turns to those among them who slighted the counsels and comforts that Jeremiah ministered to them and depended upon what the false prophets flattered them with. When this letter came from Jeremiah they would be ready to say, "Why should he make himself so busy, and take upon him to advise us? *The Lord has raised us up prophets in Babylon, v.* 15. We are satisfied with those prophets, and can depend upon them, and have no occasion to hear from any prophets in Jerusalem." See the impudent wickedness of this people; as the prophets, when they prophesied lies, said that they had them from God, so the people, when they invited those prophets thus to flatter them, fathered it upon God, and said that it was the Lord that raised them up those prophets. Whereas we may be sure that those who harden people in their sins, and deceive them with false and groundless hopes of God's mercy, are no prophets of God's raising up. These prophets of their own told them that no more should be carried captive, but that those who were in captivity should shortly return. Now, in answer to this, 1. The prophet here foretels the utter destruction of those who remained still at Jerusalem, notwithstanding what those false prophets said to the contrary: "As for the *king* and *people* that *dwell in the city*, who, you think, will be ready to bid you welcome when you return, you are deceived; they shall be followed with one judgment after another, *sword, famine,* and *pestilence,* which shall cut off multitudes; and the poor and miserable remains shall be *removed into all kingdoms of the earth,*" *v.* 16, 18. And thus God *will make them,* or rather deal with them, *like vile figs;* they have made themselves so by their wickedness, and God will use them accordingly, as the salt that has *lost its savour,* which, being good for nothing, is cast to the dunghill, and so are rotten figs. This refers to the vision and the prophecy upon it which we had *ch.* xxiv. And the reason given for these proceedings against them is the same that has often been given and will justify God in the eternal ruin of impenitent sinners (*v.* 19): *Because they have not hearkened to my words. I called, but they refused.* 2. He foretels the judgment of God upon the false prophets in Babylon, who deceived the people of God there. He calls upon all

the children of the captivity, who boasted of them as prophets of God's raising up (*v.* 20): "Stand still, and hear the doom of the prophets you are so fond of." The two prophets are named here, *Ahab* and *Zedekiah, v.* 21. Observe, (1.) The crimes charged on them—impiety and immorality: They *prophesied lies in God's name* (*v.* 21), and again (*v.* 23), They have *spoken lying words in my name.* Lying was bad, lying to the people of God to delude them into a false hope was worse, but fathering their lies upon the God of truth was worst of all. And no marvel if those that had the face to do that could allow themselves in the gratification of those vile affections to which God, in a way of righteous judgment, *gave them up.* They have done *villany in Israel,* for *they have committed adultery with their neighbours' wives.* Adultery is villany, and it is an aggravation of it if it be villany in Israel, and in such as pretend to be prophets, who by such wickednesses manifestly disprove their own pretensions. God never sent such profligate wretches on his errands. He is the *Lord God of the holy prophets,* not of such impure ones. Here it appears why they flattered others in their sins—because they could not reprove them without condemning themselves. These lewd practices of theirs they knew how to conceal from the eye of the world, that they might preserve their credit; but *I know* it *and am a witness, saith the Lord.* The most secret sins are known to God; he can see the villany that is covered with the thickest cloak of hypocrisy, and there is a day coming when he will bring to light all these hidden works of darkness and every man will appear in his own colours. (2.) The judgments threatened against them: *The king of Babylon shall slay them before your eyes;* nay, he shall put them to a miserable death, *roast them in the fire, v.* 22. We may suppose that it was not for their impiety and immorality that Nebuchadnezzar punished them thus severely, but for sedition, and some attempts of their turbulent spirits upon the public peace, and stirring up the people to revolt and rebel. So much of their wickedness shall then be detected, and in such a wretched manner they shall end their days, that their names shall be a curse among the captives in Babylon, *v.* 22. When men would imprecate the greatest evil upon one they hated they would think they could not load them with a heavier curse, in fewer words, than to say, The Lord *make thee like Zedekiah and like Ahab.* Thus were they made ashamed of the prophets they had been proud of, and convinced at last of their folly in hearkening to them. God's faithful prophets were sometimes charged with being the troublers of the land, and as such were tortured and slain; but their names were a blessing when they were gone and their memory sweet, not as these false prophets. As malefactors are attended with infamy and disgrace, so martyrs with glory and honour.

24 *Thus* shalt thou also speak to Shemaiah the Nehelamite, saying, 25 Thus speaketh the LORD of hosts, the God of Israel, saying, Because thou hast sent letters in thy name unto all the people that *are* at Jerusalem, and to Zephaniah the son of Maaseiah the priest, and to all the priests, saying, 26 The LORD hath made thee priest in the stead of Jehoiada the priest, that ye should be officers in the house of the LORD, for every man *that is* mad, and maketh himself a prophet, that thou shouldest put him in prison, and in the stocks. 27 Now therefore why hast thou not reproved Jeremiah of Anathoth, which maketh himself a prophet to you? 28 For therefore he sent unto us *in* Babylon, saying, This *captivity is* long: build ye houses, and dwell *in them;* and plant gardens, and eat the fruit of them. 29 And Zephaniah the priest read this letter in the ears of Jeremiah the prophet. 30 Then came the word of the LORD unto Jeremiah, saying, 31 Send to all them of the captivity, saying, Thus saith the LORD concerning Shemaiah the Nehelamite ; because that Shemaiah hath prophesied unto you, and I sent him not, and he caused you to trust in a lie : 32 Therefore thus saith the LORD ; Behold, I will punish Shemaiah the Nehelamite, and his seed : he shall not have a man to dwell among this people ; neither shall he behold the good that I will do for my people, saith the LORD ; because he hath taught rebellion against the LORD.

We have perused the contents of Jeremiah's letter to the captives in Babylon, who had reason, with a great deal of thanks to God and him, to acknowledge the receipt of it, and lay it up among their treasures. But we cannot wonder if the false prophets they had among them were enraged at it ; for it gave them their true character. Now here we are told concerning one of them,

I. How he manifested his malice against Jeremiah. This busy fellow is called *Shemaiah the Nehelamite,* the *dreamer* (so the margin reads it), because all his prophecies he pretended to have received from God in a dream. He had got a copy of Jeremiah's

590

letter to the captives, or had heard it read, or information was given to him concerning it, and it nettled him exceedingly ; and he will take pen in hand, and answer it, yea, that he will. But how ? He does not write to Jeremiah in justification of his own mission, nor offer any rational arguments for the support of his prophecies concerning the speedy return of the captives ; but he writes to the priests, those faithful patrons of the false prophets, and instigates them to persecute Jeremiah. He writes in his own name, not so much as pretending to have the people's consent to it ; but, as if he must be dictator to all mankind, he sends a circular letter (as it should seem) among the priests at Jerusalem and the rest of the people, probably by the same messengers that brought the letter from Jeremiah. But it is chiefly directed to Zephaniah, who was either the immediate son of Maaseiah, or of the 24th course of the priests, of which Maaseiah was the father and head. He was not the high priest, but sagan or suffragan to the high priest, or in some other considerable post of command in the temple, as Pashur, *ch.* xx. 1. Perhaps he was chairman of that committee of priests that was appointed in a particular manner to take cognizance of those that pretended to be prophets, of which there were very many at this time, and to give judgment concerning them. Now, 1. He puts him and the other priests in mind of the duty of their place (*v.* 26) : *The Lord hath made thee priest instead of Jehoiada the priest.* Some think that he refers to the famous Jehoiada, that great reformer in the days of Joash ; and (says Mr. Gataker) he would insinuate that this Zephaniah is for spirit and zeal such another as he, and raised up, as he was, for the glory of God and the good of the church ; and therefore it was expected from him that he should proceed against Jeremiah. Thus (says he) there is no act so injurious or impious, but that wicked wretches and false prophets will not only attempt it, but colour it also with some specious pretence of piety and zeal for God's glory, Isa. lxvi. 5 ; John xvi. 2. Or, rather, it was some other Jehoiada, his immediate predecessor in this office, who perhaps was carried into Babylon among the priests, *v.* 1. Zephaniah is advanced, sooner than he expected, to this place of trust and power, and Shemaiah would have him think that Providence had preferred him that he might persecute God's prophets, that he had come to this government for such a time as this, and that he was unjust and ungrateful if he did not thus improve his power, or, rather, abuse it. Their hearts are wretchedly hardened who can justify the doing of mischief by their having a power to do it. These priests' business was to examine *every man that is mad and makes himself a prophet.* God's faithful prophets are here represented as prophets of their own making, usurpers of the office, and lay-intruders, as men that were mad, actuated by some demon, and not divinely inspired, or as distracted men and men in a frenzy. Thus the characters of the false prophets are thrown upon the true ones; and, if this had been indeed their character, they would have deserved to be bound as madmen and punished as pretenders, and therefore he concludes that Jeremiah must be so treated. He does not bid them examine whether Jeremiah could produce any proofs of his mission and could make it to appear that he was not mad. No; that is taken for granted, and, when once he has had a bad name given him, he must be run down of course. 2. He informs them of the letter which Jeremiah had written to the captives (*v.* 28): *He sent unto us in Babylon,* with the authority of a prophet, saying, *This captivity is long,* and therefore resolve to make the best of it. And what harm was there in this, that it should be objected to him as a crime? The false prophets had formerly said that the captivity would never come, *ch.* xiv. 13. Jeremiah had said that it would come, and the event had already proved him in the right, which obliged them to give credit to him who now said that it would be long, rather than to those who said that it would be short, but had once before been found liars. 3. He demands judgment against him, taking it for granted that he is *mad,* and *makes himself a prophet.* He expects that they will order him to be put *in prison* and *in the stocks* (*v.* 26), that they will thus punish him, and by putting him to disgrace possess the people with prejudices against him, ruin his reputation, and so prevent the giving of any credit to his prophecies at Jerusalem, hoping that, if they could gain that point, the captives in Babylon would not be influenced by him. Nay, he takes upon him to chide Zephaniah for his neglect (*v.* 27): *Why hast thou not rebuked and restrained Jeremiah of Anathoth?* See how insolent and imperious these false prophets had grown, that, though they were in captivity, they would give law to the priests who were not only at liberty, but in power. It is common for those that pretend to more knowledge than their neighbours to be thus assuming. Now here is a remarkable instance of the hardness of the hearts of sinners, and it is enough to make us all fear *lest our hearts be at any time hardened.* For here we find, (1.) That these sinners would not be convinced by the clearest evidence. God had confirmed his word in the mouth of Jeremiah; it had *taken hold* of them (Zech. i. 6); and yet, because he does not prophesy to them the smooth things they desired, they are resolved to look upon him as not duly called to the office of a prophet. None so blind as those that will not see. (2.) That they would not be reclaimed and reformed by the most severe chastisement. They were now sent

into a miserable thraldom for *mocking the messengers of the Lord* and *misusing his prophets.* This was the sin for which God now contended with them; and yet in *their distress they trespass yet more against the Lord,* 2 Chron. xxviii. 22. This very sin they are notoriously guilty of in their captivity, which shows that afflictions will not of themselves cure men of their sins, unless the grace of God work with them, but will rather exasperate the corruptions they are intended to mortify; so true is that of Solomon (Prov. xxvii. 22), *Though thou shouldst bray a fool in a mortar, yet will not his foolishness depart from him.*

II. How Jeremiah came to the knowledge of this (*v.* 29): *Zephaniah read this letter in the ears of Jeremiah.* He did not design to do as Shemaiah would have him, but, as it should seem, had a respect for Jeremiah (for we find him employed in messages to him as a *prophet, ch.* xxi. 1, xxxvii. 3), and therefore protected him. He that continued in his dignity and power stood more in awe of God and his judgments than he that was now a captive. Nay, he made Jeremiah acquainted with the contents of the letter, that he might see what enemies he had even among the captives. Note, It is kindness to our friends to let them know their foes.

III. What was the sentence passed upon Shemaiah for writing this letter. God sent him an answer, for to him Jeremiah committed his cause: it was ordered to be sent not to him, but *to those of the captivity,* who encouraged and countenanced him as if he had been a prophet of God's raising up, *v.* 31, 32. Let them know, 1. That Shemaiah had made fools of them. He promised them peace in God's name, but God did not send him; he forged a commission, and counterfeited the broad seal of Heaven to it, and made the people *to trust in a lie,* and by preaching false comfort to them deprived them of true comfort. Nay, he had not only made fools of them, but, which was worse, he had made traitors of them; he had *taught rebellion against the Lord,* as Hananiah had done, *ch.* xxviii. 16. And, if vengeance shall be taken on those that rebel, much more on those that teach rebellion by their doctrine and example. 2. That at his end *he shall also be a fool* (as the expression is, *ch.* xvii. 11); his name and family shall be extinct and shall be buried in oblivion; he shall leave no issue behind him to bear up his name; his pedigree shall end in him: *He shall not have a man to dwell among this people;* and neither he nor any that come from him shall *behold the good that I will do for my people.* Note, Those are unworthy to share in God's favours to his church that are not willing to stay his time for them. Shemaiah was angry at Jeremiah's advice to the captives to see to the building up of their families in Babylon, that they might be increased and not diminished, and therefore justly is he written childless there. Those that slight the blessings of God's word deserve to lose the benefit of them. See Amos vii. 16, 17.

CHAP. XXX.

The sermon which we have in this and the following chapter is of a very different complexion from all those before. The prophet does indeed, by direction from God, change his voice. Most of what he had said hitherto was by way of reproof and threatening; but these two chapters are wholly taken up with precious promises of a return out of captivity, and that typical of the glorious things reserved for the church in the days of the Messiah. The prophet is told not only to preach this, but to write it, because it is intended for the comfort of the generation to come, ver. 1—3. It is here promised, I. That they should hereafter have a joyful restoration. 1. Though they were now in a great deal of pain and terror, ver. 4—7. 2. Though their oppressors were very strong, ver. 8—10. 3. Though a full end was made of other nations, and they were not restored, ver. 11. 4. Though all means of their deliverance seemed to fail and be cut off, ver. 12—14. 5. Though God himself had sent them into captivity, and justly, for their sins, ver. 15, 16. 6. Though all about them looked upon their case as desperate, ver. 17. II. That after their joyful restoration they should have a happy settlement, that their city should be rebuilt (ver. 18), their numbers increased (ver. 19, 20), their government established (ver. 21), God's covenant with them renewed (ver. 22), and their enemies destroyed and cut off, ver. 23, 24.

THE word that came to Jeremiah from the Lord, saying, 2 Thus speaketh the Lord God of Israel, saying, Write thee all the words that I have spoken unto thee in a book. 3 For, lo, the days come, saith the Lord, that I will bring again the captivity of my people Israel and Judah, saith the Lord: and I will cause them to return to the land that I gave to their fathers, and they shall possess it. 4 And these *are* the words that the Lord spake concerning Israel and concerning Judah. 5 For thus saith the Lord; We have heard a voice of trembling, of fear, and not of peace. 6 Ask ye now, and see whether a man doth travail with child? wherefore do I see every man with his hands on his loins, as a woman in travail, and all faces are turned into paleness? 7 Alas! for that day *is* great, so that none *is* like it: it *is* even the time of Jacob's trouble; but he shall be saved out of it. 8 For it shall come to pass in that day, saith the Lord of hosts, *that* I will break his yoke from off thy neck, and will burst thy bonds, and strangers shall no more serve themselves of him: 9 But they shall serve the Lord their God, and David their king, whom I will raise up unto them.

Here, I. Jeremiah is directed to *write* what God had spoken to him, which perhaps refers to all the foregoing prophecies. He must write them and publish them, in hopes that those who had not profited by what he said upon once hearing it might take more

592

notice of it when in reading it they had leisure for a more considerate review. Or, rather, it refers to the promises of their enlargement, which had been often mixed with his other discourses. He must collect them and put them together, and God will now add unto them many like words. He must write them for the generations to come, who should see them accomplished, and thereby have their faith in the prophecy confirmed. He must write them not *in a letter*, as that in the chapter before to the captives, but *in a book*, to be carefully preserved in the archives, or among the public rolls or registers of the state. Daniel understood by these books when the captivity was about coming to an end, Dan. ix. 2. He must write them in a book, not in loose papers: "*For the days come,* and are yet at a great distance, when *I will bring again the captivity of Israel and Judah,* great numbers of the ten tribes, with those of the two," *v.* 3. And this prophecy must be written, that it may be read then also, that so it may appear how exactly the accomplishment answers the prediction, which is one end of the writing of prophecies. It is intimated that they shall be *beloved for their fathers' sake* (Rom. xi. 28); for *therefore* God will bring them again to Canaan, because it was *the land that he gave to their fathers,* which therefore *they shall possess.*

II. He is directed what to write. The very words are such as the Holy Ghost teaches, *v.* 4. These are the words which God ordered to be written; and those promises which are written by his order are as truly his word as the ten commandments which were written with his finger. 1. He must write a description of the fright and consternation which the people were now in, and were likely to be still in upon every attack that the Chaldeans made upon them, which will much magnify both the wonder and the welcomeness of their deliverance (*v.* 5): *We have heard a voice of trembling* —the shrieks of terror echoing to the alarms of danger. The false prophets told them that they should have *peace,* but *there is fear and not peace,* so the margin reads it. No marvel that when *without are fightings within are fears.* The men, even the men of war, shall be quite overwhelmed with the calamities of their nation, shall sink under them, and yield to them, and shall look like *women in labour,* whose pains come upon them in great extremity and they know that they cannot escape them, *v.* 6. You never heard of a man travailing with child, and yet here you find not here and there a timorous man, but *every man with his hands on his loins,* in the utmost anguish and agony, *as women in travail,* when they see their cities burnt and their countries laid waste. But this pain is compared to that of a woman in travail, not to that of a death-bed, because it shall end in joy at last, and the pain, like that of a travailing woman, shall be forgotten. *All faces* shall be *turned into paleness.* The word signifies not only such paleness as arises from a sudden fright, but that which is the effect of a bad habit of body, the jaundice, or the green sickness. The prophet laments the calamity upon the foresight of it (*v.* 7) : *Alas : for that day is great,* a day of judgment, which is called the *great day,* the *great and terrible day of the Lord* (Joel ii. 31, Jude 6), great, so that *there has been none like it.* The last destruction of Jerusalem is thus spoken of by our Saviour as unparalleled, Matt. xxiv. 21. *It is even the time of Jacob's trouble,* a sad time, when God's professing people shall be in distress above other people. The whole time of the captivity was a time of Jacob's trouble ; and such times ought to be greatly lamented by all that are concerned for the welfare of Jacob and the honour of the God of Jacob. 2. He must write the assurances which God had given that a happy end should at length be put to these calamities. (1.) Jacob's troubles shall cease : *He shall be saved out of them.* Though the afflictions of the church may last long, they shall not last always. *Salvation belongs to the Lord,* and shall be wrought for his church. (2.) Jacob's troublers shall be disabled from doing him any further mischief, and shall be reckoned with for the mischief they have done him, *v.* 8. *The Lord of hosts,* who has all power in his hand, undertakes to do it : "*I will break his yoke from off thy neck,* which has long lain so heavy, and has so sorely galled thee. *I will burst thy bonds* and restore thee to liberty and ease, and thou shalt no more be at the beck and command of strangers, shalt no more serve them, nor shall they any more *serve themselves of thee ;* they shall no more enrich themselves either by thy possessions or by thy labours." And, (3.) That which crowns and completes the mercy is that they shall be restored to the free exercise of their religion again, *v.* 9. They shall be delivered from serving their enemies, not that they may live at large and do what they please, but that they may *serve the Lord their God and David their king,* that they may come again into order, under the established government both in church and state. *Therefore* they were brought into trouble and made to *serve their enemies* because they had not *served the Lord their God* as they ought to have done, *with joyfulness and gladness of heart,* Deut. xxviii. 47. But, when the time shall come that they should be *saved out of their trouble,* God will prepare and qualify them for it by giving them a *heart to serve him,* and will make it doubly comfortable by giving them opportunity to serve him. *Therefore* we are *delivered out of the hands of our enemies,* that we may *serve God,* Luke i. 74, 75. And *then* deliverances out of temporal calamities are mercies indeed to us when by them we find ourselves engaged to and enlarged in the service of God. They shall serve their

own God, and neither be inclined, as they had been of old in the day of their apostasy, nor compelled, as they had been of late in the day of their captivity, to serve other gods. They shall serve *David their king,* such governors as God should from time to time set over them, of the line of David (as Zerubbabel), or at least sitting on the *thrones of judgment, the thrones of the house of David,* as Nehemiah. But certainly this has a further meaning. The Chaldee paraphrase reads it, *They shall obey* (or *hearken to) the Messiah* (or *Christ), the Son of David, their king.* To him the Jewish interpreters apply it. That dispensation which commenced at their return out of captivity brought them to the Messiah. He is called *David their King* because he was the *Son of David* (Matt. xxii. 42) and he answered to the name, Matt. xx. 31, 32. David was an illustrious type of him both in his humiliation and in his exaltation. The covenant of royalty made with David had principal reference to him, and in him the promises of that covenant had their full accomplishment. God gave him the *throne of his father David ;* he *raised him up unto them, set him upon the holy hill of Zion.* God is often in the New Testament said to have *raised up Jesus,* raised him up as a King, Acts iii. 26 ; xiii. 23, 33. Observe, [1.] Those that serve the Lord as their God must also serve *David their King,* must give up themselves to Jesus Christ, to be ruled by him. For all men must *honour the Son as they honour the Father,* and come into the service and worship of God by him as Mediator. [2.] Those that are delivered out of spiritual bondage must make it appear that they are so by giving up themselves to the service of Christ. Those to whom he gives rest must take his yoke upon them.

10 Therefore fear thou not, O my servant Jacob, saith the LORD ; neither be dismayed, O Israel : for, lo, I will save thee from afar, and thy seed from the land of their captivity ; and Jacob shall return, and shall be in rest, and be quiet, and none shall make *him* afraid. 11 For I *am* with thee, saith the LORD, to save thee : though I make a full end of all nations whither I have scattered thee, yet will I not make a full end of thee : but I will correct thee in measure, and will not leave thee altogether unpunished. 12 For thus saith the LORD, Thy bruise *is* incurable, *and* thy wound *is* grievous. 13 *There is* none to plead thy cause, that thou mayest be bound up : thou hast no healing medicines. 14 All thy lovers have forgotten thee ; they seek thee not ; for I have wound-

ed thee with the wound of an enemy, with the chastisement of a cruel one, for the multitude of thine iniquity; *because* thy sins were increased. 15 Why criest thou for thine affliction? thy sorrow *is* incurable for the multitude of thine iniquity: *because* thy sins were increased, I have done these things unto thee. 16 Therefore all they that devour thee shall be devoured; and all thine adversaries, every one of them, shall go into captivity; and they that spoil thee shall be a spoil, and all that prey upon thee will I give for a prey. 17 For I will restore health unto thee, and I will heal thee of thy wounds, saith the Lord; because they called thee an Outcast, *saying,* This *is* Zion, whom no man seeketh after.

In these verses, as in those foregoing, the deplorable case of the Jews in captivity is set forth, but many precious promises are given them that in due time they should be relieved and a glorious salvation wrought for them.

I. God himself appeared against them: he *scattered* them (*v.* 11); he did *all these things unto them, v.* 15. All their calamities came from his hands; whoever were the instruments, he was the principal agent. And this made their case very sad that God, even their own God, spoke concerning them, to pull down and to destroy. Now, 1. This was intended by him as a fatherly chastisement, and no other (*v.* 11): *" I will correct thee in measure,* or *according to judgment,* with discretion, no more than thou deservest, nay, no more than thou canst well bear." What God does against his people is in a way of correction, and that correction is always moderated and always proceeds from love: *" I will not leave thee altogether unpunished,* as thou art ready to think I should, because of thy relation to me." Note, A profession of religion, though ever so plausible, will be far from securing to us impunity in sin. God is no respecter of persons, but will show his hatred of sin wherever he finds it, and that he hates it most in those that are nearest to him. God here corrects his people *for the multitude of their iniquity,* and *because their sins were increased, v.* 14, 15. Are our sorrows multiplied at any time and do they increase? We must acknowledge that it is because our sins have been multiplied and they have increased. Iniquities grow in us, and therefore troubles grow upon us. But, 2. What God intended as a fatherly chastisement they and others interpreted as an act of hostility; they looked upon him as having *wounded them with the*

wound of an enemy and *with the chastisement of a cruel one* (*v.* 14), as if he had designed their ruin, and neither mitigated the correction nor had any mercy in reserve for them. It did indeed seem as if God had dealt thus severely with them, as if he had turned to be their enemy and had fought against them, Isa. lxiii. 10. Job complains that God had become cruel to him and *multiplied his wounds.* When troubles are great and long we have need carefully to watch over our own hearts, that we entertain not such hard thoughts as these of God and his providence. His are the chastisements of a merciful one, not of a cruel one, whatever they may appear.

II. Their friends forsook them, and were shy of them. None of those who had courted them in their prosperity would take notice of them now in their distress, *v.* 13. It is commonly thus when families go to decay; those hang off from them that had been their hangers-on. In two cases we are glad of the assistance of our friends and need their service:—1. If we be impeached, accused, or reproached, we expect that our friends should appear in vindication of us, should speak a good word for us when we cannot put on a face to speak for ourselves; but here *there is none to plead thy cause,* none to stand up in thy defence, none to intercede for thee with thy oppressors; therefore God will *plead their cause,* for he might well wonder there was none to uphold a people that had been so much the favourites of Heaven, Isa. lxiii. 5. 2. If we be sick, or sore, or wounded, we expect our friends should attend us, advise us, sympathise with us, and, if occasion be, lend a hand for the applying of healing medicines; but here there is none to do that, none to bind up thy wounds, and by counsels and comforts to make proper applications to thy case; nay (*v.* 14), *All thy lovers have forgotten thee;* out of sight out of mind; instead of seeking thee, they forsake thee. Such as this has often been the case of religion and serious godliness in the world; those that from their education, profession, and hopeful beginnings, one might have expected to be its friends and lovers, its patrons and protectors, desert it, forget it, and have nothing to say in its defence, nor will do any thing towards the healing of its wounds. Observe, *Thy lovers have forgotten thee, for I have wounded thee.* When God is against a people who will be for them? Who can be for them so as to do them any kindness? See Job xxx. 11. Now, upon this account, their case seemed desperate and past relief (*v.* 12): *Thy bruise is incurable, thy wound grievous,* and (*v.* 15) *thy sorrow is incurable.* The condition of the Jews in captivity was such as no human power could redress the grievances of; there they were like a valley full of *dead and dry bones,* which nothing less than Omnipotence can put life into. Who could imagine that a people so diminished, so impoverished, should ever be restored to their own land and re-established there? So many were the aggravations of their calamity that their sorrow would not admit of any alleviation, but they seemed to be hardened in it, and their souls refused to be comforted, till divine consolations proved strong ones, too strong to be borne down even by the floods of grief that overwhelmed them. *Thy sorrow is incurable because thy sins*, instead of being repented of and forsaken, *were increased*. Note, Incurable griefs are owing to incurable lusts. Now in this deplorable condition they are looked upon with disdain (v. 17): *They called thee an outcast*, abandoned by all, abandoned to ruin; they said, *This is Zion, whom no man seeks after*. When they looked on the place where the city and temple had been built they called that an outcast; now all was in ruins, there was no resort to it, no residence in it, none asked the way to Zion, as formerly; *no man seeks after* it. .When they looked on the people that formerly dwelt in Zion, but were now in captivity (and we read of *Zion dwelling with the daughter of Babylon*, Zech. ii. 7), they called them outcasts; these are those who belong to Zion, and are wont to talk much of it and weep at the remembrance of it, but *no man seeks after* them, or enquires concerning them. Note, It is often the lot of Zion to be deserted and despised by those about her.

III. For all this God will work deliverance and salvation for them in due time. Though no other hand, nay, *because* no other hand, can cure their wound, his will, and shall. 1. Though he seemed to stand at a distance from them, yet he assures them of his presence with them, his powerful and gracious presence: *I will save thee*, v. 10. *I am with thee, to save thee*, v. 11. When they are in their troubles he is with them, to save them from sinking under them; when the time has come for their deliverance he is with them, to be ready, upon the first opportunity, to save them out of their trouble. 2. Though they were at a distance, remote from their own land, *afar off in the land of their captivity*, yet there shall salvation find them out, thence shall it fetch them, them and their *seed*, for they also shall be known among the Gentiles, and distinguished from them, that they may *return*, v. 10. 3. Though they were now full of fears, and continually alarmed, yet the time shall come when they *shall be in rest and quiet*, safe and easy, *and none shall make them afraid*, v. 10. 4. Though the nations into which they were dispersed should be brought to ruin, yet they should be preserved from that ruin (v. 11): *Though I make a full end of the nations whither I have scattered thee*, and there might be danger of thy being lost among them, *yet I will not make a full end of thee*. It was promised that in the peace of these nations they should *have peace* (ch. xxix. 7), and yet in the destruction of these nations they

should escape destruction. God's church may sometimes be brought very low, but he *will not make a full end of it, ch.* v. 10, 18. 5. Though God correct them, and justly, for their sins, their manifold transgressions and mighty sins, yet he will return in mercy to them, and even their sin shall not prevent their deliverance when God's time shall come. 6. Though their adversaries were mighty, God will bring them down, and break their power (v. 16): *All that devour thee shall be devoured*, and thus Zion's cause will be pleaded and will be made to appear to all the world a righteous cause. Thus Zion's deliverance will be brought about by the destruction of her oppressors; and thus her enemies will be recompensed for all the injury they have done her; for *there is a God that judges in the earth*, a God *to whom vengeance belongs*. "*They shall every one of them*, without exception, *go into captivity*, and the day will come when *those that* now *spoil thee shall be a spoil.*" Those that *lead into captivity shall go into captivity*, Rev. xiii. 10. This might serve to oblige the present conquerors to use their captives well, because the wheel would turn round, and the day would come when they also should be captives, and let them do now as they would then be done by. 7. Though the wound seem incurable, God will make a cure of it (v. 17): *I will restore health unto thee*. Be the disease ever so dangerous, the patient is safe if God undertakes the cure.

IV. Upon the whole matter, they are cautioned against inordinate fear and grief, for in these precious promises there is enough to silence both. 1. They must not tremble as those that have no hope in the apprehension of future further trouble that might threaten them (v. 10): *Fear thou not, O my servant Jacob! neither be dismayed*. Note, Those that are God's servants must not give way to disquieting fears, whatever difficulties and dangers may be before them. 2. They must not sorrow as those that have no hope for the troubles which at present they lie under, v. 15. "*Why criest thou for thy affliction?* It is true thy carnal confidences fail thee, creatures are physicians of no value, but *I will heal thy wound*, and therefore, *Why criest thou?* Why dost thou fret and complain thus? it is *for thy sin* (v. 14, 15), and therefore, instead of repining, thou shouldst be repenting. *Wherefore should a man complain for the punishment of his sins?* The issue will be good at last, and therefore *rejoice in hope.*"

18 Thus saith the LORD; Behold, I will bring again the captivity of Jacob's tents, and have mercy on his dwelling-places; and the city shall be builded upon her own heap, and the palace shall remain after the manner thereof. 19 And out of them shall proceed

thanksgiving and the voice of them that make merry : and I will multiply them, and they shall not be few; I will also glorify them, and they shall not be small. 20 Their children also shall be as aforetime, and their congregation shall be established before me, and I will punish all that oppress them. 21 And their nobles shall be of themselves, and their governor shall proceed from the midst of them; and I will cause him to draw near, and he shall approach unto me : for who *is* this that engaged his heart to approach unto me? saith the LORD. 22 And ye shall be my people, and I will be your God. 23 Behold, the whirlwind of the LORD goeth forth with fury, a continuing whirlwind : it shall fall with pain upon the head of the wicked. 24 The fierce anger of the LORD shall not return, until he have done *it*, and until he have performed the intents of his heart : in the latter days ye shall consider it.

We have here further intimations of the favour God had in reserve for them after the days of their calamity were over. It is promised,

I. That the city and temple should be re-built, *v.* 18. *Jacob's tents*, and *his dwelling-places*, felt the effects of *the captivity*, for they lay in ruins when the inhabitants were carried away captives; but, when they have returned, the habitations shall be repaired, and raised up out of their ruins, and therein God will *have mercy upon their dwelling-places*, that had been monuments of his justice. Then *the city* of Jerusalem *shall be built upon her own heap*, her own hill, though now it be no better than a ruinous heap. The situation was unexceptionable, and therefore it shall be rebuilt upon the same spot of ground. He that can *make of a city a heap* (Isa. xxv. 2) can when he pleases *make of a heap a city* again. *The palace* (the temple, God's palace) *shall remain after the manner thereof;* it shall be built after the old model; and the service of God shall be constantly kept up there and attended as formerly.

II. That the sacred feasts should again be solemnized (*v.* 19): *Out of* the city, and the temple, and all the dwelling-places of Jacob, *shall proceed thanksgiving and the voice of those that make merry.* They shall go with expressions of joy to the temple service, and with the like shall return from it. Observe, The voice of *thanksgiving* is the same with *the voice of those that make merry;* for whatever is the matter of our joy should be the

matter of our praise. *Is any merry? Let him sing psalms.* What makes us cheerful should make us thankful. *Serve the Lord with gladness.*

III. That the people should be multiplied, and increased, and made considerable : *They shall not be few, they shall not be small,* but shall become numerous and illustrious, and make a figure among the nations; for *I will multiply them* and *I will glorify them.* It is for the honour of the church to have many added to it that shall be saved. This would make them be of some weight among their neighbours. Let a people be ever so much diminished and despised, God can multiply and glorify them. They shall be restored to their former honour: *Their children shall be as aforetime,* playing in the streets (Zech. viii. 5); they shall inherit their parents' estates and honours as formerly; *and their congregation shall,* both in civil and sacred things, *be established before me.* There shall be a constant succession of faithful magistrates in the congregation of the elders, to establish that, and of faithful worshippers in the congregation of the saints. As one generation passes away another shall be raised up, and so the *congregation shall be established before* God.

IV. That they shall be blessed with a good government (*v.* 21) : *Their nobles* and judges *shall be of themselves,* of their own nation, and they shall no longer be ruled by strangers and enemies; *their governor shall proceed from the midst of them,* shall be one that has been a sharer with them in the afflictions of their captive state; and this has reference to Christ our *governor, David our King* (*v.* 9); he is of ourselves, *in all things made like unto his brethren. And I will cause him to draw near;* this may be understood either, 1. Of the people, Jacob and Israel : " *I will cause* them *to draw near* to me in the temple service, as formerly, to come into covenant with me, as *my people* (*v.* 22), to *approach to me* in communion; *for who* hath *engaged his heart,* made a covenant with it, and brought it into bonds, *to approach unto me?*" How few are there that do so! None can do it but by the special grace of God *causing them to draw near.* Note, Whenever we approach to God in any holy ordinance we must engage our hearts to do it; the heart must be prepared for the duty, employed in it, and kept closely to it. The heart is the main thing that God looks at and requires; but it is deceitful, and will start aside if a great deal of care and pains be not taken to engage it, to bind this *sacrifice with cords.* Or, 2. It may be understood of the governor; for it is a single person that is spoken of : *Their governor shall* be duly called to his office, shall *draw near* to God to consult him upon all occasions. God *will cause him to approach to* him, for, otherwise, who would engage to take care of so weak a people, and let this ruin come under their hand? But when God has work to do, though attended with many discouragements, he will raise up instruments to do it. But it looks further, to Christ, to him as Mediator. Note, (1.) The proper work and office of Christ, as Mediator, is *to draw near and approach unto* God, not for himself only, but for us, and in our name and stead, as the high priest of our profession. The priests are said to draw nigh to God, Lev. x. 3; xxi. 17. *Moses drew near,* Exod. xx. 21. (2.) God the Father did *cause* Jesus Christ thus *to draw near and approach to* him as Mediator. He commanded and appointed him to do it; he sanctified and sealed him, anointed him for this purpose, accepted him, and declared himself well pleased in him. (3.) Jesus Christ, being caused by the Father to approach unto him as Mediator, did *engage his heart to* do it, that is, he bound and obliged himself to it, *undertook for his heart* (so some read it), for his soul, that, in the fulness of time, it should be *made an offering for sin.* His own voluntary undertaking, in compliance with his Father's will and in compassion to fallen man, engaged him, and then his own honour kept him to it. It also intimates that he was hearty and resolute, free and cheerful, in it, and made nothing of the difficulties that lay in his way, Isa. lxiii. 3—5. (4.) Jesus Christ was, in all this, truly wonderful. We may well ask, with admiration, *Who is this that* thus *engages his heart* to such an undertaking?

V. That they shall be taken again into covenant with God, according to the covenant made with their fathers (*v.* 22): *You shall be my people;* and it is God's good work in us that makes us *to him a people, a people for his name,* Acts xv. 14. *I will be your God.* It is his good-will to us that is the summary of that part of the covenant.

VI. That their enemies shall be reckoned with and brought down (*v.* 20): *I will punish all* those *that oppress them,* so that it shall appear to all a dangerous thing to *touch God's anointed,* Ps. cv. 15. The last two verses come under this head: *The whirlwind of the Lord shall fall with pain upon the head of the wicked.* These two verses we had before (*ch.* xxiii. 19, 20); *there* they were a denunciation of God's wrath against the wicked hypocrites in Israel; *here* against the wicked oppressors of Israel. The expressions, exactly agreeing, speak the same with that (Isa. li. 22, 23), *I will take the cup of trembling out of thy hand and put it into the hand of those that afflict thee.* The wrath of God against the wicked is here represented to be, 1. Very terrible, like a whirlwind, surprising and irresistible. 2. Very grievous. It *shall fall with pain upon their heads;* they shall be as much hurt as frightened. 3. It shall pursue them. Whirlwinds are usually short, but this shall be *a continuing whirlwind.* 4. It shall accomplish that

for which it is sent: *The anger of the Lord shall not return till he have done it.* The purposes of his wrath, as well as the purposes of his love, will all be fulfilled; he will *perform the intents of his heart.* 5. Those that will not lay this to heart now will then be unable to put off the thoughts of 'it: *In the latter days you shall consider it,* when it will be too late to prevent it.

CHAP. XXXI.

This chapter goes on with the good words and comfortable words which we had in the chapter before, for the encouragement of the captives, assuring them that God would in due time restore them or their children to their own land, and make them a great and happy nation again, especially by sending them the Messiah, in whose kingdom and grace many of these promises were to have their full accomplishment. I. They shall be restored to peace and honour, and joy and great plenty, ver. 1—14. II. Their sorrow for the loss of their children shall be at an end, ver. 15—17. III. They shall repent of their sins, and God will graciously accept them in their repentance, ver. 18—20. IV. They shall be multiplied and increased, both their children and their cattle, and not be cut off and diminished as they had been, ver. 21—30. V. God will renew his covenant with them, and enrich it with spiritual blessings, ver 31—34. VI. These blessings shall be secured to theirs after them, even to the spiritual seed of Israel for ever, ver. 35 —37. VII. As an earnest of this the city of Jerusalem shall be rebuilt, ver. 38—40. These exceedingly great and precious promises were firm foundations of hope and full fountains of joy to the poor captives; and we also may apply them to ourselves and mix faith with them.

AT the same time, saith the LORD, will I be the God of all the families of Israel, and they shall be my people. 2 Thus saith the LORD, The people *which were* left of the sword found grace in the wilderness; *even* Israel, when I went to cause him to rest. 3 The LORD hath appeared of old unto me, *saying,* Yea, I have loved thee with an everlasting love: therefore with lovingkindness have I drawn thee. 4 Again I will build thee, and thou shalt be built, O virgin of Israel: thou shalt again be adorned with thy tabrets, and shalt go forth in the dances of them that make merry. 5 Thou shalt yet plant vines upon the mountains of Samaria: the planters shall plant, and shall eat *them* as common things. 6 For there shall be a day, *that* the watchmen upon the mount Ephraim shall cry, Arise ye, and let us go up to Zion unto the LORD our God. 7 For thus the LORD; Sing with gladness for Jacob, and shout among the chief of the nations: publish ye, praise ye, and say, O LORD, save thy people, the remnant of Israel. 8 Behold, I will bring them from the north country, and gather them from the coasts of the earth, *and* with them the blind and the lame, the woman with child and her that travaileth with child together: a great company shall return thither. 9 They shall come with weeping, and with supplications will I lead them : I will cause them to walk by the rivers of waters in a straight way, wherein they shall not stumble : for I am a father to Israel, and Ephraim *is* my first-born.

God here assures his people,

I. That he will again take them into a covenant relation to himself, from which they seemed to be cut off. *At the same time,* when God's anger breaks out against the wicked (*ch.* xxx. 24), his own people shall be owned by him as the children of his love: *I will be the God* (that is, I will show myself to be the God) *of all the families of Israel* (*v.* 1),—not of the two tribes only, but of all the tribes,—not of the house of Aaron only, and the families of Levi, but of all their families ; not only their state in general, but their particular families, and the interests of them, shall have the benefit of a special relation to God. Note, The families of good people, in their family capacity, may apply to God and stay themselves upon him as their God. If we and our houses serve the Lord, we and our houses shall be protected and blessed by him, Prov. iii. 33.

II. That he will do for them, in bringing them out of Babylon, as he had done for their fathers when he delivered them out of Egypt, and as he had purposed to do when he first took them to be his people.   1. He puts them in mind of what he did for their fathers when he brought them out of Egypt, *v.* 2. They were then, as these were, a *people left of the sword,* that sword of Pharaoh with which he cut off all the male children as soon as they were born (a bloody sword indeed they had narrowly escaped) and that sword with which he threatened to cut them off when he pursued them to the Red Sea. They were then *in the wilderness,* where they seemed to be lost and forgotten, as these were now in a strange land, and yet they found grace in God's sight, were owned and highly honoured by him, and blessed with wonderful instances of his peculiar favour, and he was at this time going *to cause them to rest* in Canaan.   Note, When we are brought very low, and insuperable difficulties appear in the way of our deliverance, it is good to remember that it has been so with the church formerly, and yet that it has been raised up from its low estate and has got to Canaan through all the hardships of a wilderness ; and God is still the same.   2. They put him in mind of what God had done for their fathers, intimating that they now saw not such signs, and were ready to ask, as Gideon did, *Where are all the wonders that our fathers told us of ?*   It is true, *The Lord hath appeared of old unto me* (*v.* 3), in Egypt, in the wilderness, hath ap-

598

peared with me and for me, hath been seen in his glory as my God.   The years of ancient times were glorious years ; but now it is otherwise ; what good will it do us that he *appeared of old* to us when now he is *a God that hides himself* from us ? Isa. xlv. 15. Note, It is hard to take comfort from former smiles under present frowns.   3. To this he answers with an assurance of the constancy of his love : *Yea, I have loved thee,* not only with an ancient love, but *with an everlasting love,* a love that shall never fail, however the comforts of it may for a time be suspended.   It is *an everlasting love ; therefore have I* extended or *drawn out lovingkindness unto thee* also, as well as to thy ancestors ; or, *with lovingkindness have I drawn thee* to myself as thy God, from all the idols to which thou hadst turned aside.   Note, It is the happiness of those who are through grace interested in the love of God that it is *an everlasting love* (from everlasting in the counsels of it, *to* everlasting in the continuance and consequences of it), and that nothing can separate them from that love. Those whom God loves with this love he will draw into covenant and communion with himself, by the influences of his Spirit upon their souls ; he will *draw them with lovingkindness,* with the cords of a man and bands of love, than which no attractive can be more powerful.

III. That he will again form them into a people, and give them a very joyful settlement in their own land, *v.* 4, 5.   Is the church of God his house, his temple ?   Is it now in ruins ?   It is so ; but, *Again I will build thee, and thou shalt be built.* Are the parts of this building dispersed ?   They shall be collected and put together again, each in its place.   If God undertake to build them, they shall be built, whatever opposition may be given to it ?   Is *Israel* a beautiful *virgin ?*   Is she now stripped of her ornaments and reduced to a melancholy state ?   She is so ; but *thou shalt again be adorned* and made fine, adorned *with thy tabrets,* or timbrels, the ornaments of thy chamber, and made merry.   They shall resume their harps which had been hung upon the willow-trees, shall tune them, and shall themselves be in tune to make use of them. They shall be adorned with their tabrets, for now their mirth and music shall be seasonable ; it shall be a proper time for it, God in his providence shall call them to it, and then it shall be an ornament to them ; whereas tabrets, at a time of common calamity, when God called to mourning, were a shame to them.   Or it may refer to their use of tabrets in the solemnizing of their religious feasts and their *going forth in dances* then, as the *daughters of Shiloh,* Judg. xxi. 19, 21.   Our mirth is then indeed an ornament to us when we serve God and honour him with it.   Is the joy of the city maintained by the products of the country ?   It is so ; and therefore it is promised (*v.* 5), *Thou shalt yet plant vines upon the mountains of Samaria,* which had been the head city of the kingdom of Israel, in opposition to that of Judah; but they shall now be united (Ezek. xxxvii. 22), and there shall be such perfect peace and security that men shall apply themselves wholly to the improvement of their ground: *The planters shall plant,* not fearing the soldiers' coming to eat the fruits of what they had planted, or to pluck it up; but they themselves *shall eat them* freely, *as common things,* not forbidden fruits, not forbidden by the law of God (as they were till the fifth year, Lev. xix. 23—25), not forbidden by the owners, because there shall be such plenty as to yield enough for all, enough for each.

IV. That they shall have liberty and opportunity to worship God in the ordinances of his own appointment, and shall have both invitations and inclinations to do so (*v.* 6): *There shall be a day,* and a glorious day it will be, when *the watchmen upon Mount Ephraim,* that are set to stand sentinel there, to give notice of the approach of the enemy, finding that all is very quiet and that there is no appearance of danger, shall desire for a time to be discharged from their post, that they may *go up to Zion,* to praise God for the public peace. Or *the watchmen* that tend the vineyards (spoken of *v.* 5) shall stir up themselves, and one another, and all their neighbours, to go and keep the solemn feasts at Jerusalem. Now this implies that the service of God shall be again set up in Zion, that there shall be a general resort to it, with much affection and mutual excitement, as in David's time, Ps. cxxii. 1. But that which is most observable here is *that the watchmen of Ephraim* are forward to promote the worship of God at Jerusalem, whereas formerly *the watchman of Ephraim was hatred against the house of his God* (Hos. ix. 8), and, instead of inviting people to Zion, laid snares for those that set their faces thitherward, Hos. v. 1. Note, God can make those who have been enemies to religion and the true worship of God to become encouragers of them and leaders in them. This promise was to have its full accomplishment in the days of the Messiah, when the gospel should be preached to all these countries, and a general invitation thereby given into the church of Christ, of which Zion was a type.

V. That God shall have the glory and the church both the honour and comfort of this blessed change (*v.* 7): *Sing with gladness for Jacob,* that is, let all her friends and well-wishers rejoice with her, Deut. xxxii. 43. *Rejoice, you Gentiles with his people,* Rom. xv. 10. The restoration of Jacob will be taken notice of by all the neighbours, it will be matter of joy to them all, and they shall all join with Jacob in his joys, and thereby pay him respect and put a reputation upon him. Even *the chief of the nations,* that make the greatest figure, shall think it an

honour to them to congratulate the restoration of Jacob, and shall do themselves the honour to send their ambassadors on that errand. *Publish you, praise you.* In publishing these tidings, praise the God of Israel, praise the Israel of God, speak honourably of both. The publishers of the gospel must publish it with praise, and therefore it is often spoken of in the *Psalms* as mingled with *praises,* Ps. lxvii. ii. 3; xcvi. 2, 3. What we either bring to others or take to ourselves the comfort of we must be sure to give God the praise of. *Praise you, and say, O Lord! save thy people;* that is, perfect their salvation, go on to save *the remnant of Israel,* that are yet in bondage; as Ps. cxxvi. 3, 4. Note, When we are praising God for what he has done we must call upon him for the future favours which his church is in need and expectation of; and in praying to him we really praise him and give him glory; he takes it so.

VI. That, in order to a happy settlement in their own land, they shall have a joyful return out of the land of their captivity and a very comfortable passage homeward (*v.* 8,9), and this beginning of mercy shall be to them a pledge of all the other blessings here promised. 1. Though they are scattered to places far remote, yet they shall be brought together *from the north country, and from the coasts of the earth;* wherever they are, God will find them out. 2. Though many of them are very unfit for travel, yet that shall be no hindrance to them: *The blind and the lame* shall come; such a good-will shall they have to their journey, and such a good heart upon it, that they shall not make their blindness and lameness an excuse for staying where they are. Their companions will be ready to help them, will be *eyes to the blind and legs to the lame,* as good Christians ought to be to one another in their travels heavenward, Job xxix. 15. But, above all, their God will help them; and let none plead that he is blind who has God for his guide, or lame who has God for his strength. *The women with child* are heavy, and it is not fit that they should undertake such a journey, much less those *that travail with child;* and yet, when it is to return to Zion, neither the one nor the other shall make any difficulty of it. Note, When God calls we must not plead any inability to come; for he that calls us will help us, will strengthen us. 3. Though they seem to be diminished, and to have become few in numbers, yet, when they come all together, they shall be *a great company;* and so will God's spiritual Israel be when there shall be a general rendezvous of them, though now they are but a little flock. 4. Though their return will be matter of joy to them, yet prayers and tears will be both their stores and their artillery (*v.* 9): *They shall come with weeping and with supplications,* weeping for sin, supplication for pardon; for *the goodness of God* shall *lead them to repentance;*

and they shall weep with more bitterness and more tenderness for sin, when they are delivered out of their captivity, than ever they did when they were groaning under it. Weeping and praying do well together; tears put life into prayers, and express the liveliness of them, and prayers help to wipe away tears. *With favours will I lead them* (so the margin reads it); in their journey they shall be compassed with God's favours, the fruits of his favour. 5. Though they have a perilous journey, yet they shall be safe under a divine convoy. Is the country they pass through dry and thirsty? *I will cause them to walk by the rivers of waters,* not the waters of a land-flood, which fail in summer. Is it a wilderness where there is no road, no track? *I will cause them to walk in a straight way,* which they shall not miss. Is it a rough and rocky country? Yet *they shall not stumble.* Note, Whithersoever God gives his people a clear call he will either find them or make them a ready way; and while we are following Providence we may be sure that Providence will not be wanting to us. And, *lastly,* here is a reason given why God will take all this care of his people: *For I am a Father to Israel,* a Father that begat him, and therefore will maintain him, that have the care and compassion of a father for him (Ps. ciii. 13); *and Ephraim is my first-born;* even *Ephraim,* who, having gone astray from God, was *no more worthy to be called a son,* shall yet be owned as a *first-born,* particularly dear, and heir of a double portion of blessings. The same reason that was given for their release out of Egypt is given for their release out of Babylon; they are free-born and therefore must not be enslaved, are born to God and therefore must not be the servants of men. Exod. iv. 22, 23, *Israel is my son, even my first-born; let my son go that he may serve me.* If we take God for our Father, and join ourselves to *the church of the first-born,* we may be assured that we shall want nothing that is good for us.

10 Hear the word of the Lord, O ye nations, and declare *it* in the isles afar off, and say, He that scattered Israel will gather him, and keep him, as a shepherd *doth* his flock. 11 For the Lord hath redeemed Jacob, and ransomed him from the hand of *him that was* stronger than he. 12 Therefore they shall come and sing in the height of Zion, and shall flow together to the goodness of the Lord, for wheat, and for wine, and for oil, and for the young of the flock and of the herd : and their soul shall be as a watered garden; and they shall not sorrow any more at all. 13 Then

shall the virgin rejoice in the dance, both young men and old together : for I will turn their mourning into joy, and will comfort them, and make them rejoice from their sorrow. 14 And I will satiate the soul of the priests with fatness, and my people shall be satisfied with my goodness, saith the Lord. 15 Thus saith the Lord; A voice was heard in Ramah, lamentation, *and* bitter weeping; Rachel weeping for her children refused to be comforted for her children, because they *were* not. 16 Thus saith the Lord; Refrain thy voice from weeping, and thine eyes from tears: for thy work shall be rewarded, saith the Lord; and they shall come again from the land of the enemy. 17 And there is hope in thine end, saith the Lord, that thy children shall come again to their own border.

This paragraph is much to the same purport with the last, publishing to the world, as well as to the church, the purposes of God's love concerning his people. This is a *word of the Lord* which the *nations* must *hear,* for it is a prophecy of a work of the Lord which the nations cannot but take notice of. Let them hear the prophecy, that they may the better understand and improve the performance; and let those that hear it themselves declare it to others, *declare it in the isles afar off.* It will be a piece of news that will spread all the world over. It will look very great in history; let us see how it looks in prophecy.

It is foretold, 1. That those who are dispersed shall be brought together again from their dispersions: *He that scattereth Israel will gather him;* for he knows whither he scattered them and therefore where to find them, *v.* 10. *Una eademque manus vulnus opemque tulit—The hand that inflicted the wound shall heal it.* And when he has gathered him into one body, one fold, he will *keep him, as a shepherd does his flock,* from being scattered again. 2. That those who are sold and alienated shall be redeemed and brought back, *v.* 11. Though the enemy that had got possession of him was *stronger than he,* yet *the Lord,* who is stronger than all, *has redeemed and ransomed him,* not by price, but by power, as of old out of the Egyptians' hands. 3. That with their liberty they shall have plenty and joy, and God shall be honoured and served with it, *v.* 12, 13. When they shall have returned to their own land *they shall come and sing in the high place of Zion;* on the top of that holy mountain they shall sing to the praise and glory of God. We read that they did so when the foundation of the temple was laid there; they *sang together, praising and giving thanks to the Lord,* Ezra iii. 11. They *shall flow together to the goodness of the Lord;* that is, they shall flock in great numbers and with great forwardness and cheerfulness, as streams of water, *to the goodness of the Lord,* to the temple where he causes his goodness to pass before his people. They shall come together in solemn assemblies, to *praise him for his goodness,* and to pray for the fruits of it and the continuance of it; they shall come to bless him for his goodness, in giving them *wheat, and wine, and oil, and the young of the flock and of the herd,* which, now that they have obtained their freedom, they have an uncontested property in and the quiet and peaceable enjoyment of, and which therefore they honour God with the first-fruits of and out of which they bring offerings to his altar. Note, It is comfortable to observe the goodness of the Lord in the gifts of common providence, and even in them to taste covenant-love. Having plenty (plenty out of want and scarcity) they shall greatly rejoice, *their soul shall be as a watered garden,* flourishing and fruitful (Isa. lviii. 11), pleasant and fragrant, and abounding in all good things. Note, Our souls are never valuable as gardens but when they are watered with the dews of God's Spirit and grace. It is a precious promise which follows, and which will not have its full accomplishment any where on this side the height of the heavenly Zion, that *they shall not sorrow any more at all;* for it is only in that new Jerusalem *that all tears shall be wiped away,* Rev. xxi. 4. However, so far it was fulfilled to the returned captives that they had not any more those causes for sorrow which they had formerly had; and therefore (*v.* 13) *young men and old shall rejoice together;* so grave shall the young men be in their joys as to keep company with the old men, and so transported shall the old men be as to associate with the young. *Salva res est, saltat senex—The state prospers, and the aged dance.* God *will turn their mourning into joy,* their fasts into solemn feasts, Zech. viii. 19. It was in the return out of Babylon that those *who sowed in tears* were made to *reap in joy,* Ps. cxxvi. 5, 6. Those are comforted indeed whom God comforts, and may forget their troubles when he *makes them to rejoice from their sorrow,* not only rejoice after it, but rejoice from it; their joy shall borrow lustre from their sorrow, which shall serve as a foil to it; and the more they think of their troubles the more shall they rejoice in their deliverance. 4. That both the ministers and those they minister to shall have abundant satisfaction in what God gives them (*v.* 14): *I will satiate the soul of the priests with fatness;* there shall be such a plenty of sacrifices brought to the altar that those who *live upon the altar* shall live very comfortably,

they and their families shall be *satiated with fatness,* they shall have enough, and that of the best; *and my people shall be satisfied with my goodness,* and shall think there is enough in that to make them happy; and so there is. God's people have an abundant satisfaction in God's goodness, though they have but little of this world. Let them be satisfied of God's lovingkindness, and they will be satisfied with it and desire no more to make them happy. All this is applicable to the spiritual blessings which the redeemed of the Lord enjoy by Jesus Christ, infinitely more valuable than corn, and wine, and oil, and the satisfaction of soul which they have in the enjoyment of them. 5. That those particularly who had been in sorrow for the loss of their children who were carried into captivity should have that sorrow turned into joy upon their return, *v.* 15—17. Here we have, (1.) The sad lamentation which the mothers made for the loss of their children (*v.* 15) : *In Ramah was there a voice heard,* at the time when the general captivity was, nothing but *lamentation, and bitter weeping,* more there than in other places, because there Nebuzaradan had the general rendezvous of his captives, as appears, *ch.* xl. 1, where we find him sending Jeremiah back from Ramah. *Rachel* is here said to *weep for her children.* The sepulchre of Rachel was between Ramah and Bethlehem. Benjamin, one of the two tribes, and Ephraim, head of the ten tribes, were both descendants from Rachel. She had but two sons, the elder of whom was one for whom his father grieved and *refused to be comforted* (Gen. xxxvii. 35); the other she herself called *Benoni—the son of my sorrow.* Now the inhabitants of Ramah did in like manner *grieve for their sons and their daughters* that were carried away (as 1 Sam. xxx. 6), and such a voice of lamentation was there as, to speak poetically, might even have raised Rachel out of her grave to mourn with them. The tender parents even *refused to be comforted for their children, because they were not,* were not with them, but were in the hands of their enemies; they were never likely to see them any more. This is applied by the evangelists to the great mourning that was at Bethlehem for the murder of the infants there by Herod (Matt. ii. 17—18), and this scripture is said to be then fulfilled. They wept for them, *and would not be comforted,* supposing the case would not admit any ground of comfort, *because they were not.* Note, Sorrow for the loss of children cannot but be great sorrow, especially if we so far mistake as to think *they are not.* (2.) Seasonable comfort administered to them in reference hereunto, *v.* 16, 17. They are advised to moderate that sorrow, and to set bounds to it : *Refrain thy voice from weeping and thy eyes from tears.* We are not forbidden to mourn in such a case; allowances are made for natural affection. But we must not suffer our sorrow to run into an extreme, to hinder our joy in God, or take us off from our duty to him. Though we mourn, we must not murmur, nor must we resolve, as Jacob did, to go to the grave mourning. In order to repress inordinate grief, we must consider that *there is hope in our end,* hope that there will be an end the trouble will not last always), that it will be a happy end —the end will be peace. Note, It ought to support us under our troubles that we have reason to hope they will end well. *The righteous has hope in his death ;* that will be the blessed period of his griefs and the blessed passage to his joys. *" There is hope for thy posterity "* (so some read it) ; though thou mayest not live to see these glorious days thyself, there is hope that thy posterity shall. Though one generation falls in the wilderness, the next shall enter Canaan. Two things thou mayest comfort thyself with the hope of:"—[1.] *" The reward* of thy work:—*Thy* suffering *work shall be rewarded.* The comforts of the deliverance shall be sufficient to balance all the grievances of thy captivity." God makes his people *glad according to the days wherein he has afflicted them,* and so there is a proportion between the joys and the sorrows, as between the reward and the work. The *glory to be revealed,* which the saints hope for in their end, will abundantly countervail *the sufferings of this present time,* Rom. viii. 18. [2.] "The restoration of thy children : *They shall come again from the land of the enemy* (v. 16); they *shall come again to their own border,*" *v.* 17. *There is hope* that children at a distance may be brought home. Jacob had a comfortable meeting with Joseph after he had despaired of ever seeing him. There is hope concerning children removed by death that they shall *return to their own border,* to the happy lot assigned them in the resurrection, a lot in the heavenly Canaan, that border of his sanctuary. We shall see reason to repress our grief for the death of our children that are taken into covenant with God when we consider the hopes we have of their resurrection to eternal life. They are not lost, but gone before.

18 I have surely heard Ephraim bemoaning himself *thus ;* Thou hast chastised me, and I was chastised, as a bullock unaccustomed *to the yoke :* turn thou me, and I shall be turned ; for thou *art* the LORD my God. 19 Surely after that I was turned, I repented ; and after that I was instructed, I smote upon *my* thigh: I was ashamed, yea, even confounded, because I did bear the reproach of my youth. 20 *Is* Ephraim my dear son ? *is he* a pleasant child ? for since I spake against him, I do earnestly remember him still:

therefore my bowels are troubled for him ; I will surely have mercy upon him, saith the LORD. 21 Set thee up way-marks, make thee high heaps : set thine heart toward the highway, *even* the way *which* thou wentest : turn again, O virgin of Israel, turn again to these thy cities. 22 How long wilt thou go about, O thou backsliding daughter ? for the LORD hath created a new thing in the earth, A woman shall compass a man. 23 Thus saith the LORD of hosts, the God of Israel ; As yet they shall use this speech in the land of Judah and in the cities thereof, when I shall bring again their captivity ; the LORD bless thee, O habitation of justice, *and* mountain of holiness. 24 And there shall dwell in Judah itself, and in all the cities thereof together, husbandmen, and they *that* go forth with flocks. 25 For I have satiated the weary soul, and I have replenished every sorrowful soul. 26 Upon this I awaked, and beheld ; and my sleep was sweet unto me.

We have here,

I. Ephraim's repentance, and return to God. Not only Judah, but Ephraim, the ten tribes, shall be restored, and therefore shall thus be prepared and qualified for it, Hos. xiv. 8. *Ephraim shall say, What have I to do any more with idols ?* Ephraim, the people, is here spoken of as a single person to denote their unanimity ; they shall be as one man in their repentance and shall glorify God in it with one mind and one mouth, one and all. It is likewise thus expressed that it might be the better accommodated to particular penitents, for whose directicn and encouragement this passage is intended. Ephraim is here brought in weeping for sin, perhaps because Ephraim, the person from whom that tribe had its denomination, was a man of a tender spirit, *mourned for his children many days* (1 Chron. vii. 21, 22), and sorrow for sin is compared to that *for an only son.* This penitent is here brought in, 1. Bemoaning himself and the miseries of his present case. True penitents do thus bemoan themselves. 2. Accusing himself, laying a load upon himself as a sinner, a great sinner. He charges upon himself, in the first place, that sin which his conscience told him that he was more especially guilty of at this time, and that was impatience under correction : *" Thou hast chastised me ;* I have been under the rod, and I needed it, I deserved it ; I was justly chastised, chastised *as a bullock,* who would never have felt the goad if he had not first rebelled against the yoke." True penitents look upon their afflictions as fatherly chastisements : "*Thou hast chastised me and I was chastised ;* that is, it was well that I was chastised, otherwise I should have been undone ; it did me good, or at least was intended to do me good ; and yet I have been impatient under it." Or it may intimate his want of feeling under the affliction : "*Thou hast chastised me and I was chastised,* that was all ; I was not awakened by it and quickened by it ; I looked no further than the chastisement. *I have been* under the chastisement *as a bullock unaccustomed to the yoke,* unruly and unmanageable, kicking against the pricks, *like a wild bull in a net,*" Isa. li. 20. This is the sin he finds himself guilty of now ; but (*v.* 19) he reflects upon his former sins and looks as far back as the days of his youth. The discovery of one sin should put us upon searching out more ; now he remembers *the reproach of his youth.* Ephraim, as a people, reflect upon the misconduct of their ancestors when they were first formed into a people. It is applicable to particular persons. Note, The sin of our youth was the reproach of our youth, and we ought often to remember it against ourselves and to bear it in a penitential sorrow and shame. 3. He is here brought in angry at himself, having a holy indignation at himself for his sin and folly : He *smote upon his thigh,* as the publican upon his breast. He was even amazed at himself, and at his own stupidity and frowardness : He *was ashamed, yea even confounded,* could not with any confidence look up to God, nor with any comfort reflect upon himself. 4. He is here recommending himself to the mercy and grace of God. He finds he is bent to backslide from God, and cannot by any power of his own keep himself close with God, much less, when he has revolted, bring himself back to God, and therefore he prays, *Turn thou me and I shall be turned,* which implies that unless God do turn him by his grace he shall never be turned, but wander endlessly, that therefore he is very desirous of converting grace, has a dependence upon it, and doubts not but that that grace will be sufficient for him, to help him over all the difficulties that were in the way of his return to God. See *ch.* xvii. 14, *Heal me and I shall be healed.* God works with power, can make the unwilling willing ; if he undertake the conversion of a soul, it will be converted. 5. He is here pleasing himself with the experience he had of the blessed effect of divine grace : *Surely after that I was turned I repented.* Note, All the pious workings of our heart towards God are the fruit and consequence of the powerful working of his grace in us. And observe, He was *turned,* he was *instructed,* his will was bowed to the will of God, by the right informing of his judgment concerning the truths of God. Note, The way God takes of converting souls

to himself is by opening the eyes of their understandings, and all good follows thereupon : *After that I was instructed* I yielded, *I smote upon my thigh.* When sinners come to a right knowledge they will come to a right way. Ephraim was chastised, and that did not produce the desired effect, it went no further : *I was chastised,* and that was all. But, when the instructions of God's Spirit accompanied the corrections of his providence, then the work was done, then he *smote upon his thigh,* was so humbled for sin as to have no more to do with it.

II. God's compassion on Ephraim and the kind reception he finds with God, *v.* 20. 1. God owns him for a child, though he has been an undutiful child and a prodigal : *Is Ephraim my dear son ? Is he a pleasant child ?* Thus when Ephraim bemoans himself God bemoans him, as *one whom his mother comforts,* though she had chidden him, Isa. lxvi. 13. *Is this Ephraim my dear son?* Is this that *pleasant child ?* Is it he that is thus sad in spirit and that complains so bitterly ? So it is like that of Saul (1 Sam. xxvi. 17), *Is this thy voice, my son David ?* Or, as it is sometimes supplied, *Is not Ephraim my dear son? Is he not a pleasant child ?* Yes, now he is, now he repents and returns. Note, Those that have been undutiful backsliding children, if they sincerely return and repent, however they have been under the chastisement of the rod, shall be accepted of God as dear and pleasant children. Ephraim had afflicted himself, but God thus heals him — had abased himself, but God thus honours him; as the returning prodigal who thought himself no more worthy to be *called a son,* yet, by his father, had the *best robe* put upon him and *a ring on his hand.* 2. He relents towards him, and speaks of him with a great deal of tender compassion : *Since I spoke against him,* by the threatenings of the word and the rebukes of providence, *I do earnestly remember him still,* my thoughts towards him are thoughts of peace. Note, When God afflicts his people, yet he does not forget them ; when he casts them out of their land, yet he does not cast them out of sight, nor out of mind. Even then when God is speaking against us, yet he is acting for us, and designing our good in all ; and this is our comfort in our affliction, that *the Lord thinks upon us,* though we have forgotten him. *I remember him still,* and therefore *my bowels are troubled for him,* as Joseph's yearned towards his brethren, even when he *spoke roughly* to them. When Israel's afflictions extorted a penitent confession and submission it is said that his soul was grieved for the misery of Israel (Judg. x. 16), for he always afflicts with the greatest tenderness. It was God's compassion that mitigated Ephraim's punishment : *My heart is turned within me* (Hos. xi. 8, 9) ; and now the same compassion accepted Ephraim's repentance. Ephraim had pleaded (*v.* 18), *Thou art the*

Lord my God, therefore to thee will I return, therefore on thy mercy and grace I will depend; and God shows that it was a valid plea and prevailing, for he makes it appear both that he is God and not man and that he is *his* God. 3. He resolves to do him good : *I will surely have mercy upon him, saith the Lord.* Note, God has mercy in store, rich mercy, sure mercy, suitable mercy, for all that in sincerity seek him and submit to him; and the more we are afflicted for sin the better prepared we are for the comforts of that mercy.

III. Gracious excitements and encouragements given to the people of God in Babylon to prepare for their return to their own land. Let them not tremble and lose their spirits ; let them not trifle and lose their time; but with a firm resolution and a close application address themselves to their journey, *v.* 21, 22. 1. They must think of nothing but of coming back to their own country, out of which they had been driven: *" Turn again, O virgin of Israel!* a virgin to be again espoused to thy God ; *turn again to these thy cities;* though they are laid waste and in ruins, they are *thy cities,* which thy God gave thee, and therefore *turn again* to them." They must be content in Babylon no longer than till they had liberty to return to Zion. 2. They must return the same way that they went, that the remembrance of the sorrows which attended them, or which their fathers had told them of, in such and such places upon the road, the sight of which would, by a local memory, put them in mind of them, might make them the more thankful for their deliverance. Those that have departed from God into the bondage of sin must return by the way in which they went astray, to the duties they neglected, must *do their first works.* 3. They must engage themselves and all that is within them in this affair : *Set thy heart towards the highway ;* bring thy mind to it; consider thy duty, thy interest, and go about it with a good-will. Note, The way from Babylon to Zion, from the bondage of sin to the glorious liberty of God's children, is a highway; it is right, it is plain, it is safe, it is well-tracked (Isa. xxxv. 8) ; yet none are likely to walk in it, unless they *set their hearts towards it.* 4. They must furnish themselves with all needful accommodations for the journey: *Set thee up way-marks,* and *make thee high heaps* or *pillars;* send before to have such set up in all places where there is any danger of missing the road. Let those that go first, and are best acquainted with the way, set up such directions for those that follow. 5. They must compose themselves for their journey: *How long wilt thou go about, O backsliding daughter?* Let not their minds fluctuate, or be uncertain about it, but resolve upon it: let them not distract themselves with care and fear ; let them not seek about to creatures for assistance, nor hurry hither

604

and thither in courting them, which had often been an instance of their backsliding from God ; but let them cast themselves upon God, and then let their minds be fixed. 6. They are encouraged to do this by an assurance God gives them that he would *create a new thing* (strange and surprising) *in the earth* (in that land), *a woman shall compass a man.* The church of God, that is weak and feeble as a woman, altogether unapt for military employments and of a timorous spirit (Isa. liv. 6), shall surround, besiege, and prevail against a mighty man. The church is compared to a woman, Rev. xii. 1. And, whereas we find *armies compassing the camp of the saints* (Rev. xx. 9), now the camp of the saints shall compass them. Many good interpreters understand this *new thing* created in that land to be the incarnation of Christ, which God an eye to in bringing them back to that land, and which had sometimes been given them for a sign, Isa. vii. 14 ; ix. 6. *A woman,* the virgin Mary, enclosed in her womb *the Mighty One;* for so *Geber,* the word here used, signifies ; and God is called *Gibbor, the Mighty God* (ch. xxxii. 18), as also is Christ in Isa. ix. 6, where his incarnation is spoken of, as it is supposed to be here. He is *El-Gibbor,* the *mighty God.* Let this assure them that God would not cast off this people, for that blessing was to be among them, Isa. lxv. 8.

IV. A comfortable prospect given them of a happy settlement in their own land again. 1. They shall have an interest in the esteem and good-will of all their neighbours, who will give them a good word and put up a good prayer for them (*v.* 23): *As yet,* or rather *yet again* (though Judah and Jerusalem have long been an astonishment and a hissing), *this speech shall be used,* as it was formerly, *concerning the land of Judah and the cities thereof, The Lord bless you, O habitation of justice and mountain of holiness!* This intimates that they shall return much reformed and every way better ; and this reformation shall be so conspicuous that all about them shall take notice of it. The *cities,* that used to be nests of pirates, shall be *habitations of justice;* the *mountain of Israel* (so the whole land is called, Ps. lxxviii. 54), and especially Mount Zion, shall be a *mountain of holiness.* Observe, Justice towards men, and holiness towards God, must go together. Godliness and honesty are what God has joined, and let no man think to put them asunder, nor to make one to atone for the want of the other. It is well with a people when they come out of trouble thus refined, and it is a sure presage of further happiness. And we may with great comfort pray for the blessing of God upon those houses that are *habitations of justice,* those cities and countries that are *mountains of holiness.* There the Lord will undoubtedly *command the blessing.* 2. There shall be great plenty of all good things among them (*v.* 24, 25): *There shall dwell in Judah itself,* even in it, though it has now long lain waste, both husbandmen and shepherds, the two ancient and honourable employments of Cain and Abel, Gen. iv. 2. It is comfortable dwelling in a *habitation of justice* and a *mountain of holiness.* "And the husbandmen and shepherds shall eat of the fruit of their labours; for I have *satiated the weary and sorrowful soul;*" that is, those that came weary from their journey, and have been long sorrowful in their captivity, shall now enjoy great plenty. This is applicable to the spiritual blessings God has in store for all true penitents, for all that are just and holy; they shall be abundantly satisfied with divine graces and comforts. In the love and favour of God the weary soul shall find rest and the sorrowful soul joy.

V. The prophet tells us what pleasure the discovery of this brought to his mind, *v.* 26. The foresights God had given him sometimes of the calamities of Judah and Jerusalem were exceedingly painful to him (as *ch.* iv. 19), but these views were pleasing ones, though at a distance. "*Upon this I awaked,* overcome with joy, which burst the fetters of sleep; and I reflected upon my dream, and it was such as had made *my sleep sweet to me;* I was refreshed, as men are with quiet sleep." Those may sleep sweetly that lie down and rise up in the favour of God and in communion with him. Nor is any prospect in this world more pleasing to good men, and good ministers, than that of the flourishing state of the church of God. What can we see with more satisfaction than *the good of Jerusalem, all the days of our life, and peace upon Israel?*

27 Behold, the days come, saith the LORD, that I will sow the house of Israel and the house of Judah with the seed of man, and with the seed of beast. 28 And it shall come to pass, *that* like as I have watched over them, to pluck up, and to break down, and to throw down, and to destroy, and to afflict; so will I watch over them, to build, and to plant, saith the LORD. 29 In those days they shall say no more, The fathers have eaten a sour grape, and the children's teeth are set on edge. 30 But every one shall die for his own iniquity: every man that eateth the sour grape, his teeth shall be set on edge. 31 Behold, the days come, saith the LORD, that I will make a new covenant with the house of Israel, and with the house of Judah: 32 Not according to the covenant that I made with their fathers in the day *that* I took them

by the hand to bring them out of the land of Egypt; which my covenant they brake, although I was a husband unto them, saith the LORD: 33 But this *shall be* the covenant that I will make with the house of Israel; After those days, saith the LORD, I will put my law in their inward parts, and write it in their hearts; and will be their God, and they shall be my people. 34 And they shall teach no more every man his neighbour, and every man his brother, saying, Know the LORD: for they shall all know me, from the least of them unto the greatest of them, saith the LORD: for I will forgive their iniquity, and I will remember their sin no more.

The prophet, having found his sleep sweet, made so by the revelations of divine grace, sets himself to sleep again, in hopes of further discoveries, and is not disappointed; for it is here further promised,

I. That the people of God shall become both numerous and prosperous. Israel and Judah shall be replenished both with men and cattle, as if they were sown with the seed of both, *v.* 27. They shall increase and multiply like a field sown with corn; and this is the product of God's blessing (*v.* 23), for whom God blessed, to them he said, *Be fruitful.* This should be a type of the wonderful increase of the gospel-church. God will build them, and plant them, *v.* 28. He *will watch over them* to do them good; no opportunity shall be lost that may further their prosperity. Every thing for a long time had turned so much against them, and all occurrences did so transpire to ruin them, that it seemed as if God had *watched over them to pluck up and to throw down;* but now every thing that falls out shall happily fall in to strengthen and advance their interests. God will be as ready to comfort those that repent of their sins, and are humbled for them, as he is to punish those that continue in love with their sins, and are hardened in them.

II. That they shall be reckoned with no further for the sins of their fathers (*v.* 29, 30): *They shall say no more* (they shall have no more occasion to say) that *God visits the iniquity of the parents upon the children,* which God had done in the captivity, for the sins of their ancestors came into the account against them, particularly those of Manasseh: this they had complained of as a hardship. Other scriptures justify God in this method of proceeding, and our Saviour tells the wicked Jews in his days that they should smart for their fathers' sins, because they persisted in them, Matt. xxiii. 35, 36. But it is here promised that this severe dispensation with them should now be brought to an end, that God would proceed no further in his controversy with them for their fathers' sins, but remember for them his covenant with their fathers and do them good according to that covenant: *They shall no more* complain, as they have done, that *the fathers have eaten sour grapes and the children's teeth are set on edge* (which speaks something of an absurdity, and is an invidious reflection upon God's proceedings), but *every one shall die for his own iniquity* still; though God will cease to punish them in their national capacity, yet he will still reckon with particular persons that provoke him. Note, Public salvations will give no impunity, no security, to private sinners: still every man that *eats the sour grapes* shall have his *teeth set on edge.* Note, Those that *eat* forbidden fruit, how tempting soever it looks, will find it a *sour grape,* and it will *set their teeth on edge;* sooner or later they will feel from it and reflect upon it with bitterness. There is as direct a tendency in sin to make a man uneasy as there is in sour grapes to set the teeth on edge.

III. That God will renew his covenant with them, so that all these blessings they shall have, not by providence only, but by promise, and thereby they shall be both sweetened and secured. But this covenant refers to gospel times, the latter days that *shall come;* for of gospel grace the apostle understands it (Heb. viii. 8, 9, &c.), where this whole passage is quoted as a summary of the covenant of grace made with believers in Jesus Christ. Observe, 1. Who the persons are with whom this covenant is made— *with the house of Israel and Judah,* with the gospel church, *the Israel of God* on which *peace shall be* (Gal. vi. 16), with the spiritual seed of believing Abraham and praying Jacob. Judah and Israel had been two separate kingdoms, but were united after their return, in the joint favours God bestowed upon them; so Jews and Gentiles were in the gospel church and covenant. 2. What is the nature of this covenant in general: it is a *new covenant* and *not according to the covenant made with them when they came out of Egypt;* not as if that made with them at Mount Sinai were a covenant of nature and innocency, such as was made with Adam in the day he was created; no, that was, for substance, a covenant of grace, but it was a dark dispensation of that covenant in comparison with this in gospel times. Sinners were saved by that covenant upon their repentance, and faith in a Messiah to come, whose blood, confirming that covenant, was typified by that of the legal sacrifices, Exod. xxiv. 7, 8. Yet this may upon many accounts be called new, in comparison with that; the ordinances and promises are more spiritual and heavenly, and the discoveries much more clear. That covenant God made with them when he *took them by* the hand, as if they had been blind, or lame, or weak, *to lead them out of the land of Egypt, which covenant they broke.* Observe, It was God that made this covenant, but it was the people that broke it; for our salvation is of God, but our sin and ruin are of ourselves. It was an aggravation of their breach of it that God *was a husband to them,* that he had espoused them to himself; it was a marriage-covenant that was between him and them, which they broke by idolatry, that spiritual adultery. It is a great aggravation of our treacherous departures from God that he has been a husband to us, a loving, tender, careful husband, faithful to us, and yet we false to him. 3. What are the particular articles of his covenant. They all contain spiritual blessings; not, "I will give them the land of Canaan and a numerous issue," but, "I will give them pardon, and peace, and grace, good heads and good hearts." He promises, (1.) That he will incline them to their duty: *I will put my law in their inward part and write it in their heart;* not, I will give them a new law (as Mr. Gataker well observes), for Christ *came not to destroy the law, but to fulfil it;* but the law shall be written in their hearts by the finger of the Spirit as formerly it was written in the tables of stone. God writes his law in the hearts of all believers, makes it ready and familiar to them, at hand when they have occasion to use it, as that which is *written in the heart,* Prov. iii. 3. He makes them in care to observe it, for that which we are solicitous about is said to lie near our hearts. He works in them a disposition to obedience, a conformity of thought and affection to the rules of the divine law, as that of the copy to the original. This is here promised, and ought to be prayed for, that our duty may be done conscientiously and with delight. (2.) That he will take them into relation to himself: *I will be their God,* a God all-sufficient to them, *and they shall be my people,* a loyal obedient people to me. God's being to us a God is the summary of all happiness; heaven itself is no more, Heb. xi. 16; Rev. xxi. 3. Our being to him a people may be taken either as the condition on our part (those and those only shall have God to be to them a God that are truly willing to engage themselves to be to him a people) or as a further branch of the promise that God will by his grace make us his people, a *willing people, in the day of his power;* and, whoever are his people, it is his grace that makes them so. (3.) That there shall be an abundance of the knowledge of God among all sorts of people, and this will have an influence upon all good: for those that rightly know God's name will seek him, and serve him, and put their trust in him (v. 34): *All shall know me;* all shall be welcome to the knowledge of God and shall have the means of that knowledge; *his ways shall be known upon earth,* whereas, for many ages, *in Judah only was*

God known. Many more shall know God than did in the Old-Testament times, which among the Gentiles were times of ignorance, the true God being to them an unknown God. The things of God shall in gospel times be made more plain and intelligible, and level to the capacities of the meanest, than they were while Moses had a *veil upon his face.* There shall be such a general knowledge of God that there shall not be so much need as had formerly been of teaching. Some take it as a hyperbolical expression (and the dulness of the Jews needed such expressions to awaken them), designed only to show that the knowledge of God in gospel times should vastly exceed that knowledge of him which they had under the law. Or perhaps it intimates that in gospel times there shall be such great plenty of public preaching, statedly and constantly, by men authorized and appointed to *preach the word in season and out of season,* much beyond what was under the law, that there shall be less need than there was then of fraternal teaching, by a neighbour and a brother. The priests preached but now and then, and in the temple, and to a few in comparison; but now all shall or may know God by frequenting the assemblies of Christians, wherein, through all parts of the church, the good knowledge of God shall be taught. Some give this sense of it (Mr. Gataker mentions it), That many shall have such clearness of understanding in the things of God that they may seem rather to have been taught by some immediate irradiation than by any means of instruction. In short, the things of God shall by the gospel of Christ be brought to a clearer light than ever (2 Tim. i. 10), and the people of God shall by the grace of Christ be brought to a clearer sight of those things than ever, Eph. i. 17, 18. (4.) That, in order to all these blessings, sin shall be pardoned. This is made the reason of all the rest: *For I will forgive their iniquity,* will not impute that to them, nor deal with them according to the desert of that, *will forgive* and forget: *I will remember their sin no more.* It is sin that keeps good things from us, that stops the current of God's favours; let sin be taken away by pardoning mercy, and the obstruction is removed, and divine grace runs down like a river, like a mighty stream.

35 Thus saith the LORD, which giveth the sun for a light by day, *and* the ordinances of the moon and of the stars for a light by night, which divideth the sea when the waves thereof roar; The LORD of hosts *is* his name: 36 If those ordinances depart from before me, saith the LORD, *then* the seed of Israel also shall cease from being a nation before me for ever. 37 Thus

saith the LORD; If heaven above can be measured, and the foundations of the earth searched out beneath, I will also cast off all the seed of Israel for all that they have done, saith the LORD. 38 Behold, the days come, saith the LORD, that the city shall be built to the LORD from the tower of Hananeel unto the gate of the corner. 39 And the measuring-line shall yet go forth over against it upon the hill Gareb, and shall compass about to Goath. 40 And the whole valley of the dead bodies, and of the ashes, and all the fields unto the brook of Kidron, unto the corner of the horse-gate toward the east, *shall be* holy unto the LORD; it shall not be plucked up, nor thrown down any more for ever.

Glorious things have been spoken in the foregoing verses concerning the gospel church, which that epocha of the Jewish church that was to commence at the return from captivity would at length terminate in, and which all those promises were to have their full accomplishment in. But may we depend upon these promises? Yes, we have here a ratification of them, and the utmost assurance imaginable given of the perpetuity of the blessings contained in them. The great thing here secured to us is that while the world stands God will have a church in it, which, though sometimes it may be brought very low, shall yet be raised again, and its interests re-established; it is *built upon a rock, and the gates of hell shall not prevail against it.* Now here are two things offered for the confirmation of our faith in this matter—the building of the world and the rebuilding of Jerusalem.

I. The building of the world, and the firmness and lastingness of that building, are evidences of the power and faithfulness of that God who has undertaken the establishment of his church. *He that built all things* at first *is* God (Heb. iii. 4), and the same is he that makes all things now. The constancy of the glories of the kingdom of nature may encourage us to depend upon the divine promise for the continuance of the glories of the kingdom of grace, for *this is as the waters of Noah,* Isa. liv. 9. Let us observe here,

1. The glories of the kingdom of nature, and infer thence how happy those are that have this God, the God of nature, to be their God for ever and ever. Take notice, (1.) Of the steady and regular motion of the heavenly bodies, which God is the first mover and supreme director of: *He gives the sun for a light by day* (v. 35), not only made it at first to be so, but still gives it to be so; for the light and heat, and all the

influences of the sun, continually depend upon its great Creator. He gives *the ordinances of the moon and stars for a light by night;* their motions are called *ordinances* both because they are regular and by rule and because they are determined and under rule. See Job xxxviii. 31—33. (2.) Take notice of the government of the sea, and the check that is given to its proud billows: *The Lord of hosts divides the sea,* or (as some read it) *settles the sea, when the waves thereof roar (divide et impera—divide and rule);* when it is most tossed God keeps it within compass (Jer. v. 22), and soon quiets it and makes it calm again. The power of God is to be magnified by us, not only in maintaining the regular motions of the heavens, but in controlling the irregular motions of the seas. (3.) Take notice of the vastness of the heavens and the unmeasurable extent of the firmament; he must needs be a great God who manages such a great world as this is; the *heavens above cannot be measured (v. 37),* and yet God fills them. (4.) Take notice of the mysteriousness even of that part of the creation in which our lot is cast and which we are most conversant with. *The foundations of the earth cannot be searched out beneath,* for the Creator *hangs the earth upon nothing* (Job xxvi. 7), and we *know not how the foundations thereof are fastened,* Job xxxviii. 6. (5.) Take notice of the immovable stedfastness of all these (v. 36): *These ordinances cannot depart from before God;* he. has all the hosts of heaven and earth continually under his eye and all the motions of both; he has established them, and they abide, *abide according to his ordinance, for all are his servants,* Ps. cxix. 90, 91. The heavens are often clouded, and the sun and moon often eclipsed, the earth may quake and the sea be tossed, but they all keep their place, are moved, but not removed. Herein we must acknowledge the power, goodness, and faithfulness of the Creator.

2. The securities of the kingdom of grace inferred hence : we may be confident of this very thing that *the seed of Israel shall not cease from being a nation,* for the spiritual Israel, the gospel church, shall be *a holy nation, a peculiar people,* 1 Pet. ii. 9. When Israel according to the flesh is no longer a nation the *children of the promise are counted for the seed* (Rom. ix. 8) and God *will not cast off all the seed of Israel,* no, not *for all that they have done,* though they have done very wickedly, *v.* 37. He justly might cast them off, but he will not. Though he cast them out from their land, and cast them down for a time, yet he will not cast them off. Some of them he casts off, but not all; to this the apostle seems to refer (Rom. xi. 1), *Hath God cast away his people ? God forbid* that we should think so ! For (v. 5) *at this time there is a remnant,* enough to save the credit of the promise that God *will not cast off all the seed of Israel,* though

608

many among them throw away themselves by unbelief. Now we may be assisted in the belief of this by considering, (1.) That the God that has undertaken the preservation of the church is a God of almighty power, who *upholds all things by his* almighty *word. Our help stands in his name who made heaven and earth,* and therefore can do any thing. (2.) That God would not take all this care of the world but that he designs to have some glory to himself out of it ; and how shall he have it but by securing to himself a church in it, a people that *shall be to him for a name and a praise ?* (3.) That if the order of the creation therefore continues firm because it was well-fixed at first, and is not altered because it needs no alteration, the method of grace shall for the same reason continue invariable, as it was at first well settled. (4.) That he who has promised to preserve a church for himself has approved himself faithful to the word which he has spoken concerning the stability of the world. He that is true to his covenant with Noah and his sons, because he established it for an *everlasting covenant* (Gen. ix. 9, 16), will not, we may be sure, be false to his covenant with Abraham and his seed, his spiritual seed, for that also is an *everlasting covenant.* Even that which they have done amiss, though they have done much, shall not prevail to defeat the gracious intentions of the covenant. See Ps. lxxxix. 30, &c.

II. The rebuilding of Jerusalem which was now in ruins, and the enlargement and establishment of that, shall be an earnest of these great things that God will do for the gospel church, the *heavenly Jerusalem, v.* 38—40. *The days will come,* though they may be long in coming, when, 1. Jerusalem shall be entirely built again, as large as ever it was; the dimensions are here exactly described by the places through which the circumference passed, and no doubt the wall which Nehemiah built, and which, the more punctually to fulfil the prophecy, began about the *tower of Hananeel,* here mentioned (Neh. iii. 1), enclosed as much ground as is here intended, though we cannot certainly determine the places here called *the gate of the corner, the hill Gareb,* &c. 2. When built it shall be consecrated to God and to his service. It *shall be built to the Lord (v.* 38), and even the suburbs and fields adjacent *shall be holy unto the Lord.* It shall not be polluted with idols as formerly, but God shall be praised and honoured there; the whole city shall be as it were one temple, one holy place, as the new Jerusalem is, which *therefore* has no temple, because it is all temple. 3. Being thus built by virtue of the promise of God, and then devoted to the praise of God, *it shall not be plucked up, nor thrown down, any more for ever;* that is, it shall continue very long, the time of the new city from the return to its last destruction being fully as long as that of the old from

David to the captivity. But this promise was to have its full accomplishment in the gospel church, which, as it is the spiritual Israel, and therefore God will not cast it off, so it is the holy city, and therefore all the powers of men *shall not pluck it up, nor throw it down* It may lie waste for a time, as Jerusalem did, but shall recover itself, shall weather the storm and gain its point, *and the gates of hell shall not prevail against it.*

CHAP. XXXII.

In this chapter we have, I. Jeremiah imprisoned for foretelling the destruction of Jerusalem and the captivity of king Zedekiah, ver. 1—5. II. We have him buying land, by divine appointment, as an assurance that in due time a happy end should be put to the present troubles, ver. 6—15. III. We have his prayer, which he offered up to God upon that occasion, ver. 16—25. IV. We have a message which God thereupon entrusted him to deliver to the people. 1. He must foretel the utter destruction of Judah and Jerusalem for their sins, ver. 26—35. But, 2. At the same time he must assure them that, though the destruction was total, it should not be final, but that at length their posterity should recover the peaceable possession of their own land, ver. 36—44. The predictions of this chapter, both threatenings and promises, are much the same with what we have already met with again and again, but here are some circumstances that are very particular and remarkable.

THE word that came to Jeremiah from the LORD in the tenth year of Zedekiah king of Judah, which *was* the eighteenth year of Nebuchadrezzar. 2 For then the king of Babylon's army besieged Jerusalem: and Jeremiah the prophet was shut up in the court of the prison, which *was* in the king of Judah's house. 3 For Zedekiah king of Judah had shut him up, saying, Wherefore dost thou prophesy, and say, Thus saith the LORD, Behold, I will give this city into the hand of the king of Babylon, and he shall take it; 4 And Zedekiah king of Judah shall not escape out of the hand of the Chaldeans, but shall surely be delivered into the hand of the king of Babylon, and shall speak with him mouth to mouth, and his eyes shall behold his eyes; 5 And he shall lead Zedekiah to Babylon, and there shall he be until I visit him, saith the LORD: though ye fight with the Chaldeans, ye shall not prosper. 6 And Jeremiah said, The word of the LORD came unto me, saying, 7 Behold, Hanameel the son of Shallum thine uncle shall come unto thee, saying, Buy thee my field that *is* in Anathoth: for the right of redemption *is* thine to buy *it.* 8 So Hanameel mine uncle's son came to me in the court of the prison according to the word of the LORD, and said unto me, Buy my field, I pray thee, that *is* in Anathoth, which *is* in

the country of Benjamin: for the right of inheritance *is* thine, and the redemption *is* thine; buy *it* for thyself. Then I knew that this *was* the word of the LORD. 9 And I bought the field of Hanameel my uncle's son, that *was* in Anathoth, and weighed him the money, *even* seventeen shekels of silver. 10 And I subscribed the evidence, and sealed *it,* and took witnesses, and weighed *him* the money in the balances. 11 So I took the evidence of the purchase, *both* that which was sealed *according* to the law and custom, and that which was open: 12 And I gave the evidence of the purchase unto Baruch the son of Neriah, the son of Maaseiah, in the sight of Hanameel mine uncle's *son,* and in the presence of the witnesses that subscribed the book of the purchase, before all the Jews that sat in the court of the prison. 13 And I charged Baruch before them, saying, 14 Thus saith the LORD of hosts, the God of Israel; Take these evidences, this evidence of the purchase, both which is sealed, and this evidence which is open; and put them in an earthen vessel, that they may continue many days. 15 For thus saith the LORD of hosts, the God of Israel; Houses and fields and vineyards shall be possessed again in this land.

It appears by the date of this chapter that we are now coming very nigh to that fatal year which completed the desolations of Judah and Jerusalem by the Chaldeans. God's judgments came gradually upon them, but, they not meeting him by repentance in the way of his judgments, he proceeded in his controversy till all was laid waste, which was in the eleventh year of Zedekiah; now what is here recorded happened in the tenth. The king of Babylon's army had now invested Jerusalem and was carrying on the siege with vigour, not doubting but in a little time to make themselves masters of it, while the besieged had taken up a desperate resolution not to surrender, but to hold out to the last extremity. Now,

I. Jeremiah prophesies that both the city and the court shall fall into the hands of the king of Babylon. He tells them expressly that the besiegers shall take the city as a prize, for God, whose city it was in a peculiar manner, will give it into their hands and put it out of his protection (*v.* 3),—that, though Zedekiah attempt to make his escape, he shall be overtaken, and shall be delivered a prisoner into the hands of Nebuchadnezzar, shall be brought into his presence, to his great confusion and terror, he having made himself so obnoxious by breaking his faith with him; he shall hear the king of Babylon pronounce his doom, and see with what fury and indignation he will look upon him *(His eyes shall behold his eyes, v.* 4),—that Zedekiah shall be carried to Babylon, and continue a miserable captive there, *until God visit him*, that is, till God put an end to his life by a natural death, as Nebuchadnezzar had long before put an end to his days by putting out his eyes. Note, Those that live in misery may be truly said to be visited in mercy when God by death takes them home to himself. And, *lastly*, he foretels that all their attempts to force the besiegers from their trenches shall be ineffectual: *Though you fight with the Chaldeans, you shall not prosper;* how should they, when God did not fight for them? *v.* 5. See *ch.* xxxiv. 2, 3.

II. For prophesying thus he is imprisoned, not in the common gaol, but in the more creditable prison that was within the verge of the palace, *in the king of Judah's house*, and there not closely confined, but in *custodia libera—in the court of the prison*, where he might have good company, good air, and good intelligence brought him, and would be sheltered from the abuses of the mob; but, however, it was a prison, and Zedekiah shut him up in it for prophesying as he did, *v.* 2, 3. So far was he from *humbling himself before Jeremiah*, as he ought to have done (2 Chron. xxxvi. 12), that he *hardened himself* against him. Though he had formerly so far owned him to be a prophet as to desire him to *enquire of the Lord for them* (*ch.* xxi. 2), yet now he chides him for prophesying (*v.* 3), and shuts him up in prison, perhaps not with design to punish him any further, but only to restrain him from prophesying any further, which was crime enough. Silencing God's prophets, though it is not so bad as mocking and killing them, is yet a great affront to the God of heaven. See how wretchedly the hearts of sinners are hardened by the deceitfulness of sin. Persecution was one of the sins for which God was now contending with them, and yet Zedekiah persists in it even now that he was in the depth of distress. No providences, no afflictions, will of themselves part between men and their sins, unless the grace of God work with them. Nay, some are made worse by those very judgments that should make them better.

III. Being in prison, he purchases from a near relation of his a piece of ground that lay in Anathoth, *v.* 6, 7, &c.

1. One would not have expected, (1.) That a prophet should concern himself so far in the business of this world; but why not? Though ministers must not entangle themselves, yet they may concern themselves in the affairs of

this life. (2.) That one who had neither wife nor children should buy land. We find (*ch.* xvi. 2) that he had no family of his own; yet he may purchase for his own use while he lives, and leave it to the children of his relations when he dies. (3.) One would little have thought that a prisoner should be a purchaser; how should he get money beforehand to buy land with? It is probable that he lived frugally, and saved something out of what belonged to him as a priest, which is no blemish at all to his character; but we have no reason to think that the people were kind, or that his being beforehand was owing to their generosity. Nay, (4.) It was most strange of all that he should buy a *piece of land* when he himself knew that the whole land was now to be laid waste and fall into the hands of the Chaldeans, and then what good would this do him? But it was the will of God that he should buy it, and he submitted, though the money seemed to be thrown away. His kinsman came to offer it to him; it was not of his own seeking; he coveted not to lay house to house and field to field, but Providence brought it to him, and it was probably a good bargain; besides, the *right of redemption* belonged to him (*v.* 8), and if he refused he would not do the kinsman's part. It is true he might lawfully refuse, but, being a prophet, in a thing of this nature he must do that which would be for the honour of his profession. *It became him to fulfil all righteousness.* It was land that lay within the suburbs of a priests' city, and, if he should refuse it, there was danger lest, in these times of disorder, it might be sold to one of another tribe, which was contrary to the law, to prevent which it was convenient for him to buy it. It would likewise be a kindness to his kinsman, who probably was at this time in great want of money. Jeremiah had but a little, but what he had he was willing to lay out in such a manner as might tend most to the honour of God and the good of his friends and country, which he preferred before his own private interests.

2. Two things may be observed concerning this purchase:—

(1.) How fairly the bargain was made. When Jeremiah knew by Hanameel's coming to him, as God had foretold he would, that *it was the word of the Lord*, that it was his mind that he should make this purchase, he made no more difficulty of it, but *bought the field*. And, [1.] He was very honest and exact in paying the money. He *weighed him the money*, did not press him to take it upon his report, though he was his near kinsman, but weighed it to him, current money. It was *seventeen shekels of silver*, amounting to about forty shillings of our money. The land was probably but a little field and of small yearly value, when the purchase was so low: besides, the *right of inheritance* was in Jeremiah, so that he had only to buy out his kinsman's life, the reversion being his already. Some think this was only the earnest of a greater sum; but we shall not wonder at the smallness of the price if we consider what scarcity there was of money at this time and how little lands were counted upon. [2.] He was very prudent and discreet in preserving the writings. They were subscribed *before witnesses.* One copy was *sealed up,* the other was *open.* One was the original, the other the counterpart; or perhaps that which was *sealed up* was for his own private use, the other that was *open* was to be laid up in the public register of conveyances, for any person concerned to consult. Due care and caution in things of this nature might prevent a great deal of injustice and contention. The deeds of purchase were lodged in the hands of Baruch, before witnesses, and he was ordered to lay them up in an *earthen vessel* (an emblem of the nature of all the securities this world can pretend to give us, brittle things and soon broken), that they might *continue many days,* for the use of Jeremiah's heirs, after the return out of captivity; for they might then have the benefit of this purchase. Purchasing reversions may be a kindness to those that come after us, and a good man thus *lays up an inheritance for his children's children.*

(2.) What was the design of having this bargain made. It was to signify that though Jerusalem was now besieged, and the whole country was likely to be laid waste, yet the time should come when *houses, and fields, and vineyards should be again possessed in this land, v.* 15. As God appointed Jeremiah to confirm his predictions of the approaching destruction of Jerusalem by his own practice in living unmarried, so he now appointed him to confirm his predictions of the future restoration of Jerusalem by his own practice in purchasing this field. Note, It concerns ministers to make it to appear in their whole conversation that they do themselves believe that which they preach to others; and that they may do so, and impress it the more deeply upon their hearers, they must many a time deny themselves, as Jeremiah did in both these instances. God having promised that this land should again come into the possession of his people, Jeremiah will, on behalf of his heirs, put in for a share. Note, It is good to manage even our worldly affairs in faith, and to do common business with an eye to the providence and promise of God. Lucius Florus relates it as a great instance of the bravery of the Roman citizens that in the time of the second Punic war, when Hannibal besieged Rome and was very near making himself master of it, a field on which part of his army lay, being offered to sale at that time, was immediately purchased, in a firm belief that the Roman valour would raise the siege, *lib.* ii. *cap.* 6. And have not we much more reason to ven-

ture our all upon the word of God, and to embark in Zion's interests, which will undoubtedly be the prevailing interests at last? *Non si male nunc et olim sic erit—Though now we suffer, we shall not suffer always.*

16 Now when I had delivered the evidence of the purchase unto Baruch the son of Neriah, I prayed unto the LORD, saying, 17 Ah, Lord GOD! behold, thou hast made the heaven and the earth by thy great power and stretched out arm, *and* there is nothing too hard for thee: 18 Thou showest lovingkindness unto thousands, and recompensest the iniquity of the fathers into the bosom of their children after them: the Great, the Mighty God, the LORD of hosts, *is* his name, 19 Great in counsel, and mighty in work: for thine eyes *are* open upon all the ways of the sons of men: to give every one according to his ways, and according to the fruit of his doings: 20 Which hast set signs and wonders in the land of Egypt, *even* unto this day, and in Israel, and among *other* men; and hast made thee a name, as at this day; 21 And hast brought forth thy people Israel out of the land of Egypt with signs, and with wonders, and with a strong hand, and with a stretched out arm, and with great terror; 22 And hast given them this land, which thou didst sware to their fathers to give them, a land flowing with milk and honey; 23 And they came in, and possessed it; but they obeyed not thy voice, neither walked in thy law; they have done nothing of all that thou commandedst them to do: therefore thou hast caused all this evil to come upon them: 24 Behold the mounts, they are come unto the city to take it; and the city is given into the hand of the Chaldeans, that fight against it, because of the sword, and of the famine, and of the pestilence: and what thou hast spoken is come to pass; and, behold, thou seest *it.* 25 And thou hast said unto me, O Lord GOD, Buy thee the field for money, and take witnesses; for the city is given into the hand of the Chaldeans.

We have here Jeremiah's prayer to God upon occasion of the discoveries God had made to him of his purposes concerning this nation, to pull it down, and in process of time to build it up again, which puzzled the prophet himself, who, though he delivered his messages faithfully, yet, in reflecting upon them, was greatly at a loss within himself how to reconcile them; in that perplexity he poured out his soul before God in prayer, and so gave himself ease. That which disturbed him was not the bad bargain he seemed to have made for himself in purchasing a field that he was likely to have no good of, but the case of his people, for whom he was still a kind and faithful intercessor, and he was willing to hope that, if God had so much mercy in store for them hereafter as he had promised, he would not proceed with so much severity against them now as he had threatened. Before Jeremiah went to prayer he delivered the deeds that concerned his new purchase to Baruch, which may intimate to us that when we are going to worship God we should get our minds as clear as may be from the cares and incumbrances of this world. Jeremiah was in prison, in distress, in the dark about the meaning of God's providences, and then he prays. Note, Prayer is a salve for every sore. Whatever is a burden to us, we may by prayer cast it upon the Lord and then be easy.

In this prayer, or meditation,

I. Jeremiah adores God and his infinite perfections, and gives him the glory due to his name as the Creator, upholder, and benefactor, of the whole creation, thereby owning his irresistible power, that he can do what he will, and his incontestable sovereignty, that he may do what he will, *v.* 17—19. Note, When at any time we are perplexed about the particular methods and dispensations of Providence it is good for us to have recourse to our first principles, and to satisfy ourselves with the general doctrines of God's wisdom, power, and goodness. Let us consider, as Jeremiah does here, 1. That God is the fountain of all being, power, life, motion, and perfection: He *made the heaven and the earth with his outstretched arm;* and therefore who can control him? Who dares contend with him? 2. That with him nothing is impossible, no difficulty insuperable: *Nothing is too hard for thee.* When human skill and power are quite nonplussed, *with God are strength and wisdom* sufficient to master all the opposition. 3. That he is a God of boundless bottomless mercy; mercy is his darling attribute; it is his goodness that is his glory: "Thou not only art kind, but thou *showest lovingkindness,* not to a few, to here and there one, but *to thousands,* thousands upon thousands of persons, thousands of generations." 4. That he is a God of impartial and inflexible justice. His reprieves are not pardons, but if in mercy he spares the parents, that they may be led to repentance, yet such a hatred

612

has he to sin, and such a displeasure against sinners, that he *recompenses their iniquity into the bosom of their children,* and yet does them no wrong; so hateful is the unrighteousness of man, and so jealous of its own honour is the righteousness of God. 5. That he is a God of universal dominion and command: He is *the great* God, for he is *the mighty God,* and might among men makes them great. He is *the Lord of hosts,* of all hosts, that *is his name,* and he answers to his name, for all the hosts of heaven and earth, of men and angels, are at his beck. 6. That he contrives every thing for the best, and effects every thing as he contrived it: He is *great in counsel,* so vast are the reaches and so deep are the designs of his wisdom; and he is *mighty in doing,* according to the counsel of his will. Now such a God as this is not to be quarrelled with. His service is to be constantly adhered to and all his disposals cheerfully acquiesced in.

II. He acknowledges the universal cognizance God takes of all the actions of the children of men and the unerring judgment he passes upon them (*v.* 19): *Thy eyes are open upon all the sons of men,* wherever they are, beholding the evil and the good, and upon all *their ways,* both the course they take and every step they take, not as an unconcerned spectator, but as an observing judge, *to give every one according to his ways and according* to his deserts, which are *the fruit of his doings;* for men shall find God as they are found of him.

III. He recounts the great things God had done for his people Israel formerly. 1. He brought them out of Egypt, that house of bondage, with *signs and wonders,* which remain, if not in the marks of them, yet in the memorials of them, *even unto this day;* for it would never be forgotten, not only *in Israel,* who were reminded of it every year by the ordinance of the passover, but *among other men:* all the neighbouring nations spoke of it, as that which redounded exceedingly to the glory of the God of Israel, and made him *a name as at this day.* This is repeated (*v.* 21), that God *brought them forth,* not only with comforts and joys to them, but with glory to himself, *with signs and wonders* (witness the ten plagues), *with a strong hand,* too strong for the Egyptians themselves, *and with a stretched-out arm,* that reached Pharaoh, proud as he was, *and with great terror* to them and all about them. This seems to refer to Deut. iv. 34. 2. He brought them into Canaan, that good land, that *land flowing with milk and honey.* He *swore to their fathers to give it them,* and, because he would perform his oath, he did give it to the children (*v.* 22) *and they came in and possessed it.* Jeremiah mentions this both as an aggravation of their sin and disobedience and also as a plea with God to work deliverance for them. Note, It is good for us often to reflect upon the great things that God did for his church formerly, especially in the first erecting of it, that work of wonder.

IV. He bewails the rebellions they had been guilty of against God, and the judgments God had brought upon them for these rebellions. It is a sad account he here gives of the ungrateful conduct of that people towards God. He had done every thing that he had promised to do (they had acknowledged it, 1 Kings viii. 56), but they had *done nothing of all that he commanded them to do* (v. 23); they made no conscience of any of *his laws;* they *walked not* in them, paid no respect to any of his calls by his prophets, for they *obeyed not his voice.* And therefore he owns that God was righteous in *causing all this evil to come upon them.* The city is besieged, is attacked *by the sword* without, is weakened and wasted by the *famine* and *pestilence* within, so that it is ready to fall *into the hands of the Chaldeans that fight against it* (v. 24); it is *given into their hands,* v. 25. Now, 1. He compares the present state of Jerusalem with the divine predictions, and finds that what God *has spoken* has *come to pass.* God had given them fair warning of it before; and, if they had regarded this, the ruin would have been prevented; but, if they will not do what God has commanded, they can expect no other than that he should do what he has threatened. 2. He commits the present state of Jerusalem to the divine consideration and compassion (v. 24): *Behold the mounts,* or *ramparts,* or the *engines* which they make use of to batter the city and beat down the wall of it. And again, " *Behold thou seest it,* and takest cognizance of it. Is this the city that thou hast chosen to put thy name there? And shall it be thus abandoned?" He neither complains of God for what he had done nor prescribes to God what he should do, but desires he would behold their case, and is pleased to think that he does behold it. Whatever trouble we are in, upon a personal or public account, we may comfort ourselves with this, that God sees it and sees how to remedy it.

V. He seems desirous to be let further into the meaning of the order God had now given him to purchase his kinsman's field (v. 25): " *Though the city is given into the hand of the Chaldeans,* and no man is likely to enjoy what he has, yet *thou hast said unto me, Buy thou the field.*" As soon as he understood that it was the mind of God he did it, and made no objections, was not disobedient to the heavenly vision; but, when he had done it, he desired better to understand why God had ordered him to do it, because the thing looked strange and unaccountable. Note, Though we are bound to follow God with an implicit obedience, yet we should endeavour that it may be more and more an intelligent obedience. We must never dispute God's statutes and judgments,

but we may and must enquire, *What mean these statutes and judgments?* Deut. vi. 20.

26 Then came the word of the Lord unto Jeremiah, saying, 27 Behold, I *am* the Lord, the God of all flesh : is there any thing too hard for me? 28 Therefore thus saith the Lord ; Behold, I will give this city into the hand of the Chaldeans, and into the hand of Nebuchadrezzar king of Babylon, and he shall take it : 29 And the Chaldeans, that fight against this city, shall come and set fire on this city, and burn it with the houses, upon whose roofs they have offered incense unto Baal, and poured out drink offerings unto other gods, to provoke me to anger. 30 For the children of Israel and the children of Judah have only done evil before me from their youth : for the children of Israel have only provoked me to anger with the work of their hands, saith the Lord. 31 For this city hath been to me *as* a provocation of mine anger and of my fury from the day that they built it even unto this day ; that I should remove it from before my face, 32 Because of all the evil of the children of Israel and of the children of Judah, which they have done to provoke me to anger, they, their kings, their princes, their priests, and their prophets, and the men of Judah, and the inhabitants of Jerusalem. 33 And they have turned unto me the back, and not the face : though I taught them, rising up early and teaching *them,* yet they have not hearkened to receive instruction. 34 But they set their abominations in the house, which is called by my name, to defile it. 35 And they built the high places of Baal, which *are* in the valley of the son of Hinnom, to cause their sons and their daughters to pass through *the fire* unto Molech ; which I commanded them not, neither came it into my mind, that they should do this abomination, to cause Judah to sin. 36 And now therefore thus saith the Lord, the God of Israel, concerning this city, whereof ye say, It shall be delivered into the hand of the king of Babylon by the sword, and by the

famine, and by the pestilence; 37 Behold, I will gather them out of all countries, whither I have driven them in mine anger, and in my fury, and in great wrath; and I will bring them again unto this place, and I will cause them to dwell safely: 38 And they shall be my people, and I will be their God: 39 And I will give them one heart, and one way, that they may fear me for ever, for the good of them, and of their children after them: 40 And I will make an everlasting covenant with them, that I will not turn away from them, to do them good; but I will put my fear in their hearts, that they shall not depart from me. 41 Yea, I will rejoice over them to do them good, and I will plant them in this land assuredly with my whole heart and with my whole soul. 42 For thus saith the LORD; Like as I have brought all this great evil upon this people, so will I bring upon them all the good that I have promised them. 43 And fields shall be bought in this land, whereof ye say, *It is* desolate without man or beast; it is given into the hand of the Chaldeans. 44 Men shall buy fields for money, and subscribe evidences, and seal *them*, and take witnesses in the land of Benjamin, and in the places about Jerusalem, and in the cities of Judah, and in the cities of the mountains, and in the cities of the valley, and in the cities of the south: for I will cause their captivity to return, saith the LORD.

We have here God's answer to Jeremiah's prayer, designed to quiet his mind and make him easy; and it is a full discovery of the purposes of God's wrath against the present generation and the purposes of his grace concerning the future generations. Jeremiah knew not how to *sing both of mercy and judgment*, but God here teaches to sing unto him of both. When we know not how to reconcile one word of God with another we may yet be sure that both are true, both are pure, both shall be made good, and not one iota or tittle of either shall fall to the ground. When Jeremiah was ordered to buy the field in Anathoth he was willing to hope that God was about to revoke the sentence of his wrath and to order the Chaldeans to raise the siege. " No," says God, " the execution of the sentence shall go on; Jeru-

salem shall be laid in ruins." Note, Assurances of future mercy must not be interpreted as securities from present troubles. But, lest Jeremiah should think that his being ordered to buy this field intimated that all the mercy God had in store for his people, after their return, was only that they should have the possession of their own land again, he further informs him that that was but a type and figure of those spiritual blessings which should then be abundantly bestowed upon them, unspeakably more valuable than fields and vineyards; so that in this *word of the Lord*, which came to Jeremiah, we have first as dreadful threatenings and then as precious promises as perhaps any we have in the Old Testament; life and death, good and evil, are here set before us; let us consider and choose wisely.

I. The ruin of Judah and Jerusalem is here pronounced. The decree has gone forth, and shall not be recalled. 1. God here asserts his own sovereignty and power (*v.* 27): *Behold, I am Jehovah*, a self-existent self-sufficient being; *I am that I am; I am the God of all flesh*, that is, of all mankind, here called *flesh* because weak and unable to contend with God (Ps. lvi. 4), and because wicked and corrupt and unapt to comply with God. God is the Creator of all, and makes what use he pleases of all. He that is the God of Israel is the *God of all flesh* and of *the spirits of all flesh*, and, if Israel were cast off, could raise up a people to his name out of some other nation. If he be the *God of all flesh*, he may well ask, *Is any thing too hard for me?* What cannot he do from whom all the powers of men are derived, on whom they depend, and by whom all their actions are directed and governed? Whatever he designs to do, whether in wrath or in mercy, nothing can hinder him nor defeat his designs. 2. He abides by what he had often said of the destruction of Jerusalem by the king of Babylon (*v.* 28): *I will give this city into his hand*, now that he is grasping at it, *and he shall take it* and make a prey of it, *v.* 29. *The Chaldeans shall come and set fire to it*, shall burn it and all the *houses in it*, God's house not excepted, nor the king's neither. 3. He assigns the reason for these severe proceedings against the city that had been so much in his favour. It is sin, it is that and nothing else, that ruins it. (1.) They were impudent and daring in sin. They *offered incense to Baal*, not in corners, as men ashamed or afraid of being discovered, but upon the *tops of their houses* (*v.* 29), in defiance of God's justice. (2.) They designed an affront to God herein. They did it *to provoke me to anger, v.* 29. *They have only provoked me to anger with the works of their hands, v.* 30. They could not promise themselves any pleasure, profit, or honour out of it, but did it on purpose to offend God. And again (*v.* 32), *All the evil which they have done was to provoke me to anger.*

They knew he was a jealous God in the matters of his worship, and there they resolved to try his jealousy and dare him to his face. " Jerusalem has been *to me a provocation of my anger and fury,*" *v.* 31. Their conduct in every thing was provoking. (3.) They began betimes, and had continued all along provoking to God: " They have *done evil before me from their youth,* ever since they were first formed into a people (*v.* 30), witness their murmurings and rebellions in the wilderness." And as for Jerusalem, though it was the *holy city,* it has been *a provocation* to the holy God *from the day that they built it, even to this day, v.* 31. O what reason have we to lament the little honour God has from this world, and the great dishonour that is done him, when even in Judah, where *he is known* and *his name is great,* and in Salem where his *tabernacle is,* there was always that found that was a provocation to him! (4.) All orders and degrees of men contributed to the common guilt, and therefore were justly involved in the common ruin. Not only the *children of Israel,* that had revolted from the temple, but the *children of Judah* too, that still adhered to it—not only the common people, the *men of Judah* and *inhabitants of Jerusalem,* but those that should have reproved and restrained sin in others were themselves ringleaders in it, their *kings* and *princes,* their *priests* and *prophets.* (5.) God had again and again called them to repentance, but they turned a deaf ear to his calls, and rudely turned their back on him that called them, though he was their master, to whom they were bound in duty, and their benefactor, to whom they were bound in gratitude and interest, *v.* 33. " *I taught them* better manners, with as much care as ever any tender parent taught a child, *rising up early, in teaching them,* studying to adapt the teaching to their capacities, taking them betimes, when they might have been most pliable, but all in vain ; they *turned not the face to me,* would not so much as look upon me, nay, they *turned the back upon me,*" an expression of the highest contempt. *As he called them,* like froward children, *so they went from him,* Hos. xi. 2. *They have not hearkened to receive instruction;* they regarded not a word that was said to them, though it was designed for their own good. (6.) There was in their idolatries an impious contempt of God ; for (*v.* 34) *they set their abominations* (their idols, which they knew to be in the highest degree abominable to God) *in the house which is called by my name, to defile it.* They had their idols not only in their high places and groves, but even in God's temple. (7.) They were guilty of the most unnatural cruelty to their own children ; for they *sacrificed them to Moloch, v.* 35. Thus because they *liked not to retain God in their knowledge,* but *changed his glory* into shame, they were justly given up to vile

affections and stripped of natural ones, and their glory was turned into shame. And, (8.) What was the consequence of all this? [1.] They *caused Judah to sin, v.* 35. The whole country was infected with the contagious idolatries and iniquities of Jerusalem. [2.] They brought ruin upon themselves. It was as if they had done it on purpose that God *should remove them from before his face* (v. 31); they would throw themselves out of his favour.

II. The restoration of Judah and Jerusalem is here promised, *v.* 36, &c. God will in judgment remember mercy, and there will a time come, a set time, to favour Zion. Observe, 1. The despair to which this people were now at length brought. When the judgment was threatened at a distance they had no fear ; when it attacked them they had no hope. They said concerning the city (*v.* 36), *It shall be delivered into the hand of the king of Babylon,* not by any cowardice or ill conduct of ours, but by *the sword, famine, and pestilence.* Concerning the country they said, with vexation (*v.* 43), *It is desolate, without man or beast ;* there is no relief, there is no remedy. *It is given into the hand of the Chaldeans.* Note, Deep security commonly ends in deep despair ; whereas those that keep up a holy fear at all times have a good hope to support them in the worst of times. 2. The hope that God gives them of mercy which he had in store for them hereafter. Though their carcases must fall in captivity, yet their children after them shall again see this good land and the goodness of God in it. (1.) They shall be brought up from their captivity and shall come and settle again in this land, *v.* 37. They had been under God's *anger, and fury, and great wrath ;* but now they shall partake of his grace, and love, and great favour. He had dispersed them, and *driven them into all countries.* Those that fled dispersed themselves ; those that fell into the enemies' hands were dispersed by them, in policy, to prevent combinations among them. God's hand was in both. But now God will find them out, and *gather them out of all the countries whither they were driven,* as he promised in the law (Deut. xxx. 3, 4) and the saints had prayed, Ps. cvi. 47 ; Neh. i. 9. He had banished them, but he will *bring them again to this place,* which they could not but have an affection for. For many years past, while they were in their own land, they were continually exposed, and terrified with the alarms of war ; but now *I will cause them to dwell safely.* Being reformed, and having returned to God, neither their own consciences within nor their enemies without shall be a terror to them. He promises (*v.* 41): *I will plant them in this land assuredly ;* not only I will certainly do it, but they shall here enjoy a holy security and repose, and they shall take root here, shall be *planted in stability,* and not again be unfixed and shaken. (2.) God will renew his covenant with them, a covenant of grace, the blessings of which are spiritual, and such as will work good things in them, to qualify them for the great things God intended to do for them. It is called an *everlasting covenant* (*v.* 40), not only because God will be for ever faithful to it, but because the consequences of it will be everlasting. For, doubtless, here the promises look further than to Israel according to the flesh, and are sure to all believers, to every Israelite indeed. Good Christians may apply them to themselves and plead them with God, may claim the benefit of them and take the comfort of them. [1.] God will own them for his, and make over himself to them to be theirs (*v.* 38): *They shall be my people.* He will make them his by working in them all the characters and dispositions of his people, and then he will protect, and guide, and govern them as his people. "And, to make them truly, completely, and eternally happy, *I will be their God.*" They shall serve and worship God as theirs and cleave to him only, and he will approve himself theirs. All he is, all he has, shall be engaged and employed for their good. [2.] God will give them a heart to fear him, *v.* 39. That which he requires of those whom he takes into covenant with him as his people is that they fear him, that they reverence his majesty, dread his wrath, stand in awe of his authority, pay homage to him, and give him the glory due unto his name. Now what God requires of them he here promises to work in them, pursuant to his choice of them as his people. Note, As it is God's prerogative to fashion men's hearts, so it is his promise to his people to fashion theirs aright; and a heart to fear God is indeed a good heart, and well fashioned. It is repeated (*v.* 40): *I will put my fear in their hearts*, that is, work in them gracious principles and dispositions, that shall influence and govern their whole conversation. Teachers may put good things into our heads, but it is God only that can put them into our hearts, that can work in us *both to will and to do*. [3.] He will *give them one heart and one way*. In order to their walking in one way, he will give them one heart: as the heart is, so will the way be, and both shall be one; that is, *First*, They shall be each of them one with themselves. *One heart* is the same with a *new heart*, Ezek. xi. 19. The heart is *then* one when it is fully determined for God and entirely devoted to God. When the eye is single and God's glory alone aimed at, when our hearts are fixed, trusting in God, and we are uniform and universal in our obedience to him, then the heart is one and the way one; and, unless the heart be thus steady, the goings will not be stedfast. From this promise we may take direction and encouragement to pray, with David (Ps. lxxxvi. 11), *Unite my heart to fear thy name;* for God says, *I will give them one heart, that they may fear me. Secondly,* They shall be all of them one with each

other. All good Christians shall be incorporated into one body; Jews and Gentiles shall become *one sheep-fold;* and they shall all, as far as they are sanctified, have a disposition to love one another, the gospel they profess having in it the strongest inducements to mutual love, and the Spirit that dwells in them being the Spirit of love. Though they may have different apprehensions about minor things, they shall be all one in the great things of God, being renewed after the same image. Though they may have many paths, they have but *one way*, that of serious godliness. [4.] He will effectually provide for their perseverance in grace and the perpetuating of the covenant between himself and them. They would have been happy when they were first planted in Canaan, like Adam in paradise, if they had not departed from God. And therefore, now that they are restored to their happiness, they shall be confirmed in it by the preventing of their departures from God, and this will complete their bliss. *First,* God will never leave nor forsake them: *I will not turn away from them to do them good.* Earthly princes are fickle, and their greatest favourites have fallen under their frowns; but God's *mercy endures for ever. Whom he loves he loves to the end.* God may seem to turn from this people (Isa. liv. 8), but even then he does not turn from doing and designing them good. *Secondly,* They shall never leave nor forsake him; that is the thing we are in danger of. We have no reason to distrust God's fidelity and constancy, but our own; and therefore it is here promised that God will *give them a heart to fear him for ever*, all days, to be in his fear every day and all the day long (Prov. xxiii. 17), and to continue so to the end of their days. He will put such a principle into their hearts that they *shall not depart from him.* Even those who have given up their names to God, if they be left to themselves, will depart from him; but the fear of God ruling in the heart, will prevent their departure. That, and nothing else, will do it. If we continue close and faithful to God, it is owing purely to his almighty grace and not to any strength or resolution of our own. [5.] He will entail a blessing upon their seed, will give them grace to fear him, *for the good of them and of their children after them.* As their departures from God had been to the prejudice of their children, so their adherence to God should be to the advantage of their children. We cannot better consult the good of posterity than by setting up, and keeping up, the fear and worship of God in our families. [6.] He will take a pleasure in their prosperity and will do every thing to advance it (*v.* 41): *I will rejoice over them to do them good.* God will certainly do them good because he rejoices over them. They are dear to him; he makes his boast of them, and therefore will not only do them good, but will delight in doing them good. When he punishes them it is with reluctance. *How shall I give thee up, Ephraim?* But, when he restores them, it is with satisfaction; he rejoices in doing them good. We ought therefore to serve him with pleasure and to rejoice in all opportunities of serving him. He is himself a cheerful giver, and therefore loves a cheerful servant. *I will plant them* (says God) *with my whole heart and with my whole soul.* He will be intent upon it, and take delight in it; he will make it the business of his providence to settle them again in Canaan, and the various dispensations of providence shall concur to it. All things appear at last so to have been working for the good of the church that it will be said, The governor of the world is entirely taken up with the care of his church. [7.] These promises shall as surely be performed as the foregoing threatenings were; and the accomplishment of those, notwithstanding the security of the people, might confirm their expectation of the performance of these, notwithstanding their present despair (*v.* 42:) *As I have brought all this great evil upon them,* pursuant to the threatenings, and for the glory of divine justice, *so I will bring upon them all this good,* pursuant to the promise, and for the glory of divine mercy. He that is faithful to his threatenings will much more be so to his promises; and he will comfort his people *according to the time that he has afflicted them.* The churches shall have rest after the days of adversity. [8.] As an earnest of all this, houses and lands shall again fetch a good price in Judah and Jerusalem, and, though now they are a drug, there shall again be a sufficient number of purchasers (*v.* 43, 44): *Fields shall be bought in this land,* and people will covet to have lands here rather than any where else. Lands, wherever they lie, will go off, not only in *the places about Jerusalem,* but *in the cities of Judah* and of Israel too, whether they lie *on mountains,* or in valleys, or *in the south,* in all parts of the country, *men shall buy fields, and subscribe evidences.* Trade shall revive, for they shall have money enough to buy land with. Husbandry shall revive, for those that have money shall covet to lay it out upon lands. Laws shall again have their due course, for they shall *subscribe evidences and seal them.* This is mentioned to reconcile Jeremiah to his new purchase. Though he had bought a piece of ground and could not go to see it, yet he must believe that this was the pledge of many a purchase, and those but faint resemblances of the purchased possessions in the heavenly Canaan, reserved for all those who have God's fear in their hearts and do not depart from him.

CHAP. XXXIII.

The scope of this chapter is much the same with that of the foregoing chapter—to confirm the promise of the restoration of the Jews, notwithstanding the present desolations of their country and dispersions of their people. And these promises have, both in type and tendency, a reference as far forward as to the gospel church, to which this second edition of the Jewish church was at length to resign its dignities and privileges. It is here promised, I. That the city shall be rebuilt and re-established "in statu quo—in its former state," ver. 1—6. II. That the captives, having their sins pardoned, shall be restored, ver. 7, 8. III. That this shall redound very much to the glory of God, ver. 9. IV. That the country shall have both joy and plenty, ver. 10—14. V. That that way shall be made for the coming of the Messiah, ver. 15, 16. VI. That the house of David, the house of Levi, and the house of Israel, shall flourish again, and be established, and all three in the kingdom of Christ; a gospel ministry and the gospel church shall continue while the world stands, ver. 17—26.

MOREOVER the word of the LORD came unto Jeremiah the second time, while he was yet shut up in the court of the prison, saying,

2 Thus saith the LORD the maker thereof, the LORD that formed it, to establish it; the LORD *is* his name;

3 Call unto me, and I will answer thee, and show thee great and mighty things, which thou knowest not. 4 For thus saith the LORD, the God of Israel, concerning the houses of this city, and concerning the houses of the kings of Judah, which are thrown down by the mounts, and by the sword; 5 They come to fight with the Chaldeans, but *it is* to fill them with the dead bodies of men, whom I have slain in mine anger and in my fury, and for all whose wickedness I have hid my face from this city. 6 Behold, I will bring it health and cure, and I will cure them, and will reveal unto them the abundance of peace and truth. 7 And I will cause the captivity of Judah and the captivity of Israel to return, and will build them, as at the first. 8 And I will cleanse them from all their iniquity, whereby they have sinned against me; and I will pardon all their iniquities, whereby they have sinned, and whereby they have transgressed against me. 9 And it shall be to me a name of joy, and a praise and an honour before all the nations of the earth, which shall hear all the good that I do unto them : and they shall fear and tremble for all the goodness and for all the prosperity that I procure unto it.

Observe here, I. The date of this comfortable prophecy which God entrusted Jeremiah with. It is not exact in the time, only that it was after that in the foregoing chapter, when things were still growing worse and worse; it was *the second time.* *God speaketh once, yea, twice,* for the encouragement of his people. We are not only

617

so disobedient that we have need of *precept upon precept* to bring us to our duty, but so distrustful that we have need of promise upon promise to bring us to our comfort. This word, as the former, *came to Jeremiah* when *he was in prison.* Note, No confinement can deprive God's people of his presence; no locks nor bars can shut out his gracious visits; nay, oftentimes *as their afflictions abound their consolations much more abound,* and they have the most reviving communications of his favour when the world frowns upon them. Paul's sweetest epistles were those that bore date out of a prison.

II. The prophecy itself. A great deal of comfort is wrapped up in it for the relief of the captives, to keep them from sinking into despair Observe,

1. Who it is that secures this comfort to them (*v.* 2): It is *the Lord, the maker thereof, the Lord that framed it.* He is the maker and former of heaven and earth, and therefore has all power in his hands; so it refers to Jeremiah's prayer, *ch.* xxxii. 17. He is the maker and former of Jerusalem, of Zion, built them at first, and therefore can rebuild them—built them for his own praise, and therefore *will.* He *formed it, to establish it,* and therefore it shall be established till those things be introduced which cannot be shaken, but shall remain for ever. He is the maker and former of this promise; he has laid the scheme for Jerusalem's restoration, and he that has formed it will establish it, he that has made the promise will make it good; for Jehovah *is his name,* a God giving being to his promises by the performance of them, and when he does this he is known by that name (Exod. vi. 3), a perfecting God. When the heavens and the earth were finished, then, and not till then, the Creator is called *Jehovah,* Gen. ii. 4.

2. How this comfort must be obtained and fetched in—by prayer (*v.* 3): *Call upon me, and I will answer thee.* The prophet, having received some intimations of this kind, must be humbly earnest with God for further discoveries of his kind intentions. He had prayed (*ch.* xxxii. 16), but he must pray again. Note, Those that expect to receive comforts from God must continue instant in prayer. We must call upon him, and then he will answer us. Christ himself must *ask, and it shall be given him,* Ps. ii. 8 *I will show thee great and mighty things* (give thee a clear and full prospect of them), *hidden things, which,* though in part discovered already, yet *thou knowest not,* thou canst not understand or give credit to. Or this may refer not only to the prediction of these things which Jeremiah, if he desire it, shall be favoured with, but to the performance of the things themselves which the people of God, encouraged by this prediction, must pray for. Note, Promises are given, not to supersede, but to quicken and encourage prayer. See Ezek. xxxvi. 37.

618

3. How deplorable the condition of Jerusalem was which made it necessary that such comforts as these should be provided for it, and notwithstanding which its restoration should be brought about in due time (*v.* 4, 5): *The houses of this city,* not excepting those *of the kings of Judah, are thrown down by the mounts,* or engines of battery, *and by the sword,* or axes, or hammers. It is the same word that is used Ezek. xxvi. 9, *With his axes he shall break down thy towers.* The strongest stateliest houses, and those that were best furnished, were levelled with the ground. The fifth verse comes in in a parenthesis, giving a further instance of the present calamitous state of Jerusalem. Those that *came to fight with the Chaldeans,* to beat them off from the siege, did more hurt than good, provoked the enemy to be more fierce and furious in their assaults, so that the houses in Jerusalem were filled *with the dead bodies of men,* who died of the wounds they received in sallying out upon the besiegers. God says that they were such as he had *slain in his anger,* for the enemies' sword was his sword and their anger his anger. But, it seems, the men that were slain were generally such as had distinguished themselves by their wickedness, for they were the very men *for whose wickedness* God did now *hide himself from this city,* so that he was just in all he brought upon them.

4. What the blessings are which God has in store for Judah and Jerusalem, such as will redress all their grievances.

(1.) Is their state diseased? Is it wounded? God will provide effectually for the healing of it, though the disease was thought mortal and incurable, *ch.* viii. 22. " *The whole head is sick, and the whole heart faint* (Isa. i. 5); but (*v.* 6) *I will bring it health and cure;* I will prevent the death, remove the sickness, and set all to rights again," *ch.* xxx. 17. Note, Be the case ever so desperate, if God undertake the cure, he will effect it. The sin of Jerusalem was the sickness of it (Isa. i. 6); its reformation therefore will be its recovery. And the following words tell us how that is wrought: " *I will reveal unto them the abundance of peace and truth;* I will give it to them in due time, and give them an encouraging prospect of it in the mean time." *Peace* stands here for all good; *peace and truth* are peace according to the promise and in pursuance of that: or *peace and truth* are peace and the true religion, peace and the true worship of God, in opposition to the many falsehoods and deceits by which they had been led away from God. We may apply it more generally, and observe, [1.] That peace and truth are the great subject-matter of divine revelation. These promises here lead us to the gospel of Christ, and in that God has revealed to us *peace and truth,* the method of true peace—truth to direct us, peace to make us easy. *Grace and truth,* and abundance of both, *come by Jesus Christ.* Peace and truth are the life of the soul, and Christ *came that we might have* that *life, and might have it more abundantly.* Christ rules by the power of truth (John xviii. 37) and by it he gives *abundance of peace,* Ps. lxxii. 7 ; lxxxv. 10. [2.] That the divine revelation of peace and truth brings health and cure to all those that by faith receive it : it heals the soul of the diseases it has contracted, as it is a means of sanctification, John xvii. 17. *He sent his word and healed them,* Ps. cvii. 20. And it puts the soul into good order, and keeps it in a good frame and fit for the employments and enjoyments of the spiritual and divine life.

(2.) Are they scattered and enslaved, and is their nation laid in ruins ? *" I will cause their captivity to return* (*v.* 7), both that of Israel and that of Judah" (for though those who returned under Zerubbabel were chiefly of Judah, and Benjamin, and Levi, yet afterwards many of all the other tribes returned), *" and I will rebuild them, as* I built them *at first."* When they by repentance do their first works God will by their restoration do his first works.

(3.) Is sin the procuring cause of all their troubles ? That shall be pardoned and subdued, and so the root of the judgments shall be killed, *v.* 8. [1.] By sin they have become filthy, and odious to God's holiness, but God will cleanse them, and purify *them from their iniquity.* As those that were ceremonially unclean, and were therefore shut out from the tabernacle, when they were sprinkled with the *water of purification* had liberty of access to it again, so had they to their own land, and the privileges of it, when God had *cleansed them from their iniquities.* In allusion to that sprinkling, David prays, *Purge me with hyssop.* [2.] By sin they have become guilty, and obnoxious to his justice ; but he will *pardon all their iniquities,* will remove the punishment to which for sin they were bound over. All who by sanctifying grace are cleansed from the filth of sin, by pardoning mercy are freed from the guilt of it.

(4.) Have both their sins and their sufferings turned to the dishonour of God ? Their reformation and restoration shall redound as much to his praise, *v.* 9. Jerusalem thus rebuilt, Judah thus repeopled, *shall be to me a name of joy,* as pleasing to God as ever they have been provoking, *and a praise and an honour before all the nations.* They, being thus restored, shall glorify God by their obedience to him, and he shall glorify himself by his favours to them. This renewed nation shall be as much a reputation to religion as formerly it has been a reproach to it. The nations *shall hear of all the good that* God has wrought in them by his grace and *of all the good* he has wrought for them by his providence. The wonders of their return out of Babylon shall make as great a noise in the world as ever the wonders of their deliverance out of Egypt did. And *they shall fear and tremble for all this goodness.* [1.] The people of God themselves shall fear and tremble ; they shall be much surprised at it, shall be afraid of offending so good a God and of forfeiting his favour. Hos. iii. 5, *They shall fear the Lord and his goodness.* [2.] The neighbouring nations shall fear because of the prosperity of Jerusalem, shall look upon the growing greatness of the Jewish nation as really formidable, and shall be afraid of making them their enemies. When the church is *fair as the moon,* and *clear as the sun,* she is *terrible as an army with banners.*

10 Thus saith the Lord ; Again there shall be heard in this place, which ye say *shall be* desolate without man and without beast, *even* in the cities of Judah, and in the streets of Jerusalem, that are desolate, without man, and without inhabitant, and without beast, 11 The voice of joy, and the voice of gladness, the voice of the bridegroom, and the voice of the bride, the voice of them that shall say, Praise the Lord of hosts : for the Lord *is* good ; for his mercy *endureth* for ever : *and* of them that shall bring the sacrifice of praise into the house of the Lord. For I will cause to return the captivity of the land, as at the first, saith the Lord. 12 Thus saith the Lord of hosts ; Again in this place, which is desolate without man and without beast, and in all the cities thereof, shall be an habitation of shepherds causing *their* flocks to lie down. 13 In the cities of the mountains, in the cities of the vale, and in the cities of the south, and in the land of Benjamin, and in the places about Jerusalem, and in the cities of Judah, shall the flocks pass again under the hands of him that telleth *them,* saith the Lord. 14 Behold, the days come, saith the Lord, that I will perform that good thing which I have promised unto the house of Israel and to the house of Judah. 15 In those days, and at that time, will I cause the Branch of righteousness to grow up unto David ; and he shall execute judgment and righteousness in the land. 16 In those days shall Judah be saved, and Jerusalem shall dwell

safely: and this *is the name* where-with she shall be called, The LORD our righteousness.

Here is a further prediction of the happy state of Judah and Jerusalem after their glorious return out of captivity, issuing gloriously at length in the kingdom of the Messiah.

I. It is promised that the people who were long in sorrow shall again be filled with joy. Every one concluded now that the country would lie for ever desolate, that *no beasts* would be found in the land of Judah, no inhabitant *in the streets of Jerusalem*, and consequently there would be nothing but universal and perpetual melancholy (*v.* 10); but, though weeping may endure for a time, joy will return. It was threatened (*ch.* vii. 34 and xvi. 9) that *the voice of joy and gladness should cease* there; but here it is promised that they shall revive again, that *the voice of joy and gladness shall be heard* there, because *the captivity shall be returned;* for then was *their mouth filled with laughter*, Ps. cxxvi. 1, 2. 1. There shall be common joy there, *the voice of the bridegroom and the voice of the bride;* marriages shall again be celebrated, as formerly, with songs, which in Babylon they had laid aside, for their harps were hung on the willow-trees. 2. There shall be religious joy there; temple-songs shall be revived, *the Lord's songs*, which they could not *sing in a strange land*. There shall be heard in their private houses, and in the cities of Judah, as well as in the temple, *the voice of those that shall say, Praise the Lord of hosts*. Note, Nothing is more the praise and honour of a people than to have God praised and honoured among them. This shall complete the mercy of their return and restoration, that with it they shall have hearts to be thankful for it, and give God the glory of it, the glory both of the power and of the goodness by which it is effected; they shall praise him both as *the Lord of hosts* and as the God who *is good* and whose *mercy endures for ever*. This, though a song of old, yet, being sung upon this fresh occasion, will be a new song. We find this literally fulfilled at their return out of Babylon, Ezra iii. 11. They sang together in praising the Lord, *because he is good, for his mercy endures for ever*. The public worship of God shall be diligently and constantly attended upon: *They shall bring the sacrifice of praise to the house of the Lord*. All the sacrifices were intended for the praise of God, but this seems to be meant of the spiritual sacrifices of humble adorations and joyful thanksgivings, *the calves of our lips* (Hos. xiv. 2), which *shall please the Lord better than an ox or bullock*. The Jews say that in the days of the Messiah all sacrifices shall cease but *the sacrifice of praise*, and to those days this promise has a further reference.

II. It is promised that the country, which had lain long depopulated, shall be replenished and stocked again. It was now desolate, *without man and without beast;* but, after their return, the pastures shall again be *clothed with flocks*, Ps. lxv. 13. *In all the cities of Judah and Benjamin there shall be a habitation of shepherds, v.* 12, 13. This intimates, 1. The wealth of the country, after their return. It shall not be a habitation of beggars, who have nothing, but of shepherds and husbandmen, men of substance, with good stocks upon the ground they have returned to. 2. The peace of the country. It shall not be a habitation of soldiers, nor shall there be tents and barracks set up to lodge them, but there shall be shepherds' tents; for they shall hear no more the alarms of war, nor shall there be any to make even the shepherds afraid. See Ps. cxliv. 13, 14. 3. The industry of the country, and their return to their original plainness and simplicity, from which, in the corrupt ages, they had sadly degenerated. The seed of Jacob, in their beginning, gloried in this, that they were shepherds (Gen. xlvii. 3), and so they shall now be again, giving themselves wholly to that innocent employment, *causing their flocks to lie down* (*v.* 12) and to *pass under the hands of him that telleth them* (*v.* 13); for, though their flocks are numerous, they are not numberless, nor shall they omit to number them, that they may know if any be missing and may seek after it. Note, It is the prudence of those who have ever so much of the world to keep an account of what they have. Some think that they *pass under the hand of him that telleth them* that they may be tithed, Lev. xxvii. 32. *Then* we may take the comfort of what we have when God has had his dues out of it. Now because it seemed incredible that a people, reduced as now they were, should ever recover such a degree of peace and plenty as this, here is subjoined a general ratification of these promises (*v.* 14): *I will perform that good thing which I have promised*. Though the promise may sometimes work slowly towards an accomplishment, it works surely. *The days will come*, though they are long in coming.

III. To crown all these blessings which God has in store for them, here is a promise of the Messiah, and of that everlasting righteousness which he should bring in (*v* 15, 16), and probably this is *that good thing*, that great good thing, which in the latter days, days that were yet to come, God would perform, as he had promised to Judah and Israel, and to which their return out of captivity and their settlement again in their own land was preparatory. *From the captivity to Christ* is one of the famous periods, Matt. i. 17. This promise of the Messiah we had before (*ch.* xxiii. 5, 6), and there it came in as a confirmation of the promise of the shepherds whom God would set over them, which would make one think that the promise here concerning the shepherds and their flocks, which introduces it, is to be understood figuratively. Christ is here prophesied of, 1. As a rightful King. He is a *branch of righteousness*, not a usurper, for he *grows up unto David*, descends from his loins, with whom the covenant of royalty was made, and is that seed with whom that covenant should be established, so that his title is unexceptionable. 2. As a righteous king, righteous in enacting laws, waging wars, and giving judgment, righteous in vindicating those that suffer wrong and punishing those that do wrong : *He shall execute judgment and righteousness in the land.* This may point at Zerubbabel, in the type, who governed with equity, not as Jehoiakim had done (*ch* xxii. 17); but it has a further reference to him to whom all judgment is committed and who shall *judge the world in righteousness*. 3. As a king that shall protect his subjects from all injury. By him *Judah shall be saved* from wrath and the curse, and, being so saved, *Jerusalem shall dwell safely*, quiet from the fear of evil, and enjoying a holy security and serenity of mind, in a dependence upon the conduct of this prince of peace, this prince of their peace. 4. As a king that shall be praised by his subjects : "*This is the name whereby they shall call him*" (so the Chaldee reads it, the Syriac, and vulgar Latin); "this name of his they shall celebrate and triumph in, and by this name they shall call upon him." It may be read, more agreeably to the original, *This is he who shall call her, The Lord our righteousness*. As Moses's altar is called *Jehovah-nissi* (Exod. xvii. 15), and Jerusalem *Jehovah-shammah* (Ezek. xlviii. 35), intimating that they glory in Jehovah as present with them and *their banner*, so here the city is called *The Lord our righteousness*, because they glory in Jehovah as their righteousness. That which was before said to be the name of Christ (says Mr. Gataker) is here made the name of Jerusalem, the city of the Messiah, the church of Christ. He it is that imparts righteousness to her, for he is *made of God to us righteousness*, and she, by bearing that name, professes to have her whole righteousness, not from herself, but from him. *In the Lord have I righteousness and strength*, Isa. xlv. 24. And *we are made the righteousness of God in him*. The inhabitants of Jerusalem shall have this name of the Messiah so much in their mouths that they shall themselves be called by it.

17 For thus saith the LORD; David shall never want a man to sit upon the throne of the house of Israel ; 18 Neither shall the priests the Levites want a man before me to offer burnt-offerings, and to kindle meat-offerings, and to do sacrifice continually.

19 And the word of the LORD came unto Jeremiah, saying, 20 Thus saith the LORD ; If ye can break my covenant of the day, and my covenant of the night, and that there should not be day and night in their season; 21 *Then* may also my covenant be broken with David my servant, that he should not have a son to reign upon his throne; and with the Levites the priests, my ministers. 22 As the hosts of heaven cannot be numbered, neither the sand of the sea measured : so will I multiply the seed of David my servant, and the Levites that minister unto me. 23 Moreover the word of the LORD came to Jeremiah, saying, 24 Considerest thou not what this people have spoken, saying, The two families which the LORD hath chosen, he hath even cast them off? Thus they have despised my people, that they should be no more a nation before them. 25 Thus saith the LORD; If my covenant *be* not with day and night, *and if* I have not appointed the ordinances of heaven and earth; 26 Then will I cast away the seed of Jacob, and David my servant, *so* that I will not take *any* of his seed *to be* rulers over the seed of Abraham, Isaac, and Jacob : for I will cause their captivity to return, and have mercy on them.

Three of God's covenants, that of royalty with David and his seed, that of the priesthood with Aaron and his seed, and that of peculiarity with Abraham and his seed, seemed to be all broken and lost while the captivity lasted; but it is here promised that, notwithstanding that interruption and discontinuance for a time, they shall all three take place again, and the true intents and meaning of them all shall be abundantly answered in the New-Testament blessings, typified by those conferred on the Jews after their return out of captivity.

I. The covenant of royalty shall be secured and the promises of it shall have their full accomplishment in the kingdom of Christ, the Son of David, *v.* 17. The throne of Israel was overturned in the captivity ; the crown had fallen from their head; there was not *a man to sit on the throne of Israel :* Jeconiah was written childless. After their return the house of David made a figure again; but it is in the Messiah that this promise is performed that *David shall never want a man to sit on the throne of Israel*, and that David shall have *always a son to reign upon his throne*. For as long as the man

Christ Jesus sits on the right hand of the throne of God, rules the world, and rules it for the good of the church, to which he is a quickening head, and glorified head over all things, as long as he is *King upon the holy hill of Zion,* David does not want a successor, nor is the covenant with him broken. When the first-begotten was brought into the world it was declared concerning him, *The Lord God shall give him the throne of his father David and he shall reign over the house of Jacob for ever,* Luke i. 32, 33. For the confirmation of this it is promised, 1. That the covenant with David shall be as firm as the ordinances of heaven, to the stability of which that of God's promise is compared, *ch.* xxxi. 35, 36. There is a covenant of nature, by which the common course of providence is settled and on which it is founded, here called *a covenant of the day and the night* (*v.* 20. 25), because this is one of the articles of it, That there shall be *day and night in their season,* according to the distinction put between them in the creation, when God divided between the light and the darkness, and established their mutual succession, and a government to each, that *the sun* should *rule by day* and *the moon and stars by night* (Gen. i. 4, 5, 16), which establishment was renewed after the flood (Gen. viii. 22), and has continued ever since, Ps. xix. 2. The *morning and* the *evening* have both of them their regular *outgoings* (Ps. lxv. 8); the *day-spring knows its place, knows its time,* and keeps both, so do *the shadows of the evening ;* and, while the world stands, this course shall not be altered, this covenant shall not be broken. *The ordinances of heaven and earth* (of this communication between heaven and earth, the dominion of these ordinances of heaven upon the earth), *which* God has *appointed* (*v.* 25 ; compare Job xxxviii. 33), shall never be disappointed. Thus firm shall the covenant of redemption be with the Redeemer—God's servant, but David our King, *v.* 21. This intimates that Christ shall have a church on earth to the world's end; he shall see a seed in which he shall prolong his days till time and day shall be no more. Christ's *kingdom is an everlasting kingdom ;* and when *the end cometh,* and not till then, it *shall be delivered up to God,* even *the Father.* But it intimates that the condition of it in this world shall be intermixed and counterchanged, prosperity and adversity succeeding each other, as light and darkness, day and night. But this is plainly taught us, that, as sure as we may be that, though the sun will set to-night, it will rise again to-morrow morning, whether we live to see it or no, so sure we may be that, though the kingdom of the Redeemer in the world may for a time be clouded and eclipsed by corruptions and persecutions, yet it will shine forth again, and recover its lustre, in the time appointed. 2. That *the seed of David* shall be as numerous

as the host of heaven, that is, the spiritual seed of the Messiah, that shall be born to him by the efficacy of his gospel and his Spirit working with it. *From the womb of the morning he shall have the dew of their youth,* to be his *willing people,* Ps. cx. 3. Christ's seed are not, as David's were, his successors, but his subjects; yet the day is coming when they also shall reign with him (*v.* 22) : *As the host of heaven cannot be numbered, so will I multiply the seed of David,* so that there shall be no danger of the kingdom's being extinct, or extirpated, for want of heirs. The children are numerous; *and, if children, then heirs.*

II. The covenant of priesthood shall be secured, and the promises of that also shall have their full accomplishment. This seemed likewise to be forgotten during the captivity, when there was no altar, no temple service, for the priests to attend upon ; but this also shall revive. It did so; immediately upon their coming back to Jerusalem there were priests and Levites ready *to offer burnt-offerings* and to *do sacrifice continually* (Ezra iii. 2, 3), as is here promised, *v.* 18. But that priesthood soon grew corrupt ; *the covenant of Levi* was *profaned* (as appears Mal. ii. 8), and in the destruction of Jerusalem by the Romans it came to a final period. We must therefore look elsewhere for the performance of this word, that the covenant with the Levites, the priests, God's ministers, shall be as firm, and last as long, as the covenant *with the day and the night.* And we find it abundantly performed, 1. In the priesthood of Christ, which supersedes that of Aaron, and is the substance of that shadow. While that great *high priest of our profession* is always appearing *in the presence of God for us,* presenting the virtue of his blood by which he made atonement in the incense of his intercession, it may truly be said that *the Levites do not want a man before God to offer continually,* Heb. vii. 3, 17. He is a priest for ever. The covenant of the priesthood is called *a covenant of peace* (Num. xxv. 12), of *life and peace,* Mal. ii. 5. Now we are sure that this covenant is not broken, nor in the least weakened, while Jesus Christ is himself our life and our peace. This covenant of priesthood is here again and again joined with that of royalty, for Christ is *a priest upon his throne,* as Melchizedek. 2. In a settled gospel ministry. While there are faithful ministers to preside in religious assemblies, and to offer up the spiritual sacrifices of prayer and praise, *the priests, the Levites,* do not want successors, and such as *have obtained a more excellent ministry.* The apostle makes those that preach the gospel to come in the room of those that served at the altar, 1 Cor. ix. 13, 14. 3. In all true believers, who are *a holy priesthood, a royal priesthood* (1 Peter ii. 5, 9), who are *made to our God kings and priests* (Rev. i. 6); they *offer up spiritual* sacrifices, *acceptable to God,* and themselves, in the first place, *living sacrifices.* Of these Levites this promise must be understood (v. 22), that they shall be as numerous *as the sand of the sea,* the same that is promised concerning Israel in general (Gen. xxii. 17); for all God's spiritual Israel are spiritual priests, Rev. v. 9, 10; vii. 9, 15.

III. The covenant of peculiarity likewise shall be secured and the promises of that covenant shall have their full accomplishment in the gospel Israel. Observe, 1. How this covenant was looked upon as broken during the captivity, v. 24. God asks the prophet, "Hast thou not heard, and dost *thou not consider, what this people have spoken?*" either the enemies of Israel, who triumphed in the extirpation of a people that had made such a noise in the world, or the unbelieving Israelites themselves, "*this people* among whom thou dwellest;" they have broken covenant with God, and then quarrel with him as if he had not dealt faithfully with them. *The two families which the Lord hath chosen,* Israel and Judah, whereas they were but one when he chose them, *he hath even cast them off.* "*Thus have they despised my people,* that is, despised the privilege of being my people as if it were a privilege of no value at all." The neighbouring nations despised them as now *no more a nation,* but the ruins of a nation, and looked upon all their honour as laid in the dust; but, 2. See how firm the covenant stands notwithstanding, as firm as that with day and night; sooner will God suffer day and night to cease than he will *cast away the seed of Jacob.* This cannot refer to the seed of Jacob according to the flesh, for they are cast away, but to the Christian church, in which all these promises were to be lodged, as appears by the apostle's discourse, Rom. xi. 1, &c. Christ is that seed of David that is to be perpetual dictator to the seed of Abraham, Isaac, and Jacob; and, as this people shall never want such a king, so this king shall never want such a people. Christianity shall continue in the dominion of Christ, and the subjection of Christians to him, till day and night come to an end. And, as a pledge of this, that promise is again repeated, *I will cause their captivity to return;* and, having brought them back, *I will have mercy on them.* To whom this promise refers appears Gal. vi. 16, where all that *walk according to the gospel rule* are made to be the *Israel of God,* on whom *peace and mercy* shall be.

CHAP. XXXIV.

In this chapter we have two messages which God sent by Jeremiah. I. One to foretel the fate of Zedekiah king of Judah, that he should fall into the hands of the king of Babylon, that he should live a captive, but should at last die in peace in his captivity, ver. 1—7. II. Another to read the doom both of prince and people for their treacherous dealings with God, in bringing back into bondage their servants whom they had released according to the law, and so playing fast and loose with God. They had walked at all adventures with God (ver. 8—11), and therefore God would walk at all adventures with them, in bringing the Chaldean army upon

them again when they began to hope that they had got clear of them, ver. 12—22.

THE word which came unto Jeremiah from the LORD, when Nebuchadnezzar king of Babylon, and all his army, and all the kingdoms of the earth of his dominion, and all the people, fought against Jerusalem, and against all the cities thereof, saying,

2 Thus saith the LORD, the God of Israel; Go and speak to Zedekiah king of Judah, and tell him, Thus saith the LORD; Behold, I will give this city into the hand of the king of Babylon, and he shall burn it with fire:

3 And thou shalt not escape out of his hand, but shalt surely be taken, and delivered into his hand; and thine eyes shall behold the eyes of the king of Babylon, and he shall speak with thee mouth to mouth, and thou shalt go to Babylon. 4 Yet hear the word of the LORD, O Zedekiah king of Judah; Thus saith the LORD of thee, Thou shalt not die by the sword: 5 *But* thou shalt die in peace: and with the burnings of thy fathers, the former kings which were before thee, so shall they burn *odours* for thee; and they will lament thee, - *saying,* Ah lord! for I have pronounced the word, saith the LORD. 6 Then Jeremiah the prophet spake all these words unto Zedekiah king of Judah in Jerusalem, 7 When the king of Babylon's army fought against Jerusalem, and against all the cities of Judah that were left, against Lachish, and against Azekah: for these defenced cities remained of the cities of Judah.

This prophecy concerning Zedekiah was delivered to Jeremiah, and by him to the parties concerned, before he was shut up in the prison, for we find this prediction here made the ground of his commitment, as appears by the recital of some passages out of it, ch. xxxii. 4. Observe,

I. The time when this message was sent to Zedekiah; it was *when the king of Babylon,* with all his forces, some out of *all the kingdoms of the earth* that were within his jurisdiction, *fought against Jerusalem and the cities thereof* (v. 1), designing to destroy them, having often plundered them. The cities that now remained, and yet held out, are named (v. 7), *Lachish and Azekah.* This intimates that things were now brought to the last extremity, and yet Zedekiah obstinately stood it out, his heart being hardened to his destruction.

II. The message itself that was sent to him. 1. Here is a threatening of wrath. He is told that again which he had been often told before, that the city shall be taken by the Chaldeans *and burnt with fire* (*v.* 2), that he shall himself fall into the enemy's hands, shall be made a prisoner, shall be brought before that furious prince Nebuchadnezzar, and be carried away captive into Babylon (*v.* 3); yet Ezekiel prophesied that he *should not see Babylon;* nor did he, for his eyes were put out, Ezek. xii. 13. This Zedekiah brought upon himself from God by his other sins and from Nebuchadnezzar by breaking his faith with him. 2. Here is a mixture of mercy. He shall die a captive, but he *shall not die by the sword;* he shall die a natural death (*v.* 4); he shall end his days with some comfort, *shall die in peace, v.* 5. He never had been one of the worst of the kings, but we are willing to hope that what evil he had *done in the sight of the Lord* he repented of in his captivity, as Manasseh had done, and it was forgiven to him; and, God being reconciled to him, he might truly be said to *die in peace.* Note, A man may die in a prison and yet *die in peace.* Nay, he shall end his days with some reputation, more than one would expect, all things considered. He shall be buried *with the burnings of his fathers,* that is, with the respect usually shown to their kings, especially those that had done good in Israel. It seems, in his captivity he had conducted himself so well towards his own people that they were willing to do him this honour, and towards Nebuchadnezzar that he suffered it to be done. If Zedekiah had continued in his prosperity, perhaps he would have grown worse and would have *departed* at last *without being desired;* but his afflictions wrought such a change in him that his death was looked upon as a great loss. It is better to live and die penitent in a prison than to live and die impenitent in a palace. *They will lament thee, saying, Ah lord!* an honour which his brother Jehoiakim had not, *ch.* xxii. 18. The Jews say that they lamented thus over him, *Alas! Zedekiah is dead, who drank the dregs of all the ages that went before him,* that is, who suffered for the sins of his ancestors, the measure of iniquity being filled up in his days. They shall thus lament him, *saith the Lord, for I have pronounced the word;* and what God hath spoken shall without fail be made good.

III. Jeremiah's faithfulness in delivering this message. Though he knew it would be ungrateful to the king, and might prove, as indeed it did, dangerous to himself (for he was imprisoned for it), yet he *spoke all these words to Zedekiah, v.* 6. It is a mercy to great men to have those about them that will deal faithfully with them, and tell them the evil consequences of their evil courses, that they may reform and live.

8 *This is* the word that came unto Jeremiah from the Lord, after that the king Zedekiah had made a covenant with all the people which *were* at Jerusalem, to proclaim liberty unto them; 9 That every man should let his manservant, and every man his maidservant, *being* a Hebrew or a Hebrewess, go free; that none should serve himself of them, *to wit,* of a Jew his brother. 10 Now when all the princes, and all the people, which had entered into the covenant, heard that every one should let his manservant, and every one his maidservant, go free, that none should serve themselves of them any more, then they obeyed, and let *them* go. 11 But afterward they turned, and caused the servants and the handmaids, whom they had let go free, to return, and brought them into subjection for servants and for handmaids. 12 Therefore the word of the Lord came to Jeremiah from the Lord, saying, 13 Thus saith the Lord, the God of Israel; I made a covenant with your fathers in the day that I brought them forth out of the land of Egypt, out of the house of bondmen, saying, 14 At the end of seven years let ye go every man his brother a Hebrew, which hath been sold unto thee; and when he hath served thee six years, thou shalt let him go free from thee: but your fathers hearkened not unto me, neither inclined their ear. 15 And ye were now turned, and had done right in my sight, in proclaiming liberty every man to his neighbour; and ye had made a covenant before me in the house which is called by my name: 16 But ye turned and polluted my name, and caused every man his servant, and every man his handmaid, whom he had set at liberty at their pleasure, to return, and brought them into subjection, to be unto you for servants and for handmaids. 17 Therefore thus saith the Lord; Ye have not hearkened unto me, in proclaiming liberty, every one to his brother, and every man to his neigh-

bour : behold, I proclaim a liberty for you, saith the LORD, to the sword, to the pestilence, and to the famine; and I will make you to be removed into all the kingdoms of the earth. 18 And I will give the men that have transgressed my covenant, which have not performed the words of the covenant which they had made before me, when they cut the calf in twain, and passed between the parts thereof, 19 The princes of Judah, and the princes of Jerusalem, the eunuchs, and the priests, and all the people of the land, which passed between the parts of the calf; 20 I will even give them into the hand of their enemies, and into the hand of them that seek their life : and their dead bodies shall be for meat unto the fowls of the heaven, and to the beasts of the earth. 21 And Zedekiah king of Judah and his princes will I give into the hand of their enemies, and into the hand of them that seek their life, and into the hand of the king of Babylon's army, which are gone up from you. 22 Behold, I will command, saith the LORD, and cause them to return to this city; and they shall fight against it, and take it, and burn it with fire : and I will make the cities of Judah a desolation without an inhabitant.

We have here another prophecy upon a particular occasion, the history of which we must take notice of, as necessary to give light to the prophecy.

I. When Jerusalem was closely besieged by the Chaldean army the princes and people agreed upon a reformation in one instance, and that was concerning their servants.

1. The law of God was very express, that those of their own nation should not be held in servitude above seven years, but, after they had served one apprenticeship, they should be discharged and have their liberty ; yea, though they had sold themselves into servitude for the payment of their debts, or though they were *sold by the judges* for the punishment of their crimes. This difference was put between their brethren and strangers, that those of other nations taken in war, or bought with money, might be held in perpetual slavery, they and theirs ; but their brethren must serve but for seven years at the longest. This God calls the covenant that he had made with them when he *brought them out of the land of Egypt, v.* 13, 14. This was the first of the judicial laws which God gave them (Exod. xxi. 2), and there was good reason for this law. (1.) God had put

honour upon that nation, and he would have them thus to preserve the honour of it themselves and to put a difference between it and other nations. (2.) God had brought them out of slavery in Egypt, and he would have them thus to express their grateful sense of that favour, by letting those go to whom their houses were *houses of bondage*, as Egypt had been to their forefathers. That deliverance is therefore mentioned here (*v.* 13) as the ground of that law. Note, God's compassions towards us should engage our compassions towards our brethren ; we must release as we are released, forgive as we are forgiven, and relieve as we are relieved. And this is called *a covenant ;* for our performance of the duty required is the condition of the continuance of the favours God has bestowed.

2. This law they and their fathers had broken. Their worldly profit swayed more with them than God's command or covenant. When their servants had lived seven years with them they understood their business, and how to apply themselves to it, better than they did when they first came to them, and therefore they would then by no means part with them, though God himself by his law had made them free : *Your fathers hearkened not to me* in this matter (*v.* 14), so that from the days of their fathers they had been in this trespass ; and they thought they might do it because their fathers did it, and their servants had by disuse lost the benefit of the provision God made for them ; whereas against an express law, especially against an express law of God, no custom, usage, nor prescription, is to be admitted in plea. For this sin of theirs, and their fathers, God now brought them into servitude, and justly.

3. When they were besieged, and closely shut in, by the army of the Chaldeans, they, being told of their fault in this matter, immediately reformed, and let go all their servants that were entitled to their freedom by the law of God, as Pharaoh, who, when the plague was upon him, consented to *let the people go*, and bound themselves in a covenant to do so. (1.) The prophets faithfully admonished them concerning their sin. From them they heard that they should let their Hebrew servants *go free, v.* 10. They might have read it themselves in the book of the law, but did not, or did not heed it, therefore the prophets told them what the law was. See what need there is of the preaching of the word ; people must hear the word preached because they will not make the use they ought to make of the word written. (2.) All orders and degrees of men concurred in this reformation. The *king,* and the *princes,* and *all the people,* agreed to *let go their servants,* whatever loss or damage they might sustain by so doing. When the king and princes led in this good work the people could not for shame but follow. The example and influence of great men would go

very far towards extirpating the most inveterate corruptions. (3.) They bound themselves by a solemn oath and covenant that they would do this, whereby they engaged themselves to God and one another. Note, What God has bound us to by his precept, it is good for us to bind ourselves to by our promise. This covenant was very solemn : it was made in a sacred place, *made before me, in the house which is called by my name* (*v.* 15), in the special presence of God, the tokens of which, in the temple, ought to strike an awe upon them and make them very sincere in their appeals to him. It was ratified by a significant sign ; they *cut a calf in two, and passed between the parts thereof* (*v.* 18, 19) with this dreadful imprecation, " Let us be in like manner cut asunder if we do not perform what we now promise." This calf was probably offered up in sacrifice to God, who was thereby made a party to the covenant. When God covenanted with Abram, for the ratification of it, a *smoking furnace* and a *burning lamp passed between the pieces* of the sacrifice, in allusion to this federal rite, Gen. xv. 17. Note, In order that we may effectually oblige ourselves to our duty, it is good to alarm ourselves with the apprehensions of the terror of the wrath and curse to which we expose ourselves if we live in the contempt of it, that wrath which will *cut sinners asunder* (Matt. xxiv. 51), and sensible signs may be of use to make the impressions of it deep and durable, as here. (4.) They conformed themselves herein to the command of God and their covenant with him ; they did *let their servants go*, though at this time, when the city was besieged, they could very ill spare them Thus they did *right in God's sight, v.* 15. Though it was their trouble that drove them to it, yet he was well pleased with it ; and if they had persevered in this act of *mercy to the poor*, to their poor servants, it might have been a lengthening of their tranquillity, Dan. iv. 27.

II. When there was some hope that the siege was raised and the danger over they repented of their repentance, undid the good they had done, and forced the servants they had released into their respective services again. 1. The *king of Babylon's army* had now *gone up from them, v.* 21. Pharaoh was bringing an army of Egyptians to oppose the progress of the king of Babylon's victories, upon the tidings of which the Chaldeans raised the siege for a time, as we find, *ch.* xxxvii. 5. *They departed from Jerusalem.* See how ready God was to put a stop to his judgments, upon the first instance of reformation, so slow is he to anger and so swift to show mercy. As soon as ever they let their servants go free God let them go free. 2. When they began to think themselves safe from the besiegers they made their servants come back into subjection to them, 11, and again *v.* 16. This was a great

abuse to their servants, to whom servitude would be more irksome, after they had had some taste of the pleasures of liberty. It was a great shame to themselves that they could not keep in a good mind when they were in it. But it was especially an affront to God ; in doing this they *polluted his name, v.* 16. It was a contempt of the command he had given them, as if that were of no force at all, but they might either keep it or break it as they thought fit. It was a contempt of the covenant they had made with him, and of that wrath which they had imprecated upon themselves in case they should break that covenant. It was jesting with God almighty, as if he could be imposed upon by fallacious promises, which, when they had gained their point, they would look upon themselves no longer obliged by. It was *lying to God with their mouths* and *flattering him with their tongues*. It was likewise a contempt of the judgments of God and setting them at defiance ; as if, when once the course of them was stopped a little and interrupted, they would never proceed again and the judgment would never be revived ; whereas reprieves are so far from being pardons that if they be abused thus, and sinners take encouragement from them to return to sin, they are but preparatives for heavier strokes of divine vengeance.

III. For this treacherous dealing with God they are here severely threatened. *Be not deceived ; God is not mocked.* Those that think to put a cheat upon God by a dissembled repentance, a fallacious covenant, and a partial temporary reformation, will prove in the end to have put the greatest cheat upon their own souls ; for *the Lord, whose name is Jealous, is a jealous God.* It is here threatened, with an observable air of displeasure against them, 1. That, since they had not given liberty to their servants to go where they pleased, God would give all his judgments liberty to take their course against them without control (*v.* 17): *You have not proclaimed liberty to your servants.* Though they had done it (*v.* 10), yet they might truly be said not to have done it, because they did not stand to it, but undid it again ; and *factum non dicitur quod non perseverat—that is not said to be done which does not last.* The righteousness that is forsaken and turned away from shall be forgotten, and *not mentioned* any more than if it had never been, Ezek. xviii. 24. " *Therefore I will proclaim a liberty for you ;* I will discharge you from my service, and put you out of my protection, which those forfeit that withdraw from their allegiance. You shall have liberty to choose which of these judgments you will be cut off by, *sword, famine, or pestilence ;*" such a liberty as was offered to David, which put him into a *great strait*, 2 Sam. xxiv. 14. Note, Those that will not be in subjection to the law of God put themselves into subjection to the wrath and curse of God. But this shows what liberty to *sin* really is—it is but a liberty to the sorest judgments. 2. That, since they had brought their servants back into confinement in their houses, God would *make them to be removed into all the kingdoms of the earth,* where they should live in servitude, and, being strangers, could not expect the privileges of free-born subjects. 3. That, since they had broken the covenant which they ratified by a solemn imprecation, God would bring on them the evil which they imprecated upon themselves in case they should break it. Out of their own mouth will he judge them, and so shall their doom be ; the penalty of their bond shall be recovered, because they have not performed the condition; for so some read *v.* 18, " *I will make the men which have transgressed my covenant as the calf which they cut in twain ;* I will divide them asunder as they divided it asunder.*" 4. That, since they would not let go their servants out of their hands, God would deliver them into the hands of those that hated them, even *the princes* and nobles both *of Judah and Jerusalem* (of the country and of the city), *the eunuchs* (chamberlains, or great officers of the court), *the priests, and all the people, v.* 19. They had all dealt treacherously with God, and therefore shall all be involved in the common ruin without exception. They shall all be *given into the hand of their enemies, that seek,* not their wealth only, or their service, but *their life,* and they shall have what they seek ; but neither shall that content them : when they have their lives they shall leave *their dead bodies* unburied, a loathsome spectacle to all mankind and an easy prey to *the fowls and beasts,* a lasting mark of ignominy being hereby fastened on them, *v.* 20. 5. That, since they had emboldened themselves in returning to their sin, contrary to their covenant, by the retreat of the Chaldean army from them, God would therefore bring it upon them again : " They have now *gone up from you,* and your fright is over for the present, but I *will command them* to face about as they were ; they shall *return to this city, and take it and burn it,*" *v.* 22. Note, (1.) As confidence in God is a hopeful presage of approaching deliverance, so security in sin is a sad omen of approaching destruction. (2.) When judgments are removed from a people before they have done their work, leave them, but leave them unhumbled and unreformed, it is *cum animo revertendi—with a design to return ;* they do but retreat to come on again with so much the greater force ; for when God judges he will overcome. (3.) It is just with God to disappoint those expectations of mercy which his providence had given cause for when we disappoint those expectations of duty which our professions, pretensions, and fair promises, had given cause for. If we repent of the good we had purposed, God will re-

pent of the good he had purposed. *With the froward thou wilt show thyself froward.*

CHAP. XXXV.

A variety of methods is tried, and every stone turned, to awaken the Jews to a sense of their sin and to bring them to repentance and reformation. The scope and tendency of many of the prophet's sermons was to frighten them out of their disobedience, by setting before them what would be the end thereof if they persisted in it. The scope of this sermon, in this chapter, is to shame them out of their disobedience if they had any sense of honour left in them for a discourse of this nature to fasten upon. I. He sets before them the obedience of the family of the Rechabites to the commands which were left them by Jonadab their ancestor, and how they persevered in that obedience and would not be tempted from it, ver. 1—11. II. With this he aggravates the disobedience of the Jews to God and their contempt of his precepts, ver. 12—15. III. He foretels the judgments of God upon the Jews for their impious disobedience to God, ver. 16, 17. IV. He assures the Rechabites of the blessing of God upon them for their pious obedience to their father, ver. 18, 19.

THE word which came unto Jeremiah from the LORD in the days of Jehoiakim the son of Josiah king of Judah, saying, 2 Go unto the house of the Rechabites, and speak unto them, and bring them into the house of the LORD, into one of the chambers, and give them wine to drink. 3 Then I took Jaazaniah the son of Jeremiah, the son of Habaziniah, and his brethren, and all his sons, and the whole house of the Rechabites ; 4 And I brought them into the house of the LORD, into the chamber of the sons of Hanan, the son of Igdaliah, a man of God, which *was* by the chamber of the princes, which *was* above the chamber of Maaseiah the son of Shallum, the keeper of the door : 5 And I set before the sons of the house of the Rechabites pots full of wine, and cups, and I said unto them, Drink ye wine. 6 But they said, We will drink no wine : for Jonadab the son of Rechab our father commanded us, saying, Ye shall drink no wine, *neither* ye, nor your sons for ever : 7 Neither shall ye build house, nor sow seed, nor plant vineyard, nor have *any :* but all your days ye shall dwell in tents ; that ye may live many days in the land where ye *be* strangers. 8 Thus have we obeyed the voice of Jonadab the son of Rechab our father in all that he hath charged us, to drink no wine all our days, we, our wives, our sons, nor our daughters ; 9 Nor to build houses for us to dwell in : neither have we vineyard, nor field, nor seed : 10 But we have dwelt in tents, and have obeyed, and done according to all that Jonadab our father commanded us. 11 But it came to pass, when Nebuchadrezzar king of Babylon came up into the land, that we said, Come, and let us go to Jerusalem for fear of the army of the Chaldeans, and for fear of the army of the Syrians : so we dwell at Jerusalem.

This chapter is of an earlier date than many of those before; for what is contained in it was said and done *in the days of Jehoiakim* (*v.* 1); but then it must be in the latter part of his reign, for it was after the king of Babylon with his army *came up into the land* (*v.* 11), which seems to refer to the invasion mentioned 2 Kings xxiv. 2, which was upon occasion of Jehoiakim's rebelling against Nebuchadnezzar. After the judgments of God had broken in upon this rebellious people he continued to deal with them by his prophets to turn them from sin, that his wrath might turn away from them. For this purpose Jeremiah sets before them the example of the Rechabites, a family that kept distinct by themselves and were no more numbered with the families of Israel than they with the nations. They were originally Kenites, as appears 1 Chron. ii. 55, *These are the Kenites that came out of Hemath, the father of the house of Rechab.* The Kenites, at least those of them that gained a settlement in the land of Israel, were of the posterity of Hobab, Moses's father-in-law, Judg. i. 16. We find them separated from the Amalekites, 1 Sam. xv. 6. See Judg. iv. 17. One family of these Kenites had their denomination from Rechab. His son, or a lineal descendant from him, was Jonadab, a man famous in his time for wisdom and piety. He flourished in the days of Jehu, king of Israel, nearly 300 years before this; for there we find him courted by that rising prince, when he affected to appear zealous for God (2 Kings x. 15, 16), which he thought nothing more likely to confirm people in the opinion of than to have so good a man as Jonadab ride in the chariot with him. Now here we are told,

I. What the rules of living were which Jonadab, probably by his last will and testament, in writing, and duly executed, charged his children, and his posterity after him throughout all generations, religiously to observe ; and we have reason to think that they were such as he himself had all his days observed.

1. They were comprised in two remarkable precepts:—(1.) He forbade them to *drink wine,* according to the law of the Nazarites. Wine is indeed given to *make glad the heart* of man and we are allowed the sober and moderate use of it; but we are so apt to abuse it and get hurt by it, and a good man, who has his heart made continually glad with the *light of God's countenance,* has so little need of it for that pur-

pose (Ps. iv. 6, 7), that it is a commendable piece of self-denial either not to use it at all or very sparingly and medicinally, as Timothy used it, 1 Tim. v. 23. (2.) He appointed them to *dwell in tents,* and not to build houses, nor purchase lands, nor rent or occupy either, *v.* 7. This was an instance of strictness and mortification beyond what the Nazarites were obliged to. Tents were mean dwellings, so that this would teach them to be humble ; they were cold dwellings, so that this would teach them to be hardy and not to indulge the body ; they were movable dwellings, so that this would teach them not to think of settling or taking root any where in this world. They must dwell in tents *all their days,* not for a few days, as Israel at the feast of tabernacles, not only in summer days, as soldiers and shepherds, but *all their days.* They must from the beginning thus accustom themselves to endure hardness, and then it would be no difficulty to them, no, not under the decays of old age. Now,

2. Why did Jonadab prescribe these rules of living to his posterity ? It was not merely to show his authority, and to exercise a dominion over them, by imposing upon them what he thought fit ; but it was to show his wisdom, and the real concern he had for their welfare, by recommending to them what he knew would be beneficial to them, yet not tying them by any oath or vow, or under any penalty, to observe these rules, but only advising them to conform to this discipline as far as they found it for edification, yet to be dispensed with in any case of necessity, as here, *v.* 11. He prescribed these rules to them, (1.) That they might preserve the ancient character of their family, which, however looked upon by some with contempt, he thought its real reputation. His ancestors had addicted themselves to a pastoral life (Exod. ii. 16), and he would have his posterity keep to it, and not degenerate from it, as Israel had done, who originally were shepherds and dwelt in tents, Gen. xlvi. 34. Note, We ought not to be ashamed of the honest employments of our ancestors, though they were but mean. (2.) That they might comport with their lot and bring their mind to their condition. Moses had put them in hopes that they should be naturalized (Num. x. 32); but, it seems, they were not; they were still *strangers in the land* (*v.* 7), had no inheritance in it, and therefore must live by their employments, which was a good reason why they should accustom themselves to hard fare and hard lodging ; for strangers, such as they were, must not expect to live as the landed men, so plentifully and delicately. Note, It is our wisdom and duty to accommodate ourselves to our place and rank, and not aim to live above it. What has been the lot of our fathers why may we not be content that it should be our lot, and live ac-

cording to it? *Mind not high things.* (3) That they might not be envied and disturbed by their neighbours among whom they lived. If they that were strangers should live great, raise estates, and fare sumptuously, the natives would grudge them their abundance, and have a jealous eye upon them, as the Philistines had upon Isaac (Gen. xxvi. 14), and would seek occasions to quarrel with them and do them a mischief; therefore he thought it would be their prudence to keep low, for that would be the way to continue long—to live meanly, that they might *live many days in the land where they were strangers.* Note, Humility and contentment in obscurity are often the best policy and men's surest protection. (4.) That they might be armed against temptations to luxury and sensuality, the prevailing sin of the age and place they lived in. Jonadab saw a general corruption of manners; the drunkards of Ephraim abounded, and he was afraid lest his children should be debauched and ruined by them; and therefore he obliged them to live by themselves, retired in the country; and, that they might not run into any unlawful pleasures, to deny themselves the use even of lawful delights. They must be very sober, and temperate, and abstemious, which would contribute to the health both of mind and body, and to their living many days, and easy ones, and such as they might reflect upon with comfort *in the land where they were strangers.* Note, The consideration of this, that we are strangers and pilgrims, should oblige us to abstain from all fleshly lusts, to live above the things of sense, and look upon them with a generous and gracious contempt. (5.) That they might be prepared for times of trouble and calamity. Jonadab might, without a spirit of prophecy, foresee the destruction of a people so wretchedly degenerated, and he would have his family provide, that, if they could not *in the peace thereof,* yet even in the midst of the troubles thereof, *they might have peace.* Let them therefore have little to lose, and then losing times would be the less dreadful to them: let them sit loose to what they had, and then they might with less pain be stripped of it. Note, Those are in the best frame to meet sufferings who are mortified to the world and live a life of self-denial. (6.) That in general they might learn to live by rule and under discipline. It is good for us all to do so, and to teach our children to do so. Those that have lived long, as Jonadab probably had done when he left this charge to his posterity, can speak by experience of the vanity of the world and the dangerous snares that are in the abundance of its wealth and pleasures, and therefore ought to be regarded when they warn those that come after them to stand upon their guard.

II. How strictly his posterity observed these rules, *v.* 8—10. They had in their respective generations all of them *obeyed the voice of Jonadab their father,* had *done according to all that he commanded them.* They *drank no wine,* though they dwelt in a country where there was plenty of it; their wives and children drank no wine, for those that are temperate themselves should take care that all under their charge should be so too. They built no houses, tilled no ground, but lived upon the products of their cattle. This they did partly in obedience to their ancestor, and out of a veneration they had for his name and authority, and partly from the experience they themselves had of the benefit of living such a mortified life. See the force of tradition, and the influence that antiquity, example, and great names, have upon men, and how that which seems very difficult will by long usage and custom become easy and in a manner natural. Now, 1. As to one of the particulars he had given them in charge, we are here told how in a case of necessity they dispensed with the violation of it (*v.* 11): *When the king of Babylon came into the land* with his army, though they had hitherto dwelt in tents, they now quitted their tents, and came and dwelt in Jerusalem, and in such houses as they could furnish themselves with there. Note, The rules of a strict discipline must not be made too strict, but so as to admit of a dispensation when the necessity of a case calls for it, which therefore, in making vows of that nature, it is wisdom to provide expressly for, that the way may be made the more clear, and we may not afterwards be forced to say, *It was an error,* Eccles. v. 6. Commands of that nature are to be understood with such limitations. These Rechabites would have tempted God, and not trusted him, if they had not used proper means for their own safety in a time of common calamity, notwithstanding the law and custom of their family. 2. As to the other particular, we are here told how, notwithstanding the greatest urgency, they religiously adhered to it. Jeremiah took them into the temple (*v.* 2), into a *prophet's chamber,* there, rather than into the *chamber of the princes,* that joined to it, because he had a message from God, which would look more like itself when it was delivered in the *chambers of a man of God.* There he not only asked the Rechabites whether they would drink any wine, but he set *pots full of wine before them,* and cups to drink out of, made the temptation as strong as possible, and said, "*Drink you wine,* you shall have it on free cost. You have broken one of the rules of your order, in coming to live at Jerusalem; why may you not break this too, and when you are in the city do as they there do?" But they peremptorily refused. They all agreed in the refusal. "No, *we will drink no wine;* for with us it is against the law." The prophet knew very well they would deny it, and, when they did, urged it no further, for he saw they were stedfastly resolved.

Note, Those temptations are of no force with men of confirmed sobriety which yet daily overcome such as, notwithstanding their convictions, are of no resolution in the paths of virtue.

12 Then came the word of the LORD unto Jeremiah, saying, 13 Thus saith the LORD of hosts, the God of Israel; Go and tell the men of Judah and the inhabitants of Jerusalem, Will ye not receive instruction to hearken to my words? saith the LORD. 14 The words of Jonadab the son of Rechab, that he commanded his sons not to drink wine, are performed; for unto this day they drink none, but obey their father's commandment: notwithstanding I have spoken unto you, rising early and speaking; but ye hearkened not unto me. 15 I have sent also unto you all my servants the prophets, rising up early and sending *them*, saying, Return ye now every man from his evil way, and amend your doings, and go not after other gods to serve them, and ye shall dwell in the land which I have given to you and to your fathers: but ye have not inclined your ear, nor hearkened unto me. 16 Because the sons of Jonadab the son of Rechab have performed the commandment of their father, which he commanded them; but this people hath not hearkened unto me: 17 Therefore thus saith the LORD God of hosts, the God of Israel; Behold, I will bring upon Judah and upon all the inhabitants of Jerusalem all the evil that I have pronounced against them: because I have spoken unto them, but they have not heard; and I have called unto them, but they have not answered. 18 And Jeremiah said unto the house of the Rechabites, Thus saith the LORD of hosts, the God of Israel; Because ye have obeyed the commandment of Jonadab your father, and kept all his precepts, and done according unto all that he hath commanded you: 19 Therefore thus saith the LORD of hosts, the God of Israel; Jonadab the son of Rechab shall not want a man to stand before me for ever.

The trial of the Rechabites' constancy was
630

intended but for a sign; now here we have the application of it.

I. The Rechabites' observance of their father's charge to them is made use of as an aggravation of the disobedience of the Jews to God. Let them see it and be ashamed. The prophet asks them, in God's name, " *Will you not* at length *receive instruction? v.* 13. Will nothing affect you? Will nothing fasten upon you? Will nothing prevail to discover sin and duty to you? You see how obedient the Rechabites are to their father's commandment (*v.* 14); but *you have not inclined your ear to me*" (*v.* 15), though one might much more reasonably expect that the people of God should have obeyed him than that the sons of Jonadab should have obeyed him; and the aggravation is very high, for, 1. The Rechabites were obedient to one who was but a man like themselves, who had but the wisdom and power of a man, and was only the father of their flesh; but the Jews were disobedient to an infinite and eternal God, who had an absolute authority over them, as the Father of their spirits. 2. Jonadab was long since dead, and was ignorant of them, and could neither take cognizance of their disobedience to his orders nor give correction for it; but God lives for ever, to see how his laws are observed, and is in a readiness to revenge all disobedience. 3. The Rechabites were never put in mind of their obligations to their father; but God often sent his prophets to his people, to put them in mind of their duty to him, and yet they would not do it. This is insisted on here as a great aggravation of their disobedience: "*I have* myself *spoken to you, rising early and speaking* by the written word and the dictates and admonitions of conscience (*v.* 14); nay, *I have sent unto you all my servants the prophets*, men like yourselves, whose terrors shall not make you afraid, *rising up early and sending them* (*v.* 15), and yet all in vain." 4. Jonadab never did that for his seed which God had done for his people. He left them a charge, but left them no estate to bear the charge; but God had given his people a *good land*, and promised them that, if they would be obedient, they should still dwell in it, so that they were bound both in gratitude and interest to be obedient, and yet they *would not hear*, they would not *hearken*. (5.) God did not tie up his people to so much hardship, and to such instances of mortification, as Jonadab obliged his seed to; and yet Jonadab's orders were obeyed and God's were not.

II. Judgments are threatened, as often before, against Judah and Jerusalem, for their disobedience thus aggravated. The Rechabites shall rise up in judgment against them, and shall condemn them; for they very punctually *performed the commandment of their father*, and continued and persevered in their obedience to it (*v.* 16); but *this people*, this rebellious and gainsaying people, have not hearkened unto me ; and therefore (v. 17), because they have not obeyed the precepts of the word, God will perform the threatenings of it : " *I will bring upon them,* by the Chaldean army, *all the evil pronounced against them* both in the law and in the prophets, for *I have spoken to them, I have called to them*—spoken in a still small voice to those that were near and called aloud to those that were at a distance, tried all ways and means to convince and reduce them—spoken by my word, called by my providence, both to the same purport, and yet all to no purpose; they have not *heard* nor *answered.*"

III. Mercy is here promised to the family of the Rechabites for their steady and unanimous adherence to the laws of their house. Though it was only for the shaming of Israel that their constancy was tried, yet, being unshaken, it was *found unto praise, and honour, and glory ;* and God takes occasion from it to tell them that he had favours in reserve for them (v. 18, 19) and that they should have the comfort of them. It is promised, 1. That the family shall continue as long as any of the families of Israel, among whom they were strangers and sojourners. It shall *never want a man* to inherit what they had, though they had no inheritance to leave. Note, Sometimes those that have the smallest estates have the most numerous progeny; but he that sends mouths will be sure to send meat. 2. That religion shall continue in the family : " *He shall not want a man to stand before me,* to serve me." Though they are neither priests nor Levites, nor appear to have had any post in the temple service, yet in a constant course of regular devotion, they stand before God, to minister to him. Note, (1.) The greatest blessing that can be entailed upon a family is to have the worship of God kept up in it from generation to generation. (2.) Temperance, self-denial, and mortification to the world, do very much befriend the exercises of piety, and help to transmit the observance of them to posterity. The more dead we are to the delights of sense the better we are disposed for the service of God ; but nothing is more fatal to the entail of religion in a family than pride and luxury.

CHAP. XXXVI.

Here is another expedient tried to work upon this heedless and untoward people, but it is tried in vain. A roll of a book is provided, containing an abstract or abridgement of all the sermons that Jeremiah had preached to them, that they might be put in mind of what they had heard and might the better understand it, when they had it all before them at one view. Now here we have, I. The writing of this roll by Baruch, as Jeremiah dictated it, ver. 1—4. II. The reading of the roll by Baruch to all the people publicly on a fast-day (ver. 5—10), afterwards by Baruch to the princes privately (ver. 11—19), and lastly by Jehudi to the king, ver. 20, 21. III. The burning of the roll by the king, with orders to prosecute Jeremiah and Baruch, ver. 22—26. IV. The writing of another roll, with large additions, particularly of Jehoiakim's doom for burning the former, ver. 27—32.

AND it came to pass in the fourth year of Jehoiakim the son of Josiah king of Judah, *that* this word came unto Jeremiah from the LORD, saying, 2 Take thee a roll of a book,

and write therein all the words that I have spoken unto thee against Israel, and against Judah, and against all the nations, from the day I spake unto thee, from the days of Josiah, even unto this day. 3 It may be that the house of Judah will hear all the evil which I purpose to do unto them ; that they may return every man from his evil way ; that I may forgive their iniquity and their sin. 4 Then Jeremiah called Baruch the son of Neriah : and Baruch wrote from the mouth of Jeremiah all the words of the LORD, which he had spoken unto him, upon a roll of a book. 5 And Jeremiah commanded Baruch, saying, I *am* shut up ; I cannot go into the house of the LORD : 6 Therefore go thou, and read in the roll, which thou hast written from my mouth, the words of the LORD in the ears of the people in the LORD'S house upon the fasting-day : and also thou shalt read them in the ears of all Judah that come out of their cities. 7 It may be they will present their supplication before the LORD, and will return every one from his evil way : for great *is* the anger and the fury that the LORD hath pronounced against this people. 8 And Baruch the son of Neriah did according to all that Jeremiah the prophet commanded him, reading in the book the words of the LORD in the LORD'S house.

In the beginning of Ezekiel's prophecy we meet with *a roll* written *in vision,* for discovery of the things therein contained to the prophet himself, who was to receive and digest them, Ezek. ii. 9, 10; iii. 1. Here, in the latter end of Jeremiah's prophecy, we meet with *a roll* written *in fact,* for discovery of the things contained therein to the people, who were to hear and give heed to them ; for the written word and other good books are of great use both to ministers and people. We have here,

I. The command which God gave to Jeremiah to write a summary of his sermons, of all the reproofs and all the warnings he had given in God's name to his people, ever since he first began to be a preacher, in the thirteenth year of Josiah, *to this day,* which was in the fourth year of Jehoiakim, *v.* 2, 3. What had been only spoken must now be written, that it might be reviewed, and that it might spread the further and last the longer. What had been spoken at large, with frequent repetitions of the same things, perhaps in the same words (which has its advantage one way), must now be contracted and put into less compass, that the several parts of it might be better compared together, which has its advantage another way. What they had heard once must be recapitulated, and rehearsed to them again, that what was forgotten might be called to mind again and what made no impression upon them at the first hearing might take hold of them when they heard it the second time. And what was perhaps already written, and published in single sermons, must be collected into one volume, that none might be lost. Note, The writing of the scripture is by divine appointment. And observe the reason here given for the writing of this roll (*v.* 3) : *It may be the house of Judah will hear*. Not that the divine prescience was at any uncertainty concerning the event : with that there is no peradventure ; God knew certainly *that they would deal very treacherously*, Isa. xlviii. 8. But the divine wisdom directed to this as a proper means for attaining the desired end : and, if it failed, they would be the more inexcusable. And, though God foresaw that they would not hear, he did not tell the prophet so, but prescribed this method to him as a probable one to be used, in the hopes that they would *hear*, that is, heed and regard what they heard, take notice of it and mix faith with it : for otherwise our hearing the word, though an angel from heaven were to read or preach it to us, would stand us in no stead. Now observe here, 1. What it is hoped they will thus hear : *All that evil which I purpose to do unto them.* Note, The serious consideration of the certain fatal consequences of sin will be of great use to us to bring us to God. 2. What it is hoped will be produced thereby : *They will hear, that they may return every man from his evil way.* Note, The conversion of sinners from their evil courses is that which ministers should aim at in preaching ; and people hear the word in vain if that point be not gained with them. To what purpose do we hear of the evil God will bring upon us for sin if we continue, notwithstanding, to do evil against him ? 3. Of what vast advantage their consideration and conversion will be to them : *That I may forgive their iniquity.* This plainly implies the honour of God's justice, with which it is not consistent that he should forgive the sin unless the sinner repent of it and turn from it; but it plainly expresses the honour of his mercy, that he is very ready to forgive sin and only waits till the sinner be qualified to receive forgiveness, and therefore uses various means to bring us to repentance, *that he may forgive*.

II. The instructions which Jeremiah gave to Baruch his scribe, pursuant to the command he had received from God, and the writing of the roll accordingly, *v.* 4. God bade Jeremiah write, but, it should seem,

he had not the *pen of a ready writer*, he could not write fast, or fair, so as Baruch could, and therefore he made use of him as his amanuensis. St. Paul wrote but few of his epistles with his own hand, Gal. vi. 11 ; Rom. xvi. 22. God dispenses his gifts variously ; some have a good faculty at speaking, others at writing, and neither can say to the other, We have *no need of you*, 1 Cor. xii. 21. The Spirit of God dictated to Jeremiah, and he to Baruch, who had been employed by Jeremiah as trustee for him in his purchase of the field (*ch.* xxxii. 12) and now was advanced to be his scribe and substitute in his prophetical office ; and, if we may credit the apocryphal book that bears his name, he was afterwards himself a prophet to the captives in Babylon. Those that begin low are likely to rise high, and it is good for those that are designed for prophets to have their education under prophets and to be serviceable to them. Baruch wrote what Jeremiah dictated in a *roll of a book*, on pieces of parchment, or vellum, which were joined together, the top of one to the bottom of the other, so making one long scroll, which was rolled perhaps upon a staff.

III. The orders which Jeremiah gave to Baruch to read what he had written to the people. Jeremiah, it seems, was *shut up*, and *could not go to the house of the Lord* himself, *v.* 5. Though he was not a close prisoner, for then there would have been no occasion to send officers to seize him (*v.* 26), yet he was forbidden by the king to appear in the temple, was shut out thence, where he might be serving God and doing good, which was as bad to him as if he had been shut up in a dungeon. Jehoiakim was ripening apace for ruin when he thus silenced God's faithful messengers. But, when Jeremiah could not go to the temple himself, he sent one that was deputed by him to read to the people what he would himself have said. Thus St. Paul wrote epistles to the churches which he could not visit in person. Nay, it was what he himself had often said to them. Note, The writing and repeating of the sermons that have been preached may contribute very much towards the answering of the great ends of preaching. What we have heard and known it is good for us to hear again, that we may know it better. To preach and write the same thing is safe and profitable, and many times very necessary (Phil. iii. 1), and we must be glad to hear a good word from God, though we have it, as here, at second hand. Both ministers and people must do what they can when they cannot do what they would. Observe, When God ordered the reading of the roll he said, *It may be they will hear and return from their evil ways, v.* 3. When Jeremiah orders it, he says, *It may be they will pray* (they will *present their supplications before the Lord)* and will *return from their evil way.* Note, Prayer to God for grace to turn us is necessary in order to our turning; and those that are convinced by the word of God of the necessity of returning to him will present their supplications to him for that grace. And the consideration of this, that *great is the anger which God has pronounced against us* for sin, should quicken both our prayers and our endeavours. Now, according to these orders, Baruch did read *out of the book the words of the Lord,* whenever there was a *holy convocation, v.* 8.

9 And it came to pass in the fifth year of Jehoiakim the son of Josiah king of Judah, in the ninth month, *that* they proclaimed a fast before the LORD to all the people in Jerusalem, and to all the people that came from the cities of Judah unto Jerusalem. 10 Then read Baruch in the book the words of Jeremiah in the house of the LORD, in the chamber of Gemariah the son of Shaphan the scribe, in the higher court, at the entry of the new gate of the LORD's house, in the ears of all the people. 11 When Michaiah the son of Gemariah, the son of Shaphan, had heard out of the book all the words of the LORD, 12 Then he went down into the king's house, into the scribe's chamber: and, lo, all the princes sat there, *even* Elishama the scribe, and Delaiah the son of Shemaiah, and Elnathan the son of Achbor, and Gemariah the son of Shaphan, and Zedekiah the son of Hananiah, and all the princes. 13 Then Michaiah declared unto them all the words that he had heard, when Baruch read the book in the ears of the people. 14 Therefore all the princes sent Jehudi the son of Nethaniah, the son of Shelemiah, the son of Cushi, unto Baruch, saying, Take in thine hand the roll wherein thou hast read in the ears of the people, and come. So Baruch the son of Neriah took the roll in his hand, and came unto them. 15 And they said unto him, Sit down now, and read it in our ears. So Baruch read *it* in their ears. 16 Now it came to pass, when they had heard all the words, they were afraid both one and other, and said unto Baruch, We will surely tell the king of all these words. 17 And they asked Baruch, saying, Tell us now, How didst thou write all

these words at his mouth ? 18 Then Baruch answered them, He pronounced all these words unto me with his mouth, and I wrote *them* with ink in the book. 19 Then said the princes unto Baruch, Go, hide thee, thou and Jeremiah; and let no man know where ye be.

It should seem that Baruch had been frequently reading out of the book, to all companies that would give him the hearing, before the most solemn reading of it altogether which is here spoken of; for the directions were given about it in the *fourth year of Jehoiakim,* whereas this was done *in the fifth year, v.* 9. But some think that the writing of the book fairly over took up so much time that it was another year ere it was perfected ; and yet perhaps it might not be past a month or two; he might begin in the latter end of the fourth year and finish it in the beginning of the fifth, for *the ninth month* refers to the computation of the year in general, not to the year of that reign. Now observe here, 1. The government appointed a public fast to be religiously observed (*v.* 9), on account either of the distress they were brought into by the army of the Chaldeans or of the want of rain (*ch.* xiv. 1): *They proclaimed a fast to the people;* whether the king and princes, or the priests, ordered this fast, is not certain; but it was plain that God by his providence called them aloud to it. Note, Great shows of piety and devotion may be found even among those who, though they keep up these *forms of godliness,* are strangers and enemies to *the power* of it. But what will such hypocritical services avail? Fasting, without reforming and turning away from sin, will never turn away the judgments of God, Jon. iii. 10. Notwithstanding this fast, God proceeded in his controversy with this people. 2. Baruch repeated Jeremiah's sermons publicly in the house of the Lord, on the fast-day. He stood in a chamber that belonged to Gemariah, and out of a window, or balcony, read to the people that were in the court, *v.* 10. Note, When we are speaking to God we must be willing to hear from him; and therefore, on days of fasting and prayer, it is requisite that the word be read and preached. *Hearken unto me, that God may hearken unto you.* Judg. ix. 7. For our help in suing out mercy and grace, it is proper that we should be told of sin and duty. 3. An account was brought of this to the princes that attended the court and were now together in the secretary's office, here called *the scribe's chamber, v* 12. It should seem, though the princes had called the people to meet in the house of God, to fast, and pray, and hear the word, they did not think fit to attend there themselves, which was a sign that it was not from a principle of true devotion, but merely for fashion-sake, that they proclaimed this fast. We are willing to hope that it was not with a bad design, to bring Jeremiah into trouble for his preaching, but with a good design, to bring the princes into trouble for their sins, that Michaiah informed the princes of what Baruch had read ; for his father Gemariah so far countenanced Baruch as to lend him his chamber to read out of. Michaiah finds the princes sitting in *the scribe's chamber,* and tells them they had better have been where he had been, hearing a good sermon in the temple, which he gives them the heads of. Note, When we have heard some good word that has affected and edified us we should be ready to communicate it to others that did not hear it, for their edification. *Out of the abundance of the heart the mouth speaks.* 4. Baruch is sent for, and is ordered to sit down among them and read it all over again to them (*v.* 14, 15), which he readily did, not complaining that he was weary with his public work and therefore desiring to be excused, nor upbraiding the princes with their being absent from the temple, where they might have heard it when he read it there. Note, God's ministers must *become all things to all men, if by any means they may gain some,* must comply with them in circumstances, that they may secure the substance. St. Paul preached privately to those of reputation, Gal. ii. 2. 5. The princes were for the present much affected with the word that was read to them, *v.* 16. Observe, *They heard all the words;* they did not interrupt him, but very patiently attended to the reading of the whole book; for otherwise how could they form a competent judgment of it? And, *when they had heard all, they were afraid,* were all afraid, *one* as well as *another;* like Felix, who trembled at Paul's reasonings. The reproofs were just, the threatenings terrible, and the predictions now in a fair way to be fulfilled ; so that, laying all together, they were in a great consternation. We are not told what impressions this reading of the roll made upon the people (*v.* 10), but the princes were put into a fright by it, and (as some read it) *looked one upon another,* not knowing what to say. They were all convinced that it was worthy to be regarded, but none of them had courage to second it, only they agreed to *tell the king of all these words;* and, if he think fit to give credit to them, they will, otherwise not, no, though it were to prevent the ruin of the nation. And yet at the same time they knew the king's mind so far that they advised Baruch and Jeremiah to hide themselves (*v.* 19) and to shift as they could for their own safety, expecting no other than that the king, instead of being convinced, would be exasperated. Note, It is common for sinners, under convictions, to endeavour to shake them off, by shifting off the prosecution of them to other persons, as these princes here, or to another *more convenient*

season, as Felix. 6. They asked Baruch a trifling question, *How he wrote all these words* (*v.* 17), as if they suspected there was something extraordinary in it; but Baruch gives them a plain answer, that there was nothing but what was common in the manner of the writing—Jeremiah dictated, and he wrote, *v.* 18. But thus it is common for those who would avoid the convictions of the word of God to start needless questions about the way and manner of the inspiration of it.

20 And they went in to the king into the court, but they laid up the roll in the chamber of Elishama the scribe, and told all the words in the ears of the king. 21 So the king sent Jehudi to fetch the roll: and he took it out of Elishama the scribe's chamber. And Jehudi read it in the ears of the king, and in the ears of all the princes which stood beside the king. 22 Now the king sat in the winter house in the ninth month : and *there was a fire* on the hearth burning before him. 23 And it came to pass, *that* when Jehudi had read three or four leaves, he cut it with the penknife, and cast *it* into the fire that *was* on the hearth, until all the roll was consumed in the fire that *was* on the hearth. 24 Yet they were not afraid, nor rent their garments, *neither* the king, nor any of his servants that heard all these words. 25 Nevertheless Elnathan and Delaiah and Gemariah had made intercession to the king that he would not burn the roll : but he would not hear them. 26 But the king commanded Jerahmeel the son of Hammelech, and Seraiah the son of Azriel, and Shelemiah the son of Abdeel, to take Baruch the scribe and Jeremiah the prophet : but the LORD hid them. 27 Then the word of the LORD came to Jeremiah, after that the king had burned the roll, and the words which Baruch wrote at the mouth of Jeremiah, saying, 28 Take thee again another roll, and write in it all the former words that were in the first roll, which Jehoiakim the king of Judah hath burned. 29 And thou shalt say to Jehoiakim king of Judah, Thus saith the LORD; Thou hast burned this roll, saying, Why hast thou written therein, saying, The king of Babylon

shall certainly come and destroy this land, and shall cause to cease from thence man and beast? 30 There- fore thus saith the LORD of Jehoiakim king of Judah; He shall have none to sit upon the throne of David : and his dead body shall be cast out in the day to the heat, and in the night to the frost. 31 And I will punish him and his seed and his servants for their iniquity; and I will bring upon them, and upon the inhabitants of Jeru- salem, and upon the men of Judah, all the evil that I have pronounced against them; but they hearkened not. 32 Then took Jeremiah another roll, and gave it to Baruch the scribe, the son of Neriah; who wrote therein from the mouth of Jeremiah all the words of the book which Jehoiakim king of Judah had burned in the fire : and there were added besides unto them many like words.

We have traced the roll to the people, and to the princes, and here we are to follow it to the king; and we find,

I. That, upon notice given him concern- ing it, he sent for it, and ordered it to be read to him, v. 20, 21. He did not desire that Baruch would come and read it himself, who could read it more intelligently and with more authority and affection than any one else; nor did he order one of his princes to do it (though it would have been no dispa- ragement to the greatest of them), much less would he vouchsafe to read it himself; but Jehudi, one of his pages now in waiting, who was sent to fetch it, is bidden to read it, who perhaps scarcely knew how to make sense of it. But those who thus despise the word of God will soon make it to appear, as this king did, that they hate it too, and have not only low, but ill thoughts of it.

II. That he had not patience to hear it read through as the princes had, but, when he had heard *three or four leaves* read, in a rage he *cut it with his penknife*, and threw it piece by piece *into the fire*, that he might be sure to see it *all consumed*, v. 22, 23. This was a piece of as daring impiety as a man could lightly be guilty of, and a most impudent affront to the God of heaven, whose message this was. 1. Thus he showed his impatience of reproof; being resolved to persist in sin, he would by no means bear to be told of his faults. 2. Thus he showed his indignation at Baruch and Jeremiah; he would have cut them in pieces, and burnt them, if he had had them in his reach, when he was in this passion. 3. Thus he expressed an obstinate resolution never to comply with the designs and intentions of the warnings

given him; he will do what he will, what- ever God by his prophets says to the contrary. 4. Thus he foolishly hoped to defeat the threatenings denounced against him, as if God knew not how to execute the sentence when the roll was gone in which it was written. 5. Thus he thought he had effec- tually provided that the things contained in this roll should spread no further, which was the care of the chief priests concerning the gospel, Acts iv. 17. They had told him how this roll had been read to the people and to the princes. " But," says he, " I will take a course that shall prevent its being read any more." See what an enmity there is against God in the carnal mind, and wonder at the patience of God, that he bears with such indignities done to him.

III. That neither the king himself nor any of his princes were at all affected with the word : *They were not afraid (v.* 24), no, not those princes that *trembled at the word* when they heard it the first time, v. 16. So soon, so easily, do good impressions wear off. They showed some concern till they saw how light the king made of it, and then they shook off all that concern. They *rent not their garments*, as Josiah, this Jehoia- kim's own father, did when he had the *book of the law* read to him, though it was not so particular as the contents of this roll were, nor so immediately adapted to the present posture of affairs.

IV. That there were three of the princes who had so much sense and grace left as to interpose for the preventing of the burning of the roll, but in vain, v. 25. If they had from the first shown themselves, as they ought to have done, affected with the word, perhaps they might have brought the king to a better mind and have persuaded him to bear it patiently; but frequently those that will not do the good they should put it out of their own power to do the good they would.

V. That Jehoiakim, when he had thus in effect burnt God's warrant by which he was arrested, as it were in a way of revenge, now that he thought he had got the better, signed a warrant for the apprehending of Jeremiah and Baruch, God's ministers (v. 26): *But the Lord hid them*. The princes bade them abscond (v. 19), but it was neither the princes' care for them nor theirs for themselves that secured them; it was under the divine protection that they were safe. Note, God will find out a shelter for his people, though their persecutors be ever so industrious to get them into their power, till their hour be come; nay, and then he will himself be their hiding place.

VI. That Jeremiah had orders and in- structions to write in another roll the same words that were written in the roll which Jehoiakim had burnt, v. 27, 28. Note, Though the attempts of hell against the word of God are very daring, yet not one iota or tittle of it shall fall to the ground, nor shall the unbelief of man make the word of God of no effect. Enemies may prevail to burn many a Bible, but they cannot abolish the word of God, can neither extirpate it nor defeat the accomplishment of it. Though the tables of the law were broken, they were renewed again; and so out of the ashes of the roll that was burnt arose another Phœnix. *The word of the Lord endures for ever.*

VII. That the king of Judah, though a king, was severely reckoned with by the King of kings for this indignity done to the written word. God noticed what it was in the roll that Jehoiakim took so much offence at. Jehoiakim was angry because it was *written therein, saying,* Surely *the king of Babylon shall come and destroy this land,* v. 29. And did not *the king of Babylon* come two years before this, and go far towards *the destroying of this land?* He did so (2 Chron. xxxvi. 6, 7) in his third year, Dan. i. 1. So that God and his prophets had *therefore become his enemies because they told him the truth,* told him of the desolation that was coming, but at the same time putting him into a fair way to prevent it. But, if this be the thing he takes so much amiss, let him know, 1. That the wrath of God shall come upon him and his family, in the first place, by the hand of Nebuchadnezzar. He shall be cut off, and in a few weeks his son shall be dethroned, and exchange his royal robes for prison-garments, so that *he shall have none to sit upon the throne of David;* the glory of that illustrious house shall be eclipsed, and die in him; *his dead body* shall lie unburied, or, which comes all to one, *he shall be buried with the burial of an ass,* that is, thrown into the next ditch; it shall lie exposed to all weathers, *heat and frost,* which will occasion its putrefying and becoming loathsome the sooner. "Not that his body" (says Mr. Gataker) "could be sensible of such usage, or himself, being deceased, of aught that should befal his body; but that the king's body in such a condition should be a hideous spectacle, and a horrid monument of God's heavy wrath and indignation against him, unto all that should behold it." Even *his seed and his servants* shall fare the worse for their relation to him (v. 31), for they shall be punished, not for his iniquity, but so much the sooner for their own. 2. That all the evil pronounced against Judah and Jerusalem in that roll shall be brought upon them. Though the copy be burnt, the original remains in the divine counsel, which shall again be copied out after another manner in bloody characters. Note, There is no escaping God's judgments by struggling with them. *Who ever hardened his heart against God, and prospered?*

VIII. That, when the roll was written anew, *there were added* to the former *many like words* (v. 32), many more threatenings

636

of wrath and vengeance; for, since they will yet *walk contrary to God,* he will *heat the furnace seven times hotter.* Note, As God is in one mind, and none can turn him, so he has still more arrows in his quiver; and those who contend with God's woes do but prepare for themselves heavier of the same kind.

CHAP. XXXVII.

This chapter brings us very near the destruction of Jerusalem by the Chaldeans, for the story of it lies in the latter end of Zedekiah's reign; we have in it, I. A general idea of the bad character of that reign, ver. 1, 2. II. The message which Zedekiah, notwithstanding, sent to Jeremiah to desire his prayers, ver. 3. III. The flattering hopes which the people had conceived, that the Chaldeans would quit the siege of Jerusalem, ver. 5. IV. The assurance God gave them by Jeremiah (who was now at liberty, ver. 4) that the Chaldean army should renew the siege and take the city, ver. 6—10. V. The imprisonment of Jeremiah, under pretence that he was a deserter, ver. 11—15. VI. The kindness which Zedekiah showed him when he was a prisoner, ver. 16—21.

AND king Zedekiah the son of Josiah reigned instead of Coniah the son of Jehoiakim, whom Nebuchadrezzar king of Babylon made king in the land of Judah. 2 But neither he, nor his servants, nor the people of the land, did hearken unto the words of the LORD, which he spake by the prophet Jeremiah. 3 And Zedekiah the king sent Jehucal the son of Shelemiah and Zephaniah the son of Maaseiah the priest to the prophet Jeremiah, saying, Pray now unto the LORD our God for us. 4 Now Jeremiah came in and went out among the people: for they had not put him into prison. 5 Then Pharaoh's army was come forth out of Egypt: and when the Chaldeans that besieged Jerusalem heard tidings of them, they departed from Jerusalem. 6 Then came the word of the LORD unto the prophet Jeremiah, saying, 7 Thus saith the LORD, the God of Israel; Thus shall ye say to the king of Judah, that sent you unto me to enquire of me; Behold, Pharaoh's army, which is come forth to help you, shall return to Egypt into their own land. 8 And the Chaldeans shall come again, and fight against this city, and take it, and burn it with fire. 9 Thus saith the LORD; Deceive not yourselves, saying, The Chaldeans shall surely depart from us: for they shall not depart. 10 For though ye had smitten the whole army of the Chaldeans that fight against you, and there remained *but* wounded men among them, *yet* should they rise up every man in his tent, and burn this city with fire.

Here is, 1. Jeremiah's preaching slighted, *v.* 1, 2. Zedekiah succeeded Coniah, or Jeconiah, and, though he saw in his predecessor the fatal consequences of contemning the word of God, yet he did not take warning, nor give any more regard to it than others had done before him. *Neither he, nor his courtiers, nor the people of the land, hearkened unto the words of the Lord,* though they already began to be fulfilled. Note, Those have hearts wretchedly hard indeed that see God's judgments on others, and feel them on themselves, and yet will not be humbled and brought to heed what he says. These had proof sufficient that it was the Lord who spoke by Jeremiah the prophet, and yet they would not hearken to him. 2. Jeremiah's prayers desired. Zedekiah sent messengers to him, saying, *Pray now unto the Lord our God for us.* He did so before (*ch.* xxi. 1, 2), and one of the messengers, Zephaniah, is the same there and here. Zedekiah is to be commended for this, and it shows that he had some good in him, some sense of his need of God's favour and of his own unworthiness to ask it for himself, and some value for good people and good ministers, who had an interest in Heaven. Note, When we are in distress we ought to desire the prayers of our ministers and Christian friends, for thereby we put an honour upon prayer, and an esteem upon our brethren. Kings themselves should look upon their praying people as the strength of the nation, Zech. xii. 5, 10. And yet this does but help to condemn Zedekiah out of his own mouth. If indeed he looked upon Jeremiah as a prophet, whose prayers might avail much both for him and his people, why did he not then believe him, and *hearken to the words of the Lord* which he spoke by him? He desired his good prayers, but would not take his good counsel, nor be ruled by him, though he spoke in God's name, and it appears by this that Zedekiah knew he did. Note, It is common for those to desire to be prayed for who yet will not be advised; but herein they put a cheat upon themselves, for how can we expect that God should hear others speaking to him for us if we will not hear them speaking to us from him and for him? Many who despise prayer when they are in prosperity will be glad of it when they are in adversity. Now *give us of your oil.* When Zedekiah sent to the prophet to pray for him, he had better have sent for the prophet to pray with him; but he thought that below him: and how can those expect the comforts of religion who will not stoop to the services of it? 3. Jerusalem flattered by the retreat of the Chaldean army from it. Jeremiah was now at liberty (*v.* 4); he *went in and out among the people,* might freely speak to them and be spoken to by them. Jerusalem also, for the present, was at liberty, *v.* 5. Zedekiah, though a tributary to the king of Babylon, had entered into a private league with Pharaoh king of Egypt (Ezek. xvii. 15), pursuant to which, when the king of Babylon came to chastise him for his treachery, the king of Egypt, though he came no more in person after that great defeat which Nebuchadnezzar gave him in the reign of Jehoiakim (2 Kings xxiv. 7), yet sent some forces to relieve Jerusalem when it was besieged, upon notice of the approach of which the Chaldeans raised the siege, probably not for fear of them, but in policy, to fight them at a distance, before any of the Jewish forces could join them. From this they encouraged themselves to hope that Jerusalem was delivered for good and all out of the hands of its enemies and that the storm was quite blown over. Note, Sinners are commonly hardened in their security by the intermissions of judgments and the slow proceedings of them; and those who will not be awakened by the word of God may justly be lulled asleep by the providence of God. 4. Jerusalem threatened with the return of the Chaldean army and with ruin by it. Zedekiah sent to Jeremiah to desire him to pray for them, that the Chaldean army might not return; but Jeremiah sends him word back that the decree had gone forth, and that it was but a folly for them to expect peace, for God had begun a controversy with them, which he would make an end of: *Thus saith the Lord, Deceive not yourselves, v.* 9. Note, Satan himself, though he is the great deceiver, could not deceive us if we did not deceive ourselves; and thus sinners are their own destroyers by being their own deceivers, of which this is an aggravation that they are so frequently warned of it and cautioned not to deceive themselves, and they have the word of God, the great design of which is to undeceive them. Jeremiah uses no dark metaphors, but tells them plainly, (1.) That the Egyptians shall retreat, and either give back or be forced back, into *their own land* (Ezek. xvii. 17), which was said of old (Isa. xxx. 7), and is here said again, *v.* 7. The Egyptians shall help in vain; they shall not dare to face the Chaldean army, but shall retire with precipitation. Note, If God help us not, no creature can. As no power can prevail against God, so none can avail without God nor countervail his departures from us. (2.) That the Chaldeans shall return, and shall renew the siege and prosecute it with more vigour than ever: *They shall not depart for good and all (v.* 9); *they shall come again (v.* 8); they shall *fight against the city.* Note, God has the sovereign command of all the hosts of men, even of those that know him not, that own him not, and they are all made to serve his purposes. He directs their marches, their counter-marches, their retreats, their returns, as it pleases him; and furious armies, like *stormy winds,* in all their motions are *fulfilling his word.* (3.) That Jerusalem shall certainly be delivered into the hand of the Chaldeans: *They shall take it, and burn it with fire, v.* 8. The sentence passed upon it shall be executed, and they shall be the executioners. "O but" (say they) "the Chaldeans have withdrawn; they have quitted the enterprise as impracticable." "And though they have," says the prophet, "nay, *though you had smitten* their army, so that many were slain and all the rest wounded, yet those *wounded men should rise up and burn this city," v.* 10. This is designed to denote that the doom passed upon Jerusalem is irrevocable, and its destruction inevitable; it must be laid in ruins, and these Chaldeans are the men that must destroy it, and it is now in vain to think of evading the stroke or contending with it. Note, Whatever instruments God has determined to make use of in any service for him, whether of mercy or judgment, they shall accomplish that for which they are designed, whatever incapacity or disability they may lie under or be reduced to. Those by whom God has resolved to save or to destroy, saviours they shall be and destroyers they shall be, yea, though they were all wounded; for as when God has work to do he will not want instruments to do it with, though they may seem far to seek; so when he has chosen his instruments they shall do the work, though they may seem very unlikely to accomplish it.

11 And it came to pass, that when the army of the Chaldeans was broken up from Jerusalem for fear of Pharaoh's army, 12 Then Jeremiah went forth out of Jerusalem to go into the land of Benjamin, to separate himself thence in the midst of the people. 13 And when he was in the gate of Benjamin, a captain of the ward *was* there, whose name *was* Irijah, the son of Shelemiah, the son of Hananiah; and he took Jeremiah the prophet, saying, Thou fallest away to the Chaldeans. 14 Then said Jeremiah, *It is* false; I fall not away to the Chaldeans. But he hearkened not to him: so Irijah took Jeremiah, and brought him to the princes. 15 Wherefore the princes were wroth with Jeremiah, and smote him, and put him in prison in the house of Jonathan the scribe: for they had made-that the prison. 16 When Jeremiah was entered into the dungeon, and into the cabins, and Jeremiah

638

had remained there many days; 17 Then Zedekiah the king sent, and took him out: and the king asked him secretly in his house, and said, Is there *any* word from the LORD? and Jeremiah said, There is: for, said he, thou shalt be delivered into the hand of the king of Babylon. 18 Moreover Jeremiah said unto king Zedekiah, What have I offended against thee, or against thy servants, or against this people, that ye have put me in prison? 19 Where *are* now your prophets which prophesied unto you, saying, The king of Babylon shall not come against you, nor against this land? 20 Therefore hear now, I pray thee, O my lord the king: let my supplication, I pray thee, be accepted before thee; that thou cause me not to return to the house of Jonathan the scribe, lest I die there. 21 Then Zedekiah the king commanded that they should commit Jeremiah into the court of the prison, and that they should give him daily a piece of bread out of the bakers' street, until all the bread in the city were spent. Thus Jeremiah remained in the court of the prison.

We have here a further account concerning Jeremiah, who relates more passages concerning himself than any other of the prophets; for the histories of the lives and sufferings of God's ministers have been very serviceable to the church, as well as their preaching and writing.

I. We are here told that Jeremiah, when he had an opportunity for it, attempted to retire out of Jerusalem into the country (*v.* 11, 12): *When the Chaldeans* had *broken up from Jerusalem* because *of Pharaoh's army,* upon the notice of their advancing towards them, Jeremiah determined *to go into the* country, and (as the margin reads it) *to slip away from Jerusalem in the midst of the people,* who, in that interval of the siege, went out into the country to look after their affairs there. He endeavoured to steal away in the crowd; for, though he was a man of great eminence, he could well reconcile himself to obscurity, though he was one of a thousand, he was content to be lost in the multitude and buried alive in a corner, in a cottage. Whether he designed for Anathoth or no does not appear; his concerns might call him thither, but his neighbours there were such as (unless they had mended since *ch.* xi. 21) might discourage him from coming among them; or he might intend to hide himself somewhere where he was not known, and fulfil his own wish (*ch.* ix. 2), *Oh that I had in the wilderness a lodging-place!* Jeremiah found he could do no good in Jerusalem; he laboured in vain among them, and therefore determined to leave them. Note, there are times when it is the wisdom of good men to retire into privacy, to *enter into the chamber and shut the doors about them,* Isa. xxvi. 20.

II. That in this attempt he was seized as a deserter and committed to prison (*v.* 13 —15): *He was in the gate of Benjamin,* so far he had gained his point, when *a captain of the ward,* who probably had the charge of that gate, discovered him and *took him* into custody. He was the grandson of Hananiah, who, the Jews say, was Hananiah the false prophet, who contested with Jeremiah (*ch.* xxviii. 10), and they add that this young captain had a spite to Jeremiah upon that account. He could not arrest him without some pretence, and that which he charges upon him is, *Thou fallest away to the Chaldeans*—an unlikely story, for the Chaldeans had now gone off, Jeremiah could not reach them; or, if he could, who would go over to a baffled army? Jeremiah therefore with good reason, and with both the confidence and the mildness of an innocent man, denies the charge: *It is false; I fall not away to the Chaldeans;* I am going upon my own lawful occasions." Note, It is no new thing for the church's best friends to be represented as in the interest of her worst enemies. Thus have the blackest characters been put upon the fairest purest minds, and, in such a malicious world as this is, innocency, nay, excellency itself, is no fence against the basest calumny. When at any time we are thus falsely accused we may do as Jeremiah did, boldly deny the charge and then commit our cause to him that judges righteously. Jeremiah's protestation of his integrity, though he is a prophet, a man of God, a man of honour and sincerity, though he is a priest, and is ready to say it *in verbo sacerdotis—on the word of a priest,* is not regarded; but he is brought before the privy-council, who without examining him and the proofs against him, but upon the base malicious insinuation of the captain, fell into a passion with him: they *were wroth;* and what justice could be expected from men who, being in anger, would hear no reason? They beat him, without any regard had to his coat and character, and then *put him in prison,* in the worst prison they had, that *in the house of Jonathan the scribe;* either it had been his house, and he had quitted it for the inconveniences of it, but it was thought good enough for a prison, or it was now his house, and perhaps he was a rigid severe man, that made it a house of cruel bondage to his prisoners. Into this prison Jeremiah was thrust, *into the dungeon,* which was dark and cold, damp and dirty, the most

uncomfortable unhealthy place in it; in the cells, or *cabins,* there he must lodge, among which there is no choice, for they are all alike miserable lodging-places. *There Jeremiah remained many days,* and, for aught that appears, nobody came near him or enquired after him. See what a world this is. The wicked princes, who are in rebellion against God, lie at ease, lie in state in their palaces, while godly Jeremiah, who is in the service of God, lies in pain, in a loathsome dungeon. It is well that there is a world to come.

III. That Zedekiah at length sent for him, and showed him some favour; but probably not till the Chaldean army had returned and had laid fresh siege to the city. When their vain hopes, with which they fed themselves (and in confidence of which they had re-enslaved their servants, *ch.* xxxiv. 11), had all vanished, then they were in a greater confusion and consternation than ever. " O then" (says Zedekiah) " send in all haste for the prophet; let me have some talk with him." When the Chaldeans had withdrawn, he only sent to the prophet to pray for him; but now that they had again invested the city, he sent for him to consult him. Thus gracious will men be when pangs come upon them. 1. The king sent for him to give him private audience as an ambassador from God. He *asked him secretly in his house,* being ashamed to be seen in his company, " *Is there any word from the Lord?* (*v.* 17)—any word of comfort? Canst thou give us any hopes that the Chaldeans shall again retire?" Note, Those that will not hearken to God's admonitions when they are in prosperity would be glad of his consolations when they are in adversity and expect that his ministers should then speak words of peace to them; but how can they expect it? What have they to do with peace? Jeremiah's life and comfort are in Zedekiah's hand, and he has now a petition to present to him for his favour, and yet, having this opportunity, he tells him plainly that *there is a word from the Lord,* but no word of comfort for him or his people: *Thou shalt be delivered into the hand of the king of Babylon.* If Jeremiah had consulted with flesh and blood, he would have given him a plausible answer, and, though he would not have told him a lie, yet he might have chosen whether he would tell him the worst at this time; what occasion was there for it, when he had so often told it him before? But Jeremiah was one that had *obtained mercy of the Lord to be faithful,* and would not, to obtain mercy of man, be unfaithful either to God or to his prince; he therefore tells him the truth, the whole truth. And, since there was no remedy, it would be a kindness to the king to know his doom, that, being no surprise to him, it might be the less a terror, and he might provide to make the best of bad. Jeremiah takes this occasion to upbraid him and his people with the credit they gave to the false prophets, who told them that *the king of Babylon should not come* at all, or, when he had withdrawn, should *not come* again *against* them, *v.* 19. "*Where are now your prophets*, who told you that you should have peace?" Note, Those who deceive themselves with groundless hopes of mercy will justly be upbraided with their folly when the event has undeceived them. 2. He improved this opportunity for the presenting of a private petition, as a poor prisoner, *v.* 18, 20. It was not in Jeremiah's power to reverse the sentence God had passed upon Zedekiah, but it was in Zedekiah's power to reverse the sentence which the princes had given against him; and therefore, since he thought him fit to be used as a prophet, he would not think him fit to be abused as the worst of malefactors. He humbly expostulates with the king: "*What have I offended against thee, or thy servants, or this people,* what law have I broken, what injury have I done to the common welfare, *that you have put me in prison?*" And many a one that has been very hardly dealt with has been able to make the same appeal and to make it good. He likewise earnestly begs, and very pathetically (*v.* 20), *Cause me not to return* to yonder noisome gaol, *to the house of Jonathan the scribe, lest I die there.* This was the language of innocent nature, sensible of its own grievances and solicitous for its own preservation. Though he was not at all unwilling to die God's martyr, yet, having so fair an opportunity to get relief, he would not let it slip, lest he should die his own murderer. When Jeremiah delivered God's message he spoke as one having authority, with the greatest boldness; but, when he presented his own request, he spoke as one under authority, with the greatest submissiveness: *Hear me, I pray thee, O my Lord the king! let my supplication, I pray thee, be accepted before thee.* Here is not a word of complaint of the princes that unjustly committed him, no offer to bring an action of false imprisonment against them, but all in a way of modest supplication to the king, to teach us that even when we act with the courage that becomes the faithful servants of God, yet we must conduct ourselves with the humility and modesty that become dutiful subjects to the government God hath set over us. A lion in God's cause must be a lamb in his own. And we find that God gave Jeremiah favour in the eyes of the king. (1.) He gave him his request, took care that he should not die in the dungeon, but ordered that he should have the liberty of the *court of the prison,* where he might have a pleasant walk and breathe a free air. (2.) He gave him more than his request, took care that he should not die for want, as many did that had their liberty, by reason of the straitness of the siege; he ordered

640

him his *daily bread out of the* public stock (for the prison was within the verge of the court), *till all the bread was spent.* Zedekiah ought to have released him, nay, to have preferred him, to have made him a privy-counsellor, as Joseph was taken from prison to be the second man in the kingdom. But he had not courage to do that; it was well he did as he did, and it is an instance of the care God takes of his suffering servants that are faithful to him. He can make even their confinement turn to their advantage and the court of their prison to become as green pastures to them, and raise up such friends to provide for them that *in the days of famine they shall be satisfied. At destruction and famine thou shalt laugh.*

CHAP. XXXVIII.

In this chapter, just as in the former, we have Jeremiah greatly debased under the frowns of the princes, and yet greatly honoured by the favour of the king. They used him as a criminal; he used him as a privy-counsellor. Here, I. Jeremiah for his faithfulness is put into the dungeon by the princes, ver. 1—6. II. At the intercession of Ebed-melech the Ethiopian, by special order from the king, he is taken out of the dungeon and confined only to the court of the prison, ver. 7—13. III. He has a private conference with the king upon the present conjuncture of affairs, ver. 14—23. IV. Care is taken to keep that conference private, ver. 24—28.

THEN Shephatiah the son of Mattan, and Gedaliah the son of Pashur, and Jucal the son of Shelemiah, and Pashur the son of Malchiah, heard the words that Jeremiah had spoken unto all the people, saying, 2 Thus saith the LORD, He that remaineth in this city shall die by the sword, by the famine, and by the pestilence: but he that goeth forth to the Chaldeans shall live; for he shall have his life for a prey, and shall live. 3 Thus saith the LORD, This city shall surely be given into the hand of the king of Babylon's army, which shall take it. 4 Therefore the princes said unto the king, We beseech thee, let this man be put to death: for thus he weakeneth the hands of the men of war that remain in this city, and the hands of all the people, in speaking such words unto them: for this man seeketh not the welfare of this people, but the hurt. 5 Then Zedekiah the king said, Behold, he *is* in your hand: for the king *is* not *he that* can do *any* thing against you. 6 Then took they Jeremiah, and cast him into the dungeon of Malchiah the son of Hammelech, that *was* in the court of the prison: and they let down Jeremiah with cords. And in the dungeon *there was* no water, but mire: so Jeremiah sunk in the mire. 7 Now when Ebed-melech the Ethiopian, one of the eunuchs which was in the king's house, heard that they had put Jeremiah in the dungeon; the king then sitting in the gate of Benjamin; 8 Ebed-melech went forth out of the king's house, and spake to the king, saying, 9 My lord the king, these men have done evil in all that they have done to Jeremiah the prophet, whom they have cast into the dungeon; and he is like to die for hunger in the place where he is: for *there is* no more bread in the city. 10 Then the king commanded Ebed-melech the Ethiopian, saying, Take from hence thirty men with thee, and take up Jeremiah the prophet out of the dungeon, before he die. 11 So Ebed-melech took the men with him, and went into the house of the king under the treasury, and took thence old cast clouts and old rotten rags, and let them down by cords into the dungeon to Jeremiah. 12 And Ebed-melech the Ethiopian said unto Jeremiah, Put now *these* old cast clouts and rotten rags under thine armholes under the cords. And Jeremiah did so. 13 So they drew up Jeremiah with cords, and took him up out of the dungeon: and Jeremiah remained in the court of the prison.

Here, 1. Jeremiah persists in his plain preaching; what he had many a time said, he still says (*v.* 3): *This city shall be given into the hand of the king of Babylon;* though it hold out long, it will be taken at last. Nor would he have so often repeated this unwelcome message but that he could put them in a certain way, though not to save the city, yet to save themselves; so that every man might have his own life given him for a prey if he would be advised, *v.* 2. Let him not stay in the city, in hopes to defend that, for it will be to no purpose, but let him *go forth to the Chaldeans,* and throw himself upon their mercy, before things come to extremity, and then he *shall live;* they will not put him to the sword, but give him quarter (*satis est prostrásse leoni*—it *suffices the lion to lay his antagonist prostrate*) and he shall escape *the famine and pestilence,* which will be the death of multitudes within the city. Note, Those do better for themselves who patiently submit to the rebukes of Providence than those who contend with them. And, if we cannot have our liberty, we must reckon it a mercy to have our lives,

and not foolishly throw them away upon a point of honour; they may be reserved for better times. 2. The princes persist in their malice against Jeremiah. He was faithful to his country and to his trust as a prophet, though he had suffered many a time for his faithfulness; and, though at this time he ate the king's bread, yet that did not stop his mouth. But his persecutors were still bitter against him, and complained that he abused the liberty he had of walking in the court of the prison; for, though he could not go to the temple to preach, yet he vented the same things in private conversation to those that came to visit him, and therefore (*v.* 4) they represented him to the king as a dangerous man, disaffected to his country and to the government he lived under: *He seeks not the welfare of this people, but the hurt*—an unjust insinuation, for no man had laid out himself more for the good of Jerusalem than he had done. They represent his preaching as having a bad tendency. The design of it was plainly to bring men to repent and turn to God, which would have been as much as any thing a strengthening to the hands both of the soldiery and of the burghers, and yet they represented it *as weakening their hands* and discouraging them; and, if it did this, it was their own fault. Note, It is common for wicked people to look upon God's faithful ministers as their enemies, only because they show them what enemies they are to themselves while they continue impenitent. 3. Jeremiah hereupon, by the king's permission, is put into a dungeon, with a view to his destruction there. Zedekiah, though he felt a conviction that Jeremiah was a prophet, sent of God, had not courage to own it, but yielded to the violence of his persecutors (*v.* 5): *He is in your hand;* and a worse sentence he could not have passed upon him. We found in Jehoiakim's reign that the princes were better affected to the prophet than the king was (*ch.* xxxvi. 25); but now they were more violent against him, a sign that they were ripening apace for ruin. Had it been in a cause that concerned his own honour or profit, he would have let them know that the king is he who can do what he pleases, whether they will or no; but in the cause of God and his prophet, which he was very cool in, he basely sneaks, and truckles to them: *The king is not he that can do any thing against you.* Note, Those will have a great deal to answer for who, though they have a secret kindness for good people, dare not own it in a time of need, nor will do what they might do to prevent mischief designed them. The princes, having this general warrant from the king, immediately put poor *Jeremiah into the dungeon of Malchiah, that was in the court of the prison* (*v.* 6), a deep dungeon, for they *let* him *down* into it *with cords,* and a dirty one, for there *was no water* in it, *but mire;* and he *sunk in the mire, up to the neck,* says Josephus. Those that put him here doubtless designed that he should die here, die for hunger, die for cold, and so die miserably, die obscurely, fearing, if they should put him to death openly, the people might be affected with what he would say and be incensed against them. Many of God's faithful witnesses have thus been privately made away, and starved to death, in prisons, whose blood will be brought to account in the day of discovery. We are not here told what Jeremiah did in this distress, but he tells us himself (Lam. iii. 55, 57), *I called upon thy name, O Lord! out of the low dungeon, and thou drewest near, saying, Fear not.* 4. Application is made to the king by an honest courtier, *Ebed-melech*, one of the gentlemen of the bed-chamber, in behalf of the poor sufferer. Though the princes carried on the matter as privately as they could, yet it came to the ear of this good man, who probably sought opportunities to do good. It may be he came to the knowledge of it by hearing Jeremiah's moans out of the dungeon, for it was in the king's house, *v.* 7. *Ebed-melech* was an Ethiopian, *a stranger to the commonwealth of Israel*, and yet had in him more humanity, and more divinity too, than native Israelites had. Christ found more faith among Gentiles than among Jews. Ebed-melech lived in a wicked court and in a very corrupt degenerate age, and yet had a great sense both of equity and piety. God has his remnant in all places, among all sorts. There were *saints* even in *Cæsar's household*. The king was now *sitting in the gate of Benjamin*, to try causes and receive appeals and petitions, or perhaps holding a council of war there. Thither Ebed-melech went immediately to him, for the case would not admit delay; the prophet might have perished if he had trifled or put it off till he had an opportunity of speaking to the king in private. No time must be lost when life is in danger, especially so valuable a life. He boldly asserts that Jeremiah had a great deal of wrong done him, and is not afraid to tell the king so, though they were princes that did it, though they were now present in court, and though they had the king's warrant for what they did. Whither should oppressed innocency flee for protection but to the throne, especially when great men are its oppressors? Ebed-melech appears truly brave in this matter. He does not mince the matter; though he had a place at court, which he would be in danger of losing for his plain dealing, yet he tells the king faithfully, let him take it as he will, *These men have done ill in all that they have done to Jeremiah.* They had dealt unjustly with him, for he had not deserved any punishment at all; and they had dealt barbarously with him, so as they used not to deal with the vilest malefactors. And they needed not to have put him to this miserable death; for, if they had let him alone where he was,

642

he was *likely to die for hunger in the place where he was*, in the court of the prison to which he was confined, *for there was no more bread in the city :* the stores out of which he was to have his allowance (*ch.* xxxvii. 21) were in a manner spent. See how God can raise up friends for his people in distress where they little thought of them, and animate men for his service even beyond expectation. 5. Orders are immediately given for his release, and Ebed-melech takes care to see them executed. The king, who but now durst do nothing against the princes, had his heart wonderfully changed on a sudden, and will now have Jeremiah released in defiance of the princes, for therefore he orders no less than thirty men, and those of the lifeguard, to be employed in fetching him out of the dungeon, lest the princes should raise a party to oppose it, *v.* 10. Let this encourage us to appear boldly for God— we may succeed better than we could have thought, for *the hearts of kings are in the hand of God*. Ebed-melech gained his point, and soon brought Jeremiah the good news; and it is observable how particularly the manner of his drawing him out of the dungeon is related (for *God is not unrighteous to forget* any *work or labour of love* which is shown to his people or ministers, no, nor any circumstance of it, Heb. vi. 10); special notice is taken of his great tenderness in providing old soft rags for Jeremiah to put under his arm-holes, to keep the cords wherewith he was to be drawn up from hurting him, his arm-holes being probably galled by the cords wherewith he was let down. Nor did he throw the rags down to him, lest they should be lost in the mire, but carefully let them down, *v.* 11, 12. Note, Those that are in distress should not only be relieved, but relieved with compassion and marks of respect, all which shall be placed to account and abound to a good account in the day of recompence. See what a good use even old rotten rags may be put to, which therefore should not be made waste of, any more than broken meat: even in the king's house, and *under the treasury* too, these were carefully preserved for the use of the poor or sick. Jeremiah is brought up out of the dungeon, and is now where he was, *in the court of the prison, v.* 13. Perhaps Ebed-melech could have made interest with the king to get him his discharge thence also, now that he had the king's ear; but he thought him safer and better provided for there than he would be any where else. God can, when he pleases, make a prison to become a refuge and hiding-place to his people in distress and danger.

14 Then Zedekiah the king sent, and took Jeremiah the prophet unto him into the third entry that *is* in the house of the LORD : and the king said unto Jeremiah, I will ask thee

a thing; hide nothing from me. 15 Then Jeremiah said unto Zedekiah, If I declare *it* unto thee, wilt thou not surely put me to death? and if I give thee counsel, wilt thou not hearken unto me? 16 So Zedekiah the king sware secretly unto Jeremiah, saying, *As* the Lord liveth, that made us this soul, I will not put thee to death, neither will I give thee into the hand of these men that seek thy life. 17 Then said Jeremiah unto Zedekiah, Thus saith the Lord, the God of hosts, the God of Israel; If thou wilt assuredly go forth unto the king of Babylon's princes, then thy soul shall live, and this city shall not be burned with fire; and thou shalt live, and thine house: 18 But if thou wilt not go forth to the king of Babylon's princes, then shall this city be given into the hand of the Chaldeans, and they shall burn it with fire, and thou shalt not escape out of their hand. 19 And Zedekiah the king said unto Jeremiah, I am afraid of the Jews that are fallen to the Chaldeans, lest they deliver me into their hand, and they mock me. 20 But Jeremiah said, They shall not deliver *thee.* Obey, I beseech thee, the voice of the Lord, which I speak unto thee: so it shall be well unto thee, and thy soul shall live. 21 But if thou refuse to go forth, this *is* the word that the Lord hath showed me: 22 And, behold, all the women that are left in the king of Judah's house *shall be* brought forth to the king of Babylon's princes, and those *women* shall say, Thy friends have set thee on, and have prevailed against thee: thy feet are sunk in the mire, *and* they are turned away back. 23 So they shall bring out all thy wives and thy children to the Chaldeans: and thou shalt not escape out of their hand, but shalt be taken by the hand of the king of Babylon: and thou shalt cause this city to be burned with fire. 24 Then said Zedekiah unto Jeremiah, Let no man know of these words, and thou shalt not die. 25 But if the princes hear that I have talked with thee, and they come unto thee, and say unto thee, Declare

unto us now what thou hast said unto the king, hide it not from us, and we will not put thee to death; also what the king said unto thee: 26 Then thou shalt say unto them, I presented my supplication before the king, that he would not cause me to return to Jonathan's house, to die there. 27 Then came all the princes unto Jeremiah, and asked him: and he told them according to all these words that the king had commanded. So they left off speaking with him; for the matter was not perceived. 28 So Jeremiah abode in the court of the prison until the day that Jerusalem was taken: and he was *there* when Jerusalem was taken.

In the foregoing chapter we had the king in close conference with Jeremiah, and here again, though (*v.* 5) he had given him up into the hands of his enemies; such a struggle there was in the breast of this unhappy prince between his convictions and his corruptions. Observe,

I. The honour that Zedekiah did to the prophet. When he was newly fetched out of the dungeon he sent for him to advise with him privately. He met him in *the third entry*, or (as the margin reads it) *the principal entry*, that *is in*, or leads towards, or adjoins to, *the house of the Lord, v.* 14. In appointing this place of interview with the prophet perhaps he intended to show a respect and reverence for *the house of God*, which was proper enough now that he was desiring to hear *the word of God*. Zedekiah would ask *Jeremiah a thing ;* it should rather be rendered, *a word*. "I am here asking thee for *a word of prediction*, of counsel, of comfort, *a word from the Lord, ch.* xxxvii. 17. Whatever word thou hast for me *hide it not from me ;* let me know the worst." He had been told plainly what things would come to in the foregoing chapter, but, like Balaam, he asks again, in hopes to get a more pleasing answer, as if God, who is *in one mind*, were altogether such a one as himself, who was in many minds.

II. The bargain that Jeremiah made with him before he would give him his advice, *v.* 15. He would stipulate, 1. For his own safety. Zedekiah would have him deal faithfully with him: "And if I do," says Jeremiah, "*wilt thou not put me to death ?* I am afraid *thou wilt*" (so some take it); "what else can I expect when thou art led blindfold by the princes ?" Or, Wilt thou promise that thou wilt not ?" Not that Jeremiah was backward to seal the doctrine he preached with his blood, when he was called to do so; but, in doing our duty, we ought to use all lawful means for our own preservation; even the apostles of Christ did so. 2. He would answer for the success of his advice, being no less concerned for Zedekiah's welfare than for his own. He is willing to give him wholesome advice, and does not upbraid him with his unkindness in suffering him to be put into the dungeon, nor bid him go and consult with his princes, whose judgments he had such a value for. Ministers must with meekness instruct even those that oppose themselves, and render good for evil. He is desirous that he should *hear counsel and receive instruction: "Wilt thou not hearken unto me?* Surely thou wilt; I am in hopes to find thee pliable at last, and now *in this thy day* willing to know *the things that belong to thy peace."* Note, Then, and then only, there is hope of sinners, when they are willing to hearken to good counsel. Some read it as spoken despairingly: *"If I give thee counsel, thou wilt not hearken unto me;* I have reason to fear thou wilt not, and then I might as well keep my counsel to myself."* Note, Ministers have little heart to speak to those who have long and often turned a deaf ear to them. Now, as to this latter concern of Jeremiah's, Zedekiah makes him no answer, will not promise to hearken to his advice: though he desires to know what is the mind of God, yet he will reserve himself a liberty, when he does know it, to do as he thinks fit; as if it were the prerogative of a prince not to have his ruin prevented by good counsel. But, as to the prophet's safety, he promises him, upon the word of a king, and confirms his promise with an oath, that, whatever he should say to him, no advantage should be taken against him for it: *I will neither put thee to death nor deliver thee into the hands of those that will, v. 16.* This, he thought, was a mighty favour, and yet Nebuchadnezzar and Belshazzar, when Daniel read their doom, not only protected him, but preferred and rewarded him, Dan. ii. 48; v. 29. Zedekiah's oath on this occasion is solemn, and very observable: *"As the Lord liveth, who made us this soul,* who gave me my life and thee thine, I dare not take away thy life unjustly, knowing that then I should forfeit my own to him that is the Lord of life." Note, God is the Father of spirits; souls are his workmanship, and they are more *fearfully and wonderfully made* than bodies are. The soul both of the greatest prince and of the poorest prisoner is of God's making. *He fashioneth their hearts* alike easily. In all our appeals to God, and in all our dealings both with ourselves and others, we ought to consider this, that *the living God made us these souls.*

III. The good advice that Jeremiah gave him, with good reasons why he should take it, not from any prudence or politics of his own, but in the *name of the Lord, the God of hosts* and *God of Israel.* Not as a statesman, but as a prophet, he advises him by all means to surrender himself and his city *to the king of Babylon's princes: "Go forth to them,* and make the best terms thou canst with them," *v.* 17. This was the advice he had given to the people (*v.* 2, and before, *ch.* xxi. 9), to submit to divine judgments, and not think of contending with them. Note, In dealing with God, that which is good counsel to the meanest is so to the greatest, for *there is no respect of persons* with him. To persuade him to take this counsel, he sets before him good and evil, life and death. 1. If he will tamely yield, he shall save his children from the sword and Jerusalem from the flames. The white flag is yet hung out; if he will but acknowledge God's justice, he shall experience his mercy: *The city shall not be burnt,* and thou *shalt live and thy house.* But, 2. If he will obstinately stand it out, it will be the ruin both of his house and Jerusalem (*v.* 18); for when God judges he will overcome. This is the case of sinners with God; let them humbly submit to his grace and government and they shall live; let them *take hold on his strength, that they may make peace, and they shall make peace;* but, if they harden their hearts against his proposals, it will certainly be to their destruction: they must either bend or break.

IV. The objection which Zedekiah made against the prophet's advice, *v.* 19. Jeremiah spoke to him by prophecy, in the name of God, and therefore if he had had a due regard to the divine authority, wisdom, and goodness, as soon as he understood what the mind of God was he would immediately have acquiesced in it and resolved to observe it, without disputing; but, as if it had been the dictate only of Jeremiah's prudence, he advances against it some prudential considerations of his own: but human wisdom is folly when it contradicts the divine counsels. All he suggests is, *"I am afraid,* not of the Chaldeans; their princes are men of honour, but of the Jews, that have already gone over to the Chaldeans; when they see *me* follow them, who had so much opposed their going, they will laugh at me, and say, *Hast thou also become weak as water?"* Isa. xiv. 10. Now, 1. It was not at all likely that he should be thus exposed and ridiculed, that the Chaldeans should so far gratify the Jews, or trample upon him, as to deliver him into their hands; nor that the Jews, who were themselves captives, should be in such a gay humour as to make a jest of the misery of their prince. Note, We often frighten ourselves from our duty by foolish, causeless, groundless fears, that are merely the creatures of our own fancy and imagination. 2. If he should be taunted at a little by the Jews, could he not despise it and make light of it? What harm would it do him? Note, Those have very weak and fretful spirits indeed that cannot bear to be laughed at for that which is both their duty and their interest. 3. Though it had been really the greatest personal mischief that he could imagine it to be, yet he ought to have ventured it, in obedience to God, and for the preservation of his family and city. He thought it would be looked upon as a piece of cowardice to surrender; whereas it would be really an instance of true courage cheerfully to bear a less evil, the mocking of the Jews, for the avoiding of a greater, the ruin of his family and kingdom.

V. The pressing importunity with which Jeremiah followed the advice he had given the king. He assures him that, if he would comply with the will of God herein, the thing he feared should not come upon him (*v.* 20): *They shall not deliver thee up,* but treat thee as becomes thy character. He begs of him, after all the foolish games he had played, to manage wisely the last stake, and now at length to do well for himself: *Obey, I beseech thee, the voice of the Lord,* because it is his voice, so it *shall be well unto thee.* But he tells him what would be the consequence if he would not obey. 1. He himself would *fall into the hands of the Chaldeans,* as implacable enemies, whom he might now make his friends by throwing himself into their hands. If he must fall, he should contrive how to fall easily: " *Thou shalt not escape,* as thou hopest to do," *v.* 23. 2. He would himself be chargeable with the destruction of Jerusalem, which he pretended a concern for the preservation of: " *Thou shalt cause this city to be burnt with fire,* for by a little submission and self-denial thou mightest have prevented it." Thus subjects often suffer for the pride and wilfulness of their rulers, who should be their protectors, but prove their destroyers. 3. Whereas he causelessly feared an unjust reproach for surrendering, he should certainly fall under a just reproach for standing it out, and that from women too, *v.* 22. The court ladies who were left when Jehoiakim and Jeconiah were carried away will now at length fall into the hands of the enemy, and they shall say, " *The men of thy peace,* whom thou didst consult with and confide in, and who promised thee peace if thou wouldst be ruled by them, have *set thee on,* have encouraged thee to be bold and brave and hold out to the last extremity; and see what comes of it? They, by prevailing upon thee, have *prevailed against thee,* and thou findest those thy real enemies that would be thought thy only friends. *Now thy feet are sunk in the mire,* thou art embarrassed, and hast no way to help thyself; thy feet cannot get forward, but are *turned away back.*" Thus will Zedekiah be bantered by the women, when all his wives and children shall be made a prey to the conquerors, *v.* 23. Note, What we seek to avoid by sin will be justly brought upon us by the righteousness of God. And those that decline the way of duty for fear of reproach will

certainly meet with much greater reproach in the way of disobedience. *The fear of the wicked, it shall come upon him,* Prov. x. 24.

VI. The care which Zedekiah took to keep this conference private (*v.* 24): *Let no man know of these words.* He does not at all incline to take God's counsel, nor so much as promise to consider of it; for so obstinate has he been to the calls of God, and so wilful in the ways of sin, that though he has good counsel given him he seems to be given up to walk in his own counsels. He has nothing to object against Jeremiah's advice, and yet he will not follow it. Many hear God's words, but will not do them. 1. Jeremiah is charged to let no man know of what had passed between the king and him. Zedekiah is concerned to keep it private, not so much for Jeremiah's safety (for he knew the princes could do him no hurt without his permission), but for his own reputation. Note, Many have really a better affection to good men and good things than they are willing to own. God's prophets are manifest in their consciences (2 Cor. v. 11), but they care not for manifesting that to the world; they would rather do them a kindness than have it known that they do: such, it is to be feared, *love the praise of men more than the praise of God.* 2. He is instructed what to say to the princes if they should examine him about it. He must tell them that he was petitioning the king not to remand him back to *the house of Jonathan the scribe* (*v.* 25, 26), and he did tell them so (*v.* 27), and no doubt it was true: he would not let slip so fair an opportunity of engaging the king's favour; so that this was no lie or equivocation, but a part of the truth, which it was lawful for him to put them off with when he was under no obligation at all to tell them the whole truth. Note, Though we must be harmless as doves, so as never to tell a wilful lie, yet we must be wise as serpents, so as not needlessly to expose ourselves to danger by telling all we know.

CHAP. XXXIX.

As the prophet Isaiah, after he had largely foretold the deliverance of Jerusalem out of the hands of the king of Assyria, gave a particular narrative of the story, that it might appear how exactly the event answered to the prediction, so the prophet Jeremiah, after he had largely foretold the delivering of Jerusalem into the hands of the king of Babylon, gives a particular account of that sad event for the same reason. That melancholy story we have in this chapter, which serves to disprove the false flattering prophets and to confirm the word of God's messengers. We are here told, I. That Jerusalem, after eighteen months' siege, was taken by the Chaldean army, ver. 1–3. II. That king Zedekiah, attempting to make his escape, was seized and made a miserable captive to the king of Babylon, ver. 4–7. III. That Jerusalem was burnt to the ground, and the people were carried captive, except the poor, ver. 8–10. IV. That the Chaldeans were very kind to Jeremiah, and took particular care of him, ver. 11–14. V. That Ebed-melech too, for his kindness, had a protection from God himself in this day of desolation, ver. 15–18.

I N the ninth year of Zedekiah king of Judah, in the tenth month, came Nebuchadrezzar king of Babylon and all his army against Jerusalem, and they besieged it. 2 *And* in the eleventh year of Zedekiah, in the fourth month, the ninth *day* of the month, the city was broken up. 3 And all the princes of the king of Babylon came in, and sat in the middle gate, *even* Nergal-sharezer, Samgar-nebo, Sarsechim, Rab-saris, Nergal-sharezer, Rab-mag, with all the residue of the princes of the king of Babylon. 4 And it came to pass, *that* when Zedekiah the king of Judah saw them, and all the men of war, then they fled, and went forth out of the city by night, by the way of the king's garden, by the gate betwixt the two walls: and he went out the way of the plain. 5 But the Chaldeans' army pursued after them, and overtook Zedekiah in the plains of Jericho: and when they had taken him, they brought him up to Nebuchadnezzar king of Babylon to Riblah in the land of Hamath, where he gave judgment upon him. 6 Then the king of Babylon slew the sons of Zedekiah in Riblah before his eyes: also the king of Babylon slew all the nobles of Judah. 7 Moreover he put out Zedekiah's eyes, and bound him with chains, to carry him to Babylon. 8 And the Chaldeans burned the king's house, and the houses of the people, with fire, and brake down the walls of Jerusalem. 9 Then Nebuzar-adan the captain of the guard carried away captive into Babylon the remnant of the people that remained in the city, and those that fell away, that fell to him, with the rest of the people that remained. 10 But Nebuzar-adan the captain of the guard left of the poor of the people, which had nothing, in the land of Judah, and gave them vineyards and fields at the same time.

We were told, in the close of the foregoing chapter, that *Jeremiah abode patiently in the court of the prison, until the day that Jerusalem was taken.* He gave the princes no further disturbance by his prophesying, nor they him by their persecutions; for he had no more to say than what he had said, and, the siege being carried on briskly, God found them other work to do. See here what it came to.

I. The city is at length taken by storm; for how could it hold out when God himself fought against it? Nebuchadnezzar's army sat down before it in the *ninth* year of Zede-

kiah, *in the tenth month* (*v.* 1), in the depth of winter. Nebuchednezzar himself soon after retired to take his pleasure, and left his generals to carry on the siege: they intermitted it awhile, but soon renewed it with redoubled force and vigour. At length, *in the eleventh year, in the fourth month*, about midsummer, they entered the city, the soldiers being so weakened by famine, and all their provisions being now spent, that they were not able to make any resistance, *v.* 2. Jerusalem was so strong a place that nobody would have believed the enemy could ever enter its gates, Lam. iv. 12. But sin had provoked God to withdraw his protection, and then, like Samson when his hair was cut, it was weak as other cities.

II. The princes of the king of Babylon take possession of the *middle gate, v.* 3. Some think that this was the same with that which is called the *second gate* (Zeph. i. 10), which is supposed to be in the middle wall that divided between one part of the city and the other. Here they cautiously made a halt, and durst not go forward into so large a city, among men that perhaps would sell their lives as dearly as they could, until they had given directions for the searching of all places, that they might not be surprised by any ambush. They sat in the *middle gate*, thence to take a view of the city and give orders. The princes are here named, rough and uncouth names they are, to intimate what a sad change sin had made; there, where *Eliakim* and *Hilkiah*, who bore the name of the God of Israel, used to sit, now sit *Nergal-sharezer*, and *Samgar-nebo*, &c., who bore the names of the heathen gods. *Rab-saris* and *Rab-mag* are supposed to be not the names of distinct persons, but the titles of those whose names go before. *Sarsechim* was *Rab-saris*, that is, *captain of the guard;* and *Nergal-sharezer*, to distinguish him from the other of the same name that is put first, is called *Rab-mag—camp-master*, either muster-master or quarter-master: these and the other great generals sat in the gate. And now was fulfilled what Jeremiah prophesied long since (*ch.* i. 15), that the families of the kingdoms of the north should set every one his throne at the entering of the gates of Jerusalem. Justly do the princes of the heathen set up themselves there, where the gods of the heathen had been so often set up.

III. Zedekiah, having in disguise perhaps seen the princes of the king of Babylon take possession of one of the gates of the city, thought it high time to shift for his own safety, and, loaded with guilt and fear, he *went out of the city*, under no other protection but that of *the night* (*v.* 4), which soon failed him, for he was discovered, pursued, and overtaken. Though he made the best of his way, he could make nothing of it, could not get forward, but *in the plains of Jericho* fell into the hands of the pursuers, *v.* 5. Thence he was brought prisoner to Riblah, where the king of Babylon passed sentence upon him as a rebel, not sentence of death, but, one may almost say, a worse thing. For, 1. He *slew his sons before his eyes*, and they must all be little, some of them infants, for Zedekiah himself was now but thirty-two years of age. The death of these sweet babes must needs be so many deaths to himself, especially when he considered that his own obstinacy was the cause of it, for he was particularly told of this thing: *They shall bring forth thy wives and children to the Chaldeans, ch.* xxxviii. 23. 2. He *slew all the nobles of Judah* (*v.* 6), probably not those princes of Jerusalem who had advised him to this desperate course (it would be a satisfaction to him to see them cut off), but the great men of the country, who were innocent of the matter. 3. He ordered *Zedekiah to have his eyes put out* (*v.* 7), so condemning *him* to darkness for life who had shut his eyes against the clear light of God's word, and was of those princes who *will not understand*, but *walk on in darkness*, Ps. lxxxii. 5. 4. He bound him with two brazen chains or *fetters* (so the margin reads it), to carry him away to Babylon, there to spend the rest of his days in misery. All this sad story we had before, 2 Kings xxv. 4, &c.

IV. Some time afterwards the city was burnt, temple and palace and all, and the wall of it broken down, *v.* 8. " O *Jerusalem, Jerusalem!* this comes of *killing the prophets,* and *stoning those that were sent to thee.* O *Zedekiah, Zedekiah!* this thou mightest have prevented if thou wouldst but have taken God's counsel, and yielded in time.

V. The people that were left were all *carried away captives to Babylon, v.* 9. Now they must bid a final farewell to the land of their nativity, that pleasant land, and to all their possessions and enjoyments in it, must be driven some hundreds of miles, like beasts, before the conquerors, that were now their cruel masters, must lie at their mercy in a strange land, and be servants to those who would be sure to rule them with rigour. The word *tyrant* is originally a Chaldee word, and is often used for *lords* by the Chaldee paraphrast, as if the Chaldeans, when they were lords, tyrannized more than any other : we have reason to think that the poor Jews had reason to say so. Some few were left behind, but they were *the poor of the people*, that had nothing to lose, and therefore never made any resistance. And they not only had their liberty, and were left to tarry at home, but the *captain of the guard gave them vineyards and fields at the same time*, such as they were never masters of before, *v.* 10. Observe here, 1. The wonderful changes of Providence. Some are abased, others advanced, 1 Sam. ii. 5. The *hungry are filled with good things, and the rich sent empty away.* The ruin of some proves the rise of others. Let us therefore

in our abundance *rejoice as though we rejoiced not*, and in our distresses *weep as though we wept not.* 2. The just retributions of Providence. The rich had been proud oppressors, and now they were justly punished for their injustice; the poor had been patient sufferers, and now they were graciously rewarded for their patience and amends made them for all their losses; for *verily there is a God that judges in the earth*, even in this world, much more in the other.

11 Now Nebuchadrezzar king of Babylon gave charge concerning Jeremiah to Nebuzar-adan the captain of the guard, saying, 12 Take him, and look well to him, and do him no harm; but do unto him even as he shall say unto thee. 13 So Nebuzar-adan the captain of the guard sent, and Nebushasban, Rab-saris, and Nergal-sharezer, Rab-mag, and all the king of Babylon's princes; 14 Even they sent, and took Jeremiah out of the court of the prison, and committed him unto Gedaliah the son of Ahikam the son of Shaphan, that he should carry him home: so he dwelt among the people. 15 Now the word of the LORD came unto Jeremiah, while he was shut up in the court of the prison, saying, 16 Go and speak to Ebed-melech the Ethiopian, saying, Thus saith the LORD of hosts, the God of Israel; Behold, I will bring my words upon this city for evil, and not for good; and they shall be *accomplished* in that day before thee. 17 But I will deliver thee in that day, saith the LORD: and thou shalt not be given into the hand of the men of whom thou *art* afraid. 18 For I will surely deliver thee, and thou shalt not fall by the sword, but thy life shall be for a prey unto thee: because thou hast put thy trust in me, saith the LORD.

Here we must sing of mercy, as in the former part of the chapter we sang of judgment, and must sing unto God of both. We may observe here,

I. A gracious providence concerning Jeremiah. When Jerusalem was laid in ruins, and all *men's hearts failed them for fear,* then might he *lift up his head* with comfort, *knowing that his redemption drew nigh,* as Christ's followers when the second destruction of Jerusalem was hastening on, Luke xxi. 28. Nebuchadnezzar had given particular orders that care should be taken of him, and that he should be in all respects well used, *v.* 11,

12. Nebuzar-adan and the rest of the king of Babylon's princes observed these orders, discharged him out of prison, and did every thing to make him easy, *v.* 13, 14. Now we may look upon this, 1. As a very generous act of Nebuchadnezzar, who, though he was a haughty potentate, yet took cognizance of this poor prophet. Doubtless he had received information concerning him from the deserters, that he had foretold the king of Babylon's successes against Judah and other countries, that he had pressed his prince and people to submit to him, and that he had suffered very hard things for so doing; and in consideration of all this (though perhaps he might have heard also that he had foretold the destruction of Babylon at length) he gave him these extraordinary marks of his favour. Note, It is the character of a great soul to take notice of the services and sufferings of the meanest. It was honourably done of the king to give this charge even before the city was taken, and of the captains to observe it even in the heat of action, and it is recorded for imitation. 2. As a reproach to Zedekiah and the princes of Israel. They put him in prison, and the king of Babylon and his princes took him out. God's people and ministers have often found fairer and kinder usage among strangers and infidels than among those that call themselves of the holy city. Paul found more favour and justice with king Agrippa than with Ananias the high priest. 3. As the performance of God's promise to Jeremiah, in recompence for his services. *I will cause the enemy to treat thee well in the day of evil, ch.* xv. 11. Jeremiah had been faithful to his trust as a prophet, and now God approves himself faithful to him and the promise he had made him. Now he is comforted according to the time wherein he had been afflicted, and sees thousands fall on each hand and himself safe. The false prophets fell by those judgments which they said should never come (*ch.* xiv. 15), which made their misery the more terrible to them. The true prophet escaped those judgments which he said would come, and that made his escape the more comfortable to him. The same that were the instruments of punishing the persecutors were the instruments of relieving the persecuted; and Jeremiah thought never the worse of his deliverance for its coming by the hand of the king of Babylon, but saw the more of the hand of God in it. A fuller account of this matter we shall meet with in the next chapter.

II. A gracious message to Ebed-melech, to assure him of a recompence for his kindness to Jeremiah. This message was sent to him by Jeremiah himself, who, when he returned him thanks for his kindness to him, thus turned him over to God to be his paymaster. He relieved *a prophet in the name of a prophet,* and thus he had *a prophet's reward.* This message was delivered

to him immediately after he had done that kindness to Jeremiah, but it is mentioned here after the taking of the city, to show that, as God was kind to Jeremiah at that time, so he was to Ebed-melech for his sake; and it was a token of special favour to both, and they ought so to account it, that they were not involved in any of the common calamities. Jeremiah is directed to tell him, 1. That God would certainly bring upon Jerusalem the ruin that had been long and often threatened; and, for his further satisfaction in having been kind to Jeremiah, he should see him abundantly proved a true prophet, *v.* 16. 2. That God took notice of the fear he had of the judgments coming. Though he was bravely bold in the service of God, yet he was afraid of the rod of God. The enemies were *men of whom he was afraid.* Note, God knows how to adapt and accommodate his comforts to the fears and griefs of his people, for he *knows their souls in adversity.* 3. That he shall be delivered from having a share in the common calamity : *I will deliver thee; I will surely deliver thee.* He had been instrumental to deliver God's prophet out of the dungeon, and now God promises to deliver him; for he will be behind-hand with none for any service they do, directly or indirectly, for his name: " Thou hast saved Jeremiah's life, that was precious to thee, and therefore *thy life shall be given thee for a prey.*" 4. The reason given for this distinguishing favour which God had in store for him is *because thou hast put thy trust in me, saith the Lord.* God, in recompensing men's services, has an eye to the principle they go upon in those services, and rewards according to those principles; and there is no principle of obedience that will be more acceptable to God, nor have a greater influence upon us, than a believing confidence in God. Ebed-melech trusted in God that he would own him, and stand by him, and then he was not afraid of the face of man. And those who trust God, as this good man did, in the way of duty, will find that their hope shall not make them ashamed in times of the greatest danger.

CHAP. XL.

We have attended Jerusalem's funeral pile, and have taken our leave of the captives that were carried to Babylon, not expecting to hear any more of them in this book : perhaps we may in Ezekiel ; and we must in this and the four following chapters observe the story of those few Jews that were left to remain in the land after their brethren were carried away, and it is a very melancholy story ; for, though at first there were some hopeful prospects of their welldoing, they soon appeared as obstinate in sin as ever, unhumbled and unreformed, till, all the rest of the judgments threatened in Deut. xxviii. being brought upon them, that which in the last verse of that dreadful chapter completes the threatenings was accomplished, " The Lord shall bring thee into Egypt again." In this chapter we have, I. A more particular account of Jeremiah's discharge and his settlement with Gedaliah, ver. 1—6. II. The great resort of the Jews that remained scattered in the neighbouring countries to Gedaliah, who was made their governor under the king of Babylon; and the good posture they were in for a while under him, ver. 7—12. III. A treacherous design formed against Gedaliah, by Ishmael, which we shall find executed in the next chapter, ver 13—16.

T HE word that came to Jeremiah from the LORD, after that Nebuzar-adan the captain of the guard had let him go from Ramah, when he had taken him being bound in chains among all that were carried away captive of Jerusalem and Judah, which were carried away captive unto Babylon. 2 And the captain of the guard took Jeremiah, and said unto him, The LORD thy God hath pronounced this evil upon this place. 3 Now the LORD hath brought *it,* and done according as he hath said: because ye have sinned against the LORD, and have not obeyed his voice, therefore this thing is come upon you. 4 And now, behold, I loose thee this day from the chains which *were* upon thine hand. If it seem good unto thee to come with me into Babylon, come; and I will look well unto thee: but if it seem ill unto thee to come with me into Babylon, forbear: behold, all the land *is* before thee: whither it seemeth good and convenient for thee to go, thither go. 5 Now while he was not yet gone back, *he said,* Go back also to Gedaliah the son of Ahikam the son of Shaphan, whom the king of Babylon hath made governor over the cities of Judah, and dwell with him among the people: or go wheresoever it seemeth convenient unto thee to go. So the captain of the guard gave him victuals and a reward, and let him go. 6 Then went Jeremiah unto Gedaliah the son of Ahikam to Mizpah; and dwelt with him among the people that were left in the land.

The title of this part of the book, which begins the chapter, seems misapplied *(The word which came to Jeremiah)*, for here is nothing of prophecy in this chapter, but it is to be referred to *ch.* xlii. 7, where we have a message that God sent by Jeremiah to the captains and the people that remained. The story between is only to introduce that prophecy and show the occasion of it, that it may be the better understood, and Jeremiah, being himself concerned in the story, was the better able to give an account of it.

In these verses we have Jeremiah's adhering, by the advice of Nebuzar-adan, to Gedaliah. It should seem that Jeremiah was very honourably fetched out of the court of the prison by the king of Babylon's princes (*ch.* xxxix. 13, 14), but afterwards, being found among the people in the city, when orders were given to

the inferior officers to bind all they found that were of any fashion, in order to their being carried captives to Babylon, he, through ignorance and mistake, was bound among the rest and hurried away. Poor man! he seems to have been born to hardship and abuse—*a man of sorrows* indeed! But when the captives were brought manacled to Ramah, not far off, where a council of war, or court-martial, was held for giving orders concerning them, Jeremiah was soon distinguished from the rest, and, by special order of the court, was discharged. 1. The captain of the guard solemnly owns him to be a true prophet (*v.* 2, 3): " *The Lord thy God,* whose messenger thou hast been and in whose name thou hast spoken, *has* by thee *pronounced this evil upon this place;* they had fair warning given them of it, but they would not take the warning, and *now the Lord hath brought it,* and, as by thy mouth he said it, so by my hand *he hath done what he said.*" He seems thus to justify what he had done, and to glory in it, that he had been God's instrument to fulfil that which Jeremiah had been his messenger to foretel; and upon that account it was indeed the most glorious action he had ever done. He tells all the people that were now in chains before him, *It is because you have sinned against the Lord that this thing has come upon you.* The princes of Israel would never be brought to acknowledge this, though it was as evident as if it had been written with a sun-beam; but this heathen prince plainly sees it, that a people that had been so favoured as they had been by the divine goodness would never have been abandoned thus had they not been very provoking. The people of Israel had been often told this from the pulpit by their prophets, and they would not regard it; now they are told it from the bench by their conqueror, whom they dare not contradict and who will make them regard it. Note, Sooner or later men shall be made sensible that their sin is the cause of all their miseries. 2. He gives him free leave to dispose of himself as he thought fit. He *loosed him from his chains* a second time (*v.* 4), invited him to come along with him to Babylon, not as a captive, but as a friend, as a companion; and *I will set my eye upon thee* (so the word is), not only, " *I will look well to thee,*" but " I will show thee respect, will countenance thee, and will see that thou be safe and well provided for." If he was not disposed to go to Babylon, he might dwell where he pleased in his own country, for it was all now at the disposal of the conquerors. He may go to Anathoth if he please, and enjoy the field he has purchased there. A great change with this good man! He that but lately was tossed from one prison to another may now walk at liberty from one possession to another. 3. He advises him to go to Gedaliah and settle with him. This Gedaliah, *made governor of the* land under *the king of Babylon,* was an honest Jew, who (it is probable) betimes went over with his friends to the Chaldeans, and approved himself so well that he had this great trust put into his hands, *v.* 5. *While* Jeremiah had *not yet gone back,* but stood considering what he should do, Nebuzar-adan, perceiving him neither inclined to go to Babylon nor determined whither *to go,* turned the scale for him, and bade him by all means *go to Gedaliah.* Sudden thoughts sometimes prove wise ones. But when he gave this counsel he did not design to bind him by it, nor will he take it ill if he do not follow it : *Go wheresoever it seemeth convenient unto thee.* It is friendly in such cases to give advice, but unfriendly to prescribe and to be angry if our advice be not taken. Let Jeremiah steer what course he pleases, Nebuzar-adan will agree to it, and believe he does for the best. Nor does he only give him his liberty, and an approbation of the measures he shall take, but provides for his support : He *gave him victuals and a* present, either in clothes or money, *and so let him go.* See how considerate *the captain of the guard* was in his kindness to Jeremiah. He set him at liberty, but it was in a country that was laid waste, and in which, as the posture of it now was, he might have perished, though it was his own country, if he had not been thus kindly furnished with necessaries. Jeremiah not only accepted his kindness, but took his advice, and went to Gedaliah, to Mizpah, *and dwelt with him, v.* 6. Whether we may herein commend his prudence I know not ; the event does not commend it, for it did not prove at all to his comfort. However, we may commend his pious affection to the land of Israel, that unless he were forced out of it, as Ezekiel, and Daniel, and other good men were, he would not forsake it, but chose rather to dwell with the poor in the holy land than with princes in an unholy one.

7 Now when all the captains of the forces which *were* in the fields, *even* they and their men, heard that the king of Babylon had made Gedaliah the son of Ahikam governor in the land, and had committed unto him men, and women, and children, and of the poor of the land, of them that were not carried away captive to Babylon ; 8 Then they came to Gedaliah to Mizpah, even Ishmael the son of Nethaniah, and Johanan and Jonathan the sons of Kareah, and Seraiah the son of Tanhumeth, and the sons of Ephai the Netophathite, and Jezaniah the son of a Maachathite, they and their men. 9 And Gedaliah the son of Ahikam the son of Shaphan sware

unto them and to their men, saying, Fear not to serve the Chaldeans : dwell in the land, and serve the king of Babylon, and it shall be well with you. 10 As for me, behold, I will dwell at Mizpah, to serve the Chaldeans, which will come unto us : but ye, gather ye wine, and summer fruits, and oil, and put *them* in your vessels, and dwell in your cities that ye have taken. 11 Likewise when all the Jews that *were* in Moab, and among the Ammonites, and in Edom, and that *were* in all the countries, heard that the king of Babylon had left a remnant of Judah, and that he had set over them Gedaliah the son of Ahikam the son of Shaphan ; 12 Even all the Jews returned out of all places whither they were driven, and came to the land of Judah, to Gedaliah, unto Mizpah, and gathered wine and summer fruits very much. 13 Moreover Johanan the son of Kareah, and all the captains of the forces that *were* in the fields, came to Gedaliah to Mizpah, 14 And said unto him, Dost thou certainly know that Baalis the king of the Ammonites hath sent Ishmael the son of Nethaniah to slay thee ? But Gedaliah the son of Ahikam believed them not. 15 Then Johanan the son of Kareah spake to Gedaliah in Mizpah secretly, saying, Let me go, I pray thee, and I will slay Ishmael the son of Nethaniah, and no man shall know *it :* wherefore should he slay thee, that all the Jews which are gathered unto thee should be scattered, and the remnant in Judah perish ? 16 But Gedaliah the son of Ahikam said unto Johanan the son of Kareah, Thou shalt not do this thing : for thou speakest falsely of Ishmael.

We have in these verses,

I. A bright sky opening upon the remnant of the Jews that were left in their own land, and a comfortable prospect given them of some peace and quietness after the many years of trouble and terror with which they had been afflicted. Jeremiah indeed had never in his prophecies spoken of any such good days reserved for the Jews immediately after the captivity ; but Providence seemed to raise and encourage such an expectation, and it would be to that miserable people as life from the dead. Observe the particulars.

1. Gedaliah, one of themselves, is made *governor in the land,* by *the king of Babylon, v.* 7. To show that he designed to make and keep them easy he did not give this commission to one of the princes of Babylon, but to one of their brethren, who, they might be sure, would seek their peace. He was *the son of Ahikam, the son of Shaphan,* one of the princes. We read of his father (*ch.* xxvi. 24) that he took Jeremiah's part against the people. He seems to have been a man of great wisdom and a mild temper, and under whose government the few that were left might have been very happy. The king of Babylon had a good opinion of him and reposed a confidence in him, for *to him he committed all that were* left behind.

2. There is great resort to him from all parts, and all those that were now the Jews of the dispersion came and put themselves under his government and protection. (1.) The great men that had escaped the Chaldeans by force came and quietly submitted to Gedaliah, for their own safety and common preservation. Several are here named, *v.* 8. *They came* with *their men,* their servants, their soldiers, and so strengthened one another; and the king of Babylon had such a good opinion of Gedaliah his delegate that he was not at all jealous of the increase of their numbers, but rather pleased with it. (2.) The poor men that had escaped by flight into the neighbouring countries of Moab, Ammon, and Edom, were induced by the love they bore to their own land to return to it again as soon as they heard that Gedaliah was in authority there, *v.* 11, 12. Canaan itself would be an unsafe unpleasant country if there were no government nor governors there, and those that loved it dearly would not come back to it till they heard there were. It would be a great reviving to those that were dispersed to come together again, to those that were dispersed into foreign countries to come together in their own country, to those that were under strange kings to be under a governor of their own nation. See here in wrath God remembered mercy, and yet admitted some of them upon a further trial of their obedience.

3. The model of this new government is drawn up and settled by an original contract, which Gedaliah confirmed with an oath, a solemn oath (*v.* 9): *He swore to them and to their men,* it is probable according to the warrant and instructions he had received from the king of Babylon, who empowered him to give them these assurances. (1.) They must own the property of their lands to be in the Chaldeans. "Come" (says Gedaliah), "*fear not to serve the Chaldeans.* Fear not the sin of it." Though the divine law had forbidden them to make leagues with the heathen, yet the divine sentence had obliged them to yield to the king of Babylon. "Fear not the reproach of it, and the disparagement it will be to your nation; it is what God

has brought you to, has bound you to, and it is no disgrace to any to comply with him. Fear not the consequences of it, as if it would certainly make you and yours miserable; no, you will find the king of Babylon not so hard a landlord as you apprehend him to be; if you will but live peaceably, peaceably you shall live; disturb not the government, and it will not disturb you. *Serve the king of Babylon and it shall be well with you.*" If they should make any difficulty of doing personal homage, or should be apprehensive of danger when the Chaldeans should come among them, Gedaliah, probably by instruction from the king of Babylon, undertakes upon all occasions to act for them, and make their application acceptable to the king (*v.* 10): "*As for me, behold, I will dwell at Mizpah, to serve the Chaldeans,* to do homage to them in the name of the whole body if there be occasion, to receive orders, and to pay them their tribute when they *come to us.*" All that passes between them and the Chaldeans shall pass through his hand; and, if the Chaldeans put such a confidence in him, surely his own countrymen may venture to do it. Gedaliah is willing thus to give them the assurance of an oath that he will do his part in protecting them, but, being apt to err (as many good men are) on the charitable side, he did not require an oath from them that they would be faithful to him, else the following mischief might have been prevented. However, protection draws allegiance though it be not sworn, and by joining in with Gedaliah they did, in effect, consent to the terms of government, that they should *serve the king of Babylon.* But, (2.) Though they own the property of their lands to be in the Chaldeans, yet, upon that condition, they shall have the free enjoyment of them and all the profits of them (*v.* 10): "*Gather you wine and summer fruits,* and take them for your own use; *put them in your vessels,* to be laid up for winter-store, as those do that live in a land of peace and hope to *eat the labour of your hand,* nay, the labour of other people's hands, for you reap what they sowed." Or perhaps they were the spontaneous products of that fertile soil, for which none had laboured. And accordingly we find (*v.* 12) that they *gathered wine and summer fruits very much,* such as were at present upon the ground, for their corn-harvest was over some time before Jerusalem was taken. While Gedaliah was in care for the public safety he left them to enjoy the advantages of the public plenty, and, for aught that appears, demanded no tribute from them; for he sought not his own profit, but the profit of many.

II. Here is a dark cloud gathering over this infant state, and threatening a dreadful storm. How soon is this hopeful prospect blasted! For when God begins in judgment he will make an end. It is here intimated to us, 1. That *Baalis the king of the Ammonites* had a particular spite at Gedaliah, and was contriving to take him off, either out of malice to the nation of the Jews, whose welfare he hated the thought of, or a personal pique against Gedaliah, *v.* 14. Some make Baalis to signify the queen-mother of the king of the Ammonites, or queen-dowager, as if she were the first mover of this bloody and treacherous design. One would have thought this little remnant might be safe when the great king of Babylon protected it; and yet it is ruined by the artifices of this petty prince or princess. Happy are those that have the King of kings on their side, who can take *the wise in their own craftiness;* for the greatest earthly king cannot with all his power secure us against fraud and treachery. 2. That he employed *Ishmael, the son of Nethaniah,* as the instrument of his malice, instigated him to murder Gedaliah, and, that he might have a fair opportunity to do it, directed him to go and enrol himself among his subjects and promise him fealty. Nothing could be more barbarous than the design itself, nor more base than the method of compassing it. How wretchedly is human nature corrupted and degenerated (even in those that pretend to the best blood) when it is capable of admitting the thought of such abominable wickedness! Ishmael was of the seed royal, and would therefore be easily tempted to envy and hate one that set up for a governor in Judah, who was not, as he was, of David's line, though he had ever so much of David's spirit. 3. That Johanan, a brisk and active man, having got scent of this plot, informed Gedaliah of it, yet taking it for granted he could not but know of it before, the proofs of the matter being so very plain: *Dost thou certainly know?* surely thou dost, *v.* 14. He gave him private intelligence of it (*v.* 15), hoping he would then take the more notice of it. He proffered his service to prevent it, by taking off Ishmael, whose very name was ominous to all the seed of Isaac: *I will slay* him. *Wherefore should he slay thee?* Herein he showed more courage and zeal than sense of justice; for, if it be lawful to kill for prevention, who then can be safe, since malice always suspects the worst? 4. That Gedaliah, being a man of sincerity himself, would by no means give credit to the information given him of Ishmael's treachery. He said, *Thou speakest falsely of Ishmael.* Herein he discovered more good humour than discretion, more of the innocency of the dove than the wisdom of the serpent. Princes become uneasy to themselves and all about them when they are jealous. Queen Elizabeth said that she would believe no more evil of her people than a mother would believe of her own children; yet many have been ruined by being over-confident of the fidelity of those about them.

CHAP. XLI.

It is a very tragical story that is related in this chapter, and shows

that evil pursues sinners. The black cloud that was gathering in the foregoing chapter here bursts in a dreadful storm. Those few Jews that escaped the captivity were proud to think that they were still in their own land, when their brethren had gone they knew not whither, were fond of the wine and summer-fruits they had gathered, and were very secure under Gedaliah's protectorship, when, on a sudden, even these remains prove ruins too. I. Gedaliah is barbarously slain by Ishmael, ver. 1, 2. II. All the Jews that were with him were slain likewise (ver. 3) and a pit filled with their dead bodies, ver. 9. III. Some devout men, to the number of fourscore, that were going towards Jerusalem, were drawn in by Ishmael, and murdered likewise, ver. 4—7. Only ten of them escaped, ver. 8. IV. Those that escaped the sword were taken prisoners by Ishmael, and carried off towards the country of the Ammonites, ver. 10. V. By the conduct and courage of Johanan, though the death of the slain is not revenged, yet the prisoners are recovered, and he now becomes their commander-in-chief, ver. 11 —16. VI. His project is to carry them into the land of Egypt (ver. 17, 18), which we shall hear more of in the next chapter.

NOW it came to pass in the seventh month, *that* Ishmael the son of Nethaniah the son of Elishama, of the seed royal, and the princes of the king, even ten men with him, came unto Gedaliah the son of Ahikam to Mizpah; and there they did eat bread together in Mizpah. 2 Then arose Ishmael the son of Nethaniah, and the ten men that were with him, and smote Gedaliah the son of Ahikam the son of Shaphan with the sword, and slew him, whom the king of Babylon had made governor over the land. 3 Ishmael also slew all the Jews that were with him, *even* with Gedaliah, at Mizpah, and the Chaldeans that were found there, *and* the men of war. 4 And it came to pass the second day after he had slain Gedaliah, and no man knew *it,* 5 That there came certain from Shechem, from Shiloh, and from Samaria, *even* fourscore men, having their beards shaven, and their clothes rent, and having cut themselves, with offerings and incense in their hand, to bring *them* to the house of the LORD. 6 And Ishmael the son of Nethaniah went forth from Mizpah to meet them, weeping all along as he went: and it came to pass, as he met them, he said unto them, Come to Gedaliah the son of Ahikam. 7 And it was *so,* when they came into the midst of the city, that Ishmael the son of Nethaniah slew them, *and cast them* into the midst of the pit, he, and the men that *were* with him. 8 But ten men were found among them that said unto Ishmael, Slay us not: for we have treasures in the field, of wheat, and of barley, and of oil, and of honey. So he forbare, and slew them not among their brethren. 9 Now the pit wherein Ishmael had cast all the dead bodies of the men, whom he had slain because of Gedaliah, *was* it which Asa the king had made for fear of Baasha king of Israel : *and* Ishmael the son of Nethaniah filled it with *them that were* slain. 10 Then Ishmael carried away captive all the residue of the people that *were* in Mizpah, *even* the king's daughters, and all the people that remained in Mizpah, whom Nebuzaradan the captain of the guard had committed to Gedaliah the son of Ahikam : and Ishmael the son of Nethaniah carried them away captive, and departed to go over to the Ammonites.

It is hard to say which is more astonishing, God's permitting or men's perpetrating such villanies as here we find committed. Such base, barbarous, bloody work is here done by men who by their birth should have been men of honour, by their religion just men, and this done upon those of their own nature, their own nation, their own religion, and now their brethren in affliction, when they were all brought under the power of the victorious Chaldeans, and smarting under the judgments of God, upon no provocation, nor with any prospect of advantage—all done, not only in cold blood, but with art and management. We have scarcely such an instance of perfidious cruelty in all the scripture ; so that with John, when he saw the *woman drunk with the blood of the saints,* we may well *wonder with great admiration.* But God permitted it for the completing of the ruin of an unhumbled people, and the filling up of the measure of their judgments, who had filled up the measure of their iniquities. Let it inspire us with an indignation at the wickedness of men and an awe of God's righteousness.

I. Ishmael and his party treacherously killed Gedaliah himself in the first place. Though the king of Babylon had made him a great man, had given him a commission to be *governor of the land* which he had conquered, though God had made him a good man and a great blessing to his country, and his agency for its welfare was as life from the dead, yet neither could secure him. Ishmael was of *the seed royal* (*v.* 1) and therefore jealous of Gedaliah's growing greatness, and enraged that he should merit and accept a commission under the king of Babylon. He had *ten men* with him that were *princes of the king* too, guided by the same peevish resentments that he was ; these had been with Gedaliah before, to put themselves

under his protection (*ch.* xl. 8), and now came again to make him a visit ; *and they did eat bread together in Mizpah.* He entertained them generously, and entertained no jealousy of them, notwithstanding the information given him by Johanan. They pretended friendship to him, and gave him no warning to stand on his guard ; he was in sincerity friendly to them, and did all he could to oblige them. But those that did *eat bread* with him *lifted up the heel* against him. They did not pick a quarrel with him, but watched an opportunity, when they had him alone, and assassinated him, *v.* 2.

II. They likewise put all to the sword that they found in arms there, both Jews and Chaldeans, all that were employed under Gedaliah or were in any capacity to revenge his death, *v.* 3. As if enough of the blood of Israelites had not been shed by the Chaldeans, their own princes here mingle it with the blood of the Chaldeans. The vinedressers and the husbandmen were busy in the fields, and knew nothing of this bloody massacre ; so artfully was it carried on and concealed.

III. Some good honest men, that were going all in tears to lament the desolations of Jerusalem, were drawn in by Ishmael, and murdered with the rest. Observe, 1. Whence they came (*v.* 5)—*from Shechem, Samaria,* and *Shiloh,* places that had been famous, but were now reduced ; they belonged to the ten tribes, but there were some in those countries that retained an affection for the worship of the God of Israel. 2. Whither they were going—*to the house of the Lord,* the temple at Jerusalem, which, no doubt, they had heard of the destruction of, and were going to pay their respects to its ashes, to see its ruins, that their eye might affect their heart with sorrow for them. They *favour the dust thereof,* Ps. cii. 14. They took *offerings and incense in their hand,* that if they should find any altar there, though it were but an altar of earth, and any priest ready to officiate, they might not be without something to offer ; if not, yet they showed their good-will, as Abraham, when he came to *the place of the altar,* though the altar was gone. The people of God used to go rejoicing to the *house of the Lord,* but these went in the habit of mourners, with *their clothes rent* and *their heads shaven ;* for the providence of God loudly called to weeping and mourning, because it was not with the faithful worshippers of God as in months past. 3. How they were decoyed into a fatal snare by Ishmael's malice. Hearing of their approach, he resolved to be the death of them too, so bloodthirsty was he. He seemed as if he hated every one that had the name of an Israelite or the face of an honest man. These pilgrims towards Jerusalem he had a spite to, for the sake of their errand. Ishmael went out to meet them with crocodiles' tears, pretending to bewail the desolations of Jerusalem as much as they; and, to try how they stood affected to Gedaliah and his government, he courted them into the town and found them to have a respect for him, which confirmed him in his resolution to murder them. *He said, Come to Gedaliah,* pretending he would have them come and live with him, when really he intended that they should come and die with him, *v.* 6. They had heard such a character of Gedaliah that they were willing enough to be acquainted with him; but Ishmael, when he had them *in the midst of the* town, fell upon them and *slew them* (*v.* 7), and no doubt took the offerings they had and converted them to his own use; for he that would not stick at such a murder would not stick at sacrilege. Notice is taken of his disposing of the dead bodies of these and the rest that he had slain; he tumbled them all into a great *pit* (*v.* 7), the same pit that Asa king of Judah had digged long before, either in the city or adjoining to it, when he built or fortified Mizpah (1 Kings xv. 22), to be a frontier-garrison against *Baasha king of Israel* and *for fear of* him, *v.* 9. Note, Those that dig pits with a good intention know not what bad use they may be put to, one time or other. He slew so many that he could not afford them each a grave, or would not do them so much honour, but threw them all promiscuously into one pit. Among these last that were doomed to the slaughter there were ten that obtained a pardon, by working, not on the compassion, but the covetousness, of those that had them at their mercy, *v.* 8. They *said to Ishmael,* when he was about to suck their blood, like an insatiable horseleech, after that of their companions, *Slay us not, for we have treasures in the field,* country treasures, large stocks upon the ground, abundance of such commodities as the country affords, *wheat and barley, and oil and honey,* intimating that they would discover it to him and put him in possession of it all, if he would spare them. *Skin for skin, and all that a man has, will he give for his life.* This bait prevailed. Ishmael saved them, not for the love of mercy, but for the love of money. Here were riches kept for the owners thereof, not *to their hurt* (Eccl. v. 13) and to cause them to *lose their lives* (Job xxxi. 39), but to their good and the preserving of their lives. Solomon observes that sometimes *the ransom of a man's life is his riches.* But those who think thus to bribe death, when it comes with commission, and plead with it, saying, *Slay us not, for we have treasures in the field,* will find death inexorable and themselves wretchedly deceived.

IV. He carried off the people prisoners. *The king's daughters* (whom the Chaldeans cared not for troubling themselves with when they had the king's sons) and the poor of the land, the vine-dressers and husbandmen, that were committed to Gedaliah's

charge, were all led away prisoners towards the country of *the Ammonites* (*v.* 10), Ishmael probably intending to make a present of them, as the trophies of his barbarous victory, to the king of that country, that set him on. This melancholy story is a warning to us never to be secure in this world. Worse may be yet to come when we think the worst is over; and that end of one trouble, which we fancy to be the end of all trouble, may prove to be the beginning of another, of a greater. These prisoners thought, *Surely the bitterness of death,* and of captivity, *is past;* and yet some died by the sword and others went into captivity. When we think ourselves safe, and begin to be easy, destruction may come that way that we little expected it. There is many a ship wrecked in the harbour. We can never be sure of peace on this side heaven.

11 But when Johanan the son of Kareah, and all the captains of the forces that *were* with him, heard of all the evil that Ishmael the son of Nethaniah had done, 12 Then they took all the men, and went to fight with Ishmael the son of Nethaniah, and found him by the great waters that *are* in Gibeon. 13 Now it came to pass, *that* when all the people which *were* with Ishmael saw Johanan the son of Kareah, and all the captains of the forces that *were* with him, then they were glad. 14 So all the people that Ishmael had carried away captive from Mizpah cast about and returned, and went unto Johanan the son of Kareah. 15 But Ishmael the son of Nethaniah escaped from Johanan with eight men, and went to the Ammonites. 16 Then took Johanan the son of Kareah, and all the captains of the forces that *were* with him, all the remnant of the people whom he had recovered from Ishmael the son of Nethaniah, from Mizpah, after *that* he had slain Gedaliah the son of Ahikam, *even* mighty men of war, and the women, and the children, and the eunuchs, whom he had brought again from Gibeon : 17 And they departed, and dwelt in the habitation of Chimham, which is by Beth-lehem, to go to enter into Egypt, 18 Because of the Chaldeans : for they were afraid of them, because Ishmael the son of Nethaniah had slain Gedaliah the son of Ahikam,

whom the king of Babylon made governor in the land.

It would have been well if Johanan, when he gave information to Gedaliah of Ishmael's treasonable design, though he could not obtain leave to kill Ishmael and to prevent it that way, yet had staid with Gedaliah; for he, and his captains, and their forces, might have been a life-guard to Gedaliah and a terror to Ishmael, and so have prevented the mischief without the effusion of blood: but, it seems, they were out upon some expedition, perhaps no good one, and so were out of the way when they should have been upon the best service. Those that affect to ramble are many times out of their place when they are most needed. However, at length they *hear of all the evil that Ishmael had done* (v. 11), and are resolved to try an after-game, which we have an account of in these verses. 1. We heartily wish Johanan could have taken revenge upon the murderers, but he prevailed only to rescue the captives. Those that had shed so much blood, it was a pity but their blood should have been shed; and it is strange that vengeance suffered them to live; yet it did. Johanan gathered what forces he could *and went to fight with Ishmael* (v. 12), upon notice of the murders he had committed (for though he concealed it for a time (v. 4) yet murder will out) and which way he was gone; he pursued him, and overtook him by the great *pool of Gibeon,* which we read of, 2 Sam. ii. 13. And, upon his appearing with such a force, Ishmael's heart failed him, and his guilty conscience flew in his face, and he durst not stand his ground against an enemy that was something like a match for him. The most cruel are often the most cowardly. The poor captives *were glad when they saw Johanan* and *the captains that were with him,* looking upon them as their deliverers (v. 13), and they immediately found a way to wheel about and come over to them (v. 14), Ishmael not offering to detain them when he saw Johanan. Note, Those that would be helped must help themselves. These captives staid not till their conquerors were beaten, but took the first opportunity to make their escape, as soon as they saw their friends appear and their enemies thereby disheartened. Ishmael quitted his prey to save his life, and *escaped with eight men,* v. 15. It seems, two of his ten men, that were his banditti or assassins (spoken of v. 1), either deserted him or were killed in the engagement; but he made the best of his way to the Ammonites, as a perfect renegado, that had quite abandoned all relation to the commonwealth of Israel, though he was of the seed royal, and we hear no more of him. 2. We heartily wish that Johanan, when he had rescued the captives, would have sat down quietly with them, and governed them peaceably, as Gedaliah did; but, instead of that, he is for

leading them into the land of Egypt, as Ishmael would have led them into the land of the Ammonites; so that though he got the command over them in a better way than Ishmael did, and honestly enough, yet he did not use it much better. Gedaliah, who was of a meek and quiet spirit, was a great blessing to them; but Johanan, who was of a fierce and restless spirit, was set over them for their hurt, and to complete their ruin, even after they were, as they thought, redeemed. Thus did God still walk contrary to them. (1.) The resolution of Johanan and the captains was very rash; nothing would serve them but they would *go to enter into Egypt* (v. 17), and, in order to that, they encamped for a time *in the habitation of Chimham, by Bethlehem,* David's city. Probably it was some land which David gave to Chimham, the son of Barzillai, which, though it returned to David's family at the year of Jubilee, yet still bore the name of *Chimham.* Here Johanan made his head-quarters, steering his course towards Egypt, either from a personal affection to that country or an ancient national confidence in the Egyptians for help in distress. Some of the *mighty men of war,* it seems, had escaped; those he took with him, *and the women and children, whom he had recovered from Ishmael,* who were thus emptied from vessel to vessel, because they were yet unchanged. (2.) The reason for this resolution was very frivolous. They pretended that *they were afraid of the Chaldeans,* that they would come and do I know not what with them, *because Ishmael had* killed *Gedaliah, v.* 18. I cannot think they really had any apprehensions of danger upon this account; for, though it is true that the Chaldeans had cause enough to resent the murder of their viceroy, yet they were not so unreasonable, or unjust, as to revenge it upon those who appeared so vigorously against the murderers. But they only make use of this as a sham to cover that corrupt inclination of their unbelieving ancestors, which was so strong in them, *to return into Egypt.* Those will justly lose their comfort in real fears that excuse themselves in sin with pretended fears.

CHAP. XLII.

Johanan and the captains being strongly bent upon going into Egypt, either their affections or politics advising them to take that course, they had a great desire that God should direct them to do so too like Balaam, who, when he was determined to go and curse Israel, asked God leave. Here is, I. The fair bargain that was made between Jeremiah and them about consulting God in this matter, ver. 1—6. II. The message at large which God sent them, in answer to their enquiry, in which, 1. They are commanded and encouraged to continue in the land of Judah, and assured that if they did so it should be well with them, ver. 7—12. 2. They are forbidden to go to Egypt, and are plainly told that if they did it would be their ruin, ver. 13—18. 3. They are charged with dissimulation in their asking what God's will was in this matter and disobedience when they were told what it was; and sentence is accordingly passed upon them, ver. 19—22.

THEN all the captains of the forces, and Johanan the son of Kareah, and Jezaniah the son of Hoshaiah, and all the people from the least even unto the greatest, came near, 2 And said unto Jeremiah the prophet, Let, we beseech thee, our supplication be accepted before thee, and pray for us unto the LORD thy God, *even* for all this remnant; (for we are left *but* a few of many, as thine eyes do behold us:) 3 That the LORD thy God may shew us the way wherein we may walk, and the thing that we may do. 4 Then Jeremiah the prophet said unto them, I have heard *you;* behold, I will pray unto the LORD your God according to your words; and it shall come to pass, *that* whatsoever thing the LORD shall answer you, I will declare *it* unto you; I will keep nothing back from you. 5 Then they said to Jeremiah, The LORD be a true and faithful witness between us, if we do not even according to all things for the which the LORD thy God shall send thee to us. 6 Whether *it be* good, or whether *it be* evil, we will obey the voice of the LORD our God, to whom we send thee; that it may be well with us, when we obey the voice of the LORD our God.

We have reason to wonder how Jeremiah the prophet escaped the sword of Ishmael; it seems he did escape, and it was not the first time that the Lord hid him. It is strange also that in these violent turns he was not consulted before now, and his advice asked and taken. But it should seem as if they knew not that a prophet was among them. Though this people were *as brands plucked out of the fire,* yet have they not *returned to the Lord.* This people has a *revolting and a rebellious heart;* and contempt of God and his providence, God and his prophets, is still *the sin that most easily besets* them. But now at length, to serve a turn, Jeremiah is sought out, and *all the captains, Johanan* himself not excepted, with *all the people from the least to the greatest,* make him a visit; they *came near* (v. 1), which intimates that hitherto they had kept at a distance from the prophet and had been shy of him. Now here,

I. They desire him by prayer to ask direction from God what they should do in the present critical juncture, *v.* 2, 3. They express themselves wonderfully well. 1. With great respect to the prophet. Though he was poor and low, and under their command, yet they apply to him with humility and submissiveness, as petitioners for his assistance, which yet they intimate their own unworthiness of: *Let, we beseech thee, our supplication be accepted before thee.* They

compliment him thus in hopes to persuade him to say as they would have him say. 2. With a great opinion of his interest in heaven: "*Pray for us,* who know not how to pray for ourselves. *Pray to the Lord thy God,* for we are unworthy to call him ours, nor have we reason to expect any favour from him." 3. With a great sense of their need of divine direction. They speak of themselves as objects of compassion: "*We are but a remnant, but a few of many;* how easily will such a remnant be swallowed up, and yet it is a pity that it should. *Thy eyes* see what distress we are in, what a plunge we are at; if thou canst do any thing, help us." 4. With desire of divine direction: "Let *the Lord thy God* take this ruin into his thoughts and under his hand, and *show us the way wherein we may walk* and may expect to have his presence with us, *and the thing that we may do,* the course we may take for our own safety." Note, In every difficult doubtful case our eye must be up to God for direction. They then might expect to be directed by a *spirit of prophecy,* which has now ceased; but we may still in faith pray to be guided by a *spirit of wisdom* in our hearts and the hints of Providence.

II. Jeremiah faithfully promises them to pray for direction for them, and, whatever message God should send to them by him, he would deliver it to them just as he received it without adding, altering, or diminishing, *v.* 4. Ministers may hence learn, 1. Conscientiously to pray for those who desire their prayers: *I will pray for you according to your words.* Though they had slighted him, yet, like Samuel when he was slighted, he will not *sin against the Lord in ceasing to pray for* them, 1 Sam. xii. 23. 2. Conscientiously to advise those who desire their advice as near as they can to the mind of God, not *keeping back any thing that is profitable for them,* whether it be pleasing or no, but to *declare to them the whole counsel of God,* that they may approve themselves true to their trust.

III. They fairly promise that they will be governed by the will of God, as soon as they know what it is (*v.* 5, 6), and they had the impudence to appeal to God concerning their sincerity herein, though at the same time they dissembled: "*The Lord be a true and faithful witness between us;* do thou in the fear of God tell us truly what his mind is and then we will in the fear of God comply with it, and for this the Lord the Judge be Judge between us." Note, Those that expect to have the benefit of good ministers' prayers must conscientiously hearken to their preaching and be governed by it, as far as it agrees with the mind of God. Nothing could be better said than this was: *Whether it be good, or whether it be evil, we will obey the voice of the Lord our God, that it may be well with us.* 1. They now call God *their* God, for Jeremiah had encouraged them to call him so (*v.* 4): *I will pray to the Lord your God.* He is ours, and therefore *we will obey his voice.* Our relation to God strongly obliges us to obedience. 2. They promise to *obey his voice* because they sent the prophet to him to consult him. Note, We do not truly desire to know the mind of God if we do not fully resolve to comply with it when we do know it. 3. It is an implicit universal obedience that they here promise. They will do what God appoints them to do, *whether it be good or whether it be evil:* " Though it may seem evil to us, yet we will believe that if God command it it is certainly good, and we must not dispute it, but do it. Whatever God commands, whether it be easy or difficult, agreeable to our inclinations or contrary to them, whether it be cheap or costly, fashionable or unfashionable, whether we get or lose by it in our worldly interests, if it be our duty, we will do it." 4. It is upon a very good consideration that they promise this, a reasonable and powerful one, *that it may be well with us,* which intimates a conviction that they could not expect it should be well with them upon any other terms.

7 And it came to pass after ten days, that the word of the Lord came unto Jeremiah. 8 Then called he Johanan the son of Kareah, and all the captains of the forces which *were* with him, and all the people from the least even to the greatest, 9 And said unto them, Thus saith the Lord, the God of Israel, unto whom ye sent me to present your supplication before him ; 10 If ye will still abide in this land, then will I build you, and not pull *you* down, and I will plant you, and not pluck *you* up : for I repent me of the evil that I have done unto you. 11 Be not afraid of the king of Babylon, of whom ye are afraid ; be not afraid of him, saith the Lord : for I *am* with you to save you, and to deliver you from his hand. 12 And I will show mercies unto you, that he may have mercy upon you, and cause you to return to your own land. 13 But if ye say, We will not dwell in this land, neither obey the voice of the Lord your God, 14 Saying, No ; but we will go into the land of Egypt, where we shall see no war, nor hear the sound of the trumpet, nor have hunger of bread; and there will we dwell : 15 And now therefore hear the word of the Lord, ye remnant of Judah ; Thus

saith the Lord of hosts, the God of Israel ; If ye wholly set your faces to enter into Egypt, and go to sojourn there ; 16 Then it shall come to pass, *that* the sword, which ye feared, shall overtake you there in the land of Egypt, and the famine, whereof ye were afraid, shall follow close after you there in Egypt ; and there ye shall die. 17 So shall it be with all the men that set their faces to go into Egypt to sojourn there ; they shall die by the sword, by the famine, and by the pestilence : and none of them shall remain or escape from the evil that I will bring upon them. 18 For thus saith the Lord of hosts, the God of Israel ; As mine anger and my fury hath been poured forth upon the inhabitants of Jerusalem ; so shall my fury be poured forth upon you, when ye shall enter into Egypt : and ye shall be an execration, and an astonishment, and a curse, and a reproach ; and ye shall see this place no more. 19 The Lord hath said concerning you, O ye remnant of Judah ; Go ye not into Egypt : know certainly that I have admonished you this day. 20 For ye dissembled in your hearts, when ye sent me unto the Lord your God, saying, Pray for us unto the Lord our God ; and according unto all that the Lord our God shall say, so declare unto us, and we will do *it.* 21 And *now* I have this day declared *it* to you ; but ye have not obeyed the voice of the Lord your God, nor any *thing* for the which he hath sent me unto you. 22 Now therefore know certainly that ye shall die by the sword, by the famine, and by the pestilence, in the place whither ye desire to go *and* to sojourn.

We have here the answer which Jeremiah was sent to deliver to those who employed him to ask counsel of God.

I. It did not come immediately, not till *ten days after,* v. 7. They were thus long held in suspense, perhaps, to punish them for their hypocrisy or to show that Jeremiah did not speak of himself, nor what he would, for he could not speak when he would, but must wait for instructions. However, it teaches us to continue waiting upon God for direction in our way. *The vision is for an appointed time, and at the end it shall speak.*

II. When it did come he delivered it publicly, both to the *captains* and to all the *people*, from the meanest to those in the highest station; he delivered it fully and faithfully as he received it, as he had promised that he would keep nothing back from them. If Jeremiah had been to direct them by his own prudence, perhaps he could not have told what to advise them to, the case was so difficult; but what he has to advise is what *the Lord the God of Israel saith*, to whom they had sent him, and therefore they were bound in honour and duty to observe it. And this he tells them,

1. That it is the will of God that they should stay where they are, and his promise that, if they do so, it shall undoubtedly be *well with them;* he would have them still to *abide in this land, v.* 10. Their brethren were forced out of it into captivity, and this was their affliction; let those therefore count it a mercy that they may stay in it and a duty to stay in it. Let those whose lot is in Canaan never quit it while they can keep it. It would have been enough to oblige them if God had only said, "I charge you upon your allegiance to *abide still in the land;*" but he rather persuades them to it as a friend than commands it as a prince. (1.) He expresses a very tender concern for them in their present calamitous condition: *It repenteth me of the evil that I have done unto you.* Though they had shown small sign of their repenting of their sins, yet God, as one *grieved for the misery of Israel* (Judg. x. 16), begins to repent of the judgments he had brought upon them for their sins. Not that he changed his mind, but he was very ready to change his way and to return in mercy to them. God's time to repent himself concerning his servants is when he sees that, as here, their strength is gone, and *there is none shut up or left*, Deut. xxxii. 36. (2.) He answers the argument they had against abiding in this land. They *feared the king of Babylon (ch.* xli. 18), lest he should come and avenge the death of Gedaliah upon them, though they were no way accessory to it, nay, had witnessed against it. The surmise was foreign and unreasonable; but, if there had been any ground for it, enough is here said to remove it (*v.* 11): " *Be not afraid of the king of Babylon*, though he is a man of great might and little mercy, and a very arbitrary prince, whose will is a law, and therefore you are afraid he will upon this pretence, though without colour of reason, take advantage against you; *be not afraid of him*, for that fear will bring a snare: fear not him, for *I am with you;* and, if God be for you to save you, who can be against you to hurt you?" Thus has God provided to obviate and silence even the causeless fears of his people, which discourage them in the way of their duty; there is enough in the promises to encourage them. (3.) He assures them

that if they will still abide in this land they shall not only be safe from the king of Babylon, but be made happy by the King of kings: " *I will build you and plant you;* you shall take root again, and be the new foundation of another state, a phœnix-kingdom, rising out of the ashes of the last." It is added (*v.* 12), *I will show mercies unto you*. Note, In all our comforts we may read God's mercies. God will show them mercy in this, that not only the king of Babylon shall not destroy them, but he shall *have mercy upon them* and help to settle them. Note, Whatever kindness men do us we must attribute it to God's kindness. He makes those whom he pities to be pitied even by *those who carried them captives*, Ps. cvi. 46. " The king of Babylon, having now the disposal of the country, shall *cause you to return to your own land*, shall settle you again in your own habitations and put you in possession of the lands that formerly belonged to you." Note, God has made that our duty which is really our privilege, and our obedience will be its own recompence. " *Abide in this land*, and it shall be your own land again and you shall continue in it. Do not quit it now that you stand so fair for the enjoyment of it again. Be not so unwise as to *forsake your own mercies* for *lying vanities*."

2. That as they tender the favour of God and their own happiness they must by no means think of going into Egypt, not thither of all places, not to that land out of which God had delivered their fathers and which he had so often warned them not to make alliance with nor to put confidence in. Observe here, (1.) The sin they are supposed to be guilty of (and to him that knew their hearts it was more than a supposition): " You begin to say, *We will not dwell in this land* (*v.* 13); we will never think that we can be safe in it, no, not though God himself undertake our protection. We will not continue in it, no, not *in obedience to the voice of the Lord our God.* He may say what he please, but we will do what we please. We will *go into the land of Egypt*, and *there will we dwell*, whether God give us leave and go along with us or no," *v.* 14. It is supposed that their hearts were upon it: " *If you wholly set your faces to enter into Egypt*, are obstinately resolved that you will go and *sojourn there*, though God oppose you in it both by his word and by his providence, then take what follows." Now the reason they go upon in this resolution is that " *in Egypt we shall see no war, nor have hunger of bread*, as we have had for a long time in this land," *v.* 14. Note, It is folly to quit our place, especially to quit the holy land, because we meet with trouble in it; but greater folly to think by changing our place to escape the judgments of God, and that evil which pursues sinners in every way of disobedience, and which there is no

escaping but by returning to our allegiance. (2.) The sentence passed upon them for this sin, if they will persist in it. It is pronounced in God's name (*v.* 15) : " *Hear the word of the Lord, you remnant of Judah*, who think that because you are a remnant you must be spared of course (*v.* 2) and indulged in your own humour." [1.] Did the sword and famine frighten them? Those very judgments shall pursue them into Egypt, shall overtake them, and overcome them there (*v.* 16, 17) : " You think, because war and famine have long been raging in this land, that they are entailed upon it ; whereas, if you trust in God, he can make even this land a land of peace to you ; you think they are confined to it, and, if you can get clear of this land, you shall get out of the reach of them, but God will send them after you wherever you go." Note, The evils we think to escape by sin we certainly and inevitably run ourselves upon. The men that go to Egypt in contradiction to God's will, to escape *the sword and famine*, shall *die in Egypt by sword and famine.* We may apply it to the common calamities of human life ; those that are impatient of them, and think to avoid them by changing their place, will find that they are deceived and that they do not at all better themselves. The grievances common to men will meet them wherever they go. All our removes in this world are but from one wilderness to another ; still we are where we were. [2.] Did the desolations of Jerusalem frighten them? Were they willing to get as far as they could from them? They shall meet with the second part of them too in Egypt (*v.* 18) : *As my anger and fury have been poured out* here upon Jerusalem, so they shall be *poured out upon you in Egypt.* Note, Those that have by sin made God their enemy will find him a consuming fire wherever they go. And then you shall be *an execration and an astonishment.* The Hebrews were of old an abomination to the Egyptians (Gen. xliii. 32), and now they shall be made more so than ever. When God's professing people mingle with infidels, and make their court to them, they lose their dignity and make themselves a reproach.

3. That God knew their hypocrisy in their enquiries of him, and that when they asked what he would have them to do they were resolved to take their own way ; and therefore the sentence which was before pronounced conditionally is made absolute. Having set before them good and evil, the blessing and the curse, in the close he makes application of what he had said. And here, (1.) He solemnly protests that he had faithfully delivered his message, *v.* 19. The conclusion of the whole matter is, " *Go not down into Egypt ;* you disobey the command of God if you do, and what I have said to you will be a witness against you ; for *know certainly* that, *whether you will hear or whe-*

ther *you will forbear*, I have plainly *admonished you ;* you cannot now plead ignorance of the mind of God." (2.) He charges them with base dissimulation in the application they made to him for divine direction (*v.* 20) : " *You dissembled in your hearts ;* you professed one thing and intended another, promising what you never meant to perform." *You have used deceit against your souls* (so the margin reads it) ; for those that think to put a cheat upon God will prove in the end to have put a damning cheat upon themselves. (3.) He is already aware that they are determined to go contrary to the command of God ; probably they discovered it in their countenance and secret mutterings already, before he had finished his discourse. However, he spoke from him who knew their hearts : " *You have not obeyed the voice of the Lord your God ;* you have not a disposition to obey it." Thus Moses, in the close of his farewell sermon, had told them (Deut. xxxi. 27, 29), *I know thy rebellion and thy stiff neck*, and *that you will corrupt yourselves.* Admire the patience of God, that he is pleased to speak to those who, he knows, will not regard him, and deal with those who, he knows, will *deal very treacherously*, Isa. xlviii. 8. (4.) He therefore reads them their doom, ratifying what he had said before : *Know certainly that you shall die by the sword, v.* 22. God's threatenings may be vilified, but cannot be nullified, by the unbelief of man. *Famine and pestilence* shall pursue these sinners ; for there is no place privileged from divine arrests, nor can any malefactors go out of God's jurisdiction. *You shall die in the place whither you desire to go.* Note, We know not what is good for ourselves ; and that often proves afflictive, and sometimes fatal, which we are most fond of and have our hearts most set upon.

CHAP. XLIII.

Jeremiah had faithfully delivered his message from God in the foregoing chapter, and the case was made so very plain by it that one would have thought there needed no more words about it ; but we find it quite otherwise. Here is, I. The people's contempt of this message ; they denied it to be the word of God (ver. 1—3) and then made no difficulty of going directly contrary to it. Into Egypt they went, and took Jeremiah himself along with them, ver. 4—7. II. God's pursuit of them with another message, foretelling the king of Babylon's pursuit of them into Egypt, ver. 8—13.

A ND it came to pass, *that* when Jeremiah had made an end of speaking unto all the people all the words of the LORD their God, for which the LORD their God had sent him to them, *even* all these words, 2 Then spake Azariah the son of Hoshaiah, and Johanan the son of Kareah, and all the proud men, saying unto Jeremiah, Thou speakest falsely : the LORD our God hath not sent thee to say, Go not into Egypt to sojourn there : 3 But Baruch the son of Neriah setteth thee on against us, for to deliver us into the hand of the Chaldeans, that they might put us to death, and carry us away captives into Babylon. 4 So Johanan the son of Kareah, and all the captains of the forces, and all the people, obeyed not the voice of the LORD, to dwell in the land of Judah. 5 But Johanan the son of Kareah, and all the captains of the forces, took all the remnant of Judah, that were returned from all nations, whither they had been driven, to dwell in the land of Judah; 6 *Even* men, and women, and children, and the king's daughters, and every person that Nebuzaradan the captain of the guard had left with Gedaliah the son of Ahikam, the son of Shaphan, and Jeremiah the prophet, and Baruch the son of Neriah. 7 So they came into the land of Egypt: for they obeyed not the voice of the LORD. Thus came they *even* to Tahpanhes.

What God said to the builders of Babel may be truly said of this people that Jeremiah is now dealing with : *Now nothing will be restrained from them which they have imagined to do,* Gen. xi. 6. They have a fancy for Egypt, and to Egypt they will *go,* whatever God himself says to the contrary. Jeremiah made them hear all he had to say, though he saw them uneasy at it ; it was what the Lord their God had sent him to speak to them, and they shall have it all. And now let us see what they have to say to it.

I. They deny it to be a message from God : *Johanan, and all the proud men, said to Jeremiah, Thou speakest falsely, v.* 2. See here, 1. What was the cause of their disobedience —it was pride ; only by that comes contention both with God and man. They were *proud men* that gave the lie to the prophet. They could not bear the contradiction of their sentiments and the control of their designs, no, not by the divine wisdom, but the divine will itself. Pharaoh said, *Who is the Lord, that I should obey him ?* Exod. v. 2. The proud unhumbled heart of man is one of the most daring enemies God has on this side hell. 2. What was the colour for their disobedience. They would not acknowledge it to be the word of God : *The Lord hath not sent thee* on this errand to us. Either they were not convinced that what was said came from God or (which I rather think) though they were convinced of it they would not own it. The light shone strongly in their face, but they either shut their eyes against it or would not confess that they saw it. Note, The reason why

660

men deny the scriptures to be the word of God is because they are resolved not to conform to scripture-rules, and so an obstinate infidelity is made the sorry subterfuge of a wilful disobedience. If God had spoken to them by an angel, or as he did from Mount Sinai, they would have said that it was a delusion. Had they not consulted Jeremiah as a prophet? Had he not waited to receive instructions from God what to say to them? Had not what he said all the usual marks of prophecy upon it? Was not the prophet himself embarked in the same bottom with them? What interests could he have separate from theirs? Had he not always approved himself an Israelite indeed? And had not God proved him a prophet indeed? Had any of his words ever fallen to the ground? Why, truly, they had some good thoughts of Jeremiah, but they suggest (*v.* 3), *Baruch sets thee on against us.* A likely thing, that Baruch should be in a plot to *deliver them into the hands of the Chaldeans ;* and what would he get by that? If Jeremiah and he had been so well affected to the Chaldeans as they would represent them, they would have gone away at first with Nebuzaradan, when he courted them, to Babylon, and not have staid to take their lot with this despised ungrateful remnant. But the best services are no fences against malice and slander. Or, if Baruch had been so ill disposed, could they think Jeremiah would be so influenced by him as to make God's name an authority to patronise so villanous a purpose? Note, Those that are resolved to contradict the great ends of the ministry are industrious to bring a bad name upon it. When men will persist in sin they represent those that would turn them from it as designing men for themselves, nay, as ill-designing men against their neighbours. It is well for persons who are thus misrepresented that their witness is in heaven and their record on high.

II. They determine to go to Egypt notwithstanding. They resolve not to *dwell in the land of Judah,* as God had ordered them (*v.* 4), but to go themselves with one consent and to take all that they had under their power along with them to Egypt. Those that came *from all the nations whither they had been driven, to dwell in the land of Judah,* out of a sincere affection to that land, they would not leave to their liberty, but forced them to go with them into Egypt (*v.* 5), *men, women, and children* (*v.* 6), a long journey into a strange country, an idolatrous country, a country that had never been kind or faithful to Israel ; yet thither they would go, though they deserted their own land and threw themselves out of God's protection. It is the folly of men that they know not when they are well off, and often ruin themselves by endeavouring to better themselves ; and it is the pride of great men to force those they have under their power to follow them, though ever so much against their duty and interest. These proud men compelled even Jeremiah the prophet and Baruch his scribe to go along with them to Egypt; they carried them away as prisoners, partly to punish them (and a greater punishment they could not inflict upon them than to force them against their consciences; theirs is the worst of tyranny who say to men's souls, even to good men's souls, *Bow down, that we may go over*), partly to put some reputation upon themselves and their own way. Though the prophets were under a force, they would make the world believe that they were voluntary in going along with them; and who could have blamed them for acting contrary to the word of the Lord if the prophets themselves had acted so? They *came to Tahpanhes*, a famous city of Egypt (so called from a queen of that name, 1 Kings xi. 19), the same with *Hanes* (Isa. xxx. 4); it was now the metropolis, for Pharaoh's house was there, *v.* 9. No place could serve these proud men to settle in but the royal city and near the court, so little mindful were they of Joseph's wisdom, who would have his brethren settle in Goshen. If they had had the spirit of Israelites, they would have chosen rather to dwell in the wilderness of Judah than in the most pompous populous cities of Egypt.

8 Then came the word of the LORD unto Jeremiah in Tahpanhes, saying, 9 Take great stones in thine hand, and hide them in the clay in the brick-kiln, which *is* at the entry of Pharaoh's house, in Tahpanhes, in the sight of the men of Judah; 10 And say unto them, Thus saith the LORD of hosts, the God of Israel; Behold, I will send and take Nebuchadrezzar the king of Babylon, my servant, and will set his throne upon these stones that I have hid; and he shall spread his royal pavilion over them. 11 And when he cometh, he shall smite the land of Egypt, *and deliver* such *as are* for death to death; and such *as are* for captivity to captivity; and such *as are* for the sword to the sword. 12 And I will kindle a fire in the houses of the gods of Egypt; and he shall burn them, and carry them away captives: and he shall array himself with the land of Egypt, as a shepherd putteth on his garment; and he shall go forth from thence in peace. 13 He shall break also the images of Beth-shemesh, that *is* in the land of Egypt; and the

houses of the gods of the Egyptians shall he burn with fire.

We have here, as also in the next chapter, Jeremiah prophesying in Egypt. Jeremiah was now in Tahpanhes, for there his lords and masters were; he was there among idolatrous Egyptians and treacherous Israelites; but there, 1. He received *the word of the Lord;* it *came to him.* God can find his people, with the visits of his grace, wherever they are; and, when his ministers are bound, yet the word of the Lord is not bound. The spirit of prophecy was not confined to the land of Israel. When Jeremiah went into Egypt, not out of choice, but by constraint, God withdrew not his wonted favour from him. 2. What he received of the Lord he delivered to the people. Wherever we are we must endeavour to do good, for that is our business in this world. Now we find two messages which Jeremiah was appointed and entrusted to deliver when he was in Egypt. We may suppose that he rendered what services he could to his countrymen in Egypt, at least as far as they would be acceptable, in performing the ordinary duties of a prophet, praying for them and instructing and comforting them; but only two messages of his, which he had received immediately from God, are recorded, one in this chapter, relating to Egypt itself and foretelling its destruction, the other in the next chapter, relating to the Jews in Egypt. God had told them before that if they went into Egypt the sword they feared should follow them; here he tells them further that the sword of Nebuchadrezzar, which they were in a particular manner afraid of, should follow them.

I. This is foretold by a sign. Jeremiah must take *great stones*, such as are used for foundations, and *lay them in the clay of the* furnace, or *brick-kiln*, which is in *the open way*, or *beside the way* that leads *to Pharaoh's house* (*v.* 9), some remarkable place in view of the royal palace. Egypt was famous for brick-kilns, witness the slavery of the Israelites there, whom they forced to make bricks (Exod. v. 7), which perhaps was now remembered against them. The foundation of Egypt's desolation was laid in those brick-kilns, in *that clay*. This he must do, not in the sight of the Egyptians (they knew not Jeremiah's character), but *in the sight of the men of Judah* to whom he was sent, that, since he could not prevent their going into Egypt, he might bring them to repent of their going.

II. It is foretold in express words, as express as can be, 1. That the king, the present king of Babylon, Nebuchadrezzar, the very same that had been employed in the destruction of Jerusalem, should come in person against the land of Egypt, should make himself master even of this royal city, by the same token that he should *set his throne* in

that very place where *these stones* were laid, *v.* 10. This minute circumstance is particularly foretold, that, when it was accomplished, they might be put in mind of the prophecy and confirmed in their belief of the extent and certainty of the divine prescience, to which the smallest and most contingent events are evident. God calls Nebuchadnezzar his servant, because herein he executed God's will, accomplished his purposes, and was instrumental to carry on his designs. Note, The world's princes are God's servants and he makes what use he pleases of them, and even those that know him not, nor aim at his honour, are the tools which his providence makes use of. 2. That he should destroy many of the Egyptians, and have them all at his mercy (*v.* 11): *He shall smite the land of Egypt;* and, though it has been always a warlike nation, yet none shall be able to make head against him, but whom he will he shall slay, and by what sort of death he will, whether pestilence (for that is here meant by *death,* as *ch.* xv. 2) by shutting them up in places infected, or by the sword of war or justice, in cold blood or hot. And whom he will he shall save alive and carry into *captivity.* The Jews, by going into Egypt, brought the Chaldeans thither, and so did but ill repay those that entertained them. Those who promised to protect Israel from the king of Babylon exposed themselves to him. 3. That he shall destroy the idols of Egypt, both the temples and the images of their gods (*v.* 12): *He shall burn the houses of the gods of Egypt,* but it shall be with a fire of God's kindling; the fire of God's wrath fastens upon them, and then he burns some of them and carries others captive, Isa. xlvi. 1. *Beth-shemesh,* or *the house of the sun,* was so called from a temple there built to the sun, where at certain times there was a general meeting of the worshippers of the sun. The statues or standing images there he shall *break in pieces* (*v.* 13) and carry away the rich materials of them. It intimates that he should lay all waste when even the temple and the images should not escape the fury of the victorious army. The king of Babylon was himself a great idolater and a patron of idolatry; he had his temples and images in honour of the sun as well as the Egyptians; and yet he is employed to destroy the idols of Egypt. Thus God sometimes makes one wicked man, or wicked nation, a scourge and plague to another. 4. That he shall make himself master of the land of Egypt, and none shall be able to plead its cause or avenge its quarrel (*v.* 12): *He shall array himself with the rich spoils of the land of Egypt,* both beautify and fortify himself with them. He shall array himself with them as ornaments and as armour; and this, though it shall be a rich and heavy booty, being expert in war, and expeditious, he shall slip on with as much ease and in as little time, in comparison, *as a shepherd slips*
662

on his garment, when he goes to turn out his sheep in a morning. And being loaded with the wealth of many other nations, the fruits of his conquests, he shall make no more of the spoils of the land of Egypt than of a shepherd's coat. And when he has taken what he pleases (as Benhadad threatened to do, 1 Kings xx. 6) he shall *go forth in peace,* without any molestation given him, or any precipitation for fear of it, so effectually reduced shall the land of Egypt be. This destruction of Egypt by the king of Babylon is foretold, Ezek. xxix. 19 and xxx. 10. Babylon lay at a great distance from Egypt, and yet thence the destruction of Egypt comes; for God can make those judgments strike home which are far-fetched.

CHAP. XLIV.

In this chapter we have, I. An awakening sermon which Jeremiah preaches to the Jews in Egypt, to reprove them for their idolatry, notwithstanding the warnings given them both by the word and the rod of God and to threaten the judgments of God against them for it, ver. 1—14. II. The impudent and impious contempt which the people put upon this admonition, and their declared resolution to persist in their idolatries notwithstanding, in despite of God and Jeremiah, ver. 15—19. III. The sentence passed upon them for their obstinacy, that they should all be cut off and perish in Egypt except a very small number; and, as a sign or earnest of it, the king of Egypt should shortly fall into the hands of the king of Babylon and be unable any longer to protect them, ver. 20—30.

THE word that came to Jeremiah concerning all the Jews which dwell in the land of Egypt, which dwell at Migdol, and at Tahpanhes, and at Noph, and in the country of Pathros, saying, 2 Thus saith the LORD of hosts, the God of Israel; Ye have seen all the evil that I have brought upon Jerusalem, and upon all the cities of Judah; and, behold, this day they *are* a desolation, and no man dwelleth therein, 3 Because of their wickedness which they have committed to provoke me to anger, in that they went to burn incense, *and* to serve other gods, whom they knew not, *neither* they, ye, nor your fathers. 4 Howbeit I sent unto you all my servants the prophets, rising early and sending *them,* saying, Oh, do not this abominable thing that I hate. 5 But they hearkened not, nor inclined their ear to turn from their wickedness, to burn no incense unto other gods. 6 Wherefore my fury and mine anger was poured forth, and was kindled in the cities of Judah and in the streets of Jerusalem; and they are wasted *and* desolate, as at this day. 7 Therefore now thus saith the LORD, the God of hosts, the God of Israel; Wherefore commit ye *this* great evil against your souls, to cut off from you man and woman, child and suckling, out of Judah, to leave you none to remain; 8 In that ye provoke me unto wrath with the works of your hands, burning incense unto other gods in the land of Egypt, whither ye be gone to dwell, that ye might cut yourselves off, and that ye might be a curse and a reproach among all the nations of the earth? 9 Have ye forgotten the wickedness of your fathers, and the wickedness of the kings of Judah, and the wickedness of their wives, and your own wickedness, and the wickedness of your wives, which they have committed in the land of Judah, and in the streets of Jerusalem? 10 They are not humbled *even* unto this day, neither have they feared, nor walked in my law, nor in my statutes, that I set before you, and before your fathers. 11 Therefore thus saith the LORD of hosts, the God of Israel; Behold, I will set my face against you for evil, and to cut off all Judah. 12 And I will take the remnant of Judah, that have set their faces to go into the land of Egypt to sojourn there, and they shall all be consumed, *and* fall in the land of Egypt; they shall *even* be consumed by the sword *and* by the famine: they shall die, from the least even unto the greatest, by the sword and by the famine: and they shall be an execration, *and* an astonishment, and a curse, and a reproach. 13 For I will punish them that dwell in the land of Egypt, as I have punished Jerusalem, by the sword, by the famine, and by the pestilence: 14 So that none of the remnant of Judah, which are gone into the land of Egypt to sojourn there, shall escape or remain, that they should return into the land of Judah, to the which they have a desire to return to dwell there: for none shall return but such as shall escape.

The Jews in Egypt were now dispersed into various parts of the country, into *Migdol, and Noph,* and other places, and Jeremiah was sent on an errand from God to them, which he delivered either when he had the most of them together *in Pathros*

(v. 15) or going about from place to place preaching to this purport. He delivered this message in the name of *the Lord of hosts, the God of Israel,* and in it,

I. God puts them in mind of the desolations of Judah and Jerusalem, which, though the captives *by the rivers of Babylon* were daily mindful of (Ps. cxxxvii. 1), the fugitives in the cities of Egypt seem to have forgotten and needed to be put in mind of, though, one would have thought, they had not been so long out of sight as to become out of mind '(v. 2): *You have seen* what a deplorable condition Judah and Jerusalem are brought into; now will you consider whence those desolations came? From the wrath of God; it was his fury and his anger that kindled the fire which made Jerusalem and *the cities of Judah waste and desolate* (v. 6); whoever were the instruments of the destruction, they were but instruments: it was a destruction from the Almighty.

II. He puts them in mind of the sins that brought those desolations upon Judah and Jerusalem. It was for *their wickedness.* It was this that *provoked God to anger,* and especially their idolatry, their *serving other gods* (v. 3) and giving that honour to counterfeit deities, the creatures of their own fancy and the work of their own hands, which should have been given to the true God only. They forsook the God who was known among them, and whose name was great, for gods that they knew not, upstart deities, whose original was obscure and not worth taking notice of: "*Neither they nor you, nor your fathers,* could give any rational account why *the God of Israel* was exchanged for such impostors." They knew not that they were gods; nay, they could not but know that they were no gods.

III. He puts them in mind of the frequent and fair warnings he had given them by his word not to serve other gods, the contempt of which warnings was a great aggravation of their idolatry, v. 4. *The prophets* were sent with a great deal of care to call to them, saying, *Oh! do not this abominable thing that I hate.* It becomes us to speak of sin with the utmost dread and detestation as an abominable thing; it is certainly so, for it is that which God hates, and we are sure that *his judgment is according to truth.* Call it grievous, call it odious, that we may by all means possible put ourselves and others out of love with it. It becomes us to give warning of the danger of sin, and the fatal consequences of it, with all seriousness and earnestness: "*Oh! do not* do it. If you love God, do not, for it is provoking to him; if you love your own souls do not, for it is destructive to them." Let conscience do this for us in an hour of temptation, when we are ready to yield. O take heed! *do not this abominable thing* which the Lord hates; for, if God hates it, thou shouldst hate it. But did they regard what God said to them?

No : " *They hearkened not, nor inclined their ear* (*v.* 5) ; they still persisted in their idolatries; and you see what came of it, therefore God's *anger was poured* out upon them, *as at this day.* Now this was intended for warning to you, who have not only heard the judgments of God's mouth, as they did, but have likewise seen the judgments of his hand, by which you should be startled and awakened, for they were inflicted *in terrorem*, that others might hear and fear and do no more as they did, lest they should fare as they fared."

IV. He reproves them for, and upbraids them with, their continued idolatries, now that they had come into Egypt (*v.* 8) : You *burn incense to other gods in the land of Egypt. Therefore* God forbade them to go into Egypt, because he knew it would be a snare to them. Those whom God sent into the land of the Chaldeans, though that was an idolatrous country, were there, by the power of God's grace, weaned from idolatry; but those who went against God's mind into the land of the Egyptians were there, by the power of their own corruptions, more wedded than ever to their idolatries; for, when we thrust ourselves without cause or call into places of temptation, it is just with God to leave us to ourselves. In doing this, 1. They did a great deal of injury to themselves and their families : " *You commit this great evil against your souls* (*v.* 7), you wrong them, you deceive them with that which is false, you destroy them, for it will be fatal to them." Note, In sinning against God we sin *against our own souls.* " It is the ready way to *cut yourselves off* from all comfort and hope (*v.* 8), to cut off your name and honour ; so that you will, both by your sin and by your misery, become *a curse and a reproach among all nations.* It will become a proverb, As wretched as a Jew. It is the ready way *to cut off from you* all your relations, all that you should have joy of and have your families built up in, *man and woman, child and suckling*, so that Judah shall be a land lost for want of heirs." 2. They filled up the measure of the iniquity of their fathers, and, as if that had been too little for them, added to it (*v.* 9) : " *Have you forgotten the wickedness* of those who are gone before you, that you are not humbled for it as you ought to be, and afraid of the consequences of it ?" *Have you forgotten the punishments of your fathers?* so some read it. " Do you not know how dear their idolatry cost them ? And yet dare you continue in that vain conversation received by tradition from your fathers, though you received the curse with it ?" He reminds them of the sins and punishments *of the kings of Judah*, who, great as they were, escaped not the judgments of God for their idolatry ; yea, and they should have taken warning by *the wickedness of their wives*, who had seduced them to idolatry. In the original it is, *And of his wives*, which,

Dr. Lightfoot thinks, tacitly reflects upon Solomon's wives, particularly his Egyptian wives, to whom the idolatry of the kings of Judah owed its original. " Have you forgotten this, and what came of it, that you dare venture upon the same wicked courses?" See Neh. xiii. 18, 26. " Nay, to come to your own times, *Have you forgotten your own wickedness and the wickedness of your wives*, when you lived in prosperity in Jerusalem, and what ruin it brought upon you ? But, alas ! to what purpose do I speak to them ?" (says God to the prophet, *v.* 10) " *they are not humbled unto this day*, by all the humbling providences that they have been under. *They have not feared, nor walked in my law.*" Note, Those that walk not in the law of God do thereby show that they are destitute of the fear of God.

V. He threatens their utter ruin for their persisting in their idolatry now that they were in Egypt. Judgment is given against them, as before (*ch.* xlii. 22), that they shall perish in Egypt; the decree has gone forth, and shall not be called back. They *set their faces to go into the land of Egypt* (*v.* 12), were resolute in their purpose against God, and now God is resolute in his purpose against them : *I will set my face to cut off all Judah, v.* 11. Those that think not only to affront, but to confront, God Almighty, will find themselves outfaced; for *the face of the Lord is against those that do evil*, Ps. xxxiv. 16. It is here threatened concerning these idolatrous Jews in Egypt, 1. That *they shall all be consumed*, without exception ; no degree nor order among them shall escape : *They shall fall, from the least to the greatest* (*v.* 12), *high and low, rich and poor.* 2. That *they shall be consumed by* the very same judgments which God made use of for the punishment of Jerusalem, *the sword, famine, and pestilence, v.* 12, 13. They shall not be wasted by natural deaths, as Israel in the wilderness, but by these sore judgments, which, by flying into Egypt, they thought to get out of the reach of. 3. That none (except a very few that will narrowly escape) shall ever *return to the land of Judah* again, *v.* 14. They thought, being nearer, that they stood fairer for a return to their own land than those that were carried to Babylon ; yet those shall return, and these shall not ; for the way in which God has promised us any comfort is much surer than that in which we have projected it for ourselves. Observe, Those that are fretful and discontented will be uneasy and fond of change wherever they are. The Israelites, when they were in the land of Judah, desired to go into Egypt (*ch.* xlii. 22), but when they were in Egypt they desired to *return to the land of Judah* again ; they *lifted up their soul* to it (so it is in the margin), which denotes an earnest desire. But, because they would not dwell there when God commanded it, they shall not dwell there when they desire it. If we walk

664

contrary to God, he will walk contrary to us. How can those expect to be well off who would not know when they were so, though God himself told them?

15 Then all the men which knew that their wives had burnt incense unto other gods, and all the women that stood by, a great multitude, even all the people that dwelt in the land of Egypt, in Pathros, answered Jeremiah, saying, 16 *As for* the word that thou hast spoken unto us in the name of the LORD, we will not hearken unto thee. 17 But we will certainly do whatsoever thing goeth forth out of our own mouth, to burn incense unto the queen of heaven, and to pour out drink-offerings unto her, as we have done, we, and our fathers, our kings, and our princes, in the cities of Judah, and in the streets of Jerusalem: for *then* had we plenty of victuals, and were well, and saw no evil. 18 But since we left off to burn incense to the queen of heaven, and to pour out drink-offerings unto her, we have wanted all *things*, and have been consumed by the sword and by the famine. 19 And when we burned incense to the queen of heaven, and poured out drink-offerings unto her, did we make her cakes to worship her, and pour out drink-offerings unto her, without our men?

We have here the people's obstinate refusal to submit to the power of the word of God in the mouth of Jeremiah. We have scarcely such an instance of downright daring contradiction to God himself as this, or such an avowed rebellion of the carnal mind. Observe,

I. The persons who thus set God and his judgments at defiance; it was not some one that was thus obstinate, but the generality of the Jews; and they were such as knew either themselves or their wives to be guilty of the idolatry Jeremiah had reproved, *v.* 15. We find, 1. That the women had been more guilty of idolatry and superstition than the men, not because the men stuck closer to the true God and the true religion than the women, but, I fear, because they were generally atheists, and were for no God and no religion at all, and therefore could easily allow their wives to be of a false religion, and to worship false gods. 2. That it was consciousness of guilt that made them impatient of reproof: *They knew that their wives had burnt incense to other gods,* and that they had countenanced them in it, *and the women that*

stood *by* knew that they had joined with them in their idolatrous usages; so that what Jeremiah said touched them in a sore place, which made them *kick against the pricks,* as *children of Belial,* that will not *bear the yoke.*

II. The reply which these persons made to Jeremiah, and in him to God himself; it is in effect the same with theirs who had the impudence to say to the Almighty, *Depart from us; we desire not the knowledge of thy ways.*

1. They declare their resolution not to do as God commanded them, but what they themselves had a mind to do; that is, they would go on to worship the moon, here called *the queen of heaven;* yet some understand it of the sun, which was much worshipped in Egypt (*ch.* xliii. 13) and had been so at Jerusalem (2 Kings xxiii. 11), and they say that the Hebrew word for the sun being feminine it may not unfitly be called *the queen of heaven.* And others understand it of all *the host of heaven,* or *the frame of heaven,* the whole machine, *ch.* vii. 18. These daring sinners do not now go about to make excuses for their refusal to obey, nor suggest that Jeremiah spoke from himself and not from God (as before, *ch.* xliii. 2), but they own that he spoke to them *in the name of the Lord,* and yet tell him flatly, in so many words, " *We will not hearken unto thee;* we will do that which is forbidden and run the hazard of that which is threatened." Note, Those that live in disobedience to God commonly grow worse and worse, and the heart is more and more hardened by *the deceitfulness of sin.* Here is the genuine language of the rebellious heart : *We will certainly do whatsoever thing goes forth out of our own mouth,* let God and his prophets say what they please to the contrary. What they said many think who yet have not arrived at such a degree of impudence as to speak it out. It is that which the young man would be at *in the days of his youth;* he would *walk in the way of his heart and the sight of his eyes,* and would have and do every thing he has a mind to, Eccl. xi. 9.

2. They give some sort of reasons for their resolution; for the most absurd and unreasonably wicked men will have something to say for themselves, till the day comes when *every mouth shall be stopped.*

(1) They plead many of those things which the advocates for Rome make the marks of a true church, and not only justify but magnify themselves with; and these Jews have as much right to them as the Romanists have. [1.] They plead antiquity: We are resolved *to burn incense to the queen of heaven,* for *our fathers* did so; it is a practice that pleads prescription; and why should we pretend to be wiser than our fathers? [2.] They plead authority. Those that had power practised it themselves and prescribed it to others : *Our kings and our princes* did

it, whom God set over us, and who were of the seed of David. [3.] They plead unity. It was not here and there one that did it, but *we*, we all with one consent, we that are *a great multitude* (*v.* 15), we did it. [4.] They plead universality. It was not done here and there, but *in the cities of Judah.* [5.] They plead visibility. It was not done in a corner, in dark and shady groves only, but *in the streets*, openly and publicly. [6.] They plead that it was the practice of the mother-church, the holy see; it was not now learned first in Egypt, but it had been done in *Jerusalem.* [7.] They plead prosperity: *Then had we plenty of* bread, *and* of all good things; we *were well and saw no evil.* All the former pleas, I fear, were too true in fact; God's witnesses against their idolatry were few and hid; Elijah thought that he was left alone: and this last might perhaps be true as to some particular persons, but, as to their nation, they were still under rebukes for their rebellions, and there was *no peace to those that went out or came in*, 2 Chron. xv. 5. But, supposing all to be true, yet this does not at all excuse them from idolatry; it is the law of God that we must be ruled and judged by, not the practice of men.

(2.) They suggest that the judgments they had of late been under were brought upon them for *leaving off to burn incense to the queen of heaven, v.* 18. So perversely did they misconstrue providence, though God, by his prophets, had so often explained it to them, and the thing itself spoke the direct contrary. *Since we forsook our idolatries we have wanted all things, and have been consumed by the sword*, the true reason of which was because they still retained their idols in their heart and an affection to their old sins; but they would have it thought that it was because they had forsaken the acts of sin. Thus the afflictions which should have been for their welfare, to separate between them and their sins, being misinterpreted did but confirm them in their sins. Thus, in the first ages of Christianity, when God chastised the nations by any public calamities for opposing the Christians and persecuting them, they put a contrary sense upon the calamities, as if they were sent to punish hem for conniving at the Christians and tolerating them, and cried, *Christianos ad leones—Throw the Christians to the lions.* Yet, if it had been true, as they said here, that since they returned to the service of the true God, the God of Israel, they had been in want and trouble, was that a reason why they should revolt from him again? That was as much as to say that they served not him, but their own bellies. Those who know God, and put their trust in him, will serve him, though he starve them, though he slay them, though they never see a good day with him in this world, being well assured that they shall not lose by him in the end.

666

(3.) They plead that, though the women were most forward and active in their idolatries, yet they did it with the consent and approbation of their husbands; the women were busy to *make cakes* for meat-offerings *to the queen of heaven* and to prepare *and pour out the drink-offerings, v.* 19. We found, before, that this was their work, *ch.* vii. 18. "But *did we* do it *without our husbands*, privately and unknown to them, so as to give them occasion to be jealous of us? No; the fathers kindled the fire while the women kneaded the dough; the men that were our heads, whom we were bound to learn of and to be obedient to, taught us to do it by their example." Note, It is sad when those who are in the nearest relation to each other, who should quicken each other to that which is good and so help one another to heaven, harden each other in sin and so ripen one another for hell. Some understand this as spoken by the husbands (*v.* 15), who plead that they did not do it *without their men*, that is, without their elders and rulers, their great men, and men in authority; but, because the making of the *cakes* and the pouring out of *the drink-offerings* are expressly spoken of as the women's work (*ch.* vii. 18), it seems rather to be understood as their plea: but it was a frivolous plea. What would it avail them to be able to say that it was according to their husbands' mind, when they knew that it was contrary to their God's mind?

20 Then Jeremiah said unto all the people, to the men, and to the women, and to all the people which had given him *that* answer, saying, 21 The incense that ye burned in the cities of Judah, and in the streets of Jerusalem, ye, and your fathers, your kings, and your princes, and the people of the land, did not the LORD remember them, and came it *not* into his mind? 22 So that the LORD could no longer bear, because of the evil of your doings, *and* because of the abominations which ye have committed; therefore is your land a desolation, and an astonishment, and a curse, without an inhabitant, as at this day. 23 Because ye have burned incense, and because ye have sinned against the LORD, and have not obeyed the voice of the LORD, nor walked in his law, nor in his statutes, nor in his testimonies; therefore this evil is happened unto you, as at this day. 24 Moreover Jeremiah said unto all the people, and to all the women, Hear the word of the

LORD, all Judah that *are* in the land of Egypt: 25 Thus saith the LORD of hosts, the God of Israel, saying; Ye and your wives have both spoken with your mouths, and fulfilled with your hand, saying, We will surely perform our vows that we have vowed, to burn incense to the queen of heaven, and to pour out drink-offerings unto her: ye will surely accomplish your vows, and surely perform your vows. 26 Therefore hear ye the word of the LORD, all Judah that dwell in the land of Egypt; Behold, I have sworn by my great name, saith the LORD, that my name shall no more be named in the mouth of any man of Judah in all the land of Egypt, saying, The Lord GOD liveth. 27 Behold, I will watch over them for evil, and not for good: and all the men of Judah that *are* in the land of Egypt shall be consumed by the sword and by the famine, until there be an end of them. 28 Yet a small number that escape the sword shall return out of the land of Egypt into the land of Judah, and all the remnant of Judah, that are gone into the land of Egypt to sojourn there, shall know whose words shall stand, mine, or their's. 29 And this *shall be* a sign unto you, saith the LORD, that I will punish you in this place, that ye may know that my words shall surely stand against you for evil: 30 Thus saith the LORD; Behold, I will give Pharaoh-hophra king of Egypt into the hand of his enemies, and into the hand of them that seek his life; as I gave Zedekiah king of Judah into the hand of Nebuchadrezzar king of Babylon, his enemy, and that sought his life.

Daring sinners may speak many a bold word and many a big word, but, after all, God will have the last word; for he will be justified when he speaks, and all flesh, even the proudest, shall be silent before him. Prophets may be run down, but God cannot; nay, here the prophet would not.

I. Jeremiah has something to say to them from himself, which he could say without a spirit of prophecy, and that was to rectify their mistake (a wilful mistake it was) concerning the calamities they had been under and the true intent and meaning of them.

They said that these miseries came upon them because they had now *left off burning incense to the queen of heaven.* "No," says he, "it was because you had formerly done it, not because you had now left it off." When they gave him that answer, he immediately replied (*v.* 20) that the incense which they and their fathers had burnt to other gods did indeed go unpunished a great while, for God was long-suffering towards them, and during the day of his patience it was perhaps, as they said, *well with them, and* they *saw no evil;* but at length they grew so provoking *that the Lord could no longer bear* (*v.* 22), but began a controversy with them, whereupon some of them did a little reform; their sins left them, for so it might be said, rather than that they left their sins. But their old guilt being still upon the score, and their corrupt inclinations still the same, God remembered against them the idolatries of *their fathers, their kings, and their princes, in the streets of Jerusalem,* which they, instead of being ashamed of, gloried in as a justification of them in their idolatries; they *all came into his mind* (*v.* 21), all the *abominations which they had committed* (*v.* 22) and all their disobedience to *the voice of the Lord* (*v.* 23), all were brought to account; and *therefore,* to punish them for these, *is their land a desolation and a curse, as at this day* (*v.* 22) ; *therefore,* not for their late reformation, but for their old transgressions, has all *this evil happened to them, as at this day, v.* 23. Note, The right understanding of the cause of our troubles, one would think, should go far towards the cure of our sins. Whatever *evil comes upon us, it is because we have sinned against the Lord,* and should therefore *stand in awe and sin not.*

II. Jeremiah has something to say to them, *to the women* particularly, from *the Lord of hosts, the God of Israel.* They have given their answer; now let them hear God's reply, *v.* 24. *Judah, that* dwells *in the land of Egypt,* has God speaking to them, even there; that is their privilege. Let them observe what he says; that is their duty. *v.* 26. Now God, in his reply, tells them plainly,

1. That, since they were fully determined to persist in their idolatry, he was fully determined to proceed in his controversy with them; if they would go on to provoke him, he would go on to punish them, and see which would get the better at last. God repeats what they had said (*v.* 25): "*You and your wives* are agreed in this obstinacy; *you have spoken with your mouths and fulfilled with your hands;* you have said it, and you stand to it, have said it and go on to do accordingly, *We will surely perform our vows that we have vowed, to burn incense to the queen of heaven,*" as if, though it were a sin, yet their having vowed to do it were sufficient to justify them in the doing of it;

whereas no man can by his vow make that lawful to himself, much less duty, which God has already made sin. "Well" (says God), "*you will accomplish, you will perform, your wicked vows:* now hear what is my vow, what *I have sworn by my great name;*" and, if *the Lord hath sworn,* he *will not repent,* since they have sworn and will not repent. *With the froward he will show himself froward,* Ps. xviii. 26. (1.) He had sworn that what little remains of religion there were among them should be lost, *v.* 26. Though they joined with the Egyptians in their idolatries, yet they continued upon many occasions to make mention of the name of Jehovah, particularly in their solemn oaths; they said, *Jehovah liveth,* he is *the living God,* so they owned him to be, though they worshipped dead idols; they swear, *The Lord liveth* (*ch.* v. 2), but I fear they retained this form of swearing more in honour of their nation than of their God. But God declares that his *name shall no more be* thus *named by any man of Judah in all the land of Egypt;* that is, there shall be no Jews remaining to use this dialect of their country, or, if there be, they shall have forgotten it and shall learn to swear, as the Egyptians do, *by the life of Pharaoh,* not of Jehovah. Note, Those are very miserable whom God has so far left to themselves that they have quite forgotten their religion and lost all the remains of their good education. Or this may intimate that God would take it as an affront to him, and would resent it accordingly, if they did make mention of his name and profess any relation to him. (2.) He hath sworn that what little remnant of people there was there should all be consumed (*v.* 27): *I will watch over them for evil;* no opportunity shall be let slip to bring some judgment upon them, *until there be an end of them* and they be quite rooted out. Note, To those whom God finds impenitent sinners he will be found an implacable Judge. And, when it comes to this, they *shall know* (*v.* 28) *whose word shall stand, mine or theirs.* They said that they should recover themselves when they returned to worship *the queen of heaven;* God said they should ruin themselves; and now the event will show which was in the right. The contest between God and sinners is whose word shall stand, whose will shall be done, who shall get the better. Sinners say that they shall have peace though they go on; God says they shall have no peace. But *when God judges he will overcome;* God's word shall stand, and not the sinner's.

2. He tells them that a very few of them should *escape the sword,* and in process of time *return into the land of Judah, a small number* (*v.* 28), next to none, in comparison with the great numbers that should return out of the land of the Chaldeans. This seems designed to upbraid those who boasted of their numbers that concurred in sin;

668

there were none to speak of that did not join in idolatry: "Well," says God, "and there shall be as few *that* shall *escape the sword and famine.*"

3. He gives them a sign that all these threatenings shall be accomplished in their season, that they shall be consumed here in Egypt and shall quite perish: *Pharaoh-hophra,* the present *king of Egypt,* shall be delivered *into the hand of his enemies that seek his life—of his own rebellious subjects* (so some) under Amasis, who usurped his throne—*of Nebuchadnezzar king of Babylon* (so others), who invaded his kingdom; the former is related by Herodotus, the latter by Josephus. It is likely that this Pharaoh had tempted the Jews to idolatry by promises of his favour; however, they depended upon him for his protection, and it would be more than a presage of their ruin, it would be a step towards it, if he were gone. They expected more from him than from Zedekiah king of Judah; he was a more potent and politic prince. "But," says God, "*I will give him into the hand of his enemies,* as I gave Zedekiah." Note, Those creature-comforts and confidences that we promise ourselves most from may fail us as soon as those that we promise ourselves least from, for they are all what God makes them, not what we fancy them.

The sacred history records not the accomplishment of this prophecy, but its silence is sufficient; we hear no more of these Jews in Egypt, and therefore conclude them, according to this prediction, lost there; for no word of God shall fall to the ground.

CHAP. XLV.

The prophecy we have in this chapter concerns Baruch only, yet is intended for the support and encouragement of all the Lord's people that serve him faithfully and keep closely to him in difficult trying times. It is placed here after the story of the destruction of Jerusalem and the dispersion of the Jews, but was delivered long before, in the fourth year of Jehoiakim, as was the prophecy in the next chapter, and probably those that follow. We here find, I. How Baruch was terrified when he was brought into trouble for writing and reading Jeremiah's roll, ver. 1—3. II. How his fears were checked with a reproof for his great expectations and silenced with a promise of special preservation, ver. 4, 5. Though Baruch was only Jeremiah's scribe, yet this notice is taken of his frights, and this provision made for his comfort; for God despises not any of his servants, but graciously concerns himself for the meanest and weakest, for Baruch the scribe as well as for Jeremiah the prophet.

THE word that Jeremiah the prophet spake unto Baruch the son of Neriah, when he had written these words in a book at the mouth of Jeremiah, in the fourth year of Jehoiakim the son of Josiah king of Judah, saying, 2 Thus saith the LORD, the God of Israel, unto thee, O Baruch; 3 Thou didst say, Woe is me now! for the LORD hath added grief to my sorrow; I fainted in my sighing, and I find no rest. 4 Thus shalt thou say unto him, The LORD saith thus; Behold, *that* which I have built will

I break down, and that which I have planted I will pluck up, even this whole land. 5 And seekest thou great things for thyself? seek *them* not: for, behold, I will bring evil upon all flesh, saith the LORD: but thy life will I give unto thee for a prey in all places whither thou goest.

How Baruch was employed in writing Jeremiah's prophecies, and reading them, we had an account *ch.* xxxvi., and how he was threatened for it by the king, warrants being out for him and he forced to abscond, and how narrowly he escaped under a divine protection, to which story this chapter should have been subjoined, but that, having reference to a private person, it is here thrown into the latter end of the book, as St. Paul's epistle to Philemon is put after his other epistles. Observe,

I. The consternation that poor Baruch was in when he was sought for by the king's messengers and obliged to hide his head, and the notice which God took of it. He cried out, *Woe is me now! v.* 3. He was a young man setting out in the world; he was well affected to the things of God, and was willing to serve God and his prophet; but, when it came to suffering, he was desirous to be excused. Being an ingenious man, and a scholar, he stood fair for preferment, and now to be driven into a corner, and in danger of a prison, or worse, was a great disappointment to him. When he read the roll publicly he hoped to gain reputation by it, that it would make him to be taken notice of and employed; but when he found that, instead of that, it exposed him to contempt, and brought him into disgrace, he cried out, " I am undone; I shall fall into the pursuers' hands, and be imprisoned, and put to death, or banished: *The Lord has added grief to my sorrow,* has loaded me with one trouble after another. After the grief of writing and reading the prophecies of my country's ruin, I have the sorrow of being treated as a criminal for so doing; and, though another might make nothing of this, yet for my part I cannot bear it; it is a burden too heavy for me. *I fainted in my sighing* (or *I am faint with my sighing;* it just kills me) *and I find no rest,* no satisfaction in my own mind. I cannot compose myself as I should and would to bear it, nor have I any prospect of relief or comfort." Baruch was a good man, but, we must say, this was his infirmity. Note, 1. Young beginners in religion, like fresh-water soldiers, are apt to be discouraged with the little difficulties which they commonly meet with at first in the service of God. They do but *run with the footmen,* and it *wearies them;* they *faint* upon the very dawning of *the day of adversity,* and it is an evidence that *their strength is small* (Prov. xxiv. 10), that their

faith is weak, and that they are yet but babes, who cry for every hurt and every fright. 2. Some of the best and dearest of God's saints and servants, when they have seen storms rising, have been in frights, and apt to make the worst of things, and to disquiet themselves with melancholy apprehensions more than there was cause for. 3. God takes notice of the frets and discontents of his people and is displeased with them. Baruch should have rejoiced that he was counted worthy to suffer in such a good cause and with such good company, but, instead of that, he is vexed at it, and blames his lot, nay, and reflects upon his God, as if he had dealt hardly with him; what he said was spoken in a heat and passion, but God was offended, as he was with Moses, who paid dearly for it, when, his spirit being provoked, he *spoke unadvisedly with his lips. Thou didst say* so and so, and it was not well said. God keeps account what we say, even when we speak in haste.

II. The reproof that God gave him for talking at this rate. Jeremiah was troubled to see him in such an agitation, and knew not well what to say to him. He was loth to chide him, and yet thought he deserved it, was willing to comfort him, and yet knew not which way to go about it; but God tells him what he *shall say to him, v.* 4. Jeremiah could not be certain what was at the bottom of these complaints and fears, but God sees it. They came from his corruptions. That the hurt might therefore not be healed slightly, he searches the wound, and shows him that he had raised his expectations too high in this world and had promised himself too much from it, and that made the distress and trouble he was in so very grievous to him and so hard to be borne. Note, The frowns of the world would not disquiet us as they do if we did not foolishly flatter ourselves with the hopes of its smiles and court and covet them too much. It is our over-fondness for the good things of this present time that makes us impatient under its evil things. Now God shows him that it was his fault and folly, at this time of day especially, either to desire or to look for an abundance of the wealth and honour of this world. For, 1. The ship was sinking. Ruin was coming upon the Jewish nation, an utter and universal ruin: " *That which I have built,* to be a house for myself, *I am breaking down, and that which I have planted,* to be a vineyard for myself, *I am plucking up, even this whole land,* the Jewish church and state; and dost thou now *seek great things for thyself?* Dost thou expect to be rich and honourable and to make a figure now? No." 2. " It is absurd for thee to be now painting thy own cabin. Canst thou expect to be high when all are brought low, to be full when all about thee are empty?" To seek ourselves more than the public welfare, especially to seek great things to ourselves when the public is in danger, is very unbecoming Israelites. We may apply it to this world, and our state in it; God in his providence is breaking down and pulling up; every thing is uncertain and perishing; we cannot expect any continuing city here. What folly is it then to *seek great things for ourselves* here, where every thing is little and nothing certain!

III. The encouragement that God gave him to hope that though he should not be great, yet he should be safe: " *I will bring evil upon all flesh,* all nations of men, all orders and degrees of men, *but thy life will I give to thee for a prey*" *(thy soul,* so the word is) " *in all places whither thou goest.* Thou must expect to be hurried from place to place, and, wherever thou goest, to be in danger; but thou shalt escape, though often very narrowly, shalt have thy life, but it shall be as a prey, which is got with much difficulty and danger; thou shalt be saved as by fire." Note, The preservation and continuance of life are very great mercies, and we are bound to account them such, as they are the prolonging of our opportunity to glorify God in this world and to get ready for a better; and at some times, especially when the arrows of death fly thickly about us, life is a signal favour, and what we ought to be very thankful for, and while we have it must not complain though we be disappointed of the great things we expected. *Is not the life more than meat?*

CHAP. XLVI.

How judgment began at the house of God we have found in the foregoing prophecy and history; but now we shall find that it did not end there. In this and the following chapters we have predictions of the desolations of the neighbouring nations, and those brought upon them too mostly by the king of Babylon, till at length Babylon itself comes to be reckoned with. The prophecy against Egypt is here put first and takes up this whole chapter, in which we have, I. A prophecy of the defeat of Pharaoh-necho's army by the Chaldean forces at Carchemish, which was accomplished soon after, in the fourth year of Jehoiakim, ver. 1—12. II. A prophecy of the descent which Nebuchadnezzar should make upon the land of Egypt, and his success in it, which was accomplished some years after the destruction of Jerusalem, ver. 13—26. III. A word of comfort to the Israel of God in the midst of those calamities, ver. 27, 28.

THE word of the LORD which came to Jeremiah the prophet against the Gentiles; 2 Against Egypt, against the army of Pharaoh-necho king of Egypt, which was by the river Euphrates in Carchemish, which Nebuchadrezzar king of Babylon smote in the fourth year of Jehoiakim the son of Josiah king of Judah. 3 Order ye the buckler and shield, and draw near to battle. 4 Harness the horses; and get up, ye horsemen, and stand forth with *your* helmets; furbish the spears, *and* put on the brigandines. 5 Wherefore have I seen them dismayed *and* turned away back? and their mighty ones are beaten down,

and are fled apace, and look not back : *for* fear *was* round about, saith the LORD. 6 Let not the swift flee away, nor the mighty man escape; they shall stumble, and fall towards the north by the river Euphrates. 7 Who *is* this *that* cometh up as a flood, whose waters are moved as the rivers? 8 Egypt riseth up like a flood, and *his* waters are moved like the rivers; and he saith, I will go up, *and* will cover the earth; I will destroy the city and the inhabitants thereof. 9 Come up, ye horses; and rage, ye chariots; and let the mighty men come forth; the Ethiopians and the Libyans, that handle the shield; and the Lydians, that handle *and* bend the bow. 10 For this *is* the day of the Lord GOD of hosts, a day of vengeance, that he may avenge him of his adversaries: and the sword shall devour, and it shall be satiate and made drunk with their blood : for the Lord GOD of hosts hath a sacrifice in the north country by the river Euphrates. 11 Go up into Gilead, and take balm, O virgin, the daughter of Egypt : in vain shalt thou use many medicines; *for* thou shalt not be cured. 12 The nations have heard of thy shame, and thy cry hath filled the land : for the mighty man hath stumbled against the mighty, *and* they are fallen both together.

The first verse is the title of that part of this book which relates to the neighbouring nations, and follows here. It is *the word of the Lord which came to Jeremiah against the Gentiles;* for God is King and Judge of nations, knows and will call to an account those who know him not nor take any notice of him. Both Isaiah and Ezekiel prophesied against these nations that Jeremiah here has a separate saying to, and with reference to the same events. In the Old Testament we have *the word of the Lord* against *the Gentiles;* in the New Testament we have *the word of the Lord* for *the Gentiles,* that those who were *afar off are made nigh.*

He begins with Egypt, because they were of old Israel's oppressors and of late their deceivers, when they put confidence in them. In these verses he foretels the overthrow of *the army of Pharaoh-necho,* by Nebuchadnezzar, *in the fourth year of Jehoiakim,* which was so complete a victory to the king of Babylon that thereby he recovered from the river of Egypt to *the river Euphrates, all that pertained to the king of Egypt,* and so weakened him that he *came not again any more out of his land* (as we find, 2 Kings xxiv. 7), and so made him pay dearly for his expedition against the king of Assyria four years before, in which he slew Josiah, 2 Kings xxiii. 29. This is the event that is here foretold in lofty expressions of triumph over Egypt thus foiled, which Jeremiah would speak of with a particular pleasure, because the death of Josiah, which he had lamented, was now avenged on Pharaoh-necho. Now here,

I. The Egyptians are upbraided with the mighty preparations they made for this expedition, in which the prophet calls to them to do their utmost, for so they would: " Come then, *order the buckler,* let the weapons of war be got ready," *v.* 3. Egypt was famous for *horses*—let them be *harnessed* and the cavalry well mounted : *Get up, you horsemen, and stand forth,* &c., *v.* 4. See what preparations the children of men make, with abundance of care and trouble and at a vast expense, to kill one another, as if they did not die fast enough of themselves. He compares their marching out upon this expedition to the rising of their river Nile (*v.* 7, 8): *Egypt now rises up like a flood,* scorning to keep within its own banks and threatening to overflow all the neighbouring lands. It is a very formidable army that the Egyptians bring into the field upon this occasion. The prophet summons them (*v.* 9): *Come up, you horses; rage, you chariots.* He challenges them to bring all their confederate troops together, *the Ethiopians,* that descended from the same stock with the Egyptians (Gen. x. 6), and were their neighbours and allies, *the Libyans and Lydians,* both seated in Africa, to the west of Egypt, and from them the Egyptians fetched their auxiliary forces. Let them strengthen themselves with all the art and interest they have, yet it shall be all in vain; they shall be shamefully defeated notwithstanding, for God will fight against them, and against him *there is no wisdom nor counsel,* Prov. xxi. 30, 31. It concerns those that go forth to war not only to *order the buckler,* and *harness the horses,* but to repent of their sins, and pray to God for his presence with them, and that they may have it to keep themselves from every wicked thing.

II. They are upbraided with the great expectations they had from this expedition, which were quite contrary to what God intended in bringing them together. They knew their own thoughts, and God knew them, and sat in heaven and laughed at them; *but they knew not the thoughts of the Lord, for he gathers them as sheaves into the floor,* Mic. iv. 11, 12. Egypt saith (*v.* 8): *I will go up; I will cover the earth,* and none shall hinder me; *I will destroy the city,* whatever city it is that stands in my way. Like Pharaoh of old, *I will pursue, I will*

overtake. The Egyptians say that they shall have a day of it, but God saith that it shall be his day : *This is the day of the Lord God of hosts* (*v.* 10), the day in which he will be exalted in the overthrow of the Egyptians. They meant one thing, but God meant another; they designed it for the advancement of their dignity and the enlargement of their dominion, but God designed it for the great abasement and weakening of their kingdom. It is *a day of vengeance* for Josiah's death; it is a day of sacrifice to divine justice, to which multitudes of the sinners of Egypt shall fall as victims. Note, When men think to magnify themselves by pushing on unrighteous enterprises, let them expect that God will glorify himself by blasting them and cutting them off.

III. They are upbraided with their cowardice and inglorious flight when they come to an engagement (*v.* 5, 6): " *Wherefore have I seen them,* notwithstanding all these mighty and vast preparations and all these expressions of bravery and resolution, when the Chaldean army faces them, *dismayed, turned back,* quite disheartened, and no spirit left in them." 1. They make a shameful retreat. Even *their mighty ones,* who, one would think, should have stood their ground, *flee a flight,* flee by consent, make the best of their way, flee in confusion and with the utmost precipitation; they have neither time nor heart to *look back,* but *fear is round about* them, for they apprehend it so. And yet, 2. They cannot make their escape. They have the shame of flying, and yet not the satisfaction of saving themselves by flight; they might as well have stood their ground and died upon the spot; for even *the swift shall not flee away.* The lightness of their heels shall fail them when it comes to the trial, as well as the stoutness of their hearts; the *mighty* shall not escape, nay, they *are beaten down* and broken to pieces. *They shall stumble* in their flight, *and fall towards the north,* towards their enemy's country; for such confusion were they in when they took to their feet that instead of making homeward, as men usually do in that case, they made forward. Note, *The race is not to the swift nor the battle to the strong.* Valiant men are not always victorious.

IV. They are upbraided with their utter inability ever to recover this blow, which should be fatal to their nation, *v.* 11, 12. The damsel, *the daughter of Egypt,* that lived in great pomp and state, is sorely wounded by this defeat. Let her now seek for *balm in Gilead* and physicians there; let her use all the medicines her wise men can prescribe for the healing of this hurt, and the repairing of the loss sustained by this defeat; but all in vain; *no cure shall be* to them; they shall never be able to bring such a powerful army as this into the field again. " *The nations* that rang of thy glory and strength *have* now *heard of thy shame,* how shamefully thou wast routed and how thou art weakened by it." It needs not be spread by the triumphs of the conquerors, the shrieks and outcries of the conquered will proclaim it: *Thy cry hath filled the* country about. For, when they fled several ways, one *mighty man stumbled* upon another and dashed against another, such confusion were they in, so that *both together* became a prey to the pursuers, an easy prey. A thousand such dreadful accidents there should be, which should fill the country with the cry of those that were overcome. *Let not the mighty man* therefore *glory in his might*, for the time may come when it will stand him in no stead.

13 The word that the LORD spake to Jeremiah the prophet, how Nebuchadrezzar king of Babylon should come *and* smite the land of Egypt. 14 Declare ye in Egypt, and publish in Migdol, and publish in Noph and in Tahpanhes: say ye, Stand fast, and prepare thee; for the sword shall devour round about thee. 15 Why are thy valiant *men* swept away? they stood not, because the LORD did drive them. 16 He made many to fall, yea, one fell upon another: and they said, Arise, and let us go again to our own people, and to the land of our nativity, from the oppressing sword. 17 They did cry there, Pharaoh king of Egypt *is but* a noise; he hath passed the time appointed. 18 *As* I live, saith the king, whose name *is* the LORD of hosts, Surely as Tabor *is* among the mountains, and as Carmel by the sea, *so* shall he come. 19 O thou daughter dwelling in Egypt, furnish thyself to go into captivity: for Noph shall be waste and desolate without an inhabitant. 20 Egypt *is like* a very fair heifer, *but* destruction cometh; it cometh out of the north. 21 Also her hired men *are* in the midst of her like fatted bullocks; for they also are turned back, *and* are fled away together: they did not stand, because the day of their calamity was come upon them, *and* the time of their visitation. 22 The voice thereof shall go like a serpent; for they shall march with an army, and come against her with axes, as hewers of wood. 23 They shall cut down her forest, saith the LORD, though it cannot be searched; because

they are more than the grasshoppers, and *are* innumerable. 24 The daughter of Egypt shall be confounded; she shall be delivered into the hand of the people of the north. 25 The LORD of hosts, the God of Israel, saith; Behold, I will punish the multitude of No, and Pharaoh, and Egypt, with their gods, and their kings; even Pharaoh, and *all* them that trust in him: 26 And I will deliver them into the hand of those that seek their lives, and into the hand of Nebuchadrezzar king of Babylon, and into the hand of his servants: and afterward it shall be inhabited, as in the days of old, saith the LORD. 27 But fear not thou, O my servant Jacob, and be not dismayed, O Israel: for, behold, I will save thee from afar off, and thy seed from the land of their captivity; and Jacob shall return, and be in rest and at ease, and none shall make *him* afraid. 28 Fear thou not, O Jacob my servant, saith the LORD: for I *am* with thee; for I will make a full end of all the nations whither I have driven thee: but I will not make a full end of thee, but correct thee in measure; yet will I not leave thee wholly unpunished.

In these verses we have,

I. Confusion and terror spoken to Egypt. The accomplishment of the prediction in the former part of the chapter disabled the Egyptians from making any attempts upon other nations; for what could they do when their army was routed? But still they remained strong at home, and none of their neighbours durst make any attempts upon them. Though the kings of Egypt came no more *out of their land* (2 Kings xxiv. 7), yet they kept safe and easy in their land; and what would they desire more than peaceably to enjoy their own? One would think all men should be content to do this, and not covet to invade their neighbours. But the measure of Egypt's iniquity is full, and now they shall not long enjoy their own; those that encroached on others shall now be themselves encroached on. The scope of the prophecy here is to show *how the king of Babylon should* shortly *come and smite the land of Egypt*, and bring the war into their own bosoms which they had formerly carried into his borders, v. 13. This was fulfilled by the same hand with the former, even Nebuchadnezzar's, but many years after, twenty at least, and probably the prediction of it was long after the former prediction, and perhaps much about the same time with that other prediction of the same event which we had *ch.* xlii. 10.

1. Here is the alarm of war sounded in Egypt, to their great amazement (*v.* 14), notice given to the country that the enemy is approaching, *the sword is devouring round about* in the neighbouring countries, and therefore it is time for the Egyptians to put themselves in a posture of defence, to prepare for war, that they may give the enemy a warm reception. This must be proclaimed in all parts of Egypt, particularly in Migdol, Noph, and Tahpanhes, because in these places especially the Jewish refugees, or fugitives rather, had planted themselves, in contempt of God's command (*ch.* xliv. 1), and let them hear what a sorry shelter Egypt is likely to be to them.

2. The retreat hereupon of the forces of other nations which the Egyptians had in their pay is here foretold. Some considerable number of those troops, it is probable, were posted upon the frontiers to guard them, where they were beaten off by the invaders and put to flight. Then were the *valiant men swept away* (*v.* 15) as with *a sweeping rain* (it is the word that is used Prov. xxviii. 3) ; they can none of them stand their ground, *because the Lord drives them* from their respective posts ; he drives them by his terrors; he drives them by enabling the Chaldeans to drive them. It is not possible that those should fix whom the wrath of God chases. He it was (*v* 16) that *made many to fall, yea*, when their day shall come to fall, the enemy needs not throw them down, they shall *fall one upon another*, every man shall be a stumbling-block to his fellow, to his follower; nay, if God please, they shall be made to *fall upon one another*, *every man's sword* shall be *against his fellow*. Her hired men, the troops Egypt has in her service, are indeed *in the midst of her like fatted bullocks*, lusty men, able bodied and high spirited, who were likely for action and promised to make their part good against the enemy; but *they are turned back;* their hearts failed them, and, instead of fighting, they have *fled away together.* How could they withstand their fate when *the day of their calamity had come*, the day in which God will visit them in wrath ? Some think they are compared to fatted bullocks for their luxury ; they had wantoned in pleasures, so that they were very unfit for hardships, and therefore turned back and could not stand. In this consternation, (1.) They all made homeward towards their own country (*v.* 16) : *They said, " Arise, and let us go again to our own people*, where we may be safe *from the oppressing sword* of the Chaldeans, that bears down all before it." In times of exigence little confidence is to be put in mercenary troops, that fight purely for pay, and have no interest in theirs whom they fight for. (2.) They exclaimed vehemently against

Pharaoh, to whose cowardice or bad management, it is probable, their defeat was owing. When he posted them there upon the borders of his country it is probable that he told them he would within such a time come himself with a gallant army of his own subjects to support them ; but he failed them, and, when the enemy advanced, they found they had none to back them, so that they were perfectly abandoned to the fury of the invaders. No marvel then that they quitted their post and deserted the service, crying out, *Pharaoh king of Egypt is but a noise* (*v.* 17) ; he can hector, and talk big of the mighty things he would do, but that is all ; he brings nothing to pass. All his promises to those in alliance with him, or that are employed for him, vanish into smoke. He brings not the succours he engaged to bring, or not till it is too late : *He has passed the time appointed;* he did not keep his word, nor keep his day, and therefore they bid him farewell, they will never serve under him any more. Note, Those that make most noise in any business are frequently but a noise. Great talkers are little doers.

3. The formidable power of the Chaldean army is here described as bearing down all before it. *The King* of kings, *whose name is the Lord of hosts*, and before whom the mightiest kings on earth, though gods to us, are but as grasshoppers, he hath said it, he hath sworn it, *As I live, saith* this *King, as Tabor* overtops *the mountains and Carmel* overlooks *the sea, so shall* the king of Babylon overpower all the force of Egypt, such a command shall he have, such a sway shall he bear, *v.* 18. He and his *army shall come against* Egypt *with axes, as hewers of wood* (*v.* 22), and the Egyptians shall be no more able to resist them than the tree is to resist the man that comes with an axe to *cut it down;* so that Egypt shall be felled as a *forest* is *by the hewers of wood*, which (if there be many of them, and those well provided with instruments for the purpose) will be done in a little time. Egypt is very populous, full of towns and cities, like a forest, the trees of which *cannot be searched* or numbered, and very rich, full of hidden treasures, many of which will escape the searching eye of the Chaldean soldiers; but they shall make a great spoil in the country, for *they are more than the locusts*, that come in vast swarms and overrun a country, devouring every green thing (Joel i. 6, 7), so shall the Chaldeans do, for *they are innumerable.* Note, The Lord of hosts hath numberless hosts at his command.

4. The desolation of Egypt hereby is foretold, and the waste that should be made of that rich country. *Egypt is* now *like a very fair heifer*, or calf (*v.* 20), fat and shining, and not *accustomed to the yoke* of subjection, wanton as a heifer that is well fed, and very sportful. Some think here is an allusion to Apis, the bull or calf which the

Egyptians worshipped, from whom the children of Israel learned to worship the golden calf. Egypt is as fair as a goddess, and adores herself, *but destruction comes ; cutting up comes* (so some read it) ; *it comes out of the north ;* thence the Chaldean soldiers shall come, as so many butchers or sacrificers, to kill and cut up this *fair heifer.* (1.) The Egyptians shall be brought down, shall be tamed, and their tune changed : *The daughters of Egypt shall be confounded* (v. 24), shall be filled with astonishment. *Their voice shall go like a serpent,* that is, it shall be very low and submissive ; they shall not low like a fair heifer, that makes a great noise, but hiss out of their holes like serpents. They shall not dare to make loud complaints of the cruelty of the conquerors, but vent their griefs in silent murmurs. They shall not now, as they used to do, answer roughly, but, with *the poor, use entreaties* and beg for their lives. (2.) They shall be carried away prisoners into their enemy's land (v. 19): " *O thou daughter ! dwelling* securely and delicately *in Egypt,* that fruitful pleasant country, do not think this will last always, but *furnish thyself to go into captivity ;* instead of rich clothes, which will but tempt the enemy to strip thee, get plain and warm clothes ; instead of fine shoes, provide strong ones ; and inure thyself to hardship, that thou mayest bear it the better." Note, It concerns us, among all our preparations, to prepare for trouble. We provide for the entertainment of our friends, let us not neglect to provide for the entertainment of our enemies, nor among all our furniture omit furniture for captivity. The Egyptians must prepare to flee ; for their cities shall be evacuated. Noph particularly *shall be desolate, without an inhabitant,* so general shall the slaughter and the captivity be. There are some penalties which, we say, the king and the multitude are exempted from, but here even these are obnoxious : *The multitude of No shall be punished :* it is called *populous No,* Nah. iii. 8. *Though hand join in hand,* yet they shall not escape ; nor can any think to go off in the crowd. Be they ever so many, they shall find God will be too many for them. Their kings and all their petty princes shall fall ; and their gods too (*ch* xliii. 12, 13), their idols and their great men. Those which they call their tutelar deities shall be no protection to them. Pharaoh shall be brought down, and *all those that trust in him* (v. 25), particularly the Jews that came to sojourn in his country, trusting in him rather than in God. All these shall be *delivered into the hands of the northern nations* (v. 24), into the hand not only of Nebuchadnezzar that mighty potentate, but *into the hands of his servants,* according to the curse on Ham's posterity, of which the Egyptians were, that they should be the *servants of servants.* These seek their lives, and into their hands they shall be delivered.

674

5. An intimation is given that in process of time Egypt shall recover itself again (*v.* 26) : *Afterwards it shall be inhabited,* shall be peopled again, whereas by this destruction it was almost dispeopled. Ezekiel foretels that this should be at the end of forty years, Ezek. xxix. 13. See what changes the nations of the earth are subject to, how they are emptied and increased again ; and let not nations that prosper be secure, nor those that for the present are in thraldom despair.

II. Comfort and peace are here spoken to the Israel of God, *v.* 27, 28. Some understand it of those whom the king of Egypt had carried into captivity with Jehoahaz, but we read not of any that were carried away captives with him ; it may therefore rather refer to the captives in Babylon, whom God had mercy in store for, or, more generally, to all the people of God, designed for their encouragement in the most difficult times, when the judgments of God are abroad among the nations. We had these words of comfort before, *ch.* xxx. 10, 11. 1. Let the wicked of the earth tremble, they have cause for it ; *but fear not thou, O my servant Jacob ! and be not dismayed, O Israel !* and again, *Fear thou not, O Jacob !* God would not have his people to be a timorous people. 2. The wicked of the earth *shall be put away like dross,* not to be looked after any more ; but God's people, in order to their being saved, shall be found out and gathered though they be far off, shall be redeemed though they be held fast in captivity, and shall return. 3. The wicked *is like the troubled sea when it cannot rest ;* they *flee when none pursues.* But Jacob, being at home in God, *shall be at rest and at ease, and none shall make him afraid ;* for *what time he is afraid* he has a God to trust to. 4. The wicked God *beholds afar off ;* but, wherever thou art, *O Jacob ! I am with thee, a very present help.* 5. A *full end shall be made* of the nations that oppressed God's Israel, as Egypt and Babylon ; but mercy shall be kept in store for the Israel of God : they shall be corrected, but not cast off ; the correction shall be in measure, in respect of degree and continuance. Nations have their periods ; the Jewish nation itself has come to an end as a nation ; but the gospel church, God's spiritual Israel, still continues, and will to the end of time ; in that this promise is to have its full accomplishment, that, though God correct it, he will never *make a full end of it.*

CHAP. XLVII.

This chapter reads the Philistines their doom, as the former read the Egyptians theirs and by the same hand, that of Nebuchadnezzar. It is short, but terrible ; and Tyre and Zidon, though they lay at some distance from them, come in sharers with them in the destruction here threatened. I. It is foretold that the forces of the northern crowns should come upon them, to their great terror, ver. 1—5. II. That the war should continue long, and their endeavours to put an end to it should be in vain, ver. 6—7.

T HE word of the LORD that came to Jeremiah the prophet against the Philistines, before that Pharaoh smote Gaza. 2 Thus saith the LORD; Behold, waters rise up out of the north, and shall be an overflowing flood, and shall overflow the land, and all that is therein; the city, and them that dwell therein: then the men shall cry, and all the inhabitants of the land shall howl. 3 At the noise of the stamping of the hoofs of his strong *horses,* at the rushing of his chariots, *and at* the rumbling of his wheels, the fathers shall not look back to *their* children for feebleness of hands; 4 Because of the day that cometh to spoil all the Philistines, *and* to cut off from Tyrus and Zidon every helper that remaineth: for the LORD will spoil the Philistines, the remnant of the country of Caphtor. 5 Baldness is come upon Gaza; Ashkelon is cut off *with* the remnant of their valley: how long wilt thou cut thyself? 6 O thou sword of the LORD, how long *will it be* ere thou be quiet? put up thyself into thy scabbard, rest, and be still. 7 How can it be quiet, seeing the LORD hath given it a charge against Ashkelon, and against the sea shore? there hath he appointed it.

As the Egyptians had often proved false friends, so the Philistines had always been sworn enemies, to the Israel of God, and the more dangerous and vexatious for their being such near neighbours to them. They were considerably humbled in David's time, but, it seems, they had got head again and were a considerable people till Nebuchadnezzar cut them off with their neighbours, which is the event here foretold. The date of this prophecy is observable; it was *before Pharaoh* smote Gaza. When this blow was given to Gaza by the king of Egypt is not certain, whether in his expedition against Carchemish or in his return thence, after he had slain Josiah, or when he afterwards came with design to relieve Jerusalem; but this is mentioned here to show that this word of the Lord came to Jeremiah against the Philistines when they were in their full strength and lustre, themselves and their cities in good condition, in no peril from any adversary or evil occurrent. When no disturbance of their repose was foreseen by any human probabilities, yet then Jeremiah foretold their ruin, which Pharaoh's smiting Gaza soon after would be but an earnest of, and, as it were, the beginning of sorrows to that country. It is here foretold, 1. That a

foreign enemy and a very formidable one shall be brought upon them: *Waters rise up out of the north, v.* 2. Waters sometimes signify multitudes of people and nations (Rev. xvii. 15), sometimes great and threatening calamities (Ps. lxix. 1); here they signify both. They *rise out of the north,* whence fair weather and the wind that drives away rain are said to come; but now a terrible storm comes out of that cold climate. The Chaldean army shall overflow the land like a deluge. Probably this happened before the destruction of Jerusalem, for it should seem that in Gedaliah's time, which was just after, the army of the Chaldeans was quite withdrawn out of those parts. The country of the Philistines was but of small extent, so that it would soon be overwhelmed by so vast an army. 2. That they shall all be in a consternation upon it. The men shall have no heart to fight, but shall sit down and cry like children: *All the inhabitants of the land shall howl,* so that nothing but lamentation shall be heard in all places. The occasion of the fright is elegantly described, *v.* 3. Before it comes to killing and slaying, the very *stamping of the horses* and *rattling of the chariots,* when the enemy makes his approach, shall strike a terror upon the people, to such a degree that parents in their fright shall seem void of natural affection, *for they shall not look back to their children,* to provide for their safety, or so much as to see what becomes of them. Their *hands shall be so feeble* that they shall despair of carrying them off with them, and therefore they shall not care for seeing them, but leave them to take their lot; or they shall be in such a consternation that they shall quite forget even those pieces of themselves. Let none be over-fond of their children, nor dote upon them, since such distress may come that they may either wish they had none or forget that they have, and have no heart to look upon them. 3. That the country of the Philistines shall be spoiled and laid waste, and the other countries adjoining to them and in alliance with them. It is a day *to spoil the Philistines, for the Lord will spoil them, v.* 4. Note, Those whom God will spoil must needs be spoiled; for, *if God be against them, who can be for them?* Tyre and Zidon were strong and wealthy cities, and they used to help the Philistines in a strait, but now they shall themselves be involved in the common ruin, and God will cut off from them every *helper that remains.* Note, Those that trust to help from creatures will find it cut off when they most need it and will thereby be put into the utmost confusion. Who the *remnant of the country of Caphtor* were is uncertain, but we find that the Caphtorim were near akin to the Philistines (Gen. x. 14), and probably when their own country was destroyed such as remained came and settled with their kinsmen the Philistines, and were now spoiled with them. Some particular places are here named, *Gaza, and Ashkelon, v. 5. Baldness has come upon them ;* the invaders have stripped them of all their ornaments, or they have made themselves bald in token of extreme grief, and they are *cut off*, with the other cities that were in the plain or valley about them. The products of their fruitful valley shall be *spoiled*, and made a prey of, by the conquerors. 4. That these calamities should continue long. The prophet, in the foresight of this, with his usual tenderness, asks them first (*v.* 5), *How long will you cut yourselves*, as men in extreme sorrow and anguish do? O how tedious will the calamity be! not only cutting, but long cutting. But he turns from the effect to the cause : *They cut themselves*, for the sword of the Lord cuts them. And therefore, (1.) He bespeaks that to be still (*v.* 6): *O thou sword of the Lord! how long will it be ere thou be quiet?* He begs it would *put up itself into the scabbard*, would devour no more flesh, drink no more blood. This expresses the prophet's earnest desire to see an end of the war, looking with compassion, as became a man, even upon the Philistines themselves, when their country was made desolate by the sword. Note, War is the *sword of the Lord ;* with it he punishes the crimes of his enemies and pleads the cause of his own people. When war is once begun it often lasts long ; the sword, once drawn, does not quickly find the way into the scabbard again ; nay, some when they draw the sword throw away the scabbard, for they *delight in war.* So deplorable are the desolations of war that the blessings of peace cannot but be very desirable. O that *swords might be beaten into ploughshares!* (2.) Yet he gives a satisfactory account of the continuance of the war and stops the mouth of his own complaint (*v.* 7) : *How can it be quiet, seeing the Lord hath given it a charge* against such and such places, particularly specified in its commission? *There hath he appointed it.* Note, [1.] The sword of war hath its charge from the Lord of hosts. Every bullet has its charge ; you call them blind bullets, but they are directed by an all-seeing God. The war itself has its charge ; he saith to it, *Go, and it goes— Come, and it comes—Do this, and it does it ;* for he is commander-in-chief. [2.] When the sword is drawn we cannot expect it should be sheathed till it has fulfilled its charge. As the word of God, so his rod and his sword, shall accomplish that for which he sends them.

CHAP. XLVIII.

Moab is next set to the bar before Jeremiah the prophet, whom God had constituted judge over nations and kingdoms, from his mouth to receive its doom. Isaiah's predictions concerning Moab had had their accomplishment (we had the predictions Isa. xv. and xvi. and the like Amos ii. 1), and they were fulfilled when the Assyrians, under Salmanassar, invaded and distressed Moab. But this is a prophecy of the desolations of Moab by the Chaldeans, which were accomplished under Nebuzaradan, about five years after he had destroyed Jerusalem. Here is, I. The destruction foretold, that it should be great and general, should extend itself to all parts

of the country (ver. 1—6, 8, and again ver. 21—25, 34), that spoilers should come upon them and force some to flee (ver. 9), should carry many into captivity (ver. 12, 46), that the enemy should come shortly (ver. 16), come swiftly and surprise them (ver. 40, 41), that he should make thorough work (ver. 10) and lay the country quite waste, though it was very strong (ver. 14, 15), that there should be no escaping (ver. 42, 45), that this should force them to quit their idols (ver. 13, 35) and put an end to all their joy (ver. 33, 34), that their neighbours shall lament them (ver. 17—19) and the prophet himself does, ver. 31, 36, &c. II. The causes of this destruction assigned ; it was sin that brought this ruin upon them, their pride, and security, and carnal confidence (ver. 7, 11, 14, 29), and their contempt of and enmity to God and his people, ver. 26, 27, 30. III. A promise of the restoration of Moab, ver. 47.

AGAINST Moab thus saith the Lord of hosts, the God of Israel ; Woe unto Nebo! for it is spoiled : Kiriathaim is confounded *and* taken : Misgab is confounded and dismayed. 2 *There shall be* no more praise of Moab : in Heshbon they have devised evil against it ; come, and let us cut it off from *being* a nation. Also thou shalt be cut down, O Madmen ; the sword shall pursue thee. 3 A voice of crying *shall be* from Horonaim, spoiling and great destruction. 4 Moab is destroyed ; her little ones have caused a cry to be heard. 5 For in the going up of Luhith continual weeping shall go up ; for in the going down of Horonaim the enemies have heard a cry of destruction. 6 Flee, save your lives, and be like the heath in the wilderness. 7 For because thou hast trusted in thy works and in thy treasures, thou shalt also be taken : and Chemosh shall go forth into captivity *with* his priests and his princes together. 8 And the spoiler shall come upon every city, and no city shall escape : the valley also shall perish, and the plain shall be destroyed, as the Lord hath spoken. 9 Give wings unto Moab, that it may flee and get away : for the cities thereof shall be desolate, without any to dwell therein. 10 Cursed *be* he that doeth the work of the Lord deceitfully, and cursed *be* he that keepeth back his sword from blood. 11 Moab hath been at ease from his youth, and he hath settled on his lees, and hath not been emptied from vessel to vessel, neither hath he gone into captivity : therefore his taste remained in him, and his scent is not changed. 12 Therefore, behold, the days come, saith the Lord, that I will send unto him wanderers, that shall cause him to wander, and shall empty his vessels, and break their bottles. 13 And Moab shall be ashamed of Chemosh, as the house of Israel was ashamed of Beth-el their confidence.

We may observe in these verses,

I. The author of Moab's destruction; it is *the Lord of hosts*, that has armies, all armies, at his command, and *the God of Israel* (*v.* 1), who will herein plead the cause of his Israel against a people that have always been vexatious to them, and will punish them now for the injuries done to Israel of old, though Israel was forbidden to meddle with them (Deut. ii. 9), therefore the destruction of Moab is called *the work of the Lord* (*v.* 10), for it is he that pleads for Israel; and his work will exactly agree with his word, *v.* 8.

II. The instruments of it: *Spoilers shall come* (*v.* 8), shall come with a sword, a sword that shall *pursue them, v.* 2. *" I will send unto him wanderers,* such as come from afar, as if they were vagrants, or had missed their way, but they shall *cause him to wander;* they seem as wanderers themselves, but they shall make the Moabites to be really wanderers, some to flee and others to be carried into captivity."* These destroyers stir up themselves to do execution; they *have devised evil against Heshbon,* one of the principal cities of Moab, and they aim at no less than the ruin of the kingdom: *Come, and let us cut it off from being a nation* (*v.* 2); nothing less will serve the turn of the invaders; they come, not to plunder it, but to ruin it. The prophet, in God's name, engages them to make thorough work of it (*v.* 10): *Cursed be he that does the work of the Lord deceitfully,* this bloody work, this destroying work; though it goes against the grain with men of compassion, yet it is *the work of the Lord,* and must not be done by the halves. The Chaldeans have it in charge, by a secret instinct (says Mr. Gataker), to destroy the Moabites, and therefore they must not spare, must not, out of foolish pity, *keep back their sword from blood;* they would thereby bring a sword, and a curse with it, upon themselves, as Saul did by sparing the Amalekites and Ahab by letting Benhadad go. *Thy life shall go for his life.* To this work is applied that general rule given to all that are employed in any service for God, *Cursed be he that does the work of the Lord deceitfully* or negligently, that pretends to do it, but does it not to purpose, makes a show of serving God's glory, but is really serving his own ends and carries on the work of the Lord no further than will suit his own purposes, or that is slothful in business for God and takes neither care nor pains to do it as it should be done, Mal. i. 14. Let not such de-

ceive themselves, for God will not thus be mocked.

III. The woeful instances and effects of this destruction. The cities shall be laid in ruins; they shall be *spoiled* (*v.* 1) and cut down (*v.* 2); they shall be *desolate* (*v.* 9), *without any to dwell therein;* there shall be no houses to dwell in, or no people to dwell in them, or no safety and ease to those that would dwell in them. *Every city shall be spoiled and no city shall escape.* The strongest city shall not be able to secure itself against the enemies' power, nor shall the finest city be able to recommend itself to the enemies' pity and favour. The *country* also shall be wasted, the *valley shall perish,* and the *plain be destroyed, v.* 8. The corn and the flocks, which used to cover the plains and make the valleys rejoice, shall all be destroyed, eaten up, trodden down, or carried off. The most sacred persons shall not escape: The *priests and princes shall go together into captivity.* Nay, Chemosh, the god they worship, who, they hope, will protect them, shall share with them in the ruin; his temples shall be laid in ashes and his image carried away with the rest of the spoil. Now the consequence of all this will be, 1. Great shame and confusion: *Kirjathaim is confounded,* and Misgah is so. They shall be ashamed of the mighty boasts they have sometimes made of their cities: *There shall be no more vaunting in Moab concerning Heshbon* (so it might be read, *v.* 2); they shall no more boast of the strength of that city when the evil which is designed against it is brought upon it. Nor shall they any more boast of their gods (*v.* 13); they *shall be ashamed of Chemosh* (ashamed of all the prayers they have made to and all the confidence they put in that dunghill deity), *as Israel was ashamed of Beth-el,* of the golden calf they had at Beth-el, which they confided in as their protector, but were deceived in, for it was not able to save them from the Assyrians; nor shall Chemosh be able to save the Moabites from the Chaldeans. Note, Those that will not be convinced and made ashamed of the folly of their idolatry by the word of God shall be convinced and made ashamed of it by the judgments of God, when they shall find by woful experience the utter inability of the gods they have served to do them any service. 2. There will be great sorrow; there is a *voice of crying* heard (*v.* 3) and the cry is nothing but *spoiling and great destruction.* Alas! alas! *Moab is destroyed, v.* 4. The great ones having quitted the cities to shift for their own safety, even the *little ones have caused a cry to be heard,* the meaner sort of people, or the little children, the innocent harmless ones, whose cries at such a time are the most piteous. Go up to the hills, go down to the valleys, and you meet with *weeping (weeping with weeping);* all are in tears; you meet none with dry eyes. Even the enemies have heard the cry, from whom it would have been policy to conceal it, for they will be animated and encouraged by it; but it is so great that it cannot be hid. 3. There will be great hurry; they will cry to one another, " Away, away! *flee; save your lives* (v. 6); shift for your own safety with all imaginable speed, though you escape as bare and naked as the *heath,* or grig, or dry shrub, *in the wilderness;* think not of carrying away any thing you have, for it may cost you your life to attempt it, Matt. xxiv. 16—18. Take shelter, though it be in a barren wilderness, that you may have your lives for a prey. The danger will come suddenly and swiftly; and therefore *give wings unto Moab* (v. 9); that would be the greatest kindness you could do them; that is what they will call for, *O that we had wings like a dove!* for unless they have wings, and can fly, there will be no escaping."

IV. The sins for which God will now reckon with Moab, and which justify God in these severe proceedings against them. 1. It is because they have been secure, and have trusted in their wealth and strength, *in their works* and *in their treasures, v.* 7. They had taken a great deal of pains to fortify their cities and make large works about them, and to fill their exchequer and private coffers, so that they thought themselves in as good a posture for war as any people could be and that none durst invade them, and therefore set danger at defiance. They trusted *in the abundance of their riches and strengthened themselves in their wickedness,* Ps. lii. 7. Now, for this reason, that they may have a sensible conviction of the vanity and folly of their carnal confidences, God will send an enemy that will master their works and rifle their treasures. Note, We forfeit the comfort of that creature which we repose that confidence in which should be reposed in God only. The reed will break that is leaned upon 2. It is because they have not made a right improvement of the days of their peace and prosperity, *v.* 11. (1.) They had been long undisturbed: *Moab has been at ease from his youth.* It was an ancient kingdom before Israel was, and had enjoyed great tranquillity, though a small country and surrounded with potent neighbours. God's Israel were afflicted from their youth (Ps. cxxix. 1, 2), but *Moab at ease from his youth.* He has *not been emptied from vessel to vessel,* has not known any troublesome weakening changes, but is as wine kept on the lees, and not racked or drawn off, by which it retains its strength and body. He has not been unsettled, nor any way made uneasy; he has not *gone into captivity,* as Israel have often done, and yet Moab is a wicked idolatrous nation, and one of the confederates against *God's hidden ones,* Ps. lxxxiii. 3, 6. Note, There are many that persist in unrepented iniquity and yet enjoy uninterrupted prosperity. (2.) They had

been as long corrupt and unreformed: He *has settled on his lees;* he has been secure and sensual in his prosperity, has rested in it, and fetched all the strength and life of the soul from it, as the wine from the lees. *His taste remained in him, and his scent is not changed;* he is still the same, as bad as ever he was. Note, While bad people are as happy as they used to be in the world it is no marvel if they are as bad as they used to be. They have no changes of their peace and prosperity, *therefore they fear not God,* their hearts and lives are unchanged, Ps. lv. 19.

14 How say ye, We *are* mighty and strong men for the war? 15 Moab is spoiled, and gone up *out of* her cities, and his chosen young men are gone down to the slaughter, saith the king, whose name *is* the LORD of hosts. 16 The calamity of Moab *is* near to come, and his affliction hasteth fast. 17 All ye that are about him, bemoan him; and all ye that know his name, say, How is the strong staff broken, *and* the beautiful rod! 18 Thou daughter that dost inhabit Dibon, come down from *thy* glory, and sit in thirst; for the spoiler of Moab shall come upon thee, *and* he shall destroy thy strong holds. 19 O inhabitant of Aroer, stand by the way, and espy; ask him that fleeth, and her that escapeth, *and* say, What is done? 20 Moab is confounded; for it is broken down: howl and cry; tell ye it in Arnon, that Moab is spoiled, 21 And judgment is come upon the plain country; upon Holon, and upon Jahazah, and upon Mephaath, 22 And upon Dibon, and upon Nebo, and upon Beth-diblathaim, 23 And upon Kiriathaim, and upon Beth-gamul, and upon Beth-meon, 24 And upon Kerioth, and upon Bozrah, and upon all the cities of the land of Moab, far or near. 25 The horn of Moab is cut off, and his arm is broken, saith the LORD. 26 Make ye him drunken: for he magnified *himself* against the LORD: Moab also shall wallow in his vomit, and he also shall be in derision. 27 For was not Israel a derision unto thee? was he found among thieves? for since thou spakest of him, thou skippedst for joy. 28 O ye that dwell in Moab, leave the

cities, and dwell in the rock, and be like the dove *that* maketh her nest in the sides of the hole's mouth. 29 We have heard the pride of Moab, (he is exceeding proud) his loftiness, and his arrogancy, and his pride, and the haughtiness of his heart. 30 I know his wrath, saith the Lord; but *it shall* not *be* so; his lies shall not so effect *it*. 31 Therefore will I howl for Moab, and I will cry out for all Moab; *mine heart* shall mourn for the men of Kir-heres. 32 O vine of Sibmah, I will weep for thee with the weeping of Jazer: thy plants are gone over the sea, they reach *even* to the sea of Jazer: the spoiler is fallen upon thy summer fruits and upon thy vintage. 33 And joy and gladness is taken from the plentiful field, and from the land of Moab; and I have caused wine to fail from the wine-presses: none shall tread with shouting; *their* shouting *shall be* no shouting. 34 From the cry of Heshbon *even* unto Elealeh, *and even* unto Jahaz, have they uttered their voice, from Zoar *even* unto Horonaim, *as* a heifer of three years old: for the waters also of Nimrim shall be desolate. 35 Moreover I will cause to cease in Moab, saith the Lord, him that offereth in the high places, and him that burneth incense to his gods. 36 Therefore mine heart shall sound for Moab like pipes, and mine heart shall sound like pipes for the men of Kir-heres: because the riches *that* he hath gotten are perished. 37 For every head *shall be* bald, and every beard clipped: upon all the hands *shall be* cuttings, and upon the loins sackcloth. 38 *There shall be* lamentation generally upon all the housetops of Moab, and in the streets thereof: for I have broken Moab like a vessel wherein *is* no pleasure, saith the Lord. 39 They shall howl, *saying*, How is it broken down! how hath Moab turned the back with shame! so shall Moab be a derision and a dismaying to all them about him. 40 For thus saith the Lord; Behold, he shall fly as an eagle, and shall spread his wings over Moab.

41 Kerioth is taken, and the strong holds are surprised, and the mighty men's hearts in Moab at that day shall be as the heart of a woman in her pangs. 42 And Moab shall be destroyed from *being* a people, because he hath magnified *himself* against the Lord. 43 Fear, and the pit, and the snare, *shall be* upon thee, O inhabitant of Moab, saith the Lord. 44 He that fleeth from the fear shall fall into the pit; and he that getteth up out of the pit shall be taken in the snare: for I will bring upon it, *even* upon Moab, the year of their visitation, saith the Lord. 45 They that fled stood under the shadow of Heshbon because of the force: but a fire shall come forth out of Heshbon, and a flame from the midst of Sihon, and shall devour the corner of Moab, and the crown of the head of the tumultuous ones. 46 Woe be unto thee, O Moab! the people of Chemosh perisheth: for thy sons are taken captives, and thy daughters captives. 47 Yet will I bring again the captivity of Moab in the latter days, saith the Lord. Thus far *is* the judgment of Moab.

The destruction is here further prophesied of very largely and with a great copiousness and variety of expression, and very pathetically and in moving language, designed not only to awaken them by a national repentance and reformation to prevent the trouble, or by a personal repentance and reformation to prepare for it, but to affect us with the calamitous state of human life, which is liable to such lamentable occurrences, and with the power of God's anger and the terror of his judgments, when he comes forth to contend with a provoking people. In reading this long roll of threatenings, and meditating on the terror of them, it will be of more use to us to keep this in our eye, and to get our hearts thereby possessed with a holy awe of God and of his wrath, than to enquire critically into all the lively figures and metaphors here used.

I. It is a surprising destruction, and very sudden, that is here threatened. They were very secure, thought themselves *strong for war* and able to deal with the most powerful enemy (*v.* 14), and yet the calamity is near, and he is not able to keep it off, nor so much as to keep the enemy long in parley, for the *affliction hastens fast* (*v.* 16) and will soon come to a crisis. The enemy shall *fly as an eagle*, so swiftly, so strongly shall he come

(v. 40), as an eagle flies upon his prey, and he shall *spread his wings,* the wings of his army, *over Moab;* he shall surround it, that none may escape. *The strong-holds* of Moab are taken by *surprise* (v. 41), so that all their strength stood them in no stead; and this made *the hearts* even of *their mighty men to fail,* for they had not time to recollect the considerations that might have animated them. It requires a more than ordinary degree of courage not to be *afraid of sudden fear.*

II. It is an utter destruction, and such as lays Moab all in ruins: *Moab is spoiled* (v. 15), quite spoiled, is *confounded and broken down* (v. 20); their cities are laid in ashes, or seized by the enemy, so that they are forced to quit them, v. 15. Divers cities are here named, upon which judgment has come, and the list concludes with an *et cetera—and such like.* What occasion was there for him to mention more particulars when it comes *upon all the cities of Moab* in general, *far and near?* v. 21—24. Note, When iniquity is universal we have reason to expect that calamity should be so too. The kingdom is deprived of its dignity and authority: *The horn of Moab is cut off,* the horn of its strength and power, both offensive and defensive; *his arm is broken,* that he can neither give a blow nor prevent a blow, v. 25. Is the youth of the kingdom the strength and beauty of it? *His chosen young men have gone down to the slaughter,* v. 15. They went down to the battle promising themselves that they should return victorious; but God told them that they went *down to the slaughter;* so sure are those to fall against whom God fights. In a word, *Moab shall be destroyed from being a people,* v. 42. Those that are enemies to God's people will soon be made no people.

III. It is a lamentable destruction; it will be just matter of mourning and will turn joy into heaviness. 1. The prophet that foretels it does himself lament it, and mourns at the very foresight of it, from a principle of compassion to his fellow-creatures and concern for human nature. The prophet will himself *howl for Moab;* his very *heart shall mourn for* them (v. 31); he will *weep for the vine of Sibmah* (v. 32); his *heart shall sound like pipes for Moab,* v. 36. Though the destruction of Moab would prove him a true prophet, yet he could not think of it without trouble. The ruin of sinners is no pleasure to God, and therefore should be a pain to us; even those that give warning of it should lay it to heart. These passages, and many others in this chapter, are much the same with what Isaiah had used in his prophecies against Moab (Isa. xv. 16); for, though there was a long distance of time between that prophecy and this, yet they were both dictated by one and the same Spirit, and it becomes God's prophets to speak the language of those that went before them. It is no plagiarism sometimes to

680

make use of old expressions, provided it be with new affections and applications. 2. The Moabites themselves shall lament it; it will be the greatest mortification and grief imaginable to them. Those that sat in *glory,* in the midst of wealth, and mirth, and all manner of pleasure, shall *sit in thirst,* in a dry and thirsty land, where no water, no comfort is, v. 18. It is time for them to *sit in thirst,* and inure themselves to hardship, when *the spoiler has come,* who will strip them of all, and empty them. The Moabites in the remote corners of the country, that are furthest from the danger, will be inquisitive to know how the matter goes, what news from the army, will ask every one *that escapes, What is done?* v. 19. And when they are told that all is gone, that the invader is the conqueror, they will *howl and cry,* in bitterness and anguish of spirit (v. 20); they will abandon themselves to solitude, to lament the desolations of their country; they will *leave the cities* that used to be full of mirth, and *dwell in the rock,* where they may have their fill of melancholy; they shall no more be singing birds, but mourning birds, *like the dove* (v. 28), *the doves of the valley,* Ezek. vii. 16. Let those that give themselves up to mirth know that God can soon change their note. Their sorrow shall be so very extreme that they shall make themselves *bald and cut* themselves (v. 37), which were expressions of a desperate grief, such as tempted men to be even their own destroyers. *Job* indeed *rent his mantle and shaved his head,* but he did not cut himself. When the flood of passion rises ever so high wisdom and grace must set bounds to it, set banks to it, to restrain it from such barbarities. The sorrow shall be universal (v. 38): *There shall be a general lamentation upon all the house-tops of Moab,* where they worshipped their idols, to whom they shall in vain bemoan themselves, *and in all the streets,* where they conversed with one another, for they shall be free in communicating their griefs and fears and in propagating them; for they see all lost: "*I have broken Moab like a vessel wherein is no pleasure,* which shall not be regarded and cannot be pieced again." That which Moab used to rejoice in was their pleasant fruits and the abundance of their rich wines. The delights of sense were all the matter of their joy. Take away these, destroy their gardens and vineyards, and you make *all their mirth to cease,* Hos. ii. 11, 12. There is great weeping when their plants are transplanted, *have gone over the sea* (v. 32), are carried into other countries, to be planted there. *The spoiler has fallen upon thy summer-fruits and upon thy vintage,* and it is this that makes the cry *of Heshbon* to reach *even to Elealeh,* v. 34. *Take joy and gladness from the plentiful field, and* you take it *from the land of Moab,* v. 33. If *the wine fail from the wine-presses,* that used to be trodden with acclamations of joy, all their gladness is cut off. Take away that shouting, and there shall be no shouting. Note, Those who make the delights of sense their chief joy, their exceeding joy, since these are things they may easily be deprived of in a little time, subject themselves to the tyranny of the greatest grief; whereas those who rejoice in God may do that even when *the fig-tree does not blossom and there is no fruit in the vine.* These Moabites lost not only their wine, but their water too: Even *the waters of Nimrim shall be desolate* (v. 34), and therefore their grief grew extravagantly loud and noisy, and their lamentations were heard in all places like the lowing of *a heifer of three years old.* The expressions here are borrowed from Isa. xv. 5, 6. 3. All their neighbours are called to mourn with them, and to condole with them on their ruin (v. 17): *All you that are about him bemoan him.* Let him have that allay to his grief, let him see himself pitied by the adjoining countries. Nay, let those at a distance, who do but *know his name* and have heard of his reputation, take notice of his fall, and say, *How is the strong staff broken,* whose strength was the terror of its enemies, *and the beautiful rod,* whose beauty was the pride of its friends! Let the nations take notice of this and receive instruction. Let none be puffed up with or put confidence in their strength or beauty, for neither will be a security against the judgments of God.

IV. It is a shameful destruction and such as shall expose them to contempt: *Moab is made drunk* (v. 26), and he that is made drunk is made vile; he *shall wallow in his vomit,* and become an odious spectacle, *and shall justly be in derision.* Let the Moabites be intoxicated with the cup of God's wrath till they stagger and fall, and be brought to *their wits' end,* and make themselves ridiculous by the wildness not only of their passions but of their counsels. And again (v. 39): *Moab shall be a derision and a dismaying to all about him;* they shall laugh at the fall of the pomp and power he was so proud of. Note, Those that are haughty are preparing reproach and ignominy for themselves.

V. It is the destruction of that which is dear to them, not only of their summer fruits and their vintage, but of their wealth (v. 36): *The riches that he has gotten have perished;* though he thought he had laid them up very safely, and promised himself a long enjoyment of them, yet they are gone. Note, The money that is hoarded in the chest is as liable to perishing as the summer-fruits that lie exposed in the open field. Riches are shedding things, and, like dust as they are, slip through our fingers even when we are in most care to hold them fast and gripe them hard. Yet this is not the worst; even those whose religion was false and foolish were fond of it above any thing, and, such

as it was, would not part with it; and therefore, though it was really a promise, yet to them it was a threatening (v. 35), that God *will cause to cease him that offers in the high places,* for the high places shall be destroyed, and the fields of offerings shall be laid waste, and the priests themselves, *who burnt incense to their gods,* shall be slain or carried into captivity, v. 7. Note, It is only the true religion, and the worship and service of the true God, that will stand us in stead in a day of trouble.

VI. It is a just and righteous destruction, and that which they have deserved and brought upon themselves by sin.

1. The sin which they had been most notoriously guilty of, and for which God now reckoned with them, was pride. It is mentioned six times, v. 29. *We have all heard of the pride of Moab;* his neighbours took notice of it; it has testified to his face, as Israel's did; *he is exceedingly proud,* and grows worse and worse. Observe *his loftiness, his arrogancy, his pride, his haughtiness:* the multiplying of words to the same purport intimates in how many instances he discovered his pride, and how offensive it was both to God and man. It was charged upon them Isa. xvi. 6, but here it is expressed more largely than there. Since then they had been under humbling providences, and yet were unhumbled; nay, they grew more arrogant and haughty, which plainly marked them for that utter destruction of which pride is the forerunner. Two instances are here given of the pride of Moab:—(1.) He had conducted himself insolently towards God. He must be brought down with shame (v. 26), for *he* has *magnified himself against the Lord;* and again (v. 42), he *shall be destroyed from being a people,* for this very reason. The Moabites preferred Chemosh before Jehovah, and thought themselves a match for the God of Israel, whom they set at defiance. (2.) He had conducted himself scornfully towards Israel, particularly in their late troubles; therefore Moab shall fall into the same troubles, into the same hands, and be a derision, for Israel was *a derision to him,* v. 26, 27. The generality of the Moabites, when they heard of the calamities and desolations of their neighbours the Jews, instead of lamenting them, rejoiced in them as if they had been thieves taken in the act of robbing; as often as they spoke of them, they *skipped for joy.* Many, in such a case, entertain in their minds a secret pleasure at the fall of those they had a dislike to, who yet have so much discretion as to conceal it; it is so invidious **a** thing. But the Moabites industriously proclaimed their joy, and avowed the enmity they had to Israel, triumphing over every Israelite they met with in distress and laughing at him, which was as inhuman as it was impious and an impudent affront both **to** man, whose nature they were of, and **to**

God, whose name they were called by. Note, Those that deride others in distress will justly and certainly, sooner or later, come into distress themselves, and be had in derision. Those that are *glad at calamities*, especially the calamities of God's church, *shall not long go unpunished.*

2. Besides this they had been guilty of malice against God's people, and treachery in their dealings with them, *v.* 30. They made a jest of the desolations of Judah and Jerusalem, and pretended, when they laughed at them, that it was but in sport and to make themselves merry; but, says God, " *I know his wrath;* I know it comes from the old enmity he has to the seed of Abraham and the worshippers of the true God. *I know* he thinks these calamities of the Jewish nation will end in their utter extirpation. He now tells the Chaldeans what bad people the Jews are, and irritates them against them; *but it shall not be so* as he expects; *his lies shall not so effect it.* The nation, whose fall they triumph in, shall recover itself." Some read it, *I know his rage. Is it not so?* Is he not very furious against the people of God? And *his lies I know* also. *Do they not do so?* Do they not belie them? Note, All the fury and all the falsehood of the church's enemies are perfectly known to God, whatever the pretences are with which they think to cover them, Isa. xxxvii. 28.

VII. It is a complicated destruction, and by one instance after another will at length be completed; for those that make their escape from one judgment shall perish by another: *Fear, and the pit, and the snare, shall be upon them, v.* 43. There shall be fear to drive them into the pit, and a snare to hold them fast in it when they are in it; so that they shall neither escape from the destruction nor escape out of it. What was said of sinners in general (Isa. xxiv. 17, 18), that those who *flee from the fear shall fall into the pit* and those who come *up out of the pit shall be taken in the snare,* is here particularly foretold concerning the sinners of Moab (*v.* 44); for it is the *year of their visitation,* when God comes to reckon with them, and will be *known by the judgments which he executes,* for he is *the King whose name is the Lord of hosts* (*v.* 15); he is not only *the King* who has authority to give judgment, but he is *the Lord of hosts,* who is able to do what he has determined. The figurative expressions used *v.* 44 are explained in one instance (*v.* 45): *Those that fled* out of the villages for fear of the enemy's forces put themselves *under the shadow of Heshbon,* stood there, and supposed they stood safely, as now armies sometimes retire under the cannon of a fortified city, and it is their protection; but here they should be disappointed, for, when *they flee out of the pit, they fall into the snare:* Heshbon, which they thought would shelter them, devours them as Moses had foretold long

682

since (Num. xxi. 28): *A fire has gone out of Heshbon,* and *a flame from the city of Sihon,* and devours those that come from all *the corners of Moab,* and fastens upon *the crown of the head of the tumultuous* noisy *ones,* or of the revellers, or children of noise, not meant of the rude clamorous multitude, but of the great men, who bluster, and hector, and make a noise; the judgments of God shall light on them. Shall we hear the conclusion of this whole matter? We have it (*v.* 46): *" Woe be to thee, O Moab!* thou art undone; *the people* that worship *Chemosh perish,* and are gone; farewell, Moab. *Thy sons* and *daughters,* the hopes of the next generation, have gone into captivity after the Jews, whose calamities they rejoiced in."

VIII. Yet it is not a perpetual destruction. The chapter concludes with a short promise of their return out of *captivity in the latter days.* God, who brings them into captivity, *will bring again* their *captivity, v.* 47. Thus tenderly does God deal with Moabites, much more with his own people! Even with Moabites he *will not contend for ever, nor be always wrath.* When Israel returned, Moab did; and perhaps the prophecy was intended chiefly for the encouragement of God's people to hope for that salvation which even Moabites shall share in. Yet it looks further, to gospel times; the Jews themselves refer it to the days of the Messiah; then the captivity of the Gentiles, under the yoke of sin and Satan, shall be brought back by divine grace, which shall *make them free, free indeed.* This prophecy concerning Moab is long, but here it ends; it ends comfortably: *Thus far is the judgment of Moab.*

CHAP. XLIX.

The cup of trembling still goes round, and the nations must all drink of it, according to the instructions given to Jeremiah, ch. xxv. 15. This chapter puts it into the hands, I. Of the Ammonites, ver. 1—6. II. Of the Edomites, ver. 7—22. III. Of the Syrians, ver. 23 —27. IV. Of the Kedarenes, and the kingdoms of Hazor, ver. 28 —33. V. Of the Elamites, ver. 34—39. When Israel was scarcely saved where shall all these appear?

CONCERNING the Ammonites, thus saith the LORD; Hath Israel no sons? hath he no heir? why then doth their king inherit Gad, and his people dwell in his cities? 2 Therefore, behold, the days come, saith the LORD, that I will cause an alarm of war to be heard in Rabbah of the Ammonites; and it shall be a desolate heap, and her daughters shall be burned with fire: then shall Israel be heir unto them that were his heirs, saith the LORD. 3 Howl, O Heshbon, for Ai is spoiled: cry, ye daughters of Rabbah, gird you with sackcloth; lament, and run to and fro by the hedges; for their king shall go into captivity, *and* his priests and his princes together. 4 Wherefore gloriest thou in the valleys, thy flowing valley, O backsliding daughter? that trusted in her treasures, *saying,* Who shall come unto me? 5 Behold, I will bring a fear upon thee, saith the LORD God of hosts, from all those that be about thee; and ye shall be driven out every man right forth; and none shall gather up him that wandereth. 6 And afterward I will bring again the captivity of the children of Ammon, saith the LORD.

The Ammonites were next, both in kindred and neighbourhood, to the Moabites, and therefore are next set to the bar. Their country joined to that of the two tribes and a half, on the other side Jordan, and was but a bad neighbour; however, being a neighbour, they shall have a share in these circular predictions. 1. An action is here brought, in God's name, against the Ammonites, for an illegal encroachment upon the rightful possessions of the tribe of Gad, that lay next them, *v.* 1. A writ of enquiry is brought to discover what title they had to those territories, which, upon the carrying away of the Gileadites, by the king of Assyria (2 Kings xv. 29, 1 Chron. v. 26), were left almost dispeopled, at least unguarded, and an easy prey to the next invader. "What! Does it escheat *ob defectum sanguinis*—*for want of an heir? Hath Israel no sons? Hath he no heir?* Are there no Gadites left, to whom the right of inheritance belongs? Or, if there were not, are there no Israelites, none left of Judah, that are nearer akin to them than you are? *Why then does their king,* as if he were entitled to the forfeited estates, or Milcom, their idol, as if he had the right to dispose of it to his worshippers, *inherit Gad, and his people dwell in the cities* which fell by lot to that tribe of God's people. Nay, there were sons and heirs of their own body, *en ventre de sa mere*—*in their mothers' womb,* and the Ammonites, to prevent their claim, most barbarously murdered them (Amos i. 13): *They ripped up the women with child of Gilead, that they might enlarge their border,* that, having seized it, none might rise up hereafter to recover it from them. Thus *they magnified themselves against their border* and boasted it was their own, Zeph. ii. 8. Note, Though among men might often prevails against right, yet that might shall be controlled by the Almighty, who *sits in the throne, judging right;* and those will find themselves mistaken who think every thing their own which they can lay their hands on, or which none yet appears to lay claim to. As there is justice owing to owners, so also to their heirs, when they are dead, whom it is a great sin to defraud, though they either know not

their right or know not how to come at it. This shall be reckoned for particularly, when injuries of this kind are done to God's people. 2. Judgment is here given against them for this violence. (1) Terrors shall come upon them: God *will cause an alarm of war to be heard,* even *in Rabbah,* their capital city and a very strong one, *v.* 2. *The Lord God of hosts,* who has all armies at his command, *will bring a fear upon them from all that be about them, v.* 5. Note, God has many ways to terrify those who have been a terror to his people. (2.) Their cities shall be laid in ruins: *Rabbah,* the mother-city, *shall be a desolate heap, and her daughters,* the other cities that have a dependence upon her, and receive law from her as daughters, *shall be burnt with fire;* so that the inhabitants shall be forced to quit them, and they shall *cry,* and *gird themselves with sackcloth,* as having lost all they had, and not knowing whither to betake themselves. (3.) Their country, which they were so proud of, shall be wasted *(v.* 4): *Wherefore gloriest thou in the valleys,* and *trustest in thy treasures, O backsliding daughter?* They are charged with backsliding or turning away from God and from his worship, for they were the posterity of righteous Lot. It is true, they had never been so in covenant with God as Israel was; yet all idolaters may be called *backsliders,* for the worship of the true God was prior to that of false gods. *They were untoward and refractory* (so some read it); and, when they had forsaken their God, *they gloried in their valleys,* particularly one that was called *the flowing valley,* because it flowed with all good things. These they had violently taken away from Israel, and gloried in it when they had done so. They gloried in the strength of their valleys, so surrounded with mountains that they were inaccessible, gloried in the products of them, gloried *in the treasures* they got together out of them, saying, *Who shall come unto me?* While they bathed themselves in the pleasures of their country, they flattered themselves with a conceit that they should never be disturbed in the enjoyment of them: *To-morrow shall be as this day;* therefore they set God and his judgments at defiance; they are proud, voluptuous, and secure; but wherefore dost thou do so? Note, Those who backslide and turn away from God have little reason either to take complacency or to put confidence in any worldly enjoyments whatsoever, Hos. ix. 1. (4.) Their people, from the least to the greatest, shall be forced out of the country. Some shall flee to seek for shelter, others shall be carried into captivity, so that their land shall be quite evacuated: *Their king and his princes,* nay, and Milcom, their god, *and his priests, shall go into captivity (v.* 3), *and every man shall be driven out right forth,* shall take the next way, and make the best of it in his flight *(v.* 5), forgetting the *valleys, the flowing val-*

583

leys, which now fail them. And, to complete their misery, *none shall gather up him that wanders*, none shall open their doors to them, as Jael to Sisera, to entertain them; and those that flee shall be so much in care to secure themselves that they shall not take notice of others, no, not of those that are nearest to them, that wander, and are at a loss which way to go, as *ch.* xlvii. 3. (5.) Then the country of the Ammonites shall fall into the hands of the remaining Israelites (*v.* 2): *Then shall Israel be heir to those that were his heirs*, shall possess himself of their land who had possessed themselves of his, by way of reprisal. Note, The equity of divine Providence is to be acknowledged when the losses of the injured are recompensed out of the unjust gains of the injurious. Though the enemies of God's Israel may make a prey of them for a while, the tables will shortly be turned. 3. Yet there is a prospect given them of mercy hereafter (*v.* 6), as before to Moab. The day will come when *the captivity of the children of Ammon will* be *brought again*: for so it is in human affairs: the wheel goes round.

7 Concerning Edom, thus saith the Lord of hosts; *Is* wisdom no more in Teman? is counsel perished from the prudent? is their wisdom vanished? 8 Flee ye, turn back, dwell deep, O inhabitants of Dedan; for I will bring the calamity of Esau upon him, the time *that* I will visit him. 9 If grape-gatherers come to thee, would they not leave *some* gleaning grapes? if thieves by night, they will destroy till they have enough. 10 But I have made Esau bare, I have uncovered his secret places, and he shall not be able to hide himself: his seed is spoiled, and his brethren, and his neighbours, and he *is* not. 11 Leave thy fatherless children, I will preserve *them* alive; and let thy widows trust in me. 12 For thus saith the Lord; Behold, they whose judgment *was* not to drink of the cup have assuredly drunken; and *art* thou he *that* shall altogether go unpunished? thou shalt not go unpunished, but thou shalt surely drink *of it.* 13 For I have sworn by myself, saith the Lord, that Bozrah shall become a desolation, a reproach, a waste, and a curse; and all the cities thereof shall be perpetual wastes. 14 I have heard a rumour from the Lord, and an ambassador is sent unto the heathen,

saying, Gather ye together, and come against her, and rise up to the battle. 15 For, lo, I will make thee small among the heathen, *and* despised among men. 16 Thy terribleness hath deceived thee, *and* the pride of thine heart, O thou that dwellest in the clefts of the rock, that holdest the height of the hill: though thou shouldest make thy nest as high as the eagle, I will bring thee down from thence, saith the Lord. 17 Also Edom shall be a desolation: every one that goeth by it shall be astonished, and shall hiss at all the plagues thereof. 18 As in the overthrow of Sodom and Gomorrah and the neighbour *cities* thereof, saith the Lord, no man shall abide there, neither shall a son of man dwell in it. 19 Behold, he shall come up like a lion from the swelling of Jordan against the habitation of the strong: but I will suddenly make him run away from her: and who *is* a chosen *man, that* I may appoint over her? for who *is* like me? and who will appoint me the time? and who *is* that shepherd that will stand before me? 20 Therefore hear the counsel of the Lord, that he hath taken against Edom; and his purposes, that he hath purposed against the inhabitants of Teman: surely the least of the flock shall draw them out: surely he shall make their habitations desolate with them. 21 The earth is moved at the noise of their fall, at the cry the noise thereof was heard in the Red Sea. 22 Behold, he shall come up and fly as the eagle, and spread his wings over Bozrah: and at that day shall the heart of the mighty men of Edom be as the heart of a woman in her pangs.

The Edomites come next to receive their doom from God, by the mouth of Jeremiah: they also were old enemies to the Israel of God; but their day will come to be reckoned with, and it is now at hand, and is foretold, not only for warning to them, but for comfort to the Israel of God, whose afflictions were very much aggravated by their triumphs over them and joy in their calamity, Ps. cxxxvii. 7. Many of the expressions used in this prophecy *concerning Edom* are borrowed from the prophecy of Obadiah, which is *concerning Edom*: for, all the prophets being inspired by one and the same Spirit, there must needs be a wonderful harmony and agreement in their predictions. Now here it is foretold,

I. That the country of Edom should be all wasted and made desolate, that *the calamity of Esau* should be *brought upon him,* the calamity he has deserved, and God has long designed him, for his old sins, *v.* 8. The time is at hand when God *will visit him,* and call him to an account, and then they shall *flee* from the sword, *turn back* from the battle, and *dwell deep* in some close caverns, where they shall hide themselves. All they have shall be carried off by the conqueror; whereas *grape-gatherers* will *leave some gleanings,* and even *thieves* know when *they have enough* and *will destroy* no further, those that destroy them shall never be satiated, (*v.* 9, 10); they shall make *Esau* quite *bare,* shall strip the Edomites of all they have, shall find out ways and means to come at their most hidden treasure, shall discover even the *secret places* where they thought to secure their wealth, and rifle them, so that they shall none of them save their wealth, no, nor save themselves nor their children, that might be concealed in a little room: *He shall not be able to hide himself,* and *his seed too is spoiled.* His brethren the Moabites, *and his neighbours* the Philistines, whom he might have expected succours from, or at least shelter with, are spoiled as well as he and disabled to do him any service. *And he is not,* or *there is not he, there is none to him, none left him,* that may say what follows (*v.* 11), *Leave thy fatherless children, I will preserve them alive.* When they are flying, or dying, there shall be none left, no relation, no friend, no, not so much as any parish officers to take care of their wives and children that they leave behind. Edom is not, he is cut off and gone; nor is there any to say, *Leave me thy orphans.* If the master of a family be cut off, or forced away, it is some comfort if he have a friend to leave his family with, whom he can confide in; but they shall have none such, for they shall all be involved in the same calamity. The Chaldee makes these to be the words of God to his people, distinguishing them from the Edomites in this calamity; and they read it, " *But you, O house of Israel! you shall not leave your orphans; I will secure them, and let your widows rest on my word.* Whatever becomes of the widows and fatherless of the Edomites, I will take care of yours." Note, It is an unspeakable comfort to the people of God, when they are dying, that they may leave their surviving relations with God, may, in faith, commit them to him and encourage them to trust in him; and, though they cannot promise themselves great things in the world for them, yet they may hope that he will preserve them alive, always, provided that they trust in him. Let the Edomites, for their part, count upon no other than to be made

a desolation and *a reproach;* for the decree has gone forth; God hath *sworn it by himself* (*v.* 13), that their *cities shall be wasted,* nay, they *shall be perpetual wastes,* they shall be made mean and despicable; they had made a mighty figure, but God will make *them small among the heathen;* and those that despised God's people shall themselves be *despised among men* (*v.* 15, Obad. 2), nay, they shall be made monstrous, and even a prodigy (*v.* 17): *Edom shall be* such a *desolation* that every one who goes by *shall be astonished;* nay, worse yet, they shall be made a terror; Edom shall be made like Sodom and Gomorrah, none shall care for coming near the ruins of it, *no man shall abide there* (*v.* 18), such a frightful place shall it be made.

II. That the instruments of this destruction should be very resolute and formidable. They have their commission from God; he summons them into this service (*v.* 14): *I have heard a rumour,* or report, *from the Lord,* heard it by the prophecy of Obadiah, heard it by a whisper to myself, that *an ambassador,* or herald, or messenger, *is sent to the* Gentiles, who are to lay Edom waste, saying, *Gather you together,* muster all the forces you can, *and come against her;* for (*v.* 20) this is *the counsel that he hath taken against Edom.* The matter is settled, the decree has gone forth, and there is no resisting it. God has determined that Edom shall be laid waste, and then he that is to be employed in wasting it shall come swiftly and strongly. Nebuchadnezzar is he of whom it is here foretold, 1. That he *shall come up like a lion,* with fierceness and fury, like a lion enraged by *the swelling of Jordan* overflowing his banks, which forces him out of his covert by the water-side into the higher grounds, *v.* 19. He shall come roaring, come to devour all that come in his way. He shall *come against the habitation of the strong,* the forts and castles; and I *will cause him to come suddenly into the land* (so the next words might well be read), so as to find them unprovided with necessaries for a defence; for I will look out *a chosen man to appoint over her,* to do this execution, a man fit for the purpose, one chosen out of the people; for when God has work to do he will find out the fittest instruments to be employed in doing it : " *Who is like me for* choosing the instruments, and spiriting them for the work? And *who will appoint me the time?* Who will challenge me, and fix a time and place to meet me? Who will join issue with me in battle? And, when I send a lion into the flock, *who is that shepherd* that can, or dare, stand before me, or against me, to oppose that lion, and think to rescue any of the flock?" Note, When God has work to do of any kind he will soon find those that are able to engage in it, and all the world cannot find those that are able to engage against it. Nay, if God will have Edom destroyed, and their people dislodged, there needs not a lion, a fierce lion to do it: *Even the least of the flock shall draw them out (v. 20)*; **the** meanest servant in Nebuchadnez-zar's retinue, the weakest of all that follow his camp, shall *draw them out* for the slaughter, shall force them to flee, or to surrender, and *make their habitations desolate with them.* God can bring to pass the greatest works by instruments least likely. When the Chal-dean army comes against the Edomites all hands shall be employed and the poorest soldier in it shall have a pluck at them. 2. Nebuchadnezzar shall come, not only like a lion, the king of beasts, but like an eagle, the king of birds (*v.* 22): *He shall fly as the eagle* upon his prey, so swiftly, so strongly, shall clap his wings upon Bozrah, to secure it for himself (as before, *ch.* xlviii. 40), and immediately *the hearts of the mighty men* shall fail them, for they shall see he is an enemy that it is in vain to struggle with.

III. That the Edomites' confidences should all fail them in the day of their dis-tress. 1. They trusted to their wisdom, but that shall stand them in no stead. This is the first thing fastened upon in this pro-phecy against Edom, *v.* 7. That nation used to be famous for wisdom, and their states-men were thought to excel in politics; and yet now they shall take such wrong mea-sures in all their counsels, and be so baffled in all their designs, that people shall ask, with wonder, What is the matter with the Edomites? *Is wisdom no more in Teman?* Have the wise men of the east country (1 Kings iv. 30) become fools? Are those at *their wits' end* that were thought to have the monopoly of prudence? *Has counsel perished from the understanding men?* It is so, when God is designing the ruin of a people; for whom he will destroy he infa-tuates. See Job xii. 20. *Has their wisdom vanished? Is it tired?* (so some); *is it worn out?* (so others); *has it become useless?* so others. Yes, it will do them no service when God comes forth to contend with them. 2. They trusted to their strength, but neither shall that avail them, *v.* 16. They had been a terror to all their neighbours; every body feared them and truckled to them, and this made them proud and conceited of them-selves and their own strength, and very secure; because no neighbouring nation durst meddle with them, they thought no nation in the world durst. Their country was much of it mountainous, having many passes which they thought themselves able to make good against any invader; but this terribleness of theirs deceived them, and so did their imaginary inaccessibleness; they did not prove so strong as they were formi-dable, nor so safe as they were secure. High as they are, God will bring them down; for, as *there is no wisdom*, so there is no might *against the Lord*. See these expressions, Obad. 3, 4, 8.

686

IV. That their destruction should be in-evitable and very remarkable. 1. God hath determined it (*v.* 12); he hath said it; nay (*v.* 13), he hath *sworn it*, that *the Edomites shall not go unpunished*, but they shall *drink the cup of trembling*, which is put into the hands of all their neighbours; even those *whose judgment*, or doom, *was not to drink of the cup*, who had not so well deserved it as they had done, nations that had not been such enemies to Israel as they had been, or Israel itself, that was God's peculiar people, and among whom there were many, very many, who kept his ordinances, upon which account they might have expected an ex-emption; and yet they had been made to drink of the bitter cup; and shall the Edom-ites think to pass it? No; they shall *surely drink of it*. Note, When God punishes the less guilty it is folly for the more guilty to promise themselves impunity; and when judgment begins at God's house it will reach the strangers. 2. All the world shall take notice of it (*v.* 21): *The earth is moved*, and all the nations are put into a concern, *at the noise of their fall;* the news of it shall make them tremble. *The noise of the outcry is heard to the Red Sea*, which flowed upon the coasts of Edom. So loud shall be the shouts of the conquerors and the shrieks of the conquered, and such a mighty noise shall the news of this destruction of Idumea make in the nations, that it shall be heard among the ships that lie in the Red Sea to take in lading (1 Kings ix. 26), and then they shall carry the news of it to the remotest shore. Note, The fall of those who have affected to make a noise with their pomp and power will make so much the greater noise.

23 Concerning Damascus. Ha-math is confounded, and Arpad: for they have heard evil tidings: they are fainthearted; *there is* sorrow on the sea; it cannot be quiet. 24 Da-mascus is waxed feeble, *and* turneth herself to flee, and fear hath seized on *her:* anguish and sorrows have taken her, as a woman in travail. 25 How is the city of praise not left, the city of my joy! 26 Therefore her young men shall fall in her streets, and all the men of war shall be cut off in that day, saith the LORD of hosts. 27 And I will kindle a fire in the wall of Damascus, and it shall consume the palaces of Ben-hadad.

The kingdom of Syria lay north of Canaan, as that of Edom lay south, and thither we must now remove and take a view of the approaching fate of that kingdom, which had been often vexatious to the Israel of God. Damascus was the metropolis of that kingdom, and the ruin of the whole is supposed in the ruin of that; yet Hamath and Arpad, two other considerable cities, are named (*v.* 23), and *the palaces of Ben-hadad,* which he built, are particularly marked for ruin, *v.* 27; see also Amos i. 4. Some think Ben-hadad (the son of Hadad, either their idol, or one of their ancient kings, whence the rest descended) was a common name of the kings of Syria, as Pharaoh of the kings of Egypt. Now observe concerning the judgment of Damascus, 1. It begins with a terrible fright and faint-heartedness. They *hear evil tidings,* that the king of Babylon, with all his force, is coming against them, and *they are confounded;* they know not what measures to take for their own safety, their souls are melted, *they are faint-hearted,* they have no spirit left them, they are like *the troubled sea, that cannot be quiet* (Isa. lvii. 20), or like men *in a storm* at sea (Ps. cvii. 26); or the sorrow that begins in the city shall go to the sea-coast, *v.* 23. See how easily God can dispirit those nations that have been most celebrated for valour. *Damascus* now *waxes feeble* (*v.* 24), a city that thought she could look the most formidable enemy in the face now *turns herself to flee,* and owns it is to no more purpose to think of contending with her fate than for *a woman in* labour to contend with her pains, which she cannot escape, but must yield to. It was a *city of praise* (*v.* 25), not praise to God, but to herself, a city much commended and admired by all strangers that visited it. It was a *city of joy,* where there was an affluence and confluence of all the delights of the sons of men, and abundance of mirth in the enjoyment of them. We read it (though there is no necessity for this) *the city of my joy,* which the prophet himself had sometimes visited with pleasure. Or it may be the speech of the king lamenting the ruin of *the city of* his *joy.* But now it is all overwhelmed with fear and grief. Note, Those deceive themselves who place their happiness in carnal joys; for God in his providence can soon cast a damp upon them and put an end to them. He can soon make a *city of praise* to be a reproach and a *city of joy* to be a terror to itself. 2. It ends with a terrible fall and fire. (1.) The inhabitants are slain (*v.* 26): The *young men,* who should fight the enemy and defend the city, *shall fall* by the sword *in her streets; and all the men of war,* mighty men, expert in war, and engaged in the service of their country, *shall be cut off.* (2.) The city is laid in ashes (*v.* 27): The *fire* is *kindled* by the besiegers *in the wall,* but it shall devour all before it, *the palaces of Ben-hadad* particularly, where so much mischief had formerly been hatched against God's Israel, for which it is now thus visited.

28 Concerning Kedar, and concerning the kingdoms of Hazor, which Nebuchadrezzar king of Babylon shall smite, thus saith the LORD; Arise ye, go up to Kedar, and spoil the men of the east. 29 Their tents and their flocks shall they take away: they shall take to themselves their curtains, and all their vessels, and their camels; and they shall cry unto them, Fear *is* on every side. 30 Flee, get you far off, dwell deep, O ye inhabitants of Hazor, saith the LORD; for Nebuchadrezzar king of Babylon hath taken counsel against you, and hath conceived a purpose against you. 31 Arise, get you up unto the wealthy nation, that dwelleth without care, saith the LORD, which have neither gates nor bars, *which* dwell alone. 32 And their camels shall be a booty, and the multitude of their cattle a spoil: and I will scatter into all winds them *that are* in the utmost corners; and I will bring their calamity from all sides thereof, saith the LORD. 33 And Hazor shall be a dwelling for dragons, *and* a desolation for ever: there shall no man abide there, nor *any* son of man dwell in it.

These verses foretel the desolation that Nebuchadnezzar and his forces should make among the people of Kedar (who descended from Kedar the son of Ishmael, and inhabited a part of Arabia the Stony), and of the kingdoms, the petty principalities, of Hazor, that joined to them, who perhaps were originally Canaanites, of the kingdom of Hazor, in the north of Canaan, which had Jabin for its king, but, being driven thence, settled in the deserts of Arabia and associated themselves with the Kedarenes. Concerning this people we may here observe,

I. What was their present state and posture? They dwelt in *tents* and had no walls, but *curtains* (*v.* 29), no fortified cities; they had *neither gates nor bars, v.* 31. They were shepherds, and had no treasures, but stock upon land, no money, but flocks and camels. They had no soldiers among them, for they were in no fear of invaders, no merchants, for they *dwelt alone, v.* 31. Those of other nations neither came among them nor traded with them; but they lived within themselves, content with the products and pleasures of their own country. This was their manner of living, very different from that of the nations that were round about them. And, 1. They were very rich; though they had no trade, no treasures, yet they are here said to be a *wealthy nation* (*v.* 31), because they had a sufficiency to answer all the occasions of human life and they were content with it. Note, Those are truly rich who have enough to supply their necessities, and know when they have enough. We need not go to the treasures of kings and provinces, or to the cash of merchants, to look for wealthy people; they may be found among shepherds *that dwell in tents.* 2. They were very easy: *They dwelt without care.* Their wealth was such as nobody envied them, or, if any did, they might come peaceably and enjoy the like; and therefore they feared nobody. Note, Those that live innocently and honestly may live very securely, though they have *neither gates nor bars.*

II. The design of the king of Babylon against them and the descent he made upon them: *He has taken counsel against you and has conceived a purpose against you, v.* 30. That proud man resolves it shall never be said that he, who had conquered so many strong cities, will leave those unconquered *that dwell in tents.* It was strange that that eagle should stoop to catch these flies, that so great a prince should play at such small game; but all is fish that comes to the ambitious covetous man's net. Note, It will not always secure men from suffering wrong to be able to say that they have done no wrong; not to have given offence will not be a defence against such men as Nebuchadnezzar. Yet, how unrighteous soever he was in doing it, God was righteous in directing it. These people had lived inoffensively among their neighbours, as many do, who yet, like them, are guilty before God; and it was to punish them for their offences against him that God said (*v.* 28): *Arise, go up to Kedar, and spoil the men of the east.* They will do it to gratify their own covetousness and ambition, but God orders it for the correcting of an unthankful people, and for warning to a careless world to expect trouble when they seem to be most safe. God says to the Chaldeans (*v.* 31): *"Arise, get up to the wealthy nation that dwells without care; go and give them an alarm, that none may imagine their mountain stands so strong that it cannot be moved."*

III. The great amazement that this put them into, and the great desolation hereby made among them: *They shall cry unto them;* those on the borders shall send the alarm into all parts of the country, which shall be put into the utmost confusion by it; they shall cry, *"Fear is on every side*—We are surrounded by the enemy,"* the very terror of which shall drive them all to their feet and they shall none of them have any heart to make resistance. The enemy shall *proclaim fear upon them,* or *against them, on every side.* They need not strike a stroke; they shall shout them out of their tents, *v.* 29. Upon the first alarm, they shall *flee, get far off,* and *dwell deep* (*v.* 30), as the Edomites, *v.* 8. And it will be found that this *fear on every side* is not groundless, for their calamity shall be *brought from all sides*

thereof, *v.* 32. No marvel there are *fears on every side* when there are foes on every side. The issue will be, 1. What they have will be a prey to the Chaldeans; they shall *take to themselves their curtains and vessels;* though they are but plain and coarse, and they have better of their own, yet they shall take them for spite, and spoil for spoiling sake. *They shall carry away their tents and their flocks, v.* 29. *Their camels* shall be a booty to those that came for nothing else, *v.* 32. 2. It is not said that any of them shall be slain, for they attempt not to make any resistance and their tents and flocks are accepted as a ransom for their lives; but they shall be dislodged and dispersed; though now they dwell *in the utmost corners,* out of the way, and therefore they think out of the reach, of danger (by this character those people were distinguished, *ch.* ix. 26, 25, 23), yet they shall be *scattered* thence *into all winds,* into all parts of the world. Note, Privacy and obscurity are not always a protection and security. Many that affect to be strangers to the world may yet by unthought-of providences be forced into it; and those that live most retired may have the same lot with those that thrust themselves forth and lie most exposed. 3. Their country shall lie uninhabited; for, lying remote and out of all high roads. and having neither cities nor lands inviting to strangers, none shall care to succeed them, so that *Hazor shall be a desolation for ever, v.* 33. If busy men be displaced, many strive to get into their places, because they lived great; but here are easy quiet men displaced, and *no man* cares to *abide* where they did, because they lived meanly.

34 The word of the LORD that came to Jeremiah the prophet against Elam in the beginning of the reign of Zedekiah king of Judah, saying, 35 Thus saith the LORD of hosts; Behold, I will break the bow of Elam, the chief of their might. 36 And upon Elam will I bring the four winds from the four quarters of heaven, and will scatter them toward all those winds; and there shall be no nation whither the outcasts of Elam shall not come. 37 For I will cause Elam to be dismayed before their enemies, and before them that seek their life: and I will bring evil upon them, *even* my fierce anger, saith the LORD; and I will send the sword after them, till I have consumed them: 38 And I will set my throne in Elam, and will destroy from thence the king and the princes, saith the LORD. 39 But it shall come to pass in the latter days, *that* I will

bring again the captivity of Elam, saith the LORD.

This prophecy is dated in the beginning of Zedekiah's reign; it is probable that the other prophecies against the Gentiles, going before, were at the same time. The Elamites were the Persians, descended from Elam the son of Shem (Gen. x. 22); yet some think it was only that part of Persia which lay nearest to the Jews which was called *Elymais*, and adjoined to Media-Elam, which, say they, had acted against God's Israel, *bore the quiver* in an expedition against them (Isa. xxii. 6), and therefore must be reckoned with among the rest. It is here foretold, in general, that God will *bring evil upon them, even* his *fierce anger,* and that is evil enough, it has *all evil in it, v.* 37. In particular, 1. Their forces shall be disabled, and rendered incapable of doing them any service. The Elamites were famous archers, but, *Behold, I will break the bow of Elam* (v. 35), will ruin their artillery, and then *the chief of their might* is gone. God often orders it so that that which we most trust to first fails us, and that which was *the chief of our might* proves the least of our help. 2. Their people shall be dispersed. There shall come enemies against them from all parts of the world, and they shall all carry some of them away captive into their respective countries; while others shall flee, some one way and some another, to shift for themselves, so that *there shall be no nation whither the outcasts of Elam shall not come, v.* 36. *The four winds* shall be brought upon them; the storm shall come sometimes from one point and sometimes from another, to toss and hurry them several ways. We know not from what point the wind of trouble may blow; but, if God encompass us with his favour, we are safe, and may be easy, which way soever the storm comes. Fear shall drive them into other countries; they shall *be dismayed before their enemies;* but, as if that were not enough, *I will send the sword after them, v.* 37. Note, God can make his judgments follow those that think by flight to escape them and to get out of the reach of them. *Evil pursues sinners.* 3. Their princes shall be destroyed and the government quite changed (v. 38): *I will set my throne in Elam.* The throne of Nebuchadnezzar shall be set there, or the throne of Cyrus, who began his conquests with Elymais. Or it may be meant of the throne on which God sits for judgment; he will make them know that he reigns, that he *judges in the earth,* that *kings and princes* are accountable to him, and that high as they are he is above them. The king of Elam was famous of old, Gen. xiv. 1. Chedorlaomer was king of Elam, and a mighty man he was in his day; the nations about him served him; his successors, we may suppose, made a great figure; but the king of Elam is no more to God than

another man. When God *sets his throne in Elam* he *will destroy thence the king and the princes* that are, and set up whom he pleases. 4. Yet the destruction of Elam shall not be perpetual (v. 39): *In the latter days I will bring again the captivity of Elam.* When Cyrus had destroyed Babylon, brought the empire into the hands of the Persians, the Elamites no doubt returned in triumph out of all the countries whither they were scattered, and settled again in their own country. But this promise was to have its full and principal accomplishment in the days of the Messiah, when we find Elamites particularly among those who, when the Holy Ghost was given, heard spoken *in their own tongues the wonderful works of God* (Acts ii. 9, 11), and that is the most desirable return of the captivity. *If the Son make you free, then you shall be free indeed.*

CHAP. L.

In this chapter, and that which follows, we have the judgment of Babylon, which is put last of Jeremiah's prophecies against the Gentiles because it was last accomplished; and when the cup of God's fury went round (ch.xxv. 17) the king of Sheshach, Babylon, drank last. Babylon was employed as the rod in God's hand for the chastising of all the other nations, and now at length that rod shall be thrown into the fire. The destruction of Babylon by Cyrus was foretold, long before it came to its height, by Isaiah, and now again, when it has come to its height, by Jeremiah; for, though at this time he saw that kingdom flourishing "like a green bay-tree," yet at the same time he foresaw it withered and cut down. And as Isaiah's prophecies of the destruction of Babylon and the deliverance of Israel out of it seem designed to typify the evangelical triumphs of all believers over the powers of darkness, and the great salvation wrought out by our Lord Jesus Christ, so Jeremiah's prophecies of the same events seem designed to point at the apocalyptic triumphs of the gospel church in the latter days over the New-Testament Babylon, many passages in the Revelation being borrowed hence. The kingdom of Babylon being much larger and stronger than any other of the kingdoms here prophesied against, its fall was the more considerable in itself; and, it having been more oppressive to the people of God than any of the other, the prophet is very copious upon this subject, for the comfort of the captives; and what was foretold in general often before (ch. xxv. 12 and xxvii. 7) is here more particularly described, and with a great deal of prophetic heat as well as light. The terrible judgments God had in store for Babylon, and the glorious blessings he had in store for his people that were captives there, are intermixed and counterchanged in the prophecy of this chapter; for Babylon was destroyed to make way for the turning again of the captivity of God's people. Here is, I. The ruin of Babylon, ver. 1—3, and again ver. 9—16, and again ver. 21—32, and again ver. 35—46. II. The redemption of God's people, ver. 4—8, and again ver. 17—20, and again ver. 33, 34. And, these being set the one against the other, it is easy to say which one would choose to take one's lot with, the persecuting Babylonians, who, though now in pomp, are reserved for so great a ruin, or the persecuted Israelites, who, though now in thraldom, are reserved for so great a glory.

THE word that the LORD spake against Babylon *and* against the land of the Chaldeans by Jeremiah the prophet. 2 Declare ye among the nations, and publish, and set up a standard; publish, *and* conceal not: say, Babylon is taken, Bel is confounded, Merodach is broken in pieces; her idols are confounded, her images are broken in pieces. 3 For out of the north there cometh up a nation against her, which shall make her land desolate, and none shall dwell therein: they shall remove, they shall depart, both man and beast. 4 In those days, and in that time, saith the LORD, the children of Israel shall come, they and the children of Judah together, going and weeping: they shall go, and seek the LORD their God. 5 They shall ask the way to Zion with their faces thitherward, *saying,* Come, and let us join ourselves to the LORD in a perpetual covenant *that* shall not be forgotten. 6 My people hath been lost sheep: their shepherds have caused them to go astray, they have turned them away *on* the mountains: they have gone from mountain to hill, they have forgotten their restingplace. 7 All that found them have devoured them: and their adversaries said, We offend not, because they have sinned against the LORD, the habitation of justice; even the LORD, the hope of their fathers. 8 Remove out of the midst of Babylon, and go forth out of the land of the Chaldeans, and be as the he-goats before the flocks.

I. Here is a word spoken against Babylon by him whose works all agree with his word and none of whose words fall to the ground. The king of Babylon had been very kind to Jeremiah, and yet he must foretel the ruin of that kingdom; for God's prophets must not be governed by favour or affection. Whoever are our friends, if, notwithstanding, they are God's enemies, we dare not speak peace to them. 1. The destruction of Babylon is here spoken of as a thing done, *v.* 2. Let it be published to the nations as a piece of news, true news, and great news, and news they are all concerned in; let them hang out the flag, as is usual on days of triumph, to give notice of it; let all the world take notice of it: *Babylon is taken.* Let God have the honour of it, let his people have the comfort of it, and therefore do not conceal it. Take care that it be known, that *the Lord may be known by those judgments which he executes,* Ps. ix. 16. 2. It is spoken of as a thing done thoroughly. For, (1.) The very idols of Babylon, which the people would protect with all possible care, and from which they expected protection, shall be destroyed. Bel and Merodach were their two principal deities; they shall be *confounded,* and the images of them *broken to pieces.* (2.) The country shall be laid waste (*v.* 3) out *of the north,* from Media, which lay north of Babylon, and from Assyria, through which Cyrus made his descent upon Babylon; thence the nation shall come that shall make *her land desolate.* Their land was north of the coun-
690

tries that they destroyed, who were therefore threatened with evil from the north (*Omne malum ab aquilone*—*Every evil comes from the north*); but God will find out nations yet further north to come upon them. The pomp and power of old Rome were brought down by northern nations, the Goths and Vandals.

II. Here is a word spoken for the people of God, and for their comfort, both *the children of Israel* and *of Judah;* for many there were of the ten tribes that associated with those of the two tribes in their return out of Babylon. Now here,

1. It is promised that they shall return to their God first and then to their own land; and the promise of their conversion and reformation is that which makes way for all the other promises, *v.* 4, 5. (1.) They shall *lament after the Lord* (as the whole house of Israel did in Samuel's time, 1 Sam. vii. 2); they shall *go weeping.* These tears flow not from the sorrow of the world as those when they went into captivity, but from godly sorrow; they are tears of repentance for sin, tears of joy for the goodness of God, in the dawning of the day of their deliverance, which, for aught that appears, does more towards the bringing of them to mourn for sin than all the calamities of their captivity; that prevails to *lead them to repentance* when the other did not prevail to drive them to it. Note, It is a good sign that God is coming towards a people in ways of mercy when they begin to be tenderly affected under his hand. (2.) They shall *enquire after the Lord;* they shall not sink under their sorrows, but bestir themselves to find out comfort where it is to be had: *They shall go weeping to seek the Lord their God.* Those that seek the Lord must *seek him sorrowing,* as Christ's parents sought him, Luke ii. 48. And those that sorrow must seek the Lord, and then their sorrow shall soon be turned into joy, for he will be found of those that so seek him. They shall *seek the Lord as their God,* and shall now have no more to do with idols. When they shall hear that the idols of Babylon are *confounded and broken* it will be seasonable for them to enquire after their own God and to return to him who lives for ever. *Therefore* men are deceived in false gods, that they may depend on the true God only. (3.) They shall think of returning to their own country again; they shall think of it not only as a mercy, but as a duty, because there only is the *holy hill of Zion,* on which once stood the *house of the Lord their God* (*v.* 5): *They shall ask the way to Zion with their faces thitherward.* Zion was the city of their solemnities; they often thought of it in the depth of their captivity (Ps. cxxxvii. 1); but, now that the ruin of Babylon gave them some hopes of a release, they talk of nothing else but of going back to Zion. Their hearts were upon it before,

and now they *set their faces thitherward.* They long to be there ; they set out for Zion, and resolve not to take up short of it. The journey is long and they know not the road, but they will *ask the way*, for they will press forward till they come to Zion ; and, as they are determined not to turn back, so they are in care not to miss the way. This represents the return of poor souls to God. Heaven is the Zion they aim at as their end ; on this they have set their hearts ; towards this they have *set their faces*, and therefore they *ask the way* thither. They do not ask the way to heaven and set their faces towards the world ; nor set their faces towards heaven and go on at a venture without asking the way. But in all true converts there are both a sincere desire to attain the end and a constant care to keep in the way ; and a blessed sight it is to see people thus asking the way to heaven with their faces thitherward. (4.) They shall renew their covenant to walk with God more closely for the future : *Come, and let us join ourselves to the Lord in a perpetual covenant.* They had broken covenant with God, had in effect separated themselves from him, but now they resolve to *join themselves* to him again, by engaging themselves afresh to be his. Thus, when backsliders return, they must *do their first works*, must renew the covenant they first made ; and it must be a *perpetual covenant*, that must never be broken ; and, in order to that, must never be forgotten ; for a due remembrance of it will be the means of a due observance of it.

2. Their present case is lamented as very sad, and as having been long so : " *My people"* (for he owns them as his now that they are returning to him) " *have been lost sheep* (*v.* 6) ; they have *gone from mountain to hill*, have been hurried from place to place, and could find no pasture ; *they have forgotten their resting-place* in their own country and cannot find their way to it." And that which aggravated their misery was, (1.) That they were *led astray by their own shepherds*, their own princes and priests ; they turned them from their duty, and so provoked God to turn them out of their own land. It is bad with a people when their leaders cause them to err, when those that should direct and reform them seduce and debauch them, and when those that should secure and advance their interests are the betrayers of them. (2.) That in their wanderings they lay exposed to the beasts of prey, who thought they were entitled to them, as waifs and strays that had no owner (*v.* 7) ; it is with them as with wandering sheep, *all that found them have devoured them* and made a prey of them ; and when they did them the greatest injuries they laughed at them, telling them it was what their own prophets had many a time told them they deserved ; that was far from justifying those who did them wrong,

yet they bantered them with this excuse, *We offend not, because they have sinned against the Lord ;* but they could not pretend that they had sinned against them. And see what notion they had of the Lord they had sinned against, not as the only true and living God, but only as *the habitation of justice and the hope of their fathers ;* they had put a contempt upon the temple and upon the tradition of their ancestors, and therefore deserved to suffer these hard things. And yet it was indeed an aggravation of their sin, and justified God, though it did not justify their adversaries in what was done to them, that they had *forsaken the habitation of justice* and him that was *the hope of their fathers.*

3. They are called upon to hasten away, as soon as ever the door of liberty was opened to them (*v.* 8) : " *Remove*, not only out of the borders, but *out of the midst of Babylon ;* though you be ever so well seated there, think not to settle there, but hasten to Zion, and *be as the he-goats before the flocks ;* strive which shall be foremost, which shall lead in so good a work :" a he-goat is *comely in going* (Prov. xxx. 31) because he goes first. It is a graceful thing to be forward in a good work and to set others a good example.

9 For, lo, I will raise and cause to come up against Babylon an assembly of great nations from the north country : and they shall set themselves in array against her ; from thence she shall be taken : their arrows *shall be* as of a mighty expert man ; none shall return in vain. 10 And Chaldea shall be a spoil : all that spoil her shall be satisfied, saith the LORD. 11 Because ye were glad, because ye rejoiced, O ye destroyers of mine heritage, because ye are grown fat as the heifer at grass, and bellow as bulls ; 12 Your mother shall be sore confounded ; she that bare you shall be ashamed : behold, the hindermost of the nations *shall be* a wilderness, a dry land, and a desert. 13 Because of the wrath of the LORD it shall not be inhabited, but it shall be wholly desolate : every one that goeth by Babylon shall be astonished, and hiss at all her plagues. 14 Put yourselves in array against Babylon round about : all ye that bend the bow, shoot at her, spare no arrows : for she hath sinned against the LORD. 15 Shout against her round about : she hath given her hand : her foundations are fallen, her

walls are thrown down : for it *is* the vengeance of the LORD : take vengeance upon her ; as she hath done, do unto her. 16 Cut off the sower from Babylon, and him that handleth the sickle in the time of harvest : for fear of the oppressing sword they shall turn every one to his people, and they shall flee every one to his own land. 17 Israel *is* a scattered sheep ; the lions have driven *him* away : first the king of Assyria hath devoured him ; and last this Nebuchadrezzar king of Babylon hath broken his bones. 18 Therefore thus saith the LORD of hosts, the God of Israel ; Behold, I will punish the king of Babylon and his land, as I have punished the king of Assyria. 19 And I will bring Israel again to his habitation, and he shall feed on Carmel and Bashan, and his soul shall be satisfied upon mount Ephraim and Gilead. 20 In those days, and in that time, saith the LORD, the iniquity of Israel shall be sought for, and *there shall be* none ; and the sins of Judah, and they shall not be found : for I will pardon them whom I reserve.

God is here by his prophet, as afterwards in his providence, proceeding in his controversy with Babylon. Observe,

I. The commission and charge given to the instruments that were to be employed in destroying Babylon. The army that is to do it is called *an assembly of great nations* (v. 9), the Medes and Persians, and all their allies and auxiliaries ; it is called *an assembly*, because regularly formed by the divine will and counsel to do this execution. God will *raise them up* to do it, will incline them to and fit them for this service, and then he will *cause them to come up*, for all their motions are under his conduct and direction : he shall give the word of command, shall order them to *put themselves in array against Babylon* (v. 14), and then *they shall put themselves in array* (v. 9), for what God appoints to be done shall be done ; and *thence she shall be* quickly *taken ;* from their first sitting down before it they shall be still gaining ground against it till it be taken. God shall bid them *shoot at her and spare no arrows* (v. 14), and then *their arrows shall be as of a mighty expert man*, that has both skill and strength, a good eye and a good hand (v. 9); *none shall return in vain.* When God gives commission he will give success. Nay, they are bidden not only to *shoot at her* (v. 14), but to *shout against her* (v. 15)

with a triumphant shout, as those that are already sure of victory. Those whom God directs to shoot may do so with shouting, for they are sure not to miss the mark.

II. The desolation and destruction itself that shall be brought upon Babylon. This is here set forth in a great variety of expressions. 1. The wealth of Babylon shall be a rich and easy prey to the conquerors (v. 10) : *Chaldea shall be a spoil* to all her destroyers, who shall enrich themselves by plundering her, and, which is strange, *all that spoil her shall be satisfied ;* they shall have so much that even they themselves shall say that they have enough. 2. The country of Babylon shall be depopulated and lie uninhabited : *It shall be wholly desolate* (v. 13) to such a degree that *every one who goes by* shall triumph in her fall, and, instead of condoling with them, shall *hiss at all her plagues, v.* 13. 3. Their ancestors shall be ashamed of their cowardice, in fleeing from the first onset (v. 12), or, *Your mother,* Babylon itself, the mother-city, *shall be confounded,* when she sees herself deserted by those that should have been her guards. Thus the former ages of Christians may justly be confounded and ashamed to see how unlike them the latter ages are, and how wretchedly they have degenerated ; and no sin brings a surer and sorer ruin upon persons, or people, than apostasy. 4. The great admirers of Babylon shall see it rendered very despicable : the last of kingdoms, the very tail of the nations, *shall it be, a wilderness, a dry land, a desert, v.* 12. The country that was populous shall be dispeopled, that was enriched with a fertile soil shall become barren. 5. The great city, the head of it, shall be quite ruined. *Her foundations have fallen,* and therefore *her walls are thrown down ;* for how can the walls stand when divine vengeance is at the door and shakes the very foundations ? It is the vengeance of the Lord, which nothing can contend with either in law or battle. 6. There shall not be left in Babylon so much as *the poor of the land, for vinedressers and husbandmen,* as there was in Israel (v. 16) : *The sower shall be cut off from Babylon, and he that handles the sickle ;* the country shall be so emptied of people that there shall be none to till the ground and gather in the fruits of it. Harvest shall come, and there shall be no reapers ; seedtime shall come, but there shall be no sower ; God will do his part, but there shall be no men to do theirs. 7. All their auxiliary forces, which they have hired into their service, shall desert them, as mercenary men often do upon the approach of danger (v. 16) : *For fear of the oppressing sword they shall turn every one to his people.* This was threatened before concerning Egypt, *ch.* xlvi. 16.

III. The procuring provoking cause of this destruction. It comes from God's displeasure; it is *because of the wrath of the Lord* that Babylon *shall be wholly desolate* (v. 13), and his wrath is righteous, for (v. 14) *she hath sinned against the Lord*, therefore *spare no arrows.* Note, It is sin that makes men a mark for the arrows of God's judgments. An abundance of idolatry and immorality was to be found in Babylon, yet those are not mentioned as the reason of God's displeasure against them, but the injuries they had done to the people of God, from a principle of enmity to them as his people. They have been *the destroyers of God's heritage* (v. 11); herein indeed God made use of them for the necessary correction of his people, and yet it is laid to their charge as a heinous crime, because they designed nothing but their utter destruction. 1. What they did against Jerusalem they did with pleasure (v. 11): *You were glad, you rejoiced.* God does not afflict his people willingly, and therefore takes it very ill if the instruments he employs afflict them willingly. When Titus Vespasian destroyed Jerusalem he wept over it, but these Chaldeans triumphed over it. 2. The spoils of Jerusalem they made use of to feed their own luxury: " *You have grown fat as the heifer at grass, and bellow as bulls;* your having conquered Jerusalem has made you very wanton and proud, easy to yourselves and formidable to all about you, and therefore you must *be a spoil.*" Those that have thus swallowed down riches must vomit them up again. Therefore they have *given their hand* (v. 15); they have surrendered themselves to the conqueror, have tamely yielded, so that now you may *take vengeance on her*, now you may make reprisals and *do unto her as she hath done*. 3. They aimed at nothing less than the utter ruin of God's Israel: *Israel is a scattered sheep*, as before (v. 6), that is not only barked at and worried by dogs, but even lions, the most potent adversaries, have roared upon him and *driven him away, v.* 17. One king of Assyria carried the ten tribes quite away and devoured them; another invaded Judah, and plundered and impoverished it, tore the fleece and flesh of this poor sheep; and now at last this Nebuchadnezzar, that is the terror and plague of all his neighbours, has taken advantage of the low condition to which he is reduced, and he has fallen upon him and *broken his bones*, has quite ruined him, and therefore the king of Babylon must be punished as the king of Assyria was, *v*. 18. Note, Those who pursue and prosecute the sins of their predecessors must expect to be pursued and prosecuted by their plagues; if they do as they did, let them fare as they fared.

IV. The mercy promised to the Israel of God, which shall not only accompany, but accrue from, the destruction of Babylon. 1. God will return their captivity; they shall be released out of their bondage, and *brought again to their own habitation* as sheep that

were scattered to their own fold *v.* 19. They still retained a title to the land of Canaan; it is their habitation still. The discontinuance of their possession was not the destruction of their right. But now they shall recover the enjoyment of it again. 2. He will restore their prosperity; they shall not only live, but live comfortably, in their own land again; they shall *feed upon Carmel and Bashan*, the richest and most fruitful parts of the country. These sheep shall be gathered from the deserts to which they were dispersed, and put again into good pasture, which their soul shall be satisfied with though they shall come hungry to it, having been so long stinted, and straitened, and kept short, yet they shall find enough to satiate them and shall have hearts to be satiated with it. They *enquired the way to Zion* (v. 5), where God was to be served and worshipped. This was what they chiefly aimed at in their return; but God will not only bring them thither, but bring them also to Carmel and Bashan, where they shall abundantly feed themselves. Note, Those that return to God and their duty shall find true satisfaction of soul in so doing; and those that *seek first the kingdom of God and the righteousness thereof*, that aim to make their habitation in Zion, the holy hill, shall have *other things added to them*, even all the comforts of *Ephraim and Gilead*, the fruitful hills. 3. God will pardon their iniquity; this is the root of all the rest (v. 20): *In those days the iniquity of Israel shall be sought for, and there shall be none*. Not only the punishments of their iniquity shall be taken off, but the offence which it gave to God shall be forgotten, and he will be reconciled to them. Their sin shall be before him as if it had never been; it shall be blotted out as a cloud, crossed out as a debt, shall be cast behind his back; nay, it shall be cast into the depth of the sea, shall be no longer sealed up among God's treasures, nor in any danger of appearing again or rising up against them. This denotes how fully God forgives sin; he *remembers it no more*. Note, Deliverances out of trouble are then comforts indeed when they are the fruits of the forgiveness of sin, Isa. xxxviii. 17. Judah and Israel were so fully forgiven when they were brought back out of Babylon that they are said to have *received of the Lord's hand double for all their sins*, Isa. xl. 2. This may include also a thorough reformation of their hearts and lives, as well as a full remission of their sins. If any seek for idols or any idolatrous customs among them, after their return, *there shall be none*, they *shall not find them;* their dross shall be purely purged away, and by that it shall appear that their guilt is so; *for I will pardon those whom I reserve: I will be propitious to them* (so the word is) and that must be through him who is the great propitiation. Note, Those whose sins God pardons he re-

serves for something very great ; for *whom*
he justifies them he glorifies.

21 Go up against the land of Merathaim, *even* against it, and against
the inhabitants of Pekod : waste and
utterly destroy after them, saith the
Lord, and do according to all that
I have commanded thee. 22 A sound
of battle *is* in the land, and of great
destruction. 23 How is the hammer
of the whole earth cut asunder and
broken ! how is Babylon become a
desolation among the nations ! 24 I
have laid a snare for thee, and thou
art al o taken, O Babylon, and thou
wast not aware : thou art found, and
also caught, because thou hast striven
against the Lord. 25 The Lord
hath opened his armoury, and hath
brought forth the weapons of his indignation : for this *is* the work of the
Lord God of hosts in the land of the
Chaldeans. 26 Come against her
from the utmost border, open her
store-houses : cast her up as heaps,
and destroy her utterly : let nothing
of her be left. 27 Slay all her bullocks ; let them go down to the
slaughter : woe unto them ! for their
day is come, the time of their visitation. 28 The voice of them that flee
and escape out of the land of Babylon, to declare in Zion the vengeance
of the Lord our God, the vengeance
of his temple. 29 Call together the
archers against Babylon : all ye that
bend the bow, camp against it round
about ; let none thereof escape : recompense her according to her work ;
according to all that she hath done,
do unto her : for she hath been proud
against the Lord, against the Holy
One of Israel. 30 Therefore shall
her young men fall in the streets, and
all her men of war shall be cut off in
that day, saith the Lord. 31 Behold,
I *am* against thee, O *thou* most proud,
saith the Lord God of hosts : for thy
day is come, the time *that* I will visit
thee. 32 And the most proud shall
stumble and fall, and none shall raise
him up : and I will kindle a fire in
his cities, and it shall devour all
round about him.

Here, 1. The forces are mustered and

commissioned to destroy Babylon, and every
thing is got ready for a descent upon that
potent kingdom : *Go up against* that *land
by Merathaim*, the country of the Mardi,
that lay part in Assyria and part in Armenia ;
and go among *the inhabitants of Pekod*, another country (mentioned Ezek. xxiii. 23)
which Cyrus took in his way to Babylon.
The forces of Cyrus are called to go up
against Babylon (v. 21), to *come against her
from the utmost border.* Let all come together, for there will be both work and pay
enough for them all, v. 26. Distance of
place must not be their hindrance from engaging in this work. *The archers* particularly
must be *called together against Babylon, v.
29.* Thus *the Lord hath opened his armoury*
(v. 25), *his treasury* (so the word is), *and hath
brought forth the weapons of his indignation,*
as great princes fetch out of their magazines
and stores all necessary provisions for their
armies when they undertake any great expedition. Media and Persia are now God's
armoury ; thence he fetches the weapons of
his wrath, Cyrus and his great officers and
armies, whom he will make use of for the
destruction of Babylon. Note, Great men
are but instruments which the great God
makes use of to serve his own purposes. He
has variety of instruments, has them at command, has armouries ready to be opened according as the occasion is. *This is the work
of the Lord God of hosts.* Note, When God
has work to do he will make it appear that
he is *God of hosts*, and will not want instruments to do it with. 2. Instructions are
given them what to do. In general, *Do according to all that I have commanded thee,*
v. 21. It was said of Cyrus (Isa. xliv. 28),
He shall perform all my pleasure, in his expedition against Babylon. They must *waste
and utterly destroy after them ;* when they
have destroyed once they must go over
them again, or destroy their posterity that
should come after them. They must *open
her store-houses* (v. 26), rifle her treasures,
and turn her artillery against herself. They
must *cast her up as heaps ;* let all the wealth
and pomp of Babylon be shovelled up in a
heap of ruins and rubbish. *Tread her down
as heaps* (so the margin reads it) *and destroy
her utterly.* See how little account the great
God makes of those things which men so
much value and value themselves so much
upon. Their princes and great men, who
are fat and bulky, shall fall by the sword,
not as men of war in the field of battle,
which we call a bed of honour, but as beasts
by the butcher's hand (v. 27) : *Slay all her
bullocks*, all her mighty men ; *let them go
down* sottishly and insensibly, as an ox *to
the slaughter.* *Woe unto them !* their case
is the more sad for the little sense they have
of it. *Their day has come* to fall, *the time*
when they must be reckoned with, and they
are not aware of it. 3. Assurances are given
them of success. Let them do what God

commands, and they shall accomplish what he threatens. A *great destruction* shall be made, *v.* 22. *Babylon shall become a desolation* (*v.* 23); *her young men and all her men of war shall be cut off in that day* which should have been her defence, *v.* 30. God is *against* her (*v.* 31); he has *laid a snare for* her (*v.* 24); he has formed this enterprise against her, that she should be surprised as a bird taken in a snare. Cyrus shall no doubt prevail, for he fights under God. God *will kindle a fire* in the cities of Babylon (*v.* 32); and who can stand before him when he is angry, or quench the fire that he has kindled? 4. Reasons are given for these severe dealings with Babylon. Those that are employed in this war may, if they please, know the grounds of it, and be satisfied in the justice of it, which it is fit all should be that are called to such work. (1.) Babylon has been very troublesome, vexatious, and injurious, to all its neighbours; it has been *the hammer of the whole earth* (*v.* 23), beating, beating down, and beating to pieces, all the nations far and near. It has done so long enough; it is time now that it be *cut asunder and broken.* Note, He that is the God of nations will sooner or later assert the injured rights of nations against those that unjustly and violently invade them. The God of the whole earth will break *the hammer of the whole earth.* (2.) Babylon has bidden defiance to God himself: *Thou hast striven against the Lord* (*v.* 24), *hast joined issue with him* (so the word signifies) as in law or battle, hast openly opposed him, set up rivals with him, raised rebellion against him; therefore *thou art* now *found, and caught,* as in a snare. Note, Those that strive against the Lord will soon find themselves over-matched. (3.) Babylon ruined Jerusalem, the holy city, and the holy house there, and must now be called to an account for that. This is the manifesto published in Zion, in the day of Babylon's visitation; it is *the vengeance of the Lord our God, the vengeance of his temple, v.* 28. The burning of the temple, and the carrying away of its vessels, were articles in the charge against Babylon on which greater stress was laid than upon its being *the hammer of the whole earth;* for Zion was *the joy* and glory *of the whole earth.* Note, Whatever wrong is done to God's church (his temple in the world) it will certainly be reckoned for; and no vengeance will be sorer nor heavier than *the vengeance of the temple.* (4.) Babylon has been very haughty and insolent, and therefore must have a fall; for it is the glory of God to *look upon those that are proud and to abase them,* Job xl. 12. *I am against thee, O thou most proud! v.* 31 and again *v.* 32. *Thou pride* (so the word is), as proud as pride itself. Note, The pride of men's hearts sets God against them and ripens them apace for ruin; for God *resists the proud* and will bring them down. The

most proud shall stumble and fall; they shall fall not so much by others' thrusting them down as by their own stumbling; for they hold their heads so high that they never look under their feet, to choose their way and avoid stumbling-blocks, but walk at all adventures. Babylon's pride must unavoidably be her ruin; for *she has been proud against the Lord, against the Holy One of Israel* (*v.* 29), has insulted him in insulting over his people; she has made him her enemy, and therefore, when she has *fallen, none shall raise her up, v.* 32. Who can help those up whom God will throw down?

33 Thus saith the LORD of hosts; The children of Israel and the children of Judah *were* oppressed together: and all that took them captives held them fast; they refused to let them go. 34 Their Redeemer *is* strong; the LORD of hosts *is* his name: he shall thoroughly plead their cause, that he may give rest to the land, and disquiet the inhabitants of Babylon. 35 A sword *is* upon the Chaldeans, saith the LORD, and upon the inhabitants of Babylon, and upon her princes, and upon her wise *men.* 36 A sword *is* upon the liars; and they shall dote: a sword *is* upon her mighty men; and they shall be dismayed. 37 A sword *is* upon their horses, and upon their chariots, and upon all the mingled people that *are* in the midst of her; and they shall become as women: a sword *is* upon her treasures; and they shall be robbed. 38 A drought *is* upon her waters; and they shall be dried up: for it *is* the land of graven images, and they are mad upon *their* idols. 39 Therefore the wild beasts of the desert with the wild beasts of the islands shall dwell *there,* and the owls shall dwell therein: and it shall be no more inhabited for ever; neither shall it be dwelt in from generation to generation. 40 As God overthrew Sodom and Gomorrah and the neighbour *cities* thereof, saith the LORD; *so* shall no man abide there, neither shall any son of man dwell therein. 41 Behold, a people shall come from the north, and a great nation, and many kings shall be raised up from the coasts of the earth. 42 They shall hold the bow and the lance:

they *are* cruel, and will not show mercy: their voice shall roar like the sea, and they shall ride upon horses, *every one* put in array, like a man to the battle, against thee, O daughter of Babylon. 43 The king of Babylon hath heard the report of them, and his hands waxed feeble: anguish took hold of him, *and* pangs as of a woman in travail. 44 Behold, he shall come up like a lion from the swelling of Jordan unto the habitation of the strong: but I will make them suddenly run away from her: and who *is* a chosen *man, that* I may appoint over her? for who *is* like me? and who will appoint me the time? and who *is* that shepherd that will stand before me? 45 Therefore hear ye the counsel of the LORD, that he hath taken against Babylon; and his purposes, that he hath purposed against the land of the Chaldeans: surely the least of the flock shall draw them out: surely he shall make *their* habitation desolate with them. 46 At the noise of the taking of Babylon the earth is moved, and the cry is heard among the nations.

We have in these verses,

I. Israel's sufferings, and their deliverance out of those sufferings. God takes notice of the bondage of his people in Babylon, as he did of their bondage in Egypt; he has *surely seen* it, and has *heard their cry. Israel and Judah were oppressed together, v.* 33. Those that remained of the captives of the ten tribes, upon the uniting of the kingdoms of Assyria and Chaldea, seem to have come and mingled with those of the two tribes, and to have mingled tears with them, so that they were *oppressed together.* They were humble suppliants for their liberty, and that was all; they could not attempt any thing towards it, for *all that took them captives held them fast,* and were much too hard for them. But this is their comfort in distress, that, though they are weak, *their Redeemer is strong* (v. 34), *their Avenger* (so the word signifies), he that has a right to them, and will claim his right and make good his claim. He is stronger than their enemies that hold them fast; he can overpower all the force that is against them, and put strength into his own people though they are very weak. *The Lord of hosts is his name,* and he will answer to his name, and make it to appear that he is what his people call him, and will be that to them for which they depend upon him. Note, It is the unspeakable comfort of the people of God that, though they have hosts against them, they have *the Lord of hosts* for them; and *he shall thoroughly plead their cause,* pleading he shall plead it, plead it with jealousy, plead it effectually, plead it and carry it, *that he may give rest to the land,* to his people's land, rest from all their enemies round about. This is applicable to all believers, who complain of the dominion of sin and corruption, and of their own weakness and manifold infirmities. Let them know that *their Redeemer is strong;* he is able to keep what they commit to him, and he will plead their cause. Sin shall not have dominion over them; he will *make them free,* and they shall be *free indeed;* he will give them *rest,* that *rest which remains for the people of God.*

II. Babylon's sin, and their punishment for that sin.

1. The sins they are here charged with are idolatry and persecution. (1.) They oppressed the people of God; they *held them fast,* and would not let *let them go.* They *opened not the house of his prisoners,* Isa. xiv. 17. This was God's quarrel with them, as of old with Pharaoh; it cost him dear, and yet they would not take warning. *The inhabitants of Babylon* must be *disquieted* (v. 34) because they have disquieted God's people, whose honour and comfort he is jealous for, and therefore will *recompense tribulation to those that trouble them,* as well as *rest to those that are troubled,* 2 Thess. i. 6, 7. (2.) They wronged God himself, and robbed him, giving that glory to others which is due to him alone; for (v. 38) *it is the land of graven images.* All parts of the country abounded with idols, and they were mad upon them, were in love with them and doted on them, cared not what cost and pains they were at in the worship of them, were unwearied in paying their respects to them; and in all this they were wretchedly infatuated and acted like men out of their wits; they were carried on in their idolatry without reason or discretion, like men in a perfect fury. The word here used for idols properly signifies *terrors—Enim,* the name given to giants that were formidable, because they made the images of their gods to look frightful, to strike a terror upon fools and children. Their idols were scarecrows, yet they doted on them. Babylon was *the mother of harlots* (Rev. xvii. 5), the source of idolatry. Note, It is the maddest thing in the world to make a god of any creature; and those who are proud against the Lord, the true God, are justly given up to strong delusions, to be mad upon idols that cannot profit. But this madness is wickedness, for which sinners will be certainly and severely reckoned with.

2. The judgments of God upon them for these sins are such as will quite lay them waste and ruin them.

(1.) All that should be their defence and support shall be cut off by the sword. The

Chaldeans had long been God's sword, wherewith he had done execution upon the sinful nations round about : but now, they being as bad as any of them, or worse, *a sword* is brought upon them, even *upon the inhabitants of Babylon* (*v.* 35), a sword of war ; and, as it is in God's hand, sent and directed by him, it is a sword of justice. It shall be, [1.] *Upon their princes ;* they shall fall by it, and their dignity, wealth, and power, shall not secure them. [2.] *Upon their wise men,* their philosophers, their statesmen, and privy-counsellors; their learning and policy shall neither secure them nor stand the public in any stead. [3.] *Upon* their soothsayers and astrologers, here called *the liars* (*v.* 36), for they cheated with their prognostications of peace and prosperity; the sword upon them shall make them dote, so that they shall talk like fools, and be as men that have lost all their wits. Note, God has a sword that can reach the soul and affect the mind, and bring men under spiritual plagues. [4.] *Upon their mighty men.* A sword shall be upon their spirits ; if they are not slain, yet *they shall be dismayed,* and shall be no longer *mighty men ;* for what stead will their hands stand them in when their hearts fail them ? [5.] Upon their militia (*v.* 37): *The sword shall be upon their horses and chariots ;* the invaders shall make themselves masters of all their warlike stores, shall seize their horses and chariots for themselves, or destroy them. The troops of other nations that were in their service shall be quite disheartened : *The mingled people shall become as* weak and timorous as *women.* [6.] Upon their exchequer : The *sword* shall be *upon her treasures,* which are the sinews of war, *and they shall be robbed,* and made use of by the enemy against them. See what universal destruction the sword makes when it comes with commission.

(2.) The country shall be made desolate (*v.* 38): *The waters shall be dried up,* the water that secures the city. Cyrus drew the river Euphrates into so many channels as made it passable for his army, so that they got with ease to the walls of Babylon, which, it was thought, that river had rendered inaccessible. " The water likewise that made the country fruitful shall *be dried up,* so that it shall be turned into barrenness, and shall be no more inhabited by the children of men, but by *the wild beasts of the desert,*" *v.* 39. This was foretold concerning Babylon, Isa. xiii. 19—22. It shall become like *Sodom and Gomorrah, v.* 40. The same was foretold concerning Edom, *ch.* xlix. 18. As the Chaldeans had laid Edom waste, so they shall themselves be laid waste.

(3.) The king and kingdom shall be put into the utmost confusion and consternation by the enemies' invading them, *v.* 41—43. All the expressions here used to denote the formidable power of the invaders, the terrors wherewith they should array themselves,

and the great fright which both court and country should be put into thereby, we met with before (*ch.* vi. 22—24) concerning the Chaldeans' invading the land of Judah. The battle which is there said to be *against thee, O daughter of Zion !* is here said to be *against thee, O daughter of Babylon !* to intimate that they should be paid in their own coin. God can find out such as shall be for terror and destruction to those that are for terror and destruction to others; and those who have dealt cruelly, and have shown no mercy, may expect to be cruelly dealt with, and to find no mercy. Only there is one difference between these passages ; there it is said, *We have heard the fame thereof and our hands wax feeble ;* here it is said, *The king of Babylon has heard the report and his hands waxed feeble,* which intimates that that proud and daring prince shall, in the day of his distress, be as weak and dispirited as the meanest Israelites were in the day of their distress.

(4.) That they shall be as much hurt as frightened, for the invader shall *come up like a lion* to tear and destroy (*v.* 44) and shall make them and their *habitation desolate* (*v.* 45), and the desolation shall be so astonishing that all the nations about shall be terrified by it, *v.* 46. These three verses we had before (*ch.* xlix. 19—21) in the prophecy of the destruction of Edom, which was accomplished by the Chaldeans, and they are here repeated, *mutatis mutandis—with a few necessary alterations,* in the prophecy of the destruction of Babylon, which was to be accomplished upon the Chaldeans, to show that though the distributions of Providence may appear unequal for a time its retributions will be equal at last ; when thou shalt make *an end to spoil thou shalt be spoiled,* Isa. xxxiii. 1 ; Rev. xiii. 10.

CHAP. LI.

The prophet, in this chapter, goes on with the prediction of Babylon's fall, to which other prophets also bore witness. He is very copious and lively in describing the foresight God had given him of it, for the encouragement of the pious captives, whose deliverance depended upon it and was to be the result of it. Here is, I. The record of Babylon's doom, with the particulars of it, intermixed with the grounds of God's controversy with her, many aggravations of her fall, and great encouragements given thence to the Israel of God, that suffered such hard things by her, ver. 1—58. II. The representation and ratification of this by the throwing of a copy of this prophecy into the river Euphrates, ver. 59—64.

THUS saith the LORD ; Behold, I will rise up against Babylon, and against them that dwell in the midst of them that rise up against me, a destroying wind ; 2 And will send unto Babylon fanners, that shall fan her, and shall empty her land : for in the day of trouble they shall be against her round about. 3 Against *him that* bendeth let the archer bend his bow, and against *him that* lifteth himself up in his brigandine : and spare ye not her young men ; destroy ye utterly all her host. 4 Thus the slain shall fall in the land of the Chaldeans, and *they that are* thrust through in her streets. 5 For Israel *hath* not *been* forsaken, nor Judah of his God, of the LORD of hosts; though their land was filled with sin against the Holy One of Israel. 6 Flee out of the midst of Babylon, and deliver every man his soul: be not cut off in her iniquity; for this *is* the time of the LORD's vengeance; he will render unto her a recompence. 7 Babylon *hath been* a golden cup in the LORD's hand, that made all the earth drunken: the nations have drunken of her wine; therefore the nations are mad. 8 Babylon is suddenly fallen and destroyed: howl for her; take balm for her pain, if so be she may be healed. 9 We would have healed Babylon, but she is not healed: forsake her, and let us go every one into his own country: for her judgment reacheth unto heaven, and is lifted up *even* to the skies. 10 The LORD hath brought forth our righteousness: come, and let us declare in Zion the work of the LORD our God. 11 Make bright the arrows; gather the shields: the LORD hath raised up the spirit of the kings of the Medes: for his device *is* against Babylon, to destroy it; because it *is* the vengeance of the LORD, the vengeance of his temple. 12 Set up the standard upon the walls of Babylon, make the watch strong, set up the watchmen, prepare the ambushes: for the LORD hath both devised and done that which he spake against the inhabitants of Babylon. 13 O thou that dwellest upon many waters, abundant in treasures, thine end is come, *and* the measure of thy covetousness. 14 The LORD of hosts hath sworn by himself, *saying*, Surely I will fill thee with men, as with caterpillers; and they shall lift up a shout against thee. 15 He hath made the earth by his power, he hath established the world by his wisdom, and hath stretched out the heaven by his understanding. 16 When he uttereth *his* voice, *there is* a multitude of waters in the heavens; and he causeth the

vapours to ascend from the ends of the earth: he maketh lightnings with rain, and bringeth forth the wind out of his treasures. 17 Every man is brutish by *his* knowledge; every founder is confounded by the graven image: for his molten image *is* falsehood, and *there is* no breath in them. 18 They *are* vanity, the work of errors: in the time of their visitation they shall perish. 19 The portion of Jacob *is* not like them: for he *is* the former of all things: and *Israel is* the rod of his inheritance: the LORD of hosts *is* his name. 20 Thou *art* my battle-ax *and* weapons of war: for with thee will I break in pieces the nations, and with thee will I destroy kingdoms; 21 And with thee will I break in pieces the horse and his rider; and with thee will I break in pieces the chariot and his rider; 22 With thee also will I break in pieces man and woman; and with thee will I break in pieces old and young; and with thee will I break in pieces the young man and the maid; 23 I will also break in pieces with thee the shepherd and his flock; and with thee will I break in pieces the husbandman and his yoke of oxen; and with thee will I break in pieces captains and rulers. 24 And I will render unto Babylon and to all the inhabitants of Chaldea all their evil that they have done in Zion, in your sight, saith the LORD. 25 Behold, I *am* against thee, O destroying mountain, saith the LORD, which destroyest all the earth: and I will stretch out mine hand upon thee, and roll thee down from the rocks, and will make thee a burnt mountain. 26 And they shall not take of thee a stone for a corner, nor a stone for foundations; but thou shalt be desolate for ever, saith the LORD. 27 Set ye up a standard in the land, blow the trumpet among the nations, prepare the nations against her, call together against her the kingdoms of Ararat, Minni, and Ashchenaz; appoint a captain against her; cause the horses to come up as the rough caterpillers. 28 Prepare against her the nations with the kings of the Medes, the captains thereof, and all the rulers thereof, and all the land of his dominion. 29 And the land shall tremble and sorrow: for every purpose of the LORD shall be performed against Babylon, to make the land of Babylon a desolation without an inhabitant. 30 The mighty men of Babylon have forborne to fight, they have remained in *their* holds: their might hath failed; they became as women: they have burned her dwelling-places; her bars are broken. 31 One post shall run to meet another, and one messenger to meet another, to show the king of Babylon that his city is taken at *one* end, 32 And that the passages are stopped, and the reeds they have burned with fire, and the men of war are affrighted. 33 For thus saith the LORD of hosts, the God of Israel; The daughter of Babylon *is* like a threshing-floor, *it is* time to thresh her: yet a little while, and the time of her harvest shall come. 34 Nebuchadrezzar the king of Babylon hath devoured me, he hath crushed me, he hath made me an empty vessel, he hath swallowed me up like a dragon, he hath filled his belly with my delicates, he hath cast me out. 35 The violence done to me and to my flesh *be* upon Babylon, shall the inhabitant of Zion say; and my blood upon the inhabitants of Chaldea, shall Jerusalem say. 36 Therefore thus saith the LORD; Behold, I will plead thy cause, and take vengeance for thee; and I will dry up her sea, and make her springs dry. 37 And Babylon shall become heaps, a dwelling-place for dragons, an astonishment, and a hissing, without an inhabitant. 38 They shall roar together like lions: they shall yell as lions' whelps. 39 In their heat I will make their feasts, and I will make them drunken, that they may rejoice, and sleep a perpetual sleep, and not wake, saith the LORD. 40 I will bring them down like lambs to the slaughter, like rams with he-goats. 41 How is Sheshach taken! and how is the praise of the whole earth surprised! how is Babylon become an astonishment among the nations! 42 The sea is come up upon Babylon: she is covered with the multitude of the waves thereof. 43 Her cities are a desolation, a dry land, and a wilderness, a land wherein no man dwelleth, neither doth *any* son of man pass thereby. 44 And I will punish Bel in Babylon, and I will bring forth out of his mouth that which he hath swallowed up: and the nations shall not flow together any more unto him: yea, the wall of Babylon shall fall. 45 My people, go ye out of the midst of her, and deliver ye every man his soul from the fierce anger of the LORD. 46 And lest your heart faint, and ye fear for the rumour that shall be heard in the land; a rumour shall both come *one* year, and after that in *another* year *shall come* a rumour, and violence in the land, ruler against ruler. 47 Therefore, behold, the days come, that I will do judgment upon the graven images of Babylon: and her whole land shall be confounded, and all her slain shall fall in the midst of her. 48 Then the heaven and the earth, and all that *is* therein, shall sing for Babylon: for the spoilers shall come unto her from the north, saith the LORD. 49 As Babylon *hath caused* the slain of Israel to fall, so at Babylon shall fall the slain of all the earth. 50 Ye that have escaped the sword, go away, stand not still: remember the LORD afar off, and let Jerusalem come into your mind. 51 We are confounded, because we have heard reproach: shame hath covered our faces: for strangers are come into the sanctuaries of the LORD's house. 52 Wherefore, behold, the days come, saith the LORD, that I will do judgment upon her graven images: and through all her land the wounded shall groan. 53 Though Babylon should mount up to heaven, and though she should fortify the height of her strength, *yet* from me shall spoilers come unto her, saith the LORD. 54 A sound of a cry *cometh* from Babylon, and great destruction from the land of the Chaldeans: 55 Because the LORD hath spoiled Babylon, and destroyed out of her the great voice; when her waves do roar like great waters, a noise of their voice is uttered: 56 Because the spoiler is come upon her, *even* upon Babylon, and her mighty men are taken, every one of their bows is broken: for the LORD God of recompences shall surely requite. 57 And I will make drunk her princes, and her wise *men*, her captains, and her rulers, and her mighty men: and they shall sleep a perpetual sleep, and not wake, saith the king, whose name *is* the LORD of hosts. 58 Thus saith the LORD of hosts; The broad walls of Babylon shall be utterly broken, and her high gates shall be burned with fire; and the people shall labour in vain, and the folk in the fire, and they shall be weary.

The particulars of this copious prophecy are dispersed and interwoven, and the same things left and returned to so often that it could not well be divided into parts, but we must endeavour to collect them under their proper heads. Let us then observe here,

I. An acknowledgment of the great pomp and power that Babylon had been in and the use that God in his providence had made of it (*v.* 7): *Babylon hath been a golden cup,* a rich and glorious empire, *a golden city* (Isa. xiv. 4), *a head of gold* (Dan. ii. 38), filled with all good things, as a cup with wine. Nay, she had been *a golden cup in the Lord's hand;* he had in a particular manner filled and favoured her with blessings; he had made the earth *drunk with this cup;* some were intoxicated with her pleasures and debauched by her, others intoxicated with her terrors and destroyed by her. In both senses the New-Testament Babylon is said to have made the kings of the earth drunk, Rev. xvii. 2; xviii. 3. Babylon had also been God's *battle-axe;* it was so at this time, when Jeremiah prophesied, and was likely to be yet more so, *v.* 20. The forces of Babylon were God's *weapons of war,* tools in his hand, with which he broke in pieces, and knocked down, *nations* and *kingdoms,—horses* and *chariots,* which are so much the strength of kingdoms (*v.* 21),—*man and woman, young and old,* with which kingdoms are replenished (*v.* 22),—*the shepherd and his flock, the husbandman and his oxen,* with which kingdoms are maintained and supplied, *v.* 23. Such havoc as this the Chaldeans had made when God employed them as instruments of his wrath for the chastising of the nations; and yet now Babylon itself must fall. Note, Those that have car-

ried all before them a great while will yet at length meet with their match, and their day also will come to fall; the rod will itself be thrown into the fire at last. Nor can any think it will exempt them from God's judgments that they have been instrumental in executing his judgments on others.

II. A just complaint made of Babylon, and a charge drawn up against her by the Israel of God. 1. She is complained of for her incorrigible wickedness (*v.* 9): *We would have healed Babylon, but she is not healed.* The people of God that were captives among the Babylonians endeavoured, according to the instructions given them (Jer. x. 11), to convince them of the folly of their idolatry, but they could not do it; still they doted as much as ever upon their graven images, and therefore the Israelites resolved to quit them and go to their own country. Yet some understand this as spoken by the forces they had hired for their assistance, declaring that they had done their best to save her from ruin, but that it was all to no purpose, and therefore they might as well go home to their respective countries; "for *her judgment reaches unto heaven,* and it is in vain to withstand it or think to avert it." 2. She is complained of for her inveterate malice against Israel. Other nations had been hardly used by the Chaldeans, but Israel only complains to God of it, and with confidence appeals to him (*v.* 34, 35): " *The king of Babylon has devoured me, and crushed me,* and never thought he could do enough to ruin me; *he has emptied me* of all that was valuable, has *swallowed me up as a dragon,* or whale, swallows up the little fish by shoals; *he has filled his belly,* filled his treasures, *with my delicates,* with all my pleasant things, *and has cast me out,* cast me away as a *vessel in which there is no pleasure;* and now let them be accountable for all this." *Zion and Jerusalem shall say,* "Let *the violence done to me and* my children, that are *my* own *flesh,* and pieces of myself, and all the blood of my people, which they have shed like water, *be upon* them; let the guilt of it lie upon them, and let it be required at their hands." Note, Ruin is not far off from those that lie under the guilt of wrong done to God's people.

III. Judgment given upon this appeal by the righteous Judge of heaven and earth, on behalf of Israel against Babylon. He *sits in the throne judging right,* is ready to receive complaints, and answers (*v.* 36): " *I will plead thy cause.* Leave it with me; I will in due time plead it effectually *and take vengeance for thee,* and every drop of Jerusalem's blood shall be accounted for with interest." Israel and Judah seemed to have been neglected and forgotten, but God had an eye to them, *v.* 5. It is true *their land was filled with sin against the Holy One of Israel.* They were a provoking people and their sins were a great offence to God, as a holy God, and as their God, their Holy One; and therefore he justly delivered them up into the hands of their enemies, and might justly have abandoned them and left them to perish in their hands; but God deals better with them than they deserve, and, notwithstanding their iniquities and his severities, *Israel is not forsaken*, is not cast off, though he be cast out, but is owned and looked after by his God, by the Lord of hosts. God is his God still, and will act for him as the Lord of hosts, a God of power. Note, Though God's people may have broken his laws and fallen under his rebukes, yet it does not therefore follow that they are thrown out of covenant; but God's care of them and love to them will *flourish again*, Ps. lxxxix. 30—33. The Chaldeans thought they should never be called to an account for what they had done against God's Israel; but there is *a time* fixed *for vengeance, v.* 6. We cannot expect it should come sooner than the time fixed, but then it will come; he *will render unto Babylon a recompence,* for the avenging of Israel is *the vengeance of the Lord,* who espouses their cause; it is *the vengeance of his temple, v* 11, as before, *ch.* l. 28. *The Lord God of recompences,* the *God to whom vengeance belongs, will surely requite* (*v.* 56), will pay them home; he will *render unto Babylon all the evil they have done in Zion* (*v.* 24); he will return it *in the sight* of his people. They shall have the satisfaction to see their cause pleaded with jealousy. They shall not only live to see those judgments brought upon Babylon, but they shall plainly see them to be the punishment of the wrong they have done to Zion; any man may see it, and say, *Verily there is a God that judges in the earth;* for just as *Babylon has caused the slain of Israel to fall,* has not only slain those that were found in arms, but all without distinction, even *all the land* (almost all were put to the sword), so *at Babylon shall fall* the slain not only of the city, but of *all the country, v.* 49. Cyrus shall measure to the Chaldeans the same that they measured to the Jews, so that every observer may discern that God is recompensing them for what they did against his people; but Zion's children shall in a particular manner triumph in it (*v.* 10): *The Lord has brought forth our righteousness;* he has appeared in our behalf against those that dealt unjustly with us, and has given us redress; he has also made it to appear that he is reconciled to us and that we are yet in his eyes a *righteous nation.* Let it therefore be spoken of to his praise: *Come and let us declare in Zion the work of the Lord our God,* that others may be invited to join with us in praising him.

IV. A declaration of the greatness and sovereignty of that God who espouses Zion's cause and undertakes to reckon with this proud and potent enemy, *v.* 14. It is *the Lord of hosts that has said it, that has sworn*

it, has *sworn it by himself* (for he could swear by no greater), that he will fill Babylon with vast and incredible numbers of the enemy's forces, will *fill it with men as with caterpillars,* that shall overpower it with multitudes, and need only to *lift up a shout* against it, for that shall be so terrible as to dispirit all the inhabitants and make them an easy prey to this numerous army. But who, and where, is he that can break so powerful a kingdom as Babylon? The prophet gives an account of him from the description he had formerly given of him, and of his sovereignty and victory over all pretenders (Jer. x. 12—16), which was there intended for the conviction of the Babylonian idolaters and the confirmation of God's Israel in the faith and worship of the God of Israel; and it is here repeated to show that God will convince those by his judgments who would not be convinced by his word that he is *God over all.* Let not any doubt but that he who has determined to destroy Babylon is able to make his words good, for, 1. He is the God that made the world (*v.* 15), and therefore nothing is too hard for him to do; it is in his name that our help stands, and on him our hope is built. 2. He has the command of all the creatures that he has made (*v.* 16); his providence is a continued creation. He has *wind and rain* at his disposal. If he speak the word, there is a *multitude of waters in the heavens* (and it is a wonder how they hang there), fed by *vapours out of the earth,* and it is a wonder how they ascend thence. *Lightnings and rain* seem contraries, as fire and water, and yet they are produced together; and the wind, which seems arbitrary in its motions, and we *know not whence it comes,* is yet, we are sure, brought *out of his treasuries.* 3. The idols that oppose the accomplishment of his word are a mere sham and their worshippers brutish people, *v.* 17, 18. The idols are falsehood, they are vanity, they are *the work of errors;* when they come to be visited (to be examined and enquired into) *they perish,* that is, their reputation sinks and they appear to be nothing; and those *that make them are like unto them.* But between the God of Israel and these gods of the heathen there is no comparison (*v.* 19): *The portion of Jacob is not like them;* the God who speaks this and will do it is the *former of all things* and *the Lord of all hosts,* and therefore can do what he will; and there is a near relation between him and his people, for he is *their portion* and they are his; they put a confidence in him as their portion and he is pleased to take a complacency in them and a particular care of them as the *lot of his inheritance;* and therefore he will do what is best for them. The repetition of these things here, which were said before, intimates both the certainty and the importance of them, and obliges us to take special notice of them;

God hath spoken once; yea, twice have we heard this, that power belongs to God, power to destroy the most formidable enemies of his church; and if God thus *speak once, yea, twice*, we are inexcusable if we do not perceive it and attend to it.

V. A description of the instruments that are to be employed in this service. God has *raised up the spirit of the kings of the Medes* (*v.* 11), Darius and Cyrus, who come against Babylon by a divine instinct; for *God's device is against Babylon to destroy it.* They do it, but God devised it, he designed it; they are but accomplishing his purpose, and acting as he directed. Note, God's counsel shall stand, and according to it all hearts shall move. Those whom God employs against Babylon are compared (*v.* 1) to a *destroying wind*, which either by its coldness blasts the fruits of the earth or by its fierceness blows down all before it. This wind is *brought out of God's treasuries* (*v.* 16), and it is here said to be *raised up against those that dwell in the midst of the Chaldeans*, those of other nations that inhabit among them and are incorporated with them. The Chaldeans rise up against God by falling down before idols, and against them God will raise up destroyers, for he will be too hard for those that contend with him. These enemies are compared to fanners (*v.* 2), who shall *drive them away as chaff* is driven away by the fan. The Chaldeans had been fanners to winnow God's people (*ch.* xv. 7) and to empty them, and now they shall themselves be in like manner despoiled and dispersed.

VI. An ample commission given them to destroy and lay all waste. Let them *bend their bow* against the archers of the Chaldeans (*v.* 3) and *not spare her young men*, but *utterly destroy them*, for the Lord has *both devised and done what he spoke against Babylon, v.* 12. This may animate the instruments he employs, by assuring them of success. The methods they take are such as God has devised and therefore they shall surely prosper; what he has spoken shall be done, for he himself will do it; and therefore let all necessary preparations be made. This they are called to, *v.* 27, 28. Let *a standard be set up*, under which to enlist soldiers for this expedition; *let a trumpet be blown* to call men together to it and animate them in it; let the nations, out of which Cyrus's army is to be raised, prepare their recruits; let the kingdoms of *Ararat*, and *Minni, and Ashkenaz*, of Armenia, both the higher and the lower, and of Ascania, about Phrygia and Bithynia, send in their quota of men for his service; let general officers be appointed and the cavalry advance; let the horses come up in *great numbers*, as the *caterpillars*, and come, like them, leaping and pawing in the valley; let them lay the country waste, as *caterpillars* do (Joel i. 4), especially rough caterpillars; let the kings and captains prepare nations against Babylon, for the service is great and there is occasion for many hands to be employed it.

VII. The weakness of the Chaldeans, and their inability to make head against this threatening destroying force. When God employed them against other nations they had spirit and strength to act offensively, and went on with admirable resolution, conquering and to conquer; but now that it comes to their turn to be reckoned with all their might and courage are gone, their hearts fail them, and none of all their men of might and mettle have found their hands to act so much as defensively. They are called upon here to prepare for action, but it is ironically and in an upbraiding way (*v.* 11): *Make bright the arrows*, which have grown rusty through disuse; *gather the shields*, which in a long time of peace and security have been scattered and thrown out of the way (*v.* 12); *set up the standard upon the walls of Babylon*, upon the towers on those walls, to summon all that owed suit and service to that mother-city, now to come in to her assistance; let them make the watch as strong as they can, and appoint the sentinels to their respective posts, and prepare ambushes for the reception of the enemy. This intimates that they would be found very secure and remiss, and would need to be thus quickened (and they were so to such a degree that they were in the midst of their revels when the city was taken), but that all their preparations should be to no purpose. Whoever will may call them to it, but they shall have no heart to come at the call, *v.* 29. *The* whole *land shall tremble, and sorrow* (a universal consternation) shall seize upon them; for they shall see both the irresistible arm and the irreversible counsel and decree of God against them. They shall see that God is making *Babylon a desolation*, and therein is performing what he has purposed; and then *the mighty men of Babylon have forborne to fight, v.* 30. God having taken away their strength and spirit, so that they have *remained in their holds*, not daring so much as to peep forth, the might both of their hearts and of their hands fails; they *become* as timorous *as women*, so that the enemy has, without any resistance, *burnt her dwelling-places* and *broken her bars*. It is to the same purport with *v.* 56—58. When the spoiler comes upon Babylon her mighty men, who should make head against him, are immediately taken, their weapons of war fail them, *every one of their bows is broken* and stands them in no stead. Their politics fail them; they call councils of war, but their princes and captains, who sit in council to concert measures for the common safety, are made drunk; they are as men intoxicated through stupidity or despair; they can form no right notions of things; they stagger and are unsteady in their counsels and resolves, and dash one against another, and, like drunken men, fall out among themselves. At length they *sleep a perpetual sleep*, and never *awake* from their wine, the wine of God's wrath, for it is to them an opiate that lays them into a fatal lethargy. The *walls of their city* fail them, *v.* 58. When the enemy had found ways to ford Euphrates, which was thought impassable, yet surely, think they, the walls are impregnable, they are *the broad walls of Babylon* or (as the margin reads it), *the walls of broad Babylon.* The compass of the city, within the walls, was 385 furlongs, some say 480, that is, about sixty miles; the walls were 200 cubits high, and fifty cubits broad, so that two chariots might easily pass by one another upon them. Some say that there was a threefold wall about the inner city and the like about the outer, and that the stones of the wall, being laid in pitch instead of mortar (Gen. xi. 3), were scarcely separable; and yet these shall be *utterly broken*, and *the high gates and towers shall be burnt*, and the people that are employed in the defence of the city shall *labour in vain in the fire;* they shall quite tire themselves, but shall do no good.

VIII. The destruction that shall be made of Babylon by these invaders. 1. It is a certain destruction; the doom has passed and it cannot be reversed; a divine power is engaged against it, which cannot be resisted (*v.* 8): *Babylon is fallen and destroyed*, is as sure to fall, to fall into destruction, as if it were fallen and destroyed already; though when Jeremiah prophesied this, and many a year after, it was in the height of its power and greatness. God declares, God appears against Babylon (*v.* 25): *Behold, I am against thee;* and those cannot stand long whom God is against. He will *stretch out his hand upon* it, a hand which no creature can bear the weight of nor withstand the force of. It is his purpose, which shall be performed, that *Babylon* must be a *desolation, v.* 29. 2. It is a righteous destruction. Babylon has made herself meet for it, and therefore cannot fail to meet with it. For (*v.* 25) *Babylon* has been *a destroying mountain*, very lofty and bulky as a mountain, and *destroying all the earth*, as the stones that are tumbled from high mountains spoil the grounds about them; but now it shall itself be *rolled down from its rocks*, which were as the foundations on which it stood. It shall be levelled, its pomp and power broken. It is now a burning mountain, like Ætna and the other volcanoes, that throw out fire, to the terror of all about them. But it shall be a burnt mountain; it shall at length have consumed itself, and shall remain a heap of ashes. So will this world be at the end of time. Again (*v.* 33), "*Babylon is like a threshing-floor*, in which the people of God have been long threshed, as sheaves in the floor; but now the time has come that she shall herself be threshed and her sheaves in her; her princes and great men, and all her inhabitants, shall be beaten in their own land, as in the thresh-

ing-floor. The threshing-floor is prepared. Babylon is by sin made meet to be a seat of war, and her people, like corn in harvest, are ripe for destruction," Rev. xiv. 15; Mic. iv. 12. 3. It is an unavoidable destruction. Babylon seems to be well-fenced and fortified against it : *She dwells upon many waters* (*v.* 13); the situation of her country is such that it seems inaccessible, it is so surrounded, and the march of an enemy into it so embarrassed, by rivers. In allusion to this, the New-Testament Babylon is said to *sit upon many waters*, that is, to rule over many nations, as the other Babylon did, Rev. xvii. 15. *Babylon* is *abundant in treasures;* and yet "*thy end has come*, and neither thy waters nor thy wealth shall secure thee " This end that comes shall be *the measure of thy covetousness;* it shall be the stint of thy gettings, it shall set bounds to thy ambition and avarice, which otherwise would have been boundless. God, by the destruction of Babylon, said to its proud waves, *Hitherto shall you come, and no further.* Note, If men will not set a measure to their covetousness by wisdom and grace, God will set a measure to it by his judgments. Babylon, thinking herself very safe and very great, was very proud; but she will be deceived (*v.* 53): *Though Babylon should mount* her walls and palaces *up to heaven*, and though (because what is high is apt to totter) she should take care to *fortify the height of her strength*, yet all will not do; God will send spoilers against her, that shall break through her strength and bring down her height. 4. It is a gradual destruction, which, if they had pleased, they might have foreseen and had warning of; for (*v.* 46) " *A rumour will come one year* that Cyrus is making vast preparations for war, *and after that, in another year, shall come a rumour* that his design is upon Babylon, and he is steering his course that way;" so that when he was a great way off they might have sent and desired conditions of peace; but they were too proud, too secure, to do that, and their hearts were hardened to their destruction. 5. Yet, when it comes, it is a surprising destruction : *Babylon has suddenly fallen* (*v.* 8); the destruction came upon them when they did not think of it and was perfected in a little time, as that of the New-Testament *Babylon—in one hour*, Rev. xviii. 17. The king of Babylon, who should have been observing the approaches of the enemy, was himself at such a distance from the place where the attack was made that it was a great while ere he had notice that the city was taken; so that those who were posted near the place sent one messenger, one courier, after another, with advice of it, *v.* 31. The foot-posts shall meet at the court from several quarters with this intelligence to the king of Babylon that his *city is taken at one end*, and there is nothing to obstruct the progress of the conquerors, but they will be at the other end quickly. They are to tell him that the enemy has *seized the passes* (*v.* 32), the forts or blockades upon the river, and that, having got over the river, he has set fire to the reeds on the river side, to alarm and terrify the city, so that all the men of war are affrighted and have thrown down their arms and surrendered at discretion. The messengers come, like Job's, one upon the heels of another, with these tidings, which are immediately confirmed with a witness by the enemies' being in the palace and slaying the king himself, Dan. v. 30. That profane feast which they were celebrating at the very time when the city was taken, which was both an evidence of their strange security and a great advantage to the enemy, seems here to be referred to (*v.* 38, 39) : *They shall roar together like lions*, as men in their revels do, when the wine has got into their heads. They call it *singing*; but in scripture-language, and in the language of sober men, it is called *yelling like lions' whelps*. It is probable that they were drinking confusion to Cyrus and his army with loud huzzas. Well, says God, in their heat, when they are inflamed (Isa. v. 11) and their heads are hot with hard drinking, I will *make their feasts*, I will *give them their portion*. They have passed their cup round; now *the cup of the Lord's right hand shall be turned unto them* (Hab. ii. 15, 16), a cup of fury, which shall *make them drunk that they may rejoice* (or rather *that they may revel it*) and *sleep a perpetual sleep :* let them be as merry as they can with that bitter cup, but it shall lay them to sleep never to wake more (as *v.* 57); for *on that night*, in the midst of the jollity, was *Belshazzar slain*. 6. It is to be a universal destruction. God will make thorough work of it; for, as he will perform what he has purposed, so he will perfect what he has begun. *The slain shall fall* in great abundance throughout *the land of the Chaldeans ;* multitudes shall be *thrust through in her streets*, *v.* 4. They are *brought down like lambs to the slaughter* (*v.* 40), in such great numbers, so easily, and the enemies make no more of killing them than the butcher does of killing lambs. The strength of the enemy, and their invading them, are here compared to an irruption and inundation of waters (*v.* 42): *The sea has come up upon Babylon*, which, when it has once broken through its bounds, there is no fence against, so that she is *covered with the multitude of its waves*, overpowered by a numerous army ; *her cities* then become *a desolation*, an uninhabited uncultivated desert, *v.* 43. 7. It is a destruction that shall reach the gods of Babylon, the idols and images, and fall with a particular weight upon them. " In token that *the whole land shall be confounded* and all *her slain shall fall*, and that throughout all the country *the wounded shall groan, I will do judgment upon her graven images*," *v.* 47 and again *v.* 52. All must needs perish if their gods perish, from whom

they expect protection. Though the invaders are themselves idolaters, yet they shall destroy the images and temples of the gods of Babylon, as an earnest of the abolishing of all counterfeit deities. Bel was the principal idol that the Babylonians worshipped, and therefore that is by name here marked for destruction (*v.* 44) : *I will punish Bel*, that great devourer, that image to which such abundance of sacrifices are offered and such rich spoils dedicated, and to whose temple there is such a vast resort. He shall disgorge what he has so greedily regaled himself with. God will bring forth out of his temple all the wealth laid up there, Job xx. 15. His altars shall be forsaken, none shall regard him any more, and so that idol which was thought to be a wall to Babylon shall fall and fail them. 8. It shall be a final destruction. You may *take balm for her pain*, but in vain ; she that *would not be healed* by the word of God *shall not be healed* by his providence, v. 8, 9. *Babylon* shall *become heaps* (*v.* 37), and, to complete its infamy, no use shall be made even of the ruins of Babylon, so execrable shall they be, and attended with such ill omens (*v.* 26): *They shall not take of thee a stone for a corner, nor a stone for foundations*. People shall not care for having any thing to do with Babylon, or whatever belonged to it. Or it denotes that there shall be nothing left in Babylon on which to ground any hopes or attempts of raising it into a kingdom again ; for, as it follows here, *it shall be desolate for ever*. St. Jerome says that in his time, though the ruins of Babylon's walls were to be seen, yet the ground enclosed by them was a forest of wild beasts.

IX. Here is a call to God's people to go out of Babylon. It is their wisdom, when the ruin is approaching, to quit the city and retire into the country (*v.* 6) : " *Flee out of the midst of Babylon*, and get into some remote corner, that you may save your lives, and may not be cut off in her iniquity." When God's judgments are abroad it is good to get as far as we can from those against whom they are levelled, as Israel from the tents of Korah. This agrees with the advice Christ gave his disciples, with reference to the destruction of Jerusalem. *Let those who shall be in Judea flee to the mountains*, Matt. xxiv. 16. It is their wisdom to *get out of the midst of Babylon*, lest they be involved, if not in her ruins, yet in her fears (*v.* 45, 46) : *Lest your heart faint, and you fear for the rumour that shall be heard in the land*. Though God had told them that Cyrus should be their deliverer, and Babylon's destruction their deliverance, yet they had been told also that *in the peace thereof they should have peace*, and therefore the alarms given to Babylon would put them into a fright, and perhaps they might not have faith and consideration enough to suppress those fears, for which reason they are here advised to get out of the hearing of the alarms. Note, Those who have not grace enough to keep their temper in temptation should have wisdom enough to keep out of the way of temptation. But this is not all; it is not only their wisdom to quit the city when the ruin is approaching, but it is their duty to quit the country too when the ruin is accomplished, and they are set at liberty by the pulling down of the prison over their heads. This they are told, *v.* 50, 51: "*You* Israelites, *who have escaped the sword of the Chaldeans* your oppressors, and of the Persians their destroyers, now that the year of release has come, *go away, stand not still;* hasten to your own country again, however you may be comfortably seated in Babylon, for this is not your rest, but Canaan is." 1. He puts them in mind of the inducements they had to return: "*Remember the Lord afar off,* his presence with you now, though you are here afar off from your native soil; his presence with your fathers formerly in the temple, though you are now afar off from the ruins of it." Note, Wherever we are, in the greatest depths, at the greatest distances, we may and must remember the Lord our God; and in the time of the greatest fears and hopes it is seasonable to *remember the Lord.* "And let Jerusalem come into your mind. Though it be now in ruins, yet *favour its dust* (Ps. cii. 14); though few of you ever saw it, yet believe the report you have had concerning it from those that *wept when they remembered Zion;* and think of Jerusalem until you come up to a resolution to make the best of your way thither." Note, When the city of our solemnities is out of sight, yet it must not be out of mind; and it will be of great use to us, in our journey through this world, to let the heavenly Jerusalem come often into our mind. 2. He takes notice of the discouragement which the returning captives labour under (*v.* 51); being reminded of Jerusalem, they cry out, "*We are confounded;* we cannot bear the thought of it; *shame covers our faces* at the mention of it, for *we have heard of the reproach of the sanctuary,* that is profaned and ruined by strangers; how can we think of it with any pleasure?" To this he answers (*v.* 52) that the God of Israel will now triumph over the gods of Babylon, and so that reproach will be for ever rolled away. Note, The believing prospect of Jerusalem's recovery will keep us from being ashamed of Jerusalem's ruins.

X. Here is the diversified feeling excited by Babylon's fall, and it is the same that we have with respect to the *New-Testament Babylon,* Rev. xviii. 9, 19. 1. Some shall lament the destruction of Babylon. There *is the sound of a cry,* a great outcry coming from Babylon (*v.* 54), lamenting this great destruction, the voice of mourning, because the Lord has *destroyed the voice* of the multitude, that great voice of mirth which used

to be heard in Babylon, *v.* 55. We are told what they shall say in their lamentations (*v.* 41): "*How is Sheshach taken,* and how are we mistaken concerning her! How is that city surprised and become an *astonishment among the nations* that was the praise, and glory, and admiration of the whole earth!" See how that may fall into a general contempt which has been universally cried up. 2. Yet some shall rejoice in Babylon's fall, not as it is the misery of their fellow-creatures, but as it is the manifestation of the righteous judgment of God and as it opens the way for the release of God's captives; upon these accounts *the heaven and the earth, and all that is in both, shall sing for Babylon* (*v.* 48); the church in heaven and the church on earth shall give to God the glory of his righteousness, and take notice of it with thankfulness to his praise. Babylon's ruin is Zion's praise.

59 The word which Jeremiah the prophet commanded Seraiah the son of Neriah, the son of Maaseiah, when he went with Zedekiah the king of Judah into Babylon in the fourth year of his reign. And *this* Seraiah *was* a quiet prince. 60 So Jeremiah wrote in a book all the evil that should come upon Babylon, *even* all these words that are written against Babylon. 61 And Jeremiah said to Seraiah, When thou comest to Babylon, and shalt see, and shalt read all these words; 62 Then shalt thou say, O LORD, thou hast spoken against this place, to cut it off, that none shall remain in it, neither man nor beast, but that it shall be desolate for ever. 63 And it shall be, when thou hast made an end of reading this book, *that* thou shalt bind a stone to it, and cast it into the midst of Euphrates: 64 And thou shalt say, Thus shall Babylon sink, and shall not rise from the evil that I will bring upon her: and they shall be weary. Thus far *are* the words of Jeremiah.

We have been long attending the judgment of Babylon in this and the foregoing chapter; now here we have, the conclusion of that whole matter. 1. A copy is taken of this prophecy, it should seem by Jeremiah himself, for Baruch his scribe is not mentioned here (*v.* 60): *Jeremiah wrote in a book all these words that are here written against Babylon.* He received this notice that he might give it to all whom it might concern. It is of great advantage both to the propagating and to the perpetuating of the word of God to have it written, and to have copies taken of the law, prophets, and epistles. 2. It is sent to Babylon, to the captives there, by the hand of Seraiah, who went there attendant on or ambassador for king Zedekiah, *in the fourth year of his reign, v.* 59. He *went with Zedekiah,* or (as the margin reads it) *on the behalf of Zedekiah, into Babylon.* The character given of him is observable, that this *Seraiah was a quiet prince,* a prince of rest. He was in honour and power, but not, as most of the princes then were, hot and heady, making parties, and heading factions, and driving things furiously. He was of a calm temper, studied the things that made for peace, endeavoured to preserve a good understanding between the king his master and the king of Babylon, and to keep his master from rebelling. He was no persecutor of God's prophets, but a moderate man. Zedekiah was happy in the choice of such a man to be his envoy to the king of Babylon, and Jeremiah might safely entrust such a man with his errand too. Note, It is the real honour of great men to be quiet men, and it is the wisdom of princes to put such into places of trust. 3. Seraiah is desired to read it to his countrymen that had already gone into captivity: " *When thou shalt come to Babylon, and shalt see* what a magnificent place it is, how large a city, how strong, how rich, and how well fortified, and shalt therefore be tempted to think, Surely, it will stand for ever" (as the disciples, when they observed the buildings of the temple, concluded that nothing would *throw them down* but the end of the world, Matt. xxiv. 3), " *then thou shalt read all these words* to thyself and thy particular friends, for their encouragement in their captivity: let them with an eye of faith see to the end of these threatening powers, and comfort themselves and one another herewith." 4. He is directed to make a solemn protestation of the divine authority and unquestionable certainty of that which he had read (*v.* 62): *Then thou shalt* look up to God, and say, *O Lord! it is thou that hast spoken against this place, to cut it off.* This is like the angel's protestation concerning the destruction of the New-Testament Babylon. *These are the true sayings of God,* Rev. xix. 9. *These words are true and faithful,* Rev. xxi. 5. Though Seraiah sees Babylon flourishing, having read this prophecy he must foresee Babylon falling, and by virtue of it must curse its habitation, though it be *taking root* (Job v. 3): " *O Lord! thou hast spoken against this place,* and I believe what thou hast spoken, that, as thou knowest every thing, so thou canst do every thing. Thou hast passed sentence upon Babylon, and it shall be executed. *Thou hast spoken against this place, to cut it off,* and therefore we will neither envy its pomp nor fear its power." When we see what this world is, how glittering its shows are and how flattering its proposals, let us read in the book of the Lord that its

fashion passes away, and it shall shortly be *cut off* and be *desolate for ever,* and we shall learn to look upon it with a holy contempt. Observe here, When we have been reading the word of God it becomes us to direct to him whose word it is a humble believing acknowledgment of the truth, equity, and goodness, of what we have read. 5. He must then tie a stone to the book and throw it into the midst of the river Euphrates, as a confirming sign of the things contained in it, saying, *" Thus shall Babylon sink, and not rise ;* for they *shall be weary,* they shall perfectly succumb, as men tired with a burden, under the load of *the evil that I will bring upon them,* which they shall never shake off, nor get from under," *v.* 53, 64. In the sign it was the stone that sunk the book, which otherwise would have swum. But in *the thing signified* it was rather the book that sunk the stone ; it was the divine sentence passed upon Babylon in this prophecy that sunk that city, which seemed *as firm as a stone.* The fall of the New-Testament Babylon was represented by something like this, but much more magnificent, Rev. xviii. 21. *A mighty angel cast a great millstone into the sea, saying, Thus shall Babylon fall.* Those that sink under the weight of God's wrath and curse sink irrecoverably. The last words of the chapter seal up the vision and prophecy of this book : *Thus far are the words of Jeremiah.* Not that this prophecy against Babylon was the last of his prophecies ; for it was dated in the *fourth* year of Zedekiah (*v.* 59), long before he finished his testimony ; but this is recorded last of his prophecies because it was to be last accomplished of all his prophecies against the Gentiles, *ch.* xlvi. 1. And the chapter which remains is purely historical, and, as some think, was added by some other hand.

CHAP. LII.

History is the best expositor of prophecy ; and therefore, for the better understanding of the prophecies of this book, which relate to the destruction of Jerusalem and the kingdom of Judah, we are here furnished with an account of that sad event. It is much the same with the history we had 2 Kings xxiv and xxv., and many of the particulars we had before in that book, but the matter is here repeated and put together, to give light to the book of the Lamentations, which follows next, and to serve as a key to it. That article in the close concerning the advancement of Jehoiachin in his captivity, which follows after Jeremiah's time, gives colour to the conjecture of those who suppose that this chapter was not written by Jeremiah himself, but by some man divinely inspired among those in captivity, for a constant memorandum to those who in Babylon preferred Jerusalem above their chief joy. In this chapter we have, I. The bad reign of Zedekiah, very bad in regard both of sin and of punishment, ver. 1—3. II. The besieging and taking of Jerusalem by the Chaldeans, ver. 4—7. III. The severe usage which Zedekiah and the princes met with, ver. 8—11. IV. The destruction of the temple and the city, ver. 12—14. V. The captivity of the people (ver. 15, 16) and the numbers of those that were carried away into captivity, ver. 28—30. VI. The carrying off of the plunder of the temple, ver. 17—23. VII. The slaughter of the priests, and some other great men, in cold blood, ver. 24—27. VIII. The better days which king Jehoiachin lived to see in the latter end of his time, after the death of Nebuchadnezzar, ver. 31—34.

ZEDEKIAH *was* one and twenty years old when he began to reign, and he reigned eleven years in Jerusalem. And his mother's name *was*

Hamutal the daughter of Jeremiah of Libnah. 2 And he did *that which was* evil in the eyes of the LORD, according to all that Jehoiakim had done. 3 For through the anger of the LORD it came to pass in Jerusalem and Judah, till he had cast them out from his presence, that Zedekiah rebelled against the king of Babylon. 4 And it came to pass in the ninth year of his reign, in the tenth month, in the tenth *day* of the month, *that* Nebuchadrezzar king of Babylon came, he and all his army, against Jerusalem, and pitched against it, and built forts against it round about. 5 So the city was besieged unto the eleventh year of king Zedekiah. 6 And in the fourth month, in the ninth *day* of the month, the famine was sore in the city, so that there was no bread for the people of the land. 7 Then the city was broken up, and all the men of war fled, and went forth out of the city by night by the way of the gate between the two walls, which *was* by the king's garden; (now the Chaldeans *were* by the city round about:) and they went by the way of the plain. 8 But the army of the Chaldeans pursued after the king, and overtook Zedekiah in the plains of Jericho; and all his army was scattered from him. 9 Then they took the king, and carried him up unto the king of Babylon to Riblah in the land of Hamath; where he gave judgment upon him. 10 And the king of Babylon slew the sons of Zedekiah before his eyes: he slew also all the princes of Judah in Riblah. 11 Then he put out the eyes of Zedekiah; and the king of Babylon bound him in chains, and carried him to Babylon, and put him in prison till the day of his death.

This narrative begins no higher than the beginning of the reign of Zedekiah, though there were two captivities before, one in the fourth year of Jehoiakim, the other in the first of Jeconiah; but probably it was drawn up by some of those that were carried away with Zedekiah, as a reproach to themselves for imagining that they should not go into captivity after their brethren, with which hopes they had long flattered themselves. We have here, 1. God's just displeasure against Judah and Jerusalem for their sin, *v.* 3. His anger was against them to such a degree that he determined to *cast them out from his presence*, his favourable gracious presence, as a father, when he is extremely angry with an undutiful son, bids him get out of his presence. He expelled them from that good land that had such tokens of his presence in providential bounty and that holy city and temple that had such tokens of his presence in covenant-grace and love. Note, Those that are banished from God's ordinances have reason to complain that they are in some degree *cast out of his presence;* yet none are cast out from God's gracious presence but those that by sin have first thrown themselves out of it. This fruit of sin we should therefore deprecate above any thing, as David (Ps. li. 11), *Cast me not away from thy presence.* 2. Zedekiah's bad conduct and management, to which God left him, in displeasure against the people, and for which God punished him, in displeasure against him. Zedekiah had arrived at years of discretion when he came to the throne; he *was twenty-one years old* (*v.* 1); he was none of the worst of the kings (we never read of his idolatries), yet his character is that he *did evil in the eyes of the Lord,* for he did not do the good he should have done. But that evil deed of his which did in a special manner hasten this destruction was his *rebelling against the king of Babylon,* which was both his sin and his folly, and brought ruin upon his people, not only meritoriously, but efficiently. God was greatly displeased with him for his perfidious dealing with the king of Babylon (as we find, Ezek. xvii. 15, &c.); and, because he was angry at Judah and Jerusalem, he put him into the hand of his own counsels, to do that foolish thing which proved fatal to him and his kingdom. 3. The possession which the Chaldeans at length gained of Jerusalem, after eighteen months' siege. They sat down before it, and blocked it up, in the ninth year of Zedekiah's reign, in the tenth month (*v.* 4), and made themselves masters of it in the *eleventh year in the fourth month,* *v.* 6. In remembrance of these two steps towards their ruin, while they were in captivity, they kept a *fast in the fourth month, and a fast in the tenth* (Zech. viii. 19): that in the *fifth month* was in remembrance of the burning of the temple, and that in the *seventh* of the murder of Gedaliah. We may easily imagine, or rather cannot imagine, what a sad time it was with Jerusalem, during this year and half that it was besieged, when all provisions were cut off from coming to them and they were ever and anon alarmed by the attacks of the enemy, and, being obstinately resolved to hold out to the last extremity, nothing remained but a *certain fearful looking for of judgment.* That which disabled them to hold out, and yet could not prevail with them to capitulate, was the *famine in the city* (v. 6); there was *no bread for the people of the land,* so that the soldiers could not make good their posts, but were rendered wholly unserviceable; and then no wonder that *the city was broken up, v.* 7. Walls, in such a case, will not hold out long without men, any more than men without walls; nor will both together stand people in any stead without God and his protection. 4. The inglorious retreat of the king and his mighty men. They got out of the city *by night* (v. 7) and made the best of their way, I know not whither, nor perhaps they themselves; but the king was overtaken by the pursuers *in the plains of Jericho,* his guards were dispersed, and all his army was *scattered from him, v.* 8. His fright was not causeless, for where there is guilt there will be fear in time of danger: but his flight was fruitless, for there is no escaping the judgments of God; they will *come upon the sinner,* and will *overtake him,* let him flee where he will (Deut. xxviii. 15), and these judgments particularly that are here executed were there threatened, *v.* 52, 53, &c. 5. The sad doom passed upon Zedekiah by the king of Babylon, and immediately put in execution. He treated him as a rebel, *gave judgment upon him, v.* 9. One cannot think of it without the utmost vexation and regret that a king, a king of Judah, a king of the house of David, should be arraigned as a criminal at the bar of this heathen king. But he *humbled not himself before Jeremiah* the prophet; therefore God thus humbled him. Pursuant to the sentence passed upon him by the haughty conqueror, *his sons were slain before his eyes,* and all *the princes of Judah* (v. 10); then *his eyes were put out,* and he was *bound in chains,* carried in triumph to Babylon; perhaps they made sport with him, as they did with Samson when his eyes were put out; however, he was condemned to perpetual imprisonment, wearing out the remainder of his life (I cannot say his days, for he saw day no more) in darkness and misery. He was kept in prison till *the day of his death,* but had some honour done him at his funeral, *ch.* xxxiv. 5. Jeremiah had often told him what it would come to, but he would not take warning when he might have prevented it.

12 Now in the fifth month, in the tenth *day* of the month, which *was* the nineteenth year of Nebuchadrezzar king of Babylon, came Nebuzar-adan, captain of the guard, *which* served the king of Babylon, into Jerusalem, 13 And burned the house of the LORD, and the king's house; and all the houses of Jerusalem, and all the houses of the great *men,* burned he with fire: 14 And all the army

of the Chaldeans, that *were* with the captain of the guard, brake down all the walls of Jerusalem round about. 15 Then Nebuzar-adan the captain of the guard carried away captive *certain* of the poor of the people, and the residue of the people that remained in the city, and those that fell away, that fell to the king of Babylon, and the rest of the multitude. 16 But Nebuzar-adan the captain of the guard left *certain* of the poor of the land for vine-dressers and for husbandmen. 17 Also the pillars of brass that *were* in the house of the LORD, and the bases, and the brasen sea that *was* in the house of the LORD, the Chaldeans brake, and carried all the brass of them to Babylon. 18 The caldrons also, and the shovels, and the snuffers, and the bowls, and the spoons, and all the vessels of brass wherewith they ministered, took they away. 19 And the basons, and the fire-pans, and the bowls, and the caldrons, and the candlesticks, and the spoons, and the cups; *that* which *was* of gold *in* gold, and *that* which *was* of silver *in* silver, took the captain of the guard away. 20 The two pillars, one sea, and twelve brasen bulls that *were* under the bases, which king Solomon had made in the house of the LORD: the brass of all these vessels was without weight. 21 And *concerning* the pillars, the height of one pillar *was* eighteen cubits; and a fillet of twelve cubits did compass it; and the thickness thereof *was* four fingers: *it was* hollow. 22 And a chapiter of brass *was* upon it; and the height of one chapiter *was* five cubits, with net-work and pomegranates upon the chapiters round about, all *of* brass. The second pillar also and the pomegranates *were* like unto these. 23 And there were ninety and six pomegranates on a side; *and* all the pomegranates upon the network *were* a hundred round about.

We have here an account of the woeful havoc that was made by the Chaldean army, a month after the city was taken, under the command of Nebuzaradan, who was *captain of the guard,* or general of the army, in this action. In the margin he is called the *chief* of the slaughter-men, or *executioners;* for soldiers are but slaughter-men, and God employs them as executioners of his sentence against a sinful people. Nebuzaradan was chief of those soldiers, but, in the execution he did, we have reason to fear he had no eye to God, but he served the king of Babylon and his own designs, now that he came into Jerusalem, into the very bowels of it, as captain of the slaughter-men there. And, 1. He laid the temple in ashes, having first plundered it of every thing that was valuable: He *burnt the house of the Lord,* that holy and beautiful house, where their *fathers praised him,* Isa. lxiv. 11. 2. He burnt the royal palace, probably that which Solomon built after he had built the temple, which was, ever since, *the king's house.* 3. He burnt *all the houses of Jerusalem,* that is, all the houses of the great men, or those particularly; if any escaped, it was only some sorry cottages for the poor of the land. 4. He *broke down all the walls of Jerusalem,* to be revenged upon them for standing in the way of his army so long. Thus, of a defenced city, it was made a ruin, Isa. xxv. 2. 5. He *carried away many into captivity* (*v.* 15); he took away *certain of the poor of the people,* that is, of the people in the city, for *the poor of the land* (the poor of the country) he left for *vine-dressers and husbandmen.* He also carried off *the residue of the people that remained in the city,* that had escaped the sword and famine, and the deserters, such as he thought fit, or rather such as God thought fit; for he had already determined some for the *pestilence,* some for the *sword,* some for *famine,* and some for *captivity,* ch. xv. 2. But, 6. Nothing is more particularly and largely related here than the carrying away of the appurtenances of the temple. All that were of great value were carried away before, *the vessels of silver and gold,* yet some of that sort remained, which were now carried away, *v.* 19. But most of the temple-prey that was now seized was of brass, which, being of less value, was carried off last. When the gold was gone, the brass soon went after it, because the people repented not, according to Jeremiah's prediction, *ch.* xxvii. 19, &c. When the walls of the city were demolished, the pillars of the temple were pulled down too, and both in token that God, who was the strength and stay both of their civil and their ecclesiastical government, had departed from them. No walls can protect those, nor pillars sustain those, from whom God withdraws. These pillars of the temple were not for support (for there was nothing built upon them), but for ornament and significancy. They were called *Jachin—He will establish;* and *Boaz—In him is strength;* so that the breaking of these signified that God would no longer establish his house nor be the strength of it. These pillars are here very particularly described (*v.* 21—23, from 1 Kings vii. 15),

that the extraordinary beauty and stateliness of them may affect us the more with the demolishing of them. All the vessels that belonged to the brazen altar were carried away; for the iniquity of Jerusalem, like that of Eli's house, was not to be purged by sacrifice or offering, 1 Sam. iii. 14. It is said (*v.* 20), *The brass of all these vessels was without weight;* so it was in the making of them (1 Kings vii. 47), *the weight of the brass was not* then *found out* (2 Chron. iv. 18), and so it was in the destroying of them. Those that made great spoil of them did not stand to weigh them, as purchasers do, for, whatever they weighed, it was all their own.

24 And the captain of the guard took Seraiah the chief priest, and Zephaniah the second priest, and the three keepers of the door: 25 He took also out of the city an eunuch, which had the charge of the men of war; and seven men of them that were near the king's person, which were found in the city; and the principal scribe of the host, who mustered the people of the land; and threescore men of the people of the land, that were found in the midst of the city. 26 So Nebuzar-adan the captain of the guard took them, and brought them to the king of Babylon to Riblah. 27 And the king of Babylon smote them, and put them to death in Riblah in the land of Hamath. Thus Judah was carried away captive out of his own land. 28 This *is* the people whom Nebuchadrezzar carried away captive: in the seventh year three thousand Jews and three and twenty: 29 In the eighteenth year of Nebuchadrezzar he carried away captive from Jerusalem eight hundred thirty and two persons: 30 In the three and twentieth year of Nebuchadrezzar Nebuzar-adan the captain of the guard carried away captive of the Jews seven hundred forty and five persons: all the persons *were* four thousand and six hundred.

We have here a very melancholy account, 1. Of the slaughter of some great men, in cold blood, at Riblah, seventy-two in number (according to the number of the elders of Israel, Num. xi. 24, 25), so they are computed, 2 Kings xxv. 18, 19. We read there of five out of the temple, two out of the city, five out of the court, and sixty out of the country. The account here agrees with that, except in one article; there it is said that there were five, here there were seven, of those that were *near the king,* which Dr. Lightfoot reconciles thus, that he took away seven of those that were near the king, but two of them were Jeremiah himself and Ebed-melech, who were both discharged, as we have read before, so that there were only five of them put to death, and so the number was reduced to seventy-two, some of all ranks, for they had all corrupted their way; and it is probable that such were made examples of as had been most forward to excite and promote the rebellion against the king of Babylon. *Seraiah the chief priest* is put first, whose sacred character could not exempt him from this stroke; how should it, when he himself had profaned it by sin? Seraiah the prince was *a quiet prince* (*ch.* li. 59), but perhaps Seraiah the priest was not so, but unquiet and turbulent, by which he had made himself obnoxious to the king of Babylon. The leaders of this people had caused them to err, and now they are in a particular manner made monuments of divine justice. 2. Of the captivity of the rest. Come and see how *Judah was carried away captive out of his own land* (*v.* 27), and how it spued them out as it spued out the Canaanites that went before them, which God had told them it would certainly do if they trod in their steps and copied out their abominations, Lev. xviii. 28. Now here is an account, (1.) Of two captivities which we had an account of before, one in the seventh year of Nebuchadnezzar (the same with that which is said to be in his eighth year, 2 Kings xxiv. 12), another in his eighteenth year, the same with that which is said (*v.* 12) to be in his nineteenth year. But the sums here are very small, in comparison with what we find expressed concerning the former (2 Kings xxiv. 14, 16), when there were 18,000 carried captive, whereas here they are said to be 3023; they are also small in comparison with what we may reasonably suppose concerning the latter; for, when all the residue of the people were carried away (*v.* 15), one would think there should be more than 832 souls; therefore Dr. Lightfoot conjectures that, these accounts being joined to the story of the putting to death of the great men at Riblah, all that are here said to be carried away were *put to death* as rebels. (2.) Of a third captivity, not mentioned before, which was in the twenty-third year of Nebuchadnezzar, four years after the destruction of Jerusalem (*v.* 30): Then *Nebuzaradan* came, and *carried away* 745 Jews; it is probable that this was done in revenge of the murder of Gedaliah, which was another rebellion against the king of Babylon, and that those who were now taken were aiders and abetters of Ishmael in that murder, and were not only carried away, but put to death for it; yet this is uncertain. If this be the sum

710

total of the captives (*all the persons were* 4600, *v.* 30), we may see how strangely they were reduced from what they had been, and may wonder as much how they came to be so numerous again as afterwards we find them; for it should seem that, as at first in Egypt, so again in Babylon, the Lord made them fruitful in the land of their affliction, and the more they were oppressed the more they multiplied. And the truth is, this people were often miracles both of judgment and mercy.

31 And it came to pass in the seven and thirtieth year of the captivity of Jehoiachin king of Judah, in the twelfth month, in the five and twentieth *day* of the month, *that* Evil-merodach king of Babylon in the *first* year of his reign lifted up the head of Jehoiachin king of Judah, and brought him forth out of prison, 32 And spake kindly unto him, and set his throne above the throne of the kings that *were* with him in Babylon, 33 And changed his prison-garments: and he did continually eat bread before him all the days of his life. 34 And *for* his diet, there was a continual diet given him of the king of Babylon, every day a portion until the day of his death, all the days of his life.

This passage of story concerning the reviving which king Jehoiachin had in his bondage we had likewise before (2 Kings xxv. 27—30), only there it is said to be done on *the twenty-seventh day of the twelfth month,* here on *the twenty-fifth;* but in a thing of this nature two days make a very slight difference in the account. It is probable that the orders were given for his release on the twenty-fifth day, but that he was not presented to the king till the twenty-seventh. We may observe in this story, 1. That new lords make new laws. Nebuchadnezzar had long kept this unhappy prince in prison; and his son, though well-affected to the prisoner, could not procure him any favour, not one smile, from his father, any more than Jonathan could for David from his father; but, when the old peevish man was dead, his son countenanced Jehoiachin and made him a favourite. It is common for children to undo what their fathers have done; it were well if it were always as much for the better as this was. 2. That the world we live in is a changing world. Jehoiachin, in his beginning, fell from a throne into a prison, but here he is advanced again to a throne of state (*v.* 32), though not to a throne of power. As, before, the robes were changed into prison-garments, so now they were converted into robes again. Such chequer-work is this world; prosperity and adversity are set the one over-against the other, that we may learn to *rejoice as though we rejoiced not and weep as though we wept not.* 3. That, though the night of affliction be very long, yet we must not despair but that the day may dawn at last. Jehoiachin was thirty-seven years a prisoner, in confinement, in contempt, ever since he was eighteen years old, in which time we may suppose him so inured to captivity that he had forgotten the sweets of liberty ; or, rather, that after so long an imprisonment it would be doubly welcome to him. Let those whose afflictions have been lengthened out encourage themselves with this instance ; the vision will at the end speak comfortably, and therefore wait for it. *Dum spiro spero—While there is life there is hope. Non si male nunc, et olim sic erit—Though now we suffer, we shall not always suffer.* 4. That God can make his people to find favour in the eyes of those that are their oppressors, and unaccountably turn their hearts to pity them, according to that word (Ps. cvi. 46), *He made them to be pitied of all those that carried them captives.* He can bring those that have spoken roughly to speak kindly, and those to feed his people that have fed upon them. Those therefore that are under oppression will find that it is not in vain to hope and quietly to *wait for the salvation of the Lord. Therefore* our times are in God's hand, because the hearts of all we deal with are so. 5. And now, upon the whole matter, comparing the prophecy and the history of this book together, we may learn, in general, (1.) That it is no new thing for churches and persons highly dignified to degenerate, and become very corrupt. (2.) That iniquity tends to the ruin of those that harbour it ; and, if it be not repented of and forsaken, will certainly end in their ruin. (3.) That external professions and privileges will not only not amount to an excuse for sin and an exemption from ruin, but will be a very great aggravation of both. (4.) That no word of God shall fall to the ground, but the event will fully answer the prediction ; and the unbelief of man shall not make God's threatenings, any more than his promises, of no effect. The justice and truth of God are here written in bloody characters, for the conviction or the confusion of all those that make a jest of his threatenings. Let them *not be deceived, God is not mocked.*

AN

EXPOSITION,

WITH PRACTICAL OBSERVATIONS,

OF THE

LAMENTATIONS OF JEREMIAH.

SINCE what Solomon says, though contrary to the common opinion of the world, is certainly true, that *sorrow is better than laughter,* and *it is better to go to the house of mourning than to the house of feasting,* we should come to the reading and consideration of the melancholy chapters of this book, not only willingly, but with an expectation to edify ourselves by them ; and, that we may do this, we must compose ourselves to a holy sadness and resolve to weep with the weeping prophet. Let us consider, I. The title of this book ; in the Hebrew it has none, but is called (as the books of Moses are) from the first word *Ecah—How ;* but the Jewish commentators call it, as the Greeks do, and we from them, *Kinoth—Lamentations.* As we have sacred odes or songs of joy, so have we sacred elegies or songs of lamentation ; such variety of methods has Infinite Wisdom taken to work upon us and move our affections, and so soften our hearts and make them susceptible of the impressions of divine truths, as the wax of the seal. We have not only *piped unto you,* but have *mourned* likewise, Matt. xi. 17. II. The penman of this book ; it was Jeremiah the prophet, who is here Jeremiah the poet, and *vates* signifies both ; therefore this book is fitly adjoined to the book of his prophecy, and is as an appendix to it. We had there at large the predictions of the desolations of Judah and Jerusalem, and then the history of them, to show how punctually the predictions were acccomplished, for the confirming of our faith : now here we have the expressions of his sorrow upon occasion of them, to show that he was very sincere in the protestations he had often made that he did not desire the woeful day, but that, on the contrary, the prospect of it filled him with bitterness. When he saw these calamities at a distance, he wished that his *head were waters and his eyes fountains of tears;* and, when they came, he made it to appear that he did not dissemble in that wish, and that he was far from being disaffected to his country, which was the crime his enemies charged him with. Though his country had been very unkind to him, and though the ruin of it was both a proof that he was a true prophet and a punishment of them for prosecuting him as a false prophet, which might have tempted him to rejoice in it, yet he sadly lamented it, and herein showed a better temper than that which Jonah was of with respect to Nineveh. III. The occasion of these Lamentations was the destruction of Judah and Jerusalem by the Chaldean army and the dissolution of the Jewish state both civil and ecclesiastical thereby. Some of the rabbies will have these to be the Lamentations which Jeremiah penned upon occasion of the death of Josiah, which are mentioned 2 Chron. xxxv. 25. But, though it is true that that opened the door to all the following calamities, yet these Lamentations seem to be penned in the sight, not in the foresight, of those calamities—when they had already come, not when they were at a distance; and there is nothing of Josiah in them, and his praise, as was, no question, in the lamentations for him. No, it is Jerusalem's funeral that this is an elegy upon. Others of them will have these Lamentations to be contained in the roll which Baruch wrote from Jeremiah's mouth, and which Jehoiakim burnt, and they suggest that at first there were in it only the 1st, 2d, and 4th chapters, but that the 3d and 5th were the *many like words* that were afterwards added; but this is a groundless fancy; that roll is expressly said to be a repetition and summary of the prophet's sermons, Jer. xxxvi. 2. IV. The composition of it; it is not only poetical, but alphabetical, all except the 5th chapter, as some of David's psalms are; each verse begins with a several letter in the order of the Hebrew alphabet, the first *aleph,* the second *beth, &c.,* but the 3d chapter is a triple alphabet, the first three beginning with *aleph,* the next three with *beth, &c.,* which was a help to memory (it being designed that these mournful ditties should be got by heart) and was an elegance in writing then valued and therefore not now to be despised. They observe that in the 2nd, 3d, and 4th chapters, the letter *pe* is put before *ain,* which in all the Hebrew alphabets follows it, for a reason of which Dr. Lightfoot offers this conjecture, That the letter *ajin,* which is the numeral letter for LXX., was thus, by being displaced, made remarkable, to put them in mind of the seventy years at the end of which God would turn again their captivity. V. The use of it: of great use, no doubt, it was to the pious Jews in their sufferings, furnishing them with spiritual language to express their natural grief by, helping to preserve the lively remembrance of Zion among them, and their children that never saw it, when they were in Babylon, directing their tears into the right channel (for they are here taught to mourn for sin and mourn to God), and withal encouraging their hopes that God would yet return and have mercy upon them; and it is of use to us, to affect us with godly sorrow for the calamities of the church of God, as becomes those that are living members of it and are resolved to take our lot with it.

CHAP. I.

We have here the first alphabet of this lamentation, twenty-two stanzas, in which the miseries of Jerusalem are bitterly bewailed and her present deplorable condition is aggravated by comparing it with her former prosperous state; all along, sin is acknowledged and complained of as the procuring cause of all these miseries; and God is appealed to for justice against their enemies and applied to for compassion towards them. The chapter is all of a piece, and the several remonstrances are interwoven; but here is, I. A complaint made to God of their calamities, and his compassionate consideration desired, ver. 1–11. II. The same complaint made to their friends, and their compassionate consideration desired, ver. 12–17. III. An appeal to God and his righteousness concerning it (ver. 18—22), in which he is justified in their affliction and is humbly solicited to justify himself in their deliverance.

HOW doth the city sit solitary, *that was* full of people! *how* is she become as a widow! she *that was* great among the nations, *and* princess among the provinces, *how* is she become tributary! 2 She weepeth sore in the night, and her tears *are* on her cheeks: among all her lovers she hath none to comfort *her:* all her friends have dealt treacherously with her, they are become her enemies. 3 Judah is gone into captivity because of affliction, and because of great servitude: she dwelleth among the heathen, she findeth no rest: all her persecutors overtook her between the straits. 4 The ways of Zion do mourn, because none come to the solemn feasts: all her gates are desolate: her priests sigh, her virgins are afflicted, and she *is* in bitterness. 5 Her adversaries are the chief, her enemies prosper; for the LORD hath afflicted her for the multitude of her transgressions: her children are gone into captivity before the enemy. 6 And from the daughter of Zion all her beauty is departed: her princes are become like harts *that* find no pasture, and they are gone without strength before the pursuer. 7 Jerusalem remembered in the days of her affliction and of her miseries all her pleasant things that she had in the days of old, when her people fell into the hand of the enemy, and none did help her: the adversaries saw her, *and* did mock at her sabbaths. 8 Jerusalem hath grievously sinned; therefore she is removed: all that honoured her despise her, because they have seen her nakedness: yea, she sigheth, and turneth backward. 9 Her filthiness *is* in her skirts; she remembereth not her last end; therefore she came down wonderfully: she had no comforter. O LORD, behold my affliction: for the enemy hath magnified *himself.* 10 The adversary hath spread out his hand upon all her pleasant things: for she hath seen *that* the heathen entered into her sanctuary, whom thou didst command *that* they should not enter into thy congregation. 11 All her people sigh, they seek bread; they have given their pleasant things for meat to relieve the soul: see, O LORD, and consider; for I am become vile.

Those that have any disposition to *weep with those that weep,* one would think, should scarcely be able to refrain from tears at the reading of these verses, so very pathetic are the lamentations here.

I. The miseries of Jerusalem are here complained of as very pressing and by many circumstances very much aggravated. Let us take a view of these miseries.

1. As to their civil state. (1.) A city that was populous is now depopulated, *v.* 1. It is spoken of by way of wonder—Who would have thought that ever it should come to this! Or by way of enquiry—What is it that has brought it to this? Or by way of lamentation—Alas! alas! (as Rev. xviii. 10, 16, 19) *how doth the city sit solitary that was full of people!* She was full of her own people that replenished her, and full of the people of other nations that resorted to her, with whom she had both profitable commerce and pleasant converse; but now her own people are carried into captivity, and strangers make no court to her: she *sits solitary.* The *chief places of the city* are not now, as they used to be, *places of concourse,* where *wisdom cried* (Prov. i. 20, 21); and justly are they left unfrequented, because wisdom's cry there was not heard. Note, Those that are ever so much increased God can soon diminish. *How has she become as a widow!* Her king that was, or should have been, as a husband to her, is cut off, and gone; her God has departed from her, and has given her a bill of divorce; she is emptied of her children, is solitary and sorrowful as a widow. Let no family, no state, not Jerusalem, no, nor Babylon herself, be secure, and say, *I sit as a queen,* and shall never *sit as a widow,* Isa. xlvii. 8; Rev. xviii. 7. (2.) A

city that had dominion is now in subjection. She had been *great among the nations,* greatly loved by some and greatly feared by others, and greatly observed and obeyed by both; some made her presents, and others paid her taxes; so that she was really *princess among the provinces,* and every sheaf bowed to hers; even the princes of the people entreated her favour. But now the tables are turned; she has not only lost her friends and *sits solitary,* but has lost her freedom too and sits *tributary;* she paid tribute to Egypt first and then to Babylon. Note, Sin brings a people not only into solitude, but into slavery. (3.) A city that used to be full of mirth has now become melancholy and upon all accounts full of grief. Jerusalem had been a joyous city, whither the tribes went up on purpose to rejoice before the Lord; she was *the joy of the whole earth,* but now *she weeps sorely,* her laughter is turned into mourning, her solemn feasts are all gone; she weeps *in the night,* as true mourners do who weep in secret, in silence and solitude; *in the night,* when others compose themselves to rest, her thoughts are most intent upon her troubles, and grief then plays the tyrant. What the prophet's head was for her, when she regarded it not, now her head is—*as waters, and* her *eyes fountains of tears,* so that she *weeps day and night* (Jer. ix. 1); *her tears are* continually *on her cheeks.* Though nothing dries away sooner than a tear, yet fresh griefs extort fresh tears, so that her cheeks are never free from them. Note, There is nothing more commonly seen *under the sun* than *the tears of the oppressed,* with whom *the clouds return after the rain,* Eccl. iv. 1. (4.) Those that were separated from the heathen now *dwell among the heathen;* those that were a peculiar people are now a mingled people (*v.* 3): *Judah has gone into captivity,* out of her own land into the land of her enemies, and there she abides, and is likely to abide among those that are aliens to God and the covenants of promise, with whom *she finds no rest,* no satisfaction of mind, nor any settlement of abode, but is continually hurried from place to place at the will of the victorious imperious tyrants. And again (*v.* 5): "*Her children have gone into captivity before the enemy;* those that were to have been the seed of the next generation are carried off; so that the land that is now desolate is likely to be still desolate and lost for want of heirs." Those that dwell among their own people, and that a free people, and in their own land, would be more thankful for the mercies they thereby enjoy if they would but consider the miseries of those that are forced into strange countries. (5.) Those that used in their wars to conquer are now conquered and triumphed over: *All her persecutors overlook her between the straits* (*v.* 3); they gained all possible advantages against her, so that her people unavoidably *fell into the* hand of the enemy, for there was no way to escape (*v.* 7); they were hemmed in on every side, and, which way soever they attempted to flee, they found themselves embarrassed. When they made the best of their way they could make nothing of it, but were overtaken and overcome; so that every where *her adversaries are the chief and her enemies prosper* (*v.* 5); which way soever their sword turns they get the better. Such straits do men bring themselves into by sin. If we allow that which is our greatest adversary and enemy to have dominion over us, and to be chief in us, justly will our other enemies be suffered to have dominion over us. (6.) Those that had been not only a distinguished but a dignified people, on whom God had put honour, and to whom all their neighbours had paid respect, are now brought into contempt (*v.* 8): *All that honoured her* before *despise her;* those that courted an alliance with her now value it not; those that caressed her when she was in pomp and prosperity slight her now that she is in distress, *because they have seen her nakedness.* By the prevalency of the enemies against her they perceive her weakness, and that she is not so strong a people as they thought she had been; and by the prevalency of God's judgments against her they perceive her wickedness, which now comes to light and is every where talked of. Now it appears how they have vilified themselves by their sins : *The enemies magnify themselves* against them (*v.* 9); they trample upon them, and insult over them, and in their eyes they have *become vile*, the tail of the nations, though once they were the head. Note, *Sin is the reproach of any people.* (7.) Those that lived in a fruitful land were ready to perish, and many of them did perish, for want of necessary food (*v.* 11) : *All her people sigh* in despondency and despair; they are ready to faint away; their spirits fail, and therefore they sigh, *for they seek bread* and seek it in vain. They were brought at last to that extremity that there was *no bread for the people of the land* (Jer. lii. 6), and in their captivity they had much ado to get bread, *ch.* v. 6. *They have given their pleasant things,* their jewels and pictures, and all the furniture of their closets and cabinets, which they used to please themselves with looking upon, they have sold these to buy bread for themselves and their families, have parted with them *for meat to relieve the soul,* or (as the margin is) *to make the soul come again,* when they were ready to faint away. They desired no other cordial than meat. *All that a man has will he give for life,* and for bread, which is the staff of life. Let those that abound in pleasant things not be proud of them, nor fond of them; for the time may come when they may be glad to let them go for necessary things. And let those that have competent food to relieve their soul be content with it,

714

and thankful for it, though they have not pleasant things.

2. We have here an account of their miseries in their ecclesiastical state, the ruin of their sacred interest, which was much more to be lamented than that of their secular concerns. (1.) Their religious feasts were no more observed, no more frequented (*v.* 4): *The ways of Zion do mourn;* they look melancholy, overgrown with grass and weeds. It used to be a pleasant diversion to see people continually passing and repassing in the highway that led to the temple, but now you may stand there long enough, and see nobody stir; for *none come to the solemn feasts;* a full end is put to them by the destruction of that which was the *city of our solemnities,* Isa. xxxiii. 20. *The solemn feasts* had been neglected and profaned (Isa. i. 11, 12), and therefore justly is an end now put to them. But, when thus *the ways of Zion* are made to *mourn,* all the sons of Zion cannot but mourn with them. It is very grievous to good men to see religious assemblies broken up and scattered, and those restrained from them that would gladly attend them. And, as *the ways of Zion mourned,* so *the gates of Zion,* in which the faithful worshippers used to meet, *are desolate;* for there is none to meet in them. Time was when *the Lord loved the gates of Zion more than all the dwellings of Jacob,* but now he has forsaken them, and is provoked to withdraw from them, and therefore it cannot but fare with them as it did with the temple when Christ quitted it. *Behold, your house is left unto you desolate,* Matt. xxiii. 38. (2.) Their religious persons were quite disabled from performing their wonted services, were quite dispirited : *Her priests sigh* for the desolations of the temple; their songs are turned into sighs; they sigh, for they have nothing to do, and therefore there is nothing to be had; they sigh, as the people (*v.* 11), *for want of bread,* because the offerings of the Lord, which were their livelihood, failed. It is time to sigh when the priests, the Lord's ministers, sigh. *Her virgins* also, that used, with their music and dancing, to grace the solemnities of their feasts, *are afflicted* and *in heaviness.* Notice is taken of their service in the day of Zion's prosperity (Ps. lxviii. 25, *Among them were the damsels playing with timbrels*), and therefore notice is taken of the failing of it now. *Her virgins are afflicted,* and therefore *she is in bitterness;* that is, all the inhabitants of Zion are so, whose character it is that they are *sorrowful for the solemn assembly,* and that to them *the reproach of it is a burden,* Zeph. iii. 18. (3.) Their religious places were profaned (*v.* 10): *The heathen entered into her sanctuary,* into the temple itself, into which no Israelite was permitted to enter, though ever so reverently and devoutly, but the priests only. *The stranger that comes nigh,* even to worship there, *shall be put to death.* Thither

the heathen now crowd rudely in, not to worship, but to plunder. God had commanded that *the heathen should not* so much as *enter into the congregation,* nor be incorporated with the people of the Jews (Deut. xxiii. 3); yet now they *enter into the sanctuary* without control. Note, Nothing is more grievous to those who have a true concern for the glory of God, nor is more lamented, than the violation of God's laws, and the contempt they see put upon sacred things. What *the enemy did wickedly in the sanctuary* was complained of, Ps. lxxiv. 3, 4. (4.) Their religious utensils, and all the rich things with which the temple was adorned and beautified, and which were made use of in the worship of God, were made a prey to the enemy (*v.* 10): *The adversary has spread out his hand upon all her pleasant things,* has grasped them all, seized them all, for himself. What these pleasant things are we may learn from Isa. lxiv. 11, where, to the complaint of the burning of the temple, it is added, *All our pleasant things are laid waste;* the ark and the altar, and all the other tokens of God's presence with them, these were their pleasant things above any other things, and these were now broken to pieces and carried away. Thus from *the daughter of Zion all her beauty has departed,* *v.* 6. *The beauty of holiness* was the *beauty of the daughter of Zion;* when the temple, that holy and beautiful house, was destroyed, her beauty was gone; that was the breaking *of the staff of beauty,* the taking away of the pledges and seals of the covenant, Zech. xi. 10. (5.) Their religious days were made a jest of (*v.* 7): *The adversaries saw her, and did mock at her sabbaths.* They laughed at them for observing one day in seven as a day of rest from worldly business. Juvenal, a heathen poet, ridicules the Jews in his time for losing a seventh part of their time :—

　　　——cui septima quæque fuit lux
　Ignava et vitæ partem non attigit ullam——
　They keep their sabbaths to their cost,
　For thus one day in sev'n is lost;

whereas sabbaths, if they be sanctified as they ought to be, will turn to a better account than all the days of the week besides. And whereas the Jews professed that they did it in obedience to their God, and to his honour, their adversaries asked them, "What do you get by it now? What profit have you in keeping the ordinances of your God, who now deserts you in your distress?" Note, It is a very great trouble to all that love God to hear his ordinances mocked at, and particularly his sabbaths. Zion calls them *her sabbaths,* for the sabbath was made for men; they are his institutions, but they are her privileges; and the contempt put upon sabbaths all the sons of Zion take to themselves and lay to heart accordingly; nor will they look upon sabbaths, or any other divine ordinances, as less honourable, **nor** value them less, for their being mocked

at. (6.) That which greatly aggravated all these grievances was that her state at present was just the reverse of what it had been formerly, *v.* 7. Now, *in the days of affliction and misery,* when every thing was black and dismal, *she remembers all her pleasant things that she had in the days of old,* and now knows how to value them better than formerly, when she had the full enjoyment of them. God often makes us know the worth of mercies by the want of them; and adversity is borne with the greatest difficulty by those that have fallen into it from the height of prosperity. This cut David to the heart, when he was banished from God's ordinances, that he could remember when he *went with the multitude to the house of God,* Ps. xlii. 4.

II. The sins of Jerusalem are here complained of as the procuring provoking cause of all these calamities. Whoever are the instruments, God is the author of all these troubles; it is *the Lord that has afflicted her* (*v.* 5) and he has done it as a righteous Judge, for *she has sinned.* 1. Her sins are for number numberless. Are her troubles many? Her sins are many more. It is *for the multitude of her transgressions* that *the Lord has afflicted her.* See Jer. xxx. 14. When the transgressions of a people are multiplied we cannot say, as Job does in his own case, that *wounds are multiplied without cause,* Job ix. 17. 2. They are for nature exceedingly heinous (*v.* 8): *Jerusalem has grievously sinned,* has *sinned sin* (so the word is), sinned wilfully, deliberately, has sinned that sin which of all others is the abominable thing that the Lord hates, the sin of idolatry. The sins of Jerusalem, that makes such a profession and enjoys such privileges, are of all others the most grievous sins. She has *sinned grievously* (*v.* 8), and therefore (*v.* 9) she *came down wonderfully.* Note, Grievous sins bring wondrous ruin; there are some workers of iniquity to whom there is a strange punishment, Job xxxi. 3. They are such sins as may plainly be read in the punishment. (1.) They have been very oppressive and therefore are justly oppressed (*v.* 3): *Judah has gone into captivity,* and it is *because of affliction and great servitude,* because the rich among them afflicted the poor and made them serve with rigour, and particularly (as the Chaldee paraphrases it) because they had oppressed their Hebrew servants, which is charged upon them, Jer. xxxiv. 11. Oppression was one of their crying sins (Jer. vi. 6, 7) and it is a sin that cries aloud. (2.) They have made themselves vile, and therefore are justly vilified. They all *despise her* (*v.* 8), for *her filthiness is in her skirts;* it appears upon her garments that she has rolled them in the mire of sin. None could stain our glory if we did not stain it ourselves. (3.) They have been very secure and therefore are justly surprised with this ruin (*v.* 9): *She remembers not her last end ;* she did not take the warning that was given her to *consider her latter end*, to consider what would be the end of such wicked courses as she took, and therefore she *came down wonderfully*, in an astonishing manner, that she might be made to feel what she would not fear; therefore God shall *make their plagues wonderful.*

III. Jerusalem's friends are here complained of as false and faint-hearted, and very unkind: They *have all dealt treacherously with her* (v. 2), so that, in effect, *they have become her enemies.* Her deceivers have created her as much vexation as her destroyers. The staff that breaks under us may do us as great a mischief as the *staff that beats us*, Ezek. xxix. 6, 7. *Her princes*, that should have protected her, have not courage enough to make head against the enemy for their own preservation; they *are like harts*, that, upon the first alarm, betake themselves to flight and make no resistance; nay, they *are like harts* that are famished for want of *pasture*, and therefore *are gone without strength before the pursuer*, and, having no strength for flight, are soon run down and made a prey of. Her neighbours are unneighbourly, for, 1. There is none *to help her* (v. 7); either they could not or they would not; nay, 2. *She has no comforter*, none to sympathize with her, or suggest any thing to alleviate her griefs, v. 7, 9. Like Job's friends, they saw it was to no purpose, her *grief was so great;* and *miserable comforters were they all* in such a case.

IV. Jerusalem's God is here complained to concerning all these things, and all is referred to his compassionate consideration (v. 9): " *O Lord! behold my affliction*, and take cognizance of it;" and (v. 11), " *See, O Lord! and consider*, take order about it." Note, The only way to make ourselves easy under our burdens is to cast them upon God first, and leave it to him to do with us as seemeth him good.

12 *Is it* nothing to you, all ye that pass by? behold, and see if there be any sorrow like unto my sorrow, which is done unto me, wherewith the LORD hath afflicted *me* in the day of his fierce anger. 13 From above hath he sent fire into my bones, and it prevaileth against them: he hath spread a net for my feet, he hath turned me back: he hath made me desolate *and* faint all the day. 14 The yoke of my transgressions is bound by his hand: they are wreathed, *and* come up upon my neck: he hath made my strength to fall, the LORD hath delivered me into *their* hands, *from whom* I am not able to rise up. 15 The LORD hath trodden under foot all my mighty *men* in the midst of me:

he hath called an assembly against me to crush my young men: the LORD hath trodden the virgin, the daughter of Judah, *as* in a wine-press. 16 For these *things* I weep; mine eye, mine eye runneth down with water, because the comforter that should relieve my soul is far from me: my children are desolate, because the enemy prevailed. 17 Zion spreadeth forth her hands, *and there is* none to comfort her: the LORD hath commanded concerning Jacob, *that* his adversaries *should be* round about him: Jerusalem is as a menstruous woman among them. 18 The LORD is righteous; for I have rebelled against his commandment: hear, I pray you, all people, and behold my sorrow: my virgins and my young men are gone into captivity. 19 I called for my lovers, *but* they deceived me: my priests and mine elders gave up the ghost in the city, while they sought their meat to relieve their souls. 20 Behold, O LORD; for I *am* in distress: my bowels are troubled; mine heart is turned within me; for I have grievously rebelled: abroad the sword bereaveth, at home *there is* as death. 21 They have heard that I sigh: *there is* none to comfort me: all mine enemies have heard of my trouble; they are glad that thou hast done *it :* thou wilt bring the day *that* thou hast called, and they shall be like unto me. 22 Let all their wickedness come before thee; and do unto them, as thou hast done unto me for all my transgressions: for my sighs *are* many, and my heart *is* faint.

The complaints here are, for substance, the same with those in the foregoing part of the chapter; but in these verses the prophet, in the name of the lamenting church, does more particularly acknowledge the hand of God in these calamities, and the righteousness of his hand.

I. The church in distress here magnifies her affliction, and yet no more than there was cause for; her groaning was not heavier than her strokes. She appeals to all spectators: *See if there be any sorrow like unto my sorrow*, v. 12. This might perhaps be truly said of Jerusalem's griefs; but we are apt to apply it too sensibly to ourselves when we are in trouble and more than there is cause for. Because we feel most from our own burden, and cannot be persuaded to reconcile ourselves to it, we are ready to cry out, Surely never was *sorrow like unto our sorrow;* whereas, if our troubles were to be thrown into a common stock with those of others, and then an equal dividend made, share and share alike, rather than stand to that we should each of us say, "Pray, give me my own again."

II. She here looks beyond the instruments to the author of her troubles, and owns them all to be directed, determined, and disposed of by him : " It is *the Lord that has afflicted me*, and he has *afflicted me* because he is angry with me; the greatness of his displeasure may be measured by the greatness of my distress ; it is *in the day of his fierce anger*," *v.* 12. Afflictions cannot but be very much our griefs when we see them arising from God's wrath; so the church does here. 1. She is as one in a fever, and the fever is of God's sending : "*He has sent fire into my bones* (*v.* 13), a preternatural heat, which *prevails against them*, so that they are *burnt like a hearth* (Ps. cii. 3), pained and wasted, and dried away." 2. She is as one in a net, which the more he struggles to get out of the more he is entangled in, and this net is of God's spreading. "The enemies could not have succeeded in their stratagems had not God *spread a net for my feet.*" 3. She is as one in a wilderness, whose way is embarrassed, solitary, and tiresome : "*He has turned me back*, that I cannot go on, *has made me desolate*, that I have nothing to support me with, but am *faint all the day.*" 4. She is as one in a yoke, not yoked for service, but for penance, tied neck and heels together (*v.* 14) : *The yoke of my transgressions is bound by his hand.* Observe, We never are entangled in any yoke but what is framed out of our own transgressions. The sinner is *holden with the cords of his own sins*, Prov. v. 22. The yoke of Christ's commands is an *easy yoke* (Matt. xi. 30), but that of our own transgressions is a heavy one. God is said to bind this yoke when he charges guilt upon us, and brings us into those inward and outward troubles which our sins have deserved ; when conscience, as his deputy, binds us over to his judgment, then *the yoke is bound* and *wreathed by the hand* of his justice, and nothing but the hand of his pardoning mercy will unbind it. 5. She is as one in the dirt, and he it is that has *trodden under foot all her mighty men*, that has disabled them to stand, and overthrown them by one judgment after another, and so left them to be trampled upon by their proud conquerors, *v.* 15. Nay, she is as one in a wine-press, not only trodden down, but trodden to pieces, crushed as grapes in the wine-press of God's wrath, and her blood pressed out as wine, and it is God that has thus *trodden the virgin, the daughter of Judah.* 6. She is in the hand of her enemies, and it is the Lord

that has delivered her *into their hands* (*v.* 14) : *He has made my strength to fall*, so that *I am not able to* make head against them ; nay, not only not able to rise up against them, but *not able to rise up* from them, and then *he has delivered me into their hands;* nay (*v.* 15), *he has called an assembly against me, to crush my young men*, and such an assembly as it is in vain to think of opposing; and again (*v.* 17), *The Lord has commanded concerning Jacob that his adversaries should be round about him.* He that has many a time *commanded deliverances for Jacob* (Ps. xliv. 4) now commands an invasion against Jacob, because Jacob has disobeyed the commands of his law.

III. She justly demands a share in the pity and compassion of those that were the spectators of her misery (*v.* 12) : "*Is it nothing to you, all you that pass by?* Can you look upon me without concern ? What! are your hearts as adamants and your eyes as marbles, that you cannot bestow upon me one compassionate thought, or look, or tear ? Are not you also in the body ? Is it nothing to you that your neighbour's house is on fire ?" There are those to whom Zion's sorrows and ruins are nothing ; they are not *grieved for the affliction of Joseph.* How pathetically does she beg their compassion ! (*v.* 18) : "*Hear, I pray you, all people, and behold my sorrow :* hear my complaints, and see what cause I have for them." This is a request like that of Job (*ch.* xix. 21), *Have pity upon me, have pity upon me, O you my friends !* It helps to make a burden sit lighter if our friends sympathize with us, and mingle their tears with ours, for this is an evidence that, though we are in affliction, we are not in contempt, which is commonly as much dreaded in an affliction as any thing.

IV. She justifies her own grief, though it was very extreme, for these calamities (*v.* 16) : "*For these things I weep, I weep in the night* (*v.* 2), when none sees ; *my eye, my eye, runs down with water.*" Note, This world is a vale of tears to the people of God. Zion's sons are often Zion's mourners. *Zion spreads forth her hands* (*v.* 17), which is here an expression rather of despair than of desire ; she flings out her hands as giving up all for gone. Let us see how she accounts for this passionate grief. 1. Her God has withdrawn from her ; and Micah, that had but gods of gold, when they were stolen from him cried out, *What have I more ? And what is it that you say unto me ? What aileth thee ?* The church here grieves excessively ; for, says she, *the comforter that should relieve my soul is far from me.* God is the comforter ; he used to be so to her ; he only can administer effectual comforts ; it is his word that speaks them ; it is his Spirit that speaks them to us. His are strong consolations, able to *relieve the soul*, to *bring it back* when it is gone, and we cannot of ourselves *fetch it again;* but now he has departed in displeasure, he is *far from me,* and beholds me *afar off.* Note, It is no marvel that the souls of the saints faint away, when God, who is the only Comforter that can relieve them, keeps at a distance. 2. Her children are removed from her, and are in no capacity to help her: it is for them that she weeps, as Rachel for hers, *because they were not,* and therefore she *refuses to be comforted. Her children were desolate, because the enemy prevailed* against them; there is *none of all her sons to take her by the hand* (Isa. li. 18); they cannot help themselves, and how should they help her? Both the damsels and the youths, that were her joy and hope, *have gone into captivity, v.* 18. It is said of the Chaldeans that they had *no compassion upon young men nor maidens,* not on the fair sex, not on the blooming age, 2 Chron. xxxvi. 17. 3. Her friends failed her; some would not and others could not give her any relief. She *spread forth her hands,* as begging relief, but *there is none to comfort her* (v. 17), none that can do it, none that cares to do it; she *called* for her *lovers,* and, to engage them to help her, *called* them her *lovers,* but they *deceived* her (v. 19), they proved like the brooks in summer to the thirsty traveller, Job vi. 15. Note, Those creatures that we set our hearts upon and raise our expectations from we are commonly deceived and disappointed in. Her idols were her lovers. Egypt and Assyria were her confidants. But they deceived her. Those that made court to her in her prosperity were shy of her, and strange to her, in her adversity. Happy are those that have made God their friend and keep themselves in his love, for he will not deceive them! 4. Those whose office it was to guide her were disabled from doing her any service. The *priests* and the *elders,* that should have appeared at the head of affairs, died for hunger (v. 19); they *gave up the ghost,* or were ready to expire, *while they sought their meat;* they went a begging for bread to keep them alive. *The famine is sore* indeed *in the land* when there is no bread to the wise, when priests and elders are starved. The priests and elders should have been her comforters; but how should they comfort others when they themselves were comfortless? *" They have heard that I sigh,* which should have summoned them to my assistance; but *there is none to comfort me. Lover and friend hast thou put far from me."* 5. Her enemies were too hard for her, and they insulted over her; they have *prevailed,* v. 16. *Abroad the sword bereaves* and slays all that comes in its way, and *at home* all provisions are cut off by the besiegers, so that *there is as death,* that is, famine, which is as bad as the pestilence, or worse—*the sword without and terror within,* Deut. xxxii. 25. And as the enemies, that were the instruments of the calamity, were

very barbarous, so were those that were the standers by, the Edomites and Ammonites, that bore ill will to Israel: They have *heard of my trouble, and are glad that thou hast done it* (v. 21); they rejoice in the trouble itself; they rejoice that it is God's doing; it pleases them to find that God and his Israel have fallen out, and they act accordingly with a great deal of strangeness towards them. *Jerusalem is as a menstruous woman among them,* that they are afraid of touching and are shy of, v. 17. Upon all these accounts it cannot be wondered at, nor can she be blamed, that *her sighs are many,* in grieving for what is, and that *her heart is faint* (v. 22) in fear of what is yet further likely to be.

V. She justifies God in all that is brought upon her, acknowledging that her sins had deserved these severe chastenings. The yoke that lies so heavily, and binds so hard, is *the yoke of her transgressions,* v. 14. The fetters we are held in are of our own making, and it is with our own rod that we are beaten. When the church had spoken here as if she thought the Lord severe she does well to correct herself, at least to explain herself, by acknowledging (v. 18), *The Lord is righteous.* He does us no wrong in dealing thus with us, nor can we charge him with any injustice in it; how unrighteous soever men are, we are sure that the *Lord is righteous,* and manifests his justice, though they contradict all the laws of theirs. Note, Whatever our troubles are, which God is pleased to inflict upon us, we must own that therein he *is righteous;* we understand neither him nor ourselves if we do not own it, 2 Chron. xii. 6. She owns the equity of God's actions, by owning the iniquity of her own: *I have rebelled against his commandments* (v. 18); and again (v. 20), *I have grievously rebelled.* We cannot speak ill enough of sin, and we must always speak worst of our own sin, must call it *rebellion, grievous rebellion;* and very grievous sin is to all true penitents. It is this that lies more heavily upon her than the afflictions she was under: *" My bowels are troubled; they work within me as the troubled sea; my heart is turned within me,* is restless, is turned upside down; *for I have grievously rebelled."* Note, Sorrow for sin must be great sorrow and must affect the soul.

VI. She appeals both to the mercy and to the justice of God in her present case. 1. She appeals to the mercy of God concerning her own sorrows, which had made her the proper object of his compassion (v. 20): *" Behold, O Lord! for I am in distress;* take cognizance of my case, and take such order for my relief as thou pleasest." Note, It is matter of comfort to us that the troubles which oppress our spirits are open before God's eye. 2. She appeals to the justice of God concerning the injuries that her enemies did her (v. 21, 22): *Thou wilt bring the day that thou hast called,* the day that is fixed in the counsels of God and published in the prophecies, when my enemies, that now prosecute me, *shall be like unto me,* when the cup of trembling, now put into my hands, shall be put into theirs." It may be read as a prayer, "Let the day appointed come," and so it goes on, "*Let their wickedness come before thee,* let it come to be remembered, let it come to be reckoned for; take vengeance on them for all the wrongs they have done to me (Ps. cix. 14, 15); hasten the time when thou wilt *do to them* for their trangressions *as thou hast done to me* for mine." This prayer amounts to a protestation against all thoughts of a coalition with them, and to a prediction of their ruin, subscribing to that which God had in his word spoken of it. Note, Our prayers may and must agree with God's word; and what day God has here called we are to call for, and no other. And though we are bound in charity to forgive our enemies, and to pray for them, yet we may in faith pray for the accomplishment of that which God has spoken against his and his church's enemies, that will not repent to give him glory.

CHAP. II.

The second alphabetical elegy is set to the same mournful tune with the former, and the substance of it is much the same; it begins with Ecah, as that did, "How sad is our case! Alas for us!" I. Here is the anger of Zion's God taken notice of as the cause of her calamities, ver. 1—9. II. Here is the sorrow of Zion's children taken notice of as the effect of her calamities, ver. 10—19. III. The complaint is made to God, and the matter referred to his compassionate consideration, ver. 20—22. The hand that wounded must make whole.

HOW hath the Lord covered the daughter of Zion with a cloud in his anger, *and* cast down from heaven unto the earth the beauty of Israel, and remembered not his footstool in the day of his anger! 2 The Lord hath swallowed up all the habitations of Jacob, and hath not pitied: he hath thrown down in his wrath the strong holds of the daughter of Judah; he hath brought *them* down to the ground: he hath polluted the kingdom and the princes thereof. 3 He hath cut off in *his* fierce anger all the horn of Israel: he hath drawn back his right hand from before the enemy, and he burned against Jacob like a flaming fire, *which* devoureth round about. 4 He hath bent his bow like an enemy: he stood with his right hand as an adversary, and slew all *that were* pleasant to the eye in the tabernacle of the daughter of Zion: he poured out his fury like fire. 5 The Lord was as an enemy: he hath swallowed up Israel, he hath

swallowed up all her palaces: he hath destroyed his strong holds, and hath increased in the daughter of Judah mourning and lamentation. 6 And he hath violently taken away his tabernacle, as *if it were of* a garden: he hath destroyed his places of the assembly: the Lord hath caused the solemn feasts and sabbaths to be forgotten in Zion, and hath despised in the indignation of his anger the king and the priest. 7 The Lord hath cast off his altar, he hath abhorred his sanctuary, he hath given up into the hand of the enemy the walls of her palaces; they have made a noise in the house of the Lord, as in the day of a solemn feast. 8 The Lord hath purposed to destroy the wall of the daughter of Zion: he hath stretched out a line, he hath not withdrawn his hand from destroying: therefore he made the rampart and the wall to lament; they languished together. 9 Her gates are sunk into the ground; he hath destroyed and broken her bars: her king and her princes *are* among the Gentiles: the law *is* no *more;* her prophets also find no vision from the Lord.

It is a very sad representation which is here made of the state of God's church, of Jacob and Israel, of Zion and Jerusalem; but the emphasis in these verses seems to be laid all along upon the hand of God in the calamities which they were groaning under. The grief is not so much that such and such things are done as that God has done them, that he appears angry with them; it is he that chastens them, and chastens them *in wrath* and *in his hot displeasure:* he has become their enemy, and fights against them; and this, this is the wormwood and the gall in the affliction and the misery.

I. Time was when God's delight was in his church, and he appeared to her, and appeared for her, as a friend. But now his displeasure is against her; he is angry with her, and appears and acts against her as an enemy. This is frequently repeated here, and sadly lamented. What he has done he has done *in his anger;* this makes the present day a melancholy day indeed with us, that it is *the day of his anger* (v. 1), and again (v. 2) it is *in his wrath,* and (v. 3) it is *in his fierce anger,* that he has *thrown down* and *cut off,* and (v. 6) *in the indignation of his anger.* Note, To those who know how to value God's favour nothing appears more dreadful than his anger; corrections in love are easily borne, but rebukes in love wound deeply. It is God's wrath that *burns against Jacob like a flaming fire* (v. 3), and it is a consuming fire; it *devours round about,* devours all her honours, all her comforts. This is the *fury that is poured out like fire* (v. 4), like the fire and brimstone which were rained upon Sodom and Gomorrah; but it was their sin that kindled this fire. God is such a tender Father to his children that we may be sure he is never angry with them but when they provoke him, and give him cause to be angry; nor is he ever angry more than there is cause for. God's covenant with them was that if they would *obey his voice* he would be *an enemy to their enemies* (Exod. xxiii. 22), and he had been so as long as they kept close to him; but now he is an enemy to them; at least he is *as an enemy,* v. 5. He has *bent his bow like an enemy,* v. 4. He stood *with his right hand* stretched out against them, and a sword drawn in it *as an adversary.* God is not really an enemy to his people, no, not when he is angry with them, and corrects them in anger. We may be sorely displeased against our dearest friends and relations, whom yet we are far from having an enmity to. But sometimes he is *as an enemy* to them, when all his providences concerning them seem in outward appearance to have a tendency to their ruin, when every thing makes against them and nothing for them. But, blessed be God, Christ is *our peace,* our peacemaker, who has slain the enmity, and in him we may *agree with our adversary,* which it is our wisdom to do, since it is in vain to contend with him, and he offers us advantageous conditions of peace.

II. Time was when God's church appeared very bright, and illustrious, and considerable among the nations; but now *the Lord has covered the daughter of Zion with a cloud* (v. 1), a dark cloud, which is very terrible to herself, and through which she cannot see his face; *a thick cloud* (so the word signifies), a *black cloud,* which eclipses all her glory and conceals her excellency; not such a cloud as that under which God conducted them through the wilderness, or that in which God took possession of the temple and filled it with his glory: no, that side of the cloud is now turned towards them which was turned towards the Egyptians in the Red Sea. The *beauty of Israel is now cast down from heaven to the earth;* their princes (2 Sam. i. 19), their religious worship, their beauty of holiness, all that which recommended them to the affection and esteem of their neighbours and rendered them amiable, which had *lifted them up to heaven,* was now withered and gone, because God had covered it with a cloud. He has *cut off all the horn of Israel* (v. 3), all her beauty and majesty (Ps. cxxxii. 17), all her plenty and fulness, and all her power and authority. They had, in their pride, lifted up their horn against God, and therefore justly will God *cut off their horn.* He disabled them to resist and oppose their enemies; he *turned back their right hand,* so that they were not able to follow the blow which they gave nor to ward off the blow which was given them. What can their right hand do against the enemy when God draws it back, and withers it, as he did Jeroboam's? Thus was the *beauty of Israel cast down,* when a people famed for courage were not able to stand their ground nor make good their post.

III. Time was when Jerusalem and the cities of Judah were strong and well fortified, were trusted to by the inhabitants and let alone by the enemy as impregnable. But now the Lord has in anger *swallowed them up;* they are quite gone; the forts and barriers are taken away, and the invaders meet with no opposition: the stately structures, which were their strength and beauty, are pulled down and laid waste. 1. The Lord has in anger *swallowed up all the habitations of Jacob* (v. 2), both the cities and the country houses; they are burnt, or otherwise destroyed, so totally ruined that they seem to have been *swallowed up,* and no remains left of them. He has *swallowed up, and has not pitied.* One would have thought it a pity that such sumptuous houses, so well built, so well furnished, should be quite destroyed, and that some pity should have been had for the poor inhabitants that were thus dislodged and driven to wander; but God's wonted compassions seemed to fail: *He has swallowed up Israel,* as a lion swallows up his prey, v. 5. 2. He has *swallowed up* not only her common habitations, but her palaces, *all her palaces,* the habitations of their princes and great men (v. 5), though those were most stately, and strong, and rich, and well guarded. God's judgments, when they come with commission, level palaces with cottages, and as easily swallow them up. If palaces be polluted with sin, as theirs were, let them expect to be visited with a curse, which shall *consume them, with the timber thereof and the stones thereof,* Zech. v. 4. 3. He has destroyed not only their dwelling-places, but their *strong-holds,* their castles, citadels, and places of defence. These he has *thrown down in his wrath,* and *brought them to the ground;* for shall they stand in the way of his judgments, and give check to the progress of them? No; let them drop like leaves in autumn; let them be rased to the foundations, and made to touch the *ground,* v. 2. And again (v. 5), *He has destroyed his strong-holds;* for what strength could they have against God? And thus has he *increased in the daughter of Judah mourning and lamentation,* for they could not but be in a dreadful consternation when they saw all their defence departed from them. This is again insisted on, v. 7—9. In order to the *swallowing up of her palaces,* he has *given up into the hand of the enemy the walls of her palaces,* which were their security, and, when they are *broken down,* the palaces themselves are soon broken into. The walls of palaces cannot protect them, unless God himself be a wall of fire round about them. This God did *in his anger,* and yet he has done it deliberately. It is the result of a previous purpose, and is done by a wise and steady providence; for the Lord has *purposed to destroy the wall of the daughter of Zion;* he brought the Chaldean army in on purpose to do this execution. Note, Whatever desolations God makes in his church, they are all according to his counsels; he *performs the thing that is appointed for us,* even that which makes most against us. But, when it is done, he has *stretched out a line,* a measuring line, to do it exactly and by measure: hitherto the destruction shall go, and no further; no more shall be cut off than what is marked to be so. Or it is meant of *the line of confusion* (Isa. xxxiv. 11), a levelling line; for he will go on with his work; he *has not withdrawn his hand from destroying,* that right hand which he stretched out against his people as *an adversary, v.* 4. As far as the purpose went the performance shall go, and his hand shall accomplish his counsel to the utmost, and not be withdrawn. Therefore he made the *rampart and the wall,* which the people had rejoiced in and upon which perhaps they had *made merry,* to *lament,* and they *languished together;* the *walls and the ramparts,* or bulwarks, upon them, fell together, and were left to condole with one another on their fall. *Her gates* are gone in an instant, so that one would think they were sunk into the ground with their own weight, and *he has destroyed and broken her bars,* those bars of Jerusalem's gates which formerly *he had strengthened,* Ps. cxlvii. 13. Gates and bars will stand us in no stead when God has withdrawn his protection.

IV. Time was when their government flourished, their princes made a figure, their kingdom was great among the nations, and the balance of power was on their side; but now it is quite otherwise: *He has polluted the kingdom and the princes thereof, v.* 2. They had first polluted themselves with their idolatries, and then God dealt with them as with polluted things; he threw them to the dunghill, the fittest place for them. He has given up their glory, which was looked upon as sacred (that is a character we give to majesty), to be trampled upon and profaned; and no marvel that the king and the priest, whose characters were always deemed venerable and inviolable, are despised by every body, when God has, *in the indignation of his anger, despised the king and the priest, v.* 6. He has abandoned them; he looks upon them as no longer worthy of the honours conveyed to them by the covenants of royalty and priesthood, but as having

forfeited both; and then Zedekiah the king was used despitefully, and Seraiah the chief priest put to death as a malefactor. The crown has fallen from their heads, for *her king and her princes are among the Gentiles,* prisoners among them, insulted over by them (*v.* 9), and treated not only as common persons, but as the basest, without any regard to their character. Note, It is just with God to debase those by his judgments who have by sin debased themselves.

V. Time was when the ordinances of God were administered among them in their power and purity, and they had those tokens of God's presence with them; but now those were taken from them, that part of the *beauty of Israel* was gone which was indeed their greatest beauty. 1. The ark was God's footstool, under the mercy-seat, between the cherubim; this was of all others the most sacred symbol of God's presence (it is called his *footstool,* 1 Chron. xxviii. 2; Ps. xcix. 5; cxxxii. 7); there the Shechinah rested, and with an eye to this Israel was often protected and saved; but now he *remembered not his footstool.* The ark itself was suffered, as it should seem, to fall into the hands of the Chaldeans. God, being angry, threw that away; for it shall be no longer his footstool; the earth shall be so, as it had been before the ark was, Isa. lxvi. 1. Of what little value are the tokens of his presence when his presence is gone! Nor was this the first time that God gave his ark into captivity, Ps. lxxviii. 61. God and his kingdom can stand without that footstool. 2. Those that ministered in holy things had been *pleasant to the eye in the tabernacle of the daughter of Zion* (*v.* 4); they had been *purer than snow, whiter than milk* (*ch.* iv. 7); none more pleasant in the eyes of all good people than those that did the service of the tabernacle. But now these are slain, and their *blood is mingled with their sacrifices.* Thus is the priest despised as well as the king. Note, When those that were pleasant to the eye in Zion's tabernacle are slain God must be acknowledged in it; he has done it, and the *burning which the Lord has kindled must be bewailed* by the whole house of Israel, as in the case of Nadab and Abihu, Lev. x. 6. 3. The temple was God's tabernacle (as the tabernacle, while that was in being, was called *his temple,* Ps. xxvii. 4) and this *he has violently taken away* (*v.* 6); he has plucked up the stakes of it and cut the cords; it shall be no more a tabernacle, much less his; he has *taken it away,* as the keeper *of a garden* takes away his hovel or shade, when he has done with it and has no more occasion for it; he takes it down as easily, as speedily, and with as little regret and reluctance as if it were but a *cottage in a vineyard or a lodge in a garden of cucumbers* (Isa. i. 8), but a *booth which the keeper makes,* Job xxvii. 18. When men profane God's tabernacle it is just with him to take it from them. God had justly refused to *smell in their solemn assemblies* (Amos v. 21); they had provoked him to withdraw from them, and then no marvel that he has *destroyed his places of the assembly;* what should they do with the places when the services had become an abomination? He has now *abhorred his sanctuary* (v. 7); it has been defiled with sin, that only thing which he hates, and for the sake of that he abhors even his sanctuary, which he had delighted in and called *his rest for ever*, Ps. cxxxii. 14. Thus he had *done to Shiloh.* Now the enemies have made as great *a noise* of revelling and blaspheming *in the house of the Lord* as ever had been made with the temple-songs and music *in the day of a solemn feast*, Ps. lxxiv. 4. Some, by the *places of the assembly* (v. 6), understand not only the temple, but the synagogues, and the schools of the prophets, which the enemy had *burnt up*, Ps. lxxiv. 8. 4. The solemn feasts and the sabbaths had been carefully remembered, and the people constantly put in mind of them; but now the Lord has *caused those to be forgotten*, not only in the country, among those that lived at a distance, but even in Zion itself; for there were none left to remember them, nor were there the places left where they used to be observed. Now that Zion was in ruins no difference was made between sabbath time and other times; every day was a day of mourning, so that all the *solemn feasts were forgotten.* Note, It is just with God to deprive those of the benefit and comfort of sabbaths and solemn feasts who have not duly valued them, nor conscientiously observed them, but have profaned them, which was one of the sins that the Jews were often charged with. Those that have *seen the days of the Son of man*, and slighted them, may *desire to see one of those days* and not be permitted, Luke xvii. 22. 5. The altar that had sanctified their gifts is now cast off, for God will no more accept their gifts, nor be honoured by their sacrifices, *v.* 7. The altar was *the table of the Lord*, but God will no longer keep house among them; he will neither feast them nor feast with them. 6. They had been blest with prophets and teachers of the law; but now *the law is no more* (v. 9); it is no more read by the people, no more expounded by the scribes; the tables of the law are gone with the ark; the book of the law is taken from them, and the people are forbidden to have it. What should those do with Bibles who had made no better improvement of them when they had them? *Her prophets also find no vision from the Lord;* God answers *them no more by prophets and dreams*, which was the melancholy case of Saul, 1 Sam. xxviii. 15. They had persecuted God's prophets, and despised the visions they had from the Lord, and therefore it is just with God to say that they shall have no more prophets, no more visions. Let them go to the prophets that had flattered and deceived them with visions of their own hearts, for they shall have none from God to comfort them, or tell them *how long.* Those that misuse God's prophets justly lose them.

10 The elders of the daughter of Zion sit upon the ground, *and* keep silence: they have cast up dust upon their heads; they have girded themselves with sackcloth: the virgins of Jerusalem hang down their heads to the ground. 11 Mine eyes do fail with tears, my bowels are troubled, my liver is poured upon the earth, for the destruction of the daughter of my people; because the children and the sucklings swoon in the streets of the city. 12 They say to their mothers, Where *is* corn and wine? when they swooned as the wounded in the streets of the city, when their soul was poured out into their mothers' bosom. 13 What thing shall I take to witness for thee? what thing shall I liken to thee, O daughter of Jerusalem? what shall I equal to thee, that I may comfort thee, O virgin daughter of Zion? for thy breach *is* great like the sea: who can heal thee? 14 Thy prophets have seen vain and foolish things for thee: and they have not discovered thine iniquity, to turn away thy captivity; but have seen for thee false burdens and causes of banishment. 15 All that pass by clap *their* hands at thee; they hiss and wag their head at the daughter of Jerusalem, *saying, Is* this the city that *men* call The perfection of beauty, The joy of the whole earth? 16 All thine enemies have opened their mouth against thee: they hiss and gnash the teeth: they say, We have swallowed *her* up: certainly this *is* the day that we looked for; we have found, we have seen *it.* 17 The Lord hath done *that* which he had devised; he hath fulfilled his word that he had commanded in the days of old: he hath thrown down, and hath not pitied: and he hath caused *thine* enemy to rejoice over thee, he hath set up the horn of thine adversaries. 18 Their heart cried unto the Lord, O wall of the daughter of Zion, let tears run down like a river day and night:

give thyself no rest; let not the apple of thine eye cease. 19 Arise, cry out in the night: in the beginning of the watches pour out thine heart like water before the face of the Lord: lift up thy hands toward him for the life of thy young children, that faint for hunger in the top of every street. 20 Behold, O LORD, and consider to whom thou hast done this. Shall the women eat their fruit, *and* children of a span long? shall the priest and the prophet be slain in the sanctuary of the LORD? 21 The young and the old lie on the ground in the streets: my virgins and my young men are fallen by the sword; thou hast slain *them* in the day of thine anger; thou hast killed, *and* not pitied. 22 Thou hast called as in a solemn day my terrors round about, so that in the day of the LORD's anger none escaped nor remained: those that I have swaddled and brought up hath mine enemy consumed.

Justly are these called *Lamentations*, and they are very pathetic ones, the expressions of grief in perfection, mourning and woe, and nothing else, like the contents of Ezekiel's roll, Ezek. ii. 10.

I. Copies of lamentations are here presented and they are painted to the life. 1. The judges and magistrates, who used to appear in robes of state, have laid them aside, or rather are stripped of them, and put on the habit of mourners (*v.* 10); the elders now sit no longer in the judgment-seats, the *thrones of the house of David*, but they *sit upon the ground*, having no seat to repose themselves in, or in token of great grief, as Job's friends *sat with him upon the ground*, Job ii. 13. They open not their mouth in the gate, as usual, to give their opinion, but they *keep silence*, overwhelmed with grief, and not knowing what to say. They have *cast dust upon their heads, and girded themselves with sackcloth*, as deep mourners used to do; they had lost their power and wealth, and that made them grieve thus. *Ploratur lachrymis amissa pecunia veris—Genuine are the tears which we shed over lost property.* 2. The young ladies, who used to dress themselves so richly, and *walk with stretched-forth necks* (Isa. iii. 16), now are humbled: *The virgins of Jerusalem hang down their heads to the ground;* those are made to know sorrow who seemed to bid defiance to it and were always disposed to be merry. 3. The prophet himself is a pattern to the mourners, *v.* 11. His *eyes do fail with tears;* he has wept till he can weep

no more, has almost wept his eyes out, wept himself blind. Nor are the inward impressions of grief short of the outward expressions. *His bowels are troubled*, as they were when he saw these calamities coming (Jer. iv. 19, 20), which, one would think, might have excused him now; but even he, to whom they were no surprise, felt them an insupportable grief, to such a degree that his *liver is poured out on the earth;* he felt himself a perfect colliquation; all his entrails were melted and dissolved, as Ps. xxii. 14. Jeremiah himself had better treatment than his neighbours, better than he had had before from his own countrymen, nay, their destruction was his deliverance, their captivity his enlargement; the same that made them prisoners made him a favourite; and yet his private interests are swallowed up in a concern for the public, and he bewails the *destruction of the daughter of his people* as sensibly as if he himself had been the greatest sufferer in that common calamity. Note, The judgments of God upon the land and nation are to be lamented by us, though we, for our parts, may escape pretty well.

II. Calls to lamentation are here given: *The heart of the people cried unto the Lord, v.* 18. Some fear it was a cry, not of true repentance, but of bitter complaint; their heart was as full of grief as it could hold, and they gave vent to it in doleful shrieks and outcries, in which they made use of God's name; yet we will charitably suppose that many of them did in sincerity cry unto God for mercy in their distress; and the prophet bids them go on to do so: " *O wall of the daughter of Zion!* either you that stand upon the wall, you *watchmen on the walls* (Isa. lxii. 6), when you see the enemies encamped about the walls and making their approaches towards them, or *because of the wall* (that is the subject of the lamentation), because of the *breaking down of the wall* (which was not done till about a month after the city was taken), because of this further calamity, let *the daughter of Zion lament* still." This was a thing which Nehemiah lamented long after, Neh. i. 3, 4. " *Let tears run down like a river day and night*, weep without intermission, give thyself no rest from weeping, *let not the apple of thy eye cease.*" This intimates, 1. That the calamities would be continuing, and the causes of grief would frequently recur, and fresh occasion would be given them every day and every night to bemoan themselves. 2. That they would be apt, by degrees, to grow insensible and stupid under the hand of God, and would need to be still called upon to afflict their souls yet more and more, till their proud and hard hearts were thoroughly humbled and softened.

III. Causes for lamentation are here assigned, and the calamities that are to be bewailed are very particularly and pathetically described.

1. Multitudes perish by famine, a very sore judgment, and piteous is the case of those that fall under it. God had corrected them by scarcity of provisions through want of rain some time before (Jer. xiv. 1), and they were not brought to repentance by that lower degree of this judgment, and therefore now by the straitness of the siege God brought it upon them in extremity; for, (1.) The children died for hunger in their mothers' arms: *The children and sucklings*, whose innocent and helpless state entitles them to relief as soon as any, *swoon in the streets* (v. 11) *as the wounded* (v. 12), there being no food to be had for them; those that are starved die as surely as those that are stabbed. They lie a great while crying to their poor mothers for corn to feed them and wine to refresh them, for they are such as had been bred up to the use of wine and wanted it now; but there is none for them, so that at length *their soul is poured into their mothers' bosom*, and there they breathe their last. This is mentioned again (v. 19): *They faint for hunger in the top of every street.* Yet this is not the worst, (2.) There were some little children that were slain by their mothers' hands and eaten, v. 20. Such was the scarcity of provision that the *women ate the fruit* of their own bodies, even their children when they were but of *a span long*, according to the threatening, Deut. xxviii. 53. The like was done in the siege of Samaria, 2 Kings vi. 29. Such extremities, nay, such barbarities, were they brought to by the famine. Let us, in our abundance, thank God that we have food convenient, not only for ourselves, but for our children.

2. Multitudes fall by the sword, which devours one as well as another, especially when it is in the hand of such cruel enemies as the Chaldeans were. (1.) They spared no character, no, not the most distinguished; even the *priest and the prophet*, who of all men, one would think, might expect protection from heaven and veneration on earth, *are slain*, not abroad in the field of battle, where they are out of their place, as Hophni and Phinehas, but in *the sanctuary of the Lord*, the place of their business and which they hoped would be a refuge to them. (2.) They spared no age, no, not those who, by reason of their tender or their decrepit age, were exempted from taking up the sword; for even they *perished by the sword.* "The young, who have not yet come to bear arms, and the old, who have had their *discharge*, *lie on the ground, slain in the streets*, till some kind hand is found that will bury them." (3.) They spared no sex: *My virgins and my young men have fallen by the sword.* In the most barbarous military executions that ever we read of the virgins were spared, and made part of the spoil (Num. xxxi. 18, Judges v. 30), but here the virgins were put to the sword, as well as the young men. (4.) This was the *Lord's*

doing; he suffered the sword of the Chaldeans to devour thus without distinction: *Thou hast slain them in the day of thy anger*, for it is God that *kills and makes alive*, and saves alive, as he pleases. But that which follows is very harsh: *Thou hast killed, and not pitied;* for his soul is *grieved for the misery of Israel.* The enemies that used them thus cruelly were such as he had both mustered and summoned (v. 22): "*Thou hast called in, as in a solemn day, my terrors round about*, that is, the Chaldeans, who are such a terror to me;" enemies crowded into Jerusalem now as thickly as ever worshippers used to do on a solemn festival, so that they were quite overpowered with numbers, and none escaped nor remained; Jerusalem was made a perfect slaughter-house. Mothers are cut to the heart to see those whom they have taken such care of, and pains with, and whom they have been so tender of, thus inhumanly used, suddenly cut off, though not soon reared: *Those that I have swaddled, and brought up, has my enemy consumed*, as if they were brought forth for the murderer, like lambs for the butcher, Hosea ix. 13. Zion, who was a mother to them all, lamented to see those who were brought up in her courts, and under the tuition of her oracles, thus made a prey.

3. Their false prophets cheated them, v. 14. This was a thing which Jeremiah had lamented long before, and had observed with a great concern (Jer. xiv. 13): *Ah! Lord God, the prophets say unto them, You shall not see the sword;* and here he inserts it among his lamentations: *Thy prophets have seen vain and foolish things for thee;* they pretended to discover for thee, and then to discover to thee, the mind and will of God, to see *the visions of the Almighty* and then to speak his words; but they were all vain and foolish things; their visions were all their own fancies, and, if they thought they had any, it was only the product of a crazed head or a heated imagination, as appeared by what they delivered, which was all idle and impertinent: nay, it is most likely that they themselves knew that the visions they pretended were counterfeit, and all a sham, and made use of only to colour that which they designedly imposed upon the people with, that they might make an interest in them for themselves. They are thy prophets, not God's prophets; he never sent them, nor were they pastors after his heart, but the people set them up, told them what they should say, so that they were *prophets after their hearts.* (1.) Prophets should tell people of their faults, should show them their sins, that they may bring them to repentance, and so prevent their ruin; but these prophets knew that would lose them the people's affections and contributions, and knew they could not reprove their hearers without reproaching

themselves at the same time, and therefore *they have not discovered thy iniquity;* they saw it not themselves, or, if they did, saw so little evil in it, or danger from it, that they would not tell them of it, though that might have been a means, by taking away their iniquity, to turn away their captivity. (2.) Prophets should warn people of the judgments of God coming upon them, but these *saw for them false burdens;* the messages they pretended to deliver to them from God they knew to be false, and falsely ascribed to God; so that, by soothing them up in carnal security, they caused that banishment which, by plain dealing, they might have prevented.

4. Their neighbours laughed at them (*v.* 15): *All that pass by thee clap their hands at thee.* Jerusalem had made a great figure, got a great name, and borne a great sway, among the nations; it was the envy and terror of all about; and, when that city was thus reduced; they all (as men are apt to do in such a case) triumphed in its fall; *they hissed, and wagged the head,* pleasing themselves to see how much it had fallen from its former pretensions. *Is this the city* (said they) *that men called the perfection of beauty?* Ps. l. 2. How is it now the perfection of deformity! Where is all its beauty now? *Is this the city which was called the joy of the whole earth* (Ps. xlviii. 2), which rejoiced in the gifts of God's bounty and grace more than any other place, and which all the earth rejoiced in? Where is all its joy now and all its glorying? It is a great sin thus to make a jest of others' miseries, and adds very much affliction to the afflicted.

5. Their enemies triumphed over them, *v.* 16. Those that wished ill to Jerusalem and her peace now vent their spite and malice, which before they concealed; they now *open their mouths,* nay, they widen them; they *hiss and gnash their teeth* in scorn and indignation; they triumph in their own success against her, and the rich prey they have got in making themselves masters of Jerusalem: " *We have swallowed her up;* it is our doing, and it is our gain; it is all our own now. Jerusalem shall never be either courted or feared as she has been. *Certainly this is the day that we have long looked for; we have found it; we have seen it; aha! so would we have it.*" Note, The enemies of the church are apt to take its shocks for its ruins, and to triumph in them accordingly; but they will find themselves deceived; *for the gates of hell shall not prevail against the church.*

6. Their God, in all this, appeared against them (*v.* 17): *The Lord has done that which he had devised.* The destroyers of Jerusalem could have *no power against her unless it were given them from above.* They are but the sword in God's hand; it is he that has *thrown down, and has not pitied.* " In this controversy of his with us we have not had

the usual instances of his compassion towards us." *He has caused thy enemy to rejoice over thee* (see Job xxx. 11); *he has set up the horn of thy adversaries,* has given them power and matter for pride. This is indeed the highest aggravation of the trouble, that God has become their enemy, and yet it is the strongest argument for patience under it; we are bound to submit to what God does, for, (1.) It is the performance of his purpose: *The Lord has done that which he had devised;* it is done with counsel and deliberation, not rashly, or upon a sudden resolve; it is the *evil that he has framed* (Jer. xviii. 11), and we may be sure it is framed so as exactly to answer the intention. What God devises against his people is designed for them, and so it will be found in the issue. (2.) It is the accomplishment of his predictions; it is the fulfilling of the scripture; he has now *put in execution his word that he had commanded in the days of old.* When he gave them his law by Moses he told them what judgments he would certainly inflict upon them if they transgressed that law; and now that they had been guilty of the transgression of this law he had executed the sentence of it, according to Lev. xxvi. 16, &c., Deut. xxviii. 15. Note, In all the providences of God concerning his church it is good to take notice of the fulfilling of his word; for there is an exact agreement between the judgments of God's hand and the judgments of his mouth, and when they are compared they will mutually explain and illustrate each other.

IV. Comforts for the cure of these lamentations are here sought for and prescribed.

1. They are sought for and enquired after, *v.* 13. The prophet seeks to find out some suitable acceptable words to say to her in this case: *Wherewith shall I comfort thee, O virgin! daughter of Zion?* Note, We should endeavour to comfort those whose calamities we lament, and, when our passions have made the worst of them, our wisdom should correct them and labour to make the best of them; we should study to make our sympathies with our afflicted friends turn to their consolation. Now the two most common topics of comfort, in case of affliction, are here tried, but are laid by because they would not hold. We commonly endeavour to comfort our friends by telling them, (1.) That their case is not singular, nor without precedent; there are many whose trouble is greater, and lies heavier upon them, than theirs does; but Jerusalem's case will not admit this argument: " *What thing shall I liken to thee, or what shall I equal to thee, that I may comfort thee?* What city, what country, is there, whose case is parallel to thine? What witness shall I produce to prove an example that will reach thy present calamitous state? Alas! there is none, no sorrow like thine, because there is none

whose honour was like thine. (2.) We tell them that their case is not desperate, but that it may easily be remedied; but neither will that be admitted here, upon a view of human probabilities; for *thy breach is great, like the sea,* like the breach which the sea sometimes makes upon the land, which cannot be repaired, but still grows wider and wider. Thou art wounded, and *who shall heal thee?* No wisdom nor power of man can repair the desolations of such a broken shattered state. It is to no purpose therefore to administer any of these common cordials; therefore,

2. The method of cure prescribed is to address themselves to God, and by a penitent prayer to commit their case to him, and to be instant and constant in such prayers (*v.* 19): "*Arise* out of thy dust, out of thy despondency, *cry out in the night,* watch unto prayer; when others are asleep, be thou upon thy knees, importunate with God for mercy; *in the beginning of the watches,* of each of the four watches, of the night (let thy *eyes prevent* them, Ps. cxix. 148), then *pour out thy heart like water before the Lord,* be free and full in prayer, be sincere and serious in prayer, open thy mind, spread thy case before the Lord; *lift up thy hands towards him* in holy desire and expectation; beg for *the life of thy young children.* These poor lambs, what have they done? 2 Sam. xxiv. 17. Take with you words, take with you these words (*v.* 20), *Behold, O Lord! and consider to whom thou hast done this,* with whom thou hast dealt thus. Are they not thy own, the seed of Abraham thy friend and of Jacob thy chosen? Lord, take their case into thy compassionate consideration!" Note, Prayer is a salve for every sore, even the sorest, a remedy for every malady, even the most grievous. And our business in prayer is not to prescribe, but to subscribe to the wisdom and will of God; to refer our case to him, and then to leave it with him. *Lord, behold and consider,* and *thy will be done.*

CHAP. III.

The scope of this chapter is the same with that of the two foregoing chapters, but the composition is somewhat different; that was in long verse, this is in short, another kind of metre; that was in single alphabets, this is in a treble one. Here is, I. A sad complaint of God's displeasure and the fruits of it, ver. 1—20. II. Words of comfort to God's people when they are in trouble and distress, ver. 21—36. III. Duty prescribed in this afflicted state, ver. 37—41. IV. The complaint renewed, ver. 42—54. V. Encouragement taken to hope in God, and continue waiting for his salvation, with an appeal to his justice against the persecutors of the church, ver. 55—66. Some make all this to be spoken by the prophet himself when he was imprisoned and persecuted; but it seems rather to be spoken in the person of the church now in captivity and in a manner desolate, and in the desolations of which the prophet did in a particular manner interest himself. But the complaints here are somewhat more general than those in the foregoing chapter, being accommodated to the case as well of particular persons as of the public, and intended for the use of the closet rather than of the solemn assembly. Some think Jeremiah makes these complaints, not only as an intercessor for Israel, but as a type of Christ, who was thought by some to be Jeremiah the weeping prophet, because he was much in tears (Matt. xvi. 14) and to him many of the passages here may be applied.

I AM the man *that* hath seen affliction by the rod of his wrath. 2

726

He hath led me, and brought *me into* darkness, but not *into* light. 3 Surely against me is he turned; he turneth his hand *against me* all the day. 4 My flesh and my skin hath he made old; he hath broken my bones. 5 He hath builded against me, and compassed *me* with gall and travel. 6 He hath set me in dark places, as *they that be* dead of old. 7 He hath hedged me about, that I cannot get out: he hath made my chain heavy. 8 Also when I cry and shout, he shutteth out my prayer. 9 He hath inclosed my ways with hewn stone, he hath made my paths crooked. 10 He *was* unto me *as* a bear lying in wait, *and as* a lion in secret places. 11 He hath turned aside my ways, and pulled me in pieces: he hath made me desolate. 12 He hath bent his bow, and set me as a mark for the arrow. 13 He hath caused the arrows of his quiver to enter into my reins. 14 I was a derision to all my people; *and* their song all the day. 15 He hath filled me with bitterness, he hath made me drunken with wormwood. 16 He hath also broken my teeth with gravel stones, he hath covered me with ashes. 17 And thou hast removed my soul far off from peace: I forgat prosperity. 18 And I said, My strength and my hope is perished from the LORD: 19 Remembering mine affliction and my misery, the wormwood and the gall. 20 My soul hath *them* still in remembrance, and is humbled in me.

The title of the 102d Psalm might very fitly be prefixed to this chapter—*The prayer of the afflicted, when he is overwhelmed, and pours out his complaint before the Lord;* for it is very feelingly and fluently that the complaint is here poured out. Let us observe the particulars of it. The prophet complains, 1. That God is angry. This gives both birth and bitterness to the affliction (*v.* 1): *I am the man,* the remarkable man, *that has seen affliction,* and has felt it sensibly, *by the rod of his wrath.* Note, God is sometimes angry with his own people; yet it is to be complained of, not as a sword to cut off, but only as a rod to correct; it is to them *the rod of his wrath,* a chastening which, though grievous for the present, will in the issue be advantageous. By this rod we must expect to *see affliction,* and, if we be made to see more than ordinary affliction by that rod, we must not quarrel, for we are sure that the anger is just and the affliction mild and mixed with mercy. 2. That he is at a loss and altogether in the dark. Darkness is put for great trouble and perplexity, the want botr. of comfort and of direction; this was the case of the complainant (*v.* 2): " *He has led me* by his providence, and an unaccountable chain of events, *into darkness and not into light,* the darkness I feared and not into the light I hoped for." And (*v.* 6), *He has set me in dark places,* dark as the grave, *like those that are dead of old,* that are quite forgotten, nobody knows who or what they were. Note, The Israel of God, though children of light, sometimes *walk in darkness.* 3. That God appears against him as an enemy, as a professed enemy. God had been for him, but now " *Surely against me is he turned* (*v.* 3), as far as I can discern; for *his hand is turned against me all the day. I am chastened every morning,*" Ps. lxxiii. 14. And, when God's hand is continually turned against us, we are tempted to think that his heart is turned against us too. God had said once (Hos. v. 14), *I will be as a lion to the house of Judah,* and now he has made his word good (*v.* 10): " *He was unto me as a bear lying in wait,* surprising me with his judgments, *and as a lion in secret places;* so that which way soever I went I was in continual fear of being set upon and could never think myself safe." Do men shoot at those they are enemies to? *He has bent his bow,* the bow that was ordained against the church's persecutors, that is bent against her sons, *v.* 12. *He has set me as a mark for his arrow,* which he aims at, and will be sure to hit, and then *the arrows of his quiver enter into my reins,* give me a mortal wound, an inward wound, *v.* 13. Note, God has many arrows in his quiver, and they fly swiftly and pierce deeply. 4. That he is as one sorely afflicted both in body and mind. The Jewish state may now be fitly compared to a man wrinkled with age, for which there is no remedy (*v.* 4): " *My flesh and my skin has he made old;* they are wasted and withered, and I look like one that is ready to drop into the grave; nay, *he has broken my bones,* and so disabled me to help myself, *v.* 15. *He has filled me with bitterness,* a bitter sense of these calamities." God has access to the spirit, and can so embitter that as thereby to embitter all the enjoyments; as, when the stomach is foul, whatever is eaten sours in it: " *He has made me drunk with wormwood,* so intoxicated me with the sense of my afflictions that I know not what to say or do. *He has* mingled *gravel* with my bread, so that *my teeth are broken* with it (*v.* 16) and what I eat is neither pleasant nor nourishing. *He has covered me with ashes,* as mourners used to be, or (as some read it) *he has fed me with ashes. I have eaten ashes like bread,*" Ps. cii. 9. 5. That

he is not able to discern any way of escape or deliverance (*v.* 5): " *He has built against me,* as forts and batteries are built against a besieged city. Where there was a way open it is now quite made up: *He has compassed me* on every side *with gall and travel;* I vex, and fret, and tire myself, to find a way of escape, but can find none, *v.* 7. *He has hedged me about, that I cannot get out.*" When Jerusalem was besieged it was said to be *compassed in on every side,* Luke xix. 43. " I am chained; and as some notorious malefactors are double-fettered, and loaded with irons, so he *has made my chain heavy. He has* also (*v.* 9) *enclosed my ways with hewn stone,* not only hedged up my way *with thorns* (Hos. ii. 6), but stopped it up with a stone wall, which cannot be broken through, so that *my paths are made crooked;* I traverse to and fro, to the right hand, to the left, to try to get forward, but am still turned back." It is just with God to make those who walk in the crooked paths of sin, crossing God's laws, walk in the crooked paths of affliction, crossing their designs and breaking their measures. So (*v.* 11), *He has turned aside my ways;* he has blasted all my counsels, ruined my projects, so that I am necessitated to yield to my own ruin. He has *pulled me in pieces;* he has torn and is gone away (Hos. v. 14), and has *made me desolate,* has deprived me of all society and all comfort in my own soul." 6. That God turns a deaf ear to his prayers (*v.* 8): " *When I cry and shout,* as one in earnest, as one that would make him hear, yet he *shuts out my prayer* and will not suffer it to have access to him." God's ear is wont to be open to the prayers of his people, and his door of mercy to those that knock at it; but now both are shut, even to one that *cries and shouts.* Thus sometimes God seems to be angry even against *the prayers of his people* (Ps. lxxx. 4), and their case is deplorable indeed when they are denied not only the benefit of an answer, but the comfort of acceptance. 7. That his neighbours make a laughing matter of his troubles (*v.* 14): *I was a derision to all my people,* to all the wicked among them, who made themselves and one another merry with the public judgments, and particularly the prophet Jeremiah's griefs. I am their song, their *neginath,* or hand-instrument of music, their *tabret* (Job xvii. 6), that they play upon, as Nero on his harp when Rome was on fire. 8. That he was ready to despair of relief and deliverance: " 'Thou hast not only taken peace from me, but hast *removed my soul far off from peace* (*v.* 17), so that it is not only not within reach, but not within view. *I forget prosperity;* it is so long since I had it, and so unlikely that I should ever recover it, that I have lost the idea of it. I have been so inured to sorrow and servitude that I know not what joy and liberty mean. I have even given up all for gone, concluding,

727

My strength and my hope have perished from the Lord (*v.* 18); I can no longer stay myself upon God as my support, for I do not find that he gives me encouragement to do so; nor can I look for his appearing in my behalf, so as to put an end to my troubles, for the case seems remediless, and even my God inexorable." Without doubt it was his infirmity to say this (Ps. lxxvii. 10), for with God there is *everlasting strength,* and he is his people's never-failing hope, whatever they may think. 9. That grief returned upon every remembrance of his troubles, and his reflections were as melancholy as his prospects, *v.* 19, 20. Did he endeavour, as Job did (Job ix. 27), to *forget his complaint?* Alas! it was to no purpose; he remembers, upon all occasions, *the affliction and the misery, the wormwood and the gall.* Thus emphatically does he speak of his affliction, for thus did he think of it, thus heavily did it lie when he reviewed it! It was an affliction that was misery itself. *My affliction and my transgression* (so some read it), my trouble and my sin that brought it upon me; this was *the wormwood and the gall* in *the affliction and the misery.* It is sin that makes the cup of affliction a bitter cup. *My soul has them still in remembrance.* The captives in Babylon had all the miseries of the siege in their mind continually and the flames and ruins of Jerusalem still before their eyes, and *wept when* they *remembered Zion;* nay, they could *never forget Jerusalem,* Ps. cxxxvii. 1, 5. *My soul,* having *them in remembrance, is humbled in me,* not only oppressed with a sense of the trouble, but in bitterness for sin. Note, It becomes us to have humble hearts under humbling providences, and to renew our penitent humiliations for sin upon every remembrance of our afflictions and miseries. Thus we may get good by former corrections and prevent further.

21 This I recall to my mind, therefore have I hope. 22 *It is of* the LORD's mercies that we are not consumed, because his compassions fail not. 23 *They are* new every morning: great *is* thy faithfulness. 24 The LORD *is* my portion, saith my soul; therefore will I hope in him. 25 The LORD *is* good unto them that wait for him, to the soul *that* seeketh him. 26 *It is* good that *a man* should both hope and quietly wait for the salvation of the LORD. 27 *It is* good for a man that he bear the yoke in his youth. 28 He sitteth alone and keepeth silence, because he hath borne *it* upon him. 29 He putteth his mouth in the dust; if so be there

728

may be hope. 30 He giveth *his* cheek to him that smiteth him: he is filled full with reproach. 31 For the LORD will not cast off for ever: 32 But. though he cause grief, yet will he have compassion according to the multitude of his mercies. 33 For he doth not afflict willingly nor grieve the children of men. 34 To crush under his feet all the prisoners of the earth, 35 To turn aside the right of a man before the face of the most High, 36 To subvert a man in his cause, the LORD approveth not.

Here the clouds begin to disperse and the sky to clear up; the complaint was very melancholy in the former part of the chapter, and yet here the tune is altered and the mourners in Zion begin to look a little pleasant. But for hope, the heart would break. To save the heart from being quite broken, here is something *called to mind,* which gives ground for *hope* (*v.* 21), which refers to what comes after, not to what goes before. *I make to return to my heart* (so the margin words it); what we have had in our hearts, and have laid to our hearts, is sometimes as if it were quite lost and forgotten, till God by his grace make it return to our hearts, that it may be ready to us when we have occasion to use it. "*I recal* it *to mind; therefore have I hope,* and am kept from downright despair." Let us see what these things are which he calls to mind.

I. That, bad as things are, it is owing to the mercy of God that they are not worse. We are *afflicted by the rod of his wrath, but it is of the Lord's mercies that we are not consumed, v.* 22. When we are in distress we should, for the encouragement of our faith and hope, observe what makes for us as well as what makes against us. Things are bad but they might have been worse, and therefore there is hope that they may be better Observe here, 1. The streams of mercy acknowledged: *We are not consumed.* Note, The church of God is like Moses's bush, burning, yet *not consumed;* whatever hardships it has met with, or may meet with, it shall have a being in the world to the end of time. It is *persecuted* of men, *but not forsaken* of God, and therefore, though it is *cast down,* it is *not destroyed* (2 Cor. iv. 9), corrected, yet *not consumed,* refined in the furnace as silver, but *not consumed* as dross. 2. These streams followed up to the fountain: *It is of the Lord's mercies.* Here are mercies in the plural number, denoting the abundance and variety of those mercies. God is an inexhaustible *fountain of mercy, the Father of mercies.* Note, We all owe it to the sparing mercy of God *that we are not consumed.* Others have been consumed round about us, and we ourselves have been in the consuming, and yet *we are not consumed;* we are out of the grave; we are out of hell. Had we been dealt with *according to our sins,* we should have been consumed long ago; but we have been dealt with *according to God's mercies,* and we are bound to acknowledge it to his praise.

II. That even in the depth of their affliction they still have experience of the tenderness of the divine pity and the truth of the divine promise. They had several times complained that God had not pitied (*ch.* ii. 17, 21), but here they correct themselves, and own, 1. That *God's compassions fail not;* they do not really fail, no, not even when in anger he seems to have *shut up his tender mercies.* These rivers of mercy run fully and constantly, but never run dry. No; *they are new every morning;* every morning we have fresh instances of God's compassion towards us; he visits us with them *every morning* (Job vii. 18); *every morning does he bring his judgment to light,* Zeph. iii. 5. When our comforts fail, yet God's compassions do not. 2. That *great is his faithfulness.* Though the covenant seemed to be broken, they owned that it still continued in full force; and, though Jerusalem be in ruins, *the truth of the Lord endures for ever.* Note, Whatever hard things we suffer, we must never entertain any hard thoughts of God, but must still be ready to own that he is both kind and faithful.

III. That God is, and ever will be, the all-sufficient happiness of his people, and they have chosen him and depend upon him to be such (*v.* 24): *The Lord is my portion, saith my soul;* that is, 1. "When I have lost all I have in the world, liberty, and livelihood, and almost life itself, yet I have not lost my interest in God." Portions on earth are perishing things, but God is a *portion for ever.* 2. "While I have an interest in God, therein I have enough; I have that which is sufficient to counterbalance all my troubles and make up all my losses." Whatever we are robbed of our portion is safe. 3. "This is that which I depend upon and rest satisfied with: *Therefore will I hope in him.* I will stay myself upon him, and encourage myself in him, when all other supports and encouragements fail me." Note, It is our duty to make God the portion of our souls, and then to make use of him as our portion and to take the comfort of it in the midst of our lamentations.

IV. That those who deal with God will find it is not in vain to trust in him; for, 1. He is good to those who do so, *v.* 25. He is good to all; *his tender mercies are over all his works;* all his creatures taste of his goodness. But he is in a particular manner *good to those that wait for him, to the soul that seeks him.* Note, While trouble is prolonged, and deliverance is deferred, we must patiently wait for God and his gracious returns to us. While we *wait for him* by faith,

we must *seek him* by prayer: our *souls* must *seek him,* else we do not seek so as to find. Our seeking will help to keep up our waiting. And to those who thus wait and seek God will be gracious; he will show them his *marvellous lovingkindness.* 2. Those that do so will find it good for them (*v.* 26): *It is good* (it is our duty, and will be our unspeakable comfort and satisfaction) *to hope and quietly to wait for the salvation of the Lord,* to hope that it will come, though the difficulties that lie in the way of it seem insupportable, to wait till it does come, though it be long delayed, and while we wait to be quiet and silent, not quarrelling with God nor making ourselves uneasy, but acquiescing in the divine disposals. *Father, thy will be done.* If we call this to mind, we may have hope that all will end well at last.

V. That afflictions are really good for us, and, if we bear them aright, will work very much for our good. It is not only good to hope and wait for the salvation, but it is good to be under the trouble in the mean time (*v.* 27): *It is good for a man that he bear the yoke in his youth.* Many of the young men were carried into captivity. To make them easy in it, he tells them that it was good for them to *bear the yoke* of that captivity, and they would find it so if they would but accommodate themselves to their condition, and labour to answer God's ends in laying that heavy yoke upon them. It is very applicable to the yoke of God's commands. It is good for young people to take that yoke upon them in their youth; we cannot begin too soon to be religious. It will make our duty the more acceptable to God, and easy to ourselves, if we engage in it when we are young. But here it seems to be meant of the yoke of affliction. Many have found it good to bear this in youth; it has made those humble and serious, and has weaned them from the world, who otherwise would have been proud and unruly, and *as a bullock unaccustomed to the yoke.* But when do we *bear the yoke* so that it is really *good for us to bear it in our youth?* He answers in the following verses, 1. When we are sedate and quiet under our afflictions, when we *sit alone and keep silence,* do not run to and fro into all companies with our complaints, aggravating our calamities, and quarrelling with the disposals of Providence concerning us, but retire into privacy, that we may *in a day of adversity consider, sit alone,* that we may converse with God and *commune with our own hearts,* silencing all discontented distrustful thoughts, and laying our hand upon our mouth, as Aaron, who, under a very severe trial, held his peace. We must keep silence under the yoke as those that have borne it upon us, not wilfully pulled it upon our own necks, but patiently submitted to it when God laid it upon us. When those who are afflicted in their youth accommodate themselves to their afflictions, fit their necks to the yoke and study to answer God's end in afflicting them, then they will find it good for them to bear it, for it yields *the peaceable fruit of righteousness to those who are* thus *exercised thereby.* 2. When we are humble and patient under our affliction. *He* gets good by the yoke who *puts his mouth in the dust,* not only *lays his hand upon his mouth,* in token of submission to the will of God in the affliction, but *puts it in the dust,* in token of sorrow, and shame, and self-loathing, at the remembrance of sin, and as one perfectly reduced and reclaimed, and brought as those that are vanquished to *lick the dust,* Ps. lxxii. 9. And we must thus humble ourselves, *if so be there may be hope,* or (as it is in the original) *peradventure there is hope.* If there be any way to acquire and secure a good hope under our afflictions, it is this way, and yet we must be very modest in our expectations of it, must look for it with an *it may be,* as those who own ourselves utterly unworthy of it. Note, Those who are truly humbled for sin will be glad to obtain a good hope, through grace, upon any terms, though they *put their mouth in the dust* for it; and those who would have hope must do so, and ascribe it to free grace if they have any encouragements, which may keep their hearts from sinking into the dust when they put their mouth there. 3. When we are meek and mild towards those who are the instruments of our trouble, and are of a forgiving spirit, *v.* 30. *He* gets good by the yoke who *gives his cheek to him that smites him,* and rather *turns the other cheek* (Matt. v. 39) than returns the second blow. Our Lord Jesus has left us an example of this, for he *gave his back to the smiter,* Isa. l. 6. He who can bear contempt and reproach, and not *render railing for railing* and bitterness for bitterness, who, when he is *filled full with reproach,* keeps it to himself, and does not retort it and empty it again upon those who filled him with it, but *pours it out before the Lord* (as those did, Ps. cxxiii. 4, whose *souls were exceedingly filled with the contempt of the proud),* he shall find that *it is good to bear the yoke,* that it shall turn to his spiritual advantage. The sum is, *If tribulation work patience,* that *patience* will work *experience,* and that *experience a hope that makes not ashamed.*

VI. That God will graciously return to his people with seasonable comforts *according to the time that he has afflicted them, v.* 31, 32. *Therefore* the sufferer is thus penitent, thus patient, because he believes that God is gracious and merciful, which is the great inducement both to evangelical repentance and to Christian patience. We may bear ourselves up with this, 1. That, when we are cast down, yet we are not cast off; the father's correcting his son is not a disinheriting of him. 2. That though we may seem to be cast off for a time, while sensible comforts are suspended and desired salva-

tions deferred, yet we are not really cast off, because not *cast off for ever;* the controversy with us shall not be perpetual. 3 That, whatever sorrow we are in, it is what God has allotted us, and his hand is in it. It is he that causes grief, and therefore we may be assured it is ordered wisely and graciously; and it is but *for a season,* and when need is, that we *are in heaviness,* 1 Pet. i. 6. 4. That God has compassions and comforts in store even for those whom he has himself grieved. We must be far from thinking that, though God cause grief, the world will relieve and help us. No; the very same that caused the grief must bring in the favour, or we are undone. *Una eademque manus vulnus opemque tulit—The same hand inflicted the wound and healed it.* He has torn, and he will heal us, Hos. vi. 1. 5. That, when God returns to deal graciously with us, it will not be according to our merits, but according to his mercies, *according to the multitude,* the abundance, *of his mercies.* So unworthy we are that nothing but an abundant mercy will relieve us; and from that what may we not expect? And God's causing our grief ought to be no discouragement at all to those expectations.

VII. That, when God does cause grief, it is for wise and holy ends, and he takes not delight in our calamities, *v.* 33. He does indeed *afflict, and grieve the children of men;* all their grievances and afflictions are from him. But he does not do it *willingly,* not *from the heart;* so the word is. 1. He never afflicts us but when we give him cause to do it. He does not dispense his frowns as he does his favours, *ex mero motu —from his mere good pleasure.* If he show us kindness, it is because *so it seems good* unto him; but, if he write bitter things against us, it is because we both deserve them and need them. 2. He does not afflict with pleasure. He delights not in the death of sinners, or the disquiet of saints, but punishes with a kind of reluctance. He comes out of his place to punish, for his place is the mercy-seat. He delights not in the misery of any of his creatures, but, as it respects his own people, he is so far from it that in all their afflictions he is afflicted and his soul is grieved for the misery of Israel. 3. He retains his kindness for his people even when he afflicts them. If he does not *willingly grieve the children of men,* much less his own children. However it be, yet *God is good* to them (Ps. lxxiii. 1), and they may by faith see love in his heart even when they see frowns in his face and a rod in his hand.

VIII. That though he makes use of men as his hand, or rather instruments in his hand, for the correcting of his people, yet he is far from being pleased with the injustice of their proceedings and the wrong they do them, *v.* 34—36. Though God serves his own purposes by the violence of wicked and unreasonable men, yet it does not therefore follow that he countenances that violence, as his oppressed people are sometimes tempted to think. Hab. i. 13, *Wherefore lookest thou upon those that deal treacherously?* Two ways the people of God are injured and oppressed by their enemies, and the prophet here assures us that God does not approve of either of them :—1. If men injure them by force of arms, God does not approve of that. He does not himself *crush under his feet the prisoners of the earth,* but he regards the cry of the prisoners ; nor does he approve of men's doing it ; nay, he is much displeased with it. It is barbarous to trample on those that are down, and to crush those that are bound and cannot help themselves. 2. If men injure them under colour of law, and in the pretended administration of justice,— if they *turn aside the right of a man,* so that he cannot discover what his rights are or cannot come at them, they are out of his reach,— if they *subvert a man in his cause,* and bring in a wrong verdict, or give a false judgment, let them know, (1.) That God sees them. It is *before the face of the Most High* (v. 35); it is in his sight, under his eye, and is very displeasing to him. They cannot but know it is so, and therefore it is in defiance of him that they do it. He is *the Most High,* whose authority over them they contemn by abusing their authority over their subjects, not considering that *he that is higher than the highest regardeth,* Eccl. v. 8. (2.) That God does not approve of them. More is implied than is expressed. The perverting of justice, and the subverting of the just, are a great affront to God ; and, though he may make use of them for the correction of his people, yet he will sooner or later severely reckon with those that do thus. Note, However God may for a time suffer evil-doers to prosper, and serve his own purposes by them, yet he does not therefore approve of their evil doings. *Far be it from God that he should do iniquity,* or countenance those that do it.

37 Who *is* he *that* saith, and it cometh to pass, *when* the LORD commandeth *it* not? 38 Out of the mouth of the most High proceedeth not evil and good? 39 Wherefore doth a living man complain, a man for the punishment of his sins? 40 Let us search and try our ways, and turn again to the LORD. 41 Let us lift up our heart with *our* hands unto God in the heavens.

That we may be entitled to the comforts administered to the afflicted in the foregoing verses, and may taste the sweetness of them, we have here the duties of an afflicted state prescribed to us, in the performance of which we may expect those comforts.

I. We must see and acknowledge the hand of God in all the calamities that befal

us at any time, whether personal or public, v. 37, 38. This is here laid down as a great truth, which will help to quiet our spirits under our afflictions and to sanctify them to us. 1. That, whatever men's actions are, it is God that overrules them : *Who is he that saith, and it cometh to pass* (that designs a thing and bring his designs to effect), if *the Lord commandeth it not?* Men can do nothing but according to the counsel of God, nor have any power or success but what is given them from above. *A man's heart devises his way ;* he projects and purposes ; he says that he will do so and so (Jam. iv. 13); *but the Lord directs his steps* far otherwise than he designed them, and what he contrived and expected does not *come to pass,* unless it be what God's hand and his counsel had determined before to be done, Prov. xvi. 9; Jer. x. 23. The Chaldeans said that they would destroy Jerusalem, and it came to pass, not because they said it, but because God commanded it and commissioned them to do it. Note, Men are but tools which the great God makes use of, and manages as he pleases, in the government of this lower world; and they cannot accomplish any of their designs without him. 2. That, whatever men's lot is, it is God that orders it : *Out of the mouth of the Most High do not evil and good proceed?* Yes, certainly they do ; and it is more emphatically expressed in the original: *Do not* this *evil, and* this *good, proceed out of the mouth of the Most High?* Is it not what he has ordained and appointed for us? Yes, certainly it is ; and for the reconciling of us to our own afflictions, whatever they be, this general truth must thus be particularly applied. This comfort I receive *from the hand of God, and shall I not receive* that *evil* also? so Job argues, *ch.* ii. 10. Are we healthful or sickly, rich or poor? Do we succeed in our designs, or are we crossed in them? It is all what God orders; *every man's judgment proceeds from him. The Lord gave, and the Lord has taken away ;* he forms the light and creates the darkness, as he did at first. Note, All the events of divine Providence are the products of a divine counsel; whatever is done God has the directing of it, and the works of his hands agree with the words of his mouth ; *he speaks, and it is done,* so easily, so effectually are all his purposes fulfilled.

II. We must not quarrel with God for any affliction that he lays upon us at any time (v. 39): *Wherefore does a living man complain?* The prophet here seems to check himself for the complaint he had made in the former part of the chapter, wherein he seemed to reflect upon God as unkind and severe. "Do I well to be angry? Why do I fret thus?" Those who in their haste have chidden with God must, in the reflection, chide themselves for it. From the doctrine of God's sovereign and universal providence, which he had asserted in the verses before, he draws this inference, *Wherefore does a living man complain?* What God does we must not open our mouths against, Ps. xxxix. 9. Those that blame their lot reproach him that allotted it to them. The sufferers in the captivity must submit to the will of God in all their sufferings. Note, Though we may pour out our complaints before God, we must never exhibit any complaints against God. What! Shall *a living man complain, a man for the punishment of his sins?* The reasons here urged are very cogent. 1. We are men; let us herein show ourselves men. Shall *a man complain?* And again, *a man!* We are men, and not brutes, reasonable creatures, who should act with reason, who should look upward and look forward, and both ways may fetch considerations enough to silence our complaints. We are men, and not children that cry for every thing that hurts them. We are men, and not gods, subjects, not lords; we are not our own masters, not our own carvers; we are bound, and must obey, must submit. We are men, and not angels, and therefore cannot expect to be free from troubles as they are; we are not inhabitants of that world where there is no sorrow, but this where there is nothing but sorrow. We are men, and not devils, are not in that deplorable, helpless, hopeless, state that they are in, but have something to comfort ourselves with which they have not. 2. We are living men. Through the good hand of our God upon us we are alive yet, though dying daily; and shall *a living man complain?* No; he has more reason to be thankful for life than to complain of any of the burdens and calamities of life. Our lives are frail and forfeited, and yet we are alive; now *the living, the living, they* should *praise*, and not complain (Isa. xxxviii. 19); while there is life there is hope, and therefore, instead of complaining that things are bad, we should encourage ourselves with the hope that they will be better. 3. We are sinful men, and that which we complain of is the just *punishment of our sins;* nay, it is far less than our iniquities have deserved. We have little reason to complain of our trouble, for it is our own doing; we may thank ourselves. Our own wickedness corrects us, Prov. xix. 3. We have no reason to quarrel with God, for he is righteous in it; he is the governor of the world, and it is necessary that he should maintain the honour of his government by chastising the disobedient. Are we suffering for our sins? Then let us not complain; for we have other work to do; instead of repining, we must be repenting; and, as an evidence that God is reconciled to us, we must be endeavouring to reconcile ourselves to his holy will. Are we *punished for our sins?* It is our wisdom then to submit, and to kiss the rod; for, if we still walk contrary to

732

God, he will punish us yet seven times more; for *when he judges he will overcome.* But, if we accommodate ourselves to him, though we be *chastened of the Lord* we shall not be *condemned with the world.*

III. We must set ourselves to answer God's intention in afflicting us, which is to bring sin to our remembrance, and to bring us home to himself, *v.* 40. These are the two things which our afflictions should put us upon. 1. A serious consideration of ourselves and a reflection upon our past lives. *Let us search and try our ways,* search what they have been, and then try whether they have been right and good or no; search as for a malefactor in disguise, that flees and hides himself, and then try whether guilty or not guilty. Let conscience be employed both to search and to try, and let it have leave to deal faithfully, to accomplish a diligent search and to make an impartial trial. *Let us try our ways,* that by them we may try ourselves, for we are to judge of our state not by our faint wishes, but by our steps, not by one particular step, but by our ways, the ends we aim at, the rules we go by, and the agreeableness of the temper of our minds and the tenour of our lives to those ends and those rules. When we are in affliction it is seasonable to *consider our ways* (Hag. i. 5), that what is amiss may be repented of and amended for the future, and so we may answer the intention of the affliction. We are apt, in times of public calamity, to reflect upon other people's ways, and lay blame upon them; whereas our business is to *search and try our* own *ways.* We have work enough to do at home; we must each of us say, "What have I done? What have I contributed to the public flames?" that we may each of us mend one, and then we should all be mended. 2. A sincere conversion to God: "Let us *turn again to the Lord,* to him who is turned against us and whom we have turned from; to him let us turn by repentance and reformation, as to our owner and ruler. We have been with him, and it has never been well with us since we forsook him; let us therefore now turn again to him." This must accompany the former and be the fruit of it; *therefore* we must *search and try our ways,* that we may turn from the evil of them to God. This was the method David took. Ps. cxix. 59, *I thought on my ways, and turned my feet unto thy testimonies.*

IV. We must offer up ourselves to God, and our best affections and services, in the flames of devotion, *v.* 41. When we are in affliction, 1. We must look up to God as a *God in the heavens,* infinitely above us, and who has an incontestable dominion over us; for *the heavens do rule,* and are therefore not to be quarrelled with, but submitted to. 2. We must pray to him, with a believing expectation to receive mercy from him; for that is implied in our *lifting up our hands* to him (a gesture commonly used in prayer and sometimes put for it, as Ps. cxli. 2, *Let the lifting up of my hands be as the evening sacrifice*); it signifies our requesting mercy from him and our readiness to receive that mercy. (3.) Our hearts must go along with our prayers. We must *lift up our hearts with our hands*, as we must pour out our souls with our words. It is the heart that God looks at in that and every other service; for what will a sacrifice without a heart avail? If inward impressions be not in some measure answerable to outward expressions, we do but mock God and deceive ourselves. Praying is lifting up the soul to God (Ps. xxv. 1) as to *our Father in heaven;* and the soul that hopes to be with God in heaven for ever will thus, by frequent acts of devotion, be still learning the way thither and pressing forward in that way.

42 We have transgressed and have rebelled: thou hast not pardoned. 43 Thou hast covered with anger, and persecuted us: thou hast slain, thou hast not pitied. 44 Thou hast covered thyself with a cloud, that *our* prayer should not pass through. 45 Thou hast made us *as* the off-scouring and refuse in the midst of the people. 46 All our enemies have opened their mouths against us. 47 Fear and a snare is come upon us, desolation and destruction. 48 Mine eye runneth down with rivers of water for the destruction of the daughter of my people. 49 Mine eye trickleth down, and ceaseth not, without any intermission, 50 Till the LORD look down, and behold from heaven. 51 Mine eye affecteth mine heart because of all the daughters of my city. 52 Mine enemies chased me sore, like a bird, without cause. 53 They have cut off my life in the dungeon, and cast a stone upon me. 54 Waters flowed over mine head; *then* I said, I am cut off.

It is easier to chide ourselves for complaining than to chide ourselves out of it. The prophet had owned that a living man should not complain, as if he checked himself for his complaints in the former part of the chapter; and yet here the clouds return after the rain and the wound bleeds afresh; for great pains must be taken with a troubled spirit to bring it into temper.

I. They confess the righteousness of God in afflicting them (*v.* 42): *We have transgressed and have rebelled.* Note, It becomes us, when we are in trouble, to justify God, by owning our sins, and laying the load upon ourselves for them. Call sin a transgression, call it a rebellion, and you do not miscal it. This is the result of their searching and trying their ways; the more they enquired into them the worse they found them. Yet,

II. They complain of the afflictions they are under, not without some reflections upon God, which we are not to imitate, but, under the sharpest trials, must always think and speak highly and kindly of him.

1. They complain of his frowns and the tokens of his displeasure against them. Their sins were repented of, and yet (*v.* 42), *Thou hast not pardoned.* They had not the assurance and comfort of the pardon; the judgments brought upon them for their sins were not removed, and therefore they thought they could not say the sin was pardoned, which was a mistake, but a common mistake with the people of God when their souls are cast down and disquieted within them. Their case was really pitiable, yet they complain, *Thou hast not pitied, v.* 43. Their enemies persecuted and slew them, but that was not the worst of it; they were but the instruments in God's hand: "*Thou hast persecuted us, and thou hast slain us,* though we expected thou wouldst protect and deliver us." They complain that there was a wall of partition between them and God, and, (1.) This hindered God's favours from coming down upon them. The reflected beams of God's kindness to them used to be the beauty of Israel; but now "*thou hast covered* us *with anger,* so that our glory is concealed and gone; now God is angry with us, and we do not appear that illustrious people that we have formerly been thought to be." Or, "*Thou hast covered us* up as men that are buried are covered up and forgotten." (2.) It hindered their prayers from coming up unto God (*v.* 44): "*Thou hast covered thyself with a cloud,*" not like that bright cloud in which he took possession of the temple, which enabled the worshippers to draw near to him, but like that in which he came down upon Mount Sinai, which obliged the people to stand at a distance. "This cloud is so thick *that our prayers* seem as if they were lost in it; they cannot *pass through;* we cannot obtain an audience." Note, The prolonging of troubles is sometimes a temptation, even to praying people, to question whether God be what they have always believed him to be, a prayer-hearing God.

2. They complain of the contempt of their neighbours and the reproach and ignominy they were under (*v.* 45): "*Thou hast made us as the off-scouring,* or scrapings, of the first floor, which are thrown to the dunghill." This St. Paul refers to in his account of the sufferings of the apostles. 1 Cor. iv. 13, *We are made as the filth of the world and are the off-scouring of all things.* "We are the *refuse,* or dross, *in the midst of the people,* trodden upon by every body, and looked

upon as the vilest of the nations, and good for nothing but to be cast out as *salt* which *has lost its savour. Our enemies have opened their mouths against us (v.* 46), have *gaped upon us as roaring lions,* to swallow us up, or made mouths at us, or have taken liberty to say what they please of us." These complaints we had before, *ch.* ii. 15, 16. Note, It is common for base and ill-natured men to run upon, and run down, those that have fallen into the depths of distress from the height of honour. But this they brought upon themselves by sin. If they had not made themselves vile, their enemies could not have made them so : but *therefore men call them reprobate silver, because the Lord has rejected them* for rejecting him.

3. They complain of the lamentable destruction that their enemies made of them (*v.* 47): *Fear and a snare have come upon us ;* the enemies have not only terrified us with those alarms, but prevailed against us by their stratagems, and surprised us with the ambushes they laid for us; and then follows nothing but *desolation and destruction,* the *destruction of the daughter of my people* (*v.* 48), *of all the daughters of my city, v.* 51. The enemies, having taken some of them *like a bird* in a snare, *chased* others as a harmless bird is chased by a bird of prey (*v.* 52): *My enemies chased me sorely like a bird* which is beaten from bush to bush, as Saul hunted David *like a partridge.* Thus restless was the enmity of their persecutors, and yet causeless. They have done it *without cause,* without any provocation given them. Though God was righteous, they were unrighteous. David often complains of those that *hated him without cause ;* and such are the enemies of Christ and his church, John xv. 25. Their enemies chased them till they had quite prevailed over them (*v.* 53): *They have cut off my life in the dungeon.* They have shut up their captives in close and dark prisons, where they are as it were cut off *from the land of the living* (as *v.* 6), or the state and kingdom are sunk and ruined, the life and being of them are gone, and they are as it were thrown into the dungeon or grave and a *stone cast upon them,* such as used to be *rolled to the door of the sepulchres.* They look upon the Jewish nation as dead and buried, and imagine that there is no possibility of its resurrection. Thus Ezekiel saw it, in vision, *a valley full of dead and dry bones.* Their destruction is compared not only to the burying of a dead man, but to the sinking of a living man into the water, who cannot long be a living man there, *v.* 54. *Waters of affliction flowed over my head.* The deluge prevailed and quite overwhelmed them. The Chaldean forces broke in upon them *as the breaking forth of waters,* which rose so high as to *flow over their heads ;* they could not wade, they could not swim, and therefore must unavoidably sink. Note, The distresses

734

of God's people sometimes prevail to such a degree that they cannot find any footing for their faith, nor keep their head above water, with any comfortable expectation.

4. They complain of their own excessive grief and fear upon this account. (1.) The afflicted church is drowned in tears, and the prophet for her (*v.* 48, 49): *My eye runs down with rivers of water,* so abundant was their weeping; *it trickles down and ceases not,* so constant was their weeping, *without any intermission,* there being no relaxation of their miseries. The distemper was in continual extremity, and they had no better day. It is added (*v.* 51), *" My eye affects my heart.* My seeing eye affects my heart. The more I look upon the desolations of the city and country the more I am grieved. Which way soever I cast my eye, I see that which renews my sorrow, even *because of all the daughters of my city,"* all the neighbouring towns, which were as daughters to Jerusalem the mother-city. Or, *My weeping eye affects my heart ;* the venting of the grief, instead of easing it, did but increase and exasperate it. Or, *My eye melts my soul ;* I have quite wept away my spirits; not only *my eye is consumed with grief, but my soul and my life are spent with it,* Ps. xxxi. 9, 10. Great and long grief exhausts the spirits, and brings not only many a *gray head,* but many a green head too, *to the grave.* I weep, says the prophet, *more than all the daughters of my city* (so the margin reads it); he outdid even those of the tender sex in the expressions of grief. And it is no diminution to any to be much in tears for the sins of sinners and the sufferings of saints; our Lord Jesus was so; for, *when he came near, he beheld* this same *city and wept over it,* which the daughters of Jerusalem did not. (2.) She is overwhelmed with fears, not only grieves for what is, but fears worse, and gives up all for gone (*v.* 54): *" Then I said, I am cut off,* ruined, and see no hope of recovery; I am as one dead." Note, Those that are cast down are commonly tempted to think themselves cast off, Ps. xxxi. 22 ; Jon. ii. 4.

5. In the midst of these sad complaints here is one word of comfort, by which it appears that their case was not altogether so bad as they made it, *v.* 50. We continue thus weeping *till the Lord look down and behold from heaven.* This intimates, (1.) That they were satisfied that God's gracious regard to them in their miseries would be an effectual redress of all their grievances. " If God, who now *covers himself with a cloud,* as if he took no notice of our troubles (Job xxii. 13), would but shine forth, all would be well ; if he look upon us, *we shall be saved,"* Ps. lxxx. 19 ; Dan. ix. 17. Bad as the case is, one favourable look from heaven will set all to rights. (2.) That they had hopes that he would at length look graciously upon them and relieve them ; nay, they take it for

granted that he will: "Though he contend long, he will not contend for ever, though we deserve that he should." (3.) That while they continued weeping they continued waiting, and neither did nor would expect relief and succour from any hand but his; nothing shall comfort them but his gracious returns, nor shall any thing wipe tears from their eyes *till he look down.* Their eyes, which now *run down with water,* shall still *wait upon the Lord their God until he have mercy upon them,* Ps. cxxiii. 2.

55 I called upon thy name, O Lord, out of the low dungeon. 56 Thou hast heard my voice: hide not thine ear at my breathing, at my cry. 57 Thou drewest near in the day *that* I called upon thee: thou saidst, Fear not. 58 O Lord, thou hast pleaded the causes of my soul; thou hast redeemed my life. 59 O Lord, thou hast seen my wrong: judge thou my cause. 60 Thou hast seen all their vengeance *and* all their imaginations against me. 61 Thou hast heard their reproach, O Lord, *and* all their imaginations against me; 62 The lips of those that rose up against me, and their device against me all the day. 63 Behold their sitting down, and their rising up; I *am* their musick. 64 Render unto them a recompence, O Lord, according to the work of their hands. 65 Give them sorrow of heart, thy curse unto them. 66 Persecute and destroy them in anger from under the heavens of the Lord.

We may observe throughout this chapter a struggle in the prophet's breast between sense and faith, fear and hope; he complains and then comforts himself, yet drops his comforts and returns again to his complaints, as Ps. xlii. But, as there, so here, faith gets the last word and comes off a conqueror; for in these verses he concludes with some comfort. And here are two things with which he comforts himself:—

I. His experience of God's goodness even in his affliction. This may refer to the prophet's personal experience, with which he encourages himself in reference to the public troubles. He that has seasonably succoured particular saints will not fail the church in general. Or it may include the remnant of good people that were among the Jews, who had found that it was not in vain to wait upon God. In three things the prophet and his pious friends had found God good to them:—1. He had *heard their prayers;* though they had been ready to fear that the cloud of wrath was such as their *prayers could not pass through* (v. 44), yet upon second thoughts, or at least upon further trial, they find it otherwise, and that God had not said unto them, *Seek you me in vain.* When they were *in the low dungeon,* as *free among the dead,* they *called upon God's name* (v. 55); their weeping did not hinder praying. Note, Though we are cast into ever so low a dungeon, we may thence find a way of access to God in the highest heavens. *Out of the depths have I cried unto thee* (Ps. cxxx. 1), as Jonah out of the whale's belly. And could God hear them out of the low dungeon, and would he? Yes, he did: *Thou hast heard my voice;* and some read the following words as carrying on the same thankful acknowledgment: *Thou didst not hide thy ear at my breathing, at my cry;* and the original will bear that reading. We read it as a petition for further audience: *Hide not thy ear.* God's having heard our voice when we *cried to him,* even out of *the low dungeon,* is an encouragement for us to hope that he will not at any time *hide his ear.* Observe how he calls prayer *his breathing;* for in prayer we breathe towards God, we breathe after him. Though we be but weak in prayer, cannot cry aloud, but only *breathe* in *groanings that cannot be uttered,* yet we shall not be neglected if we be sincere. Prayer is the breath of the new man, sucking in the air of mercy in petitions and returning it in praises; it is both the evidence and the maintenance of the spiritual life. Some read it, *at my gasping.* "When I lay gasping for life, and ready to expire, and thought I was breathing my last, then thou tookest cognizance of my distressed case." 2. He had silenced their fears and quieted their spirits (v. 57): "*Thou drewest near in the day that I called upon thee;* thou didst graciously assure me of thy presence with me, and give me to see thee nigh unto me, whereas I had thought thee to be at a distance from me." Note, When we draw nigh to God in a way of duty we may by faith see him drawing nigh to us in a way of mercy. But this was not all: *Thou saidst, Fear not.* This was the language of God's prophets preaching to them not to fear (Isa. xli. 10, 13, 14), of his providence preventing those things which they were afraid of, and of his grace quieting their minds, and making them easy, by the witness of his Spirit with their spirits that they were his people still, though in distress, and therefore ought not to fear. 3. He had already begun to appear for them (v. 58): "*O Lord! thou hast pleaded the causes of my soul*" (that is, as it follows), "*thou hast redeemed my life,* hast rescued that out of the hands of those who would have taken it away, hast saved that when it was ready to be swallowed up, hast given me that for a prey." And this is an encouragement to them to hope that he would yet further appear for them: "*Thou hast delivered my soul from death,* and therefore wilt deliver *my feet from falling;* thou hast *pleaded the causes of my life*, and therefore will plead my other causes."

II. He comforts himself with an appeal to God's justice, and (in order to the sentence of that) to his omniscience.

1. He appeals to God's knowledge of the matter of fact, how very spiteful and malicious his enemies were (*v.* 59): "O Lord! thou hast seen my wrong, that I have done no wrong at all, but suffer a great deal." He that knows all things knew, (1.) The malice they had against him: "*Thou hast seen all their vengeance*, how they desire to do me a mischief, as if it were by way of reprisal for some great injury I had done them." Note, We should consider, to our terror and caution, that God knows all the revengeful thoughts we have in our minds against others, and therefore we should not allow of those thoughts nor harbour them, and that he knows all the revengeful thoughts others have causelessly in their minds against us, and therefore we should not be afraid of them, but leave it to him to protect us from them. (2.) The designs and projects they had laid to do him a mischief: *Thou hast seen all their imaginations against me* (*v.* 60), and again, "*Thou hast heard all their imaginations against me* (*v.* 61), both the desire and the device they have to ruin me; whether it show itself in word or deed, it is known to thee; nay, though the products of it are not to be seen nor heard, yet their device against me all the day is perceived and understood by him to whom all things are naked and open." Note, The most secret contrivances of the church's enemies are perfectly known to the church's God, from whom they can hide nothing. (3.) The contempt and calumny wherewith they loaded him, all that they spoke slightly of him, and all that they spoke reproachfully: "*Thou hast heard their reproach* (*v.* 61), all the bad characters they give me, laying to my charge things that I know not, all the methods they use to make me odious and contemptible, even the *lips of those that rose up against me* (*v.* 62), the contumelious language they use whenever they speak of me, and that at their sitting down and rising up, when they lie down at night and get up in the morning, when they sit down to their meat and with their company, and when they rise from both, still I am their music; they make themselves and one another merry with my miseries, as the Philistines made sport with Samson." Jerusalem was the tabret they played upon. Perhaps they had some tune or play, some opera or interlude, that was called *the destruction of Jerusalem*, which, though in the nature of a tragedy, was very entertaining to those who wished ill to the holy city. Note, God will one day call sinners to an account for all the hard speeches which they have spoken against him and his people, Jude 15.

2. He appeals to God's judgment upon this fact: "Lord, thou hast seen my wrong; there is no need of any evidence to prove it, nor any prosecutor to enforce and aggravate it; thou seest it in its true colours; and now I leave it with thee. *Judge thou my cause*, *v.* 59. Let them be dealt with," (1.) "As they deserve (*v.* 64): *Render to them a recompence according to the work of their hands.* Let them be dealt with as they have dealt with us; let thy hand be against them as their hand has been against us. They have created us a great deal of vexation; now, Lord, *give them sorrow of heart* (*v.* 65), *perplexity of heart*" (so some read it); "let them be surrounded with threatening mischiefs on all sides, and not be able to see their way out. Give them *despondency of heart*" (so others read it); "let them be driven to despair, and give themselves up for gone." God can entangle the head that thinks itself clearest, and sink the heart that thinks itself stoutest. (2.) "Let them be dealt with according to the threatenings: *Thy curse unto them;* that is, let thy curse come upon them, all the evils that are pronounced in thy word against the enemies of thy people, *v.* 65. They have loaded us with curses; as they loved cursing, so let it come unto them, thy curse which will make them truly miserable. Theirs is causeless, and therefore fruitless, it shall not come; but thine is just, and shall take effect. Those whom thou cursest are cursed indeed. Let the curse be executed, *v.* 66. *Persecute and destroy them in anger*, as they persecute and destroy us in their anger. *Destroy them from under the heavens of the Lord;* let them have no benefit of the light and influence of the heavens. Destroy them in such a manner that all who see it may say, It is a destruction from the Almighty, who *sits in the heavens and laughs at them* (Ps. ii. 4), and may own *that the heavens do rule*," Dan. iv. 26. What is said of the idols is here said of their worshippers (who in this also shall be like unto them), *They shall perish from under these heavens*, Jer. x. 11. They shall be not only excluded from the happiness of the invisible heavens, but cut off from the comfort even of these visible ones, which are the *heavens of the Lord* (Ps. cxv. 16) and which those therefore are unworthy to be taken under the protection of who rebel against him.

CHAP. IV.

This chapter is another single alphabet of Lamentations for the destruction of Jerusalem, like those in the first two chapters. I. The prophet here laments the injuries and indignities done to those to whom respect used to be shown, ver. 1, 2. II. He laments the direful effects of the famine to which they were reduced by the siege, ver. 3–10. III. He laments the taking and sacking of Jerusalem and its amazing desolations, ver. 11, 12. IV. He acknowledges that the sins of their leaders were the cause of all these calamities, ver. 13–16. V. He gives up all as doomed to utter ruin, for their enemies were every way too hard for them, ver. 17–20. VI. He foretels the destruction of the Edomites who triumphed in Jerusalem's fall, ver. 21. VII. He foretels the return of the captivity of Zion at last, ver. 22.

H OW is the gold become dim! *how* is the most fine gold changed!

the stones of the sanctuary are poured out in the top of every street. 2 The precious sons of Zion, comparable to fine gold, how are they esteemed as earthen pitchers, the work of the hands of the potter ! 3 Even the sea monsters draw out the breast, they give suck to their young ones : the daughter of my people *is become* cruel, like the ostriches in the wilderness. 4 The tongue of the sucking child cleaveth to the roof of his mouth for thirst : the young children ask bread, *and* no man breaketh *it* unto them. 5 They that did feed delicately are desolate in the streets: they that were brought up in scarlet embrace dunghills. 6 For the punishment of the iniquity of the daughter of my people is greater than the punishment of the sin of Sodom, that was overthrown as in a moment, and no hands stayed on her. 7 Her Nazarites were purer than snow, they were whiter than milk, they were more ruddy in body than rubies, their polishing *was* of sapphire : 8 Their visage is blacker than a coal ; they are not known in the streets : their skin cleaveth to their bones ; it is withered, it is become like a stick. 9 *They that be* slain with the sword are better than *they that be* slain with hunger : for these pine away, stricken through for *want of* the fruits of the field. 10 The hands of the pitiful women have sodden their own children : they were their meat in the destruction of the daughter of my people. 11 The LORD hath accomplished his fury ; he hath poured out his fierce anger, and hath kindled a fire in Zion, and it hath devoured the foundations thereof. 12 The kings of the earth, and all the inhabitants of the world, would not have believed that the adversary and the enemy should have entered into the gates of Jerusalem.

The elegy in this chapter begins with a lamentation of the very sad and doleful change which the judgments of God had made in Jerusalem. The city that was formerly *as gold,* as *the most fine gold,* so rich and splendid, *the perfection of beauty and the joy of the whole earth,* has become dim, and is changed, has lost its lustre, lost its value, is

not what it was ; it has become dross. Alas ! what an alteration is here !

I. The temple was laid waste, which was the glory of Jerusalem and its protection. It is given up into the hands of the enemy. And some understand the gold spoken of (*v.* 1) to be the *gold of the temple,* the fine gold with which it was overlaid (1 Kings vi. 22) ; when the temple was burned the gold of it was smoked and sullied, as if it had been of little value. It was thrown among the rubbish ; it *was changed,* converted to common uses and made nothing of. *The stones of the sanctuary,* which were curiously wrought, were thrown down by the Chaldeans, when they demolished it, or were brought down by the force of the fire, and were *poured out,* and thrown about *in the top of every street ;* they lay mingled without distinction among the common ruins. When the God of the sanctuary was by sin provoked to withdraw no wonder that the stones of the sanctuary were thus profaned.

II. The princes and priests, who were in a special manner the *sons of Zion,* were trampled upon and abused, *v.* 2. Both the house of God and the house of David were in Zion. The sons of both those houses were upon this account precious, that they were heirs to the privileges of those two covenants of priesthood and royalty. They were *comparable to fine gold.* Israel was more rich in them than in treasures of gold and silver. But now they are *esteemed as earthen pitchers;* they are broken as *earthen pitchers,* thrown by as vessels in which there is no pleasure. They have grown poor, and are brought into captivity, and thereby are rendered mean and despicable, and every one treads upon them and insults over them. Note, The contempt put upon God's people ought to be matter of lamentation to us.

III. Little children were starved for want of bread and water, *v.* 3, 4. The nursing-mothers, having no meat for themselves, had no milk for the babes at their breast, so that, though in disposition they were really compassionate, yet in fact they seemed to be cruel, *like the ostriches in the wilderness, that leave their eggs in the dust* (Job xxxix. 14, 15); having no food for their children, they were forced to neglect them and do what they could to forget them, because it was a pain to them to think of them when they had nothing for them; in this they were worse than the seals, or *sea-monsters,* or *whales* (as some render it), for they *drew out the breast, and gave suck to their young,* which *the daughter of my people* will not do. Children cannot shift for themselves as grown people can; and therefore it was the more painful to see *the tongue of the sucking-child cleave to the roof of his mouth for thirst,* because there was not a drop of water to moisten it; and to hear the young children, that could but just speak, *ask bread* of their parents, who had none to give them, no, nor any friend that could supply them. As doleful as our thoughts are of this case, so thankful should our thoughts be of the great plenty we enjoy, and the food convenient we have for ourselves and for our children, and for *those of our own house.*

IV. Persons of good rank were reduced to extreme poverty, *v.* 5. Those who were well-born and well bred, and had been accustomed to the best, both for food and clothing, who had *fed delicately*, had every thing that was curious and nice (they call it *eating well*, whereas those only eat well who eat to the glory of God), and *fared sumptuously every day;* they had not only been *advanced to the scarlet*, but from their beginning were *brought up in scarlet*, and were never acquainted with any thing mean or ordinary. They were *brought up upon scarlet* (so the word is); their foot-cloths, and the carpets they walked on, were scarlet, yet these, being stripped of all by the war, are *desolate in the streets*, have not a house to put their head in, nor a bed to lie on, nor clothes to cover them, nor fire to warm them. They *embrace dunghills;* on them they were glad to lie to get a little rest, and perhaps raked in the dunghills for something to eat, as the prodigal son who *would fain have filled his belly with the husks.* Note, Those who live in the greatest pomp and plenty know not what straits they may be reduced to before they die; as sometimes the *needy* are *raised out of the dunghill* (Ps. cxiii. 7), so there are instances of the *wealthy* being brought *to the dunghill. Those who were full have hired out themselves for bread*, 1 Sam. ii. 5. It is therefore the wisdom of those who have abundance not to use themselves too nicely, for then hardships, when they come, will be doubly hard, Deut. xxviii. 56.

V. Persons who were eminent for dignity, nay, perhaps for sanctity, shared with others in the common calamity, *v.* 7, 8. *Her Nazarites* are extremely changed. Some understand it only of her honourable ones, the young gentlemen, who were very clean, and neat, and well-dressed, washed and perfumed; but I see not why we may not understand it of those devout people among them who *separated themselves to the Lord* by the *Nazarites'* vow, Num. vi. 2. That there were such among them in the most degenerate times appears from Amos ii. 11, *I raised up of your young men for Nazarites.* These *Nazarites*, though they were not to cut their hair, yet by reason of their temperate diet, their frequent washings, and especially the pleasure they had in devoting themselves to God and conversing with him, which made their faces to shine as *Moses's*, were *purer than snow* and *whiter than milk;* drinking no wine nor strong drink, they had a more healthful complexion and cheerful countenance than those who regaled themselves daily with the blood of the grape, as

Daniel and his fellows with *pulse and water*. Or it may denote the great respect and veneration which all good people had for them; though perhaps to the eye they had *no form nor comeliness*, yet, being separated to the Lord, they were valued as if they had been *more ruddy than rubies and their polishing had been of sapphire.* But now *their visage is marred* (as is said of Christ, Isa. lii. 14); it is *blacker than a coal;* they look miserably, partly through hunger and partly through grief and perplexity. *They are not known in the streets;* those who respected them now take no notice of them, and those who had been intimately acquainted with them now scarcely knew them, their countenance was so altered by the miseries that attended the long siege. *Their skin cleaves to their bones*, their flesh being quite consumed and wasted away; it is *withered;* it has *become like a stick*, as dry and hard as a piece of wood. Note, It is a thing to be much lamented that even those who are separated to God are yet, when desolating judgments are abroad, often involved with others in the common calamity.

VI. Jerusalem came down slowly, and died a lingering death; for the famine contributed more to her destruction than any other judgment whatsoever. Upon this account the destruction of *Jerusalem was greater than that of Sodom* (v. 6), for that was *overthrown in a moment;* one shower of fire and brimstone dispatched it; *no hand staid on her;* she did not endure any long siege, as Jerusalem has done; she fell immediately into the *hands of the Lord*, who strikes home at a blow, and did not *fall into the hands of man*, who, being weak, is long in doing execution, Judg. viii. 21. Jerusalem is kept many months upon the rack, in pain and misery, and dies by inches, dies so as to feel herself die. And, when the iniquity of Jerusalem is more aggravated than that of Sodom, no wonder that the punishment of it is so. Sodom never had the means of grace that Jerusalem had, the oracles of God and his prophets, and therefore the condemnation of Jerusalem will be *more intolerable* than that of Sodom, Matt. xi. 23, 24. The extremity of the famine is here set forth by two frightful instances of it:—1. The tedious deaths that it was the cause of (v. 9); many were slain with hunger, were famished to death, their stores being spent, and the public stores so nearly spent that they could not have any relief out of them. They were *stricken through, for want of the fruits of the field;* those who were starved were as sure to die as if they had been stabbed and stricken through; only their case was much more miserable. *Those who are slain with the sword* are soon put out of their pain; *in a moment they go down to the grave*, Job xxi. 13. They have not the terror of seeing death make its advances towards them, and scarcely feel it when the blow is given; it is but one sharp struggle, and the work is done. And, if we be ready for another world, we need not be afraid of a short passage to it; the quicker the better. But those who die by famine pine away; hunger preys upon their spirits and wastes them gradually; nay, and it frets their spirits, and fills them with vexation, and is as great a torture to the mind as to the body. There are *bands in their death,* Ps. lxxiii. 4. 2. The barbarous murders that it was the occasion of (*v.* 10): *The hands of the pitiful women have* first slain and then *sodden their own children.* This was lamented before (*ch.* ii. 20); and it was a thing to be greatly lamented that any should be so wicked as to do it and that they should be brought to such extremities as to be tempted to it. But this horrid effect of long sieges had been threatened in general (Lev. xxvi. 29, Deut. xxviii. 53), and particularly against Jerusalem in the siege of the Chaldeans, Jer. xix. 9; Ezek. v. 10. The case was sad enough that they had not wherewithal to feed their children and make meat for them (*v.* 4), but much worse that they could find in their hearts to feed upon their children and make meat of them. I know not whether to make it an instance of the power of necessity or of the power of iniquity; but, as the Gentile idolaters were justly *given up to vile affections* (Rom. i. 26), so these Jewish idolaters, and the women particularly, who had *made cakes to the queen of heaven* and taught their children to do so too, were *stripped of natural affection* and that to their own children. Being thus left to *dishonour their own nature* was a righteous judgment upon them for the dishonour they had done to God.

VII. Jerusalem comes down utterly and wonderfully. 1. The destruction of Jerusalem is a complete destruction (*v.* 11): *The Lord has accomplished his fury;* he has made thorough work of it, has executed all that he purposed in wrath against Jerusalem, and has remitted no part of the sentence. He has poured out the full vials of his fierce anger, poured them out to the bottom, even the dregs of them. He has *kindled a fire in Zion,* which has not only consumed the houses, and levelled them with the ground, but, beyond what other fires do, has *devoured the foundations thereof,* as if they were to be no more built upon. 2. It is an amazing destruction, *v.* 12. It was a surprise to the kings of the earth, who are acquainted with, and inquisitive about, the state of their neighbours; nay, it was so to *all the inhabitants of the world* who knew Jerusalem, or had ever heard or read of it; they *could not have believed that the adversary and enemy would* ever *enter into the gates of Jerusalem;* for, (1.) They knew that Jerusalem was strongly fortified, not only by walls and bulwarks, but by the numbers and strength of its inhabitants; the strong hold of Zion was thought

to be impregnable. (2.) They knew that it was the *city of the great King,* where the Lord of the whole earth had in a more peculiar manner his residence; it was the holy city, and therefore they thought that it was so much under the divine protection that it would be in vain for any of its enemies to make an attack upon it. (3.) They knew that many an attempt made upon it had been baffled, witness that of Sennacherib. They were therefore amazed when they heard of the Chaldeans making themselves masters of it, and concluded that it was certainly by an immediate hand of God that Jerusalem was given up to them; it was by a commission from him that the enemy broke through and entered the gates of Jerusalem.

13 For the sins of her prophets, *and* the iniquities of her priests, that have shed the blood of the just in the midst of her, 14 They have wandered *as* blind *men* in the streets, they have polluted themselves with blood, so that men could not touch their garments. 15 They cried unto them, Depart ye; *it is* unclean; depart, depart, touch not: when they fled away and wandered, they said among the heathen, They shall no more sojourn *there.* 16 The anger of the LORD hath divided them; he will no more regard them: they respected not the persons of the priests, they favoured not the elders. 17 As for us, our eyes as yet failed for our vain help: in our watching we have watched for a nation *that* could not save *us.* 18 They hunt our steps, that we cannot go in our streets: our end is near, our days are fulfilled; for our end is come. 19 Our persecutors are swifter than the eagles of the heaven: they pursued us upon the mountains, they laid wait for us in the wilderness. 20 The breath of our nostrils, the anointed of the LORD, was taken in their pits, of whom we said, Under his shadow we shall live among the heathen.

We have here,

I. The sins they were charged with, for which God brought this destruction upon them, and which served to justify God in it (*v.* 13, 14): It is *for the sins of her prophets,* and the *iniquities of her priests.* Not that the people were innocent; no, they *loved to have it so* (Jer. v. 31), and it was to please them that the prophets and priests did as they did; but the fault is chiefly laid upon them, who should have taught them better, should have reproved and admonished them, and told them what would be in the end hereof; of the hands of those watchmen who did not give them warning will their blood be required. Note, Nothing ripens a people more for ruin, nor fills the measure faster, than the sins of their priests and prophets. The particular sin charged upon them is persecution; the false prophets and corrupt priests joined their power and interest to *shed the blood of the just in the midst of her,* the blood of God's prophets and of those that adhered to them. They not only shed the blood of their innocent children, whom they sacrificed to Moloch, but the blood of the righteous men that were among them, whom they sacrificed to that more cruel idol of enmity to the truth and true religion. This was that sin which the Lord would not pardon (2 Kings xxiv. 4) and which brought the last destruction upon Jerusalem (Jam. v. 6): *You have condemned and killed the just.* And the priests and prophets were the ringleaders in persecution, as in Christ's time the chief priests and scribes were the men that incensed the people against him, who otherwise would have persisted in their hosannas. Now these are those that *wandered as blind men in the streets, v.* 14. They strayed from the paths of justice, were blind to every thing that is good, but to do evil they were quick-sighted. God says of corrupt judges, *They know not, neither do they understand; they walk in darkness* (Ps. lxxxii. 5); and Christ says of the corrupt teachers, *They are blind leaders of the blind,* Matt. xv. 14. They have *so polluted themselves with* innocent *blood,* the blood of the saints, that *men could not touch their garments;* they made themselves odious to all about them, so that good men were as shy of touching them as of touching a dead body, which contracted a ceremonial pollution, or of touching the bloody clothes of one slain, which tender spirits care not to do. There is nothing that will make prophets and priests to be abhorred so much as a spirit of persecution.

II. The testimony of their neighbours produced in evidence against them, both to convict them of sin and to show the equity of God's proceedings against them. Some that have grown very impudent in sin boast that they *care not what people say of them;* but God, by the prophet, would have the Jews to take notice of what people said of them and what was the opinion of the standers by concerning them (v. 15, 16), what they said, nay, what *they cried unto them,* especially to the corrupt priests and prophets, *among the heathen.* 1. They upbraided them with their pretended purity, while they lived in all manner of real iniquity. They cried to them, " *Depart you; it is unclean.* You were so precise that you would not touch a Gentile, but cried, *Depart, depart; stand by thyself; I am holier than thou,"* Isa. lxv. 5. Thus the prosecutors of Christ would not go *into the judgment-hall, lest they should be defiled.* "But can you now keep the Gentiles from touching you, when God has delivered you into their hands? When you flee away and wander you will bid them stand off and not touch you, because they are unclean. But in vain; these serpents will not be charmed or enchanted thus; no, they will not *respect the persons of the priests,* nor *favour the elders;* the most venerable persons will to them be despicable." 2. They upbraided them with their sins, and the anger of God against them for their sins, and the direful effects of that anger. *They cried to them, Depart you; it is unclean.* They all cried out shame on them, and could easily foresee that God would not long suffer so provoking a people to continue in so good a land. They knew their *statutes and judgments were righteous,* and expected they should be *a wise and understanding people,* Deut. iv. 6. But, when they saw them quite otherwise, they cried, *Depart, depart;* they soon read their doom, that the land would spue them out, as it had done their predecessors, and, when they saw the dispersed of *Jacob fleeing and wandering,* they told them of it. They said, Now *the anger of the Lord has divided them,* has dispersed them into all countries, because *they respected not the persons of the priests,* the pious priests that were among them, such as Zechariah the son of Jehoiada, Jeremiah, and others; neither did they *favour the elders,* but despised them and their authority when they went about to check them for their vicious courses. The very heathen foresaw that this would ruin them. 3. They triumphed in their ruin as irrecoverable. They said, when they saw them expelled out of their own land, " Now *they shall no more sojourn there;* they have bidden it a final farewell, never more to return to it, for *God will no more regard them,* and how then can they help themselves?" Herein they were mistaken. God had not cast them off, for all this. Yet thus much is intimated, that all about them observed them to be so very provoking to their God that there was no reason to expect any other than that they should be quite abandoned.

III. The despair which they themselves were almost brought to under their calamities. Having heard what they said concerning them *among the heathen,* let us now hear what they say concerning themselves (v. 17): " *As for us,* we look upon our case to be in a manner helpless. *Our end is near* (v. 18), the end both of our church and of our state; we are just at the brink of the ruin of both; nay, *our end has come;* we are utterly undone; a fatal final period is put to all our comforts; the days of our prosperity are fulfilled; they are numbered and finished."

Thus their fears concurred with the hopes of their enemies that the *Lord would no more regard them.* For, 1. The refuges they fled to disappointed them. They looked for help from this and the other powerful ally, but to no purpose; it proved vain help. The succours they expected did not come in, or at least they had not the success they expected, and their eyes failed with looking for that which never came (*v.* 17); they *watched in watching;* they watched long, and with a great deal of earnestness and impatience, *for a nation* that promised them assistance, but failed them, and frustrated their expectations. They *could not save them;* they were too weak to contend with the Chaldean army and therefore retired. Help from creatures is vain help (Ps. lx. 11), and we may look for it till our eyes fail, till our hearts fail, and come short of it at last. 2. The persecutors they fled from overtook them and overcame them (*v.* 18): *They hunt our steps, that we cannot go in our streets.* When the Chaldeans besieged the city they raised their batteries so high above the walls that they could command the town, and shoot at people as they went along the streets. They *hunted them* with their arrows from place to place. When the city was broken up, and all the men of war fled, their *persecutors were swifter than the eagles of heaven* when they fly upon their prey, *v.* 19. There was no escaping them; they *pursued them upon the mountains,* and, when they thought they had got clear of them, they fell into the hands of those that *laid wait for them in the wilderness,* to cut off their retreat, and to pick up stragglers. Nay, the king himself, though he may be supposed to have had all the advantages the exigence of the case would admit to favour his flight, yet could not escape, for divine vengeance pursued him with them, and then (*v.* 20), *The breath of our nostrils, the anointed of the Lord, was taken in their pits.* Some apply it to Josiah, who was killed in battle by the king of Egypt; but it is rather to be understood of Zedekiah, who was the last king of the house of David, and who was pursued by the Chaldeans and seized in the plains of Jericho, Jer. xxxix. 5. He was *the anointed of the Lord,* heir of that family which God had appointed to the government. He was very much confided in by the Jewish state: *They said, Under his shadow we shall live among the heathen.* They promised themselves that the remnant which were left after Jeconiah's captivity should, under the protection of his government, yet again *take root downward and bear fruit upward.* They thought, though they were so reduced that they could not think of reigning over the heathen, as they had done, yet they might make a shift to live among them and not be insulted and pulled to pieces by them. Thus apt are sinking interests not only to catch at

every twig, but to think it will recover them. Jerusalem died of a consumption, a flattering distemper. Even when she was ready to expire she formed some hopeful symptoms to herself, and on them grounded a hope that she should recover; but what came of it? The shadow under which they thought they should live proved like that of Jonah's gourd, which *withered in a night.* He that was *the anointed of the Lord was taken in their pits,* as if he had been but a beast of prey; so little account did they make of a person deemed sacred and not to be violated. Note, When we make any creature *the breath of our nostrils,* and promise ourselves that we shall live by it, it is just with God to stop that breath, and deprive us of the life we expected by it; for God will have the honour of being himself alone *our life and the length of our days.*

21 Rejoice and be glad, O daughter of Edom, that dwellest in the land of Uz; the cup also shall pass through unto thee: thou shalt be drunken, and shalt make thyself naked. 22 The punishment of thine iniquity is accomplished, O daughter of Zion; he will no more carry thee away into captivity: he will visit thine iniquity, O daughter of Edom; he will discover thy sins.

David's psalms of lamentation commonly conclude with some word of comfort, which is as life from the dead and light shining out of darkness; so does this lamentation here in this chapter. The people of God are now in great distress, their aspects all doleful, their prospects all frightful, and their ill-natured neighbours the Edomites insult over them and do all they can to exasperate their destroyers against them. Such was their violence against their brother Jacob (Obad. 10), such their spleen at Jerusalem, of which they cried, *Rase it, rase it,* Ps. cxxxvii. 7. Now it is here foretold, for the encouragement of God's people,

I. That an end shall be put to Zion's troubles (*v.* 22): *The punishment of thy iniquity is accomplished, O daughter of Zion!* not the fulness of that punishment which it deserves, but of that which God has designed and determined to inflict, and which was necessary to answer the end, the glorifying of God's justice and the taking away of their sin. The captivity, which is *the punishment of thy iniquity, is accomplished* (Isa. xl. 2), and *he will no longer keep thee in captivity;* so it may be read, as well as, *he will no more carry thee into captivity;* he will turn again thy captivity and work a glorious release for thee. Note, The troubles of God's people shall be continued no longer than till they have done their work for which they were sent.

II. That an end shall be put to Edom's triumphs. It is spoken ironically (*v.* 21): *Rejoice and be glad, O daughter of Edom!* go on to insult over Zion in distress, till thou hast filled up the measure of thy iniquity. Do so; rejoice in thy own present exemption from the common fate of thy neighbours." This is like Solomon's upbraiding the young man with his ungoverned mirth (Eccl. xi. 9): " *Rejoice, O young man! in thy youth;* rejoice, if thou canst, when God comes to reckon with thee, and that he will do ere long. *The cup* of trembling, which it is now Jerusalem's turn to drink deeply of, *shall pass through unto thee;* it shall go round till it comes to be thy lot to pledge it." Note, This is a good reason why we should not insult over any who are in misery, because we ourselves also are in the body, and we know not how soon their case may be ours. But those who please themselves in the calamities of God's church must expect to have their doom, as aiders and abettors, with those that are instrumental in those calamities. The destruction of the Edomites was foretold by this prophet (Jer. xlix. 7. &c.), and the people of God must encourage themselves against their present rudeness and insolence with the prospect of it. 1. It will be a shameful destruction : " *The cup* that *shall pass unto thee* shall intoxicate thee" (and that is shame enough to any man); " *thou shalt be drunken*, quite infatuated, and at thy wits' end, shalt stagger in all thy counsels and stumble in all thy enterprises, and then, as Noah when he was drunk, *thou shalt make thyself naked* and expose thyself to contempt." Note, Those who ridicule God's people will justly be left to themselves to do that, some time or other, by which they will be made ridiculous. 2. It will be a righteous destruction. God will herein *visit thy iniquity* and *discover thy sins;* he will punish them, and, to justify himself therein, he will discover them, and make it to appear that he has just cause thus to proceed against them. Nay, the punishment of the sin shall so exactly answer the sin that it shall itself plainly discover it. Sometimes God does so visit the iniquity that he that runs may read the sin in the punishment. But, sooner or later, sin will be visited and discovered, and all the hidden works of darkness brought to light.

CHAP. V.

This chapter, though it has the same number of verses with the 1st, 2d, and 4th, is not alphabetical, as they were, but the scope of it is the same with that of all the foregoing elegies. We have in it, I. A representation of the present calamitous state of God's people in their captivity, ver. 1- 16. II. A protestation of their concern for God's sanctuary, as that which lay nearer their heart than any secular interest of their own, ver. 17, 18. III. A humble supplication to God and expostulation with him, for the returns of mercy (ver. 19—22); for those that lament and do not pray sin in their lamentations. Some ancient versions call this chapter, " The Prayer of Jeremiah."

REMEMBER, O Lord, what is come upon us: consider, and

behold our reproach. 2 Our inheritance is turned to strangers, our houses to aliens. 3 We are orphans and fatherless, our mothers *are* as widows. 4 We have drunken our water for money; our wood is sold unto us. 5 Our necks *are* under persecution : we labour, *and* have no rest. 6 We have given the hand *to* the Egyptians, *and to* the Assyrians, to be satisfied with bread. 7 Our fathers have sinned, *and are* not; and we have borne their iniquities. 8 Servants have ruled over us : *there is* none that doth deliver *us* out of their hand. 9 We gat our bread with *the peril of* our lives because of the sword of the wilderness. 10 Our skin was black like an oven because of the terrible famine. 11 They ravished the women in Zion, *and* the maids in the cities of Judah. 12 Princes are hanged up by their hand : the faces of elders were not honoured. 13 They took the young men to grind, and the children fell under the wood. 14 The elders have ceased from the gate, the young men from their musick. 15 The joy of our heart is ceased; our dance is turned into mourning. 16 The crown is fallen *from* our head : woe unto us, that we have sinned!

Is any afflicted? let him *pray;* and let him in prayer pour out his complaint to God, and make known before him his trouble. The people of God do so here; being overwhelmed with grief, they give vent to their sorrows at the footstool of the throne of grace, and so give themselves ease. They complain not of evils feared, but of evils felt : " *Remember what has come upon us, v.* 1. What was of old threatened against us, and was long in the coming, has now at length *come upon us,* and we are ready to sink under it. *Remember what is* past, *consider and behold* what is present, and *let not all the trouble* we are in *seem little to thee,* and not worth taking notice of," Neh. ix. 32. Note, As it is a great comfort to us, so it ought to be a sufficient one, in our troubles, that God sees, and considers, and remembers, all that *has come upon us;* and in our prayers we need only to recommend our case to his gracious and compassionate consideration. The one word in which all their grievances are summed up is *reproach: Consider, and behold, our reproach.* The troubles they were in, compared with their former dignity and plenty, were a greater reproach to them than they would have been to any other people, especially considering their relation to God and dependence upon him, and his former appearances for them; and therefore this they complain of very sensibly, because, as it was a reproach, it reflected upon the name and honour of that God who had owned them for his people. *And what wilt thou do unto thy great name ?*

I. They acknowledge the reproach of sin which they bear, *the reproach of their youth* (which Ephraim bemoans himself for, Jer. xxxi. 19), of the early days of their nation. This comes in in the midst of their complaints (*v.* 7), but may well be put in the front of them: *Our fathers have sinned and are not ;* they are dead and gone, but *we have borne their iniquities.* This is not here a peevish complaint, nor an imputation of unrighteousness to God, like that which we have, Jer. xxxi. 29, Ezek. xviii. 2. *The fathers did eat sour grapes, and the children's teeth are set on edge,* and therefore *the ways of the Lord are not equal.* But it is a penitent confession of the sins of their ancestors, which they themselves also had persisted in, for which they now justly suffered; the judgments God brought upon them were so very great that it appeared that God had in them an eye to the sins of their ancestors (because they had not been remarkably punished in this world) as well as to their own sins; and thus God was justified both in his connivance at their ancestors (he *laid up their iniquity for their children)* and in his severity with them, on whom he visited that iniquity, Matt. xxiii. 35, 36. Thus they do here, 1. Submit themselves to the divine justice: " Lord, thou art just in all that is brought upon us, for we are a seed of evil doers, children of wrath, and heirs of the curse; we are sinful, and we have it by kind." Note, The sins which God looks back upon in punishing we must look back upon in repenting, and must take notice of all that which will help to justify God in correcting us. 2. They refer themselves to the divine pity: " Lord, *our fathers have sinned,* and we justly smart for their sins; but *they are not ;* they were taken away from the evil to come; they lived not to see and share in these miseries that have *come upon us,* and we are left to *bear their iniquities.* Now, though herein God is righteous, yet it must be owned that our case is pitiable, and worthy of compassion." Note, If we be penitent and patient under what we suffer for the sins of our fathers, we may expect that he who punishes will pity, and will soon return in mercy to us.

II. They represent the reproach of trouble which they bear, in divers particulars, which tend much to their disgrace.

1. They are disseised of that good land which God gave them, and their enemies have got possession of it, *v.* 2. Canaan was their inheritance; it was theirs by promise. God gave it to them and their seed, and they held it by grant from his crown, Ps.

cxxxvi. 21, 22) ; but now, '' It is turned to strangers; those possess it who have no right to it, who are *strangers to the commonwealth of Israel and aliens from the covenants of promise ;* they dwell in the houses that we built, and this is our reproach." It is the happiness of all God's spiritual Israel that the heavenly Canaan is an inheritance that they cannot be disseised of, that shall never be turned to strangers.

2. Their state and nation are brought into a condition like that of widows and orphans (*v.* 3) : " *We are fatherless* (that is, helpless); we have none to protect us, to provide for us, to take any care of us. Our king, who is the father of the country, is cut off; nay, God our Father seems to have forsaken us and cast us off; *our mothers,* our cities, that were as fruitful mothers in Israel, *are* now *as widows,* are as wives whose husbands are dead, destitute of comfort, and exposed to wrong and injury, and this is our reproach; for we who made a figure are now looked on with contempt."

3. They are put hard to it to provide necessaries for themselves and their families, whereas once they lived in abundance and had plenty of every thing. Water used to be free and easily come by, but now (*v.* 4), *We have drunk our water for money,* and the saying is no longer true, *Usus communis aquarum—Water is free to all.* So hardly did their oppressors use them that they could not have a draught of fair water but they must purchase it either with money or with work. Formerly they had fuel too for the fetching; but now, '' *Our wood is sold to us,* and we pay dearly for every faggot." Now were they punished for employing their children to gather wood for fire with which to *bake cakes for the queen of heaven,* Jer. vii. 18. They were perfectly proscribed by their oppressors, were forbidden the use both of fire and water, according to the ancient form, *Interdico tibi aqua et igni— I forbid thee the use of water and fire.* But what must they do for bread ? Truly that was as hard to come at as any thing, for (1.) Some of them sold their liberty for it (*v.* 6) : " *We have given the hand to the Egyptians and to the Assyrians,* have made the best bargain we could with them, to serve them, that we might *be satisfied with bread.* We were glad to submit to the meanest employment, upon the hardest terms, to get a sorry livelihood; we have yielded ourselves to be their vassals, have parted with all to them, as the Egyptians did to Pharaoh in the years of famine, that we might have something for ourselves and families to subsist on." The neighbouring nations used to trade with Judah for wheat (Ezek. xxvii. 17), for it was a fruitful land; but now it *eats up the inhabitants,* and they are glad to make court to the Egyptians and Assyrians. (2.) Others of them ventured their lives for it (*v.* 9) : *We got our bread with the peril of our lives ;*

when, being straitened by the siege and all provisions cut off, they either sallied or stole out of the city, to fetch in some supply, they were in danger of falling into the hands of the besiegers and being put to the sword, *the sword of the wilderness* it is called, *or of the plain* (for so the word signifies), the besiegers lying dispersed every where in the plains that were about the city. Let us take occasion hence to bless God for the plenty that we enjoy, that we get our bread so easily, scarcely with the sweat of our face, much less *with the peril of our lives;* and for the peace we enjoy, that we can go out, and enjoy not only the necessary productions, but the pleasures of the country, without any fear of *the sword of the wilderness.*

4. Those are brought into slavery who were a free people, and not only their own masters, but masters of all about them, and this is as much as any thing their reproach (*v.* 5): *Our necks are under* the grievous and intolerable yoke of *persecution* (the iron yoke which Jeremiah foretold should be laid upon them, Jer. xxviii. 14); we are used like beasts in the yoke, that wholly serve their owners, and are at the command of their drivers. That which aggravated the servitude was, (1.) That their labours were incessant, like those of Israel in Egypt, who were daily tasked, nay, overtasked: *We labour and have no rest,* neither leave nor leisure to rest. The oxen in the yoke are unyoked at night and have rest; so they have, by a particular provision of the law, on the sabbath day; but the poor captives in Babylon, who were compelled to work for their living, *laboured and had no rest,* no night's rest, no sabbath-rest; they were quite tired out with continual toil. (2.) That their masters were insufferable (*v.* 8): *Servants have ruled over us;* and nothing is more vexatious than *a servant when he reigns,* Prov. xxx. 22. They were not only the great men of the Chaldeans that commanded them, but even the meanest of their servants abused them at pleasure, and insulted over them; and they must be at their beck too. The curse of Canaan had now become the doom of Judah: *A servant of servants shall he be.* They would not be ruled by their God, and by his servants the prophets, whose rule was gentle and gracious, and therefore justly are they ruled with rigour by their enemies and their servants. (3.) That they saw no probable way for the redress of their grievances: " *There is none that doth deliver us out of their hand;* not only none to rescue us out of our captivity, but none to check and restrain the insolence of the servants that abuse us and trample upon us," which one would think their masters should have done, because it was a usurpation of their authority; but, it should seem, they connived at it and encouraged it, and, as if they were not worthy of the correction of gentlemen, they are turned

over to the footmen to be spurned by them. Well might they pray, Lord, *consider and behold our reproach.*

5. Those who used to be feasted are now famished (*v.* 10): *Our skin was black like an oven,* dried and parched too, *because of the terrible famine,* the *storms of famine* (so the word is); for, though famine comes gradually upon a people, yet it comes violently, and bears down all before it, and there is no resisting it; and this also is their disgrace; hence we read of *the reproach of famine,* which in captivity they received among the heathen, Ezek. xxxvi. 30.

6. All sorts of people, even those whose persons and characters were most inviolable, were abused and dishonoured. (1.) The *women* were *ravished,* even *the women in Zion,* that holy mountain, *v.* 11. The committing of such abominable wickednesses there is very justly and sadly complained of. (2.) The great men were not only put to death, but put to ignominious deaths. *Princes were hanged,* as if they had been slaves, *by the hands* of the Chaldeans (*v.* 12), who took a pride in doing this barbarous execution with *their own hands.* Some think that the dead bodies of the princes, after they were slain with the sword, were hung up, as the bodies of Saul's sons, in disgrace to them, and as it were to expiate the nation's guilt. (3.) No respect was shown to magistrates and those in authority: *The faces of elders,* elders in age, elders in office, *were not honoured.* This will be particularly remembered against the Chaldeans another day. Isa. xlvii. 6, *Upon the ancient hast thou very heavily laid thy yoke.* (4.) The tenderness of youth was no more considered than the gravity of old age (*v.* 13): *They took the young men to grind* at the hand-mills, nay, perhaps at the horse-mills. *The young men have carried the grist* (so some), *have carried the mill,* or *mill-stones,* so others. They loaded them as if they had been beasts of burden, and so broke their backs when they were young, and made the rest of their lives the more miserable. Nay, they made *the little children* carry their wood home for fuel, and laid such burdens upon them that they *fell* down *under* them, so very inhuman were these cruel taskmasters!

7. An end was put to all their gladness, and their joy was quite extinguished (*v.* 14): *The young men,* who used to be disposed to mirth, have ceased *from their music,* have hung their harps upon the willow-trees. It does indeed well become old men to cease from their music; it is time to lay it by with a gracious contempt when *all the daughters of music are brought low;* but it speaks some great calamity upon a people when their young men are made to cease from it. It was so with the body of the people (*v.* 15): *The joy of their heart ceased;* they never knew what joy was since the enemy came in upon them like a flood, for ever since

deep called unto deep, and one wave flowed in upon the neck of another, so that they were quite overwhelmed: *Our dance is turned into mourning*, instead of leaping for joy, as formerly, we sink and lie down in sorrow. This may refer especially to the joy of their solemn feasts, and the dancing used in them (Judg. xxi. 21), which was not only modest, but sacred, dancing; this was *turned into mourning*, which was doubled on their festival days, in remembrance of their former pleasant things.

8. An end was put to all their glory. (1.) The public administration of justice was their glory, but that was gone : *The elders have ceased from the gate* (v. 14); the course of justice, which used to run down like a river, is now stopped ; the courts of justice, which used to be kept with so much solemnity, are put down ; for the judges are slain, or carried captive. (2.) The royal dignity was their glory, but that also was gone : *The crown has fallen from our head*, not only the *king* himself fallen into disgrace, but *the crown*; he has no successor ; the regalia are all lost. Note, Earthly crowns are fading falling things; but, blessed be God, there is *a crown of glory that fades not away*, that never falls, *a kingdom that cannot be moved*. Upon this complaint, but with reference to all the foregoing complaints, they make that penitent acknowledgment, " *Woe unto us that we have sinned !* Alas for us ! Our case is very deplorable, and it is all owing to ourselves ; we are undone, and, which aggravates the matter, we are undone by our own hands. God is righteous, for *we have sinned.*" Note, All our woes are owing to our own sin and folly. If *the crown of our head be fallen* (for so the words run), if we lose our excellency and become mean, we may thank ourselves, we have by our own iniquity profaned our crown and *laid our honour in the dust*.

17 For this our heart is faint; for these *things* our eyes are dim. 18 Because of the mountain of Zion, which is desolate, the foxes walk upon it. 19 Thou, O LORD, remainest for ever ; thy throne from generation to generation. 20 Wherefore dost thou forget us for ever, *and* forsake us so long time ? 21 Turn thou us unto thee, O LORD, and we shall be turned; renew our days as of old. 22 But thou hast utterly rejected us ; thou art very wroth against us.

Here, I. The people of God express the deep concern they had for the ruins of the temple, more than for any other of their calamities ; the interests of God's house lay nearer their hearts than those of their own (v. 17, 18): *For this our heart is faint*, and sinks under the load of its own heaviness; *for these things our eyes are dim*, and our sight is gone, as is usual in a deliquium, or fainting fit. " It is *because of the mountain of Zion, which is desolate*, the holy mountain, and the temple built upon that mountain. For other desolations our hearts grieve and our eyes weep ; but for this our hearts faint and our eyes are dim." Note, Nothing lies so heavily upon the spirits of good people as that which threatens the ruin of religion or weakens its interests ; and it is a comfort if we can appeal to God that that afflicts us more than any temporal affliction to ourselves. "The people have polluted the *mountain of Zion* with their sins, and therefore God has justly made it *desolate*, to such a degree that *the foxes walk upon it* as freely and commonly as they do in the woods." It is sad indeed when the *mountain of Zion* has become *a portion for foxes* (Ps. lxiii. 10); but sin had first made it so, Ezek. xiii. 4.

II. They comfort themselves with the doctrine of God's eternity, and the perpetuity of his government (v. 19): But *thou, O Lord ! remainest for ever*. This they are taught to do by that psalm which is entitled, *A prayer of the afflicted*, Ps. cii. 27, 28. When all our creature-comforts are removed from us, and our hearts fail us, we may then encourage ourselves with the belief, 1. Of God's eternity : *Thou remainest for ever*. What shakes the world gives no disturbance to him who made it ; whatever revolutions there are on earth there is no change in the Eternal Mind ; God is still the same, and *remains for ever* infinitely wise and holy, just and good ; with him there is *no variableness nor shadow of turning*. 2. Of the never-failing continuance of his dominion : *Thy throne is from generation to generation ;* the throne of glory, the throne of grace, and the throne of government, are all unchangeable, immovable ; and this is matter of comfort to us when *the crown has fallen from our head*. When the thrones of princes, that should be our protectors, are brought to the dust, and buried in it, God's throne continues still ; he still rules the world, and rules it for the good of the church. The Lord reigns, reigns for ever, even *thy God, O Zion !*

III. They humbly expostulate with God concerning the low condition they were now in, and the frowns of heaven they were now under (v. 20): " *Wherefore dost thou forget us for ever*, as if we were quite cast out of mind ? *Wherefore dost thou forsake us so long time*, as if we were quite deprived of the tokens of thy presence ? Wherefore dost thou defer our deliverance, as if thou hadst utterly abandoned us ? Thou art the same, and, though the throne of thy sanctuary is demolished, thy throne in heaven is unshaken. But wilt thou not be the same to us ?" Not as if they thought God had forgotten and forsaken them, much less feared his forgetting and forsaking them for ever ; but thus they express the value they had for his favour and presence, which they thought it long that they were deprived of the evidence and comfort of. The last verse may be read as such an expostulation, and so the margin reads it : " *For wilt thou utterly reject us ? Wilt thou be perpetually wroth with us,* not only not smile upon us and remember us in mercy, but frown upon us and lay us under the tokens of thy wrath, not only not draw nigh to us, but cast us out of thy presence and forbid us to draw nigh unto thee ? How will this be reconciled with thy goodness and faithfulness, and the stability of thy covenant ?" We read it, " *But thou hast rejected us ;* thou hast given us cause to fear that thou hast. Lord, how long shall we be in this temptation ?" Note, Though we may not quarrel with God, yet we may plead with him ; and, though we may not conclude that he has cast off, yet we may (with the prophet, Jer. xii. 1) humbly reason with him concerning his judgments, especially the continuance of the desolations of his sanctuary.

IV. They earnestly pray to God for mercy and grace : " Lord, do not reject *us for ever,* but *turn thou us unto thee; renew our days,*" *v.* 21. Though these words are not put last, yet the Rabbin, because they would not have the book to conclude with those melancholy words (*v.* 22), repeat this prayer again, that the sun may not set under a cloud, and so make these the last words both in writing and reading this chapter. They here pray, 1. For converting grace to prepare and qualify them for mercy : *Turn us to thee, O Lord !* They had complained that God had forsaken and forgotten them, and then their prayer is not, *Turn thou to us,* but, *Turn us to thee,* which implies an acknowledgment that the cause of the dis-

tance was in themselves. God never leaves any till they first leave him, nor stands afar off from any longer than while they stand afar off from him ; if therefore he turn them to him in a way of duty, no doubt but he will quickly return to them in a way of mercy. This agrees with that repeated prayer (Ps. lxxx. 3, 7, 19), *Turn us again, and then cause thy face to shine. Turn us from our idols to thyself, by a sincere repentance and reformation, and then we shall be turned.* This implies a further acknowledgment of their own weakness and inability to turn themselves. There is in our nature a proneness to backslide from God, but no disposition to return to him till his grace works in us both *to will and to do.* So necessary is that grace that we may truly say, *Turn us or we shall not be turned,* but shall wander endlessly ; and so powerful and effectual is that grace that we may as truly say, *Turn us, and we shall be turned ;* for it is a day of power, almighty power, in which God's people are made a *willing people,* Ps. cx. 3. 2. For restoring mercy : *Turn us to thee,* and then *renew our days as of old,* put us into the same happy state that our ancestors were in long ago and that they continued long in ; let it be with us as it was *at the first,* and *at the beginning,* Isa. i. 26. Note, If God by his grace renew our hearts, he will by his favour *renew our days,* so that we shall *renew our youth as the eagle,* Ps. ciii. 5. Those that *repent, and do their first works,* shall rejoice, and recover their first comforts. God's mercies to his people have been *ever of old* (Ps. xxv. 6) ; and therefore they may hope, even then when he seems to have forsaken and forgotten them, that the mercy which was *from everlasting* will be *to everlasting.*

AN

EXPOSITION,

WITH PRACTICAL OBSERVATIONS,

OF THE BOOK OF THE PROPHET

E Z E K I E L.

WHEN we entered upon the writings of the prophets, which speak of the *things that should be hereafter,* we seemed to have the same call that St. John had (Rev. iv. 1), *Come up hither ;* but, when we enter upon the prophecy of this book, it is as if the voice said, *Come up higher ;* as we go forward in time (for Ezekiel prophesied in the captivity, as Jeremiah prophesied just before it), so we soar upward in discoveries yet more sublime of the divine glory. These waters of the sanctuary still grow deeper ; so far are they from being fordable that in some places they are scarcely fathomable ; yet, deep as they are, out of them flow streams which *make glad the city of our God, the holy place of the tabernacles of the Most High.* As to this prophecy now before us, we may enquire, I. Concerning the penman of it—it was Ezekiel ; his name signifies, *The strength of God*, or one *girt* or *strengthened of God.* He girded up the loins of his mind to the service, and God put strength into him. Whom God calls to any service he will himself enable for it; if he give commission, he will give power to execute it. Ezekiel's name was answered when God said (and no doubt did as he said), *I have made thy face strong against their faces.* The learned Selden, in his book *De Diis Syris,* says that it was the opinion of some of the ancients that the prophet Ezekiel was the same with that Nazaratus Assyrius whom Pythagoras (as himself relates) had for his tutor for some time, and whose lectures he attended. It is agreed that they lived much about the same time; and we have reason to think that many of the Greek philosophers were acquainted with the sacred writings and borrowed some of the best of their notions from them. If we may give credit to the tradition of the Jews, he was put to death by the captives in Babylon, for his faithfulness and boldness in reproving them; it is stated that they dragged him upon the stones till his brains were dashed out. An Arabic historian says that he was put to death and was buried in the sepulchre of Shem the son of Noah. So Hottinger relates, *Thesaur. Philol. lib.* ii. *cap.* 1. II. Concerning the date of it—the place whence it is dated and the time when. The scene is laid in Babylon, when it was a *house of bondage* to the *Israel of God;* there the prophecies of this book were preached, there they were written, when the prophet himself, and the people to whom he prophesied, were captives there. Ezekiel and Daniel are the only writing prophets of the Old Testament who lived and prophesied any where but in the land of Israel, except we add Jonah, who was sent to Nineveh to prophesy. Ezekiel prophesied in the beginning of the captivity, Daniel in the latter end of it. It was an indication of God's good-will to them, and his gracious designs concerning them in their affliction, that he raised up prophets among them, both to convince them when, in the beginning of their troubles, they were secure and unhumbled, which was Ezekiel's business, and to comfort them when, in the latter end of their troubles, they were dejected and discouraged. If the Lord had been pleased to kill them, he would not have used such apt and proper means to cure them. III. Concerning the matter and scope of it. 1. There is much in it that is very mysterious, dark, and hard to be understood, especially in the beginning and the latter end of it, which therefore the Jewish rabbin forbade the reading of to their young men, till they came to be thirty years of age, lest by the difficulties they met with there they should be prejudiced against the scriptures; but if we read these difficult parts of scripture with humility and reverence, and search them diligently, though we may not be able to untie all the knots we meet with, any more than we can solve all the phenomena in the book of nature, yet we may from them, as from the book of nature, gather a great deal for the confirming of our faith and the encouraging of our hope in the God we worship. 2. Though the visions here be intricate, such as an elephant may swim in, yet the sermons are mostly plain, such as a lamb may wade in; and the chief design of them is to *show God's people their transgressions,* that in their captivity they might be repenting and not repining. It should seem, the prophet was constantly attended (for we read of their *sitting before him as God's people sat to hear his words, ch.* xxxiii. **31**), and that he was occasionally consulted, for we read of the elders of Israel who came to *enquire of the Lord* by him, *ch.* xiv. 1, 3. And, as it was of great use to the oppressed captives themselves to have a prophet with them, so it was a testimony to their holy religion against their oppressors who ridiculed it and them. 3. Though the reproofs and the threatenings here are very sharp and bold, yet towards the close of the book very comfortable assurances are given of great mercy God had in store for them; and there, at length, we shall meet with something that has reference to gospel times, and which was to have its accomplishment in the kingdom of the Messiah, of whom indeed this prophet speaks less than almost any of the prophets. But by opening the *terrors of the Lord* he prepares Christ's way. By the law is the knowledge of sin, and so it becomes our *school-master to bring us to Christ.* The visions which were the prophet's credentials we have *ch.* i.—iii., the reproofs and threatenings *ch.* iv.—xxiv. betwixt which and the comforts which we have in the latter part of the book we have messages sent to the nations that bordered upon the land of Israel, whose destruction is foretold (*ch.* xxv.—xxxv.), to make way for the restoration of God's Israel and the re-establishment of their city and temple, which are foretold *ch.* xxxvi. to the end. Those who would apply the comforts to themselves must apply the convictions to themselves.

CHAP. I.

In this chapter we have, I. The common circumstances of the prophecy now to be delivered, the time when it was delivered (ver. 1), the place where (ver. 2), and the person by whom, ver. 3. II. The uncommon introduction to it by a vision of the glory of God, 1. In his attendance and retinue in the upper world, where his throne is surrounded with angels, here called "living creatures," ver. 4—14. 2. In his providences concerning the lower world, represented by the wheels and their motions, ver. 15—25. 3. In the face of Jesus Christ sitting upon the throne, ver. 26—28. And the more we are acquainted, and the more intimately we converse, with the glory of God in these three branches of it, the more commanding influence will divine revelation have upon us and the more ready shall we be to submit to it, which is the thing aimed at in prefacing the prophecies of this book with these visions. When such a God of glory speaks, it concerns us to hear with attention and reverence; it is at our peril if we do not.

NOW it came to pass in the thirtieth year, in the fourth *month,* in the fifth *day* of the month, as I *was* among the captives by the river of Chebar, *that* the heavens were opened, and I saw visions of God. 2 In the fifth *day* of the month, which *was* the fifth year of king Jehoiachin's captivity, 3 The word of the LORD came expressly unto Ezekiel the priest, the son of Buzi, in the land of the Chaldeans by the river Chebar; and the hand of the LORD was there upon him.

The circumstances of the vision which Ezekiel saw, and in which he received his commission and instructions, are here very particularly set down, that the narrative may appear to be authentic and not romantic. It may be of use to keep an account when and where God has been pleased to manifest himself to our souls in a peculiar manner, that the *return of the day*, and our return to *the place of the altar* (Gen. xiii. 4), may revive the pleasing grateful remembrance of God's favour to us. "Remember, O my soul! and never forget what communications of divine love thou didst receive at such a time, at such a place; tell others what God did for thee."

I. The time when Ezekiel had this vision is here recorded. It was *in the thirtieth year, v.* 1. Some make it the thirtieth year of the prophet's age; being a priest, he was at that age to enter upon the full execution of the priestly office, but being debarred from that by the iniquity and calamity of the times, now that they had neither temple nor altar, God at that age called him to the dignity of a prophet. Others make it to be the thirtieth year from the beginning of the reign of Nabopolassar, the father of Nebuchadnezzar, from which the Chaldeans began a new computation of time, as they had done from Nabonassar 123 years before. Nabopolassar reigned nineteen years, and this was the eleventh of his son, which makes the thirty. And it was proper enough for Ezekiel, when he was in Babylon, to use the computation they there used, as we in foreign countries date by the new style; and he afterwards uses the melancholy computation of his own country, observing (*v.* 2) that it was the fifth year of Jehoiachin's captivity. But the Chaldee paraphrase fixes upon another era, and says that this was the thirtieth year after *Hilkiah the priest found the book of the law in the house of the sanctuary, at midnight, after the setting of the moon, in the days of Josiah the king.* And it is true that this was just thirty years from that time; and that was an event so remarkable (as it put the Jewish state upon a new trial) that it was proper enough to date from it; and perhaps therefore the prophet speaks indefinitely of thirty years, as having an eye both to that event and to the Chaldean computation, which were coincident. It was in the *fourth month,* answering to our June, and in the *fifth day of the month,* that Ezekiel had this vision, *v.* 2. It is probable that it was on the sabbath day, because we read (*ch.* iii. 16) that *at the end of seven days,* which we may well suppose to be the next sabbath, the word of the Lord came to him again. Thus *John was in the Spirit on the Lord's day,* when he *saw the visions of the Almighty,* Rev. i. 10. God would hereby put an honour upon his sabbaths, when *the enemies mocked at them,* Lam. i. 7. And he would thus encourage his people to keep up their

748

attendance on the ministry of his prophets every sabbath day, by the extraordinary manifestations of himself on some sabbath days.

II. The melancholy circumstances he was in when God honoured him, and thereby favoured his people, with this vision. He was *in the land of the Chaldeans, among the captives, by the river of Chebar, and it was in the fifth year of king Jehoiachin's captivity.* Observe,

1. The people of God were now, some of them, *captives in the land of the Chaldeans.* The body of the Jewish nation yet remained in their own land, but these were the first-fruits of the captivity, and they were some of the best; for in Jeremiah's vision these were the *good figs,* whom God had *sent into the land of the Chaldeans for their good* (Jer. xxiv. 5); and, that it might be for their good, God raised up a prophet among them, to *teach them out of the law,* then when he chastened them, Ps. xciv. 12. Note, It is a great mercy to have the word of God brought to us, and a great duty to attend to it diligently, when we are in affliction. The word of instruction and the rod of correction may be of great service to us, in concert and concurrence with each other, the word to explain the rod and the rod to enforce the word: both together give wisdom. It is happy for a man, when he is sick and in pain, to have a messenger with him, an interpreter, *one among a thousand,* if he have but his *ear open to discipline,* Job xxiii. 23. One of the quarrels God had with the Jews, when he sent them into captivity, was for *mocking his messengers* and *misusing his prophets;* and yet, when they were suffering for this sin, he favoured them with this forfeited mercy. It were ill with us if God did not sometimes graciously thrust upon us those means of grace and salvation which we have foolishly thrust from us. In their captivity they were destitute of ordinary helps for their souls, and therefore God raised them up these extraordinary ones; for God's children, if they be hindered in their education one way, shall have it made up another way. But observe, *It was in the fifth year of the captivity* that Ezekiel was raised up among them, and not before. So long God left them without any prophet, till they began to *lament after the Lord* and to complain that they *saw not their signs* and there was none to *tell them how long* (Ps. lxxiv. 9), and then they would know how to value a prophet, and God's discoveries of himself to them by him would be the more acceptable and comfortable. The Jews that remained in their own land had Jeremiah with them, those that had gone into captivity had Ezekiel with them; for wherever the children of God are scattered abroad he will find out tutors for them.

2. The prophet was himself among the captives, those of them that were posted by *the river Chebar;* for it was *by the rivers of*

Babylon that they *sat down,* and on the willow-trees by the river's side that they *hanged their harps,* Ps. cxxxvii. 1, 2. The planters in America keep along by the sides of the rivers, and perhaps those captives were employed by their masters in improving some parts of the country by the rivers' sides that were uncultivated, the natives being generally employed in war; or they employed them in manufactures, and therefore chose to fix them by the sides of rivers, that the goods they made might the more easily be conveyed by water-carriage. Interpreters agree not what river this of Chebar was, but *among the captives* by that river Ezekiel was, and himself a captive. Observe here, (1.) The best men, and those that are dearest to God, often share, not only in the common calamities of this life, but in the public and national judgments that are inflicted for sin; those feel the smart who contributed nothing to the guilt, by which it appears that the difference between good and bad arises not from the events that befal them, but from the temper and disposition of their spirits under them. And since not only righteous men, but prophets, share with the worst in present punishments, we may infer thence, with the greatest assurance, that there are rewards reserved for them in the future state. (2.) Words of conviction, counsel, and comfort, come best to those who are in affliction from their fellow sufferers. The captives will be best instructed by one who is a captive among them and experimentally knows their sorrows. (3.) The spirit of prophecy was not confined to the land of Israel, but some of the brightest of divine revelations were revealed *in the land of the Chaldeans,* which was a happy presage of the carrying of the church, with that divine revelation upon which it is built, into the Gentile world; and, as now, so afterwards, when the gospel kingdom was to be set up, the dispersion of the Jews contributed to the spreading of the knowledge of God. (4.) Wherever we are we may keep up our communion with God. *Undique ad cœlos tantundem est viæ —From the remotest corners of the earth we may find a way open heavenward.* (5.) When God's ministers are bound *the word of the Lord is not bound,* 2 Tim. ii. 9. When St. Paul was a prisoner the gospel had a free course. When St. John was banished into the Isle of Patmos Christ visited him there. Nay, God's suffering servants have generally been treated as favourites, and their consolations have much more abounded when affliction has abounded, 2 Cor. i. 5.

III. The discovery which God was pleased to make of himself to the prophet when he was in these circumstances, to be by him communicated to his people. He here tells us what he saw, what he heard, and what he felt. 1. He *saw visions of God, v.* 1. No man can *see God and live;* but many have seen visions of God, such displays of the divine glory as have both instructed and affected them; and commonly, when God first revealed himself to any prophet, he did it by an extraordinary vision, as to Isaiah (*ch.* vi.), to Jeremiah (*ch.* i.), to Abraham (Acts vii. 2), to settle a correspondence and a satisfactory way of intercourse, so that there needed not afterwards a vision upon every revelation. Ezekiel was employed in turning the hearts of the people to the Lord their God, and therefore he must himself see the visions of God. Note, It concerns those to be well acquainted with God themselves, and much affected with what they know of him, whose business it is to bring others to the knowledge and love of him. That he might see the *visions of God the heavens were opened;* the darkness and distance which hindered his visions were conquered, and he was let into the light of the glories of the upper world, as near and clear as if heaven had been opened to him. 2. He heard the voice of God (*v.* 3): *The word of the Lord came expressly* to him, and what he saw was designed to prepare him for what he was to hear. The expression is emphatic. *Essendo fuit verbum Dei—The word of the Lord was as really it was to him.* There was no mistake in it; it came to him in the fulness of its light and power, in the evidence and demonstration of the Spirit; it came close to him, nay, it came into him, took possession of him and dwelt in him richly. It *came expressly,* or accurately, to him; he did himself clearly understand what he said and was abundantly satisfied of the truth of it. *The essential Word* (so we may take it), *the Word who is, who is what he is, came to Ezekiel,* to send him on his errand. 3. He felt the power of God opening his eyes to see the visions, opening his ear to hear the voice, and opening his heart to receive both: *The hand of the Lord was there upon him.* Note, *The hand of the Lord* goes along with *the word of the Lord,* and so it becomes effectual; those only understand and *believe the report to whom the arm of the Lord is revealed. The hand of God was upon him,* as upon Moses, to cover him, that he should not be overcome by the dazzling light and lustre of the visions he saw, Exod. xxxiii. 22. It *was upon him* (as upon St. John, Rev. i. 17), to revive and support him, that he might bear up, and not faint, under these discoveries, that he might neither be lifted up nor cast down with the abundance of the revelations. *God's grace is sufficient for him,* and, in token of that, his *hand is upon him.*

4 And I looked, and, behold, a whirlwind came out of the north, a great cloud, and a fire infolding itself, and a brightness *was* about it, and out of the midst thereof as the colour

of amber, out of the midst of the fire. 5 Also out of the midst thereof *came* the likeness of four living creatures. And this *was* their appearance; they had the likeness of a man. 6 And every one had four faces, and every one had four wings. 7 And their feet *were* straight feet; and the sole of their feet *was* like the sole of a calf's foot: and they sparkled like the colour of burnished brass. 8 And *they had* the hands of a man under their wings on their four sides; and they four had their faces and their wings, 9 Their wings *were* joined one to another; they turned not when they went; they went every one straight forward. 10 As for the likeness of their faces, they four had the face of a man, and the face of a lion, on the right side: and they four had the face of an ox on the left side; they four also had the face of an eagle. 11 Thus *were* their faces: and their wings *were* stretched upward; two *wings* of every one *were* joined one to another, and two covered their bodies. 12 And they went every one straight forward: whither the spirit was to go, they went; *and* they turned not when they went. 13 As for the likeness of the living creatures, their appearance *was* like burning coals of fire, *and* like the appearance of lamps: it went up and down among the living creatures; and the fire was bright, and out of the fire went forth lightning. 14 And the living creatures ran and returned as the appearance of a flash of lightning.

The visions of God which Ezekiel here saw were very glorious, and had more particulars than those which other prophets saw. It is the scope and intention of these visions, 1. To possess the prophet's mind with very great, and high, and honourable thoughts of that God by whom he was commissioned and for whom he was employed. It is *the likeness of the glory of the Lord* that he sees (*v.* 28), and hence he may infer that it is his honour to serve him, for he is one whom angels serve. He may serve him with safety, for he has power sufficient to bear him out in his work. It is at his peril to draw back from his service, for he has power to pursue him, as he did Jonah. So great a God as this must be served *with reverence and godly fear;* and with assur-

750

ance may Ezekiel foretel what this God will do, for he is able to make his words good. 2. To strike a terror upon the sinners who remained in Zion, and those who had already come to Babylon, who were secure, and bade defiance to the threatenings of Jerusalem's ruin, as we have found in Jeremiah's prophecy, and shall find in this, many did. "Let those who said, *We shall have peace though we go on*, know that *our God is a consuming fire*, whom they cannot stand before." That this vision had a reference to the destruction of Jerusalem seems plain from *ch.* xliii. 3, where he says that it was *the vision which he saw when he came to destroy the city*, that is, to prophesy the destruction of it. 3. To speak comfort to those that feared God, and trembled at his word, and humbled themselves under his mighty hand. "Let them know that, though they are captives in Babylon, yet they have God nigh unto them; though they have not *the place of the sanctuary* to be their glorious high throne, they have the God of the sanctuary." Dr. Lightfoot observes, "Now that the church is to be planted for a long time in another country, the Lord shows a glory in the midst of them, as he had done at their first constituting into a church in the wilderness; and out of *a cloud and fire*, as he had done there, he showed himself; and from between *living creatures*, as from between the cherubim, he gives his oracles." This put an honour upon them, by which they might value themselves when the Chaldeans insulted over them, and this might encourage their hopes of deliverance in due time.

Now, to answer these ends, we have in these verses the first part of the vision, which represents God as attended and served by an innumerable company of angels, who are all his messengers, his ministers, *doing his commandments* and *hearkening to the voice of his word.* This denotes his grandeur, as it magnifies an earthly prince to have a splendid retinue and numerous armies at his command, which engages his allies to trust him and his enemies to fear him.

I. The introduction to this vision of the angels is very magnificent and awakening, *v.* 4. The prophet, observing the heavens to open, *looked*, looked up (as it was time), to see what discoveries God would make to him. Note, When the heavens are opened it concerns us to have our eyes open. To clear the way, *behold, a whirlwind came out of the north*, which would drive away the interposing mists of this lower region. Fair weather *comes out of the north*, and thence *the wind* comes that *drives away rain.* God can by a whirlwind clear the sky and air, and produce that serenity of mind which is necessary to our communion with Heaven. Yet this whirlwind was attended with *a great cloud.* When we think that the clouds which arise from this earth are dispelled, and we can see beyond them, yet still there is a cloud which heavenly things are wrapped in, a cloud from above, so that *we cannot order our speech* concerning them *by reason of darkness.* Christ here descended, as he ascended, *in a cloud.* Some by this *whirlwind and cloud* understand the Chaldean army coming *out of the north* against the land of Judah, bearing down all before them as a tempest; and so it agrees with that which was signified by one of the first of Jeremiah's visions (Jer. i. 14, *Out of the north an evil shall break forth);* but I take it here as an introduction rather to the vision than to the sermons. This whirlwind came to Ezekiel (as that to Elijah, 1 Kings xix. 11), to *prepare the way of the Lord,* and to demand attention. *He that has eyes, that has ears,* let him see, *let him hear.*

II. The vision itself. *A great cloud* was the vehicle of this vision, in which it was conveyed to the prophet; for God's pavilion in which he rests, his chariot in which he rides, is *darkness and thick clouds,* Ps. xviii. 11; civ. 3. Thus he *holds back the face of his throne,* lest its dazzling light and lustre should overpower us, by *spreading a cloud upon it.* Now,

1. The cloud is accompanied with *a fire,* as upon Mount Sinai, where God resided in a *thick cloud;* but *the sight of his glory was like devouring fire* (Exod. xxiv. 16, 17), and his first appearance to Moses was *in a flame of fire in the bush;* for *our God is a consuming fire.* This was *a fire enfolding itself,* a globe, or orb, or wheel of fire. God being his own cause, his own rule, and his own end, if he be as *a fire,* he is as *a fire enfolding itself,* or (as some read it) *kindled by itself.* The fire of God's glory shines forth, but it quickly enfolds itself; for he lets us know but part of his ways; the fire of God's wrath breaks forth, but it also quickly enfolds itself, for the divine patience suffers not all his wrath to be stirred up. If it were not a fire thus enfolding itself, *O Lord! who shall stand?*

2. The fire is surrounded with a glory: *A brightness was about it,* in which it enfolded itself, yet it made some discovery of itself. Though we cannot see into the fire, cannot by searching find out God to perfection, yet we see the brightness that is round about it, the reflection of this fire from the thick cloud. Moses might see God's back parts, but not his face. We have some light concerning the nature of God, from the brightness which encompasses it, though we have not an insight into it, by reason of the cloud spread upon it. Nothing is more easy than to determine that God is, nothing more difficult than to describe what he is. When God displays his wrath as fire, yet there is a brightness about it; for his holiness and justice appear very illustrious in the punishment of sin and sinners: even about the devouring fire there is a brightness, which glorified saints will for ever admire

3. Out of this fire there shines *the colour of amber.* We are not told who or what it was that had this colour of amber, and therefore I take it to be the whole frame of the following vision, which came into Ezekial's view *out of the midst of the fire and brightness;* and the first thing he took notice of before he viewed the particulars was that it was *of the colour of amber,* or *the eye of amber;* that is, it looked as amber does to the eye, of a bright flaming fiery colour, the colour of *a burning coal;* so some think it should be read. The *living creatures* which he saw coming *out of the midst of the fire* were *seraphim—burners;* for *he maketh his angels spirits, his ministers a flaming fire.*

4. That which comes out of the fire, of a fiery amber colour, when it comes to be distinctly viewed, is *the likeness of four living creatures;* not the *living creatures* themselves (angels are spirits, and cannot be seen), but *the likeness* of them, such a hieroglyphic, or representation, as God saw fit to make use of for the leading of the prophet, and us with him, into some acquaintance with the world of angels (a matter purely of divine revelation), so far as is requisite to possess us with an awful sense of the greatness of that God who has angels for his attendants, and the goodness of that God who has appointed them to be attendants on his people. *The likeness of these living creatures came out of the midst of the fire;* for angels derive their being and power from God; they are in themselves, and to us, what he is pleased to make them; their glory is a ray of his. The prophet himself explains this vision (*ch.* x. 20): *I knew that the living creatures were the cherubim,* which is one of the names by which the angels are known in scripture. To Daniel was made known their number, *ten thousand times ten thousand,* Dan. vii. 10. But, though they are many, yet they are one, and that is made known to Ezekiel here; they are one in nature and operation, as an army, consisting of thousands, is yet called a body of men. We have here an account of,

(1.) Their nature. They are living creatures; they are the creatures of God, the work of his hands; their being is derived; they have not life in and of themselves, but receive it from him who is *the fountain of life.* As much as the living creatures of this lower world excel the vegetables that are the ornaments of earth, so much do the angels, the living creatures of the upper world, excel the sun, moon, and stars, the ornaments of the heavens. The sun (say some) is a flame of *fire enfolding itself,* but it is not a living creature, as angels, those flames of fire, are. Angels are living creatures, living beings, emphatically so. Men on earth are dying creatures, dying daily *(in the midst of life we are in death),* but angels in heaven are living creatures; they live indeed, live to good purpose; and, when saints come to be *equal unto the angels,* they shall not *die any more,* Luke xx. 36.

(2.) Their number. They are four; so they appear here, though they are innumerable; not as if these were four particular angels set up above the rest, as some have fondly imagined, Michael and Gabriel, Raphael and Uriel, but for the sake of the four faces they put on, and to intimate their being sent forth towards *the four winds of heaven,* Matt. xxiv. 31. Zechariah saw them as four chariots going forth east, west, north, and south, Zech. vi. 1. God has messengers to send every way; for his kingdom is universal, and reaches to all parts of the world.

(3.) Their qualifications, by which they are fitted for the service of their Maker and Master. These are set forth figuratively and by similitude, as is proper in visions, which are parables to the eye. Their description here is such, and so expressed, that I think it is not possible by it to form an exact idea of them in our fancies, or with the pencil, for that would be a temptation to worship them; but the several instances of their fitness for the work they are employed in are intended in the several parts of this description. Note, It is the greatest honour of God's creatures to be in a capacity of answering the end of their creation; and the more ready we are to every good work the nearer we approach to the dignity of angels. These living creatures are described here, [1.] By their general appearance: *They had the likeness of a man;* they appeared, for the main, in a human shape, *First,* To signify that these living creatures are reasonable creatures, intelligent beings, who have that *spirit of a man* which is the *candle of the Lord. Secondly,* To put an honour upon the nature of man, who is made lower, yet but *a little lower, than the angels,* in the very next rank of beings below them. When the invisible intelligences of the upper world would make themselves visible, it is in *the likeness of man. Thirdly,* To intimate that their *delights are with the sons of men,* as their Master's are (Prov. viii. 31), that they do service to men, and men may have spiritual communion with them by faith, hope, and holy love. *Fourthly,* The angels of God appear in *the likeness of man* because in *the fulness of time* the Son of God was not only to appear in that likeness, but to assume that nature; they therefore show this love to it. [2.] By their faces: *Every one had four faces,* looking four several ways. In St. John's vision, which has a near affinity with this, each of the four living creatures has one of these faces here mentioned (Rev. iv. 7); here each of them has all four, to intimate that they have all the same qualifications for service; though, perhaps, among the angels of heaven, as among the angels of the churches, some excel in one gift and others in another, but

752

all for the common service. Let us contemplate their faces till we be in some measure changed into the same image, that we may do the will of God as the angels do it in heaven. They *all four had the face of a man* (for in that likeness they appeared, *v.* 5), but, besides that, they had *the face of a lion, an ox,* and *an eagle,* each masterly in its kind, *the lion* among *wild* beasts, *the ox* among *tame* ones, and *the eagle* among fowls, *v.* 10. Does God make use of them for the executing of judgments upon his enemies? They are fierce and strong as the lion and the eagle in tearing their prey. Does he make use of them for the good of his people? They are as *oxen strong for labour* and inclined to serve. And in both they have *the understanding of a man.* The scattered perfections of the living creatures on earth meet in the angels of heaven. They have *the likeness of man;* but, because there are some things in which man is excelled even by the inferior creatures, they are therefore compared to some of them. They have *the understanding of a man,* and such as far exceeds it; they also resemble man in tenderness and humanity. But, *First, A lion* excels man in strength and boldness, and is much more formidable; therefore the angels, who in this resemble them, put on the *face of a lion. Secondly, An ox* excels man in diligence, and patience, and painstaking, and an unwearied discharge of the work he has to do; therefore the angels, who are constantly employed in the service of God and the church, put on *the face of an ox. Thirdly, An eagle* excels man in quickness and piercingness of sight, and in soaring high; and therefore the angels, who seek things above, and see far into divine mysteries, put on *the face of a flying eagle.* [3.] By their wings: *Every one had four wings, v.* 6. In the vision Isaiah had of them they appeared with six, now with four; for they appeared above the throne, and had occasion for two to cover their faces with. The angels are fitted with wings to fly swiftly on God's errands; whatever business God sends them upon they lose no time. Faith and hope are the soul's wings, upon which it soars upward; pious and devout affections are its wings on which it is carried forward with vigour and alacrity. The prophet observes here, concerning their wings, *First,* That they were *joined one to another, v.* 9 and again *v.* 11. They did not make use of their wings for fighting, as some birds do; there is no contest among the angels. God makes *peace,* perfect peace, *in his high places.* But their wings were joined, in token of their perfect unity and unanimity and the universal agreement there is among them. *Secondly,* That *they were stretched upward,* extended, and ready for use, not folded up, or flagging. Let an angel receive the least intimation of the divine will, and he has nothing to seek, but is upon the wing immediately; while our poor dull souls are like the ostrich, that with much difficulty lifts up herself on high. *Thirdly,* That two of their wings were made use of in covering their bodies, the spiritual bodies they assumed. The clothes that cover us are our hindrance in work; angels need no other covering than their own wings, which are their furtherance. They cover their bodies from us, so forbidding us needless enquiries concerning them. Ask not after them, for they are wonderful, Judg. xiii. 18. They cover them before God, so directing us, when we approach to God, to see to it that we be so clothed with Christ's righteousness *that the shame of our nakedness may not appear.* [4.] By their feet, including their legs and thighs: They were *straight feet* (*v.* 7); they stood straight, and firm, and steady; no burden of service could make their legs to bend under them. The spouse makes this part of the description of her beloved, that *his legs were as pillars of marble set upon sockets of fine gold* (Cant. v. 15); such are the angels' legs. *The sole of their feet was like* that *of a calf's foot,* which divides the hoof and is therefore clean: *as it were the sole of a round foot* (as the Chaldee words it); they were ready for motion any way. *Their feet were winged* (so the LXX.); they went so swiftly that it was as if they flew. And their very feet *sparkled like the colour of burnished brass;* not only the faces, but the very feet, of those are beautiful whom God sends on his errands (Isa. lii. 7); every step the angels take is glorious. In the vision John had of Christ it is said, *His feet were like unto fine brass, as if they burned in a furnace,* Rev. i. 15. [5.] By their hands (*v.* 8): *They had the hands of a man under their wings on their four sides,* an arm and a hand under every wing. They had not only wings for motion, but hands for action. Many are quick who are not active; they hurry about a great deal, but do nothing to purpose, bring nothing to pass; they have wings, but no hands: whereas God's servants, the angels, not only go when he sends them and come when he calls them, but do what he bids them. They are *the hands of a man,* which are wonderfully made and fitted for service, which are guided by reason and understanding; for what angels do they do intelligently and with judgment. They have calves' feet; this denotes the swiftness of their motion (the cedars of Lebanon are said to *skip like a calf,* Ps. xxix. 6); but they have a man's hand, which denotes the niceness and exactness of their performances, as the heavens are said to be the work of God's fingers. Their hands were *under their wings,* which concealed them, as they did the rest of their bodies. Note, The agency of angels is a secret thing and their work is carried on in an invisible way. In working for God, though we must not, with *the sluggard,* hide

our hand in our bosom, yet we must, with the humble, *not let our left hand know what our right hand doeth.* We may observe that where these wings were their hands were *under their wings;* wherever their wings carried them they carried hands along with them, to be still doing something suitable, something that the duty of the place requires. (4.) Their motions. The living creatures are moving. Angels are active beings; it is not their happiness to sit still and do nothing, but to be always well employed; and we must reckon ourselves then best when we are doing good, doing it as the angels do it, of whom it is here observed, [1.] That whatever service they went about *they went every one straight forward* (*v.* 9, 12), which intimates, *First,* That they sincerely aimed at the glory of God, and had a single eye to that, in all they did. Their going *straight forward* supposes that they looked straight forward, and never had any sinister intentions in what they did. And, if thus *our eye be single,* our *whole body will be full of light.* The singleness of the eye is the sincerity of the heart. *Secondly,* That they were intent upon the service they were employed in, and did it with a close application of mind. They went forward with their work; for what their hand found to do they did *with all their might* and did not loiter in it. *Thirdly,* That they were unanimous in it: *They went straight forward,* every one about his own work; they did not thwart or jostle one another, did not stand in one another's light, in one another's way. *Fourthly,* That they perfectly understood their business, and were thoroughly apprised of it, so that they needed not to stand still, to pause or hesitate, but pursue their work with readiness, as those that knew what they had to do and how to do it. *Fifthly,* They were steady and constant in their work. They did not fluctuate, did not tire, did not vary, but were of a piece with themselves. They moved in a direct line, and so went the nearest way to work in all they did and lost no time. When we go straight we go forward; when we serve God with one heart we rid ground, we rid work. [2.] *They turned not when they went,* v. 9, 12. *First,* They made no blunders or mistakes, which would give them occasion to turn back to rectify them; their work needed no correction, and therefore needed not to be gone over again. *Secondly,* They minded no diversions; as they turned not back, so they turned not aside, to trifle with any thing that was foreign to their business. [3.] *They went whither the Spirit was to go* (*v.* 12), either, *First, Whither* their own *spirit was* disposed *to go;* thither *they* went, having no bodies, as we have, to clog or hinder them. It is our infelicity and daily burden that, when *the spirit is willing,* yet *the flesh is weak* and cannot keep pace with it, so that *the good which we would do we do it not;* but angels and glorified saints labour under no such impotency; whatever they incline or intend to do they do it, and never come short of it. Or, rather, *Secondly,* Whithersoever *the Spirit* of God would have them *go,* thither *they went.* Though they had so much wisdom of their own, yet in all their motions and actions they subjected themselves to the guidance and government of the divine will. Whithersoever the divine Providence *was to go they went,* to serve its purposes and to execute its orders. The Spirit of God (says Mr. Greenhill) is the great agent that sets angels to work, and it is their honour that they are led, they are easily *led, by the Spirit.* See how tractable and obsequious these noble creatures are. Whithersoever *the Spirit* is *to go* they go immediately, with all possible alacrity. Note, Those that *walk after the Spirit* do the will of God as the angels do it. [4.] They *ran and returned like a flash of lightning, v.* 14. This intimates, *First,* That they made haste; they were quick in their motions, as quick as lightning. Whatever business they went about they despatched it immediately, in a moment, in the twinkling of an eye. Happy they that have no bodies to retard their motion in holy exercises. And happy shall we be when we come to have spiritual bodies for spiritual work. Satan *falls like lightning* into his own ruin, Luke x. 18. Angels fly *like lightning* in their Master's work. The angel Gabriel flew swiftly. *Secondly,* That they made haste back : They *ran and returned;* ran to do their work and execute their orders, and then returned to give an account of what they had done and receive new instructions, that they might be always doing. They *ran* into the lower world, to do what was to be done there; but, when they had done it, they *returned like a flash of lightning* to the upper world again, to the beatific vision of their God, which they could not with any patience be longer from than their service did require. Thus we should be in the affairs of this world as out of our element. Though we run into them, we must not repose in them, but our souls must quickly return like lightning to God their rest and centre.

5. We have an account of the light by which the prophet saw these living creatures, or the looking-glass in which he saw them, *v.* 13. (1.) He saw them by their own light, for *their appearance was like burning coals of fire;* they are *seraphim—burners,* denoting the ardour of their love to God, their fervent zeal in his service, their splendour and brightness, and their terror against God's enemies. When God employs them to fight his battles they are as *coals of fire* (Ps. xviii. 12) to *devour the adversaries,* as lightnings shot out to discomfit them. (2.) He saw them by the light of some *lamps,* which *went up and down among* them, the shining whereof *was* very *bright.* Satan's works

are works of darkness; he is *the ruler of the darkness of this world.* But the angels of light are in the light, and, though they conceal their working, they show their work, for it will bear the light. But we see them and their works only by candle-light, by the dim light *of lamps* that go *up and down among* them; when *the day breaks, and the shadows flee away,* we shall see them clearly. Some make the *appearance* of these *burning coals,* and of the *lightning* that issues *out of the fire,* to signify the wrath of God, and his judgments, that were now to be executed upon Judah and Jerusalem for their sins, in which angels were to be employed; and accordingly we find afterwards *coals of fire scattered upon the city* to consume it, which were *fetched from between the cherubim, ch.* x. 2. But by *the appearance of the lamps* then we may understand the light of comfort which shone forth to the people of God in the darkness of this present trouble. If the ministry of the angels is as a consuming fire to God's enemies, it is as a rejoicing light to his own children. To the one this *fire* is *bright,* it is very reviving and refreshing; to the other, *out of the fire* comes fresh *lightning* to destroy them. Note, Good angels are our friends, or enemies, according as God is.

15 Now as I beheld the living creatures, behold one wheel upon the earth by the living creatures, with his four faces. 16 The appearance of the wheels and their work *was* like unto the colour of a beryl: and they four had one likeness: and their appearance and their work *was* as it were a wheel in the middle of a wheel. 17 When they went, they went upon their four sides: *and* they turned not when they went. 18 As for their rings, they were so high that they were dreadful; and their rings *were* full of eyes round about them four. 19 And when the living creatures went, the wheels went by them: and when the living creatures were lifted up from the earth, the wheels were lifted up. 20 Whithersoever the spirit was to go, they went, thither *was* their spirit to go; and the wheels were lifted up over against them: for the spirit of the living creature *was* in the wheels. 21 When those went, *these* went; and when those stood, *these* stood; and when those were lifted up from the earth, the wheels were lifted up over against them: for the spirit of the living creature *was* in

the wheels. 22 And the likeness of the firmament upon the heads of the living creature *was* as the colour of the terrible crystal, stretched forth over their heads above. 23 And under the firmament *were* their wings straight, the one toward the other: every one had two, which covered on this side, and every one had two, which covered on that side, their bodies. 24 And when they went, I heard the noise of their wings, like the noise of great waters, as the voice of the Almighty, the voice of speech, as the noise of a host: when they stood, they let down their wings. 25 And there was a voice from the firmament that *was* over their heads, when they stood, *and* had let down their wings.

The prophet is very exact in making and recording his observations concerning this vision. And here we have,

I. The notice he took of the *wheels, v.* 15—21. The glory of God appears not only in the splendour of his retinue in the upper world, but in the steadiness of his government here in this lower world. Having seen how God does according to his will in the armies of heaven, let us now see how he does according to it among the inhabitants of the earth; for there, *on the earth,* the prophet saw the *wheels, v.* 15. *As he beheld the living creatures,* and was contemplating the glory of that vision and receiving instruction from it, this other vision presented itself to his view. Note, Those who make a good use of the discoveries God has favoured them with may expect further discoveries; for *to him that hath shall be given.* We are sometimes tempted to think there is nothing glorious but what is in the upper world, whereas, could we with an eye of faith discern the beauty of Providence and the wisdom, power, and goodness, which shine in the administration of that kingdom, we should see, and say, *Verily he is a God that judgeth in the earth* and acts like himself. There are many things in this vision which give us some light concerning the divine Providence. 1. The dispensations of Providence are compared to *wheels,* either the wheels of a chariot, in which the conqueror rides in triumph, or rather the wheels of a clock or watch, which all contribute to the regular motion of the machine. We read of *the course* or *wheel of nature* (James iii. 6), which is here set before us as under the direction of the God of nature. *Wheels,* though they move not of themselves, as *the living creatures* do, are yet made movable and are almost continually kept in action.

Providence, represented by these *wheels,* produces changes; sometimes one spoke of the wheel is uppermost and sometimes another; but the motion of the wheel on its own axletree, like that of the orbs above, is very regular and steady. The motion of the wheels is circular; by the revolutions of Providence things are brought to the same posture and pass which they were in formerly; for *the thing that is is that which has been, and there is no new thing under the sun,* Eccl. i. 9, 10. 2. The wheel is said to be *by the living creatures,* who attended it to direct its motion; for the angels are employed as the ministers of God's providence, and have a greater hand in directing the motions of second causes to serve the divine purpose than we think they have. Such a close connexion is there between *the living creatures* and the *wheels* that they moved and rested together. Were angels busily employed? Men were busily employed as instruments in their hand, whether of mercy or judgment, though they themselves were not aware of it. Or, Are men active to compass their designs? Angels at the same time are acting to control and overrule them. This is much insisted on here (*v.* 19): *When the living creatures went,* to bring about any business, *the wheels went by them;* when God has work to do by the ministry of angels second causes are all found, or made, ready to concur in it; and (*v.* 21) *when those stood these stood;* when the angels had done their work the second causes had done theirs. If *the living creatures were lifted up from the earth,* were elevated to any service above the common course of nature and out of the ordinary road (as suppose in the working of miracles, the dividing of the water, the standing still of the sun), *the wheels,* contrary to their own natural tendency, which is towards the earth, move in concert with them, and *are lifted up over against them;* this is thrice mentioned, *v.* 19—21. Note, All inferior creatures are, and move, and act, as the Creator, by the ministration of angels, directs and influences them. Visible effects are managed and governed by invisible causes. The reason given of this is because *the spirit of the living creatures was in the wheels;* the same wisdom, power, and holiness of God, the same will and counsel of his, that guides and governs the angels and all their performances, does, by them, order and dispose of all the motions of the creatures in this lower world and the events and issues of them. God is the soul of the world, and animates the whole, both that above and that beneath, so that they move in perfect harmony, as the upper and lower parts of the natural body do, so that *whithersoever the Spirit is to go* (whatever God wills and purposes to be done and brought to pass) *thither their spirit is to go;* that is, the angels, knowingly and designedly, set themselves to bring it about. And *their* spirit is in the wheels, which are therefore *lifted up over against them;* that is, both the powers of nature and the wills of men are all made to serve the intention, which they infallibly and irresistibly effect, though perhaps *they mean not so, neither doth their heart think so,* Isa. x. 7; Mic. iv. 11, 12. Thus, though the will of God's precept be not *done on earth as it is done in heaven,* yet the will of his purpose and counsel is, and shall be. 3. The wheel is said to have four *faces,* looking four several ways (*v.* 15), denoting that the providence of God exerts itself in all parts of the world, east, west, north, and south, and extends itself to the remotest corners of it. Look which way you will upon the wheel of Providence, and it has a face towards you, a beautiful one, which you may admire the features and complexion of; it looks upon you as ready to speak to you, if you be but ready to hear the voice of it; like a well-drawn picture, it has an eye upon all that have an eye upon it. The wheel had so four *faces* that it had in it four *wheels,* which *went upon their four sides, v.* 17. At first Ezekiel saw it as *one wheel* (*v.* 15), one sphere; but afterwards he saw it was four, but *they* four *had one likeness* (*v.* 16); not only they were like one another, but they were as if they had been one. This intimates, (1.) That one event of providence is like another; what happens to us is *that which is common to men* and what we are not to think strange. (2.) That various events have a tendency to the same issue and concur to answer the same intention. 4. *Their appearance and their work* are said to be *like the colour of a beryl* (*v.* 16), *the colour of Tarshish* (so the word is), that is, of the sea; the beryl is of that colour, sea-green; *blue Neptune* we call it. The nature of things in this world is like that of the sea, which is in a continual flux and yet there is a constant coherence and succession of its parts. There is a chain of events which is always drawing one way or other. The sea ebbs and flows, so does Providence in its disposals, but always in the stated appointed times and measures. The sea looks blue, as the air does, because of the shortness and feebleness of our sight, which can see but a little way of either; to that colour therefore are *the appearance and work* of Providence fitly compared, because we cannot find out that which God does *from the beginning to the end,* Eccl. iii. 11. We see but *parts of his ways* (Job xxvi. 14), and all beyond looks blue, which gives us to understand no more concerning it but that in truth we know it not; it is *far above out of our sight.* 5. *Their appearance and their work* are likewise said to be *as it were a wheel in the middle of a wheel.* Observe here again, Their *appearance* to the prophet is designed to set forth what *their work* really is. Men's appearance and their work often differ, but the appearance of God's providence and its work

agree; if they seem to differ, it is through our ignorance and mistake. Now both *were as a wheel in a wheel,* a less wheel moved by a greater. We pretend not to give a mathematical description of it. The meaning is that the disposals of Providence seem to us intricate, perplexed, and unaccountable, and yet that they will appear in the issue to have been all wisely ordered for the best; so that though *what God does we know not now,* yet *we shall know hereafter,* John xiii. 7. 6. The motion of these wheels, like that of the living creatures, was steady, regular, and constant: *They returned not when they went* (*v.* 17), because they never went amiss, nor otherwise than they should do. God, in his providence, takes his work before him, and he will have it forward; and it is going on even when it seems to us to be going backward. *They went* as the Spirit directed them, and therefore *returned not.* We should not have occasion to return back as we have, and to undo that by repentance which we have done amiss, and to do it over again, if we were but *led by the Spirit* and followed his direction. *The Spirit of life* (so some read it) *was in the wheels,* which carried them on with ease and evenness, and then *they returned not when they went.* 7. The *rings,* or rims, *of the wheels were so high that they were dreadful, v.* 18. They were of a vast circumference, so that when they were reared, and put in motion, the prophet was even afraid to look upon them. Note, The vast compass of God's thought, and the vast reach of his design, are really astonishing; when we go about to describe the circle of Providence we are struck with amazement and are even swallowed up. O the height and depth of God's councils! The consideration of them should strike an awe upon us. 8. They were *full of eyes round about.* This circumstance of the vision is most surprising of all, and yet most significant, plainly denoting that the motions of Providence are all directed by infinite wisdom. The issues of things are not determined by a blind fortune, but by those *eyes of the Lord* which *run to and fro through the earth,* and *are in every place, beholding the evil and the good.* Note, It is a great satisfaction to us, and ought to be so, that, though we cannot account for the springs and tendencies of events, yet they are all under the cognizance and direction of an all-wise all-seeing God.

II. The notice he took of *the firmament* above *over the heads of the living creatures.* When he saw *the living creatures* moving, and *the wheels by* them, he looked up, as it is proper for us to do when we observe the various motions of providence in this lower world; looking up, he saw *the firmament stretched forth over the heads of the living creatures, v.* 22. What is done on earth is done under the heaven (as the scripture often speaks), under its inspection and influence.

Observe, 1. What he saw: *The firmament was as the colour of the terrible crystal,* truly glorious, but terribly so; the vastness and brightness of it put the prophet into an amazement and struck him with an awful reverence. *The terrible ice,* or *frost* (so it may be read), the colour of snow congealed, or as mountains of ice in the northern seas, which are very frightful. Daring sinners ask, *Can God judge through the dark cloud?* Job xxii. 13. But that which we take to be a dark cloud is to him transparent as crystal, through which, *from the place of his habitation, he looks upon all the inhabitants of the earth,* Ps. xxxiii. 14. *Under the firmament* he saw *the wings of the living creatures* erect, *v.* 23. When they pleased they used them either for flight or for covering, or two for flight and two for covering. God is on high, *above the firmament;* the angels are *under the firmament,* which denotes their subjection to God's dominion and their readiness to fly on his errands *in the open firmament of heaven,* and to serve him unanimously. 2. What he heard. (1.) He heard the *noise of the angels' wings, v.* 24. Bees and other insects make a great noise with the vibration of their wings; here the angels do so, to awaken the attention of the prophet to that which God was about to say to him from *the firmament, v.* 25. Angels, by the providences they are employed in, sound God's alarms to the children of men and stir them up to *hear his voice;* for that is it that *cries in the city* and is heard and understood by *the men of wisdom. The noise of their wings* was loud and terrible, *as the noise of great waters* (like the rout or roaring of the sea), and *as the noise of a host,* the noise of war; but it was articulate and intelligible, and did not *give an uncertain sound;* for it was *the voice of speech;* nay, it was *as the voice of the Almighty,* for *God,* by his providences, *speaks once, yea, twice,* if we could but *perceive it,* Job. xxxiii. 14. The *Lord's voice cries,* Mic. vi. 9. (2.) He heard a *voice from the firmament,* from him that sits upon the throne there, *v.* 25. When the angels moved they *made a noise with their wings;* but, when with that they had roused a careless world, they stood still, and *let down their wings,* that there might be a profound silence, and so God's voice might be the better heard. The voice of Providence is designed to open men's ears to the voice of the word, to do the office of the crier, who with a loud voice charges silence while the judge passes sentence. *He that has ears to hear, let him hear.* Note, Noises on earth should awaken our attention to the *voice from the firmament;* for *how shall we escape if we turn away from him that speaks from heaven!*

26 And above the firmament that *was* over their heads *was* the likeness of a throne, as the appearance of a sapphire stone: and upon the like-

ness of the throne *was* the likeness as the appearance of a man above upon it. 27 And I saw as the colour of amber, as the appearance of fire round about within it, from the appearance of his loins even upward, and from the appearance of his loins even downward, I saw as it were the appearance of fire, and it had brightness round about. 28 As the appearance of the bow that is in the cloud in the day of rain, so *was* the appearance of the brightness round about. This *was* the appearance of the likeness of the glory of the LORD. And when I saw *it,* I fell upon my face, and I heard a voice of one that spake.

All the other parts of this vision were but a preface and introduction to this. God in them had made himself known as Lord of angels and supreme director of all the affairs of this lower world, whence it is easy to infer that whatever God by his prophets either promises or threatens to do he is able to effect it. Angels are his servants; men are his tools. But now that a divine revelation is to be given to a prophet, and by him to the church, we must look higher than the living creatures or the wheels, and must expect that from the eternal Word, of whom we have an account in these verses. Ezekiel, hearing a voice from the firmament, looked up, as John did, to *see the voice that spoke with him,* and he *saw one like unto the Son of man,* Rev. i. 12, 13. The second person sometimes tried the *fashion of a man* occasionally before he clothed himself with it for good and all; and the Spirit of prophecy is called the *Spirit of Christ* (1 Pet. i. 11) and the *testimony of Jesus,* Rev. xix. 10. 1. This glory of Christ that the prophet saw *was above the firmament* that was *over the heads* of the living creatures, *v.* 26. Note, The heads of angels themselves are under the feet of the Lord Jesus; for the firmament that is over their heads is under his feet. *Angels, principalities, and powers are made subject to him,* 1 Pet. iii. 22. This dignity and dominion of the Redeemer before his incarnation magnify his condescension in his incarnation, when he was *made a little lower than the angels,* Heb. ii. 9. 2. The first thing he observed was a *throne;* for divine revelation comes backed and supported with a royal authority. We must have an eye of faith to God and Christ as upon a throne. The first thing that John discovered in his visions was *a throne set in heaven* (Rev. iv. 2), which commands reverence and subjection. It is a throne of glory, a throne of grace, a throne of triumph, a throne of government, a throne of judgment. *The Lord has prepared his throne in* the heavens, has prepared it for his Son, whom he has set *King on his holy hill of Zion.* 3. On the throne he saw *the appearance of a man.* This is good news to the children of men, that the throne above the firmament is filled with one that is not ashamed to appear, even there, in the likeness of man. Daniel, in vision, saw the kingdom and dominion given to one *like the Son of man,* who *therefore* has *authority given him to execute judgment because he is the Son of man* (John v. 27), so appearing in these visions. 4. He saw him as a prince and judge upon this throne. Though he appeared *in fashion as a man,* yet he appeared in more than human glory, v. 27. (1.) Is God a *shining light?* So is he : when the prophet saw him he saw *as the colour of amber,* that is, a *brightness round about ;* for God dwells in light, and *covers himself with light as with a garment.* How low did the Redeemer stoop for us when, to bring about our salvation, he suffered his glory to be eclipsed by the veil of his humanity ! (2.) Is God a *consuming fire ?* So is he : from his loins, both upward and downward, there was the *appearance of fire.* The fire above the loins was *round about within the amber ;* it was inward and involved. That below the loins was more outward and open, and yet that also had *brightness round about.* Some make the former to signify Christ's divine nature, the glory and virtue of which are hidden within the *colour of amber ;* it is what no man has seen nor can see. The latter they suppose to be his human nature, the glory of which there were those who saw ; the glory as of *the only begotten of the Father, full of grace and truth,* John i. 14. He had *rays coming out of his hand,* and yet *there was the hiding of his power,* Hab. iii. 4. The fire in which the Son of man appeared here might be intended to signify the judgments that were ready to be executed upon Judah and Jerusalem, coming from that *fiery indignation* of the Almighty which *devours the adversaries.* Nothing is more dreadful to the most daring sinners than *the wrath of him that sits upon the throne, and of the Lamb,* Rev. vi. 16. The day is coming when *the Lord Jesus shall be revealed in flaming fire,* 2 Thess. i. 7, 8. It concerns us therefore *to kiss the Son lest he be angry.* 5. The throne is surrounded with a rainbow, v. 28. It is so in St. John's vision, Rev. iv. 3. The brightness about it was of divers colours, *as the bow that is in the cloud in the day of rain,* which, as it is a display of majesty, and looks very great, so it is a pledge of mercy, and looks very kind ; for it is a confirmation of the gracious promise God has made that he will not drown the world again, and he has said, *I will look upon the bow and remember the covenant,* Gen. ix. 16. This intimates that he who *sits upon the throne* is the *Mediator of the covenant,* that his dominion is for our protection, not our destruction, that he in-

terposes between us and the judgments our sins have deserved, and that *all the promises of God are in him yea and amen.* Now that the fire of God's wrath was breaking out against Jerusalem bounds should be set to it, and he would not make an utter destruction of it, for he would *look upon the bow and remember the covenant,* as he promised in such a case, Lev. xxvi. 42.

Lastly, We have the conclusion of this vision. Observe, 1. What notion the prophet himself had of it : *This was the appearance of the likeness of the glory of the Lord.* Here, as all along, he is careful to guard against all gross corporeal thoughts of God, which might derogate from the transcendent purity of his nature. He does not say, *This was the Lord* (for he is invisible), but, *This was the glory of the Lord,* in which he was pleased to manifest himself a glorious being ; yet it is not *the glory of the Lord,* but *the likeness of that glory,* some faint resemblance of it ; nor is it any adequate likeness of that glory, but only *the appearance of that likeness,* a shadow of it, and not the very *image of the thing,* Heb. x. 1. 2. What impressions it made upon him : *When I saw it, I fell upon my face.* (1.) He was overpowered by it ; the dazzling lustre of it conquered him and threw him upon his face ; for *who is able to stand before this holy Lord God ?* Or, rather, (2.) He prostrated himself in a humble sense of his own unworthiness of the honour now done him, and of the infinite distance which he now, more than ever, perceived to be between him and God ; he fell upon his face in token of that holy awe and reverence of God with which his mind was possessed and filled. Note, The more God is pleased to make known of himself to us the more low we should be before him. He *fell upon his face* to adore the majesty of God, to implore his mercy and to deprecate the wrath he saw ready to break out against the children of his people. 3. What instructions he had from it. All he saw was only to prepare him for that which he was to hear ; for *faith comes by hearing.* He therefore *heard a voice of one that spoke ;* for we are taught by words, not merely by hieroglyphics. When *he fell on his face,* ready to receive the word, then he *heard the voice of one that spoke ;* for God delights to teach the humble.

CHAP. II.

What our Lord Jesus said to St. Paul (Acts xxvi. 16) may fitly be applied to the prophet Ezekiel, to whom the same Jesus is here speaking, " Rise and stand upon thy feet, for I have appeared unto thee for this purpose, to make thee a minister." We have here Ezekiel's ordination to his office, which the vision was designed to fit him for, not to entertain his curiosity with uncommon speculations, but to put him into business. Now here, I. He is commissioned to go as a prophet to the house of Israel, now captives in Babylon, and to deliver God's messages to them from time to time, ver. 1—5. II. He is cautioned not to be afraid of them, ver. 6. III. He is instructed what to say to them, and has words put into his mouth, signified by the vision of a roll, which he was ordered to eat (ver. 7—10), and which, in the next chapter, we find he did eat.

AND he said unto me, Son of man, stand upon thy feet, and I will speak unto thee. 2 And the spirit entered into me when he spake unto me, and set me upon my feet, that I heard him that spake unto me. 3 And he said unto me, Son of man, I send thee to the children of Israel, to a rebellious nation that hath rebelled against me: they and their fathers have transgressed against me, *even* unto this very day. 4 For *they are* impudent children and stiff-hearted. I do send thee unto them; and thou shalt say unto them, Thus saith the Lord God. 5 And they, whether they will hear, or whether they will forbear, (for they *are* a rebellious house,) yet shall know that there hath been a prophet among them.

The title here given to Ezekiel, as often afterwards, is very observable. God, when he speaks to him, calls him, Son *of man* (*v.* 1, 3), Son *of Adam,* Son *of the earth.* Daniel is once called so (Dan. viii. 17) and but once; the compellation is used to no other of the prophets but to Ezekiel all along. We may take it, 1. As a humble diminishing title. Lest Ezekiel should be lifted up with the abundance of the revelations, he is put in mind of this, that still he is a *son of man,* a mean, weak, mortal creature. Among other things made known to him, it was necessary he should be made to know this, that he was a *son of man,* and therefore that it was wonderful condescension in God that he was pleased thus to manifest himself to him. Now he is among the living creatures, the angels; yet he must remember that he is himself a man, a dying creature. *What is man, or the son of man,* that he should be thus visited, thus dignified? Though God had here a splendid retinue of holy angels about his throne, who were ready to go on his errands, yet he passes them all by, and pitches on Ezekiel, a *son of man,* to be his messenger to the *house of Israel;* for we *have this treasure in earthen vessels,* and God's messages sent us by men like ourselves, whose terror shall not *make us afraid* nor *their hand be heavy upon us.* Ezekiel was a priest, but the priesthood was brought low and the honour of it laid in the dust. It therefore became him, and all of his order, to humble themselves, and to lie low, as sons of men, common men. He was now to be employed as a prophet, God's ambassador, and a ruler over the kingdoms (Jer. i. 10), a post of great honour, but he must remember that he is a *son of man,* and, whatever good he did, it was not by any might of his own, for he was a *son of man,* but in the strength of divine grace, which must therefore have all the glory. Or, 2. We may take it as an honourable

dignifying title; for it is one of the titles of the Messiah in the Old Testament (Dan. vii. 13, *I saw one like the Son of man come with the clouds of heaven),* whence Christ borrows the title he often calls himself by. *The Son of man.* The prophets were types of him, as they had near access to God and great authority among men; and therefore as David the king is called the *Lord's anointed,* or *Christ,* so Ezekiel the prophet is called *son of man.*

I. Ezekiel is here set up, and made to stand, that he might receive his commission, *v.* 1, 2. He is set up,

1. By a divine command: *Son of man, stand upon thy feet.* His lying prostrate was a posture of greater reverence, but his standing up would be a posture of greater readiness and fitness for business. Our adorings of God must not hinder, but rather quicken and excite, our actings for God. He *fell on his face* in a holy fear and awe of God, but he was quickly raised up again; for those that *humble themselves shall be exalted.* God delights not in the dejections of his servants, but the same that brings them low will raise them up; the same that is a Spirit of bondage will be a Spirit of adoption. *Stand, and I will speak to thee.* Note, We may expect that God will speak to us when we stand ready to do what he commands us.

2. By a divine power going along with that command, *v.* 2. God bade him *stand up;* but, because he had not strength of his own to recover his feet nor courage to face the vision, *the Spirit entered into him* and *set him upon his feet.* Note, God is graciously pleased to work that in us which he requires of us and raises those whom he bids rise. We must stir up ourselves, and then God will put strength into us; we must *work out our salvation,* and then God will *work in us.* He observed that the Spirit entered into him when Christ spoke to him; for Christ conveys his Spirit by his word as the ordinary means and makes the word effectual by the Spirit. *The Spirit set* the prophet *upon his feet,* to raise him up from his dejections, for *he is the Comforter.* Thus, in a similar case, Daniel was strengthened by a divine touch (Dan. x. 18) and John was raised by the right hand of Christ laid upon him, Rev. i. 17. The *Spirit set him upon his feet,* made him willing and forward to do as he was bidden, and then he *heard him that spoke* to him. He heard the voice before (*ch.* i. 28), but now he heard it more distinctly and clearly, heard it and submitted to it. The Spirit sets us upon our feet by inclining our will to our duty, and thereby disposes the understanding to receive the knowledge of it.

II. Ezekiel is here sent, and made to go, with a message to the children of Israel (*v.* 3): *I send thee to the children of Israel.* God had for many ages been sending to them his servants the prophets, rising up betimes and sending them, but to little purpose; they were now sent into captivity for abusing God's messengers, and yet even there God sends this prophet among them, to try if their ears were open to discipline, now that they were holden in the cords of affliction. As the supports of life, so the means of grace, are continued to us after they have been a thousand times forfeited. Now observe,

1. The rebellion of the people to whom this ambassador is sent; he is sent to reduce them to their allegiance, to bring back the children of Israel to the Lord their God. Let the prophet know that there is occasion for his going on this errand, for they are a *rebellious nation* (v. 3), *a rebellious house,* v. 5. They are called *children of Israel;* they retain the name of their pious ancestors, but they have wretchedly degenerated, they have become *Goim*—*nations,* the word commonly used for the Gentiles. The *children of Israel* have become as the *children of the Ethiopian* (Amos ix. 7), for they are *rebellious;* and rebels at home are much more provoking to a prince than enemies abroad. Their idolatries and false worships were the sins which, more than any thing, denominated them a *rebellious nation;* for thereby they set up another prince in opposition to their rightful Sovereign, and did homage and paid tribute to the usurper, which is the highest degree of rebellion that can be. (1.) They had been all along a rebellious generation and had persisted in their rebellion: *They and their fathers have transgressed against me.* Note, Those are not always in the right that have antiquity and the fathers on their side; for there are errors and corruptions of long standing: and it is so far from being an excuse for walking in a bad way that our fathers walked in it that it is really an aggravation, for it is justifying the sin of those that have gone before us. They have continued in their rebellion *even unto this very day;* notwithstanding the various means and methods that have been made use of to reclaim them, *to this day,* when they are under divine rebukes for their rebellion, they continue *rebellious;* many among them, like Ahaz, even *in their distress, trespass yet more;* they are not the better for all the changes that have befallen them, but still remain unchanged. (2.) They were now hardened in their rebellion. They are *impudent children,* brazen-faced, and cannot blush; they are stiff-hearted, self-willed, and cannot bend, cannot stoop, neither ashamed nor afraid to sin; they will not be wrought upon by the sense either of honour or duty. We are willing to hope this was not the character of all, but of many, and those perhaps the leading men. Observe, [1.] God knew this concerning them, how inflexible, how incorrigible, they were. Note, God is perfectly

acquainted with every man's true character, whatever his pretensions and professions may be. [2.] He told the prophet this, that he might know the better how to deal with them and what handle to take them by. He must rebuke such men as those sharply, cuttingly, must deal plainly with them, though they call it *dealing roughly.* God tells him this, that it might be no surprise or stumbling-block to him if he found that his preaching should not make that impression upon them, which he had reason to think it would.

2. The dominion of the prince by whom this ambassador is sent. (1.) He has authority to command him whom he sends : *" I do send thee unto them,* and therefore *thou shalt say* thus and thus unto them,"* v. 4. Note, It is the prerogative of Christ to send prophets and ministers and to enjoin them their work. St. Paul thanked Christ Jesus who put him into the ministry (1 Tim. i. 12); for, as he was sent of the Father, ministers are sent by him; and as he received the Spirit without measure he gives the Spirit by measure, saying, *Receive you the Holy Ghost.* They are *impudent* and *rebellious,* and yet *I send thee unto them.* Note, Christ gives the means of grace to many who he knows will not make a good use of those means, puts many a price into the hand of fools to get wisdom, who not only have no heart to it, but have their hearts turned against it. Thus he will magnify his own grace, justify his own judgment, leave them inexcusable, and make their condemnation more intolerable. (2.) He has authority by him to command those to whom he sends him : *Thou shalt say unto them, Thus saith the Lord God.* All he said to them must be spoken in God's name, enforced by his authority, and delivered as from him. Christ delivered his doctrines as a Son—*Verily, verily, I say unto you;* the prophets as *servants*—*Thus saith the Lord God,* our Master and yours. Note, The writings of the prophets are the word of God, and so are to be regarded by every one of us. (3.) He has authority to call those to an account to whom he sends his ambassadors. *Whether they will hear or whether they will forbear,* whether they will attend to the word or turn their backs upon it, *they shall know that there has been a prophet among them,* shall know by experience. [1.] If they hear and obey, they will know by comfortable experience that the word which did them good was brought to them by one that had a commission from God and a divine power going along with him in the execution of it. Thus those who were converted by St. Paul's preaching are said to be *the seals of his apostleship,* 1 Cor. ix. 2. When men's hearts are made to burn under the word, and their wills to bow to it, then they know and bear the witness in themselves that it is not the *word of men, but of God.*

[2.] If they forbear, if they turn a deaf ear to the word (as it is to be feared they will, *for they are a rebellious house*), yet they shall be made to know that he whom they slighted was indeed a prophet, by the reproaches of their own consciences and the just judgments of God upon them for refusing him; they shall know it to their cost, know it to their confusion, know it by sad experience, what a pernicious dangerous thing it is to despise God's messengers. They shall know by the accomplishment of the threatenings that the prophet who denounced them was sent of God; thus the word will *take hold of men*, Zech. i. 6. Note, *First*, Those to whom the word of God is sent are upon their trial *whether they will hear* or *whether they will forbear*, and accordingly will their doom be. *Secondly*, Whether we be edified by the word or no, it is certain that God will be glorified and his word magnified and made honourable. Whether it be a *savour of life unto life* or *of death unto death*, either way it will appear to be of divine original.

6 And thou, son of man, be not afraid of them, neither be afraid of their words, though briers and thorns *be* with thee, and thou dost dwell among scorpions: be not afraid of their words, nor be dismayed at their looks, though they *be* a rebellious house. 7 And thou shalt speak my words unto them, whether they will hear, or whether they will forbear: for they *are* most rebellious. 8 But thou, son of man, hear what I say unto thee; Be not thou rebellious like that rebellious house: open thy mouth, and eat that I give thee. 9 And when I looked, behold, a hand *was* sent unto me; and, lo, a roll of a book *was* therein; 10 And he spread it before me: and it *was* written within and without: and *there was* written therein lamentations, and mourning, and woe.

The prophet, having received his commission, here receives a charge with it. It is a post of honour to which he is advanced, but withal it is a post of service and work, and it is here required of him,

I. That he be bold. He must act in the discharge of this trust with an undaunted courage and resolution, and not be either driven off from his work or made to drive on heavily, by the difficulties and oppositions that he would be likely to meet with in it: *Son of man, be not afraid of them*, v. 6. Note, Those that will do any thing to purpose in the service of God must not be afraid of the face of man; for the fear of men will bring a snare, which will be very entangling to us in the work of God. 1. God tells the prophet what was the character of those to whom he sent him, as before, v. 3, 4. They are *briers and thorns*, scratching, and tearing, and vexing a man, which way soever he turns. They are continually teazing God's prophets and entangling them in their *talk* (Matt. xxii. 15); they are *pricking briers* and *grieving thorns*. The best of them is as a brier, and *the most upright sharper than a thorn-hedge*, Mic. vii. 4. Thorns and briers are the fruit of sin and the curse, and of equal date with the enmity between the seed of the woman and the seed of the serpent. Note, Wicked men, especially the persecutors of God's prophets and people, are as briers and thorns, which are hurtful to the ground, choke the good seed, hinder God's husbandry, are vexatious to his husbandmen; but they are *nigh unto cursing* and *their end is to be burned*. Yet God makes use of them sometimes for the correction and instruction of his people, as *Gideon taught the men of Succoth with thorns and briers*, Judg. viii. 16. Yet this is not the worst of their character: they are *scorpions*, venomous and malignant. The sting of a scorpion is a thousand times more hurtful than the scratch of a brier. Persecutors are a *generation of vipers*, are of the serpent's seed, and the *poison of asps is under their tongue*; and they are *more subtle than any beast of the field*. And, which makes the prophet's case the more grievous, he dwells among these scorpions; they are continually about him, so that he cannot be safe nor quiet in his own house; these bad men are his bad neighbours, who thereby have many opportunities, and will let slip none, to do him a mischief. God takes notice of this to the prophet, as Christ to the angel of one of the churches, Rev. ii. 13. *I know thy works, and where thou dwellest, even where Satan's seat is*. Ezekiel had been, in vision, conversing with angels, but when he comes down from this mount he finds he *dwells with scorpions*. 2. He tells him what would be their conduct towards him, that they would do what they could to frighten him with *their looks* and *their words;* they would hector him and threaten him, would look scornfully and spitefully at him, and do their utmost to face him down and put him out of countenance, that they might drive him off from being a prophet, or at least from telling them of their faults and threatening them with the judgments of God; or, if they could not prevail in this, that they might vex and perplex him, and disturb the repose of his mind. They were now themselves in subjection, divested of all power, so that they had no other way of persecuting the prophet than with *their looks and their words;* and so they did persecute him. *Behold, thou hast spoken and done evil things as thou couldest*, Jer. iii. 5. If they had had more power, they would have done more mischief. They were now in captivity, smarting for their rebellion, and particularly their misusing God's prophets; and yet they are as bad as ever. *Though thou bray a fool in a mortar, yet will not his foolishness depart from him ;* no providences will of themselves humble and reform men, unless the grace of God work with them. But, how malicious soever they were, Ezekiel must not be *afraid of them* nor *dismayed*, he must not be deterred from his work, or any part of it, nor be disheartened or dispirited in it by all their menaces, but go on in it with resolution and cheerfulness, assuring himself of safety under the divine protection.

II. It is required that he be faithful, *v.* 7. 1. He must be faithful to Christ who sent him: *Thou shalt speak my words unto them.* Note, As it is the honour of prophets that they are entrusted to speak God's words, so it is their duty to cleave closely to them and to speak nothing but what is agreeable to the words of God. Ministers must always speak according to that rule. 2. He must be faithful to the souls of those to whom he was sent: *Whether they will hear or whether they will forbear*, he must deliver his message to them as he received it. He must bring them to comply with the word, and not study to accommodate the word to their humours. " It is true they are *most rebellious*, they are rebellion itself; but, however, *speak my words* to them, whether they are pleasing or unpleasing." Note, The untractableness and unprofitableness of people under the word are no good reason why ministers should leave off preaching to them; nor must we decline an opportunity by which good may be done, though we have a great deal of reason to think no good will be done.

III. It is required that he be observant of his instructions.

1. Here is a general intimation what the instructions were that were given him, in the contents of the book which was *spread before him, v.* 10. (1.) His instructions were large; for the roll was *written within and without*, on the inside and on the outside of the roll. It was as a sheet of paper written on all the four sides. One side contained their sins; the other side contained the judgments of God coming upon them for those sins. Note, God has a great deal to say to his people when they have degenerated and become rebellious. (2.) His instructions were melancholy. He was sent on a sad errand; the matter contained in the book was, *lamentations, and mourning, and woe.* The idea of his message is taken from the impression it would make upon the minds of those that carefully attended to it; it would set them a weeping and crying out, *Woe! and, Alas!* Both the discoveries of sin and the denunciations of wrath would

be matter of lamentation. What could be more lamentable, more mournful, more woeful, than to see a holy happy people sunk into such a state of sin and misery as it appears by the prophecy of this book the Jews were at this time? Ezekiel echoes to Jeremiah's lamentations. Note, Though God is rich in mercy, yet impenitent sinners will find there are even among his words *lamentations and woe.*

2. Here is an express charge given to the prophet to observe his instructions, both in receiving his message and delivering it. He is now to receive it and is here commanded, (1.) To attend diligently to it: *Son of man, hear what I say unto thee, v.* 8. Note, Those that speak from God to others must be sure to hear from God themselves and be obedient to his voice: " *Be not thou rebellious;* do not refuse to go on this errand, or to deliver it; do not fly off, as Jonah did, for fear of disobliging thy countrymen. They are a *rebellious house*, among whom thou livest; but be not thou like them, do not comply with them in any thing that is evil. If ministers, who are reprovers by office, connive at sin and indulge sinners, either show them not their wickedness or show them not the fatal consequences of it, for fear of displeasing them and getting their ill-will, they hereby make themselves partakers of their guilt and are rebellious like them. If people will not do their duty in reforming, yet let ministers do theirs in reproving, and they will have the comfort of it in the reflection, whatever the success be, as that prophet had, Isa. l. 5. *The Lord God has opened my ear, and I was not rebellious.* Even the best of men, when their lot is cast in bad times and places, have need to be cautioned against the worst of crimes. (2.) To digest it in his own mind by an experience of the favour and power of it: " *Do not only hear what I say unto thee,* but *open thy mouth, and eat that which I give thee.* Prepare to eat it, and eat it willingly and with an appetite." All God's children are content to be at their heavenly Father's finding, and to eat whatever he gives them. That which God's hand reached out to Ezekiel was *a roll of a book,* or *the volume of a book,* a book or scroll of paper or parchment fully written and rolled up. Divine revelation comes to us from the hand of Christ; he gave it to the prophets, Rev. i. 1. When we look at *the roll of the book* we must have an eye to the hand by which it is sent to us. He that brought it to the prophet *spread it before him,* that he might not swallow it with an implicit faith, but might fully understand the contents of it, and then receive it and make it his own. *Be not rebellious,* says Christ, but *eat what I give thee.* If we receive not what Christ in his ordinances and providences allots for us, if we submit not to his word and rod, and reconcile not ourselves to both, we shall be accounted rebellious.

CHAP. III.

In this chapter we have the further preparation of the prophet for the work to which God called him. I. His eating the roll that was presented to him in the close of the foregoing chapter, ver. 1—3. II. Further instructions and encouragements given him to the same purport with those in the foregoing chapter, ver. 4—11. III. The mighty impulse he was under, with which he was carried to those that were to be his hearers, ver. 12—15. IV. A further explication of his office and business as a prophet, under the similitude of a watchman, ver. 16—21. V. The restraining and restoring of the prophet's liberty of speech, as God pleased, ver. 22—27.

MOREOVER he said unto me, Son of man, eat that thou findest; eat this roll, and go speak unto the house of Israel. 2 So I opened my mouth, and he caused me to eat that roll. 3 And he said unto me, Son of man, cause thy belly to eat, and fill thy bowels with this roll that I give thee. Then did I eat *it;* and it was in my mouth as honey for sweetness. 4 And he said unto me, Son of man, go, get thee unto the house of Israel, and speak with my words unto them. 5 For thou *art* not sent to a people of a strange speech and of a hard language, *but* to the house of Israel; 6 Not to many people of a strange speech and of a hard language, whose words thou canst not understand. Surely, had I sent thee to them, they would have hearkened unto thee. 7 But the house of Israel will not hearken unto thee; for they will not hearken unto me: for all the house of Israel *are* impudent and hard-hearted. 8 Behold, I have made thy face strong against their faces, and thy forehead strong against their foreheads. 9 As an adamant harder than flint have I made thy forehead: fear them not, neither be dismayed at their looks, though they *be* a rebellious house. 10 Moreover he said unto me, Son of man, all my words that I shall speak unto thee receive in thine heart, and hear with thine ears. 11 And go, get thee to them of the captivity, unto the children of thy people, and speak unto them, and tell them, Thus saith the Lord God; whether they will hear, or whether they will forbear. 12 Then the spirit took me up, and I heard behind me a voice of a great rushing, *saying,* Blessed *be* the glory of the Lord from his place. 13 *I heard* also the noise of the wings of the living creatures that touched one

another, and the noise of the wheels over against them, and a noise of a great rushing. 14 So the spirit lifted me up, and took me away, and I went in bitterness, in the heat of my spirit; but the hand of the Lord was strong upon me. 15 Then I came to them of the captivity at Tel-abib, that dwelt by the river of Chebar, and I sat where they sat, and remained there astonished among them seven days.

These verses are fitly joined by some translators to the foregoing chapter, as being of a piece with it and a continuation of the same vision. The prophets received the word from God that they might deliver it to the people of God, furnished themselves that they might furnish them with the knowledge of the mind and will of God. Now here the prophet is taught,

I. How he must receive divine revelation himself, *v.* 1. Christ (whom he saw *upon the throne, ch.* i. 26) said to him, " *Son of man, eat this roll,* admit this revelation into thy understanding, take it, take the meaning of it, understand it aright, admit it into thy heart, apply it, and be affected with it; imprint it in thy mind, ruminate and chew the cud upon it; take it as it is entire, and make no difficulty of it, nay, take a pleasure in it as thou dost in thy meat, and let thy soul be nourished and strengthened by it; let it be meat and drink to thee, and as thy necessary food; be full of it, as thou art of the meat thou hast eaten." Thus ministers should in their studies and meditations take in that word of God which they are to preach to others. *Thy words were found, and I did eat them,* Jer. xv. 16. They must be both well acquainted and much affected with the things of God, that they may speak of them both clearly and warmly, with a great deal of divine light and heat. Now observe, 1. How this command is inculcated upon the prophet. In the foregoing chapter, *Eat what I give thee;* and here (*v.* 1), " *Eat that thou findest,* that which is presented to thee by the hand of Christ." Note, Whatever we find to be the word of God, whatever is brought to us by him who is the Word of God, we must receive it without disputing. What we find set before us in the scripture, that we must eat. And again (*v.* 3), " *Cause thy belly to eat, and fill thy bowels with this roll;* do not eat it and bring it up again, as that which is nauseous, but eat it and retain it, as that which is nourishing and grateful to the stomach. Feast upon this vision till thou be *full of matter,* as Elihu was, Job xxxii. 18. Let the word have a place in thee, the innermost place." We must take pains with our own hearts, that we may cause them duly to receive and entertain the word of God, that every faculty may do its office, in order to the due digesting of the word of God, that it may be turned *in succum et sanguinem—into blood and spirits.* We must empty ourselves of worldly things, that we may *fill our bowels with this roll.* 2. How this command is explained (*v.* 10): " *All my words that I shall speak unto thee,* to be spoken unto the people, *thou must receive in thy heart,* as well as *hear with thy ears,* receive them in the love of them." *Let these sayings sink down into your ears,* Luke ix. 44. Christ demands the prophet's attention not only to what he now says, but to all that he shall at any time hereafter speak: *Receive* it all *in thy heart; meditate on these things and give thyself wholly to to them,* 1 Tim. iv. 15. 3. How this command was obeyed in vision. He *opened his mouth* and Christ *caused him to eat the roll, v.* 2. If we be truly willing to receive the word into our hearts, Christ will by his Spirit bring it into them and cause it to *dwell in us richly.* If he that *opens the roll,* and by his Spirit, as a *Spirit of revelation,* spreads it before us, did not also *open our understanding,* and by his Spirit, as a *Spirit of wisdom,* give us the knowledge of it and *cause us to eat* it, we should be for ever strangers to it. The prophet had reason to fear that the roll would be an unpleasant morsel and a sorry dish to make a meal of, but it proved to be in his *mouth as honey for sweetness.* Note, If we readily obey even the most difficult commands, we shall find that comfort in the reflection which will make us abundant amends for all the hardships we meet with in the way of our duty. Though *the roll was filled with lamentations, and mourning, and woe,* yet it was to the prophet *as honey for sweetness.* Note, Gracious souls can receive those truths of God with great delight which speak most terror to wicked people. We find St. John let into some **part** of the revelation by such a sign as this, Rev. x. 9, 10. He *took the book out of the angel's hand, and ate it up, and it was,* as this, *in* his *mouth sweet as honey;* but it was *bitter in the belly;* and we shall find that this was so too, for (*v.* 14) the prophet *went in bitterness.*

II. How he must deliver that divine revelation to others which he himself had received (*v.* 1): *Eat this roll, and* then *go, speak to the house of Israel.* He must not undertake to preach the things of God to others till he did himself fully understand them; let him not go without his errand, nor take it by the halves. But when he does himself fully understand them he must be both busy and bold to preach them for the good of others. We must not *conceal the words of the Holy One* (Job vi. 10), for that is burying a talent which was given us to trade with. He must *go and speak to the house of Israel;* for it is their privilege to have God's statutes and judgments made known to them; as *the giving of the law*

(the lively oracles), so prophecy (the living oracle) *pertains to them.* He is not sent to the Chaldeans to reprove them for their sins, but *to the house of Israel* to reprove them for theirs; for the father corrects his own child if he do amiss, not the child of a stranger.

1. The instructions given him in speaking to them are much the same with those in the foregoing chapter.

(1.) He must speak to them all that, and that only, which God spoke to him. He had said before (*ch.* ii. 7): *Thou shalt speak my words to them;* here he says (*v.* 4), *Thou shalt speak with my words unto them,* or *in my words.* He must not only say that which for substance is the same that God had said to him, but as near as may be in the same language and expressions. Blessed Paul, though a man of a very happy invention, yet speaks of the things of God *in the words which the Holy Ghost teaches,* 1 Cor. ii. 13. Scripture truths look best in scripture language, their native dress; and how can we better speak God's mind than with his words?

(2.) He must remember that they are *the house of Israel* whom he is sent to speak to, God's house and his own; and therefore such as he ought to have a particular concern for and to deal faithfully and tenderly with. They were such as he had an intimate acquaintance with, being not only their countryman, but their *companion in tribulation;* they and he were fellow-sufferers, and had lately been fellow-travellers, in very melancholy circumstances, from Judea to Babylon, and had often mingled their tears, which could not but knit their affections to each other. It was well for the people that they had a prophet who knew experimentally how to sympathize with them, and could not but be touched with the feeling of their infirmities. It was well for the prophet that he had to do with those of his own nation, not *with a people of strange speech and a hard language,* deep of lip, so that thou canst not fathom their meaning, and heavy of tongue, whom it is intolerable and impossible to converse with. Every strange language seems to us to be deep and heavy. " Thou art not sent to *many such people,* whom thou couldst neither speak to nor hear from, neither understand nor be understood among but by an interpreter." The apostles indeed were sent to *many people of a strange speech,* but they could not have done any good among them if they had not had *the gift of tongues;* but Ezekiel was sent only to one people, those but a few, and his own, whom having acquaintance with he might hope to find acceptance with.

(3.) He must remember what God had already told him of the bad character of those to whom he was sent, that, if he met with discouragement and disappointment in them, he might not be offended. They *are impudent and hard-hearted* (v. 7), no convictions of sin would make them blush, no denunciations of wrath would make them tremble. Two things aggravated their obstinacy:—[1.] That they were more obstinate than their neighbours would have been if the prophet had been sent to them. Had God sent him to any other people, though of a *strange speech, surely they would have hearkened* to him; they would at least have given him a patient hearing and shown him that respect which he could not obtain of his own countrymen. The Ninevites were wrought upon by Jonah's preaching when the house of Israel, that was compassed about with so great a cloud of prophets, was unhumbled and unreformed. But what shall we say to these things? The means of grace are given to those that will not improve them and withheld from those that would have improved them. We must resolve this into the divine sovereignty, and say, Lord, *thy judgments are a great deep.* [2.] That they were obstinate against God himself: "They *will not hearken unto thee,* and no marvel, *for they will not hearken unto me;*" they will not regard the word of the prophet, for they will not regard the rod of God, by which the *Lord's voice cries in the city.* If they believe not God speaking to them by a minister, neither would they believe though he should speak to them by *a voice from heaven;* nay, *therefore* they reject what the prophet says, because it comes from God, whom *the carnal mind is enmity to.* They are prejudiced against the law of God, and for that reason turn a deaf ear to his prophets, whose business it is to enforce his law.

(4.) He must resolve to put on courage, and Christ promises to steel him with it, *v.* 8, 9. He is sent to such as *are impudent and hard-hearted,* who will receive no impressions nor be wrought upon either by fair means or foul, who will take a pride in affronting God's messenger and confronting the message. It will be a hard task to know how to deal with them; but, [1.] God will enable him to put a good face on it: "*I have made thy face strong against their faces,* endued thee with all the firmness and boldness that the case calls for." Perhaps Ezekiel was naturally bashful and timorous, but, if God did not find him fit, yet by his grace he made him fit, to encounter the greatest difficulties. Note, The more impudent wicked people are in their opposition to religion the more openly and resolutely should God's people appear in the practice and defence of it. Let the *innocent stir up himself against the hypocrite,* Job xvii. 8. When vice is daring let not virtue be sneaking. And, when God has work to do, he will animate men for it and give them strength according to the day. If there be occasion, God can and will by his grace make the *foreheads* of faithful ministers *as an ada-*

mant, so that the most threatening powers shall not dash them out of countenance. The *Lord God will help me, therefore have I set my face like a flint,* Isa. l. 7. [2.] He is therefore commanded to have a good heart on it, and to go on in his work with a holy security, not valuing either the censures or the threats of his enemies: "*Fear not, neither be dismayed at their looks;* let not the menaces of their impotent malice cast either a damp upon thee or a stumbling-block before thee." Bold sinners must have bold reprovers; *evil beasts* must be *rebuked* cuttingly (Tit. i. 12, 13), must be *saved with fear,* Jude 23. Those that keep closely to the service of God may be sure of the favour of God, and then they need not be dismayed at the proud looks of men. Let not the angry countenance that drives away a backbiting tongue give any check to a reproving tongue.

(5.) He must continue instant with them in his preaching, whatever the success was, *v.* 11. He must *go to those of the captivity.* who, being in affliction, it was to be hoped would receive instruction; he must look upon them as *the children of his people,* to whom he was nearly allied, and for whom he therefore ought to have a very tender concern, as Paul for his kinsmen, Rom. ix. 3. And he must *tell them* not only what the Lord said, but that the Lord said it; let him speak in God's name, and back what he said with his authority: *Thus saith the Lord God; tell them* so, *whether they will hear or whether they will forbear.* Not that it may be indifferent to us what success our ministry has, but, whatever it be, we must go on with our work and leave the issue to God. We must not say "Here are some so good that we do not need to speak to them," or, "Here are others so bad that it is to no purpose to speak to them;" but, however it be, deliver thy message faithfully, *tell them, The Lord God saith* so and so, let them reject it at their peril.

2. Full instructions being thus given to the prophet, pursuant to his commission, we are here told,

(1.) With what satisfaction this mission of his was applauded by the holy angels, who were very well pleased to see one of a nature inferior to their own thus honourably employed and entrusted. He *heard a voice of a great rushing* (v. 12), as if the angels thronged and crowded to see the inauguration of a prophet; for to them *is known by the church* (that is, by reflection from the church) *the manifold wisdom of God,* Eph. iii. 10. They seemed to strive who should get nearest to this great sight. He *heard the noise of their wings that touched,* or (as the word is) *kissed one another,* denoting the mutual affections and assistances of the angels. He heard also *the noise of the wheels* of Providence moving *over-against* the angels and in concert with them. All this was to engage his attention and to convince him that the God who sent him, having such a glorious train of attendants, no doubt had power sufficient to bear him out in his work. But all this noise ended in the voice of praise. He heard them saying, *Blessed be the glory of the Lord from his place.* [1.] From heaven, his place above, whence his glory was now in vision descending, or whither perhaps it was now returning. Let the innumerable company of angels above join with those employed in this vision in saying, *Blessed be the glory of the Lord. Praise you the Lord from the heavens. Praise him, all his angels,* Ps. cxlviii. 1, 2. [2.] From the temple, his place on earth, whence his glory was now departing. They lament the departure of the glory, but adore the righteousness of God in it: however it be, yet God is blessed and glorious, and ever will be so. The prophet Isaiah heard God thus praised when he received his commission (Isa. vi. 3); and a comfort it is to all the faithful servants of God, when they see how much God is dishonoured in this lower world, to think how much he is admired and glorified in the upper world. *The glory of the Lord* has many slights from our place, but many *praises from his place.*

(2.) With what reluctance of his own spirit, and yet with what a mighty efficacy of *the Spirit of God,* the prophet was himself brought to the execution of his office. *The grace given to him was not in vain;* for, [1.] The Spirit led him with a strong hand. God bade him go, but he stirred not till *the Spirit took him up. The Spirit of the living creatures* that was *in the wheels* now was in the prophet too, and *took him up,* first to hear more distinctly the acclamations of the angels (v. 12), but afterwards (v. 14) *lifted him up, and took him away* to his work, which he was backward to, being very loth either to bring trouble upon himself or foretel it to his people. He would gladly have been excused, but must own, as another prophet does (Jer. xx. 7), *Thou wast stronger than I, and hast prevailed.* Ezekiel would willingly have kept all he heard and saw to himself, that it might go no further, *but the hand of the Lord was strong upon him* and overpowered him; he was carried on contrary to his own inclinations by the prophetical impulse, so that he could not *but speak the things which he had heard and seen,* as the apostles, Acts iv. 20. Note, Those whom God calls to the ministry, as he furnishes their heads for it, so he bows their hearts to it. [2.] He followed with a sad heart: *The Spirit took me away,* says he, *and* then *I went,* but it was *in bitterness, in the heat of my spirit.* He had perhaps seen what a hard task Jeremiah had at Jerusalem when he appeared as a prophet, what pains he took, what opposition he met with, how he was abused by hand and tongue, and what ill treatment he met with, and all *to*

no purpose. "And" (thinks Ezekiel) "must I be set up for a mark like him?" The life of a captive was bad enough; but what would the life of a prophet in captivity be? Therefore he went in this fret and under this discomposure. Note, There may in some cases be a great reluctance of corruption even where there is a manifest predominance of grace. "*I went,* not *disobedient to the heavenly vision,* or shrinking from the work, as Jonah, but *I went in bitterness,* not at all pleased with it." When he received the divine revelation himself, it was to him *sweet as honey* (v. 3); he could with abundance of pleasure have spent all his days in meditating upon it; but when he is to preach it to others, who, he foresees, will be hardened and exasperated by it, and have their condemnation aggravated, then he goes *in bitterness.* Note, It is a great grief to faithful ministers, and makes them go on in their work with a heavy heart, when they find people untractable and hating to be reformed. He *went in the heat of his spirit,* because of the discouragements he foresaw he should meet with; *but the hand of the Lord was strong upon* him, not only to compel him to his work, but to fit him for it, to carry him through it, and animate him against the difficulties he would meet with (so we may understand it); and, when he found it so, he was better reconciled to his business and applied himself to it: *Then he came to those of the captivity* (v. 15), to some place where there were many of them together, *and sat where they sat,* working, or reading, or talking, and continued *among them seven days* to hear what they said and observe what they did; and all that time he was waiting for *the word of the Lord* to come to him. Note, Those that would speak suitably and profitably to people about their souls must acquaint themselves with them and with their case, must do as Ezekiel did here, must *sit where they sit,* and speak familiarly to them of the things of God, and put themselves into their condition, yea, though they *sit by the rivers of Babylon.* But observe, He was *there astonished,* overwhelmed with grief for the sins and miseries of his people and overpowered by the pomp of the vision he had seen. He was *there desolate* (so some read it); God showed him no visions, men made him no visits. Thus was he left to digest his grief, and come to a better temper, before *the word of the Lord* should come to him. Note, Those whom God designs to exalt and enlarge he first humbles and straitens for a time.

16 And it came to pass at the end of seven days, that the word of the LORD came unto me, saying, 17 Son of man, I have made thee a watchman unto the house of Israel: therefore hear the word at my mouth and give

them warning from me. 18 When I say unto the wicked, Thou shalt surely die; and thou givest him not warning, nor speakest to warn the wicked from his wicked way, to save his life; the same wicked *man* shall die in his iniquity; but his blood will I require at thine hand. 19 Yet if thou warn the wicked, and he turn not from his wickedness, nor from his wicked way, he shall die in his iniquity; but thou hast delivered thy soul. 20 Again, When a righteous *man* doth turn from his righteousness, and commit iniquity, and I lay a stumbling-block before him, he shall die: because thou hast not given him warning, he shall die in his sin, and his righteousness which he hath done shall not be remembered; but his blood will I require at thine hand. 21 Nevertheless if thou warn the righteous *man*, that the righteous sin not, and he doth not sin, he shall surely live, because he is warned; also thou hast delivered thy soul.

These further instructions God gave to the prophet *at the end of seven days*, that is, on the seventh day after the vision he had; and it is very probable that both that and this were on the sabbath day, which *the house of Israel*, even in their captivity, observed as well as they could in those circumstances. We do not find that their conquerors and oppressors tied them to any constant service, as their Egyptian taskmasters had formerly done, but that they might observe the sabbath-rest for a sign to distinguish between them and their neighbours; but for the sabbath-work they had not the convenience of temple or synagogue, only it should seem they had a *place by the river side where prayer was wont to be made* (as Acts xvi. 13); there they met on the sabbath day; there their enemies upbraided them with *the songs of Zion* (Ps. cxxxvii. 1, 3); there Ezekiel met them, and *the word of the Lord* then and there *came to* him. He that had been musing and meditating on the things of God all the week was fit to speak to the people in God's name on the sabbath day, and disposed to hear God speak to him. This sabbath day Ezekiel was not so honoured with visions of the glory of God as he had been the sabbath before; but he is plainly, and by a very common similitude, told his duty, which he is to communicate to the people. Note, Raptures and transports of joy are not the daily bread of God's children, however they may upon special occasions be feasted with

them. We must not deny but that we have truly communion with God (1 John i. 3) though we have it not always so sensibly as at some times. And, though the mysteries of the kingdom of heaven may sometimes be looked into, yet ordinarily it is plain preaching that is most for edification. God here tells the prophet what his office was, and what the duty of that office; and this (we may suppose) he was to tell the people, that they might attend to what he said and improve it accordingly. Note, It is good for people to know and consider what a charge their ministers have of them and what an account they must shortly give of that charge. Observe,

I. What the office is to which the prophet is called: *Son of man, I have made thee a watchman to the house of Israel, v.* 17. The vision he saw astonished him: he knew not what to make of that, and therefore God used this plain comparison, which served better to lead him to the understanding of his work and so to reconcile him to it. He sat among the captives, and said little, but God comes to him, and tells him that will not do; he is *a watchman*, and has something to say to them; he is appointed to be as *a watchman* in the city, to guard against fire, robbers, and disturbers of the peace, as *a watchman* over the flock, to guard against thieves and beasts of prey, but especially as *a watchman* in the camp, in an invaded country or a besieged town, that is to watch the motions of the enemy, and to sound an alarm upon the approach, nay, upon the first appearance, of danger. This supposes *the house of Israel* to be in a military state, and exposed to enemies, who are subtle and restless in their attempts upon it; yea, and each of the particular members of that house to be in danger and concerned to stand upon their guard. Note, Ministers are *watchmen on the church's walls* (Isa. lxii. 6), *watchmen that go about the city,* Cant. iii. 3. It is a toilsome office. Watchmen must keep awake, be they ever so sleepy, and keep abroad, be it ever so cold; they must stand all weathers *upon the watch-tower,* Isa. xxi. 8; Gen. xxxi. 40. It is a dangerous office. Sometimes they cannot keep their post, but are in peril of death from the enemy, who gain their point if they kill the sentinel; and yet they dare not quit their post upon pain of death from their general. Such a dilemma are the church's watchmen in; men will curse them if they be faithful, and God will curse them if they be false. But it is a needful office; *the house of Israel* cannot be safe without watchmen, and yet, *except the Lord keep it, the watchman waketh but in vain,* Ps. cxxvii. 1, 2.

II. What is the duty of this office. The work of a watchman is to take notice and to give notice.

1. The prophet, as a watchman, must

take notice of what God said concerning this people, not only concerning the body of the people, to which the prophecies of Jeremiah and other prophets had most commonly reference, but concerning particular persons, according as their character was. He must not, as other watchmen, look round to spy danger and gain intelligence, but he must look up to God, and further he need not look : *Hear the word at my mouth, v.* 17. Note, Those that are to preach must first hear; for how can those teach others who have not first learned themselves?

2. He must give notice of what he heard. As a watchman must have eyes in his head, so he must have a tongue in his head; if he be dumb, it is as bad as if he were blind, Isa. lvi. 10. Thou shalt *give them warning from me,* sound an alarm in the *holy mountain;* not in his own name, or as from himself, but in God's name, and from him. Ministers are God's mouth to the children of men. The scriptures are written for our admonition. *By them is thy servant warned,* Ps. xix. 11. But, because that which is delivered *vivâ voce—by the living voice,* commonly makes the deepest impression, God is pleased, by men like ourselves, who are equally concerned, to enforce upon us the warnings of the written word. Now the prophet, in his preaching, must distinguish between the wicked and the righteous, the precious and the vile, and in his applications must suit his alarms to each, giving every one his portion; and, if he did this, he should have the comfort of it, whatever the success was, but, if not, he was accountable.

(1.) Some of those he had to do with were wicked, and he must warn them not to go on in their wickedness, but to turn from it, *v.* 18, 19. We may observe here, [1.] That the God of heaven has said, and does say, to every wicked man, that if he go on still in his trespasses he *shall surely die. His iniquity* shall undoubtedly be his ruin; it tends to ruin and will end in ruin. Dying *thou shalt die, thou shalt die* so great a death, *shalt die* eternally, be ever dying, but never dead. *The wicked man shall die in his iniquity, shall die* under the guilt of it, *die* under the dominion of it. [2.] That if a *wicked man turn from his wickedness,* and *from his wicked way, he shall live,* and the ruin he is threatened with shall be prevented; and, that he may do so, he is warned of the danger he is in. *The wicked man shall die* if he go on, but *shall live* if he repent. Observe, He is to turn *from his wickedness* and *from his wicked way.* It is not enough for a man to turn *from his wicked way* by an outward reformation, which may be the effect of his sins leaving him rather than of his leaving his sins, but he must *turn from his wickedness,* from the love of it and the inclination to it, by an inward regeneration; if he do not so much as turn *from his wicked way,* there is little hope that

768

he will turn *from his wickedness.* [3.] That it is the duty of ministers both to warn sinners of the danger of sin and to assure them of the benefit of repentance, to set before them how miserable they are if they go on in sin, and how happy they may be if they will but repent and reform. Note, The ministry of the word is concerning matters of *life and death,* for those are the things it sets before us, *the blessing and the curse,* that we may escape the curse and inherit the blessing. [4.] That, though ministers do not warn wicked people as they ought of their misery and danger, yet that shall not be admitted as an excuse for those that go on still in their trespasses; for, though the watchman did not *give them warning, yet* they *shall die in their iniquity,* for they had sufficient warning given them by the providence of God and their own consciences; and, if they would have taken it, they might have *saved* their *lives.* [5.] That if ministers be not faithful to their trust, if they do not warn sinners of the fatal consequences of sin, but suffer them to go on unreproved, the *blood* of those that perish through their carelessness *will be required at their hand.* It shall be charged upon them in the day of account that it was owing to their unfaithfulness that such and such precious souls perished in sin; for who knows but if they had had fair warning given them they might have fled in time *from the wrath to come?* And, if it contract so heinous a guilt as it does to be accessory to the murder of a dying body, what is it to be accessory to the ruin of an immortal soul? [6.] That if ministers do their duty in giving warning to sinners, though the warning be not taken, yet they may have this satisfaction, that they are *clear from* their *blood,* and have *delivered their own souls,* though they cannot prevail to deliver theirs. Those that are faithful shall have their reward, though they be not successful.

(2.) Some of those he had to deal with were *righteous,* at least he had reason to think, in a judgment of charity, that they were so; and he must warn them not to apostatize and *turn away from their righteousness, v.* 20, 21. We may observe here, [1.] That the best men in the world have need to be warned against apostasy, and to be told of the danger they are in of it and the danger they are in by it. God's servants must be warned (Ps. xix. 11) that they do not neglect his work and quit his service. One good means to keep us from falling is to keep up a holy fear of falling, Heb. iv. 1. *Let us therefore fear;* and (Rom. xi. 20) even those that *stand by faith* must *not be high-minded, but fear,* and must therefore be warned. [2.] There is a *righteousness* which a man may *turn from,* a seeming *righteousness,* and, if men turn from this, it thereby appears that it was never sincere, how passable, nay, how plausible soever it was; for, *if they had been of us, they would no doubt have continued with us,* 1 John ii. 19. There are many that *begin in the spirit,* but *end in the flesh,* that set their faces heavenward, but look back; that had a first love, but have lost it, and *turned from the holy commandment.* [3.] When men *turn from their righteousness* they soon learn to commit iniquity. When they grow careless and remiss in the duties of God's worship, neglect them, or are negligent in them, they become an easy prey to the tempter. Omissions make way for commissions. [4.] *When men turn from their righteousness, and commit iniquity,* it is just with God to lay *stumbling-blocks before them,* that they may grow worse and worse, till they are ripened for destruction. When Pharaoh hardened his heart God hardened it. When sinners turn their back upon God, desert his service, and so cast a reproach upon it, he does, in a way of righteous judgment, not only withdraw his restraining grace and give them up to their own hearts' lusts, but order them by his providence into such circumstances as occasion their sin and hasten their ruin. There are those to whom Christ himself is *a stone of stumbling and a rock of offence,* 1 Pet. ii. 8. [5.] The righteousness which men relinquish shall never be remembered to their honour or comfort; it will stand them in no stead in this world or the other. Apostates lose all that they have wrought; their services and sufferings are all in vain, and shall never be brought to an account, because not continued in. It is a rule in the law, *Factum non dicitur, quod non perseverat—We are said to do only that which we do perseveringly,* Gal. iii. 3, 4. [6.] If ministers do not give fair warning, as they ought, of the weakness of the best, their aptness to stumble and fall, the particular temptations they are in and the fatal consequences of apostasy, the ruin of those that do apostatize will be laid at their door, and they shall answer for it. Not but that there are those who are warned against it, and yet *turn from their righteousness;* but that case is not put here, as was concerning the wicked man, but, on the contrary, that a *righteous man,* being warned, takes the warning and *does not sin* (v. 21); for, if you *give instruction to a wise man, he will be yet wiser.* We must not only not flatter the wicked, but not flatter even the righteous as if they were perfectly safe any where on this side heaven. [7.] If ministers give warning, and people take it, it is well for both. Nothing is more beautiful than *a wise reprover upon an obedient ear;* the one *shall live because he is warned* and the other *has delivered his soul.* What can a good minister desire more than to *save himself and those that hear him?* 1 Tim. iv. 16.

22 And the hand of the LORD was there upon me; and he said unto me, Arise, go forth into the plain, and I will there talk with thee. 23 Then I arose, and went forth into the plain: and, behold, the glory of the LORD stood there, as the glory which I saw by the river of Chebar: and I fell on my face. 24 Then the spirit entered into me, and set me upon my feet, and spake with me, and said unto me, Go, shut thyself within thine house. 25 But thou, O son of man, behold, they shall put bands upon thee, and shall bind thee with them, and thou shalt not go out among them: 26 And I will make thy tongue cleave to the roof of thy mouth, that thou shalt be dumb, and shalt not be to them a reprover: for they *are* a rebellious house. 27 But when I speak with thee, I will open thy mouth, and thou shalt say unto them, Thus saith the Lord GOD; He that heareth, let him hear; and he that forbeareth, let him forbear: for they *are* a rebellious house.

After all this large and magnificent discovery which God had made of himself to the prophet, and the full instructions he had given him how to deal with those to whom he sent him with an ample commission, we should have expected presently to see him preaching the word of God to a great congregation of Israel; but here we find it quite otherwise. His work here, at first, seems not at all proportionable to the pomp of his call.

I. We have him here retired for further learning. By his unwillingness to go it should seem as if he were not so thoroughly convinced as he might have been of the ability of him that sent him to bear him out; and therefore, to encourage him against the difficulties he foresaw, God will favour him with another vision of his glory, which (if any thing) would put life into him and animate him for his work. In order to this, God calls him out *to the plain* (v. 22) and there he will have some *talk with him.* See and admire the condescension of God in conversing thus familiarly with a man, a *son of man,* a poor captive, nay, with a sinful man, who, when God sent him, *went in bitterness of spirit,* and was at this time out of humour with his work. And let us own ourselves for ever indebted to the mediation of Christ for this blessed intercourse and communion between God and man, between heaven and earth. See here the benefit of solitude, and how much it befriends contemplation. It is very comfortable to be alone with God, withdrawn from the world for converse with him, to hear from him, to speak to him; and a good man will say that he is never less alone than when thus alone. Ezekiel *went forth into the plain* more willingly than he went *among those of the captivity* (*v.* 15); for those that know what it is to have communion with God cannot but prefer that before any converse with this world, especially such as is commonly met with. He *went out into the plain,* and there he saw the same vision that he had seen *by the river of Chebar;* for God is not tied to places. Note, Those who follow God shall meet with his consolations, wherever they go. God called him out to *talk with him,* but did more than that: he showed him his *glory, v.* 23. We are not now to expect such visions, but we must own that we have a favour done us no way inferior if we so by faith *behold the glory of the Lord* as to be *changed into the same image, by the Spirit of the Lord;* and this *honour have all his saints. Praise you the Lord,* 2 Cor. iii. 18.

II. We have him here restrained from further teaching for the present. When he saw *the glory of the Lord* he *fell on his face,* being struck with an awe of God's majesty and a dread of his displeasure; but *the Spirit entered into* him to raise him up, and then he recovered himself and got *upon his feet* and heard what the Spirit whispered to him, which is very surprising. One would have expected now that God would send him directly to the chief place of concourse, would give him favour in the eyes of his brethren, and make him and his message acceptable to them, that he would have a wider door of opportunity opened to him and that God would give him a door of utterance to open his mouth boldly; but what is here said to him is the reverse of all this.

1. Instead of sending him to a public assembly, he orders him to confine himself to his own lodgings: *Go, shut thyself within thy house, v.* 24. He was not willing to appear in public, and, when he did, the people did not regard him, nor show him the respect he deserved, and as a just rebuke both to him and them, to him for his shyness of them and to them for their coldness towards him, God forbids him to appear in public. Note, Our choice is often made our punishment; and it is a righteous thing with God to remove teachers into corners when they, or their people, or both, grow indifferent to solemn assemblies. Ezekiel must shut up himself, some think, to give a sign of the besieging of Jerusalem, in which the people should be closely shut up as he was in his house, and which he speaks of in the next chapter. He must *shut himself within his house,* that he might receive further discoveries of the mind of God and might abundantly furnish himself with something to say to the people when he went abroad. We find that *the elders of Judah* visited him and *sat before* him sometimes *in his house* (*ch.* viii. 1), to be witnesses of

his ecstasies; but it was not till *ch.* xi. 25 that he *spoke to those of the captivity all the things that the Lord had shown him.* Note, Those that are called to preach must find time to study, and a great deal of time too, must often shut themselves up in their houses, that they may give attendance to reading and meditation, and so their profiting may appear to all.

2. Instead of securing him an interest in the esteem and affections of those to whom he sent him he tells him that *they shall put bands upon him and bind him* (*v.* 25), either (1.) As a criminal. *They shall bind him* in order to the further punishing of him as a disturber of the peace; though they were themselves sent into bondage in Babylon for persecuting the prophets, yet there they continue to persecute them. Or, rather, (2.) As a distracted man. *They* would go about to *bind him* as one beside himself; for to that they imputed his violent motions in his raptures. The captains asked Jehu, *Wherefore came this mad fellow unto thee?* Festus said to Paul, *Thou art beside thyself;* and so the Jews said of our Lord Jesus, Mark iii. 21. Perhaps this was the reason why he must keep within doors, because otherwise they would bind him, under pretence of his being mad, and therefore he must not *go out among them.* Justly are prophets forbidden to go to those that will abuse them.

3. Instead of opening his lips that his mouth might show forth God's praise, God silenced him, made his *tongue cleave to the roof of his mouth,* so that he was dumb for a considerable time, *v.* 26. The pious captives in Babylon used this imprecation upon themselves, that, *if* they should *forget Jerusalem,* their *tongue* might *cleave to the roof of their mouth,* Ps. cxxxvii. 6. Ezekiel remembers Jerusalem more than any of them, and yet his *tongue cleaves to the roof of his mouth,* and he that can speak best is forbidden to speak at all; and the reason given is because *they are a rebellious house* to whom he is sent, and they are not worthy to have him for *a reprover.* He shall not give them instructions and admonitions, for they are lost and thrown away upon them. He is before commanded to speak boldly to them because *they are most rebellious* (*ch.* ii. 7); but, since that proves to no purpose, he is now for that reason enjoined silence and shall not speak at all to them. Note, Those whose hearts are hardened against conviction are justly deprived of the means of conviction. Why should not the reprovers be dumb, if, after long trials, it be found that the reproved resolve to be deaf? If Ephraim *be joined to idols, let him alone. Thou shalt be dumb, and not be a reprover,* implying that unless he were dumb he would be reproving; if he could speak at all, he would witness against the wickedness of the wicked. *But when God speaks with* him, and designs to speak by him, he *will open* his *mouth,*

v. 27. Note, Though God's prophets may be silenced awhile, there will come a time when God will give them the opening of the mouth again. And, when God speaks to his ministers, he not only opens their ears to hear what he says, but opens their mouth to return an answer. Moses, who had a veil on his face when he went down to the people, took it off when he went up again to God, Exod. xxxiv. 34.

4. Instead of giving him assurance of success when he should at any time speak to the people, he here leaves the matter very doubtful, and Ezekiel must not perplex and disquiet himself about it, but let it be as it will. *He that hears, let him hear,* and he is welcome to the comfort of it; *let him hear, and his soul shall live;* but *he that forbears, let him forbear* at his peril, and take what comes. *If thou scornest, thou alone shalt bear it;* neither God nor his prophet shall be any losers by it; but the prophet shall be rewarded for his faithfulness in reproving the sinner, and God will have the glory of his justice in condemning him for not taking the reproof.

CHAP. IV.

Ezekiel was now among the captives in Babylon, but they there had Jerusalem still upon their hearts; the pious captives looked towards it with an eye of faith (as Daniel, ch. vi. 10), the presumptuous ones looked towards it with an eye of pride, and flattered themselves with a conceit that they should shortly return thither again; those that remained corresponded with the captives, and, it is likely, buoyed them up with hopes that all would be well yet, as long as Jerusalem was standing in its strength, and perhaps upbraided those with their folly who had surrendered at first; therefore, to take down this presumption, God gives the prophet, in this chapter, a very clear and affecting foresight of the besieging of Jerusalem by the Chaldean army and the calamities which would attend that siege. Two things are here represented to him in vision:—I. The fortifications that should be raised against the city; this is signified by the prophet's laying siege to the portraiture of Jerusalem (ver. 1—3) and lying first on one side and then on the other side before it, ver. 4—8. II. The famine that should rage within the city; this is signified by his eating very coarse fare, and confining himself to a little of it, so long as this typical representation lasted, ver. 9—17.

THOU also, son of man, take thee a tile, and lay it before thee, and portray upon it the city, *even* Jerusalem: 2 And lay siege against it, and build a fort against it, and cast a mount against it; set the camp also against it, and set *battering*-rams against it round about. 3 Moreover take thou unto thee an iron pan, and set it *for* a wall of iron between thee and the city: and set thy face against it, and it shall be besieged, and thou shalt lay siege against it. This *shall be* a sign to the house of Israel. 4 Lie thou also upon thy left side, and lay the iniquity of the house of Israel upon it: *according* to the number of the days that thou shalt lie upon it thou shalt bear their iniquity. 5 For I have laid upon thee the years of their iniquity, according to the num-

ber of the days, three hundred and ninety days: so shalt thou bear the iniquity of the house of Israel. 6 And when thou hast accomplished them, lie again on thy right side, and thou shalt bear the iniquity of the house of Judah forty days: I have appointed thee each day for a year. 7 Therefore thou shalt set thy face toward the siege of Jerusalem, and thine arm *shall be* uncovered, and thou shalt prophesy against it. 8 And, behold, I will lay bands upon thee, and thou shalt not turn thee from one side to another, till thou hast ended the days of thy siege.

The prophet is here ordered to represent to himself and others, by signs which would be proper and powerful to strike the fancy and to affect the mind, *the siege of Jerusalem;* and this amounted to a prediction.

I. He was ordered to engrave a draught of Jerusalem upon a tile, *v.* 1. It was Jerusalem's honour that while she kept her integrity God had *graven her upon the palms of his hands* (Isa. xlix. 16), and the names of the tribes were engraven in precious stones on the breast-plate of the high priest; but, now that *the faithful city has become a harlot,* a worthless brittle tile or brick is thought good enough to *portray it upon.* This the prophet must lay before him, that the eye may affect the heart.

II. He was ordered to build little forts against this portraiture of the city, resembling the batteries raised by the besiegers, *v.* 2. Between the city that was besieged and himself that was the besieger he was to set up an *iron pan,* as an *iron wall, v.* 3. This represented the inflexible resolution of both sides; the Chaldeans resolved, whatever it cost them, that they would make themselves masters of the city and would never quit it till they had conquered it; on the other side, the Jews resolved never to capitulate, but to hold out to the last extremity.

III. He was ordered to lie upon his side before it, as it were to surround it, representing the Chaldean army lying before it to block it up, to keep the meat from going in and the mouths from going out. He was to lie on his left side 390 *days* (*v.* 5), about thirteen months; the siege of Jerusalem is computed to last eighteen months (Jer. lii. 4—6), but if we deduct from that five months' interval, when the besiegers withdrew upon the approach of Pharaoh's army (Jer. xxxvii. 5—8), the number of the days of the close siege will be 390. Yet that also had another signification. The 390 days, according to the prophetic dialect, signified 390 years; and, when the prophet lies so many days on his side, he bears the guilt of that iniquity which *the house of Israel*, the ten tribes, had borne 390 years, reckoning from their first apostasy under Jeroboam to the destruction of Jerusalem, which completed the ruin of those small remains of them that had incorporated with Judah. He is then to lie forty days *upon his right side*, and so long to bear *the iniquity of the house of Judah*, the kingdom of the two tribes, because the measure-filling sins of that people were those which they were guilty of during the last forty years before their captivity, since the thirteenth year of Josiah, when Jeremiah began to prophesy (Jer. i. 1, 2), or, as some reckon it, since the eighteenth, when the book of the law was found and the people renewed their covenant with God. When they persisted in their impieties and idolatries, notwithstanding they had such a prophet and such a prince, and were brought into the bond of such a covenant, what could be expected but ruin without remedy? Judah, that had such helps and advantages for reformation, fills the measure of its iniquity in less time than Israel does. Now we are not to think that the prophet lay constantly night and day upon his side, but every day, for so many days together, at a certain time of the day, when he received visits, and company came in, he was found lying 390 *days on his left side* and *forty days on his right side* before his portraiture of Jerusalem, which all that saw might easily understand to mean the close besieging of that city, and people would be flocking in daily, some for curiosity and some for conscience, at the hour appointed, to see it and to make their different remarks upon it. His being found constantly on the same side, as if *bands were laid upon him* (as indeed they were by the divine command), so that he could not *turn himself from one side to another till he had ended the days of the siege*, did plainly represent the close and constant continuance of the besiegers about the city during that number of days, till they had gained their point.

IV. He was ordered to prosecute the siege with vigour (*v.* 7) : *Thou shalt set thy face towards the siege of Jerusalem*, as wholly intent upon it and resolved to carry it; so the Chaldeans would be, and neither bribed nor forced to withdraw from it. Nebuchadnezzar's indignation at Zedekiah's treachery in breaking his league with him made him very furious in pushing on this siege, that he might chastise the insolence of that faithless prince and people ; and his army promised themselves a rich booty of that pompous city ; so that both set their faces against it, for they were very resolute. Nor were they less active and industrious, exerting themselves to the utmost in all the operations of the siege, which the prophet was to represent by the *uncovering of his arm*, or, as some read it, the *stretching out* of his arm,

as it were to deal blows about without mercy. When God is about to do some great work he is said to *make bare his arm*, Isa. lii. 10. In short, The Chaldeans will go about their business, and go on in it, as men in earnest, who resolve to go through with it. Now, 1. This is intended to be a *sign to the house of Israel* (*v.* 3), both to those in Babylon, who were eye-witnesses of what the prophet did, and to those also who remained in their own land, who would hear the report of it. The prophet was *dumb* and *could not speak* (*ch.* iii. 26) ; but as his silence had a voice, and upbraided the people with their deafness, so even then God *left not himself without witness*, but ordered him to make signs, as dumb men are accustomed to do, and as Zacharias did when he was dumb, and by them to *make known his mind* (that is, the mind of God) to the people. And thus likewise the people were upbraided with their stupidity and dulness, that they were not capable of being taught as men of sense are, by words, but must be taught as children are, by pictures, or as deaf men are, by signs. Or, perhaps, they are hereby upbraided with their malice against the prophet. Had he spoken in words at length what was signified by these figures, they would have entangled him in his talk, would have indicted him for treasonable expressions, for they knew how to *make a man an offender for a word* (Isa. xxix. 21), to avoid which he is ordered to make use of signs. Or the prophet made use of signs for the same reason that Christ made use of parables, that *hearing they might hear and not understand*, and *seeing they might see and not perceive*, Matt. xiii. 14, 15. They would not understand what was plain, and therefore shall be taught by that which is difficult ; and herein the Lord was righteous. 2. Thus the prophet *prophesies against Jerusalem* (*v.* 7) ; and there were those who not only understood it so, but were the more affected with it by its being so represented, for images to the eye commonly make deeper impressions upon the mind than words can, and for this reason sacraments are instituted to represent divine things, that we might see and believe, might see and be affected with those things ; and we may expect this benefit by them, and a blessing to go along with them, while (as the prophet here) we make use only of such signs as God himself has expressly appointed, which, we must conclude, are the fittest. Note, The power of imagination, if it be rightly used, and kept under the direction and correction of reason and faith, may be of good use to kindle and excite pious and devout affections, as it was here to Ezekiel and his attendants. "*Methinks I see* so and so, myself dying, time expiring, the world on fire, the dead rising, the great tribunal set, and the like, may have an exceedingly good influence upon us : for fancy is like fire, a *good ser-*

vant, *but a bad master.* 3. This whole transaction has that in it which the prophet might, with a good colour of reason, have hesitated at and excepted against, and yet, in obedience to God's command, and in execution of his office, he did it according to order. (1.) It seemed childish and ludicrous, and beneath his gravity, and there were those that would ridicule him for it; but he knew the divine appointment put honour enough upon that which otherwise seemed mean to save his reputation in the doing of it. (2.) It was toilsome and tiresome to do as he did; but our ease as well as our credit must be sacrificed to our duty, and we must never call God's service in any instance of it a hard service. (3.) It could not but be very much against the grain with him to appear thus against Jerusalem, the city of God, the holy city, to act as an enemy against a place to which he was so good a friend; but he is a prophet, and must follow his instructions, not his affections, and must plainly preach the ruin of a sinful place, though its welfare is what he passionately desires and earnestly prays for. 4. All this that the prophet sets before the children of his people concerning the destruction of Jerusalem is designed to bring them to repentance, by showing them sin, the provoking cause of this destruction, sin the ruin of that once flourishing city, than which surely nothing could be more effectual to make them hate sin and turn from it; while he thus in lively colours describes the calamity with a great deal of pain and uneasiness to himself, he is *bearing the iniquity of Israel and Judah.* "Look here" (says he) "and see what work sin makes, what an *evil and bitter thing it is to depart from God;* this comes of sin, your sin and the sin of your fathers; let that therefore be the daily matter of your sorrow and shame now in your captivity, that you may make your peace with God and he may return in mercy to you." But observe, It is a day of punishment for a year of sin: *I have appointed thee each day for a year.* The siege is a calamity of 390 days, in which God reckons for the iniquity of 390 years; justly therefore do they acknowledge that God had *punished them less than their iniquity deserved,* Ezra ix. 13. But let impenitent sinners know that, though now God is longsuffering towards them, in the other world there is an everlasting punishment. When God *laid bands* upon the prophet, it was to show them how they were *bound with the cords of their own transgression* (Lam. i. 14), and therefore they were now *holden in the cords of affliction.* But we may well think of the prophet's case with compassion, when God laid upon him the bands of duty, as he does on all his ministers (1 Cor. ix. 16, *Necessity is laid upon me, and woe unto me if I preach not the gospel) ;* and yet men laid upon him bonds of restraint (*ch.* iii. 25); but under both it is satisfaction enough that

they are serving the interests of God's kingdom among men.

9 Take thou also unto thee wheat, and barley, and beans, and lentiles, and millet, and fitches, and put them in one vessel, and make thee bread thereof, *according* to the number of the days that thou shalt lie upon thy side, three hundred and ninety days shalt thou eat thereof. 10 And thy meat which thou shalt eat *shall be* by weight, twenty shekels a day: from time to time shalt thou eat it. 11 Thou shalt drink also water by measure, the sixth part of a hin: from time to time shalt thou drink. 12 And thou shalt eat it *as* barley-cakes, and thou shalt bake it with dung that cometh out of man, in their sight. 13 And the LORD said, Even thus shall the children of Israel eat their defiled bread among the Gentiles, whither I will drive them. 14 Then said I, Ah Lord GOD! behold, my soul hath not been polluted: for from my youth up even till now have I not eaten of that which dieth of itself, or is torn in pieces; neither came there abominable flesh into my mouth. 15 Then he said unto me, Lo, I have given thee cow's dung for man's dung, and thou shalt prepare thy bread therewith. 16 Moreover he said unto me, Son of man, behold, I will break the staff of bread in Jerusalem: and they shall eat bread by weight, and with care; and they shall drink water by measure, and with astonishment: 17 That they may want bread and water, and be astonished one with another, and consume away for their iniquity.

The best exposition of this part of Ezekiel's prediction of Jerusalem's desolation is Jeremiah's lamentation of it, Lam. iv. 3, 4, &c., and v. 10, where he pathetically describes the terrible famine that was in Jerusalem during the siege and the sad effects of it.

I. The prophet here, to affect the people with the foresight of it, must confine himself for 390 days to coarse fare and short commons, and that ill-dressed, for they should want both food and fuel.

1. His meat, for the quality of it, was to be of the worst bread, made of but little wheat and barley, and the rest of beans, and

lentiles, and millet, and fitches, such as we feed horses or fatted hogs with, and this mixed, as mill corn, or as that in the beggar's bag, that has a dish full of one sort of corn at one house and of another at another house; of such corn as this must the prophet's bread be made while he underwent the fatigue of lying on his side, and needed something better to support him, *v.* 9. Note, It is our wisdom not to be too fond of dainties and pleasant bread, because we know not what hard meat we may be tied to, nay, and may be glad of, before we die. The meanest sort of food is better than we deserve, and therefore must not be despised nor wasted, nor must those that use it be looked upon with disdain, because we know not what may be our own lot.

2. For the quantity of it, it was to be of the least that a man could be kept alive with, to signify that the besieged should be reduced to short allowance and should hold out till all *the bread in the city was spent*, Jer. xxxvii. 21. The prophet must eat but twenty *shekels'* weight of bread a day (*v.* 10), that was about ten ounces; and he must drink but the *sixth part of a hin of water*, that was half a pint, about eight ounces, *v.* 11. The stint of the Lessian diet is fourteen ounces of meat and sixteen of drink. The prophet in Babylon had bread enough and to spare, and was by the river side, where there was plenty of water; and yet, that he might confirm his own prediction and be a sign to the children of Israel, God obliges him to live thus sparingly, and he submits to it. Note, God's servants must learn to endure hardness, and to deny themselves the use of lawful delights, when they may thereby serve the glory of God, evidence the sincerity of their faith, and express their sympathy with their brethren in affliction. The body must be *kept under and brought into subjection*. Nature is content with a little, grace with less, but lust with nothing. It is good to stint ourselves of choice, that we may the better bear it if ever we should come to be stinted by necessity. And in times of public distress and calamity it ill becomes us to make much of ourselves, as those that *drank wine in bowls* and *were not grieved for the affliction of Joseph*, Amos vi. 4—6.

3. For the dressing of it, he must *bake it with man's dung* (*v.* 12); that must be dried, and serve for fuel to heat his oven with. The thought of it would almost turn one's stomach; yet the coarse bread, thus baked, he must *eat as barley-cakes*, as freely as if it were the same bread he had been used to. This nauseous piece of cookery he must exercise publicly *in their sight*, that they might be the more affected with the calamity approaching, which was signified by it, that in the extremity of the famine they should not only have nothing that was dainty, but nothing that was cleanly, about them; they must take up with what they could get. To

the hungry soul every bitter thing is sweet. This circumstance of the sign, the baking of his bread with man's dung, the prophet with submission humbly desired might be dispensed with (*v.* 14); it seemed to have in it something of a ceremonial pollution, for there was a law that man's dung should *be covered with earth*, that God might *see no unclean thing in their camp*, Deut. xxiii. 13, 14. And must he go and gather a thing so offensive, and use it in the dressing of his meat in the sight of the people? "*Ah! Lord God,*" says he, "*behold, my soul has not been polluted*, and I am afraid lest by this it be polluted." Note, The pollution of the soul by sin is what good people dread more than any thing; and yet sometimes tender consciences fear it without cause, and perplex themselves with scruples about lawful things, as the prophet here, who had not yet learned that it is not that which *goes into the mouth that defiles the man*, Matt. xv. 11. But observe he does not plead, "Lord, from my youth I have been brought up delicately and have never been used to any thing but what was clean and nice" (and there were those who were so brought up, who in the siege of Jerusalem did *embrace dunghills*, Lam. iv. 5), but that he had been brought up conscientiously, and had never eaten any thing that was forbidden by the law, that *died of itself* or was *torn in pieces;* and therefore, "Lord, do not put this upon me now." Thus Peter pleaded (Acts x. 14), *Lord, I have never eaten any thing that is common or unclean.* Note, It will be comfortable to us, when we are reduced to hardships, if our hearts can witness for us that we have always been careful to abstain from sin, even from little sins, and the *appearances of evil*. Whatever God commands us, we may be sure, is good; but, if we be put upon any thing that we apprehend to be evil, we should argue against it, from this consideration, that hitherto we have preserved our purity—and shall we lose it now? Now, because Ezekiel with a manifest tenderness of conscience made this scruple, God dispensed with him in this matter. Note, Those who have power in their hands should not be rigorous in pressing their commands upon those that are dissatisfied concerning them, yea, though their dissatisfactions be groundless or arising from education and long usage, but should recede from them rather than grieve or offend the weak, or put a stumbling-block before them, in conformity to the example of God's condescension to Ezekiel, though we are sure his authority is incontestable and all his commands are wise and good. God allowed Ezekiel to use *cow's dung* instead of *man's dung, v.* 15. This is a tacit reflection upon man, as intimating that he being polluted with sin his filthiness is more nauseous and odious than that of any other creature. *How much more abominable and filthy is man!* Job xv. 16.

II. Now this sign is particularly explained here; it signified,

1. That those who remained in Jerusalem should be brought to extreme misery for want of necessary food. All supplies being cut off by the besiegers, the city would soon find the want of the country, for *the king himself is served of the field;* and thus *the staff of bread* would be *broken in Jerusalem, v.* 16. God would not only take away from the bread its power to nourish, so that *they should eat and not be satisfied* (Lev. xxvi. 26), but would take away the bread itself (Isa. iii. 1), so that what little remained should be *eaten by weight,* so much a day, so much a head, that they might have an equal share and might make it last as long as possible. But to what purpose, when they could not make it last always, and the besieged must be tired out before the besiegers? They should eat and drink *with care,* to make it go as far as might be, and with *astonishment,* when they saw it almost spent and knew not which way to look for a recruit. They should *be astonished one with another;* whereas it is ordinarily some alleviation of a calamity to have others share with us in it *(Solamen miseris socios habuisse doloris),* and some ease to the spirit to complain of the burden, it should be an aggravation of the misery that it was universal, and their complaining to one another should but make them all the more uneasy and increase the *astonishment.* And the event shall be as bad as their fears; they cannot make it worse than it is, for *they shall consume away for their iniquity;* multitudes of them shall die of famine, a lingering death, worse than that by *the sword* (Lam. iv. 9); they shall die so as to *feel themselves die.* And it is sin that brings all this misery upon them: *They shall consume away in their iniquity* (so it may be read); they shall continue hardened and impenitent, and shall die in their sins, which is more miserable than to die on a dunghill. Now, (1.) Let us see here what woeful work sin makes with a people, and acknowledge the righteousness of God herein. Time was when *Jerusalem was filled with the finest of the wheat* (Ps. cxlvii. 14); but now it would be glad of the coarsest, and cannot have it. *Fulness of bread,* as it was one of Jerusalem's mercies, so it had become one of her sins, Ezek. xvi. 49. The plenty was abused to luxury and excess, which were therefore thus justly punished with famine. It is a righteous thing with God to deprive us of those enjoyments which we have made the food and fuel of our lusts. (2.) Let us see what reason we have to bless God for plenty, not only for the fruits of the earth, but for the freedom of commerce, that the husbandman can have money for his bread and the tradesman bread for his money, that there is abundance not only in the field, but in the market, that those who live in cities and great towns, though they *sow not,* nei-

ther do they *reap,* are yet fed from day to day with food convenient.

2. It signified that those who were carried into captivity should be forced to *eat their defiled bread among the Gentiles (v.* 13), to eat meat made up by Gentile hands otherwise than according to the law of the Jewish church, which they were always taught to call *defiled,* and which they would have as great an aversion to as a man would have to bread prepared with dung, that is (as perhaps it may be understood) kneaded and moulded with dung. Daniel and his fellows confined themselves to *pulse and water,* rather than they would *eat the portion of the king's meat* assigned them, because they apprehended it would defile them, Dan. i. 8. Or they should be forced to eat putrid meat, such as their oppressors would allow them in their slavery, and such as formerly they would have scorned to touch. Because they *served not God* with cheerfulness in the abundance of all things, God will make them serve their enemies in the want of all things.

CHAP. V.

In this chapter we have a further, and no less terrible, denunciation of the judgments of God, which were coming with all speed and force upon the Jewish nation, which would utterly ruin it; for when God judges he will overcome. This destruction of Judah and Jerusalem is here, I. Represented by a sign, the cutting, and burning, and scattering of hair, ver. 1—4. II. That sign is expounded, and applied to Jerusalem. 1. Sin is charged upon Jerusalem as the cause of this desolation—contempt of God's law (ver. 5—7) and profanation of his sanctuary, ver. 11. 2. Wrath is threatened, great wrath (ver. 8—10), a variety of miseries (ver. 12, 16, 17), such as should be their reproach and ruin, ver. 13—15.

AND thou, son of man, take thee a sharp knife, take thee a barber's razor, and cause *it* to pass upon thine head and upon thy beard: then take thee balances to weigh, and divide the *hair.* 2 Thou shalt burn with fire a third part in the midst of the city, when the days of the siege are fulfilled: and thou shalt take a third part, *and* smite about it with a knife: and a third part thou shalt scatter in the wind; and I will draw out a sword after them. 3 Thou shalt also take thereof a few in number, and bind them in thy skirts. 4 Then take of them again, and cast them into the midst of the fire, and burn them in the fire; *for* thereof shall a fire come forth into all the house of Israel.

We have here the sign by which the utter destruction of Jerusalem is set forth; and here, as before, the prophet is himself the sign, that the people might see how much he affected himself with, and interested himself in, the case of Jerusalem, and how near it lay to his heart, even when he foretold the desolations of it. He was so much concerned about it as to take what was done to it as done to himself, so far was he from desiring the woeful day

I. He must *shave off the hair of his head and beard* (v. 1), which signified God's utter rejecting and abandoning that people, as a useless worthless generation, such as could well be spared, nay, such as it would be his honour to part with ; his judgments, and all the instruments he made use of in cutting them off, were this *sharp knife* and this *razor*, that were proper to be made use of, and would do execution. Jerusalem had been the head, but, having degenerated, had become as the *hair*, which, when it grows thick and long, is but a burden which a man wishes to get clear of, as God of the sinners in Zion. *Ah! I will ease me of my adversaries*, Isa. i. 24. Ezekiel must not cut off that hair only which was superfluous, but *cut it all off*, denoting the full end that God would make of Jerusalem. The hair that would not be trimmed and kept neat and clean by the admonitions of the prophets must be all shaved off by utter destruction. Those will be ruined that will not be reformed.

II. He must *weigh the hair* and *divide it into three parts*. This intimates the very exact directing of God's judgments according to equity (by him men and their actions are *weighed* in the unerring balance of truth and righteousness) and the proportion which divine justice observes in punishing some by one judgment and others by another; one way or other, they shall all be met with. Some make the shaving of the hair to denote the loss of their liberty and of their honour: it was looked upon as a mark of ignominy, as in the disgrace Hanun put on David's ambassadors. It denotes also the loss of their joy, for they shaved their heads upon occasion of great mourning; I may add the loss of their Nazariteship, for the shaving of the head was a period to that vow (Num. vi. 18), and Jerusalem was now no longer looked upon as a *holy city*.

III. He must dispose of the hair so that it might all be destroyed or dispersed, *v.* 2. 1. One *third part* must *be burnt in the midst of the city*, denoting the multitudes that should perish by famine and pestilence, and perhaps many in the conflagration of the city, *when the days of the siege were fulfilled.* Or the laying of that glorious city in ashes might well be looked upon as a third part of the destruction threatened. 2. Another third part was to be *cut in pieces with a knife*, representing the many who, during the siege, were slain by the sword, in their sallies out upon the besiegers, and especially when the city was taken by storm, the Chaldeans being then most furious and the Jews most feeble. 3. Another third part was to be *scattered in the wind*, denoting the carrying away of some into the land of the conqueror and the flight of others into the neighbouring countries for shelter ; so that they were hurried, some one way and some another, like loose hairs in the wind. But, lest they should

think that this dispersion would be their escape, God adds, *I will draw out a sword after them*, so that wherever they go evil shall pursue them. Note, God has variety of judgments wherewith to accomplish the destruction of a sinful people and to make an end when he begins.

IV. He must preserve a small quantity of the third sort that were to be *scattered in the wind*, and *bind them in his skirts*, as one would bind that which he is very mindful and careful of, *v.* 3. This signified perhaps that little handful of people which were left under the government of Gedaliah, who, it was hoped, would keep possession of the land when the body of the people was carried into captivity. Thus God would have done well for them if they would have done well for themselves. But these few that were reserved must be taken and *cast into the fire, v.* 4. When Gedaliah and his friends were slain the people that put themselves under his protection were scattered, some gone into Egypt, others carried off by the Chaldeans, and in short the land totally cleared of them; then this was fulfilled, for out of those combustions *a fire came forth into all the house of Israel*, who, as fuel upon the fire, kindled and consumed one another. Note, It is ill with a people when those are taken away in wrath that seemed to be marked for monuments of mercy ; for then there is no remnant or escaping, none shut up or left.

5 Thus saith the Lord God ; This *is* Jerusalem : I have set it in the midst of the nations and countries *that are* round about her. 6 And she hath changed my judgments into wickedness more than the nations, and my statutes more than the countries that *are* round about her: for they have refused my judgments and my statutes, they have not walked in them. 7 Therefore thus saith the Lord God ; Because ye multiplied more than the nations that *are* round about you, *and* have not walked in my statutes, neither have kept my judgments, neither have done according to the judgments of the nations that *are* round about you ; 8 Therefore thus saith the Lord God ; Behold, I, even I, *am* against thee, and will execute judgments in the midst of thee in the sight of the nations. 9 And I will do in thee that which I have not done, and whereunto I will not do any more the like, because of all thine abominations. 10 Therefore the fathers shall eat the sons in the

midst of thee, and the sons shall eat their fathers; and I will execute judgments in thee, and the whole remnant of thee will I scatter into all the winds. 11 Wherefore, *as* I live, saith the Lord God; Surely, because thou hast defiled my sanctuary with all thy detestable things, and with all thine abominations, therefore will I also diminish *thee;* neither shall mine eye spare, neither will I have any pity. 12 A third part of thee shall die with the pestilence, and with famine shall they be consumed in the midst of thee: and a third part shall fall by the sword round about thee; and I will scatter a third part into all the winds, and I will draw out a sword after them. 13 Thus shall mine anger be accomplished, and I will cause my fury to rest upon them, and I will be comforted: and they shall know that I the Lord have spoken *it* in my zeal, when I have accomplished my fury in them. 14 Moreover I will make thee waste, and a reproach among the nations that *are* round about thee, in the sight of all that pass by. 15 So it shall be a reproach and a taunt, an instruction and an astonishment unto the nations that *are* round about thee, when I shall execute judgments in thee in anger and in fury and in furious rebukes. I the Lord have spoken *it*. 16 When I shall send upon them the evil arrows of famine, which shall be for *their* destruction, *and* which I will send to destroy you: and I will increase the famine upon you, and will break your staff of bread: 17 So will I send upon you famine and evil beasts, and they shall bereave thee; and pestilence and blood shall pass through thee; and I will bring the sword upon thee. I the Lord have spoken *it*.

We have here the explanation of the foregoing similitude: *This is Jerusalem.* Thus it is usual in scripture language to give the name of the thing signified to the sign; as when Christ said, *This is my body.* The prophet's head, which was to be shaved, signified Jerusalem, which by the judgments of God was now to be stripped of all its ornaments, to be emptied of all its inhabit-

ants, and to be set *naked and bare*, to be *shaved with a razor that is hired*, Isa. vii. 20. The head of one that was a priest, a prophet, a holy person, was fittest to represent Jerusalem the holy city. Now the contents of these verses are much the same with what we have often met with, and still shall, in the writings of the prophets. Here we have,

I. The privileges Jerusalem was honoured with (*v.* 5): *I have set it in the midst of the nations and countries that are round about her*, and those famous nations and very considerable. Jerusalem was not situated in a remote obscure corner of the world, far from neighbours, but in the midst of kingdoms that were populous, polite, and civilized, famed for learning, arts, and sciences, and which then made the greatest figure in the world. But there seems to be more in it than this. 1. Jerusalem was dignified and preferred above the neighbouring nations and their cities. It was *set in the midst* of them as excelling them all. This *holy mountain was exalted above all the hills*, Isa. ii. 2. *Why leap you, you high hills? This is the hill which God desires to dwell in*, Ps. lxviii. 16. Jerusalem was a city upon a hill, conspicuous and illustrious, and which all the neighbouring nations had an eye upon, some for good-will, some for ill-will. 2. Jerusalem was designed to have a good influence upon *the nations and countries round about*, was set in the midst of them as a candle upon a candlestick, to spread the light of divine revelation, which she was blessed with, to all the dark corners of the neighbouring nations, that from them it might diffuse itself further, even to the ends of the earth. Jerusalem was set *in the midst* of the nations, to be as the heart in the body, to invigorate this dead world with a divine life as well as to enlighten this dark world with a divine light, to be an example of every thing that was good. The nations that observed what excellent *statutes and judgments* they had concluded them to be *a wise and understanding people* (Deut. iv. 6), fit to be consulted as an oracle, as they were in Solomon's time, 1 Kings iv. 34. And, had they preserved this reputation and made a right use of it, what a blessing would Jerusalem have been to all the nations about! But, failing to be so, the accomplishment of this intention was reserved for its latter days, *when out of Zion went forth the gospel law and the word of the Lord* Jesus *from Jerusalem*, and there *repentance and remission* began to be preached, and thence the preachers of them *went forth into all nations.* And, when that was done, Jerusalem was levelled with the ground. Note, When places and persons are made great, it is with design that they may do good and that those about them may be the better for them, that their *light may shine before men.*

II. The provocations Jerusalem was guilty of. A very high charge is here drawn up against that city, and proved beyond contradiction sufficient to justify God in seizing its privileges and putting it under military execution. 1. She had *not walked in God's statutes,* nor *kept his judgments* (v. 7); nay, the inhabitants of Jerusalem had *refused his judgments and his statutes* (v. 6); they did not do their duty, nay, they *would not,* they said that they would not. Those *statutes and judgments* which their neighbours admired they despised, which they should have set before their face they cast behind their back. Note, A contempt of the word and law of God opens a door to all manner of iniquity. God's statutes are the terms on which he deals with men; those that refuse his terms cannot expect his favours. 2. She had *changed God's judgments into wickedness* (v. 6), a very high expression of profaneness, that the people had not only broken God's laws, but had so perverted and abused them that they had made them the excuse and colour of their wickedness. They introduced the abominable customs and usages of the heathen, instead of God's institutions; this was changing *the truth of God into a lie* (Rom. i. 25) and the *glory of God into shame,* Ps. iv. 2. Note, Those that have been well educated, if they live ill, put the highest affront imaginable upon God, as if he were the patron of sin and *his judgments* were *turned into wickedness.* 3. She had been worse than the neighbouring nations, to whom she should have set a good example: *She has changed my judgments,* by idolatries and false worship, *more than the nations* (v. 6), and she has *multiplied* (that is, multiplied idols and altars, gods and temples, multiplied those things the unity of which was their praise) *more than the nations that were round about.* Israel's God is one, and his name one, his altar one; but they, not content with this one God, multiplied their gods to such a degree that *according to the number of their cities so were their gods,* and their altars were *as heaps in the furrows of the field;* so that they exceeded all their neighbours in having *gods many and lords many.* They corrupted revealed religion more than the Gentiles had corrupted natural religion. Note, If those who have made a profession of religion, and have had a pious education, apostatize from it, they are commonly more profane and vicious than those who never made any profession; they have *seven other spirits more wicked.* 4. She had *not done according to the judgments of the nations,* v. 7. Israel had not acted towards their God, though he is the only true God, as the nations had acted towards their gods, though they were false gods; they had not been so observant of him nor so constant to him. Has a nation *changed its gods,* or slighted them, so as they have? Jer. ii. 11. Or it may refer to their morals; instead of reforming their neighbours, they came short of them; and

many who were of the *uncircumcision kept the righteousness of the law* better than those who were *of the circumcision,* Rom. ii. 26, 27. Those who had the light of scripture did not *according to the judgments* of many who had only the light of nature. Note, There are those who are called *Christians* who will in the great day be condemned by the better tempers and better lives of sober heathens. 5. The particular crime charged upon Jerusalem is profaning the holy things, which she had been both entrusted and honoured with (v. 11): *Thou hast defiled my sanctuary with all thy detestable things,* with thy idols and idolatries. The images of their pretended deities, and the groves erected in honour of them, were brought into the temple; and the ceremonies used by idolaters were brought into the worship of God. Thus every thing that is sacred was polluted. Note, Idols are detestable things any where, but more especially so in the sanctuary.

III. The punishments that Jerusalem should fall under for these provocations: *Shall not God visit for these things?* No doubt he shall. The matter of the sentence here passed upon Jerusalem is very dreadful, and the manner of expression makes it yet more so; the judgments are various, and the threatenings of them varied, reiterated, inculcated, that one may well say, *Who is able to stand in God's sight when once he is angry?*

1. God will take this work of punishing Jerusalem into his own hands; and *who knows the power of his anger* and what *a fearful thing it is to fall into his hands?* Observe what a strong emphasis is laid upon it (v. 8): *I, even I, am against thee.* God had been for Jerusalem, to defend and save it; but miserable is its case when he has turned to be its enemy and fights against it. If God be against us, the whole creation is at war with us, and nothing can be for us so as to stand us in any stead: "You think it is only the Chaldean army that is against you, but they are God's hand, or rather the staff in his hand; it is *I, even I,* that *am against thee,* not only to speak against thee by prophets, but to act against thee by providence. *I will execute judgments in thee* (v. 10), *in the midst of thee* (v. 8), not only in the suburbs, but in the heart of the city, not only in the borders, but in the bowels of the country." Note, Those who will not observe the judgments of God's mouth shall not escape the judgments of his hand; and God's judgments, when they come with commission, will penetrate into the midst of a people, will enter into the soul, *into the bowels like water* and *like oil into the bones.* *I will execute judgments.* Note, God himself undertakes to execute his own judgments, according to the true and full intent of them; whatever are the instruments, he is the principal agent. 2. These punishments shall come from

his displeasure. As to the body of the people, it shall not be a correction in love, but he will *execute judgments in anger, and in fury, and in furious rebukes* (v. 15), strange expressions to come from a God who has said, *Fury is not in me,* and who has declared himself *gracious, and merciful,* and *slow to anger.* But they are designed to show the malignity of sin, and the offence it gives to the just and holy God. That must needs be a very evil thing which provokes him to such resentments, and against his own people too, that had been so high in his favour, and expressed with so much satisfaction (v. 13): "*My anger,* which has long been withheld, *shall* now *be accomplished, and I will cause my fury to rest upon them;* it shall not only light upon them, but lie upon them, and fill them as vessels of wrath fitted by their own wickedness to destruction; *and,* justice being hereby glorified, *I will be comforted,* I will be entirely satisfied in what I have done." As, when God is dishonoured by the sins of men, he is said to be *grieved* (Ps. xcv. 10), so when he is honoured by their destruction he is said to *be comforted.* The struggle between mercy and judgment is over, and in this case judgment triumphs, triumphs indeed; for mercy that has been so long abused is now silent and gives up the cause, has not a word more to say on the behalf of such an ungrateful incorrigible people: *My eye shall not spare, neither will I have any pity, v.* 11. Divine compassion defers the punishment, or mitigates it, or supports under it, or shortens it; but here is *judgment without mercy,* wrath without any mixture or allay of pity. These expressions are thus sharpened and heightened perhaps with design to look further, to the vengeance of eternal fire, which some of the destructions we read of in the Old Testament were typical of, and particularly that of Jerusalem; for surely it is nowhere on this side hell that this word has its full accomplishment, *My eye shall not spare, but I will cause my fury to rest.* Note, Those who live and die impenitent will perish for ever unpitied; there is a day coming when *the Lord will not spare.*

3. Punishments shall be public and open: *I will execute these judgments in the sight of the nations* (v. 8); the judgments themselves shall be so remarkable that all the nations far and near shall take notice of them; they shall be all the talk of that part of the world, and the more for the conspicuousness of the place and people on which they are inflicted. Note, Public sins, as they call for public reproofs *(those that sin rebuke before all),* so, if those prevail not, they call for public judgments. *He strikes them as wicked men in the open sight of others* (Job xxxiv. 26), that he may maintain and vindicate the honour of his government, for (as Grotius descants upon it here) *why should he suffer it to be said, See what wicked lives those lead*

who *profess to be the worshippers of the only true God!* And, as the publicity of the judgments will redound to the honour of God, so it will serve, (1.) To aggravate the punishment, and to make it lie the more heavily. Jerusalem, being made *waste,* becomes *a reproach among the nations in the sight of all that pass by, v.* 14. The more conspicuous and the more peculiar any have been in the day of their prosperity the greater disgrace attends their fall; and that was Jerusalem's case. The more Jerusalem had been *a praise in the earth* the more it is now *a reproach and a taunt, v.* 15. This she was warned of as much as any thing when her glory commenced (1 Kings ix. 8), and this was lamented as much as any thing when it was laid in the dust, Lam. ii. 15. (2.) To teach the nations to fear before the God of Israel, when they see what a jealous God he is, and how severely he punishes sin even in those that are nearest to him. *It shall be an instruction to the nations, v.* 15. Jerusalem should have taught her neighbours the fear of God by her piety and virtue, but, she not doing that, God will teach it to them by her ruin; for they have reason to say, *If this be done in the green tree, what shall be done in the dry?* If *judgment begin at the house of God,* where will it end? If those be thus punished who only had some idolaters among them, what will become of us who are all idolaters? Note, The destruction of some is designed for the instruction of others. Malefactors are publicly punished *in terrorem—that others may take warning.*

4. These punishments, in the kind of them, shall be very severe and grievous. (1.) They shall be such as have no precedent or parallel. Their sins being more provoking than those of others, the judgments executed upon them should be uncommon (v. 9): "*I will do in thee that which I have not done* in thee before, though thou hast long since deserved it; nay, that which I have not done in any other city.*" This punishment of Jerusalem is said to be *greater than that of Sodom* (Lam. iv. 6). which was more grievous than all that went before it; nay, it is such as "*I will not do any more the like,* all the circumstances taken in, to any other city, till the like come to be done again to this city, in its final overthrow by the Romans." This is a rhetorical expression of the most grievous judgments, like that character of Hezekiah, that there was *none like him, before or after him.* (2.) They shall be such as will force them to break the strongest bonds of natural affection to one another, which will be a just punishment of them for their wilfully breaking the bonds of their duty to God (v. 10): *The fathers shall eat the sons, and the sons shall eat the fathers,* through the extremity of the famine, or shall be compelled to do it by their barbarous conquerors. (3.) There shall be a compli-

cation of judgments, any one of them terrible enough, and desolating; but what then would they be when they came all together and in perfection? Some shall be taken away by the plague (*v.* 12); the *pestilence shall pass through thee* (*v.* 17), sweeping all before it, as the destroying angel; others *shall be consumed with famine,* shall gradually waste away as men in a consumption (*v.* 12); this is again insisted on (*v.* 16): *I will send upon them the evil arrows of famine;* hunger shall make them pine, and shall pierce them to the heart, as if arrows, *evil arrows,* poisoned darts, were shot into them. God has many arrows, *evil arrows,* in his quiver; when some are discharged, he has still more in reserve. *I will increase the famine upon you.* A famine in a bereaved country may *decrease* as fruits spring forth; but a famine in a besieged city will *increase* of course; yet God speaks of it as his act: " *I will increase it, and will break your staff of bread,* will take away the necessary supports of life, will disappoint you of all that which you depend upon, so that there is no remedy, but you must fall to the ground." Life is frail, is weak, is burdened, so that, if it have not daily bread for its staff to lean upon, it cannot but sink, and is soon gone if that staff be broken. Others *shall fall by the sword round about* Jerusalem, when they sally out upon the besiegers; it is a *sword* which God *will bring, v.* 17. The sword of the Lord, that used to be drawn for Jerusalem's defence, is now drawn for its destruction. Others are devoured by *evil beasts,* which will make a prey of those that fly for shelter to the deserts and mountains. They shall meet their ruin where they expected refuge, for there is no escaping the judgments of God, *v.* 17. And, *lastly,* those who escape shall be *scattered into* all parts of the world, *into all the winds* (so it is expressed, *v.* 10, 12), intimating that they should not only be dispersed, but hurried, and tossed, and driven to and fro, as *chaff before the wind.* Nay, and Cain's curse (to be fugitives and vagabonds) is not the worst of it neither; their restless life shall be cut off by a bloody death : " *I will draw out a sword after them,* which shall follow them wherever they go. *Evil pursues sinners;* and the curse shall come upon them and overtake them.

5. These punishments will prove their ruin by degrees. They shall be *diminished* (*v.* 11); their strength and glory shall grow less and less. They shall be *bereaved* (*v.* 17), emptied of all that which was their joy and confidence. God sends these judgments on purpose to destroy them, *v.* 16. The arrows are not sent (as those which Jonathan shot) for their direction, but *for their destruction;* for God will *accomplish his fury upon them* (*v.* 13); the day of God's patience is over, and the ruin is remediless. Though this prophecy was to have its accomplish-

ment now quickly, in the destruction of Jerusalem by the Chaldeans, yet the executioners not being named here, but the criminal only *(this is Jerusalem),* we may well suppose that it looks further, to the final destruction of that great city by the Romans when God made a full end of the Jewish nation, and *caused his fury to rest upon them.*

6. All this is ratified by the divine authority and veracity : *I the Lord have spoken it, v.* 15 and again *v.* 17. The sentence is passed by him that is Judge of heaven and earth, whose *judgment is according to truth,* and the judgments of whose hand are according to the judgments of his mouth. He has spoken it who can do it, for with him nothing is impossible. He has spoken it who will do it, for *he is not a man that he should lie.* He has spoken it whom we are bound to hear and heed, whose *ipse dixit*—*word* commands the most serious attention and submissive assent: *And they shall know that I the Lord have spoken it, v.* 13. There were those who thought it was only the prophet that spoke it in his delirium ; but God will make them know, by the accomplishment of it, that he has spoken it in his zeal. Note, Sooner or later, God's word will prove itself.

CHAP. VI.

In this chapter we have, I. A threatening of the destruction of Israel for their idolatry, and the destruction of their idols with them, ver. 1—7. II. A promise of the gracious return of a remnant of them to God, by true repentance and reformation, ver. 8—10. III. Directions given to the prophet and others, the Lord's servants, to lament both the iniquities and the calamities of Israel, ver. 11—14

AND the word of the LORD came unto me, saying, 2 Son of man, set thy face toward the mountains of Israel, and prophesy against them, 3 And say, Ye mountains of Israel, hear the word of the Lord GOD; Thus saith the Lord GOD to the mountains, and to the hills, to the rivers, and to the valleys; Behold, I, *even* I, will bring a sword upon you, and I will destroy your high places. 4 And your altars shall be desolate, and your images shall be broken : and I will cast down your slain *men* before your idols. 5 And I will lay the dead carcases of the children of Israel before their idols; and I will scatter your bones round about your altars. 6 In all your dwelling-places the cities shall be laid waste, and the high places shall be desolate; that your altars may be laid waste and made desolate, and your idols may be broken and cease, and your images may be cut down, and your works may be abolished. 7 And the slain shall fall in the midst of you, and ye shall know that I *am* the LORD.

Here, I. The prophecy is directed to *the mountains of Israel* (v. 1, 2); the prophet must *set his face towards* them. If he could see so far off as the land of Israel, *the mountains* of that land would be first and furthest seen ; towards them therefore he must look, and look boldly and stedfastly, as the judge looks at the prisoner, and directs his speech to him, when he passes sentence upon him. Though *the mountains of Israel* be ever so high and ever so strong, he must *set his face against* them, as having judgments to denounce that should shake their foundation. *The mountains of Israel* had been *holy mountains*, but now that they had polluted them with their high places God set his face against them and therefore the prophet must. Israel is here put, not, as sometimes, for the ten tribes, but for the whole land. *The mountains* are called upon to *hear the word of the Lord*, to shame the inhabitants that would not hear. The prophets might as soon gain attention from the *mountains* as from that *rebellious and gainsaying people*, to whom they all day long *stretched out their hands in vain. Hear, O mountains ! the Lord's controversy* (Mic. vi. 1, 2), for God's cause will have a hearing, whether we hear it or no. But from *the mountains the word of the Lord* echoes *to the hills, to the rivers, and to the valleys ;* for to them also the Lord God speaks, intimating that the whole land is concerned in what is now to be delivered and shall be witnesses against this people that they had fair warning given them of the judgments coming, but they would not take it ; nay, they contradicted the message and persecuted the messengers, so that God's prophets might more safely and comfortably speak to *the hills and mountains* than to them.

II. That which is threatened in this prophecy is the utter destruction of the idols and the idolaters, and both by the sword of war. God himself is commander-in-chief of this expedition against *the mountains of Israel*. It is he that says, *Behold, I, even I, will bring a sword upon you* (v. 3) ; the sword of the Chaldeans is at God's command, goes where he sends it, comes where he brings it, and lights as he directs it. In the desolations of that war,

1. The idols and all their appurtenances should be destroyed. The *high places*, which were on the tops of mountains (v. 3), shall be levelled *and made desolate* (v. 6) ; they shall not be beautified, shall not be frequented as they had been. The *altars*, on which they offered sacrifice and burnt incense to strange gods, *shall be broken* to pieces and *laid waste ;* the *images* and *idols* shall be defaced, *shall be broken and cease*, and be cut down, and all the fine costly works about them shall be abolished, v. 4, 6. Observe here, (1.) That war makes woeful de-

solations, which those persons, places, and things that were esteemed most sacred cannot escape ; for *the sword devours one as well as another.* (2.) That God sometimes ruins idolatries even by the hands of idolaters, for such the Chaldeans themselves were ; but, as if the deity were a local thing, the greatest admirers of the gods of their own country were the greatest despisers of the gods of other countries. (3.) It is just with God to make that a desolation which we make an idol of ; for he is a jealous God and will not bear a rival. (4.) If men do not, as they ought, destroy idolatry, God will, first or last, find out a way to do it. When Josiah had destroyed the high places, altars, and images, with the sword of justice, they set them up again ; but God will now destroy them with the sword of war, and let us see who dares re-establish them.

2. The worshippers of idols and all their adherents should be destroyed likewise. As *all their high places shall be laid waste*, so shall all *their dwelling-places* too, even *all their cities*, v. 6. Those that profane God's dwelling-place as they had done can expect no other than that he should abandon theirs, ch. v. 11. *If any man defile the temple of God, him will God destroy*, 1 Cor. iii. 17. It is here threatened that *their slain shall fall in the midst of them* (v. 7) ; there shall be abundance slain, even in those places which were thought most safe ; but it is added as a remarkable circumstance that they shall fall *before their idols* (v. 4), that their *dead carcases* should be *laid*, and their *bones scattered, about their altars*, v. 5. (1.) Thus their idols should be polluted, and those places profaned by the dead bodies which they had had in veneration. If they will not *defile the covering of their graven images*, God will, Isa. xxx. 22. The throwing of the carcases among them, as upon the dunghill, intimates that they were but dunghill-deities. (2.) Thus it was intimated that they were but dead things, unfit to be rivals with *the living God ;* for the carcases of dead men, that, like them, *have eyes and see not, ears and hear not*, were the fittest company for them. (3.) Thus the idols were upbraided with their inability to help their worshippers, and idolaters were upbraided with the folly of trusting in them ; for, it should seem, they fell by the sword of the enemy when they were actually before their idols imploring their aid and putting themselves under their protection. Sennacherib was slain by his sons when he was *worshipping in the house of his god.* (4.) The sin might be read in this circumstance of the punishment ; the *slain men* are *cast before the idols*, to show that *therefore* they are slain, because they worshipped those idols ; see Jer. viii. 1, 2. Let the survivors observe it, and take warning not to worship images ; let them see it, and know that *God is the Lord*, that *the Lord he is God* and he alone.

8 Yet will I leave a remnant, that ye may have *some* that shall escape the sword among the nations, when ye shall be scattered through the countries. 9 And they that escape of you shall remember me among the nations whither they shall be carried captives, because I am broken with their whorish heart, which hath departed from me, and with their eyes, which go a whoring after their idols : and they shall loathe themselves for the evils which they have committed in all their abominations. 10 And they shall know that I *am* the LORD, *and that* I have not said in vain that I would do this evil unto them.

Judgment had hitherto triumphed, but in these verses mercy rejoices against judgment. A sad end is made of this provoking people, but not a full end. The ruin seems to be universal, and *yet will I leave a remnant*, a little remnant, distinguished from the body of the people, a few of many, such as are left when the rest perish ; and it is God that leaves them. This intimates that they deserved to be cut off with the rest, and would have been cut off if God had not left them. See Isa. i. 9. And it is God who by his grace works that in them which he has an eye to in sparing them. Now,

I. It is a preserved remnant, saved from the ruin which the body of the nation is involved in (*v.* 8): *That you may have some who shall escape the sword.* God said (*ch.* v. 12) that he would *draw a sword after those* who were *scattered*, that destruction should pursue them in their dispersions ; but here is *mercy remembered in the midst of* that *wrath*, and a promise that some of *the Jews of the dispersion*, as they were afterwards called, should *escape the sword.* None of those who were to *fall by the sword about* Jerusalem *shall escape ;* for they trust to Jerusalem's walls for security, and shall be made ashamed of that vain confidence. But some of them *shall escape the sword among the nations*, where, being deprived of all other stays, they stay themselves upon God only. They are said to *have* those who shall *escape ;* for they shall be the seed of another generation, out of which Jerusalem shall flourish again.

II. It is a penitent remnant (*v.* 9) : *Those who escape of you shall remember me.* Note, To those whom God designs for life he will give *repentance unto life.* They are reprieved, and *escape the sword*, that they may have time to return to God. Note, God's patience both leaves room for repentance and is an encouragement to sinners to repent. Where God designs grace to repent he allows space to repent ; yet many who have the space want the grace, many who

escape the sword do not forsake the sin, as it is promised that these shall do. This remnant, here marked for salvation, is a type of the remnant reserved out of the body of mankind to be monuments of mercy, who are made safe in the same way that these were, by being brought to repentance. Now observe here,

1. The occasion of their repentance, and that is a mixture of judgment and mercy— judgment, that they were *carried captives*, but mercy, that they *escaped the sword* in the land of their captivity. They were driven out of their own land, but not out of the land of the living, *not chased out of the world*, as others were and they deserved to be. Note, The consideration of the just rebukes of Providence we are under, and yet of the mercy mixed with them, should engage us to repent, that we may answer God's end in both. And true repentance shall be accepted of God, though we are brought to it by our troubles ; nay, sanctified afflictions often prove means of conversion, as to Manasseh.

2. The root and principle of their repentance : *They shall remember me among the nations.* Those who *forgot God* in the land of their peace and prosperity, who *waxed fat and kicked*, were brought to remember him in the land of their captivity. The prodigal son never bethought himself of his father's house till he was ready to perish for hunger in the far country. Their remembering God was the first step they took in returning to him. Note, Then there begins to be some hopes of sinners when they begin to think of him whom they have sinned against, and to enquire, *Where is God my Maker?* Sin takes rise in forgetting God, Jer. iii. 21. Repentance takes rise from the remembrance of him and of our obligations to him. God says, *They shall remember me*, that is, " I will give them grace to do so ;" for otherwise they would for ever forget him. That grace shall find them out wherever they are, and by bringing God to their mind shall bring them to their right mind. The prodigal, when he remembered his father, remembered how he had *sinned against Heaven and before* him ; so do these penitents. (1.) They remember the base affront they had put upon God by their idolatries, and this is that which an ingenuous repentance fastens upon and most sadly laments. They had departed from God to idols, and given that honour to pretended deities, the creatures of men's fancies and the work of men's hands, which they should have given to the God of Israel. They *departed from* God, from his word, which they should have made their rule, from his work, which they should have made their business. *Their hearts departed from* him. The heart, which he requires and insists upon, and without which *bodily exercise profits nothing*, the *heart*, which should be set upon him, and

carried out towards him, when that *departs from* him, is as the treacherous elopement of a wife from her husband or the rebellious revolt of a subject from his sovereign. *Their eyes* also *go after their idols;* they doted on them, and had great expectations from them. Their hearts followed their eyes in the choice of their gods (they must have gods that they could see), and then their eyes followed their hearts in the adoration of them. Now the malignity of this sin is that it is spiritual whoredom; it is a *whorish heart* that *departs from* God; and they are *eyes* that *go a whoring after their idols.* Note, Idolatry is spiritual whoredom; it is the breach of a marriage-covenant with God; it is the setting of the affections upon that which is a rival with him, and the indulgence of a base lust, which deceives and defiles the soul, and is a great wrong to God in his honour, (2.) They remember what a grief this was to him and how he resented it. They shall remember *that I am broken with their whorish heart and their eyes* that are full of this spiritual adultery, not only angry at it, but grieved, as a husband is at the lewdness of a wife whom he dearly loved, grieved to such a degree that he is broken with it; it breaks his heart to think that he should be so disingenuously dealt with; he is broken as an aged father is with the undutiful behaviour of a rebellious and disobedient son, which sinks his spirits and makes him to stoop. *Forty years long was I grieved with this generation,* Ps. xcv. 10. *God's measures were broken* (so some); a stop was put to the current of his favours towards them, and he was even compelled to punish them. This they shall remember in the day of their repentance, and it shall affect and humble them more than any thing, not so much that their peace was broken, and their country broken, as *that God was broken* by their sin. Thus *they shall look on him whom they have pierced and shall mourn,* Zech. xii. 10. Note, Nothing grieves a true penitent so much as to think that his sin has been a grief to God and to the Spirit of his grace.

3. The product and evidence of their repentance : *They shall loathe themselves for the evils which they have committed in all their abominations.* Thus God will give them grace to qualify them for pardon and deliverance. Though he had been *broken by their whorish heart,* yet he would not quite cast them off. See Isa. lvii. 17, 18 ; Hos. ii. 13, 14. His goodness takes occasion from their badness to appear the more illustrious. Note, (1.) True penitents see sin to be an abominable thing, that *abominable thing which the Lord hates* and which makes sinners, and even their services, odious to him, Jer. xliv. 4 ; Isa. i. 11. It defiles the sinner's own conscience, and makes him, unless he be past feeling, an abomination to himself. An idol is particularly called *an abomination,* Isa. xliv. 19. Those gratifica-

tions which the hearts of sinners were set upon as delectable things the hearts of penitents are turned against as detestable things. (2.) There are many *evils committed in these abominations,* many included in them, attendant on them, and flowing from them, many transgressions in one sin, Lev. xvi. 21. In their idolatries they were sometimes guilty of whoredom (as in the worship of Peor), sometimes of murder (as in the worship of Moloch) ; these were *evils committed in their abominations.* Or it denotes the great malignity there is in sin; it is an abomination that has abundance of evil in it. (3.) Those that truly loathe sin cannot but loathe themselves because of sin ; self-loathing is evermore the companion of true repentance. Penitents quarrel with themselves, and can never be reconciled to themselves till they have some ground to hope that God is reconciled to them ; nay, *then* they shall lie down in their shame, when he is pacified towards them, ch. xvi. 63.

4. The glory that will redound to God by their repentance (v. 10) : " *They shall know that I am the Lord ;* they shall be convinced of it by experience, and shall be ready to own it, *and that I have not said in vain that I would do this evil unto them,* finding that what I have said is made good, and made to work for good, and to answer a good intention, and that it was not without just provocation that they were thus threatened and thus punished." Note, (1.) One way or other God will make sinners to know and own that he is the Lord, either by their repentance or by their ruin. (2.) All true penitents are brought to acknowledge both the equity and the efficacy of the word of God, particularly the threatenings of the word, and to justify God in them and in the accomplishment of them.

11 Thus saith the Lord GOD; Smite with thine hand, and stamp with thy foot, and say, Alas for all the evil abominations of the house of Israel! for they shall fall by the sword, by the famine, and by the pestilence. 12 He that is far off shall die of the pestilence; and he that is near shall fall by the sword; and he that remaineth and is besieged shall die by the famine: thus will I accomplish my fury upon them. 13 Then shall ye know that I *am* the LORD, when their slain *men* shall be among their idols round about their altars, upon every high hill, in all the tops of the mountains, and under every green tree, and under every thick oak, the place where they did offer sweet savour to all their idols.

14 So will I stretch out my hand upon them, and make the land desolate, yea, more desolate than the wilderness toward Diblath, in all their habitations: and they shall know that I *am* the LORD.

The same threatenings which we had before in the foregoing chapter, and in the former part of this, are here repeated, with a direction to the prophet to lament them, that those he prophesied to might be the more affected with the foresight of them. I. He must by his gestures in preaching express the deep sense he had both of the iniquities and of the calamities of the house of Israel (*v.* 11): *Smite with thy hand and stamp with thy foot.* Thus he must make it to appear that he was in earnest in what he said to them, that he firmly believed it and laid it to heart. Thus he must signify the just displeasure he had conceived at their sins, and the just dread he was under of the judgments coming upon them. Some would reject this use of these gestures, and call them antic and ridiculous; but God bids him use them because they might help to enforce the word upon some and give it the setting on; and those that know the worth of souls will be content to be laughed at by the wits, so they may but edify the weak. Two things the prophet must thus lament: —1. National sins. *Alas! for all the evil abominations of the house of Israel.* Note, The sins of sinners are the sorrows of God's faithful servants, especially the *evil abominations of the house of Israel*, whose sins are more abominable and have more evil in them than the sins of others. Alas! *What will be in the end hereof?* 2. National judgments. To punish them for these abominations *they shall fall by the sword, by the famine, and by the pestilence.* Note, It is our duty to be affected not only with our own sins and sufferings, but with the sins and sufferings of others; and to look with compassion upon the miseries that wicked people bring upon themselves; as Christ *beheld Jerusalem and wept over it.* II. He must inculcate what he had said before concerning the destruction that was coming upon them. 1. They shall be run down and ruined by a variety of judgments which shall find them out and follow them wherever they are (*v.* 12): *He that is far off,* and thinks himself out of danger, because out of the reach of the Chaldeans' arrows, shall find himself not out of the reach of God's arrows, which fly day and night (Ps. xci. 5): *He shall die of the pestilence.* He *that is near* a place of strength, which he hopes will be to him a place of safety, *shall fall by the sword,* before he can retreat. He *that* is so cautious as not to venture out, but *remains* in the city, *shall* there *die by the famine,* the saddest death of all. *Thus will*

784

God *accomplish his fury,* that is, do all that against them which he had purposed to do. 2. They shall read their sin in their punishment; for *their slain men shall be among their idols, round about their altars,* as was threatened before, *v.* 5—7. There, where they had prostrated themselves in honour of their idols, God will lay them dead, to their own reproach and the reproach of their idols. They lived among them and shall die among them. They had offered sweet odours to their idols, but there shall their dead carcases send forth an offensive smell, as it were to atone for that misplaced incense. 3. The country shall be all laid waste, as, before, *the cities* (*v.* 6): *I will make the land desolate.* That fruitful, pleasant, populous country, that has been as the garden of the Lord, the glory of all lands, shall be *desolate, more desolate than the wilderness towards Diblath,* *v.* 14. It is called Diblathaim (Num. xxxiii. 46; Jer. xlviii. 22), that *great and terrible wilderness* which is described Deut. viii. 15, wherein were *fiery serpents and scorpions.* The land of Canaan is at this day one of the most barren desolate countries in the world. City and country are thus depopulated, *that the altars may be laid waste and made desolate, v.* 6. Rather than their idolatrous altars shall be left standing, both town and country shall be laid in ruins. Sin is a desolating thing; therefore *stand in awe and sin not.*

CHAP. VII.

In this chapter the approaching ruin of the land of Israel is most particularly foretold in affecting expressions often repeated, that if possible they might be awakened to repentance to prevent it. The prophet must tell them, I. That it will be a final ruin, a complete utter destruction, which would make an end of them, a miserable end, ver. 1—6. II. That it is an approaching ruin, just at the door, ver. 7—10. III. That it is an unavoidable ruin, because they had by sin brought it upon themselves, ver. 10—15. IV. That their strength and wealth should be no fence against it, ver. 16—19. V. That the temple, which they trusted in, should itself be ruined, ver. 20—22. VI. That it should be a universal ruin, the sin that brought it having been universal, ver. 23—27.

MOREOVER the word of the LORD came unto me, saying, 2 Also, thou son of man, thus saith the Lord GOD unto the land of Israel; An end, the end is come upon the four corners of the land. 3 Now *is* the end *come* upon thee, and I will send mine anger upon thee, and will judge thee according to thy ways, and will recompense upon thee all thine abominations. 4 And mine eye shall not spare thee, neither will I have pity: but I will recompense thy ways upon thee, and thine abominations shall be in the midst of thee: and ye shall know that I *am* the LORD. 5 Thus saith the Lord GOD; An evil, an only evil, behold, is come. 6 An end is come, the end is come: it watcheth for thee; behold, it is come. 7 The morning is come unto thee, O thou that dwellest in the land: the time is come, the day of trouble *is* near, and not the sounding again of the mountains. 8 Now will I shortly pour out my fury upon thee, and accomplish mine anger upon thee: and I will judge thee according to thy ways, and will recompense thee for all thine abominations. 9 And mine eye shall not spare, neither will I have pity: I will recompense thee according to thy ways and thine abominations *that* are in the midst of thee; and ye shall know that I *am* the LORD that smiteth. 10 Behold the day, behold it is come: the morning is gone forth; the rod hath blossomed, pride hath budded. 11 Violence is risen up into a rod of wickedness: none of them *shall remain*, nor of their multitude, nor of any of their's: neither *shall there be* wailing for them. 12 The time is come, the day draweth near: let not the buyer rejoice, nor the seller mourn: for wrath *is* upon all the multitude thereof. 13 For the seller shall not return to that which is sold, although they were yet alive: for the vision *is* touching the whole multitude thereof, *which* shall not return; neither shall any strengthen himself in the iniquity of his life. 14 They have blown the trumpet, even to make all ready; but none goeth to the battle: for my wrath *is* upon all the multitude thereof. 15 The sword *is* without, and the pestilence and the famine within: he that *is* in the field shall die with the sword; and he that *is* in the city, famine and pestilence shall devour him.

We have here fair warning given of the destruction of the land of Israel, which was now hastening on apace. God, by the prophet, not only sends notice of it, but will have it inculcated in the same expressions, to show that the thing is certain, that it is near, that the prophet is himself affected with it and desires they should be so too, but finds them deaf, and stupid, and unaffected. When the town is on fire men do not seek for fine words and quaint expressions in which to give an account of it, but cry about the streets, with a loud and lamentable voice, "Fire! fire!" So the prophet here proclaims, *An end! an end! it has come, it has*

come; *behold, it has come. He that hath ears to hear let him hear.*

I. *An end has come, the end has come* (v. 2), and again (v. 3, 6), *Now has the end come upon thee*—the end which all their wickedness had a tendency to, and which God had often told them it would come to at last, when by his prophets he had asked them, *What will you do in the end hereof?*—the end which all the foregoing judgments had been working towards, as means to bring it about (their ruin shall now be completed)—or *the end*, that is, the period of their state, the final destruction of their nation, as the deluge was *the end of all flesh*, Gen. vi. 13. They had flattered themselves with hopes that they should shortly *see an end* of their troubles. "Yea," says God, "*An end has come*, but a miserable one, not *the expected end*" (which is promised to the pious remnant among them, Jer. xxix. 11); "*it is the end, that end* which you have been so often warned of, *that last end* which Moses wished you to *consider* (Deut. xxxii. 29), and which, because *Jerusalem remembered not, therefore she came down wonderfully*," Lam. i. 9. This end was long in coming, but *now it has come*. Though the ruin of sinners comes slowly, it comes surely. "*It has come;* it watches for thee, ready to receive thee." This perhaps looks further, to the last destruction of that nation by the Romans, which that by the Chaldeans was an earnest of; and still further to the final destruction of the world of the ungodly. *The end of all things is at hand;* and Jerusalem's last end was a type of *the end of the world*, Matt. xxiv. 3. Oh that we could all see that end of time and days very near, and the end of our own time and days much nearer, that we may secure a happy lot *at the end of the days!* Dan. xii. 13. This *end comes upon the four corners of the land*. The ruin, as it shall be final, so it shall be total; no part of the land shall escape; no, not that which lies most remote. Such will the destruction of the world be; all these things shall be dissolved. Such will the destruction of sinners be; none can avoid it. *Oh that the wickedness of the wicked* might *come to an end*, before it bring them to *an end!*

II. *An evil, an only evil, behold, has come,* v. 5. Sin is *an evil, an only evil, an evil* that has no good in it; it is the worst of evils. But this is spoken of the evil of trouble; it is *an evil*, one *evil*, and that one shall suffice to affect and complete the ruin of the nation; there needs no more to do its business; this one shall *make an utter end*, affliction needs not *rise up a second time*, Nah. i. 9. It is *an evil* without precedent or parallel, *an evil* that stands alone; you cannot produce such another instance. It is to the impenitent *an evil, an only evil;* it hardens their hearts and irritates their corruptions, whereas there were those to whom it was sanctified by the grace of God and made a means of **much** good; they were *sent into Babylon for their good*, Jer. xxiv. 5. The wicked have *the dregs of that cup* to drink which to the righteous is full of *mixtures of mercy*, Ps. lxxv. 8. The same affliction is to us either a half *evil* or *an only evil* according as we conduct ourselves under it and make use of it. But when *an end, the end, has come* upon the wicked world, then *an evil, an only evil*, comes upon it, and not till then. The sorest of temporal judgments have their allays, but the torments of the damned are *an evil, an only evil*.

III. *The time has come*, the set time, for the inflicting of this *only evil* and the making of this *full end;* for to all God's purposes *there is a time*, a proper time, and that prefixed, in which the purpose shall have its accomplishment; particularly the time of reckoning with wicked people, and rendering to them according to their deserts, is fixed, *the day of the revelation of the righteous judgment of God;* and *he sees*, whether we see it or no, that *his day is coming*. This they are here told of again and again (v. 10): *Behold, the day* that has lingered so long *has come* at last, *behold, it has come. The time has come, the day draws near, the day of trouble is near, v.* 7, 12. Though threatened judgments may be long deferred, yet they shall not be dropped; the time for executing them will come. Though God's patience may put them off, nothing but man's sincere repentance and reformation will put them by. *The morning has come unto thee* (v. 7), and again (v. 10), *The morning has gone forth;* the day of trouble dawns, the day of destruction is already begun. *The morning* discovers that which was hidden; they thought their secret sins would never come to light, but now they will be brought to light. They used to try and execute malefactors in the morning, and such a morning of judgment and execution is now coming upon them, *a day of trouble* to sinners, *the year of their visitation*. See how stupid these people were, that, though the day of their destruction was already begun, yet they were not aware of it, but must be thus told of it again and again. *The day of trouble*, real trouble, *is near, and not the sounding again of the mountains*, that is, not a mere echo or report of troubles, as they were willing to think it was, nothing but a groundless surmise; as if the *men that came against them* were but *the shadow of the mountains* (as Zebul suggested to Gaal, Judg. ix. 36) and the intelligence they received were but *an empty sound*, reverberated from the mountains. No; the trouble is not a fancy, and so you will soon find.

IV. All this comes from God's wrath, not allayed, as sometimes it has been, with mixtures of mercy. This is the fountain from which all these calamities flow; and this is *the wormwood and the gall* in *the affliction and the misery*, which make it bitter indeed (v. 3): *I will send my anger upon thee*. Observe,

786

God is Lord of his anger; it does not break out but when he pleases, nor fasten upon any but as he directs it and gives it commission. The expression rises higher (v. 8): *Now will I shortly pour out my fury upon thee* in full vials, *and accomplish my anger*, all the purposes and all the products of it, *upon thee*. This wrath does not single out here and there one to be made examples, but it *is upon all the multitude thereof* (v. 12, 14); the whole body of the nation has become a *vessel of wrath, fitted for destruction*. God does sometimes *in wrath remember mercy*, but now he says, *My eye shall not spare thee, neither will I have pity, v.* 4 and again *v.* 9. Those shall *have judgment without mercy* who made light of mercy when it was offered them.

V. All this is the just punishment of their sins, and it is what they have by their own folly brought upon themselves. This is much insisted on here, that they might be brought to justify God in all he had brought upon them. God never sends his anger but in wisdom and justice; and therefore it follows, "*I will judge thee according to thy ways, v.* 3. I will examine what thy ways have been, compare them with the law, and then deal with thee according to the merit of them, and *recompense* them to *thee," v.*4. Note, In the heaviest judgments God inflicts upon sinners he does but *recompense their own ways upon them;* they are beaten with their own rod. And, when God comes to reckon with a sinful people, he will bring every provocation to account: "*I will recompense upon thee all thy abominations* (v. 3); and now *thy iniquity shall be found to be hateful* (Ps. xxxvi. 2) *and thy abominations shall be in the midst of thee* (v. 4); that is, the secret wickedness shall now be brought to light, and that shall appear to have been in the midst of thee which before was not suspected; and thy sin shall now become an *abomination* to thyself. So the abomination of iniquity will be when it comes to be an *abomination of desolation*, Matt. xxiv. 15. Or, *Thy abominations* (that is, the punishments of them) *shall be in the midst of thee;* they shall *reach to thy heart*. See Jer. iv. 18. Or therefore God *will not spare, nor have pity*, because, even when he is *recompensing their ways* upon them, yet *in their distress they trespass yet more;* their *abominations* are still *in the midst of them*, indulged and harboured in their hearts. It is repeated again (v. 8, 9), *I will judge thee, I will recompense thee*. Two sins are particularly specified as provoking God to bring these judgments upon them—pride and oppression. 1. God will humble them by his judgments, for they have magnified themselves. *The rod of af-fliction has blossomed*, but it was *pride* that *budded, v.* 10. What buds in sin will blossom in some judgment or other. The pride of Judah and Jerusalem appeared among all orders and degrees of men, as buds upon the tree in spring. 2. Their enemies shall deal hardly with them, for they have dealt hardly with one another (v. 11): *Violence has risen up into a rod of wickedness;* that is, their injuriousness to one another is protected and patronised by the power of the magistrate. The rod of government had become a *rod of wickedness,* to such a degree of impudence was *violence risen up. I saw the place of judgment, that wickedness was there,* Eccl. iii. 16; Isa. v. 7. Whatever are the fruits of God's judgments, it is certain that our sin is the root of them.

VI. There is no escape from these judgments nor fence against them, for they shall be universal and shall bear down all before them, without remedy. 1. Death in its various shapes shall ride triumphantly, both in town and in country, both within the city and without it, v. 15. Men shall be safe nowhere; for *he that is in the field shall die by the sword* (every field shall be to them a field of battle) *and he that is in the city,* though it be a holy city, yet it shall not be his protection, but *famine and pestilence shall devour him.* Sin had abounded both in city and country, *Iliacos intra muros peccator et extra—Trojans and Greeks offend alike;* and therefore among both desolations are made. 2. None of those that are marked for death shall escape: There *shall none of them remain.* None of those proud oppressors that did violence to their poor neighbours with *the rod of wickedness,* none of them shall be left, but they shall be all swept away by the desolation that is coming (v. 11): *None of their multitude,* that is, of the rabble, whom they set on to do mischief, and to countenance them in doing it, to cry, " Crucify, crucify," when they were resolved on the destruction of any, *none of them shall remain, nor any of theirs;* their families shall all be destroyed, and neither root nor branch left them. This multitude, this mob, divine vengeance will in a particular manner fasten upon; *for wrath is upon all the multitude thereof* (v. 12, 14) and *the vision was touching the whole multitude thereof* (v. 13), the bulk of the common people. The judgments coming shall carry them away by wholesale, and they shall neither secure themselves nor their masters whose creatures and tools they were. God's judgments, when they come with commission, cannot be overpowered by multitudes. *Though hand join in hand, yet shall not the wicked go unpunished.* 3. Those that fall shall not be lamented (v. 11): *There shall be no wailing for them,* for there shall be none left to bewail them, but such as are hastening apace after them. And the times shall be so bad that men shall rather congratulate than lament the death of their friends, as reckoning those happy that are taken away from seeing these desolations and sharing in them, Jer. xvi. 4, 5. 4. They shall not be able to make any resistance. The decree has gone forth, and *the vision* concerning them *shall not return,* v. 13. God will not

recal it, and they cannot defeat it; and therefore it *shall not return re infectâ—without having accomplished any thing,* but shall *accomplish that for which he sends it.* God's word will take place, and then, (1.) Particular persons cannot make their part good against God: No man *shall strengthen himself in the iniquity of his life;* it will be to no purpose for sinners to set God and his judgments at defiance as they used to do. *None ever hardened his heart against God and prospered.* Those that strengthen themselves in their wickedness will be found not only to weaken, but to ruin, themselves, Ps. lii. 7. (2.) *The multitude* cannot resist the torrent of these judgments, nor make head against them (v 14): *They have blown the trumpet,* to call their soldiers together, and to animate and encourage those whom they have got together, and thus they think *to make all ready;* but all in vain; none enlist themselves, or those that do have not courage to face the enemy. Note, If God be against us, none can be for us to do us any service. 5. They shall have no hope of the return of their prosperity, with which to support themselves in their adversity; they shall have given up all for gone; and therefore, " *Let not the buyer rejoice* that he is increasing his estate and has become a purchaser; nor let *the seller mourn* that he is lessening his estate and has become a bankrupt," v. 12. See the vanity of the things of this world, and how worthless they are—that in a time of trouble, when we have most need of them, we may perhaps make least account of them. Those that have sold are the more easy, having the less to lose, and those that have bought have but increased their own cares and fears. Because *the fashion of this world passes away,* let *those that buy be as though they possessed not,* because they know not how soon they may be dispossessed, 1 Cor. vii. 29—31. It is added (v. 13), " *The seller shall not return,* at the year of jubilee, *to that which is sold,* according to the law, though he should escape the sword and pestilence, and live till that year comes; for no inheritances shall be enjoyed here till the seventy years be accomplished, and then men shall return to their possessions, shall claim and have their own again." In the belief of this, Jeremiah, about this time, *bought his uncle's field,* yet, according to the charge, the buyer did not rejoice, but complain, Jer. xxxii. 25. 6. God will be glorified in all: " *You shall know that I am the Lord* (v. 4), *that I am the Lord that smiteth,* v. 9. You look at second causes, and think it is Nebuchadnezzar that smites you, but you shall be made to know he is but the staff: it is the hand of the Lord that smiteth you, and who knows the weight of his hand?" Those who would not know it was the *Lord that did them good* shall be made to know it is *the Lord that smiteth* them; for, one way or other, he will be owned.

16 But they that escape of them shall escape, and shall be on the mountains like doves of the valleys, all of them mourning, every one for his iniquity. 17 All hands shall be feeble, and all knees shall be weak *as* water. 18 They shall also gird *themselves* with sackcloth, and horror shall cover them; and shame *shall be* upon all faces, and baldness upon all their heads. 19 They shall cast their silver in the streets, and their gold shall be removed: their silver and their gold shall not be able to deliver them in the day of the wrath of the LORD: they shall not satisfy their souls, neither fill their bowels: because it is the stumbling-block of their iniquity. 20 As for the beauty of his ornament, he set it in majesty: but they made the images of their abominations *and* of their detestable things therein: therefore have I set it far from them. 21 And I will give it into the hands of the strangers for a prey, and to the wicked of the earth for a spoil; and they shall pollute it. 22 My face will I turn also from them, and they shall pollute my secret *place:* for the robbers shall enter into it, and defile it.

We have attended the fate of those that are cut off, and are now to attend the flight of those that have an opportunity of escaping the danger; some of them *shall escape (v. 16)*, but what the better? As good die once as, in a miserable life, die a thousand deaths, and escape only like Cain to be *fugitives and vagabonds*, and afraid of being slain by every one they meet; so shall these be.

I. They shall have no comfort or satisfaction in their own minds, but be in continual anguish and terror; for, wherever they go, they carry about with them guilty consciences, which make them a burden to themselves. 1. They shall be always solitary and under prevailing melancholy; they shall not be in the cities, or places of concourse, but all alone *upon the mountains*, not caring for society, but shy of it, as being ashamed of the low circumstances to which they are reduced. 2. They shall be always sorrowful. Those have reason to be so that are under the tokens of God's displeasure; and God can make those so that have been most jovial and have set sorrow at defiance. Those that once thought themselves as the lions of the mountains, so daring were they, now become as the *doves of the valleys*, so timid are they, and so dispirited, ready to

flee when none pursues and to tremble at the shaking of a leaf. They are all of them mourning (not with a *godly sorrow*, but with the *sorrow of the world*, which *works death*), *every one for his iniquity*, that is, for those calamities which they now see their iniquity has brought upon them, not only the iniquity of the land, but their own: they shall then be brought to acknowledge what they have each of them contributed to the national guilt. Note, Sooner or later sin will have sorrow of one kind or other; and those that will not repent of their iniquity may justly be left to pine away in it; those that will not mourn for it as it is an offence to God shall be made to mourn for it as it is a shame and ruin to themselves, to *mourn at the last, when the flesh and the body are consumed, and to say, How have I hated instruction!* Prov. v. 11, 12. 3. They shall be deprived of all their strength of body and mind (*v.* 17): *All hands shall be feeble*, so that they shall not be able to fight, or defend themselves, and *all knees shall be weak as water*, so that they shall neither be able to flee nor to stand their ground; they shall feel a universal colliquation: their knees *shall flow as water*, so that they must fall of course. Note, It is folly for the *strong man to glory in his strength*, for God can soon weaken it. 4. They shall be deprived of all their hopes and shall abandon themselves to despair (*v.* 18); they shall have nothing to hold up their spirits with; their aspects shall show what are their prospects, all dreadful, for they shall *gird themselves with sackcloth*, as having no expectation ever to wear better clothing. *Horror shall cover them*, and *shame*, and *baldness*, all the expressions of a desperate sorrow, Isa. xvii. 11. Note, Those that will not be kept from sin by fear and shame shall by fear and shame be punished for it; such is the confusion that sin will end in.

II. They shall have no benefit from their wealth and riches, but shall be perfectly sick of them, *v.* 19. Those that were reduced to this distress were such as had had abundance of *silver and gold*, money, and plate, and jewels, and other valuable goods, from which they promised themselves a great deal of advantage in times of public trouble. They thought their wealth would be *their strong city*, that with it they could bribe enemies and buy friends, that it would be the ransom of their lives, that they could never want bread as long as they had money, and that *money would answer all things;* but see how it proved. 1. Their wealth had been a great temptation to them in the *day of their prosperity;* they set their affections upon it, and put their confidence in it. By their eager pursuit of it they were drawn into sin, and by their plentiful enjoyment of it they were hardened in sin; and thus it was the stumbling-block of their iniquity; it occasioned their falling into sin and obstructed their return to God. Note, There are many whose wealth is their snare and ruin. The gaining of the world is the losing of their souls; it makes them proud, secure, covetous, oppressive, voluptuous; and that which, if well used, might have been the servant of their piety, being abused, becomes *the stumbling-block of their iniquity.* 2. It was no relief to them now in the day of their adversity; for, (1.) Their *gold and silver* could not protect them from the judgments of God. They *shall not be able to deliver them in the day of the wrath of the Lord;* they shall not serve to atone his justice, or turn away his wrath, nor to screen them from the judgments he is bringing upon them. Note, *Riches profit not in the day of wrath,* Prov. xi. 4. They neither set them so high that God's judgments cannot reach them nor make them so strong that they cannot conquer them. There is a day of wrath coming, when it will appear that men's wealth is utterly unable to deliver them or do them any service. What the better was the rich man for his full barns when his soul was required of him, or that other rich man for his *purple, and scarlet, and sumptuous fare,* when in hell he could not procure a drop of water to *cool his tongue?* Money is no defence against the arrests of death, nor any alleviation to the miseries of the damned. (2.) Their *gold and silver* could not give them any content under their calamities. [1.] They could not fill their bowels; when there was no bread left in the city, none to be had for love or money, their silver and gold could not satisfy their hunger, nor serve to make one meal's meat for them. Note, We could better be without mines of gold than fields of corn; the products of the earth, which may easily be gathered from the surface of it, are much greater blessings to mankind than its treasures, which are with so much difficulty and hazard dug out of its bowels. If God give us daily bread, we have reason to be thankful, and no reason to complain, though silver and gold we have none. [2.] Much less could they satisfy their souls, or yield them any inward comfort. Note, The wealth of this world has not that in it which will answer the desires of the soul, or be any satisfaction to it in a day of distress. *He that loves silver shall not be satisfied with silver,* much less he that loses it. (3.) Their *gold and silver shall be thrown into the streets,* either by the hands of the enemy, who shall have more spoil than they care for or can carry away (silver shall be nothing accounted of; they shall *cast that in the streets;* but the *gold,* which is more valuable, shall be removed and brought to Babylon); or they themselves shall *throw away their silver and gold,* because it would be an incumbrance to them and retard their flight, or because it would expose them and be a temptation to the enemy to cut their throats for their money, or in indignation at it, because, after all the care and pains they had taken

to scrape it together and hoard it up, they found that it would stand them in no **stead**, but do them a mischief rather. Note, *The world passes away, and the lusts thereof,* 1 John ii. 17. The time may come when worldly men will be as weary of their wealth as now they are wedded to it, when those will fare best that have least.

III. God's temple shall stand them in no stead, *v.* 20—22. This they had prided themselves in, and promised themselves security from (Jer. vii. 4; Mic. iii. 11); but this confidence of theirs shall fail them. Observe, 1. The great honour God had done to that people in setting up his sanctuary among them (*v.* 20): *As for the beauty of his ornament,* that *holy and beautiful house,* where *they and their fathers praised God* (Isa. lxiv. 11), which was therefore beautiful because holy (it was called the *beauty of holiness,* and holiness is the beauty of its ornament; it was also adorned with gold and gifts)—as for this, *he set it in majesty;* every thing was contrived to make it magnificent, that it might help to make the people of Israel the more illustrious among their neighbours. *He built his sanctuary like high palaces,* Ps. lxxviii. 69. It was a *glorious high throne from the beginning,* Jer. xvii. 12. But, 2. Here is the great dishonour they had done to God in profaning his sanctuary; they *made the images of their* counterfeit deities, which they set up in rivalship with God, and which are here called *their abominations* and *their detestable things* (for so they were to God, and so they should have been to them), and these they set up in God's temple, than which a greater affront could not be put upon him. And therefore, 3. It is here threatened that they shall be deprived of the temple, and it shall be no succour to them: *Therefore have I set it far from them,* that is, sent them far from it, so that it is out of the reach of their services and they are out of the reach of its influences. Note, God's ordinances, and the privileges of a profession of religion, will justly be taken away from those that despise and profane them. Nay, they shall not only be kept at a distance from the temple, but the temple itself shall be involved in the common desolation (*v.* 21); the Chaldeans, who are *strangers,* and therefore have no veneration for it, who are *the wicked of the earth,* and therefore have an antipathy to it, shall *have it for a prey* and for *a spoil;* all the ornaments and treasures of it shall fall into their hands, who will make no difference between that and other plunder. This was a grief to the saints in Zion, who complained of nothing so much as of that which *the enemy did wickedly in the sanctuary* (Ps. lxxiv. 3); but it was the punishment of the sinners in Zion, who, by profaning the temple with *strange gods,* provoked God to suffer it to be profaned by *strange nations,* and to *turn his face from those that* did it as if he had not seen them and their crimes and from those that deprecated it as not regarding them and their prayers. Let the soldiers do as they will; let them *enter into the secret place*, into the holy of holies, as robbers; let them strip it, let them pollute it; its defence has departed, and then farewell all its glory. Note, Those are unworthy to be honoured with the form of godliness who will not be governed by the power of godliness.

23 Make a chain: for the land is full of bloody crimes, and the city is full of violence. 24 Wherefore I will bring the worst of the heathen, and they shall possess their houses: I will also make the pomp of the strong to cease; and their holy places shall be defiled. 25 Destruction cometh; and they shall seek peace, and *there shall be* none. 26 Mischief shall come upon mischief, and rumour shall be upon rumour; then shall they seek a vision of the prophet; but the law shall perish from the priest, and counsel from the ancients. 27 The king shall mourn, and the prince shall be clothed with desolation, and the hands of the people of the land shall be troubled: I will do unto them after their way, and according to their deserts will I judge them; and they shall know that I *am* the LORD.

Here is, I. The prisoner arraigned: *Make a chain*, in which to drag the criminal to the bar, and set him before the tribunal of divine justice; let him stand in fetters (as a notorious malefactor), stand pinioned to receive his doom. Note, Those that break the bands of God's law *asunder*, and *cast away those cords from them*, will find themselves bound and held by the chains of his judgments, which they cannot break nor cast from them. The chain signified the siege of Jerusalem, or the slavery of those that were carried into captivity, or that they were all bound over to the righteous judgment of God, *reserved in chains*.

II. The indictment drawn up against the prisoner: *The land is full of bloody crimes*, full of *the judgments of blood* (so the word is), that is, of the guilt of blood which they had shed under colour of justice and by forms of law, with the solemnity of a judgment. The innocent blood which Manasseh shed, probably thus shed, by the *judgment of the blood*, was the measure-filling sin of Jerusalem, 2 Kings xxiv. 4. Or, It is full of such crimes as by the law were to be punished with death, *the judgment of blood*. Idolatry, blasphemy, witchcraft, Sodomy,

and the like, were *bloody crimes*, for which particular sinners were to die; and therefore, when they had become national, there was no remedy but the nation must be cut off. Note, Bloody crimes will be punished with bloody judgments. *The city*, the city of David, the holy city, that should have been the pattern of righteousness, the protector of it, and the punisher of wrong, *is now full of violence;* the rulers of that city, having greater power and reputation, are greater oppressors than any others. This was sadly to be lamented. *How has the faithful city become a harlot!*

III. Judgment given upon this indictment. God will reckon with them not only for the profaning of his sanctuary, but for the perverting of justice between man and man; for, as *holiness becomes his house*, so the *righteous Lord loves righteousness* and is the avenger of unrighteousness. Now the judgment given is, 1. That since they had walked in the way of the heathen, and done worse than they, God would *bring the worst of the heathen upon them* to destroy them and lay them waste, the most barbarous and outrageous, that have the least compassion to mankind and the greatest antipathy to the Jews. Note, Of the heathen some are worse than others, and God sometimes picks out the worst to be a scourge to his own people, because he intends them for the fire when the work is done. 2. That since they had filled their houses with goods unjustly gotten, and used their pomp and power for the crushing and oppressing of the weak, God would give their houses to be possessed and all the furniture of them to be enjoyed by strangers, and *make the pomp of the strong to cease*, so that their great men should not dazzle the eyes of the weak-sighted with their pomp, nor with their might at any time prevail against right, as they had done. 3. That, since they had *defiled the holy places* with their idolatries, God would defile them with his judgments, since they had set up the images of other gods in the temple, God would remove thence the tokens of the presence of their own God. When the holy places are deserted by their God they will soon be defiled by their enemies. 4. Since they had followed one sin with another, God would pursue them with one judgment upon another: "*Destruction comes, utter destruction* (v. 25); for there shall come *mischief upon mischief* to ruin you, and *rumour upon rumour* to frighten you, like the waves in a storm, one upon the neck of another." Note, Sinners that are marked for ruin shall be prosecuted to it; for God will overcome when he judges. 5. Since they had disappointed God's expectations from them, he would disappoint their expectations from him; for, (1.) They shall not have the *deliverance out of their troubles* that they expect. They shall *seek peace;* they shall desire it and pray for it; they shall aim at and expect it: but *there shall be none;* their attempts both to court their enemies and to conquer them shall be in vain, and their troubles shall grow worse and worse. (2.) They shall not have the direction in the trouble that they expect (*v.* 26): *They shall seek a vision of the prophet,* shall desire, for their support under their troubles, to be assured of a happy issue out of them. They did not desire a vision to reprove them for sin, nor to warn them of danger, but to promise them deliverance. Such messages they longed to hear. But *the law shall perish from the priest;* he shall have no words either of counsel or comfort to say to them. They would not hear what God had to say to them by way of conviction, and therefore he has nothing to say to them by way of encouragement. *Counsel shall perish from the ancients;* the elders of the people, that should advise them what to do in this difficult juncture, shall be infatuated and at their wits' end. It is bad with a people when those that should be their counsellors know not how to consider within themselves, consult with one another, or counsel them. 6. Since they had animated and encouraged one another to sin, God would dispirit and dishearten them all, so that they should not be able to make head against the judgments of God that were breaking in upon them. All orders and degrees of men shall lie down by consent under the load (*v.* 27): *The king,* that should inspire life into them, and *the prince,* that should lead them on to attack the enemy, *shall mourn* and be *clothed with desolation;* their heads and hearts shall fail, their politics and their courage; and then no wonder if *the hands of the people of the land,* that should fight for them, be *troubled.* None of the men of might shall *find their hands.* What can men contrive or do for themselves when God has departed from them and appears against them? All must needs be in *tears,* all in *trouble,* when God comes to *judge them according to their deserts,* and so make them know, to their cost, that he is the Lord, the *God to whom vengeance belongs.*

CHAP. VIII.

God, having given the prophet a clear foresight of the people's miseries that were hastening on, here gives him a clear insight into the people's wickedness, by which God was provoked to bring these miseries upon them, that he might justify God in all his judgments, might the more particularly reprove the sins of the people, and with the more satisfaction foretel their ruin. Here God, in vision, brings him to Jerusalem, to show him the sins that were committed there, though God had begun to contend with them (ver. 1—4), and there he sees, I. The image of jealousy set up at the gate of the altar, ver. 5, 6. II. The elders of Israel worshipping all manner of images in a secret chamber, ver. 7—12. III. The women weeping for Tammuz, ver. 13, 14. IV. The men worshipping the sun, ver. 15, 16. And then appeals to him whether such a provoking people should have any pity shown them, ver. 17, 18.

AND it came to pass in the sixth year, in the sixth *month,* in the fifth *day* of the month, *as* I sat in mine house, and the elders of Judah sat before me, that the hand of the

Lord GOD fell there upon me. 2 Then I beheld, and lo a likeness as the appearance of fire: from the appearance of his loins even downward, fire; and from his loins even upward, as the appearance of brightness, as the colour of amber. 3 And he put forth the form of a hand, and took me by a lock of mine head; and the spirit lifted me up between the earth and the heaven, and brought me in the visions of God to Jerusalem, to the door of the inner gate that looketh toward the north; where *was* the seat of the image of jealousy, which provoketh to jealousy. 4 And, behold, the glory of the God of Israel *was* there, according to the vision that I saw in the plain. 5 Then said he unto me, Son of man, lift up thine eyes now the way toward the north. So I lifted up mine eyes the way toward the north, and behold northward at the gate of the altar this image of jealousy in the entry. 6 He said furthermore unto me, Son of man, seest thou what they do? *even* the great abominations that the house of Israel committeth here, that I should go far off from my sanctuary? but turn thee yet again, *and* thou shalt see greater abominations.

Ezekiel was now in Babylon; but the messages of wrath he had delivered in the foregoing chapters related to Jerusalem, for in the peace or trouble thereof the captives looked upon themselves to have peace or trouble, and therefore here he has a vision of what was done at Jerusalem, and this vision is continued to the close of the 11th chapter.

I. Here is the date of this vision. The first vision he had was in *the fifth year of the captivity, in the fourth month* and *the fifth day of the month,* ch. i. 1, 2. This was just fourteen months after. Perhaps it was after he had lain 390 days on his left side, to bear the iniquity of Israel, and before he began the forty days on his right side, to bear the iniquity of Judah; for now he was sitting in the house, not lying. Note, God keeps a particular account of the messages he sends to us, because he will shortly call us to account about them.

II. The opportunity is taken notice of, as well as the time. 1. The prophet was himself *sitting in his house,* in a sedate composed frame, deep perhaps in contemplation. Note, The more we retreat from the world, and retire into our own hearts, the better frame we are in for communion with God: those that sit down to consider what they have learned shall be taught more. Or, He *sat in his house,* ready to preach to the company that resorted to him, but waiting for instructions what to say. God will communicate more knowledge to those who are communicative of what they do know. 2. *The elders of Judah,* that were now in captivity with him, *sat before him.* It is probable that it was on the sabbath day, and that it was usual for them to attend on the prophet every sabbath day, both to hear the word from him and to join with him in prayer and praise: and how could they spend the sabbath better, now that they had neither temple nor synagogue, neither priest nor altar? It was a great mercy that they had opportunity to spend it so well, as the good people in Elisha's time, 2 Kings iv. 23. But some think it was on some extraordinary occasion that they attended him, to enquire of the Lord, and *sat down* at his feet to *hear his word.* Observe here, (1.) When the *law had perished from the priests* at Jerusalem, whose *lips should keep knowledge* (ch. vii. 26), those in Babylon had a prophet to consult. God is not tied to places or persons. (2.) Now that the elders of Judah were in captivity they paid more respect to God's prophets, and his word in their mouth, than they did when they lived in peace in their own land. When God brings men into the *cords of affliction,* then he *opens their ears to discipline,* Job xxxvi. 8, 10; Ps. cxli. 6. Those that despised vision in the *valley of vision* prized it now that the word of the Lord was precious and there was *no open vision.* (3.) When our teachers are driven into corners, and are forced to preach in private houses, we must diligently attend them there. A minister's house should be a church for all his neighbours. Paul preached in his own hired house at Rome, and God owned him there, and *no man forbad him.*

III. The divine influence and impression that the prophet was now under: *The hand of the Lord fell there upon me.* God's hand took hold of him, and arrested him, as it were, to employ him in this vision, but at the same time supported him to bear it.

IV. The vision that the prophet saw, *v.* 2. He *beheld a likeness,* of a man we may suppose, for that was the likeness he saw before, but it was all *brightness* above the girdle and all *fire* below, fire and flame. This agrees with the description we had before of the apparition he saw, *ch.* i. 27. It is probable that it was the same person, the man Christ Jesus. It is probable that the elders that *sat with him* (as the men that journeyed with Paul) saw a light and were afraid, and this happy sight they gained by attending the prophet in a private meeting, but they had no distinct view of him that spoke to him, Acts xxii. 9.

792

V. The prophet's remove, in vision, to Jerusalem. The apparition he saw *put forth the form of a hand,* which *took him by a lock of his head,* and the Spirit was that hand which was put forth, for the Spirit of God is called *the finger of God.* Or, The spirit within him *lifted him up,* so that he was borne up and carried on by an internal principle, not an external violence. A faithful ready servant of God will be drawn by a hair, by the least intimation of the divine will, to his duty; for he has that within him which inclines him to a compliance with it, Ps. xxvii. 8. He was miraculously *lifted up between heaven and earth,* as if he were to fly away upon eagles' wings. This, it is probable (so Grotius thinks), the elders that sat with him saw; they were witnesses of *the hand taking him by the lock* of hair, and *lifting him up,* and then perhaps laying he had the following visions, *whether in the body or out of the body,* we may suppose, he *could not tell,* any more than Paul in a like case, much less can we. Note, Those are best prepared for communion with God and the communications of divine light that by divine grace are raised up above the earth and the things of it, to be out of their attractive force. But, being lifted up towards heaven, he was carried in vision to Jerusalem, and to God's sanctuary there; for those that would go to heaven must take that in their way. The Spirit represented to his mind the city and temple as plainly as if he had been there in person. O that by faith we could thus enter into the Jerusalem, the holy city, above, and see the things that are invisible!

VI. The discoveries that were made to him there.

1. There he saw the glory of God (*v.* 4): *Behold, the glory of the God of Israel was there,* the same appearance of the living creatures, and the wheels, and the throne, that he had seen, *ch.* i. Note, God's servants, wherever they are and whithersoever they go, ought to carry about with them a believing regard to the glory of God and to set that always before them; and those that have seen God's power and glory in the sanctuary should desire to see them again, so as they have seen them, Ps. lxiii. 2. Ezekiel has this repeated vision of the glory of God both to give credit to and to put honour upon the following discoveries. But it seems to have a further intention here; it was to aggravate this sin of Israel, in changing their own God, the God of Israel (who is a God of so much glory as here he appears to be), for dunghill gods, scandalous gods, false gods, and indeed no gods. Note, The more glorious we see God to be the more odious we shall see sin to be, especially idolatry, which turns his truth into a lie, his glory into shame. It was also to aggravate their approaching misery, when this

glory of the Lord should remove from them (*ch.* xi. 23) and leave the house and city desolate.

2. There he saw the reproach of Israel—and that was *the image of jealousy,* set *northward, at the gate of the altar, v.* 3, 5. What image this was is uncertain, probably an image of Baal, or of the grove, which Manasseh made and set in the temple (2 Kings xxi. 7, 2 Chron. xxxiii. 3), which Josiah removed, but his successors, it seems, replaced there, as probably they did the *chariots of the sun* which he found *at the entering in of the house of the Lord* (2 Kings xxiii. 11), and this is here said to be *in the entry.* But the prophet, instead of telling us what image it was, which might gratify our curiosity, tells us that it was *the image of jealousy,* to convince our consciences that, whatever image it was, it was in the highest degree offensive to God and *provoked him to jealousy.* He resented it as a husband would resent the whoredoms of his wife, and would certainly revenge it; for *God is jealous, and the Lord revenges,* Nah. i. 2.

(1.) The very setting up of this image *in the house of the Lord* was enough to *provoke him to jealousy;* for it is in the matters of his worship that we are particularly told, *I the Lord thy God am a jealous God.* Those that placed this image at *the door of the inner gate,* where the people assembled, called *the gate of the altar* (*v.* 5), thereby plainly intended, [1.] To affront God, to provoke him to his face, by advancing an idol to be a rival with him for the adoration of his people, in contempt of his law and in defiance of his justice. [2.] To debauch the people, and pick them up as they were entering into the courts of the Lord's house to bring their offerings to him, and to tempt them to offer them to this image; like the adulteress Solomon describes, that *sits at the door of her house, to call passengers who go right on their ways, Whoso is simple, let him turn in hither,* Prov. ix. 14—16. With good reason therefore is this called *the image of jealousy.*

(2.) We may well imagine what a surprise and what a grief it was to Ezekiel to see this image in the house of God, when he was in hopes that the judgments they were under had, by this time, wrought some reformation among them; but there is more wickedness in the world, in the church, than good men think there is. And now, [1.] God appeals to him whether this was not bad enough, and a sufficient ground for God to go upon in casting off this people and abandoning them to ruin. Could he, or any one else, expect any other than *that God should go far from his sanctuary,* when there were such abominations committed there, in that very place; nay, was he not perfectly driven thence? They did these things designedly, and on purpose that he should leave his sanctuary, and so shall their doom

be; they have hereby, in effect, like the Gadarenes, desired him *to depart out of their coasts,* and therefore he will depart; he will no more dignify and protect his sanctuary, as he has done, but will give it up to reproach and ruin. But, [2.] Though this is bad enough, and serves abundantly to justify God in all that he brings upon them, yet the matter will appear to be much worse: *But turn thyself yet again,* and thou wilt be amazed *to see greater abominations than these.* Where there is one abomination it will be found that there are many more. Sins do not go alone.

7 And he brought me to the door of the court; and when I looked, behold a hole in the wall. 8 Then said he unto me, Son of man, dig now in the wall: and when I had digged in the wall, behold a door. 9 And he said unto me, Go in, and behold the wicked abominations that they do here. 10 So I went in and saw; and behold every form of creeping things, and abominable beasts, and all the idols of the house of Israel, portrayed upon the wall round about. 11 And there stood before them seventy men of the ancients of the house of Israel, and in the midst of them stood Jaazaniah the son of Shaphan, with every man his censer in his hand; and a thick cloud of incense went up. 12 Then said he unto me, Son of man, hast thou seen what the ancients of the house of Israel do in the dark, every man in the chambers of his imagery? for they say, The LORD seeth us not; the LORD hath forsaken the earth.

We have here a further discovery of the abominations that were committed at Jerusalem, and within the confines of the temple too. Now observe,

I. How this discovery is made. God, in vision, brought Ezekiel to the *door of the court,* the outer court, along the sides of which the priests' lodgings were. God could have introduced him at first into *the chambers of imagery,* but he brings him to them by degrees, partly to employ his own industry in searching out these mysteries of iniquity, and partly to make him sensible with what care and caution those idolaters concealed their idolatries. Before the priests' apartments they had run up a wall, to make them the more private, that they might not lie open to the observation of those who passed by—a shrewd sign that they did something which they had reason to be ashamed of. *He that doeth evil hates the light*. They were not willing that those who saw them in God's house should see them in their own, lest they should see them contradict themselves and undo in private what they did in public. But, *behold, a hole in the wall* (*v.* 7), a spy-hole, by which you might see that which would give cause to suspect them. When hypocrites screen themselves behind the wall of an external profession, and with it think to conceal their wickedness from the eye of the world and carry on their designs the more successfully, it is hard for them to manage it with so much art but that there is some hole or other left in the wall, something that betrays them, to those who look diligently, not to be what they pretend to be. The ass's ears in the fable appeared from under the lion's skin. This *hole in the wall* Ezekiel made wider, and *behold a door, v.* 8. This door he goes in by into *the treasury,* or some of the apartments of the priests, and sees *the wicked abominations that they do there, v.* 9. Note, Those that would discover the mystery of iniquity in others, or in themselves, must accomplish a diligent search ; for Satan has his wiles, and depths, and devices, which we should not be ignorant of, and *the heart is deceitful above all things ;* in the examining of it therefore we are concerned to be very strict.

II. What the discovery is. It is a very melancholy one. 1. He sees a chamber set round with idolatrous pictures (*v.* 10): *All the idols of the house of Israel,* which they had borrowed from the neighbouring nations, were *portrayed upon the wall round about,* even the vilest of them, *the forms of creeping things,* which they worshipped, and *beasts,* even *abominable ones,* which are poisonous and venomous ; at least they were abominable when they were worshipped. This was a sort of pantheon, a collection of all the idols together which they paid their devotions to. Though the second commandment, in the letter of it, forbids only graven images, yet painted ones are as bad and as dangerous. 2. He sees this chamber filled with idolatrous worshippers (*v.* 11): There were *seventy men of the elders of Israel* offering incense to these painted idols. Here was a great number of idolaters strengthening one another's hands in this wickedness ; though it was in a private chamber, and the meeting industriously concealed, yet here were seventy men engaged in it. I doubt these elders were many more than those in Babylon that sat before the prophet in his house, *v.* 1. They were *seventy men,* the number of the great Sanhedrim, or chief council of the nation, and, we have reason to fear, the same men ; for they were *the ancients of the house of Israel,* not only in age, but in office, who were bound, by the duty of their place, to restrain and punish idolatry and to destroy and abolish all superstitious images wherever they found 794

them ; yet these were those that did themselves worship them in private, so undermining that religion which in public they professed to own and promote only because by it they held their preferments. They had *every man his censer in his hand ;* so fond were they of the idolatrous service that they would all be their own priests, and very prodigal they were of their perfumes in honour of these images, for *a thick cloud of incense went up,* that filled the room. O that the zeal of these idolaters might shame the worshippers of the true God out of their indifference to his service ! The prophet took particular notice of one whom he knew, who *stood in the midst of* these idolaters, as chief among them, being perhaps president of the great council at this time or most forward in this wickedness. No wonder the people were corrupt when the elders were so. The sins of leaders are leading sins.

III. What the remark is that is made upon it (*v.* 12): "*Son of man, hast thou seen this?* Couldst thou have imagined that there was such wickedness committed?" It is here observed concerning it, 1. That it was done *in the dark;* for sinful works are *works of darkness.* They concealed it, lest they should lose their places, or at least their credit. There is a great deal of secret wickedness in the world, which the day will declare, *the day of the revelation of the righteous judgment of God.* 2. That this one idolatrous chapel was but a specimen of many the like. Here they met together, to worship their images in concert, but, it should seem, they had *every man the chamber of his imagery* besides, a room in his own house for this purpose, in which every man gratified his own fancy with such pictures as he liked best. Idolaters had their household gods, and their family worship of them in private, which is a shame to those who call themselves Christians and yet have no church in their house, no worship of God in their family. Had they *chambers of imagery,* and shall not we have chambers of devotion? 3. That atheism was at the bottom of their idolatry. They worship images *in the dark,* the images of the gods of other nations, and *they say,* "Jehovah, the God of Israel, whom we should serve, *seeth us not.* Jehovah *hath forsaken the earth,* and we may worship what God we will ; he regards us not." (1.) They think themselves out of God's sight: *They say, The Lord seeth us not.* They imagined, because the matter was carried on so closely that men could not discover it, nor did any of their neighbours suspect them to be idolaters, that therefore it was hidden from the eye of God ; as if there were any *darkness, or shadow of death, where the workers of iniquity may hide themselves.* Note, A practical disbelief of God's omniscience is at the bottom of our treacherous departures from him ; but the church argues justly, as to this very sin of idolatry (Ps. xliv. 20, 21), *If we have forgotten the name of our God, and stretched forth our hand to a strange god, will not God search this out?* No doubt he will. (2.) They think themselves out of God's care: "*The Lord has forsaken the earth,* and looks not after the affairs of it; and then we may as well worship any other god as him." Or, "He has forsaken our land, and left it to be a prey to its enemies; and therefore it is time for us to look out for some other god, to whom to commit the protection of it. Our one God cannot, or will not, deliver us; and therefore let us have many." This was a blasphemous reflection upon God, as if he had forsaken them first, else they would not have forsaken him. Note, Those are ripe indeed for ruin who have arrived at such a pitch of impudence as to lay the blame of their sins upon God himself.

13 He said also unto me, Turn thee yet again, *and* thou shalt see greater abominations that they do. 14 Then he brought me to the door of the gate of the LORD's house which *was* toward the north; and, behold, there sat women weeping for Tammuz. 15 Then said he unto me, Hast thou seen *this,* O son of man? turn thee yet again, *and* thou shalt see greater abominations than these. 16 And he brought me into the inner court of the LORD's house, and, behold, at the door of the temple of the LORD, between the porch and the altar, *were* about five and twenty men, with their backs toward the temple of the LORD, and their faces toward the east; and they worshipped the sun toward the east. 17 Then he said unto me, Hast thou seen *this,* O son of man? Is it a light thing to the house of Judah that they commit the abominations which they commit here? for they have filled the land with violence, and have returned to provoke me to anger: and, lo, they put the branch to their nose. 18 Therefore will I also deal in fury: mine eye shall not spare, neither will I have pity: and though they cry in mine ears with a loud voice, *yet* will I not hear them.

Here we have,

I. More and greater abominations discovered to the prophet. He thought that what he had seen was bad enough and yet (*v.* 13): *Turn thyself again, and thou shalt see yet*

greater abominations, and greater still, *v.* 15, as before, *v.* 6. There are those who live in retirement who do not think what wickedness there is in this world; and the more we converse with it, and the further we go abroad into it, the more corrupt we see it. When we have seen that which is bad we may have our wonder at it made to cease by the discovery of that which, upon some account or other, is a great deal worse. We shall find it so in examining our own hearts and searching into them; there is a world of iniquity in them, a great abundance and variety of abominations, and, when we have found out much amiss, still we shall find more; for *the heart is desperately wicked, who can know it* perfectly? Now the abominations here discovered were, 1. *Women weeping for Tammuz, v.* 14. An abominable thing indeed, that any should choose rather to serve an idol in tears than to serve the true God *with joyfulness and gladness of heart!* Yet such absurdities as these are those guilty of who *follow after lying vanities* and *forsake their own mercies.* Some think it was for Adonis, an idol among the Greeks, others for Osiris, an idol of the Egyptians, that they shed these tears. The image, they say, was made to weep, and then the worshippers wept with it. They bewailed the death of this Tammuz, and anon rejoiced in its returning to life again. These mourning women *sat at the door of the gate of the Lord's house,* and there shed their idolatrous tears, as it were in defiance of God and the sacred rites of his worship, and some think, with their idolatry, prostrating themselves also to corporeal whoredom; for these two commonly went together, and those that dishonoured the divine nature by the one were justly *given up to vile affections* and a reprobate sense to dishonour the human nature, which nowhere ever sunk so far below itself as in these idolatrous rites. 2. *Men worshipping the sun, v.* 16. And this was so much the greater an abomination that it was practised *in the inner court of the Lord's house at the door of the temple of the Lord, between the porch and the altar.* There, where the most sacred rites of their holy religion used to be performed, was this abominable wickedness committed. Justly might God in jealousy say to those who thus affronted him at his own door, as the king to Haman, *Will he force the queen also before me in the house?* Here *were about twenty-five men* giving that honour to the sun which is due to God only. Some think they were the king and his princes; it should rather seem that they were priests, for this was the court of the priests, and the proper place to find them in. Those that were entrusted with the true religion, had it committed to their care and were charged with the custody of it, they were the men that betrayed it. (1.) They turned *their backs towards the temple of the Lord,* resolvedly forgetting it and designedly slighting it and putting contempt upon it. Note, When men turn their backs upon God's institutions, and despise them, it is no marvel if they wander endlessly after their own inventions. Impiety is the beginning of idolatry and all iniquity. (2.) They turned *their faces towards the east, and worshipped the sun,* the rising sun. This was an ancient instance of idolatry; it is mentioned in Job's time (Job xxxi. 26), and had been generally practised among the nations, some worshipping the sun under one name, others under another. These priests, finding it had antiquity and general consent and usage on its side (the two pleas which the papists use at this day in defence of their superstitious rites, and particularly this of worshipping towards the east), practised it in the court of the temple, thinking it an omission that it was not inserted in their ritual. See the folly of idolaters in worshipping that as a god, and calling it *Baal*—a lord, which God made to be a servant to the universe (for such the sun is, and so his name *Shemesh* signifies, Deut. iv. 19), and in adoring the borrowed light and despising the *Father of lights.*

II. The inference drawn from these discoveries (*v.* 17): "*Hast thou seen this, O son of man!* and couldst thou have thought ever to see such things done in the temple of the Lord?" Now, 1. He appeals to the prophet himself concerning the heinousness of the crime. Can he think it *is a light thing to the house of Judah,* who know and profess better things, and are dignified with so many privileges above other nations? Is it an excusable thing in those that have God's oracles and ordinances *that they commit the abominations which they commit here?* Do not those deserve to suffer that thus sin? Should not such abominations as these *make desolate?* Dan. ix. 27. 2. He aggravates it from the fraud and oppression that were to be found in all parts of the nations: *They have filled the land with violence.* It is not strange if those that wrong God thus make no conscience of wronging one another, and with all that is sacred trample likewise upon all that is just. And their wickedness in their conversations made even the worship they paid to their own God an abomination (Isa. i. 11, &c.): "*They fill the land with violence,* and then they return to the temple *to provoke me to anger* there; for even their sacrifices, instead of making an atonement, do but add to their guilt. They *return to provoke me* (they repeat the provocation, do it, and do it again), *and, lo, they put the branch to their nose*"—a proverbial expression denoting perhaps their scoffing at God and having him in derision; they snuffed at his service, as men do when they *put a branch to their nose.* Or it was some custom used by idolaters in honour of the idols they served. We read of garlands used in their idolatrous worships (Acts xiv. 13), out of

796

which every zealot took a branch which they smelled to as a nosegay. Dr. Lightfoot (*Hor. Heb. in John* xv. 6) gives another sense of this place: *They put the branch to their wrath,* or *to his wrath,* as the Masorites read it; that is, they are still bringing more fuel (such as the withered branches of the vine) to the fire of divine wrath, which they have already kindled, as if that wrath did not burn hot enough already. Or putting the branch to the nose may signify the giving of a very great affront and provocation either to God or man; they are an abusive generation of men. 3. He passes sentence upon them that they shall be utterly cut off: *Therefore,* because they are thus furiously bent upon sin, *I will also deal in fury* with them, *v.* 18. *They filled the land with their violence,* and God will fill it with the violence of their enemies; and he will not lend a favourable ear to the suggestions either, (1.) Of his own pity: *My eye shall not spare, neither will I have pity;* repentance shall be hidden from his eyes; or, (2.) Of their prayers: *Though they cry in my ears with a loud voice, yet will I not hear them;* for still their sins cry more loudly for vengeance than their prayers cry for mercy. God will now be as deaf to their prayers as their own idols were, on whom they cried aloud, but in vain, 1 Kings xviii. 26. Time was when God was ready to hear even *before they cried* and to *answer while they were yet speaking;* but now *they shall seek me early and not find me,* Prov. i. 28. It is not the loud voice, but the upright heart, that God will regard.

CHAP. IX.

The prophet had, in vision, seen the wickedness that was committed at Jerusalem, in the foregoing chapter, and we may be sure that it was not represented to him worse than really it was; now here follows, of course, a representation of their ruin approaching; for when sin goes before judgments come next. Here is, I. Preparation made of instruments that were to be employed in the destruction of the city, ver. 1, 2. II. The removal of the Shechinah from the cherubim to the threshold of the temple, ver. 3. III. Orders given to one of the persons employed, who is distinguished from the rest, for the marking of a remnant to be preserved from the common destruction, ver. 3, 4. IV. The warrant signed for the execution of those that were not marked, and the execution begun accordingly, ver. 5—7. V. The prophet's intercession for the mitigation of the sentence, and a denial of any mitigation, the decree having now gone forth, ver. 8—10. VI. The report made by him that was to mark the pious remnant of what he had done in that matter, ver. 11. And this shows a usual method of Providence in the government of the world.

HE cried also in mine ears with a loud voice, saying, Cause them that have charge over the city to draw near, even every man *with* his destroying weapon in his hand. 2 And, behold, six men came from the way of the higher gate, which lieth toward the north, and every man a slaughter weapon in his hand; and one man among them *was* clothed with linen, with a writer's inkhorn by his side: and they went in, and stood beside the brazen altar. 3 And the glory of the God of Israel was gone up from the cherub, whereupon he was, to the threshold of the house. And he called to the man clothed with linen, which *had* the writer's inkhorn by his side ; 4 And the Lord said unto him, Go through the midst of the city, through the midst of Jerusalem, and set a mark upon the foreheads of the men that sigh and that cry for all the abominations that be done in the midst thereof.

In these verses we have,

I. The summons given to Jerusalem's destroyers to come forth and give their attendance. He that appeared to the prophet (*ch.* viii. 2), that had brought him to Jerusalem and had shown the wickedness that was done there, *he cried, Cause those that have charge over the city to draw near* (*v.* 1), or, as it might better be read, and nearer the original, *Those that have charge over the city are drawing near.* He had said (*ch.* viii. 18), *I will deal in fury ;* now, says he to the prophet, thou shalt see who are to be employed as the instruments of my wrath. *Appropinquaverunt visitationes civitatis—The visitations* (or visitors) *of the city are at hand.* They would not *know the day of their visitations* in mercy, and now they are to be visited in wrath. Observe, 1. How the notice of this is given to the prophet : *He cried it in my ears with a loud voice,* which intimates the vehemency of him that spoke ; when men are highly provoked, and threaten in anger, they speak aloud. Those that regard not the counsels God gives them in a still small voice shall be made to hear the threatenings, to hear and tremble. It denotes also the prophet's unwillingness to be told this ; he was deaf on that ear, but there is no remedy, their sin will not admit an excuse and therefore their judgment will not admit a delay : " *He cried it in my ears with a loud voice ;* he made me hear it, and I heard it with a sad heart." 2. What this notice is. There are those *that have charge over the city* to destroy it, not the Chaldean armies, they are to be indeed employed in this work, but they are not the visitors, they are only the servants, or tools rather. God's angels have received a charge now to lay that city waste, which they had long had a charge to protect and watch over. They are at hand, as destroying angels, as ministers of wrath, for *every man has his destroying weapon in his hand,* as the angel that kept the way of the tree of life with a flaming sword. Note, Those that have by sin made God their enemy have made the good angels their enemies too. These visitors are called and *caused to draw near.* Note, God has ministers of wrath always within call, always at command, invisible powers, by whom he ac-

complishes his purposes. The prophet is made to see this in vision, that he might with the greater assurance in his preaching denounce these judgments. God told it him with a loud voice, *taught it him with a strong hand* (Isa. viii. 11), that it might make the deeper impression upon him and that he might thus proclaim it in the people's ears.

II. Their appearance, upon this summons, is recorded. Immediately *six men came* (*v.* 2), one for each of the principal gates of Jerusalem. Two destroying angels were sent against Sodom, but six against Jerusalem ; for Jerusalem's doom in the judgment will be thrice as heavy as that of Sodom. There is an angel watching at every gate to destroy, to bring in judgments from every quarter, and to take heed that none escape. One angel served to destroy the first-born of Egypt, and the camp of the Assyrians, but here are six. In the Revelation we find seven that were to *pour out the vials of God's wrath,* Rev. xvi. 1. They came with every one a *slaughter-weapon in his hand,* prepared for the work to which they were called. The nations of which the king of Babylon's army was composed, which some reckon to be six, and the commanders of his army (of whom *six* are named as principal, Jer. xxxix. 3), may be called *the slaughter-weapons* in the hands of the angels. The angels are thoroughly furnished for every service. 1. Observe whence they came—*from the way of the higher gate, which lies towards the north* (*v.* 2), either because the Chaldeans came from the north (Jer. i. 14, *Out of the north an evil shall break forth)* or because the image of jealousy was set up *at the door of the inner gate that looks towards the north, ch.* viii. 3, 5. At that gate of the temple the destroying angels entered, to show what it was that opened the door to them. Note, That way that sin lies judgments may be expected to come. 2. Observe where they placed themselves : *They went in and stood beside the brazen altar,* on which sacrifices were wont to be offered and atonement made. When they acted as destroyers they acted as sacrificers, not from any personal revenge or ill-will, but with a pure and sincere regard to the glory of God ; for to his justice all they slew were offered up as victims. *They stood by the altar,* as it were to protect and vindicate that, and plead its righteous cause, and avenge the horrid profanation of it. At the altar they were to receive their commission to destroy, to intimate that the iniquity of Jerusalem, like that of Eli's house, was *not to be purged by sacrifice.*

III. The notice taken of one among the destroying angels distinguished in his habit from the rest, from whom some favour might be expected ; it should seem he was not one of the six, but *among them,* to see that mercy was mixed with judgment, *v.* 2. This *man was clothed with linen,* as the priests were, and he had *a writer's inkhorn* hanging at his side, as anciently attorneys and lawyers' clerks had, which he was to make use of, as the other six were to make use of their *destroying weapons.* Here the honours of the pen exceeded those of the sword; they were angels that bore the sword, but he was the Lord of angels that made use of the *writer's inkhorn;* for it is generally agreed, among the best interpreters, that this man represented Christ as Mediator saving those that are his from the flaming sword of divine justice. He is our *high priest,* clothed with holiness, for that was signified by the *fine linen,* Rev. xix. 8. As prophet he wears the *writer's inkhorn.* The book of life is the Lamb's book. The great things of the law and gospel which God has written to us are of his writing; for it is the Spirit of Christ, in the writers of the scripture, that testifies to us, and the Bible is *the revelation of Jesus Christ.* Note, It is a matter of great comfort to all good Christians that, in the midst of the destroyers and the destructions that are abroad, there is a Mediator, a great high priest, who has an interest in heaven, and whom saints on earth have an interest in.

IV. The removal of the appearance of the divine glory from over the cherubim. Some think this was that usual display of the divine glory which was between the cherubim over the mercy seat, in the most holy place, that took leave of them now, and never returned; for it is supposed that it was not in the second temple. Others think it was that display of the divine glory which the prophet now saw over the cherubim in vision; and this is more probable, because this is called *the glory of the God of Israel* (ch. viii. 4), and this is it which he had now his eye upon; this was gone *to the threshold of the house,* as it were to call to the servants that attended without the door, to send them on their errand and give them their instructions. And the removal of this, as well as the former, might be significant of God's departure from them, and leaving them their house desolate; and when God goes all good goes, but he goes from none till they first drive him from them. He went at first no further than *the threshold,* that he might show how loth he was to depart, and might give them both time and encouragement to invite his return to them and his stay with them. Note, God's departures from a people are gradual, but gracious souls are soon aware of the first step he takes towards a remove. Ezekiel immediately observed that *the glory of the God of Israel had gone up from the cherub:* and what is a vision of angels if God be gone?

V. The charge given *to the man clothed in linen* to secure the pious remnant from the general desolation. We do not read that this Saviour was summoned and sent for, as the destroyers were; for he is always

798

ready, *appearing in the presence of God for us;* and to him, as the most proper person, the care of those that are marked for salvation is committed, *v.* 4. Now observe, 1. The distinguishing character of this remnant that is to be saved. They are such as *sigh and cry,* sigh in themselves, as men in pain and distress, cry to God in prayer, as men in earnest, because of *all the abominations that* are committed in Jerusalem. It was not only the idolatries they were guilty of, but all their other enormities, that were abominations to God. These pious few had witnessed against those abominations and had done what they could in their places to suppress them; but, finding all their attempts for the reformation of manners fruitless, they sat down, and *sighed, and cried,* wept in secret, and complained to God, because of the dishonour done to his name by their wickedness and the ruin it was bringing upon their church and nation. Note, It is not enough that we do not delight in the sins of others, and that we have not fellowship with them, but we must mourn for them, and lay them to heart; we must grieve for that which we cannot help, as those that hate sin for its own sake, and have a tender concern for the souls of others, as David (Ps. cxix. 136), and Lot, who *vexed his righteous soul* with the wicked conversation of his neighbours. The abominations committed in Jerusalem are to be in a special manner lamented, because they are in a particular manner offensive to God. 2. The distinguishing care taken of them. Orders are given to find those all out that are of such a pious public spirit: " *Go through the midst of the city* in quest of them, and though they are ever so much dispersed, and ever so closely hid from the fury of their persecutors, yet see that you discover them, *and set a mark upon their foreheads,*" (1.) To signify that God owns them for his, and he will confess them another day. A work of grace in the soul is to God *a mark upon the forehead,* which he will acknowledge as his mark, and by which *he knows those that are his.* (2.) To give to them who are thus marked an assurance of God's favour, that they may know it themselves; and the comfort of knowing it will be the most powerful support and cordial in calamitous times. Why should we perplex ourselves about this temporal life if we know by the mark that we have eternal life? (3.) To be a direction to the destroyers whom to pass by, as the blood upon the door-posts was an indication that that was an Israelite's house, and the first-born there must not be slain. Note, Those who keep themselves pure in times of common iniquity God will keep safe in times of common calamity. Those that distinguish themselves shall be distinguished; those that cry for other men's sins shall not need to cry for their own afflictions, for they shall be either delivered from them or comforted under them. God will set a mark upon his mourners, will book their sighs and bottle their tears. The *sealing of the servants of God in their foreheads* mentioned Rev. vii. 3 was the same token of the care God has of his own people with this related here; only this was to secure them from being destroyed, that from being seduced, which is equivalent.

5 And to the others he said in mine hearing, Go ye after him through the city, and smite: let not your eye spare, neither have ye pity: 6 Slay utterly old *and* young, both maids, and little children, and women: but come not near any man upon whom *is* the mark; and begin at my sanctuary. Then they began at the ancient men which *were* before the house. 7 And he said unto them, Defile the house, and fill the courts with the slain: go ye forth. And they went forth, and slew in the city. 8 And it came to pass, while they were slaying them, and I was left, that I fell upon my face, and cried, and said, Ah Lord GOD! wilt thou destroy all the residue of Israel in thy pouring out of thy fury upon Jerusalem? 9 Then said he unto me, The iniquity of the house of Israel and Judah *is* exceeding great, and the land is full of blood, and the city full of perverseness: for they say, The LORD hath forsaken the earth, and the LORD seeth not. 10 And as for me also, mine eye shall not spare, neither will I have pity, *but* I will recompense their way upon their head. 11 And, behold, the man clothed with linen, which *had* the inkhorn by his side, reported the matter, saying, I have done as thou hast commanded me.

In these verses we have,

I. A command given to the destroyers to do execution according to their commission. *They stood by the brazen altar,* waiting for orders; and orders are here given them to cut off and destroy all that were either guilty of, or accessory to, the abominations of Jerusalem, and that did not *sigh and cry* for them. Note, When God has *gathered his wheat into his garner* nothing remains but to *burn up the chaff,* Matt. iii. 12.

1. They are ordered to destroy all, (1.) Without exception. They must *go through the city, and smite:* they must *slay utterly,*

slay to destruction, give them their death's wound. They must make no distinction of age or sex, but cut off *old and young;* neither the beauty of the virgins, nor the innocency of the babes, shall secure them. This was fulfilled in the death of multitudes by famine and pestilence, especially by the sword of the Chaldeans, as far as the military execution went. Sometimes even such bloody work as this has been God's work. But what an evil thing is sin, then, which provokes the God of infinite mercy to such severity! (2.) Without compassion: "*Let not your eye spare, neither have you pity (v. 5);* you must not save any whom God has doomed to destruction, as Saul did Agag and the Amalekites, for that is *doing the work of God deceitfully,* Jer. xlviii. 10. None need to be more merciful than God is; and he had said (*ch.* viii. 18), *My eye shall not spare, neither will I have pity.* Note, Those that live in sin, and hate to be reformed, will perish in sin, and deserve not to be pitied; for they might easily have prevented the ruin, and would not.

2. They are warned not to do the least hurt to those that were marked for salvation: "*Come not near any man upon whom is the mark;* do not so much as threaten or frighten any of them; it is promised them that there shall no evil come nigh them, and therefore you must keep at a distance from them." The king of Babylon gave particular orders that Jeremiah should be protected. Baruch and Ebed-melech were secured, and, it is likely, others of Jeremiah's friends, for his sake. God had promised that *it should go well with his remnant* and they *should be well treated* (Jer. xv. 11); and we have reason to think that none of the mourning praying remnant fell by the sword of the Chaldeans, but that God found out some way or other to secure them all, as, in the last destruction of Jerusalem by the Romans, the Christians were all secured in a city called *Pella,* and none of them perished with the unbelieving Jews. Note, None of those shall be lost whom God has marked for life and salvation; for the foundation of God stands sure.

3. They are directed to *begin at the sanctuary (v. 6),* that sanctuary which, in the chapter before, he had seen the horrid profanation of; they must begin there because there the wickedness began which provoked God to send these judgments. The debaucheries of the priests were the poisoning of the springs, to which all the corruption of the streams was owing. The wickedness of the sanctuary was of all wickedness the most offensive to God, and therefore there the slaughter must begin: "*Begin* there, to try if the people will take warning by the judgments of God upon their priests, and will repent and reform; *begin* there, that all the world may see and know that the Lord, whose name is *Jealous,* is *a jealous God,* and hates sin most in those that are nearest to him."

Note, When judgments are abroad they commonly *begin at the house of God*, 1 Pet. iv. 17. *You only have I known, and therefore I will punish you*, Amos iii. 2. God's temple is a sanctuary, a refuge and protection for penitent sinners, but not for any that *go on still in their trespasses;* neither the sacredness of the place nor the eminency of their place in it will be their security. It should seem the destroyers made some difficulty of putting men to death in the temple, but God bids them not hesitate at that, but (*v.* 7), *Defile the house, and fill the courts with the slain.* They will not be *taken from the altar* (as was appointed by the law, Exod. xxi. 14), but think to secure themselves by *keeping hold of the horns of* it, like Joab, and therefore, like him, let them *die there*, 1 Kings ii. 30, 31. There the blood of one of God's prophets had been shed (Matt. xxiii. 35) and therefore let their blood be shed. Note, If the servants of God's house defile it with ther idolatries, God will justly suffer the enemies of it to defile it with their violences, Ps. lxxix. 1. But these acts of necessary justice were really, whatever they were ceremonially, rather a purification than a pollution of the sanctuary; it was *putting away evil from among them.*

4. They are appointed to *go forth into the city, v.* 6, 7. Note, Wherever sin has gone before judgment will follow after; and, though *judgment begins at the house of God*, yet it shall not end there. The holy city shall be no more a protection to the wicked people than the holy house was to the wicked priests.

II. Here is execution done accordingly. They observed their orders, and, 1. *They began at the elders, the ancient men that were before the house*, and slew them first, either those seventy ancients who worshipped idols in their chambers (*ch.* viii. 12) or those twenty-five who *worshipped the sun between the porch and the altar*, who might more properly be said to be *before the house*. Note, Ringleaders in sin may expect to be first met with by the judgments of God; and the sins of those who are in the most eminent and public stations call for the most exemplary punishments. 2. They proceeded to the common people : *They went forth and slew in the city;* for, when the decree has gone forth, there shall be no delay; if God begin, he will make an end.

III. Here is the prophet's intercession for a mitigation of the judgment, and a reprieve for some (*v.* 8): *While they were slaying them, and I was left, I fell upon my face.* Observe here, 1. How sensible the prophet was of God's mercy to him, in that he was spared when so many round about him were cut off. *Thousands fell on his right hand, and on his left,* and yet *the destruction did not come nigh him; only with his eyes did he behold the just reward of the wicked*, Ps. xci. 7, 8. He speaks as one that narrowly es-

caped the destruction, attributing it to God's goodness, not his own deserts. Note, The best saints must acknowledge themselves indebted to sparing mercy that they are not consumed. And when desolatin judgments are abroad, and multitudes fall by them, it ought to be accounted a great favour if we have our *lives ~ven us for a prey;* for we might justly have perished with those that perish. 2, Observe how he improved this mercy; he looked upon it that *therefore* he was left that he might stand in the gap to turn away the wrath of God. Note, We must look upon it that for this reason we are spared, that we may do good in our places, may do good by our prayers. Ezekiel did not triumph in the slaughter he made, but his *flesh trembled for fear of God* (as David's, Ps. cxix. 120); he *fell on* his *face, and cried*, not in fear for himself (he was one of those that were marked), but in compassion to his fellow-creatures. Those that sigh and cry for the sins of sinners cannot but sigh and cry for their miseries too; yet the day is coming when all this concern will be entirely swallowed up in a full satisfaction in this, that God is glorified; and those that now *fall on their faces, and cry, Ah ! Lord God*, will lift up their heads, and sing, *Hallelujah*, Rev. xix. 1, 3. The prophet humbly expostulates with God : " *Wilt thou destroy all the residue of Israel*, and shall there be none left but the few that are marked? Shall the Israel of God be destroyed, utterly destroyed? When there are but a few left shall those few be cut off, who might have been the seed of another generation? And will the God of Israel be himself their destroyer? Wilt thou now destroy Israel, who wast wont to protect and deliver Israel? Wilt thou so *pour out thy fury upon Jerusalem* as by the total destruction of the city to ruin the whole country too? Surely thou wilt not !" Note, Though we acknowledge that *God is righteous*, yet we have leave to *plead with him concerning his judgments*, Jer. xii. 1.

IV. Here is God's denial of the prophet's request for a mitigation of the judgment and his justification of himself in that denial, *v.* 9, 10. 1. Nothing could be said in extenuation of this sin. God was as willing to show mercy as the prophet could desire; he always is so. But here the case will not admit of it; it is such that mercy cannot be granted without wrong to justice; and it is not fit that one attribute of God should be glorified at the expense of another. Is it any pleasure to the Almighty that he should destroy, especially that he should destroy Israel? By no means. But the truth is their crimes are so flagrant that the reprieve of the sinners would be a connivance at the sin : " *The iniquity of the house of Judah and Israel is exceedingly great;* there is no suffering them to go on at this rate. *The land is filled with innocent blood*, and, when the city courts are appealed to for the defence of injured innocency, the remedy is as bad as the disease, for *the city is full of perverseness, or wresting of judgment ;* and that which they support themselves with in this iniquity is the same atheistical profane principle with which they flattered themselves in their idolatry, *ch.* viii. 12. *The L-rd has forsaken the earth,* and left it to us to do what we will in it; he will not intermeddle in the affairs of it; and, whatever wrong we do, he *sees not ;* he either knows it not, or will not take cognizance of it." Now how can those expect benefit by the mercy of God who thus bid defiance to his justice? No; nothing can be offered by an advocate in excuse of the crimes while the criminal puts in such a plea as this in his own vindication; and therefore, 2. Nothing can be done to mitigate the sentence (*v.* 10): "Whatever thou thinkest of it, *as for me, my eye shall not spare, neither will I have pity ;* I have borne with them as long as it was fit that such impudent sinners should be borne with; and therefore now *I will recompense their way on their head."* Note, Sinners sink and perish under the weight of their own sins; it is their own way, which they deliberately chose rather than the way of God, and which they obstinately persisted in, in contempt of the word of God, that is *recompensed on* them. Great iniquities justify God in great severities; nay, he is ready to justify himself, as he does here to the prophet, for he will be *clear when he judges.*

V. Here is a return made of the writ of protection which was issued out for the securing of those that mourned in Zion (*v.* 11): *The man clothed with linen reported the matter,* gave an account of what he had done in pursuance of his commission ; he had found out all that mourned in secret for the sins of the land, and cried out against them by a public testimony, and had marked them all in the forehead. Lord, *I have done as thou hast commanded me.* We do not find that those who were commissioned to destroy reported what destruction they had made, but he who was appointed to protect reported his matter; for it would be more pleasing both to God and to the prophet to hear of those that were saved than of those that perished. Or this report was made now because the thing was finished, whereas the destroying work would be a work of time, and when it was brought to an end then the report should be made. See how faithful Christ is to the trust reposed in him. Is he commanded to secure eternal life to the chosen remnant? He has done as was commanded him. *Of all that thou hast given me I have lost none.*

CHAP. X.

The prophet had observed to us (ch. viii. 4) that when he was in vision at Jerusalem he saw the same appearance of the glory of God there that he had seen by the river Chebar; now, in this chapter, he gives us some account of the appearance there, as far as was requisite for the clearing up of two further indications of the approaching destruction of Jerusalem, which God here gave the prophet:—I. The scattering of the coals of fire upon the city, which were taken from between the cherubim, ver. 1—7. II. The removal of the glory of God from the temple, and its being upon the wing to be gone, ver. 8—22. When God goes out from a people all judgments break in upon them.

THEN I looked, and, behold, in the firmament that was above the head of the cherubims there appeared over them as it were a sapphire-stone, as the appearance of the likeness of a throne. 2 And he spake unto the man clothed with linen, and said, Go in between the wheels, *even* under the cherub, and fill thine hand with coals of fire from between the cherubims, and scatter *them* over the city. And he went in in my sight. 3 Now the cherubims stood on the right side of the house, when the man went in; and the cloud filled the inner court. 4 Then the glory of the LORD went up from the cherub, *and stood* over the threshold of the house; and the house was filled with the cloud, and the court was full of the brightness of the LORD's glory. 5 And the sound of the cherubims' wings was heard *even* to the outer court, as the voice of the Almighty God when he speaketh. 6 And it came to pass, *that* when he had commanded the man clothed with linen, saying, Take fire from between the wheels, from between the cherubims ; then he went in, and stood beside the wheels. 7 And *one* cherub stretched forth his hand from between the cherubims unto the fire that *was* between the cherubims, and took *thereof,* and put *it* into the hands of *him that was* clothed with linen : who took *it,* and went out.

To inspire us with a holy awe and dread of God, and to fill us with his fear, we may observe, in this part of the vision which the prophet had,

I. The glorious appearance of his majesty. Something of the invisible world is here made visible, some faint representations of its brightness and beauty, some shadows, but such as are no more to be compared with the truth and substance than a picture with the life ; yet here is enough to oblige us all to the utmost reverence in our thoughts of God and approaches to him, if we will but admit the impressions this discovery of him will make. 1. He is here *in the firmament above the head of the cherubim, v.* 1. He manifests his glory in the upper world, where purity and brightness are both in perfection;

and the vast expanse of the firmament aims to speak the God that dwells there infinite. It is *the firmament of his power* and of his prospect too; for thence *he beholds* all *the children of men.* The divine nature infinitely transcends the angelic nature, and God is *above the head of the cherubim*, in respect not only of his dignity above them, but of his dominion over them. Cherubim have great power, and wisdom, and influence, but they are all subject to God and Christ. 2. He is here upon the throne, or that which had *the appearance of the likeness of a throne* (for God's glory and government infinitely transcend all the brightest ideas our minds can either form or receive concerning them); and it was *as it were a sapphire-stone*, pure and sparkling; such a throne has God *prepared in the heavens*, far exceeding the thrones of any earthly potentates. 3. He is here attended with a glorious train of holy angels. When God came into his temple *the cherubim stood on the right side of the house* (v. 3), as the prince's life-guard, attending the gate of his palace. Christ has angels at command. The orders given to all the angels of God are, to *worship him.* Some observe that they *stood on the right side of the house*, that is, the south side, because on the north side the image of jealousy was, and other instances of idolatry, from which they would place themselves at as great a distance as might be. 4. The appearance of his glory is veiled with a cloud, and yet out of that cloud darts forth a dazzling lustre; in *the house* and *inner court* there was *a cloud* and darkness, which filled them, and yet either the outer court, or the same court after some time, *was full of the brightness of the Lord's glory*, v. 3, 4. There was a darting forth of light and brightness; but, if any over curious eye pried into it, it would find itself lost in a cloud. His righteousness is conspicuous *as the great mountains*, and the brightness of it *fills the court*; but *his judgments are a great deep*, which we cannot fathom, *a cloud* which we cannot see through. *The brightness* discovers enough to awe and direct our consciences, but the *cloud* forbids us to expect the gratifying of our curiosity; for *we cannot order our speech by reason of darkness.* Thus (Hab. iii. 4) *he had rays coming out of his hand, and yet there was the hiding of his power.* Nothing is more clear than that God *is*, nothing more dark than *what* he is. God *covers himself with light*, and yet, as to us, *makes darkness his pavilion.* God took possession of the tabernacle and temple in a cloud, which was always the symbol of his presence. In the temple above there will be no cloud, but we shall *see face to face.* 5. The cherubim made a dreadful sound with their wings, v. 5. The vibration of them, as of the strings of musical instruments, made a curious melody; bees, and other winged insects, make a noise with their wings. Probably this intimated their pre-

paring to remove, by stretching forth and lifting up their wings, which made this noise as it were to give warning of it. This noise is said to be *as the voice of the almighty God when he speaks*, as the thunder, which is called *the voice of the Lord* (Ps. xxix. 3), or *as the voice of the Lord* when he spoke to Israel on Mount Sinai; and *therefore* he then gave the law with abundance of terror, to signify with what terror he would reckon for the violation of it, which he was now about to do. This noise of their *wings was heard even to the outer court*, the court of the people; for the Lord's voice, in his judgments, *cries in the city*, which those may hear that do not, as Ezekiel, see the visions of them.

II. The terrible directions of his wrath This vision has a further tendency than merely to set forth the divine grandeur; further orders are to be given for the destruction of Jerusalem The greatest devastations are made by fire and sword. For a general slaughter of the inhabitants of Jerusalem orders were given in the foregoing chapter; now here we have a command to lay the city in ashes, by *scattering coals of fire* upon it, which in the vision were fetched *from between the cherubim.*

1. For the issuing out of orders to do this *the glory of the Lord* was lifted *up from the cherub* (as in the chapter before for the giving of orders there, v. 3) *and stood* upon *the threshold of the house*, in imitation of the courts of judgment, which they kept in the gates of their cities. The people would not hear the oracles which God delivered to them from his holy temple, and therefore they shall thence be made to hear their doom.

2. *The man clothed in linen* who had marked those that were to be preserved is to be employed in this service; for *the same Jesus* that is the protector and Saviour of those that believe, having *all judgment committed to him*, that of condemnation as well as that of absolution, will *come in flaming fire to take vengeance on those that obey not his gospel.* He that sits on the throne calls *to the man clothed in linen to go in between the wheels, and fill his hand with coals of fire from between the cherubim, and scatter them over the city.* This intimates, (1.) That the burning of the city and temple by the Chaldeans was a consumption determined, and that therein they executed God's counsel, did what he designed before should be done. (2.) That the fire of divine wrath, which kindles judgment upon a people, is just and holy, for it is fire fetched *from between the cherubim.* The fire on God's altar, where atonement was made, had been slighted, to avenge which fire is here fetched from heaven, like that by which Nadab and Abihu were killed for offering strange fire. If a city, or town, or house, be burnt, whether by design or accident, if we trace it in its original, we shall find that the *coals* which kindled the *fire* came from *between the wheels:*

for there is not any evil of that kind in the city, but the Lord has done it. (3.) That Jesus Christ acts by commission from the Father, for from him he *receives authority to execute judgment, because he is the Son of man.* Christ came to *send fire on the earth* (Luke xii. 49) and in the great day will speak this world into ashes. By fire from his hand, the earth, and all the works that are therein, will be burnt up.

3. This *man clothed with linen* readily attended to this service; though, being *clothed with linen*, he was very unfit to go among the burning *coals*, yet, being called, he said, *Lo, I come;* this commandment he had received of his Father, and he complied with it; the prophet saw him go in, *v. 2. He went in, and stood beside the wheels,* expecting to be furnished there with the coals he was to scatter; for what Christ was to give he first received, whether for mercy or judgment. He was directed to take fire, but he staid till he had it given him, to show how slow he is to execute judgment, and how long-suffering to us-ward.

4. One of the cherubim reached him a handful of fire from the midst of the living creatures. The prophet, when he first saw this vision, observed that there were *burning coals of fire,* and *lamps, that went up and down among the living creatures* (ch. i. 13); thence this fire was taken, *v. 7.* The *spirit of burning, the refiner's fire,* by which Christ purifies his church, is of a divine original. It is by a celestial fire, *fire* from *between the cherubim,* that wonders are wrought. The *cherubim put it into* his *hand;* for the angels are ready to be employed by the Lord Jesus and to serve all his purposes.

5. When he had taken the fire he *went out,* no doubt to *scatter* it up and down upon *the city,* as he was directed. And *who can abide the day of his coming?* Who can stand before him when he goes out in his anger?

8 And there appeared in the cherubims the form of a man's hand under their wings. 9 And when I looked, behold the four wheels by the cherubims, one wheel by one cherub, and another wheel by another cherub: and the appearance of the wheels *was* as the colour of a beryl-stone. 10 And *as for* their appearances, they four had one likeness, as if a wheel had been in the midst of a wheel. 11 When they went, they went upon their four sides; they turned not as they went, but to the place whither the head looked they followed it; they turned not as they went. 12 And their whole body, and their backs, and their hands, and their wings, and the wheels, *were* full

of eyes round about, *even* the wheels that they four had. 13 As for the wheels, it was cried unto them in my hearing, O wheel. 14 And every one had four faces: the first face *was* the face of a cherub, and the second face *was* the face of a man, and the third the face of a lion, and the fourth the face of an eagle. 15 And the cherubims were lifted up. This *is* the living creature that I saw by the river of Chebar. 16 And when the cherubims went, the wheels went by them: and when the cherubims lifted up their wings to mount up from the earth, the same wheels also turned not from beside them. 17 When they stood, *these* stood; and when they were lifted up, *these* lifted up themselves *also:* for the spirit of the living creature *was* in them. 18 Then the glory of the LORD departed from off the threshold of the house, and stood over the cherubims. 19 And the cherubims lifted up their wings, and mounted up from the earth in my sight: when they went out, the wheels also *were* beside them, and *every one* stood at the door of the east gate of the LORD's house; and the glory of the God of Israel *was* over them above. 20 This *is* the living creature that I saw under the God of Israel by the river of Chebar; and I knew that they *were* the cherubims. 21 Every one had four faces a-piece, and every one four wings; and the likeness of the hands of a man *was* under their wings. 22 And the likeness of their faces *was* the same faces which I saw by the river of Chebar, their appearances and themselves: they went every one straight forward.

We have here a further account of the vision of God's glory which Ezekiel saw, here intended to introduce that direful omen of the departure of that glory from them, which would open the door for ruin to break in.

I. Ezekiel sees the glory of God shining in the sanctuary, as he had seen it *by the river of Chebar,* and gives an account of it, that those who had by their wickedness provoked God to depart from them might know what they had lost and might lament after the Lord, groaning out their Ichabod, *Where is the glory?* Ezekiel here sees the operations of divine Providence in the government of the lower world, and the affairs of it, represented by the *four wheels;* and the perfections of the holy angels, the inhabitants of the upper world, and their ministrations, represented by the *four living creatures,* every one of which had *four faces.* The agency of the angels in directing the affairs of this world is represented by the close communication that was between the *living creatures* and the *wheels,* the wheels being guided by them in all their motions, as the chariot is by him that drives it. But the same Spirit being both in the *living creatures* and in the *wheels* denotes that infinite wisdom which serves its own purposes by the ministration of angels and all the occurrences of this lower world. So that this vision gives our faith a view of that throne which the Lord has *prepared in the heavens,* and that kingdom of his which *rules over all,* Ps. ciii. 19. The prophet observes that this was *the same vision* with that he saw by the river of Chebar (*v.* 15, 22), and yet in one thing there seems to be a material difference, that that which was there *the face of an ox,* and was *on the left side* (*ch.* i. 10), is here the *face of a cherub,* and is the *first face* (*v.* 14), whence some have concluded that the peculiar face of a cherub was that of an ox, which the Israelites had an eye to when they made the golden calf. I rather think that in this latter vision the first face was the proper appearance or figure of a cherub, which Ezekiel knew very well, being a priest, by what he had seen in the temple of the Lord (1 Kings vi. 29), but which we now have no certainty of at all; and by this Ezekiel knew assuredly, whereas before he only conjectured it, that they were all cherubim, though putting on different faces, *v.* 20. And this first appearing in the proper figure of a cherub, and yet it being proper to retain the number of four, that of the ox is left out and dropped, because the face of the cherubim had been most abused by the worship of an ox. As sometimes when God appeared to deliver his people, so now when he appeared to depart from them, *he rode upon a cherub, and did fly.* Now observe here, 1. That this world is subject to turns, and changes, and various revolutions. The course of affairs in it is represented by *wheels* (*v.* 9); sometimes one spoke is uppermost and sometimes another; they are still ebbing and flowing like the sea, waxing and waning like the moon, 1 Sam. ii. 4, &c. Nay, their appearance is as if there were a *wheel in the midst of a wheel* (*v.* 10), which intimates the mutual references of providences to each other, their dependences on each other, and the joint tendency of all to one common end, while their motions as to us are intricate, and perplexed, and seemingly contrary. 2. That there is an admirable harmony and uniformity in the various occurrences of providence (*v.* 13): *As for the wheels,* though they

moved several ways, yet *it was cried to them, O wheel !* they were all as one, being guided by one Spirit to one end; for God works all according to the counsel of his own will, which is one, for his own glory, which is one. And this makes the disposals of Providence truly admirable, and to be looked upon with wonder. As the works of his creation, considered separately, were *good,* but all together *very good,* so the wheels of Providence, considered by themselves, are wonderful, but put them together and they are very wonderful. *O wheel !* 3. That the motions of Providence are steady and regular, and whatever the Lord pleases that he does and is never put upon new counsels. *The wheels turned not as they went* (*v.* 11), and the *living creatures went every one straight forward,* *v.* 22. Whatever difficulties lay in their way, they were sure to get over them, and were never obliged to stand still, turn aside, or go back. So perfectly known to God are all his works that he is never put upon new counsels. 4. That God makes more use of the ministration of angels in the government of this lower world than we are aware of: *The four wheels were by the cherubim, one wheel by one cherub and another wheel by another cherub,* *v.* 9. What has been imagined by some concerning the spheres above, that every orb has its intelligence to guide it, is here intimated concerning the wheels below, that every wheel has its cherub to guide it. We think it a satisfaction to us if under the wise God there are wise men employed in managing the affairs of kingdoms and churches; whether there be so or no, it appears by this that there are wise angels employed, *a cherub to every wheel.* 5. That all the motions of Providence and all the ministrations of angels are under the government of the great God. They are all *full of eyes,* those eyes of the Lord which run to and fro through the earth and which the angels have always an eye to, *v.* 12. The *living creatures* and *the wheels* concur in their motions and rests (*v.* 17); for *the Spirit of life,* as it may be read, or *the Spirit of the living creatures, is in the wheels.* The Spirit of God directs all the creatures, both upper and lower, so as to make them serve the divine purpose. Events are not determined by the *wheel of fortune,* which is blind, but by the *wheels of Providence,* which are full of eyes.

II. Ezekiel sees the glory of God removing out of the sanctuary, the place where God's honour had long dwelt, and this sight is as sad as the other was grateful. It was pleasant to see that God had not *forsaken the earth* (as the idolaters suggested, *ch.* ix. 9), but sad to see that he was forsaking his sanctuary. The *glory of the Lord stood over the threshold, v.* 4. But now it *departed from off the threshold,* having thence given the necessary orders for the destruction of the city, and it *stood over the cherubim,* not those in the most holy place, but those that Ezekiel now saw in vision, v. 18. It ascended that stately chariot, as the judge, when he comes off the bench, goes into his coach and is gone. And immediately *the cherubim lifted up their wings (v. 19),* as they were directed, and they *mounted up from the earth,* as birds upon the wing ; and, *when they went out,* the wheels of this chariot were not drawn, but went by instinct, *beside them,* by which it appeared that *the Spirit of the living creatures was in the wheels.* Thus, when God is leaving a people in displeasure, angels above, and all events here below, shall concur to further his departure. But observe here, In the courts of the temple where the people of Israel had dishonoured their God, had cast off his yoke and withdrawn the shoulder from it, blessed angels appear very ready to serve him, to draw in his chariot, and to *mount upwards* with it. God had shown the prophet how the will of God was disobeyed by men on earth (*ch.* viii.) ; here he shows him how readily it is obeyed by angels and inferior creatures ; and it is a comfort to us, when we grieve for the wickedness of the wicked, to think how his angels do his commandments, *hearkening to the voice of his word,* Ps. ciii. 20. Let us now, 1. Take a view of this chariot in which *the glory of the God of Israel rides triumphantly.* He that is the God of Israel is the God of heaven and earth, and has the command of all the powers of both. Let the faithful Israelites comfort themselves with this, that he who is their God is above the cherubim ; their Redeemer is so (1 Pet. iii. 22) and has the sole and sovereign disposal of all events ; *the living creatures* and *the wheels* agree to serve him, so that he is *head over all things to the church.* The rabbin call this vision that Ezekiel had *Mercabah*—the *vision of the chariot ;* and thence they call the more abstruse part of divinity, which treats concerning God and spirits, *Opus currûs*—*The work of the chariot,* as they do the other part, that is more plain and familiar, *Opus bereshith*—*The work of the creation.*—2. Let us attend the motions of this chariot : The *cherubim, and the glory of God above them, stood at the door of the east gate of the Lord's house,* ready to depart and leave the house, *v.* 19. But observe with how many stops and pauses God departs, as loth to go, as if to see if there be any that will intercede with him to return. None of the priests in the inner court, between the temple and the altar, would court his stay ; therefore he leaves their court, and stands at the *east gate,* which led into the *court of the people,* to see if any of them would yet at length stand in the gap. Note, God removes by degrees from a provoking people ; and, when he is ready to depart in displeasure, would return to them in mercy if they were but a repenting praying people.

CHAP. XI.

This chapter concludes the vision which Ezekiel saw, and this part of it furnishes him with two messages :—I. A message of wrath against those who continued still at Jerusalem, and were there in the height of presumption, thinking they should never fall, ver. 1—13. II. A message of comfort to those who were carried captives into Babylon and were there in the depth of despondency, thinking they should never rise. And, as the former are assured that God has judgments in store for them notwithstanding their present security, so the latter are assured that God has mercy in store for them notwithstanding their present distress, ver. 14—21. And so the glory of God removes further, ver. 22, 23. The vision disappears (ver. 24), and Ezekiel faithfully gives his hearers an account of it, ver. 25.

MOREOVER the spirit lifted me up, and brought me unto the east gate of the LORD's house, which looketh eastward : and behold at the door of the gate five and twenty men ; among whom I saw Jaazaniah the son of Azur, and Pelatiah the son of Benaiah, princes of the people. 2 Then said he unto me, Son of man, these *are* the men that devise mischief, and give wicked counsel in this city : 3 Which say, *It is* not near ; let us build houses : this *city is* the caldron, and we *be* the flesh. 4 Therefore prophesy against them, prophesy, O son of man. 5 And the Spirit of the LORD fell upon me, and said unto me, Speak ; Thus saith the LORD ; Thus have ye said, O house of Israel : for I know the things that come into your mind, *every one of* them. 6 Ye have multiplied your slain in this city, and ye have filled the streets thereof with the slain. 7 Therefore thus saith the Lord GOD ; Your slain whom ye have laid in the midst of it, they *are* the flesh, and this *city is* the caldron : but I will bring you forth out of the midst of it. 8 Ye have feared the sword ; and I will bring a sword upon you, saith the Lord GOD. 9 And I will bring you out of the midst thereof, and deliver you into the hands of strangers, and will execute judgments among you. 10 Ye shall fall by the sword ; I will judge you in the border of Israel ; and ye shall know that I *am* the LORD. 11 This *city* shall not be your caldron, neither shall ye be the flesh in the midst thereof ; *but* I will judge you in the border of Israel : 12 And ye shall know that I *am* the LORD : for ye have not walked in my statutes, neither executed my judgments, but have done after the manners of the heathen that *are* round about you. 13 And it came to pass, when I prophesied, that Pelatiah the son of Benaiah died. Then fell I down upon my face, and cried with a loud voice, and said, Ah Lord God! wilt thou make a full end of the remnant of Israel?

We have here,

I. The great security of the princes of Jerusalem, notwithstanding the judgments of God that were upon them. The prophet was brought, in vision, to the gate of the temple where these princes sat in council upon the present arduous affairs of the city: *The Spirit lifted me up, and brought me to the east gate of the Lord's house, and behold twenty-five men were there.* See how obsequious the prophet was to the Spirit's orders and how observant of all the discoveries that were made to him. It should seem, these twenty-five men were not the same with those twenty-five whom he saw at the door of the temple, *worshipping towards the east* (*ch.* viii. 16); those seem to have been priests or Levites, for they were between the porch and the altar, but these were princes sitting *in the gate of the Lord's house*, to try causes (Jer. xxvi. 10), and they are here charged, not with corruptions in worship, but with mal-administration in the government; two of them are named, because they were the most leading active men, and perhaps because the prophet knew them, though he had been some years absent—*Pelatiah* and *Jaazaniah*, not that mentioned *ch.* viii. 11, for he was the son of *Shaphan*, this is the *son of Azur*. Some tell us that Jerusalem was divided into twenty-four wards, and that these were the governors or aldermen of those wards, with their mayor or president. Now observe, 1. The general character which God gives of these men to the prophet (*v.* 2): *"These are the men that devise mischief;* under pretence of concerting measures for the public safety they harden people in their sins, and take off their fear of God's judgments which they are threatened with by the prophets; they *give wicked counsel in this city,* counselling them to restrain and silence the prophets, to rebel against the king of Babylon, and to resolve upon holding *the city* out to the last extremity." Note, It is bad with a people when the things that belong to their peace are hidden from the eyes of those who are entrusted with their counsels. And, when mischief is done, God knows at whose door to lay it, and, in the day of discovery and recompence, will be sure to lay it at the right door, and will say, *These are the men that devised it,* though they are great men, and pass for wise men, and must not now be contradicted or controlled. 2. The particular charge exhibited against them in proof of this character. They are indicted

for words spoken at their council-board, which he that *stands in the congregation of the mighty* would take cognizance of (*v.* 3); they said to this effect, *"It is not near;* the destruction of our city, that has been so often threatened by the prophets, *is not near,* not so near as they talk of." They are conscious to themselves of such an enmity to reformation that they cannot but conclude it will come at last; but they have such an opinion of God's patience (though they have long abused it) that they are willing to hope it will not come this great while. Note, Where Satan cannot persuade men to look upon the judgment to come as a thing doubtful and uncertain, yet he gains his point by persuading them to look upon it as a thing at a distance, so that it loses its force: if it be sure, yet *it is not near;* whereas, in truth, *the Judge stands before the door.* Now, if the destruction is not near, they conclude, *Let us build houses;* let us count upon a continuance, for *this city is the caldron and we are the flesh.* This seems to be a proverbial expression, signifying no more than this, "We are as safe in this city as flesh in a boiling pot; the walls of the city shall be to us as *walls of brass,* and shall receive no more damage from the besiegers about it than the *caldron* does from *the fire under it.* Those that think to force us out of our city into captivity shall find it to be as much at their peril as it would be to take the flesh out of a boiling pot with their hands." This appears to be the meaning of it, by the answer God gives to it (*v.* 9): *" I will bring you out of the midst of the city,* where you think yourselves safe, and then it will appear (*v.* 11) that *this is not your caldron, neither are you the flesh."* Perhaps it has a particular reference to *the flesh of the peace-offerings,* which it was so great an offence for the priests themselves to take out of the *caldron* while it was in seething (as we find 1 Sam. ii. 13, 14), and then it intimates that they were the more secure because Jerusalem was the holy city, and they thought themselves a holy people in it, not to be meddled with. Some think this was a banter upon Jeremiah, who in one of his first visions saw Jerusalem represented by a *seething pot,* Jer. i. 13. "Now," say they, in a way of jest and ridicule, " if it be a seething pot, we are as the flesh in it, and who dares meddle with us?" Thus they continued mocking the messengers of the Lord, even while they suffered for so doing; but *be you not mockers, lest your bands be made strong.* Those hearts are hard indeed which are made more secure by those words of God which were designed for warning to them.

II. The method taken to awaken them out of their security. One would think that the providences of God which related to them were enough to startle them; but, to help them to understand and improve those, the word of God is sent to them to give them warning (*v.* 4): *Therefore prophesy against them,* and try to undeceive them; *prophesy, O son of man!* upon these dead and dry bones. Note, The greatest kindness ministers can do to secure sinners is to preach against them, and to show them their misery and danger, though they are ever so unwilling to see them. We then act most for them when we appear most against them. But the prophet, being at a loss what to say to men that were hardened in sin, and that bade defiance to the judgments of God, *the Spirit of the Lord fell upon him,* to make him full of power and courage, and *said unto him, Speak.* Note, When sinners are flattering themselves into their own ruin it is time to speak, and to tell them that they shall have no peace if they go on. Ministers are sometimes so bashful and timorous, and so much at a loss, that they must be put on to speak, and to speak boldly. But he that commands the prophet to speak gives him instructions what to say; and he must address himself to them as *the house of Israel* (*v.* 5), for not the princes only, but all the people, were concerned to know the truth of their cause, to know the worst of it. They are the *house of Israel,* and therefore the *God of Israel* is concerned, in kindness to them, to give them warning; and they are concerned in duty to him to take the warning. And what is it that he must say to them in God's name? 1. Let them know that the God of heaven takes notice of the vain confidences with which they support themselves (*v.* 5): " *I know the things which come into your minds every one of them,* what secret reasons you have for these resolutions, and what you aim at in putting so good a face upon a matter you know to be bad." Note, God perfectly knows not only the things that come out of our mouths, but the things that come into our minds, not only all we say, but all we think; even those thoughts that are most suddenly darted into our minds, and that as suddenly slip out of them again, so that we ourselves are scarcely aware of them, yet God knows them. He knows us better than we know ourselves; *he understands our thoughts afar off.* The consideration of this should oblige us to keep our hearts with all diligence, that no vain thoughts come into them or lodge within them. 2. Let them know that those who advised the people to stand it out should be accounted before God the murderers of all who had fallen, or should yet fall, in Jerusalem, by the sword of the Chaldeans; and those slain were the only ones that should *remain in the city,* as the *flesh in the caldron.* " *You have multiplied your slain in the city,* not only those whom you have by the sword of justice unjustly put to death under colour of law, but those whom you have by your wilfulness and pride unwisely exposed to the sword of war,

though you were told by the prophets that you should certainly go by the worst. Thus you, with your stubborn humour, have *filled the streets of Jerusalem with the slain,*" *v.* 6. Note, Those who are either unrighteous or imprudent in beginning or carrying on a war bring upon themselves a great deal of the guilt of blood; and those who are slain in the battles or sieges which they, by such a reasonable peace as the war aimed at, might have prevented, will be called *their slain.* Now these slain are the only flesh that shall be left in this *caldron, v.* 7. There shall none remain to keep possession of the city but those that are buried in it. There shall be no inhabitants of Jerusalem but the inhabitants of the graves there, no freemen of the city but the free among the dead. 3. Let them know that, how impregnable soever they thought their city to be, they should be forced out of it, either driven to flight or dragged into captivity: *I will bring you forth out of the midst of it,* whether you will or no, *v.* 7, 9. They had provoked God to forsake the city, and thought they should do well enough by their own policy and strength when he was gone; but God will make them know that there is no peace to those that have left their God. If they have by their sins driven God from his house, he will soon by his judgments drive them from theirs; and it will be found that those are least safe that are most secure: "This city shall not be your *caldron, neither shall you be the flesh;* you shall not soak away in it as you promise yourselves, and die in your nest; you think yourself safe *in the midst thereof,* but you shall not be long there." 4. Let them know that when God has got them out of the midst of Jerusalem he will pursue them with his judgments wherever he finds them, the judgments which they thought to shelter themselves from by keeping close in Jerusalem. They feared the sword if they should go out to the Chaldeans, and therefore would abide in their *caldron,* but, says God, I will *bring a sword upon you* (*v.* 8) and *you shall fall by the sword, v.* 10. Note, The fear of the wicked shall come upon him. And there is no fence against the judgments of God when they come with commission, no, not in walls of brass. They were afraid of trusting to the mercy of strangers. "But," says God, " *I will deliver you into the hands of strangers,* whose resentments you shall feel, since you were not willing to lie at their mercy." See Jer. xxxviii. 17, 18. They thought to escape the judgments of God, but God says that he will *execute judgments upon them;* and whereas they resolved, if they must be judged, that it should be in Jerusalem, God tells them (*v.* 10 and again *v.* 11) that he will judge them *in the borders of Israel,* which was fulfilled when Nebuchadnezzar slew all the nobles of Judah at Riblah in the land of Hamath, on the utmost border of the land of Canaan. Note, Those who have taken ever so deep root in the place where they live cannot be sure that in that place they shall die. 5. Let them know that all this is the due punishment of their sin, and *the revelation of the righteous judgment of God* against them : *You shall know that I am the Lord, v.* 10 and again *v.* 12. Those shall be made to know by the sword of the Lord who would not be taught by his word what a hatred he has to sin, and what a fearful thing it is for impenitent sinners to fall into his hands. *I will execute judgments,* and then you shall *know that I am the Lord,* for the Lord is known by the judgments which he executes upon those *that have not walked in his statutes.* Hereby it is known that he made the law, because he punishes the breach of it. *I will execute judgments among you* (says God) because *you have not execut- ed my judgments, v.* 12. Note, The execut- ing of the judgments of God's mouth by us, in a uniform steady course of obedience to his law, is the only way to prevent the executing of the judgments of his hand upon us in our ruin and confusion. One way or other. God's judgments will be executed; the law will take place either in its precept or in its penalty. If we do not give honour to God by executing his judgments as he has commanded, he will *get him honour* upon us by executing his judgments as he has threatened ; and thus we shall know that he is the Lord, the sovereign Lord of all, that will not be mocked. And observe, When they cast off God's statutes, and walked not in them, they did *after the man- ners of the heathen that were round about them,* and introduced into their worship all their impure, ridiculous, and barbarous usages. When men leave the settled rule of divine institutions, they wander endlessly. Justly therefore was this made the reason why they should *keep God's ordinances,* that they might not *commit the abominable cus- toms of the heathen,* Lev. xviii. 30.

III. This awakening word is here imme- diately followed by an awakening providence, *v.* 13. Here we may observe, 1. With what power Ezekiel prophesied, or, rather, what a divine power went along with it : *It came to pass, when I prophesied, that Pelatiah the son of Benaiah died;* he was mentioned (*v.* 1) as a principal man among the twenty-five princes that made all the mischief in Jerusalem. It should seem, this was done in vision now, as the slaying of the ancient men (*ch.* ix. 6) upon occasion of which Ezekiel prayed (*v.* 8) as he did here; but it was an assurance that when this prophecy should be published it should be done in fact. The death of Pelatiah was an earnest of the complete accomplishment of this prophecy. Note, God is pleased often- times to single out some sinners, and to make them monuments of his justice, for warning to others of what is coming ; and

some that thought themselves very safe are snatched away suddenly, and drop down dead in an instant, as Ananias and Sapphira at Peter's feet when he prophesied. 2. With what pity Ezekiel prayed. Though the sudden death of Pelatiah was a confirmation of Ezekiel's prophecy, and really an honour to him, yet he was in deep concern about it, and laid it to heart as if he had been his relation or friend : *He fell on his face and cried with a loud voice,* as one in earnest, " *Ah! Lord God, wilt thou make a full end of the remnant of Israel?* Many are swept away by the judgments we have been under ; and shall the remnant which have escaped the sword die thus by the immediate hand of heaven ? Then thou wilt indeed make a full end." Perhaps it was Ezekiel's in- firmity to bewail the death of this wicked prince thus, as it was Samuel's to mourn so long for Saul ; but thus he showed how far he was from desiring the woeful day he foretold. David lamented the sickness of those that hated and persecuted him. And we ought to be much affected with the sudden death of others, yea, though they are wicked.

14 Again the word of the LORD came unto me, saying, 15 Son of man, thy brethren, *even* thy brethren, the men of thy kindred, and all the house of Israel wholly, *are* they unto whom the inhabitants of Jerusalem have said, Get you far from the LORD : unto us is this land given in posses- sion. 16 Therefore say, Thus saith the Lord GOD ; Although I have cast them far off among the heathen, although I have scattered them among the countries, yet will I be to them as a little sanctuary in the countries where they shall come. 17 Therefore say, Thus saith the Lord GOD ; I will even gather you from the people, and assemble you out of the countries where ye have been scattered, and I will give you the land of Israel. 18 And they shall come thither, and they shall take away all the detestable things thereof and all the abominations thereof from thence. 19 And I will give them one heart, and I will put a new spirit within you; and I will take the stony heart out of their flesh, and will give them a heart of flesh : 20 That they may walk in my statutes, and keep mine ordinances, and do them : and they shall be my people, and I will be

their God. 21 But *as for them* whose heart walketh after the heart of their detestable things and their abominations, I will recompense their way upon their own heads, saith the the Lord GOD.

Prophecy was designed to exalt *every valley* as well as to bring low *every mountain and hill* (Isa. xl. 4), and prophets were to speak not only conviction to the presumptuous and secure, but comfort to the despised and desponding that trembled at God's word. The prophet Ezekiel, having in the former part of this chapter received instructions for the awakening of those that were *at ease in Zion*, is in these verses furnished with comfortable words for those that mourned in Babylon and *by the rivers* there sat *weeping* when they *remembered Zion.* Observe,

I. How the pious captives were trampled upon and insulted over by those who continued in Jerusalem, *v.* 15. God tells the prophet what the inhabitants of Jerusalem said of him and the rest of them that were already carried away to Babylon. God had owned them as *good figs*, and declared it was for their good that he had sent them into Babylon; but the inhabitants of Jerusalem abandoned them, supposing those that were really all the best saints to be the greatest sinners of all men that dwelt in Jerusalem. Observe, 1. How they are described: They are *thy brethren* (says God to the prophet), whom thou hast a concern and affection for; they are *the men of thy kindred (the men of thy redemption,* so the word is), thy next of kin, to whom the right of redeeming the alienated possession belongs, but who are so far from being able to do it that they have themselves gone into captivity. They are *the whole house of Israel;* God so accounts of them because they only have retained their integrity, and are bettered by their captivity. They were not only of the same family and nation with Ezekiel, but of the same spirit; they were his hearers, and he had communion with them in holy ordinances; and perhaps upon that account they are called *his brethren and the men of his kindred.* 2. How they were disowned by *the inhabitants of Jerusalem;* they said of them, *Get you far from the Lord.* Those that were at ease and proud themselves scorned their brethren that were humbled and under humbling providences. (1.) They cut them off from being members of their church. Because they had separated themselves from their rulers, and in compliance with the will of God had surrendered themselves to the king of Babylon, they excommunicated them, and said, "*Get you far from the Lord;* we will have nothing to do with you." Those that were superstitious were very willing to shake off those that were conscientious, and were severe in their censures of them and sentences against

them, as if they were forsaken and forgotten of the Lord and were cut off from the communion of the faithful. (2.) They cut them off from being members of the commonwealth too, as if they had no longer any part or lot in the matter: "*Unto us is this land given in possession,* and you have forfeited your estates by surrendering to the king of Babylon, and we have thereby become entitled to them." God takes notice of, and is much displeased with, the contempt which those that are in prosperity put upon their brethren that are in affliction.

II. The gracious promises which God made to them in consideration of the insolent conduct of their brethren towards them. Those that hated them and cast them out said, *Let the Lord be glorified;* but *he shall appear to their joy,* Isa. lxvi. 5. God owns that his hand had gone out against them, which had given occasion to their brethren to triumph over them (*v.* 16): "It is true *I have cast them far off among the heathen* and *scattered them among the countries;* they look as if they were an abandoned people, and so mingled with the nations that they will be lost among them; but I have mercy in store for them." Note, God takes occasion from the contempts which are put upon his people to speak comfort to them, as David hoped God would reward him good for Shimei's cursing. His time to support his people's hopes is when their enemies are endeavouring to drive them to despair. Now God promises,

1. That he will make up to them the want of the temple and the privileges of it (*v.* 16): *I will be to them as a little sanctuary, in the countries where they shall come.* Those at Jerusalem have the temple, but without God; those in Babylon have God, though without the temple. (1.) God *will be a sanctuary to them;* that is, a place of refuge; to him they shall flee, and in him they shall be safe, as he was that took hold on *the horns of the altar.* Or, rather, they shall have such communion with God in the land of their captivity as it was thought could be had nowhere but in the temple. They shall there *see God's power and his glory,* as they used *to see them in the sanctuary;* they shall have the tokens of God's presence with them, and his grace in their hearts shall sanctify their prayers and praises, as well as ever the altar sanctified the gift, so that they shall *please the Lord better than an ox or bullock.* (2.) He *will be a little sanctuary,* not seen or observed by their enemies, who looked with an evil and an envious eye upon *that house* at Jerusalem which was high and great, 1 Kings ix. 8. They were but few and mean, and a little sanctuary was fittest for them. God regards the low estate of his people, and suits his favours to their circumstances. Observe the condescensions of divine grace. The great God will be to his people a little sanctuary. Note, Those that are deprived of

the benefit of public ordinances, if it be not their own fault, may have the want of them abundantly made up in the immediate communications of divine grace and comforts.

2. That God would in due time put an end to their afflictions, bring them out of the land of their captivity, and settle them again, them or their children, in their own land (*v.* 17): " *I will gather* even *you* that are thus dispersed, thus despised, and given over for lost by your own countrymen; *I will gather you from the people*, distinguish you from those with whom you are mingled, deliver you from those by whom you are held captives, *and assemble you* in a body out of the countries *where you have been scattered*; you shall not come back one by one, but all together, which will make your return more honourable, safe, and comfortable; and then *I will give you the land of Israel*, which now your brethren look upon you as for ever shut out from." Note, It is well for us that men's severe censures cannot cut us off from God's gracious promises. There are many that will be found to have a place in the holy land whom uncharitable men, by their monopolies of it to themselves, had secluded from it. *I will give you the land of Israel*, give it to you again by a new grant, *and they shall come thither*. If there be any thing in the change of the person from *you* to *them*, it may signify the posterity of those to whom the promise is made. " *You* shall have the title as the patriarchs had, and *those* that come after shall have the possession."

3. That God by his grace would part between them and their sins, *v.* 18. Their captivity shall effectually cure them of their idolatry : *When they come thither* to their own land again *they shall take away all the detestable things thereof*. Their idols, that had been their delectable things, should now be looked upon with detestation, not only the idols of Babylon, where they were captives, but the idols of Canaan, where they were natives; they should not only not worship them as they had done, but they should not suffer any monuments of them to remain : *They shall take all the abominations thereof thence*. Note, *Then* it is in mercy that we return to a prosperous estate, when we return not to the sins and follies of that state. *What have I to do any more with idols?*

4. That God would powerfully dispose them to their duty; they shall not only *cease to do evil*, but they shall *learn to do well*, because there shall be not only an end of their troubles, but a return to their peace.

(1.) God will plant good principles in them; he will make the tree good, *v.* 19. This is a gospel promise, and is made good to all those whom God designs for the heavenly Canaan; for God prepares all for heaven whom he has prepared heaven for. It is promised, [1.] That God *will give them*

810

one heart, a heart entire for the true God and not divided as it had been among many gods, a heart firmly fixed and resolved for God and not wavering, steady and uniform, and not inconstant with itself. *One heart* is a sincere and upright heart, its intentions of a piece with its professions. [2.] That he *will put a new spirit within them*, a temper of mind agreeable to the new circumstances into which God in his providence would bring them. All that are sanctified have *a new spirit*, quite different from what it was; they act from new principles, walk by new rules, and aim at new ends. A new name, or a new face, will not serve without a new spirit. *If any man be in Christ, he is a new creature.* [3.] That he *will take* away *the stony heart out of their flesh*, out of their corrupt nature. Their hearts shall no longer be, as they have been, dead and dry, and hard and heavy, as a stone, no longer incapable of bearing good fruit, so that the good seed is lost upon it, as it was on the *stony ground*. [4.] That he *will give them a heart of flesh*, not dead or proud flesh, but living flesh; he will make their hearts sensible of spiritual pains and spiritual pleasures, will make them tender, and apt to receive impressions. This is God's work, it is his gift, his gift by promise; and a wonderful and happy change it is that is wrought by it, from death to life. This is promised to those whom God would bring back to their own land; for *then* such a change of the condition is for the better indeed when it is accompanied with such a change of the heart; and such a change must be wrought in all those that shall be brought to the *better country*, that is, the heavenly.

(2.) Their practices shall be consonant to those principles : *I will give them a new spirit*, not that they may be able to discourse well of religion and to dispute for it, but *that they may walk in my statutes* in their whole conversation *and keep my ordinances* in all acts of religious worship, *v.* 20. These two must go together; and those to whom God has given *a new heart and a new spirit* will make conscience of both; and then *they shall be my people and I will be their God*. The ancient covenant, which seemed to be broken and forgotten, shall be renewed. By their idolatry, it should seem, they had cast God off; by their captivity, it should seem, God had cast them off. But when they were cured of their idolatry, and delivered out of their captivity, God and his Israel own one another again. God, by his good work in them, will make them his *people;* and then, by the tokens of his good-will towards them, he will show that he is *their God*.

III. Here is a threatening of wrath against those who hated to be reformed. As, when judgments are threatened, the righteous are distinguished so as not to share in the evil of those judgments, so, when favours are promised, the wicked are distinguished so as not to share in the comfort of those favours; they have no part nor lot in the matter, *v.* 21. *But, as for those* that have no grace, what have they *to do with peace?* Observe, 1. Their description. Their *heart walks after the heart of their detestable things;* they have as great a mind to worship devils as devils have to be worshipped. Or, in opposition to the *new heart* which God gives his people, which is a heart after his own heart, they have a *heart after the heart of their idols;* in their temper and practice they conformed to the characters and accounts given them of their idols, and the ideas they had of them, and of them they learned lewdness and cruelty. Here lies the root of all their wickedness, the corruption of the heart; as the root of their reformation is laid in the renovation of the heart. The heart has its walks, and according as those are the man is. 2. Their doom. It carries both justice and terror in it: *I will recompense their way upon their own heads;* I will deal with them as they deserve. There needs no more than this to speak God righteous, that he does but render to men according to their deserts: and yet such are the deserts of sin that there needs no more than this to speak the sinner miserable.

22 Then did the cherubims lift up their wings, and the wheels beside them; and the glory of the God of Israel *was* over them above. 23 And the glory of the LORD went up from the midst of the city, and stood upon the mountain which *is* on the east side of the city. 24 Afterwards the spirit took me up, and brought me in a vision by the Spirit of God into Chaldea, to them of the captivity. So the vision that I had seen went up from me. 25 Then I spake unto them of the captivity all the things that the LORD had showed me.

Here is, 1. The departure of God's presence from the city and temple. When the message was committed to the prophet, and he was fully apprized of it, fully instructed how to separate between *the precious and the vile,* then *the cherubim lifted up their wings and the wheels beside them* (*v.* 22) as before, *ch.* x. 19. Angels, when they have done their errands in this lower world, are upon the wing to be gone, for they lose no time. We left *the glory of the Lord* last at *the east gate of the temple* (ch. x. 19), which is here said to be in the *midst of the city.* Now here we are told that, finding and wondering that there was none to intercede, none to uphold, none to invite its return, it removed next to *the mountain which is on the east side of the city* (*v.* 23); that was the *mount of Olives.* On this mountain they had set up

their idols, to confront God in his temple, when he dwelt there (1 Kings xi. 7), and thence it was called *the mount of corruption* (2 Kings xxiii. 13); therefore there God does as it were set up his standard, his tribunal, as it were to confront those who thought to keep possession of the temple for themselves now that God had left it. From that mountain there was a full prospect of the city; thither God removed, to make good what he had said (Deut. xxxii. 20), *I will hide my face from them, I will see what their end shall be.* It was from this mountain that Christ *beheld the city and wept over it,* in the foresight of its last destruction by the Romans. *The glory of the Lord* removed thither, to be as it were yet within call, and ready to return if now at length, *in this their day,* they would have *understood the things that belonged to their peace.* Loth to depart bids oft farewell. God, by going away thus slowly, thus gradually, intimated that he left them with reluctance, and would not have gone if they had not perfectly forced him from them. He did now, in effect, say, *How shall I give thee up, Ephraim? How shall I deliver thee, Israel?* But, though he bear long, he will not bear always, but will at length forsake those, and cast them off for ever, who have forsaken him and cast him off. 2. The departure of this vision from the prophet. At length it *went up from him* (*v.* 24); he saw it mount upwards, till it went out of sight, which would be a confirmation to his faith that it was a heavenly vision, that it descended from above, for thitherward it returned. Note, The visions which the saints have of the glory of God will not be constant till they come to heaven. They have glimpses of that glory, which they soon lose again, visions which go up from them, tastes of divine pleasures, but not a continual feast. It was from the mount of Olives that the vision went up, typifying the ascension of Christ to heaven from that very mountain, when those that had seen him *manifested in the flesh* saw him no more. It was foretold (Zech. xiv. 4) that *his feet should stand upon the mount of Olives,* stand last there. 3. The prophet's return to those of the captivity. The same spirit that had carried him in a trance or ecstasy to Jerusalem brought him back to Chaldea; for there the bounds of his habitation are at present appointed, and that is the place of his service. The Spirit came to him, not to deliver him out of captivity, but (which was equivalent) to support and comfort him in his captivity. 4. The account which he gave to his hearers of all he had seen and heard, *v.* 25. He received that he might give, and he was *faithful to him that appointed him;* he delivered his message very honestly: he *spoke all that,* and that only, which God *had shown* him. He told them of the great wickedness he had seen at Jerusalem, and the ruin that was hastening towards that city, that they might not repent of their surrendering themselves to the king of Babylon as Jeremiah advised them, and blame themselves for it, nor envy those that staid behind, and laughed at them for going when they did, nor wish themselves there again, but be content in their captivity. Who would covet to be in a city so full of sin and so near to ruin? It is better to be in Babylon under the favour of God than in Jerusalem under his wrath and curse. But, though this was delivered immediately to those of the captivity, yet we may suppose that they sent the contents of it to those at Jerusalem, with whom they kept up a correspondence; and well would it have been for Jerusalem if she had taken the warning hereby given.

CHAP. XII.

Though the vision of God's glory had gone up from the prophet, yet his word comes to him still, and is by him sent to the people, and to the same purport with that which was discovered to him in the vision, namely, to set forth the terrible judgments that were coming upon Jerusalem, by which the city and temple should be entirely laid waste. In this chapter, I. The prophet, by removing his stuff, and quitting his lodgings, must be a sign to set forth Zedekiah's flight out of Jerusalem in the utmost confusion when the Chaldeans took the city, ver. 1—16. II. The prophet, by eating his meat with trembling, must be a sign to set forth the famine in the city during the siege, and the consternation that the inhabitants should be in, ver. 17—20. III. A message is sent from God to the people, to assure them that all these predictions should have their accomplishment very shortly, and not be deferred, as they flattered themselves they would be, ver. 21—28.

THE word of the LORD also came unto me, saying, 2 Son of man, thou dwellest in the midst of a rebellious house, which have eyes to see, and see not; they have ears to hear, and hear not: for they *are* a rebellious house. 3 Therefore, thou son of man, prepare thee stuff for removing, and remove by day in their sight; and thou shalt remove from thy place to another place in their sight: it may be they will consider, though they *be* a rebellious house. 4 Then shalt thou bring forth thy stuff by day in their sight, as stuff for removing: and thou shalt go forth at even in their sight, as they that go forth into captivity. 5 Dig thou through the wall in their sight, and carry out thereby. 6 In their sight shalt thou bear *it* upon *thy* shoulders, *and* carry *it* forth in the twilight: thou shalt cover thy face, that thou see not the ground: for I have set thee *for* a sign unto the house of Israel. 7 And I did so as I was commanded: I brought forth my stuff by day, as stuff for captivity, and in the even I digged through the wall with mine hand; I brought *it* forth in the twilight, *and* I bare *it*

upon *my* shoulder in their sight. 8 And in the morning came the word of the LORD unto me, saying, 9 Son of man, hath not the house of Israel, the rebellious house, said unto thee, What doest thou? 10 Say thou unto them, Thus saith the Lord GOD; This burden *concerneth* the prince in Jerusalem, and all the house of Israel that *are* among them. 11 Say, I *am* your sign: like as I have done, so shall it be done unto them: they shall remove *and* go into captivity. 12 And the prince that *is* among them shall bear upon *his* shoulder in the twilight, and shall go forth: they shall dig through the wall to carry out thereby: he shall cover his face, that he see not the ground with *his* eyes. 13 My net also will I spread upon him, and he shall be taken in my snare: and I will bring him to Babylon *to* the land of the Chaldeans; yet shall he not see it, though he shall die there. 14 And I will scatter toward every wind all that *are* about him to help him, and all his bands; and I will draw out the sword after them. 15 And they shall know that I *am* the LORD, when I shall scatter them among the nations, and disperse them in the countries. 16 But I will leave a few men of them from the sword, from the famine, and from the pestilence; that they may declare all their abominations among the heathen whither they come; and they shall know that I *am* the LORD.

Perhaps Ezekiel reflected with so much pleasure upon the vision he had had of the glory of God that often, since it went up from him, he was wishing it might come down to him again, and, having seen it once and a second time, he was willing to hope he might be a third time so favoured; but we do not find that he ever saw it any more, and yet *the word of the Lord comes to* him; for God did *in divers manners speak to the fathers* (Heb. i. 1) and they often *heard the words of God* when they did not *see the visions of the Almighty.* Faith comes by hearing that word of prophecy which is more sure than vision. We may keep up our communion with God without raptures and ecstasies. In these verses the prophet is directed,

I. By what signs and actions to express the approaching captivity of Zedekiah king of Judah; that was the thing to be foretold, and it is foretold to those that are already in captivity, because as long as Zedekiah was upon the throne they flattered themselves with hopes that he would make his part good with the king of Babylon, whose yoke he was now projecting to shake off, from which, it is probable, these poor captives promised themselves great things; and it may be, when he was forming that design, he privately sent encouragement to them to hope that he would rescue them shortly, or procure their liberty by exchange of prisoners. While they were fed with these vain hopes they could not set themselves either to submit to their affliction or to get good by their affliction. It was therefore necessary, but very difficult, to convince them that Zedekiah, instead of being their deliverer, should very shortly be their fellow-sufferer. Now, one would think it might have been sufficient if the prophet had only told them this in God's name, as he does afterwards (*v.* 10); but, to prepare them for the prophecy of it, he must first give them a sign of it, must speak it to their eyes first and then to their ears: and here we have, 1. The reason why he must take this method (*v.* 2): It is because they are a stupid, dull, unthinking people, that will not heed or will soon forget what they only hear of, or at least will not be at all affected with it; it will make no impression at all upon them: *Thou dwellest in the midst of a rebellious house*, whom it is next to impossible to work any good upon. *They have eyes and ears*, they have intellectual powers and faculties, but they *see not*, they *hear not*. They were idolaters, whose character it was that they were like the idols they worshipped, which *have eyes and see not, ears and hear not*, Ps. cxv. 5, 6, 8. Note, Those are to be reckoned rebellious that shut their eyes against the divine light and stop their ears to the divine law. The ignorance of those that are wilfully ignorant, that have faculties and means and will not use them, is so far from being their excuse that it adds rebellion to their sin. None so blind, so deaf, as those that will not see, that will not hear. They *see not*, they *hear not; for they are a rebellious house.* The cause is all from themselves: the darkness of the understanding is owing to the stubbornness of the will. Now this is the reason why he must speak to them by signs, as deaf people are taught, that they might be either instructed or ashamed. Note, Ministers must accommodate themselves not only to the weakness, but to the wilfulness of those they deal with, and deal with them accordingly: if they dwell among those that are rebellious they must speak to them the more plainly and pressingly, and take that course that is most likely to work upon them, that they may be left inexcusable. 2. The method he must take to awaken and affect them; he must furnish himself with all necessaries *for re-*

moving (*v.* 3), provide for a journey clothes and money; he must *remove from one place to another*, as one unsettled and forced to shift; this he must do *by day, in the sight* of the people; he must bring out all his household goods, to be packed up and sent away (*v.* 4); and, because all the doors and gates were either locked up that they could not pass through them or so guarded by the enemy that they durst not, he must therefore *dig through the wall*, and convey his goods away clandestinely through that breach in the wall, *v.* 5. He must carry his goods away himself upon his own shoulders, for want of a servant to attend him; he must do this *in the twilight*, that he might not be discovered; and, when he has made what shift he can to secure some of the best of his effects, he must himself steal away *at evening in their sight*, with fear and trembling, and must go *as those that go forth into captivity* (*v.* 4); that is, he must *cover* his *face* (*v.* 6) as being ashamed to be seen and afraid to be known, or in token of very great sorrow and concern; he must go away as a poor broken tradesman, who, when he is forced to shut up shop, hides his head, or quits his country. Thus Ezekiel must be himself a sign to them; and when perhaps he seemed somewhat backward to put himself to all this trouble, and to expose himself to be bantered and ridiculed for it, to reconcile him to it God says (*v.* 3) " *It may be they will consider*, and will by it be taken off from their vain confidences, *though they be a rebellious house.*" Note, We must not despair even of the worst, but that yet they may be brought to bethink themselves and repent; and therefore we must continue the use of proper means for their conviction and conversion, because, while there is life, there is hope. And ministers must be willing to go through the most difficult and inconvenient offices (for such was this of Ezekiel's removing), though there be but the *it may be* of success. If but one soul be awakened to consider, our care and pains will be well bestowed. 3. Ezekiel's ready and punctual obedience to the orders God gave him (*v.* 7): *I did so as I was commanded.* Hereby he teaches us all, and ministers especially, (1.) To obey with cheerfulness every command of God, even the most difficult. Christ himself *learned obedience*, and so we must all. (2.) To do all we can for the good of the souls of others, to put ourselves to any trouble or pains for the conviction of those that are unconvinced. *We do all things* (that is, we are willing to do any thing), *dearly beloved, for your edifying.* (3.) To be ourselves affected with those things wherewith we desire to affect others. When Ezekiel would give his hearers a melancholy prospect he does himself put on a melancholy aspect. (4.) To sit loose to this world, and prepare to leave it, to carry out our *stuff for removing*, because *we have here no continuing city. Arise, depart, this is not your rest, for it is polluted.* Thou dwellest *in a rebellious house*, therefore prepare for removing ; for who would not be willing to leave such a house, such a wicked world as this is ?

II. He is directed by what words to explain those signs and actions, as Agabus, when he bound his own hands and feet, told whose binding was thereby signified. But observe, It was not till morning that God gave him an exposition of the sign, till the next morning, to keep up in him a continual dependence upon God for instruction. As what God does, so what he directs us to do, perhaps we know not now, but shall know hereafter.

1. It was supposed that the people would ask the meaning of this sign, or at least they should (*v.* 9) : " *Hath not the house of Israel said unto thee, What doest thou ?* Yes, I know they have. *Though they* are *a rebellious house*, yet they are inquisitive concerning the mind of God," as those (Isa. lviii. 2) who *sought God daily. Therefore* the prophet must do such a strange uncouth thing, that they might enquire what it meant ; and then, it may be hoped, people will take notice of what is told them, and profit by it, when it comes to them in answer to their enquiries. But some understand it as an intimation that they had not made any such enquiries : " *Hath not this rebellious house* so much as asked thee, *What doest thou ?* No ; they take no notice of it ; but tell them the meaning of it, though they do not ask." Note, When God sends to us by his ministers he observes what entertainment we give to the messages he sends us ; he hearkens and hears what we say to them, and what enquiries we make upon them, and is much displeased if we pass them by without taking any notice of them. When we have heard the word we should apply to our ministers for further instruction ; and then we shall know if we thus follow on to know.

2. The prophet is to tell them the meaning of it. In general (*v.* 10), *This burden concerns the prince in Jerusalem ;* they knew who that was, and gloried in it now that they were in captivity that they had a prince of their own in Jerusalem, and that *the house of Israel* was yet entire there, and therefore doubted not but in time to do well enough. " But tell them," says God, " that in what thou hast done they may read the doom of their friends at Jerusalem. *Say, I am your sign*," *v.* 11. As the conversation of ministers should teach the people what they should do, so the providences of God concerning them are sometimes intended to tell them what they must expect. The unsettled state and removals of ministers give warning to people what they must expect in this world, no continuance, but constant changes. When times of trouble are coming on Christ tells his disciples, *They shall first lay their hands on you,* Luke xxi. 12.

(1.) The people shall be led away into captivity (*v.* 11) : *As I have done, so shall it be done unto them ;* they shall be forced away from their own houses, no more to return to them, neither shall *their place know them any more.* We cannot say concerning our dwelling-place that it is our resting-place ; for how far we may be tossed from it before we die we cannot foresee. (2.) The prince shall in vain attempt to make his escape ; for he also shall go into captivity. Jeremiah had told Zedekiah the same to his face (Jer. xxxiv. 3) : *Thou shalt not escape, but shalt surely be taken.* Ezekiel here foretels it to those who made him their confidence and promised themselves relief from him. [1.] That he shall himself carry away his own goods : *He shall bear upon his shoulder* some of his most valuable effects. Note, The judgments of God can turn a prince into a porter. He that was wont to have the regalia carried before him, and to march through the city at noon-day, shall now himself carry his goods on his back and steal away out of the city in the twilight. See what a change sin makes with men ! All the avenues to the palace being carefully watched by the enemy, *they shall dig through the wall to carry out thereby.* Men shall be their own house-breakers, and steal away their own goods ; so it is when the sword of war has cancelled all right and property. [2.] That he shall attempt to escape in a disguise, with a mask or a visor on, which *shall cover his face,* so that he shall be able only to look before him, and shall *not see the ground with his eyes.* He who, when he was in pomp, affected to be seen, now that he is in his flight is afraid to be seen ; let none therefore either be proud of being looked at or overmuch pleased with looking about them, when they see a king with *his face covered, that he cannot see the ground.* [3.] That he shall be made a prisoner and carried captive into Babylon (*v.* 13) : *My net will I spread upon him and he shall be taken in my snare.* It seemed to be the Chaldeans' net and their snare, but God owns them for his. Those that think to escape the sword of the Lord will find themselves taken in his net. Jeremiah had said that king Zedekiah should *see the king of Babylon* and that he should *go to Babylon ;* Ezekiel says, He shall be *brought to Babylon,* yet he *shall not see it,* though *he shall die there.* Those that were disposed to cavil would perhaps object that these two prophets contradicted one another ; for one said, He shall *see the king of Babylon,* the other said, He shall *not see Babylon ;* and yet both proved true : he did *see the king of Babylon* at Riblah, where he passed sentence upon him for his rebellion, but there he had his eyes put out, so that he did *not see Babylon* when he was brought thither. These captives expected to see their prince come to Babylon as a conqueror, to bring them out of their trouble ; but he shall come thither a prisoner, and his disgrace will be a great addition to their troubles. Little joy could they have in seeing him when he could not see them. [4.] That all his guards should be dispersed and utterly disabled for doing him any service (*v.* 14): *I will scatter all that are about him to help him*, so that he shall be left helpless; *I will scatter them among the nations and disperse them in the countries* (*v.* 15), to be monuments of divine justice wherever they go But are there not hopes that they may rally again? (he that flies one time may fight another time); no: *I will draw out the sword after them*, which shall cut them off wherever it finds them; for the sword that God draws out will be sure to do the execution designed. Yet of Zedekiah's scattered troops some shall escape (*v.* 16): *I will leave a few men of them.* Though they shall all be scattered, yet they shall not all be cut off; some shall have their *lives given them for a prey.* And the end for which they are thus remarkably spared is very observable: *That they may declare all their abominations among the heathen whither they come;* the troubles they are brought into will bring them to themselves and to their right mind, and then they will acknowledge the justice of God in all that is brought upon them and will make an ingenuous confession of their sins, which provoked God thus to contend with them; and, as by this it shall appear that they were spared in mercy, so hereby they will make a suitable grateful return to God for his favours to them in sparing them. Note, When God has remarkably delivered us from the deaths wherewith we were surrounded we must look upon it that for this end, among others, we were spared, that we might glorify God and edify others by making a penitent acknowledgment of our sins. Those that by their afflictions are brought to this are then made to know *that God is the Lord* and may help to bring others to the knowledge of him. See how God brings good out of evil. The dispersion of sinners, who had done God much dishonour and disservice in their own country, proves the dispersion of penitents, who shall do him much honour and service in other countries. The Levites are by a curse *divided in Jacob* and *scattered in Israel*, yet it is turned into a blessing, for thereby they have the fairest opportunity to *teach Jacob God's laws.*

17 Moreover the word of the LORD came to me, saying, 18 Son of man, eat thy bread with quaking, and drink thy water with trembling and with carefulness; 19 And say unto the people of the land, Thus saith the Lord GOD of the inhabitants of Jerusalem, *and* of the land of Israel; They shall eat their bread

with carefulness, and drink their water with astonishment, that her land may be desolate from all that is therein, because of the violence of all them that dwell therein. 20 And the cities that are inhabited shall be laid waste, and the land shall be desolate; and ye shall know that I *am* the LORD.

Here again the prophet is made a sign to them of the desolations that were coming on Judah and Jerusalem. 1. He must himself eat and drink in care and fear, especially when he was in company, *v.* 17, 18. Though he was under no apprehension of danger to himself, but lived in safety and plenty, yet he must *eat his bread with quaking* (the bread of sorrows, Ps. cxxvii. 2) *and drink his water with trembling and with carefulness*, that he might express the calamitous condition of those that should be in Jerusalem during the siege; not that he must dissemble and pretend to be in fear and care when really he was not; but having to foretel this judgment, to show that he firmly believed it himself, and yet was far from desiring it, in the prospect of it he was himself affected with grief and fear. Note, When ministers speak of the ruin coming upon impenitent sinners they must endeavour to speak feelingly, as those that *know the terrors of the Lord;* and they must be content to endure hardness, so that they may but do good. 2. He must tell them that *the inhabitants of Jerusalem* should in like manner eat and drink with care and fear, *v.* 19, 20. Both those that have their home in Jerusalem and those *of the land of Israel* that come to shelter themselves there, *shall eat their bread with carefulness and drink their water with astonishment*, either because they are afraid it will not hold out, but they shall want shortly, or because they are continually expecting the alarms of the enemy, *their life hanging in doubt before them* (Deut. xxviii. 66), so that what they have they shall have no enjoyment of nor will it do them any good. Note, Care and fear, if they prevail, are enough to embitter all our comforts and are themselves very sore judgments. They shall be reduced to these straits that thus by degrees, and by the hand of those that thus straiten them, both city and country may be laid in ruins; for it is no less than an utter destruction of both that is aimed at in these judgments—*that her land may be desolate from all* the fulness thereof, may be stripped of all its ornaments and robbed of all its fruits, and then of course *the cities that are inhabited shall be laid waste*, for they are served by the *field.* This universal desolation was coming upon them, and then no wonder that they eat their bread with care and fear. Now we are here told, (1.) How bad the cause of this judgment was; it is *because of the violence of all those that dwell therein*, their injustice and oppression, and the mischief they did one another, for which God would reckon with them, as well as for the affronts put upon him in his worship. Note, The decay of virtue in a nation brings on a decay of every thing else; and when neighbours devour one another it is just with God to bring enemies upon them to devour them all. (2.) How good the effect of this judgment should be: *You shall know that I am the Lord;* and if, by these judgments, they learn to know him aright, that will make up the loss of all they are deprived of by these desolations. Those are happy afflictions, how grievous soever to flesh and blood, that help to introduce us into and improve us in an acquaintance with God.

21 And the word of the Lord came unto me, saying, 22 Son of man, what *is* that proverb *that* ye have in the land of Israel, saying, The days are prolonged, and every vision faileth? 23 Tell them, therefore, Thus saith the Lord God; I will make this proverb to cease, and they shall no more use it as a proverb in Israel; but say unto them, The days are at hand, and the effect of every vision. 24 For there shall be no more any vain vision nor flattering divination within the house of Israel. 25 For I *am* the Lord: I will speak, and the word that I shall speak shall come to pass; it shall be no more prolonged: for in your days, O rebellious house, will I say the word, and will perform it, saith the Lord God. 26 Again the word of the Lord came to me, saying, 27 Son of man, behold, *they of* the house of Israel say, The vision that he seeth *is* for many days *to come*, and he prophesieth of the times *that are* far off. 28 Therefore say unto them, Thus saith the Lord God: There shall none of my words be prolonged any more, but the word which I have spoken shall be done, saith the Lord God.

Various methods had been used to awaken this secure and careless people to an expectation of the judgments coming, that they might be stirred up, by repentance and reformation, to prevent them. The prophecies of their ruin were confirmed by visions, and illustrated by signs, and all with such evidence and power that one would think they must needs be wrought upon; but here we are told how they evaded the conviction, and guarded against it, namely, by telling themselves, and one another, that though these judgments threatened should come at last yet they would not come of a long time. This suggestion, with which they bolstered themselves up in their security, is here answered, and shown to be vain and groundless, in two separate messages which God sent to them by the prophet at different times, both to the same purport; such care, such pains, must the prophet take to undeceive them, *v.* 21, 26. Observe,

I. How they flattered themselves with hopes that the judgments should be delayed. One saying they had, which had become proverbial *in the land of Israel, v.* 22. They said, "*The days are prolonged;* the judgments have not come when they were expected to come, but seem to be still put off *de die in diem—from day to day*, and therefore we may conclude that *every vision fails*, because it should seem that some do, that because the destruction has not come yet it will never come; we will never trust a prophet again, for we have been more frightened than hurt." And another saying they had which, if it would not conquer their convictions, yet would cool their affections and abate their concern, and that was, "*The vision* is *for* a great while *to come;* it refers to events at a vast distance, *and he prophesies of* things which, though they may be true, are yet very *far off*, so that we need not trouble our heads about them (*v.* 27); we may die in honour and peace before these troubles come." And, if indeed the troubles had been thus adjourned, they might have made themselves easy, as Hezekiah did. *Is it not well if peace and truth shall be in my days?* But it was a great mistake, and they did but deceive themselves into their own ruin; and God is here much displeased at it; for, 1. It was a wretched abuse of the patience of God, who, because for a time he kept silence, was thought to be *altogether such a one as themselves*, Ps. l. 21. That forbearance of God which should have led them to repentance hardened them in sin. They were willing to think their works were not *evil because sentence against* them was *not executed speedily;* and therefore concluded the *vision* itself *failed*, because *the days were prolonged.* 2. It received countenance from the false prophets that were among them, as should seem from the notice God takes (*v.* 24) of the *vain visions*, and *flattering divinations*, even *within the house of Israel*, to whom *were committed the oracles of God.* No marvel if those that deceived themselves by worshipping pretended deities deceived themselves also by crediting pretended prophecies, to which *strong delusions* God justly *gave them up* for their idolatries. 3. These sayings had become proverbial; they were industriously spread among the people, so that they had got into every one's mouth, and not only so, but were generally assented to, as proverbs usually are, not only the proverbs of the ancients, but those of the moderns too. Note, It is a token of universal degeneracy in a nation when corrupt and wicked sayings have grown proverbial; and it is an artifice of Satan by them to confirm men in their prejudices against the word and ways of God, and a great offence to the God of heaven. It will not serve for an excuse, in saying ill, to plead that it is a common saying.

II. How they are assured that they do but deceive themselves, for the judgments shall be hastened, these profane proverbs shall be confronted: *Tell them, therefore, The days are at hand* (v. 23), and again, *There shall none of my words be prolonged any more, v. 28.* Their putting the evil day far from them does but provoke God to bring it the sooner upon them; and it will be so much the sorer, so much the heavier, so much the more a surprise and terror to them when it does come. He must tell them,

1. That God will certainly silence the lying proverbs, and the lying prophecies, with which they buoyed up their vain hopes, and will make them ashamed of both (1): *I will make this proverb to cease;* for when they find the days of vengeance have come, and not one iota or tittle of the prediction falls to the ground, they will be ashamed to *use it as a proverb in Israel, The days are prolonged, and the vision fails.* Note, Those that will not have their eyes opened and their mistakes rectified, by the word of God, shall be undeceived by his judgments: for *every mouth* that speaks perverse things *shall be stopped.* (2.) *There shall be no more any vain vision, v. 24.* The false prophets, who told the people they should have peace and should soon see an end of their troubles, shall be disproved by the event, and then shall be ashamed of their pretensions, and shall hide their heads and impose silence upon themselves. Note, As truth was older than error, so it will survive it; it got the start, and it will get the race. The true prophets' visions and predictions stand, and are in full force, power, and virtue; they give law, and receive credit, when the *vain visions,* and the *flattering divinations,* are lost and forgotten, and *shall be no more in the house of Israel;* for great is the truth, and will prevail.

2. That God will certainly, and very shortly, accomplish every word that he has spoken. With what majesty does he say it (v. 25): I am the Lord! *I am Jehovah!* That glorious name of his speaks him a God giving being to his word by the performance of it, and therefore to the patriarchs, who lived by faith in a promise not yet performed, he was not known by his name *Jehovah,* Exod. vi. 3. But, as he is Jehovah in making good his promise, so he is in making good his threatenings. Let them know then that God, *with whom they have to do,* is the great Jehovah,

and therefore, (1.) He will speak, *whether they will hear or whether they will forbear:* I am the Lord, I will speak. God will have his saying, whoever gainsays it. God's oracles are called *lively* ones, for they still speak when the pagan oracles are long ago struck dumb. There has been, and shall be, a succession of God's ministers to the end of the world, by whom he will speak; and, though contempt may be put upon them, that shall not put a period to their ministration: *In your days, O rebellious house! will I say the word.* Even in the worst ages of the church God *left not himself without witness,* but raised up men that spoke for him, that spoke from him. *I will say the word,* the word that shall stand. (2.) The word that he speaks shall come to pass; it shall infallibly be accomplished according to the true intent and meaning of it, and according to the full extent and compass of it: *I will say the word and will perform it* (v. 25), for his mind is never changed, nor his arm shortened, nor is Infinite Wisdom ever nonplussed. With men saying and doing are two things, but they are not so with God; with him it is *dictum, factum—said, and done.* In the works of providence, as in those of creation, *he speaks and it is done;* for he said, Let there be light, and there was light—Let there be a *firmament, and there was a firmament,* Num. xxiii. 19; 1 Sam. xv. 29. Whereas they had said, *Every vision fails* (v. 22), God says, "No, there shall be the effect of every vision (v. 23); it shall not return void, but every sign shall be answered by the thing signified." Those that *see the visions of the Almighty* do not see *vain visions;* God *confirms the word of his servants* by performing it. (3.) It shall be accomplished very shortly: "*The days are at hand* when you shall see the effect *of every vision, v. 23.* It is said, it is sworn, that delay *shall be no longer* (Rev. x. 6); the year of God's patience has now just expired, and he will no longer defer the execution of the sentence. *It shall be no more prolonged* (v. 25); he has borne with you a great while, but he will not bear always. *In your days, O rebellious house!* shall the word that is said be *performed,* and you shall see the threatened judgments and share in them. *Behold, the Judge stands at the door.* The *righteous are taken away from the evil to come,* but this *rebellious house* shall not be so quietly taken away; no, they shall live to be hurried away, to *be chased out of the world.*" This is repeated (v. 28): *There shall none of my words be prolonged any more,* but judgment shall now hasten on apace; and the longer the bow has been in the drawing the deeper shall the arrow pierce." When we tell sinners of death and judgment, heaven and hell, and think by them to persuade them to a holy life, though we do not find them downright infidels (they will own that they do believe there is a state of rewards and punishments in the other world), yet they put by the force of those great truths, and avoid the impressions of them, by looking upon the things of the other world as very remote; they tell us, " *The vision you see is for many days to come, and* you *prophesy of the times that are very far off;* it will be time enough to think of them when they come nearer," whereas really there is but a step between us and death, between us and an awful eternity; *yet a little while and the vision shall speak and not lie,* and therefore it concerns us to redeem time, and get ready with all speed for a future state; for, though it is future, it is very near, and while impenitent sinners slumber their *damnation slumbers not.*

CHAP. XIII.

Mention had been made, in the chapter before, of the vain visions and flattering divinations with which the people of Israel suffered themselves to be imposed upon (ver. 24); now this whole chapter is levelled against them. God's faithful prophets are nowhere so sharp upon any sort of sinners as upon the false prophets, not because they were the most spiteful enemies to them, but because they put the highest affront upon God and did the greatest mischief to his people. The prophet here shows the sin and punishment, I. Of the false prophets, ver. 1—16. II. Of the false prophetesses, ver. 17—23. Both agreed to sooth men up in their sins, and, under pretence of comforting God's people, to flatter them with hopes that they should yet have peace; but the prophets shall be proved liars, their prophecies mere shams, and the expectations of the people illusions; for God will let them know that " the deceived and the deceiver are his," are both accountable to him, Job xii. 16.

AND the word of the LORD came unto me, saying, 2 Son of man, prophesy against the prophets of Israel that prophesy, and say thou unto them that prophesy out of their own hearts, Hear ye the word of the LORD; 3 Thus saith the Lord GOD; Woe unto the foolish prophets, that follow their own spirit, and have seen nothing! 4 O Israel, thy prophets are like the foxes in the deserts. 5 Ye have not gone up into the gaps, neither made up the hedge for the house of Israel to stand in the battle in the day of the LORD. 6 They have seen vanity and lying divination, saying, The LORD saith : and the LORD hath not sent them : and they have made *others* to hope that they would confirm the word. 7 Have ye not seen a vain vision, and have ye not spoken a lying divination, whereas ye say, The LORD saith *it;* albeit I have not spoken? 8 Therefore thus saith the Lord GOD; Because ye have spoken vanity, and seen lies, therefore, behold, I *am* against you, saith the Lord GOD. 9 And mine hand shall be upon the prophets that see vanity, and that divine lies: they shall not be in the assembly of my people, neither shall

818

they be written in the writing of the house of Israel, neither shall they enter into the land of Israel; and ye shall know that I *am* the Lord GOD.

The false prophets, who are here prophesied against, were some of them at Jerusalem (Jer. xxiii. 14): *I have seen in the prophets at Jerusalem a horrible thing;* some of them among the captives in Babylon, for to them Jeremiah writes (Jer. xxix. 8), *Let not your diviners, that be in the midst of you, deceive you.* And as God's prophets, though at a distance from each other in place or time, yet preached the same truths, which was an evidence that they were guided by one and the same good Spirit, so the false prophets prophesied the same lies, being actuated by one and the same spirit of error. There were little hopes of bringing them to repentance, they were so hardened in their sin; yet Ezekiel must prophesy against them, in hopes that the people might be cautioned not to hearken to them; and thus a testimony will be left upon record against them, and they will thereby be left inexcusable.

Ezekiel had express orders to *prophesy against the prophets of Israel;* so they called themselves, as if none but they had been worthy of the name of Israel's prophets, who were indeed Israel's deceivers. But it is observable that Israel was never imposed upon by pretenders to prophecy till after they had rejected and abused the true prophets; as, afterwards, they were never deluded by counterfeit messiahs till after they had refused the true Messiah and rejected him. These false prophets must be required to *hear the word of the Lord.* They took upon them to speak what concerned others as from God; let them now hear what concerned themselves as from him. And two things the prophet is directed to do :—

I. To discover their sin to them, and to convince them of that if possible, or thereby to prevent their proceeding any further, by making *manifest their folly unto all men,* 2 Tim. iii. 9. They are here called *foolish prophets* (v. 3), men that did not at all understand the business they pretended to; to make fools of the people they made fools of themselves, and put the greatest cheat upon their own souls. Let us see what is here laid to their charge. 1. They pretend to have a commission from God, whereas he never sent them. They thrust themselves into the prophetic office, without warrant from him who is *the Lord God* of the holy prophets, which was a foolish thing; for how could they expect that God should own them in a work to which he never called them? They are *prophets out of their own hearts* (so the margin reads it, *v.* 2), prophets of their own making, *v.* 6. *They say,* The *Lord saith;* they pretend to be his messengers, but *the Lord has not sent them,* has not given them any orders. They counterfeit the broad seal of heaven, than which they cannot do a greater indignity to mankind, for hereby they put a reproach upon divine revelation, lessen its credit, and weaken its credibility. When these pretenders are found to be deceivers atheists and infidels will thence infer, They are all so. *The Lord has not sent them;* for though crafty enough in other things *like the foxes,* and very wise for the world, yet they are *foolish prophets* and have no experimental acquaintance with the things of God. Note, Foolish prophets are not of God's sending, for whom he sends he either finds fit or makes fit. Where he gives warrant he gives wisdom. 2. They pretend to have instructions from God, whereas he never made himself and his mind known to them: *They followed their own spirit* (*v.* 3); they delivered that as a message from God which was the product either of their subtle invention, to serve a turn for themselves, or of their own crazed and heated imagination, to give vent to a fancy. For *they have seen nothing,* they have not really had any heavenly vision; they pretend that what they say *the Lord saith it,* but God disowns it: "*I have not spoken it,* I never said it, never meant any such thing." What they delivered was not what they had seen or heard, as that is which the ministers of Christ deliver (1 John i. 1), but either what they had dreamed or what they thought would please those they coveted to make an interest in; this is called their *seeing vanity and lying divination* (*v.* 6); they pretended to have seen that which they did not see, and produced that as a divine truth which they knew to be false. To the same purport (*v.* 7): *You have seen a vain vision and spoken a lying divination,* which had no divine original and would have no effect, but would certainly be disproved by the event; the words are changed (*v.* 8): *You have spoken vanity and seen lies;* what they saw and what they said was all alike, a mere sham; they saw nothing, they said nothing, to the purpose, nothing that could be relied on or that deserved regard. Again (*v.* 9), They *see vanity and divine lies;* they pretended to have had visions, as the true prophets had, whereas really they had none, but either it was the creature of their own fancy (they thought they had a vision, as men in a delirium do, that was *seeing vanity)* or it was a fiction of their own politics, and they knew they had none, and then they *saw lies, and divined lies.* See Jer. xxiii. 16, &c. Note, Since the devil is universally known to be the father of lies, those put the highest affront imaginable upon God who tell lies, and then father them upon him. But those that had put God's character upon Satan, in worshipping devils, arrived at length at such a pitch of impiety as to put Satan's character upon God. 3. They took no care to prevent the judgments of God that were breaking in upon the kingdom. They are like *the foxes*

in the deserts, running to and fro, and seeming to be in a great hurry, but it was to get away and shift for their own safety, not to do any good: *The hireling flees, and leaves the sheep.* They are like foxes that are greedy of prey for themselves, crafty and cruel to feed themselves. But (*v.* 5), "You *have not gone up into the gaps, nor made up the hedge of the house of Israel.* A breach is made in their fences, at which judgments are ready to pour in upon them, and then, if ever, is the time to do them service; but you have done nothing to help them." They should have made intercession for them, to turn away the wrath of God; but they were not praying prophets, had no interest in heaven nor intercourse with heaven (as prophets used to have, Gen. xx. 7) and so could do them no service that way. They should have made it their business by preaching and advice to bring people to repentance and reformation, and so have *made up the hedge,* and put a stop to the judgments of God; but this was none of their care: they contrived how to please people, not how to profit them. They saw a deluge of profaneness and impiety breaking in upon the land, waging war with virtue and holiness, and threatening to crush them and bear them down, and then they should have come in *to the help of the Lord, to the help of the Lord against the mighty,* by witnessing against the wickedness of the time and place they lived in; but they thought that would be as dangerous a piece of service as standing in a breach to make it good against the besiegers, and therefore they declined it, did nothing to stem the tide, stood not in the battle against vice and immorality, but basely deserted the cause of religion and reformation, *in the day of the Lord,* when it was proclaimed, *Who is on the Lord's side? Who will rise up for me against the evil-doers?* Ps. xciv. 16. Those were unworthy the name of prophets that could think so favourably of sin, and had so little zeal for God and the public welfare. 4. They flattered people into a vain hope that the judgments God had threatened would never come, whereby they hardened those in sin whom they should have endeavoured to turn from sin (*v.* 6): *They have made others to hope* that all should be well, and they should have peace, though they went on still in their trespasses, and that the event would confirm the word. They were still ready to say, "We will warrant you that these troubles will be at an end quickly, and we shall be in prosperity again," as if their warrants would confirm false prophecies, in defiance of God himself.

II. He is directed to denounce the judgments of God against them for these sins, from which their pretending to the character of prophets would not exempt them. 1. In general, here is a *woe* against them (*v.* 3), and what that woe is we are told (*v.* 8). *Behold, I am against you, saith the Lord God.* Note, Those are in a woeful condition that have God against them. Woe, and a thousand woes, to those that have made him their enemy. 2. In particular, they are sentenced to be excluded from all the privileges of the commonwealth of Israel, for they are adjudged to have forfeited them all (*v.* 9): God's *hand shall be upon them,* to seize them and bring them to his bar, to shut them out from his presence, and they will find it a *fearful thing to fall into his hands.* They pretend to be prophets, particular favourites of heaven, and authorized to preside in the congregation of his church on earth; but, by pretending to the honours they were not entitled to, they lost those that otherwise they might have enjoyed, Matt. v. 19. Their doom is, (1.) To be expelled from the communion of saints, and not to be looked upon as belonging to it: *They shall not be in the secret of my people;* their folly shall be so clearly manifested that they shall never be consulted, nor their advice asked; they shall not be present at any debates about public affairs. Or, rather, they shall not be in the assembly of God's people for religious worship, for they shall be ashamed to show their heads there, when they are proved by the events to be false prophets, and, like Cain, shall *go out from the presence of the Lord.* The people that are deceived by them shall abandon them, and resolve to have no more to do with them. Those that usurped Moses's chair shall not be allowed so much as a door-keeper's place. In the great day they shall *not stand in the congregation of the righteous* (Ps. i. 5), when God *gathers his saints together to him* (Ps. l. 5, 16), *to be for ever with him.* (2.) To be expunged out of the book of the living. They shall die in their captivity, and shall die childless, shall leave no posterity to take their denomination from them, and so their names shall not be found among those who either themselves or their posterity returned out of Babylon, of whom a particular account was kept in a public register, which was called *the writing of the house of Israel,* such as we have Ezra ii. They shall not be found among the living in Jerusalem, Isa. iv. 3. Or they shall not be found written among those whom God has from eternity chosen to be vessels of his mercy to eternity. We read of those who *prophesied in Christ's name,* and yet he will tell them that he *never knew them* (Matt. vii. 22, 23), because they were not among those that were *given to him.* The Chaldee paraphrase reads it, *They shall not be written in the writing of eternal life, which is written for the righteous of the house of Israel.* See Ps. lxix. 28. (3.) To be for ever excluded from the land of Israel. God has *sworn in his wrath* concerning them that *they shall never enter* with the returning captives into the land of Canaan, which a second time remains a rest for them. Note, Those who oppose the design of God's threatenings, and will not be awed and in-

820

fluenced by them, forfeit the benefit of his promises, and cannot expect to be comforted and encouraged by them.

10 Because, even because they have seduced my people, saying, Peace; and *there was* no peace; and one built up a wall, and, lo, others daubed it with untempered *mortar:* 11 Say unto them which daub *it* with untempered *mortar,* that it shall fall: there shall be an overflowing shower; and ye, O great hailstones, shall fall; and a stormy wind shall rend *it.* 12 Lo, when the wall is fallen, shall it not be said unto you, Where *is* the daubing wherewith ye have daubed *it?* 13 Therefore thus saith the Lord God; I will even rend *it* with a stormy wind in my fury; and there shall be an overflowing shower in mine anger, and great hailstones in *my* fury to consume *it.* 14 So will I break down the wall that ye have daubed with untempered *mortar,* and bring it down to the ground, so that the foundation thereof shall be discovered, and it shall fall, and ye shall be consumed in the midst thereof: and ye shall know that I *am* the Lord. 15 Thus will I accomplish my wrath upon the wall, and upon them that have daubed it with untempered *mortar,* and will say unto you, The wall *is* no *more,* neither they that daubed it; 16 *To wit,* the prophets of Israel which prophesy concerning Jerusalem, and which see visions of peace for her, and *there is* no peace, saith the Lord God.

We have here more plain dealing with the false prophets, and some further articles of their doom. We have seen the people made ashamed of the false prophets (though sometimes they had been fond of them) and casting them away, as they shall do their false gods, with indignation; now here we find them as much ashamed of their false prophecies, which they had sometimes depended upon with much assurance. Observe,

I. How the people are deceived by the false prophets. Those flatterers seduce them, saying, *Peace, and there was no peace,* v. 10. They pretended to have *seen visions of peace,* v. 16. But that could not be, for *there was no peace, saith the Lord God.* There was no prosperity designed for them, and therefore there could be no ground for their security;

yet they told them that God was at peace with them, and had mercy in reserve for them, and that the war they were engaged in with the Chaldeans should soon end in an honourable peace, and their land should enjoy a happy repose and tranquillity. They told the idolaters and other sinners that there was neither harm nor danger in the way they were in. Thus they *seduced God's people;* they put a cheat upon them, led them into mistakes, and drew them aside out of that way of repentance and reformation which the other prophets were endeavouring to bring them into. Note, Those are the most dangerous seducers who suggest to sinners that which tends to lessen their dread of sin and their fear of God. Now this is compared to the building of a slight rotten wall, or, according to our Saviour's similitude, which is to the same purport with this (Matt. vii. 26), the *building of a house upon the sand,* which seems to be a shelter and protection for a while, but will fall when a storm comes. One false prophet built the wall, set up the notion that God was not at all displeased with Jerusalem, but that the city should be confirmed in its flourishing state, and be victorious over the powers that now threatened it. This notion was very pleasing, and he that started it made himself very acceptable by it and was caressed by every body, which invited others to say the same. They made the matter look yet more plausible and promising; they *daubed the wall,* which the first had built, but it was with *untempered mortar,* sorry stuff, that will not bind nor hold the bricks together; they had no ground for what they said, nor had it any consistency with itself, but was like ropes of sand. They did not strengthen the wall, were in no care to make it firm, to see that they went upon sure grounds; they only daubed it to hide the cracks and make it look well to the eye. And the wall thus built, when it comes to any stress, much more to any distress, will bulge and totter, and come down by degrees. Note, Doctrines that are groundless, though ever so grateful, that are not built upon a scripture foundation nor fastened with a scripture cement, though ever so plausible, ever so pleasing, are not of any worth, nor will stand men in any stead; and those hopes of peace and happiness which are not warranted by the word of God will but cheat men, like a wall that is well daubed indeed, but ill-built.

II. How they will be soon undeceived by the judgment of God, which, we are sure, is according to truth. 1. God will in anger bring a terrible storm that shall beat fiercely and furiously upon the wall. The descent which the Chaldean army shall make upon Judah, and the siege which they shall lay to Jerusalem, will be as *an overflowing shower,* or inundation (such as Solomon calls a *sweeping rain that leaves no food,* Prov. xxviii. 3), will bear down all before it, as the deluge

did in Noah's time: *You, O great hailstones! shall fall,* the artillery of heaven, every hailstone like a cannon-ball, battering this wall, and with these a *stormy wind,* which is sometimes so strong as to *rend the rocks* (1 Kings xix. 11), much more an ill-built wall, *v.* 11. But that which makes this *rain,* and *hail,* and *wind,* most terrible is that they arise from the wrath of God, and are enforced by that; it is that which sends them; it is that which gives them the setting on (*v.* 13); it is *a stormy wind in my fury,* and *an overflowing shower in my anger,* and *great hailstones in my fury.* The fury of Nebuchadnezzar and his princes, who highly resented Zedekiah's treachery, made the invasion very formidable, but that was nothing in comparison with God's displeasure. *The staff in their hand is my indignation,* Isa. x. 5. Note, An angry God has winds and storms at command wherewith to alarm secure sinners; and his wrath makes them frightful and forcible indeed; for *who can stand before him when he is angry?* 2. This storm shall overturn the wall: *it shall fall,* and the wind shall *rend it* (*v.* 11), the *hailstones shall consume it* (*v.* 13); I will *break it down* (*v.* 14) and *bring it to the ground,* so that the *foundation thereof shall be discovered;* it will appear how false, how rotten it was, to the prophetical reproach of the builders. When the Chaldean army has made Judah and Jerusalem desolate then this credit of the prophets, and the hopes of the people, will both sink together; the former will be found false in flattering the people and the latter foolish in suffering themselves to be imposed upon by them, and so exposed to so much the greater confusion, when the judgment shall surprise them in their security. Note, Whatever men think to shelter themselves with against the judgments of God, while they continue unreformed, will prove but a *refuge of lies* and will not profit them *in the day of wrath.* See Isa. xxviii. 17. Men's anger cannot shake that which God has built (for *the blast of the terrible ones is but as a storm against the wall,* which makes a great noise, but never stirs the wall; see Isa. xxv. 4), but God's anger will overthrow that which men have built in opposition to him. They and all their attempts, they and all the securities wherein they intrench themselves, shall be *as a bowing wall and as a tottering fence* (Ps. lxii. 3, 10); and when their vain predictions are disproved, and their vain expectations disappointed, then it will be discovered that there was no ground for either, Hab. iii. 13. The *day will declare* what every man's work is, and *the fire will try* it, 1 Cor. iii. 13. 3. The builders of the wall, and those that daubed it, will themselves be buried in the ruins of it: *It shall fall, and you shall* be *consumed in the midst thereof, v.* 14. And thus the threatenings of God's wrath, and all the just intentions of it, shall be accomplished to the uttermost, both upon *the wall* and upon those *that have* daubed it, v. 15. The same judgments that will prove the false prophets to be false will punish them for their falsehood; and they themselves shall be involved in the calamity which they made the people believe there was no danger of, and become monuments of that justice which they bade defiance to. Thus, if *the blind lead the blind,* both the blind leaders and the blind followers will *fall together into the ditch.* Note, Those that deceive others will in the end prove to have deceived themselves; and no doom will be more fearful than that of unfaithful ministers, that flattered sinners in their sins. 4. Both the deceivers and the deceived, when they thus perish together, will justly be ridiculed and triumphed over (v. 12): *When the wall has fallen shall it not be said unto you,* by those that gave credit to the true prophets, and feared the word of the Lord, " Now *where is the daubing wherewith you have daubed the wall?* What has become of all the fine soft words and fair promises wherewith you flattered your wicked neighbours, and all the assurances you gave them that the troubles of the nation should soon be at an end? The *righteous shall laugh at them,* the righteous God shall, righteous men shall, saying, *Lo, this is the man that made not God his strength,* Ps. lii. 6, 7. *I also will laugh at your calamity,* Prov. i. 26. They will say unto you (v. 15), " *The wall is no more, neither he that daubed it;* your hopes have vanished, and those that supported them, even *the prophets of Israel,"* v. 16. Note, Those that usurp the honours that do not belong to them will shortly be filled with the shame that does.

17 Likewise, thou son of man, set thy face against the daughters of thy people, which prophesy out of their own heart; and prophesy thou against them, 18 And say, Thus the Lord God; Woe to the *women* that sew pillows to all armholes, and make kerchiefs upon the head of every stature to hunt souls! Will ye hunt the souls of my people, and will ye save the souls alive *that come* unto you? 19 And will ye pollute me among my people for handfuls of barley and for pieces of bread, to slay the souls that should not die, and to save the souls alive that should not live, by your lying to my people that hear *your* lies? 20 Wherefore thus saith the Lord God; Behold, I *am* against your pillows, wherewith ye there hunt the souls to make *them* fly, and I will tear them from your arms, and will let the souls go, *even*

822

the souls that ye hunt to make *them* fly. 21 Your kerchiefs also will I tear, and deliver my people out of your hand, and they shall be no more in your hand to be hunted; and ye shall know that I *am* the Lord. 22 Because with lies ye have made the heart of the righteous sad, whom I have not made sad; and strengthened the hands of the wicked, that he should not return from his wicked way, by promising him life: 23 Therefore ye shall see no more vanity, nor divine divinations: for I will deliver my people out of your hand: and ye shall know that I *am* the Lord.

As God has promised that when he pours out his Spirit upon his people both *their sons and their daughters shall prophesy,* so the devil, when he acts as a spirit of lies and falsehood, is so in the mouth not only of false prophets, but of false prophetesses too, and those are the deceivers whom the prophet is here directed to prophesy against; for they are not such despicable enemies to God's truths as deserve not to be taken notice of, nor yet will either the weakness of their sex excuse their sin or the tenderness and respect that are owing to it exempt them from the reproaches and threatenings of the word of God. No: *Son of man, set thy face against the daughters of thy people,* v. 17. God takes no pleasure in owning them for his people. They are *thy people,* as Exod. xxxii. 7. The women pretend to a spirit of prophecy, and are in the same song with the men, as Ahab's prophets were: *Go on, and prosper.* They *prophesy out of their own heart* too; they say what comes uppermost and what they know nothing of. Therefore *prophesy against them* from God's own mouth. The prophet must *set his face against them,* and try if they can look him in the face and stand to what they say. Note, When sinners grow very impudent it is time for reprovers to be very bold. Now observe,

I. How the sin of these false prophetesses is described, and what are the particulars of it. 1. They told deliberate lies to those who consulted them, and came to them to be advised, and to be told their fortune: " You do mischief *by your lying to my people that hear your lies* (v. 19); they come to be told the truth, but you tell them lies; and, because you humour them in their sins, they are willing to hear you." Note, It is ill with those people who can better hear pleasing lies than unpleasing truths; and it is a temptation to those who lie in wait to deceive to tell lies when they find people willing to hear them and to excuse themselves with this, *Si populus vult decipi, decipiatur—If the people will be deceived, let them.* 2. They profaned the name of God by pretending to have received those lies from him (v. 19): *You pollute my name among my people,* and make use of that for the patronising of your lies and the gaining of credit to them." Note, Those greatly pollute God's holy name that make use of it to give countenance to falsehood and wickedness. Yet this they did *for handfuls of barley and pieces of bread.* They did it for gain; they cared not what dishonour they did to God's name by their lying, so they could but make a hand of it for themselves. There is nothing so sacred which men of mercenary spirits, in whom the love of this world reigns, will not profane and prostitute, if they can but get money by the bargain. But they did it for poor gain; if they could get no more for it, rather than break they would sell you a false prophecy that should please you to a nicety for the beggar's dole, a *piece of bread* or *a handful of barley;* and yet that was more than it was worth. Had they asked it as an alms, for God's sake, surely they might have had it, and God would have been honoured; but, taking it as a fee for a false prophecy, God's name is polluted, and the smallness of the reward heightens the offence. *For a piece of bread that man will transgress,* Prov. xxviii. 21. Had their poverty been their temptation to *steal, and so to take the name of the Lord in vain,* it would not have been nearly so bad as when it tempted them to *prophesy lies in his name* and so to profane it. 3. They kept people in awe, and terrified them with their pretensions: " *You hunt the souls of my people* (v. 18), *hunt them to make them flee* (v. 20), *hunt them into gardens* (so the margin reads it); you use all the arts you have to court or compel them into those places where you deliver your pretended predictions, or you have got such an influence upon them that you make them do just as you would have them to do, and tyrannise over them." It was indeed the people's fault that they did regard them, but it was their fault by lies and falsehoods to command that regard; they pretended to *save the souls alive that came to them, v.* 18. If they would but be hearers of them, and contributors to them, they might be sure of salvation; thus they beguiled unstable souls that had a concern about salvation as their end but did not rightly understand the way, and therefore hearkened to those who were most confident in promising it to them. " But will you pretend to save souls, or secure salvation to your party?" Those are justly suspected that make such pretensions. 4. They discouraged those that were honest and good, and encouraged those that were wicked and profane: *You slay the souls that should not die, and save those alive that should not live, v.* 19. This is explained (v. 22): *You have made the heart of the righteous sad, whom I have not made sad;* because they would not, they durst not, countenance your preten-

sions, you thundered out the judgments of God against them, to their great grief and trouble; you put them under invidious characters, to make them either despicable or odious to the people, and pretended to do it in God's name, which made them go many a time with a sad heart; whereas it was the will of God that they should be comforted, and by having respect put upon them should have encouragement given them. But on the other side, and which is still worse, you have *strengthened the hands of the wicked* and emboldened them to go on in their *wicked ways* and not to return from them, which was the thing the true prophets with earnestness called them to. " You have promised sinners life in their sinful ways, have told them that they shall have peace though they go on, by which their *hands have been strengthened* and their hearts hardened." Some think this refers to the severe censures they passed upon those who had already gone into captivity (who were humbled under their affliction, by *which their hearts were made sad),* and the commendations they gave to those who rebelled against the king of Babylon, who were hardened in their impieties, by which their *hands were strengthened;* or by their polluting the name of God they saddened the hearts of good people who have a value and veneration for the word of God, and confirmed atheists and infidels in their contempt of divine revelation and furnished them with arguments against it. Note, Those have a great deal to answer for who grieve the spirits, and weaken the hands, of good people, and who gratify the lusts of sinners, and animate them in their opposition to God and religion. Nor can any thing strengthen the hands of sinners more than to tell them that they may be saved in their sins without repentance, or that there may be repentance though they do not return from their wicked ways. 5. They mimicked the true prophets, by giving signs for the illustrating of their false predictions (as Hananiah did, Jer. xxviii. 10), and they were signs agreeable to their sex; they *sewed little pillows to the people's arm-holes,* to signify that they might be easy and repose themselves, and needed not be disquieted with the apprehensions of trouble approaching. And they *made kerchiefs upon the head of every stature,* of persons of every age, young and old, distinguishable by their stature, v. 18. These kerchiefs were badges of liberty or triumph, intimating that they should not only be delivered from the Chaldeans, but be victorious over them. Some think these were some superstitious rites which they used with those to whom they delivered their divinations, preparing them for the reception of them by putting enchanted pillows under their arms and handkerchiefs on their heads, to raise their fancies and their expectations of something great. Or perhaps the expressions are figurative: they did all they could to make people secure, which is signified by laying them easy, and to make people proud, which is signified by dressing them fine with handkerchiefs, perhaps laid or embroidered on their heads.

II. How the wrath of God against them is expressed. Here is a woe to them (*v.* 18), and God declares himself against the methods they took to delude and deceive, *v.* 20. But what course will God take with them? 1. They shall be confounded in their attempts, and shall proceed no further; for (*v.* 23) you shall *see no more vanity nor divine revelations;* not that they shall themselves lay down their pretensions in a way of repentance, but when the event gives them the lie they shall be silent for shame; or their fancies and imaginations shall not be disposed to receive impressions which assist them in their divinations as they have been; or they themselves shall be cut off. 2. God's people shall be delivered out of their hands. When they see themselves deluded by them into a false peace and a fool's paradise, and that though they would not leave their sin their sin has left them, and they *see no more vanity nor divine divinations,* they shall turn their back upon them, shall slight their predictions. The righteous shall be no more saddened by them, no, nor the wicked strengthened: The *pillows shall be torn from their arms,* and the *kerchiefs from their heads;* the fallacies shall be discovered, their frauds detected, and the people of God shall no more be in their hand, to be hunted as they had been. Note, It is a great mercy to be delivered from a servile regard to, and fear of, those who, under colour of a divine authority, impose upon and tyrannise over the consciences of men, and say to their souls, *Bow down, that we may go over.* But it is a sore grief to those who delight in such usurpations to have their power broken and the prey delivered; such was the reformation to the church of Rome. And, when God does this, he makes it to appear that he is the Lord, that it is his prerogative to give law to souls.

CHAP. XIV.

Hearing the word, and prayer, are two great ordinances of God, in which we are to give honour to him and may hope to find favour and acceptance with him; and yet in this chapter, to our great surprise, we find some waiting upon God in the one and some in the other and yet not meeting with success as they expected. I. The elders of Israel come to hear the word, and enquire of the prophet, but, because they are not duly qualified, they meet with a rebuke instead of acceptance (ver. 1—5) and are called upon to repent of their sins and reform their lives, else it is at their peril to enquire of God, ver. 6—11. II. Noah, Daniel, and Job, are supposed to pray for this people, and yet, because the decree has gone forth, and the destruction of them is determined by a variety of judgments, their prayers shall not be answered, ver. 12—21. And yet it is promised, in the close, that a remnant shall escape, ver. 22, 23.

THEN came certain of the elders of Israel unto me, and sat before me. 2 And the word of the Lord came unto me, saying, 3 Son of man, these men have set up their idols in their heart, and put the stumbling-

824

block of their iniquity before their face: should I be enquired of at all by them? 4 Therefore speak unto them, and say unto them, Thus saith the Lord God; Every man of the house of Israel that setteth up his idols in his heart, and putteth the stumbling-block of his iniquity before his face, and cometh to the prophet; I the Lord will answer him that cometh according to the multitude of his idols; 5 That I may take the house of Israel in their own heart, because they are all estranged from me through their idols. 6 Therefore say unto the house of Israel, Thus saith the Lord God; Repent, and turn *yourselves* from your idols; and turn away your faces from all your abominations. 7 For every one of the house of Israel, or of the stranger that sojourneth in Israel, which separateth himself from me, and setteth up his idols in his heart, and putteth the stumbling-block of his iniquity before his face, and cometh to a prophet to enquire of him concerning me; I the Lord will answer him by myself: 8 And I will set my face against that man, and will make him a sign and a proverb, and I will cut him off from the midst of my people; and ye shall know that I *am* the Lord. 9 And if the prophet be deceived when he hath spoken a thing, I the Lord have deceived that prophet, and I will stretch out my hand upon him, and will destroy him from the midst of my people Israel. 10 And they shall bear the punishment of their iniquity: the punishment of the prophet shall be even as the punishment of him that seeketh *unto him;* 11 That the house of Israel may go no more astray from me, neither be polluted any more with all their transgressions; but that they may be my people, and I may be their God, saith the Lord God.

Here is, I. The address which some of the elders of Israel made to the prophet, as an oracle, to enquire of the Lord by him. They *came, and sat before him, v.* 1. It is probable that they were not of those who were now his fellow-captives, and constantly attended his ministry (such as those we read of *ch*

viii. 1), but some occasional hearers, some of the grandees of Jerusalem who had come upon business to Babylon, perhaps public business, on an embassy from the king, and in their way called on the prophet, having heard much of him and being desirous to know if he had any message from God, which might be some guide to them in their negociation. By the severe answer given them one would suspect they had a design to ensnare the prophet, or to try if they could catch hold of any thing that might look like a contradiction to Jeremiah's prophecies, and so they might have occasion to reproach them both. However, they feigned themselves just men, complimented the prophet, and sat before him gravely enough, as God's people used to sit. Note, It is no new thing for bad men to be found employed in the external performances of religion.

II. The account which God gave the prophet privately concerning them. They were strangers to him; he only knew that they were *elders of Israel;* that was the character they wore, and as such he received them with respect, and, it is likely, was glad to see them so well disposed. But God gives him their real character (v. 3); they were idolaters, and did only consult Ezekiel as they would any oracle of a pretended deity, to gratify their curiosity, and therefore he appeals to the prophet himself whether they deserved to have any countenance or encouragement given them: " *Should I be enquired of at all by them?* Should I accept their enquiries as an honour to myself, or answer them for satisfaction to them? No; they have no reason to expect it;" for, 1. They *have set up their idols in their heart;* they not only have idols, but they are in love with them, they dote upon them, are wedded to them, and have laid them so near tneir hearts, and have given them so great a room in their affections, that there is no parting with them. The idols they have set up in their houses, though they are now at a distance from *the chambers of their imagery*, yet they have them in their hearts, and they are ever and anon worshipping them in their fancies and imaginations. *They have made their idols to ascend upon their hearts* (so the word is); they have subjected their hearts to their idols, they are upon the throne there. Or when they came to enquire of the prophet they pretended to put away their idols, but it was in pretence only; they still had a secret reserve for them. They kept them *up in their hearts;* and, if they left them for a while, it was *cum animo revertendi—with an intention to return to them*, not a final farewell. Or it may be understood of spiritual idolatry; those whose affections are placed upon the wealth of the world and the pleasures of sense, whose god is their money, *whose god is their belly*, they *set up their idols in their heart*. Many who have no idols in their sanctuary have idols in their hearts,

which is no less a usurpation of God's throne and a profanation of his name. *Little children, keep yourselves from* those idols. 2. They *put the stumbling-block of their iniquity before their face*. Their *silver and gold* were called *the stumbling-block of their iniquity* (ch. vii. 19), their *idols of silver and gold,* by the beauty of which they were allured to idolatry, and so it was the block at which they stumbled, and fell into that sin; or *their iniquity* is their *stumbling-block*, which throws them down, so that they fall into ruin. Note, Sinners are their own tempters *(every man is tempted when he is drawn aside of his own lust)*, and so they are their own destroyers. *If thou scornest, thou alone shalt bear it;* and thus *they put the stumbling-block of their iniquity before their own faces,* and stumble upon it though they⋅see it before their eyes. It intimates that they are resolved to go on in sin, whatever comes of it. *I have loved strangers, and after them I will go;* that is the language of their hearts. And *should* God *be enquired of* by such wretches? Do they not hereby rather put an affront upon him than do him any honour, as those did who *bowed the knee* to Christ in mockery? Can those expect an answer of peace from God who thus continue their acts of hostility against him? " Ezekiel, what thinkest thou of it?"

III. The answer which God, in just displeasure, orders Ezekiel to give them, v. 4. Let them know that it is not out of any disrespect to their persons that God refuses to give them an answer, but it is laid down as a rule for *every man of the house of Israel*, whoever he be, that if he continue in love and league with his idols, and come to enquire of God, God will resent it as an indignity done to him, and will answer him according to his real iniquity, not according to his pretended piety. He *comes to the prophet*, who, he expects, will be civil to him, but God will give him his answer, by punishing him for his impudence: *I the Lord*, who *speak and it is done, I will answer him that cometh, according to the multitude of his idols.* Observe, Those who *set up idols in their hearts*, and set their hearts upon their idols, commonly have a multitude of them. Humble worshippers God answers *according to the multitude of his mercies*, but bold intruders he answers *according to the multitude of their idols*, that is, 1. According to the desire of their idols; he will give them up *to their own hearts' lust*, and leave them to themselves to be as bad as they have a mind to be, till they *have filled up the measure of their iniquity*. Men's corruptions are *idols in their hearts*, and they are of their own setting up; their temptations are *the stumbling-block of their iniquity*, and they are of their own putting, and God will answer them accordingly; let them take their course. 2. According to the desert of their idols; they shall have such an answer as it is just that such idolaters should have. God will punish them as he usually punishes idolaters, that is, when they stand in need of his help he will *send them to the gods whom they have chosen,* Judg. x. 13, 14. Note, The judgment of God will dwell with men according to what they are really (that is, according to what their hearts are), not according to what they are in show and profession. And what will be the end of this? What will this threatened answer amount to? He tells them (*v.* 5): *That I may take the house of Israel in their own heart,* may lay them open to the world, that they may be ashamed; nay, lay them open to the curse, that they may be ruined. Note, The sin and shame, and pain and ruin, of sinners, are all from themselves, and their own hearts are the snares in which they are taken; they seduce them, they betray them; their own consciences witness against them, condemn them, and are a terror to them. If God take them, if he discover them, if he convict them, if he bind them over to his judgment, it is all by *their own hearts.* *O Israel! thou hast destroyed thyself.* The *house of Israel* is ruined by its own hands, *because they are all estranged from me through their idols.* Note, (1.) The ruin of sinners is owing to their estrangement from God. (2.) It is through some idol or other that the hearts of men are estranged from God; some creature has gained that place and dominion in the heart that God should have.

IV. The extent of this answer which God had given them—to all *the house of Israel,* *v.* 7, 8. The same thing is repeated, which intimates God's just displeasure against hypocrites, who mock him with the shows and forms of devotion, while their hearts are estranged from him and at war with him. Observe, 1. To whom this declaration belongs. It concerns not only every one of the house of Israel (as before, *v.* 4), but *the stranger that sojourns in Israel;* let him not think it will be an excuse for him in his idolatries that he is but a stranger and a sojourner in Israel, and does but worship the gods that his father served and that he himself was bred up in the service of; no, let him not expect any benefit from Israel's oracles or prophets unless he thoroughly renounce his idolatry. Note, Even proselytes shall not be countenanced if they be not sincere: a dissembled conversion is no conversion. 2. The description here given of hypocrites: They *separate themselves from* God by their fellowship with idols; they cut themselves off from their relation to God and their interest in him; they break off their acquaintance and intercourse with him, and set themselves at a distance from him. Note, Those that join themselves to idols separate themselves from God; nor shall any be for ever separated from the vision and fruition of God, but such as now separate themselves from his service and

826

wilfully withdraw their allegiance from him. But there are those who thus separate themselves from God, and yet come to the prophets with a seeming respect and deference to their office, *to enquire of them concerning* God, in order to satisfy a vain curiosity, to stop the mouth of a clamorous conscience, or to get or save a reputation among men, but without any desire to be acquainted with God or any design to be ruled by him. 3. The doom of those who thus trifle with God and think to impose upon him: " *I the Lord will answer him by myself;* let me alone to deal with him; I will give him an answer that shall fill him with confusion, that shall make him repent of his daring impiety." He shall have his answer, not by the words of the prophet, but by the judgments of God. *And I will set my face against that man,* which denotes great displeasure against him and a fixed resolution to ruin him. God can outface the most impenitent sinner. The hypocrite thought to save his credit, nay, and to gain applause, but, on the contrary, God *will make him a sign and a proverb,* will inflict such judgments upon him as shall make him remarkable and contemptible in the eyes of all about him; his misery shall be made use of to express the greatest misery, as when the worst of sinners are said to have *their portion appointed them with hypocrites,* Matt. xxiv. 51. God will make him an example; his judgments upon him shall be for warning to others to take heed of mocking God: for *thus shall it be done to the man that separates himself from* God, and yet pretends to *enquire concerning him.* The hypocrite thought to pass for one of God's people, and to crowd into heaven among them; but God *will cut him off from the midst of his people,* will discover him, and pluck him out from the thickest of them; and by this, says God, *you shall know that I am the Lord.* By the discovery of hypocrites it appears that God is omniscient: ministers know not how people stand affected when they come to hear the word, but God does. And by the punishment of hypocrites it appears that he is a jealous God, and one that cannot and will not be imposed upon.

V. The doom of those pretenders to prophecy who give countenance to these pretenders to piety, *v.* 9, 10. These hypocritical enquirers, though Ezekiel will not give them a comfortable answer, yet hope to meet with some other prophets that will; and if they do, as perhaps they may, let them know that God permits those lying prophets to deceive them in part of punishment: " *If the prophet* that flatters them *be deceived,* and gives them hopes which there is no ground for, *I the Lord have deceived that prophet,* have suffered the temptation to be laid before him, and suffered him to yield to it, and overruled it for the hardening of those in their wicked courses who were resolved to go on in them."

We are sure that God is not the author of sin, but we are sure that he is the Lord of all and the Judge of sinners, and that he often makes use of one wicked man to destroy another, and so of one wicked man to deceive another. Both are sins in him who does them, and so they are *not* from God; both are punishments to him to whom they are done, and so they *are* from God. We have a full instance of this in the story of Ahab's prophets, who were deceived by a lying spirit, which God put into their mouths (1 Kings xxii. 23), and another in those whom God *gives up to strong delusions, to believe a lie, because they received not the love of the truth,* 2 Thess. ii. 10, 11. But read the fearful doom of the lying prophet: *I will stretch out my hand upon him and will destroy him.* When God has served his own righteous purposes by him he shall be reckoned with for his unrighteous purposes. As, when God had made use of the Chaldeans for the wasting of a sinful people, he justly punished them for their rage, so when he had made use of *false prophets,* and afterwards of *false Christs,* for the deceiving of a sinful people, he justly punished them for their falsehood. But herein we must acknowledge (as Calvin upon this place reminds us) that God's *judgments are a great deep,* that we are incompetent judges of them, and that, though we cannot account for the equity of God's proceedings to the satisfying and silencing of every caviller, yet there is a day coming when he will be justified before all the world, and particularly in this instance, when *the punishment of the prophet* that flattereth the hypocrite in his evil way shall be as the punishment of the hypocrite that seeketh to him and bespeaks *smooth things* only, Isa. xxx. 10. The ditch shall be the same to the blind leader and the blind followers.

VI. The good counsel that is given them for the preventing of this fearful doom (*v.* 6): " *Therefore repent, and turn yourselves from your idols.* Let *this* separate between you and them, that they separate between you and God; because they set God's face against you, do you *turn away your faces from them,*" which denotes, not only forsaking them, but forsaking them with loathing and detestation: "Turn from them as from abominations that you are sick of; and then you will be welcome to enquire of the Lord. *Come now, and let us reason together.*"

VII. The good issue of all this as to the house of Israel; *therefore* the pretending prophets, and the pretending saints, shall perish together by the judgments of God, that, some being made examples, the body of the people may be reformed, *that the house of Israel may go no more astray from me, v.* 11. Note, The punishments of some are designed for the prevention of sin, that others may hear, and fear, and take warning. When we see what becomes of those that go astray from God we should thereby be engaged to keep close to

him. And, if *the house of Israel go not astray, they will not be polluted any more.* Note, Sin is a polluting thing; it renders the sinner odious in the eyes of the pure and holy God, and in his own eyes too whenever conscience is awakened; and therefore they shall *no more be polluted, that they may be my people and I may be their God.* Note, Those whom God takes into covenant with himself must first be cleansed from the pollutions of sin; and those who are so cleansed shall not only be saved from ruin, but be entitled to all the privileges of God's people.

12 The word of the LORD came again to me, saying, 13 Son of man, when the land sinneth against me by trespassing grievously, then will I stretch out mine hand upon it, and will break the staff of the bread thereof, and will send famine upon it, and will cut off man and beast from it: 14 Though these three men, Noah, Daniel, and Job, were in it, they should deliver *but* their own souls by their righteousness, saith the Lord GOD. 15 If I cause noisome beasts to pass through the land, and they spoil it, so that it be desolate, that no man may pass through because of the beasts: 16 *Though* these three men *were* in it, *as* I live, saith the Lord GOD, they shall deliver neither sons nor daughters; they only shall be delivered, but the land shall be desolate. 17 Or *if* I bring a sword upon that land, and say, Sword, go through the land; so that I cut off man and beast from it: 18 Though these three men *were* in it, *as* I live, saith the Lord GOD, they shall deliver neither sons nor daughters, but they only shall be delivered themselves. 19 Or *if* I send a pestilence into that land, and pour out my fury upon it in blood, to cut off from it man and beast: 20 Though Noah, Daniel, and Job, *were* in it, *as* I live, saith the Lord GOD, they shall deliver neither son nor daughter; they shall *but* deliver their own souls by their righteousness. 21 For thus saith the Lord GOD; How much more when I send my four sore judgments upon Jerusalem, the sword, and the famine, and the noisome beast, and the pestilence, to cut off from it man and beast? 22 Yet, behold, therein shall be left a remnant that shall be

brought forth, *both* sons and daughters: behold, they shall come forth unto you, and ye shall see their way and their doings: and ye shall be comforted concerning the evil that I have brought upon Jerusalem, *even* concerning all that I have brought upon it. 23 And they shall comfort you, when ye see their ways and their doings: and ye shall know that I have not done without cause all that I have done in it, saith the Lord God.

The scope of these verses is to show,

I. That national sins bring national judgments. When virtue is ruined and laid waste every thing else will soon be ruined and laid waste too (*v.* 13): *When the land sins against me,* when vice and wickedness become epidemical, *when the land sins by trespassing grievously,* when the sinners have become very numerous and their sins very heinous, when gross impieties and immoralities universally prevail, *then will I stretch forth my hand upon it,* for the punishment of it. The divine power shall be vigorously and openly exerted; the judgments shall be extended and stretched forth to all the corners of the land, to all the concerns and interests of the nation. Grievous sins bring grievous plagues.

II. That God has a variety of sore judgments wherewith to punish sinful nations, and he has them all at command and inflicts which he pleases. He did indeed give David his choice what judgment he would be punished with for his sin in numbering the people; for any of them would serve to answer the end, which was to lessen the numbers he was proud of; but David, in effect, referred it to God again: " *Let us fall into the hands of the Lord;* let him choose with what rod we shall be beaten." But he uses a variety of judgments that it may appear he has a universal dominion, and that in all our concerns we may see our dependence on him. *Four sore judgments* are here specified:—1. *Famine, v.* 13. The denying and withholding of common mercies is itself judgment enough, there needs no more to make a people miserable. God needs not bring the staff of oppression, it is but *breaking the staff of bread* and the work is soon done; he *cuts off man and beast* by cutting off the provisions which nature makes for both in the annual products of the earth. God *breaks the staff of bread* when, though we have bread, yet we are not nourished and strengthened by it. Hag. i. 6, *You eat, but you have not enough.* 2. Hurtful *beasts, noisome* and noxious, either as poisonous or as ravenous. God can make these *to pass through the land* (*v.* 15), to increase in all parts of it, and to bereave it, not only of the tame cattle, preying upon their flocks and 828

herds, but of their people, devouring men, women, and children, so *that no man may pass through because of the beasts;* none dare travel even in the high roads for fear of being pulled in pieces by lions, or other beasts of prey, as the children of Beth-el by two bears. Note, When men revolt from their allegiance to God, and rebel against him, it is just with God that the inferior creatures should rise up in arms against man, Lev. xxvi. 22. 3. War. God often chastises sinful nations by bringing a sword upon them, the sword of a foreign enemy, and he gives it its commission and orders what execution it shall do (*v.* 17): he says, *Sword, go through the land.* It is bad enough if the sword do but enter into the borders of a land, but much worse when it goes through the bowels of a land. By it God *cuts off man and beast,* horse and foot. What execution the sword does God does by it; for it is his sword, and it acts as he directs. 4. *Pestilence* (*v.* 19), a dreadful disease, which has sometimes depopulated cities; by it God *pours out his fury in blood* (that is, in death); the pestilence kills as effectually as if the blood were shed by the sword, for it is poisoned by the disease, *the sickness* we call it. See how miserable the case of mankind is that lies thus exposed to deaths in various shapes. See how dangerous the case of sinners is against whom God has so many ways of fighting, so that, though they escape one judgment, God has another waiting for them.

III. That when God's professing people revolt from him, and rebel against him, they may justly expect a complication of judgments to fall upon them. God has various ways of contending with a sinful nation; but if Jerusalem, the holy city, *become a harlot,* God will send upon her all his *four sore judgments* (*v.* 21); for the nearer any are to God in name and profession the more severely will he reckon with them if they reproach that worthy name by which they are called and give the lie to that profession. They shall be punished *seven times more.*

IV. That there may be, and commonly are, some few very good men, even in those places that by sin are ripened for ruin. It is no foreign supposition that, even in a land that has *trespassed grievously,* there may be *three* such *men* as *Noah, Daniel, and Job.* Daniel was now living, and at this time had scarcely arrived at the prime of his eminency, but he was already famous (at least this word of God concerning him would without fail make him so); yet he was carried away into captivity with the first of all, Dan. i. 6. Some of the better sort of people in Jerusalem might perhaps think that, if Daniel (of whose fame in the king of Babylon's court they had heard much) had but continued in Jerusalem, it would have been spared for his sake, as the magicians in Babylon were. " No," says God, " though you had him, who was as eminently good in bad times and places as Noah in the old world and Job in the land of Uz, yet a reprieve should not be obtained." In the places that are most corrupt, and in the ages that are most degenerate, *there is a remnant* which God reserves to himself, and which *still hold fast their integrity* and stand fair for the honour of *delivering the land*, as *the innocent* are said to do, Job xxii. 30.

V. That God often spares very wicked places for the sake of a few godly people in them. This is implied **here** as the expecta-tion of Jerusalem's friends in the day of its distress : " Surely God will stay his contro-versy with us ; for are there not some among us that are emptying the measure of na-tional guilt by their prayers, as others are filling it by their sins ? And, rather than God will *destroy the righteous with the wicked*, he will preserve *the wicked with the right-eous.* If Sodom might have been spared for the sake of ten good men, surely Jeru-salem may."

VI. That such men as Noah, Daniel, and Job, will prevail, if any can, to turn away the wrath of God from a sinful people. Noah was a perfect man, and kept his in-tegrity when all flesh had corrupted their way ; and, for his sake, his family, though one of them was wicked (Ham), was saved in the ark. Job was a great example of piety, and mighty in prayer for his children, for his friends ; and God turned his captivity when he prayed. Those were very ancient examples, before Moses, that great interces-sor ; and therefore God mentions them, to intimate that he had some very peculiar fa-vourites long before the Jewish nation was formed or founded, and would have such when it was ruined, for which reason, it should seem, those names were made use of, rather than Moses, Aaron, or Samuel ; and yet, lest any should think that God was partial in his respects to the ancient days, here is a modern instance, a living one, placed be-tween those two that were the glories of an-tiquity, and he now a captive, and that is Daniel, to teach us not to lessen the useful good men of our own day by over-magnify-ing the ancients. Let the children of the captivity know that Daniel, their neighbour, and *companion in tribulation*, being a man of great humility, piety, and zeal for God, and instant and constant in prayer, had as good an interest in heaven as Noah or Job had. Why may not God raise up as great and good men now as he did formerly, and do as much for them?

VII. That when the sin of a people has come to its height, and the decree has gone forth for their ruin, the piety and prayers of the best men shall not prevail to finish the controversy. This is here asserted again and again, that, *though these three men were in* Jerusalem at this time, yet they should *de-liver neither son nor daughter;* not so much as the little ones should be spared for their

sakes, as the little ones of Israel were upon the prayer of Moses, Num. xiv. 31. No ; *the land shall be desolate*, and God would not hear their prayers for it, though *Moses and Samuel stood before him*, Jer. xv. 1. Note, Abused patience will turn at last into inex-orable wrath ; and it should seem as if God would be more inexorable in Jerusalem's case than in another (*v.* 6), because, besides the divine patience, they had enjoyed greater privileges than any other people, which were the aggravations of their sin.

VIII. That, though pious praying men may not prevail to deliver others, yet *they shall deliver their own souls by their righte-ousness*, so that, though they may suffer in the common calamity, yet to them the pro-perty of it is altered ; it is not to them what it is to the wicked ; it is unstrung, and does them no hurt ; it is sanctified, and does them good. Sometimes *their souls* (their lives) are remarkably *delivered*, and *given them for a prey ;* at least *their souls* (their spiritual interests) are secured. If their bodies be not *delivered*, yet *their souls* are. *Riches* indeed *profit not in the day of wrath*, but *righteousness delivers from death*, from so great a death, so many deaths as are here threatened. This should encourage us to keep our integrity in times of common apos-tasy, that, if we do so, we shall be *hidden in the day of the Lord's anger.*

IX. That, even when God makes the greatest desolations by his judgments, he reserves some to be the monuments of his mercy, *v.* 22, 23. In Jerusalem itself, though marked for utter ruin, yet *there shall be left a remnant*, who shall not be cut off by any of those *sore judgments* before mentioned, but shall be carried into captivity, both *sons and daughters*, who shall be the seed of a new generation. The young ones, who had not grown up to such an obstinacy in sin as their fathers had who were therefore cut off as incurable, these *shall be brought forth* out of the ruins of Jerusalem by the victo-rious enemy, and *behold they shall come forth to you* that are in captivity, they shall make a virtue of a necessity, and shall come the more willingly to Babylon because so many of their friends have gone thither before them and are there ready to receive them ; and, when they come, *you shall see their ways and their doings;* you shall hear them make a free and ingenuous confession of the sins they had formerly been guilty of, and a humble profession of repentance for them, with promises of reformation ; and you shall see instances of their reformation, shall see what good their affliction has done them, and how prudently and patiently they con-duct themselves under it. Their narrow escape shall have a good effect upon them ; it shall change their temper and conversa-tion, and make them new men. And this will redound, 1. To the satisfaction of their brethren : *They shall comfort you when you see their ways.* Note, It is a very comfortable sight to see people, when they are under the rod, repenting and humbling themselves, justifying God and accepting the punishment of their iniquity. When we sorrow (as we ought to do) for the afflictions of others, it is a great comfort to us in our sorrow to see them improving their afflictions and making a good use of them. When those captives told their friends how bad they had been, and how righteous God was in bringing these judgments upon them, it made them very easy, and helped to reconcile them to the calamities of Jerusalem, to the justice of God in punishing his own people so, and to the goodness of God, which now appeared to have had kind intentions in all; and thus " *You shall be comforted concerning all the evil that I have brought upon Jerusalem,* and, when you better understand the thing, shall not have such direful apprehensions concerning it as you have had.'' Note, It is a debt we owe to our brethren, if we have got good by our afflictions, to comfort them by letting them know it. 2. It will redound to the honour of God: " *You shall know that I have not done without cause,* not without a just provocation, and yet not without a gracious design, *all that I have done in it.*" Note, When afflictions have done their work, and have accomplished that for which they were sent, then will appear the wisdom and goodness of God in sending them, and God will be not only justified, but glorified in them.

CHAP. XV.

Ezekiel has again and again, in God's name, foretold the utter ruin of Jerusalem; but, it should seem, he finds it hard to reconcile himself to it, and to acquiesce in the will of God in this severe dispensation; and therefore God takes various methods to satisfy him not only that it shall be so, but that there is no remedy: it must be so; it is fit that it should be so. Here, in this short chapter, he shows him (probably with design that he should tell the people) that it was as requisite Jerusalem should be destroyed as that the dead and withered branches of a vine should be cut off and thrown into the fire. I. The similitude is very elegant (ver. 1—5), but, II. The explanation of the similitude is very dreadful, ver. 6—8.

AND the word of the LORD came unto me, saying, 2 Son of man, what is the vine-tree more than any tree, *or than* a branch which is among the trees of the forest? 3 Shall wood be taken thereof to do any work? or will *men* take a pin of it to hang any vessel thereon? 4 Behold, it is cast into the fire for fuel; the fire devoureth both the ends of it, and the midst of it is burned. Is it meet for *any* work? 5 Behold, when it was whole, it was meet for no work: how much less shall it be meet yet for *any* work, when the fire hath devoured it, and it is burned? 6 Therefore thus saith the Lord GOD; As the vine-tree among the trees of the forest, which I have given to the fire for fuel, so

830

will I give the inhabitants of Jerusalem. 7 And I will set my face against them; they shall go out from *one* fire, and *another* fire shall devour them; and ye shall know that I *am* the LORD, when I set my face against them. 8 And I will make the land desolate, because they have committed a trespass, saith the Lord GOD.

The prophet, we may suppose, was thinking what a glorious city Jerusalem was, above any city in the world; it was the crown and *joy of the whole earth;* and therefore what a pity it was that it should be destroyed; it was a noble structure, the city of God, and the city of Israel's solemnities. But, if these were the thoughts of his heart, God here returns an answer to them by comparing Jerusalem to a vine. 1. It is true, if a vine be fruitful, it is a most valuable tree, none more so; it was one of those that were courted to have dominion over the trees, and the fruit of it is such as *cheers God and man* (Judg. ix. 12, 13); it *makes glad the heart,* Ps. civ. 15. So Jerusalem was *planted a choice and noble vine, wholly a right seed* (Jer. ii. 21); and, if it had brought forth fruit suitable to its character as a holy city, it would have been the glory both of God and Israel. It was a vine which *God's right hand had planted,* a *branch out of a dry ground,* which, though its original was mean and despicable, God had *made strong for himself* (Ps. lxxx. 15), to be *to him for a name and for a praise.* 2. But, if it be not fruitful, it is good for nothing, it is as worthless and useless a production of the earth as even thorns and briers are: *What is the vine-tree,* if you take the tree by itself, without consideration of the fruit? *What is it more than any tree,* that it should have so much care taken of it and so much cost laid out upon it? What is a branch of the vine, though it spread *more than a branch which is among the trees of the forest,* where it grows neglected and exposed? Or, as some read it, *What is the vine more than any tree if the branch of it be as the trees of the forest;* that is, if it bear no fruit, as forest-trees seldom do, being designed for timber-trees, not fruit-trees? Now there are some fruit-trees which, if they do not bear, are nevertheless of good use, as the wood of them may be made to turn to a good account; but the vine is not of this sort: if that do not answer its end as a fruit-tree, it is worth nothing as a timber-tree. Observe,

I. How this similitude is expressed here. The wild vine, that *is among the trees of the forest,* or the empty vine (which Israel is compared to, Hos. x. 1), that bears no more fruit than a forest-tree, is good for nothing; it is as useless as a brier, and more so, for that will add some sharpness to the thorny hedge, which the vine-branch will not do.

He shows, 1. That it is fit for no use. The wood of it is not *taken to do any work;* one cannot so much as make *a pin of it to hang a vessel upon, v. 3.* See how variously the gifts of nature are dispensed for the service of man. Among the plants, the roots of some, the seeds or fruits of others, the leaves of others, and of some the stalks, are most serviceable to us; so, among trees, some are strong and not fruitful, as the oaks and cedars; others are weak but very fruitful, as the vine, which is unsightly, low, and depending, yet of great use. Rachel is comely but barren, Leah homely but fruitful. 2. That therefore it is made use of *for fuel;* it will serve to heat the oven with. Because *it is* not *meet for any work, it is cast into the fire, v. 4.* When it is good for nothing else it is useful this way, and answers a very needful intention, *for fuel* is a thing we must have, and to burn any thing for fuel which is good for other work is bad husbandry. *To what purpose is this waste?* The unfruitful vine is disposed of in the same way with the briers and thorns, which are rejected, and *whose end is to be burnt,* Heb. vi. 8. And what care is taken of it then? If a piece of solid timber be kindled, somebody perhaps may snatch it *as a brand out of the burning,* and say, " It is a pity to burn it, for it may be put to some better use;" but if the branch of a vine be on fire, and, as usual, both the ends of it and the middle be kindled together, nobody goes about to save it. *When it was whole it was meet for no work, much less when the fire has devoured it* (v. 5); even the ashes of it are not worth saving.

II. How this similitude is applied to Jerusalem. 1. That holy city had become unprofitable and good for nothing. It had been as *the vine-tree among the trees of the* vineyard, abounding in the fruits of righteousness to the glory of God. When religion flourished there, and the pure worship of God was kept up, many a joyful vintage was then gathered in from it; and, while it continued so, God made a hedge about it; it was his *pleasant plant* (Isa. v. 7); he *watered it every moment* and *kept it night and day* (Isa. xxvii. 3); but it had now become *the degenerate plant of a strange vine,* of a wild vine (such as we read of 2 Kings iv. 39), *a vine-tree among the trees of the forest,* which, being wild, *brings forth wild grapes* (Isa. v. 4), which are not only of no use, but are nauseous and noxious (Deut. xxxii. 32), *their grapes are grapes of gall, and their clusters are bitter.* It is explained (v. 8): " *They have trespassed a trespass,* that is, they have treacherously prevaricated with God and perfidiously apostatized from him;" for so the word signifies. Note, Professors of religion, if they do not live up to their profession, but contradict it, if they degenerate and depart from it, are the most unprofitable creatures in the world, like the salt that has *lost its savour* and is thenceforth *good for nothing,* Mark ix. 50. Other nations were famed for valour or politics, some for war, others for trade, and retained their credit; but the Jewish nation, being famous as a holy people, when they lost their holiness, and became wicked, were thenceforth *good for nothing;* with that they lost all their credit and usefulness, and became the most base and despicable people under the sun, *trodden under foot of the Gentiles.* Daniel, and other pious Jews, were of great use in their generation; but the idolatrous Jews then, and the unbelieving Jews now since the preaching of the gospel, have been, and are, of no common service, not fit *for any work.* 2. Being so, it is *given to the fire for fuel, v. 6.* Note, Those who are not fruitful to the glory of God's grace will be fuel to the fire of his wrath; and thus, if they give not honour to him, he will *get himself honour upon them,* honour that will shine brightly in that flaming fire by which impenitent sinners will be for ever consumed. He will not be a loser at last by any of his creatures. *The Lord has made all things for himself,* yea, *even the wicked,* that would not otherwise be for him, *for the day of evil* (Prov. xvi. 4); and in those who would not glorify him as *the God to whom* duty *belongs* he will be glorified as *the God to whom vengeance belongs.* The fire of God's wrath had before *devoured both the ends of* the Jewish nation (v. 4), Samaria and the cities of Judah; and now Jerusalem, that was *the midst of it,* was thrown *into the fire,* to be *burnt* too, for *it is meet for no work;* it will not be wrought upon, by any of the methods God has taken, to be serviceable to him. *The inhabitants of Jerusalem* were like a vine-branch, rotten and awkward; and therefore (v. 7), " *I will set my face against them,* to thwart all their counsels," as they set their faces against God, to contradict his word and defeat all his designs. It is decreed; the consumption is determined: *I will make the land* quite *desolate,* and therefore, when they *go out from one fire, another fire shall devour them* (v. 7); the end of one judgment shall be the beginning of another, and their escape from one only a reprieve till another comes; they shall go from misery in their own country to misery in Babylon. Those who kept out of the way of the sword perished by famine or pestilence. When one descent of the Chaldean forces upon them was over, and they thought, *Surely the bitterness of death is past,* yet soon after they returned again with double violence, till they had made a full end. Thus *they shall know that I am the Lord,* a God of almighty power, *when I set my face against them.* Note, God shows himself to be *the Lord,* by perfecting the destruction of his implacable enemies as well as the deliverances of his obedient people. Those against whom God *sets his face,* though they may come out of one trouble little hurt, will fall into another; though they *come out of the pit,* they will be *taken in the snare* (Isa. xxiv. 18); though they escape *the sword of Hazael,* they will fall by that of Jehu (1 Kings xix. 17); for *evil pursues sinners.* Nay, though *they go out from the fire* of temporal judgments, and seem to die in peace, yet there is an everlasting fire that will *devour them;* for, *when God judges,* first or last *he will overcome,* and he will be *known by the judgments which he executes.* See Matt. iii. 10; John xv. 6.

CHAP. XVI.

Still God is justifying himself in the desolations he is about to bring upon Jerusalem; and very largely, in this chapter, he shows the prophet, and orders him to show the people, that he did but punish them as their sins deserved. In the foregoing chapter he had compared Jerusalem to an unfruitful vine, that was fit for nothing but the fire; in this chapter he compares it to an adulteress, that, in justice, ought to be abandoned and exposed, and he must therefore show the people their abominations, that they might see how little reason they had to complain of the judgments they were under. In this long discourse are set forth, I. The despicable and deplorable beginnings of that church and nation, ver. 3—5. II. The many honours and favours God had bestowed upon them, ver. 6—14. III. Their treacherous and ungrateful departures from him to the services and worship of idols, here represented by the most impudent whoredom, ver. 15—34. IV. A threatening of terrible destroying judgments, which God would bring upon them for this sin, ver. 35—43. V. An aggravation both of their sin and of their punishment, by comparison with Sodom and Samaria, ver. 44—59. VI. A promise of mercy in the close, which God would show to a penitent remnant, ver. 60—63. And this is designed for admonition to us.

A GAIN the word of the LORD came unto me, saying, 2 Son of man, cause Jerusalem to know her abominations, 3 And say, Thus saith the Lord GOD unto Jerusalem; Thy birth and thy nativity *is* of the land of Canaan; thy father *was* an Amorite, and thy mother a Hittite. 4 And *as for* thy nativity, in the day thou wast born thy navel was not cut, neither wast thou washed in water to supple *thee;* thou wast not salted at all, nor swaddled at all. 5 None eye pitied thee, to do any of these unto thee, to have compassion upon thee; but thou wast cast out in the open field, to the loathing of thy person, in the day that thou wast born.

Ezekiel is now among the captives in Babylon; but, as Jeremiah at Jerusalem wrote for the use of the captives though they had Ezekiel upon the spot with them (ch. xxix.), so Ezekiel wrote for the use of Jerusalem, though Jeremiah himself was resident there; and yet they were far from looking upon it as an affront to one another, or an interference with one another's business; for ministers have need of one another's help both by preaching and writing. Jeremiah wrote to the captives for their consolation, which was the thing they needed; Ezekiel here is directed to write to the inhabitants of Jerusalem for their conviction and humiliation, which was the thing they needed. I. This is his commission (v. 2): "Cause

Jerusalem to know her abominations (that is, her sins); set them in order before her." Note, 1. Sins are not only *provocations* which God is angry at, but *abominations* which he hates, as contrary to his nature, and which we ought to hate, Jer. xliv. 4. 2. The sins of Jerusalem are in a special manner so. The practice of profaneness appears most odious in those that make a profession of religion. 3. Though Jerusalem is a place of great knowledge, yet she is loth *to know her abominations;* so partial are men in their own favour that they are hardly made to see and own their own badness, but deny it, palliate or extenuate it. 4. It is requisite that we should know our sins, that we may confess them, and may justify God in what he brings upon us for them. 5. It is the work of ministers to cause sinners, sinners in Jerusalem, *to know their abominations,* to set before them the glass of the law, that in it they may see their own deformities and defilements, to tell them plainly of their faults. *Thou art the man.*

II. That Jerusalem may be made *to know her abominations,* and particularly the abominable ingratitude she had been guilty of, it was requisite that she should be put in mind of the great things God had done for her, as the aggravations of her bad conduct towards him; and, to magnify those favours, she is in these verses made to know the meanness and baseness of her original, from what poor beginnings God raised her, and how unworthy she was of his favour and of the honour he had put upon her. Jerusalem is here put for the Jewish church and nation, which is here compared to an outcast child, base-born and abandoned, which the mother herself has no affection nor concern for. 1. The extraction of the Jewish nation was mean: "*Thy birth is of the land of Canaan* (v. 3); thou hadst from the very first the spirit and disposition of a Canaanite." The patriarchs dwelt in Canaan, and they were there but *strangers and sojourners,* had no possession, no power, not one foot of ground of their own but a burying-place. Abraham and Sarah were indeed their *father and mother,* but they were only inmates with the Amorites and Hittites, who, having the dominion, seemed to be as parents to the seed of Abraham, witness the court Abraham made to the *children of Heth* (Gen. xxiii. 4, 8), the dependence they had upon their neighbours the Canaanites, and the fear they were in of them, Gen. xiii. 7; xxxiv. 30. If the patriarchs, at their first coming to Canaan, had conquered it, and made themselves masters of it, this would have put an honour upon their family and would have looked great in history; but, instead of that, they *went from one nation to another* (Ps. cv. 13), as tenants from one farm to another, almost as beggars from one door to another, when they *were but few in number,* yea, very few. And yet this was not the worst;

their fathers had *served other gods in Ur of the Chaldees* (Josh. xxiv. 2) ; even in Jacob's family there were *strange gods,* Gen. xxxv. 2. Thus early had they a genius leading them to idolatry; and upon this account their ancestors were Amorites and Hittites. 2. When they first began to multiply their condition was really very deplorable, like that of a new-born child, which must of necessity die from the womb if the knees prevent it not, Job iii. 11, 12. The children of Israel, when they began to increase into a people and became considerable, were thrown out from the country that was intended for them ; a famine drove thence them. Egypt was *the open field* into which they were cast; there they had no protection or countenance from the government they were under, but, on the contrary, were ruled with rigour, and their lives embittered ; they had no encouragement given them to build up their families, no help to build up their estates, no friends or allies to strengthen their interests. Joseph, who had been the *shepherd and stone of Israel,* was dead ; the king of Egypt, who should have been kind to them for Joseph's sake, set himself to *destroy this man-child as soon as it was born* (Rev. xii. 4), ordered all the males to be slain, which, it is likely, occasioned the exposing of many as well as Moses, to which perhaps the similitude here has reference. The founders of nations and cities had occasion for all the arts and arms they were masters of, set their heads on work, by policies and stratagems, to preserve and nurse up their infant states. *Tantæ molis erat Romanam condere gentem—So vast were the efforts requisite to the establishment of the Roman name.* Virgil. But the nation of Israel had no such care taken of it, no such pains taken with it, as Athens, Sparta, Rome, and other commonwealths had when they were first founded, but, on the contrary, was doomed to destruction, like an infant newborn, exposed to wind and weather, *the navel-string not cut,* the poor babe *not washed,* not clothed, *not swaddled,* because not pitied, *v.* 4, 5. Note, We owe the preservation of our infant lives to the natural pity and compassion which the God of nature has put into the hearts of parents and nurses towards new-born children. This infant is said to be *cast out, to the loathing of her person ;* it was a sign that she was loathed by those that bore her, and she appeared loathsome to all that looked upon her. *The Israelites were an abomination to the Egyptians,* as we find Gen xliii. 32 ; xlvi. 34. Some think that this refers to the corrupt and vicious disposition of that people from their beginning : they were not only the weakest and *fewest of all people* (Deut. vii. 7), but the worst and most ill-humoured of all people. *God giveth thee this good land, not for thy righteousness, for thou art a stiffnecked people,* Deut. ix. 6. And Moses tells them there (*v.* 24), *You have been rebellious*

against the Lord *from the day that I knew you.* They were not *suppled,* nor *washed,* nor *swaddled ;* they were not at all tractable or manageable, nor cast into any good shape. God took them to be his people, not because he saw any thing in them inviting or promising, but *so it seemed good in his sight.* And it is a very apt illustration of the miserable condition of all the children of men by nature. *As for* our *nativity, in the day that* we *were born* we were shapen in iniquity and conceived in sin, our understandings darkened, our minds alienated from the life of God, polluted with sin, which rendered us loathsome in the eyes of God. *Marvel not* then that we are told, *You must be born again.*

6 And when I passed by thee, and saw thee polluted in thine own blood, I said unto thee *when thou wast* in thy blood, Live ; yea, I said unto thee *when thou wast* in thy blood, Live. 7 I have caused thee to multiply as the bud of the field, and thou hast increased and waxen great, and thou art come to excellent ornaments: *thy* breasts are fashioned, and thine hair is grown, whereas thou *wast* naked and bare. 8 Now when I passed by thee, and looked upon thee, behold, thy time *was* the time of love; and I spread my skirt over thee, and covered thy nakedness: yea, I sware unto thee, and entered into a covenant with thee, saith the Lord GOD, and thou becamest mine. 9 Then washed I thee with water ; yea, I thoroughly washed away thy blood from thee, and I anointed thee with oil. 10 I clothed thee also with broidered work, and shod thee with badgers' skin, and I girded thee about with fine linen, and I covered thee with silk. 11 I decked thee also with ornaments, and I put bracelets upon thy hands, and a chain on thy neck. 12 And I put a jewel on thy forehead, and ear-rings in thine ears, and a beautiful crown upon thine head. 13 Thus wast thou decked with gold and silver; and thy raiment *was of* fine linen, and silk, and broidered work ; thou didst eat fine flour, and honey, and oil : and thou wast exceeding beautiful, and thou didst prosper into a kingdom. 14 And thy renown went forth among the heathen for thy beauty : for it *was* perfect through my

comeliness, which I had put upon thee, saith the Lord God.

In these verses we have an account of the great things which God did for the Jewish nation in raising them up by degrees to be very considerable. 1. God saved them from the ruin they were upon the brink of in Egypt (v. 6): " When I passed by thee, and saw thee polluted in thy own blood, loathed and abandoned, and appointed to die, as sheep for the slaughter, then I said unto thee, Live. I designed thee for life when thou wast doomed to destruction, and resolved to save thee from death." Those shall live to whom God commands life. God looked upon the world of mankind as thus cast off, thus cast out, thus polluted, thus weltering in blood, and his thoughts towards it were thoughts of good, designing it life, and that more abundantly. By converting grace, he says to the soul, Live. 2. He looked upon them with kindness and a tender affection, not only pitied them, but set his love upon them, which was unaccountable, for there was nothing lovely in them; but I looked upon thee, and, behold, thy time was the time of love, v. 8. It was the kindness and love of God our Saviour that sent Christ to redeem us, that sends the Spirit to sanctify us, that brought us out of a state of nature into a state of grace. That was a time of love indeed, distinguishing love, when God manifested his love to us, and courted our love to him. Then was I in his eyes as one that found favour, Cant. viii. 10. 3. He took them under his protection: " I spread my skirt over thee, to shelter thee from wind and weather, and to cover thy nakedness, that the shame of it might not appear." Boaz spread his skirt over Ruth, in token of the special favour he designed her, Ruth iii. 9. God took them into his care, as an eagle bears her young ones upon her wings, Deut. xxxii. 11, 12. When God owned them for his people, and sent Moses to Egypt to deliver them, which was an expression of the good-will of him that dwelt in the bush, then he spread his skirt over them. 4. He cleared them from the reproachful character which their bondage in Egypt laid them under (v. 9): " Then washed I thee with water, to make thee clean, and anointed thee with oil, to make thee sweet and supple thee." All the disgrace of their slavery was rolled away when they were brought, with a high hand and a stretched-out arm, into the glorious liberty of the children of God. When God said, Israel is my son, my first-born—Let my people go, that they may serve me, that word, backed as it was with so many works of wonder, thoroughly washed away their blood; and when God led them under the convoy of the pillar of cloud and fire he spread his skirt over them. 5. He multiplied them and built them up into a people. This is here mentioned (v. 7) before his spreading

834

his skirt over them, because their numbers increased exceedingly while they were yet bond-slaves in Egypt. They multiplied as the bud of the field in spring time; they waxed great, exceedingly mighty, Exod. i. 7, 20. Their breasts were fashioned when they were formed into distinct tribes and had officers of their own (Exod. v. 19); their hair grew when they grew numerous, whereas they had been naked and bare, very few and therefore contemptible. 6. He admitted them into covenant with himself. See what glorious nuptials this poor forlorn infant is preferred to at last. How she is dignified who at first had scarcely her life given her for a prey: I swore unto thee and entered into covenant with thee. This was done at Mount Sinai; "when the covenant between God and Israel was sealed and ratified then thou becamest mine." God called them his people, and himself the God of Israel. Note, Those to whom God gives spiritual life he takes into covenant with himself; by that covenant they become his subjects and servants, which intimates their duty—his portion, his treasure, which intimates their privilege; and it is confirmed with an oath, that we might have strong consolation. 7. He beautified and adorned them. This maid cannot forget her ornaments, and she is gratified with abundance of them, v. 10—13. We need not be particular in the application of these. Her wardrobe was well furnished with rich apparel; they had embroidered work to wear, shoes of fine badgers' skins, linen girdles, and silk veils, bracelets and necklaces, jewels and ear-rings, and even a beautiful crown, or coronet. Perhaps this may refer to the jewels and other rich goods which they took from the Egyptians, which might well be spoken of thus long after as a merciful circumstance of their deliverance, when it was spoken of long before, Gen. xv. 14. They shall come out with great substance. Or it may be taken figuratively for all those blessings of heaven which adorned both their church and state. In a little time they came to excellent ornaments, v. 7. The laws and ordinances which God gave them were to them as ornaments of grace to the head and chains about the neck, Prov. i. 9. God's sanctuary, which he set up among them, was a beautiful crown upon their head; it was the beauty of holiness. 8. He fed them with abundance, with plenty, with dainty: Thou didst eat fine flour, and honey, and oil—manna, angels' food—honey out of the rock, oil out of the flinty rock. In Canaan they did eat bread to the full, the finest of the wheat, Deut. xxxii. 13, 14. Those whom God takes into covenant with himself are fed with the bread of life, clothed with the robe of righteousness, adorned with the graces and comforts of the spirit. The hidden man of the heart is that which is incorruptible. 9. He gave them great reputation among their neighbours, and made them considerable, acceptable to their friends and allies and formidable to their adversaries : *Thou didst prosper into a kingdom* (*v.* 13), which speaks both dignity and dominion; and, *Thy renown went forth among the heathen for thy beauty, v.* 14. The nations about had their eye upon them, and admired them for the excellent laws by which they were governed, the privilege they had of access to God, Deut. iv. 7, 8. Solomon's wisdom, and Solomon's temple, were very much *the renown* of that nation ; and, if we put all the privileges of the Jewish church and kingdom together, we must own that it was the most accomplished beauty of all the nations of the earth. The beauty of it was perfect ; you could not name the thing that would be the honour of a people but it was to be found in Israel, in David's and Solomon's time, when that kingdom was in its zenith—piety, learning, wisdom, justice, victory, peace, wealth, and all sure to continue if they had kept close to God. *It was perfect, saith God, through my comeliness which I had put upon thee,* through the beauty of their holiness, as they were a people set apart for God, and devoted to him, to be to him *for a name, and for a praise, and for a glory.* It was this that put a lustre upon all their other honours and was indeed the perfection of their beauty. We may apply this spiritually. Sanctified souls are truly beautiful ; they are so in God's sight, and they themselves may take the comfort of it. But God must have all the glory, for they were by nature deformed and polluted, and, whatever comeliness they have, it is that which God has put upon them and beautified them with, and he will be well pleased with the work of his own hands.

15 But thou didst trust in thine own beauty, and playedst the harlot because of thy renown, and pouredst out thy fornications on every one that passed by; his it was. 16 And of thy garments thou didst take, and deckedst thy high places with divers colours, and playedst the harlot thereupon : *the like things* shall not come, neither shall it be *so.* 17 Thou hast also taken thy fair jewels of my gold and of my silver, which I had given thee, and madest to thyself images of men, and didst commit whoredom with them, 18 And tookest thy broidered garments, and coveredst them : and thou hast set mine oil and mine incense before them. 19 My meat also which I gave thee, fine flour, and oil, and honey, *wherewith* I fed thee, thou hast even set it before them for a sweet savour : and *thus* it was, saith the

Lord God. 20 Moreover thou hast taken thy sons and thy daughters, whom thou hast borne unto me, and these hast thou sacrificed unto them to be devoured. *Is this* of thy whoredoms a small matter, 21 That thou hast slain my children, and delivered them to cause them to pass through *the fire* for them? 22 And in all thine abominations and thy whoredoms thou hast not remembered the days of thy youth, when thou wast naked and bare, *and* wast polluted in thy blood. 23 And it came to pass after all thy wickedness, (Woe, woe unto thee ! saith the Lord God;) 24 *That* thou hast also built unto thee an eminent place, and hast made thee a high place in every street. 25 Thou hast built thy high place at every head of the way, and hast made thy beauty to be abhorred, and hast opened thy feet to every one that passed by, and multiplied thy whoredoms. 26 Thou hast also committed fornication with the Egyptians thy neighbours, great of flesh ; and hast increased thy whoredoms, to provoke me to anger. 27 Behold, therefore I have stretched out my hand over thee, and have diminished thine ordinary *food,* and delivered thee unto the will of them that hate thee, the daughters of the Philistines, which are ashamed of thy lewd way. 28 Thou hast played the whore also with the Assyrians, because thou wast unsatiable; yea, thou hast played the harlot with them, and yet couldest not be satisfied. 29 Thou hast moreover multiplied thy fornication in the land of Canaan unto Chaldea; and yet thou wast not satisfied herewith. 30 How weak is thine heart, saith the Lord God, seeing thou doest all these *things,* the work of an imperious whorish woman; 31 In that thou buildest thine eminent place in the head of every way, and makest thine high place in every street; and hast not been as a harlot, in that thou scornest hire ; 32 *But as* a wife that committeth adultery, *which* taketh strangers instead of her husband! 33 They give gifts to all whores : but thou givest thy gifts to all thy lovers, and hirest them, that they may come unto thee on every side for thy whoredom. 34 And the contrary is in thee from *other* women in thy whoredoms, whereas none followeth thee to commit whoredoms : and in that thou givest a reward, and no reward is given unto thee, therefore thou art contrary.

In these verses we have an account of the great wickedness of the people of Israel, especially in worshipping idols, notwithstanding the great favours that God had conferred upon them, by which, one would think, they should have been for ever engaged to him. This wickedness of theirs is here represented by the lewd and scandalous conversation of that beautiful maid which was rescued from ruin, brought up and well provided for by a kind friend and benefactor, that had been in all respects as a father and a husband to her. Their idolatry was the great provoking sin that they were guilty of; it began in the latter end of Solomon's time (for from Samuel's till then I do not remember that we read any thing of it), and thenceforward continued more or less the crying sin of that nation till the captivity; and, though it now and then met with some check from the reforming kings, yet it was never totally suppressed, and for the most part appeared to a high degree impudent and barefaced. They not only worshipped the true God by images, as the ten tribes by the calves at Dan and Bethel, but they worshipped false gods, Baal and Moloch, and all the senseless rabble of the pagan deities.

This is that which is here all along represented (as often elsewhere) under the similitude of whoredom and adultery, 1. Because it is the violation of a marriage-covenant with God, forsaking him and embracing the bosom of a stranger; it is giving that affection and that service to his rivals which are due to him alone. 2. Because it is the corrupting and defiling of the mind, and the enslaving of the spiritual part of the man, and subjecting it to the power and dominion of sense, as whoredom is. 3. Because it debauches the conscience, sears and hardens it; and those who by their idolatries dishonour the divine nature, and change the truth of God into a lie and his glory into shame, God justly punishes by giving them over to a reprobate mind, to dishonour the human nature with vile affections, Rom. i. 23, &c. It is a besotting bewitching sin; and, when men are given up to it, they seldom recover themselves out of the snare. 4. Because it is a shameful scandalous sin for those that have joined themselves to the Lord to join themselves to an idol. Now observe here,

I. What were the causes of this sin. How

came the people of God to be drawn away to the service of idols? How came a virgin so well taught, so well educated, to be debauched? Who would have thought it? But, 1. They grew proud (*v.* 15): *Thou trustedst to thy beauty*, and didst expect that that should make thee an interest, and didst *play the harlot because of thy renown.*" They thought, because they were so complimented and admired by their neighbours, that, further to ingratiate themselves with them and return their compliments, they must join with them in their worship and conform to their usages. Solomon admitted idolatry, to gratify his wives and their relations. Note, Abundance of young people are ruined by pride and particularly pride in their beauty. *Rara est concordia formæ atque pudicitiæ— Beauty and chastity are seldom associated* 2. They forgot their beginning (*v.* 22) " *Thou hast not remembered the days of thy youth*, how poor, and mean, and despicable thou wast, and what great things God did for thee and what lasting obligations he laid upon thee thereby." Note, It would be an effectual check to our pride and sensuality to consider what we are and how much we are beholden to the free grace of God. 3. They were weak in understanding and in resolution (*v.* 30): *How weak is thy heart, seeing thou dost all these things.* Note, The strength of men's lusts is an evidence of the weakness of their hearts; they have no acquaintance with themselves, nor government of themselves. She is weak, and yet an imperious whorish woman. Note, Those that are most foolish are commonly most imperious, and think themselves fit to manage others when they are far from being able to manage themselves.

II. What were the particulars of it. 1. They worshipped all the idols that came in their way, all that they were ever courted to the worship of; they were at the beck of all their neighbours (*v.* 15) : *Thou pouredst out thy fornications on every one that passed by : his it was.* They were ready to close with every temptation of this kind, though ever so absurd. No foreign idol could be imported, no new god invented, but they were ready to catch at it, as a common strumpet that prostitutes herself to all comers and *multiplies her whoredoms, v.* 25. Thus some common drunkards will be company for every one that puts up the finger to them; how weak are the hearts of such ! 2. They adorned their idol-temples, and groves, and high places, with the fine rich clothing that God had given them (*v.* 16, 18): *Thou deckedst thy high places with divers colours*, with the coats of divers colours, like Joseph's, which God had given them as particular marks of his favour, *and hast played the harlot* (that is, worshipped idols) *thereupon.* Of this he saith, " *The like things shall not come, neither shall it be so : that is,* this is a thing by no means to be suffered; I will never endure such practices as these without showing my resentments." 3. They made images for worship of the jewels which God had given them (*v.* 17): *The jewels of my gold and my silver which I had given thee.* Note, It is God that gives us our gold and silver; the products of trade, of art and industry, are the gifts of God's providence to us, as well as the fruits of the earth. And what God gives us the use of he still retains a property in. It is *my silver* and *my gold,* though I have *given it to thee.*" It is his still, so that we ought to serve and honour him with it, and are accountable to him for the disposal of it. Every penny has God's image upon it as well as Cæsar's. Should we make our silver and gold, our plate, money, and jewels, the matter of our pride and contention, our covetousness and prodigality, if we duly considered that they were God's silver and his gold? The Israelites began betimes to turn their jewels into idols, when Aaron made the golden calf of their earrings. 4. They served their idols with the good things which God gave them for their own use and to serve him with (*v.* 18): " *Thou hast set my oil and my incense before them,* upon their altars, as perfumes to these dunghill-deities; *my meat, and fine flour, and oil,* and that honey which Canaan flowed with, and *wherewith I fed thee,* thou hast regaled them and their hungry priests with, hast made an offering of it to them for *a sweet savour,* to purify them, and procure acceptance with them: and *thus it was, saith the Lord God;* it is too plain to be denied, too bad to be excused. *These things thou hast done.* He that knows all things knows it." See how fond they were of their idols, that they would part with that which was given them for the necessary subsistence of themselves and their families to honour them with, which may shame our niggardliness and strait-handedness in the service of the true and living God. 5. They had sacrificed their children to their idols. This is insisted upon here, and often elsewhere, as one of the worst instances of their idolatry, as indeed there was none in which the devil triumphed so much over the children of men, both their natural reason and their natural affection, as in this (see Jer. vii. 31; xix. 5; xxxii. 35): *Thou hast taken thy sons and thy daughters,* and not only made them to pass through the fire, or between two fires, in token of their being dedicated to Moloch, but thou hast *sacrificed them to be devoured,* *v.* 20. Never was there such an instance of the degenerating of the paternal authority into the most barbarous tyranny as this was. Yet that was not the worst of it: it was an irreparable wrong to God himself, who challenged a special property in their children more than in their gold and silver and their meat: They are *my children* (*v.* 21), the *sons and daughters which thou hast borne unto me,* *v.* 20. He is the *Father of spirits,* and rational souls are in a particular manner his; and therefore the taking away of life, human

life, unjustly, is a high affront to the *God of life.* But the children of Israelites were his by a further right; they were the *children of the covenant,* born in God's house. He had said to Abraham, *I will be a God to thee and to thy seed;* they had the seal of the covenant in their flesh from eight days old; they were to bear God's name, and keep up his church; to murder them was in the highest degree inhuman, but to murder them in honour of an idol was in the highest degree impious. One cannot think of it without the utmost indignation: to see the pitiless hands of the parents shedding the guiltless blood of their own children, and by offering those pieces of themselves to the devil for dying sacrifices openly avowing the offering up of themselves to him for living sacrifices! How absurd was this, that the children which were born to God should be *sacrificed to devils!* Note, The children of parents that are members of the visible church are to be looked upon as born unto God, and his children; as such, and under that character, we are to love them, and pray for them, bring them up for him, and, if he calls for them, cheerfully part with them to him; for *may he not do what he will with his own?* Upon this instance of their idolatry, which indeed ought not to pass without a particular brand, this remark is made (*v.* 20), *Is this of thy whoredoms a small matter?* which intimates that there were those who made a small matter of it, and turned it into a jest. Note, There is no sin so heinous, so apparently heinous, which men of profligate consciences will not make a mock at. But is whoredom, is spiritual whoredom, a small matter? Is it a small matter for men to make their children brutes and the devil their god? It will be a great matter shortly. 6. They built temples in honour of their idols, that others might be invited to resort thither and join with them in the worship of their idols: " *After all thy wickedness* of this kind committed in private, for which, *woe, woe, unto thee*" (that comes in in a sad parenthesis, denoting those to be in a woeful condition who are going on in sin, and giving them warning in time, if they would but take it), "thou hast at length arrived at such a pitch of impudence as to proclaim it; thou hast long had a whore's heart, but now thou hast come to have a whore's forehead, and canst not blush," *v.* 23—25. *Thou hast built there an eminent place,* a *brothel-house* (so the margin reads it), and such their idol temples were. *Thou hast made for thyself a high place,* for one idol or other, *in every street,* and *at every head of the way;* and again *v.* 31. They did all they could to seduce and debauch others, and to spread the contagion, by making the temptations to idolatry as strong as possibly they could; and hereby the ringleaders in idolatry did but *make themselves vile,* and even those that had courted them to it, finding themselves outdone by them, began to be surfeited with the abundance and violence of their idolatries: *Thou hast made thy beauty to be abhorred,* even by those that had admired it. The Jewish nation, by leaving their own God, and doting on the gods of the nations round about them, had made themselves mean and despicable in the eyes even of their heathen neighbours; much more was their *beauty abhorred* by all that were wise and good, and had any concern for the honour of God and religion. Note, Those shame themselves that bring a reproach on their profession. And justly will that beauty, that excellency, at length be made the object of the loathing of others which men have made the matter of their own pride.

III. What were the aggravations of this sin.

1. They were fond of the idols of those nations which had been their oppressors and persecutors. As, (1.) The Egyptians. They were a people notorious for idolatry, and for the most sottish senseless idolatries; they had of old abused Israel by their barbarous dealings, and of late by their treacherous dealings—were always either cruel or false to them; and yet so infatuated were they that *they committed fornication with the Egyptians their neighbours,* not only by joining with them in their idolatries, but by entering into leagues and alliances with them, and depending upon them for help in their straits, which was an adulterous departure from God. (2.) The Assyrians. They had also been vexatious to Israel: " And yet *thou hast played the whore with them* (*v.* 28); though they lived at a greater distance, yet thou hast entertained their idols and their superstitious usages, and so *hast multiplied thy fornications unto Chaldea,* hast borrowed images of gods, patterns of altars, rites of sacrificing, and one foolery or other of that kind, from that remote country, that enemy's country, and hast imported them *into the land of Canaan,* enfranchised and established them there." Thus Mr. George Herbert long since foretold, or feared at least,

That Seine shall swallow Tiber, and the Thames
By letting in them both pollute her streams.

2. They had been under the rebukes of Providence for their sins, and yet they persisted in them (*v.* 27): *I have stretched out my hand over thee,* to threaten and frighten thee. So God did before he *laid his hand upon them* to ruin and destroy them; and that is his usual method, to try to bring men to repentance first by less judgments. He did so here. Before he brought such a famine upon them as broke the staff of bread he *diminished their ordinary food,* cut them short before he cut them off. When the overplus is abused, it is just with God to diminish that which is for necessity. Before he delivered them to the Chaldeans to be destroyed he delivered them *to the daughters of the Philistines* to be ridiculed for their

idolatries; for they hated them, and, though they were idolaters themselves, yet were ashamed of the lewd way of the Israelites, who had grown more profane in their idolatries than any of their neighbours, who changed their gods, whereas other nations did not change theirs, Jer. ii. 10, 11. For this they were justly chastised by the Philistines. Or it may refer to the inroads which the Philistines made upon the south of Judah in the reign of Ahaz, by which it was weakened and impoverished, and which was the beginning of sorrows to them (2 Chron. xxviii. 18); but they did not take warning by those judgments, and therefore were justly abandoned to ruin at last. Note, In the account which impenitent sinners shall be called to they will be told not only of the mercies for which they have been ungrateful, but of the afflictions under which they have been incorrigible, Amos iv. 11.

3. They were insatiable in their spiritual whoredom: Thou *couldst not be satisfied,* *v.* 28 and again *v.* 29. When they had multiplied their idols and superstitious usages beyond measure, yet still they were enquiring after new gods and new fashions in worship. Those that in sincerity join themselves to the true God find enough in him for their satisfaction; and, though they still desire more of God, yet they never desire more than God. But those that forsake this living fountain for broken cisterns will find themselves soon surfeited, but never satisfied; they have soon enough of the gods they have, and are still enquiring after more.

4. They were at great expense with their idolatry, and laid out a great deal of wealth in purchasing patterns of images and altars, and hiring priests to attend upon them from other countries. Harlots generally had their hire; but this impudent adulteress, instead of being hired to serve idols, hired idols to protect her and accept her homage. This is much insisted on, *v.* 31—34. " In this respect *the contrary is in thee from other women in thy whoredoms:* others are courted, but thou makest court to those that do not follow thee, art fond of making leagues and alliances with those heathen nations that despise thee; others have gifts given them, but thou givest thy gifts, the gifts which God had graciously given thee, to thy idols; herein thou art like a wife that commits adultery, not for gain, as harlots do, but entirely for the sin's sake." Note, Spiritual lusts, those of the mind, such as theirs after idols were, are often as strong and impetuous as any carnal lusts are. And it is a great aggravation of sin when men are their own tempters, and, instead of proposing to themselves any worldly advantage by their sin, are at great expense with it; such are *transgressors without cause* (Ps. xxv. 3), wicked transgressors indeed.

And now is not Jerusalem in all this made to know her abominations? For what greater abominations could she be guilty of than these? Here we may see with wonder and horror what the corrupt nature of men is when God leaves them to themselves, yea, though they have the greatest advantages to be better and do better. And the way of sin is down-hill. *Nitimur in vetitum— We incline to what is forbidden.*

35 Wherefore, O harlot, hear the word of the LORD: 36 Thus saith the Lord GOD; Because thy filthiness was poured out, and thy nakedness discovered through thy whoredoms with thy lovers, and with all the idols of thy abominations, and by the blood of thy children, which thou didst give unto them; 37 Behold, therefore I will gather all thy lovers, with whom thou hast taken pleasure, and all *them* that thou hast loved, with all *them* that thou hast hated; I will even gather them round about against thee, and will discover thy nakedness unto them, that they may see all thy nakedness. 38 And I will judge thee, as women that break wedlock and shed blood are judged; and I will give thee blood in fury and jealousy. 39 And I will also give thee into their hand, and they shall throw down thine eminent place, and shall break down thy high places: they shall strip thee also of thy clothes, and shall take thy fair jewels, and leave thee naked and bare. 40 They shall also bring up a company against thee, and they shall stone thee with stones, and thrust thee through with their swords. 41 And they shall burn thine houses with fire, and execute judgments upon thee in the sight of many women: and I will cause thee to cease from playing the harlot, and thou also shalt give no hire any more. 42 So will I make my fury toward thee to rest, and my jealousy shall depart from thee, and I will be quiet, and will be no more angry. 43 Because thou hast not remembered the days of thy youth, but hast fretted me in all these *things;* behold, therefore I also will recompense thy way upon *thine* head, saith the Lord GOD: and thou shalt not commit this lewdness above all thine abominations.

Adultery was by the law of Moses made a capital crime. This notorious adulteress,

the criminal at the bar, being in the foregoing verses found guilty, here has sentence passed upon her. It is ushered in with solemnity, v. 35. The prophet, as the judge, in God's name calls to her, *O harlot! hear the word of the Lord.* Our Saviour preached to harlots, for their conversion, to bring them into the kingdom of God, not as the prophet here, to expel them out of it. Note, An apostate church is a harlot. Jerusalem is so if she become idolatrous. *How has the faithful city become a harlot!* Rome is so represented in the Revelation, when it is marked for ruin, as Jerusalem here. Rev. xvii. 1, *Come, and I will show thee the judgments of the great whore.* Those who will not hear the commanding word of the Lord and obey it shall be made to hear the condemning word of the Lord and shall tremble at it. Let us attend while judgment is given.

I. The crime is stated and the articles of the charge are summed up (v. 36) and (as is usual) with the attendant aggravations (v. 43); for when God speaks in wrath he will be justified, and clear when he judges, clear when he is judged; and sinners, when they are condemned, shall have their sins so set in order before them that their mouth shall be stopped and they shall not have a word to object against the equity of the sentence. The crimes which this harlot stands convicted of, and is now to be condemned for, are, 1. The violation of the first two commandments of the first table by idolatry, which is here called her *whoredoms with her lovers* (so she called them, Hos. ii. 12, because she loved them as if they had been indeed her benefactors), that is, with *all the idols of her abominations,* the abominable idols which she served and worshipped. This was the sin which provoked God to jealousy. 2. The violation of the first two commandments of the second table by the murder of their own innocent infants: *The blood of thy children which thou didst give unto them.* It is not strange if those that have cast off God and his fear break through the strongest and most sacred bonds of natural affection. Their sins are aggravated from the consideration, (1.) Of the dishonour they had thereby done to themselves: " Hereby *thy filthiness was poured out:* the uncleanness that was in thy heart was hereby discovered and brought to light, and thy nakedness was exposed to view, and thou wast thereby exposed to contempt." God is displeased with his professing people for shaming themselves by their sins. (2.) Their base ingratitude is another aggravation of their sins: " *Thou hast not remembered the days of thy youth,* and the kindness that was done thee then, when otherwise thou wouldst have perished," v. 43. And, (3.) The vexation which their sins gave to God, whom they ought to have pleased: " *Thou hast fretted me in all these things,*
839

not only angered me, but grieved me." It is a strange expression, and, one would think, enough to melt a heart of stone, that the great God, who cannot admit any uneasiness, is pleased to speak of the sins and follies of his professing people as *fretting* to him. *Forty years long was I grieved with this generation.*

II. The sentence is passed in general: *I will judge thee as women that break wedlock and shed blood are judged* (v. 38), and those two crimes were punished with death, with an ignominious death. "Thou hast *shed blood*, and therefore I will *give thee blood;* thou hast *broken wedlock*, and therefore I will give it thee, not only in justice, but in jealousy, not only as a righteous Judge, but as an injured and incensed husband, who *will not spare in the day of vengeance*," Prov. vi. 34, 35. He will *recompense their way upon their head, v. 43.* In all the judgments God executes upon sinners we must see *their own way recompensed upon their head;* they are dealt with not only as they deserved, but as they procured. It is the end which their sin, as a way, had a direct tendency to. More particularly, 1. This criminal must be (as is usually done with criminals) exposed to public shame, *v. 37.* Malefactors are not executed privately, but are made a spectacle to the world. Care is here taken to bring spectators together: *All those whom thou hast loved, with whom thou hast taken pleasure,* shall come to be witnesses of the execution, that they may take warning and prevent their own like ruin; and those also *whom thou hast hated,* who will insult over thee and triumph in thy fall." Both ways the calamities of Jerusalem will be aggravated, that they will be the grief of her friends and the joy of her foes. These shall not only be gathered *around her,* but *gathered against her;* even those with whom she took unlawful pleasure, with whom she contracted unlawful leagues, the Egyptians and Assyrians, shall now contribute to her ruin. As, *when a man's ways please the Lord, he makes even his enemies to be at peace with him,* so when a man's ways displease the Lord he makes even his friends to be at war with him; and justly makes those a scourge and a plague to sinners, and instruments of their destruction, who were their tempters, and with whom they were partakers in wickedness. Those whom they have suffered to strip them of their virtue shall see them stripped, and perhaps help to strip them, of all their other ornaments; to *see the nakedness of the land* will they come. It is added, to the same purport (v. 41), *I will execute judgments upon thee in the sight of many women;* thou shalt be made an example of *in terrorem* —*that others may see and fear* and do no more presumptuously. 2. The criminal is condemned to die, for her sins are such as death is the wages of (v. 40): *They shall*

bring up a company (that is, a company shall be brought up) *against thee,* and *they shall stone thee with stones,* and *thrust thee through with their swords;* so great a death, so many deaths in one, is this adulteress adjudged to. When the walls of Jerusalem were battered down with stones shot against them, and the inhabitants of Jerusalem were put to the sword, then this sentence was executed in the letter of it. 3. The estate of the criminal is confiscated, and all that belonged to her destroyed with her (v. 39): *They shall throw down thy eminent place,* and (v. 41) they *shall burn thy houses,* as the habitations of bad women are destroyed, in detestation of their lewdness. Their high places, erected in honour of their idols, by which they thought to ingratiate themselves with their neighbours, shall be an offence to them, and even *they* shall *break them down.* It was long the complaint, even in some of the best reigns of the kings of Judah, that *the high places were not taken away;* but now the army of the Chaldeans, when they lay all waste, shall break them down. If iniquity be not taken away by the justice of the nation, it shall be taken away by the judgments of God upon the nation. 4. Thus both the sin and the sinners shall be abolished together, and an end put to both: *Thou shalt cease from playing the harlot;* there shall be no remainders of idolatry in the land, because the inhabitants shall be wholly extirpated, and they shall *give no more hire* because they shall have no more to give. Some that will not leave their sins live till their sins leave them. When all that with which they honoured their idols is taken from them they shall not *give hire any more* (v. 41): "Then *thou shalt not commit this lewdness* of sacrificing thy children, which was a crime provoking *above all thy abominations,* for thy children shall all be cut off by the sword or carried into captivity, so that thou shalt have none to sacrifice," *v. 43.* Or it may be meant of the reformation of those of them that escape and survive the punishment; they shall take warning, and shall *do no more presumptuously.* The captivity in Babylon made the people of Israel to cease for ever *from playing the harlot;* it effectually cured them of their inclination to idolatry. And then all shall be well, when this is the fruit, even the *taking away of sin;* then (v. 42) *my jealousy shall depart. I will be quiet, and no more angry.* When we begin to be at war with sin God will be at peace with us; for he continues the affliction no longer than till it has done its work. When sin departs God's jealousy will soon depart, for he is never jealous but when we give him just cause to be so. Yet some understand this as a threatening of utter ruin, that God will *make a full end* and the fire of his anger shall burn as long as there is any fuel for it. *His fury shall rest upon them,* and not remove. Compare this with that doom of unbelievers, John iii. 36. *The wrath of God abideth on them.* They shall drink the dregs of the cup, and then God will be *no more angry*, for he is *eased of his adversaries* (Isa. i. 24), is satisfied in the abandoning of them, and therefore will be *no more angry*, because there are no more for his anger to fasten upon. They had fretted him, when judgment and mercy were contesting; but now *he is quiet*, as he will be in the eternal damnation of sinners, wherein he will be glorified, and therefore he will be satisfied.

44 Behold, every one that useth proverbs shall use *this* proverb against thee, saying, As *is* the mother, *so is* her daughter. 45 Thou *art* thy mother's daughter, that loatheth her husband and her children; and thou *art* the sister of thy sisters, which loathed their husbands and their children: your mother *was* a Hittite, and your father an Amorite. 46 And thine elder sister *is* Samaria, she and her daughters that dwell at thy left hand: and thy younger sister, that dwelleth at thy right hand, *is* Sodom and her daughters. 47 Yet hast thou not walked after their ways, nor done after their abominations: but, as *if that were* a very little *thing*, thou wast corrupted more than they in all thy ways. 48 *As* I live, saith the Lord GOD, Sodom thy sister hath not done, she nor her daughters, as thou hast done, thou and thy daughters. 49 Behold, this was the iniquity of thy sister Sodom, pride, fulness of bread, and abundance of idleness was in her and in her daughters, neither did she strengthen the hand of the poor and needy. 50 And they were haughty, and committed abomination before me: therefore I took them away as I saw *good.* 51 Neither hath Samaria committed half of thy sins; but thou hast multiplied thine abominations more than they, and hast justified thy sisters in all thine abominations which thou hast done. 52 Thou also, which hast judged thy sisters, bear thine own shame for thy sins that thou hast committed more abominable than they: they are more righteous than thou: yea, be thou confounded also, and bear thy shame, in that thou hast

justified thy sisters. 53 When I shall bring again their captivity, the captivity of Sodom and her daughters, and the captivity of Samaria and her daughters, then *will I bring again* the captivity of thy captives in the midst of them: 54 That thou mayest bear thine own shame, and mayest be confounded in all that thou hast done, in that thou art a comfort unto them. 55 When thy sisters, Sodom and her daughters, shall return to their former estate, and Samaria and her daughters shall return to their former estate, then thou and thy daughters shall return to your former estate. 56 For thy sister Sodom was not mentioned by thy mouth in the day of thy pride, 57 Before thy wickedness was discovered, as at the time of *thy* reproach of the daughters of Syria, and all *that are* round about her, the daughters of the Philistines, which despise thee round about. 58 Thou hast borne thy lewdness and thine abominations, saith the LORD. 59 For thus saith the Lord GOD; I will even deal with thee as thou hast done, which hast despised the oath in breaking the covenant.

The prophet here further shows Jerusalem her abominations, by comparing her with those places that had gone before her, and showing that she was worse than any of them, and therefore should, like them, be utterly and irreparably ruined. We are all apt to judge of ourselves by comparison, and to imagine that we are sufficiently good if we are but as good as such and such, who are thought passable; or that we are not dangerously bad if we are no worse than such and such, who, though bad, are not of the worst. Now God by the prophet shows Jerusalem,

I. That she was as bad as *her mother*, that is, as the accursed devoted Canaanites that were the possessors of this land before her. Those that use proverbs, as most people do, shall apply that proverb to Jerusalem, *As is the mother, so is her daughter, v.* 44. She is her *mother's own child.* The Jews are as like the Canaanites in temper and inclination as if they had been their own children. The character of the mother was that she *loathed her husband and her children*, she had all the marks of an adulteress; and that is the character of the daughter: she *forsakes the guide of her youth*, and is barbarous to the children of her own bowels. When God brought Israel into Canaan he particularly warned them not to do according to the abominations of *the men of that land, who went before them* (for which *it had spued them out,* Lev. xviii. 27, 28), the monuments of whose idolatry, with the remains of the idolaters themselves, would be a continual temptation to them; but they learned their way, and trod in their steps, and were as well affected to the *idols of Canaan* as ever they were (Ps. cvi. 38), and thus, in respect of imitation, it might truly be said that *their mother* was a *Hittite* and their *father* an *Amorite* (*v.* 45), for they resembled them more than Abraham and Sarah.

II. That she was worse than her sisters Sodom and Samaria, that were adulteresses too, that *loathed their husbands and their children,* that were weary of the gods of their fathers, and were for introducing new gods, *à-la-mode—quite in style,* that came newly up, and new fashions in religion, and were given to change. On this comparison between Jerusalem and *her sisters* the prophet here enlarges, that he might either shame them into repentance or justify God in their ruin. Observe,

1. Who Jerusalem's sisters were, *v.* 45. Samaria and Sodom. Samaria is called the *elder* sister, or rather the *greater,* because it was a much larger city and kingdom, richer and more considerable, and more nearly allied to Israel. If Jerusalem look northward, this is partly *on her left hand.* This city of Samaria, and the towns and villages, that were as *daughters* to that *mother-city,* these had been *lately* destroyed for their *spiritual whoredom.* Sodom, and the adjacent towns and villages that were her daughters, dwelt at Jerusalem's *right hand,* and was her *less sister,* less than Jerusalem, less than Samaria, and these were of old destroyed for their corporeal whoredom, Jude 7.

2. Wherein Jerusalem's sins resembled her sisters', particularly Sodom's (*v.* 49): *This was the iniquity of Sodom* (it is implied, and this is *thy* iniquity too), *pride, fulness of bread, and abundance of idleness.* Their *going after strange flesh,* which was Sodom's most flagrant wickedness, is not mentioned, because notoriously known, but those sins which did not look so black, but opened the door and led the way to these more enormous crimes, and began to fill that measure of her sins, which was filled up at length by their unnatural filthiness. Now these initiating sins were, (1.) Pride, in which the heart lifts up itself above and against both God and man. Pride was the first sin that turned angels into devils, and the *garden of the Lord* into a *hell upon earth.* It was the pride of the Sodomites that they despised *righteous Lot,* and would not bear to be reproved by him; and this ripened them for ruin. (2.) Gluttony, here called *fulness of bread.* It was God's great mercy that they had plenty, but their great sin that they abused it, glutted themselves with it, ate to excess and drank to excess, and made that

the gratification of their lusts which was given them to be the support of their lives. (3.) Idleness, *abundance of idleness,* a dread of labour and a love of ease. Their country was fruitful, and the abundance they had they came easily by, which was a temptation to them to indulge themselves in sloth, which disposed them to all that abominable filthiness which kindled their flames. Note, Idleness is an inlet to much sin. The men of Sodom, who were idle, were *wicked,* and *sinners before the Lord exceedingly,* Gen. xiii. 13. The standing waters gather filth and the sitting bird is the fowler's mark. When David *arose from off his bed at evening* he saw Bathsheba. *Quæritur, Ægisthus quare sit factus adulter? In promptu causa est: desidiosus erat—What made Ægisthus an adulterer? Indolence.* (4.) Oppression: Neither did she *strengthen the hands of the poor and needy;* probably it is implied that she weakened their hands and *broke* their arms; however, it was bad enough that, when she had so much wealth, and consequently power and interest and leisure, she did nothing for the relief of the poor, in providing for whose wants those that themselves are *full of bread* may employ their time well; they need not be so abundantly idle as too often they are. These were the sins of the Sodomites, and these were Jerusalem's sins. Their pride, the cause of their sins, is mentioned again (*v.* 50): *They were haughty,* with the horrid effects of their sins, their *abominations* which they *committed before God.* Men arrive gradually at the height of impiety and wickedness. *Nemo repente fit turpissimus—No man reaches the height of vice at once.* But, where pride has got the ascendant in a man, he is in the high road to all abominations.

3. How much the sins of Jerusalem exceeded those of Sodom and Samaria; they were more heinous in the sight of God, either in themselves or by reason of several aggravations: " *Thou hast not only walked after their ways,* and trod in their steps, but hast quite outdone them in wickedness, *v.* 47. Thou thoughtest it *a very little thing* to do as they did; didst laugh at them as sneaking sinners and silly ones; thou wouldst be more cunning, more daring, in wickedness, wouldst triumph more boldly over thy convictions, and bid more open defiance to God and religion: ' if a man will break, let him break for *something.*' Thus *thou wast corrupted more than they in all thy ways.*" Jerusalem was more polite, and therefore sinned with more wit, more art and ingenuity, than Sodom and Samaria could. Jerusalem had more wealth and power, and its government was more absolute and arbitrary, and therefore had the more opportunity of oppressing the poor, and shedding malignant influences around her, than Sodom and Samaria had. Jerusalem had the temple, and the ark, and the priesthood, and kings of the house of

David; and therefore the wickedness of that holy city, that was so dignified, so near, so dear to God, was more provoking to him than the wickedness of Sodom and Samaria, that had not Jerusalem's privileges and means of grace. Sodom has *not done as thou hast done, v.* 48. This agrees with what Christ says. Matt. xi. 24, *It shall be more tolerable for the land of Sodom in the day of judgment than for thee.* The kingdom of the ten tribes had been very wicked; and yet *Samaria has not committed half thy sins* (*v.* 51), has not worshipped half so many idols, nor slain half so many prophets. It was bad enough that those of Jerusalem were guilty of Sodom's sins, Sodomy itself not excepted, 1 Kings xiv. 24; 2 Kings xxiii. 7. And though the Dead Sea, the standing monument of Sodom's sin and ruin, bordered upon their country (Num. xxxiv. 12), and that sulphureous lake was always under their nose (God having *taken away Sodom and her daughters* in such way and manner as he *saw good*, as he says here, *v.* 50, so as that one thing should effectually make their *overthrow* an *ensample to those that afterwards should live ungodly*, 2 Pet. ii. 6), yet they did not take warning, but *multiplied their abominations more than they;* and, (1.) By this they *justified Sodom and Samaria, v.* 51. They pretended, in their haughtiness and superciliousness, to *judge them*, and in the days of old, when they retained their integrity, they did judge them, *v.* 52. But now they justify them comparatively: *Sodom and Samaria* are *more righteous than thou*, that is, less wicked. It will look like some extenuation of their sins that, bad as they were, Jerusalem was worse, though it was God's own city. Not that it will serve for a plea to justify Sodom, but it condemns Jerusalem, against which Sodom and Samaria will *rise up in judgment.* (2.) For this they ought themselves to be greatly ashamed: "Thou who hast *judged thy sisters*, and cried out shame on them, now *bear thy own shame, for thy sins which thou hast committed*, which, though of the same kind with theirs, yet, being committed *by thee*, are *more abominable than theirs," v.* 52. This may be taken either as foretelling their ruin *(Thou shalt bear thy shame)* or as inviting them to repentance: "*Be thou confounded and bear thy shame;* take the shame to thyself that is due to thee." It may be hoped that sinners will forsake their sins when they begin to be heartily ashamed of them. And therefore they shall go into captivity, and there they shall lie, that they may be *confounded in all that they have done*, because they had been a comfort and encouragement to Sodom and Samaria, *v.* 54. Note, There is nothing in sin which we have more reason to be ashamed of than this, that by our sin we have encouraged others in sin, and comforted them in that for which they must be grieved or they are undone. Another reason why they must now

be ashamed is because in the day of their prosperity they had looked with so much disdain upon their neighbours: *Thy sister Sodom was not mentioned by thee in the day of thy pride, v.* 56. They thought Sodom not worthy to be named the same day with Jerusalem, little dreaming that Jerusalem would at length lie under a worse and more scandalous character than Sodom herself. Those that are high may perhaps come to stand upon a level with those they contemn. Or "Sodom was *not mentioned*, that is, the warning designed to be given to thee by Sodom's ruin was not regarded." If the Jews had but talked more frequently and seriously to one another, and to their children, concerning *the wrath of God revealed from heaven* against *Sodom's ungodliness and unrighteousness*, it might have kept them in awe, and prevented their treading in their steps; but they kept the thought of it at a distance, would not bear the mention of it, and (as the ancients say) put Isaiah to death for putting them in mind of it, when he called them *rulers of Sodom* and *people of Gomorrah*, Isa. i. 10. Note, Those are but preparing judgments for themselves that will not take notice of God's judgments upon others.

4. What desolations God had brought and was bringing upon Jerusalem for these wickednesses, wherein they had exceeded Sodom and Samaria. (1.) She has already long ago been disgraced, and has fallen into contempt, among her neighbours (*v.* 57): *Before her wickedness was discovered*, before she came to be so grossly and openly flagitious, she bore the just punishment of her secret and more concealed lewdness, when she fell under *the reproach of the daughters of Syria, of the Philistines*, who were said to *despise her* and *be ashamed of her* (*v.* 27), and under the reproach of *all that were round about her*, which seems to refer to the descent made upon Judah by the Syrians in the days of Ahaz, and soon after another by the Philistines, 2 Chron. xxviii. 5, 18. Note, Those that disgrace themselves by yielding to their lusts will justly be brought into disgrace by being made to yield to their enemies; and it is observable that before God brought potent enemies upon them, for *their destruction*, he brought enemies upon them that were less formidable, *for their reproach.* If less judgments would do the work, God would not send greater. In this *thou hast borne thy lewdness, v.* 58. Those that will not cast off their sins by repentance and reformation shall be made to bear their sins to their confusion. (2.) She is now *in captivity*, or hastening into captivity, and therein is reckoned with, not only for her lewdness (*v.* 58), but for her perfidiousness and covenant-breaking (*v.* 59): "*I will deal with thee as thou hast done;* I will forsake thee as thou hast forsaken me, and cast thee off as thou hast cast me off, for thou hast *despised*

the oath, in breaking the covenant." This seems to be meant of the covenant God made with their fathers at Mount Sinai, whereby he took them and theirs to be a peculiar people to himself. They flattered themselves with a conceit that because God had hitherto continued his favour to them, notwithstanding their provocations, he would do so still. "No," says God, "you have *broken covenant with me,* have despised both the promises of the covenant and the obligations of it, and therefore I will *deal with thee as thou hast done.*" Note, Those that will not adhere to God as their God have no reason to expect that he should continue to own them as his people. (3.) The captivity of the wicked Jews, and their ruin, shall be as irrevocable as that of Sodom and Samaria. In this sense, as a threatening, most interpreters take *v.* 53, 55. "*When I shall bring again the captivity of Sodom and Samaria, and when they shall return to their former estate, then I will bring again the captivity of thy captives in the midst of them,* and as it were for their sakes, and under their shadow and protection, because they are *more righteous than thou,* and *then thou shalt return to thy former estate.*" But Sodom and Samaria were never brought back, nor ever returned to their former estate, and therefore let not Jerusalem expect it, that is, those who now remained there, whom God would *deliver to be removed into all the kingdoms of the earth for their hurt,* Jer. xxiv. 9, 10. Sooner shall the Sodomites arise out of the salt sea, and the Samaritans return out of the land of Assyria, than they enjoy their peace and prosperity again; for, to their shame be it spoken, it is *a comfort* to those of the ten tribes, who are dispersed and in captivity, to see those of the two tribes who had been as bad as they, or worse, in like manner dispersed and in captivity; and therefore they shall live and die, shall stand and fall, together. The bad ones of both shall perish together; the good ones of both shall return together. Note, Those who do as the worst of sinners do must expect to fare as they fare. *Let my enemy be as the wicked.*

60 Nevertheless I will remember my covenant with thee in the days of thy youth, and I will establish unto thee an everlasting covenant. 61 Then thou shalt remember thy ways, and be ashamed, when thou shalt receive thy sisters, thine elder and thy younger: and I will give them unto thee for daughters, but not by thy covenant. 62 And I will establish my covenant with thee; and thou shalt know that I *am* the LORD: 63 That thou mayest remember, and be confounded, and never open thy mouth

any more because of thy shame, when I am pacified toward thee for all that thou hast done, saith the Lord GOD.

Here, in the close of the chapter, after a most shameful conviction of sin and a most dreadful denunciation of judgments, mercy is remembered, mercy is reserved, for those who shall come after. As was when God swore in his wrath concerning those who came out of Egypt that they should not enter Canaan, "Yet" (says God) "your little ones shall;" so here. And some think that what is said of the return of Sodom and Samaria (*v.* 53, 55), and of Jerusalem with them, is a promise; it may be understood so, if by Sodom we understand (as Grotius and some of the Jewish writers do) the Moabites and Ammonites, the posterity of Lot, who once dwelt in Sodom; their captivity was returned (Jer. xlviii. 47; xlix. 6), as was that of many of the ten tribes, and Judah's with them. But these closing verses are, without doubt, a precious promise, which was in part fulfilled at the return of the penitent and reformed Jews out of Babylon, but was to have its full accomplishment in gospel-times, and in that *repentance and* that *remission of sins* which should then be *preached* with success *to all nations, beginning at Jerusalem.* Now observe here,

I. Whence this mercy should take rise—from *God himself,* and his *remembering his covenant* with them (*v.* 60): *Nevertheless,* though they had been so provoking, and God had been provoked to such a degree that one would think they could never be reconciled again, yet "*I will remember my covenant with thee,* that covenant which I made with thee *in the days of thy youth,* and will revive it again. Though thou hast *broken the covenant* (*v.* 59), I will remember it, and it shall flourish again." See how much it is our comfort and advantage that God is pleased to deal with us in a covenant-way, for thus the mercies of it come to be *sure mercies* and *everlasting* (Isa. lv. 3); and, while this root stands firmly in the ground, there is *hope of the tree,* though it be *cut down,* that *through the scent of water it will bud again.* We do not find that they put him in mind of the covenant, but *ex mero motu—from his own mere good pleasure,* he *remembers* it as he had promised. Lev. xxvi. 42, *Then will I remember my covenant, and will remember the land.* He that bids us to be ever mindful of the covenant no doubt will himself be ever mindful of it, the word *which he commanded* (and what he commands stands fast for ever) to *a thousand generations.*

II. How they should be prepared and qualified for this mercy (*v.* 61): "*Thou shalt remember thy ways,* thy evil ways; God will put thee in mind of them, will set them in order before thee, that thou mayest be *ashamed of them.*" Note, God's good work in us commences and keeps pace with his good-will towards us. When he remembers his covenant for us, that he may not remember our sins against us, he puts us upon remembering our sins against ourselves. And if we will but be brought to remember our ways, how crooked and perverse they have been and how we have walked contrary to God in them, we cannot but be ashamed; and, when we are so, we are best prepared to receive the honour and comfort of a sealed pardon and a settled peace.

III. What the mercy is that God has in reserve for them. 1. He will take them into covenant with himself (*v.* 60): *I will establish unto thee an everlasting covenant;* and again (*v.* 62), *I will establish,* re-establish, and establish more firmly than ever, *my covenant with thee.* Note, It is an unspeakable comfort to all true penitents that the covenant of grace is so well ordered in all things that every transgression in the covenant does not throw us out of the covenant, for that is inviolable. 2. He will bring the Gentiles into church-communion with them (*v.* 61): *"Thou shalt receive thy sisters,* the Gentile nations that are round about thee, *thy elder and thy younger,* greater than thou art and less, ancient nations and modern, and *I will give them unto thee for daughters;* they shall be founded, nursed, taught, and educated, by that gospel, that *word of the Lord,* which shall *go forth from* Zion and from *Jerusalem;* so that all the neighbours shall call Jerusalem *mother,* while the church continues there, and shall acknowledge the Jerusalem which is from above, and *which is free,* to be *the mother of us all,* Gal. iv. 26. They shall be thy *daughters,* but *not by thy covenant,* not by the covenant of peculiarity, not as being proselytes to the Jewish religion and subject to the yoke of the ceremonial law, but as being converts with thee to the Christian religion." Or *not by thy covenant* may mean, " not upon such terms as thou shalt think fit to impose upon them as conquered nations, as captives and homagers to whom thou mayest give law at pleasure" (such a dominion as that the carnal Jews hope to have over the nations); " no, they shall be. thy daughters *by my covenant,* the covenant of grace made with thee and them in concert, as an *indenture tripartite.* I will be a Father, a common Father, both to Jews and Gentiles, and so they shall become sisters to one another. And, when thou *shalt receive them,* thou shalt be *ashamed of thy own evil ways* wherein thou wast conformed to them. Thou shalt blush to look a Gentile in the face, remembering how much worse than the Gentiles thou wast in the day of thy apostasy."

IV. What the fruit and effect of this will be. 1. God will hereby be glorified (*v.* 62): *" Thou shalt know that I am the Lord.* It shall hereby be known that the God of Israel is Jehovah, a God of power, and faith-

ful to his covenant; and thou shalt know it who hast hitherto lived as if thou didst not know or believe it." It had often been said in wrath, *You shall know that I am the Lord,* shall know it to your cost; here it is said in mercy, You shall know it to your comfort; and it is one of the most precious promises of the new covenant which God has made with us that *all shall know him from the least to the greatest.* 2. They shall hereby be more humbled and abased for sin (*v.* 63): *" That thou mayest be the* more *confounded* at the *remembrance of all that thou hast done* amiss, mayest reproach thyself for it and call thyself a thousand times unwise, undutiful, ungrateful, and unlike what thou wast, and mayest never *open thy mouth any more* in contradiction to God, reflection on him, or complaints of him, but mayest be for ever silent and submissive *because of thy shame."* Note, Those that rightly remember their sins will be truly ashamed of them; and those that are truly ashamed of their sins will see great reason to be patient under their afflictions, to be dumb, and not open their mouths against what God does. But that which is most observable is, that all this shall be *when I am pacified towards thee, saith the Lord God.* Note, It is the gracious ingenuousness of true penitents that the clearer evidences and the fuller instances they have of God's being reconciled to them the more grieved and ashamed they are that ever they have offended God. God is in Jesus Christ *pacified towards us;* he is our peace, and it is by his cross that we are reconciled, and in his gospel that God is reconciling the world to himself. Now the consideration of this should be powerful to melt our hearts into a godly sorrow for sin. This is repenting because *the kingdom of heaven is at hand.* The prodigal, after he had received the kiss which assured him that his father was *pacified towards him,* was ashamed and confounded, and said, *Father, I have sinned against heaven and before thee.* And the more our shame for sin is increased by the sense of pardoning mercy the more will our comfort in God be increased.

CHAP. XVII.

God was, in the foregoing chapter, reckoning with the people of Judah, and bringing ruin upon them for their treachery in breaking covenant with him; in this chapter he is reckoning with the king of Judah for his treachery in breaking covenant with the king of Babylon; for when God came to contend with them he found many grounds of his controversy. The thing was now in doing: Zedekiah was practising with the king of Egypt underhand for assistance in a treacherous project he had formed to shake off the yoke of the king of Babylon, and violate the homage and fealty he had sworn to him. For this God by the prophet here, I. Threatens the ruin of him and his kingdom, by a parable of two eagles and a vine (ver. 1—10), and the explanation of that parable, ver. 11—21. But, in the close, II. He promises hereafter to raise the royal family of Judah again, the house of David, in the Messiah and his kingdom, ver. 22—24.

A ND the word of the LORD came unto me, saying, 2 Son of man, put forth a riddle, and speak a parable unto the house of Israel; 3 And say,

Thus saith the Lord GOD; A great eagle with great wings, long-winged, full of feathers, which had divers colours, came unto Lebanon, and took the highest branch of the cedar: 4 He cropped off the top of his young twigs, and carried it into a land of traffick; he set it in a city of merchants. 5 He took also of the seed of the land, and planted it in a fruitful field; he placed *it* by great waters, *and* set it *as* a willow-tree. 6 And it grew, and became a spreading vine of low stature, whose branches turned toward him, and the roots thereof were under him: so it became a vine, and brought forth branches, and shot forth sprigs. 7 There was also another great eagle with great wings and many feathers: and, behold, this vine did bend her roots toward him, and shot forth her branches toward him, that he might water it by the furrows of her plantation. 8 It was planted in a good soil by great waters, that it might bring forth branches, and that it might bear fruit, that it might be a goodly vine. 9 Say thou, Thus saith the Lord GOD; Shall it prosper? shall he not pull up the roots thereof, and cut off the fruit thereof, that it wither? it shall wither in all the leaves of her spring, even without great power or many people to pluck it up by the roots thereof. 10 Yea, behold, *being* planted, shall it prosper? shall it not utterly wither, when the east wind toucheth it? it shall wither in the furrows where it grew. 11 Moreover the word of the LORD came unto me, saying, 12 Say now to the rebellious house, Know ye not what these *things mean?* tell *them,* Behold, the king of Babylon is come to Jerusalem, and hath taken the king thereof, and the princes thereof, and led them with him to Babylon; 13 And hath taken of the king's seed, and made a covenant with him, and hath taken an oath of him: he hath also taken the mighty of the land: 14 That the kingdom might be base, that it might not lift itself up, *but* that by keeping of his covenant it might stand. 15 But he rebelled against him in sending his ambassadors into Egypt,

846

that they might give him horses and much people. Shall he prosper? shall he escape that doeth such *things?* or shall he break the covenant, and be delivered? 16 *As* I live, saith the Lord GOD, surely in the place *where* the king *dwelleth* that made him king, whose oath he despised, and whose covenant he brake, *even* with him in the midst of Babylon he shall die. 17 Neither shall Pharaoh with *his* mighty army and great company make for him in the war, by casting up mounts, and building forts, to cut off many persons: 18 Seeing he despised the oath by breaking the covenant, when, lo, he had given his hand, and hath done all these *things,* he shall not escape. 19 Therefore thus saith the Lord GOD; *As* I live, surely mine oath that he hath despised, and my covenant that he hath broken, even it will I recompense upon his own head. 20 And I will spread my net upon him, and he shall be taken in my snare, and I will bring him to Babylon, and will plead with him there for his trespass that he hath trespassed against me. 21 And all his fugitives with all his bands shall fall by the sword, and they that remain shall be scattered toward all winds: and ye shall know that I the LORD have spoken *it.*

We must take all these verses together, that we may have the parable and the explanation of it at one view before us, because they will illustrate one another. 1. The prophet is appointed to *put forth a riddle* to the *house of Israel* (*v.* 2), not to puzzle them, as Samson's riddle was put forth to the Philistines, not to hide the mind of God from them in obscurity, or to leave them in uncertainty about it, one advancing one conjecture and another another, as is usual in expounding riddles; no, he is immediately to tell them the meaning of it. *Let him that speaks in an unknown tongue pray that he may interpret,* 1 Cor. xiv. 13. But he must deliver this message in a riddle or parable that they might take the more notice of it, might be the more affected with it themselves, and might the better remember it and tell it to others. For these reasons God often used similitudes by his servants the prophets, and Christ himself *opened his mouth in parables.* Riddles and parables are used for an amusement to ourselves and an entertainment to our friends. The prophet must make use of these to see if in this dress the things of God might find acceptance, and insinuate themselves into the minds of a careless people. Note, Ministers should study to find out acceptable words, and try various methods to do good; and, as far as they have reason to think will be for edification, should both bring that which is familiar into their preaching and their preaching too into their familiar discourse, that there may not be so vast a dissimilitude as with some there is between what they say in the pulpit and what they say out. 2. He is appointed to expound this riddle to *the rebellious house, v.* 12. Though being *rebellious* they might justly have been left in ignorance, to see and hear and not perceive, yet the thing shall be explained to them: *Know you not what these things mean?* Those that knew the story, and what was now in agitation, might make a shrewd guess at the meaning of this riddle, but, that they might be left without excuse, he is to give it to them in plain terms, stripped of the metaphor. But the enigma was first propounded for them to study on awhile, and to send to their friends at Jerusalem, that they might enquire after and expect the solution of it some time after.

Let us now see what the matter of this message is.

I. Nebuchadnezzar had some time ago carried off Jehoiachin, the same that was called *Jeconiah,* when he was but eighteen years of age and had reigned in Jerusalem but *three months,* him and his princes and great men, and had brought them captives to Babylon, 2 Kings xxiv. 12. This in the parable is represented by an eagle's cropping the top and tender branch of *a cedar,* and carrying it into *a land of traffic,* a *city of merchants* (v. 3, 4), which is explained, *v.* 12. The *king of Babylon* took the *king of Jerusalem,* who was no more able to resist him than a young twig of a tree is to contend with the strongest bird of prey, that easily crops it off, perhaps towards the making of *her nest.* Nebuchadnezzar, in Daniel's vision, is *a lion,* the king of beasts (Dan. vii. 4); there he has *eagle's wings,* so swift were his motions, so speedy were his conquests. Here, in this parable, he is *an eagle,* the king of birds, a *great eagle,* that lives upon spoil and rapine, whose young ones *suck up blood,* Job xxxix. 30. His dominion extends itself far and wide, like the great and long wings of an eagle; the people are numerous, for it is *full of feathers;* the court is splendid, for it has *divers colours,* which look like *embroidering,* as the word is. Jerusalem is Lebanon, a forest of houses, and very pleasant. The royal family is *the cedar;* Jehoiachin is the *top branch,* the *top of the young twigs,* which he crops off. Babylon is the *land of traffic* and *city of merchants* where it is set. And the king of Judah, being of the house of David, will think himself much degraded and disgraced to be lodged among tradesmen; but he must make the best of it.

II. When he carried him to Babylon he made his uncle Zedekiah king in his room, *v.* 5, 6. His name was *Mattaniah—the gift of the Lord,* which Nebuchadnezzar changed into *Zedekiah—the justice of the Lord,* to remind him to be just like the God he called his, for fear of his justice. This was *one of the seed of the land,* a native, not a foreigner, not one of his Babylonian princes; he was *planted in a fruitful field,* for so Jerusalem as yet was; he *placed it by great waters,* where it would be likely to grow, like *a willow-tree,* which grows quickly, and grows best in moist ground, but is never designed nor expected to be a stately tree. He *set it with* care and *circumspection* (so some read it); he wisely provided that it might grow, but that it might not grow too big. *He took of the king's seed* (so it is explained, *v.* 13) and *made a covenant with him* that he should have the kingdom, and enjoy the regal power and dignity, provided he held it as his vassal, dependent on him and accountable to him. He *took an oath of him,* made him swear allegiance to him, swear by his own God, the God of Israel, that he would be a faithful tributary to him, 2 Chron. xxxvi. 13. He also *took away the mighty of the land,* the chief of the men of war, partly as hostages for the performance of the covenant, and partly that, the land being thereby weakened, the king might be the less able, and therefore the less in temptation, to break his league. What he designed we are told (*v.* 14): *That the kingdom might be base,* in respect both of honour and strength, might neither be a rival with its powerful neighbours, nor a terror to its feeble ones, as it had been, that *it might not lift up itself* to vie with the kingdom of Babylon, or to bear down any of the petty states that were in subjection to it. But yet he designed that by the *keeping of this covenant it might stand,* and continue a kingdom. Hereby the pride and ambition of that haughty potentate would be gratified, who aimed to be *like the Most High* (Isa. xiv. 14), to have all about him subject to him. Now see here, 1. How sad a change sin made with the royal family of Judah. Time was when all the nations about were tributaries to that; now that has not only lost its dominion over other nations, but has itself become a tributary. *How has the gold become dim!* Nations by sin sell their liberty, and princes their dignity, and *profane their crowns by casting them to the ground* 2. How wisely Zedekiah did for himself in accepting these terms, though they were dishonourable, when necessity brought him to it. A man may live very comfortably and contentedly, though he cannot bear a part, and make a figure, as formerly. A kingdom may stand firmly and safely, though it do not stand so high as it has sometimes done; and so may a family.

III. Zedekiah, while he continued faithful to the king of Babylon, did very well, and, if he would but have reformed his kingdom, and returned to God and his duty, he would have done better, and by that means might soon have recovered his former dignity, *v.* 6. This plant grew, and though it was *set as a willow-tree*, and little account was made of it, yet it became *a spreading vine of low stature*, a great blessing to his own country, and his fruits *made glad their hearts ;* and it is better to be a spreading vine of low stature than a lofty cedar of no use. Nebuchadnezzar was pleased, for *the branches turned towards him*, and rested on him as the vine on the wall, and he had his share of the fruits of this vine ; *the roots thereof* too were *under him*, and at his disposal. The Jews had reason to be pleased, for they sat under their own vine, which *brought forth branches, and shot forth sprigs*, and looked pleasant and promising. See how gradually the judgments of God came upon this provoking people, how God gave them respite and so gave them space to repent. He made *their kingdom base*, to try if that would humble them, before he made it no kingdom ; yet left it easy for them, to try if that would win upon them to return to him, that the troubles threatened might be prevented.

IV. Zedekiah knew not when he was well off, but grew impatient of the disgrace of being a tributary to the king of Babylon, and, to get clear of it, entered into a private league with the king of Egypt. He had no reason to complain that the king of Babylon put any new hardships upon him or improved his advantages against him, that he oppressed or impoverished his country, for, as the prophet had said before (*v.* 6) to aggravate his treachery, he shows again (*v.* 8) what a fair way he was in to be considerable : *He was planted in a good soil by great waters ;* his family was likely enough to be built up, and his exchequer to be filled, in a little time, so that, if he had dealt faithfully, he might have been *a goodly vine.* But there was *another great eagle* that he had an affection for, and put a confidence in, and that was the *king of Egypt, v.* 7. Those two great potentates, the kings of Babylon and Egypt, were but two great eagles, *birds of prey.* This great eagle of Egypt is said to have *great wings*, but not to be *long-winged* as the king of Babylon, because, though the kingdom of Egypt was strong, yet it was not of such a vast extent as that of Babylon was. The great eagle is said to have *many feathers*, much wealth and many soldiers, which he depended upon as a substantial defence, but which really were no more than so *many feathers.* Zedekiah, promising himself liberty, made himself a vassal to the king of Egypt, foolishly expecting ease by changing his master. Now *this vine* did secretly and under-hand *bend her roots towards* the king of Egypt, that great eagle, and after awhile did openly *shoot forth her branches towards him*, give him an intimation how much she coveted an alliance with him, *that he might*

848

water it by the furrows of her plantation, whereas it was *planted by great waters*, and did not need any assistance from him. This is expounded, *v.* 15. Zedekiah rebelled against the king of Babylon in *sending his ambassadors into Egypt*, that they might *give him horses and much people*, to enable him to contend with the king of Babylon. See what a change sin had made with the people of God ! God promised that they should be a numerous people, as the sand of the sea ; yet now, if their king had occasion for *much people*, he must send to Egypt for them, they being for sin *diminished and brought low*, Ps. cvii. 39. See also the folly of fretful discontented spirits, that ruin themselves by striving to better themselves, whereas they might be easy and happy enough if they would but *make the best of that which is.*

V. God here threatens Zedekiah with the utter destruction of him and his kingdom, and, in displeasure against him, passes that doom upon him for his treacherous revolt from the king of Babylon. This is represented in the parable (*v.* 9, 19) by the *plucking up of this vine by the roots, the cutting off of the fruit*, and *the withering of the leaves*, the leaves *of her spring*, when they are in their greenness (Job viii. 12), before they begin in autumn to wither of themselves. The project shall be blasted ; it shall *utterly wither.* The affairs of this perfidious prince shall be ruined past retrieve ; as a vine when the east wind blasts it, so that it shall be fit for nothing but the fire (as we had it in that parable, *ch.* xv. 4), it shall wither even *in the furrows where it grew*, though they were ever so well watered. It shall be destroyed *without great power or many people to pluck it up ;* for what need is there of raising the militia to pluck up a vine ? Note, God can bring great things to pass without much ado. He needs not great power and many people to effect his purposes ; a handful will serve if he pleases. He can without any difficulty ruin a sinful king and kingdom, and make no more of it than we do of rooting up a tree that cumbers the ground. In the explanation of the parable the sentence is very largely recorded : *Shall he prosper ? v.* 15. Can he expect to do ill and fare well ? Nay, shall he that does such wicked things *escape ?* Shall he *break the covenant, and be delivered* from that vengeance which is the just punishment of his treachery ? No ; can he expect to do ill and not suffer ill ? Let him hear his doom.

1. It is ratified by the oath of God (*v.* 16) : *As I live, saith the Lord God, he shall die* for it. This intimates how highly God resented the crime, and how sure and severe the punishment of it would be. God *swears in his wrath*, as he did Ps. xcv. 11. Note, As God's promises are confirmed with an oath, for comfort to the saints, so are his threatenings, for terror to the wicked. As sure as God lives and is happy (I may add, and as long),

so sure, so long, shall impenitent sinners die and be miserable.

2. It is justified by the heinousness of the crime he had been guilty of. (1.) He had been very ungrateful to his benefactor, who had *made him king,* and undertook to protect him, had made him a prince when he might as easily have made him a prisoner. Note, It is a sin against God to be unkind to our friends and to lift up the heel against those that have helped to raise us. (2.) He had been very false to him whom he had covenanted with. This is mostly insisted on: He *despised the oath.* When his conscience or friends reminded him of it he made a jest of it, put on a daring resolution, and *broke it, v.* 15, 16, 18, 19. He broke through it, and took a pride in making nothing of it, as a great tyrant in our own day, whose maxim (they say) it is, *That princes ought not to be slaves to their word any further than it is for their interest.* That which aggravated Zedekiah's perfidiousness was that the oath by which he had bound himself to the king of Babylon was, [1.] A solemn oath. An emphasis is laid upon this (*v.* 18) : *When, lo, he had given his hand,* as a confederate with the king of Babylon, not only as his subject, but as his friend, the joining of hands being a token of the joining of hearts. [2.] A sacred oath. God says (*v.* 19): It is *my oath* that he has despised and *my covenant that he has broken.* In every solemn oath God is appealed to as a witness of the sincerity of him that swears, and invocated as a judge and revenger of his treachery if he now swear falsely or at any time hereafter break his oath. But the oath of allegiance to a prince is particularly called *the oath of God* (Eccl. viii. 2), as if that had something in it more sacred than another oath; for princes are *ministers of God to us for good,* Rom. xiii. 4. Now Zedekiah's breaking this oath and covenant is the sin which God will *recompense upon his own head* (*v.* 19), the *trespass which he has trespassed against God,* for which God will *plead with him, v.* 20. Note, Perjury is a heinous sin and highly provoking to the God of heaven. It would not serve for an excuse, *First,* That he who took this oath was a king, a king of the house of David, whose liberty and dignity might surely set him above the obligation of oaths. No; though kings are gods to us, they are men to God, and not exempt from his law and judgment. The prince is doubtless as firmly bound before God to the people by his coronation-oath as the people are to the prince by the oath of allegiance. *Secondly,* Nor that this oath was sworn to the king of Babylon, a heathen prince, worse than a heretic, with whom the church of Rome says, *No faith is to be kept.* No; though Nebuchadnezzar was a worshipper of false gods, yet the true God will avenge this quarrel when one of his worshippers breaks his league with him; for truth is a debt due to all men; and, if the

professors of the true religion deal perfidiously with those of a false religion, their profession will be so far from excusing, much less justifying them, that it aggravates their sin, and God will the more surely and severely punish it, because by it they give occasion to the enemies of the Lord to blaspheme; as that Mahometan prince, who, when the Christians broke their league with him, cried out, *O Jesus! are these thy Christians? Thirdly,* Nor would it justify him that the oath was extorted from him by a conqueror, for the covenant was made upon a valuable consideration. He held his life and crown upon this condition, that he should be faithful and bear true allegiance to the king of Babylon; and, if he enjoy the benefit of his bargain, it is very unjust if he do not observe the terms. Let him know then that, having *despised the oath,* and *broken the covenant,* he *shall not escape.* And if the contempt and violation of such an oath, such a covenant as this, would be so punished, of how much sorèr punishment shall those be thought worthy who break covenant with God (when, *lo, they had given their hand* upon it that they would be faithful), who *tread under foot the blood* of that *covenant* as an unholy thing? Between the covenants there is no comparison.

3. It is particularized in divers instances, wherein the punishment is made to answer the sin. (1.) He had rebelled against the king of Babylon, and the king of Babylon should be his effectual conqueror. In the place where that king *dwells* whose *covenant he broke,* even *with him in the midst of Babylon he shall die, v.* 16. He thinks to get out of his hands, but he shall fall, more than before, into his hands. God himself will now take part with the king of Babylon against him : *I will spread my net upon him, v.* 20. God has a net for those who deal perfidiously and think to escape his righteous judgments, in which those shall be taken and held who would not be held by the bond of an oath and covenant. Zedekiah dreaded Babylon : " Thither I will bring him," says God, " and *plead with him there."* Men will justly be forced upon that calamity which they endeavour by sin to flee from. (2.) He had *relied upon the king of Egypt,* and the king of Egypt should be his ineffectual helper : *Pharaoh with his mighty army shall not make for him in the war* (*v.* 17), shall do him no service, nor give any check to the progress of the Chaldean forces; he shall not assist him in the *siege* by *casting up mounts and building forts,* nor in battle by *cutting off many persons.* Note, Every creature is that to us which God makes it to be; and he commonly weakens 'and withers that *arm of flesh* which we trust in and stay ourselves upon. Now was again fulfilled what was spoken on a former similar occasion (Isa. xxx. 7), *The Egyptians shall help in vain.* They did so; for though, upon the approach

of the Egyptian army, the Chaldeans withdrew from the siege of Jerusalem, upon their retreat they returned to it again and took it. It should seem, the Egyptians were not hearty, had strength enough, but no good-will, to help Zedekiah. Note, Those who deal treacherously with those who put a confidence in them will justly be dealt treacherously with by those they put a confidence in. Yet the Egyptians were not the only states Zedekiah stayed himself upon; he had bands of his own to stand by him, but those bands, though we may suppose they were veteran troops and the best soldiers his kingdom afforded, shall become *fugitives*, shall quit their posts, and make the best of their way, and shall *fall by the sword* of the enemy, and the *remains of them shall be scattered, v.* 21. This was fulfilled *when the city was broken up and all the men of war fled,* Jer. lii. 7. Then *you shall know that I the Lord have spoken it.* Note, Sooner or later God's word will prove itself; and those who will not believe shall find by experience the reality and weight of it.

22 Thus saith the Lord God; I will also take of the highest branch of the high cedar, and will set *it;* I will crop off from the top of his young twigs a tender one, and will plant *it* upon a high mountain and eminent: 23 In the mountain of the height of Israel will I plant it: and it shall bring forth boughs, and bear fruit, and be a goodly cedar: and under it shall dwell all fowl of every wing; in the shadow of the branches thereof shall they dwell. 24 And all the trees of the field shall know that I the Lord have brought down the high tree, have exalted the low tree, have dried up the green tree, and have made the dry tree to flourish: I the Lord have spoken and have done *it.*

When the royal family of Judah was brought to desolation by the captivity of Jehoiachin and Zedekiah it might be asked, "What has now become of the covenant of royalty made with David, that *his children should sit upon his throne for evermore?* Do the *sure mercies of David* prove thus unsure?" To this it is sufficient for the silencing of the objectors to answer that the promise was conditional. If *they will keep my covenant,* then they shall continue, Ps. cxxxii. 12. But David's posterity broke the condition, and so forfeited the promise. But the unbelief of man shall not invalidate the promise of God. He will find out another *seed of David* in which it shall be accomplished; and that is promised in these verses.

I. The house of David shall again be

magnified, and out of its ashes another phœnix shall arise. The metaphor of a tree, which was made use of in the threatening, is here presented in the promise, *v.* 22, 23. This promise had its accomplishment in part when Zerubbabel, a branch of the house of David, was raised up to head the Jews in their return out of captivity, and to rebuild the city and temple and re-establish their church and state; but it was to have its full accomplishment in the kingdom of the Messiah, who was a root out of a dry ground, and to whom God, according to promise, gave *the throne of his father David,* Luke i. 32. 1. God himself undertakes the reviving and restoring of the house of David. Nebuchadnezzar was the *great eagle* that had attempted the re-establishing of the house of David in a dependence upon him, *v.* 5. But the attempt miscarried; his plantation withered and was plucked up. "Well," says God, "the next shall be of my planting: *I will also take of the highest branch of the high cedar and I will set it.*" Note, As men have their designs, God also has his designs; but his will prosper when theirs are blasted. Nebuchadnezzar prided himself in setting up kingdoms at his pleasure, Dan. v. 19. But those kingdoms soon had an end, whereas the *God of heaven sets up a kingdom that shall never be destroyed,* Dan. ii. 44. 2. The house of David is revived in a *tender one cropped from the top of his young twigs.* Zerubbabel was so; that which was hopeful in him was but the *day of small things* (Zech. iv. 10), yet before him *great mountains* were *made plain.* Our Lord Jesus was *the highest branch of the high cedar,* the furthest of all from *the root* (for soon after he appeared the *house of David* was all cut off and extinguished), but the nearest of all to heaven, for his kingdom was not of this world. He was *taken from the top of the young twigs,* for he is *the man, the branch, a tender* plant, and a *root out of a dry ground* (Isa. liii. 2), but a *branch of righteousness, the planting of the Lord, that he may be glorified.* 3. This branch is planted *in a high mountain* (*v.* 22), in the *mountain of the height of Israel, v.* 23. Thither he brought Zerubbabel in triumph; there he raised up his son Jesus, sent him to gather the *lost sheep of the house of Israel* that were *scattered upon the mountains,* set him *his king* upon his *holy hill of Zion,* sent forth the gospel from *Mount Zion, the word of the Lord from Jerusalem;* there, in the *height of Israel,* a nation which all its neighbours had an eye upon as conspicuous and illustrious, was the Christian church first planted. The churches of Judea were the most primitive churches. The unbelieving Jews did what they could to prevent its being planted there; but who can pluck up what God will plant? 4. Thence it spreads far and wide. The Jewish state, though it began very low in Zerubbabel's time, was set as a tender branch, which might easily be plucked up, yet took root, spread strangely, and after some time became very considerable ; those of other nations, *fowl of every wing*, put themselves under the protection of it. The Christian church was at first like a grain of mustard-seed, but became, like this tender branch, a great tree, its beginning small, but its latter end increasing to admiration. When the Gentiles flocked into the church then did the *fowl of every wing* (even the birds of prey, which those preyed upon, as the *wolf and the lamb* feeding together, Isa. xi. 6) come and *dwell under the shadow of this goodly cedar.* See Dan. iv. 21.

II. God himself will herein be glorified, *v.* 24. The setting up of the Messiah's kingdom in the world shall discover more clearly than ever to the children of men that *God is the King of all the earth*, Ps. xlvii. 7. Never was there a more full conviction given of this truth, that all things are governed by an infinitely wise and mighty Providence, than that which was given by the exaltation of Christ and the establishment of his kingdom among men ; for by that it appeared that God has all hearts in his hand, and the sovereign disposal of all affairs. *All the trees of the field shall know*, 1. That the tree which God will have to be *brought down*, and *dried up*, shall be so, though it be ever so high and stately, ever so green and flourishing. Neither honour nor wealth, neither external advancements nor internal endowments, will secure men from humbling withering providences. 2. That the trees which God will have to be exalted, and to flourish, shall so be, shall so do, though ever so low, and ever so dry. The house of Nebuchadnezzar, that now makes so great a figure, shall be extirpated, and the house of David, that now makes so mean a figure, shall become famous again ; and the Jewish nation, that is now despicable, shall be considerable. The kingdom of Satan, that has borne so long, so large, a sway, shall be broken, and the kingdom of Christ, that was looked upon with contempt, shall be established. The Jews, who, in respect of church-privileges, had been high and green, shall be thrown out, and the Gentiles, who had been low and dry trees, shall be taken in their room, Isa. liv. 1. All the enemies of Christ shall be abased and made his footstool, and his interests shall be confirmed and advanced : *I the Lord have spoken* (it is the decree, the declared decree, that Christ must be exalted, must be the headstone of the corner), and *I have done it*, that is, I will do it in due time, but it is as sure to be done as if it were done already. With men *saying and doing are two things*, but they are not so with God. What he has spoken we may be sure that he will do, nor shall one iota or tittle of his word fall to the ground, for *he is not a man, that he should lie, or the son of man, that he should repent* either of his threatenings or of his promises.

CHAP. XVIII.

Perhaps, in reading some of the foregoing chapters, we may have been tempted to think ourselves not much concerned in them (though they also were written for our learning) ; but this chapter, at first view, appears highly and nearly to concern us all, very highly, very nearly ; for, without particular reference to Judah and Jerusalem, it lays down the rule of judgment according to which God will deal with the children of men in determining them to their everlasting state, and it agrees with that very ancient rule laid down, Gen. iv. 7, " If thou doest well, shalt thou not be accepted?" But, "if not, sin," the punishment of sin, " lies at the door." Here is, I. The corrupt proverb used by the profane Jews, which gave occasion to the message here sent them, and made it necessary for the justifying of God in his dealings with them, ver. 1—3. II. The reply given to this proverb, in which God asserts in general his own sovereignty and justice, ver. 4. Woe to the wicked ; it shall be ill with them, ver. 4, 20. But say to the righteous, It shall be well with them, ver. 5—9. In particular, as to the case complained of, he assures us, 1. That it shall be ill with a wicked man, though he had a good father, ver. 10—13. 2. That it shall be well with a good man, though he had a wicked father, ver. 14—18. And therefore in this God is righteous, ver. 19, 20. 3. That it shall be well with penitents, though they began ever so ill, ver. 21—23, and again ver. 27, 28. 4. That it shall be ill with apostates, though they began ever so well, ver. 24, 26. And the use of all this is, (1.) To justify God and clear the equity of all his proceedings, ver. 25, 29. (2.) To engage and encourage us to repent of our sins and turn to God, ver. 30—32. And these are things which belong to our everlasting peace. O that we may understand and regard them before they be hidden from our eyes !

THE word of the LORD came unto me again, saying, 2 What mean ye, that ye use this proverb concerning the land of Israel, saying, The fathers have eaten sour grapes, and the children's teeth are set on edge ? 3 *As* I live, saith the Lord GOD, ye shall not have *occasion* any more to use this proverb in Israel. 4 Behold, all souls are mine ; as the soul of the father, so also the soul of the son is mine : the soul that sinneth, it shall die. 5 But if a man be just, and do that which is lawful and right, 6 *And* hath not eaten upon the mountains, neither hath lifted up his eyes to the idols of the house of Israel, neither hath defiled his neighbour's wife, neither hath come near to a menstruous woman, 7 And hath not oppressed any, *but* hath restored to the debtor his pledge, hath spoiled none by violence, hath given his bread to the hungry, and hath covered the naked with a garment ; 8 He *that* hath not given forth upon usury, neither hath taken any increase, *that* hath withdrawn his hand from iniquity, hath executed true judgment between man and man, 9 Hath walked in my statutes, and hath kept my judgments, to deal truly ; he *is* just, he shall surely live, saith the Lord GOD.

Evil manners, we say, beget good laws ; and in like manner sometimes unjust reflections occasion just vindications ; evil proverbs beget good prophecies. Here is,

I. An evil proverb commonly used by the

Jews in their captivity. We had one before (*ch.* xii. 22) and a reply to it; here we have another. *That* sets God's justice at defiance: "*The days are prolonged and every vision fails;* the threatenings are a jest." *This* charges him with injustice, as if the judgments executed were a wrong: "You use this proverb *concerning the land of Israel,* now that it is laid waste by the judgments of God, saying, *The fathers have eaten sour grapes and the children's teeth are set on edge;* we are punished for the sins of our ancestors, which is as great an absurdity in the divine regimen as if the children should have their teeth set on edge, or stupified, by the fathers' eating sour grapes, whereas, in the order of natural causes, if men eat or drink any thing amiss, they only themselves shall suffer by it." Now, 1. It must be owned that there was some occasion given for this proverb. God had often said that he would *visit the iniquity of the fathers upon the children,* especially the sin of idolatry, intending thereby to express the evil of sin, of that sin, his detestation of it, and just indignation against it, and the heavy punishments he would bring upon idolaters, that parents might be restrained from sin by their affection to their children and that children might not be drawn to sin by their reverence for their parents. He had likewise often declared by his prophets that in bringing the present ruin upon Judah and Jerusalem he had an eye to the sins of Manasseh and other preceding kings; for, looking upon the nation as a body politic, and punishing them with national judgments for national sins, and admitting the maxim in our law that *a corporation never dies,* reckoning with them now for the iniquities of former ages was but like making a man, *when he is old,* to *possess the iniquities of his youth,* Job xiii. 26. And there is no unrighteousness with God in doing so. But, 2. They intended it as a reflection upon God, and an impeachment of his equity in his proceedings against them. Thus far that is right which is implied in this proverbial saying, That those who are guilty of wilful sin *eat sour grapes;* they do that which they will feel from, sooner or later. The grapes may look well enough in the temptation, but they will be bitter as bitterness itself in the reflection. They will set the sinner's teeth on edge. When conscience is awake, and sets the sin in order before them, it will spoil the relish of their comforts as when the teeth are set on edge. But they suggest it as unreasonable that the children should smart for the fathers' folly and feel the pain of that which they never tasted the pleasure of, and that God was unrighteous in thus taking vengeance and could not justify it. See how wicked the reflection is, how daring the impudence; yet see how witty it is, and how sly the comparison. Many that are impious in their jeers are ingenious in their jests; and thus the malice

of hell against God and religion is insinuated and propagated. It is here put into a proverb, and that proverb used, commonly used; they had it up ever and anon. And, though it had plainly a blasphemous meaning, yet they sheltered themselves under the similitude from the imputation of downright blasphemy. Now by this it appears that they were unhumbled under the rod, for, instead of condemning themselves and justifying God, they condemned him and justified themselves; but *woe to him that* thus *strives with his Maker.*

II. A just reproof of, and reply to, this proverb: *What mean you* by using it? That is the reproof. "Do you intend hereby to try it out with God? Or can you think any other than that you will hereby provoke him to be *angry with you till he has consumed you?* Is this the way to reconcile yourselves to him and make your peace with him?" The reply follows, in which God tells them,

1. That the use of the proverb should be taken away. This is said, it is sworn (*v.* 3): *You shall not have occasion any more to use this proverb;* or (as it may be read), *You shall not have the use of this parable.* The taking away of this parable is made the matter of a promise, Jer. xxxi. 29. Here it is made the matter of a threatening. There it intimates that God will return to them in ways of mercy; here it intimates that God would proceed against them in ways of judgment. He will so punish them for this impudent saying that they shall not dare to use it any more; as in another case, Jer. xxiii. 34, 36. God will find out effectual ways to silence those cavillers. Or God will so manifest both to themselves and others that they have wickedness of their own enough to bring all these desolating judgments upon them that they shall no longer for shame lay it upon the sins of their fathers that they were thus dealt with: "Your own consciences shall tell you, and all your neighbours shall confirm it, that you yourselves have eaten the same sour grapes that your fathers ate before you, or else your teeth would not have been set on edge."

2. That really the saying itself was unjust and a causeless reflection upon God's government. For,

(1.) God does not punish the children for the fathers' sins unless they tread in their fathers' steps and *fill up the measure of their iniquity* (Matt. xxiii. 32), and then they have no reason to complain, for, whatever they suffer, it is less than their own sin has deserved. And, when God speaks of *visiting the iniquity of the fathers upon the children,* that is so far from putting any hardship upon the children, to whom he only renders *according to their works,* that it accounts for God's patience with the parents, whom he therefore does not punish immediately, because he *lays up their iniquity for their children,* Job xxi. 19.

(2.) It is only in temporal calamities that

children (and sometimes innocent ones) fare the worse for their parents' wickedness, and God can alter the property of those calamities, and make them work for good to those that are visited with them; but as to spiritual and eternal misery (and that is the death here spoken of) the children shall by no means smart for the parents' sins. This is here shown at large; and it is a wonderful piece of condescension that the great God is pleased to reason the case with such wicked and unreasonable men, that he did not immediately strike them dumb or dead, but vouchsafed to state the matter before them, that he may be clear when he is judged. Now, in his reply,

[1.] He asserts and maintains his own absolute and incontestable sovereignty: *Behold, all souls are mine, v.* 4. God here claims a property in all the souls of the children of men, one as well as another. *First,* Souls are his. He that is the Maker of *all things* is in a particular manner the *Father of spirits,* for his image is stamped on the souls of men; it was so in their creation; it is so in their renovation. He *forms the spirit of man within him,* and is therefore called *the God of the spirits of all flesh,* of embodied spirits. *Secondly,* All souls are his, all created by him and for him, and accountable to him. *As the soul of the father, so the soul of the son, is mine.* Our earthly parents are only the *fathers of our flesh;* our souls are not theirs; God challenges them. Now hence it follows, for the clearing of this matter, 1. That God may certainly do what he pleases both with fathers and children, and none may say unto him, *What doest thou?* He that gave us our being does us no wrong if he takes it away again, much less when he only takes away some of the supports and comforts of it; it is as absurd to quarrel with him as for *the thing formed to say to him that formed it, Why hast thou made me thus?* 2. That God as certainly bears a good-will both to father and son, and will put no hardship upon either. We are sure that God hates nothing that he has made, and therefore (speaking of the adult, who are capable of acting for themselves) he has such a kindness for all souls that none die but through their own default. *All souls are his,* and therefore he is not partial in his judgment of them. Let us subscribe to his interest in us and dominion over us. He says, *All souls are mine;* let us answer, " Lord, my soul is thine; I devote it to thee to be employed for thee and made happy in thee." It is with good reason that God says, " *My son, give me thy heart,* for it is my own," to which we must yield, " *Father, take my heart,* it is thy own."

[2.] Though God might justify himself by insisting upon his sovereignty, yet he waives that, and lays down the equitable and unexceptionable rule of judgment by which he will proceed as to particular per-

sons; and it is this :—*First,* The sinner that persists in sin shall certainly die, his iniquity shall be his ruin: *The soul that sins shall die,* shall die as a soul can die, shall be excluded from the favour of God, which is the life and bliss of the soul, and shall lie for ever under his wrath, which is its death and misery. Sin is the act of the *soul,* the body being only the *instrument of unrighteousness;* it is called the *sin of the soul,* Mic. vi. 7. And therefore the punishment of sin is the *tribulation and the anguish of the soul,* Rom. ii. 9. *Secondly,* The righteous man that perseveres in his righteousness shall certainly live. *If a man be just,* have a good principle, a good spirit and disposition, and, as an evidence of that, *do judgment and justice* (v. 5), *he shall surely live,* saith the Lord God, v. 9. He that makes conscience of conforming in every thing to the will of God, that makes it his business to serve God and his aim to glorify God, shall without fail be happy here and for ever in the love and favour of God; and, wherein he comes short of his duty, it shall be forgiven him, through a Mediator. Now here is part of the character of this just man. 1. He is careful to keep himself clean from the pollutions of sin, and at a distance from all the appearances of evil. (1.) From sins against the second commandment. In the matters of God's worship he is jealous, for he knows God is so. He has not only not sacrificed in the high places to the images there set up, but he has not so much as *eaten upon the mountains,* that is, not had any communion with idolaters by *eating things sacrificed to idols,* 1 Cor. x. 20. He would not only not kneel with them at their altars, but not sit with them at their tables in their high places. He detests not only the idols of the heathen but *the idols of the house of Israel,* which were not only allowed of, but generally applauded and adored, by those that were accounted the professing people of God. He has not only not worshipped those idols, but he has not so much as *lifted up his eyes* to them; he has not given them a favourable look, has had no regard at all to them, neither desired their favour nor dreaded their frowns. He has observed so many bewitched by them that he has not dared so much as to look at them, lest he should be taken in the snare. The eyes of idolaters are said to *go a whoring,* Ezek. vi. 9. See Deut. iv. 19. (2.) From sins against the seventh commandment. He is careful to possess his vessel in *sanctification and honour,* and not *in the lusts of uncleanness;* and therefore he has not dared to *defile his neighbour's wife,* nor said or done any thing which had the least tendency to corrupt or debauch her, no, nor will he make any undue approaches to his own wife when she is *put apart for her uncleanness,* for it was forbidden by the law, Lev. xviii. 19; xx. 18. Note, It is an essential branch of wisdom and justice to keep the appetites of the body always in subjection to reason and virtue. (3.) From sins against the eighth commandment. He is a *just man*, who has not, by fraud and under colour of law and right, *oppressed any*, and who has not with force and arms *spoiled any by violence*, not spoiled them of their goods or estates, much less of their liberties and lives, *v.* 7. Oppression and violence were the sins of the old world, that brought the deluge, and are sins of which still God is and will be the avenger. Nay, he is one that has not lent his money *upon usury*, nor *taken increase* (*v.* 8), though, being done by contract, it may seem free from injustice (*Volenti non fit injuria*—*What is done to a person with his own consent is no injury to him*), yet, as far as it is forbidden by the law, he dares not do it. A moderate usury they were allowed to receive from strangers, but not from their brethren. A just man will not take advantage of his neighbour's necessity to make a prey of him, nor indulge himself in ease and idleness to live upon the sweat and toil of others, and therefore will not take increase from those who cannot make increase of what he lends them, nor be rigorous in exacting what was agreed for from those who by the act of God are disabled to pay it; but he is willing to share in loss as well as profit. *Qui sentit commodum, sentire debet et onus*— *He who enjoys the benefit should bear the burden.* 2. He makes conscience of doing the duties of his place. He has *restored the pledge* to the poor debtor, according to the law. Exod. xxii. 26, " *If thou take thy neighbour's raiment* for a pledge, the raiment that is for necessary use, thou shalt *deliver it* to him again, that he may sleep in his own bedclothes." Nay, he has not only restored to the poor that which was their own, but has *given his bread to the hungry.* Observe, It is called *his bread*, because it is honestly come by; that which is given to some is not unjustly taken from others; for God has said, *I hate robbery for burnt-offerings.* Worldly men insist upon it that their bread is *their own*, as Nabal, who therefore would not give of it to David (1 Sam. xxv. 11); yet let them know that it is not so their own but that they are bound to do good to others with it. Clothes are necessary as well as food, and therefore this just man is so charitable as *to cover the naked* also *with a garment, v.* 7. The coats which Dorcas had made for the poor were produced as witnesses of her charity, Acts ix. 39. This just man has *withdrawn his hands from iniquity, v.* 8. If at any time he has been drawn in through inadvertency to that which afterwards has appeared to him to be a wrong thing, he does not persist in it because he has begun it, but *withdraws his hand* from that which he now perceives to be *iniquity ;* for he *executes true judgment between man and man*, according as his opportunity is of doing it (as a judge,

as a witness, as a juryman, as a referee), and in all commerce is concerned that justice be done, that no man be wronged, that he who is wronged be righted, and that every man have his own, and is ready to interpose himself, and do any good office, in order hereunto. This is his character towards his neighbours; yet it will not suffice that he be just and true to his brother, to complete his character he must be so to his God likewise (*v.* 9): *He has walked in my statutes*, those which relate to the duties of his immediate worship; *he has kept* those and all his other *judgments*, has had respect to them all, has made it his constant care and endeavour to conform and come up to them all, to deal truly, that so he may approve himself faithful to his covenant with God, and, having joined himself to God, he does not treacherously *depart from him*, nor *dissemble with him.* This is a just man, and *living he shall live ;* he shall certainly live, shall have life and shall have it more abundantly, shall live truly, live comfortably, live eternally. *Keep the commandments*, and thou shalt *enter into life*, Matt. xix. 17.

10 If he beget a son *that is* a robber, a shedder of blood, and *that* doeth the like to *any* one of these *things*, 11 And that doeth not any of those *duties*, but even hath eaten upon the mountains, and defiled his neighbour's wife, 12 Hath oppressed the poor and needy, hath spoiled by violence, hath not restored the pledge, and hath lifted up his eyes to the idols, hath committed abomination, 13 Hath given forth upon usury, and hath taken increase : shall he then live ? He shall not live : he hath done all these abominations ; he shall surely die ; his blood shall be upon him. 14 Now, lo, *if* he beget a son, that seeth all his father's sins which he hath done, and considereth, and doeth not such like, 15 *That* hath not eaten upon the mountains, neither hath lifted up his eyes to the idols of the house of Israel, hath not defiled his neighbour's wife, 16 Neither hath oppressed any, hath not withholden the pledge, neither hath spoiled by violence, *but* hath given his bread to the hungry, and hath covered the naked with a garment, 17 *That* hath taken off his hand from the poor, *that* hath not received usury nor increase, hath executed my judgments, hath walked in my statutes ; he shall not

die for the iniquity of his father, he shall surely live. 18 *As for* his father, because he cruelly oppressed, spoiled his brother by violence, and did *that* which *is* not good among his people, lo, even he shall die in his iniquity. 19 Yet say ye, Why? doth not the son bear the iniquity of the father? When the son hath done that which is lawful and right, *and* hath kept all my statutes, and hath done them, he shall surely live. 20 The soul that sinneth, it shall die. The son shall not bear the iniquity of the father, neither shall the father bear the iniquity of the son : the righteousness of the righteous shall be upon him, and the wickedness of the wicked shall be upon him.

God, by the prophet, having laid down the general rule of judgment, that he will render eternal life to those that *patiently continue in well-doing*, but indignation and wrath to those that do not *obey the truth*, but *obey unrighteousness* (Rom. ii. 7, 8), comes, in these verses, to show that men's parentage and relation shall not alter the case either one way or other.

I. He applies it largely and particularly both ways. As it was in the royal line of the kings of Judah, so it often happens in private families, that godly parents have wicked children and wicked parents have godly children. Now here he shows,

1. That a wicked man shall certainly perish in his iniquity, though he be the son of a pious father. If that righteous man before described *beget a son* whose character is the reverse of his father's, his condition will certainly be so too. (1.) It is supposed as no uncommon case, but a very melancholy one, that the child of a very godly father, notwithstanding all the instructions given him, the good education he has had and the needful rebukes that have been given him, and the restraints he has been laid under, after all the pains taken with him and prayers put up for him, may yet prove notoriously wicked and vile, the grief of his father, the shame of his family, and the curse and plague of his generation. He is here supposed to allow himself in all those enormities which his good father dreaded and carefully avoided, and to shake off all those good duties which his father made conscience of and took satisfaction in ; he undoes all that his father did, and goes counter to his example in every thing. He is here described to be a highwayman—*a robber and a shedder of blood.* He is an idolater: *He has eaten upon the mountains* (v. 11) and has *lifted up his eyes to the idols,* which his good father

never did, and has come at length not only to feast with the idolaters, but to sacrifice with them, which is here called *committing abomination,* for the way of sin is down-hill. He is an adulterer, has *defiled his neighbour's wife.* He is an oppressor even of *the poor and needy ;* he robs the spital, and squeezes those who, he knows, cannot defend themselves, and takes a pride and pleasure in trampling upon the weak and impoverishing those that are poor already. He *takes away* from those to whom he should *give.* He has *spoiled by violence* and open force ; he has *given forth upon usury,* and so spoiled by contract ; and he *has not restored the pledge,* but unjustly detained it even when the debt was paid. Let those good parents that have wicked children not look upon their case as singular ; it is a case put here ; and by it we see that grace does not run in the blood, nor always attend the means of grace. The race is not always to the swift, nor the battle to the strong, for then the children that are well taught would do well, but God will let us know that his grace is his own and his Spirit a free-agent, and that though we are tied to give our children a good education he is not tied to bless it. In this, as much as any thing, appears the power of original sin and the necessity of special grace. (2.) We are here assured that this wicked man shall perish for ever in his iniquity, notwithstanding his being the son of a good father: He may perhaps prosper awhile in the world, for the sake of the piety of his ancestors, but, having *committed all these abominations,* and never repented of them, *he shall not live,* he shall not be happy in the favour of God ; though he may escape the sword of men, he shall not escape the curse of God. *He shall surely die ;* he shall be for ever miserable ; *his blood shall be upon him.* He may thank himself ; he is his own destroyer. And his relation to a good father will be so far from standing him in stead that it will aggravate his sin and his condemnation. It made his sin the more heinous, nay, it made him really the more vile and profligate, and, consequently, will make his misery hereafter the more intolerable.

2. That a righteous man shall be certainly happy, though he be the son of a wicked father. Though the father did eat the sour grapes, if the children do not meddle with them, they shall fare never the worse for that. Here, (1.) It is supposed (and, blessed be God, it is sometimes a case in fact) that the son of an ungodly father may be godly, that, observing how fatal his father's errors were, he may be so wise as to *take warning,* and not tread in his father's steps, v. 14. Ordinarily, children partake of the parents' temper and are drawn in to imitate their example ; but here the son, instead of *seeing his father's sins,* and, as is usual, doing the like, sees them and dreads doing the like. *Men* indeed do not *gather grapes of thorns,* but

God sometimes does, takes a branch from a wild olive and grafts it into a good one. Wicked Ahaz begets a good Hezekiah, who *sees all his father's sins which he has done,* and though he will not, like Ham, proclaim his father's shame, or make the worst of it, yet he loathes it, and blushes at it, and thinks the worse of sin because it was the reproach and ruin of his own father. *He considers and does not such like;* he considers how ill it became his father to do such things, what an offence it was to God and all good men, what a wound and dishonour he got by it, and what calamities he brought into his family, and therefore he *does not such like.* Note, If we did but duly *consider the ways* of wicked men, we should all dread being associates with them and followers of them. The particulars are here again enumerated almost in the same words with that character given of the just man (*v.* 6, &c.), to show how good men *walk in the same spirit and in the same steps.* This just man here, when he took care to avoid his father's sins, took care to imitate his grandfather's virtues; and, if we look back, we shall find some examples for our imitation, as well as others for our admonition. This just man can not only say, as the Pharisee, *I am no adulterer, no extortioner,* no oppressor, no usurer, no idolater; but he has *given his bread to the hungry* and *covered the naked.* He has *taken off his hand from the poor;* where he found his father had put hardships upon poor servants, tenants, neighbours, he eased their burden. He did not say, "What my father has done I will abide by, and if it was a fault it was his and not mine;" as Rehoboam, who contemned the taxes his father had imposed. No; he *takes his hand off from the poor,* and restores them to their rights and liberties again, *v.* 15—17. Thus he has *executed God's judgments* and *walked in his statutes,* not only done his duty for once, but gone on in a course and way of obedience. (2.) We are assured that the graceless father alone shall die in his iniquity, but his gracious son shall fare never the worse for it. As for his father (*v.* 18), because he was a cruel oppressor, and *did hurt,* nay, because, though he had wealth and power, he did not with them do good among his people, lo, *even he,* great as he is, *shall die in his iniquity,* and be undone for ever; but he that kept his integrity *shall surely live,* shall be easy and happy, and he shall *not die for the iniquity of his father.* Perhaps his father's wickedness has lessened his estate and weakened his interest, but it shall be no prejudice at all to his acceptance with God and his eternal welfare.

II. He appeals to themselves then whether they did not wrong God with their proverb. "Thus plain the case is, and *yet you say, Does not the son bear the iniquity of the father?* No, he does not; he shall not if he will himself *do that which is lawful and right,*" *v.* 19. But this people that bore the iniquity

of their fathers had not done that which is lawful and right, and therefore justly suffered for their own sin and had no reason to complain of God's proceedings against them as at all unjust, though they had reason to complain of the bad example their fathers had left them as very unkind. *Our fathers have sinned and are not, and we have borne their iniquity,* Lam. v. 7. It is true that there is a curse entailed upon wicked families, but it is as true that the entail may be cut off by repentance and reformation; let the impenitent and unreformed therefore thank themselves if they fall under it. The settled rule of judgment is therefore repeated (*v.* 20): *The soul that sins shall die,* and not another for it. What direction God has given to earthly judges (Deut. xxiv. 16) he will himself pursue: *The son shall not die,* not die eternally, *for the iniquity of the father,* if he do not tread in the steps of it, nor the father *for the iniquity of the son,* if he endeavour to do his duty for the preventing of it. In *the day of the revelation of the righteous judgment of God,* which is now clouded and eclipsed, *the righteousness of the righteous shall* appear before all the world to be *upon him,* to his everlasting comfort and honour, upon him as a robe, upon him as a crown; and *the wickedness of the wicked* shall be *upon him,* to his everlasting confusion, upon him as a chain, upon him as a load, as a mountain of lead to sink him to the bottomless pit.

21 But if the wicked will turn from all his sins that he hath committed, and keep all my statutes, and do that which is lawful and right, he shall surely live, he shall not die. 22 All his transgressions that he hath committed, they shall not be mentioned unto him: in his righteousness that he hath done he shall live. 23 Have I any pleasure at all that the wicked should die? saith the Lord GOD: *and* not that he should return from his ways, and live? 24 But when the righteous turneth away from his righteousness, and committeth iniquity, *and* doeth according to all the abominations that the wicked *man* doeth, shall he live? All his righteousness that he hath done shall not be mentioned: in his trespass that he hath trespassed, and in his sin that he hath sinned, in them shall he die. 25 Yet ye say, The way of the LORD is not equal. Hear now, O house of Israel; is not my way equal? are not your ways unequal? 26 When a righteous *man* turneth away from his righteousness, and committeth iniquity, and

dieth in them; for his iniquity that he hath done shall he die. 27 Again, when the wicked *man* turneth away from his wickedness that he hath committed, and doeth that which is lawful and right, he shall save his soul alive. 28 Because he considereth, and turneth away from all his transgressions that he hath committed, he shall surely live, he shall not die. 29 Yet saith the house of Israel, The way of the LORD is not equal. O house of Israel, are not my ways equal? are not your ways unequal?

We have here another rule of judgment which God will go by in dealing with us, by which is further demonstrated the equity of his government. The former showed that God will reward or punish according to the change made in the family or succession, for the better or for the worse; here he shows that he will reward or punish according to the change made in the person himself, whether for the better or the worse. While we are in this world we are in a state of probation; the time of trial lasts as long as the time of life, and according as we are found at last it will be with us to eternity. Now see here,

I. The case fairly stated, much as it had been before (*ch.* iii. 18, &c.), and here it is laid down once (*v.* 21—24) and again (*v.* 26 —28), because it is a matter of vast importance, a matter of life and death, of life and death eternal. Here we have,

1. A fair invitation given to wicked people, to turn from their wickedness. Assurance is here given us that, *if the wicked will turn,* he shall *surely live, v.* 21, 27. Observe,

(1.) What is required to denominate a man a true convert, how he must be qualified that he may be entitled to this act of indemnity. [1.] The first step towards conversion is consideration (*v.* 28): *Because he considers and turns.* The reason why sinners go on in their evil ways is because they do not consider what will be *in the end thereof;* but if the prodigal once *come to himself,* if he sit down and consider a little how bad his state is and how easily it may be bettered, he will soon *return to his father* (Luke xv. 17), and the adulteress *to her first husband* when she considers that *then it was better with her than now,* Hos. ii. 7. [2.] This consideration must produce an aversion to sin. When he considers he must turn *away from his wickedness,* which denotes a change in the disposition of the heart; he must turn from *his sins and his transgressions,* which denotes a change in the life; he must break off from all his evil courses, and, wherein he has done iniquity, must resolve to do so no more, and this from a principle of hatred to sin. *What have I to do any more with idols?* [3.] This

aversion to sin must be universal; he must turn from *all* his sins and *all* his transgressions, without a reserve for any Delilah, any house of Rimmon. We do not rightly turn from sin unless we truly hate it, and we do not truly hate sin, as sin, if we do not hate all sin. [4.] This must be accompanied with a conversion to God and duty; he must *keep all God's statutes* (for the obedience, if it be sincere, will be universal) and must *do that which is lawful and right,* that which agrees with the word and will of God, which he must take for his rule, and not the will of the flesh and the way of the world.

(2.) What is promised to those that do thus turn from sin to God. [1.] They shall *save their souls alive, v.* 27. They shall *surely live, they shall not die, v.* 21 and again *v.* 28. Whereas it was said, *The soul that sins it shall die,* yet let not those that have sinned despair but that the threatened death may be prevented if they will but turn and repent in time. When David penitently acknowledges, *I have sinned,* he is immediately assured of his pardon: "*The Lord has taken away thy sin, thou shalt not die* (2 Sam. xii. 13), thou shalt not die eternally." He shall *surely live;* he shall be restored to the favour of God, which is the life of the soul, and shall not lie under *his wrath,* which is as *messengers of death* to the soul. [2.] The sins they have repented of and forsaken shall not rise up in judgment against them, nor shall they be so much as upbraided with them: *All his transgressions that he has committed,* though numerous, though heinous, though very provoking to God, and redounding very much to his dishonour, yet *they shall not be mentioned unto him* (*v.* 22), not mentioned against him; not only they shall not be imputed to him to ruin him, but in the great day they shall not be remembered against him to grieve or shame him; they shall be covered, shall be sought for and not found. This intimates the fulness of pardoning mercy; when sin is forgiven it is *blotted out,* it is remembered no more. [3.] In *their righteousness they shall live;* not for their righteousness, as if that were the purchase of their pardon and bliss and an atonement for their sins, but in their righteousness, which qualifies them for all the blessings purchased by the Mediator, and is itself one of those blessings.

(3.) What encouragement a repenting returning sinner has to hope for pardon and life according to this promise. He is conscious to himself that his obedience for the future can never be a valuable compensation for his former disobedience; but he has this to support himself with, that God's nature, property, and delight, is to have mercy and to forgive, for he has said (*v.* 23): "*Have I any pleasure at all that the wicked should die?* No, by no means; you never had any cause given you to think so." It is true God has determined to punish sinners;

857

his justice calls for their punishment, and, pursuant to that, impenitent sinners will lie for ever under his wrath and curse; that is the will of his decree, his consequent will, but it is not his antecedent will, the will of his delight. Though the righteousness of his government requires that sinners die, yet the goodness of his nature objects against it. *How shall I give thee up, Ephraim?* It is spoken here comparatively; he has not pleasure in the ruin of sinners, for he would rather they should *turn from their ways and live:* he is better pleased when his mercy is glorified in their salvation than when his justice is glorified in their damnation.

2. A fair warning given to righteous people not to turn from their righteousness, *v.* 24—26. Here is, (1.) The character of an apostate, that *turns away from his righteousness.* He never was in sincerity a righteous man (as appears by that of the apostle, 1 John ii. 19, *If they had been of us, they would, no doubt, have continued with us*), but he passed for a righteous man. He had the denomination and all the external marks of a righteous man; he thought himself one, and others thought him one. But he throws off his profession, leaves his first love, disowns and forsakes the truth and ways of God, and so *turns away from his righteousness* as one sick of it, and now shows, what he always had, a secret aversion to it; and, having *turned away from his righteousness,* he *commits iniquity,* grows loose, and profane, and sensual, intemperate, unjust, and, in short, *does according to all the abominations that the wicked man does;* for, when the unclean spirit recovers his possession of the heart, he *brings with him seven other spirits more wicked than himself and they enter in and dwell there,* Luke xi. 26. (2.) The doom of an apostate: *Shall he live* because he was once a *righteous man?* No; *factum non dicitur quod non perseverat—that which does not abide is not said to be done. In his trespass* (*v.* 24) and for his iniquity (that is the meritorious cause of his ruin), *for the iniquity that he has done, he shall die,* shall die eternally, *v.* 26. *The backslider in heart shall be filled with his own ways.* But will not his former professions and performances stand him in some stead—will they not avail at least to mitigate his punishment? No: *All his righteousness that he has done,* though ever so much applauded by men, *shall not be mentioned* so as to be either a credit or a comfort to him; the righteousness of an apostate is forgotten, as the wickedness of a penitent is. Under the law, if a Nazarite was polluted he lost all the foregoing days of his separation (Num. vi. 12), so those that have *begun in the spirit and end in the flesh* may reckon all their past services and sufferings *in vain* (Gal. iii. 3, 4); unless we persevere we *lose what we have gained,* 2 John 8.

II. An appeal to the consciences even of the house of Israel, though very corrupt, concerning God's equity in all these proceedings; for he will be justified, as well as sinners judged, out of their own mouths. 1. The charge they drew up against God is blasphemous, *v.* 25, 29. The *house of Israel* has the impudence to say, *The way of the Lord is not equal,* than which nothing could be more absurd as well as impious. *He that formed the eye, shall he not see?* Can his ways be unequal whose will is the eternal rule of good and evil, right and wrong? *Shall not the Judge of all the earth do right?* No doubt he shall; he cannot do otherwise. 2. God's reasonings with them are very gracious and condescending, for even these blasphemers God would rather have convinced and saved than condemned. One would have expected that God would immediately vindicate the honour of his justice by making those that impeached it eternal monuments of it. Must those be suffered to draw another breath that have once breathed out such wickedness as this? Shall that tongue ever speak again any where but in hell that has once said, *The ways of the Lord are not equal?* Yes, because this is the day of God's patience, he vouchsafes to argue with them; and he requires them to own, for it is so plain that they cannot deny, (1.) The equity of his ways: *Are not my ways equal?* No doubt they are. He never lays upon man more than is right. In the present punishments of sinners and the afflictions of his own people, yea, and in the eternal damnation of the impenitent, *the ways of the Lord are equal.* (2.) The iniquity of their ways: "*Are not your ways unequal?* It is plain that they are, and the troubles you are in you have brought upon your own heads. God does you no wrong, but you have wronged yourselves." *The foolishness of man perverts his way,* makes that unequal, and then *his heart frets against the Lord,* as if his ways were unequal, Prov. xix. 3. In all our disputes with God, and in all his controversies with us, it will be found that his ways are equal, but ours are unequal, that he is in the right and we are in the wrong.

30 Therefore I will judge you, O house of Israel, every one according to his ways, saith the Lord God. Repent, and turn *yourselves* from all your transgressions; so iniquity shall not be your ruin. 31 Cast away from you all your transgressions, whereby ye have transgressed; and make you a new heart and a new spirit: for why will ye die, O house of Israel? 32 For I have no pleasure in the death of him that dieth, saith the Lord God: wherefore turn *yourselves,* and live ye.

We have here the conclusion and application of this whole matter. After a fair trial at the bar of right reason the verdict is brought in on God's side; it appears that *his ways are equal.* Judgment therefore is next to be given; and one would think it should be a judgment of condemnation, nothing short of *Go, you cursed, into everlasting fire.* But, behold, a miracle of mercy; the day of grace and divine patience is yet lengthened out; and therefore, though God will at last judge *every one according to his ways,* yet he waits to be gracious, and closes all with a call to repentance and a promise of pardon upon repentance.

I. Here are four necessary duties that we are called to, all amounting to the same :— 1. We must repent; we must change our mind and change our ways; we must be sorry for what we have done amiss and ashamed of it, and go as far as we can towards the undoing of it again. 2. We must *turn ourselves from all our transgressions, v.* 30 and again *v.* 32. *Turn yourselves,* face about; turn from sin, nay, turn against it as the enemy you loathe, turn to God as the friend you love. 3. We must *cast away from us all our transgressions;* we must abandon and forsake them with a resolution never to return to them again, give sin a bill of divorce, break all the leagues we have made with it, throw it overboard, as the mariners did Jonah (for it has raised the storm), cast it out of the soul, and crucify it as a malefactor. 4. We must *make us a new heart and a new spirit.* This was the matter of a promise, *ch.* xi. 19. Here it is the matter of a precept. We must do our endeavour, and then God will not be wanting to us to give us his grace. St. Austin well explains this precept. *Deus non jubet impossibilia, sed jubendo monet et facere quod possis et petere quod non possis—God does not enjoin impossibilities, but by his commands admonishes us to do what is in our power and to pray for what is not.*

II. Here are four good arguments used to enforce these calls to repentance :—1. It is the only way, and it is a sure way, to prevent the ruin which our sins have a direct tendency to: *So iniquity shall not be your ruin,* which implies that, if we do not repent, iniquity will be our ruin, here and for ever, but that, if we do, we are safe, we are snatched as brands out of the burning. 2. If we repent not, we certainly perish, and our blood will be upon our own heads. *Why will you die, O house of Israel?* What an absurd thing it is for you to choose death and damnation rather than life and salvation. Note, The reason why sinners die is because they *will die;* they will go down the way that leads to death, and not come up to the terms on which life is offered. Herein sinners, especially sinners of the house of Israel, are most unreasonable and act most unaccountably. 3. The God of heaven has no delight in our ruin, but desires our welfare (*v.* 32): *I have no pleasure in the death of him that dies,* which implies that he has pleasure in the recovery of those that repent; and this is both an engagement and an en-

couragement to us to repent. 4. We are made for ever if we repent : *Turn yourselves, and live.* He that says to us, *Repent,* thereby says to us, *Live,* yea, he says to us, *Live ;* so that life and death are here set before us.

CHAP. XIX.

The scope of this chapter is much the same with that of the 17th, to foretel and lament the ruin of the house of David, the royal family of Judah, in the calamitous exit of the four sons and grandsons of Josiah—Jehoahaz, Jehoiakim, Jeconiah, and Zedekiah, in whom that illustrious line of kings was cut off, which the prophet is here ordered to lament, ver. 1. And he does it by similitudes. I. The kingdom of Judah and house of David are here compared to a lioness, and those princes to lions, that were fierce and ravenous, but were hunted down and taken in nets, ver. 2—9. II. That kingdom and that house are here compared to a vine, and these princes to branches, which had been strong and flourishing, but were now broken off and burnt, ver. 10—14. This ruin of that monarchy was now in the doing, and this lamentation of it was intended to affect the people with it, that they might not flatter themselves with vain hopes of the lengthening out of their tranquillity.

MOREOVER take thou up a lamentation for the princes of Israel, 2 And say, What *is* thy mother ? A lioness : she lay down among lions, she nourished her whelps among young lions. 3 And she brought up one of her whelps : it became a young lion, and it learned to catch the prey ; it devoured men. 4 The nations also heard of him ; he was taken in their pit, and they brought him with chains unto the land of Egypt. 5 Now when she saw that she had waited, *and* her hope was lost, then she took another of her whelps, *and* made him a young lion. 6 And he went up and down among the lions, he became a young lion, and learned to catch the prey, *and* devoured men. 7 And he knew their desolate palaces, and he laid waste their cities ; and the land was desolate, and the fulness thereof, by the noise of his roaring. 8 Then the nations set against him on every side from the provinces, and spread their net over him : he was taken in their pit. 9 And they put him in ward in chains, and brought him to the king of Babylon : they brought him into holds, that his voice should no more be heard upon the mountains of Israel.

Here are, I. Orders given to the prophet to bewail the fall of the royal family, which had long made so great a figure by virtue of a covenant of royalty made with David and his seed, so that the eclipsing and extinguishing of it are justly lamented by all who know what value to put upon the *covenant of our God,* as we find, after a very large account of that covenant with David (Ps. lxxxix. 3, 20, &c.), a sad lamentation for the decays and desolations of his family (*v.* 38, 39):

But thou hast cast off and abhorred, hast made void the covenant of thy servant and profaned his crown, &c. The kings of Judah are here called *princes of Israel;* for their glory was diminished and they had become but as princes, and their purity was lost; they had become corrupt and idolatrous as the *kings of Israel,* whose ways they had learned. The prophet must *take up a lamentation* for them; that is, he must describe their lamentable fall as one that did himself lay it to heart, and desired that those he preached and wrote to might do so to. And how can we expect that others should be affected with that which we ourselves are not affected with? Ministers, when they boldly foretel, must yet bitterly lament the destruction of sinners, as those that have not *desired the woeful day.* He is not directed to give advice to the princes of Israel (that had been long and often done in vain), but, the decree having gone forth, he must *take up a lamentation* for them.

II. Instructions given him what to say. 1. He must compare the kingdom of Judah to a *lioness,* so wretchedly degenerated was it from what it had been formerly, when it sat as a queen among the nations, *v.* 2. *What is thy mother?* thine, O king? (we read of Solomon's crown wherewith his mother crowned him, that is, his people, Cant. iii. 11), thine, O Judah? The royal family is as a mother to the kingdom, a nursing mother. She is a *lioness,* fierce, and cruel, and ravenous. When they had left their divinity they soon lost their humanity too; and, when they *feared not God,* neither did they *regard man.* She *lay down among lions.* God had said, *The people shall dwell alone,* but they *mingled with the nations* and *learned their works.* She *nourished her whelps among young lions,* taught the young princes the way of tyrants, which was then used by the arbitrary kings of the east, filled their heads betimes with notions of their absolute despotic power, and possessed them with a belief that they had a right to enslave their subjects, that their liberty and property lay at their mercy: thus *she nourished her whelps among young lions.* 2. He must compare the kings of Judah to *lions' whelps, v.* 3. Jacob had compared Judah, and especially the house of David, to a *lion's whelp,* for its being strong and formidable to its enemies abroad (Gen. xlix. 9, *He is an old lion; who shall stir him up?)* and, if they had adhered to the divine law and promise, God would have preserved to them the might, and majesty, and dominion of a lion, and does it in Christ, the *Lion of the tribe of Judah.* But these *lions' whelps* were so to their own subjects, were cruel and oppressive to them, preyed upon their estates and liberties; and, when they thus by their tyranny made themselves a terror to those whom they ought to have protected, it was just with God to make those a terror to them whom otherwise they might have subdued. Here is lamented, (1.) The

sin and fall of Jehoahaz, one of the whelps of this lioness. He *became a young lion (v.* 3); he was made king, and thought he was made so that he might do what he pleased, and gratify his own ambition, covetousness, and revenge, as he had a mind; and so he was soon master of all the arts of tyranny; he *learned to catch the prey and devoured men.* When he got power into his hand, all that had before in any thing disobliged him were made to feel his resentments and become a sacrifice to his rage. But what came of it? He did not prosper long in his tyranny: *The nations heard of him (v.* 4), heard how furiously he drove at his first coming to the crown, how he trampled upon all that is just and sacred, and violated all his engagements, so that they looked upon him as a dangerous neighbour, and prosecuted him accordingly, *as a multitude of shepherds is called forth against a lion roaring on his prey,* Isa. xxxi. 4. And *he was taken,* as a beast of prey, *in their pit.* His own subjects durst not stand up in defence of their liberties, but God raised up a foreign power that soon put an end to his tyranny, and *brought him in chains to the land of Egypt.* Thither Jehoahaz was carried captive, and never heard of more. (2.) The like sin and fall of his successor Jehoiakim. The *kingdom of Judah* for some time expected the return of Jehoahaz out of Egypt, but at length despaired of it, and then *took another* of the *lion's* whelps, and *made him a young lion, v.* 5. And he, instead of taking warning by his brother's fate to use his power with equity and moderation, and to seek the good of his people, trod in his brother's steps: *He went up and down among the lions, v.* 6. He consulted and conversed with those that were fierce and furious like himself, and took his measures from them, as Rehoboam took the advice of the rash and hot-headed young men. And he soon learned to *catch the prey,* and he *devoured men (v.* 6); he seized his subjects' estates, fined and imprisoned them, filled his treasury by rapine and injustice, sequestrations and confiscations, fines and forfeitures, and swallowed up all that stood in his way. He had got the art of discovering what effects men had that lay concealed, and where the treasures were which they had hoarded up; he *knew their desolate places (v.* 7), where they hid *their money* and sometimes hid *themselves;* he knew where to find both out; and by his oppression he *laid waste their cities,* depopulated them by forcing the inhabitants to remove their families to some place of safety. *The land was desolate,* and the country villages were deserted; and though there was great plenty, and a fulness of all good things, yet people quitted it all for fear of *the noise of his roaring.* He took a pride in making all his subjects afraid of him, as the lion makes all the beasts of the forest to tremble (Amos iii. 8), and by his terrible roaring so astonished them that they fell down for fear, and, having not spirit to make their escape, became an easy prey to him, as they say the lions do. He hectored, and threatened, and talked big, and bullied people out of what they had. Thus he thought to establish his own power, but it had a contrary effect, it did but hasten his own ruin (*v.* 8): *The nations set against him on every side*, to restrain and reduce his exorbitant power, which they joined in confederacy to do for their common safety; and *they spread their net over him*, formed designs against him. God brought against Jehoiakim bands of the Syrians, Moabites, and Ammonites, with the Chaldees (2 Kings xxiv. 2), and he was *taken in their pit*. Nebuchadnezzar *bound him in fetters to carry him to Babylon*, 2 Chron. xxxvi. 6. They put this lion within grates, bound him *in chains*, and *brought him to the king of Babylon*, *v.* 9. What became of him we know not; but *his voice was nowhere heard* roaring upon the mountains of Israel. There was an end of his tyranny: he was *buried with the burial of an ass* (Jer. xxii. 19), though he had been as a lion, *the terror of the mighty in the land of the living*. Note, The righteousness of God is to be acknowledged when those who have terrified and enslaved others are themselves terrified and enslaved, when those who by the abuse of their power to destruction which was given them for edification make themselves as wild beasts, as *roaring lions and ranging bears* (for such, Solomon says, *wicked rulers* are *over the poor people*, Prov. xxviii. 15); are treated as such —when those who, like Ishmael, have their *hand against every man*, come at last to have *every man's hand against them*. It was long since observed that bloody tyrants seldom die in peace, but have blood given them to drink, for they are worthy.

Ad generum Cereris sine cæde et sanguine pauci
Descendunt reges et siccâ morte tyranni—

How few of all the boastful men that reign
Descend in peace to Pluto's dark domain!
                 JUVENAL.

10 Thy mother *is* like a vine in thy blood, planted by the waters: she was fruitful and full of branches by reason of many waters. **11** And she had strong rods for the sceptres of them that bare rule, and her stature was exalted among the thick branches, and she appeared in her height with the multitude of her branches. **12** But she was plucked up in fury, she was cast down to the ground, and the east wind dried up her fruit: her strong rods were broken and withered; the fire consumed them. **13** And now she *is* planted in the wilderness, in a dry and thirsty ground. **14** And fire is gone out of a rod of her branches,

which hath devoured her fruit, so that she hath no strong rod *to be* a sceptre to rule. This *is* a lamentation, and shall be for a lamentation.

Jerusalem, the mother-city, is here represented by another similitude; she is a vine, and the princes are her branches. This comparison we had before, ch. xv. 1. Jerusalem is as *a vine;* the Jewish nation is so: *Like a vine in thy blood* (*v.* 10), the blood-royal, like a vine set in blood and watered with blood, which contributes very much to the flourishing and fruitfulness of vines, as if the blood which had been shed had been designed for the fattening and improving of the soil, in such plenty was it shed; and for a time it seemed to have that effect, for she was *fruitful and full of branches* by reason of the waters, the *many waters* near which she was *planted*. Places of great wickedness may prosper for a while; and a vine set in blood may be full of branches. Jerusalem was full of able magistrates, men of sense, men of learning and experience, that were *strong rods*, branches of this vine of uncommon bulk and strength, or poles for the support of this vine, for such magistrates are. The boughs of this vine had grown to such maturity that they were fit to make white staves of for *the sceptres of those that bore rule, v.* 11. And those are *strong rods* that are fit for *sceptres*, men of strong judgments and strong resolutions that are fit for magistrates. When the royal family of Judah was numerous, and the courts of justice were filled with men of sense and probity, then *Jerusalem's stature was exalted among thick branches;* when the government is in good able hands a nation is thereby made considerable. Then she was not taken for a weak and lowly vine, but *she appeared in her height*, a distinguished city, *with the multitude of her branches*. *Tanquam lenta solent inter viburna cupressi—Midst humble withies thus the cypress soars.* "*In thy quietness*" (so some read that, *v.* 10, which we translate *in thy blood*) "thou wast such a vine as this." When Zedekiah was quiet and easy under the king of Babylon's yoke his kingdom flourished thus. See how slow God is to anger, how he defers his judgments, and waits to be gracious. 2. This vine is now quite destroyed. Nebuchadnezzar, being highly provoked by Zedekiah's treachery, *plucked it up in fury* (*v.* 12), ruined the city and kingdom, and cut off all the branches of the royal family that fell in his way. The vine was *cut off close to the ground*, though not plucked up by the roots. The *east wind dried up the fruit* that was blasted. The young people fell by the sword, or were carried into captivity. The aspect of it had nothing that was pleasing, the prospect nothing that was promising. Her *strong rods were broken and withered;* her great men were cut off, judges and magistrates deposed. *The vine itself is planted in the wilderness, v.* 13. Babylon was as a wilderness to those of the people that were carried captives thither; the land of Judah was as a wilderness to Jerusalem, now that the whole country was ravaged and laid waste by the Chaldean army—a *fruitful land turned into barrenness.* "It is *burnt with fire* (Ps. lxxx. 16) and that fire has *gone out of a rod of her branches* (v. 14); the king himself, by rebelling against the king of Babylon, has given occasion to all this mischief. She may thank herself for the fire that consumes her; she has by her wickedness made herself like tinder to the sparks of God's wrath, so that her own branches serve as fuel for her own consumption; in them the fire is kindled which *devoured the fruit,* the sins of the elder being the judgments which destroy the younger; her *fruit* is burned with her own branches, so that she *has no strong rod to be a sceptre to rule,* none to be found now that are fit for the government or dare take *this ruin under their hand,* as the complaint is (Isa. iii. 6, 7), none of the house of David left that have a right to rule, no wise men, or men of sense, that are able to rule." It goes ill with any state, and is likely to go worse, when it is thus deprived of the blessings of government and has *no strong rods for sceptres. Woe unto thee, O land! when thy king is a child,* for it is as well to have no rod as not a strong rod. Those strong rods, we have reason to fear, had been instruments of oppression, assistant to the king in *catching the prey and devouring men,* and now they are destroyed with him. Tyranny is the inlet to anarchy; and, when the rod of government is turned into the serpent of oppression, it is just with God to say, "There shall be no strong rod to be a sceptre to rule; but let men be as *are the fishes of the sea,* where the greater devour the less." Note, *This is a lamentation and shall be for a lamentation.* The prophet was bidden (v. 1) *to take up a lamentation;* and, having done so, he leaves it to be made use of by others. *"It is a lamentation* to us of this age, and, the desolations continuing long, it *shall be for a lamentation* to those that shall come after us; the child unborn will rue the destruction made of Judah and Jerusalem by the present judgments. They were a great while in coming; the bow was long in the drawing; but now that they have come they will continue, and the sad effects of them will be entailed upon posterity." Note, Those who fill up the measure of their fathers' sins are laying up in store for their children's sorrows and furnishing them with matter for lamentation; and nothing is more so than the overthrow of government.

CHAP. XX.

In this chapter, I. The prophet is consulted by some of the elders of Israel, ver. 1. II. He is instructed by his God what answer to give them. He must, 1. Signify God's displeasure against them, ver. 2, 3. And, 2. He must show them what just cause he had for that displeasure, by giving them a history of God's gracious dealings with their fathers and their treacherous dealings with God. (1.) In Egypt, ver. 5—9. (2.) In the wilderness, ver. 10—26. (3.) In Canaan, ver. 27—32. 3. He must denounce the judgments of

862

God against them, ver. 33—36. 4. He must tell them likewise what mercy God had in store for them, when he would bring a remnant of them to repentance, re-establish them in their own land, and set up his sanctuary among them again, ver. 37—44. 5. Here is another word dropped towards Jerusalem, which is explained and enlarged upon in the next chapter, ver. 45—49.

AND it came to pass in the seventh year, in the fifth *month,* the tenth *day* of the month, *that* certain of the elders of Israel came to enquire of the LORD, and sat before me. 2 Then came the word of the LORD unto me, saying, 3 Son of man, speak unto the elders of Israel, and say unto them, Thus saith the Lord GOD; Are ye come to enquire of me? *As* I live, saith the Lord GOD, I will not be enquired of by you. 4 Wilt thou judge them, son of man, wilt thou judge *them?* cause them to know the abominations of their fathers:

Here is, 1. The occasion of the message which we have in this chapter. That sermon which we had *ch.* xviii. was occasioned by their presumptuous reflections upon God; this was occasioned by their hypocritical enquiries after him. Each shall have his own. This prophecy is exactly dated, in the *seventh year of the* captivity, about two years after Ezekiel began to prophesy. God would have them to keep account how long their captivity lasted, that they might see how the years went on towards their deliverance, though very slowly. *Certain of the elders of Israel came to enquire of the Lord,* not statedly (as those *ch.* viii. 1), but, as it should seem, occasionally, and upon a particular emergency. Whether they were of those that were now in captivity, or elders lately come from Jerusalem upon business to Babylon, is not certain; but, by what the prophet says to them (v. 32), it should seem, their enquiry was whether now that they were captives in Babylon, at a distance from their own country, where they had not only no temple, but no synagogue, for the worship of God, it was not lawful for them, that they might ingratiate themselves with their lords and masters, to join with them in their worship and do *as the families of these countries* do, that *serve wood and stone.* This matter was palliated as well as it would bear, like Naaman's pleading with Elisha for leave to bow in the house of Rimmon, in compliment to the king; but we have reason to suspect that their enquiry drove at this. Note, Those hearts are wretchedly hardened which ask God leave to go on in sin, and that when they are suffering for it. They came and *sat* very demurely and with a show of devotion *before the prophet, ch.* xxxiii. 31. 2. The purport of this message. (1.) They must be made to know that *God is angry with them;* he takes it as an affront that they come to enquire of him when they are resolved to go on still in their trespasses:

As I live, saith the Lord God, I will not be enquired of by you, v. 3. Their shows of devotion shall be neither acceptable to God nor advantageous to themselves. God will not take notice of their enquiries, nor give them any satisfactory answers. Note, A hypocritical attendance on God and his ordinances is so far from being pleasing to him that it is provoking. (2.) They must be made to know that God is justly angry with them (*v.* 4): *" Wilt thou judge them, son of man, wilt thou judge them ?"* Thou art a prophet, surely thou wilt not *plead for them,* as an intercessor with God; but surely thou wilt *pass sentence* on them as a judge for God. *See, I have set thee over the nation;* wilt thou not declare to them the judgments of the Lord? Cause them therefore *to know the abominations of their fathers."* So the orders run now, as before (*ch.* xvi. 2) he must cause them to *know their own abominations.* Though their own abominations were sufficient to justify God in the severest of his proceedings against them, yet it would be of use for them to know the *abominations of their fathers,* that they might see what a righteous thing it was with God now at last to cut them off from being a people, who from the first were such a provoking people.

5 And say unto them, Thus saith the Lord GOD; In the day when I chose Israel, and lifted up mine hand unto the seed of the house of Jacob, and made myself known unto them in the land of Egypt, when I lifted up mine hand unto them, saying, I *am* the LORD your God; 6 In the day *that* I lifted up mine hand unto them, to bring them forth of the land of Egypt into a land that I had espied for them, flowing with milk and honey, which *is* the glory of all lands: 7 Then said I unto them, Cast ye away every man the abominations of his eyes, and defile not yourselves with the idols of Egypt: I *am* the LORD your God. 8 But they rebelled against me, and would not hearken unto me: they did not every man cast away the abominations of their eyes, neither did they forsake the idols of Egypt: then I said, I will pour out my fury upon them, to accomplish my anger against them in the midst of the land of Egypt. 9 But I wrought for my name's sake, that it should not be polluted before the heathen, among whom they *were,* in whose sight I made myself known unto them, in

bringing them forth out of the land of Egypt.

The history of the ingratitude and rebellion of the people of Israel here begins as early as their beginning; so does the history of man's apostasy from his Maker. No sooner have we read the story of our first parents' creation than we immediately meet with that of their rebellion; so we see here it was with Israel, a people designed to represent the body of mankind both in their dealings with God and in his with them. Here is,

I. The gracious purposes of God's law concerning Israel in Egypt, where they were bond-slaves to Pharaoh. Be it spoken, be it written, to the immortal honour of free grace, that then and there, 1. He chose Israel to be a peculiar people to himself, though their condition was bad and their character worse, that he might have the honour of mending both. He *therefore* chose them, because they were *the seed of the house of Jacob,* the posterity of that prince with God, *that he might keep the oath which he had sworn unto their fathers,* Deut. vii. 7, 8. 2. He *made himself known to them* by his name *Jehovah* (a new name, Exod. vi. 3), when by reason of their servitude they had almost lost the knowledge of that name by which he was known to their fathers, *God Almighty.* Note, As the foundation of our blessedness is laid in God's choosing us, so the first step towards it is God's making himself known to us. And whatever distance we are at, whatever distress we are in, he that made himself known to Israel even in the land of Egypt can find us out, and follow us with the gracious discoveries and manifestations of his favour. 3. He made over himself to them as their God in covenant: *I lifted up my hand unto them,* saying it, and confirming it with an oath, " *I am the Lord your God,* to whom you are to pay your homage, and from whom and in whom you are to expect your bliss." 4. He promised to bring them out of Egypt; and made good what he promised. He *lifted up his hand,* that is, he swore unto them, that he would deliver them; and, they being very unworthy, and their deliverance very unlikely, it was requisite that the promise of it should be *confirmed by an oath.* Or, He *lifted up his hand,* that is, he put forth his almighty power to do it; he did it with an *outstretched arm,* Ps. cxxxvi. 12. 5. He assured them that he would put them in possession of the land of Canaan. He *therefore* brought them out of Egypt, *that he might bring them into a land that he had spied out for them,* a second garden of Eden, which was *the glory of all lands.* So he found it, the climate being temperate, the soil fruitful, the situation pleasant, and every thing agreeable (Deut. viii. 7; xi. 12); or, however this might be, so he made it, by setting up his sanctuary in it.

II. The reasonable commands he gave them, and the easy conditions of his covenant with them at that time. Having told them what they might expect from him, he next tells them what was all he expected from them ; it was no more than this (*v.* 7) : " *Cast you away every man* his images that he uses for worship, that are the adorations, but should be the *abominations, of his eyes.* Let him abominate them, and put them out of his sight, and *defile not yourselves with the idols of Egypt.*" Of these, it seems, many of them were fond ; the golden calf was one of them. It was just, and what might reasonably be expected, that, being delivered from the Egyptian slavery, they should quit the Egyptian idolatry, especially when God, at bringing them out, *executed judgment upon the gods of Egypt* (Num. xxxiii. 4) and thereby showed himself above them. And, whatever other idols they might have an inclination to, one would think they should have had a rooted aversion to the gods of Egypt for Egypt's sake, which had been to them a house of bondage. Yet, it seems, they needed this caution, and it is backed with a good reason : *I am the Lord your God,* who neither need an assistant nor will admit a rival.

III. Their unreasonable disobedience to these commands, for which God might justly have cut them off as soon as ever they were formed into a people (*v.* 8) : *They rebelled against God,* not only refused to comply with his particular precepts, but shook off their allegiance, and in effect told him that they would be at liberty to worship what God they pleased. And even then when God came down to deliver them, and sent Moses for that purpose, yet they would not *forsake the idols of Egypt,* which perhaps made them speak so affectionately of the *onions of Egypt* (Num. xi. 5), for among other things the Egyptians worshipped an onion. It was strange that all the plagues of Egypt would not prevail to cure them of their affection to the *idols of Egypt.* For this God said he would *pour out his fury upon them,* even while they were yet *in the midst of the land of Egypt.* Justly might he have said, " Let them die with the Egyptians." This magnifies the riches of God's goodness, that he was pleased to work so great a salvation for them even when he saw them ripe for ruin. Well might Moses tell them, It is *not for your righteousness,* Deut. ix. 4, 5.

IV. The wonderful deliverance which God wrought for them, notwithstanding. Though they forfeited the favour while it was in the bestowing, and when God *would have healed them* then their *iniquity was discovered* (Hos. vii. 1), yet *mercy rejoiced against judgment,* and God did what he designed purely *for his own name's sake, v.* 9. When nothing in us will furnish him with a reason for his favours he furnishes himself with one. God *made himself known* to them *in the sight of*

the heathen when he ordered Moses publicly to say to Pharaoh, Israel is *my son, my firstborn,* let them go, *that they may serve me.* Now, if he had left them to perish for their wickedness as they deserved, the Egyptians would have reflected upon him for it, and his name would have been polluted, which ought to be sanctified and shall be so. Note, The church is secured, even when it is corrupt, because God will secure his own honour.

10 Wherefore I caused them to go forth out of the land of Egypt, and brought them into the wilderness. 11 And I gave them my statutes, and showed them my judgments, which *if* a man do, he shall even live in them. 12 Moreover also I gave them my sabbaths, to be a sign between me and them, that they might know that I *am* the LORD that sanctify them. 13 But the house of Israel rebelled against me in the wilderness : they walked not in my statutes, and they despised my judgments, which *if* a man do, he shall even live in them ; and my sabbaths they greatly polluted : then I said, I would pour out my fury upon them in the wilderness, to consume them. 14 But I wrought for my name's sake, that it should not be polluted before the heathen, in whose sight I brought them out. 15 Yet also I lifted up my hand unto them in the wilderness, that I would not bring them into the land which I had given *them,* flowing with milk and honey, which *is* the glory of all lands ; 16 Because they despised my judgments, and walked not in my statutes, but polluted my sabbaths : for their heart went after their idols. 17 Nevertheless mine eye spared them from destroying them, neither did I make an end of them in the wilderness. 18 But I said unto their children in the wilderness, Walk ye not in the statutes of your fathers, neither observe their judgments, nor defile yourselves with their idols : 19 I *am* the LORD your God ; walk in my statutes, and keep my judgments, and do them ; 20 And hallow my sabbaths ; and they shall be a sign between me and you, that ye may know that I *am* the LORD your God. 21 Notwithstanding the children rebell ℃d

against me : they walked not in my statutes, neither kept my judgments to do them, which *if* a man do, he shall even live in them ; they polluted my sabbaths : then I said, I would pour out my fury upon them, to accomplish my anger against them in the wilderness. 22 Nevertheless I withdrew mine hand and wrought for my name's sake, that it should not be polluted in the sight of the heathen, in whose sight I brought them forth. 23 I lifted up mine hand unto them also in the wilderness, that I would scatter them among the heathen, and disperse them through the countries ; 24 Because they had not executed my judgments, but had despised my statutes, and had polluted my sabbaths, and their eyes were after their fathers' idols. 25 Wherefore I gave them also statutes *that were* not good, and judgments whereby they should not live ; 26 And I polluted them in their own gifts, in that they caused to pass through *the fire* all that openeth the womb, that I might make them desolate, to the end that they might know that I *am* the LORD.

The history of the struggle between the sins of Israel, by which they endeavoured to ruin themselves, and the mercies of God, by which he endeavoured to save them and make them happy, is here continued : and the instances of that struggle in these verses have reference to what passed between God and them in the wilderness, in which God honoured himself and they shamed themselves. The story of Israel in the wilderness is referred to in the New Testament (1 Cor. x. and Heb. iii.), as well as often in the Old, for warning to us Christians ; and therefore we are particularly concerned in these verses. Observe,

I. The great things God did for them, which he puts them in mind of, not as grudging them his favours, but to show how ungrateful they had been. And we say, If you call a man ungrateful, you can call him no worse. It was a great favour, 1. That God *brought them forth out of Egypt* (v. 10), though, as it follows, he *brought them into the wilderness* and not into Canaan immediately. It is better to be at liberty in a wilderness than bond-slaves in a land of plenty, to enjoy God and ourselves in solitude than to lose both in a crowd ; yet there were many of them who had such base servile spirits as not to understand this, but, when they met with the difficulties of a desert,

wished themselves in Egypt again. 2. That he gave them the law upon Mount Sinai (v. 11), not only instructed them concerning good and evil, but by his authority bound them from the evil and to the good. He *gave them his statutes,* and a valuable gift it was. *Moses commanded them a law that was the inheritance of the congregation of Israel,* Deut. xxxiii. 4. God *made them to know his judgments,* not only enacted laws for them, but showed them the reasonableness and equity of those laws, with what judgment they were formed. The laws he gave them they were encouraged to observe and obey ; for, *if a man do them, he shall even live in them ;* in keeping God's commandments there is abundance of comfort and a great reward. Christ says, *If thou wilt into enter life,* and enjoy it, *keep the commandments.* Though those who are the most strict in their obedience are thus far unprofitable servants that they do no more than is their duty to do, yet it is thus richly recompensed : *This do, and thou shalt live.* The Chaldee says, *He shall live an eternal life in them.* St. Paul quotes this (Gal. iii. 12) to show that *the law is not of faith,* but proposes life upon condition of perfect obedience, which we are not capable of rendering, and therefore must have recourse to the grace of the gospel, without which we are all undone. 3. That he revived the ancient institution of the sabbath day, which was lost and forgotten while they were bond-slaves in Egypt ; for their task-masters there would by no means allow them to rest one day in seven. In the wilderness indeed every day was a day of rest ; for what need had those to labour who lived upon manna, and whose raiment waxed not old ? But one day in seven must be a holy rest (v. 12) : *I gave them my sabbaths to be a sign between me and them* (the institution of the sabbath was a sign of God's good-will to them, and their observance of it a sign of their regard to him), *that they might know that I am the Lord that sanctify them.* By this God made it to appear that he had distinguished them from the rest of the world, and designed to model them for a peculiar people to himself ; and by their attendance on God in solemn assemblies on sabbath days they were made to increase in the knowledge of God, in an experimental knowledge of the powers and pleasures of his sanctifying grace. Note, (1.) Sabbaths are privileges, and are so to be accounted ; the church acknowledges as a great favour, in that chapter which is parallel to this and seems to have a reference to this (Neh. ix. 14), *Thou madest known unto them thy holy sabbaths.* (2.) Sabbaths are signs ; it is a sign that men have a sense of religion, and that there is some good correspondence between them and God, when they make conscience of keeping holy the sabbath day. (3.) Sabbaths, if duly sanctified, are the means of our sanctification ; if we do the duty of the day, we shall find, to our comfort, *it is the Lord that sanctifies us,* makes us holy (that is, truly happy) here, and prepares us to be happy (that is, perfectly holy) hereafter.

II. Their disobedient undutiful conduct towards God, for which he might justly have thrown them out of covenant as soon as he had taken them into covenant (*v.* 13): *They rebelled in the wilderness.* There where they received so much mercy from God, and had such a dependence upon him, and were in their way to Canaan, yet there they broke out in many open rebellions against the God that led them and fed them. They did not only not *walk in God's statutes,* but they *despised his judgments* as not worth observing; instead of sanctifying the sabbaths, they polluted them, greatly polluted them; one gathered sticks, many went out to gather manna on this day. Hereupon God was ready sometimes to cut them off; he said, more than once, that he would *consume them in the wilderness.* But Moses interceded, so did God's own mercy more powerfully, and most of all a concern for his own glory, that *his name might not be polluted and profaned among the heathen* (*v.* 14), that the Egyptians might not say that for mischief he brought them thus far, or that he was not able to bring them any further, or that he had no such good land as was talked of to bring them to, Exod. xxxii. 12; Num. xiv. 13, &c. Note, God's strongest reasons for his sparing mercy are those which are fetched from his own glory.

III. God's determination to cut off that generation of them in the wilderness. He who *lifted up his hand* for them (*v.* 6) now *lifted up his hand against them ;* he who by an oath confirmed his promise to bring them out of Egypt now by an oath confirmed his threatenings that he would not bring them into Canaan (*v.* 15, 16): *I lifted up my hand unto them,* saying, As truly as I live, these men who have tempted me these ten times shall never see the land which I swore unto their fathers, Num. xiv. 22, 23; Ps. xcv. 11. By their contempt of God's laws, and particularly of his sabbaths, they put a bar in their own door; and that which was at the bottom of their disobedience to God, and their neglect of his institutions, was a secret affection to the gods of Egypt: *Their heart went after their idols.* Note, The bias of the mind towards the world and the flesh, the money and the belly (those two great objects of spiritual idolatry), is the root of bitterness from which springs all disobedience to the divine law. The heart that goes after those idols despises God's judgments.

IV. The reservation of a seed that should be admitted upon a new trial, and the instructions given to that seed, *v.* 17. Though they thus deserved ruin, and were doomed to it, yet *my eye spared them.* When he looked upon them he had compassion on
866

them, and did not *make an end of them,* but reprieved them till a new generation was reared. Note, It is owing purely to the mercy of God that he has not long ago *made an end of us.* This new generation is well educated. Moses in Deuteronomy reported and enforced the laws which had been given to those that came out of Egypt, that their children might have them as it were sounding in their ears afresh when they entered Canaan (*v.* 18): *"I said unto their children in the wilderness,* in the plains of Moab, Walk in the statutes of your God and *walk not in the statutes of your fathers ;* do not imitate their superstitious usages nor retain their foolish wicked customs; away with their vain conversation, which has nothing else to say for itself but that it was *received by the tradition of your fathers,* 1 Pet. i. 18. *Defile not yourselves with their idols,* for you see how odious they rendered themselves to God by them. But *keep my judgments* and *hallow my sabbaths,"* v. 19, 20. Note, If parents be careless, and do not give their children good instructions as they ought, the children ought to make up the want by studying the word of God so much the more carefully and diligently themselves when they grow up ; and the bad examples of parents must be made use of by their children for admonition, and not for imitation.

V. The revolt of the next generation from God, by which they also made themselves obnoxious to the wrath of God (*v.* 21): *The children rebelled against me* too. And the same that was said of the fathers' rebellion is here said *of the children's,* for they were a seed of evil-doers. Moses told them that he *knew their rebellion and their stiff neck,* Deut. xxxi. 27. And Deut. ix. 24, *You have been rebellious against the Lord from the day that I knew you.* They walked not in my statutes (*v.* 21); nay, *they despised my statutes,* v. 24. Those who disobey God's statutes despise them, they show that they have a mean opinion of them and of him whose statutes they are. They *polluted God's sabbaths,* as their fathers. Note, The profanation of the sabbath day is an inlet to all impiety; those who pollute holy time will keep nothing pure. It was said of the fathers (*v.* 16) that *their heart went after their idols ;* they worshipped idols because they had an affection for them. It is said of the children (*v.* 24) that *their eyes went after their fathers' idols ;* they had grown atheistical, and had no affection for any gods at all, but they worshipped *their fathers' idols* because they were their fathers' and they had them before their eyes. They were used to them; and, if they must have gods, they would have such as they could see, such as they could manage. And that which aggravated their disobedience to God's statutes was that, *if they had done them, they might have lived in them* (*v.* 21), might have been a happy thriving people. Note, Those that go contrary to their duty go contrary to their interest; they will not obey, will not come to Christ, that they may have life, John v. 40. And it is therefore just that those who will not live and flourish as they might in their obedience should die and perish in their disobedience. Now the great instance of that generation's rebellion and inclination to idolatry was the *iniquity of Peor,* as that of their fathers was the *golden calf.* Then *the anger of the Lord was kindled against Israel,* Num, xxv. 3. Then there was a plague in the congregation of the Lord, which, if it had not been seasonably stayed by Phinehas's zeal, had cut them all off; and yet they owned, in Joshua's time, We are not *cleansed from that iniquity unto this day,* Josh. xxii. 17; Ps. cvi. 29. Then it was that God said he would *pour out his fury upon them* (v. 21), that he *lifted up his hand unto them in the wilderness,* when they were a second time just ready to enter Canaan, *that he would scatter them among the heathen.* This very thing he said to them by Moses in his parting song, Deut. xxxii. 20. Because they *provoked him to jealousy with strange gods,* he said, *I will hide my face from them;* and (v. 26, 27) he said, *I would scatter them into corners, were it not that I feared the wrath of the enemy,* which explains this (v. 21, 22), *I said I would pour out my fury upon them,* but *I withdrew* my hand *for my name's sake.* Note, When the corruptions of the visible church are such, and so provoking, that we have reason to fear its total extirpation, yet then we may be confident of this, to our comfort, that God will secure his own honour, by making good his purpose, that while the world stands he will have a church in it.

VI. The judgments of God upon them for their rebellion. They would not regard the statutes and judgments by which God prescribed them their duty, but despised them, and therefore God *gave them statutes and judgments* which *were not good,* and *by which they should not live, v.* 25. By this we may understand the several ways by which God punished them while they were in the wilderness—the plague that broke in upon them, the fiery serpent, and the like—which, in allusion to the law they had broken, are called *judgments,* because inflicted by the justice of God, and *statutes,* because he gave orders concerning them and commanded desolations as sometimes he had commanded deliverances, and appointed Israel's plagues as he had done the plagues of Egypt. When God said, *I will consume them in a moment* (Num. xvi. 21), when he said, *Take the heads of the people and hang them up* (Num. xxv. 4), when he threatened them with the curse and obliged them to say *Amen* to every curse (Deut. xxvii. 28), then he gave them judgments by *which they should not live.* More is implied than is expressed; they are judgments by which they should

die. Those that will not be bound by the precepts of the law shall be bound by the sentence of it; for one way or other the word of God will *take hold* of men, Zech. i. 6. Spiritual judgments are the most dreadful; and these God punished them with. The statutes and judgments which the heathen observed in the worship of their idols were not good, and in practising them they could not live; and God gave them up to those. He made their sin to be their punishment, gave them up to a *reprobate mind,* as he did the Gentile idolaters (Rom. i. 24, 26), gave them up to their own heart's lusts (Ps. lxxxi. 12), punished them for those superstitious customs which were against the written law by giving them up to those which were against the very light and law of nature; he left them to themselves to be guilty of the most impure idolatries, as in the worship of Baal-peor (he *polluted them,* that is, he permitted them to pollute themselves, *in their own gifts, v.* 26), and of the most barbarous idolatries, as in the worship of Moloch, when they *caused their children,* especially their firstborn, which God challenged a particular property in *(the first-born of thy sons shalt thou give unto me),* to pass *through the fire,* to be sacrificed to their idols; that thus he might *make them desolate,* not only that he might justly do it, but that he might do it by their own hands; for this must needs be a great weakening to their families and a diminution of the honour and strength of their country. Note, God sometimes makes sin to be its own punishment, and yet is not the author of sin; and there needs no more to make men miserable than to give them up to their own vile appetites and passions. Let them be put into the hand of their own counsels, and they will ruin themselves and make themselves desolate. And thus God makes them know that he is the Lord, and that he is a righteous God, which they themselves will be compelled to own when they see how much their wilful transgressions contribute to their own desolations. Note, Those who will not acknowledge God as the Lord their ruler shall be made to acknowledge him as the Lord their judge when it is too late.

27 Therefore, son of man, speak unto the house of Israel, and say unto them, Thus saith the Lord God; Yet in this your fathers have blasphemed me, in that they have committed a trespass against me. 28 *For* when I had brought them into the land, *for* the which I lifted up mine hand to give it to them, then they saw every high hill, and all the thick trees, and they offered there their sacrifices, and there they presented

the provocation of their offering: there also they made their sweet savour, and poured out there their drink-offerings. 29 Then I said unto them, What *is* the high place whereunto ye go? and the name thereof is called Bamah unto this day. 30 Wherefore say unto the house of Israel, Thus saith the Lord GOD; Are ye polluted after the manner of your fathers? and commit ye whoredom after their abominations? 31 For when ye offer your gifts, when ye make your sons to pass through the fire, ye pollute yourselves with all your idols, even unto this day: and shall I be enquired of by you, O house of Israel? *As* I live, saith the Lord GOD, I will not be enquired of by you. 32 And that which cometh into your mind shall not be at all, that ye say, We will be as the heathen, as the families of the countries, to serve wood and stone.

Here the prophet goes on with the story of their rebellions, for their further humiliation, and shows,

I. That they had persisted in them after they were settled in the land of Canaan. Though God had so many times testified his displeasure against their wicked courses, " yet *in this* (that is, in the very same thing) *your fathers have blasphemed me*, continued to affront me, that they *also have trespassed a trespass against me*," v. 27. Note, It is a great aggravation of sin when men will not take warning by the mischievous consequences of sin in those that have gone before them: this is *blaspheming God;* it is speaking reproachfully of his judgments, as if they were of no significancy and were not worth regarding. 1. God had made good his promise: *I brought them into the land* that I had sworn to give them. Though their unbelief and disobedience had made the performance slow, and much retarded it, yet it did not *make the promise of no effect.* They were often very near being cut off in the wilderness, but a step between them and ruin, and yet they came to Canaan at last. Note, Even God's Israel get to heaven by hell-gates; so many are their transgressions, and so strong their corruptions, that it is a miracle of mercy they are happy at last; as hypocrites go to hell by heaven-gates. *The righteous scarcely are saved. Per tot discrimina rerum tendimus ad cœlum —Ten thousand dangers fill the road to heaven.* 2. They had broken his precept by their abominable idolatries. God had appointed them to destroy all the monuments of idolatry, that they might not be tempted

to desert his sanctuary; but, instead of defacing them, they fell in love with them, and when they *saw every high hill* whence they had the most delightful prospects, and all the *thick trees* where they had the most delightful shades (the former to show forth their pompous idolatries, the latter to conceal their shameful ones), *there they offered their sacrifices* and *made their sweet savour*, which should have been presented upon God's altar only. *There they presented the provocation of their offering* (v. 28), that is, their offerings, which, instead of pacifying God, or pleasing him, were highly provoking—sacrifices which, though costly, yet, being misplaced, were an abomination to the Lord. 3. They obstinately persisted herein notwithstanding all the admonitions that were given them (v. 29): " *Then I told them,* by my servants the prophets, told them *where the high place was, to which they went;* nay, I put them upon considering it, and asking their own consciences concerning it, by putting this question to them, *Which is the high place whereunto you go?* What do you find there so inviting that you will leave God's altars, where he requires your attendance, to frequent such places as he has forbidden you to worship in? Do you not know that those high places are of a heathenish extraction, and that the things which the Gentiles sacrificed they sacrificed to devils and not to God? Did not Moses tell you so? Deut. xxxii. 17. *And will you have fellowship with devils? What is that high place to which you go* when you turn your back on God's altars? *O foolish* Israelites, *who* or what *has bewitched you,* that you will forsake the fountain of life for broken cisterns, that worship which God appoints, and will accept, for that which he forbids, which he abhors, and which he will punish?" And yet *the name is called Bamah unto this day;* they will have their way, let God and his prophets say what they please to the contrary. They are wedded to their *high places;* even in the best reigns those were not taken away; you could not prevail to take away the name of *Bamah— the high place,* out of their mouths, but still they would have that in the place of their worship. The sin and the sinner are with difficulty parted.

II. That this generation, after they were unsettled, continued under the dominion of the same corrupt inclinations to idolatry, v. 30. He must *say to the present house of Israel,* some of whose elders were now sitting before him, " *Are you polluted after the manner of your fathers?* After all that God has said against you by a succession of prophets, and done against you by a series of judgments, yet will you take no warning? Will you still be as bad as your fathers were, and commit the same abominations that they committed? I see you will; you are bent upon returning to the old abominations; you *offer your gifts* in the high places, and you *make your sons to pass through the fire;* either you actually do it or you do it in purpose and imagination, and so you continue idolaters *to this day.*" These elders seem now to have been projecting a coalition with the heathen ; their hearts they will reserve for the God of Israel, but their knees they will be at liberty to bow to the gods of the nations among whom they live, that they may have the more respect and the fairer quarter among them.   Now the prophet is here ordered to tell those who were forming this scheme, and were for compounding the matter between God and Baal, that they should have no comfort or benefit from either.   1. They should have no benefit by their consulting in private with the prophets of the Lord; for, because they were hearkening after idols, God would have nothing to do with them (*v.* 31): *As I live, saith the Lord God, I will not be enquired of by you.* What he had said before (*v.* 3), having largely shown how just it was, he here repeats, as that which he would abide by.   Let them not think that they honoured him by their enquiries, nor expect an answer of peace from him, as long as they continued in love and league with their idols.   Note, Those reap no benefit by their religion that are not entire and sincere in it; nor can we have any comfortable communion with God in ordinances of worship unless we be inward and upright with him therein.   We make nothing of our profession if it be but a profession.   Nay, 2. They should have no benefit from their conforming in public to the practice of their neighbours (*v* 32): "*That which comes into your mind* as a piece of refined politics in the present difficult juncture, and which you would be advised to for your own preservation, and that you may not by being singular expose yourselves to abuses, it *shall not be at all,* it shall turn to no account to you.   You say, '*We will be as the heathen,* we will join with them in worshipping their gods, though at the same time we do not believe them to be gods, but *wood and stone,* and then we should be taken *as the families of the countries;* they will not know, or in a little while will have forgotten, that we are Jews, and will allow us the same privileges with their own countrymen.'   Tell them," says God, " that this project shall *never prosper.*   Either their neighbours will not admit them to join with them in their worship, or, if they do, will think never the better, but the worse, of them for it, and will look upon them as dissemblers, and not fit to be trusted, who are thus false to their God, and put a cheat upon their neighbours."   Note, There is nothing got by sinful compliances; and the carnal projects of hypocrites will stand them in no stead.   It is only integrity and uprightness that will preserve men, and recommend them to God and man.

33 *As* I live, saith the Lord God, surely with a mighty hand, and with a stretched-out arm, and with fury poured out, will I rule over you : 34 And I will bring you out from the people, and will gather you out of the countries wherein ye are scattered, with a mighty hand, and with a stretched-out arm, and with fury poured out. 35 And I will bring you into the wilderness of the people, and there will I plead with you face to face. 36 Like as I pleaded with your fathers in the wilderness of the land of Egypt, so will I plead with you, saith the Lord God. 37 And I will cause you to pass under the rod, and I will bring you into the bond of the covenant : 38 And I will purge out from among you the rebels, and them that transgress against me : I will bring them forth out of the country, where they sojourn, and they shall not enter into the land of Israel : and ye shall know that I *am* the Lord. 39 As for you, O house of Israel, thus saith the Lord God ; Go ye, serve ye every one his idols, and hereafter *also,* if ye will not hearken unto me : but pollute ye my holy name no more with your gifts, and with your idols. 40 For in mine holy mountain, in the mountain of the height of Israel, saith the Lord God, there shall all the house of Israel, all of them in the land, serve me : there will I accept them, and there will I require your offerings, and the first-fruits of your oblations, with all your holy things. 41 I will accept you with your sweet savour, when I bring you out from the people, and gather you out of the countries wherein ye have been scattered ; and I will be sanctified in you before the heathen. 42 And ye shall know that I *am* the Lord, when I shall bring you into the land of Israel, into the country *for* the which I lifted up mine hand to give it to your fathers. 43 And there shall ye remember your ways, and all your doings, wherein ye have been defiled ; and ye shall loathe yourselves in your own sight for all your evils that ye have committed. 44 And ye shall know that I

am the LORD, when I have wrought with you for my name's sake, not according to your wicked ways, nor according to your corrupt doings, O ye house of Israel, saith the Lord GOD.

The design which was now on foot among the elders of Israel was that the people of Israel, being scattered among the nations, should lay aside all their peculiarities and conform to those among whom they lived; but God had told them that the design should not take effect, *v.* 32. Now, in these verses, he shows particularly how it should be frustrated. They aimed at the *mingling* of the families of *Israel with the families of the countries;* but it will prove in the issue that the wicked Israelites, notwithstanding their compliances, shall not mingle with them in their prosperity, but shall be distinguished from them for destruction; for idolatrous Israelites, that are apostates from God, shall be sooner and more sorely punished than idolatrous Babylonians that never knew the way of righteousness. Read and tremble at the doom here passed upon them; it is backed with an oath not to be reversed: *As I live, saith the Lord God,* thus and thus will I deal with you. They think to make both Jerusalem and Babylon their friends by halting between two; but God threatens that neither of them shall serve for a rest or refuge for them.

I. Babylon shall not protect them, nor any of the countries of the heathen; for God will cast them out of his protection and then what prince, what people, what place, can serve to be a sanctuary to them? God was Israel's King of old, and had they continued his loyal subjects he would have *ruled over them* with care and tenderness for their good, but now *with a stretched-out arm, and with fury poured out, will I rule over them, v.* 33. That power which should have been exerted for their protection shall be exerted for their destruction. Note, There is no shaking off God's dominion; rule he will, either with the golden sceptre or with the iron rod; and those that will not yield to the power of his grace shall be made to sink under the power of his wrath. Now when God is angry with them, though they may think that they shall be lost in the crowd of the heathen among whom they are scattered, they will be disappointed; for (*v.* 34) *I will gather you out of the countries wherein you are scattered,* as, when the rebels are dispersed in battle, those that have escaped the sword of war are pursued and brought together out of all the places whither they were scattered, to be punished by the sword of justice. They shall be brought *into the wilderness of the people* (*v.* 35), either into Babylon, which is called a *wilderness* (*ch.* xix. 13), and the *desert of the sea* (Isa. xxi. 1), or into some place which, though full of people, shall be

870

to them as the wilderness was to Israel after they came out of Egypt, a place where God will *plead with them face to face,* as he *pleaded with their fathers in the wilderness of Egypt* (*v.* 36),—where their carcases shall fall and where he will swear concerning them that they shall never return to Canaan, as he did swear concerning their fathers that they should never come into Canaan,—where he will avenge the breach of his law with as much terror as that with which he gave it in the wilderness of Sinai. Note, God has a good action against apostates, and will find not only time, but a proper place, to plead with them in upon that action, a wilderness even in the midst of the people for that purpose.

II. Israel shall be no more able to protect them than Babylon could; nor shall their relation to God's people stand them in any more stead for the other world than their compliance with idolaters shall for this world; nor shall they stand *in the congregation of the righteous* any more than in the congregation of evil-doers; for there will come a distinguishing day, when God will separate between the precious and the vile; he will *cause them,* as the shepherd causes his sheep, to *pass under the rod,* when he tithes them (Lev. xxvii. 32), that he may mark which is for God. God will take particular notice of each of them, one by one, as sheep are counted, and *he will bring them into the bond of the covenant* (*v.* 37); he will try them and judge of them according to the tenour of the covenant, and the difference made between some and others by the blessings and curses of the covenant. Or it may refer to those among them that repented and reformed; he will cause them to pass under the rod of affliction, and, having done them good by it, he will bring them again *into the bond of the covenant,* will be to them a God in covenant, and use them again as *heirs of promise.*

1. He will separate the wicked from among them (*v.* 38): " *I will purge out from among you the rebels,* who have been a grief and scandal to you, and who have by their rebellions brought all these calamities upon you." The judgments of God shall find them out, and their naming the name of Israel shall be no shelter to them. They shall be *brought out of the countries where they sojourn,* and shall not have that rest in them which they promised themselves. But they *shall not enter into the land of Israel,* nor enjoy the benefit of that rest which God has promised to his people. Note, Though godly people may share with the wicked in the calamities of the world, yet wicked people shall have no share with the godly in the heavenly Canaan; but it shall be part of the blessedness of that world that they shall be *purged out from among them,* the tares from the wheat, the chaff from the corn, *ch.* xiii. 9. But wherever these idolaters of *the house of Israel* were contriving to worship both God

and their idols, thinking to please both, God here protests against it (*v.* 39), as Elijah had done in his name: "*If the Lord be God, then follow him, but, if Baal, then follow him;* if you will serve your idols, do, and take what comes of it; but then do not pretend relation to God and a religious regard to him, nor *pollute his holy name with your gifts* at his altar." Spiritual judgments are the sorest judgments. Two of that kind of judgments are threatened in this verse against those that were for dividing between the God of Israel and the gods of the nations :—(1.) That they should be given up to the service of their idols. To them he said ironically, "*Since you will not hearken unto me, go you, serve every one his idols,* now that you think it will be for your interest, *and hereafter also.* You shall go on in it. *Ephraim is joined to idols, let him alone;* let him take his course, and see what he will get by it at last." Note, Those who think to serve themselves by sin will find in the end that they have but enslaved themselves to sin. (2.) That they should be cut off from the service of God and communion with God: "You *shall not pollute my holy name* with your *vain oblations,* Isa. i. 11. You bring your gifts in your hands, wherewith you pretend to honour me, but at the same time you bring your idols in your hearts, and therefore you do but pollute me, which I will not suffer any more," Amos v. 21, 22. Note, Those are justly forbidden God's house that profane his house.

2. He will separate them to himself again. (1.) He will *gather them* in mercy *out of the countries whither they were scattered,* to be monuments of mercy, as the incorrigible were gathered to be vessels of wrath, *v.* 41. Not one of God's jewels shall be lost in the lumber of this world. (2.) He will *bring them to the land of Israel,* which he had promised to *give to their fathers;* and the discontinuance of their possession shall be no defeasance of their right; it is the *land of Israel* still, and thither God will bring them safely again, *v.* 42. (3.) He will re-establish his ordinances among them, will set up his sanctuary in his holy mountain, which is here called *the mountain of the height of Israel;* for, though the Mount Zion was none of the highest mountains, yet the temple there was one of the highest honours of Israel. It is promised that those who preserved their integrity, and would not serve idols, in other lands, shall return to their prosperity and shall serve the true God in their own land: *All of them in the land shall serve me.* Note, It is the true happiness of a people, and a sure token for good to them, when there is a prevailing disposition in them to serve God. Whereas God had forbidden the idolaters to bring their gifts to his altar, of these he will *require offerings and first-fruits,* and will accept them, *v.* 40. What he does not require he will not accept,

but what is done with a regard to his precepts he will be well pleased with. He will *accept them with their sweet savour,* or *savour of rest* (*v.* 41), as being very grateful to him and what he takes a complacency in; whereas, to hypocritical worshippers, he says, *I will not smell in your solemn assemblies.* (4.) He will give them true repentance for their sins, *v.* 43. When they find how gracious God is to them they will be overcome with his kindness, and blush to think of their bad behaviour towards so *good a God:* "There, in *my holy mountain,* when you come to enjoy the privileges of that again, *there* shall you *remember your doings,* wherein you have been defiled." Note, The more conversant we are with God's holiness the more we shall see of the odious nature of sin. There *you shall loathe yourselves in your own sight.* Note, Ingenuous evangelical repentance makes people loathe themselves for their sins, as Job xlii. 5, 6. (5.) He will give them the knowledge of himself: *They shall know* by experience that *he is the Lord,* that he is a God of almighty power and inexhaustible goodness, kind to his people and faithful to his covenant with them. Note, All the favours we receive from God should lead us into a more intimate acquaintance with him. (6.) He will do all this for his own name's sake, notwithstanding their undeservings and ill-deservings (*v.* 44); he has *wrought with them,* that is, wrought for them, wrought in favour of them, wrought in concurrence with them, they doing their endeavour; he has wrought with them purely *for his name's sake.* His reasons were all fetched from himself. Had he dealt with them *according to their wicked ways and their corrupt doings,* though they were the better and sounder part of the house of Israel, he would have left them to be scattered and lost with the rest; but he recovered and restored them for the sake of his own name, not only that it might not be *polluted* (*v.* 14), but that he might be *sanctified in them before the heathen* (*v.* 41), that he might *sanctify himself* (so the word is); for it is God's work to glorify his own name. He will do well for his people that he may have the glory of it, that he may manifest himself to be a God pardoning sin and so keeping promise, that his people may praise him, and that their neighbours may likewise take notice of him, as they did when God *turned again their captivity,* Ps. cxxvi. 3. *Then said they among the heathen, The Lord has done great things for them.*

45 Moreover the word of the Lord came unto me, saying, 46 Son of man, set thy face toward the south, and drop *thy word* toward the south, and prophesy against the forest of the south field; 47 And say to the forest of the south, Hear the word of the Lord; Thus saith the Lord God; Behold,

I will kindle a fire in thee, and it shall devour every green tree in thee, and every dry tree : the flaming flame shall not be quenched, and all faces from the south to the north shall be burned therein. 48 And all flesh shall see that I the LORD have kindled it : it shall not be quenched. 49 Then said I, Ah Lord GOD! they say of me, Doth he not speak parables?

We have here a prophecy of wrath against Judah and Jerusalem, which would more fitly have begun the next chapter than conclude this ; for it has no dependence on what goes before, but that which follows in the beginning of the next chapter is the explication of it, when the people complained that this was a parable which they understood not. In this parable, 1. It is a forest that is prophesied against, *the forest of the south field*, Judah and Jerusalem. These lay south from Babylon, where Ezekiel now was, and therefore he is directed to *set his face towards the south* (v. 46), to intimate to them that God had set his face against them, was displeased with them, and determined to destroy them. But, though it be a message of wrath which he has to deliver, he must deliver it with mildness and tenderness ; he must *drop his word towards the south ;* his doctrine must *distil as the rain* (Deut. xxxii. 2), that people's hearts might be softened by it, as the earth by the *river of God*, which *drops upon the pastures of the wilderness* (Ps. lxv. 12) and which a south land more especially calls for, Josh. xv. 19. Judah and Jerusalem are called *forests*, not only because they had been full of people, as a wood of trees, but because they had been empty of fruit, for fruit-trees grow not in a forest ; and a forest is put in opposition to a fruitful field, Isa. xxxii. 15. Those that should have been as the garden of the Lord, and his vineyard, had become like a forest, all overgrown with *briers and thorns ;* and those that are so, that bring not forth the fruits of righteousness, God's word prophesies against 2. It is a fire kindled in his forest that is prophesied of, v. 47. All those judgments which wasted and consumed both the city and the country—sword, famine, pestilence, and captivity, are signified by this fire. (1.) It is a fire of God's own kindling : *I will kindle a fire in thee ;* the *breath of the Lord* is not as a drop, but *as a stream, of brimstone* to set it on fire, Isa. xxx. 33. He that had been himself a protecting fire about Jerusalem is now a consuming fire in it. *All flesh shall see* by the fury of this fire, and the desolations it shall make, especially when they compare it with the sins which had made them fuel for this fire, that it is *the Lord* that *has kindled it* (v. 48), as a just avenger of his own injured honour. (2.) This conflagration shall be general : all orders

and degrees of men shall be devoured by it —young and old, rich and poor, high and low. Even *green trees*, which the fire does not easily fasten upon, shall be devoured by this fire ; even good people shall some of them be involved in these calamities ; and *if this be done in the green trees, what shall be done in the dry?* The dry trees shall be as tinder and touch-wood to this fire. *All faces* (that is, all that covers the face of the earth) *from the south* of Canaan to the north, from Beersheba to Dan, shall be *burnt therein.* (3.) The fire *shall not be quenched ;* no attempts to give check to the dissolution shall prevail. When God will ruin a nation, who or what can save it?

Now observe, 1. The people's reflection upon the prophet on occasion of this discourse. They said, *Does he not speak parables?* This was the language either of their ignorance or infidelity (the plainest truths were as parables to them), or of their malice and ill-will to the prophet. Note. It is common for those who will not be wrought upon by the word to pick quarrels with it ; it is either too plain or too obscure, too fine or too homely, too common or too singular ; something or other is amiss in it. 2. The prophet's complaint to God : *Ah, Lord God! they say* so and so of me. Note, It is a comfort to us, when people speak ill of us unjustly, that we have a God to complain to.

CHAP. XXI.

In this chapter we have, I. An explication of the prophecy in the close of the foregoing chapter concerning the fire in the forest, which the people complained they could not understand (ver. 1—5), with directions to the prophet to show himself deeply affected with it, ver. 6, 7. II. A further prediction of the sword that was coming upon the land, by which all should be laid waste ; and this expressed very emphatically, ver. 8—17. III. A prospect given of the king of Babylon's approach to Jerusalem, to which he was determined by divination, ver. 18—24. IV. Sentence passed upon Zedekiah king of Judah, ver. 25—27. \. The destruction of the Ammonites by the sword foretold, ver. 28—32. Thus is this chapter all threatenings.

AND the word of the LORD came unto me, saying, 2 Son of man, set thy face toward Jerusalem, and drop *thy word* toward the holy places, and prophesy against the land of Israel, 3 And say to the land of Israel, Thus saith the LORD ; Behold, I *am* against thee, and will draw forth my sword out of his sheath, and will cut off from thee the righteous and the wicked. 4 Seeing then that I will cut off from thee the righteous and the wicked, therefore shall my sword go forth out of his sheath against all flesh from the south to the north : 5 That all flesh may know that I the LORD have drawn forth my sword out of his sheath : it shall not return any more. 6 Sigh therefore, thou son of man, with the breaking of *thy* loins ; and with bitterness sigh before their eyes.

7 And it shall be, when they say unto thee, Wherefore sighest thou? that thou shalt answer, For the tidings; because it cometh: and every heart shall melt, and all hands shall be feeble, and every spirit shall faint, and all knees shall be weak *as* water: behold, it cometh, and shall be brought to pass, saith the Lord GOD.

The prophet had faithfully delivered the message he was entrusted with, in the close of the foregoing chapter, in the terms wherein he received it, not daring to add his own comment upon it; but, when he complained that the people found fault with him for speaking parables, the word of the Lord came to him again, and gave him a key to that figurative discourse, that with it he might let the people into the meaning of it and so silence that objection. For all men shall be rendered inexcusable at God's bar and every mouth shall be stopped. Note, He that *speaks with tongues* should *pray that he may interpret*, 1 Cor. xiv. 13. When we speak to people about their souls we should study plainness, and express ourselves as we may be the best understood. Christ *expounded his parables to his disciples*, Mark iv. 34. 1. The prophet is here more plainly directed against whom to level the arrow of this prophecy. He must *drop his word towards the holy places* (v. 2), towards Canaan the holy land, Jerusalem the holy city, the temple the holy house. These were highly dignified above other places; but, when they polluted them, that word which used to drop in the holy places shall now drop against them: *Prophesy against the land of Israel*. It was the honour of Israel that it had prophets and prophecy; but these, being despised by them, are turned against them. And justly is Zion battered with her own artillery, which used to be employed against her adversaries, seeing she knew not how to value it. 2. He is instructed, and is to instruct the people, in the meaning of the fire that was threatened to consume the forest of the south: it signified a sword drawn, the sword of war which should make the land desolate (v. 3): *Behold, I am against thee, O land of Israel!* There needs no more to make a people miserable than to have God against them; for as, if he be for us, we need not fear, whoever are against us, so, if he be against us, we cannot hope, whoever are for us. And God's professing people, when they revolt from him, set him against them, who used to be for them. Was the fire there of God's kindling? The sword here is his sword, which he has prepared, and which he will give commission to; it is he that will *draw it out of its sheath*, where it had lain quiet and threatened no harm. Note, When the sword is unsheathed among the nations God's hand must be eyed and

owned in it. Did the fire devour *every green tree* and *every dry tree?* The sword in like manner shall *cut off the righteous and the wicked*. Good and bad were involved in the common calamities of the nation; the righteous were *cut off from the land of Israel* when they were sent captives in Babylon, though perhaps few or none of them were cut off from the land of the living; and it was a threatening omen to the land of Israel that in the beginning of its troubles such excellent men as Daniel and his fellows, and Ezekiel, were cut off from it and conveyed to Babylon. But though the sword *cut off the righteous and the wicked* (for it *devours one as well as another*, 2 Sam. xi. 25), yet far be it from us to think that *the righteous are as the wicked*, Gen. xviii. 25. No; God's graces and comforts make a great difference when his providence seems to make none. The *good figs* are sent into Babylon *for their good*, Jer. xxiv. 5, 6. It is only in outward appearance that there is *one event to the righteous and to the wicked*, Eccl. ix. 2. But it speaks the greatness of God's displeasure against the land of Israel. Well might it be said, *His eye shall not spare*, when it shall not spare, no, not the *righteous* in it. Since there are not righteous men sufficient to save the land, to make the justice of God the more illustrious the few that there are shall suffer with it, and God's mercy shall make it up to them some other way. Did the fire *burn up all faces from the south to the north?* The sword shall go *forth against all flesh from the south to the north*, shall go forth, as God's sword, with a commission that cannot be contested, with a force that cannot be resisted. Were all flesh made to know that God kindled the fire? They shall be made to know that he has *drawn forth the sword*, v. 5. And, *lastly*, Shall the fire that is *kindled never be quenched?* So when this sword of the Lord is drawn against Judah and Jerusalem the scabbard is thrown away, and it shall never be sheathed: It *shall not return any more*, till it has made a full end. 3. The prophet is ordered, by expressions of his own grief and concern for these calamities that were coming on, to try to make impressions of the like upon the people. When he has delivered his message he must *sigh* (v. 6), must fetch many deep sighs, *with the breaking of his loins;* he must sigh as if his heart would burst, *sigh with bitterness*, with other expressions of bitter sorrow, and this publicly, *in the sight* of those to whom he delivered the foregoing message, that this might be a sermon to their eyes as that was to their ears; and it was well if both would work upon them. The prophet must sigh, though it was painful to himself and made his breast sore, and though it is probable that the profane among the people would ridicule him for it and call him a whining canting preacher. But, *if we be beside ourselves it is to God;* and, *if this be to be vile, we will be yet more so.* Note, Ministers, if they would affect others with the things they speak of, must show that they are themselves in the greatest sincerity affected with them, and must submit to that which may create uneasiness to themselves, so that it will promote the ends of their ministry. The people, observing the prophet to sigh so much and seeing no visible occasion for it, would ask, *" Wherefore sighest thou?* These sighs have some mystical meaning; let us know what it is." And he must answer them (*v.* 7): *" It is for the tidings,* the heavy tidings, that we shall hear shortly; the *tidings come* (the judgments come which we hear the tidings of), they come apace, and then you will all sigh; nay, that will not serve. *every heart shall melt* and *every spirit fail;* your courage will all be gone and you will have no animating considerations to support yourselves with. And, when *heart* and *spirit* fail, it will follow of course that *all hands will be feeble* and unable to fight, and all *knees will* be *weak as water* and unable to flee or to stand their ground." Those who have God for them when flesh and heart fail have him to be *the strength of their heart;* but those who have God against them have no cordial for a fainting spirit, but are as Belshazzar when *his thoughts troubled him,* Dan. v. 6. But some people are worse frightened than hurt; may not the case be so here and the event prove better than likely? No: *Behold it cometh,* and *shall be brought to pass.* It is not a bugbear that they are frightened with, but *according to the fear so is the wrath,* and more grievous than is feared.

8 Again the word of the LORD came unto me, saying, 9 Son of man, prophesy, and say, Thus saith the LORD; Say, a sword, a sword is sharpened, and also furbished: 10 It is sharpened to make a sore slaughter; it is furbished that it may glitter: should we then make mirth? it contemneth the rod of my son, *as* every tree. 11 And he hath given it to be furbished, that it may be handled: this sword is sharpened, and it is furbished, to give it into the hand of the slayer. 12 Cry and howl, son of man: for it shall be upon my people, it *shall be* upon all the princes of Israel: terrors by reason of the sword shall be upon my people: smite therefore upon *thy* thigh. 13 Because *it is* a trial, and what if *the sword* contemn even the rod? it shall be no *more,* saith the Lord GOD. 14 Thou therefore, son of man, prophesy, and smite *thine* hands together, and let

the sword be doubled the third time, the sword of the slain: it *is* the sword of the great *men that are* slain, which entereth into their privy chambers. 15 I have set the point of the sword against all their gates, that *their* heart may faint, and *their* ruins be multiplied: ah! *it is* made bright, *it is* wrapped up for the slaughter. 16 Go thee one way or other, *either* on the right hand, *or* on the left, whithersoever thy face *is* set. 17 I will also smite mine hands together, and I will cause my fury to rest: I the LORD have said *it.*

Here is another prophecy of the sword, which is delivered in a very affecting manner; the expressions here used are somewhat intricate, and perplex interpreters. The sword was unsheathed in the foregoing verses; here it is fitted up to do execution, which the prophet is commanded to lament. Observe,

I. How the sword is here described. 1. It is *sharpened,* that it may cut and wound, and make *a sore slaughter.* The wrath of God will put an edge upon it; and, whatever instruments God shall please to make use of in executing his judgments, he will fill them with strength, courage, and fury, according to the service they are employed in. Out of the mouth of Christ goes a *sharp sword,* Rev. xix. 15. 2. It is *furbished,* that *it may glitter,* to the terror of those against whom it is drawn. It shall be a kind of *flaming sword.* If it have rusted in the scabbard for want of use, it shall be rubbed and brightened; for though the glory of God's justice may seem to have been eclipsed for a while, during the day of his patience and the delay of his judgments, yet it will shine out again and be made to glitter. 3. It is a victorious sword, nothing shall stand before it (*v.* 10): *It contemneth the rod of my son as every tree.* Israel,* said God once, *is my son, my first-born.* The government of that people was called a *rod,* a *strong rod;* we read (*ch.* xix. 11) of the *strong rods* they had *for sceptres.* But when the sword of God's justice is drawn it *contemns this rod,* makes nothing of it; though it be a *strong rod,* and the *rod of his son,* it is no more than *any other tree.* When God's professing people have revolted from him, and are in rebellion against him, his sword *despises* them. What are they to him more than another people? The marginal reading gives another notion of this sword: *It is the rod of my son;* and we know of whom God has said (Ps. ii. 7), *Thou art my Son, this day have I begotten thee,* and (*v.* 9) *Thou shalt break them with a rod of iron.* This sword is *that rod of iron* which *contemns every tree* and will bear it down. Or, This sword is *the rod of my son,* a correcting rod, for the chastening of the transgression of God's people (2 Sam. vii. 14), not to cut them off from being a people. It is a sword to others, a rod to my son.

II. How the sword is here put into the hand of the executioners: It is *the rod of my Son*, and he has *given it that it may be handled* (v. 11), that it may be made use of for the end for which it was drawn. *It is given into the hand*, not of the fencer to be played with, but *of the slayer* to do execution with. The sword of war my Son makes use of as a sword of justice, and to him *all judgment is committed*. It is *made bright* (v. 15), *it is wrapped up*, that it may be kept safe, and clean, and sharp *for the slaughter*, not as Goliath's sword was wrapped *up in a cloth* only for a memorial," 1 Sam. xxi. 9.

III. How the sword is directed, and against whom it is sent (v. 12): *It shall be upon my people ;* they shall fall by this sword. It is repeated again, as that which is scarcely credible, that *the sword* of the heathen shall be upon God's own people; nay, it shall be *upon all the princes of Israel ;* their dignity and power as princes shall be no more their security than their profession of religion as princes of Israel. But, if the sword be at any time upon God's people, have they not comfort within sufficient to arm them against everything in it that is frightful? Yes, they have, while they conduct themselves as becomes his people; but these had not done so, and therefore *terrors, by reason of the sword*, shall be upon those that call themselves *my people*. Note, While good men are quiet, not only from evil, but from the fear of it, wicked men are disturbed not only with the sword, but with the terrors of it, arising from a consciousness of their own guilt. This sword is directed particularly *against the great men*, for they had been the greatest sinners among them; they had *altogether broken the yoke and burst the bonds* (Jer. v. 5), and therefore with them in a special manner God's controversy is, who had been the ringleaders in sin. The *sword of the slain* is *the sword of the great men that are slain*, v. 14. Though they have furnished themselves with places of retirement, places of concealment, where they flatter themselves with hopes that they shall be safe, they will find that the sword will *enter into their privy chambers*, and find them out there, as the *frogs*, when they were one of Egypt's plagues, found admission into the *chambers of their kings*. The sword, the *point of this sword*, is directed *against their gates*, against all *their gates* (v. 15), against all those things with which they thought to keep it out and fortify themselves against it. Note, The strongest gates, though they be *gates of brass*, ever so well barred, ever so well guarded, are no fence against the point of the sword of God's judgments. But when that is pointed against sinners, 1. They are ready to fear the worst; *their hearts faint*, so that they are

not able to make any resistance. 2. The worst comes; whatever resistance they make, it is to no purpose, but they are ruined, and *their ruins are multiplied*. But what need have we to observe the particular directions of this sword when it has a general commission, is sent with a running warrant? (v. 16): " *Go thee, one way or other*, which way thou wilt, turn *to the right hand or to the left*, thou wilt find those that are obnoxious, for there are none free from guilt; and thou hast authority against them, for there are none exempt from punishment; and therefore, *whithersoever thy face is set*, that way do thou proceed, and, like Jonathan's sword, *from the blood of the slain, from the fat of the mighty, thou shalt never return empty*," 2 Sam. i. 22. Note, So full is the world of wicked people that, which way soever God's judgments go forth, they will find work, will find matter to work upon. That fire will never go out on this earth for want of fuel. And such various methods God has of meeting with sinners that the sword of his justice is still as it was at first when it flamed in the hand of the cherubim: it *turns every way*, Gen. iii. 24.

IV. What is the nature of this sword, and what are the intentions and limitations of it as to the people of God, v. 13. It is a correction; it is designed to be so; the sword to others is a rod to them. This is a comfortable word which comes in in the midst of these terrible ones, though it be expressed somewhat obscurely. 1. The people of God begin to be afraid that *the sword will contemn even the rod*, that the sword will go on with such fury that it will despise its commission to be a rod only, will forget its bounds and become a sword indeed, even to God's own people. They fear lest the Chaldeans' sword, which is the rod of God's anger, contemn its being called a rod, and become as the *axe* that *boasts itself against him that heweth therewith* or *the staff that lifts up itself as if it were no wood*, Isa. x. 15. Or, " *What if the sword contemn even the rod ?* that is, what if this sword make the former rods, as that of Sennacherib, to be contemned as nothing to this? What if this should prove not a correcting rod, but a destroying sword, to make a full end of our church and nation ?" This is that which the thinking, but timorous, few are apprehensive of. Note, When threatening judgments are abroad it is good to suppose the worst that may be the consequences of them, that we may provide accordingly. *What if the sword contemn the tribe or sceptre ?* namely, that of Judah and the house of David (so some think *Shebet* here signifies); what if it should aim at the ruin of our government? If it do, *the Lord is righteous* and *will be gracious* notwithstanding. But, 2. These fears are silenced with an assurance that it is not so; the sword shall not forget itself, nor the errand on which it is sent: *It is a trial*, and it is *no more than a trial.* He that sends it makes what use of it, and sets what bounds to it, he pleases. Here shall its proud waves be stayed. Note, It is matter of comfort to the people of God, when his judgments are abroad, and they are ready to tremble for fear of them, that, whatever they are to others, to them they are but trials ; and, *when they are tried, they shall come forth as gold,* and the proving of their faith shall be the improving of it.

V. Here the prophet and the people must show themselves affected with these judgments threatened. 1. The prophet must be very serious in denouncing these judgments. He must say, *A sword ! a sword ! v.* 9. Let him not study for fine words, and a variety of quaint expressions; when the town is on fire people do not so give notice of it, but cry, with a frightful doleful voice, *Fire ! fire !* So must the prophet cry, *A sword ! a sword !* and (*v.* 14), *Let the sword be doubled* the *third time* in thy preaching. God speaks once, yea, twice, yea, thrice; it were well if men, after all, would perceive and regard it. It shall be *doubled the third time* in God's providence ; for it was Nebuchadnezzar's third descent upon Jerusalem that *made a full end* of it. Ruin comes gradually, but at last comes effectually, upon a provoking people. Yet this is not all : the prophet is not only as a herald at arms to proclaim war, and to cry, *A sword ! a sword !* once and again, and a third time, but, as a person nearly concerned, he must *cry and howl* (*v.* 12), must sadly lament the desolations that the sword would make, as one that did himself not only sympathize with the sufferers, but feel from the sufferings. Again (*v.* 14), *Prophesy, and smite thy hands together,* wring *thy hands,* as lamenting the desolation, or clap thy hands, as by thy prophecy instigating and encouraging those that were to be the instruments of it, or as one standing amazed at the suddenness and severity of the judgment. The prophet must *smite his hands together ;* for (says God) *I will also smite my hands together, v.* 17. God is in earnest in pronouncing this sentence upon them, and therefore the prophet must show himself in earnest in publishing it. God's *smiting his hands together,* as well as the prophet's smiting, is in token of a holy indignation at their wickedness, which was really very astonishing. When Balak's anger was kindled against Balaam he *smote his hands together,* Num. xxiv. 10. Note, God and his ministers are justly angry at those who might be saved and yet will be ruined. Some make it an expression of triumph and exultation, agreeing with that (Isa. i. 24)), *Ah ! I will ease me of my adversaries ;* and that (Prov. i. 26), *I also will laugh at their calamity.* And so it follows here, *I will cause my fury to rest,* not only it shall be perfected, but it shall be pleased. And observe with what solemnity, with what authority, this sentence is ratified : "*I the Lord have said it,* who can and will make good

what I have said. I have said it, and will never unsay it. I have said it, and who can gainsay it ?" 2. The people must be very serious in the prospect of these judgments. An intimation of this comes in in a parenthesis (*v.* 10) : *Should we then make mirth ?* Seeing God has drawn the sword, and the prophet sighs and cries, *Should we then make mirth ?* The prophet seems to give this as a reason why he sighs ; as Neh. ii. 3, *Why should not my countenance be sad,* when Jerusalem lies waste? Note, Before we allow ourselves to be merry, we ought to consider whether we should be merry or no. Should we make mirth, we who are sentenced to the sword, who lie under the wrath and curse of God ? Shall we *make mirth as other people,* who have *gone a whoring from our God ?* Hos. ix. 1. Should we now make mirth, when the hand of God has gone out against us, when God's judgments are abroad in the land and he by them *calls to weeping and mourning ?* Isa. xxii. 11, 13. Shall we now make mirth as the king and Haman, when the church is in perplexity (Esther iii. 15), when we should be *grieving for the affliction of Joseph ?* Amos vi. 6.

18 The word of the LORD came unto me again, saying, 19 Also, thou son of man, appoint thee two ways, that the sword of the king of Babylon may come : both twain shall come forth out of one land : and choose thou a place, choose *it* at the head of the way to the city. 20 Appoint a way, that the sword may come to Rabbath of the Ammonites, and to Judah in Jerusalem the defenced. 21 For the king of Babylon stood at the parting of the way, at the head of the two ways, to use divination : he made *his* arrows bright, he consulted with images, he looked in the liver. 22 At his right hand was the divination for Jerusalem, to appoint captains, to open the mouth in the slaughter, to lift up the voice with shouting, to appoint *battering* rams against the gates, to cast a mount, *and* to build a fort. 23 And it shall be unto them as a false divination in their sight, to them that have sworn oaths : but he will call to remembrance the iniquity, that they may be taken. 24 Therefore thus saith the Lord GOD ; Because ye have made your iniquity to be remembered, in that your transgressions are discovered, so that in all your doings your sins do

appear; because, *I say,* that ye are come to remembrance, ye shall be taken with the hand. 25 And thou, profane wicked prince of Israel, whose day is come, when iniquity *shall have* an end, 26 Thus saith the Lord GOD; Remove the diadem, and take off the crown: this *shall* not *be* the same: exalt *him that is* low, and abase *him that is* high. 27 I will overturn, overturn, overturn, it: and it shall be no *more,* until he come whose right it is; and I will give it *him.*

The prophet, in the verses before, had shown them the sword coming; he here shows them that sword coming against them, that they might not flatter themselves that by some means or other it should be diverted a contrary way.

I. He must see and show the Chaldean army coming against Jerusalem and determined by a supreme power so to do. The prophet must *appoint him two ways,* that is, he must upon a paper draw out two roads (v. 19), as sometimes is done in maps; and he must bring the king of Babylon's army to the place where the roads part, for there they will make a stand. They both *come out of the same land;* but when they come to the place where one road leads to Rabbath, the head city of the Ammonites, and the other to Jerusalem, he makes a pause; for, though he is resolved to be the ruin of both, yet he is not determined which to attack first; here his politics and his politicians leave him at a loss. The sword must go either to Rabbath or *to Judah in Jerusalem.* Many of the inhabitants of Judah had now taken shelter in Jerusalem, and all the interests of the country were bound up in the safety of the city, and therefore it is called *Judah in Jerusalem the defenced;* so strongly fortified was it, both by nature and art, that it was thought impregnable, Lam. iv. 12. The prophet must describe this dilemma that the king of Babylon is at (v. 21); for *the king of Babylon stood* (that is, he shall stand considering what course to take) *at the head of the two ways.* Though he was a prince of great foresight and great resolution, yet, it seems, he knew neither his own interest nor his own mind. Let not the wise man then glory in his wisdom nor the mighty man in his arbitrary power, for even those that may do what they will seldom know what to do for the best. Now observe, 1. The method he took to come to a resolution; he *used divination,* applied to a higher and invisible power, perhaps to the determination of Providence by a lot, in order to which he *made his arrows bright,* that were to be drawn for the lots, in honour of the solemnity. Perhaps *Jerusalem* was written on one arrow and *Rabbath* on the other, and that which

was first drawn out of the quiver he determined to attack first. Or he applied to the direction of some pretended oracle: he *consulted with images* or *teraphim,* expecting to receive audible answers from them. Or to the observations which the augurs made upon the entrails of the sacrifices: *he looked in the liver,* whether the position of that portended good or ill luck. Note, It is a mortification to the pride of the wise men of the earth that in difficult cases they have been glad to make their court to heaven for direction; as it is an instance of their folly that they have taken such ridiculous ways of doing it, when in cases proper for an appeal to Providence it is sufficient that *the lot be cast into the lap,* with that prayer, *Give a perfect lot,* and a firm belief that the *disposal thereof* is not fortuitous, but *of the Lord,* Prov. xvi. 33. 2. The resolution he was hereby brought to. Even by these sinful practices God served his own purposes and directed him to go to Jerusalem, *v.* 22. *The divination for Jerusalem* happened to be *at his right hand,* which, according to the rules of divination, determined him *that way.* Note, What services God designs men for he will be sure in his providence to lead them to, though perhaps they themselves are not aware what guidance they are under. Well, Jerusalem being the mark set up, the campaign is presently opened with the siege of that important place. *Captains* are appointed for the command of the forces to be employed in the siege, who must *open the mouth in the slaughter,* must give directions to the soldiers what to do and make speeches to animate them. Orders are given to provide every thing necessary for carrying on the siege with vigour; *battering rams* must be prepared and *forts built.* O what pains, what cost, are men at to destroy one another!

II. He must show both the people and the prince that they bring this destruction upon themselves by their own sin.

1. The people do so, *v.* 23, 24. They slight the notices that are given them of the judgment coming. Ezekiel's prophecy is to them a *false divination;* they are not moved or awakened to repentance by it. When they hear that Nebuchadnezzar by his divinations is directed to Jerusalem, and assured of success in that enterprise, they laugh at it and continue *secure,* calling it a *false divination;* because *they have sworn oaths,* that is, they have joined in a solemn league with the Egyptians, and they depend upon the promise they have made them to *raise the siege,* or upon the assurances which the false prophets have given them that it shall be raised. Or it may refer to the oaths of allegiance they had sworn to the king of Babylon, but had violated, for which treachery of theirs God had given them up to a judicial blindness, so that the fairest warnings given them were slighted by them as false divinations. Note, It is not strange if those who make a

jest of the most sacred oaths can make a jest likewise of the most sacred oracles; for where will a profane mind stop? But shall their unbelief invalidate the counsel of God? Are they safe because they are secure? By no means; nay, the contempt they put upon divine warnings is a sin that brings to remembrance their other sins, and they may thank themselves if they be now remembered against them. (1.) Their present wickedness is discovered. Now that God is contending with them so perverse and obstinate are they that whatever they offer in their own defence does but add to their offence; they never conducted themselves so ill as they did now that they had the loudest call given them to repent and reform: " *So that in all your doings your sins do appear.* Turn yourselves which way you will, you show a black side." This is too true of every one of us; for not only there is *none that lives and sins not,* but *there is not a just man upon earth that does good and sins not.* Our best services have such allays of weakness, and folly, and imperfection, and so much *evil* is *present with us* even when we *would do good,* that we may say, with sorrow and shame, *In all our doings,* and in all our sayings too, *our sins do appear,* and witness against us, so that if we were under the law we were undone. (2.) This brings to mind their former wickedness: " *You have made your iniquity to be remembered,* not by yourselves that it might be repented of, but by the justice of God that it might be reckoned for. Your own sins make the sins of your fathers to be remembered against you, which otherwise you should never have smarted for." Note, God remembers former iniquities against those only who by the present discoveries of their wickedness show that they do not repent of them (3.) That they may suffer for all together, they are turned over to the destroyer, that they may be taken (*v.* 23): " *You shall be taken with the hand* that God had appointed to seize you and to hold you and out of which you cannot escape." Men are said to be *God's hand* when they are made use of as the ministers of his justice, Ps. xvii. 14. Note, Those who will not be taken with the word of God's grace shall at last be taken by the hand of his wrath.

2. The prince likewise brings his ruin upon himself. Zedekiah is the *prince of Israel,* to whom the prophet here, in God's name, addresses himself; and, if he had not spoken in God's name, he would not have spoken so boldly, so bluntly; for *is it fit to say to a king, Thou art wicked?* (1.) He gives him his character, *v.* 25. Thou profane and *wicked prince of Israel!* He was not so bad as some of his predecessors, and yet bad enough to merit his character. He was himself profane, lost to every thing that is virtuous and sacred. And he was wicked, as he promoted sin among his people; he sinned, and *made Israel to sin.* Note, Pro-

faneness and wickedness are bad in any, but worst of all in a prince, a prince of Israel, who as an Israelite should know better himself, and as a prince should set a better example and have a better influence on those about him. (2.) He reads him his doom. His iniquity *has an end;* the measure of it is full, and therefore *his day has come,* the day of his punishment, the day of divine vengeance. Note, Though those who are wicked and profane may flourish awhile, yet *their day will come* to fall. The sentence here passed is, [1.] That Zedekiah shall be deposed. He has forfeited his crown, and he shall no longer wear it; he has by his profaneness profaned his crown, and it shall be *cast to the ground* (*v.* 26): *Remove the diadem.* Crowns and diadems are loseable things; it is only in the other world that there is a crown of glory that fades not away, a *kingdom that cannot be moved.* The Chaldee paraphrase expounds it thus: *Take away the diadem from Seraiah the chief priest, and I will take away the crown from Zedekiah the king; neither this nor that shall abide in his place, but shall be removed.* This shall not be the same, not the same that he has been; *this not this* (so the word is); profane and wicked perhaps he is as he has been, but not prince of Israel as he has been. Note, Men lose their dignity by their iniquity. Their profaneness and wickedness remove their diadem, and take off their crown, and make them the reverse of what they were. [2.] That great confusion and disorder in the state shall follow hereupon. Every thing shall be turned upside down. The conqueror shall take a pride in *exalting him that is low* and *abasing him that is high,* preferring some and degrading others, at his pleasure, without any regard either to right or merit. [3.] Attempts to re-establish the government shall be blasted and come to nothing, Gedaliah's particularly, and Ishmael's who was *of the seed-royal* (to which the Chaldee paraphrase refers this); neither of them shall be able to make any thing of it. *I will overturn, overturn, overturn,* first one project and then another; for who can build up what God will throw down? [4.] This monarchy shall never be restored till it is fixed for perpetuity in the hands of the Messiah. There *shall be no more* kings of the house of David after Zedekiah, till Christ comes, *whose right the kingdom is,* who is that seed of David in whom the promise was to have its full accomplishment, and *I will give it to him.* He shall have *the throne of his father David,* Luke i. 32. Immediately before the coming of Christ there was a long eclipse of the royal dignity, as there was also a failing of the spirit of prophecy, that his shining forth in the fulness of time both as king and prophet might appear the more illustrious. Note, Christ has an incontestable title to the dominion and sovereignty both in the church and in the world; the kingdom is his right. And, having the right, he shall in due time have the possession: *I will give it to him;* and there shall be a general overturning of all rather than he shall come short of his right, and a certain overturning of all the opposition that stands in his way to make room for him, Dan. ii. 45; 1 Cor. xv. 25. This is mentioned here for the comfort of those who feared that the promise made in David would fail for evermore. "No," says God, "that promise is sure, for the Messiah's kingdom shall last for ever."

28 And thou, son of man, prophesy and say, Thus saith the Lord God concerning the Ammonites, and concerning their reproach; even say thou, The sword, the sword *is* drawn: for the slaughter *it is* furbished, to consume because of the glittering: 29 Whiles they see vanity unto thee, whiles they divine a lie unto thee, to bring thee upon the necks of *them that are* slain, of the wicked, whose day is come, when their iniquity *shall have* an end. 30 Shall I cause *it* to return into his sheath? I will judge thee in the place where thou wast created, in the land of thy nativity. 31 And I will pour out mine indignation upon thee, I will blow against thee in the fire of my wrath, and deliver thee into the hand of brutish men, *and* skilful to destroy. 32 Thou shalt be for fuel to the fire; thy blood shall be in the midst of the land; thou shalt be no *more* remembered: for I the Lord have spoken *it.*

The prediction of the destruction of the Ammonites, which was effected by Nebuchadnezzar about five years after the destruction of Jerusalem, seems to come in here upon occasion of the king of Babylon's diverting his design against Rabbath, when he turned it upon Jerusalem. Upon this the Ammonites grew very insolent, and triumphed over Jerusalem; but the prophet must let them know that forbearance is no acquittance; the reprieve is not a pardon; their day also is at hand; their turn comes next, and it will be but a poor satisfaction to them that they are to be devoured last, to be last executed.

I. The sin of the Ammonites is here intimated; it is *their reproach, v.* 28. 1. The reproach they put upon themselves when they hearkened to their false prophets (for such it seems there were among them as well as among the Jews), who pretended to foretel their perpetual safety in the midst of the desolations that were made of the countries round about them: "They *see vanity unto*

thee *and divine a lie, v.* 29. They flatter thee with promises of peace, and thou art such a fool as to suffer thyself to be imposed upon by them and to encourage them therein by giving credit to them." Note, Those that feed themselves with a self-conceit in the day of their prosperity prepare matter for a self-reproach in the day of their calamity. 2. The reproach they put upon the Israel of God, when they triumphed in their afflictions, and thereby added affliction to them, which was very barbarous and inhuman. Their divines, by puffing them up with a conceit that they were a better people than Israel, being spared when they were cut off, and with a confidence that their prosperity should always continue, made them so very haughty and insolent that they did even *tread on the necks of the Israelites that were slain, slain by the wicked Chaldeans,* who had commission to execute God's judgments upon them when their *iniquity had an end,* that is, when the measure of it was full. We shall meet with this again, *ch.* xxv. 3, &c. Note, Those are ripening apace for misery who trample upon the people of God in their distress, whereas they ought to tremble when *judgment begins at the house of God.*

II. The utter destruction of the Ammonites is threatened. For the reproach cast on the church by her neighbours will be returned into their own bosom, Ps. lxxix. 12. Let us see how terrible the threatening is and the destruction will be. 1. It shall come *from the wrath of God,* who resents the indignities and injuries done to his people as done to himself (v. 31): *I will pour out my indignation* as a shower of fire and brimstone *upon thee.* The least drop of divine *indignation and wrath* will create *tribulation and anguish* enough to the *soul of man that does evil;* what then would a full stream of that indignation and wrath do? "*I will blow against thee in the fire of my wrath;* that is, I will blow up the fire of my wrath against thee; it shall burn with the utmost vehemence." *Thou shalt be for fuel to this fire, v.* 32. Note, Wicked men make themselves fuel to the fire of God's wrath; they are consumed by it, and it is inflamed by them. 2. It shall be effected by the sword of war; to them he must cry, as before to Israel, because they had triumphed in Israel's overthrow: *The sword, the sword is drawn* (v. 28, compare v. 9, 10); it is drawn *to consume because of the glittering,* because it is brandished and glitters, and is fit to be made use of. God's executions will answer his preparations. This sword, when it is drawn, *shall not return into its sheath* (v. 30) till it has done the work for which it was drawn. When the sword is drawn it does not return till *God causes it to return,* and *he is in one mind and who can turn him?* Who can change his purpose? 3. The persons employed in it are *brutish men, and skilful to destroy.* Men of such a bad character as this, who have the wit *of* men to do the work of wild beasts—human reason, which makes them skilful, but no human compassion, which makes them skilful only to destroy—though they are the scandal of mankind, yet sometimes are made use of to serve God's purposes. God *delivers the Ammonites into the hands of such,* and justly, for they themselves were brutish, and delighted in the destruction of God's Israel. We have reason to pray, as Paul desired to be prayed for, that we may be *delivered from wicked and unreasonable men* (2 Thess. iii. 2), men that seem made for doing mischief. 4. The place where they should thus be reckoned with : "*I will judge thee where thou wast created,* where thou wast first formed into a people, and where thou hast been settled ever since, and therefore where thou seemest to have taken root ; *the land of thy nativity* shall be the land of thy destruction." Note, God can bring ruin upon us even where we are most secure, and turn us out of that land which we thought we had a title to not to be disputed and a possession of not to be disturbed. *Thy blood shall be shed* not only in thy borders, but *in the midst of thy land. Lastly,* It shall be an irreparable ruin : "Though thou mayest think to recover thyself, it is in vain to think of it ; thou *shalt be no more remembered* with any respect, Ps. ix. 6. Justly is their name blotted out who would have Israel's name for ever lost.

CHAP. XXII.

Here are three separate messages which God entrusts the prophet to deliver concerning Judah and Jerusalem, and all to the same purport, to show them their sins and the judgments that were coming upon them for those sins. I. Here is a catalogue of their sins, by which they had exposed themselves to shame and for which God would bring them to ruin, ver. 1—16. II. They are here compared to dross, and are condemned as dross to the fire, ver. 17—22. III. All orders and degrees of men among them are here found guilty of the neglect of the duty of their place and of having contributed to the national guilt, which therefore, since none appeared as intercessors, they must all expect to share in the punishment of, ver. 23—31.

MOREOVER the word of the Lord came unto me, saying, 2 Now, thou son of man, wilt thou judge, wilt thou judge the bloody city? yea, thou shalt show her all her abominations. 3 Then say thou, Thus saith the Lord God ; The city sheddeth blood in the midst of it, that her time may come, and maketh idols against herself to defile herself. 4 Thou art become guilty in thy blood that thou hast shed ; and hast defiled thyself in thine idols which thou hast made : and thou hast caused thy days to draw near, and art come *even* unto thy years : therefore have I made thee a reproach unto the heathen, and a mocking to all countries. 5 *Those that be* near, and *those that be* far from thee, shall mock thee, *which*

art infamous *and* much vexed. 6 Behold, the princes of Israel, every one were in thee to their power to shed blood. 7 In thee have they set light by father and mother : in the midst of thee have they dealt by oppression with the stranger : in thee have they vexed the fatherless and the widow. 8 Thou hast despised mine holy things, and hast profaned my sabbaths. 9 In thee are men that carry tales to shed blood : and in thee they eat upon the mountains : in the midst of thee they commit lewdness. 10 In thee have they discovered their fathers' nakedness : in thee have they humbled her that was set apart for pollution. 11 And one hath committed abomination with his neighbour's wife ; and another hath lewdly defiled his daughter in law ; and another in thee hath humbled his sister, his father's daughter. 12 In thee have they taken gifts to shed blood ; thou hast taken usury and increase, and thou hast greedily gained of thy neighbours by extortion, and hast forgotten me, saith the Lord God. 13 Behold, therefore I have smitten mine hand at thy dishonest gain which thou hast made, and at thy blood which hath been in the midst of thee. 14 Can thine heart endure, or can thine hands be strong, in the days that I shall deal with thee? I the Lord have spoken *it,* and will do *it.* 15 And I will scatter thee among the heathen, and disperse thee in the countries, and will consume thy filthiness out of thee. 16 And thou shalt take thine inheritance in thyself in the sight of the heathen, and thou shalt know that I *am* the Lord.

In these verses the prophet by a commission from Heaven sits as a judge upon the bench, and Jerusalem is made to hold up her hand as a prisoner at the bar ; and, if prophets were set over other nations, much more over God's nation, Jer. i. 10. This prophet is authorized to *judge the bloody city,* the *city of bloods.* Jerusalem is so called, not only because she had been guilty of the particular sin of blood-shed, but because her crimes in general were bloody crimes (*ch.* vii. 23), such as polluted her in her blood, and for which she deserved to have blood given her to drink. Now the business of a judge with a malefactor is to convict him of his crimes, and then to pass sentence upon him for them. These two things Ezekiel is to do here.

I. He is to find Jerusalem guilty of many heinous crimes here enumerated in a long bill of indictment, and it is *billa vera—a true bill;* so he writes upon it whose judgment we are sure is according to truth. He must *show her all her abominations* (*v.* 2), that God may be justified in all the desolations brought upon her. Let us take a view of all the particular sins which Jerusalem here stands charged with; and they are all exceedingly sinful.

1. Murder: *The city sheds blood,* not only in the suburbs, where the strangers dwell, but *in the midst of it,* where, one would think, the magistrates would, if any where, be vigilant. Even there people were murdered either in duels or by secret assassinations and poisonings, or in the courts of justice under colour of law, and there was no care taken to discover and punish the murderers according to the law (Gen. ix. 6), no, nor so much as the ceremony used to expiate an uncertain murder (Deut. xxi. 1), and so the guilt and pollution remains upon the city. Thus *thou hast become guilty in thy blood that thou hast shed, v.* 4. This crime is insisted most upon, for it was Jerusalem's measure-filling sin more than any; it is said to be that *which the Lord would not pardon,* 2 Kings xxiv. 4. (1.) The *princes of Israel,* who should have been the protectors of injured innocence, *every one were to their power to shed blood, v.* 6. They thirsted for it, and delighted in it, and whoever came within their power were sure to feel it; whoever lay at their mercy were sure to find none. (2.) There were those who *carried tales to shed blood, v.* 9. They told lies of men to the princes, to whom they knew it would be pleasing, to incense them against them; or they betrayed what passed in private conversation, to make mischief among neighbours, and set them together by the ears, to bite, and devour, and worry one another, even to death. Note, Those who, by giving invidious characters and telling ill-natured stories of their neighbours, sow discord among brethren, will be accountable for all the mischief that follows upon it; as he that kindles a fire will be accountable for all the hurt it does. (3.) There were those who *took gifts to shed blood* (*v.* 12), who would be hired with money to swear a man out of his life, or, if they were upon a jury, would be bribed to find an innocent man guilty. When so much barbarous bloody work of this kind was done in Jerusalem we may well conclude, [1.] That men's consciences had become wretchedly profligate and seared and their hearts hardened; for those would stick at no wickedness who would not stick at this. [2.] That abundance of quiet, harmless, good people were made away with, whereby, as the guilt

of the city was increased, so the number of those that should have stood in the gap to turn away the wrath of God was diminished.

2. Idolatry: *She makes idols against herself to destroy herself, v.* 3. And again (*v.* 4), *Thou hast defiled thyself in thy idols which thou hast made.* Note, Those who make idols for themselves will be found to have made them against themselves, for idolaters put a cheat upon themselves and prepare destruction for themselves; besides that thereby they pollute themselves, they render themselves odious in the eyes of the just and jealous God, and even *their mind and conscience are defiled,* so that to them *nothing is pure.* Those who did not make idols themselves were yet found guilty of *eating upon the mountains,* or high places (*v.* 9), in honour of the idols and in communion with idolaters.

3. Disobedience to parents (*v.* 7): *In thee have* the children *set light by their father and mother,* mocked them, cursed them, and despised to obey them, which was a sign of a more than ordinary corruption of nature as well as manners, and a disposition to all manner of disorder, Isa. iii. 5. Those that set light by their parents are in the highway to all wickedness. God had made many wholesome laws for the support of the paternal authority, but no care was taken to put them in execution; nay, the Pharisees in their day taught children, under pretence of respect to the Corban, to set light by their parents and refuse to maintain them, Matt. xv. 5.

4. Oppression and extortion. To enrich themselves they wronged the poor (*v.* 7): *They dealt by oppression* and *deceit with the stranger,* taking advantage of his necessities, and his ignorance of the laws and customs of the country. In Jerusalem, that should have been a sanctuary to the oppressed, *they vexed the fatherless and widows* by unreasonable demands and inquisitions, or troublesome law-suits, in which might prevails against right. " *Thou hast taken usury and increase* (*v.* 12); not only there are those in thee that do it, but thou hast done it." It was an act of the city or community; the public money, which should have been employed in public charity, was put out to usury, with extortion. *Thou hast greedily gained of thy neighbours* by *violence* and *wrong.* For neighbours to gain by one another in a way of fair trading is well, but those who are *greedy of gain* will not be held within the rules of equity.

5. Profanation of the sabbath and other holy things. This commonly goes along with the other sins for which they here stand indicted (*v.* 8): *Thou hast despised my holy things,* holy oracles, holy ordinances. The rites which God appointed were thought too plain, too ordinary; they despised them, and therefore were fond of the customs of the

heathen. Note, Immorality and dishonesty are commonly attended with a contempt of religion and the worship of God. *Thou hast profaned my sabbaths.* There was not in Jerusalem that face of sabbath-sanctification that one would have expected in the *holy city.* Sabbath-breaking is an iniquity that is an inlet to all iniquity. Many have owned it to contribute as much to their ruin as any thing.

6. Uncleanness and all manner of seventh-commandment sins, fruits of those vile affections to which God in a way of righteous judgment gives men up, to punish them for their idolatry and profanation of holy things. Jerusalem had been famous for its purity, but now *in the midst of thee they commit lewdness (v. 9);* lewdness goes bare-faced, though in the most scandalous instances, as that of a man's having his father's wife, which is the *discovery of the father's nakedness (v.* 10) and is a sin not *to be named among Christians* without the utmost detestation (1 Cor. v. 1), and was made a capital crime by the law of Moses, Lev. xx. 11. The time *to refrain from embracing* has not been observed (Eccles. iii. 6), for *they have humbled her that was set apart for her pollution.* They made nothing of committing lewdness with a *neighbour's wife,* with a *daughter-in-law,* or a sister, *v.* 11. And *shall not God visit for these things?*

7. Unmindfulness of God was at the bottom of all this wickedness *(v.* 12): " *Thou hast forgotten me,* else thou wouldst not have done thus." Note, Sinners do that which provokes God because they forget him; they forget their descent from him, dependence on him, and obligations to him; they forget how valuable his favour is, which they make themselves unfit for, and how formidable his wrath, which they make themselves obnoxious to. Those that *pervert their ways forget the Lord their God,* Jer. iii. 21.

II. He is to pass sentence upon Jerusalem for these crimes.

1. Let her know that she has filled up the measure of her iniquity, and that her sins are such as forbid delays and call for speedy vengeance. She has made *her time to come (v.* 3), *her days to draw near;* and she has *come to her years* of maturity for punishment *(v.* 4), as an heir that has *come to age* and is ready for his inheritance. God would have borne longer with them, but they had arrived at such a pitch of impudence in sin that God could not in honour give them a further day. Note, Abused patience will at last be weary of forbearing. And, when sinners (as Solomon speaks) grow *overmuch wicked,* they *die before their time* (Eccl. vii. 17) and shorten their reprieves.

2. Let her know that she has exposed herself, and therefore God has justly exposed her, to the contempt and scorn of all her neighbours *(v.* 4): *I have made thee a reproach to the heathen,* both *those who are near,* who are eye-witnesses of Jerusalem's apostasy and degeneracy, and *those afar off,* who, though at a distance, will think it worth taking notice of *(v.* 5); they shall all *mock thee.* While they were reproached by their neighbours for their adherence to God it was their honour, and they might be sure that God would roll away their reproach. But, now that they are laughed at for their revolt from God, they must lie down in their shame, and must say, *The Lord is righteous.* They make a mock at Jerusalem, both because her sins had been very *scandalous* (she is *infamous, polluted in name,* and has quite lost her credit), and because her punishment is very *grievous*—she is *much vexed* and frets without measure at her troubles. Note, Those who fret most at their troubles have commonly those about them who will be so much the more apt to make a jest of them.

3. Let her know that God is displeased, highly displeased, at her wickedness, and does and will witness against it *(v.* 13): *I have smitten my hand at thy dishonest gain.* God, both by his prophets and by his providence, revealed his wrath from heaven against their *ungodliness* and *unrighteousness,* the oppressions they were guilty of, though they got by them, and *their murders* (the *blood which has been in the midst of thee),* and all their other sins. Note, God has sufficiently discovered how angry he is at the wicked courses of his people; and, that they may not say that they have not had fair warning, he *smites his hand* against the sin before he *lays his hand* upon the sinner. And this is a good reason why we should despise dishonest gain, even the *gain of oppressions,* and *shake our hands from holding bribes,* because these are sins against which God *shakes his hands,* Isa. xxxiii. 15.

4. Let her know that, proud and secure as she is, she is no match for God's judgments, *v.* 14. (1.) She is assured that the destruction she has deserved will come: *I the Lord have spoken it, and will do it.* He that is true to his promises will be true to his threatenings too, for he is not a man that he should repent. (2.) It is supposed that she thinks herself able to contend with God, and to stand a siege against his judgments. She bade defiance to the day of the Lord, Isa. v. 19. But, (3.) She is convinced of her utter inability to make her part good with him: " *Can thy heart endure, or can thy hand be strong, in the days that I shall deal with thee?* Thou thinkest thou hast to do only with men like thyself, but shalt be made to know that thou fallest into the hands of a living God." Observe here, [1.] There is a day coming when God will *deal with sinners,* a day of visitation. He deals with some to bring them to repentance, and there is no resisting the force of convictions when he sets them on; he deals with others to bring them to ruin. He deals with sinners in this life, when he brings upon them his

sore judgments; but the days of eternity are especially the days in which God will deal with them, when the full vials of God's wrath will be poured out without mixture. [2.] The wrath of God against sinners, when he comes to deal with them, will be found both intolerable and irresistible. There is no heart stout enough to endure it; it is none of the infirmities which *the spirit of a man will sustain.* Damned sinners can neither forget nor despise their torments, nor have they any thing wherewith to support themselves under their torments. There are no hands strong enough either to ward off the strokes of God's wrath or to break the chains with which sinners are bound over to the day of wrath. *Who knows the power of God's anger?*

5. Let her know that, since she has walked in the way of the heathen, and learned their works, she shall have enough of them (*v.* 15): " *I will* not only send thee *among the heathen,* out of thy own land, but *I will scatter thee* among them and *disperse thee in the countries,* to be abused and insulted over by strangers." And since her *filthiness* and *filthy ones* continued in her, notwithstanding all the methods God had taken to *refine* her (she *would not be made clean,* Jer. xiii. 27), he will by his judgments *consume her filthiness out of her:* he will destroy those that are incurably bad and reform those that are inclined to be good.

6. Let her know that God has disowned her and cast her off. He had been her heritage and portion; but now (*v.* 16), " *Thou shalt take thy inheritance in thyself,* shift for thyself, make the best hand thou canst for thyself, for God will no longer undertake for thee." Note, Those that give up themselves to be ruled by their lusts will justly be given up to be portioned by them. Those that resolve to be their own masters, let them expect no other comfort and happiness than what their own hands can furnish them with, and a miserable portion it will prove. *Verily, I say unto you, They have their reward. Thou in thy life-time receivedst thy good things.* These are the same with this, " *Thou shalt take thy inheritance in thyself*', and then, when it is too late, shalt own *in the sight of the heathen that I am the Lord,* who alone am a portion sufficient for my people." Note, Those that have lost their interest in God will know how to value it.

17 And the word of the Lord came unto me, saying, 18 Son of man, the house of Israel is to me become dross: all they *are* brass, and tin, and iron, and lead, in the midst of the furnace; they are *even* the dross of silver. 19 Therefore thus saith the Lord God; Because ye are all become dross, behold, therefore I will gather you into the midst of Jerusalem. 20 *As*

they gather silver, and brass, and iron, and lead, and tin, into the midst of the furnace, to blow the fire upon it, to melt *it;* so will I gather *you* in mine anger and in my fury, and I will leave *you there,* and melt you. 21 Yea, I will gather you, and blow upon you in the fire of my wrath, and ye shall be melted in the midst thereof. 22 As silver is melted in the midst of the furnace, so shall ye be melted in the midst thereof; and ye shall know that I the Lord have poured out my fury upon you.

The same melancholy string is still harped upon, and various turns are given it, to make it affecting, that it may be influencing. The prophet must here show, or at least it is here shown him, that the whole house of Israel has become as dross and that as dross they shall be consumed. What David has said concerning the wicked ones of the world is here said concerning the wicked ones of the church, now that it is corrupt and degenerate (Ps. cxix. 119): *Thou puttest away all the wicked of the earth like dross.*

I. See here how the wretched degeneracy of the house of Israel is described. Tha state, in David's and Solomon's time, had been *a head of gold;* when the kingdoms were divided it was as the *arms of silver.* But now, 1. It has degenerated into baser metal, of no value in comparison with what it formerly was: *They are all brass, and tin, and iron, and lead,* which some make to signify divers sorts of sinners among them. Their being brass denotes the impudence of some in their wickedness; they are *brazen-faced,* and cannot blush; their *shoes* had been *iron and brass* (Deut. xxxiii. 25), but now their brow is so, Isa. xlviii. 4. Their being tin denotes the hypocritical profession of piety with which many of them cover their iniquity; they have a specious show, but no intrinsic worth. Their being iron denotes the cruel disposition of some, and their delight in war, according to the character of the *iron age.* Their being lead denotes their dulness, sottishness, and stupidity: though soft and pliable to evil, yet heavy and not movable to good. *How has the gold become dross! How has the most fine gold changed!* So is Jerusalem's degeneracy bewailed, Lam. iv. 1. Yet this is not the worst; these metals, though of less value, are yet of good use. But, 2. The *house of Israel has become dross to me.* So she is in God's account, whatever she is in her own and her neighbours' account. They were silver, but now they are *even the dross of silver;* the word signifies all the dirt, and rubbish, and worthless stuff, that are separated from the silver in the washing, melting, and refining of it.

883

Note, Sinners, and especially degenerate professors, are in God's account as dross, vile, and contemptible, and of no account, as the *evil figs* which *could not be eaten, they were so evil.* They are useless and fit for nothing; of no consistency with themselves and no service to man.

II. How the woeful destruction of this degenerate house of Israel is foretold. They are all gathered together in Jerusalem; thither people fled from all parts of the country as to a city of refuge, not only because it was a strong city, but because it was the holy city. Now God tells them that their flocking into Jerusalem, which they intended for their security, should be as the gathering of various sorts of metal into the furnace or crucible, to be melted down, and to have the dross separated from them. They are *in the midst of Jerusalem,* surrounded by the forces of the enemy; and, being thus enclosed, 1. The *fire of God's wrath* shall be kindled upon this furnace, and it shall be *blown,* to make it burn fiercely and strongly, *v.* 20, 21. God will *gather them in his anger and fury.* The blowing of the fire makes a great noise, so will the judgments of God upon Jerusalem. When God stirs up himself to execute judgments upon a provoking people, from the consideration of his own glory and the necessity of making some examples, then he may be said to *blow the fire of his wrath* against sin and sinners, to *heat the furnace seven times hotter.* 2. The several sorts of metal gathered in it shall be melted; by a complication of judgments, as by a raging fire, their constitution shall be dissolved, they shall lose all their former shape and strength, and shall be utterly unable to stand before the wrath of God. The various sorts of sinners shall be melted down together, and united in a common overthrow, as *brass* and *lead* in the same furnace, as trees are *bound in bundles for the fire.* They came together into Jerusalem as a place of defence, but God brought them together there as unto a place of execution. 3. God will leave them in the furnace (*v.* 20): I will *gather you into the furnace* and will *leave you there.* When God brings his own people into the furnace he sits by them, as the refiner by his gold, to see that they be not continued there any longer than is fitting and needful; but he will bring these people into the furnace, as men throw dross into it, which they design shall be consumed, and therefore are in no care about it, but *leave it there.* Compare with this Hos. v. 14, *I will tear and go away.* 4. Hereby the dross shall be wholly separated and the good metal purified, the impenitent shall be destroyed and the penitent reformed and fitted for deliverance. *Take away the dross from the silver, and there shall come forth a vessel for the finer,* Prov. xxv. 4. This judgment shall do that in the house of Israel for the doing of which other methods had been tried in vain, and *repro-*

884

bate silver shall they no more be called, Jer. vi. 30.

23 And the word of the LORD came unto me, saying, 24 Son of man, say unto her, Thou *art* the land that is not cleansed, nor rained upon in the day of indignation. 25 *There is* a conspiracy of her prophets in the midst thereof, like a roaring lion ravening the prey; they have devoured souls; they have taken the treasure and precious things; they have made her many widows in the midst thereof. 26 Her priests have violated my law, and have profaned mine holy things: they have put no difference between the holy and profane, neither have they showed *difference* between the unclean and the clean, and have hid their eyes from my sabbaths, and I am profaned among them. 27 Her princes in the midst thereof *are* like wolves ravening the prey, to shed blood, *and* to destroy souls, to get dishonest gain. 28 And her prophets have daubed them with untempered *mortar,* seeing vanity, and divining lies unto them, saying, Thus saith the Lord GOD, when the LORD hath not spoken. 29 The people of the land have used oppression, and exercised robbery, and have vexed the poor and needy: yea, they have oppressed the stranger wrongfully. 30 And I sought for a man among them, that should make up the hedge, and stand in the gap before me for the land, that I should not destroy it: but I found none. 31 Therefore have I poured out mine indignation upon them; I have consumed them with the fire of my wrath: their own way have I recompensed upon their heads, saith the Lord GOD.

Here is, I. A general idea given of the land of Israel, how well it deserved the judgments coming to destroy it and how much it needed these judgments to refine it. Let the prophet tell her plainly, "*Thou art the land that is not cleansed,* not refined as metal is, and therefore needest to be again put into the furnace. Means and methods of reformation have been ineffectual; thou art *not rained upon in the day of indignation.*" This was one of the judgments which God brought upon them in the day of his wrath, he *withheld the rain* from them, Jer. xiv. 4. Or,

" When thou art under the tokens of God's displeasure, even in the day of indignation thou art *not rained upon ;* thou hast not received instruction by the prophets, whose doctrine is said to *descend as the rain.*" Or, " When thou art corrected thou art not cleansed ; thy filth is not carried away as that in the streets is by a sweeping rain. Nay, though it be a *day of indignation* with thee, yet thy filthiness, which should be done away, has become more *offensive,* as that of a city is in dry weather, when it is not rained upon." Or, " Thou hast nothing to refresh and comfort thyself with *in the day of indignation ;* thou art not rained upon by divine consolations." So the rich man in torment had not a *drop of water,* or rain, *to cool his tongue.*

II. A particular charge drawn up against the several orders and degrees of men among them, which shows that they had all helped to fill the measure of the nation's guilt, but none had done any thing towards the emptying of it; they are therefore all alike.

1. They have every one *corrupted his way,* and those who should have been the brightest examples of virtue were ringleaders in iniquity and patterns of vice.

(1.) The *prophets,* who pretended to make known the mind of God to them, were not only *deceivers,* but *devourers* (v. 25), and hardened them in their wickedness both by their preaching, wherein they promised them impunity and prosperity, and by their conversation, in which they were as profligate as any. *There is a conspiracy of her prophets* against God and religion, against the true prophets and all good men; they conspired together to be all in one song, as Ahab's prophets were, to assure them of peace in their sinful ways. Note, The unity which is found among pretenders to infallibility, and which they so much boast of, is only the result of a secret *conspiracy* against the truth. Satan is not *divided against himself.* The prophets are *in conspiracy* with the murderers and oppressors, to patronise and protect them in their wickedness, and justify what they did with their false prophecies, provided they may come in sharers with them in the profits of it. They are like *a roaring lion ravening the prey ;* they thunder out threats against those whose ruin is aimed at, terrify them, or make them odious to the people, and so make themselves masters, [1.] Of their lives : They *have devoured souls,* have been accessory to the shedding of the blood of many an innocent person, and so have made many to become sorrowful widows who were comfortable wives. They have persecuted those to death who witnessed against their pretensions to prophecy and would not be imposed upon by their counterfeit commission. Or, They devoured souls by flattering sinners into a false peace and a vain hope, and seducing them into the paths of sin, which would be their eternal ruin. Note, Those who draw

men to wickedness, and encourage them in it, are the devourers and murderers of their souls. [2.] Of their estates. When Naboth is slain they take possession of his vineyard ; *They have seized the treasure and precious things,* as forfeited ; some way or other they had of *devouring the widows' houses,* as the Pharisees, Matt. xxiii. 14. Or, They got this *treasure,* and all these *precious things,* as fees for false and flattering prophecies ; for *he that puts not into their mouths, they even prepare war against him,* Mic. iii. 5. It was sad with Jerusalem when such men as these passed for prophets.

(2.) The priests, who were teachers by office, and had the custody of the sacred things, and should have called the false prophets to account, were as bad as they, v. 26. [1.] They violated the law of God, which they should have observed and taught others to observe. They made no conscience of the law of the priesthood, but openly broke it, and with contempt, as Hophni and Phinehas. They did what they had a mind, with an express *non obstante—notwithstanding* to the word of God. And how should those teach the people their duty who lived in contradiction to their own ? [2.] They *profaned God's holy things,* about which they were to minister, and which they ought to have restrained others from the profanation of. They suffered those to eat of the holy things who were unqualified by the law. The table of the Lord was contemptible with them. By dealing in holy things with such unhallowed hands they did themselves profane them. [3.] They did not themselves put a difference, nor did they show the people how to *put a difference, between the holy and profane, the clean and the unclean,* according to the directions and distinctions of the law. They did not exclude those from God's courts who were excluded by the law, nor teach the people to observe the difference the law had made between food clean and unclean, between times and places holy and common ; but they lived at large themselves and encouraged the people to do so too. [4.] They *hid their eyes from God's sabbaths ;* they took no care about them ; it was all one to them whether God's sabbaths were kept holy or no ; they neither gave countenance to those who observed them nor check to those who profaned them, nor did they themselves show any regard to them or veneration for them. They winked at those who did servile works on that day, and looked another way when they should have inspected the behaviour of the people on sabbath days. God's sabbaths have such a beauty and glory put upon them by the divine institution as may command respect ; but they *hid their eyes* from them and would not see that excellency in them. [5.] By all this God himself was *profaned among them ;* his authority was slighted, his goodness made light of, and the highest affront and contempt imaginable were put upon his holiness. Note,

The profanation of the honour of the scriptures, of sabbaths and sacred things, is a profanation of the honour of God himself, who is interested in them.

(3.) The princes, who should have interposed with their authority to redress these grievances, were as daring transgressors of the law as any (*v.* 27) : *They are like wolves ravening the prey;* for such is power without justice and goodness to direct it. All their business was to gratify, [1.] Their own pride and ambition, by making themselves arbitrary and formidable. [2.] Their own malice and revenge, by *shedding blood* and *destroying souls*, sacrificing to their cruelty all those that stood in their way or had in any thing disobliged them. [3.] Their own avarice; all they aim at is to *get dishonest gain*, by crushing and oppressing their subjects. *Lucri bonus est odor ex re qualibet. Rem, rem, quocunque modo rem—Sweet is the odour of gain, from whatever substance it ascends. Money, money, by fairness or by fraud, get money.* But, though they had power sufficient to carry them on in their oppressive courses, yet how could they answer it both to their credit and to their consciences? We are told how (*v.* 28) : The prophets *daubed them with untempered mortar*, told them in God's name (horrid wickedness!) that there was no harm in what they did, that they might dispose of the lives and estates of their subjects as they pleased, and could do no wrong, nay, that in prosecuting such and such whom they had marked out they did God service; and thus they stopped the mouth of their consciences. They also justified what they did, to the people, nay, and *magnified* it as if it were all for the public good, and so saved their reputation, and kept their oppressed subjects from murmuring. Note, Daubing prophets are the great supporters of ravening princes, but will prove at last their great deceivers, for they daub with untempered mortar which will not hold, nor will the wall stand long that is built up with it. They pretend to be seers, but they *see vanity;* they pretend to be diviners, but they *divine lies;* they pretend a warrant from Heaven for what they say, and that it is all as true as gospel; they say, *Thus saith the Lord God*, but it is all a sham, for *the Lord has not spoken any such thing.*

(4.) The people that had any power in their hands learned of their princes to abuse it, *v.* 29. Those that should have complained of the oppression of the subject, and have put in a *claim of rights* on behalf of the injured, that should have stood up for liberty and property, were themselves invaders of them : *The people of the land have used oppression and exercised robbery.* The rich oppress the poor, masters their servants, landlords their tenants, and even parents their own children; nay, the buyers and sellers will find some way to oppress one another. This is such a sin as, when it is

886

national, is indeed a national judgment, and is threatened as such. Isa. iii. 5, *The people shall be oppressed every one by his neighbour.* It is an aggravation of the sin that they have *vexed the poor and needy*, whom they should have relieved, and have *oppressed the stranger* and deprived him of *his right*, to whom they ought to have been not only just, but kind. Thus was the apostasy universal and the disease epidemical.

2. There is none that appears as an intercessor for them (*v.* 30) : *I sought for a man among them that should stand in the gap, but I found none.* Note, (1.) Sin makes a gap in the hedge of protection that is about a people at which good things run out from them and evil things pour in upon them, a gap by which God enters to destroy them. (2.) There is a way of standing in the gap, and making up the breach against the judgments of God, by repentance, and prayer, and reformation. Moses stood in the gap when he made intercession for Israel to *turn away the wrath of God*, Ps. cvi. 23. (3.) When God is coming forth against a sinful people to destroy them he expects some to intercede for them, and enquires if there be but one that does; so much is it his desire and delight to show mercy. If there be but a man that stands in the gap, as Abraham for Sodom, he will discover him and be well pleased with him. (4.) It bodes ill to a people when judgments are breaking in upon them, and the spirit of prayer is restrained, so that *not one is found* that will either give them a good word or speak a good word for them. (5.) When it is so, what can be expected but utter ruin? *Therefore have I poured out my indignation upon them* (*v.* 31), have given it full scope, that it may come upon them in a full stream; yet, whatever God's wrath inflicts upon a people, it is *their own way* that is therein *recompensed upon their heads*, and God deals with them no worse, but even much better, than their iniquity deserves.

CHAP. XXIII.

This long chapter (as before, ch. xvi. and xx.) is a history of the apostasies of God's people from him and the aggravations of those apostasies under the similitude of corporal whoredom and adultery. Here the kingdoms of Israel and Judah, the ten tribes and the two, with their capital cities, Samaria and Jerusalem, are considered distinctly. Here is, I. The apostasy of Israel and Samaria from God (ver. 1—8) and their ruin for it, ver. 9, 10. II. The apostasy of Judah and Jerusalem from God (ver. 11—21) and sentence passed upon them, that they shall in like manner be destroyed for it, ver. 22—35. III. The joint wickedness of them both together (ver. 36—44) and the joint ruin of them both, ver. 45—49. And all that is written for warning against the sins of idolatry, and confidence in an arm of flesh, and sinful leagues and confederacies with wicked people (which are the sins here meant by committing whoredom), is that others may hear and fear, and not sin after the similitude of the transgressions of Israel and Judah.

THE word of the LORD came again unto me, saying, 2 Son of man, there were two women, the daughters of one mother : 3 And they committed whoredoms in Egypt; they committed whoredoms in their youth: there were their breasts pressed, and there they bruised the teats of their virginity. 4 And the names of them *were* Aholah the elder, and Aholibah her sister: and they were mine, and they bare sons and daughters. Thus *were* their names; Samaria *is* Aholah, and Jerusalem Aholibah. 5 And Aholah played the harlot when she was mine; and she doted on her lovers, on the Assyrians *her* neighbours, 6 *Which were* clothed with blue, captains and rulers, all of them desirable young men, horsemen riding upon horses. 7 Thus she committed her whoredoms with them, with all them *that were* the chosen men of Assyria, and with all on whom she doted: with all their idols she defiled herself. 8 Neither left she her whoredoms *brought* from Egypt: for in her youth they lay with her, and they bruised the breasts of her virginity, and poured their whoredom upon her. 9 Wherefore I have delivered her into the hand of her lovers, into the hand of the Assyrians, upon whom she doted. 10 These discovered her nakedness: they took her sons and her daughters, and slew her with the sword: and she became famous among women; for they had executed judgment upon her.

God had often spoken to Ezekiel, and by him to the people, to this effect, but now his word *comes again;* for *God speaks* the same thing *once, yea, twice,* yea, many a time, and all little enough, and too little, for *man perceives it not.* Note, To convince sinners of the evil of sin, and of their misery and danger by reason of it, there is need of *line upon line,* so loth we are to know the worst of ourselves. The sinners that are here to be exposed are *two women,* two kingdoms, sister-kingdoms, Israel and Judah, *daughters of one mother,* having been for a long time but *one people.* Solomon's kingdom was so large, so populous, that immediately after his death it divided into two. Observe, 1. Their character when they were one (*v.* 3): *They committed whoredoms in Egypt,* for there they were guilty of idolatry, as we read before, *ch.* xx. 8. The representing of those sins which are most provoking to God and most ruining to a people by the sin of whoredom plainly intimates what an exceedingly sinful sin uncleanness is, how offensive, how destructive. Doubtless it is itself one of the worst of sins, for the worst of other sins are compared to it here and often elsewhere, which should increase our detestation and dread of all manner of *fleshly lusts,* all appearances

of them and approaches to them, as *warring against the soul,* infatuating sinners, bewitching them, alienating their minds from God and all that is good, debauching conscience, rendering them odious in the eyes of the pure and holy God, and drowning them at last in destruction and perdition. 2. Their names when they became two, *v.* 4. The kingdom of Israel is called the *elder sister,* because that first made the breach, and separated from the family both of kings and priests that God had appointed—the *greater sister* (so the word is), for ten tribes belonged to that kingdom and only two to the other. God says of them both, *They were mine,* for they were the seed of Abraham *his friend* and of Jacob *his chosen;* they were in covenant with God, and carried about with them the sign of *their circumcision,* the seal of the covenant. *They were mine;* and therefore their apostasy was the highest injustice. It was alienating God's property, it was the basest ingratitude to the best of benefactors, and a perfidious treacherous violation of the most sacred engagements. Note, Those who have been in profession the people of God, but have revolted from him, have a great deal to answer for more than those who never made any such profession. "*They were mine;* they were espoused to me, and to me *they bore sons and daughters;*" there were many among them that were devoted to God's honour, and employed in his service, and were the strength and beauty of these kingdoms, as children are of the families they are born in. In this parable Samaria and the kingdom of Israel shall bear the name of *Aholah—her own tabernacle,* because the places of worship which that kingdom had were of their own devising, their own choosing, and the worship itself was their own invention; God never owned it. *Her tabernacle to herself* (so some render it); "let her take it to herself, and make her best of it." Jerusalem and the kingdom of Judah bear the name of *Aholibah—my tabernacle is in her,* because *their* temple was the place which God himself had *chosen* to *put his name there.* He acknowledged it to be his, and honoured them with the tokens of his presence in it. Note, Of those that stand in relation to God, and make profession of his name, some have greater privileges and advantages than others; and, as those who have greater are thereby rendered the more inexcusable if they revolt from God, so those who have less will not thereby be rendered excusable. 3. The treacherous departure of the kingdom of Israel from God (*v.* 5): *Aholah played the harlot when she was mine.* Though the ten tribes had deserted the house of David, yet God owned them for *his* still; though Jeroboam, in setting up the golden calves, *sinned, and made Israel to sin,* yet, as long as they worshipped the God of Israel only, though by images, he did not quite cast them off. But the way of sin is down-hill. Aholah played the harlot, brought in the worship of Baal (1 Kings xvi. 31), set up that other god, that dunghill-god, in competition with Jehovah (1 Kings xviii. 21), as a vile adulteress *dotes on her lovers*, because they are well dressed and make a figure, because they are young and handsome (*v.* 6), *clothed with blue, captains and rulers, desirable young* men, genteel, and that pass for men of honour, so she doted upon her neighbours, particularly the Assyrians, who had extended their conquests near them; she admired their idols and worshipped them, admired the pomp of their courts and their military strength and courted alliances with them upon any terms, as if her own God were not sufficient to be depended upon. We find one of the kings of Israel giving a *thousand talents* to the *king of Assyria*, to engage him in his interests, 2 Kings xv. 19. She doted on the *chosen men of Assyria*, as worthy to be trusted and employed in the service of the state (*v.* 7), and *on all their idols with which she defiled herself*. Note, Whatever creature we dote upon, pay homage to, and put a confidence in, we make an idol of that creature; and whatever we make an idol of we defile ourselves with. And now again the conviction looks back as far as the original of their nation: *Neither left she her whoredoms which she brought from Egypt, v.* 8. Their being idolaters in Egypt was a thing never to be forgotten—that they should be in love with Egypt's idols even when they were continually in fear of Egypt's tyrants and task-masters! But (as some have observed) therefore, at that time, when Satan boasted of his having *walked through the earth* as all his own, to disprove his pretensions God did not say, Hast thou considered *my people Israel in Egypt?* (for they had become idolaters, and were not to be boasted of), but, *Hast thou considered my servant Job in the land of Uz?* And this corrupt disposition in them, when they were first formed into a people, is an emblem of that original corruption which is born with us and is woven into our constitution, a strong bias towards the world and the flesh, like that in the Israelites towards idolatry; it was *bred in the bone* with them, and was charged upon them long after, that they *left not their whoredoms brought from Egypt.* It would never *out of the flesh*, though Egypt had been a house of bondage to them. Thus the corrupt affections and inclinations which we brought into the world with us we have not lost, nor got clear of, but still retain them, though the iniquity we were born in was the source of all the calamities which human life is liable to. 4 The destruction of the kingdom of Israel for their apostasy from God (*v.* 9, 10): *I have delivered her into the hand of her lovers.* God first justly gave her up to her lust *(Ephraim is joined to idols, let him alone)*, and then gave her up to her lovers. The neighbouring nations,

whose idolatries she had conformed to and whose friendship she had confided in, and in both had affronted God, are now made use of as the instruments of her destruction. The *Assyrians, on whom she doted*, soon spied out the *nakedness of the land*, discovered her blind side, on which to attack her, stripped her of all her ornaments and all her defences, and so *uncovered* her, and *made her naked and bare*, carried her *sons and daughters* into captivity, *slew her with the sword*, and quite destroyed that kingdom and put an end to it. We have the story at large 2 Kings xvii. 6, &c., where the cause of the ruin of that once flourishing kingdom by the Assyrians is shown to be their forsaking the God of Israel, *fearing other gods*, and *walking in the statutes of the heathen;* it was for this that God was very *angry with them and removed them out of his sight, v.* 18. And that the Assyrians, whom they had been so fond of, should be employed in *executing judgments* upon them was very remarkable, and shows how God, in a way of righteous judgment, often makes that a scourge to sinners which they have inordinately set their hearts upon. The devil will for ever be a tormentor to those impenitent sinners who now hearken to him and comply with him as a tempter. Thus Samaria became *famous among women*, or *infamous* rather; she *became a name* (so the word is); not only she came to be the subject of discourse, and much talked of, as the desolations of cities and kingdoms fill the newspapers, but she was thus ruined for her idolatries *in terrorem—for warning* to all people to take heed of doing likewise; as the public execution of notorious malefactors makes them such *a name*, such an ill name, as may serve to frighten others from those wicked courses which have brought them to a miserable and shameful end. Deut. xxi. 21, *All Israel shall hear and fear.*

11 And when her sister Aholibah saw *this*, she was more corrupt in her inordinate love than she, and in her whoredoms more than her sister in *her* whoredoms. 12 She doted upon the Assyrians *her* neighbours, captains and rulers clothed most gorgeously, horsemen riding upon horses, all of them desirable young men. 13 Then I saw that she was defiled, *that* they *took* both one way, 14 And *that* she increased her whoredoms: for when she saw men portrayed upon the wall, the images of the Chaldeans portrayed with vermilion, 15 Girded with girdles upon their loins, exceeding in dyed attire upon their heads, all of them princes to look to, after the manner of the Babylonians of

Chaldea, the land of their nativity: 16 And as soon as she saw them with her eyes, she doted upon them, and sent messengers unto them into Chaldea. 17 And the Babylonians came to her into the bed of love, and they defiled her with their whoredom, and she was polluted with them, and her mind was alienated from them. 18 So she discovered her whoredoms, and discovered her nakedness: then my mind was alienated from her, like as my mind was alienated from her sister. 19 Yet she multiplied her whoredoms, in calling to remembrance the days of her youth, wherein she had played the harlot in the land of Egypt. 20 For she doted upon their paramours, whose flesh *is as* the flesh of asses, and whose issue *is like* the issue of horses. 21 Thus thou calledst to remembrance the lewdness of thy youth, in bruising thy teats by the Egyptians for the paps of thy youth.

The prophet Hosea, in his time, observed that the two tribes retained their integrity, in a great measure, when the ten tribes had apostatized (Hos. xi. 12, *Ephraim indeed compasses me about with lies, but Judah yet rules with God and is faithful with the saints;* and this was justly expected from them: Hos. iv. 15, *Though thou Israel play the harlot, yet let not Judah offend);* but this lasted 'not long. By some unhappy matches made between the house of David and the house of Ahab the worship of Baal had been brought into the kingdom of Judah, but had been by the reforming kings worked out again; and at the time of the captivity of the ten tribes, which was in the reign of Hezekiah, things were in a good posture: but it lasted not long. In the reign of Manasseh, soon after the kingdom of Judah had seen the destruction of the kingdom of Israel, they became more corrupt than Israel had been in their inordinate love of idols, *v.* 11. Instead of being made better by the warning which that destruction gave them, they were made worse by it, as if they were *displeased because the Lord had made that breach upon Israel,* and for that reason became disaffected to him and to his service. Instead of being made to stand in awe of him as a *jealous God,* they therefore grew strange to him, and liked those gods better that would admit of partners with them. Note, Those may justly expect God's judgments upon themselves who do not take warning by his judgments upon others, who see in others what is the end of sin and yet continue to make a light matter of it. But it is bad indeed with those who are made worse by

that which should make them better, and have their lusts irritated and exasperated by that which was designed to suppress and subdue them. Jerusalem grew worse *in her whoredoms* than her sister Samaria had been *in her whoredoms.* This was observed before (*ch.* xvi. 51), *Neither has Samaria committed half of thy sins.*

I. Jerusalem, that had been a *faithful city, became a harlot,* Isa. i. 21. She also *doted upon the Assyrians* (*v.* 12), joined in league with them, joined in worship with them, grew to be in love with their *captains and rulers,* and cried them up as finer and more accomplished gentlemen than any that ever the land of Israel produced. "See how richly, how neatly, they are dressed, *clothed most gorgeously;* how well they sit a horse; they are *horsemen riding on horses;* how charmingly they look, *all of them desirable young men."* And thus they grew to affect every thing that was foreign and to despise their own nation; and even the religion of it was mean and homely, and not to be compared with the curiosity and gaiety of the heathen temples. Thus she *increased her whoredoms;* she fell in love, fell in league, with the Chaldeans. Hezekiah himself was faulty this way when he was proud of the court which the king of Babylon made to him and complimented his ambassadors with the sight of all his treasures, Isa. xxxix. 2. And the humour increased (*v.* 14); she doted upon the pictures of the Babylonian captains (*v.* 15, 16), joined in alliance with that kingdom, invited them to come and settle in Jerusalem, that they might refine the genius of the Jewish nation and make it more polite; nay, they sent for patterns of their images, altars, and temples, and made use of them in their worship. Thus was she *polluted with her whoredoms* (*v.* 17), and thereby she *discovered her own whoredom* (*v.* 18), her own strong inclination to idolatry. And when she had had enough of the Chaldeans, and grew tired of them and disposed to break her league with them, as Jehoiakim and Zedekiah did, *her mind being alienated from them,* she courted the *Egyptians, doted upon their paramours* (*v.* 20), would come into an alliance with them, and, to strengthen the alliance, would join with them in their idolatries and then depend upon them to be their protectors from all other nations; for so wise, so rich, so strong, was the Egyptian nation, and came to such perfection in idolatry, that there was no nation now which they could take such satisfaction in as in Egypt. Thus they *called to remembrance the days of their youth* (*v.* 19), the *lewdness of their youth, v.* 21. 1. They pleased themselves with the remembrance of it. When they began to set their affections upon Egypt, they encouraged themselves to put a confidence in that kingdom, because of the old acquaintance they had with it, as if they still retained the gust and relish of the *leeks and onions* they ate there, or rather of the idolatrous worship they learned there, and brought up with them thence. When they began an acquaintance with Egypt they remembered how merrily their fathers worshipped the golden calf, what music and dancing they had at that sport, which they learned in Egypt; and they hoped they should now have a fair pretence to come to that again. Thus *she multiplied her whoredoms,* repeated her former whoredoms, and encouraged herself to close with present temptations, by calling *to remembrance the days of her youth.* Note, Those who, instead of reflecting upon their former sins with sorrow and shame, reflect upon them with pleasure and pride, contract new guilt thereby, strengthen their own corruptions, and in effect bid defiance to repentance. This is returning *with the dog to his vomit.* 2. They called it *God's remembrance,* and provoked him to remember it against them. God had said indeed that he would reckon with them for *the golden calf,* that *idol of Egypt* (Exod. xxxii. 34); but such was his patience that he seemed to have forgotten it till they, by their league now with the Egyptians against the Chaldeans, did, as it were, put him in mind of it; and in the day *when he visits he will now,* as he has said, *visit for that.* It is very observable how this adulteress changes her lovers: she dotes first on the Assyrians; then she thought the Chaldeans finer and courted them; after a while her mind was alienated from them, and she thought the Egyptians more powerful (*v.* 20) and she must contract an intimacy with them. This shows the folly, (1.) Of fleshly lusts; when they are indulged they grow humoursome and fickle, are soon surfeited but never satisfied; they must have variety, and what is loved one day is loathed the next. *Unius adulterium matrimonium vocant—One adultery is called marriage,* as Seneca observes. (2.) Of idolatry. Those who think one God too little will not think a hundred sufficient, but will still be for trying more, as finding all insufficient. (3.) Of seeking to creatures for help; we go from one to another, but are disappointed in them all, and can never rest till we have made the God of Israel our help.

II. The faithful God justly gives a bill of divorce to this now faithless city, that has *become a harlot.* His jealousy soon discovered her lewdness (*v.* 13): *I saw that she was defiled,* that she was debauched, and saw which way her inclination was, that the *two sisters both took one way,* and that Jerusalem grew worse than Samaria. For, *if we stretch out our hand to a strange god, will not God search this out?* No doubt he will; and when he has found it can he be pleased with it? No (*v.* 18): *Then my mind was alienated from her, as it was from her sister.* How could the pure and holy God any longer take delight in such a lewd generation? Note,

890

Sin alienates God's mind from the sinner, and justly, for it is the alienation of the sinner's mind from God; but woe, and a thousand woes, to those from whom God's mind is alienated; for whom he turns from he will turn against.

22 Therefore, O Aholibah, thus saith the Lord GOD; Behold, I will raise up thy lovers against thee, from whom thy mind is alienated, and I will bring them against thee on every side; 23 The Babylonians, and all the Chaldeans, Pekod, and Shoa, and Koa, *and* all the Assyrians with them: all of them desirable young men, captains and rulers, great lords and renowned, all of them riding upon horses. 24 And they shall come against thee with chariots, waggons, and wheels, and with an assembly of people, *which* shall set against thee buckler and shield and helmet round about: and I will set judgment before them, and they shall judge thee according to their judgments. 25 And I will set my jealousy against thee, and they shall deal furiously with thee: they shall take away thy nose and thine ears; and thy remnant shall fall by the sword: they shall take thy sons and thy daughters; and thy residue shall be devoured by the fire. 26 They shall also strip thee out of thy clothes, and take away thy fair jewels. 27 Thus will I make thy lewdness to cease from thee, and thy whoredom *brought* from the land of Egypt: so that thou shalt not lift up thine eyes unto them, nor remember Egypt any more. 28 For thus saith the Lord GOD; Behold, I will deliver thee into the hand *of them* whom thou hatest, into the hand *of them* from whom thy mind is alienated: 29 And they shall deal with thee hatefully, and shall take away all thy labour, and shall leave thee naked and bare: and the nakedness of thy whoredoms shall be discovered, both thy lewdness and thy whoredoms. 30 I will do these *things* unto thee, because thou hast gone a whoring after the heathen, *and* because thou art polluted with their idols. 31 Thou hast walked in the way of thy sister; therefore will I give her cup into

thine hand. 32 Thus saith the Lord God; Thou shalt drink of thy sister's cup deep and large: thou shalt be laughed to scorn and had in derision; it containeth much. 33 Thou shalt be filled with drunkenness and sorrow, with the cup of astonishment and desolation, with the cup of thy sister Samaria. 34 Thou shalt even drink it and suck *it* out, and thou shalt break the sherds thereof, and pluck off thine own breasts: for I have spoken *it*, saith the Lord God. 35 Therefore thus saith the Lord God; Because thou hast forgotten me, and cast me behind thy back, therefore bear thou also thy lewdness and thy whoredoms.

Jerusalem stands indicted by the name of *Aholibah*, for that she, as a false traitor to her sovereign Lord the God of heaven, not having his fear before her eyes, but moved by the instigation of the devil, had revolted from her allegiance to him, had compassed and imagined to shake off his government, had kept up a correspondence and joined in confederacy with his enemies, and the pretenders to a deity, in contempt of his crown and dignity. To this indictment she has pleaded, Not guilty: *I am not polluted; I have not gone after Baalim.* But it is found against her by the notorious evidence of the fact, and she stands convicted of it, nor has any thing material to offer why judgment should not be given and execution awarded according to law. In these verses, therefore, we have the sentence.

I. Her old confederates must be her executioners; and those whom she had courted to be her leaders in sin are now to be employed as instruments of her punishment (*v.* 22): "*I will raise up thy lovers against thee*, the Chaldeans, whom formerly thou didst so much admire and covet an acquaintance with, but from whom thy mind is since alienated and with whom thou hast perfidiously broken covenant." They are called *thy lovers* (*v.* 22) and yet (*v.* 28) *those whom thou hatest*, It is common for sinful love soon to turn into hatred; as Amnon's to Tamar. Those of headstrong and unreasonable passions are often very hot against those persons and things that a little before they were as hot for. Fools run into extremes; nay, and wise men may see cause to change their sentiments. And therefore, as we should rejoice and weep as if we rejoiced not and wept not, so we should love and hate as if we loved not and hated not. *Ita ama tanquam osurus—Love as one who may have cause to feel aversion.*

II. The execution to be done upon her is very terrible.

1. Her enemies shall come against her on *every side* (*v.* 22), those of the several nations that constituted the Chaldean army (*v.* 23), all of them *great lords and renowned*, whose pomp, and grandeur, and splendid appearance made them look the more amiable when they came as friends to protect and patronise Jerusalem, but the more formidable when they came to chastise its treachery and aimed at no less than its ruin. (1.) They shall come with a great deal of military force (*v.* 24), with *chariots and waggons* furnished with all necessary provisions for a camp, with arms and ammunition, bag and baggage, with a vast army, and well armed. (2.) They shall have justice on their side: "*I will set judgment before them*" (they shall have right with them as well as might; for the king of Babylon had just cause to make war upon the king of Judah, because he had broken his league with him), "and therefore they *shall judge thee*, not only according to God's judgments, as the instruments of his justice, to punish thee for the indignities done to him, but *according to their judgments*, according to the law of nations, to punish thee for thy perfidious dealings with them." (3.) They shall prosecute the war with a great deal of fury and resentment. It being a war of revenge, *they shall deal with thee hatefully, v.* 29. This will make the execution the more severe that their swords will be dipped in poison. Thou hatest them, and they shall deal hatefully with thee; those that hate will be hated and will be hatefully dealt with. (4.) God himself will lead them on, and his anger shall be mingled with theirs (*v.* 25): *I will set my jealousy against thee;* that shall kindle this fire, and then *they shall deal furiously with thee.* If men deal ever so hatefully, ever so furiously, with us, yet, if we have God on our side, we need not fear them; they can do us no real hurt. But if men deal furiously with us, and God set his jealousy against us too, what will become of us?

2. The particulars of the sentence here passed upon this notorious adulteress are, (1.) That all she has shall be seized on. The *clothes* and the *fair jewels*, with which she had endeavoured to recommend herself to her lovers, these she shall be stripped of, *v.* 26. All those things that were the ornaments of their state shall be taken away: "*They shall take away all thy labour*, all that thou hast gotten by thy labour, and shall *leave thee naked and bare*," *v.* 29. Both city and country shall be impoverished and all the wealth of both swept away. (2.) That her children shall go into captivity. "They shall *take thy sons and thy daughters*, and make slaves of them (*v.* 25); for they are *children of whoredoms*, unworthy the dignities and privileges of Israelites," Hos. ii. 4. (3.) That she shall be stigmatized and deformed: "They shall *take away thy nose and thy ears*, shall mark thee for a harlot,

and render thee for ever odious," *v.* 25. This intimates the many cruelties of the Chaldean soldiers towards the Jews that fell into their hands, whom, it is probable, they used barbarously. Some will have this to be understood figuratively; and by the nose they think is meant the kingly dignity, and by the ears that of the priesthood. (4.) That she shall be exposed to shame: *Thy lewdness and thy whoredoms shall be discovered* (*v.* 29), as, when a malefactor is punished, all his crimes are ripped up, and repeated to his disgrace; what was secret then comes to light, and what was done long since is then called to mind. (5.) That she shall be quite cut off and ruined: " *The remnant of thy people that have escaped the famine and pestilence shall fall by the sword; and the residue of thy houses that have not been battered down about thy ears shall be devoured by the fire,*" *v.* 25. And this shall be the end of Jerusalem.

III. Because she has trod in the steps of Samaria's sins, she must expect no other than Samaria's fate. It is common, in giving judgment, to have an eye to precedents; so has God in passing this sentence on Jerusalem (*v.* 31, &c.): " *Thou hast walked in the way of thy sister,* notwithstanding the warning thou hast had given thee, by the fatal consequences of her wickedness; and therefore I *will give her cup,* her portion of miseries, *into thy hand,* the cup of the Lord's fury, which will be to thee a *cup of trembling.*" Now, 1. This cup is said to be *deep and large,* and to *contain much* (*v.* 32), abundance of God's wrath and abundance of miseries, the fruits of that wrath. It is such a cup as that which we read of, Jer. xxv. 15, 16. The cup of divine vengeance holds a great deal, and so those will find into whose hand it shall be put. 2. They shall be made to drink the very dregs of this cup, as the *wicked* are said to do (Ps. lxxv. 8): " *Thou shalt drink it and suck it out,* not because it is pleasant, but because it is forced upon thee (*v.* 34); *thou shalt break the shreds thereof,* and *pluck off thy own breasts,* for indignation at the extreme bitterness of this cup, being *full of the fury of the Lord* (Isa. li. 20), as men in great anguish tear their hair, and throw every thing from them. Finding there is no remedy, but it must be drank (for *I have spoken it, saith the Lord God),* thou shalt have no manner of patience in the drinking of it." 3. They shall be intoxicated by it, made sick, and be at their wits' end, as men in drink are, staggering, and stumbling, and ready to fall (*v.* 33): *Thou shalt be filled with drunkenness and sorrow.* Note, Drunkenness has sorrow attending it, to such a degree that the utmost confusion and astonishment are here represented by it. Who would think that that which is such a force upon nature, such a scandal to it, which deprives men of their reason, disorders them to the last degree, and is therefore expressive of the greatest

892

misery, should yet be with many a beloved sin, that they should damn their own souls to distemper their own bodies? *Who has woe and sorrow* like them? Prov. xxiii. 29. 4. Being so intoxicated, they shall become, as drunkards deserve to be, a laughing-stock to all about them (*v.* 32): *Thou shalt be laughed to scorn and had in derision,* as acting ridiculously in every thing thou goest about. When God is about to ruin a people he *makes their judges fools* and *pours contempt on their princes,* Job xii. 17, 21.

IV. In all this God will be justified, and by all this they will be reformed; and so the issue even of this will be God's glory and their good. 1. They have been bad, very bad, and that justifies God in all that is brought upon them (*v.* 30): I *will do these things unto thee because thou hast gone a whoring after the heathen,* and (*v.* 35) *because thou hast forgotten me and cast me behind thy back.* Note, Forgetfulness of God, and a contempt of him, of his eye upon us and authority over us, are at the bottom of all our treacherous adulterous departures from him. *Therefore* men wander after idols, because they forget *God,* and their obligations to him; nor could they look with so much desire and delight upon the baits of sin if they did not first cast God *behind their back,* as not worthy to be regarded. And those who put such an affront upon God, how can they think but that it should turn upon themselves at last? *Therefore bear thou also thy lewdness and thy whoredoms;* that is, thou shalt *suffer the punishment* of them, and thou alone must *bear the blame.* Men need no more to sink them than the weight of their own sins; and those who will not part with their lewdness and their whoredoms must bear them. 2. They shall be better, much better, and this fire, though consuming to many, shall be refining to a remnant (*v.* 27): *Thus will I make thy lewdness to cease from thee.* The judgments which were brought upon them by their sins parted between them and their sins, and taught them at length to say, *What have we to do any more with idols?* Observe, (1.) How inveterate the disease was: *Thy whoredoms were brought from the land of Egypt.* Their disposition to idolatry was early and innate, their practice of it was ancient, and had gained a sort of prescription by long usage. (2.) How complete the cure was notwithstanding: "Though it has taken root, yet it shall be made to cease, so that thou shalt not so much as *lift up thy eyes* to the idols again, nor *remember Egypt* with pleasure *any more.*" They shall avoid the occasions of this sin, for they shall not so much as look upon an idol, lest their hearts should unawares *walk after their eyes.* And they shall abandon all inclinations to it: " They shall *not remember Egypt;* they shall not retain any of that affection for idols which they had from the very infancy of their nation. They got it, through the corruption of nature, in their bondage in Egypt, and lost it, through the grace of God, in their captivity in Babylon, which this was the blessed fruit of, even *the taking away of sin,* of *that* sin; so that whereas, before the captivity, no nation (all things considered) was more impetuously bent upon idols and idolatry than they were, after that captivity no nation was more vehemently set against idols and idolatry than they were, insomuch that at this day the image-worship which is practised in the church of Rome confirms the Jews as much as any thing in their prejudices against the Christian religion.

36 The Lord said moreover unto me; Son of man, wilt thou judge Aholah and Aholibah? yea, declare unto them their abominations; 37 That they have committed adultery, and blood *is* in their hands, and with their idols have they committed adultery, and have also caused their sons, whom they bare unto me, to pass for them through *the fire,* to devour *them.* 38 Moreover this they have done unto me: they have defiled my sanctuary in the same day, and have profaned my sabbaths. 39 For when they had slain their children to their idols, then they came the same day into my sanctuary to profane it; and, lo, thus have they done in the midst of mine house. 40 And furthermore, that ye have sent for men to come from far, unto whom a messenger *was* sent; and, lo, they came: for whom thou didst wash thyself, paintedst thy eyes, and deckedst thyself with ornaments, 41 And satest upon a stately bed, and a table prepared before it, whereupon thou hast set mine incense and mine oil. 42 And a voice of a multitude being at ease *was* with her: and with the men of the common sort *were* brought Sabeans from the wilderness, which put bracelets upon their hands, and beautiful crowns upon their heads. 43 Then said I unto *her that was* old in adulteries, Will they now commit whoredoms with her, and she *with them?* 44 Yet they went in unto her, as they go in unto a woman that playeth the harlot: so went they in unto Aholah and unto Aholibah, the lewd women. 45 And the righteous men, they shall judge them after the manner of adulteresses, and after the manner of

women that shed blood; because they *are* adulteresses, and blood *is* in their hands. 46 For thus saith the Lord God; I will bring up a company upon them, and will give them to be removed and spoiled. 47 And the company shall stone them with stones, and dispatch them with their swords; they shall slay their sons and their daughters, and burn up their houses with fire. 48 Thus will I cause lewdness to cease out of the land, that all women may be taught not to do after your lewdness. 49 And they shall recompense your lewdness upon you, and ye shall bear the sins of your idols: and ye shall know that I *am* the Lord God.

After the ten tribes were carried into captivity, and that kingdom was made quite desolate, the remains of it by degrees incorporated with the kingdom of Judah, and gained a settlement (many of them) in Jerusalem; so that the *two sisters* had in effect become *one* again; and therefore, in these verses, the prophet takes those to task jointly who were thus conjoined: " *Wilt thou judge Aholah and Aholibah* together? *v.* 36. Wilt thou go about to frame an excuse for them? Thou seest the matter is so bad as not to bear an excuse." Or, rather, "Thou shalt now be employed, in God's name, to *judge them, ch.* xx. 4. The matter is rather worse than better since the union."

I. Let them be made to see the sins they are guilty of: *Declare unto them* openly and boldly *their abominations.* 1. They have been guilty of gross idolatry, here called *adultery. With their idols they have committed adultery* (v. 37), have broken their marriage-covenant with God, have lusted after the gratifications of a carnal sensual mind in the worship of God. This is the first and worst of the abominations he is to charge them with. 2. They have committed the most barbarous murders, in sacrificing their children to Moloch, a sin so unnatural that they deserve to hear of it upon all occasions: *Blood is in their hands,* innocent blood, the blood of their own children, which they have *caused to pass through the fire* (v. 37), not that they might be dedicated to the idols, but that they might be devoured, a sign that they loved their idols better than that which was dearest to them in the world. 3. They have profaned the sacred things with which God had dignified and distinguished them: This *they have done unto me,* this indignity, this injury, *v.*38. Every contempt put upon that which is holy reflects upon him who is the fountain of holiness, and from a relation to whom whatever is called holy has its denomination. God had set up his sanctuary among them, but they defiled it, by making it a house of merchandise, a den of thieves; nay, and much worse; there they set up their idols and worshipped them, and there they shed the blood of God's prophets. God had revealed to them his holy sabbaths, but they profaned them, by doing all manner of servile work therein, or perhaps by sports and recreations on that day, not only practised, but allowed and encouraged by authority. They *defiled the sanctuary* on *the same day* that they *profaned the sabbath.* To defile the sanctuary was bad enough on any day, but to do it on the sabbath day was an aggravation. We commonly say, *The better day the better deed;* but here, the better day the worse deed. God takes notice of the circumstances of sin which add to the guilt. He shows (*v.* 39) what was their profanation both of the sanctuary and of the sabbath. *They slew their children,* and sacrificed them *to their idols,* to the great dishonour both of God and of human nature; and then came, on *the same day,* their hands imbrued with the blood of their children and their clothes stained with it, to attend in *God's sanctuary,* not to ask pardon for what they had done, but to present themselves before him, as other Israelites did, expecting acceptance with him, notwithstanding these villanies which they were guilty of; as if God either did not know their wickedness or did not hate it. Thus they *profaned the sanctuary,* as if that were a protection to the worst of malefactors; for thus they did *in the midst of his house.* Note, It is a profanation of God's solemn ordinances when those that are grossly and openly profane and vicious impudently and impenitently so intrude upon the services and privileges of them. *Give not that which is holy unto dogs. Friend, how camest thou in hither?* 4. They have courted foreign alliances, been proud of them, and reposed a confidence in them. This also is represented by the sin of adultery, for it was a departure from God, not only *to whom* alone they ought to pay their homage and not to idols, but *in* whom alone they ought to put their trust, and not in creatures. Israel was a peculiar people, must *dwell alone* and not be *reckoned among the nations;* and they profane their crown, and lay their honour in the dust, when they covet to be like them or in *league* with them. But this they have now done; they have entered into strict alliances with the Assyrians, Chaldeans, and Egyptians, the most renowned and potent kingdoms at that time; but they scorned alliances with the petty kingdoms and states that lay near them, which yet might have been of more real service to them. Note, Affecting an acquaintance and correspondence with great people has often been a snare to good people. Let us see how Jerusalem courts her high allies, thinking thereby to make herself considerable. (1.) She privately requested that a public embassy might be sent to her (*v.* 40): *You sent a messenger for men to come from*

894

far. It seems, then, that the neighbours had no desire to come into a confederacy with Jerusalem, but she thrust herself upon them, and sent under-hand to desire them to court her: and, *lo, they came.* The wisest and best may be drawn unavoidably into company and conversation with profane and wicked people: but it is no sign either of wisdom or goodness to covet an intimacy with such and to court it. (2.) Great preparation was made for the reception of these foreign ministers, for their public entry and public audience, which is compared to the pains that an adulteress takes to make herself look handsome. Jezebel-like, thou *paintedst thy face* and *deckedst thyself with ornaments, v.* 40. The king and princes made themselves new clothes, fitted up the rooms of state, beautified the furniture, and made it look fresh. Thou *sattest upon a stately bed* (*v.* 41), a stately throne; *a table was prepared, whereon thou has set my oil and my incense.* This was either, [1.] A feast for the ambassadors, a noble treat, agreeable to the other preparations. There was incense to perfume the room and oil to anoint their heads. Or, [2.] An altar already furnished for the ambassadors' use in the worship of their idols, to let them know that the Israelites were not so strait-laced but that they could allow foreigners the free exercise of their religion among them, and furnish them with chapels, yea, and complimented them so far as to join with them in their devotions; though the law of their God was against it, yet they could easily dispense with themselves to oblige a friend. The oil and incense God calls *his,* not only because they were the gift of his providence, but because they should have been offered at his altar, which was an aggravation of their sin in serving idols and idolaters with them. See Hos. ii. 8. (3.) There was great joy at their coming, as if it were such a blessing as never happened to Jerusalem before (*v.* 42): *A voice of a multitude being at ease was with her.* The people were very easy, for they tnought themselves very safe and happy now that they had such powerful allies; and therefore attended the ambassadors with loud huzzas and acclamations of joy. A great confluence of people there was to the court upon this occasion. The *men of the common sort* were there to grace the solemnity, and to increase the crowd; and *with them were brought Sabeans from the wilderness.* The margin reads it *drunkards from the wilderness,* that would drink healths to the prosperity of this grand alliance, and force them upon others, and be most noisy in shouting upon this occasion. Whoever they were, in honour of the ambassadors they put *bracelets upon their hands and beautiful crowns upon their heads,* which made the cavalcade appear very splendid. (4.) God by his prophets warned them against making these dangerous leagues with foreigners (*v.* 43): " *Then said I unto her that*

was old in adulteries, that from the first was
fond of leagues with the heathen, of matching with their families (Judg. iii. 6), and
afterwards of making alliances with their
kingdoms, and, though often disappointed
therein, would never be dissuaded from it
(this was the adultery she was old in), I said,
*Will they now commit whoredoms with her
and she with them?* Surely experience and
observation will by this time have convinced
both them and her that an alliance between
the nation of the Jews and a heathen nation
can never be for the advantage of either."
They are *iron and clay,* that will not mix,
nor will God bless such an alliance, or smile
upon it. But, it seems, her being old in
these adulteries, instead of weaning her from
them, as one would expect, does but make
her the more impudent and insatiable in
them; for, though she was thus admonished
of the folly of it, *yet they went in unto her,*
v. 44. A bargain was soon clapped up, and
a league made, first with this, and then with
the other, foreign state. Samaria did so,
Jerusalem did so, like lewd women. They
could not rest satisfied in the embraces of
God's laws and care, and the assurances of
protection he gave them; they could not think
his covenant with them security enough.
But they must by treaties and leagues, politic ones (they thought) and well-concerted,
throw themselves into the arms of foreign
princes, and put their interests under their
protection. Note, Those hearts go a whoring from God that take a complacency in
the pomp of the world and put a confidence
in its wealth, and in an *arm of flesh,* Jer.
xvii. 5.

II. Let them be made to foresee the judgments that are coming upon them for these
sins (*v.* 45): *The righteous men, they shall
judge them.* Some make the instruments
of their destruction to be the righteous men
that shall judge them. The Assyrians that
destroyed Samaria, the Chaldeans that destroyed Jerusalem, those were comparatively
righteous, had a sense of justice between man
and man and justly resented the treachery of
the Jewish nation; however, they executed
God's judgments, which, we are sure, are all
righteous. Others understand it of the prophets, whose office it was, in God's name, to
judge them and pass sentence upon them. Or
we may take it as an appeal to all righteous
men, to all that have a sense of equity; they
shall all judge concerning these cities, and
agree in their verdict, that forasmuch as they
have been notoriously guilty of adultery and
murder, and the guilt is national, therefore
they ought to suffer the pains and penalties
which by law are inflicted upon women in
their personal capacity that shed blood and
are adulteresses. Righteous men will say,
" Why should bloody filthy cities escape any
better than bloody filthy persons? *Judge, I
pray thee,*" Isa. v. 3. This judgment being
given by the righteous men, the righteous

God will award execution. See here, 1.
What the execution will be. *v.* 46, 47. The
same as before, *v.* 23, &c. God will *bring a
company* of enemies *upon them,* who shall be
made to serve his holy purposes even when
they are serving their own sinful appetites
and passions. These enemies shall easily
prevail, for God will *give them* into their
hands *to be removed and spoiled;* this company shall *stone them with stones* as malefactors, shall *single them out* and *dispatch
them with their swords;* and, as was sometimes done in severe executions (witness that
of Achan), they shall *slay their children and
burn their houses.* 2. What will be the effects
of it. (1.) Thus they shall suffer for their
sins: Their *lewdness shall be recompensed upon
them* (*v.* 49); and they shall *bear the sins of
their idols, v.* 35, 49. Thus God will assert
the honour of his broken law and injured
government, and let the world know what a
just and jealous God he is. (2.) Thus they
shall be broken off from their sins: *I will
cause lewdness to cease out of the land, v.* 27,
48. The destruction of God's city, like the
death of God's saints, shall do that for them
which ordinances and providences before
could not do; it shall quite take away their
sin, so that Jerusalem shall rise out of its
ashes a new lump, as gold comes out of the
furnace purified from its dross. (3.) Thus
other cities and nations will have fair warning
given them to keep themselves from idols.
That *all women may be taught not to do after
your lewdness.* This is the end of the punishment of malefactors, that they may be made
examples to others, who will *see and fear.*
Smite the scorner and the simple will beware.
The judgments of God upon some are designed to teach others, and happy are those
who receive instruction from them not to
tread in the steps of sinners, lest they be
taken in their snares; those who would be
taught this must *know God is the Lord* (*v.*
49), that he is the governor of the world, a
God that judges in the earth, and with whom
there is *no respect of persons.*

CHAP. XXIV.

Here are two sermons in this chapter, preached on a particular occasion, and they are both from Mount Sinai, the mount of terror,
both from Mount Ebal, the mount of curses; both speak the approaching fate of Jerusalem. The occasion of them was the king
of Babylon's laying siege to Jerusalem, and the design of them is
to show that in the issue of that siege he should be not only master of the place, but destroyer of it. I. By the sign of flesh boiling
in a pot over the fire are shown the miseries that Jerusalem should
suffer during the siege, and justly, for her filthiness, ver. 1—14.
II. By the sign of Ezekiel's not mourning for the death of his wife
is shown that the calamities coming upon Jerusalem were too
great to be lamented, so great that they should sink down under
them into a silent despair, ver. 15—27.

AGAIN in the ninth year, in the
tenth month, in the tenth *day* of
the month, the word of the LORD
came unto me, saying, 2 Son of man,
write thee the name of the day, *even*
of this same day: the king of Babylon
set himself against Jerusalem this
same day. 3 And utter a parable unto

the rebellious house, and say unto them, Thus saith the Lord GOD; Set on a pot, set *it* on, and also pour water into it: 4 Gather the pieces thereof into it, *even* every good piece, the thigh, and the shoulder; fill *it* with the choice bones. 5 Take the choice of the flock, and burn also the bones under it, *and* make it boil well, and let them seethe the bones of it therein. 6 Wherefore thus saith the Lord GOD; Woe to the bloody city, to the pot whose scum *is* therein, and whose scum is not gone out of it! bring it out piece by piece; let no lot fall upon it. 7 For her blood is in the midst of her: she set it upon the top of a rock; she poured it not upon the ground, to cover it with dust; 8 That it might cause fury to come up to take vengeance; I have set her blood upon the top of a rock, that it should not be covered. 9 Therefore thus saith the Lord GOD; Woe to the bloody city! I will even make the pile for fire great. 10 Heap on wood, kindle the fire, consume the flesh, and spice it well, and let the bones be burned. 11 Then set it empty upon the coals thereof, that the brass of it may be hot, and may burn, and *that* the filthiness of it may be molten in it, *that* the scum of it may be consumed. 12 She hath wearied *herself* with lies, and her great scum went not forth out of her: her scum *shall be* in the fire. 13 In thy filthiness *is* lewdness: because I have purged thee, and thou wast not purged, thou shalt not be purged from thy filthiness any more, till I have caused my fury to rest upon thee. 14 I the LORD have spoken *it:* it shall come to pass, and I will do *it;* I will not go back, neither will I spare, neither will I repent; according to thy ways, and according to thy doings, shall they judge thee, saith the Lord GOD.

We have here,

I. The notice God gives to Ezekiel in Babylon of Nebuchadnezzar's laying siege to Jerusalem, just at the time when he was doing it (*v.* 2): " *Son of man,* take notice, *the king of Babylon,* who is now abroad with his army, thou knowest not where, *set himself against Jerusalem this same day.*" It

896

was many miles, it was many days' journey, from Jerusalem to Babylon, Perhaps the last intelligence they had from the army was that the design was upon Rabbath of the children of Ammon and that the campaign was to be opened with the siege of that city. But God knew, and could tell the prophet, " *This day,* at this time, Jerusalem is invested, and the Chaldean army has sat down before it." Note, As all times, so all places, even the most remote, are present with God and under his view. He tells the prophet, that the prophet might tell the people, that so when it proved to be punctually true, as they would find by the public intelligence in a little time, it might be a confirmation of the prophet's mission, and they might infer that, since he was right in his news, he was so in his predictions, for he owed both to the same correspondence he had with Heaven.

II. The notice which he orders him to take of it. He must enter it in his book, *memorandum,* that *in the ninth year* of Jehoiachin's captivity (for thence Ezekiel dated, *ch.* i. 2, which was also the ninth year of Zedekiah's reign, for he began to reign when Jehoiachin was carried off), in the tenth month, on the tenth day of the month, the king of Babylon laid siege to Jerusalem; and the date here agrees exactly with the date in the history, 2 Kings xxv. 1. See how God reveals things to his servants the prophets, especially those things which serve to confirm their word, and so to confirm their own faith. Note, It is good to keep an exact account of the date of remarkable occurrences, which may sometimes contribute to the manifesting of God's glory so much the more in them, and the explaining and confirming of scripture prophecies. *Known unto God are all his works.*

III. The notice which he orders him to give to the people thereupon, the purport of which is that this siege of Jerusalem, now begun, will infallibly end in the ruin of it. This he must say *to the rebellious house,* to those of them that were in Babylon, to be by them communicated to those that were yet in their own land. A rebellious house will soon be a ruinous house.

1. He must show them this by a sign; for that stupid people needed to be taught as children are. The comparison made use of is that of a *boiling pot.* This agrees with Jeremiah's vision many years before, when he first began to be a prophet, and probably was designed to put them in mind of that (Jer. i. 13, *I see a seething pot, with the face towards the north;* and the explanation of it (*v.* 15) makes it to signify the besieging of Jerusalem by the *northern* nations); and, as this comparison is intended to confirm Jeremiah's vision, so also to confront the vain confidence of the princes of Jerusalem, who had said (*ch.* xi. 3), *This city is the caldron and we are the flesh,* meaning, " We are as safe here as if we were surrounded with walls

of brass." " Well," says God, " it shall be so; you shall be boiled in Jerusalem, as the *flesh in the caldron,* boiled to pieces; let the pot be set on with water in it (*v* 4); let it be filled with the flesh of the *choice of the flock* (*v*. 5), with the choice pieces (*v*. 4), and the marrow-bones, and let the other bones serve for fuel, that, one way or other, either in the pot or under it, the whole beast may be made use of." A fire of bones, though it be a slow fire (for the siege was to be long), is yet a sure and lasting fire; such was God's wrath against them, and not like the *crackling of thorns under a pot,* which has noise and blaze, but no intense heat. Those that from all parts of the country fled into Jerusalem for safety would be sadly disappointed when the siege laid to it would soon make the place too hot for them; and yet there was no getting out of it, but they must be forced to abide by it, as the flesh in a boiling pot.

2. He must give them a comment upon this sign. It is to be construed as a *woe to the bloody city,* v. 6. And again (*v*. 9), being *bloody,* let it *go to pot,* to be boiled; that is the fittest place for it. Let us here see,

(1.) What is the course God takes with it. Jerusalem, during the siege, is like a pot boiling over the fire, all in a heat, all in a hurry. [1.] Care is taken to keep a good fire under the pot, which signifies the closeness of the siege, and the many vigorous attacks made upon the city by the besiegers, and especially the continued wrath of God burning against them (*v*. 9): *I will make the pile for fire great.* Commission is given to the Chaldeans (*v*. 10) to *heap on wood, and kindle the fire,* to make Jerusalem more and more hot to the inhabitants. Note, The fire which God kindles for the consuming of impenitent sinners shall never abate, much less go out, for want of fuel. *Tophet has fire and much wood,* Isa. xxx. 33. [2.] The meat, as it is boiled, is taken out, and given to the Chaldeans for them to feast upon. " *Consume the flesh;* let it be thoroughly boiled, boiled to rags. *Spice it well,* and make it savoury, for those that will feed sweetly upon it. *Let the bones be burnt,*" either the bones *under* the pot (" let them be consumed with the other fuel") or, as some think, the bones *in* the pot—" let it boil so furiously that not only the flesh may be sodden, but even the bones softened; let all the inhabitants of Jerusalem be by sickness, sword, and famine, reduced to the extremity of misery." And then (*v*. 6), " *Bring it out piece by piece;* let every man be delivered into the enemy's hand, to be either put to the sword or made a prisoner. Let them be an easy prey to them, and let the Chaldeans fall upon them as eagerly as a hungry man does upon a good dish of meat when it is set before him. *Let no lot fall upon it;* every piece in the pot shall be fetched out and devoured, first or last, and therefore it is no

matter for casting lots which shall be fetched out first." It was a very severe military execution when David measured Moab with *two lines to put to death and one full line to keep alive,* 2 Sam. viii. 2. But here is no line, no lot of mercy, made use of; all goes one way, and that is to destruction. [3.] When all the broth is boiled away the pot is set empty upon the coals, that it may burn too, which signifies the setting of the city on fire, *v*. 11. The scum of the meat, or (as some translate it) *the rust of the metal,* has so got into the pot that there is no making it clean by washing or scouring it, and therefore it must be done by fire; so let the filthiness be burnt out of it, or, rather, *melted in it* and burnt with it. Let the vipers and their nest be consumed together.

(2.) What is the quarrel God has with it. He would not take these severe methods with Jerusalem but that he is provoked to it; she deserves to be thus dealt with, for, [1.] It is a bloody city (*v*. 7, 8): *Her blood is in the midst of her.* Many a barbarous murder has been committed in the very heart of the city; nay, and they have a disposition to cruelty in their hearts; they inwardly delight in blood-shed, and so it is *in the midst of them.* Nay, they commit their murders in the face of the sun, and openly and impudently avow them, in defiance of the justice both of God and man. She did not *pour out* the blood she shed *upon the ground, to cover it with dust,* as being ashamed of the sin or afraid of the punishment. She did not look upon it as a filthy thing, proper to be concealed (Deut. xxiii. 13), much less dangerous. Nay, she poured out the innocent blood she shed upon a rock, where it would not soak in, upon *the top of a rock,* in despite of divine views and vengeance. They shed innocent blood under colour of justice; so that they gloried in it, as if they had done God and the country good service, so put it, as it were, *on the top of a rock.* Or it may refer to the sacrificing of their children on their high places, perhaps on the top of rocks Now thus they *caused fury to come up and take vengeance,* v. 8. It could not be avoided but that God *must* in anger *visit for these things; his soul must be avenged on such a nation as this.* If such impudent murderers as these, that even dare divine vengeance, go unpunished, it will be said that God has *forsaken the earth.* It is absolutely necessary that such a bloody city as this should have blood given her to drink, for she is worthy, for the vindicating of the honour of divine justice. And, the crime having been public and notorious, it is fit that the punishment should be so too: *I have set her blood on the top of a rock.* Jerusalem was to be made an example, and therefore was made a spectacle, to the world; God dealt with her according to the law of retaliation. It is fit that those who *sin before all* should be *rebuked before all;* and that the reputation of those should not be consulted by the concealment of their punishment who were so impudent as not to desire the concealment of their sin. [2.] It is a filthy city. Great notice is taken, in this explanation of the comparison, of the *scum of this pot*, which signifies the sin of Jerusalem, working up and appearing when the judgments of God were upon her. It is the pot *whose scum is therein* and has *not gone out of it, v.* 6. The *great scum* that *went not forth out of her* (*v.* 12), that stuck to the pot when all was boiled away, and was *molten in it* (*v.* 11), some of this runs over *into the fire* (*v.* 12), inflames that, and makes it burn the more furiously, but *it shall all be consumed* at last, *v.* 11. When the hand of God had gone out against them, instead of humbling themselves under it, repenting and reforming, and accepting the punishment of their iniquity, they grew more impudent and outrageous in sin, quarrelled with God, persecuted his prophets, were fierce to one another, enraged to the last degree against the Chaldeans, snarled at the stone, gnawed their chain, and were like a wild bull in a net. This was *their scum;* in their distress they *trespassed yet more against the Lord*, like *that king Ahaz*, 2 Chron. xxviii. 22. There is little hope of those who are made worse by that which should make them better, whose corruptions are excited and exasperated by those rebukes both of the word and of the providence of God which were designed for the suppressing and subduing of them, or of those whose scum boiled up once in convictions, and confessions of sin, as if it would be taken off by reformation, but afterwards returned again, in a revolt from their good overtures; and the heart that seemed softened is hardened again. This was Jerusalem's case: *She has wearied with lies*, wearied her God with purposes and promises of amendment, which she never stood to, wearied herself with her carnal confidences, which have all deceived her, *v.* 12. Note, Those that follow after lying vanities weary themselves with the pursuit. Now see her doom, *v.* 13, 14. Because she is incurably wicked she is abandoned to ruin, without remedy. *First*, Methods and means of reformation had been tried in vain (*v.* 13): " *In thy filthiness is lewdness;* thou hast become obstinate and impudent in it; thou hast got a habit of it, which is confirmed by frequent acts. *In thy filthiness* there is a rooted lewdness; as appears by this, *I have purged thee and thou wast not purged*. I have given thee medicine, but it has done thee no good. I have used the means of cleansing thee, but they have been ineffectual; the intention of them has not been answered." Note, It is sad to think how many there are on whom ordinances and providences are all lost. *Secondly*, It is therefore resolved that no more such methods shall be used: *Thou shalt not be purged from thy filthiness any more*. The fire shall no longer be a refining

fire, but a consuming fire, and therefore shall not be mitigated and shortened, as it has been, but shall be continued in extremity, till it has done its destroying work. Note, Those that will not be healed are justly given up and their case adjudged desperate. There is a day coming when it will be said, *He that is filthy, let him be filthy still. Thirdly*, Nothing remains then but to bring them to utter ruin : *I will cause my fury to rest upon thee.* This is the same with what is said of the later Jews, that *wrath has come upon them to the uttermost*, 1 Thess. ii. 16. They deserve it : *According to thy doings they shall judge thee, v.* 14. And God will do it. The sentence is bound on with repeated ratifications, that they might be awakened to see how certain their ruin was : " *I the Lord have spoken it*, who am able to make good what I have spoken ; *it shall come to pass*, nothing shall prevent it, for *I will do it* myself, *I will not go back* upon any entreaties ; the decree has gone forth, and *I will not spare* in compassion to them, *neither will I repent.*" He will neither change his mind nor his way. Hereby the prophet was forbidden to intercede for them, and they were forbidden to flatter themselves with hopes of an escape. God hath said it, and he will do it. Note, The declarations of God's wrath against sinners are as inviolable as the assurances he has given of favour to his people ; and the case of such is sad indeed, who have brought it to this issue, that either God must be false or they must be damned.

15 Also the word of the LORD came unto me, saying, 16 Son of man, behold, I take away from thee the desire of thine eyes with a stroke : yet neither shalt thou mourn nor weep, neither shall thy tears run down. 17 Forbear to cry, make no mourning for the dead, bind the tire of thine head upon thee, and put on thy shoes upon thy feet, and cover not *thy* lips, and eat not the bread of men. 18 So I spake unto the people in the morning : and at even my wife died ; and I did in the morning as I was commanded. 19 And the people said unto me, Wilt thou not tell us what these *things are* to us, that thou doest *so?* 20 Then I answered them, The word of the LORD came unto me, saying, 21 Speak unto the house of Israel, Thus saith the Lord GOD ; Behold, I will profane my sanctuary, the excellency of your strength, the desire of your eyes, and that which your soul pitieth ; and your sons and your daughters whom ye have left shall fall

by the sword. 22 And ye shall do as I have done: ye shall not cover *your* lips, nor eat the bread of men. 23 And your tires *shall be* upon your heads, and your shoes upon your feet: ye shall not mourn nor weep; but ye shall pine away for your iniquities, and mourn one toward another. 24 Thus Ezekiel is unto you a sign: according to all that he hath done shall ye do: and when this cometh, ye shall know that I *am* the Lord God. 25 Also, thou son of man, *shall it* not *be* in the day when I take from them their strength, the joy of their glory, the desire of their eyes, and that whereupon they set their minds, their sons and their daughters, 26 *That* he that escapeth in that day shall come unto thee, to cause *thee* to hear *it* with *thine* ears? 27 In that day shall thy mouth be opened to him which is escaped, and thou shalt speak, and be no more dumb: and thou shalt be a sign unto them; and they shall know that I *am* the Lord.

These verses conclude what we have been upon all along from the beginning of this book, to wit, Ezekiel's prophecies of the destruction of Jerusalem; for after this, though he prophesied much concerning other nations, he said no more concerning Jerusalem, till he heard of the destruction of it, almost three years after, *ch.* xxxiii. 21. He had assured them, in the former part of this chapter, that there was no hope at all of the preventing of the trouble; here he assures them that they should not have the ease of weeping for it. Observe here,

I. The sign by which this was represented to them, and it was a sign that cost the prophet very dear; the more shame for them that when he, by a divine appointment, was at such an expense to affect them with what he had to deliver, yet they were not affected by it.

1. He must lose a good wife, that should suddenly be taken from him by death. God gave him notice of it before, that it might be the less surprise to him (*v.* 16): *Behold, I take away from thee the desire of thy eyes with a stroke.* Note, (1.) A married state may very well agree with the prophetical office; it is *honourable in all,* and therefore not sinful in ministers. (2.) Much of the comfort of human life lies in agreeable relations. No doubt Ezekiel found a prudent tender yokefellow, that shared with him in his griefs and cares, to be a happy companion in his captivity. (3.) Those in the conjugal relation must be to each other not only a *covering of*

the eyes (Gen. xx. 16), to restrain wandering looks after others; but a *desire of the eyes,* to engage pleasing looks on one another. A beloved wife is the *desire of the eyes,* which find not any object more grateful. (4.) That is least safe which is most dear; we know not how soon the desire of our eyes may be removed from us and may become the sorrow of our hearts, which is a good reason why those that *have wives* should be *as though they had none,* and those *who rejoice* in them *as though they rejoiced not,* 1 Cor. vii. 29, 30. Death is a stroke which the most pious, the most useful, the most amiable, are not exempted from. (5.) When the desire of our eyes is taken away with a stroke we must see and own the hand of God in it: *I take away the desire of thy eyes.* He takes our creature-comforts from us when and how he pleases; he gave them to us, but reserved to himself a property in them; and *may he not do what he will with his own?* (6.) Under afflictions of this kind it is good for us to remember that we are *sons of men;* for so God calls the prophet. If thou art a *son of Adam,* thy wife is a daughter of *Eve,* and therefore a dying creature. It is an affliction which the children of men are liable to; and *shall the earth be forsaken for us?* According to this prediction, he tells us (*v.* 18), *I spoke unto the people in the morning:* for God sent his prophets, *rising up early* and sending them; then he thought, if ever, they would be disposed to hearken to him. Observe, [1.] Though God had given Ezekiel a certain prospect of this affliction coming upon him, yet it did not take him off from his work, but he resolved to go on in that. [2.] We may the more easily bear an affliction if it find us in the way of our duty; for nothing can hurt us, nothing come amiss to us, while we keep ourselves in the love of God.

2. He must deny himself the satisfaction of mourning for his wife, which would have been both an honour to her and an ease to the oppression of his own spirit. He must not use the natural expressions of sorrow, *v.* 16. He must not give vent to his passion by *weeping,* or letting *his tears run down,* though tears are a tribute due to the dead, and, when the body is sown, it is fit that it should thus be watered. But Ezekiel is not allowed to do this, though he thought he had as much reason to do it as any man and would perhaps be ill thought of by the people if he did it not. Much less might he use the customary formalities of mourners. He must dress himself in his usual attire, must bind his turban on him, here called the *tire of his head,* must *put on his shoes,* and not go barefoot, as was usual in such cases; he must not *cover his lips,* not throw a veil over his face (as mourners were wont to do, Lev xiii. 45), must not be of a *sorrowful countenance, appearing unto men to fast,* Matt. vi. 18. He must not *eat the bread of men,* nor expect that his neighbours and friends should

send him in provisions, as usually they did in such cases, presuming the mourners had no heart to provide meat for themselves; but, if it were sent, he must not eat of it, but go on in his business as at other times. It could not but be greatly against the grain to flesh and blood not to lament the death of one he loved so dearly, but so God commands; and *I did in the morning as I was commanded.* He appeared in public, in his usual habit, and looked as he used to do, without any signs of mourning. (1.) Here there was something peculiar, and Ezekiel, to make himself a sign to the people, must put a force upon himself and exercise an extraordinary piece of self-denial. Note, Our dispositions must always submit to God's directions, and his command must be obeyed even in that which is most difficult and displeasing to us. (2.) Though mourning for the dead be a duty, yet it must always be kept under the government of religion and right reason, and we must not *sorrow as those that have no hope,* nor lament the loss of any creature, even the most valuable, and that which we could worst spare, as if we had lost our God, or as if all our happiness were gone with it; and, of this moderation in mourning, ministers, when it is their case, ought to be examples. We must at such a time study to improve the affliction, to accommodate ourselves to it, and to get our acquaintance with the other world increased, by the removal of our dear relations, and learn with holy Job *to bless the name of the Lord* even when he takes as well as when he gives.

II. The explication and application of this sign. The people enquired the meaning of it (*v.* 19): *Wilt thou not tell us what these things are to us that thou doest so?* They knew that Ezekiel was an affectionate husband, that the death of his wife was a great affliction to him, and that he would not appear so unconcerned at it but for some good reason and for instruction to them; and perhaps they were in hopes that it had a favourable signification, and gave them an intimation that God would now comfort them again according to the time he had afflicted them, and make them look pleasant again. Note, When we are enquiring concerning the things of God our enquiry must be, "What are those things *to us?* What are we concerned in them? What conviction, what counsel, what comfort, do they speak to us? Wherein do they reach our case?" Ezekiel gives them an answer *verbatim*—*word for word* as he had received it from the Lord, who had told him what he must *speak to the house of Israel.*

1. Let them know that as Ezekiel's wife was taken from him by a stroke so would God take from them all that which was dearest to them, *v.* 21. If this was *done to the green tree, what shall be done to the dry?* If a faithful servant of God was thus afflicted

900

only for his trial, shall such a generation of rebels against God go unpunished? By this awakening providence God showed that he was in earnest in his threatenings, and inexorable. We may suppose that Ezekiel prayed that, if it were the will of God, his wife might be spared to him, but God would not hear him; and should he be heard then in his intercessions for this provoking people? No, it is determined: *God will take away the desire of your eyes.* Note, The removal of the comforts of others should awaken us to think of parting with ours too; for *are we better than they?* We know not how soon the same cup, or a more bitter one, may be put into our hands, and should therefore weep with those that weep, as being ourselves also in the body. God will *take away that which their soul pities,* that is, of which they say, What a pity is it that it should be cut off and destroyed! That *for which your souls are afraid* (so some read it); you shall lose that which you most dread the loss of. And what is that? (1.) That which was their public pride, the temple: "*I will profane my sanctuary,* by giving that into the enemy's hand, to be plundered and burnt." This was signified by the death of a wife, a dear wife, to teach us that God's sanctuary should be dearer to us, and more *the desire of our eyes,* than any creature-comfort whatsoever. Christ's church, that is his spouse, should be ours too. Though this people were very corrupt, and had themselves profaned the sanctuary, yet it is called *the desire of their eyes.* Note, Many that are destitute of the *power of godliness* are yet very fond of *the form* of it; and it is just with God to punish them for their hypocrisy by depriving them of that too. The sanctuary is here called the *excellency of their strength;* they had many strong-holds and places of defence, but the temple excelled them all. It was the *pride of their strength;* they prided in it as their strength that they were *the temple of the Lord,* Jer. vii. 4. Note, The church-privileges that men are proud of are profaned by their sins, and it is just with God to profane them by his judgments. And with these God will take away, (2.) That which was their family-pleasure, which they looked upon with delight: "*Your sons and your daughters* (which are the dearer to you because they are but a few left of many, the rest having perished by famine and pestilence) shall *fall by the sword* of the Chaldeans." What a dreadful spectacle would it be to see their own children, pieces, pictures, of themselves, whom they had taken such care and pains to bring up, and whom they loved as their own souls, sacrificed to the rage of merciless conquerors! This, this, was the punishment of sin.

2. Let them know that as Ezekiel wept not for his affliction so neither should they weep for theirs. He must say, You shall *do as I have done,* v. 22. *You shall not mourn nor*

weep, v. 23. Jeremiah had told them the same, that men *shall not lament for the dead nor cut themselves* (Jer. xvi. 6); not that there shall be any such merciful circumstance without, or any such degrees of wisdom and grace within, as shall mitigate and moderate the sorrow; but they *shall not mourn,* for, (1.) Their grief shall be so great that they shall be quite overwhelmed with it; their passions shall stifle them, and they shall have no power to ease themselves by giving vent to it. (2.) Their calamities shall come so fast upon them, one upon the neck of another, that by long custom they shall be *hardened in their sorrows* (Job vi. 10) and perfectly stupified, and moped (as we say), with them. (3.) They shall not dare to express their grief, for fear of being deemed disaffected to the conquerors, who would take their lamentations as an affront and disturbance to their triumphs. (4.) They shall not have hearts, nor time, nor money, wherewith to put themselves in mourning, and accommodate themselves with the ceremonies of grief : "You will be so entirely taken up with solid substantial grief that you will have no room for the shadow of it." (5.) Particular mourners shall not need to distinguish themselves by *covering their lips,* and laying aside their ornaments, and *going barefoot;* for it is well known that every body is a mourner. (6.) There shall be none of that sense of their affliction and sorrow for it which would help to bring them to repentance, but that only which shall drive them to despair; so it follows : "*You shall pine away for your iniquities,* with seared consciences and reprobate minds, and *you shall mourn,* not to God in prayer and confession of sin, but *one towards another,*" murmuring, and fretting, and complaining of God, thus making their burden heavier and their wound more grievous, as impatient people do under their afflictions by mingling their own passions with them.

III. An appeal to the event, for the confirmation of all this (*v.* 24): "*When this comes,* as it is foretold, when Jerusalem, which is this day besieged, is quite destroyed and laid waste, which now you cannot believe will ever be, *then you shall know that I am the Lord God,* who have given you this fair warning of it. Then you will remember that Ezekiel was to you a sign." Note, Those who regard not the threatenings of the word when they are preached will be made to remember them when they are executed. Observe,

1. The great desolation which the siege of Jerusalem should end in (*v.* 25): *In that day,* that terrible day, when the city shall be broken up, *I will take from them,* (1.) That which they depended on—*their strength,* their walls, their treasures, their fortifications, their men of war; none shall stand them in stead. (2.) That which they boasted of—the *joy of their glory,* that which they looked

upon as most their glory, and which they most rejoiced in, the temple of their God and the palaces of their princes. (3.) That which they delighted in, which was the *desire of their eyes,* and on which they *set their minds.* Note, Carnal people set their minds upon that on which they can set their eyes; they look at, and dote upon, *the things that are seen ;* and it is their folly to *set their minds* upon that which they have no assurance of and which may be taken from them in a moment, Prov. xxiii. 5. *Their sons and their daughters* were all this—*their strength, and joy, and glory ;* and these shall go into captivity.

2. The notice that should be brought to the prophet, not by revelation, as the notice of the siege was brought to him (*v.* 2), but in an ordinary way (*v.* 26): "*He that escapes in that day* shall, by a special direction of Providence, *come to thee,* to bring thee intelligence of it," which we find was done, *ch.* xxxiii. 21. The ill-news came slowly, and yet to Ezekiel and his fellow-captives it came too soon.

3. The divine impression which he should be under upon receiving that notice, *v.* 27. Whereas, from this time to that, Ezekiel was thus far dumb that he prophesied no more against the land of Israel, but against the neighbouring nations, as we shall find in the following chapters, then he shall have orders given him to *speak again to the children of his people* (*ch.* xxxiii. 2, 22); then *his mouth shall be opened.* He was suspended from prophesying against them in the mean time, because, Jerusalem being besieged, his prophecies could not be sent into the city,— because, when God was speaking so loudly by the rod, there was the less need of speaking by the word,—and because then the accomplishment of his prophecies would be the full confirmation of his mission, and would the more effectually clear the way for him to begin again. It being referred to that issue, that issue must be waited for. Thus Christ forbade his disciples to preach openly that he was Christ till after his resurrection, because that was to be the full proof of it. "But then *thou shalt speak* with the greater assurance, and the more effectually, either to their conviction or to their confusion." Note, God's prophets are never silenced but for wise and holy ends. And when God gives them the opening of the mouth again (as he will in due time, for even the witnesses that are *slain* shall *arise*) it shall appear to have been for his glory that they were for a while silent, that people may the more certainly and fully *know* that God *is the Lord.*

Judgment began at the house of God, and therefore with them the prophets began, who were the judges; but it must not end there, and therefore they must not. Ezekiel had finished his testimony which related to the destruction of Jerusalem. As to that he was ordered to say no more, but stand upon his watch-tower and wait the issue ; and yet he must not be silent ; there are divers nations bordering upon the land of Israel, which he must prophesy against, as Isaiah and Jeremiah had done before; and must pro-claim God's controversy with them, chiefly for the injuries and in-dignities which they had done to the people of God in the day of their calamity. In this chapter we have his prophecy, I. Against the Ammonites, ver. 1–7. II. Against the Moabites, ver. 8–11. III. Against the Edomites, ver. 11–14. IV. Against the Philis-tines, ver. 15–17. That which is laid to the charge of each of them is their barbarous and insolent conduct towards God's Israel, for which God threatens to put the same cup of trembling into their hand. God's resenting it thus would be an encouragement to Israel to believe that though he had dealt thus severely with them yet he had not cast them off, but would still own them and plead their cause.

THE word of the LORD came again unto me, saying, 2 Son of man, set thy face against the Ammonites, and prophesy against them; 3 And say unto the Ammonites, Hear the word of the Lord GOD; Thus saith the Lord GOD; Because thou saidst, Aha, against my sanctuary, when it was profaned; and against the land of Israel, when it was desolate; and against the house of Judah, when they went into captivity; 4 Behold, there-fore I will deliver thee to the men of the east for a possession, and they shall set their palaces in thee, and make their dwellings in thee: they shall eat thy fruit, and they shall drink thy milk. 5 And I will make Rabbah a stable for camels, and the Ammonites a couchingplace for flocks: and ye shall know that I *am* the LORD. 6 For thus saith the Lord GOD; Because thou hast clapped *thine* hands, and stamped with the feet, and rejoiced in heart with all thy despite against the land of Israel; 7 Behold, therefore I will stretch out mine hand upon thee, and will deli-ver thee for a spoil to the heathen; and I will cut thee off from the peo-ple, and I will cause thee to perish out of the countries: I will destroy thee; and thou shalt know that I *am* the LORD.

Here, I. The prophet is ordered to ad-dress himself to the Ammonites, in the name of *the Lord Jehovah* the *God of Israel*, who is also the God of the whole earth. But what can Chemosh, the god of the children of Ammon, say, in answer to it? He is bidden to *set his face against the Ammonites*, for he is God's representative as a prophet, and thus he must signify that God *set his face against them*, for *the face of the Lord is against those that do evil*, Ps. xxxiv. 16. He must speak with boldness and assurance, as one that knew whose errand he went upon, and that he should be borne out in delivering it. He must therefore *set his face as a flint*, Isa. l. 7. He must show his displeasure against

these proud enemies of Israel, and face them down, though they were very impudent, and thus must show that, though he had prophesied so much and so long *against Israel*, yet still he was for Israel, and, while he witnessed against their corruptions, he adhered to and gloried in God's covenant with them. Note, Those are miserable that have the preaching and praying of God's prophets against them, against whom their faces are set.

II. He is directed what to say to them. Ezekiel is now a captive in Babylon, and has been so many years, and knows little of the state of his own nation, much less of the nations that were about it; but God tells him both what they were doing and what he was about to do with them. And thus by the spirit of prophecy he is enabled to speak as pertinently to their case as if he had been among them.

1. He must upbraid the Ammonites with their insolent and barbarous triumphs over the people of Israel in their calamities, *v.* 3. The Ammonites said, when all went against the Jews, *Aha! so would we have it*. They were glad to see, (1.) The temple burned, *the sanctuary profaned* by the victorious Chaldeans. This is put first, to intimate what was the cause of the controversy; they had an enmity to the Jews for the sake of their religion, though it was only some poor remains of the profession of it that were to be found among them. (2.) The nation ruined. They rejoiced when *the land of Is-rael was made desolate*, the cities burnt, the country wasted, and both depopulated, and when the house of *Judah went into captivity*. When they had not power to oppress God's Israel themselves they were pleased to see the Chaldeans oppress them, partly because they envied their wealth and the good land they enjoyed, partly because they feared their growing power, and partly because they hated their religion and the divine oracles they were favoured with. It is repeated again (*v.* 6): *They clapped with their hands*, to irritate the rage of the Chaldeans, and to set them on as dogs upon the game; or they clapped their hands in triumph, attended this tragedy with their *Plaudite—Give us your applause*, thinking it well acted; never was there any thing more diverting or enter-taining to them. They *stamped with their feet*, ready to leap and dance for joy upon this occasion; they not only *rejoiced in heart*, but they could not forbear showing it, though every one that had any sense of honour and humanity would cry shame upon them for it, especially considering that they rejoiced thus, not for any thing they got by Israel's fall (if so, they would have been the more excusable: most people are for themselves); but this was purely from a principle of ma-lice and enmity: *Thou hast rejoiced in heart with all thy despite* (which signifies both scorn and hatred) *against the land of Israel.*

Note, The people of God have always had a great deal of ill-will borne them by this wicked world; and their calamities have been their neighbours' entertainments. See to what unnatural instances of malice the enmity that is in the seed of the serpent against the seed of the woman will carry them. The Ammonites, of all people, should not have rejoiced in Jerusalem's ruin, but should rather have trembled, because they themselves had such a narrow escape at the same time; it was but "cross or pile" [the toss of a halfpenny] which should be besieged first, Rabbath or Jerusalem, *ch.* xxi. 20. And they had reason to think that the king of Babylon would set upon them next. But thus were their hearts hardened to their ruin, and their insolence against Jerusalem was to them an *evident token of perdition*, Phil. i. 28. It is a very wicked thing to be glad at the calamities of any, especially of God's people, and a sin that God will surely reckon for; such delight has God in showing mercy, and so backward is he to punish, that nothing is more pleasing to him than to be stopped in the ways of his judgments by intercessions, nor any thing more provoking than to *help forward the affliction* when he is but *a little displeased*, Zech. i. 15.

2. He must threaten the Ammonites with utter ruin for this insolence which they were guilty of. God turns away his wrath from Israel against them, as is said, Prov. xxiv. 17, 18. God is jealous for his people's honour, because his own is so nearly interested in it. And therefore those that touch that shall be made to know that they touch the apple of his eye. He had before predicted the destruction of the Ammonites, *ch.* xxi. 28. Had they repented, that would have been revoked; but now it is ratified. (1.) A destroying enemy is brought against them: *I will deliver thee to the men of the east*, first to the Chaldeans, who came from the northeast, and whose army, under the command of Nebuchadnezzar, destroyed the country of the Ammonites, about five years after the destruction of Jerusalem (as Josephus relates, *Antiq. lib.* x. *cap.* 11), and then to the Arabians, who were properly the *children of the east*, who, when the Chaldeans had made the country desolate, and quitted it, came and took possession of it for themselves, probably with the consent of the conquerors. Shepherds' tents were their palaces; these they set up in the country of the Ammonites; there they *made their dwellings*, *v.* 4. They enjoyed the products of the country: *They shall eat thy fruit and drink thy milk;* and the milk from the cattle is the fruit of the ground at second-hand. They made use even of the royal city for their cattle (*v.* 5): *I will make Rabbath*, that was a nice and splendid city, to be *a stable for camels;* for its new masters, whose wealth lies all in cattle, will not think they can put the palaces of Rabbath to a better use. Rab-

bath had been a habitation of brutish men; justly therefore is it now made a *stable for camels* and the country a *couching-place for flocks*, more innocent beasts than those with which it had been before replenished. (2.) God himself acts as an enemy to them (*v.* 7): *I will stretch out my hand upon thee*, a hand that will reach far and strike home, which there is no resisting the blow of, for it is a mighty hand, nor bearing the weight of, for it is a heavy hand. God's hand stretched out against the Ammonites will not only deliver them *for a spoil to the heathen*, so that all their neighbours shall prey upon them, but will *cut them off from the people* and *make them perish out of the countries*, so that there shall be no remains of them in that place. Compare with this, Jer. xlix. 1, &c. What can sound more terrible than that resolution (*v.* 7), *I will destroy thee?* For the almighty God is able both *to save and to destroy*, and it is *a fearful thing to fall into his hands*. Both the threatenings here (*v.* 5 and *v.* 7) conclude with this, *You shall know that I am the Lord*. For, [1.] Thus God will maintain his own honour, and will make it appear that he is the God of Israel, though he suffers them for a time to be captives in Babylon. [2.] Thus he will bring those that were strangers to him into an acquaintance with him, and it will be a blessed effect of their calamities. Better know God and be poor than be rich and ignorant of him.

8 Thus saith the Lord GOD; Because that Moab and Seir do say, Behold, the house of Judah *is* like unto all the heathen; 9 Therefore, behold, I will open the side of Moab from the cities, from his cities *which are* on his frontiers, the glory of the country, Beth-jeshimoth, Baal-meon, and Kiriathaim, 10 Unto the men of the east with the Ammonites, and will give them in possession, that the Ammonites may not be remembered among the nations. 11 And I will execute judgments upon Moab; and they shall know that I *am* the LORD. 12 Thus saith the Lord GOD; Because that Edom hath dealt against the house of Judah by taking vengeance, and hath greatly offended, and revenged himself upon them; 13 Therefore thus saith the Lord GOD; I will also stretch out mine hand upon Edom, and will cut off man and beast from it; and I will make it desolate from Teman; and they of Dedan shall fall by the sword. 14 And I will lay my vengeance upon Edom by the hand

of my people Israel: and they shall do in Edom according to mine anger and according to my fury; and they shall know my vengeance, saith the Lord God. 15 Thus saith the Lord God; Because the Philistines have dealt by revenge, and have taken vengeance with a despiteful heart, to destroy *it* for the old hatred; 16 Therefore thus saith the Lord God; Behold, I will stretch out mine hand upon the Philistines, and I will cut off the Cherethims, and destroy the remnant of the sea coast. 17 And I will execute great vengeance upon them with furious rebukes; and they shall know that I *am* the Lord, when I shall lay my vengeance upon them.

Three more of Israel's ill-natured neighbours are here arraigned, convicted, and condemned to destruction, for contributing to and triumphing in Jerusalem's fall.

I. The Moabites. Seir, which was the seat of the Edomites, is joined with them (*v.* 8), because they said the same as the Moabites; but they were afterwards reckoned with by themselves, *v.* 12. Now observe,

1. What was the sin of the Moabites; they said, *Behold, the house of Judah is like unto all the heathen.* They triumphed, (1.) In the apostasies of Israel, were pleased to see them forsake their God and worship idols, and hoped that in a while their religion would be quite lost and forgotten and the *house of Judah* would be *like all the heathen,* perfect idolaters. When those that profess religion walk unworthy of their profession they encourage the enemies of religion to hope that it will in time sink, and be run down, and quite abandoned; but let the Moabites know that, though there are those of the house of Judah who have made themselves *like the heathen,* yet there is a remnant that retain their integrity, the religion of the house of Judah shall recover itself, its peculiarities shall be preserved, it shall not lose itself *among the heathen,* but distinguish itself from them, till it deliver itself honourably into a better institution. (2.) In the calamities of Israel. They said, " *The house of Judah is like all the heathen,* in as bad a state as they; their God is no more able to deliver them from this *overflowing scourge* of these parts of the world than the gods of the heathen are to deliver them. Where are the promises they gloried in and all the wonders which they and their fathers told us of? What the better are they for the covenant of peculiarity, upon which they so much valued themselves? Those that looked with so much scorn upon *all the heathen* are now set upon a level with them, or rather sunk below them." Note, Those who judge

only by outward appearance are ready to conclude that the people of God have lost all their privileges when they have lost their worldly prosperity, which does not follow, for good men, even in affliction, in captivity among the heathen, have graces and comforts within sufficient to distinguish them from all the heathen. Though the event seem one to the *righteous and wicked,* yet indeed it is vastly different.

2. What should be the punishment of Moab for this sin; because they triumphed in the overthrow of Judah, their country shall be in like manner overthrown with that of the Ammonites, who were guilty of the same sin (*v.* 9, 10): " *I will open the side of Moab,* will uncover its shoulder, will take away all its defences, that it may become an easy prey to any that will make a prey of it." (1.) See here how it shall be exposed; the frontier-towns, that were its strength and guard, shall be demolished by the Chaldean forces, and laid open. Some of the cities are here named, which are said to be *the glory of the country,* which they trusted in, and boasted of as impregnable; these shall decay, be deserted, or betrayed, or fall into the enemies' hands, so that Moab shall lie exposed, and whoever will may penetrate into the heart of the country. Note, Those who glory in any other defence and protection than that of the divine power, providence, and promise, will sooner or later see cause to be ashamed of their glorying. (2.) See here to whom it shall be exposed: *The men of the east,* when they come to take possession of the country of the Ammonites, shall seize that of the Moabites too. God, the Lord of all lands, will give them that land; for the kingdoms of men he gives to whomsoever he will. The Arabians, who are shepherds, and live quietly, plain men dwelling in tents, shall by an overruling Providence be put in possession of the land of the Moabites, who are soldiers, men of war, and cunning hunters, that live turbulently. The Chaldeans shall get it by war, and the Arabians shall enjoy it in peace. Concerning the Ammonites it is said, They shall no *more be remembered among the nations* (*v.* 10), for they had been accessory to the murder of Gedaliah, Jer. xl. 14. But of the Moabites it is said, *I will execute judgments upon Moab:* they shall feel the weight of God's displeasure, but perhaps not to that degree that the Ammonites shall; however, so far as that *they shall know that I am the Lord,* that the God of Israel is a God of power, and that his covenant with his people is not broken.

II. The Edomites, the posterity of Esau, between whom and Jacob there had been an old enmity. And here is,

1. The sin of the Edomites, *v.* 12. They not only triumphed in the ruin of Judah and Jerusalem, as the Moabites and Ammonites had done, but they took advantage from the present distressed state to which the Jews

were reduced to do them some real mischiefs, probably made inroads upon their frontiers and plundered their country : *Edom has dealt against the house of Judah by taking vengeance.* The Edomites had of old been tributaries to the Jews, according to the sentence that the elder should serve the younger. In Jehoram's time they revolted. Amaziah severely chastised them (2 Kings xiv. 7), and for this they *took vengeance.* Now they would pay off all the old scores, and not only incensed the Babylonians against Jerusalem, crying, *Rase it, rase it* (Ps. cxxxvii. 7), but cut *off those that escaped,* as we find in the prophecy of Obadiah, which is wholly directed against Edom, *v.* 11, 12, &c. It is called here *revenging a revenge,* which intimates that they were not only eager upon it, but very cruel in it, and recompensed to the Jews more than double. " Herein he *has greatly offended.*" Note, It is a great offence to God for us to revenge ourselves upon our brother; for God has said, *Vengeance is mine.* We are forbidden to *revenge* or to *bear a grudge.* Suppose Judah had been hard upon Edom formerly, it was a base thing for the Edomites now, in revenge for it, *to smite them secretly.* But the Jews had a divine warrant to reign over the Edomites, for that therefore they ought not to have made reprisals; and it was the more disingenuous for them to retain the old enmity when God had particularly commanded his people to forget it. Deut. xxiii. 7, *Thou shalt not abhor an Edomite.*

2. The judgments threatened against them for this sin. God will take them to task for it (*v.* 13): *I will stretch out my hand upon Edom.* Their country shall be desolate *from Teman,* which lay in the south part of it; and *they shall fall by the sword unto Dedan,* which lay north; the desolations of war should go through the nation. (1.) They had taken vengeance, and therefore God will *lay his vengeance* upon them (*v.* 14): *They shall know my vengeance.* Those that will not leave it to God to take vengeance for them may expect that he will take vengeance on them; and those that will not believe and fear his vengeance shall be made to know and feel his vengeance; they shall be dealt with *according to God's anger* and *according to his fury,* not according to the weakness of the instruments that are employed in it, but according to the strength of the arm that employs them. (2.) They had taken vengeance on Israel, and God will lay his vengeance on them *by the hand of his people Israel.* They suffered much by the Chaldeans, which seems to be referred to, Jer. xlix. 8. But besides that there were *saviours* to come *upon Mount Zion,* who should judge the mount of Esau (Obad. 21), and Israel's Redeemer comes *with dyed garments from Bozrah* (Isa. lxiii. 1), this implies a promise that Israel should recover itself again to such a degree as to be in a

capacity of curbing the insolence of its neighbours. And we find (1 Mac. v. 3) that *Judas Maccabeus fought against the children of Esau in Idumea, gave them a great overthrow, abated their courage, and took their spoil ;* and Josephus says *(Antiq. lib.* 13 *cap.* 17), that Hircanus made the Edomites tributaries to Israel. Note, The equity of God's judgments is to be observed when he not only avenges injuries upon those that did them, but by those against whom they were done.

III. The Philistines. And, 1. Their sin is much the same with that of the Edomites : They have *dealt by revenge* with the people of Israel, and have *taken vengeance with a despiteful heart,* not to disturb them only, but to *destroy them,* for *the old hatred* (*v.* 15), the old grudge they bore them, or (as the margin reads it) *with perpetual hatred,* a hatred that began long since and which they resolved to continue. The anger was implacable : they *dealt by revenge,* traded in the acts of malice; it was their constant practice, and their heart, their spiteful heart, was upon it. 2. Their punishment likewise is much the same, *v.* 16. Those that were for destroying God's people shall themselves be cut off and destroyed; and (*v.* 17) those that were for avenging themselves shall find that God will *execute great vengeance upon them.* This was fulfilled when that country was wasted by the Chaldean army, not long after the destruction of Jerusalem, which is foretold, Jer. xlvii. It was strange that these nations, which bordered upon the land of Israel, were not alarmed by the success of the Chaldean army, and made to tremble in the apprehension of their own danger; when their neighbour's house was on fire it was time to look to their own; but their impiety and malice made them forget their politics, till God by his judgments convinced them that the cup was going round, and they were the less safe for being secure.

CHAP. XXVI.

The prophet had soon done with those four nations that he set his face against in the foregoing chapters; for they were not at that time very considerable in the world, nor would their fall make any great noise among the nations nor any figure in history. But the city of Tyre is next set to the bar; this, being a place of vast trade, was known all the world over; and therefore here are three whole chapters, this and the two that follow, spent in the prediction of the destruction of Tyre. We have " the burden of Tyre," Isa. xxiii. It is but just mentioned in Jeremiah, as sharing with the natives in the common calamity, ch. xxv. 22 ; xxvii. 3 ; xlvii. 4. But Ezekiel is ordered to be copious upon that head. In this chapter we have, I. The sin charged upon Tyre, which was triumphing in the destruction of Jerusalem, ver. 2. II. The destruction of Tyrus itself foretold. 1. The extremity of this destruction : it shall be utterly ruined, ver. 4—6, 12—14. 2. The instruments of this destruction, many nations (ver. 3), and the king of Babylon by name with his vast victorious army, ver. 7—11. 3. The great surprise that this should give to the neighbouring nations, who would all wonder at the fall of so great a city and be alarmed at it, ver. 15—21.

AND it came to pass in the eleventh year, in the first *day* of the month, *that* the word of the LORD came unto me, saying, 2 Son of man, because that Tyrus hath said against

Jerusalem, Aha, she is broken *that was* the gates of the people: she is turned unto me: I shall be replenished, *now* she is laid waste: 3 Therefore thus saith the Lord GOD; Behold, I *am* against thee, O Tyrus, and will cause many nations to come up against thee, as the sea causeth his waves to come up. 4 And they shall destroy the walls of Tyrus, and break down her towers: I will also scrape her dust from her, and make her like the top of a rock. 5 It shall be *a place for* the spreading of nets in the midst of the sea: for I have spoken *it*, saith the Lord GOD: and it shall become a spoil to the nations. 6 And her daughters which *are* in the field shall be slain by the sword; and they shall know that I *am* the LORD. 7 For thus saith the Lord GOD; Behold, I will bring upon Tyrus Nebuchadrezzar king of Babylon, a king of kings, from the north, with horses, and with chariots, and with horsemen, and companies, and much people. 8 He shall slay with the sword thy daughters in the field: and he shall make a fort against thee, and cast a mount against thee, and lift up the buckler against thee. 9 And he shall set engines of war against thy walls, and with his axes he shall break down thy towers. 10 By reason of the abundance of his horses their dust shall cover thee: thy walls shall shake at the noise of the horsemen, and of the wheels, and of the chariots, when he shall enter into thy gates, as men enter a city wherein is made a breach. 11 With the hoofs of his horses shall he tread down all thy streets: he shall slay thy people by the sword, and thy strong garrisons shall go down to the ground. 12 And they shall make a spoil of thy riches, and make a prey of thy merchandise: and they shall break down thy walls, and destroy thy pleasant houses: and they shall lay thy stones and thy timber and thy dust in the midst of the water. 13 And I will cause the noise of thy songs to cease; and the sound of thy harps shall be no more heard. 14 And I will make thee like the top of

a rock: thou shalt be *a place* to spread nets upon; thou shalt be built no more: for I the LORD have spoken *it*, saith the Lord GOD.

This prophecy is dated in the eleventh year, which was the year that Jerusalem was taken, and *in the first day of the month*, but it is not said what month, some think the month in which Jerusalem was taken, which was the fourth month, others the month after; or perhaps it was the first month, and so it was the first day of the year. Observe here,

I. The pleasure with which the Tyrians looked upon the ruins of Jerusalem. Ezekiel was a great way off, in Babylon, but God told him what Tyrus said against Jerusalem (*v.* 2): "*Aha! she is broken*, broken to pieces, that was *the gates of the people*, to whom there was a great resort and where there was a general rendezvous of all nations, some upon one account and some upon another, and I shall get by it; all the wealth, power, and interest, which Jerusalem had, it is hoped, shall be turned to Tyre, and so *now* that *she is laid waste I shall be replenished*." We do not find that the Tyrians had such a hatred and enmity to Jerusalem and the sanctuary as the Ammonites and Edomites had, or were so spiteful and mischievous to the Jews. They were men of business, and of large acquaintance and free conversation, and therefore were not so bigoted, and of such a persecuting spirit, as the narrow souls that lived retired and knew not the world. All their care was to get estates, and enlarge their trade, and they looked upon Jerusalem not as an enemy, but as a rival. Hiram, king of Tyre, was a good friend to David and Solomon, and we do not read of any quarrels the Jews had with the Tyrians; but Tyre promised herself that the fall of Jerusalem would be an advantage to her in respect of trade and commerce, that now she shall have Jerusalem's customers, and the great men from all parts that used to come to Jerusalem for the accomplishing of themselves, and to spend their estates there, will now come to Tyre and spend them there; and whereas many, since the Chaldean army became so formidable in those parts, had retired into Jerusalem, and brought their estates thither for safety, as the Rechabites did, now they will come to Tyre, which, being in a manner surrounded with the sea, will be thought a place of greater strength than Jerusalem, and thus the prosperity of Tyre will rise out of the ruins of Jerusalem. Note, To be secretly pleased with the death or decay of others, when we are likely to get by it, with their fall when we may thrive upon it, is a sin that does most easily beset us, but is not thought to be such a bad thing, and so provoking to God, as really it is. We are apt to say, when those who stand in our light, in our way, are removed, when they break or fall into disgrace, "We shall be *replenished* now that they are *laid waste.*" But this comes from a selfish covetous principle, and a desire to be *placed alone in the midst of the earth,* as if we grudged that any should live by us. This comes from a want of that love to our neighbour as to ourselves which the law of God so expressly requires, and from that inordinate love of the world as our happiness which the love of God so expressly forbids. And it is just with God to blast the designs and projects of those who thus contrive to raise themselves upon the ruins of others; and we see they are often disappointed.

II. The displeasure of God against them for it. The providence of God had done well for Tyrus. Tyrus was a pleasant and wealthy city, and might have continued so if she had, as she ought to have done, sympathized with Jerusalem in her calamities and sent her an address of condolence; but when, instead of that, she showed herself pleased with her neighbour's fall, and perhaps sent an address of congratulation to the conquerors, then God says, *Behold, I am against thee, O Tyrus! v.* 3. And let her not expect to prosper long if God be against her.

1. God will bring formidable enemies upon her: *Many nations shall come against thee,* an army made up of many nations, or one nation that shall be as strong as many. Those that have God against them may expect all the creatures against them; for what peace can those have with whom God is at war? They shall come pouring in as *the waves of the sea,* one upon the neck of another, with an irresistible force. The person is named that shall bring this army upon them—*Nebuchadnezzar king of Babylon, a king of kings,* that had many kings tributaries to him and dependents on him, besides those that were his captives, Dan. ii. 37, 38. He is that *head of gold.* He shall come with a vast army, *horses and chariots,* &c., all landforces. We do not find that he had any naval force, or any thing wherewith he might attack it by sea, which made the attempt the more difficult, as we find *ch.* xxix. 18, where it is called a *great service which he served against Tyrus.* He shall besiege it in form (*v.* 8), *make a fort, and cast a mount,* and (*v.* 9) shall *set engines of war against the walls.* His troops shall be so numerous as to raise a dust that shall cover the city, *v.* 10. They shall make a noise that shall even *shake the walls;* and they shall shout at every attack, as soldiers do when they *enter a city* that is *broken up;* the horses shall prance with so much fury and violence that they shall even *tread down the streets* though so ever well paved.

2. They shall do terrible execution. (1.) The enemy shall make themselves masters of all their fortifications, shall *destroy the walls* and *break down the towers, v.* 4. For

what walls are so strongly built as to be a fence against the judgments of God? Her *strong garrisons shall go down to the ground, v.* 11. And the walls shall be broken down, *v.* 12. The city held out a long siege, but it was taken at last. (2.) A great deal of blood shall be shed: *Her daughters who are in the field,* the cities upon the continent, which were subject to Tyre as the mother-city, the inhabitants of them *shall be slain by the sword, v.* 6. The invaders begin with those that come first in their way. And (*v.* 11) *he shall slay thy people with the sword;* not only the soldiers that are found in arms, but the burghers, shall be *put to the sword,* the king of Babylon being highly incensed against them for holding out so long. (3.) The wealth of the city shall all become a spoil to the conqueror (*v.* 12): They *shall make a prey of the merchandise.* It was in hope of the plunder that the city was set upon with so much vigour. See the vanity of riches, that they are *kept for the owners to their hurt;* they entice and recompense thieves, and not only cease to benefit those who took pains for them and were duly entitled to them, but are made to serve their enemies, who are thereby put into a capacity of doing them so much the more mischief. (4.) The city itself shall be laid in ruins. All the *pleasant houses* shall be *destroyed* (*v.* 12), such as were pleasantly situated, beautified, and furnished, shall become a heap of rubbish. Let none please themselves too much in their pleasant houses, for they know no how soon they may see the desolation of them. Tyre shall be utterly ruined; the enemy shall not only pull down the houses, but shall carry away *the stones and the timber,* which might serve for the rebuilding of it, and shall *lay them in the midst of the water,* not to be recovered, or ever made use of again. Nay (*v.* 4), *I will scrape her dust from her;* not only shall the loose dust be blown away, but the very ground it stands upon shall be torn up by the enraged enemy, carried off, and laid *in the midst of the water, v.* 12. The *foundation* is *in the dust;* that dust shall be all taken away, and then the city must fall of course. When Jerusalem was destroyed it was *ploughed like a field,* Mic. iii. 12. But the destruction of Tyre is carried further than that; the very soil of it shall be scraped away, and it shall be made *like the top of a rock* (*v.* 4, 14), pure rock that has no earth to cover it; it shall only be a place *for the spreading of nets* (*v.* 5, 14); it shall serve fishermen to dry their nets upon and mend them. (5.) There shall be a full period to all its mirth and joy (*v.* 13): *I will cause the noise of thy songs to cease.* Tyre had been a joyous city (Isa. xxiii. 7); with her songs she had courted customers to deal with her in a way of trade. But now farewell all her profitable commerce and pleasant conversation; Tyre is no more a place either of business or of sport. *Lastly,* It shall be built no more (v. 14), not built any more as it had been, with such state and magnificence, nor built any more in the same place, within the sea, nor built any where for a long time; the present inhabitants shall be destroyed or dispersed, so that this Tyre shall be *no more.* For *God has spoken it* (v. 5, 14); and when what he has said is accomplished *they shall know* thereby that *he is the Lord,* and *not a man that he should lie nor the son of man that he should repent.*

15 Thus saith the Lord God to Tyrus; Shall not the isles shake at the sound of thy fall, when the wounded cry, when the slaughter is made in the midst of thee? 16 Then all the princes of the sea shall come down from their thrones, and lay away their robes, and put off their broidered garments: they shall clothe themselves with trembling; they shall sit upon the ground, and shall tremble at *every* moment, and be astonished at thee. 17 And they shall take up a lamentation for thee, and say to thee, How art thou destroyed, *that wast* inhabited of seafaring men, the renowned city, which was strong in the sea, she and her inhabitants, which cause their terror *to be* on all that haunt it! 18 Now shall the isles tremble in the day of thy fall; yea, the isles that *are* in the sea shall be troubled at thy departure. 19 For thus saith the Lord God; When I shall make thee a desolate city, like the cities that are not inhabited; when I shall bring up the deep upon thee, and great waters shall cover thee; 20 When I shall bring thee down with them that descend into the pit, with the people of old time, and shall set thee in the low parts of the earth, in places desolate of old, with them that go down to the pit, that thou be not inhabited; and I shall set glory in the land of the living; 21 I will make thee a terror, and thou *shalt be* no *more:* though thou be sought for, yet shalt thou never be found again, saith the Lord God.

The utter ruin of Tyre is here represented in very strong and lively figures, which are exceedingly affecting.

1. See how high, how great, Tyre had been, how little likely ever to come to this. The remembrance of men's former grandeur

and plenty is a great aggravation of their present disgrace and poverty. Tyre was *a renowned city* (v. 17), famous among the nations, the *crowning* city (so she is called Isa. xxiii. 8), a city that had crowns in her gift, honoured all she smiled upon, crowned herself and all about her. She was *inhabited of seas,* that is, of those that trade at sea, of those who from all parts came thither by sea, bringing with them the *abundance of the seas* and *the treasures hidden in the sand.* She was *strong in the sea,* easy of access to her friends, but to her enemies inaccessible, fortified by a *wall of water,* which made her impregnable. So that *she* with her pomp, *and her inhabitants* with their pride, *caused their terror to be on all that haunted* that city, and upon any account frequented it. It was well fortified, and formidable in the eyes of all that acquainted themselves with it. Every body stood in awe of the Tyrians and was afraid of disobliging them. Note, Those who know their strength are too apt to cause terror, to pride themselves in frightening those they are an over-match for.

2. See how low, how little, Tyre is made, v. 19, 20. This *renowned city* is made a *desolate city,* is no more frequented as it has been; there is no more resort of merchants to it; it is *like the cities not inhabited,* which are no cities, and, having none to keep them in repair, will go to decay of themselves. Tyre shall be like a city overflowed by an inundation of waters, which *cover* it, and upon which the *deep* is *brought up.* As the waves had formerly been its defence, so now they shall be its destruction. She shall be *brought down with those that descend into the pit,* with the cities of the old world that were under water, and with *Sodom and Gomorrah,* that lie in the bottom of the Dead Sea. Or, she shall be in the condition of those who have been long buried, of the *people of old time,* who are old inhabitants of the silent grave, who are quite rotted away under ground and quite forgotten above ground; such shall *Tyre be, free among the dead, set in the lower parts of the earth,* humbled, mortified, reduced. It shall be *like the places desolate of old,* as well as like persons dead of old; it shall be like other cities that have formerly been in like manner deserted and destroyed. It shall *not be inhabited* again; none shall have the courage to attempt the rebuilding of it upon that spot, so that *it shall be no more;* the Tyrians shall be lost among the nations, so that people will look in vain for Tyre in Tyre: *Thou shalt be sought for, and never found again.* New persons may build a new city upon a new spot of ground hard by, which they may call *Tyre,* but Tyre, as it is, shall never be any more. Note, The strongest cities in this world, the best-fortified and best-furnished, are subject to decay, and may in a little time be brought to nothing. In the history of our own island many cities are spoken of as in being when

the Romans were here which now our antiquaries scarcely know where to look for, and of which there remains no more evidence than Roman urns and coins digged up there sometimes accidentally. But in the other world we look for a city that shall stand for ever and flourish in perfection through all the ages of eternity.

3. See what a distress the inhabitants of Tyre are in (*v.* 15): *There is a great slaughter made in the midst of thee,* many slain, and great men. It is probable that, when the city was taken, the generality of the inhabitants were put to the sword. Then did *the wounded cry,* and they cried in vain, to the pitiless conquerors; they cried *quarter,* but it would not be given them; the wounded are *slain* without mercy, or, rather, that is the only mercy that is shown them, that the second blow shall rid them out of their pain.

4. See what a consternation all the neighbours are in upon the fall of Tyre. This is elegantly expressed here, to show how astonishing it should be. (1.) The *islands shall shake at the sound of thy fall* (*v.* 15), as, when a great merchant breaks, all that he deals with are shocked by it, and begin to look about them; perhaps they had effects in his hands, which they are afraid they shall lose. Or, when they see one fail and become bankrupt of a sudden, in debt a great deal more than he is worth, it makes them afraid for themselves, lest they should do so too. Thus *the isles,* which thought themselves safe in the embraces of the sea, when they see Tyrus fall, shall *tremble* and *be troubled,* saying, "What will become of us?" And it is well if they make this good use of it, to take warning by it not to be secure, but to stand in awe of God and his judgments. The sudden fall of a great tower shakes the ground round about it; thus all the islands in the Mediterranean Sea shall feel themselves sensibly touched by the destruction of Tyre, it being a place they had so much knowledge of, such interests in, and such a constant correspondence with. (2.) The *princes of the sea* shall be affected with it, who ruled in those islands. Or the rich merchants, who live like princes (Isa. xxiii. 8), and the masters of ships, who command like princes, these shall condole the fall of Tyre in a most compassionate and pathetic manner (*v.* 16): *They shall come down from their thrones,* as neglecting the business of their thrones and despising the pomp of them. They shall *lay away their robes* of state, *their broidered garments,* and shall *clothe themselves* all over with *tremblings,* with sackcloth that will make them shiver. Or they shall by their own act and deed make themselves to tremble upon this occasion; they shall *sit upon the ground* in shame and sorrow; they shall *tremble every moment* at the thought of what has happened to Tyre, and for fear of what may happen to themselves; for what island is safe if Tyre be not? They shall *take up a*

lamentation for thee, shall have elegies and mournful poems penned upon the fall of Tyre, *v.* 17. *How art thou destroyed!* [1.] It shall be a great surprise to them, and they shall be affected with wonder, that a place so well fortified by nature and art, so famed for politics and so full of money, which is the sinews of war, that held out so long and with so much bravery, should be taken at last (*v.* 21): *I make thee a terror.* Note, It is just with God to make those a terror to their neighbours, by the suddenness and strangeness of their punishment, who make themselves a terror to their neighbours by the abuse of their power. Tyre had *caused her terror* (*v.* 17) and now is made a terrible example. [2.] It shall be a great affliction to them, and they shall be affected with sorrow (*v.* 17); they shall *take up a lamentation for Tyre,* as thinking it a thousand pities that such a rich and splendid city should be thus laid in ruins. When Jerusalem, the holy city, was destroyed, there were no such lamentations for it; it was *nothing* to *those that passed by* (Lam. i. 12); but when Tyre, the trading city, fell, it was universally bemoaned. Note, Those who have the world in their hearts lament the loss of great men more than the loss of good men. [3.] It shall be a loud alarm to them: *They shall tremble in the day of thy fall,* because they shall have reason to think that their own turn will be next. If Tyre fall, who can stand? *Howl, fir-trees, if such a cedar be shaken.* Note, The fall of others should awaken us out of our security. The death or decay of others in the world is a check to us, when we dream that our mountain *stands strongly and shall not be moved.*

5. See how the irreparable ruin of Tyre is aggravated by the prospect of the restoration of Israel. Thus shall Tyre sink *when I shall set glory in the land of the living, v.* 20. Note, (1.) The holy land is the *land of the living:* for none but holy souls are properly living souls. Where living sacrifices are offered to the living God, and where the lively oracles are, there *the land of the living* is; there David hoped to *see the goodness of the Lord,* Ps. xxvii. 13. That was a type of heaven, which is indeed the *land of the living.* (2.) Though this land of the living may for a time lie under disgrace, yet God will again *set glory* in it; the glory that had departed shall return, and the restoration of what they had been deprived of shall be so much more their glory. God will himself be the glory of the lands that are the lands of the living. (3.) It will aggravate the misery of those that have their portion in the land of the dying, of those that are for ever dying, to behold the happiness of those, at the same time, that shall have their everlasting portion in the land of the living. When the rich man was himself in torment he saw Lazarus in the bosom of Abraham, and glory set for him in the land of the living.

CHAP. XXVII.

Still we are attending the funeral of Tyre and the lamentations made for the fall of that renowned city. In this chapter we have, I. A large account of the dignity, wealth, and splendour of Tyre, while it was in its strength, the vast trade it drove, and the interest it had among the nations (ver. 1—25), which is designed to make its ruin the more lamentable. II. A prediction of its fall and ruin, and the confusion and consternation which all its neighbours shall thereby be put into, ver. 26—36. And this is intended to stain the pride of all worldly glory, and, by setting the one over-against the other, to let us see the vanity and uncertainty of the riches, honours, and pleasures of the world, and what little reason we have to place our happiness in them or to be confident of the continuance of them; so that all this is written for our learning.

THE word of the LORD came again unto me, saying, 2 Now, thou son of man, take up a lamentation for Tyrus; 3 And say unto Tyrus, O thou that art situate at the entry of the sea, *which art* a merchant of the people for many isles, Thus saith the Lord GOD; O Tyrus, thou hast said, I *am* of perfect beauty. 4 Thy borders *are* in the midst of the seas, thy builders have perfected thy beauty. 5 They have made all thy *ship* boards of fir trees of Senir: they have taken cedars from Lebanon to make masts for thee. 6 *Of* the oaks of Bashan have they made thine oars; the company of the Ashurites have made thy benches *of* ivory, *brought* out of the isles of Chittim. 7 Fine linen with broidered work from Egypt was that which thou spreadest forth to be thy sail; blue and purple from the isles of Elishah was that which covered thee. 8 The inhabitants of Zidon and Arvad were thy mariners: thy wise *men*, O Tyrus, *that* were in thee, were thy pilots. 9 The ancients of Gebal and the wise *men* thereof were in thee thy calkers: all the ships of the sea with their mariners were in thee to occupy thy merchandise. 10 They of Persia and of Lud and of Phut were in thine army, thy men of war: they hanged the shield and helmet in thee; they set forth thy comeliness. 11 The men of Arvad with thine army *were* upon thy walls round about, and the Gammadims were in thy towers: they hanged their shields upon thy walls round about; they have made thy beauty perfect. 12 Tarshish *was* thy merchant by reason of the multitude of all *kind of* riches; with silver, iron, tin, and lead, they traded in thy fairs. 13 Javan, Tubal, and Meshech, they *were* thy merchants: they traded the persons

910

of men and vessels of brass in thy market. 14 They of the house of Togarmah traded in thy fairs with horses and horsemen and mules. 15 The men of Dedan *were* thy merchants; many isles *were* the merchandise of thine hand: they brought thee *for* a present horns of ivory and ebony. 16 Syria *was* thy merchant by reason of the multitude of the wares of thy making: they occupied in thy fairs with emeralds, purple, and broidered work, and fine linen, and coral, and agate. 17 Judah, and the land of Israel, they *were* thy merchants: they traded in thy market wheat of Minneth, and Pannag, and honey, and oil, and balm. 18 Damascus *was* thy merchant in the multitude of the wares of thy making, for the multitude of all riches; in the wine of Helbon, and white wool. 19 Dan also and Javan going to and fro occupied in thy fairs: bright iron, cassia, and calamus, were in thy market. 20 Dedan *was* thy merchant in precious clothes for chariots. 21 Arabia, and all the princes of Kedar, they occupied with thee in lambs, and rams, and goats: in these *were they* thy merchants. 22 The merchants of Shebah and Raamah, they *were* thy merchants: they occupied in thy fairs with chief of all spices, and with all precious stones, and gold. 23 Haran, and Canneh, and Eden, the merchants of Sheba, Ashur, *and* Chilmad, *were* thy merchants. 24 These *were* thy merchants in all sorts *of things*, in blue clothes, and broidered work, and in chests of rich apparel, bound with cords, and made of cedar, among thy merchandise. 25 The ships of Tarshish did sing of thee in thy market: and thou wast replenished, and made very glorious in the midst of the seas.

Here, I. The prophet is ordered to take up a lamentation for Tyrus, *v.* 2. It was yet in the height of its prosperity, and there appeared not the least symptom of its decay; yet the prophet must lament it, because its prosperity is its snare, is the cause of its pride and security, which will make its fall the more grievous. Even those that live at ease are to be lamented if they be not preparing for trouble. He must lament it because its ruin is hastening on apace; it is sure, it is near; and though the prophet foretel it, and justify God in it, yet he must lament it. Note, We ought to mourn for the miseries of other nations, as well as for our own, out of an affection for mankind in general; it is a part of the honour we owe to all men to bewail their calamities, even those which they have brought upon themselves by their own folly.

II. He is directed what to say, and to say it in the name of *the Lord Jehovah*, a name not unknown in Tyre, and which shall be better known, *ch*. xxvi. 6.

1. He must upbraid Tyre with her pride: *O Tyrus! thou hast said, I am of perfect beauty* (*v*. 3), of *universal beauty* (so the word is), every way accomplished, and therefore every where admired. Zion, that had the *beauty of holiness*, is called indeed the *perfection of beauty* (Ps. l. 2); that is the *beauty of the Lord*. But Tyre, because well-built and well-filled with money and trade, will set up for a perfect beauty. Note, It is the folly of the children of this world to value themselves on the pomp and pleasure they live in, to call themselves beauties for the sake of them, and, if in these they excel others, to think themselves perfect. But God takes notice of the vain conceits men have of themselves in their prosperity when the mind is lifted up with the condition, and often, for the humbling of the spirit, finds a way to bring down the estate. Let none reckon themselves beautified any further than they are sanctified, nor say that they are of perfect beauty till they come to heaven.

2. He must upbraid Tyre with her prosperity, which was the matter of her pride. In elegies it is usual to insert encomiums of those whose fall we lament; the prophet, accordingly, praises Tyre for all that she had that was praiseworthy. He has nothing to say of her religion, her piety, her charity, her being a refuge to the distressed or using her interest to do good offices among her neighbours; but she lived great, and had a great trade, and all the trading part of mankind made court to her. The prophet must describe her height and magnificence, that God may be the more glorified in her fall, as the God who *looks upon every one that is proud and abases him, hides the proud in the dust together, and binds their faces in secret*, Job xl. 12.

(1.) The city of Tyre was advantageously situated, *at the entry of the sea* (*v*. 3), having many commodious harbours each way, not as cities seated on rivers, which the shipping can come but one way to. It stood at the east end of the Mediterranean, very convenient for trade by land into all the Levant parts; so that she became a *merchant of the people for many isles*. Lying between Greece and Asia, it became the great emporium, or mart-town, the rendezvous of merchants from all parts: *Thy borders are in the heart of the seas, v*. 4. It was surrounded with water, which was a great advantage to its trade; it was the darling of the sea, laid in its bosom,

in its heart. Note, It is a great convenience, upon many accounts, to live in an island: seas are the most *ancient land-mark*, not *which our fathers have set*, but the God of our fathers, and which cannot be removed as other land-marks may, nor so easily got over. The people so situated may the more easily *dwell alone*, if they please, as *not reckoned among the nations*, and yet, if they please, may the more easily traffic abroad and keep a correspondence with the nations. We therefore of this island must own that he who determines the bounds of men's habitations has determined well for us.

(2.) It was curiously built, according as the fashion then was; and, being a city on a hill, it made a glorious show and tempted the ships that sailed by into her ports (*v*. 4): *Thy builders have perfected thy beauty;* they have so improved in architecture that nothing appears in the buildings of Tyre that can be found fault with; and yet it wants that perfection of beauty into which the Lord does and will build up his Jerusalem.

(3.) It had its haven replenished with abundance of *gallant ships*, Isa. xxxiii. 21. The ship-carpenters did their part, as well as the house-carpenters theirs. The Tyrians are thought to be the first that invented the art of navigation; at least they improved it, and brought it to as great a perfection perhaps as it could be without the loadstone. [1.] They made the *boards*, or planks, for the hulk of the ship, of *fir-trees* fetched from *Senir*, a mount in the land of Israel, joined with Hermon, Cant. iv. 8. Planks of fir were smooth and light, but not so lasting as our English oak. [2.] They had cedars from Lebanon, another mountain of Israel, for their masts, *v*. 5. [3.] They had oaks from Bashan (Isa. ii. 13), to make oars of; for it is probable that their ships were mostly galleys, that go with oars. The people of Israel built few ships for themselves, but they furnished the Tyrians with timber for shipping. Thus one country uses what another produces, and so they are serviceable one to another, and cannot say to each other, *I have no need of thee*. [4.] Such magnificence did they affect in building their ships that they made the very *benches* of *ivory*, which they fetched from *the isles of Chittim*, from Italy or Greece, and had workmen from the Ashurites or Assyrians to make them, so rich would they have their state-rooms in their ships to be. [5.] So very prodigal were they that they made their *sails* of *fine linen* fetched from Egypt, and that *embroidered* too, *v*. 7. Or it may be meant of their *flags* (which they hoisted to notify what city they belonged to), which were very costly. The word signifies a *banner* as well as a *sail*. [6.] They hung those rooms on ship-board with *blue and purple*, the richest cloths and richest colours they could get from the isles they traded with. For though Tyre was itself famous for purple, which is therefore called the

Tyrian dye, yet they must have that which was far-fetched.

(4.) These gallant ships were well-manned, by men of great ingenuity and industry. The pilots and masters of the ships, that had command in their fleets, were of their own city, such as they could put a confidence in (*v.* 8) : *Thy wise men, O Tyrus ! that were in thee, were thy pilots.* But, for common sailors, they had men from other countries : *The inhabitants of Arvad and Zidon were thy mariners.* These came from cities near them ; Zidon was sister to Tyre, not two leagues off, to the northward ; there they bred able seamen, which it is the interest of the maritime powers to support and give all the countenance they can to. They sent to Gebal in Syria for *calkers,* or *strengtheners of the clefts* or *chinks,* to stop them when the ships come home, after long voyages, to be repaired. To do this they had the *ancients* and *wise men* (*v.* 9) ; for there is more need of wisdom and prudence to repair what has gone to decay than to build anew. In public matters there is occasion for the *ancients* and *wise men* to be the *repairers of the breaches and the restorers of paths to dwell in.* Nay, all the countries they traded with were at their service, and were willing to send men into their pay, to put their youths apprentice in Tyre, or to put them on board their fleets ; so that *all the ships in the sea with their mariners were* ready *to occupy thy merchandise.* Those that give good wages shall have hands at command.

(5.) Their city was guarded by a military force that was very considerable, *v.* 10, 11. The Tyrians were themselves wholly given to trade ; but it was necessary that they should have a good army on foot, and therefore they took those of other states into their pay, such as were fittest for service, though they had them from afar (which perhaps was their policy), from Persia, Lud, and Phut. These bore their arms when there was occasion, and in time of peace *hung up the shield and buckler* in the armoury, as it were to proclaim peace, and let the world know that they had at present no need of them, but they were ready to be taken down whenever there was occasion for them. Their *walls* were *guarded* by the *men of Arvad ;* their *towers* were garrisoned by *the Gammadim,* robust men, that had a great deal of strength in *their arms ;* yet the vulgar Latin renders it *pygmies,* men no longer than one's arm. They *hung their shields upon the walls* in their magazines or places of arms ; or hung them out upon the walls of the city, that none might dare to approach them, seeing how well provided they were with all things necessary for their own defence. " Thus *they set forth thy comeliness* (v. 10), and *made thy beauty perfect," v.* 11 It contributed as much as any thing to the glory of Tyre that it had those of all the surrounding nations in its service, except the land of Israel (though it lay

next them), which furnished them with timber, but we do not find that it furnished them with men ; that would have trenched upon the liberty and dignity of the Jewish nation, 2 Chron. ii. 17, 18. It was also the glory of Tyre that it had such a militia, so fit for service, and in constant pay, and such an armoury, like that in the tower of David, where hung the *shields of mighty men,* Cant. iv. 4. It is observable that there and here the armouries are said to be furnished with *shields* and *helmets,* defensive arms, not with swords and spears, offensive, though it is probable that there were such, to intimate that the military force of a people must be intended only for their own protection and not to invade and annoy their neighbours, to secure their own right, not to encroach upon the rights of others.

(6.) They had a vast trade and a correspondence with all parts of the known world. Some nations they dealt with in one commodity and some in another, according as either its products or its manufactures were, and the fruits of nature or art were, with which it was blessed. This is very much enlarged upon here, as that which was the principal glory of Tyre, and which supported all the rest. We do not find any where in scripture so many nations named together as are here ; so that this chapter, some think, gives much light to the first account we have of the settlement of the nations after the flood, Gen. x. The critics have abundance of work here to find out the several places and nations spoken of. Concerning many of them their conjectures are different and they leave us in the dark and at much uncertainty ; it is well that it is not material. Modern surveys come short of explaining the ancient geography. And therefore we will not amuse ourselves here with a particular enquiry either concerning the traders or the goods they traded in. We leave it to the critical expositors, and observe that only which is improvable. [1.] We have reason to think that Ezekiel knew little, of his own knowledge, concerning the trade of Tyre. He was a priest, carried away captive far enough from the neighbourhood of Tyre, we may suppose when he was young, and there he had been eleven years. And yet he speaks of the particular merchandises of Tyre as nicely as if he had been comptroller of the custom-house there, by which it appears that he was divinely inspired in what he spoke and wrote. It is God that *saith this, v.* 3. [2.] This account of the trade of Tyre intimates to us that God's eye is upon men, and that he takes cognizance of what they do when they are employed in their worldly business, not only when they are at church, praying and hearing, but when they are in their markets and fairs, and upon the exchange, buying and selling, which is a good reason why we should in all our dealings *keep a conscience void of offence,* and have our eye always upon him whose eye is always upon us. [3.] We may here observe the wisdom of God, and his goodness, as the common Father of mankind, in making one country to abound in one commodity and another in another, and all more or less serviceable either to the necessity or to the comfort or ornament of human life. *Non omnis fert omnia tellus—One land does not supply all the varieties of produce.* Providence dispenses its gifts variously, some to each, and all to none, that there may be a mutual commerce among those whom God has *made of one blood,* though they are made *to dwell on all the face of the earth,* Acts xvii. 26. Let every nation therefore thank God for the productions of its country; though they be not so rich as those of others, yet there is use for them in the public service of the world. [4.] See what a blessing trade and merchandise are to mankind, especially when followed in the fear of God, and with a regard not only to private advantage, but to a common benefit. *The earth is full of God's riches,* Ps. civ. 24. There is a *multitude of all kinds of riches* in it (as it is here, *v.* 12), gathered off its surface and dug out of its bowels. The earth is also full of the fruits of men's ingenuity and industry, according as their genius leads them. Now by exchange and barter these are made more extensively useful; thus what can be spared is helped off, and what is wanted is fetched in, in lieu of it, from the most distant countries. Those that are not tradesmen themselves have reason to thank God for tradesmen and merchants, by whom the productions of other countries are brought to our hands, as those of our own are by our husbandmen. [5.] Besides the necessaries that are here traded in, see what abundance of things are here mentioned that only serve to please fancy, and are made valuable only by men's humour and custom; and yet God allows us to use them, and trade in them, and part with those things for them which we can spare that are of an intrinsic worth much beyond them. Here are *horns of ivory and ebony* (*v.* 15), that are *brought for a present,* exposed to sale, and offered in exchange, or (as some think) presented to the city, or the great men of it, to obtain their favour. Here are *emeralds, coral,* and *agate* (*v.* 16), all *precious stones, and gold* (*v.* 22), which the world could better be without than iron and common stones. Here are, to please the taste and smell, the *chief of all spices* (*v.* 22), *cassia and calamus* (*v.* 19); and, for ornament, *purple, broidered work, and fine linen* (*v.* 16), *precious clothes for chariots* (*v.* 20), *blue clothes* (which Tyre was famous for), *broidered work,* and *chests of rich apparel, bound with* rich *cords,* and *made of cedar,* a sweet wood to perfume the garments kept in them, *v.* 24. Upon the review of this invoice, or bill of parcels, we may justly say, What a great many things are here that we have no need of, and can live very comfortably with-

out! [6.] It is observable that Judah and the *land of Israel* were merchants in Tyre too; in a way of trade they were allowed to converse with the heathen. But they traded mostly *in wheat,* a substantial commodity, and necessary, *wheat of Minnith and Pannag,* two countries in Canaan famous for the best wheat, as some think. The whole land indeed was a *land of wheat* (Deut. viii. 8); it had *the fat of kidneys of wheat,* Deut. xxxii. 14. Tyre was maintained by corn fetched from the land of Israel. They traded likewise in *honey, and oil,* and *balm,* or *rosin;* all useful things, and not serving to pride or luxury. And the land which these were the staple commodities of was that which was the *glory of all lands,* which God reserved for his peculiar people, not those that traded in spices and *precious stones;* and the Israel of God must reckon themselves well provided for if they have *food convenient;* for those that are acquainted with the delights of the children of God will not set their hearts on the *delights of the sons and daughters of men,* or the *treasures of kings and provinces.* We find indeed that the New-Testament Babylon trades in such things as Tyre traded in, Rev. xviii. 12, 13. For, notwithstanding its pretensions to sanctity, it is a mere worldly interest. [7.] Though Tyre was a city of great merchandise, and they got abundance by buying and selling, importing commodities from one place and exporting them to another, yet manufacture-trades were not neglected. The *wares of their own making,* and a *multitude of such wares,* are here spoken of, *v.* 16, 18. It is the wisdom of a nation to encourage art and industry, and not to bear hard upon the handicraft-tradesmen; for it contributes much to the wealth and honour of a nation to send abroad *wares of their own making,* which may bring them in the *multitude of all riches.* [8.] All this made Tyrus very great and very proud: *The ships of Tarshish did sing of thee in thy market* (*v.* 25); thou wast admired and cried up by all the nations that had dealings with thee; for *thou wast replenished* in wealth and number of people, wast beautified, and *made very glorious, in the midst of the seas.* Those that grow very rich are cried up as very glorious; for riches are glorious things in the eyes of carnal people, Gen. xxxi. 1.

26 Thy rowers have brought thee into great waters : the east wind hath broken thee in the midst of the seas. 27 Thy riches, and thy fairs, thy merchandise, thy mariners, and thy pilots, thy calkers, and the occupiers of thy merchandise, and all thy men of war, that *are* in thee, and in all thy company which *is* in the midst of thee, shall fall into the midst of the seas in the day of thy ruin. 28 The suburbs

shall shake at the sound of the cry of thy pilots. 29 And all that handle the oar, the mariners, *and* all the pilots of the sea, shall come down from their ships, they shall stand upon the land; 30 And shall cause their voice to be heard against thee, and shall cry bitterly, and shall cast up dust upon their heads, they shall wallow themselves in the ashes : 31 And they shall make themselves utterly bald for thee, and gird them with sackcloth, and they shall weep for thee with bitterness of heart *and* bitter wailing. 32 And in their wailing they shall take up a lamentation for thee, and lament over thee, *saying,* What *city is* like Tyrus, like the destroyed in the midst of the sea? 33 When thy wares went forth out of the seas, thou filledst many people; thou didst enrich the kings of the earth with the multitude of thy riches and of thy merchandise. 34 In the time *when* thou shalt be broken by the seas in the depths of the waters thy merchandise and all thy company in the midst of thee shall fall. 35 All the inhabitants of the isles shall be astonished at thee, and their kings shall be sore afraid, they shall be troubled in *their* countenance. 36 The merchants among the people shall hiss at thee; thou shalt be a terror, and never *shalt be* any more.

We have seen Tyre flourishing; here we have Tyre falling, and great is the fall of it, so much the greater for its having made such a figure in the world. Note, The most mighty and magnificent kingdoms and states, sooner or later, have their day to come down. They have their period; and, when they are in their zenith, they will begin to decline. But the destruction of Tyre was sudden. Her *sun went down at noon.* And all her wealth and grandeur, pomp and power, did but aggravate her ruin, and make it the more grievous to herself and astonishing to all about her. Now observe here, 1. How the ruin of Tyrus will be brought about, *v.* 26. She is as a great ship richly laden, that is split or sunk by the indiscretion of her steersmen : *Thy rowers have* themselves *brought thee into great* and dangerous *waters ;* the governors of the city, and those that had the management of their public affairs, by some mismanagement or other involved them in that war with the Chaldeans which was the ruin of their state. By their insolence, by

some affront given to the Chaldeans or some attempt made upon them, in confidence of their own ability to contend with them, they provoked Nebuchadnezzar to make a descent upon them, and, by their obstinacy in standing it out to the last, enraged him to such a degree that he determined on the ruin of their state, and, *like an east wind, broke them in the midst of the seas.* Note, It is ill with a people when those that sit at the stern, instead of putting them into the harbour, run them aground. 2. How great and general the ruin will be. All her wealth shall be buried with her, *her riches, her fairs, and her merchandise* (*v.* 27) ; all that had any dependence upon her, and dealings with her, in trade, in war, in conversation, shall *fall with her into the midst of the seas, in the day of her ruin.* Note, Those who make creatures their confidence, place their happiness in their interest in them and rest their hopes upon them, will of course fall with them; *happy* therefore *are those that have the God of Jacob for their help,* and *whose hope is in the Lord their God,* who lives for ever. 3. What sad lamentation would be made for the destruction of Tyre. The pilots, her princes and governors, when they see how wretchedly they have mismanaged and how much they have contributed to their own ruin, shall *cry out* so loud as to make even the *suburbs shake* (*v.* 28), such a vexation shall it be to them to reflect upon their own bad conduct. The inferior officers, that were as the mariners of the state, shall be forced to come down from their respective posts (*v.* 29), and they shall *cry out against thee,* as having deceived them, in not proving so well able to hold out as they thought thou hadst been; they shall *cry bitterly* for the common ruin, and their own share in it. They shall use all the most solemn expressions of grief; they shall *cast dust on their heads,* in indignation against themselves, shall *wallow themselves in ashes,* as having bid a final farewell to all ease and pleasure; they shall *make themselves bald* (*v.* 31), with *tearing their hair ;* and, according to the custom of great mourners, those shall *gird themselves with sackcloth* who used to wear fine linen, and, instead of merry songs, they shall *weep with bitterness of heart.* Note, Losses and crosses are very grievous, and hard to be borne, to those that have long been wallowing in pleasure and sleeping in carnal security. 4. How Tyre should be upbraided with her former honour and prosperity (*v.* 32, 33) ; she that was Tyrus the *renowned* shall now be called *Tyrus the destroyed* in the *midst of the sea.* " *What city is like Tyre?* Did ever any city come down from such a height of prosperity to such a depth of adversity? Time was when *thy wares,* those of thy own making and those that passed through thy hands, *went forth out of the seas,* and were exported to all parts of the world; then *thou filledst many people,* and didst *enrich the kings of the earth* and their kingdoms." The Tyrians, though they bore such a sway in trade, were yet, it seems, fair merchants, and let their neighbours not only live, but thrive by them. All that dealt with them were gainers; they did not cheat or oppress the people, but did enrich them with *the multitude of their merchandise.* " But now those that used to be enriched by thee shall be ruined with thee (as is usual in trade); " *when thou shalt be broken,* and all thou hast is seized on, *all thy company shall fall too," v.* 34. There is an end of Tyre, that made such a noise and bustle in the world. This great blaze goes out in a snuff. 5. How the fall of Tyre should be matter of terror to some and laughter to others, according as they were differently interested and affected. Some shall be *sorely afraid,* and shall *be troubled* (*v.* 35), concluding it will be their own turn to fall next. Others shall *hiss at her* (*v.* 36), shall ridicule her pride, and vanity, and bad management, and think her ruin just. She triumphed in Jerusalem's fall, and there are those that will triumph in hers. When God casts his judgments on the sinner *men* also *shall clap their hands at him* and *shall hiss him out of his place,* Job xxvii. 22, 23. *Is this the city which men called the perfection of beauty ?*

CHAP. XXVIII.

In this chapter we have, I. A prediction of the fall and ruin of the king of Tyre, who, in the destruction of that city, is particularly set up as a mark for God's arrows, ver. 1—10. II. A lamentation for the king of Tyre, when he has thus fallen, though he falls by his own iniquity, ver. 11—19. III. A prophecy of the destruction of Zidon, which was in the neighbourhood of Tyre and had a dependence upon it, ver. 20—23. IV. A promise of the restoration of the Israel of God, though in the day of their calamity they were insulted over by their neighbours, ver. 24—26.

THE word of the Lord came again unto me, saying, 2 Son of man, say unto the prince of Tyrus, Thus saith the Lord God; Because thine heart *is* lifted up, and thou hast said, I *am* a God, I sit *in* the seat of God, in the midst of the seas; yet thou *art* a man, and not God, though thou set thine heart as the heart of God: 3 Behold, thou *art* wiser than Daniel; there is no secret that they can hide from thee: 4 With thy wisdom and with thine understanding thou hast gotten thee riches, and hast gotten gold and silver into thy treasures: 5 By thy great wisdom *and* by thy traffick hast thou increased thy riches, and thine heart is lifted up because of thy riches: 6 Therefore thus saith the Lord God; Because thou hast set thine heart as the heart of God; 7 Behold, therefore I will bring strangers upon thee, the terrible of the nations: and they shall draw their swords against the beauty of thy wisdom,

and they shall defile thy brightness. 8 They shall bring thee down to the pit, and thou shalt die the deaths of *them that are* slain in the midst of the seas. 9 Wilt thou yet say before him that slayeth thee, I *am* God? but thou *shalt be* a man, and no God, in the hand of him that slayeth thee. 10 Thou shalt die the deaths of the uncircumcised by the hand of strangers: for I have spoken *it,* saith the Lord God.

We had done with Tyrus in the foregoing chapter, but now the prince of Tyrus is to be singled out from the rest. Here is something to be said to him by himself, a *message to him from God,* which the prophet must send him, whether he will hear or whether he will forbear.

I. He must tell him of his pride. His people are proud (*ch.* xxvii. 3) and so is he; and they shall both be made to know that *God resists the proud.* Let us see, 1. What were the expressions of his pride: *His heart was lifted up, v.* 2. He had a great conceit of himself, was puffed up with an opinion of his own sufficiency, and looked with disdain upon all about him. Out of the abundance of the pride of his heart he said, *I am a god;* he did not only say it in his heart, but had the impudence to speak it out. God has said of princes, *They are gods* (Ps. lxxxii. 6); but it does not become them to say so of themselves; it is a high affront to him who is *God alone,* and will not give his glory to another. He thought that the city of Tyre had as necessary a dependence upon him as the world has upon the God that made it, and that he was himself independent as God and unaccountable to any. He thought himself to have as much wisdom and strength as God himself, and as incontestable an authority, and that his prerogatives were as absolute and his word as much a law as the word of God. He challenged divine honours, and expected to be praised and admired as a god, and doubted not to be deified, among other heroes, after his death as a great benefactor to the world. Thus the king of Babylon said, *I will be like the Most High* (Isa. xiv. 14), not like the *Most Holy.* " *I am the strong God,* and therefore will not be contradicted, because I cannot be controlled. *I sit in the seat of God;* I sit *as high* as God, my throne equal with his. *Divisum imperium cum Jove Cæsar habet—Cæsar divides dominion with Jove.* I sit as safely as God, as safely *in the heart of the seas,* and as far out of the reach of danger, as he in the *height of heaven.*" He thinks his guards of men of war about his throne as pompous and potent as the hosts of angels that are about the throne of God. He is put in mind of his meanness and mortality, and, since he needs to be told, he shall

915

be told, that self-evident truth, *Thou art a man, and not God*, a depending creature, a dying creature; thou art *flesh, and not spirit*, Isa. xxxi 3. Note, Men must be made to know that they are *but men*, Ps. ix. 20. The greatest wits, the greatest potentates, the greatest saints, are *men, and not gods*. Jesus Christ was both God and man. The king of Tyre, though he has such a mighty influence upon all about him, and with the help of his riches bears a mighty sway, though he has tribute and presents brought to his court with as much devotion as if they were sacrifices to his altar, though he is flattered by his courtiers and made a god of by his poets, yet, after all, he is *but a man;* he knows it; he fears it. But *he sets his heart as the heart of God:* "Thou hast conceited thyself to be a god, hast compared thyself with God, thinking thyself as wise and strong, and as fit to govern the world, as he." It was the ruin of our first parents, and ours in them, that they would be *as gods*, Gen. iii. 5. And still that corrupt nature which inclines men to set up themselves as their own masters, to do what they will, and their own carvers, to have what they will, their own end, to live to themselves, and their own felicity, to enjoy themselves, *sets their hearts as the heart of God*, invades his prerogatives, and catches at the flowers of his crown—a presumption that cannot go unpunished.

2. We are here told what it was that he was proud of. (1.) His wisdom. It is probable that this prince of Tyre was a man of very good natural parts, a philosopher, and well read in all the parts of learning that were then in vogue, at least a politician, and one that had great dexterity in managing the affairs of state. And then he thought himself *wiser than Daniel, v.* 3. We found, before, that Daniel, though now but a young man, was celebrated for his prevalency in prayer, *ch.* xiv. 14. Here we find he was famous for his prudence in the management of the affairs of this world, a great scholar and statesman, and withal a great saint, and yet not a prince, but a poor captive. It was strange that under such external disadvantages his lustre should shine forth, so that he had become *wise to a proverb*. When the king of Tyre dreams himself to be a god he says, I am *wiser than Daniel. There is no secret that they can hide from thee.* Probably he challenged all about him to *prove him with questions*, as Solomon was proved, and he had unriddled all their enigmas, had solved all their problems, and none of them all could puzzle him He had perhaps been successful in discovering plots, and diving into the counsels of the neighbouring princes, and therefore thought himself omniscient, and that no thought could be withholden from him; therefore he said, *I am a god.* Note, *Knowledge puffeth up;* it is hard to know much and not to know it too well and

916

to be elevated with it. He that was *wiser than Daniel* was prouder than Lucifer. Those therefore that are knowing must study to be humble and to evidence that they are so. (2.) His wealth. That way his wisdom led him; it is not said that by his wisdom he searched into the arcana either of nature or government, modelled the state better than it was, or made better laws, or advanced the interests of the commonwealth of learning; but his *wisdom and understanding* were of use to him in *traffic.* As some of the kings of Judah *loved husbandry* (2 Chron. xxvi. 10), so the king of Tyre loved merchandise, and by it he *got riches, increased his riches, and filled his treasures with gold and silver, v.* 4, 5. See what the wisdom of this world is; those are cried up as the wisest men that know how to get money and by right or wrong to raise estates; and yet really *this their way is their folly*, Ps. xlix. 13. It was the folly of the king of Tyre, [1.] That he attributed the increase of his wealth to himself and not to the providence of God, forgetting him who *gave him power to get wealth*, Deut. viii. 17, 18. [2.] That he thought himself a wise man because he was a rich man; whereas a fool may have an estate (Eccl. ii. 19), yea, and a fool may get an estate, for the world has been often observed to favour such, *when bread is not to the wise*, Eccl. ix. 11. [3.] That *his heart was lifted up because of his riches*, because of the increase of his wealth, which made him so haughty and secure, so insolent and imperious, and which *set his heart as the heart of God.* The *man of sin*, when he had a great deal of worldly pomp and power, *showed himself as a god*, 2 Thess. ii. 4. Those who are rich in this world have therefore need to charge that upon themselves which the word of God charges upon them, *that they be not high-minded*, 1 Tim. vi. 17.

II. Since *pride goes before destruction, and a haughty spirit before a fall*, he must tell him of that destruction, of that fall, which was now hastening on as the just punishment of his presumption in setting up himself a rival with God. "Because thou hast pretended to be a god (*v.* 6), therefore thou shalt not be long a man," *v.* 7. Observe here,

1. The instruments of his destruction: *I will bring strangers upon thee*—the Chaldeans, whom we do not find mentioned among the many nations and countries that traded with Tyre, *ch.* xxvii. If any of those nations had been brought against it, they would have had some compassion upon it, for old acquaintance-sake; but these strangers will have none. They are people of a *strange language*, which the king of Tyre himself, wise as he is, perhaps understands not. They are the *terrible of the nations;* it was an army made up of many nations, and it was at this time the most formidable both for strength and fury. These God has at command, and these he will bring upon the king of Tyre.

2. The extremity of the destruction : *They shall draw their swords against the beauty of thy wisdom* (*v.* 7), against all those things which thou gloriest in as thy beauty and the production of thy wisdom. Note, It is just with God that our enemies should make that their prey which we have made our pride. The king of Tyre's palace, his treasury, his city, his navy, his army, these he glories in as his brightness, these, he thinks, make him illustrious and glorious as a god on earth. But all these the victorious enemy shall defile, shall deface, shall deform. He thought them sacred, things that none durst touch; but the conquerors shall seize them as common things, and spoil the brightness of them. But, whatever becomes of what he has, surely his person is sacred. No (*v.* 8) : *They shall bring thee down to the pit,* to the grave; thou shalt *die the death.* And, (1.) It shall not be an honourable death, but an ignominious one. He shall be so vilified in his death that he may despair of being deified after his death. He shall die *the deaths of those that are slain in the midst of the seas,* that have no honour done them at their death, but their dead bodies are immediately thrown overboard, without any ceremony or mark of distinction, to be a feast for the fish. Tyre is *likely to be destroyed in the midst of the sea* (*ch.* xxvii. 32) and the prince of Tyre shall fare no better than the people. (2.) It shall not be a happy death, but a miserable one. He shall *die the deaths of the uncircumcised* (*v.* 10), of those that are strangers to God and not in covenant with him, and therefore die under his wrath and curse. It is *deaths,* a double death, temporal and eternal, the death both of body and soul. He shall die the *second death;* that is dying miserably indeed. The sentence of death here passed upon the king of Tyre is ratified by a divine authority : *I have spoken it, saith the Lord God.* And what he has said he will do. None can gainsay it, nor will he unsay it.

3. The effectual disproof that this will be of all his pretensions to deity (*v.* 9) : " When the conqueror sets his sword to thy breast, and thou seest no way of escape, *wilt thou then say, I am God?* Wilt thou then have such a conceit of thyself and such a confidence in thyself as thou now hast? No; thy being overpowered by death, and by the fear of it, will force thee to own that thou art not a god, but a weak, timorous, trembling, dying man. *In the hand of him that slays thee* (in the hand of God, and of the instruments that he employed) *thou shalt be a man, and not God,* utterly unable to resist, and help thyself." *I have said, You are gods ; but you shall die like men,* Ps. lxxxii. 6, 7. Note, Those who pretend to be rivals with God shall be forced one way or other to let fall their claims. Death at furthest, when we come into his hand, will make us know that we are men.

11 Moreover the word of the Lord came unto me, saying, 12 Son of man, take up a lamentation upon the king of Tyrus, and say unto him, Thus saith the Lord God; Thou sealest up the sum, full of wisdom, and perfect in beauty. 13 Thou hast been in Eden the garden of God; every precious stone *was* thy covering, the sardius, topaz, and the diamond, the beryl, the onyx, and the jasper, the sapphire, the emerald, and the carbuncle, and gold : the workmanship of thy tabrets and of thy pipes was prepared in thee in the day that thou wast created. 14 Thou *art* the anointed cherub that covereth ; and I have set thee *so :* thou wast upon the holy mountain of God; thou hast walked up and down in the midst of the stones of fire. 15 Thou *wast* perfect in thy ways from the day that thou wast created, till iniquity was found in thee. 16 By the multitude of thy merchandise they have filled the midst of thee with violence, and thou hast sinned : therefore I will cast thee as profane out of the mountain of God : and I will destroy thee, O covering cherub, from the midst of the stones of fire. 17 Thine heart was lifted up because of thy beauty, thou hast corrupted thy wisdom by reason of thy brightness : I will cast thee to the ground, I will lay thee before kings, that they may behold thee. 18 Thou hast defiled thy sanctuaries by the multitude of thine iniquities, by the iniquity of thy traffick ; therefore will I bring forth a fire from the midst of thee, it shall devour thee, and I will bring thee to ashes upon the earth in sight of all them that behold thee. 19 All they that know thee among the people shall be astonished at thee : thou shalt be a terror, and never *shalt* thou *be* any more.

As after the prediction of the ruin of Tyre (*ch.* xxvi) followed a pathetic lamentation for it (*ch.* xxvii), so after the ruin of the king of Tyre is foretold it is bewailed.

I. This is commonly understood of the prince who then reigned over Tyre, spoken to, *v.* 2. His name was *Ethbaal,* or *Ithobalus,* as Diodorus Siculus calls him that was king of Tyre when Nebuchadnezzar destroyed it. He was, it seems, upon all external accounts an accomplished man, very great and famous; but his iniquity was his ruin. Many expositors have suggested that besides the literal sense of this lamentation there is an allegory in it, and that it is an allusion to the fall of the angels that sinned, who undid themselves by their pride. And (as is usual in texts that have a mystical meaning) some passages here refer primarily to the king of Tyre, as that of his merchandises, others to the angels, as that of being *in the holy mountain of God*. But, if there be any thing mystical in it (as perhaps there may), I shall rather refer it to the fall of Adam, which seems to be glanced at, *v.* 13. *Thou hast been in Eden the garden of God, and that in the day thou wast created.*

II. Some think that by *the king of Tyre* is meant the whole royal family, this including also the foregoing kings, and looking as far back as Hiram, king of Tyre. The then governor is called *prince* (*v.* 2); but he that is here lamented is called *king*. The court of Tyre with its kings had for many ages been famous; but sin ruins it. Now we may observe two things here :—

1. What was the renown of the king of Tyre. He is here spoken of as having lived in great splendour, *v.* 12—15. He was a man, but it is here owned that he was a very considerable man and one that made a mighty figure in his day. (1.) He far exceeded other men. Hiram and other kings of Tyre had done so in their time; and the reigning king perhaps had not come short of any of them: *Thou sealest up the sum full of wisdom and perfect in beauty.* Both the powers of human nature and the prosperity of human life seemed in him to be at the highest pitch. He was looked upon to be as wise as the reason of men could make him, and as happy as the wealth of this world and the enjoyment of it could make him; in him you might see the utmost that both could do; and therefore *seal up the sum*, for nothing can be added; he is a complete man, perfect *in suo genere—in his kind*. (2.) He seemed to be as wise and happy as Adam in innocency (*v.* 13): *" Thou hast been in Eden, even in the garden of God; thou hast lived as it were in paradise all thy days, hast had a full enjoyment of every thing that is good for food* or *pleasant to the eyes*, and an uncontroverted dominion over all about thee, as Adam had."* One instance of the magnificence of the king of Tyre is, that he outdid all other princes in jewels, which those have the greatest plenty of that trade most abroad, as he did: *Every precious stone was his covering.* There is a great variety of precious stones; but he had of every sort and in such plenty that besides what were treasured up in his cabinet, and were the ornaments of his crown, he had his clothes trimmed with them; they were his *covering*. Nay (*v.* 14), he *walked up and down*

918

in the midst of the stones of fire, that is, these precious stones, which glittered and sparkled like fire. His rooms were in a manner set round with jewels, so that he walked in the midst of them, and then fancied himself as glorious as if, like God, he had been surrounded by so many angels, who are compared to a *flame of fire*. And, if he be such an admirer of precious stones as to think them as bright as angels, no wonder that he is such an admirer of himself as to think himself as great as God. Nine several sorts of precious stones are here named, which were all in the high priest's ephod. Perhaps they are particularly named because he, in his pride, used to speak particularly of them, and tell those about him, with a great deal of foolish pleasure, " This is such a precious stone, of such a value, and so and so are its virtues." Thus is he upbraided with his vanity. *Gold* is mentioned last, as far inferior in value to those precious stones; and he used to speak of it accordingly. Another thing that made him think his palace a paradise was the curious music he had, the *tabrets and pipes*, hand-instruments and wind-instruments. The *workmanship* of these was extraordinary, and they were prepared for him on purpose; prepared *in thee*, the pronoun is feminine— *in thee*, O Tyre! or it denotes that the king was effeminate in doting on such things. They were prepared *in the day he was created*, that is, either born, or created king; they were made on purpose to celebrate the joys either of his birth-day or of his coronation-day. These he prided himself much in, and would have all that came to see his palace take notice of them. (3.) He looked like an incarnate angel (*v.* 14): *Thou art the anointed cherub that covers* or *protects;* that is, he looked upon himself as a guardian angel to his people, so bright, so strong, so faithful, appointed to this office and qualified for it. Anointed kings should be to their subjects as anointed cherubim, that cover them with the wings of their power; and, when they are such, God will own them. Their advancement was from him: *I have set thee so.* Some think, because mention was made of Eden, that it refers to the cherub set on the east of Eden to cover it, Gen. iii. 24. He thought himself as able to guard his city from all invaders as that angel was for his charge. Or it may refer to the cherubim in the most holy place, whose wings covered the ark; he thought himself as bright as one of them. (4.) He appeared in as much splendour as the high priest when he was clothed with his garments for glory and beauty: *" Thou wast upon the holy mountain of God*, as president of the temple built on that holy mountain; thou didst look as great, and with as much majesty and authority, as ever the high priest did when he walked in the temple, which was *garnished with pre-*

cious stones (2 Chron. iii. 6), and had his habit on, which had precious stones both in the breast and on the shoulders; in that he seemed to *walk in the midst of the stones of fire.*" Thus glorious is the king of Tyre; at least he thinks himself so.

2. Let us now see what was the ruin of the king of Tyre, what it was that stained his glory and laid all this honour in the dust (*v.* 15): " *Thou wast perfect in thy ways; thou didst prosper in all thy affairs and every thing went well with thee; thou hadst not only a clear, but a bright reputation, from the day thou wast created,* the day of thy accession to the throne, *till iniquity was found in thee;* and that spoiled all." This may perhaps allude to the deplorable case of the angels that fell, and of our first parents, both of whom *were perfect in their ways till iniquity was found in them.* And when iniquity was once *found in him* it increased; he grew worse and worse, as appears (*v.* 18): " *Thou hast defiled thy sanctuaries;* thou hast lost the benefit of all that which thou thoughtest sacred, and in which, as in a sanctuary, thou thoughtest to take refuge; these thou hast *defiled,* and so exposed thyself *by the multitude of thy iniquities.*" Now observe,

(1.) What the iniquity was that was the ruin of the king of Tyre. [1.] The *iniquity of his traffic* (so it is called, *v.* 18), both his and his people's, for their sin is charged upon him, because he connived at it and set them a bad example (*v.* 16): *By the multitude of thy merchandise they have filled the midst of thee with violence,* and thus *thou hast sinned.* The king had so much to do with his merchandise, and was so wholly intent upon the gains of that, that he took no care to do justice, to give redress to those that suffered wrong and to protect them from violence; nay, in the multiplicity of business, wrong was done to many by oversight; and in his dealings he made use of his power to invade the rights of those he dealt with. Note, Those that have much to do in the world are in great danger of doing much amiss; and it is hard to deal with many without violence to some. Trades are called mysteries; but too many make them mysteries of iniquity. [2.] His pride and vain-glory (*v.* 17): " *Thy heart was lifted up because of thy beauty;* thou wast in love with thyself, and thy own shadow. And thus *thou hast corrupted thy wisdom by reason of the brightness,* the pomp and splendour, wherein thou livedst." He gazed so much upon this that it dazzled his eyes and prevented him from seeing his way. He appeared so puffed up with his greatness that it bereaved him both of his wisdom and of the reputation of it. He really became a *fool in glorying.* Those make a bad bargain for themselves that part with their wisdom for the gratifying of their gaiety, and, to please a vain humour, lose a real excellency.

(2.) What the ruin was that this iniquity brought him to. [1.] He was thrown out of his dignity and dislodged from his palace, which he took to be his paradise and temple (*v.* 16): *I will cast thee as profane out of the mountain of God.* His kingly power was high as a *mountain,* setting him above others; it was a *mountain of God,* for the powers that be are ordained of God, and have something in them that is sacred; but, having abused his power, he is reckoned profane, and is therefore deposed and expelled. He disgraces the crown he wears, and so has forfeited it, and shall be destroyed *from the midst of the stones of fire,* the precious stones with which his palace was garnished, as the temple was; and they shall be no protection to him. [2.] He was exposed to contempt and disgrace, and trampled upon by his neighbours: " *I will cast thee to the ground* (*v.* 17), will cast thee among the *pavement-stones,* from the midst of the *precious stones,* and will *lay thee* a rueful spectacle *before kings, that they may behold thee* and take warning by thee not to be proud and oppressive." [3.] He was quite consumed, his city and he in it: *I will bring forth a fire from the midst of thee.* The conquerors, when they have plundered the city, will kindle a fire in the heart of it, which shall lay it, and the palace particularly, in ashes. Or it may be taken more generally for the fire of God's judgments, which shall devour both prince and people, and bring all the glory of both *to ashes upon the earth;* and this fire shall be *brought forth from the midst of thee.* All God's judgments upon sinners take rise from themselves; they are devoured by a fire of their own kindling. [4.] He was hereby made a terrible example of divine vengeance. Thus he is reduced *in the sight of all those that behold him* (*v.* 18): *Those that know him shall be astonished at him,* and shall wonder how one that stood so high could be brought so low. The king of Tyre's palace, like the temple at Jerusalem, when it is destroyed shall be *an astonishment and a hissing,* 2 Chron. vii. 20, 21. So fell the king of Tyre.

20 Again the word of the Lord came unto me, saying, 21 Son of man, set thy face against Zidon, and prophesy against it, 22 And say, Thus saith the Lord God; Behold, I *am* against thee, O Zidon; and I will be glorified in the midst of thee: and they shall know that I *am* the Lord, when I shall have executed judgments in her, and shall be sanctified in her. 23 For I will send into her pestilence, and blood into her streets: and the wounded shall be judged in the midst of her by the sword upon

her on every side; and they shall know that I *am* the Lord. 24 And there shall be no more a pricking brier unto the house of Israel, nor *any* grieving thorn of all *that are* round about them, that despised them; and they shall know that I *am* the Lord God. 25 Thus saith the Lord God; When I shall have gathered the house of Israel from the people among whom they are scattered, and shall be sanctified in them in the sight of the heathen, then shall they dwell in their land that I have given to my servant Jacob. 26 And they shall dwell safely therein, and shall build houses, and plant vineyards; yea, they shall dwell with confidence, when I have executed judgments upon all those that despise them round about them; and they shall know that I *am* the Lord their God.

God's glory is his great end, both in all the good and in all the evil which *proceed out of the mouth of the Most High;* so we find in these verses. 1. God will be glorified in the destruction of Zidon, a city that lay near to Tyre, was more ancient, but not so considerable, had a dependence upon it and stood and fell with it. God says here, *I am against thee, O Zidon! and I will be glorified in the midst of thee, v.* 22. And again, " Those that would not know by gentler methods shall be made to *know that I am the Lord,* and I alone, and that I am a just and jealous God, *when I shall have executed judgments in her,* destroying judgments, when I shall have done execution according to justice and according to the sentence passed, and so shall be *sanctified in her.*" The Zidonians, it should seem, were more addicted to idolatry than the Tyrians were, who, being men of business and large conversation, were less under the power of bigotry and superstition. The Zidonians were noted for the worship of Ashtaroth; Solomon introduced it, 1 Kings xi. 5. Jezebel was daughter to the king of Zidon, who brought the worship of Baal into Israel (1 Kings xvi. 31); so that God had been much dishonoured by the Zidonians. Now, says he, *I will be glorified, I will be sanctified.* The Zidonians were borderers upon the land of Israel, where God was known, and where they might have got the knowledge of him and have learned to glorify him; but, instead of that, they seduced Israel to the worship of their idols. Note, When God is sanctified he is glorified, for his holiness is his glory; and those whom he is not sanctified and glorified by he will be sanctified and glorified upon, by executing

judgments upon them, which declare him a just avenger of his own and his people's injured honour. The judgments that shall be executed upon Zidon are war and pestilence, two wasting depopulating judgments, *v.* 23. They are God's messengers, which he sends on his errands, and they shall accomplish that for which he sends them. *Pestilence* and *blood* shall be sent *into her streets;* there the dead bodies of those shall lie who perished, some by the plague, occasioned perhaps through ill diet when the city was besieged, and some by the sword of the enemy, most likely the Chaldean armies, when the city was taken, and all were put to the sword. Thus the wounded shall be judged; when they are dying of their wounds they shall judge themselves, and others shall say, They justly fall. Or, as some read it, *They shall be punished by the sword,* that sword which has commission to destroy *on every side.* It is God that judges, and he will overcome. Nor is it Tyre and Zidon only on which God would execute judgments, but on all those that despised his people Israel, and triumphed in their calamities; for this was now God's controversy with the nations that were *round about them, v.* 26. Note, When God's people are under his correcting hand for their faults he takes care, as he did concerning malefactors that were scourged, *that they shall not seem vile* to those that are about them, and therefore takes it ill of those who despise them and so *help forward the affliction* when he is but *a little displeased,* Zech. i. 15. God regards them even in their low estate; and therefore let not men despise them. 2. God will be glorified in the restoration of his people to their former safety and prosperity. God had been dishonoured by the sins of his people, and their sufferings too had given occasion to the enemy to blaspheme (Isa. lii. 5); but God will now both cure them of their sins and ease them of their troubles, and so *will be sanctified in them in the sight of the heathen,* will recover the honour of his holiness, to the satisfaction of all the world, *v.* 25. For, (1.) They shall return to the possession of their own land again : *I will gather the house of Israel* out of their dispersions, in answer to that prayer (Ps. cvi. 47), *Save us, O Lord our God! and gather us from among the heathen;* and in pursuance of that promise (Deut. xxx. 4), Thence will *the Lord thy God gather thee.* Being gathered, they shall be brought in a body, to *dwell in the land that I have given to my servant Jacob.* God had an eye to the ancient grant, in bringing them back, for that remained in force, and the discontinuance of the possession was not a defeasance of the right. He that gave it will again give it. (2.) They shall enjoy great tranquillity there. When those that have been vexatious to them are taken off they shall live in quietness; there shall be no more *a pricking brier nor a grieving thorn, v.* 24. They shall have a happy settlement, for they shall *build houses,* and *plant vineyards;* and they shall enjoy a happy security and serenity there; they shall *dwell safely,* shall *dwell with confidence,* and there shall be none to disquiet them or make them afraid, *v.* 26. This never had a full accomplishment in the body of that people, for after their return out of captivity they were ever and anon molested by some bad neighbour or other. Nor has the gospel-church been ever quite free from pricking briers and grieving thorns; yet sometimes *the church has rest,* and believers always dwell safely under the divine protection and may be *quiet from the fear of evil.* But the full accomplishment of this promise is reserved for the heavenly Canaan, when all the saints shall be gathered together, and every thing that offends shall be removed, and all griefs and fears for ever banished.

CHAP. XXIX.

Three chapters we had concerning Tyre and its king; next follow four chapters concerning Egypt and its king. This is the first of them. Egypt had formerly been a house of bondage to God's people; of late they had had but too friendly a correspondence with it, and had depended too much upon it; and therefore, whether the prediction reached Egypt or no, it would be of use to Israel, to take them off from their confidence in their alliance with it. The prophecies against Egypt, which are all laid together in these four chapters, were of five several dates; the first in the 10th year of the captivity (ver. 1), the second in the 27th (ver. 17), the third in the 11th year and the first month (ch. xxx. 20), the fourth in the 11th year and the third month (ch. xxxi. 1), the fifth in the 12th year (ch. xxxii. 1), and another in the same year, ver. 17. In this chapter we have, I. The destruction of Pharaoh foretold, for his dealing deceitfully with Israel, ver. 1—7. II. The desolation of the land of Egypt foretold, ver. 8—12. III. A promise of the restoration thereof, in part, after forty years, ver. 13—16. IV. The possession that should be given to Nebuchadnezzar of the land of Egypt, ver. 17—20. V. A promise of mercy to Israel, ver. 21.

IN the tenth year, in the tenth *month,* in the twelfth *day* of the month, the word of the LORD came unto me, saying, 2 Son of man, set thy face against Pharaoh king of Egypt, and prophesy against him, and against all Egypt: 3 Speak, and say, Thus saith the Lord GOD; Behold, I *am* against thee, Pharaoh king of Egypt, the great dragon that lieth in the midst of his rivers, which hath said, My river *is* mine own, and I have made *it* for myself. 4 But I will put hooks in thy jaws, and I will cause the fish of thy rivers to stick unto thy scales, and I will bring thee up out of the midst of thy rivers, and all the fish of thy rivers shall stick unto thy scales. 5 And I will leave thee *thrown* into the wilderness, thee and all the fish of thy rivers: thou shalt fall upon the open fields; thou shalt not be brought together, nor gathered: I have given thee for meat to the beasts of the field and to the

fowls of the heaven. 6 And all the inhabitants of Egypt shall know that I *am* the LORD, because they have been a staff of reed to the house of Israel. 7 When they took hold of thee by thy hand, thou didst break, and rend all their shoulder: and when they leaned upon thee, thou brakest, and madest all their loins to be at a stand.

Here is, I. The date of this prophecy against Egypt. It was in the *tenth year of the captivity,* and yet it is placed after the prophecy against Tyre, which was delivered in the eleventh year, because, in the accomplishment of the prophecies, the destruction of Tyre happened before the destruction of Egypt, and Nebuchadnezzar's gaining Egypt was the reward of his service against Tyre; and *therefore* the prophecy against Tyre is put first, that we may the better observe that. But particular notice must be taken of this, that the first prophecy against Egypt was just at the time when the king of Egypt was coming to relieve Jerusalem and raise the siege (Jer. xxxvii. 5), but did not answer the expectations of the Jews from them. Note, It is good to foresee the failing of all our creature-confidences, then when we are most in temptation to depend upon them, that we may *cease from man.*

II. The scope of this prophecy. It is directed against *Pharaoh king of Egypt, and against all Egypt, v.* 2. The prophecy against Tyre began with the people, and then proceeded against the prince. But this begins with the prince, because it began to have its accomplishment in the insurrections and rebellions of the people against the prince, not long after this.

III. The prophecy itself. Pharaoh Hophrah (for so was the reigning Pharaoh surnamed) is here represented by a *great dragon,* or crocodile, that *lies in the midst of his rivers,* as Leviathan in the waters, to *play therein, v.* 3. Nilus, the river of Egypt, was famed for crocodiles. And what is the king of Egypt, in God's account, but a *great dragon,* venomous and mischievous? Therefore says God, *I am against thee. I am above thee;* so it may be read. How high soever the princes and potentates of the earth are, there is a *higher than they* (Eccl. v. 8), a God above them, that can control them, and, if they be tyrannical and oppressive, a God against them, that will be free to reckon with them. Observe here,

1. The pride and security of Pharaoh. He *lies in the midst of his rivers,* rolls himself with a great deal of satisfaction in his wealth and pleasures; and he says, *My river is my own.* He boasts that he is an absolute prince (his subjects are his vassals; Joseph bought them long ago, Gen. xlvii. 23),—that he is a sole prince, and has neither partner

in the government nor competitor for it,—that he is out of debt (what he has is his *own*, and none of his neighbours have any demands upon him),—that he is independent, neither tributary nor accountable to any. Note, Worldly carnal minds please themselves with, and pride themselves in, their property, forgetting that whatever we have we have only the use of it, the property is in God. We ourselves are not our own, but his. Our *tongues are not our own*, Ps. xii. 4. Our river is not *our own*, for its springs are in God. The most potent prince cannot call what he has his own, for, though it be so against all the world, it is not so against God. But Pharaoh's reason for his pretensions is yet more absurd : *My river is my own*, for *I have made it for myself.* Here he usurps two of the divine prerogatives, to be the author and the end of his own being and felicity. He only that is the great Creator can say of this world, and of every thing in it, *I have made it for myself.* He calls his river his own because he *looks not unto the Maker thereof, nor has respect unto him that fashioned it long ago*, Isa. xxii. 11. What we have we have received from God and must use for God, so that we cannot say, We made it, much less, We made it for ourselves ; and why then do we boast? Note, Self is the great idol that all the world worships, in contempt of God and his sovereignty.

2. The course God will take with this proud man, to humble him. He is a great dragon in the waters, and God will accordingly deal with him, *v.* 4, 5. (1.) He will draw him out of his rivers, for he has *a hook and a cord* for this *leviathan*, with which he can manage him, though none on earth can (Job xli. 1) : " *I will bring thee up out of the midst of thy rivers*, will cast thee out of thy palace, out of thy kingdom, out of all those things in which thou takest such a complacency and placest such a confidence." Herodotus relates of this Pharaoh, who was now king of Egypt, that he had reigned in great prosperity for twenty-five years, and was so elevated with his successes that he said that *God himself could not cast him out of his kingdom;* but he shall soon be convinced of his mistake, and what he depended on shall be no defence. God can force men out of that in which they are most secure and easy. (2.) *All his fish* shall be drawn out with him, his servants, his soldiers, and all that had a dependence on him, as he thought, but really such as he had dependence upon. These shall *stick to his scales*, adhere to their king, resolving to live and die with him. But, (3.) The king and his army, the dragon and all the fish that stick to his scales, shall perish together, as fish cast upon dry ground, and shall be *meat to the beasts and fowls, v.* 5. Now this is supposed to have had its accomplishment soon after, when this Pharaoh, in defence of Aricius king of Libya, who had been expelled

922

his kingdom by the Cyrenians, levied a great army, and went out aganst the Cyrenians, to re-establish his friend, but was defeated in battle, and all his forces were put to flight, which gave such disgust to his kingdom that they rose in rebellion against him. Thus was he left *thrown into the wilderness, he and all the fish of the river* with him. Thus issue men's pride, and presumption, and carnal security. Thus men justly lose what they might call their own, under God, when they call it their own against him.

3. The ground of the controversy God has with the Egyptians ; it is because they have cheated his people. They encouraged them to expect relief and assistance from them when they were in distress, but failed them (*v.* 6, 7) : *Because they have been a staff of reed to the house of* Israel. They pretended to be a staff for them to lean upon, but, when any stress was laid upon them, they were either weak and could not or treacherous and would not do that for them which was expected. They *broke under them*, to their great disappointment and amazement, so that they *rent their shoulder* and *made all their loins to be at a stand*. The king of Egypt, it is probable, had encouraged Zedekiah to break his league with the king of Babylon, with a promise that he would stand by him, which, when he failed to do, to any purpose, it could not but put them into a great consternation. God had told them, long since, that the Egyptians were broken reeds, Isa. xxx. 6, 7. Rabshakeh had told them so, Isa. xxxvi. 6. And now they found it so. It was indeed the folly of Israel to trust them, and they were well enough served when they were deceived in them. God was righteous in suffering them to be so. But that is no excuse at all for the Egyptians' falsehood and treachery, nor shall it secure them from the judgments of that God who is and will be the avenger of all such wrongs. It is a great sin, and very provoking to God, as well as unjust, ungrateful, and very dishonourable and unkind, to put a cheat upon those that put a confidence in us.

8 Therefore thus saith the Lord God ; Behold, I will bring a sword upon thee, and cut off man and beast out of thee. 9 And the land of Egypt shall be desolate and waste ; and they shall know that I *am* the Lord : because he hath said, The river *is* mine, and I have made *it*. 10 Behold, therefore I *am* against thee, and against thy rivers, and I will make the land of Egypt utterly waste *and* desolate, from the tower of Syene even unto the border of Ethiopia. 11 No foot of man shall pass through it, nor foot

of beast shall pass through it, neither shall it be inhabited forty years. 12 And I will make the land of Egypt desolate in the midst of the countries *that are* desolate, and her cities among the cities *that are* laid waste shall be desolate forty years: and I will scatter the Egyptians among the nations, and will disperse them through the countries. 13 Yet thus saith the Lord GOD; At the end of forty years will I gather the Egyptians from the people whither they were scattered: 14 And I will bring again the captivity of Egypt, and will cause them to return *into* the land of Pathros, into the land of their habitation; and they shall be there a base kingdom. 15 It shall be the basest of the kingdoms; neither shall it exalt itself any more above the nations: for I will diminish them, that they shall no more rule over the nations. 16 And it shall be no more the confidence of the house of Israel, which bringeth *their* iniquity to remembrance, when they shall look after them: but they shall know that I *am* the Lord GOD.

This explains the foregoing prediction, which was figurative, and looks something further. Here is a prophecy,

I. Of the ruin of Egypt. The threatening of this is very full and particular; and the sin for which this ruin shall be brought upon them is their pride, *v.* 9. They said, *The river is mine and I have made it;* therefore their land shall spue them out. 1. God is against them, both against the king and against the people, *against thee and against thy rivers.* Waters signify *people and multitudes,* Rev. xvii. 15. 2. Multitudes of them shall be cut off by the sword of war, a sword which God will bring upon them to destroy *both man and beast,* the sword of civil war. 3. The country shall be depopulated. The *land of Egypt shall be desolate and waste* (*v.* 9), the country not cultivated, the cities not inhabited. The wealth of both was their pride, and that God will take away. It *shall be utterly waste (wastes of waste,* so the margin reads it), *and desolate* (*v.* 10); *neither men nor beasts shall pass through it, nor shall it be inhabited* (*v.* 11); it shall be *desolate in the midst of the countries that are so, v.* 12. This was the effect not so much of those wars spoken of before, which were made by them, but of the war which the king of Babylon made upon them. It shall be desolate from one end of the land to the other, *from the tower of Syene even unto the border of Ethiopia.*

The sin of pride is enough to ruin a whole nation. 4. The people shall be dispersed and scattered among the nations (*v.* 12), so that those who thought the balance of power was in their hand should now become a contemptible people. Such a fall does a haughty spirit go before.

II. Of the restoration of Egypt after awhile, *v.* 13. Egypt shall lie *desolate forty years* (*v.* 12) and then *I will bring again the captivity of Egypt, v.* 14. Some date the forty years from Nebuchadnezzar's destroying Egypt, others from the desolation of Egypt some time before; however, they end about the first year of Cyrus, when the seventy years' captivity of Judah ended, or soon after. Then this prediction was accomplished, 1. That God will gather the Egyptians out of all the countries into which they were dispersed, and make them to *return to the land of their habitation,* and give them a settlement there again, *v.* 14. Note, Though God will find out a way to humble the proud, yet he will not contend for ever, no, not with them in this world. 2. That yet they shall not make a figure again as they have done. Egypt shall be *a kingdom* again, but it shall be the *basest of the kingdoms* (*v.* 15); it shall have but little wealth and power, and shall not extend its conquests as formerly; it shall be the tail of the nations, and not the head. It is a mercy that it shall become a kingdom again, but, to humble it, it shall be a despicable kingdom; it shall be a long time before it recover any thing like its ancient lustre. For two reasons it shall be thus mortified:—(1.) That it may not domineer over its neighbours, that it may not *exalt itself above the nations,* nor *rule over the nations,* as it has done, but that it may know what it is to be low and despised. Note, Those who abuse their power will justly be stripped of it; and God, as King of nations, will find out a way to maintain the injured rights and liberties, not only of his own, but of other nations. (2.) That it may not deceive the people of God (*v.* 16): *It shall no more be the confidence of the house of Israel;* they shall no more be in temptation to trust in it as they have done, which is a sin that *brings their iniquity to remembrance,* that is, provokes God to punish them not for that only, but for all their other sins. Or it *puts them in mind* of their idolatries to return to them, *when they look* to the idolaters, to repose a confidence in them. Note, The creatures we confide in are often *therefore* ruined, because there is no other way effectually to cure us of our confidence in them. Rather than Israel shall be ensnared again, the whole land of Egypt shall be laid waste. He that once *gave Egypt for their ransom* (Isa. xliii. 3) will now give Egypt for their cure; and it shall be destroyed rather than Israel shall not in this particular be reformed. God, not only in justice, but in wisdom and goodness to us, breaks those creature-stays which we lean too much upon, and makes them to be no more, that they may be no more our confidence.

17 And it came to pass in the seven and twentieth year, in the first *month*, in the first *day* of the month, the word of the Lord came unto me, saying, 18 Son of man, Nebuchadrezzar king of Babylon caused his army to serve a great service against Tyrus: every head *was* made bald, and every shoulder *was* peeled : yet had he no wages, nor his army, for Tyrus, for the service that he had served against it : 19 Therefore thus saith the Lord God ; Behold, I will give the land of Egypt unto Nebuchadrezzar king of Babylon ; and he shall take her multitude, and take her spoil, and take her prey ; and it shall be the wages for his army. 20 I have given him the land of Egypt *for* his labour wherewith he served against it, because they wrought for me, saith the Lord God. 21 In that day will I cause the horn of the house of Israel to bud forth, and I will give thee the opening of the mouth in the midst of them ; and they shall know that I *am* the Lord.

The date of this prophecy is observable ; it was in the twenty-seventh year of Ezekiel's captivity, sixteen years after the prophecy in the former part of the chapter, and almost as long after those which follow in the next chapters ; but it comes in here for the explication of all that was said against Egypt. After the destruction of Jerusalem Nebuchadnezzar spent two or three campaigns in the conquest of the Ammonites and Moabites and making himself master of their countries. Then he spent thirteen years in the siege of Tyre. During all that time the Egyptians were embroiled in war with the Cyrenians and one with another, by which they were very much weakened and impoverished ; and just at the end of the siege of Tyre God delivers this prophecy to Ezekiel, to signify to him that that utter destruction of Egypt which he had foretold fifteen or sixteen years before, which had been but in part accomplished hitherto, should now be completed by Nebuchadnezzar. The prophecy which begins here, it should seem, is continued to the twentieth verse of the next chapter. And Dr. Lightfoot observes that it is the last prophecy we have of this prophet, and should have been last in the book, but is laid here, that all the prophecies against Egypt might come together. The particular destruction of Pharaoh-Hophrah, foretold in the former

924

part of this chapter, was likewise foretold Jer. xliv. 30. This general devastation of Egypt by Nebuchadnezzar was foretold Jer. xliii. 10. Observe,

I. What success God would give to Nebuchadnezzar and his forces against Egypt. God gave him *that land*, that he might *take the spoil* and *prey* of it, *v.* 19, 20. It was a cheap and easy prey. He subdued it with very little difficulty ; the blood and treasure expended upon the conquest of it were inconsiderable. But it was a rich prey, and he carried off a great deal from it that was of value. Their having been divided among themselves, no doubt, gave a common enemy great advantage against them, who, when they had been so long preying upon one another, soon made a prey of them all. *En! quo discordia cives perduxit miseros—What wretchedness does civil discord bring!* Jeremiah foretold that Nebuchadnezzar should *array himself with the land of Egypt as a shepherd puts on his coat*, which intimates what a rich and cheap prey it should be.

II. Upon what considerations God would give Nebuchadnezzar this success against Egypt ; it was to be a recompence to him for the hard service with which he had caused his army to serve against Tyre, *v.* 18, 20. 1. The taking of Tyre was a tedious piece of work ; it cost Nebuchadnezzar abundance of blood and treasure. It held out thirteen years ; all that time the Chaldean army was hard at it, to make themselves masters of it. A large current of the sea, between Tyre and the continent, was filled up with earth, and many other difficulties which were thought insuperable they had to struggle with ; but so great a prince, having begun such an undertaking, thought himself bound in honour to push it on, whatever it cost him. How many thousand lives have been sacrificed to such points of honour as this was ! In prosecuting this siege *every head was made bald, and every shoulder peeled*, with carrying burdens and labouring in the water when they had a strong tide and a strong town to contend with. Egypt, a large kingdom, being divided within itself, is easily conquered ; Tyre, a single city, being unanimous, is with difficulty subdued. Those that have much to do in the world find some affairs go on a great deal more readily and easily than others. But, 2. In this service God owns that they *wrought for him, v.* 20. He set them at work, for the humbling of a proud city and its king, though *they meant not so, neither did their heart think so*, who were employed in it. Note, Even great men and bad men are tools that God makes use of, and are *working for him* even when they are pursuing their own covetous and ambitious designs ; so wonderfully does God overrule all to his own glory. Yet, 3. For this service he had *no wages* nor *his army.* He was at a vast expense to take Tyre ; and when he had it, though it was a very rich city, and he promised himself good plunder for his army from it, he was disappointed; the Tyrians sent away by ship their best effects, and threw the rest into the sea, so that they had nothing but bare walls. Thus are the children of this world ordinarily frustrated in their highest expectations from it. Therefore, 4. He shall have the spoil of Eygpt to recompense him for his service against Tyre. Note, God will be behind-hand with none for any service they do for him, but, one way or other, will recompense them for it; none shall kindle a fire on his altar for nought. The service done for him by worldly men, with worldly designs, shall be recompensed with a mere worldly reward, which his faithful servants, that have a sincere regard to his will and glory, would not be put off with. This accounts for the prosperity of wicked men in this world; God is in it paying them for some service or other, in which he has made use of them. *Verily they have their reward.* Let none envy it them. The conquest of Egypt is spoken of as Nebuchadnezzar's *full reward*, for that completed his dominion over the then known world in a manner; that was the last of the kingdoms he subdued; when he was master of that he became the *head of gold*.

III. The mercy God had in store for the house of Israel soon after. When the tide is at the highest it will turn, and so it will when it is at the lowest. Nebuchadnezzar was in the zenith of his glory when he had conquered Egypt, but within a year after he ran mad (Dan. iv.), was so seven years, and within a year or two after he had recovered his senses he resigned his life. When he was at the highest Israel was at the lowest; then were they in the depth of their captivity, their bones dead and dry; but *in that day the horn of the house of Israel shall bud forth, v. 21.* The day of their deliverance shall begin to dawn, and they shall have some little reviving in their bondage, in the honour that shall be done, 1. To their princes; they are the *horns of the house of Israel*, the seat of their glory and power. These began to bud forth when Daniel and his fellows were highly preferred in Babylon; Daniel *sat in the gate of the city; Shadrach, Meshach, and Abednego, were set over the affairs of the province* (Dan. ii. 49); these were all *of the king's seed, and of the princes*, Dan. i. 3. And it was within a year after the conquest of Egypt that they were thus preferred; and, soon after, three of them were made famous by the honour God put upon them in bringing them alive out of the burning fiery furnace. This might very well be called the *budding forth of the horn of the house of Israel*. And, some years after, this promise had a further accomplishment in the enlargement and elevation of Jehoiachin king of Judah, Jer. lii. 31, 32. They were both tokens of God's favour to Israel, and happy omens. 2. To their prophets. And *I will give thee the open-*

ing of the mouth. Though none of Ezekiel's prophecies, after this, are recorded, yet we have reason to think he went on prophesying, and with more liberty and boldness, when Daniel and his fellows were in power, and would be ready to protect him not only from the Babylonians, but from the wicked ones of his own people. Note, It bodes well to a people when God enlarges the liberties of his ministers and they are countenanced and encouraged in their work.

CHAP. XXX.

In this chapter we have, I. A continuation of the prophecy against Egypt, which we had in the latter part of the foregoing chapter, just before the desolation of that once flourishing kingdom was completed by Nebuchadnezzar, in which is foretold the destruction of all her allies and confederates, all her interests and concerns, and the several steps which the king of Babylon should take in pushing on this destruction, ver. 1—19. II. A repetition of a former prophecy against Egypt, just before the desolation of it begun by their own bad conduct, which gradually weakened them and prepared the way for the king of Babylon, ver. 20—26. It is all much to the same purport with what we had before.

THE word of the LORD came again unto me, saying, 2 Son of man, prophesy and say, Thus saith the Lord GOD; Howl ye, Woe worth the day! 3 For the day is near, even the day of the LORD is near, a cloudy day; it shall be the time of the heathen. 4 And the sword shall come upon Egypt, and great pain shall be in Ethiopia, when the slain shall fall in Egypt, and they shall take away her multitude, and her foundations shall be broken down. 5 Ethiopia, and Libya, and Lydia, and all the mingled people, and Chub, and the men of the land that is in league, shall fall with them by the sword. 6 Thus saith the LORD; They also that uphold Egypt shall fall; and the pride of her power shall come down: from the tower of Syene shall they fall in it by the sword, saith the Lord GOD. 7 And they shall be desolate in the midst of the countries *that are* desolate, and her cities shall be in the midst of the cities *that are* wasted. 8 And they shall know that I *am* the LORD, when I have set a fire in Egypt, and *when* all her helpers shall be destroyed. 9 In that day shall messengers go forth from me in ships to make the careless Ethiopians afraid, and great pain shall come upon them, as in the day of Egypt: for, lo, it cometh. 10 Thus saith the Lord GOD; I will also make the multitude of Egypt to cease by the hand of Nebuchadrezzar king of Babylon. 11 He and his people with him, the terrible of the nations, shall be brought to destroy the land : and they shall draw their swords against Egypt, and fill the land with the slain. 12 And I will make the rivers dry, and sell the land into the hand of the wicked : and I will make the land waste, and all that is therein, by the hand of strangers : I the LORD have spoken *it*. 13 Thus saith the Lord GOD; I will also destroy the idols, and I will cause *their* images to cease out of Noph; and there shall be no more a prince of the land of Egypt : and I will put a fear in the land of Egypt. 14 And I will make Pathros desolate, and will set fire in Zoan, and will execute judgments in No. 15 And I will pour my fury upon Sin, the strength of Egypt; and I will cut off the multitude of No. 16 And I will set fire in Egypt : Sin shall have great pain, and No shall be rent asunder, and Noph *shall have* distresses daily. 17 The young men of Aven and of Pi-beseth shall fall by the sword : and these *cities* shall go into captivity. 18 At Tehaphnehes also the day shall be darkened, when I shall break there the yokes of Egypt : and the pomp of her strength shall cease in her : as for her, a cloud shall cover her, and her daughters shall go into captivity. 19 Thus will I execute judgments in Egypt : and they shall know that I *am* the LORD.

The prophecy of the destruction of Egypt is here very full and particular, as well as, in the general, very frightful. What can protect a provoking people when the righteous God comes forth to contend with them? I. It shall be a very lamentable destruction, and such as shall occasion great sorrow (*v.* 2, 3): "*Howl you;* you may justly shriek now that it is coming, for you will be made to shriek and make hideous outcries when it comes. Cry out, *Woe worth the day!* or, *Ah the day! alas because of the day!* the terrible day! *Woe and alas!* For the day *is near;* the day we have so long dreaded, so long deserved. It is the *day of the Lord,* the day in which he will manifest himself as a God of vengeance. You have your day now, when you carry all before you, and trample on all about you, but God will have his day shortly, the day of the revelation of his righteous judgment," Ps. xxxvii. 13. It will be *a cloudy day,* that is, dark and dismal, without the shining forth of any comfort; and it shall threaten a storm—*fire, and*
926

brimstone, and a horrible tempest. It shall be the time of the heathen, of reckoning with the heathen for all their heathenish practices, that time which David spoke of when God would *pour out his fury upon the heathen* (Ps. lxxix. 6), when *they should sink,* Ps. ix. 15.

II. It shall be the destruction of Egypt, and of all the states and countries in confederacy with her and in her neighbourhood. 1. Egypt herself shall fall (*v.* 4) : The *sword shall come upon Egypt,* the sword of the Chaldeans, and it shall be a victorious sword, for the *slain shall fall in Egypt,* fall by it, fall before it. Is the country populous? They shall *take away her multitude.* Is it strong, and well-fixed? *Her foundations shall be broken down,* and then the fabric, though built ever so fine, ever so high, will fall of course. 2. Her neighbours and inmates shall fall with her. When the slain fall so thickly in Egypt *great pain shall be in Ethiopia,* both that in Africa, which is in the neighbourhood of Egypt on one side, and that in Asia, which is near to it on the other side. When their neighbour's house was on fire they could not but apprehend their own in danger; nor were their fears groundless, for they shall all *fall with them by the sword, v.* 5. *Ethiopia and Libya* (Cush and Phut, so the Hebrew names are, two of the sons of Ham who are mentioned, and Mizraim, that is, Egypt, between them, Gen. x. 6), *and the Lydians* (who were famous archers, and are spoken of as confederates with Egypt, Jer. xlvi. 9), these shall fall with Egypt and *Chub* (the Chaldeans, the inhabitants of the inner Libya); these and others were the *mingled people;* there were those of all these and other countries who upon some account or other resided in Egypt, as did also *the men of the land that is in league,* some of the remains of the people of Israel and Judah, the *children of the covenant,* or league, as they are called (Acts iii. 25), the *children of the promise,* Gal. iv. 28. These sojourned in Egypt contrary to God's command, and these shall *fall with them.* Note, Those that will take their lot with God's enemies shall have their lot with them, yea, though they be in profession the men of the land that is in league with God.

III. All that pretend to support the sinking interests of Egypt shall come down under her, shall come down with her (*v.* 6) : *Those that uphold Egypt shall fall,* and then Egypt must fall of course. See the justice of God; Egypt pretended to uphold Jerusalem when that was tottering, but proved a deceitful reed; and now those that pretended to uphold Egypt shall prove no better. Those that deceive others are commonly paid in their own coin; they are themselves deceived. 1. Does Egypt think herself upheld by the absolute authority and dominion of her king? The *pride of her power* shall *come down, v.* 6. The power of the king of Egypt was his pride; but that shall be broken, and humbled. 2. Is the multitude of her people her support? These shall *fall by the sword,* even *from the tower of Syene,* which is in the utmost corner of the land, from that side of it by which the enemy shall enter. Both the *countries* and the *cities,* the husbandmen and the merchants, shall be desolate, *v.* 7, as before, *ch.* xxix. 12. Even *the multitude of Egypt shall be made to cease, v.* 10. That populous country shall be depopulated. The land shall be even *filled with the slain, v.* 11. 3. Is the river Nile her support, and are the several channels of it a defence to her? "*I will make the rivers dry* (*v.* 12), so that those natural fortifications which were thought impregnable, because impassable, shall stand them in no stead." 4. Are her idols a support to her? They shall be destroyed; those imaginary upholders shall appear more than ever to be imaginary, for so images are when they pretend to be deliverers and strongholds (*v.* 13): *I will cause their images to cease out of Noph.* 5. Is her royal family her support? *There shall be no more a prince in the land of Egypt;* the royal family shall be extirpated and extinguished, which had continued so long. 6. Is her courage her support, and does she think to uphold herself by the bravery of her men of war, who have now of late been inured to service? That shall fail: *I will put a fear in the land of Egypt.* 7. Is the rising generation her support? is she upheld by her children, and does she think herself happy because she has her quiver full of them? Alas! *the young men shall fall by the sword* (*v.* 17) and *the daughters shall go into captivity* (*v.* 18), and so she shall be robbed of all her hopes.

IV. God shall inflict these desolating judgments on Egypt (*v.* 8): *They shall know that I am the Lord,* and greater than all gods, than all *their* gods, when I have *set a fire in Egypt.* The fire that consumes nations is of God's kindling; and, when he sets fire to a people, *all their helpers shall be destroyed.* Those that go about to quench the fire shall themselves be devoured by it; for who can stand before him when he is angry? When he *pours out his fury* upon a place, when he sets fire to it (*v.* 15, 16), neither its strength nor its multitude can stand it in any stead.

V. The king of Babylon and his army shall be employed as instruments of this destruction: *The multitude of Egypt shall be made to cease* and be quite cut off *by the hand of the king of Babylon, v.* 10. Those that undertook to protect Israel from the king of Babylon shall not be able to protect themselves. It is said of the Chaldeans, who should destroy Egypt, 1. That they are *strangers* (*v.* 12), who therefore shall show no compassion for old acquaintance-sake, but shall behave strangely towards them. 2. That they are *the terrible of the nations* (*v.* 11), both in respect of force and in re-

spect of fierceness; and, being terrible, they shall *make terrible work.* (3.) That they are *the wicked,* who will not be restrained by reason and conscience, the laws of nature or the laws of nations, for they are without law: *I will sell the land into the hand of the wicked.* They do violence *unjustly,* as they are wicked; yet, so far as they are instruments in God's hand of executing his judgments, it is on his part justly done. Note, God often makes one wicked man a scourge to another; and even wicked men acquire a title to prey, *jure belli*—by the laws of war, for God *sells it into their hands.*

VI. No place in the land of Egypt shall be exempted from the fury of the Chaldean army, not the strongest, not the remotest: *The sword shall go through the land.* Various places are here named: *Pathros, Zoan, and No* (*v.* 14), *Sin and Noph* (*v.* 15, 16), *Aven and Pi-beseth* (*v.* 17), and *Tehaphnehes, v.* 18. These shall be made desolate, shall be fired, and God's judgments shall be executed upon them, and his fury poured out upon them. Their strength and multitude shall be *cut off;* they shall have *great pain,* shall be *rent asunder* with fear, and shall *have distresses daily.* Their *day shall be darkened;* their honours, comforts, and hopes, shall be extinguished. Their *yokes* shall be *broken,* so that they shall no more oppress and tyrannize as they have done. The *pomp of their strength shall cease,* and *a cloud shall cover them,* a cloud so thick that through it they shall not see any hopes, nor shall their glory *be seen,* or *shine further.* And, *lastly,* the Ethiopians, who are at a distance from them, as well as those who are mingled with them, shall share in their pain and terror. God will by his providence spread the rumour, and the *careless Ethiopians* shall be *made afraid, v.* 9. Note, God can strike a terror upon those that are most secure; fearfulness shall, when he pleases, surprise the most presumptuous hypocrites.

The close of this prediction leaves, 1. The land of Egypt mortified: *Thus will I execute judgments on Egypt, v.* 19. The destruction of Egypt is the *executing of judgments,* which intimates not only that it is done justly, for its sins, but that it is done regularly and legally, by a judicial sentence. All the executions God does are according to his judgments. 2. The God of Israel herein glorified: *They shall know that I am the Lord.* The Egyptians shall be made to know it and the people of God shall be made to know it better. *The Lord is known by the judgments which he executes.*

20 And it came to pass in the eleventh year, in the first *month,* in the seventh *day* of the month, *that* the word of the LORD came unto me, saying, 21 Son of man, I have broken the arm of Pharaoh king of Egypt;

and, lo, it shall not be bound up to be healed, to put a roller to bind it, to make it strong to hold the sword. 22 Therefore thus saith the Lord GOD; Behold, I *am* against Pharaoh king of Egypt, and will break his arms, the strong, and that which was broken; and I will cause the sword to fall out of his hand. 23 And I will scatter the Egyptians among the nations, and will disperse them through the countries. 24 And I will strengthen the arms of the king of Babylon, and put my sword in his hand: but I will break Pharaoh's arms, and he shall groan before him with the groanings of a deadly wounded *man*. 25 But I will strengthen the arms of the king of Babylon, and the arms of Pharaoh shall fall down; and they shall know that I *am* the LORD, when I shall put my sword into the hand of the king of Babylon, and he shall stretch it out upon the land of Egypt. 26 And I will scatter the Egyptians among the nations, and disperse them among the countries; and they shall know that I *am* the LORD.

This short prophecy of the weakening of the power of Egypt was delivered about the time that the army of the Egyptians, which attempted to raise the siege of Jerusalem, was frustrated in its enterprises, and returned *re infectâ*—*without accomplishing their purpose;* whereupon the king of Babylon renewed the siege and carried his point. The kingdom of Egypt was very ancient, and had been for many ages considerable. That of Babylon had but lately arrived at its great pomp and power, being built upon the ruins of the kingdom of Assyria. Now it is with them as it is with families and states, some are growing up, others are declining and going back; one must increase and the others must of course decrease.

I. It is here foretold that the king of Egypt shall grow weaker and weaker. The extent of his territories shall be abridged, his wealth and power shall be diminished, and he shall become less able than ever to help either himself or his friend. 1. This was in part done already (*v.* 21): *I have broken the arm of Pharaoh,* some time ago. One arm of that kingdom might well be reckoned broken when the king of Babylon routed the forces of Pharaoh-Necho at Carchemish (Jer. xlvi. 2), and made himself master of *all that pertained to Egypt from the river of Egypt to Euphrates,* 2 Kings xxiv. 7. Egypt had been long in gathering strength and extending its dominions, and therefore, that there

928

may be a proportion observed in providence, it loses its strength slowly and by degrees. It was soon after the king of Egypt slew good king Josiah, and in the same reign, that its arm was thus broken, and it received that fatal blow which it never recovered. Before Egypt's heart and neck were broken its arm was. God's judgments come upon a people by steps, that they may meet him repenting. When the arm of Egypt is broken *it shall not be bound up to be healed,* for none can heal the wounds that God gives but he himself. Those whom he disarms, whom he disables, cannot again hold the sword. 2. This was to be done again. One arm was broken before, and something was done towards the setting of it, towards the healing of the deadly wound that was given to the beast. But now (*v.* 22), *I am against Pharaoh, and will break both his arms,* both *the strong* and that *which was broken* and set again. Note, If less judgments do not prevail to humble and reform sinners, God will send greater. Now God will *cause the sword to fall out of his hand,* which he caught hold of as thinking himself strong enough to hold it. It is repeated (*v.* 24), *I will break Pharaoh's arms.* He had been a cruel oppressor to the people of God formerly, and of late the *staff of a broken rod* to them; and now God by breaking his arms reckons with him for both. God justly breaks that power which is abused either to put wrongs upon people or to put cheats upon them. But this is not all; (1.) The king of Egypt shall be dispirited when he finds himself in danger of the king of Babylon's forces: he *shall groan before him with the groaning of a deadly wounded man.* Note, It is common for those that are most elated in their prosperity to be most dejected and disheartened in their adversity. Pharaoh, even before the sword touches him, shall groan as if he had received his death's wound. (2.) The people of Egypt shall be dispersed (*v.* 23 and again *v.* 26): *I will scatter them among the nations.* Other nations had mingled with them (*v.* 5); now they shall be mingled with other nations, and seek shelter in them, and so be made to know that the Lord is righteous.

II. It is here foretold that the king of Babylon shall grow stronger and stronger, *v.* 24, 25. It is said, and repeated, that God will, 1. *Put strength* into the king of Babylon's arms, that he may be able to go through the service he is designed for. 2. That he will *put a sword,* his sword, into the king of Babylon's hand, which signified his giving him a commission and furnishing him with arms for carrying on a war, particularly against Egypt. Note, As judges on the bench, like Pilate (John xix. 11), so generals in the field, like Nebuchadnezzar, have no power but what is given them from above.

CHAP. XXXI.

The prophecy of this chapter, as the two chapters before, is against

Egypt, and designed for the humbling and mortifying of Pharaoh. In passing sentence upon great criminals it is usual to consult precedents, and to see what has been done to others in the like case, which serves both to direct and to justify the proceedings. Pharaoh stands indicted at the bar of divine justice for his pride and haughtiness, and the injuries he had done to God's people; but he thinks himself so high, so great, as not to be accountable to any authority, so strong, and so well guarded, as not to be conquerable by any force. The prophet is therefore directed to make a report to him of the case of the king of Assyria, whose head city was Nineveh. I. He must show him how great a monarch the king of Assyria had been, what a vast empire he had, what a mighty sway he bore ; the king of Egypt, great as he was, could not go beyond him, ver. 3—9. II. He must then show him how like he was to the king of Assyria in pride and carnal security, ver. 10. III. He must next read him the history of the fall and ruin of the king of Assyria, what a noise it made among the nations and what a warning it gave to all potent princes to take heed of pride, ver. 11—17. IV. He must leave the king of Egypt to apply all this to himself, to see his own face in the looking-glass of the king of Assyria's sin, and to foresee his own fall through the perspective glass of his ruin, ver. 18.

A ND it came to pass in the eleventh year, in the third *month*, in the first *day* of the month, *that* the word of the LORD came unto me, saying, 2 Son of man, speak unto Pharaoh king of Egypt, and to his multitude ; Whom art thou like in thy greatness ? 3 Behold, the Assyrian *was* a cedar in Lebanon with fair branches, and with a shadowing shroud, and of a high stature ; and his top was among the thick boughs. 4 The waters made him great, the deep set him up on high with her rivers running round about his plants, and sent out her little rivers unto all the trees of the field. 5 Therefore his height was exalted above all the trees of the field, and his boughs were multiplied, and his branches became long because of the multitude of waters, when he shot forth. 6 All the fowls of heaven made their nests in his boughs, and under his branches did all the beasts of the field bring forth their young, and under his shadow dwelt all great nations. 7 Thus was he fair in his greatness, in the length of his branches : for his root was by great waters. 8 The cedars in the garden of God could not hide him : the fir-trees were not like his boughs, and the chesnut-trees were not like his branches ; nor any tree in the garden of God was like unto him in his beauty. 9 I have made him fair by the multitude of his branches : so that all the trees of Eden, that *were* in the garden of God, envied him.

This prophecy bears date the month before Jerusalem was taken, as that in the close of the foregoing chapter about four months before. When God's people were in the depth of their distress, it would be some comfort to them, as it would serve likewise for a check to the pride and malice of their neighbours, that insulted over them, to be told from heaven that the cup was going round, even the cup of trembling, that it would shortly be taken out of the hands of God's people and put into the hands of those that hated them, Isa. li. 22, 23. In this prophecy,

I. The prophet is directed to put Pharaoh upon searching the records for a case parallel to his own (*v.* 2) : *Speak to Pharaoh and to his multitude*, to the multitude of his attendants, that contributed so much to his magnificence, and the multitude of his armies, that contributed so much to his strength. These he was proud of, these he put a confidence in ; and they were as proud of him and trusted as much in him. Now ask him, *Whom art thou like in thy greatness?* We are apt to judge of ourselves by comparison. Those that think highly of themselves fancy themselves as great and as good as such and such, that have been mightily celebrated. The flatterers of princes tell them whom they equal in pomp and grandeur. " Well," says God, " let him pitch upon the most famous potentate that ever was, and it shall be allowed that he is *like him in greatness* and no way inferior to him ; but, let him pitch upon whom he will, he will find that *his day came to fall ;* he will see there was an *end* of all *his perfection*, and must therefore expect the end of his own in like manner." Note, The falls of others, both into sin and ruin, are intended as admonitions to us not to be secure or *high-minded*, nor to think we stand out of danger.

II. He is directed to show him an instance of one whom he resembles in greatness, and that was the Assyrian (*v.* 3), whose monarchy had continued from Nimrod. Sennacherib was one of the mighty princes of that monarchy ; but it sunk down soon after him, and the monarchy of Nebuchadnezzar was built upon its ruins, or rather grafted upon its stock. Let us now see what a flourishing prince the king of Assyria was. He is here compared to a stately cedar, *v.* 3. The glory of the house of David is illustrated by the same similitude, *ch.* xvii. 3. The olive-tree, the fig-tree, and the vine, which were all fruit-trees, had refused to be *promoted over the trees* because they would not leave their fruitfulness (Judg. ix. 8, &c.), and therefore the choice falls upon the cedar, that is stately and strong, and casts a great shadow, but bears no fruit. 1. The Assyrian monarch was a tall cedar, such as the cedars in Lebanon generally were, of a *high stature*, and *his top among the thick boughs ;* he was attended by other princes that were tributaries to him, and was surrounded by a life-guard of brave men. He surpassed all the princes in his neighbourhood ; they were all shrubs to him (*v.* 5) : *His height was exalted above all the trees of the field;* they were many of them very high, but he overtopped them all, *v.* 8. The cedars, even those in the garden of Eden, which we may suppose were the best of the kind, *would not hide him,* but his top branches outshot theirs. 2. He was a spreading cedar; his branches did not only run up in height, but run out in breadth, denoting that this mighty prince was not only exalted to great dignity and honour, and had a name above the names of the great men of the earth, but that he obtained great dominion and power; his territories were large, and he extended his conquests far and his influences much further. This cedar, like *a vine,* sent forth *his branches to the sea, to the river,* Ps. lxxx. 11. *His boughs were multiplied; his branches became long (v.* 5); so that *he had a shadowing shroud, v.* 3. This contributed very much to his beauty, that he grew proportionally large as well as high. He was *fair in his greatness, in the length of his branches (v.* 7), very comely as well as very stately, *fair by the multitude of his branches, v.* 9. His large dominions were well managed, like a spreading tree that is kept in shape and good order by the skill of the gardener, so as to be very beautiful to the eye. His government was as amiable in the eyes of wise men as it was admirable in the eyes of all men. The *fir-trees* were not *like his boughs,* so straight, so green, so regular; nor were the branches of *the chestnut-trees like his branches,* so thick, so spreading. In short, *no tree in the garden of God,* in Eden, in Babylon (for that stood where paradise was planted), where there was every tree that was *pleasant to the sight* (Gen. ii. 9), was like *to this cedar in beauty;* that is, in all the surrounding nations there was no prince so much admired, so much courted, and whom every body was so much in love with, as the king of Assyria. Many of them *did virtuously,* but he *excelled them all,* outshone them all. *All the trees of Eden envied him, v.* 9. When they found they could not compare with him they were angry and grieved that he so far outdid them, and secretly grudged him the praise due to him. Note, It is the unhappiness of those who in any thing excel others that thereby they make themselves the objects of envy; and *who can stand before envy?* 3. He was serviceable, as far as a standing growing cedar could be, and that was only by his shadow (*v.* 6): *All the fowls of heaven,* some of all sorts, *made their nests in his boughs,* where they were sheltered from the injuries of the weather. The *beasts of the field* put themselves under the protection of *his branches.* There they were *levant—rising up,* and *couchant—lying down;* there they *brought forth their young;* for they had there a natural covert from the heat and from the storm. The meaning of all is, *Under his shadow dwelt all great nations;* they all fled to him for safety, and were willing to swear allegi-

ance to him if he would undertake to protect them, as travellers in a shower come under thick trees for shelter. Note, Those who have power ought to use it for the protection and comfort of those whom they have power over; for to that end they are entrusted with power. Even the bramble, if he be anointed king, invites the trees to come and *trust in his shadow,* Judg. ix. 15. But the utmost security that any creature, even the king of Assyria himself, can give, is but like the shadow of a tree, which is but a scanty and slender protection, and leaves a man many ways exposed. Let us therefore flee to God for protection, and he will take us *under the shadow of his wings,* where we shall be warmer and safer than under the shadow of the strongest and stateliest cedar, Ps. xvii. 8; xci. 4. 4. He seemed to be settled and established in his greatness and power. For, (1.) It was God that *made him fair, v.* 9. For by him kings reign. He was comely with the comeliness that God put upon him. Note, God's hand must be eyed and owned in the advancement of the great men of the earth, and therefore we must not envy them; yet that will not secure the continuance of their prosperity, for he that gave them their beauty, if they be deprived of it, knows how to turn it into deformity. (2.) He seemed to have a good bottom. This cedar was not like the *heath in the desert, made to inhabit the parched places* (Jer. xvii. 6); it was not *a root in a dry ground,* Isa. liii. 2. No; he had abundance of wealth to support his power and grandeur (*v.* 4): *The waters made him great;* he had vast treasures, large stores and magazines, which were as the *deep that set him up on high,* constant revenues coming in by taxes, customs, and crown-rents, which were *as rivers running round about his plants;* these enabled him to strengthen and secure his interests every where, for he *sent out his little rivers,* or conduits, *to all the trees of the field,* to water them; and when they had *maintenance from the king's palace* (Ezra iv. 14), and *their country was nourished by the king's country* (Acts xii. 20), they would be serviceable and faithful to him. Those that have wealth flowing upon them in great rivers find themselves obliged to send it out again in little rivers; for, *as goods are increased, those are increased that eat them,* and the more men have the more occasion they have for it; yea, and still the more they have occasion for. The *branches* of this cedar *became long,* because of *the multitude of waters* which fed them (*v.* 5 and 7); *his root was by great waters,* which seemed to secure it that *its leaf should never wither* (Ps. i. 3), that it should not *see when heat came,* Jer. xvii. 8. Note, Worldly people may seem to have an established prosperity, yet it only seems so, Job v. 3; Ps. xxxvii. 35.

10 Therefore thus saith the Lord God; Because thou hast lifted up

thyself in height, and he hath shot up his top among the thick boughs, and his heart is lifted up in his height; 11 I have therefore delivered him into the hand of the mighty one of the heathen; he shall surely deal with him: I have driven him out for his wickedness. 12 And strangers, the terrible of the nations, have cut him off, and have left him: upon the mountains and in all the valleys his branches are fallen, and his boughs are broken by all the rivers of the land; and all the people of the earth are gone down from his shadow, and have left him. 13 Upon his ruin shall all the fowls of the heaven remain, and all the beasts of the field shall be upon his branches: 14 To the end that none of all the trees by the waters exalt themselves for their height, neither shoot up their top among the thick boughs, neither their trees stand up in their height, all that drink water: for they are all delivered unto death, to the nether parts of the earth, in the midst of the children of men, with them that go down to the pit. 15 Thus saith the Lord God; In the day when he went down to the grave I caused a mourning: I covered the deep for him, and I restrained the floods thereof, and the great waters were stayed: and I caused Lebanon to mourn for him, and all the trees of the field fainted for him. 16 I made the nations to shake at the sound of his fall, when I cast him down to hell with them that descend into the pit: and all the trees of Eden, the choice and best of Lebanon, all that drink water, shall be comforted in the nether parts of the earth. 17 They also went down into hell with him unto *them that be* slain with the sword; and *they that were* his arm, *that* dwelt under his shadow in the midst of the heathen. 18 To whom art thou thus like in glory and in greatness among the trees of Eden? yet shalt thou be brought down with the trees of Eden unto the nether parts of the earth: thou shalt lie in the midst of the uncircumcised with *them that be* slain by the sword. This *is* Pharaoh and all his multitude, saith the Lord God.

We have seen the king of Egypt resembling the king of Assyria in pomp, and power, and prosperity, how like he was to him in his greatness; now here we see,

I. How he does likewise resemble him in his pride, *v.* 10. For, as face answers to face in a glass, so does one corrupt carnal heart to another; and the same temptations of a prosperous state by which some are overcome are fatal to many others too. "*Thou,* O king of Egypt! *hast lifted up thyself in height,* hast been proud of thy wealth and power, *ch.* xxix. 3. And just so *he* (that is, the king of Assyria); when he had *shot up his top among the thick boughs his heart* was immediately *lifted up in his height,* and he grew insolent and imperious, set God himself at defiance, and trampled upon his people;" witness the messages and letter which *the great king, the king of Assyria,* sent to Hezekiah, Isa. xxxvi. 4. How haughtily does he speak of himself and his own achievements! how scornfully of that great and good man! There were other sins in which the Egyptians and the Assyrians did concur, particularly that of oppressing God's people, which is charged upon them both together (Isa. lii. 4); but here that sin is traced up to its cause, and that was pride; for it is the *contempt of the proud* that they are *filled with.* Note, When men's outward condition rises their minds commonly rise with it; and it is very rare to find a humble spirit in the midst of great advancements.

II. How he shall therefore resemble him in his fall; and for the opening of this part of the comparison,

1. Here is a history of the fall of the king of Assyria. For his part, says God (*v.* 11), *I have therefore,* because he was thus lifted up, *delivered him into the hand of the mighty one of the heathen.* Cyaxares, king of the Medes, in the twenty-sixth year of his reign, in conjunction with Nebuchadnezzar king of Babylon in the first year of his reign, destroyed Nineveh, and with it the Assyrian empire. Nebuchadnezzar, though he was not then, yet afterwards became, very emphatically, the *mighty one of the heathen,* most mighty among them and most mighty over them, to prevail against them.

(1.) Respecting the fall of the Assyrian three things are affirmed:—[1.] It is God himself that orders his ruin : *I have delivered him into the hand* of the executioner; *I have driven him out.* Note, God is the Judge, who puts down one and sets up another (Ps. lxxv. 7); and when he pleases he can extirpate and expel those who think themselves, and seem to others, to have taken deepest root. And the mightiest ones of the heathens could not gain their point against those they contended with if the Almighty did not himself deliver them into their hands. [2.] It is his own sin that procures his ruin : *I have driven him out for his wickedness.* None are driven out from their honour, power, and possessions, but it is *for their wickedness.* None of our comforts are ever lost but what have been a thousand times forfeited. If the wicked are *driven away,* it is *in their wickedness.* [3.] It is a *mighty one of the heathen* that shall be the instrument of his ruin ; for God often employs one wicked man in punishing another. *He shall surely deal with him,* shall know how to manage him, great as he is. Note, Proud imperious men will, sooner or later, meet with their match.

(2.) In this history of the fall of the Assyrian observe, [1.] A continuation of the similitude of the cedar. He grew very high, and extended his boughs very far ; but his day comes to fall. *First,* This stately cedar was cropped : *The terrible of the nations cut him off.* Soldiers, who being both armed and commissioned to kill, and slay, and destroy, may well be reckoned among *the terrible of the nations.* They have lopped off his branches first, have seized upon some parts of his dominion and forced them out of his hands ; so that in all *mountains* and *valleys* of the nations about, in the high-lands and low-lands, and *by all the rivers,* there were cities or countries that were broken off from the Assyrian monarchy, that had been subject to it, but had either revolted or were recovered from it. Its feathers were borrowed ; and, when every bird had fetched back its own, it was naked like the stump of a tree. *Secondly,* It was deserted : *All the people of the earth,* that had fled to him for shelter, have *gone down from his shadow and have left him.* When he was disabled to give them protection they thought they no longer owed him allegiance. Let not great men be proud of the number of those that attend them and have a dependence upon them ; it is only for what they can get. When Providence frowns upon them their retinue is soon dispersed and scattered from them. *Thirdly,* It was insulted over, and its fall triumphed in (*v.* 13) : *Upon his ruin shall all the fowls of the heaven remain,* to tread upon the broken branches of this cedar. Its fall is triumphed in by the other trees, who were angry to see themselves overtopped so much : *All the trees of Eden,* that were cut down and had fallen before him, *all that drank water* of the rain of heaven, as the stump of the tree that is left in the *south* is said to be *wet with the dew of heaven* (Dan. iv. 23) and to bud *through the scent of water* (Job xiv. 9), *shall be comforted in the nether parts of the earth* when they see this proud cedar brought as low as themselves. *Solamen miseris socios habuisse doloris—To have companions in woe is a solace to those who suffer.* But, on the contrary, the trees of Lebanon, that are yet standing in their height and strength, *mourned for him,* and *the trees of the field fainted for him,* because they could
932

not but read their own destiny in his fall. *Howl, fir-trees, if the cedar be shaken,* for they cannot expect to stand long, Zech. xi. 2. [2.] An explanation of the similitude of the cedar. By the cutting down of this cedar is signified the slaughter of this mighty monarch and all his adherents and supporters ; they are all *delivered to death,* to fall by the sword, as the cedar by the axe. He and his princes, who, he said, were *altogether kings,* go down to the grave, *to the nether parts of the earth, in the midst of the children of men,* as common persons of no quality or distinction. *They died like men* (Ps. lxxxii. 7) ; they were carried away with *those that go down to the pit,* and their pomp did neither protect them nor *descend after them.* Again (*v.* 16), He was *cast down to hell with those that descend into the pit ;* he went into the state of the dead, and was buried as others are, in obscurity and oblivion. Again (*v.* 17), *They all that were his arm,* on whom he stayed, by whom he acted and exerted his power, all *that dwelt under his shadow,* his subjects and allies, and all that had any dependence on him, they all *went down* into ruin, down into the grave *with him, unto those that were slain with the sword,* to those that were cut off by untimely deaths before them, under the load of guilt and shame. When great men fall a great many fall with them, as a great many in like manner have fallen before them. [3.] What God designed, and aimed at, in bringing down this mighty monarch and his monarchy. He designed thereby, *First,* To give an alarm to the nations about, to put them all to a stand, to put them all to a gaze (*v.* 16) : *I made the nations to shake at the sound of his fall.* They were all struck with astonishment to see so mighty a prince brought down thus. It give a shock to all their confidences, every one thinking his turn would be next. *When he went down to the grave* (*v.* 15) *I caused a mourning,* a general lamentation, as the whole kingdom goes into mourning at the death of the king. In token of this general grief, *I covered the deep for him,* put that into black, gave a stop to business, in complaisance to this universal mourning. *I restrained the floods, and the great waters were stayed,* that they might run into another channel, that of lamentation. Lebanon particularly, the kingdom of Syria, that was sometimes in confederacy with the Assyrian, mourned for him ; as the allies of Babylon, Rev. xviii. 9. *Secondly,* To give an admonition to the nations about, and to their kings (*v.* 14) : *To the end that none of all the trees by the waters,* though ever so advantageously situated, *may exalt themselves for their height,* may be proud and conceited of themselves and *shoot up their top among the thick boughs,* looking disdainfully upon others, nor *stand upon themselves for their height,* confiding in their own politics and powers, as if they could never be brought down. Let them all take warning by the Assyrian, for he once held up his head as high, and thought he kept his footing as firm, as any of them; but his pride went before his destruction, and his confidence failed him. Note, The fall of proud presumptuous men is intended for warning to others to keep humble. It would have been well for Nebuchadnezzar, who was himself active in bringing down the Assyrian, if he had taken the admonition.

2. Here is a prophecy of the fall of the king of Egypt in like manner, *v.* 18. He thought himself like the Assyrian *in glory and greatness,* over-topping *all the trees of Eden,* as the cypress does the shrubs. "But *thou* also *shalt be brought down,* with the other trees that are pleasant to the sight, as those in Eden. Thou shalt be *brought to the grave,* to the nether or lower *parts of the earth;* thou shalt *lie in the midst of the uncircumcised,* that die in their uncleanness, die ingloriously, die under a curse and at a distance from God; then shall those whom thou hast trampled upon triumph over thee, saying, *This is Pharaoh and all his multitude.* See how mean he looks, how low he lies; see what all his pomp and pride have come to; here is all that is left of him." Note, Great men and great multitudes, with the great figure and great noise they make in the world, when God comes to contend with them, will soon become little, less than nothing, such as Pharaoh and all his multitude.

CHAP. XXXII.

Still we are upon the destruction of Pharaoh and Egypt, which is wonderfully enlarged upon, and with a great deal of emphasis. When we read so very much of Egypt's ruin, no less than six several prophecies at divers times delivered concerning it, we are ready to think, Surely there is some special reason for it. And, I. Perhaps it may look as far back as the book of Genesis, where we find (ch. xv. 14) that God determined to judge Egypt for oppressing his people; and, though that was in part fulfilled in the plagues of Egypt and the drowning of Pharaoh, yet, in this destruction, here foretold, those old scores were reckoned for, and that was to have its full accomplishment. II. Perhaps it may look as far forward as the book of the Revelation, where we find that the great enemy of the gospel-church, that makes war with the Lamb, is spiritually called Egypt, Rev. xi. 8. And, if so, the destruction of Egypt and its Pharaoh was a type of the destruction of that proud enemy; and between this prophecy of the ruin of Egypt and the prophecy of the destruction of the antichristian generation there is some analogy. We have two distinct prophecies in this chapter relating to Egypt, both in the same month, one on the 1st day, the other that day fortnight, probably both on the sabbath day. They are both lamentations, not only to signify how lamentable the fall of Egypt should be, but to intimate how much the prophet himself should lament it, from a generous principle of love to mankind. The destruction of Egypt is here represented under two similitudes:—1. The killing of a lion, or a whale, or some such devouring creature, ver. 1—16. 2. The funeral of a great commander or captain-general, ver. 17—32. The two prophecies of this chapter are much of the same length.

AND it came to pass in the twelfth year, in the twelfth month, in the first *day* of the month, *that* the word of the LORD came unto me, saying, 2 Son of man, take up a lamentation for Pharaoh king of Egypt, and say unto him, Thou art like a young lion of the nations, and thou *art* as a whale in the seas: and thou camest forth with thy rivers, and troubledst the waters with thy feet, and fouledst their rivers. 3 Thus saith the Lord GOD; I will therefore spread out my net over thee with a company of many people; and they shall bring thee up in my net. 4 Then will I leave thee upon the land, I will cast thee forth upon the open field, and will cause all the fowls of the heaven to remain upon thee, and I will fill the beasts of the whole earth with thee. 5 And I will lay thy flesh upon the mountains, and fill the valleys with thy height. 6 I will also water with thy blood the land wherein thou swimmest, *even* to the mountains; and the rivers shall be full of thee. 7 And when I shall put thee out, I will cover the heaven, and make the stars thereof dark; I will cover the sun with a cloud, and the moon shall not give her light. 8 All the bright lights of heaven will I make dark over thee, and set darkness upon thy land, saith the Lord GOD. 9 I will also vex the hearts of many people, when I shall bring thy destruction among the nations, into the countries which thou hast not known. 10 Yea, I will make many people amazed at thee, and their kings shall be horribly afraid for thee, when I shall brandish my sword before them; and they shall tremble at *every* moment, every man for his own life, in the day of thy fall. 11 For thus saith the Lord GOD; The sword of the king of Babylon shall come upon thee. 12 By the swords of the mighty will I cause thy multitude to fall, the terrible of the nations, all of them: and they shall spoil the pomp of Egypt, and all the multitude thereof shall be destroyed. 13 I will destroy also all the beasts thereof from beside the great waters; neither shall the foot of man trouble them any more, nor the hoofs of beasts trouble them. 14 Then will I make their waters deep, and cause their rivers to run like oil, saith the Lord GOD. 15 When I shall make the land of Egypt desolate, and the country shall be destitute of that whereof it was full, when I shall smite all them that dwell therein, then shall they know that I *am* the LORD. 16 This *is* the lamentation wherewith they shall lament her: the daughters of the nations shall lament her: they shall lament for her, *even* for Egypt, and for all her multitude, saith the Lord GOD.

Here, I. The prophet is ordered to *take up a lamentation for Pharaoh king of Egypt, v.* 2. It concerns ministers to be much of a serious spirit, and, in order thereunto, to be frequent in taking up lamentations for the fall and ruin of sinners, as those that have not desired, but dreaded, the woeful day. Note, Ministers that would affect others with the things of God must make it appear that they are themselves affected with the miseries which sinners bring upon themselves by their sins. It becomes us to weep and tremble for those that will not weep and tremble for themselves, to try if thereby we may set them a weeping, set them a trembling.

II. He is ordered to show cause for that lamentation.

1. Pharaoh has been a troubler of the nations, even of his own nation, which he should have procured the repose of: He is *like a young lion of the nations (v.* 2), loud and noisy, hectoring and threatening as a lion when he roars. Great potentates, if they be tyrannical and oppressive, are in God's account no better than beasts of prey. He is like *a whale,* or dragon, like a crocodile (so some) *in the seas,* very turbulent and vexatious, as the *leviathan* that *makes the deep to boil like a pot,* Job xli. 31. When Pharaoh engaged in an unnecessary war with the Cyrenians he *came forth with his rivers,* with his armies, *troubled the waters,* disturbed his own kingdom and the neighbouring nations, *fouled the rivers,* and made them muddy. Note, A great deal of disquiet is often given to the world by the restless ambition and implacable resentments of proud princes. Ahab is he that troubles Israel, and not Elijah.

2. He that has troubled others must expect to be himself troubled; for the Lord is righteous, Josh. vii. 25.

(1.) This is set forth here by a comparison. Is Pharaoh like a *great whale,* which, when it comes up the river, gives great disturbance, a leviathan which Job cannot *draw out with a hook?* (Job xli. 1), yet God has a net for him which is large enough to enclose him and strong enough to secure him *(v.* 3): *I will spread my net over thee,* even the army of the Chaldeans, a *company of many people;* they shall force him out of his fastnesses, dislodge him out of his possessions, throw him like a great fish upon dry ground, *upon the open field (v.* 4), where, being out of his element, he must die of course, and be a prey to the birds and beasts, as was foretold, *ch.* xxix. 5. What can the strongest fish do to help itself when it is out of the water and lies gasping? *The flesh* of this great whale

shall be *laid upon the mountains (v.* 5) and the *valleys* shall be *filled with his height.* Such numbers of Pharaoh's soldiers shall be slain that the dead bodies shall be scattered upon the hills and there shall be heaps of them piled up in the valleys. Blood shall be shed in such abundance as to swell the rivers in the valleys. Or, Such shall be the bulk, such the height, of this leviathan, that, when he is laid upon the ground, he shall fill a valley. Such vast quantities of blood shall issue from this *leviathan* as shall *water the land of Egypt,* the land wherein *now he swims,* now he sports himself, *v.* 6. It shall reach *to the mountains,* and the waters of Egypt shall again be *turned into blood* by this means: *The rivers shall be full of thee.* The judgments executed upon Pharaoh of old are expressed by the *breaking* of *the heads of leviathan in the waters,* Ps. lxxiv. 13, 14. But now they go further; this old serpent not only has now his head bruised, but is all crushed to pieces.

(2.) It is set forth by a prophecy of the deep impression which the destruction of Egypt should make upon the neighbouring nations; it would put them all into a consternation, as the fall of the Assyrian monarchy did, *ch.* xxxi. 15, 16. When Pharaoh, who had been like a blazing burning torch, is *put out* and *extinguished* it shall make all about him look black, *v.* 7. The heavens shall be hung with black, the *stars darkened,* the sun eclipsed, and the moon be deprived of her borrowed light. It is from the upper world that this lower receives its light; and therefore *(v.* 8), when the *bright lights of heaven* are *made dark* above, darkness by consequence is *set upon the land,* upon the earth; so it shall be on the land of Egypt. Here the plague of darkness, which was upon Egypt of old for three days, seems to be alluded to, as, before, the turning of the waters into blood. For, when former judgments are forgotten, it is just that they should be repeated. When their privy-counsellors, and statesmen, and those that have the direction of the public affairs, are deprived of wisdom and made fools, and the things that belong to their peace are hidden from their eyes, then their lights are darkened and the land is in a mist. This is foretold, Isa. xix. 13. *The princes of Zoan have become fools.* Now upon the spreading of the report of the fall of Egypt, and the bringing of the news to remote countries, *countries which they had not known (v.* 9), people shall be much affected, and shall feel themselves sensibly touched by it. [1.] It shall fill them with vexation to see such an ancient, wealthy, potent kingdom thus humbled and brought down, and the pride of worldly glory, which they have such a value for, stained. The *hearts of many people* will be *vexed* to see the word of the God of Israel fulfilled in the destruction of Egypt, and that all the *gods of Egypt* were not able to relieve it. Note, The destruction of some wicked people is a vexation to others. [2.] It shall fill them with admiration (*v.* 10): They shall be *amazed at thee,* shall wonder to see such *great riches* and power *come to nothing,* Rev. xviii. 17. Note, Those that admire with complacency the pomp of this world will admire with consternation the ruin of that pomp, which to those that know the vanity of all things here below is no surprise at all. [3.] It shall fill them with fear: even *their kings* (that think it their prerogative to be secure) shall be *horribly afraid for thee,* concluding their own house to be in danger when their neighbour's is on fire. *When I shall brandish my sword before them they shall tremble every man for his own life.* Note, When the sword of God's justice is drawn against some, to cut them off, it is thereby brandished before others, to give them warning. And those that will not be admonished by it, and made to reform, shall yet be frightened by it and made to tremble. They shall *tremble at every moment, because of thy fall.* When others are ruined by sin we have reason to quake for fear, as knowing ourselves guilty and obnoxious. *Who is able to stand before this holy Lord God?*

(3.) It is set forth by a plain and express prediction of the desolation itself that should come upon Egypt. [1.] The instruments of the desolation appear here very formidable. It is the *sword of the king of Babylon,* that warlike, that victorious prince, that shall *come upon thee* (*v.* 11), the *swords of the mighty,* even the *terrible of the nations, all of them* (*v.* 12), an army that there is no standing before. Note, Those that delight in war, and are upon all occasions entering into contention, may expect, some time or other, to be engaged with those that will prove too hard for them. Pharaoh had been forward to quarrel with his neighbour and to come forth *with his rivers,* with his armies, *v.* 2. But God will now give him enough of it. [2.] The instances of the desolation appear here very frightful, much the same with what we had before, *ch.* xxix. 10—12; xxx. 7. *First,* The multitude of Egypt shall be destroyed, not decimated, some picked out to be made examples, but all cut off. Note, The numbers of sinners, though they be a multitude, will neither secure them against God's power nor entitle them to his pity. *Secondly,* The pomp of Egypt shall be spoiled, the pomp of their court, what they have been proud of. Note, In renouncing the pomps of this world we did ourselves a great kindness, for they are things that are soon spoiled and that cheat their admirers. *Thirdly,* The cattle of Egypt, that used to feed by the rivers, shall be destroyed (*v.* 13), either cut off by the sword or carried off for a prey. Egypt was famous for horses, which would be an acceptable booty to the Chaldeans. The rivers shall be no more frequented as they have been by man and beast,

that came thither to drink. *Fourthly,* The *waters of Egypt,* that used to flow briskly, shall now grow deep, and slow, and heavy, and shall *run like oil* (*v.* 14), a figurative expression signifying that there should be such universal sadness and heaviness upon the whole nation that even the rivers should go softly and silently like mourners, and quite forget their rapid motion. *Fifthly,* The whole country of Egypt shall be stripped of its wealth; it shall be *destitute of that whereof it was full* (*v.* 15), corn, and cattle, and all the pleasant fruits of the earth; when those are *smitten that dwell therein* the ground is untilled, and that which is gathered becomes an easy prey to the invader. Note, God can soon empty those of this world's goods that have the greatest fulness of those things and are full of them, that enjoy most and have their hearts set upon those enjoyments. The Egyptians were full of their pleasant and plentiful country, and its rich productions. Every one that talked with them might perceive how much it filled them. But God can soon make their *country destitute of that whereof it is full;* it is therefore our wisdom to be full of treasures in heaven. When the country is made destitute, 1. It shall be an instruction to them: *Then shall they know that I am the Lord.* A sensible conviction of the vanity of the world, and the fading perishing nature of all things in it, will contribute much to our right knowledge of God as our portion and happiness. 2. It shall be a lamentation to all about them: *The daughters of the nations shall lament her* (*v.* 16), either because, being in alliance with her, they share in her grievances and suffer with her, or, being admirers of her, they at least share in her grief and sympathize with her. They shall lament *for Egypt and all her multitude;* it shall excite their pity to see so great a devastation made. By enlarging the matters of our joy we increase the occasions of our sorrow.

17 It came to pass also in the twelfth year, in the fifteenth *day* of the month, *that* the word of the LORD came unto me, saying, 18 Son of man, wail for the multitude of Egypt, and cast them down, *even* her, and the daughters of the famous nations, unto the nether parts of the earth, with them that go down into the pit. 19 Whom dost thou pass in beauty? go down, and be thou laid with the uncircumcised. 20 They shall fall in the midst of *them that are* slain by the sword: she is delivered to the sword: draw her and all her multitudes. 21 The strong among the mighty shall speak to him out of the midst of hell with them that help him: they are

gone down, they lie uncircumcised, slain by the sword. 22 Asshur *is* there and all her company: his graves *are* about him: all of them slain, fallen by the sword: 23 Whose graves are set in the sides of the pit, and her company is round about her grave: all of them slain, fallen by the sword, which caused terror in the land of the living. 24 There *is* Elam and all her multitude round about her grave, all of them slain, fallen by the sword, which are gone down uncircumcised into the nether parts of the earth, which caused their terror in the land of the living; yet have they borne their shame with them that go down to the pit. 25 They have set her a bed in the midst of the slain with all her multitude: her graves *are* round about him: all of them uncircumcised, slain by the sword: though their terror was caused in the land of the living, yet have they borne their shame with them that go down to the pit: he is put in the midst of *them that be* slain. 26 There *is* Meshech, Tubal, and all her multitude: her graves *are* round about him: all of them uncircumcised, slain by the sword, though they caused their terror in the land of the living. 27 And they shall not lie with the mighty *that are* fallen of the uncircumcised, which are gone down to hell with their weapons of war: and they have laid their swords under their heads, but their iniquities shall be upon their bones, though *they were* the terror of the mighty in the land of the living. 28 Yea, thou shalt be broken in the midst of the uncircumcised, and shalt lie with *them that are* slain with the sword. 29 There *is* Edom, her kings, and all her princes, which with their might are laid by *them that were* slain by the sword: they shall lie with the uncircumcised, and with them that go down to the pit. 30 There *be* the princes of the north, all of them, and all the Zidonians, which are gone down with the slain; with their terror they are ashamed of their might; and they lie uncircumcised with *them that be* slain by the sword,

936

and bear their shame with them that go down to the pit. 31 Pharaoh shall see them, and shall be comforted over all his multitude, *even* Pharaoh and all his army slain by the sword, saith the Lord GOD. 32 For I have caused my terror in the land of the living: and he shall be laid in the midst of the uncircumcised with *them that are* slain with the sword, *even* Pharaoh and all his multitude, saith the Lord GOD.

This prophecy concludes and completes the burden of Egypt, and leaves it and all its multitude in the pit of destruction.

I. We are here invited to attend the funeral of that once flourishing kingdom, to lament its fall, and to take a view of those who attend it to the grave and accompany it in the grave.

1. This dead corpse of a kingdom is here brought to the grave. The prophet is ordered to *cast them down* to the pit (*v.* 18), to foretel their destruction as one that had authority, as Jeremiah was set over the kingdoms, Jer. i. 10. He must speak in God's name, and as from him who will cast them down. Yet he must foretel it as one that had an affectionate concern for them; he must *wail for the multitude of Egypt,* even when he *casts them down.* When Egypt is slain, let her have an honourable funeral, befitting her quality; let her be buried *with the daughters of the famous nations,* in their burying-places and with the same ceremony. It is but a poor allay to the reproach and terror of death to be buried with those that were famous; yet this is all that is allowed to Egypt. Shall Egypt think to exempt herself from the common fate of proud and imperious nations? No; she must take her lot with them (*v.* 19): "*Whom dost thou surpass in beauty?* Art thou so much fairer than any other nation that thou shouldst expect therefore to be excused? No; others as fair as thou have sunk into the pit; *go down* therefore, and *be thou laid with the uncircumcised.* Thou art like them and art likely to lie among them. The multitude of Egypt shall all *fall in the midst of those that are slain with the sword,* now that there is a general slaughter made among the nations." Egypt with the rest must drink of the bloody cup, and therefore she is *delivered to the sword,* to the sword of war (but, in God's hand, the sword of justice), is delivered to be publicly executed. *Draw her and all her multitude;* draw them either as the dead bodies of great men are drawn in honour to the grave, in a hearse, or as malefactors are drawn in disgrace to the place of execution, on a sledge; draw them to the pit, and let them be made a spectacle to the world.

2. This corpse of a kingdom is bid welcome to the grave, and Pharaoh is made free

of the congregation of the dead, and admitted into their regions, not without some pomp and ceremony. As the surprising fall of the king of Babylon is thus illustrated, *Hell from beneath is moved for thee to meet thee at thy coming,* and to introduce thee into those mansions of darkness (Isa. xiv. 9, &c.), so here (v. 21), *They shall speak to him out of the midst of hell,* as it were congratulating his arrival and calling him to join with them in acknowledging that which neither he nor they would be brought to own when they were in their pomp and pride, that it is in vain to think of contesting with God, and none ever hardened their hearts against him and prospered. They shall say to him, and to those that pretended to help him, Where are you now? What have you brought your attempts to at last? Divers nations are here mentioned as gone down to the grave before Egypt that are ready to give her a scornful reception and upbraid her with coming to them at last. These nations here spoken of were probably such as had been of late years ruined and wasted by the king of Babylon, and their princes cut off; let Egypt know that she has *neighbour's fare.* When she goes to the grave she does but *migrare ad plures—migrate to the majority;* there are *innumerable before her.* But it is observable that though Judah and Jerusalem were just about this time, or a little before, utterly ruined and laid waste, yet they are not mentioned here among the nations that welcome Egypt to the pit; for though they suffered the same things that these nations suffered, and by the same hand, yet the kind intentions of their affliction, and its happy issue at last, and the mercy God had yet in reserve for them, altered the property of it; it was not to them a *going down to the pit,* as it was to the heathen; they were not *smitten as others were,* nor *slain according to the slaughter of other nations,* Isa. xxvii. 7. But let us see who those are that have *gone to the grave* before Egypt, that *lie uncircumcised, slain by the sword,* with whom she must now take up her lodging. (1.) There lie the Assyrian empire, and all the princes and mighty men of that monarchy (v. 22): *Asshur is there and all her company,* all the countries that were tributaries to and had dependence upon that crown. That mighty potentate who used to lie in state, with his guards and grandees about him, now lies in obscurity, with his *graves about him* and his soldiers in them, unable any longer to do him service or honour; they are *all of them slain, fallen by the sword.* The number of their months was *cut off in the midst,* and, being *bloody* and *deceitful men,* they were not suffered to *live out half their days.* Their *graves were set in the sides of the pit,* all in a row, like beds in a common chamber, v. 23. All their company is such as were *slain, fallen by the sword;* a vast congregation there is of such, who had *caused terror in the land of the liv-*

ing. But as the death of those to whom they were a terror put an end to their fears (in the grave *the prisoners rest together* and *hear not the voice of the oppressor,* Job iii. 18), so the death of these mighty men puts an end to their terrors. Who is afraid of *a dead lion?* Note, Death will be a king of terrors to those who, instead of making themselves blessings, make themselves terrors, in their generation. (2.) There lies the kingdom of Persia, which perhaps within the memory of man at that time had been wasted and brought down: *There is Elam and all her multitude,* the king of Elam and his numerous armies, v. 24, 25. They also had *caused their terror in the land of the living,* had made a fearful noise and bluster among the nations in their day. But Elam has now a grave by herself, and the graves of the common people *round about her, fallen by the sword;* she has *her bed in the midst of the slain* that went down *uncircumcised, unsanctified,* unholy, and not in covenant with God. They have *borne their shame with those that go down to the pit;* they have fallen under the common disgrace and mortification of mankind, that they die and are buried; nay, they die under particular marks of ignominy, which God and man put upon them. Note, Those who cause their terror shall, sooner or later, bear their *shame,* and be made a terror to themselves. The king of Elam is *put in the midst of those that are slain.* All the honour he can now pretend to is to be buried in the chief sepulchre. (3.) There lies the Scythian power, which, about this time, was busy in the world. *Meshech* and *Tubal,* those barbarous northern nations, had lately made a descent upon the Medes, and *caused their terror* among them, lived among them upon free quarter for some years, making every thing their own that they could lay their hands on; but at length Cyaxares, king of the Medes, drew them by a wile into his power, cut off abundance of them, and obliged them to quit his country, v. 26. There lie Meshech and Tubal, and all their multitude; there is a burying place for them, with their chief commander in the midst of them, *all of them uncircumcised, slain by the sword.* These Scythians, dying ingloriously as they lived, are not laid, as the other nations spoken of before, in the bed of honour (v. 27): *They shall not lie with the mighty,* shall not be buried in state, as those are, even by consent of the enemy, that are slain in the field of battle, that *go down to their graves with their weapons of war* carried before the hearse, or trailed after it, that have particularly *their swords laid under their heads,* as if they could sleep the sweeter in the grave when they laid their heads on such a pillow. These Scythians are not buried with these marks of honour, but *their iniquities shall be upon their sons;* they shall, for their iniquity, be left unburied, though they were the *terror* even *of the mighty in the land of the living.*

(4.) There lies the kingdom of Edom, which had flourished long, but about this time, at least before the destruction of Egypt, was made quite desolate, as was foretold, *ch.* xxv. 13. Among the sepulchres of the nations *there is Edom, v.* 29. There lie, not dignified with monuments or inscriptions, but mingled with common dust, *her kings and all her princes,* her wise statesmen (which Edom was famous for), and her brave soldiers. These *with their might are laid by those that were slain by the sword;* their might could not prevent it, nay, their might helped to procure it, for that both encouraged them to engage in war and incensed their neighbours against them, who thought it necessary to curb their growing greatness. A great deal of pains they took to ruin themselves, as many do, who *with their might,* with all their might, are *laid by those that were slain with the sword.* The Edomites retained circumcision, being of the seed of Abraham. But that shall stand them in no stead; they shall *lie with the uncircumcised.* (5.) There lie the *princes of the north, and all the Zidonians.* These were as well acquainted with maritime affairs as the Egyptians were, who relied much upon that part of their strength, but they have *gone down with the slain* (*v.* 30), down to the pit. Now they are *ashamed of their might,* ashamed to think how much they boasted of it and trusted to it; and, as the *Edomites with their might,* so these *with their terror,* are laid with those that are *slain by the sword* and are forced to take their lot with them. They *bear their shame with those that go down to the pit,* die in as much disgrace as those that are cut off by the hand of public justice. (6.) All this is applied to Pharaoh and the Egyptians, who have no reason to flatter themselves with hopes of tranquillity when they see how the wisest, and wealthiest, and strongest, of their neighbours have been laid waste (*v.* 28): "Yea, thou shalt be broken in the midst of the uncircumcised; when God is pulling down the unhumbled and unreformed nations thou must expect to come down with them." [1.] It will be some extenuation of the miseries of Egypt to observe that it has been the case of so many great and mighty nations before (*v.* 31): *Pharaoh shall see them and be comforted;* it will be some ease to his mind that he is not the first king that has been slain in battle—his not the first army that has been routed, his not the first kingdom that has been made desolate. Mr. Greenhill observes here, "The comfort which wicked ones have after death is poor comfort, not real, but imaginary." They will find little satisfaction in having so many fellow-sufferers; the rich man in hell dreaded it. It is only in point of honour that Pharaoh can *see and be comforted.* [2.] But nothing will be an exemption from these miseries; for (*v.* 32) *I have caused my terror in the land of the living.* Great men have caused their terror, have

938

studied how to make every body *fear them. Oderint dum metuant—Let them hate, so that they do but fear.* But now the great God has *caused his terror in the land of the living;* and therefore he laughs at theirs, because he sees that *his day is coming,* Ps. xxxvii. 13. In this day of terror Pharaoh *and all his multitude* shall be *laid with those that are slain by the sword.*

II. The view which this prophecy gives us of ruined states may show us something, 1. Of this present world, and the empire of death in it. Come, and see the calamitous state of human life; see what a dying world this is. The strong die, the mighty die, Pharaoh and all his multitude. See what a killing world this is. They are all *slain with the sword.* As if men did not die fast enough of themselves, men are ingenious at finding out ways to destroy one another. It is not only a great pit, but a great cock-pit. 2. Of the other world. Though it is the destruction of nations as such that perhaps is principally intended here, yet here is a plain allusion to the final and everlasting ruin of impenitent sinners, of those that are uncircumcised in heart; they are *slain by the sword* of divine justice; their *iniquity is upon them,* and with it they *bear their shame.* Those, Christ's enemies, that would not have him to reign over them, *shall be brought forth* and *slain before him,* though they be as pompous, though they be as numerous, as Pharaoh and *all his multitude.*

CHAP. XXXIII.

The prophet has now come off his circuit, which he went as judge, in God's name, to try and pass sentence upon the neighbouring nations, and, having finished with them, and read them all their doom, in the eight chapters foregoing, he now returns to the children of his people, and receives further instructions what to say to them. I. He must let them know what office he was in among them as a prophet, that he was a watchman, and had received a charge concerning them, for which he was accountable, ver. 1—9. The substance of this we had before, ch. iii. 17, &c. II. He must let them know upon what terms they stand with God, that they are upon their trial, upon their good behaviour, that if a wicked man repent he shall not perish, but that if a righteous man apostatize he shall perish, ver. 10—20. III. Here is a particular message sent to those who yet remained in the land of Israel, and (which is very strange) grew secure there, and confident that they should take root there again, to tell them that their hopes would fail them because they persisted in their sins, ver. 21—29. IV. Here is a rebuke to those who personally attended Ezekiel's ministry, but were not sincere in their professions of devotion, ver. 30—33.

AGAIN the word of the LORD came unto me, saying, 2 Son of man, speak to the children of thy people, and say unto them, When I bring the sword upon a land, if the people of the land take a man of their coasts, and set him for their watchman: 3 If when he seeth the sword come upon the land, he blow the trumpet, and warn the people; 4 Then whosoever heareth the sound of the trumpet, and taketh not warning; if the sword come, and take him away, his blood shall be upon his own head. 5 He heard the sound of the trumpet, and took not warning; his blood shall be upon him. But he that taketh warning shall deliver his soul. 6 But if the watchman see the sword come, and blow not the trumpet, and the people be not warned; if the sword come, and take *any* person from among them, he is taken away in his iniquity; but his blood will I require at the watchman's hand. 7 So thou, O son of man, I have set thee a watchman unto the house of Israel; therefore thou shalt hear the word at my mouth, and warn them from me. 8 When I say unto the wicked, O wicked *man*, thou shalt surely die; if thou dost not speak to warn the wicked from his way, that wicked *man* shall die in his iniquity; but his blood will I require at thine hand. 9 Nevertheless, if thou warn the wicked of his way to turn from it; if he do not turn from his way, he shall die in his iniquity; but thou hast delivered thy soul.

The prophet had been, by express order from God, taken off from prophesying to the Jews, just then when the news came that Jerusalem was invested, and close siege laid to it, *ch.* xxiv. 27. But now that Jerusalem is taken, two years after, he is appointed again to direct his speech to them; and here his commission is renewed. If God had abandoned them quite, he would not have sent prophets to them; nor, if he had not had mercy in store for them, would he have *shown them such things as these.* In these verses we have,

I. The office of a watchman laid down, the trust reposed in him, the charge given him, and the conditions adjusted between him and those that employ him, *v.* 2, 6. 1. It is supposed to be a public danger that gives occasion for the appointing of a watchman—when *God brings the sword upon a land, v.* 2. The sword of war, whenever it comes upon a land, is of God's bringing; it is the *sword of the Lord*, of his justice, how unjustly soever men draw it. At such a time, when a country is in fear of a foreign invasion, that they may be informed of all the motions of the enemy, may not be surprised with an attack, but may have early notice of it, in order to their being at their arms and in readiness to give the invader a warm reception, they *set a man of their coast*, some likely person, that lives upon the borders of their country, where the threatened danger is expected, and is therefore well acquainted with all the avenues of it, and make him *their watchman.* Thus *wise* are the *children*

of this world in their generation. Note, One man may be of public service to a whole country. Princes and statesmen are the watchmen of a kingdom; they are continually to employ themselves, and, if occasion be, as watchmen, to expose themselves for the public safety. 2. It is supposed to be a public trust that is lodged in the watchman and that he is accountable to the public for the discharge of it. His business is, (1.) To discover the approaches and advances of the enemy; and therefore he must not be blind nor asleep, for then he cannot *see the sword coming.* (2.) To give notice of them immediately by sound of trumpet, or, as sentinels among us, by the discharge of a gun, as a signal of danger. A special trust and confidence is reposed in him by those that set him to be their watchman that he will faithfully do these two things; and they venture their lives upon his fidelity. Now, [1.] If he do his part, if he be betimes aware of all the dangers that fall within his cognizance, and give warning of them, he has discharged his trust, and has not only *delivered his soul*, but earned his wages. If the people do not take warning, if they either will not believe the notice he gives them, will not believe the danger to be so great or so near as really it is, or will not regard it, and so are surprised by the enemy in their security, it is their own fault; the blame is not to be laid upon the watchman, but their blood is upon their own head. If any person goes presumptuously into the mouth of danger, though he heard the sound of the trumpet, and was told by it where the danger was, and *so the sword comes* and *takes him away* in his folly, he is *felo de se—a suicide*: foolish man, he has *destroyed himself.* But, [2.] If the watchman do not do his duty, if he might have seen the danger, and did not, but was asleep, or heedless, or looking another way, or if he did *see the danger* (for so the case is put here) and shifted only for his own safety, and *blew not the trumpet* to *warn the people*, so that some are surprised and cut off *in their iniquity (v.* 6), cut off suddenly, without having time to cry, *Lord, have mercy upon me*, time to repent and make their peace with God (which makes the matter much the worse, that the poor creature is *taken away in his iniquity)*, his blood shall be required *at the watchman's hand*; he shall be found guilty of his death, because he did not *give him warning* of his danger. But if the watchman do his part, and the people do theirs, all is well; both he that gives warning and he that takes warning have delivered their souls.

II. The application of this to the prophet, *v.* 7, 9.

1. He is a *watchman to the house of Israel.* He had occasionally given warning to the nations about, but to the house of Israel he was a watchman by office, for they were the *children of the prophets and the covenant*

They did not *set him for a watchman,* as the people of the land, *v.* 2 (for they were not so wise for their souls as to secure the welfare of them, as they would have been for the protection of their temporal interests) ; but God did it for them ; he appointed them a watchman.

2. His business as a watchman is to give warning to sinners of their misery and danger by reason of sin. This is the word he must *hear from God's mouth* and *speak to them.* (1.) God has said, *The wicked man shall surely die ;* he shall be miserable. Unless he repent, he shall be cut off from God and all comfort and hope in him, shall be cut off from all good. He shall fall and lie for ever under the wrath of God, which is the death of the soul, as his favour is its life. The righteous God has said it, and will never unsay it, nor can all the world gainsay it, that the *wages of sin is death. Sin, when it is finished, brings forth death.* The wrath of God is revealed from heaven, not only against wicked nations, speaking ruin to them as nations, but against wicked persons, speaking ruin to them in their personal capacity, their personal interests, which pass into the other world and last to eternity, as national interests do not. (2.) It is the will of God that the wicked man should be warned of this : *Warn them from me.* This intimates that there is a possibility of preventing it, else it were a jest to give warning of it ; nay, and that God is desirous it should be prevented. Sinners are *therefore* warned of the wrath to come, that they may *flee from it,* Matt. iii. 7. (3.) It is the work of ministers to give him warning, to say to the wicked, *It shall be ill with thee,* Isa. iii. 11. God says in general, *The soul that sinneth it shall die.* The minister's business is to apply this to particular persons, and to say, " *O wicked man ! thou shalt surely die,* whoever thou art ; if thou go on still in thy trespasses, they will inevitably be thy ruin. O adulterer ! O robber ! O drunkard ! O swearer ! O sabbath-breaker ! *thou shalt surely die.*" And he must say this, not in passion, to provoke the sinner, but in compassion, to *warn the wicked from his way,* warn him to *turn from it,* that he may live. This is to be done by the faithful preaching of the word in public, and by personal application to those whose sins are open.

3. If souls perish through his neglect of his duty, he brings guilt upon himself. " If the prophet do not warn the wicked of the ruin that is at the end of his wicked way, that *wicked man shall die in his iniquity ;* for, though the watchman did not do his part, yet the sinner might have taken warning from the written word, from his own conscience, and from God's judgments upon others, by which his mouth shall be stopped, and God will be justified in his destruction." Note, It will not serve impenitent sinners to plead in the great day that their watchmen

did not give them warning, that they were careless and unfaithful ; for, though they were so, it will be made to appear that *God left not himself without witness.* " But he shall not perish alone in his iniquity ; the watchman also shall be called to an account : *His blood will I require at thy hand.* The blind leader shall fall with the blind follower into the ditch." See what a desire God has of the salvation of sinners, in that he resents it so ill if those concerned do not what they can to prevent their destruction. And see what a great deal those ministers have to answer for another day who palliate sin, and flatter sinners in their evil way, and by their wicked lives countenance and harden them in their wickedness, and encourage them to believe that they shall have peace though they go on.

4. If he do his duty, he may take the comfort of it, though he do not see the success of it (*v.* 9) : " *If thou warn the wicked of his way,* if thou tell him faithfully what will be the end thereof, and call him earnestly to turn from it, and he do not turn, but persist in it, *he shall die in his iniquity,* and the fair warning given him will be an aggravation of his sin and ruin ; but *thou hast delivered thy soul.*" Note, It is a comfort to ministers that they may through grace save themselves, though they cannot be instrumental to save so many as they wish of those that hear them.

10 Therefore, O thou son of man, speak unto the house of Israel ; Thus ye speak, saying, If our transgressions and our sins *be* upon us, and we pine away in them, how should we then live? 11 Say unto them, *As* I live, saith the Lord God, I have no pleasure in the death of the wicked ; but that the wicked turn from his way and live : turn ye, turn ye from your evil ways ; for why will ye die, O house of Israel ? 12 Therefore, thou son of man, say unto the children of thy people, The righteousness of the righteous shall not deliver him in the day of his transgression : as for the wickedness of the wicked, he shall not fall thereby in the day that he turneth from his wickedness ; neither shall the righteous be able to live for his *righteousness* in the day that he sinneth. 13 When I shall say to the righteous, *that* he shall surely live ; if he trust to his own righteousness, and commit iniquity, all his righteousnesses shall not be remembered ; but for his iniquity that he hath committed, he shall die for it. 14 Again, when I say

unto the wicked, Thou shalt surely die; if he turn from his sin, and do that which is lawful and right; 15 *If* the wicked restore the pledge, give again that he had robbed, walk in the statutes of life, without committing iniquity; he shall surely live, he shall not die. 16 None of his sins that he hath committed shall be mentioned unto him: he hath done that which is lawful and right; he shall surely live. 17 Yet the children of thy people say, The way of the Lord is not equal: but as for them, their way is not equal. 18 When the righteous turneth from his righteousness, and committeth iniquity, he shall even die thereby. 19 But if the wicked turn from his wickedness, and do that which is lawful and right, he shall live thereby. 20 Yet ye say, The way of the Lord is not equal. O ye house of Israel, I will judge you every one after his ways.

These verses are the substance of what we had before (*ch.* xviii. 20, &c.) and they are so full and express a declaration of the terms on which people stand with God (as the former were of the terms on which ministers stand) that it is no wonder that they are here repeated, as those were, though we had the substance of them before. Observe here,

I. The cavils of the people against God's proceedings with them. God was now in his providence contending with them, but their uncircumcised hearts were not as yet humbled, for they were industrious to justify themselves, though thereby they reflected on God. Two things they insisted upon, in their reproaches of God, and in both they added iniquity to their sin and misery to their punishment:—1. They quarrelled with his promises and favours, as having no kindness nor sincerity in them, *v.* 10. God had *set life before them,* but they plead that he had set it out of their reach, and therefore did but mock them with the mention of it. The prophet had said, some time ago (*ch.* xxiv. 23), *You shall pine away for your iniquities;* with that word he had concluded his threatenings against Judah and Jerusalem; and this they now upbraided him with, as if it had been spoken absolutely, to drive them to despair; whereas it was spoken conditionally, to bring them to repentance. Thus are the sayings of God's ministers perverted by men of corrupt minds, who are inclined to pick quarrels. He puts them in hopes of life and happiness; and herein they would make him contradict himself;

"for" (say they) "*if our transgressions and our sins be upon us,* as thou hast often told us they are, and if we must, as thou sayest, *pine away in them,* and wear out a miserable captivity in a fruitless repentance, *how shall we then live?* If this be our doom, there is no remedy. *We die, we perish, we all perish.*" Note, It is very common for those that have been hardened with presumption when they were warned against sin to sink into despair when they are called to repent, and to conclude there is no hope of life for them. 2. They quarrelled with his threatenings and judgments, as having no justice or equity in them. They said, *The way of the Lord is not equal* (*v.* xvii. 20), suggesting that God was partial in his proceedings, that with him there was respect of persons and that he was more severe against sin and sinners than there was cause.

II. Here is a satisfactory answer given to both these cavils.

1. Those that despaired of finding mercy with God are here answered with a solemn declaration of God's readiness to show mercy, *v.* 11. When they spoke of *pining away in their iniquity* God sent the prophet to them, with all speed, to tell them that though their case was sad it was not desperate, but there was yet *hope in Israel.* (1.) It is certain that God has no delight in the ruin of sinners, nor does he desire it. If they will destroy themselves, he will glorify himself in it, but he has no pleasure in it, but would rather they should *turn and live,* for his goodness is that attribute of his which is most his glory, which is most his delight. He would rather sinners should turn and live than go on and die. He has said it, he has sworn it, that by these two immutable things, in both which it is impossible for God to lie, we might have strong consolation. We have his word and his oath ; and, since he could *swear by no greater, he swears by himself: As I live.* They questioned whether they should *live,* though they did repent and reform; yea, says God, as sure *as I live,* true penitents shall live also; for *their life is hid with Christ in God.* (2.) It is certain that God is sincere and in earnest in the calls he gives sinners to repent: *Turn you, turn you, from your evil way.* To repent is to turn from our evil way; this God requires sinners to do; this he urges them to do by repeated pressing instances: *Turn you, turn you.* O that they would be prevailed with to turn, to turn quickly, without delay! This he will enable them to do if they will but *frame their doings to turn to the Lord,* Hos. v. 4. For he has said, *I will pour out my Spirit unto you,* Prov. i. 23. And in this he will accept of them; for it is not only what he commands, but what he counts them to. (3.) It is certain that, if sinners perish in their impenitency, it is owing to themselves; they die because they will die; and herein they act most absurdly and unreasonably: *Why*

will you die, O house of Israel ?   God would have heard them, and they would not be heard.

2. Those that despaired of finding justice with God are here answered with a solemn declaration of the rule of judgment which God would go by in dealing with the children of men, which carries along with it the evidence of its own equity ; he that runs may read the justice of it. The Jewish nation, as a nation, was now *dead ;* it was ruined to all intents and purposes. The prophet must therefore deal with particular persons, and the rule of judgment concerning them is much like that concerning a nation, Jer. xviii. 7—10. If God speak concerning it to build and to plant, and it do wickedly, he will recal his favours and leave it to ruin. But if he speak concerning it to pluck up and destroy, and it repent, he will revoke the sentence and deliver it. So it is here. In short, The most plausible professors, if they apostatize, shall certainly perish for ever in their apostasy from God ; and the most notorious sinners, if they repent, shall certainly be happy for ever in their return to God. This is here repeated again and again, because it ought to be again and again considered, and preached over to our own hearts. This was necessary to be inculcated upon this stupid senseless people, that said, *The way of the Lord is not equal ;* for these rules of judgment are so plainly just that they need no other confirmation of them than the repetition of them

(1.) If those that have made a great profession of religion throw off their profession, quit the good ways of God and grow loose and carnal, sensual and worldly, the profession they made and all the religious performances with which they had for a great while kept up the credit of their profession shall stand them in no stead, but they shall certainly perish in their iniquity, *v.* 12, 13, 18. [1.] God says to the *righteous man* that *he shall surely live, v.* 13. He says it by his word, by his ministers. He that lives regularly, his own heart tells him, his neighbours tell him, He shall live. Surely such a man as this cannot but be happy. And it is certain, if he proceed and persevere in his righteousness, and if, in order to that, he be upright and sincere in it, if he be really as good as he seems to be, he shall live ; he shall continue in the love of God and be for ever happy in that love. [2.] Righteous men, who have very good hopes of themselves and whom others have a very good opinion of, are yet in danger of turning to iniquity by trusting to their righteousness. So the case is put here : *If he trust to his own righteousness, and commit iniquity,* and come to make a trade of sin—if he not only take a false step, but turn aside into a false way and persist in it. This may possibly be the case of a righteous man, and it is the effect of his trusting to his own righteousness. Note, Many eminent professors have been ruined

by a proud conceitedness of themselves and confidence in themselves. He trusts to the merit of his own righteousness, and thinks he has already made God so much his debtor that now he may venture to commit iniquity, for he has righteousness enough in stock to make amends for it ; he fancies that whatever evil deeds he may do hereafter he can be in no danger from them, having so many good deeds beforehand to counterbalance them. Or, He trusts to the strength of his own righteousness, thinks himself now so well established in a course of virtue that he may thrust himself into any temptation and it cannot overcome him, and so by presuming on his own sufficiency he is brought to commit iniquity. By making bold on the confines of sin he is drawn at length into the depths of hell. This ruined the Pharisees ; they *trusted to themselves that they were righteous,* and that their long prayers, and fasting twice in the week, would atone for their devouring widows' houses. [3.] If righteous men *turn to iniquity,* and return not to their righteousness, they shall certainly perish in their iniquity, and all the righteousness they have formerly done, all their prayers, and all their alms, shall be forgotten. No mention shall be made, no remembrance had, of their good deeds ; they shall be overlooked, as if they had never been. The *righteousness of the righteous shall not deliver him* from the wrath of God, and the curse of the law, *in the day of his transgression.* When he becomes a traitor and a rebel, and takes up arms against his rightful Sovereign, it will not serve for him to plead in his own defence that formerly he was a loyal subject, and did many good services to the government. No ; *he shall not be able to live.* The remembrance of his former righteousness shall be no satisfaction either to God's justice or his own conscience *in the day that he sins,* but rather shall, in the estimate of both, highly aggravate the sin and folly of his apostasy. And therefore *for his iniquity that he committed he shall die, v.* 13. And again (*v.* 18), *He shall even die thereby ;* and it is owing to himself.

(2.) If those that have lived a wicked life repent and reform, forsake their wicked ways and become religious, their sins shall be pardoned, and they shall be justified and saved, if they persevere in their reformation. [1.] God says *to the wicked, " Thou shalt surely die.* The way that thou art in leads to destruction. The wages of thy sin is death, and thy iniquity will shortly be thy ruin." It was said to the righteous man, *Thou shalt surely live,* for his encouragement to proceed and persevere in the way of righteousness ; but he made an ill use of it, and was emboldened by it to commit iniquity. It was said to the wicked man, *Thou shalt surely die,* for warning to him not to persist in his wicked ways ; and he makes a good use of it, and is quickened thereby to return to God and duty. Thus even the threatenings of the word are to some, by the grace of God, a savour of life unto life, while even the promises of the word become to others, by their own corruption, a savour of death unto death. When God says to the wicked man, *Thou shalt surely die,* die eternally, it is to frighten him, not out of his wits, but out of his sins. [2.] There is many a wicked man who was hastening apace to his own destruction who yet is wrought upon by the grace of God to return and repent, and live a holy life. He *turns from his sin* (v. 14), and is resolved that he will have no more to do with it; and, as an evidence of his repentance for wrong done, he *restores the pledge* (v. 15) which he had taken uncharitably from the poor, *he gives again that which he had robbed* and taken unjustly from the rich. Nor does he only *cease to do evil,* but he *learns to do well ;* he *does that which is lawful and right,* and makes conscience of his duty both to God and man—a great change, since, awhile ago, he neither feared God nor regarded man. But many such amazing changes, and blessed ones, have been wrought by the power of divine grace. He that was going on in the paths of death and the destroyer now walks in *the statutes of life,* in the way of God's commandments, which has both life in it (Prov. xii. 28) and life at the end of it, Matt. xix. 17. And in this good way he perseveres *without committing iniquity,* though not free from remaining infirmity, yet under the dominion of no iniquity. He repents not of his repentance, nor returns to the commission of those gross sins which he before allowed himself in. [3.] He that does thus repent and return shall escape the ruin he was running into, and his former sins shall be no prejudice to his acceptance with God. Let him not pine away in his iniquity, for, if he confess and forsake it, he shall find mercy. He *shall surely live ; he shall not die,* v. 15. Again (v. 16), *He shall surely live.* Again (v. 19), *He has done that which is lawful and right,* and *he shall live thereby.* But will not his wickednesses be remembered against him? No; he shall not be punished for them (v. 12): *As for the wickedness of the wicked,* though it was very heinous, *yet he shall not fall thereby in the day that he turns from his wickedness.* Now that it has become his grief it shall not be his ruin. Now that there is a settled separation between him and sin there shall be no longer a separation between him and God. Nay, he shall not be so much as upbraided with them (v. 16): *None of his sins that he has committed shall be mentioned unto him,* either as a clog to his pardon or an allay to the comfort of it, or as any blemish and diminution to the glory that is prepared for him.

Now lay all this together, and then judge whether the *way of the Lord be not equal,* whether this will not justify God in the destruction of sinners and glorify him in the

salvation of penitents. The conclusion of the whole matter is (v. 20): " *O you house of Israel,* though you are all involved now in the common calamity, yet there shall be a distinction of persons made in the spiritual and eternal state, and *I will judge you every one after his ways.*" Though they were sent into captivity by the lump, good fish and bad enclosed in the same net, yet there he will separate between the precious and the vile and will *render to every man according to his works.* Therefore God's way is equal and unexceptionable ; but, as for the *children of thy people,* God turns them over to the prophet, as he did to Moses (Exod. xxxii. 7): " They are thy people ; I can scarcely own them for mine." As for them, *their way is unequal ;* this way which they have got of quarrelling with God and his prophets is absurd and unreasonable. In all disputes between God and his creatures it will certainly be found that he is in the right and they are in the wrong.

21 And it came to pass in the twelfth year of our captivity, in the tenth *month,* in the fifth *day* of the month, *that* one that had escaped out of Jerusalem came unto me, saying, The city is smitten. 22 Now the hand of the LORD was upon me in the evening, afore he that was escaped came ; and had opened my mouth, until he came to me in the morning ; and my mouth was opened, and I was no more dumb. 23 Then the word of the LORD came unto me, saying, 24 Son of man, they that inhabit those wastes of the land of Israel speak, saying, Abraham was one, and he inherited the land : but we *are* many ; the land is given us for inheritance. 25 Wherefore say unto them, Thus saith the Lord GOD ; Ye eat with the blood, and lift up your eyes toward your idols, and shed blood : and shall ye possess the land ? 26 Ye stand upon your sword, ye work abomination, and ye defile every one his neighbour's wife : and shall ye possess the land? 27 Say thou thus unto them, Thus saith the Lord GOD ; *As* I live, surely they that *are* in the wastes shall fall by the sword, and him that *is* in the open field will I give to the beasts to be devoured, and they that *be* in the forts and in the caves shall die of the pestilence. 28 For I will lay the land most desolate, and the pomp of her strength shall cease ; and the moun-

tains of Israel shall be desolate, that none shall pass through. 29 Then shall they know that I *am* the LORD, when I have laid the land most desolate because of all their abominations which they have committed.

Here we have,

I. The tidings brought to Ezekiel of the burning of Jerusalem by the Chaldeans. The city was burnt in the eleventh year of the captivity and the fifth month, Jer. lii. 12, 13. Tidings hereof were brought to the prophet by one that was an eye-witness of the destruction, in the twelfth year, and the tenth month (*v.* 21), which was a year and almost five months after the thing was done; we may well suppose that, there being a constant correspondence at this time more than ever kept up between Jerusalem and Babylon, he had heard the news long before. But this was the first time he had an account of it from a refugee, from one who escaped, who could be particular, and would be pathetic, in the narrative of it. And the sign given him was the coming of such a one to him as had himself narrowly escaped the flames (*ch.* xxiv. 26): *He that escapes in that day shall come unto thee,* to *cause thee to hear it with thy ears,* to hear it more distinctly than ever, from one that could say, *Quæque ipse miserrima vidi—These miserable scenes I saw.*

II. The divine impressions and influences he was under, to prepare him for those heavy tidings (*v.* 22): *The hand of the Lord was upon me before he came, and had opened my mouth* to speak to the house of Israel what we had in the former part of this chapter. And now *he was no more dumb;* he prophesied now with more freedom and boldness, being by the event proved a true prophet, to the confusion of those that contradicted him. All the prophecies from *ch.* xxiv. to this chapter having relation purely to the nations about, it is probable that the prophet, when he received them from the Lord, did not deliver them by word of mouth, but in writing; for he could not *Say to the Ammonites, Say unto Tyrus, Say unto Pharaoh,* &c., so and so, but by letters directed to the persons concerned, as Zacharias, when he could not speak, wrote; and herein he was as truly executing his prophetic office as ever. Note, Even silenced ministers may be doing a great deal of good by writing letters and making visits. But now the prophet's *mouth is opened,* that he may *speak to the children of his people.* It is probable that he had, during these three years, been continually speaking to them as a friend, putting them in mind of what he had formerly delivered to them, but that he never spoke to them as a prophet, by inspiration, till now, when *the hand of the Lord came upon him,* renewed his commission, gave him

944

fresh instructions, and *opened his mouth,* furnished him with power to speak to the people *as he ought to speak.*

III. The particular message he was entrusted with, relating to these Jews that yet remained in the *land of Israel,* and *inhabited the wastes* of that land, *v.* 24. See what work sin had made. *The cities of* Israel had now become the wastes of Israel, for they lay all in ruins; some few that had escaped the sword and captivity still continued there and began to think of re-settling. This was so long after the destruction of Jerusalem that it was some time before this that Gedaliah (a modest humble man) and his friends were slain; but probably at this time Johanan, and the *proud men* that joined with him, were at the height (Jer. xliii. 2); and before they came to a resolution to go into Egypt, wherein Jeremiah opposed them, it is probable that the project was to establish themselves in the wastes of the land of Israel, in which Ezekiel here opposed them, and probably despatched the message away by the person that brought him the news of Jerusalem's destruction. Or, perhaps, those here prophesied against might be some other party of Jews, that remained in the ₁land, hoping to take root there and to be sole masters of it, after Johanan and his forces had gone into Egypt. Now here we have,

1. An account of the pride of these remaining Jews, who dwelt in the *wastes of the land of* Israel. Though the providence of God concerning them had been very humbling, and still was very threatening, yet they were intolerably haughty and secure, and promised themselves peace. He that brought the news to the prophet that Jerusalem was smitten could not tell him (it is likely) what these people said, but God tells him, *They say,* " *The land is given us for inheritance,* *v.* 24. Our partners being gone, it is now all our own by survivorship, or, for want of heirs, it comes to us as occupants; we shall now be placed alone in the midst of the earth and have it all to ourselves." This argues great stupidity under the weighty hand of God, and a reigning selfishness and narrow-spiritedness; they pleased themselves in the ruin of their country as long as they hoped to find their own account in it, cared not though it were *all waste,* so that they might have the sole property—a poor inheritance to be proud of! They have the impudence to compare their case with Abraham's, glorying in this, *We have Abraham to our father.* " Abraham," say they, " *was one,* one family, and *he inherited the land,* and lived many years in the peaceable enjoyment of it; *but we are many,* many families, more numerous than he; *the land is given us for inheritance.*" (1.) They think they can make out as good a title from God to this land as Abraham could: " If God *gave this land* to him, who was but one worshipper of him, as a reward of his service,

much more will he give it to us, who are many worshippers of him, as the reward of our service." This shows the great conceit they had of their own merits, as if they were greater than those of Abraham their father, who yet was not justified by works. (2.) They think they can make good the possession of this land against the Chaldeans and all other invaders, as well as Abraham could against those that were competitors with him for it : " If he, who was but one, could hold it, much more shall we, who are many, and have many more at command than his 300 *trained servants.*" This shows the confidence they had in their own might; they had got possession, and were resolved to keep it.

2 A check to this pride. Since God's providences did neither humble them nor terrify them, he sends them a message sufficient to do both.

(1.) To humble them, he tells them of the wickedness they still persisted in, which rendered them utterly unworthy to possess this land, so that they could not expect God should give it to them. They had been followed with one judgment after another, but they had not profited by those means of grace as might be expected; they were still unreformed, and how could they expect *that they should possess the land ? " Shall you possess the land ?* What! such wicked people as you are ? *How shall I put thee among the children, and give thee a pleasant land ?* Jer. iii. 19. Surely you never reflect upon yourselves, else you would rather wonder that you are in the land of the living than expect to possess this land. For do you not know how bad you are ?" [1.] " You make no conscience of forbidden fruit, forbidden food: *You eat with the blood,*" directly contrary to one of the precepts given to Noah and his sons when God gave them possession of the earth, Gen. ix. 4. [2.] " Idolatry, that covenant-breaking sin, that sin which the jealous God has been in a particular manner provoked by to lay your country waste, is still the sin that most easily besets you and which you have a strong inclination to : *You lift up your eyes towards your idols,* which is a sign that though perhaps you do not bow your knee to them so much as you have done, yet you set your hearts upon them and hanker after them " [3] " You are as fierce, and cruel, and barbarous as ever: *You shed blood,* innocent blood." [4.] " You confide in your own strength, your own arm, your own bow, and have no dependence on, or regard to, God and his providence : *You stand upon your sword* (*v.* 26); you think to carry all before you, and make all your own, by force of arms." How can those expect the inheritance of Isaac (as these did) who are of Ishmael's disposition, that had *his* hand *against every man* (Gen. xvi. 12), and Esau's resolution to *live by his sword ?* Gen xxvii. 40. We met with those (*ch* xxxii. 27) who,

when they died, thought they could not lie easy underground unless they had their swords under their heads. Here we meet with those who, while they live, think they cannot stand firmly above ground unless they have their swords under their feet, as if swords were both the softest pillows and the strongest pillars; though it was sin, it was sin, that first drew the sword. But, blessed be God, there are those who know better, who stand upon the support of the divine power and promise and lay their heads in the bosom of divine love, *not trusting in their own sword,* Ps. xliv. 3. [5.] "You are guilty of all manner of abominations, and, particularly, *you defile every one his neighbour's wife,* which is an abomination of the first magnitude, *and shall you possess the land ?* What! such vile miscreants as you ?" Note, Those cannot expect to *possess the land,* nor to enjoy any true comfort or happiness here or hereafter, who live in rebellion against the Lord.

(2) To terrify them, he tells them of the further judgments God had in store for them, which should make them utterly unable to possess this land, so that they could not stand it out against the enemy. Do they say that they shall possess the land ? God has said they shall not, he has sworn it, *As I live, saith the Lord.* Though he has sworn that he delights not *in the death of sinners,* yet he has sworn also that those who persist in impenitency and unbelief *shall not enter into his rest.* [1.] Those that are in the cities, here called the *wastes,* shall *fall by the sword,* either by the sword of the Chaldeans, who come to avenge the murder of Gedaliah, or by one another's swords, in their intestine broils. [2.] Those that are in the open field shall be *devoured by* wild *beasts,* which swarmed, of course, in the country when it was dispeopled, and there were none to master them and keep them under, Exod. xxiii. 29. When the army of the enemy had quitted the country still there was no safety in it. *Noisome beasts* constituted one of the four *sore judgments, ch.* xiv. 15. [3.] Those that are *in the forts and in the caves,* that think themselves safe in artificial or natural fastnesses, because men's eyes cannot discover them nor men's darts reach them, there the arrows of the Almighty shall find them out; they shall *die of the pestilence.* [4.] The whole land, even the land of Israel, that had been the glory of all lands, shall be *most desolate, v.* 28. *It shall be desolation, desolation,* all over as desolate as desolation itself can make it. The *mountain of Israel,* the fruitful mountains, Zion itself the holy mountain not excepted, *shall be desolate,* the roads unfrequented, the houses uninhabited, that *none shall pass through ;* as it was threatened (Deut. xxviii. 62), *You shall be left few in number.* [5.] The *pomp of her strength,* whatever she glories in as her pomp and trusts to as her strength, shall be made to cease. [6.] The

cause of all this was very bad; it is for *all their abominations which they have committed.* It is sin that does all this mischief, that makes nations desolate; and therefore we ought to call it an abomination. [7.] Yet the effect of all this will be very good: *Then shall they know that I am the Lord,* am their Lord, and shall return to their allegiance, *when I have made the land most desolate.* Those are untractable unteachable indeed that are not made to know their dependence upon God when all their creature-comforts fail them and are made desolate.

30 Also, thou son of man, the children of thy people still are talking against thee by the walls and in the doors of the houses, and speak one to another, every one to his brother, saying, Come, I pray you, and hear what is the word that cometh forth from the LORD. 31 And they come unto thee as the people cometh, and they sit before thee *as* my people, and they hear thy words, but they will not do them: for with their mouth they show much love, *but* their heart goeth after their covetousness. 32 And, lo, thou *art* unto them as a very lovely song of one that hath a pleasant voice, and can play well on an instrument: for they hear thy words, but they do them not. 33 And when this cometh to pass, (lo, it will come,) then shall they know that a prophet hath been among them.

The foregoing verses spoke conviction to the Jews who remained in the land of Israel, who were monuments of sparing mercy and yet returned not to the Lord; in these verses those are reproved who were now in captivity in Babylon, under divine rebukes, and yet were not reformed by them. They are not indeed charged with the same gross enormities that the others are charged with. They made some show of religion and devotion; but their hearts were not right with God. The thing they are here accused of is *mocking the messengers of the Lord,* one of their measure-filling sins, which brought this ruin upon them, and yet they were not cured of it. Two ways they mocked the prophet Ezekiel:—

I. By invidious ill natured reflections upon him, privately among themselves, endeavouring by all means possible to render him despicable. The prophet did not know it, but charitably thought that those who spoke so well to him to his face, with so much seeming respect and deference, would surely not speak ill of him behind his back. But God comes and tells him, *The children of thy people are still talking against thee* (v.

30), or *talking of thee,* no good, I doubt. Note, Public persons are a common theme or subject of discourse; every one takes a liberty to censure them at pleasure. Faithful ministers know not how much ill is said of them every day; it is well that they do not; for, if they did, it might prove a discouragement to them in their work not to be easily got over. But God takes notice of all that is said against his ministers, not only what is decreed against them, or sworn against them, not only what is written against them, or spoken with solemnity and deliberation, but of what is said against them in common talk, among neighbours when they meet in an evening, *by the walls and in the doors of their houses,* where whatever freedom of speech they use, if they reproach and slander any of God's ministers, God will reckon with them for it; his prophets shall not be made the song of the drunkards always. They had no crime to lay to the prophet's charge, but they loved to talk of him in a careless, scornful, bantering way; they said, jokingly, " *Come, and let us hear what is the word that comes forth from the Lord;* perhaps it will be something new, and will entertain us, and furnish us with matter for discourse." Note, Those have arrived at a great pitch of profaneness who can make so great a privilege, and so great a duty, as the preaching and hearing of the word of God, a matter of sport and ridicule, yea though it be not done publicly, but in private conversation among themselves. Serious things should be spoken of seriously.

II. By dissembling with him in their attendance upon his ministry. Hypocrites mock God and mock his prophets. But their hypocrisy is open before God, and the day is coming when, as here, it will be laid open. Observe here,

1. The plausible profession which these people made and the speciousness of their pretensions. They are like those (Matt. xv. 8) who *draw nigh to God with their mouths and honour him with their lips, but their hearts are far from him.* (1.) They were diligent and constant in their attendance upon the means of grace: *They come unto thee as the people come.* In Babylon they had no temple or synagogue, but they went to the prophet's house (*ch.* viii. 1), and there, it is probable, they spent their *new moons and their sabbaths* in religious exercises, 2 Kings iv. 23. When the prophet was bound the word of the Lord was not bound; and the people, when they had not the help for their souls that they wished for, were thankful for what they had; it was a reviving in their bondage. Now these hypocrites came, *according to the coming of the people,* as duly and as early as any of the prophet's hearers. Their being said to come *as the people came* seems to intimate that the reason why they came was because other people came; they did not come out of conscience towards God,

but only for company, for fashion-sake, and because it was now the custom of their countrymen. Note, Those that have no inward principle of love to God's ordinances may yet be found much in the external observance of them. Cain brought his sacrifice as well as Abel; and the Pharisee went up to the temple to pray as well as the publican. (2.) They behaved themselves very decently and reverently in the public assembly; there were none of them whispering, or laughing, or gazing about them, or sleeping. But *they sit before thee as my people,* with all the shows of gravity, and sereneness, and composure of mind. They sit out the time, without weariness, or wishing the sermon done. (3.) They were very attentive to the word preached : " They are not thinking of something else, but they *hear thy words,* and take notice of what thou sayest." (4.) They pretended to have a great kindness and respect for the prophet. Though, behind his back, they could not give him a good word, yet, to his face, *they showed much love* to him and his doctrine; they pretended to have a great concern lest he should spend himself too much in preaching or expose himself to the Chaldeans, for they would be thought to be some of his best friends and well-wishers. (5.) They took a great deal of pleasure in the word; they *delighted to know God's word,* Isa. lviii. 2. *Herod heard John Baptist gladly,* Mark vi. 20. *Thou art unto them as a very lovely song.* Ezekiel's matter was surprising, his language fine, his expressions elegant, his similitudes apt, his voice melodious, and his delivery graceful; so that they could sit with as much pleasure to hear him preach as (if I may speak in the language of our times) to see a play or an opera, or to hear a concert of music. Ezekiel was to them as one *that had a pleasant voice* and could sing well, *or play well on an instrument.* Note, Men may have their fancies pleased by the word, and yet not have their consciences touched nor their hearts changed, the itching ear gratified and yet not the corrupt nature sanctified.

2. The hypocrisy of these professions and pretensions; it is all a sham, it is all a jest. (1.) They have no cordial affection for the word of God. While they *show much love* it is only *with the mouth,* from the teeth outward, but *their heart goes after their covetousness;* they are as much set upon the world as ever, as much in love and league with it as ever. Hearing the word is only their diversion and recreation, a pretty amusement now and then for an hour or two. But still their main business is with their farm and merchandise; the bent and bias of their souls are towards them, and their *inward thoughts* are employed in projects about them. Note, Covetousness is the ruining sin of multitudes that make a great profession of religion; it is the love of

the world that secretly eats the love of God out of their hearts. *The cares of* this world and the deceitfulness of riches are the *thorns* that *choke the seed,* and choke the soul too. And those neither please God nor profit themselves who, when they are hearing the word of God, are musing upon their worldly affairs. God has his eye on the hearts that do so. (2.) They yield no subjection to it. They *hear thy words,* but it is only a hearing that they *give thee,* for they *will not do them, v.* 31. And again (*v.* 32), they *do them not.* They will not be persuaded by all the prophet can say, either by authority or argument, to cross themselves in any instance, to part with any one beloved sin, or apply themselves to any one duty that is against the grain to flesh and blood. Note, There are many who take pleasure in hearing the word, but make no conscience of doing it; and so they build upon the sand, and deceive themselves.

3. Let us see what will be in the end hereof : *Shall their unbelief* and carelessness *make the word of God of no effect?* By no means. (1.) God will confirm the prophet's word, though they contemn it, and make light of it, *v.* 33. What he says will come to pass, and not one jot or one tittle shall fall to the ground. Note, The curses of the law, though they may be bantered by profane wits, cannot be baffled. (2.) They themselves shall rue their folly when it is too late. When it comes to pass *they shall know,* shall know to their cost, know to their confusion, that *a prophet has been among them,* though they made no more of him than as one that *had a pleasant voice.* Note, Those who will not consider that a prophet is among them, and who improve not the day of their visitation while it is continued, will be made to remember that a prophet has been among them when the things that belong to their peace are *hidden from their eyes.* The day is coming when vain and worldly men will have other thoughts of things than now they have, and will feel a weight in that which they made light of. They shall know that *a prophet has been among them* when they see the event exactly answer the prediction, and the prophet himself shall be a witness against them that they had fair warning given them, but would not take it. When Ezekiel is gone, whom now they speak against, and *there is no more any prophet,* nor any *to show them how long,* then they will remember that once they had a prophet, but knew not how to use him well. Note, Those who will not know the worth of mercies by the improvement of them will justly be made to know the worth of them by the want of them, as those who should desire to see one of the days of the Son of man, which now they slighted, and might not see it.

CHAP. XXXIV.

The iniquities and calamities of God's Israel had been largely and pathetically lamented before, in this book. Now in this chapter the shepherds of Israel, their rulers both in church and state, are called to an account, as having been very much accessory to the sin and ruin of Israel, by their neglecting to do the duty of their place. Here is, I. A high charge exhibited against them for their negligence, their unskilfulness, and unfaithfulness in the management of public affairs, ver. 1—6 and again ver. 8. II. Their discharge from their trust, for their insufficiency and treachery, ver. 7—10. III. A gracious promise that God would take care of his flock, though they did not, and that it should not always suffer as it had done by their mal-administrations, ver. 11—16. IV. Another charge exhibited against those of the flock that were fat and strong, for the injuries they did to those that were weak and feeble, ver. 17—22. V. Another promise that God would in the fulness of time send the Messiah, to be the great and good Shepherd of the sheep, who should redress all grievances and set every thing to rights with the flock, ver. 23—31.

AND the word of the LORD came unto me, saying, 2 Son of man, prophesy against the shepherds of Israel, prophesy, and say unto them, Thus saith the Lord GOD unto the shepherds; Woe *be* to the shepherds of Israel that do feed themselves! should not the shepherds feed the flocks? 3 Ye eat the fat, and ye clothe you with the wool, ye kill them that are fed: *but* ye feed not the flock. 4 The diseased have ye not strengthened, neither have ye healed that which was sick, neither have ye bound up *that which was* broken, neither have ye brought again that which was driven away, neither have ye sought that which was lost; but with force and with cruelty have ye ruled them. 5 And they were scattered, because *there is* no shepherd: and they became meat to all the beasts of the field, when they were scattered. 6 My sheep wandered through all the mountains, and upon every high hill: yea, my flock was scattered upon all the face of the earth, and none did search or seek *after them.*

The prophecy of this chapter is not dated, nor any of those that follow it, till chap. xl. It is most probable that it was delivered after the completing of Jerusalem's destruction, when it would be very seasonable to enquire into the causes of it.

I. The prophet is ordered to *prophesy against the shepherds of Israel*—the princes and magistrates, the priests and Levites, the great Sanhedrim or council of state, or whoever they were that had the direction of public affairs in a higher or lower sphere, the kings especially, for there were two of them now captives in Babylon, who, as well as the people, must have their transgressions shown them, that they might repent, as Manasseh in his captivity. God has something to *say to the shepherds*, for they are but undershepherds, accountable to him who is the great *Shepherd of Israel*, Ps. lxxx. 1. And that which he says is, *Woe to the shepherds of Israel!* Though they are shepherds, and

shepherds of Israel, yet he must not spare them, must not flatter them. Note, If men's dignity and power do not, as they ought, keep them from sin, they will not serve to exempt them from reproof, to excuse their repentance, or to secure them from the judgments of God if they do not repent. We had a *woe to the pastors*, Jer. xxiii. 1. God will in a particular manner reckon with them if they be false to their trust.

II. He is here directed what to charge the shepherds with, in God's name, as the ground of God's controversy with them; for it is not a causeless quarrel. Two things they are charged with:—1. That all their care was to advance and enrich themselves and to make themselves great. Their business was to take care of those that were committed to their charge: *Should not the shepherds feed the flocks?* No doubt they should; they betray their trust if they do not. Not that they are to put the meat into their mouths, but to provide it for them and bring them to it. But *these* shepherds made this the least of their care; they *fed themselves*, contrived every thing to gratify and indulge their own appetite, and to make themselves rich and great, fat and easy. They made sure of the profits of their places; they did *eat the fat*, the *cream* (so some), for he *that feeds a flock eats of the milk of it* (1 Cor. ix. 7), and they made sure of the best of the milk. They made sure of the fleece, and *clothed themselves with the wool*, getting into their hands as much as they could of the estates of their subjects, yea, and *killed those that were well fed*, that what they had might be fed upon, as Naboth was put to death for his vineyard. Note, There is a woe to those who are in public trusts, but consult only their own private interest, and are more inquisitive about the benefice than about the office, what money is to be got than what good to be done. It is an old complaint, *All seek their own*, and too many *more than their own.* 2. That they took no care for the benefit and welfare of those that were committed to their charge: *You feed not the flock.* They neither knew how to do it, so ignorant were they, nor would they take any pains to do it, so lazy and slothful were they; nay, they never desired nor designed it, so treacherous and unfaithful were they. (1.) They did not do their duty to those of the flock that were distempered, did not strengthen them, nor heal them, nor bind them up, *v* 4. When any of the flock were sick or hurt, worried or wounded, it was all one to them whether they lived or died; they never looked after them. The princes and judges took no care to right those that suffered wrong or to shelter injured innocency. They took no care of the poor to see them provided for; they might starve, for them. The priests took no care to instruct the ignorant, to rectify the mistakes of those that were in error, to warn the unruly, or to comfort the feeble-minded. The ministers of state took no care to check the growing distempers of the kingdom, which threatened the vitals of it. Things were amiss, and out of course, every where, and nothing was done to rectify them. (2.) They did not do their duty to those of the flock that were dispersed, that were driven away by the enemies that invaded the country, and were forced to seek for shelter where they could find a place, or that *wandered* of choice upon *the mountains and hills* (*v.* 6), where they were exposed to the beasts of prey and became *meat to them, v.* 5. Every one is ready to seize a waif and stray. Some went abroad and begged, some went abroad and traded, and thus the country became thin of inhabitants, and was weakened and impoverished, and wanted hands both in the fields of corn and in the fields of battle, both in harvest and in war : *My flock was scattered upon all the face of the earth, v.* 6. And they were never enquired after, were never encouraged to return to their own country : *None did search or seek after them.* Nay, *with force and cruelty they ruled them,* which drove more away, and discouraged those that were driven away from all thoughts of returning. *Their* case is bad who have reason to expect better treatment among strangers than in their own country. It may be meant of those of the flock that went astray from God and their duty; and the priests, that should have taught the good knowledge of the Lord, used no means to convince and reclaim them, so that they became an easy prey to seducers. Thus were *they scattered because there was no shepherd, v.* 5. There were those that called themselves shepherds, but really they were not. Note, Those that do not do the work of shepherds are unworthy of the name. And if those that undertake to be shepherds are *foolish shepherds* (Zech. xi. 15), if they are proud and above their business, idle and do not love their business, or faithless and unconcerned about it, the case of the flock is as bad as if it were without a shepherd. Better no shepherd than such shepherds. Christ complains that his flock were *as sheep having no shepherd,* when yet the scribes and Pharisees *sat in Moses' seat,* Matt. ix. 36. It is ill with the patient when his physician is his worst disease, ill with the flock when the shepherds drive them away and disperse them, *by ruling them with force.*

7 Therefore, ye shepherds, hear the word of the Lord ; 8 *As* I live, saith the Lord God, surely because my flock became a prey, and my flock became meat to every beast of the field, because *there was* no shepherd, neither did my shepherds search for my flock, but the shepherds fed themselves, and fed not my flock ; 9 There-

fore, O ye shepherds, hear the word of the Lord ; 10 Thus saith the Lord God ; Behold, I *am* against the shepherds ; and I will require my flock at their hand, and cause them to cease from feeding the flock ; neither shall the shepherds feed themselves any more ; for I will deliver my flock from their mouth, that they may not be meat for them. 11 For thus saith the Lord God ; Behold, I, *even* I, will both search my sheep, and seek them out. 12 As a shepherd seeketh out his flock in the day that he is among his sheep *that are* scattered ; so will I seek out my sheep, and will deliver them out of all places where they have been scattered in the cloudy and dark day. 13 And I will bring them out from the people, and gather them from the countries, and will bring them to their own land, and feed them upon the mountains of Israel by the rivers, and in all the inhabited places of the country. 14 I will feed them in a good pasture, and upon the high mountains of Israel shall their fold be : there shall they lie in a good fold, and *in* a fat pasture shall they feed upon the mountains of Israel. 15 I will feed my flock, and I will cause them to lie down, saith the Lord God. 16 I will seek that which was lost, and bring again that which was driven away, and will bind up *that which was* broken, and will strengthen that which was sick : but I will destroy the fat and the strong ; I will feed them with judgment.

Upon reading the foregoing articles of impeachment drawn up, in God's name, against the shepherds of Israel, we cannot but look upon the shepherds with a just indignation, and upon the flock with a tender compassion. God, by the prophet, here expresses both in a high degree; and the shepherds are called upon (*v.* 7, 9) to *hear the word of the Lord,* to hear this word. Let them hear how little he regards them, who made much of themselves, and how much he regards the flock, which they made nothing of; both will be humbling to them. Those that will not *hear the word of the Lord* giving them their direction shall be made to hear the word of the Lord reading them their doom. Now see here,

I. How much displeased God is at the shepherds. Their crimes are repeated, *v.* 8.

God's flock became a prey to the deceivers first that drew them to idolatry, and then to the destroyers that carried them into captivity; and these shepherds took no care to prevent either the one or the other, but were as if there had been *no shepherds;* and therefore God says (*v.* 10), and confirms it with an oath (*v.* 8), *I am against the shepherds.* They had a commission from God to feed the flock, and made use of his name in what they did, expecting he would stand by them. "No," says God, "so far from that, *I am against them.*" Note, It is not our having the name and authority of shepherds that will engage God for us, if we do not the work enjoined us, and be not faithful to the trust reposed in us. God is *against them,* and they shall know it; for, 1. They shall be made to account for the manner in which they have discharged their trust: *"I will require my flock at their hands,* and charge it upon them that so many of them are missing." Note, Those will have a great deal to answer for in the judgment-day who take upon them the care of souls and yet take no care of them. Ministers must *watch* and work as those that *must give account,* Heb. xiii. 17. 2. They shall be deprived *officio et beneficio*—both *of the work and of the wages. They shall cease from feeding the flock,* that is, from pretending to feed it. Note, It is just with God to take out of men's hands that power which they have abused and that trust which they have betrayed. But, if this were all their punishment, they could bear it well enough; therefore it is added, " *Neither shall the shepherds feed themselves any more,* for *I will deliver my flock from their mouth,* which, instead of protecting, they had made a prey of." Note, Those that are enriching themselves with the spoils of the public cannot expect that they shall always be suffered to do so. Nor will God always permit his people to be trampled upon by those that should support them, but will find a time to deliver them from the shepherds their false friends, as well as from the lions their open enemies.

II. How much concerned God is for the flock; he speaks as if he were the more concerned for them because he saw them thus neglected, for *with him the fatherless finds mercy.* Precious promises are made here upon the occasion, which were to have their accomplishment in the return of the Jews out of their captivity and their re-establishment in their own land. Let the shepherds *hear this word of the Lord,* and know that they have no part nor lot in the matter. But let the poor sheep hear it and take the comfort of it. Note, Though magistrates and ministers fail in doing their part, for the good of the church, yet God will not fail in doing his; he will take the flock into his own hand rather than the church shall come short of any kindness he has designed for it. The under-shepherds may prove careless,

but the chief Shepherd *neither slumbers nor sleeps.* They may be false, but God *abides faithful.*

1. God will gather his sheep together that were scattered, and bring those back to the fold that had wandered from it: *"I, even I,* who alone can do it, will do it, and will have all the glory of it. *I will both search my sheep and find them out* (*v.* 11) as a shepherd does (*v.* 12), and bring them back as he does the stray-sheep, upon his shoulders, *from all the places where they have been scattered in the cloudy and dark day.*" There are cloudy and dark days, windy and stormy ones, which scatter God's sheep, which send them hither and thither, to divers and distant places, in quest of secresy and safety. But, (1.) Wherever they are the eye of God will *find them out;* for his eyes run to and fro through the earth, in favour of them. *I will seek out my sheep;* and not one that belongs to the fold, though driven ever so far off, shall be lost. *The Lord knows those that are his;* he *knows their work* and *where they dwell* (Rev. ii. 13), and where they are hidden. (2.) When his time shall come his arms will *fetch them home* (*v.* 13): *I will bring them out from the people.* God will both incline their hearts to come by his grace and will by his providence open a door for them and remove every difficulty that lies in the way. They shall not return one by one, clandestinely stealing away, but they shall return in a body: *"I will gather them from the countries* into which they are dispersed, not only the most considerable families of them, but every particular person. *I will seek that which was lost and bring again that which was driven away,*" *v.* 16. This was done when so many thousand Jews returned triumphantly out of Babylon, under the conduct of Zerubbabel, Ezra, and others. When those that have gone astray from God into the paths of sin are brought back by repentance, when those that erred come to the acknowledgment of the truth, when God's outcasts are gathered and restored, and religious assemblies, that were dispersed, rally again, upon the ceasing of persecution, and when the churches have rest and liberty, then this promise has a further accomplishment.

2. God will feed his people as the *sheep of his pasture,* that had been famished. God will bring the returning captives safely to their own land (*v.* 13), *will feed them upon the mountains of Israel,* and that is a *good pasture,* and a *fat pasture* (*v.* 14); there shall their *feeding* be, and there shall be *their fold;* and it is a *good fold.* There God will not only *feed them,* but *cause them to lie down* (*v.* 15), which denotes a comfortable rest after they had tired themselves with their wanderings, and a constant continuing residence; they shall not be driven out again from these green pastures, as they have been, nor shall they be disturbed, but shall lie down in a sweet repose and there shall be

none to make them afraid. Ps. xxiii. 2, *He makes me to lie down in green pastures.* Compare this with the like promise (Jer. xxiii. 3, 4), when God restored them not only to the milk and honey of their own land, to the enjoyment of its fruits, but to the privileges of his sanctuary on Mount Zion, the chief of the mountains of Israel. When they had an altar and a temple again, and the benefit of a settled priesthood, then they were fed in a good pasture.

3. He will succour those that are hurt, will *bind up that which was broken and strengthen that which was sick,* will comfort those that *mourn in Zion* and with Zion. If ministers, who should speak peace to those who are of a sorrowful spirit, neglect their duty, yet the Holy Ghost the Comforter will be faithful to his office. But, as it follows, the *fat and the strong shall be destroyed.* He that has rest for disquieted saints has terror to speak to presumptuous sinners. As *every valley* shall be *filled,* so *every mountain and hill shall be brought low,* Luke iii. 5.

17 And *as for* you, O my flock, thus saith the Lord God; Behold, I judge between cattle and cattle, between the rams and the he-goats. 18 *Seemeth it* a small thing unto you to have eaten up the good pasture, but ye must tread down with your feet the residue of your pastures? and to have drunk of the deep waters, but ye must foul the residue with your feet? 19 And *as for* my flock, they eat that which ye have trodden with your feet; and they drink that which ye have fouled with your feet. 20 Therefore thus saith the Lord God unto them; Behold, I, *even* I, will judge between the fat cattle and between the lean cattle. 21 Because ye have thrust with side and with shoulder, and pushed all the diseased with your horns, till ye have scattered them abroad; 22 Therefore will I save my flock, and they shall no more be a prey; and I will judge between cattle and cattle. 23 And I will set up one shepherd over them, and he shall feed them, *even* my servant David; he shall feed them, and he shall be their shepherd. 24 And I the Lord will be their God, and my servant David a prince among them; I the Lord have spoken *it.* 25 And I will make with them a covenant of peace, and will cause the evil beasts to cease out of the land: and they shall dwell safely in the wilderness, and sleep in the woods. 26 And I will make them and the places round about my hill a blessing; and I will cause the shower to come down in his season; there shall be showers of blessing. 27 And the tree of the field shall yield her fruit, and the earth shall yield her increase, and they shall be safe in their land, and shall know that I *am* the Lord, when I have broken the bands of their yoke, and delivered them out of the hand of those that served themselves of them. 28 And they shall no more be a prey to the heathen, neither shall the beast of the land devour them; but they shall dwell safely, and none shall make *them* afraid. 29 And I will raise up for them a plant of renown, and they shall be no more consumed with hunger in the land, neither bear the shame of the heathen any more. 30 Thus shall they know that I the Lord their God *am* with them, and *that* they, *even* the house of Israel, *are* my people, saith the Lord God. 31 And ye my flock, the flock of my pasture, *are* men, *and* I *am* your God, saith the Lord God.

The prophet has no more to say to the shepherds, but he has now a message to deliver to the flock. God had ordered him to speak tenderly to them, and to assure them of the mercy he had in store for them. But here he is ordered to make a difference between some and others of them, to separate between the precious and the vile and then to give them a promise of the Messiah, by whom this distinction should be effectually made, partly at his first coming (for *for judgment he came into this world,* John ix. 39, to *fill the hungry with good things and to send the rich empty away,* Luke i. 53), but completely at his second coming, when he shall, as it is here said, *judge between cattle and cattle, as a shepherd divides between the sheep and the goats, and shall set the sheep on his right hand and the goats on his left* (Matt. xxv. 32, 33), which seems to have reference to this. We have here,

I. Conviction spoken to those of the flock that were fat and strong, the *rams and the he-goats* (v. 17), those that, though they had not power, as shepherds and rulers, to oppress with, yet, being rich and wealthy, made use of the opportunity which this gave them to bear hard upon their poor neighbours. Those that have much would have more, and, if they set to it, will have more,

951

so many ways have they of encroaching upo their poor neighbours, and forcing from them the one ewe-lamb, 2 Sam. xii. 4. Do not the rich oppress the poor merely with the help of their riches, and *draw them before the judgment-seats?* Jam. ii. 6. Poor servants and tenants are hardly used by their rich lords and masters. The *rams* and the *he-goats* not only kept all the good pasture to themselves, ate the fat and drank the sweet, but they would not let the poor of the flock have any comfortable enjoyment of the little that was left them; they *trod down the residue of the pastures and fouled the residue of the waters,* so that the flock was obliged to eat that which they had trodden into the dirt, and drink that which they had muddied, *v.* 18, 19. This intimates that the great men not only by extortion and oppression made and kept their neighbours poor, and scarcely left them enough to subsist on, but were so vexatious to them that what little coarse fare they had was embittered to them. And this *seemed a small thing* to them; they thought there was no harm in it, as if it were the privilege of their quality to be injurious to all their neighbours. Note, Many that live in pomp and at ease themselves care not what straits those about them are reduced to, so they may but have every thing to their mind. Those that *are at ease,* and *the proud,* grudge that any body should live by them with any comfort. But this was not all; they not only robbed the poor, to make them poorer, but were troublesome to the sick and weak of the flock (*v.* 21): They *thrust with side and shoulder* those that were feeble (for the weakest goes to the wall) and *pushed the diseased with their horns,* because they knew they could be too hard for them, when they durst not meddle with their match. It has been observed concerning sheep that if one of the flock be sick and faint the rest will secure it as well as they can, and shelter it from the scorching heat of the sun; but these, on the contrary, were most injurious to the diseased. Those that they could not serve themselves of they did what they could to rid the country of, and so *scattered them abroad,* as if the poor, whom, Christ says, we must have always with us, were public nuisances, not to be relieved, but sent far away from us. Note, It is a barbarous thing to *add affliction to the afflicted.* Perhaps these *rams* and *he-goats* are designed to represent the scribes and Pharisees, for they are such troublers of the church as Christ himself must come to deliver it from, *v.* 23. They devoured widows' houses, took away the key of knowledge, corrupted the pure water of divine truths, and oppressed the consciences of men with the traditions of the elders, besides that they were continually vexatious and injurious to *the poor of the flock* that *waited on the Lord,* Zech. xi. 11. Note, It is no new thing for the flock of God to receive a great deal of damage and mischief from those that are

themselves of the flock, and in eminent stations in it, Acts xx. 30.

II. Comfort spoken to those of the flock that are poor and feeble, and that wait for the consolation of Israel (*v.* 22): " *I will save my flock,* and they shall no more be spoiled as they have been by the beasts of prey, by their own shepherds or by the rams and he-goats among themselves." Upon this occasion, as is usual in the prophets, comes in a prediction of the coming of the Messiah, and the setting up of his kingdom, and the exceedingly great and precious benefits which the church should enjoy under the protection and influence of that kingdom. Observe what is here foretold,

1. Concerning the Messiah himself. (1.) He shall have his commission from God himself: I will *set him up* (*v.* 23); *I will raise him up, v.* 29. He sanctified and sealed him, appointed and anointed him. (2.) He shall be the great *Shepherd* of the sheep, who shall do that for his flock which no one else could do. He is the *one Shepherd,* under whom Jews and Gentiles should be *one fold.* (3.) He is *God's servant,* employed by him and for him, and doing all in obedience to his will, with an eye to his glory—his servant, to re-establish his kingdom among men and advance the interests of that kingdom. (4.) He is David, one after God's own heart, set as his King upon the holy hill of Zion, made the head of the corner, with whom the covenant of royalty is made, and to whom God would *give the throne of his father David.* He is both the *root and offspring of David.* (5.) He is the *plant of renown,* because a *righteous branch* (Jer. xxiii. 5), a branch of the Lord, that is *beautiful* and *glorious,* Isa. iv. 2. He has a name above every name, a throne above every throne, and may therefore well be called a *branch of renown.* Some understand it of the church, the *planting of the Lord,* Isa. lxi. 3. *Its name shall be remembered* (Ps. xlv. 17) and Christ's in it.

2. Concerning the great charter by which the kingdom of the Messiah should be incorporated, and upon which it should be founded (*v.* 25): *I will make with them a covenant of peace.* The covenant of grace is a covenant of peace. In it God is at peace with us, speaks peace to us, and assures us of peace, of all good, all the good we need to make us happy. The tenour of this covenant is: " *I the Lord will be their God,* a God all-sufficient to them (*v.* 24), will own them and will be owned by them; in order to this *my servant David shall be a prince among them,* to reduce them to their allegiance, to receive their homage, and to reign over them, in them, and for them." Note, Those, and those only, that have the Lord Jesus for *their prince* have the Lord Jehovah for *their God.* And then *they, even the house of Israel, shall be my people.* If we take God to be *our God,* he will take us to be *his people.* From this covenant between God and Israel

there results communion : " *I the Lord their God am with them*, to converse with them; and *they shall know it*, and have the comfort of it."

3. Concerning the privileges of those that are the faithful subjects of this kingdom of the Messiah and interested in the covenant of peace. These are here set forth figuratively, as the blessings of the flock. But we have a key to it, *v.* 31. Those that belong to this flock, though they are spoken of as *sheep*, are really men, men that have the Lord for *their God*, and are in covenant with him. Now to them it is promised,

(1.) That they shall enjoy a holy security under the divine protection. Christ, our good Shepherd, has *caused the evil beasts to cease out of the land* (*v.* 25), having vanquished all our spiritual enemies, broken their power, and triumphed over them ; the roaring lion is not a roaring devouring lion to them ; *they shall no more be a prey to the heathen* nor the heathen a terror to them, *neither shall the beasts of the land devour them*. Sin and Satan, death and hell, are conquered. And then *they shall dwell safely*, not only in the folds, but in the fields, *in the wilderness, in the woods*, where the beasts of prey are ; they shall not only dwell there, but they shall sleep there, which denotes not only that the beasts being *made to cease* there shall be no danger, but, their consciences being purified and pacified, they shall be in no apprehension of danger ; not only safe from evil, but quiet from the fear of evil. Note, Those may lay down and sleep securely, sleep at ease, that have Christ for their prince ; for he will be their protector, and make them to dwell in safety. None shall hurt them, nay, *none shall make them afraid*. If God be for us, who can be against us? *Therefore will not we fear, though the earth be removed*. Through Christ, God delivers his people not only from the things they have reason to fear, but from their fear even of death itself, from all that fear that has torment. This safety from evil is promised (*v.* 27) : *They shall be safe in their land*, in no danger of being invaded and enslaved, though their great plenty be a temptation to their neighbours to *desire their land ;* and that which shall make them think themselves safe is their confidence in the wisdom, power, and goodness of God : *They shall know that I am the Lord*. All our disquieting fears arise from our ignorance of God and mistakes concerning him. Their experience of his particular care concerning them encourages their confidence in him : " *I have broken the bands of their yoke*, with which they have been brought and held down under oppression, and have *delivered them out of the hand of those that served themselves of them*, whence they shall argue, He that has delivered does and will, therefore will we dwell safely." This is explained, and applied to our gospel-state, Luke i. 74. *That*

we, being delivered out of the hand of our enemies, might serve him without fear, as those may do that serve him in faith.

(2.) That they shall enjoy a spiritual plenty of all good things, the best things, for their comfort and happiness : *They shall no more be consumed with hunger in the land, v.* 29. Famine and scarcity, when Israel was punished with that judgment, turned as much to their reproach among the heathen as any other, because the fruitfulness of Canaan was so much talked of. But now *they shall not bear that shame of the heathen any more*. For the *showers shall come down in their season*, even *showers of blessing, v.* 26. Christ is a Shepherd that will feed his people ; and they shall *go in and out, and find pasture*. [1.] They shall not be consumed with hunger ; for they shall not be put off with the world for a portion, which is not bread, which satisfies not, and which leaves those that are put off with it to be *consumed with hunger*. The ordinances of the ceremonial law are called *beggarly elements*, for there was little in them, compared with the Christian institutes, *wherewith the mower fills his hand and he that binds sheaves his bosom*. Those that *hunger and thirst after righteousness* shall not be consumed with that hunger, for *they shall be filled*. And he that drinks of the water that Christ gives him, the still waters by which he leads his sheep, shall *never thirst*. [2.] *Showers of blessings* shall come upon them, *v.* 26, 27. The heavens shall yield their dews ; the *trees of the field* also shall *yield their fruit*. The seat of this plenty is *God's hill*, his holy hill of Zion, for on that mountain, in the gospel church, it is, that God has *made to all nations a feast ;* to that those must join themselves who would partake of gospel benefits. The cause of this plenty is the *showers that come down in their season*, that descend upon the mountains of Zion, the graces of Christ, his doctrine that drops as the dew, the graces of Christ, and the gifts and comforts of his Spirit, by which we are made fruitful in the fruits of righteousness. The instances of this plenty are the blessings of heaven poured down upon us and the productions of grace brought forth by us, our comfort in God's favour and God's glory in our fruit-bearing. The extent of this plenty is very large, to all the *places round about my hill ;* for *out of Zion shall go forth the law*, shall go forth light to a dark world, and the river that shall water a dry and desert world ; all that are in the neighbourhood of Zion shall fare the better for it ; and the nearer the church the nearer its God. And, *lastly*, The *effect of this plenty* is, *I will make them a blessing*, eminently and exemplarily blessed, patterns of happiness, Isa. xix. 24. Or, They shall be blessings to all about them, diffusively useful. Note, Those that are the *blessed of the Lord* must study to make themselves blessings to the world. He that is good, let him do *good;* he that has received the gift, the grace, let him minister the same.

Now this promise of the Messiah and his kingdom spoke much comfort to those to whom it was then made, for they might be sure that God would not utterly *destroy* their nation, how low soever it might be brought, as long as that *blessing* was *in* the womb of *it*, Isa. lxv. 8. But it speaks much more comfort to us, to whom it is fulfilled, who are the sheep of this good Shepherd, are fed in his pastures, and *blessed with all spiritual blessings in heavenly things* by him.

CHAP. XXXV.

It was promised, in the foregoing chapter, that when the time to favour Zion, yea, the set time, should come, especially the time for sending the Messiah and setting up his kingdom in the world, God would cause the enemies of his church to cease and the blessings and comforts of the church to abound. This chapter enlarges upon the former promise, concerning the destruction of the enemies of the church; the next chapter upon the latter promise, the replenishing of the church with blessings. Mount Seir (that is, Edom) is the enemy prophesied against in this chapter, but fitly put here, as in the prophecy of Obadiah, for all the enemies of the church; for, as those all walked in the way of Cain that hated Abel, so those all walked in the way of Esau who hated Jacob, but over whom Jacob, by virtue of a particular blessing, was to have dominion. Now here we have, I. The sin charged upon the Edomites, and that was their spite and malice to Israel, ver. 5, 10—13. II. The ruin threatened, that should come upon them for this sin. God will be against them (ver. 3) and then their country shall be laid waste (ver. 4), depopulated, and made quite desolate (ver. 6—9), and left so when other nations that had been wasted should recover themselves, ver. 14, 15.

MOREOVER the word of the LORD came unto me, saying, 2 Son of man, set thy face against mount Seir, and prophesy against it, 3 And say unto it, Thus saith the Lord GOD; Behold, O mount Seir, I *am* against thee, and I will stretch out mine hand against thee, and I will make thee most desolate. 4 I will lay thy cities waste, and thou shalt be desolate, and thou shalt know that I *am* the LORD. 5 Because thou hast had a perpetual hatred, and hast shed *the blood of* the children of Israel by the force of the sword in the time of their calamity, in the time *that their* iniquity *had* an end: 6 Therefore, *as* I live, saith the Lord GOD, I will prepare thee unto blood, and blood shall pursue thee: sith thou hast not hated blood, even blood shall pursue thee. 7 Thus will I make mount Seir most desolate, and cut off from it him that passeth out and him that returneth. 8 And I will fill his mountains with his slain *men:* in thy hills, and in thy valleys, and in all thy rivers, shall they fall that are slain with the sword. 9 I will make thee perpetual desolations, and thy cities shall not return: and ye shall know that I *am* the LORD.

Mount Seir was mentioned as partner with

954

Moab in one of the threatenings we had before (*ch.* xxv. 8); but here it is convicted and condemned by itself, and has woes of its own. The prophet must boldly *set his face against Edom*, and *prophesy* particularly *against it;* for the God of Israel has said, *O Mount Seir! I am against thee.* Note, Those that have God against them have the word of God against them, and the face of his ministers, nor dare they prophesy any good to them, but evil. The prophet must tell the Edomites that God has a controversy with them, and let them know,

I. What is the cause and ground of that controversy, *v.* 5. God espouses his people's cause, and will plead it, takes what is done against them as done against himself, and will reckon for it; and it is upon their account that God now contends with the Edomites. 1. Because of the enmity they had against the people of God, that was rooted in the heart. "Thou hast had a *perpetual hatred* to them, to the very name of an Israelite." The Edomites kept up an *hereditary* malice against Israel, the same that Esau bore to Jacob, because he got the birth-right and the blessing. Esau had been reconciled to Jacob, had embraced and kissed him (Gen. xxxiii.), and we do not find that ever he quarrelled with him again. But the posterity of Esau would never be reconciled to the seed of Jacob, but hated them with a perpetual hatred. Note, Children will be more apt to imitate the vices than the virtues of their parents, and to tread in the steps of their sin than in the steps of their repentance. Parents should therefore be careful not to set their children any bad example, for though, through the grace of God, they may return, and prevent the mischief of what they have done amiss to themselves, they may not be able to obviate the bad influence of it upon their children. It is strange how deeply-rooted national antipathies sometimes are, and how long they last; but it is not to be wondered at that profane Edomites hate pious Israelites, since the old *enmity* that was put between the *seed of the woman* and the seed of the serpent (Gen. iii. 15) will continue to the end. *Marvel not if the world hate you.* 2. Because of the injuries they had done to the people of God. They *shed their blood by the force of the sword, in the time of their calamity;* they did not attack them as fair and open enemies, but laid wait for them, to *cut off* those of them that had escaped (Obad. 14), or they drove them back upon the sword of the pursuers, by which they fell. It was cowardly, as well as barbarous, to take advantage of their distress; and for neighbours, with whom they had lived peaceably, to *smite them secretly* when strangers openly invaded them. It was in the time *that their iniquity had an end,* when the measure of it was full and destruction came. Note, Even those that suffer justly, and for their sins, are yet to be pitied and not trampled upon. If the father corrects one child, he expects the rest should tremble at it, not triumph in it.

II. What should be the effect and issue of that controversy. If God stretch out his hand against the country of Edom, he will *make it most desolate, v. 3. Desolation and desolation.* 1. The inhabitants shall be slain with the sword (*v.* 6) : *I will prepare thee unto blood.* Edom shall be gradually weakened, and so be the more easily conquered, and the enemy shall gather strength the more effectually to subdue it. Thus preparation is in the making a great while before for this destruction. *Thou hast not hated blood;* it implies, " Thou hast delighted in it and thirsted after it." Those that do not keep up a rooted hatred of sin, when a temptation to it is very strong, will be in danger of yielding to it. Some read it, " *Unless thou hatest blood"* (that is, " unless thou dost repent, and put off this bloody disposition) *blood shall pursue thee."* And then it is an intimation that the judgment may yet be prevented by a thorough reformation. *If he turn not, he will whet his sword,* Ps. vii. 12. But, if he turn, he will lay it by. *Blood shall pursue thee,* the *guilt* of the blood which thou hast shed or the *judgment* of blood; thy blood-thirsty enemies shall pursue thee, which way soever thou seekest to make thy escape. A great and general slaughter shall be made of the Idumeans, such as had been foretold (Is. xxxiv. 6) : The *mountains and hills, the valleys and rivers,* shall be *filled with the slain, v.* 8. The pursuers shall overtake those that flee and shall give no quarter, but put them all to the sword. Note, When God comes to make inquisition for blood those that have shed the blood of his Israel shall have blood given them to drink, for they are worthy. *Satia te sanguine quem sitisti—Glut thyself with blood, after which thou hast thirsted.* 2. The country shall be laid waste. The cities shall be destroyed (*v.* 4), the *country made most desolate* (*v.* 7); for God will *cut off* from both him that *passes out* and *him that returns;* and when the inhabitants are cut off that should keep the cities in repair they will decay and go into ruins, and when those are cut off that should till the land that will soon be over-run with briers and thorns and become a wilderness. Note, Those that help forward the desolations of Israel may expect to be themselves made desolate. And that which completes the judgment is that Edom shall be made *perpetual desolations* (*v.* 9) and the cities shall never return to their former state, nor the inhabitants of them come back from their captivity and dispersion. Note, Those that have a perpetual enmity to God and his people, as the carnal mind has, can expect no other than to be made a perpetual desolation. Implacable malice will justly be punished with irreparable ruin.

10 Because thou hast said, These

two nations and these two countries shall be mine, and we will possess it; whereas the LORD was there : 11 Therefore, *as* I live, saith the Lord GOD, I will even do according to thine anger, and according to thine envy which thou hast used out of thy hatred against them; and I will make myself known among them, when I have judged thee. 12 And thou shalt know that I *am* the LORD, *and that* I have heard all thy blasphemies which thou hast spoken against the mountains of Israel, saying, They are laid desolate, they are given us to consume. 13 Thus with your mouth ye have boasted against me, and have multiplied your words against me : I have heard *them.* 14 Thus saith the Lord GOD; When the whole earth rejoiceth, I will make thee desolate. 15 As thou didst rejoice at the inheritance of the house of Israel, because it was desolate, so will I do unto thee : thou shalt be desolate, O mount Seir, and all Idumea, *even* all of it : and they shall know that I *am* the LORD.

Here is, I. A further account of the sin of the Edomites, and their bad conduct towards the people of God. We find the church complaining of them for setting on the Babylonians, and irritating them against Jerusalem, saying, *Rase it, rase it,* down with it, down with it (Ps. cxxxvii. 7), inflaming a rage that needed no spur; here it is further charged upon them that they triumphed in Jerusalem's ruin and in the desolations of the country. Many *blasphemies* they spoke against the *mountains of Israel,* saying, with pride and pleasure, *They are laid desolate, v.* 12. Note, The troubles of God's church, as they give proofs of the constancy and fidelity of its friends, so they discover and draw out the corruptions of its enemies, in whom there then appears more brutish malice than one would have thought of. Now their triumphing in Jerusalem's ruin is here said to proceed, 1. From a sinful passion against the people of Israel; from *anger* and *envy,* and *hatred against them* (*v.* 11), that *perpetual hatred* spoken of *v.* 5. Though they were not a match for them, and therefore could not do them a mischief themselves, yet they were glad when the Chaldeans did them a mischief. 2. From a sinful appetite to the land of Israel. They pleased themselves with hopes that when the people of Israel were destroyed they should be let into the possession of their country, which they had so often grudged and envied them. They thought they could make out something of a title to it, *ob defectum sanguinis—for want of other heirs.* If Jacob's issue fail, they think that they are next in the entail, and that the remainder will be to his brother's issue : *"These two nations of Judah and Israel shall be mine.* Now is the time for me to put in for them."* At least they hope to come in as first occupants, being near neighbours : *We will possess it* when it is deserted. *Ceditur occupanti—Let us get possession and that will be title enough.* Note, Those have the spirit of Edomites who desire the death of others because they hope to get by it, or are pleased with their failing because they expect to come into their business. When we see the vanity of the world in the disappointments, losses, and crosses, that others meet with in it, instead of showing ourselves, upon such an occasion, greedy of it, we should rather be made thereby to sit more loose to it, and both take our affections off it and lower our expectations from it. But in this case of the Edomites' coveting the land of Israel, and gaping for it, there was a particular affront to God, when they said, *" These lands are given us to devour,* and we shall have our bellies full of their riches." God says, *You have boasted against me and have multiplied your words against me ;* for they expected possession upon a vacancy, because Israel was driven out, *whereas the Lord was* still *there, v.* 10. His temple indeed was burnt, and the other tokens of his presence were gone ; but his promise to give that land to the seed of Jacob for an inheritance was not made void, but remained in full force and virtue ; and by that promise he did in effect still keep possession for Israel, till they should in due time be restored to it. That was Immanuel's land (Isa. viii. 8) ; in that land he was to be born, and therefore that people shall continue in it of whom he is to be born, till he has passed his time in it, and then let who will take it. *The Lord is there,* the Lord Jesus is to be there ; and therefore Israel's discontinuance of possession is no defeasance of their right, but it shall be kept for them, and they shall have, hold, and enjoy it by virtue of the divine grant, till the promise of this Canaan shall by the Messiah be changed into the promise of a far better. Note, It is a piece of presumption highly offensive to God for Edomites to lay claim to those privileges and comforts that are peculiar to God's chosen Israel and are reserved for them. It is *blasphemy against the mountains of Israel,* the holy mountains, to say, because they are for the present made a prey of and *trodden under foot of the Gentiles* (Rev. xi. 2), even the *holy city* itself, that therefore the *Lord has forsaken them,* their *God has forgotten them.* The apostle will by no means admit such a thought as this, that *God hath cast away his people,* Rom. xi. 1. No ; though they are cast down for a time, they are not cast off for ever. Those *reproach the Lord* who say they are.

II. The notice God took of the barbarous insolence of the Edomites, and the doom passed upon them for it : *I have heard all thy blasphemies, v.* 12. And again (*v.* 13), *You have multiplied your words against me,* and *I have heard them,* I have observed them, I have kept an account of them. Note, In the multitude of words, not one escapes God's cognizance ; let men speak ever so much, ever so fast, though they multiply words, which they themselves regard not, but forget immediately, yet none of them are lost in the crowd, not the most idle words ; but God hears them, and will be able to charge the sinner with them. All the haughty and hard speeches, particularly, which are spoken against the Israel of God, the words which are *magnified* (as it is in the margin, *v.* 13) as well as the words which are multiplied, God takes notice of. For, as the most trifling words are not below his cognizance, so the most daring are not above his rebuke. *I have heard all thy blasphemies.* This is a good reason why we should bear reproach as if we heard it not, because *God will hear,* Ps. xxxviii. 13, 15. God has heard the Edomites' blasphemy ; let them therefore hear their doom, *v.* 14, 15. It was a national sin (the blasphemies charged upon them were the sense and language of all the Edomites), and therefore shall be punished with a national desolation. And, 1. It shall be a distinguishing punishment. As God has peculiar favours for Israelites, so he has peculiar plagues for Edomites : so that *" When the whole earth rejoices I will make thee desolate ;* when other nations have their desolations repaired, to their joy, thine shall be *perpetual," v.* 9. 2. The punishment shall answer to the sin : *" As thou didst rejoice in the desolation of the house of Israel,* God will give thee enough of desolation ; since thou art so fond of it, *thou shalt be desolate ; I will make thee so."* Note, Those who, instead of weeping with the mourners, make a jest of their grievances, may justly be made to weep like the mourners, and themselves to feel the weight, to feel the smart, of those grievances which they set so light by. Some read *v.* 14 so as to complete the resemblance between the sin and the punishment : *The whole earth shall rejoice when I make thee desolate, as thou didst rejoice when Israel* was made desolate. Those that are glad at the death and fall of others may expect that others will be glad of their death, of their fall. 3. In the destruction of the enemies of the church God designs his own glory, and we may be sure that he will not come short of his design. (1.) That which he intends is to manifest himself, as a just and jealous God, firm to his covenant and faithful to his people and their injured cause (*v.* 11) : *I will make myself known among them when I have judged thee.* The Lord is and will be known by the judgments which he executes. (2.) His intention shall be fully answered ; not only his own people shall be made to know it to their comfort, but even the Edomites themselves, and all the other enemies of his name and people, *shall know that he is the Lord, v.* 4, 9, 15. As the works of creation and common providence demonstrate that there is a God, so the care taken of Israel shows that Jehovah, the God of Israel, is that God alone, the true and living God.

CHAP. XXXVI.

We have done with Mount Seir, and left it desolate, and likely to continue so, and must now turn ourselves, with the prophet, to the mountains of Israel, which we find desolate too, but hope before we have done with the chapter to leave in better plight. Here are two distinct prophecies in this chapter:—I. Here is one that seems chiefly to relate to the temporal estate of the Jews, wherein their present deplorable condition is described and the triumphs of their neighbours in it; but it is promised that their grievances shall be all redressed and that in due time they shall be settled again in their own land, in the midst of peace and plenty, ver. 1—15. II. Here is another that seems chiefly to concern their spiritual estate, wherein they are reminded of their former sins and God's judgments upon them, to humble them for their sins and under God's mighty hand, ver. 16—20. But it is promised, 1. That God would glorify himself in showing mercy to them, ver. 21—24. 2. That he would sanctify them, by giving them his grace and fitting them for his service; and this for his own name's sake and in answer to their prayers, ver. 25—38.

ALSO, thou son of man, prophesy unto the mountains of Israel, and say, Ye mountains of Israel, hear the word of the Lord: 2 Thus saith the Lord God; Because the enemy hath said against you, Aha, even the ancient high places are our's in possession: 3 Therefore prophesy and say, Thus saith the Lord God; Because they have made *you* desolate, and swallowed you up on every side, that ye might be a possession unto the residue of the heathen, and ye are taken up in the lips of talkers, and *are* an infamy of the people: 4 Therefore, ye mountains of Israel, hear the word of the Lord God; Thus saith the Lord God to the mountains, and to the hills, to the rivers, and to the valleys, to the desolate wastes, and to the cities that are forsaken, which became a prey and derision to the residue of the heathen that *are* round about; 5 Therefore thus saith the Lord God; Surely in the fire of my jealousy have I spoken against the residue of the heathen, and against all Idumea, which have appointed my land into their possession with the joy of all *their* heart, with despiteful minds, to cast it out for a prey. 6 Prophesy therefore concerning the land of Israel, and say unto the mountains, and to the hills, to the rivers, and to the valleys, Thus saith the Lord God; Behold, I have spoken

in my jealousy and in my fury, because ye have borne the shame of the heathen: 7 Therefore thus saith the Lord God; I have lifted up mine hand, Surely the heathen that *are* about you, they shall bear their shame. 8 But ye, O mountains of Israel, ye shall shoot forth your branches, and yield your fruit to my people of Israel; for they are at hand to come. 9 For, behold, I *am* for you, and I will turn unto you, and ye shall be tilled and sown: 10 And I will multiply men upon you, all the house of Israel, *even* all of it: and the cities shall be inhabited, and the wastes shall be builded: 11 And I will multiply upon you man and beast; and they shall increase and bring fruit: and I will settle you after your old estates, and will do better *unto you* than at your beginnings: and ye shall know that I *am* the Lord. 12 Yea, I will cause men to walk upon you, *even* my people Israel; and they shall possess thee, and thou shalt be their inheritance, and thou shalt no more henceforth bereave them *of men.* 13 Thus saith the Lord God; Because they say unto you, Thou *land* devourest up men, and hast bereaved thy nations; 14 Therefore thou shalt devour men no more, neither bereave thy nations any more, saith the Lord God. 15 Neither will I cause *men* to hear in thee the shame of the heathen any more, neither shalt thou bear the reproach of the people any more, neither shalt thou cause thy nations to fall any more, saith the Lord God.

The prophet had been ordered to set his face *towards the mountains of Israel* and *prophesy against them,* ch. vi. 2. Then God was coming forth to contend with his people; but now that God is returning in mercy to them he must speak good words and comfortable words to these mountains, *v.* 1 and again *v.* 4. *You mountains of Israel, hear the word of the Lord;* and what he says to them he says *to the hills, to the rivers, to the valleys, to the desolate wastes* in the country, and to the cities *that are forsaken, v.* 4 and again *v.* 6. The people were gone, some one way and some another; nothing remained there to be spoken to but the places, the mountains and valleys; these the Chaldeans could not carry away with them. *The earth abides for ever.* Now, to show the mercy God had in reserve for the people, he is to speak of him as having a dormant kindness for the place, which, if the Lord had been pleased for ever to abandon, he would not have called upon to *hear the word of the Lord*, nor *would he as at this time have shown it such things as these.* Here is,

I. The compassionate notice God takes of the present deplorable condition of the land of Israel. It has become both a *prey* and a *derision to the heathen that are round about*, *v.* 4. 1. It has become a prey to them; and they are all enriched with the plunder of it. When the Chaldeans had conquered them all their neighbours flew to the spoil as to a shipwreck, every one thinking all his own that he could lay his hands on (*v.* 3): *They have made you desolate, and swallowed you up on every side, that you might be a possession to the heathen*, to the *residue* of them, even such as had themselves narrowly escaped the like desolation. No one thought it any crime to strip an Israelite. *Turba Romæ sequitur fortunam ut semper—The mob of Rome still praise the elevated and despise the fallen.* It is the common cry, when a man is down, *Down with him.* 2. It has become a derision to them. They took all they had and laughed at them when they had done. *The enemy said, "Aha! even the ancient high places are ours in possession, v.* 2. Neither the antiquity, nor the dignity, neither the sanctity nor the fortifications, of the land of Israel, are its security, but we have become masters of it all." The more honours that land had been adorned with, and the greater figure it had made among the nations, the more pride and pleasure did they take in making a spoil of it, which is an instance of a base and sordid spirit; for the more glorious the prosperity was the more piteous is the adversity. God takes notice of it here as an aggravation of the present calamity of Israel: *You are taken up in the lips of talkers and are an infamy of the people, v.* 3. All the talk of the country about was concerning the overthrow of the Jewish nation; and every one that spoke of it had some peevish ill-natured reflection or other upon them. They were the *scorning of those that were at ease and the contempt of the proud*, Ps. cxxiii. 4. There are some that are noted for talkers, that have something to say of every body, but cannot find in their hearts to speak well of any body; God's people, among such people, were sure to be a reproach when the crown had fallen from their head. Thus it was the lot of Christianity, in its suffering days, to be *every where spoken against.*

II. The expressions of God's just displeasure against those who triumphed in the desolations of the land of Israel, as many of its neighbours did, even the residue of the brethren, and Idumea particularly. Let us see, 1. How they dealt with the Israel of God. They carved out large possessions to themselves out of their land, out of God's land;

for so indeed it was: "*They have appointed my land into their possession* (*v.* 5), and so not only invaded their neighbour's property, but intrenched upon God's prerogative." It was the holy land which they laid their sacrilegious hands upon. They did not own any dependence upon God, as the God of that land, nor acknowledge any remaining interest that Israel had in it, but *cast it out for a prey*, as if they had won it in a lawful war. And this they did without any dread of God and his judgments and without any compassion for Israel and their calamities, but with the *joy of all their hearts*, because they got by it, and *with despiteful minds* to Israel that lost by it. Increasing wealth, by right or wrong, is all the joy of a worldly heart; and the calamities of God's people are all the joy of a despiteful mind. And those that had not an opportunity of making a prey of God's people made a reproach of them; so that they were *the shame of the heathen, v.* 6. Every body ridiculed them and made a jest of them; and the truth is they had by their own sin made themselves vile; so that God was righteous herein, but men were unrighteous and very barbarous. 2. How God would deal with those who were thus in word and deed abusive to his people. He has *spoken against the heathen;* he has passed sentence upon them; he has determined to reckon with them for it, and this *in the fire of his jealousy*, both for his own honour and for the honour of his people, *v.* 5. Having a *love* for both as *strong as death*, he has a *jealousy* for both as *cruel as the grave*. They spoke in their malice against God's people, and he will speak in his jealousy against them; and it is easy to say which will speak most powerfully. God will speak *in his jealousy and in his fury, v.* 6. Fury is not in God; but he will exert his power against them and handle them as severely as men do when they are in a fury. He will so *speak to them in his wrath as to vex them in his sore displeasure.* What he says he will stand to, for it is backed with an oath. He has *lifted up his hand* and sworn by himself, has sworn and will not repent. And what is it that is said with so much heat, and yet with so much deliberation? It is this (*v.* 7), *Surely the heathen that are about you, they shall bear their shame.* Note, The righteous God, to whom vengeance belongs, will render shame for shame. Those that put contempt and reproach upon God's people will, sooner or later, have it *turned upon themselves*, perhaps in this world (either their follies or their calamities, their miscarriages or their mischances, shall be their reproach), at furthest in that day when all the impenitent shall *rise to shame and everlasting contempt.*

III. The promises of God's favour to his Israel and assurances given of great mercy God had in store for them. God takes occasion from the outrage and insolence of their enemies to show himself so much the more concerned for them and ready to do them good, as David hoped that God would recompense him good for Shimei's cursing him. *Let them curse, but bless thou.* In this way, as well as others, the enemies of God's people do them real service, even by the injuries they do them, against their will and beyond their intention. We shall have no reason to complain if, the more unkind men are, the more kind God is—if, the more kindly he speaks to us by his word and Spirit, the more kindly he acts for us in his providence. The prophet must say so to the *mountains of Israel,* which were now *desolate and despised,* that God is *for them* and will *turn to them, v.* 9. As the curse of God reaches the ground for man's sake, so does the blessing. Now that which is promised is, 1. That their rightful owners should return to the possession of them: *My people Israel are at hand to come, v.* 8. Though they are at a great distance from their own country, though they are dispersed in many countries, and though they are detained by the power of their enemies, yet they shall *come again to their own border,* Jer. xxxi. 17. The time is at hand for their return. Though there were above forty years of the seventy (perhaps fifty) yet remaining, it is spoken of as near, because it is sure, and there were some among them that should live to see it. A *thousand years are* with God but *as one day.* The mountains of Israel are now desolate ; but God will *cause men to walk upon them* again, *even his people Israel,* not as travellers passing over them, but as inhabitants —not tenants, but freeholders: *They shall possess thee,* not for term of life, but for themselves and their heirs; *thou shalt be their inheritance.* It was a type of the heavenly Canaan, to which all God's children are heirs, every Israelite indeed, and into which they shall shortly be all brought together, out of the countries where they are now scattered. 2. That they should afford a plentiful comfortable maintenance for their owners at their return. When the land had *enjoyed her sabbaths* for so many years, it should be so much the more fruitful afterwards, as we should be after rest, especially a sabbath rest : *You shall be tilled and sown* (v. 9) and shall *yield your fruit to my people Israel, v.* 8. Note, It is a blessing to the earth to be made serviceable to men, especially to good men, that will serve God with cheerfulness in the use of those good things which the earth serves up to them. 3. That the people of Israel should have not only a comfortable sustenance, but a comfortable settlement, in their own land : The *cities shall be inhabited ; the wastes shall be builded, v.* 10 And *I will settle you after your old estates, v.* 11. Their own sin had unsettled them, but now God's favour shall resettle them. When the prodigal son has become a penitent he is settled again in his father's

house, according to his former estate. Bring hither the *first robe,* and put it on him. Nay, *I will do better unto you* now *than at your beginnings.* There is more joy for the sheep that is brought back than there would have been if it had never gone astray. And God sometimes multiplies his people's comforts in proportion to the *time that he has afflicted them.* Thus God blessed the latter end of Job more than his beginning, and doubled to him all he had. 4. That the people, after their return, should be *fruitful, and multiply, and replenish the land,* so that it should not only be inhabited again, but as thickly inhabited, and as well peopled, as ever. God will bring back to it *all the house of Israel, even all of it* (observe what an emphasis is laid upon that, *v.* 10), all *whose spirits God stirred up* to return ; and those only were reckoned of *the house of Israel,* the rest had cut themselves off from it ; or, though but few, in comparison, returned at first, yet afterwards, at divers times, they *all* returned ; and then (says God) *I will multiply these men* (*v.* 10), *multiply man and beast ; and they shall increase, v.* 11. Note, God's kingdom in the world is a growing kingdom ; and his church, though for a time it may be diminished, shall recover itself and be again replenished. 5. That the reproach long since cast upon the land of Israel by the evil spies, and of late revived, that *it was a land that ate up the inhabitants* of it by famine, sickness, and the sword, should be quite rolled away, and there should never be any more occasion for it. Canaan had got into a bad name. It had of old *spued out the inhabitants* (Lev. xviii. 28), the natives, the aborigines, which was turned to its reproach by those that should have put another construction upon it, Num. xiii. 32. It had of late devoured the Israelites, and spued them out too ; so that it was commonly said of it, It is a land which, instead of supporting its nations or tribes that inhabit it, *bereaves* them, *overthrows* them, and *causes them to fall ;* it is a tenement which breaks all the tenants that come upon it. This character it had got among the neighbours ; but God now promises that it shall be so no more : *Thou shalt no more bereave them of men* (*v.* 12), shalt *devour men no more, v.* 14. But the inhabitants shall live to a good old age, and not have the number of their months cut off in the midst. Compare this with that promise, Zech. viii. 4. Note, God will take away the reproach of his people by taking away that which was the occasion of it. When the nation is made to flourish in peace, plenty, and power, then they *hear no more the shame of the heathen* (*v.* 15), especially when it is reformed ; when sin, which is the reproach of any people, particularly of God's professing people, is taken away, then they *hear no more the reproach of the people.* Note, When God returns in mercy to a people that return to him in duty, all their grievances will be soon redressed and their honour retrieved.

16 Moreover the word of the Lord came unto me, saying, 17 Son of man, when the house of Israel dwelt in their own land, they defiled it by their own way and by their doings: their way was before me as the uncleanness of a removed woman. 18 Wherefore I poured my fury upon them for the blood that they had shed upon the land, and for their idols *wherewith* they had polluted it: 19 And I scattered them among the heathen, and they were dispersed through the countries: according to their way and according to their doings I judged them. 20 And when they entered unto the heathen, whither they went, they profaned my holy name, when they said to them, These *are* the people of the Lord, and are gone forth out of his land. 21 But I had pity for mine holy name, which the house of Israel had profaned among the heathen, whither they went. 22 Therefore say unto the house of Israel, Thus saith the Lord God; I do not *this* for your sakes, O house of Israel, but for mine holy name's sake, which ye have profaned among the heathen, whither ye went. 23 And I will sanctify my great name, which was profaned among the heathen, which ye have profaned in the midst of them; and the heathen shall know that I *am* the Lord, saith the Lord God, when I shall be sanctified in you before their eyes. 24 For I will take you from among the heathen, and gather you out of all countries, and will bring you into your own land.

When God promised the poor captives a glorious return, in due time, to their own land, it was a great discouragement to their hopes that they were unworthy, utterly unworthy, of such a favour; therefore, to remove that discouragement, God here shows them that he would do it for them purely *for his own name's sake,* that he might be glorified in them and by them, that he might manifest and magnify his mercy and goodness, that attribute which of all others is most his glory. And, the restoration of that people being typical of our redemption by Christ, this is intended further to show that the ultimate end aimed at in our salvation,

to which all the steps of it were made subservient, was the glory of God. To this end Christ directed all he did in that short prayer, *Father, glorify thy name;* and God declared it was his end in all he did in the immediate answer given to that prayer, by a voice from heaven: *I have glorified it, and I will glorify it yet again,* John xii. 28. Now observe here,

1. How God's name had suffered both by the sins and by the miseries of Israel; and this was more to be regretted than all their sorrow, which they had brought upon themselves; for the honour of God lies nearer the hearts of good men than any interests of their own. 1. God's glory had been injured by the sin of Israel when they were in their own land, *v.* 17. It was a good land, a holy land, a land that had the eye of God upon it. *But they defiled it by their own way,* their wicked way; that is *our own* way, the way of our own choice; and we ourselves must bear the blame and shame of it. The sin of a people defiles their land, renders it abominable to God and uncomfortable to themselves; so that they cannot have any holy communion with him nor with one another. What was unclean might not be made use of. By the abuse of the gifts of God's bounty to us we forfeit the use of them; and, the mind and conscience being defiled with guilt, no comfort is allowed us, *nothing is pure* to us. Their way in the eye of God was like the pollution of a woman during the days of her separation, which shut her out from the sanctuary and made every thing she touched ceremonially unclean, Lev. xv. 19. Sin is that *abominable thing which the Lord hates,* and which he cannot endure to look upon. They *shed blood* and *worshipped idols* (*v.* 18) and with those sins *defiled the land.* For this God *poured out his fury* upon them, *scattered them among the heathen.* Their own land was sick of them, and they were sent into other lands. Herein God was righteous, and was justified in what he did; none could say that he did them any wrong, nay, he did justice to his own honour, for he *judged them according to their way and according to their doings, v.* 19. And yet, the matter being not rightly understood, he was not glorified in it; for the enemies did say, as Moses pleaded the Egyptians would say if he had destroyed them in the wilderness, that *for mischief he brought them forth.* Their neighbours considered them rather as a holy people than as a sinful people, and therefore took occasion from the calamities they were in, instead of glorifying God, as they might justly have done, to reproach him and put contempt upon him; and God's name was *continually every day blasphemed* by their oppressors, Isa. lii. 5. 2. When they *entered into the land of the heathen* God had no glory by them there; but, on the contrary, his holy name was profaned, *v.* 20. (1.) It was profaned by the sins of Israel; they were no credit to their profession wherever they

went, but, on the contrary, a reproach to it. The *name of God* and his holy religion was *blasphemed through them*, Rom. ii. 24. When those that pretended to be in relation to God, in covenant and communion with him, were found corrupt in their morals, slaves to their appetites and passions, dishonest in their dealings, and false to their words and the trusts reposed in them, the enemies of the Lord had thereby great occasion given them to blaspheme, especially when they quarrelled with their God for correcting them, than which nothing could be more scandalous. (2.) It was profaned by the sufferings of Israel; for from them the enemies of God took occasion to reproach God, as unable to protect his own worshippers and to make good his own grants. They said, in scorn, "*These are the people of the land,* these wicked people (you see he could not keep them in their obedience to his precepts), these *miserable people*—you see he could not keep them in the enjoyment of his favours. These are *the people that came out of Jehovah's land,* they are the very scum of the nations. Are these those that had statutes so righteous whose lives are so unrighteous? Is this the nation that is so much celebrated for a *wise and understanding people,* and that is said to have *God so nigh unto them?* Do these belong to that brave, that holy nation, who appear here so vile, so abject?" Thus God sold his people and did not *increase his wealth by their price,* Ps. xliv. 12. The reproach they were under reflected upon him.

II. Let us now see how God would retrieve his honour, secure it, and advance it, by working a great reformation upon them and then working a great salvation for them. He would have *scattered them among the heathen, were it not that he feared the wrath of the enemy,* Deut. xxxii. 26, 27. But, though they were unworthy of his compassion, yet *he had pity for his own holy name,* and a thousand pities it was that that should be trampled upon and abused. He looked with compassion on his own honour, which lay bleeding among the heathen, on that jewel which was trodden into the dirt, which *the house of Israel,* even in the land of their captivity, *had profaned,* v. 21. In pity to that God brought them out from the heathen, because their sins were more scandalous there than they had been in their own land. "Therefore I *will gather you out of all countries and bring you into your own land,* v. 24. *Not for your sake,* because you are worthy of such a favour, for you are most unworthy, but *for my holy name's sake* (v. 22), that *I may sanctify my great name,*" v. 23. Observe, by the way, God's holy name is his great name. His holiness is his greatness; so he reckons it himself. Nor does any thing make a man truly great but being truly good, and partaking of God's holiness. God will magnify his name as a holy name, for he will sanctify it: *I will sanctify my name which*

you have profaned. When God performs that which he has sworn by his holiness, then he sanctifies his name. The effect of this shall be very happy: *The heathen shall know that I am the Lord when I shall be sanctified in you before their eyes* and yours. When God proves his own holy name, and his saints praise it, then he is sanctified in them, and this contributes to the propagating of the knowledge of him. Observe, 1. God's reasons of mercy are all fetched from within himself; he will bring his people out of Babylon, not for their sakes, but *for his own name's sake,* because he will be glorified. 2. God's goodness takes occasion from man's badness to appear so much the more illustrious; *therefore* he will sanctify his name by the pardon of sin, because it has been profaned by the commission of sin.

25 Then will I sprinkle clean water upon you, and ye shall be clean: from all your filthiness, and from all your idols, will I cleanse you. 26 A new heart also will I give you, and a new spirit will I put within you: and I will take away the stony heart out of your flesh, and I will give you a heart of flesh. 27 And I will put my Spirit within you, and cause you to walk in my statutes, and ye shall keep my judgments, and do *them.* 28 And ye shall dwell in the land that I gave to your fathers; and ye shall be my people, and I will be your God. 29 I will also save you from all your uncleannesses: and I will call for the corn, and will increase it, and lay no famine upon you. 30 And I will multiply the fruit of the tree, and the increase of the field, that ye shall receive no more reproach of famine among the heathen. 31 Then shall ye remember your own evil ways, and your doings that *were* not good, and shall loathe yourselves in your own sight for your iniquities and for your abominations. 32 Not for your sakes do I *this,* saith the Lord God, be it known unto you: be ashamed and confounded for your own ways, O house of Israel. 33 Thus saith the Lord God; In the day that I shall have cleansed you from all your iniquities I will also cause *you* to dwell in the cities, and the wastes shall be builded. 34 And the desolate land shall be tilled, whereas it lay desolate in the sight of all that passed by. 35 And

they shall say, This land that was desolate is become like the garden of Eden; and the waste and desolate and ruined cities *are become* fenced, *and* are inhabited. 36 Then the heathen that are left round about you shall know that I the LORD build the ruined *places, and* plant that that was desolate: I the LORD have spoken *it*, and I will do *it*. 37 Thus saith the Lord GOD; I will yet *for* this be enquired of by the house of Israel, to do *it* for them; I will increase them with men like a flock. 38 As the holy flock, as the flock of Jerusalem in her solemn feasts; so shall the waste cities be filled with flocks of men : and they shall know that I *am* the LORD.

The people of God might be discouraged in their hopes of a restoration by the sense not only of their unworthiness of such a favour (which was answered, in the foregoing verses, with this, that God, in doing it, would have an eye to his own glory, not to their worthiness), but of their unfitness for such a favour, being still corrupt and sinful; and that is answered in these verses, with a promise that God would by his grace prepare and qualify them for the mercy and then bestow it on them. And this was in part fulfilled in that wonderful effect which the captivity in Babylon had upon the Jews there, that it effectually cured them of their inclination to idolatry. But it is further intended as a draught of the covenant of grace, and a specimen of those spiritual blessings with which we are blessed in heavenly things by that covenant. As (*ch.* xxxiv.) after a promise of their return the prophecy insensibly slid into a promise of the coming of Christ, the great Shepherd, so here it insensibly slides into a promise of the Spirit, and his gracious influences and operations, which we have as much need of for our sanctification as we have of Christ's merit for our justification.

I. God here promises that he will work a good work in them, to qualify them for the good work he intended to bring about for them, *v.* 25—27. We had promises to the same purport, *ch.* xi. 18—20. 1. That God would cleanse them from the pollutions of sin (*v.* 25): *I will sprinkle clean water upon you,* which signifies both the blood of Christ sprinkled upon the conscience to purify that and to take away the sense of guilt (as those that were sprinkled with the water of purification were thereby discharged from their ceremonial uncleanness) and the grace of the Spirit sprinkled on the whole soul to purify it from all corrupt inclinations and dispositions, as Naaman was cleansed from his leprosy by dipping in Jordan. Christit

was himself clean, else his blood could not have been cleansing to us; and it is a Holy Spirit that makes us holy: *From all your filthiness and from all your idols will I cleanse you.* And (*v.* 29) *I will save you from all your uncleannesses.* Sin is defiling, idolatry particularly is so; it renders sinners odious to God and burdensome to themselves. When guilt is pardoned, and the corrupt nature sanctified, then we are cleansed from our filthiness, and there is no other way of being saved from it. This God promises his people here, in order to his being sanctified in them, *v.* 23. We cannot sanctify God's name unless he sanctify our hearts, nor live to his glory, but by his grace. 2. That God would give them a *new heart,* a disposition of mind excellent in itself and vastly different from what it was before. God will work an inward change in order to a universal change. Note, All that have an interest in the new covenant, and a title to the new Jerusalem, have a new heart and a new spirit, and these are necessary in order to their walking in *newness of life.* This is that *divine nature* which believers are by the promises made partakers of. 3. That, instead of a *heart of stone,* insensible and inflexible, unapt to receive any divine impressions and to return any devout affections, God would give a *heart of flesh,* a soft and tender heart, that has spiritual senses exercised, conscious to itself of spiritual pains and pleasures, and complying in every thing with the will of God. Note, Renewing grace works as great a change in the soul as the turning of a dead stone into living flesh. 4. That since, besides our inclination to sin, we complain of an inability to do our duty, God will *cause them to walk in his statutes,* will not only show them the way of his statutes before them, but incline them to walk in it, and thoroughly furnish them with wisdom and will, and active powers, for every good work. In order to this he will *put his Spirit within them,* as a teacher, guide, and sanctifier. Note, God does not force men to walk in his statutes by external violence, but causes them to walk in his statutes by an internal principle. And observe what use we ought to make of this gracious power and principle promised us, and put within us : *You shall keep my judgments.* If God will do his part according to the promise, we must do ours according to the precept. Note, The promise of God's grace to enable us for our duty should engage and quicken our constant care and endeavour to do our duty. God's promises must drive us to his precepts as our rule, and then his precepts must send us back to his promises for strength, for without his grace we can do nothing.

II. God here promises that he will take them into covenant with himself. The sum of the covenant of grace we have, *v.* 28. *You shall be my people, and I will be your God.* It is not, "If you will be my people, I will be your God" (though it is very true that we cannot expect to have God to be to us a God unless we be to him a people), but he has chosen us, and loved us, first, not we him; therefore the condition is of grace, is by promise, as well as the reward; not of merit, not of works: "*You shall be my people; I will make you so;* I will give you the nature and spirit of my people, and then *I will be your God.*" And this is the foundation and top-stone of a believer's happiness; it is heaven itself, Rev. xxi. 3, 7.

III. He promises that he will bring about all that good for them which the exigence of their case calls for. When they are thus prepared for mercy, 1. Then they shall return to their possessions and be settled again in them (*v.* 28): *You shall dwell in the land that I gave to your fathers.* God will, in bringing them back to it, have an eye not to any merit of theirs, but to the promise made to the fathers; for therefore he gave it to them at first, Deut. vii. 7, 8. *Therefore* he is gracious, because he has said that he will be so. This shall follow upon the blessed reformation God would work among them (*v.* 33): "*In the day that I shall have cleansed you from all your iniquities,* and so shall have made you meet for the inheritance, *I will cause you to dwell in the cities,* and so put you in possession of the inheritance." This is God's method of mercy indeed, first to part men from their sins, and then to restore them to their comforts. 2. Then they shall enjoy a plenty of all good things. When they are saved *from their uncleanness,* from their sins which kept good things from them, then *I will call for the corn and will increase it, v.* 29. Plenty comes at God's call, and the plenty he calls for shall be still growing; and when he speaks the word the fruit both of the tree and of the field shall multiply. As the inhabitants multiply the productions shall multiply for their maintenance; for he that sends mouths will send meat. Famine was one of the judgments which they had laboured under, and it had been as much as any a reproach to them, that they should be starved in a land so famed for fruitfulness. But now *I will lay no famine upon you;* and none are under that rod without having it laid on by him. Then they *shall receive no more reproach of famine,* shall never be again upbraided with that, nor shall it ever be said that God is a Master that keeps his servants to short allowance. Nay, they shall not only be cleared from the reproach of famine, but they shall have the credit of abundance. The land that had long *lain desolate in the sight of all that passed by,* that looked upon it, some with contempt and some with compassion, shall again *be tilled* (*v.* 34), and, having long lain fallow, it will now be the more fruitful. Observe, God will *call for the corn* and yet they must *till the ground* for it. Note, Even promised mercies must be laboured for; for the promise is not to super-

sede, but to quicken and encourage our industry and endeavour. And such a blessing will God command on the *hand of the diligent* that all who pass by shall take notice of it, with wonder, *v.* 35. They shall say, "See what a blessed change here is, how *this land that was desolate* has *become like the garden of Eden,* the desert turned again into a paradise." Note, God has honours in reserve for his people to be crowned with sufficient to counterbalance the contempt they are now loaded with, and in them he will be honoured. This wonderful increase both of the people of the land and of its products is compared (*v.* 38) to the large flocks of cattle that are brought to Jerusalem, to be sacrificed at one of the solemn feasts. Even the cities that now lie waste shall be filled with *flocks of men,* not like the flocks with which the pastures are *covered over* (Ps. lxv. 13), but like the holy flock which is brought to the courts of the Lord's house. Note, *Then* the increase of the numbers of a people is honourable and comfortable indeed when they are all dedicated to God as a holy flock, to be presented to him for *living sacrifices.* Crowds are a lovely sight in God's temple.

IV. He shows what shall be *the happy effects of this blessed change.* 1. It shall have a happy effect upon the people of God themselves, for it shall bring them to an ingenuous repentance for their sins (*v.* 31): *Then shall you remember your own evil ways and shall loathe yourselves.* See here what sin is; it is an *abomination,* a loathsome thing, that abominable thing which the Lord hates. See what is the first step towards repentance; it is *remembering our own evil ways,* reflecting seriously upon the sins we have committed and being particular in recapitulating them. We must remember against ourselves not only our gross enormities, *our own evil ways,* but our defects and infirmities, *our doings that were not good,* not so good as they should have been; not only our direct violations of the law, but our coming short of it. See what is evermore a companion of true repentance, and that is self-loathing, a holy shame and confusion of face: "*You shall loathe yourselves in your own sight,* seeing how loathsome you have made yourselves in the sight of God." Self-love is at the bottom of sin, which we cannot but blush to see the absurdity of; but our quarrelling with ourselves is in order to our being, upon good grounds, reconciled to ourselves. And, *lastly,* see what is the most powerful inducement to an evangelical repentance, and that is a sense of the mercy of God; when God settles them in the midst of plenty, *then they shall loathe themselves for their iniquities.* Note, The goodness of God should overcome our badness and *lead us to repentance.* The more we see of God's readiness to receive us into favour upon our repentance the more reason we shall see to be ashamed of ourselves that we could ever sin against so much love. That heart is hard indeed that will not be thus melted. 2. It shall have a happy effect upon their neighbours, for it shall bring them to a more clear knowledge of God (v. 36): " *Then the heathen that are left round about you,* that spoke ignorantly of God (for so all those do that speak *ill* of him) when they saw the land of Israel desolate, shall begin to know better, and to speak more intelligently of God, being convinced that he is able to rebuild the most desolate cities and to replant the most desolate countries, and that, though the course of his favours to his people may be obstructed for a time, they shall not be cut off for ever. They shall be made to know the truth of divine revelation by the exact agreement which they shall discern between God's word which he has spoken to Israel and his works which he has done for them : *I the Lord have spoken it, and I will do it.* With us saying and doing are two things, but they are not so with God.

V. He proposes these things to them, not as the *recompence* of their merits, but as the return of their prayers.

1. Let them not think that they have deserved it : *Not for your sakes do I this, be it known to you* (v. 22, 32) ; no, *be you ashamed and confounded for your own ways.* God is *doing* this, all this which he has promised; it is as sure to be done as if it were done already, and present events have a tendency towards it. But then, (1.) They must renounce the merit of their own good works, and be brought to acknowledge that it is not for their sakes that it is done; so, when God brought Israel into Canaan the first time, an express *caveat* was entered against this thought. Deut. ix. 4—6, *It is not for thy righteousness.* It is not for the sake of any of their good qualities or good deeds, not because God had any need of them, or expected any benefit by them. No, in showing mercy he acts by prerogative, not for our deserts, but for his own honour. See how emphatically this is expressed : *Be it known to you,* it is *not for your sakes,* which intimates that we are apt to entertain a high conceit of our own merits and are with difficulty persuaded to disclaim a confidence in them. But, one way or other, God will make all his favourites to know and own that it is his grace, and not their goodness, his mercy, and not their merit, that made them so ; and that therefore not unto them, not unto them, but unto him, is all the glory due. (2.) They must repent of the sin of their own evil ways. They must own that the mercies they receive from God are not only not merited, but that they are a thousand times forfeited ; and therefore they must be so far from boasting of their good works that they must be ashamed and confounded for their evil ways, and then they are best prepared for mercy.

2. Yet let them know that they must desire and expect it (v. 37): *I will yet for this be*

964

enquired of by the house of Israel. God has spoken, and he will do it, and he will be sought unto for it. He requires that his people should *seek unto him,* and he will incline their hearts to do it, when he is coming towards them in ways of mercy. (1.) They must pray for it, for by prayer God is sought unto, and enquired after. What is the matter of God's promises must be the matter of our prayers. By asking for the mercy promised we must give glory to the donor, express a value for the gift, own our dependence, and put honour upon prayer which God has put honour upon. Christ himself must ask, and then God will *give him the heathen for his inheritance,* must *pray the Father,* and then he will *send the Comforter;* much more must we ask that we may receive. (2.) They must consult the oracles of God, and thus also God is sought unto and enquired after. The mercy must be, not an act of providence only, but a child of promise ; and therefore the promise must be looked at, and prayer made for it with an eye of faith fastened upon the promise, which must be both the guide and the ground of our expectations. Both these ways we find God enquired of by Daniel, in the name of the house of Israel, when he was about to do those great things for them ; he consulted the oracles of God, for he *understood by books,* the book of the prophet Jeremiah, both what was to be expected and when ; and then he *set his face* to seek God by prayer, Dan. ix. 2, 3. Note, Our communion with God must be kept up by the word and prayer in all the operations of his providence concerning us and in both he must be enquired of.

CHAP. XXXVII.

The threatenings of the destruction of Judah and Jerusalem for their sins, which we had in the former part of this book, were not so terrible, but the promises of their restoration and deliverance for the glory of God, which we have here in the latter part of the book, are as comfortable ; and as those were illustrated with many visions and similitudes, for the awakening of a holy fear, so are these, for the encouraging of a humble faith. God had assured them, in the foregoing chapter, that he would gather the house of Israel, even all of it, and would bring them out of their captivity, and return them to their own land ; but there were two things that rendered this very unlikely :—I. That they were so dispersed among their enemies, so destitute of all helps and advantages which might favour or further their return, and so dispirited likewise in their own minds ; upon all these accounts they are here, in vision, compared to a valley full of the dry bones of dead men, which should be brought together and raised to life. The vision of this we have (ver. 1—10) and the explication of it, with its application to the present case, ver. 11—14. II. That they were so divided among themselves, too much of the old enmity between Judah and Ephraim remaining even in their captivity. But, as to this, by a sign of two sticks made one in the hand of the prophet is foreshown the happy coalition that should be, at their return, between the two nations of Israel and Judah, ver. 15—22. In this there was a type of the uniting of Jews and Gentiles, Jews and Samaritans, in Christ and his church. And so the prophet slides into a prediction of the kingdom of Christ, which should be set up in the world with God's tabernacle in it, and of the glories and graces of that kingdom, ver. 23—28.

THE hand of the LORD was upon me, and carried me out in the Spirit of the LORD, and set me down in the midst of the valley which *was* full of bones, 2 And caused me to pass by them round about: and, behold, *there were* very many in the open valley, and, lo, *they were* very dry. 3 And he said unto me, Son of man, can these bones live? And I answered, O Lord GOD, thou knowest. 4 Again he said unto me, Prophesy upon these bones, and say unto them, O ye dry bones, hear the word of the LORD. 5 Thus saith the Lord GOD unto these bones; Behold, I will cause breath to enter into you, and ye shall live: 6 And I will lay sinews upon you, and will bring up flesh upon you, and cover you with skin, and put breath in you, and ye shall live; and ye shall know that I *am* the LORD. 7 So I prophesied as I was commanded: and as I prophesied, there was a noise, and behold a shaking, and the bones came together, bone to his bone. 8 And when I beheld, lo, the sinews and the flesh came up upon them, and the skin covered them above: but *there was* no breath in them. 9 Then said he unto me, Prophesy unto the wind, prophesy, son of man, and say to the wind, Thus saith the Lord GOD; Come from the four winds, O breath, and breathe upon these slain, that they may live. 10 So I prophesied as he commanded me, and the breath came into them, and they lived, and stood up upon their feet, an exceeding great army. 11 Then he said unto me, Son of man, these bones are the whole house of Israel: behold, they say, Our bones are dried, and our hope is lost: we are cut off for our parts. 12 Therefore prophesy and say unto them, Thus saith the Lord GOD; Behold, O my people, I will open your graves, and cause you to come up out of your graves, and bring you into the land of Israel. 13 And ye shall know that I *am* the LORD, when I have opened your graves, O my people, and brought you up out of your graves, 14 And shall put my spirit in you, and ye shall live, and I shall place you in your own land: then shall ye know that I the LORD have spoken *it*, and performed *it*, saith the LORD.

Here is, I. The vision of a resurrection from death to life, and it is a glorious resurrection. This is a thing so utterly unknown

to nature, and so contrary to its principles *(a privatione ad habitum non datur regressus —from privation to possession there is no return)*, that we could have no thought of it but *by the word of the Lord;* and that it is certain by that word that there shall be a general resurrection of the dead some have urged from this vision, "For" (say they) "otherwise it would not properly be made a sign for the confirming of their faith in the promise of their deliverance out of Babylon, as the coming of the Messiah is mentioned for the confirming of their faith touching a former deliverance," Isa. vii. 14. But,

1. Whether it be a confirmation or no, it is without doubt a most lively representation of a threefold resurrection, besides that which it is primarily intended to be the sign of. (1.) The resurrection of souls from the death of sin to the life of righteousness, to a holy, heavenly, spiritual, and divine life, by the power of divine grace going along with the word of Christ, John v. 24, 25. (2.) The resurrection of the gospel church, or any part of it, from an afflicted persecuted state, especially under the yoke of the New-Testament Babylon, to liberty and peace. (3.) The resurrection of the body at the great day, especially the bodies of believers that shall rise to life eternal.

2. Let us observe the particulars of this vision.

(1.) The deplorable condition of these dead bones. The prophet was made, [1.] to take an exact view of them. By a prophetic impulse and a divine power he was, in vision, carried out and set *in the midst of a valley,* probably that plain spoken of *ch.* iii. 22, where God then *talked with him;* and it was *full of bones,* of dead men's bones, not piled up on a heap, as in a charnel-house, but scattered upon the face of the ground, as if some bloody battle had been fought here, and the slain left unburied till all the flesh was devoured or putrefied, and nothing left but the bones, and those disjointed from one another and dispersed. He *passed by them round about,* and he observed not only that they were very many (for there are multitudes gone to the congregation of the dead), but that, *lo, they were very dry,* having been long exposed to the sun and wind. The bones that have been *moistened with marrow* (Job xxi. 24), when they have been any while dead, lose all their moisture, and are dry as dust. The body is now fenced with bones (Job x. 11), but then they will themselves be defenceless. The Jews in Babylon were like those dead and dry bones, unlikely ever to come together, to be so much as a skeleton, less likely to be formed into a body, and least of all to be a living body. However, they lay *unburied* in the open *valley,* which encouraged the hopes of their resurrection, as of the two witnesses, Rev. xi. 8, 9. The bones of Gog and Magog shall be buried (*ch.* xxxix. 12, 15), for their destruction is final;

but the bones of Israel are in the *open valley*, under the eye of Heaven, for there is *hope in their end*. [2.] He was made to own their case deplorable, and not to be helped by any power less than that of God himself (*v.* 3): " Son of man, *can these bones live?* Is it a thing likely? Canst thou devise how it should be done? Can thy philosophy reach to put life into dry bones, or thy politics to restore a captive nation?" " No," says the prophet, " I know not how it should be done, but *thou knowest.*" He does not say, " They cannot live," lest he should seem to limit the Holy One of Israel; but, " Lord, thou knowest whether they can and whether they shall; if thou dost not put life into them, it is certain that they cannot live." Note, God is perfectly acquainted with his own power and his own purposes, and will have us to refer all to them, and to see and own that his wondrous works are such as could not be effected by any counsel or power but his own.

(2.) The means used for the bringing of these dispersed bones together and these dead and dry bones to life. It must be done by prophecy. Ezekiel is ordered to *prophesy upon these bones* (*v.* 4 and again *v.* 9), to *prophesy to the wind.* So he *prophesied as he was commanded, v.* 7, 10. [1.] He must preach, and he did so; and the dead bones lived by a power that went along with the word of God which he preached. [2.] He must pray, and he did so; and the dead bones were made to live in answer to prayer; for *a spirit of life* entered into them. See the efficacy of the word and prayer, and the necessity of both, for the raising of dead souls. God bids his ministers *prophesy upon the dry bones.* Say unto them, *Live;* yea, say unto them, *Live;* and they do as they are commanded, calling to them again and again, *O you dry bones! hear the word of the Lord.* But we call in vain, still they are dead, still they are very dry; we must therefore be earnest with God in prayer for the working of the Spirit with the word: *Come, O breath!* and breathe upon them. God's grace can save souls without our preaching, but our preaching cannot save them without God's grace, and that grace must be sought by prayer. Note, Ministers must faithfully and diligently use the means of grace, even with those that there seems little probability of gaining upon. To prophesy upon dry bones seems as great a penance as to water a dry stick; and yet, whether they will hear or forbear, we must discharge our trust, must *prophesy as we are commanded,* in the name of him who raises the dead and is the fountain of life.

(3.) The wonderful effect of these means. Those that do as they are commanded, as they are commissioned, in the face of the greatest discouragements, need not doubt of success, for God will own and enrich his own appointments. [1.] Ezekiel looked down and prophesied upon the bones in the valley, 966

and they became human bodies. *First,* That which he had to *say to them* was that God would infallibly raise them to life: *Thus saith the Lord God unto these bones, You shall live, v.* 5 and again *v.* 6. And he that speaks the word will thereby do the work; he that says, They *shall live,* will make them alive: He will *clothe them with skin and flesh* (*v.* 6), as he did at first, Job x. 11. He that made us so fearfully and wonderfully, and curiously wrought us, can in like manner new-make us, for *his arm is not shortened. Secondly,* That which was immediately done for them was that they were moulded anew into shape. We may well suppose it was with great liveliness and vigour that the prophet prophesied, especially when he found what he said begin to take effect. Note, The opening, sealing, and applying of the promises, are the ordinary means of our participation of a new and divine nature. As Ezekiel prophesied in this vision *there was a noise,* a word of command, from heaven, seconding what he said; or it signified the motion of the angels that were to be employed as the ministers of the divine Providence in the deliverance of the Jews, and we read of the *noise of their wings* (Ezek. i. 24) and the *sound of their going,* 2 Sam. v. 24. *And, behold, a shaking,* or commotion, among the bones. Even dead and dry bones begin to move when they are called to hear the word of the Lord. This was fulfilled when, upon Cyrus's proclamation of liberty, those whose spirits God had stirred up began to think of making use of that liberty, and getting ready to be gone. When *there was a noise, behold, a shaking;* when David heard *the sound of the going on the tops of the mulberry-trees* then he bestirred himself; then there was a *shaking.* When Paul heard the voice saying, *Why persecutest thou me?* behold, a shaking of the dry bones; he *trembled* and was *astonished.* But this was not all: *The bones came together bone to his bone,* under a divine direction; and, though there is in man a multitude of bones, yet of all the bones of those numerous slain not one was missing, not one missed its way, not one missed its place, but, as it were by instinct, each knew and found its fellow. The dispersed bones came together and the displaced bones were knit together, the divine power supplying that to these dry bones which in a living body *every joint supplies.* Thus shall it be in the resurrection of the dead; the scattered atoms shall be ranged and marshalled in their proper place and order, and *every bone come to his bone,* by the same wisdom and power by which the bones were first *formed in the womb of her that is with child.* Thus it was in the return of the Jews; those that were scattered in several parts of the province of Babylon came to their respective families, and all as it were by consent to the general rendezvous, in order to their return. By degrees *sinews* and *flesh* came upon these bones, and the *skin covered them, v.* 8. This was fulfilled when the captives got their effects about them, and the *men of their place helped them* with *silver,* and *gold,* and whatever they needed for their remove, Ezra i. 4. But still there was *no breath in them;* they wanted spirit and courage for such a difficult and hazardous enterprise as this was of returning to their own land. [2.] Ezekiel then looked up and prophesied to the *wind,* or *breath,* or *spirit,* and said, *Come, O breath! and breathe upon these slain.* As good have been still dry bones as dead bodies: but as for God *his work is perfect;* he is not the God of the dead, but of the living; therefore *breathe upon them that they may live.* In answer to this request, *the breath* immediately came *into them, v.* 10. Note, the spirit of life is from God; he at first in the creation breathed into man the breath of life, and so he will at last in the resurrection. The dispirited despairing captives were wonderfully animated with resolution to break through all the discouragements that lay in the way of their return and applied themselves to it with all imaginable vigour And then they *stood upon their feet, an exceedingly great army;* not only living men, but effective men, fit for service in the wars and formidable to all that gave them any opposition. Note, With God nothing is impossible. He can *out of stones raise up children unto Abraham* and out of dead and dry bones levy an exceedingly great army to fight his battles and plead his cause.

II. The application of this vision to the present calamitous condition of the Jews in captivity: *These bones are the whole house of Israel,* both the ten tribes and the two. See in this what they are and what they shall be. 1. The depth of despair to which they are now reduced, *v.* 11. They all give up themselves for lost and gone; they say, "*Our bones are dried,* our strength is exhausted, our spirits are gone, *our hope is* all *lost;* every thing we looked for succour and relief from fails us, and *we are cut off for our parts.* Let who will cherish some hope, we see no ground for any." Note, When troubles continue long, hopes have been often frustrated, and all creature-confidences fail, it is not strange if the spirits sink; and nothing but an active faith in the power, promise, and providence of God will keep them from quite dying away. 2. The height of prosperity to which, notwithstanding this, they shall be advanced: "*Therefore,* because things have come thus to the last extremity, *prophesy to them,* and tell them, now is God's time to appear for them. *Jehovah-jireh—in the mount of the Lord it shall be seen, v.* 12—14. Tell them," (1.) "That they shall be brought out of the land of their enemies, where they are as it were buried alive: *I will open your graves.*" Those shall be restored, not only whose *bones* are *scattered at the grave's mouth* (Ps. cxli. 7), but who are buried in the grave; though the power of the enemy is like the *bars of*

the pit, which one would think it impossible to break through, strong as death and cruel as the grave, yet it shall be conquered. God can *bring* his people *up from the depths of the earth,* Ps. lxxi. 20. (2.) "That they shall be brought into their own land, where they shall live in prosperity: *I will bring you into the land of Israel (v.* 12) and *place you there (v.* 14), and will *put my spirit in you* and then *you shall live.*" Note, *Then* God puts spirit in us to good purpose, and so that we shall indeed live, when he puts his Spirit in us. And *(lastly)* in all this God will be glorified: *You shall know that I am the Lord (v.* 13), that I have *spoken it and performed it, v.* 14. Note, God's quickening the dead redounds more than any thing to his honour, and to the honour of his word, which he has magnified above all his name, and will magnify more and more by the punctual accomplishment of every tittle of it.

15 The word of the Lord came again unto me, saying, 16 Moreover, thou son of man, take thee one stick, and write upon it, For Judah, and for the children of Israel his companions: then take another stick, and write upon it, For Joseph, the stick of Ephraim, and *for* all the house of Israel his companions: 17 And join them one to another into one stick; and they shall become one in thine hand. 18 And when the children of thy people shall speak unto thee, saying, Wilt thou not show us what thou *meanest* by these? 19 Say unto them, Thus saith the Lord God; Behold, I will take the stick of Joseph, which *is* in the hand of Ephraim, and the tribes of Israel his fellows, and will put them with him, *even* with the stick of Judah, and make them one stick, and they shall be one in mine hand. 20 And the sticks whereon thou writest shall be in thine hand before their eyes. 21 And say unto them, Thus saith the Lord God; Behold, I will take the children of Israel from among the heathen, whither they be gone, and will gather them on every side, and bring them into their own land: 22 And I will make them one nation in the land upon the mountains of Israel; and one king shall be king to them all: and they shall be no more two nations, neither shall they be divided into two kingdoms any more at all: 23 Neither shall they defile themselves any

967

more with their idols, nor with their detestable things, nor with any of their transgressions: but I will save them out of all their dwelling-places, wherein they have sinned, and will cleanse them: so shall they be my people, and I will be their God. 24 And David my servant *shall be* king over them; and they all shall have one shepherd: they shall also walk in my judgments, and observe my statutes, and do them. 25 And they shall dwell in the land that I have given unto Jacob my servant, wherein your fathers have dwelt; and they shall dwell therein, *even*they, and their children, and their children's children for ever: and my servant Daniel *shall be* their prince for ever. 26 Moreover I will make a covenant of peace with them; it shall be an everlasting covenant with them: and I will place them, and multiply them, and will set my sanctuary in the midst of them for evermore. 27 My tabernacle also shall be with them: yea, I will be their God, and they shall be my people. 28 And the heathen shall know that I the LORD do sanctify Israel, when my sanctuary shall be in the midst of them for evermore.

Here are more exceedingly great and precious promises made of the happy state of the Jews after their return to their own land; but they have a further reference to the kingdom of the Messiah and the glories of gospel-times.

I. It is here promised that Ephraim and Judah shall be happily united in brotherly love and mutual serviceableness; so that whereas, ever since the desertion of the ten tribes from the house of David under Jeroboam, there had been continual feuds and animosities between the two kingdoms of Israel and Judah, and it is to be feared there had been some clashings between them even in the land of their captivity (Ephraim upon all occasions envying Judah and Judah vexing Ephraim), now it should be no longer, but there should be a coalition between them, and, notwithstanding the old differences that had been between them, they should agree to love one another and to do one another all good offices. This is here illustrated by a sign. The prophet was to take *two sticks*, and write upon one, For *Judah* (including Benjamin, those of the *children of Israel* that were *his companions*), upon the other, *For Joseph*, including the rest of the tribes, *v.* 16. These two sticks must be so framed as to fall into *one in his*

968

hand, v. 17. The people took notice of this, and desired him to *tell them the meaning of it,* for they knew he did not play with sticks for his diversion, as children do. Those that would know the meaning should ask the meaning of the word of God which they read and hear, and of the instituted signs by which spiritual and divine things are represented to us; the ministers' *lips* should *keep the knowledge* hereof and the people should *ask it at their mouth,* Mal. ii. 7. It is a necessary question for grown people, as well as children, to ask, *What mean you by this service,* by this sign? Exod. xii. 26. The meaning was that Judah and Israel should become *one in the hand of God, v.* 19. 1. They shall be one, one nation, *v.* 22. They shall have no separate interests, and, consequently, no divided affections. There shall be no mutual jealousies and animosities, no remembrance, no remains, of their former discord. But there shall be a perfect harmony between them, a good understanding one of another, a good disposition one to another, and a readiness to all good offices and services for one another's credit and comfort. They had been two sticks crossing and thwarting one another, nay, beating and bruising one another; but now they shall become one, supporting and strengthening one another. *Vis unita fortior—Force added to force is proportionally more efficient.* Behold, how good and how *pleasant a thing it is* to see Judah and Israel, that had long been at variance, now *dwelling together in unity.* Then they shall become acceptable to their God, amiable to their friends, and formidable to their enemies, Isa. xi. 13, 14. 2. They shall be one in *God's hand;* by his power they shall be united, and, being by his hand brought together, his hand shall keep them together, so that they shall not fly off, to be separated again. They shall be one in his hand, for his glory shall be the centre of their unity and his grace the cement of it. In him, in a regard to him and in his service and worship, they shall unite, and so shall become one. Both sides shall agree to put themselves into his hand, and so they shall be one. *Qui conveniunt in aliquo tertio inter se conveniunt—Those who agree in a third agree with each other.* Note, Those are best united that are one in God's hand, whose union with each other results from their union with Christ and their communion with God through him, Eph. i. 10. *One in us,* John xvii. 21. 3. They shall be one in their return out of captivity (*v.* 21): *I will take them from among the heathen,* and *gather them on every side,* and *bring them* together incorporated into one body *to their own land.* They shall be one in their separation from the heathen with whom they had mingled themselves: they shall both agree to part from them, and take their affections off from them, and no longer to comply with their usages, and then they will soon agree to join together in walking according to the rule of God's word. Their having been joint-sufferers will contribute to this blessed comprehension, when they begin to come to themselves and to consider things. Put many pieces of metal together into the furnace, and, when they are melted, they will run all together. It was time for them to strengthen one another when their oppressors were so busy to weaken and ruin them all. Likewise their being joint-sharers in the favour of God, and the great and common deliverance wrought out for them all, should help to unite them. God's loving them all was a good reason why they should love one another. Times of common joy, as well as times of common suffering, should be healing loving times. 4. They shall all be the subjects of one king, and so they shall become one. The Jews, after their return, were under one government, and not divided as formerly. But this certainly looks further, to the kingdom of Christ; he is that one King in allegiance to whom all God's spiritual Israel shall cheerfully unite, and under whose protection they shall all be gathered. All believers unite in *one Lord, one faith,* and *one baptism.* And the uniting of Jews and Gentiles in the gospel church, their becoming one fold under Christ the one great Shepherd, is doubtless the union that is chiefly looked at in this prophecy. By Christ the partition-wall between them was taken down, and the enmity slain, and of them *twain* was made *one new man,* Eph. ii. 14, 15.

II. It is here promised that the Jews shall by their captivity be cured of their inclination to idolatry; this shall be the happy fruit of that affliction, even the taking away of their sin (*v.* 23): *Neither shall they defile themselves any more with their idols,* those detestable defiling things, no, nor *with any of their* former *transgressions.* Note, When one sin is sincerely parted with all sin is abandoned too, for he that hates sin, as sin, will hate all sin. And those that are cured of their spiritual idolatry, their inordinate affection to the world and the flesh, that no longer make a god of their money or their belly, have a happy blow given to the root of all their transgressions. Two ways God will take to cure them of their idolatry:—
1. By bringing them out of the way of temptation to it: " *I will save them out of all their dwelling-places wherein they have sinned,* because there they met with the occasion of sin and allurements to it." Note, It is our wisdom to avoid the places where we have been overcome by temptations to sin, not to remain in them, or return to them, but to *save ourselves* out of them, as we would out of infected places; see Zech. ii. 7; Rev. xviii. 4. And it is a great mercy when God, in his providence, *saves us out of the dwelling-places where we have sinned,* and

keeps us from harm by keeping us out of harm's way, in answer to our prayer, *Lead us not into temptation, but deliver us from evil.* 2. By changing the disposition of their mind : " *I will cleanse them* (*v.* 28); that is, I will sanctify them, will work in them an aversion to the pollutions of sin and a complacency in the pleasures of holiness, and then you may be sure they will not defile themselves any more with their idols." Those whom God has cleansed he will keep clean.

III. It is here promised that they shall be the people of God, as *their God,* and the subjects and sheep of Christ their King and Shepherd. These promises we had before, and they are here repeated (*v.* 23, 24) for the encouragement of the faith of Israel : *They shall be my people,* to serve me, and *I will be their God,* to save them and to make them happy. *David, my servant, shall be king over them,* to fight their battles, to protect them from injury, and to rule them, to overrule all things that concern them for their good. He shall be *their shepherd,* to guide them and provide for them. Christ is this David, Israel's King of old; and those whom he subdues to himself, and makes willing in the day of his power, he makes to *walk in his judgments and to keep his statutes.*

IV. It is here promised that they shall dwell comfortably, *v.* 25, 26. They shall dwell in the land of Israel; for where else should Israelites dwell? And many things will concur to make their dwelling agreeable. 1. They shall have it by covenant; they shall come in again upon their old title, by virtue of the grant made unto *Jacob,* God's *servant.* As Christ was David, God's servant, so the church is Jacob, his servant too; and the members of the church shall come in for a share, as born in God's house. He will make a *covenant of peace* with them (*v.* 26), and in pursuance of that covenant he will *place them, and multiply them.* Note, Temporal mercies are doubly sweet when they come from the promise of the covenant, and not merely from common providence. 2. They shall come to it by prescription : " It is *the land wherein your fathers have dwelt,* and for that reason you cannot but have a special kindness for it, which God will graciously gratify." It was the inheritance of their ancestors, and therefore shall be theirs. They are *beloved for their fathers' sakes.* 3. They shall have it entailed upon them and the heirs of their body, and shall have their families built up, so that it shall not be lost for want of heirs. *They shall dwell therein* all their time, and never be turned out of possession, and they shall leave it for an inheritance to *their children and their children's children for ever,* who shall enjoy it when they are gone, the prospect of which will be a satisfaction to them. 4. They shall live under a good government, which will contribute very much to the comfort of their lives: *My servant David shall be their prince for ever.* This can be no other than Christ, of whom it was said, when he was brought into the world, *He shall reign over the house of Jacob for ever,* Luke i. 33. Note, It is the unspeakable comfort of all Christ's faithful subjects that, as his *kingdom* is *everlasting,* so he is an *everlasting King,* he lives to reign for ever; and, as sure and as long as he lives and reigns, they shall live and reign also. 5. The charter by which they hold all their privileges is indefeasible. God's covenant with them shall be an *everlasting covenant;* so the covenant of grace is, for it secures to us an everlasting happiness.

V. It is here promised that God will dwell among them; and this will make them dwell comfortably indeed: *I will set my sanctuary in the midst of them for evermore; my tabernacle also shall be with them,* v. 26, 27. 1. They shall have the tokens of God's special presence with them and his gracious residence among them. God will *in very deed dwell with them upon the earth,* for where his sanctuary is he is; when they profaned his sanctuary he took it from them (Isa. lxiv. 11), but now that they are purified God will dwell with them again. 2. They shall have opportunity of conversing with God, of hearing from him, speaking to him, and so keeping up communion with him, which will be the comfort of their lives. 3. They shall have the means of grace. By the oracles of God in his tabernacle they shall be made wiser and better, and all their children shall be taught of the Lord. 4. Thus their covenant relation to God shall be improved and the bond of it strengthened: *"I will be their God and they shall be my people,* and they shall know it by having my sanctuary among them, and shall have the comfort of it."

VI. Both God and Israel shall have the honour of this among the heathen, *v.* 26. "Now the heathen observe how Israel have profaned their own crown by their sins, and God has profaned it by his judgments; but then, when Israel is reformed and God has returned in mercy to them, the very heathen shall be made to know that *the Lord sanctifies* Israel, has a title to them and an interest in them more than other people, because his sanctuary is, and shall be, in the midst of them." Note, God designs the sanctification of those among whom he sets up his sanctuary. And blessed and holy are those who, enjoying the privileges of the sanctuary, give such proofs and evidences of their sanctification that the heathen may know it is no less than the almighty grace of God that sanctifies them. Such have God's sanctuary in the midst of them, the kingdom of God within them, in the principles of the spiritual life, and shall have it so for evermore in the enjoyments of an eternal life.

970

CHAP. XXXVIII.

This chapter, and that which follows it, are concerning Gog and Magog, a powerful enemy to the people of Israel, that should make a formidable descent upon them, and put them into a consternation, but their army should be routed and their design defeated; and this prophecy, it is most probable, had its accomplishment some time after the return of the people of Israel out of their captivity, whether in the struggles they had with the kings of Syria, especially Antiochus Epiphanes, or perhaps in some other way not recorded, we cannot tell. If the sacred history of the Old Testament had reached as far as the prophecy, we should have been better able to understand these chapters, but, for want of that key, we are locked out of the meaning of them. God had by the prophet assured his people of happy times after their return to their own land; but lest they should mistake the promises which related to the kingdom of the Messiah and the spiritual privileges of that kingdom, as if from them they might promise themselves an uninterrupted temporal prosperity, he here tells them, as Christ told his disciples to prevent the like mistake, that in the world they shall have tribulation, but they may be of good cheer, for they shall be victorious at last. This prophecy here of Gog and Magog is without doubt alluded to in that prophecy which relates to the latter days, and which seems to be yet unfulfilled (Rev. xx. 8), that Gog and Magog shall be gathered to battle against the camp of the saints, as the Old-Testament prophecies of the destruction of Babylon are alluded to, Rev. xviii. But, in both, the Old-Testament prophecies had their accomplishment in the Jewish church as the New-Testament prophecies shall have when the time comes in the Christian church. In this chapter we have intermixed, I. The attempt that Gog and Magog should make upon the land of Israel, the vast army they should bring into the field, and their vast preparations (ver. 4—7), their project and design in it (ver. 8 —13), God's hand in it, ver. 4. II. The great terror that this should strike upon the land of Israel, ver. 15, 16, 18—20. III. The divine restraint that these enemies should be under, and the divine protection that Israel should be under, ver. 2—4, and again ver. 14. IV. The defeat that should be given to those enemies by the immediate hand of God (ver. 21—23), which we shall hear more of in the next chapter.

AND the word of the LORD came unto me, saying, 2 Son of man, set thy face against Gog, the land of Magog, the chief prince of Meshech and Tubal, and prophesy against him, 3 And say, Thus saith the Lord GOD; Behold, I *am* against thee, O Gog, the chief prince of Meshech and Tubal: 4 And I will turn thee back, and put hooks into thy jaws, and I will bring thee forth, and all thine army, horses and horsemen, all of them clothed with all sorts *of armour, even* a great company *with* bucklers and shields, all of them handling swords: 5 Persia, Ethiopia, and Libya with them; all of them with shield and helmet: 6 Gomer, and all his bands; the house of Togarmah of the north quarters, and all his bands: *and* many people with thee. 7 Be thou prepared, and prepare for thyself, thou, and all thy company that are assembled unto thee, and be thou a guard unto them. 8 After many days thou shalt be visited: in the latter years thou shalt come into the land *that is* brought back from the sword, *and is* gathered out of many people, against the mountains of Israel, which have been always waste: but it is brought forth out of the nations, and they shall dwell safely all of them. 9 Thou shalt ascend and come like a storm, thou shalt be like a cloud to cover the land, thou, and all thy bands, and many people with thee. 10 Thus saith the Lord GOD; It shall also come to pass, *that* at the same time shall things come into thy mind, and thou shalt think an evil thought: 11 And thou shalt say, I will go up to the land of unwalled villages; I will go to them that are at rest, that dwell safely, all of them dwelling without walls, and having neither bars nor gates, 12 To take a spoil, and to take a prey; to turn thine hand upon the desolate places *that are now* inhabited, and upon the people *that are* gathered out of the nations, which have gotten cattle and goods, that dwell in the midst of the land. 13 Sheba, and Dedan, and the merchants of Tarshish, with all the young lions thereof, shall say unto thee, Art thou come to take a spoil? hast thou gathered thy company to take a prey? to carry away silver and gold, to take away cattle and goods, to take a great spoil?

The critical expositors have enough to do here to enquire out Gog and Magog. We cannot pretend either to add to their observations or to determine their controversies. Gog seems to be the king and Magog the kingdom; so that Gog and Magog are like Pharaoh and the Egyptians. Some think they find them afar off, in Scythia, Tartary, and Russia. Others think they find them nearer the land of Israel, in Syria, and Asia the Less. Ezekiel is appointed to prophesy against Gog, and to tell him that *God is against him, v.* 2, 3. Note, God does not only see those that are now the enemies of his church and set himself against them, but he foresees those that will be so and lets them know by his word that he is against them too, and yet is pleased to make use of them to serve his own purposes, for the glory of his own name; surely *their wrath* shall *praise him,* and the *remainder thereof he will restrain,* Ps. lxxvi. 10. Let us observe here,

I. The confusion which God designed to put this enemy to. It is remarkable that this is put first in the prophecy; before it is foretold that God will *bring him forth* against Israel it is foretold that God will *put hooks into his jaws* and *turn him back* (v. 4), that they might have assurance of their deliverance before they had the prospect given them of their danger. Thus tender is God of the comfort of his people, thus careful that they may not be frightened; even before the trouble begins he tells them it will end well.

II. The undertaking which he designed to engage him in, in order to this defeat and disappointment. 1. The nations that shall be confederate in this enterprise against Israel are many, and great, and mighty (*v.* 5, 6), *Persia, Ethiopia,* &c. Antiochus had an army made up of all the nations here named, and many others. These people had been at variance with one another, and yet in combination against Israel. How are those increased that trouble God's people! 2. They are well furnished with arms and ammunition, and bring a good train of artillery into the field—*horses and horsemen* (v. 4) bravely equipped *with all sorts of armour, bucklers and shields* for defence, *and all handling swords* for offence. Orders are given to make all imaginable preparation for this expedition (*v.* 7): "*Be thou prepared, and do thou prepare.* See what warlike preparations thou hast already in store, and, lest that should not suffice, make further preparation, *thou and all thy company.*" Let Gog himself be a guard to the rest of the confederates. As commander-in-chief, let him engage to take care of them and their safety; let him pass his word for their security, and take them under his particular protection. The leaders of an army, instead of exposing their soldiers needlessly and presumptuously, and throwing away their lives upon desperate undertakings, should study to be a guard to them, and, whenever they send them forth in danger, should contrive to support and cover them. This call to prepare seems to be ironical—*Do thy worst,* but I will *turn thee back;* like that Isa. viii. 9. *Gird yourselves, and you shall be broken in pieces.* 3. Their design is against *the mountains of Israel* (v. 8), against *the land that is brought back from the sword.* It is not long since it was harassed with the sword of war, and it has been always wasted, more or less, with one judgment or other; it is but newly *gathered out of many people,* and *brought forth out of the nations;* it has enjoyed comparatively but a short breathing-time, has scarcely recovered any strength since it was brought down by war and captivity; and therefore its neighbours need not fear its being too great, nay, and therefore it is very barbarous to pick a quarrel with it so soon. It is a people that *dwell safely, all of them, in unwalled villages,* very secure, and *having neither bars nor gates, v.* 11. It is a certain sign that they intend no mischief to their neighbours, for they fear no mischief from them. It cannot be thought that those will offend others who do not take care to defend themselves; and this aggravates the sin of these invaders. It is base and barbarous to *devise evil against thy neighbour while he dwells securely by thee,* and has no distrust of thee, Prov. iii. 29. But see here how *the clouds return after the rain* in this world, and what little reason we have ever to be secure till we come to heaven. It is not long since

Israel was brought back from the sword of one enemy, and behold the sword of another is drawn against it. Former troubles will not excuse us from further troubles; but when we think we have *put off the harness*, at least for some time, by a fresh and sudden alarm we may be called to *gird it on again;* and therefore we must never boast nor be off our guard. 4. That which the enemy has in view, in forming this project, is to enrich himself and to make himself master, not of the country, but of the wealth of it, to spoil and plunder it, and make a prey of it: *At the same* time that God intends to bring this matter about *things shall come into the mind* of this enemy, and *he shall think an evil thought*, v. 10. Note, All the mischief men do, and particularly the mischief they do to the church of God, arises from evil thoughts that come into their mind, ambitious thoughts, covetous thoughts, spiteful thoughts against those that are good, for the sake of their goodness. It came into Antiochus's mind what a singular people these religious Jews were, and how their worship witnessed against and condemned the idolatries of their neighbours, and therefore, in enmity to their religion, he would plague them. It came into his mind what a wealthy people they were, that they had *gotten cattle and goods in the midst of the land* (v. 12), and withal how weak they were, how unable to make any resistance, how easy it would be to carry off what they had, and how much glory this rapine would add to his victorious sword; these things coming into his mind, and one evil thought drawing on another, he came at last to this resolve (v. 11, 12): " *I will go up to the land of unwalled villages;* yea, that that I will; it will cost me nothing to make them all my own. I will go and disturb *those that are at rest*, without giving them any notice, not to crush their growing greatness, or chastise their insolence, or make reprisals upon them for any wrong they have done us (they had none of these pretences to make war upon them), but purely *to take a spoil and to take a prey*" (v. 12), in open defiance to all the laws of justice and equity, as much as the highwayman's killing the traveller that he may take his money. These were the thoughts that came into the mind of this wicked prince, and God knew them; nay, he knew them before they came into his mind, for he *understands our thoughts afar off*, Ps. cxxxix. 2. 5. According to the project thus formed he pours in all his forces upon the land of Israel, and finds those that are ready to come in to his assistance with the same prospects (v. 9): " *Thou shalt ascend and come like a storm*, with all the force, and fury, and fierceness imaginable, and *thou shalt be like a cloud to cover the land*, to darken it, and to threaten it, *thou and* not only *all thy bands*, all the force thou canst bring into the field, but *many people with thee*" (such as are spoken of v. 13), " *Sheba*

and Dedan, the Arabians and the Edomites, *and the merchants of Tarshish*, of Tyre and Sidon and other maritime cities, they and their *young lions* that are greedy of spoil and live upon it, *shall say*, Hast thou come to take the spoil of this land?" Yes he has; and therefore they wish him success. Or perhaps they envy him, or grudge it to him. "Hast thou come for riches who art thyself so rich already?" Or, knowing that God was on Israel's side, they thus ridicule his attempts, foreseeing that they would be baffled and that he would be disappointed of the prey he promised himself. Or, if he come to *take the prey*, they will come and join with him, and add to his forces. When Lysias, who was general of Antiochus's army, came against the Jews, the neighbouring nations joined with him (1 Mac. iii. 41), to share in the guilt, in hopes to share in the prey. *When thou sawest a thief then thou consentedst with him.*

14 Therefore, son of man, prophesy and say unto Gog, Thus saith the Lord God; In that day when my people of Israel dwelleth safely, shalt thou not know *it?* 15 And thou shalt come from thy place out of the north parts, thou, and many people with thee, all of them riding upon horses, a great company, and a mighty army: 16 And thou shalt come up against my people of Israel, as a cloud to cover the land; it shall be in the latter days, and I will bring thee against my land, that the heathen may know me, when I shall be sanctified in thee, O Gog, before their eyes. 17 Thus saith the Lord God; *Art* thou he of whom I have spoken in old time by my servants the prophets of Israel, which prophesied in those days *many* years that I would bring thee against them? 18 And it shall come to pass at the same time when Gog shall come against the land of Israel, saith the Lord God, *that* my fury shall come up in my face. 19 For in my jealousy, *and* in the fire of my wrath have I spoken, Surely in that day there shall be a great shaking in the land of Israel; 20 So that the fishes of the sea, and the fowls of the heaven, and the beasts of the field, and all creeping things that creep upon the earth, and all the men that *are* upon the face of the earth, shall shake at my presence, and the mountains shall be thrown down, and the steep

places shall fall, and every wall shall fall to the ground. 21 And I will call for a sword against him throughout all my mountains, saith the Lord God : every man's sword shall be against his brother. 22 And I will plead against him with pestilence and with blood ; and I will rain upon him, and upon his bands, and upon the many people that *are* with him, an overflowing rain, and great hailstones, fire, and brimstone. 23 Thus will I magnify myself, and sanctify myself ; and I will be known in the eyes of many nations, and they shall know that I *am* the Lord.

This latter part of the chapter is a repetition of the former ; the dream is doubled, for the thing is certain and to be very carefully regarded.

I. It is here again foretold that this spiteful enemy should make a formidable descent upon the land of Israel (*v.* 15) : " *Thou shalt come out of the north parts* (Syria lay on the north of Canaan) with *a mighty army,* shalt come like *a cloud,* and *cover the land of my people Israel, v.* 16. These words (*v.* 14), *When my people Israel dwell safely, shalt thou not know it ?* may be taken two ways :—1. As intimating his inducements to this attempt. "Thou shalt have intelligence brought thee how securely, and therefore how carelessly, the people of Israel dwell, which shall give rise to thy project against them ; for when thou knowest not only what a rich, but what an easy prey they are likely to be, thou wilt soon determine to fall upon them." Note, God's providence is to be acknowledged in the occasion, the small occasion perhaps, that is given, and that not designedly neither, to those first thoughts from which great enterprises take their original. God, to bring about his own purposes, lets men know that which yet he knows they will make a bad use of, as here. Or, 2. As intimating his disappointment in this attempt, which here, as before, the prophecy begins with : " *When my people Israel dwell safely,* not in their own apprehension only, but in reality, forasmuch as they dwell safely under the divine protection, shalt not thou be made to know it by the fruitlessness of thy endeavours to destroy them ? Thou shalt soon find that there is *no enchantment against Jacob,* that *no weapon formed against them shall prosper ;* thou shalt know to thy cost, shalt know to thy shame, that though they have no walls, nor bars, nor gates, they have God himself, a *wall of fire, round about them,* and that he who *touches them touches the apple of his eye ;* whosoever meddles with them meddles to his own hurt. And it is for the demonstrating of this to all the world that God will bring this mighty enemy against his people. Those

that *gathered themselves against Israel* said, *Let us take the spoil and take the prey,* but they *knew not the thoughts of the Lord,* Mic. iv. 11, 12. *I will bring thee against my land.* This is strange news, that God will not only permit his enemies to come against his own children, but will himself bring them ; but, if we understand what he aims at, we shall be well reconciled even to this : it is "*that the heathen may know me* to be the only living and true God *when I shall be sanctified in thee,* O Gog ! that is, in thy defeat and destruction *before their eyes,* that all the nations may see, and say, *There is none like unto the God of Jeshurun, that rides on the heavens for the help of his people.*" Note, God brings his people into danger and distress that he may have the honour of bringing about their deliverance, and suffers the enemies of his church to prevail awhile, though they profane his name by their sin, that he may have the honour of prevailing at last and sanctifying his own name in their ruin. Now it is said, This shall be *in the latter days,* namely, in the latter days of the Old-Testament church ; so the mischief that Antiochus did to Israel was ; but in the latter days of the New-Testament church another like enemy should arise, that should in like manner be defeated. Note, Effectual securities are treasured up in the word of God against the troubles and dangers the church may be brought into a great while hence, even in the latter days.

II. Reference is herein had to the predictions of the former prophets (*v.* 17) : *Art thou he of whom I have spoken in old time,* of whom Moses spoke in his prophecy of the latter days (Deut. xxxii. 43, *He will render vengeance to his adversaries),* and David, Ps. ix. 15 *(The heathen are sunk down into the pit that they made)* and often elsewhere in the Psalms ? This is the leviathan of whom Isaiah spoke (Isa. xxvii. 1), that congress of the nations of which Joel spoke, Joel iii. 1. Many of the prophets had perhaps spoken particularly of this event, though it be not written, as they all had spoken and written too that which is applicable to it. Note, There is an amiable admirable harmony and agreement between the Lord's prophets, though they lived in several ages, for they were all guided by one and the same Spirit.

III. It is here foretold that this furious formidable enemy should be utterly cut off in this attempt upon Israel, and that it should issue in his own ruin. This is supposed by many to have its accomplishment in the many defeats given by the Maccabees to the forces of Antiochus and the remarkable judgments of God executed upon his own person, for he died of sore diseases. But these things are here foretold, as usual, in figurative expressions, which we are not to look for the literal accomplishment of, and yet they might be fulfilled nearer the letter than we know of. 1. God will be highly displeased with this bold invader : *When he comes up* in pride and anger *against the land of Israel,* and thinks to carry all before him with a high hand, then *God's fury shall come up in his face,* which is an allusion to the manner of men, whose colour rises in their faces when some high affront is offered them and they are resolved to show their resentment of it, *v.* 18. God will speak against them in his *jealousy* for his people and in *the fire of his wrath* against his and their enemies, *v.* 19. See how God's permitting sin, his laying occasions of sin before men, and his making use of it to serve his own purposes, consist with his hatred of sin and his displeasure against it. God *brings this enemy against his land,* letting him know what an easy prey it might be and determining thereby to glorify himself ; and yet, *when he comes against the land,* God's *fury comes up,* and *he speaks to him in the fire of his wrath.* If any ask, Why does he thus find fault ? for who has resisted his will ? It is easy to answer, *Nay, but, O man ! who art thou that repliest against God ?* 2. His forces shall be put into the greatest confusion and consternation imaginable (*v.* 19): *There shall be a great shaking of them in the land of Israel,* a universal concussion (*v.* 20), such as shall affect the *fishes* and *fowls,* the *beasts* and *creeping things,* and much more *the men that are upon the face of the earth,* who sooner receive impressions of fear. There shall be such an earthquake as shall *throw down the mountains,* those natural heights, and the *steep places,* towers and *walls,* those artificial heights ; they shall all *fall to the ground.* Some understand this of the fright which the land of Israel should be put into by the fury of the enemy. But it is rather to be understood of the fright which the enemy should be put into by the wrath of God ; all those things which they both raise themselves and stay themselves upon shall be shaken down, and their hearts shall fail them. 3. He shall be routed and utterly ruined ; both earth and heaven shall be armed against him. (1.) The earth shall muster up its forces to destroy him. If the people of Israel have not strength and courage to resist him, God will *call for a sword against him, v.* 21. And he has swords always at command, that are *bathed in heaven,* Isa. xxxv. 5. Throughout all the mountains of Israel, where he hoped to meet with spoil to enrich him, he shall meet with swords to destroy him, and, rather than fail, *every man's sword shall be against his brother,* as in *the day of Midian,* Ps. lxxxiii. 9. The great men of Syria shall undermine and overthrow one another, shall accuse one another, shall fight duels with one another. Note, God can, and often does, make the destroyers of his people to be their own destroyers and the destroyers of one another. However, he will himself be their destroyer, will take the work into his own hand, that it may be done thoroughly (*v.* 22): *I will plead against him with pesti-*

974

lence and blood. Note, Whom God acts against he pleads against ; he shows them the ground of his controversy with them, that their mouths may be stopped, and he may be clear when he judges. (2.) The artillery of heaven shall also be drawn out against them : *I will rain upon him an overflowing rain, v.* 22. He comes like a storm upon Israel, *v.* 9. But God will come like a storm upon him, will rain upon him *great hailstones* as upon the Canaanites (Josh. x. 11), fire and brimstone as upon Sodom, and a *horrible tempest,* Ps. xi. 6. Thus the Gog and Magog in the New Testament shall be devoured with *fire from heaven,* and cast into the *lake of brimstone,* Rev. xx. 9, 10. That will be the everlasting portion of all the impenitent implacable enemies of God's church and people. 4. God, in all this, will be glorified. The end he aimed at (*v.* 16) shall be accomplished (*v.* 23): *Thus will I magnify myself and sanctify myself.* Note, In the destruction of sinners God makes it to appear that he is a great and holy God, and he will do so to eternity. And, if men do not magnify and sanctify him as they ought, he will magnify himself, and sanctify himself ; and this we should desire and pray for daily, *Father, glorify thy own name.*

CHAP. XXXIX.

This chapter continues and concludes the prophecy against Gog and Magog, in whose destruction God crowns his favour to his people Israel, which shines very brightly after the scattering of that black cloud in the close of this chapter. Here is, I. An express prediction of the utter destruction of Gog and Magog, agreeing with what we had before, ver. 1—7. II. An illustration of the vastness of that destruction, in three consequences of it : the burning of their weapons (ver. 8—10), the burying of their slain (ver. 11—16), and the feasting of the fowls with the dead bodies of those that were unburied, ver. 17—22. III. A declaration of God's gracious purposes concerning his people Israel, in this and his other providences concerning them, and a promise of further mercy that he had yet in store for them, ver. 23—29.

T**HEREFORE,** thou son of man, prophesy against Gog, and say, Thus saith the Lord G**OD** ; Behold, I *am* against thee, O Gog, the chief prince of Meshech and Tubal : 2 And I will turn thee back, and leave but the sixth part of thee, and will cause thee to come up from the north parts, and will bring thee upon the mountains of Israel : 3 And I will smite thy bow out of thy left hand, and will cause thine arrows to fall out of thy right hand. 4 Thou shalt fall upon the mountains of Israel, thou, and all thy bands, and the people that *is* with thee : I will give thee unto the ravenous birds of every sort, and *to* the beasts of the field to be devoured. 5 Thou shalt fall upon the open field : for I have spoken *it,* saith the Lord G**OD.** 6 And I will send a fire on Magog, and among them that dwell carelessly in the isles: and they shall know that I *am* the LORD. 7 So will I make my holy name known in the midst of my people Israel; and I will not *let them* pollute my holy name any more: and the heathen shall know that I *am* the LORD, the Holy One in Israel.

This prophecy begins as that before (*ch.* xxxviii. 3, 4, *I am against thee, and I will turn thee back*); for there is need of line upon line, both for the conviction of Israel's enemies and the comfort of Israel's friends. Here, as there, it is foretold that God will bring this enemy *from the north parts*, as formerly the Chaldeans were fetched from the north, Jer. i. 14 (*Omne malum ab aquilone—Every evil comes from the north*), and, long after, the Roman empire was overrun by the northern nations, that he will bring him *upon the mountains of Israel* (*v.* 2), first as a place of temptation, where the measures of his iniquity shall be filled up, and then as a place of execution, where his ruin shall be completed. And that is it which is here enlarged upon. 1. His soldiers shall be disarmed and so disabled to carry on their enterprise. Though the men of might may *find their hands*, yet to what purpose, when they find it is put out of their power to do mischief, when God shall smite their *bow out of their left hand* and their *arrow out of their right? v.* 3. Note, The weapons formed against Zion shall not prosper. 2. He and the greatest part of his army shall be slain in the field of battle (*v.* 4): *Thou shalt fall upon the mountains of Israel;* there they sinned, and there they shall perish, even upon the holy *mountains of Israel*, for *there broke he the arrows of the bow*, Ps. lxxvi. 3. The mountains of Israel shall be moistened, and fattened, and made fruitful, with the blood of the enemies. " Thou shalt *fall upon the open field* (*v.* 5) and shalt not be able even there to make thy escape." Even upon the mountains he shall not find a pass that he shall be able to maintain, and upon the open field he shall not find a road that he shall be able to make his escape by. He and *his bands :* his regular troops, and the people that are *with him* that follow the camp to share in the plunder, shall all *fall with him.* Note, Those that *cast in their lot* among wicked people (Prov. i. 14), that they *may have one purse* with them, must expect to *take their lot with them,* and fare as they fare, taking the worse with the better. There shall be such a general slaughter made that but *a sixth part shall be left* (*v.* 2), the other five shall all be cut off. Never was army so totally routed as this. And, for its greater infamy and reproach, their bodies shall be a feast to the birds of prey, *v.* 4. Compare *v.* 17, *Thou shalt fall*, for *I have spoken it.* Note, Rather shall the most illustrious princes (Antiochus **was** called *Epiphanes—the illustrious*) and

the most numerous armies *fall to the ground* than any word of God; for he that has spoken will *make it good.* 3. His country also shall be made desolate: *I will send a fire on Magog* (*v.* 6) and *among those that dwell carelessly,* or confidently, *in the isles,* that is, the nations of the Gentiles. He designed to destroy the land of Israel, but shall not only be defeated in that design, but shall have his own destroyed by some fire, some consuming judgment or other. Note, Those who invade other people's rights justly lose their own. 4. God will by all this advance the honour of his own name, (1.) Among his people Israel; they shall hereby know more of God's name, of his power and goodness, his care of them, his faithfulness to them. His providence concerning them shall lead them into a better acquaintance with him; every providence should do so, as well as every ordinance: *I will make my holy name known in the midst of my people.* In Judah is God known; but those that know much of God should know more of him; we should especially increase in the knowledge of his name as a holy name. They shall know him as a God of perfect purity and rectitude and that hates all sin, and then it follows, *I will not let them pollute my holy name any more.* Note, Those that rightly know God's holy name will not dare to profane it; for it is through ignorance of it that men make light of it and make bold with it. And this is God's method of dealing with men, first to enlighten their understandings, and by that means to influence the whole man; he first makes us to know his holy name, and so keeps us from polluting it and engages us to honour it. And this is here the blessed effect of God's glorious appearances on the behalf of his people. Thus he completes his favours, thus he sanctifies them, thus he makes them blessings indeed ; by them he instructs his people and reforms them. *When the Almighty scattered kings for her she was white as snow in Salmon,* Ps. lxviii. 14. (2.) Among the heathen; those that never knew it, or would not own it, shall *know that I am the Lord, the Holy One in Israel.* They shall be made to know by dearbought experience that he is a God of power, and his people's God and Saviour; and it is in vain for the greatest potentates to contend with him; none ever hardened their heart against him and prospered.

8 Behold, it is come, and it is done, saith the Lord GOD; this *is* the day whereof I have spoken. 9 And they that dwell in the cities of Israel shall go forth, and shall set on fire and burn the weapons, both the shields and the bucklers, the bows and the arrows, and the hand-staves, and the spears, and they shall burn them with fire

seven years: 10 So that they shall take no wood out of the field, neither cut down *any* out of the forests; for they shall burn the weapons with fire: and they shall spoil those that spoiled them, and rob those that robbed them, saith the Lord God. 11 And it shall come to pass in that day, *that* I will give unto Gog a place there of graves in Israel, the valley of the passengers on the east of the sea: and it shall stop the *noses* of the passengers: and there shall they bury Gog and all his multitude: and they shall call *it* The valley of Hamon-gog. 12 And seven months shall the house of Israel be burying of them, that they may cleanse the land. 13 Yea, all the people of the land shall bury *them;* and it shall be to them a renown the day that I shall be glorified, saith the Lord God. 14 And they shall sever out men of continual employment, passing through the land to bury with the passengers those that remain upon the face of the earth, to cleanse it: after the end of seven months shall they search. 15 And the passengers *that* pass through the land, when *any* seeth a man's bone, then shall he set up a sign by it, till the buriers have buried it in the valley of Hamon-gog. 16 And also the name of the city *shall be* Hamonah. Thus shall they cleanse the land. 17 And, thou son of man, thus saith the Lord God; Speak unto every feathered fowl, and to every beast of the field, Assemble yourselves, and come; gather yourselves on every side to my sacrifice that I do sacrifice for you, *even* a great sacrifice upon the mountains of Israel, that ye may eat flesh, and drink blood. 18 Ye shall eat the flesh of the mighty, and drink the blood of the princes of the earth, of rams, of lambs, and of goats, of bullocks, all of them fatlings of Bashan. 19 And ye shall eat fat till ye be full, and drink blood till ye be drunken, of my sacrifice which I have sacrificed for you. 20 Thus ye shall be filled at my table with horses and chariots, with mighty men, and with all men of war, saith the Lord God. 21 And I will set my glory among the heathen,

976

and all the heathen shall see my judgment that I have executed, and my hand that I have laid upon them. 22 So the house of Israel shall know that I *am* the Lord their God from that day and forward.

Though this prophecy was to have its accomplishment in the latter days, yet it is here spoken of as if it were already accomplished, because it is certain (*v.* 8): " *Behold it has come, and it is done;* it is as sure to be done when the time shall come as if it were done already; *this is the day whereof I have* long and often *spoken,* and, though it has been long in coming, yet at length *it has come.*" Thus it was said unto John (Rev. xxi. 6), *It is done.* To represent the routing of the army of Gog as very great, here are three things specified as the consequences of it. It was God himself that gave the defeat; we do not find that the people of Israel drew a sword or struck a stroke: but,

I. They shall *burn their weapons,* their *bows and arrows,* which *fell out of their hands* (*v.* 3), *their shields and bucklers,* their *javelins, spears, leading staves, truncheons,* and *half-pikes,* every thing that is combustible. They shall not lay them up in their armouries, nor reserve them for their own use, lest they should be tempted to put a confidence in them, but they shall burn them; not all at once, for a bonfire (to what purpose would be that waste?) but as they had occasion to use them for fuel in their houses, instead of other fire-wood, so that they should have no occasion to *take wood out of the field or forests* for *seven years* together (*v.* 10), such vast quantities of weapons shall there be left upon the open field where the enemy fell, and in the roads which they passed in their flight. The weapons were dry and fitter for fuel than green wood; and, by saving the wood in their coppices and forests, they gave it time to grow. Though the mountains of Israel produce plenty of all good things, yet it becomes the people of Israel to be good husbands of their plenty and to save what they can for the benefit of those that come after them, as Providence shall give them opportunity to do so. We may suppose that when those who dwelt in the cities of Israel came forth to *spoil those who spoiled them,* and make reprisals upon them, they found upon them silver, and gold, and ornaments; yet no mention is made of any thing particularly that they converted to their own use but the wood of the weapons for fuel, which is one of the necessaries of human life, to teach us to think it enough if we be well supplied with those, though we have but little of the delights and gaieties of it and of those things which we may very well live without. And every time they put fuel to the fire, and warmed themselves at it, they would be put in mind of the number and strength of their enemies, and the imminent peril they were in of falling into their hands, which would help to enlarge their hearts in thankfulness to that God who had so wonderfully, so seasonably, delivered them. As they sat by *the fire* with their children about them (their fire-side), they might from it take occasion to tell them what great things God had done for them.

II. They shall bury their dead. Usually, after a battle, when many are slain, the enemy desire time to bury their own dead. But here the slaughter shall be so general that there shall not be a sufficient number of the enemies left alive to bury the dead. And, besides, the slain lie so dispersed on the mountains of Israel that it would be a work of time to find them out; and therefore it is left to the house of Israel to bury them as a piece of triumph in their overthrow. 1. A place shall be appointed on purpose for the burying of them, *the valley of the passengers, on the east of the sea,* either the salt sea or the sea of Tiberias, a valley through which there was great passing and repassing of travellers between Egypt and Chaldea. There shall be such a multitude of dead bodies, putrefying above ground, with such a loathsome stench, that the travellers who go that way shall be forced to *stop their noses.* See what vile bodies ours are; when the soul has been a little while from them the smell of them becomes offensive, no smell more nauseous or more noxious. There therefore where the greatest number lay slain shall the burying-place be appointed. In the place where the tree falls there let it lie. And it shall be called, *The valley of Hamon-gog,* that is, *of the multitude of Gog;* for that was the thing which was in a particular manner to be had in remembrance. How numerous the forces of the enemy were which God defeated and destroyed for the defence of his people Israel! 2. A considerable time shall be spent in burying them, no less than *seven months* (*v.* 12), which is a further intimation that the *slain of the Lord* in this action should be many and that great care should be taken by the house of Israel to leave none unburied, that so *they might cleanse the land* from the ceremonial pollution it contracted by the lying of so many dead corpses unburied in it, for the prevention of which it was appointed that those who were *hanged on a tree* should be speedily *taken down and buried,* Deut. xxi. 23. This is an intimation that times of eminent deliverances should be times of reformation. The more God has done for the saving of a land from ruin the more the inhabitants should do for the cleansing of the land from sin. 3. Great numbers shall be employed in this work: *All the people of the land* shall be ready to lend a helping hand to it, *v.* 13. Note, Every one should contribute the utmost he can in his place towards the cleansing of

the land from the pollutions of it, and from every thing that is a reproach to it. Sin is a common enemy, which every man should take up arms against. *In publico discrimine unusquisque homo miles est—In the season of public danger every man becomes a soldier.* And whoever shall assist in this work *it shall be to them a renown;* though the office of grave-makers, or common scavengers of the country, seem but mean, yet, when it is for the cleansing and purifying of the land from dead works, it shall be mentioned to their honour. Note, Acts of humanity add much to the renown of God's Israel; it is a credit to religion when those that profess it are ready to every good work; and a good work it is to bury the dead, yea, though they be strangers and enemies to the commonwealth of Israel, for even they shall rise again. *It shall be a renown* to them in *the day when God will be glorified.* Note, It is for the glory of God when his Israel do that which adorns their profession; others *will see their good works and glorify their Father,* Matt. v. 16. And when God is honoured he will put honour upon his people. His glory is their renown. 4. Some particular persons shall make it their business to search out the dead bodies, or any part of them that should remain unburied. The *people of the land* will soon grow weary of burying the pollutions of the country, and therefore they shall appoint *men of continual employment,* that shall apply themselves to it and do nothing else till the land be thoroughly cleansed; for, otherwise, that which is every one's work would soon become nobody's work. Note, Those that are engaged in public work, especially for the cleansing and reforming of a land, ought to be *men of continual employments,* men that will stick to what they undertake and go through with it, men that will apply themselves to it; and those that will do good according to their opportunities will find themselves *continually employed.* 5. Even the passengers shall be ready to give information to those whose business it is to cleanse the land of what public nuisances they meet with, which call for their assistance. Those that *pass through the land,* though they will not stay to bury the dead themselves, lest they should contract a ceremonial pollution, will yet give notice of those that they find unburied. If they but discover a bone, they will *set up a sign,* that *the buriers may come and bury it,* and that, till it is buried, others may take heed of touching it, for which reason their sepulchres among the Jews were whitened, that people might keep at a distance from them. Note, When good work is to be done every one should lend a hand to further it, even the passengers themselves, who must not think themselves unconcerned, in a common calamity, or a common iniquity, to put a stop to it. Those whose work it is to cleanse the land must not countenance any thing in it that is defiling; though it were not the body, but only *the bone, of a man,* that was found unburied, they must encourage those who will give information of it (private information, by a sign, concealing the informer), that they may take it away, and bury it out of sight. Nay, *after the end of seven months,* which was allowed them for this work, when all is taken away that appeared at first view, *they shall search* for more, that what is hidden may be brought to light; they shall *search out iniquity till they find none.* In memory of this they shall give a new name to their city. It shall be called *Hamonah—The multitude.* O what a multitude of our enemies have we of this city buried! *Thus shall they cleanse the land,* with all this care, with all this pains, *v.* 16. Note, After conquering there must be cleansing. Moses appointed those Israelites that had been employed in the war with the Midianites to *purify themselves,* Num. xxxi. 24. Having received special favours from God, *let us cleanse ourselves from all filthiness.*

III. The birds and beasts of prey shall rest upon the carcases of the slain while they remain unburied and it shall be impossible to prevent them, *v.* 17, &c. We find a great slaughter represented by this figure, Rev. xix. 17, &c., which is borrowed from this.

1. There is a general invitation given, *v.* 17. It is *to the fowl of every wing* and to *every beast of the field,* from the greatest to the least, that preys upon carcases, from the eagle to the raven, from the lion to the dog; let them all gather themselves on every side; here is meat enough for them, and they are all welcome. Let them come to God's *sacrifice,* to his *feast;* so the margin reads it. Note, The judgments of God, executed upon sin and sinners, are both a sacrifice and a feast, a sacrifice to the justice of God and a feast to the faith and hope of God's people. When God *broke the head of leviathan,* he gave him to be *meat to Israel,* Ps. lxxiv. 14. *The righteous shall rejoice* as at a feast *when he sees the vengeance,* and shall *wash his foot,* as at a feast, *in the blood of the wicked.* This sacrifice is *upon the mountains of Israel;* these are the high places, the altars, where God has been dishonoured by the idolatries of the people, but where he will now glorify himself in the destruction of his enemies.

2. There is great preparation made: They shall *eat the flesh of the mighty* and *drink the blood of the princes of the earth, v.* 18, 19. (1.) It is the flesh and blood of men that they shall be treated with. This has sometimes been an instance of the rebellion of the inferior creatures against man their master, which is an effect of his rebellion against God his Maker. (2.) It is the flesh and blood of great men, here called *rams,* and *bullocks,* and *great goats, all of them fatlings of Bashan.* It is the blood of *the princes of the earth* that they shall regale themselves

with. What a mortification is this to the princes of the blood, as they call themselves, that God can make that blood, that royal blood, which swells their veins, a feast for the birds and beasts of prey! (3.) It is the flesh and blood of wicked men, the enemies of God's church and people, that they are invited to. They had accounted the Israel of God as *sheep for the slaughter,* and now they shall themselves be so accounted; they had thus used the *dead bodies of God's servants* (Ps. lxxix. 2), or would have done, and now it shall come upon themselves.

3. They shall all be fed, they shall all be feasted to the full (*v.* 19, 20): "*You shall eat fat, and drink blood,* which are satiating surfeiting things. The sacrifice is great and the feast upon the sacrifice is accordingly: *You shall be filled at my table.* Note, God keeps a table for the inferior creatures; he *provides food for all flesh.* The *eyes of all wait upon him,* and he *satisfies their desires,* for he keeps a plentiful table. And if the birds and beasts shall be filled at God's table, which he has prepared for them, much more shall his children be abundantly satisfied with the goodness of his house, even of his holy temple. They shall be filled *with horses and chariots;* that is, those who ride in the chariots, *mighty men and men of war,* who triumphed over nations, are now themselves triumphed over by the *ravens of the valley* and the *young eagles,* Prov. xxx. 17. They thought to make an easy prey of God's Israel, and now they are themselves an easy prey to the birds and beasts. See how *evil pursues sinners* even after death. This exposing of their bodies to be a prey is but a type and sign of those terrors which, after death, shall prey upon their consciences (which the poetical fictions represented by a vulture continually pecking at the heart), and this shame is but an earnest of the everlasting shame and contempt they shall rise to.

IV. This shall redound very much both to the glory of God and to the comfort and satisfaction of his people. 1. It shall be much for the honour of God, for the heathen shall hereby be made to know that he is the Lord (*v.* 21): *All the heathen shall see* and observe *my judgments that I have executed,* and thereby my *glory shall be set among them.* This principle shall be admitted and established among them more than ever, that the God of Israel is a great and glorious God. He is known to be so even among the heathen, that have not, or read not, his written word, by *the judgments which he executes.* 2. It shall be much for the satisfaction of his people; for they shall hereby be made to know that he is their God (*v.* 22): *The house of Israel shall know,* abundantly to their comfort, that *I am the Lord their God from that day and forward.* (1.) He will be so from that day and forward. God's present mercies are pledges and assurances of further mercies. If God evidence to us that he is our God he assures us that he will never leave us. *This God is our God for ever and ever.* (2.) They shall know it with more satisfaction from that day and forward. They had sometimes been ready to question whether the Lord was with them or no; but the events of this day shall silence their doubts, and, the matter being thus settled and made clear, it shall not be doubted of for the future. As boasting in themselves is hereby for ever excluded, so boasting in God is hereby for ever secured.

23 And the heathen shall know that the house of Israel went into captivity for their iniquity: because they trespassed against me, therefore hid I my face from them, and gave them into the hand of their enemies: so fell they all by the sword. 24 According to their uncleanness and according to their transgressions have I done unto them, and hid my face from them. 25 Therefore thus saith the Lord God; Now will I bring again the captivity of Jacob, and have mercy upon the whole house of Israel, and will be jealous for my holy name; 26 After that they have borne their shame, and all their trespasses whereby they have trespassed against me, when they dwelt safely in their land, and none made *them* afraid. 27 When I have brought them again from the people, and gathered them out of their enemies' lands, and am sanctified in them in the sight of many nations; 28 Then shall they know that I *am* the Lord their God, which caused them to be led into captivity among the heathen: but I have gathered them unto their own land, and have left none of them any more there. 29 Neither will I hide my face any more from them: for I have poured out my Spirit upon the house of Israel, saith the Lord God.

This is the conclusion of the whole matter going before, and has reference not only to the predictions concerning Gog and Magog, but to all the prophecies of this book concerning the captivity of the house of Israel, and then concerning their restoration and return out of their captivity.

I. God will let the heathen know the meaning of his people's troubles, and rectify the mistake of those concerning them who took occasion from the troubles of Israel to reproach the God of Israel, as unable to pro-

tect them and untrue to his covenant with them. When God, upon their reformation and return to him, turned again their captivity, and brought them back to their own land, and, upon their perseverance in their reformation, wrought such great salvations for them as that from the attempts of Gog upon them, then it would be made to appear, even to the heathen that would but consider and compare things, that there was no ground at all for their reflection, that Israel went into captivity, not because God could not protect them, but because they had by sin forfeited his favour and thrown themselves out of his protection (*v.* 23, 24): *The heathen shall know that the house of Israel went into captivity for their iniquity,* that iniquity which they learned from the heathen their neighbours, *because they trespassed against God.* That was the true reason why God *hid his face from them* and *gave them into the hand of their enemies.* It was *according to their uncleanness* and *according to their transgressions.* Now the evincing of this will not only silence their reflections on God, but will redound greatly to his honour; when the troubles of God's people are over, and we see the end of them, we shall better understand them than we did at first. And it will appear much for the glory of God when the world is made to know, 1. That God punishes sin even in his own people, because he hates it most in those that are nearest and dearest to him, Amos iii. 2. It is the praise of justice to be impartial. 2. That, when God gives up his people for a prey, it is to correct them and reform them, not to gratify their enemies, Isa. x. 7; xlii. 24. Let not them therefore exalt themselves. 3. That no sooner do God's people humble themselves under the rod than he returns in mercy to them.

II. God will give his own people to know what great favour he has in store for them notwithstanding the troubles he had brought them into (*v.* 25, 26): *Now will I bring again the captivity of Jacob.*

1. Why now? Now God will *have mercy upon the whole house of Israel,* (1.) Because it is time for him to stand up for his own glory, which suffers in their sufferings: *Now will I be jealous for my holy name,* that that may no longer be reproached. (2.) Because now they repent of their sins: They *have borne their shame, and all their trespasses.* When sinners repent, and take shame to themselves, God will be reconciled and put honour upon them. It is particularly pleasing to God that these penitents look a great way back in their penitential reflections, and are ashamed of all their trespasses which they were guilty of *when they dwelt safely in their land and none made them afraid.* The remembrance of the mercies they enjoyed in their own land, and the divine protection they were under there, shall be improved as an aggravation of the sins they committed in that land; they dwelt safely, and might have

continued to dwell so, and none should have given them any disquiet or disturbance if they had continued in the way of their duty. Nay, *therefore* they trespassed because *they dwelt safely.* Outward safety is often a cause of inward security, and that is an inlet to all sin, Ps. lxxiii. Now this they are willing to bear the shame of, and acknowledge that God has justly brought them into a land of trouble, where every one makes them afraid, because they had trespassed against him in a land of peace, where none made them afraid. And, when they thus humble themselves under humbling providences, God will bring again their captivity: and,

2. What then? When God has gathered them out of their enemies' hands, and brought them home again, (1.) Then God will have the praise of it: I will be *sanctified in them in the sight of many nations, v.* 27. As God was reproached in the reproach they were under during their captivity, so he will be sanctified in their reformation and the making of them a holy people again, and will be glorified in their restoration and the making of them a happy glorious people again. (2.) Then they shall have the benefit of it (*v.* 28): *They shall know that I am the Lord their God.* Note, The providences of God concerning his people, that are designed for their good, have the grace of God going along with them to teach them to eye God as the Lord, and their God, in all; and then they do them good. They shall eye him as the Lord and their God, [1.] In their calamities, that it was he who *caused them to be led into captivity;* and therefore they must not only submit to his will, but endeavour to answer his end in it. [2.] In their comfort, that it is he who has *gathered them to their own land,* and left none of them among the heathen. Note, By the variety of events that befal us, if we look up to God in all, we may come to acquaint ourselves better with his various attributes and designs. (3.) Then God and they will never part, *v.* 29. [1.] God will *pour out his Spirit* upon them, to prevent their departures from him and returns to folly again, and to keep them close to their duty. And then, [2.] He will *never hide his face any more from them,* will never suspend his favour as he had done; he will never turn from doing them good, and, in order to that, he will effectually provide that they shall never turn from doing him service. Note, The indwelling of the Spirit is an infallible pledge of the continuance of God's favour. He will hide his face no more from those on whom he has *poured out his Spirit.* When therefore we pray that God would never *cast us away from his presence* we must as earnestly pray that, in order to that, he would *never take his Holy Spirit away from us,* Ps. li. 11.

CHAP. XL.

The waters of the sanctuary which this prophet saw in ᵥision (ch. xlvii. l) are a proper representation of this prophecy. Hitherto the

waters have been sometimes but to the ancles, in other places to the knees, or to the loins, but now the waters have risen, and have become "a river which cannot be passed over." Here is one continued vision, beginning at this chapter, to the end of the book, which is justly looked upon to be one of the most difficult portions of scripture in all the book of God. The Jews will not allow any to read it till they are thirty years old, and tell those who do read it that, though they cannot understand every thing in it, "when Elias comes he will explain it." Many commentators, both ancient and modern, have owned themselves at a loss what to make of it and what use to make of it. But because it is hard to be understood we must not therefore throw it by, but humbly search concerning it, get as far as we can into it and as much as we can out of it, and, when we despair of satisfaction in every difficulty we meet with, bless God that our salvation does not depend upon it, but that things necessary are plain enough, and wait till God shall reveal even this unto us. These chapters are the more to be regarded because the last two chapters of the Revelation seem to have a plain allusion to them, as Rev. xx. has to the foregoing prophecy of Gog and Magog. Here is the vision of a glorious temple (in this chapter and ch. xli. and xlii.), of God's taking possession of it (ch. xliii.), orders concerning the priests that are to minister in this temple (ch. xliv.), the division of the land, what portion should be allotted for the sanctuary, what for the city, and what for the prince, both in his government of the people and his worship of God (ch. xlv.), and further instructions for him and the people, ch. xlvi. After the vision of the holy waters we have the borders of the holy land, and the portions assigned to the tribes, and the dimensions and gates of the holy city, ch. xlvii., xlviii. Some make this to represent what had been during the flourishing state of the Jewish church, how glorious Solomon's temple was in its best days, that the captives might see what they had lost by sin and might be the more humbled. But that seems not probable. The general scope of it I take to be, 1. To assure the captives that they should not only return to their own land, and be settled there, which had been often promised in the foregoing chapters, but that they should have, and therefore should be encouraged to build, another temple, which God would own, and where he would meet them and bless them, that the ordinances of worship should be revived, and the sacred priesthood should there attend; and, though they should not have a king to live in such splendour as formerly, yet they should have a prince or ruler (who is often spoken of in this vision), who should countenance the worship of God among them and should himself be an example of diligent attendance upon it, and that prince, priests, and people, should have a very comfortable settlement and subsistence in their own land. 2. To direct them to look further than all this, and to expect the coming of the Messiah, who had before been prophesied of under the name of David because he was the man that projected the building of the temple and that should set up a spiritual temple, even the gospel-church, the glory of which should far exceed that of Solomon's temple, and which should continue to the end of time. The dimensions of these visionary buildings being so large (the new temple more spacious than all the old Jerusalem and the new Jerusalem of greater extent than all the land of Canaan) plainly intimates, as Dr. Lightfoot observes, that these things cannot be literally, but must be spiritually, understood. And the gospel-temple, erected by Christ and his apostles, was so closely connected with the second material temple, was erected so carefully just at the time when that fell into decay, that it might be ready to receive its glories when it resigned them, that it was proper enough that they should both be referred to in one and the same vision. Under the type and figure of a temple and altar, priests and sacrifices, is foreshown the spiritual worship that should be performed in gospel times, more agreeably to the nature both of God and man, and that perfected at last in the kingdom of glory, in which perhaps these visions will have their full accomplishment, and some think in some happy and glorious state of the gospel-church on this side heaven, in the latter days.

In this chapter we have, I. A general account of this vision of the temple and city, ver. 1—4. II. A particular account of it entered upon; and a description given, 1. Of the outside wall, ver. 5. 2. Of the east gate, ver. 6—19. 3. Of the north gate, ver. 20—23. 4. Of the south gate (ver. 24—31) and the chambers and other appurtenances belonging to these gates. 5. Of the inner court, both towards the east and towards the south, ver. 32—38. 6. Of the tables, ver. 39—43. 7. Of the lodgings for the singers and the priests, ver. 44—47. 8. Of the porch of the house, ver. 48, 49.

IN the five and twentieth year of our captivity, in the beginning of the year, in the tenth *day* of the month, in the fourteenth year after that the city was smitten, in the selfsame day the hand of the LORD was upon me, and brought me thither. 2 In the visions of God brought he me into the land of Israel, and set me upon a very high mountain, by which *was* as the frame of a city on the south. 3 And he brought me thither, and, behold, *there was* a man, whose appearance *was* like the appearance of brass, with a line of flax in his hand, and a measuring-reed; and he stood in the gate. 4 And the man said unto me, Son of man, behold with thine eyes, and hear with thine ears, and set thine heart upon all that I shall show thee; for to the intent that I might show *them* unto thee *art* thou brought hither: declare all that thou seest to the house of Israel.

Here is, 1. The date of this vision. It was in the twenty-fifth year of Ezekiel's captivity (v. 1), which some compute to be the thirty-third year of the first captivity, and is here said to be the *fourteenth year after the city was smitten.* See how seasonably the clearest and fullest prospects of their deliverance were given, when they were in the depth of their distress, and an assurance of the return of the morning when they were in the midnight of their captivity: "Then *the hand of the Lord was upon me* and *brought me thither* to Jerusalem, now that it was in ruins, desolate and deserted"—a pitiable sight to the prophet. 2. The scene where it was laid. The prophet was brought, *in the visions of God, to the land of Israel, v.* 2. And it was not the first time that he had been brought thither in vision. We had him carried to Jerusalem to see it in its iniquity and shame (*ch.* viii. 3); here he is carried thither to have a pleasing prospect of it in its glory, though its present aspect, now that it was quite depopulated, was dismal. He was set *upon a very high mountain,* as Moses upon the top of Pisgah, to view this land, which was now a second time a *land of promise,* not yet in possession. From the top of this mountain he saw *as the frame of a city,* the plan and model of it; but this city was a temple as large as a city. The *New Jerusalem* (Rev. xxi. 22) had *no temple therein;* this which we have here is *all temple,* which comes much to one. It is a city for men to dwell in; it is a temple for God to dwell in; for in the church on earth God dwells with men, in that in heaven men dwell with God. Both these are framed in the counsel of God, framed by infinite wisdom, and all very good. 3. The particular discoveries of this city (which he had at first a general view of) were made to him by *a man whose appearance was like the appearance of brass (v.* 3), not a created angel, but Jesus Christ, who should be found in fashion as a man, that he might both discover and build the gospel-temple. He brought him to this city, for it is through Christ that we have both acquaintance with and access to the benefits and privileges of God's house. He it is that *shall build the temple of the Lord,* Zech. vi. 13. His ap-

pearing like brass intimates both his brightness and his strength. John, in vision, saw *his feet like unto fine brass,* Rev. i. 15. 4. The dimensions of this city or temple, and the several parts of it, were taken with a *line of flax* and a *measuring reed,* or *rod (v.* 3), as carpenters have both their line and a wooden measure. The temple of God is built by line and rule; and those that would let others into the knowledge of it must do it by that line and rule. The church is formed according to the scripture, *the pattern in the mount.* That is the line and the measuring reed that is in the hand of Christ. With that doctrine and laws ought to be measured, and examined by that; for then peace is upon the Israel of God when they *walk according to that rule.* 5. Directions are here given to the prophet to receive this revelation from the Lord and transmit it pure and entire to the church, *v.* 4. (1.) He must carefully observe every thing that was said and done in this vision. His attention is raised and engaged (*v.* 4): "*Behold with thy eyes* all that is *shown thee* (do not only see it, but look intently upon it), and *hear with thy ears* all that is *said to thee;* diligently hearken to it, and be sure *to set thy heart upon it;* attend with a fixedness of thought and a close application of mind." What we see of the works of God, and what we hear of the word of God, will do us no good unless we set our hearts upon it, as those that reckon ourselves nearly concerned in it, and expect advantage to our souls by it. (2.) He must faithfully *declare it to the house of Israel,* that they may have the comfort of it. Therefore he receives, that he may give. Thus the *Revelation of Jesus Christ* was lodged in the hands of John, that he might signify it to the churches, Rev. i. 1. And, because he is to declare it as a message from God, he must therefore be fully apprised of it himself and much affected with it. Note, Those who are to preach God's word to others ought to study it well themselves and set their hearts upon it. Now the reason given why he must both observe it himself and declare it to the house of Israel is because to this intent he is brought hither, and has it shown to him. Note, When the things of God are shown to us it concerns us to consider to what intent they are shown to us, and when we are sitting under the ministry of the word, to consider to what intent we are brought thither, that we may answer the end of our coming, and may not receive the grace of God, in showing us such things, in vain.

5 And behold a wall on the outside of the house round about, and in the man's hand a measuring-reed of six cubits *long* by the cubit and a handbreadth: so he measured the breadth of the building, one reed; and the height, one reed. 6 Then came he

unto the gate which looketh toward the east, and went up the stairs thereof, and measured the threshold of the gate, *which was* one reed broad; and the other threshold *of the gate, which was* one reed broad. 7 And *every* little chamber *was* one reed long, and one reed broad; and between the little chambers *were* five cubits; and the threshold of the gate by the porch of the gate within *was* one reed. 8 He measured also the porch of the gate within, one reed. 9 Then measured he the porch of the gate, eight cubits; and the posts thereof, two cubits; and the porch of the gate *was* inward. 10 And the little chambers of the gate eastward *were* three on this side, and three on that side; they three *were* of one measure: and the posts had one measure on this side and on that side. 11 And he measured the breadth of the entry of the gate, ten cubits; *and* the length of the gate, thirteen cubits. 12 The space also before the little chambers *was* one cubit *on this side,* and the space *was* one cubit on that side: and the little chambers *were* six cubits on this side, and six cubits on that side. 13 He measured then the gate from the roof of *one* little chamber to the roof of another: the breadth *was* five and twenty cubits, door against door. 14 He made also posts of threescore cubits, even unto the post of the court round about the gate. 15 And from the face of the gate of the entrance unto the face of the porch of the inner gate *were* fifty cubits. 16 And *there were* narrow windows to the little chambers, and to their posts within the gate round about, and likewise to the arches: and windows *were* round about inward: and upon *each* post *were* palm-trees. 17 Then brought he me into the outward court, and, lo, *there were* chambers, and a pavement made for the court round about: thirty chambers *were* upon the pavement. 18 And the pavement by the side of the gates over against the length of the gates *was* the lower pavement. 19 Then he measured the breadth from the fore-front of the lower gate unto the fore-front of the

inner court without, a hundred cubits eastward and northward. 20 And the gate of the outward court that looked toward the north, he measured the length thereof, and the breadth thereof. 21 And the little chambers thereof *were* three on this side and three on that side; and the posts thereof and the arches thereof were after the measure of the first gate: the length thereof *was* fifty cubits, and the breadth five and twenty cubits. 22 And their windows, and their arches, and their palm-trees, *were* after the measure of the gate that looketh toward the east; and they went up unto it by seven steps; and the arches thereof *were* before them. 23 And the gate of the inner court *was* over against the gate toward the north, and toward the east; and he measured from gate to gate a hundred cubits. 24 After that he brought me toward the south, and behold a gate toward the south: and he measured the posts thereof and the arches thereof according to these measures. 25 And *there were* windows in it and in the arches thereof round about, like those windows: the length *was* fifty cubits, and the breadth five and twenty cubits. 26 And *there were* seven steps to go up to it, and the arches thereof *were* before them: and it had palm-trees, one on this side, and another on that side, upon the posts thereof.

The measuring-reed which was in the hand of the surveyor-general was mentioned before, *v.* 3. Here we are told (*v.* 5) what was the exact length of it, which must be observed, because the house was measured by it. It was *six cubits long,* reckoning, not by the common cubit, but the *cubit of the sanctuary,* the sacred cubit, by which it was fit that this holy house should be measured, and that was a hand-breadth (that is, four inches) longer than the common cubit: the common cubit was eighteen inches, this twenty-two, see *ch.* xliii. 13. Yet some of the critics contend that this *measuring-reed* was but six common cubits in length, and one hand-breadth added to the whole. The former seems more probable. Here is an account,

I. Of the outer wall of the house, which encompassed it round, which was three yards thick and three yards high, which denotes the separation between the church and the world on every side and the divine protection which the church is under. If a wall of this vast thickness will not secure it, God himself will be *a wall of fire round about it ;* whoever attack it will do so at their peril.

II. Of the several gates with the chambers adjoining to them. Here is no mention of the outer court of all, which was called the *court of the Gentiles,* some think because in gospel-times there should be such a vast confluence of Gentiles to the church that their court should be left unmeasured, to signify that the worshippers in that court should be unnumbered, Rev. vii. 9, 11, 12.

1. He begins with the *east gate,* because that was the usual way of entering into the lower end of the temple, the holy of holies being at the west end, in opposition to the idolatrous heathen that worshipped towards the east. Now, in the account of this gate, observe, (1.) That he went up to it by *stairs* (*v.* 6), for the gospel-church was exalted above that of the Old Testament, and when we go to worship God we must ascend; so is the call, Rev. iv. 1. Come up hither. *Sursum corda—Up with your hearts.* (2.) That the chambers adjoining to the gates were but *little chambers,* about ten feet square, *v.* 7. These were for those to lodge in who attended the service of the house. And it becomes such as are made spiritual priests to God to content themselves with little chambers and not to seek great things to themselves; so that we may but have a place within the verge of God's court we have reason to be thankful though it be in a little chamber, a mean apartment, though we be but door-keepers there. (3.) The chambers, as they were each of them four-square, denoting their stability and due proportion and their exact agreement with the rule (for they were each of them one reed long and one reed broad), so they were all of *one measure,* that there might be an equality among the attendants on the service of the house. (4.) The chambers were very many; for in our Father's house there are *many mansions* (John xiv. 2), in his house above, and in that here on earth. In the secret of his tabernacle shall those be hid, and in a safe pavilion, whose desire is to dwell in the house of the Lord all the days of their life, Ps. xxvii. 4, 5. Some make these chambers to represent the particular congregations of believers, which are parts of the great temple, the universal church, which are, and must be, framed by the scripture-line and rule, and which Jesus Christ takes the measure of, that is, takes cognizance of, for he walks in the midst of the seven golden candlesticks. (5.) It is said (*v.* 14), *He made also the posts.* He that now measured them was the same that made them ; for Christ is the builder of his church and therefore is best able to give us the knowledge of it. And his reducing them to the rule and standard is called his making them, for no account is made of them further than they agree with that. *To the law and to the testimony.*

(6.) Here are posts of sixty cubits, which, some think, was literally fulfilled when Cyrus, in his edict for rebuilding the temple at Jerusalem, ordered that the height thereof should be sixty cubits, that is, thirty yards and more, Ezra vi. 3. (7.) Here were windows to the little chambers, and windows to *the posts and arches* (that is, to the cloisters below), and *windows round about* (*v.* 16), to signify the light from heaven with which the church is illuminated; divine revelation is let into it for instruction, direction, and comfort, to those that dwell in God's house, light to work by, light to walk by, light to see themselves and one another by. There were lights to the little chambers; even the least, and least considerable, parts and members of the church, shall have light afforded them. *All thy children shall be taught of the Lord.* But they are *narrow windows,* as those in the temple, 1 Kings vi. 4. The discoveries made to the church on earth are but narrow and scanty compared with what shall be in the future state, when we shall no longer *see through a glass darkly.* (8.) Divers courts are here spoken of, an outermost of all, then an outer court, then an inner, and then the innermost of all, into which the priests only entered, which (some think) may put us in mind "of the diversities of gifts, and graces, and offices, in the several members of Christ's mystical body here, as also of the several degrees of glory in the courts and mansions of heaven, as there are stars in several spheres and stars of several magnitudes in the fixed firmament." *English Annotations.* Some draw nearer to God than others and have a more intimate acquaintance with divine things ; but to a child of God a day in any of his courts is *better than a thousand* elsewhere. These courts had porches, or piazzas, round them, for the shelter of those that attended in them from wind and weather ; for when we are in the way of our duty to God we may believe ourselves to be under his special protection, that he will graciously provide for us, nay, that he will himself be to us *a covert from the storm and tempest,* Isa. iv. 5, 6. (9.) On the posts were palm-trees engraven (*v.* 16), to signify that *the righteous shall flourish like the palm-tree* in the courts of God's house, Ps. xcii. 12. The more they are depressed with the burden of affliction the more strongly do they grow, as they say of the palm-trees. It likewise intimates the saints' victory and triumph over their spiritual enemies ; they have *palms in their hands* (Rev. vii. 9) ; but lest they should drop these, or have them snatched out of their hands, they are here engraven upon the posts of the temple as perpetual monuments of their honour. *Thanks be to God, who always causes us to triumph.* Nay, believers shall themselves be made pillars in the temple of our God, and shall *go no more out,* and shall have his name engraven on them, which will be their brightest ornament and honour,

Rev. iii. 12. (10) Notice is here taken of the pavement of the court, *v.* 17, 18. The word intimates that the pavement was made of *porphyry-stone,* which was of the colour of *burning coals;* for the brightest and most sparkling glories of this world should be put and kept under our feet when we draw near to God and are attending upon him. The stars are, as it were, the *burning coals,* or stones of a *fiery colour,* with which the pavement of God's celestial temple is laid; and, if the pavement of the court be so bright and glittering, how glorious must we conclude the mansions of that house to be!

2. The gates that looked towards the north (*v.* 20) and towards the south (*v.* 24), with their appurtenances, are much the same with that towards the east, *after the measure of the first gate, v.* 21. But the description is repeated very particularly. And thus largely was the structure of the tabernacle related in Exodus, and of the temple in the books of Kings and Chronicles, to signify the special notice God does take, and his ministers should take, of all that belong to his church. His delight is in them; his eye is upon them. He knows all that are his, all his living temples and all that belongs to them. Observe, (1.) This temple had not only a gate towards the east, to let into it the *children of the east,* that were famous for their wealth and wisdom, but it had a gate to the north, and another to the south, for the admission of the poorer and less civilized nations. The new Jerusalem has *twelve gates,* three towards each quarter of the world (Rev. xxi. 13); for many shall come from all parts to sit down there, Matt. viii. 11. (2.) To those gates they went up by steps, *seven steps* (*v.* 22—26), which, as some observe, may remind us of the necessity of advancing in grace and holiness, adding one grace to another, going from step to step, *from strength to strength,* still pressing forward towards perfection— upward, upward, towards heaven, the temple above.

27 And *there was* a gate in the inner court toward the south: and he measured from gate to gate toward the south a hundred cubits. 28 And he brought me to the inner court by the south gate: and he measured the south gate according to these measures; 29 And the little chambers thereof, and the posts thereof, and the arches thereof, according to these measures: and *there were* windows in it and in the arches thereof round about: *it was* fifty cubits long, and five and twenty cubits broad. 30 And the arches round about *were* five and twenty cubits long, and five cubits broad. 31 And the arches thereof

984

were toward the utter court; and palm-trees *were* upon the posts thereof: and the going up to it *had* eight steps. 32 And he brought me into the inner court toward the east: and he measured the gate according to these measures. 33 And the little chambers thereof, and the posts thereof, and the arches thereof, *were* according to these measures: and *there were* windows therein and in the arches thereof round about: *it was* fifty cubits long, and five and twenty cubits broad. 34 And the arches thereof *were* toward the outward court; and palm-trees *were* upon the posts thereof, on this side, and on that side: and the going up to it *had* eight steps. 35 And he brought me to the north gate, and measured *it* according to these measures; 36 The little chambers thereof, the posts thereof, and the arches thereof, and the windows to it round about: the length *was* fifty cubits, and the breadth five and twenty cubits. 37 And the posts thereof *were* toward the utter court; and palm-trees *were* upon the posts thereof, on this side, and on that side: and the going up to it *had* eight steps. 38 And the chambers and the entries thereof *were* by the posts of the gates, where they washed the burnt-offering.

In these verses we have a delineation of the inner court. The survey of the outer court ended with the south side of it. This of the inner court begins with the south side (*v.* 27), proceeds to the east (*v.* 32), and so to the north (*v.* 35); for here is no gate either of the outer or inner court towards the *west.* It should seem that in Solomon's temple there were gates westward, for we find porters towards the west, 1 Chron. ix. 24; xxvi. 8. But Josephus says that in the second temple there was no gate on the west side. Observe, 1. These gates into the inner court were exactly uniform with those into the outer court, the dimensions the same, the chambers adjoining the same, the galleries or rows round the court the same, and the very engravings on the posts the same. The work of grace, and its workings, are the same, for substance, in grown Christians that they are in young beginners, only that the former have got so much nearer their perfection. The faith of all the saints is alike precious, though it be not alike strong. There is a great resemblance between one child of God and another; for *all they are brethren* and bear the same image. 2. The ascent into the outer court at each gate was by *seven steps,* but the ascent into the inner court at each gate was by *eight steps.* This is expressly taken notice of (*v.* 31, 34, 37), to signify that the nearer we approach to God the more we should rise above this world and the things of it. The people, who worshipped in the outer court, must rise seven steps above other people, but the priests, who attended in the inner court, must rise eight steps above them, must exceed them at least one step more than they exceed other people.

39 And in the porch of the gate *were* two tables on this side, and two tables on that side, to slay thereon the burnt-offering and the sin-offering and the trespass-offering. 40 And at the side without, as one goeth up to the entry of the north gate, *were* two tables ; and on the other side, which *was* at the porch of the gate, *were* two tables. 41 Four tables *were* on this side, and four tables on that side, by the side of the gate ; eight tables, whereupon they slew *their sacrifices.* 42 And the four tables *were* of hewn stone for the burnt-offering, of a cubit and a half long, and a cubit and a half broad, and one cubit high : whereupon also they laid the instruments wherewith they slew the burnt-offering and the sacrifice. 43 And within *were* hooks, a hand broad, fastened round about : and upon the tables *was* the flesh of the offering. 44 And without the inner gate *were* the chambers of the singers in the inner court, which *was* at the side of the north gate ; and their prospect *was* toward the south : one at the side of the east gate *having* the prospect toward the north. 45 And he said unto me, This chamber, whose prospect *is* toward the south, *is* for the priests, the keepers of the charge of the house. 46 And the chamber whose prospect *is* toward the north *is* for the priests, the keepers of the charge of the altar : these *are* the sons of Zadok among the sons of Levi, which come near to the LORD to minister unto him. 47 So he measured the court, a hundred cubits long, and a hundred cubits broad, four-square ; and the altar *that was* before the house. 48 And he

brought me to the porch of the house, and measured *each* post of the porch, five cubits on this side, and five cubits on that side : and the breadth of the gate *was* three cubits on this side, and three cubits on that side. 49 The length of the porch *was* twenty cubits, and the breadth eleven cubits ; and *he brought me* by the steps whereby they went up to it : and *there were* pillars by the posts, one on this side, and another on that side.

In these verses we have an account,

I. Of the tables that were in the porch of the gates of the inner court. We find no description of the altars of burnt-offerings in the midst of that court till *ch.* xliii. 13. But, because the one altar under the law was to be exchanged for a multitude of tables under the gospel, here is *early notice* taken of the tables, at our entrance into the inner court ; for till we come to partake of the *table of the Lord* we are but professors at large ; our admission to that is our entrance into the inner court. But in this gospel-temple we meet with no altar till after the glory of the Lord has taken possession of it, for Christ is our altar, that sanctifies every gift. Here were eight tables provided, whereon to *slay the sacrifices, v.* 41. We read not of any tables for this purpose either in the tabernacle or in Solomon's temple. But here they are provided, to intimate the multitude of spiritual sacrifices that should be brought to God's house in gospel-times, and the multitude of hands that should be employed in offering up those sacrifices. Here were the shambles for the altar ; here were the dressers on which they laid the flesh of the sacrifice, the knives with which they cut it up, and the hooks on which they hung it up, that it might be ready to be offered on the altar (*v.* 43), and there also they washed the burnt-offerings (*v.* 38), to intimate that before we draw near to God's altar we must have every thing in readiness, must wash our hands, our hearts, those spiritual sacrifices, and so *compass God's altar.*

II. The use that some of the chambers mentioned before were put to. 1. Some were for the *singers, v.* 44. It should seem they were first provided for before any other that attended this temple-service, to intimate, not only that the singing of psalms should still continue a gospel-ordinance, but that the gospel should furnish all that embrace it with abundant matter for joy and praise, and give them occasion to *break forth into singing,* which is often foretold concerning gospel times, Ps. xcvi. 1 ; xcviii. 1. Christians should be singers. *Blessed are those that dwell in God's house,* they will be *still praising him.* 2. Others of them were for *the priests*, both those that kept *the charge of the house*, to cleanse it, and to see that none came into it to pollute it, and to keep it in good repair (*v.* 45), and those that *kept the charge of the altar* (*v.* 46), that *came near to the Lord to minister to him.* God will find convenient lodging for all his servants. Those that do the work of his house shall enjoy the comforts of it.

III. Of the inner court, the court of the priests, which was fifty yards square, *v.* 47. The altar that *was before the house* was placed in the midst of this court, overagainst the three gates, and, standing in a direct line with the three gates of the outer court, when the gates were set open all the people in the outer court might through them be spectators of the service done at the altar. Christ is both our altar and our sacrifice, to whom we must look with an eye of faith in all our approaches to God, and he is salvation in the midst of the earth (Ps. lxxiv. 12), to be looked unto from all quarters.

IV. Of the porch of the house. The temple is called the house, emphatically, as if no other house were worthy to be called so. Before this house there was a porch, to teach us not to rush hastily and inconsiderately into the presence of God, but gradually, that is, gravely, and with solemnity, passing first through the outer court, then the inner, then the porch, ere we enter into the house. Between this porch and the altar was a place where the priests used to pray, Joel ii. 17. In the porch, besides the posts on which the doors were hung, there were pillars, probably for state and ornament, like *Jachin* and *Boaz—He will establish; in him is strength, v.* 49. In the gospel church every thing is strong and firm, and every thing ought to be kept in its place and to be done decently and in order.

CHAP. XLI.

An account was given of the porch of the house in the close of the foregoing chapter; this brings us to the temple itself, the description of which here given creates much difficulty to the critical expositors and occasions differences among them. Those must consult them who are nice in their enquiries into the meaning of the particulars of this delineation; it shall suffice us to observe, I. The dimensions of the house, the posts of it (ver. 1), the door (ver. 2), the wall and the side-chambers (ver. 5, 6), the foundations and wall of the chambers, their doors (ver. 8—11), and the house itself, ver. 13. II. The dimensions of the oracle, or most holy place, ver. 3, 4. III. An account of another building over against the separate place, yer. 12—15. IV. The manner of the building of the house, ver. 7, 16, 17. V. The ornaments of the house, ver. 18—20. VI. The altar of incense and the table, ver. 22. VII. The doors between the temple and the oracle, ver. 23—26. There is so much difference both in the terms and in the rules of architecture between one age and another, one place and another, that it ought not to be any stumbling-block to us that there is so much in these descriptions dark and hard to be understood, about the meaning of which the learned are not agreed. To one not skilled in mathematics the mathematical description of a modern structure would be scarcely intelligible; and yet to a common carpenter or mason among the Jews at that time we may suppose that all this, in the literal sense of it, was easy enough.

A FTERWARD he brought me to the temple, and measured the posts, six cubits broad on the one side, and six cubits broad on the other side, *which was* the breadth of the taber-

986

nacle. 2 And the breadth of the door *was* ten cubits; and the sides of the door *were* five cubits on the one side, and five cubits on the other side : and he measured the length thereof, forty cubits : and the breadth, twenty cubits. 3 Then went he inward, and measured the post of the door, two cubits; and the door, six cubits; and the breadth of the door, seven cubits. 4 So he measured the length thereof, twenty cubits; and the breadth, twenty cubits, before the temple : and he said unto me, This *is* the most holy *place.* 5 After he measured the wall of the house, six cubits; and the breadth of *every* side-chamber, four cubits, round about the house on every side. 6 And the side-chambers *were* three, one over another, and thirty in order; and they entered into the wall which *was* of the house for the side-chambers round about, that they might have hold, but they had not hold in the wall of the house. 7 And *there was* an enlarging, and a winding about still upward to the side-chambers : for the winding about of the house went still upward round about the house : therefore the breadth of the house *was still* upward, and so increased *from* the lowest *chamber* to the highest by the midst. 8 I saw also the height of the house round about : the foundations of the side-chambers *were* a full reed of six great cubits. 9 The thickness of the wall, which *was* for the side-chamber without, *was* five cubits : and *that* which *was* left *was* the place of the side-chambers that *were* within. 10 And between the chambers *was* the wideness of twenty cubits round about the house on every side. 11 And the doors of the side-chambers *were* toward *the place that was* left, one door toward the north, and another door toward the south : and the breadth of the place that was left *was* five cubits round about.

We are still attending a prophet that is under the guidance of an angel, and therefore attend with reverence, though we are often at a loss to know both what this is and what it is to us. Observe here, 1. After the prophet had observed the courts he was at length *brought to the temple, v.* 1. If we diligently attend to the instructions given us in the plainer parts of religion, and profit by them, we shall be led further into an acquaintance with the mysteries of the kingdom of heaven. Those that are willing to dwell in God's courts shall at length be brought into his temple. Ezekiel was himself a priest, but by the iniquity and calamity of the times was cut short of his birthright privilege of ministering in the temple; but God makes up the loss to him by introducing him into this prophetical, evangelical, celestial temple, and employing him to transmit a description of it to the church, in which he was dignified above all the rest of his order. 2. When our Lord Jesus spoke of the destroying of *this temple*, which his hearers understood of this second temple of Jerusalem, he spoke of the temple of his body (John ii. 19, 21); and with good reason might he speak so ambiguously when Ezekiel's vision had a joint respect to them both together, including also his mystical body the church, which is called the *house of God* (1 Tim. iii. 15), and all the members of that body, which are *living temples*, in which the Spirit dwells. 3. The very posts of this temple, the door-posts, were as far one from the other, and consequently the door was as wide, as *the* whole *breadth of the tabernacle* of Moses (*v.* 1), namely, twelve cubits, Exod. xxvi. 16, 22, 25. In comparison with what had been under the law we may say, *Wide is the gate* which leads into the church, the ceremonial law, that wall of partition which had so much straitened the gate, being taken down. 4. The most holy place was an exact square, twenty cubits each way, *v.* 4. For the new Jerusalem is exactly square (Rev. xxi. 16), denoting its stability; for we look for a city that cannot be moved. 5. The upper stories were larger than the lower, *v.* 7. The walls of the temple were six cubits thick at the bottom, five in the middle story, and four in the highest, which gave room to enlarge the chambers the higher they went; but care was taken that the timber might have *fast hold* (though God builds high, he builds firmly), yet so as not to weaken one part for the strengthening of another; they had hold, but not *in the wall of the house.* By this spreading gradually, the *side-chambers* that were on *the height of the house* (in the uppermost story of all) were six cubits, whereas the lowest were but four; they gained a cubit every story. The higher we build up ourselves in our most holy faith the more should our hearts, those living temples, be enlarged.

12 Now the building that *was* before the separate place at the end toward the west *was* seventy cubits broad; and the wall of the building *was* five cubits thick round about, and the length thereof ninety cubits. 13

So he measured the house, a hundred cubits long; and the separate place, and the building, with the walls thereof, a hundred cubits long; 14 Also the breadth of the face of the house, and of the separate place toward the east, a hundred cubits. 15 And he measured the length of the building over against the separate place which *was* behind it, and the galleries thereof on the one side and on the other side, a hundred cubits, with the inner temple, and the porches of the court; 16 The door-posts, and the narrow windows, and the galleries round about on their three stories, over against the door, ceiled with wood round about, and from the ground up to the windows, and the windows *were* covered; 17 To that above the door, even unto the inner house, and without, and by all the wall round about within and without, by measure. 18 And *it was* made with cherubims and palm-trees, so that a palm-tree *was* between a cherub and a cherub; and *every* cherub had two faces; 19 So that the face of a man *was* toward the palm-tree on the one side, and the face of a young lion toward the palm-tree on the other side: *it was* made through all the house round about. 20 From the ground unto above the door *were* cherubims and palm-trees made, and *on* the wall of the temple. 21 The posts of the temple *were* squared, *and* the face of the sanctuary; the appearance *of the one* as the appearance *of the other*. 22 The altar of wood *was* three cubits high, and the length thereof two cubits; and the corners thereof, and the length thereof, and the walls thereof, *were* of wood: and he said unto me, This *is* the table that *is* before the LORD. 23 And the temple and the sanctuary had two doors. 24 And the doors had two leaves *a-piece*, two turning leaves; two *leaves* for the one door, and two leaves for the other *door*. 25 And *there were* made on them, on the doors of the temple, cherubims and palm-trees, like as *were* made upon the walls; and *there were* thick planks upon the face of the porch without. 26 And *there were* narrow windows and palm-trees on the one side and on the other side, on the sides of the porch, and *upon* the side-chambers of the house, and thick planks.

Here is, 1. An account of a building that was *before the separate place* (that is, before the temple), *at the end towards the west* (*v.* 12), which is here measured, and compared (*v.* 13) with the measure of the house, and appears to be of equal dimensions with it. This stood in a court by itself, which is measured (*v.* 15) and its galleries, or chambers belonging to it, its posts and windows, and the ornaments of them, *v.* 15—17. But what use was to be made of this other building we are not told; perhaps, in this vision, it signified the setting up of a church among the Gentiles not inferior to the Jewish temple, but of quite another nature, and which should soon supersede it. 2. A description of the ornaments of the temple, and the other building. The walls on the inside from top to bottom were adorned with *cherubim and palm-trees*, placed alternately, as in Solomon's temple, 1 Kings vi. 29. Each cherub is here said to have two *faces*, the *face of a man* towards the palm tree on one side and the *face of a young lion towards the palm-tree* on the other side, *v.* 19. These seem to represent the angels, who have more than the wisdom of a man and the courage of a lion; and in both they have an eye to the palms of victory and triumph which are set before them, and which they are sure of in all their conflicts with the powers of darkness. And in the assemblies of the saints angels are in a special manner present, 1 Cor. xi. 10. 3. A description of the posts of the doors both of the temple and of the sanctuary; they were *squared* (*v.* 21), not round like pillars; and *the appearance of the one was as the appearance of the other.* In the tabernacle, and in Solomon's temple, the door of the sanctuary, or most holy, was narrower than that of the temple, but here it was fully as broad; for in gospel-times *the way into the holiest of all is made* more *manifest* than it was under the Old Testament (Heb. ix. 8) and therefore the door is wider. These doors are described, *v.* 23, 24. The temple and the sanctuary had each of them its door, and they were *two-leaved*, folding doors. 4. We have here the description of the altar of incense, here said to be an *altar of wood, v.* 22. No mention is made of its being *overlaid with gold;* but surely it was intended to be so, else it would not bear the fire with which the incense was to be burned, unless we will suppose that it served only to put the censers upon. Or else it intimates that the incense to be offered in the gospel-temple shall be purely spiritual, and the fire spiritual, which will not consume an altar of wood. Therefore this altar is called a table. *This is the table that is before the Lord.*

Here, as before, we find the altar turned into a table; for, the great sacrifice being now offered, that which we have to do is to feast upon the sacrifice at the Lord's table. 5. Here is the adorning of the doors and windows with palm-trees, that they might be of a piece with the walls of the house, *v.* 25, 26. Thus the living temples are adorned, not with gold, or silver, or costly array, but with *the hidden man of the heart, in that which is not corruptible.*

CHAP. XLII.

This chapter continues and concludes the describing and measuring of this mystical temple, which it is very hard to understand the particular architecture of, and yet more hard to comprehend the mystical meaning of. Here is, I. A description of the chambers that were about the courts, their situation and structure (ver. 1—13), and the uses for which they were designed, ver. 13, 14. II. A survey of the whole compass of ground which was taken up with the house, and the courts belonging to it, ver. 15—20.

THEN he brought me forth into the utter court, the way toward the north: and he brought me into the chamber that *was* over against the separate place, and which *was* before the building toward the north. 2 Before the length of a hundred cubits *was* the north door, and the breadth *was* fifty cubits. 3 Over against the twenty *cubits* which *were* for the inner court, and over against the pavement which *was* for the utter court, *was* gallery against gallery in three *stories.* 4 And before the chambers *was* a walk of ten cubits breadth inward, a way of one cubit; and their doors toward the north. 5 Now the upper chambers *were* shorter: for the galleries were higher than these, than the lower, and than the middlemost of the building. 6 For they *were* in three *stories,* but had not pillars as the pillars of the courts: therefore *the building* was straitened more than the lowest and the middlemost from the ground. 7 And the wall that *was* without over against the chambers, toward the utter court on the forepart of the chambers, the length thereof *was* fifty cubits. 8 For the length of the chambers that *were* in the utter court *was* fifty cubits: and, lo, before the temple *were* a hundred cubits. 9 And from under these chambers *was* the entry on the east side, as one goeth into them from the utter court. 10 The chambers *were* in the thickness of the wall of the court toward east, over against the separate place, and over against the building. 11

And the way before them *was* like the appearance of the chambers which *were* toward the north, as long as they, *and* as broad as they: and all their goings out *were* both according to their fashions, and according to their doors. 12 And according to the doors of the chambers that *were* toward the south *was* a door in the head of the way, *even* the way directly before the wall toward the east, as one entereth into them. 13 Then said he unto me, The north chambers *and* the south chambers, which *are* before the separate place, they *be* holy chambers, where the priests that approach unto the LORD shall eat the most holy things: there shall they lay the most holy things, and the meat-offering, and the sin-offering, and the trespass-offering; for the place *is* holy. 14 When the priests enter therein, then shall they not go out of the holy *place* into the utter court, but there they shall lay their garments wherein they minister; for they *are* holy; and shall put on other garments, and shall approach to *those things* which *are* for the people.

The prophet has taken a very exact view of the temple and the buildings belonging to it, and is now brought again into the outer court, to observe the chambers that were in that square.

I. Here is a description of these chambers, which (as that which went before) seems to us very perplexed and intricate, through our unacquaintedness with the Hebrew language and the rules of architecture at that time. We shall only observe, in general, 1. That about the temple, which was the place of public worship, there were private chambers, to teach us that our attendance upon God in solemn ordinances will not excuse us from the duties of the closet. We must not only worship in the courts of God's house, but must, both before and after our attendance there, enter into our chambers, enter into our closets, and read and meditate, and *pray to our Father in secret;* and a great deal of comfort the people of God have found in their communion with God in solitude. 2. That these chambers were many; there were *three stories* of them, and, though the higher stories were not so large as the lower, yet they served as well for retirement, *v.* 5, 6. There were many, that there might be conveniences for all such devout people as Anna the prophetess, who *departed not from the temple night or day,* Luke ii. 37. *In my Fa-*

ther's house are many mansions. In his house on earth there are so; multitudes by faith have taken lodgings in his sanctuary, and *yet there is room.* 3. That these chambers, though they were private, yet were near the temple, within view of it, within reach of it, to teach us to prefer public worship before private *(the Lord loves the gates of Zion more than all the dwellings of Jacob,* and so must we), and to refer our private worship to the public. Our religious performances in our chambers must be to prepare us for the exercises of devotion in public, and to further us in our improvement of them, as our opportunities are. 4. That before these chambers there were *walks of five yards broad* (*v.* 4), in which those that had lodgings in these chambers might meet for conversation, might walk and talk together for their mutual edification, might communicate their knowledge and experiences. For we are not to spend all our time between church and the chamber, though a great deal of time may be spent to very good purpose in both. But man is made for society, and Christians for the communion of saints; and the duties of that communion we must make conscience of, and the privileges and pleasures of that communion we must take the comfort of. It is promised to Joshua, who was high priest in the second temple, that God will *give him places to walk in among those that stand by,* Zech. iii. 7.

II. Here is the use of these chambers appointed, *v.* 13, 14. 1. They were *for the priests* that approach unto the Lord, that they may be always near their business and may not be non-residents. *Therefore* they are called *holy chambers,* because they were for use of those that ministered in holy things during their ministration. Those that have public work to do for God and the souls of men have need to be much in private, to fit themselves for it. Ministers should spend much time in their chambers, in reading, meditation, and prayer, that their *profiting may appear;* and they ought to be provided with conveniences for this purpose. 2. There the priests were to deposit *the most holy things,* those parts of the offerings which fell to their share; and there they were to *eat them,* they and their families, in a religious manner, for *the place is holy;* and thus they must make a difference between those feasts upon the sacrifice and other meals. 3. There (among other uses) they were to lay their vestments, which God had appointed them to wear when they ministered at the altar, their linen ephods, coats, girdles, and bonnets. We read of the providing of priests garments after their return out of captivity, Neh. vii. 70, 72. When they had ended their service at the altar they must lay by those garments, to signify that the use of them should continue only during that dispensation; but they must *put on other garments,* such as other people wear, when they approached to those things which were for the people, that is, to do that part of their service which related to the people, to teach them the law and to answer their enquiries. Their holy garments must be *laid up*, that they may be kept clean and decent for the credit of their service.

15 Now when he had made an end of measuring the inner house, he brought me forth toward the gate whose prospect *is* toward the east, and measured it round about. 16 He measured the east side with the measuring-reed, five hundred reeds, with the measuring-reed round about. 17 He measured the north side, five hundred reeds, with the measuring-reed round about. 18 He measured the south side, five hundred reeds, with the measuring-reed. 19 He turned about to the west side, *and* measured five hundred reeds, with the measuring-reed. 20 He measured it by the four sides : it had a wall round about, five hundred *reeds* long, and five hundred broad, to make a separation between the sanctuary and the profane place.

We have attended the measuring of this mystical temple and are now to see how far the holy ground on which we tread extends; and that also is here measured, and found to take in a great compass. Observe, 1. What the dimensions of it were. It extended each way 500 reeds (*v.* 16—19), each reed above three yards and a half, so that it reached every way about an English measured mile, which, the ground lying square, was above four miles round. Thus large were the suburbs (as I may call them) of this mystical temple, signifying the great extent of the church in gospel-times, when all nations should be discipled and the kingdoms of the world made Christ's kingdoms. Room should be made in God's courts for the numerous forces of the Gentiles that shall flow into them, as was foretold, Isa. xlix. 18; lx. 4. It is in part fulfilled already in the accession of the Gentiles to the church; and we trust it shall have a more full accomplishment when the *fulness of the Gentiles shall come in* and *all Israel shall be saved.* 2. Why the dimensions of it were made thus large. It was to *make a separation*, by putting a very large distance *between the sanctuary* and *the profane place:* and therefore there was a wall surrounding it, to keep off those that were unclean and to separate between the *precious and the vile.* Note, A difference is to be put between common and sacred things, between God's name and other names, between his day and other days, his

book and other books, his institutions and other observances; and a distance is to be put between our worldly and religious actions, so as still to go about the worship of God with a solemn pause.

CHAP. XLIII.

The prophet, having given us a view of the mystical temple, the gospel-church, as he received it from the Lord, that it might appear not to be erected in vain, comes to describe, in this and the next chapter, the worship that should be performed in it, but under the type of the Old-Testament services. In this chapter we have, I. Possession taken of this temple, by the glory of God filling it, ver. 1—6. II. A promise given of the continuance of God's presence with his people upon condition of their return to, and continuance in, the instituted way of worship, and their abandoning idols and idolatry, ver. 7—12. III. A description of the altar of burnt-offerings, ver. 13—17. IV. Directions given for the consecration of that altar, ver. 18—27. Ezekiel seems here to stand between God and Israel, as Moses the servant of the Lord did when the sanctuary was first set up.

AFTERWARD he brought me to the gate, *even* the gate that looketh toward the east : 2 And, behold, the glory of the God of Israel came from the way of the east : and his voice *was* like a noise of many waters : and the earth shined with his glory. 3 And *it was* according to the appearance of the vision which I saw, *even* according to the vision that I saw when I came to destroy the city : and the visions *were* like the vision that I saw by the river Chebar; and I fell upon my face. 4 And the glory of the LORD came into the house by the way of the gate whose prospect *is* toward the east. 5 So the spirit took me up, and brought me into the inner court; and, behold, the glory of the LORD filled the house. 6 And I heard *him* speaking unto me out of the house; and the man stood by me.

After Ezekiel has patiently surveyed the temple of God, the greatest glory of this earth, he is admitted to a higher form, and honoured with a sight of the glories of the upper world; it is said to him, *Come up hither.* He has seen the temple, and sees it to be very spacious and splendid ; but, till the glory of God comes into it, it is but like the dead bodies he had seen in vision (*ch.* xxxvii.), that had *no breath* till the Spirit of life entered into them. Here therefore he sees the house filled with God's glory.

I. He has a vision of *the glory of God* (*v.* 2), *the glory of the God of Israel*, that God who is in covenant with Israel, and whom they serve and worship. The idols of the heathen have no glory but what they owe to the goldsmith or the painter ; but this is the glory of the God of Israel. This glory *came from the way of the east*, and therefore he was brought to the *gate that leads towards the east*, to expect the appearance and approach of it. Christ's *star was seen in the east*, and he is that *other angel that ascends out of the east,* Rev. vii. 2. For he is the morning star, he is the sun of righteousness. Two things he observed in this appearance of the glory of God :—1. The power of his word which he heard : *His voice was like a noise of many waters,* which is heard very far, and makes impressions; the noise of purling streams is grateful, of a roaring sea dreadful, Rev. i. 15 ; xiv. 2. Christ's gospel, in the glory of which he shines, was to be proclaimed aloud, the report of it to be heard far ; to some it is a savour of life, to others of death, according as they are. 2. The brightness of his appearance which he saw : *The earth shone with his glory ;* for God is light, and none can bear the lustre of his light, none *has seen* nor *can see it.* Note, That glory of God which shines in the church shines on the world. When God appeared for David *the brightness that was before him* dispersed the clouds, Ps. xviii. 12. This appearance of the glory of God to Ezekiel he observed to be the same with the vision he saw when he first received his commission (*ch.* i. 4), *according to that by the river Chebar* (*v.* 3) ; because God is the same, he was pleased to manifest himself in the same manner, for with him is *no variableness.* "It was the same" (says he) "as that which I saw *when I came to destroy the city,* that is, to foretel the city's destruction," which he did with such authority and efficacy, and the event did so certainly answer the prediction, that he might be said to destroy it. As a judge, in God's name, he passed a sentence upon it, which was soon executed. God appeared in the same manner when he sent him to speak words of terror and when he sent him to speak words of comfort; for in both God is and will be glorified. *He kills and he makes alive ;* he *wounds and he heals,* Deut. xxxii. 39. To the same hand that destroyed we must look for deliverance. *He has smitten, and he will bind up. Una eademque manus vulnus opemque tulit—The same hand inflicted the wound and healed it.*

II. He has a vision of the entrance of this glory into the temple. When he saw this glory he *fell upon his face* (*v.* 3), as not *able* to bear the lustre of God's glory, or rather as one willing to give him the glory of it by a humble and reverent adoration. But the Spirit *took him up* (*v.* 5) when the *glory of the Lord* had *come into the house* (*v.* 4), that he might see how the house was filled with it. He saw how the glory of the Lord in this same appearance departed from the temple, because it was profaned, to his great grief; now he shall see it return to the temple to his great satisfaction. See *ch.* x. 18, 19 ; xi. 23. Note, Though God may forsake his people for a small moment, he will return with everlasting loving-kindness. God's glory *filled the house* as it had filled the tabernacle which Moses set up and the temple of Solomon, Exod. xl. 34 ; 1 Kings

viii. 10. Now we do not find that ever the Shechinah did in that manner take possession of the second temple, and therefore this was to have its accomplishment in that glory of the divine grace which shines so brightly in the gospel church, and fills it. Here is no mention of a cloud filling the house as formerly, for we now *with open face behold the glory of the Lord,* in the face of Christ, and not as of old through the cloud of types.

III. He receives instructions more immediately from the glory of the Lord, as Moses did when God had taken possession of the tabernacle (Lev. i. 1) : *I heard him speaking to me out of the house, v.* 6. God's glory shining in the church, we must thence expect to receive divine oracles. *The man stood by me ;* we could not bear to hear the voice of God any more than to see the face of God if Jesus Christ did not stand by us as Mediator. Or, if this was a created angel, it is observable that when God began to speak to Ezekiel he stood by and gave way, having no more to say. Nay, he stood by the prophet, as a learner with him ; for *to the principalities and powers,* to the angels themselves, who *desire to look into* these things, *is known by the church the manifold wisdom of God,* Eph. iii 10. The man stood by him to conduct him thither where he might receive further discoveries, *ch.* xliv. 1.

7 And he said unto me, Son of man, the place of my throne, and the place of the soles of my feet, where I will dwell in the midst of the children of Israel for ever, and my holy name, shall the house of Israel no more defile, *neither* they, nor their kings, by their whoredom, nor by the carcases of their kings in their high places. 8 In their setting of their threshold by my thresholds, and their post by my posts, and the wall between me and them, they have even defiled my holy name by their abominations that they have committed : wherefore I have consumed them in mine anger. 9 Now let them put away their whoredom, and the carcases of their kings, far from me, and I will dwell in the midst of them for ever. 10 Thou son of man, show the house to the house of Israel, that they may be ashamed of their iniquities : and let them measure the pattern. 11 And if they be ashamed of all that they have done, show them the form of the house, and the fashion thereof, and the goings out thereof, and the comings in there-

of, and all the forms thereof, and all the ordinances thereof, and all the forms thereof, and all the laws thereof: and write *it* in their sight, that they may keep the whole form thereof, and all the ordinances thereof, and do them. 12 This *is* the law of the house; Upon the top of the mountain the whole limit thereof round about *shall be* most holy. Behold, this *is* the law of the house.

God does here, in effect, renew his covenant with his people Israel, upon his retaking possession of the house, and Ezekiel negociates the matter, as Moses formerly. This would be of great use to the captives at their return both for direction and encouragement; but it looks further, to those that are blessed with the privileges of the gospel-temple, that they may understand how they are before him on their good behaviour.

I. God, by the prophet, puts them in mind of their former provocations, for which they had long lain under the tokens of his displeasure. This conviction is spoken to them to make way for the comforts designed them. Though God *gives and upbraids not*, it becomes us, when he forgives, to upbraid ourselves with our unworthy conduct towards him. Let them now remember therefore, 1. That they had formerly *defiled God's holy name*, had profaned and abused all those sacred things by which he had made himself known among them, *v.* 7. *They and their kings* had brought contempt on the religion they professed, and their relation to God, by their spiritual whoredom, their idolatry, and by worshipping images, which they called *their kings* (for so *Moloch* signifies) or lords (for so *Baal* signifies), but which were really the *carcases of kings*, not only lifeless and useless, but loathsome and abominable as dead carcases, *in their high places*, set up in honour of them. They had defiled God's name by their abominations. And what were they? It was *in setting their threshold by my thresholds, and their post by my posts*, that is, adding their own inventions to God's institutions, and urging all to a compliance with them, as if they had been of equal authority and efficacy, *teaching for doctrines the commandments of men* (Isa. xxix.13); or, rather, setting up altars to their idols even in the courts of the temple, than which a more impudent affront could not be put upon the divine Majesty. Thus they set up a separation *wall between him and them*, which stopped the current of his favours to them and spoiled the acceptableness of their services to him. See what an indignity sinners do to God, setting up their walls in opposition to his, and thrusting him out from what is his right; and see what injury they do to themselves, for the nearer

any come to God with their sins the further they set him at a distance from them. Some give this sense of it: Though their houses joined close to God's house, their posts and thresholds to his, so that they were in a manner his next neighbours, *there was but a wall between me and them* (so it is in the margin), so that it might have been expected they would acquaint themselves with him and be in care to please him, yet they were not so much as neighbourly. Note, It often proves too true, *The nearer the church the further from God.* They were, by profession, in covenant with God, and yet they had *defiled the place of his throne* and of *the soles of his feet*, his temple, where he did both reside and reign. Jerusalem is called the *city of the great king* (Ps. xlviii. 2) and his *footstool*, Ps. xcix. 5; cxxxii. 7. Note, When God's ordinances are profaned his holy name is polluted. 2. That for this God had had a controversy with them in their late troubles. They could not condemn him, for he had but brought upon them the desert of their sins: *Wherefore I have consumed them in my anger.* Note, Those that pollute God's holy name fall under his just displeasure.

II. He calls upon them to repent and reform, and, in order to that, to be ashamed of their iniquities (*v.* 9): "*Now let them put away their whoredom;* now that they have smarted so severely for it, and now that God is returning in mercy to them and setting up his sanctuary again in the midst of them, now let them cast away their idols and have no more to do with them, that they may not again forfeit the privileges which they have been taught to know the worth of by the want of them. Let them put away their idols, those loathsome *carcases of their kings, far from me,* from being a provocation to me." This was seasonable counsel now that the prophet had the model or pattern of the temple to set before them; for, 1. If *they see that pattern,* they will surely be ashamed of their sins (*v.* 10): when they see what mercy God has in store for them, notwithstanding their utter unworthiness of it, they will be ashamed to think of their disingenuous conduct towards him. Note, The goodness of God to us should lead us to repentance, especially to a penitential shame. Let *them measure the pattern* themselves, and see how much it exceeds the former pattern, and guess by that what great things God has in store for them; and surely it will put them out of countenance to think what the desert of their sins was. And then, 2. If *they be ashamed* of their sins, they shall surely see more of the pattern, *v.* 11. If they *be ashamed of all that they have done,* upon a general view of the goodness of God, let them have a more distinct particular account of the temple. Note, Those that improve what they see and know of the goodness of God shall see and know more of it. And then, and not till then, we are qualified for

God's favours, when we are truly humbled for our own follies. "*Show them the form of the house;* let them see what a stately structure it will be; and withal show them the ordinances and laws of it." Note, With the foresights of our comforts it is fit that we should get the knowledge of our duty; with the privileges of God's house we must acquaint ourselves with the rules of it. *Show them* these ordinances, that they may *keep them* and *do them.* Note, *Therefore* we are made to know our duty, that we may do it, and be blessed in our deed.

III. He promises that they shall be such as they should be, and then he will be to them such as they would have him to be, *v.* 7. 1. The house of *Israel shall no more defile my holy name.* This is pure gospel. The precept of the law says, You must not defile my name: the grace of the gospel says, You shall not. Thus what is required in the covenant is promised in the covenant, Jer. xxxii. 40. 2. Then *I will dwell in the midst of them for ever;* and the same again *v.* 9. God secures to us his good-will by confirming in us his good work. If we do not defile his name, we may be sure that he will not depart from us.

IV. The general law of God's house is laid down (*v.* 12), That, whereas formerly only the chancel, or sanctuary, was *most holy,* now the whole *mountain of the house* shall be so; the *whole limit thereof,* including all the courts and all the chambers, shall be as the most holy place, signifying that in gospel-times, 1. The whole church shall have the privilege of the *holy of holies,* that of a near access to God. All believers have now, under the gospel, *boldness to enter into the holiest* (Heb. x. 19), with this advantage, that whereas the high priest entered in the virtue of the blood of bulls and goats, we enter in the virtue of the blood of Jesus, and, wherever we are, we have through him *access to the Father.* 2. The whole church shall be under a mighty obligation to press towards the perfection of holiness, *as he who has called us is holy.* All must now be most holy. *Holiness becomes God's house* for ever, and in gospel-times more than ever. Behold this is the *law of the house;* let none expect the protection of it that will not submit to this law.

13 And these *are* the measures of the altar after the cubits: the cubit *is* a cubit and a hand-breadth; even the bottom *shall be* a cubit, and the breadth a cubit, and the border thereof by the edge thereof round about *shall be* a span: and this *shall be* the higher place of the altar. 14 And from the bottom *upon* the ground *even* to the lower settle *shall be* two cubits, and the breadth one cubit; and from

the lesser settle *even* to the greater settle *shall be* four cubits, and the breadth *one* cubit. 15 So the altar *shall be* four cubits; and from the altar and upward *shall be* four horns. 16 And the altar *shall be* twelve *cubits* long, twelve broad, square in the four squares thereof. 17 And the settle *shall be* fourteen *cubits* long and fourteen broad in the four squares thereof; and the border about it *shall be* half a cubit; and the bottom thereof *shall be* a cubit about; and his stairs shall look toward the east. 18 And he said unto me, Son of man, Thus saith the Lord GOD; These *are* the ordinances of the altar in the day when they shall make it, to offer burnt-offerings thereon, and to sprinkle blood thereon. 19 And thou shalt give to the priests the Levites that be of the seed of Zadok, which approach unto me, to minister unto me, saith the Lord GOD, a young bullock for a sin-offering. 20 And thou shalt take of the blood thereof, and put *it* on the four horns of it, and on the four corners of the settle, and upon the border round about: thus shalt thou cleanse and purge it. 21 Thou shalt take the bullock also of the sin-offering, and he shall burn it in the appointed place of the house, without the sanctuary. 22 And on the second day thou shalt offer a kid of the goats without blemish for a sin-offering; and they shall cleanse the altar, as they did cleanse *it* with the bullock. 23 When thou hast made an end of cleansing *it,* thou shalt offer a young bullock without blemish, and a ram out of the flock without blemish. 24 And thou shalt offer them before the LORD, and the priests shall cast salt upon them, and they shall offer them up *for* a burnt-offering unto the LORD. 25 Seven days shalt thou prepare every day a goat *for* a sin-offering: they shall also prepare a young bullock, and a ram out of the flock, without blemish. 26 Seven days shall they purge the altar, and purify it; and they shall consecrate themselves. 27 And when these days are expired, it shall be, *that* upon the eighth day, and *so* forward, the priests shall make your burnt-offerings upon the altar, and your peace-offerings; and I will accept you, saith the Lord GOD.

This relates to the altar in this mystical temple, and that is mystical too; for Christ is our altar. The Jews, after their return out of captivity, had an altar long before they had a temple, Ezra iii. 3. But this was an altar in the temple. Now here we have,

I. The measures of the altar, *v.* 13. It was six yards square at the top and seven yards square at the bottom; it was four yards and a half high; it had a lower bench or shelf, here called a *settle*, a yard from the ground, on which some of the priests stood to minister, and another two yards above that, on which others of them stood, and these had each of them half a yard broad, and had ledges on either side, that they might stand firmly upon them. The sacrifices were killed at the table spoken of before, *ch.* xl. 39. What was to be burnt on the altar was given up to those on the lower bench, and handed by them to those on the higher, and they laid it on the altar. Thus in the service of God we must be assistant to one another.

II. The ordinances of the altar. Directions are here given, 1. Concerning the dedication of the altar at first. *Seven days* were to be spent in the dedication of it, and every day sacrifices were to be offered upon it, and particularly a goat for a *sin-offering* (*v.* 25), besides a young bullock for a *sin-offering* on the first day (*v.* 19), which teaches us in all our religious services to have an eye to Christ the great sin-offering. Neither our persons nor our performances can be acceptable to God unless sin be taken away, and that cannot be taken away but by the blood of Christ, which both sanctifies the altar (for Christ entered by his own blood, Heb. ix. 12) and the gift upon the altar. There were also to be a *bullock* and a ram offered for a *burnt-offering* (*v.* 24), which was intended purely for the glory of God, to teach us to have an eye to that in all our services; we present ourselves as living sacrifices, and our devotions as spiritual sacrifices, that we and they may be to him for a name, and for a praise, and for a glory. The dedication of the altar is here called the *cleansing* and *purging* of it, *v.* 20, 26. Christ, our altar, though he had no pollution to be cleansed from, yet sanctified himself (John xvii. 19); and when we consecrate the altars of our hearts to God, to have the fire of holy love always burning upon them, we must see that they be purified and cleansed from the love of the world and the lusts of the flesh. It is observable that there are several differences between the rites of dedication here and those which were appointed Exod. xxix., to intimate that the ceremonial institutions were mutable things, and the changes in them were earnests of their period in Christ. Only

here, according to the general law, that all the sacrifices must be seasoned with salt (Lev. ii. 13), particular orders are given (*v.* 24) that the priests shall *cast salt upon the sacrifices. Grace* is the *salt* with which all our religious performances must be seasoned, Col. iv. 6. An everlasting covenant is called a *covenant of salt*, because it is incorruptible. The *glory* reserved for us is incorruptible and undefiled; and the *grace* wrought in us is the hidden man of the heart in that *which is not corruptible.* 2. Concerning the constant use that should be made of it, when it was dedicated: *Henceforward* the priests shall *make their burnt-offerings and peace-offerings upon this altar* (*v.* 27), for *therefore* it was *sanctified*, that it might *sanctify the gift* that was offered upon it. Observe further, (1.) Who were to serve at the altar: The *priests of the seed of Zadok, v.* 19. That family was substituted in the room of Abiathar by Solomon, and God confirms it. His name signifies *righteous*, for they are the righteous seed that are priests to God, through Christ *the Lord our righteousness.* (2.) How they should prepare for this service (*v.* 26): *They shall consecrate themselves,* shall *fill their hand* with the offerings, in token of the giving up of themselves with their offerings to God and to his service. Note, Before we minister to the Lord in holy things we must consecrate ourselves by getting our hands and hearts filled with those things. (3.) How they should speed in it (*v.* 27): *I will accept you.* And if God now accept our works, if our services be pleasing to him, it is enough, we need no more. Those that give themselves to God shall be accepted of God, their persons first and then their performances, through the Mediator.

CHAP. XLIV.

In this chapter we have, I. The appropriating of the east gate of the temple to the prince, ver. 1—3. II. A reproof sent to the house of Israel for their former profanations of God's sanctuary, with a charge to them to be more strict for the future, ver. 4—9 III. The degrading of those Levites that had formerly been guilty of idolatry and the establishing of the priesthood in the family of Zadok, which had kept their integrity, ver. 10—16. IV. Divers laws and ordinances concerning the priests, ver. 17—31.

THEN he brought me back the way of the gate of the outward sanctuary which looketh toward the east; and it *was* shut. 2 Then said the LORD unto me; This gate shall be shut, it shall not be opened, and no man shall enter in by it; because the LORD, the God of Israel, hath entered in by it, therefore it shall be shut. 3 *It is* for the prince; the prince, he shall sit in it to eat bread before the LORD; he shall enter by the way of the porch of *that* gate, and shall go out by the way of the same.

The prophet is here brought to review what he had before once surveyed; for, though we have often looked into the things of God, they will yet bear to be looked over again, such a copiousness there is in them. The lessons we have learned we should still repeat to ourselves. Every time we review the sacred fabric of holy things, which we have in the scriptures, we shall still find something new which we did not before take notice of. The prophet is brought a third time to the east gate, and finds it shut, which intimates that the rest of the gates were open at all times to the worshippers. But such an account is given of this gate's being shut as puts honour, 1. Upon the God of Israel. It is for the honour of him that the gate of the inner court, at which his glory entered when he took possession of the house, was ever after kept shut, and no man was allowed to enter in by it, *v.* 2. The difference ever after made between this and the other gates, that this was shut when the others were open, was intended both to perpetuate the remembrance of the solemn entrance of the glory of the Lord into the house (which it would remain a traditional evidence of the truth of) and also to possess the minds of people with a reverence for the Divine Majesty, and with very awful thoughts of his transcendent glory, which was designed in God's charge to Moses at the bush, *Put off thy shoe from off thy foot.* God will have a way by himself. 2. Upon the prince of Israel, *v.* 3. It is an honour to him that though he may not enter in by this gate, for no man may, yet, (1.) He shall *sit in this gate* to *eat* his share of the peace-offerings, that sacred food, *before the Lord.* (2.) He shall *enter by the way of the porch of that gate*, by some little door or wicket, either in the gate or adjoining to it, which is called the *way of the porch.* This was to signify that God puts some of his glory upon magistrates, upon the princes of his people, for he has said, *You are gods.* Some by the prince here understand the high priest, or the sagan or second priest; and that he only was allowed to enter by this gate, for he was God's representative. Christ is the high priest of our profession, who entered himself into the holy place, and *opened the kingdom of heaven to all believers.*

4 Then brought he me the way of the north gate before the house: and I looked, and, behold, the glory of the LORD filled the house of the LORD: and I fell upon my face. 5 And the LORD said unto me, Son of man, mark well, and behold with thine eyes, and hear with thine ears all that I say unto thee concerning all the ordinances of the house of the LORD, and all the laws thereof; and mark well the entering in of the house, with every going forth of the sanctuary. 6 And thou shalt say to the rebellious, *even*

to the house of Israel, Thus saith the Lord GOD; O ye house of Israel, let it suffice you of all your abominations, 7 In that ye have brought *into my sanctuary* strangers, uncircumcised in heart, and uncircumcised in flesh, to be in my sanctuary, to pollute it, *even* my house, when ye offer my bread, the fat and the blood, and they have broken my covenant because of all your abominations. 8 And ye have not kept the charge of mine holy things: but ye have set keepers of my charge in my sanctuary for yourselves. 9 Thus saith the Lord GOD; No stranger, uncircumcised in heart, nor uncircumcised in flesh, shall enter into my sanctuary, of any stranger that *is* among the children of Israel.

This is much to the same purport with what we had in the beginning of *ch.* xliii. As the prophet must look again upon what he had before seen, so he must be told again what he had before heard. Here, as before, he sees the house *filled with the glory of the Lord,* which strikes an awe upon him, so that he falls prostrate at the sight, the humblest posture of adoration and the expression of a holy awe: *I fell upon my face, v.* 4. Note, The more we see of the glory of God the more low we shall lie in our own eyes. Now here,

I. God charges the prophet to take a very particular notice of all he saw, and all that was said to him (*v.* 5): "*Mark well,* set thy heart, apply thy mind, to the discoveries now made thee." 1. "*Behold with thy eyes* what is *shown* thee, particularly the *entering in of the house* and *every going forth* of it, all the inlets and all the outlets of the sanctuary;" those he must take special notice of. Note, In acquainting ourselves with divine things we must not aim so much at an abstract speculation of the things themselves as at finding the plain appointed way of converse and communion with those things, that we may *go in and out and find pasture.* 2. *Hear with thy ears all that I say unto thee* about *the laws* and *ordinances of the house,* which he was to instruct the people in. Note, Those who are appointed to be teachers have need to be very diligent careful learners, that they may neither forget any of the things they are entrusted with nor mistake concerning them.

II. He sends him upon an errand to the people, *to the rebellious, even to the house of Israel, v.* 6. It is sad to think that the house of Israel should deserve this character from him who perfectly knew them, that a people in covenant with God should be rebellious against him. Who are his subjects if the house of Israel be rebels? But it is an instance of God's rich mercy that, though they had been *rebellious*, yet, being the *house of Israel*, he does not cast them off, but sends an ambassador to them, to invite and encourage them to return to their allegiance, which he would not have done if he had been pleased to kill them. The whole race of mankind has fallen under the character here given of the house of Israel; but our Lord Jesus, when he ascended on high, received gifts for men, *yea, even for the rebellious also, that, as here, the Lord God might dwell among them*, Ps. lxviii. 18.

1. He must tell them of their faults, must show them their rebellions, must show the house of Jacob their sins. Note, Those that are sent to comfort God's people must first convince them, and so prepare them for comfort. *Let it suffice you of all your abominations*, v. 6. Note, It is time for those that have continued long in sin to reckon it long enough, and too long, and to begin to think of taking up in time, and leaving off their evil courses. *" Let the time past of your lives suffice*, for by this time, surely, you have surfeited upon your abominations and have become sick of them,"* 1 Pet. iv.
3. That which is here charged upon them is, (1.) That they had admitted those to the privileges of the sanctuary that were not entitled to them; whereas God had said, *The stranger that comes nigh shall be put to death*, they had not only connived at the intrusion of strangers into the sanctuary, but had themselves introduced them (v. 7): *You brought in strangers uncircumcised in flesh*, and therefore under a legal incapacity to enter into the sanctuary, which was a *breaking of the covenant* of circumcision, throwing down the hedge of their peculiarity, and laying themselves in common with the rest of the world. Yet if these strangers had been devout and good, though they were not circumcised, the crime would not have been so great; but they were *uncircumcised in heart* too, unhumbled, unreformed, and strangers indeed to God and all goodness. When they came to offer sacrifice they brought these with them to feast with them upon the sacrifice, because they were fond of their company, and this was one of their abominations, wherewith they *polluted God's sanctuary;* it was *giving that which was holy unto dogs*, Matt. vii. 6. Note, The admission of those who are openly wicked and profane to special ordinances is a polluting of God's sanctuary and a great provocation to him. (2.) That they had employed those in the service of the sanctuary who were not fit for it. Though none but priests and Levites were to minister in the sanctuary, yet we may suppose that all who were priests and Levites did not immediately attend there, but chosen men of them, who were best qualified, who were most wise, serious, and conscientious, and most likely to keep the charge of the holy

996

things carefully; but, in making this choice, they had not regard to merit and qualification for the work: *" You have set keepers of my charge in my sanctuary for yourselves*, such as you had some favour or affection for, such as you either had got, or hoped to get, money by, or such as would comply with your humours and would dispense with the laws of the sanctuary to please you; *thus you have not kept the charge of my holy things."* Note, Those who have the choice of the keepers of the holy things, if, to serve some secular selfish purpose, they choose such as are unfit and unfaithful, will justly have it laid at their door, that they have betrayed holy things by lodging them in bad hands.

2. He must tell them their duty (v. 9): *" No stranger shall enter into my sanctuary till he has first submitted to the laws of it."* But, lest any should think that this excluded the penitent believing Gentiles from the church, the stranger here is described to be one that is *uncircumcised in heart*, not in sincerity consenting to the covenant, nor putting away the filth of the flesh; whereas the believing Gentiles were *circumcised with the circumcision made without hands*, Col. ii. 11. This circumcision of the heart, in the *spirit, not in the letter*, was what the unbelieving Jews were strangers to and unconcerned about, while yet they were zealous to keep out of the sanctuary uncircumcised Gentiles, witness their rage against Paul when they did but suspect him to have brought *Greeks into the temple*, Acts xxi. 28.

10 And the Levites that are gone away far from me, when Israel went astray, which went astray away from me after their idols; they shall even bear their iniquity. 11 Yet they shall be ministers in my sanctuary, *having* charge at the gates of the house, and ministering to the house: they shall slay the burnt-offering and the sacrifice for the people, and they shall stand before them to minister unto them. 12 Because they ministered unto them before their idols, and caused the house of Israel to fall into iniquity; therefore have I lifted up mine hand against them, saith the Lord God, and they shall bear their iniquity. 13 And they shall not come near unto me, to do the office of a priest unto me, nor to come near to any of my holy things, in the most holy *place:* but they shall bear their shame, and their abominations which they have committed. 14 But I will make them keepers of the charge of the house, for all the service thereof,

and for all that shall be done therein. 15 But the priests the Levites, the sons of Zadok, that kept the charge of my sanctuary when the children of Israel went astray from me, they shall come near to me to minister unto me, and they shall stand before me to offer unto me the fat and the blood, saith the Lord God: 16 They shall enter into my sanctuary, and they shall come near to my table, to minister unto me, and they shall keep my charge.

The Master of the house, being about to set up house again, takes account of his servants the priests, and sees who are fit to be turned out of their places and who to be kept in, and takes a course with them accordingly. I. Those who have been treacherous are degraded and put lower those Levites—or priests who were carried down the stream of the apostasy of Israel formerly, who *went astray from God after their idols* (*v.* 10), who had complied with the idolatrous kings of Israel or Judah, who *ministered to them before their idols* (*v.* 12), bowed with them in the house of Rimmon, or set up altars for them, as Urijah did for Ahaz, and so *caused the house of Israel to fall into iniquity,* led them to sin and hardened them in sin; for, if the priests go astray, many will follow *their pernicious ways.* Perhaps in Babylon some of the Jewish priests had complied with the idolaters of the place, to the great scandal of their religion. Now these priests who had thus prevaricated were justly put under the mark of God's displeasure; or, if they were dead (as it is probable that they were, if the crime were committed before the captivity), the iniquity was visited upon their children. Or perhaps it was the whole family of Abiathar that had been guilty of this trespass, which was now called to account for it. And, 1. They are sentenced to be deprived, in part, of their office, and from the dignity of priests are put down into the condition of ordinary Levites. God has *lifted up his hand against them,* has said it, and sworn it, that *they shall bear their iniquity* (*v.* 12); assuredly they shall suffer for it, shall suffer disgrace for it; *they shall bear their shame* (*v.* 13), for though they have (we charitably hope) repented of it, *yet they shall not come near to do the office of a priest,* that is, those parts of the office that were peculiar to them, they shall not come near to *any of the holy things* within the sanctuary, *v.* 13. Note, those who have robbed God of his honour will justly be deprived of their honour. And it is really a great punishment to be forbidden to come near to God; and justly might those who have once gone away from him be rejected as unworthy ever to come near to him and put at an everlasting distance. 2. Yet there is a mixture of mercy in this

sentence. God deals not in severity, as he might have done, with those who had dealt treacherously with him, but mitigates the sentence, *v.* 11, 14. They are deprived but in part, *ab officio—of their office,* and, it should seem, not at all *à beneficio—of their emoluments.* They shall help to *slay the sacrifice,* which the Levites were permitted to do, and which in this temple was done, not at the altar, but *at the tables, ch.* xl. 39. They shall be porters *at the gates of the house,* and they shall be *keepers of the charge of the house, for all the service thereof.* Note, Those who may not be fit to be employed in one kind of service may yet be fit to be employed in another; and even those who have offended may yet be made use of, and not quite thrown aside, much less thrown away.

II. Those who have been faithful are honoured and established, *v.* 15, 16. These are remarkably distinguished from the other: *"But the sons of Zadok,* who kept their integrity in a time of general apostasy, who *went not astray* when others did, *they shall come near to me, shall come near to my table."* Note, God will put marks of honour upon those who give proofs of their fidelity and constancy to him in shaking trying times, and will employ those in his service who have kept close to his service when others deserted it and drew back. And it ought to be reckoned a true and great reward of stability in duty to be established in it. If we keep close to God, God will keep us close to him.

17 And it shall come to pass, *that* when they enter in at the gates of the inner court, they shall be clothed with linen garments; and no wool shall come upon them, whiles they minister in the gates of the inner court, and within. 18 They shall have linen bonnets upon their heads, and shall have linen breeches upon their loins; they shall not gird *themselves* with any thing that causeth sweat. 19 And when they go forth into the utter court, *even* into the utter court to the people, they shall put off their garments wherein they ministered, and lay them in the holy chambers, and they shall put on other garments; and they shall not sanctify the people with their garments. 20 Neither shall they shave their heads, nor suffer their locks to grow long; they shall only poll their heads. 21 Neither shall any priest drink wine, when they enter into the inner court. 22 Neither shall they take for their wives a widow, nor her that is put away: but they shall take maidens of the seed of

the house of Israel, or a widow that had a priest before. 23 And they shall teach my people *the difference* between the holy and profane, and cause them to discern between the unclean and the clean. 24 And in controversy they shall stand in judgment; *and* they shall judge it according to my judgments: and they shall keep my laws and my statutes in all mine assemblies; and they shall hallow my sabbaths. 25 And they shall come at no dead person to defile themselves: but for father, or for mother, or for son, or for daughter, for brother, or for sister that hath had no husband, they may defile themselves. 26 And after he is cleansed, they shall reckon unto him seven days. 27 And in the day that he goeth into the sanctuary, unto the inner court, to minister in the sanctuary, he shall offer his sin offering, saith the Lord GOD. 28 And it shall be unto them for an inheritance: I *am* their inheritance: and ye shall give them no possession in Israel: I *am* their possession. 29 They shall eat the meat offering, and the sin offering, and the trespass offering; and every dedicated thing in Israel shall be their's. 30 And the first of all the firstfruits of all *things,* and every oblation of all, of every *sort* of your oblations, shall be the priest's: ye shall also give unto the priest the first of your dough, that ye may cause the blessing to rest in thine house. 31 The priests shall not eat of any thing that is dead of itself, or torn, whether it be fowl or beast.

God's priests must be *regulars,* not *seculars;* and therefore here are rules laid down for them to govern themselves by and due encouragement given them to live up to those rules. Directions are here given,

I. Concerning their clothes; they must wear *linen garments* when they *went in to minister* or do any service in the inner court, or in the sanctuary, and nothing that was *woollen,* because it would *cause sweat, v.* 17, 18. They must dress themselves cool, that they might go the more readily about their work; and they had the more need to do so because they were to attend the altars, which had constant fires upon them. And they must dress themselves clean and sweet, and avoid every thing that was sweaty and filthy, **to signify** the purity of mind with

998

which the service of God is to be attended to. Sweat came in with sin and was part of the curse. *In the sweat of thy face shalt thou eat bread.* Clothes came in with sin, coats of skins did; and therefore the priests must use as little and as light clothing as possible, and not such as caused sweat. When they had finished their service they must change their clothes again, and lay up their linen garments in the chambers appointed for that purpose, *v.* 19, as before, *ch.* xlii. 14. They must not go among the people with their holy garments on, lest they should imagine themselves sanctified by the touch of them; or, *They shall sanctify the people,* that is (as it is explained, *ch.* xlii. 14), they shall *approach to those things which are for the people,* in their ordinary *garments.*

II. Concerning their hair; in that they must avoid extremes on both hands (*v.* 20): *They must not shave their heads,* in imitation of the Gentile priests, and as the priests of the Romish church do; nor, on the other hand, must they *suffer their locks to grow long,* as the *beaux,* or that they might be thought Nazarites, when really they were not; but they must be grave and modest, must *poll their heads* and keep their hair short. If a *man,* especially a minister, wear *long hair,* it is not becoming (1 Cor. xi. 14); it is effeminate.

III. Concerning their diet; they must be sure to *drink no wine* when they went in to minister, lest they should drink to excess, should drink and forget the law, *v.* 21. *It is not for kings to drink wine,* more than will do them good, much less for priests. See Lev. x. 9; Prov. xxxi. 4, 5.

IV. Concerning their marriages, *v.* 22. Here they must consult the credit of their office, and not marry one that had been *divorced,* that was at least under the suspicion of immodesty, nor a *widow,* unless she were a priest's widow, that had been accustomed to the usages of the priests' families. Others may do that which ministers may not do, but must deny themselves in, in honour of their character. Their wives as well as themselves must be of good report.

V. Concerning their preaching and church-government. 1. It was part of their business to teach the people; and herein they must approve themselves both skilful and faithful (*v.* 23): *They shall teach my people the difference between the holy and the profane,* between good and evil, lawful and unlawful, that they may neither scruple what is lawful nor venture upon what is unlawful, that they may not pollute what is holy nor pollute themselves with what is profane. Ministers must take pains to cause *people to discern between the clean and the unclean,* that they may not confound the distinctions between right and wrong, nor mistake concerning them, so as to *put darkness for light and light for darkness,* but may have a good judgment of discretion concerning their own actions. 2. It was part of their business to judge upon appeals made to them (Deut. xvii. 8, 9); and *in controversy they shall stand in judgment*, v. 24. They shall have the honesty to stand up for what is right, and, when they have passed a right judgment, shall have the courage to stand to it and stand by it. They must judge, not according to their own fancies, or inclinations, or secular interests, but *according to my judgments;* that must be their rule and standard. Note, Ministers must decide controversies according to the word of God, *to the law and to the testimony. Sit liber judex—Let the judge be unbiassed.* Their business is to keep courts in God's name, to preside in the congregations of his people. And herein they must go to the statute-book : They shall *keep my statutes in all my assemblies.* God calls the assemblies of his people *his* assemblies, because they are held in his name, to his glory. Ministers are the masters of those assemblies, are to preside in them, and in all their acts must keep close to God's laws. Another part of their work, as church governors, is to *hallow God's sabbaths,* to do the public work of that day with a becoming care and reverence, as the work of a holy day should be done, and to see that God's people also sanctify that day and do nothing to pollute it.

VI. Concerning their mourning for dead relations; the rule here agrees with the law of Moses, Lev. xxi. 1, 11. A priest shall not come near any *dead body* (for they must be purified *from dead works*) except of his next relations, v. 25. Decent expressions of a pious sorrow for dear relations, when they are removed by death, are not disagreeable to the character of a minister. Yet by this approach to the dead body of a relation they contracted a ceremonial pollution, from which they must be cleansed by a *sin-offering* before they went in again to minister, v. 26, 27. Note, Though sorrow for the dead is very allowable and commendable, yet there is danger of sinning in it, either by excess or dissimulation; and those tears have too often need to be *wept over again.*

VII. Concerning their maintenance; they must live upon the altar at which they served, and live comfortably (v. 28) : " *You shall give them no possession in Israel,* no lands or tenements, lest they should be entangled with the affairs of this life;" for God has said, *I am their inheritance,* and they need no other in reserve; *I am their possession,* and they need no other in hand. Some land was allowed them (*ch.* xlviii. 10), but their principal subsistence was by their office. What God appropriated to himself they were the receivers of, for their own proper use and behoof; they lived upon the holy things, and so God himself was the portion both of their inheritance and of their cup. Note, Those who have God for their inheritance and their possession may be content with a little, and ought not to covet a great deal of the possessions and inheritances

of this earth. If we have God, we have *all ;* and therefore may well reckon that we have enough. Observe,

1. What the priests were to have from the people, for their maintenance and encouragement. (1.) They must have the flesh of many of the offerings, the *sin-offering and trespass-offering,* which would supply them and their families with flesh-meat, and the *meat-offerings,* which would supply them with bread. What we offer to God will redound to our own advantage. (2.) They must have every dedicated devoted thing in Israel, which was in many cases to be turned into money and given to the priest. This is explained, v. 30. *Every oblation* or freewill-offering (which in times of reformation and devotion would be many and considerable) *of all, of every sort of your oblations, shall be the priest's.* We have the law concerning them Lev. xxvii. (3.) They were to have *the first of the dough* when it was going to the oven, as well as the first of their fruits when they were going to the barn. God, who is the first, must have the first; and, if it belong to him, his priests must have it. We may *then* comfortably enjoy what we have, when a share of it has been first set apart for works of piety and charity. To this the apostle's rule bears some analogy, to *begin the week* with laying by for pious uses, 1 Cor. xvi. 2. The priests being so well provided for, it would be inexcusable in them if they (contrary to the law which every Israelite is bound by) should *eat that which is torn or which died of itself,* v. 31. Those that were in want of necessary food might perhaps expect to be dispensed with in such a case. Poverty has its temptations, but the priests were so well provided for that they could have no pretence for it.

2. What the people might expect from the priest for their recompence. Those that are kind to a prophet, to a priest, shall have a prophet's, a priest's reward : *That he may cause the blessing to rest in thy house* (v. 30), that God may cause it by commanding it, that the priest may cause it by praying for it; and it was part of the priest's work to *bless the people in the name of the Lord,* not only their congregations, but their families. Note, It is all in all to the comfort of any house to have the blessing of God upon it and to have the blessing to rest in it, to dwell where we dwell and to attend the entail of it upon those that shall come after us. And the way to have the blessing of God abide upon our estates is to honour God with them, and to give him and his ministers, him and his poor, their share out of them. God blesses, he surely blesses, the habitation of those who are thus just, Prov. iii. 33. And ministers, by instructing and praying for the families that are kind to them, should do their part towards causing the blessing to rest there. *Peace be to this house.*

CHAP. XLV.

In this chapter is further represented to the prophet, in vision, I. The division of the holy land, so much for the temple, and the priests that attended the service of it (ver. 1—4), so much for the Levites (ver. 5), so much for the city (ver. 6), so much for the prince, and the residue to the people, ver. 7, 8. II. The ordinances of justice that were given both to prince and people, ver. 9—12. III. The oblations they were to offer, and the prince's part in those oblations, ver. 13—17. Particularly in the beginning of the year (ver. 18—20) and in the passover, and the feast of tabernacles, ver. 21—25. And all this seems to point at the new church-state that should be set up under the gospel, which, both for extent and for purity, should far exceed that of the Old Testament.

MOREOVER, when ye shall divide by lot the land for inheritance, ye shall offer an oblation unto the LORD, a holy portion of the land: the length *shall be* the length of five and twenty thousand *reeds*, and the breadth *shall be* ten thousand. This *shall be* holy in all the borders thereof round about. 2 Of this there shall be for the sanctuary five hundred *in length*, with five hundred *in breadth*, square round about; and fifty cubits round about for the suburbs thereof. 3 And of this measure shalt thou measure the length of five and twenty thousand, and the breadth of ten thousand : and in it shall be the sanctuary *and* the most holy *place*. 4 The holy *portion* of the land shall be for the priests, the ministers of the sanctuary, which shall come near to minister unto the LORD: and it shall be a place for their houses, and a holy place for the sanctuary. 5 And the five and twenty thousand of length, and the ten thousand of breadth, shall also the Levites, the ministers of the house, have for themselves, for a possession for twenty chambers. 6 And ye shall appoint the possession of the city five thousand broad, and five and twenty thousand long, over against the oblation of the holy *portion :* it shall be for the whole house of Israel. 7 And *a portion shall be* for the prince on the one side and on the other side of the oblation of the holy *portion*, and of the possession of the city, before the oblation of the holy *portion*, and before the possession of the city, from the west side westward, and from the east side eastward : and the length *shall be* over against one of the portions, from the west border unto the east border. 8 In the land shall be his possession in Israel: and my

princes shall no more oppress my people ; and *the rest of* the land shall they give to the house of Israel according to their tribes.

Directions are here given for the dividing of the land after their return to it ; and, God having warranted them to do it, it would be an act of faith, and not of folly, thus to divide it before they had it. And it would be welcome news to the captives to hear that they should not only return to their own land, but that, whereas they were now but few in number, they should *increase and multiply*, so as to *replenish* it. But this never had its accomplishment in the Jewish state after the return out of captivity, but was to be fulfilled in the model of the Christian church, which was perfectly new (as this division of the land was quite different from that in Joshua's time) and much enlarged by the accession of the Gentiles to it ; and it will be perfected in the heavenly kingdom, of which the land of Canaan had always been a type. Now, 1. Here is the portion of land assigned to *the sanctuary*, in the midst of which the temple was to be built, with all its courts and purlieus ; the rest round about it was for the priests. This is called (v. 1) *an oblation to the Lord ;* for what is given in works of piety, for the maintenance and support of the worship of God and the advancement of religion, God accepts as given to him, if it be done with a single eye. It is a *holy portion of the land*, which is to be set out first, as the *first-fruits* that sanctify the lump. The appropriating of lands for the support of religion and the ministry is an act of piety that bids as fair for perpetuity, and the benefit of posterity, as any. This *holy portion of the land* was to be measured, and the borders of it fixed, that the sanctuary itself might not have more than its share and in time engross the whole land. So far the lands of the church shall extend and no further ; as in our own kingdom donations to the church were of old limited by the *statute* of *mortmain*. The lands here allotted to the sanctuary were 25,000 *reeds* (so our translation makes it, though some make them only *cubits*) in length, and 10,000 in breadth—about eighty miles one way and thirty miles another way (say some) ; twenty-five miles one way and ten miles the other way, so others. The priests and Levites that were to come near to minister were to have their dwellings in this *portion of the land* that was round about the sanctuary, that they might be near their work ; whereas by the distribution of the land in Joshua's time the cities of the priests and Levites were dispersed all the nation over. This intimates that gospel ministers should reside upon their charge ; where their service lies there must they live 2. Next to the lands of the sanctuary the city-lands are assigned, in which the holy city was to be built, and with the issues and profits of which the citizens were to be maintained (*v.* 6): *It shall be for the whole house of Israel*, not appropriated, as before, to one tribe or two, but some of all the tribes shall dwell in the city, as we find they did, Neh. xi. 1, 2. The portion for the city was fully as long, but only half as broad, as that for the sanctuary; for the city was enriched by trade and therefore had the less need of lands. 3. The next allotment after the church-lands and the city-lands is of the crown-lands, *v.* 7, 8. Here is no admeasurement of these, but they are said to lie *on the one side and on the other side* of the church-lands and city-lands, to intimate that the prince with his wealth and power was to be a protection to both. Some make the prince's share equal to the church's and city's share both together; others make it to be a thirteenth part of the rest of the land, the other twelve parts being for the twelve tribes. The prince that attends continually to the administration of public affairs must have wherewithal to support his dignity, and have abundance, that he may not be in temptation to oppress the people, which yet with many does not prevent that; but the grace of God shall prevent it, for it is promised here, *My princes shall no more oppress my people:* for God will make the *officers peace* and the *exactors righteousness.* Notwithstanding this, we find that after the return of the Jews to their own land the princes were complained of for their exactions. But Nehemiah was one that did not do as the *former governors*, and yet kept a handsome court, Neh. v. 15, 18. But so much is said of the prince in this mystical holy state, to intimate that in the gospel-church magistrates should be as *nursing fathers* to it and Christian princes its patrons and protectors; and the holy religion they profess, as far as they are subject to the power of it, will restrain them from oppressing God's people, because they are more his people than theirs. 4. The rest of the lands were to be distributed to the people *according to their tribes*, who had reason to think themselves well settled, when they had both the *testimony of Israel* and the *throne of judgment* so near them.

9 Thus saith the Lord GOD; Let it suffice you, O princes of Israel: remove violence and spoil, and execute judgment and justice, take away your exactions from my people, saith the Lord GOD. 10 Ye shall have just balances, and a just ephah, and a just bath. 11 The ephah and the bath shall be of one measure, that the bath may contain·the tenth part of a homer, and the ephah the tenth part of a homer: the measure thereof shall be after the homer. 12 And the shekel *shall be* twenty gerahs: twenty shekels, five and twenty shekels, fifteen shekels, shall be your maneh.

We have here some general rules of justice laid down both for prince and people, the rules of distributive and commutative justice; for godliness without honesty is but a form of godliness, will neither please God nor avail to the benefit of any people. Be it therefore enacted, by the authority of the church's King and God, 1. That *princes do not oppress their subjects*, but duly and faithfully administer justice among them (*v.* 9): *"Let it suffice you, O princes of Israel!* that you have been oppressive to the people and have enriched yourselves by spoil and violence, that you have so long fleeced the flock instead of feeding them, and henceforward do so no more."* Note, Even princes and great men that have long done amiss must at length think it time, high time, to reform and amend; for no prescription will justify a wrong. Instead of saying that they have been long accustomed to oppress, and therefore may persist in it, for the custom will bear them out, they should say that they have been long accustomed to it and therefore, as here, *Let the time past suffice*, and let them now remove *violence and spoil:* let them drop wrongful demands, cancel wrongful usages, and turn out those from employments under them that do violence. Let them *take away their exactions*, ease their subjects of those taxes which they find lie heavily upon them, and let them *execute judgment and justice* according to law, as the duty of their place requires. Note, All princes, but especially the princes of Israel, are concerned to do justice; for of their people God says, They are my people, and they in a special manner *rule for God.* 2. That one neighbour do not cheat another in commerce (*v.* 10): *You shall have just balances*, in which to weigh both money and goods, a *just ephah* for dry measure of corn and flour, a *just bath* for the measure of liquids, wine, and oil; and the *ephah* and *bath* shall be *one measure*, the tenth part of a *chomer*, or *cor*, *v.* 11. So that the ephah and bath contained (as the learned Dr. Cumberland has computed) seven wine gallons and four pints, and something more. An omer was but the tenth part of an ephah (Exod. xvi. 36) and the one hundredth part of a *chomer*, or *homer*, and contained about six pints. The *shekel* is here settled (*v.* 13); it is twenty *gerahs*, just half a *Roman* ounce, in our money 2s. 4¼d. and almost the eighth part of a farthing, as the aforesaid learned man exactly computes it. By the shekels the *maneh*, or pound, was reckoned, which, when it was set for a mere weight (says bishop Cumberland), without respect to coinage, contained just 100 shekels, as appears by comparing 1 Kings x. 17, where it is said three *manehs*, or *pounds, of gold, went to one shield*, with the parallel place, 2 Chron. ix. 16, where it is said 300 *shekels of gold went to one shield.* But when the *maneh* is set for a sum of money or coin it contains but sixty shekels, as appears here, where twenty shekels, twenty-five shekels, and fifteen shekels, which in all make sixty, shall be the *maneh.* But it is thus reckoned because they had one piece of money that weighed twenty shekels, another twenty-five, another fifteen, all of which made up one pound, as a learned writer here observes. Note, It concerns God's Israel to be very honest and just in all their dealings, very punctual and exact in rendering to all their due, and very cautious to do wrong to none, because otherwise they spoil the acceptableness of their profession with God and the reputation of it before men.

13 This *is* the oblation that ye shall offer; the sixth part of an ephah of a homer of wheat, and ye shall give the sixth part of an ephah of a homer of barley: 14 Concerning the ordinance of oil, the bath of oil, *ye shall offer* the tenth part of a bath out of the cor, *which is* a homer of ten baths; for ten baths *are* a homer: 15 And one lamb out of the flock, out of two hundred, out of the fat pastures of Israel; for a meat-offering, and for a burnt-offering, and for peace-offerings, to make reconciliation for them, saith the Lord GOD. 16 All the people of the land shall give this oblation for the prince in Israel. 17 And it shall be the prince's part *to give* burnt-offerings, and meat-offerings, and drink-offerings, in the feasts, and in the new moons, and in the sabbaths, in all solemnities of the house of Israel: he shall prepare the sin-offering, and the meat-offering, and the burnt-offering, and the peace-offerings, to make reconciliation for the house of Israel. 18 Thus saith the Lord GOD; In the first *month*, in the first *day* of the month, thou shalt take a young bullock without blemish, and cleanse the sanctuary: 19 And the priest shall take of the blood of the sin-offering, and put *it* upon the posts of the house, and upon the four corners of the settle of the altar, and upon the posts of the gate of the inner court. 20 And so thou shalt do the seventh *day* of the month for every

1002

one that erreth, and for *him that is* simple: so shall ye reconcile the house. 21 In the first *month*, in the fourteenth day of the month, ye shall have the passover, a feast of seven days; unleavened bread shall be eaten. 22 And upon that day shall the prince prepare for himself and for all the people of the land a bullock *for* a sin-offering. 23 And seven days of the feast he shall prepare a burnt-offering to the LORD, seven bullocks and seven rams without blemish daily the seven days; and a kid of the goats daily *for* a sin-offering. 24 And he shall prepare a meat-offering of an ephah for a bullock, and an ephah for a ram, and a hin of oil for an ephah. 25 In the seventh *month*, in the fifteenth day of the month, shall he do the like in the feast of the seven days, according to the sin-offering, according to the burnt-offering, and according to the meat-offering, and according to the oil.

Having laid down the rules of righteousness towards men, which is really a branch of true religion, he comes next to give some directions for their religion towards God, which is a branch of universal righteousness.

I. It is required that they offer an oblation to the Lord out of what they have (*v.* 13): *All the people of the land* must give an oblation, *v.* 16. As God's tenants, they must pay a quitrent to their great landlord. They had offered an oblation out of their real estates (*v.* 1), a *holy portion of their land;* now they are directed to offer an oblation out of their personal estates, their goods and chattels, as an acknowledgment of their receivings from him, their dependence on him, and their obligations to him. Note, Whatever our substance is we must honour God with it, by giving him his dues out of it. Not that God has need of or may be benefited by any thing that we can give him, Ps. l. 9. No; it is but an *oblation;* we only *offer it* to him; the benefit of it returns back to ourselves, to his poor, who, as our neighbours, are ourselves, or to his ministers who serve continually for our good.

II. The proportion of this oblation is here determined, which was not done by the law of Moses. No mention is made of the tithe, but only of this oblation. And the *quantum* of this is thus settled:—1. Out of their corn they were to offer a sixtieth part; out of every *homer* of *wheat* and *barley*, which contained ten ephahs, they were to offer the sixth part of one ephah, which was a sixtieth part of the whole, *v.* 13. 2. Out of their oil (and probably their wine too) they were to offer a hundredth part, for this oblation; out of every cor, or homer, which contained ten baths, they were to offer the tenth part of one bath, *v.* 14. This was given to the altar; for in every meat-offering there was *flour mingled with oil.* 3. Out of their flocks they were to give *one lamb* out of 200; that was the smallest proportion of all, *v.* 15. But it must be *out of the fat pastures of Israel.* They must not offer to God that which was taken up from the common, but the fattest and best they had, for *burnt-offerings* and *peace-offerings:* the former were offered for the giving of glory to God, the latter for the fetching in of mercy, grace, and peace, from God, and in our spiritual sacrifices these are our two great errands at the throne of grace; but, in order to the acceptance of both, these sacrifices were to *make reconciliation* for them. Christ is our sacrifice of atonement, by whom reconciliation is made, and to him we must have an eye in our sacrifices of acknowledgment.

III. This oblation must be given *for the prince in Israel, v.* 16. Some read it *to the prince,* and understand it of Christ, who is indeed the prince in Israel, to whom we must offer our oblations, and into whose hands we must put them, to be presented to the Father. Or, They shall give it *with* the prince; every private person shall bring his oblation, to be offered with that of the prince; for it follows (*v.* 17), It *shall be the prince's part to provide* all the offerings, *to make reconciliation for the house of Israel.* The people were to bring their oblations to him according to the foregoing rules, and he was to bring them to the sanctuary, and to make up what fell short out of his own. Note, It is the duty of rulers to take care of religion, and to see that the duties of it be regularly and carefully performed by those under their charge, and that nothing be wanting that is requisite thereto: the magistrate is the keeper of both tables; and it is a happy thing when those that are above others in power and dignity go before them in the service of God.

IV. Some particular solemnities are here appointed.

1. Here is one in the beginning of the year, which seems to be altogether new, and not instituted by the law of Moses; it is the annual solemnity of cleansing the sanctuary. (1.) *On the first day of the first month* (upon new-year's day) they were to offer a sacrifice for the *cleansing of the sanctuary* (*v.* 18), that is, to make atonement for the iniquity of the holy things the year past, that they might bring none of the guilt of them into the services of the new year, and to implore grace for the preventing of that iniquity, and for the better performance of the service of the sanctuary the ensuing year. And, in token of this, the blood of this *sin-offering* was to be put upon *the posts* of the temple, the four corners, not of the altar, but the *settle of the altar,* and the *posts of the gate of the inner*

court (*v.* 19), to signify that by it atonement was intended to be made for the sins of all the servants that attended that house, priests, Levites, and people, even the sins that were found in all their services. Note, Even sanctuaries on earth need cleansing, frequent cleansing; that above needs none. Those that worship God together should often join in renewing their repentance for their manifold defects, and applying the blood of Christ for the pardon of them, and in renewing their covenants to be more careful for the future; and it is very seasonable to begin the year with this work, as Hezekiah did when it had been long neglected, 2 Chron. xxix. 17. They were here appointed to *cleanse the sanctuary* upon the first day of the month, because on the fourteenth day of the month they were to eat the *passover,* an ordinance which, of all Old-Testament institutions, had most in it of Christ and gospel grace, and therefore it was very fit that they should begin to prepare for it a fortnight before by cleansing the sanctuary. (2.) This sacrifice was to be repeated *on the seventh day of the first month, v.* 20. And then it was intended to make atonement *for every one that errs, and for him that is simple.* Note, He that sins *errs* and is *simple:* he mistakes, he goes out of the way, and shows himself to be foolish and unwise. But here it is spoken of those sins which are committed through ignorance, mistake, or inadvertency, whether by any of the priests, or of the Levites, or of the people. Sacrifices were appointed to atone for such sins as men were surprised into, or did before they were aware, which they would not have done if they had known and remembered aright, which they were overtaken in, and for which, afterwards, they condemn themselves. But for presumptuous sins, committed with a high hand, there was no sacrifice appointed, Num. xv. 30. By these repeated sacrifices you shall *reconcile the house,* that is, God will be reconciled to it, and continue the tokens of his presence in it, and will *let it alone this year also.*

2. The passover was to be religiously observed at the time appointed, *v.* 21. Christ is *our passover, that is sacrificed for us.* We celebrate the memorial of that sacrifice and feast upon it, triumphing in our deliverance out of the Egyptian slavery of sin and our preservation from the sword of the destroying angel, the sword of divine justice, in the Lord's supper, which is our passover-feast, as the whole Christian life is, and must be, the feast of unleavened bread. It is here appointed that the prince shall prepare a *sin-offering,* to be offered *for himself and the people,* a bullock on the *first* day (*v.* 22) and a *kid of the goats* every other day (*v.* 23), to teach us, in all our attendance upon God for communion with him, to have an eye to the great sin-offering, by which *transgression* was *finished* and an *everlasting righteousness* brought in. On every day of the feast there was

to be a *burnt-offering*, purely for the honour of God, of no less than seven bullocks and seven rams, with their meat-offering, which were wholly consumed upon the altar, and yet *no waste, v.* 23, 24.

3. The feast of tabernacles; that is spoken of next (*v.* 25), and there is no mention of the feast of pentecost, which came between that of the passover and that of tabernacles. Orders are here given (above what were given by the law of Moses) for the same sacrifices to be offered during the seven days of the passover. See the deficiency of the legal sacrifices for sin; they were therefore often repeated, not only every year, but every feast, every day of the feast, because *they could not make the comers thereunto perfect,* Heb. x. 1, 3. See the necessity of our frequently repeating the same religious exercises. Though the sacrifice of atonement is offered *once for all,* yet the sacrifices of acknowledgment, that of a broken heart, that of a thankful heart, those spiritual sacrifices which are acceptable to God through Christ Jesus, must be every day offered. We should, as here, fall into a method of holy duties, and keep to it.

CHAP. XLVI.

In this chapter we have, I. Some further rules given both to the priests and to the people, relating to their worship, ver. 1—15. II. A law concerning the prince's disposal of his inheritance, ver. 16—18. III. A description of the places provided for the boiling of the sacrifices and the baking of the meat-offerings, ver. 19—24.

THUS saith the Lord God; The gate of the inner court that looketh toward the east shall be shut the six working days; but on the sabbath it shall be opened, and in the day of the new moon it shall be opened. 2 And the prince shall enter by the way of the porch of *that* gate without, and shall stand by the post of the gate, and the priest shall prepare his burnt-offering and his peace-offerings, and he shall worship at the threshold of the gate: then he shall go forth; but the gate shall not be shut until the evening. 3 Likewise the people of the land shall worship at the door of this gate before the LORD in the sabbaths and in the new moons. 4 And the burnt-offering that the prince shall offer unto the LORD in the sabbath-day *shall be* six lambs without blemish, and a ram without blemish. 5 And the meat-offering *shall be* an ephah for a ram, and the meat-offering for the lambs as he shall be able to give, and a hin of oil to an ephah. 6 And in the day of the new moon *it shall be* a young bullock without blemish, and six lambs, and a ram : they

shall be without blemish. 7 And he shall prepare a meat-offering, an ephah for a bullock, and an ephah for a ram, and for the lambs according as his hand shall attain unto, and a hin of oil to an ephah. 8 And when the prince shall enter, he shall go in by the way of the porch of *that* gate, and he shall go forth by the way thereof. 9 But when the people of the land shall come before the LORD in the solemn feasts, he that entereth in by the way of the north gate to worship shall go out by the way of the south gate; and he that entereth by the way of the south gate shall go forth by the way of the north gate : he shall not return by the way of the gate whereby he came in, but shall go forth over against it. 10 And the prince in the midst of them, when they go in, shall go in; and when they go forth, shall go forth. 11 And in the feasts and in the solemnities the meat-offering shall be an ephah to a bullock, and an ephah to a ram, and to the lambs as he is able to give, and a hin of oil to an ephah. 12 Now when the prince shall prepare a voluntary burnt-offering or peace-offerings voluntarily unto the LORD, *one* shall then open him the gate that looketh toward the east, and he shall prepare his burnt-offering and his peace-offerings, as he did on the sabbath-day : then he shall go forth; and after his going forth *one* shall shut the gate. 13 Thou shalt daily prepare a burnt-offering unto the LORD *of* a lamb of the first year without blemish : thou shalt prepare it every morning. 14 And thou shalt prepare a meat-offering for it every morning, the sixth part of an ephah, and the third part of a hin of oil, to temper with the fine flour; a meat-offering continually by a perpetual ordinance unto the LORD. 15 Thus shall they prepare the lamb, and the meat-offering, and the oil, every morning *for* a continual burnt-offering.

Whether the rules for public worship here laid down were designed to be observed, even in those things wherein they differed from the law of Moses, and were so observed under the second temple, is not certain; we find not in the history of that latter part of the Jewish church that they governed themselves in their worship by these ordinances, as one would think they should have done, but only by the law of Moses, looking upon this *then* in the next age after as mystical, and not literal. We may observe, in these verses,

I. That the place of worship was fixed, and rules were given concerning that, both to prince and people.

1. The east gate, which was kept shut at other times, was to be opened on the sabbath days, on the new moons (*v.* 1), and whenever the prince offered a voluntary offering, *v.* 12. Of the keeping of this gate ordinarily shut we read before (*ch.* xliv. 2); whereas the other gates of the court were opened every day, this was opened only on high days and on special occasions, when it was opened for the prince, who was to *go in by the way of the porch of that gate, v.* 2, 8. Some think he went in with the priests and Levites into the *inner court* (for into that court this gate was the entrance), and they observe that magistrates and ministers should join forces, and go the same way, hand in hand, in promoting the service of God. But it should rather seem that he did not go *through* the gate (as the glory of the Lord had done), though it was open, but he went *by the way of the porch of the gate,* stood *at the post of the gate,* and *worshipped at the threshold of the gate* (*v.* 2), where he had a full view of the priests' performances at the altar, and signified his concurrence in them, for himself and for the people of the land, that stood behind him *at the door of that gate, v.* 3. Thus must every prince show himself to be of David's mind, who would very willingly be *a door-keeper in the house of his God,* and, as the word there is, *lie at the threshold,* Ps. lxxxiv. 10. Note, The greatest of men are less than the least of the ordinances of God. Even princes themselves, when they draw near to God, must worship *with reverence and godly fear,* owning that even they are unworthy to approach to him. But Christ is *our prince,* whom God causes to *draw near* and *approach to him,* Jer. xxx. 21.

2. As to the north gate and south gate, by which they entered into the *court of the people* (not into the inner court), there was this rule given, that whoever came in at the *north gate* should go out at the *south gate,* and whoever came in at the *south gate* should go out at the *north gate, v.* 9. Some think this was to prevent thrusting and jostling one another; for God is *the God of order, and not of confusion.* We may suppose that they came in at the gate that was next their own houses, but, when they went away, God would have them go out at that gate which would lead them *the furthest way about,* that they might have time for meditation; being thereby obliged to go a great way round the

sanctuary, they might have an opportunity to *consider the palaces* of it, and, if they improved their time well in fetching this circuit, they would call it the nearest way home. Some observe that this may remind us, in the service of God, to be still pressing forward (Phil. iii. 13) and not to *look back,* and, in our attendance upon ordinances, not to go back as we came, but more holy, and heavenly, and spiritual.

3. It is appointed that *the people shall worship at the door of the east gate,* where the prince does, he at the head and they attending him, both *on the sabbath and on the new moons* (*v.* 3), and that, when they come in and go out, the prince shall be *in the midst of them, v.* 10. Note, Great men should, by their constant and reverent attendance on God in public worship, give a good example to their inferiors, both engaging them and encouraging them to do likewise. It is a very graceful becoming thing for persons of quality to go to church with their servants, and tenants, and poor neighbours about them, and to behave themselves there with an air of seriousness and devotion; and those who thus honour God with their honour he will delight to honour.

II. That the ordinances of worship were fixed. Though the prince is supposed himself to be a very hearty zealous friend to the sanctuary, yet it is not left to him, no, not in concert with the priests, to appoint what sacrifices shall be offered, but God himself appoints them; for it is his prerogative to institute the rites and ceremonies of religious worship. 1. Every morning, as duly as the morning came, they must offer *a lamb* for a *burnt-offering, v.* 13. It is strange that no mention is made of the evening sacrifice; but Christ having come, and having offered himself now *in the end of the world* (Heb. ix. 26), we are to look upon him as the evening sacrifice, about the time of the offering up of which he died. 2. On the sabbath days, whereas by the law of Moses four lambs were to be offered (Num. xxviii. 9), it is here appointed that (at the prince's charge) there shall be *six lambs* offered, *and a ram* besides (*v.* 4), to intimate how much we should abound in sabbath work, now in gospel-time, and what plenty of the spiritual sacrifices of prayer and praise we should offer up to God on that day; and, if *with such sacrifices God is well-pleased,* surely we have a great deal of reason to be so. 3. On the new moons, in the beginning of their months, there was over and above the usual sabbath-sacrifices the additional offering of a young bullock, *v.* 6. Those who do much for God and their souls, stately and constantly, must yet, upon some occasions, do still more. 4. All the sacrifices were to be *without blemish;* so Christ, the great sacrifice, was (1 Pet. i. 19), and so Christians, who are to present themselves to God as living sacrifices, should aim and endeavour to be—*blameless, and harmless, and without rebuke.* 5. All the sacrifices were to have their meat-offerings annexed to them, for so the law of Moses had appointed, to show what a good table God keeps in his house and that we ought to honour him with the fruit of our ground as well as with the fruit of our cattle, because in both he has blessed us, Deut. xxviii. 4. In the beginning, Cain offered the one and Abel the other. Some observe that the meat-offerings here are much larger in proportion than they were by the law of Moses. Then the proportion was *three tenth-deals to a bullock,* and *two to a ram* (so many tenth parts of an ephah) and half a hin of oil at the most (Num. xv. 6—9); but here, for every bullock and every ram, a whole ephah and a whole hin of oil (*v.* 7), which intimates that under the gospel, the great atoning sacrifice having been offered, these unbloody sacrifices shall be more abounded in; or, in general, it intimates that as now, under the gospel, God abounds in the gifts of his grace to us, more than under the law, so we should abound in the returns of praise and duty to him. But it is observable that in the meat-offering *for the lambs* the prince is allowed to offer *as he shall be able to give* (v. 5, 7, 11), *as his hand shall attain unto.* Note, Princes themselves must spend as they can afford; and even in that which is laid out in works of piety God expects and requires but that we should do according to our ability, every man *as God has prospered him,* 1 Cor. xvi. 2. God has not *made us to serve with an offering* (Isa. xliii. 23), but considers our frame and state. Yet this will not countenance those who pretend a disability that is not real, or those who by their extravagances in other things disable themselves to do the good they should. And we find those praised who, in an extraordinary case of charity, went not only *to their power,* but *beyond their power.*

16 Thus saith the Lord God; If the prince give a gift unto any of his sons, the inheritance thereof shall be his sons'; it *shall be* their possession by inheritance. 17 But if he give a gift of his inheritance to one of his servants, then it shall be his to the year of liberty; after it shall return to the prince: but his inheritance shall be his sons' for them. 18 Moreover the prince shall not take of the people's inheritance by oppression, to thrust them out of their possession; *but* he shall give his sons inheritance out of his own possession: that my people be not scattered every man from his possession.

We have here a law for the limiting of the power of the prince in the disposing of the

crown-lands. 1. If he have a *son* that is a favourite, or has merited well, he may, if he please, as a token of his favour and in recompence for his services, settle some parts of his lands upon him and his heirs for ever (*v.* 16), provided it do not go out of the family. There may be a cause for parents, when their children have grown up, to be more kind to one than to another, as Jacob gave to Joseph one portion *above his brethren,* Gen. xlviii. 22. 2. Yet, if he have a servant that is a favourite, he may not in like manner settle lands upon him, v. 17. But if he see cause he may give him lands to the year of jubilee, and then they must return to the family again, *v.* 17. The servant might have the rents, issues, and pro ts, for such a term, but the inheritance, the *jus proprietarium—the right of proprietorship,* shall remain in the prince and his heirs. It was fit that a difference should be put between a child and a servant, like that John viii. 35. *The servant abides not in the house for ever,* as the son does. 3. What estates he gives his children must be of his own (*v.* 18): He *shall not take of the people's inheritance,* under pretence of having many children to provide for; he shall not find ways to make them forfeit their estates, or to force them to sell them and so *thrust his subjects out of their possession;* but let him and his sons be content with their own. It is far from being a prince's honour to increase the wealth of his family and crown by encroaching upon the rights and properties of his subjects; nor will he himself be a gainer by it at last, for he will be but a poor prince when the people are *scattered every man from his possession,* when they quit their native country, being forced out of it by oppression, choosing rather to live among strangers that are free people, and where what they have they can call their own, be it ever so little. It is the interest of princes to rule in the hearts of their subjects, and then all they have is, in the best manner, at their service. It is better for themselves to gain their affections by protecting their rights than to gain their estates by invading them.

19 After he brought me through the entry, which *was* at the side of the gate, into the holy chambers of the priests, which looked toward the north : and, behold, there *was* a place on the two sides westward. 20 Then said he unto me, This *is* the place where the priests shall boil the trespass-offering and the sin-offering, where they shall bake the meat-offering; that they bear *them* not out into the utter court, to sanctify the people. 21 Then he brought me forth into the utter court, and caused me to pass by

the four corners of the court ; and, behold, in every corner of the court *there was* a court. 22 In the four corners of the court *there were* courts joined of forty *cubits* long and thirty broad : these four corners *were* of one measure. 23 And *there was* a row *of building* round about in them, round about them four, and *it was* made with boiling-places under the rows round about. 24 Then said he unto me, These *are* the places of them that boil, where the ministers of the house shall boil the sacrifice of the people.

We have here a further discovery of buildings about the temple, which we did not observe before, and those were places to boil the flesh of the offerings in, *v.* 20. He that kept such a plentiful table at his altar needed large kitchens; and a wise builder will provide conveniences of that kind. Observe, 1. Where those boiling-places were situated. There were some at the entry into the inner court (*v.* 19) and others under the rows, in the four corners of the outer court, *v.* 21 —23. These were the places where, it is likely, there was most room to spare for this purpose; and this purpose was found for the spare room, that none might be lost. It is a pity that holy ground should be waste ground. 2. What use they were put to. In those places they were to *boil the trespass-offering and the sin-offering,* those parts of them which were allotted to the priests and which were more sacred than the flesh of the peace-offerings, of which the offerers also had a share. There also they were to *bake the meat-offering,* their share of it, which they had from the altar for their own tables, *v.* 20. Care was taken that they should not *bear them out into the outer court, to sanctify the people.* Let them not pretend to sanctify the people with this holy flesh, and so impose upon them; or let not the people imagine that by touching these sacred things they were sanctified, and made any the better or more acceptable to God. It should seem (from Hag. ii. 12) that there were those who had such a conceit; and therefore the priests must not carry any of the holy flesh away with them, lest they should encourage that conceit. Ministers must take heed of doing any thing to bolster up ignorant people in their superstitious vanities.

CHAP. XLVII.

In this chapter we have, I. The vision of the holy waters, their rise, extent, depth, and healing virtue, the plenty of fish in them, and an account of the trees growing on the banks of them, ver. 1—12. II. An appointment of the borders of the land of Canaan, which was to be divided by lot to the tribes of Israel and the strangers that sojourned among them, ver. 13—23.

AFTERWARD he brought me again unto the door of the house; and, behold, waters issued out from under the threshold of the house eastward : for the forefront of the house *stood toward* the east, and the waters came down from under from the right side of the house, at the south *side* or the altar. 2 Then brought he me out of the way of the gate northward, and led me about the way without unto the utter gate by the way that looketh eastward ; and, behold, there ran out waters on the right side. 3 And when the man that had the line in his hand went forth eastward, he measured a thousand cubits, and he brought me through the waters ; the waters *were* to the ancles. 4 Again he measured a thousand, and brought me through the waters ; the waters *were* to the knees. Again he measured a thousand, and brought me through ; the waters *were* to the loins. 5 Afterward he measured a thousand ; *and it was* a river that I could not pass over : for the waters were risen, waters to swim in, a river that could not be passed over. 6 And he said unto me, Son of man, hast thou seen *this?* then he brought me, and caused me to return to the brink of the river. 7 Now when I had returned, behold, at the bank of the river *were* very many trees on the one side and on the other. 8 Then said he unto me, These waters issue out toward the east country, and go down into the desert, and go into the sea : *which being* brought forth into the sea, the waters shall be healed. 9 And it shall come to pass, *that* every thing that liveth, which moveth, whithersoever the rivers shall come, shall live : and there shall be a very great multitude of fish, because these waters shall come thither : for they shall be healed; and every thing shall live whither the river cometh. 10 And it shall come to pass, *that* the fishers shall stand upon it from En-gedi, even unto En-eglaim ; they shall be a *place* to spread forth nets ; their fish shall be according to their kinds, as the fish of the great sea, exceeding many. 11 But the miry places thereof and the marishes thereof shall not be healed ; they shall be given to salt. 12 And by the river upon the bank thereof, on this side and on that side, shall grow all trees for meat, whose leaf shall not fade, neither shall the fruit thereof be consumed: it shall bring forth new fruit according to his months, because their waters they issued out of the sanctuary: and the fruit thereof shall be for meat, and the leaf thereof for medicine.

This part of Ezekiel's vision must so necessarily have a mystical and spiritual meaning that thence we conclude the other parts of his vision have a mystical and spiritual meaning also; for it cannot be applied to the waters brought by pipes into the temple for the washing of the sacrifices, the keeping of the temple clean, and the carrying off of those waters, for that would be to turn this pleasant river into a sink or common sewer. That prophecy, Zech. xiv. 8, may explain it, of *living waters* that shall *go out* from Jerusalem, *half of them towards the former sea and half of them towards the hinder sea.* And there is plainly a reference to this in St. John's vision of *a pure river of water of life,* Rev. xxii. 1. That seems to represent the glory and joy which are grace perfected. This seems to represent the grace and joy which are glory begun. Most interpreters agree that these waters signify the gospel of Christ, which went forth from Jerusalem, and spread itself into the countries about, and the gifts and powers of the Holy Ghost which accompanied it, and by virtue of which it spread far and produced strange and blessed effects. Ezekiel had walked round the house again and again, and yet did not till now take notice of those waters; for God makes known his mind and will to his people, not all at once, but by degrees. Now observe,

I. The rise of these waters. He is not put to trace the streams to the fountain, but has the fountain-head first discovered to him (v. 1): *Waters issued out from the threshhold of the house eastward,* and from *under the right side of the house,* that is, the south side of *the altar.* And again (v. 2), *There ran out waters on the right side,* signifying that *from Zion should go forth the law and the word of the Lord from Jerusalem,* Isa. ii. 3. There it was that the Spirit was poured out upon the apostles, and endued them with the gift of tongues, that they might carry these waters to all nations. In the temple first they were to stand and *preach the words of this life,* Acts v. 20. They must preach the gospel to all nations, but must *begin at Jerusalem,* Luke xxiv. 47. But that is not all: Christ is the temple; he is the door; from him those living waters flow, out of his pierced side. It is the water that he gives us that is *the well of water which springs up,* John iv. 14. And it is by believing in him that we receive from him *rivers of living*

water; and *this spoke he of the Spirit,* John vii. 38, 39. The original of these waters was not above-ground, but they sprang up from under the threshold; for the fountain of a believer's life is a mystery; it is *hid with Christ in God,* Col. iii. 3. Some observe that they came forth *on the right side of the house* to intimate that gospel-blessings are right-hand blessings. It is also an encouragement to those who attend at Wisdom's gates, at the posts of her doors, who are willing to lie at the threshold of God's house, as David was, that they lie at the fountain-head of comfort and grace; the very entrance into God's word gives light and life, Ps. cxix. 130. David speaks it to the praise of Zion, *All my springs are in thee,* Ps. lxxxvii. 7. They came *from the side of the altar,* for it is in and by Jesus Christ, the great altar (who *sanctifies our gifts* to God), that God has *blessed us with spiritual blessings in* holy *heavenly places.* From God as the fountain, in him as the channel, flows the river which *makes glad the city of our God, the holy place of the tabernacles of the Most High,* Ps. xlvi. 4. But observe how much the blessedness and joy of glorified saints in heaven exceed those of the best and happiest saints on earth; here the streams of our comfort arise *from under the threshold;* there they proceed *from the throne,* the throne *of God and of the Lamb,* Rev. xxii. 1.

II. The progress and increase of these waters: They *went forth eastward* (v. 3), *towards the east country* (v. 8), for so they were directed. The prophet and his guide followed the stream as it ran down from the holy mountains, and when they had followed it about *a thousand cubits* they went over across it, to try the depth of it, and it was *to the ancles, v.* 3. Then they walked along on the bank of the river on the other side, a thousand cubits more, and then, to try the depth of it, they waded through it the second time, and it was up to *their knees, v.* 4. They walked along by it a thousand cubits more, and then forded it the third time, and then it was up to their middle—*the waters were to the loins.* They then walked a thousand cubits further, and attempted to repass it the fourth time, but found it impracticable: *The waters had risen,* by the addition either of brooks that fell into it above ground or by springs under ground, so that they were *waters to swim in, a river that could not be passed over, v.* 5. Note, 1. The waters of the sanctuary are running waters, as those of a river, not standing waters, as those of a pond. The gospel, when it was first preached, was still spreading further. Grace in the soul is still pressing forward; it is an active principle, *plus ultra—onward still,* till it comes to perfection. 2. They are increasing waters. This river, as it runs constantly, so the further it goes the fuller it grows. The gospel-church was very small in its beginnings, like a little purling brook;

but by degrees it came to be *to the ancles, to the knees:* many were added to it daily, and the *grain of mustard seed* grew up to be a *great tree.* The gifts of the Spirit increase by being exercised, and grace, where it is true, is growing, like the light of the morning, which *shines more and more to the perfect day.* 3. It is good for us to follow these waters, and go along with them. Observe the progress of the gospel in the world; observe the process of the work of grace in the heart; attend the motions of the blessed Spirit, and walk after them, under a divine guidance, as Ezekiel here did. 4. It is good to be often searching into the things of God, and trying the depth of them, not only to look on the surface of those waters, but to go to the bottom of them as far as we can, to be often digging, often diving, into the mysteries of the kingdom of heaven, as those who covet to be intimately acquainted with those things. 5. If we search into the things of God, we shall find some things very plain and easy to be understood, as the waters that were but to the ancles, others more difficult, and which require a deeper search, as the water to the knees or the loins, and some quite beyond our reach, which we cannot penetrate into, or account for, but, despairing to find the bottom, must, as St. Paul, sit down at the brink, and adore the *depth,* Rom. xi. 33. It has been often said that in the scripture, like these waters of the sanctuary, there are some places so shallow that a lamb may wade through them, and others so deep that an elephant may swim in them. And it is our wisdom, as the prophet here, to begin with that which is most easy, and get our hearts washed with those things before we proceed to that which is *dark and hard to be understood;* it is good to take our work before us.

III. The extent of this river: *It issues towards the east country,* but thence it either divides itself into several streams or fetches a compass, so that it *goes down into the desert,* and so *goes into the sea,* either into the *dead sea,* which lay *south-east,* or the sea of Tiberias, which lay *north-east,* or the great sea, which lay *west, v.* 8. This was accomplished when the gospel was preached with success throughout all the regions of Judea and Samaria (Acts viii. 1), and afterwards the nations about, nay, and those that lay most remote, even in the isles of the sea, were enlightened and leavened by it. The sound of it went forth *to the end of the world;* and the enemies of it could no more prevail to stop the progress of it than that of a mighty river.

IV. The healing virtue of this river. The waters of the sanctuary, wherever they come and have a free course, will be found a wonderful restorative. Being *brought forth into the sea,* the sulphureous lake of Sodom, that standing monument of divine vengeance, even those *waters shall be healed (v.* 8), shall

become sweet, and pleasant, and healthful. This intimates the wonderful and blessed change that the gospel would make, wheresoever it came in its power, as great a change, in respect both of character and condition, as the turning of the dead sea into a fountain of gardens. When children of wrath became children of love, and those that were dead in trespasses and sins were made alive, then this was fulfilled. The gospel was as that salt which Elisha cast into the spring of the waters of Jericho, with which he *healed them,* 2 Kings ii. 20, 21. Christ, coming into the world to be its physician, sent his gospel as the great medicine, the *panpharmacon;* there is in it a remedy for every malady. Nay, wherever these rivers come, they *make things to live (v.* 9), both plants and animals; they are *the water of life,* Rev. xxii. 1, 17. Christ came, *that we might have life,* and for that end he sends his gospel. *Every thing shall live whither the river comes.* The grace of God makes dead sinners alive and living saints lively; every thing is made fruitful and flourishing by it. But its effect is according as it is received, and as the mind is prepared and disposed to receive it; for (*v.* 11) with respect to the marshes and *miry places thereof,* that are settled in the mire of their own sinfulness, and will not be healed, or settled in the moisture of their own righteousness, and think they need no healing, their doom is, *They shall not be healed;* the same gospel which to others is a savour of life unto life shall to them be a savour of death unto death: *they shall be given to salt,* to perpetual barrenness, Deut. xxix. 23. Those that will not be watered with the grace of God, and made fruitful, shall be abandoned to their own hearts' lusts, and left for ever unfruitful. *He that is filthy, let him be filthy still. Never fruit grow on thee more for ever.* They shall be given to *salt,* that is, to be monuments of divine justice, as Lot's wife that was turned into *a pillar of salt,* to season others.

V. The great plenty of fish that should be in this river. Every living moving thing shall be found here, shall *live here (v.* 9), shall come on and prosper, shall be the best of the kind, and shall increase greatly; so that there shall be a *very great multitude of fish, according to their kinds, as the fish of the great sea, exceedingly many.* There shall be as great plenty of the river fish, and as vast shoals of them, as there is of salt-water fish, *v.* 10. There shall be great numbers of Christians in the church, and those multiplying like fishes in the rising generations and *the dew of their youth.* In the creation the *waters brought forth* the fish *abundantly* (Gen. i. 20, 21), and they still live in and by the waters that produced them; so believers are *begotten by the word of truth* (James i. 18), and *born by it* (1 Pet. i. 23), that river of God; by it they live, from it they have their maintenance and subsistence; in the waters of the sanctuary they are as in their element, out of them they are as fish *upon dry ground ;* so David was when he thirsted and panted for God, for the living God. Where the fish are known to be in abundance, thither will the fishers flock, and there they will *cast their nets ;* and therefore, to intimate the replenishing of these waters and their being made every way useful, it is here foretold that the fishers shall stand upon the banks of this river, from *En-gedi,* which lies on the border of the dead sea, to *En-eglaim,* another city, which joins to that sea, and all along shall *spread their nets.* The dead sea, which before was shunned as noisome and noxious, shall be frequented. Gospel-grace makes those persons and places which were unprofitable and good for nothing to become serviceable to God and man.

VI. The trees that were on the banks of this river—*many trees on the one side and on the other* (v. 7), which made the prospect very pleasant and agreeable to the eye; the shelter of these trees also would be a convenience to the fishery. But that is not all (v. 12); they *are trees for meat,* and the *fruit* of them *shall not be consumed,* for it shall produce fresh fruit *every month.* The *leaf* shall be *for medicine,* and it *shall not fade.* This part of the vision is copied out into St. John's vision very exactly (Rev. xxii. 2), where, on either side of the river, is said to grow the *tree of life,* which *yielded her fruit every month,* and *the leaves* were *for the healing of the nations.* Christians are supposed to be these trees, ministers especially, *trees of righteousness, the planting of the Lord* (Isa. lxi. 3), set by *the rivers of water,* the waters of the sanctuary (Ps. i. 3), grafted into Christ the tree of life, and by virtue of their union with him made trees of life too, *rooted* in him, Col. ii. 7. There is a great variety of these trees, through the diversity of gifts with which they are endued by that *one Spirit* who *works all in all.* They grow *on the bank* of the river, for they keep close to holy ordinances, and through them derive from Christ sap and virtue. They are *fruit-trees,* designed, as the fig-tree and the olive, with their fruits to *honour God and man,* Judg. ix. 9. *The fruit thereof shall be for meat,* for the *lips of the righteous feed many.* The fruits of their righteousness are one way or other beneficial. The very leaves of these trees *are for medicine,* for *bruises and sores, margin.* Good Christians with their good discourses, which are as their leaves, as well as with their charitable actions, which are as their fruits, do good to those about them; they *strengthen the weak,* and bind up the broken-hearted. Their cheerfulness *does good like a medicine,* not only to themselves, but to others also. They shall be enabled by the grace of God to persevere in their goodness and usefulness; their *leaf shall not fade,* or lose its medicinal virtue, having not only life in their root, but

sap in all their branches; their profession *shall not wither* (Ps. i. 3), *neither shall the fruit thereof be consumed ;* that is, they shall not lose the principle of their fruitfulness, but *shall still bring forth fruit in old age,* to *show that the Lord is upright* (Ps. xcii. 14, 15), or the reward of their fruitfulness shall abide for ever; they bring forth fruit that shall abound to their account in the great day, *fruit to life eternal ;* that is indeed *fruit which shall not be consumed.* They bring new *fruit according to their months,* some in one month and others in another: so that still there shall be one or other found to serve the glory of God for the purpose he designs. Or each one of them shall bring forth fruit monthly, which denotes an abundant disposition to fruit-bearing (they shall never be weary of well-doing), and a very happy climate, such that there shall be a perpetual spring and summer. And the reason of this extraordinary fruitfulness is *because their waters issued out of the sanctuary ;* it is not to be ascribed to any thing in themselves, but to the continual supplies of divine grace, with which they are *watered every moment* (Isa. xxvii. 3); for, whoever planted them, it was that which *gave the increase.*

13 Thus saith the Lord GOD; This *shall be* the border, whereby ye shall inherit the land according to the twelve tribes of Israel: Joseph *shall have two* portions. 14 And ye shall inherit it, one as well as another : *concerning* the which I lifted up mine hand to give it unto your fathers : and this land shall fall unto you for inheritance. 15 And this *shall be* the border of the land toward the north side, from the great sea, the way of Hethlon, as men go to Zedad; 16 Hamath, Berothah, Sibraim, which *is* between the border of Damascus and the border of Hamath; Hazar-hatticon, which *is* by the coast of Hauran. 17 And the border from the sea shall be Hazar-enan, the border of Damascus, and the north northward, and the border of Hamath. And *this is* the north side. 18 And the east side ye shall measure from Hauran, and from Damascus, and from Gilead, and from the land of Israel *by* Jordan, from the border unto the east sea. And *this is* the east side. 19 And the south side southward, from Tamar *even* to the waters of strife *in* Kadesh, the river to the great sea. And *this is* the south side southward. 20 The west side also *shall be* the great sea from the

border, till a man come over against Hamath. This *is* the west side. 21 So shall ye divide this land unto you according to the tribes of Israel. 22 And it shall come to pass, *that* ye shall divide it by lot for an inheritance unto you, and to the strangers that sojourn among you, which shall beget children among you : and they shall be unto you as born in the country among the children of Israel ; they shall have inheritance with you among the tribes of Israel. 23 And it shall come to pass, *that* in. what tribe the stranger sojourneth, there shall ye give *him* his inheritance, saith the Lord God.

We are now to pass from the affairs of the sanctuary to those of the state, from the city to the country. 1. The land of Canaan is here secured to them for an inheritance (*v.* 14): *I lifted up my hand to give it unto your fathers,* that is, promised it upon oath to them and their posterity. Though the possession had been a great while discontinued, yet God had not forgotten his oath which he swore to their fathers. Though God's providences may for a time seem to contradict his promises, yet the promise will certainly take place at last, for God will be *ever mindful of his covenant. I lifted up my hand to give it,* and therefore it shall without fail *fall to you for an inheritance.* Thus the heavenly Canaan is sure to all the seed, because it is what *God, who cannot lie, has promised.* 2. It is here circumscribed, and the bounds and limits of it are fixed, which they must not pass over to encroach upon their neighbours and which their neighbours shall not break through to encroach upon them. We had such a draught of the borders of Canaan when Joshua was to put the people in possession of it, Num. xxxiv. 1, &c. That begins with the salt sea in the south, goes round and ends there. This begins with Hamath about Damascus in the north, and so goes round and ends there, *v.* 20. Note, It is God that *appoints the bounds of our habitation ;* and his Israel shall always have cause to say that *the lines have fallen to them in pleasant places.* The lake of Sodom is here called *the east sea,* for, it being healed by the waters of the sanctuary, it is no more to be called a *salt sea,* as it was in Numbers. 3. It is here ordered to be divided among the tribes of Israel, reckoning Joseph for two tribes, to make up the number of twelve, when Levi was taken out to attend the sanctuary, and had his lot adjoining to that (*v.* 13, 21): *You shall inherit it, one as well as another, v.* 14. The tribes shall have an equal share, one as much as another. As the tribes returned out of Babylon, this

seems unequal, because some tribes were much more numerous than the other, and indeed the most were of Judah and Benjamin and very few of the other ten tribes ; but as the twelve tribes stand, in type and vision, for the gospel-church, the Israel of God, it was very equal, because we find in another vision an equal number of each of the twelve tribes *sealed* for the *living God,* just 12,000 of each, Rev. vii. 5, &c. And to those sealed ones these allotments did belong. It intimates likewise that all the subjects of Christ's kingdom have *obtained like precious faith.* Male and female, Jew and Gentile, bond and free, are all alike welcome to Christ and made partakers of him. 4. The strangers who sojourn among them, *who shall beget children* and be built up into families, and so help to people their country, *shall have inheritance among* the tribes, as if they had been native Israelites (*v.* 22, 23), which was by no means allowed in Joshua's division of the land. This is an act for a general naturalization, which would teach the Jews who was their neighbour, not those only of their own nation and religion, but those, whoever they were, that they had an opportunity of showing kindness to, because from them they would be willing to receive kindness. It would likewise invite strangers to come and settle among them, and put themselves under the wings of the divine Majesty. But it certainly looks at gospel-times, when the partition-wall between Jew and Gentile was taken down, and both were put upon a level before God, both made one in Christ, in whom *there is no difference,* Rom. x. 12. This land was a type of the heavenly Canaan, that *better country* (Heb. xi. 16), in which believing Gentiles shall have a blessed lot, as well as believing Jews, Isa. lvi. 3.

CHAP. XLVIII.

In this chapter we have particular directions given for the distribution of the land, of which we had the metes and bounds assigned in the foregoing chapter. I. The portions of the twelve tribes, seven to the north of the sanctuary (ver. 1—7) and five to the south, ver. 23—29. II. The allotment of land for the sanctuary, and the priests (ver. 8—11), for the Levites (ver. 12—14), for the city (ver. 15—20), and for the prince, ver. 21, 22. Much of this we had before, ch. xlv. III. A plan of the city, its gates, and the new name given to it (ver. 30—35), which seals up, and concludes, the vision and prophecy of this book.

NOW these *are* the names of the tribes. From the north end to the coast of the way of Hethlon, as one goeth to Hamath, Hazar-enan, the border of Damascus northward, to the coast of Hamath ; for these are his sides east *and* west ; a *portion for* Dan. 2 And by the border of Dan, from the east side unto the west side, a *portion for* Asher. 3 And by the border of Asher, from the east side even unto the west side, a *portion for* Naphtali. 4 And by the border of Naphtali, from the east side unto the west side, a *portion for* Manasseh. 5 And by the border of Manasseh, from the east side unto the west side, a *portion for* Ephraim. 6 And by the border of Ephraim, from the east side even unto the west side, a *portion for* Reuben. 7 And by the border of Reuben, from the east side even unto the west side, a *portion for* Judah. 8 And by the border of Judah, from the east side unto the west side, shall be the offering which ye shall offer of five and twenty thousand *reeds in* breadth, and *in* length as one of the *other* parts, from the east side unto the west side: and the sanctuary shall be in the midst of it. 9 The oblation that ye shall offer unto the Lord *shall be* of five and twenty thousand in length, and of ten thousand in breadth. 10 And for them, *even* for the priests, shall be *this* holy oblation; toward the north five and twenty thousand *in length*, and toward the west ten thousand in breadth, and toward the east ten thousand in breadth, and toward the south five and twenty thousand in length: and the sanctuary of the Lord shall be in the midst thereof. 11 *It shall be* for the priests that are sanctified of the sons of Zadok; which have kept my charge, which went not astray when the children of Israel went astray, as the Levites went astray. 12 And *this* oblation of the land that is offered shall be unto them a thing most holy by the border of the Levites. 13 And over against the border of the priests the Levites *shall have* five and twenty thousand in length, and ten thousand in breadth: all the length *shall be* five and twenty thousand, and the breadth ten thousand. 14 And they shall not sell of it, neither exchange, nor alienate the firstfruits of the land: for *it is* holy unto the Lord. 15 And the five thousand, that are left in the breadth over against the five and twenty thousand, shall be a profane *place* for the city, for dwelling, and for suburbs: and the city shall be in the midst thereof. 16 And these *shall be* the measures thereof; the north side four thousand and five hundred, and the south side four thou-

sand and five hundred, and on the east side four thousand and five hundred, and the west side four thousand and five hundred. 17 And the suburbs of the city shall be toward the north two hundred and fifty, and toward the south two hundred and fifty, and toward the east two hundred and fifty, and toward the west two hundred and fifty. 18 And the residue in length over against the oblation of the holy *portion shall be* ten thousand eastward, and ten thousand westward: and it shall be over against the oblation of the holy *portion;* and the increase thereof shall be for food unto them that serve the city. 19 And they that serve the city shall serve it out of all the tribes of Israel. 20 All the oblation *shall be* five and twenty thousand by five and twenty thousand: ye shall offer the holy oblation foursquare, with the possession of the city. 21 And the residue *shall be* for the prince, on the one side and on the other of the holy oblation, and of the possession of the city, over against the five and twenty thousand of the oblation toward the east border, and westward over against the five and twenty thousand toward the west border, over against the portions for the prince: and it shall be the holy oblation; and the sanctuary of the house *shall be* in the midst thereof. 22 Moreover from the possession of the Levites, and from the possession of the city, *being* in the midst *of that* which is the prince's, between the border of Judah and the border of Benjamin, shall be for the prince. 23 As for the rest of the tribes, from the east side unto the west side, Benjamin *shall have* a *portion.* 24 And by the border of Benjamin, from the east side unto the west side, Simeon *shall have* a *portion.* 25 And by the border of Simeon, from the east side unto the west side, Issachar a *portion.* 26 And by the border of Issachar, from the east side unto the west side, Zebulun a *portion.* 27 And by the border of Zebulun, from the east side unto the west side, Gad a *portion.* 28 And by the border of Gad, at the south side southward, the border shall be even from Tamar *unto* the waters of strife *in* Kadesh, *and* to the river toward the great sea. 29 This *is* the land which ye shall divide by lot unto the tribes of Israel for inheritance, and these *are* their portions, saith the Lord GOD. 30 And these *are* the goings out of the city on the north side, four thousand and five hundred measures.

We have here a very short and ready way taken for the dividing of the land among the twelve tribes, not so tedious and so far about as the way that was taken in Joshua's time; for in the distribution of spiritual and heavenly blessings there is not that danger of murmuring and quarrelling that there is in the participation of temporal blessings. When God gave to the labourers every one his penny those that were uneasy at it were soon put to silence with, *May I not do what I will with my own?* And such is the equal distribution here among the tribes. In this distribution of the land we may observe, 1. That it differs very much from the division of it in Joshua's time, and agrees not with the order of their birth, nor with that of their blessing by Jacob or Moses. Simeon here is not *divided* in Jacob, nor is Zebulun a *haven of ships*, a plain intimation that it is not so much to be understood literally as spiritually, though the mystery of it is very much hidden from us. In gospel times old things have passed away; *behold, all things have become new.* The Israel of God is cast into a new method. 2. That the tribe of Dan, which was last provided for in the first division of Canaan (Josh. xix. 40), is first provided for here, *v.* 1. Thus in the gospel the last shall be first, Matt. xix. 30. God, in the dispensation of his grace, does not follow the same method that he does in the disposals of his providence. But Dan had now his portion thereabouts where he had only one city before, northward, on the border of Damascus, and furthest of all from the sanctuary, because that tribe had revolted to idolatry. 3. That all the ten tribes that were carried away by the king of Assyria, as well as the two tribes that were long afterwards carried to Babylon, have their allotment in this visionary land, which some think had its accomplishment in the particular persons and families of those tribes who returned with Judah and Benjamin, of which we find many instances in Ezra and Nehemiah; and it is probable that there were returns of many more afterwards at several times, which are not recorded; and the Jews having Galilee, and other parts, that had been the possessions of the ten tribes, put into their hands, in common with them, they enjoyed them. Grotius says, If the ten tribes had repented and returned to

God, as the *chief fathers of Judah and Benjamin did, and the priests and Levites* (Ezra i. 5), they would have fared as those two tribes did, but they forfeited the benefit of this glorious prophecy by sin. However, we believe it has its designed accomplishment in the establishment and enlargement of the gospel church, and the happy settlement of all those who are Israelites indeed in the sure and sweet enjoyment of the privileges of the new covenant, in which there is enough for all and enough for each. 4. That every tribe in this visionary distribution had its particular lot assigned it by a divine appointment; for it was never the intention of the gospel to pluck up the hedge of property and lay all in common; it was in a way of charity, not of legal right, that the first Christians had all things common (Acts ii. 44), and many precepts of the gospel suppose that every man should know his own. We must not only acknowledge, but acquiesce in, the hand of God appointing us our lot, and be well pleased with it, believing it fittest for us. *He shall choose our inheritance for us,* Ps. xlvii. 4. 5. That the tribes lay contiguous. By *the border* of one tribe was *the portion* of another, all in a row, in exact order, so that, like stones in an arch, they fixed, and strengthened, and wedged in one another. *Behold how good and how pleasant a thing it is for brethren* thus *to dwell together!* It was a figure of the communion of churches and saints under the gospel-government; thus, though they are many, yet they are one, and should hold together in holy love and mutual assistance. 6. That the lot of Reuben, which before lay at a distance beyond Jordan, now lies next to Judah, and next but one to the sanctuary; for the scandal he lay under, for which he was told *he should not excel,* began by this time to wear off. What has turned to the reproach of any person or people ought not to be remembered for ever, but should at length be kindly forgotten. 7. That the sanctuary was *in the midst* of them There were seven tribes to the north of it, and the Levites, the prince's, and the city's portion, with that of five tribes more, to the south of it; so that it was, as it ought to be, *in the heart of the kingdom,* that it might diffuse its benign influences to the whole, and might be the centre of their unity. The tribes that lay most remote from each other would meet there in a mutual acquaintance and fellowship. Those of the same parish or congregation, though dispersed, and having no occasion otherwise to know each other, yet by meeting statedly to worship God together should have their hearts knit to each other in holy love. 8. That where the sanctuary was the priests were: *For them, even for the priests, shall this holy oblation be, v.* 10. As, on the one hand, this denotes honour and comfort to ministers, that what is given for their support and maintenance is reckoned *a holy oblation to* the Lord, so it intimates their duty, which is that, since they are appointed and maintained for the service of the sanctuary, they ought to *attend continually to this very thing,* to reside on their cures. Those that live upon the altar must serve at the altar, not take the wages to themselves and devolve the work upon others; but how can they serve the altar, his altar they live upon, if they do not live near it? 9. Those priests had the priests' share of these lands that had approved themselves faithful to God in times of trial (v. 11): *It shall be for the sons of Zadok,* who, it seems, had signalized themselves in some critical juncture, and *went not astray* when the *children of Israel,* and the other *Levites, went astray.* God will put honour upon those who keep their integrity in times of general apostasy, and he has special favours in reserve for them. Those are swimming upwards, and so they will find at last, that are swimming against the stream. 10. The land which was appropriated to the ministers of the sanctuary might by no means be alienated. It was in the nature of the *first-fruits of the land,* and was therefore *holy to the Lord ;* and, though the priests and Levites had both the use of it and the inheritance of it to them and their heirs, yet they might not *sell it nor exchange it, v. 14.* It is sacrilege to convert that to other uses which is dedicated to God. 11. The land allotted for the city and its suburbs is called a *profane place (v. 15),* or *common:* not but that the city was a holy city above other cities, for the Lord was there, but, in comparison with the sanctuary, it was a profane place. Yet it is too often true in the worst sense that great cities, even those which, like this, have the sanctuary near them, are profane places, and it ought to be deeply lamented. It was the complaint of old, *From Jerusalem has profaneness gone forth into all the land,* Jer. xxiii. 15. 12. The city is made to be exactly square, and the suburbs extending themselves equally on all sides, as the Levites' cities did in the first division of the land (v. 16, 17), which, never being literally fulfilled in any city, intimates that it is to be understood spiritually of the beauty and stability of the gospel church, that *city of the living God,* which is formed according to the wisdom and counsel of·God, and is made firm and immovable by his promise. 13. Whereas, before, the inhabitants of Jerusalem were principally of Judah and Benjamin, in whose tribe it lay, now the head city lies not in the particular lot of any of the tribes, but *those that serve the city,* and bear office in it, *shall serve it out of all the tribes of Israel, v. 19.* The most eminent men must be picked out of all the tribes of Israel for the service of the city, because many eyes were upon it, and there was great resort to it from all parts of the nation and from other nations. Those that live in the city are said to serve the city,

for, wherever we are, we must study to be serviceable to the place, some way or other, according as our capacity is. They must not come out of the tribes of Israel to the city to take their ease, and enjoy their pleasures, but to serve the city, to do all the good they can there, and in so doing they would have a good influence upon the country too. 14. Care was taken that those who applied themselves to public business in the city, as well as in the sanctuary, should have an honourable comfortable maintenance; lands are appointed, *the increase* whereof *shall be food unto those that serve the city, v.* 18. Who goes a warfare at his own charges? Magistrates, that attend the service of the state, as well as ministers, that attend the service of the church, should have all due encouragement and support in so doing; and *for this cause pay we tribute also.* 15. The prince had a lot for himself, suited to the dignity of his high station (v. 21); we took an account of it before, *ch.* xlv. He was seated near the sanctuary, where the testimony of Israel was, and near the city, where the *thrones of judgment* were, that he might be a protection to both and might see that the duty of both was carefully and faithfully done; and herein he was a minister of God for good to the whole community. Christ is the church's prince, that defends it on every side, and creates a defence; nay, he is himself a defence upon all its glory and encompasses it with his favour. 16. As Judah had his lot next the sanctuary on one side, so Benjamin had, of all the tribes, his lot nearest to it on the other side, which honour was reserved for those who adhered to the house of David and the temple at Jerusalem when the other ten tribes went astray from both. It is enough if treachery and apostasy, upon repentance, be pardoned, but constancy and fidelity shall be rewarded and preferred.

31 And the gates of the city *shall be* after the names of the tribes of Israel: three gates northward; one gate of Reuben, one gate of Judah, one gate of Levi. 32 And at the east side four thousand and five hundred: and three gates; and one gate of Joseph, one gate of Benjamin, one gate of Dan. 33 And at the south side four thousand and five hundred measures: and three gates; one gate of Simeon, one gate of Issachar, one gate of Zebulun. 34 At the west side four thousand and five hundred, *with* their three gates; one gate of Gad, one gate of Asher, one gate of Naphtali. 35 *It was* round about eighteen thousand *measures:* and the name of the city

from *that* day *shall be,* The LORD *is* there.

We have here a further account of the city that should be built for the metropolis of this glorious land, and to be the receptacle of those who should come from all parts to worship in the sanctuary adjoining. It is nowhere called Jerusalem, nor is the land which we have had such a particular account of the dividing of any where called the land of Canaan; for the old names are forgotten, to intimate that the *old things are done away, behold all things have become new.* Now, concerning this city, observe here, 1. The measures of its out-lets, and the grounds belonging to it, for its several conveniences; each way its appurtenances extended 4500 *measures,* 18,000 in all, *v.* 35. But what these measures were is uncertain. It is never said, in all this chapter, whether so many *reeds* (as our translation determines by inserting that word, *v.* 8, each reed containing six cubits and a span, *ch.* xl. 5, and why should the measurer appear with the measuring reed in his hand of that length if he did not measure with *that,* except where it is expressly said he measured by cubits?) or whether, as others think, it is so many cubits, because those are mentioned *ch.* xlv. 2 and *ch.* xlvii. 3. Yet that makes me incline rather to think that where cubits are not mentioned it must be intended so many lengths of the measuring reed. But those who understand it of so many cubits are not agreed whether it be meant of the common cubit, which was half a yard, or the geometrical cubit, which, for better expedition, is supposed to be mostly used in surveying lands, which, some say, contained six cubits, others about three cubits and a half, so making 1000 cubits the same with 1000 paces, that is, an English mile. But our being left at this uncertainty is an intimation that these things are to be understood spiritually, and that what is principally meant is that there is an exact and just proportion observed by Infinite Wisdom in modelling the gospel church, which though now we cannot discern we shall when we come to heaven. 2. The number of its gates. It had twelve gates in all, three on each side, which was very agreeable when it lay four square; and these twelve gates were inscribed to the twelve tribes. Because the city was to be served *out of all the tribes of Israel* (*v.* 19) it was fit that each tribe should have its gate; and, Levi being here taken in, to keep to the number twelve Ephraim and Manasseh are made one in Joseph, *v.* 32. On the north side were the gates of Reuben, Judah, and Levi (*v.* 31), on the east the gates of Joseph, Benjamin, and Dan (*v.* 32), on the south the gates of Simeon, Issachar, and Zebulun (*v.* 33), and on the west the gates of Gad, Asher, and Naphtali, *v.* 34. Conformable to this, in St. John's vision, the new Jerusalem (for so the holy city is called there, though not here) has *twelve gates,* three on a side, and on them are written *the names of the twelve tribes of the children of Israel,* Rev. xxi. 12, 13. Note, Into the church of Christ, both militant and triumphant, there is a free access by faith for all that come of every tribe, from every quarter. Christ has *opened the kingdom of heaven for all believers.* Whoever will may come and *take of the water of life,* of the tree of life, *freely.* 3. The name given to this city: *From that day,* when it shall be newly-erected according to this model, the name of it shall be, not, as before, *Jerusalem—The vision of peace,* but, which is the original of that, and more than equivalent to it, *Jehovah Shammah—The Lord is there,* v. 35. This intimated, (1) That the captives, after their return, should have manifest tokens of God's presence with them and his residence among them, both in his ordinances and in his providences. They shall have no occasion to ask, as their fathers did, *Is the Lord among us, or is he not?* for they shall see and say that he is with them of a truth. And then, though their troubles were many and threatening, they were like the bush which burned but was not consumed, because *the Lord was there.* But when God departed from their temple, when he said, *Migremus hinc—Let us go hence,* their house was soon *left unto them desolate.* Being no longer his, it was not much longer theirs. (2.) That the gospel-church should likewise have the presence of God in it, though not in the *Shechinah,* as of old, yet in a token of it no less sure, that of his Spirit. Where the gospel is faithfully preached, gospel ordinances are duly administered, and God is worshipped in the name of Jesus Christ only, it may truly be said, *The Lord is there;* for faithful is he that has said, and he will be as good as his word, *Lo, I am with you always even unto the end of the world. The Lord is there* in his church, to rule and govern it, to protect and defend it, and graciously to accept and own his sincere worshippers, and to be *nigh unto them in all that they call upon him for.* This should engage us to keep close to the communion of saints, for *the Lord is there;* and then whither shall we go to better ourselves? Nay, it is true of every good Christian; he dwells in God, and God in him; whatever soul has in it a living principle of grace, it may be truly said, *The Lord is there.* (3.) That the glory and happiness of heaven should consist chiefly in this, that *the Lord is there.* St. John's representation of that blessed state does indeed far exceed this in many respects. That is all gold, and pearls, and precious stones; it is much larger than this, and much brighter, for it *needs not the light of the sun.* But, in making the presence of God the principal matter of its bliss, they both agree. There the happiness of the glorified saints is made to be that *God himself shall be with* them (Rev. xxi. 3), that *he who sits on the throne shall dwell among them,* Rev. vii. 15. And here it is made to crown the bliss of this holy city that *the Lord is there.* Let us therefore give all diligence to make sure to ourselves a place in that city, that we may be *for ever with the Lord.*

AN

EXPOSITION,

WITH PRACTICAL OBSERVATIONS,

OF THE BOOK OF THE PROPHET

DANIEL.

THE book of Ezekiel left the affairs of Jerusalem under a doleful aspect, all in ruins, but with a joyful prospect of all in glory again. This of Daniel fitly follows. Ezekiel told us what was seen, and what was foreseen, by him in the former years of the captivity: Daniel tells us what was seen, and foreseen, in the latter years of the captivity. When God employs different hands, yet it is about the same work. And it was a comfort to the poor captives that they had first one prophet among them and then another, to show them *how long,* and a sign that God had not quite cast them off. Let us enquire, I. Concerning this prophet. His Hebrew name was *Daniel,* which signifies the *judgment of God;* his Chaldean name was *Belteshazzar.* He was of the tribe of Judah, and, as it should seem, of the royal family. He was betimes eminent for wisdom and piety. Ezekiel, his contemporary, but much his senior, speaks of him as an oracle when thus he upbraids the king of Tyre with his conceitedness of himself: *Thou art wiser than Daniel,* Ezek. xxviii. 3. He is likewise there celebrated for success in prayer, when Noah, Daniel, and Job are reckoned as three men that had the greatest interest in heaven of any, Ezek. xiv. 14. He began betimes to be famous, and continued long so. Some of the Jewish rabbin are loth to acknowledge him to be a prophet of the higher form, and therefore rank his book among the *Hagiographa,* not among the prophecies, and would not have their disciples pay much regard to it. One reason they pretend is because he did not live such a mean mortified life as Jeremiah and some other of the prophets did, but lived like a prince, and was a prime-minister of state; whereas we find him persecuted as other prophets were (*ch.* vi.), and mortifying himself as other prophets did, when he *ate no pleasant bread* (*ch.* x. 3), and fainting and sick when he was under the power of the Spirit of prophecy, *ch.* viii. 27. Another reason they pretend is because he wrote his book in a heathen country, and *there* had his visions, and not in the land of Israel; but, for the same reason, Ezekiel also must be expunged out of the roll of prophets. But the true reason is that he speaks so plainly of the time of the Messiah's coming that the Jews cannot avoid the conviction of it and therefore do not care to hear of it. But Josephus calls him one of the *greatest* of *the prophets,* nay, the angel Gabriel calls him a *man greatly beloved.* He lived long an active life in the courts and councils of some of the greatest monarchs the world ever had, Nebuchadnezzar, Cyrus, Darius; for we mistake if we confine the privilege of an intercourse with heaven to speculative men, or those that spend their time in contemplation; no, who was more intimately acquainted with the mind of God than Daniel, a courtier, a statesman, and a man of business? The Spirit, as the wind, blows where it lists. And, if those that have much to do in the world plead that as an excuse for the infrequency and slightness of their converse with God, Daniel will condemn them. Some have thought that he returned to Jerusalem, and was one of the masters of the Greek synagogue; but nothing of that appears in scripture; it is therefore generally concluded that he died in Persia at Susan, where he lived to be very old. II. Concerning this book. The first six chapters of it are historical, and are plain and easy; the last six are prophetical, and in them are many things dark, and hard to be understood, which yet would be more intelligible if we had a more complete history of the nations, and especially the Jewish nation, from Daniel's time to the coming of the Messiah. Our Saviour intimates the difficulty of apprehending the sense of Daniel's prophecies when, speaking of them, he says, *Let him that readeth understand,* Matt. xxiv. 15. The first chapter, and the first three verses of the second chapter, are in Hebrew; thence to the eighth chapter is in the Chaldee dialect; and thence to the end is in Hebrew. Mr. Broughton observes that, as the Chaldeans were kind to Daniel, and gave cups of cold water to him when he requested it, rather than the king's wine, God would not have them lose their reward, but made that language which they taught him to have honour in his writings through all the world, unto this day. Daniel, according to his computation, continues the holy story from the first surprising of Jerusalem by the Chaldean Babel, when he himself was carried away captive, until the last destruction of it by Rome, the mystical Babel, for so far forward his predictions look, *ch.* ix. 27. The fables of Susannah, and of Bel and the Dragon, in both which Daniel is made a party, are apocryphal stories, which we think we have no reason to give any credit to, they being never found in the Hebrew or Chaldee, but only in the Greek, nor ever admitted by the Jewish church. There are some both of the histories and of the prophecies of this book that bear date in the latter end of the Chaldean monarchy, and others of both that are dated in the beginning of the Persian monarchy. But both Nebuchadnezzar's dream, which Daniel interpreted, and his own visions, point at the Grecian and Roman monarchies, and very particularly at the Jews' troubles under Antiochus, which it would be of great use to them to prepare for; as his fixing the very time for the coming of the Messiah was of use to all those that waited for the consolation of Israel, and is to us, for the confirming of our belief, That this is he who should come, and we are to look for no other.

CHAP. I.

This chapter gives us a more particular account of the beginning of Daniel's life, his original and education, than we have of any other of the prophets. Isaiah, Jeremiah, and Ezekiel, began immediately with divine visions; but Daniel began with the study of human learning, and was afterwards honoured with divine visions; such variety of methods has God taken in training up men for the service of his church. We have here, I. Jehoiakim's first captivity (ver. 1, 2), in which Daniel, with others of the seed-royal, was carried to Babylon. II. The choice made of Daniel, and some other young men, to be brought up in the Chaldean literature, that they might be fitted to serve the government, and the provision made for them, ver. 3–7. III. Their pious refusal to eat the portion of the king's meat, and their determining to live upon pulse and water, which, having tried it, the master of the eunuchs allowed them to do, finding that it agreed very well with them, ver. 8–16. IV. Their wonderful improvement, above all their fellows, in wisdom and knowledge, ver. 17–21.

IN the third year of the reign of Jehoiakim king of Judah came Nebuchadnezzar king of Babylon unto Jerusalem, and besieged it. 2 And the LORD gave Jehoiakim king of Judah into his hand, with part of the vessels of the house of God: which he carried into the land of Shinar to the house of his god; and he brought the vessels into the treasure-house of his god. 3 And the king spake unto Ashpenaz the master of his eunuchs, that he should bring *certain* of the children of Israel, and of the king's seed, and of the princes; 4 Children in whom *was* no blemish, but well-favoured, and skilful in all wisdom, and cunning in knowledge, and understanding science, and such as *had* ability in them to stand in the king's palace, and whom they might teach the learning and the tongue of the Chaldeans. 5 And the king appointed them a daily provision of the king's meat, and of the wine which he drank: so nourishing them three years, that at the end thereof they might stand before the king. 6 Now among these were of the children of Judah, Daniel, Hananiah, Mishael, and Azariah: 7 Unto whom the prince of the eunuchs gave names: for he gave unto Daniel

the name of Belteshazzar; and to Hananiah, of Shadrach; and to Mishael, of Meshach; and to Azariah, of Abed-nego.

We have in these verses an account,

I. Of the first descent which Nebuchadnezzar, king of Babylon, in the first year of his reign, made upon Judah and Jerusalem, in the third year of the reign of Jehoiakim, and his success in that expedition (*v.* 1, 2): He *besieged Jerusalem*, soon made himself master of it, seized the king, took whom he pleased and what he pleased away with him, and then left Jehoiakim to reign as tributary to him, which he did about eight years longer, but then rebelled, and it was his ruin. Now from this *first* captivity most interpreters think the seventy years are to be dated, though Jerusalem was not destroyed, nor the captivity completed, till about nineteen years after. In that first year Daniel was carried to Babylon, and there continued the whole seventy years (see *v.* 21), during which time all nations shall serve Nebuchadnezzar, and his son, and his son's son, Jer. xxv. 11. This one prophet therefore saw within the compass of his own time the rise, reign, and ruin of that monarchy; so that it was *res unius ætatis—the affair of a single age*, such short-lived things are the kingdoms of the earth; but the kingdom of heaven is everlasting. The righteous, that see them taking root, shall *see their fall*, Job v. 3; Prov. xxix. 16. Mr. Broughton observes the proportion of times in God's government since the coming out of Egypt: thence to their entering Canaan forty years, thence seven years to the dividing of the land, thence seven Jubilees to the first year of Samuel, in whom prophecy began, thence to this first year of the captivity seven seventies of years, 490 (ten Jubilees), thence to the return one seventy, thence to the death of Christ seven seventies more, and thence to the destruction of Jerusalem forty years.

II. The improvement he made of this success. He did not destroy the city or kingdom, but did that which just accomplished the first threatening of mischief by Babylon. It was denounced against Hezekiah, for showing his treasures to the king of Babylon's ambassadors (Isa. xxxix. 6, 7), that the treasures and the children should be carried away, and, if they had been humbled and reformed by this, hitherto the king of Babylon's power and success should have gone, but *no further.* If less judgments do the work, God will not send greater; but, if not, he will heat the furnace seven times hotter. Let us see what was now done. 1. The vessels of the sanctuary were carried away, *part* of them, *v.* 2. They fondly trusted to the temple to defend them, though they went on in their iniquity. And now, to show them the vanity of that confidence, the temple is first plundered. Many of the holy vessels which used to be employed in the service of God were taken away by the king of Babylon, those of them, it is likely, which were most valuable, and he brought them as trophies of victory to the *house of his god,* to whom, with a blind devotion, he gave the praise of his success; and having appropriated these vessels, in token of gratitude, to his god, he *put them in the treasury* of his temple. See the righteousness of God; his people had brought the images of other gods into his temple, and now he suffers the vessels of the temple to be carried into the treasuries of those other gods. Note, When men profane the vessels of the sanctuary with their sins it is just with God to profane them by his judgments. It is probable that the treasures of the king's house were rifled, as was foretold, but particular mention is made of the taking away of the *vessels of the sanctuary* because we shall find afterwards that the profanation of them was that which filled up the measure of the Chaldeans' iniquity, *ch.* v. 3. But observe, It was only *part of them* that went now; some were left them yet upon trial, to see if they would take the right course to prevent the carrying away of the remainder. See Jer. xxvii. 18. 2. The children and young men, especially such as were of noble or royal extraction, that were sightly and promising, and of good natural parts, were carried away. Thus was the iniquity of the fathers visited upon the children. These were taken away by Nebuchadnezzar, (1.) As trophies, to be made a show of for the evidencing and magnifying of his success. (2.) As hostages for the fidelity of their parents in their own land, who would be concerned to conduct themselves well that their children might have the better treatment. (3.) As a seed to serve him. He took them away to train them up for employments and preferments under him, either out of an unaccountable affectation, which great men often have, to be attended by foreigners, though they be blacks, rather than by those of their own nation, or because he knew that there were no such witty, sprightly, ingenious young men to be found among his Chaldeans as abounded among the youth of Israel; and, if that were so, it was much for 1018

the honour of the Jewish nation, as of an uncommon genius above other people, and a fruit of the blessing. But it was a shame that a people who had so much wit should have so little wisdom and grace. Now observe, [1] The directions which the king of Babylon gave for the choice of these youths, *v.* 4. They must not choose such as were deformed in body, but comely and well-favoured, whose countenances were indexes of ingenuity and good humour. But that is not enough; they must be *skilful in all wisdom,* and *cunning,* or *well-seen in knowledge,* and *understanding science,* such as were quick and sharp, and could give a ready and intelligent account of their own country and of the learning they had hitherto been brought up in. He chose such as were young, because they would be pliable and tractable, would forget their own people and incorporate with the Chaldeans. He had an eye to what he designed them for; they must be such as had ability in them to *stand in the king's palace,* not only to attend his royal person, but to preside in his affairs. This is an instance of the policy of this rising monarch, now in the beginning of his reign, and was a good omen of his prosperity, that he was in care to raise up a succession of persons fit for public business. He did not, like Ahasuerus, appoint them to choose him out young women for the service of his lusts, but young men for the service of his government. It is the interest of princes to have wise men employed under them; it is therefore their wisdom to take care for the finding out and training up of such. It is the misery of this world that so many who are fit for public stations are buried in obscurity, and so many who are unfit for them are preferred to them. [2.] The care which he took concerning them. *First,* For their education. He ordered that they should be taught *the learning and tongue of the Chaldeans.* They are supposed to be wise and knowing young men, and yet they must be further taught. *Give instructions to a wise man and he will increase in learning.* Note, Those that would do good in the world when they grow up must learn when they are young. That is the learning age; if that time be lost, it will hardly be redeemed. It does not appear that Nebuchadnezzar designed they should learn the unlawful arts that were used among the Chaldeans, magic and divination; if he did, Daniel and his fellows would not defile themselves with them. Nay, we do not find that he ordered them to be taught the religion of the Chaldeans, by which it appears that he was at this time no bigot; if men were skilful and faithful, and fit for his business, it was not material to him what religion they were of, provided they had but some religion. They must be trained up in the language and laws of the country, in history, philosophy, and mathematics, in the arts of husbandry, war, and navigation, in such learning as might qualify them to serve their generation. Note. It is real service to the public to provide for the good education of youth. *Secondly*, For their maintenance. He provided for them *three years*, not only necessaries, but dainties for their encouragement in their studies. They had *daily provision of the king's meat, and of the wine which he drank, v. 5.* This was an instance of his generosity and humanity; though they were his captives, he considered their birth and quality, their spirit and genius, and treated them honourably, and studied to make their captivity easy to them. There is a respect due to those who are well-born and bred when they have fallen into distress. With a liberal education there should be a liberal maintenance.

III. A particular account of Daniel and his fellows. They were of the *children of Judah*, the royal tribe, and probably of the house of David, which had grown a numerous family; and God told Hezekiah that of the children that should *issue from him* some should be taken and made eunuchs, or chamberlains, *in the palace of the king of Babylon.* The *prince of the eunuchs* changed the names of Daniel and his fellows, partly to show his authority over them and their subjection to him, and partly in token of their being naturalized and made Chaldeans. Their Hebrew names, which they received at their circumcision, had something of God, or Jah, in them: *Daniel—God is my Judge; Hananiah—The grace of the Lord; Mishael —He that is the strong God; Azariah—The Lord is a help.* To make them forget the God of their fathers, the guide of their youth, they give them names that savour of the Chaldean idolatry. *Belteshazzar* signifies the *keeper of the hidden treasures of Bel; Shadrach*—The *inspiration of the sun,* which the Chaldeans worshipped; *Meshach—Of the goddess Shach,* under which name Venus was worshipped; *Abed-nego,* The *servant of the shining fire,* which they worshipped also. Thus, though they would not force them from the religion of their fathers to that of their conquerors, yet they did what they could by fair means insensibly to wean them from the former and instil the latter into them. Yet see how comfortably they were provided for; though they suffered for their fathers' sins they were preferred for their own merits, and the land of their captivity was made more comfortable to them than the land of their nativity at this time would have been.

8 But Daniel purposed in his heart that he would not defile himself with the portion of the king's meat, nor with the wine which he drank : therefore he requested of the prince of the eunuchs that he might not defile him-

self. 9 Now God had brought Daniel into favour and tender love with the prince of the eunuchs. 10 And the prince of the eunuchs said unto Daniel, I fear my lord the king, who hath appointed your meat and your drink : for why should he see your faces worse liking than the children which *are* of your sort ? then shall ye make *me* endanger my head to the king. 11 Then said Daniel to Melzar, whom the prince of the eunuchs had set over Daniel, Hananiah, Mishael, and Azariah, 12 Prove thy servants, I beseech thee, ten days ; and let them give us pulse to eat, and water to drink. 13 Then let our countenances be looked upon before thee, and the countenance of the children that eat of the portion of the king's meat: and as thou seest, deal with thy servants. 14 So he consented to them in this matter, and proved them ten days. 15 And at the end of ten days their countenances appeared fairer and fatter in flesh than all the children which did eat the portion of the king's meat. 16 Thus Melzar took away the portion of their meat, and the wine that they should drink; and gave them pulse.

We observe here, very much to our satisfaction,

I. That Daniel was a favourite with the *prince of the eunuchs (v. 9)*, as Joseph was with the keeper of the prison ; he had a *tender love* for him. No doubt Daniel deserved it, and recommended himself by his ingenuity and sweetness of temper (he was *greatly beloved, ch.*ix. 23) ; and yet it is said here that it was God that *brought him into favour with the prince of the eunuchs,* for every one does not meet with acceptance according to his merits. Note, The interest which we think we make for ourselves we must acknowledge to be God's gift, and must ascribe to him the glory of it. Whoever are in favour, it is God that has brought them into favour; and it is by him that they *find good understanding.* Herein was again verified that word (Ps. cvi. 46), *He made them to be pitied of all those that carried them captives.* Let young ones know that the way to be acceptable is to be tractable and dutiful.

II. That Daniel was still firm to his religion. They had changed his name, but they could not change his nature. Whatever they pleased to call him, he still retained the spirit of an Israelite indeed. He would apply his mind as closely as any of them to his books, and took pains to make himself master of the *learning and tongue of the Chal-deans*, but he was resolved that *he would not defile himself with the portion of the king's meat*, he would not meddle with it, nor *with the wine which he drank, v.* 8. And having communicated his purpose, with the reasons of it, to his fellows, they concurred in the same resolution, as appears, *v.* 11. This was not out of sullenness, or peevishness, or a spirit of contradiction, but from a principle of conscience. Perhaps it was not in itself unlawful for them to *eat of the king's meat* or to *drink of his wine.* But, 1. They were scrupulous concerning the meat, lest it should be sinful. Sometimes such meat would be set before them as was expressly forbidden by their law, as swine's flesh; or they were afraid lest it should have been offered in sacrifice to an idol, or blessed in the name of an idol. The Jews were distinguished from other nations very much by their meats (Lev. xi. 45, 46), and these pious young men, being in a strange country, thought themselves obliged to keep up the honour of their being a peculiar people. Though they could not keep up their dignity as princes, they would not lose it as Israelites; for on that they most valued themselves. Note, When God's people are in Babylon they have need to take special care that they *partake not in her sins.* Providence seemed to lay this meat before them; being captives they must eat what they could get and must not disoblige their masters; yet, if the command be against it, they must abide by that. Though Providence says, *Kill and eat*, conscience says, *Not so, Lord, for nothing common or unclean has come into my mouth.* 2. They were jealous over themselves, lest, though it should not be sinful in itself, it should be an *occasion of sin* to them, lest, by indulging their appetites with these dainties, they should grow sinful, and voluptuous, and in love with the pleasures of Babylon. They had learned David's prayer, *Let me not eat of their dainties* (Ps. cxli. 4), and Solomon's precept, *Be not desirous of dainties, for they are deceitful meat* (Prov. xxiii. 3), and accordingly they form their resolution. Note, It is very much the praise of all, and especially of young people, to be dead to the delights of sense, not to covet them, not to relish them, but to look upon them with indifference. Those that would excel in wisdom and piety must learn betimes to *keep under the body and bring it into subjection.* 3. However, they thought it unseasonable now, when Jerusalem was in distress, and they themselves were in captivity. They had no heart to *drink wine in bowls*, so much were they *grieved for the affliction of Joseph.* Though they had royal blood in their veins, yet they did not think it proper to have royal dainties in their mouths when they were thus brought low. Note, It becomes us to be humble under humbling providences. *Call me not Naomi; call me*

1020

Marah. See the benefit of affliction; by the account Jeremiah gives of the princes and great men now at Jerusalem it appears that they were very corrupt and wicked, and defiled themselves with things offered to idols, while these young gentlemen that were in captivity would not defile themselves, no, not with their *portion of the king's meat.* How much better is it with those that retain their integrity in the depths of affliction than with those that retain their iniquity in the heights of prosperity! Observe, The great thing that Daniel avoided was defiling himself with the pollutions of sin; that is the thing we should be more afraid of than of any outward trouble. Daniel, having taken up this resolution, *requested of the prince of the eunuchs that he might not defile himself*, not only that he might not be compelled to do it, but that he might not be tempted to do it, that the bait might not be laid before him, that he might not see the portion appointed him of the king's meat, nor look upon the wine when it was red. It will be easier to keep the temptation at a distance than to suffer it to come near and then be forced to *put a knife to our throat.* Note, We cannot better improve our interest in any with whom we have found favour than by making use of them to keep us from sin.

III. That God wonderfully owned him herein. When Daniel requested that he might have none of the king's meat or wine set before him the prince of the eunuchs objected that, if he and his fellows were not found in as good case as any of their companions, he should be in danger of having anger and of losing his head, *v.* 10. Daniel, to satisfy him that there would be no danger of any bad consequence, desires the matter might be put to a trial. He applies himself further to the under-officer, Melzar, or the steward: " *Prove us for ten days;* during that time let us have nothing but *pulse to eat*, nothing but herbs and fruits, or parched peas or lentils, and nothing but *water to drink*, and see how we can live upon that, and proceed accordingly," *v.* 13. People will not believe the benefit of abstemiousness and a spare diet, nor how much it contributes to the health of the body, unless they try it. Trial was accordingly made. Daniel and his fellows lived for ten days upon *pulse and water*, hard fare for young men of genteel extraction and education, and which one would rather expect they should have indented against than petitioned for; but *at the end of the ten days* they were compared with the other children, and were found *fairer and fatter in flesh*, of a more healthful look and a better complexion, than *all those who did eat the portion of the king's meat, v.* 15. This was in part a natural effect of their temperance, but it must be ascribed to the special blessing of God, which will make a little to go a great way, a *dinner of herbs* better than a *stalled ox.* By this it appears that *man lives not by bread alone ;* pulse and water shall be the most nourishing food if God speak the word. See what it is to keep ourselves pure from the pollutions of sin; it is the way to have that comfort and satisfaction which will be *health to the navel* and *marrow to the bones,* while the pleasures of sin are *rottenness to the bones.*

IV. That his master countenanced him. The steward did not force them to eat against their consciences, but, as they desired, *gave them pulse and water* (v. 16), the pleasures of which they enjoyed, and we have reason to think were not envied the enjoyment. Here is a great example of temperance and contentment with mean things; and (as Epicurus said) "he that lives according to nature will never be poor, but he that lives according to opinion will never be rich." This wonderful abstemiousness of these young men in the days of their youth contributed to the fitting of them, 1. For their eminent services. Hereby they kept their minds clear and unclouded, and fit for contemplation, and saved for the best employments a great deal both of time and thought; and thus they prevented those diseases which indispose men for the business of age that owe their rise to the intemperances of youth. 2. For their eminent sufferings. Those that had thus inured themselves to hardship, and lived a life of self-denial and mortification, could the more easily venture upon the fiery furnace and the den of lions, rather than sin against God.

17 As for these four children, God gave them knowledge and skill in all learning and wisdom: and Daniel had understanding in all visions and dreams. 18 Now at the end of the days that the king had said he should bring them in, then the prince of the eunuchs brought them in before Nebuchadnezzar. 19 And the king communed with them; and among them all was found none like Daniel, Hananiah, Mishael, and Azariah: therefore stood they before the king. 20 And in all matters of wisdom *and* understanding, that the king enquired of them, he found them ten times better than all the magicians *and* astrologers that *were* in all his realm. 21 And Daniel continued *even* unto the first year of king Cyrus.

Concerning Daniel and his fellows we have here,

I. Their great attainments in learning, *v.* 17. They were very sober and diligent, and studied hard; and we may suppose their tutors, finding them of an uncommon capacity, took a great deal of pains with them,

but, after all, their achievements are ascribed to God only. It was he that *gave them knowledge and skill in all learning and wisdom;* for *every good and perfect gift is from above, from the Father of lights.* It is the Lord our God that *gives men power to get* this wealth; the mind is furnished only by him that formed it. The great learning which God gave these four children was, 1. A balance for their losses. They had, for the iniquity of their fathers, been deprived of the honours and pleasures that would have attended their noble extraction; but, to make them amends for that, God, in giving them learning, gave them better honours and pleasures than those they had been deprived of. 2. A recompence for their integrity. They kept to their religion, even in the minutest instances of it, and would not so much as defile themselves with the king's meat or wine, but became, in effect, Nazarites; and now God rewarded them for it with an eminency in learning; for God *gives to a man that is good in his sight wisdom, and knowledge, and joy* with them, Eccl. ii. 26. To Daniel he gave a double portion; he had *understanding in visions and dreams ;* he knew how to interpret dreams, as Joseph, not by rules of art, such as are pretended to be given by the oneirocritics, but by a divine sagacity and wisdom which God gave him. Nay, he was endued with a prophetic spirit, by which he was enabled to converse with God, and to receive the notices of divine things in dreams and visions, Num. xii. 6. According to this gift given to Daniel, we find him, in this book, all along employed about dreams and visions, interpreting or entertaining them; for, *as every one has received the gift,* so shall he have an opportunity, and so should he have a heart, to *minister the same,* 1 Pet. iv. 10.

II. Their great acceptance with the king. After *three years* spent in their education (they being of some maturity, it is likely, when they came, perhaps about twenty years old) they were presented to the king with the rest that were of their standing, *v.* 18. And the king examined them and *communed with them* himself, *v.* 19. He could do it, being a man of parts and learning himself, else he would not have come to be so great; and he would do it, for it is the wisdom of princes, in the choice of the persons they employ, to see with their own eyes, to exercise their own judgment, and not trust too much to the representation of others. The king examined them not so much in the languages, in the rules of oratory or poetry, as *in all matters of wisdom and understanding,* the rules of prudence and true politics; he enquired into their judgment about the due conduct of human life and public affairs; not, "Were they wits?" but, "Were they wise?" And he not only found them to excel the young candidates for preferment that were of their own standing, but found that they had *more understanding than the ancients, than all their teachers,* Ps. cxix. 99, 100. So far was the king from being partial to his own countrymen, to seniors, to those of his own religion and of an established reputation, that he freely owned that, upon trial, he found those poor young captive Jews ten times wiser and *better than all the magicians that were in all his realm,* v. 20. He was soon aware of something extraordinary in these young men, and, which gave him a surprising satisfaction, was soon aware that a little of their true divinity was preferable to a great deal of the divination he had been used to. *What is the chaff to the wheat?* what are the magicians' rods to Aaron's? There was no comparison between them. These four young students were better, were *ten times* better, than all the old practitioners, put them all together, that were *in all his realm,* and we may be sure that they were not a few. This contempt did God pour upon the pride of the Chaldeans, and this honour did he put upon the low estate of his own people; and thus did he make not only these persons, but the rest of their nation for their sakes, the more respected in the land of their captivity. *Lastly,* This judgment being given concerning them, they *stood before the king* (v. 19); they attended in the presence-chamber, nay, and in the council-chamber, for to *see the king's face* is the periphrasis of a privy-counsellor, Esth. i. 14. This confirms Solomon's observation, *Seest thou a man diligent in his business,* sober and humble? *he shall stand before kings; he shall not stand before mean men.* Industry is the way to preferment. How long the other three were about the court we are not told; but Daniel, for his part, *continued to the first year of Cyrus* (v. 21), though not always alike in favour and reputation. He lived and prophesied after the first year of Cyrus; but that is mentioned to intimate that he lived to see the deliverance of his people out of their captivity and their return to their own land. Note, Sometimes God favours his servants that mourn with Zion in her sorrows to let them live to see better times with the church than they saw in the beginning of their days and to share with her in her joys.

CHAP. II.

It was said (ch. i. 17) that Daniel had understanding in dreams; and here we have an early and eminent instance of it, which soon made him famous in the court of Babylon, as Joseph by the same means came to be so in the court of Egypt. This chapter is a history, but it is the history of a prophecy, by a dream and the interpretation of it. Pharaoh's dream, and Joseph's interpretation of it, related only to the years of plenty and famine and the interest of God's Israel in them; but Nebuchadnezzar's dream here, and Daniel's interpretation of that, look much higher, to the four monarchies, and the concerns of Israel in them, and the kingdom of the Messiah, which should be set up in the world upon the ruins of them. In this chapter we have, I. The great perplexity that Nebuchadnezzar was put into by a dream which he had forgotten, and his command to the magicians to tell him what it was, which they could not pretend to do, ver. 1—11. II. Orders given for the destroying of all the wise men of Babylon, and of Daniel among the rest, with his fellows, ver. 12—15. III. The discovery of this secret to him, in answer to prayer, and the thanksgiving he offered up to God thereupon, ver. 16—23. IV. His admission to the king, and the discovery he made to him both of his dream and of the interpretation of it, ver. 24—45. V. The great honour which Nebu-

1022

chadnezzar put upon Daniel, in recompence for this service, and the preferment of his companions with him, ver. 46—49.

AND in the second year of the reign of Nebuchadnezzar Nebuchadnezzar dreamed dreams, wherewith his spirit was troubled, and his sleep brake from him. 2 Then the king commanded to call the magicians, and the astrologers, and the sorcerers, and the Chaldeans, for to show the king his dreams. So they came and stood before the king. 3 And the king said unto them, I have dreamed a dream, and my spirit was troubled to know the dream. 4 Then spake the Chaldeans to the king in Syriac, O king, live for ever: tell thy servants the dream, and we will show the interpretation. 5 The king answered and said to the Chaldeans, The thing is gone from me: if ye will not make known unto me the dream, with the interpretation thereof, ye shall be cut in pieces, and your houses shall be made a dunghill. 6 But if ye show the dream, and the interpretation thereof, ye shall receive of me gifts and rewards and great honour: therefore show me the dream, and the interpretation thereof. 7 They answered again and said, Let the king tell his servants the dream, and we will show the interpretation of it. 8 The king answered and said, I know of certainty that ye would gain the time, because ye see the thing is gone from me. 9 But if ye will not make known unto me the dream, *there is but* one decree for you: for ye have prepared lying and corrupt words to speak before me, till the time be changed: therefore tell me the dream, and I shall know that ye can show me the interpretation thereof. 10 The Chaldeans answered before the king, and said, There is not a man upon the earth that can show the king's matter: therefore *there is* no king, lord, nor ruler, *that* asked such things at any magician, or astrologer, or Chaldean. 11 And *it is* a rare thing that the king requireth, and there is none other that can show it before the king, except the gods, whose dwelling is not with flesh. 12 For this cause the king was angry and very furious, and commanded to destroy all the wise *men* of Babylon. 13 And the decree went forth that the wise *men* should be slain; and they sought Daniel and his fellows to be slain.

We meet with a great difficulty in the date of this story; it is said to be in the second year of the reign of Nebuchadnezzar, *v.* 1. Now Daniel was carried to Babylon in his first year, and, it should seem, he was three years under tutors and governors before he was presented to the king, *ch.* i. 5. How then could this happen in *the second year?* Perhaps, though three years were appointed for the education of other children, yet Daniel was so forward that he was taken into business when he had been but one year at school, and so in the second year he became thus considerable. Some make it to be the second year after he began to reign alone, but the fifth or sixth year since he began to reign in partnership with his *father*. Some read it, *and in the second year* (the second after Daniel and his fellows stood before the king), *in the kingdom of Nebuchadnezzar*, or *in his reign*, this happened; as Joseph, in the second year after his skill in dreams, showed and expounded Pharaoh's, so Daniel, in the second year after he commenced master in that art, did this service. I would much rather take it some of these ways than suppose, as some do, that it was in the second year after he had conquered Egypt, which was the thirty-sixth year of his reign, because it appears, by what we meet with in Ezekiel, that Daniel was famous both for wisdom and prevalence in prayer long before that; and therefore this passage, or story, which shows how he came to be so eminent for both these must be laid early in Nebuchadnezzar's reign. Now here we may observe,

I. The perplexity that Nebuchadnezzar was in by reason of a dream which he had dreamed but had forgotten (*v.* 1): *He dreamed dreams*, that is, a dream consisting of divers distinct parts, or which filled his head as much as if it had been many dreams. Solomon speaks of a *multitude of dreams*, strangely incoherent, in which *there are divers vanities*, Eccl. v. 7. This dream of Nebuchadnezzar's had nothing in the thing itself but what might be paralleled in many a common dream, in which are often represented to men things as foreign as are here mentioned; but there was something in the impression it made upon him which carried with it an incontestable evidence of its divine original and its prophetic significancy. Note, The greatest of men are not exempt from, nay, they lie most open to, those cares and troubles of mind which disturb their repose in the night, while *the sleep of the labouring man is sweet* and sound, and the sleep of the sober temperate man free from confused dreams. The abundance of the rich will

not suffer them to sleep at all for care, and the excesses of gluttons and drunkards will not suffer them to sleep quietly for dreaming. But this recorded here was not from natural causes. Nebuchadnezzar was a troubler of God's Israel, but God here troubled him; for he that made the soul can *make his sword to approach to it.* He had his guards about him, but they could not keep trouble from his spirit. We know not the uneasiness of many that live in great pomp, and, one would think, in pleasure too. We look into their houses, and are tempted to envy them; but, could we look into their hearts, we should pity them rather. All the treasures and all the delights of the children of men, which this mighty monarch had the command of, could not procure him a little repose, when by reason of the trouble of his mind his *sleep broke from him.* But God *gives his beloved sleep*, who return to him as their rest.

II. The trial that he made of his magicians and astrologers whether they could tell him what his dream was, which he had forgotten. They were immediately sent for, to *show the king his dreams, v.* 2. There are many things which we retain the impressions of, and yet have lost the images of the things; though we cannot tell what the matter was, we know how we were affected with it; so it was with this king. His dream had slipped out of his mind, and he could not possibly recollect it, but he was confident he should know it if he heard it again. God ordered it so that Daniel might have the more honour, and, in him, the God of Daniel. Note, God sometimes serves his own purposes by putting things out of men's minds as well as by putting things into their minds. The magicians, it is likely, were proud of their being sent for into the king's bed-chamber, to give him a taste of their office, not doubting but it would be for their honour. He tells them that he had *dreamed a dream, v.* 3. They speak to him in the Syriac tongue, which was then the same with the Chaldee, but now they differ much. And henceforward Daniel uses that language, or dialect of the Hebrew, for the same reason that those words, Jer. x. 11, are in that language, because designed to convince the Chaldeans of the folly of their idolatry and to bring them to the knowledge and worship of the true and living God, which the stories of these chapters have a direct tendency to. But *ch.* viii. and forward, being intended for the comfort of the Jews, is written in their peculiar language. They, in their answer, complimented the king with their good wishes, desired him to tell his dream, and undertook with all possible assurance to interpret it, *v.* 4. But the king insisted upon it that they must tell him the dream itself, because he had forgotten it and could not tell it to them. And, if they could not do this, they should all be put to death as deceivers (*v.* 5), themselves cut *to pieces* and *their houses made a dung-hill.* If they could, they should be rewarded and preferred, *v.* 6. And they knew, as Balaam did concerning Balak, that he was able to *promote them to great honour,* and give them that *wages of unrighteousness* which, like him, *they loved* so dearly. No question therefore that they will do their utmost to gratify the king; if they do not, it is not for want of good-will, but for want of power, Providence so ordering it that the magicians of Babylon might now be as much confounded and put to shame as of old the magicians of Egypt had been, that, how much soever his people were both in Egypt and Babylon vilified and made contemptible, his oracles might in both be magnified and made honourable, by the silencing of those that set up in competition with them. The magicians, having reason on their side, insist upon it that the king must tell them the dream, and then, if they do not tell him the interpretation of it, it is their fault, *v.* 7. But arbitrary power is deaf to reason. The king falls into a passion, gives them hard words, and, without any colour of reason, suspects that they could tell him but would not; and instead of upbraiding them with impotency, and the deficiency of their art, as he might justly have done, he charges them with a combination to affront him : *You have prepared lying and corrupt words to speak before me.* How unreasonable and absurd is this imputation! If they had undertaken to tell him what his dream was, and had imposed upon him with a sham, he might have charged them with lying and corrupt words; but to say this of them when they honestly confessed their own weakness only shows what senseless things indulged passions are, and how apt great men are to think it is their prerogative to pursue their humour in defiance of reason and equity, and all the dictates of both. When the magicians begged of him to tell them the dream, though the request was highly rational and just, he tells them that they did but dally with him, to gain time (*v.* 8), *till the time be changed* (*v.* 9), either till the king's desire to know his dream be over, and he grown indifferent whether he be told it or no, though now he is so hot upon it, or till they may hope he has so perfectly forgotten his dream (the remaining shades of which are slipping from him apace as he catches at them) that they may tell him what they please and make him believe it was his dream, and, when the thing which is going, is quite *gone from him,* as it will be in a little time, he will not be able to disprove them. And therefore, without delay, they must tell him the dream. In vain do they plead, 1. That there is *no man on earth* that can retrieve the king's dream, *v.* 10. There are settled rules by which to discover what the meaning of the dream was; whether they will hold or no is the question. But never were any rules offered to be given

by which to discover what the dream was; they cannot work unless they have something to work upon. They acknowledge that the gods may indeed *declare unto man what is his thought* (Amos iv. 13), for God *understands our thoughts afar off* (Ps. cxxxix. 2), what they will be before we think them, what they are when we do not regard them, and what they have been when we have forgotten them. But those who can do this are gods, that *have not their dwelling with flesh* (*v.* 11), and it is they alone that can do this. As for men, their *dwelling is with flesh ;* the wisest and greatest of men are clouded with a veil of flesh, which quite obstructs and confounds all their acquaintance with spirits, and their powers and operations; but the gods, that are themselves pure spirits, know what is in man. See here an instance of the ignorance of these magicians, that they speak of many gods, whereas there is but one and can be but one infinite; yet see their knowledge of that which even the light of nature teaches and the works of nature prove, that there is a God, who is a Spirit, and perfectly knows the spirits of men and all their thoughts, so as it is not possible that any man should. This confession of the divine omniscience is here extorted from these idolaters, to the honour of God and their own condemnation, who though they knew there is a God in heaven, *to whom all hearts are open, all desires known, and from whom no secret is hid,* yet offered up their prayers and praises to dumb idols, that have *eyes and see not, ears and hear not.* 2. That there is no king on earth that would expect or require such a thing, *v.* 10. This intimates that they were *kings, lords,* and *potentates,* not ordinary people, that the magicians had most dealings with, and at whose devotion they were, while the oracles of God and the gospel of Christ are dispensed *to the poor.* Kings and potentates have often required unreasonable things of their subjects, but they think that never any required so unreasonable a thing as this, and therefore hope his imperial majesty will not insist upon it. But it is all in vain; when passion is in the throne reason is under foot : He was *angry and very furious, v.* 12. Note, It is very common for those that will not be convinced by reason to be provoked and exasperated by it, and to push on with fury what they cannot support with equity.

III. The doom passed upon all the magicians of Babylon. There is but *one decree for them all* (*v.* 9); they all stand condemned without exception or distinction. The decree has gone forth, they must every man of them be slain (*v.* 13), Daniel and his fellows (though they knew nothing of the matter) not excepted. See here, 1. What are commonly the unjust proceedings of arbitrary power. Nebuchadnezzar is here a tyrant in true colours, speaking death when he cannot speak sense, and treating those as traitors whose only fault is that they would serve him, but cannot. 2. What is commonly the just punishment of pretenders. How unrighteous soever Nebuchadnezzar was in this sentence, as to the ringleaders in the imposture, God was righteous. Those that imposed upon men, in pretending to do what they could not do, are now sentenced to death for not being able to do what they did not pretend to.

14 Then Daniel answered with counsel and wisdom to Arioch the captain of the king's guard, which was gone forth to slay the wise *men* of Babylon: 15 He answered and said to Arioch the king's captain, Why *is* the decree *so* hasty from the king? Then Arioch made the thing known to Daniel. 16 Then Daniel went in, and desired of the king that he would give him time, and that he would show the king the interpretation. 17 Then Daniel went to his house, and made the thing known to Hananiah, Mishael, and Azariah, his companions: 18 That they would desire mercies of the God of heaven concerning this secret; that Daniel and his fellows should not perish with the rest of the wise *men* of Babylon. 19 Then was the secret revealed unto Daniel in a night-vision. Then Daniel blessed the God of heaven. 20 Daniel answered and said, Blessed be the name of God for ever and ever: for wisdom and might are his: 21 And he changeth the times and the seasons: he removeth kings, and setteth up kings: he giveth wisdom unto the wise, and knowledge to them that know understanding: 22 He revealeth the deep and secret things: he knoweth what *is* in the darkness, and the light dwelleth with him. 23 I thank thee, and praise thee, O thou God of my fathers, who hast given me wisdom and might, and hast made known unto me now what we desired of thee: for thou hast *now* made known unto us the king's matter.

When the king sent for his wise men to tell them his dream, and the interpretation of it (*v.* 2), Daniel, it seems, was not summoned to appear among them; the king, though he was highly pleased with him when he examined him, and thought him *ten times* wiser than the rest of his wise men, yet forgot him when he had most occasion for him; and no wonder, when all was done in a

heat, and nothing with a cool and deliberate thought. But Providence so ordered it; that the magicians being nonplussed might be the more taken notice of, and so the more glory might redound to the God of Daniel. But, though Daniel had not the honour to be consulted with the rest of the wise men, contrary to all law and justice, by an undistinguishing sentence, he stands condemned with them, and till he has notice brought him to prepare for execution he knows nothing of the matter. How miserable is the case of those who live under an arbitrary government, as this of Nebuchadnezzar's! How happy are we, whose lives are under the protection of the law and methods of justice, and lie not thus at the mercy of a peevish and capricious prince!

We have found already, in Ezekiel, that Daniel was famous both for prudence and prayer; as a prince he had power with God and man; by prayer he had power with God, by prudence he had power with man, and in both he prevailed. Thus did he *find favour and good understanding* in the sight of both, and in these verses we have a remarkable instance of both.

I. Daniel by prudence knew how to deal with men, and he prevailed with them. When *Arioch, the captain of the guard,* that was appointed to slay all the wise men of Babylon, the whole college of them, seized Daniel (for the sword of tyranny, like the sword of war, *devours one as well as another*), he *answered with counsel and wisdom* (*v.* 14); he did not fall into a passion, and reproach the king as unjust and barbarous, much less did he contrive how to make resistance, but mildly asked, *Why is the decree so hasty? v.* 15. And whereas the rest of the wise men had insisted upon it that it was utterly impossible for him ever to have his demand gratified, which did but make him more outrageous, Daniel undertakes, if he may but have a little time allowed him, to give the king all the satisfaction he desired, *v.* 16. The king, being now sensible of his error in not sending for Daniel sooner, whose character he began to recollect, was soon prevailed upon to respite the judgment, and make trial of Daniel. Note, The likeliest method to turn away wrath, even the wrath of a king, which is as the messenger of death, is by a *soft answer,* by that yielding which *pacifies great offences;* thus, though *where the word of a king is there is power,* yet even that word may be repelled, and that so as to be repealed; and so some read it here (*v.* 14): *Then Daniel returned,* and stayed *the counsel and edict, through Arioch, the king's provost-marshal.*

II. Daniel knew how by prayer to converse with God, and he found favour with him, both in petition and in thanksgiving, which are the two principal parts of prayer. Observe,

1. His humble petition for this mercy, that

God would discover to him what was the king's dream, and the interpretation of it. When he had gained time he did not go to consult with the rest of the wise men whether there was any thing in their art, in their books, that might be of use in this matter, but *went to his house,* there to be alone with his God, for from him alone, who is the Father of lights, he expected this great gift. Observe, (1.) He did not only pray for this discovery himself, but he engaged his companions to pray for it too. He *made the thing known* to those who had been all along his bosom-friends and associates, requesting *that they would desire mercy of God concerning this secret,* v. 17, 18. Though Daniel was probably their senior, and every way excelled them, yet he engaged them as partners with him in this matter, *Vis unita fortior—The union of forces produces greater force.* See Esth. iv. 16. Note, Praying friends are valuable friends; it is good to have an intimacy with and an interest in those that have fellowship with God and an interest at the throne of grace; and it well becomes the greatest and best of men to desire the assistance of the prayers of others for them. St. Paul often entreats his friends to pray for him. Thus we must show that we put a value upon our friends, upon prayer, upon their prayers. (2.) He was particular in this prayer, but had an eye to, and a dependence upon, the general mercy of God: *That they would desire mercies of the God of heaven concerning this secret,* v. 18. We ought in prayer to look up to God as the *God of heaven,* a God above us, and who has dominion over us, to whom we owe adoration and allegiance, a God of power, who can do every thing. Our Saviour has taught us to pray to God as *our Father in heaven.* And, whatever good we pray for, our dependence must be upon the *mercies of God* for it, and an interest in those mercies we must desire; we can expect nothing by way of recompence for our merits, but all as the gift of God's mercies. They desired mercy *concerning this secret.* Note, Whatever is the matter of our care must be the matter of our prayer; we must desire mercy of God concerning this thing and the other thing that occasions us trouble and fear. God gives us leave to be humbly free with him, and in prayer to enter into the detail of our wants and burdens. *Secret things belong to the Lord our God,* and therefore, if there be any mercy we stand in need of that concerns a secret, to him we must apply; and, though we cannot in faith pray for miracles, yet we may in faith pray to him who has all hearts in his hand, and who in his providence does wonders without miracles, for the discovery of that which is out of our view and the obtaining of that which is out of our reach, as far as is for his glory and our good, believing that to him nothing is hidden, nothing is hard. (3.) Their plea with God was

the imminent peril they were in; they desired mercy of God in this matter, that so Daniel and his *fellows might not perish with the rest of the wise men of Babylon,* that the righteous might not be destroyed with the wicked. Note, When the lives of good and useful men are in danger it is time to be earnest with God for mercy for them, as for Peter in prison, Acts xii. 5. (4.) The mercy which Daniel and his fellows prayed for was bestowed. The *secret* was *revealed unto Daniel* in a *night-vision,* v. 19. Some think he dreamed the same dream, when he was asleep, that Nebuchadnezzar had dreamed; it should rather seem that when he was awake, and continuing *instant in prayer,* and *watching in the same,* the dream itself, and the interpretation of it, were communicated to him by the ministry of an angel, abundantly to his satisfaction. Note, The *effectual fervent prayer of righteous men avails much.* There are mysteries and secrets which by prayer we are let into; with that key the cabinets of heaven are unlocked, for Christ has said, Thus *knock, and it shall be opened unto you.*

2. His grateful thanksgiving for this mercy when he had received it: *Then Daniel blessed the God of heaven,* v. 19. He did not stay till he had told it to the king, and seen whether he would own it to be his dream or no, but was confident that it was so, and that he had gained his point, and therefore he immediately turned his prayers into praises. As he had prayed in a full assurance that God would do this for him, so he gave thanks in a full assurance that he had done it; and in both he had an eye to God as the *God of heaven.* His prayer was not recorded, but his thanksgiving is. Observe,

(1.) The honour he gives to God in this thanksgiving, which he studies to do in a great variety and copiousness of expression: *Blessed be the name of God for ever and ever.* There is that *for ever* in God which is to be blessed and praised; it is unchangeably and eternally in him. And it is to be blessed *for ever and ever:* as the matter of praise is God's eternal perfection, so the work of praise shall be everlastingly in the doing. [1.] He gives to God the glory of what he is in himself: *Wisdom and might are his, wisdom and courage* (so some); whatever is fit to be done he will do; whatever he will do he can do, he dares do, and he will be sure to do it in the best manner, for he has infinite wisdom to design and contrive and infinite power to execute and accomplish. *With him are strength and wisdom,* which in men are often parted. [2.] He gives him the glory of what he is to the world of mankind. He has a universal influence and agency upon all the children of men, and all their actions and affairs. Are the times changed? Is the posture of affairs altered? Does every thing lie open to mutability? It is God that *changes the times and the seasons,* and the face of them. No change comes to pass by chance, but according to the will and counsel of God. Are those that were kings removed and deposed? Do they abdicate? Are they laid aside? It is God that *removes kings.* Are the *poor raised out of the dust, to be set among princes?* It is God that *sets up kings;* and the making and unmaking of kings is a flower of his crown who is the fountain of all power, *King of kings* and *Lord of lords.* Are there men that excel others in wisdom, philosophers and statesmen, that think above the common rate, contemplative penetrating men? It is *God that gives wisdom to the wise,* whether they be so wise as to acknowledge it or no; they have it not of themselves, but it is he that *gives knowledge to those that know understanding,* which is a good reason why we should not be proud of our knowledge, and why we should serve and honour God with it and make it our business to know him. [3.] He gives him the glory of this particular discovery. He praises him, *First,* For that he could make such a discovery (*v.* 22) : *He reveals the deep and secret things* which are hidden from the eyes of all living. It was he that revealed to man what is true wisdom when none else could (Job xxviii. 27, 28) ; it is he that reveals things to come to his servants the prophets. He does himself perfectly discern and distinguish that which is most closely and most industriously concealed, for he will *bring into judgment every secret thing;* the truth will be evident in the great day. He *knows what is in the darkness,* and what is done in the darkness, for that *hides not from him,* Ps. cxxxix. 11, 12. *The light dwells with him,* and he *dwells in the light* (1 Tim. vi. 16), and yet, as to us, he *makes darkness his pavilion.* Some understand it of the light of prophecy and divine revelation, which dwells with God and is derived from him; for he is the *Father of lights,* of all lights; they are all at home in him. *Secondly,* For that he had made this discovery to him. Here he has an eye to God as the *God of his fathers;* for, though the Jews were now captives in Babylon, yet they were *beloved for their fathers' sake.* He praises God, who is the fountain of wisdom and might, for the wisdom and might he had given him, wisdom to know this great secret and might to bear the discovery. Note, What wisdom and might we have we must acknowledge to be God's gift. *Thou hast made this known to me, v.* 23. What was hidden from the celebrated Chaldeans, who made the interpreting of dreams their profession, is revealed to Daniel, a captive-Jew, a babe, much their junior. God would hereby put honour upon the *Spirit of prophecy* just when he was putting contempt upon the *spirit of divination.* Was Daniel thus thankful to God for making known that to him which was the saving of the lives of him and his fellows? Much more reason

have we to be thankful to him for making known to us the great salvation of the soul, to us and *not to the world,* to us and *not to the wise and prudent.*

(2.) The respect he puts upon his companions in this thanksgiving. Though it was by his prayers principally that this discovery was obtained, and to him that it was made, yet he owns their partnership with him, both in praying for it (it is what *we desired of thee*) and in enjoying it—Thou hast *made known unto us the king's matter.* Either they were present with Daniel when the discovery was made to him, or as soon as he knew it he told it them (εὕρηκα, εὕρηκα—*I have found it, I have found it),* that those who had assisted him with their prayers might assist him in their praises; his joining them with him is an instance of his humility and modesty, which well become those that are taken into communion with God. Thus St. Paul sometimes joins Sylvanus, Timotheus, or some other minister, with himself in the inscriptions to many of his epistles. Note, What honour God puts upon us we should be willing that our brethren may share with us in.

24 Therefore Daniel went in unto Arioch, whom the king had ordained to destroy the wise *men* of Babylon : he went and said thus unto him ; Destroy not the wise *men* of Babylon : bring me in before the king, and I will show unto the king the interpretation. 25 Then Arioch brought in Daniel before the king in haste, and said thus unto him, I have found a man of the captives of Judah, that will make known unto the king the interpretation. 26 The king answered and said to Daniel, whose name *was* Belteshazzar, Art thou able to make known unto me the dream which I have seen, and the interpretation thereof? 27 Daniel answered in the presence of the king, and said, The secret which the king hath demanded cannot the wise *men,* the astrologers, the magicians, the soothsayers, show unto the king ; 28 But there is a God in heaven that revealeth secrets, and maketh known to the king Nebuchadnezzar what shall be in the latter days. Thy dream, and the visions of thy head upon thy bed, are these; 29 As for thee, O king, thy thoughts came *into thy mind* upon thy bed, what should come to pass hereafter : and he that revealeth secrets maketh

known to thee what shall come to pass. 30 But as for me, this secret is not revealed to me for *any* wisdom that I have more than any living, but for *their* sakes that shall make known the interpretation to the king, and that thou mightest know the thoughts of thy heart.

We have here the introduction to Daniel's declaring the dream, and the interpretation of it.

I. He immediately bespoke the reversing of the sentence against the wise men of Babylon, *v.* 24. He went with all speed to Arioch, to tell him that his commission was now superseded : *Destroy not the wise men of Babylon.* Though there were those of them perhaps that deserved to die, as magicians, by the law of God, yet here that which they stood condemned for was not a crime worthy of death or of bonds, and therefore let them not die, and be *unjustly destroyed,* but let them live, and be justly shamed, as having been nonplussed and unable to do that which a prophet of the Lord could do. Note, Since God shows common kindness to the evil and good, we should do so too, and be ready to save the lives even of bad men, Matt. v. 45. A good man is a common good. To Paul in the ship God gave the souls of all that sailed with him ; they were saved for his sake. To Daniel was owing the preservation of all the wise men, who yet rendered not according to the benefit done to them, *ch.* iii. 8.

II. He offered his service, with great assurance, to go to the king, and tell him his dream and the interpretation of it, and was admitted accordingly, *v.* 24, 25. Arioch brought him in haste to the king, hoping to ingratiate himself by introducing Daniel; he pretends he had sought him to interpret the king's dream, whereas really it was to execute upon him the king's sentence that he sought him. But courtiers' business is every way to humour the prince and make their own services acceptable.

III. He contrived as much as might be to reflect shame upon the magicians, and to give honour to God, upon this occasion. The king owned that it was a bold undertaking, and questioned whether he could make it good (*v.* 26): *Art thou able to make known unto me the dream?* What! Such a babe in this knowledge, such a stripling as thou art, wilt thou undertake that which thy seniors despair of doing? The less likely it appeared to the king that Daniel should do this the more God was glorified in enabling him to do it. Note, In transmitting divine revelation to the children of men it has been God's usual way to make use of the *weak and foolish things* and persons *of the world,* and such as were *despised* and despaired of, *to confound the wise and mighty,* that the

1028

excellency of the power might be of him, 1 Cor. i. 27, 28. Daniel from this takes occasion, 1. To put the king out of conceit with his magicians and soothsayers, whom he had such great expectations from (*v.* 27) : " *This secret they cannot show to the king ;* it is out of their power ; the rules of their art will not reach to it. Therefore let not the king be angry with them for not doing that which they cannot do ; but rather despise them, and cast them off, because they cannot do it." Broughton reads it generally : " This secret *no sages, astrologers, enchanters, or entrail-cookers, can show unto the king ;* let not the king therefore consult them any more." Note, The experience we have of the inability of all creatures to give us satisfaction should lessen our esteem of them, and lower our expectations from them. They are baffled in their pretensions; we are baffled in our hopes from them. Hitherto they come, and no further; let us therefore say to them, as Job to his friends, *Now you are nothing ; miserable comforters are you all.* 2. To bring him to the knowledge of the one only living and true God, the God whom Daniel worshipped : "Though they cannot find out the secret, let not the king despair of having it found out, for *there is a God in heaven that reveals secrets," v.* 28. Note, The insufficiency of creatures should drive us to the all-sufficiency of the Creator. *There is a God in heaven* (and it is well for us there is) who can do that for us, and make known that to us, which none on earth can, particularly the secret history of the work of redemption and the secret designs of God's love to us therein, the mystery which was *hidden from ages and generations ;* divine revelation helps us out where human reason leaves us quite at a loss, and makes known that, not only to kings, but to the poor of this world, which none of the philosophers or politicians of the heathens, with all their oracles and arts of divination to help them, could ever pretend to give us any light into, Rom. xvi. 25, 26.

IV. He confirmed the king in his opinion that the dream he was thus solicitous to recover the idea of was really well worth enquiring after, that it was of great value and of vast consequence, not a common dream, the idle disport of a ludicrous and luxuriant fancy, which was not worth remembering or telling again, but that it was a divine discovery, a ray of light darted into his mind from the upper world, relating to the great affairs and revolutions of this lower world. God in it *made known to the king what should be in the latter days* (*v.* 28), that is, in the times that were to come, reaching as far as the setting up of Christ's kingdom in the world, which was to be *in the latter days,* Heb. i. 1. And again (*v.* 29) : " *The thoughts which came into thy mind* were not the repetitions of what had been before, as our dreams usually are"—

Omnia quæ sensu volvuntur vota diurno
  Tempore sopito reddit amica quies—
The sentiments which we indulge throughout the
  day often mingle with the grateful slumbers of
  the night.   CLAUDIAN.

" But they were predictions of *what should
come to pass hereafter,* which he that *reveals
secrets makes known unto thee;* and therefore thou art in the right in taking the hint
and pursuing it thus." Note, Things that
are to come to pass hereafter are secret
things, which God only can reveal; and
what he has revealed of those things, especially with reference to the last days of all,
to the end of time, ought to be very seriously
and diligently enquired into and considered
by every one of us. Some think that the
thoughts which are said to have *come into the
king's mind upon his bed, what should come to
pass hereafter,* were his own thoughts when
he was awake. Just before he fell asleep,
and dreamed this dream, he was musing in
his own mind what would be the issue of his
growing greatness, what his kingdom would
hereafter come to; and so the dream was
an answer to those thoughts. What discoveries God intends to make he thus prepares men for.

V. He solemnly professes that he could
not pretend to have merited from God the
favour of this discovery, or to have obtained
it by any sagacity of his own (*v.* 30): " *But,
as for me,* this secret is not found out by me,
but is *revealed to me,* and that *not for any
wisdom that I have more than any living,* to
qualify me for the receiving of such a discovery." Note, It well becomes those whom
God has highly favoured and honoured to be
very humble and low in their own eyes, to
lay aside all opinion of their own wisdom
and worthiness, that God alone may have all
the praise of the good they are, and have,
and do, and that all may be attributed to the
freeness of his good-will towards them and
the fulness of his good work in them. The
secret was made known to him not for his
own sake, but, 1. For the sake of his people,
for *their sakes that shall make known the interpretation to the king,* that is, for the sake
of his brethren and companions in tribulation, who had by their prayers helped him
to obtain this discovery, and so might be
said to make known the interpretation—
that their lives might be spared, that they
might come into favour and be preferred,
and all the people of the Jews might fare the
better, in their captivity, for their sakes.
Note, Humble men will be always ready to
think that what God does for them and by
them is more for the sake of others than for
their own. 2. For the sake of *his prince;*
and some read the former clause in this
sense, "Not for any wisdom of mine, *but
that the king may know the interpretation, and
that thou mightest know the thoughts of thy
heart,* that thou mightest have satisfaction
given thee as to what thou wast before

considering, and thereby instruction given
thee how to behave towards the church of
God." God revealed this thing to Daniel
that he might make it known to the king.
Prophets receive that they may give, that the
discoveries made to them may not be lodged
with themselves, but communicated to the
persons that are concerned.

31 Thou, O king, sawest, and behold a great image. This great image,
whose brightness *was* excellent, stood
before thee; and the form thereof *was*
terrible. 32 This image's head *was*
of fine gold, his breast and his arms
of silver, his belly and his thighs of
brass, 33 His legs of iron, his feet
part of iron and part of clay. 34 Thou
sawest till that a stone was cut out
without hands, which smote the image
upon his feet *that were* of iron and
clay, and brake them to pieces. 35
Then was the iron, the clay, the brass,
the silver, and the gold, broken to
pieces together, and became like the
chaff of the summer threshing-floors;
and the wind carried them away, that
no place was found for them: and the
stone that smote the image became a
great mountain, and filled the whole
earth. 36 This *is* the dream; and we
will tell the interpretation thereof
before the king. 37 Thou, O king,
art a king of kings: for the God of
heaven hath given thee a kingdom,
power, and strength, and glory. 38
And wheresoever the children of men
dwell, the beasts of the field and the
fowls of the heaven hath he given
into thine hand, and hath made thee
ruler over them all. Thou *art* this
head of gold. 39 And after thee shall
arise another kingdom inferior to thee,
and another third kingdom of brass,
which shall bear rule over all the
earth. 40 And the fourth kingdom
shall be strong as iron: forasmuch as
iron breaketh in pieces and subdueth
all *things:* and as iron that breaketh
all these, shall it break in pieces and
bruise. 41 And whereas thou sawest
the feet and toes, part of potters' clay,
and part of iron, the kingdom shall
be divided; but there shall be in it
of the strength of the iron, forasmuch
as thou sawest the iron mixed with
miry clay. 42 And *as* the toes of the

feet *were* part of iron, and part of clay, *so* the kingdom shall be partly strong, and partly broken. 43 And whereas thou sawest iron mixed with miry clay, they shall mingle themselves with the seed of men: but they shall not cleave one to another, even as iron is not mixed with clay. 44 And in the days of these kings shall the God of heaven set up a kingdom, which shall never be destroyed: and the kingdom shall not be left to other people, *but* it shall break in pieces and consume all these kingdoms, and it shall stand for ever. 45 Forasmuch as thou sawest that the stone was cut out of the mountain without hands, and that it brake in pieces the iron, the brass, the clay, the silver, and the gold; the great God hath made known to the king what shall come to pass hereafter: and the dream *is* certain, and the interpretation thereof sure.

Daniel here gives full satisfaction to Nebuchadnezzar concerning his dream and the interpretation of it. That great prince had been kind to this poor prophet in his maintenance and education; he had been brought up at the king's cost, preferred at court, and the land of his captivity had hereby been made much easier to him than to others of his brethren. And now the king is abundantly repaid for all the expense he had been at upon him; and for receiving this prophet, though not in the name of a prophet, he had a prophet's reward, such a reward as a prophet only could give, and for which that wealthy mighty prince was now glad to be beholden to him. Here is,

I. The dream itself, *v.* 31, 45. Nebuchadnezzar perhaps was an admirer of statues, and had his palace and gardens adorned with them; however, he was a worshipper of images, and now behold a *great image* is set before him in a dream, which might intimate to him what the images were which he bestowed so much cost upon, and paid such respect to; they were mere dreams. The creatures of fancy might do as well to please the fancy. By the power of imagination he might shut his eyes, and represent to himself what forms he thought fit, and beautify them at his pleasure, without the expense and trouble of sculpture. This was the image of a man erect: *It stood before him,* as a living man; and, because those monarchies which were designed to be represented by it were admirable in the eyes of their friends, the *brightness* of this image *was excellent;* and because they were formidable to their enemies, and dreaded by all about them, the *form* of this image is said to be *terrible;* both the

features of the face and the postures of the body made it so. But that which was most remarkable in this image was the different metals of which it was composed—the *head of gold* (the richest and most durable metal), the *breast and arms of silver* (the next to it in worth), the *belly and sides* (or *thighs) of brass,* the *legs of iron* (still baser metals), and lastly the feet *part of iron and part of clay.* See what the things of this world are; the further we go in them the less valuable they appear. In the life of man youth is a head of gold, but it grows less and less worthy of our esteem; and old age is half clay; a man is then *as good as dead.* It is so with the world; later ages degenerate. The first age of the Christian church, of the reformation, was a head of gold; but we live in an age that is iron and clay. Some allude to this in the description of a hypocrite, whose practice is not agreeable to his knowledge. He has a head of gold, but feet of iron and clay: he knows his duty, but does it not. Some observe that in Daniel's visions the monarchies were represented by four beasts (*ch.* vii.), for he looked upon that wisdom from beneath, by which they were turned to be earthly and sensual, and a tyrannical power, to have more in it of the beast than of the man, and so the vision agreed with his notions of the thing. But to Nebuchadnezzar, a heathen prince, they were represented by a gay and pompous image of a man, for he was an admirer of the *kingdoms of this world and the glory of them.* To him the sight was so charming that he was impatient to see it again. But what became of this image? The next part of the dream shows it to us calcined, and brought to nothing. He saw a stone cut out of the quarry by an unseen power, without hands, and this stone fell upon the *feet of the image,* that were of *iron and clay,* and *broke them to pieces:* and then the image must fall of course, and so the gold, and silver, and brass, and iron, were all broken to pieces together, and beaten so small that they became like the *chaff of the summer threshing-floors,* and there were not to be found any the least remains of them; but the stone *cut out of the mountain* became itself a *great mountain, and filled the earth.* See how God can bring about great effects by weak and unlikely causes; when he pleases a *little one shall become a thousand.* Perhaps the destruction of this image of gold, and silver, and brass, and iron, might be intended to signify the abolishing of idolatry out of the world in due time. The *idols of the heathen are silver and gold,* as this image was, and *they shall perish from off the earth and from under these heavens,* Jer. x. 11; Isa. ii. 18. And whatever power destroys idolatry is in the ready way to magnify and exalt itself, as this stone, when it had broken the image to pieces, became a great mountain.

II The interpretation of this dream. Let

us now see what is the meaning of this. It was from God, and therefore from him it is fit that we take the explication of it. It should seem, Daniel had his fellows with him, and speaks for them as well as for himself, when he says, *We will tell the interpretation, v.* 36. Now,

1. This image represented the kingdoms of the earth that should successively bear rule among the nations and have influence on the affairs of the Jewish church. The four monarchies were not represented by four distinct statues, but by one image, because they were all of one and the same spirit and genius, and all more or less against the church. It was the same power, only lodged in four different nations, the two former lying eastward of Judea, the two latter westward. (1.) The *head of gold* signified the Chaldean monarchy, which was now in being (*v.* 37, 38) : *Thou, O king! art* (or, rather, *shalt be*) *a king of kings,* a universal monarch, to whom many kings and kingdoms shall be tributaries ; or, Thou art the *highest of kings* on earth at this time (as a *servant of servants* is the meanest servant) ; thou dost outshine all other kings. But let him not attribute his elevation to his own politics or fortitude. No ; it is *the God of heaven* that has *given thee a kingdom, power, and strength, and glory,* a kingdom that exercises great authority, stands firmly, and shines brightly, acts by a puissant army with an arbitrary power. Note, The greatest of princes have no power but what is given them from above. The extent of his dominion is set forth (*v.* 38), that *wheresoever the children of men dwell,* in all the nations of that part of the world, he was *ruler over them all,* over them and all that belonged to them, all their cattle, not only those which they had a property in, but those that were *feræ naturæ—wild,* the *beasts of the field* and *the fowls of the heaven.* He was lord of all the woods, forests, and chases, and none were allowed to hunt or fowl without his leave. Thus " *thou art the head of gold ;* thou, and thy son, and thy son's son, for seventy years." Compare this with Jer. xxv. 9. 11, especially Jer. xxvii. 5—7. There were other powerful kingdoms in the world at this time, as that of the Scythians ; but it was the kingdom of Babylon that reigned over the Jews, and that began the government which continued in the succession here described till Christ's time. It is called a *head,* for its wisdom, eminency, and absolute power, a head of *gold* for its wealth (Isa. xiv. 4) ; it was a golden city. Some make this monarchy to begin in Nimrod, and so bring into it all the Assyrian kings, about fifty monarchs in all, and compute that it lasted above 1600 years. But it had not been so long a monarchy of such vast extent and power as is here described, nor any thing like it ; therefore others make only Nebuchadnezzar, Evil-merodach, and Belshazzar, to belong to this *head of gold ;*

and a glorious high throne they had, and perhaps exercised a more despotic power than any of the kings that went before them. Nebuchadnezzar reigned forty-five years current, Evil-merodach twenty-three years current, and Belshazzar three. Babylon was their metropolis, and Daniel was with them upon the spot during the seventy years. (2.) The *breast and arms of silver* signified the monarchy of the Medes and Persians, of which the king is told no more than this, *There shall arise another kingdom inferior to thee* (*v.* 39), not so rich, powerful, or victorious. This kingdom was founded by Darius the Mede and Cyrus the Persian, in alliance with each other, and therefore represented by two arms, meeting in the breast. Cyrus was himself a Persian by his father, a Mede by his mother. Some reckon that this second monarchy lasted 130 years, others 204 years. The former computation agrees best with the scripture chronology. (3.) The *belly and thighs of brass* signified the monarchy of the Grecians, founded by Alexander, who conquered Darius Codomannus, the last of the Persian emperors. This is the *third kingdom, of brass,* inferior in wealth and extent of dominion to the Persian monarchy, but in Alexander himself it shall by the power of the sword *bear rule over all the earth ;* for Alexander boasted that he had conquered the world, and then sat down and wept because he had not another world to conquer. (4.) The *legs and feet of iron* signified the Roman monarchy. Some make this to signify the latter part of the Grecian monarchy, the two empires of Syria and Egypt, the former governed by the family of the Seleucidæ, from Seleucus, the latter by that of the Lagidæ, from Ptolemæus Lagus ; these they make the two legs and feet of this image : Grotius, and Junius, and Broughton, go this way. But it has been the more received opinion that it is the Roman monarchy that is here intended, because it was in the time of that monarchy, and when it was at its height, that the kingdom of Christ was set up in the world by the preaching of the everlasting gospel. The Roman kingdom was strong as iron (*v.* 40), witness the prevalency of that kingdom against all that contended with it for many ages. That kingdom *broke in pieces* the Grecian empire and afterwards quite destroyed the nation of the Jews. Towards the latter end of the Roman monarchy it grew very weak, and branched into ten kingdoms, which were as the toes of these feet. Some of these were weak as clay, others strong as iron, *v.* 42. Endeavours were used to unite and cement them for the strengthening of the empire, but in vain : *They shall not cleave one to another, v.* 43. This empire divided the government for a long time between the senate and the people, the nobles and the commons, but they did not entirely coalesce. There were civil wars between Marius and

Sylla, Cæsar and Pompey, whose parties were as iron and clay. Some refer this to the declining times of that empire, when, for the strengthening of the empire against the irruptions of the barbarous nations, the branches of the royal family intermarried; but the politics had not the desired effect, when the day of the fall of that empire came.

2. The stone *cut out without hands* represented the kingdom of Jesus Christ, which should be set up in the world in the time of the Roman empire, and upon the ruins of Satan's kingdom in the *kingdoms of the world.* This is *the stone cut out of the mountain without hands,* for it should be neither raised nor supported by human power or policy; no visible hand should act in the setting of it up, but it should be done invisibly by the *Spirit of the Lord of hosts.* This was *the stone which the builders refused,* because it was not cut out by their hands, but it has now become the *head-stone of the corner.* (1.) The gospel-church is a kingdom, which Christ is the sole and sovereign monarch of, in which he rules by his word and Spirit, to which he gives protection and law, and from which he receives homage and tribute. It is a kingdom *not of this world,* and yet set up in it; it is the kingdom of God among men. (2.) The *God of heaven* was to set up this kingdom, to give authority to Christ to execute judgment, to set him as *King upon his holy hill of Zion,* and to bring into obedience to him a willing people. Being set up by the God of heaven, it is often in the *New Testament* called the *kingdom of heaven,* for its original is from above and its tendency is upwards. (3.) It was to be set up *in the days of these kings,* the kings of the fourth monarchy, of which particular notice is taken (Luke ii. 1), that Christ was born when, by the decree of the emperor of Rome, *all the world was taxed,* which was a plain indication that that empire had become as universal as any earthly empire ever was. When these kings are contesting with each other, and in all the struggles each of the contending parties hopes to find its own account, God will do his own work and fulfil his own counsels. *These kings* are all enemies to Christ's kingdom, and yet it shall be set up in defiance of them. (4.) It is a kingdom that knows no decay, is in no danger of destruction, and will not admit any succession or revolution. It shall *never be destroyed* by any foreign force invading it, as many other kingdoms are; fire and sword cannot waste it; the combined powers of earth and hell cannot deprive either the subjects of their prince or the prince of his subjects; nor shall this *kingdom be left to other people,* as the kingdoms of the earth are. As Christ is a monarch that has no successor (for he himself shall reign for ever), so his kingdom is a monarchy that has no revolution. The kingdom of God was indeed taken from the Jews and given to the Gentiles (Matt. xxi.

43), but still it was Christianity that ruled, the kingdom of the Messiah. The Christian church is still the same; it is fixed on a rock, much fought against, but never to be prevailed against, by the gates of hell. (5.) **It** is a kingdom that shall be victorious over all opposition. It shall *break in pieces and consume all those kingdoms,* as the *stone cut out of the mountain without hands* broke in pieces the image, *v.* 44, 45. The kingdom of Christ shall *wear out* all other kingdoms, shall outlive them, and flourish when they are sunk with their own weight, and so wasted that their place *knows them no more.* All the kingdoms that appear against the kingdom of Christ shall be broken with a *rod of iron,* as a *potter's vessel,* Ps. ii. 9. And in the kingdoms that submit to the kingdom of Christ tyranny, and idolatry, and every thing that is their reproach, shall, as far as the gospel of Christ gets ground, be broken. The day is coming when Jesus Christ shall have *put down all rule, principality, and power,* and have made *all his enemies his footstool;* and then this prophecy will have its full accomplishment, and not till then, 1 Cor. xv. 24, 25. Our Saviour seems to refer to this (Matt. xxi. 44,) when, speaking of himself as the stone set at nought by the Jewish builders, he says, *On whomsoever* this stone *shall fall, it will grind him to powder.* (6.) It shall be an everlasting kingdom. Those kingdoms of the earth that had *broken in pieces* all about them at length came, in their turn, to be in like manner broken; but the kingdom of Christ shall break other kingdoms in pieces and shall itself *stand for ever.* His throne shall be as the days of heaven, his seed, his subjects, as the stars of heaven, not only so innumerable, but so immutable. Of the *increase* of Christ's *government and peace* there shall be *no end. The Lord shall reign for ever,* not only to the end of time, but when time and days shall be no more, and *God shall be all in all* to eternity.

III. Daniel having thus interpreted the dream, to the satisfaction of Nebuchadnezzar, who gave him no interruption, so full was the interpretation that he had no question to ask, and so plain that he had no objection to make, he closes all with a solemn assertion, 1. Of the divine original of this dream: *The great God* (so he calls him, to express his own high thoughts of him, and to beget the like in the mind of this great king) has *made known to the king what shall come to pass hereafter,* which the gods of the magicians could not do. And thus a full confirmation was given to that great argument which Isaiah had long before urged against idolaters, and particularly the idolaters of Babylon, when he challenged the gods they worshipped to *show things that are to come hereafter, that we may know that you are gods* (Isa. xli. 23), and by *this* proved the God of Israel to be the true God, that he *declares the end from the beginning,* Isa. xlvi. 10. 2. Of the undoubted certainty of the things foretold by this dream. He who makes known these things is the same that has himself designed and determined them, and will by his providence effect them; and we are sure that *his counsel shall stand,* and cannot be altered, and therefore *the dream is certain and the interpretation thereof sure.* Note, Whatever God has made known we may depend upon.

46 Then the king Nebuchadnezzar fell upon his face, and worshipped Daniel, and commanded that they should offer an oblation and sweet odours unto him. 47 The king answered unto Daniel, and said, Of a truth *it is* that your God *is* a God of gods, and a Lord of kings, and a revealer of secrets, seeing thou couldest reveal this secret. 48 Then the king made Daniel a great man, and gave him many great gifts, and made him ruler over the whole province of Babylon, and chief of the governors over all the wise *men* of Babylon. 49 Then Daniel requested of the king, and he set Shadrach, Meshach, and Abed-nego, over the affairs of the province of Babylon: but Daniel *sat* in the gate of the king.

One might have expected that when Nebuchadnezzar was contriving to make his own kingdom everlasting he would be enraged at Daniel, who foretold the fall of it and that another kingdom of another nature should be the everlasting kingdom; but, instead of resenting it as an affront, he received it as an oracle, and here we are told what the expressions were of the impressions it made upon him. 1. He was ready to look upon Daniel as a little god. Though he saw him to be a man, yet from this wonderful discovery which he had made both of his secret thoughts, in telling him the dream, and of things to come, in telling him the interpretation of it, he concluded that he had certainly a divinity lodged in him, worthy his adoration; and therefore he *fell upon his face and worshipped Daniel,* v. 46. It was the custom of the country by prostration to give honour to kings, because they have something of a divine power in them *(I have said, You are gods);* and therefore this king, who had often received such veneration from others, now paid the like to Daniel, whom he supposed to have in him a divine knowledge, which he was so struck with an admiration of that he could not contain himself, but forgot both that Daniel was a man and that himself was a king. Thus did God magnify divine revelation *and make it ho-*

nourable, extorting from a proud potentate such a veneration but for one glimpse of it. He *worshipped Daniel,* and *commanded that they should offer an oblation to him,* and burn incense. Herein he cannot be justified, but may in some measure be excused, when Cornelius was thus ready to worship Peter, and John the angel, who both knew better. But, though it is not here mentioned, yet we have reason to think that Daniel refused these honours that he paid him, and said, as Peter to Cornelius, *Stand up, I myself also am a man,* or, as the angel to St. John, *See thou do it not;* for it is not said that the oblation was offered unto him, though the king commanded it, or rather *said* it, for so the word is. He said, in his haste, *Let an oblation be offered to him.* And that Daniel did say something to him which turned his eyes and thoughts another way is intimated in what follows (v. 47), *The king answered Daniel.* Note, It is possible for those to express a great honour for the ministers of God's word who yet have no true love for the word. *Herod feared John,* and *heard him gladly,* and yet went on in his sins, Mark vi. 20. 2. He readily acknowledged the God of Daniel to be the great God, the true God, the only living and true God. If Daniel will not suffer himself to be worshipped, he will (as Daniel, it is likely, directed him) *worship God,* by confessing (v. 47), *Of a truth your God is a God of gods,* such a God as there is no other, above all gods in dignity, over all gods in dominion. He is a LORD *of kings,* from whom they derive their power and to whom they are accountable; and he is both a discoverer and a *revealer of secrets;* what is most secret he sees and can reveal, and what he has revealed is what was secret and which none but himself could reveal, 1 Cor. ii. 10. 3. He preferred Daniel, made him a great man, *v.* 48. God made him a great man indeed when he took him into communion with himself, a greater man than Nebuchadnezzar could make him; but, because God had magnified him, therefore the king magnified him. Does wealth make men great? The king *gave him many great gifts;* and he had no reason to refuse them, when they all put him into so much the greater capacity of doing good to his brethren in captivity. These gifts were grateful returns for the good services he had done, and not aimed at, nor bargained for, by him, as the rewards of divination were by Balaam. Does power make a man great? He made him *ruler over the whole province of Babylon,* which no doubt had great influence upon the other provinces; he made him likewise chancellor of the university, *chief of the governors over all the wise men of Babylon,* to instruct those whom he had thus outdone; and, since they could not do what the king would have them do, they shall be obliged to do what Daniel would have them do. Thus it is fit that *the fool should be servant to the wise in heart.* Seeing Daniel *could reveal this secret* (v. 47), the king thus advanced him. Note, It is the wisdom of princes to advance and employ those who receive divine revelation, and are much conversant with it, who, as Daniel here, show themselves to be well acquainted with the kingdom of heaven. Joseph, like Daniel here, was advanced in the court of the king of Egypt for his interpreting his dreams; and he called him *Zaphnath-paaneah—a revealer of secrets,* as the king of Babylon here calls Daniel; so that the preambles to their patents of honour are the same—for, and in consideration of, their good services done to the crown in *revealing secrets.* 4. He preferred his companions for his sake, and upon his special instance and request, *v.* 49. Daniel himself *sat in the gate of the king,* as president of the council, chief-justice, or prime-minister of state, or perhaps chamberlain of the household; but he used his interest for his friends as became a good man, and procured places in the government for Shadrach, Meshach, and Abednego. Those that helped him with their prayers shall share with him in his honours, such a grateful sense had he even of that service. The preferring of them would be a great stay and help to Daniel in his place and business. And these pious Jews, being thus preferred in Babylon, had great opportunity of serving their brethren in captivity, and of doing them many good offices, which no doubt they were ready to do. Thus, sometimes, before God brings his people into trouble, he prepares it, that it may be easy to them.

CHAP. III.

In the close of the foregoing chapter we left Daniel's companions, Shadrach, Meshach, and Abednego, in honour and power, princes of the provinces, and preferred for their relation to the God of Israel and the interest they had in him. I know not whether I should say, It were well if this honour had all the saints. No; there are many whom it would not be good for; the saints' honour is reserved for another world. But here we have those same three men as much under the king's displeasure as then they were in his favour, and yet more truly, more highly, honoured by their God than there they were honoured by their prince, both by the grace wherewith he enabled them rather to suffer than to sin and by the miraculous and glorious deliverance which he wrought for them out of their sufferings. It is a very memorable story, a glorious instance of the power and goodness of God, and a great encouragement to the constancy of his people in trying times. The apostle refers to it when he mentions, among the believing heroes, those who by faith "quenched the violence of fire," Heb. xi. 34. We have here, I. Nebuchadnezzar's erecting and dedicating a golden image, and his requiring all his subjects, of what rank or degree scever, to fall down and worship it, and the general compliance of his people with that command, ver. 1—7. II. Information given against the Jewish princes for refusing to worship this golden image, ver. 8—12. III. Their constant persisting in that refusal, notwithstanding his rage and menaces, ver. 13—18. IV. The casting of them into the fiery furnace for their refusal, ver. 19—23. V. Their miraculous preservation in the fire by the power of God, and their invitation out of the fire by the favour of the king, who was by this miracle convinced of his error in casting them in, ver. 24—27. VI. The honour which the king gave to God hereupon, and the favour he showed to those faithful worthies, ver. 28—30.

NEBUCHADNEZZAR the king made an image of gold, whose height *was* threescore cubits, *and* the breadth thereof six cubits: he set it up in the plain of Dura, in the pro-
1034

vince of Babylon. 2 Then Nebuchadnezzar the king sent to gather together the princes, the governors, and the captains, the judges, the treasurers, the counsellors, the sheriffs, and all the rulers of the provinces, to come to the dedication of the image which Nebuchadnezzar the king had set up. 3 Then the princes, the governors, and captains, the judges, the treasurers, the counsellors, the sheriffs, and all the rulers of the provinces, were gathered together unto the dedication of the image that Nebuchadnezzar the king had set up; and they stood before the image that Nebuchadnezzar had set up. 4 Then an herald cried aloud, To you it is commanded, O people, nations, and languages, 5 *That* at what time ye hear the sound of the cornet, flute, harp, sackbut, psaltery, dulcimer, and all kinds of music, ye fall down and worship the golden image that Nebuchadnezzar the king hath set up: 6 And whoso falleth not down and worshippeth shall the same hour be cast into the midst of a burning fiery furnace. 7 Therefore at that time, when all the people heard the sound of the cornet, flute, harp, sackbut, psaltery, and all kinds of music, all the people, the nations, and the languages, fell down *and* worshipped the golden image that Nebuchadnezzar the king had set up.

We have no certainty concerning the date of this story, only that if this image, which Nebuchadnezzar dedicated, had any relation to that which he dreamed of, it is probable that it happened not long after that; some reckon it to be about the seventh year of Nebuchadnezzar, a year before Jehoiachin's captivity, in which Ezekiel was carried away. Observe,

I. A *golden image set up* to be worshipped. Babylon was full of idols already, yet nothing will serve this imperious prince but they must have one more; for those who have forsaken the one only living God, and begin to set up many gods, will find the gods they set up so unsatisfying, and their desire after them so insatiable, that they will multiply them without measure, wander after them endlessly, and never know when they have sufficient. Idolaters are fond of novelty and variety. *They choose new gods.* Those that have many will wish to have more. Nebuchadnezzar the king, that he might exert the prerogative of his crown, to make what god he thought fit, *set up* this image, *v.* 1. Observe, 1. The *valuableness* of it; it was *an image of gold,* not all gold surely; rich as he was, it is probable that he could not afford that, but overlaid with gold. Note, The worshippers of false gods are not wont to mind charges in setting up images and worshipping them; they *lavish gold out of the bag* for that purpose (Isa. xlvi. 6), which shames our niggardliness in the worship of the true God. 2. The vastness of it; it was *threescore cubits high and six cubits broad.* It exceeded the ordinary stature of a man fifteen times (for that is reckoned but four cubits, or six feet), as if its being monstrous would make amends for its being lifeless. But why did Nebuchadnezzar set up this image? Some suggest that it was to clear himself from the imputation of having turned a Jew, because he had lately spoken with great honour of the God of Israel and had preferred some of his worshippers. Or perhaps he set it up as an image of himself, and designed to be himself worshipped in it. Proud princes affected to have divine honours paid them; Alexander did so, pretending himself to be the son of Jupiter Olympius. He was told that in the image he had seen in his dream he was represented by the *head of gold,* which was to be succeeded by kingdoms of baser metal; but here he sets up to be himself the whole image, for he makes it all of gold. See here, (1.) How the good impressions that were then made upon him were quite lost, and quickly. He then acknowledged that the God of Israel is of a truth a *God of gods* and a *Lord of kings;* and yet now, in defiance of the express law of that God, he sets up an image to be worshipped, not only continues in his former idolatries, but contrives new ones. Note, Strong convictions often come short of a sound conversion. Many in a pang have owned the absurdity and dangerousness of sin, and yet have gone on in it. (2.) How that very dream and the interpretation of it, which then made such good impressions upon him, now had a quite contrary effect. Then it made him fall down as a humble worshipper of God; now it made him set up for a bold competitor with God. Then he thought it a great thing to be the golden head of the image, and owned himself obliged to God for it; but, his mind rising with his condition, now he thinks that too little, and, in contradiction to God himself and his oracle, he will be *all in all.*

II. A general convention of the states summoned to attend the solemnity of the dedication of this image, *v.* 2, 3. Messengers are despatched to all parts of the kingdom to *gather together the princes,* dukes, and lords, all the peers of the realm, with all officers civil and military, *the captains and commanders of the forces, the judges,*

the treasurers or general receivers, *the counsellors,* and *the sheriffs, and all the rulers of the provinces;* they must all *come to the dedication of this image* upon pain and peril of what shall fall thereon. He summons the great men, for the great honour of his idol; it is therefore mentioned to the glory of Christ that *kings shall bring presents unto him.* If he can bring them to pay homage to his golden image, he doubts not but the inferior people will follow of course. In obedience to the king's summons all the magistrates and officers of that vast kingdom leave the services of their particular countries, and come to Babylon, to the dedication of this golden image; long journeys many of them took, and expensive ones, upon a very foolish errand; but, as the idols are sensless things, such are the worshippers.

III. A proclamation made, commanding all manner of persons present before the image, upon the signal given, to fall down prostrate, and worship the image, under the style and title of *The golden image which Nebuchadnezzar the king has set up.* A herald proclaims this aloud throughout this vast assembly of grandees, with their numerous train of servants and attendants, and a great crowd of people, no doubt, that were not sent for; let them all take notice, 1. That the king does strictly charge and command all manner of persons to fall down and *worship the golden image;* whatever other gods they worship at other times, now they must worship this. 2. That they must all do this just at the same time, in token of their communion with each other in this idolatrous service, and that, in order hereunto, notice shall be given by a concert of music, which would likewise serve to adorn the solemnity and to sweeten and soften the minds of those that were loth to yield and bring them to comply with the king's command. This mirth and gaiety in the worship would be very agreeable to carnal sensual minds, that are strangers to that spiritual worship which is due to God who is a spirit.

IV. The general compliance of the assembly with this command, *v.* 7. They heard the sound of the musical instruments, both wind-instruments and hand-instruments, *the cornet* and *flute,* with the *harp, sackbut, psaltery,* and *dulcimer,* the melody of which they thought was ravishing (and fit enough it was to excite such a devotion as they were then to pay), and immediately they all, as one man, as soldiers that are wont to be exercised by beat of drum, *all the people, nations, and languages, fell down and worshipped the golden image.* And no marvel when it was proclaimed, That whosoever would not *worship this golden image* should be immediately thrown *into the midst of a burning fiery furnace,* ready prepared for that purpose, *v.* 6. Here were the charms of music to allure them into a compliance and the terrors of the fiery furnace to frighten them into a compliance. Thus beset with temptation, they all yielded. Note, That way that sense directs the most will go; there is nothing so bad which the careless world will not be drawn to by a concert of music, or driven to by a fiery furnace. And by such methods as these false worship has been set up and maintained.

8 Wherefore at that time certain Chaldeans came near, and accused the Jews. 9 They spake and said to the king Nebuchadnezzar, O king, live for ever. 10 Thou, O king, hast made a decree, that every man that shall hear the sound of the cornet, flute, harp, sackbut, psaltery, and dulcimer, and all kinds of music, shall fall down and worship the golden image : 11 And whoso falleth not down and worshippeth, *that* he should be cast into the midst of a burning fiery furnace. 12 There are certain Jews whom thou hast set over the affairs of the province of Babylon, Shadrach, Meshach, and Abed-nego ; these men, O king, have not regarded thee : they serve not thy gods, nor worship the golden image which thou hast set up. 13 Then Nebuchadnezzar in *his* rage and fury commanded to bring Shadrach, Meshach, and Abed-nego. Then they brought these men before the king. 14 Nebuchadnezzar spake and said unto them, *Is it* true, O Shadrach, Meshach, and Abed-nego, do not ye serve my gods, nor worship the golden image which I have set up? 15 Now if ye be ready that at what time ye hear the sound of the cornet, flute, harp, sackbut, psaltery, and dulcimer, and all kinds of music, ye fall down and worship the image which I have made; *well :* but if ye worship not, ye shall be cast the same hour into the midst of a burning fiery furnace ; and who *is* that God that shall deliver you out of my hands ? 16 Shadrach, Meshach, and Abed-nego, answered and said to the king, O Nebuchadnezzar, we *are* not careful to answer thee in this matter. 17 If it be *so,* our God whom we serve is able to deliver us from the burning fiery furnace, and he will deliver *us* out of thine hand, O king. 18 But if not, be it known unto thee, O king, that

1036

we will not serve thy gods, nor worship the golden image which thou hast set up.

It was strange that Shadrach, Meshach, and Abednego, would be present at this assembly, when, it is likely, they knew for what intent it was called together. Daniel, we may suppose, was absent, either his business calling him away or having leave from the king to withdraw, unless we suppose that he stood so high in the king's favour that none durst complain of him for his non-compliance. But why did not his companions keep out of the way? Surely because they would obey the king's orders as far as they could, and would be ready to bear a public testimony against this gross idolatry. They did not think it enough not to bow down to the image, but, being in office, thought themselves obliged to stand up against it, though it was the image which the king their master set up, and would be a golden image to those that worshipped it. Now,

I. Information is brought to the king by *certain Chaldeans* against these three gentlemen that they did not obey the king's edict, *v.* 8. Perhaps these Chaldeans that accused them were some of those *magicians or astrologers* that were particularly called *Chaldeans* (*ch.* ii. 2, 4) who bore a grudge to Daniel's companions for his sake, because he had eclipsed them, and so had these his companions. They by their prayers had obtained the mercy which saved the lives of these Chaldeans, and, behold, how they requite them evil for good ! for their love they are their adversaries. Thus Jeremiah *stood before God,* to *speak good for those* who afterwards *dug a pit for his life,* Jer. xviii. 20. We must not think it strange if we meet with such ungrateful men. Or perhaps they were such of the Chaldeans as expected the places to which they were advanced, and envied them their preferments; *and who can stand before envy ?* They appeal to the king himself concerning the edict, with all due respect to his majesty, and the usual compliment, O *king! live for ever* (as if they aimed at nothing but his honour, and to serve his interest, when really they were putting him upon that which would endanger the ruin of him and his kingdom); they beg leave, 1. To put him in mind of the law he had lately made, That all manner of persons, without exception of nation or language, should *fall down and worship this golden image ;* they put him in mind also of the penalty which by the law was to be inflicted upon recusants, that they were to be *cast into the midst of the burning fiery furnace, v.* 10, 11. It cannot be denied but that this was the law; whether a righteous law or no ought to be considered. 2. To inform him that these three men, Shadrach, Meshach, and Abednego, had not conformed to this edict, *v.* 12. It is probable that Nebuchadnezzar had no particular design to ensnare them in making the law, for then he would himself have had his eye upon them, and would not have needed this information; but their enemies, that sought an occasion against them, laid hold on this, and were forward to accuse them. To aggravate the matter, and incense the king the more against them, (1.) They put him in mind of the dignity to which the criminals had been preferred. Though they were Jews, foreigners, captives, men of a despised nation and religion, yet the king had *set them over the affairs of the province of Babylon.* It was therefore very ungrateful, and an insufferable piece of insolence, for them to disobey the king's command, when they had shared so much of the king's favour. And, besides, the high station they were in would make their refusal the more scandalous; it would be a bad example, and have a bad influence upon others; and therefore it was necessary that it should be severely animadverted upon. Thus princes that are incensed enough against innocent people commonly have but too many about them who do all they can to make them worse. (2.) They suggest that it was done maliciously, contumaciously, and in contempt of him and his authority: They have *set no regard upon thee;* for they *serve not the gods* which thou servest, and which thou requirest them to serve, nor *worship the golden image which thou hast set up.*"

II. These three pious Jews are immediately brought before the king, and arraigned and examined upon this information. Nebuchadnezzar fell into a great passion, and *in his rage and fury commanded* them to be seized, *v.* 13. How little was it the honour of this mighty prince that he had rule over so many nations when at the same time he had no *rule over his own spirit*, that there were so many who were subjects and captives to him when he was himself a perfect slave to his own brutish passions and led captive by them! How unfit was he to rule reasonable men who could not himself be ruled by reason! It needed not be a surprise to him to hear that these three men did not now serve his gods, for he knew very well they never had served them, and that their religion, which they had always adhered to, forbade them to do it. Nor had he any reason to think that they designed any contempt of his authority, for they had in all instances shown themselves respectful and dutiful to him as their prince. But it was especially unseasonable at this time, when he was in the midst of his devotions, dedicating his golden image, to be in such a rage and fury, and so much to discompose himself. The *discretion of a man*, one would think, should at least have *deferred this anger.* True devotion calms the spirit, quiets and meekens it; but superstition, and a devotion to false gods, inflame men's passions, inspire them with rage, and fury, and turn them into brutes.

The wrath of a king is as the roaring of a lion; so was the wrath of this king; and yet, when he was in such a heat, these three men were *brought before him*, and appeared with an undaunted courage, an unshaken constancy.

III. The case is laid before them in short, and it is put to them whether they will comply or no. 1. The king asked them whether it was true that they had not worshipped the golden image when others did, *v.* 14. "*Is it of purpose?*" so some read it. "Was it designedly and deliberately done, or was it only through inadvertency, that you have not *served my gods?* What! you that I have nourished and brought up, that have been educated and maintained at my charge, that I have been so kind to and done so much for, you that have been in such reputation for wisdom, and therefore should better have known your duty to your prince; what! do not you *serve my gods nor worship the golden image which I have set up?*" Note, The faithfulness of God's servants to him has often been the wonder of their enemies and persecutors, who *think it strange* that they *run not with them to the same excess of riot.* 2. He was willing to admit them to a new trial; if they did on purpose not do it before, yet, it may be, upon second thoughts, they will change their minds; it is therefore repeated to them upon what terms they now stand, *v.* 15. (1.) The king is willing that music shall play again, only for their sakes, to soften them into a compliance; and if they will not, like the deaf adder, stop their ears, but will hearken to the voice of the charmers and will *worship the golden image*, well and good; their former omission shall be pardoned. But, (2.) The king is resolved, if they persist in their refusal, that they shall immediately be *cast into the fiery furnace*, and shall not have so much as an hour's reprieve. Thus does the matter lie in a little compass—*Turn, or burn;* and, because he knew they buoyed themselves up in their refusal with a confidence in their God, he insolently set him at defiance: "*And who is that God that shall deliver you out of my hands?* Let him, if he can." Now he forgot what he himself once owned, that their God was a *God of gods* and a *Lord of kings*, ch. ii. 47. Proud men are still ready to say, as Pharaoh, *Who is the Lord that I should obey his voice?* or, as Nebuchadnezzar, Who is the Lord, that I should *fear his power?*

IV. They give in their answer, which they all agree in, that they still adhere to their resolution not to worship the golden image, *v.* 16—18. We have here such an instance of fortitude and magnanimity as is scarcely to be paralleled. We call these the *three children* (and they were indeed *young men*), but we should rather call them the three champions, the *first three* of the *worthies* of God's *kingdom among men.* They did not break out into any intemperate heat or passion against those that did worship the golden image, did not insult or affront them; nor did they rashly thrust themselves upon the trial, or go out of their way to court martyrdom; but, when they were duly called to the fiery trial, they acquitted themselves bravely, with a conduct and courage that became sufferers for so good a cause. The king was not so daringly bad in making this idol, but they were as daringly good in witnessing against it. They keep their temper admirably well, do not call the king a tyrant or an idolater (the cause of God needs not the wrath of man), but, with an exemplary calmness and sedateness of mind, they deliberately give in their answer, which they resolve to abide by. Observe,

1. Their gracious and generous contempt of death, and the noble negligence with which they look upon the dilemma that they are put to: *O Nebuchadnezzar! we are not careful to answer thee in this matter.* They do not in sullenness deny him an answer, nor stand mute; but they tell him that they are in no care about it. *There needs not an answer* (so some read it); they are resolved not to comply, and the king is resolved they shall die if they do not; the matter therefore is determined, and why should it be disputed? But it is better read, "*We want not an answer for thee*, nor have it to seek, but come prepared." (1.) They needed no time to deliberate concerning the matter of their answer; for they did not in the least hesitate whether they should comply or no. It was a matter of life and death, and one would think they might have considered awhile before they had resolved; life is desirable, and death is dreadful. But when the sin and duty that were in the case were immediately determined by the letter of the second commandment, and no room was left to question what was right, the life and death that were in the case were not to be considered. Note, Those that would avoid sin must not parley with temptation. When that which we are allured or affrighted to is manifestly evil the motion is rather to be rejected with indignation and abhorrence than reasoned with; stand not to pause about it, but say, as Christ has taught us, *Get thee behind me, Satan.* (2.) They needed no time to contrive how they should *word* it. While they were advocates for God, and were called out to witness in his cause, they doubted not but it should be *given them in that same hour what they should speak*, Matt. x. 19. They were not contriving an evasive answer, when a direct answer was expected from them; no, nor would they seem to court the king not to insist upon it. Here is nothing in their answer that looks like compliment; they begin not, as their accusers did, with, *O king! live for ever*, no artful insinuation, *ad captandam benevolentiam*—to put him into a good humour, but every thing that is plain and downright: O Nebuchadnezzar! *we are not*

1038

careful to answer thee. Note, Those that make their duty their main care need not be careful concerning the event.

2. Their believing confidence in God and their dependence upon him, *v.* 17. It was this that enabled them to look with so much contempt upon death, death in pomp, death in all its terrors: they trusted in the living God, and by that faith chose rather to suffer than to sin; they therefore *feared not the wrath of the king*, but endured, because by faith they had an eye to *him that is invisible* (Heb. xi. 25, 27): "*If it be so*, if we are brought to this strait, if we must be thrown into the fiery furnace unless we serve thy gods, know then," (1.) "That though we worship not *thy gods* yet we are not atheists; there is a God whom we can call ours, to whom we faithfully adhere." (2.) "That we serve this God; we have devoted ourselves to his honour; we employ ourselves in his work, and depend upon him to protect us, provide for us, and reward us." (3.) "That we are well assured that this God is *able to deliver us from the burning fiery furnace;* whether he will or no, we are sure that he can either prevent our being cast into the furnace or rescue us out of it." Note, The faithful servants of God will find him a Master able to bear them out in his service, and to control and overrule all the powers that are armed against them. *Lord, if thou wilt, thou canst.* (4.) "That we have reason to hope *he will deliver us*," partly because, in such a vast appearance of idolaters, it would be very much for the honour of his great name to deliver them, and partly because Nebuchadnezzar had defied him to do it—*Who is that God that shall deliver you?* God sometimes appears wonderfully for the silencing of the blasphemies of the enemy, as well as for the answering of the prayers of his people, Ps. lxxiv. 18—22; Deut. xxxii. 27. "But, if he do not deliver us from the fiery furnace, he will *deliver us out of thy hand.*" Nebuchadnezzar can but torment and kill the body, and, after that, there is no more that he can do; then they are got out of his reach, delivered out of his hand. Note, Good thoughts of God, and a full assurance that he is with us while we are with him, will help very much to carry us through sufferings; and, if he be for us, we need not fear what man can do unto us; let him do his worst. God will deliver us either from death or in death.

3. Their firm resolution to adhere to their principles, whatever might be the consequence (*v.* 18): "But, *if not*, though God should not think fit to deliver us from the fiery furnace (which yet we know he can do), if he should suffer us to *fall into thy hand*, and fall by thy hand, yet *be it known unto thee, O king! we will not serve* these gods, though they are *thy gods, nor worship this golden image*, though thou thyself hast *set it up.*" They are neither ashamed nor afraid to own their religion, and tell the king to his face

that they do not fear him, they will not yield to him; had they consulted with flesh and blood, much might have been said to bring them to a compliance, especially when there was no other way of avoiding death, *so great a death.* (1.) They were not required to abjure their own God, or to renounce his worship, no, nor by any verbal profession or declaration to own this golden image to be a god, but only to bow down before it, which they might do with a secret reserve of their hearts for the God of Israel, inwardly detesting this idolatry, as Naaman bowed in the house of Rimmon. (2.) They were not to fall into a course of idolatry; it was but one single act that was required of them, which would be done in a minute, and the danger was over, and they might afterwards declare their sorrow for it. (3.) The king that commanded it had an absolute power; they were under it, not only as subjects, but as captives; and, if they did it, it was purely by coercion and duress, which would serve to excuse them. (4.) He had been their benefactor, had educated and preferred them, and in gratitude to him they ought to go as far as they could, though it were to strain a point, a point of conscience. (5.) They were now driven into a strange country, and to those that were so driven out it was, in effect, said, *Go, and serve other gods,* 1 Sam. xxvi. 19. It was taken for granted that in their disposition they would *serve other gods,* and it was made a part of the judgment, Deut. iv. 28. They might be excused if they should go down the stream, when it is so strong. (6.) Did not their kings, and their princes, and their fathers, yea, and their priests too, set up idols even in God's temple, and worship them there, and not only bow down to them, but erect altars, burn incense, and offer sacrifices, even their own children, to them? Did not all the ten tribes, for many ages, worship gods of gold at Dan and Bethel? And shall they be more precise than their fathers? *Communis error facit jus—What all do must be right.* (7.) If they should comply, they would save their lives and keep their places, and so be in a capacity to do a great deal of service to their brethren in Babylon, and to do it long; for they were young men, and rising men. But there is enough in that one word of God wherewith to answer and silence these and many more such like carnal reasonings: *Thou shalt not bow down thyself to any images, nor worship them.* They know they must obey God rather than man; they must rather suffer than sin, and must not do evil that good may come. And therefore none of these things move them; they are resolved rather to die in their integrity than live in their iniquity. While their brethren, who yet remained in their own land, were worshipping images by choice, they in Babylon would not be brought to it by constraint, but, as if they were good by *antiperistasis,* were most zealous against idolatry in

an idolatrous country. And truly, all things considered, the saving of them from this sinful compliance was as great a miracle in the kingdom of grace as the saving of them out of the fiery furnace was in the kingdom of nature. These were those who formerly resolved not to defile themselves with the *king's meat,* and now they as bravely resolve not to defile themselves with his gods. Note, A stedfast self-denying adherence to God and duty in less instances will qualify and prepare us for the like in greater. And in this we must be resolute, never, under any pretence whatsoever, to worship images, or to say "A confederacy" with those that do so.

19 Then was Nebuchadnezzar full of fury, and the form of his visage was changed against Shadrach, Meshach, and Abed-nego: *therefore* he spake, and commanded that they should heat the furnace one seven times more than it was wont to be heated. 20 And he commanded the most mighty men that *were* in his army to bind Shadrach, Meshach, and Abed-nego, *and* to cast *them* into the burning fiery furnace. 21 Then these men were bound in their coats, their hosen, and their hats, and their *other* garments, and were cast into the midst of the burning fiery furnace. 22 Therefore because the king's commandment was urgent, and the furnace exceeding hot, the flame of the fire slew those men that took up Shadrach, Meshach, and Abed-nego. 23 And these three men, Shadrach, Meshach, and Abed-nego, fell down bound into the midst of the burning fiery furnace. 24 Then Nebuchadnezzar the king was astonied, and rose up in haste, *and* spake, and said unto his counsellers, Did not we cast three men bound into the midst of the fire? They answered and said unto the king, True, O king. 25 He answered and said, Lo, I see four men loose, walking in the midst of the fire, and they have no hurt; and the form of the fourth is like the Son of God. 26 Then Nebuchadnezzar came near to the mouth of the burning fiery furnace, *and* spake, and said, Shadrach, Meshach, and Abed-nego, ye servants of the most high God, come forth, and come *hither.* Then Shadrach, Meshach, and Abed-nego, came forth or the midst of the fire. 27 And the

princes, governors, and captains, and the king's counsellors, being gathered together, saw these men, upon whose bodies the fire had no power, nor was a hair of their head singed, neither were their coats changed, nor the smell of fire had passed on them.

In these verses we have,

I. The casting of these three faithful servants of God into the fiery furnace. Nebuchadnezzar had himself known and owned so much of the true God that, one would have thought, though his pride and vanity induced him to make this golden image, and set it up to be worshipped, yet what these young men now said (whom he had formerly found to be wiser than all his wise men) would revive his convictions, and at least engage him to excuse them; but it proved quite otherwise. 1. Instead of being convinced by what they said, he was exasperated, and made more outrageous, *v.* 19. It made him *full of fury*, and the *form of his visage was changed* against these men. Note, Brutish passions the more they are indulged the more violent they grow, and even change the countenance, to the great reproach of the wisdom and reason of a man. Nebuchadnezzar, in this heat, exchanged the awful majesty of a prince upon his throne, or a judge upon the bench, for the frightful fury of a *wild bull in a net.* Would men in a passion but view their faces in a glass, they would blush at their own folly and turn all their displeasure against themselves. 2. Instead of mitigating their punishment, in consideration of their quality and the posts of honour they were in, he ordered it to be heightened, that they should *heat the furnace seven times more than it was wont to be heated* for other malefactors, that is, that they should put seven times more fuel to it, which, though it would not make their death more grievous, but rather dispatch them the sooner, was designed to signify that the king looked upon their crime as seven times more heinous than the crimes of others, and so made their death more ignominious. But God brought glory to himself out of this foolish instance of the tyrant's rage; for, though it would not have made their death the more grievous, yet it did make their deliverance much the more illustrious. 3. He ordered them to be bound in their clothes, and cast into the midst of the burning fiery furnace, which was done accordingly, *v.* 20, 21. They were bound, that they might not struggle, or make any resistance, were bound in their clothes, for haste, or that they might be consumed the more slowly and gradually. But God's providence ordered it for the increase of the miracle, in that their clothes were not so much as singed. They were bound in their *coats* or mantles, their *hosen* or breeches, and their *hats* or turbans, as if, in detestation of their crime, they would have

their clothes to be burnt with them. What a terrible death was this—to be *cast bound into the midst of a burning fiery furnace! v.* 23. It makes one's flesh tremble to think of it, and horror to take hold on one. It is amazing that the tyrant was so hard-hearted as to inflict such a punishment, and that the confessors were so stout-hearted as to submit to it rather than sin against God. But what is this to the *second death*, to that furnace into which the tares shall be cast in bundles, to that lake which burns eternally with fire and brimstone? Let Nebuchadnezzar heat his furnace as hot as he can, a few minutes will finish the torment of those who are cast into it; but hell-fire tortures and does not kill. The pain of damned sinners is more exquisite, and *the smoke of their torment ascends for ever and ever,* and *those have no rest,* no intermission, no cessation of their pains, *who have worshipped the beast and his image* (Rev. xiv. 10, 11), whereas their pain would be soon over that were cast into this furnace for not worshipping this Babylonian beast and his image. 4. It was a remarkable providence that the men, the *mighty men,* that bound them, and threw them into the furnace, were themselves consumed or suffocated by the flame, *v.* 22. The *king's commandment was urgent,* that they should dispatch them quickly, and be sure to do it effectually; and therefore they resolved to go to the very mouth of the furnace, that they might throw them *into the midst* of it, but they were in such haste that they would not take time to arm themselves accordingly. The apocryphal additions to Daniel say that the flame ascended forty-nine cubits above the mouth of the furnace. Probably God ordered it so that the wind blew it directly upon them with such violence that it smothered them. God did thus immediately plead the cause of his injured servants, and take vengeance for them on their persecutors, whom he punished, not only in the very act of their sin, but by it. But these men were only the instruments of cruelty; he that bade them do it had the greater sin; yet they suffered justly for executing an unjust decree, and it is very probable that they did it with pleasure and were glad to be so employed. Nebuchadnezzar himself was reserved for a further reckoning. There is a day coming when proud tyrants will be punished, not only for the cruelties they have been guilty of, but for employing those about them in their cruelties, and so exposing them to the judgments of God.

II. The deliverance of these three faithful servants of God out of the furnace. When they were cast bound into the midst of that devouring fire we might well conclude that we should hear no more of them, that their very bones would be calcined; but, to our amazement, we here find that Shadrach, Meshach, and Abednego, are yet alive.

1. Nebuchadnezzar finds them walking in the fire. *He was astonished, and rose up in*

haste, v. 24. Perhaps the slaying of the men that executed his sentence was that which astonished him, as well it might, for he had reason to think his own turn would be next; or it was some unaccountable impression upon his own mind that astonished him, and made him rise up in haste, and go to the furnace, to see what had become of those he had cast into it. Note, God can strike those with astonishment whose hearts are most hardened both against him and against his people. He that made the soul can make his sword to approach to it, even to that of the greatest tyrant. In his astonishment he calls his counsellors about him, and appeals to them. *Did we not cast three men bound into the fire?* It seems, it was done by order, not only of the king, but of the council. They durst not but concur with him, which he forced them to do, that they might share with him in the guilt and odium? "*True, O king!*" say they; "we did order such an execution to be done, and it was done." "But now," says the king, "I have been looking into the furnace, and *I see four men, loose, walking in the midst of the fire,*" *v.* 25. (1.) They were loosed from their bonds. The fire that did not so much as singe their clothes burnt the cords wherewith they were bound, and set them at liberty; thus God's people have their hearts enlarged, through the grace of God, by those very troubles with which their enemies designed to straiten and hamper them. (2.) They had no hurt, made no complaint, felt no pain or uneasiness in the least; the flame did not scorch them; the smoke did not stifle them; they were alive and as well as ever in the midst of the flames. See how the God of nature can, when he pleases, control the powers of nature, to make them serve his purposes. Now was fulfilled in the letter that gracious promise (Isa. xliii. 2), *When thou walkest through the fire thou shalt not be burnt, neither shall the flame kindle upon thee.* By faith they *quench the violence of the fire, quench the fiery darts of the wicked.* (3.) They *walked in the midst of the fire.* The furnace was large, so that they had room to walk; they were unhurt, so that they were able to walk; their minds were easy, so that they were disposed to walk, as in a paradise or garden of pleasure. *Can a man walk upon hot coals and his feet not be burnt?* Prov. vi. 28. Yes, they did it with as much pleasure as the king of Tyrus *walked up and down in the midst of his stones of fire,* his precious stones that sparkled as fire, Ezek. xxviii. 14. They were not striving to get out, finding themselves unhurt; but, leaving it to that God who preserved them in the fire to bring them out of it, they walked up and down *in the midst of it* unconcerned. One of the apocryphal writings relates at large the prayer which Azariah, one of the three, prayed in the fire (wherein he laments the calamities and iniquities of Israel, and entreats God's favour to his people), and the song of praise which they all three sang in the midst of the flames, in both which there are remarkable strains of devotion; but we have reason to think, with Grotius, that they were composed by some Jew of a later age, not as what were used, but only as what might have been used, on this occasion, and therefore we justly reject them as no part of holy writ. (4.) There was a fourth seen with them in the fire, whose form, in Nebuchadnezzar's judgment, was *like the Son of God;* he appeared as a divine person, a messenger from heaven, not as a servant, but as a son. *Like an angel* (so some); and angels are called *sons of God,* Job xxxviii. 7. In the apocryphal narrative of this story it is said, *The angel of the Lord came down into the furnace;* and Nebuchadnezzar here says (*v.* 28), God *sent his angel and delivered them;* and it was an angel that shut the lions' mouths when Daniel was in the den, *ch.* vi. 22. But some think it was the eternal Son of God, the angel of the covenant, and not a created angel. He appeared often in our nature before he assumed it in his incarnation, and never more seasonably, nor to give a more proper indication and presage of his great errand into the world in the fulness of time, than now, when, to deliver his chosen out of the fire, he came and walked with them in the fire. Note, Those that suffer for Christ have his gracious presence with them in their sufferings, even in the fiery furnace, even in the valley of the shadow of death, and therefore even there they need *fear no evil.* Hereby Christ showed that what is done against his people he takes as done against himself; whoever throws them into the furnace does, in effect, throw him in. *I am Jesus, whom thou persecutest,* Isa. lxiii. 9.

2. Nebuchadnezzar calls them out of the furnace (*v.* 26): He *comes near to the mouth of the burning fiery furnace,* and bids them *come forth and come hither. Come forth, come* (so some read it); he speaks with a great deal of tenderness and concern, and stands ready to lend them his hand and help them out. He is convinced by their miraculous preservation that he did evil in casting them into the furnace; and therefore he does not *thrust them out privily; no verily, but he will come himself and fetch them out,* Acts xvi. 37. Observe the respectful title that he gives them. When he was in the heat of his fury and rage against them it is probable that he called them rebels, and traitors, and all the ill names he could invent; but now he owns them for *the servants of the most high God,* a God who now appears *able to deliver them out of his hand.* Note, Sooner or later, God will convince the proudest of men that he is the most high God, and above them, and too hard for them, even in those things wherein they deal proudly and presumptuously, Exod. xviii. 11. He will likewise let them know

who are his servants, and that he owns them and will stand by them. Elijah prayed (1 Kings xviii. 36), *Let it be known that thou art God and that I am thy servant.* Nebuchadnezzar now embraces those whom he had abandoned, and is very officious about them, now that he perceives them to be the favourites of Heaven. Note, What persecutors have done against God's servants, when God opens their eyes, they must as far as they can undo again. How the *fourth,* whose *form was like the Son of God,* withdrew, and whether he vanished away or visibly ascended, we are not told, but of the other three we are informed, (1.) That they *came forth out of the midst of the fire,* as Abraham their father out of Ur (that is, *the fire) of the Chaldees,* into which, says this tradition of the Jews, he was cast, for refusing to worship idols, and out of which he was delivered, as those his *three children* were. When they had their discharge they did not tempt God by staying in any longer, but came forth as brands out of the burning. (2.) That it was made to appear, to the full satisfaction of all the amazed spectators, that they had not received the least damage by the fire, *v.* 27. All the great men came together to view them, and found that there was not so much as *a hair of their head singed.* Here that was true in the letter which our Saviour spoke figuratively, for an assurance to his suffering servants that they should sustain no real damage (Luke xxi. 18), *There shall not a hair of your head perish.* Their clothes did not so much as change colour, nor smell of fire, much less were their bodies in the least scorched or blistered; no, *the fire had no power on them.* The Chaldeans worshipped the fire, as a sort of image of the sun, so that, in restraining the fire now, God put contempt, not only upon their king, but upon their god too, and showed that *his voice divides the flames of fire* as well as the floods of water (Ps. xxix. 7), when he pleases to make a way for his people through the midst of it. It is our God only that is *the consuming fire* (Heb. xii. 29); other fire, if he but speak the word, shall not consume.

28 *Then* Nebuchadnezzar spake, and said, Blessed *be* the God of Shadrach, Meshach, and Abed-nego, who hath sent his angel, and delivered his servants that trusted in him, and have changed the king's word, and yielded their bodies, that they might not serve nor worship any God, except their own God. 29 Therefore I make a decree, that every people, nation, and language, which speak any thing amiss against the God of Shadrach, Meshach, and Abed-nego, shall be cut in

pieces, and their houses shall be made a dunghill: because there is no other God that can deliver after this sort. 30 Then the king promoted Shadrach, Meshach, and Abed-nego, in the province of Babylon.

The strict observations that were made, *super visum corporis—on inspecting their bodies,* by the princes and governors, and all the great men who were present upon this public occasion, and who could not be supposed partial in favour of the confessors, contributed much to the clearing of this miracle and the magnifying of the power and grace of God in it. *That indeed a notable miracle has been done is manifest, and we cannot deny it,* Acts iv. 16. Let us now see what effect it had upon Nebuchadnezzar.

I. He gives glory to the God of Israel as a God able and ready to protect his worshippers (*v.* 28): " *Blessed be the God of Shadrach, Meshach, and Abednego.* Let him have the honour both of the faithful allegiance which his subjects bear to him and the powerful protection he grants to them, neither of which can be paralleled by any other nation and their gods." The king does himself acknowledge and adore him, and thinks it is fit that he should be acknowledged and adored by all. *Blessed be the God of Shadrach.* Note, God can extort confessions of his blessedness even from those that have been ready to curse him to his face. 1. He gives him the glory of his power, that he was able to protect his worshippers against the most mighty and malignant enemies: *There is no other God that can deliver after this sort* (*v.*29), no, not this golden image which he had set up. For this reason there was no other god that obliged his worshippers to cleave to him only, and to suffer death rather than worship any other, as the God of Israel did, for they could not engage to bear them out in so doing, as he could. If God can work such deliverance as no other can, he may demand such obedience as no other may. 2. He gives him the glory of his goodness, that he was ready to do it (*v.* 28): *He has sent his angel and delivered his servants.* Bel could not save his worshippers from being burnt at the mouth of the furnace, but the God of Israel saved his from being burnt when they were cast into the midst of the furnace because they refused to *worship any other god.* By this Nebuchadnezzar was plainly given to understand that all the great success which he had had, and should yet have, against the people of Israel, which he gloried in, as if he had therein overpowered the God of Israel, was owing purely *to their sin:* if the body of that nation had faithfully adhered to their own God and the worship of him only, as these three men did, they would all have been delivered out of his hand as these three men were. And this was a necessary instruction for him at this time.

II. He applauds the constancy of these three men in their religion, and describes it to their honour, *v.* 28. Though he is not himself persuaded to own their God for his and to worship him, because, if he do so, he knows he must worship him only and renounce all others, and he calls him *the God of Shadrach*, not *my* God, yet he commends them for cleaving to him, and *not serving nor worshipping any other God but their own*. Note, There are many who are not religious themselves, and yet will own that those are clearly in the right that are religious and are stedfast in their religion. Though they are not themelves persuaded to close with it, they will commend those who, having closed with it, cleave to it. If men have given up their names to that God who will alone be served, let them keep to their principles, and serve him only, whatever it cost them. Such a constancy in the true religion will turn to men's praise, even among those that are without, when unsteadiness, treachery, and double dealing, are what all men will cry shame on. He commends them that they did this, 1. With a generous contempt of their lives, which they valued not, in comparison with the favour of God and the testimony of a good conscience. They *yielded their* own *bodies* to be cast into the fiery furnace rather than they would not only not forsake their God, but not affront him, by once paying that homage to any other which is due to him alone. Note, Those shall have their praise, if not of men, yet of God, who prefer their souls before their bodies, and will rather lose their lives than forsake their God. Those know not the worth and value of religion who do not think it worth suffering for. 2. They did it with a glorious contradiction to their prince: They *changed the king's word*, that is, they were contrary to it, and thereby put contempt upon both his precepts and threatenings, and made him repent and revoke both. Note, Even kings themselves must own that, when their commands are contrary to the commands of God, he is to be obeyed and not they. (3.) They did it with a gracious confidence in their God. They *trusted in him* that he would stand by them in what they did, that he would either bring them out of the fiery furnace back to their place on earth or lead them through the fiery furnace forward to their place in heaven; and in this confidence they became fearless of the king's wrath and regardless of their own lives. Note, A stedfast faith in God will produce a stedfast faithfulness to God. Now this honourable testimony, thus publicly borne by the king himself to these servants of God, we may well think, would have a good influence upon the rest of the Jews that were, or should be, captives in Babylon. Their

neighbours could not with any confidence urge them to do that, nor could they for shame do that, which their brethren were so highly applauded by the king himself for not doing. Nay, and what God did for these his servants would help not only to keep the Jews close to their religion while they were in captivity, but to cure them of their inclination to idolatry, for which end they were sent into captivity; and, when it had had that blessed effect upon them, they might be assured that God would deliver them out of that furnace, as now he delivered their brethren out of this.

III. He issues a royal edict, strictly forbidding any to speak evil of the God of Israel, *v.* 29. We have reason to think that both the sins and the troubles of Israel had given great occasion, though no just occasion, to the Chaldeans to blaspheme the God of Israel, and, it is likely, Nebuchadnezzar himself had encouraged it; but now, though he is no true convert, nor is wrought upon to worship him, yet he resolves never to speak ill of him again, nor to suffer others to do so: " *Whoever shall speak any thing amiss*, any *error* (so some), or rather any reproach or blasphemy, whoever shall speak with contempt of *the God of Shadrach, Meshach, and Abednego*, they shall be counted the worst of malefactors, and dealt with accordingly, they shall be *cut in pieces*, as Agag was by the sword of Samuel, and their houses shall be demolished and made a *dunghill.*" The miracle now wrought by the power of this God in defence of his worshippers, publicly in the sight of the thousands of Babylon, was a sufficient justification of this edict. And it would contribute much to the ease of the Jews in their captivity to be by this law screened from the fiery darts of reproach and blasphemy, with which otherwise they would have been continually annoyed. Note, It is a great mercy to the church, and a good point gained, when its enemies, though they have not their hearts turned, yet have their mouths stopped and their tongues tied. If a heathen prince laid such a restraint upon the proud lips of blasphemers, much more should Christian princes do it; nay, in this thing, one would think that men should be a law to themselves, and that those who have so little love to God that they care not to speak well of him, yet could never find in their hearts, for we are sure they could never find cause, to *speak any thing amiss* of him.

IV. He not only reverses the attainder of these three men, but restores them to their places in the government *(makes them to prosper*, so the word is), and prefers them to greater and more advantageous trusts than they had been in before: He *promoted them in the province* of Babylon, which was much to their honour and the comfort of their brethren in captivity there. Note, It is the wisdom of princes to prefer and employ men of stedfastness in religion; for those are most likely to be faithful to them who are faithful to God, and it is likely to be well with them when God's favourites are made theirs.

CHAP. IV.

The penman of this chapter is Nebuchadnezzar himself: the story here recorded concerning him is given us in his own words, as he himself drew it up and published it; but Daniel, a prophet, by inspiration, inserts it in his history, and so it has become a part of sacred writ and a very memorable part. Nebuchadnezzar was as daring a rival with God Almighty for the sovereignty as perhaps any mortal man ever was; but here he fairly owns himself conquered, and gives it under his hand that the God of Israel is above him. Here is, I. The preface to his narrative, wherein he acknowledges God's dominion over him, ver. 1—3. II. The narrative itself, wherein he relates, 1. His dream, which puzzled the magicians, ver. 1—3. 2. The interpretation of his dream by Daniel, who showed him that it was a prognostication of his own fall, advising him therefore to repent and reform, ver. 19—27. 3. The accomplishment of it in his running stark mad for seven years, and then recovering the use of his reason again, ver. 28—36. 4. The conclusion of the narrative, with a humble acknowledgment and adoration of God as Lord of all, ver. 37. This was extorted from him by the overruling power of that God who has all men's hearts in his hand, and stands upon record a lasting proof of God's supremacy, a monument of his glory, a trophy of his victory, and a warning to all not to think of prospering while they lift up or harden their hearts against God.

NEBUCHADNEZZAR the king, unto all people, nations, and languages, that dwell in all the earth; Peace be multiplied unto you. 2 I thought it good to show the signs and wonders that the high God hath wrought toward me. 3 How great *are* his signs! and how mighty *are* his wonders! his kingdom *is* an everlasting kingdom, and his dominion *is* from generation to generation.

Here is, I. Something of form, which was usual in writs, proclamations, or circular letters, issued by the king, *v.* 1. The royal style which Nebuchadnezzar makes use of has nothing in it of pomp or fancy, but is plain, short, and unaffected—*Nebuchadnezzar the king.* If at other times he made use of great swelling words of vanity in his title, now he laid them all aside; for he was old, he had lately recovered from a distraction which had humbled and mortified him, and was now in the actual contemplation of God's greatness and sovereignty. The declaration is directed not only to his own subjects, but to all to whom this present writing shall come—*to all people, nations, and languages, that dwell in all the earth.* He is not only willing that they should all hear of it, though it carry the account of his own infamy (which perhaps none durst have published if he had not done it himself, and therefore Daniel published the original paper), but he strictly charges and commands all manner of persons to take notice of it; for all are concerned, and it may be profitable to all. He salutes those to whom he writes, in the usual form, *Peace be multiplied unto you.* Note, It becomes kings with their commands to disperse their good wishes, and, as fathers of their country, to bless their subjects. So the common form with

1044

us. We send greeting, *Omnibus quibus hæ præsentes literæ pervenerint, salutem—To all to whom these presents shall come, health;* and sometimes *Salutem sempiternam—Health and salvation everlasting.*

II. Something of substance and matter. He writes this, 1. To acquaint others with the providences of God that had related to him (*v.* 2): *I thought it good to show the signs and wonders that the high God* (so he calls the true God) *has wrought towards me.* He thought it *seemly* (so the word is), that it was his duty, and did well become him, that it was a debt he owed to God and the world, now that he had recovered from his distraction, to relate to distant places, and record for future ages, how justly God had humbled him and how graciously he had at length restored him. All the nations, no doubt, had heard what had befel Nebuchadnezzar, and rang of it; but he thought it fit that they should have a distinct account of it from himself, that they might know the hand of God in it, and what impressions were made upon his own spirit by it, and might speak of it not as a matter of news, but as a matter of religion. The events concerning him were not only wonders to be admired, but signs to be instructed by, signifying to the world that Jehovah is greater than all gods. Note, We ought to show to others God's dealings with us, both the rebukes we have been under and the favours we have received; and though the account hereof may reflect disgrace upon ourselves, as this did upon Nebuchadnezzar, yet we must not conceal it, as long as it may redound to the glory of God. Many will be forward to tell what God has done *for their souls,* because that turns to their own praise, who care not for telling what God has done against them, and how they deserved it; whereas we ought to give glory to God, not only by praising him for his mercies, but by confessing our sins, accepting the punishment of our iniquity, and in both taking shame to ourselves, as this mighty monarch here does. 2. To show how much he was himself affected with them and convinced by them, *v.* 3. We should always speak of the word and works of God with concern and seriousness and show ourselves affected with those great things of God which we desire others should take notice of. (1.) He admires God's doings. He speaks of them as one amazed: *How great are his signs, and how mighty are his wonders!* Nebuchadnezzar was now old, had reigned above forty years, and had seen as much of the world and the revolutions of it as most men ever did; and yet never till now, when himself was nearly touched, was he brought to admire surprising events as God's signs and his wonders. Now, *How great, how mighty,* are they! Note. The more we see events to be *the Lord's doing,* and see in them the product of a divine power and the conduct of a divine wisdom, the more marvellous they will appear in our eyes, Ps. cxviii. 23; lxvi. 2. (2.) He thence infers God's dominion. This is that which he is at length brought to subscribe to: *His kingdom is an everlasting kingdom;* and not like his own kingdom, which he saw, and long since foresaw, in a dream, hastening towards a period. He now owns that there is a God that governs the world and has a universal, incontestable, absolute dominion in and over all the affairs of the children of men. And it is the glory of this kingdom that it is everlasting. Other reigns are confined to one generation, and other dynasties to a few generations, but God's *dominion is from generation to generation.* It should seem, Nebuchadnezzar here refers to what Daniel had foretold of a kingdom which the God of heaven would set up, that should *never be destroyed* (ch. ii. 44), which, though meant of the kingdom of the Messiah, he understood of the providential kingdom. Thus we may make a profitable practical use and application of those prophetical scriptures which yet we do not fully, and perhaps not rightly, comprehend the meaning of.

4 I Nebuchadnezzar was at rest in mine house, and flourishing in my palace: 5 I saw a dream which made me afraid, and the thoughts upon my bed and the visions of my head troubled me. 6 Therefore made I a decree to bring in all the wise *men* of Babylon before me, that they might make known unto me the interpretation of the dream. 7 Then came in the magicians, the astrologers, the Chaldeans, and the soothsayers: and I told the dream before them; but they did not make known unto me the interpretation thereof. 8 But at the last Daniel came in before me, whose name *was* Belteshazzar, according to the name of my God, and in whom *is* the spirit of the holy gods: and before him I told the dream, *saying,* 9 O Belteshazzar, master of the magicians, because I know that the spirit of the holy gods *is* in thee, and no secret troubleth thee, tell me the visions of my dream that I have seen, and the interpretation thereof. 10 Thus *were* the visions of mine head in my bed; I saw, and behold a tree in the midst of the earth, and the height thereof *was* great. 11 The tree grew, and was strong, and the height thereof reached unto heaven, and the sight

thereof to the end of all the earth: 12 The leaves thereof *were* fair, and the fruit thereof much, and in it *was* meat for all: the beasts of the field had shadow under it, and the fowls of the heaven dwelt in the boughs thereof, and all flesh was fed of it. 13 I saw in the visions of my head upon my bed, and, behold, a watcher and a holy one came down from heaven; 14 He cried aloud, and said thus, Hew down the tree, and cut off his branches, shake off his leaves, and scatter his fruit: let the beasts get away from under it, and the fowls from his branches: 15 Nevertheless leave the stump of his roots in the earth, even with a band of iron and brass, in the tender grass of the field; and let it be wet with the dew of heaven, and *let* his portion *be* with the beasts in the grass of the earth: 16 Let his heart be changed from man's, and let a beast's heart be given unto him; and let seven times pass over him. 17 This matter *is* by the decree of the watchers, and the demand by the word of the holy ones: to the intent that the living may know that the most High ruleth in the kingdom of men, and giveth it to whomsoever he will, and setteth up over it the basest of men. 18 This dream I king Nebuchadnezzar have seen. Now thou, O Belteshazzar, declare the interpretation thereof, forasmuch as all the wise *men* of my kingdom are not able to make known unto me the interpretation: but thou *art* able; for the spirit of the holy gods *is* in thee.

Nebuchadnezzar, before he relates the judgments of God that had been wrought upon him for his pride, gives an account of the fair warning he had of them before they came, a due regard to which might have prevented them. But he was *told of them,* and of the issue of them, *before they came to pass, that, when they did come to pass,* by comparing them with the prediction of them, he might see, and say, that they were the Lord's doing, and might be brought to believe that there is a divine revelation in the world, as well as a divine Providence, and that the works of God agree with his word.

Now, in the account he here gives of his dream, by which he had notice of what was coming, we may observe,

I. The time when this alarm was given to

him (*v.* 4) ; it was when he was *at rest in his house, and flourishing in his palace.* He had lately conquered Egypt, and with it completed his victories, and ended his wars, and made himself monarch of all those parts of the world, which was about the thirty-fourth or thirty-fifth year of his reign, Ezek. xxix. 17. Then he had this dream, which was accomplished about a year after. Seven years his distraction continued, upon his recovery from which he penned this declaration, lived about two years after, and died in his forty-fifth year. He had undergone a long fatigue in his wars, had made many a tedious and dangerous campaign in the field ; but now at length he is *at rest in his house,* and there is *no adversary, nor* any *evil occurrent.* Note, God can reach the greatest of men with his terrors even when they are most secure, and think themselves at rest and flourishing.

II. The impression it made upon him (*v.* 5): *I saw a dream which made me afraid.* One would think no little thing would frighten him that had been a man of war from his youth, and used to look the perils of war in the face without change of countenance ; yet, when God pleases, a dream strikes a terror upon him. His bed, no doubt, was soft, and easy, and well-guarded, and yet his own *thoughts upon his bed* made him uneasy, and the *visions of his head,* the creatures of his own imagination, *troubled him.* Note, God can make the greatest of men uneasy even when they say to their souls, *Take your ease, eat, drink, and be merry ;* he can make those that have been the troublers of the world, and have tormented thousands, to be their own troublers, their own tormentors, and those that have been *the terror of the mighty* a terror to themselves. By the consternation which this dream put him into, and the impression it made upon him, he perceived it to be, not an ordinary dream, but sent of God on a special errand.

III. His consulting, in vain, with the magicians and astrologers concerning the meaning of it. He had not now forgotten the dream, as before, *ch.* ii. He had it ready enough, but he wanted to know the interpretation of it and what was prefigured by it, *v.* 6. Orders are immediately given to summon *all the wise men of Babylon* that were such fools as to pretend by magic, divination, inspecting the entrails of beasts, or observations of the stars, to predict things to come : they must all come together, to see if any, or all of them in consultation, could interpret the king's dream. It is probable that these people had sometimes, in a like case, given the king some sort of satisfaction, and by the rules of their art had answered the king's queries so as to please him, whether it were right or wrong, hit or missed ; but now his expectation from them was disappointed: He *told them the dream* (*v.* 7),

but they *could not tell him the interpretation of it,* though they had boasted, with great assurance (*ch.* ii. 4, 7), that, if they had but the dream told them, they would without fail interpret it. But the key of this dream was in a sacred prophecy (Ezek. xxxi. 3, &c.), where the Assyrian is compared, as Nebuchadnezzar here, to a *tree cut down,* for his pride ; and that was a book they had not studied, nor acquainted themselves with, else they might have been let into the mystery of this dream. Providence ordered it so that they should be first puzzled with it, that Daniel's interpreting it afterwards might redound to the glory of the God of Daniel. Now was fulfilled what Isaiah foretold (*ch.* xlvii. 12, 13), that when the ruin of Babylon was drawing on her *enchantments* and *sorceries,* her *astrologers* and *star-gazers,* should not be able to do her any service.

IV. The court he made to Daniel, to engage him to expound his dream to him : *At the last Daniel came in, v.* 8. Either he declined associating with the rest because of their badness, or they declined his company because of his goodness ; or perhaps the king would rather that his own magicians should have the honour of doing it if they could than that Daniel should have it ; or Daniel, being *governor* of the wise men (*ch.* ii. 48), was, as is usual, last consulted. Many make God's word their last refuge, and never have recourse to it till they are driven off from all other succours. He compliments Daniel very highly, takes notice of the name which he had himself given him, in the choice of which he thinks he was very happy and that it was a good omen : "His *name was Belteshazzar,* from *Bel, the name of my god.*" He applauds his rare endowments : He has *the spirit of the holy gods,* so he tells him to his face (*v.* 9), with which we may suppose that Daniel was so far from being puffed up that he was rather very much grieved to hear that which he had by gift from the God of Israel, the true and living God, ascribed to Nebuchadnezzar's god, a dunghill deity. Here is a strange medley in Nebuchadnezzar, but such as is commonly found in those that side with their corruptions against their convictions. 1. He retains the language and dialect of his idolatry, and therefore, it is to be feared, is no convert to the faith and worship of the living God. He is an idolater, and his speech betrayeth him. For he speaks of many gods, and is not brought to acquiesce in one as sufficient, no, not in him who is all-sufficient. And some think, when he speaks of *the spirit of the holy gods,* that he supposes there are some evil malignant deities, whom men are concerned to worship, only to prevent their doing them a mischief, and some who are good beneficent deities, and that by the spirit of the latter Daniel was animated. He also owns that Bel was his god still, though he had once and again acknowledged the *God of Israel* to be Lord of all, *ch.* ii. 47 ; iii. 29. He also applauds Daniel, not as *a servant of God*, but as *master of the magicians* (*v.* 9), supposing his knowledge to differ from theirs, not in kind, but only in degree; and he consulted him not as a prophet, but as a celebrated magician, so endeavouring to save the credit of the art when those blundered and were nonplussed who were masters of the art. See how close his idolatry sat to him. He has got a notion of many gods, and has chosen Bel for his god, and he cannot persuade himself to quit either his notion or his choice, though the absurdity of both had been evidenced to him, more than once, beyond contradiction. He, like other heathens, would not change his gods, though they were no gods, Jer. ii. 11. Many persist in a false way only because they think they cannot in honour leave it. See how loose his convictions sat, and how easily he had dropped them. He once called the God of Israel a *God of gods, ch.* ii. 47. Now he sets him upon a level with the rest of those whom he calls the *holy gods.* Note, If convictions be not speedily prosecuted, it is a thousand to one but in a little time they will be quite lost and forgotten. Nebuchadnezzar, not going forward with the acknowledgments he had been brought to make of the sovereignty of the true God, soon *went backwards*, and relapsed to the same veneration he had always had for his false gods. And yet, 2. He professes a great opinion of Daniel, whom he knows to be a servant of the true God, and of him only. He looked upon him as one that had such an insight, such a foresight, as none of his magicians had : *I know that no secret troubles thee.* Note, The spirit of prophecy quite outdoes the spirit of divination, even the enemies themselves being judges ; for so it was adjudged here, upon a fair trial of skill.

V. The particular account he gives him of his dream.

1. He saw a stately flourishing tree, remarkable above all the trees of the wood. This tree was *planted in the midst of the earth* (*v.* 10), fitly representing him who reigned in Babylon, which was about the midst of the then known world. His dignity and eminency above all his neighbours were signified by the height of this tree, which was *exceedingly great ; it reached unto heaven.* He over-topped those about him, and aimed to have divine honours given him ; nay, he over-powered those about him, and the potent armies he had the command of, with which he carried all before him, are signified by the strength of this tree : it *grew and was strong.* And so much were Nebuchadnezzar and his growing greatness the talk of the nations, so much had they their eye upon him (some a jealous eye, all a wondering eye), that the sight of this tree is said to be *to the end of all the earth.* This tree had every thing in it that was pleasant to

the eye and good for food (*v.* 12) : *The leaves thereof were fair*, denoting the pomp and splendour of Nebuchadnezzar's court, which was the wonder of strangers and the glory of his own subjects. Nor was this tree for sight and state only, but for use. (1.) For protection ; the boughs of it were for shelter both to the beasts and to the fowls. Princes should be a screen to their subjects *from the heat* and *from the storm*, should expose themselves to secure them, and study how to make them safe and easy. If the bramble be *promoted over the trees*, he invites them to come and *trust in his shadow*, such as it is, Judg. ix. 15. It is protection that draws allegiance. The kings of the earth are to their subjects but as the shadow of a great tree; but Christ is to his subjects as the *shadow of a great rock*, Isa. xxxii. 2. Nay, because that, though strong, may be cold, they are said to be hidden under the *shadow of his wings* (Ps. xvii. 8), where they are not only safe, but warm. (2.) For provision. The Assyrian was compared to a *cedar* (Ezek. xxxi. 6), which affords shadow only ; but this tree here had much fruit—in it was *meat for all* and *all flesh was fed of it.* This mighty monarch, it should seem by this, not only was great, but did good; he did not impoverish, but enrich his country, and by his power and interest abroad brought wealth and trade to it. Those that *exercise authority* would be called *benefactors* (Luke xxii. 25), and the most effectual course they can take to support their authority is to be really benefactors. And see what is the best that great men, with their wealth and power can attain to, and that is to have the honour of having many to live upon them and to be maintained by them ; for, *as goods are increased, those are increased that eat them.*

2. He heard the doom of this tree read, which he perfectly remembered, and relates here, perhaps word for word as he heard it. The sentence was passed upon it by an angel, whom he saw *come down from heaven*, and heard proclaim this sentence aloud. This angel is here called a *watcher*, or *watchman*, not only because angels by their nature are spirits, and therefore neither slumber nor sleep, but because by their office they are *ministering spirits*, and attend continually to their ministrations, watching all opportunities of serving their great Master. They, as watchers, encamp round those that fear God, to deliver them, and *bear them up in their hands.* This angel was a *messenger*, or *ambassador* (so some read it), and *a holy one. Holiness becomes God's house ;* therefore angels that attend and are employed by him are *holy ones ;* they preserve the purity and rectitude of their nature, and are in every thing conformable to the divine will. Let us review the doom passed upon the tree

(1.) Orders are given that it be cut down (*v.* 14) ; now also *the axe is laid to the root* of this tree. Though it is ever so high, ever so strong, that cannot secure it when its day comes to fall; the beasts and fowls, that are sheltered in and under the boughs of it, are driven away and dispersed; the branches are cropped, the leaves shaken off, and the fruit scattered. Note, Worldly prosperity in its highest degree is a very uncertain thing; and it is no uncommon thing for those that have lived in the greatest pomp and power to be stripped of all that which they trusted to and gloried in. By the turns of providence, those who made a figure become captives, those who lived in plenty, and above what they had, are reduced to straits, and live far below what they had, and those perhaps are brought to be beholden to others who once had many depending upon them and making suit to them. But the *trees of righteousness,* that are *planted in the house of the Lord* and bring forth fruit to him, shall not be cut down, nor shall their leaf wither.

(2.) Care is taken that the root be preserved (*v.* 15): "*Leave the stump of it in the earth,* exposed to all weathers. There let it lie neglected and buried in the grass. Let the beasts that formerly sheltered themselves under the boughs now repose themselves upon the stump; but that it may not be raked to pieces, nor trodden to dirt, and to show that it is yet reserved for better days, let it be hooped round with *a band of iron and brass,* to keep it firm." Note, God in judgment remembers mercy; and may yet have good things in store for those whose condition seems most forlorn. There is *hope of a tree, if it be cut down, that it will sprout again, that through the scent of water it will bud,* Job xiv. 7—9.

(3.) The meaning of this is explained by the angel himself to Nebuchadnezzar, *v.* 16. Whoever is the person signified by this tree he is sentenced to be deposed from the honour, state, and dignity of a man, to be deprived of the use of his reason, and to be and live like a brute, till *seven times pass over him. Let a beast's heart be given unto him.* This is surely the saddest and sorest of all temporal judgments, worse a thousand times than death, and though, like it, least felt by those that lie under it, yet to be dreaded and deprecated more than any other. Nay, whatever outward affliction God is pleased to lay upon us, we have reason to bear it patiently, and to be thankful that he continues to us the use of our reason and the peace of our consciences. But those proud tyrants who *set their heart as the heart of God* (Ezek. xxviii. 2) may justly be deprived of the heart of man, and have a beast's heart given them.

(4.) The truth of it is confirmed (*v.* 17): *This matter is by the decree of the watchers and the demand by the word of the holy ones.* God has determined it, as a righteous Judge; he has signed this edict; pursuant to his eternal counsel, the decree has gone forth.

And, [1.] The angels of heaven have subscribed to it, as attesting it, approving it, and applauding it. It is by *the decree of the watchers;* not that the great God needs the counsel or concurrence of the angels in any thing he determines or does, but, as he uses their ministration in executing his counsels, so he is sometimes represented, after the manner of men, as if he consulted them. *Whom shall I send?* Isa. vi. 8. *Who shall persuade Ahab?* 1 Kings xxii. 20. So it denotes the solemnity of this sentence. The king's breves, or short writs, pass, *Teste me ipso—In my presence;* but charters used to be signed, *His testibus—In presence of us whose names are under-written;* such was Nebuchadnezzar's doom; it was by the *decree of the watchers.* [2.] The saints on earth petitioned for it, as well as the angels in heaven: *The demand is by the word of the holy ones.* God's suffering people, that had long groaned under the heavy yoke of Nebuchadnezzar's tyranny, cried to him for vengeance; they made the demand, and God gave this answer to it; for, when the *oppressed cry to God, he will hear,* Exod. xxii. 27. Sentence was passed, in Ahab's time, that there should be no more rain, at Elijah's word, when he *made intercession against Israel,* 1 Kings xvii. 1.

(5.) The design of it is declared. Orders are given for the cutting down of this tree, *to the intent that the living may know that the Most High rules.* This judgment must be executed, to convince the unthinking, unbelieving, world, that *verily there is a God that judges in the earth,* a God that governs the world, that not only has a kingdom of his own in it, and administers the affairs of that kingdom, but rules also *in the kingdom of men,* in the dominion that one man has over another, and *gives that to whomsoever he will;* from him promotion comes, Ps. lxxv. 6, 7. He advances men to power and dominion that little expected it, and crosses the projects of the ambitious and aspiring. Sometimes he *sets up the basest of men,* and serves his own purposes by them. He sets up mean men, as David from the sheepfold; *he raises the poor out of the dust,* to *set them among princes,* Ps. cxiii. 7, 8. Nay, sometimes he sets up bad men, to be a scourge to a provoking people. Thus he can do, thus he may do, thus he often does, and *gives not account of any of his matters.* By humbling Nebuchadnezzar it was designed that the living should be made to know this. The dead know it, that have gone to the world of spirits, the world of retribution; they know that *the Most High rules;* but the living must be made to know it and lay it to heart, that they may make their peace with God before it be too late.

Thus has Nebuchadnezzar fully and faithfully related his dream, what he saw and what he heard, and then demands of Daniel the interpretation of it (*v.* 18), for he found that no one else was able to interpret it, but was confident that he was : *For the spirit of the holy gods is in thee,* or of the *Holy God,* the proper title of the God of Israel. Much may be expected from those that have in them the *Spirit of the Holy God.* Whether Nebuchadnezzar had any jealousy that it was his own doom that was read by this dream does not appear; perhaps he was so vain and secure as to imagine that it was some other prince that was a rival with him, whose fall he had the pleasing prospect of given him in this dream ; but, be it for him or against him, he is very solicitous to know the true meaning of it and depends upon Daniel to give it to him. Note, When God gives us general warnings of his judgments we should be desirous to understand his mind in them, to hear *the Lord's voice crying in the city.*

19 Then Daniel, whose name *was* Belteshazzar, was astonied for one hour, and his thoughts troubled him. The king spake, and said, Belteshazzar, let not the dream, or the interpretation thereof, trouble thee. Belteshazzar answered and said, My lord, The dream *be* to them that hate thee, and the interpretation thereof to thine enemies. 20 The tree that thou sawest, which grew, and was strong, whose height reached unto the heaven, and the sight thereof to all the earth ; 21 Whose leaves *were* fair, and the fruit thereof much, and in it *was* meat for all ; under which the beasts of the field dwelt, and upon whose branches the fowls of the heaven had their habitation : 22 It *is* thou, O king, that art grown and become strong : for thy greatness is grown, and reacheth unto heaven, and thy dominion to the end of the earth. 23 And whereas the king saw a watcher and a holy one coming down from heaven, and saying, Hew the tree down, and destroy it ; yet leave the stump of the roots thereof in the earth, even with a band of iron and brass, in the tender grass of the field ; and let it be wet with the dew of heaven, and *let* his portion *be* with the beasts of the field, till seven times pass over him ; 24 This *is* the interpretation, O king, and this *is* the decree of the Most High, which is come upon my lord the king : 25 That they shall drive thee from men, and thy dwelling shall be with the

beasts of the field, and they shall make thee to eat grass as oxen, and they shall wet thee with the dew of heaven, and seven times shall pass over thee, till thou know that the Most High ruleth in the kingdom of men, and giveth it to whomsoever he will. 26 And whereas they commanded to leave the stump of the tree roots ; thy kingdom shall be sure unto thee, after that thou shalt have known that the heavens do rule. 27 Wherefore, O king, let my counsel be acceptable unto thee, and break off thy sins by righteousness, and thine iniquities by showing mercy to the poor ; if it may be a lengthening of thy tranquillity.

We have here the interpretation of Nebuchadnezzar's dream ; and when once it is applied to himself, and it is declared that he is the tree in the dream *(Mutato nomine de te fabula narratur—Change but the name, the fable speaks of thee),* when once it is said, *Thou art the man,* there needs little more to be said for the explication of the dream. *Out of his own mouth he is judged ; so shall his doom be, he himself has decided it.* The thing was so plain that Daniel, upon hearing the dream, was *astonished for one hour, v.* 19. He was struck with amazement and terror at so great a judgment coming upon so great a prince. *His flesh trembled for fear of God.* He was likewise struck with confusion when he found himself under a necessity of being the man that must bring to the king *these heavy tidings,* which, having received so many favours from the king, he had rather he should have heard from any one else ; so far is he from desiring the woeful day that he dreads it, and the thoughts of it trouble him. Those that come after the ruined sinner are said to be *astonished at his day,* as *those that went before,* and saw it coming (as Daniel here), *were affrighted,* Job xviii. 20.

I. The preface to the interpretation is a civil compliment which, as a courtier, he passes upon the king. The king observed him to stand as one astonished, and, thinking he was loth to speak out for fear of offending him, he encouraged him to deal plainly and faithfully with him : *Let not the dream, nor the interpretation thereof, trouble thee.* This he speaks either, 1. As one that sincerely desired to know the truth. Note, Those that consult the oracles of God must be ready to receive them as they are, whether they be for them or against them, and must accordingly give their ministers leave to be free with them. Or, 2. As one that despised the truth, and set it at defiance. When we see how regardless he was of this warning afterwards we are tempted to think that this was his meaning: "*Let it not trouble thee,* for I am resolved it shall not trouble me; nor will I lay it to heart." But, whether he have any concern for himself or no, Daniel is concerned for him, and therefore wishes, "*The dream be to those that hate thee.* Let the ill it bodes light on the head of thy enemies, not on thy head." Though Nebuchadnezzar was an idolater, a persecutor, and an oppressor of the people of God, yet he was, at present, Daniel's prince; and therefore, though Daniel foresees, and is now going to foretel, ill concerning him, he dares not wish ill to him.

II. The interpretation itself is only a repetition of the dream, with application to the king. "As for *the tree* which thou sawest *flourishing* (v. 20, 21), *it is thou, O king!*" *v.* 22. And willing enough would the king be to hear this (as, before, to hear, *Thou art the head of gold*), but for that which follows. He shows the king his present prosperous state in the glass of his own dream: "*Thy greatness has grown and reaches* as near *to heaven* as human greatness can do, and *thy dominion is to the end of the earth,*" *ch.* ii. 37, 38. "As for the doom passed upon the tree (v. 23), it is *the decree of the Most High, which comes upon my lord the king,*" v. 24. He must not only be deposed from his throne, *but driven from men,* and being deprived of his reason, and having a beast's heart given him, his dwelling shall be *with the beasts of the field,* and with them he shall be a fellow-commoner: he shall *eat grass as oxen,* and, like them, lie out all weathers, and be *wet with the dew of heaven,* and this till *seven times* pass over him, that is, *seven years;* and then he shall know that the *Most High rules,* and when he is brought to know and own this he shall be restored to his dominion again (v. 26): "*Thy kingdom shall be sure unto thee,* shall remain as firm as the *stump of the tree* in the ground, and thou shalt have it, *after thou shalt have known* that *the heavens do rule.*" God is here called *the heavens,* because it is in heaven that he has *prepared his throne* (Ps. ciii. 19), thence he *beholds all the sons of men,* Ps. xxxiii. 13. The *heavens, even the heavens, are the Lord's;* and the influence which the visible heavens have upon this earth is intended as a faint representation of the dominion the God of heaven has over this lower world; we are said to *sin against heaven,* Luke xv. 18. Note, Then only we may expect comfortably to enjoy our right in, and government of, both ourselves and others, when we dutifully acknowledge God's title to, and dominion over, us and all we have.

III. The close of the interpretation is the pious counsel which Daniel, as a prophet, gave the king, *v.* 27. Whether he appeared concerned or not at the interpretation of the dream, a word of advice would be very seasonable—if careless, to awaken him, if

1050

troubled, to comfort him; and it is not inconsistent with the dream and the interpretation of it, for Daniel knew not but it might be conditional, like the prediction of Nineveh's destruction. Observe, 1. How humbly he gives his advice, and with what tenderness and respect: "*O king! let my counsel be acceptable unto thee;* take it in good part, as coming from love, and well-meant, and let it not be misinterpreted." Note, Sinners need to be courted to their own good, and respectfully entreated to do well for themselves. The apostle beseeches men to *suffer the word of exhortation,* Heb. xiii. 22. We think it a good point gained if people will be persuaded to take good counsel kindly; nay, if they will take it patiently. 2. What his advice is. He does not counsel him to enter into a course of physic, for the preventing of the distemper in his head, but to break off a course of sin that he was in, to reform his life. He wronged his own subjects, and dealt unfairly with his allies; and he must *break off* this *by righteousness,* by rendering to all their due, making amends for wrong done, and not triumphing over right with might. He had been cruel to the poor, to God's poor, to the poor Jews; and he must *break off* this *iniquity* by *showing mercy* to those poor, pitying those oppressed ones, setting them at liberty or making their captivity easy to them. Note, It is necessary, in repentance, that we not only *cease to do evil, but learn to do well,* not only do no wrong to any, but do good to all. 3. What the motive is with which he backs this advice: *If it may be a lengthening of thy tranquillity.* Though it should not wholly prevent the judgment, yet by this means a reprieve may be obtained, as by *Ahab's humbling himself,* 1 Kings xxi. 29. Either the trouble may be the longer before it comes or the shorter when it does come; yet he cannot assure him of this, but *it may be,* it may prove so. Note, The mere probability of preventing a temporal judgment is inducement enough to a work so good in itself as the leaving off of our sins and reforming of our lives, much more the certainty of preventing our eternal ruin. "*That will be a healing of thy error*" (so some read it); "thus the quarrel will be taken up, and all will be well again."

28 All this came upon the king Nebuchadnezzar. 29 At the end of twelve months he walked in the palace of the kingdom of Babylon. 30 The king spake, and said, Is not this great Babylon, that I have built for the house of the kingdom by the might of my power, and for the honour of my majesty? 31 While the word *was* in the king's mouth, there fell a voice from heaven, *saying,* O king Nebu-

chadnezzar, to thee it is spoken ; The kingdom is departed from thee. 32 And they shall drive thee from men, and thy dwelling *shall be* with the beasts of the field : they shall make thee to eat grass as oxen, and seven times shall pass over thee, until thou know that the Most High ruleth in the kingdom of men, and giveth it to whomsoever he will. 33 The same hour was the thing fulfilled upon Nebuchadnezzar : and he was driven from men, and did eat grass as oxen, and his body was wet with the dew of heaven, till his hairs were grown like eagles' *feathers,* and his nails like birds' *claws.*

We have here Nebuchadnezzar's dream accomplished, and Daniel's application of it to him justified and confirmed. How he took it we are. not told, whether he was pleased with Daniel or displeased ; but here we have,

I. God's patience with him : *All this came upon him,* but not till *twelve months after* (v. 29), so long there was a *lengthening of his tranquillity,* though it does not appear that he *broke off his sins,* or showed any *mercy to the poor* captives, for this was still God's quarrel with him, that he *opened not the house of his prisoners,* Isa. xiv. 17. Daniel having counselled him to repent, God so far confirmed his word that he gave him space to repent ; he *let him alone this year also,* this one year more, before he brought this judgment upon him. Note, God is long-suffering with provoking sinners, because he is not willing that *any should perish, but that all should come to repentance,* 2 Pet. iii. 9.

II. His pride, and haughtiness, and abuse of that patience. He walked *in the palace of the kingdom of Babylon,* in pomp and pride, pleasing himself with the view of that vast city, which, with all the territories thereunto belonging, was under his command, and *he said,* either to himself or to those about him, perhaps some foreigners to whom he was showing his kingdom and the glory of it, *Is not this great Babylon ?* Yes, it is great, of vast extent, no less than forty-five miles compass within the walls. It is full of inhabitants, and they are full of wealth. It is a *golden city,* and that is enough to proclaim it great, Isa. xiv. 4. See the grandeur of the houses, walls, towers, and public edifices. Every thing in Babylon he thinks looks great ; " and this *great Babylon I have built.*" Babylon was built many ages before he was born, but because he had fortified and beautified it, and we may suppose much of it was rebuilt during his long and prosperous reign, he boasts that he has built it, as Augustus Cæsar boasted concerning Rome,

Lateritiam inveni, marmoream reliqui—I found it brick, but I left it marble. He boasts that he built it *for the house of the kingdom,* that is, the metropolis of his empire. This vast city, compared with the countries that belonged to his dominions, was but as one house. He built it with the assistance of his subjects, yet boasts that he did it *by the might of his power ;* he built it for his security and convenience, yet, as if he had no occasion for it, boasts that he built it purely *for the honour of his majesty.* Note, Pride and self-conceitedness are sins that most easily beset great men, who have great things in the world. They are apt to take the glory to themselves which is due to God only.

III. His punishment for his pride. When he was thus strutting, and vaunting himself, and adoring his own shadow, *while the* proud *word was in the king's mouth* the powerful word came from heaven, by which he was immediately deprived, 1. Of his honour as a king : *The kingdom has departed from thee.* When he thought he had erected impregnable bulwarks for the preserving of his kingdom, now, in an instant, it *has departed from him ;* when he thought it so well guarded that none could take it from him, behold, it departs of itself. As soon as he becomes utterly incapable to manage it, it is of course taken out of his hands. 2. He is deprived of his honour as a man. He loses his reason, and by that means loses his dominion : *They shall drive thee from men,* v. 32. And it was fulfilled (v. 33) : he was *driven from men the same hour.* On a sudden he fell stark mad, distracted in the highest degree that ever any man was. His understanding and memory were gone, and all the faculties of a rational soul broken, so that he became a perfect brute in the shape of a man. He went naked, and on all four, like a brute, did himself shun the society of reasonable creatures and run wild into the fields and woods, and was driven out by his own servants, who, after some time of trial, despairing of his return to his right mind, abandoned him, and looked after him no more. He had not the spirit of a beast of prey (that of the royal lion), but of the abject and less honourable species, for he was made to *eat grass as oxen ;* and, probably, he did not speak with human voice, but lowed like an ox. Some think that his body was all covered with hair ; however, *the hair* of his head and beard, being never cut nor combed, grew like *eagles' feathers,* and *his nails like birds' claws.* Let us pause a little, and view this miserable spectacle ; and let us receive instruction from it. (1.) Let us see here what a mercy it is to have the use of our reason, how thankful we ought to be for it, and how careful we ought to be not to do any thing which may either provoke God or may have a natural tendency to put us out of the possession of our own souls. Let us learn how to value our own reason, and to pity the case of those that are under the prevailing power of melancholy or distraction, or are delirious, and to be very tender in our censures of them and conduct towards them, for it is a trial common to men, and a case which, some time or other, may be our own. (2.) Let us see here the vanity of human glory and greatness. Is this Nebuchadnezzar the Great? What this despicable animal that is meaner than the poorest beggar? Is this he that looked so glorious on the throne, so formidable in the camp, that had politics enough to subdue and govern kingdoms, and now has not so much sense as to keep his own clothes on his back? *Is this the man that made the earth to tremble, that did shake kingdoms?* Isa. xiv. 16. Never let the *wise man* then *glory in his wisdom,* nor *the mighty man in his strength.* (3.) Let us see here how God resists the proud, and delights to abase them and put contempt upon them. Nebuchadnezzar would be more than a man, and therefore God justly makes him less than a man, and puts him upon a level with the beasts who set up for a rival with his Maker. See Job xl. 11—13.

34 And at the end of the days I Nebuchadnezzar lifted up mine eyes unto heaven, and mine understanding returned unto me, and I blessed the Most High, and I praised and honoured him that liveth for ever, whose dominion *is* an everlasting dominion, and his kingdom *is* from generation to generation: 35 And all the inhabitants of the earth *are* reputed as nothing: and he doeth according to his will in the army of heaven, and *among* the inhabitants of the earth: and none can stay his hand, or say unto him, What doest thou? 36 At the same time my reason returned unto me; and for the glory of my kingdom, mine honour and brightness returned unto me; and my counsellors and my lords sought unto me; and I was established in my kingdom, and excellent majesty was added unto me. 37 Now I Nebuchadnezzar praise and extol and honour the King of heaven, all whose works *are* truth, and his ways judgment: and those that walk in pride he is able to abase.

We have here Nebuchadnezzar's recovery from his distraction, and his return to his right mind, *at the end of the days* prefixed, that is, of the seven years. So long he continued a monument of God's justice and a trophy of his victory over the children of pride, and he was made more so by being struck mad than if he had been in an instant
1052

struck dead with a thunderbolt; yet it was a mercy to him that he was kept alive, for while there is life there is hope that we may yet praise God, as he did here: *At the end of the days* (says he), *I lifted up my eyes unto heaven* (v. 34), looked no longer down towards the earth as a beast, but began to look up as a man. *Os homini sublime dedit—Heaven gave to man an erect countenance.* But there was more in it than this; he looked up as a devout man, as a penitent, as a humble petitioner for mercy, being perhaps never till now made sensible of his own misery. And now,

I. He has the use of his reason so far restored to him that with it he glorifies God, and humbles himself under his mighty hand. He was told that he should continue in that forlorn case till he should know that the Most High rules, and here we have him brought to the knowledge of this: *My understanding returned to me, and I blessed the Most High.* Note, Those may justly be reckoned void of understanding that do not bless and praise God; nor do men ever rightly use their reason till they begin to be religious, nor live as men till they live to the glory of God. As reason is the substratum or subject of religion (so that creatures which have no reason are not capable of religion), so religion is the crown and glory of reason, and we have our reason in vain, and shall one day wish we had never had it, if we do not glorify God with it. This was the first act of Nebuchadnezzar's returning reason; and, when this became the employment of it, he was then, and not till then, qualified for all the other enjoyments of it. And till he was for a great while disabled to exercise it in other things he never was brought to apply it to this, which is the great end for which our reason is given us. His folly was the means whereby he became wise; he was not recovered by his dream of this judgment (that was soon forgotten like a dream), but he is made to feel it, and then his *ear is opened to discipline.* To bring him to himself, he must first be *beside himself.* And by this it appears that what good thoughts there were in his mind, and what good work was wrought there, were not of himself (for he was not his own man), but it was the gift of God. Let us see what Nebuchadnezzar is now at length effectually brought to the acknowledgment of; and we may learn from it what to believe concerning God. 1. That the *most high* God *lives for ever,* and his being knows neither change nor period, for he has it of himself. His flatterers often complimented him with, *O king! live for ever.* But he is now convinced that no king lives for ever, but the God of Israel only, who is still the same. 2. That his kingdom is like himself, *everlasting,* and his *dominion from generation to generation;* there is no succession, no revolution, in his kingdom. As he lives, so he reigns, for ever, and of his government there is no end. 3. That *all nations* before him are *as nothing.* He has no need of them; he makes no account of them. The greatest of men, in comparison with him, are less than nothing. Those that think highly of God think meanly of themselves. 4. That his kingdom is universal, and both *the armies of heaven* and *the inhabitants of the earth* are his subjects, and under his check and control. Both angels and men are employed by him, and are accountable to him; the highest angel is not above his command, nor the meanest of the children of men beneath his cognizance. The angels of heaven are his armies, the inhabitants of the earth his tenants. 5. That his power is irresistible, and his sovereignty uncontrollable, for he *does according to his will,* according to his design and purpose, according to his decree and counsel; whatever he pleases that he does; whatever he appoints that he performs; and none can resist his will, change his counsel, nor *stay his hand, nor say unto him, What doest thou?* None can arraign his proceedings, enquire into the meaning of them, nor demand a reason for them. Woe to him that strives with his Maker, that says to him, *What doest thou?* Or, *Why doest thou so?* 6. That every thing which God does is well done: His *works are truth,* for they all agree with his word. *His ways are judgment,* both wise and righteous, exactly consonant to the rules both of prudence and equity, and no fault is to be found with them. 7. That the has power to humble the haughtiest of his enemies that act in contradiction to him or competition with him: *Those that walk in pride he is able to abase* (v. 37); he is able to deal with those that are most confident of their own sufficiency to contend with him.

II. He has the use of his reason so far restored to him as with it to re-enjoy himself, and the pleasures of his re-established prosperity (v. 36): *At the same time my reason returned to me;* he had said before (v. 34) that his *understanding returned* to him, and here he mentions it again, for the use of our reason is a mercy we can never be sufficiently thankful for. Now his *lords sought to him;* he did not need to seek to them, and they soon perceived, not only that he had recovered his reason and was fit to rule, but that he had recovered it with advantage, and was more fit to rule than ever. It is probable that the dream and the interpretation of it were well known, and much talked of, at court; and the former part of the prediction being fulfilled, that he should go distracted, they doubted not but that, according to the prediction, he should come to himself again at seven years' end, and, in confidence of that, when the time that expired they were ready to receive him; and then *his honour and brightness returned to him,* the same that he had before his madness seized him. He is now established in his kingdom as firmly as if there had been no interruption given

him. *He becomes a fool, that he may be wise,* wiser than ever; and he that but the other day was in the depth of disgrace and ignominy has now *excellent majesty added to him,* beyond what he had when he went from kingdom to kingdom conquering and to conquer. Note, 1. When men are brought to honour God, particularly by a penitent confession of sin and a believing acknowledgment of his sovereignty, then, and not till then, they may expect that God will put honour upon them, will not only restore them to the dignity they lost by the sin of the first Adam, but *add excellent majesty to them* from the righteousness and grace of the second Adam. 2. Afflictions shall last no longer than till they have done the work for which they were sent. When this prince is brought to own God's dominion over him he is then restored to a dominion over himself. 3. All the accounts we take and give of God's dealing with us ought to conclude with praises to him. When Nebuchadnezzar is restored to his kingdom he *praises, and extols, and honours the King of heaven* (v. 37), before he applies himself to his secular business. Therefore we have our reason, that we may be in a capacity of praising him, and therefore our prosperity, that we may have cause to praise him.

It was not long after this that Nebuchadnezzar ended his life and reign. Abydenus, quoted by Eusebius (*Præp. Evang.* i. 9), reports, from the tradition of the Chaldeans, that upon his death-bed he foretold the taking of Babylon by Cyrus. Whether he continued in the same good mind that here he seems to have been in we are not told, nor does any thing appear to the contrary but that he did: and, if so great a *blasphemer and persecutor* did find mercy, he was not the last. And, if our charity may reach so far as to hope he did, we must admire free grace, by which he lost his wits for a while, that he might save his soul for ever.

CHAP. V.

The destruction of the kingdom of Babylon had been long and often foretold when it was at a distance; in this chapter we have it accomplished, and a prediction of it the very same night that it was accomplished. Belshazzar now reigned in Babylon; some compute he had reigned seventeen years, others but three; we have here the story of his exit and the period of his kingdom. We must know that about two years before this Cyrus king of Persia, a growing monarch, came against Babylon with a great army; Belshazzar met him, fought him, and was routed by him in a pitched battle. He and his scattered forces retired into the city, where Cyrus besieged them. They were very secure, because the river Euphrates was their bulwark, and they had twenty years' provision in the city; but in the second year of the siege he took it, as is here related. We have in this chapter, I. The riotous, idolatrous, sacrilegious feast which Belshazzar made, in which he filled up the measure of his iniquity, ver. 1—4. II. The alarm given him in the midst of his jollity by a hand-writing on the wall, which none of his wise men could read or tell him the meaning of, ver. 5—9. III. The interpretation of the mystical characters by Daniel, who was at length brought in to him, and dealt plainly with him, and showed him his doom written, ver. 10—28. IV. The immediate accomplishment of the interpretation in the slaying of the king and seizing of the kingdom, ver. 30, 31.

BELSHAZZAR the king made a great feast to a thousand of his lords, and drank wine before the thousand. 2 Belshazzar, whiles he tasted the wine, commanded to bring the golden and silver vessels which his father Nebuchadnezzar had taken out of the temple which *was* in Jerusalem; that the king, and his princes, his wives, and his concubines, might drink therein. 3 Then they brought the golden vessels that were taken out of the temple of the house of God which *was* at Jerusalem; and the king, and his princes, his wives, and his concubines, drank in them. 4 They drank wine, and praised the gods of gold, and of silver, of brass, of iron, of wood, and of stone. 5 In the same hour came forth fingers of a man's hand, and wrote over against the candlestick upon the plaster of the wall of the king's palace: and the king saw the part of the hand that wrote. 6 Then the king's countenance was changed, and his thoughts troubled him, so that the joints of his loins were loosed, and his knees smote one against another. 7 The king cried aloud to bring in the astrologers, the Chaldeans, and the soothsayers. *And* the king spake, and said to the wise *men* of Babylon, Whosoever shall read this writing, and show me the interpretation thereof, shall be clothed with scarlet, and *have* a chain of gold about his neck, and shall be the third ruler in the kingdom. 8 Then came in all the king's wise *men :* but they could not read the writing, nor make known to the king the interpretation thereof. 9 Then was king Belshazzar greatly troubled, and his countenance was changed in him, and his lords were astonied.

We have here Belshazzar the king very gay, but all of a sudden very gloomy, and in straits in the fulness of his sufficiency. See how he affronts God, and God affrights him; and wait what will be the issue of this contest; and whether he that hardened his heart against God prospered.

I. See how the king affronted God, and put contempt upon him. He *made a great feast,* or *banquet of wine;* probably it was some anniversary solemnity, in honour of his birth-day or coronation-day, or in honour of some of their idols. Historians say that Cyrus, who was now with his army besieging Babylon, knew of this feast, and presuming that they then would be off their guard, *somno vinoque sepulti—buried in sleep*

and wine, took that opportunity to attack the city, and so with the more ease made himself master of it. Belshazzar upon this occasion invited *a thousand of his lords* to come and drink with him. Perhaps they were such as had signalized themselves in defence of the city against the besiegers; or these were his great council of war, with whom, when they had well drunk, he would advise what was further to be done. And they were to look upon it as a great favour that he *drank wine before* them, for it was the pride of those eastern kings to be seldom seen. He drank wine before them, for he made this feast, as Ahasuerus did, to show the *honour of his majesty.* Now in this sumptuous feast, 1. He put an affront upon the providence of God and bade defiance to his judgments. His city was now besieged; a powerful enemy was at his gates; his life and kingdom lay at stake. In all this the hand of the Lord had gone out against him, and by it he called him to *weeping, and mourning, and girding with sackcloth.* God's voice cried in the city, as Jonah to Nineveh, *Yet forty days,* or fewer, *and Babylon shall be destroyed.* He should therefore, like the king of Nineveh, have proclaimed a fast; but, as one resolved to walk contrary to God, he proclaims a feast, and behold *joy and gladness, slaying oxen, killing sheep, eating flesh, and drinking wine,* as if he dared the Almighty to do his worst, Isa. xxii. 12, 13. To show how little fear he had of being forced to surrender, for want of provisions, he spent thus extravagantly. Note, Security and sensuality are sad presages of approaching ruin. Those that will not be warned by the judgments of God may expect to be wounded by them. 2. He put an affront upon the temple of God, and bade defiance to his sanctuary, *v.* 2. *While he tasted the wine, he commanded to bring the vessels* of the temple, that they might drink in them. When he tasted how rich and fine the wine was, " O," said he, " it is a pity but we should have holy vessels to drink such delicious wine as this in," which was looked upon as a piece of wit, and, to carry on the humour, the vessels of the temple were immediately sent for. Nay, there seems to have been something more in it than a frolic, and that it was done in a malicious despite to the God of Israel. The heart of his people was very much upon these sacred vessels, as appears from Jer. xxvii. 16, 18. Their principal care, at their return, was about these, Ezra i. 7. Now, we may suppose, they had an expectation of their deliverance approaching, reckoning the seventy years of their captivity near a period ; and some of them might perhaps have given out some words to that purport, that shortly they should have the vessels of the sanctuary restored to them, in defiance of which Belshazzar here proclaims them to be his own, will keep them in store no longer, but will make use of them among his own plate. Note, That mirth is sinful indeed, and fills the measure of men's iniquity apace, which profanes sacred things and jests with them. This ripened Babylon for ruin—that no songs would serve them but the *songs of Zion* (Ps. cxxxvii. 3), no vessels but the vessels of the sanctuary. Let those who thus sacrilegiously alienate what is dedicated to God and his honour know that he *will not be mocked.* 3. He put an affront upon God himself, and bade defiance to his deity; for *they drank wine, and praised the gods of gold and silver, v. 4.* They gave that glory to images, the work of their own hands and creatures of their own fancy, which is due to the true and living God only. They praised them either with sacrifices offered to them or with songs sung in honour of them. When their heads were giddy, and their hearts merry, with wine, they were in the fittest frame to *praise the gods of gold and silver, wood and stone;* for one would think that men in their senses, who had the command of a clear and sober thought, could not be guilty of so gross an absurdity; they must be intoxicated ere they could be so infatuated. Drunken worshippers, who are not men, but beasts, are the most proper for the service of dunghill deities, that are not gods, but devils. *They have erred through wine,* Isa. xxviii. 7. They drank wine, and praised their idol-gods, as if they had been the founders of their feast and the givers of all good things to them. Or, when they were drinking wine, they praised their gods by drinking healths to them; and the king *drank wine before* them (*v.* 1), that is, he began the health, first to this god, and then to the other, till they went through the *bead-roll* or *farrago* of them, those of *wood and stone* not excepted. Note, Immorality and impiety, vice and profaneness, strengthen the hands and advance the interests one of another. Drunken frolics were an introduction to idolatry, and then idolatrous healths were a shoeing-horn to further drunkenness.

II. See how God affrighted the king, and struck a terror upon him. Belshazzar and his lords are in the midst of their revels, the cups going round apace, and all upon the merry pin, drinking confusion, it may be, to Cyrus and his army, and roaring out huzzas, in confidence of the speedy raising of the siege; but the hour had come when that must be fulfilled which had been long ago said of the king of Babylon, when his city should be besieged by the Persians and Medes, Isa. xxi. 2—4. *The night of my pleasures has he turned into fear to me.* The mirth of this ball at court must be spoiled, and a damp cast upon their jollity, though the king himself be master of the revels; immediately, when God speaks the word, we have him and all his guests in the utmost confusion, and the end of their mirth is heaviness. 1. There appear the *fingers of a man's hand writing on the plaster of the wall,* before the king's face (*v.* 5), "the angel Gabriel," say the rabbin, "directing these fingers and writing by them." "That divine hand" (says a rabbi of our own, Dr. Lightfoot) "that had written the two tables for a law to his people now writes the doom of Babel and Belshazzar upon the wall." Here was nothing sent to frighten them which made a noise, or threatened their lives, no claps of thunder nor flashes of lightning, no destroying angel with his sword drawn in his hand, only a pen in the hand, writing upon the wall, *over-against the candlestick,* where they might all see it by the light of their own candle. Note, God's written word is sufficient to put the proudest boldest sinners into a fright, when he is pleased to give it the setting on. The king saw *the part of the hand that wrote,* but saw not the person whose hand it was, which made the thing more frightful. Note, What we see of God, the part of the hand that writes in the book of the creatures and the book of the scriptures *(Lo, these are parts of his ways,* Job xxvi. 14), may serve to possess us with awful thoughts concerning that of God which we do not see. If this be *the finger of God,* what is his arm made bare? And what is he? 2. The king is immediately seized with a panic fear (*v.* 6): *His countenance was changed* (his colour went and came); *the joints of his loins were loosed,* so that he had no strength in them, but was struck with a pain in his back, as is usual in a great fright; *his knees smote one against another,* so violently did he tremble like an aspen leaf. But what was the matter? Why is he in such a fright? He perceives not what is written, and how does he know but it may be some happy presage of deliverance to him and to his kingdom? But the business was *his thoughts troubled him;* his own guilty conscience flew in his face, and told him that he had no reason to expect any good news from Heaven, and that the hand of an angel could write nothing but terror to him. He that knew himself liable to the justice of God immediately concluded this to be an arrest in his name, a summons to appear before him. Note, God can soon awaken the most secure and make the heart of the stoutest sinner to tremble; and there needs no more to do it than to let loose his own thoughts upon him; they will soon play the tyrant, and give him trouble enough. 3. The wise men of Babylon are immediately called in, to see what they can make of this writing upon the wall, *v.* 7. The king *cried aloud,* as one in haste, as one in earnest, to bring the whole college of magicians, to try if they can *read this writing,* and *show the interpretation of it;* for the king and all his lords cannot pretend to it, it is out of their sphere. The study of divine revelation (such as they had, or thought they had) and converse with the world of spirits were by the heathen confined to one profession, and no other meddled with it; but what is written to us by the finger of God is legible to all; whoever will may read the mind of God in the scriptures. To engage these wise men to exert the utmost of their skill in this matter, and provoke them to an emulation in the attempt, he promised that whoever would give him a satisfactory account of this writing should be dignified with the highest honours of the court. He knew what these pretenders to wisdom aimed at, and what would please them, and therefore promised them a *scarlet robe* and a *gold chain*, glorious things in the eyes of those that know no better. Nay, he should be *primus par regni* —*chief minister of state, the third ruler* in the kingdom, next to the king and his heir apparent. 4. The king is disappointed in his expectations from them; they can none of them *read the writing*, much less interpret it (*v.* 8), which increases the king's confusion, *v.* 9. He likes the thing yet worse and worse, and fears that mischief is towards him. *His lords* also, that had been partners with him in his jollity, are now sharers with him in his terrors; they also were *astonished* and at their wits' end; and neither their numbers nor their refreshment by wine would serve to keep up their spirits. The reason why the wise men could not read the writing was not because it was written in any language or characters unknown to them, but God either cast a mist before their eyes or put such confusion upon their spirits that they could not read it, that the honour of expounding this mystical writing might be reserved for Daniel. Note, The terror of an awakened convinced conscience may justly be increased by the utter insufficiency of all creatures to give it ease or satisfaction.

10 *Now* the queen by reason of the words of the king and his lords came into the banquet-house: *and* the queen spake and said, O king, live for ever: let not thy thoughts trouble thee, nor let thy countenance be changed: 11 There is a man in thy kingdom, in whom *is* the spirit of the holy gods; and in the days of thy father light and understanding and wisdom, like the wisdom of the gods, was found in him; whom the king Nebuchadnezzar thy father, the king, *I say*, thy father, made master of the magicians, astrologers, Chaldeans, *and* soothsayers; 12 Forasmuch as an excellent spirit, and knowledge, and understanding, interpreting of dreams, and showing of hard sentences, and dissolving of doubts, were found in the same Daniel, whom the king named Belteshazzar: now let Daniel be called, and

1056

he will show the interpretation. 13 Then was Daniel brought in before the king. *And* the king spake, and said unto Daniel, *Art* thou that Daniel, which *art* of the children of the captivity of Judah, whom the king my father brought out of Jewry? 14 I have even heard of thee, that the spirit of the gods *is* in thee, and *that* light and understanding and excellent wisdom is found in thee. 15 And now the wise *men*, the astrologers, have been brought in before me, that they should read this writing, and make known unto me the interpretation thereof: but they could not show the interpretation of the thing: 16 And I have heard of thee, that thou canst make interpretations, and dissolve doubts: now if thou canst read the writing, and make known to me the interpretation thereof, thou shalt be clothed with scarlet, and *have* a chain of gold about thy neck, and shalt be the third ruler in the kingdom. 17 Then Daniel answered and said before the king, Let thy gifts be to thyself, and give thy rewards to another; yet I will read the writing unto the king, and make known to him the interpretation. 18 O thou king, the most high God gave Nebuchadnezzar thy father a kingdom, and majesty, and glory, and honour: 19 And for the majesty that he gave him, all people, nations, and languages, trembled and feared before him: whom he would he slew; and whom he would he kept alive; and whom he would he set up; and whom he would he put down. 20 But when his heart was lifted up, and his mind hardened in pride, he was deposed from his kingly throne, and they took his glory from him: 21 And he was driven from the sons of men; and his heart was made like the beasts, and his dwelling *was* with the wild asses: they fed him with grass like oxen, and his body was wet with the dew of heaven; till he knew that the most high God ruled in the kingdom of men, and *that* he appointeth over it whomsoever he will. 22 And thou his son, O Belshazzar, hast not humbled thine heart, though thou knewest all this; 23 But hast lifted up thyself against the Lord of heaven; and they have brought the vessels of his house before thee, and thou, and thy lords, thy wives, and thy concubines, have drunk wine in them; and thou hast praised the gods of silver, and gold, of brass, iron, wood, and stone, which see not, nor hear, nor know: and the God in whose hand thy breath *is*, and whose *are* all thy ways, hast thou not glorified: 24 Then was the part of the hand sent from him; and this writing was written. 25 And this *is* the writing that was written, MENE, MENE, TEKEL, UPHARSIN. 26 This *is* the interpretation of the thing: MENE; God hath numbered thy kingdom, and finished it. 27 TE-KEL; thou art weighed in the balances, and art found wanting. 28 PERES; thy kingdom is divided, and given to the Medes and Persians. 29 Then commanded Belshazzar, and they clothed Daniel with scarlet, and *put* a chain of gold about his neck, and made a proclamation concerning him, that he should be the third ruler in the kingdom.

Here is, I. The information given to the king, by the queen-mother, concerning Daniel, how fit he was to be consulted in this difficult case. It is supposed that this queen was the widow of Evil-Merodach, and was that famous Nitocris whom Herodotus mentions as a woman of extraordinary prudence. She was not present at the feast, as the king's *wives and concubines were* (v. 2); it was not agreeable to her age and gravity to keep a merry night. But, tidings of the fright which the king and his lords were put into being brought to her apartment, she came herself to the banqueting-house, to recommend to the king a physician for his melancholy. She entreated him not to be discouraged by the insufficiency of his wise men to solve this riddle, for that there was *a man in his kingdom* that had more than once helped his grandfather at such a dead lift, and, no doubt, could help him, *v.* 11, 12. She could not undertake to read the writing herself, but directed him to one that could; let *Daniel be called* now, who should have been called first. Now observe, 1. The high character she gives of Daniel: He is a *man in whom is the spirit of the holy gods*, who has something in him more than human, not only the *spirit of a man*, which, in all, is the *candle of the Lord*, but a divine spirit. Accord-

ing to the language of her country and reli-gion, she could not give a higher encomium of any man; she speaks honourably of him as a man that had, (1) An admirably good head: *Light, and understanding, and wisdom, like the wisdom of the gods, were found in him.* Such an insight had he into things secret, and such a foresight of things to come, that it was evident he was divinely inspired; he had *knowledge* and *understanding* beyond all the other wise men for *interpreting dreams*, explaining enigmas or hard sentences, unty-ing knots, and resolving doubts. Solomon had a wonderful sagacity of this kind; but it should seem that in these things Daniel had more of an immediate divine direction. *Behold, a greater than Solomon* himself *is here.* Yet what was the wisdom of them both compared with the treasures of wisdom hidden in Christ? (2.) He had an admira-bly good heart: *An excellent spirit was found in him,* which was a great ornament to his wisdom and knowledge, and qualified him to receive that gift; for God *gives to a man that is good in his sight wisdom, and knowledge, and joy.* He was of a humble, holy, heavenly spirit, had a devout and gracious spirit, a spirit of zeal for the glory of God and the good of men. This was indeed an excellent spirit. 2. The account she gives of the re-spect that Nebuchadnezzar had for him; he was much in his favour, and was preferred by him: "*The king thy father*" (that is, thy grandfather, but even to many generations Nebuchadnezzar might well be called the fa-ther of that royal family, for he it was that raised it to such a pitch of grandeur), "*the king*, I say, *thy father, made him master of the magicians.*" Perhaps Belshazzar had some-times, in his pride, spoken slightly of Nebu-chadnezzar, and his politics, and the methods of his government, and the ministers he em-ployed, and thought himself wiser than he; and therefore his mother harps upon that. "*The king*, I say, *thy father*, to whose good management all thou hast is owing, he pro-nounced him chief of, and gave him domi-nion over, all the wise men of Babylon, and *named him Belteshazzar*, according to the name of his god, thinking thereby to put ho-nour upon him;" but Daniel, by constantly making use of his Jewish name himself (which he resolved to keep, in token of his faithful adherence to his religion), had worn out that name; only the queen-dowager re-membered it, otherwise he was generally called *Daniel.* Note, It is a very good office to revive the remembrance of the good services of worthy men, who are themselves modest, and willing that they should be for-gotten. 3. The motion she makes concern-ing him: *Let Daniel be called, and he will show the interpretation.* By this it appears that Daniel was now forgotten at court. Belshazzar was a stranger to him, knew not that he had such a jewel in his kingdom. With the new king there came in a new ministry, and the old one was laid aside. Note, There are a great many valuable men, and such as might be made very useful, that lie long buried in obscurity, and some that have done eminent services that live to be overlooked and taken no notice of ; but, whatever men are, God is not unrighteous to forget the services done to his kingdom. Daniel, being turned out of his place, lived privately, and sought not any opportunity to come into notice again ; yet he lived near the court and within call, though Babylon was now besieged, that he might be ready, if there were occasion, to do any good office, by what interest he had among the great ones, for the children of his people. But Providence so ordered it that now, just at the fall of that monarchy, he should by the queen's means be brought to court again, that he might lie there ready for preferment in the ensuing government. Thus do *the righteous shine forth out of obscurity*, and *before honour is humility*.

II. The introducing of Daniel to the king, and his request to him to read and expound the writing. Daniel was *brought in before the king*, *v.* 13. He was now nearly ninety years of age, so that his years, and honours, and former preferments, might have entitled him to a free admission into the king's presence ; yet he was willing to be conducted in, as a stranger, by the master of the ceremonies. Note, 1. The king asks, with an air of haughtiness : *Art thou that Daniel who art of the children of the captivity ?* Being a Jew, and a captive, he was loth to be beholden to him if he could help it. 2. He tells him what an encomium he had heard of him (*v.* 14), *that the spirit of the gods was in him ;* and he had sent for him to try whether he deserved so high a character or no. 3. He acknowledges that all the wise men of Babylon were baffled ; they could not *read this writing*, nor *show the interpretation*, *v.* 16. But, 4. He promises him the same rewards that he had promised them if he would do it, *v.* 16. It was strange that the magicians, when now, and in Nebuchadnezzar's time, once and again, they were nonplussed, did not attempt something to save their credit ; if they had with a good assurance said, " This is the meaning of such a dream, such a writing," who could disprove them ? But God so ordered it that they had nothing at all to say, as, when Christ was born, the heathen oracles were struck dumb.

III. The interpretation which Daniel gave of these mystic characters, which was so far from easing the king of his fears that we may suppose it increased them rather. Daniel was now in years, and Belshazzar was young ; and therefore he seems to take a greater liberty of dealing plainly and roundly with him than he had done upon the like occasions with Nebuchadnezzar. In reproving any man, especially great men, there is need of wisdom to consider all circumstances ; for

1058

they are *the reproofs of instruction* that are *the way of life.* In Daniel's discourse here, 1. He undertakes to read the writing which gave them this alarm, and to show them the interpretation of it, *v.* 17. He slights the offer he made him of rewards, is not pleased that it was mentioned, for he is not one of those that *divine for money ;* what gratuities Nebuchadnezzar gave him afterwards he gladly accepted, but he scorned to bargain for them, or to read the *writing to the king* for and in consideration of such and such honours promised him. No : " *Let thy gifts be to thyself*, for they will not be long thine, and *give thy fee to another*, to any of the wise men whom thou wouldst have most wished to earn it ; I value it not." Daniel sees his kingdom now at its last gasp, and therefore looks with contempt upon his gifts and rewards. And thus should we despise all the gifts and rewards that this world can give did we see, as we may by faith, its final period hastening on. Let it give its perishing gifts to another ; there are better gifts which we have our eyes and hearts upon ; but let us do our duty in the world, do it all the real service we can, read God's writing to it in a profession of religion, and by an agreeable conversation make known the interpretation of it, and then trust God for his gifts, his rewards, in comparison with which all the world can give is mere trash and trifles.

2. He largely recounts to the king God's dealings with his father Nebuchadnezzar, which were intended for instruction and warning to him, *v.* 18, 21. This is not intended for a flourish or an amusement, but is a necessary preliminary to the interpretation of the writing. Note, That we may understand aright what God is doing with us, it is of use to us to review what he has done with others.

(1.) He describes the great dignity and power to which the divine Providence had advanced Nebuchadnezzar, *v.* 18, 19. He had *a kingdom, and majesty, and glory, and honour*, for aught we know, above what any heathen prince ever had before him ; he thought that he got his glory by his own extraordinary conduct and courage, and ascribed his successes to a projecting active genius of his own ; but Daniel tells him who now enjoyed what he had laboured for that it was the *most high God*, the *God of gods and Lord of kings* (as Nebuchadnezzar himself had called him), that gave him *that kingdom*, that vast dominion, that majesty wherewith he presided in the affairs of it, and that *glory and honour* which by his prosperous management he acquired. Note, Whatever degree of outward prosperity any arrive at, they must own that it is of God's giving, not their own getting. Let it never be said, *My might, and the power of my hand, have gotten me this wealth*, this preferment ; but let it always be remembered that it is *God that gives men power to get wealth*, and gives success to their endeavours. Now the power which God gave to Nebuchadnezzar is here described to be very great in respect both of ability and of authority. [1.] His ability was so strong that it was irresistible; such was the majesty that God gave him, so numerous were the forces he had at command, and such an admirable dexterity he had at commanding them, that, which way soever his sword turned, it prospered. He could captivate and subdue nations by threatening them, without striking a stroke, for *all people trembled and feared before him*, and would compound with him for their lives upon any terms. See what force is, and what the fear of it does. It is that by which the brutal part of the world, even of the world of mankind, both governs and is governed. [2.] His authority was so absolute that it was uncontrollable. The power which was allowed him, which descended upon him, or which, at least, he assumed, was without contradiction, was absolute and despotic, none shared with him either in the legislative or in the executive part of it. In dispensing punishments he condemned or acquitted at pleasure: *Whom he would he slew, and whom he would he saved alive*, though both were equally innocent or equally guilty. The *jus vitæ et necis—the power of life and death* was entirely in his hand. In dispensing rewards he granted or denied preferment at pleasure: *Whom he would he set up, and whom he would he put down*, merely for a humour, and without giving a reason so much as to himself; but it is all *ex mero motu—of his own good pleasure*, and *stat pro ratione voluntas—his will stands for a reason.* Such was the constitution of the eastern monarchies, such the manner of their kings.

(2.) He sets before him the sins which Nebuchadnezzar had been guilty of, whereby he had provoked God against him. [1.] He behaved insultingly towards those that were under him, and grew tyrannical and oppressive. The description given of his power intimates his abuse of his power, and that he was directed in what he did by humour and passion, not by reason and equity; so that he often condemned the innocent and acquitted the guilty, both which are an *abomination to the Lord.* He deposed men of merit and preferred unworthy men, to the great detriment of the public, and for this he was accountable to the most high God, that gave him his power. Note, It is a very hard and rare thing for men to have an absolute arbitrary power, and not to make an ill use of it. Camden has a distich of Giraldus, wherein he speaks of it as a rare instance, concerning our king Henry II. of England, that never any man had so much power and did so little hurt with it.

Glorior hoc uno, quòd nunquam vidimus unum,
  Nec potuisse magis, nec nocuisse minus—

Of him I can say, exulting, that with the same power to do harm no one was ever more inoffensive.

But that was not all. [2.] He behaved insolently towards the God above him, and grew proud and haughty (v. 20): *His heart was lifted up*, and there his sin and ruin began; his *mind* was *hardened* in pride, hardened against the commands of God and his judgments; he was wilful and obstinate, and neither the word of God nor his rod made any lasting impression upon him. Note, Pride is a sin that hardens the heart in all other sin and renders the means of repentance and reformation ineffectual.

(3.) He reminds him of the judgments of God that were brought upon him for his pride and obstinacy, how he was deprived of his reason, and so *deposed from his kingly throne* (v. 20), *driven from among men*, to *dwell with the wild asses, v. 21.* He that would not govern his subjects by rules of reason had not reason sufficient for the government of himself. Note, Justly does God deprive men of their reason when they become unreasonable and will not use it, and of their power when they become oppressive and use it ill. He continued like a brute till *he knew* and embraced that first principle of religion, *That the most high God rules.* And it is rather by religion than reason that man is distinguished from, and dignified above, the beasts; and it is more his honour to be a subject to the supreme Creator than to be lord of the inferior creatures. Note, Kings must know, or shall be made to know, that the most high God rules in their kingdoms (that is an *imperium in imperio—an empire within an empire*, not to be excepted against), and that he appoints over them whomsoever he will. As he makes heirs, so he makes princes.

3. In God's name, he exhibits articles of impeachment against Belshazzar. Before he reads him his doom, from the hand-writing on the wall, he shows him his crime, that God may be *justified when he speaks, and clear when he judges.* Now that which he lays to his charge is, (1.) That he had not taken warning by the judgments of God upon his father (v. 22): *Thou his son, O Belshazzar! hast not humbled thy heart, though thou knewest all this.* Note, It is a great offence to God if our hearts be not humbled before him to comply both with his precepts and with his providences, humbled by repentance, obedience, and patience; nay, he expects from the greatest of men that their hearts should be humbled before him, by an acknowledgment that, great as they are, to him they are accountable. And it is a great aggravation of the unhumbledness of our hearts when we know enough to humble them but do not consider and improve it, particularly when we know how others have been broken that would not bend, how others have fallen that would not stoop, and yet we continue stiff and inflexible. It makes the sin of children the more heinous if they tread in the steps of their parents' wickedness, though

they have seen how dearly it has cost them, and how pernicious the consequences of it have been. Do we know this, do we know all this, and yet are we not humbled? (2.) That he had affronted God more impudently than Nebuchadnezzar himself had done, witness the revels of this very night, in the midst of which he was seized with this horror (*v.* 23): " *Thou hast lifted up thyself against the Lord of heaven,* hast swelled with rage against him, and taken up arms against his crown and dignity, in this particular instance, that thou hast profaned the *vessels of his house,* and made the utensils of his sanctuary instruments of thy iniquity, and, in an actual designed contempt of him, hast *praised the gods of silver and gold, which see not, nor hear, nor know* any thing, as if they were to be preferred before the God that sees, and hears, and knows every thing." Sinners that are resolved to go on in sin are well enough pleased with gods that *neither see, nor hear, nor know,* for then they may sin securely; but they will find, to their confusion, that though those are the gods they choose those are not the gods they must be judged by, but one to whom *all things are naked and open.* (3.) That he had not answered the end of his creation and maintenance : *The God in whose hand thy breath is, and whose are all thy ways, hast thou not glorified.* This is a general charge, which stands good against us all; let us consider how we shall answer it. Observe, [1.] Our dependence upon God as our Creator, preserver, benefactor, owner, and ruler; not only from his hand our breath was at first, but *in his hand our breath is* still; it is he that *holds our souls in life,* and, if he *take away our breath, we die.* Our times being *in his hand,* so is our breath, by which our times are measured. *In him we live, and move, and have our being;* we live by him, live upon him, and cannot live without him. *The way of man is not in himself,* not at his own command, at his own disposal, *but his are all our ways;* for our hearts are in his hand, and so are the hearts of all men, even of kings, who seem to act most as free-agents. [2.] Our duty to God, in consideration of this dependence; we ought to glorify him, to devote ourselves to his honour and employ ourselves in his service, to make it our care to please him and our business to praise him. [3.] Our default in this duty, notwithstanding that dependence; we have not done it; for we have *all sinned, and have come short of the glory of God.* This is the indictment against Belshazzar; there needs no proof, it is made good by the notorious evidence of the fact, and his own conscience cannot but plead guilty to it. And therefore,

4. He now proceeds to read the sentence, as he found it *written upon the wall:* "*Then*" (says Daniel) " when thou hast come to such a height of impiety as thus to trample upon the most sacred things, *then* when thou wast

1060

in the midst of thy sacrilegious idolatrous feast, then was *the part of the hand,* the writing fingers, sent *from him,* from that God whom thou didst so daringly affront, and who had borne so long with thee, but would bear no longer; he *sent them,* and *this writing,* thou now seest, *was written, v.* 24. It is he that now *writes bitter things against thee,* and *makes thee to possess thy iniquities,*" Job xiii. 26. Note, As the sin of sinners is written in the book of God's omniscience, so the doom of sinners is written in the book of God's law; and the day is coming when those *books shall be opened,* and they shall be judged by them. Now the writing was, *Mene, Mene, Tekel, Upharsin, v.* 25. It is well that we have an authentic exposition of these words annexed, else we could make little of them, so concise are they; the signification of them is, *He has numbered, he has weighed, and they divide.* The Chaldean wise men, because they knew not that there is but one God only, could not understand who this *He* should be, and for that reason (some think) the writing puzzled them. (1.) *Mene;* that is repeated, for the thing is certain—*Mene, mene;* that signifies, both in Hebrew and Chaldee, *He has numbered and finished,* which Daniel explains thus (*v.* 26): " *God has numbered thy kingdom,* the years and days of the continuance of it; these were numbered in the counsel of God, and now they are finished; the term has expired for and during which thou wast to hold it, and now it must be surrendered. Here is an end of thy kingdom." (2.) *Tekel;* that signifies, in Chaldee, *Thou art weighed,* and, in Hebrew, *Thou art too light.* So Dr. Lightfoot. For this king and his actions are weighed in the just and unerring balances of divine equity. God does as perfectly know his true character as the goldsmith knows the weight of that which he has weighed in the nicest scales. God does not give judgment against him till he has first pondered his actions, and considered the merits of his case. " But thou art *found wanting,* unworthy to have such a trust lodged in thee, a vain, light, empty man, a man of no weight or consideration." (3.) *Upharsin,* which should be rendered, *and Pharsin,* or *Peres. Parsin,* in Hebrew, signifies the *Persians; Paresin,* in Chaldee, signifies *dividing;* Daniel puts both together (*v.* 28): " *Thy kingdom is divided,* is rent from thee, and *given to the Medes and Persians,* as a prey to be divided among them." Now this may, without any force, be applied to the doom of sinners. *Mene, Tekel, Peres,* may easily be made to signify *death, judgment,* and *hell.* At death, the sinner's days are *numbered* and *finished;* after death the judgment, when he will be *weighed in the balance and found wanting;* and after judgment the sinner will be *cut asunder,* and given as a prey to the devil and his angels. Daniel does not here give Belshazzar such advice and encouragement to repent as he had given Nebuchadnezzar, because he saw the decree had gone forth and he would not be allowed any space to repent.

One would have thought that Belshazzar would be exasperated against Daniel, and, seeing his own case desperate, would be in a rage against him. But he was so far convicted by his own conscience of the reasonableness of all he said that he objected nothing against it; but, on the contrary, gave Daniel the reward he promised him, put on him the *scarlet gown* and the *gold chain*, and proclaimed him the *third ruler in the kingdom* (*v.* 29), because he would be as good as his word, and because it was not Daniel's fault if the exposition of the hand-writing was not such as he desired. Note, Many show great respect to God's prophets who yet have no regard to his word. Daniel did not value these titles and ensigns of honour, yet would not refuse them, because they were tokens of his prince's good-will: but we have reason to think that he received them with a smile, foreseeing how soon they would all wither with him that bestowed them. They were like Jonah's gourd, which came up in a night and perished in a night, and therefore it was folly for him to be *exceedingly glad* of them.

30 In that night was Belshazzar the king of the Chaldeans slain. 31 And Darius the Median took the kingdom, *being* about threescore and two years old.

Here is, 1. The death of the king. Reason enough he had to tremble, for he was just falling into the hands of the *king of terrors, v.* 30. *In that night,* when his heart was merry with wine, the besiegers broke into the city, aimed at the palace; there they found the king, and gave him his death's wound. He could not find any place so secret as to conceal him, or so strong as to protect him. Heathen writers speak of Cyrus's taking Babylon by surprise, with the assistance of two deserters that showed him the best way into the city. And it was foretold what a consternation it would be to the court, Jer. li. 11, 39. Note, Death comes as a snare upon those whose hearts are overcharged with surfeiting and drunkenness. 2. The transferring of the kingdom into other hands. From the head of gold we now descend to the breast and arms of silver. *Darius the Mede took the kingdom* in partnership with, and by the consent of, Cyrus, who had conquered it, *v.* 31. They were partners in war and conquest, and so they were in dominion, *ch.* vi. 28. Notice is taken of his age, that he was now sixty-two years old, for which reason Cyrus, who was his nephew, gave him the precedency. Some observe that being now sixty-two years old, in the last year of the captivity, he was born in the eighth year of it, and that was the year when Jeconiah was carried captive and all the no-

bles, &c. See 2 Kings xxiv. 13—15. Just at that time when the most fatal stroke was given was a prince born that in process of time should avenge Jerusalem upon Babylon, and heal the wound that was now given. Thus deep are the counsels of God concerning his people, thus kind are his designs towards them.

CHAP. VI.

Daniel does not give a continued history of the reigns in which he lived, nor of the state-affairs of the kingdoms of Chaldea and Persia, though he was himself a great man in those affairs; for what are those to us? But he selects such particular passages of story as serve for the confirming of our faith in God and the encouraging of our obedience to him, for the things written aforetime were written for our learning. It is a very observable improvable story that we have in this chapter, how Daniel by faith "stopped the mouths of lions," and so "obtained a good report," Heb. xi. 33. The three children were cast into the fiery furnace for not committing a known sin, Daniel was cast into the lions' den for not omitting a known duty, and God's miraculously delivering both them and him is left upon record for the encouragement of his servants in all ages to be resolute and constant both in their abhorrence of that which is evil and in their adherence to that which is good, whatever it cost them. In this chapter we have, I. Daniel's preferment in the court of Darius, ver. 1—3. II. The envy and malice of his enemies against him, ver. 4, 5. III. The decree they obtained against prayer for thirty days, ver. 6—9. IV. Daniel's continuance and constancy in prayer, notwithstanding that decree, ver. 10. V. Information given against him for it, and the casting of him into the den of lions, ver. 11—17. VI. His miraculous preservation in the lions' den, and deliverance out of it, ver. 18—23. VII. The casting of his accusers into the den, and their destruction there, ver. 24. VIII. The decree which Darius made upon this occasion, in honour of the God of Daniel, and the prosperity of Daniel afterwards, ver. 25—28. And this God is our God for ever and ever.

IT pleased Darius to set over the kingdom a hundred and twenty princes, which should be over the whole kingdom; 2 And over these three presidents; of whom Daniel *was* first: that the princes might give accounts unto them, and the king should have no damage. 3 Then this Daniel was preferred above the presidents and princes, because an excellent spirit *was* in him; and the king thought to set him over the whole realm. 4 Then the presidents and princes sought to find occasion against Daniel concerning the kingdom; but they could find none occasion nor fault; forasmuch as he *was* faithful, neither was there any error or fault found in him. 5 Then said these men, We shall not find any occasion against this Daniel, except we find *it* against him concerning the law of his God.

We are here told concerning Daniel,

I. What a *great man* he was. When Darius, upon his accession to the crown of Babylon by conquest, new-modelled the government, he made Daniel prime-minister of state, set him at the helm, and made him first commissioner both of the treasury and of the great seal. Darius's dominion was very large; all he got by his conquests and acquests was that he had so many more countries to take care of; no more can be expected from himself than what one man can do, and therefore others must be employed under him. He *set over the kingdom* 120 *princes* (v. 1), and appointed them their districts, in which they were to administer justice, preserve the public peace, and levy the king's revenue. Note, Inferior magistrates are ministers of God to us for good as well as the sovereign; and therefore we must submit ourselves both to the king as supreme and to the governors that are constituted and commissioned by him, 1 Pet. ii. 13, 14. Over these princes there was a *triumvirate*, or *three presidents*, who were to take and state the public accounts, to receive appeals from the princes, or complaints against them in case of mal-administration, *that the king should have no damage* (v. 2), that he should not sustain loss in his revenue and that the power he delegated to the princes might not be abused to the oppression of the subject, for by that the king (whether he thinks so or no) receives real damage, both as it alienates the affections of his people from him and as it provokes the displeasure of his God against him. Of these three Daniel was the chief, because he was found to go beyond them all in all manner of princely qualifications. He was *preferred above the presidents and princes* (v. 3), and so wonderfully well pleased the king was with his management that *he thought to set him over the whole realm,* and let him place and displace at his pleasure. Now, 1. We must take notice of it to the praise of Darius that he would prefer a man thus purely for his personal merit, and his fitness for business; and those sovereigns that would be well served must go by that rule. Daniel had been a great man in the kingdom that was conquered, and for that reason, one would think, should have been looked upon as an enemy, and as such imprisoned or banished. He was a native of a foreign kingdom, and a ruined one, and upon that account might have been despised as a stranger and captive. But Darius, it seems, was very quick-sighted in judging of men's capacities, and was soon aware that this Daniel had something extraordinary in him, and therefore, though no doubt he had creatures of his own, not a few, that expected preferment in this newly-conquered kingdom, and were gaping for it, and those that had been long his confidants would depend upon it that they should be now his presidents, yet so well did he consult the public welfare that, finding Daniel to excel them all in prudence and virtue, and probably having heard of his being divinely inspired, he made him his right hand. 2. We must take notice of it, to the glory of God, that, though Daniel was now very old (it was above seventy years since he was brought a captive to Babylon), yet he was as able as ever for business both in body and mind, and that he who had continued faithful to his religion through all the temptations of the foregoing reigns in a new government

was as much respected as ever. He kept in by being an oak, not by being a willow, by a constancy in virtue, not by a pliableness to vice. Such honesty is the best policy, for it secures a reputation; and those who thus honour God he will honour.

II. What a good man he was: *An excellent spirit was in him, v.* 3. And he was faithful to every trust, dealt fairly between the sovereign and the subject, and took care that neither should be wronged, so that there was *no error,* or *fault, to be found in him, v.* 4. He was not only not chargeable with any treachery or dishonesty, but not even with any mistake or indiscretion. He never made any blunder, nor had any occasion to plead inadvertency or forgetfulness for his excuse. This is recorded for an example to all that are in places of public trust to approve themselves both careful and conscientious, that they may be free, not only from fault, but from error, not only from crime, but from mistake.

III. What ill-will was borne him, both for his greatness and for his goodness. The presidents and princes envied him because he was advanced above them, and probably hated him because he had a watchful eye upon them and took care they should not wrong the government to enrich themselves. See here, 1. The cause of envy, and that is every thing that is good. Solomon complains of it as a vexation that *for every right work a man is envied of his neighbour* (Eccl. iv. 4), that the better a man is the worse he is thought of by his rivals. Daniel is envied because he has a more excellent spirit than his neighbours. 2. The effect of envy, and that is every thing that is bad. Those that envied Daniel sought no less than his ruin. His disgrace would not serve them; it was his death that they desired. *Wrath is cruel, and anger is outrageous, but who can stand before envy?* Prov. xxvii. 4. Daniel's enemies set spies upon him, to observe him in the management of his place; they *sought to find occasion against him,* something on which to ground an accusation *concerning the kingdom,* some instance of neglect or partiality, some hasty word spoken, some person borne hard upon, or some necessary business overlooked. And if they could but have found the mote, the mole-hill, of a mistake, it would have been soon improved to the beam, to the mountain, of an unpardonable misdemeanour. But *they could find no occasion against* him; they owned that they could not. Daniel always acted honestly, and now the more warily, and stood the more upon his guard, *because of his observers,* Ps. xxvii. 11. Note, We have all need to walk circumspectly, because we have many eyes upon us, and some that watch for our halting. Those especially have need to carry their cup even that have it full. They concluded, at length, that they should not find any occasion against him except *concerning the law of his God v.* 5. It seems then that

Daniel kept up the profession of his religion, and held it fast without wavering or shrinking, and yet that was no bar to his preferment; there was no law that required him to be of the king's religion, or incapacitated him to bear office in the state unless he were. It was all one to the king what God he prayed to, so long as he did the business of his place faithfully and well. He was at the king's service *usque ad aras—as far as the altars;* but there he left him. In this matter therefore his enemies hoped to ensnare him. *Quærendum est crimen læsæ religionis ubi majestatis deficit—When treason could not be charged upon him he was accused of impiety.* Grotius. Note, It is an excellent thing, and much for the glory of God, when those who profess religion conduct themselves so inoffensively in their whole conversation that their most watchful spiteful enemies may find no occasion of blaming them, save only in the matters of their God, in which they walk according to their consciences. It is observable that, when Daniel's enemies could find no occasion against him concerning the kingdom, they had so much sense of justice left that they did not suborn witnesses against him to accuse him of crimes he was innocent of, and to swear treason upon him, wherein they shame many that were called Jews and are called Christians.

6 Then these presidents and princes assembled together to the king, and said thus unto him, King Darius, live for ever. 7 All the presidents of the kingdom, the governors, and the princes, the counsellors, and the captains, have consulted together to establish a royal statute, and to make a firm decree, that whosoever shall ask a petition of any God or man for thirty days, save of thee, O king, he shall be cast into the den of lions. 8 Now, O king, establish the decree, and sign the writing, that it be not changed, according to the law of the Medes and Persians, which altereth not. 9 Wherefore king Darius signed the writing and the decree. 10 Now when Daniel knew that the writing was signed, he went into his house; and his windows being open in his chamber toward Jerusalem, he kneeled upon his knees three times a day, and prayed, and gave thanks before his God, as he did aforetime.

Daniel's adversaries could have no advantage against him from any law now in being; they therefore contrive a new law, by which they hope to ensnare him, and in a matter in which they knew they should be sure of

him; and such was his fidelity to his God that they gained their point. Here is,

I. Darius's impious law. I call it *Darius's,* because he gave the royal assent to it, and otherwise it would not have been of force; but it was not properly his: he contrived it not, and was perfectly wheedled to consent to it. The presidents and princes framed the edict, brought in the bill, and by their management it was agreed to by the convention of the states, who perhaps were met at this time upon some public occasion. It is pretended that this bill which they would have to pass into a law was the result of mature deliberation, that *all the presidents of the kingdom, the governors, princes, counsellors, and captains, had consulted together* about it, and that they not only agreed to it, but *advised it,* for *divers good causes and considerations,* that they had done what they could to *establish it for a firm decree;* nay, they intimate to the king that it was carried *nemine contradicente—unanimously:* "*All the presidents* are of this mind;*" and yet we are sure that Daniel, the chief of the three presidents, did not agree to it, and have reason to think that many more of the princes excepted against it as absurd and unreasonable. Note, It is no new thing for that to be represented, and with great assurance too, as the sense of the nation, which is far from being so; and that which few approve of is sometimes confidently said to be that which all agree to. But, O the infelicity of kings, who, being under a necessity of seeing and hearing with other people's eyes and ears, are often wretchedly imposed upon! These designing men, under colour of doing honour to the king, but really intending the ruin of his favourite, press him to pass this into a law, and make it a royal statute, that *whosoever shall ask a petition of any god or man for thirty days, save of the king, shall be* put to death after the most barbarous manner, shall be *cast into the den of lions, v.* 7. This is the bill they have been hatching, and they lay it before the king to be signed and passed into a law. Now, 1. There is nothing in it that has the least appearance of good, but that it magnifies the king, and makes him seem both very great and very kind to his subjects, which, they suggest, will be of good service to him now that he has newly come to his throne, and will confirm his interests. All men must be made to believe that the king is so rich, and withal so ready to all petitioners, that none in any want or distress need to apply either to God or man for relief, but to him only. And for thirty days together he will be ready to give audience to all that have any petition to present to him. It is indeed much for the honour of kings to be benefactors to their subjects and to have their ears open to their complaints and requests; but if they pretend to be their sole benefactors, and undertake to be to them instead of God, and challenge that respect from them which is due to God only, it is their disgrace, and not their honour. But, 2. There is a great deal in it that is apparently evil. It is bad enough to forbid asking a petition of any man. Must not a beggar ask an alms, or one neighbour beg a kindness of another? If the child want bread, must he not ask it of his parents, or be cast into the den of lions if he do? Nay, those that have business with the king, may they not petition those about him to introduce them? But it was much worse, and an impudent affront to all religion, to forbid asking a petition *of any god.* It is by prayer that we give glory to God, fetch in mercy from God, and so keep up our communion with God; and to interdict prayer for thirty days is for so long to rob God of all the tribute he has from man and to rob man of all the comfort he has in God. When the light of nature teaches us that the providence of God has the ordering and disposing of all our affairs does not the law of nature oblige us by prayer to acknowledge God and seek to him? Does not every man's heart direct him, when he is in want or distress, to call upon God, and must this be made high treason? We could not live a day without God; and can men live thirty days without prayer? Will the king himself be tied up for so long from praying to God; or, if it be allowed him, will he undertake to do it for all his subjects? Did ever any nation thus slight their gods? But see what absurdities malice will drive men to. Rather than not bring Daniel into trouble for praying to his God, they will deny themselves and all their friends the satisfaction of praying to theirs. Had they proposed only to prohibit the Jews from praying to their God, Daniel would have been as effectually ensnared; but they knew the king would not pass such a law, and therefore made it thus general. And the king, puffed up with a fancy that this would set him up as a little god, was fond of the *feather in his cap* (for so it was, and not a *flower in his crown*) and *signed the writing and the decree* (*v.* 9), which, being once done, according to the constitution of the united kingdom of the Medes and Persians, was not upon any pretence whatsoever to be altered or dispensed with, or the breach of it pardoned.

II. Daniel's pious disobedience to this law, *v.* 10. He did not retire into the country, nor abscond for some time, though he knew the law was levelled against him; but, because he knew it was so, therefore he stood his ground, knowing that he had now a fair opportunity of honouring God before men, and showing that he preferred his favour, and his duty to him, before life itself. *When Daniel knew that the writing was signed* he might have gone to the king, and expostulated with him about it; nay, he might have remonstrated against it, as grounded upon a misinformation that *all the presidents* had

consented to it, whereas he that was chief of them had never been consulted about it; but *he went to his house,* and applied himself to his duty, cheerfully trusting God with the event. Now observe,

1. Daniel's constant practice, which we were not informed of before this occasion, but which we have reason to think was the general practice of the pious Jews. (1.) He *prayed in his house,* sometimes himself alone and sometimes with his family about him, and made a solemn business of it. Cornelius was a man that *prayed in his house,* Acts x. 30. Note, Every house not only may be, but ought to be, a house of prayer; where we have a tent God must have an altar, and on it we must offer spiritual sacrifices. (2.) In every prayer he gave thanks. When we pray to God for the mercies we want we must praise him for those we have received. Thanksgiving must be a part of every prayer. (3.) In his prayer and thanksgiving he had an eye to God as his God, his in covenant, and set himself as in his presence. He did this *before his God,* and with a regard to him. (4.) When he prayed and gave thanks he *kneeled upon his knees,* which is the most proper gesture in prayer, and most expressive of humility, and reverence, and submission to God. Kneeling is a begging posture, and we come to God as beggars, beggars for our lives, whom it concerns to be importunate. (5.) He *opened the windows of his chamber,* that the sight of the visible heavens might affect his heart with an awe of that God who dwells above the heavens; but that was not all: he *opened them towards Jerusalem,* the holy city, though now in ruins, to signify the affection he had for its very stones and dust (Ps. cii. 14) and the remembrance he had of its concerns daily in his prayers. Thus, though he himself lived great in Babylon, yet he testified his concurrence with the meanest of his brethren the captives, in remembering Jerusalem and preferring it before his *chief joy,* Ps. cxxxvii. 5, 6. Jerusalem was the place which God had chosen to put his name there; and, when the temple was dedicated, Solomon's prayer to God was that if his people should *in the land of their enemies* pray unto him with their eye towards the land which he gave them, and the city he had chosen, and the house which was built to his name, then he would *hear* and *maintain their cause* (1 Kings viii. 48, 49), to which prayer Daniel had reference in this circumstance of his devotions. (6.) He did this *three times a day,* three times every day according to the example of David (Ps. lv. 17), *Morning, evening, and at noon, I will pray.* It is good to have our hours of prayer, not to bind, but to remind conscience; and, if we think our bodies require refreshment by food thrice a day, can we think seldomer will serve our souls? This is surely as little as may be to answer the command of *praying always.* (7.) He

did this so openly and avowedly that all who knew him knew it to be his practice; and he thus showed it, not because he was proud of it (in the place where he was there was no room for that temptation, for it was not reputation, but reproach, that attended it), but because he was not ashamed of it. Though Daniel was a great man, he did not think it below him to be thrice a day upon his knees before his Maker and to be his own chaplain; though he was an old man, he did not think himself past it; nor, though it had been his practice from his youth up, was he weary of this well doing. Though he was a man of business, vast business, for the service of the public, he did not think that would excuse him from the daily exercises of devotion. How inexcusable then are those who have but little to do in the world, and yet will not do thus much for God and their souls! Daniel was a man famous for prayer, and for success in it (Ezek. xiv. 14), and he came to be so by thus making a conscience of prayer and making a business of it daily; and in thus doing God blessed him wonderfully.

2. Daniel's constant adherence to this practice, even when it was made by the law a capital crime. When he knew that *the writing was signed* he continued to do *as he did aforetime*, and altered not one circumstance of the performance. Many a man, yea, and many a good man, would have thought it prudence to omit it for these thirty days, when he could not do it without hazard of his life; he might have prayed so much the oftener when those days had expired and the danger was over, or he might have performed the duty at another time, and in another place, so secretly that it should not be possible for his enemies to discover it; and so he might both satisfy his conscience and keep up his communion with God, and yet avoid the law, and continue in his usefulness. But, if he had done so, it would have been thought, both by his friends and by his enemies, that he had thrown up the duty for this time, through cowardice and base fear, which would have tended very much to the dishonour of God and the discouragement of his friends. Others who moved in a lower sphere might well enough act with caution; but Daniel, who had so many eyes upon him, must act with courage; and the rather because he knew that the law, when it was made, was particularly levelled against him. Note, We must not omit duty for fear of suffering, no, nor so much as *seem to come short* of it. In trying times great stress is laid upon our *confessing Christ before men* (Matt. x. 32), and we must take heed lest, under pretence of discretion, we be found guilty of cowardice in the cause of God. If we do not think that this example of Daniel obliges us to do likewise, yet I am sure it forbids us to censure those that do, for God owned him in it. By his constancy to his duty it now appears that he had never been used to admit any excuse for the omission of it; for, if ever any excuse would serve to put it by, this would have served now, (1.) That it was forbidden by the king his master, and in honour of the king too; but it is an undoubted maxim, in answer to that, We are to obey God rather than men. (2.) That it would be the loss of his life, but it is an undoubted maxim, in answer to that, Those who throw away their souls (as those certainly do that live without prayer) to save their lives make but a bad bargain for themselves; and though herein they make themselves, like the king of Tyre, *wiser than Daniel*, at their end they will be fools.

11 Then these men assembled, and found Daniel praying and making supplication before his God. 12 Then they came near, and spake before the king concerning the king's decree; Hast thou not signed a decree, that every man that shall ask *a petition* of any God or man within thirty days, save of thee, O king, shall be cast into the den of lions? The king answered and said, The thing *is* true, according to the law of the Medes and Persians, which altereth not. 13 Then answered they and said before the king, That Daniel, which *is* of the children of the captivity of Judah, regardeth not thee, O king, nor the decree that thou hast signed, but maketh his petition three times a day. 14 Then the king, when he heard *these* words, was sore displeased with himself, and set *his* heart on Daniel to deliver him: and he laboured till the going down of the sun to deliver him. 15 Then these men assembled unto the king, and said unto the king, Know, O king, that the law of the Medes and Persians *is*, that no decree nor statute which the king establisheth may be changed. 16 Then the king commanded, and they brought Daniel, and cast *him* into the den of lions. *Now* the king spake and said unto Daniel, Thy God, whom thou servest continually, he will deliver thee. 17 And a stone was brought, and laid upon the mouth of the den; and the king sealed it with his own signet, and with the signet of his lords; that the purpose might not be changed concerning Daniel.

Here is, 1. Proof made of Daniel's praying to his God, notwithstanding the late edict to the contrary (*v.* 11): *These men assembled;* they *came tumultuously together,* so the word is, the same that was used *v.* 6, borrowed from Ps. ii. 1, *Why do the heathen rage?* They came together to visit Daniel, perhaps under pretence of business, at that time which they knew to be his usual hour of devotion; and, if they had not found him so engaged, they would have upbraided him with his faint-heartedness and distrust of his God, but (which they rather wished to do) they *found him on his knees praying* and *making supplication before his God.* For *his love they are his adversaries;* but, like his father David, he *gives himself unto prayer,* Ps. cix. 4. 2. Complaint made of it to the king. When they had found occasion against Daniel concerning *the law of his God* they lost no time, but applied to the king (*v.* 12), and having appealed to him whether there was not such a law made, and gained from him a recognition of it, and that it was so ratified that it might not be altered, they proceeded to accuse Daniel, *v.* 13. They so describe him, in the information they give, as to exasperate the king and incense him the more against him : " He is *of the children of the captivity of Judah;* he is of Judah, that despicable people, and now a captive in a despicable state, that can call nothing his own but what he has by the king's favour, and yet he *regards not thee, O king! nor the decree that thou hast signed.* Note, It is no new thing for that which is done faithfully, in conscience towards God, to be misrepresented as done obstinately and in contempt of the civil powers, that is, for the best saints to be reproached as the worst men. Daniel regarded God, and therefore prayed, and we have reason to think prayed for the king and his government, yet this is construed as not regarding the king. That excellent spirit which Daniel was endued with, and that established reputation which he had gained, could not protect him from these poisonous darts. They do not say, He makes his petition to his God, lest Darius should take notice of that to his praise, but only, *He makes his petition,* which is the thing the law forbids. 3. The great concern the king was in hereupon. He now perceived that, whatever they pretended, it was not to honour him, but in spite to Daniel, that they had proposed that law, and now he is *sorely displeased with himself* for gratifying them in it, *v.* 14. Note, When men indulge a proud vain-glorious humour, and please themselves with that which feeds it, they know not what vexations they are preparing for themselves; their flatterers may prove their tormentors, and are but *spreading a net for their feet.* Now the king *sets his heart to deliver Daniel;* both by argument and by authority he labours *till the going down of the sun* to deliver him, that is,

to persuade his accusers not to insist upon his prosecution. Note, We often do that, through inconsideration, which afterwards we see cause a thousand times to wish undone again, which is a good reason why we should *ponder the path of our feet,* for then *all our ways will be established.* 4. The violence with which the prosecutors demanded judgment, *v.* 15. We are not told what Daniel said; the king himself is his advocate, he needs not plead his own cause, but silently commits himself and it to him that judges righteously. But the prosecutors insist upon it that the law must have its course; it is a fundamental maxim in the constitution of the government of the Medes and Persians, which had now become the universal monarchy, that *no decree or statute which the king establishes may be changed.* The same we find Esth. i. 19; viii. 8. The Chaldeans magnified the will of their king, by giving him a power to make and unmake laws at his pleasure, to slay and keep alive whom he would. The Persians magnified the wisdom of their king, by supposing that whatever law he solemnly ratified it was so well made that there could be no occasion to alter it, or dispense with it, as if any human foresight could, in framing a law, guard against all inconveniences. But, if this maxim be duly applied to Daniel's case (as I am apt to think it is not, but perverted), while it honours the king's legislative power it hampers his executive power, and incapacitates him to show that mercy which upholds the throne, and to pass acts of indemnity, which are the glories of a reign. Those who allow not the sovereign's power to dispense with a disabling statute, yet never question his power to pardon an offence against a penal statute. But Darius is denied this power. See what need we have to pray for princes that God would give them wisdom, for they are often embarrassed with great difficulties, even the wisest and best are. 5. The executing of the law upon Daniel. The king himself, with the utmost reluctance, and against his conscience, signs the warrant for his execution; and Daniel, that venerable grave man, who carried such a mixture of majesty and sweetness in his countenance, who had so often looked great upon the bench, and at the council-board, and greater upon his knees, who had power with God and man, and had prevailed, is brought, purely for worshipping his God, as if he had been one of the vilest of malefactors, and *thrown into the den of lions,* to be devoured by them, *v.* 16. One cannot think of it without the utmost compassion to the gracious sufferer and the utmost indignation at the malicious prosecutors. To make sure work, the stone *laid upon the mouth of the den is sealed,* and the king (an over-easy man) is persuaded to seal it *with his own signet* (*v.* 17), that unhappy signet with which he had confirmed the law that Daniel falls by. But his lords cannot trust him, unless they add their signets too. Thus, when Christ was buried, his adversaries *sealed the stone* that was rolled to the door of his sepulchre.   6. The encouragement which Darius gave to Daniel to trust in God: *Thy God whom thou servest continually, he will deliver thee, v.* 16. Here, (1.) He justifies Daniel from guilt, owning all his crime to be serving his God continually, and continuing to do so even when it was made a crime.   (2.) He leaves it to God to free him from punishment, since he could not prevail to do it: *He will deliver thee.* He is sure that his God can deliver him, for he believes him to be an almighty God, and he has reason to think he will do it, having heard of his delivering Daniel's companions in a like case from the fiery furnace, and concluding him to be always faithful to those who approve themselves faithful to him   Note, Those who serve God continually he will continually preserve, and will bear them out in his service.

18 Then the king went to his palace, and passed the night fasting; neither were instruments of music brought before him: and his sleep went from him. 19 Then the king arose very early in the morning, and went in haste unto the den of lions. 20 And when he came to the den, he cried with a lamentable voice unto Daniel: *and* the king spake and said to Daniel, O Daniel, servant of the living God, is thy God, whom thou servest continually, able to deliver thee from the lions? 21 Then said Daniel unto the king, O king, live for ever. 22 My God hath sent his angel, and hath shut the lions' mouths, that they have not hurt me: forasmuch as before him innocency was found in me; and also before thee, O king, have I done no hurt. 23 Then was the king exceeding glad for him, and commanded that they should take Daniel up out of the den. So Daniel was taken up out of the den, and no manner of·hurt was found upon him, because he believed in his God. 24 And the king commanded, and they brought those men which had accused Daniel, and they cast *them* into the den of lions, them, their children, and their wives; and the lions had the mastery of them, and brake all their bones in pieces or ever they came at the bottom of the den.

Here is, I. The melancholy night which the king had, upon Daniel's account, *v.* 18. He had said, indeed, that God would deliver him out of the danger, but at the same time he could not forgive himself for throwing him into the danger; and justly might God deprive him of a friend whom he had himself used so barbarously. He *went to his palace,* vexed at himself for what he had done, and calling himself unwise and unjust for not adhering to the law of God and nature, with a *non obstante—a negative* to the law of the Medes and Persians. He ate no supper, but *passed the night fasting;* his heart was already full of grief and fear. He forbade the music; nothing is more unpleasing than songs sung to a heavy heart. He went to bed, but got no sleep, was full of *tossings to and fro* till the dawning of the day. Note, The best way to have a good night is to keep a good conscience, then we may lie down in peace.

II. The solicitous enquiry he made concerning Daniel the next morning, *v.* 19, 20. He was up early, *very early;* for how could he lie in bed when he could not sleep for dreaming of Daniel, nor lie awake quietly for thinking of him? And he was no sooner up than he *went in haste to the den of lions,* for he could not satisfy himself to send a servant (that would not sufficiently testify his affection for Daniel), nor had he patience to stay so long as till a servant would return. When he comes to the den, not without some hopes that God had graciously undone what he had wickedly done, he cries, *with a lamentable voice,* as one full of concern and trouble, *O Daniel!* art thou alive? He longs to know, yet trembles to ask the question, fearing to be answered with the roaring of the lions after more prey: *O Daniel! servant of the living God,* has *thy God whom thou servest* made it to appear that he is *able to deliver thee from the lions?* If he rightly understood himself when he called him *the living God,* he could not doubt of his ability to keep Daniel alive, for he that has life in himself quickens whom he will; but has he thought fit in this case to exert his power? What he doubted of we are sure of, that the *servants of the living God* have a Master who is well able to protect them and bear them out in his service.

III. The joyful news he meets with—that Daniel is alive, is safe, and well, and unhurt in the lions' den, *v.* 21, 22. Daniel knew the king's voice, though it was now a lamentable voice, and spoke to him with all the deference and respect that were due to him: *O king! live for ever.* He does not reproach him for his unkindness to him, and his easiness in yielding to the malice of his persecutors; but, to show that he has heartily forgiven him, he meets him with his good wishes. Note, We should not upbraid those with the diskindnesses they have done us who, we know, did them with reluctance, and are very ready to upbraid themselves with them. The account Daniel gives the king is very pleasant; it is triumphant. 1. God has preserved his life by a miracle. Darius had called him Daniel's God *(thy God whom thou servest)*, to which Daniel does as it were echo back, Yea, he is *my God*, whom I own, and who owns me, for *he has sent his angel.* The same bright and glorious being that was seen in *the form of the Son of God* with the three children in the fiery furnace had visited Daniel, and, it is likely, in a visible appearance had enlightened the dark den, and kept Daniel company all night, and had *shut the lions' mouths, that they* had not in the least *hurt him.* The angel's presence made even the lions' den his strong-hold, his palace, his paradise; he had never had a better night in his life. See the power of God over the fiercest creatures, and believe his power to restrain the roaring lion that *goes about continually seeking to devour* from hurting those that are his. See the care God takes of his faithful worshippers, especially when he calls them out to suffer for him. If he keeps their souls from sin, comforts their souls with his peace, and receives their souls to himself, he does in effect *stop the lions' mouths*, that they cannot hurt them. See how ready the angels are to minister for the good of God's people, for they own themselves their *fellow servants.* 2. God has therein pleaded his cause. He was represented to the king as disaffected to him and his government. We do not find that he said any thing in his own vindication, but left it to God to clear up his integrity as the light; and he did it effectually, by working a miracle for his preservation. Daniel, in what he had done, had not offended either God or the king: *Before him* whom I prayed to *innocency was found in me.* He pretends not to a meritorious excellence, but the testimony of his conscience concerning his sincerity is his comfort—*As also that before thee, O king! I have done no hurt*, nor designed thee any affront.

IV. The discharge of Daniel from his confinement. His prosecutors cannot but own that the law is satisfied, though they are not, or, if it be altered, it is by a power superior to that of the Medes and Persians; and therefore no cause can be shown why Daniel should not be fetched out of the den (*v 23*): *The king was exceedingly glad* to find him alive, and gave orders immediately that they should *take him out of the den*, as Jeremiah out of the dungeon; and, when they searched, *no manner of hurt was found upon him;* he was nowhere crushed nor scarred, but was kept perfectly well, *because he believed in his God.* Note, Those who boldly and cheerfully trust in God to protect them in the way of their duty shall never be made ashamed of their confidence in him, but shall always find him a present help.

1068

V. The committing of his prosecutors to the same prison, or place of execution rather, *v.* 24. Darius is animated by this miracle wrought for Daniel, and now begins to take courage and act like himself. Those that would not suffer him to show mercy to Daniel shall, now that God has done it for him, be made to feel his resentments; and he will do justice for God who had shown mercy for him. Daniel's accusers, now that his innocency is cleared, and Heaven itself has become his compurgator, have the same punishment inflicted upon them which they designed against him, according to the law of retaliation made against false accusers, Deut. xix. 18, 19. Such they were to be reckoned now that Daniel was proved innocent; for, though the fact was true, yet it was not a fault. They were *cast into the den of lions*, which perhaps was a punishment newly invented by themselves; however, it was what they maliciously designed for Daniel. *Nec lex est justior ulla quàm necis artifices arte perire suâ—No law can be more just than that which adjudges the devisers of barbarity to perish by it*, Ps. vii. 15, 16; ix. 15, 16. And now Solomon's observation is verified (Prov. xi. 8), *The righteous is delivered out of trouble*, and *the wicked cometh in his stead.* In this execution we may observe, 1. The king's severity, in ordering their wives and children to be thrown to the lions with them. How righteous are God's statutes above those of the nations! For God commanded that the children should not die for the fathers' crimes, Deut. xxiv. 16. Yet they were put to death in extraordinary cases, as those of Achan, and Saul, and Haman. 2. The lions' fierceness. They had the *mastery of them* immediately, and tore them to pieces *before they came to the bottom of the den.* This verified and magnified the miracle of their sparing Daniel; for hereby it appeared that it was not because they had not appetite, but because they had not leave. Mastiffs that are kept muzzled are the more fierce when the muzzle is taken off; so were these lions. And the Lord is known by those judgments which he executes.

25 Then king Darius wrote unto all people, nations, and languages, that dwell in all the earth; Peace be multiplied unto you. 26 I make a decree, that in every dominion of my kingdom men tremble and fear before the God of Daniel: for he *is* the living God, and stedfast for ever, and his kingdom *that* which shall not be destroyed, and his dominion *shall be even* unto the end. 27 He delivereth and rescueth, and he worketh signs and wonders in heaven and in earth, who hath delivered Daniel from the power

of the lions. 28 So this Daniel prospered in the reign of Darius, and in the reign of Cyrus the Persian.

Darius here studies to make some amends for the dishonour he had done both to God and Daniel, in casting Daniel into the lions' den, by doing honour to both.

I. He gives honour to God by a decree published to all nations, by which they are required to fear before him. And this is a decree which is indeed fit to be made unalterable, according to the laws of the Medes and Persians, for it is the *everlasting gospel*, preached to those that *dwell on the earth*, Rev. xiv. 7. *Fear God, and give glory to him.* Observe, 1. To whom he sends this decree—*to all people, nations, and languages, that dwell in all the earth, v. 25.* These are great words, and it is true that all the inhabitants of the earth are obliged to that which is here decreed; but here they mean no more than *every dominion of his kingdom*, which, though it contained many nations, did not contain all nations; but so it is, those that have much are ready to think they have all. 2. What the matter of the decree is—that *men tremble and fear before the God of Daniel.* This goes further than Nebuchadnezzar's decree upon a similar occasion, for that only restrained people from *speaking amiss* of this God, but this requires them to *fear before him*, to keep up and express awful reverent thoughts of him. And well might this decree be prefaced, as it is, with *Peace be multiplied unto you*, for the only foundation of true and abundant peace is laid in the fear of God, for that is true wisdom. If we live in the fear of God, and walk according to that rule, peace shall be upon us, peace shall be multiplied to us. But, though this decree goes far, it does not go far enough; had he done right, and come up to his present convictions, he would have commanded all men not only to tremble and fear before this God, but to love him and trust in him, to forsake the service of their idols, and to worship him only, and call upon him as Daniel did. But idolatry had been so long and so deeply rooted that it was not to be extirpated by the edicts of princes, nor by any power less than that which went along with the glorious gospel of Christ. 3. What are the causes and considerations moving him to make this decree. They are sufficient to have justified a decree for the total suppression of idolatry, much more will they serve to support this. There is good reason why all men should fear before this God, for, (1.) His being is transcendant. "He is the *living God*, lives as a God, whereas the gods we worship are dead things, have not so much as an animal life." (2.) His government is incontestable. He has a *kingdom*, and a *dominion;* he not only lives, but reigns as an absolute sovereign. (3.) Both his being and his government are

unchangeable. He is himself *stedfast for ever*, and with him is no shadow of turning. And his *kingdom* too is *that which shall not be destroyed* by any external force, nor has his *dominion* any thing in itself that threatens a decay or tends towards it, and therefore it shall be *even to the end.* (4.) He has an ability sufficient to support such an authority, *v.* 27. He delivers his faithful servants from trouble and rescues them out of trouble; he *works signs and wonders*, quite above the utmost power of nature to effect, both *in heaven and on earth*, by which it appears that he is sovereign Lord of both. (5.) He has given a fresh proof of all this in *delivering* his servant *Daniel from the power of the lions.* This miracle, and that of the delivering of the three children, were wrought in the eyes of the world, were seen, published, and attested by two of the greatest monarchs that ever were, and were illustrious confirmations of the first principles of religion, abstracted from the narrow scheme of Judaism, effectual confutations of all the errors of heathenism, and very proper preparations for pure catholic Christianity.

II. He puts honour upon Daniel (*v.* 28): *So this Daniel prospered.* See how God brought to him good out of evil. This bold stroke which his enemies made at his life was a happy occasion of taking them off, and their children too, who otherwise would still have stood in the way of his preferment, and have been upon all occasions vexatious to him; and now he *prospered more than ever*, was more in favour with his prince and in reputation with the people, which gave him a great opportunity of doing good to his brethren. Thus *out of the eater* (and that was a lion too) *came forth meat, and out of the strong sweetness.*

CHAP. VII.

The six former chapters of this book were historical; we now enter with fear and trembling upon the six latter, which are prophetical, wherein are many things dark and hard to be understood, which we dare not positively determine the sense of, and yet many things plain and profitable, which I trust God will enable us to make a good use of. In this chapter we have, I. Daniel's vision of the four beasts, ver. 1—8. II. His vision of God's throne of government and judgment, ver. 9—14. III. The interpretation of these visions, given him by an angel that stood by, ver. 15—28. Whether those visions look as far forward as the end of time, or whether they were to have a speedy accomplishment, is hard to say, nor are the most judicious interpreters agreed concerning it.

IN the first year of Belshazzar king of Babylon Daniel had a dream and visions of his head upon his bed : then he wrote the dream, *and* told the sum of the matters. 2 Daniel spake and said, I saw in my vision by night, and, behold, the four winds of the heaven strove upon the great sea. 3 And four great beasts came up from the sea, diverse one from another. 4 The first *was* like a lion, and had eagle's wings : I beheld till the wings thereof were plucked, and it was lifted up from the earth, and made stand upon the feet as a man, and a man's heart was given to it. 5 And behold another beast, a second, like to a bear, and it raised up itself on one side, and *it had* three ribs in the mouth of it between the teeth of it : and they said thus unto it, Arise, devour much flesh. 6 After this I beheld, and lo another, like a leopard, which had upon the back of it four wings of a fowl ; the beast had also four heads ; and dominion was given to it. 7 After this I saw in the night visions, and behold a fourth beast, dreadful and terrible, and strong exceedingly ; and it had great iron teeth : it devoured and brake in pieces, and stamped the residue with the feet of it : and it *was* diverse from all the beasts that *were* before it ; and it had ten horns. 8 I considered the horns, and, behold, there came up among them another little horn, before whom there were three of the first horns plucked up by the roots : and, behold, in this horn *were* eyes like the eyes of man, and a mouth speaking great things.

The date of this chapter places it before *ch.* v., which was in the last year of Belshazzar, and *ch.* vi., which was in the first of Darius ; for Daniel had those visions in the first year of Belshazzar, when the captivity of the Jews in Babylon was drawing near a period. Belshazzar's name here is, in the original, spelt differently from what it used to be ; before it was *Bel-she-azar—Bel is he that treasures up riches.* But this is *Bel-eshe-zar —Bel is on fire by the enemy.* Bel was the god of the Chaldeans ; he had prospered, but is now to be consumed.

We have, in these verses, Daniel's vision of the four monarchies that were oppressive to the Jews. Observe,

I. The circumstances of this vision. Daniel had interpreted Nebuchadnezzar's dream, and now he is himself honoured with similar divine discoveries (*v.* 1) : He *had visions of his head upon his bed,* when he was asleep ; so God sometimes revealed himself and his mind to the children of men, when deep sleep fell upon them (Job xxxiii. 15) ; for when we are most retired from the world, and taken off from the things of sense, we are most fit for communion with God. But when he was awake he *wrote the dream* for his own use, lest he should forget it as a dream which passes away ; and he *told the sum of the matters* to his brethren the Jews for their use, and gave it to them in writing, 1070

that it might be communicated to those at a distance and preserved for their children after them, who shall see these things accomplished. The Jews, misunderstanding some of the prophecies of Jeremiah and Ezekiel, flattered themselves with hopes that, after their return to their own land, they should enjoy a complete and uninterrupted tranquillity ; but that they might not so deceive themselves, and their calamities be made doubly grievous by the disappointment, God by this prophet lets them know that they shall have tribulation : those promises of their prosperity were to be accomplished in the spiritual blessings of the kingdom of grace ; as Christ has told his disciples they must expect persecution, and the promises they depend upon will be accomplished in the eternal blessings of the kingdom of glory. Daniel both wrote these things and spoke them, to intimate that the church should be taught both by the scriptures and by ministers' preaching, both by the written word and by word of mouth ; and ministers in their preaching are to *tell the sum of the matters* that are written.

II. The vision itself, which foretels the revolutions of government in those nations which the church of the Jews, for the following ages, was to be under the influence of. 1. He observed the *four winds to strive upon the great sea, v.* 2. They strove which should blow strongest, and, at length, blow alone. This represents the contests among princes for empire, and the shakings of the nations by these contests, to which those mighty monarchies, which he was now to have a prospect of, owed their rise. One wind from any point of the compass, if it blow hard, will cause a great commotion in the sea ; but what a tumult must needs be raised when the four winds strive for mastery ! That is it which the kings of the nations are contending for in their wars, which are as noisy and violent as the battle of the winds ; but how is the poor sea tossed and torn, how terrible are its concussions, how violent its convulsions, while the winds are at strife which shall have the sole power of troubling it ! Note, This world is like a stormy tempestuous sea ; thanks to the proud ambitious winds that vex it. 2. He saw *four great beasts come up from the sea,* from the *troubled waters,* in which aspiring minds love to fish. The monarchs and monarchies are represented by *beasts,* because too often it is by brutish rage and tyranny that they are raised and supported. These beasts were *diverse one from another (v.* 3), of different shapes, to denote the different genius and complexion of the nations in whose hands they were lodged. (1.) *The first* beast *was like a lion, v.* 4. This was the Chaldean monarchy, that was fierce and strong, and made the kings absolute. This lion had *eagle's wings,* with which to fly upon the prey, denoting the wonderful speed that

Nebuchadnezzar made in his conquest of kingdoms. But Daniel soon sees the *wings plucked*, a full stop put to the career of their victorious arms. Divers countries that had been tributaries to them revolt from them, and make head against them; so that this monstrous animal, this winged lion, is made to *stand upon the feet as a man, and a man's heart is given to it.* It has lost the heart of a lion, which it had been famous for (one of our English kings was called *Cœur de Lion* —*Lion-heart*), has lost its courage and become feeble and faint, dreading every thing and daring nothing; they are put in fear, and made to know themselves to be but men. Sometimes the valour of a nation strangely sinks, and it becomes cowardly and effeminate, so that what was the head of the nations in an age or two becomes the tail. (2.) The *second* beast was *like a bear, v. 5.* This was the Persian monarchy, less strong and generous than the former, but no less ravenous. This bear *raised up itself on one side* against the lion, and soon mastered it. It *raised up one dominion;* so some read it. Persia and Media, which in Nebuchadnezzar's image were the *two arms* in one breast, now set up a joint government. This bear had *three ribs in the mouth of it between the teeth,* the remains of those nations it had devoured, which were the marks of its voraciousness, and yet an indication that though it had devoured much it could not devour all; some ribs still stuck in the teeth of it, which it could not conquer. Whereupon it was said to it, " *Arise, devour much flesh;* let alone the bones, the ribs, that cannot be conquered, and set upon that which will be an easier prey." The princes will stir up both the kings and the people to push on their conquests, and let nothing stand before them. Note, Conquests, unjustly made, are but like those of the beasts of prey, and in *this* much worse, that the beasts prey not upon those of their own kind, as wicked and unreasonable men do. (3.) The third beast was *like a leopard, v. 6.* This was the Grecian monarchy, founded by *Alexander the Great,* active, crafty, and cruel, like a *leopard.* He had *four wings of a fowl;* the lion seems to have had but two wings, but the leopard had four, for though Nebuchadnezzar made great despatch in his conquests Alexander made much greater. In six years' time he gained the whole empire of Persia, a great part besides of Asia, made himself master of Syria, Egypt, India, and other nations. This beast had *four heads;* upon Alexander's death his conquests were divided among his four chief captains; Seleucus Nicanor had Asia the Great; Perdiccas, and after him Antigonus, had Asia the Less; Cassander had Macedonia; and Ptolemeus had Egypt. *Dominion* was *given* to this *beast;* it was given of God, from whom alone promotion comes. (4.) The fourth beast was more fierce, and formidable, and mischievous,

than any of them, unlike any of the other, nor is there any among the beasts of prey to which it might be compared, *v.* 7. The learned are not agreed concerning this anonymous beast; some make it to be the Roman empire, which, when it was in its glory, comprehended ten kingdoms, Italy, France, Spain, Germany, Britain, Sarmatia, Pannonia, Asia, Greece, and Egypt; and then the little horn which rose by the fall of three of the other horns (*v.* 8) they make to be the Turkish empire, which rose in the room of Asia, Greece, and Egypt. Others make this fourth beast to be the kingdom of Syria, the family of the Seleucidæ, which was very cruel and oppressive to the people of the Jews, as we find in Josephus and the history of the Maccabees. And herein that empire was diverse from those which went before, that none of the preceding powers compelled the Jews to renounce their religion, but the kings of Syria did, and used them barbarously. Their armies and commanders were the *great iron teeth* with which they *devoured and broke in pieces* the people of God, and they *trampled upon the residue* of them. The *ten horns* are then supposed to be ten kings that reigned successively in Syria; and then the *little horn* is Antiochus Epiphanes, the last of the ten, who by one means or other undermined three of the kings, and got the government. He was a man of great ingenuity, and therefore is said to have eyes *like the eyes of a man;* and he was very bold and daring, had *a mouth speaking great things.* We shall meet with him again in these prophecies.

9 I beheld till the thrones were cast down, and the Ancient of days did sit, whose garment *was* white as snow, and the hair of his head like the pure wool: his throne *was like* the fiery flame, *and* his wheels *as* burning fire. 10 A fiery stream issued and came forth from before him: thousand thousands ministered unto him, and ten thousand times ten thousand stood before him: the judgment was set, and the books were opened. 11 I beheld then because of the voice of the great words which the horn spake: I beheld *even* till the beast was slain, and his body destroyed, and given to the burning flame. 12 As concerning the rest of the beasts, they had their dominion taken away: yet their lives were prolonged for a season and time. 13 I saw in the night visions, and, behold, *one* like the Son of man came with the clouds of heaven, and came to the Ancient

of days, and they brought him near before him. 14 And there was given him dominion, and glory, and a kingdom, that all people, nations, and languages, should serve him : his dominion *is* an everlasting dominion, which shall not pass away, and his kingdom *that* which shall not be destroyed.

Whether we understand the fourth beast to signify the Syrian empire, or the Roman, or the former as the figure of the latter, it is plain that these verses are intended for the comfort and support of the people of God in reference to the persecutions they were likely to sustain both from the one and from the other, and from all their proud enemies in every age; for it is written for their learning on whom the ends of the world have come, that they also, through patience and comfort of this scripture, might have hope. Three things are here discovered that are very encouraging :—

I. That there is a judgment to come, and God is the Judge. Now men have their day, and every pretender thinks he should have his day, and struggles for it. But *he that sits in heaven laughs at them,* for he sees that *his day is coming,* Ps. xxxvii. 13. *I beheld* (v. 9) *till the thrones were cast down,* not only the thrones of these beasts, but *all rule, authority, and power,* that are set up in opposition to the kingdom of God among men (1 Cor. xv. 24): such are the thrones of the kingdoms of the world, in comparison with God's kingdom; those that see them set up need but wait awhile, and they will see them cast down. *I beheld till thrones were set up* (so it may as well be read), Christ's throne and the throne of his Father. One of the rabbin confesses that these thrones are *set up,* one for *God,* another for the *Son of David.* It is the *judgment* that is here set, *v.* 10. Now, 1. This is intended to proclaim God's wise and righteous government of the world by his providence; and an unspeakable satisfaction it gives to all good men, in the midst of the convulsions and revolutions of states and kingdoms, that *the Lord has prepared his throne in the heavens and his kingdom rules over all* (Ps. ciii. 19), *that verily there is a God that judges in the earth,* Ps. lviii. 11. 2. Perhaps it points at the destruction brought by the providence of God upon the empire of Syria, or that of Rome, for their tyrannizing over the people of God. But, 3. It seems principally designed to describe the last judgment, for though it follow not immediately upon the dominion of the fourth beast, nay, though it be yet to come, perhaps many ages to come, yet it was intended that in every age the people of God should encourage themselves, under their troubles, with the belief and prospect of it. Enoch, the seventh from Adam, prophesied of it, Jude 14. Does the

mouth of the enemy *speak great things, v.* 8. Here are far greater things which the mouth of the Lord has spoken. Many of the New-Testament predictions of the judgment to come have a plain allusion to this vision, especially St. John's vision of it, Rev. xx. 11, 12. (1.) The Judge is *the Ancient of days* himself, *God the Father,* the glory of whose presence is here described. He is called *the Ancient of days,* because he is God *from everlasting to everlasting.* Among men we reckon that *with the ancient is wisdom,* and *days shall speak;* shall not all flesh then be silent before him who is *the Ancient of days?* The glory of the Judge is here set forth by his garment, which was *white as snow,* denoting his splendour and purity in all the administrations of his justice; and the *hair of his head* clean and white, *as the pure wool,* that, as the white and hoary head, he may appear venerable. (2.) The throne is very formidable. It is *like the fiery flame,* dreadful to the wicked that shall be summoned before it. And the throne being movable upon wheels, or at least the chariot in which he rode the circuit, the *wheels* thereof are as *burning fire,* to devour the adversaries; for *our God is a consuming fire,* and with him are *everlasting burnings,* Isa xxxiii. 14. This is enlarged upon, *v.* 10. As to all his faithful friends there *proceeds out of the throne of God and the Lamb a pure river of water of life* (Rev. xxii. 1), so to all his implacable enemies there *issues and comes forth from* his throne a *fiery stream,* a *stream of brimstone* (Isa. xxx. 33), a *fire* that shall *devour before him.* He is a swift witness, and his word a word upon the wheels. (3.) The attendants are numerous and very splendid. The Shechinah is always attended with angels; it is so here (*v.* 10) : *Thousand thousands minister to him,* and *ten thousand times ten thousand stand before him.* It is his glory that he has such attendants, but much more his glory that he neither needs them nor can be benefited by them. See how numerous the heavenly hosts are (there are *thousands of angels*), and how obsequious they are—they *stand before God,* ready to go on his errands and to take the first intimation of his will and pleasure. They will particularly be employed as ministers of his justice in the last judgment day, when the *Son of man shall come, and all the holy angels with him.* Enoch prophesied that the Lord should come *with his holy myriads.* (4.) The process is fair and unexceptionable : *The judgment is set,* publicly and openly, that all may have recourse to it; and *the books are opened.* As in courts of judgment among men the proceedings are in writing and upon record, which is laid open when the cause comes to a hearing, the examination of witnesses is produced, and affidavits are read, to clear the matter of fact, and the statute and common-law books are consulted to find out what is the law, so, in the judgment of the great day, the equity of the sentence will be as incontestably evident as if there were books opened to justify it.

II. That the proud and cruel enemies of the church of God will certainly be reckoned with and brought down in due time, *v.* 11, 12. This is here represented to us, 1. In the destroying of the fourth beast. God's quarrel with this beast is *because of the voice of the great words which the horn spoke,* bidding defiance to Heaven, and triumphing over all that is sacred; this provokes God more than any thing, for the *enemy to behave himself proudly,* Deut. xxxii. 27. Therefore Pharaoh must be humbled, because he has said, *Who is the Lord?* and has said, *I will pursue, I will overtake.* Enoch foretold that *therefore* the Lord would come to *judge the world,* that he might *convince all that are ungodly of their hard speeches,* Jude 15. Note, Great words are but idle words, for which men must give account in the great day. And see what becomes of this beast that talks so big: He *is slain,* and *his body destroyed and given to the burning flame.* The Syrian empire, after Antiochus, was destroyed. He himself died of a miserable disease, his family was rooted out, the kingdom wasted by the Parthians and Armenians, and at length made a province of the Roman empire by Pompey. And the Roman empire itself (if we take that for the fourth beast), after it began to persecute Christianity, declined and wasted away, and the body of it was destroyed. *So shall all thy enemies perish, O Lord!* and be *slain before thee.* 2. In the diminishing and weakening of the other three beasts (*v.* 12): They had *their dominion taken away,* and so were disabled from doing the mischiefs they had done to the church and people of God; but *a prolonging in life was given them, for a time and a season,* a set time, the bounds of which they could not pass. The power of the foregoing kingdoms was quite broken, but the people of them still remained in a mean, weak, and low condition. We may allude to this in describing the remainders of sin in the hearts of good people; they have corruptions in them, the lives of which are prolonged, so that they are not perfectly free from sin, but the dominion of them is taken away, so that sin does not *reign in their mortal bodies.* And thus God deals with his church's enemies; sometimes he breaks the teeth of them (Ps. iii. 7), when he does not break the neck of them, crushes the persecution, but reprieves the persecutors, that they may have space to repent. And it is fit that God, in doing his own work, should take his own time and way.

III. That the kingdom of the Messiah shall be set up, and kept up, in the world, in spite of all the opposition of the powers of darkness. Let the heathen rage and fret as long as they please, God will *set his King upon his holy hill of Zion.* Daniel sees this in vision, and comforts himself and his friends with the prospect of it. This is the same with Nebuchadnezzar's foresight of the *stone cut out of the mountain without hands,* which broke in pieces the image; but in this vision there is much more of pure gospel than in that. 1. The Messiah is here called the Son of man—*one like unto the Son of man;* for he was *made in the likeness of sinful flesh,* was *found in fashion as a man.* I saw one like *unto the Son of man,* one exactly agreeing with the idea formed in the divine counsels of him that in the fulness of time was to be the Mediator between God and man. He is *like unto the son of man,* but is indeed the Son of God. Our Saviour seems plainly to refer to this vision when he says (John v. 27) that the *Father* has therefore *given him authority to execute judgment* because he is *the Son of man,* and because he is the person whom Daniel saw in vision, to whom a kingdom and dominion were to be given. 2. He is said to *come with the clouds of heaven.* Some refer this to his incarnation; he descended *in the clouds of heaven,* came into the world unseen, as the glory of the Lord took possession of the temple in a cloud. The empires of the world were beasts that *rose out of the sea;* but Christ's kingdom is from above: he is the *Lord from heaven.* I think it is rather to be referred to his ascension; when he returned to the Father the eye of his disciples followed him, till *a cloud received him out of their sight,* Acts i. 9. He made that cloud his chariot, wherein he rode triumphantly to the upper world. He comes swiftly, irresistibly, and comes in state, for he *comes with the clouds of heaven.* 3. He is here represented as having a mighty interest in Heaven. When the cloud received him out of the sight of his disciples, it is worth while to enquire (as the sons of the prophets concerning Elijah in a like case) whither it carried him, where it lodged him; and here we are told, abundantly to our satisfaction, that *he came to the Ancient of days;* for he ascended to *his Father and our Father,* to *his God and our God* (John xx. 17); from him he came forth, and to him he returns, to be glorified with him, and to sit down at his right hand. It was with a great deal of pleasure that he said, *Now I go to him that sent me.* But was he welcome? Yes, no doubt, he was, for *they brought him near before him;* he was introduced into his Father's presence, with the attendance and adorations of *all the angels of God,* Heb. i. 6. God *caused him to draw near and approach to him,* as an advocate and undertaker for us (Jer. xxx. 21), that we through him might be *made nigh.* By this solemn near approach which he made to the Ancient of days it appears that the Father accepted the sacrifice he offered, and the satisfaction he made, and was entirely well pleased with all he had done. He was *brought near,* as our high priest, who for us enters within the veil, and as our forerunner, 4. He is here represented as having a mighty influence upon this earth, *v.* 14. When he went to be glorified with his Father he had a *power given him over all flesh,* John xvii. 2, 5. With the prospect of this Daniel and his friends are here comforted, that not only the dominion of the church's enemies shall be taken away (*v.* 12), but the church's head and best friend shall have *the dominion given him;* to him *every knee shall bow* and *every tongue confess,* Phil. ii. 9, 10. To him are given *glory and a kingdom,* and they are given by him who has an unquestionable right to give them, which, some think with an eye to these words, our Saviour teaches us to acknowledge in the close of the Lord's prayer, *For thine is the kingdom, the power, and the glory.* It is here foretold that the kingdom of the exalted Redeemer shall be, (1.) A universal kingdom, the only universal monarchy, whatever others have pretended to, or aimed at: *All people, nations, and languages,* shall *fear him,* and be under his jurisdiction, either as his willing subjects or as his conquered captives, to be either ruled or overruled by him. One way or other, the kingdoms of the world shall all become his kingdoms. (2.) An everlasting kingdom. His *dominion* shall not *pass away* to any successor, much less to any invader, and his kingdom is *that* which *shall not be destroyed.* Even the gates of hell, or the infernal powers and policies, shall not prevail against it. The church shall continue militant to the end of time, and triumphant to the endless ages of eternity.

15 I Daniel was grieved in my spirit in the midst of *my* body, and the visions of my head troubled me. 16 I came near unto one of them that stood by, and asked him the truth of all this. So he told me, and made me know the interpretation of the things. 17 These great beasts, which are four, *are* four kings, *which* shall arise out of the earth. 18 But the saints of the Most High shall take the kingdom, and possess the kingdom for ever, even for ever and ever. 19 Then I would know the truth of the fourth beast, which was diverse from all the others, exceeding dreadful, whose teeth *were of* iron, and his nails *of* brass; *which* devoured, brake in pieces, and stamped the residue with his feet; 20 And of the ten horns that *were* in his head, and *of* the other which came up, and before whom three fell; even *of* that horn that had eyes, and a mouth that spake very great things, whose look *was* more

stout than his fellows. 21 I beheld, and the same horn made war with the saints, and prevailed against them; 22 Until the Ancient of days came, and judgment was given to the saints of the Most High; and the time came that the saints possessed the kingdom. 23 Thus he said, The fourth beast shall be the fourth kingdom upon earth, which shall be diverse from all kingdoms, and shall devour the whole earth, and shall tread it down, and break it in pieces. 24 And the ten horns out of this kingdom *are* ten kings *that* shall arise: and another shall rise after them; and he shall be diverse from the first, and he shall subdue three kings. 25 And he shall speak *great* words against the Most High, and shall wear out the saints of the Most High, and think to change times and laws: and they shall be given into his hand until a time and times and the dividing of time. 26 But the judgment shall sit, and they shall take away his dominion, to consume and to destroy *it* unto the end. 27 And the kingdom and dominion, and the greatness of the kingdom under the whole heaven, shall be given to the people of the saints of the Most High, whose kingdom *is* an everlasting kingdom, and all dominions shall serve and obey him. 28 Hitherto *is* the end of the matter. As for me Daniel, my cogitations much troubled me, and my countenance changed in me: but I kept the matter in my heart.

Here we have, I. The deep impressions which these visions made upon the prophet. God in them put honour upon him, and gave him satisfaction, yet not without a great allay of pain and perplexity (*v.* 15): *I Daniel was grieved in my spirit, in the midst of my body.* The word here used for the *body* properly signifies a *sheath* or *scabbard,* for the body is no more to the soul; that is the weapon; it is that which we are principally to take care of. The *visions of my head troubled me,* and again (*v.* 28), *my cogitations much troubled me.* The manner in which these things were discovered to him quite overwhelmed him, and put his thoughts so much to the stretch that his spirits failed him, and the trance he was in tired him and made him faint. The things themselves that were discovered amazed and astonished him, and put him into a confusion, till by degrees he recollected and conquered himself, and set the comforts of the vision over against the terrors of it.

II. His earnest desire to understand the meaning of them (*v.* 16): *I came near to one of those that stood by, to* one of the angels that appeared attending the *Son of man* in his glory, and *asked him the truth* (the true intent and meaning) *of all this.* Note, It is a very desirable thing to take the right and full sense of what we see and hear from God; and those that would know must ask by faithful and fervent prayer and by *accomplishing a diligent search.*

III. The key that was given him, to let him into the understanding of this vision. The angel *told him,* and told him so plainly that he made him *know the interpretation of the thing,* and so made him somewhat more easy.

1. *The great beasts* are great *kings* and their kingdoms, great monarchs and their monarchies, *which shall arise out of the earth,* as those beasts did *out of the sea, v.* 17. They are but *terræfilii—from beneath;* they savour of the earth, and their foundation is *in the dust;* they are of the earth earthy, and they are written in the dust, and to the dust they shall return.

2. Daniel pretty well understands the first three beasts, but concerning the fourth he desires to be better informed, because it differed so much from the rest, and was *exceedingly dreadful,* and not only so, but very mischievous, for it *devoured and broke in pieces, v.* 19. Perhaps it was this that put Daniel into such a fright, and this part of the visions of his head troubled him more than any of the rest. But especially he desired to know what the *little horn* was, that *had eyes,* and a *mouth that spoke very great things,* and whose countenance was more fearless and formidable than that of *any of his fellows, v.* 20. And this he was most inquisitive about because it was this horn that *made war with the saints, and prevailed against them, v.* 21. While no more is intimated than that the children of men make war with one another, and prevail against one another, the prophet does not show himself so much concerned *(let the potsherds strive with the potsherds of the earth,* and be dashed in pieces one against another); but when they *make war with the saints,* when the *precious sons of Zion,* comparable to *fine gold,* are broken as *earthen pitchers,* it is time to ask, " What is the meaning of this? Will the Lord cast off his people? Will he suffer their enemies to trample upon them and triumph over them? What is this same horn that shall prevail so far against the saints?" To this his interpreter answers (*v.* 23—25) that this *fourth beast* is a *fourth kingdom,* that *shall devour the whole earth,* or (as it may be read) *the whole land.* That the *ten horns are ten kings,* and the *little horn* is another king that shall subdue three kings, and shall be very abusive to God and his people, shall act, (1) Very impiously towards God. He shall *speak great words against the Most High,* setting him,

and his authority and justice, at defiance. (2.) Very imperiously towards the people of God. He shall *wear out the saints of the Most High;* he will not cut them off at once, but wear them out by long oppressions and a constant course of hardships put upon them, ruining their estates and weakening their families. The design of Satan has been to *wear out the saints of the Most High,* that they may be no more in remembrance; but the attempt is vain, for while the world stands God will have a church in it. He shall *think to change times and laws,* to abolish all the ordinances and institutions of religion, and to bring every body to say and do just as he would have them. He shall trample upon laws and customs, human and divine. *Diruit, ædificat, mutat quadrata rotundis— He pulls down, he builds, he changes square into round,* as if he meant to alter even the ordinances of heaven themselves. And in these daring attempts he shall for a time prosper and have success; they shall be given into his hand *until time, times, and half a time* (that is, for three years and a half), that famous prophetical measure of time which we meet with in the Revelation, which is sometimes called forty-two months, sometimes 1260 days, which come all to one. But at the end of that time the *judgment shall sit and take away his dominion* (*v.* 26), which he expounds (*v.* 11) of the beast being *slain and his body destroyed.* And (as Mr. Mede reads *v.* 12) *as to the rest of the beast,* the ten horns, especially the little *ruffling* horn (as he calls it), they had their dominion taken away. Now the question is, Who is this enemy, whose rise, reign, and ruin, are here foretold? Interpreters are not agreed. Some will have the fourth kingdom to be that of the Seleucidæ, and the little horn to be Antiochus, and show the accomplishment of all this in the history of the Maccabees; so Junius, Piscator, Polanus, Broughton, and many others: but others will have the fourth kingdom to be that of the Romans, and the *little horn* to be Julius Cæsar, and the succeeding emperors (says Calvin), the antichrist, the papal kingdom (says Mr. Joseph Mede), that *wicked one,* which, as this *little horn,* is to be consumed by the *brightness of Christ's second coming.* The pope assumes a power to *change times and laws, potestas αὐτοκρατορικὴ—an absolute and despotic power,* as he calls it. Others make the *little horn* to be the *Turkish empire;* so Luther, Vatablus, and others. Now I cannot prove either side to be in the wrong; and therefore, since prophecies sometimes have many fulfillings, and we ought to give scripture its full latitude (in this as in many other controversies), I am willing to allow that they are both in the right, and that this prophecy has primary reference to the Syrian empire, and was intended for the encouragement of the Jews who suffered under Antiochus, that they might see even these melancholy times foretold, but might foresee a glorious issue of them at last, and the final overthrow of their proud oppressors ; and, which is best of all, might foresee, not long after, the setting up of the kingdom of the Messiah in the world, with the hopes of which it was usual with the former prophets to comfort the people of God in their distresses. But yet it has a further reference, and foretels the like persecuting power and rage in Rome heathen, and no less in Rome papal, against the Christian religion, that was in Antiochus against the pious Jews and their religion. And St. John, in his visions and prophecies, which point primarily at Rome, has plain reference, in many particulars, to these visions of Daniel.

3. He has a joyful prospect given him of the prevalency of God's kingdom among men, and its victory over all opposition at last. And it is very observable that in the midst of the predictions of the force and fury of the enemies this is brought in abruptly (*v.* 18 and again *v.* 22), before it comes, in the course of the vision, to be interpreted, *v.* 26, 27. And this also refers, (1.) To the prosperous days of the Jewish church, after it had weathered the storm under Antiochus, and the power which the Maccabees obtained over their enemies. (2.) To the setting up of the kingdom of the Messiah in the world by the preaching of his gospel. *For judgment Christ comes into this world,* to rule by his Spirit, and to make all his saints *kings and priests to their God.* (3.) To the second coming of Jesus Christ, when the saints shall judge the world, shall sit down with him on his throne and triumph in the complete downfal of the devil's kingdom. Let us see what is here foretold. [1.] *The Ancient of days shall come, v.* 22. God shall judge the world by his Son, to whom he has *committed all judgment,* and, as an earnest of that, he *comes* for the deliverance of his oppressed people, comes for the setting up of his kingdom in the world. [2.] *The judgment shall sit, v.* 26. God will make it to appear that he *judges in the earth,* and will, both in wisdom and in equity, plead his people's righteous cause. At the great day he will *judge the world in righteousness by that man whom he has ordained.* [3.] The *dominion* of the enemy shall be *taken away, v.* 26. All Christ's enemies shall be made his footstool, and shall be *consumed and destroyed* to the end : these words the apostle uses concerning the man of sin, 2 Thess. ii. 8. He shall be *consumed* with the *spirit of Christ's mouth* and *destroyed with the brightness of his coming.* [4.] *Judgment is given to the saints of the Most High.* The apostles are entrusted with the preaching of a gospel by which the *world shall be judged.* All the saints by their faith and obedience condemn an unbelieving disobedient world ; in Christ their head they shall judge the world, shall *judge the twelve tribes of Israel,* Matt. xix. 28. See what reason

we have to honour those that fear the Lord ; how mean and despicable soever the saints now appear in the eye of the world, and how much contempt soever is poured upon them, they are the *saints of the Most High ;* they are near and dear to God, and he owns them for his, and *judgment* is *given to them.* [5.] That which is most insisted upon is that *the saints of the Most High shall take the kingdom, and possess the kingdom for ever, v.* 18. And again (*v.* 22), The *time came that the saints possessed the kingdom.* And again (*v.* 27), The *kingdom and dominion, and the greatness of the kingdom under the whole heavens, shall be given to the people of the saints of the Most High.* Far be it from us to infer hence that dominion is founded on grace, or that this will warrant any, under pretence of saintship, to usurp kingship. No ; *Christ's kingdom is not of this world ;* but this intimates the spiritual dominion of the saints over their own lusts and corruptions, their victories over Satan and his temptations, and the triumphs of the martyrs over death and its terrors. It likewise promises that the gospel kingdom shall be set up, a kingdom of light, holiness, and love, a kingdom of grace, the privileges and comforts of which now, *under the heavens,* shall be the earnest and first-fruits of the kingdom of *glory in the heavens.* When the empire became Christian, and princes used their power for the defence and advancement of Christianity, then the *saints possessed the kingdom.* The saints rule by the Spirit's ruling in them (and *this is the victory overcoming the world, even their faith*) and by making the kingdoms of this world to become Christ's kingdom. But the full accomplishment of this will be in the everlasting happiness of the saints, the kingdom that cannot be moved, which we, according to his promise, look for (that is the *greatness of the kingdom*), the crown of glory that fades not away—that is the *everlasting kingdom.* See what an emphasis is laid upon this (*v.* 18): The saints shall possess the kingdom *for ever, even for ever and ever ;* and the reason is because he whose saints they are is the *Most High* and *his kingdom is an everlasting kingdom, v.* 27. His is so, and therefore theirs shall be so. *Because I live, you shall live also,* John xiv. 19. His kingdom is theirs ; they reckon themselves exalted in his exaltation, and desire no greater honour and satisfaction to themselves than that *all dominions* should *serve and obey him,* as they shall do, *v.* 27. They shall either be brought into subjection to his golden sceptre or brought to destruction by his iron rod.

Daniel, in the close, when he ends that matter, tells us what impressions this vision made upon him ; it overwhelmed his spirits to such a degree that his *countenance* was *changed,* and it made him look pale ; but he *kept the matter in his heart.* Note, The heart must be the treasury and store-house of divine things ; there we must hide God's word, as the Virgin Mary kept the sayings of Christ, Luke ii. 51. Daniel kept *the matter in his heart,* with a design, not to keep it from the church, but to keep it for the church, that what he had received from the Lord he might fully and faithfully deliver to the people. Note, It concerns God's prophets and ministers to treasure up the things of God in their minds, and there to digest them well. If we would have God's word ready in our mouths when we have occasion for it, we must keep it in our hearts at all times.

CHAP. VIII.

The visions and prophecies of this chapter look only and entirely at the events that were then shortly to come to pass in the monarchies of Persia and Greece, and seem not to have any further reference at all. Nothing is here said of the Chaldean monarchy, for that was now just at its period; and therefore this chapter is written not in Chaldee, as the six foregoing chapters were, for the benefit of the Chaldeans, but in Hebrew, and so are the rest of the chapters to the end of the book, for the service of the Jews, that they might know what troubles were before them and what the issue of them would be, and might provide accordingly. In this chapter we have, I. The vision itself of the ram, and the he-goat, and the little horn that should fight and prevail against the people of God, for a certain limited time, ver. 1—14. II. The interpretation of this vision by an angel, showing that the ram signified the Persian empire, t͟he ne-goat the Grecian, and the little horn a king of the Grecian monarchy, that should set himself against the Jews and religion, which was Antiochus Epiphanes, ver. 15—27. The Jewish church, from its beginning, had been all along, more or less, blessed with prophets, men divinely inspired to explain God's mind to them in his providences and give them some prospect of what was coming upon them; but, soon after Ezra's time, divine inspiration ceased, and there was no more any prophet till the gospel day dawned. And therefore the events of that time were here foretold by Daniel, and left upon record, that even then God might not leave himself without witness, nor them without a guide.

IN the third year of the reign of king Belshazzar a vision appeared unto me, *even unto* me Daniel, after that which appeared unto me at the first. 2 And I saw in a vision; and it came to pass, when I saw, that I *was* at Shushan *in* the palace, which *is* in the province of Elam; and I saw in a vision, and I was by the river of Ulai. 3 Then I lifted up mine eyes, and saw, and, behold, there stood before the river a ram which had *two* horns: and the *two* horns *were* high; but one *was* higher than the other, and the higher came up last. 4 I saw the ram pushing westward, and northward, and southward; so that no beasts might stand before him, neither *was there any* that could deliver out of his hand; but he did according to his will, and became great. 5 And as I was considering, behold, a he-goat came from the west on the face of the whole earth, and touched not the ground: and the goat *had* a notable horn between his eyes. 6 And he came to the ram that had *two* horns, which I had seen standing before the river, and ran unto him in

the fury of his power. 7 And I saw him come close unto the ram, and he was moved with choler against him, and smote the ram, and brake his two horns: and there was no power in the ram to stand before him, but he cast him down to the ground, and stamped upon him: and there was none that could deliver the ram out of his hand. 8 Therefore the he-goat waxed very great: and when he was strong, the great horn was broken; and for it came up four notable ones toward the four winds of heaven. 9 And out of one of them came forth a little horn, which waxed exceeding great, toward the south, and toward the east, and toward the pleasant *land.* 10 And it waxed great, *even* to the host of heaven; and it cast down *some* of the host and of the stars to the ground, and stamped upon them. 11 Yea, he magnified *himself* even to the prince of the host, and by him the daily *sacrifice* was taken away, and the place of his sanctuary was cast down. 12 And a host was given *him* against the daily *sacrifice* by reason of transgression, and it cast down the truth to the ground; and it practised, and prospered. 13 Then I heard one saint speaking, and another saint said unto that certain *saint* which spake, How long *shall be* the vision *concerning* the daily *sacrifice,* and the transgression of desolation, to give both the sanctuary and the host to be trodden under foot? 14 And he said unto me, Unto two thousand and three hundred days; then shall the sanctuary be cleansed.

Here is, I. The date of this vision, *v.* 1. It was *in the third year of the reign of Belshazzar,* which proved to be his last year, as many reckon; so that this chapter also should be, in order of time, before the fifth. That Daniel might not be surprised at the destruction of Babylon, now at hand, God gives him a foresight of the destruction of other kingdoms hereafter, which in their day had been as potent as that of Babylon. Could we foresee the changes that shall be hereafter, when we are gone, we should the less admire, and be less affected with, the changes in our own day; for *that which is done* is *that which shall be done,* Eccl. i. 9. Then it was that a *vision appeared to me, even to me, Daniel.* Here he solemnly attests the truth of it: it was to him, even to him, that the vision was shown; he was the eye-witness of it. And this vision puts him in mind of a former vision which *appeared to him at the first*, in the first year of this reign, which he makes mention of because this vision was an explication and confirmation of that, and points at many of the same events. That seems to have been a dream, a vision in his sleep; this seems to have been when he was awake.

II. The scene of this vision. The place where that was laid was in *Shushan the palace*, one of the royal seats of the kings of Persia, situated on the banks of the river Ulai, which surrounded the city; it was in the province of Elam, that part of Persia which lay next to Babylon. Daniel was not there in person, for he was now in Babylon, a captive, in some employment under Belshazzar, and might not go to such a distant country, especially being now an enemy's country. But he was there in vision; as Ezekiel, when a captive in Babylon, was often brought, in the spirit, to the land of Israel. Note, The soul may be at liberty when the body is in captivity; for, when we are bound, the Spirit of the Lord is not bound. The vision related to that country, and therefore there he was made to fancy himself to be as strongly as if he had really been there.

III. The vision itself and the process of it.

1. He saw a *ram* with *two horns, v. 3*. This was the second monarchy, of which the kingdoms of Media and Persia were the two horns. The horns were *very high;* but that which came up last was the higher, and got the start of the former. So the last shall be first, and the first last. The kingdom of Persia, which rose last, in Cyrus, became more eminent than that of the Medes.

2. He saw this *ram pushing* all about him with his horns (*v.* 4), *westward* (towards Babylon, Syria, Greece, and Asia the less), *northward* (towards the Lydians, Armenians, and Scythians), and *southward* (towards Arabia, Ethiopia, and Egypt), for all these nations did the Persian empire, one time or other, make attempts upon for the enlarging of their dominion. And at last he became so powerful that *no beasts might stand before him*. This *ram*, though of a species of animal often preyed upon, became formidable even to the beasts of prey themselves, so that there was *no standing* before him, no escaping him, none that *could deliver out of his hand*, but all must yield to him : the kings of Persia did according *to their will*, prospered in all their ways abroad, had an uncontrollable power at home, and *became great*. He thought himself great because he did what he would; but to do good is that which makes men truly great.

3. He saw this ram overcome by a he-goat. He was considering the *ram* (wondering that so weak an animal should come to be so prevalent) and thinking what would be the

issue; and, *behold, a he-goat came, v.* 5. This was Alexander the Great, the son of Philip king of Macedonia He *came from the west*, from Greece, which lay west from Persia. He fetched a great compass with his army : he came *upon the face of the whole earth ;* he did in effect conquer the world, and then sat down and wept because there was not another world to be conquered. *Unus Pellæo juveni non sufficit orbis—One world was too little for the youth of Pellæ.* This he-goat (a creature famed for comeliness in going, Prov. xxx. 31) went on with incredible swiftness, so that he *touched not the ground*, so lightly did he move; he rather seemed to fly above the ground than to go upon the ground; or *none touched him in the earth*, that is, he met with little or no opposition. This *he-goat*, or buck, had a *notable horn between his eyes*, like a unicorn. He had strength, and knew his own strength; he saw himself a match for all his neighbours. Alexander pushed his conquests on so fast, and with so much fury, that none of the kingdoms he attacked had courage to make a stand, or give check to the progress of his victorious arms. In six years he made himself master of the greatest part of the then known world. Well might he be called a *notable horn*, for his name still lives in history as the name of one of the most celebrated commanders in war that ever the world knew. Alexander's victories and achievements are still the entertainment of the ingenious. This *he-goat* came to the *ram that had two horns, v.* 6. Alexander with his victorious army attacked the kingdom of Persia, an army consisting of no more than 30,000 foot and 5000 horse. He *ran unto him*, to surprise him ere he could get intelligence of his motions, *in the fury of his power*. He came *close to the ram*. Alexander with his army came up with Darius Codomannus, then emperor of Persia, being *moved with choler against him, v.* 7. It was with the greatest violence that Alexander pushed on his war against Darius, who, though he brought vast numbers into the field, yet, for want of skill, was an unequal match for him, so that Alexander was too hard for him whenever he engaged him, *smote him, cast him down to the ground*, and *stamped upon him*, which three expressions, some think, refer to the three famous victories that Alexander obtained over Darius, at Granicus, at Issus, and at Arbela, by which he was at length totally routed, having, in the last battle, had 600,000 men killed, so that Alexander became absolute master of all the Persian empire, *broke his two horns*, the kingdoms of Media and Persia. The ram that had destroyed *all before him* (*v.* 4) now is himself destroyed; Darius has *no power to stand* before Alexander, nor has he any friends or allies to help to *deliver him out of his hand*. Note, Those kingdoms which, when they had power, abused it, and, because none could oppose them, withheld not themselves from the doing of any wrong, may expect to have their power at length taken from them, and to be served in their own kind, Isa. xxxiii. 1.

4. He saw the he-goat made hereby very considerable; but the *great horn*, that had done all this execution, *was broken, v.* 8. Alexander was about twenty years old when he began his wars. When he was about twenty-six he conquered Darius, and became master of the whole Persian empire; but when he was about thirty-two or thirty-three *years of age*, when he was *strong*, in his full strength, he was *broken*. He was not killed in war, in the bed of honour, but died of a drunken surfeit, or, as some suspect, by poison, and left no child living behind him to enjoy that which he had endlessly laboured for, but left a lasting monument of the vanity of worldly pomp and power, and their insufficiency to make a man happy.

5. He saw this kingdom divided into four parts, and that instead of that one great horn there came up *four notable ones*, Alexander's four captains, to whom he bequeathed his conquests; and he had so much that, when it was divided among four, they had each of them enough for any one man. These *four notable horns* were towards the *four winds of heaven*, the same with the *four heads* of the leopard (*ch.* vii. 6), the kingdoms of Syria and Egypt, Asia and Greece—Syria lying to the *east*, Greece to the *west*, Asia Minor to the *north*, and Egypt to the *south*. Note, Those that heap up riches know not who shall gather them, nor whose all those things shall be which they have provided.

6. He saw a *little horn* which became a great persecutor of the church and people of God; and this was the principal thing that was intended to be shown to him in this vision, as afterwards, *ch.* xi. 30, &c. All agree that this was *Antiochus Epiphanes* (so he called himself)—*the illustrious*, but others called him *Antiochus Epimanes—Antiochus the furious.* He is called here (as before, *ch.* vii. 8) a *little horn*, because he was in his original contemptible; there were others between him and the kingdom, and he was of a base servile disposition, had nothing in him of princely qualities, and had been for some time a hostage and prisoner at Rome, whence he made his escape, and, though the youngest brother, and his elder living, got the kingdom. He waxed exceedingly great *towards the south*, for he seized upon Egypt, and towards *the east*, for he invaded Persia and Armenia. But that which is here especially taken notice of is the mischief that he did to the people of the Jews. They are not expressly named, for prophecies must not be too plain; but they are here so described that it would be easy for those who understood scripture-language to know who were meant; and the Jews, having notice of this before, might be awakened to prepare themselves and their children beforehand for these suffering trying times. (1.) He set himself against *the pleasant land*, the land of Israel, so called because it was the *glory of all lands*, for fruitfulness and all the delights of human life, but especially for the tokens of God's presence in it, and its being blessed with divine revelations and institutions; it was Mount Zion that was *beautiful for situation*, and the *joy of the whole earth*, Ps. xlviii. 2. The pleasantness of that land was that there the Messiah was to be born, who would be both the consolation and *the glory of his people Israel.* Note, We have reason to reckon that a pleasant place which is a holy place, in which God dwells, and where we may have opportunity of communing with him. Surely, *It is good to be here.* (2.) He fought against the *host of heaven*, that is, the people of God, the church, which is the kingdom of heaven, the church-militant here on earth. The saints, being born from above, and citizens of heaven, and doing the will of God, by his grace, in some measure, as the angels of heaven do it, may be well called a *heavenly host.* Or the priests and Levites, who were employed in the service of the tabernacle, and there *warred a good warfare*, were this *host of heaven.* These Antiochus set himself against; he *waxed great to the host of heaven*, in opposition to them and in defiance of them. (3.) He *cast down some of the host* (that is, *of the stars*, for they are called the host of heaven) *to the ground, and stamped upon them.* Some of those that were most eminent both in church and state, that were burning and shining lights in their generation, he either forced to comply with his idolatries or put them to death; he got them into his hands, and then trampled upon them and triumphed over them; as good old Eleazar, and the *seven brethren*, whom he put to death with cruel tortures, because they would not eat swine's flesh, 2 Mac. vi. 7. He gloried in it that herein he insulted Heaven itself and *exalted his throne above the stars of God*, Isa. xiv. 13. (4.) He *magnified himself even to the prince of the host.* He set himself against the high priest, Onias, whom he deprived of his dignity, or rather against God himself, who was Israel's *King of old*, who *reigns for ever* Zion's King, who himself heads his own host that fight his battles. Against him Antiochus magnified himself; as Pharaoh, when he said, *Who is the Lord?* Note, Those who persecute the people of God persecute God himself. (5.) He *took away the daily sacrifice.* The morning and evening lamb, which God appointed to be offered every day upon his altar to his honour, Antiochus forbade and restrained the offering of. No doubt he took away all other sacrifices, but only the *daily sacrifice* is mentioned, because that was the greatest loss of all, for in that they kept up their constant communion with God, which they preferred before that which is only occasional. God's people reckon their daily sacrifices,

their morning and evening exercises of devotion, the most needful of their daily business and the most delightful of their daily comforts, and would not for all the world part with them. (6.) He *cast down the place of his sanctuary*. He did not burn and demolish the temple, but he cast it down, when he profaned it, made it the temple of Jupiter Olympius, and set up his image in it. He also *cast down the truth to the ground*, trampled upon the book of the law, that word of truth, tore it, and burnt it, and did what he could to destroy it quite, that it might be lost and forgotten for ever. These were the projects of that wicked prince. In these he practised. And (would you think it?) in these he prospered. He carried the matter very far, seemed to have gained his point, and went near to extirpate that holy religion which God's right hand had planted. But lest he or any other should triumph, as if herein he had prevailed against God himself and been too hard for him, the matter is here explained and set in a true light. [1.] He could not have done this if God had not permitted him to do it, could have had no power against Israel unless it had been given him from above. God put this power into his hand, and *gave him a host against the daily sacrifice*. God's providence put that sword into his hand by which he was enabled thus to bear down all before him. Note, We ought to eye and own the hand of God in all the enterprises and all the successes of the church's enemies against the church. They are but the rod in God's hand. [2.] God would not have permitted it if his people had not provoked him to do so. It is *by reason of transgression*, the transgression of Israel, to correct them for that, that Antiochus is employed to give them all this trouble. Note, When the pleasant land and all its pleasant things are laid waste, it must be acknowledged that sin is the procuring cause of all the desolation. *Who gave Jacob to the spoil? Did not the Lord, he against whom we have sinned?* Isa. xlii. 24. The great transgression of the Jews after the captivity (when they were cured of idolatry) was a contempt and profanation of the holy things, *snuffing* at the service of God, *bringing the torn and the lame for sacrifice*, as if the *table of the Lord* were a *contemptible* thing (so we find Mal. i. 7, 8, &c., and that the priests were guilty of this Mal. ii. 1, 8), and therefore God sent Antiochus to *take away the daily sacrifice* and *cast down the place of his sanctuary*. Note, It is just with God to deprive those of the privileges of his house who despise and profane them, and to make those know the worth of ordinances by the want of them who would not know it by the enjoyment of them.

7. He heard the time of this calamity limited and determined, not the time *when it should come* (that is not here fixed, because God would have his people always prepared for it), but *how long it should last*, that, when
1080

they had no more any *prophets* to *tell them how long* (Ps. lxxiv. 9, which psalm seems to have been calculated for this dark and doleful day), they might have this prophecy to give them a prospect of deliverance in due time Now concerning this we have here,

(1.) The question asked concerning it, *v.* 13. Observe [1.] By whom the question was put: *I heard one saint speaking* to this purport, and then *another saint* seconded him. " O that we knew how long this trouble will last !" The angels here are called *saints*, for they are *holy ones* (ch. iv. 13), the *holy myriads*, Jude 14. The angels concern themselves in the affairs of the church, and enquire concerning them, if, as here, concerning its temporal salvations, much more do they desire to *look into the great salvation*, 1 Pet. i. 12. One saint *spoke* of the thing, and another *enquired* concerning it. Thus John, who lay in Christ's bosom, was beckoned to by Peter to ask Christ a question, John xiii. 23, 24. [2.] To whom the question was put. He said *unto Palmoni that spoke*. Some make this *certain saint* to be a superior angel who understood more than the rest, to whom therefore they came with their enquiries. Others make it to be the *eternal Word*, the *Son of God*. He is the *unknown One*. *Palmoni* seems to be compounded of *Peloni Almoni*, which is used (Ruth iv. 1) for *Ho, such a one*, and (2 Kings vi. 8) for *such a place*. Christ was yet the *nameless One*. *Wherefore askest thou after my name, seeing it is secret?* Judg. xiii. 18. He is the *numberer of secrets* (as some translate it), for from him there is nothing hidden —*the wonderful numberer*, so others ; his name is called *Wonderful*. Note, If we would know the mind of God, we must apply to Jesus Christ, who lay in the bosom of the Father, and *in whom are hidden all the treasures of wisdom and knowledge*, not hidden from us, but hidden for us. [3.] The question itself that was asked : " *How long shall be the vision concerning the daily sacrifice?* How long shall the prohibition of it continue? How long shall the pleasant land be made unpleasant by that severe interdict? How long shall *the transgression of desolation* (the image of Jupiter), that great transgression which makes all our sacred things desolate, how long shall that stand in the temple? How long shall *the sanctuary and the host*, the holy place and the holy persons that minister in it, be *trodden under foot* by the oppressor?" Note, Angels are concerned for the prosperity of the church on earth and desirous to see an end of its desolations. The angels asked, for the satisfaction of Daniel, not doubting but he was desirous to know, how long these calamities should last? The question takes it for granted that they should not last always. *The rod of the wicked shall not rest upon the lot of the righteous*, though it may come upon their lot. Christ comforted himself in his sufferings with this, *The things concerning me have an end* (Luke xxii. 37), and so may the church in hers. But it is desirable to know how long they shall last, that we may provide accordingly.

(2.) The answer given to this question, *v.* 14. Christ gives instruction to the holy angels, for they are our fellow-servants; but here the answer was given to Daniel, because for his sake the question was asked: *He said unto me.* God sometimes gives in great favours to his people, in answer to the enquiries and requests of their friends for them. Now, [1.] Christ assures him that the trouble shall end; it shall continue 2300 *days and no longer,* so many *evenings and mornings* (so the word is), so many νυχϑήμεραι, so many *natural* days, reckoned, as in the beginning of Genesis, by the evenings and mornings, because it was the evening and the morning sacrifice that they most lamented the loss of, and thought the time passed very slowly while they were deprived of them. Some make the morning and the evening, in this number, to stand for two, and then 2300 evenings and as many mornings will make but 1150 days; and about so many days it was that the daily sacrifice was interrupted: and this comes nearer to the computation (*ch.* vii. 25) of a *time, times,* and the *dividing of a time.* But it is less forced to understand them of so many natural days; 2300 days make *six years* and *three months,* and about eighteen days; and just so long they reckon from the defection of the people, procured by Menelaus the high priest in the 142nd year of the kingdom of the Seleucidæ, the sixth month of that year, and the 6th day of the month (so Josephus dates it), to the cleansing of the sanctuary, and the re-establishment of religion among them, which was in the 148th year, the 9th month, and the 25th *day of the month,* 1 Mac. iv. 52. God reckons the time of his people's affliction by *days,* for in all their afflictions he is afflicted. Rev. ii. 10, Thou shalt have *tribulation ten days.* [2.] He assures him that they shall see better days afterwards: *Then shall the sanctuary be cleansed.* Note, The cleansing of the sanctuary is a happy token for good to any people; when they begin to be reformed they will soon be relieved. Though the righteous God may, for the correction of his people, suffer his sanctuary to be profaned for a while, yet the jealous God will, for his own glory, see to the cleansing of it in due time. Christ died to cleanse his church, and he will so cleanse it as at length to present it blameless to himself.

15 And it came to pass, when I, *even* I Daniel, had seen the vision, and sought for the meaning, then, behold, there stood before me as the appearance of a man. 16 And I heard a man's voice between *the banks of*

Ulai, which called, and said, Gabriel, make this *man* to understand the vision. 17 So he came near where I stood: and when he came, I was afraid, and fell upon my face: but he said unto me, Understand, O son of man: for at the time of the end *shall be* the vision. 18 Now as he was speaking with me, I was in a deep sleep on my face toward the ground: but he touched me, and set me upright. 19 And he said, Behold, I will make thee know what shall be in the last end of the indignation: for at the time appointed the end *shall be.* 20 The ram which thou sawest having *two* horns *are* the kings of Media and Persia. 21 And the rough goat *is* the king of Grecia: and the great horn that *is* between his eyes *is* the first king. 22 Now that being broken, whereas four stood up for it, four kingdoms shall stand up out of the nation, but not in his power. 23 And in the latter time of their kingdom, when the transgressors are come to the full, a king of fierce countenance, and understanding dark sentences, shall stand up. 24 And his power shall be mighty, but not by his own power: and he shall destroy wonderfully, and shall prosper, and practise, and shall destroy the mighty and the holy people. 25 And through his policy also he shall cause craft to prosper in his hand; and he shall magnify *himself* in his heart, and by peace shall destroy many: he shall also stand up against the Prince of princes; but he shall be broken without hand. 26 And the vision of the evening and the morning which was told *is* true: wherefore shut thou up the vision; for it *shall be* for many days. 27 And I Daniel fainted, and was sick *certain* days; afterward I rose up, and did the king's business; and I was astonished at the vision, but none understood *it.*

Here we have,

I. Daniel's earnest desire to have this vision explained to him (*v.* 15): *I sought the meaning.* Note, Those that rightly know the things of God cannot but desire to know more and more of them, and to be led further into the mystery of them; and those that would find the meaning of what they have seen or heard from God must seek it, and seek it diligently. *Seek and you shall find.* Daniel considered the thing, compared it with the former discoveries, to try if he could understand it; but especially he sought by prayer (as he had done *ch.* ii. 18), and he did not seek in vain.

II. Orders given to the angel Gabriel to inform him concerning this vision. One *in the appearance of a man* (who, some think, was Christ himself, for who besides could command angels?) orders Gabriel to *make Daniel understand this vision.* Sometimes God is pleased to make use of the ministration of angels, not only to protect his children, but to instruct them, to serve the kind intentions, not only of his providence, but of his grace.

III. The consternation that Daniel was in upon the approach of his instructor (*v.* 17): *When he came near I was afraid.* Though Daniel was a man of great prudence and courage, and had been conversant with the visions of the Almighty, yet the approach of an extraordinary messenger from heaven put him into this fright. He *fell upon his face,* not to worship the angel, but because he could no longer bear the dazzling lustre of his glory. Nay, being prostrate upon the ground, he *fell into a deep sleep* (*v.* 18), which came not from any neglect of the vision, or indifference towards it, but was an effect of his faintness and the oppression of spirit he was under, through the abundance of revelations. The disciples in the garden slept for sorrow; and, as there, so here, *the spirit was willing, but the flesh was weak.* Daniel would have kept awake, and could not.

IV. The relief which the angel gave to Daniel, with great encouragement to him to expect a satisfactory discovery of the meaning of this vision. 1. He *touched him,* and *set him upon his feet, v.* 18. Thus when John, in a similar case, was in similar consternation, Christ *laid his right hand upon him,* Rev. i. 17. It was a gentle touch that the angel here gave to Daniel, to show that he came not to hurt him, not to *plead against him with his great power,* or with a hand *heavy upon him,* but to help him, to *put strength into him* (Job xxiii. 6), which God can do with a touch. When we are slumbering and grovelling on this earth we are very unfit to hear from God, and to converse with him. But, if God design instruction for us, he will by his grace awaken us out of our slumber, raise us from things below, and *set us upright.* 2. He promised to inform him: "*Understand, O son of man! v.* 17. Thou shalt understand, if thou wilt but apply thy mind to understand." He calls him *son of man* to intimate that he would consider his frame, and would deal tenderly with him, accommodating himself to his capacity as a man. Or thus he preaches humility to him; though he be admitted to converse with angels, he

1082

must not be puffed up with it, but must remember that he is a son of man. Or perhaps this title puts an honour upon him: the Messiah was lately called the *Son of man* (*ch.* vii. 13), and Daniel is akin to him, and is a figure of him as a prophet and one *greatly beloved.* He assures him that he shall be made to know *what shall be in the last end of the indignation, v.* 19. Let it be laid up for a comfort to those who shall live to see these calamitous times that there shall be an end of them; *the indignation shall cease* (Isa. x. 25); it *shall be overpast,* Isa. xxvi. 20. It may intermit and return again, but the *last end* shall be glorious; good will follow it, nay, and good will be brought out of it. He tells him (*v.* 17), "*At the time of the end shall be the vision;* when the last end of the indignation comes, when the course of this providence is completed, then the vision shall be made plain and intelligible by the event, as the event shall be made plain and intelligible by the vision." Or, "*At the time of the end* of the Jewish church, in the latter days of it, *shall this vision* be accomplished, 300 or 400 years hence; understand it therefore, that thou mayest leave it on record for the generations to come." But if he ask more particularly, "When is the time of the end? And how long will it be before it arrive?" let this answer suffice (*v.* 19): *At the time appointed the end shall be;* it is fixed in the divine counsel, which cannot be altered and which must not be pried into.

V. The exposition which he gave him of the vision.

1. Concerning the two monarchies of Persia and Greece, *v.* 20—22. The *ram* signified the succession of the kings of Media and Persia; the *rough goat* signified the kings of Greece; the *great horn* was Alexander; the *four horns* that rose in his room were the four kingdoms into which his conquests were cantoned, of which before, *v.* 8. They are said to *stand up out of the nations,* but *not in his power;* none of them ever made the figure that Alexander did. Josephus relates that when Alexander had taken Tyre, and subdued Palestine, and was upon his march to Jerusalem, Jaddas, who was then high priest (Nehemiah mentions one of his name, *ch.* xii. 11), fearing his rage, had recourse to God by prayer and sacrifice for the common safety, and was by him warned in a dream that upon Alexander's approach he should throw open the gates of the city, and that he and the rest of the priests should go forth to meet him in their habits, and all the people in white. Alexander, seeing this company at a distance, went himself alone to the high priest, and, having prostrated himself before that God whose name was engraven in the golden plate of his mitre, he first saluted him; and, being asked by one of his own captains why he did so, he said that while he was yet in Macedon, musing on the conquest of Asia, there appeared to him

a man like unto this, and thus attired, who invited him into Asia, and assured him of success in the conquest of it. The priests led him to the temple, where he offered sacrifice to the God of Israel as they directed him; and there they showed him this book of the prophet Daniel, that it was there foretold that a Grecian should come and destroy the Persians, which animated him very much in the expedition he was now meditating against Darius. Hereupon he took the Jews and their religion under his protection, promised to be kind to those of their religion in Babylon and Media, whither he was now marching, and in honour of him all the priests that had sons born that year called them *Alexander. Joseph. lib.* 11.

2. Concerning Antiochus, and his oppression of the Jews. This is said to be in the *latter time of the* kingdom of the Greeks, *when the transgressors are come to the full* (*v.* 23); that is, when the degenerate Jews have filled up the measure of their iniquity, and are ripe for this destruction, so that God cannot in honour bear with them any longer, then shall *stand up* this king, to be *flagellum Dei*—the rod in God's hand for the chastising of the Jews. Now observe here, (1.) His character : He shall be a *king of fierce countenance,* insolent and furious, neither fearing God nor regarding man, *understanding dark sentences,* or (rather) *versed in dark practices,* the *hidden things of dishonesty;* he was master of all the arts of dissimulation and deceit, and knew the *depths of Satan* as well as any man. He was *wise to do evil.* (2.) His success. He shall make dreadful havoc of the nations about him : *His power shall be mighty,* bear down all before it, but not *by his own power* (*v.* 24), but partly by the assistance of his allies, Eumenes and Attalus, partly by the baseness and treachery of many of the Jews, even of the priests that came into his interests, and especially by the divine permission. It was not by his own power, but by a power given him from above, that he *destroyed wonderfully,* and thought he made himself a great man by being a great destroyer. He destroys wonderfully indeed, for he destroys, [1.] The *mighty people,* and they cannot resist him by their power. The princes of Egypt cannot stand before him with all their forces, but he practises against them and prospers. Note, The mighty ones of the earth commonly meet with those at length that are too hard for them, that are more mighty than they. Let not the strong man then glory in his strength, be it ever so great, unless he could be sure that there were none stronger than he. [2.] He destroys the *holy people,* or *the people of the holy ones;* and their sacred character does neither assure him from destroying them nor defend them from being destroyed. *All things come alike to all,* and there is one event to the mighty and to the holy in this world. [3.] The methods by

which he will gain this success, not by true courage, wisdom, or justice, but by his *policy* and *craft* (*v.* 25), by fraud and deceit, and serpentine subtlety : He shall *cause craft to prosper;* so cunningly shall he carry on his projects that he shall gain his point by the art of wheedling. *By peace he shall destroy many,* as others do by war; under the pretence of treaties, leagues, and alliances, with them, he shall encroach on their rights, and trick them into a subjection to him. Thus sometimes what a nation truly brave has gained in a righteous war a nation truly base has regained in a treacherous peace, and craft has been caused to prosper. [4] The mischief that he shall do to religion : *He shall magnify himself in his heart,* and think himself fit to prescribe and give law to every body, so that he shall *stand up against the Prince of princes,* that is, against God himself. He will profane his temple and altar, prohibit his worship, and persecute his worshippers. See what a height of impudence some men's impiety brings them to; they openly bid defiance to God himself though he is the King of kings. [5.] The ruin that he shall be brought to at last: *He shall be broken without hand,* that is, without the hand of man. He shall not be slain in war, nor shall he be assassinated, as tyrants commonly were, but he shall fall into the hand of the living God and die by an immediate stroke of his vengeance. He, hearing that the Jews had cast the image of Jupiter Olympius out of the temple, where he had placed it, was so enraged at the Jews that he vowed he would make Jerusalem *a common burial-place,* and determined to march thither immediately; but no sooner had he spoken these proud words than he was struck with an incurable plague in his bowels; worms bred so fast in his body that whole flakes of flesh sometimes dropped from him; his torments were violent, and the stench of his disease such that none could endure to come near him. He continued in this misery very long. At first he persisted in his menaces against the Jews; but at length, despairing of his recovery, he called his friends together, and acknowledged all those miseries to have fallen upon him for the injuries he had done to the Jews and his profaning the temple at Jerusalem. Then he wrote courteous letters to the Jews, and vowed that if he recovered he would let them have the free exercise of their religion. But, finding his disease grow upon him, when he could no longer endure his own smell, he said, *It is meet to submit to God, and for man who is mortal not to set himself in competition with God,* and so died miserably in a strange land, on the mountains of Pacata near Babylon: so Usher's Annals, *A. M.* 3840, about 160 years before the birth of Christ.

3. As to the time fixed for the continuance of the cessation of the daily sacrifice, it is not explained here, but only confirmed (*v.*

26) · That *vision of the evening and morning is true,* in the proper sense of the words, and needs no explication. How unlikely soever it might be that God should suffer his own sanctuary to be thus profaned, yet it is true, it is too true, so it shall be.

VI. Here is the conclusion of this vision, and here, 1. The charge given to Daniel to keep it private for the present: *Shut thou up the vision;* let it not be publicly known among the Chaldeans, lest the Persians, who were now shortly to possess the kingdom, should be incensed against the Jews by it, because the downfal of their kingdom was foretold by it, which would be unseasonable now that the edict for their release was expected from the king of Persia. *Shut it up, for it shall be for many days.* It was about 300 years from the time of this vision to the time of the accomplishment of it; therefore he must *shut it up* for the present, even from the people of the Jews, lest it should amaze and perplex them, but let it be kept safely for the generations to come, that should live about the time of the accomplishment of it, for to them it would be both most intelligible and most serviceable. Note, What we know of the things of God should be carefully laid up, that hereafter, when there is occasion, it may be faithfully laid out; and what we have not now any use for, yet we may have another time. Divine truths should be sealed up among our treasures, that we may find them again after many days. 2. The care he took to keep it private, having received such a charge, *v.* 27. He *fainted, and was sick,* with the multitude of his thoughts within him occasioned by this vision, which oppressed and overwhelmed him the more because he was forbidden to publish what he had seen, so that *his belly was as wine which has no vent,* he was *ready to burst like new bottles,* Job xxxii. 19. However, he kept it to himself, stifled and smothered the concern he was in; so that those he conversed with could not perceive it, but he *did the king's business* according to the duty of his place, whatever it was. Note, As long as we live in this world we must have something to do in it; and even those whom God has most dignified with his favours must not think themselves above their business; nor must the pleasure of communion with God take us off from the duties of our particular callings, but still we must in them *abide with God.* Those especially that are entrusted with public business must see to it that they conscientiously discharge their trust.

CHAP. IX.

In this chapter we have, I. Daniel's prayer for the restoration of the Jews who were in captivity, in which he confesses sin, and acknowledges the justice of God in their calamities, but pleads God's promises of mercy which he had yet in store for them, v. 1—19. II. An immediate answer sent him by an angel to his prayer, in which, I. He is assured of the speedy release of the Jews out of their captivity, v. 20—23. And, 2. He is informed concerning the redemption of the world by Jesus Christ (of which that was a type), what should be the nature of it and when it should be accomplished, v. 24—27. And it is the clearest, brightest, prophecy of the Messiah, in all the Old Testament.

1084

IN the first year of Darius the son of Ahasuerus, of the seed of the Medes, which was made king over the realm of the Chaldeans ; 2 In the first year of his reign I Daniel understood by books the number of the years, whereof the word of the LORD came to Jeremiah the prophet, that he would accomplish seventy years in the desolations of Jerusalem. 3 And I set my face unto the Lord God, to seek by prayer and supplications, with fasting, and sackcloth, and ashes :

We left Daniel, in the close of the foregoing chapter, employed in the *king's business;* but here we have him employed in better business than any the king had for him, speaking to God and hearing from him, not for himself only, but for the church, whose mouth he was to God, and for whose use the *oracles* of God were *committed to him,* relating to the days of the Messiah. Observe, 1. When it was that Daniel had this communion with God (*v.* 1), *in the first year of Darius the Mede,* who was newly made king of the Chaldeans, Babylon being conquered by him and his nephew, or grandson, Cyrus. In this year the seventy years of the Jews' captivity ended, but the decree for their release was not yet issued out ; so that this address of Daniel's to God seems to have been ready in that year, and, probably, before he was cast into the lions' den. And one powerful inducement, perhaps, it was to him then to keep so close to the duty of prayer, though it cost him his life, that he had so lately experienced the benefit and comfort of it. 2. What occasioned his address to God by prayer (*v.* 2) : He *understood by books* that seventy years was the time fixed for the continuance of *the desolations of Jerusalem, v.* 2. The *book* by which he understood this was the book of the prophecies of Jeremiah, in which he found it expressly foretold (Jer. xxix. 10), *After seventy years be accomplished in Babylon* (and therefore they must be reckoned from the first captivity, in the *third year* of Jehoiakim, which Daniel had reason to remember by a good token, for it was in that captivity that he was carried away himself, *ch.* i. 1), *I will visit you, and perform my good word towards you.* It was likewise said (Jer. xxv. 11), *This whole land shall be seventy years a desolation (chorbath),* the same word that Daniel here uses for the *desolations of Jerusalem,* which shows that he had that prophecy before him when he wrote this. Though Daniel was himself a great prophet, and one that was well acquainted with the visions of God, yet he was a diligent student in the scripture, and thought it no disparagement to him to consult Jeremiah's prophecies. He was a great politician, and prime-minister of state to one of the greatest monarchs upon earth, and yet could find both heart and time to converse with the word of God. The greatest and best men in the world must not think themselves above their Bibles. 3. How serious and solemn his address to God was when he understood that the seventy years were just upon expiring (for it appears, by Ezekiel's dating of his prophecies, that they exactly computed the years of their captivity), then he *set his face to seek God by prayer.* Note, God's promises are intended, not to supersede, but to excite and encourage, our prayers; and, when we see the day of the performance of them approaching, we should the more earnestly plead them with God and put them in suit. So Daniel did here; he prayed three times a day, and, no doubt, in every prayer made mention of the desolations of Jerusalem; yet he did not think that enough, but even in the midst of his business set time apart for an extraordinary application to Heaven on Jerusalem's behalf. God had said to Ezekiel that though Daniel, among others, stood before him, his intercession should not prevail to prevent the judgment (Ezek. xiv. 14), yet he hopes, now that *the warfare is accomplished* (Isa. xl. 2), his prayer may be heard for the removing of the judgment. When the day of deliverance dawns it is time for God's praying people to bestir themselves; something extraordinary is then expected and required from them, besides their daily sacrifice. Now *Daniel sought by prayer and supplications,* for fear lest the sins of the people should provoke him to defer their deliverance longer than was intended, or rather that the people might be prepared by the grace of God for the deliverance now that the providence of God was about to work it out for them. Now observe, (1.) The intenseness of his mind in this prayer: *I set my face unto the Lord God to seek him,* which denotes the fixedness of his thoughts, the firmness of his faith, and the fervour of his devout affections, in the duty. We must, in prayer, set God before us, and set ourselves as in his presence; to him we must *direct our prayer* and must *look up.* Probably, in token of his setting his face towards God, he did, as usual, set his face towards Jerusalem, to affect his own heart the more with the desolations of it. (2.) The mortification of his body in this prayer. In token of his deep humiliation before God for his own sins, and the sins of his people, and the sense he had of his unworthiness, when he prayed he *fasted,* put on *sackcloth,* and lay in *ashes,* the more to affect himself with the desolations of Jerusalem, which he was praying for the repair of, and to make himself sensible that he was now about an extraordinary work.

4 And I prayed unto the Lord my God, and made my confession, and said, O Lord, the great and dreadful God, keeping the covenant and mercy to them that love him, and to them that keep his commandments; 5 We have sinned, and have committed iniquity, and have done wickedly, and have rebelled, even by departing from thy precepts and from thy judgments: 6 Neither have we hearkened unto thy servants the prophets, which spake in thy name to our kings, our princes, and our fathers, and to all the people of the land. 7 O Lord, righteousness *belongeth* unto thee, but unto us confusion of faces, as at this day; to the men of Judah, and to the inhabitants of Jerusalem, and unto all Israel, *that are* near, and *that are* far off, through all the countries whither thou hast driven them, because of their trespass that they have trespassed against thee. 8 O Lord, to us *belongeth* confusion of face, to our kings, to our princes, and to our fathers, because we have sinned against thee. 9 To the Lord our God *belong* mercies and forgivenesses, though we have rebelled against him; 10 Neither have we obeyed the voice of the Lord our God, to walk in his laws, which he set before us by his servants the prophets. 11 Yea, all Israel have transgressed thy law, even by departing, that they might not obey thy voice; therefore the curse is poured upon us, and the oath that *is* written in the law of Moses the servant of God, because we have sinned against him. 12 And he hath confirmed his words, which he spake against us, and against our judges that judged us, by bringing upon us a great evil: for under the whole heaven hath not been done as hath been done upon Jerusalem. 13 As *it is* written in the law of Moses, all this evil is come upon us: yet made we not our prayer before the Lord our God, that we might turn from our iniquities, and understand thy truth. 14 Therefore hath the Lord watched upon the evil, and brought it upon us: for the Lord our God *is* righteous in all his works which he doeth: for we obeyed not his voice. 15 And now, O Lord our God, that hast brought thy people

forth out of the land of Egypt with a mighty hand, and hast gotten thee renown, as at this day; we have sinned, we have done wickedly. 16 O LORD, according to all thy righteousness, I beseech thee, let thine anger and thy fury be turned away from thy city Jerusalem, thy holy mountain: because for our sins, and for the iniquities of our fathers, Jerusalem and thy people *are become* a reproach to all *that are* about us. 17 Now therefore, O our God, hear the prayer of thy servant, and his supplications, and cause thy face to shine upon thy sanctuary that is desolate, for the Lord's sake. 18 O my God, incline thine ear, and hear; open thine eyes, and behold our desolations, and the city which is called by thy name: for we do not present our supplications before thee for our righteousness, but for thy great mercies. 19 O Lord, hear; O Lord, forgive; O Lord, hearken and do; defer not, for thine own sake, O my God: for thy city and thy people are called by thy name.

We have here Daniel's prayer to God as his God, and the confession which he joined with that prayer: I *prayed, and made my confession.* Note, In every prayer we must make confession, not only of the sins we have been guilty of (which we commonly call *confession*), but of our faith in God and dependence upon him, our sorrow for sin and our resolutions against it. It must be our confession, must be the language of our own convictions and that which we ourselves do heartily subscribe to.

Let us go over the several parts of this prayer, which we have reason to think that he offered up much more largely than is here recorded, these being only the heads of it.

I. Here is his humble, serious, reverent address to God, in which he gives glory to God, 1. As a God to be feared, and whom it is our duty always to stand in awe of: "*O Lord! the great and dreadful God,* that art able to deal with the greatest and most terrible of the church's enemies." 2. As a God to be trusted, and whom it is our duty to depend upon and put a confidence in: *Keeping the covenant and mercy to those that love him,* and, as a proof of their love to him, *keep his commandments.* If we fulfil our part of the bargain, he will not fail to fulfil his. He will be to his people as good as his word, for he keeps covenant with them, and not one iota of his promise shall fall to the ground; nay, he will be better than his word, for he keeps mercy to them, something more than

1086

was in the covenant. It was proper for Daniel to have his eye upon God's mercy now that he was to lay before him the miseries of his people, and upon God's covenant now that he was to sue for the performance of a promise. Note, We should, in prayer, look both at God's greatness and his goodness, his majesty and his mercy in conjunction.

II. Here is a penitent confession of sin, the procuring cause of all the calamities which his people had for so many years been groaning under, v. 5, 6. When we seek to God for national mercies we ought to humble ourselves before him for national sins. These are the sins Daniel here laments; and we may here observe the variety of words he makes use of to set forth the greatness of their provocations (for it becomes penitents to lay load upon themselves): *We have sinned* in many particular instances, nay, *we have committed iniquity,* we have driven a trade of sin, *we have done wickedly* with a hard heart and a stiff neck, and herein we have *rebelled,* have taken up arms against the King of kings, his crown and dignity. Two things aggravated their sins:—1. That they had violated the express laws God had given them by Moses: "We have *departed from thy precepts and from thy judgments,* and have not conformed to them. And (*v.*10) *we have not obeyed the voice of the Lord our God.*" That which speaks the nature of sin, that it is *the transgression of the law,* does sufficiently speak the malignity of it; if sin be made to *appear sin,* it cannot be made to appear worse; its *sinfulness* is its greatest hatefulness, Rom. vii. 13. God has *set his laws before us* plainly and fully, as the copy we should write after, yet *we have not walked in* them, but turned aside, or turned back. 2. That they had slighted the fair warnings God had given them by the prophets, which in every age he had sent to them, *rising up betimes and sending them* (*v.* 6): "*We have not hearkened to thy servants the prophets,* who have put us in mind of thy laws, and of the sanctions of them; though they *spoke in thy name,* we have not regarded them; though they delivered their message faithfully, with a universal respect to all orders and degrees of men, to *our kings and princes,* whom they had the courage and confidence to speak to, *to our fathers,* and to all the *people of the land,* whom they had the condescension and compassion to speak to, yet *we have not hearkened to them,* nor heard them, or not heeded them, or not complied with them." Mocking God's messengers, and despising his words, were Jerusalem's measure-filling sins, 2 Chron. xxxvi. 16. This confession of sin is repeated here, and much insisted on; penitents should again and again accuse and reproach themselves till they find their hearts thoroughly broken. *All Israel have transgressed thy law,* v. 11. It is *Israel,* God's professing people, who have known better, and from whom better is expected—

Israel, God's peculiar people, whom he has surrounded with his favours; not here and there one, but it is *all* Israel, the generality of them, the body of the people, that *have transgressed by departing* and getting out of the way, *that they might not* hear, and so might not *obey, thy voice.* This disobedience is that which all true penitents do most sensibly charge upon themselves (v. 14): *We obeyed not his voice, and* (v. 15) *we have sinned, we have done wickedly.* Those that would find mercy must thus confess their sins.

III. Here is a self-abasing acknowledgment of the righteousness of God in all the judgments that were brought upon them; and it is evermore the way of true penitents thus to justify God, that he may be clear when he judges, and the sinner may bear all the blame. 1. He acknowledges that it was sin that plunged them in all these troubles. Israel is *dispersed* through *all the countries* about, and so weakened, impoverished, and exposed. God's hand has *driven them* hither and thither, some *near*, where they are known and therefore the more ashamed, others *afar off*, where they are not known and therefore the more abandoned, and it is *because of their trespass that they have trespassed* (v. 7); they mingled themselves with the nations that they might be debauched by them, and now God mingles them with the nations that they might be stripped by them. 2. He owns the righteousness of God in it, that he had done them no wrong in all he had brought upon them, but had dealt with them as they deserved (v. 7): " *O Lord! righteousness belongs to thee;* we have no fault to find with thy providence, no exceptions to make against thy judgments, for (v. 14) *the Lord our God is righteous in all his works which he does,* even in the sore calamities we are now under, for *we obeyed not the words* of his mouth, and therefore justly feel the weight of his hand." This seems to be borrowed from Lam. i. 18. 3. He takes notice of the fulfilling of the scripture in what was brought upon them. *In very faithfulness he afflicted them;* for it was according to the word which he had spoken. *The curse is poured upon us and the oath,* that is, the curse that was ratified by an oath in the law of Moses, v. 11. This further justifies God in their troubles, that he did but inflict the penalty of the law, which he had given them fair notice of. It was necessary for the preserving of the honour of God's veracity, and saving his government from contempt, that the threatenings of his word should be accomplished, otherwise they look but as bugbears, nay, they seem not at all frightful. Therefore *he has confirmed his words which he spoke against us* because we broke his laws, *and against our judges that judged us* because they did not according to the duty of their place punish the breach of God's laws. He told them many a time that if they did not execute

justice, as terrors to evil-workers, he must and would take the work into his own hands; and now he has *confirmed* what he said *by bringing upon us a great evil*, in which the princes and judges themselves deeply shared. Note, It contributes very much to our profiting by the *judgments of God's hand* to observe how exactly they agree with the *judgments of his mouth.* 4. He aggravates the calamities they were in, lest they should seem, having been long used to them, to make light of them, and so to lose the benefit of the chastening of the Lord by despising it. " It is not some of the common troubles of life that we are complaining of, but that which has in it some special marks of divine displeasure; for *under the whole heaven has not been done as has been done upon Jerusalem,*" v. 12. It is Jeremiah's lamentation in the name of the church, *Was ever sorrow like unto my sorrow?* which must suppose another similar question, *Was ever sin like unto my sin?* 5. He puts shame upon the whole nation, from the highest to the lowest; and if they will say *Amen* to his prayer, as it was fit they should if they would come in for a share in the benefit of it, they must all put their hand upon their mouth, and their mouth in the dust: " *To us belongs confusion of faces as at this day* (v. 7); we lie under the shame of the punishment *at this day*, and we ought to accommodate ourselves to it, and to accept of the punishment of our iniquity, for shame is our due." If Israel had retained their character, and had continued a holy people, they would have been *high above all nations in praise, and name, and honour* (Deut. xxvi. 19); but now that they have *sinned and done wickedly* confusion and disgrace belong to them, to *the men of Judah and the inhabitants of Jerusalem*, the inhabitants both of the country and of the city, for they have been all alike guilty before God; it belongs to *all Israel*, both to the two tribes, *that are near*, by the rivers of Babylon, and to the ten tribes, *that are afar off*, in the land of Assyria. " Confusion belongs not only to the common people of our land, but to *our kings, our princes*, and *our fathers* (v. 8), who should have set a better example, and have used their authority and influence for the checking of the threatening torrent of vice and profaneness." 6. He imputes the continuance of the judgment to their incorrigibleness under it (v. 13, 14): " *All this evil has come upon us*, and has lain long upon us, *yet made we not our prayer before the Lord our God*, not in a right manner, as we should have made it, *with a humble, lowly, penitent, and obedient heart.* We have been smitten, but have not returned to him that smote us. *We have not entreated the face of the Lord our God* (so the word is); " we have taken no care to make our peace with God and reconcile ourselves to him." Daniel set his brethren a good example of praying continually, but he was sorry to see how few there were that followed his example; in their *affliction* it was expected that they would *seek God early*, but they sought him not, that they might *turn from their iniquities* and *understand his truth.* The errand upon which afflictions are sent is to bring men to *turn from their iniquities* and to *understand God's truth;* so Elihu had explained them, Job xxxvi. 10. God by them *opens men's ears to discipline* and *commands that they return from iniquity.* And if men were brought rightly to *understand God's truth*, and to submit to the power and authority of it, they would turn from the error of their ways. Now the first step towards this is to *make our prayer before the Lord our God*, that the affliction may be sanctified before it is removed, and that the grace of God may go along with the providence of God, to make it answer the end. Those who in their affliction *make not their prayer to God*, who *cry not when he binds them*, are not likely to *turn from iniquity* or to *understand his truth.* " *Therefore*, because we have not improved the affliction, *the Lord has watched upon the evil*, as the judge takes care that execution be done according to the sentence. Because we have not been melted, he has kept us still in the furnace, and *watched over it*, to make the heat yet more intense;" for when God judges he will overcome, and will be justified in all his proceedings.

IV. Here is a believing appeal to the mercy of God, and to the ancient tokens of his favour to Israel, and the concern of his own glory in their interests. 1. It is some comfort to them (and not a little) that God has been always ready to pardon sin (*v.* 9): *To the Lord our God belong mercies and forgivenesses;* this refers to that proclamation of his name, Exod. xxxiv. 6, 7, *The Lord God, gracious and merciful, forgiving iniquity.* Note, It is very encouraging to poor sinners to recollect that *mercies belong to God*, as it is convincing and humbling to them to recollect that righteousness belongs to him; and those who give him the glory of his righteousness may take to themselves the comfort of his mercies, Ps. lxii. 12. There are abundant mercies in God, and not only forgiveness but *forgivenesses;* he is a *God of pardons* (Neh. ix. 17, marg.); he *multiplies to pardon*, Isa. lv. 7. *Though we have rebelled against him*, yet with him there is mercy, pardoning mercy, even *for the rebellious.* 2. It is likewise a support to them to think that God had formerly glorified himself by delivering them out of Egypt; so far he looks back for the encouragement of his faith (*v.* 15): " *Thou hast* formerly *brought thy people out of Egypt with a mighty hand*, and wilt thou not now with the same mighty hand bring them out of Babylon? Were they then formed into a people, and shall they not now be reformed and new-formed? Are they now sinful and unworthy, and were they not so then? Are their oppressors now

1088

mighty and haughty, and were they not so then? And has not God said that their deliverance out of Babylon shall outshine even that out of Egypt?" Jer. xvi. 14, 15. The force of this plea lies in that, " *Thou hast gotten thyself renown*, hast *made thyself a name*" (so the word is) " *as at this day*, even to this day, by bringing us out of Egypt; and wilt thou lose the credit of that by letting us perish in Babylon? Didst thou get a renown by that deliverance which we have so often commemorated, and wilt thou not now get thyself a renown by this which we have so often prayed for, and so long waited for?"

V. Here is a pathetic complaint of the reproach that God's people lay under, and the ruins that God's sanctuary lay in, both which redounded very much to the dishonour of God and the diminution of that name and renown which God had gained by bringing them out of Egypt. 1. God's holy people were despised. By *their sins and the iniquities of their fathers* they had profaned their crown and made themselves despicable, and then though they are, in name and profession, God's people, and upon that account truly great and honourable, yet they become *a reproach to all that are round about them.* Their neighbours laugh them to scorn, and triumph in their disgrace. Note, *Sin is a reproach to any people*, but especially to God's people, that have more eyes upon them and have more honour to lose than other people. 2. God's holy place was desolate. Jerusalem, the holy city, was a reproach (*v.* 16) when it lay in ruins; it was an *astonishment* and a hissing to all that passed by. The sanctuary, the holy house, was desolate (*v.* 17), the altars were demolished, and all the buildings laid in ashes. Note, The desolations of the sanctuary are the grief of all the saints, who reckon all their comforts in this world buried in the ruins of the sanctuary.

VI. Here is an importunate request to God for the restoring of the poor captive Jews to their former enjoyments again. The petition is very pressing, for God gives us leave in prayer to wrestle with him: " *O Lord! I beseech thee, v.* 16. If ever thou wilt do any thing for me, do this; it is my heart's desire and prayer. *Now therefore, O our God! hear the prayer of thy servant and his supplication* (*v.* 17), and grant an answer of peace." Now what are his petitions? What are his requests? 1. That God would turn away his wrath from them; that is it which all the saints dread and deprecate more than any thing: O let *thy anger be turned away from thy Jerusalem, thy holy mountain! v.* 16. He does not pray for the turning again of their captivity (let the Lord do with them as seems good in his eyes), but he prays first for the *turning away of God's wrath.* Take away the cause, and the effect will cease. 2. That he would lift up the light of his countenance upon them (*v.* 17): " *Cause thy face to shine upon thy sanctuary that is desolate;* return in mercy to us, and show that thou art reconciled to us, and then all shall be well." Note, The shining of God's face upon the desolations of the sanctuary is all in all towards the repair of it ; and upon that foundation it must be rebuilt. If therefore its friends would begin their work at the right end, they must first be earnest with God in prayer for his favour, and recommend his desolate sanctuary to his smiles. *Cause thy face to shine* and then *we shall be saved,* Ps. lxxx. 3. 3. That he would forgive their sins, and then hasten their deliverance (*v.* 19): *O Lord! hear ; O Lord! forgive.* "That the mercy prayed for may be granted in mercy, let the sin that threatens to come between us and it be removed : *O Lord ! hearken and do,* not hearken and speak only, but hearken and do ; do that for us which none else can, and that speedily—*defer not, O my God !*" Now that he saw the appointed day approaching he could in faith pray that God would make haste to them and not defer. David often prays, *Make haste, O God ! to help me.*

VII. Here are several pleas and arguments to enforce the petitions. God gives us leave not only to pray, but to plead with him, which is not to move him (he himself knows what he will do), but to move ourselves, to excite our fervency and encourage our faith. 1. They disdain a dependence upon any righteousness of their own ; they pretend not to merit any thing at God's hand but wrath and the curse (*v.* 18) : *" We do not present our supplications before thee* with hope to speed *for our righteousness,* as if we were worthy to receive thy favour for any good in us, or done by us, or could demand any thing as a debt ; we cannot insist upon our own justification, no, though we were more righteous than we are ; nay, though we knew nothing amiss of ourselves, yet are we not thereby justified, nor *would we answer,* but we would *make supplication to our Judge.*" Moses had told Israel long before that, whatever God did for them, it was *not for their righteousness,* Deut. ix. 4, 5. And Ezekiel had of late told them that their return out of Babylon would be *not for their sakes,* Ezek. xxxvi. 22, 32. Note, Whenever we come to God for mercy we must lay aside all conceit of, and confidence in, our own righteousness. 2. They take their encouragement in prayer from God only, as knowing that his reasons of mercy are fetched from within himself, and therefore from him we must borrow all our pleas for mercy, and so give honour to him when we are suing for grace and mercy from him. (1.) " Do it *for thy own sake* (*v.* 19), for the accomplishment of thy own counsel, the performance of thy own promise, and the manifestation of thy own glory." Note, God will do his own work, not only in his own way and time, but for his own sake, and so we must take it. (2.) " Do it *for the Lord's sake,* that is,

for the Lord Christ's sake," for the sake of the Messiah promised, who is the Lord (so the most and best of our Christian interpreters understand it), *for the sake of Adonai,* so David called the Messiah (Ps. cx. 1), and mercy is prayed for for the church for the sake of the *Son of man* (Ps. lxxx. 17), and *for thy Word's sake,* 2 Sam. vii. 21. Note, Christ is *the Lord ;* he is Lord of all. It is for his sake that God causes his face to shine upon sinners when they repent and turn to him, because of the satisfaction he has made. In all our prayers that therefore must be our plea ; we must *make mention of his righteousness, even of his only,* Ps. lxxi. 16. *Look upon the face of the anointed.* He has himself directed us to *ask in his name.* (3.) " Do it *according to all thy righteousness* (*v.* 16), that is, plead for us against our persecutors and oppressors *according to thy righteousness.* Though we are ourselves unrighteous before God, yet with reference to them we have a righteous cause, which we leave it with the righteous God to appear in the defence of." Or, rather, by the *righteousness of God* here is meant his faithfulness to his promise. God had, *according to his righteousness,* executed the threatening, *v.* 11. " Now, Lord, wilt thou not do according to *all* thy righteousness ? Wilt thou not be as true to thy promises as thou hast been to thy threatenings and accomplish them also ?" (4.) " Do it *for thy great mercies* (*v.* 18), to make it to appear that thou art a merciful God." The good things we ask of God we call *mercies,* because we expect them purely from God's mercy. And, because misery is the proper object of mercy, the prophet here spreads the deplorable condition of the church before God, as it were to move his compassion : " *Open thy eyes and behold our desolations,* especially the desolations of the sanctuary. O look with pity upon a pitiable case !" Note, The desolations of the church must in prayer be laid before God and then left with him. (5.) " Do it for the sake of the relation we stand in to thee. The sanctuary that is desolate is thy sanctuary (*v.* 17), dedicated to thy honour, employed in thy service, and the place of thy residence. Jerusalem is *thy* city and *thy holy mountain* (*v.* 16) ; it is *the city which is called by thy name,*" *v.* 18. It was the city which God had *chosen out of all the tribes of Israel, to put his name there.* " The people that have *become a reproach* are *thy people,* and thy name suffers in the reproach cast upon them (*v.* 16) ; they are *called by thy name,* v. 19. Lord, thou hast a property in them, and therefore art interested in their interests ; wilt thou not provide for thy own, for those of thy own house ? They are *thine, save them,*" Ps. cxix. 94.

20 And whiles I was speaking, and praying, and confessing my sin and the sin of my people Israel, and pre-

senting my supplication before the LORD my God for the holy mountain of my God; 21 Yea, whiles I *was* speaking in prayer, even the man Gabriel, whom I had seen in the vision at the beginning, being caused to fly swiftly, touched me about the time of the evening oblation. 22 And he informed *me*, and talked with me, and said, O Daniel, I am now come forth to give thee skill and understanding. 23 At the beginning of thy supplications the commandment came forth, and I am come to show *thee;* for thou *art* greatly beloved: therefore understand the matter, and consider the vision. 24 Seventy weeks are determined upon thy people and upon thy holy city, to finish the transgression, and to make an end of sins, and to make reconciliation for iniquity, and to bring in everlasting righteousness, and to seal up the vision and prophecy, and to anoint the most Holy. 25 Know therefore and understand, *that* from the going forth of the commandment to restore and to build Jerusalem unto the Messiah the Prince *shall be* seven weeks, and threescore and two weeks: the street shall be built again, and the wall, even in troublous times. 26 And after threescore and two weeks shall Messiah be cut off, but not for himself: and the people of the prince that shall come shall destroy the city and the sanctuary; and the end thereof *shall be* with a flood, and unto the end of the war desolations are determined. 27 And he shall confirm the covenant with many for one week: and in the midst of the week he shall cause the sacrifice and the oblation to cease, and for the overspreading of abominations he shall make *it* desolate, even until the consummation, and that determined shall be poured upon the desolate.

We have here the answer that was immediately sent to Daniel's prayer, and it is a very memorable one, as it contains the most illustrious prediction of Christ and gospel-grace that is extant in all the *Old Testament*. If John Baptist was the morning-star, this was the day-break to the Sun of righteousness, the *day-spring from on high*. Here is,

I. The time when this answer was given.

1. It was while Daniel was at prayer.

This he observed and laid a strong emphasis upon: *While I was speaking* (v. 20), yea, *while I was speaking in prayer* (v. 21), before he rose from his knees, and while there was yet more which he intended to say.

(1.) He mentions the two heads he chiefly insisted upon in prayer, and which perhaps he designed yet further to enlarge upon. [1.] He was confessing sin and lamenting that—"both *my sin and the sin of my people Israel.*" Daniel was a very great and good man, and yet he finds sin of his own to confess before God and is ready to confess it; for there is not a *just man upon earth that does good and sins not*, nor that sins and repents not. St. John puts himself into the number of those who deceive themselves if they say that they *have no sin*, and who therefore *confess their sins*, 1 John i. 8. Good men find it an ease to their consciences to pour out their complaints before the Lord against themselves; and that is *confessing sin*. He also confessed the *sin of his people*, and bewailed that: Those who are heartily concerned for the glory of God, the welfare of the church, and the souls of men, will mourn for the sins of others as well as for their own. [2.] He was *making supplication before the Lord his God*, and presenting it to him as an intercessor for Israel; and in this prayer his concern was for *the holy mountain of his God*, Mount Zion. The desolations of the sanctuary lay nearer his heart than those of the city and the land; and the repair of that, and the setting up of the public worship of the God of Israel again, were the things he had in view, in the deliverance he was preparing for, more than the re-establishment of their civil interests. Now,

(2.) While Daniel was thus employed, [1.] He had a grant made him of the mercy he prayed for. Note, God is very ready to hear prayer and to give an answer of peace. Now was fulfilled what God had spoken Isa. lxv. 24, *While they are yet speaking, I will hear*. Daniel grew very fervent in prayer, and his affections were very strong, v. 18, 19. And, *while he was speaking* with such fervour and ardency, the angel came to him with a gracious answer. God is well pleased with lively devotions. We cannot now expect that God should send us answers to our prayer by angels, but, if we pray with fervency for that which God has promised, we may by faith take the promise as an immediate answer to the prayer; for *he is faithful that has promised*. [2.] He had a discovery made to him of a far greater and more glorious redemption which God would work out for his church in the latter days. Note, Those that would be brought acquainted with Christ and his grace must be *much in prayer*.

2. It was *about the time of the evening oblation*, v. 21. The altar was in ruins, and there was no oblation offered upon it, but, it should seem, the pious Jews in their captivity were daily thoughtful of the time when

it should have been offered, and at that hour were ready to weep at the remembrance of it, and desired and hoped that their prayer should be *set forth before God as incense,* and the *lifting up of their hands,* and their hearts with their hands, should be acceptable in his sight *as the evening-sacrifice,* Ps. cxli. 2. The evening oblation was a type of the great sacrifice which Christ was to offer in the evening of the world, and it was in the virtue of that sacrifice that Daniel's prayer was accepted when he prayed *for the Lord's sake;* and for the sake of that this glorious discovery of redeeming love was made to him. The Lamb *opened the seals* in the virtue of his own blood.

II. The messenger by whom this answer was sent. It was not given him in a dream, nor by a voice from heaven, but, for the greater certainty and solemnity of it, an angel was sent on purpose, appearing in a human shape, to give this answer to Daniel. Observe,

1. Who this angel, or messenger, was; it was *the man Gabriel.* If Michael the archangel be, as many suppose, no other than Jesus Christ, this Gabriel is the only created angel that is named in scripture. Gabriel signifies the *mighty one of God;* for the angels are *great in power and might,* 2 Pet. ii. 11. It was he *whom I had seen in the vision at the beginning.* Daniel heard him called by his name, and thence learned it (Dan. viii. 16); and, though then he trembled at his approach, yet he observed him so carefully that now he knew him again, knew him to be the same that he had seen at the beginning, and, being somewhat better acquainted with him, was not now so terrified at the sight of him as he had been at first. When this angel said to *Zacharias, I am Gabriel* (Luke i. 19), he intended thereby to put him in mind of this notice which he had given to Daniel of the Messiah's coming when it was at a distance, for the confirming of his faith in the notice he was then about to give of it as at the door.

2. The instructions which this messenger received from the Father of lights to whom Daniel prayed (*v.* 23): *At the beginning of thy supplications* the word, *the commandment, came forth* from God. Notice was given to the angels in heaven of this counsel of God, which they were desirous to look into; and orders were given to Gabriel to go immediately and bring the notice of it to Daniel. By this it appears that it was not any thing which Daniel said that moved God, for the answer was given as he began to pray; but God was well pleased with his serious solemn address to the duty, and, in token of that, sent him this gracious message. Or perhaps it was *at the beginning of Daniel's supplications* that *Cyrus's word,* or *commandment, went forth to restore and to build Jerusalem,* that going forth spoken of *v.* 25. "The thing was done *this very day;* the pro-

clamation of liberty to the Jews was signed this morning, just when thou wast praying for it;" and now, at the close of this fastday, Daniel had notice of it, as, at the close of the *day of atonement,* the jubilee-trumpet sounded to proclaim liberty.

3. The haste he made to deliver his message: He was *caused to fly swiftly, v.* 21. Angels are winged messengers, quick in their motions, and delay not to execute the orders they receive; they run and *return like a flash of lightning,* Ezek. i. 14. But, it should seem, sometimes they are more expeditious than at other times, and make a quicker despatch, as here the angel was *caused to fly swiftly;* that is, he was ordered and he was enabled to fly swiftly. Angels do their work in obedience to divine command and in dependence upon divine strength. Though they excel in wisdom, they fly swifter or slower as God directs; and, though they excel in power, they fly but as God causes them to fly. Angels themselves are to us what he makes them to be; they are *his ministers,* and *do his pleasure,* Ps. ciii. 21.

4. The prefaces or introductions to his message. (1.) He *touched him* (*v.* 21), as before (*ch.* viii. 18), not to awaken him out of sleep as then, but to give him a hint to break off his prayer and to attend to that which he has to say in answer to it. Note, In order to the keeping up of our communion with God we must not only be forward to speak to God, but as forward to hear what he has to say to us; when we have prayed we must look up, must look after our prayers, must set ourselves upon our watch-tower. (2.) He *talked with him* (*v.* 22), talked familiarly with him, as one friend talks with another, that *his terror might not make him afraid.* He informed him on what errand he came, that he was sent from heaven on purpose with a kind message to him: "*I have come to show thee* (*v.* 23), to tell thee that which thou didst not know before." He had shown him the troubles of the church under Antiochus, and the period of those troubles (*ch.* viii. 19); but now he has greater things to show him, for he that is faithful in a little shall be entrusted with more. "Nay, *I have now come forth to give thee skill and understanding* (*v.* 22), not only to show thee these things, but to *make thee understand* them." (3.) He assured him that he was a favourite of Heaven, else he would not have had this intelligence sent him, and he must take it for a favour: "*I have come to show thee, for thou art greatly beloved.* Thou art *a man of desires,* acceptable to God, and whom he has a favour for." Note, Though God loves all his children, yet there are some that are more than the rest *greatly beloved.* Christ had one disciple that lay in his bosom; and that *beloved disciple* was he that was entrusted with the prophetical visions of the New Testament, as Daniel was with those of the Old. For what greater token can there be of God's

favour to any man than for the secrets of the Lord to be with him? Abraham is the *friend of God;* and therefore *Shall I hide from Abraham that thing which I do?* Gen. xviii. 17. Note, Those may reckon themselves greatly beloved of God to whom, and in whom, he *reveals his Son.* Some observe that the title which this angel Gabriel gives to the Virgin Mary is much the same with this which he here gives to Daniel, as if he designed to put her in mind of it—*Thou that art highly favoured;* as Daniel, *greatly beloved.* (4.) He demands his serious attention to the discovery he was now about to make to him: *Therefore understand the matter, and consider the vision, v.* 23. This intimates that it was a thing well worthy of his regard, above any of the visions he had been before favoured with. Note, Those who would understand the things of God must consider them, must apply their minds to them, ponder upon them, and compare spiritual things with spiritual. The reason why we are so much in the dark concerning the revealed will of God, and mistake concerning it, is want of consideration. This vision both requires and deserves consideration.

III. The message itself. It was delivered with great solemnity, received no doubt with great attention, and recorded with great exactness; but in it, as is usual in prophecies, there are things dark and hard to be understood. Daniel, who understood by the book of the prophet Jeremiah the expiration of the seventy years of the captivity, is now honourably employed to make known to the church another more glorious release, which that was but a shadow of, at the end of another seventy, not years, but weeks of years. He prayed over that prophecy, and received this in answer to that prayer. He had prayed for *his people* and the *holy city*—that *they* might be released, that *it* might be rebuilt; but God answers him *above what he was able to ask or think.* God not only grants, but outdoes, the desires of those that fear him, Ps. xxi. 4.

1. The times here determined are somewhat hard to be understood. In general, it is *seventy weeks,* that is, *seventy times seven years,* which makes just 490 years. The great affairs that are yet to come concerning the people of Israel, and the city of Jerusalem, will lie within the compass of these years.

(1.) These years are thus described by weeks, [1.] In conformity to the prophetic style, which is, for the most part, abstruse, and out of the common road of speaking, that the things foretold might not lie too obvious. [2.] To put an honour upon the division of time into weeks, which is made purely by the sabbath day, and to signify that that should be perpetual. [3.] With reference to the seventy years of the captivity; as they had been so long kept out of the possession of their own land, so, being now restored to it they should seven times as long be kept

1092

in the possession of it. So much more does God delight in showing mercy than in punishing. The land had *enjoyed its sabbaths,* in a melancholy sense, seventy years, Lev. xxvi. 34. But now the people of the Lord shall, in a comfortable sense, enjoy their sabbaths seven times seventy years, and in them seventy sabbatical years, which makes ten jubilees. Such proportions are there in the disposals of Providence, that we might see and admire the wisdom of him who has determined the times before appointed.

(2.) The difficulties that arise about these seventy weeks are, [1.] Concerning the time when they commence and whence they are to be reckoned. They are here dated *from the going forth of the commandment to restore and to build Jerusalem, v.* 25. I should most incline to understand this of the edict of Cyrus mentioned Ezra i. 1, for by it the people were *restored;* and, though express mention be not made there of the building of Jerusalem, yet that is supposed in the building of the temple, and was foretold to be done by Cyrus, Isa. xliv. 28. He shall *say to Jerusalem, Thou shalt be built.* That was, both in prophecy and in history, the most famous decree for the building of Jerusalem; nay, it should seem, this *going forth of the commandment* (which may as well be meant of God's command concerning it as of Cyrus's) is the same with that going forth of the commandment mentioned *v.* 23, which was *at the beginning of Daniel's supplications.* And it looks very graceful that the seventy weeks should begin immediately upon the expiration of the seventy years. And there is nothing to be objected against this but that by this reckoning the *Persian monarchy,* from the taking of Babylon by Cyrus to Alexander's conquest of Darius, lasted but 130 years; whereas, by the particular account given of the reigns of the Persian emperors, it is computed that it continued 230 years. So Thucydides, Xenophon, and others reckon. Those who fix it to that first edict set aside these computations of the heathen historians as uncertain and not to be relied upon. But others, willing to reconcile them, begin the 490 years, not at the edict of Cyrus (Ezra i. 1), but at the second edict for the building of Jerusalem, issued out by Darius Nothus above 100 years after, mentioned Ezra vi. Others fix on the seventh year of Artaxerxes Mnemon, who sent Ezra with a commission, Ezra vii. 8—12. The learned Mr. Poole, in his Latin Synopsis, has a vast and most elaborate collection of what has been said, *pro* and *con,* concerning the different beginnings of these weeks, with which the learned may entertain themselves. [2.] Concerning the termination of them; and here likewise interpreters are not agreed. Some make them to end at the death of Christ, and think the express words of this famous prophecy will warrant us to conclude that from this very hour when Gabriel spoke to Daniel, at the time of the evening oblation, to the hour when Christ died, which was towards evening too, it was exactly 490 years; and I am willing enough to be of that opinion. But others think, because it is said that *in the midst of the weeks* (that is, the last of the seventy weeks) he *shall cause the sacrifice and the oblation to cease,* they end *three years and a half* after the death of Christ, when, the Jews having rejected the gospel, the apostles turned to the Gentiles. But those who make them to end precisely at the death of Christ read it thus, " He shall *make strong the testament to the many; the last seven,* or the last week, yea, *half that seven,* or *half that week* (namely, the latter half, the three years and a half which Christ spent in his public ministry), shall bring to an end sacrifice and oblation." Others make these 490 years to end with the destruction of Jerusalem, about thirty-seven years after the death of Christ, because these seventy weeks are said to be *determined upon the people* of the Jews *and the holy city;* and much is said here concerning the destruction of the city and the sanctuary. [3.] Concerning the division of them into seven weeks, and sixty-two weeks, and one week; and the reason of this is as hard to account for as any thing else. In the first seven weeks, or forty-nine years, the temple and city were built; and in the last single week Christ preached his gospel, by which the Jewish economy was taken down, and the foundations were laid of the gospel city and temple, which were to be built upon the ruins of the former.

(3.) But, whatever uncertainty we may labour under concerning the exact fixing of these times, there is enough clear and certain to answer the two great ends of determining them. [1.] It did serve them to raise and support the expectations of believers. There were general promises of the coming of the Messiah made to the patriarchs; the preceding prophets had often spoken of him as *one that should come,* but never was the time fixed for his coming until now. And, though there might be so much doubt concerning the date of this reckoning that they could not ascertain the time just to a year, yet by the light of this prophecy they were directed about what time to expect him. And we find, accordingly, that when Christ came he was generally *looked for* as the *consolation of Israel,* and *redemption in Jerusalem* by him, Luke ii. 25, 38. There were those that for this reason thought the *kingdom of God should immediately appear* (Luke xix. 11), and some think it was this that brought a more than ordinary concourse of people to Jerusalem, Acts ii. 5. [2.] It does serve still to refute and silence the expectations of unbelievers, who will not own that Jesus is he who *should come,* but still *look for another.* This prediction should silence them, and will condemn them; for, reckon these seventy weeks from which of the com-

mandments to build Jerusalem we please, it is certain that they have expired above 1500 years ago; so that the Jews are for ever *without excuse,* who will not own that the Messiah has come when they have gone so far beyond their utmost reckoning for his coming. But by this we are confirmed in our belief of the Messiah's being come, and that our Jesus is he, that he came just at the time prefixed, a time worthy to be had in everlasting remembrance.

2. The events here foretold are more plain and easy to be understood, at least to us now. Observe what is here foretold,

(1.) Concerning the return of the Jews now speedily to their own land, and their settlement again there, which was the thing that Daniel now principally prayed for; and yet it is but briefly touched upon here in the answer to his prayer. Let this be a comfort to the pious Jews, that a *commandment* shall *go forth to restore and to build Jerusalem, v.* 25. And the commandment shall not be in vain; for though the times will be very troublous, and this good work will meet with great opposition, yet it shall be carried on, and brought to perfection at last. The *street* shall be *built again,* as spacious and splendid as ever it was, and *the walls, even in troublous times.* Note, as long as we are here in this world we must expect *troublous times,* upon some account or other. Even when we have *joyous times* we must rejoice with trembling; it is but a gleam, it is but a lucid interval of peace and prosperity; the clouds will *return after the rain.* When the Jews are restored in triumph to their own land, yet there they must expect troublous times, and prepare for them. But this is our comfort, that God will carry on his own work, will build up his Jerusalem, will beautify it, will fortify it, *even in troublous times;* nay, the troublousness of the times may by the grace of God contribute to the advancement of the church. The more it is afflicted the more it multiplies.

(2.) Concerning the Messiah and his undertaking. The carnal Jews looked for a Messiah that should deliver them from the Roman yoke and give them temporal power and wealth, whereas they were here told that the Messiah should come upon another errand, purely spiritual, and upon the account of which he should be the more welcome. [1.] Christ came to *take away sin,* and to abolish that. Sin had made a quarrel between God and man, had alienated man from God and provoked God against man; it was this that put dishonour upon God and brought misery upon mankind; this was the great mischief-maker. He that would do God a real service, and man a real kindness, must be the destruction of this. Christ undertakes to be so, and *for this purpose* he is *manifested, to destroy the works of the devil.* He does not say to *finish your* transgressions and your sins, but *transgression and sin in*

1093

general, for he is the propitiation not only for our sins, that are Jews, but *for the sins of the whole world.* He came, First, To *finish transgression,* to *restrain* it (so some), to break the power of it, to *bruise the head* of that serpent that had done so much mischief, to take away the usurped dominion of that tyrant, and to set up a kingdom of holiness and love in the hearts of men, upon the ruins of Satan's kingdom there, that, where *sin and death* had *reigned, righteousness* and *life* through grace might *reign.* When he died he said, *It is finished;* sin has now had its death-wound given it, like Samson's, *Let me die with the Philistines. Animamque in vulnere ponit—He inflicts the wound and dies Secondly,* To *make an end of sin,* to abolish it, that it may not rise up in judgment against us, to obtain the pardon of it, that it may not be our ruin, to *seal up sins* (so the margin reads it), that they may not appear or break out against us, to accuse and condemn us, as, when Christ cast the devil into the bottomless pit, he *set a seal upon him,* Rev. xx. 3. When sin is pardoned it is *sought for and not found,* as that which is *sealed up. Thirdly,* To *make reconciliation for iniquity,* as by a sacrifice, to satisfy the justice of God and so to *make peace* and bring God and man together, not only as an arbitrator, or referee, who only brings the contending parties to a good understanding one of another, but as a surety, or undertaker, for us. He is not only the *peace-maker,* but the *peace.* He is the *atonement.* [2.] He came to *bring in an everlasting righteousness.* God might justly have made an end of the sin by making an end of the sinner; but Christ found out another way, and so made an end of sin as to save the sinner from it, by providing a righteousness for him. We are all guilty before God, and shall be condemned as guilty, if we have not a righteousness wherein to appear before him. Had we stood, our innocency would have been our righteousness, but, having fallen, we must have something else to plead; and Christ has provided us a plea. The merit of his sacrifice is *our righteousness;* with this we answer all the demands of the law: *Christ has died, yea, rather, has risen again.* Thus Christ is *the Lord our righteousness,* for he is *made of God to us righteousness,* that we might be *made the righteousness of God in him.* By faith we apply this to ourselves and plead it with God, and our *faith is imputed to us for righteousness,* Rom. iv. 3, 5. This is an *everlasting* righteousness, for Christ, who is *our righteousness,* and the *prince* of our *peace,* is the *everlasting Father.* It was from everlasting in the counsels of it and will be to everlasting in the consequences of it. The application of it was from the beginning, for Christ was *the Lamb slain from the foundation of the world;* and it will be to the end, for he is *able to save to the uttermost.* It is of everlasting

virtue (Heb. x. 12); it is the *rock that follows us* to Canaan. [3.] He came to *seal up the vision and prophecy,* all the prophetical visions of the Old Testament, which had reference to the Messiah. He *sealed them up,* that is, he accomplished them, answered to them to a tittle; all things that were written in the law, the prophets, and the psalms, concerning the Messiah, were fulfilled in him. Thus he confirmed the truth of them as well as his own mission. He *sealed them up,* that is, he put an end to that method of God's discovering his mind and will, and took another course by completing the scripture-canon in the New Testament, which is the more sure word of prophecy than that *by vision,* 2 Pet. i. 19; Heb. i. 1. [4.] He came to *anoint the most holy,* that is, himself, the Holy One, who was *anointed* (that is, appointed to his work and qualified for it) by the Holy Ghost, that oil of gladness which he received *without measure,* above his fellows; or to *anoint* the gospel-church, his spiritual temple, or holy place, to sanctify and cleanse it, and appropriate it to himself (Eph. v. 26), or to consecrate for us *a new and living way into the holiest,* by his own blood (Heb. x. 20), as the sanctuary was *anointed,* Exod. xxx. 25, &c. He is called *Messiah* (v. 25, 26), which signifies *Christ—Anointed* (John i. 41), because he received the unction both for himself and for all that are his. [5.] In order to all this the Messiah must be *cut off,* must die a violent death, and so be *cut off from the land of the living,* as was foretold, Isa. liii. 8. Hence, when Paul preaches the death of Christ, he says that he preached nothing but *what the prophet said should come,* Acts xxvi. 22, 23. And *thus it behoved Christ to suffer.* He must be *cut off, but not for himself*—not for any sin of his own, but, as Caiaphas prophesied, he must *die for the people,* in our stead and for our good,—not for any *advantage of his own* (the glory he purchased for himself was no more than the glory he had before, John xvii. 4, 5); no; it was to atone for our sins, and to purchase life for us, that he was *cut off.* [6.] He must *confirm the covenant with many.* He shall introduce a new covenant between God and man, a covenant of grace, since it had become impossible for us to be saved by a covenant of innocence. This covenant he shall confirm by his doctrine and miracles, by his death and resurrection, by the ordinances of baptism and the Lord's supper, which are the *seals* of the New Testament, assuring us that God is willing to accept us upon gospel-terms. His death made *his testament* of force, and enabled us to claim what is bequeathed by it. He confirmed it to *the many,* to the common people; the poor were *evangelized,* when the *rulers* and *Pharisees believed not on him.* Or, he confirmed it *with many,* with the Gentile world. The New Testament was not (like the Old) confined to the Jewish church, but was committed to all nations. Christ gave his life a *ransom for many.* [7.] He must *cause the sacrifice and oblation to cease.* By offering himself a sacrifice once for all he shall put an end to all the Levitical sacrifices, shall supersede them and set them aside; when the substance comes the shadows shall be done away. He causes all the peace-offerings to cease when he has made peace by the blood of his cross, and by it confirmed the covenant of peace and reconciliation. By the preaching of his gospel to the world, with which the apostles were entrusted, he took men off from expecting remission by the blood of bulls and goats, and so *caused the sacrifice and oblation to cease.* The apostle in his epistle to the Hebrews shows what a better priesthood, altar, and sacrifice, we have now than they had under the law, as a reason why we should *hold fast our profession.*

(3.) Concerning the final destruction of Jerusalem, and of the Jewish church and nation; and this follows immediately upon the cutting off of the Messiah, not only because it was the *just punishment* of those that put him to death, which was the sin that filled up the measure of their iniquity and brought ruin upon them, but because, as things were, it was necessary to the perfecting of one of the great intentions of his death. He died to take away the ceremonial law, quite to abolish *that law of commandments,* and to vacate the obligation of it. But the Jews would not be persuaded to quit it; still they kept it up with more zeal than ever; they would hear no talk of parting with it; they stoned Stephen (the first Christian martyr) for saying that Jesus should *change the customs which Moses delivered them* (Acts vi. 14); so that there was no way to abolish the Mosaic economy but by destroying the temple, and the holy city, and the Levitical priesthood, and that whole nation which so incurably doted on them. This was effectually done in less than forty years after the death of Christ, and it was a desolation that could *never be repaired* to this day. And this is it which is here largely foretold, that the Jews who returned out of captivity might not be overmuch lifted up with the rebuilding of their city and temple, because in process of time they would be finally destroyed, and not as now for seventy years only, but might rather rejoice in hope of the coming of the Messiah, and the setting up of his spiritual kingdom in the world, which should *never be destroyed.* Now, [1.] It is here foretold that *the people of the prince that shall come* shall be the instruments of this destruction, that is, the Roman armies, belonging to a monarchy yet to come (Christ is *the prince that shall come,* and they are employed by him in this service; they are *his armies,* Matt. xxii. 7), or the Gentiles (who, though now strangers, shall become the people of the Messiah) shall destroy the Jews [2.]

That the destruction shall be *by war,* and the *end* of that *war* shall be this *desolation determined.* The *wars of the Jews* with the Romans were by their own obstinacy made very long and very bloody, and they issued at length in the utter extirpation of that people. [3.] That the *city* and *sanctuary* shall in a particular manner be *destroyed* and laid quite waste. Titus the Roman general would fain have saved the temple, but his soldiers were so enraged against the Jews that he could not restrain them from burning it to the ground, that this prophecy might be fulfilled. [4.] That all the resistance that shall be made to this destruction shall be in vain: *The end of it shall be with a flood.* It shall be a deluge of destruction, like that which swept away the old world, and which there will be no making head against. [5.] That hereby the *sacrifice and oblation* shall be *made to cease.* And it must needs cease when the family of the priests was so extirpated, and the genealogies of it were so confounded, that (they say) there is no man in the world that can prove himself of the seed of Aaron. [6.] That there shall be *an overspreading of abominations,* a general corruption of the Jewish nation and an abounding of iniquity among them, for which it shall be *made desolate,* 1 Thess. ii. 16. Or it is rather to be understood of the armies of the Romans, which were abominable to the Jews (they could not endure them), which *overspread the nation,* and by which it was *made desolate;* for these are the words which Christ refers to, Matt. xxiv. 15, *When you shall see the abomination of desolation, spoken of by Daniel, stand in the holy place, then let those who shall be in Judea flee,* which is explained Luke xxi. 20, *When you shall see Jerusalem encompassed with armies then flee.* [7.] That the desolation shall be total and final: *He shall make it desolate, even until the consummation,* that is, he shall make it completely desolate. It is a *desolation determined,* and it will be accomplished to the utmost. And when it is made desolate, it should seem, there is something more determined that is to be *poured upon the desolate* (v. 27), and what should that be but the *spirit of slumber* (Rom. xi. 8, 25), that blindness which has happened to Israel until the fulness of the Gentiles shall come in? And *then all Israel shall be saved.*

CHAP. X.

This chapter and the two next (which conclude this book) make up one entire vision and prophecy, which was communicated to Daniel for the use of the church, not by signs and figures, as before (ch. vii. and viii.), but by express words; and this was about two years after the vision in the foregoing chapter. Daniel prayed daily, but had a vision only now and then. In this chapter we have some things introductory to the prophecy, in the eleventh chapter the particular predictions, and ch. xii. the conclusion of it. This chapter shows us, I. Daniel's solemn fasting and humiliation, before he had this vision, ver. 1—3. II. A glorious appearance of the Son of God to him, and the deep impression it made upon him, ver. 4—9. III. The encouragement that was given him to expect such a discovery of future events as should be satisfactory and useful both to others and to himself, and that he should be enabled both to understand the meaning of this discovery, though difficult, and to bear up under the lustre of it, though dazzling and dreadful, ver. 10—21.

I N the third year of Cyrus king of Persia a thing was revealed unto Daniel, whose name was called Belteshazzar; and the thing *was* true, but the time appointed *was* long: and he understood the thing, and had understanding of the vision. 2 In those days I Daniel was mourning three full weeks. 3 I ate no pleasant bread, neither came flesh nor wine in my mouth, neither did I anoint myself at all, till three whole weeks were fulfilled. 4 And in the four and twentieth day of the first month, as I was by the side of the great river, which *is* Hiddekel; 5 Then I lifted up mine eyes, and looked, and behold a certain man clothed in linen, whose loins *were* girded with fine gold of Uphaz: 6 His body also *was* like the beryl, and his face as the appearance of lightning, and his eyes as lamps of fire, and his arms and his feet like in colour to polished brass, and the voice of his words like the voice of a multitude. 7 And I Daniel alone saw the vision: for the men that were with me saw not the vision; but a great quaking fell upon them, so that they fled to hide themselves. 8 Therefore I was left alone, and saw this great vision, and there remained no strength in me: for my comeliness was turned in me into corruption, and I retained no strength. 9 Yet heard I the voice of his words: and when I heard the voice of his words, then was I in a deep sleep on my face, and my face toward the ground.

This vision is dated in the *third year of Cyrus*, that is, of his reign after the conquest of Babylon, his third year since Daniel became acquainted with him and a subject to him. Here is,

I. A general idea of this prophecy (*v.* 1): *The thing was true;* every word of God is so; it was true that Daniel had such a vision, and that such and such things were said. This he solemnly attests upon the word of a prophet. *Et hoc paratus est verificare—* He was prepared to verify it; and, if it was a word *spoken from heaven,* no doubt it is stedfast and may be depended upon. *But the time appointed was long,* as long as to the end of the reign of Antiochus, which was 300 years, a long time indeed when it is looked upon as to come. Nay, and because it is usual with the prophets to glance at things

spiritual and eternal, there is that in this prophecy which looks in type as far forward as to the end of the world and the resurrection of the dead; and then he might well say, *The time appointed was long.* It was, however, made as plain to him as if it had been a history rather than a prophecy; he *understood the thing;* so distinctly was it delivered to him, and received by him, that he could say he *had understanding of the vision.* It did not so much operate upon his fancy as upon his understanding.

II. An account of Daniel's mortification of himself before he had this vision, not in expectation of it, nor, when he prayed that solemn prayer *ch.* ix., does it appear that he had any expectation of the vision in answer to it, but purely from a principle of devotion and pious sympathy with the afflicted people of God. He *was mourning full three weeks* (*v.* 2), for his own sins and the sins of his people, and their sorrows. Some think that the particular occasion of his mourning was the slothfulness and indifference of many of the Jews, who, though they had liberty to return to their own land, continued still in the land of their captivity, not knowing how to value the privileges offered them; and perhaps it troubled him the more because those that did so justified themselves by the example of Daniel, though they had not that reason to stay behind which he had. Others think that it was because he heard of the obstruction given to the building of the temple by the enemies of the Jews, who *hired counsellors against them, to frustrate their purpose* (Ezra iv. 4, 5), *all the days of Cyrus,* and gained their point from his son Cambyses, or Artaxerxes, who governed while Cyrus was absent in the Scythian war. Note, Good men cannot but mourn to see how slowly the work of God goes on in the world and what opposition it meets with, how weak its friends are and how active its enemies. During the days of Daniel's mourning he *ate no pleasant bread;* he could not live without meat, but he ate little, and very sparingly, and mortified himself in the quality as well as the quantity of what he ate, which may truly be reckoned fasting, and a token of humiliation and sorrow. He did not eat the pleasant bread he used to eat, but that which was coarse and unpalatable, which he would not be tempted to eat any more of than was just necessary to support nature. As ornaments, so delicacies, are very disagreeable to a day of humiliation. *Daniel ate no flesh, drank no wine, nor anointed himself,* for these three weeks' time, *v.* 3. Though he was now a very old man, and might plead that the decay of his nature required what was nourishing, though he was a very great man, and might plead that, being used to dainty meats, he could not do without them, it would prejudice his health if he were, yet, when it was both to testify and to assist his devotion, he could thus deny himself; let this be noted to the shame of many young people in the common ranks of life who cannot persuade themselves thus to deny themselves.

III. A description of that glorious person whom Daniel saw in vision, which, it is generally agreed, could be no other than Christ himself, the eternal Word. He was by the side of the river Hiddekel (*v.* 4), probably walking there, not for diversion, but devotion and contemplation, as Isaac walked in the field, to meditate ; and, being a person of distinction, he had his servants attending him at some distance. There he *looked up,* and saw *one man,* one alone, *a certain man,* even *the man Christ Jesus.* It must be he, for he appears in the same resemblance wherein he appeared to St. John in the isle of Patmos, Rev. i. 13—15. His dress was priestly, for he is the high priest of our profession, *clothed in linen,* as the high priest himself was on the day of atonement, that great day; *his loins were girded* (in St. John's vision his *paps* were *girded) with a golden girdle* of the finest gold, that of Uphaz, for every thing about Christ is the best in its kind. The *girding of the loins* denotes his ready and diligent application to his work, as his Father's servant, in the business of our redemption. His shape was amiable, *his body like the beryl,* a precious stone of a sky-colour. His countenance was awful, and enough to strike a terror on the beholders, for his face was *as the appearance of lightning,* which dazzles the eyes, both frightens and threatens. His *eyes* were bright and sparkling, *as lamps of fire.* His *arms and feet* shone *like polished brass, v.* 6. His *voice* was loud, and strong, and very piercing, *like the voice of a multitude.* The *vox Dei*—*voice of God* can overpower the *vox populi*—*voice of the people.* Thus glorious did Christ appear, and it should engage us, 1. To think highly and honourably of him. *Now consider how great this man is,* and in all things let him have the pre-eminence. 2. To admire his condescension for us and our salvation. Over all this splendour he drew a veil when he took upon him the form of a servant, and *emptied himself.*

IV. The wonderful influence that this appearance had upon Daniel and his attendants, and the terror that it struck upon him and them.

1. His attendants *saw not the vision ;* it was not fit that they should be honoured with the sight of it. There is a divine revelation vouchsafed to all, from converse with which none are excluded who do not exclude themselves ; but such a vision must be peculiar to Daniel, who was a favourite. Paul's companions were aware of the *light,* but *saw no man,* Acts ix. 7 ; xxii. 9. Note, It is the honour of those who are beloved of God that, what is hidden from others, is known to them. Christ *manifests himself to them, but not to the world,* John xiv. 22. But, though they saw not the vision, they were

seized with an unaccountable trembling ; either from the voice they heard, or from some strange concussion or vibration of the air they felt, so it was that *a great quaking fell upon them, so that they fled to hide themselves,* probably among the willows that grew by the river's side. Note, Many have a *spirit of bondage to fear* who never receive a *spirit of adoption,* to whom Christ has been, and will be, never otherwise than a terror. Now the fright that Daniel's attendants were in is a confirmation of the truth of the vision ; it could not be Daniel's fancy, or the product of a heated imagination of his own, for it had a real, powerful, and strange effect upon those about him.

2. He himself saw it, and saw it alone, but he was not able to bear the sight of it. It not only dazzled his eyes, but overwhelmed his spirit, so that *there remained no strength in him, v.* 8. He said, as Moses himself, *I exceedingly fear and quake.* His spirits were all so employed, either in an intense speculation of the glory of this vision or in the fortifying of his heart against the terror of it, that his body was left in a manner lifeless, and spiritless. He had no vigour in him, and was but one remove from a dead carcase ; he looked as pale as death, his colour was gone, his *comeliness* in him was *turned into corruption,* and he *retained no strength.* Note, The greatest and best of men cannot bear the immediate discoveries of the divine glory ; no man can see it and live ; it is next to death to see a glimpse of it, as Daniel here ; but glorified saints see Christ as he is and can bear the sight. But, though Daniel was thus dispirited with the vision of Christ, yet he *heard the voice of his words* and knew what he said. Note, We must take heed lest our reverence of God's glory, by which we should be awakened to hear his voice both in his word and in his providence, should degenerate into such a dread of him as will disable or indispose us to hear it. It should seem that when the vision of Christ terrified Daniel the voice of his words soon pacified and composed him, silenced his fear, and laid him to sleep in a holy security and serenity of mind : *When I heard the voice of his words I fell into a slumber,* a sweet slumber, *on my face,* and *my face towards the ground.* When he saw the vision he threw himself prostrate, into a posture of the most humble adoration, and dropped asleep, not as careless of what he heard and saw, but charmed with it. Note, How dreadful soever Christ may appear to those who are under convictions of sin, and in terror by reason of it, there is enough in his word to quiet their spirits and make them easy, if they will but attend to it and apply it.

10 And, behold, a hand touched me, which set me upon my knees and *upon* the palms of my hands. 11 And he said unto me, O Daniel, a man

greatly beloved, understand the words that I speak unto thee, and stand upright: for unto thee am I now sent. And when he had spoken this word unto me, I stood trembling. 12 Then said he unto me, Fear not, Daniel: for from the first day that thou didst set thine heart to understand, and to chasten thyself before thy God, thy words were heard, and I am come for thy words. 13 But the prince of the kingdom of Persia withstood me one and twenty days: but, lo, Michael, one of the chief princes, came to help me; and I remained there with the kings of Persia. 14 Now I am come to make thee understand what shall befal thy people in the latter days: for yet the vision *is* for *many* days. 15 And when he had spoken such words unto me, I set my face toward the ground, and I became dumb. 16 And, behold, *one* like the similitude of the sons of men touched my lips: then I opened my mouth, and spake, and said unto him that stood before me, O my lord, by the vision my sorrows are turned upon me, and I have retained no strength. 17 For how can the servant of this my lord talk with this my lord? for as for me, straightway there remained no strength in me, neither is there breath left in me. 18 Then there came again and touched me *one* like the appearance of a man, and he strengthened me, 19 And said, O man greatly beloved, fear not: peace *be* unto thee, be strong, yea, be strong. And when he had spoken unto me, I was strengthened, and said, Let my lord speak; for thou hast strengthened me. 20 Then said he, Knowest thou wherefore I come unto thee? and now will I return to fight with the prince of Persia: and when I am gone forth, lo, the prince of Grecia shall come. 21 But I will show thee that which is noted in the scripture of truth: and *there is* none that holdeth with me in these things, but Michael your prince.

Much ado here is to bring Daniel to be able to bear what Christ has to say to him. Still we have him in a fright, hardly and very slowly recovering himself; but he is still

answered and *supported* with *good words* and *comfortable words.* Let us see how Daniel is by degrees brought to himself, and gather up the several passages that are to the same purport.

I. Daniel is in a great consternation and finds it very difficult to get clear of it. The hand that *touched him* set him at first *upon his knees and the palms of his hands, v.* 10. Note, Strength and comfort commonly come by degrees to those that have been long cast down and disquieted; they are first helped up a little, and then more. *After two days he will revive us, and* then *the third day he will raise us up.* And we must not *despise the day of small things,* but be thankful for the beginnings of mercy. Afterwards he is helped up, but he *stands trembling (v.* 11), for fear lest he fall again. Note, Before God *gives strength and power unto his people* he makes them sensible of their own weakness. *I trembled in myself, that I might rest in the day of trouble,* Hab. iii. 16. But when, afterwards, Daniel recovered so much strength in his limbs that he could stand steadily, yet he tells us (*v.* 15) that he *set his face towards the ground and became dumb ;* he was as a man astonished, who knew not what to say, struck dumb with admiration and fear, and was loth to enter into discourse with one so far *above him ;* he *kept silence,* yea, *even from good,* till he had recollected himself a little. Well, at length he recovered, not only the use of his feet, but the use of his tongue; and, when he *opened his mouth (v.* 16), that which he had to say was to excuse his having been so long silent, for really he durst not speak, he could not speak: " *O my lord*" (so, in great humility, this prophet calls the angel, though the angels, in great humility, called themselves *fellow-servants to the prophets,* Rev. xxii. 9), " *by the vision my sorrows are turned upon me ;* they break in upon me with violence; the sense of my sinful sorrowful state *turns upon me* when I see thy purity and brightness." Note, Man, who has lost his integrity, has reason to blush, and be ashamed of himself, when he sees or considers the glory of the blessed angels that keep their integrity. " *My sorrows are turned upon me, and I have retained no strength* to resist them or bear up a head against them." And again (*v.* 17), like one half dead with the fright, he complains, " As for me, *straightway there remained no strength in me* to receive these displays of the divine glory and these discoveries of the divine will; nay, *there is no breath left in me.*" Such a *deliquium* did he suffer that he could not draw one breath after another, but panted and languished, and was in a manner breathless. See how well it is for us that the treasure of divine revelation is put into *earthen vessels,* that God speaks to us *by men like ourselves* and not by angels. Whatever we may wish, in a peevish dislike of the method God takes in dealing with us, it is certain that if we were tried we should all be of Israel's mind at Mount Sinai, when they said to Moses, *Speak thou to us, and we will hear, but let not God speak to us lest we die,* Exod. xx. 19. If Daniel could not bear it, how could we? Now this he insists upon as an excuse for his irreverent silence, which otherwise would have been blame-worthy: *How can the servant of this my lord talk with this my lord? v.* 17. Note, Whenever we enter into communion with God it becomes us to have a due sense of the vast distance and disproportion that there are between us and the holy angels, and of the infinite distance, and no proportion at all, between us and the holy God, and to acknowledge that we cannot *order our speech by reason of darkness.* How shall we that are dust and ashes speak to the Lord of glory?

II. The blessed angel that was employed by Christ to converse with him gave him all the encouragement and comfort that could be. It should seem, it was not he whose glory he saw in vision (*v.* 5, 6) that here *touched him,* and *talked with him;* that was Christ, but this seems to have been the angel Gabriel, whom Christ had once before ordered to instruct Daniel, *ch.* viii. 16. That glorious appearance (as that of the *God of glory* to Abraham, Acts vii. 2) was to give authority and to gain attention to what the angel should say. Christ himself comforted John when he in a like case *fell at his feet as dead* (Rev. i. 17); but here he did it by *the angel,* whom Daniel saw in a glory much inferior to that of the vision in the verses before; for he was *like the similitude of the sons of men* (*v.* 16), one like the appearance *of a man, v.* 18. When *he* only *appeared,* as he had done before (*ch.* ix. 21), we do not find that Daniel was put into any disorder by it, as he was by this vision; and therefore he is here employed a third time with Daniel.

1. He lent him his hand to help him, *touched him, and set him upon his hands and knees* (*v.* 10), else he would still have lain grovelling, *touched his lips* (*v.* 16), else he would have been still dumb; again he *touched him* (*v.* 18), and put strength into him, else he would still have been staggering and trembling. Note, The hand of God's power going along with the word of his grace is alone effectual to redress all our grievances, and to rectify whatever is amiss in us. One touch from heaven brings us to our knees, sets us on our feet, opens our lips, and strengthens us; for it is God that works on us, and *works in us, both to will and to do* that which is good.

2. He assured him of the great favour that God had for him: Thou art *a man greatly beloved* (*v.* 11); and again (*v.* 19), *O man greatly beloved!* Note, Nothing is more likely, nothing more effectual, to revive the drooping spirits of the saints than to be assured of God's love to them. Those are greatly beloved indeed whom God loves; and it is comfort enough to know it.

3. He silenced his fears, and encouraged his hopes, with good words and comfortable words. He said unto him, *Fear not, Daniel* (*v.* 12); and again (*v.* 19), *O man greatly beloved! fear not; peace be unto thee; be strong, yea, be strong.* Never did any tender mother quiet her child, when any thing had grieved or frightened it, with more compassion and affection than the angel here quieted Daniel. Those that are beloved of God have no reason to be afraid of any evil; peace is to them; God himself speaks peace to them; and they ought, upon the warrant of that, to speak peace to themselves; and that peace, that *joy of the Lord,* will be *their strength.* Will God *plead against us with his great power?* will he take the advantage against us of our being overcome by his terror? *No, but he will put strength into us,* Job xxiii. 6. So he did into Daniel here, when, by reason of the lustre of the vision, *no strength* of his own *remained in him;* and he acknowledges it (*v.* 19): *When he had spoken to me I was strengthened.* Note, God by his word puts life, and strength, and spirit into his people; for if he says, *Be strong,* power goes along with the word. And, now that Daniel has experienced the efficacy of God's strengthening word and grace, he is ready for any thing: "*Now let my lord speak,* and I can hear it, I can bear it, and am ready to do according to it, *for thou hast strengthened me.*" Note, To those that (like Daniel here) have no might God *increases strength,* Isa. xl. 29. And we cannot keep up our communion with God but by strength derived from him; but, when he is pleased to put strength into us, we must make a good use of it, and say, Speak, Lord, *for thy servant hears.* Let God enable us to comply with his will, and then, whatever it is, we will stand complete in it. *Da quod jubes, et jube quod vis—Give what thou commandest, and then command what thou wilt.*

4. He assured him that his fastings and prayers had come up for a memorial before God, as the angel told Cornelius (Acts x. 4): *Fear not, Daniel, v.* 12. It is natural to fallen man to be afraid of an extraordinary messenger from heaven, as dreading to hear evil tidings thence; but Daniel need not fear, for he has by his three weeks' humiliation and supplication sent *extraordinary* messengers to heaven, which he may expect to return with an olive-branch of peace: "*From the first day that thou didst set thy heart to understand* the word of God, which is to be the rule of thy prayers, and to *chasten thyself before thy God,* that thou mightest put an edge upon thy prayers, *thy words were heard,*" as, before, *at the beginning of thy supplication, ch.* ix. 23. Note, As the *entrance of God's word is enlightening* to the upright, so the entrance of their prayers is pleasing to God, Ps. cxix. 130. From the first day that we begin to look towards God in a way of duty he is ready to meet us in a

way of mercy. Thus ready is God to hear prayer. *I said, I will confess, and thou forgavest.*

5. He informed him that he was sent to him on purpose to bring him a prediction of the future state of the church, as a token of God's accepting his prayers for the church : " *Knowest thou wherefore I come unto thee?* If thou knewest on what errand I come, thou wouldst not be put into such a consternation by it." Note, If we rightly understood the meaning of God's dealings with us, and the methods of his providence and grace concerning us, we should be better reconciled to them. " *I have come for thy words* (*v.* 12), to bring thee a gracious answer to thy prayers." Thus, when God's praying people call to him, he says, *Here I am* (Isa. lviii. 9); *what would you* have with me? See the power of prayer, what glorious things it has, in its time, fetched from heaven, what strange discoveries! On what errand did this angel come to Daniel? He tells him (*v.* 14): *I have come to make thee understand what shall befal thy people in the latter days.* Daniel was a curious inquisitive man, that had all his days been searching into secret things, and it would be a great gratification to him to be let into the knowledge of things to come. Daniel had always been concerned for the church; its interests lay much upon his heart, and it would be a particular satisfaction to him to know what its state should be, and he would know the better what to pray for as long as he lived. He was now lamenting the difficulties which his people met with in the present day; but, that he might not be offended in those, the angel must tell him what greater difficulties are yet before them; and, if they be *wearied* now that they only *run with the footmen, how will they contend with horses?* Note, It would abate our resentment of present troubles to consider that we know not but much greater are before us, which we are concerned to provide for. Daniel must be made to know what shall befal his people *in the latter days* of the church, after the cessation of prophecy, and when the time drew nigh for the Messiah to appear, *for yet the vision is for many days;* the principal things that this vision was intended to give the church the foresight of would come to pass in the days of Antiochus, nearly 300 years after this. Now that which the angel is entrusted to communicate to Daniel, and which Daniel is encouraged to expect from him, is not any curious speculations, moral prognostications, nor rational prospects of his own, though he is an angel, but what he has *received from the Lord.* It was the *revelation of Jesus Christ* that the angel gave to St. John to be *delivered to the churches,* Rev. i. 1. So here (*v.* 21): *I will show thee what is written in the scriptures of truth,* that is, what is fixed in the determinate counsel and foreknowledge of God. The *decree of God* is a thing
1100

written, it is a *scripture* which remains and cannot be altered. *What I have written I have written.* As there are scriptures for the revealed will of God, the letters-patent, which are published to the world, so there are scriptures for the secret will of God, the close rolls, which are *sealed among his treasures,* the book of his decrees. Both are *scriptures of truth;* nothing shall be added to nor taken from either of them. The *secret things belong not to us,* only now and then some few paragraphs have been copied out from the book of God's counsels, and delivered to the prophets for the use of the church, as here to Daniel; but they are the *things revealed,* even the *words of this law,* which belong *to us and to our children;* and we are concerned to study what is written in these *scriptures of truth,* for they are things which *belong to our everlasting peace.*

6. He gave him a general account of the adversaries of the church's cause, from whom it might be expected that troubles would arise, and of its patrons, under whose protection it might be assured of safety and victory at last. (1.) The *kings of the earth* are and will be its adversaries; for they set themselves against the Lord, and against his Anointed, Ps. ii. 2. The angel told Daniel that he was to have come to him with a gracious answer to his prayers, but that the *prince of the kingdom of Persia withstood him one and twenty days,* just the three weeks that Daniel had been fasting and praying. Cambyses king of Persia had been very busy to embarrass the affairs of the Jews, and to do them all the mischief he could, and the angel had been all that time employed to counter-work him; so that he had been constrained to defer his visit to Daniel till now, for angels can be but in one place at a time. Or, as Dr. Lightfoot says, This new king of Persia, by hindering the temple, had hindered those good tidings which otherwise he should have brought him. The kings and kingdoms of the world were indeed sometimes helpful to the church, but more often they were injurious to it. " When *I have gone forth* from the kings of Persia, when their monarchy is brought down for their unkindness to the Jews, then *the prince of Grecia shall come,*" *v.* 20. The Grecian monarchy, though favourable to the Jews at first, as the Persian was, will yet come to be vexatious to them. Such is the state of the church-militant; when it has got clear of one enemy it has another to encounter: and such a hydra's head is that of the old serpent; when one storm has *blown over* it is not long before another rises. (2.) The *God of heaven* is, and will be, its protector, and, under him, the angels of heaven are its patrons and guardians. [1.] Here is the angel Gabriel busy in the service of the church, making his part good in defence of it twenty-one days, *against the prince of Persia,* and *remaining there with the kings of Persia,* as consul, or liege-am-

bassador, to take care of the affairs of the
Jews in that court, and to do them service,
v. 13. And, though much was done against
them by the kings of Persia (God permitting
it), it is probable that much more mischief
would have been done them, and they would
have been quite ruined (witness Haman's
plot), if God had not prevented it by the
ministration of angels. Gabriel resolves,
when he has despatched this errand to
Daniel, that he will return *to fight with the
prince of Persia*, will continue to oppose
him, and will at length humble and bring
down that proud monarchy (*v.* 20), though
he knows that another as mischievous, even
that of Grecia, will rise instead of it.	[2.]
Here is Michael our prince, the great protector of the church, and the patron of its
just but injured cause: *The first of the chief
princes, v.* 13. Some understand it of a created angel, but an archangel of the highest
order, 1 Thess. iv. 16; Jude 9. Others
think that *Michael the archangel* is no other
than Christ himself, the *angel of the covenant,* and the Lord of the angels, he whom
Daniel saw in vision, *v.* 5. He *came to help
me* (*v.* 13); and there is *none but he that holds
with me in these things, v.* 21. Christ is the
church's prince; angels are not, Heb. ii. 5.
He presides in the affairs of the church and
effectually provides for its good. He is said
to *hold with the angels,* for it is he that makes
them serviceable to the *heirs of salvation;*
and, if he were not on the church's side, its
case were bad. But, says David, and so says
the church, *The Lord takes my part with
those that help me,* Ps. cxviii. 7. *The Lord
is with those that uphold my soul,* Ps. liv. 4.

CHAP. XI.

The angel Gabriel, in this chapter, performs his promise made to
Daniel in the foregoing chapter, that he would " show him what
should befal his people in the latter days," according to that which
was " written in the scriptures of truth:" very particularly does he
here foretel the succession of the kings of Persia and Grecia, and
the affairs of their kingdoms, especially the mischief which Antiochus Epiphanes did in his time to the church, which was foretold
before, ch. viii. 11—12. Here is, I. A brief prediction of the setting
up of the Grecian monarchy upon the ruins of the Persian monarchy, which was now newly begun, ver. 1—4. II. A prediction of
the affairs of the two kingdoms of Egypt and Syria, with reference
to each other, ver. 5—20. III. Of the rise of Antiochus Epiphanes,
and his actions and successes, ver.21—29. IV. Of the great mischief
that he should do to the Jewish nation and religion, and his contempt of all religion, ver. 30—39. V. Of his fall and ruin at last,
when he is in the heat of his pursuit, ver. 40—45.

ALSO I in the first year of Darius
the Mede, *even* I, stood to confirm and to strengthen him. 2 And
now will I show thee the truth. Behold, there shall stand up yet three
kings in Persia; and the fourth shall
be far richer than *they* all: and by
his strength through his riches he
shall stir up all against the realm of
Grecia. 3 And a mighty king shall
stand up, that shall rule with great
dominion, and do according to his
will. 4 And when he shall stand up

his kingdom shall be broken, and
shall be divided toward the four winds
of heaven; and not to his posterity,
nor according to his dominion which
he ruled: for his kingdom shall be
plucked up, even for others beside
those.

Here, 1. The angel Gabriel lets Daniel
know the good service he has done to the
Jewish nation (*v.* 1): " *In the first year of
Darius the Mede,* who destroyed Babylon and
released the Jews out of that house of bondage, *I stood a strength and fortress to him,*
that is, I was instrumental to protect him,
and give him success in his wars, and, after
he had conquered Babylon, to confirm him
in his resolution to release the Jews," which,
it is likely, met with much opposition. Thus
by the angel, and at the request of *the
watcher,* the golden head was broken, and
the axe laid to the root of the tree. Note,
We must acknowledge the hand of God in
the strengthening,of those that are friends to
the church for the service they are to do it,
and confirming them in their good resolutions; herein he uses the ministry of angels
more than we are aware of. And the many
instances we have known of God's care of
his church formerly encourage us to depend
upon him in further straits and difficulties.
2. He foretels the reign of four Persian
kings (*v.* 2): *Now I will tell thee the truth,*
that is, the true meaning of the visions of
the great image, and of the four beasts, and
expound in plain terms what was before represented by dark types. (1.) There shall
stand up *three kings in Persia,* besides Darius, in whose reign this prophecy is dated,
ch. ix. 1. Mr. Broughton makes these three
to be Cyrus, Artaxasta or Artaxerxes, called
by the Greeks *Cambyses,* and Ahasuerus
that married Esther, called *Darius son of
Hystaspes.* To these three the Persians
gave these attributes—Cyrus was a father,
Cambyses a master, and Darius a hoarder
up. So Herodotus. (2.) There shall be a
fourth, *far richer than they all,* that is,
Xerxes, of whose wealth the Greek authors
take notice. By *his strength* (his vast army,
consisting of 800,000 men at least) and *his
riches,* with which he maintained and paid
that vast army, he *stirred up all* against *the
realm of Greece.* Xerxes's expedition against
Greece is famous in history, and the shameful defeat that he met with. He who when
he went out was the terror of Greece in his
return was the scorn of Greece. Daniel
needed not to be told what disappointment he
would meet with, for he was a hinderer of
the building of the temple; but soon after,
about thirty years after the first return from
captivity, Darius, a young king, revived the
building of the temple, owning the hand of
God against his predecessors for hindering
it, Ezra vi. 7. 3. He foretels Alexander's

conquests and the partition of his kingdom, v. 3. He is that *mighty king* that shall *stand up* against the kings of Persia, and he shall *rule with great dominion*, over many kingdoms, and with a despotic power, for he shall *do according to his will*, and undo likewise, which, by the law of the Medes and Persians, their kings could not. When Alexander, after he had conquered Asia, would be worshipped as a god, then this was fulfilled, that he shall *do according to his will*. That is God's prerogative, but was his pretension. But (v. 4) his *kingdom* shall soon be *broken*, and *divided* into four parts, *but not to his posterity*, nor shall any of his successors reign *according to his dominion;* none of them shall have such large territories nor such an absolute power. His *kingdom was plucked up for others besides those* of his own family. Arideus, his brother, was made king in Macedonia; Olympias, Alexander's mother, killed him, and poisoned Alexander's two sons, Hercules and Alexander. Thus was his family rooted out by its own hands. See what decaying perishing things worldly pomp and possessions are, and the powers by which they are got. Never was the vanity of the world and its greatest things shown more evidently than in the story of Alexander. *All is vanity and vexation of spirit.*

5 And the king of the south shall be strong, and *one* of his princes; and he shall be strong above him, and have dominion; his dominion *shall be* a great dominion. 6 And in the end of years they shall join themselves together; for the king's daughter of the south shall come to the king of the north to make an agreement: but she shall not retain the power of the arm; neither shall he stand, nor his arm: but she shall be given up, and they that brought her, and he that begat her, and he that strengthened her in *these* times. 7 But out of a branch of her roots shall *one* stand up in his estate, which shall come with an army, and shall enter into the fortress of the king of the north, and shall deal against them, and shall prevail: 8 And shall also carry captives into Egypt their gods, with their princes, *and* with their precious vessels of silver and of gold; and he shall continue *more* years than the king of the north. 9 So the king of the south shall come into *his* kingdom, and shall return into his own land. 10 But his sons shall be stirred up, and shall assemble a multitude of

1102

great forces: and *one* shall certainly come, and overflow, and pass through: then shall he return, and be stirred up, *even* to his fortress. 11 And the king of the south shall be moved with choler, and shall come forth and fight with him, *even* with the king of the north: and he shall set forth a great multitude; but the multitude shall be given into his hand. 12 *And* when he hath taken away the multitude, his heart shall be lifted up; and he shall cast down *many* ten thousands: but he shall not be strengthened *by it.* 13 For the king of the north shall return, and shall set forth a multitude greater than the former, and shall certainly come after certain years with a great army and with much riches. 14 And in those times there shall many stand up against the king of the south: also the robbers of thy people shall exalt themselves to establish the vision; but they shall fall. 15 So the king of the north shall come, and cast up a mount, and take the most fenced cities: and the arms of the south shall not withstand, neither his chosen people, neither *shall there be any* strength to withstand. 16 But he that cometh against him shall do according to his own will, and none shall stand before him: and he shall stand in the glorious land, which by his hand shall be consumed. 17 He shall also set his face to enter with the strength of his whole kingdom, and upright ones with him; thus shall he do: and he shall give him the daughter of women, corrupting her: but she shall not stand *on his side*, neither be for him. 18 After this shall he turn his face unto the isles, and shall take many: but a prince for his own behalf shall cause the reproach offered by him to cease; without his own reproach he shall cause *it* to turn upon him. 19 Then he shall turn his face toward the fort of his own land: but he shall stumble and fall, and not be found. 20 Then shall stand up in his estate a raiser of taxes *in* the glory of the kingdom: but within few days he shall be destroyed, neither in anger, nor in battle.

Here are foretold,

I. The rise and power of two great king-doms out of the remains of Alexander's con-quests, *v.* 5. 1. The kingdom of Egypt, which was made considerable by Ptolemæus Lagus, one of Alexander's captains, whose successors were, from him, called the *La-gidæ.* He is called the king of the *south,* that is, Egypt, named here, *v.* 8, 42, 43. The countries that at first belonged to Pto-lemy are reckoned to be Egypt, Phœnicia, Arabia, Libya, Ethiopia, &c. Theocr. Idyl. 17. 2. The kingdom of Syria, which was set up by Seleucus Nicanor, or the *conqueror;* he was one of Alexander's princes, and be-came stronger than the other, and *had the greatest dominion of all,* was the most power-ful of all Alexander's successors. It was said that he had no fewer than seventy-two kingdoms under him. Both these were strong against Judah (the affairs of which are particularly eyed in this prediction); Pto-lemy, soon after he gained Egypt, invaded Judea, and took Jerusalem *on a sabbath,* pretending a friendly visit. Seleucus also gave disturbance to Judea.

II. The fruitless attempt to unite these two kingdoms as iron and clay in Nebu-chadnezzar's image (*v.* 6): "*At the end of certain years,* about seventy after Alexander's death, the Lagidæ and the Seleucidæ shall associate, but not in sincerity. Ptolemy Philadelphus, king of Egypt, shall marry his daughter Berenice to Antiochus Theos, king of Syria," who had already a wife called *La-odice.* "Berenice shall come to the king *of the north,* to make an agreement, but it shall not hold: *She shall not retain the power of the arm;* neither she nor her posterity shall establish themselves in the kingdom of the north, neither shall Ptolemy her father, nor Antiochus her husband (between whom there was to be a great alliance), *stand,* nor their arm, but *she shall be given up and those that brought her,*" all that projected that unhappy marriage between her and Antiochus, which occasioned so much mischief, instead of pro-ducing a coalition between the northern and southern crowns, as was hoped. Antiochus divorced Berenice, took his former wife La-odice again, who soon after poisoned him, procured Berenice and her son to be mur-dered, and set up her own son by Antiochus to be king, who was called *Seleucus Cal-linicus.*

III. A war between the two kingdoms, *v.* 7, 8. A branch from the same root with Berenice *shall stand up in his estate.* Ptole-mæus Euergetes, the son and successor of Ptolemæus Philadelphus, shall come with an army against Seleucus Callinicus, king of Syria, to avenge his sister's quarrel, and shall prevail; and he shall carry away a rich booty both of persons and goods into Egypt, and shall *continue more years than the king of the north.* This Ptolemy reigned forty-six years; and Justin says that if his own affairs

had not called him home he would, in this war, have made himself master of the whole kingdom of Syria. But (*v.* 9) he shall be forced to *come into his kingdom* and *return into his own land,* to keep peace there, so that he can no longer carry on the war abroad. Note, It is very common for a treacherous peace to end in a bloody war.

IV. The long and busy reign of *Antiochus the Great,* king of Syria. Seleucus Calli-nicus, that king of the north that was over-come (*v.* 7) and died miserably, left two sons, Seleucus and Antiochus; these are his sons, the sons of the *king of the north,* that shall be *stirred up, and shall assemble a multitude of great forces,* to recover what their father had lost, *v.* 10. But Seleucus the elder, being weak, and unable to rule his army, was poisoned by his friends, and reigned only two years; and his brother Antiochus succeeded him, who reigned thirty-seven years, and was called *the Great.* And there-fore the angel, though he speaks of *sons* at first, goes on with the account of *one only,* who was but fifteen years old when he began to reign, and he shall *certainly come, and overflow,* and *over-run,* and shall *be restored* at length to what his father lost. 1. The *king of the south,* in this war, shall at first have very great success. Ptolemæus Phi-lopater, moved with indignation at the in-dignities done by *Antiochus the Great,* shall (though otherwise a slothful prince) *come forth, and fight with him,* and shall bring a vast army into the field of 70,000 foot, and 5000 horse, and seventy-three ele-phants. And the *other multitude* (the army of Antiochus, consisting of 62,000 foot, and 6000 horse, and 102 elephants) shall *be given into his hand.* Polybius, who lived with Scipio, has given a particular account of this battle of Raphia. Ptolemæus Philopater, having gained this victory, grew very inso-lent; *his heart was lifted up;* then he went into the temple of God at Jerusalem, and, in defiance of the law, entered the most holy place, for which God has a controversy with him, so that, though he shall *cast down many myriads,* yet he shall *not be strengthened by it,* so as to secure his interest. For, 2. The *king of the north, Antiochus the Great,* shall *return* with a *greater army* than *the former;* and, at the *end of times (that is, years)* he shall *come with a mighty army, and great riches,* against the *king of the south,* that is, Ptolemæus Epiphanes, who succeeded Pto-lemæus Philopater his father, when he was a child, which gave advantage to Antiochus the Great. In this expedition he had some powerful allies (*v.* 14): *Many shall stand up against the king of the south.* Philip of Ma-cedon was confederate with Antiochus against the king of Egypt, and Scopas his general, whom he sent into Syria; Antiochus routed him, destroyed a great part of his army; whereupon the Jews willingly yielded to Antiochus, joined with him, helped him to besiege Ptolemæus's garrisons. Then *the robbers of thy people shall exalt themselves to establish the vision*, to help forward the accomplishment of this prophecy; but *they shall fall, and shall come to nothing, v.* 14. Hereupon (*v.* 15) the *king of the north*, this same Antiochus Magnus, shall carry on his design against the king of the south another way. (1.) He shall surprise his strong-holds; all that he has got in Syria and Samaria, and the arms of the south, all the power of the king of Egypt, shall not be able to withstand him. See how dubious and variable the turns of the scale of war are; like buying and selling, it is winning and losing; sometimes one side gets the better and sometimes the other; yet neither by chance; it is not, as they call it, the *fortune of war*, but according to the will and counsel of God, who brings some low and raises others up. (2.) He shall make himself master of the land of Judea (*v.* 16): *He that comes against him* (that is, the king of the north) shall carry all before him and do what he pleases, and *he shall stand* and get footing *in the glorious land:* so the land of Israel was, and *by his hand* it was wasted and consumed, for with the spoil of that good land he victualled his vast army. The land of Judea lay between these two potent kingdoms of Egypt and Syria, so that in all the struggles between them that was sure to suffer, for to it they both bore *ill will.* Yet some read this, *By his hand it shall be perfected;* as if it intimated that the land of Judea, being taken under the protection of this Antiochus, shall flourish, and be in better condition than it had been. (3.) He shall still push on his war against the king of Egypt, and *set his face* to *enter with the strength of his whole kingdom*, taking advantage of the infancy of Ptolemy Epiphanes, and the *upright ones*, many of the pious Israelites, siding with him, *v.* 17. In prosecution of his design, he shall give him his daughter Cleopatra to wife, designing, as Saul in giving his daughter to David, that she should be a *snare to him*, and do him a mischief; but she *shall not stand on her father's* side, nor be *for him*, but for her husband, and so that plot failed him. (4.) His war with the Romans is here foretold (*v.* 18): He shall *turn his face to the isles* (*v.* 18), the isles of the Gentiles (Gen. x. 5), Greece and Italy. He took many of the isles about the Hellespont—Rhodes, Samos, Delos, &c., which by war or treaty he made himself master of; but a *prince*, or *state* (so some), even the Roman senate, or a *leader*, even the Roman general, shall *return his reproach* with which he abused the Romans *upon himself*, or shall *make his shame rest on himself*, and *without his own shame*, or any disgrace to himself, shall *pay him again.* This was fulfilled when the two Scipios were sent with an army against Antiochus. Hannibal was then with him, and advised him to invade Italy and waste it as

1104

he had done; but he did not take his advice; and Scipio joined battle with him, and gave him a total defeat, though Antiochus had 70,000 men and the Romans but 30,000. Thus he caused the *reproach offered by him to cease.* (5.) His fall. When he was totally routed by the Romans, and was forced to abandon to them all he had in Europe, and had a very heavy tribute exacted from him, he *turned to his own land*, and, not knowing which way to raise money to pay his tribute, he plundered a temple of Jupiter, which so incensed his own subjects against him that they set upon him, and killed him; so he was overthrown, and *fell*, and *was no more found, v.* 19. (6.) His next successor, *v.* 20. There rose up one in his place, a *raiser of taxes*, a *sender forth of the extortioner*, or extorter. This character was remarkably answered in Seleucus Philopater, the elder son of Antiochus the Great, who was a great oppressor of his own subjects, and exacted abundance of money from them; and, when he was told he would thereby lose his friends, he said he knew no better friend he had than money. He likewise attempted to rob the temple at Jerusalem, which this seems especially to refer to. But *within a few days he shall be destroyed, neither in anger nor in battle*, but poisoned by Heliodorus, one of his own servants, when he had reigned but twelve years, and done nothing remarkable.

V. From all this let us learn, 1. That God in his providence sets up one, and pulls down another, as he pleases, advances some from low beginnings and depresses others that were very high. Some have called great men the *foot-balls of fortune;* or, rather, they are the *tools of Providence.* 2. This world is full of *wars and fightings*, which come *from men's lusts*, and make it a theatre of sin and misery. 3. All the changes and revolutions of states and kingdoms, and every event, even the most minute and contingent, were plainly and perfectly foreseen by the God of heaven, and to him nothing is *new.* 4. No word of God shall fall to the ground; but what he has designed, what he has declared, shall infallibly come to pass; and even the sins of men shall be made to serve his purpose, and contribute to the bringing of his counsels to birth in their season; and yet *God is not the author of sin.* 5. That, for the right understanding of some parts of scripture, it is necessary that heathen authors be consulted, which give light to the scripture, and show the accomplishment of what is there foretold; we have therefore reason to bless God for the human learning with which many have done great service to divine truths.

21 And in his estate shall stand up a vile person, to whom they shall not give the honour of the kingdom: but he shall come in peaceably, and obtain the kingdom by flatteries. 22

And with the arms of a flood shall they be overflown from before him, and shall be broken; yea, also the prince of the covenant. 23 And after the league *made* with him he shall work deceitfully: for he shall come up, and shall become strong with a small people. 24 He shall enter peaceably even upon the fattest places of the province; and he shall do *that* which his fathers have not done, nor his fathers' fathers; he shall scatter among them the prey, and spoil, and riches: *yea*, and he shall forecast his devices against the strong holds, even for a time. 25 And he shall stir up his power and his courage against the king of the south with a great army; and the king of the south shall be stirred up to battle with a very great and mighty army; but he shall not stand: for they shall forecast devices against him. 26 Yea, they that feed of the portion of his meat shall destroy him, and his army shall overflow: and many shall fall down slain. 27 And both these kings' hearts *shall be* to do mischief, and they shall speak lies at one table; but it shall not prosper: for yet the end *shall be* at the time appointed. 28 Then shall he return into his land with great riches; and his heart *shall be* against the holy covenant; and he shall do *exploits*, and return to his own land. 29 At the time appointed he shall return, and come toward the south; but it shall not be as the former, or as the latter. 30 For the ships of Chittim shall come against him: therefore he shall be grieved, and return, and have indignation against the holy covenant: so shall he do; he shall even return, and have intelligence with them that forsake the holy covenant. 31 And arms shall stand on his part, and they shall pollute the sanctuary of strength, and shall take away the daily *sacrifice*, and they shall place the abomination that maketh desolate. 32 And such as do wickedly against the covenant shall be corrupt by flatteries: but the people that do know their God shall be strong, and do *exploits*. 33 And they that understand among the people shall instruct many: yet they shall fall by the sword, and by flame, by captivity, and by spoil, *many* days. 34 Now when they shall fall, they shall be holpen with a little help: but many shall cleave to them with flatteries. 35 And *some* of them of understanding shall fall, to try them, and to purge, and to make *them* white, *even* to the time of the end: because *it is* yet for a time appointed. 36 And the king shall do according to his will; and he shall exalt himself, and magnify himself above every god, and shall speak marvellous things against the God of gods, and shall prosper till the indignation be accomplished: for that that is determined shall be done. 37 Neither shall he regard the God of his fathers, nor the desire of women, nor regard any god: for he shall magnify himself above all. 38 But in his estate shall he honour the God of forces: and a god whom his fathers knew not shall he honour with gold, and silver, and with precious stones, and pleasant things. 39 Thus shall he do in the most strong holds with a strange god, whom he shall acknowledge *and* increase with glory: and he shall cause them to rule over many, and shall divide the land for gain. 40 And at the time of the end shall the king of the south push at him: and the king of the north shall come against him like a whirlwind, with chariots, and with horsemen, and with many ships; and he shall enter into the countries, and shall overflow and pass over. 41 He shall enter also into the glorious land, and many *countries* shall be overthrown: but these shall escape out of his hand, *even* Edom, and Moab, and the chief of the children of Ammon. 42 He shall stretch forth his hand also upon the countries: and the land of Egypt shall not escape. 43 But he shall have power over the treasures of gold and of silver, and over all the precious things of Egypt: and the Libyans and the Ethiopians *shall be* at his steps. 44 But tidings out of the east and out of the north shall trouble him: therefore he shall go forth with great **fury** to destroy, and utterly to make away many. 45 And he shall plant the tabernacles of his palaces between the seas in the glorious holy mountain; yet he shall come to his end, and none shall help him.

All this is a prophecy of the reign of Antiochus Epiphanes, the *little horn* spoken of before (*ch.* viii. 9) a sworn enemy to the Jewish religion, and a bitter persecutor of those that adhered to it. What troubles the Jews met with in the reigns of the Persian kings were not so particularly foretold to Daniel as these, because then they had living prophets with them, Haggai and Zechariah, to encourage them; but these troubles in the days of Antiochus were foretold, because, before that time, prophecy would cease, and they would find it necessary to have recourse to the written word. Some things in this prediction concerning Antiochus are alluded to in the New-Testament predictions of the antichrist, especially *v.* 36, 37. And as it is usual with the prophets, when they foretel the prosperity of the Jewish church, to make use of such expressions as were applicable to the *kingdom of Christ,* and insensibly to slide into a prophecy of that, so, when they foretel the troubles of the church, they make use of such expressions as have a further reference to the kingdom of the antichrist, the rise and ruin of that. Now concerning Antiochus, the angel foretels here,

I. His character : He shall be a *vile person.* He called himself *Epiphanes—the illustrious,* but his character was the reverse of his surname. The heathen writers describe him to be an *odd-humoured* man, rude and boisterous, base and sordid. He would sometimes steal out of the court into the city, and herd with any infamous company *incognito—in disguise;* he made himself a companion of the common sort, and of the basest strangers that came to town. He had the most unaccountable whims, so that some took him to be silly, others to be mad. Hence he was called *Epimanes—the madman.* He is called a *vile person,* for he had been a long time a hostage at Rome for the fidelity of his father when the Romans had subdued him; and it was agreed that, when the other hostages were exchanged, he should continue a prisoner at large.

II. His accession to the crown. By a trick he got his elder brother's son, Demetrius, to be sent a hostage to Rome, in exchange for him, contrary to the cartel; and, his elder brother being made away with by Heliodorus (*v.* 20), he took the kingdom. The states of Syria did not *give it to him* (*v.* 21), because they knew it belonged to his elder brother's son, nor did he get it by the sword, but *came in peaceably,* pretending to reign for his brother's son, Demetrius, then a hostage at Rome. But with the help of

Eumenes and Attalus, neighbouring princes, he gained an interest in the people, and *by flatteries obtained the kingdom,* established himself in it, and crushed Heliodorus, who made head against him *with the arms of a flood;* those that opposed him were *overflown* and *broken before him,* even *the prince of the covenant,* his nephew, the rightful heir, whom he pretended to covenant with that he would resign to him whenever he should return, *v.* 22. But (*v.* 23) *after the league made with him he shall work deceitfully,* as one whose avowed maxim it is that princes ought not to be bound by their word any longer than it is for their interest. And *with a small people,* that at first cleave to him, he shall *become strong,* and (*v.* 24) *he shall enter peaceably upon the fattest places* of the kingdom of Syria, and, very unlike his predecessors, shall *scatter* among the people the *prey, and the spoil, and riches,* to insinuate himself into their affections; but, at the same time, he shall *forecast his devices against the strong-holds,* to make himself master of them, so that his generosity shall last but for a time; when he has got the garrisons into his hands he will scatter his spoil no more, but rule by force, as those commonly do that come in by fraud. He that comes in like a fox reigns like a lion. Some understand these verses of his first expedition into Egypt, when he came not as an enemy, but as a friend and guardian to the young king Ptolemæus Philometer, and therefore brought with him but few followers, yet those stout men, and faithful to his interest, whom he placed in divers of the strong-holds in Egypt, thereby making himself master of them.

III. His war with Egypt, which was his second expedition thither. This is described, *v.* 25, 27. Antiochus shall *stir up his power and courage* against Ptolemæus Philometer king of Egypt. Ptolemy, thereupon, shall *be stirred up to battle* against him, shall come against him *with a very great and mighty army;* but Ptolemy, though he has such a vast army, shall not be able to stand before him; for Antiochus's army shall *overthrow* his, and overpower it, and great multitudes of the Egyptian army shall *fall down slain.* And no marvel, for the king of Egypt shall be betrayed by his own counsellors; those that *feed of the portion of his meat,* that eat of his bread and live upon him, being bribed by Antiochus, shall *forecast devices against him,* and even *they shall destroy him;* and what fence is there against such treachery ? After the battle, a treaty of peace shall be set on foot, and these two kings shall meet *at one council-board,* to adjust the articles of peace between them; but they shall neither of them be sincere in it, for they shall, in their pretences and promises of amity and friendship, *lie to one another,* for their hearts shall be at the same time to do one another all the mischief they can. And then no marvel that *it shall not prosper.* The peace shall not last; but *the end* of it shall be *at the time appointed* in the divine Providence, and then the war shall break out again, as a sore that is only skinned over.

IV. Another expedition against Egypt. From the former he *returned with great riches* (*v.* 28), and therefore took the first occasion to invade Egypt again, *at the time appointed* by the divine Providence, two years after, in the eighth year of his reign, *v.* 29. He shall come *towards the south.* But this attempt shall not succeed, as the two former did, nor shall he gain his point, as he had done before once and again; for (*v.* 30) *the ships of Chittim shall come against him,* that is, the navy of the Romans, or only ambassadors from the Roman senate, who came in ships. Ptolemæus Philometer, king of Egypt, being now in a strict alliance with the Romans, craved their aid against Antiochus, who had besieged him and his mother Cleopatra in the city of Alexandria. The Roman senate thereupon sent an embassy to Antiochus, to command him to raise the siege, and, when he desired some time to consider of it and consult with his friends about it, Popilius, one of the ambassadors, with his staff drew a circle about him, and told him, as one having authority, he should give a positive answer before he came out of that circle; whereupon, fearing the Roman power, he was forced immediately to give orders for the raising of the siege and the retreat of his army out of Egypt. So Livy and others relate the story which this prophecy refers to. *He shall be grieved, and return;* for it was a great vexation to him to be forced to yield thus.

V. His rage and cruel practices against the Jews. This is that part of his government, or mis-government rather, which is most enlarged upon in this prediction. In his return from his expedition into Egypt (which is prophesied of, *v.* 28) he *did exploits* against the Jews, in the sixth year of his reign; then he spoiled the city and temple. But the most terrible storm was in his return from Egypt, two years after, prophesied of *v.* 30. Then he took Judea in his way home; and, because he could not gain his point in Egypt by reason of the Romans interposing, he wreaked his revenge upon the poor Jews, who gave him no provocation, but had greatly provoked God to permit him to do it, Dan. viii. 23.

1. He had a rooted antipathy to the Jews' religion: *His heart* was *against the holy covenant, v.* 28. And (*v.* 30) *he had indignation against the holy covenant,* that covenant of peculiarity by which the Jews were incorporated a people distinct from all other nations, and dignified above them. He hated the law of Moses and the worship of the true God, and was vexed at the privileges of the Jewish nation and the promises made to them. Note, That which is the hope and joy of the people of God is the

envy of their neighbours, and that is *the holy covenant.* Esau hated Jacob because he had got the blessing. Those that are strangers to the covenant are often enemies to it.

2. He carried on his malicious designs against the Jews by the assistance of some perfidious apostate Jews. He kept up *intelligence with those that forsook the holy covenant* (*v.* 30), some of the Jews that were false to their religion, and introduced the customs of the heathen, with whom they made a covenant. See the fulfilling of this, 1 Mac. i. 11—15, where it is expressly said, concerning those renegado Jews, that they *made themselves uncircumcised and forsook the holy covenant.* We read (2 Mac. iv. 9) of Jason, the brother of Onias the high priest, who by the appointment of Antiochus set up a school at Jerusalem, *for the training up of youth in the fashions of the heathen;* and (2 Mac. iv. 23, &c.) of Menelaus, who fell in with the interests of Antiochus, and was the man that helped him into Jerusalem, now in his last return from Egypt. We read much in the book of the Maccabees of the mischief done to the Jews by these treacherous men of their own nation, Jason and Menelaus, and their party. These upon all occasions he made use of. *" Such as do wickedly against the covenant,* such as throw up their religion, and comply with the heathen, he shall *corrupt with flatteries,* to harden them in their apostasy, and to make use of them as decoys to draw in others," *v.* 32. Note, It is not strange if those who do not live up to their religion, but in their conversations *do wickedly against the covenant,* are easily *corrupted by flatteries* to quit their religion. Those that make shipwreck of a good conscience will soon *make shipwreck of the faith.*

3. He profaned the temple. *Arms stand on his part* (*v.* 31), not only his own army which he now brought from Egypt, but a great party of deserters from the Jewish religion that joined with them; and they *polluted the sanctuary of strength,* not only the holy city, but the temple. The story of this we have, 1 Mac. i. 21, &c. He *entered proudly into the sanctuary,* took *away the golden altar, and the candlestick,* &c. And therefore (*v.* 25) *there was a great mourning in Israel; the princes and elders mourned,* &c. And (2 Mac. v. 15, &c.) *Antiochus went into the most holy temple, Menelaus, that traitor to the laws and to his own country, being his guide.* Antiochus, having resolved to bring all about him to be of his religion, *took away the daily sacrifice, v.* 31. Some observe that the word *Tammidh,* which signifies no more than *daily,* is only here, and in the parallel place, used for the *daily sacrifice,* as if there were a designed liberty left to supply it either with *sacrifice,* which was suppressed by Antiochus, or with *gospel-worship,* which was suppressed by the Antichrist. Then he *set up the abomi-*

nation of desolation upon the altar (1 Mac. i. 54), even an *idol altar* (v. 59), and called the temple the temple of *Jupiter Olympius,* 2 Mac. vi. 2.

4. He persecuted those who retained their integrity. Though there are many who *forsake the covenant* and *do wickedly* against it, yet there is a people who do *know their God* and retain the knowledge of him, and *they shall be strong and do exploits,* v. 32. When others yield to the tyrant's demands, and surrender their consciences to his impositions, they bravely keep their ground, resist the temptation, and make the tyrant himself ashamed of his attempt upon them. Good old Eleazar, one of the *principal scribes,* when he had swine's flesh thrust into his mouth, did bravely spit it out again, though he knew he must be tormented to death for so doing, and was so, 2 Mac. vi. 19. The mother and her seven sons were put to death for adhering to their religion, 2 Mac. vii. This might well be called *doing exploits ;* for to choose suffering rather than sin is a great exploit. And it was *by faith,* by being *strong in faith,* that they did those exploits, that *they were tortured, not accepting deliverance,* as the apostle speaks, probably with reference to that story, Heb. xi. 35. Or it may refer to the military courage and achievements of Judas Maccabæus and others in opposition to Antiochus. Note, The right knowledge of God is, and will be, the strength of the soul, and, in the strength of that, gracious souls do exploits. *Those that know his name will put their trust in him,* and by that trust will do great things. Now, concerning this people that knew their God, we are here told, (1.) That *they shall instruct many,* v. 33. They shall make it their business to show others what they have learned themselves of the difference between truth and falsehood, good and evil. Note, Those that have the knowledge of God themselves should communicate their knowledge to those about them, and this spiritual charity must be extensive : they must *instruct many.* Some understand this of a society newly erected for the propagating of divine knowledge, called *Assideans,* godly men, *pietists* (so the name signifies), that were both knowing and zealous in the law ; these instructed many. Note, In times of persecution and apostasy, which are trying times, those that have knowledge ought to make use of it for the strengthening and establishing of others. Those that understand aright themselves ought to do what they can to bring others to understand ; for knowledge is a talent that must be traded with. Or, They shall instruct many by their perseverance in their duty and their patient suffering for it. Good examples instruct many, and with many are the most powerful instructions. (2.) *They shall fall* by the cruelty of Antiochus, shall be put to the torture, and put to death, by his rage. Though they are so excellent and
1108

intelligent themselves, and so useful and serviceable to others, yet Antiochus shall show them no mercy, but *they shall fall for some days ;* so it may be read, Rev. ii. 10, *Thou shalt have tribulation ten days.* We read much, in the books of the Maccabees, of Antiochus's barbarous usage of the pious Jews, how many he slew in wars and how many he murdered in cold blood. Women were *put to death* for having their children *circumcised,* and their *infants were hanged about their necks,* 1 Mac. i. 60, 61. But why did God suffer this? How can this be reconciled with the justice and goodness of God? I answer, Very well, if we consider what it was that God aimed at in this (v. 35) : *Some of those of understanding shall fall,* but it shall be for the good of the church and for their own spiritual benefit. *It shall* be to *try them, and to purge, and to make them white.* They *needed* these afflictions themselves. The best have their spots, which must be washed off, their dross, which must be purged out ; and their troubles, particularly their *share in the public troubles,* help to do this ; being sanctified to them by the grace of God, they are means of mortifying their corruptions, weaning them from the world, and awakening them to greater seriousness and diligence in religion. They try them, as silver in the furnace is refined from its dross ; they purge them, as wheat in the barn is winnowed from the chaff ; and they *make them white,* as cloth by the fuller is cleared from its spots. See 1 Pet. i. 7. Their sufferings *for righteousness' sake* would try and purge the nation of the Jews, would convince them of the truth, excellency, and power of that holy religion which these *understanding* men died for their adherence to. The blood of the martyrs is the seed of the church ; it is precious blood, and not a drop of it should be shed but upon such a valuable consideration. (3.) The cause of religion, though it be thus run upon, shall not be run down. *When they shall fall* they shall not be utterly cast down, but *they shall be holpen with a little help,* v. 34. Judas Maccabæus, and his brethren, and a few with them, shall *make head* against the tyrant, and assert the injured cause of their religion ; they *pulled down* the idolatrous *altars, circumcised the children that they found uncircumcised, recovered the law out of the hand of the Gentiles, and the work prospered in their hands,* 1 Mac. ii. 45, &c. Note, Those that stand by the cause of religion when it is threatened and struck at, though they may not immediately be delivered and made victorious, shall yet have *present help.* And a *little help* must not be despised ; but, when times are very bad, we must be thankful for *some reviving.* It is likewise foretold that *many shall cleave to them with flatteries ;* when they see the Maccabees prosper some Jews shall join with them that are no true friends to religion, but will only pretend friendship either with design to *betray them* or in hope to *rise with them;* but the *fiery trial* (v. 35) will separate between the *precious and the vile,* and by it *those that are perfect will be made manifest* and those that are not. (4.) Though these troubles may continue long, yet they will have *an end.* They are *for a time appointed,* a limited time, fixed in the divine counsels. This warfare shall be accomplished. *Hitherto* the power of the enemy shall come, and *no further;* here shall its *proud waves* be *stayed.*

5. He grew very proud, insolent, and profane, and, being puffed up with his conquests, bade defiance to Heaven, and trampled upon every thing that was sacred, v. 36. &c. And here some think begins a prophecy of the antichrist, the papal kingdom. It is plain that St. Paul, in his prophecy of the rise and reign of the man of sin, alludes to this (2 Thess. ii. 4), which shows that Antiochus was a type and figure of that enemy, as Babylon also was; but, this being joined in a continued discourse with the foregoing prophecies concerning Antiochus, to me it seems probable that it principally refers to him, and in him had its primary accomplishment, and has reference to the other only by way of accommodation. (1.) He shall impiously dishonour the God of Israel, the only living and true God, called here the *God of gods.* He shall, in defiance of him and his authority, *do according to his will* against his people and his holy religion; he shall *exalt himself* above him, as Sennacherib did, and shall *speak marvellous things against him* and against his laws and institutions. This was fulfilled when Antiochus forbade *sacrifices* to be *offered* in God's temple, and ordered the *sabbaths* to be *profaned,* the *sanctuary* and the *holy people* to be *polluted,* &c., to *the end that they might forget the law and change all the ordinances,* and this upon pain of death, 1 Mac. i. 45. (2.) He shall proudly put contempt upon *all other gods,* shall *magnify himself above every god,* even the gods of the nations. Antiochus wrote to his own kingdom that every one should leave the gods he had worshipped, and worship such as he ordered, contrary to the practice of all the conquerors that went before him, 1 Mac. i. 41, 42. And *all the heathen agreed according to the commandment of the king;* fond as they were of their gods, they did not think them worth suffering for, but, their gods being idols, it was all alike to them what gods they worshipped. Antiochus did not *regard any god,* but *magnified himself above all,* v. 37. He was so proud that he thought himself above the condition of a mortal man, that he could *command the waves of the sea, and reach to the stars of heaven,* as his insolence and haughtiness are expressed, 2 Mac. ix. 8, 10. Thus he carried all before him, *till the indignation was accomplished* (v. 36), till he had run his length, and filled up the measure of his

iniquity; for *that which is determined shall be done,* and nothing more, nothing short. (3) He shall, contrary to the way of the heathen, disregard the god of his fathers, v. 37. Though an affection to the religion of their ancestors was, among the heathen, almost as natural to them as *the desire of women* (for, if you search through *the isles of Chittim,* you will not find an instance of a nation that has *changed its gods,* Jer. ii. 10, 11), yet Antiochus shall not *regard the god of his fathers;* he made laws to abolish the religion of his country, and to bring in the idols of the Greeks. And though his predecessors had honoured the God of Israel, and given great gifts to the temple at Jerusalem (2 Mac. iii. 2, 3), he offered the greatest indignities to God and his temple. His not regarding the *desire of women* may denote his barbarous cruelty (he shall spare no age or sex, no, not the tender ones) or his unnatural lusts, or, in general, his contempt of every thing which men of honour have a concern for, or it might be accomplished in something we meet not with in history. Its being joined to his not *regarding the god of his fathers* intimates that the idolatries of his country had in them more of the gratifications of the flesh than those of other countries (Lucian has written of the Syrian goddesses), and yet that would not prevail to keep him to them. (4.) He shall set up an unknown god, a new god, v. 38. *In his estate,* in the room of the god of his fathers (Apollo and Diana, deities of pleasure), he shall *honour the god of forces,* a supposed deity of power, a *god whom his fathers knew not,* nor worshipped; because he will be thought in wisdom and strength to excel his fathers, he shall *honour this god with gold, and silver, and precious stones,* thinking nothing too good for the god he has taken a fancy to. This seems to be Jupiter Olympius, known among the Phœnicians by the name of *Baal-Semen, the lord of heaven,* but never introduced among the Syrians till Antiochus introduced it. Thus shall he do *in the most strong holds,* in the temple of Jerusalem, which is called the *sanctuary of strength* (v. 31), and here the *fortresses of munitions; there* he shall set up the image of this *strange god.* Some read it, *He shall commit the munitions of strength,* or of the most strong God (that is, the city Jerusalem), to *a strange god;* he put it under the protection and government of Jupiter Olympius. This god he shall not only acknowledge, but shall *increase with glory,* by setting his image even upon God's altar. And he shall *cause those* that minister to this idol *to rule over many,* shall put them into places of power and trust, and they shall *divide the land for gain,* shall be maintained richly out of the profits of the country. Some by the *Mahuzzim,* or *god of forces,* that Antiochus shall worship, understand *money,* which is said to *answer all things*, and which is the great idol of worldly people.

Now here is very much that is applicable to the *man of sin;* he *exalts himself above all that is called god or that is worshipped; magnifies himself above all;* his flatterers call him *our lord god the pope.* By forbidding marriage, and magnifying the single life, he pretends not to regard the desire of women ; and honours the *god of forces,* the god *Mahuzzim,* or *strong holds,* saints and angels, whom his followers take for their protectors, as the heathen did of old their demons ; these they make presidents of several countries, &c. These they honour with vast treasures dedicated to them, and therein the learned Mr. Mede thinks that this prophecy was fulfilled, and that it is referred to 1 Tim. iv. 1, 2.

VI. Here seems to be another expedition into Egypt, or, at least, a struggle with Egypt. The Romans had tied him up from invading Ptolemy, but now that *king of the south pushes at him* (v. 40), makes an attempt upon some of his territories, whereupon Antiochus, the *king of the north, comes against him like a whirlwind,* with incredible swiftness and fury, *with chariots, and horses, and many ships,* a great force. He shall *come through countries, and shall overflow and pass over.* In this flying march *many countries shall be overthrown by him;* and he shall enter into *the glorious land,* the land of Israel ; it is the same word that is translated *the pleasant land,* ch. viii. 9. He shall make dreadful work among the nations thereabout ; yet some shall escape his fury, particularly Edom and Moab, and *the chief of the children of Ammon,* v. 41. He did not put these countries under contribution, because they had joined with him against the Jews. But especially the land of Egypt *shall not escape,* but he will quite beggar that, so bare will he strip it. This some reckon his fourth and last expedition against Egypt, in the tenth or eleventh year of his reign, under pretence of assisting the younger brother of Ptolemæus Philometer against him. We read not of any great slaughter made in this expedition, but great plunder ; for, it should seem, that was what he came for : He shall *have power over the treasures of gold and silver, and all the precious things of Egypt,* v. 43. Polybius, in Athenæus, relates that Antiochus, having got together abundance of wealth, by spoiling young Philometer, and breaking league with him, and by the contributions of his friends, bestowed a vast deal upon a triumph, in imitation of Paulus Æmilius, and describes the extravagance of it ; here we are told how he got that money which he spent so profusely. Notice is here taken likewise of the use he made of the Lybians and Ethiopians, who bordered upon Egypt ; they *were at his steps;* he had them at his foot, had them at his beck, and they made inroads upon Egypt to serve him.

VII. Here is a prediction of the fall and ruin of Antiochus, as before (*ch.* viii. 25), when he is in the height of his honour, flushed with victory, and laden with spoils, tidings *out of the east* and *out of the north* (out of the north-east) shall trouble him, *v.* 44. Or, He shall have intelligence, both from the eastern and northern parts, that the king of Parthia is invading his kingdom. This obliged him to drop the enterprises he had in hand, and to go against the Persians and Parthians that were revolting from him ; and this *vexed* him, for now he thought utterly to ruin and extirpate the Jewish nation, when that expedition called him off, in which he perished. This is explained by a passage in Tacitus (though an impious one) where he commends Antiochus for his attempt to *take away the superstition of the Jews,* and *bring in the manners of the Greeks,* among them (*ut teterrimam gentem in melius mutaret—to meliorate an odious nation),* and laments that he was hindered from accomplishing it by the Parthian war. Now here is, 1. The last effort of his rage against the Jews. When he finds himself perplexed and embarrassed in his affairs he shall *go forth with great fury to destroy and utterly to make away many,* v. 44. The story of this we have 1 Mac. iii. 27, &c., what a rage Antiochus was in when he heard of the successes of Judas Maccabæus, and the orders he gave to Lysias to destroy Jerusalem. Then *he planted the tabernacles of his palace,* or *tents of his court, between the seas,* between the Great Sea and the Dead Sea. He set up his royal pavilion at Emmaus near Jerusalem, in token that, though he could not be present himself, yet he gave full power to his captains to prosecute the war against the Jews with the utmost rigour. He placed his tent there, as if he had taken possession *of the glorious holy mountain* and called it *his own.* Note, When impiety grows very impudent we may see its ruin near. 2. His exit : *He shall come to his end and none shall help him;* God shall cut him off in the midst of his days and none shall be able to prevent his fall. This is the same with that which was foretold *ch.* viii. 25 (*He shall be broken without hand),* where we took a view of his miserable end. Note, When God's time shall come to bring proud oppressors to their end none shall be able to help them, nor perhaps inclined to help them ; for those that covet to be feared by all when they are in their grandeur, when they come to be in distress will find themselves loved by none ; none will lend them so much as a hand or a prayer to help them ; and, if the Lord do not help, who shall ?

Of the kings that came after Antiochus nothing is here prophesied, for that was the most malicious mischievous enemy to the church, that was a type of the son of perdition, whom the Lord shall consume with the breath of his mouth and destroy with the brightness of his coming, and none shall help him.

CHAP. XII.

After the prediction of the troubles of the Jews under Antiochus, prefiguring the troubles of the Christian church under the antichristian power, we have here, I. Comforts, and very precious ones, prescribed as cordials for the support of God's people in those times of trouble; and they are such as may indifferently serve both for those former times of trouble under Antiochus and those latter which were prefigured by them, ver. 1—4. II. A conference between Christ and an angel concerning the time of the continuance of these events, designed for Daniel's satisfaction, ver. 5—7. III. Daniel's enquiry for his own satisfaction, ver. 8. And the answer he received to that enquiry, ver. 9—13.

AND at that time shall Michael stand up, the great prince which standeth for the children of thy people : and there shall be a time of trouble, such as never was since there was a nation *even* to that same time : and at that time thy people shall be delivered, every one that shall be found written in the book. 2 And many of them that sleep in the dust of the earth shall awake, some to everlasting life, and some to shame *and* everlasting contempt. 3 And they that be wise shall shine as the brightness of the firmament ; and they that turn many to righteousness as the stars for ever and ever. 4 But thou, O Daniel, shut up the words, and seal the book, *even* to the time of the end : many shall run to and fro, and knowledge shall be increased.

It is usual with the prophets, when they foretel the grievances of the church, to furnish it at the same time with proper antidotes, a remedy for every malady. And no relief is so sovereign, of such general application, so easily accommodated to every case, and of such powerful efficacy, as those that are fetched from Christ and the future state ; thence the comforts here are fetched.

I. Jesus Christ shall appear his church's patron and protector : *At that time,* when the persecution is at the hottest, *Michael shall stand up, v.* 1. The angel had told Daniel what a firm friend Michael was to the church, *ch.* x. 21. He all along showed this friendship in the upper world ; the angels knew it ; but now *Michael shall stand* up in his providence, and work deliverance for the Jews, *when he sees that their power is gone,* Deut. xxxii. 36. Christ is *that great prince,* for he is the *prince of the kings of the earth,* Rev. i. 5. And, if he stand up for his church, who can be against it ? But this is not all : *At that time* (that is, soon after) Michael shall stand up for the working out of our eternal salvation ; the Son of God shall be incarnate, shall be *manifested to destroy the works of the devil.* Christ *stood for the children of our people* when he was made sin and a curse for them, stood in their stead as a

sacrifice, bore the curse for them, to bear it from them. He stands for them in the intercession he ever lives to make within the veil, stands up for them, and stands their friend. And after the destruction of antichrist, of whom Antiochus was a type, Christ shall *stand at the latter day upon the earth,* shall appear for the complete redemption of all his.

II. When Christ appears he will recompense tribulation to those that trouble his people. There shall *be a time of trouble,* threatening to all, but ruining to all the implacable enemies of God's kingdom among men, such *trouble as never was since there was a nation.* This is applicable, 1. To the destruction of Jerusalem, which Christ calls (perhaps with an eye to this prediction) such a *great tribulation as was not since the beginning of the world to this time,* Matt. xxiv. 21. This the angel had spoken much of (*ch.* ix. 26, 27) ; and it happened about the same time that Christ set up the gospel-kingdom in the world, that Michael our prince *stands up.* Or, 2. To the judgment of the great day, that day that shall *burn as an oven,* and consume the proud and all that do wickedly ; that will be such a *day of trouble* as never was to all those whom Michael our prince stands against.

III. He will work salvation for his people : " *At that time thy people shall be delivered,* delivered from the mischief and ruin designed them by Antiochus, even all those that were marked for preservation, that were *written among the living,*" Isa. iv. 3. When Christ comes into the world he will save his spiritual Israel from sin and hell, and will, at his second coming, complete their salvation, even the salvation of as many as were given him, as many as have *their names in the book of life,* Rev. xx. 15. They were written there before the world, and will be *found written* there at the end of the world, when the books shall be opened.

IV. There shall be a distinguishing resurrection of those that *sleep in the dust, v.* 2. 1. When God works deliverance for his people from persecution it is a kind of resurrection ; so the Jews' release out of Babylon was represented in vision (Ezek. xxxvii) and so the deliverance of the Jews from Antiochus, and other restorations of the church to outward prosperity ; they were as *life from the dead. Many of those* who had long slept in the dust of obscurity and calamity shall then awake, some to that life, and honour, and comfort which will be lasting, everlasting ; but to others, who, when they return to their prosperity, will return to their iniquity, it will be a resurrection to shame and contempt, for the *prosperity of fools* will but expose them and destroy them. 2. When, upon the appearing of Michael our prince, his gospel is preached, many of those who *sleep in the dust,* both Jews and Gentiles, shall be awakened by it to take upon them a profession of religion, and shall rise out of their heathenism or Judaism; but, since there will be always a mixture of hypocrites with true saints, it is but some of those who are *raised to life* to whom the gospel is a *savour of life unto life,* but others will be raised by it *to shame and contempt,* to whom the gospel of Christ will be a *savour of death unto death,* and Christ himself set for their fall. The net of the gospel encloses both good and bad. But, 3. It must be meant of the general resurrection at the last day: *The multitude of those that sleep in the dust shall awake,* that is, all, which shall be a great many. Or, *Of those that sleep in the dust* many shall arise to life and many to shame. The Jews themselves understand this of the resurrection of the dead at the end of time; and Christ seems to have an eye to it when he speaks of the *resurrection of life* and the *resurrection of damnation* (John v. 29); and upon this the Jews are said by St. Paul to expect a *resurrection of the dead both of the just and of the unjust,* Acts xxiv. 15. And nothing could come in more seasonably here, for, under Antiochus's persecution, some basely betrayed their religion, others bravely adhered to it. Now it would be a trouble to them that, when the storm was over, they could neither reward the one nor punish the other; this therefore would be a satisfaction to them, that they would both be recompensed according to their works in the resurrection. And the apostle, speaking of the pious Jews that suffered martyrdom under Antiochus, tells us that though they were tortured yet they *accepted not deliverance,* because they *hoped to obtain this better resurrection,* Heb. xi. 35.

V. There shall be a glorious reward conferred on those who, in the day of trouble and distress, being themselves *wise,* did *instruct many.* Such were taken particular notice of in the prophecy of the persecution (ch. xi. 33), that they should do eminent service, and yet should *fall by the sword and by flame;* now, if there were not another life after this, they would be *of all men most miserable,* and therefore we are here assured that they shall be recompensed *in the resurrection of the just* (v. 3); *Those that are wise* (that are *teachers,* so some read it, for teachers have need of wisdom, and those that have wisdom themselves should communicate it to others) *shall shine as the brightness of the firmament,* shall shine in glory, heavenly glory, the glory of the upper world; and those that by the wisdom they have, and the instructions they give, are instrumental *to turn* any, especially to *turn many to righteousness,* shall shine as the stars for ever and ever. Note, 1. There is a glory reserved for all the saints in the future state, for all that are wise, wise for their souls and eternity. A man's wisdom now *makes his face to shine* (Eccles. viii. 1), but much more will it do so in that state where its power shall be perfected and its

services rewarded. 2. The more good any do in this world, especially to the souls of men, the greater will be their glory and reward in the other world. Those that turn *men to righteousness,* that *turn sinners from the errors of their ways* and help to *save their souls from death* (Jam. v. 20), will share in the glory of those they have helped to heaven, which will be a great addition to their own glory. 3. Ministers of Christ, who have obtained mercy of him to be faithful and successful, and so are made *burning and shining lights* in this world, shall shine very brightly in the other world, shall shine *as the stars.* Christ is *the sun,* the fountain, of the lights both of grace and glory; ministers, as stars, shine in both, with a light derived from him, and a diminutive light in comparison of him; yet to those that are *earthen vessels* it will be a glory infinitely transcending their deserts. They shall *shine as the stars* of different magnitudes, some in less, others in greater lustre; but, whereas the day is coming when the stars shall fall from heaven as leaves in autumn, these stars shall *shine for ever and ever,* shall never set, never be eclipsed.

VI. That this prophecy of those times, though sealed up now, would be of great use to those that should live then, *v.* 4. Daniel must now *shut up the words and seal the book* because the *time would be long* ere these things would be accomplished: and it was some comfort that the Jewish nation, though, in the infancy of their return from Babylon, while they were few and weak, they met with obstructions in their work, were not persecuted for their religion till a long time after, when they had grown to some strength and maturity. He must *seal the book,* because it would not be *understood,* and therefore would not be regarded, till the things contained in it were accomplished; but he must keep it safely, as a treasure of great value, laid up for the ages to come, to whom it would be of great service; for *many shall then run to and fro, and knowledge shall be increased.* Then this hidden treasure shall be opened, and many shall search into it, and dig for the knowledge of it, as for silver. They shall *run to and fro,* to enquire out copies of it, shall collate them, and see that they be true and authentic. They shall read it over and over, shall meditate upon it, and run it over in their minds; *discurrent—they shall discourse* of it, and talk it over among themselves, and compare notes about it, if by any means they may *sift out* the meaning of it; and thus *knowledge shall be increased.* By consulting this prophecy on this occasion they shall be led to *search* other *scriptures,* which shall contribute much to their advancement in useful knowledge; for *then shall we know if we follow on to know the Lord,* Hos. vi. 3. Those that would have their knowledge increased must take pains, must not sit still in slothfulness and bare wishes but *run to and fro*, must make use of all the means of knowledge and improve all opportunities of getting their mistakes rectified, their doubts resolved, and their acquaintance with the things of God improved, to know more and to know better what they do know. And let us here see reason to hope that, 1. Those things of God which are now dark and obscure will hereafter be made clear, and easy to be understood. *Truth is the daughter of time.* Scripture prophecies will be expounded by the accomplishment of them; *therefore* they are given, and for that explication they are reserved. *Therefore* they are *told us before*, that, *when they do come to pass*, we may believe. 2. Those things of God which are despised and neglected, and thrown by as useless, shall be brought into reputation, shall be found to be of great service, and be brought into request; for divine revelation, however slighted for a time, shall be *magnified and made honourable*, and, above all, in the *judgment of the great day*, when the books shall be opened, and that book among the rest.

5 Then I Daniel looked, and, behold, there stood other two, the one on this side of the bank of the river, and the other on that side of the bank of the river. 6 And *one* said to the man clothed in linen, which *was* upon the waters of the river, How long *shall it be to* the end of these wonders? 7 And I heard the man clothed in linen, which *was* upon the waters of the river, when he held up his right hand and his left hand unto heaven, and sware by him that liveth for ever that *it shall be* for a time, times, and a half; and when he shall have accomplished to scatter the power of the holy people, all these *things* shall be finished. 8 And I heard, but I understood not: then said I, O my lord, what *shall be* the end of these *things?* 9 And he said, Go thy way, Daniel: for the words *are* closed up and sealed till the time of the end. 10 Many shall be purified and made white, and tried; but the wicked shall do wickedly: and none of the wicked shall understand; but the wise shall understand. 11 And from the time *that* the daily *sacrifice* shall be taken away, and the abomination that maketh desolate set up, *there shall be* a thousand two hundred and ninety days. 12 Blessed *is* he that waiteth, and cometh to the thousand three hundred

and five and thirty days. 13 But go thou thy way till the end *be*: for thou shalt rest, and stand in thy lot at the end of the days.

Daniel had been made to foresee the amazing revolutions of states and kingdoms, as far as the Israel of God was concerned in them; in them he foresaw troublous times to the church, suffering trying times, the prospect of which much affected him and filled him with concern. Now there were two questions proper to be asked upon this head:—*When* shall the *end be?* And, *What* shall the *end be?* These two questions are asked and answered here, in the close of the book; and though the comforts prescribed in the foregoing verses, one would think, were satisfactory enough, yet, for more abundant satisfaction, this is added.

I. The question, *When shall the end be?* is asked by an angel, *v.* 5, 6. Concerning this we may observe,

1. Who it was that asked the question. Daniel had had a vision of Christ in his glory, the *man clothed in linen, ch.* x. 5. But his discourse had been with the angel Gabriel, and now he *looks*, and *behold other two* (*v.* 5), two angels that he had not seen before, *one upon the bank of the river on one side and the other on the other side*, that, the river being between them, they might not whisper to one another, but what they said might be heard. Christ stood *on the waters of the river* (*v.* 6), *between the banks of Ulai*: it was therefore proper that the angels his attendants should stand on either bank, that they might be ready to go, one one way and the other the other way, as he should order them. These angels appeared, (1.) To adorn the vision, and make it the more illustrious; and to add to the glory of the Son of man, Heb. i. 6. Daniel had not seen them before, though it is probable that they were there; but now, when they began to speak, he looked up, and saw them. Note, The further we look into the things of God, and the more we converse with them, the more we shall see of those things, and still new discoveries will be made to us; those that know much, if they improve it, shall know more. (2.) To confirm the discovery, that *out of the mouth of two or three witnesses the word might be established.* Three angels appeared to Abraham. (3.) To inform themselves, to hear and ask questions; for the mysteries of God's kingdom are things which the *angels desire to look into* (1 Pet. i. 12) and they are *known to the church*, Eph. iii. 10. Now one of these two angels said, *When shall the end be?* Perhaps they both asked, first one and then the other, but Daniel heard only one.

2. To whom this question was put, to the *man clothed in linen*, of whom we read before (*ch.* x. 5), to Christ our great high priest, *who was upon the waters of the river*, and whose spokesman, or interpreter, the angel

Gabriel had all this while been. This river was Hiddekel (*ch.* x. 4), the same with Tigris, the place whereabout many of the events prophesied of would happen; there therefore is the scene laid. Hiddekel was mentioned as one of the rivers that watered the garden of Eden (Gen. ii. 14); fitly therefore does Christ stand upon that river, for by him the trees in the paradise of God are watered. *Waters* signify *people*, and so his standing upon the waters denotes his dominion over all; he *sits upon the flood* (Ps. xxix. 10); *he treads upon the waters of the sea*, Job ix. 8. And Christ, to show that this was he, in the days of his flesh *walked upon the waters*, Matt. xiv. 25. He was *above the waters of the river* (so some read it); he appeared in the air over the river.

3. What the question was: *How long shall it be to the end of these wonders?* Daniel would not ask the question, because he would not pry into what was hidden, nor seem inquisitive concerning the times and the seasons, which the Father has *put in his own power*, Acts i. 7. But, that he might have the satisfaction of the answer, the angel put the question in his hearing. Our Lord Jesus sometimes answered the questions which his disciples were afraid or ashamed to ask, John xvi. 19. The angel asked as one concerned, *How long shall it be?* What is the time prefixed in the divine counsels for the *end of these wonders*, these suffering trying times, that are to pass over the people of God? Note, (1.) The troubles of the church are the *wonder* of angels. They are astonished that God will suffer his church to be thus afflicted, and are anxious to know what good he will do his church by its afflictions. (2.) Good angels know no more of things to come than God is pleased to discover to them, much less do evil angels. (3.) The holy angels in heaven are concerned for the church on earth, and lay to heart its afflictions; how much more then should we, who are more immediately related to it, and have so much of our peace in its peace?

4. What answer was returned to it by him who is indeed the *numberer of secrets*, and knows things to come.

(1.) Here is a more general account given of the continuance of these troubles to the angel that made the enquiry (*v.* 7), that they shall continue *for a time, times, and a half*, that is, a year, two years, and half a year, as was before intimated (*ch.* vii. 25), but the one half of a prophetical week. Some understand it indefinitely, a certain time for an uncertain; it shall be *for a time* (a considerable time), for *times* (a longer time yet, double what it was thought at first that it would be), and yet indeed it shall be but *half a time*, or a part of a time; when it is over it shall seem not half so much as was feared. But it is rather to be taken for a certain time; we meet with it in the Revelation, under the title sometimes of three days

1114

and a half, put for three years and a half, sometimes forty-two months, sometimes 1260 days. Now this determination of the time is here, [1.] Confirmed by an oath. The man *clothed in linen* lifted up both his hands *to heaven, and swore by him that lives for ever and ever* that it should be so. Thus the *mighty angel* whom St. John saw is brought in, with a plain reference to this vision, standing with his *right foot on the sea* and *his left foot on the earth*, and with his hand lifted up to heaven, swearing *that there shall be no longer delay*, Rev. x. 5, 6. This Mighty One that Daniel saw stood with *both feet* on the water, and swore with *both hands* lifted up. Note, An oath is of use for confirmation; God only is to be sworn by, for he is the proper Judge to whom we are to appeal; and lifting up the hand is a very proper and significant sign to be used in a solemn oath. [2.] It is illustrated with a reason. God will suffer him to prevail *till he shall have accomplished to scatter the power of the holy people*. God will suffer him to do his worst, and run his utmost length, and then *all these things shall be finished*. Note, God's time to succour and relieve his people is when their affairs are brought to the last extremity; *in the mount of the Lord it shall be seen* that Isaac is saved just when he lies ready to be sacrificed. Now the event answered the prediction; Josephus says expressly, in his book of the *wars of the Jews*, that Antiochus, surnamed Epiphanes, surprised Jerusalem by force, *and held it three years and six months*, and was then *cast out of the country* by the Asmoneans or Maccabees. Christ's public ministry continued *three years and a half*, during which time he endured the contradiction of sinners against himself, and lived in poverty and disgrace; and then when his power seemed to be quite scattered at his death, and his enemies triumphed over him, he obtained the most glorious victory and said, *It is finished*.

(2.) Here is something added more particularly concerning the time of the continuance of those troubles, in what is said to Daniel, *v.* 11, 12, where we have, [1.] The event fixed from which the time of the trouble is to be dated, from the *taking away of the daily sacrifice* by Antiochus, and the *setting up* of the image of Jupiter upon the altar, which was the *abomination of desolation*. They must reckon their troubles to begin indeed when they were deprived of the benefit of public ordinances; that was to them the *beginning of sorrows*; that was what they laid most to heart. [2.] The continuance of their trouble; it shall last 1290 days, *three years* and *seven months*, or (as some reckon) *three years, six months*, and *fifteen days*; and then, it is probable, the daily sacrifice was restored, and the abomination of desolation taken away, in remembrance of which the *feast of dedication* was observed even to our Saviour's time, John x. 22. Though it does not appear by the history that it was exactly so long to a day, yet it appears that the beginning of the trouble was in the 145th year of the Seleucidæ, and the end of it in the 148th year; and either the restoring of the sacrifice, and the taking away of the image, were just so many days after, or some other previous event that was remarkable, which is not recorded. There are many particular times fixed in the scripture-prophecies, which it does not appear by any history, sacred or profane, that the event answered, and yet no doubt it did punctually; as Isa. xvi. 14. [3.] The completing of their deliverance, or at least a further advance towards it, which is here set forty-five days after the former, and, some think, points at the death of Antiochus, 1335 days after his profaning the temple. *Blessed is he that waits and comes* to that time. It is said (1 Mac. vi. 16) that Antiochus died *in the 149th year of the kingdom of the Greeks*, and (2 Mac. ix. 28; x. 1) that the Maccabees, under a divine conduct, *recovered the temple and the city.* Many good interpreters make these to be prophetical days (that is, so many years), and date them from the destruction of Jerusalem by the Romans; but what events they then fall upon they are not agreed. Others date them from the corruption of the gospel-worship by the antichrist, whose reign is confined in the Apocalypse to 1260 days (that is, years), at the end of which he shall begin to fall; but thirty years after he shall be quite fallen, at the end of 1290 days; and whoever lives forty years longer, to 1335 days, will see glorious times indeed. Whether it looks so far forward or no I cannot tell; but this, however, we may learn, *First,* That there is a time fixed for the termination of the church's troubles, and the bringing about of her deliverance, and that this time will be punctually observed to a day. *Secondly,* That this time must be waited for with faith and patience. *Thirdly,* That, when it comes, it will abundantly recompense us for our long expectations of it. *Blessed is he* who, having waited long, comes to it at last, for he will then have reason to say, *Lo, this is our God, and we have waited for him.*

II. The question, *What shall the end be?* is asked by Daniel, and an answer given to it. Observe,

1. Why Daniel asked this question; it was because, though he *heard what was said* to the angel, yet he did not *understand* it, *v.* 8. Daniel was a very intelligent man, and had been conversant in visions and prophecies, and yet here he was puzzled; he did not understand the meaning of the *time, times, and the part of a time,* at least not so clearly and with so much certainty as he wished Note, The best men are often much at a loss in their enquiries concerning divine things, and meet with that which they do not *understand.* But the better they are the more sensible they are of their own weak-

ness and ignorance, and the more ready to acknowledge them.

2. What the question was: *O my Lord! What shall be the end of these things?* He directs his enquiry not to the angel that talked with him, but immediately to Christ, for to whom else should we go with our enquiries? "What shall be the final issue of these events? What do they tend to? What will they end in?" Note, When we take a view of the affairs of this world, and of the church of God in it, we cannot but think, What will be the end of these things? We see things move as if they would end in the utter ruin of God's kingdom among men. When we observe the prevalence of vice and impiety, the decay of religion, the sufferings of the righteous, and the triumphs of the ungodly over them, we may well ask, *O my Lord! what will be the end of these things?* But this may satisfy us in general, that all will end well at last. Great is the truth, and will prevail at long-run. All opposing rule, principality, and power, will be put down, and holiness and love will triumph, and be in honour, to eternity. The end, this end, will come.

3. What answer is returned to this question. Besides what refers to the time (*v.* 11, 12), of which before, here are some general instructions given to Daniel, with which he is dismissed from further attendance.

(1.) He must content himself with the discoveries that had been made to him, and not enquire any further: "*Go thy way, Daniel;* let it suffice thee that thou hast been admitted thus far to the foresight of things to come, but stop here. *Go thy way* about the king's business again, *ch.* viii. 27. *Go thy way,* and record what thou hast seen and heard, for the benefit of posterity, and covet not to see and hear more at present." Note, Communion with God is not our continual feast in this world; we sometimes are taken to be witnesses of Christ's glory, and we say, *It is good to be here;* but we must go down from the mount, and have there no continuing city. Those that know much *know but in part,* and still see there is a great deal that they are kept in the dark about, and are likely to be so till the veil is rent; hitherto their knowledge shall go, but no further. "*Go thy way, Daniel,* satisfied with what thou hast."

(2.) He must not expect that what had been said to him would be fully understood till it was accomplished: *The words are closed up and sealed,* are involved in perplexities, and are likely to be so, *till the time of the end,* till the end of these things; nay, till the end of all things. Daniel was ordered to *seal the book to the time of the end, v.* 4. The Jews used to say, *When Elias comes he will tell us all things.* "They are *closed up and sealed,* that is, the discovery designed to be made by them is now fully settled and completed; nothing is to be added to it nor taken from it, for it is *closed up* and *sealed;* ask not therefore after more." *Nescire velle quæ magister maximus docere non vult erudita inscitia est—He has learned much who is willing to be ignorant of those things which the great teacher does not choose to impart.*

(3.) He must count upon no other than that, as long as the world stands, there will still be in it such a mixture as now we see there is of good and bad, *v.* 10. We long to see all wheat and no tares in God's field, all corn and no chaff in God's floor; but it will not be till the time of ingathering, till the winnowing day, comes; both must *grow together until the harvest.* As it has been, so it is, and will be, *The wicked shall do wickedly,* but *the wise shall understand.* In this, as in other things, St. John's Revelation closes as Daniel did. Rev. xxii. 11, *He that is filthy, let him be filthy still; and he that is holy, let him be holy still.* [1.] There is no remedy but that wicked people *will do wickedly;* and such people there are and will be in the world to the end of time. *So said the proverb of the ancients, Wickedness proceeds from the wicked* (1 Sam. xxiv. 13); and the observation of the moderns says the same. Bad men will do bad things; and a *corrupt tree* will *never bring forth good fruit.* Do men *gather grapes of thorns,* or bring forth good things from an evil treasure in the heart? No; wicked practices are the natural products of wicked principles and dispositions. *Marvel not at the matter* then, Eccl. v. 8. We are told, before, that the *wicked will do wickedly;* we can expect no better from them: but, which is worse, *none of the wicked shall understand.* This is either, *First,* A part of their sin. They *will not understand;* they shut their eyes against the light, and none so blind as those that will not see. *Therefore* they are *wicked* because they *will not understand.* If they did but rightly know the truths of God, they would readily obey the laws of God, Ps. lxxxii. 5. Wilful sin is the effect of wilful ignorance; they *will not understand* because *they are wicked;* they *hate the light,* and come not to the light, *because their deeds are evil,* John iii. 19. Or, *Secondly,* It is a part of their punishment; they will do wickedly, and therefore God has given them up to *blindness of mind,* and has said concerning them, *They shall not understand,* nor be *converted and healed,* Matt. xiii. 14, 15. God will not *give them eyes to see,* because they will do wickedly, Deut. xxix. 4. [2.] Yet, bad as the world is, God will secure to himself a remnant of good people in it; still there shall be some, there shall be many, to whom the providences and ordinances of God shall be *a savour of life unto life,* while to others they are *a savour of death unto death. First,* The providences of God shall do them good: *Many shall be purified, and made white, and tried,* by their troubles (compare *ch.* xi. 35), by the same troubles which will but stir up

the corruptions of the wicked and make them do more wickedly. Note, The afflictions of good people are designed for their trial; but by these trials they are *purified* and *made white,* their corruptions are purged out, their graces are brightened, and made both more vigorous and more conspicuous, and are *found to praise, and honour, and glory,* 1 Pet. i. 7. To those who are themselves sanctified and good every event is sanctified, and works for good, and helps to make them better. *Secondly,* The word of God shall do them good. When the *wicked understand not,* but stumble at the word, the *wise shall understand.* Those who are wise in practice shall understand doctrine; those who are influenced and governed by the divine law and love shall be illuminated with a divine light. For if any man will *do his will* he shall *know the truth,* John vii. 17. *Give instruction to a wise man, and he will be yet wiser.*

(4.) He must comfort himself with the pleasing prospect of his own happiness in death, in judgment, and to eternity, *v.* 13. Daniel was now very old, and had been long engaged both in an intimate acquaintance with heaven and in a great deal of public business on this earth. And now he must think of bidding farewell to this present state: *Go thou thy way till the end be.* [1.] It is good for us all to think much of going away from this world; we are still going, and must be gone shortly, gone the way of all the earth. That must be our way; but this is our comfort, We shall not go till God calls for us to another world, and till he has done with us in this world, till he says, " Go thou thy way; thou hast finished thy testimony, done thy work, and accomplished as a hireling thy day, therefore now, Go thy way, and leave it to others to take thy room." [2.] When a good man goes his way from this world he enters into rest: " *Thou shalt rest* from all thy present toils and agitations, and shalt not see the evils that are coming on the next generation." Never can a child of God say more pertinently than in his dying moments, *Return unto thy rest, O my soul!* [3.] Time and days will have an end; not only our time and days will end very shortly, but all times and days will have an end at length; yet a little while, and time shall be no more, but all its revolutions will be numbered and finished. [4.] Our rest in the grave will be but *till the end of the days;* and then the peaceful rest will be happily disturbed by a joyful resurrection. Job foresaw this when he said of the dead, *Till the heavens be no more,* they *shall not awake, nor be raised out of their sleep,* implying that then they shall, Job xiv. 12. [5.] We must every one of us *stand in our lot at the end of the days.* In the judgment of the great day we must have our allotment according to what we were, and what we did, in the body, either, *Come, you blessed* or,

Go, you cursed; and we must *stand for ever in that lot.* It was a comfort to Daniel, it is a comfort to all the saints, that, whatever their lot is in the days of time, they shall have a happy lot in *the end of the days,* shall have their *lot among the chosen.* And it ought to be the great care and concern of every one of us to secure a happy lot at last in the *end of the days,* and then we may well be content with our present lot, welcome the will of God. [6.] A believing hope and prospect of a blessed lot in the heavenly Canaan, at the end of the days, will be an effectual support to us when we are going our way out of this world, and will furnish us with living comforts in dying moments.

AN

EXPOSITION,

WITH PRACTICAL OBSERVATIONS,

OF THE BOOK OF THE PROPHET

HOSEA.

I. WE have now before us the twelve minor prophets, which some of the ancients, in reckoning up the books of the Old Testament, put all together, and reckon but as *one book.* They are called the minor prophets, not because their writings are of any less authority or usefulness than those of the greater prophets, or as if these prophets were less in God's account or might be so in ours than the other, but only because they are shorter, and less in bulk, than the other. We have reason to think that these prophets preached as much as the others, but that they did not write so much, nor is so much of their preaching kept upon record. Many excellent prophets wrote nothing, and others but little, who yet were very useful in their day. And so in the Christian church there have been many burning and shining lights, who are not known to posterity by their writings, and yet were no way inferior in gifts, and graces, and serviceableness to their own generation, than those who are; and some who have left but little behind them, and make no great figure among authors, were yet as valuable men as the more voluminous writers. These twelve small prophets, Josephus says, were put into one volume by the *men of the great synagogue* in Ezra's time, of which learned and pious body of men the last three of these twelve prophets are supposed to have been themselves members. These are what remained of the scattered pieces of inspired writing. Antiquaries value the *fragmenta veterum—the fragments of antiquity;* these are the fragments of prophecy, which are carefully gathered up by the divine Providence and the care of the church, that nothing might be lost, as St. Paul's short epistles after his long ones. The son of Sirach speaks of these twelve prophets with honour, as men that *strengthened Jacob, Ecclus.* xlix. 10. Nine of these prophets prophesied before the captivity, and the last three after the return of the Jews to their own land. Some difference there is in the order of these books. We place them as the ancient Hebrew did; and all agree to put Hosea first; but the ancient Septuagint places the first six in this order—Hosea, Amos, Micah, Joel, Obadiah, and Jonah. The thing is not material. And, if we covet to place them according to their seniority, as to some of them we shall find no certainty.

II. We have before us the prophecy of Hosea, who was the first of all the writing prophets, being raised up somewhat before the time of Isaiah. The ancients say, He was of Bethshemesh, and of the tribe of Issachar. He continued very long a prophet; the Jews reckoned that he prophesied nearly fourscore and ten years; so that, as Jerome observes, he prophesied of the destruction of the kingdom of the ten tribes when it was at a great distance, and lived himself to see and lament it, and to improve it when it was over, for warning to its sister kingdom. The scope of his prophecy is to discover sin, and to denounce the judgments of God against a people that would not be reformed. The style is very concise and sententious, above any of the prophets; and in some places it seems to be like the book of Proverbs, without connexion, and rather to be called Hosea's *sayings* than Hosea's *sermons.* And a weighty adage may sometimes do more service than a laboured discourse. Huetius observes that many passages in the prophecies of Jeremiah and Ezekiel seem to refer to, and to be borrowed from, the prophet Hosea, who wrote a good while before them. As Jer. vii. 34; xvi. 9; xxv. 10; and Ezek. xxvi. 13, speak the same with Hos. ii. 11; so Ezek. xvi. 16, &c., is taken from Hos. ii. 8. And that promise of *serving the Lord their God,* and *David their king,* Jer. xxx. 8, 9, Ezek. xxxiv. 23, *Hosea* had before, *ch.* iii. 5. And Ezek. xix. 12 is taken from Hos. xiii. 15. Thus one prophet confirms and corroborates another; and all these worketh that one and the self-same Spirit.

CHAP. I.

The mind of God is revealed to this prophet, and by him to the people, in the first three chapters, by signs and types, but afterwards only by discourse. In this chapter we have, I. The general title of the whole book, ver. 1. II. Some particular instructions which he was ordered to give to the people of God. 1. He must convince them of their sin in going a whoring from God, by marrying a wife of whoredoms, ver. 2, 3. 2. He must foretel the ruin coming upon them for their sin, in the names of his sons, which signified God's disowning and abandoning them, ver. 4—6, 8, 9. 3. He must speak comfortably to the kingdom of Judah, which still retained the pure worship of God, and assure them of the salvation of the Lord, ver. 7. 4. He must give an intimation of the great mercy God had in store both for Israel and Judah, in the latter days (ver. 10, 11), for in this prophecy many precious promises of mercy are mixed with the threatenings of wrath.

THE word of the LORD that came unto Hosea, the son of Beeri, in the days of Uzziah, Jotham, Ahaz, *and* Hezekiah, kings of Judah, and in the days of Jeroboam the son of Joash, king of Israel.

1. Here is the prophet's name and surname, which he himself, as other prophets, prefixes to his prophecy, for the satisfaction of all that he is ready to attest what he writes to be of God; he sets his hand to it, as that which he will stand by. His name, *Hosea,* or *Hoshea* (for it is the very same with Joshua's original name), signifies a *saviour;* for prophets were instruments of salvation to the people of God, so are faithful ministers; they help to save many a soul from death, by saving it from sin. His surname was *Ben-Beeri,* or *the son of Beeri.* As with us now, so with them then, some had their surname from their place, as Micah the Morashite, Nahum the Elkoshite; others from their parents, as Joel the son of Bethuel, and here Hosea the son of Beeri. And perhaps they made use of that distinction when the eminence of their parents was such as would bring honour upon them; but it is a groundless conceit of the Jews that where a prophet's father is named he also was a prophet. *Beeri* signifies a *well,* which may put us in mind of the fountain of life and living waters from which prophets are drawn and must be continually drawing. 2. Here are his authority and commission : *The word of the Lord came to him.* It *was to him;* it came with power and efficacy to him ; it was revealed to him as a real thing, and not a fancy or imagination of his own, in some such way as God then discovered himself to his servants the prophets. What he said and wrote was by divine inspiration ; it was *by the word of the Lord,* as St. Paul speaks concerning that which he had purely by revelation, 1 Thess. iv. 15. Therefore this book was always received among the canonical books of the Old Testament, which is confirmed by what is quoted out of it in the New Testament, Matt. ii. 15 ; ix. 13 ; xii. 7 ; Rom. ix. 25, 26 ; 1 Pet. ii. 10. For the word of the Lord endures for ever. 3. Here is a particular account of the times in which he prophesied—*in the days of Uzziah, Jotham, Ahaz, and Hezekiah, kings of Judah, and in the days of Jeroboam the son of Joash, king*

of Israel. We have only this general date of his prophecy, and not the date of any particular part of it, as, before, in Isaiah, Jeremiah, Ezekiel, and Daniel, and, afterwards, in Haggai and Zechariah. Here is only one king of Israel named, though there were many more within this time, because, having mentioned the kings of Judah, there was no necessity of naming the other ; and, they being all wicked, he took no pleasure in naming them, nor would he do them the honour. Now by this account here given of the several reigns in which Hosea prophesied (and it should seem the word of the Lord still came to him, more or less, at times, throughout all these reigns) it appears, (1.) That he prophesied a long time, that he began when he was very young, which gave him the advantage of strength and sprightliness, and that he continued at his work till he was very old, which gave him the advantage of experience and authority. It was a great honour to him to be thus long employed in such good work, and a great mercy to the people to have a minister so long among them that so well knew their state, and naturally cared for it, one they had been long used to and who therefore was the more likely to be useful to them. And yet, for aught that appears, he did but little good among them ; the longer they enjoyed him the less they regarded him ; they despised his youth first, and afterwards his age. (2.) That he passed through a variety of conditions. Some of these kings were very good, and, it is likely, countenanced and encouraged him ; others were very bad, who (we may suppose) frowned upon him and discouraged him ; and yet he was still the same. God's ministers must expect to pass through *honour and dishonour, evil report and good report,* and must resolve in both to hold fast their integrity and keep close to their work. (3.) That he began to prophesy at a time when the judgments of God were abroad, when God was himself contending in a more immediate way with that sinful people, who *fell into the hands of the Lord,* before they were turned over *into the hands of man;* for in the days of Uzziah, and of Jeroboam his contemporary, the dreadful earthquake was, mentioned Zech. xiv. 5 and Amos i. 1. And then was the plague of locusts, Joel i. 2—4; Amos vii. 1; Hos. iv. 3. The rod of God is sent to enforce the word and the word of God is sent to explain the rod, yet neither prevails till God by his Spirit opens the ear to instruction and discipline. (4.) That he began to prophesy in Israel at a time when their kingdom was in a flourishing prosperous condition, for so it was in the reign of Jeroboam the second, as we find 2 Kings xiv. 25, *He restored the coast of Israel,* and God *saved them by his hand;* yet then Hosea boldly tells them of their sins and foretels their destruction. Men are not to be flattered in their sinful ways because they prosper in the world, but even then must be faithfully reproved, and plainly told that their prosperity will not be their security, nor will it last long if they *go on still in their trespasses.*

2 The beginning of the word of the Lord by Hosea. And the Lord said to Hosea, Go, take unto thee a wife of whoredoms and children of whoredoms: for the land hath committed great whoredom, *departing* from the Lord. 3 So he went and took Gomer the daughter of Diblaim; which conceived, and bare him a son. 4 And the Lord said unto him, Call his name Jezreel; for yet a little *while*, and I will avenge the blood of Jezreel upon the house of Jehu, and will cause to cease the kingdom of the house of Israel. 5 And it shall come to pass at that day, that I will break the bow of Israel in the valley of Jezreel. 6 And she conceived again, and bare a daughter. And *God* said unto him, Call her name Lo-ruhamah: for I will no more have mercy upon the house of Israel; but I will utterly take them away. 7 But I will have mercy upon the house of Judah, and will save them by the Lord their God, and will not save them by bow, nor by sword, nor by battle, by horses, nor by horsemen.

These words, *The beginning of the word of the Lord by Hosea,* may refer either, 1. To that glorious set of prophets which was raised up about this time. About this time there lived and prophesied Joel, Amos, Micah, Jonah, Obadiah, and Isaiah; but Hosea was the first of them that foretold the destruction of Israel; the *beginning of this word of the Lord was by him.* We read in the history of this Jeroboam here named (2 Kings xiv. 27) that *the Lord had not yet said he would blot out the name of Israel,* but soon after he said he would, and Hosea was the man that began to say it, which made it so much the harder task to him, to be the first that should carry an unpleasing message and some time before any were raised up to second him. Or, rather, 2. To Hosea's own prophecies. This was the first message God sent him upon to this people, to tell them that they were *an evil and an adulterous generation.* He might have desired to be excused from dealing so roughly with them till he had gained authority and reputation, and some interest in their affections. No; he must *begin with this,* that they might know what to expect from a prophet of the Lord. Nay, he must not only preach this to them, but he must write it, and publish

it, and leave it upon record as a witness against them. Now here,

I. The prophet must, as it were in a looking-glass, show them *their sin,* and show it to be exceedingly sinful, exceedingly hateful. The prophet is ordered to *take unto him a wife of whoredoms and children of whoredoms, v. 2.* And he did so, *v. 3.* He married a woman of ill fame, *Gomer the daughter of Diblaim,* not one that had been married and had committed adultery, for then she must have been put to death, but one that had lived scandalously in the single state. To marry such a one was not *malum in se—evil in itself,* but only *malum per accidens—incidentally an evil,* not prudent, decent, or expedient, and therefore forbidden to the priests, and which, if it were really done, would be an affliction to the prophet (it is threatened as a curse on Amaziah that his wife should be a harlot, Amos vii. 17), but not a sin when God commanded it for a holy end; nay, if commanded, it was his duty, and he must trust God with his reputation. But most commentators think that it was done *in vision,* or that it is no more than a parable; and that was a way of teaching commonly used among the ancients, particularly prophets; what they meant of others they *transferred to themselves in a figure,* as St. Paul speaks, 1 Cor. iv. 6. He must take a *wife of whoredoms,* and have such children by her as every one would suspect, though born in wedlock, to be *children of whoredoms,* begotten in adultery, because it is too common for those who have lived lewdly in the single state to live no better in the married state. " Now" (saith God) " Hosea, this people is to me such a dishonour, and such a grief and vexation, as a *wife of whoredoms* and *children of whoredoms* would be to thee. *For the land has committed great whoredoms.*" In all instances of wickedness they had departed from the Lord; but their idolatry especially is the whoredom they are here chaged with. Giving that glory to any creature which is due to God alone is such an injury and affront to God as for a wife to embrace the bosom of a stranger is to her husband. It is especially so in those that have made a profession of religion, and have been taken into covenant with God; it is breaking the marriage-bond; it is a heinous odious sin, and, as much as any thing, besots the mind and takes away the heart. *Idolatry* is *great whoredom,* worse than any other; it is departing from *the Lord,* to whom we lie under greater obligations than any wife does or can do to her husband. *The land has committed whoredom :* it is not here and there a particular person that is guilty of idolatry, but the whole land is polluted with it; the sin has become national, the disease epidemical. What an odious thing would it be for the prophet, a *holy man,* to have a whorish wife, and children whorish like her!

What an exercise would it be of his patience, and, if she persisted in it, what could be expected but that he should give her a bill of divorce! And is it not then much more offensive to the *holy God* to have such a people as this to be called by his name and have a place in his house? How great is his patience with them! And how justly may he cast them off! It was as if he should have married Gomer the daughter of Diblaim, who probably was at that time a noted harlot. The land of Israel was like Gomer the daughter of Diblaim. *Gomer* signifies *corruption; Diblaim* signifies *two cakes,* or *lumps of figs;* this denotes that Israel was near to ruin, and that their luxury and sensuality were the cause of it. They were as the *evil figs* that could not be eaten, they were so evil. It intimates sin to be the daughter of plenty and destruction the daughter of the abuse of plenty. Some give this sense of the command here given to the prophet: " Go, take thee a wife of *whoredoms,* for, if thou shouldst go to seek for an honest modest woman, thou wouldst not find any such, for the whole land, and all the people of it, are given to whoredom, the usual concomitant of idolatry."

II. The prophet must, as it were through a perspective glass, show them their ruin; and this he does in the names given to the children born of this adulteress; for as *lust,* when it has *conceived, brings forth sin,* so *sin, when it is finished, brings forth death.*

1. He foretels the fall of the royal family in the name he is appointed to give to his first child, which was a son : *Call his name Jezreel, v.* 4. We find that the prophet Isaiah gave prophetical names to his children (Isa. vii. 3 ; viii. 3), so this prophet here. Jezreel signifies *the seed of God* (so they should have been); but it signifies also the *scattered of God;* they shall be as sheep on the mountains, that have no shepherds. *Call them not Israel,* which signifies *dominion,* they have lost all the honour of that name; but call them Jezreel, which signifies *dispersion,* for those that have departed from the Lord will wander endlessly. Hitherto they have been scattered as seed; let them now be scattered as chaff. Jezreel was the name of one of the royal seats of the kings of Israel; it was a beautiful city, seated in a pleasant valley, and it is with allusion to that city that this child is called *Jezreel,* for *yet a little while and I will avenge the blood of Jezreel upon the house of Jehu.* Observe here, (1.) Who it is that God has a controversy with; it is *the house of Jehu,* from whom the present king, Jeroboam, was lineally descended. The house of Jehu smarted for the sins of Jehu, for God often lays up men's iniquity for their children and visits it upon them. It is *the kingdom of the house of Israel,* which may be meant either of the present royal family, that of Jehu, which God did quickly *cause to cease* (for

1120

the son of this Jeroboam, Zechariah, reigned but *six months,* and he was the last of Jehu's race), or of the whole kingdom in general, which continued corrupt and wicked, and which was *made to cease* in the reign of Hoshea, about seventy years after; and with God that is but a *little while.* Note, Neither the pomp of kings nor the power of kingdoms can secure them from God's destroying judgments, if they continue to rebel against him. (2.) What is the ground of this controversy : *I will revenge the blood of Jezreel upon the house of Jehu,* the blood which Jehu shed at Jezreel, when, by commission from God and in obedience to his command, he utterly destroyed the house of Ahab, and all that were in alliance with it, with all the worshippers of Baal. God approved of what he did (2 Kings x. 30): *Thou hast done well in executing that which is right in my eyes;* and yet here God will avenge that *blood upon the house of Jehu,* when the time has expired during which it was promised that his family should reign, even to the fourth generation. But how comes the same action to be both rewarded and punished? Very justly; the matter of it was good; it was the execution of a righteous sentence passed upon the house of Ahab, and, as such, it was rewarded; but Jehu did it not in a right manner; he aimed at his own advancement, not at the glory of God, and mingled his own resentments with the execution of God's justice. He did it with a malice against the sinners, but not with any antipathy to the sin; for he kept up the worship of the golden calves, and *took no heed to walk in the law of God,* 2 Kings x. 31. And therefore when the measure of the iniquity of his house was full, and God came to reckon with them, the first article in the account is (and, being first, it is put for all the rest) for the blood of the house of Ahab, here called the *blood of Jezreel.* Thus when the house of Baasha was rooted out it was because he did *like the house of Jeroboam, and because he killed him,* 1 Kings xvi. 7. Note, Those that are entrusted with the administration of justice are concerned to see to it that they do it from a right principle and with a right intention, and that they do not themselves live in those sins which they punish in others, lest even their just executions should be reckoned for, another day, as little less than murders. (3.) How far the controversy shall proceed; it shall be not a correction, but a destruction. Some make those words, *I will visit, or appoint, the blood of Jezreel upon the house of Jehu,* to signify, not as we read it the revenging of that bloodshed, but the repeating of that bloodshed : " I will punish the house of Jehu, as I punished the house of Ahab, because Jehu did not take warning by the punishment of his predecessors, but trod in the steps of their idolatry. And after the house of Jehu is destroyed *I will cause to* cease the kingdom of the house of Israel; I will begin to bring it down, though now it flourish." After the death of Zechariah, the last of the house of Jehu, the kingdom of the ten tribes went to decay, and dwindled sensibly. And, in order to the ruin of it, it is threatened (v. 5), *I will break the bow of Israel in the valley of Jezreel;* the *strength of the warriors of Israel,* so the Chaldee. God will disable them either to defend themselves or to resist their enemies. As the *bow abiding in strength,* and being *renewed in the hand,* intimates a growing power, so the *breaking of the bow* intimates a sinking ruined power. The bow shall be broken *in the valley of Jezreel,* where, probably, the armoury was; or, it may be, in that valley some battle was fought, wherein the kingdom of Israel was very much weakened. Note, There is no fence against God's controversy; when he comes forth against a people their strong bows are soon broken and their strong-holds broken down. In the valley of Jezreel they shed that blood which the righteous God would in that very place avenge upon them; as some notorious malefactors are hanged in chains just where the villany they suffer for was perpetrated, that the punishment may answer the sin.

2. He foretels God's abandoning the whole nation in the name he gives to the second child. This was a daughter, as the former was a son, to intimate that both sons and daughters had corrupted their way. Some make it to signify that Israel grew effeminate, and was thereby enfeebled and made weak. Call the name of this daughter *Lo-ruhamah* —*not beloved* (so it is translated Rom. ix. 25), or *not having obtained mercy,* so it is translated 1 Pet. ii. 10. It comes all to one. This reads the doom of the *house of Israel: I will no more have mercy* upon them. It intimates that God had shown them great mercy, but they had abused his favours, and forfeited them, and now he would show them favour no more. Note, Those that forsake their own mercies for lying vanities have reason to expect that their own mercies should forsake them, and that they should be left to their *lying vanities,* Jonah ii. 8. Sin turns away the mercy of God even from *the house of Israel,* his own professing people, whose case is sad indeed when God says that he will no more have mercy upon them. And then it follows, *I will utterly take them away,* will utterly *remove them* (so some), will utterly *pluck them up,* so others. Note, When the streams of mercy are stopped we can expect no other than that the vials of wrath should be opened. Those whom God will no more have mercy upon shall be utterly taken away, as dross and dung. The word for *taking away* sometimes signifies to *forgive* sin; and some take it in that sense here: *I will no more have mercy upon them, though in pardoning I have pardoned them* heretofore. Though God has borne long, he will not bear always, with a people that hate to be reformed. Or, *I will no more have mercy upon them, that I should in any wise pardon them,* or (as our margin reads it) *that I should altogether pardon them.* If pardoning mercy is denied, no other mercy can be expected, for that opens the door to all the rest. Some make this to speak comfort: *I will no more have mercy upon them till in pardoning I shall pardon them,* that is, till the Redeemer comes to Zion to turn away ungodliness from Jacob. The Chaldee reads it, *But, if they repent, in pardoning I will pardon them.* Even the greatest sinners, if in time they bethink themselves and return, will find that there is forgiveness with God.

III. He must show them what mercy God had in store for the house of Judah, at the same time that he was thus contending with the house of Israel (v. 7): *But I will have mercy upon the house of Judah.* Note, Though some are justly cast off for their disobedience, yet God will always secure to himself a remnant that shall be the vessels and monuments of mercy. When divine justice is glorified in some, yet there are others in whom free grace is glorified. And, though some through unbelief are broken off, yet God will have a church in this world till the end of time. It aggravates the rejection of Israel that God will have mercy on Judah, and not on them, and magnifies God's mercy to Judah that, though they also have done wickedly, yet God did not reject them, as he rejected Israel: *I will have mercy upon them and will save them.* Note, Our salvation is owing purely to God's mercy, and not to any merit of our own. Now,

1. This, without doubt, refers to the temporal salvations which God wrought for Judah in a distinguishing way, the favours shown to them and not to Israel. When the Assyrian armies had destroyed Samaria, and carried the ten tribes away into captivity, they proceeded to besiege Jerusalem; but God had mercy on the house of Judah, and saved them by the vast slaughter which an angel made, in one night, in the camp of the Assyrians; then they were *saved by the Lord their God* immediately, and not by sword or bow. When the ten tribes were continued in their captivity, and their land was possessed by others, they being *utterly taken away,* God *had mercy on the house of Judah* and *saved them,* and, after seventy years, brought them back, *not by might or power, but by the Spirit of the Lord of hosts,* Zech. iv. 6. *I will save them by the Lord their God,* that is, by myself. God will be exalted *in his own strength,* will take the work into his own hands. That salvation is sure which he undertakes to be the author of; for, if he will work, none shall hinder. And that salvation is most acceptable which he does *by himself. So the Lord alone did lead him.* The less there is of man in any salvation, and the more of God, the brighter it shines and the

sweeter it tastes. I will save them *in the word of the Lord* (so the Chaldee), for the sake of Christ, the eternal word, and by his power. *I will save them not by bow nor by sword,* that is, (1.) They shall be saved when they are reduced to so low an ebb that they have neither bow nor sword to defend themselves with, Judg. v. 8; 1 Sam. xiii. 22. (2.) They shall be saved by the Lord when they are brought off from trusting to their own strength and their weapons of war, Ps. xliv. 6. (3.) They shall be saved easily, without the trouble of sword and bow, *v.* 7. Isa. ix. 5, *I will save them by the Lord their God.* In calling him *their God,* he upbraids the ten tribes who had *cast him off* from being *theirs,* for which reason he had *cast them off,* and intimates what was the true reason why he had mercy, distinguishing mercy, for the house of Judah, and saved them: it was in pursuance of his covenant with them as the Lord their God, and in recompence for their faithful adherence to him and to his word and worship. But,

2. This may refer also to the salvation of Judah from idolatry, which qualified and prepared them for their other salvations. And this is indeed a salvation *by the Lord their God;* it is wrought only by the power of his grace, and can never be wrought by *sword or bow.* Just at the time that the kingdom of Israel was *utterly taken away,* under Hoshea, the kingdom of Judah was gloriously reformed, under Hezekiah, and was therefore preserved; and in Babylon God saved them from their idolatry first, and then from their captivity.

3. Some make this promise to look forward to the great salvation which, in the fulness of time, was to be wrought out *by the Lord our God,* Jesus Christ, who came into the world to *save his people from their sins.*

8 Now when she had weaned Lo-ruhamah, she conceived, and bare a son. 9 Then said *God,* Call his name Lo-ammi : for ye *are* not my people, and I will not be your *God.* 10 Yet the number of the children of Israel shall be as the sand of the sea, which cannot be measured nor numbered; and it shall come to pass, *that* in the place where it was said unto them, Ye *are* not my people, *there* it shall be said unto them, Ye *are* the sons of the living God. 11 Then shall the children of Judah and the children of Israel be gathered together, and appoint themselves one head, and they shall come up out of the land: for great *shall be* the day of Jezreel.

We have here a prediction,

I. Of the rejection of Israel for a time, which is signified by the name of another child that Hosea had by his adulterous spouse, *v.* 8, 9. And still we must observe that those children whose names carried these direful omens in them to Israel were all *children of whoredoms* (*v.* 2), all born of the harlot that Hosea married, to intimate that the ruin of Israel was the natural product of the sin of Israel. If they had not first revolted from God, they would never have been rejected by him; God never leaves any till they first leave him. Here is, 1. The birth of this child: *When she had weaned her daughter, she conceived and bore a son.* Notice is taken of the delay of the birth of this child, which was to carry in its name a certain presage of their utter rejection, to intimate God's patience with them, and his unwillingness to proceed to extremity. Some think that her bearing another son signifies that people's persisting in their wickedness; lust still *conceived* and *brought forth sin.* They *added to do evil* (so the Chaldee paraphrase expounds it); they were old in adulteries, and obstinate. 2. The name given him: *Call him Lo-ammi—Not my people.* When they were told that God would *no more have mercy on them* they regarded it not, but buoyed up themselves with this conceit, that they were God's people, whom he could not but have mercy on. And therefore he plucks that staff from under them, and disowns all relation to them: *You are not my people, and I will not be your God.* "*I will not be yours* (so the word is); I will be in no relation to you, will have nothing to do with you; I will not be *your King, your* Father, *your* patron and protector." We supply it very well with that which includes all, "*I will not be your God; I will not be to you* what I have been, nor what you vainly expect I should be, nor what I would have been if you had kept close to me." Observe, "*You are not my people;* you do not act as becomes my people; you are not observant of me and obedient to me, as my people should be; you are not my people, but the people of this and the other dunghill-deity; and therefore I will not own you for my people, will not protect you, will not put in any claim to you, not demand you, not deliver you out of the hands of those that have seized you; let them take you; you are none of mine. You will not have me to be your God, but pay your homage to the pretenders, and therefore *I will not be your God;* you shall have no interest in me, shall expect no benefit from me." Note, Our being taken into covenant with God is owing purely to his grace, for then it begins on his side: *I will be to them a God,* and then they shall be *to me a people; we love him because he first loved us.* But our being cast out of covenant is owing purely to ourselves and our own folly. The breach is on man's side: *You are not my people,* and therefore *I will not be your God;* if God *hate any,* it is because they *first hated him.* This was fulfilled in Israel when they were *utterly taken away* into the *land of Assyria,* and their place knew them no more. They were no longer *God's people,* for they lost the knowledge and worship of him; no prophets were sent to them, no promises made to them, as were to the two tribes in their captivity; nay, they were no longer *a people,* but, for aught that appears, were mingled with the nations into which they were carried, and lost among them.

II. Of the reduction and restoration of Israel in the fulness of time. Here, as before, mercy is remembered in the midst of wrath; the rejection, as it shall not be total, so it shall not be final (*v.* 10, 11): *Yet the number of the children of Israel shall be as the sand of the sea.* See how the same hand that wounded is stretched forth to heal, and how tenderly he that has *torn binds up;* though God *cause grief* by his threatenings, yet *he will have compassion,* and will gather with everlasting kindness. They are very precious promises which are here made concerning the Israel of God, and which may be of use to us now.

1. Some think that these promises had their accomplishment in the return of the Jews out of their captivity in Babylon, when many of the ten tribes joined themselves to Judah, and took the benefit of the liberty which Cyrus proclaimed, came up in great numbers out of the several countries into which they were dispersed, to their own land, appointed Zerubbabel their head, and coalesced into one people, whereas before they had been two distinct nations. And in their own land, where God had by his prophets disowned and rejected them as none of his, he would by his prophets own them and appear for them as his children; and from all parts of the country they should come up to the temple to worship. And we have reason to think that, though this promise has a further reference, yet it was graciously intended and piously used for the support and comfort of the captives in Babylon, as giving them a general assurance of mercy which God had in store for them and their land; their nation could not be destroyed so long as this blessing was in it, was in reserve for it.

2. Some think that these promises will not have their accomplishment, at least not in full, till the general conversion of the Jews in the latter days, which is expected yet to come, when the vast incredible numbers of Jews, that are now dispersed as the sand of the sea, shall be brought to embrace the faith of Christ and be incorporated in the gospel-church. Then, and not till then, God will own them as his people, his children, even there where they had lain under the dismal tokens of their rejection. The Jewish doctors look upon this promise as not having had its accomplishment yet. But,

3. It is certain that this promise had its accomplishment in the setting up of the kingdom of Christ, by the preaching of the gospel, and the bringing in both of Jews and Gentiles to it, for to this these words are applied by St. Paul (Rom. ix. 25, 26), and by St. Peter when he writes to the Jews of the dispersion, 1 Pet. ii. 10. Israel here is the gospel-church, the spiritual Israel (Gal. vi. 16), all believers who follow the steps, and inherit the blessing of faithful Abraham, who is the father of all that believe, whether Jews or Gentiles, Rom. iv. 11, 12. Now let us see what is promised concerning this Israel.

(1.) That it shall greatly multiply, and the numbers of it be increased; it shall be *as the sand of the sea, which cannot be measured nor numbered.* Though Israel according to the flesh be diminished and made few, the spiritual Israel shall be numerous, shall be innumerable. In the vast multitudes that by the preaching of the gospel have been brought to Christ, both in the first ages of Christianity and ever since, this promise is fulfilled, thousands out of every tribe in Israel, and out of other nations, *a multitude which no man can number,* Rev. vii. 4, 9; Gal. iv. 27. In this the promise made to Abraham, when God called him Abraham the *high father of a multitude,* had its full accomplishment (Gen. xvii. 5), and that Gen. xxii. 17. Some observe that they are here compared to the *sand of the sea,* not only for their numbers, but as the sand of the sea serves for a boundary to the waters, that they shall not overflow the earth, so the Israelites indeed are a wall of defence to the places where they live, to keep off judgments. God can do nothing against Sodom while Lot is there.

(2.) That God will renew his covenant with the gospel-Israel, and will incorporate it a church to himself, by as full and ample a charter as that whereby the Old-Testament church was incorporated; nay, and its privileges shall be much greater: *" In the place where it was said unto them, You are not my people,* there shall you be again admitted into covenant, and owned as my people." The *abandoned Gentiles* in their respective places, and the *rejected Jews* in theirs, shall be favoured and blessed. There, where the fathers were cast off for their unbelief, the children, upon their believing, shall be taken in. This is a blessed resurrection, the making of those the people of God that were *not a people.* Nay, but the privilege is enlarged; now it is not only, *You are my people,* as formerly, but *You are the sons of the living God,* whether by birth you were Jews or Gentiles. Israel under the law was God's *son, his first-born,* but then they were as children *under age;* now, under the gospel, they have grown up both to greater understanding and greater liberty, Gal. iv. 1, 2. Note, [1.] It is the unspeakable privilege of all believers that they have the living God for their Father, the ever-living God, and may look upon themselves as his children by grace and adoption. [2.] The sonship of believers shall be owned and acknowledged; it shall be *said to them*, for their comfort and satisfaction, nay, and it shall be said for their honour in the hearing of the world, *You are the sons of the living God.* Let not the saints disquiet themselves; let not others despise them; for, sooner or later, there shall be a manifestation of the children of God, and all the world shall be made to know their excellency and the value God has for them. [3.] It will add much to their comfort, very much to their honour, when they are dignified with the tokens of God's favour in that very place where they had long lain under the tokens of his displeasure. This speaks comfort to the believing Gentiles, that they need not go up to Jerusalem, to be received and owned as God's children; no, they may stay where they are, and *in that place*, though it be in the remotest corner of the earth, *in that place* where they were at a distance, where it was said to them, *You are not God's people*, but are separated from them (Isa. lvi. 3, 6), even there, without leaving their country and kindred, they may by faith receive the *Spirit of adoption*, witnessing with their spirits that *they are the children of God.*"

(3.) That those who had been at variance should be happily brought together (*v.* 11): *Then shall the children of Judah and the children of Israel be gathered together.* This uniting of Judah and Israel, those two kingdoms that were now so much at variance, biting and devouring one another, is mentioned only as a specimen, or one instance, of the happy effect of the setting up of Christ's kingdom in the world, the bringing of those that had been at the greatest enmity one against another to a good understanding one of another and a good affection one to another. This was literally fulfilled when the Galileans, who inhabited that part of the country which belonged to the ten tribes, and probably for the most part descended from them, so heartily joined with those that were probably called *Jews* (that were of Judea) in following Christ and embracing his gospel; and his first disciples were partly Jews and partly Galileans. The first that were blessed with the light of the gospel were of the *land of Zebulun and Naphtali* (Matt. iv. 15); and, though there was no good-will at all between the Jews and the Galileans, yet, upon their believing in Christ, they were happily consolidated, and there were no remains of the former disaffection they had to one another; nay, when the Samaritans believed, though between them and the Jews there was a much greater enmity, yet in Christ there was a perfect unanimity, Acts viii. 14. Thus Judah and Israel were *gathered together;* yet this was but a type of the much more celebrated coalition between Jews and Gentiles, when, by the death of Christ, the partition-wall of the ce-

remonial law was taken down. See Eph. ii. 14—16. Christ died, to *gather together in one all the children of God that were scattered abroad,* John xi. 52; Eph. i. 10.

(4.) That Jesus Christ should be the centre of unity to all God's spiritual Israel. They shall all agree to *appoint to themselves one head,* which can be no other than he whom God has appointed, even Christ. Note, Jesus Christ is the head of the church, the one only head of it, not only a head of government, as of the body politic, but a head of vital influence, as of the natural body. To believe in Christ is to appoint him to ourselves for our head, that is, to consent to God's appointment, and willingly commit ourselves to his guidance and government; and this in concurrence and communion with all good Christians that make him their head; so that, though they are many, yet in him they are one, and so become one with each other. *Qui conveniunt in aliquo tertio inter se conveniunt—Those who agree with a third agree with each other.*

(5.) That, having appointed Christ for their head, *they shall come up out of the land;* they shall come, some of all sorts, from all parts, to join themselves to the church, as, under the Jewish economy, they came up from all corners of the land of Israel to Jerusalem, to worship (Ps. cxxii. 4), *Thither the tribes go up,* to which there is a plain allusion in that prophecy of the accession of the Gentiles to the church (Isa. ii. 3), *Come, and let us go up to the mountain of the Lord.* It denotes not a local remove (for they are said to be in the same place, *v.* 10), but a change of their mind, a spiritual ascent to Christ. They shall *come up from the earth* (so it may be read); for those who have given up themselves to Christ as their head take their affections off from *this earth,* and the things of it, to set them upon *things above* (Col. iii. 1, 2); for they are not of the world (John xv. 19), but have their conversation in heaven. They shall *come up out of the land,* though it be the land of their nativity; they shall, in affection, come out from it, that they may *follow the Lamb whithersoever he goes.* Thus the learned Dr. Pocock takes it.

(6.) That, when all this comes to pass, *great shall be the day of Jezreel.* Though *great* is *the day of Jezreel's* affliction (so some understand it), yet *great shall be the day* of Jezreel's glory. This shall be Israel's day; the day shall be *their own,* after their enemies have long had their day. Israel is here called *Jezreel,* the *seed of God,* the *holy seed* (Isa. vi. 13), the *substance* of the land. This seed is now sown in the earth, and buried under the clods; but great shall be its day when the harvest comes. Great was the church's day when there were *added to it daily such as should be saved;* then did the Almighty *do great things* for it.

CHAP. II.

The scope of this chapter seems to be much the same with that of the foregoing chapter, and to point at the same events, and the causes of them. As there, so here, I. God, by the prophet, discovers sin to them, and charges it home upon them, the sin of their idolatry, their spiritual whoredom, their serving idols and forgetting God and their obligations to him, ver. 1, 2, 5, 8. II. He threatens to take away from them that plenty of all good things with which they had served their idols, and to abandon them to ruin without remedy, ver. 3, 4, 6, 7, 9—13. III. Yet he promises at last to return in ways of mercy to them for his own sake (ver. 14), to restore them to their former plenty (ver. 15), to cure them of their inclination to idolatry (ver. 16, 17), to renew his covenant with them (ver. 18—20), and to bless them with all good things, ver. 21—23.

SAY ye unto your brethren, Ammi; and to your sisters, Ruhamah. 2 Plead with your mother, plead: for she *is* not my wife, neither *am* I her husband: let her therefore put away her whoredoms out of her sight, and her adulteries from between her breasts; 3 Lest I strip her naked, and set her as in the day that she was born, and make her as a wilderness, and set her like a dry land, and slay her with thirst. 4 And I will not have mercy upon her children; for they *be* the children of whoredoms. 5 For their mother hath played the harlot: she that conceived them hath done shamefully: for she said, I will go after my lovers, that give *me* my bread and my water, my wool and my flax, mine oil and my drink.

The first words of this chapter some make the close of the foregoing chapter, and add them to the promises which we have here of the great things God would do for them. When they shall have appointed Christ their head, and centered in him, then let them say to one another, with triumph and exultation *(let the prophets say it* to them, so the Chaldee—*Comfort you, comfort you, my people,* is now their commission), "say to them, *Ammi,* and *Ruhamah;* call them so again, for they shall no longer lie under the reproach and doom of *Lo-ammi* and *Lo-ruhamah;* they shall now be *my people* again, and shall *obtain mercy.*" God's spiritual Israel, made up of Jews and Gentiles without distinction, shall call one another brethren and sisters, shall own one another for the people of God and beloved of him, and, for that reason, shall embrace one another, and stir up one another both to give thanks for and to walk worthy of this *common salvation* which they partake of. Or rather, because the following words seem to have a coherence with these, these also are designed for conviction and humiliation. The *mother* (*v.* 2) seems to be the same with the *brethren* and *sisters* (*v.* 1), the church of the ten tribes, the body of the people, who were brethren, and in a special manner with the heads and leaders, who were as the mother by whom the rest were brought up and nursed. But who are the children that must *plead with their mother* thus? Either, 1. The godly that were among

them, that witnessed against the iniquities of the times, let them boldly go on to bear their testimony against the idolatries and gross corruptions that prevail among them. Let those that had not bowed the knee to Baal reason the case with those that had, and endeavour to convince them with such arguments as are here put into their mouths. Note, Private persons may, and ought, in their places, to appear and plead against the public profanations of God's name and worship. Children may humbly and modestly argue with their parents when they do amiss: *Plead with your mother, plead,* as Jonathan with Saul concerning David. Or, 2. The sufferers among them, that shared in the calamities of the times, let them not complain of God, let them not quarrel with him, nor lay the blame on him, as if he had dealt hardly with them, and not like a tender father. No; let them *plead with their mother,* and lay the fault on her, where it ought to be laid; compare Isa. l. 1. "*For her transgressions is your mother put away;* she may thank herself, and you may thank her for all your miseries.*" Let us see now how they must plead with her.

I. They must put her in mind of the relation wherein she had stood to God, the kindness he had had for her, the many favours he had bestowed upon her, and the further favours he had designed her. Let them tell their *brethren* and *sisters* that they had been *Ammi* and *Ruhamah,* that they had been God's people and vessels of his mercy, and might have been so still if it had not been their own fault, *v.* 1. Note, Our relation to God and dependence on him are a great aggravation of our revolts from him and rebellions against him.

II. They must, in God's name, charge her with the violation of the marriage-covenant between her and God. Let them tell her that God does not look upon her as his wife, nor upon himself as her husband any longer. Tell her (*v.* 2) that *she is not my wife, neither am I her husband,* that by her spiritual whoredom she has forfeited all the honour and comfort of her relation to God, and provoked him to give her a bill of divorce. Note, No consideration can be more powerful to awaken us to repentance than the provocation we have by sin given to God to disown and cast us off. It is time to look about us, and to think what course we must take, when God threatens to reject us; for woe unto us if he be not *our husband.* They must charge this home upon her (*v.* 5): *Their mother has played the harlot; their congregation has run a whoring after false prophets* (so the Chaldee), or, rather, *after idols,* wherein they were encouraged by their false prophets; *she that conceived them has done shamefully,* in making and worshipping idols. An idol is called a *shame* (ch. ix. 10) and idolatry is a *shameful thing.* It is not only an affront to God, but a reproach to men, to *fall down to the stock of a tree*, as the prophet speaks. Or it denotes that the sinner was shameless, impudent in sin, and could not blush; Jer. vi. 15. Or, *She has made ashamed*, has made all that see her ashamed of her; her own children are ashamed of their relation to her.

III. They must upbraid her with her horrid ingratitude to God her benefactor, in ascribing to her idols the glory of the gifts he had given her, and then giving that for a reason why she paid them the homage due to him only, *v.* 5. In this she *did shamefully* indeed, that *she said, I will go after my lovers that give me my bread and my water.* Observe here, 1. Her wicked resolution to persist in idolatry, notwithstanding all that God said, both by his prophets and by his providences, to draw her from it. *She said*, Whatever is offered to the contrary, *I will go after my lovers*, or *those that cause me to love them*, whom I cannot but be in love with. The Chaldee understands it of the nations whose alliance Israel courted and depended upon, who supplied them with what they needed. But it is rather to be understood of the idols they worshipped, to justify their love of which they called them their lovers. See who do shamefully; those that are wilful and resolute in sin, and those that openly profess and own their resolution to go on in it. See the folly of idolaters, to call those their lovers that had not so much as life; yet let us learn to call our God our lover; let us keep up good thoughts of him, and put a high value upon our interest in him and in his love. 2. The gross mistake upon which this resolution was grounded: " I will go after my lovers, because they give me my *bread and my water*, which are necessary to sustain the body, *my wool and my flax*, which are necessary to clothe the body, and pleasant things, *my oil*, and *my drink*, my liquors" (so the word is), " wine and strong drink." Note, (1.) The things of sense are the best things with carnal hearts, and the most powerful attractives, in pursuit of which they care not what they follow after. The God of Israel set before them his *statutes* and *judgments* (Deut. iv. 8), *more to be desired than gold, and sweeter than honey* (Ps. cxix. 10), promised them his favour, which would *put gladness in their hearts more than corn, wine, and oil* (Ps. iv. 7); but they had no relish at all for these things. Whence they thought their oil and their drink came, thither they would return their best affections. *O curvæ in terram animæ et cœlestium inanes !* —*O degenerate minds, bending towards the earth, and devoid of every thing heavenly !* (2.) It is a great abuse and injury to God, in pursuance of the pleasures and delights of sense to forsake him, who not only gives us better things, but gives us even those things too. The idolaters made Ceres the goddess of their corn, Bacchus the god of their wine, &c., and then foolishly fancied they had their corn and wine from these, forgetting the Lord their God, who both gave them that good land and *gave them power to get wealth* out of it. (3.) Many are hardened in sin by their worldly prosperity. They had an abundance of those things when they served their idols, and then imagined them to be given them by their idols, which kept them to their service; thus they argued (Jer. xliv. 17, 18), *While we burnt incense to the queen of heaven we had plenty of victuals.*

IV. They must persuade her to repent and reform. God will disown her if she persist in her whoredoms; *let her therefore put away her whoredoms, v.* 2. Let her be convinced that it is possible for her to reform; the idols, dear as they are, may yet be parted with; and it will certainly be well with her if she do reform. Note, Our pleading with sinners must be to drive them to repentance, not to drive them to despair. Let her *put away her whoredoms and her adulteries;* the doubling of words to the same purport, and both plural, denotes the abundance of idolatries they were guilty of, all which must be abandoned ere God would be reconciled to them. Let her put them *out of her sight*, as detestable things which she cannot endure to look upon; let her say unto them, *Get you hence*, Isa. xxx. 22. Let her put them *from her face* and from *between her breasts*, that is, let her not do as harlots use to do, that both discover their own wicked disposition, and allure others to wickedness, by painting their faces, and exposing their naked breasts, and adorning them; let her not thus, by annexing all possible gaieties and pleasures to the worship of idols, engage herself and allure others to it. Let her put away all these. Every sinful course, persisted in, is an adulterous departure from God. And here we may see what it is truly to repent of it and turn from it. 1. True penitents will forsake both open sins and secret sins, will put away not only the whoredoms that lie in sight, but those that lie in secret *between their breasts*, the sin that is *rolled under the tongue as a sweet morsel*. 2. They will both avoid the outward occasions of sin and mortify the inward disposition to it. Idolaters walked after their own eyes, which *went a whoring* after their idols (Ezek. vi. 9, Deut. iv. 19), and *therefore* they must put them away *out of their sight*, lest they should be tempted to worship them. *Look not upon the wine when it is red.* But that is not enough: the axe must be *laid to the root ;* the corrupt bent and inclination of the heart must be changed, and it must be put away *from between the breasts*, that Christ alone may have the innermost and uppermost place there. Cant. i. 13.

V. They must show her the utter ruin that will certainly be the fatal consequence of her sin if she do not repent and reform (*v.* 3): *Lest I strip her naked.* This comes in here not by way of sentence passed upon her, but by way of warning given to her, that she may prevent it: *Let her put away her whoredoms, that I may not strip her naked* (so it may be read), intimating that God waits to show mercy to sinners, if they would but qualify themselves for / that mercy. It is here threatened that God will deal with her as the just and jealous husband at length does with an adulterous wife, that has filled his house with a spurious brood, and will not be reclaimed; he turns her and her children out of doors and sends them a begging; *I will not have mercy upon her children* (v. 4); the particular persons that share in the calamity of the nation, and the rising generation, shall be ruined by it, for they are *children of whoredoms*, and keep up the *vain conversation received by tradition from their fathers.* Now it is here threatened that they shall be both stripped and starved. They thought their idols gave them *their bread and their water, their wool and their flax;* but God, by taking them away, will let them know that it was he that gave them. 1. She shall be stripped: *Lest I strip her* of all her ornaments which she is proud of, and with which she courts her lovers, *strip her* and set her *as in the day that she was born,* send her as naked out of the world as she came into it; this death does, Job i. 21. *I will strip her,* and so expose her to cold, and expose her to shame; and justly is she exposed to shame that *did shamefully, v.* 5. The day when God brought them out of Egypt, where they were no better than slaves and beggars, was *the day in which they were born;* and God threatens to bring them back to as low and miserable a condition as he then found them in. Whatever they had that either gained them respect or screened them from contempt, among their neighbours, should be taken from them. See Ezek. xvi. 4, 39. 2. She shall be starved, shall be deprived not only of her honours, but of her comforts and necessary supports. She shall be famished, shall be made *as a wilderness* and *a dry land,* and *slain with thirst.* She that boasted so much of her bread and water, her oil and her drinks, which her lovers had *given her,* shall not have so much as necessary food. The land shall not afford subsistence for the inhabitants, for want of the rain of heaven; or, if it do, it shall be taken from them by the enemy, so that the rightful owners shall perish for want of it. Some understand it thus: *I will make her as* she was in the *wilderness,* and set her as she was *in the desert land,* where she was sometimes ready to perish *for thirst.* So it explains the former part of the verse: I will set her *as in the day that she was born;* for it was in the vast howling wilderness that Israel was first formed into a people. They shall be in as deplorable a condition as their fathers were, whose carcases fell in the wilderness, and in this respect, worse, that then the

children were reserved to be heirs of the land of promise, but now *I will not have mercy upon her children,* for *their mother has played the harlot.*

6 Therefore, behold, I will hedge up thy way with thorns, and make a wall, that she shall not find her paths. 7 And she shall follow after her lovers, but she shall not overtake them; and she shall seek them, but shall not find *them:* then shall she say, I will go and return to my first husband; for then *was it* better with me than now. 8 For she did not know that I gave her corn, and wine, and oil, and multiplied her silver and gold, *which* they prepared for Baal. 9 Therefore will I return, and take away my corn in the time thereof, and my wine in the season thereof, and will recover my wool and my flax *given* to cover her nakedness. 10 And now will I discover her lewdness in the sight of her lovers, and none shall deliver her out of mine hand. 11 I will also cause all her mirth to cease, her feast-days, her new moons, and her sabbaths, and all her solemn feasts. 12 And I will destroy her vines and her fig-trees, whereof she hath said, These *are* my rewards that my lovers have given me: and I will make them a forest, and the beasts of the field shall eat them. 13 And I will visit upon her the days of Baalim, wherein she burned incense to them, and she decked herself with her ear-rings and her jewels, and she went after her lovers, and forgat me, saith the LORD.

God here goes on to threaten what he would do with this treacherous idolatrous people; and he warns that he may not wound, he threatens that he may not strike. *If he turn not, he will whet his sword* (Ps. vii. 12); but, if he turn, he will sheathe it. They did not turn, and therefore all this came upon them: and its being threatened before shows that it was the execution of a divine sentence upon them for their wickedness; and it is written for admonition to us.

I. They shall be perplexed and embarrassed in all their counsels, and disappointed in all their expectations. This is threatened *v.* 6, 7. But to the threatening is annexed a promise that this shall be a means to convince them of their folly, and bring them home to their duty; and so good shall be brought out of evil, in token of the mercy God has yet in reserve for them. And, this being the happy fruit and effect of the distress, it is hard to say whether the prediction, or the distress itself, should be called a threatening or a promise.

1. God will raise up difficulties and troubles in their way, so that their public counsels and affairs shall have no success, nor shall they be able to get forward in them: *I will hedge up thy way with thorns*, with such crosses as, like thorns and briers, are the product of sin and the curse, and are scratching, and tearing, and vexing, and, when the way we are in is hedged up with them, stop our progress, and force us to turn back. She said, *" I will go after my lovers;* I will pursue my leagues and alliances with foreign powers, and depend upon them."* But God says, " She shall be frustrated in these projects, and not be able to proceed in them. *I will hedge up thy way with thorns*, and, if that do not serve, *I will make a wall."* If some smaller difficulties be got over, and prevail not to break her measures, God will raise greater, for he will overcome when he judges. It shall be such a hedge, and such a wall, that *she shall not find her paths*. The change of the person here, I will hedge up *thy way*, and then, *She* shall not find *it*, is usual in scripture, especially in an earnest way of speaking. " Sinner, do thou take notice, *I will hedge up thy way*, and all you that are by-standers take notice what will be the effect of this, you may observe that *she* cannot find her paths."* She shall be as a traveller that not only knows not which way to go, of many that are before him, but that finds no way at all to go forward. And then *she shall follow after her lovers, but she shall not overtake them;* she shall endeavour to make an interest in the Assyrians and Egyptians, and to have them for her protectors, but she shall not gain her point; they shall either not come into confederacy with her or not do her any service, shall *help in vain* and be as the *staff of a broken reed*. *She shall seek them, but shall not find them,* shall seek to her idols, but shall not find that satisfaction in them which she promised herself; the gods whom she trusted and courted not only can do nothing for her, but have nothing to say to her to encourage her. Now, (1.) This is such a just judgment as the Sodomites met with, that were *struck with blindness*, and *wearied themselves to find the door* (Gen. xix. 11), and the Syrians, 2 Kings vi. 18. Note, Those that are most resolute in their sinful pursuits are commonly most crossed in them. *Thorns and snares are in the way of the froward* (Prov. xxii. 5); and thus with them God *shows himself froward* (Ps. xviii. 26), and *walks contrary to those that walk contrary to him,* Lev. xxvi. 23, 24. The lamenting prophet complains, *He has enclosed my ways,* Lam. iii. 7, 9. The way of God and duty is often hedged about with thorns, but we have

reason to think it is a sinful way that is hedged up with thorns. (2.) This is such a kind rebuke, and indeed such a mercy, as Balaam met with, when the angel stood in his way, to hinder his going forward to *curse Israel,* Num. xxii. 22. Note, Crosses and obstacles in an evil course are great blessings, and are so to be accounted. They are God's hedges, to keep us from transgressing, to restrain us from wandering out of the green pastures, to *withdraw man from his purpose* (Job xxxiii. 17), to make the way of sin difficult, that we may not go on in it, and to keep us from it whether we will or not. We have reason to bless God both for restraining grace and for restraining providences.

2. These difficulties that God raises up in their way shall raise up in their minds thoughts of turning back : " *Then shall she say,* Since I cannot overtake my lovers, I will even *go and return to my first husband,* that is, will return to God, and humble myself to him, and desire him to take me in again; for, when I kept close to him, it was every way *better with me than now."* Two things are here extorted from this degenerate apostate people :—(1.) A just acknowledgment of the folly of their apostasy. They are now brought to own that it was better with them while they kept close to their God than ever it was since they forsook him. Note, Whoever have exchanged the service of God for the service of the world and the flesh have, sooner or later, been made to own that they *changed for the worse,* and that while they continued in good company, and went on in the way of good duties, and made conscience how they spent their time and what they said or did, it was better with them; they had more true comfort and enjoyment of themselves than ever they had since they went astray. (2.) A good purpose, to come back again to their duty : *I will go, and return to my first husband;* and she knows so much of his goodness and readiness to forgive that she speaks without any doubt of his receiving her again into favour and making her condition as good as ever. Note, The disappointments we meet with in our pursuits of satisfaction in the creature should, if nothing else will do it, drive us at length to the Creator, in whom alone it is to be had. When Moab is *weary of the high place* he shall *go to the sanctuary,* Isa. xvi. 12. And when the prodigal son is reduced to husks, short allowance indeed, and remembers that *in his father's house there is bread enough,* then he says, *I will arise and go to my father's house,* Luke xv. 17, 18.

II. The necessary supports and comforts of life shall be taken from them, because they had dishonoured God with them, *v.* 8, 9. Their land was plenteous. Now see here,

1. How graciously their plenty was given to them. God gave them not only corn for

necessity, but wine for delight, and oil for ornament. Nay, he *multiplied their silver and gold*, wherewith to traffic with other nations and bring home their products, and which they might hoard up for posterity. *Silver and gold* will keep longer than *corn, and wine, and oil*. He gave them *wool* and *flax* too, to *cover their nakedness*, and to serve for ornament enough to them, Ezek. xvi. 10. Note, God is a bountiful benefactor even to those who, he foresees, will be ungrateful and unthankful to him.

2. How basely their plenty was abused by them. (1.) They robbed God of the honour of his gifts: *She did not know that I gave her corn and wine:* she did not remember it. The law and the prophets had told them, again and again, that all their comforts they received from God's bountiful providence; but they were so often told by their false prophets and idolatrous priests that they had their corn from such an idol, and their wine from such an idol, &c., that they had quite forgotten their relation to their great benefactor and their obligations to him. She did not consider it; she would not acknowledge it. This they were *willingly ignorant of*, and more brutish than the ox, that *knows his owner*, and the *ass, that knows his master's crib*. *She did not know it*, for she did not return thanks to him for his gifts, nor study what she should render; nor did she give him his dues out of them, but acted as if she were ignorant who was the donor. (2.) They served and honoured his enemies with them: *They prepared them for Baal;* they adorned their images with *gold and silver* (Jer. x. 4), and adorned themselves for the worship of their images, v. 13. See Ezek. xvi. 17—19. *Wherewith they made Baal* (so the margin reads it), that is, the image of Baal. Note, It is a very great dishonour to the God of heaven to make those gifts of his providence the food and fuel of our lusts which he gave us for our support in his service, and to be oil to the wheels of our obedience.

3. How justly their plenty should be taken from them: "*Therefore will I return;* I will alter my dealings with them, will take another course, *and will take away my corn* and other good things that I gave her." I will *recover* them, a law term, as a man by due course of law recovers what is unjustly detained from him, or as, when the tenant has committed waste, the landlord recovers *locum vastatum—dilapidations*. Observe, God calls their abundance *my corn* and *my wine, my wool* and *my flax*. They called it theirs *(my bread* and *my water*, v. 5), but God lets them know that it is not theirs; he only allowed them the use of it as tenants, entrusted them with the management of it as stewards, but still reserved the property in himself. " It is *my* corn and *my* wine." God will have us to know, not only that we have all our creature-comforts and enjoyments from him,

but that he has still an incontestable right and title to them, that they are more his than ours, and therefore are to be used for him, and accounted for to him. He will therefore take their plenty away from them, because they have forfeited it by disowning his right, as a tenant by copy of court-roll, who holds at the will of his lord, forfeits his estate if he makes a feoffment of it as though he were a freeholder. He will *recover* it, will *free* or *deliver* it, that it may be no longer abused, as the creature is said to be *delivered from the bondage of corruption* under which *it groans*, Rom. viii. 21. He will take it away *in the time thereof*, and *in the season thereof*, just when they expected it, and thought that they were sure of it. It shall suffer shipwreck in the harbour; and *the harvest shall be a heap*. He will take it away by unseasonable weather or by unreasonable men. Note, Those that abuse the mercies God gives them, to his dishonour, cannot expect to enjoy them long.

III. They shall lose *all their honour*, and be exposed to contempt (v. 10): "*I will discover her lewdness*, will bring to light all her secret wickedness, and make it public, to her shame; I will show by the punishment of it how heinous, how odious, how offensive it is. The fact has been denied, but now it shall appear; the fault has been diminished, but now it shall appear exceedingly sinful. And this *in the sight of her lovers*, in the sight of the neighbouring nations, with whom she courted an alliance, and on whom she had a dependence; they shall despise her and be ashamed of her because of her weakness, and poverty, and ill conduct; they shall not think her any longer worthy of their friendship." See this fulfilled, Lam. i. 8, *All that honoured her despise her, because they have seen her nakedness*. Or in the sight of *the sun and moon*, which she worshipped as *her lovers;* before them shall *her lewdness be discovered*. Compare this with Jer. viii. 1, 2, *They shall bring out the bones of their kings and princes, and spread them before the sun and moon, whom they have loved and served*. Note, Sin will have shame; let those expect it that have done shamefully. What other lot can this impudent adulteress expect but that of a common harlot, to be carted through the town? And, when God comes to deal thus with her, *none shall deliver her out of his hands*, neither the gods nor the men they confide in. Note, Those who will not deliver themselves into the hand of God's mercy cannot be delivered out of the hand of his justice.

IV. They shall lose all their pleasure, and shall be left melancholy (v. 11): *I will cause her mirth to cease*. It seems, then, though they had *gone a whoring from their God*, yet they could find in their hearts to *rejoice as other people*, which is forbidden, *ch.* ix. 1. Note, Many who lie under guilt and wrath are yet very jocund and merry, and live jovially; but, whether in their laughter their hearts be sad or no, it is certain that the *end of their mirth* will be *heaviness;* for God *will cause all their mirth to cease.* It is as Mr. Burroughs observes here, *Sin and mirth can never hold long together;* but, *if men will not take away sin from their mirth, God will take away mirth from their sin.*

1. God will take away the occasions of their sacred mirth—*their feast-days, their new moons, their sabbaths, and all their solemn feasts.* These God instituted to be observed in a religious manner, and they were to be observed with rejoicing; and, it seems, though they had departed from the pure worship of God, yet they kept up the observance of these, not at God's temple at Jerusalem, for they had long since forsaken that, but probably at Dan and Bethel, where the calves were, or in some other places of meeting that they had. They observed them, not for the honour of God, nor with any true devotion towards him, but only because they were times of mirth and feasting, music and dancing, and meeting of friends, received by tradition from their fathers. Thus, when they had lost the power of godliness, and denied that, yet, for the pleasing of a vain and carnal mind, they kept up the form of it; and by this means their new-moons and their sabbaths became an iniquity which God *could not away with,* Isa. i. 13. Now observe, (1.) God calls them their new-moons and their sabbaths, not his (he disowns them), but theirs. (2.) He will *cause them to cease.* Note, When men by their sins have caused the life and substance of ordinances to cease it is just with God by his judgments to cause the remaining show and shadow of them to cease.

2. He will take away the supports of their carnal mirth. They loved the new-moons and the sabbaths only for the sake of the good cheer that was stirring then, not for the sake of any religious exercises then performed; these they had dropped long ago; and now God will take away their provisions for these solemnities (*v.* 12): *I will destroy her vines and her fig-trees.* Note, If men destroy God's words and ordinances, by which he should be honoured on their feast-days, it is just with him to destroy their vines and fig-trees, with which they regale themselves. While they took the pleasure of these, they gave their lovers the praise of them: "*These are my rewards which my lovers have given me;* I may thank my stars for these, and my worship of them; I may thank my neighbours for these, and my alliance with them." And therefore God will destroy them, will wither them with a blast, or bring in a foreign enemy that shall lay the country waste, so that their vineyards shall become *a forest;* the enclosures shall be thrown down, as is usual in war; all shall be laid in common, so that the *beasts of the field* shall eat their grapes and their

1130

figs. Or they shall be so blasted with the east wind that fruit-trees shall be of no more use than forest-trees; but, being withered and good for nothing, what fruit there is shall be left to the *beasts of the field.* Or it shall be devoured by their enemies, by men as barbarous as wild beasts. Now, (1.) This shall be the ruin of their mirth: God will *cause all her mirth to cease.* How will he do it? Taking away the new-moons and the sabbaths will not do it; they can very easily part with them, and find no loss; but "I will *destroy her vines and her fig-trees,* will take away her sensual pleasures, and then she will think herself undone indeed." Note, The destruction of the vines and the fig-trees causes all the mirth of a carnal heart to cease; it will say, as Micah, You have *taken away my gods, and what have I more?* (2.) This shall be the punishment of her idolatry (*v.* 13): "*I will visit upon her the days of Baalim;* I will reckon with her for all the worship of all the Baals they have made gods of, from the days of their fathers unto this day." We read of their worshipping Baal as long ago as the time of the Judges, and, for aught I know, this may look as far back as those times, those *days of Baalim;* for it is in the second commandment, which forbids idolatry, that God threatens to *visit the iniquities of the fathers upon the children;* and justly is that sin so visited, more than any other, because it commonly supports itself by prescription and long usage. Now that the measure of the iniquity of Israel was full all their former sins came into the account, and shall be *required of this generation.* Or the *days of Baalim* are the solemn festival days which they kept in honour of their idols. Days of sinful mirth must be visited in days of mourning. These were the days wherein she *burnt incense* to idols, and, to grace the solemnity, *decked herself with her ear-rings and her jewels,* that, appearing honourable, the honour she did to Baal might be thought the greater. Or she was as a wife that decks herself with the ear-rings and jewels that her husband gave her, to make herself amiable to her lovers, whom she follows after, and is ever mindful of. But *she forgot me, saith the Lord.* Note, Our treacherous departures from God are owing to our forgetfulness of him, of his nature and attributes, his relation to us and our obligations to him. Many who plead that they have weak memories, and forget the things of God, can remember other things well enough; nay, it is because they are so mindful of lying vanities that they are so forgetful of their own mercies.

14 Therefore, behold, I will allure her, and bring her into the wilderness, and speak comfortably unto her. 15 And I will give her her vineyards

from thence, and the valley of Achor for a door of hope: and she shall sing there, as in the days of her youth, and as in the day when she came up out of the land of Egypt. 16 And it shall be at that day, saith the LORD, *that* thou shalt call me Ishi; and shalt call me no more Baali. 17 For I will take away the names of Baalim out of her mouth, and they shall no more be remembered by their name. 18 And in that day will I make a covenant for them with the beasts of the field, and with the fowls of heaven, and *with* the creeping things of the ground: and I will break the bow and the sword and the battle out of the earth, and will make them to lie down safely. 19 And I will betroth thee unto me for ever; yea, I will betroth thee unto me in righteousness, and in judgment, and in lovingkindness, and in mercies. 20 I will even betroth thee unto me in faithfulness: and thou shalt know the LORD. 21 And it shall come to pass in that day, I will hear, saith the LORD, I will hear the heavens, and they shall hear the earth; 22 And the earth shall hear the corn, and the wine, and the oil; and they shall hear Jezreel. 23 And I will sow her unto me in the earth; and I will have mercy upon her that had not obtained mercy; and I will say to *them which were* not my people, Thou *art* my people; and they shall say, *Thou art* my God.

The state of Israel ruined by their own sin did not look so black and dismal in the former part of the chapter, but that the state of Israel, restrained by the divine grace, looks as bright and pleasant here in the latter part of the chapter, and the more surprisingly so as the promises follow thus close upon the threatenings; nay, which is very strange, they are by a note of connexion joined to, and inferred from, that declaration of their sinfulness upon which the threatenings of their ruin are grounded: *She went after her lovers, and forgot me, saith the Lord; therefore I will allure her.* Fitly therefore is that *therefore* which is the note of connexion immediately followed with a note of admiration: *Behold I will allure her!* When it was said, *She forgot me,* one would think it should have followed, "Therefore I will abandon her, I will forget her, I will never look after her more." No, *There-*

fore I will allure her. Note, God's thoughts and ways of mercy are infinitely above ours; his reasons are all fetched from within himself, and not from any thing in us; nay, his goodness takes occasion from man's badness to appear so much the more illustrious, Isa. lvii. 17, 18. *Therefore,* because she will not be restrained by the denunciations of wrath, God will try whether she will be wrought upon by the offers of mercy. Some think it may be translated, *Afterwards,* or *nevertheless,* I will allure her. It comes all to one; the design is plainly to magnify free grace to those on whom God will have mercy purely for mercy's sake. Now that which is here promised to Israel is,

I. That though now they were disconsolate, and ready to despair, they should again be revived with comforts and hopes, v. 14, 15. This is expressed here with an allusion to God's dealings with that people when he brought them out of Egypt, through the wilderness to Canaan, as their forlorn and deplorable condition in their captivity was compared to their state in *Egypt in the day that they were born,* v. 3. They shall be new-formed by such miracles of love and mercy as they were first-formed by, and such a transport of joy shall they be in as they were in then. It is hard to say when this had its accomplishment in the kingdom of the ten tribes; but it principally aims, no doubt, at the bringing in both of Jews and Gentiles into the church by the gospel of Christ; and it is applicable, nay, we have reason to think it was designed that it should be applied, to the conversion of particular souls to God. Now observe,

1. The gracious methods God will take with them. (1.) He will *bring them into the wilderness,* as he did at first when he brought them out of Egypt, where he instructed them, and took them into covenant with himself. The land of their captivity shall be to them now, as that wilderness was then, the *furnace of affliction,* in which God will *choose them.* See Ezek. xx. 35, 36, *I will bring you into the wilderness of the people, and there will I plead with you.* God had said that he would *make them as a wilderness* (v. 3), which was a threatening; now, when it is here made part of a promise that he would bring them into the wilderness, the meaning may be that he would by his grace bring their minds to their condition: "They shall have humble hearts under humbling providences; being poor, they shall be poor in spirit, shall *accept of the punishment of their iniquity,* and then they are prepared to have comfort spoken to them." When God delivered Israel out of Egypt he led them into the wilderness, to *humble them and prove them, that he might do them good* (Deut. viii. 2, 3, 15, 16), and so he will do again. Note, Those whom God has mercy in store for he first *brings into a wilderness*—into solitude and retirement,

that they may the more freely converse with him out of the noise of this world,—into distress of mind, through sense of guilt and dread of wrath, which brings a soul to be quite at a loss in itself and bewildered, and by those convictions he prepares for consolations,—and sometimes into outward distress and trouble, thereby to open the ear to discipline. (2.) He will then *allure them and speak comfortably to them*, will *persuade them* and *speak to their hearts*, that is, he will by his word and Spirit incline their hearts to return to him, and encourage them to do so. He will allure them with the promises of his favour, as before he had terrified them with the threatenings of his wrath, will speak friendly to them, both by his prophets and by his providences, as before he had spoken roughly, Isa. xl. 1, 2. *By the hand of my servants the prophets I will speak comfort to her heart;* so the Chaldee. This refers to the gospel of Christ, and the offers of divine grace in the gospel, by which we are allured to forsake our sins and to turn to God, and which speaks to the heart of a convinced sinner that which is every way suited to his case, speaks abundant consolation to those that sorrow for sin and lament after the Lord. And when by the Spirit it is indeed spoken to the heart effectually, and so as to reach the conscience (which it is God's prerogative to do), O what a blessed change is wrought by it! Note, The best way of reducing wandering souls to God is by fair means. By the promise of rest in Christ we are invited to take his yoke upon us; and the work of conversion may be forwarded by comforts as well as by convictions. (3.) *He will give her her vineyards thence.* From that time and from that place where he has afflicted her, and brought her to see her folly and to humble herself, thenceforward he will *do her good;* not only speak comfortably to her, but do well for her, and undo what he had done against her. He had *destroyed her vines* (v. 12), but now he will give her whole *vineyards*, as if for every vine destroyed she should have a vineyard restored, and so be repaid with interest; she shall not only have corn for necessity, but vineyards for delight. These denote the privileges and comforts of the gospel, which are prepared for those that *come up out of the wilderness leaning upon* Christ as *their beloved*, Cant. viii. 5. Note, God has vineyards of consolation ready to bestow on those who repent and return to him; and he can give vineyards *out of a wilderness*, which are of all others the most welcome, as rest to the weary. (4.) He will give her *the valley of Achor for a door of hope. The valley of Achor* was that in which Achan was stoned; it signifies *the valley of trouble*, because he troubled Israel, and there God troubled him. This was the beginning of the wars of Canaan; and their putting away the accursed thing in that place gave them

1132

ground to hope that God would continue his presence with them and complete their victories. So when God returns to his people in mercy, and they to him in duty, it will be to them as happy an omen as any thing. If they put away the accursed thing from among them, if by mortifying sin they stone the Achan that has troubled their camp, their subduing that enemy within themselves is an earnest to them of victory over all the kings of Canaan. Or, if the allusion be to the name, it intimates that trouble for sin, if it be sincere, opens a door of hope; for that sin which truly troubles us shall not ruin us. The valley of Achor was a very fruitful pleasant valley, some think the same with the valley of Engedi, famous for vineyards, Cant. i. 14. This God gave to Israel as a pattern and pledge of the whole land of Canaan; so "God will by his gospel give to all believers such gifts, graces, and comforts in this life, as shall be a taste of those more perfect good things of the kingdom of heaven, and shall give them an assured hope of a full possession of them in due time." So the learned Dr. Pocock expounds it; and, to the same purport, this whole context.

2. The great rejoicing with which they shall receive God's gracious returns towards them: *She shall sing there as in the days of her youth.* This plainly refers to that triumphant and prophetic song which Moses and the children of Israel sang at the *Red Sea*, Exod. xv. 1. When they are delivered out of captivity they shall repeat that song, and to them it shall be a new song, because sung upon a new occasion, not inferior to the former. God had said (v. 11) that he would *cause all her mirth to cease*, but now he would cause it to revive : She shall sing *as in the day that she came out of Egypt.* Note, When God repeats former mercies we must repeat former praises; we find the song of Moses sung in the New Testament, Rev. xv. 3. This promise of Israel's singing has its accomplishment in the gospel of Christ, which furnishes us with abundant matter for joy and praise, and wherever it is received in its power enlarges the heart in joy and praise; and this is that land flowing with milk and honey which *the valley of Achor* opens *a door of hope to.* We *rejoice in tribulation.*

II. That, though they had been much addicted to the worship of Baal, they should now be perfectly weaned from it, should relinquish and abandon all appearances of idolatry and approaches towards it, and cleave to God only, and worship him as he appoints, v. 16, 17. Note, The surest pledge and token of God's favour to any people is his effectual parting between them and their beloved sins. The worship of Baal was the sin that did most easily beset the people of Israel; it was their own iniquity, the sin that had dominion over them; but now that idolatry shall be quite abolished, and there shall not be the least remains of it among them. 1. The idols of Baal shall not be mentioned, not any of the Baals that *in the days of Baalim* had made so great a noise with, *O Baal! hear us; O Baal! hear us.* The very *names of Baalim* shall be *taken out of their mouths;* they shall be so disused that they shall be quite forgotten, as if their names had never been known in Israel; they shall be so detested that people will not bear to mention them themselves, nor to hear others mention them, so that posterity shall scarcely know that ever there were such things. They shall be so ashamed of their former love to Baal that they shall do all they can to blot out the remembrance of it. They shall tie themselves up to the strictest literal meaning of that law against idolatry (Exod. xxiii. 13), *Make no mention of the names of other gods, neither let it be heard out of thy mouth,* as David, Ps. xvi. 4. Thus the apostle expresses the abhorrence we ought to have of all fleshly lusts: *Let them not be once named among you,* Eph. v. 3. But how can such a change of the Ethiopian's skin be wrought? It is answered, The power of God can do it, and will. *I will take away the names of Baalim;* as Zech. xiii. 2, *I will cut off the names of the idols.* Note, God's grace in the heart will change the language by making that iniquity to be loathed which was beloved. Zeph. iii. 9, *I will turn to the people a pure language.* One of the rabbin says, This promise relates to the Gentiles as well as to Israel; and we know it had its accomplishment in the turning of the Gentiles, by the gospel of Christ, from the idolatries which they had been wedded to, 1 Thess. i. 9. 2. The very word Baal shall be laid aside, even in its innocent signification. God says, *Thou shalt call me Ishi, and call me no more Baali;* both signify *my husband,* and both had been made use of concerning God. Isa. liv. 5, *Thy Maker is thy husband,* thy *Baal* (so the word is), thy owner, patron, and protector. It is probable that many good people had, accordingly, made use of the word *Baali* in worshipping the God of Israel; when their wicked neighbours bowed the knee to Baal they gloried in this, that God was their Baal. "But," says God, "you shall call me so no more, because I will have the very names of Baalim taken away." Note, That which is very innocent in itself should, when it has been abused to idolatry, be abolished, and the very use of it taken away, that nothing may be done to keep idols in remembrance, much less to keep them in reputation. When calling God *Ishi* will do as well, and signify as much, as *Baali,* let that word be chosen rather, lest, by calling him Baali, others should be put in mind of their *quondam* Baals. Some think that there is another reason intimated why God would be called *Ishi* and not *Baali;* they both signify *my husband,* but *Ishi* is a compellation of love,

and sweetness, and familiarity, *Baali* of reverence and subjection. Ishi is *vir meus—my man;* Baali is *dominus meus—my lord.* In gospel-times God has so revealed himself to us as to encourage us to come boldly to the throne of his grace, and to use a holy humble freedom there; we ought to call God our Master, for so he is, but we are more taught to call him our Father. *Ishi* is *a man the Lord* (Gen. iv. 1), and intimates that in gospel-times the church's husband shall be *the man Christ Jesus,* made like unto his brethren, and therefore they shall call him *Ishi,* not *Baali.*

III. That though they had been in continual troubles, as if the whole creation had been at war with them, now they shall enjoy perfect peace and tranquillity, as if they were in a league of friendship with the whole creation (*v.* 18): *In that day,* when they have forsaken their idols, and put themselves under the divine protection, *I will make a covenant for them.* 1. They shall be protected from evil; nothing shall hurt them, nor do them any mischief. *Tranquillus Deus tranquillat omnia—When God is at peace with us he makes every creature to be so too.* The inferior creatures shall do them no harm, as they had done when the *beasts of the field* ate up their vineyards (*v.* 12) and when *noisome beasts* were one of God's *sore judgments,* Ezek. xiv. 15. The *fowl* and the *creeping things* are taken into this covenant; for they also, when God makes use of them as the instruments of his justice, may become very hurtful, but they shall be no more so; nay, by virtue of this covenant, they shall be made serviceable to them and brought into their interests. Note, God has the command of the inferior creatures, and brings them into what covenant he pleases; he can make *the beasts of the field* to *honour* him (so he has promised, Isa. xliii. 20) and to contribute to his people's comfort. And, if the inferior creatures are thus laid under an engagement to serve us, it is our part of the covenant not to abuse them, but to serve God with them. Some think that this had its accomplishment in the miraculous power Christ gave his disciples to *take up serpents,* Mark xvi. 17, 18. It agrees with the promises made particularly to Israel, in their return out of captivity (Ezek. xxxiv. 25, *I will cause the evil beasts to cease out of the land*), and the more general ones to all the saints. Job v. 22, 23, *The beasts of the field shall be at peace with thee;* and Ps. xci. 13, *Thou shalt tread upon the lion and adder.* But this is not all; men are more in danger from one another than from the brute beast, and therefore it is further promised that God will *make wars to cease,* will disarm the enemy: *I will break the bow, and sword, and battle.* He can do it when he pleases (Ps. xlvi. 9), and will do it for those whose *ways please him,* for he *makes even their enemies to be at peace with them,* Prov. xvi. 7. This agrees with the promise that in gospel-times swords shall be beaten into plough-shares, Isa. ii. 4. 2. They shall be quiet from the fear of evil. God will not only keep them safe, but *make them to lie down safely,* as those that know themselves to be under the protection of Heaven, and therefore are not afraid of the powers of hell.

IV. That, though God had given them a bill of divorce for their whoredoms, yet, upon their repentance, he would again take them into covenant with himself, into a marriage-covenant, *v.* 19, 20. God's making a covenant for them with the inferior creatures was a great favour; but it was nothing to this, that he took them into covenant with himself and engaged himself to do them good. Observe,

1. The nature of this covenant; it is a *marriage-covenant,* founded in choice and love, and founding the nearest relation : *I will betroth thee unto me;* and again, and a third time, *I will betroth thee.* Note, All that are sincerely devoted to God are betrothed to him; God gives them the most sacred and inviolable security imaginable that he will love them, protect them, and provide for them, that he will do the part of a husband to them, and that he will incline their hearts to join themselves to him and will graciously accept of them in so doing. Believing souls are espoused to Christ, 2 Cor. xi. 2. The gospel-church is *the bride, the Lamb's wife;* and they would never come into that relation to him if he did not by the power of his grace betroth them to himself. The separation begins on our side; we alienate ourselves from God. The coalition begins on his side; he betroths us to himself.

2. The duration of this covenant : " *I will betroth thee for ever.* The covenant itself shall be inviolable; God will not break it on his part, and you shall not on yours; and the blessings of it shall be everlasting." One of the Jewish rabbin says, This is a promise that *she shall attain to the life of the world to come, which is absolute eternity or perpetuity.*

3. The manner in which this covenant shall be made. (1.) In *righteousness and judgment,* that is, God will deal sincerely and uprightly in covenant with them; they have broken covenant, and God is righteous. "But," says God, "I will renew the covenant *in righteousness.*" The matter shall be so ordered that God may receive even these backsliding children into his family again, without any reflection upon his justice, nay, his justice being satisfied by the Mediator of this covenant, very much to the honour of it. But what reason can there be why God should take a people into covenant with him that had so often dealt treacherously? Will it not reflect upon his wisdom? "No," says God; "I will do it *in judgment,* not rashly, but upon due consideration; let me alone to give a reason for it and to justify my own con-

duct." (2.) *In lovingkindness and in mercies.* God will deal tenderly and graciously in covenanting with them; and will be not only as good as his word, but better; and, as he will be just in keeping covenant with them, so he will be merciful in keeping them in the covenant. They are subject to many infirmities, and, if he be extreme to mark what they do amiss, they will soon lose the benefit of the covenant. He therefore promises that it shall be a covenant of grace, made in a compassionate consideration of their infirmities, so that every transgression in the covenant shall not throw them out of covenant; he will *gather with everlasting lovingkindness.* (3.) *In faithfulness.* Every article of the covenant shall be punctually performed. *Faithful is he that has called them, who also will do it ;* he cannot *deny himself.*

4. The means by which they shall be kept tight and faithful to the covenant on their part : *Thou shalt know the Lord.* This is not only a promise that God will reveal himself to them more fully and clearly than ever, but that he will give them *a heart to know him;* they shall know more of him, and shall know him in another manner than ever yet. The ground of their apostasy was their not knowing God to be their benefactor (*v.* 8); therefore, to prevent the like, they shall all be *taught of God* to know him. Note, God keeps up his interest in men's souls by giving them a good understanding and a right knowledge of things, Heb. viii. 11.

V. That, though the heavens had been to them as brass, and the earth as iron, now the heavens shall yield their dews, and by that means the earth its fruits, *v.* 21, 22. God having betrothed the gospel-church and in it all believers to himself, how shall he not with himself and with his Son freely *give them all things,* all things pertaining both to life and godliness, all things they need or can desire? *All is theirs,* for they are *Christ's,* betrothed to him; and with the righteousness of the kingdom of God, which they *seek first,* all *other things* shall be *added unto them.* And yet this promise of *corn and wine* is to be taken also in a spiritual sense (so the learned Dr. Pocock thinks) : it is an effusion of those blessings and graces which relate to the soul that is here promised under the metaphor of temporal blessings, the dew of heaven, as well as the fatness of the earth, and that put first, as in the blessing of Jacob, Gen. xxvii. 28. God had threatened (*v.* 9) that he would *take away the corn and the wine;* but now he promises to restore them, and that in the common course and order of nature. While they lay under the judgment of famine they called to the earth for *corn and wine* for the support of themselves and their families. Very gladly would the earth have supplied them, but she cannot give unless she receive, cannot produce *corn and wine* unless she be *enriched with the river of God* (Ps. lxv. 9); and therefore she calls to the heavens for rain, the former and latter rain in their season, gapes for it, and by her melancholy aspect when rain is denied pleads for it. "But," say the heavens, "we have no rain to give unless he who has the key of the clouds unlock them, and open these bottles; so that, *if the Lord do not help you,* we cannot." But, when God takes them into covenant with himself, then the wheel of nature shall be set a-going again in favour of them, and the streams of mercy shall flow in the usual channel: Then *I will hear, saith the Lord; I will receive your prayers* (so the Chaldee interprets the first *hearing*); God will graciously take notice of their addresses to him. And then *I will hear the heavens;* I will *answer* them (so it may be read); and then they shall *hear and answer the earth,* and pour down seasonable rain upon it; and then the *earth* shall *hear the corn and vines,* and supply them with moisture, and *they shall hear Jezreel,* and be nourishment and refreshment for those that inhabit Jezreel. See here the coherence of second causes with one another, as links in a chain, and the necessary dependence they all have upon God, the first Cause. Note, We must expect all our comforts from God in the usual method and by the appointed means; and, when we are at any time disappointed in them, we must look up to God, *above the hills and the mountains,* Ps. cxxi. 1, 2. See how ready the creatures are to serve the people of God, how desirous of the honour: the corn cries to the earth, the earth to the heavens, the heavens to God, and all that they may supply them. And see how ready God is to give relief: *I will hear,* saith the Lord, yea, *I will hear.* And, if God will hear the cry of the heavens for his people, much more will he hear the intercession of his Son for them, who is made *higher than the heavens.* See what a peculiar delight those that are in covenant with God may take in their creature-comforts, as seeing them all come to them from the hand of God; they can trace up all the streams to the fountain, and taste covenant-love in common mercies, which makes them doubly sweet.

VI. That whereas they were now dispersed, not only, as Simeon and Levi, divided in Jacob and scattered in Israel, but divided and scattered all the world over, God will turn this curse, as he did that, into a blessing: "I will not only water the earth for her, but will *sow her unto me in the earth;* her dispersion shall be not like that of the chaff in the floor, which *the wind drives away,* but like that of the seed in the field, in order to its greater increase; wherever they are scattered they shall *take root downward and bear fruit upward. The good seed are the children of the kingdom. I will sow her unto me.*" This alludes to the name Jezreel, which signifies *sown of God,* or *for God;* as she was scattered of him (which is one signification of the words) so she shall be sown

of him; and to what he sows he will give the increase. When in all parts of the world Christianity got footing, and every where there were professors of it, then this promise was fulfilled, *I will sow her unto me in the earth.* Note, The greatest blessing of this earth is that God has a church in it, and from that arises all the tribute of glory which he has out of it; it is what he has sown to himself, and what he will therefore secure to himself.

VII. That, whereas they had been *Lo-ammi—not a people,* and *Lo-ruhamah—not finding mercy* with God, now they shall be restored to his favour and taken again into covenant with him (*v.* 23): They *had not obtained mercy,* but seemed to be abandoned; they were *not my people,* not distinguished, not dealt with, as my people, but left to lie in common with the nations. This was the case with the rejected Jews; and the same, or more deplorable, was that of the Gentile world (to whom the apostle applies this, Rom. ix. 24, 25), that had *no hope,* and was *without God in the world;* but when great multitudes both of Jews and Gentiles were, upon their believing in Christ, incorporated into a Christian church, then, 1. God had mercy on those who *had not obtained mercy.* Those found favour with God, and became the children of his love, who had been long out of favour and the children of his wrath, and, if infinite mercy had not interposed, would have been for ever so. Note, God's mercy must not be despaired of any where on this side hell. 2. He took those into a covenant-relation to himself who had been strangers and foreigners. He says to them, " *Thou art my people,* whom I will own and bless, protect and provide for;" and they shall say, " *Thou art my God,* whom I will serve and worship, and to whose honour I will be entirely and for ever devoted." Note, (1.) The sum total of the happiness of believers is the mutual relation that is between them and God, that he is theirs and they are his; this is the crown of all the promises. (2.) This relation is founded in free grace. We have not chosen him, but he has chosen us. He first says, They are my people, and makes them willing to be so in the day of his power, and then they avouch him to be theirs. (3.) As we need desire no more to make us happy than to be the people of God, so we need desire no more to make us easy and cheerful than to have him to assure us that we are so, to say unto us, by his Spirit witnessing with ours, *Thou art my people.* (4.) Those that have accepted the Lord for their God must avouch him to be so, must go to him in prayer and tell him so, *Thou art my God,* and must be ready to make profession before men. (5.) It adds to the comfort of our covenant with God that in it there is a communion of saints, who, though *they are many,* yet here are one. It is not, I will *say to them, You are my people,* but,

Thou art; for he looks upon them as all *one in Christ*, and, as such in him, he speaks to them and covenants with them; and they also do not say, Thou art *our God*, for they look upon themselves as one body, and desire with one mind and one mouth to glorify him, and therefore say, *Thou art my God.* Or it intimates that such a covenant as God made of old with his people Israel, in general, now under the gospel he makes with particular believers, and says to *each of them*, even the meanest, with as much pleasure as he did of old to the *thousands of Israel*, *Thou art my people*, and invites and encourages each of them to say, *Thou art my God*, and to triumph therein, as Moses and all Israel did. Exod. xv. 2, He is *my God*, and my *father's God.*

CHAP. III.

God is still by the prophet inculcating the same thing upon this careless people, and much in the same manner as before, by a type or sign, that of the dealings of a husband with an adulterous wife: In this chapter we have, I. The bad character which the people of Israel now had; they were, as is said of the Athenians (Acts xvii. 16), "wholly given to idolatry," ver. 1. II. The low condition which they should be reduced to by their captivity, and the other instances of God's controversy with them, ver. 2—4. III. The blessed reformation that should at length be wrought upon them in the latter days, ver. 5.

THEN said the LORD unto me, Go yet, love a woman beloved of *her* friend, yet an adulteress, according to the love of the LORD toward the children of Israel, who look to other gods, and love flagons of wine. 2 So I bought her to me for fifteen *pieces* of silver, and *for* a homer of barley, and a half homer of barley: 3 And I said unto her, Thou shalt abide for me many days; thou shalt not play the harlot, and thou shalt not be for *another* man: so *will* I also *be* for thee. 4 For the children of Israel shall abide many days without a king, and without a prince, and without a sacrifice, and without an image, and without an ephod, and *without* teraphim: 5 Afterward shall the children of Israel return, and seek the LORD their God, and David their king; and shall fear the LORD and his goodness in the latter days.

Some think that this chapter refers to Judah, the two tribes, as the adulteress the prophet married (*ch.* i. 3) represented the *ten tribes;* for this was not to be divorced, as the ten tribes were, but to be left desolate for a long time, and then to return, as the two tribes did. But these are called the *children of Israel*, which was the ten tribes, and therefore it is more probable that of them this parable, as well as that before, is to be understood. *Go*, and repeat it, says God to the prophet; *Go yet again.* Note, For the conviction and reduction of sinners

it is necessary that precept be upon precept, and line upon line. If they will not believe one sign, try another, Exod. iv. 8, 9. Now,

I. In this parable we may observe,

1. God's goodness and Israel's badness strangely serving for a foil to each other, *v.* 1. Israel is as a woman *beloved of her friend*, either of him that has married her or of him that only courts her, and *yet an adulteress;* such is the case between God and Israel. We say of those whose affection is mutual that there is *no love lost* between them; but here we find a great deal of the love even of God himself lost and thrown away upon an unworthy ungrateful people. The God of Israel retains a very great love for the *children of Israel*, and yet they are an evil and adulterous generation. *Be astonished, O heavens! at this, and wonder, O earth!* (1.) That God's goodness has not put an end to their badness; the Lord loves them, has a kindness for them, and is continually showing kindness to them; they know it, they cannot but own it, that he has been as a friend and Father to them; and yet they *look to other gods*, gods that they can see, and to the love of which they are draw by the eye; they look to them with an eye of adoration (they offer up all their services to them) and with an eye of dependence (they expect all their comforts from them); if they were restrained from bowing the knee to idols, yet they gave them an amorous glance, and had *eyes full of that* spiritual *adultery.* And they loved *flagons of wine;* they joined with idolaters because they lived merrily and drank hard; they had a kindness for *other gods* for the sake of the plenty of good wine with which they had been sometimes treated in their temples. Idolatry and sensuality commonly go together; those that make a god of their belly, as drunkards do, will easily be brought to make a god of any thing else. God's priests were to *drink no wine* when they went in to minister, and his Nazarites none at all. But the worshippers of other gods *drank wine in bowls;* nay, no less than *flagons of wine* would content them. (2.) That their badness had not put an end to God's goodness, and stopped the current of his favours to them. This is a wonder of mercy indeed, that she is thus *beloved of her friend, though an adulteress;* such is the *love of the Lord towards the children* of Israel. "Go," says God, "*love* such a woman; see if thou canst find in thy heart to do it. No, thou canst not, the breast of no man would admit such a love; yet such is my *love to the children of Israel;* it is love to the loveless, to the unlovely, to those that have a thousand times forfeited it." Note, In God's goodwill to poor sinners his thoughts and ways are infinitely above ours, and his love is more condescending and compassionate than ours is, or can be; in this, as much as any thing, he is *God, and not man,* Hos. xi. 9.

2. The method found for the bringing of

a God so very good and a people so very bad together again; this is the thing aimed at, and what God aims at he will accomplish. To our great surprise, we find a breach thus wide as the sea effectually healed; miracles cease not so long as divine mercy does not cease. Observe here, (1.) The course God takes to humble them and make them know themselves (v. 2): *I bought her to me for fifteen pieces of silver, and a homer and a half of barley*, that is, I courted her to be reconciled, to leave her ill courses, and return to her first husband, as *ch.* ii. 14. I *allured* her, and *spoke comfortably* to her; as the *Levite who went after* his concubine that had *played the harlot* from him, and had run away with another man, *spoke friendly to her*, Judg. xix. 3. But here the present which the prophet brought her for the purchasing of her favour is observed to be a very small one; but it was all that was intended for her separate maintenance, and in it she is reduced to a short allowance, and, to punish her for her pride, is made to look very mean. When Samson went to be reconciled to his wife that had disobliged him he *visited her with a kid* (Judg. xv. 1), which was a genteel entertainment. But the prophet here visited his wife with *fifteen pieces of silver*, a small sum, which yet she must be content to live upon a great while, so long as till her husband thought fit to restore her to her first estate. She shall also have *a homer and a half of barley*, for bread-corn, and that is all she must expect till she be sufficiently humbled, and, by a competent time of trial, satisfactory proof given that she is indeed reformed. Let her be made sensible that it is not for her own merit that her husband makes court to her; it is but a lame price that he values her at. The price of a servant was thirty shekels, Exod. xxi. 32. This was but half so much; yet let her know that it is more than she is worth. God had given Egypt for Israel's ransom once, so precious were they then in his sight, and so honourable, Isa. xliii. 3, 4. But now that they have gone a whoring from him he will give but fifteen pieces of silver for them, so much have they lost in their value by their iniquity. Note, Those whom God designs honour and comfort for he first makes sensible of their own worthlessness, and brings them to acknowledge, with the prodigal, I am no more worthy to be called thy son. Time was when Israel was *fed with the finest of the wheat*, but they grew wanton, *and loved flagons of wine*, and therefore, in order to the humbling and reducing of them, they must be brought in the land of their captivity to eat barley-bread, and be thankful they can get it, and to eat that too by weight and measure, whereas they did not use to be stinted. Note, Poverty and disgrace sometimes prove a happy means of making great sinners true penitents. (2.) The new terms upon which God is willing to come with them (v. 3):

Thou shalt abide for me many days, and shalt not be for another, so will I be for thee. He might justly have given them a bill of divorce, and have resolved to have no more to do with them; but he is willing to show them kindness, and that the matter should be compromised; he deals not with them in strict justice, according to the rigour of the law, but according to the multitude of his mercies; and it represents God's gracious dealings with the apostate race of mankind, that had gone a whoring from him; he bought them indeed with an inestimable price, not for their honour, but for the honour of his own justice; and now this is the proposal he makes to them, the covenant of grace he is willing to enter into with them—they must be to him a people, and he will be to them a God, the same with the proposal here made to Israel. [1.] They must take to themselves the shame of their apostasy from him, must submit to, and accept of, the punishment of their iniquity: *Thou shalt abide for me many days* in *solitude* and *silence*, as a widow that' is *desolate* and in sorrow; they must *lay aside their ornaments*, and wait with patience and submission to know what God will do with them, and whether he will please to admit such unworthy wretches into his favour again, as they did Exod. xxxiii. 4, 5. *Their father*, their husband, has *spit in their face* (as God said concerning Miriam), has put them under the marks of his displeasure, and therefore, like her, they must be *ashamed seven days*, and be *shut out of the camp* (Num. xii. 14), till *their uncircumcised hearts be humbled*, Lev. xxvi. 41. Let them *sit alone* and *keep silence, waiting for the salvation of the Lord*, and in the mean time let them *bear the yoke*, Lam. iii. 26—28. Let them not expect that God should speedily return in mercy to them, as sometimes he has done, that comfort should come over cheap and easy to them; no, let them want it, let them wait for it *many days*, during all the days of their captivity, and reckon it a miracle of mercy, and well worth waiting for, if it come at last. Note, Those whom God designs mercy for he will first bring to abase themselves and to put a high value upon his favours. [2.] They must never return to folly again; that is the condition upon which God will *speak peace to his people and to his saints* (Ps. lxxxv. 8), and to no other. " *Thou shalt not play the harlot*, shalt not worship idols in the land of thy captivity, while thou art there set apart for thy uncleanness." Note, It is not enough to take shame to ourselves for the sins we have committed, and to justify God in correcting us for them, but we must resolve, in the strength of God's grace, that we will not offend any more, that we will not again go a whoring from God, after the world and the flesh. Blessed be God, though it is the law of the covenant, it is not the condition of it that we shall never in any thing do amiss : " But thou shalt not *play the harlot;* thou shalt not serve other gods, *shalt not be for another man."* In the land of their captivity they would be courted to worship the idols of the country; that would be a trial for them, a *long* trial, many days: " But if thou keep thy ground, and hold fast thy integrity, if, when *all this comes upon thee,* thou dost not *stretch out thy hand to a strange god,* thou wilt be qualified for the returns of God's favour." Note, It is a certain sign that our afflictions are means of much good to us, and earnests of more, when we are kept by the grace of God from being overcome by the temptations of an afflicted state. [3.] Upon these terms their Maker will again be their husband: *So will I also be for thee.* This is the covenant between God and returning sinners, that, if they will be for him to serve him, he will be for them to save them. Let them renounce and abjure all rivals with God for the throne in the heart, and devote themselves entirely to him and him only, and he will be to them a God all-sufficient. If we be faithful and constant to God in a way of duty, and will never leave nor forsake him, he will be so to us in a way of mercy, and will never leave nor forsake us. And a fairer proposal could not be made.

II. In the last two verses we have the interpretation of the parable and the application of it to Israel.

1. They must long *sit like a widow,* stripped of all their joys and honours, Lam. iv. 1, 2. *They shall abide many days without a king, and without a prince;* and a nation in this condition may well be called *a widow.* They want the blessing, (1.) Of civil government: They shall abide *without a king,* and *without a prince,* of their own. There were kings and princes over them to oppress them and rule them with rigour, but they had no king nor prince to protect them, to fight their battles for them, to administer justice to them, and to take care of their common safety and welfare. Note, Magistracy is a very great blessing to a people, and it is a sad and sore judgment to want it. (2.) Of public worship: *They shall* abide *without a sacrifice,* and *without an image* (or a *statue,* or *pillar;* the word is used concerning the pillars Jacob erected, Gen. xxviii. 18; xxxi. 45; xxxv. 20), and *without an ephod and teraphim.* The *teraphim* being here closely joined to the *ephod,* some think the *urim* and *thummim* were meant by it in the breast-plate of the high priest. The meaning is that in their captivity they should not only have no face of a nation upon them, but no face of a church; they should not have (as a learned expositor speaks) liberty of any public profession or exercise of religion, either true or false, according to their choice. They shall have *no sacrifice or altar* (so the LXX.), and therefore no sacrifice because no altar. They shall have *no ephod,* nor *teraphim,* no legal priesthood, no means of knowing God's

mind, no oracle to consult in doubtful cases, but shall be all in the dark. Note, The case of those is very melancholy that are deprived of all opportunities to worship God in public. This was the case of the Jews in their captivity; and it is so far the case of the scattered Jews at this day that, though they have their synagogues, they have no temple-service. Desolate indeed is their condition that are shut out from communion with God, that have no opportunity of directing their addresses to God by sacrifice and altar, and of receiving instructions from him by ephod and teraphim.

2. They shall at length be received again as a wife (*v.* 5): *Afterwards,* in process of time, when they have gone through this discipline, *they shall return,* that is, they shall repent of their idolatries and forsake them, they shall apply themselves to God and adhere to him, and herein they shall be accepted of him. Two things are here promised as instances of their return, and steps towards their acceptance with God in their return :—
(1.) The enquiries they shall make after God: *They shall seek the Lord their God, and David their king.* Note, Those that would find God, and find favour with him, must seek him, must ask after him, covet acquaintance with him, desire to be reconciled to him, set their love on him, and labour in this that they may be accepted of him. Their seeking him implies that they had lost him, that they were lamenting their loss, and that they were solicitous to retrieve what they had lost. They shall seek him as *their God;* for *should not a people seek unto their God?* And they shall seek *David their King,* who can be no other than the Messiah, our Lord Jesus Christ, the Son of David, the *root and offspring of David,* whom David himself called *Lord* (Ps. cx. 1), and to whom God gave the *throne of his father David,* Luke i. 32. The Chaldee reads it, They shall *seek the service of the Lord their God,* and *shall obey Messiah, the Son of David their king.* Compare this with Jer. xxx. 9; Ezek. xxxiv. 23; xxxvii. 25. Note, Those that would seek the Lord so as to find him must apply to Jesus Christ, and must seek to him as their King, and become his willing people, and take an oath of fealty and allegiance to him. (2.) The reverence they shall have of God: *They shall fear the Lord and his goodness.* Some by his *goodness* here understand the temple, towards which they shall look, in worshipping God. The Jews say, There were three things which Israel cast off in the days of Rehoboam—the *kingdom of heaven,* the *family of David,* and the *house of the sanctuary;* and it will never be well with them till they return, and seek them all three, which is here promised. They shall seek the kingdom of heaven in *the Lord their God,* the royal family in *David their King,* and the temple in *the goodness of the Lord.* Others by *his goodness* under-

stand Christ, the same *with David their King*. But it is rather to be taken for that attribute of God which he showed as his glory, and by which he proclaimed his name. Note, It is not only the Lord and his greatness that we are to fear, but the Lord and his goodness, not only his majesty, but his mercy. They shall *flee for fear to the Lord and his goodness* (so some take it), shall flee to it as their city of refuge. We must *fear God's goodness*, that is, we must admire it, and stand amazed at it, must adore it, and *worship* as Moses did at the proclaiming of this name, Exod. xxxiv. 6. We must be afraid of offending his goodness, of making any ungrateful returns for it, and so forfeiting it. *There is forgiveness with God, that he may be feared*, Ps. cxxx. 4. We must *rejoice with trembling* in the goodness of God, must not be *high-minded, but fear*. Now this promise had its accomplishment when by the gospel of Christ great multitudes both of Jews and Gentiles were brought home to God, and incorporated in the New-Testament church, served God in Christ, with a filial fear of divine grace, and were accepted of God as his Israel. And some think it is to be yet further accomplished in the conversion of those Jews to the faith of Christ who shall remain in unbelief, when they shall seek their Messiah as *David their King*, and by him *all Israel shall be saved*, when the *fulness of the Gentiles is brought in*. Time was when they sought him to put him to death, saying, *We have no king but Cæsar ;* but the day is coming when they shall seek him to *appoint him their head*, and to lay their necks under his yoke. He that has here promised that they shall do it will enable them to do it, and bring about this great work in his own way and time, *in the latter days* of the *last times*, the times of the Messiah : but, alas ! who shall live when God does this ? How far we are to expect a general conversion of that nation I cannot say ; but I am sure we ought to pray that the Jews may be converted.

CHAP. IV.

Prophets were sent to be reprovers, to tell people of their faults, and to warn them of the judgments of God, to which by sin they exposed themselves; so the prophet is employed in this and the following chapters. He is here, as counsel for the King of kings, opening an indictment against the people of Israel, and labouring to convince them of sin, and of their misery and danger because of sin, that he might prevail with them to repent and reform. I. He shows them what were the grounds of God's controversy with them, a general prevalency of vice and profaneness (ver. 1, 2), ignorance and forgetfulness of God (ver. 6, 7), the worldly-mindedness of the priests (ver. 8), drunkenness and uncleanness (ver. 11), using divination and witchcraft (ver. 12), offering sacrifice in the high places (ver. 13), whoredoms (ver. 14, 18), and bribery among magistrates, ver. 18. II. He shows them what would be the consequences of God's controversy. God would punish them for these things, ver. 9. The whole land should be laid waste (ver. 3), all sorts of people cut off (ver. 5), their honour lost (ver. 7), their creature-comforts unsatisfying (ver. 10), and themselves made ashamed, ver. 19. And, which is several times mentioned here as the sorest judgment of all, they should be let alone in their sins (ver. 17); they shall not reprove one another (ver. 4), God will not punish them (ver. 14), nay, he will let them prosper, ver. 16. III. He gives warning to Judah not to tread in the steps of Israel, because they saw their steps went down to hell, ver. 15.

HEAR the word of the Lord, ye children of Israel: for the Lord

hath a controversy with the inhabitants of the land, because *there is* no truth, nor mercy, nor knowledge of God in the land. 2 By swearing, and lying, and killing, and stealing, and committing adultery, they break out, and blood toucheth blood. 3 Therefore shall the land mourn, and every one that dwelleth therein shall languish, with the beasts of the field, and with the fowls of heaven; yea, the fishes of the sea also shall be taken away. 4 Yet let no man strive, nor reprove another : for thy people *are* as they that strive with the priest. 5 Therefore shalt thou fall in the day, and the prophet also shall fall with thee in the night, and I will destroy thy mother.

Here is, I. The court set, and both attendance and attention demanded : " *Hear the word of the Lord, you children of Israel*, for to you is the word of this conviction sent, whether you will hear or whether you will forbear." Whom may God expect to give him a fair hearing, and take from him a fair warning, but the children of Israel, his own professing people ? Yea, they will be ready enough to hear when God speaks comfortably to them; but are they willing to hear when he has a controversy with them ? Yes, they must hear him when he pleads against them, when he has something to lay to their charge : *The Lord has a controversy with the inhabitants of the land*, of this land, of this holy land. Note, Sin is the great mischief-maker; it sows discord between God and Israel. God sees sin in his own people, and a good action he has against them for it. Some more particular actions lie against his own people, which do not lie against other sinners. He has a controversy with them for breaking covenant with him, for bringing a reproach upon him, and for an ungrateful return to him for his favours. God's controversy will be pleaded, pleaded by the judgments of his mouth before they are pleaded by the judgments of his hand, that he may be justified in all he does and may make it appear that he desires not the death of sinners ; and God's pleadings ought to be attended to, for, sooner or later, they shall have a hearing.

II. The indictment read, by which the whole nation stands charged with crimes of a heinous nature, by which God is highly provoked. 1. They are charged with national omissions of the most important duties : *There is no truth nor mercy*, neither justice nor charity, these most *weighty matters of the law*, as our Saviour accounts them (Matt. xxiii. 23), *judgment, mercy, and faith*. The generality of the people seemed to have no sense at all of the thing called honesty; they made no conscience of what they said and did, though ever so contrary to the truth and injurious to their neighbour. Much less had they any sense of mercy, or any obligation they were under to pity and help the poor. And it is not strange that there is no truth and mercy when there is *no knowledge of God in the land.* What good can be expected where there is no knowledge of God? It was the privilege of that land that *in Israel God was* made *known,* and his *name* was *great,* which was an aggravation of their sin, that they did not *know him,* Ps. lxxvi. 1. 2. Hence follow national commissions of the most enormous sins against both the first and second table, for they had no regard at all to either. *Swearing,* and *lying,* and *killing,* and *stealing,* and *committing adultery,* against the third, ninth, sixth, eighth, and seventh commandments, were to be found in all corners of the land, and among all orders and degrees of men among them, *v.* 2. The corruption was universal; what good people there were among them were either lost or hid, or they hid themselves. By these they *break out,* that is, they transgress all bounds of reason and conscience, and the divine law; *they have exceeded* (Job xxxvi. 9); they have been *overmuch wicked* (Eccl. vii. 17); they suffer their corruptions to break out; they themselves break over, and break through, all that stands in their way and would stop them in their sinful career, as water overflows the banks. Note, Sin is a violent thing and its power exorbitant; when men's hearts are *fully set in them to do evil* (Eccl. viii. 11) *what will be restrained from them?* Gen. xi. 6. When they break out thus *blood touches blood,* that is, abundance of murders are committed in all parts of the country, and, as it were, in a constant series and succession. *Cædes aliæ aliis sunt contiguæ — Murders touch murders;* a stream of blood runs down among them, even royal blood. It was about this time that there was so much blood shed in grasping at the crown; Shallum slew Zechariah, and Menahem slew Shallum, Pekah slew Pekahiah, and Hoshea slew Pekah; and the like bloody work, it is likely, there was among other contenders, so that the land was *polluted with blood* (Ps. cvi. 38); *it was filled with blood from one end to the other,* 2 Kings xxi. 16.

III. Sentence passed upon this guilty and polluted land, *v.* 3. It shall be utterly destroyed and laid waste. The whole land is infected with sin, and therefore *the whole land shall mourn* under God's sore judgments, shall sit in mourning, being stripped of all its wealth and beauty. As the valleys are said to *shout for joy, and sing,* when there are plenty and peace, so here they are said to *mourn* when by war and famine they are made desolate. The *whole land shall be*

brimstone, *and* salt, *and* burning, was as threatened in the law, Deut. xxix. 33. They had broken all God's commandments, and now God threatens to take away all their comforts. The *land mourns* when there is neither *grass for the cattle nor herbs for the service of man;* and then *every one that dwells therein shall languish* for want of nice food to support a wasting life, and fret for want of the usual dainties for delight. The *beasts of the field* will languish, Jer. xiv. 5, 6. Nay, the destruction of the fruits of the earth shall be so great that there shall not be picking for the *fowls of the air,* to keep them alive; they shall suffer with man, and their dying, or growing lean, will be a punishment to those who used to have their tables replenished with wild-fowl. Nay, *the fishes of the sea shall be taken away,* or *gathered together,* that they may go away in shoals to some other coast, and then the fishing trade will be worth nothing. This desolation shall be in that respect more general than that by Noah's flood, for that did not affect the fishes of the sea, but this shall. It was part of one of the plagues of Egypt that he *slew their fish* (Ps. cv. 29); when the waters are dried the *fish die,* Isa. l. 2; Zeph. i. 2, 3. Note, When man becomes disobedient to God, it is just that the inferior creatures should be made unserviceable to man. Oh what reason have we to admire God's patience and mercy to our land, that though there is in it so much swearing, and lying, and killing, and stealing, and adultery, yet there is plenty of flesh, and fish, and fowl, on our tables!

IV. An order of court that no pains should be taken with the condemned criminal to bring him to repentance, with the reason for that order. Observe, 1. The order itself (*v.* 4): *Yet let no man strive nor reprove another;* let no means be used to reduce and reclaim them; let their physicians give them up as desperate and past cure. It intimates that as long as there is any hope we ought to reprove sinners for their sins; it is a duty we owe to one another to give and to take reproofs; it was one of the laws of Moses (Lev. xix. 17), *Thou shalt in any wise rebuke thy neighbour;* it is an instance of brotherly love. Sometimes there is need to rebuke sharply, not only to reprove, but to strive, so loth are men to part with their sins. But it is a sign that persons and people are abandoned to ruin when God says, *Let them not be reproved.* Yet this is to be understood as God's commands sometimes to the prophets not to *pray for them,* notwithstanding which they did pray for them; but the meaning is, They are so hardened in sin, and so ripened for ruin, that it will be to little purpose either to deal with them or to deal with God for them. Note, It bodes ill to a people when reprovers are silenced, and when those who should witness against the sins of the times, retire into a corner, and give up the cause. See 2 Chron. xxv. 16. 2. The reasons of this order. Let them not reprove one another; for, (1.) They are determined to *go on in sin*, and no reproofs will cure them of that: *Thy people are as those that strive with the priests;* they have grown so very impudent in sin, so very insolent, and impatient of reproof, that they will fly in the face even of a priest himself if he should but give them the least check, without any regard to his character and office; and how then can it be thought that they should take a reproof from a private person? Note, Those sinners have their hearts wickedly hardened who quarrel with their ministers for dealing faithfully with them; and those who rebel against ministerial reproof, which is an ordinance of God for their reformation, have forfeited the benefit of brotherly reproof too. Perhaps this may refer to the late wickedness of Joash king of Judah, and his people, who stoned Zechariah, the son of Jehoiada, for delivering them a message from God, 2 Chron. xxiv. 21. He was a *priest;* with him they *strove* when he was officiating *between the temple and the altar;* and Dr. Lightfoot thinks the prophet had an eye to his case when he spoke (v. 2) of *blood touching blood;* the blood of the *sacrificer was mingled with the blood of the sacrifice,* That, says he, was the *apex* of *their wickedness*—thence their ruin was to be dated (Matt. xxiii. 35), as this is of *their incorrigibleness,* that they are as those who *strive with the priest,* therefore let no man reprove them; for, (2.) God also is determined to *proceed in their ruin* (v. 5): " *Therefore,* because thou wilt take no reproof, no advice, *thou shalt fall,* and it is in vain for any to think of preventing it, for the *decree* has *gone forth.* Thou shalt stumble and *fall in the day,* and *the prophet,* the false prophet that flattered and seduced thee, shall *fall with thee in the night;* both thou and thy prophet shall fall *night and day,* shall be continually falling into one calamity or other; the darkness of the night shall not help to cover thee from trouble nor the light of the day help thee to flee from it." The prophets are blind leaders and the people blind followers; and to the blind day and night are alike, so that whether it be day or night both shall *fall together into the ditch.* "Thou shalt fall *in the day,* when thy fall is least feared by thyself and thou art very *secure;* and *in the day,* when it will be seen and observed by others, and turn most to thy shame; and the prophet shall *fall in the night,*" when to himself it will be most terrible." Note, The ruin of those who have helped to ruin others will, in a special manner, be intolerable. And did the children think that when they were in danger of falling their mother would help them? It shall be in vain to expect it, for *I will destroy thy mother,* Samaria, the mother-city, the whole state, or *kingdom,* which is as a mother to

every part. It shall all be *made silent.* Note, When all are involved in guilt nothing less can be expected than that all should be involved in ruin.

6 My people are destroyed for lack of knowledge: because thou hast rejected knowledge, I will also reject thee, that thou shalt be no priest to me: seeing thou hast forgotten the law of thy God, I will also forget thy children. 7 As they were increased, so they sinned against me: *therefore* will I change their glory into shame. 8 They eat up the sin of my people, and they set their heart on their iniquity. 9 And there shall be, like people, like priest: and I will punish them for their ways, and reward them their doings. 10 For they shall eat, and not have enough: they shall commit whoredom, and shall not increase: because they have left off to take heed to the LORD. 11 Whoredom and wine and new wine take away the heart.

God is here proceeding in his controversy both with the priests and with the people. *The people* were as those *that strove with the priests* (v. 4) when they had priests that did their duty; but the generality of them lived in the neglect of their duty, and here is a word for those priests, and for the people that love to have it so, Jer. v. 31. And it is observable here how the punishment answers to the sin, and how, for the justifying of his own proceedings, God sets the one overagainst the other.

I. The people *strove with the priests* that should have taught them the knowledge of God; justly therefore were they *destroyed for lack of knowledge,* v. 6. Note, Those that rebel against the light can expect no other than to perish in the dark. Or it is a charge upon the priests, who should have been still *teaching the people knowledge* (Eccl. xii. 9), but they did not, or did it in such a manner that it was as if they had not done it at all, so there was *no knowledge of God in the land;* and because there was no vision, or none to any purpose, the people *perished,* Prov. xxix. 18. Note, Ignorance is so far from being the mother of devotion that it is the mother of destruction; lack of knowledge is ruining to any person or people. They are *my people* that are thus *destroyed;* their relation to God as his people aggravates both their sin in not taking pains to get the knowledge of that God whose command they were under and with whom they were taken into covenant, and likewise the sin of those who should have taught them; God set his children to school to them, and they never minded them. nor took any pains with them.

II. Both priests and people rejected knowledge; and justly therefore will God *reject them.* The reason why the people did not learn, and the priests did not teach, was not because they had not the light, but because they hated it—not because they had not ways of coming to the knowledge of God and of communicating it, but because they had no heart to it; they *rejected* it. They *desired not the knowledge of God's ways,* but put it from them, and shut their eyes against the light; and therefore " *I will also reject thee;* I will refuse to take cognizance of thee and to own thee; you will not know me, but bid me *depart;* I will therefore say, *Depart from me, I know you not. Thou* shalt be *no priest to me.*" 1. The priests shall be no longer admitted to the privileges, or employed in the services, of the priesthood, nor shall they ever be received again, as we find, Ezek. xliv. 13. Note, Ministers that reject knowledge, that are grossly ignorant and scandalous, ought not to be owned as ministers; but that which they *seem to have* should be *taken away,* Luke viii. 18. 2. The people shall be no longer as they have been, a *kingdom of priests,* a royal priesthood, Exod. xix. 6. God's people, by rejecting knowledge, forfeit their honour and profane their own crown.

III. They *forgot the law of God,* neither desired nor endeavoured to retain it in mind, nor to transmit the remembrance of it to their posterity, and therefore justly will God *forget* them and *their children,* the people's children; they did not educate them, as they ought to have done, in the knowledge of God and their duty to him, and therefore God will disown them, as not in covenant with him. Note, If parents do not teach their children, when they are young, to *remember their Creator,* they cannot expect that their Creator should remember them. Or it may be meant of the priests' children; they shall not succeed them in the priests' office, but shall be reduced to poverty, as is threatened against Eli's house, 1 Sam. ii. 20.

IV. They dishonoured God with that which was their honour, and justly therefore will God strip them of it, *v.* 7. It was their honour that they were increased in number, wealth, power, and dignity. The beginning of their nation was small, but in process of time it *greatly increased,* and grew very considerable; the family of the priests increased wonderfully. But, *as they were increased, so they sinned* against God. The more populous the nation grew, the more sin was committed and the more profane they were; their wealth, honour, and power, did but make them the more daring in sin. Therefore, says God, *will I change their glory into shame.* Are their numbers their glory? God will diminish them and make them few. Is their wealth their glory? God will impoverish them and bring them low; so that they

1142

shall themselves be ashamed of that which they gloried in. Their priests shall be made *contemptible and base,* Mal. ii. 9. Note, That which is our honour, if we dishonour God with it, will sooner or later be turned into shame to us: for *those that despise God shall be lightly esteemed,* 1 Sam. ii. 30.

V. The priests ate up the sin of God's people, and therefore *they shall eat and not have enough.* 1. They abused the maintenance that was allowed to the priests, to the priests of the house of Aaron, by the law of God, and to the mock-priests of the calves by their constitution (*v.* 8): *They eat up the sin of my people,* that is, their sin-offerings. If it be meant of the priests of the calves, it intimates their seizing that which they had no right to; they usurped the revenues of the priests, though they were no priests. If it be meant of those who were legal priests, it intimates their greediness of the profits and perquisites of their office, when they took no care at all to do the duty of it. They feasted upon their part of the offerings of the Lord, but forgot the work for which they were so well paid. They *set their hearts* upon the people's *iniquities;* they *lifted up their soul* to them, that is, they were glad when people did commit iniquity, that they might be obliged to bring an offering to make atonement for it, which they should have their share of; the more sins the more sacrifices, and therefore they cared not how much sin people were guilty of. Instead of warning the people against sin, from the consideration of the sacrifices, which showed them what an offence sin was to God, since it needed such an expiation, they emboldened and encouraged the people to sin, since an atonement might be made at so small an expense. Thus they glutted themselves upon the sins of the people, and helped to keep up that which they should have beaten down. Note, It is a very wicked thing to be well pleased with the sins of others because, in some way or other, they may turn to our advantage. 2. God will therefore deny them his blessing upon their maintenance (*v.* 10): *They shall eat and not have enough.* Though they have great plenty by the abundance of offerings that are brought in, yet they shall have no satisfaction in it. Either their food shall yield no good nourishment or their greedy appetites shall not be satisfied with it. Note, What is unlawfully gained cannot be comfortably used; no, nor that which is inordinately coveted; it is just that the desires which are insatiable should always be unsatisfied, and that those should never have enough who never know when they have enough. See Mic. vi. 14; Hag. i. 6.

VI. The more they increased the more they sinned (*v.* 7), and therefore though they *commit whoredom,* though they take the most wicked methods to multiply their people, yet *they shall not increase.* Though they have many wives and concubines, as Solomon had, yet they shall not have their families built up thereby in a numerous progeny, any more than he had. Note, Those that hope any way to increase by unlawful means will be disappointed. And therefore God will thus blast all their projects *because they have left off to take heed to the Lord;* time was when they had some regard to God, and to his authority over them and interest in them, but they have *left it off;* they take no heed to his word nor to his providences; they do not eye him in either. They *forsake him, so as not to take heed to him;* they have apostatized to such a degree that they have no manner of regard to God, but are perfectly *without God in the world.* Note, Those that leave off to take heed to the Lord leave off all good, and can expect no other than that all good should leave them.

VII. The people and the priests did harden one another in sin; and therefore justly shall they be sharers in the punishment (v. 9): *There shall be, like people, like priest.* So they were in character; people and priest were both alike ignorant and profane, regardless of God and their duty, and addicted to idolatry: and so they shall be in condition; God will bring judgments upon them, that shall be the destruction both of priest and people; the famine that deprives the people of their meat shall deprive the priests of their *meat-offerings,* Joel i. 9. It is part of the description of a universal desolation that it shall be *as with the people, so with the priest,* Isa. xxiv. 2. God's judgments, when they come with commission, will make no difference. Note, Sharers in sin must expect to be sharers in ruin. Thus God will *punish them* both *for their ways,* and *reward them for their doings.* God will *cause their doings to return upon them* (so the word is); when a sin is committed the sinner thinks *it is gone* and he shall hear no more of it, but he shall find it *called over again,* and made to *return,* either to his humiliation or to his condemnation.

VIII. They indulged themselves in the delights of sense, to hold up their hearts; but they shall find that they *take away their hearts* (v. 11): *Whoredom, and wine, and new wine take away the heart.* Some join this with the foregoing words, *They have forsaken the Lord,* to *take heed to whoredom, and wine, and new wine.* Or, *Because* these *have taken away their heart.* Their sensual pleasures have taken them off from their devotions and drowned all that is good in them. Or we may take it as a distinct sentence, containing a great truth which we see confirmed by every day's experience, that drunkenness and uncleanness are sins which besot and infatuate men, weaken and enfeeble them. They take away both the understanding and the courage.

12 My people ask counsel at their stocks, and their staff declareth unto

them: for the spirit of whoredoms hath caused *them* to err, and they have gone a whoring from under their God. 13 They sacrifice upon the tops of the mountains, and burn incense upon the hills, under oaks and poplars and elms, because the shadow thereof *is* good: therefore your daughters shall commit whoredom, and your spouses shall commit adultery. 14 I will not punish your daughters when they commit whoredom, nor your spouses when they commit adultery: for themselves are separated with whores, and they sacrifice with harlots: therefore the people *that* doth not understand shall fall. 15 Though thou, Israel, play the harlot, *yet* let not Judah offend; and come not ye unto Gilgal, neither go ye up to Beth-aven, nor swear, The LORD liveth. 16 For Israel slideth back as a backsliding heifer: now the LORD will feed them as a lamb in a large place. 17 Ephraim *is* joined to idols: let him alone. 18 Their drink is sour: they have committed whoredom continually: her rulers *with* shame do love, Give ye. 19 The wind hath bound her up in her wings, and they shall be ashamed because of their sacrifices.

In these verses we have, as before,
I. The sins charged upon the people of Israel, for which God had a controversy with them, and they are,
1. Spiritual whoredom, or idolatry. They have in them a *spirit of whoredoms,* a strong inclination to that sin; the bent and bias of their hearts are that way; it is *their own iniquity;* they are carried out towards it with an unaccountable violence, and this *causes them to err.* Note, The errors and mistakes of the judgment are commonly owing to the corrupt affections; *men therefore* have a good opinion of sin, because they have a disposition towards it. And having such erroneous notions of idols, and such passionate motions towards them, no marvel that with such a head and such a heart they have *gone a whoring from under their God, v.* 12. They ought to have been in subjection to him as their head and husband, to have been under his guidance and command, but they revolted from their allegiance, and put themselves under the guidance and protection of false gods. So (*v.* 15) Israel has *played the harlot;* their conduct in the worship of their idols was like that of a harlot, wanton and impudent. And (*v.* 16), *Israel slideth back as a backsliding heifer,* as an *untamed* heifer

(so some), or as a *perverse* or *refractory* one (so others), as a heifer that is turned loose runs madly about the pasture, or, if put under the yoke (which seems rather to be alluded to here), will draw back instead of going forward, will struggle to get her neck out of the yoke and her feet out of the furrow. Thus unruly, ungovernable, untractable, were the people of Israel. They had begun to draw in the yoke of God's ordinances, but they drew back, as *children of Belial*, that will not endure the yoke; and when the prophets were sent with the goads of reproof, to put them forward, they *kicked against the pricks*, and ran backwards. The sum of all is (*v.* 17), *Ephraim is joined to idols*, is perfectly wedded to them; his affections are glued to them, and his heart is upon them. There are two instances given of their spiritual whoredom, in both which they gave that honour to their idols which is due to God only:—(1.) They consulted them as oracles, and used those arts of divination which they had learned from their idolatrous priests (*v.* 12): *My people ask counsel at their stocks,* their wooden gods; they apply to them for advice and direction in what they should do and for information concerning the event. They *say to a stock, Thou art my father* (Jer. ii. 27); and, if it were indeed a father, it were worthy of this honour; but it was a great affront to God, who was indeed their Father, and whose lively oracles they had among them, with which they had liberty to consult at any time, thus to *ask counsel at their stocks.* And they expect that their *staff* should *declare to them* what course they should take and what the event should be. It is probable that this refers to some wicked methods of divination used among the Gentiles, and which the Jews learned from them, by a *piece of wood,* or by *a staff,* like Nebuchadnezzar's divining by *his arrows,* Ezek. xxi. 21. Note, Those who forsake the oracles of God, to take their measures from the world and the flesh, do in effect but consult with their stocks and their staves. (2.) They offered sacrifice to them as gods, whose favour they wanted and whose wrath they dreaded and deprecated (*v.* 13): *They sacrifice to them,* to atone and pacify them, and *burn incense* to them, to please and gratify them, and hope by both to recommend themselves to them. God had pitched upon the place where he would record his name; but they, having forsaken that, chose places for their irreligious rites which pleased their own fancies; they chose, [1.] High places, *upon the tops of the mountains* and *upon the hills,* foolishly imagining that the height of the ground gave them some advantage in their approaches towards heaven. [2.] Shady places, *under oaks, and poplars, and elms, because the shadow thereof* is pleasant to them, especially in those hot countries, and therefore they thought it was pleasing to their gods; or they fancied that a thick shade befriends contemplation, possesses the mind with something of awe, and therefore is proper for devotion.

2. Corporal whoredom is another crime here charged upon them: *They have committed whoredom continually,* v. 18. They drove a trade of uncleanness; it was not a single act now and then, but their constant practice, as it is of many that have *eyes full of adultery* and *which cannot cease from* that sin, 2 Pet. ii. 14. Now the abominable filthiness and lewdness that was found in Israel is here spoken of, (1.) As a concomitant of their idolatry; their false gods drew them to it; for the devil whom they worshipped, though a spirit, is an unclean spirit. Those that worshipped idols were *separated with harlots,* and they *sacrificed with harlots;* for because they *liked not to retain God in their knowledge,* but dishonoured him, therefore God *gave them up to vile affections,* by the indulging of which they *dishonoured themselves,* Rom. i. 24, 28. (2.) As a punishment of it. The *men* that worshipped idols were *separated with harlots* that attended the idolatrous rites, as in the worship of *Baal-peor,* Num. xxv. i. 2. To punish them for that God gave up their wives and daughters to the like vile affections: They *committed whoredom and adultery* (*v.* 13), which could not but be a great grief and reproach to their husbands and parents; for those that are not chaste themselves desire to have their wives and daughters so. But thus they might read their sin in their punishment, as David's adultery was punished in the debauching of his concubines by his own son, 2 Sam. xii. 11. Note, When the same sin in others is made men's grief and affliction which they have themselves been guilty of they must own that the Lord is righteous.

3. The perverting of justice, *v.* 18. *Their rulers* (be it spoken to their shame) *do love, Give ye,* that is, they love bribes, and have it continually in their mouths, *Give, give.* They are given to *filthy lucre;* every one that has any business with them must expect to be asked, What will you give? Though, as rulers, they are bound by office to do justice, yet none can have justice done them without a fee; and you may be sure that for a fee they will do injustice. Note, The love of money is the ruin of equity and the root of all iniquity. But of all men it is a shame for rulers (who should be men *fearing God* and *hating covetousness)* to love *Give ye.* Perhaps this is intended in that part of the charge here, *Their drink is sour;* it is *dead;* it is *gone.* Justice, duly administered, is refreshing, like drink to the thirsty, but when it is perverted, and rulers take rewards either to acquit the guilty or to condemn the innocent, the *drink is sour;* they *turn judgment into wormwood,* Amos v. 7. Or it may refer in general to the depraved morals of the whole nation; they had lost all their life and spirit, and were as offensive to God as dead

and sour drink is to us. See Deut. xxxi. 32, 33.

II. The tokens of God's wrath against them for their sins. 1. Their wives and daughters should not be punished for the injury and disgrace they did to their families (v. 14): *I will not punish your daughters;* and, not being punished for their sin, they would go on in it. Note, The impunity of one sinner is sometimes made the punishment of another. Or, " *I will not punish* them as I will punish you; for you must own, as Judah did concerning his daughter-in-law, that *they are more righteous than you,*" Gen. xxxviii. 26. 2. They themselves should prosper for a while, but their prosperity should help to destroy them. It comes in as a token of God's wrath (v. 16): *The Lord will feed them as a lamb in a large place;* they shall have a fat pasture, and a large one, in which they shall be fed to the full, and fed of the best, but it shall be only to prepare them for the slaughter, as a lamb is that is so fed. If they *wax fat and kick,* they do but wax fat for the butcher. But others make them feed as *a lamb on the common,* a large place indeed, but where it has short grass and lies exposed. The Shepherd of Israel will turn them both out of his pastures and out of his protection. 3. No means should be used to bring them to repentance (v. 17): "*Ephraim is joined to idols,* is in love with them and addicted to them, and therefore *let him alone,* as v. 4, *Let no man reprove* him. Let him be given up to *his own heart's lusts,* and walk *in his own counsels;* we *would have healed* him, and he *would not be healed,* therefore *forsake* him." See *what their end will be,* Deut. xxxii. 20. Note, It is a sad and sore judgment for any man to be let alone in sin, for God to say concerning a sinner, "He is joined to his idols, the world and the flesh; he is incurably proud, covetous, or profane, an incurable drunkard or adulterer; *let him alone;* conscience, let him alone; minister, let him alone; providences, let him alone. Let nothing awaken him till the flames of hell do it." The father corrects not the rebellious son any more when he determines to disinherit him. Those that are not disturbed in their sin will be destroyed for their sin." 4. They should be hurried away with a swift and shameful destruction (v. 19): *The wind has bound her up in her wings,* to carry her away into captivity, suddenly, violently, and irresistibly; he shall take *them away as with a whirlwind,* Ps. lviii. 9. And then *they shall be ashamed because of their sacrifices,* ashamed of their sin in offering sacrifice to idols, ashamed of their folly in putting themselves to such an expense upon gods that have no power to help them, and thereby making that God their enemy who has almighty power to destroy them. Note, There are sacrifices that men will one day be ashamed of. Those that have sacrificed their time, strength, honour, and all their comforts, to

the world and the flesh, will shortly be ashamed of it. Yea, and those that bring to God blind, and lame, and heartless sacrifices, will be ashamed of them too.

III. The warning given to Judah not to sin after the similitude of Israel's transgression. It is said in the close of v. 14, *Those that do not understand shall fall;* those must needs fall that do not understand how to avoid, or get over, the stumbling-blocks they meet with (and therefore *let him that thinks he stands take heed lest he fall*), particularly the two tribes (v. 15): *Though thou, Israel, play the harlot, yet let not Judah offend.* Though Israel be given to idolatry, yet let not Judah take the infection. Now, 1. This was a very needful caution. The men of Israel were brethren, and near neighbours, to the men of Judah; Israel was more numerous, and at this time in a prosperous condition, and therefore there was danger lest the men of Judah should learn their way and get a snare to their souls. Note, The nearer we are to the infection of sin the more need we have to stand upon our guard. 2. It was a very rational caution: " *Let Israel play the harlot,* yet let not Judah do so; for Judah has greater means of knowledge than Israel, has the temple and priesthood, and a king of the house of David; from Judah Shiloh is to come; and for Judah God has reserved great blessings in store; therefore *let not Judah offend,* for more is expected from them than from Israel, they will have more to answer for if they do offend, and from them God will take it more unkindly. If *Israel play the harlot,* let not Judah do so too, for then God will have no professing people in the world." God bespeaks Judah here, as Christ does the twelve, when many turned their backs upon him, *Will you also go away?* John vi. 67. Note, Those that have hitherto kept their integrity should, for that reason, still hold it fast, even in times of general apostasy. Now, to preserve Judah from offending as Israel had done, two rules are here given :—(1.) That they might not be guilty of idolatry they must keep at a distance from the places of idolatry: *Come not you unto Gilgal,* where *all their wickedness was* (ch. ix. 15; xii. 11); there they *multiplied transgression* (Amos iv. 4); and perhaps they contracted a veneration for that place because there it was said to Joshua, The place *where thou standest is holy ground* (Josh. v. 15); therefore they are forbidden to *enter into Gilgal,* Amos v. 5. And for the same reason they must *not go up to Bethel,* here called the *house of vanity,* for so *Bethaven* signifies, not the *house of God,* as *Bethel* signifies. Note, Those that would be kept from sin, and not fall into the devil's hands, must studiously avoid the occasions of sin and not come upon the devil's ground. (2.) That they might not be guilty of idolatry they must take heed of profaneness, and *not swear, The Lord liveth.* They are commanded to swear, *The Lord liveth in truth and righteousness* (Jer. iv. 2) ; and therefore that which is here forbidden is swearing so in untruth and unrighteousness, swearing rashly and lightly, or falsely and with deceit, or swearing by the Lord and the idol, Zeph. i. 5. Note, Those that would be steady in their adherence to God must possess themselves with an awe and reverence of God, and always speak of him with solemnity and seriousness ; for those that can make a jest of the true God will make a god of any thing.

CHAP. V.

The scope of this chapter is the same with that of the foregoing chapter, to discover the sin both of Israel and Judah, and to denounce the judgments of God against them. I. They are called to hearken to the charge, ver. 1, 8. II. They are accused of many sins, which are here aggravated. 1. Persecution, ver. 1, 2. 2. Spiritual whoredom, ver. 3, 4. 3. Pride, ver. 5. 4. Apostasy from God, ver. 7. 5. The tyranny of the princes, and the tameness of the people in submitting to it, ver. 10, 11. III. They are threatened with God's displeasure for their sins ; he knows all their wickedness (ver. 3) and makes known his wrath against them for it, ver. 9. 1. They shall fall in their iniquity, ver. 5. 2. God will forsake them, ver. 6. 3. Their portions shall be devoured, ver. 7. 4. God will rebuke them, and pour out his wrath upon them, ver. 9, 10. 5. They shall be oppressed, ver. 11. 6. God will be as a moth to them in secret judgments (ver. 12) and as a lion in public judgments, ver. 14. IV. They are blamed for the wrong course they took under their afflictions, ver. 13. V. It is intimated that they shall at length take a right course, ver. 15. The more generally these things are expressed of so much the more general use they are for our learning, and particularly for our admonition.

HEAR ye this, O priests; and hearken, ye house of Israel ; and give ye ear, O house of the king ; for judgment *is* toward you, because ye have been a snare on Mizpah, and a net spread upon Tabor. 2 And the revolters are profound to make slaughter, though I *have been* a rebuker of them all. 3 I know Ephraim, and Israel is not hid from me : for now, O Ephraim, thou committest whoredom, *and* Israel is defiled. 4 They will not frame their doings to turn unto their God : for the spirit of whoredoms *is* in the midst of them, and they have not known the LORD. 5 And the pride of Israel doth testify to his face : therefore shall Israel and Ephraim fall in their iniquity ; Judah also shall fall with them. 6 They shall go with their flocks and with their herds to seek the LORD ; but they shall not find *him ;* he hath withdrawn himself from them. 7 They have dealt treacherously against the LORD : for they have begotten strange children : now shall a month devour them with their portions.

Here, I. All orders and degrees of men are cited to appear and answer to such things as shall be laid to their charge (v. 1) : *Hear you this, O priests !* whether *in holy orders*

1146

(as those in Judah, and perhaps many in Israel too, for in the ten tribes there were divers cities of priests and Levites, who, it is probable, staid in their own lot after the revolt of the ten tribes and did so much of their office as might be done at a distance from the temple) or *pretending holy orders,* as the priests of the calves, who, some think, are included here. " Hearken, *you house of Israel,* the common people, and *give ear, O house of the king !*" let them all take notice, for they have all contributed to the national guilt, and they shall all share in the national judgments. Note, If neither the sanctity of the priesthood nor the dignity of the royal family will prevail to keep out sin, it cannot be expected that they should avail to keep out wrath. If the priests, and the house of the king, though they bear such noble characters, sin like others, their noble characters will not excuse them, but they must smart like others. Nor shall it be any plea for *the house of Israel* that they were misled by their priests and princes, but they shall receive their doom with them, and neither their meanness nor their multitude shall be their exemption.

II. Witness is produced against them, one instead of a thousand ; it is God's omniscience (v. 3) : *I know Ephraim, and Israel is not hidden from me.* They have *not known the Lord* (v. 4), but the Lord has known them, knows their true character however disguised, knows their secret wickedness however concealed. Note, Men's rejecting the knowledge of God will not secure them from his knowledge of them ; and when he contends with them he will prove their sins upon them by his own knowledge, so that it will be in vain to plead *Not guilty.*

III. Very bad things are laid to their charge. 1. They had been very ingenious and very industrious to draw people either into sin or into trouble : You have been *a snare on Mizpah, and a net spread upon Tabor* (v. 1), that is, such snares and nets as the huntsmen used to lay upon those mountains in pursuit of their game. When the worship of the calves was set up in Israel the patrons of that idolatry, and sticklers for it, contrived by all possible arts and wiles to draw men into it and reconcile those to it that at first had a dread of it. Note, Those that allure and entice men to sin, however they may pretend friendship and good-will, are to be looked upon as *snares and nets* to them, and *their hands as bands,* Eccl. vii. 26. But to those whom they could not seduce into sin they were as a net and a snare to bring them into trouble. Some think it was their practice to set spies in the road, and particularly upon the mountains of Mizpah and Tabor, at the times of the solemn feasts at Jerusalem, to watch if any of their people who were piously affected went thither, and to inform against them, that they might be prosecuted for it, thus doing the devil's work, who disquiets those whom he cannot debauch. 2. They had been both very crafty and very cruel in carrying on their designs (*v.* 2): *The revolters are profound to make slaughter.* Note, Those who have themselves apostatized from the truths of God are often the most subtle and barbarous persecutors of those who still adhere to them. Nothing will serve them but to *make slaughter* (it is the blood of the saints that they thirst after) : and with the serpent's sting they have his head ; they are *profound* to do it. O the depth of *the depths of Satan,* of the wickedness of his agents, of those that have *deeply revolted!* Isa. xxxi. 6. Now that which aggravated this was the many reproofs and warnings that had been given them : *Though I have been a rebuker of them all.* The prophet had been so, a reprover by office. He had many a time told them of the evil of their ways and doings, had dealt plainly *with them all,* and had not spared either the priests or the house of the king. God himself had been *a rebuker of them all* by their own consciences and by his providences. Note, Sins against reproof are doubly sinful, Prov. xxix. 1. 3. They had committed *whoredom,* had defiled their own bodies with fleshly lusts, had defiled their own souls with the worship of idols, *v.* 3. This God was a witness to, though secretly committed and artfully palliated. Nay, the piercing eye of God saw *the spirit of whoredom* that was *in the midst of them,* their secret inclination and disposition to those sins, the love they had to their sins, and the dominion their sins had over them, how much they were under the power of a *spirit of whoredom,* that *root of bitterness* which bore all this gall and wormwood, that corrupt and poisoned fountain. 4. They had no disposition at all to come into acquaintance and communion with God. The *spirit of whoredoms,* having *caused them to err* from him, keeps them wandering endlessly, *v.* 4. (1.) They *have not known the Lord,* nor desire to know him, but have rather declined, nay, dreaded, the knowledge of him, for that would disturb them in their sinful ways. (2.) Therefore *they will not frame their doings to turn to their God,* by which it appeared that they did not know him aright. This intimates their obstinate persistance in their apostasy from God ; they would not *turn to God,* though he was *their God,* theirs in covenant, by whose name they had been called, and whom they were bound to *serve.* They would not return to the worship of him, from which they had turned aside. Nay, *they would not frame their doings to turn to God.* They would not *consider their ways,* nor dispose themselves into a serious temper, nor apply their minds to think of those things that would bring them to God. It is true we cannot by our own power, without the special grace of God, turn to him ; but we may by the due improvement of our own

faculties, and the common aids of his Spirit, *frame our doings* to turn to him. Those that will not do this, that *prepare not their hearts to seek the Lord* (2 Chron. xii. 14), owe it to themselves that they are not turned ; they die because they will die ; and to those that will do this further grace shall not be wanting. (5.) They were guilty of notorious arrogancy, and insolence in sin (*v.* 5): *The pride of Israel doth testify to his face,* doth witness against him that he is a rebel to God and his government. The *spirit of whoredoms* which was *in the midst of them* showed itself in the gaiety and gaudiness of their worship, as a harlot is known by her attire, Prov. vii. 10. The wantonness of her dress testifies to her face that she is not a modest woman. Or their pride in confronting the prophets God sent them and the message they brought (Jer. xliii. 2), or a haughty scornful conduct towards their brethren and those that were under them, *witnessed against* them that they were not God's people and justified God in all the humbling judgments he brought upon them. His pride testifies *in his face :* so some read it, agreeing with Isa. iii. 9, *The show of their countenance doth witness against them.* They have that *proud look* which *the Lord hates.* (6.) They departed from God to idols, and bred up their children in idolatry (*v.* 7) : *They have dealt treacherously against the Lord,* as a wife, who, in contempt of the marriage covenant, forsakes her husband, and lives in adultery with another. Thus those who are guilty of spiritual idolatry, whose god is their money, whose god is their belly, *deal treacherously against the Lord ;* they violate their engagements to him and frustrate his expectations from them. Note, Wilful sinners are treacherous dealers. *They have begotten strange children,* that is, their children which they have begotten are estranged from God, and trained up in a false way of worship ; they are a spurious brood, as *children of fornication* (John viii. 41), whom God will disown. Note, Those deal treacherously with God indeed who not only turn from following him themselves but train up their children in wicked ways.

IV. Very sad things are made to be their doom. In general (*v.* 1), "*Judgment is towards you.* God is coming forth to contend with you, and to testify his displeasure against you for your sins." It is time to hearken when judgment is towards us. In particular,

1. They shall *fall in their iniquity.* This follows upon their *pride testifying to their face* (*v.* 5) *Therefore shall Israel and Ephraim fall in their iniquity.* Note, Pride will have a fall ; it is the certain presage and forerunner of it. Those that exalt themselves shall be abased. The face in which pride testifies shall be filled with confusion. They shall not only fall, but fall in their iniquity, the saddest fall of any. Their pride kept them from repenting of their iniquity,

and therefore they shall fall in it. Note, Those that are not humbled for their sins are likely to perish for ever in their sins. It is added, *Judah also shall fall with them* in her iniquity. As the ten tribes were carried captive into Assyria, for their idolatry, so the two tribes, in process of time, were carried into Babylon for following their bad example; but the former fell and were utterly cast down, the latter fell and were raised up again. Judah had the temple and priesthood, and yet these shall not secure them, but, if they sin with Israel and Ephraim, with them they shall fall.

2. They shall fall short of God's favour when they profess to seek it (v. 6): *They shall go with their flocks and with their herds to seek the Lord,* but in vain ; *they shall not find him.* This seems to be spoken principally of Judah, when they fell into their iniquity, and when they fell in their iniquity. (1.) When they fell into their iniquity they *sought the Lord;* but they did not *seek him only,* and therefore he was not *found of them.* When they worshipped strange gods, yet they kept up the show and shadow of the worship of the true God; they went as usual, at the solemn feasts, *with their flocks and herds* to *seek the Lord;* but their hearts were not *upright with him,* because they were not *entire for him,* and therefore he would not accept them ; for *then* only shall we find him when we *seek him with our whole heart,* not divided between God and Baal, Ezek. xiv. 3. (2.) When they fell in their iniquity, or found themselves falling by it, they *sought the Lord;* but they did not seek him *early,* and therefore he will not be found of them. They shall see ruin coming upon them, and shall then, in their distress, flee to God, and think to make him their friend with burnt-offerings and sacrifices; but it will be too late then to turn away his wrath when *the decree has gone forth.* Even Josiah's reformation did not prevail to *turn away the wrath of God,* 2 Kings xxiii. 25, 26. Those that go *with their flocks and their herds* only to seek the Lord, and not with their hearts and souls, cannot expect to find him, for his favour is not to be purchased with *thousands of rams.* Nor shall those speed who do not seek the Lord *while he may be found,* for there is a time when he will not be found. They shall not find him, for he has withdrawn himself; he will not be enquired of by them, but will turn a deaf ear to their prayers and have no regard to their sacrifices. See how much it is our concern to seek God early, now while the accepted time is, and the day of salvation.

3. They and their portions shall all be swallowed up. They have *dealt treacherously against the Lord,* and have thought to strengthen themselves in it by their alliances with strange children ; but *now shall a month devour them with their portions,* that is, their estates and inheritances all those things

1148

which they have taken, and taken up with, as their portion ; or by their *portions* is meant their idols, whom they chose for their portion instead of God. Note, Those that make an idol of the world, by taking it for their portion, will themselves perish with it. A *month* shall *devour* them, or eat them up— a certain time prefixed, and a short time. When God's judgments begin with them they shall soon make an end ; one month will do their business. How much may a body be weakened by one month's sickness, or a kingdom wasted by one month's war! *Three shepherds* (says God) *I cut off in one month,* Zech. xi. 8. Note, The judgments of God sometimes make quick work with a sinful people. A month devours more, and more portions, than many years can repair.

8 Blow ye the cornet in Gibeah, *and* the trumpet in Ramah : cry aloud *at* Beth-aven, after thee, O Benjamin. 9 Ephraim shall be desolate in the day of rebuke : among the tribes of Israel have I made known that which shall surely be. 10 The princes of Judah were like them that remove the bound : *therefore* I will pour out my wrath upon them like water. 11 Ephraim *is* oppressed *and* broken in judgment, because he willingly walked after the commandment. 12 Therefore *will* I *be* unto Ephraim as a moth, and to the house of Judah as rottenness. 13 When Ephraim saw his sickness, and Judah *saw* his wound, then went Ephraim to the Assyrian, and sent to king Jareb : yet could he not heal you, nor cure you of your wound. 14 For I *will be* unto Ephraim as a lion, and as a young lion to the house of Judah : I, *even* I, will tear and go away ; I will take away, and none shall rescue *him.* 15 I will go *and* return to my place, till they acknowledge their offence, and seek my face : in their affliction they will seek me early.

Here is, I. A loud alarm sounded, giving notice of judgments coming (v. 8): *Blow you the cornet in Gibeah* and *in Ramah,* two cities near together in the confines of the two kingdoms of Judah and Israel, Gibeah a frontier-town of the kingdom of Judah, Ramah of Israel; so that the warning is hereby sent into both kingdoms. " *Cry aloud at Beth-aven,* or Bethel, which place seems to be already seized upon by the enemy, and therefore the trumpet is not sounded there, but you hear the outcries of those that shout for mastery, mixed with theirs that are overcome." Let them *cry aloud, " After thee, O Benjamin !* comes the enemy. The tribe of Ephraim is already vanquished, and the enemy will be upon thy back, O Benjamin ! in a little time ; thy turn comes next. The cup of trembling shall go round." The prophet had described God's controversy with them as a trial at law (*ch.* iv. 1) ; here he describes it as a trial by battle ; and here also *when he judges he will overcome.* Let all therefore prepare to meet their God. He had before spoken of the judgments as certain ; here he speaks of them as near ; and, when they are apprehended as just at the door, they are very startling and awakening. The blowing of this cornet is explained, *v.* 9. *Among the tribes of Israel have I made known that which shall surely be,* that which is *true* or *certain,* so the word is. Note, The destruction of impenitent sinners is a thing which shall surely be ; it is not mere talk, to frighten them, but it is an irrevocable sentence. And it is a mercy to us that it is *made known* to us, that we have timely warning given us of it, that we may *flee from the wrath to come.* It is the privilege of the tribes of Israel that, as they are told their duty, so they are told their danger, by the oracles of God committed to them.

II. The ground of God's controversy with them. 1. He has a quarrel with *the princes of Judah,* because they were daring leaders in sin, *v.* 10. They are *like those that remove the bound,* or the ancient land-marks. God has given them his law, to be a fence about his own property ; but they have sacrilegiously broken through it, and set it aside ; they have encroached even upon God's rights, have trampled upon the distinctions between good and evil, and the most sacred obligations of reason and equity, thinking, because they were princes, that they might do any thing, *Quicquid libet, licet—Their will was a law.* Or it may be understood of their invading the liberty and property of the subject for the advancing of the prerogative, which was like removing the ancient landmarks. Some have observed that the princes of Judah were more absolute, and assumed a more arbitrary power, than the princes of Israel did ; now, for this, God has a controversy with them : *I will pour out my wrath upon them like water,* in great abundance, like the waters of the flood, which were poured upon the *giants* of the *old world,* for the violence which the earth was filled with through them, Gen. vi. 13. Note, There are *bounds* which even princes themselves must not remove, bounds both of religion and justice, which they are limited by, and, if they break through them, they must know that there is a God above them that will call them to account for it. 2. He has a quarrel with the *people of Ephraim,* because they were sneaking followers in sin (*v.* 11) : *He willingly walked after the commandment,* that is, the commandment of Jeroboam and the

succeeding kings of Israel, who obliged all their subjects by a law to worship the calves at Dan and Bethel, and never to go up to Jerusalem to worship. This was *the commandment ;* it was the law of the land, and backed with reasons of state ; and the people not only walked after it in a blind implicit obedience to authority, but they willingly walked after it, from a secret antipathy they had to the worship of God and a strong bias to the worship of idols. Note, An easy compliance with the commandments of men that thwart the commandments of God ripens a people for ruin as much as any thing. And the punishment of the sequacious disobedience (if I may so call it) answers to the sin ; for it is for this that *Ephraim is oppressed and broken in judgment,* has all his civil rights and liberties broken in upon and trodden down ; and, (1.) It is just with God that it should be so, that those who betray God's property should lose their own, that those who subject their consciences to an infallible judge, and an arbitrary power, should have enough of both. (2.) There is a natural tendency in the thing itself towards it. *Those that willingly walk after the commandment,* even when it walks contrary to the command of God, will find the commandment an encroaching thing, and that the more power is given it the more it will claim. Note, Nothing gives greater advantage to a mastiff-like tyranny, that is fierce and furious, than a spaniel-like submission, that is fawning and flattering. Thus is *Ephraim oppressed and broken in judgment,* that is, he is wronged under a face and colour of right. Note, It is a sad and sore judgment upon any people to be oppressed under pretence of having justice done them. This explains the threatening *v.* 9, *Ephraim shall be desolate in the day of rebuke.* Note, Daring sinners must expect that a day of rebuke will come, and such a day of rebuke as will make them desolate, will deprive them of the comfort of all they have and all they hope for.

III. The different methods that God would take both with Judah and Ephraim, sometimes one method and sometimes the other, and sometimes both together, or rather by which, first the one and then the other, he would advance towards their complete ruin.

1. He would begin with less judgments, which should sometimes work silently and insensibly (*v.* 12) : *I will be* (that is, my providences shall be) *unto Ephraim as a moth ;* nay (as it might better be supplied), they *are unto Ephraim as a moth,* for it is such *a sickness* as Ephraim now sees, *v.* 13. Note, The judgments of God are sometimes to a sinful people *as a moth,* and *as rottenness,* or as *a worm.* The former signifies the little animals that breed in clothes, the latter those that breed in wood ; as these consume the clothes and the wood, so shall the judgments of God consume them. (1.) Silently, so as not to make any noise in the world,

nay, so as they themselves shall not be sensible of it; they shall think themselves safe and thriving, but, when they come to look more narrowly into their state, shall find themselves wasting and decaying. (2.) Slowly, and with long delays and intervals, that he may give them *space to repent.* Many a nation, as well as many a person, in the prime of its time, dies of a consumption. (3.) Gradually. God comes upon sinners with less judgments, so to prevent greater, if they will be wise and take warning; he comes upon them step by step, to show he is not willing that they should perish. (4.) The moth breeds in the clothes, and the worm or rottenness in the wood; thus sinners are consumed by a fire of their own kindling

2. When it appeared that those had not done their work he would come upon them with greater (*v.* 14) : *I will be unto Ephraim as a lion, and to the house of Judah as a young lion,* though Judah is himself, in Jacob's blessing, a *lion's whelp.* Lest any should think his power weakened, because he was said to be *as a moth* to them, he says that he will now be as *a lion* to them, not only to frighten them with his roaring, but to pull them to pieces. Note, If less judgments prevail not to do their work, it may be expected that God will send greater. *Christ* is sometimes a lion of the tribe of Judah, here he is a lion against that tribe. See what God will do to a people that are secure in sin : *Even I will tear.* He seems to glory in it, as his prerogative, to be able to *destroy,* as the *alone lawgiver,* Jam. iv. 12. " *I, even I,* will take the work into my own hands; I *say it* that will *do it.*" There is a more immediate work of God in some judgments than in others. *I will tear, and go away.* He will go away, (1.) As not fearing them; he will go away in state, and with a majestic face, as the lion from his prey. (2.) As not helping them. If God tear by afflicting providences, and yet by his graces and comforts stays with us, it is well enough; but our condition is sad indeed if he *tear* and *go away,* if, when he deprives us of our creature comforts, he does himself depart from us. When he goes away he will take away all that is valuable and dear, for, when God goes, all good goes along with him. He will take away, *and none shall rescue him,* as the prey cannot be rescued from the lion, Mic. v. 8. Note, None can be delivered out of the hands of God's justice but those that are delivered into the hands of his grace. It is in vain for a man to strive with his Maker.

IV. The different effects of those different methods. 1. When God contended with them by less judgments they neglected him, and sought to creatures for relief, but sought in vain, *v.* 13. When God was to them *as a moth,* and as *rottenness,* they perceived *their sickness* and *their wound;* after a while they found themselves going down the hill, and that they

were behind-hand in their affairs, their estate was sensibly decaying, and then they sent *to the Assyrian,* to come in to their assistance, made their court to king Jareb, which, some think, was one of the names of Pul, or Tiglathpileser, kings of Assyria, to whom both Israel and Judah applied for relief in their distress, hoping by an alliance with them to repair and re-establish their declining interests. Note, Carnal hearts, in time of trouble, see their sickness and see their wound, but do not see the sin that is the cause of it, nor will be brought to acknowledge that, no, nor to acknowledge the hand of God, his *mighty hand,* much less his righteous hand, in their trouble; and therefore, instead of going the next way to the Creator, who could relieve them, they take a great deal of pains to go about to creatures, who can do them no service. Those who repent not that they have offended God by their sins are loth to be beholden to him in their afflictions, but would rather seek relief any where than with him. And what is the consequence ? *Yet could he not heal you, nor cure you of your wound.* Note, Those who neglect God, and seek to creatures for help, will certainly be disappointed; those who depend upon them for support will find them, not *foundations,* but *broken reeds;* those who depend upon them for supply will find them, not *fountains,* but *broken cisterns;* those who depend upon them for comfort and a cure will find them *miserable comforters,* and *physicians of no value.* The kings of Assyria, whom Judah and Israel sought unto, *distressed them* and *helped them not,* 2 Chron. xxviii. 16, 28. Some make king *Jareb* to signify the *great, potent,* or *magnificent king,* for they built much upon his power; others *the king that will plead,* or *should plead,* for they built much upon his wisdom and eloquence, and in his interesting himself in their affairs. They had sent him *a present* (*ch.* x. 6), a good fee, and, having so retained him of counsel for them, they doubted not of his fidelity to them; but he deceived them, as an arm of flesh does those that trust in it, Jer. xvii. 5, 6.

2. When, to convince them of their folly, God brought greater judgments upon them, then they would at length be forced to apply to him, *v.* 15. When he has *torn* as a *lion,* (1.) He will leave them : *I will go and return to my place,* to heaven, or to the mercy-seat, the throne of grace, which is his glory. When God punishes sinners he *comes out of his place* (Isa. xxvi. 21); but, when he designs them favour, he *returns to his place,* where he *waits to be gracious,* upon their submission. Or he will *return to his place* when he has corrected them, as not regarding them, hiding his face from them, and not taking notice of their troubles or prayers; and this for their further humiliation, till they are qualified in some measure for the returns of his favour. (2.) He will

at length work upon them, and bring them home to himself, by their afflictions, which is the thing he waits for; and then he will no longer withdraw from them. Two things are here mentioned as instances of their return :—[1.] Their penitent confession of sin : *Till they acknowledge their offence ;* marg. *Till they be guilty,* that is, till they be sensible of their guilt, and be brought to own it, and humble themselves before God for it. Note, When men begin to complain more of their sins than of their afflictions then there begins to be some hope of them ; and this is that which God requires of us, when we are under his correcting hand, that we own ourselves in a fault and justly corrected. [2.] Their humble petition for the favour of God : Till they *seek my face,* which, it may be expected, they will do when they are brought to the last extremity, and they have tried other helpers in vain. *In their affliction they will seek me early,* that is, diligently and earnestly, and with great importunity ; and if they seek him thus, and be sincere in it, though it might be called seeking him late, because it was long ere they were brought to it, yet it is not too late, nay, he is pleased to call it seeking him early, so willing is he to make the best of true penitents in their return to him. Note, When we are under the convictions of sin, and the corrections of the rod, our business is to seek God's face ; we must desire the knowledge of him, and an acquaintance with him, that he may manifest himself to us, and for us, in token of his being at peace with us. And it may reasonably be expected that affliction will bring those to God that had long gone astray from him, and kept at a distance. *Therefore* God for a time turns away from us, that he may turn us to himself, and then return to us. *Is any among you afflicted? Let him pray.*

CHAP. VI.

The closing words of the foregoing chapter gave us some hopes that God and his Israel, notwithstanding their sins and his wrath, might yet be happily brought together again, that they would seek him and he would be found of them ; now this chapter carries that matter further, and some join the beginning of this chapter with the end of that, " They will seek me early," saying, " Come and let us return." But God doth again complain of the wickedness of this people ; for, though some did repent and reform, the greater part continued obstinate. Observe, I. Their resolution to return to God, and the comforts wherewith they encourage themselves in their return, ver. 1—3. II. The instability of many of them in their professions and promises of repentance, and the severe course which God therefore took with them, ver. 4, 5. III. The covenant God made with them, and his expectations from them (ver. 6); their violation of that covenant and frustrating those expectations, ver. 7—11.

COME, and let us return unto the LORD : for he hath torn, and he will heal us ; he hath smitten, and he will bind us up. 2 After two days will he revive us : in the third day he will raise us up, and we shall live in his sight. 3 Then shall we know, *if* we follow on to know the LORD : his going forth is prepared as the

morning ; and he shall come unto us as the rain, as the latter *and* former rain unto the earth.

These may be taken either as the words of the prophet to the people, calling them to repentance, or as the words of the people to one another, exciting and encouraging one another to *seek the Lord,* and to humble themselves before him, in hopes of finding mercy with him. God had said, *In their affliction they will seek me ;* now the prophet, and the good people his friends, would strike while the iron was hot, and set in with the convictions their neighbours seemed to be under. Note, Those who are disposed to turn to God themselves should do all they can to excite, and engage, and encourage others to return to him. Observe,

I. What it is they engage to do : "*Come, and let us return to the Lord, v.* 1. Let us go no more to the Assyrian, nor send to king Jareb ; we have had enough of that. But let us *return to the Lord,* return to the worship of him from our idolatries, and to our hope in him from all our confidences in the creature." Note, It is the great concern of those who have revolted from God to return to him. And those who have gone from him by consent, and in a body, drawing one another to sin, should by consent, and in a body, return to him, which will be for his glory and their mutual edification.

II. What inducements and encouragements to do this they fasten upon, to stir up one another with.

1. The experience they had had of his displeasure : " Let us return to him, for *he has torn, he has smitten.* We have been torn, and it was he that tore us ; we have been smitten, and it was he that smote us. *Therefore* let us return to him, because it is for our revolts from him that he has torn and smitten us in anger, and we cannot expect that he should be reconciled to us till we return to him ; and for this end he has afflicted us thus, that we might be wrought upon to return to him. His hand will be stretched out still against us if the people *turn not to him that smites them,*" Isa. ix. 12, 13. Note, The consideration of the judgments of God upon us and our land, especially when they are tearing judgments, should awaken us to return to God by repentance, and prayer, and reformation.

2. The expectation they had of his favour : " He that has torn will *heal us,* he that has smitten will *bind us up,*" as the skilful surgeon with a tender hand binds up the broken bone or bleeding wound. Note, The same providence of God that afflicts his people relieves them, and the same Spirit of God that convinces the saints comforts them ; that which is first *a Spirit of bondage* is afterwards *a Spirit of adoption.* This is an acknowledgment of the power of God (he can heal though we be ever so ill torn), and

of his mercy (he will do it); nay, *therefore* he has torn that he may heal. Some think this points particularly to the return of the Jews out of Babylon, when they sought the Lord, and joined themselves to him, in the prospect of his gracious return to them in a way of mercy. Note, It will be of great use to us, both for our support under our afflictions and for our encouragement in our repentance, to keep up good thoughts of God and of his purposes and designs concerning us. Now this favour of God which they are here in expectation of is described in several instances:—

(1.) They promise themselves that their deliverance out of their troubles should be to them as *life from the dead* (*v.* 2): " *After two days he will revive us* (that is, in a short time, in a day or two), *and the third day,* when it is expected that the dead body should putrefy and corrupt, and be buried *out of our sight,* then will he *raise us up,* and *we shall live in his sight,* we shall see his face with comfort and it shall be reviving to us. Though he *forsake* for *a small moment,* he will *gather* with *everlasting kindness.*" Note, The people of God may not only be torn and smitten, but left for dead, and may lie so a great while; but they shall not always lie so, nor shall they long lie so; God will in a little time revive them; and the assurance given them of this should engage them to return and adhere to him. But this seems to have a further reference to the resurrection of Jesus Christ; and the time limited is expressed by *two days* and the *third day,* that it may be a type and figure of Christ's rising the *third day,* which he is said to do *according to the scriptures,* according to this scripture; for all the prophets testified of *the sufferings of Christ and the glory that should follow.* Let us see and admire the wisdom and goodness of God, in ordering the prophet's words so that when he foretold the deliverance of the church out of her troubles he should at the same time point out our salvation by Christ, which other salvations were both figures and fruits of; and, though they might not be aware of this mystery in the words, yet now that they are fulfilled in the letter of them in the resurrection of Christ it is a confirmation to our faith that *this is he that should come,* and we are to *look for no other.* And it is every way suitable that a prophecy of Christ's rising should be thus expressed, " He will raise *us* up, and *we* shall live," for Christ rose as the first-fruits, and we revive with him, we live through him; he rose for our justification, and all believers are said to be *risen with Christ.* See Isa. xxvi. 19. And it would serve for a comfort to the church then, and an assurance that God would raise them out of their low estate, for in his fulness of time he would raise his Son from the grave, who would be the life and glory of his people Israel. Note, A regard by faith to a rising

1152

Christ is a great support to a suffering Christian, and gives abundant encouragement to a repenting returning sinner; for he has said, *Because I live, you shall live also.*

(2.) That then they shall improve in the knowledge of God (*v.* 3): *Then shall we know, if we follow on to know, the Lord.* *Then,* when God returns in mercy to his people and designs favour for them, he will, as a pledge and fruit of his favour, give them more of the knowledge of himself; the earth shall be *full of that knowledge,* Isa. xi. 9. *Knowledge shall be increased,* Dan. xii. 4. *All shall know God,* Jer. xxxi. 34. *We shall know, we shall follow to know, the Lord* (so the words are); and it may be taken as the fruit of Christ's resurrection, and the life we live in God's sight by him, that we shall have not only greater means of knowledge, but grace to improve in knowledge by those means. Note, When God designs mercy for a people he gives them *a heart to know him,* Jer. xxiv. 7. Those that have *risen with Christ* have the spirit of wisdom and revelation given them. And if we understand our living in his sight, as the Chaldee paraphrast does, of the day of the resurrection of the dead, it fitly follows, *We shall know, we shall follow to know, the Lord;* for in that day we shall see him as he is, and our knowledge of him shall be perfected, and yet be eternally increasing. Or, taking it as we read it, *If we follow on to know,* we have here, [1.] A precious blessing promised: *Then shall we know,* shall *know the Lord,* then when we *return to God;* those that come to God shall be brought into an acquaintance with him. When we are designed to *live in his sight,* then he gives us to know him; for this is *life eternal to know God,* John xvii. 3. [2.] The way and means of obtaining this blessing. We must *follow on to know* him. We must value and esteem the knowledge of God as the best knowledge, we must *cry after it,* and *dig for it* (Prov. ii. 3, 4), must *seek and intermeddle with all wisdom* (Prov. xviii. 1), and must proceed in our enquiries after this knowledge and our endeavours to improve in it. And, if we do the prescribed duty, we have reason to expect the promised mercy, that we shall know more and more of God, and be at last perfect in this knowledge.

(3.) That then they shall abound in divine consolations: *His going forth is prepared as the morning,* that is, the returns of his favour, which he had withdrawn from us when he went and *returned to his place.* His outgoings again are prepared and secured to us as firmly as the return of the morning after a dark night, and we expect it, as those do that *wait for the morning* after a long night, and are sure that it will come at the time appointed and will not fail; and the light of his countenance will be both welcome to us and growing upon us, unto the perfect day, as the light of the morning is. *He shall come to us,* and be welcome to us, *as the rain, as the latter and former rain unto the earth,* which refreshes it and makes it fruitful. Now this looks further than their deliverance out of captivity, and, no doubt, was to have its full accomplishment in Christ, and the grace of the gospel. The Old-Testament saints *followed on to know him,* earnestly looked for redemption in Jerusalem; and at length the out-goings of divine grace in him, in his going forth to visit this world, were [1.] As the morning to this earth when it is dark; for he went forth as the *sun of righteousness,* and in him *the day-spring from on high visited us. His going forth was prepared as the morning,* for he came in the fulness of time; John Baptist was his forerunner, nay, he was himself the *bright and morning star.* [2.] As the rain to this earth when it is *dry. He shall come down as the rain upon the mown grass,* Ps. lxxii. 6. In him showers of blessings descend upon this world, which *give seed to the sower and bread to the eater,* Isa. lv. 10. And the favour of God in Christ is what is said of the king's favour, *like the cloud of the latter rain,* Prov. xvi. 15. The grace of God in Christ is both the *latter and the former rain,* for by it the good work of our fruit-bearing is both begun and carried on.

4 O Ephraim, what shall I do unto thee? O Judah, what shall I do unto thee? for your goodness *is* as a morning cloud, and as the early dew it goeth away. 5 Therefore have I hewed *them* by the prophets; I have slain them by the words of my mouth: and thy judgments *are as* the light *that* goeth forth. 6 For I desired mercy, and not sacrifice; and the knowledge of God more than burnt-offerings. 7 But they like men have transgressed the covenant: there have they dealt treacherously against me. 8 Gilead *is* a city of them that work iniquity, *and is* polluted with blood. 9 And as troops of robbers wait for a man, *so* the company of priests murder in the way by consent: for they commit lewdness. 10 I have seen a horrible thing in the house of Israel: there *is* the whoredom of Ephraim, Israel is defiled. 11 Also, O Judah, he hath set a harvest for thee, when I returned the captivity of my people.

Two things, two evil things, both Judah and Ephraim are here charged with, and justly accused of:—

I. That they were not firm to their own convictions, but were unsteady, *unstable as*

water, v. 4, 5. *O Ephraim! what shall I do unto thee? O Judah! what shall I do unto thee?* This is a strange expression. Can Infinite Wisdom be at a loss what to do? Can it be nonplussed, or put upon taking new measures? By no means; but God speaks after the manner of men, to show how absurd and unreasonable they were, and how just his proceedings against them were. Let them not complain of him as harsh and severe in tearing them, and smiting them, as he has done; for what else should he do? What other course could he take with them? God had tried various methods with them *(What could have been done more to his vineyard than he had done?* Isa. v. 4), and very loth he was to let things go to extremity; he reasons with himself (as *ch.* xi. 9), *How shall I give thee up, Ephraim?* God would have done them good, but they were not qualified for it: " *What shall I do unto thee?* What else can I do but cast thee off, when I cannot in honour save thee?" Note, God never destroys sinners till he sees there is no other way with them. See here, 1. What their conduct was towards God: *Their goodness,* or *kindness,* was *as the morning cloud.* Some understand it of their kindness to themselves and their own souls, in their repentance; it is indeed mercy to ourselves to repent of our sins, but they soon retracted that kindness to themselves, undid it again, and wronged their own souls as much as ever. But it is rather to be taken for their piety and religion; what good appeared in them sometimes, it soon vanished and disappeared again, *as the morning cloud and the early dew.* Such was the goodness of Israel in Jehu's time, and of Judah in Hezekiah's and Josiah's time; it was soon gone. In time of drought the *morning-cloud* promises rain, and the *early dew* is some present refreshment to the earth; but the cloud is dispersed (and hypocrites are compared to *clouds without water,* Jude 12) and the dew does not soak into the ground, but is drawn back again into the air, and the earth is parched still. What shall he do with them? Shall he accept their goodness? No, for it *passes away;* and *factum non dicitur quod non perseverat—that which does not continue can scarcely be said to be done.* Note, That goodness will never be either pleasing to God or profitable to ourselves which is as the morning cloud and the early dew. When men promise fair and do not perform, when they begin well in religion and do not hold on, when they leave their first love and their first works, or, though they do not quite cast off religion, are yet unsteady, uneven, and inconstant in it, then is their *goodness as the morning cloud and the early dew.* 2. What course God had taken with them (v. 5): " *Therefore,* because they were so rough and ill-shapen, *I have hewn them by the prophets,* as timber or stone is hewn for use; *I have slain them by the words of my mouth.*" What the prophets did was done by the word of God in their mouths, which never returned void. By it they thought themselves slain, were ready to say that the prophets killed them, or cut them to the heart when they dealt faithfully with them. (1.) The prophets hewed them by convictions of sin, endeavouring to cut off their transgressions from them. They were uneven in religion (*v.* 4), therefore God hewed them. The hearts of sinners are not only as stone, but as rough stone, which requires a great deal of pains to bring it into shape, or as knotty timber, that is not squared without a great deal of difficulty; ministers' work is to hew them, and God by the minister hews them, *for with the froward will he show himself froward.* And there are those whom ministers must rebuke sharply; every word should cut, and though the chips fly in the face of the workman, though the reproved fly in the face of the reprover and reckon him an enemy because he tells the truth, yet he goes on with his work (2.) They slew them by the denunciations of wrath, foretelling that they should be slain, as Ezekiel is said to destroy the city when he prophesied of the destruction of it, Ezek. xliii. 3. And God accomplished that which was foretold: "*I have slain them* by my judgments, according to the words of my mouth." Note, The word of God will be the death either of the sin or of the sinner, a savour either of life unto life or of death unto death. Some read it, "*I have hewn the prophets, and slain them by the words of my mouth,* that is, I have employed them in laborious service for the people's good, which has wasted their strength; they have spent themselves, and hewn away all their spirits, in their work, and in hazardous service, which has cost many of them their lives." Note, Ministers are the tools which God makes use of in working upon people ; and, though with many they labour in vain, yet God will reckon for the wearing out of his tools. (3.) God was hereby justified in the severest proceedings against them afterwards. His prophets had taken a great deal of pains with them, had admonished them of their sin and warned them of their danger, but the means used had not the desired effect ; some good impressions perhaps were made for the present, but they wore off, and passed away as the morning cloud, and now they cannot charge God with severity if he bring upon them the miseries threatened. The prophet turns to him and acknowledges, *Thy judgments are as the light that goes forth,* evidently just and righteous. Note, Though sinners be not reclaimed by the pains that ministers take with them, yet thereby God will be *justified when he speaks and clear when he judges.* See Matt. xi. 17—19.

II. That they were not faithful to God's covenant with them, *v.* 6, 7. Here observe,

1. What the covenant was that God made with them, and upon what terms they should obtain his favour and be accepted of him (*v.* 6) : *I desired mercy and not sacrifice* (that is, rather than sacrifice), and insisted upon *the knowledge of God more than* upon *burnt-offerings. Mercy* here is the same word which in *v.* 4 is rendered *goodness—chesed—piety, sanctity ;* it is put for all practical religion ; it is the same with *charity* in the New Testament, the reigning love of God and our neighbour, and this accompanied with and flowing from the *knowledge of God,* as he has revealed himself in his word, a firm belief that he is, and is the *rewarder of those that diligently seek him,* a good affection to divine things guided by a good judgment, which cannot but produce a very good conversation; this is that which God by his covenant requires, and *not sacrifice and offering.* This is fully explained, Jer. vii. 22, 23. *I spoke not to your fathers concerning burnt-offerings* (that was the smallest of the matters I spoke to them of, and on which the least stress was laid), but *this I said, Obey my voice,* Mic. vi. 6—8. To love God and our neighbour is *better than all burnt offering and sacrifice,* Mark xii. 33 ; Ps. li. 16, 17. Not but that sacrifice and offering were required, and to be paid, and had their use, and, when they were accompanied with mercy and the knowledge of God, were acceptable to him, but, without them, God regarded them not, he despised them, Isa. i. 10, 11. Perhaps this is mentioned here to show a difference between the God whom they deserted and the gods whom they went over to. The true God aimed at nothing but that they should be good men, and live good lives for their own good, and the ceremony of honouring him with sacrifices was one of the smallest matters of his law ; whereas the false gods required that only ; let their priests and altars be regaled with sacrifices and offerings, and the people might live as they listed. What fools were those then that left a God who aimed at giving his worshippers a new nature, for gods who aimed at nothing but making themselves a new name ! It is mentioned likewise to show that God's controversy with them was not for the omission of sacrifices (*I will not reprove thee for them,* Ps. l. 8), but because there was no *justice, nor mercy,* nor *knowledge of God,* among them (*ch.* iv. 1), and to teach us all that the *power of godliness* is the main thing God looks at and requires, and without it the *form of godliness* is of no avail. Serious piety in the heart and life is the *one thing needful,* and, separate from that, the performances of devotion, though ever so plausible, ever so costly, are of no account. Our Saviour quotes this to show that moral duties are to be preferred before rituals whenever they come in competition, and to justify himself in *eating with publicans and sinners,* because it was in mercy to the souls of men, and in healing on the

sabbath day, because it was in mercy to the bodies of men, to which the ceremony of singularity in eating and the sabbath-rest must give way, Matt. ix. 13; xii. 7.

2. How little they had regarded this covenant, though it was so well ordered in all things, though they, and not God, would be the gainers by it. See here what came of it.

(1.) In general, they broke with God, and proved unfaithful; there were *good things committed* to them to keep, the jewels of mercy and piety, and the knowledge of God, in the cabinet of sacrifice and burnt-offering, but they betrayed their trust, kept the cabinet, but pawned the jewels for the gratification of a base lust, and this is that for which God has justly a quarrel with them (*v.* 7): *They, like men, have transgressed the covenant,* that covenant which God made with them; they have broken the conditions of it, and so forfeited the benefit of it. By casting off mercy and the knowledge of God, and other instances of disobedience, [1.] They had contracted the guilt of perjury and covenant-breaking; they were like men that transgress a covenant by which they had solemnly bound themselves, which is a thing that all the world cries out shame on; men that have done so deserve not again to be valued, or trusted, or dealt with. "*There,* in that thing, *they have dealt treacherously against me;* they have been perfidious, base, and false children, in whom is no faith, though I depended upon their being *children that would not lie.*" [2.] In this they had but acted like themselves, *like men,* who are generally false and fickle, and in whose nature (their corrupt nature) it is to deal treacherously; *all men are liars,* and they are like the rest of that degenerate race, *all gone aside,* Ps. xiv. 2, 3. They have *transgressed the covenant* like *men* (like the Gentiles that transgressed the covenant of nature), like *mean men* (the word here used is sometimes put for *men of low degree*); they have dealt deceitfully, like base men that have no sense of honour. [3.] Herein they trod in the steps of our first parents: *They, like Adam, have transgressed the covenant* (so it might very well be read); as he transgressed the covenant of innocency, so they transgressed the covenant of grace, so treacherously, so foolishly; *there* in paradise he violated his engagements to God, and there in Canaan, another paradise, they violated their engagements. And by their treacherous dealing they, like Adam, have ruined themselves and theirs. Note, Sin is so much the worse the more there is in it of the *similitude of Adam's transgression,* Rom. v. 14. [4.] Low thoughts of God and of his authority and favour were at the bottom of all this; for so some read it: *They have transgressed the covenant, as of a man,* as if it had been but the covenant of a man, that stood upon even ground with them, as if the commands of the covenant were but like those of a man like themselves, and the kindness conveyed by it no more valuable than that of a man. There is something sacred and binding in *a man's covenant* (as the apostle shows, Gal. iii. 15), but much more in the covenant of God, which yet they made small account of; and *there* in that covenant they *dealt treacherously,* promised fair, but performed nothing. Dealing treacherously with God is here called dealing treacherously against him, for it is both an affront and an opposition. Deserters are traitors, and will be so treated; the revolting heart is a rebellious heart.

(2.) Some particular instances of their treachery are here given: *There they dealt treacherously,* that is, in the places hereafter named. [1.] Look on the other side Jordan, to the country which lay most exposed to the insults of the neighbouring nations, and where therefore the people were concerned to keep themselves under the divine protection, and yet there you will find the most daring provocations of the divine Majesty, *v.* 8. Gilead, which lay in the lot of Gad and the half tribe of Manasseh, was *a city of the workers of iniquity.* Wickedness was the trade that was driven there; the country was called *Gilead,* but it was all called a *city,* because they were all as it were incorporated in one society of rebels against God. Or (as most think) Ramoth Gilead is the city here meant, one of the three cities of refuge on the other side Jordan, and a Levites' city; the inhabitants of it, though of the sacred tribe, were *workers of iniquity,* contrived it, and practised it. Note, It is bad indeed when a Levites' city is *a city of those that work iniquity,* when those that are to preach good doctrine live bad lives. Particularly it is *polluted with blood,* as if that were a sin which the wicked Levites were in a special manner guilty of. In popish countries the clergy are observed to be the most bloody persecutors. Or, as it was a *city of refuge,* by abusing the power it had to judge of murders it became *polluted with blood.* They would, for a bribe, protect those that were guilty of wilful murder, whom they ought to have put to death, and would deliver those to the avenger of blood who were guilty but of chance-medley, if they were poor and had nothing to give them; and both these ways they were *polluted with blood.* Note, Blood defiles the land where it is shed, and where no inquisition is made or no vengeance taken for it. See how the best institutions, that are ever so well designed to keep the balance even between justice and mercy, are capable of being abused and perverted to the manifest prejudice and violation of both. [2.] Look among those whose business it was to minister in holy things, and they were as bad as the worst and as vile as the vilest (*v.* 9): *The company of priests* are so, not here and there one that is the scandal of his order, but the whole order and body of them, the *priests* go all one way *by consent, with one shoulder* (as the word is), one and all; and they make one another worse, more daring, and fierce, and impudent, in sin, more crafty and more cruel. A *company of priests* will say and do that in conspiracy which none of them would dare to say or do singly. The *companies of priests* were as *troops of robbers,* as *banditti,* or gangs of highwaymen, that cut men's throats to get their money. *First,* They were cruel and blood-thirsty. They *murder* those that they have a pique against, or that stand in their way; nothing less will satisfy them. *Secondly,* They were cunning. They *laid wait* for men, that they might have a fair opportunity to compass their mischievous malicious designs; thus the company of priests laid wait for Christ to take him, saying, *Not on the feast-day.* *Thirdly,* They were concurring as one man: *They murder in the way;* in the highway, where travellers should be safe, there *they murder by consent,* aiding and abetting one another in it. See how unanimous wicked people are in doing mischief; and should not good people be so then in doing good? *They murder in the way to Shechem* (so the margin reads it, as a proper name) such as were going to Jerusalem (for that way Shechem lay) to worship. Or *in the way to Shechem* (some think) means in the same manner that their father Levi, with Simeon his brother, murdered the Shechemites (Gen. xxxiv.), by fraud and deceit; and some understand it of their destroying the souls of men by drawing them to sin. *Fourthly,* They did it with contrivance: *They commit lewdness;* the word signifies such wickedness as is committed with deliberation, and of malice prepense, as we say. The more there is of device and design in sin the worse it is. [3.] Look into the body of the people, take a view of the whole house of Israel, and they are all alike (v. 10): *I have seen a horrible thing in the house of Israel,* and, though it be ever so artfully managed, God discovers it, and will discover it to them; and who can deny that which God himself says that he has seen? *There is the whoredom of Ephraim,* both corporal and spiritual whoredom; there it is too plain to be denied. Note, The sin of sinners, especially sinners of the house of Israel, has enough in it to make them tremble, for it is a horrible thing, it is amazing, and it is threatening, enough to make them blush, for Israel is thereby defiled and rendered odious in the sight of God. [4.] Look into Judah, and you find them sharing with Israel (v. 11): *Also, O Judah! he has set a harvest for thee;* thou must be reckoned with as well as Ephraim; thou art ripe for destruction too, and the time, even the set time, of thy destruction is hastening on, when thou that hast *ploughed iniquity,* and *sown wickedness,* shalt *reap the same.* The general judgment is compared to *a harvest* (Matt. xiii. 39), so are particular judgments,

Joel iii. 13; Rev. xiv. 15. I have appointed a time to call thee to account, even *when I returned the captivity of my people,* that is, when those captives of Judah which were taken by the men of Israel were restored, in obedience to the command of God sent them by Oded the prophet, 2 Chron. xxviii. 8—15. When God spared them that time he *set them a harvest,* that is, he designed to reckon with them another time for all together. Note, Preservations from present judgments, if a good use be not made of them, are but reservations for greater judgments.

CHAP. VII.

In this chapter we have, I. A general charge drawn up against Israel for those high crimes and misdemeanors by which they had obstructed the course of God's favours to them, ver. 1, 2. II. A particular accusation, 1. Of the court—the king, princes, and judges, ver. 3–7. 2. Of the country. Ephraim is here charged with conforming to the nations (ver. 8), senselessness and stupidity under the judgments of God (ver. 9—11), ingratitude to God for his mercies (ver. 13), incorrigibleness under his judgments (ver. 14), contempt of God (ver. 15), and hypocrisy in their pretences to return to him, ver. 16. They are also threatened with a severe chastisement, which shall humble them (ver. 12), and, if that prevail not, then with an utter destruction (ver. 13), particularly their princes, ver. 16.

WHEN I would have healed Israel, then the iniquity of Ephraim was discovered, and the wickedness of Samaria: for they commit falsehood; and the thief cometh in, *and* the troop of robbers spoileth without. 2 And they consider not in their hearts *that* I remember all their wickedness: now their own doings have beset them about; they are before my face. 3 They make the king glad with their wickedness, and the princes with their lies. 4 They *are* all adulterers, as an oven heated by the baker, *who* ceaseth from raising after he hath kneaded the dough, until it be leavened. 5 In the day of our king the princes have made *him* sick with bottles of wine; he stretched out his hand with scorners. 6 For they have made ready their heart like an oven, whiles they lie in wait: their baker sleepeth all the night; in the morning it burneth as a flaming fire. 7 They are all hot as an oven, and have devoured their judges; all their kings are fallen: *there is* none among them that calleth unto me.

Some take away the last words of the foregoing chapter, and make them the beginning of this: "*When I returned,* or *would have returned, the captivity of my people,* when I was about to come towards them in ways of mercy, even *when I would have healed Israel then the iniquity of Ephraim* (the country and common people) *was discovered, and the wickedness of Samaria,* the court and the chief city." Now, in these verses, we may observe,

I. A general idea given of the present state of Israel, *v.* 1, 2. See how the case now stood with them.

1. God graciously designed to do well for them : *I would have healed Israel.* Israel were sick and wounded; their disease was dangerous and malignant, and likely to be fatal, Isa. i. 6. But God offered to be their physician, to undertake the cure, and there was balm in Gilead sufficient to recover the health of the daughter of his people; their case was bad, but it was not desperate, nay, it was hopeful, when God *would have healed Israel.* (1.) He would have reformed them, would have separated between them and their sins, would have purged out the corruptions that were among them, by his laws and prophets. (2.) He would have delivered them out of their troubles, and restored to them their peace and prosperity. Several healing attempts were made, and their declining state seemed sometimes to be in a hopeful way of recovery; but their own folly put them back again. Note, If sinful miserable souls be not healed and helped, but perish in their sin and misery, they cannot lay the blame on God, for he both could and *would have healed them;* he offered to take the ruin under his hand. And there are some special seasons when God manifests his readiness to heal a distempered church and nation, now and then a hopeful crisis, which, if carefully watched and improved, might, even when the case is very bad, turn the scale for life and health.

2. They stood in their own light and put a bar in their own door. When God *would have healed them,* when they bade fair for reformation and peace, then their *iniquity* was *discovered* and their *wickedness,* which stopped that current of God's favours, and undid all again. (1.) *Then,* when their case came to be examined and enquired into, in order to their cure, that wickedness which had been concealed and palliated was *found out;* not that it was ever hid from God, but he speaks after the manner of men; as a surgeon, when he probes a wound in order to the cure of it and finds that it touches the vitals and is incurable, goes no further in his endeavour to cure it, so, when God *came down to see* the case of Israel (as the expression is, Gen. xviii. 21), with kind intentions towards them, he found their wickedness so very flagrant, and them so hardened in it, so impudent and impenitent, that he could not in honour show them the favour he designed them. Note, Sinners are not healed because they would not be healed. Christ *would have gathered* them, and they *would not.* (2.) *Then,* when some endeavours were used to reform and reclaim them, that wickedness which had been restrained and kept

under *broke out;* and from God's steps towards the healing of them they took occasion to be so much the more provoking. When endeavours were used to reform them vice grew more impetuous, more outrageous, and swelled so much the higher, as a stream when it is dammed up. When they began to prosper they grew more proud, wanton, and secure, and so stopped the progress of their cure. Note, It is sin that turns away good things from us when they are coming towards us; and it is the folly and ruin of multitudes that, when God would do well for them, they do ill for themselves. And what was it that did them this mischief? In one word, *they commit falsehood;* they worship idols (so some), defraud one another (so others), or, rather, they dissemble with God in their professions of repentance and regard to him. They say that they are desirous to be healed by him, and, in order to that, willing to be ruled by him; but they *lie unto him with their mouth and flatter him with their tongue.*

3. A practical disbelief of God's omniscience and government was at the bottom of all their wickedness (*v.* 2) : " *They consider not in their hearts,* they never say it to their own hearts, never think of this, *that I remember all their wickedness.*" As if God could not see it, though he is all eye, or did not heed it, though his name is Jealous, or had forgotten it, though he is an eternal mind that can never be unmindful, or would not reckon for it, though he is the *Judge of heaven and earth.* This is the sinner's atheism; as good say that there is *no God* as say that he is either ignorant or forgetful, that there is *none that judges in the earth* as that he remembers not the things he is to give judgment upon. It is a high affront they put upon God; it is a damning cheat they put upon themselves; they say, *The Lord shall not see,* Ps. xciv. 7. They cannot but know that God remembers all their works; they have been told it many a time; nay, if you ask them, they cannot but own it, and yet they do not *consider it;* they do not think of it when they should, and with application to themselves and their own works, else they would not, they durst not, do as they do. But the time will come when those who thus deceive themselves shall be undeceived: " *Now their own doings have beset them about,* that is, they have come at length to such a pitch of wickedness that their sins appear on every side of them; all their neighbours see how bad they are, and can they think that God does not see it ?" Or, rather, " The punishment of their doings besets them about; they are surrounded and embarrassed with troubles, so that they cannot get out, by which it appears that the sins they smart for are *before my face,* not only that I have seen them, but that I am displeased at them;" for, till God by pardoning our sins has cast them behind his

back, they are still before his face. Note, Sooner or later, God will convince those who do not now consider it that he *remembers all their works.*

4. God had begun to contend with them by his judgments, in earnest of what was further coming : *The thief comes in, and the troop of robbers spoils without.* Some take this as an instance of their wickedness, that they robbed and spoiled one another. *Nec hospes ab hospite tutus—The host and the guest stand in fear of each other.* It seems rather to be a punishment of their sin ; they were infested with secret thieves among themselves, that robbed their houses and shops and picked their pockets, and *troops of robbers,* foreign invaders, that with open violence *spoiled abroad*; so far was Israel from being healed that they had fresh wounds given them daily by robbers and spoilers ; and all this the effect of sin, all to punish them for robbing God, Isa. xlii. 24 ; Mal. iii. 8, 11.

II. A particular account of the sins of the court, of the king and princes, and those about them, and the tokens of God's displeasure that they were under for them.

1. Their king and princes were pleased with the wickedness and profaneness of their subjects, who were emboldened thereby to be so much the more wicked (*v.* 3) : *They make the king and princes glad with their wickedness.* It pleased them to see the people conform to their wicked laws and examples, in the worship of their idols, and other instances of impiety and immorality, and to hear them flatter and applaud them in their wicked ways. When Herod saw that his wickedness pleased the people he proceeded further in it, much more will the people do so when they see that it pleases the prince, Acts xii. 3. Particularly, they made them glad *with their lies,* with the lying praises with which they crowned the favourites of the prince and the lying calumnies and censures with which they blackened those whom they knew the princes had a dislike to. Those who show themselves pleased with slanders and ill-natured stories shall never want those about them who will fill their ears with such stories. Prov. xxix. 12, *If a ruler hearken to lies, all his servants are wicked,* and will make him glad with their lies.

2. Drunkenness and revelling abound much at the court, *v.* 5. The *day of our king* was a merry day with them, either his birth-day or his inauguration-day, of which it is probable that they had an anniversary observation, or perhaps it was some holiday of his appointing, which was therefore called *his day :* on that day the princes met to drink the king's health, and got him among them, to be merry, and *made him sick with bottles of wine.* It should seem the king did not ordinarily drink to excess, but he was now upon a high day brought to it by the artifices of the princes, tempted by

1158

the goodness of the wine, the gaiety of the company, or the healths they urged ; and so little was he used to it that it *made him sick :* and it is justly charged as a crime, as *crimen læsæ majestatis—treason,* upon those who thus imposed upon him and *made him sick :* nor would it serve for an excuse that it was *the day of their king,* but was rather an aggravation of the crime, that, when ey pretended to do him honour, they dishonoured him to the highest degree. If it is a great affront and injury to a common person to make him drunk, and there is a woe to those that do it (Hab. ii. 15), much more to a crowned head ; for the greater any man's dignity is the greater disgrace it is to him to be drunk. *It is not for kings, O Lemuel! it is not for kings, to drink wine,* Prov. xxxi. 4, 5. See what a prejudice the sin of drunkenness is to a man, to a king. (1.) In his health ; it *made him sick.* It is a force upon nature ; and strange it is by what charms men, otherwise rational enough, can be drawn to that which besides the offence it gives to God, and the damage it does to their spiritual and eternal welfare, is a present disorder and distemper to their own bodies. (2.) In his honour ; for, when he was thus intoxicated, he *stretched out his hand with scorners :* then he that was entrusted with the government of a kingdom lost the government of himself, and so far forgot, [1.] The dignity of a king that he made himself familiar with players and buffoons, and those whose company was a scandal. [2.] The duty of a king that he joined in confederacy with atheists, and the profane scoffers at religion, whom he ought to have silenced and put to shame ; he *sat in the seat of the scornful,* of those that had arrived at the highest pitch of impiety ; he struck in with them, said as they said, did as they did, and exerted his power, and *stretched forth the hand* of his government, in concurrence with them. Goodness and good men are often made *the song of the drunkards* (Ps. lxix. 12 ; xxxv. 16); but *woe unto thee, O land!* when *thy king is such a child* as to *stretch forth his hand* with those that make them so, Eccl. x. 16.

3. Adultery and uncleanness prevailed much among the courtiers. This is spoken of *v.* 4, 6, 7, and the charge of drunkenness comes in in the midst of this article ; for wine is oil to the fire of lust, Prov. xxiii. 33. Those that are inflamed with fleshly lusts, that are *adulterers* (*v.* 4), are here again and again compared to an oven heated by the baker (*v.* 4): *They have made ready their heart like an oven* (*v.* 6); *they are all hot as an oven, v.* 7. Note, [1.] An unclean heart is like an oven heated ; and the unclean lusts and affections of it are as the fuel that makes it hot. It is an inward fire, it keeps the heat within itself ; so adulterers and fornicators secretly *burn in lust,* as the expression is, Rom. i. 27. The heat of the oven is an in-

tense heat, especially as it is here described; he that heats it *stirs up* the fire, and *ceases not from raising* it up, till the bread is ready to be put in, being *kneaded* and *leavened,* all which only signifies that they are like an oven when it is at the hottest; nay, when it is *too hot for the baker* (so the learned Dr. Pocock), when it is *hotter than he would have it,* so that the raiser up of the fire ceases as long as while the dough that is kneaded is in the fermenting, that the heat may abate a little. Thus fiery hot are the lusts of an unclean heart. (2.) The unclean wait for an opportunity to compass their wicked desires; having made ready their heart like an oven, they lie in wait to catch their prey. *The eye of the adulterer waits for the twilight,* Job xxiv. 15. *Their baker sleeps all the night, but in the morning it burns as a flaming fire.* As the baker, having kindled a fire in his oven and laid sufficient fuel to it, goes to bed, and sleeps all night, and in the morning finds his oven well heated, and ready for his purpose, so these wicked people, when they have laid some wicked plot, and formed a design for the gratifying of some covetous, ambitious, revengeful, or unclean lusts, have their hearts so fully set in them to do evil that, though they may stifle them for a while, yet the fire of corrupt affections is still glowing within, and, as soon as ever there is an opportunity for it, their purposes which they have compassed and imagined break out into overt acts, as a fire flames out when it has vent given it. Thus *they are all hot as an oven.* Note, Lust in the heart is like fire in an oven, puts it into a heat; but the day is coming when those who thus make themselves like a fiery oven with their own vile affections, if that fire be not extinguished by divine grace, shall be made as a fiery oven by divine wrath (Ps. xxi. 9), when *the day comes* that shall *burn as an oven,* Mal. iv. 1.

4. They resist the proper methods of reformation and redress: *They have devoured their judges,* those few good judges that were among them, that would have put out these fires with which they were heated; they fell foul upon them, and would not suffer them to do justice, but were ready to stone them, and perhaps did so; or, as some think, they provoked God to deprive them of the blessing of magistracy and to leave all in confusion: *All their kings* have *fallen* one after another, and their families with them, which could not but put the kingdom into confusion, crumble it into contending parties, and occasion a great deal of bloodshed. There are heart-burnings among them; they are *hot as an oven* with rage and malice at one another, and this occasions the *devouring of their judges,* the *falling* of their *kings.* For *the transgressions of a land many are the princes thereof,* Prov. xxviii. 2. But in the midst of all this trouble and disorder *there is none among them that calls unto God,* that sees

his hand stretched out against them in these judgments, and deprecates the strokes of it, none, or next to none, that stir up themselves to take hold on God, Isa. lxiv. 7. Note, Those are not only heated with sin, but hardened in sin, that continue to live without prayer even when they are in trouble and distress.

8 Ephraim, he hath mixed himself among the people; Ephraim is a cake not turned. 9 Strangers have devoured his strength, and he knoweth *it* not : yea, gray hairs are here and there upon him, yet he knoweth not. 10 And the pride of Israel testifieth to his face : and they do not return to the LORD their God, nor seek him for all this. 11 Ephraim also is like a silly dove without heart: they call to Egypt, they go to Assyria. 12 When they shall go, I will spread my net upon them; I will bring them down as the fowls of the heaven; I will chastise them, as their congregation hath heard. 13 Woe unto them! for they have fled from me : destruction unto them! because they have transgressed against me : though I have redeemed them, yet they have spoken lies against me. 14 And they have not cried unto me with their heart, when they howled upon their beds : they assemble themselves for corn and wine, *and* they rebel against me. 15 Though I have bound *and* strengthened their arms, yet do they imagine mischief against me. 16 They return, *but* not to the Most High : they are like a deceitful bow : their princes shall fall by the sword for the rage of their tongue : this *shall be* their derision in the land of Egypt.

Having seen how vicious and corrupt the court was, we now come to enquire how it is with the country, and we find that to be no better; and no marvel if the distemper that has so seized the head affect the whole body, so that there is *no soundness* in it; the *iniquity of Ephraim is discovered,* as well as *the sin of Samaria,* of the people as well as the princes, of which here are divers instances.

I. They were not peculiar and entire for God, as they should have been, *v.* 8. 1. They did not distinguish themselves from the heathen, as God had distinguished them : *Ephraim, he has mingled himself among the people,* has associated with them, and conformed himself to them, and has in a manner confounded himself with them and lost his

1159

character among them. Gód had said, *The people shall dwell alone;* but they *mingled themselves with the heathen and learned their works,* Ps. cvi. 35. They went up and down among the heathen, to beg help of one of them against another (so some); whereas, if they had kept close to God, they would not have needed the help of any of them. 2. They were not entirely devoted to God: *Ephraim is a cake not turned,* and so is burnt on one side and dough on the other side, but good for nothing on either side. As in Ahab's time, so now, they *halted between God and Baal;* sometimes they seemed zealous for God, but at other times as hot for Baal. Note, It is sad to think how many, who, after a sort, profess religion, are made up of contraries and inconsistencies, *as a cake not turned,* a constant self-contradiction, and always in one extreme or the other.

II. They were strangely insensible of the judgments of God, which they were under, and which threatened their ruin, *v.* 9. Observe, 1. The condition they were in. God was now to them, in his judgments, as *a moth* and as *rottenness;* they were silently and slowly drawing towards the ruin of their state partly by the encroachments of foreigners upon them: *Strangers have devoured his strength,* and eaten him up; they have wasted his wealth and treasure, lessened his numbers, and consumed the fruits of the earth. Some devoured them by open wars (as 2 Kings xiii. 7, when the king of Syria made them *like the dust by threshing*), others by pretending treaties of peace and amity, in which they extorted abundance of wealth from them, and made them pay dearly for that which did them no good, but which afterwards they paid more dearly for, as 2 Kings xvi. 9. This Ephraim got by mingling with the heathen, and suffering them to mingle with him; they devoured that which he rested upon and supported himself with. Note, Those that make not God their strength (Ps. lii. 7) make that their strength which will soon be devoured by strangers. They were thus reduced partly by their own mal-administrations among themselves: *Yea, gray hairs are here and there upon him* (are *sprinkled* upon him, so the word is), that is, the sad symptoms of a decaying declining state, which is *waxing old* and *ready to vanish away,* and the effects of trouble and vexation. *Cura facit canos—Care turns gray.* The *almond-tree* does not as yet *flourish,* but it begins to turn colour, which speaks aloud to him that the *evil days* are coming, and the years *of which he shall say, I have no pleasure in them,* Eccl. xii. 1, 5. 2. Their regardlessness of these warnings: *He knows it not;* he is not aware of the hand of God gone out against him; it is lifted up, but he *will not see,* Isa. xxvi. 11. He does not know how near his ruin is, and takes no care to prevent it. Note, Stupidity under less judgments is a presage of greater coming.

1160

III. They went on frowardly in their wicked ways, and were not reclaimed by the rebukes they were under (*v.* 10): *The pride of Israel* still *testifies to his face,* as it had done before (*ch.* v. 5); under humbling providences their hearts were still unhumbled, their lusts unmortified; and it is *through the pride of their countenance* that they *will not seek after God* (Ps. x. 4); they *do not return to the Lord their God* by repentance and reformation, *nor do they seek him* by faith and prayer *for all this;* though they suffer for going astray from him, though it can never be well with them till they come back to him, and though they have in vain sought to others for relief, yet they think not of applying to God.

IV. They were infatuated in their counsels, and took very wrong methods when they were in distress (*v.* 11, 12): *Ephraim is like a silly dove without heart.* To be harmless as a dove, without gall, and not to hurt or injure others, is commendable; but to be sottish as a dove, without heart, that knows not how to defend herself and provide for her own safety, is a shame.

1. The silliness of this dove is, (1.) That she laments not the loss of her young that are taken from her, but will make her nest again in the same place; so they have their people carried away by the enemy, and are not affected with it, but continue their dealings with those that deal barbarously with them. (2.) That she is easily enticed by the bait into the net, and has *no heart,* no understanding, to discern her danger, as many other fowls do, Prov. i. 17. She *hastes to the snare, and knows not that it is for her life* (Prov. vii. 23); so they were drawn into leagues with neighbouring nations that were their ruin. (3.) That, when she is frightened, she has not courage to stay in the dove-house, where she is safe, and under the careful protection of her owner, but flutters and hovers, seeking shelter first in one place, then in another, and thereby exposes herself so much the more; so this people, when they were in distress, sought not to God, did not fly *like the doves to their windows,* where they might have been secured from all the birds of prey that struck at them, but threw themselves out of God's protection, and then *called to Egypt* to help them, and went in all haste *to Assyria,* to seek for that aid in vain which they might, by repentance and prayer, have found nearer home, in their God. Note, It is a silly senseless thing for those who have a God in heaven to trust to creatures for the refuge and relief which are to be had in him only; and those that do so are a *people of no understanding,* they are *without heart.* Now,

2. See what becomes of this *silly dove* (*v.* 12): *When they shall go* to Egypt and Assyria, *I will spread my net upon them.* Note, Those that will not abide by the mercy of God must expect to be pursued by the jus-

tice of God. Here, (1.) They are ensnared: "*I will spread my net upon them,* bring them into straits, that they may see their folly and think of returning." Note, It is common for those that go away from God to find snares where they expected shelters. (2.) They are humbled; they soar upward, proud of their foreign alliances and confiding in them; but *I will bring them down,* let them fly ever so high, *as the fowls of heaven,* that are shot flying. Note, God can and will *bring those down* that *exalt themselves as the eagle,* Obad. 3, 4. (3.) They are made to smart for their folly: *I will chastise them.* Note, The disappointments we meet with in the creature, when we put a confidence in it, are a necessary chastisement, or discipline, that we may learn to be wiser another time. (4.) In all this the scripture is fulfilled. It is *as their congregation has heard;* they have been many a time told by the word of God, read, and preached, and sung, in their religious assemblies, that *vain is the help of man,* that *in the son of man there is no help;* they have heard both from the law and from the prophets what judgments God would bring upon them for their wickedness; and *as they have heard* now *they shall see,* they shall feel." Note, It concerns us to take notice of the word of God which we hear from time to time *in the congregation,* and to be governed by it, for we must shortly be judged by it; and it will justify God in the condemnation of sinners, and aggravate it to them, that they have had plain public warning given them of it; it is what their congregation has heard many a time, but they would not take warning. "*Son, remember* thou wast told what would come of it; and now thou seest they were not vain words." See Zech. i. 6.

V. They revolted from God and rebelled against him, notwithstanding the various methods he took to retain them in their allegiance, *v.* 13—15. Here observe,

1. How kindly and tenderly God had dealt with them, as a gracious sovereign towards a people dear unto him, and whose prosperity he had much at heart. He had *redeemed them* (*v.* 13), brought them, at first, out of the land of Egypt, and, since, delivered them out of many a distress. He had *bound and strengthened their arms, v.* 15. When their power was weakened, like an arm broken or out of joint, God set it again, and bound it, as a surgeon does a broken bone, to make it knit. God had given Israel victories over the Syrians (2 Kings xiii. 16, 17), had *restored their coast* (2 Kings xiv. 25, 26), had *girded them with strength for battle.* "Though *I have chastened* them" (so the margin reads it), "sometimes corrected them for their faults and thereby taught them, at other times *strengthened their arms* and relieved them, though I have used both fair means and foul to work upon them, it was all to no purpose; they were mercy-proof and judgment-proof."

2. How impudent their conduct had been towards him notwithstanding, which is described here for the conviction and humiliation of all those who have gone on in any way of wickedness, that they may see how exceedingly sinful their sin is, how heinous, how the God of heaven interprets it, how he resents it. (1.) He had courted them to him, and taken them into covenant with himself; but *they fled from him,* as if he had been their dangerous enemy who had always approved himself their faithful friend. They wandered from him, as the silly dove from her nest, for those who forsake God will find no rest nor settlement in the creature, but wander endlessly. They fled from God when they forsook the worship of him, and ran away from his service, and withdrew themselves from their allegiance to him. (2.) He had given them his laws, which were all holy, just, and good, by which he designed to keep them in the right way; but they *transgressed against him;* they sinned with a high hand and a stiff neck, wilfully and presumptuously (so the word signifies); they broke through the fence of the divine law, and therein thwarted the design of the divine love. (3.) He had made known his truths to them, and given them all possible proofs of the sincerity of his good-will to them; and yet they *spoke lies against him.* They set up false gods in competition with him; they denied his providence and power: thus they *belied the Lord,* Jer. v. 12. They rejected his messages sent them by his prophets, and said that they should have peace, though they went on in sin, directly against what he said. In their hypocritical professions of religion, shows of devotion, and promises of amendment, they lied to the Lord, which he took as lying against him. (4.) He was their rightful Lord and King, and had always ruled in Jacob with equity, and for the public good; and yet they *rebelled against him, v.* 14. They not only went off from him, but took up arms against him, would have deposed him if they could and set up another. (5.) He designed well for them, but they *imagined mischief against him, v.* 15. Sin is a mischievous thing; it is mischief against God, for it is treason against his crown and dignity; not that the sinners can do any thing to hurt their Creator (as one of the ancients observes on these words), but *what they can they do;* and it is so much the worse when it is not done by surprise, or through inadvertency, but designedly and with contrivance. The Jews have a saying, which Dr. Pocock quotes here, *The thoughts of transgression are worse than the transgression.* The designing of mischief is doing it, in God's account. *Compassing and imagining* the death of the king is treason by our law. Those that imagine an evil thing, though it prove a vain thing (Ps. ii. 1), will be reckoned with for the imagination.

3. How they shall be punished for this (v. 13): *Woe unto them! for they have fled from me.* Note, Those who flee from God have woes sent after them, and are, without doubt, in a woeful case. The wrath of God is revealed from heaven against them; the word of God says, *Woe to them!* And observe what follows immediately, *Destruction unto them!* Note, The woes of God's word have real effects; destruction makes them good. The judgments of his hand shall verify the judgments of his mouth. Those 'whom he curses, and pronounces woeful, they are cursed, they are woeful indeed.

VI. Their shows of devotion and reformation were but shows, and in them they did but mock God.

1. They pretended devotion, but it was not sincere, *v.* 14. When the hand of God had gone forth against them they made some sort of application to him. *When he slew them, then they sought him.* Lord, in trouble have they visited thee. But it was all in hypocrisy. (1.) When they were under personal troubles, and called upon God in secret, they were not sincere in that: *They have not cried unto me with their heart, when they howled upon their beds.* When they were *chastened with pain upon their beds,* and the *multitude of their bones with strong pains,* perhaps ill of the wounds they received in war, they cried, and groaned, and complained in the forms of devotion, and, it may be, they used many good words, proper enough for the circumstances they were in; they cried, *God help us,* and, *Lord, look upon us.* But they did not *cry with their heart,* and therefore God reckons it as no crying to him. Moses is said to *cry unto God* when he spoke not a word, only his heart prayed with faith and fervency, Exod. xiv. 15. These made a great noise, and said a great deal, and yet did not *cry to God,* because their hearts were not *right with him,* not subjected to his will, devoted to his honour, nor employed in his service. To pray is to *lift up the soul* to God, this is the essence of prayer. If this be not done, *words,* though ever so well chosen, *are but wind;* but, if it be, it is an acceptable prayer, though the *groanings cannot be uttered.* Note, Those do not pray to God at all that do not pray *in the spirit.* Nay, God is so far from approving their prayer and accepting it that he calls it *howling.* Some think it intimates the *noisiness* of their prayers (they cried to God as they used to cry to Baal, when they thought he must be awaked), or the brutish violent passions which they vented in their prayers; they snarled at the stone, and howled under the whip, but regarded not the hand. Or it denotes that their hypocritical prayers were so far from being pleasing to God that they were offensive to him; he *was angry at their prayers.* The *songs of the temple shall be howlings,* Amos viii. 3. God will be so

far from pitying them that he will justly *laugh at their calamity,* who have so often laughed at his authority. (2.) When they were under public troubles, and met together to implore God's favour, in that also they were hypocritical; they *assembled themselves,* for fashion-sake, because it was usual to *call a solemn assembly* in times of general mourning, Zeph. ii. 1. But it was only to pray *for corn and wine* that they came together, which were the things they wanted, and feared being deprived of by the want of rain, the judgment they now laboured under. They did not pray for the favour or grace of God, that God would give them repentance, pardon their sins, and turn away his wrath, but only that he would not take away from them *their corn and wine.* Note, Carnal hearts, in their prayers to God, covet temporal mercies only, and dread and deprecate no other but temporal judgments, for they have no sense of any other.

2. They pretended reformation, but neither was that sincere, *v.* 16. Here is, (1.) The sin of Israel: *They return,* that is, they make as if they would return; they pretend to repent and amend their doings, but they make nothing of it; they do not come home to God nor return to their allegiance, whereas God says (Jer. iv. 1), *If thou wilt return, O Israel! return to me;* do not only *turn towards me,* but *return to me.* This dissimulation of theirs makes them like a *deceitful bow,* which looks as if it were fit for business, and is bent and drawn accordingly, but, when strength comes to be laid to it, either the bow or the string breaks, and the arrow, instead of flying to the mark, drops at the archer's foot. Such were their essays towards repentance and reformation. (2.) The sin of the princes of Israel. That which is charged upon them is *the rage of their tongue,* quarrelling with God and his providence and with all about them when they are crossed. Princes think they may say what they will, and that it is their prerogative to huff and bluster, to curse and rail, and to call names at their pleasure, but let them know there is a God above them that will call them to an account for the *rage of their tongues* and make *their own tongues to fall upon them.* (3.) The punishment of Israel and their princes for their sin. As for the princes, they shall *fall by the sword* either of their enemies or of their own people, some by one and some by the other; and *this shall be their derision,* this is that for which they shall be derided *in the land of Egypt,* when they flee to the Egyptians for succour, *v.* 11. Their sin and punishment shall make them a laughing-stock to all about them. Note, Those that are treacherous and deceitful in their dealings with God, and passionate and outrageous in their conduct towards men, will justly be made a derision to their neighbours, for they make themselves ridiculous.

CHAP. VIII.

This chapter, as that before, divides itself into the sins and punishments of Israel; every verse almost declares both, and all to bring them to repentance. When they saw the malignant nature of their sin, in the descriptions of that, they could not but be convinced how much it was their duty to repent of what was so bad in itself; and when they saw the mischievous consequences of their sin, in the predictions of them, they could not but see how much it was their interest to repent for the preventing of them. I. The sin of Israel is here set forth, 1. In many general expressions, ver. 1, 3, 12, 14. 2. In many particular instances; setting up kings without God (ver. 4), setting up idols against God (ver. 4—6, 11), and courting alliances with the neighbouring nations, ver. 8—10. 3. In this aggravation of it, that they still kept up a profession of religion and relation to God, ver. 2, 13, 14. II. The punishment of Israel is here set forth as answering to the sin. God would bring an enemy upon them, ver. 1, 3. All their projects should be blasted, ver. 7. Their confidence both in their idols and in their foreign alliances should disappoint them, ver. 6, 8, 10. Their strength at home should fail them, ver. 14. Their sacrifices should have no reckoning made of them, and their sins should have a reckoning made for them, ver. 13.

*S*ET the trumpet to thy mouth. *He shall come* as an eagle against the house of the LORD, because they have transgressed my covenant, and trespassed against my law. 2 Israel shall cry unto me, My God, we know thee. 3 Israel hath cast off *the thing that is* good: the enemy shall pursue him. 4 They have set up kings, but not by me: they have made princes, and I knew *it* not: of their silver and their gold have they made them idols, that they may be cut off. 5 Thy calf, O Samaria, hath cast *thee* off; mine anger is kindled against them: how long *will it be* ere they attain to innocency? 6 For from Israel *was* it also: the workman made it; therefore it *is* not God: but the calf of Samaria shall be broken in pieces. 7 For they have sown the wind, and they shall reap the whirlwind: it hath no stalk: the bud shall yield no meal: if so be it yield, the stranger shall swallow it up.

The reproofs and threatenings here are introduced with an order to the prophet to *set the trumpet to his mouth* (v. 1), thus to call a solemn assembly, that all might take notice of what he had to deliver and take warning by it. He must sound an alarm, must, in God's name, proclaim war with this rebellious nation. An enemy is coming with speed and fury to seize their land, and he must awaken them to expect it. Thus the prophet must do the part of a watchman, that was by sound of trumpet to call the besieged to stand to their arms, when he saw the besiegers making their attack, Ezek. xxxiii. 3. The prophet must *lift up his voice like a trumpet* (Isa. lviii. 1), and the people must hearken to the sound of the trumpet, Jer. vi. 17. Now,

I. Here is a general charge drawn up against them as rebels and traitors against their sovereign Lord. 1. They have *transgressed my covenant, v.* 1. They have

not only transgressed the command (every sin does that), but they have *transgressed the covenant;* they have been guilty of such sins as break the original contract; they have revolted from their allegiance, and violated the marriage-covenant by their spiritual whoredom; they have, in effect, declared that they will be no longer God's people, nor take him for their God; that is *transgressing the covenant.* They have not only done foolishly, but have dealt deceitfully. 2. They have *trespassed against my law* in many particular instances. God's law is the rule by which we are to walk; and this is the malignity of sin, that it trespasses upon the bounds set us by that law. 3. They have *cast off the thing that is good.* They have *put away* and *rejected good,* that is, God himself; so some understand it, and very fitly. He is good, and does good, and is our goodness. *There is none good but one, that is God,* the fountain of all good. They have *cast him off,* as not desiring to have any thing more to do with him. God was abandoning them to ruin, and here gives the reason for it. Note, God never casts off any till they first cast him off. Or, as we read it, They have cast off *the thing that is good;* they have cast off the service and worship of God, which is, in effect, *casting God off.* They have cast off that which denominates men good; they have cast off the fear of God, and the regard of man, and all sense of virtue and honesty. Observe, They have *transgressed my covenant;* it has come to this at last; for *they trespassed against my law.* Breaking the command made way for breaking the covenant; and they did that, for they *cast off that which was good;* there it began first. They *left off to be wise and to do good,* and then they went all to naught, Ps. xxxvi. 3. See the method of apostasy; men first cast off that which is good; then those omissions make way for commissions; and frequent actual transgressions of God's law bring men at length to an habitual renunciation of his covenant. When men cast off praying, and hearing, and sabbath-sanctification, and other things that are good, they are in the high road to a total forsaking of God.

II. Here are general threatenings of wrath and ruin for their sin: *The enemy shall come as an eagle against the house of the Lord,* and (v. 3) *shall pursue him.* If by *the house of the Lord* we understand the temple at Jerusalem, by the eagle that comes against it we must suppose to be meant either Sennacherib, who had taken all the fenced cities of Judah, laid siege to Jerusalem (and, no doubt, aimed at the house of the Lord, to lay that waste, as he had done the temples of the gods of other nations), or Nebuchadnezzar, who burnt the temple and made a prey of the vessels of the temple. But, if we make it to point at the destruction of the kingdom of the ten tribes by the king of Assyria, we must reckon it is

1163

the body of that people which as Israelites, to whom *pertained the adoption, the glory, and the covenants,* is here called the *house of the Lord.* They thought their being so would be their protection; but the prophet is directed to tell them that now they had lost the life and spirit of their religion, though they still retained the name and form of it, they were but as a carcase to which the eagles and other birds of prey should be gathered together. The enemy shall pursue them *as an eagle,* so swiftly, so strongly, so furiously. Note, Those who break their covenant of friendship with God expose themselves to the enmity of all about them, to whom they make themselves a cheap and easy prey; and their having been *the house of the Lord,* and his living temples, will be no excuse nor refuge to them. See Amos iii. 2.

III. Here is the people's hypocritical claim of relation to God, when they were in trouble and distress (*v.* 2): *Israel shall cry unto me;* when either they are threatened with these judgments, and would plead an exemption, or when the judgments are inflicted on them and they apply to God for relief, *pouring out a prayer when God's chastening is upon them,* they will plead that among them *God is known* and his *name is great* (Ps. lxxvi. 1) and in their distress will pretend to that knowledge of God's ways which in their prosperity they *desired not,* but *despised.* They will then cry unto God, will call him their God, and (as impudent beggars) will tell him they are well acquainted with him, and have known him long. Note, There are many who in works deny God, and disown him, yet, to serve a turn, will profess that they *know him,* that they know more of him than some of their neighbours do. But what stead will it stand a man in to be able to say, *My God, I know thee,* when he cannot say, "My God, I love thee," and "My God, I serve thee, and cleave to thee only?"

IV. Here is the prophet's expostulation with them, in God's name (*v.* 5): *How long will it be ere they attain to innocency?* It is not meant of absolute innocency (that is what the guilty can never attain to); but how long will it be ere they repent and reform, ere they become innocent in this matter, and free from the sin of idolatry? They are wedded to their idols; how long will it be ere they are weaned from them, ere *they are able to get clear of them?* so it might be rendered. This intimates that custom in sin makes it very difficult for men to part with it. It is hard to cleanse from that filthiness, either of flesh or spirit, which has been long wallowed in. But God speaks as if he thought the time long till sinners cast away their iniquities and come to live a new life. He complains of their obstinacy; it is that which keeps his anger against them burning, which would soon be turned away if they did but *attain to innocency* from those sins that kindled it. They in trouble cry, *How long* will
1164

it be ere God return to us in a way of mercy? but they do not hear him ask, *How long* will it be ere they return to God in a way of duty?

V. Here are some particular sins which they are charged with, are convicted of the folly of, and warned of the fatal consequences of, and for which God's *anger is kindled against them.*

1. In their civil affairs. They set *up kings without God,* and in contempt of him, *v.* 4. So they did when they rejected Samuel, in whom the Lord was their king, and chose Saul, that they might be *like the nations.* So they did when they revolted from their allegiance to the house of David, and set up Jeroboam, wherein, though they fulfilled God's secret counsel, yet they aimed not at his glory, nor consulted his oracle, nor applied to him by prayer for direction, nor had any regard to his providence, but were led by their own humour and hurried on by the impetus of their own passions. So they did now about the time when Hosea prophesied, when it seems to have grown fashionable to *set up kings,* and depose them again, according as the contenders for the crown could make an interest, 2 Kings xv. 8, &c. Note, We cannot expect comfort and success in our affairs when we go about them, and go on in them, without consulting God and acknowledge not him in all our ways : "They *set up kings,* and *I knew it not,* that is, I did not know it from them, they did not ask *counsel at my mouth,* whether they might lawfully do it or whether it would be best for them to do it, though they had prophets and oracles with whom they might have advised." They *looked not to the Holy One of Israel,* Isa. xxxi. 1. Nor did the princes do as Jephthah, who, before he took upon him the government, *uttered all his words before the Lord in Mizpeh,* Judg. xi. 11. Note, Those that are entrusted with public concerns, and particularly with the election and nomination of magistrates, ought to take God along with them therein, by desiring his direction and designing his honour.

2. In their religious matters they did much worse; for they *set up calves against God,* in competition with him and contradiction to him. "Of *their silver and their gold* which God *gave them,* and *multiplied* to them, that they might serve and honour him with them, they have *made them idols."* They called them *gods* (1 Kings xii. 28, *Behold thy gods, O Israel!*) but God calls them *idols;* the word signifies *griefs,* or *troubles,* because they are offensive to God and will be ruining to those that worship them. *Their silver and their gold they have made to them idols;* so the words are, referring primarily to the images of their gods, which they made of gold and silver, especially the golden calves at Dan and Bethel. Idolaters spare no cost in worshipping their idols. But they are very applicable to the spiritual idolatry of the covetous : *Their silver and their gold* are the

gods they place their happiness in, set their hearts upon, to which they pay their homage, and in which they put their confidence. Now, to show them the folly of their idolatry, he tells them,

(1.) Whence their gods came. Trace them to their original, and they will be found the creatures of their own fancies and the work of their own hands, *v.* 6. The calf they worshipped is here called *the calf of Samaria,* because it is probable that when Samaria, in Ahab's time, became the metropolis of the kingdom, a calf was set up there to be near the court, besides those at Dan and Bethel, or perhaps one of those was removed thither; for those that are for new gods will still be for newer. Now let them consider what this god of theirs owed its rise and being to. [1.] To their own invention and institution : *From Israel was it also,* not from the God of Israel (he expressly forbade it), but from Israel ; it was a device of their own (some think), not borrowed from any of their neighbours, no, not from the Egyptians, for, though they worshipped Apis in a living cow, they never worshipped a *golden calf:* that was from Israel ; it was *their own iniquity.* Now could that be worthy of their worship which was a contrivance of their own ? It was *from Israel,* that is, the gold and silver of which it was made were collected from the people of Israel by a brief : it was a poor god that was framed by contribution. [2.] It was owing to the skill and labour of the craftsman, Deut. xxvii. 15. *The workmen made it, therefore it is not God, v.* 6. This is a very cogent conclusive argument, and the inference so very plain that one would think their own thoughts should have suggested it to them, so as to make them ashamed of their idolatry. What can be more absurd than for men to worship that as a god, giving being and good to them, which they themselves gave being to (both matter and form), but could not give-life to ? A made god is no God. This is a self-evident truth ; and yet St. Paul was accused as a criminal for preaching that *those are no gods which are made with hands,* Acts xix. 26. And, here, this which should have turned them from their idols comes in as a reason why they were inseparably wedded to them ; therefore they could not attain to innocency because it was *from themselves:* they were willing to have gods of their own to do what they pleased with, that they themselves might do what they pleased.

(2.) What their gods would come to. If they are not gods, they will not last ; nay, if they pretend to be gods, they will be reckoned with : *The calf of Samaria shall be broken to pieces,* and those that would not yield to the force of the former argument shall be convinced by this that it is not God, but an *unprofitable idol,* as the Chaldee calls it. It shall be *broken to shivers,* like a potter's vessel, though it be a golden calf. It shall be *chips* or *saw-dust;* it shall be a *spider's web;*

so St. Jerome. It seems to allude to Moses's grinding to powder the golden calf that was in his time. This shall be served as that was. Sennacherib boasted what he had done to *Samaria and her idols,* Isa. x. 11. Note, Deifying any creature makes way for the destruction of it. If they had made vessels and ornaments for themselves of their silver and gold, they might have remained ; but, if they make gods of them, they shall be *broken to pieces.*

(3.) What their gods would bring them to. The breaking of them to pieces would be a disappointment to those who trusted in them. But that was not all : *They have* made to themselves idols, *that they may be cut off* (*v.* 4), that their gold and silver, which they so abused, may be cut off (so some take it), nay, that they may themselves be cut off from God, from their own land, from the land of the living. Their idolatry will as certainly end in their extirpation as if they had purposely designed it. And, when this proves to be the effect of their sin, what relief will they have from the gods wherein they trusted ? None at all : " *Thy calf, O Samaria ! has cast thee off;* it cannot give thee any help in thy distress, and the pleasure thou now takest in it will vanish, and be no pleasure to thee." Those that were justly sent to the gods whom they had chosen found them *miserable comforters,* Judg. x. 14. If men will not quit the love and service of sin, yet they shall certainly lose all the delights and profits of it. If Samaria had continued firm and faithful to the God of Israel, he would have been a present powerful help to her ; but the calf she preferred before him was a broken reed. The case will be the same with those that make their silver and their gold their god. It will *cast them off,* and not *profit them in the day of wrath,* Ezek. vii. 12. Note, Those that suffer themselves to be deceived into any idolatries will certainly find themselves deceived in them. Cardinal Wolsey owned that if he had served his God as faithfully as he had served his prince he would not have *cast him off,* as his prince did, in his old age. Their disappointment in their idols is illustrated (*v.* 7) by a similitude which intimates both that and the destruction which God brought upon them for their idolatry. [1.] They got no good to themselves by worshipping idols : *They have sown the wind.* They have put themselves to a great deal of trouble and expense to make and worship their idols, have made a business of it as much as the husbandman does of sowing his corn, in expectation of reaping some mighty advantage from it, and that they should be as prosperous and victorious as the neighbouring nations were, that worshipped idols. But it is all a cheat; it is like *sowing the wind,* which can yield no increase ; they *labour in vain, labour for the wind,* Eccl. v. 16. They take great pains to no purpose, and *weary themselves for very* vanity, Hab. ii. 13. Those that make an idol of this world do so; they *set their eyes on that which is not*, which, like the wind, makes a great noise, but has nothing substantial in it [2.] They brought ruin upon themselves by it: They shall *reap the whirlwind*, a *great whirlwind* (so the word signifies), which shall hurry them away and dash them to pieces. They not only have not their false gods for them, but they set the true God against them; their favour will stand them in no more stead than the wind, but his wrath will do them more mischief than a whirlwind. As a man sows, so shall he reap. " If it may be supposed that a man should sow the wind, and cover it with earth, or keep it there for a while penned up, what could he expect but that it should be forced by its being shut up, and the accession of what might increase its strength, to break forth again in greater quantities with greater violence?" So Dr. Pocock. They promise themselves plenty, peace, and victory, by worshipping idols, but their expectations come to nothing. What they sow never comes up; it has *no stalk*, no blade, or, if it have, *the bud shall yield no meal;* it shall be as the thin ears in Pharaoh's dream, that were blasted with the *east wind*, and there was nothing in them. Or *if it yield*, if they do prosper for a while in their idolatrous courses, *the strangers shall swallow it up;* it shall be so far from doing them any service that it shall be but as a bait to invite strangers to invade them, and as a spoil to enrich those strangers and enable them to do so much the more mischief. Note, The service of idols is an unprofitable service, and the works of darkness are unfruitful; nay, in the end they will be pernicious. Rom. vi. 21, *The end of those things is death.* Those that *sow iniquity* reap *vanity :* nay, those that *sow the flesh, reap corruption.* The hopes of sinners will be cheats, and their gains will be snares.

8 Israel is swallowed up: now shall they be among the Gentiles as a vessel wherein *is* no pleasure. 9 For they are gone up to Assyria, a wild ass alone by himself: Ephraim hath hired lovers. 10 Yea, though they have hired among the nations, now will I gather them, and they shall sorrow a little for the burden of the king of princes. 11 Because Ephraim hath made many altars to sin, altars shall be unto him to sin. 12 I have written to him the great things of my law, *but* they were counted as a strange thing. 13 They sacrifice flesh *for* the sacrifices of mine offerings, and eat *it ; but* the Lord accepteth them not; now will he remember

their iniquity, and visit their sins: they shall return to Egypt. 14 For Israel hath forgotten his Maker, and buildeth temples; and Judah hath multiplied fenced cities: but I will send a fire upon his cities, and it shall devour the palaces thereof.

It was the honour and happiness of Israel that they had but one God to trust to and he all-sufficient in every strait, and but one God to serve, and he well worthy of all their devotions. But it was their sin, and folly, and shame, that they knew not when they were well off, that they forsook their own mercies for lying vanities; for,

I. They multiplied their alliances (*v.* 9): *They have hired lovers*, or (as the margin reads it) *they have hired loves.* They were at great expense to purchase the friendship of the nations about them, that otherwise had no value nor affection at all for them, nor cared for having any thing to do with them but only upon the Shechemites' principles— *Shall not their cattle and their substance be ours?* Gen. xxxiv. 23. Had Israel maintained the honour of their peculiarity, the surrounding nations would have continued to admire them *as a wise and understanding people ;* but, when they profaned their own crown, their neighbours despised them, and they had no interest in them further than they paid dearly for it. But those surely have behaved ill among their neighbours who have no loves, no lovers, but what they hire. See here, 1. The contempt that Israel lay under among the nations (*v.* 8): *Israel is swallowed up*, devoured by strangers, their land eaten up (*v.* 7), and themselves too, and, being impoverished, they have quite lost their credit and reputation, like a merchant that has become a bankrupt, so that they are *among the Gentiles as a vessel wherein is no pleasure*, a vessel of *dishonour* (2 Tim. ii. 20), a *despised broken vessel*, Jer. xxii. 28. None of their neighbours have any value for them, nor care to have any thing to do with them. Note, Those that have professed religion, if they degenerate and grow profane, are of all men the most contemptible. *If the salt have lost its savour*, it is fit for nothing but to be *trodden under foot of men.* Or it denotes their dispersion and captivity *among the Gentiles ;* they shall be among them poor and prisoners; and who has pleasure in such? 2. The court that Israel made to the nations notwithstanding (*v.* 9): They have *gone to Assyria*, to engage the king of Assyria to help them; and herein they are as a *wild ass alone by himself*, foolish, head-strong, and unruly; they will have their way, and nothing shall *hold them in*, no, not the bridle of God's laws, nothing shall *turn them back*, no, not the sword of God's wrath. They take a course by themselves, and the effect will be that, like a *wild ass by himself,* they will be the easier and surer prey to the lion. See Job xi. 12; Jer. ii. 24. Note, Man is in nothing more like the wild ass's colt than in seeking for that succour and that satisfaction in the creature which are to be had in God only. 3. The crosses that they were likely to meet with in their alliances with the neighbouring nations (*v.* 10): *Though they have hired among the nations,* and hoped thereby to prevent their own ruin, yet *now will I gather them,* as *the sheaves in the floor* (Mic. iv. 12); so that what they provided for their own safety shall but make them the easier prey to their enemies. Note, There is no fence against the judgments of God, when they come with commission; nay, that which men hire for their own preservation often contributes to their own destruction. See Isa. vii. 20. The king of Assyria, whose friendship they courted, called himself a *king of princes,* Isa. x. 8. *Are not my princes altogether kings?* He laid *burdens* upon Israel, levied taxes upon them, 2 Kings xv. 19, 20. And for these *they shall sorrow a little;* this shall be but a little burden to them in comparison of what they may further expect; or they will be but little sensible of this grievance, will not lay it to heart, and therefore may expect heavier judgments. *They have begun to be diminished* (so some read it), *by the burden of the king of princes;* but this is only the *beginning of sorrows* (Matt. xxiv. 8), *the beginning of revenges,* Deut. xxxii. 42. Note, God often comes gradually with his judgments upon a provoking people, that he may show how slow he is to wrath, and may awaken them to repentance; but those that are made to *sorrow a little,* if they are not thereby brought to sorrow after a godly sort, will, another day, be made to sorrow a great deal, to sorrow everlastingly.

II. They multiplied their altars and temples. Observe,

1. How they denied *the power of godliness,* and wholly cast that off (*v.* 12): *I have written to him the great things of my law;* this intimates the privilege they enjoyed, as having God's statutes and judgments made known to them, and being entrusted with the lively oracles. Note, (1.) The things of God's law are *magnalia Dei*—*the great things of God.* They are things that proclaim the greatness of the Law-maker, and things of great use and great importance to us; they are our life, and our eternal welfare depends upon our observance of them and obedience to them; they will make us great if we make a right use of them; and they are things which God will magnify and make honourable. (2.) It is a great privilege to have the things of God's law written; thus they are reduced to a greater certainty, spread the further, and last the longer, with much less danger of being embezzled and corrupted than if they were transmitted by word of mouth only. (3.) The things of God's law

are of his own writing; for Moses and the prophets were his amanuenses, and holy men wrote as they were moved by the Holy Ghost. (4.) It is the advantage of those that are members of the visible church that these great things are written *to them,* are intended for their direction, and so they must receive them; what things were written in former ages *were written for our learning,* and are profitable for us. And, if those were happy who had the *great things of God's law* written to them, how much happier are we who have the much greater things of his gospel written to us! But see how this privilege was slighted; these great things of the law were *counted as a strange thing,* as unintelligible and unreasonable (which might *therefore* be slighted, because not to be fathomed, not to be accounted for), or as foreign, and things of no concernment to them, things that they had nothing to do with nor were to be governed by; they used those things as strangers, which they were shy of, and knew not how to bid welcome. *We desire not the knowledge of thy ways.* Note, [1.] God having written to us the great things of his law, we ought to make them familiar to us, as our nearest relations (Prov. vii. 3, 4); for *therefore* we have them written, that they may *talk with us,* Prov. vi. 22. [2.] We make nothing of the things of God's law if we make strange of them, as if they did not affect us and therefore we need not be affected with them.

2. How they kept up the form of godliness notwithstanding, and to what little purpose they did so.

(1.) They multiplied their altars (*v.* 11): *Ephraim made many altars to sin.* God appointed that there should be but one altar for sacrifice (Deut. xii. 3, 5); but the ten tribes, having forsaken that, would still be thought very devout, and zealous for the honour of God, and, as if they would make amends for the affront they put on God's altar, they made *many altars,* dedicated to the God of Israel, whom hereby they intended, or at least pretended, to give glory to; but that would not justify their violation of God's express command, nor would the example of the patriarchs, who before the law of Moses had many altars. No, they *made many altars to sin* (that is, they did that which turned into sin to them), and therefore these *altars shall be unto* them *to sin,* that is, God will charge it upon them as a heinous sin, and put that upon the score of their crimes which they designed to be for the expiation of their crimes. Or they shall be to them an occasion of further sin. Their multiplying of altars dedicated to the God of Israel would introduce altars dedicated to other gods. Note, It is a great sin to corrupt the worship of God, and it will be charged as sin upon those that do it, how plausible soever their pretensions may be. And the way of this, as other sins, is down-hill; those that once deviate from the fixed rule of God's commands will wander endlessly.

(2.) They multiplied their sacrifices, *v.* 13. Their altars were smoking altars : They *sacrificed flesh for the sacrifices of God's offerings*, and they celebrated their feasts upon their sacrifices; they were at a great expense upon their devotions, and (as those commonly are who set up their own inventions in the room of divine institutions) were very zealous in their way; as if they hoped by their impositions on themselves to atone for the contempt of the great atonement, and by their observing a ceremonial law of their own to excuse themselves from the obligation of all God's moral precepts. But how did they speed ? [1.] God makes no reckoning of their services: *The Lord accepts them not.* How should he, when they did not offer their sacrifice upon that altar which alone *sanctified the gift*, and when they only sacrificed flesh, but not the spiritual sacrifice of a penitent believing heart? Note, Those services only are acceptable to God which are performed according to the rule of his word, and *through Jesus Christ*, 1 Pet. ii. 5. [2.] He takes that occasion to reckon with them for their sins; now will he, instead of pardoning their iniquity and blotting out their sins, as they expected, *remember their iniquity and visit their sins.* Such an *abomination to the Lord* are the *sacrifices of the wicked* that they provoke him to call them to an account for all their other abominations. When they think by their sacrifices to bribe the Judge of heaven and earth into a connivance at their wickedness he will resent that as the highest affront they can put upon him, and it shall be the measure-filling sin. Note, A petition for leave to sin amounts to an imprecation of the curse for sin, and so it shall be answered, *according to the multitude of the idols.* " I will punish their sins, *for they shall return to Egypt;*" they shall be carried captive into Assyria, which shall be to them a house of bondage, as Egypt was to their fathers. Or it refers to Deut. xxviii. 68, where returning to Egypt is made to close and complete the miseries of that sinful nation.

(3.) They multiplied their temples, and these also in honour of the true God, as they pretended, but really in contempt of the choice he had made of Jerusalem to *put his name there.* *Israel has forgotten his Maker, v.* 14. They pretended to know him, and yet forgot him, for they *liked not to retain God in their knowledge,* when the remembrance of him would give check to their lusts. It was an aggravation of their sin in forgetting God that he was *their Maker* (Deut. xxxii. 15, 18 ; Job xxxv. 10), as nothing obliges us more to remember him than that he is *our Creator,* Eccl. xii. 1. " He has *forgotten his Maker, and builds temples;* he seems by the temples he builds to be mindful of his Maker, and to be desirous still to keep him in mind, and

1168

yet really he has forgotten him, because he has cast off the fear of him." Some by temples here understand *palaces,* for so the word sometimes signifies. " *He has forgotten his Maker,* and yet is so secure and haughty that he sets his judgments at defiance, as Nebuchadnezzar did when he said, *Is not this great Babylon that I have built ?*" Judah is likewise charged with *multiplying fenced cities,* and trusting in them for safety, when the judgments of God were abroad. To fortify their cities in subjection and subordination to God was well enough ; but to fortify them in opposition to God, and without any regard to him or his providence (Isa. xxii. 11), shows their hearts to be desperately *hardened through the deceitfulness of sin.* But *none ever hardened his heart against God and prospered,* nor shall they. *God will send a fire upon his cities,* upon the cities both of Judah and Israel, not only the head-cities of Jerusalem and Samaria, but all the other cities of those two kingdoms, and it shall devour not only the cottages, but *the palaces thereof;* though ever so strong, the fire shall master them; though ever so stately and sumptuous, the fire shall not spare them. This was fulfilled when all the cities of Israel were laid in ashes by the king of Assyria, and all the cities of Judah by the king of Babylon. The fires they both kindled were of his sending; and when he judges he will overcome.

CHAP. IX.

In this chapter, I. God threatens to deprive this degenerate seed of Israel of all their worldly enjoyments, because by sin they had forfeited their title to them; so that they should have no comfort either in receiving them themselves or in offering them to God, ver. 1—5. II. He dooms them to utter ruin, for their own sins and the sins of their prophets, ver. 6—8. III. He upbraids them with the wickedness of their fathers before them, whose steps they trod in, ver. 9, 10. IV. He threatens them with the destruction of their children and the rooting out of their posterity, ver. 11—17.

REJOICE not, O Israel, for joy, as *other* people : for thou hast gone a whoring from thy God, thou hast loved a reward upon every cornfloor. 2 The floor and the wine-press shall not feed them, and the new wine shall fail in her. 3 They shall not dwell in the LORD's land; but Ephraim shall return to Egypt, and they shall eat unclean *things* in Assyria. 4 They shall not offer wine-*offerings* to the LORD, neither shall they be pleasing unto him : their sacrifices *shall be* unto them as the bread of mourners ; all that eat thereof shall be polluted : for their bread for their soul shall not come into the house of the LORD. 5 What will ye do in the solemn day, and in the day of the feast of the LORD ? 6 For, lo, they are gone because of destruction : Egypt shall gather them up, Memphis shall bury them; the pleasant *places* for their silver, nettles shall possess them: thorns *shall be* in their tabernacles.

Here, I. The people of Israel are charged with spiritual adultery: *O Israel! thou hast gone a whoring from thy God,* v. 1. Their covenant with God was a marriage-covenant, by which they were joined to him as their God, renouncing all others. But when they set up idols and worshipped them, when they fled to creatures for succour and put a confidence in them, they *went a whoring from God* as their God, and honoured the pretenders and rivals with the affection, adoration, and confidence, which were due to God only. Other people were idolaters, but that sin was not, in them, going a whoring from God, as it was in Israel that had been married to him. Note, The sins of those who have made a profession of religion and relation to God are more provoking to him than the sins of others. As a proof of their going a whoring from God, it is charged upon them that *they loved a reward upon every corn-floor.* 1. They loved to give rewards to their idols, in the offerings and first-fruits they presented to them out of every corn-floor. They took a strange pleasure in serving their idols with that which they would have grudged to consecrate to God and employ in his service. Note, It is common for those that are niggardly in the expenses of their religion to be very prodigal in spending upon their lusts. Or, 2. They loved to receive rewards from their idols; and such they reckoned the fruits of the earth to be: *These are my rewards, which my lovers have given me,* ch. ii. 12. Note, Those are directly disposed to spiritual idolatry that love a reward in the corn-floor better than a reward in the favour of God and eternal life.

II. They are forbidden to rejoice as other people do: "*Rejoice not, O Israel! for joy.* Do not expect to rejoice. *What peace,* what joy, what hast thou to do with either, while thy whoredoms and witchcrafts are so many?" 2 Kings ix. 19—22. Be not disposed to rejoice, for it does not become thee, but rather to *be afflicted, and mourn, and weep,* Jam. iv. 9. Judah, that keeps close to the true God, nay, and other people that never knew him, nor could ever be charged with revolting from him, may be allowed to rejoice, as not having so much cause to be ashamed as Israel has, that has gone a whoring from him. Some think that they had at this time particular occasions for joy, probably upon the account of some losses recovered, or some advantages gained, or some league made with a potent ally, for which they had public rejoicings, as other people used to have upon such occasions; but God sends to them not to rejoice. Note, Joy is forbidden fruit to wicked people. They must not rejoice, because they have gone a whoring from their God; and therefore, 1. Whatever it was

that they rejoiced in, it would be no security nor advantage to them, so long as they were at a distance from God and at war with him. Note, We are likely to have small joy of any of our creature-comforts if we make not God our chief joy. 2. The sense of sin and dread of wrath ought to be a damp upon their joy and a strong alloy to all their comforts. Note, Those who by departing from God have made work for repentance have thereby marred their own mirth, till they return and make their peace with God.

III. They are threatened with destroying judgments for their spiritual whoredoms, according to what was said long before. Ps. lxxiii. 27, *Thou hast destroyed all those that go a whoring from thee.* It is here threatened,

1. That their land shall not yield its wonted increase. Canaan, that *fruitful land,* shall be *turned into barrenness for the wickedness of those that dwell therein.* They *love the reward in the corn-floor,* and are so full of the *joy of harvest* that they have no disposition at all to mourn for their sins; and therefore God will, for their effectual humiliation, take away from them, not only their delights and dainties, but even their necessary food (*v.* 2): *The floor and the wine-press shall not feed them,* much less feast them; they shall either be blasted by the hand of God or plundered by the hand of man. The *new wine* with which they used to make merry shall *fail in her.* Note, When we make the world, and the things of it, our idol and portion, above what they were designed for, it is just with God to deny us even support and nourishment from them, according to that which they were designed for, to show us our folly and correct us for it. Let those miss of their food in the corn-floor that look for their reward in the corn-floor. We forfeit the good things of this world if we love them as the best things.

2. That their land shall not only cease to feed them, but cease to lodge them and to be a habitation for them; it shall *spue them out,* as it had done the Canaanites before them (*v.* 3): *They shall not dwell any longer in the Lord's land.* The land of Canaan was in a peculiar manner *the Lord's land, the land of the Shechinah* (so the Chaldee), *the land of the Lord of the world* (so the Arabic); he whose all the earth is (Ps. xxiv. 1) took that for his demesne. *The land is mine,* says God, Lev. xxv. 23. They had used it, or abused it rather, as if it had been their own, had not paid the rent, nor done the services, due to God as their landlord, and therefore God justly *enters,* and takes possession of it, they having forfeited their lease. " It is *my land*" (says God) " and I will make it appear, for they shall be turned off, as bad tenants, and be made to know that, though they thought themselves freeholders, they were but tenants at will." Note, It is for the honour of God's justice and holiness that those who go a whoring from God

should not be suffered to dwell upon his land; and therefore, sooner or later, the wicked shall be *chased out of the world.* Or it is called the Lord's land because it was the holy land, *Immanuel's land,* the land that had peculiar tokens of God's favour to it, and presence in it, where God was known and his name was great, where God's prophets and oracles were; it was a kind of copy of the earthly paradise, and a type of the heavenly one. It was a great privilege to have a lot in such a land as this. It was a great sin and folly to rebel against God, and go a whoring from him, in such a land as this, to *deal unjustly in a land of uprightness,* Isa. xxvi. 10. And it was a sad and sore judgment to be driven out from such a land as this; it was like driving our first parents out of the garden of Eden, and almost amounted to an exclusion out of the heavenly Canaan. Note, Those cannot expect to dwell in the Lord's land that will not be subject to the Lord's laws, nor be influenced by his love. Those have forfeited the privileges of the church that conform not to the rules of it.

3. That, when they are turned out from the Lord's land, they shall have no rest nor satisfaction in any other land. When Cain was *driven out from the presence of the Lord* he was *a fugitive and a vagabond* ever after, and dwelt in the land of *trembling.* So Israel here. Some shall *return into Egypt,* the old house of bondage; thither they shall flee from the Assyrian (*ch.* viii. 13) and they shall lose and ruin themselves where they thought to hide and help themselves. Others shall be carried captives to Assyria and there shall be forced to *eat unclean things,* either (1.) Such things as were not fit for men to eat, that which is rotten and putrefied, intimating that they shall be reduced to the utmost poverty, as the prodigal that would fain have filled his belly *with the husks.* Or, (2) Such things as were not fit for Jews to eat, being prohibited by their law. It is probable that while they were in their own land, however disobedient in other things, they kept up the distinction of meats, and prided themselves in that; but, since they would not keep the law of God in other things, they should not be suffered to keep it in that, and it was a just punishment of their sin in eating things offered to idols. Note, When at any time we suffer in our food, and either through want or for our health are forced to eat or drink that which is unpleasing, we must acknowledge that God is righteous, because we have sinned about our food, and have indulged ourselves too much in that which is pleasing.

4. That in the land of their enemies, to which they shall be driven, they shall have no opportunity either of giving honour to God or obtaining favour with God, by offering any acceptable sacrifice to him; they should not be in a capacity of keeping up any face or show of religion among them; "and

1170

so" (as Dr. Pocock expresses it) "should be as it were quite cut off from any expression of relation to him, from all signs of grace, and means of reconciliation with him, which would be to them a token of their being rejected of God, estranged from him, and no more owned by him as his people." (1.) They shall have no sacrifices to offer, nor any altar to offer them on, nor priests to offer them; they shall not so much as *offer drink-offerings* to the Lord, much less any other sacrifices. (2.) If they should offer them, neither they nor their sacrifices shall be pleasing to him, for they cannot have any legal offerings, nor are their hearts humbled. (3.) Instead of their sacrifices of joy and praise, they shall *eat the bread of mourners;* they shall live desolate, and disconsolate, mourning for the death of their relations and their own miseries, so that if they had opportunity of sacrificing they should never be themselves in a frame fit for it; for they were forbidden to eat of the holy things *in their mourning,* Deut. xxvi. 14. *All that eat* of the bread of mourners *are polluted,* and incapacitated to *partake of the altar.* (4.) Their *bread for their soul,* the bread which they must either eat or starve, the bread which they shall have for the support of their lives, *shall not come into the house of the Lord;* they shall have no house of the Lord to bring it to, or, if they had, it is such as is not fit to be brought, nor are they rightly disposed to bring it. (5.) The return of the days of their sacred and solemn feasts would therefore be very melancholy and uncomfortable to them (*v.* 5): *What will you do in the solemn day,* in the sabbath, *the solemn day* of every week, in the *new moons,* the solemn days of every month, at the return of the times for keeping the passover, pentecost, and feast of tabernacles, the solemn days of every year, the *days of the feasts of the Lord?* Note, The feasts of the Lord are solemn days; and, when we are invited to those feasts, we ought to consider seriously what we shall do. But the question is here put to those who were to be deprived of the benefit and comfort of those solemn feasts, " *What will you do then?* You will then spend those days in sorrow and lamentation which, if it had not been your own fault, you might have been spending in joy and praise. You will then be made to know the worth of mercies by the want of them and to prize spiritual bread by being made to feel a famine of it." Note, When we enjoy the means of grace we ought to consider what we shall do if ever we should know the want of them, if either they should be taken from us or we be disabled to attend upon them.

5. That they should perish in the land of their dispersion (*v.* 6): *For, lo, they have gone* out of the Lord's land, where they might have spent both their sabbath days and other days with comfort, *gone because of destruction,* gone to Egypt because of the destruc-

tion of their own country by the Assyrians, flattering themselves with hopes that they shall return when the storm is over; but those hopes also shall fail them; they shall find there are *graves in Egypt,* as their murmuring ancestors said (Exod. xiv. 11), graves for them; for *Egypt shall gather them up,* as dead men are gathered up and carried forth to the grave, and Memphis (one of the chief cities of Egypt) *shall bury them. Gathering* and *burying* are put together, Jer. viii. 2; Job xxvii. 19. Note, Those that think presumptuously to flee from the judgments of God are likely enough to meet their death where they hoped to save their lives.

6. That their land, which they left behind and to which they hoped to return, should become a desolation: As for *their tabernacles,* where they formerly dwelt and where they kept their stores, *the pleasant places for their silver,* they shall be demolished and laid in ruins, to such a degree that they shall be overgrown with *nettles;* so that if they should survive the trouble, and return to their own land again, they would find it neither fruitful nor habitable; it would afford them neither food nor lodging. Note, Those that make their money their god reckon the *places of their silver* their *pleasant places,* as those that make the Lord their God reckon his tabernacles amiable and his ordinances their pleasant things, Isa. lxiv. 11. But, while the pleasures of communion with God are out of the reach of chance and change, the *pleasant places of men's silver,* which were purchased with silver, or in which they deposited their silver, or which were beautified and adorned with silver, are liable to be laid in ruins, in nettles, and therewith all the pleasure men took in them.

7 The days of visitation are come, the days of recompence are come; Israel shall know *it :* the prophet *is* a fool, the spiritual man *is* mad, for the multitude of thine iniquity, and the great hatred. 8 The watchman of Ephraim *was* with my God: *but* the prophet *is* a snare of a fowler in all his ways, *and* hatred in the house of his God. 9 They have deeply corrupted *themselves,* as in the days of Gibeah: *therefore* he will remember their iniquity, he will visit their sins. 10 I found Israel like grapes in the wilderness; I saw your fathers as the first ripe in the fig-tree at her first time: *but* they went to Baalpeor, and separated themselves unto *that* shame; and *their* abominations were according as they loved.

For their further awakening, it is here threatened,

I. That the destruction spoken of shall come speedily. They shall have no reason to hope for a long reprieve, for the judgment slumbers not; it is at the door (*v.* 7): *The days of visitation have come,* and there shall be no more delay; *the days of recompence have come,* which they have been so often warned to expect; their prophets have told them that destruction *would come,* and now it has come, and the time of the divine patience has expired. Note, 1. The day of God's judgment is both a *day of visitation,* in which men's sins are enquired into and brought to light, and a *day of recompence,* in which men's doom will be passed, and a reward given to every man according to his work; the strict visitation is in order to a just retribution. 2. This day of visitation and recompence is hastening on apace. It is sure; it is near; as if it had already come.

II. That hereby they shall be made ashamed of their sentiments concerning their prophets. When the day of visitation comes *Israel shall know it,* shall be made to know that by sad experience which they would not know by instruction. *Israel shall know* then what an *evil and bitter thing it* is to *depart from God,* and what a *fearful thing* it is to *fall into his hands. When thy hand is lifted up they will not see, but they shall see.* Israel shall know the difference between true prophets and false. 1. They shall know then that the pretenders to prophecy, who flattered them in their sins, and rocked them asleep in their security, and told them that they should have peace though they went on, however they pretended to be *spiritual men* (as Ahab's prophets did, 1 Kings xxii. 24), were *fools* and *madmen,* and not true prophets; they deceived themselves and those to whom they prophesied. But why would God suffer his people Israel to be imposed upon by those false prophets? He answers, *" It is for the multitude of thy iniquity* which, in contempt of the divine law, thou hast persisted in, *and, for the great hatred of* the true prophets, that reproved thee, in God's name, for it."* Note, Because men receive not the love of the truth, but conceive a hatred of it, and by the multitude of their iniquities bid defiance to it, therefore God shall *send them strong delusions, to believe a lie,* so strong that they shall not be undeceived till the day of visitation and recompence comes, which will convince them of the folly and madness of those that seduced them and of their own folly and madness in suffering themselves to be seduced by them. 2. They shall know then whether the *true prophets,* that were really *spiritual men,* guided by the Spirit of God, were such as they called and counted them, *fools and madmen;* and they shall be convinced that they were so far from being so that they were the wise men of their times, and God's faithful ambassadors to them. When Israel saw that none of Samuel's words *fell to the ground* they knew he was *established to be a prophet* (1 Sam. iii. 20); and so here, when God fulfils the word of his messengers, by bringing the days of recompence they foretold, then those that despised and ridiculed them, and thought Bedlam the fittest place for them, will be ashamed of *the multitude of their iniquities* of that kind, and of *their great hatred,* for which God brings upon them this swift destruction. Mocking the messengers of the Lord was the sin they were punished for, and so made ashamed of.

III. That hereby the wickedness of the false prophets themselves shall be manifested to their shame (v. 8) : " *The watchman of Ephraim was with my God;* he had been formerly. They had a set of worthy good ministers, that kept close to God and maintained communion with him; but now they have a race of corrupt, malignant, persecuting prophets, that are the ring-leaders of all mischief." Or, " The *watchman of Ephraim* now pretends to have been *with my God,* and prefaces his lies with, *Thus saith the Lord;* but he is *a snare of a fowler in all his ways,* and is cunning to draw the simple into sin and the upright into trouble ; and he is so full of hatred and enmity to goodness and good men that he has become *hatred* itself *in the house of his God,* or *against the house of his God."* Note, Wicked prophets are the worst of men; their sins against God are most heinous, and their plots against religion most dangerous. They may boast that they are *watchmen, speculators,* and, as far as speculation goes, they may be right, and *with my God,* may have their heads full of good notions; but look into their lives, and they are the *snare of a fowler in all their ways,* catching for themselves and making a prey of others; look into *their hearts,* and they are *hatred in the house of my God,* very malicious and spiteful against good ministers and good people. Woe unto thee, O land ! unto thee, O church ! that hast such watchmen, such prophets, that are seers, but not doers ! *Corruptio optimi est pessima—The best things, when corrupted, become the worst.*

IV. That God will now reckon with them for the sins of their fathers, which they have trod in the steps of, v. 9, 10. 1. They were as bad as their fathers : *They have deeply corrupted themselves;* they are rooted and rivetted in sin; they are far gone in the *depths of Satan* (Isa. xxxi. 6), so that it is next to impossible that they should be recovered; the stain of their corruption is deep, not to be got out; it is as scarlet and crimson, or as the spots of the leopard : and it is their own fault; they have *corrupted themselves,* have polluted and hardened their own hearts, as *in the days of Gibeah,* when the Levite's concubine was abused to death by the men of Gibeah and the whole tribe of Benjamin patronised the villany ; that was a time of deep corruption indeed, and such were the present days. Lewdness and wickedness

1172

were as impudent and daring now as in the days of Gibeah ; and therefore what can be expected but such a vengeance as was then taken on Gibeah ? Every tribe is now as bad as the tribe of Benjamin then was, and therefore may expect to be brought as low as that tribe then was. 2. They shall therefore be reckoned with for their fathers' sins : *He will remember their iniquity and visit their sins,* the iniquity they have by kind and by entail, the sin that runs in the blood; the *sin of the father* shall now be *visited upon the children.* Hence God takes occasion to upbraid them with the degeneracy and apostasy of their ancestors, their perfidiousness and base ingratitude, v. 10. Here observe, (1.) The great honour God put upon Israel when he first formed them into a people : *I found Israel like grapes in the wilderness.* He took as much delight and pleasure in them as a poor traveller would do if he found grapes in a wilderness, where he most needed them and least expected them. Or when they were *in the wilderness* he *found them as grapes,* not precious in themselves, but precious to him, and pleasant as the first-ripe grapes to the lord of the vineyard. They were *precious in his sight, and honourable* (Isa. xliii. 4); he planted them a *choice vine,* a *right seed* (Jer. ii. 21), and found them no better than he himself made them, good grapes at first. *I saw them* with pleasure, *as the first-ripe in the fig-tree at the first time.* Good people are compared to the *good things that are first ripe,* Jer. xxiv. 2. One then is worth more than many afterwards. This intimates the delight God took in them and in doing them good, not for their sakes, but because he loved their fathers. He preserved them carefully, as a man does the first and choicest fruits of his vineyard. Now when he put all this honour upon them, and they stood so fair for preferment, one would think they should have maintained their excellency; but, (2.) See the great disgrace they put upon themselves. God set them apart for himself as a peculiar people, but they went to Baal-peor, joined with the Moabites in sacrificing to that dirty dunghill deity (Num. xxv. 2, 3), and they *separated themselves unto that shame,* that shameful idol, so Baal-peor was in a particular manner, if (as should seem) the *whoredom* which the people *committed with the daughters of Moab* was a part of the service done to Baal-peor. Note, Whatever those separate themselves to that forsake God it will certainly be a shame to them, first or last. *Their abominations* are here said to be *as they loved;* their practices which were an abomination to God were as the best-beloved of their souls. Or when they had once forsaken God they multiplied *their abominations,* their idols and abominable idolatries, at their pleasure. This was the way of their fathers; God had done well for them, but they had acted ungratefully towards him, and in the same manner had the present generation *deeply corrupted them-selves.*

11 As for Ephraim, their glory shall fly away like a bird, from the birth, and from the womb, and from the conception. 12 Though they bring up their children, yet will I bereave them, *that there shall* not *be* a man *left :* yea, woe also to them when I depart from them! 13 Ephraim, as I saw Tyrus, *is* planted in a pleasant place : but Ephraim shall bring forth his children to the murderer. 14 Give them, O LORD : what wilt thou give ? give them a miscarrying womb and dry breasts. 15 All their wickedness *is* in Gilgal : for there I hated them : for the wickedness of their doings I will drive them out of mine house, I will love them no more : all their princes *are* revolters. 16 Ephraim is smitten, their root is dried up, they shall bear no fruit : yea, though they bring forth, yet will I slay *even* the beloved *fruit* of their womb. 17 My God will cast them away, because they did not hearken unto him : and they shall be wanderers among the nations.

In the foregoing verses we saw the sin of Israel derived from their fathers; here we see the punishment of Israel derived to their children; for, as death entered by sin at first, so it is still entailed with it. We may observe, in these verses,

I. The sin of Ephraim. Some expressions are here which describe that. 1. *They did not hearken to God* (*v.* 17); they did not give attention to the voice either of his word or of his rod; they did not believe what he said, nor would they be ruled by him. He told them their duty, their interest, their danger, but they regarded him not ; all he said to them by his words and by his prophets was to them as a tale that is told ; and then no wonder that we hear, 2. Of the *wickedness of their doings* (*v.* 15), the downright malice that was in their sins ; they were not infirmities, but daring presumptions. How can those but do wickedly who will not hearken to the word of God, that would teach and persuade them to do well ? And no wonder that there were wicked doings among them when, 3. Their worship was corrupt (*v.* 15) : *All their wickedness is in Gilgal,* which was a place infamous for idolatry, as appears, *ch.* iv. 15 ; xii. 11 ; Amos iv. 4 ; v. 5. It is probable that the idolaters chose that place for their head-quarters because it had been famous in other ages for solemn transactions between God and

Israel, as Josh. v. 2, 10 ; 1 Sam. x. 8 ; xi. 15. There, where the source of idolatry was, whence it spread through the kingdom, there it might be said that *all their wickedness* was, for all other wickedness owed its origin to that. Corruptions in worship make way for corruptions in morals. The *mother of harlots* is the *mother of* all other *abominations,* Rev. xvii. 5. The learned Grotius conjectures that there is a mystical sense here. Golgotha in Syriac is the same with Gilgal in Hebrew, and therefore he thinks this may have reference to the putting of Christ to death at Golgotha, which was the greatest sin of the Jewish nation, and of which it might truly be said, *All their wickedness* was summed up in that. And no wonder that the people did wickedly, both in worship and conversation, when, 4. *All their princes were revolters;* the whole succession of the kings of the ten tribes did evil in the sight of the Lord, or all the set of judges and magistrates at this time were wicked ; they turned aside to sinful ways and persisted in those ways.

II. The displeasure of God against Ephraim for sin. This is variously expressed here, to show what a provocation sin is to the pure eyes of his glory, and how odious it makes the sinner to him. 1. He *departs from them, v.* 12. When they revolt from him, and withdraw from their allegiance to him, how can they expect but that he should depart from them and withdraw both his protection and his bounty ? And well may his threatening be enforced as it is, and made terrible : *Woe also unto them when I depart from them !* Note, Those are in a woeful condition indeed whom God has forsaken. Our weal or woe depends upon the gracious presence of God with us ; and, if he goes, all weal goes with him and all woes come upon us. *God has forsaken him ; persecute and take him.* Saul knew this when he laid such an emphasis upon this part of his complaint, *The Philistines make war against me, and God has departed from me.* Nay, he does not only depart from them, but, 2. He hates them. *In Gilgal,* where *all their wickedness is, there I hated them.* There, where the abominations of sin are committed, there God abominates the sinners. In Gilgal he had bestowed many tokens of his favour upon their ancestors, but now that is the place where he hates them for their base ingratitude. Nay, he not only hates them, but, 3. He *will love them no more,* will never take them into his favour again ; the breach between God and Israel is wide as the sea, which cannot be healed. This agrees with what he had said, (*ch.* i. 6, 7), *I will no more have mercy upon the house of Israel,* the ten tribes. 4. He will discard them, and have no more to do with them : *For the wickedness of their doings, I will drive them out of my house.* He will no longer own them as his, or as belonging to his family in the world; he will turn them out of doors as unfaithful tenants that pay him no rent, as unprofitable servants that do him neither credit nor work. Note, Those that profane God's house can expect no other than to be expelled his house, and no longer suffered to be either lodgers in it or retainers to it. Nay, he will not only drive them out of his house, but, 5. He will drive them far enough (v. 17): *My God will cast them away*, not only out of his house, but out of his sight; he will quite abandon and reject them; they shall be *cast-aways*. God said that he would *drive them out of his house*, and here the prophet seconds it, as one that knew his Master's mind very well: *My God will cast them away*. See with what comfort and pleasure he calls God his God. Note, When others disown God, and are disowned by him, it is a very great satisfaction to good people that they can call God their God, can cheerfully own him and see themselves owned by him—all revolters, all ruined, yet God is *my God*.

III. The fruit of this displeasure, in the cutting off and abandoning of their posterity, which is the judgment here threatened again and again. Observe here,

1. How numerous Ephraim seemed likely to be. The name *Ephraim* is derived from *fruitfulness*, Gen. xli. 52. Joseph is a *fruitful bough*, Gen. xlix. 22. And Moses's blessing foretold the *ten thousands of Ephraim*, Deut. xxxiii. 17. This was his glory, v. 11. For this he seemed designed by him that appoints the bounds of men's habitation; for *Ephraim, as I saw Tyrus, is planted in a pleasant place*, to encourage his increase, which one may expect as from a tree planted by the river's side. Ephraim is as strong and rich as ever Tyre was, and as proud and secure. The Chaldee paraphrase gives this sense of it, *The congregation of Israel, while they observed the law, was like to Tyrus in prosperity and security*.

2. How few Ephraim should be (v. 11): *Their glory shall fly away like a bird;* their children shall be taken away and the hopes of their families cut off. All their glory shall fly *as an eagle towards heaven*, swiftly and irrecoverably. Note, Worldly glory is glory that will *fly away;* but those that have their God their glory have in him an unfading everlasting glory. Ephraim has been as a fruitful tree. But now *Ephraim is smitten*, is blasted; *their root is dried up; they shall bear no fruit*, v. 16. If the root be dried, the branch must wither of course. Observe,

(1.) God's threatening this judgment of the destroying of their children. [1.] They shall perish of themselves by the immediate hand of God (v. 11): They shall *fly away from the birth, and from the womb, and from the conception*. Some of their children shall die as soon as they are born; the cradle shall

1174

be presently turned into a coffin. Others of them shall be *still-born*, or the womb shall be their grave, and their death there their mothers' death too. Of others their mothers shall miscarry almost as soon as they have conceived, and they shall be as untimely fruit. See how easily God can, and how justly we are sure he might, root out the whole race of mankind, that degenerate, guilty, obnoxious race, and blot out the name of it from under heaven; it is but doing as he does by Ephraim here, writing them all childless, making all their glory to *fly away from the birth, the womb, and the conception*, drying up their root, that they bear no fruit, and their business is done in a few years. [2.] They shall perish by the hand of their enemies; they shall die violent deaths (v. 12): "*Though they bring up their children* to some maturity, though they escape the diseases and deaths which the infant age is liable to, and are thought to be reared past danger, *yet will I bereave them* (v. 12), by one judgment or other, so that *there shall not be a man left* to build up their families and bear up their name." Again (v. 13), *Ephraim shall bring forth his children to the murderer*. The mothers shall travail with pain to bear their children, and a great deal of care, and pains, and cost shall be bestowed upon the nursing of them, and when a cruel enemy comes and puts all to the sword, young and old, without mercy, then they seem but as lambs that were all this while fed for the slaughter. Note, It is a great alloy to the comfort parents have in their children that they know not what they have brought them forth and brought them up for, perhaps *for the murderer*, or, which is worse, to be themselves the plagues of their generation. It is threatened again (v. 16), *Though they bring forth, yet will I slay even the beloved fruit of their womb*, those children that they are most fond of. Note, The parents' love is no security to the children's lives; nay, sometimes death is commissioned to take the darlings of the family and leave the burdens of it. When sentence was passed upon Israel in the wilderness, that they should all perish there, this mercy was mixed with the wrath, that their children should nevertheless enter into that rest which they through unbelief could not enter into. But this is a total and final rejection; even their children shall all be cut off, and the land shall escheat to the crown, *ob defectum sanguinis—shall be lost for want of heirs*. The Chaldee-paraphrase, and many of the rabbin, by the *murderers* to whom the children were brought forth, understand those that sacrificed their children to Moloch, a sin which was its own punishment, which showed the parents void of bowels and justly left them void of blessings. [3.] Those few that escape and remain shall be dispersed (v. 17): They shall be *wanderers among the nations;* so the remains of the Jews are at this day, and there is no place in the world where they are a distinct nation.

(2.) The prophet's prayer relating to it (*v.* 14): *Give them, O Lord! what wilt thou give?* What shall I ask for a people thus doomed to destruction? It is this; since the decree has gone forth, that they must either die from the womb or be brought forth for the murderer, of the two let them rather *die from the womb.* Rather let them have no children than have them to be made miserable; for the same reason, when a total ruin was coming on the Jewish nation, Christ said, *Blessed is the womb that never bore and the paps that never gave suck,* Luke xxiii. 29. " Give therefore *a miscarrying womb and dry breasts;* for it is better to fall into the hands of the Lord, whose mercies are great, than into the hands of man." Note, Those that are childless may with this reconcile themselves to the will of God herein, that the time may come when, if they were not so, they would wish they had been so.

CHAP. X.

In this chapter, I. The people of Israel are charged with gross corruptions in the worship of God and are threatened with the destruction of their images and altars, ver. 1, 2, 5, 6, 8. II. They are charged with corruptions in the administration of the civil government and are threatened with the ruin of that, ver. 3, 4, 7. III. They are charged with imitating the sins of their fathers, and with security in their own sins, and are threatened with smarting humbling judgments, ver. 9—11. IV. They are earnestly invited to repent and reform, and are threatened with ruin if they did not, ver. 12—15.

ISRAEL *is* an empty vine, he bringeth forth fruit unto himself: according to the multitude of his fruit he hath increased the altars; according to the goodness of his land they have made goodly images. 2 Their heart is divided; now shall they be found faulty: he shall break down their altars, he shall spoil their images. 3 For now they shall say, We have no king, because we feared not the LORD; what then should a king do to us? 4 They have spoken words, swearing falsely in making a covenant: thus judgment springeth up as hemlock in the furrows of the field. 5 The inhabitants of Samaria shall fear because of the calves of Bethaven: for the people thereof shall mourn over it, and the priests thereof *that* rejoiced on it, for the glory thereof, because it is departed from it. 6 It shall be also carried unto Assyria *for* a present to king Jareb: Ephraim shall receive shame, and Israel shall be ashamed of his own counsel. 7 *As for* Samaria, her king is cut off as the foam upon the water. 8 The high places also of Aven, the

sin of Israel, shall be destroyed: the thorn and the thistle shall come up on their altars; and they shall say to the mountains, Cover us; and to the hills, Fall on us.

Observe, I. What the sins are which are here laid to Israel's charge, the national sins which bring down national judgment. The prophet deals plainly with them; for what good would it do them to be flattered?

1 They were not fruitful in the fruits of righteousness to the glory of God. Here all their other wickedness began (*v.* 1): *Israel is an empty vine.* The church of God is fitly compared to a *vine*, weak, and of an unpromising outside, yet spreading and fruitful; believers are branches of that vine, and partake of its root and fatness. But this was the character of Israel, they were as *an empty vine*, a vine that had no sap or virtue in it, and therefore none of those good fruits produced by it that were expected from it, with which God and man should be honoured. Note, There are many who, though they have not become *degenerate* vines, are yet *empty vines*, have no good in them. A vine is of all trees least serviceable if it do not bear fruit. It is thenceforth good for nothing, Ezek. xv. 3, 5. And those that bring forth no grapes will soon come to bring forth wild grapes; those that do no good will do hurt. He is an *empty vine*, for *he brings forth fruit to himself.* What good there is in him is not directed to the glory of God, but he takes the praise of it to himself, and prides himself in it. Christians live not to themselves (Rom. xiv. 6), but hypocrites make self their centre; they *eat and drink to themselves,* Zech. vii. 5, 6. Or Israel is by the judgments of God *emptied* and *spoiled* of all his wealth, because he made use of it in the service of his lusts, and not to the honour of God who gave it to him. Note, What we do not rightly employ we may justly expect to be emptied of.

2. They multiplied their altars and images, and the more bountiful God's providence was to them the more prodigal they were in serving their idols: *According to the multitude of his fruit* which his land brought forth *he has increased the altars,* and *according to the goodness of his land they have made goodly images.* Note, It is a great affront to God, and an abuse of his goodness, when the more mercies we receive from him the more sins we commit against him, and when the more wealth men have the more mischief they do. Should not we be thus abundant in the service of our God, as they were in the service of their idols? As we find our estates increasing, we should proportionably abound the more in works of piety and charity.

3. Their hearts were divided, *v.* 2. (1.) They were divided among themselves. They were at variance about their idols, some for one, some for another, at variance about their kings, whose separate interests made

parties in the kingdom, and in them their very hearts were divided, and alienated one from another, and there was no such thing as cordial friendship to be found among them; it follows therefore, *Now shall they be found faulty.* Note, The divisions and animosities of a people are the causes of much sin and the presages of ruin. (2.) They were divided between God and their idols. They had a remaining affection in their hearts for God, but a reigning affection for their idols. They *halted between God and Baal,* that was the dividing of their heart. But God is the sovereign of the heart and he will by no means endure a rival; he will either have all or none. Satan, like the pretended mother, says, *Let it be neither mine nor thine, but divide it;* but, if this be yielded to, God says, Nay, *let him take it all.* A heart thus divided will be *found faulty,* and be rejected as treacherous in covenanting with God. Note, A heart divided between God and mammon, though it may trim the matter so as to appear plausible, will, in the day of discovery, be *found faulty.*

4. They made no conscience of what they said and what they did in the most solemn manner, *v.* 4. (1.) Not of what they said in swearing, which is the most solemn speaking: *They have spoken words,* and words only, for they meant not as they said; they did *verba dare—give words.* They *swore falsely in making a covenant;* they were deceitful in their covenanting with God, the covenant of circumcision, the fair promises they made of reformation when they were in distress; and no marvel if those that were false to their God were false to all mankind. They contracted such a habit of treachery that they broke through the most sacred bonds, and made nothing of them; subjects violated their oaths of allegiance and their kings their coronation-oaths; they broke their leagues with the nations they were in alliance with, nor was any conscience made of contracts between private persons. (2.) Nor of what they did in judgment, which is the most solemn acting. Justice could not take place when men made nothing of forswearing themselves; for thus *judgment,* which should have been a healing medicinal plant and of a sweet smell, *sprang up as hemlock,* which is both nauseous and noxious, *in the furrows of the field,* in the field that was ploughed and furrowed for good corn. Note, God is greatly offended with corruptions, not only in his own worship, but in the administration of justice between man and man, and the dishonesty of a people shall be the ground of his controversy with them as well as their idolatry and impiety; for God's laws are intended for man's benefit and the good of the community, as well as for God's honour, and the profanation of courts of justice shall be avenged as surely as the profanation of temples.

II. What the judgments are with which

1176

Israel should be punished for these sins; they sinned both in civil and religious matters, and in both they shall be punished. 1. They shall have no joy of their kings and of their government. Because justice is turned into oppression, therefore those who are entrusted with the administration of it, and should be blessings to the state, shall be complained of as the burdens of it (*v.* 3), and those that would not rule their people well shall not be able to protect them : *Now they shall say,* " *We have no king,* that is, we are as if we had none, we have none to do us any good nor stand us in any stead, none to keep us from destroying ourselves or being destroyed by our enemies, none to preserve the public peace nor to fight our battles; and justly has this come to us. *Because we feared not the Lord,* when we were safe under the protection of our kings, therefore we are rejected by him, and then *what shall a king do for us?* What good can we expect from a king when we have forfeited the favour of our God?" Note, Those that cast off the fear of God are not likely to have joy of any of their creature-comforts; nor will men's loyalty to their prince befriend them without religion, for, though that may engage him to be for them, what good will that do them if God be against them ? Those that keep themselves in the fear and favour of God may say, with triumph, " What can the greatest of men do against us?" But those that throw themselves out of his protection must say, with despair, " What can the greatest of men do for us?" He was a king that said, *If the Lord do not help thee, whence should I help thee?* Yet he is a fool that says, If a king cannot help us, we must perish (as these intimate here), for God can do that for us which kings cannot. Time was when they doted upon having a king: but now what can a king (who, they thought, could do any thing) do for them? God can make people sick of those creature-confidences which they were most fond of. This is their complaint when their king is disabled to help them, yet this is not the worst; their civil government shall not only be weakened, but quite destroyed (*v.* 7): *As for Samaria,* the royal city, which is now almost all that is left, *her king is cut off as the foam from the water.* The foam swims uppermost, and makes a great show upon the face of the water, yet it is but a heap of bubbles raised by the troubling of the water. Such were the kings of Israel, after their revolt from the house of David, a mere scum; their government had no foundation. No better are the greatest of kings when they set up in opposition to God; when God comes to contend with them by his judgments he can as easily disperse and dissolve them, and bring them to nothing, as the froth upon the water. 2. They shall have no joy of their idols and of their worship of them. And miserable is the case of that people whose gods fail them when their kings do. (1.) The idols they had made, and the altars they had set up in honour of them, should be broken down, and spoiled, and carried away, as common plunder, by the victorious enemy : He *shall break down their altars.* God shall do it by the hand of the Assyrians : the Assyrians shall do it by order from God. *He shall spoil their images, v.* 2. Note, What men make idols of it is just with God to *break down* and *spoil.* But the calf at Bethel was the sovereign idol; it was this that the inhabitants of Samaria doted most upon; now it is here foretold that this should be destroyed: *The glory of it has departed from it* (*v.* 5) when it is thrown down and defaced, no more to be worshipped; but this is not all: *It shall also be carried to Assyria* (as some think that the calf at Dan was some time before) *for a present to king Jareb.* It was carried to him as a rich booty (for it was a golden calf, and probably adorned with the gifts and offerings of its worshippers) and as a trophy of victory over their enemies : and what more glorious trophy could they bring than this, or more incontestable proof of an absolute conquest ? Thus it is said, *The sin of Israel shall be destroyed* (*v.* 8), that is, the idols which they made the matter of their sin; it is said of them, *They became a sin to all Israel,* 1 Kings xii. 30. Note, If the grace of God prevail not to destroy the love of sin in us, it is just that the providence of God should destroy the food and fuel of sin about us. With the idols, *the high places* shall be destroyed, the *high places of Aven,* that is, of *Bethaven* (*v.* 5) or *Bethel;* it was called *the house of God* (so Bethel signifies), but now it is called *the house of iniquity,* nay, *iniquity* itself. The kings did not, as they ought to have done, *take away the high places* by the sword of justice, and therefore God will take them away by the sword of war; so that *the thorn and the thistle* shall *come up on their altars,* that is, they shall lie in ruins. Their altars, while they stood, were as thorns and thistles, offensive to God and good men, and fruits of sin and the curse; justly therefore are they buried in thorns and thistles. (2.) The destruction of their idols, their altars, and their high places, shall be the occasion of sorrow, and shame, and terror to them. [1.] It shall be an occasion of sorrow to them. When the calf at Bethel. is broken *the people thereof shall mourn over it.* They looked upon the calf to be the protector of their nation, and, when that was gone, thought they must all be undone, which made the poor ignorant people that were deluded into the love of it lament bitterly, as Micah did (Judg. xviii. 24), *You have taken away my gods, and what have I more?* The priests that had rejoiced in it shall now mourn for it with the people. Note, Whatever men make a god of they will mourn

for the loss of; and an inordinate sorrow for the loss of any worldly good is a sign we made an idol of it. They used to be very merry in the worship of their idols, but now they shall mourn over them; for sinful mirth shall, sooner or later, be turned into mourning. [2.] It shall be an occasion of shame to them (*v.* 6) : *Ephraim shall receive shame* when he sees the gods he trusted to carried into captivity, and *Israel shall be ashamed of his own counsel,* in putting such confidence in them and paying such adoration to them. God's ark and altars were never thrown down till the people rejected them; but the idolatrous altars were thrown down when the people were doting on them, which shows that the contempt of the former, and the veneration for the latter, were the sins for which God visited them. [3.] It shall be an occasion of fear to them (*v.* 5): *The inhabitants of Samaria shall fear ;* they shall be in pain for their gods and afraid of losing them; or, rather, they shall be in pain for themselves and their children and families, when they see the judgments of God breaking in upon them and beginning with their idols, as he *executed judgment against the gods of Egypt,* Exod. xii. 12. Thus idolaters are brought in trembling when God arises to *shake terribly the earth,* Isa. ii. 21. And here (*v.* 8), *They shall say to the mountains, Cover us ; and to the hills, Fall on us.* The supporters of idolatry (Rev. vi. 15, 16) are brought in calling thus in vain to rocks and mountains to shelter them from God's wrath.

9 O Israel, thou hast sinned from the days of Gibeah : there they stood : the battle in Gibeah against the children of iniquity did not overtake them. 10 *It is* in my desire that I should chastise them; and the people shall be gathered against them, when they shall bind themselves in their two furrows. 11 And Ephraim *is as* a heifer *that is* taught, *and* loveth to tread out *the corn;* but I passed over upon her fair neck : I will make Ephraim to ride ; Judah shall plough, *and* Jacob shall break his clods. 12 Sow to yourselves in righteousness, reap in mercy ; break up your fallow ground : for *it is* time to seek the LORD, till he come and rain righteousness upon you. 13 Ye have ploughed wickedness, ye have reaped iniquity ; ye have eaten the fruit of lies : because thou didst trust in thy way, in the multitude of thy mighty men. 14 Therefore shall a tumult arise among thy people, and all thy fortresses shall be

1177

spoiled, as Shalman spoiled Beth-ar-bel in the day of battle: the mother was dashed in pieces upon *her* children. 15 So shall Beth-el do unto you because of your great wickedness: in a morning shall the king of Israel utterly be cut off.

Here, I. They are put in mind of the sins of their fathers and predecessors, for which God would now reckon with them. It was told them (*ch.* ix. 9) that they had *corrupted themselves, as in the days of Gibeah,* and here (*v.* 9), *O Israel! thou hast sinned from the days of Gibeah.* Not only the wickedness that was committed in that age is revived in this, and reacted, a copy from that original, but the wickedness that was committed in that age has been continued in a constant series and succession through all the intervening ages down to this; so that the measure of iniquity had been long in filling; and still there had been made additions to it. Or, " *Thou hast sinned more than in the days of Gibeah*" (so it may be read); " the sins of this age exceed those of the worst of former ages. The case was bad then, for *there they stood;* the criminals stood in their own defence, and the tribes of Israel, who undertook to chastise them for their wickedness, were *at a stand,* when both in the first and in the second battle the malefactors were the victors; and *the battle in Gibeah against the children of iniquity did not overtake them* till the third engagement, and then did not overtake them all, for 600 made their escape. But thy sin is worse than theirs, and therefore thou canst not expect but that the battle against the children of iniquity should overtake thee, and overcome thee."

II. They have warning given them, fair warning, of the judgments of God that were coming upon them, *v.* 10. God had hitherto pitied and spared them. Though they had been very provoking, he had a mind to try whether they would be wrought upon by patience and forbearance; but now, " *It is in my desire that I should chastise them;* it is what I have a purpose of and will take pleasure in." He will *rejoice over them to do them hurt,* Deut. xxviii. 63. Note, Because God does not desire the death and ruin of sinners, therefore he does desire their chastisement. And see what the chastisement is: *The people shall be gathered against them,* as all the other tribes were against Benjamin in the battle of Gibeah. One of the rabbin thus descants upon it: " Because they receive not chastisement from me by my prophets, who in my name rebuke them, I will chastise them by the hands of the people who shall be *gathered against them, when they shall bind themselves in their two furrows,*" that is, when they shall think to fortify themselves, as it were, within a double

entrenchment. Or, *When I shall bind them for their two transgressions* (so the margin reads it), meaning their corporal and spiritual whoredom, which they are so often charged with, or the *two calves* at Dan and Bethel, or those two great evils mentioned Jer. ii. 13. Or, *When I shall bind them to their two furrows,* that is, bring them into servitude to the Assyrians, who shall keep them under the yoke as oxen in the plough, who are bound to the two furrows up the field and down it, and dare not, for fear of the goad, stir a step out of them. The Chaldee says, Those that are *gathered against them shall exercise dominion over them, in like manner as a pair of heifers are tied to their two furrows.* Thus those that would not be God's freemen shall be their enemies' slaves, and shall be made to know the difference between *God's service* and *the service of the kingdoms of the countries,* 2 Chron. xii. 8.

III. They are made to know that their unacquaintedness with sufferings and hardships should not excuse them from a very miserable captivity, *v.* 11. See how nice, and tender, and delicate, Ephraim is; he is *as a heifer that is taught to tread out the corn, and loves* that work, because, being not allowed to be muzzled, she has liberty to eat at pleasure, and the work itself was dry and easy, and both its own diversion and its own wages. " But," says God, " I have a yoke to put upon *her fair neck,* fair as it is. *I will make Ephraim to ride,* that is, I will tame them, or cause them to be ridden by the Assyrians and other conquerors that shall rule them with rigour, as men do the beasts they ride upon (Ps. lxvi. 12); and *Judah* too shall be made to *plough,* and *Jacob to break the clods,*" that is, they shall be used hardly, but not so hardly as Ephraim. Note, It is just with God to make those know what hardships mean that indulge themselves too much in their own ease and pleasure. The learned Dr. Pocock inclines to another sense of these words, as intimating the tender gentle methods God took with this people, to bring them into obedience to his law, as a reason why they should return to that obedience; he had managed them as the husbandman does his cattle that he trains up for service. Ephraim being as a docile heifer, fit to be employed, God took hold of *her fair neck,* to accustom her to the hand, *harnessed her,* or put the yoke of his commandments upon her, gave his people Israel a law, that, being trained up in his institutions, they might not be tempted by the usages of the heathen; he had used all fair and likely means with them to keep them in their obedience, had set *Judah to plough* and *Jacob to break the clods,* had employed them in the observance of precepts proper for them; and yet they would not be retained in their obedience, but started aside.

IV. They are invited and encouraged to return to God by prayer, repentance, and reformation, *v.* 12, 13. See here,

1. The duties they are called to. They are *God's husbandry* (1 Cor. iii. 9), and the duties are expressed in language borrowed from the husbandman's calling. If they would not be brought into bondage by their oppressors, let them return to God's service. (1.) Let them *break up the fallow ground;* let them cleanse their hearts from all corrupt affections and lusts, which are as weeds and thorns, and let them be humbled for their sins, and be of a broken and contrite spirit in the sense of them; let them be full of sorrow and shame at the remembrance of them, and prepare to receive the divine precepts, as the ground that is ploughed is to receive the seed, that it may take root. See Jer. iv. 3. (2.) Let them *sow to themselves in righteousness;* let them return to the practice of good works, according to the law of God, which is the rule of righteousness; let them abound in works of piety towards God, and of justice and charity towards one another, and herein let them *sow to the Spirit,* as the apostle speaks, Gal. vi. 7, 8. Every action is seed sown. Let them *sow in righteousness;* let them sow what they should sow, do what they should do, and they themselves shall have the benefit of it. (3.) Let them *seek the Lord;* let them look up to him for his grace, and beg of him to bless the *seed sown.* The husbandman must plough and sow with an eye to God, asking of him rain in the season thereof.

2. The arguments used for the pressing of these duties. Consider, (1.) It is time to do it; it is *high time.* The husbandman sows in seed-time, and, if that time be far spent, he applies to the work with the more diligence. Note, Seeking the Lord is to be every day's work, but there are some special occasions given by the providence and grace of God when it is, in a particular manner, time to seek him. (2.) If we do our part, God will do his. If we *sow to ourselves in righteousness*—if we be careful and diligent to do our duty, in a dependence upon his grace—he will shower down his grace upon us, will *rain righteousness,* the very thing that those need most who are to sow *in righteousness;* for *by the grace of God we are what we are.* Some apply it to Christ, who should come in the fulness of time, and for whose coming they must prepare themselves; he shall come as *the Lord our righteousness,* and shall *rain righteousness upon us,* that everlasting righteousness which he has brought in; he will grant us of it abundantly. It is foretold (Ps. lxxii. 6) that *he shall come down like rain.* (3.) If we *sow in righteousness,* we shall *reap in mercy,* which agrees with that promise, If we *sow to the Spirit,* we shall *of the Spirit reap life everlasting.* We shall reap *according to the measure of mercy* (so the word is); it shall be a great reward, according to the

riches of mercy, such a reward, not as becomes such mean creatures as we are to receive, but as becomes a God of infinite mercy to give, a reward, *not of debt,* but *of grace.* We reap not in merit, but in mercy. It is what is sown; God gives a body as it has pleased him. (4.) We have *ploughed wickedness and reaped iniquity;* and the time *past of our life may suffice* that we have done so, *v.* 13. "You have taken a great deal of pains in the service of sin, have laboured at it in the very fire; and will you grudge to bear the burden and heat of the day in God's service and in doing that which will be for your own advantage? You have done much to damn your souls; will you not undo it again, and do something to save them?" (5.) We never got any thing in the service of sin. They have *ploughed wickedness* (that is, they have done the drudgery of sin), and they have *reaped iniquity,* that is, they have got all that is to be got by it; they have carried it on to the *harvest,* and what the better? It is all a cheat. *They have eaten the fruit of lies,* fruit that is but a lie, which looks fair, but is rotten within; the *works of darkness* are *unfruitful works,* Eph. v. 11; Rom. vi. 21. Even the gains of sin yield the sinner no satisfaction. (6.) As our comforts, so our confidences, in the service of sin will certainly fail us: "*Thou didst trust in thy ways, in the multitude of thy mighty men;* thou hast stayed thyself upon creatures, thy own power and policy, and therefore hast ventured to plough wickedness, and thy hopes have deceived thee; come therefore, and seek the Lord, and thy hope in him shall not deceive thee."

V. They are threatened with utter destruction, both for their carnal practices and for their carnal confidences, *v.* 14, 15. *Therefore,* because thou hast sown wickedness, and trusted in thy own way, *a tumult shall arise among thy people,* either by insurrections at home or invasions from abroad, either of which will put a kingdom into confusion and make a noise, much more both together. 1. Their cities and strongholds shall be a prey to the enemy: The *fortresses* which they confided in, and in which they had laid up their effects, shall be seized and rifled, as *Shalman spoiled Beth-arbel in the day of battle.* This refers to some event that had lately happened, not elsewhere recorded; and probably Shalman is the same with Shalmaneser king of Assyria, who had lately put some town, or castle, or house *(Beth-arbel is the house of Arbel),* under *military execution,* which perhaps he used with severity in the beginning of his conquests, to terrify other garrisons into a speedy surrender at the first summons. God tells them that thus Samaria should be *spoiled.* 2. The inhabitants shall be put to the *sword,* as it was at *Beth-arbel;* when it was taken *the mother was dashed in pieces upon her children,* that is, they were both dashed in pieces together by the fury of the soldiers. See what cruel work war makes. *Jusque datum sceleri—Wickedness has free course.* It is strange that any of the human race could be so inhuman; but see what comes of sin. *Homo homini lupus—Man is a wolf to man,* and then, *Homo homini agnus —Man is a lamb to man.* 3. Even royal blood shall be mingled with common gore : *In a morning shall the king of Israel utterly be cut off, v.* 15. Hoshea was the last king of Israel; in him the whole kingdom was *cut off* and came to a period; it may refer either to him or to some of his predecessors that were cut off by treachery. It shall be done *in a morning,* in a very little time, as suddenly as the dawning of the morning, or at the time appointed, for so the morning comes, punctually at its time. Or *in the morning,* when they think the night of calamity is over, and expect a returning day, then shall all their hopes be dashed by the sudden cutting off of their king, *v.* 7. Kings, though gods to us, are men to God, and shall die like men. And *(lastly)* what does all this desolation owe its rise to? What is the spring of this bloodshed? He tells us (*v.* 15) : *So shall Bethel do unto you.* Bethel was the place where one of the calves was; Gilgal, where *all their wickedness* is said to have been, was hard by; there was their *great wickedness,* the *evil of their evil* (so the word is), the sum and quintessence of their sin; and that was it that *did this to them,* that made all this havoc, for that was it that provoked God to bring it upon them. He does not say, " So shall the *king of Assyria* do to you;" but, " So shall *Bethel* do to you." Note, Whatever mischief is done to us it is sin that does it. Are the fortresses spoiled? Are the women and children murdered? Is the king cut off? It is sin that does all this. It is sin that ruins soul, body, estate, all. *So shall Bethel do unto you.* It is *thy own wickedness* that *corrects thee* and *thy backslidings* that *reprove thee.*

CHAP. XI.

In this chapter we have, I. The great goodness of God towards his people Israel, and the great things he had done for them, ver. 1, 3, 4. II. Their ungrateful conduct towards him, notwithstanding his favours towards them, ver. 2—4, 7, 12. III. Threatenings of wrath against them for their ingratitude and treachery, ver. 5, 6. IV. Mercy remembered in the midst of wrath, ver. 8, 9. V. Promises of what God would yet do for them, ver. 10, 11. VI. An honourable character given of Judah, ver. 12.

WHEN Israel *was* a child, then I loved him, and called my son out of Egypt. 2 *As* they called them, so they went from them : they sacrificed unto Baalim, and burned incense to graven images. 3 I taught Ephraim also to go, taking them by their arms ; but they knew not that I healed them. 4 I drew them with cords of a man, with bands of love : and I was to them as they that take off the yoke on their jaws, and I laid

meat unto them. 5 He shall not return into the land of Egypt, but the Assyrian shall be his king, because they refused to return. 6 And the sword shall abide on his cities, and shall consume his branches, and devour *them,* because of their own counsels. 7 And my people are bent to backsliding from me : though they called them to the Most High, none at all would exalt *him.*

Here we find,

I. God very gracious to Israel. They were a people for whom he had done more than for any people under heaven, and to whom he had given more, which they are here, I will not say upbraided with (for God gives, and upbraids not), but put in mind of, as an aggravation of their sin and an encouragement to repentance. 1. He had a kindness for them when they were young (*v.* 1) : *When Israel was a child then I loved him ;* when they first began to multiply into a nation in Egypt God then *set his love upon them,* and *chose them because he loved them,* because he would love them, Deut. vii. 7, 8. When they were weak and helpless as children, foolish and froward as children, when they were outcasts, and children exposed, then God *loved them ;* he pitied them, and testified his goodwill to them ; he bore them as the nurse does the sucking child, nourished them, and suffered their manners. Note, Those that have grown up, nay, those that have grown old, ought often to reflect upon the goodness of God to them in their childhood. 2. He delivered them out of the house of bondage : *I called my son out of Egypt,* because a son, because a beloved son. When God demanded Israel's discharge from Pharaoh he called them *his son,* his *first-born.* Note, Those whom God loves he calls out of the bondage of sin and Satan into the glorious liberty of his children. These words are said to have been fulfilled in Christ, when, upon the death of Herod, he and his parents were *called out of Egypt* (Matt. ii. 15), so that the words have a double aspect, speaking historically of the calling of Israel out of Egypt and prophetically of the bringing of Christ thence ; and the former was a type of the latter, and a pledge and earnest of the many and great favours God had in reserve for that people, especially the sending of his Son into the world, and the bringing him again into the land of Israel when they had unkindly driven him out, and he might justly never have returned. The calling of Christ out of Egypt was a figure of the calling of all that are his, through him, out of spiritual slavery. 3. He gave them a good education, took care of them, took pains with them, not only as a father or tutor, but, such is the condescension of divine grace, as a mother or nurse (*v.* 3) : *I taught Ephraim also to go,* as a child in leading-strings is taught. When they were in the wilderness God led them by the pillar of cloud and fire, showed them the way in which they should go, and bore them up, *taking them by the arms. He taught them to go* in the way of his commandments, by the institutions of the ceremonial law, which were as tutors and governors to that people under age. He took them by the arms, to guide them, that they might not stray, and to hold them up, that they might not stumble and fall. God's spiritual Israel are thus supported. *Thou hast holden me by my right hand,* Ps. lxxiii. 23. 4. When any thing was amiss with them, or they were ever so little out of order, he was their physician : "*I healed them;* I not only took a tender care of them (a friend may do that), but wrought an effectual cure : it is a God only that can do that. *I am the Lord that healeth thee* (Exod. xv. 26), that redresseth all thy grievances." 5. He brought them into his service by mild and gentle methods (*v.* 4) : *I drew them with cords of a man, with bands of love.* Note, It is God's work to draw poor souls to himself; and none can come to him except he draw them, John vi. 44. He draws, (1.) *With the cords of a man,* with such cords as men draw with that have a principle of humanity, or such cords as men are drawn with ; he dealt with them *as men,* in an equitable rational way, in an easy gentle way, *with the cords of Adam.* He dealt with them as with Adam in innocency, bringing them at once into a paradise, and into covenant with himself. (2.) *With bands of love,* or *cart-ropes* of love. This word signifies stronger cords than the former. He did not drive them by force into his service, whether they would or no, nor rule them with rigour, nor detain them by violence, but his attractives were all loving and endearing, all sweet and gentle, that he might overcome them with kindness. Moses, whom he made their guide, was the meekest man in the world. *Kindnesses* among men we commonly call *obligations,* or *bonds,* bonds of love. Thus God *draws with the savour of his good ointments* (Cant. i. 4), draws *with lovingkindness,* Jer. xxxi. 3. Thus God deals with us, and we must deal in like manner with those that are under our instruction and government, deal rationally and mildly with them. 6. He eased them of the burdens they had been long groaning under : *I was to them as those that take off the yoke on their jaws,* alluding to the care of the good husbandman, who is merciful to his beast, and will not tire him with hard and constant labour. Probably, in those times, the yoke on the neck of the oxen was fastened with some bridle, or headstall, over the jaws, which *muzzled the mouth of the ox.* Israel in Egypt were thus restrained from the enjoyments of their comforts and constrained to hard labour ; but God eased them, *removed their shoulder from the burden,* Ps.

lxxxi. 6. Note, Liberty is a great mercy, especially out of bondage. 7. He supplied them with food convenient. In Egypt they fared hard, but, when God brought them out, he *laid meat unto them,* as the husbandman, when he has unyoked his cattle, fodders them. God rained manna about their camp, bread from heaven, angels' food ; other creatures *seek their meat,* but God laid meat to his own people, as we do to our children, was himself their caterer and carver, anticipated *them with the blessings of goodness.*

II. Here is Israel very ungrateful to God. 1. They were deaf and disobedient to his voice. He spoke to them by his messengers, Moses and his other prophets, called them from their sins, called them to himself, to their work and duty ; but *as they called them so they went from them;* they rebelled in those particular instances wherein they were admonished ; the more pressing and importunate the prophets were with them, to persuade them to that which was good, the more refractory they were, and the more resolute in their evil ways, disobeying for disobedience-sake. This foolishness is bound in the hearts of children, who, as soon as they are taught to go, will go from those that call them.

2. They were fond of idols, and worshipped them : They *sacrificed to Baalim,* first one Baal and then another, and *burnt incense to graven images,* though they were called to by the prophets of the Lord again and again not to do this abominable thing which he hated. Idolatry was the sin which from the beginning, and all along, had most easily beset them.

3. They were regardless of God, and of his favours to them : *They knew not that I healed them.* They looked only at Moses and Aaron, the instruments of their relief, and, when any thing was amiss, quarrelled with them, but looked not through them to God who employed them. Or, When God corrected them, and kept them under a severe discipline, they understood not that it was for their good, and that God thereby *healed them,* and it was necessary for the perfecting of their cure, else they would have been better reconciled to the methods God took. Note, Ignorance is at the bottom of ingratitude, *ch.* ii. 8.

4. They were strongly inclined to apostasy. This is the blackest article in the charge (*v.* 7) : *My people are bent to backsliding from me.* Every word here is aggravating. (1.) They *backslide.* There is no hold of them, no stedfastness in them ; they seem to come forward, towards God, but they quickly slide back again, and are as a deceitful bow. (2.) They backslide *from me,* from God, the chief good, the fountain of life and living waters, from their God, their owner, ruler, and benefactor, from God who never turned from them, nor was as a wilderness to them. (3.) They are *bent to backslide;*

they are ready to sin; there is in their natures a propensity to that which is evil; at the best they hang in suspense between God and the world, so that a little thing serves to draw them the wrong way; they are forward to close with every temptation. It also intimates that they are resolute in sin; their hearts are *fully set in them to do evil;* the bias is strong that way; and they persist in their backslidings, whatever is said or done to stop them; and yet, (4.) "They are, in profession, *my people.* They are *called by my name,* and profess relation to me; they are mine, whom I have done much for and expect much from, whom I have *nourished* and *brought up, as children,* and yet they backslide *from me."* Note, In our repentance we ought to lament not only our backslidings, but our *bent to backslide,* not only our actual transgressions, but our original corruption, the sin that dwells in us, the carnal mind.

5. They were strangely averse to repentance and reformation. Here are two expressions of their obstinacy:—(1.) *They refused to return, v. 5.* So much were they bent to backslide that, though they could not but find, upon trial, the folly of their backslidings, and that when they forsook God they changed for the worse, yet they went on frowardly. *I have loved strangers, and after them I will go.* They were commanded to return, were courted and entreated to return, were promised that if they would they should be kindly received, but they refused. (2.) Though *they called them to the Most High.* God's prophets and ministers called them to return to the God from whom they had revolted, to the most high God, from whom they had sunk into this wretched degeneracy; they called them from the worship of the idols, which were so much below them, and the worship of which was therefore their disparagement, to the true God, who was so much above them, and the worship of whom was therefore their preferment; they called them from this earth to high and heavenly things; but they called in vain. *None at all would exalt him.* Though he is the most high God they would not acknowledge him to be so, would do nothing to honour him nor give him the glory due to his name. Or, They would not *exalt themselves,* would not rise out of that state of apostasy and misery into which they had precipitated themselves; but there they contentedly lay still, would not lift up their heads nor lift up their souls. Note, God's faithful ministers have taken a great deal of pains, to no purpose, with backsliding children, have called them to the Most High; but none would stir, *none at all would exalt him.*

III. Here is God very angry, and justly so, with Israel; see what are the tokens of God's displeasure with which they are here threatened. 1. God, who brought them out of Egypt, to take them for a people to himself, since they would not be faithful to him,

shall bring them into a worse condition than he at first found them in (*v.* 5): "*He shall not return into the land of Egypt,* though that was a house of bondage grievous enough; but he shall go into a harder service, for *the Assyrian shall be his king,* who will use him worse than ever Pharaoh did." They shall not return into Egypt, which lies near, where they may hear often from their own country, and whence they may hope shortly to return to it again; but they shall be carried into Assyria, which lies much more remote, and where they shall be cut off from all correspondence with their own land and from all hopes of returning to it, and justly, because *they refused to return.* Note, Those that will not return to the duties they have left cannot expect to return to the comforts they have lost. 2. God, who gave them Canaan, that good land, and a very safe and comfortable settlement in it, shall bring his judgments upon them there, which shall make their habitation unsafe and uncomfortable (*v.* 6): *The sword* shall come upon them, the sword of war, the sword of a foreign enemy, prevailing against them and triumphing over them. (1.) This judgment shall spread far. The sword shall fasten upon their *cities,* those nests of people and store-houses of wealth; it shall likewise reach to their *branches,* the country villages (so some), the citizens themselves (so others), or the *bars* (so the word signifies) and gates of their city, or all the branches of their revenue and wealth, or their children, the branches of their families. (2.) It shall last long: It shall *abide on their cities.* David thought *three months* flying before his enemies was the only judgment of the three that was to be excepted against; but this *sword* shall abide much longer than three months on the cities of Israel. They continued their rebellions against God, and therefore God continued his judgments on them. (3.) It shall *make a full end:* It shall *consume their branches, and devour them,* and lay all waste, and this *because of their own counsels,* that is, because they would have their own way, both in worship and conversation, would do as they listed, and pursue their own projects, which God therefore, in a way of righteous judgment, gave them up to. Note, The confusion of sinners is owing to their contrivance. God's counsels would have saved them, but their own counsels ruined them.

8 How shall I give thee up, Ephraim? *how* shall I deliver thee, Israel? how shall I make thee as Admah? *how* shall I set thee as Zeboim? mine heart is turned within me, my repentings are kindled together. 9 I will not execute the fierceness of mine anger, I will not return to destroy Ephraim: for I *am* God, and not man; the Holy One in the midst

of thee: and I will not enter into the city. 10 They shall walk after the LORD: he shall roar like a lion: when he shall roar, then the children shall tremble from the west. 11 They shall tremble as a bird out of Egypt, and as a dove out of the land of Assyria: and I will place them in their houses, saith the LORD. 12 Ephraim compasseth me about with lies, and the house of Israel with deceit: but Judah yet ruleth with God, and is faithful with the saints.

In these verses we have,

I. God's wonderful backwardness to destroy Israel (v. 8, 9): *How shall I give thee up?* Here observe,

1. God's gracious debate within himself concerning Israel's case, a debate between justice and mercy, in which victory plainly inclines to mercy's side. Be astonished, O heavens! at this, and wonder, O earth! at the glory of God's goodness. Not that there are any such struggles in God as there are in us, or that he is ever fluctuating or unresolved; no, he is in one mind, and knows it; but they are expressions after the manner of men, designed to show what severity the sin of Israel had deserved, and yet how divine grace would be glorified in sparing them notwithstanding. The connexion of this with what goes before is very surprising; it was said of Israel (v. 7) that they were *bent to backslide from God,* that though they were called to him they *would not exalt him,* upon which, one would think, it should have followed, "Now I am determined to destroy them, and never show them mercy any more." No, such is the sovereignty of mercy, such the freeness, the fulness, of divine grace, that it follows immediately, *How shall I give thee up?* See here, (1.) The proposals that justice makes concerning Israel, the suggestion of which is here implied. Let Ephraim be given up, as an incorrigible son is given up to be disinherited, as an incurable patient is given over by his physician. Let him be given up to ruin. Let Israel be delivered into the enemy's hand, as a lamb to the lion to be torn in pieces; let them be made as Admah and set as Zeboim, the two cities that with Sodom and Gomorrah were destroyed by fire and brimstone rained from heaven upon them; let them be utterly and irreparably ruined, and be made as like these cities in desolation as they have been in sin. Let that curse which is written in the law be executed upon them, that the *whole land* shall be *brimstone and salt, like the overthrow of Sodom and Gomorrah, Admah and Zeboim,* Deut. xxix. 23. Ephraim and Israel deserve to be thus abandoned, and God will do them no wrong if he deal thus with them. (2.) The opposition that mercy makes to these

proposals: *How shall I do it?* As the tender father reasons with himself, "How can I cast off my untoward son? for he is my son, though he be untoward; how can I find in my heart to do it?" Thus, "Ephraim has been a dear son, a pleasant child: *How can I do it?* He is ripe for ruin; judgments stand ready to seize him; there wants nothing but *giving him up,* but I cannot do it. They have been a people near unto me; there are yet some good among them; theirs are the children of the covenant; if they be ruined, the enemy will triumph; it may be they will yet repent and reform; and therefore how can I do it?" Note, The God of heaven is slow to anger, and is especially loth to abandon a people to utter ruin that have been in special relation to him. See how mercy works upon the mention of those severe proceedings: *My heart is turned within me,* as we say, Our heart fails us, when we come to do a thing that is against the grain with us. God speaks as if he were conscious to himself of a strange striving of affections in compassion to Israel; as Lam. i. 20, *My bowels are troubled; my heart is turned within me.* As it follows here, *My repentings are kindled together.* His bowels yearned towards them, and *his soul was grieved* for their sin and *misery,* Judg. x. 16. Compare Jer. xxxi. 20. *Since I spoke against him my bowels are troubled for him.* When God was to give up his Son to be a sacrifice for sin, and a Saviour for sinners, he did not say, How shall I give him up? No, he *spared not his own Son;* it *pleased the Lord to bruise him;* and *therefore* God spared not him, that he might spare us. But this is only the language of the day of his patience; when men have sinned that away, and the great day of his wrath comes, then no difficulty is made of it; nay, *I will laugh at their calamity.*

2. His gracious determination of this debate. After a long contest mercy in the issue rejoices against judgment, has the last word, and carries the day, *v.* 9. It is decreed that the reprieve shall be lengthened out yet longer, and *I will not* now *execute the fierceness of my anger,* though I am angry; though they shall not go altogether unpunished, yet he will mitigate the sentence and abate the rigour of it. He will show himself to be justly angry, but not implacably so; they shall be corrected, but not consumed. *I will not return to destroy Ephraim;* the judgments that have been inflicted shall not be repeated, shall not go so deep as they have deserved. He will not *return to destroy,* as soldiers, when they have pillaged a town once, return a second time, to take more, as when *what the palmer-worm has left the locust has eaten.* It is added, in the close of the verse, "*I will not enter into the city,* into Samaria, or any other of their cities; I will not enter into them as an enemy, utterly to destroy them and lay them waste, as I did the cities of Admah and Zeboim."

3. The ground and reason of this determination : *For I am God and not man, the Holy One of Israel.* To encourage them to hope that they shall find mercy, consider, (1.) What he is in himself : *He is God, and not man*, as in other things, so in pardoning sin and sparing sinners. If they had offended a man like themselves, he would not, he could not have borne it ; his passion would have overpowered his compassion, and he would have executed the fierceness of his anger ; but *I am God, and not man.* He is *Lord of his anger*, whereas men's anger commonly lords it over them. If an earthly prince were in such a strait between justice and mercy, he would be at a loss how to compromise the matter between them ; but he who is God, and not man, knows how to find out an expedient to secure the honour of his justice and yet advance the honour of his mercy. Man's compassions are nothing in comparison with the tender mercies of our God, whose thoughts and ways, in receiving returning sinners, are as much above ours as heaven is above the earth, Isa. lv. 9. Note, It is a great encouragement to our hope in God's mercies to remember that he is *God, and not man.* He is *the Holy One.* One would think this were a reason why he should reject such a provoking people. No ; God knows how to spare and pardon poor sinners, not only without any reproach to his holiness, but very much to the honour of it, as he is *faithful and just to forgive us our sins*, and therein *declares his righteousness*, now Christ has purchased the pardon and he has promised it. (2.) What he is to them ; he is the *Holy One in the midst of thee* ; his holiness is engaged for the good of his church, and even in this corrupt and degenerate land and age there were some that gave thanks at the remembrance of his holiness, and he required of them all to be *holy as he is*, Lev. xix. 2. As long as we have the *Holy One in the midst of us* we are safe and well ; but woe to us when he leaves us ! Note, Those who submit to the influence may take the comfort of God's holiness.

II. Here is his wonderful forwardness to do good for Israel, which appears in this, that he will qualify them to receive the good he designs for them (v. 10, 11) : *They shall walk after the Lord.* This respects the same favour with that (ch. iii. 5), *They shall return, and seek the Lord their God ;* it is spoken of the ten tribes, and had its accomplishment, in part, in the return of some of them with those of the two tribes in Ezra's time ; but it had its more full accomplishment in God's spiritual Israel, the gospel-church, brought together and incorporated by the gospel of Christ. The ancient Jews referred it to the time of the Messiah ; the learned Dr. Pocock looks upon it as a prophecy of Christ's coming to preach the gospel to the dispersed children of Israel, the children of God that were scattered abroad. And then

observe, 1. How they were to be called and brought together : *The Lord shall roar like a lion.* The *word of the Lord* (so says the Chaldee) *shall be as a lion that roars.* Christ is called *the lion of the tribe of Judah*, and his gospel, in the beginning of it, was *the voice of one crying in the wilderness*, When Christ cried with a loud voice it was as *when a lion roared*, Rev. x. 3. The voice of the gospel was heard afar, as the *roaring of a lion*, and it was a *mighty voice.* See Joel iii. 16. 2. What impression this call should make upon them, such an impression as the roaring of a lion makes upon all the beasts of the forest : *When he shall roar then the children shall tremble.* See Amos iii. 8, *The lion has roared ; the Lord God has spoken ;* and then *who will not fear ?* When those whose hearts the gospel reached trembled, and were astonished, and cried out, *What shall we do ?*—when they were by it put upon working out their salvation, and worshipping God with fear and trembling, then this promise was fulfilled. *The children shall tremble from the west.* The dispersed Jews were carried eastward, to Assyria and Babylon, and those that returned came from the east ; therefore this seems to have reference to the calling of the Gentiles that lay westward from Canaan, for that way especially the gospel spread. They shall *tremble ;* they shall move and come with trembling, with care and haste, *from the west*, from the nations that lay that way, to the mountain of the Lord (Isa. ii. 3), to the gospel-Jerusalem, upon hearing the alarm of the gospel. The apostle speaks of *mighty signs and wonders* that were wrought by the preaching of the gospel from *Jerusalem round about to Illyricum*, Rom. xv. 19. Then the children trembled from the west. And, whereas Israel after the flesh was dispersed in Egypt and Assyria, it is promised that they shall be effectually summoned thence (v. 11) : *They shall tremble ;* they shall come trembling, and with all haste, *as a bird* upon the wing, *out of Egypt*, and *as a dove out of the land of Assyria ;* a dove is noted for swift and constant flight, especially when she flies *to her windows*, which the flocking of Jews and Gentiles to the church is here compared to, as it is Isa. lx. 8. Wherever those are that belong to the election of grace—east, west, north, or south—they shall *hear the joyful sound*, and be wrought upon by it ; those of Egypt and Assyria shall come together ; those that lay most remote from each other shall meet in Christ, and be incorporated in the church. Of the uniting of Egypt and Assyria, it was prophesied, Isa. xix. 23. 3. What effect these impressions should have upon them. Being *moved with fear*, they shall flee to the ark : *They shall walk after the Lord*, after *the service of the Lord* (so the Chaldee) ; they shall take the Lord Christ for their *leader and commander ;* they shall enlist themselves under him as the captain of their salvation, and give up themselves to the direction of the Spirit as their guide by the word; they shall *leave all to follow Christ,* as becomes *disciples.* Note, Our holy trembling at the word of Christ will draw us to him, not drive us from him. When he *roars like a lion* the slaves tremble and flee from him, the children tremble and flee to him. 4. What entertainment they shall meet with at their return (*v.* 11): *I will place them in their houses* (all those that come at the gospel-call shall have a place and a name in the gospel-church, in the particular churches which are their houses, to which they pertain; they shall dwell in God, and be at home in him, both easy and safe, as a man in his own house; they shall have mansions, for there are many in *our Father's house),* in his tabernacle on earth and his temple in heaven, in *everlasting habitations,* which may be called *their houses,* for they are *the lot* they shall stand in *at the end of the days.*

III. Here is a sad complaint of the treachery of Ephraim and Israel, which may be an intimation that it is not Israel after the flesh, but the spiritual Israel, to whom the foregoing promises belong, for as for this Ephraim, this Israel, they *compass God about with lies and deceit;* all their services of him, when they pretended to compass his altar, were feigned and hypocritical; when they surrounded him with their prayers and praises, every one having a petition to present to him, they *lied to him with their mouth and flattered him with their tongue;* their pretensions were so fair, and yet their intentions so foul, that they would, if possible, have imposed upon God himself. Their professions and promises were all a cheat, and yet with these they thought to compass God about, to enclose him as it were, to keep him among them, and prevent his leaving them.

IV. Here is a pleasant commendation of the integrity of the two tribes, which they held fast, and this comes in as an aggravation of the perfidiousness of the ten tribes, and a reason why God had that mercy in store for Judah which he had not for Israel (*ch.* i. 6, 7), for *Judah yet rules with God and is faithful with the saints,* or *with the Most Holy.* 1. *Judah rules with God,* that is, he serves God, and the service of God is not only true liberty and freedom, but it is dignity and dominion. *Judah rules,* that is, the princes and governors of Judah *rule with God;* they use their power for him, for his honour, and the support of his interest. Those *rule with God* that *rule in the fear of God* (2 Sam. xxiii. 3), and it is their honour to do so, and their praise shall be *of God,* as Judah's here is. Judah is *Israel—a prince with God.* 2. He is *faithful with the holy God,* keeps close to his worship and *to his saints*—to his priests, to his people; *faithful with the saints,* with Abraham, Isaac, and Jacob, whose steps they faithfully tread in. They *walk in the way of good*

men; and those that do so *rule with God,* they have a mighty interest in Heaven. Judah yet does thus, which intimates that the time would come when Judah also would revolt and degenerate. Note, When we see how many there are that compass God about *with lies and deceit* it may be a comfort to us to think that God has his remnant that cleave to him with purpose of heart, and are faithful to his saints; and for those who are thus faithful unto death is reserved a crown of life, when hypocrites and all liars shall have their portion without.

CHAP. XII.

In this chapter we have, I. A high charge drawn up against both Israel and Judah for their sins, which were the ground of God's controversy with them, ver. 1, 2. Particularly the sin of fraud and injustice, which Ephraim is charged with (ver. 7), and justifies himself in, ver. 8. And the sin of idolatry (ver. 11), by which God is provoked to contend with them, ver. 14. II. The aggravations of the sins they are charged with, taken from the honour God put upon their father Jacob (ver. 3—5), the advancement of them into a people from low and mean beginnings (ver. 12, 13), and the provision he had made them of helps for their souls by the prophets he sent them, ver. 10. III. A call to the unconverted to turn to God, ver. 6. IV. An intimation of mercy that God had in store for them, ver. 9.

EPHRAIM feedeth on wind, and followeth after the east wind: he daily increaseth lies and desolation; and they do make a covenant with the Assyrians, and oil is carried into Egypt. 2 The LORD hath also a controversy with Judah, and will punish Jacob according to his ways; according to his doings will he recompense him. 3 He took his brother by the heel in the womb, and by his strength he had power with God: 4 Yea, he had power over the angel, and prevailed: he wept, and made supplication unto him: he found him *in* Bethel, and there he spake with us; 5 Even the LORD God of hosts; the LORD *is* his memorial. 6 Therefore turn thou to thy God: keep mercy and judgment, and wait on thy God continually.

In these verses,

I. Ephraim is convicted of folly, in staying himself upon Egypt and Assyria, when he was in straits (*v.* 1): *Ephraim feeds on wind,* that is, feeds himself with vain hopes of assistance from man, when he is at variance with God; and, when he meets with disappointments, he still pursues the same game, and greedily pants and *follows after the east wind,* which he cannot catch hold of, nor, if he could, would it be nourishing, nay, it would be noxious. We say of the *wind in the east,* It is *good neither for man nor beast.* It was said (*ch.* viii. 7), He *sows the wind;* and as he sows so he reaps (He *reaps the whirlwind;* and as he reaps so he feeds—He feeds on the wind, the *east wind.* Note, Those that make creatures their confidence make fools of themselves, and take a great deal of pains to put a cheat upon their own souls and to prepare vexation for themselves: *He daily increaseth lies,* that is, multiplies his correspondences and leagues with his neighbours, which will all prove deceitful to him; nay, they will prove desolation to him. Those very nations that he makes his refuge will prove his ruin. Those that stay themselves upon lies will be still coveting to increase them, that they may build their hopes firmly upon them; as if many lies twisted together would make one truth, or many broken reeds and rotten supports one sound one, which is a great delusion and will prove to them a great desolation; for those that *observe lying vanities* the more they increase them the more disappointments they prepare for themselves and the further they run from *their own mercies.* The men of Ephraim did so when they thought to secure the Assyrians in their interests by a *solemn league,* signed, sealed, and sworn to: *They make a covenant with the Assyrians,* but they will find there is no hold of them; that potent prince will be a slave to his word no longer than he pleases. They thought to secure the Egyptians for their confederates by a rich present of the commodities of their country, not only to purchase their favour, but to show that their friendship was worth having: *Oil is carried into Egypt.* But the Egyptians, when they had got the bribe, dropped the cause, and Ephraim was never the better for them. *Oleum perdidit et operam—The oil and the labour are both lost.* This was *feeding on wind;* this was *increasing lies and desolation.*

II. Judah is contended with too, and Jacob, which includes both Ephraim and Judah (*v.* 2): *The Lord has also a controversy with Judah;* for though he had awhile ago *ruled with God,* and been *faithful with the saints,* yet now he begins to degenerate. Or though, in keeping close to the house of David and the house of Aaron, and in them to the covenants of royalty and priesthood, they were so far *in the right,* in the former they *ruled with God* and in the latter were *faithful to the saints,* yet upon other accounts God *had a controversy* with them, and would punish them. Note, Men's being in the right in some things, in the main things, will not exempt them from correction, and therefore should not exempt them from reproof, for those things wherein they are in the wrong. There were those of the seven churches of Asia whom Christ approved and commended, and yet he adds, *Nevertheless I have something against thee.* So here; though the seed of Jacob are a people near to God, yet God will punish them according to the evil ways they are found in and the evil doings they are found guilty of; for God sees sin even in his own people, and will reckon with them for it.

III. Both Ephraim and Judah are put in mind of their father Jacob, whose seed they were and whose name they bore (and it was their honour), of the extraordinary things which he did and which God did for him, that they might be the more ashamed of themselves for degenerating from so illustrious a progenitor and staining the lustre of so great a name, and yet that they might be engaged and encouraged to return to God, the God of their father Jacob, in hopes for his sake to find favour with him. He had called this people Jacob (*v.* 2), threatening to punish them; but *how shall I give them up?* How shall that dear name be forgotten?

1. Three glorious things concerning Jacob the person Jacob the people are here put in mind of; but by brief hints only, for it is presumed that they knew the story:—(1.) His struggling with Esau in the womb: There *he took his brother by the heel, v.* 3. We have the story Gen. xxv. 26. It was an early act of bravery, and an effort for the best precedency, a pious ambition for that birthright in the covenant which Esau is justly branded as profane for despising. But his degenerate seed, by mingling with the nations, and making leagues with them, profaned that crown, and laid that honour in the dust, which he so gloriously put in for. Then it was that the dominion was given to him: *The elder shall serve the younger.* Then he was owned of God as his beloved: *Jacob have I loved, but Esau have I hated.* But they had by their sin forfeited both the love of God and dominion over their neighbours. (2.) His wrestling with the angel. "Remember how your father Jacob had *power with God by his* own *strength,* the strength he had by the gift of God, who *pleaded* not *against him by his great power,* but *put strength into him,"* Job xxiii. 6. The angel he wrestled with is called *God,* and therefore is supposed to be the *Son of God,* the angel of the covenant. "God was both a combatant with Jacob and an assistant of him, showing, in the latter respect, greater strength than in the former, fighting as it were against him with his left hand and for him with his right, and to that putting greater force." So Dr. Pocock. The providence of God fought against him when he met with one danger after another, in his return homewards; but the grace of God enabled him to go on cheerfully in his way, and, when his faith acted upon the divine promise that was for him prevailed above his fears that arose from the divine providences that were against him, then *by his strength he had power with God.* But it refers especially to his prayer for deliverance from Esau, and for a blessing: *He had power over the angel and prevailed,* for he *wept and made supplication.* Here was a mixture of the greatest courage and the greatest tenderness, Jacob wrestling like a champion and yet weeping like a child. Note, Prayers and tears are the weapons with which the saints have obtained the most glorious victories. Thus

Jacob commenced *Israel—a prince with God;* his posterity was called *Israel,* but they were unworthy the name, for they had forfeited and lost their communion with God, and their interest in him, by revolting from their duty to him. (3.) His meeting with God at Bethel: God *found him* in Bethel, *and there he spoke with us.* God found him the first time in Bethel, as he went to Padanaram (Gen. xxviii. 10), and a second time after his return, Gen. xxxv. 9, &c. It is probable that this refers to both; for in both God spoke to Jacob, and renewed the covenant with him, and the prophet might very well say, *There he spoke with us* who are the seed of Jacob, for both times that God spoke with Jacob at Bethel he spoke with him concerning his seed. Gen. xxviii. 14, *Thy seed shall be as the dust of the earth;* and Gen. xxxv. 12, *This land I will give unto thy seed.* Thus God then covenanted with him and his seed after him. Now justly are they upbraided with this; for in that very place which their father Jacob called *Bethel—the house of God,* in remembrance of the communion he there had with God, did they set up one of the calves, and worship it; thus they turned that Bethel into a *Beth-aven—a house of iniquity.* There God *spoke with them* exceedingly great and precious promises, which they had despised and lost the benefit of.

2. Two inferences are here drawn from these stories concerning Jacob, for instruction to his seed:—

(1.) Here is a use of information. From what passed between God and Jacob we may learn that *Jehovah, the Lord God of hosts,* is *the God of Israel;* he was the God of Jacob, and this is *his memorial* throughout all the generations of the seed of Jacob (*v.* 5)—the more shame for those who forgot the memorial of their church, deserted the God of their fathers, and exchanged a *Lord of hosts* for Baalim. Note, Those only are accounted the people of God that keep up a memorial of God, such a memorial of him as he himself has instituted, by which he makes himself known and will have us to remember him. Here are two memorials of his, by which he is distinguished from all others, and is to be acknowledged and adored by us. [1.] The former denotes his *existence of himself.* He is Jehovah, much the same with *I AM,* the same that *was, and is, and is to come,* infinite, eternal, and unchangeable. Jehovah is *his memorial,* his peculiar name. [2.] The latter denotes his dominion over all: He is the *God of hosts,* that has all the hosts of heaven and earth at his beck and command, and makes what use he pleases of them. Jacob saw *Mahanaim—*God's *two hosts,* about the time that he *wrestled with the angel* (Gen. xxxii. 1, 2), and so learned to call God the *God of hosts,* and transmitted it to us as his memorial. God's names, titles, and attributes, are the memorials of him; there is no need for images to be such. And

that which was a revelation of God to one is his memorial to many, to all generations.

(2.) Here is a use of exhortation, *v.* 6. "Is this so, that Jacob thy father had this communion with the Lord God of hosts, and is this still his memorial?" Then, [1.] Let those that have gone astray from God be converted to him: *Therefore turn thou to thy God.* He that was the God of Jacob is the God of Israel, is *thy God;* from him thou hast unjustly and unkindly revolted; therefore turn thou to him by repentance and faith, turn to him as thine, to love him, obey him, and depend upon him. [2.] Let those that are converted to him walk with him in all holy conversation and godliness: "*Keep mercy and judgment,* mercy in relieving and succouring the poor and distressed, judgment in rendering to all their due; be kind to all; do wrong to none. *Keep piety and judgment*" (so it may be read); "live *righteously and godly in this present world;* be devout and be honest. Do not only practise these occasionally, but be careful, and constant, and conscientious in the practice of them." [3.] Let those that walk with God be encouraged to live a life of dependence upon him: "*Wait on thy God continually,* with a believing expectation to receive from him all the succours and supplies thou standest in need of." Those that live a life of conformity to God may live a life of confidence and comfort in him, if it be not their own fault. Let our *eyes* be *ever towards the Lord,* and let us preserve a holy security and serenity of mind under the protection of the divine power and the influence of the divine favour, looking, without anxiety, for a dubious event, and by faith keeping our spirits sedate and even; this is waiting on God as our God in covenant, and this we must do continually.

7 *He is* a merchant, the balances of deceit *are* in his hand: he loveth to oppress. 8 And Ephraim said, Yet I am become rich, I have found me out substance: *in* all my labours they shall find none iniquity in me that *were* sin. 9 And I *that am* the LORD thy God from the land of Egypt will yet make thee to dwell in tabernacles, as in the days of the solemn feasts. 10 I have also spoken by the prophets, and I have multiplied visions, and used similitudes, by the mini∴ ∵y of the prophets. 11 *Is there* iniquity *in* Gilead? surely they are vanity: they sacrifice bullocks in Gilgal; yea, their altars *are* as heaps in the furrows of the fields. 12 And Jacob fled into the country of Syria, and Israel served for a wife, and for a wife he kept *sheep.* 13 And by a

prophet the LORD brought Israel out of Egypt, and by a prophet was he preserved. 14 Ephraim provoked *him* to anger most bitterly : therefore shall he leave his blood upon him, and his reproach shall his Lord return unto him.

Here are intermixed, in these verses,

I. Reproofs for sin. When God is coming forth to contend with a people, that he may demonstrate his own righteousness, he will demonstrate their unrighteousness. Ephraim was called to turn to his God and *keep judgment* (*v.* 6) ; now, to show that he had need of that call, he is charged with turning from his God by idolatry, and breaking the laws of justice and judgment.

1. He is here charged with injustice against the precepts of the second table, *v.* 7, 8. Here observe,

(1.) What the sin is wherewith he is charged : *He is a merchant.* The margin reads it as a proper name, *He is Canaan,* or a Canaanite, unworthy to be denominated from Jacob and Israel, and worthy to be cast out with a curse from this good land, as the Canaanites were. See Amos ix. 7. But Canaan sometimes signifies *a merchant,* and therefore is most likely to do so here, where Ephraim is charged with deceit in trade. Though God had given his people a land flowing with milk and honey, yet he did not forbid them to enrich themselves by merchandise, and they succeeded the Canaanites in that as well as in their husbandry; they sucked *the abundance of the seas and the treasures hidden in the sand,* Deut. xxxiii. 19. And, if they had been fair merchants, it would have been no reproach at all to them, but an honour and a blessing. But he is such a merchant as the Canaanites were, who were honest only with good looking to, and, if they could, cheated all they dealt with. Ephraim does so ; he deceives and thereby oppresses. Note, There is oppression by fraud as well as oppression by force. It is not only princes, lords, and masters, that oppress their subjects, tenants, and servants, but merchants and traders are often guilty of oppressing those they deal with, when they impose upon their ignorance, or take advantage of their necessity, to make hard bargains with them, or are rigorous and severe in exacting their debts. Ephraim cheated, [1.] With a great deal of art and cunning : *The balances of deceit are in his hand.* He uses balances, and delivers his goods by weight and measure, as if he would be very exact, but they are balances of deceit, false weights and false measures, and thus, under colour of doing right, he does the greatest wrong. Note, God has his eye upon merchants and traders, when they are weighing their goods and paying their money, whether they do honestly or deceitfully. He observes what

1188

balances they have in their hand, and how they hold them ; and, though those they deal with may not be aware of that sleight of hand with which they make them balances of deceit, God sees it, and knows it. Trades by the wit of man are made *mysteries,* but it is a pity that by the sin of man they should ever be made *mysteries of iniquity.* [2.] With a great deal of pleasure and pride : *He loves to oppress.* To oppress is bad enough, but to love to do so is much worse. His conscience does not check and reprove him for it, as it ought to do ; if it did, though he committed the sin, he could not delight in it ; but his corruptions are so strong, and have so triumphed over his convictions, that he not only loves the gain of oppression, but he loves to oppress, sins for sinning-sake, and takes a pleasure in out-witting and over-reaching those that suspect him not.

(2.) How he justifies himself in this sin, *v.* 8. Wicked men will have something to say for themselves now when they are told of their faults, some frivolous turn-off or other wherewith to evade the convictions of the word. Ephraim stands indicted for a common cheat. Now see what he pleads to the indictment. He does not deny the charge, nor plead, Not guilty, yet does not make a penitent confession of it and ask pardon, but insists upon his own justification. Suppose it were so that he did use balances of deceit, yet, [1.] He pleads that he had got a good estate. Let the prophet say what he pleased of his deceit, of the sin of it and the curse of God that attended it, he could not be convinced there was any harm or danger in it, for this he was sure of that he had thriven in it : "*Yet I have become rich, I have found me out substance.* Whatever you make of it, I have made a good hand of it." Note, Carnal hearts are often confirmed in a good opinion of their evil ways by their worldly prosperity and success in those ways. But it is a great mistake. Every word in what Ephraim says here proclaims his folly. *First,* It is folly to call the riches of this world substance, for they are things that are not, Prov. xxiii. 5. *Secondly,* It is folly to think that we have them of ourselves, to say (as some read it), *I have made myself rich :* what *substance* I have is owing purely to my ingenuity and industry —*I have found it : my might and the power of my hand have gotten me this wealth. Thirdly,* It is folly to think that what we have is for ourselves. *I have found me out substance,* as if we had it for our own proper use and behoof, whereas we hold it in trust, only as stewards. *Fourthly,* It is folly to think that riches are things to be gloried in, and to say with exultation, *I have become rich.* Riches are not the honours of the soul, are not peculiar to the best men, nor sure to us ; and therefore *let not the rich man glory in his riches,* Jam. i. 9, 10. *Fifthly,* It is folly to think that growing rich in a sinful way makes us innocent, or will make us safe, or may make us easy, in that way; for the prosperity of fools deceives and destroys them. See Isa. xlvii. 10; Prov. i. 32. [2.] He pleads that he had kept a good reputation. It is common for sinners, when they are justly reproved by their ministers, to appeal to their neighbours, and because they know no ill of them, or will say none, or think well of what the prophets charge them with as bad, fly in the face of their reprovers: *In all my labours* (says Ephraim) *they shall find no iniquity in me that were sin.* Note, Carnal hearts are apt to build a good opinion of themselves upon the fair character they have among their neighbours. Ephraim was very secure; for, *First*, All his neighbours knew him to be diligent in his business; they had an eye upon *all his labours*, and commended him for them. *Men will praise thee when thou doest well for thyself.* *Secondly*, None of them knew him to be deceitful in his business. He acted with so much policy that nobody could say to the contrary but that he acted with integrity. For either, 1. He concealed the fraud, so that none discovered it: "Whatever iniquity there is, *they shall find* none;" as if no iniquity were displeasing to God, and damning to the soul, but that which is open and scandalous before men. What will it avail us that men shall find no iniquity in us, when God finds a great deal, and will bring every secret work, even secret frauds, into judgment? Or, 2. He excused the fraud, so that none condemned it: "*They shall find no iniquity in me that were sin*, nothing very bad, nothing but what is very excusable, only some venial sins, sins not worth speaking of," which they think God will make nothing of because they do not. It is a fashionable iniquity; it is customary; it is what every body does; it is pleasant; it is gainful; and this, they think, is no iniquity that is sin; nobody will think the worse of them for it. But God sees not as man sees; he judges not as man judges.

2. He is here charged with idolatry, against the precepts of the first table, with that iniquity which is in a special manner vanity, the making and worshipping of images, which are vanities (*v.* 11): *Surely they are vanity;* they do not profit, but deceive. Now the prophet mentions two places notorious for idolatry:—(1.) Gilead on the other side Jordan, which had been branded for it before (*ch.* vi. 8): *Is there iniquity in Gilead?* It is a thing to be wondered at; it is a thing to be sadly lamented. What! iniquity in Gilead? idolatry there? Gilead was a fruitful pleasant country (pleasant to a proverb, Jer. xxii. 6), and does it so ill requite the Lord? It was a frontier-country, and lay much exposed to the insults of enemies, and therefore stood in special need of the divine protection; what! and yet by iniquity throw itself out of that protection? *Is there ini-*

quity *in Gilead?* Yea, (2.) And in Gilgal too; there they *sacrifice bullocks* (*ch.* ix. 15), and there *their altars* which they have set up, either to strange gods in opposition to God himself or to the God of Israel in opposition to his own appointed altar, are as thick *as heaps* of manure *in the furrows of the field* that is to be sown, *ch.* viii. 11. *Is there iniquity in Gilead* only? so some. Is it only in those remote parts of the nation that people are so superstitious, where they border upon other nations? No; they are as bad at Gilgal. In Gilead God protected Jacob their father (of whom he had been speaking) from the rage of Laban; and will you there commit iniquity?

II. Here are threatenings of wrath for sin. Some make that to be so (*v.* 9), *I will make thee to dwell in tabernacles as in the days of the appointed time*, that is, I will bring thee into such a condition as the Israelites were in when they dwelt in tents and wandered for forty years; that was the *time appointed* in *the wilderness.* Ephraim forgot that God brought him out of Egypt and brought him up to be what he was, and was proud of his wealth, and took sinful courses to increase it; and therefore God threatens to bring him to a tabernacle-state again, to a poor, mean, desolate, unsettled condition. Note, It is just with God, when men have by their sins turned their tents into houses, by his judgments to turn their houses into tents again. However, that is certainly a threatening (*v.* 14), *Ephraim provoked him to anger most bitterly.* See how men are deceived in their opinion of themselves, and how they will one day be undeceived. Ephraim thought that there was no iniquity in him that deserved to be called sin (*v.* 8); but God told him that there was that in him which was sin, and would be found so if he did not repent and reform; for, 1. It was extremely offensive to his God: *Ephraim provoked him to anger most bitterly* with his iniquities, which were so distasteful to God, and to him too would be *bitterness in the latter end.* He was so wilful in sinning against his knowledge and convictions that any one might see, and say, that he designed no other than to provoke God in the highest degree. 2. It would certainly be destructive to himself; that cannot be otherwise which provokes God against him, and kindles the fire of his wrath. Therefore, (1.) He shall take away his forfeited life: *He shall leave his blood upon him*, that is, he shall not hold him guiltless, but bring upon him that death which is the wages of sin. *His blood shall be upon his own head* (2 Sam. i. 16), for his own iniquity has testified against him and he alone shall bear it. Note, When sinners perish their blood is left upon them. (2.) He shall take away his forfeited honour: *His reproach shall his Lord return upon him.* God is *his Lord;* he had by idolatry and other sins reproached the Lord, and done dishonour to him, and to his name and family, and had given occasion to others to reproach him ; and now God will return the reproach upon him, according to the word he has spoken, that *those who despise him shall be lightly esteemed.* Note, Shameful sins shall have shameful punishments. If Ephraim put contempt on his God, he shall be so reduced that all his neighbours shall look with contempt upon him.

III. Here are memorials of former mercy, which come in to convict them of base ingratitude in revolting from God. Let them blush to remember,

1. That God had raised them from meanness. When Ephraim had become rich, and was proud of that, he forgot that which God (that he might not forget it) obliged them every year to acknowledge (Deut. xxvi. 5), *A Syrian ready to perish was my father.* But God here puts them in mind of it, *v.* 12. Let them remember, not only the honours of their father Jacob, what a *mighty prince* he was with God, *v.* 3 (an honour which they had no share in while they were in rebellion against God), but what a poor servant he was to Laban, which was sufficient to mortify those that were puffed up with the estates they had raised. *Jacob fled into Syria* from a malicious brother, and there served a covetous uncle *for a wife,* and *for a wife he kept sheep,* because he had no estate to endow a wife with. Jacob was poor, and low, and a fugitive ; therefore his posterity ought not to be proud. He was a plain man, dwelling in tents, and keeping sheep; therefore *balances of deceit* ill became them. He *served for a wife* that was not a Canaanitess, as Esau's wives were; therefore it was a shame for them to degenerate into Canaanites, and mingle with the nations. God wonderfully preserved him in his flight and preserved him in his service, so that he multiplied exceedingly, and from that root in a dry ground sprang an illustrious nation, that bore his name, which magnifies the goodness of God both to him and them and leaves them under the stain of base ingratitude to that God who was their founder and benefactor.

2. That God had rescued them from misery, had raised them to what they were, not only out of poverty, but out of slavery (*v.* 13), which laid them under much stronger obligations to serve him and under a yet deeper guilt in serving other gods. (1.) God *brought Israel out of Egypt* on purpose that they might serve him, and by redeeming them out of bondage acquired a special title to them and to their service. (2.) He preserved them, as sheep are kept by the shepherd's care. He preserved them from Pharaoh's rage at the sea, even at the Red Sea, protected them from all the perils of the wilderness, and provided for them. (3.) He did this *by a prophet,* Moses, who, though he is called *king in Jeshurun* (Deut. xxxiii. 5), yet

did what he did for Israel *as a prophet,* by direction from God and by the power of his word. The ensign of his authority was not a royal sceptre, but the *rod of God;* with that he summoned both Egypt's plagues and Israel's blessings. Moses, as a prophet, was a type of Christ (Acts iii. 22), and it is by Christ as a prophet that we are brought out of the Egypt of sin and Satan by the power of his truth. Now this shows how very unworthy and ungrateful this people were, [1.] In rejecting their God, who had brought them out of Egypt, which, in the preface to the commandments, is particularly mentioned as a reason for the first, why they should have no other gods before him. [2.] In despising and persecuting his prophets, whom they should have loved and valued, and have studied to answer God's end in sending them, for the sake of that prophet by whom God had brought them out of Egypt and preserved them in the wilderness. Note, The benefit we have had by the word of God greatly aggravates our sin and folly if we put any slight upon the word of God.

3. That God had taken care of their education as they grew up. This instance of God's goodness we have, *v.* 10. As by a prophet he delivered them, so *by prophets* he still continued to speak to them. Man, who is formed out of the earth, is fed out of the earth ; so that nation, that was formed by prophecy, by prophecy was fed and taught ; *beginning at Moses,* and so going on *to all the prophets* through the several ages of that church, we find that divine revelation was all along their tuition. (1.) They had prophets raised up among themselves (Amos ii. 11), a succession of them, were scarcely ever without a Spirit of prophecy among them more or less, from Moses to Malachi. (2.) These prophets were *seers;* they had *visions,* and *dreams,* in which God discovered his mind to them immediately, with a full assurance that it was his mind, Num. xii. 6. (3.) These visions were multiplied; God spoke not only *once, yea, twice,* but many a time; if one vision was not regarded, he sent another. The prophets had variety of visions, and frequent repetitions of the same. (4.) God *spoke* to them *by the prophets.* What the prophets *received from the Lord* they plainly and faithfully delivered to them. The people at Mount Sinai begged that God would speak to them by men like themselves, and he did so. (5.) In speaking to them by the prophets he *used similitudes,* to make the messages he sent by them intelligible, more affecting, and more likely to be remembered. The visions they saw were often similitudes, and their discourses were embellished with very apt comparisons. And, as God by his prophets, so by his Son, he *used similitudes,* for *he opened his mouth in parables.* Note, God keeps an account, whether we do or no, of the sermons we hear ; and those that have long enjoyed the means of grace in purity,

plenty, and power, that have been frequently, faithfully, and familiarly, told the mind of God, will have a great deal to answer for another day if they persist in a course of iniquity.

IV. Here are intimations of further mercy, and this remembered too in the midst of sin and wrath (as some understand v. 9): " *I that am the Lord thy God from the land of Egypt,* who then and there took thee to be my people, and have approved myself thy God ever since, in a constant series of merciful providences, have yet a kindness for thee, bad as thou art; and I will *make thee to dwell in tabernacles,* not as in the wilderness, but *as in the days of the solemn feast,*" the feast of tabernacles, which was celebrated with great joy, Lev. xxiii. 40. 1. They shall be made to see, by the grace of God, that though they are rich, and have found out substance, yet they are but in a tabernacle-state, and have in their worldly wealth *no continuing city.* 2. They shall yet have cause to rejoice in God, and have opportunity to do it in public ordinances. The feast of tabernacles was the first solemn feast the Jews kept after their return out of Babylon, Ezra iii. 4. 3. This, as other promises, was to have its full accomplishment in the grace of the gospel, which provides tabernacles for believers in their way to heaven, and furnishes them with matter of joy, holy joy, joy in God, such as was in the feast of tabernacles, Zech. xiv. 18, 19.

CHAP. XIII.

The same strings, though generally unpleasing ones, are harped upon in this chapter that were in those before. People care not to be told either of their sin or of their danger by sin; and yet it is necessary, and for their good, that they should be told of both, nor can they better hear of either than from the word of God and from their faithful ministers, while the sin may be repented of and the danger prevented. Here, I. The people of Israel are reproved and threatened for their idolatry, ver. 1—4. II. They are reproved and threatened for their wantonness, pride, and luxury, and other abuses of their wealth and prosperity, ver. 5—8. III. The ruin that is coming upon them for these and all their other sins is foretold as very terrible, ver. 12, 13, 15, 16. IV. Those among them that yet retain a respect for their God are here encouraged to hope that he will yet appear for their relief, though their kings and princes, and all their other supports and succours, fail them, ver. 9—11, 14.

WHEN Ephraim spake trembling, he exalted himself in Israel; but when he offended in Baal, he died. 2 And now they sin more and more, and have made them molten images of their silver, *and* idols according to their own understanding, all of it the work of the craftsmen: they say of them, Let the men that sacrifice kiss the calves. 3 Therefore they shall be as the morning cloud, and as the early dew that passeth away, as the chaff *that* is driven with the whirlwind out of the floor, and as the smoke out of the chimney. 4 Yet I *am* the LORD thy God from the land of Egypt, and thou shalt know no god but me: for *there is* no saviour beside me.

Idolatry was the sin that did most easily beset the Jewish nation till after the captivity; the ten tribes from the first were guilty of it, but especially after the days of Ahab; and this is the sin which, in these verses, they are charged with. Observe,

I. The provision that God made to prevent their falling into idolatry. This we have, v. 4. God did what was fit to be done to keep them close to himself; what could have been done more? 1. He made known himself to them as *the Lord their God,* and took them to be his people in a peculiar manner. Both by his word and by his works all along *from the land of Egypt* he declared, *I am the Lord thy God;* he told them so from heaven at Mount Sinai, that he was *the Lord* and *their God,* who *brought them out of the land of Egypt.* This he continued both to declare and to prove to them by his prophets and by his providences. 2. He gave them a law forbidding them to worship any other: " *Thou shalt know no God but me;* not only shalt not own and worship any other, but shalt not acquaint thyself with any other, nor make the rites and usages of the Gentiles familiar to thee." Note, It is a happy ignorance not to know that which we ought not to meddle with. We find those commended who *have not known the depths of Satan.* 3. He gave them a good reason for it : *There is no saviour besides me.* Whatever we take for our God we expect to have for our saviour, to make us happy here and hereafter; as, where we have protection, we owe allegiance, so where we have salvation, and hope for it, we owe adoration.

II. The honour that Ephraim had, while he kept himself clear from idolatry (v. 1): *While Ephraim spoke trembling,* or *with trembling* (that is, as Dr. Pocock understands it, while he behaved himself towards God as his father Jacob did, with *weeping and supplications,* and spoke not proudly and insolently against God and his prophets, while he kept up a holy fear of God, and worshipped him in that fear), so long *he exalted himself in Israel,* that is, he was very considerable among the tribes and made a figure. Jeroboam, who was of that tribe, exalted himself and his family. *When he spoke there was trembling,* that is, all about him stood in awe of him; so some understand it. Note, *Those that humble themselves,* especially that humble themselves before God, *shall be exalted.* When people speak with modesty and jealousy of themselves, with a diffidence of their own judgment and a deference to others, they exalt themselves, they gain a reputation. But as for Ephraim he soon lost himself: *When he offended in Baal he died,* that is, he lost his reputation, his honour soon dwindled and sunk, and was laid in the dust. Baal is here put for all idolatry; when Ephraim forsook God, and took to worship images, the state received its death's wound and was never good for any thing afterwards. Note, Deserting God is the death of any person or persons.

III. The lamentable growth of idolatry among them (*v.* 2) : *Now they sin more and more.* When once he began to *offend in Baal* the ice was broken, and he grew worse and worse, coveted more idols, doted more upon those he had, and grew more ridiculous in the worship of them. Note, The way of idolatry, as of other sins, is down-hill, and men cannot easily stop themselves. It is the sad case of all those who have forsaken God that they sin yet more and more. Let us trace them in their apostasy. 1. They made themselves *molten images,* proud to have gods that they could cast into what mould they pleased ; probably these were the calves in miniature like the silver shrines for Diana ; the zealots for the calf-worship carried about with them, it may be, images of the gods they worshipped, made on purpose *for themselves.* 2. They made them of *their silver,* and then doubted not of their property in them, when they purchased them with their own money or made them of their own plate melted down for that purpose. See what cost they put themselves to in the service of their idols, which they honoured with the best they had, and therefore made their molten images of silver. 3. They made them *according to their own understanding,* according to their own fancy. They consulted with themselves what shape they should make their idol in, and made it accordingly, *a god* according to the *best of their judgment.* Or *according to their own likeness,* in the form of a man. And, when they made their idols men like themselves in shape, they made themselves stocks and stones like them in reality ; for *those that make them are like unto them, and so is every one that trusts in them.* 4. It was *all the work of the craftsmen.* Their images did not pretend, like that of Diana, to have come down from Jupiter (Acts xix. 35) ; no, perhaps the workmen stamped their names upon them, such an idol was such a man's work. See *ch.* viii. 6 ; Isa. xliv. 9, &c. 5. Though they were thus the work of their hands, yet they were the beloved of their souls ; for they say of them, *Let the men that sacrifice kiss the calves.* Either the priests called upon the people thus to pay their homage, or the people, who were not allowed to come so near themselves, called upon the *men that sacrificed,* the priests that attended for them, to *kiss the calves* in their name and stead, because they could not reach to do it, so very fond were they of paying their utmost respects to such an idol as they were taught to have a veneration for. Though they were calves, yet, if they were gods, the worshippers, by themselves or their proxies, thus made their honours to them. They *kissed*

the calves, in token of the adoration of them, affection for them, and allegiance to them, as theirs. Thus we are directed to *kiss the Son,* to take him for our Lord and our God.

IV. Threatenings of wrath for their idolatry. The Lord, whose name is *Jealous,* is a jealous God, and will not give his glory to another ; and therefore all those that *worship images* shall be *confounded,* especially if Ephraim do it, Ps. xcvii. 7. Because they are so fond of kissing their calves, therefore God will give them sensible convictions of their folly, *v.* 3. They promise themselves a great deal of safety and satisfaction in the worship of their idols, and that their prosperity will thereby be established ; but God tells them that they shall be disappointed, and *driven away in their wickedness.* This is illustrated by four similitudes :—They shall be, 1. As the *morning cloud,* which promises showers of rain to the parched ground. 2. As the *early dew,* which seems to be an earnest of such showers. But both *pass away,* and the day proves as dry and hot as ever ; so fleet and transitory their profession of piety was (*ch.* vi. 4), and so had they disappointed God's expectation from them, and therefore it is just that so their prosperity should be, and so their expectations from their idols should be disappointed, and so will all theirs be that make an idol of this world. 3. They are *as the chaff,* light and worthless ; and they shall be driven *as the chaff is driven with the whirlwind out of the floor,* Ps. i. 4 ; xxxv. 5 ; Job xxi. 18. Nay, 4. They are *as the smoke,* noisome and offensive (see Isa. lxv. 5), and they shall be driven away *as the smoke out of the chimneys,* that is soon dissipated and disappears, Ps. lxviii. 2. Note, No solid lasting comfort is to be expected any where but in God.

5 I did know thee in the wilderness, in the land of great drought. 6 According to their pasture, so were they filled ; they were filled, and their heart was exalted ; therefore have they forgotten me. 7 Therefore I will be unto them as a lion : as a leopard by the way will I observe *them :* 8 I will meet them as a bear *that is* bereaved *of her whelps,* and will rend the caul of their heart, and there will I devour them like a lion : the wild beast shall tear them.

We may observe here, 1. The plentiful provision God had made for Israel and the seasonable supplies he had blessed them with (*v.* 5) : " *I did know thee in the wilderness,* took cognizance of thy case and made provision for thee, even in *a land of great drought,* when thou wast in extreme distress, and when no relief was to be had in an ordinary way." See a description of this wilderness, Deut. viii. 15. Jer. ii. 6. and say.

The God that knew them, and owned them, and fed them there, was a *friend indeed*, for he was a *friend at need* and an all-sufficient friend, that could victual so vast an army when all ordinary ways of provision were cut off, and where, if miracles had not been their daily bread, they must all have perished. Note, Help at an exigency lays under peculiar obligations and must never be forgotten. 2. Their unworthy ungrateful abuse of God's favour to them. God not only took care of them in the wilderness, but put them in possession of Canaan, a good land, a large and fat pasture. And (*v.* 6) *according to their pasture so were they filled.* God gave them both plenty and dainties, and they did not spare it, but, having been long confined to manna, when they came into Canaan they fed themselves *to the full.* And this was no hopeful presage; it would have looked better, and promised better, if they had been more modest and moderate in the use of their plenty, and had learned to deny themselves; but what was the effect of it? *They were filled, and their heart was exalted.* Their luxury and sensuality made them proud, insolent, and secure. The best comment upon this is that of Moses, Deut. xxxii. 13—15. But *Jeshurun waxed fat and kicked.* When the body was stuffed up with plenty the soul was puffed up with pride. Then they began to think their religion a thing below them, and they could not persuade themselves to stoop to the services of it. *The wicked, through the pride of his countenance, will not seek after God.* When they were poor and lame in the wilderness they thought it was necessary for them to keep in with God; but when they were replenished and established in Canaan they began to think they had no further need of him: *Their heart was exalted, therefore have they forgotten me.* Note, Worldly prosperity, when it feeds men's pride, makes them forgetful of God; for they remember him only when they want him. When Israel was filled, what more could the Almighty do for them? And therefore they said to him, *Depart from us*, Job xxii. 17. It is sad that those favours which ought to make us mindful of God, and studious what we shall render to him, should make us unmindful of him, and regardless what we do against him. We ought to know that we live upon God when we live upon common providence, though we do not, as Israel in the wilderness, live upon miracles. 3. God's just resentment of their base ingratitude, *v.* 7, 8. The judgments threatened (*v.* 3) intimated the departure of all good from them. The threatenings here go further, and intimate the breaking in of all evils upon them; for God, who had so much befriended them, now *turns to be their enemy and fights against them*, which is expressed here very terribly: *I will be unto them as a lion* and *as a leopard.* The lion is strong, and there is no resisting him. The

leopard is here taken notice of to be crafty and vigilant: *As a leopard by the way will I observe them.* As that beast of prey lies in wait by the road-side to catch travellers, and devour them, so will God by his judgments *watch over them* to do them hurt, as he had watched over them to do them good, Jer. xliv. 27. No opportunity shall be let slip that may accelerate or aggravate their ruin (Jer. v. 6): *A leopard shall watch over their cities.* A lynx, or spotted beast (and such the leopard is), is noted for quicksightedness above any creature *(lynx visu—the eyes of a lynx)*, and so it intimates that not only the power, but the wisdom of God is engaged against those whom he has a controversy with. Some read it (and the original will bear it), *I will be as a leopard in the way of Assyria.* The judgments of God shall surprise them just when they are going to the Assyrians to seek for protection and help from them. It is added, *I will meet them as a bear that is bereaved*, and thereby exasperated and made more cruel (2 Sam. xvii. 8, Prov. xxviii. 15), which intimates how highly God was provoked, and he would make them feel it: He will *rend the caul of their heart.* The lion is observed to aim at the heart of the beasts he preys upon, and thus will God *devour them like a lion.* He will send such judgments upon them as shall prey upon their spirits and consume their vitals. Their heart was exalted (*v.* 6), but God will take an effectual course to bring it down: *The wild beast shall tear them;* not only God will be as a lion and leopard to them, but the metaphor shall be fulfilled in the letter, for *noisome beasts* are one of the *four sore judgments* with which God will destroy a provoking people, Ezek. xiv. 15.

Now all this teaches us, 1. That abused goodness turns into the greater severity. Those who despise God and affront him, when he is to them as a careful tender shepherd, shall find he will be even to his own flock as the beasts of prey are. Those whom God has in vain *endured with much long-suffering*, and invited with much affection, in them he will *show his wrath* and make them *vessels* of it, Rom. ix. 22. *Patientia læsa fit furor—Despised patience will turn into fury.* 2. That the judgments of God, when they come with commission against impenitent sinners, will be irresistible and very terrible. They will *rend the caul of the heart*, will fill the soul with confusion, and tear that in pieces; and we are as unable to grapple with them as a lamb is to make his part good against a roaring lion, for *who knows the power of God's anger? Knowing therefore the terror of the Lord*, let us be persuaded to make peace with him; for are we stronger than he?

9 O Israel, thou hast destroyed thyself; but in me *is* thine help. 10 I will be thy king: where *is any other* that may save thee in all thy

cities ? and thy judges of whom thou saidst, Give me a king and princes ? 11 I gave thee a king in mine anger, and took *him* away in my wrath.　12 The iniquity of Ephraim *is* bound up; his sin *is* hid.　13 The sorrows of a travailing woman shall come upon him : he *is* an unwise son; for he should not stay long in *the place of* the breaking forth of children.　14 I will ransom them from the power of the grave; I will redeem them from death : O death, I will be thy plagues; O grave, I will be thy destruction : repentance shall be hid from mine eyes.　15 Though he be fruitful among *his* brethren, an east wind shall come, the wind of the LORD shall come up from the wilderness, and his spring shall become dry, and his fountain shall be dried up : he shall spoil the treasure of all pleasant vessels.　16 Samaria shall become desolate; for she hath rebelled against her God : they shall fall by the sword : their infants shall be dashed in pieces, and their women with child shall be ripped up.

The first of these verses is the summary, or contents, of all the rest (*v.* 9), where we have, 1. All the blame of Israel's ruin laid upon themselves : *O Israel! thy perdition is thence;* it is of and from thyself; or, "*It has destroyed thee, O Israel!* that is, all that sin and folly of thine which thou art before charged with. As *thy own wickedness* has many a time *corrected thee,* so that has now at length destroyed thee." Note, Wilful sinners are self-destroyers. Obstinate impenitence is the grossest self-murder. Those that are *destroyed of the destroyer* have their blood upon their own head ; they have *destroyed themselves.* 2. All the glory of Israel's relief ascribed to God : *But in me is thy help.* That is, (1.) It might have been : " I would have helped thee and healed thee, but thou wouldst not be healed and helped, but wast resolutely set upon thy own destruction." This will aggravate the condemnation of sinners, not only that they did that which tended to their own ruin, but that they opposed the offers God made them and the methods he took with them to prevent it : *I would have gathered them,* and they *would not.* They might have been easily and effectually helped, but they put the help away from them.　Nay, (2.) It may be : " Thy case is bad, but it is not desperate.　*Thou hast destroyed thyself;* but come to me, and I will help thee." This is a plank thrown
1194

out after shipwreck, and greatly magnifies not only the power of God, that he can help when things are at the worst, can help those that cannot help themselves, but the riches of his grace, that he will help those that have destroyed themselves and therefore might justly be left to perish, that he will help those that have long refused his help. Dr. Pocock gives a different reading and sense of this verse : " *O Israel! this has destroyed thee, that in me is thy help.* Presuming upon God and his favour has emboldened thee in those wicked ways which have been thy ruin."

Now, in the rest of these verses, we may see,

I. How Israel destroyed themselves. It is said (*v.* 16), They *rebelled against God,* revolted from their allegiance to him, entered into a confederacy with his enemies, and took up arms against him ; and this was the thing that ruined them, for never any hardened themselves against God and prospered.　Note, Those that rebel against their God destroy themselves, for they make him their enemy for whom they are an unequal match.

1. They treasure up wrath against the day of wrath, and so they destroy themselves. They are doing that, every day, which will be remembered against them another day (*v.* 12): *The iniquity of Ephraim is bound up, and his sin is hid;* God took notice of it, kept it upon record, and will produce it against him and reckon with him for it afterwards. Their former sins contributed to their present destruction ; for they were *laid up in store with God,* Deut. xxxii. 34, 35 ; Job xiv. 17.　It is laid up in safety, and will not be forgotten, nor the evidence against him lost ; but it is laid up in secret ; it is hid ; the sinner himself is not aware of it. It is bound up in God's omniscience, in the sinner's own conscience.　Note, The sin of sinners is not forgotten till it is pardoned, but an exact account is kept of it, which will be opened in proper time.

2. They make no haste to repent and help themselves when they are under divine rebukes ; they are their own ruin because they will not do what they should do towards their own salvation, *v.* 13.　(1.) They are brought into trouble and distress by sin : *The sorrows of a travailing woman shall come upon him.* They shall smart for sin, and so be made sensible of it ; they shall be thrown into pangs and agonies by it, very sharp and severe, and yet, like the pains of a woman in labour, hopeful and promising, and in order to deliverance ; and by these, though God corrects them, yet he designs their good. They are chastened, that they may not be destroyed. But, (2.) They are not by these forwarded as they ought to be towards repentance and reformation, which would cause their sorrows to issue in true joy : *He is an unwise son, for he should not stay long,* as he does, *in the place of the breaking forth of children,* but,

being *brought to the birth,* should struggle to *get forth,* lest he be stifled and *still-born at last.* Were the child which the mother is in travail of capable of understanding its own case, we should reckon it an unwise child that would choose to stay long in the birth; for the *captive exile hasteth to be loosed, lest he die in the pit,* Isa. li. 14. Note, Those may justly be reckoned their own destroyers who defer and put off their repentance, by which alone they might help themselves. Those are in danger of miscarrying in conversion who delay it, and will not put forth themselves to speed the work and bring it to an issue.

3. *Therefore* they are destroyed because they have done that which will be their certain ruin and neglected that which would have been their only relief. Here is a sad description of the desolation they are doomed to, *v.* 15, 16. It is here taken for granted that *Ephraim* is *fruitful among his children;* his name signifies *fruitfulness.* He is fruitful in respect of the plentiful products of his country and the great numbers of its inhabitants; it was both a rich and a populous tribe, as was foretold concerning it; but sin turns this fruitful tribe into barrenness. *Joseph* was a *fruitful bough,* but for sin it was blasted. The instrument is an *east wind,* representing a foreign enemy that should invade it. It is called the *wind of the Lord,* not only because it shall be a very great and strong wind, but because it shall be sent by divine direction; it shall come *from the Lord,* and do whatever he appoints; and see what effect it shall have upon that flourishing tribe, what desolations war shall make. (1.) Was it a rich tribe? The foreign enemy shall make it poor enough. This *wind of the Lord* shall come up *from the wilderness,* a freezing blasting wind, and shall *dry up* the *springs* and *fountains* with which this tree is watered, shall exhaust the sources of its wealth. The invader shall waste the country and so impoverish the husbandman, shall intercept trade and commerce and so impoverish the merchant; and let not the great men, whose wealth lies in their rich furniture, think that they shall be exempted from the judgment, for he shall *spoil the treasure of all pleasant vessels.* See the folly of those that lay up their treasure on earth, that lay it up in *pleasant vessels (vessels of desire,* so the word is), on which they set their affections, and in which they place their comfort and satisfaction. This is treasure that may be spoiled and that they may be spoiled of; it is what either moth or rust may corrupt, or what thieves and soldiers may steal and carry away. But wise and happy are those who have laid up their treasure in heaven, and in the pleasant things of that world, which cannot be spoiled, which they cannot be stripped of; ever happy are they, and therefore truly wise. (2.) Was it a populous tribe, and numerous? The enemy shall depopulate it and make its

men few: *Samaria shall become desolate,* without inhabitants. [1.] Those shall be cut off who are the guard and joy of the present generation; the men who bear arms shall bear them to no purpose, for *they shall fall by the sword,* so that there shall be none to make head against the fury of the conqueror nor to take care of the concerns either of the public or of private families. [2.] Those shall be cut off who are the seed and hope of the next generation, who should rise up in the places of those who fell by the sword; the whole nation must be rooted out, and therefore *the infants shall be dashed to pieces,* in the most cruel and barbarous manner, and, which is if possible yet more inhuman, *the women with child shall be ripped up.* Thus shall the glory of *Samaria flee away from the birth, and from the womb, ch.* ix. 11; x. 14. See instances of this cruelty, 2 Kings viii. 12; xv. 16; Amos i. 13.

II. Let us now see how God was the help of this self-destroying people, how he was their only help (*v.* 10): *I will be thy King,* to rule and save thee. Though they had refused to be his subjects and had rebelled against him, yet he would still be their King and would not abandon them. The business and care of a good king is to keep his people, not only from being ruined by foreign enemies, but from ruining themselves and one another. Thus will God yet be Israel's King, as he was *their King of old.* Note, Our case would be sad indeed if God were not better to us than we are to ourselves.

1. God will be their King when they have no other king; he will protect and save them when those are cut off and gone who should have been their protectors and saviours: *I will be he* (so *v.* 10 may be read), he that shall help thee. " *Where is the king that may save thee in all thy cities,* that may go in and out before thee, and fight thy battles, when thy cities are invaded by a foreign power, and suppress the more dangerous quarrels of thy citizens among themselves? *Where are thy judges,* who by administering public justice should preserve the public peace? For it is *righteousness* and *peace* that *kiss each other. Where are thy judges* that thou hadst such a desire of and such a dependence upon, of whom thou saidst, *Give me a king and princes?* This refers, (1.) To the foolish wicked desire which the whole nation had of a kingly government, being weary of the theocracy, or divine government, which they had been under during the time of the *Judges,* because it looked too mean for them. They rejected Samuel, and in him *the Lord,* when they said, *Give us a king* like the nations, whereas the *Lord was their King.* (2.) To the desire which the ten tribes had of a kingly government different from that of the house of David, because they thought that was too absolute and bore too hard upon them, and they hoped to better themselves by setting

up Jeroboam. Both these are instances, [1.] Of men's improvidence for themselves. When they are uneasy with their present lot they are fond of novelty, and think to better themselves by a change; but they are commonly disappointed, and do not find that advantage in the alteration which they promised themselves. [2.] Of men's impiety towards God, in thinking to refine upon his appointments and amend them. God gave Israel judges and prophets for their guidance; but they were weary of them, and cried, *Give us a king and princes.* God gave them the house of David, established it by a covenant of royalty; but they were soon weary of that too, and cried, *We have no part in David.* Those destroy themselves who are not pleased with what God does for them, but think they can do better for themselves. Well, in both these requests, Providence humoured them, gave them Saul first, and afterwards Jeroboam. And what the better were they for them? Saul was *given in anger* (given in *thunder,* 1 Sam. xii. 18, 19) and soon after was *taken away in wrath,* upon Mount Gilboa. The kingly government of the ten tribes was given in anger, not only against Solomon for his defection, but against the ten tribes that desired it, for their discontent and disaffection to the house of David; and God was now about to take that away in wrath by the power of the king of Assyria. And then, *where is thy king?* He is gone, and thou shalt abide many days *without a king, and without a prince* (ch. iii. 4), shalt have none to save thee, none to rule thee. Note, *First,* God often gives in anger what we sinfully and inordinately desire, gives it with a curse, and with it gives us up to our own hearts' lusts. Thus he gave Israel quails. *Secondly,* What we inordinately desire we are commonly disappointed in, and it cannot save us, as we expected it should. *Thirdly,* What God gives in anger he takes away in wrath; what he gives because we did not desire it well he takes away because we did not use it well. It is the happiness of the saints that, whether God gives or takes, it is all in love, and furnishes them with matter for praise. *To the pure all things are pure.* It is the misery of the wicked that, whether God gives or takes, it is all in wrath; to them nothing is pure, nothing is comfortable.

2. God will do that for them which no other king could do if they had one (*v.* 14): *I will ransom them from the power of the grave.* Though Israel, according to the flesh, be abandoned to destruction, God has mercy in store for his spiritual Israel, in whom all the promises were to have their accomplishment, and this among the rest, for to them the apostle applies it (1 Cor. xv. 55), and particularly to the blessed resurrection of believers at the great day, yet not excluding their spiritual resurrection from the death of sin to a holy, heavenly,

1196

spiritual, and divine life. It is promised, (1.) That the captives shall be delivered, *shall be ransomed, from the power of the grave.* Their deliverance shall be by ransom; and we know who it was that paid their ransom, and what the ransom was, for it was the Son of man that *gave his life a ransom for many,* Matt. xx. 28. It is he that thus redeemed them. Those who, upon their repenting and believing, are, for the sake of Christ's righteousness, acquitted from the guilt of sin and saved from death and hell, which are the *wages of sin,* are those *ransomed of the Lord* that shall, in the great day, be brought out of the grave in triumph, and it shall be as impossible for the bands of death to hold them as it was to hold their Master. (2.) That the conqueror shall be destroyed: *O death! I will be thy plagues.* Jesus Christ was the plague and destruction of death and the grave when by death he *destroyed him that had the power of death,* and when in his own resurrection he triumphed over the grave. But the complete destruction of them will be in the resurrection of believers at the great day, when death shall for ever be swallowed up in victory, and it is the last enemy that shall be destroyed. But the word which we translate *I will* may as well be rendered *Ubi nunc—Where now* are thy plagues? And so the apostle took it: " *O death! where is thy plague,* or *sting,* with which thou hast so long pestered the world? *O grave! where is thy victory,* or thy *destruction,* wherewith thou hast destroyed mankind?" Christ has abolished death, has broken the power of it and altered the property of it, and so enabled us to triumph over it. This promise he has made, and it shall be made good to all that are his; for *repentance shall be hidden from his eyes;* he will never recal this sentence passed on death and the grave, for he is not a man that he should repent. Thanks be to God therefore who gives us the victory.

CHAP. XIV.

The strain of this chapter differs from that of the foregoing chapters. Those were generally made up of reproofs for sin and threatenings of wrath; but this is made up of exhortations to repentance and promises of mercy, and with these the prophet closes; for all the foregoing convictions and terrors he had spoken were designed to prepare and make way for these. He wounds that he may heal. The Spirit convinces that he may comfort. This chapter is a lesson for penitents; and some such there were in Israel at this day, bad as things were. We have here, I. Directions in repenting, what to do and what to say, ver. 1—3. II. Encouragements to repent, taken from God's readiness to receive returning sinners (ver. 4, 8) and the comforts he has treasured up for them, ver. 5—7. III. A solemn recommendation of these things to our serious thoughts, ver. 9.

O ISRAEL, return unto the LORD thy God; for thou hast fallen by thine iniquity. 2 Take with you words, and turn to the LORD: say unto him, Take away all iniquity, and receive *us* graciously: so will we render the calves of our lips. 3 Asshur shall not save us; we will not ride upon horses: neither will we say any more to the work of our hands, *Ye are* our gods : for in thee the fatherless findeth mercy.

Here we have,

I. A kind invitation given to sinners to repent. *v.* 1. It is directed to Israel, God's professing people. They are called to *return.* Note, Conversion must be preached even to those that are within the pale of the church as well as to heathen. " Thou art Israel, and therefore art bound to thy God in duty, gratitude, and interest ; thy revolt from him is so much the more heinous, and thy return to him so much the more necessary." Let Israel see, 1. What work he has made for repentance: " *Thou hast fallen by thy iniquity.*" *Thou hast stumbled;* so some read it. Their idols were their *stumblingblocks.* " Thou hast fallen from God into sin, fallen off from all good, fallen down under the load of guilt and the curse." Note, Sin is a fall; and it concerns those that have fallen by sin to get up again by repentance. 2. What work he has to do in his repentance : " *Return to the Lord thy God;* return to him as *the Lord* whom thou hast a dependence upon, as *thy God,* thine in covenant, whom thou hast an interest in." Note, It is the great concern of those that have revolted from God to *return to God,* and so to do their *first works.* " Return to him from whom thou hast fallen, and who alone is able to raise thee up. Return *even to the Lord,* or *quite home* to the Lord ; do not only look to him, or take some steps towards him, but make thorough work of it." The ancient Jews had a saying, grounded on this, *Repentance is a great thing, for it brings men quite up to the throne of glory.*

II. Necessary instructions given them how to repent. 1. They must bethink themselves what to say to God when they come to him : *Take with you words.* They are required to bring, not sacrifices and offerings, but penitential prayers and supplications, the *fruit of thy lips,* yet not of the lips only, but of the heart, else words are but wind. One of the rabbin says, They must be such words as proceed *from what is spoken first in the inner man;* the heart must dictate to the tongue. We must take good words with us, by taking good thoughts and good affections with us. *Verbaque prævisam rem non invita sequentur—Those who master a subject are seldom at a loss for language.* Note, When we come to God we should consider what we have to say to him ; for, if we come without an errand, we are likely to go without an answer. Ezra ix. 10, *What shall we say?* We must take with us words from the scripture, take them from the Spirit of grace and supplication, who teaches us to cry, Abba, Father, and makes intercession in us. 2. They must bethink themselves what to do. They must not only take with them words, but must *turn to the Lord;*

inwardly in their hearts, outwardly in their lives.

III. For their assistance herein, and encouragement, God is pleased to put words into their mouths, to teach them what they shall say. Surely we may hope to speed with God, when he himself has ordered our address to be drawn up ready to our hands, and his own Spirit has indited it for us; and no doubt we shall speed if the workings of our souls agree with the words here recommended to us. They are,

1. Petitioning words. Two things we are here directed to petition for :—(1.) To be acquitted from guilt. When we return to the Lord we must say to him, Lord, *take away all iniquity.* They were now smarting for sin, under the load of affliction, but are taught to pray, not as Pharaoh, Take away *this death,* but, *Take away this* sin. Note, When we are in affliction we should be more concerned for the forgiveness of our sins than for the removal of our trouble. " *Take away iniquity,* lift it off as a *burden* we are ready to sink under or as the stumbling-block which we have often fallen over. Lord, take it away, that it may not appear against us, to our confusion and condemnation. Take it all away by a free and full remission, for we cannot pretend to strike any of it off by a satisfaction of our own." When God pardons sin he pardons *all,* that *great debt;* and when we pray against sin we must pray against it all and not except any. (2.) To be accepted as righteous in God's sight : " *Receive us graciously.* Let us have thy favour and love, and have thou respect to us and to our performances. Receive our prayer graciously ; be well pleased with that good which by thy grace we are enabled to do." *Take good* (so the word is) ; take it to bestow upon us, so the margin reads it— *Give good.* This follows upon the petition for the taking away of iniquity ; for, till iniquity is taken away, we have no reason to expect any good from God, but the taking away of iniquity makes way for the conferring of good *removendo prohibens—by taking that out of the way which hindered.* Give *good;* they do not say what good, but refer themselves to God ; it is not good of the world's showing (Ps. iv. 6), but good of God's giving. " *Give good,* that good which we have forfeited, and which thou hast promised, and which the necessity of our case calls for." Note, God's gracious acceptance, and the blessed fruits and tokens of that acceptance, are to be earnestly desired and prayed for by us in our returning to God. " *Give good,* that good which will make us good and keep us from returning to iniquity again."

2. Promising words. These also are put into their mouths, not to move God, or to oblige him to show them mercy, but to move themselves, and oblige themselves to returns of duty. Note, Our prayers for pardon and

acceptance with God should be always ac-companied with sincere purposes and vows of new obedience. Two things they are to promise and vow:—(1.) Thanksgiving. " Pardon our sins, and accept of us, so *will we render the calves of our lips.*" The *fruit of our lips* (so the LXX.), a word they used for *burnt-offerings*, and so it agrees with the Hebrew. The apostle quotes this phrase (Heb. xiii. 15), and by the *fruit of our lips* understands the *sacrifice of praise to God, giving thanks to his name.* Note, Praise and thanksgiving are our spiritual sacrifice, and, if they come from an upright heart, shall please the Lord *better than an ox or bullock,* Ps. lxix. 30, 31. And the sense of our par-don and acceptance with God will enlarge our hearts in praise and thankfulness. Those that are *received graciously* may, and must, *render the calves of their lips*—poor returns for rich receivings, yet, if sincere, more ac-ceptable than the calves of the stall. (2.) Amendment of life. They are taught to pro-mise, not only verbal acknowledgments, but a real reformation. And we are taught here, [1.] In our returns to God to covenant against sin. We cannot expect that God should take it away by forgiving it if we do not put it away by forsaking it. [2.] To be particular in our covenants and resolutions against sin, as we ought to be in our con-fession, because deceit lies in generals. [3.] To covenant especially and expressly against those sins which we have been most subject to, which have most easily beset us, and which we have been most frequently over-come by. We must keep ourselves from, and therefore must thus fortify ourselves against, *our own iniquity,* Ps. xviii. 23. The sin they here covenant against, owning there-by that they had been guilty of it, is giving that glory to another which is due to God only; this they promise they will never do, *First,* By putting that confidence in crea-tures which should be put in God only. They will not trust to their alliances abroad: *Asshur* (that is, Assyria) *shall not save us.* " We will not court the help of the Assy-rians when we are in distress, as we have done (*ch.* v. 13; vii. 11; viii. 9); we will not contract for it, nor will we confide in it, or depend upon it. Having a God to go to, a God all-sufficient to trust to, we scorn to be beholden to the Assyrians for help." They will not trust to their warlike preparations at home, especially not those which they were forbidden to multiply: " *We will not ride upon horses,* that is, we will not make court to Egypt," for thence they fetched their horses, Deut. xvii. 16; Isa. xxx. 16; xxxi. 1, 3. " When our enemies invade us we will depend upon our God to succour our infantry, and will be in no care to remount our cavalry." Or, "We will not *post on horse-back,* for haste, from one creature to an-other, to seek relief, but will take the nearest way, and the only sure way, by addressing

ourselves to God," Isa. xx. 5. Note, True repentance takes us off from trusting to an arm of flesh, and brings us to rely on God only for all the good we stand in need of. *Secondly,* Nor will they do it by paying that homage to creatures which is due to God only. We *will not say any more to the works of our hands, You are our gods.* They must promise never to worship idols again, and for a good reason, because it is the most ab-surd and senseless thing in the world to pray to that as a god which is the work of our hands. We must promise that we will not set our hearts upon the gains of this world, nor pride ourselves in our external per-formances in religion, for that is, in effect, to say to the work of our hands, *You are our gods.*

3. Pleading words are here put into their mouths: For *in thee the fatherless find mercy.* We must take our encouragement in prayer, not from any merit God finds in us, but purely from the mercy we hope to find in God. This contains in itself a great truth, that God takes special care of fatherless children, Ps. lxviii. 4, 5. So he did in his law, Exod. xxii. 22. So he does in his pro-vidence, Ps. xxvii. 10. It is God's prero-gative to help the helpless. In him there is mercy for such, for they are proper objects of mercy. In him they find it; there it is laid up for them, and there they must seek it; *seek and you shall find.* It comes in here as a good plea for mercy and grace and an encouraging one to their faith. (1.) They plead the distress of their state and condi-tion: " We are fatherless orphans, destitute of help." Those may expect to find help in God that are truly sensible of their help-lessness in themselves and are willing to ac-knowledge it. This is a good step towards comfort. "If we have not yet boldness to call God *Father,* yet we look upon ourselves as fatherless without him, and therefore lay ourselves at his feet, to be looked upon by him with compassion." (2.) They plead God's wonted lovingkindness to such as were in that condition: *With thee the fatherless* not only may find, but *does find,* and shall find, *mercy.* It is a great encouragement to our faith and hope, in returning to God, that it is his glory to father the fatherless and help the helpless.

4 I will heal their backsliding, I will love them freely : for mine anger is turned away from him. 5 I will be as the dew unto Israel : he shall grow as the lily, and cast forth his roots as Lebanon. 6 His branches shall spread, and his beauty shall be as the olive-tree, and his smell as Lebanon. 7 They that dwell under his shadow shall return ; they shall revive *as* the corn, and grow as the

vine: the scent thereof *shall be* as the wine of Lebanon.

We have here an answer of peace to the prayers of returning Israel. They seek God's face, and they shall not *seek in vain.* God will be sure to meet those in a way of mercy who return to him in a way of duty. If we speak to God in good prayers, God will speak to us in good promises, as he *answered the angel with good words and comfortable words,* Zech. i. 13. If we take with us the foregoing words in our coming to God, we may take home with us these following words for our faith to feast upon; and see how these answer those.

I. Do they dread and deprecate God's displeasure, and therefore return to him? He assures them that, upon their submission, his *anger is turned away from them.* This is laid as the ground of all the other favours here promised. I will do so and so, for my *anger is turned away,* and thereby a door is opened for all good to flow to them, Isa. xii. 1. Note. Though God is justly and greatly angry with sinners, yet he is not implacable in his anger; it may be turned away; it shall be turned away, from those that turn away from their iniquity. God will be reconciled to those that are reconciled to him and to his whole will.

II. Do they pray for the *taking away of iniquity?* He assures them that he will *heal their backslidings;* so he promised, Jer. iii. 22. Note, Though backslidings from God are the dangerous diseases and wounds of the soul, yet they are not incurable, for God has graciously promised that if backsliding sinners will apply to him as their physician, and comply with his methods, he will heal their backslidings. He will heal the guilt of their backslidings by pardoning mercy and their *bent to backslide* by renewing grace. Their *iniquity* shall *not be their ruin.*

III. Do they pray that God will receive them graciously? In answer to that, behold, it is promised, *I will love them freely.* God had hated them while they went on in sin (*ch.* ix. 15); but now that they return and repent he loves them, not only ceases to be *angry* with them, but takes complacency in them and designs their good. He *loves them freely,* with an *absolute entire* love (so some), so that there are no remains of his former displeasure, with a *liberal bountiful* love (so others); he will be open-handed in his love to them, and will think nothing too much to bestow upon them or to do for them. Or with a *cheerful willing* love; he will love them without reluctancy or renitency. He will not say in the day of thy repentance, *How shall I receive thee again?* as he said in the day of thy apostasy, *How shall I give thee up?* Or with an *unmerited preventing* love. Whom God loves he loves *freely,* not because they deserve it, but of his own good pleasure. He loves because he *will* love, Deut. vii. 7, 8.

IV. Do they pray that God will *give good,* will make them good? In answer to that, behold, it is promised, *I will be as the dew unto Israel, v.* 5. Observe,

1. What shall be the favour God will bestow upon them. It is the blessing of their father Jacob, *God give thee the dew of heaven,* Gen. xxvii. 28. Nay, what they need God will not only give them, but he will himself be *that* to them, all that which they need: I *will be as the dew unto Israel.* This ensures *spiritual blessings in heavenly things;* and it follows upon the healing of their backslidings, for pardoning mercy is always accompanied with renewing grace. Note, To Israelites indeed God himself will be *as the dew.* He will instruct them; his doctrine shall drop upon them as the dew, Deut. xxxii. 2. They shall know more and more of him, for he will come to them *as the rain,* Hos. vi. 3. He will refresh them with his comforts, so that their souls shall be as a *watered garden,* Isa. lviii. 11. He will be to true penitents *as the dew to Israel* when they were in the wilderness, dew that had manna in it, Exod. xvi. 14; Num. xi. 9. The graces of the Spirit are the hidden manna, hidden in the dew; God will give them bread from heaven, as he did to Israel in the dew in abundance, John i. 16.

2. What shall be the fruit of that favour which shall be produced in them. The grace thus freely bestowed on them *shall not be in vain.* Those souls, those Israelites, to whom God is as the dew, on whom his grace distils,

(1.) Shall be growing. The bad being by the grace of God made good, they shall by the same grace be made better; for grace, wherever it is true, is growing. [1.] They shall grow upwards, and be more flourishing, *shall grow as the lily,* or (as some read it) shall *blossom as the rose.* The growth of the lily, as that of all bulbous roots, is very quick and speedy. The root of the lily seems lost in the ground all winter, but, when it is refreshed with the dews of the spring, it starts up in a little time; so the grace of God improves young converts sometimes very fast. The lily, when it has come to its height, is a lovely flower (Matt. vi. 29), so grace is the comeliness of the soul, Ezek. xvi. 14. It is the *beauty of holiness* that is produced by the *dew of the morning,* Ps. cx. 3. [2.] They shall grow downwards, and be more firm. The lily indeed grows fast, and grows fine, but it soon fades and is easily plucked up; and therefore it is here promised to Israel that with the flower of the lily he shall have the root of the cedar: He shall *cast forth his roots as Lebanon,* as the *trees of Lebanon,* which, having taken deep root, cannot be plucked up, Amos ix. 15. Note, Spiritual growth consists most in the growth of the root, which is out of sight. The more we depend upon Christ and draw sap and virtue from him, the more we act in religion from a principle and the more stedfast and resolved we are in it, the more we *cast forth our roots.* [3.] They shall grow round about (*v.* 6) : *His branches shall spread* on all sides. And (*v.* 7) he shall *grow as the vine,* whose branches extend furthest of any tree. Joseph was to be *a fruitful bough,* Gen. xlix. 22. When many are added to the church from without, when a hopeful generation rises up, then Israel's branches spread. When particular believers abound in good works, and increase in the knowledge of God and in every good gift, then their branches may be said to spread. The *inward man is renewed day by day.*

(2.) They shall be graceful and acceptable both to God and man. Grace is an amiable thing, and makes those that have it truly amiable. They are here compared to such trees as are pleasant, [1.] To the sight: *His beauty shall be as the olive-tree,* which is always green. *The Lord called thy name a green olive-tree,* Jer. xi. 16. Ordinances are the beauty of the church, and in them it is, and shall be, ever green. Holiness is the beauty of a soul; when those that believe with the heart make profession with the mouth, and justify and adorn that profession with an agreeable conversation, then their beauty is as the olive-tree, Ps. lii. 8. It is a promise to the trees of righteousness that their leaf shall not wither. [2.] To the smell: *His smell shall be as Lebanon* (*v.* 6) and his *scent* as *the wine of Lebanon, v.* 7. This was the praise of their father Jacob, *The smell of my son is as the smell of a field which the Lord has blessed,* Gen. xxvii. 27. The church is compared to a *garden of spices* (Cant. iv. 12, 14), which *all her garments smell of.* True believers are *acceptable to God* and *approved of men.* God *smells a sweet savour* from their *spiritual sacrifices* (Gen. viii. 21), and they are *accepted of the multitude of their brethren.* Grace is the perfume of the soul, the perfume of the name, makes it like precious ointment, Eccl. vii. 1. *The memorial thereof shall be as the wine of Lebanon* (so the margin reads it), not only their reviving comforts now, but their surviving honours when they are gone, shall be as *the wine of Lebanon,* that has a delicate flavour. Flourishing churches have *their faith spoken of throughout the world* (Rom. i. 8) and *leave their name to be remembered* (Ps. xlv. 17) ; and *the memory* of flourishing saints is *blessed,* and shall be so, as theirs who *by faith obtained a good report.*

(3.) They shall be fruitful and useful. The church is compared here to the vine and the olive, which bring forth useful fruits, to the honour of God and man. Nay, the very shadow of the church shall be agreeable (*v.* 7): *Those that dwell under his shadow shall return*—under God's *shadow* (so some), under the shadow of the Messias, so the Chaldee. Believers *dwell under God's shadow* (Ps. xci. 1), and there they are and may be safe and easy. But it is rather *under the*

shadow of Israel, under the shadow of the church. Note, God's promises pertain to those, and those only, that dwell under the church's shadow, that attend on God's ordinances and adhere to his people, not those that flee to that shadow only for shelter in a hot gleam, but those that *dwell under it,* Ps. xxvii. 4. We may apply it to particular believers; when a man is effectually brought home to God all that *dwell under his shadow* fare the better for it—children, servants, subjects, friends. *This day has salvation come to this house.* Those that dwell under the shadow of this church shall return; their drooping spirits shall return, and they shall be refreshed and comforted. He *restores my soul,* Ps. xxiii. 3. *They shall revive as the corn,* which, when it is sown, dies first, and then revives, and *brings forth much fruit,* John xii. 24. It is promised that God's people shall be blessings to the world, as corn and wine are. And a very great and valuable mercy it is to be serviceable to our generation. Comfort and honour attend it.

8 Ephraim *shall say,* What have I to do any more with idols? I have heard *him,* and observed him: I *am* like a green fir-tree. From me is thy fruit found. 9 Who *is* wise, and he shall understand these *things?* prudent, and he shall know them? for the ways of the LORD *are* right, and the just shall walk in them: but the transgressors shall fall therein.

Let us now hear the conclusion of the whole matter.

I. Concerning Ephraim; he is spoken of and spoken to, *v.* 8. Here we have,

1. His repentance and reformation: *Ephraim shall say, What have I to do any more with idols?* As some read it, God here reasons and argues with him, why he should renounce idolatry: " *O Ephraim! what to me and idols? What concord* or agreement can there be *between me and idols? What communion between light and darkness, between Christ and Belial?* 2 Cor. vi. 14, 15. Therefore thou must break off thy league with them if thou wilt come into covenant with me." As we read it, God promises to bring Ephraim and keep him to this: *Ephraim shall say,* God will put it into his heart to say it, *What have I to do any more with idols?* He had promised (*v.* 3) not to *say any more to the works of his hands, You are my gods.* But God's promises to us are much more our security and our strength for the mortifying of sin than our promises to God; and therefore God himself is here *surety for his servant to good,* will put it into his heart and into his mouth. And, whatever good we say or do at any time, it is he that works it in us. Ephraim had solemnly engaged not to call his idols *his gods;* but God here

engages further for him that he shall resolve to have *no more to do with them.* He shall abolish them, he shall abandon them, and that with the utmost detestation; for it is necessary not only that in our lives we be turned from sin, but that in our hearts we be turned against sin. See here, (1.) The power of divine grace. Ephraim had been *joined to idols* (ch. iv. 17), was so fond of them that one would have thought he could never fall out with them; and yet God will work such a change in him that he shall loathe them as much as ever he loved them. (2.) See the benefit of sanctified afflictions. Ephraim had smarted for his idolatry; it had brought one judgment after another upon hi n, and this at length is the fruit, even the *taking away of his sin,* Isa. xxvii. 9. (3.) See the nature of repentance; it is a firm and fixed resolution to have no more to do with sin. This is the language of a penitent: "I am ashamed that ever I had to do with sin; but I have had enough of it; I hate it, and by the grace of God I will never have any thing to do with it again, no, not with the occasions of it." Thou shalt say to thy idol, *Get thee hence* (Isa. xxx. 22), shalt say to the tempter, *Get thee behind me, Satan.*

2. The gracious notice God is pleased to take of it: *I have heard him, and observed him. I have heard, and will look upon him;* so some read it. Note, The God of heaven takes cognizance of the penitent reflections and resolutions of returning sinners. He expects and desires the repentance of sinners, because he has no pleasure in their ruin. *He looks upon men* (Job xxxiii. 27), *hearkens and hears,* Jer. viii. 6. And, if there be any disposition to repent, he is well pleased with it. When *Ephraim bemoans himself* before God, he is a *dear son,* he is a *pleasant child,* Jer. xxxi. 20. He meets penitents with mercy, as the father of the prodigal met his returning son. God *observed* Ephraim, to see whether he would bring forth fruits meet for this profession of repentance that he made, and whether he would continue in this good mind. He observed him to do him good, and comfort him, according to the exigences of his case.

3. The mercy God designed for him, in order to his comfort and perseverance in his resolutions; still God will be all in all to him. Before, Israel was compared to a tree, now God compares himself to one. He will be to his people, (1) As the branches of a tree: "*I am like a green fir-tree,* and will be so to thee." The fir-trees, in those countries, were exceedingly large and thick, and a shelter against sun and rain. God will be to all true converts both a delight and a defence; under his protection and influence they shall both dwell in safety and dwell at ease. He will be either *a sun and a shield* or *a shade and a shield,* according as their case requires. They shall sit down *under his shadow with delight,* Cant. ii. 3. He will be

so all weathers, Isa. iv. 6. (2.) As the root of a tree: *From me is thy fruit found,* which may be understood either of the fruit brought forth to us (to him we owe all our comforts) or of the fruit brought forth by us—from him we receive grace and strength to enable us to do our duty. Whatever fruits of righteousness we bring forth, all the praise of them is due to God; for he works in us both to will and to do that which is good.

II. Concerning every one that hears and reads the words of the prophecy of this book (v. 9): *Who is wise? and he shall understand these things.* Perhaps the prophet was wont to conclude the sermons he preached with these words, and now he closes with them the whole book, in which he had committed to writing some fragments of the many sermons he had preached. Observe, 1. The character of those that do profit by the truths he delivered: *Who is wise* and *prudent? He shall understand these things, he shall know them.* Those that set themselves to understand and know these things thereby make it to appear that they are truly wise and prudent, and will thereby be made more so; and, if any do not understand and know them, it is because they are foolish and unwise. Those that are wise in the doing of their duty, that are prudent in practical religion, are most likely to know and understand both the truths and providences of God, which are a mystery to others, John vii. 17. *The secret of the Lord is with those that fear him,* Ps. xxv. 14. *Who is wise?* This intimates a desire that those who read and hear these things would understand them *(O that they were wise!)* and a complaint that few were so—*Who has believed our report?* 2. The excellency of the things concerning which we are here instructed: *The ways of the Lord are right;* and therefore it is our wisdom and duty to know and understand them. The way of God's precepts, in which he requires us to walk, is right, agreeing with the rules of eternal reason and equity and having a direct tendency to our eternal felicity. The ways of God's providence, in which he walks towards us, are all right; no fault is to be found with any thing that God does, for it is all well done. His judgments upon the impenitent, his favours to the penitent, are all right; however they may be perverted and misinterpreted, God will at last be justified and glorified in them all. His *ways are equal.* 3. The different use which men make of them. (1.) The right ways of God to those that are good are, and will be, a savour of life unto life: *The just shall walk in them;* they shall conform to the will of God both in his precepts and in his providences, and shall have the comfort of so doing. They shall well understand the mind of God both in his word and in his works; they shall be well reconciled to both, and shall accommodate themselves to God's intention in both. *The just shall walk* in *those ways* towards their great end, and shall not come short of it. (2.) The right ways of God will be to those that are wicked a savour of death unto death : *The transgressors shall fall* not only in their own wrong ways, but even *in the right ways of the Lord.* Christ, who is a foundation stone to some, is to others a *stone of stumbling* and a *rock of offence.* That which was *ordained to life* becomes, through their abuse of it, death to them. God's providences, being not duly improved by them, harden them in sin and contribute to their ruin. God's discovery of

himself both in the judgments of his mouth and in the judgments of his hand is to us according as we are affected under it. *Recipitur ad modum recipientis—What is received influences according to the qualities of the receiver.* The same sun softens wax and hardens clay. But of all transgressors those certainly have the most dangerous fatal falls that fall *in the ways of God,* that split on the rock of ages, and suck poison out of the balm of Gilead. *Let the sinners in Zion be afraid* of this.

AN

EXPOSITION,

WITH PRACTICAL OBSERVATIONS,

OF THE BOOK OF THE PROPHET

JOEL.

WE are altogether uncertain concerning the time when this prophet prophesied ; it is probable that it was about the same time that Amos prophesied, not for the reason that the rabbin give, " Because Amos begins his prophecy with that wherewith Joel concludes his, *The Lord shall roar out of Zion,*" but for the reason Dr. Lightfoot gives, " Because he speaks of the same judgments of locusts, and drought, and fire, that Amos laments, which is an intimation that they appeared about the same time, Amos in Israel and Joel in Judah. Hosea and Obadiah prophesied about the same time ; and it appears that Amos prophesied in the days of Jeroboam, the second king of Israel, Amos vii. 10. God sent a variety of prophets, that they might strengthen the hands one of another, and that out of the mouth of two or three witnesses every word might be established. In this prophecy, I. The desolations made by hosts of noxious insects is described, *ch.* i. and part of *ch.* ii. II. The people are hereupon called to repentance, *ch.* ii. III. Promises are made of the return of mercy upon their repentance (*ch.* ii.), and promises of the pouring out of the Spirit in the latter days. IV. The cause of God's people is pleaded against their enemies, whom God would in due time reckon with (*ch.* iii.) ; and glorious things are spoken of the gospel-Jerusalem and of the prosperity and perpetuity of it.

CHAP. I.

This chapter is the description of a lamentable devastation made of the country of Judah by locusts and caterpillars. Some think that the prophet speaks of it as a thing to come and gives warning of it beforehand, as usually the prophets did of judgments coming. Others think that it was now present, and that his business was to affect the people with it and awaken them by it to repentance. I. It is spoken of as a judgment which there was no precedent of in former ages, ver. 1—7. II. All sorts of people sharing in the calamity are called upon to lament it, ver. 8—13. III. They are directed to look up to God in their lamentations, and to humble themselves before him, ver. 14—20.

THE word of the LORD that came to Joel the son of Pethuel. 2 Hear this, ye old men, and give ear, all ye inhabitants of the land. Hath this been in your days, or even in the days of your fathers? 3 Tell ye your children of it, and *let* your children *tell* their children, and their children

another generation. 4 That which the palmer-worm hath left hath the locust eaten ; and that which the locust hath left hath the canker-worm eaten ; and that which the canker-worm hath left hath the caterpillar eaten. 5 Awake, ye drunkards, and weep ; and howl, all ye drinkers of wine, because of the new wine ; for it is cut off from your mouth. 6 For a nation is come up upon my land, strong, and without number, whose teeth *are* the teeth of a lion, and he hath the cheek-teeth of a great lion. 7 He hath laid my vine waste, and barked my fig-tree : he hath made it clean bare, and cast *it* away ; the branches thereof are made white.

It is a foolish fancy which some of the Jews have, that this Joel the prophet was the same with that Joel who was the son of Samuel (1 Sam. viii. 2) ; yet one of their rabbin very gravely undertakes to show why Samuel is here called *Pethuel.* This Joel was long after that. He here speaks of a sad and sore judgment which was now brought, or to be brought, upon Judah, for their sins. Observe,

I. The greatness of the judgment, expressed here in two things :—1. It was such as could not be paralleled in the ages that were past, in history, or in the memory of any living, *v.* 2. The *old men* are appealed to, who could remember what had happened long ago ; nay, and *all the inhabitants of the land* are called on to testify, if they could any of them remember the like. Let them go further than any man's memory, and *prepare themselves for the search of their fathers* (Job viii. 8), and they would not find an account of the like in any record. Note, Those that outdo their predecessors in sin may justly expect to fall under greater and sorer judgments than any of their predecessors knew. 2. It was such as would not be forgotten in the ages to come (*v.* 3) : " *Tell you your children of it ;* let them know what dismal tokens of the wrath of God you have been under, that they may take warning, and may learn obedience by the things which you have suffered, for it is designed for warning to them also. Yea, let *your children tell their children, and their children another generation ;* let them tell it not only as a strange thing, which may serve for matter of talk" (as such uncommon accidents are recorded in our almanacs—It is so long since the plague, and fire—so long since the great frost, and the great wind), " but let them tell it to *teach their children* to stand in awe of God and of his judgments, and to tremble before him." Note, We ought to transmit to posterity the memorial of God's judgments as well as of his mercies.

II. The judgment itself ; it is an invasion of the country of Judea by a great army. Many interpreters both ancient and modern understand it of armies of men, the forces of the Assyrians, which, under Sennacherib, *took all the defenced cities of Judah,* and then, no doubt, made havoc of the country and destroyed the products of it ; nay, some make the four sorts of animals here named (*v.* 4) to signify the four monarchies which, in their turns, were oppressive to the people of the Jews, one destroying what had escaped the fury of the other. Many of the Jewish expositors think it is a parabolical expression of the coming of enemies, and their multitude, to lay all waste. So the Chaldee paraphrast mentions these animals (*v.* 4) ; but

afterwards (*ch.* ii. 25) puts instead of them, *Nations, peoples, tongues, languages, potentates,* and *revenging kingdoms.* But it seems much rather to be understood literally of armies of insects coming upon the land and eating up the fruits of it. Locusts were one of the plagues of Egypt. Of them it is said, There never were any like them, nor should be (Exod. x. 14), none such as those in Egypt, none such as these in Judah—none like those locusts for bigness, none like these for multitude and the mischief they did. The plague of locusts in Egypt lasted but for a few days ; this seems to have continued for four years successively (as some think), because here are four sorts of insects mentioned (*v.* 4), one destroying what the other left ; but others think they came all in one year. We are not told, in the history of the Old Testament, when this happened, but we are sure that no word of God fell to the ground ; and, though a devastation by these insects is primarily intended here, yet it is expressed in such language as is very applicable to the destruction of the country by a foreign enemy invading it, because, if the people were not humbled and reformed by that less judgment which devoured the land, God would send this greater upon them, which would devour the inhabitants ; and by the description of that they are bidden to take it for a warning. If this nation of worms do not subdue them, another nation shall come to ruin them. Observe, 1. What these animals are that are sent against them—*locusts* and *caterpillars, palmer-worms* and *canker-worms, v.* 4. We cannot now describe how these differed one from another ; they were all little insects, any one of them despicable, and which a man might easily crush with his foot or with his finger ; but when they came in vast swarms, or shoals, they were very formidable and ate up all before them. Note, God is Lord of hosts, has all creatures at his command, and, when he pleases, can humble and mortify a proud and rebellious people by the weakest and most contemptible creatures. Man is said to be a worm ; and by this it appears that he is *less than a worm,* for, when God pleases, worms are too hard for him, plunder his country, eat up that for which he laboured, destroy the forage, and cut off the subsistence of a potent nation. The weaker the instrument is that God employs the more is his power magnified. 2. What force and fury they came with. They are here called a *nation* (*v.* 6), because they are embodied, and act by consent, and as it were with a common design ; for, though *the locusts have no king, yet go they forth all of them by bands* (Prov. xxx. 27), and it is there mentioned as an instance of their *wisdom.* It is prudence for those that are weak severally to unite and act jointly. They are *strong,* for they are *without number.* The *small dust of the balance* is light, and easily blown away, but a heap of dust is weighty; so a worm can do little (yet one worm served to destroy Jonah's gourd), but numbers of them can do wonders. They are said to have the *teeth of a lion*, of a *great lion*, because of the great and terrible execution they do. Note, Locusts become as lions when they come armed with a divine commission. We read of the locusts out of the bottomless pit, that *their teeth were as the teeth of lions*, Rev. ix. 8. 3. What mischief they do. They *eat up* all before them (*v.* 4); what one leaves the other devours; they destroy not only the grass and corn, but the trees (*v.* 7): The *vine is laid waste*. These vermin eat the leaves which should be a shelter to the fruit while it ripens, and so that also perishes and comes to nothing. They eat the very bark of the fig-tree, and so kill it. Thus the *fig-tree does not blossom*, nor is there *fruit in the vine*.

III. A call to the drunkards to lament this judgment (*v.* 5): *Awake and weep, all you drinkers of wine.* This intimates, 1. That they should suffer very sensibly by this calamity. It should touch them in a tender part; the *new wine* which they loved so well should be *cut off from their mouth*. Note, It is just with God to take away those comforts which are abused to luxury and excess, to *recover* the *corn and wine* which are *prepared* for Baal, which are made the food and fuel of a base lust. And to them judgments of that kind are most grievous. The more men place their happiness in the gratifications of sense the more pressing temporal afflictions are upon them. The drinkers of water needed not to care when the vine was laid waste; they could live as well without it as they had done; it was no trouble to the Nazarites. But the *drinkers of wine* will *weep and howl*. The more delights we make necessary to our satisfaction the more we expose ourselves to trouble and disappointment. 2. It intimates that they had been very senseless and stupid under the former tokens of God's displeasure; and therefore they are here called to *awake and weep*. Those that will not be roused out of their security by the word of God shall be roused by his rod; those that will not be startled by judgments at a distance shall be themselves arrested by them; and when they are going to partake of the forbidden fruit a prohibition of another nature shall come *between the cup and the lip*, and *cut off the wine from their mouth*.

8 Lament like a virgin girded with sackcloth for the husband of her youth. 9 The meat-offering and the drink-offering is cut off from the house of the LORD; the priests, the LORD's ministers, mourn. 10 The field is wasted, the land mourneth; for the corn is wasted: the new wine is dried up, the oil languisheth. 11 Be ye ashamed,

O ye husbandmen; howl, O ye vinedressers, for the wheat and for the barley; because the harvest of the field is perished. 12 The vine is dried up, and the fig-tree languisheth; the pomegranate-tree, the palm-tree also, and the apple-tree, *even* all the trees of the field, are withered: because joy is withered away from the sons of men. 13 Gird yourselves, and lament, ye priests: howl, ye ministers of the altar: come, lie all night in sackcloth, ye ministers of my God: for the meat-offering and the drink-offering is withholden from the house of your God.

The judgment is here described as very lamentable, and such as all sorts of people should share in; it shall not only rob the drunkards of their pleasure (if that were the worst of it, it might be the better borne), but it shall deprive others of their necessary subsistence, who are therefore called to lament (*v.* 8), as a virgin laments the death of her lover to whom she was espoused, but not completely married, yet so that he was in effect her husband, or as a young woman lately married, from whom the *husband of her youth*, her young husband, or the husband to whom she was married when she was young, is suddenly taken away by death. Between a new-married couple that are young, that married for love, and that are every way amiable and agreeable to each other, there is great fondness, and consequently great grief if either be taken away. Such lamentation shall there be for the loss of their corn and wine. Note, The more we are wedded to our creature-comforts the harder it is to part with them. See that parallel place, Isa. xxxii. 10—12. Two sorts of people are here brought in, as concerned to lament this devastation, countrymen and clergymen.

I. Let the husbandmen and vine-dressers lament, *v.* 11. Let them be ashamed of the care and pains they have taken about their vineyards, for it will be all labour lost, and they shall gain no advantage by it; they shall see the fruit of their labour eaten up before their eyes, and shall not be able to save any of it. Note, Those who labour only *for the meat that perishes* will, sooner or later, be ashamed of their labour. The *vine-dressers* will then express their extreme grief by *howling*, when they see their vineyards stripped of leaves and fruit, and the vines withered, so that nothing is to be had or hoped for from them, wherewith they might pay their rent and maintain their families. The destruction is particularly described here: *The field is laid waste* (*v.* 10); all is consumed that it produced; *the land mourns;* the ground has a melancholy aspect, and looks ruefully; all the inhabitants of the land are in tears for what they have lost, are in fears of perishing for want, Isa. xxiv. 4; Jer. iv. 28. " The *corn,* the bread-corn, which is the staff of life, is *wasted;* the *new wine,* which should be brought into the cellars for a supply when the old is drunk, is *dried up,* is *ashamed* of having promised so fair what it is not now able to perform; the oil *languishes,* or is *diminished,* because (as the Chaldee renders it) *the olives have fallen off.*" The people were not thankful to God as they should have been for the *bread that strengthens man's heart,* the *wine* that *makes glad the heart,* and the *oil that makes the face to shine* (Ps. civ. 14, 15); and therefore they are justly brought to lament the loss and want of them, of all the products of the earth, which God had given them either for necessity or for delight (this is repeated, *v.* 11, 12)—the *wheat and barley,* the two principal grains bread was then made of, wheat for the rich and barley for the poor, so that the rich and poor meet together in the calamity. The trees are destroyed, not only the *vine and the fig-tree* (as before, *v.* 7), which were more useful and necessary, but other trees also that were for delight—the *pomegranate, palm-tree,* and *apple-tree,* yea, all the *trees of the field,* as well as those of the orchard, timber-trees as well as fruit-trees. In short, all *the harvest of the field has perished, v.* 11. And by this means *joy has withered away from the children of men* (*v.* 11); the *joy of harvest,* which is used to express great and general joy, has come to nothing, is turned into shame, is turned into lamentation. Note, The perishing of the harvest is the withering of the joy of the children of men. Those that place their happiness in the delights of sense, when they are deprived of them, or in any way disturbed in the enjoyment of them, lose all their joy; whereas the children of God, who look upon the pleasures of sense with holy indifference and contempt, and know what it is to make God their hearts' delight, can rejoice in him as the *God of their salvation* even when the *fig-tree does not blossom;* spiritual joy is so far from withering then, that it flourishes more than ever, Hab. iii. 17, 18. Let us see here, 1. What perishing uncertain things all our creature-comforts are. We can never be sure of the continuance of them. Here the heavens had given their rains in due season, the earth had yielded her strength, and, when the appointed weeks of harvest were at hand, they saw no reason to doubt but that they should have a very plentiful crop; yet then they are invaded by these unthought-of enemies, that lay all waste, and not by fire and sword. It is our wisdom not to lay up our treasure in those things which are liable to so many untoward accidents. 2. See what need we have to live in a continual dependence upon

God and his providence, for our own hands are not sufficient for us. When we see the *full corn in the ear,* and think we are sure of it—nay, when we have *brought it home,* if he *blow upon it,* nay, if he do not bless it, we are not likely to have any good of it. 3. See what ruinous work sin makes. A paradise is turned into a wilderness, a fruitful land, the most fruitful land upon earth, *into barrenness,* for the *iniquity of those that dwelt therein.*

II. Let the priests, the Lord's ministers, lament, for they share deeply in the calamity: *Gird yourselves* with sackcloth (*v.* 13); nay, they *do mourn, v.* 9. Observe, The priests are called the *ministers of the altar,* for on that they attended, and the *ministers of the Lord* (of *my God,* says the prophet), for in attending on the altar they served him, did his work, and did him honour. Note, Those that are employed in holy things are therein God's ministers, and on him they attend. The ministers of the altar used to rejoice before the Lord, and to spend their time very much in singing; but now they must *lament and howl,* for the *meat-offering* and *drink-offering* were *cut off from the house of the Lord* (*v.* 9), and the same again (*v.* 13), *from the house of your God.* " He is your God in a particular manner; you are in a nearer relation to him than other Israelites are; and therefore it is expected that you should be more concerned than others for that which is a hindrance to the service of his sanctuary." It is intimated, 1. That the people, as long as they had the fruits of the earth brought in in their season, presented to the Lord his dues out of them, and brought the offerings to the altar and tithes to those that served at the altar. Note, A people may be filling up the measure of their iniquity apace, and yet may keep up a course of external performances in religion. 2. That, when the meat and drink failed, the meat-offering and drink-offering failed of course; and this was the sorest instance of the calamity. Note, As far as any public trouble is an obstruction to the course of religion it is to be upon that account, more than any other, sadly lamented, especially by the priests, the Lord's ministers. As far as poverty occasions the decay of piety and the neglect of divine offices, and starves the cause of religion among a people, it is indeed a sore judgment. When the famine prevailed God could not have his sacrifices, nor could the priests have their maintenance; and therefore let *the Lord's ministers mourn.*

14 Sanctify ye a fast, call a solemn assembly, gather the elders *and* all the inhabitants of the land *into* the house of the LORD your God, and cry unto the LORD, 15 Alas for the day! for the day of the LORD *is* at hand, and

as a destruction from the Almighty shall it come. 16 Is not the meat cut off before our eyes, *yea*, joy and gladness from the house of our God? 17 The seed is rotten under their clods, the garners are laid desolate, the barns are broken down; for the corn is withered. 18 How do the beasts groan! the herds of cattle are perplexed, because they have no pasture; yea, the flocks of sheep are made desolate. 19 O LORD, to thee will I cry: for the fire hath devoured the pastures of the wilderness, and the flame hath burned all the trees of the field. 20 The beasts of the field cry also unto thee: for the rivers of waters are dried up, and the fire hath devoured the pastures of the wilderness.

We have observed abundance of tears shed for the destruction of the fruits of the earth by the locusts; now here we have those tears turned into the right channel, that of repentance and humiliation before God. The judgment was very heavy, and here they are directed to own the hand of God in it, his *mighty hand*, and to *humble themselves* under it. Here is,

I. A proclamation issued out for a general fast. The priests are ordered to appoint one; they must not only mourn themselves, but they must call upon others to mourn too: "*Sanctify a fast;* let some time be set apart from all worldly business to be spent in the exercises of religion, in the expressions of repentance and other extraordinary instances of devotion." Note, Under public judgments there ought to be public humiliations; for by them the *Lord God calls to weeping and mourning.* With all the marks of sorrow and shame sin must be confessed and bewailed, the righteousness of God must be acknowledged, and his favour implored. Observe what is to be done by a nation at such a time. 1. A day is to be appointed for this purpose, a *day of restraint* (so the margin reads it), a day in which people must be restrained from their other ordinary business (that they may the more closely attend God's service), and from all bodily refreshments; for, 2. It must be a *fast*, a religious abstaining from meat and drink, further than is of absolute necessity. The king of Nineveh appointed a fast, in which they were to *taste nothing*, Jonah iii. 7. Hereby we own ourselves unworthy of our necessary food, and that we have forfeited it and deserve to be wholly deprived of it, we punish ourselves and mortify the body, which has been the occasion of sin, we keep it in a frame fit to serve the soul in serving God, and, by the appetite's craving

food, the desires of the soul towards that which is better than life, and all the supports of it, are excited. This was in a special manner seasonable now that God was depriving them of their *meat and drink;* for hereby they accommodated themselves to the affliction they were under. When God says, *You shall fast*, it is time to say, *We will fast.* 3. There must be a solemn assembly. The *elders* and the *people*, magistrates and subjects, must be *gathered together*, even *all the inhabitants of the land*, that God might be honoured by their public humiliations, that they might thereby take the more shame to themselves, and that they might excite and stir up one another to the religious duties of the day. All had contributed to the national guilt, all shared in the national calamity, and therefore they must all join in the professions of repentance. 4. They must come together in the temple, *the house of the Lord their God*, because that was the house of prayer, and there they might hope to meet with God because it was the place which he had *chosen to put his name there*, there they might hope to speed because it was a type of Christ and his mediation. Thus they interested themselves in Solomon's prayer for the acceptance of all the requests that should be put up in or towards this house, in which their present case was particularly mentioned. 1 Kings viii. 37, *If there be locust, if there be caterpillar.* 5. They must *sanctify* this fast, must observe it in a religious manner, with sincere devotion. What is a fast worth if it be not sanctified? 6. They must *cry unto the Lord.* To him they must make their complaint and offer up their supplication. When we cry in our affliction we must *cry to the Lord;* this is *fasting to him*, Zech. vii. 5.

II. Some considerations suggested to induce them to proclaim this fast and to observe it strictly.

1. God was beginning a controversy with them. It is time to *cry unto the Lord*, for *the day of the Lord is at hand, v.* 15. Either they mean the continuance and consequences of this present judgment which they now saw but breaking in upon them, or some greater judgments which this was but a preface to. However it be, this they are taught to make the matter of their lamentation: *Alas, for the day! for the day of the Lord is at hand.* Therefore *cry to God.* For, (1.) "The day of his judgment is very near, it is *at hand;* it *will not slumber*, and therefore you should not. It is time to fast and pray, for you have but a little time to turn yourselves in." (2.) It will be very terrible; there is no escaping it, no resisting it: *As a destruction from the Almighty shall it come.* See Isa. xiii. 6. It is not a correction, but a destruction; and it comes from the hand, not of a weak creature, but *of the Almighty:* and *who knows* (nay, who does not know) *the power of his anger?* Whither should we

go with our cries but to him from whom the judgment we dread comes? There is no fleeing from him but by fleeing to him, no escaping destruction from the Almighty but by making our submission and supplication to the Almighty; this is *taking hold on his strength, that we may make peace,* Isa. xxvii. 5.

2. They saw themselves already under the tokens of his displeasure. It is time to fast and pray, for their distress is very great, *v.* 16. (1.) Let them look into their own houses, and there was no plenty there, as used to be. Those who kept a good table were now obliged to retrench: *Is not the meat cut off before our eyes?* We see it wherever we go. Note, Though it is common for the heart not to rue what the eye sees not, yet that heart is hard indeed which trembles not, and humbles not itself, when God's judgments are *before the eyes.* If, when God's hand is lifted up, men *will not see,* when his hand is laid on *they shall see.* Is not the meat many a time cut off before our eyes? Let us then labour for that spiritual meat which is not before our eyes, and which cannot be cut off. (2.) Let them look into God's house, and see the effects of the judgment there; joy and gladness were *cut off from the house of God.* Note, The house of our God is the proper place of joy and gladness; when David goes to the *altar of God,* it is to God *my exceeding joy;* but when *joy and gladness* are *cut off from God's house,* either by the corruption of holy things or the persecution of holy persons, when serious godliness decays and love waxes cold, then it is time to cry to the Lord, time to cry, *Alas!*

3. The prophet returns to describe the grievousness of the calamity, in some particulars of it. Corn and cattle are the husbandman's staple commodities; now here he is deprived of both these. (1.) The caterpillars have devoured the corn, *v.* 17. The *garners,* which they used to fill with corn, *are laid desolate,* and *the barns broken down,* because *the corn has withered,* and the owners think it not worth while to be at the charge of repairing them when they have nothing to put in them, nor are likely to have any thing; for *the seed is rotten under the clods,* either through too much rain or (which was the more common case in Canaan) for want of rain, or perhaps some insects under ground ate it up. When one crop fails the husbandman hopes the next may make it up; but here they despair of that, the seedness being as bad as the harvest. (2.) The cattle perish too for want of grass (*v.* 18): *How do the beasts groan!* This the prophet takes notice of, that the people might be affected with it and lay to heart the judgment. The groans of the cattle should soften their hard and impenitent hearts. *The herds of cattle,* the large cattle (black cattle we call them), *are perplexed;* nay, even *the flocks of sheep,* which will live upon a common and be con-

tent with very short grass, *are made desolate.* See here the inferior creatures suffering for our transgression, and groaning under the double burden of being serviceable to the sin of man and subject to the curse of God for it. *Cursed is the ground for thy sake.*

III. The prophet stirs them up to cry to God, with the consideration of the examples given them for it.

1. His own example (*v.* 19): *O Lord! to thee will I cry.* He would not put them upon doing that which he would not resolve to do himself; nay, whether they would do it or no, he would. Note, If God's ministers cannot prevail to affect others with the discoveries of divine wrath, yet they ought to be themselves affected with them; if they cannot bring others to cry to God, yet they must themselves be much in prayer. In time of trouble we must not only pray, but cry, must be fervent and importunate in prayer; and to God, from whom both the destruction is and the salvation must be, ought our cry to be always directed. That which engaged him to *cry to God* was, not so much any personal affliction, as the national calamity: The *fire has devoured the pastures of the wilderness,* which seems to be meant of some parching scorching heat of the sun, which was as fire to the fruits of the earth; it consumed them all. Note, When God *calls to contend by fire* it concerns those that have any interest in heaven to cry mightily to him for relief. See Num. xi. 2; Amos vii. 4, 5.

2. The example of the inferior creatures: " *The beasts of the field* do not only *groan,* but *cry unto thee, v.* 20. They appeal to thy pity, according to their capacity, and as if, though they are not capable of a rational and revealed religion, yet they had something of dependence upon God by natural instinct." At least, when they groan by reason of their calamity, he is pleased to interpret it as if they cried to him; much more will he put a favourable construction upon the groanings of his own children, though sometimes so feeble that they *cannot be uttered,* Rom. viii. 26. The beasts are here said to *cry unto God,* as from him the *lions seek their meat* (Ps. civ. 21) and the young *ravens,* Job xxxviii. 41. The complaints of the brute-creatures here are for want of water (*The rivers are dried up,* through the excessive heat), and for want of grass, for the *fire has devoured the pastures of the wilderness.* And what better are those than beasts who never cry to God but for corn and wine, and complain of nothing but the want of the delights of sense? Yet their crying to God in those cases shames the stupidity of those who cry not to God in any case.

CHAP. II.

In this chapter we have, I. A further description of that terrible desolation which should be made in the land of Judah by the locusts and caterpillars, ver. 1—11. II. A serious call to the people, when they are under this sore judgment, to return and repent, to fast and pray, and to seek unto God for mercy, with directions how to

do this aright, ver. 12—17. III. A promise that, upon their repentance, God would remove the judgment, would repair the
breaches made upon them by it, and restore unto them plenty of
all good things, ver. 18—27. IV. A prediction of the setting up of
the kingdom of the Messiah in the world, by the pouring out of
the Spirit in the latter days, ver. 28—32. Thus the beginning of
this chapter is made terrible with the tokens of God's wrath, but
the latter end of it made comfortable with the assurances of his
favour, and it is in the way of repentance that this blessed change
is made; so that, though it is only the last paragraph of the chapter that points directly at gospel-times, yet the whole may be improved as a type and figure, representing the curses of the law invading men for their sins, and the comforts of the gospel flowing
in to them upon their repentance

BLOW ye the trumpet in Zion,
and sound an alarm in my holy
mountain : let all the inhabitants of
the land tremble : for the day of the
LORD cometh, for *it is* nigh at hand;
2 A day of darkness and of gloominess, a day of clouds and of thick darkness, as the morning spread upon
the mountains : a great people and a
strong ; there hath not been ever the
like, neither shall be any more after
it, *even* to the years of many generations. 3 A fire devoureth before them ;
and behind them a flame burneth : the
land *is* as the garden of Eden before
them, and behind them a desolate wilderness ; yea, and nothing shall escape them. 4 The appearance of them
is as the appearance of horses ; and
as horsemen, so shall they run. 5
Like the noise of chariots on the tops
of mountains shall they leap, like the
noise of a flame of fire that devoureth
the stubble, as a strong people set in
battle array. 6 Before their face the
people shall be much pained : all faces
shall gather blackness. 7 They shall
run like mighty men ; they shall climb
the wall like men of war ; and they
shall march every one on his ways,
and they shall not break their ranks :
8 Neither shall one thrust another ;
they shall walk every one in his path :
and *when* they fall upon the sword,
they shall not be wounded. 9 They
shall run to and fro in the city ; they
shall run upon the wall, they shall
climb up upon the houses ; they shall
enter in at the windows like a thief.
10 The earth shall quake before them ;
the heavens shall tremble : the sun and
the moon shall be dark, and the stars
shall withdraw their shining : 11 And
the LORD shall utter his voice before
his army : for his camp *is* very great :
for *he is* strong that executeth his
word : for the day of the LORD *is*

great and very terrible ; and who can
abide it ?

Here we have God contending with his
own professing people for their sins and executing upon them the judgment written in
the law (Deut. xxviii. 42), *The fruit of thy
land shall the locust consume,* which was one
of those diseases of Egypt that God would
bring upon them, *v.* 60.

I. Here is the war proclaimed (*v.* 1) :
Blow the trumpet in Zion, either to call the
invading army together, and then the trumpet sounds a charge, or rather to give notice
to Judah and Jerusalem of the approach of
the judgment, that they might *prepare to
meet their God* in the way of his judgments
and might endeavour by prayers and tears,
the church's best artillery, to put by the
stroke. It was the priests' business to sound
the trumpet (Num. x. 8), both as an appeal
to God in the day of their distress and a
summons to the people to come together to
seek his face. Note, It is the work of ministers to give warning from the word of God
of the fatal consequences of sin, and to reveal
his wrath from heaven against the ungodliness and unrighteousness of men. And
though it is not the privilege of Zion and
Jerusalem to be exempted from the judgments of God, if they provoke him, yet it is
their privilege to be warned of them, that
they may make their peace with him. Even
in *the holy mountain* the *alarm* must be *sounded,* and then it sounds most dreadful, Amos
iii. 2. Now, *shall a trumpet be blown in the
city,* in the holy city, *and the people not be
afraid?* Surely they will. Amos iii. 6. *Let
all the inhabitants of the land tremble ;* they
shall be made to tremble by the judgment
itself ; let them therefore tremble at the
alarm of it.

II. Here is a general idea given of the
day of battle, which *cometh,* which is *nigh
at hand,* and there is no avoiding it. It is
the *day of the Lord,* the day of his judgment, in which he will both manifest and
magnify himself. It is *a day of darkness
and gloominess* (*v.* 2), literally so, the swarms
of locusts and caterpillars being so large and
so thick as to darken the sky (Exod. x. 15),
or rather figuratively ; it will be a melancholy
time, a time of grievous affliction. And it
will come *as the morning spread upon the
mountains ;* the darkness of this day will
come as suddenly as the morning light, as
irresistibly, will spread as far, and grow upon
them as the morning light.

III. Here is the army drawn up in array
(*v.* 2) : They are a *great people, and a strong.*
Any one that sees the vast numbers that there
shall be of locusts and caterpillars, destroying the land, will say (as we are all apt to be
most affected with what is present), " Surely,
never was the like before, nor ever will be
the like again." Note, Extraordinary judgments are rare things, and seldom happen,

which is an instance of God's patience. When God had drowned the world once he promised never to do it again. The army is her described to be, 1. Very bold and daring: They *are as horses,* as war-horses, that rush into the battle and *are not affrighted* (Job xxxix. 22); and *as horsemen,* carried on with martial fire and fury, *so they shall run, v.* 4. Some of the ancients have observed that the head of a locust is very like, in shape, to the head of a horse. 2. Very loud and noisy—*like the noise of chariots,* of many chariots, when driven furiously over rough ground, *on the tops of the mountains, v.* 5. Hence is borrowed part of the description of the locusts which St. John saw rise ut of the bottomless pit. Rev. ix. 7, 9, *The shapes of the locusts were like unto horses prepared to the battle; and the sound of their wings was as the sound of chariots, of many horses running to the battle.* Historians tell us that the noise made by swarms of locusts in those countries that are infested with them has sometimes been heard six miles off. The noise is likewise compared to that of a *roaring fire;* it is like the *noise of a flame* that *devours the stubble,* which noise is the more terrible because that which it is the indication of is devouring. Note, When God's judgments are abroad they make a great noise; and it is necessary for the awakening of a secure and stupid world that they should do so. (3.) They are very regular, and keep ranks in their march; though numerous and greedy of spoil, yet they are *as a strong people set in battle array* (*v.* 5): *They shall march every one on his ways,* straight forward, as if they had been trained up by the discipline of war to keep their post and observe their right-hand man. *They shall not break their ranks, nor one thrust another, v.* 7, 8. Their number and swiftness shall breed no confusion. See how God can make creatures to act by rule that have no reason to act by, when he designs to serve his own purposes by them. And see how necessary it is that those who are employed in any service for God should observe order, and keep ranks, should diligently go on in their own work and not stand in one another's way. 4. They are very *swift;* they *run like horsemen* (*v.* 4), run *like mighty men* (*v.* 7); they *run to and fro in the city,* and *run upon the wall, v.* 9. When God *sends forth his command on earth* his word *runs very swiftly,* Ps. cxlvii. 15. Angels have wings, and so have locusts, when God makes use of them.

IV. Here is the terrible execution done by this formidable army, 1. In the country, *v.* 3. View the army in the front, and you will see a *fire devouring before them;* they consume all as if they breathed fire. View it in the rear, and you will see those that come behind as furious as the foremost: *Behind them a flame burns.* When they are gone, then it will appear what destruction they have made. Look upon the fields that

they have not yet invaded, and they are *as the garden of Eden,* pleasant to the eye, and full of good fruits; they are the pride and glory of the country. But look upon the fields that they have eaten up and they are *as a desolate wilderness;* one would not think that these had ever been like the former, and yet so they were perhaps but the day before, or that those should ever be made like these, and yet so they shall be perhaps by to-morrow night; yea, and *nothing shall escape them* that can possibly be made food for them. Let none be proud of the beauty of their grounds any more than of their bodies, for God can soon change the face of both. 2. In the city. They shall *climb the wall* (*v.* 7), they shall *run upon the houses,* and *enter in at the windows like a thief* (*v.* 9); when Egypt was plagued with locusts, they filled *Pharaoh's houses* and the *houses of his servants,* Exod. x. 5, 6. The locusts out of the bottomless pit, Satan's emissaries, and missionaries of the man of sin, do as these locusts. God's judgments too, when they come with commission, cannot be kept out with bars and bolts; they will find or force their way.

V. The impressions that should hereby be made upon the people. They shall find it to no purpose to make opposition. These enemies are invulnerable and therefore irresistible: *When they fall upon the sword they shall not be wounded, v.* 8. And those that cannot be hurt cannot be stopped; and therefore *before their faces the people shall be much pained* (*v.* 6), as the merchants are in pain for their trading ships when they hear that they are just in the mouth of a squadron of the enemies. "One is in pain for his field, another for his vineyard, *and all faces gather blackness,*" which denotes the utmost consternation imaginable. Men in fear look pale, but men in despair look black; the whiteness of a sudden fright, when it is settled, turns into blackness. What is the matter of our pride and pleasure God can soon make the matter of our pain. The terror that the country should be in is described (*v.* 10) by figurative expressions: *The earth shall quake and the heavens tremble;* even the hearts that seemed undaunted, so firm that nothing would frighten them, as immoveable as heaven or earth, shall be seized with astonishment. Or when the inhabitants of the land are made to quake it seems to them as if all about them trembled too. Through the prevalency of their fear, or for want of the supports of life which they used to have, their eye shall wax dim and their sight fail them, so that to them *the sun and moon shall seem* to be *dark,* and the stars to *withdraw their shining.* Note, When God frowns upon men the lights of heaven will be small joy to them; for man, by rebelling against his Creator, has forfeited the benefit of all the creatures. But, though this is to be understood figuratively, there is

1209

a day coming when it will be accomplished in the letter, when the _heavens_ shall be _rolled together like a scroll,_ and _the earth, and all the works that are therein,_ shall be _burnt up._ Particular judgments should awaken us to think of the general judgment.

VI. We are here directed to look up to him who is the commander-in-chief of this formidable army, and that is God himself, _v._ 11. It is _his army; it is his camp._ He raised it; he gives it commission; he _utters his voice before it,_ as the general gives orders to his army what to do and makes a speech to animate the soldiers; it is the Lord that gives the word of command to all these animals, which they exactly observe. Some think that with this cloud of locusts God sent terrible thunder, for that is called, _The voice of the Lord,_ and was another of the plagues of Egypt, and this made the heavens and the earth tremble. It is the _day of the Lord_ (as it was called, _v._ 1), for in this war we are sure he carries the day; it must needs be his, for _his camp is great_ and numerous. Those whom he makes war upon he can, as here, overpower with numbers; and whoever he employs to _execute his word,_ as the minister of his justice, is sure to be made _strong_ and _par negotio—equal to what he undertakes;_ whom God gives commission to he girds with strength for the executing of that commission. And this makes the _great day_ of the Lord _very terrible_ to all those who in that day are to be made the monuments of his justice; for _who can abide it?_ None can escape the arrests of God's wrath, can make head against the force of it, or bear up under the weight of it, 1 Sam. vi. 20; Ps. lxxvi. 7.

12 Therefore also now, saith the Lord, Turn ye _even_ to me with all your heart, and with fasting, and with weeping, and with mourning: 13 And rend your heart, and not your garments, and turn unto the Lord your God: for he _is_ gracious and merciful, slow to anger, and of great kindness, and repenteth him of the evil. 14 Who knoweth _if_ he will return and repent, and leave a blessing behind him; _even_ a meat-offering and a drink-offering unto the Lord your God? 15 Blow the trumpet in Zion, sanctify a fast, call a solemn assembly: 16 Gather the people, sanctify the congregation, assemble the elders, gather the children, and those that suck the breasts: let the bridegroom go forth of his chamber, and the bride out of her closet. 17 Let the priests, the ministers of the Lord, weep between the porch and the altar, and let

them say, Spare thy people, O Lord, and give not thine heritage to reproach, that the heathen should rule over them: wherefore should they say among the people, Where _is_ their God?

We have here an earnest exhortation to repentance, inferred from that desolating judgment described and threatened in the foregoing verses: _Therefore now turn you to the Lord._ 1. "Thus you must answer the end and intention of the judgment; for it was sent for this end, to convince you of your sins, to humble you for them, to reduce you to your right minds and to your allegiance." God brings us into straits, that he may bring us to repentance and so bring us to himself. 2. "Thus you may stay the progress of the judgment. Things are bad with you, but thus you may prevent their growing worse; nay, if you take this course, they will soon grow better." Here is a gracious invitation,

I. To a personal repentance, exercised in the soul, _every family apart, and their wives apart,_ Zech. xii. 12. When the judgments of God are abroad, each person is concerned to contribute his _quota_ to the common supplications, having contributed to the common guilt. Every one must mend one and mourn for one, and then we should all be mended and all found among God's mourners. Observe,

1. What we are here called to, which will teach us what it is to repent, for it is the same that the Lord our God still requires of us, we having all made work for repentance. (1.) We must be truly humbled for our sins, must be sorry we have by sin offended God, and ashamed we have by sin wronged ourselves, both wronged our judgments and wronged our interests. There must be outward expressions of sorrow and shame, _fasting,_ and _weeping,_ and _mourning;_ tears for the trouble must be turned into tears for the sin that procured it. But what will the outward expressions of sorrow avail if the inward impressions be not agreeable, and not only accompany them, but be the root and spring of them, and give rise to them? And therefore it follows, _Rend your heart, and not your garments;_ not but that, according to the custom of that age, it was proper for them to rend their garments, in token of great grief for their sins and a holy indignation against themselves for their folly; but, "Rest not in the doing of that, as if that were sufficient, but be more in care to accommodate your spirits than to accommodate your dress to a day of fasting and humiliation; nay, rend not your garments at all, unless withal you rend your hearts, for the sign without the thing signified is but a jest and a mockery, and an affront to God." Rending the heart is that which God looks for and requires; that is

the *broken and contrite heart* which he *will not despise*, Ps. li. 17. When we are greatly grieved in soul for sin, so that it even *cuts us to the heart* to think how we have dishonoured God and disparaged ourselves by it, when we conceive an aversion to sin, and earnestly desire and endeavour to get clear of the principles of it and never to return to the practice of it, then we rend our hearts for it, and then will God *rend the heavens* and come down to us with mercy. (2.) We must be thoroughly converted to our God, and come home to him when we fall out with sin. *Turn you even to me, saith the Lord* (v. 12), and again (v. 13), *Turn unto the Lord your God.* Our fasting and weeping are worth nothing if we do not with them turn to God as our God. When we are fully convinced that it is our duty and interest to keep in with him, and are heartily sorry we have ever turned the back upon him, and thereupon, by a firm and fixed resolution, make his glory our end, his will our rule, and his favour our felicity, then we *return to the Lord our God*, and this we are all commanded and invited to do, and to do it quickly.

2. What arguments are here used to persuade this people thus to turn to the Lord, and to turn to him *with all their hearts*. When the heart is rent for sin, and rent from it, then it is prepared to turn entirely to God, and to be devoted entirely to him, and he will have it all or none. Now, to bring ourselves to this, let us consider, (1.) We are sure that he is, in general, a good God. We must *turn to the Lord our God*, not only because he has been just and righteous in punishing us for our sins, the fear of which should drive us to him, but because he is *gracious and merciful*, in receiving us upon our repentance, the hope of which should draw us to him. He is gracious and merciful, delights not in the death of sinners, but desires they may turn and live. *He is slow to anger* against those that offend him, but of *great kindness* towards those that desire to please him. These very expressions are used in God's proclamation of his name when he caused *his goodness*, and with it all his glory, to *pass before Moses*, Exod. xxxiv. 6, 7. *He repents him of the evil*, not that he changes his mind, but, when the sinner's mind is changed, God's way towards him is changed; the sentence is reversed, and the curse of the law is taken off. Note, That is genuine, ingenuous, and evangelical repentance, which arises from a firm belief of the mercy of God, which we have sinned against, and yet are not in despair. *Repent, for the kingdom of heaven is at hand.* The goodness of God, if it be rightly understood, instead of emboldening us to go on in sin, will be the most powerful inducement to repentance, Ps. cxxx. 4. The act of indemnity brings those to God whom the act of attainder frightened from him. (2.) We have reason to hope that he will, upon our repentance, give us

that good which by sin we have forfeited and deprived ourselves of (v. 14), that he will *return and repent*, that he will not proceed against us as he has done, but will act in favour of us. *Therefore* let us repent of our sins against him, and return to him in a way of duty, because then we may hope that he will repent of his judgments against us and return to us in a way of mercy. Now observe, [1.] The manner of the expectation is very humble and modest: *Who knows if he will?* Some think it is expressed thus doubtfully to check the presumption and security of the people, and to quicken them to a holy carefulness and liveliness in their repentance, as Josh. xxiv. 19. Or, rather, it is expressed doubtfully because it is the removal of a temporal judgment that they here promise themselves, of which we cannot be so confident as we can that, in general, God is gracious and merciful. There is no question at all to be made but that if we truly repent of our sins God will forgive them, and be reconciled to us; but whether he will remove this or the other affliction which we are under may well be questioned, and yet the probability of it should encourage us to repent. Promises of temporal good things are often made with a peradventure. *It may be, you shall be hid*, Zeph. ii. 3. David's sin is pardoned, and yet the child shall die, and, when David prayed for its life, he said, as here, *Who can tell whether God will be gracious to me* in this matter likewise? 2 Sam. xii. 22. The Ninevites repented and reformed upon such a consideration as this, Jonah iii. 9. [2.] The matter of the expectation is very pious. They hope God will return and repent, and *leave a blessing behind him*, not as if he were about to go from them, and they could be content with any blessing in lieu of his presence, but *behind him*, that is, "After he has ceased his controversy with us, he will bestow a blessing upon us;" and what is it? It is a *meat-offering and a drink-offering to the Lord our God.* The fruits of the earth are called *a blessing* (Isa. lxv. 8) because they depend upon God's blessing and are necessary blessings to us. They had been deprived of these, and that which grieved them most while they were so was that God's altar was deprived of its offerings and God's priests of their maintenance; that therefore which they comfort themselves with the prospect of in their return of plenty is that then there shall be meat-offerings and drink-offerings in abundance brought to God's altar, which they more desired than to see the wonted abundance of meat and drink brought to their own tables. Thus when Hezekiah was in hopes that he should recover of his sickness he asked, *What is the sign that I shall go up*, not to the thrones of judgment, or to the council-board, but *to the house of the Lord?* Isa. xxxviii. 22. Note, The plentiful enjoyment of God's ordinances in their power and purity is the most valuable instance of a nation's prosperity and the greatest blessing that can be desired. If God give the blessing of the meat-offering and the drink-offering, that will bring along with it other blessings, will sanctify them, sweeten them, and secure them.

II. They are here called to a public national repentance, to be exercised in the solemn assembly, as a national act, for the glory of God and the excitement of one another, and that the neighbouring nations might know and observe what it was that qualified them for God's gracious returns in mercy to them, which they would be the admiring witnesses of. Let us see here, 1. How the congregation must be called together, *v.* 15, 16. The trumpet was blown (*v.* 1), to sound an *alarm of war;* but now it must be blown in order to a treaty of peace. God is willing to show mercy to his people if he do but find them in a frame fit for it; and therefore, Call them together; *sanctify a fast.* By the law many annual feasts were appointed, but only one day in the year was to be observed as a fast, the *day of atonement,* a day to *afflict the soul;* and, if they had kept close to God and their duty, there would have been no occasion to observe any more; but now that they had by sin brought the judgments of God upon them they are often called to fasting. What was said *ch.* i. 14 is here repeated: " *Call a solemn assembly; gather the people* (press them to come together upon this errand); *sanctify the congregation;* appoint a time for solemn preparation beforehand and put them in mind to prepare themselves. Let not the greatest be excused, but *assemble the elders,* the judges and magistrates. Let not the meanest be passed by, but *gather the children, and those that suck the breasts.*" It is good to bring little children, as soon as they are capable of understanding any thing, to religious assemblies, that they may be trained up betimes in the way wherein they should go; but these were brought even when they were at the breast and were kept fasting, that by their cries for the breast the hearts of the parents might be moved to repent of sin, which God might justly so visit upon their children that the *tongue of the sucking child* might *cleave to the roof of his mouth* (Lam. iv. 4), and that on them God might have compassion, as he had on the infants of Nineveh, Jonah iv. 11. New-married people must not be exempted: *Let the bridegroom go forth of his chamber and the bride out of her closet;* let them not take state upon them as usual, not put on their ornaments, nor indulge themselves in mirth, but address themselves to the duties of the public fast with as much gravity and sadness as any of their neighbours. Note, Private joys must always give way to public sorrows, both those for affliction and those for sin.

1212

2. How the work of the day must be carried on, *v.* 17. (1.) The priests, *the Lord's ministers,* must preside in the congregation, and be God's mouth to the people, and theirs to God; who should stand in the gap to turn away the wrath of God but those whose business it was to make intercession upon ordinary occasions? (2.) They must officiate *between the porch and the altar.* There they used to attend about the sacrifices, and therefore now that they have no sacrifices to offer, or next to none, there they must offer up spiritual sacrifices. There the people must see them weeping and wrestling, like their father Jacob, and be helped into the same devout frame. Ministers must themselves be affected with those things wherewith they desire to affect others. It was *between the porch and the altar* that Zechariah the son of Jehoiada was put to death for his faithfulness; that precious blood God would require at their hands, and therefore, to turn away the judgment threatened for it, there they must *weep.* (3.) They must pray. Words are here put into their mouths, which they might in their prayers enlarge upon. Their petition must be, *Spare thy people, O Lord!* God's people, when they are in distress, can expect no relief against God's justice but what comes from his mercy. They cannot say, Lord, *right us,* but, Lord, *spare us.* We deserve the correction; we need it; but, Lord, mitigate it. The sinner's supplication is, *Spare us, good Lord.* Their plea must be taken from the relation wherein they stand to God ("They are *thy people,* and *thy heritage,* therefore have compassion on them"), but especially from the concern of God's glory in their trouble—" Lord, *give not thy heritage to reproach,* to the reproach of famine; let not the land of Canaan, that has so long been celebrated as the glory of all lands, now be made the scorn of all lands; let not *the heathen rule over them,* as they will easily do when thy heritage is thus impoverished and disabled to subsist. Let not the heathen make them *a proverb,* or a *by-word*" (so some read it); "let it never be said, *As poor and beggarly as an Israelite.*" Note, The maintaining of the credit of the nation among its neighbours is a blessing to be desired and prayed for by all that wish well to it. But that reproach of the church is especially to be dreaded and deprecated which reflects upon God: " Let them not *say among the people, Where is their God*—that God who has promised to help them, whom they have boasted so much of and put such a confidence in?" If God's heritage be destroyed, the neighbours will say, " God was either weak and could not relieve them or unkind and would not." God thus triumphs over the pretended deities. Deut. xxxii. 37, *Where are now their gods in whom they trusted?* And Sennacherib thus triumphs over them. *Where are the gods of Hamath and Arpad?* But it must by no means be

suffered that they should say of Israel, *Where is their God?* For we are sure that our God is in the heavens (Ps. cxv. 2, 3), is in his temple, Ps. xi. 4.

18 Then will the Lord be jealous for his land, and pity his people. 19 Yea, the Lord will answer and say unto his people, Behold, I will send you corn, and wine, and oil, and ye shall be satisfied therewith : and I will no more make you a reproach among the heathen : 20 But I will remove far off from you the northern *army,* and will drive him into a land barren and desolate, with his face toward the east sea, and his hinder part toward the utmost sea, and his stink shall come up, and his ill savour shall come up, because he hath done great things. 21 Fear not, O land; be glad and rejoice : for the Lord will do great things. 22 Be not afraid, ye beasts of the field : for the pastures of the wilderness do spring, for the tree beareth her fruit, the fig-tree and the vine do yield their strength. 23 Be glad then, ye children of Zion, and rejoice in the Lord your God : for he hath given you the former rain moderately, and he will cause to come down for you the rain, the former rain, and the latter rain in the first *month.* 24 And the floors shall be full of wheat, and the fats shall overflow with wine and oil. 25 And I will restore to you the years that the locust hath eaten, the canker-worm, and the caterpillar, and the palmer-worm, my great army which I sent among you. 26 And ye shall eat in plenty, and be satisfied, and praise the name of the Lord your God, that hath dealt wondrously with you : and my people shall never be ashamed. 27 And ye shall know that I *am* in the midst of Israel, and *that* I *am* the Lord your God, and none else : and my people shall never be ashamed.

See how ready God is to succour and relieve his people, how he *waits to be gracious;* as soon as ever they humble themselves under his hand, and pray, and seek his face, he immediately meets them with his favours. They prayed that God would *spare them,* and see here with what *good words and comfortable words* he answered them; for God's promises are real answers to the prayers of

faith, because with him saying and doing are not two things. Now observe,

I. Whence this mercy promised shall take rise (*v.* 18) : God will be *jealous for his land* and *pity his people.* He will have an eye, 1. To his own honour, and the reputation of his covenant with Israel, by which he had conveyed to them that good land and had given in the value of it very high; now he will not suffer it to be despised nor disparaged, but will be jealous for the credit of his land, and the inhabitants of it, who had been praised as a happy people and therefore must not lie open to reproach as a miserable people. 2. To their distress : He will *pity his people,* and, in pity to them, he will restore them their forfeited comforts. God's compassion is a great encouragement to those that come humbly to him as penitents and as petitioners.

II. What his mercy shall be, in several instances :—1. The destroying army shall be dispersed and defeated (*v.* 20) : " *I will remove far off from you the northern army,* that army of locusts and caterpillars that invaded you from the north, brought in upon the wings of a north wind, an army which you could put no stop to the progress of; but, when you have made your peace with God, he will ease you of these soldiers that are quartered upon you and will *drive them into a land barren and desolate,* into that vast howling wilderness that Israel wandered in, where, after having surfeited upon the plenty of Canaan, they shall perish for want of sustenance. Those that have their *face to the east sea* (the Dead Sea, which lay east of Judea) shall perish in that, and the rear of the army shall be lost in the Great Sea," called here the *utmost sea.* They had made the land barren and desolate, and now God will cast them into a land barren and desolate. Thus those whom God employs for the correction of his people come afterwards to be themselves reckoned with; and the rod is thrown into the fire. Nothing shall remain of these swarms of insects but the ill savour of them. When Egypt was eased of the plague of locusts they were carried away to the Red Sea, Exod. x. 19. Note, When an affliction has done its work it shall be removed in mercy, as the locusts of Canaan were from a penitent people, not as the locusts of Egypt were removed, in wrath, from an impenitent prince, only to make room for another plague. Many interpreters, by this northern army, understand that of Sennacherib, which was dispersed when God by it had *accomplished his whole work upon Mount Zion and upon Jerusalem,* Isa. x. 12. This enemy shall be driven away, because *he has done great things,* has done a great deal of mischief, and has *magnified* to do it, has done it in the pride of his heart; therefore it follows (*v.* 21), *The Lord will do great things for* his people, as the enemy has done great things against them, to convince them that wherein they deal proudly he is, and will be, above them, that, what great things soever they did, they did no more than God commissioned them to do; and as, when he said to them, Go, they went, so, when he said to them, Come, they came, to show that they were *soldiers under him.* 2. The destroyed land shall be watered and made fruitful. When the army is scattered, yet what shall we do if the desolation they have made continue? It is therefore promised (*v.* 22) that *the pastures of the wilderness,* the pastures which the locusts had left as bare as the wilderness, shall again *spring* and the *trees shall again bear their fruit,* particularly the *fig-tree and the vine.* But, when we see how the country is wasted, we are tempted to say, *Can these dry bones live?* If *the Lord should make windows in heaven,* it cannot be; but it shall be, for (*v.* 23) *the Lord has given* and will give you *the former rain and the latter rain,* and, if he give them in mercy, he will give them moderately, so that the rain shall not turn into a judgment, and he will give them in due season, the *latter rain in the first month,* when it was wanted and expected. It would make it comfortable to them to see it coming from the hand of God, and ordered by his wisdom, for then we are sure it is well ordered. *He has given you a teacher of righteousness* (so the margin reads it, for the same word that signifies the *rain* signifies a *teacher,* and that which we translate *moderately* is *according to righteousness),* and this *teacher of righteousness,* says one of the rabbin, is the King Messias, and of him many others understand this; for he is a *teacher come from God,* and he shows us the way of *righteousness.* But others understand it of any prophet that *instructs unto righteousness,* and some of Hezekiah particularly, others of Isaiah. Note, It is a good sign that God has mercy in store for a people when he sends them teachers of righteousness, pastors after his own heart. 3. All their losses shall be repaired (*v.* 25): "*I will restore to you the years that the locust has eaten;* you shall be comforted according to the time that you have been afflicted, and shall have years of plenty to balance the years of famine." Thus does it *repent the Lord concerning his servants,* when they repent, and, to show how perfectly he is reconciled to them, he makes good the damage they have sustained by his judgments, and, like the jailer, *washes their stripes.* Though, in justice, he distrained upon them, and did them no wrong, yet, in compassion, he makes restitution; as the father of the prodigal, upon his return, made up all he had lost by his sin and folly, and took him into his family, as in his former estate. The locusts and caterpillars are here called *God's great army which he sent among them,* and he will repair what they had devoured because they were his army. 4. They shall have great abundance of all good things.

The earth shall yield her increase, and they shall enjoy it. Look into the stores where they lay up, and you shall find *the floors full of wheat, and the fats overflowing with wine and oil* (*v.* 24), whereas, in the day of their distress, the *wine and oil languished* and *the barns were broken down, ch.* i. 10, 17. Look upon their tables, where they lay out what they have laid up, and you shall find that they *eat in plenty and are satisfied, v.* 26. They do not eat to excess, nor are surfeited; we hope the *drunkards* are cured by the late affliction of their inordinate love of wine and strong drink, for, though they were brought in howling for their scarcity (*ch.* i. 5), they are not brought in again here singing for the plenty of it; but now all shall have enough, and shall know when they have enough, for God will make their food nourishing and give to them to be content with it.

These are the mercies promised, and in these *God does great things* (*v.* 21), *He deals wondrously with his people, v.* 26. Herein he glorifies his power, and shows that he can relieve his people though their distress be ever so great, and glorifies his goodness, that he will do it upon their repentance though their provocations were ever so great. Note, When God deals graciously with poor sinners that return to him it must be acknowledged that he deals wondrously and does great things. Some expositors understand these promises figuratively, as pointing at gospel-grace, and having their accomplishment in the abundant comforts that are treasured up for believers in the covenant of grace and the satisfaction of soul they have therein. When God sends us his promises to be the matter of our comfort, his graces to be the grounds of it, and his Spirit to be the author of it, we may well own that he has sent us (according to his promise here, *v.* 19) *corn, and wine, and oil,* or that which is unspeakably better, and we have reason to be satisfied therewith.

III. What use shall be made of these returns of God's mercy to them and the good account they shall turn to.

1. God shall have the glory thereof, for they shall *rejoice in the Lord their God* (*v.* 23), and what is the matter of their rejoicing shall be the matter of their thanksgiving; they shall *praise the name of the Lord their God* (*v.* 26) and not praise their idols, nor call their corn and wine the *rewards that their lovers had given them.* Note, The plenty of our creature-comforts is a mercy indeed to us when by them our hearts are enlarged in love and thankfulness to God, who gives us all things richly to enjoy, though we serve him but poorly. When God restores to us plenty after we have known scarcity, as it is doubly pleasant to us, so it should make us the more thankful to God. When Israel comes out of a wilderness into a Canaan, and there eats and is full, surely he will then *bless the Lord,* with a very sensible pleasure,

for *that good land* which *he has given him,*
Deut. viii. 10.

2. They shall have the credit, and comfort, and spiritual benefit, thereof. When
God gives them plenty again, and gives them
to be satisfied with it, (1.) Their reputation
shall be retrieved; they and their God shall
be no more reflected upon as unfaithful to
one another when they have returned to him
in a way of duty and he to them in a way of
mercy (*v.* 19): "*I will no more make you a
reproach among the heathen,* that triumphed
in your calamities and insulted over you;
and *v.* 26, 27, "*My people shall never be
ashamed,* as they have been, of their good
land which they used to boast of, but shall
again and ever have the same occasion to
boast of it." Note, It redounds much to the
honour of God when he does that which
saves the honour of his people; and those
that are his people indeed, though they may
be for a time, shall not be always, a *reproach
among the heathen;* if we be rightly ashamed
of our sins against God, we shall never be
ashamed of our glorying in God. (2.) Their
joys shall be revived (*v.* 23): *Be glad and
rejoice, O land!* and all the inhabitants of it.
Times of plenty are commonly times of joy;
yet the favour of God *puts gladness into the
heart* more than those have whose *corn, and
wine, and oil increase.* But especially *be glad
then, you children of Zion, and rejoice in the
Lord your God, v.* 23. They *mourned in
Zion* (*v.* 15), and therefore there in a particular manner they shall rejoice; for those
that sow in penitential tears shall certainly
reap in thankful joys. The children of Zion,
who led the rest in fasting, must lead the
rest in rejoicing. But observe, They shall
rejoice in the Lord their God, not so much in
the good things themselves that are given
them as in the good hand that gives them
and in the return of his favour to them, as
theirs in covenant, which these good things
are the tokens and pledges of. The *joy of harvest* and the joy of a feast must both terminate
in God, whose love we should taste in all the
gifts of his bounty, that we may make him
our chief joy, as he is our chief good, and
the fountain of all good to us. (3.) Their
faith in God shall be confirmed and increased. When temporal mercies are made
by the grace of God to be of spiritual advantage to us, and plenty for the body is so far
from being an enemy (as with many it
proves) that it becomes a friend to the prosperity of the soul, then they are mercies indeed to us. This is promised here (*v.* 27):
You shall know that I am in the midst of Israel, the *Holy One in the midst of thee* (Hos.
xi. 9), *and that I am the Lord your God, and
none else.* As it proves that the Lord is God,
and there is none other, because he *wounds*
and he *heals,* he *forms light and darkness,* he
does *good and evil* (Isa. xlv. 7; Deut. xxxii.
39), so it proves him to be *God of Israel,* a
God in covenant with his people and a

father to them, that as a father he both corrects them when they offend and comforts
them when they repent. It was the burden
of the threatenings in Ezekiel's prophecy,
Such and such evils I will bring upon you,
and you shall know that I am the Lord; and
the same is here made the crown of the promises: You shall *eat, and be satisfied,* and rejoice, and thus *you shall know that I am the
Lord.* Note, We should labour to grow in
our acquaintance with God by all providences,
both merciful and afflictive. When God
gives to his people plenty, and peace, and
joy, upon their return to him, he thereby
gives them to understand that he is pleased
with their repentance, that he has pardoned
their sins, and that he is theirs as much as
ever—that they are taken into the same covenant with him, for he is the Lord their
God, and into the same communion, for he
is in the midst of them, *nigh unto them in
all that they call upon him for,* and, as the
sun in the centre of the worlds, so in the
midst of them as to diffuse his benign influences to all the parts of his land.

3. Even the inferior creatures shall share
therein and be made easy thereby: *Fear not,
O land! v.* 21. *Be not afraid, you beasts of the
field, v.* 22. They had suffered for the sin
of man, and for God's quarrel with him;
and now they shall fare the better for man's
repentance and God's reconciliation to him.
Nay, the beasts were said to *cry unto God*
(*ch.* i. 20); and now that cry is answered,
and they are directed not to *be afraid,* for
they shall have plenty of all that which their
nature craves. God, in sparing Nineveh,
had an eye to the cattle (Jonah iv. 11), for
the cattle had fasted, *ch.* iii. 8. This may
lead us to think of the restitution of all
things, when the *creature,* that is now *made
subject to vanity* and *groans* under it, *shall
be brought,* though not into the glorious joy,
yet *into the glorious liberty, of the children of
God,* Rom. viii. 21.

28 And it shall come to pass afterward, *that* I will pour out my Spirit
upon all flesh; and your sons and
your daughters shall prophesy, your
old men shall dream dreams, your
young men shall see visions: 29 And
also upon the servants and upon the
handmaids in those days will I pour
out my Spirit. 30 And I will show
wonders in the heavens and in the
earth, blood, and fire, and pillars of
smoke. 31 The sun shall be turned
into darkness, and the moon into
blood, before the great and the terrible day of the LORD come. 32 And
it shall come to pass, *that* whosoever
shall call on the name of the LORD
shall be delivered: for in mount Zion

and in Jerusalem shall be deliverance, as the LORD hath said, and in the remnant whom the LORD shall call.

The promises of corn, and wine, and oil, in the foregoing verses, would be very acceptable to a wasted country; but here we are taught that we must not rest in those things. God has reserved some better things for us, and these verses have reference to those better things, both the kingdom of grace and the kingdom of glory, with the happiness of true believers in both. We are here told,

I. How the kingdom of grace shall be introduced by a plentiful *effusion of the Spirit,* *v.* 28, 29. We are not at a loss about the meaning of this promise, nor in doubt what it refers to and wherein it had its accomplishment, for the apostle Peter has given us an infallible explication and application of it, assuring us that when the Spirit was poured out upon the apostles, on the day of Pentecost (Acts ii. 1, &c.), that was the very thing *which was spoken of here by the prophet Joel,* *v.* 16, 17. That was the gift of the Spirit, which, according to this prediction, was *to come,* and we are not to *look for any other,* any more than for another accomplishment of the promise of the Messiah. Now, 1. The blessing itself here promised is the *pouring out of the Spirit of God,* his gifts, graces, and comforts, which the blessed Spirit is the author of. We often read in the Old Testament of the Spirit of the Lord coming by drops, as it were, upon the judges and prophets whom God raised up for extraordinary services; but now the Spirit shall be poured out plentifully in a full stream, as was promised with an eye to gospel-times, Isa. xliv. 3. *I will pour my Spirit upon thy seed.* 2. The time fixed for this is *afterwards;* after the fulfilling of the foregoing promises this shall be fulfilled. St. Peter expounds this of *the last days,* the days of the Messiah, by whom the world was to have its last revelation of the divine will and grace in the last days of the Jewish church, a little before its dissolution. 3. The extent of this blessing, in respect of the persons on whom it shall be bestowed. The Spirit shall be *poured out upon all flesh,* not as hitherto upon Jews only, but upon Gentiles also; for in Christ there is no distinction between Jew and Greek, Rom. x. 11, 12. Hitherto divine revelation was confined to the seed of Abraham, none but those of the land of Israel had the Spirit of prophecy; but, in the last days, *all flesh shall see the glory of God* (Isa. xl. 5) and shall come to *worship before him,* Isa. lxvi. 23. The Jews understand it of all flesh in the land of Israel, and Peter himself did not fully understand it as speaking of the Gentiles till he saw it accomplished in the descent of the Holy Ghost upon Cornelius and his friends, who were Gentiles (Acts x. 44, 45), which was

but a continuation of the same gift which was bestowed on the day of Pentecost. The Spirit shall be poured out *upon all flesh,* that is, upon all those whose hearts are made hearts of flesh, soft and tender, and so prepared to receive the impressions and influences of the Holy Ghost. *Upon all flesh,* that is, upon some of all sorts of men; the gifts of the Spirit shall not be so sparing, or so much confined, as they have been, but shall be more general and diffusive of themselves. (1.) The Spirit shall be poured out upon some of each sex. Not *your sons* only, but *your daughters,* shall prophesy: we read of four sisters in one family that were prophetesses, Acts xxi. 9. Not the parents only, but the children, shall be filled with the Spirit, which intimates the continuance of this gift for some ages successively in the church. (2.) Upon some of each age: "*Your old men,* who are past their vigour and whose spirits begin to decay, *your young men,* who have yet but little acquaintance with and experience of divine things, shall yet *dream dreams* and *see visions;* God will reveal himself by dreams and visions both to young and old. (3.) Upon those of the meanest rank and condition, even *upon the servants and the handmaids.* The Jewish doctors say, *Prophecy does not reside on any* but such as are *wise, valiant, and rich,* not upon the soul of a *poor man,* or a man *in sorrow.* But in Christ Jesus there is *neither bond nor free,* Gal. iii. 28. There were many that *were called being servants* (1 Cor. vii. 21), but that was no obstruction to their receiving the Holy Ghost. (4.) The effect of this blessing: *They shall prophesy;* they shall receive new discoveries of divine things, and that not for their own use only, but for the benefit of the church. They shall interpret scripture, and speak of things secret, distant, and future, which by the utmost sagacities of reason, and their natural powers, they could not have any insight into nor foresight of. By these extraordinary gifts the Christian church was first founded and set up, and the scriptures were written, and the ministry settled, by which, with the ordinary operations and influences of the Spirit, it was to be afterwards maintained and kept up.

II. How the kingdom of glory shall be introduced by the universal change of nature, *v.* 30, 31. The pouring out of the Spirit will be very comfortable to the righteous; but let the unrighteous hear this, and tremble. There is a *great and terrible day of the Lord* coming, which shall be ushered in with *wonders* in *heaven and earth, blood, and fire, and pillars of smoke,* the turning of *the sun into darkness and the moon into blood.* This is to have its full accomplishment (as the learned Dr. Pocock thinks) in the day of judgment, at the end of time, before which these signs will be performed in the letter of them, yet so that it was accomplished in part in the death of Christ (which is called the *judgment of this world*, when the earth quaked and the sun was darkened, and a *great and terrible day* it was), and more fully in the destruction of Jerusalem, which was a type and figure of the general judgment, and before which there were many amazing prodigies, besides the convulsions of states and kingdoms prophesied of under the figurative expressions of turning *the sun into darkness and the moon into blood*, and the *wars and rumours of wars*, and *distress of nations*, which our Saviour spoke of as the *beginning of* these *sorrows*, Matt. xxiv. 6, 7. But before the last judgment there will be *wonders* indeed *in heaven and earth*, the dissolution of both, without a metaphor. The judgments of God upon a sinful world, and the frequent destruction of wicked kingdoms by fire and sword, are prefaces to and presages of the judgment of the world in the last day. Those on whom the Spirit is poured out shall foresee and foretel that *great and terrible day of the Lord*, and expound the *wonders in heaven and earth* that go before it; for, as to his first coming, so to his second, all the prophets did and do bear witness, Rev. x. 7.

III. The safety and happiness of all true believers both in the first and second coming of Jesus Christ, v. 32. This speaks of particular persons, for to them the New Testament has more respect, and less to kingdoms and nations, than the Old. Now observe here, 1. That there is a salvation wrought out. Though the day of the Lord will be great and terrible, yet *in Mount Zion and in Jerusalem there shall be deliverance* from the terror of it. It is the day of the Lord, the day of his judgment, who knows how to separate between the precious and the vile. In the everlasting gospel, which *went from Zion*, in the church of the first-born typified by Mount Zion, and which is the Jerusalem that is from above, there is *deliverance ;* a way of escaping the *wrath to come* is found out and laid open. Christ is himself not only the *Saviour*, but *the salvation ;* he is so *to the ends of the earth*. This deliverance, laid up for us in the covenant of grace, is in performance of the promises made to the fathers. *There shall be deliverance, as the Lord has said.* See Luke i. 72. Note, This is ground of comfort and hope to sinners, that, whatever danger there is in their case, there is also deliverance, deliverance for them, if it be not their own fault. And, if we would share in this deliverance, we must ourselves apply to the gospel-Zion, to God's Jerusalem. 2. That there is a remnant interested in this salvation, and for whom the deliverance is wrought. It is *in that remnant* (that is, among them) that the deliverance is, or in their souls and spirits; there are the earnests and evidences of it. *Christ in you, the hope of glory.* They are called a *remnant*, because they are but a few in comparison with the multitudes that are left to perish;

a little remnant but a chosen one, a *remnant according to the election of grace.* And here we are told who they are that shall be delivered in the great day. (1.) Those that sincerely call upon God : *Whosoever shall call on the name of the Lord*, whether Jew or Gentile (for the apostle so expounds it, Rom. x. 13, where he lays this down as the great rule of the gospel by which we must all be judged), *shall be delivered.* This calling on God supposes knowledge of him, faith in him, desire towards him, dependence on him, and, as an evidence of the sincerity of all this, a conscientious obedience to him ; for, without that, crying Lord, Lord, will not stand us in any stead. Note, It is the praying remnant that shall be the saved remnant. And it will aggravate the ruin of those who perish that they might have been saved on such easy terms. (2.) Those that are effectually called to God. The deliverance is sure to the *remnant whom the Lord shall call*, not only with the common call of the gospel, with which many are called that are not chosen, but with a special call into the fellowship of Jesus Christ, whom *the Lord predestinates*, or *prepares*, so the Chaldee. St. Peter borrows this phrase, Acts ii. 39. Note, Those only shall be delivered in the great day that are now effectually called from sin to God, from self to Christ, from things below to things above.

CHAP. III.

In the close of the foregoing chapter we had a gracious promise of deliverance in Mount Zion and Jerusalem ; now this whole chapter is a comment upon that promise, showing what that deliverance shall be, how it shall be wrought by the destruction of the church's enemies, and how it shall be perfected in the everlasting rest and joy of the church. This was in part accomplished in the deliverance of Jerusalem from the attempt that Sennacherib made upon it in Hezekiah's time, and afterwards in the return of the Jews out of their captivity in Babylon, and other deliverances wrought for the Jewish church between that and Christ's coming. But it has a further reference, to the great redemption wrought out for us by Jesus Christ, and the destruction of our spiritual enemies and all their agents, and will have its full accomplishment in the judgment of the great day. Here is a prediction, I. Of God's reckoning with the enemies of his people for all the injuries and indignities that they had done them, and returning them upon their own head, ver. 1—8. II. Of God's judging all nations when the measure of their iniquity is full, and appearing publicly, to the everlasting confusion of all impenitent sinners and the everlasting comfort of all his faithful servants, ver. 9—17. III. Of the provision God has made for the refreshment of his people, for their safety and purity, when their enemies shall be made desolate, ver. 18—21. These promises were not of private interpretation only, but were written for our learning, " that we, through patience and comfort of this scripture, might have hope."

FOR, behold, in those days, and in that time, when I shall bring again the captivity of Judah and Jerusalem, 2 I will also gather all nations, and will bring them down into the valley of Jehoshaphat, and will plead with them there for my people and *for* my heritage Israel, whom they have scattered among the nations, and parted my land. 3 And they have cast lots for my people ; and have given a boy for a harlot, and sold a girl for wine, that they might drink. 4 Yea, and what have ye to do with me, O Tyre, and Zidon, and all the coasts of Palestine? will ye render me a recompence? and if ye recompense me, swiftly *and* speedily will I return your recompence upon your own head; 5 Because ye have taken my silver and my gold, and have carried into your temples my goodly pleasant things: 6 The children also of Judah and the children of Jerusalem have ye sold unto the Grecians, that ye might remove them far from their border. 7 Behold, I will raise them out of the place whither ye have sold them, and will return your recompence upon your own head: 8 And I will sell your sons and your daughters into the hand of the children of Judah, and they shall sell them to the Sabeans, to a people far off: for the LORD hath spoken *it*.

We have often heard of the *year of the redeemed*, and the *year of recompences for the controversy of Zion;* now here we have a description of the transactions of that year, and a prophecy of what shall be done when it comes, whenever it comes, for it comes often, and at the end of time it will come once for all.

I. It shall be the *year of the redeemed*, for God will *bring again the captivity of Judah and Jerusalem, v.* 1. Though the bondage of God's people may be grievous and very long, yet it shall not be everlasting. That in Egypt ended at length in their deliverance into the glorious liberty of the children of God. *Let my son go, that he may serve me.* That in Babylon shall likewise end well. And the Lord Jesus will provide for the effectual redemption of poor enslaved souls from under the dominion of sin and Satan, and will proclaim that *acceptable year*, the year of jubilee, the release of debts and servants, and the *opening of the prison to those that were bound.* There is a day, there is a time, fixed for the *bringing again of the captivity* of God's children, for the redeeming of them *from the power of the grave;* and it shall be the *last day* and the end of all time.

II. It shall be the *year of recompences for the controversy of Zion.* Though God may suffer the enemies of his people to prevail against them very far and for a long time, yet he will call them to an account for it, and will lead captivity captive (Ps. lxviii. 18), will lead those captive that led his people captive, Rev. xiii. 10. Observe,

1. Who those are that shall be reckoned with—*all nations, v.* 2. This intimates, (1.) That all the nations had made themselves liable to the judgment of God for wrong done to his people. Persecution is the reigning crying sin of the world; that *lying in*

1218

wickedness itself is set against godliness. The enmity that is in the old serpent, *the god of this world*, against the seed of the woman, appears more or less in the *children of this world.* *Marvel not if the world hate you.* (2.) That, whatsoever nation injured God's nation, they should not go unpunished; for he that touches the Israel of God shall be made to know that he touches the apple of his eye. Jerusalem will be a *burdensome stone to all people*, Zech. xii. 3. But the neighbouring nations shall be particularly reckoned with—*Tyre, and Sidon, and all the coasts of Palestine*, or the Philistines, who have been troublesome neighbours to the Israel of God, *v.* 4. When the more remote and potent nations that laid Israel waste are reckoned with the impotent malice of those that lay near them, and *helped forward the affliction*, (Zech. i. 15), and made a hand of it (Ezek. xxvi. 2), shall not be passed by. Note, Little persecutors shall be called to an account as well as great ones; and, though they could not do much mischief, shall be reckoned with according to the *wickedness of their endeavours* and the mischief they would have done.

2. The sitting of this court for judgment. They shall all be *gathered* (v. 2), that those who have combined together against God's people, *with one consent* (Ps. lxxxiii. 5), may together receive their doom. They shall be *brought down into the valley of Jehoshaphat*, which lay near Jerusalem, and there *God will plead with them,* (1.) Because it is fit that criminals should be tried in the same country where they did the fact. (2.) For their greater confusion, when they shall see that Jerusalem which they have so long endeavoured and hoped for the ruin of, in spite of all their rage, made a *praise in the earth.* (3.) For the greater comfort and honour of God's Jerusalem, which shall see God pleading their cause. (4.) Then shall be re-acted what God did for Jehoshaphat when he gave him victory over those that invaded him, and furnished him and his people with matter of joy and praise, in *the valley of Berachah.* See 2 Chron. xx. 26. (5.) It was in this valley of Jehoshaphat (as Dr. Lightfoot suggests) that Sennacherib's army, or part of it, lay, when it was destroyed by an angel. They came together to ruin Jerusalem, but God brought them together for their own ruin, *as sheaves into the floor*, Mic. iv. 12.

3. The plaintiff called, on whose behalf this prosecution is set on foot; it is *for my people*, and *for my heritage Israel.* It is their cause that God will now plead with jealousy. Note, God's people are *his heritage*, his *peculiar*, his *portion*, his *treasure*, above all people, Exod. xix. 5; Deut. xxxii. 9. They are his demesne, and therefore he has a good action against those that trespass upon them.

4. The charge exhibited against them, which is very particular. Many affronts they had put upon God by their idolatries,

but that for which God has a quarrel with them is the affront they have put upon his people and upon the vessels of his sanctuary. (1.) They had been very abusive to the people of Israel, had *scattered them among the nations* and forced them to seek for shelter where they could find a place, or carried them captive into their respective countries and there industriously dispersed them, for fear of their incorporating for their common safety. They *parted their land*, and took every one his share of it as their own; nay, they have *cast lots for my people*, and *sold them*. When they had taken them prisoners, [1.] They made a jest of them, made a scorn of them as of no value. They would not release them and yet thought them not worth the keeping; they made nothing of playing them away at dice. Or they made a dividend of the prisoners *by lot*, as the soldiers did of Christ's garments. [2.] They made a gain of them. When they had them they *sold* them, yet with so much contempt that they did *not increase their wealth by their price*, but sold them for their pleasure rather than their profit; they *gave a boy* taken in war for the *hire of a harlot*, and *a girl* for so many bottles of wine as would serve them for one sitting, a *goodly price* at which they valued them, and goodly preferment for a son and daughter of Israel to be a slave and a drudge in a tavern or a brothel. Observe, here, how that which is got by one sin is commonly spent upon another. The spoil which these enemies of the Jews gathered by injustice and violence they scattered and threw away in drinking and whoring; such is frequently the character, and such the conversation, of the enemies and persecutors of the people of God. The Tyrians and Philistines, when they seized any of the children of Judah and Jerusalem, either took them prisoners in war or kidnapped them, they sold them to the Grecians (with whom the men of Tyre traded in the *persons of men*, Ezek. xxvii. 13), that they *might remove them far from their* own *border, v.* 6. It was a great reproach to Israel, God's first-born, his free-born, to be thus bought and sold among the heathen.

(2.) They had unjustly seized *God's silver and gold* (*v.* 5), by which some understand the wealth of Israel. The silver and gold which God's people had he calls his, because they had received it from him and devoted it to him; and whosoever robbed them God took it as if they had robbed him and would make reprisals accordingly. Those who take away the estates of good men for well-doing will be found guilty of sacrilege; they take God's *silver and gold*. But it seems rather to be meant of the *vessels* and *treasures of the temple*, which God here calls his *goodly pleasant things*, precious and desirable to him and all that are his. These they *carried into their temples* as trophies of their victory over God's Israel, thinking that therein they

triumphed over Israel's God, nay, and that their idols triumphed over him. Thus the ark was put in Dagon's temple. Thus they did unjustly. *"What have you to do with me* (*v.* 4), with my people; what wrong have they done you? What provocation have they given you? You had nothing to do with them, and yet you do all this against them. Devices are devised against the *quiet in the land*, and those offended and harmed that are harmless and inoffensive : *Will you render me a recompence?"* Can they pretend that either God or his people have done them any injury, for which they may justify themselves by the law of retaliation in doing them these mischiefs? No; they have no colour for it. Note, It is no new thing for those who have been very civil and obliging to their neighbours to find them very unkind and unneighbourly and for those who do no injuries to suffer many.

5. The sentence passed upon them. In general (*v.* 4), " If *you recompense me*, if you pretend a quarrel with me, if you provoke me thus to jealousy, if you touch the apple of my eye, *I will swiftly and speedily return your recompence upon your own head."* Those that contend with God will find themselves unable to make their part good with him. He will recompense them *suddenly*, when they little think of it, and have not time to prevent it; if he take them to task, he will soon effect their ruin. Particularly, it is threatened, (1.) That they shall not gain their end in the mischief they designed against God's people. They thought to *remove them so far from their border* that they should never return to it again, *v.* 6. But (says God) *" I will raise them out of the place whither you have sold them, and they shall not, as you* intended, be buried alive there." Men's selling the people of God will not deprive him of his property in them. (2.) That they shall be paid in their own coin, as Adonibezek was (*v.* 8): *" I will sell your sons and your daughters into the hands of the children of Judah;* you shall lie as much at their mercy as they have been at yours," Isa. lx. 14. Thus the Jews *had rule over those that hated them*, Esther ix. 1. And then they shall justly be *sold to the Sabeans, to a people far off.* This (some think) had its accomplishment in the victories obtained by the Maccabees over the enemies of the Jews; others think it looks as far forward as the last day, when the *upright shall have dominion* (Ps. xlix. 14) and *the saints shall judge the world.* It is certain that none ever hardened his heart against God, or his church, and prospered long; no, not Pharaoh himself, for *the Lord has spoken it*, for the comfort of all his suffering servants, that *vengeance is his and he will repay.*

9 Proclaim ye this among the Gentiles; Prepare war, wake up the mighty men, let all the men of war

draw near ; let them come up : 10 Beat your plough-shares into swords, and your pruning-hooks into spears : let the weak say, I *am* strong. 11 Assemble yourselves, and come, all ye heathen, and gather yourselves together round about : thither cause thy mighty ones to come down, O LORD. 12 Let the heathen be wakened, and come up to the valley of Jehoshaphat : for there will I sit to judge all the heathen round about. 13 Put ye in the sickle, for the harvest is ripe : come, get you down ; for the press is full, the fats overflow ; for their wickedness *is* great. 14 Multitudes, multitudes in the valley of decision : for the day of the LORD *is* near in the valley of decision. 15 The sun and the moon shall be darkened, and the stars shall withdraw their shining. 16 The LORD also shall roar out of Zion, and utter his voice from Jerusalem ; and the heavens and the earth shall shake : but the LORD *will be* the hope of his people, and the strength of the children of Israel. 17 So shall ye know that I *am* the LORD your God dwelling in Zion, my holy mountain : then shall Jerusalem be holy, and there shall no strangers pass through her any more.

What the psalmist had long before ordered to be *said among the heathen* (Ps. xcvi. 10) the prophet here will have in like manner to be published to all nations, That *the Lord reigns,* and that *he comes, he comes to judge the earth,* as he had long been judging in the earth. The notice here given of God's judging the nations may have reference to the destruction of Sennacherib, Nebuchadnezzar, Antiochus, and to the Antichrist especially, and all the proud enemies of the Christian church ; but some of the best interpreters, ancient and modern (particularly the learned Dr. Pocock), think the scope of these verses is to set forth the day of the last judgment under the similitude of God's making war upon the enemies of his kingdom, and his gathering in the harvest of the earth, both which similitudes we find used in the Revelation, *ch.* xix. 11 ; xiv. 18. Here we have,

I. A challenge given to all the enemies of God's kingdom to do their worst. To signify to them that God is preparing war against them, they are called upon to prepare war against him, *v.* 9—11. When the

hour of God's judgment shall come effectual methods shall be taken to gather all nations *to the battle of that great day of God Almighty,* Rev. xvi. 14 ; xx. 8. It seems to be here spoken ironically : *" Proclaim you this among the Gentiles ;* let all the forces of the nations be summoned to join in confederacy against God and his people." It is like that, Isa. viii. 9, " *Associate yourselves, O you people!* and *gird yourselves,* but you shall be *broken to pieces. Prepare war ;* muster up all your strength ; *wake up the mighty men ;* call them into your service ; excite them to vigilance and resolution ; *let all the men of war draw near. Let them come* and enter the lists with Omnipotence if they dare ; let them not complain for want of weapons, but let them *beat their ploughshares into swords* and their *pruning-hooks into spears.* Let them resolve, if they will, never to return to their husbandry again, but either to conquer or die ; let none plead unfitness to bear arms, but *let the weak say, I am strong* and will venture into the field of battle." Thus does a God of almighty power bid defiance to all the opposition of the powers of darkness ; let the *heathen rage,* and the *kings of the earth take counsel together, against the Lord and his Christ ;* let them *assemble, and come,* and *gather themselves together ;* but he that sits in heaven shall laugh at them, and, while he thus calls them, he has them in derision, Ps. ii. 1, 4. The heathen must be wakened, must be raised from the dead, that they may *come up to the valley of Jehoshaphat,* to receive their doom (*v.* 12), may come up out of their graves, come up *into the air,* to meet the Lord there. Jehoshaphat signifies *the judgment of the Lord.* Let them come to the place of God's judgment, which perhaps is the chief reason for the using of this name here, but it is put together as a proper name for the sake of allusions to the place so called, which we observed before ; let them come thither where God will *sit to judge the heathen,* to that *throne of glory* before which shall be *gathered all nations* (Matt. xxv. 32), for before the judgment-seat of Christ *we must all appear.* The challenge (*v.* 9) is turned into a summons, *v.* 12. It is not only, *Come if you dare,* but, *You shall come* whether you will or no, for there is no escaping the judgments of God.

II. A charge given to the ministers of God's justice to appear and act against these daring enemies of his kingdom among men : And therefore *cause thy mighty ones to come down, O Lord! v.* 11. When they bring their forces into the field, let God bring his, let the archangel's trumpet sound a charge, to call together his *mighty ones,* that is, his angels. Perhaps it is with reference to this that Christ's coming from heaven at the last day is said to be *with his mighty angels,* 2 Thess. i. 7. These are the *hosts of the Lord,* that shall fight his battles when he shall put down all opposing rule, principality, and power, when he shall *judge among the heathen,* Ps. cx. 6. Some think these words (*v.* 9, 10), *Prepare war, wake up the mighty men,* are not a challenge to the enemies' hosts, but a charge to God's hosts; let them *draw near, and come up.* When God's cause is to be pleaded, either by the law or by the sword, he has those ready that shall plead it effectually, witnesses ready to appear for him in the court of judgment, soldiers ready to appear for him in the field of battle. They shall *beat ploughshares into swords,* if need be. However, it is plain that to them the charge is given (*v.* 13), *Put you in the sickle, for the harvest is ripe;* that is, *their wickedness is great,* the measure of it is full, and they are ripe for ruin. Our Saviour has expounded this, Matt. xiii. 39. *The harvest is the end of the world, and the reapers are the angels.* And they are commanded to *thrust* in their *sickle, their sharp sickle,* and gather in both the *harvest* and the *vintage,* Rev. xiv. 15, 18. Note, The greatness of men's wickedness makes them ripe for God's judgment.

III. The vast appearance that shall be in that great and solemn day (*v.* 14): *Multitudes, multitudes, in the valley of decision,* the same which before was called the *valley of Jehoshaphat,* or *of the judgment of the Lord,* for the *day of the Lord is near* in that valley. Note, 1. The judgment-day, that day of the Lord, has all along been looked upon, and spoken of, as *nigh at hand.* Enoch said, *Behold, the Lord comes,* as if the Judge were then standing before the door, because it is certain that that day will come and will come according to the appointment, and a *thousand years with God are but as one day;* things are ripening apace for it; we ought always to be ready for it, because our judgment is at hand. 2. The day of judgment will be the *day of decision,* when every man's eternal state will be determined, and the controversy that has been long depending between the kingdom of Christ and that of Satan shall be finally decided, and an end put to the struggle. *The valley of the distribution of judgment* (so the Chaldee), when *every man shall receive according to the things done in the body. The valley of threshing* (so the margin), carrying on the metaphor of the harvest, *v.* 13. The proud enemies of God's people will then be crushed and broken to pieces, and made as the *dust of the summer threshing-floors.* 3. Innumerable multitudes will be gathered together to receive their final doom in that day, as in the destruction of Gog we read of the valley of *Hamon-Gog,* and the city of *Hamonah* (Ezek. xxxix. 15, 16), both signifying the *multitude* of the vanquished enemies; it is the word here used, *Hamonim, Hamonim,* expressed by way of admiration—O what vast multitudes of sinners will divine justice be glorified in the ruin of at that day! *A multitude of living* (says one of the rabbin) *and a multitude of*

dead, for Christ shall come *to judge both the quick and the dead.*

IV. The amazing change that shall then be made in the kingdom of nature (*v.* 15): *The sun and moon shall be darkened,* as before, *ch.* ii. 31. Their glory and lustre shall be eclipsed by the far greater brightness of that glory in which the Judge shall then appear. Nay, they shall themselves be set aside in the dissolution of all things; for damned sinners in hell shall not be allowed their light, being cast into utter darkness, and glorified saints in heaven shall not need their light, for God himself will be *their everlasting light,* Isa. lx. 19. Those that fall under the wrath of God in that day of wrath shall be cut off from all comfort and joy, signified by the darkening not only of sun and moon, but of the stars also.

V. The different impressions which that day will make upon the children of this world and the children of God, according as it will be to them. 1. To the wicked it will be a terrible day. *The Lord* shall then speak *from Zion and Jerusalem,* from the throne of his glory, from heaven, where he manifests himself in a peculiar manner, as sometimes he had done in the *glorious high throne of his sanctuary,* which yet was but a faint resemblance of the glory of that day. He shall speak *from heaven,* from *the midst* of his saints and angels (so some understand it), the holy society of which may be called *Zion* and *Jerusalem;* for, when we come to the *heavenly Jerusalem,* we come to the *innumerable company of angels;* see Heb. xii. 22, 25. Now his speaking in that day will be to the wicked as *roaring,* terrible as the roaring of a lion (for so the word signifies); he long kept silence, but now *our God shall come, and shall not keep silence,* Ps. l. 3, 21. Note, The judgment of the great day will make the ears of those to tingle that continue the implacable enemies of God's kingdom. God's voice will then *shake terribly* both *heaven and earth* (Isa. ii. 21), yet *once more,* Hag. ii. 6; Heb. xii. 26. This denotes that the voice of God will in the great day speak such terror to the wicked as were enough to put even heaven and earth into a consternation. When God comes to pull down and destroy his enemies, and make them all his footstool, though heaven and earth should stand up in defence of them and undertake their protection, it shall be all in vain. Even they shall shake before him and be an insufficient shelter to those whom he comes forth to contend with. Note, As blessings out of Zion are the sweetest blessings, and enough to make heaven and earth sing, so terrors out of Zion are the sorest terrors, and enough to make heaven and earth shake. 2. To the righteous it will be a joyful day. When heaven and earth shall tremble, and be dissolved and burnt up, then will the Lord be the *hope of his people* and the *strength of the children of Israel* (v. 16), and *then shall Jerusalem be holy,* v. 17. The saints are the Israel of God; they are *his people;* the church is his Jerusalem. They are in covenant and communion with him; now in the great day, (1.) Their longings shall be satisfied: *The Lord will be the hope of his people.* As he always was the founder and foundation of their hopes, so he then will be the crown of their hopes. He will be the *harbour* of his people (so the word is), their receptacle, refuge, and home. The saints in the great day shall arrive at the desired haven, shall put to shore after a stormy voyage; they shall go to be for ever at home with God, to their Father's house, the house *not made with hands.* (2.) Their happiness shall be confirmed. God will be in that day the *strength of the children of Israel,* enabling them to bid that day welcome and to bear up under the weight of its glories and joys. In this world, when the judgments of God are abroad, and sinners are falling under them, God is and will be the hope and strength of his people, the strength of their heart, and their portion, when other men's hearts fail them for fear. (3.) Their holiness shall be completed (v. 17): *Then shall Jerusalem be holy,* the *holy city* indeed; such shall the heavenly Jerusalem be, such the glorious church, *without spot, or wrinkle, or any such thing. Jerusalem shall be holiness* (so the word is); it shall be perfectly holy; there shall be no remainder of sin in it. The gospel-church is a holy society, even in its militant state, but will never be holiness itself till it comes to be triumphant. Then *no stranger shall pass through her any more;* there shall not enter into the New Jerusalem any thing that defiles or works iniquity; none shall be there but those who have a right to be there, none but its own citizens; for it shall be an unmixed society. (4.) God shall in all this be manifested and magnified: *So shall you know that I am the Lord your God.* By the sanctifying and glorifying of the church God will be known in his holiness and glory, as the God that dwells in his holy mountain and makes it holy by dwelling in it; and those that are sanctified and glorified are so *through the knowledge of him* that called them. The knowledge which true believers have of God is, [1.] An appropriating knowledge. They know that he is *the Lord their God,* yet not theirs only, but theirs in common with the whole church, that he is their God, but *dwelling in Zion his holy mountain;* for, though faith appropriates, it does not engross or monopolize the privileges of the covenant. [2.] It is an experimental knowledge. They shall find him their *hope and strength* in the worst of times, and so they shall *know that he is the Lord their God.* Those know best the goodness of God who have tasted and seen it, and have found him good to them.

18 And it shall come to pass in that day, *that* the mountains shall drop down new wine, and the hills shall flow with milk, and all the rivers of Judah shall flow with waters, and a fountain shall come forth of the house of the LORD, and shall water the valley of Shittim. 19 Egypt shall be a desolation, and Edom shall be a desolate wilderness, for the violence *against* the children of Judah, because they have shed innocent blood in their land. 20 But Judah shall dwell for ever, and Jerusalem from generation to generation. 21 For I will cleanse their blood *that* I have not cleansed: for the LORD dwelleth in Zion.

These promises with which this prophecy concludes have their accomplishment in part in the kingdom of grace, and the comforts and graces of all the faithful subjects of that kingdom, but will have their full accomplishment in the kingdom of glory; for, as to the Jewish church, we know not of any event concerning that which answers to the extent of these promises, and what instances of peace and prosperity they were blessed with, which these may be supposed to be a hyperbolical description of, they were but figures of *better things* reserved *for us, that they* in their best estate *without us might not be made perfect.*

I. It is promised that the enemies of the church shall be vanquished and brought down, v. 19. Egypt, that old enemy of Israel, and Edom, which had an inveterate enmity to Israel, derived from Esau, these *shall be a desolation,* a *desolate wilderness,* no more to be inhabited; they have become the *people of God's curse;* so the Idumeans were, Isa. xxxiv. 5. No strength nor wealth of a nation is a defence against the judgments of God. But what is the quarrel God has with these potent kingdoms? It is for their *violence against the children of Judah,* and the injuries they had done them; see Ezek. xxv. 3, 8, 12, 15; xxvi. 2. They had *shed* the *innocent blood* of the Jews that fled to them for shelter or were making their escape through their country. Note, The innocent blood of God's people is very precious to him, and not a drop of it shall be shed but it shall be reckoned for. In the last day this earth, which has been filled with violence against the people of God, shall be made a desolation, when it and all the works that are therein shall be burnt up. And, sooner or later, the oppressors and persecutors of God's Israel shall be brought down and laid in the dust, nay, they will at length be brought down and laid in the flames.

II. It is promised that the church shall be very happy; and truly happy it is in spiritual privileges, even during its militant state, but much more when it comes to be triumphant. Three things are here promised it:—

1. Purity. This is put last here, as a reason for the rest (*v.* 21); but we may consider it first, as the ground and foundation of the rest: *I will cleanse their blood that I have not cleansed,* that is, their bloody heinous sins, especially shedding innocent blood; that filth and guilt they had contracted by sin, which rendered them unfit for communion with God, and made them odious to his holiness and obnoxious to his justice; this they shall be washed from in the *fountain opened,* Zech. xiii. 1. That shall be cleansed by the blood of Christ which could not be cleansed by the sacrifices and purifications of the ceremonial law. Or, if we apply it to the happiness of a future state, it intimates the cleansing of the saints from all these corruptions from which they were not cleansed either by ordinances or providences in this world; there shall not be the least remains of sin in them there. Here, though they are washing daily, there is still something that is not cleansed; but in heaven, even that also shall be done away. And the reason is because *the Lord dwells in Zion,* dwells with his church, and much more gloriously with that in heaven, and *holiness becomes his house for ever,* for which reason, where he dwells there must be, there shall be, a perfection of holiness. Note, Though the refining and reforming of the church is work that goes on slowly, and still there is something we complain of that is not *cleansed,* yet there is a day coming when every thing that is amiss shall be amended, and the church shall be all fair, and no spot, no stain in her; and we must wait for that day.

2. Plenty, *v.* 18. This is put first, because it is the reverse of the judgment threatened in the foregoing chapters. (1.) The streams of this plenty overflow the land and enrich it: *The mountains shall drop new wine* and *the hills shall flow with milk,* such great abundance shall they have of suitable provision, both for *babes* and *strong men.* It intimates the abundance of vineyards, and all fruitful; and the abundance of cattle in the pastures that fill them with milk. And, to make the corn-land fruitful, the *rivers of Judah shall flow with water,* so that the country shall be like the garden of Eden, well-watered every where and greatly enriched, Ps. lxv. 9. But this seems to be meant spiritually; the graces and comforts of the new covenant are compared to *wine and milk* (Isa. lv. 1), and the Spirit to *rivers of living water,* John vii. 38. And these gifts abound much more under the New Testament than they did under the Old; when believers receive *grace for grace* from Christ's fulness, when they are enriched

with *everlasting consolations,* and *filled with joy and peace in believing,* then *the mountains drop new wine,* and *the hills flow with milk. Drink you,* drink abundantly, *O beloved!* When there is a plentiful effusion of the Spirit of grace, then the *rivers of Judah flow with water,* and make glad, not only *the city of our God* (Ps. xlvi. 4), but the whole land. (2.) The fountain of this plenty is in the *house of God,* whence the streams take their rise, as those *waters of the sanctuary* (Ezek. xlvii. 1) from *under the threshold of the house,* and the river of life *out of the throne of God and the Lamb,* Rev. xxii. 1. The psalmist, speaking of Zion, says, *All my springs are in thee,* Ps. lxxxvii. 7. Those that take temporal blessings to be meant in the former part of the verse, yet by this *fountain* out of *the house of the Lord* understand the grace of God, which, if we abound in temporal blessings, we have so much the more need of, that we may not abuse them. Christ himself is this fountain; his merit and grace cleanse us, refresh us, and make us fruitful. This is said to water *the valley of Shittim,* which lay a great way off from the temple at Jerusalem, on the other side of Jordan, and was a dry and barren valley, which intimates that gospel-grace, flowing from Christ, shall reach far, even to the Gentile world, to the most remote regions of it, and shall make those to abound in the fruits of righteousness who had long lain as the barren wilderness. This grace is a fountain overflowing, ever-flowing, from which we may be continually drawing, and yet need not fear its being drawn dry. This fountain comes *out of the house of the Lord;* for those that would partake of the promised graces and comforts must diligently and constantly attend upon instituted ordinances; and *from the house of the Lord* above, from his temple in heaven, flows all that good which here we are daily tasting the streams of, but hope to be shortly, hope to be eternally, drinking at the fountain-head of.

3. Perpetuity. This crowns all the rest (*v.* 20): *Judah shall dwell for ever* (when Egypt and Edom are made a *desolation),* and Jerusalem shall continue *from generation to generation.* This is a promise, and a precious promise it is, (1.) That the church of Christ shall continue in the world to the end of time. As one generation of professing Christians passes away, another shall come, in whom the *throne* of Christ *shall endure for ever,* and *the gates of hell shall not prevail* against it. (2.) That all the living members of that church (Judah and Jerusalem are put for the *inhabitants* of that city and country, Matt. iii. 5) shall be established in their happiness to the utmost ages of eternity. This new Jerusalem shall be *from generation to generation,* for it is a city that has foundations, not made with hands, but eternal in the heavens.

AN

EXPOSITION,

WITH PRACTICAL OBSERVATIONS,

OF THE PROPHECY OF

A M O S.

THOUGH this prophet appeared a little before Isaiah, yet he was not, as some have mistaken, that Amos who was the Father of Isaiah (Isa. i. 1), for in the Hebrew their names are very different; their families too were of a different character, for Isaiah was a courtier, Amos a country-farmer. Amos signifies a *burden*, whence the Jews have a tradition that he was of a slow tongue and spoke with stammering lips ; we may rather, in allusion to his name, say that his speech was *weighty* and his word *the burden of the Lord*. He was (as most think) of Judah, yet prophesied chiefly against Israel, and at Bethel, *ch.* vii. 13. Some think his style savours of his extraction, and is more plain and rustic than that of some other of the prophets; I do not see it so ; but it is plain that his matter agreed with that of his contemporary Hosea, that *out of the mouth of these two witnesses the word might be established.* It appears by his contest with Amaziah the priest of Bethel that he met with opposition in his work, but was a man of undaunted resolution in it, faithful and bold in reproving sin and denouncing the judgments of God for it, and pressing in his exhortations to repentance and reformation. He begins with threatenings against the neighbouring nations that were enemies to Israel, *ch.* i. and ii. He then calls Israel to account, and judges them for their idolatry, their unworthy walking under the favours God had bestowed upon them, and their incorrigibleness under his judgments, *ch.* iii. and iv. He calls them to repentance (*ch.* v.), rejecting their hypocritical sacrifices unless they did repent. He foretels the desolations that were coming upon them notwithstanding their security (*ch.* vi.), some particular judgments (*ch.* vii.), particularly on Amaziah ; and, after other reproofs and threatenings (*ch.* viii. and ix.), concludes with a promise of the setting up of the Messiah's kingdom and the happiness of God's spiritual Israel therein, just as the prophecy of Joel concluded. These prophets, having opened the wound in their reproofs and threatenings, which show all wrong, in the promises of gospel-grace open the remedy, which alone will set all to rights.

CHAP. I.

In this chapter we have, I. The general title of this prophecy (ver. 1), with the general scope of it, ver. 2. II. God's particular controversy with Syria (ver. 3—5), with Palestine (ver. 6—8), with Tyre (ver. 9, 10), with Edom (ver. 11, 12), and with Ammon (ver. 13—15), for their cruelty to his people and the many injuries they had done them. This explains God's pleading with the nations, Joel iii. 2.

THE words of Amos, who was among the herdmen of Tekoa, which he saw concerning Israel in the days of Uzziah king of Judah, and in the days of Jeroboam the son of Joash king of Israel, two years before the earthquake. 2 And he said, The LORD will roar from Zion, and utter his voice from Jerusalem ; and the habitations of the shepherds shall mourn, and the top of Carmel shall wither.

Here is, I. The general character of this prophecy. It consists of *the words which the prophet saw.* Are words to be seen ? Yes, God's words are ; the apostles speak of the

word of life, which they had not only *heard*, but *which they had seen with their eyes, which they had looked upon, and which their hands had handled* (1 John i. 1), such a real substantial thing is the word of God. The prophet saw these words, that is, 1. They were revealed to him in a *vision*, as John is said to see *the voice* that spoke to him, Rev. i. 12. 2. That which was foretold by them was to him as certain as if he had seen it with his bodily eyes. It intimates how strong he was in that faith which is *the evidence of things not seen.*

II. The person by whom this prophecy was sent—*Amos, who was among the herdmen of Tekoa*, and was one of them. Some think he was a rich dealer in cattle; the word is used concerning the king of Moab (2 Kings iii. 4, *He was a sheep-master) ;* it is probable that he got money by that business, and yet he must quit it, to follow God as a prophet. Others think he was a poor keeper of cattle, for we find (*ch.* vii. 14, 15) that he was withal *a gatherer of wild figs*, a poor employment by which we may suppose he could but just get his bread, and that God took him, as he did David, from following the flock, and Elisha from following the plough. Many were trained up for great employments, in the quiet, innocent, contemplative business of shepherds. When God would send a prophet to reprove and warn his people, he employed a shepherd, a herdsman, to do it; for they had made themselves *as the horse and mule that have no understanding,* nay, worse than the *ox that knows his owner.* God sometimes *chooses the foolish things of the world to confound the wise,* 1 Cor. i. 27. Note, Those whom God has endued with abilities for his service ought not to be despised nor laid aside for the meanness either of their origin or of their beginnings. Though Amos himself is not ashamed to own that he was a herdsman, yet others ought not to upbraid him with it nor think the worse of him for it.

III. The persons concerned in the prophecy of this book; it is *concerning Israel,* the *ten tribes,* who were now ripened in sin and ripening apace for ruin. God had raised them up prophets among themselves (*ch.* ii. 11), but they regarded them not; therefore God sends them one from Tekoa, in the land of Judah, that, coming from another country, he might be the more valued, and perhaps he was the rather sent out of his own country because there he was despised for his having been a herdsman. See Matt. xiii. 55—57.

IV. The time when these prophecies were delivered. 1. The book is dated, as laws used to be, by the reigns of the kings under whom the prophet prophesied. It was in the days of *Uzziah king of Judah,* when the affairs of that kingdom went very well, and of Jeroboam the second king of Israel, when the affairs of that kingdom went pretty well; yet then they must both be told both of the sins they were guilty of and of the judgments that were coming upon them for those sins, that they might not with the present gleam of prosperity flatter themselves either into an opinion of their innocence or a confidence of their perpetual security. 2. It is dated by a particular event to which his prophecy had a reference; it was *two years before the earthquake,* that earthquake which is mentioned to have been *in the days of Uzziah* (Zech. xiv. 5), which put the nation into a dreadful fright, for it is there said, They *fled before* it. But how could they flee from it? Some conjecture that this earthquake was at the time of Isaiah's vision, when the *posts of the door were moved,* Isa. vi. 4. The tradition of the Jews is that it happened just at the time when Uzziah presumptuously invaded the priest's office and went in to burn incense, 2 Chron. xxvi. 16. Josephus mentions this earthquake, *Antiq.* ix. 11, and says, " By it half of a mountain was removed and carried to a plain four furlongs off; and it spoiled the king's gardens." God by

this prophet gave warning of it *two years* before, that God by it would shake down their houses, *ch.* iii. 15.

V. The introduction to these prophecies, containing the general scope of them (*v.* 2): *The Lord will roar from Zion.* His threatenings by his prophets, and the executions of those threatenings in his providence, will be as terrible as the roaring of a lion is to the shepherds and their flocks. Amos here speaks the same language with his contemporaries, Hosea (*ch.* xi. 10) and Joel, *ch.* iii. 16. The lion roars before he tears; God gives warning before he strikes. Observe, 1. Whence this warning comes—*from Zion* and Jerusalem, from the oracles of God there delivered; for *by them is thy servant warned,* Ps. xix. 11. Our God, whose special residence is there, will issue out warrants, *given at that court,* as it were, for the executing of judgments on the land. See Jer. xxv. 30. In Zion was the mercy-seat; thence the Lord roars, intimating that God's acts of justice are consistent with mercy, allayed and mitigated by mercy, nay, as they are warnings, they are really acts of mercy. We are chastened, that we may not be condemned. 2. What effect the warning has: *The habitations of the shepherds mourn,* either because they fear the roaring lion or because they feel what is signified by that comparison, the consequences of a *great drought* (*ch.* iv. 7), which made *the top of Carmel* (of the most fruitful fields) to *wither* and become as a desert, Joel i. 12—17.

3 Thus saith the LORD; For three transgressions of Damascus, and for four, I will not turn away *the punishment* thereof; because they have threshed Gilead with threshing instruments of iron: 4 But I will send a fire into the house of Hazael, which shall devour the palaces of Ben-hadad. 5 I will break also the bar of Damascus, and cut off the inhabitant from the plain of Aven, and him that holdeth the sceptre from the house of Eden: and the people of Syria shall go into captivity unto Kir, saith the LORD. 6 Thus saith the LORD; For three transgressions of Gaza, and for four, I will not turn away *the punishment* thereof; because they carried away captive the whole captivity, to deliver *them* up to Edom: 7 But I will send a fire on the wall of Gaza, which shall devour the palaces thereof: 8 And I will cut off the inhabitant from Ashdod, and him that holdeth the sceptre from Ashkelon, and I will turn mine hand against Ekron: and

the remnant of the Philistines shall perish, saith the Lord GOD. 9 Thus saith the LORD; For three transgressions of Tyrus, and for four, I will not turn away *the punishment* thereof; because they delivered up the whole captivity to Edom, and remembered not the brotherly covenant: 10 But I will send a fire on the wall of Tyrus, which shall devour the palaces thereof. 11 Thus saith the LORD; For three transgressions of Edom, and for four, I will not turn away *the punishment* thereof; because he did pursue his brother with the sword, and did cast off all pity, and his anger did tear perpetually, and he kept his wrath for ever: 12 But I will send a fire upon Teman, which shall devour the palaces of Bozrah. 13 Thus saith the LORD; For three transgressions of the children of Ammon, and for four, I will not turn away *the punishment* thereof; because they have ripped up the women with child of Gilead, that they might enlarge their border: 14 But I will kindle a fire in the wall of Rabbah, and it shall devour the palaces thereof, with shouting in the day of battle, with a tempest in the day of the whirlwind: 15 And their king shall go into captivity, he and his princes together, saith the LORD.

What the Lord says here may be explained by what he says Jer. xii. 14, *Thus saith the Lord, against all my evil neighbours that touch the inheritance of my people Israel, Behold, I will pluck them out.* Damascus was a near neighbour to Israel on the north, Tyre and Gaza on the west, Edom on the south, Ammon and (in the next chapter) Moab on the east; and all of them had been, one time, one way, or other, *pricking briers and grieving thorns* to Israel, evil neighbours to them; and, because God espouses his people's cause, he there calls them *his evil neighbours,* and here comes forth to reckon with them. The method taken in dealing with each of them is, in part, the same, and therefore we put them together, and yet in each there is something peculiar.

I. Let us see what is repeated, both by way of charge and by way of sentence, concerning them all. The controversy God has with each of them is prefaced with, *Thus saith the Lord,* Jehovah the God of Israel. Though those nations will not worship him as their God, yet they shall be made to know

1226

that they are accountable to him as their Judge. The God of Israel is *the God of the whole earth,* and has something to say to them that shall make them tremble. Against them the Lord *roars out of Zion.* And before God, by the prophet, threatens Israel and Judah, he denounces judgments against those nations whom he made use of as scourges to them for their being so, which might serve for a check to their pride and insolence and a relief to his people under their dejections; for hereby they might see that God had not quitted his interest in them, and therefore might hope they had not lost their interest in him. Now as to all these nations here arraigned,

1. The indictment drawn up against them all is thus far the same, (1.) That they are charged in general with *three transgressions, and with four,* that is, with many transgressions (as by one or two we mean *a few,* so by three or four we mean many, as in Latin a man that is very happy is said to be *terque quaterque beatus—three and four times happy)*: or *with three and four,* that is, with seven transgressions, a number of perfection, intimating that they have *filled up the measure of their iniquities,* and are ripe for ruin; or *with three* (that is, a variety of sins) *and with a fourth* especially, which is specified concerning each of them, though the other three are not, as Prov. xxx. 15, 18, 21, 29, where we read of *three things, yea, four,* generally one seems to be more especially intended. (2.) That the particular sin which is fastened upon as the fourth, and which alone is specified, is the sin of persecution: it is some mischief or other done to the people of God that is particularly charged upon every one of them, for persecution is the measure-filling sin of any people, and it is this sin that will be particularly reckoned for —*I was hungry, and you gave me no meat;* much more if it may be said, *I was hungry, and you took my meat from me.*

2. The judgment given against them all is thus far the same, (1.) That, their sin having risen to such a height, *God will not turn away the punishment thereof.* Though he has granted them a long reprieve, and has often *turned away their punishment,* yet now he will turn it away no longer, but justice shall take its course. *"I will not revoke it* (so some read it); I will not recal *the voice* which has *gone forth* from Zion and Jerusalem (*v.* 2), speaking death and terror to the sinful nations." It is an irrevocable sentence. God has spoken it, and he will not *call it back.* Note, Though God bear long, he will not bear always, with those that provoke him; and, when the decree brings forth, it will bring up. (2.) That God will *kindle a fire* among them; this is said concerning all these *evil neighbours, v.* 4, 7, 10, 12, 14. God will *send a fire* into their cities. When fires are kindled that lay cities, towns, and houses in ashes, whether designedly or casually

God must be acknowledged in it; they are of his sending. Sin stirs up the fire of his jealousy, and that kindles other fires.

II. Let us see what is mentioned, both by way of charge and by way of sentence, that is peculiar to each of them, that every one may take his portion.

1. Concerning Damascus, the head-city of Syria, a kingdom that was often vexatious to Israel. (1.) The peculiar sin of Damascus was using the Gileadites barbarously : *They threshed Gilead with threshing-instruments of iron* (v. 3), which may be understood literally of their putting to the torture, or to cruel deaths, the inhabitants of Gilead whom they got into their hands, as David put the Ammonites under *saws and harrows*, 2 Sam. xii. 31. We read with what inhumanity Hazael king of Syria prosecuted his wars with Israel (2 Kings viii. 12); he *dashed their children*, and *ripped up their women with child ;* and see what desolations he made in their land, 2 Kings x. 32, 33. Or it may be taken figuratively, for his laying the country waste, and this very similitude is used in the history of it. 2 Kings xiii. 7, He *destroyed them, and made them like the dust by threshing.* Note, Men often do that unjustly and wickedly, and shall be severely reckoned with for it, which yet God justly permits them to do. The church is called *God's threshing, and the corn of his floor* (Isa. xxi. 10); but if men make it their threshing, and the chaff of their floor, they shall be sure to hear of it. (2.) The peculiar punishment of Damascus is, [1.] That the fire which shall be sent shall fasten upon the court in the first place, not on the chief city, nor the country towns, but on *the house of Hazael*, which he built; and *it shall devour the palaces of Ben-hadad*, the royal palaces inhabited by the kings of Syria, many of whom were of that name. Note, Even royal palaces are no defence against the judgments of God, though ever so richly furnished, though ever so strongly fortified. [2.] That the enemy shall force his way into the city (v. 5): *I will break the bar of Damascus*, and then the gate flies open. Or it may be understood figuratively : all that which is depended upon as the strength and safety of that great city shall fail, and prove insufficient. When God's judgments come with commission it is in vain to think of turning them out. [3.] That the people shall be destroyed with the sword: *I will cut off the inhabitant from the plain of Aven*, the *valley of idolatry*, for the gods of the Syrians were *gods of the valleys* (1 Kings xx. 23), were worshipped in valleys; as the idols of Israel were worshipped on *the hills : him also that holdeth the sceptre* of power, some petty king or other that used to boast of the sceptre he held from Beth-Eden, the *house of pleasure.* Both those that were given to idolatry and those that were given to sensuality should be cut off together. [4.] That the body of the nation shall be carried off.

The *people shall go into captivity unto Kir*, which was in the country of the Medes. We find this fulfilled (2 Kings xvi. 9) about fifty years after this, when *the king of Assyria went up against Damascus*, and *took it*, and *carried the people of it captive to Kir, and slew Rezin*, at the instigation of Ahaz king of Judah.

2. Concerning Gaza, a city of the Philistines, and now the metropolis of that country. (1.) The peculiar sin of the Philistines was *carrying away captive the whole captivity*, either of Israel or Judah, which some think refers to that inroad made upon Jehoram when they took away *all the king's sons* and *all his substance* (2 Chron. xxi. 17), or, perhaps, it refers to their seizing those that fled to them for shelter when Sennacherib invaded Judah, and *selling them to the Grecians* (Joel iii. 4—6), or (as here) to the Edomites, who were always sworn enemies to the people of God. They spared none, but carried off all they could lay their hands on, designing, if possible, to *cut off the name of Israel*, Ps. lxxxiii. 4—7. (2.) The peculiar punishment of the Philistines is that the fire which God will send shall devour the palaces of Gaza, and that the *inhabitants* of the other cities of the Philistines, Ashdod (or Azotus), Ashkelon, and Ekron, shall all be *cut off*, and God will make as thorough work with them in their ruin as they would have made with God's people when they carried away the whole captivity; for even the *remnant* of them *shall perish*, v. 8. Note, God will make a full end of those that think to make a full end of his church and people.

3. Concerning Tyre, that famous city of wealth and strength, that was itself a kingdom, v. 9. (1.) The peculiar sin of Tyre is *delivering up the whole captivity to Edom*, that is, selling to the Edomites those of Israel that fled to them for shelter, or in any way fell into their hands; not caring what hardships they put upon them, so that they could but make gain of them to themselves. Herein they forgot the *brotherly covenant*, the league that was between Solomon and Hiram king of Tyre (1 Kings v. 12), which was so intimate that Hiram called Solomon his *brother*, 1 Kings ix. 13. Note, It is a great aggravation of enmity and malice when it is the violation of friendship and of a *brotherly covenant*. (2.) Here is nothing peculiar in the punishment of Tyrus but that *the palaces thereof* shall be *devoured*, which was done when Nebuchadnezzar took it after thirteen years' siege. Their merchants were all princes, and their private houses were as palaces; but the fire shall make no more of them than of cottages.

4. Concerning Edom, the posterity of Esau. (1.) Their peculiar sin was an unmerciful, unwearied, pursuit of the people of God, and their taking all advantages against them to do them a mischief, v. 11. He did *pursue his brother with the sword*, not

only of old, when the king of Edom took up arms to oppose the children of Israel's passage *through his border* (Num. xx. 18), but ever since upon all occasions ; they had not strength and courage enough to face them in the field of battle, but, whenever any other enemy had put Judah or Israel to flight, then the Edomites set in with the pursuers, fell upon the rear, slew those that were half dead already, and (as is usual with cowards when they have an enemy at an advantage) they did *cast off all pity.* Those that are least courageous are commonly most cruel. Edom was so ; his malice *destroyed his compassion* (so the word is) ; he stripped himself of the tenderness of a man, and put on the fierceness of a beast of prey ; and, as such a one, he did tear, his *anger did tear perpetually.* His cruelty was insatiable, and he never knew when he had sucked enough of the blood of Israel, but, like the horse-leech, still cried, *Give, give.* Nay, he *kept his wrath for ever ;* when he wanted objects of his wrath, and opportunity to show it, yet he kept it in reserve (it *rested in his bosom*), he rolled it under his tongue as a sweet morsel, and had it ready to spit in the face of Israel upon the next occasion. Cursed be such cruel wrath, and anger so fierce, so outrageous, which makes men like the devil, who *continually seeks to devour*, and unlike to God, who *keeps not his anger for ever.* Edom's malice was unnatural, for thus he pursued his brother, whom he ought to have protected : it was hereditary, as if it had been entailed upon the family ever since Esau hated Jacob, and time itself could not wear it out, no, nor the brotherly conduct of Israel towards them (Deut. ii. 4), and the express law given to Israel (Deut. xxiii. 7), *Thou shalt not abhor an Edomite, for he is thy brother.* (2.) Here is nothing peculiar in their punishment ; but (*v.* 12) a *fire* shall be *sent to devour their palaces.* Note, The fire of our anger against our brethren kindles the fire of God's anger against us.

5. Concerning the Ammonites, *v.* 13—15. (1.) See how violently the fire of their anger turned against the people of God ; they not only triumphed in their calamities (as we find, Ezek. xxv. 2, 6), but they did themselves use them barbarously ; they *ripped up the women with child of Gilead*, a piece of cruelty the very mention of which strikes a horror upon one's mind ; one would think it not possible that any of the human race should be so inhuman. Hazael was guilty of it, 2 Kings viii. 12. It was done not only in a brutish rage, which falls without consideration upon all that comes before it, but with a devilish design to extirpate the race of Israel by killing not only all that were born, but all that were to be born, worse than Egyptian cruelty. It was *that they might enlarge their border*, that they might make the land of Gilead their own, and there might be none to lay claim to it or

1228

give them any disturbance in the possession of it. We find (Jer. xlix. 1) that the Ammonites inherited *Gad* (that is, Gilead) under pretence that Israel had no sons, no heirs. We know how heavy the doom of those was, and how heinous their crime, who said, *This is the heir ; come, let us kill him, and the inheritance shall be ours* by occupancy. See what cruelty covetousness is the cause of, and what horrid practices those are often put upon that are greedy to *enlarge their own border.* (2.) See how violently the fire of God's anger burned against them ; shall not God *visit for these things* done to any of mankind, especially when they are done to his own people ? *Shall not his soul be avenged on such a nation as this?* No doubt, it shall. The fire shall be kindled *with shouting in the day of battle*, that is, war shall kindle the fire ; it shall be a fire accompanied with the sword, or a roaring fire, which shall make a noise like that of soldiers ready to engage, and it shall be as a *tempest* in the *day of the whirlwind*, which comes swiftly, furiously, and bears down all before it. Or this tempest and whirlwind shall be as bellows to the fire, to make it burn the stronger, and spread the further. It is particularly threatened that *their king and his princes shall go together into captivity*, carried away by the king of Babylon, not long after Judah was. See what changes God's providence often makes with men, or rather their own sin ; kings become captives, and princes prisoners. *Milchom shall go into captivity ;* some understand it of the god of the Ammonites, whom they called *Moloch*—*a king. He, and his princes*, and his priests that attended him, shall go *into captivity ;* their idol shall be so far from protecting them that it shall itself go into captivity with them. Note, Those who by violence and fraud seek to enlarge their own border will justly be expelled and excluded their own border ; nor is it strange if those who make no conscience of invading the rights of others be able to make no resistance against those who invade theirs.

CHAP. II.

In this chapter, I. God, by the prophet, proceeds in a like controversy with Moab as before with other nations, ver. 1—3. II. He shows what quarrel he had with Judah, ver. 4, 5. III. He at length begins his charge against Israel, to which all that goes before is but an introduction. Observe, 1. The sins they are charged with—injustice, oppression, whoredom, ver. 6—8. 2. The aggravations of those sins—the temporal and spiritual mercies God had bestowed upon them, for which they had made him such ungrateful returns, ver. 9—12. 3. God's complaint of them for their sins (ver. 13) and his threatenings of their ruin, and their utter inability to prevent it, ver. 14—16.

THUS saith the LORD ; For three transgressions of Moab, and for four, I will not turn away *the punishment* thereof ; because he burned the bones of the king of Edom into lime :

2 But I will send a fire upon Moab, and it shall devour the palaces of Kirioth : and Moab shall die with

tumult, with shouting, *and* with the sound of the trumpet : 3 And I will cut off the judge from the midst thereof, and will slay all the princes thereof with him, saith the LORD. 4 Thus saith the LORD; For three transgressions of Judah, and for four, I will not turn away *the punishment* thereof; because they have despised the law of the LORD, and have not kept his commandments, and their lies caused them to err, after the which their fathers have walked : 5 But I will send a fire upon Judah, and it shall devour the palaces of Jerusalem. 6 Thus saith the LORD; For three transgressions of Israel, and for four, I will not turn away *the punishment* thereof; because they sold the righteous for silver, and the poor for a pair of shoes; 7 That pant after the dust of the earth on the head of the poor, and turn aside the way of the meek : and a man and his father will go in unto the *same* maid, to profane my holy name : 8 And they lay *themselves* down upon clothes laid to pledge by every altar, and they drink the wine of the condemned *in* the house of their god.

Here is, I. The judgment of Moab, another of the nations that bordered upon Israel. They are reckoned with and shall be punished *for three transgressions and for four,* as those before. Now, 1. Moab's fourth transgression, as theirs who were before set to the bar, was cruelty. The instance given refers not to the people of God, but to a heathen like themselves : The king of Moab *burnt the bones of the king of Edom into lime.* We find there was war between the Edomites and the Moabites, in which the king of Moab, in distress and rage, offered his own son for a burnt-offering, to appease his deity, 2 Kings iii. 26, 27. And it should seem that afterwards he, or some of his successors, in revenge upon the Edomites for bringing him to that extremity, having an advantage against the *king of Edom,* seized him alive and burnt him to ashes, or slew him and burnt his body, or dug up the bones of their dead king, of that particularly who had so straitened him, and, in token of his rage and fury, *burnt them to lime,* and perhaps made use of the powder of his bones for the white-washing of the walls and ceiling of his palace, that he might please himself with the sight of that monument of his revenge. *Est vindicta bonum vitâ jucundius ipsâ—Revenge is sweeter than life itself.*

It is barbarous to abuse human bodies, for we ourselves also are *in the body;* it is senseless to abuse dead bodies, nay, it is impious, for we believe and look for their resurrection; and to abuse the dead bodies of kings (whose persons and names ought to be in a particular manner respected and had in veneration) is an affront to majesty; it is an argument of a base spirit for those to trample upon a dead lion who, were he alive, would tremble before him. 2. Moab's doom for this transgression is, (1.) A judgment of death. Those that deal cruelly shall be cruelly dealt with (*v.* 2) : *Moab shall die;* the Moabites shall be cut off with the sword of war, which kills *with tumult, with shouting, and with sound of trumpet,* circumstances that make it so much the more terrible, as the lion's roaring aggravates his tearing. *Every battle of the warrior is with confused noise,* Isa. ix. 5. (2.) It is a judgment upon their judge, who had passed the sentence upon the bones of the king of Edom that they should be burnt to lime : *I will cut him off,* says God (*v.* 3); he shall know there is a judge that is higher than he. The king, the chief judge, and all the inferior judges and princes, shall be cut off together. If the people sometimes suffer for the sin of their princes, yet the princes themselves shall not escape, Jer. xlviii. 47. *Thus far is the judgment of Moab.*

II. Judah also is a near neighbour to Israel, and therefore, now that justice is riding the circuit, that shall not be passed by; that nation had made itself like the heathen and mingled with them, and therefore the indictment here runs against them in the same form in which it had run against all the rest : *For three transgressions of Judah, and for four, I will not turn away the punishment thereof;* their sins are as many as the sins of other nations, and we find them huddled up with them in the same character, Jer. ix. 26, " As for *Egypt, and Judah, and Edom,* jumble them together; they are all alike;" the sentence here also is the same (*v.* 5) : " *I will send a fire upon Judah,* though it is the land where God is known, and it shall *devour the palaces of Jerusalem,* though it is the holy city, and God has formerly been *known in its palaces for a refuge,*" Ps. xlviii. 3. But the sin here charged upon Judah is different from all the rest. The other nations were reckoned with for injuries done to men, but Judah is reckoned with for indignities done to God, *v.* 4. 1. They put contempt upon his statutes and persisted in disobedience to them : *They have despised the law of the Lord,* as if it were not worth taking notice of, nor had any thing in it valuable; and herein they despised the wisdom, justice, and goodness, as well as the authority and sovereignty, of the Lawmaker; this they did, in effect, when they *kept not his commandments,* made no conscience of them, took no care about them.

2. They put honour upon his rivals, their idols, here called *their lies*, which *caused them to err;* for *an image is a teacher of lies*, Hab. ii. 18. And those that are led away into the error of idolatry are by that led into a multitude of other errors, *Uno dato absurdo mille sequuntur—One absurdity draws after it a thousand.* God is an infinite eternal Spirit ; but, when that *truth of God* is by idolatry *changed into a lie*, all his other truths are in danger of being so changed likewise ; thus their idols caused them to err, and God justly gave them up to strong delusions ; nor was it any excuse for their sin that they were the lies *after which their fathers walked*, for they should rather have taken warning than taken pattern by those that perished with these *lies in their right hand.*

III. We now at length come to *the words* which *Amos saw concerning Israel.* The reproofs and threatenings having walked the round, here they centre, here they settle. He begins with them as with the rest : *For three transgressions of Israel, and for four, I will not turn away the punishment thereof ;* if all these nations must be punished for their iniquities, shall Israel go unpunished? Observe here what their sins were, for which God would reckon with them. 1. Perverting justice. This was the sin of those who were entrusted with the administration of justice, the judges and magistrates, and all parties concerned. They made nothing of selling a righteous man, and his righteous cause when it came to be tried before them, for a piece of silver ; sentence was passed, not according to the merits of the cause, but the bribe always turned the scale, and judgment was set to sale by auction to the highest bidder. They would sell the life and livelihood of a *poor* man *for a pair of shoes*, for the least advantage to themselves that could be proposed to them ; give them but a *pair of shoes*, and the cause of a poor man, who could not give them as much as that, should be betrayed, and left at the mercy of those that will have no mercy. They will rather play at small game than sit out. *For a piece of bread such a man will transgress.* Note, Those who will wrong their consciences for any thing will come at length to do it for next to nothing ; those who begin to sell justice for silver will in time be so sordid as to sell it *for a pair of shoes*, for a pair of old shoes. 2. Oppressing the poor, and seeking to benefit themselves by doing them a mischief : *They pant after the dust of the earth on the head of the poor ;* they swallow up the poor with the utmost greediness, and make a prey of those that are in sorrow with dust on their heads, poor orphans that are in mourning for their parents ; they catch at them to get their estates into their hands ; they never rest till they have got the heads of the poor in the dust, to be trodden on. Or, They *pant after the dust of the earth*, that is, silver and gold, white and yellow dust ; they covet it earnestly, and levy it *upon the head of the poor*, by their unjust exactions. Note, Men's seeking to enrich themselves by the impoverishing of others is a transgression which God will not long *turn away the punishment of.* This is *turning aside the way of the meek*, contriving to do injury to those who, they know, are mild and patient and will bear injury. They invade their rights, break their measures, and obstruct the course of justice in favour of them, not suffering them to go on with their righteous cause; this is *turning aside their way.* Note, The more patiently men bear the injuries that are done them the greater is the sin of those that injure them, and the more occasion they have to expect that God will give them redress, and take vengeance for them. I, *as a deaf man, heard not*, and then *thou wilt hear.* 3. Abominable uncleanness, even incest itself, such as is not named among the Gentiles, that *a man should have his father's wife*, (1 Cor. v. 1), his father's concubine : *A man and his father will go in unto the same young woman*, as black an instance as any other of an unbounded promiscuous lust ; and yet where the former iniquities of oppression and extortion are this also is found ; for laws of modesty seldom hold those that have broken the bands of justice and *cast away its cords* from them. This wickedness is such a scandal to religion, and the profession of it, that those who are guilty of it are looked upon as designing thereby to *profane God's holy name*, and to render it odious among the heathen, as if he countenanced the villanies which those who pretend relation to him allow themselves in, and were altogether such a one as they. 4. Regaling themselves, and yet pretending to honour their God with that which they had got by oppression and extortion, *v.* 8. They add idolatry to their injustice, and then think to atone for their injustice with their idolatry. (1.) They make merry with that which they have unjustly squeezed from the poor. They *lay themselves down* at ease, and in state, and stretch themselves upon *clothes laid to pledge*, which they ought to have restored the same night, according to the law, Deut. xxiv. 12, 13. And they *drink the wine of the condemned*, of such as they have fined and laid heavy mulcts upon, spending that in sensuality which they have got by injustice. (2.) They think to make atonement for this by feasting on the gains of oppression *before their altars*, and *drinking this wine in the house of their God*, in the temples where they worshipped their calves, as if they would make God a *partner in their crimes* by making him a *partner of the profits* of them—service good enough for false gods ; but the true God will not thus be mocked ; he has declared that he *hates robbery for burnt-offerings*, and cannot be served acceptably but with that which is got honestly.

9 Yet destroyed I the Amorite before them, whose height *was* like the height of the cedars, and he *was* strong as the oaks; yet I destroyed his fruit from above, and his roots from beneath. 10 Also I brought you up from the land of Egypt, and led you forty years through the wilderness, to possess the land of the Amorite. 11 And I raised up of your sons for prophets, and of your young men for Nazarites. *Is it* not even thus, O ye children of Israel? saith the Lord. 12 But ye gave the Nazarites wine to drink; and commanded the prophets, saying, Prophesy not. 13 Behold, I am pressed under you, as a cart is pressed *that is* full of sheaves. 14 Therefore the flight shall perish from the swift, and the strong shall not strengthen his force, neither shall the mighty deliver himself: 15 Neither shall he stand that handleth the bow; and *he that is* swift of foot shall not deliver *himself:* neither shall he that rideth the horse deliver himself. 16 And *he that is* courageous among the mighty shall flee away naked in that day, saith the Lord.

Here, I. God puts his people Israel in mind of the great things he had done for them, in putting them into possession of the land of Canaan, the greatest part of which these ten tribes now enjoyed, *v.* 9, 10. Note, We need often to be reminded of the mercies we have received, which are the heaviest aggravations of the sins we have committed. God gives liberally, and upbraids us not with our meanness and unworthiness, and the disproportion between his gifts and our merits; but he justly upbraids us with our ingratitude, and ill requital of his favours, and tells us what he has done for us, to shame us for not rendering again according to the benefit done to us. " *Son, remember;* Israel, remember, 1. That God brought thee out of a house of bondage, rescued thee out of the *land of Egypt,* where thou wouldst otherwise have perished in slavery." 2. That he *led thee forty years* through a desert land, and fed thee in a *wilderness,* where thou wouldst otherwise have perished with hunger. Mercies to our ancestors were mercies to us, for, if they had been cut off, we should not have been. 3. That he made room for them in Canaan, by extirpating the natives by a series of wonders little inferior to those by which they were redeemed out of Egypt: *I destroyed the Amorite before them,* here put for all the devoted nations. Ob-

serve the magnificence of the enemies that stood in their way, which is taken notice of, that God may be the more magnified in the subduing of them. They were of great stature *(whose height was like the height of the cedars)* and the people of Israel were as shrubs to them; and they were also of great strength, not only tall, but well-set: *He was strong as the oaks.* Their kingdom was eminent among the nations, and over-topped all its neighbours. The supports and defences of it seemed impregnable; it was as fine as the stately cedar; it was as firm as the sturdy oak; yet, when God had a vine to plant there (Ps. lxxx. 8, 9), this Amorite was not only cut down, but plucked up: *I destroyed his fruit from above and his roots from beneath,* so that the Amorites were no more a nation, nor ever read of any more. Thus highly did God value Israel. He gave men *for them and people for their life,* Isa. xliii. 4. How ungrateful then were those who put such contempt upon him! 4. That he made them *possess the land of the Amorite,* not only put it into their hands, so that they became masters of it *jure belli—by right of conquest,* but gave them a better title to it, so that it became theirs by promise.

II. He likewise upbraids them with the spiritual privileges and advantages they enjoyed as a holy nation, *v.* 11. They had helps for their souls, which taught them how to make good use of their temporal enjoyments and were therefore more valuable. It is true the *ten tribes* had not God's temple, altar, and priesthood, and it was their own fault that they deserted them, and for that they might justly have been left in utter darkness; but God *left not himself without witness,* nor them without guides to show them the way. 1. They had prophets that were powerful instructors in piety, divinely inspired, and commissioned to make known the mind of God to them, to show them what is pleasing to God and what displeasing, to reprove them for their faults and warn them of their danger, to direct them in their difficulties and comfort them in their troubles. God raised them up prophets, animated them for that work and employed them in it. He *raised* them *up of their sons,* from among themselves, as Moses and Christ were raised up *from among their brethren,* Deut. xviii. 15. It was an honour put upon their nation, and upon their families, that they had children of their own to be God's messengers to them, of their own language, not strangers sent from another country, whom they might suspect to be prejudiced against them and their land, but those who, they knew, wished well to them. Note, Faithful ministers are great blessings to any people, and it is God that raises them up to be so, that they may justly be reckoned an honour to the families they are of. 2. They had Nazarites that were bright examples of piety: *I raised up of your young men for Nazarites,* men that bound themselves by a vow to God and his service, and, in pursuance of that, denied themselves many of the lawful delights of sense, as drinking wine and eating grapes. There were some of their young men that were in their prime for the enjoyment of the pleasures of this life and yet voluntarily abridged themselves of them; these God raised up by the power of his grace, to be *monuments of his grace,* to his glory, and to be his witnesses against the impieties of that degenerate age. Note, It is as great a blessing to any place to have eminent good Christians in it as to have eminent good ministers in it; for so they have examples to their rules. We must acknowledge that it bodes well to any people when God raises up numbers of hopeful young people among them, when he makes their young men Nazarites, devout, and conscientious, and mortified to the pleasures of sense; and those that are such Nazarites are *purer than snow, whiter than milk;* they are indeed the polite young men, for their *polishing is of sapphires,* Lam. iv. 7. Those that have such men, such young men, among them, have therein such an advantage, both for direction and encouragement, to be religious, as they will be called to an account for another day if they do not improve. Israel is here reckoned with, not only for the prophets, but for the Nazarites, raised up among them. Concerning the truth of this, he appeals to themselves: " *Is it not even thus, O you children of Israel?* Can you deny it? Have not you yourselves been sensible of the advantage you had by the prophets and Nazarites raised up among you?" Note, Sinners' own consciences will be witnesses for God that he has not been wanting to them in the means of grace, so that, if they perish, it is because they have been wanting to themselves in not improving those means. The men of Judah shall themselves *judge between God and his vineyard,* whether he could have done more for it, Isa. v. 3, 4.

III. He charges them with the abuse of the means of grace they enjoyed, and the opposition they gave to God's designs in affording them those means, *v.* 12. They were so far from walking in the light that they rebelled against it, and did what they could to extinguish it, that it might not shine in their faces, to their conviction. 1. They did what they could to debauch good people, to draw them off from their seriousness in devotion and their strictness in conversation: *You gave the Nazarites wine to drink,* contrary to their vow, that, having broken it in that instance, they might not pretend to keep it in any other. Some they surprised, or allured into it, and *with their much fair speech caused them to yield;* others they forced and frightened into it, reproached and threatened them if they were more precise than their neighbours; and, by drawing them in to drink wine, they spoiled them for

1232

Nazarites. Note, Satan and his agents are very busy to corrupt the minds of young people that look heavenward; and many that we thought would have been Nazarites they have overcome by giving them wine to drink, by drawing them in to the love of mirth and pleasure, and drinking company. Multitudes of young men that bade fair for eminent professors of religion have *erred through wine,* and been undone for ever. And how do the factors for hell triumph in the debauching of a Nazarite! 2. They did what they could to silence good ministers, and to stop their mouths: " *You commanded the prophets, saying, Prophesy not,* and threatened them if they did prophesy (*ch.* vii. 12), as if God's messengers were bound to observe your orders, and might not deliver their errand unless you gave them leave, and so you not only *received the grace of God,* in raising up those prophets, *in vain,* but put the highest affront imaginable upon that God in whose name the prophets spoke." Note, Those have a great deal to answer for that cannot bear faithful preaching, and those much more that suppress it.

IV. He complains of the wrong they did him by their sins (*v.* 13): " *I am pressed under you,* I am *straitened* by you, and know not what to do, Hos. xi. 8, 9. I am loaded and burdened by you, and can no longer bear it, and therefore *I will ease myself of my adversaries,* Isa. i. 24. *I am pressed under you* and the load of your sins *as a cart is pressed that is full of sheaves,* is loaded with corn, in the midst of the *joy of harvest,* as long as any will lie on." Note, The great God complains of sin, especially the sins of his professing people, as a burden to him. He is *grieved with this generation* (Ps. xcv. 10), *is broken with their whorish heart* (Ezek. vi. 9), a consideration which, if it make not the sinner's repentance very deep, will make his ruin very great. The great God that upholds the world, and never complains that he is pressed under the weight of it (he *fainteth not, neither is weary),* yet complains of the sins of Israel, yea, and of their hypocritical services too, that he is *weary of bearing them,* Isa. i. 14. No wonder the *creature groans being burdened* (Rom. viii. 22), when the Creator says, *I am pressed under them.*

V. He threatens them with unavoidable ruin. And so some read, *v.* 13, " *Behold I will press,* or straiten, *your place, as a cart full of sheaves presses;* they shall be loaded with judgments till they shall sink under them, and shall make a noise, as a cart overloaded does." Those that will not submit to the convictions of the word, that will neither be won by that nor by the conversation of those about them, shall be made to sink under the weight of God's judgments. If God load us daily with his benefits, and we, notwithstanding that, load him with our sins, how can we expect any other than that he should load us with his judgments? And it is here threatened in the last three verses that, when God comes forth to contend with this provoking people, they shall not be able to stand before him, to flee from him, nor to make their part good with him; for when God judges he will overcome. Though his patience be tired out, his power is not, and so the sinner shall find, to his cost. When the Assyrian army comes to lay the country waste by sword and captivity none shall escape, but every one shall have his share in the common desolation. 1. It will be in vain to think of fleeing from the enemy that comes armed with a commission to make all desolate: *The flight shall perish from the swift;* those that have been famed for happy escapes and happy retreats shall now find their arts fail them; they shall have no time to flee, or shall find no way to take, or they shall have no strength or spirit to attempt it; they shall be at their wits' end, and then they are soon at their flight's end. Are they, as Asahel, as *swift of foot as a wild roe?* (2 Sam. ii. 18), yet, like him, they shall run the faster upon their own destruction: *He that is swift of foot shall not deliver himself,* v. 15. Or do they say (as those, Isa. xxx. 16), *We will flee upon horses,* and *we will ride upon the swift?* Yet they shall be overtaken: *Neither shall he that rides the horse deliver himself* from his pursuers. *A horse is a vain thing for safety.* 2. It will be in vain to think of fighting it out. God is at war with them; and *are they stronger than he?* Is there any military force that can pretend to be a match for Omnipotence? No: *The strong shall not strengthen his force.* He that has a habit of strength shall not be able to exert it when he has occasion for it. And *the mighty,* who should protect and deliver others, shall not be able to *deliver himself,* to deliver *his soul* (so the word is), shall not save his life. Let not the *strong man* then *glory in his strength,* nor trust in it, but *strengthen himself in the Lord his God,* for in him is *everlasting strength.* And, as the bodily strength shall fail, so shall the weapons of war. The armour as well as the arm shall become insufficient: *Neither shall he stand that handles the bow,* though he stand at a distance, but shall betake himself to flight, and not trust to his own bow to save him. Though the arm be ever so strong, and the armour ever so well fixed, neither will avail when the spirit fails (v. 16): *He that is courageous among the mighty,* that used to look danger in the face, and not be dismayed at it, shall *flee away naked in that day,* not only disarmed, having thrown away his weapons both offensive and defensive, but plundered of his treasure, which he thought to carry away with him, and he shall think it as much as he could expect that he has *his life for a prey.* Thus when God pleases *he takes away the heart of the chief of the people of the earth,* and causes those who used to boast of their

courage, and their daring enterprises in the field, to *wander* and sneak *in a wilderness where there is no way,* Job xii. 24.

CHAP. III.

A stupid, senseless, heedless people, are, in this chapter, called upon to take notice, I. Of the judgments of God denounced against them and the warnings he gave them of those judgments, and to be hereby awakened out of their security, ver. 1—8. II. Of the sins that were found among them, by which God was provoked thus to threaten, thus to punish, that they might justify God in his controversy with them, and, unless they repented and reformed, might expect no other than that God should proceed in his controversy, ver. 9—15.

HEAR this word that the LORD hath spoken against you, O children of Israel, against the whole family which I brought up from the land of Egypt, saying, 2 You only have I known of all the families of the earth: therefore I will punish you for all your iniquities. 3 Can two walk together, except they be agreed? 4 Will a lion roar in the forest, when he hath no prey? will a young lion cry out of his den, if he have taken nothing? 5 Can a bird fall in a snare upon the earth, where no gin *is* for him? shall *one* take up a snare from the earth, and have taken nothing at all? 6 Shall a trumpet be blown in the city, and the people not be afraid? shall there be evil in a city, and the LORD hath not done *it?* 7 Surely the Lord GOD will do nothing, but he revealeth his secret unto his servants the prophets. 8 The lion hath roared, who will not fear? the Lord GOD hath spoken, who can but prophesy?

The scope of these verses is to convince the people of Israel that God had a controversy with them. That which the prophet has to say to them is to let them know that the Lord has something to say against them, v. 1. They were his peculiar people above others, knew his name, and were called by it; *nevertheless he had something against them,* and they were called to hear what it was, that they might consider what answer they should make, as the prisoner at the bar is told to hearken to his indictment. The *children of Israel* would not regard the words of counsel and comfort that God had many a time spoken to them, and now they shall be made to hear the word of reproof and threatening that the Lord has spoken against them; for he will act as he has spoken.

I. Let them know that the gracious cognizance God had taken of them, and the favours he had bestowed upon them, should not exempt them from the punishment due to them for their sins. Israel is a *family* that *God brought up out of the land of Egypt,* (*v.* 1), and it was no more than a family when it went down thither; thence God delivered it; thence he fetched it to be a family to himself. It is not only the ten tribes, the kingdom of Israel, that must take notice of this, but that of Judah also, for it is spoken against the whole *family* that *God brought up out of Egypt.* It is a family that God has bestowed distinguishing favours upon, has owned in a peculiar manner. *You only have I known of all the families of the earth.* Note, God's church in the world is a family dignified above all the families of the earth. Those that know God are known of him. *In Judah is God known,* and therefore Judah is more than any people known of God. God has *known* them, that is, he has chosen them, covenanted with them, and conversed with them as his acquaintance. Now, one would think, it should follow, "Therefore I will spare you, will connive at your faults, and excuse you." No: *Therefore I will punish you for all your iniquities.* Note, The distinguishing favours of God to us, if they do not serve to restrain us from sin, shall not serve to exempt us from punishment; nay, the nearer any are to God in profession, and the kinder notice he has taken of them, the more surely, the more quickly, and the more severely will he reckon with them, if they by a course of wilful sin profane their character, disgrace their relation to him, violate their engagements, and put a slight upon the favours and honours with which they have been distinguished. *Therefore* they shall be punished, because their sins dishonour him, affront him, and grieve him, more than the sins of others, and because it is necessary that God should vindicate his own honour by making it appear that he hates sin and hates it most in those that are nearest to him; if they be but as bad as others, they shall be punished worse than others, because it is justly expected that they should be so much better than others. *Judgment begins at the house of God,* begins at the sanctuary; for God will be sanctified either by or upon those that *come nigh unto him,* Lev. x. 3.

II. Let them know that they could not expect any comfortable communion with God unless they first made their peace with him (*v.* 3): *Can two walk together except they be agreed?* No; how should they? Where there is not friendship there can be no fellowship; if two persons be at variance, they must first accommodate the matters in difference between them before there can be any interchanging of good offices. Israel had affronted God, had broken their covenant with him, and ill-requited his favours to them; and yet they expected that he should continue to walk with them, should take their part, act for them, and give them assurances of his presence with them, though they took no care by repentance and reformation to *agree with their adversary* and to turn
1234

away his wrath. "But how can that be?" says God. "While you continue to *walk contrary to God* you can look for no other than that he should *walk contrary to you,*" Lev. xxvi. 23, 24. Note, We cannot expect that God should be present with us, or act for us, unless we be reconciled to him. God and man cannot *walk together except they be agreed.* Unless we agree with God in our end, which is his glory, we cannot walk with him by the way.

III. Let them know that the warnings God gave them of judgments approaching were not causeless and groundless, merely to amuse them, but certain declarations of the wrath of God against them, which (if they did not speedily repent) they would infallibly feel the effects of (*v.* 4): "*Will a lion roar in the forest when he has no prey* in view? No; he roars upon his prey. Nor will a *young lion cry out of his den* if the old lion *have taken nothing* to bring home to him; nor would God thus give you warning both by the threatenings of his word, and by less judgments, if you had not by your sins made yourselves a prey to his wrath, nor if he were not really about to fall upon you with desolating destroying judgments." Note, The threatenings of the word and providence of God are not bugbears, to frighten children and fools, but are certain inferences from the sin of man and certain presages of the judgments of God.

IV. Let them know that, as their own wickedness was the procuring cause of these judgments, so they shall not be removed till they have done their work, *v.* 5. When God has come forth to contend with a sinful people it is necessary that they should understand, 1. That it is their own sin that has entangled them; for *can a bird fall in a snare upon the earth where no gin is for him?* No, nature does not lay snares for the creatures, but the art of men; a bird is not taken in a snare by chance, but with the fowler's design; so the providence of God prepares trouble for sinners, and it is *in the work of their own hands* that they *are snared.* Affliction does not *spring out of the dust,* but it is God's justice, and *our own wickedness,* that *correct us.* 2. It is nothing but their own repentance that can disentangle them; for *shall one take up a snare from the earth,* which he laid with design, except he have *taken something* as he designed? So neither will God remove the affliction he has sent till it have done its work and accomplished that for which he sent it. If our hearts be duly humbled, and we are brought by our afflictions to confess and forsake our sins, then the snare has taken something, then the point is gained, the end is answered, and then, and not till then, the *snare is broken,* is taken up from the earth, and *we are delivered* in love and mercy.

V. Let them know that all their troubles came from the hand of God's providence and from the counsel of his will (*v.* 6): *Shall there be evil in a city*, in a family, in a nation, *and the Lord has not done it*, appointed it, and performed what he appointed? The evil of sin is from ourselves; it is our own doing. But the evil of trouble, personal or public, is from God, and is his doing; whoever are the instruments, God is the principal agent. *Out of his mouth both evil and good proceed.* This consideration, that, whatever evil is in the city, the Lord has done it, should engage us patiently to bear our share in public calamities and to study to answer God's intention in them.

VI. Let them know that their prophets, who give them warning of judgments approaching, deliver nothing to them but what they have *received from the Lord* to be delivered to his people. 1. God makes it known beforehand to the prophets (*v.* 7): *Surely the Lord Jehovah will do nothing*, none of that evil in the city spoken of (*v.* 6), *but he reveals it to his servants the prophets*, though to others it is a secret. Therefore those know not what they do who make light of the warnings which the prophets give them, in God's name. Observe, God's prophets are *his servants*, whom he employs to go on his errands to the children of men. The *secret* of God is with them; it is in some sense with all *the righteous* (Prov. iii. 32), with *all that fear God* (Ps. xxv. 14), but in a peculiar manner with the prophets, to whom the Spirit of prophecy is a Spirit of revelation. It would have put honour enough upon prophets if it had been only said that sometimes God is pleased to reveal to his prophets what he designs to do, but it speaks something very great to say that he *does nothing* but what he *reveals to them*, as if they were *the men of his counsel. Shall I hide from Abraham, who is a prophet, the thing which I do?* Gen. xviii. 17. God will therefore be sure to reckon with those who put contempt on the prophets, whom he puts this honour upon. 2. The prophets cannot but make that known to the people which God has made known to them (*v.* 8): *The Lord God has spoken; who can but prophesy?* His prophets, to whom he has spoken in secret by dreams and visions, cannot but speak in public to the people what they have heard from God. They are so full of those things themselves, so well assured concerning them, and so much affected with them, that they cannot but speak of them; for *out of the abundance of the heart* the mouth will speak. *I believed; therefore have I spoken*, Acts iv. 20. Nay, and besides the prophetic impulse which went along with the inspiration, and made the word *like a fire in their bones* (Jer. xx. 9), they received a command from God to deliver what they had been charged with; and they would have been false to their trust if they had not done it. *Necessity was laid upon them*, as upon the preachers of the gospel, 1 Cor. ix. 16.

VII. Let them know that they ought to tremble before God upon the fair warning he had given them, as they would, 1. Upon the sounding of a trumpet, to give notice of the approach of the enemy, that all may stand upon their guard and stand to their arms: *Shall a trumpet be blown in the city, and the people not be afraid*, or *run together?* so some read it, *v.* 6. Will they not immediately come together in a fright, to consider what is best to be done for the common safety? Yet when God by his prophets gives them notice of their danger, and summons them to come and enlist themselves under his banner, it makes no impression; they will sooner give credit to a watchman on their walls than to a prophet sent of God, will sooner obey the summons of the governor of their city than the orders given them by the Governor of the world. God says, *Hearken to the voice of the trumpet;* but *they will not hearken*, nay, and they tell him plainly that they will not, Jer. vi. 17. 2. Upon the roaring of a lion. God is sometimes *as a lion, and a young lion, to the house of Judah*, Hos. v. 14. The lion roars before he tears; thus God warns before he wounds. If therefore the lion roars upon a poor traveller (as he did against Samson, Judg. xiv. 5), he cannot but be put into great consternation; yet the *Lord roars out of Zion* (*ch.* i. 2), and none are afraid, but they go on securely as if they were in no danger. Note, The fair warning given to a careless world, if it be not taken, will aggravate its condemnation another day. The lion roared, and they were not moved with fear to prepare an ark. O the amazing stupidity of an unbelieving world, that will not be wrought upon, no, not by the *terrors of the Lord!*

9 Publish in the palaces at Ashdod, and in the palaces in the land of Egypt, and say, Assemble yourselves upon the mountains of Samaria, and behold the great tumults in the midst thereof, and the oppressed in the midst thereof. 10 For they know not to do right, saith the LORD, who store up violence and robbery in their palaces. 11 Therefore thus saith the Lord GOD; An adversary *there shall be* even round about the land; and he shall bring down thy strength from thee, and thy palaces shall be spoiled. 12 Thus saith the LORD; As the shepherd taketh out of the mouth of the lion two legs, or a piece of an ear; so shall the children of Israel be taken out that dwell in Samaria in the corner of a bed, and in Damascus in a couch. 13 Hear ye, and testify in the house of Jacob, saith the Lord

GOD, the God of hosts, 14 That in the day that I shall visit the transgressions of Israel upon him, I will also visit the altars of Beth-el: and the horns of the altar shall be cut off, and fall to the ground. 15 And I will smite the winter-house with the summer-house; and the houses of ivory shall perish, and the great houses shall have an end, saith the LORD.

The Israelites are here again convicted and condemned, and particular notice given of the crimes they are convicted of and the punishment they are condemned to.

I. Notice is given of it to their neighbours. The prophet is ordered to *publish it in the palaces of Ashdod,* one of the chief cities of the Philistines; nay, the summons must go further, even to *the palaces in the land of Egypt.* "The great men of both those nations, that dwell in the palaces, that are inquisitive concerning the affairs of the neighbouring nations, and are conversant with the public intelligence, let them *assemble themselves upon the mountains of Samaria,*" v. 9. There, upon *a throne high and lifted up,* the judgment is set. Samaria is the criminal that is to be tried; let them be present at the trial, for it shall be (as other trials are) public, in the face of the country; let them make an appointment to meet there from all parts, to judge between God and his vineyard. God appeals to all impartial righteous men, Ezek. xxiii. 45. They will all subscribe to the equity of his proceedings when they see how the case stands. Note, God's controversies with sinners do not fear a scrutiny; even Philistines and Egyptians will be made to see, and say, that *the ways of the Lord are equal,* but *our ways are unequal.* They are likewise summoned to attend, not only that they may justify God and be witnesses for him that he deals fairly, but that they may themselves take warning; for, if *judgment begin at the house of God,* as they see it does, what shall be the end of those that are strangers to him? 1 Pet. iv. 17. *If this be done in a green tree, what shall be done in a dry?* Or this intimates that the sin of Israel had been so notorious that the neighbouring nations could come in witnesses against them, and therefore it was fit that their punishment should be so. "If it could have been concealed, we would have said, *Tell it not in Gath; publish it not in the streets of Ashkelon;*" but why should their friends consult their reputation, when they themselves do not consult it? If they have grown impudent in sin, let them bear the shame: "*Publish* it in *Ashdod,* in *Egypt.*"

1. Let them see how black the charge is, and how well proved. Let them observe the behaviour of the inhabitants of Samaria; let them look off from the adjacent hills, and they may see how rude and boisterous they are, and hear how loud the cry of their sin is, as was that of Sodom. (1.) Look into their streets and you will see nothing but riot and disorder, *great tumults in the midst thereof;* reason and justice are upon all occasions run down by the noise and fury of an outrageous mob, the dominion of which is the sin and shame of any people, and is likely to be their ruin. (2.) Look into their prisons, and you will see them filled with injured innocents: *The oppressed* are *in the midst thereof,* thrown down and crushed by their oppressors, overpowered and overwhelmed, and *they had no comforter,* Eccl. iv. 1. (3.) Look into their courts of justice, and you will see that those who preside in those courts *know not to do right,* because they have always been accustomed to do wrong; they act as if they had no notion at all of the thing called justice, are in no care to do justice themselves nor to see that others do justice. (4.) Look into their treasures and stores, and you will see them replenished with *violence and robbery,* with that which was unjustly got and is still unjustly kept. Thus *they have heaped treasures together for the last days,* but it will prove a *treasure of wrath against the day of wrath.* It may well be said, Those *know not to do right* who think to enrich themselves by doing wrong.

2. Let them see how heavy the doom is, and how well executed, v. 11, 12.

(1.) Their country shall be invaded and ruined; and observe how the punishment answers to the sin. [1.] *Great tumults* are *in the midst of the land,* and therefore *an adversary shall be even round about the land;* the Assyrian forces shall surround it and break in upon it on every side. Note, When sin is harboured and indulged in the midst of a people they can expect no other than that adversaries should be round about them, so that, go which way they will, they go into the mouth of danger, Luke xix. 43. [2.] They strengthened themselves in their wickedness, but the enemy shall *bring down their strength* from them, that strength which they abused in oppressing the poor, and doing violence to all about them. Note, That power which is made an instrument of unrighteousness will justly be brought down and broken. [3.] They *stored up robbery in their palaces,* and therefore their *palaces shall be spoiled;* for what is got and kept wrongfully will not be kept long. Even palaces will be no protection to fraud and oppression; but the greatest of men, if they have spoiled others, shall themselves be spoiled, for *the Lord is the avenger of all such.*

(2.) Their countrymen shall not escape, v. 12. They shall be in the hands of the enemy, as a lamb in the mouth of a lion, all devoured and eaten up, and they shall be utterly unable to make any resistance; and if any do make their escape, so as neither to fall by the sword nor go into captivity, yet they shall be very few, and those of the meanest and least considerable, like *two legs,* or *shanks,* of a lamb, *or,* it may be, *a piece of an ear,* which the lion drops, or *the shepherd* takes from him, when he has eaten the whole body; so, perhaps, here and there one may escape from Samaria and from Damascus, when the king of Assyria shall fall upon them both, but none to make any account of; and those that do escape shall do so with the utmost difficulty and hazard, by hiding themselves in the *corner of a bed* or under the *bed's feet,* which intimates that their spirits shall be quite cowed and broken, and they shall sneak shamefully in the time of danger. They shall not hide themselves in dens and caves, but in the *corner of a bed,* or the *piece of a bed,* such as poor people must be content with. They shall very narrowly escape, as it is foretold concerning the last destruction of Jerusalem that there shall be *two in a bed together, one taken and the other left.* Note, When God's judgments come forth against a people with commission it will be in vain to think of escaping them. Some make their *dwelling in the corner of a bed,* and *in a couch,* to denote their present security and sensuality; they are at ease, as *in a bed,* or *on a couch,* but, when God comes to contend with them, he shall make them uneasy, shall take them away out of the bed of their sloth and slumber. Those that stretch themselves lazily upon their couches when God's judgments are abroad shall *go captive with the first that go captive.*

II. Notice is given of it to themselves, *v.* 13. Let this be *testified,* and *heard, in the house of Jacob,* among all the seed of Israel, for it is spoken *by the Lord God, the God of hosts,* who has authority to pass this sentence and ability to execute it; let them know from him that the day is at hand when God will *visit the transgressions of Israel upon him,* when he will enquire into them and reckon for them: there will come *a day of visitation,* a day of punishment, and in that day all those things they are proud of, and put confidence in, shall fail them, and so they shall smart for the sins they have been guilty of about them. 1. Woe to *their altars,* for God will *visit* them. He will enquire into the sins they have been guilty of at their altars, and bring into the account all their superstition and idolatry, all their expenses on their false gods, and all their expectations from them; and he will lay the altars themselves under the marks of his displeasure, *for the horns of the altar shall be cut off,* and *fall to the ground,* and with them the altar itself demolished and broken to pieces. We find the altar at Bethel prophesied against (1 Kings xiii. 2), and immediately *rent* (*v.* 3), and that prophecy fulfilled when *Josiah burnt men's bones upon it,* 2 Kings xxiii. 15, 16. This seconds that prophecy, and seems to point at the same event. Note, If men will not destroy idolatrous altars, God will, and those with them that had them in veneration. Some make *the horns of the altar* to signify all those things which they flee to for refuge, and trust in, and which they make their sanctuary: they shall all be cut off, so that they shall have nothing to take hold of. 2. Woe to their houses, for God will visit them too. He will enquire into the sins they have been guilty of in their houses, the robbery they have stored up in their houses, and the luxury in which they lived: *and I will smite the winter-house with the summer-house, v.* 15. Their nobility, and gentry, and rich merchants, had their winter-houses in the city and their summer-houses in the country, so nice were they in guarding against the inconveniences of the winter when the country was thought too cold, and of the summer when the city was thought too hot, though the climate of that good land was so temperate, like that of ours, that neither the cold nor heat was ever in extremity. They indulged a foolish affectation of change and variety; but God will, either by war or by the earthquake, smite both the winter-house and the summer-house; neither shall serve to shelter them from his judgments. *The houses of ivory* (so called because the ceiling, or wainscot, or some of the ornaments of them, were edged or inlaid with ivory) *shall perish,* shall be burnt or pulled down; *and the great houses shall have an end;* the most splendid and spacious houses, the houses of their great men, shall no longer be, or at least be no longer theirs. Note, The pomp or pleasantness of men's houses will be so far from fortifying them against God's judgments that it will make them the more grievous and vexatious, as their extravagance about them will be put to the score of their sins and follies.

CHAP. IV.

In this chapter, I. The oppressors in Israel are threatened for their oppression of the poor, ver. 1—3. II. The idolaters in Israel, being joined to idols, are given up to their own heart's lusts, ver. 4, 5. III. All the sins of Israel are aggravated from their incorrigibleness in them, and their refusal to return and reform, notwithstanding the various rebukes of Providence which they had been under, ver. 6—11. IV. They are invited yet at length to humble themselves before God, since it is impossible for them to make their part good against him, ver. 12, 13.

HEAR this word, ye kine of Bashan, that *are* in the mountain of Samaria, which oppress the poor, which crush the needy, which say to their masters, Bring, and let us drink. 2 The Lord GOD hath sworn by his holiness, that, lo, the days shall come upon you, that he will take you away with hooks, and your posterity with fish-hooks. 3 And ye shall go out at the breaches, every *cow at that which is* before her; and ye shall cast *them* into the palace, saith the LORD.

4 Come to Beth-el, and transgress; at Gilgal multiply transgression; and bring your sacrifices every morning, *and* your tithes after three years : 5 And offer a sacrifice of thanksgiving with leaven, and proclaim *and* publish the free-offerings : for this liketh you, O ye children of Israel, saith the Lord GOD.

It is here foretold, in the name of God, that oppressors shall be humbled and idolaters shall be hardened.

I. That proud oppressors shall be humbled for their oppressions ; for *he that does wrong shall receive according to the wrong that he has done.* Now observe,

1. How their sin is described, *v.* 1. They are compared to the *kine of Bashan,* which were a breed of cattle very large and strong, especially if, though bred there, they were fed upon *the mountain of Samaria,* where the pastures were extraordinarily fat. Amos had been a herdsman, and he speaks in the dialect of his calling, comparing the rich and great men, that lived in luxury and wantonness, to the *kine of Bashan,* which were wanton and unruly, would not be kept within the bounds of their own pasture, but broke through the hedges, broke down all the fences, and trespassed upon the neighbouring grounds ; and not only so, but pushed and gored the smaller cattle that were not a match for them. Those that had their summer-houses upon the mountains of Samaria when they went thither for fresh air were as mischievous as the kine upon the mountains of Bashan and as injurious to those about them. (1.) They oppress the poor and needy themselves; they *crush* them, to squeeze something to themselves out of them. They took advantage of their poverty, and necessity, and inability to help themselves, to make them poorer and more necessitous than they were. They made use of their power as judges and magistrates for the invading of men's rights and properties, the poor not excepted; for they made no conscience of robbing even the hospital. (2.) They are in confederacy with those that do so. They *say to their masters* (to the masters of the poor, that abuse them and violently take from them what they have, when they ought to relieve them), " *Bring, and let us drink;* let us feast with you upon the gains of your oppression, and then we will protect you, and stand by you in it, and reject the appeals of the poor against you." Note, What is got by extortion is commonly made use of as *provision for the flesh, to fulfil the lusts thereof;* and *therefore* men are tyrants to the poor because they are slaves to their appetites. *Bring, and let us drink,* is the language of those that *crush the needy,* as if the *tears of the oppressed,* mingled with their wine, made it drink the better. And
1238

by their associations for drinking and revelling, and an excess of riot, they strengthen their combinations for persecution and oppression, and harden the hearts of one another in it.

2. How their punishment is described, *v.* 2, 3. God will *take them away with hooks, and their posterity with fish-hooks;* he will send the Assyrian army upon them, that shall make a prey of them, shall not only enclose the body of the nation in their net, but shall angle for particular persons, and take them prisoners and captives as with hooks and fish-hooks, shall draw them out of their own land as fish are drawn out of the water, which is their element, them and their children with them, or, They in their day shall be drawn out by one victorious enemy, and their posterity in their day by another, so that by a succession of destroying judgments they shall at length be wholly extirpated. These *kine of Bashan* thought they could no more be drawn out with a hook and a cord than the Leviathan can, Job xli. 1, 2. But God will make them know that he has a *hook for their nose* and a *bridle for their jaws,* Isa. xxxvii. 29. The enemy shall take them away as easily as the fisherman takes away the little fish, and shall make it their sport and recreation. When the enemy has made himself master of Samaria, then, (1.) Some shall attempt to escape by flight : *You shall go out at the breaches* made in the wall of the city, *every cow at that which is before her,* to shift for her own safety, and make the best of her way; and now the unruly kine of Bashan are tamed, and are themselves crushed, as they crushed the poor and needy. Note, Those to whom God has given a good pasture, if they are wanton in it, will justly be turned out of it; and those who will not be kept within the hedge of God's precept forfeit the benefit of the hedge of God's protection, and will be forced in vain to flee through the breaches they have themselves fearfully made in that hedge. (2.) Others shall think to shelter themselves, or at least their best effects, in the palace, because it is a castle well fortified and a garrison well manned : *You shall throw yourselves* (so some read it), or *throw them* (that is, your posterity, your children, or whatever is dear to you), *into the palace,* where the enemy will find it ready to be seized. Note, What is got by oppression cannot long be enjoyed with satisfaction.

3. How their sentence to this punishment is ratified : *The Lord God has sworn it by his holiness.* He had often said it, and they regarded it not; they thought God and his prophets did but jest with them; therefore he *swears* it *in his wrath,* and what he has sworn he will not revoke. He swears by *his holiness,* that attribute of his which is so much his glory, and which is so much glorified in the punishment of wicked people; for, as sure as God is a holy God, those that *plough*

iniquity and sow wickedness shall reap the same.

II. That obstinate idolaters shall be hardened in their idolatries (*v.* 4, 5): *Come to Bethel, and transgress.* It is spoken ironically: " Do so; take your course; *multiply* your *transgressions* by multiplying your sacrifices, *for this liketh you;* but what will you do in the end hereof?" Here we see, 1. How intent they were upon the service of their idols, and how willing they were to be at cost upon them; they *brought their sacrifices,* and their *tithes,* and their *free-will offerings,* hoping that therein they should be accepted of God, but it was all an abomination to him. The profuseness of idolaters in the service of their false gods may shame our strait-handedness in the service of the true and living God. 2. How they mimicked God's institutions. They had their *daily sacrifice* at the altar of Bethel, as God had at his altar; they had their *thank-offerings* as God had, only they allowed *leaven* in them, which God had forbidden, because their priests did not like to have the bread so heavy and tasteless as it would be if it had not leaven in it, or something to ferment it. Holy bread would not serve them, unless it were pleasant bread. 3. How well pleased they were with these services themselves: *This liketh you, O you children of Israel! So you love.* What was their own invention they were fond of and wedded to, and thought it must be pleasing to God because it was agreeable to their own fancy. 4. How they are upbraided with it: " *Come to Bethel, to Gilgal; bring the sacrifices* and *tithes* yourselves; *proclaim* and *publish* to the nation the *free-offerings,* pressing them to bring in abundance of such; *go on* in this way;" that is, (1.) " It is plain that you are resolved to do it, whatever God and conscience say to the contrary." (2.) " Your prophets shall let you alone in it, and not admonish you as they have done, for it is to no purpose. *Let no man strive nor rebuke his neighbour.*" (3.) " Your foolish hearts shall be more and more darkened and besotted, and you shall be quite *given up to* these *strong delusions, to believe a lie.*" (4.) " What will you get by it? *Come to Bethel* and *multiply* your *sacrifices,* and see what the better you will be, what returns you will have to your sacrifices, what stead they will stand you in in the day of distress. *You shall be ashamed of Bethel your confidence,*" Jer. xlviii. 13. (5.) " *Come, and transgress,* come, and *multiply your transgression,* that you may *fill up the measure* of your iniquity and be ripened for ruin." Thus Christ said to Judas, *What thou doest do quickly;* and to the Jews, *Fill you up the measure of your fathers,* Matt. xxiii. 32.

6 And I also have given you cleanness of teeth in all your cities, and want of bread in all your places: yet have ye not returned unto me, saith the LORD. 7 And also I have withholden the rain from you, when *there were* yet three months to the harvest: and I caused it to rain upon one city, and caused it not to rain upon another city: one piece was rained upon, and the piece whereupon it rained not withered. 8 So two *or* three cities wandered unto one city, to drink water; but they were not satisfied: yet have ye not returned unto me, saith the LORD. 9 I have smitten you with blasting and mildew: when your gardens and your vineyards and your fig-trees and your olive-trees increased, the palmer-worm devoured *them:* yet have ye not returned unto me, saith the LORD. 10 I have sent among you the pestilence after the manner of Egypt: your young men have I slain with the sword, and have taken away your horses; and I have made the stink of your camps to come up unto your nostrils: yet have ye not returned unto me, saith the LORD. 11 I have overthrown *some* of you, as God overthrew Sodom and Gomorrah, and ye were as a firebrand plucked out of the burning: yet have ye not returned unto me, saith the LORD. 12 Therefore thus will I do unto thee, O Israel: *and* because I will do this unto thee, prepare to meet thy God, O Israel. 13 For, lo, he that formeth the mountains, and createth the wind, and declareth unto man what *is* his thought, that maketh the morning darkness, and treadeth upon the high places of the earth, The LORD, The God of Hosts, *is* his name.

Here, I. God complains of his people's incorrigibleness under the judgments which he had brought upon them in order to their humiliation and reformation. He had by several tokens intimated to them his displeasure, with this design, that they might by repentance make their peace with him; but it had not that effect.

1. It is five times repeated in these verses, as the burden of the charge, " *Yet have you not returned unto me, saith the Lord:* you have been several times corrected, but in vain; you are not reclaimed, there is no sign of amendment. You have been sent for by one messenger after another, but you have

not come back, you have not come home." (1.) This intimates that that which God designed in all his providential rebukes was to reduce them to their allegiance, to influence them to return to him. (2.) That, if they had returned to their God, they would have been accepted, he would have bidden them welcome, and the troubles they were in would have been removed. (3.) That the reason why God sent further troubles was because former troubles had not done the work, otherwise it is *no pleasure to the Almighty that he should afflict.* (4.) That God was grieved at their obstinacy, and took it unkindly that they should force him to do that which he did so unwillingly : " *You have not returned to me* from whom you have revolted, *to me* with whom you are in covenant, *to me* who stand ready to receive you, *to me* who have so often called you." Now,

2. To aggravate their incorrigibleness, and to justify himself in inflicting greater judgments, he recounts the less judgments with which he had tried to bring them to repentance.

(1.) There had sometimes been a scarcity of provisions, though there was no visible cause of it (*v.* 6) : " *I have given you cleanness of teeth in all your cities,* for you had no meat to chew, whereby your teeth might be fouled," especially no flesh, which dirties the teeth. Or, *I have given you emptiness of teeth,* nothing to fill your mouths with. " *Bread,* the staff of life, has been wanting, for you have *sown much* and *brought in little,*" as Hag. i. 9. Some think this refers to that *seven years' famine* that was in Elisha's time, which we read of 2 Kings viii. 1. Now when God thus *took away their corn in the season thereof,* because they had prepared it for Baal, they should have said, We will *go and return to our first husband,* having paid dearly for leaving him ; but it had not that effect. *They have not returned to me,* saith the Lord.

(2.) Sometimes they had wanted rain, and then of course they wanted the fruits of the earth. This evil was of the Lord : *I have withholden the rain from you.* God has the key of the clouds, and, if he shut up, who can open? *v.* 7. The rain was withheld *when there were yet three months to the harvest,* at the time when they used to have it, and therefore the withholding of it was an extraordinary thing, and, if the course of nature was altered, they must therein own the hand of the God of nature ; and it was at a time when they most needed it, and therefore the want of it was a very sore judgment, and blasted their expectations of a crop at harvest. And one circumstance which made this very remarkable was that when there were some places that wanted rain, and withered for want of it, there were other places near adjoining that had it in abundance. God *caused it to rain upon one city, and not upon another,* in the same

country ; nay, he caused it to rain *upon one field,* one *piece* of a field, and it was thereby made fruitful and flourishing, but on the next field, on the other side of the hedge, nay, on another part of the same field, *it rained not* at all, and it was so long without rain that all the products of it *withered.* No doubt this was literally true, and there were many instances of it which were generally taken notice of. Now, [1.] By this it appeared that the withholding of the rain was not casual, but by a divine direction and disposal, and that the cloud which waters the earth is *turned round about by the counsels of God, to do whatsoever he commands it, whether for correction, or for his land, or for mercy,* Job xxxvii. 12—18. Rain does not go by planets (as common people speak), but as God sends it by his winds. [2.] We have reason to think that those cities on which it rained not were the most infamous for wickedness, such as Bethel and Gilgal (*v.* 4), and that those on which it rained were such as retained something of religion and virtue among them. And so in the town-fields it rained or rained not, upon the piece, according as the owner was ; for we are sure *the curse of the Lord is in the house,* and upon the ground, *of the wicked, but he blesses the habitation of the just,* and his field is a *field that the Lord has blessed.* [3.] It would be the greater grief and vexation to those whose fields withered for want of rain to see their neighbours' fields well watered and flourishing. *My servants shall eat, but you shall be hungry,* Isa. lxv. 13. The *wicked shall see it, and be grieved.* Probably those that were oppressed were rained upon, and so they recovered their losses, while the oppressors withered, and so lost their gains. [4.] Yet, as to the nation in general, it was a mixture of mercy with the judgment, and, consequently, strengthened the call to repentance and reformation, and encouraged them to hope for all mercy, in their returns to God, since there was so much mercy even in God's rebukes of them. But, because they did not make a good use of this gracious allay to the extremity of the judgment, they had not the benefit of it, which otherwise they might have had, for (*v.* 8) *two or three cities wandered* at uncertainty, as beggars, *unto one city, to drink water,* and, if possible, to have some to carry home with them, but *they were not satisfied ;* it was but here and there one city that had water, while many wanted, and then it was not; as usual, *Usus communis aquarum—Water is free to all.* Those that had it had occasion for it, or knew not how soon they might, and therefore could afford but little to those that wanted, saying, *Lest there be not enough for us and you.* Those that came *drank water,* but *they were not satisfied,* because they drank it *by measure, and with astonishment ;* and those that *drink of this water shall thirst again,* John iv. 13. They were not satisfied, because their desires were greedy, and what they had God did not bless to them, Hag. i. 6. And now, one would think, when they met with all this disappointment, they should have considered their ways and repented; but it had not that effect: "*Yet have you not returned to me,* no, not so much as to pray in a right manner for the former and latter rain," Zech. x. 1. See the folly of carnal hearts; they will wander from city to city, from one creature to another, in pursuit of satisfaction, and still they miss of it; they *labour for that which satisfies not* (Isa. lv. 2), and yet, after all, they *will not return to God,* will not incline their ear to him in whom they might have satisfaction. The preaching of the gospel is as rain; God sometimes blesses one place with it more than another; some countries, some cities, are, like Gideon's fleece, wet with this dew, while the ground about is dry; all withers where this rain is wanting. But it were well if people were but as wise for their souls as they are for their bodies, and, when they have not this rain near them, would go and seek it where it is to be had; and, if they seek aright, they shall not seek in vain.

(3.) Sometimes the fruits of their ground were eaten up by caterpillars, or blasted with mildew, *v.* 9. Heaven and earth are armed against those who have made God their enemy. When God pleased, that is, when he was displeased, [1.] They suffered by a malignant air, the influence of which, either too hot or too cold, blasted their fruits, with a force that could be neither discerned nor resisted, and against which there was no defence. [2.] They suffered by malignant animals. Their *vineyards* and *gardens* yielded their increase in great abundance, so did their *fig-trees* and *olive-trees;* but the *palmer-worm devoured them* before the fruits were ripe, and fit to be gathered in. This was either the same judgment with that which we read of Joel i. 4—6, or a less judgment of the same nature, sent before to give warning of that. But they did not take warning: *Yet have you not returned unto me.*

(4.) Sometimes the plague had raged among them, and the sword of war had cut off multitudes, *v.* 10. *The pestilence* is God's messenger; this he *sent among* them, with directions whom to strike dead, and it was done. It was a *pestilence after the manner of Egypt;* deaths were scattered among them by the hand of a *destroying angel at midnight.* And perhaps this pestilence, as that of Egypt, fastened upon the first-born. *In the way of Egypt* (so the margin); when they were making their escape to Egypt, or going thither to seek for aid, the pestilence seized them by the way and stopped their journey. The sword of war is likewise *the sword of the Lord;* this was drawn among them with commission; and then it *slew their young men,* the strength of the present generation and the seed of the next. God

says, *I have slain them;* he avows the execution. *The slain of the Lord are many.* The enemy *took away their horses,* and converted them to their own use; and the dead carcases of those that were slain either with sword or pestilence were so many, and for want of surviving friends were left so long unburied, that the *stench of their camps came up into their nostrils,* and was both noisome and dangerous, and might put them in mind of the offensiveness of their sin to God. And yet this did not prevail to humble and reclaim them: *You have not returned to* him that smites you. Such a rueful woeful sight as this prevailed not to make them religious.

(5.) In these and other judgments some were remarkably cut off, and made monuments of justice, others were remarkably spared, and made monuments of mercy, the setting of which the one over against the other one would have thought likely to work upon them, but it had not its effect, *v.* 11. [1.] Some were quite ruined, their families destroyed, and themselves in them: *I have overthrown some of you, as God overthrew Sodom and Gomorrah.* Perhaps they were consumed with lightning, as Sodom was, or the houses were, in some other way, burnt to the ground, and the inhabitants in them. Sodom and Gomorrah are said to be *condemned with an overthrow, and so made an example,* 2 Pet. ii. 6. God had threatened to destroy the whole land with such an overthrow as that of Sodom, Deut. xxix. 23. But he began with some particular places first, to give them warning, or perhaps with some particular persons, whose *sins went beforehand to judgment.* [2.] Others very narrowly escaped: "You *were* many of you as a *firebrand plucked out of the burning,* like Lot out of Sodom, when the fire had already kindled upon you; and yet you hate sin never the more for the danger it has brought you to, nor love God ever the more for the deliverance he wrought for you. You that have been so signally delivered, and in such a distinguishing way, *have not returned unto me.*

II. God, in the close, calls upon his people, now at length, in this their day, to understand the things that belong to their peace, before they were hidden from their eyes, *v.* 12, 13. Observe here,

1. How God threatens them with sorer judgments than any they had yet been under: "Therefore, seeing you have not been wrought upon by correction hitherto, *thus will I do unto thee, O Israel!*" He does not say how he will do, but it shall be something worse than had come yet, John v. 14. Or, "*Thus I will* go on to *do unto thee,* following one judgment with another, like the plagues of Egypt, till I have made a full end." Nothing but reformation will prevent the ruin of a sinful people. If they turn not to him, his anger is not *turned away,* but *his hand is stretched out still. I will punish you yet seven times more, if you will*

not be reformed; so it was written in the law, Lev. xxvi. 23, 24.

2. How he awakens them therefore to think of making their peace with God : " *Seeing I will do this unto thee*, and there is no remedy, *prepare to meet thy God, O Israel !*" that is, (1.) " Consider how unable thou art to meet him as a combatant." Some make it to be spoken by way of irony or challenge : " Prepare to meet God, who is coming forth to contend with thee. What armour of proof canst thou put on ? What courage canst thou steel thyself with? Alas ! it is but putting *briers and thorns* before a consuming fire, Isa. xxvii. 4, 5. Art thou able with less than 10,000 to meet him that comes forth against thee with more than 20,000 ?" Luke xiv. 31. (2.) " Resolve therefore to meet him as a penitent, as a humble suppliant, to meet him as *thy God*, in covenant with thee, to submit, and stand it out no longer." We must prepare to *meet God in the way of his judgments* (Isa. xxvi. 8), to *take hold on his strength, that we may make peace*. Note, Since we cannot flee from God we are concerned to prepare to meet him ; and therefore he gives us warning, that we may prepare. When we are to meet him in his ordinances we must prepare to meet him, prepare to seek him.

3. How he sets forth the greatness and power of God as a reason why we should prepare to meet him, v. 13. If he be such a God as he is here described to be, it is folly to contend with him, and our duty and interest to make our peace with him ; it is good having him our friend and bad having him our enemy. (1.) He *formed the mountains*, made the earth, the strongest stateliest parts of it, and by the word of his power still upholds it and them. Whatever are the products of the everlasting mountains, he formed them ; whatever *salvation* is *hoped for from hills and mountains*, he is the founder of it, Ps. lxxxix. 11, 12. He that formed the *great mountains* can *make them plain*, when they stand in the way of his people's salvation. (2.) He *creates the wind*. The power of the air is derived from him, and directed by him ; he brings the wind out of his treasures, and orders from what point of the compass it shall blow ; and he that made it rules it ; even *the winds and the seas obey him*. (3.) He *declares unto man what is his thought*. He makes known his counsel by his servants the prophets to the children of men, the thought of his justice against impenitent sinners, and the thought of good he thinks towards those that repent. He can also make known, for he perfectly knows, the thought that is in man's heart ; he *understands it afar off*, and in the day of conviction will set the evil thoughts among the other sins of sinners *in order before them*. (4.) He often *makes the morning darkness*, by thick clouds overspreading the sky immediately after the sun rose bright and glori-

ous ; so when we look for prosperity and joy he can dash our expectations with some unlooked-for calamity. (5.) He *treads upon the high places of the earth*, is not only higher than the highest, but has dominion over all, tramples upon proud men, and upon the idols that were worshipped in the highest places. (6.) *Jehovah the God of hosts is his name*, for he has his being of himself, and is the fountain of all being, and all the hosts of heaven and earth are at his command. Let us humble ourselves before this God, prepare to meet him, and give all diligence to make him our God, for happy are the people whose God he is, who have all this power engaged for them.

CHAP. V.

The scope of this chapter is to prosecute the exhortation given to Israel in the close of the foregoing chapter to prepare to meet their God ; the prophet here tells them, I. What preparation they must make ; they must " seek the Lord," and not seek any more to idols (ver. 4—8) ; they must seek good, and love it, ver. 14, 15. II. Why they must make this preparation to meet their God. 1. Because of the present deplorable condition they were in, ver. 1— 3. 2. Because it was by sin that they were brought into such a condition, ver. 7, 10—12. 3. Because it would be their happiness to seek God, and he was ready to be found of them, ver. 8, 9, 14. 4. Because he would proceed, in his wrath, to their utter ruin, if they did not seek him, ver. 5, 6, 13, 16, 17. 5. Because all their confidences would fail them if they did not seek unto God, and make him their friend. (1.) Their profane contempt of God's judgments, and setting them at defiance, would not secure them, ver. 18—20. (2.) Their external services in religion, and the shows of devotion, would not avail to turn away the wrath of God, ver. 21 —24. (3.) Their having been long in possession of church-privileges, and in a course of holy duties, would not be their protection, while all along they had kept up their idolatrous customs, ver. 25 —27. They have therefore no way left them to save themselves, but by repentance and reformation.

HEAR ye this word which I take up against you, *even* a lamentation, O house of Israel. 2 The virgin of Israel is fallen ; she shall no more rise : she is forsaken upon her land ; *there is* none to raise her up. 3 For thus saith the Lord God ; The city that went out *by* a thousand shall leave a hundred, and that which went forth *by* a hundred shall leave ten, to the house of Israel.

This chapter begins, as those two next foregoing began, with, *Hear this word*. Where God has a mouth to speak we must have an ear to hear ; it is our duty, it is our interest ; yet so stupid are most men that they need to be again and again called upon to *hear the word of the Lord*, to give audience, to give attention. *Hear this word*. This convincing awakening word must be heard and heeded, as well as words of comfort and peace ; the word that is taken up against us, as well as that which makes for us ; for, whether we hear or forbear, the word of God shall take effect, and not a tittle of it shall fall to the ground. It is the *word which I take up*—not the prophet only, but the God that sent him. It is the *word that the Lord has spoken, ch.* iii. 1. The word to be heard is *a lamentation*, a lamentable account of the present calamitous state of the kingdom of Israel, and a lamentable prediction of its utter destruction. Their condition is sad: *The virgin of Israel has fallen* (*v.* 2), has come down from what she was; that state, though not pure and chaste as a virgin, yet was beautiful and gay, and had its charms; she looked high herself, and was courted by many as a virgin; but *she has fallen* into contempt and poverty, and is universally slighted. Nay, and their condition is helpless: *She shall no more rise,* shall never recover her former dignity again. God had lately begun to *cut Israel short* (2 Kings x. 32), and, because they repented not, it was not long before he *cut Israel down.* 1. Their princes, that should have helped them up, were disabled: *She is forsaken upon her land.* Not only those she was in alliance with abroad failed her, but her friends at home deserted her; she would not have been carried captive into a strange land if she had not first been *forsaken upon her own land* and *thrown to the ground* there, and all her true interests abandoned by those that should have had them at heart. *There is none to raise her up,* none that can do it, none that cares to lend her a hand. 2. Their people, that should have helped them up, were diminished, *v.* 3. "The city that had a militia, 1000 strong, and, in the beginning of the war, had furnished out 1000 effective men, able-bodied and well-armed, when they come to review their troops after the battle, shall find but 100 *left;* and, in proportion, the city that sent out 100 shall have but *ten* come back, so great a slaughter shall be made, and so few left to the house of Israel for the public service and safety. Scarcely one in ten shall escape of the hands that should relieve this abject, this dejected, nation. Note, The lessening of the numbers of God's spiritual Israel, by death or desertion, is just matter for lamentation; for *by whom shall Jacob arise,* by whom shall the decays of piety be repaired, when he is thus *made small?*

4 For thus saith the LORD unto the house of Israel, Seek ye me, and ye shall live: 5 But seek not Beth-el, nor enter into Gilgal, and pass not to Beer-sheba: for Gilgal shall surely go into captivity, and Beth-el shall come to nought. 6 Seek the LORD, and ye shall live; lest he break out like fire in the house of Joseph, and devour *it,* and *there be* none to quench *it* in Beth-el. 7 Ye who turn judgment to wormwood, and leave off righteousness in the earth, 8 *Seek him* that maketh the seven stars and Orion, and turneth the shadow of death into the morning, and maketh the day dark with night: that calleth for the waters of the sea, and poureth them out upon

the face of the earth: the LORD *is* his name: 9 That strengtheneth the spoiled against the strong, so that the spoiled shall come against the fortress. 10 They hate him that rebuketh in the gate, and they abhor him that speaketh uprightly. 11 Forasmuch therefore as your treading *is* upon the poor, and ye take from him burdens of wheat: ye have built houses of hewn stone, but ye shall not dwell in them; ye have planted pleasant vineyards, but ye shall not drink wine of them. 12 For I know your manifold transgressions and your mighty sins: they afflict the just, they take a bribe, and they turn aside the poor in the gate *from their right.* 13 Therefore the prudent shall keep silence in that time; for it *is* an evil time. 14 Seek good, and not evil, that ye may live: and so the LORD, the God of hosts, shall be with you, as ye have spoken. 15 Hate the evil, and love the good, and establish judgment in the gate: it may be that the LORD God of hosts will be gracious unto the remnant of Joseph.

This is a message from God to the house of Israel, in which,

I. They are told of their faults, that they might see what occasion there was for them to repent and reform, and that, when they were called to return, they might not need to ask, *Wherein shall we return?*

1. God tells them, in general (*v.* 12), " *I know your manifold transgressions, and your mighty sins;* and you shall be made to know them too." In our penitent reflections upon our sins we must consider, as God does in his judicial remarks upon them, and will do in the great day, (1.) That they are very numerous; they are our *manifold transgressions,* sins of various kinds and often repeated. Oh what a multitude of vain and vile thoughts lodge within us! What a multitude of idle, foolish, wicked words have been spoken by us! In what a multitude of instances have we gratified and indulged our corrupt appetites and passions! And how many are our omissions of duty and in duty! Who can understand his errors? Who can tell how often he offends? God knows how many, just how many, our transgressions are; none of them pass him unobserved; we know that they are to us innumerable, *more than the hairs of our head;* and we have reason to see what danger we have brought ourselves into, and what abundance of work we have made for repentance, by our

manifold transgressions, by the numberless number of our sins of daily incursion. (2.) That some of them are very heinous; they are *our mighty* sins; sins that are more exceedingly sinful in their own nature and by being committed presumptuously and with a high hand, sins against the light of nature, flagrant crimes, that are mighty to overpower your convictions and to pull down judgments upon you.

2. He specifies some of these mighty sins. (1.) They corrupted the worship of God, and turned to idols; this is implied *v.* 5. They had *sought to Bethel,* where one of the golden calves was; they had frequented Gilgal, a place which they chose to set up idols in, because it had been made famous in the days of Joshua by God's wonderful appearances to and for his people. Beer-sheba likewise, a place that had been famous in the days of the patriarchs, was now another rendezvous of idols; as we find also, *ch.* viii. 14. And thither *they passed,* though it lay at a distance, in the land of Judah. Now, having thus shamefully gone a whoring from God, no doubt they should have felt themselves concerned to return to him. (2.) They perverted justice among themselves (*v.* 7): " *You turn judgment to wormwood,* that is, you make your administrations of justice bitter and nauseous, and highly displeasing both to God and man." That fruit has become a *weed,* a weed in the garden; as nothing is more venerable, nothing more valuable, than justice duly administered, so nothing is more hurtful, nothing more abominable, than designedly doing wrong under colour and pretence of doing right. *Corruptio optimi est pessima*—*The best, when corrupted, becomes the worst.* " *You leave off righteousness in the earth,* as if those that do wrong were accountable to the God of heaven only, and not to the princes and *judges of the earth.*" Thus it was as before the flood, when the *earth was filled with violence.* (3.) They were very oppressive to the poor, and made them poorer; they trod upon the poor (*v.* 11), trampled upon them, hectored over them, made them their footstool, and were most imperious and barbarous to those that were most obsequious and submissive; they cared not what shame and slavery they put those to who were poor and such as they could get nothing by. The judges aimed at nothing but to enrich themselves; and therefore they *took from* the poor *burdens of wheat,* took it by extortion, either by way of bribe or by usury. The poor had no other way to save themselves from being trodden upon, and trodden to dirt, by them, than by presenting to them horse-loads of that corn which they and their families should have had to subsist upon, and they forced them to do it. They took from the poor *debts of wheat,* so some read it. It was legally due either for rent or for corn lent, but they exacted it with rigour from those who were disabled by the

1244

providence of God to pay it, as Neh. v. 2, 5. In demanding and recovering even a just debt we must take heed lest we act either unjustly or uncharitably. This sin of oppression they are again charged with (*v.* 12): *They afflict the just,* by turning the edge of the law and of the sword of justice against those that are the innocent and *quiet in the land;* they hated men because they were more righteous than themselves, and he that *departed from evil* thereby *made himself a prey* to them. They take a bribe from the rich to patronize and protect them in oppressing the poor, so that he who has money in his hand is sure to have the judgment on his side, be his cause ever so bad. Thus they *turn aside the poor in the gate,* in the courts of justice, *from their right.* If the poor sue for their right, who cannot bribe them, or are so honest that they will not, though they have it ever so clear in view and ever so *near,* yet they are turned away from it by their unrighteous sentence and cannot come at it. And *therefore the prudent will keep silence, v.* 13. Men will reckon it their prudence, when they are wronged and injured, to be silent, and make no complaints to the magistrates, for it will be to no purpose; they shall not have justice done them. (4.) They were malicious persecutors of God's faithful ministers and people, *v.* 10. Their hearts were so fully set in them to do evil that they could not bear to be reproved, [1.] By the ministry of the word, by the reading and expounding of the law, and the messages which the prophets delivered to them in the name of the Lord. *They hate him that rebukes in the gate,* in the gate of the Lord's house, or in their courts of justice, or in the places of concourse, where Wisdom is lifting up her voice, Prov. i. 21. Reprovers in the gate are reprovers by office; these they hated, counting them their *enemies because they told them the truth,* as Ahab hated Micaiah. They not only despised them, but had an enmity to them, and sought to do them mischief. Those that hate reproof love ruin. [2.] By the conversation of their honest neighbours. Though things were generally very bad, yet there were some among them that *spoke uprightly,* that made conscience of what they said, and, as it was their praise, so it was the shame of those that spoke deceitfully, and condemned them, as Noah's faith condemned the unbelief of the old world, and for that reason *they abhorred them;* they were such inveterate enemies to the thing called honesty that they could not endure the sight of an honest man. All that have any sense of the common interest of mankind will love and value such as speak uprightly, for veracity is the bond of human society; to what a pitch of folly and madness then have those arrived who, having banished all notions of justice out of their own hearts, would have them banished out of the world too, and so put mankind into a state of war, for they *abhor him that* speaks *uprightly!* And for this reason *the prudent shall keep silence in that time, v.* 13. Prophets cannot, dare not, keep silence; the impulse they are under will not allow them to act on prudential considerations; they must *cry aloud, and not spare.* But as for other wise and good men they shall keep silence, and shall reckon it is their prudence to do so, because it is an evil time. *First,* They shall think it dangerous to complain, and therefore shall keep silence; this was one way in which they afflicted the just, that by false suggestions and strained innuendos they made men *offenders for a word* (Isa. xix. 21); and therefore *the prudent,* who were *wise as serpents,* because they knew not how what they said might be misinterpreted and misrepresented, were so cautious as to say nothing, lest they should run themselves into a premunire, because it was an evil time. Note, Through the iniquity of the times, as good men are hidden, so good men are silent, and it is their wisdom to be so; *little said soon amended.* But it is their comfort that they may speak freely to God when they know not to whom else they can speak freely. *Secondly,* They shall think it fruitless to reprove. They see what wickedness is committed, and their spirits are stirred up, as Paul's at Athens; but they shall think it prudent not to bear an open testimony against it, because it is to no purpose. They are *joined to their idols; let them alone. Let no man strive or rebuke another;* for it is but *casting pearls before swine.* The cautious men will say to a bold reprover, as Erasmus to Luther, *"Abi in cellam, et dic, Miserere mei, Domine—Away to thy cell, and cry, Have mercy on me, O Lord!"* Let grave lessons and counsels be kept for better men and better times. And there is *a time to keep silence* as well as *a time to speak,* Eccl. iii. 7. *Evil times* will not bear plain dealing, that is, *evil men* will not; and the men the prophet here speaks of had reason to think themselves evil men indeed, when wise and good men thought it in vain to speak to them and were afraid of having any thing to do with them.

II. They are told of their danger and what judgments they lay exposed to for their sins. 1. The places of their idolatry are in danger of being ruined in the first place, *v.* 5. *Gilgal,* the head-quarters of idolatry, *shall go into captivity,* not only its inhabitants, but its images, *and Bethel* with its golden calf *shall come to nought.* The victorious enemy shall make nothing of it, so easily shall it be spoiled, and shall bring it to nothing, so effectually shall it be spoiled. Idols were always vanity, and *things of nought,* and so they shall prove when God appears to abolish them. 2. The body of the kingdom is in danger of being ruined with them, *v.* 6. There is danger lest, if you seek him not in time, he *break out like a fire in the house of Joseph and devour it;* for our God is a right-

eous Judge, is a *consuming fire,* and the men of Israel, as criminals, are stubble before him; woe to those that make themselves fuel to the fire of God's wrath! It follows, *And there shall be none to quench it in Bethel.* There their idols were, and their idolatrous priests; thither they brought their sacrifices, and there they offered up their prayers. But God tells them that when the fire of his judgments should kindle upon them all the gods they served at Bethel should not be able to quench it, should not turn away the judgment, nor be any relief to them under it. Thus those that make an idol of the world will find it insufficient to protect them when God comes to reckon with them for their spiritual idolatry. 3. What they have got by oppression and extortion shall be taken from them (*v.* 11): *" You have built houses of hewn stone,* which you thought would be lasting; *but you shall not dwell in them,* for your enemies shall burn them down, or possess them for themselves, or take you into captivity. *You have planted pleasant vineyards,* have contrived how to make them every way agreeable, and have promised yourselves many a pleasant walk in them; but you shall be forced to walk off, and shall never *drink wine of them."* The law had tenderly provided that if a man had *built a house,* or *planted a vineyard,* he should be at his liberty to return from the wars, Deut. xx. 5, 6. But now the necessity would be so urgent that it would not be allowed; all must go to the battle, and many of those who had lately been building and planting should fall in battle, and never enjoy what they had been labouring for. What is not honestly got is not likely to be long enjoyed.

III. They are told their duty, and have great encouragement to set about it in good earnest, and good reason. The duties here prescribed to them are godliness and honesty, seriousness in their applications to God and justice in their dealings with men; and each of these is here pressed upon them with proper arguments to enforce the exhortation. 1. They are here exhorted to be sincere and devout in their addresses to God, *v.* 4. God says to the *house of Israel, Seek you me,* and with good reason, for *should not a people seek unto their God?* Isa. viii. 19. Whither else should they go but to their protector? Israel was a *prince with God;* let his descendants *seek the Lord,* as he did, and they shall be so too. Now, in order to their doing this, they must abandon their idolatries. God is not sought truly if he be not sought exclusively, for he will endure no rivals: *"Seek you the Lord, and seek not Bethel* (*v.* 5), consult not your idol-oracles, nor ask at the mouth of the priests of Bethel; seek not to the golden calf there for protection, nor bring your prayers and sacrifices any longer thither, or to Gilgal, for you *forsake your own mercies* if you observe those *lying vanities.* But *seek the Lord* (*v.* 6, 8); enquire after him;
1245

enquire of him; seek to know his mind as your rule, to secure his favour as your felicity." To press this exhortation we are told to consider, (1.) What we shall get by seeking God; it will be *our life;* we shall find him, and shall be happy in him. So he tells them himself (*v.* 4): *Seek you me, and you shall live.* So the prophet tells them (*v.* 6): *Seek the Lord, and you shall live.* Those that seek perishing gods shall perish with them (*v.* 5), but those that seek the living God shall live with him : " You shall be delivered from the killing judgments which you are threatened with; your nation shall live, shall recover from its present languishings; your souls shall live; you shall be sanctified and comforted, and made for ever blessed. *You shall live.*" (2.) What a God he is whom we are to *seek, v.* 8, 9. [1.] He is a God of almighty power himself. The idols were impotent things, could do neither good nor evil, and therefore it was folly either to fear or trust them; but the God of Israel does every thing, and can do any thing, and therefore we ought to seek to him; he challenges our homage who has all power in his hand, and it is our interest to have him on our side. Divers proofs and instances are here given of God's power, as Creator, in the kingdom of nature, as both founding and governing that kingdom. Compare *ch.* iv. 13. *First,* The stars are the work of his hands; those stars which the heathens worshipped (*v.* 26), the *stars of your god,* those stars are God's creatures and servants. He *makes the seven stars and Orion,* two very remarkable constellations, which Amos, a herdsman, while he kept his cattle by night, had particularly observed the motions of. He made them at the first, he still makes them to be what they are to this earth and either *binds* or *looses* the *sweet influences* of *Pleiades* and *Orion,* the two constellations here mentioned. See Job xxxviii. 31; ix. 9, to which passages Amos seems here to refer, putting them in mind of those ancient discoveries of the glory of God before he was called the *God of Israel. Secondly,* The constant succession of day and night is under his direction, and is kept up by his power and providence. It is he that *turns* the night (which is dark as *the shadow of death) into the morning* by the rising of the sun, and by the setting of the sun *makes the day dark with night;* and the same power can, for humble penitents, easily turn affliction and sorrow into prosperity and joy, but can as easily turn the prosperity of presumptuous sinners into darkness, into utter darkness. *Thirdly,* The rain rises and falls as he appoints. He *calls for the waters of the sea;* out of them vapours are drawn up by the heat of the sun, which gather into clouds, and are *poured out upon the face of the earth,* to water it and make it fruitful. This was the mercy that had been *withholden from them* of late (*ch.* iv. 7); and therefore to whom should they apply but to

him who had power to give it? For all the *vanities of the heathen* could not *give rain,* nor could *the heavens give showers,* Jer. xiv. 22. It is God that has *made these things; Jehovah is his name,* the name by which the God of nature, the God of the whole earth, has made himself known to his people Israel and covenanted with them. [2.] As he is a God of almighty power himself, so he *gives strength and power unto his people* that seek him, and *renews strength* to those that had lost it, if they *wait upon him* for it; for (*v.* 9) he *strengthens the spoiled against the strong* to such a degree that the spoiled come *against the fortress* and make bold and brave attacks upon those that had spoiled them. This is an encouragement to the people to *seek the Lord,* that, if they do so, they shall find him able to retrieve their affairs, when they are brought to the lowest ebb; though they are the spoiled, and their enemies are the strong, if they can but engage God for them, they shall soon recruit so as the next time to be not only the aggressors, but the conquerors; they *come against the fortress,* to make reprisals and become masters of it.

2. They are here exhorted to be honest and just in their dealings with men, *v.* 14, 15, where observe, (1.) The duty required: *Seek good, and not evil. Hate the evil, and love the good, and establish judgment in the gate;* re-establish it there, whence it has been banished, *v.* 7. Note, Things are not so bad but that they may be amended if the right course be taken; we must not despair but that grievances may be redressed and abuses rectified : justice may yet triumph where injustice tyrannizes. In order to this, good must be loved and sought, evil must be hated and no longer sought. We must love good principles and adhere to them, love to do good and abound in doing it, love good people, and good converse, and good duties; and, whatever good we do, we must do it from a principle of love, do it of choice and with delight. Those who thus *love good* will *seek it,* will contrive to do all the good they can, enquire for opportunities of doing it, and endeavour to do it to the utmost of their power. They will also *hate evil,* will abhor the thought of doing an unjust thing, and abstain from all appearance of it. In vain do we pretend to seek God in our devotions if we do not seek good in our whole conversations. (2.) The reasons annexed. [1.] This is the sure way to be happy ourselves and to have the continual presence of God with us : " *Seek good, and not evil, that you may live,* may escape the punishment of the evil you have sought and loved *(righteousness delivereth from death),* that you may have the favour of God, which is your life, which is better than life itself, that you may have comfort in yourselves and may live to some good purpose. You shall live, for *so the Lord God of hosts shall be with you* and be

your life." Note, Those that keep in the way of duty have the presence of God with them, as the *God of hosts*, a God of almighty power. " He will be with you *as you have spoken*, that is, as you have *gloried;* you shall have that really which, while you went on in unrighteous ways, you only seemed to have and boasted of as if you had." Those that truly repent and reform enter into the enjoyment of that comfort which before they had only flattered themselves with the imagination of. Or, "As you have prayed when *you sought the Lord*. Live up to your prayers, and you shall have what you pray for." [2.] This is the likeliest way to make the nation happy : " If you seek and love that which is good, you may contribute to the saving of the land from ruin." *It may be, the Lord God of hosts will be gracious to the remnant of Joseph;* though there is but a remnant left, yet, if God be gracious to that remnant, it will rise to a great nation again; and if some among them turn from sin, especially if *judgment* be *established in the gate*, though we cannot be certain, yet there is great probability that public affairs will take a new and happy turn, and every thing will mend if men mend their lives. Temporal promises are made with an *It may be ;* and our prayers must be made accordingly.

16 Therefore the LORD, the God of hosts, the Lord, saith thus ; Wailing *shall be* in all streets ; and they shall say in all the highways, Alas ! alas ! and they shall call the husbandman to mourning, and such as are skilful of lamentation to wailing. 17 And in all vineyards *shall be* wailing : for I will pass through thee, saith the LORD. 18 Woe unto you that desire the day of the LORD! to what end *is* it for you? the day of the LORD *is* darkness, and not light. 19 As if a man did flee from a lion, and a bear met him ; or went into the house, and leaned his hand on the wall, and a serpent bit him. 20 *Shall* not the day of the LORD *be* darkness, and not light? even very dark, and no brightness in it ?

Here is, I. A very terrible threatening of destruction approaching, *v.* 16, 17. Since they would not take the right course to obtain the favour of God, God would take an effectual course to make them feel the weight of his displeasure. The threatening is introduced with more than ordinary solemnity, to strike an awe upon them ; it is not the word of the prophet only (if so, it might be made light of), but it is the *Lord Jehovah*, who has an infinite eternal being ; it is the *God of hosts*, who has a boundless irresistible power, and it is *Adonai—the Lord*, who has

an absolute incontestable sovereignty, and a univeral dominion ; it is he who says it, who can and will make his words good, and he has said, 1. That the land of Israel shall be put in mourning, true mourning, that all places shall be filled with lamentation for the calamities coming upon them. Look into the cities, and *wailing shall be in all streets*, in the great streets, in the by-streets. Look into the country, and *they shall say in all the highways, Alas ! alas !* we are all undone ! The lamentation shall be so great as not to be confined within doors, nor kept within the bounds of decency, but it shall be proclaimed in the streets and highways, and shall run wild. The husbandman shall be called from the plough by the calamities of his country to the natural expressions of mourning ; and, because those will come short of the merits of the cause, such as are skilful of lamentation shall be called to artificial mourning, to put accents upon the lamentations of the real mourners with their *Ahone, ahone*. Even in all vineyards, where there used to be nothing but mirth and pleasure, there shall be general wailing, when a foreign force invades the country, lays all waste, and there is no making any head against it, no weapons left but prayers and tears. 2. That the land of Israel shall be brought to ruin, and the advances of that ruin are the the occasion of all this wailing : *I will pass through thee*, as the destroying angel passed through the land of Egypt to destroy the first-born, but then passed over the houses of the Israelites. God's judgments had often passed by them, but now they shall pass through them, shall run them through.

II. A just and severe reproof to those who made light of these threatenings, and impudently bade defiance to the justice of God and his judgments, *v.* 18. Woe unto you that *desire the day of the Lord*, that really wish for times of war and confusion, as some do who have restless spirits, and long for changes, or who choose to *fish in troubled waters*, hoping to raise their families, as some had done, upon the ruins of their country ; but the prophet tells them that this should be so great a desolation that nobody could get by it. Or it is spoken to those who, in their wailings and lamentations for the calamities they were in, wished they might die, and be delivered out of their misery, as Job did, with passion. The prophet shows them the folly of this. Do they know what death is to those who are unprepared for it, and how much more terrible it will be than any thing that can befal them in this life? Or, rather, it is spoken to those who speak jestingly of that day of the Lord which the prophet spoke so seriously of ; they desired it, that is, they challenged it ; they said, Let him do his worst; *let him make speed*, and *hasten his work*, Isa. v. 19. *Where is the promise of his coming?* 2 Pet. iii. 4. It intimates, 1. That they do not believe it. They say that they wish it would come because they do not believe it will ever come; nor will they believe it unless they see it. 2. That they do not fear it; though they may have some belief of it, yet they have so little consideration of it, and their mind is so intent upon other things, that they are under no apprehension at all of peril from it; instead of having the conscience to dread it, they have the curiosity to desire it. In answer to this, (1.) He shows the folly of those who impudently wished for any of God's judgments, and made a jest of any of the terrors of the Lord: " *To what end is it for you* that the day of the Lord should come ? You will find it both certain and sad; not a thing to be bantered, for it is neither a thing to be questioned whether it will come or no nor a thing to be turned off with a slight when it does come. *The day of the Lord is darkness, and not light, v.* 18. *Shall it not be so ? v.* 20. Do not your own consciences tell you that it will be so, that it will be *very dark,* and *no brightness in it ?*" Note, The *day of the Lord* will be a dark, dismal, gloomy day to all impenitent sinners; the *day of judgment* will be so ; and sometimes the day of their present trouble. And, when God makes a day dark, all the world cannot make it light. (2.) He shows the folly of those who impatiently wished for a change of God's judgments, in hopes that the next would be better and more tolerable. They desire *the day of the Lord,* in hopes to better themselves (though their hearts and lives be not amended), or, at least, to know the worst. But the prophet tells them that they know not what they ask, *v.* 19. It is *as if a man did flee from a lion and a bear met him,* a beast of prey more cruel and ravenous than a lion, or as if a man, to escape all dangers abroad, *went into the house for security,* and *leaned his hand on the wall* to rest himself, and there a *serpent bit him.* Note, Those who are not reformed by the judgments of God will be pursued by them; and, if they escape one, another stands ready to seize them; *fear and the pit and snare* surround them, Isa. xxiv. 17, 18. It is madness therefore to *defy the day of the Lord.*

21 I hate, I despise your feast days, and I will not smell in your solemn assemblies. 22 Though ye offer me burnt-offerings and your meat-offerings, I will not accept *them :* neither will I regard the peace-offerings of your fat beasts. 23 Take thou away from me the noise of thy songs ; for I will not hear the melody of thy viols. 24 But let judgment run down as waters, and righteousness as a mighty stream. 25 Have ye offered unto me sacrifices and offerings in the wilder-

ness forty years, O house of Israel ? 26 But ye have borne the tabernacle of your Moloch and Chiun your images, the star of your god, which ye made to yourselves. 27 Therefore will I cause you to go into captivity beyond Damascus, saith the LORD, whose name *is* The God of hosts.

The scope of these verses is to show how little God valued their shows of devotion, nay, how much he detested them, while they went on in their sins. Observe,

I. How unpleasing, nay, how displeasing, their hypocritical services were to God. They had their *feast-days* at Bethel, in imitation of those at Jerusalem, in which they pretended to rejoice before God. They had their *solemn assemblies* for religious worship, in which they put on the gravity of those who *come before God as his people come, and sit before him as his people sit.* They offered to God *burnt-offerings,* to the honour of God, together with the *meat-offerings* which by the law were to be offered with them ; they offered the *peace-offerings,* to implore the favour of God, and they offered them of the *fat beasts* that they had, *v.* 21, 22. In imitation likewise of the temple-music, they had the *noise of their songs* and the *melody of their viols (v.* 23), vocal and instrumental music, with which they praised God. With these services they hoped to make God amends for the sins they had committed, and to obtain leave to go on in sin ; and therefore they were so far from being acceptable to God that they were abominable. He *hated,* he *despised,* their *feast-days,* not only despised them as no valuable services done to him, but hated them as an affront and provocation to him, as we hate to see men dissemble with us, pretend a respect for us when really they have none. Nothing more hateful, more despicable, than hypocrisy. *He that blesseth his friend with a loud voice, it shall be counted a curse,* when it appears that his heart is not with him. God will not *smell* in *their solemn assemblies,* for there is nothing in them that is grateful to him, but a great deal that is offensive. Their sacrifices are not to him *of a sweet smelling savour,* as Noah's was, Gen. viii. 21. He will not accept them ; he will not regard them, will not take any notice of them ; he will not hear the melody of their viols ; for, when sin is a jar in the harmony, it grates in his ears : " *Take it away,*" says God, " I cannot bear it." Now this intimates, 1. That sacrifice itself is of small account with God in comparison with moral duties ; to love God and our neighbour is *better than all burnt offering and sacrifice.* 2. That the sacrifice of the wicked is really an abomination to him, Prov. xv. 8. Dissembled piety is double iniquity, and so it will be found when, if any place in hell be hotter than another, that will be the hypocrite's portion.

II. What it was that he required in order to the acceptableness of their sacrifices and without which no sacrifice would be acceptable (*v.* 24): *Let judgment run down as waters, among you, and righteousness as a mighty stream,* that is, 1. "Let there be a general reformation of manners among you; let religion (God's *judgment)* and *righteousness* have their due influence upon you; let your land be watered with it, and let it bear down all the opposition of vice and profaneness; let it run wide as overflowing waters, and yet run strong as a mighty stream." (2.) "In particular, let justice be duly administered by magistrates and rulers; let not the current of it be stopped by partiality and bribery, but let it come freely as waters do, in the natural course; let it be pure as running waters, not muddied with corruption or whatever may pervert justice; let it run *like a mighty stream,* and not suffer itself to be obstructed, or its course retarded, by the fear of man; let all have free access to it as to a common stream, and have benefit by it as *trees planted by the rivers of waters."* The great thing laid to Israel's charge was *turning judgment into wormwood (v.* 7); in that matter therefore they must reform, Zech. vii. 9. This was what God desired *more than sacrifices,* Hos. vi. 6; 1 Sam. xv. 22.

III. What little stress God had laid upon the law of sacrifices, though it was his own law, in comparison with the moral precepts (*v.* 25): "*Did you offer unto me sacrifices in the wilderness forty years?* No, you did not." For the greatest part of that time sacrifice was very much neglected, because of the unsettledness of their state; after the second year, the passover was not kept till they came into Canaan, and other institutions were in like manner intermitted; and yet, because God will have mercy and not sacrifice, he never imputed the omission to them as their fault, but continued his care of them and kindness to them: it was not that, but their murmuring and unbelief, for which God was displeased with them. He that so owned his people, though they did not sacrifice, when in other things they kept close to him, will certainly disown them, though they do sacrifice, if in other things they depart from him. But, though ritual sacrifices may thus be dispensed with, spiritual sacrifices will not; even justice and honesty will not excuse for the want of prayer and praise, a broken heart and the love of God. Stephen quotes this passage (Acts vii. 42), to show the Jews that they ought not to think it strange that the ceremonial law was repealed, when from the beginning it was comparatively made light of. Compare Jer. vii. 22, 23.

IV. What little reason they had to expect that their sacrifices should be acceptable to God, when they and their fathers had been all along addicted to the worship of other gods. So some take *v.* 25, "*Did you offer to me sacrifices,* that is, to me only? No, and therefore not at all to me acceptably;" for the law of worshipping the Lord our God is, *Him only we must serve.* "*But you have borne the tabernacle of your Moloch* (*v.* 26), little shrines that you made to carry about with you, pocket-idols for your private superstition, when you durst not be seen to do it publicly. You have had the images of your *Moloch—your king*" (probably representing *the sun,* that sits king among the heavenly bodies), "*and Chiun, or Remphan*" (as Stephen calls it, Acts vii. 43, after the LXX.), which, it is supposed, represented Saturn, the highest of the seven planets. The worship of the sun, moon, and stars, was the most ancient, most general, and most plausible idolatry. They *made to themselves* the *star of their God,* some particular star which they took to be their god, or the name of which they gave to their god. This idolatry Israel was from the beginning prone to (Deut. iv. 19); and those that retain an affection for false gods cannot expect the favour of the true God.

V. What punishment God would inflict upon them for their persisting in idolatry (*v.* 27): *I will cause you to go into captivity beyond Damascus.* They were led captive by Satan into idolatry, and therefore God caused them to go into captivity among idolaters, and hurried them into a strange land, since they were so fond of strange gods. They were carried *beyond Damascus.* Their captivity by the Assyrians was far beyond that by the Syrians; for, if less judgments do not work that for which they were sent, God will send greater. Or the captivity of Israel under Shalmaneser was far beyond that of Damascus under Tiglath-pileser, and much more grievous and destructive, which was foretold *ch.* i. 5. For, as the sins of God's professing people are greater than the sins of others, so it may be expected that their punishments will be proportionable. We find the spoil of Damascus and that of Samaria carried off together by the king of Assyria, Isa. viii. 4. Stephen reads it, *I will carry you away beyond Babylon* (Acts vii. 43), further than Judah shall be carried, so far further as not to return. And, to make this sentence appear both the more certain and the more dreadful, he that passes it calls himself *the Lord, whose name is, The God of hosts,* and who is therefore able to execute the sentence, having hosts at command.

CHAP. VI.

In this chapter we have, 1. A sinful people studying to put a slight upon God's threatenings and to make them appear trivial, confiding in their privileges and pre-eminences above other nations (ver. 2, 3), and their power (ver. 13), and wholly addicted to their pleasures, ver. 4—6. II. A serious prophet studying to put a weight upon God's threatenings and to make them appear terrible, by setting forth the severity of those judgments that were coming upon these sensualists (ver. 7), God's abhorring them, and abandoning them and theirs to death (ver. 8—11), and bringing utter desolation upon them, since they would not be wrought upon by the methods he had taken for their conviction, ver. 12—14.

WOE to them *that are* at ease in Zion, and trust in the mountain of Samaria, *which are* named chief of the nations, to whom the house of Israel came! 2 Pass ye unto Calneh, and see; and from thence go ye to Hamath the great: then go down to Gath of the Philistines: *be they* better than these kingdoms? or their border greater than your border? 3 Ye that put far away the evil day, and cause the seat of violence to come near; 4 That lie upon beds of ivory, and stretch themselves upon their couches, and eat the lambs out of the flock, and the calves out of the midst of the stall; 5 That chant to the sound of the viol, *and* invent to themselves instruments of music, like David; 6 That drink wine in bowls, and anoint themselves with the chief ointments: but they are not grieved for the affliction of Joseph. 7 Therefore now shall they go captive with the first that go captive, and the banquet of them that stretched themselves shall be removed.

The first words of the chapter are the contents of these verses; but they sound very strangely, and contrary to the sentiments of a vain world: *Woe to those that are at ease!* We are ready to say, *Happy are those that are at ease,* that neither feel any trouble nor fear any, that lie soft and warm, and lay nothing to heart; and wise we think are those that do so, that bathe themselves in the delights of sense and care not how the world goes. Those are looked upon as doing well for themselves that do well for their bodies and make much of them; but against them this woe is denounced, and we are here told what their ease is, and what the woe is.

I. Here is a description of their pride, security, and sensuality, for which God would reckon with them.

1. They were vainly conceited of their own dignities, and thought those would secure them from the judgments threatened and be their defence against the wrath both of God and man. (1). Those that dwelt in Zion thought that was honour and protection enough for them, and they might there be quiet from all fear of evil, because it was a strong city, well fortified both by nature and art (we read of Zion's *strong-holds* and her *bulwarks)*, and because it was a royal city, where were set the thrones of the house of David (it was the head-city of Judah, and therefore truly great), and especially because it was the holy city, where the temple was, and the testimony of Israel; those that
1250

dwelt there doubted not but that God's sanctuary would be a sanctuary to them and would shelter them from his judgments. The *temple of the Lord are these,* Jer. vii. 4. They are *haughty because of the holy mountain,* Zeph. iii. 11. Note, Many are puffed up with pride, and rocked asleep in carnal security, by their church-privileges, and the place they have in Zion. (2.) Those that dwelt *in the mountain of Samaria,* though it was not a holy hill, like that of Zion, yet they trusted in it, because it was the metropolis of a potent kingdom, and perhaps, in imitation of Jerusalem, was the head-quarters of its religion; and by lapse of time the hill of Shemer became with them in as good repute as the hill of Zion ever was. They hoped for salvation from these hills and mountains. (3.) Both these two kingdoms valued themselves upon their relation to Israel, that prince with God, which they looked upon as making them the *chief of the nations,* more ancient and honourable than any of them; the *first-fruits of the nations* (so the word is), dedicated to God and sanctifying the whole harvest. The *house of Israel* came to them, that is, was divided into those kingdoms, of which Zion and Samaria were the mother cities. Those that were at ease were the princes and rulers, the great men, that were *chief of the nations,* chief of those two kingdoms, and to whom, having their residence in Zion and Samaria, the whole house of Israel applied for judgment. Note, It is hard to be great and not to be proud. Great nations and great men are apt to overvalue themselves, and to overlook their neighbours, because they think they a little overtop them. But, for a check to their pride and security, the prophet bids them take notice of those cities that were within the compass of their knowledge, that had been as illustrious in their time as ever Zion or Samaria was, and yet were destroyed, *v.* 2. " Go *to Calneh* (which was an ancient city built by Nimrod, Gen. x. 10), and see what has become of that; it is now in ruins; so is *Hamath the great,* one of the chief cities of Syria. Sennacherib boasts of *destroying the gods of Hamath.* Gath was likewise made desolate by Hazael, and not long ago, 2 Kings xii. 17. Now *were they better than these kingdoms* of Judah and Israel? Yes, they were, and *their border greater than your border,* so that they had more reason than you to be confident of their own safety; yet you see what has become of them, and dare you be secure? *Art thou better than populous No?"* Nah. iii. 8. Note, The examples of others' ruin forbid us to be secure.

2. They persisted in their wicked courses upon a presumption that they should never be called to an account for them (*v.* 3): " *You put far away the evil day,* the day of reckoning, as a thing that shall never come, or you look upon it as at such a distance

that it makes no impression at all upon you; you *put it far away*, and think you can still put it yet further, and adjourn it *de die in diem*—*from day to day*, and therefore you *cause the seat of violence to draw near;* you venture upon all acts of injustice and oppression, and have *fellowship with the throne of iniquity, which frames mischief by a law*, Ps. xciv. 20. You cause that to come near, as if that would be your protection from these judgments which really ripens you for them." Note, *Therefore* men take sin to be near them, because they take judgment to be far off from them; but those deceive themselves who thus mock God.

3. They indulged themselves in all manner of sensual pleasures and delights, *v.* 4—6. These Israelites were perfect epicures and slaves to their appetites. Their dignities (in consideration of which they ought to have been examples of self-denial and mortification), they thought, would justify them in their sensuality; the gains of their oppression and violence, they thought, would bear the charge of it; and they put the evil day at a distance, that that might give them no disturbance in it. That which they are here charged with is not in itself sinful (these things might be soberly and moderately used), but they placed their happiness in the gratification of their carnal appetites; and though they were men in office, that had business to mind, they gave themselves up to their pleasures, spent their time in them, and threw away their thoughts, and cares, and estates upon them. They were in these enjoyments as in their element. Their hearts were upon them; they exceeded all bounds in them, and this at a time when God in his providence was calling them to *weeping and mourning*, Isa. xxii. 12, 13. When they were under guilt and wrath, and the judgments of God were ready to break in upon them, they called for *wine and strong drink*, presuming that *to-morrow shall be as this day, and much more abundant* (Isa. lvi. 12), thus walking contrary to God and setting his justice at defiance. (1.) They were extravagant in their furniture. Nothing would serve them but *beds of ivory* to sleep upon, or to sit on at their meat, when sackcloth and ashes would have become them better. (2.) They were lazy, and humoured themselves in the love of ease. They did not only lie down, but *stretched themselves* upon their couches, when they should have stirred up themselves to their business; they were willingly slothful, and took a pride in doing nothing; they *abound in superfluities* (so the margin reads it), when many of their poor brethren wanted necessaries. (3.) They were nice and curious in their diet, must have every thing of the best and abundance of it: They ate *the lambs out of the flock* (lambs by wholesale) and the *calves out of the midst of the stall*, the fattest they could lay their hand on; and these perhaps not out of their own flock and their own stall, but taken by oppression from the poor. (4.) They were merry and jovial, and diverted themselves at their feasts with music and singing: They *chant to the sound of the viol*, sing and play in concert, and they invent new-fashioned *instruments of music*, striving herein, more than in any thing else, to excel their ancestors; they set their wits on work to contrive how to please their fancy. Some men never show their ingenuity but in their luxury; on that they bestow all their faculty of invention and contrivance. They invent *instruments of music, like David*, entertain themselves with that which formerly used to be the entertainment of kings only. Or it intimates their profaneness in their mirth; they mimicked the temple-music, and made a jest of that, because, it may be, it was old-fashioned, and they took a pride in bantering it as the Babylonians did when they urged the captives to sing to them the *songs of Zion;* such was Belshazzar's profaneness when he drank wine in temple-bowls, and such is theirs that sing vain and loose songs in psalm-tunes, on purpose to ridicule a divine institution. (5.) They drank to excess, and never thought they could pour down enough: They *drink wine in bowls*, not in glasses, or cups (as Jer. xxxv. 5); they hate to be stinted, and must have large draughts, and therefore make use of vessels that they can steal a draught out of (6.) They affected the strongest perfumes: They *anoint themselves with the chief ointments*, to please the smell, and to make them more in love with their own bodies, and to guard against those presages of putrefaction which they carry about with them while they live. No ordinary ointments would serve their turn; they must have the chief, such as were far-fetched and dear-bought, when cheaper would have served as well.

4. They had no concern at all for the interests of the church of God, and of the nation, that were sinking and going to decay: *They are not grieved for the affliction of Joseph;* the church of God, including both the kingdoms of Judah and Israel (which are called *Joseph*, Ps. lxxx. 1), was in distress, invaded, insulted, and broken in upon. As to their own kingdom which they were entrusted with the government of, the affairs of which they were the directors of, the peace of which they were the conservators of, great breaches were made upon it, upon its peace and welfare; and they were so besotted that they were not aware of them, so indulgent of their pleasures that they never laid them to heart, and had such an aversion to the thing called business that they were in no care or concern to get them repaired. It is all one to them whether the nation sink or swim, so that they can but lie at ease and live in pleasure. Particular persons that belonged to Joseph were in affliction, and they took no cognizance of their case of the

wrongs and hardships they sustained and the troubles they were in, nor took any care to relieve them, and right them, contrary to the temper of holy Job, who, when he was in prosperity, *wept with him* that *was in misery* and his *soul* was *grieved for the poor,* Job xxx. 25. Some think that, in calling the afflicted church *Joseph,* there is an allusion to the story of Pharaoh's butler, who, when he was preferred to give the cup again into his master's hand, *remembered not Joseph, but forgot him,* Gen. xl. 21, 23. Thus they *drank wine in bowls,* but *were not grieved for the affliction of Joseph.* Note, Those are commonly careless of the troubles of others who are set upon their own pleasures; and it is a great offence to God when his church is in affliction and we are not grieved for it, nor lay it to heart.

II. Here is the doom passed upon them (*v.* 7): *Therefore now shall they go captive with the first that go captive,* and shall fall into all the miseries that attend captives; and the *banquet of those* that *stretched themselves* upon their couches *shall be removed.* Their plenty shall be taken from them, and they from it, because they made it the food and fuel of their lusts. 1. Those who lived in luxury shall lose even their liberty; and by being brought into servitude shall be justly punished for the abuse of their dignity and dominion. 2. Those who trusted in the delights and pleasures of their own land shall be carried away into a strange land, and so made ashamed of their pride and confidence; they shall *go captive.* 3. Those who placed their happiness in the pleasures of sense, and set their hearts upon them, shall be deprived of those pleasures; their banquet shall be removed, and they shall know what it is to fare hard. 4. Those who *stretched themselves* shall be made to contract themselves, and to come into a less compass. 5. Those who *put the evil day far from them* shall find it nearer to them than it is to others; *those shall go captive with the first* who flattered themselves with hopes that if trouble did come they should be the last who should be seized by it. Those are ripening apace for trouble themselves who lay not to heart the troubles of others and of the church of God. Those who give themselves to mirth, when God calls them to mourning, will find it is a sin that shall not go unpunished, Isa. xxii. 14.

8 The Lord GOD hath sworn by himself, saith the LORD the God of hosts, I abhor the excellency of Jacob, and hate his palaces: therefore will I deliver up the city with all that is therein. 9 And it shall come to pass, if there remain ten men in one house, that they shall die. 10 And a man's uncle shall take him up, and

1252

he that burneth him, to bring out the bones out of the house, and shall say unto him that *is* by the sides of the house, *Is there* yet *any* with thee? And he shall say, No. Then shall he say, Hold thy tongue: for we may not make mention of the name of the LORD. 11 For, behold, the LORD commandeth, and he will smite the great house with breaches, and the little house with clefts. 12 Shall horses run upon the rock? will *one* plough *there* with oxen? for ye have turned judgment into gall, and the fruit of righteousness into hemlock: 13 Ye which rejoice in a thing of nought, which say, Have we not taken to us horns by our own strength? 14 But, behold, I will raise up against you a nation, O house of Israel, saith the LORD the God of hosts; and they shall afflict you from the entering in of Hamath unto the river of the wilderness.

In the former part of the chapter we had these secure Israelites loading themselves with pleasures, as if they could never be made merry enough; here we have God loading them with punishments, as if they could never be made miserable enough. And observe,

I. How strongly this burden is bound on, not to be shaken off by their presumption and security; for it is bound by *the Lord the God of hosts,* by his mighty, his almighty, hand, which none can resist; it is bound with an oath, which puts the sentence past revocation: *The Lord God has sworn, and he will not repent,* and, since he could swear by no greater, he has sworn by himself. How dreadful, how miserable, is the case of those whose ruin, whose eternal ruin, God himself has sworn, who can execute his purpose and cannot alter it!

II. How heavily this burden lies! Let us see the particulars. 1. God will abhor and abandon them, and that implies misery enough, all misery: *I abhor the excellency of Jacob,* all that which they are proud of, and value themselves upon, and for which they call and count themselves the *chief of the nations.* Their visible church-membership, and the privileges of that, their temple, altar, and priesthood, these were, more than any thing, the excellencies of Jacob; but, when these were profaned and polluted by sin, God abhorred them; he hated and despised them, *ch.* v. 21. Note, God abhors that form of godliness which hypocrites keep up, while they abhor the power of it. And if he abhors their temple, for the iniquity of that, no marvel that he hates their palaces, for the injustice and oppression he finds there. Note, That creature which we take such a complacency and put such a confidence in as to make it a rival with God is thereby made abominable to him. He *hates the palaces* of sinners, for the sake of the wickedness of those who dwell therein. Prov. iii. 33, *The curse of the Lord is in the house of the wicked.* And, if God abhor them, immediately it follows, He will *deliver up the city with all that is therein,* deliver it up into the hands of the enemy, that will lay it waste, and make a prey of all its wealth. Note, Those that are abhorred and abandoned of God are undone to all intents and purposes. 2. There shall be a great and general mortality among them (*v.* 9): *If there remain ten men in one house,* that have escaped the sword of the enemy, yet they shall be met with another way; *they shall all die* by famine or pestilence. In the most sickly times, if there be ten in a house, one may hope that at least the one-half of them will escape, according to the proportion of two in a bed, *one taken and the other left;* but here not one of ten shall live to bury the rest. Another instance of the greatness of the mortality is (*v.* 10) that the nearest relations of the dead shall be forced with their own hands to wind up their bodies, and bury them, for want of other hands to be employed in it; that is all that the *next of kin,* to whom the right of redemption belongs, can do for them, and with great reluctance will they do that. It intimates that the young people shall be cut off soonest; for the uncle that survives is, ordinarily, the senior relation. " When the uncle comes with the sexton (or *him that burns*), *to bring out the bones out of the house,* he *shall say* to him that he sees next about the house, ' *Is there yet any with thee?* Are there any left alive?' And he shall say, ' No, this is the last; now the whole family is cut off by death, and neither root nor branch remains.'" But that which makes this judgment the more grievous is that their hearts seem to be hardened under it. " When he that is found by the sides of the house begin to enter into discourse with those that are carrying off the dead, they shall say, ' *Hold thy tongue;* do not stand preaching to us about the hand of Providence in this calamity, for *we may not make mention of the name of the Lord;* God is so angry with us that there is no speaking to him; he is so extreme to mark what we do amiss that we dare not so much as make mention of his name.'" Thus *the foolishness of men perverts their way,* and brings them into distress, and then *their heart frets against the Lord.* Even then they will not take notice of his hand, nor suffer those about them to do it. Perhaps it was forbidden by some of the idolatrous kings to make mention of the name of Jehovah, as by the law of Moses it was for-

bidden to make mention of the names of the heathen-gods: " We may not do it without incurring the penalty." Note, Those hearts are wretchedly hardened indeed that will not be brought to make mention of God's name, and to worship him, when the hand of God has gone out against them, and when, as here, sickness and death are in their families. Thus those *heap up wrath* who *cry not when God binds them.* 3. Their houses shall be destroyed, *v.* 11. God *will smite the great house with breaches, and the little house with clefts;* they shall both be cracked so as to lose their beauty and strength, and to be hastening towards a fall. The princes' palaces are not above the rebuke of divine justice, nor the poor men's cottages beneath it; neither shall escape. When sin has marked them for ruin God will find ways to bring it about. It is by order from him that breaches are made.

III. How justly they are thus burdened. If we understand the matter aright, we shall say, *The Lord is righteous.* 1. The methods used for their reformation had been all fruitless and ineffectual (*v.* 12): *Shall horses run upon the rock,* to hurl or harrow the ground there? Or will *one plough there with oxen?* No, for there will be no profit to countervail the pains. God had sent them his prophets, to *break up their fallow-ground;* but they found them as hard and inflexible as the rock, rough and rugged, and they could do no good with them, nor work upon them, and therefore they shall not attempt it any more. They will not be reclaimed, and therefore shall not be reproved, but quite abandoned. Note, Those who will not be cultivated as fields and vineyards shall be rejected as barren rocks and deserts, Heb. vi. 7, 8. 2. They had abused their power to the wrong and oppression of many, whose injured cause the sovereign Judge would not only right, but revenge: *You have turned judgment into gall,* which is nauseous, and *the fruit of righteousness into hemlock,* which is noxious; it would make one sick to see how those that were entrusted with the administration of public justice bore down equity with that power with which they ought to have defended and supported it, and so turned its own artillery against itself. Note, When our services of God are soured with sin his providences will justly be embittered to us. 3. They had set the judgments of God at defiance, and, confiding in their own strength, thought themselves a match for Omnipotence, *v.* 13. They *rejoiced in a thing of nought,* pleased themselves with a fancy that no evil should befal them, though they had no ground at all for that confidence, nothing to trust to that would bear any weight. They said, " *Have we not taken to us horns;* have we not arrived to great dignity and dominion, have we not pushed down our enemies and pushed on our victories, and this *by our own strength,* our own skill and courage, our own wealth and military force? Who then need we be afraid of? Who then need we make court to? Not God himself." Note, Prosperity and success commonly make men secure and haughty; and those that have done much think they can do any thing, any thing without God, nay, any thing against him. But those who trust in their own strength rejoice in *a thing of nought,* and so they will find. Probably they did not say this with their lips, *totidem verbis—in so many words,* but it was the language of their hearts and of their actions, both which God understands.

IV. How easily and effectually this burden shall be brought upon them, *v.* 14. He that brings it upon them is *the Lord the God of hosts,* who both may do and can do what he pleases, who has all creatures at his command, and who, when he has work to do, will not be at a loss for instruments to do it with; though they are the house of Israel, yet he will *raise up against them a nation* which they feared not, but had many a time hoped in, even the Assyrians, and this nation shall *afflict them,* bring them into straits, and put them to pain, from the *entering in of Hamath,* in the north, to *the river of the wilderness,* the river of Egypt, Sihor or Nile, in the south. The whole nation has shared in the iniquity, and therefore must expect to share in the calamity. Note, When men are in any way instruments of affliction to us we must see God raising them up against us, for they are his hand—the rod, the sword, in his hand. The Lord has bidden Shimei curse David.

CHAP. VII.

In this chapter we have, I. God contending with Israel, by the judgments brought on their land. 1. They are threatened with less judgments, but are reprieved, and the judgments turned away at the prayer of Amos, ver. 1—6. 2. God's patience is at length worn out by their obstinacy, and they are rejected, and sentenced to utter ruin, ver. 7—9. II. Israel contending with God, by the opposition given to his prophet. 1. Amaziah informs against Amos (ver. 10, 11) and does what he can to rid the country of him as a public nuisance, ver. 12, 13. 2. Amos justifies himself in what he did as a prophet (ver. 14, 15) and denounces the judgments of God against Amaziah his prosecutor (ver. 16, 17); for, when the contest is between God and man, it is easy to foresee; it is very easy to foretel, who will come off with the worst of it.

THUS hath the Lord GOD showed unto me; and, behold, he formed grasshoppers in the beginning of the shooting up of the latter growth; and, lo, *it was* the latter growth after the king's mowings. 2 And it came to pass, *that* when they had made an end of eating the grass of the land, then I said, O Lord GOD, forgive, I beseech thee: by whom shall Jacob arise? for he *is* small. 3 The LORD repented for this: it shall not be, saith the LORD. 4 Thus hath the Lord GOD showed unto me: and, behold, the Lord GOD called to contend by fire, and it devoured the great deep,

1254

and did eat up a part. 5 Then said I, O Lord GOD, cease, I beseech thee: by whom shall Jacob arise? for he *is* small. 6 The LORD repented for this: this also shall not be, saith the Lord GOD. 7 Thus he showed me: and, behold, the Lord stood upon a wall *made* by a plumb-line, with a plumb-line in his hand. 8 And the LORD said unto me, Amos, what seest thou? And I said, A plumb-line. Then said the Lord, Behold, I will set a plumb-line in the midst of my people Israel: I will not again pass by them any more: 9 And the high places of Isaac shall be desolate, and the sanctuaries of Israel shall be laid waste; and I will rise against the house of Jeroboam with the sword.

We here see that God bears long, but that he will not bear always, with a provoking people; both these God here showed the prophet: *Thus hath the Lord God showed me, v.* 1, 4, 7. He showed him what was present, foreshowed him 'what was to come, gave him the knowledge both of what he did and of what he designed; for the *Lord God reveals his secret unto his servants the prophets, ch.* iii. 7.

I. We have here two instances of God's sparing mercy, remembered in the midst of judgment, the narratives of which are so much like one another that they will be best considered together, and very considerable they are.

1. God is here coming forth against this sinful nation, first by one judgment and then by another. (1.) He begins with the judgment of famine. The prophet saw this in vision He saw God *forming grasshoppers,* or *locusts,* and bringing them upon the land, to eat up the fruits of it, and so to strip it of its beauty and starve its inhabitants, *v.* 1. God formed these grasshoppers, not only as they were his creatures (and much of the wisdom and power of God appears in the formation of minute animals, as much in the structure of an ant as of an elephant), but as they were instruments of his wrath. God is said to *frame evil* against a sinful people, Jer. xviii 11. These grasshoppers were framed on purpose to *eat up the grass of the land;* and vast numbers of them were prepared accordingly. They were sent *in the beginning of the shooting up of the latter growth, after the king's mowings.* See here how the judgment was mitigated by the mercy that went before it. God could have sent these insects to eat up the grass at the beginning of the first growth, in the spring, when the grass was most needed, was most plentiful, and was the best in its kind; but God suffered that to grow, and suffered

them to gather it in; the king's mowings were safely housed, for *the king himself is served from the field* (Eccl. v. 9), and could as ill be without his mowings as without any other branch of his revenues. Uzziah, who was now king of Judah, *loved husbandry*, 2 Chron. xxvi. 10. But the grasshoppers were commissioned to eat up only the *latter growth* (the edgrew we call it in the country), the after-grass, which is of little value in comparison with the former. The mercies which God gives us, and continues to us, are more numerous and more valuable than those he removes from us, which is a good reason why we should be thankful and not complain. The remembrance of the mercies of the former growth should make us submissive to the will of God when we meet with disappointments in the latter growth. The prophet, in vision, saw this judgment prevailing far. These grasshoppers *ate up the grass of the land*, which should have been for the cattle, which the owners must of course suffer by. Some understand this figuratively of a wasting destroying army brought upon them. In the days of Jeroboam the kingdom of Israel began to recover itself from the desolations it had been under in the former reigns (2 Kings xiv. 25); the latter growth shot up, after the mowings of the kings of Syria, which we read of 2 Kings xiii. 3. And then God commissioned the king of Assyria with an army of caterpillars to come upon them and lay them waste, that nation spoken of *ch.* vi. 14, which afflicted them *from the entering of Hamath to the river of the wilderness*, which seems to refer to 2 Kings xiv. 25, where Jeroboam is said to have restored their coast *from the entering of Hamath to the sea of the plain.* God can bring all to ruin when we think all is in some good measure repaired. (2). He proceeds to the judgment of fire, to show that he has many arrows in his quiver, many ways of humbling a sinful nation (*v.* 4): *The Lord God called to contend by fire.* He contended, for God's judgments upon a people are his controversies with them; in them he prosecutes his action against them; and his controversies are neither causeless nor groundless. He *called to contend;* he did by his prophets give them notice of his controversy, and drew up a declaration, setting forth the meaning of it. Or he called for his angels, or other ministers of his justice, that were to be employed in it. A fire was kindled among them, by which perhaps is meant a great drought (the heat of the sun, which should have warmed the earth, scorched it, and burnt up the roots of the grass which the locusts had eaten the spires of), or a raging fever, which was as a fire in their bones, which devoured and ate up multitudes, or lightning, fire from heaven, which consumed their houses, as Sodom and Gomorrah were consumed (*ch.* iv. 11), or it was the burning

of their cities, either by accident or by the hand of the enemy, for fire and sword used to go together; thus were the towns wasted, as the country was by the grasshoppers. This fire, which God called for, did terrible execution; it *devoured the great deep*, as the fire that fell from heaven on Elijah's altar licked up the water that was in the trench. Though the water designed for the stopping and quenching of this fire was as the water of the great deep, yet it devoured it; for who, or what, can stand before a fire kindled by the wrath of God? It did *eat up a part*, a great part, of the cities where it was sent; or it was as the fire at Taberah, which *consumed the outermost parts of the camp* (Num. xi. 1); when some were overthrown others were as *brands plucked out of the fire.* All deserved to be devoured, but it ate up only a part, for God does not stir up all his wrath.

2. The prophet goes forth to meet him in the way of his judgments, and by prayer seeks to turn away his wrath, *v.* 2. When he saw, in vision, what dreadful work these caterpillars made, that they had eaten up in a manner *all the grass of the land* (he foresaw they would do so, if suffered to go on), then he said, *O Lord God! forgive, I beseech thee* (*v.* 2); *cease, I beseech thee, v.* 5. He that foretold the judgment in his preaching to the people, yet deprecated it in his intercessions for them. *He is a prophet, and he shall pray for thee.* It was the business of prophets to pray for those to whom they prophesied, and so to make it appear that though they denounced they did not *desire the woeful day. Therefore* God showed his prophets the evils coming, that they might befriend the people, not only by warning them, but by praying for them, and *standing in the gap*, to turn away God's wrath, as Moses, that great prophet, often did. Now observe here,

(1.) The prophet's prayer: *O Lord God! [1.] Forgive, I beseech thee*, and take away the sin, *v.* 2. He sees sin at the bottom of the trouble, and therefore concludes that the pardon of sin must be at the bottom of the deliverance, and prays for that in the first place. Note, Whatever calamity we are under, personal or public, the forgiveness of sin is that which we should be most earnest with God for. [2.] *Cease, I beseech thee*, and take away the judgment; cease the fire, cease the controversy; *cause thy anger towards us to cease.* This follows upon the forgiveness of sin. Take away the cause and the effect will cease. Note, Those whom God contends with will soon find what need they have to cry for a cessation of arms; and there are hopes that though God has begun, and proceeded far, in his controversy, yet it may be obtained.

(2.) The prophet's plea to enforce this prayer: *By whom shall Jacob arise, for he is small? v.* 2. And it is repeated (*v.* 5) and yet no vain repetition. Christ, *in his agony*, prayed earnestly, *saying the same words,* again and again. [1.] It is Jacob that he is interceding for, the professing people of God, called by his name, calling on his name, the seed of Jacob, his chosen, and in covenant with him. It is Jacob's case that is in this prayer spread before the God of Jacob. [2.] *Jacob is small,* very small already, weakened and brought low by former judgments; and therefore, if these come, he will be quite ruined and brought to nothing. The people are few; *the dust of Jacob,* which was once innumerable, is now soon counted. Those few are feeble (it is *the worm Jacob,* Isa. xli. 14); they are unable to help themselves or one another. Sin will soon make a great people small, will diminish the numerous, impoverish the plenteous, and weaken the courageous. [3.] *By whom shall he arise?* He has fallen, and cannot help himself up, and he has no friend to help him, none to raise him, unless the hand of God do it; what will become of him, then, if the hand that should raise him be stretched out against him? Note, When the state of God's church is very low and very helpless it is proper to be recommended by our prayers to God's pity.

3. God graciously lets fall his controversy, in answer to the prophet's prayer, once and again (v. 3): *The Lord repented for this.* He did not change his mind, for he is in one mind and who can turn him? But he changed his way, took another course, and determined to deal in mercy and not in wrath. He said, *It shall not be.* And again (v. 6), *This also shall not be.* The caterpillars were countermanded, were remanded; a stop was put to the progress of the fire, and thus a reprieve was granted. See the power of prayer, of *effectual fervent* prayer, and how much it *avails,* what great things it prevails for. A stop has many a time been put to a judgment by making *supplication to the Judge.* This was not the first time that Israel's life was begged, and so saved. See what a blessing praying people, praying prophets, are to a land, and therefore how highly they ought to be valued. Ruin would many a time have broken in if they had not stood in the breach, and made good the pass. See how ready, how swift, God is to show mercy, how he *waits to be gracious.* Amos moves for a reprieve, and obtains it, because God inclines to grant it and looks about to see if there be any that will intercede for it, Isa. lix. 16. Nor are former reprieves objected against further instances of mercy, but are rather encouragements to pray and hope for them. This also shall not be, any more than that. It is the glory of God that he *multiplies to pardon,* that he spares, and forgives, to more than seventy times seven times.

II. We have here the rejection of those at last who had been often reprieved and yet never reclaimed, reduced to straits and yet never reduced to their God and their duty This is represented to the prophet by a vision (v. 7, 8) and an express prediction of utter ruin, v. 9.

1. The vision is of a *plumb-line,* a line with a plummet at the end of it, such as masons and bricklayers use to run up a wall by, that they may work it straight and true, and by rule. (1.) Israel was a wall, a strong wall, which God himself had reared, as a bulwark, or wall of defence, to his sanctuary, which he set up among them. The Jewish church says of herself (Cant. viii. 10), *I am a wall, and my breasts are like towers.* This wall was *made by a plumb-line,* very exact and firm. So happy was its constitution, so well compacted, and every thing so well ordered according to the model; it had long stood fast as a wall of brass. But, (2.) God now *stands upon* this wall, not to hold it up, but to tread it down, or, rather, to consider what he should do with it. He *stands upon it with a plumb-line in his hand,* to take measure of it, that it may appear to be a bowing, bulging wall. *Recti est index sui et obliqui—This plumb-line would discover where it was crooked.* Thus God would bring the people of Israel to the trial, would discover their wickedness, and show wherein they erred; and he would likewise bring his judgments upon them according to equity, would set a *plumb-line in the midst of them,* to mark how far their wall must be pulled down, as David measured the *Moabites with a line* (2 Sam. viii. 2) to *put them to death.* And, when God is coming to the ruin of a people, he is said to *lay judgment to the line and righteousness to the plummet;* for when he punishes it is with exactness. It is now determined: "*I will not again pass by them any more;* they shall not be spared and reprieved as they have been; their punishment shall not be *turned away,*" ch. i. 3. Note, God's patience, which has long been sinned against, will at length be sinned away; and the time will come when those that have been spared often shall be no longer spared. *My spirit shall not always strive.* After frequent reprieves, yet a day of execution will come.

2. The prediction is of utter ruin, v. 9. (1.) The body of the people shall be destroyed, with all those things that were their ornament and defence. They are here called *Isaac* as well as *Israel, the house of Isaac* (v. 16), some think in allusion to the signification of Isaac's name; it is *laughter;* they shall become a jest among all their neighbours; their neighbours shall *laugh at them.* The desolation shall fasten upon their high places and their *sanctuaries,* either their *castles* or their *temples,* both built on high places. Their castles they thought safe, and their temples sacred as sanctuaries. These shall be *laid waste,* to punish them for their idolatry and to make them ashamed of their carnal confidences, which were the two things for which

God had a controversy with them. When these were made desolate they might read their sin and folly in their punishment. (2.) The royal family shall sink first, as an earnest of the ruin of the whole kingdom : *I will rise against the house of Jeroboam,* Jeroboam the second, who was now king of the ten tribes; his family was extirpated in his son Zecharias, who was *slain with the sword before the people,* by Shallum who *conspired against him,* 2 Kings xv. 10. How unrighteous soever the instruments were, God was righteous, and in them God rose up against that idolatrous family. Even king's houses will be no shelter against the sword of God's wrath.

10 Then Amaziah the priest of Beth-el sent to Jeroboam king of Israel, saying, Amos hath conspired against thee in the midst of the house of Israel : the land is not able to bear all his words. 11 For thus Amos saith, Jeroboam shall die by the sword, and Israel shall surely be led away captive out of their own land. 12 Also Amaziah said unto Amos, O thou seer, go, flee thee away into the land of Judah, and there eat bread, and prophesy there : 13 But prophesy not again any more at Beth-el : for it *is* the king's chapel, and it *is* the king's court. 14 Then answered Amos, and said to Amaziah, I *was* no prophet, neither *was* I a prophet's son ; but I *was* a herdman, and a gatherer of sycamore fruit : 15 And the LORD took me as I followed the flock, and the LORD said unto me, Go, prophesy unto my people Israel. 16 Now therefore hear thou the word of the LORD : Thou sayest, Prophesy not against Israel, and drop not *thy word* against the house of Isaac. 17 Therefore thus saith the LORD ; Thy wife shall be a harlot in the city, and thy sons and thy daughters shall fall by the sword, and thy land shall be divided by line ; and thou shalt die in a polluted land : and Israel shall surely go into captivity forth of his land.

One would have expected, 1. That what we met with in the former part of the chapter would awaken the people to repentance, when they saw that they were reprieved in order that they might have *space to repent* and that they could not obtain a pardon unless they did repent. 2. That it would endear the prophet Amos to them, who had not only shown his good-will to them in praying against the judgments that invaded them, but had prevailed to turn away those judgments, which, if they had had any sense of gratitude, would have gained him an interest in their affections. But it fell out quite contrary ; they continue impenitent, and the next news we hear of Amos is that he is persecuted. Note, As it is the praise of great saints that they pray for those that are enemies to them, so it is the shame of many great sinners that they are enemies to those who pray for them, Ps. xxxv. 13, 15 ; cix. 4. We have here,

I. The malicious information brought to the king against the prophet Amos, *v.* 10, 11. The informer was *Amaziah the priest of Bethel,* the chief of the priests that ministered to the golden calf there, the *president of Bethel* (so some read it), that had the principal hand in civil affairs there. He complained against Amos, not only because he prophesied without license from him, but because he prophesied against his altars, which would soon be deserted and demolished if Amos's preaching could but gain credit. Thus the shrine-makers at Ephesus hated Paul, because his preaching tended to spoil their trade. Note, Great pretenders to sanctity are commonly the worst enemies to those who are really sanctified. Priests have been the most bitter persecutors. Amaziah brings an information to Jeroboam against Amos. Observe, 1. The crime he is charged with is no less than treason : *"Amos has conspired against thee,* to depose and murder thee ; he aims at succeeding thee, and therefore is taking the most effectual way to weaken thee. He sows the seeds of sedition in the hearts of the good subjects of the king, and makes them disaffected to him and his government, that he may draw them by degrees from their allegiance ; upon this account *the land is not able to bear his words."* It is slyly insinuated to the king that the country was exasperated against him, and it is given in as their sense that his preaching was intolerable, and such as nobody could be reconciled to, such as the times would by no means bear, that is, the men of the times would not. Both the impudence of his supposed treason, and the bad influence it would have upon the country, are intimated in that part of the charge, that he conspired against the king in the midst of the house of Israel. Note, It is no new thing for the accusers of the brethren to misrepresent them as enemies to the king and kingdom, as traitors to their prince and troublers of the land, when really they are the best friends to both. And it is common for designing men to assert that as the sense of the country which is far from being so. And yet here, I doubt, it was too true, that the people could not bear plain dealing any more than the priests. 2. The words laid in the indictment for the support of this charge (*v.* 11) : *Amos says* (and they have witnesses ready to prove it) *Jeroboam shall die by the sword, and Israel shall be led away captive;* and hence they infer that he is an enemy to his king and country, and not to be tolerated. See the malice of Amaziah; he does not tell the king how Amos had interceded for Israel, and by his intercession had turned away first one judgment and then another, and did not let fall his intercession till he saw the decree had gone forth; he does not tell him that these threatenings were conditional, and that he had often assured them that if they would repent and reform the ruin should be prevented. Nay, it was not true that he said, *Jeroboam shall die by the sword,* nor did he so die (2 Kings xiv. 28), but that God would *rise against the house of Jeroboam with the sword, v.* 9. God's prophets and ministers have often had occasion to make David's complaint (Ps. lvi. 5), *Every day they wrest my words.* But shall it be made the watchman's crime, when he sees the sword coming, to give warning to the people, that they may get themselves secured? or the physician's crime to tell his patient of the danger of his disease, that he may use means for the cure of it? What enemies are foolish men to themselves, to their own peace, to their best friends! It does not appear that Jeroboam took any notice of this information; perhaps he reverenced a prophet, and stood more in awe of the divine authority than Amaziah his priest did.

II. The method he used to persuade Amos to withdraw and quit the country (*v.* 12, 13); when he could not gain his point with the king to have Amos imprisoned, banished, or put to death, or at least to have him frightened into silence or flight, he tried what he could do by fair means to get rid of him; he insinuated himself into his acquaintance, and with all the arts of wheedling endeavoured to persuade him to go and prophesy in the *land of Judah,* and not at Bethel. He owns him to be a seer, and does not pretend to enjoin him silence, but suggests to him,

1. That Bethel was not a proper place for him to exercise his ministry in, for it was *the king's chapel,* or *sanctuary,* where he had his idols and their altars and priests; and it was *the king's court,* or *the house of the kingdom,* where the royal family resided and where were set the thrones of judgment; and therefore *prophesy not any more* here. And why not? (1.) Because Amos is too plain and blunt a preacher for the court and the king's chapel. Those *that wear silk and fine clothing,* and speak silken soft words, are fit for king's palaces. (2.) Because the worship that is in the king's chapel will be a continual vexation and trouble to Amos; let him therefore get far enough from it, and what the eye sees not the heart grieves not for. (3.) Because it was not fit that the king and his house should be affronted in their own court and chapel by the reproofs

and threatenings which Amos was continually teazing them with in the name of the Lord; as if it were the prerogative of the prince, and the privilege of the peers, when they are running headlong upon a precipice, not to be told of their danger. (4.) Because he could not expect any countenance or encouragement there, but, on the contrary, to be bantered and ridiculed by some and to be threatened and brow-beaten by others; however, he could not think to make any converts there, or to persuade any from that idolatry which was supported by the authority and example of the king. To preach his doctrine there was but (as we say) to run his head against a post; and therefore *prophesy no more* there. But,

2. He persuades him that the land of Judah was the fittest place for him to set up in: *Flee thee away* thither with all speed, and *there eat bread,* and *prophesy there.* There thou wilt be safe; there thou wilt be welcome; the king's court and chapel there are on thy side; the prophets there will second thee; the priests and princes there will take notice of thee, and allow thee an honourable maintenance. See here, (1.) How willing wicked men are to get clear of their faithful reprovers, and how ready to *say to the seers, See not,* or See not for us; the two witnesses were a torment to those that dwelt on the earth (Rev. xi. 10), and it were indeed a pity that men should be *tormented before the time,* but that it is in order to the preventing of eternal torment. (2.) How apt worldly men are to measure others by themselves. Amaziah, as a priest, aimed at nothing but the profits of his place, and he thought Amos, as a prophet, had the same views, and therefore advised him to prophesy where he might *eat bread,* where he might be sure to have as much as he chose; whereas Amos was to prophesy where God appointed him, and where there was most need of him, not where he would get most money. Note, Those that make gain their godliness, and are governed by the hopes of wealth and preferment themselves, are ready to think these the most powerful inducements with others also.

III. The reply which Amos made to these suggestions of Amaziah's. He did not *consult with flesh and blood,* nor was it his care to enrich himself, but to *make full proof of his ministry,* and to be found faithful in the discharge of it, not to sleep in a whole skin, but to keep a good conscience; and therefore he resolved to abide by his post, and, in answer to Amaziah,

1. He justified himself in his constant adherence to his work and to his place (*v.* 14, 15); and that which he was sure would not only bear him out, but bind him to it, was that he had a divine warrant and commission for it: " *I was no prophet, nor prophet's son,* neither born nor bred to the office, not originally designed for a prophet, as Samuel and Jeremiah, not educated in the schools of

the prophets, as many others were; but *I was a herdman,* a keeper of cattle, and a *gatherer of sycamore-fruit."* Our sycamores bear no fruit, but, it seems, theirs did, which Amos gathered either for his cattle or for himself and his family, or to sell. He was a plain country-man, bred up and employed in country work and used to country fare. He *followed the flocks* as well as the herds, and thence God *took him,* and bade him *go* and *prophesy to his people Israel,* deliver to them such messages as he should from time to time *receive from the Lord.* God made him a prophet, and a prophet to them, appointed him his work and appointed him his post. Therefore he ought not to be silenced, for, (1.) He could produce a divine commission for what he did. He did not run before he was sent, but pleads, as Paul, that he was *called to be an apostle;* and men will find it is at their peril if they contradict and oppose any that come in God's name, if they say to his *seers, See not,* or silence those whom he has bidden to speak; such *fight against God.* An affront done to an ambassador is an affront to the prince that sends him. Those that have a warrant from God ought not to *fear the face of man.* (2.) The mean character he wore before he received that commission strengthened his warrant, so far was it from weakening it. [1.] He had no thoughts at all of ever being a prophet, and therefore his prophesying could not be imputed to a raised expectation or a heated imagination, but purely to a divine impulse. [2.] He was not educated nor instructed in the art or mystery of prophesying, and therefore he must have his abilities for it immediately from God, which is an undeniable proof that he had his mission from him. The apostles, being originally unlearned and ignorant men, evidenced that they owed their knowledge to their having *been with Jesus,* Acts iv. 13. When the treasure is put into such earthen vessels, it is thereby made to appear that the *excellency of the power is of God, and not of man,* 2 Cor. iv. 7. [3.] He had an honest calling, by which he could comfortably maintain himself and his family, and therefore did not need to prophesy for bread, as Amaziah suggested (*v.* 12), did not take it up as a trade to live by, but as a trust to honour God and do good with. [4.] He had all his days been accustomed to a plain homely way of living among poor husbandmen, and never affected either gaieties or dainties, and therefore would not have thrust himself so near the king's court and chapel if the business God had called him to had not called him thither. [5.] Having been so meanly bred, he could not have had courage to speak to kings and great men, especially to speak such bold and provoking things to them, if he had not been animated by a greater spirit than his own. If God, that sent him, had not strengthened him, he could not thus have *set his face as a flint,* Isa. l. 7. Note,

God often chooses the *weak and foolish things of the world* to confound the wise and mighty; and a herdman of Tekoa puts to shame a priest of Bethel, when he receives from God authority and ability to act for him.

2. He condemns Amaziah for the opposition he gave him, and denounces the judgments of God against him, not from any private resentment or revenge, but in the name of the Lord and by authority from him, *v.* 16, 17. Amaziah would not suffer Amos to preach at all, and therefore he is particularly ordered to preach against him: *Now therefore hear thou the word of the Lord,* hear it and tremble. Those that cannot bear general woes may expect woes of their own. The sin he is charged with is forbidding Amos to prophesy; we do not find that he beat him, or put him in the stocks, only he enjoined him silence: *Prophesy not against Israel, and drop not thy word against the house of Isaac;* he must not only not thunder against them, but he must not so much as drop a word against them; he cannot bear, no, not the most gentle distilling of that rain, that small rain. Let him therefore hear his doom.

(1.) For the opposition he gave to Amos God will bring ruin upon himself and his family. This was the sin that filled the measure of his iniquity. [1.] He shall have no comfort in any of his relations, but be afflicted in those that were nearest to him: *His wife shall be a harlot;* either she shall be forcibly abused by the soldiers, as the Levite's concubine by the men of Gibeah (they *ravish the women in Zion,* Lam. v. 11), or she shall herself wickedly play the harlot, which, though her sin, her great sin, would be his affliction, his great affliction and reproach, and a just punishment upon him for promoting spiritual whoredom. Sometimes the sins of our relations are to be looked upon as the judgments of God upon us. His children, though they keep honest, yet shall not keep alive: His *sons and his daughters shall fall by the sword* of war, and he himself shall live to see it. He had trained them up in iniquity, and therefore God will cut them off in it. [2.] He shall be stripped of all his estate; it shall fall into the hand of the enemy, and be *divided by line,* by lot, among the soldiers. What is ill gotten will not be long kept. [3.] He shall himself perish in a strange country, not in the *land of Israel,* which had been holiness to the Lord, but in a *polluted land,* in a heathen country, the fittest place for such a heathen to end his days in, that hated and silenced God's prophets and contributed so much to the polluting of his own land with idolatry.

(2.) Notwithstanding the opposition he gave to Amos, God will bring ruin upon the land and nation. He was accused for saying, *Israel shall be led away captive* (*v.* 11), but he stands to it, and repeats it; for the unbelief of man shall not make the word of God of no effect. The *burden of the word of the* Lord may be striven with, but it cannot be shaken off. Let Amaziah rage, and fret, and say what he will to the contrary, *Israel shall surely go into captivity forth of his land.* Note, It is to no purpose to contend with the judgments of God; for when God judges he will overcome. Stopping the mouths of God's ministers will not stop the progress of God's word, for it shall not return void.

CHAP. VIII.

Sinful times are here attended with sorrowful times, so necessary is the connexion between them; it is threatened here again and again that the laughter shall be turned into mourning. I. By the vision of "a basket of summer-fruit" is signified the hastening on of the ruin threatened (ver. 1—3) and that shall change their note. II. Oppressors are here called to an account for their abusing the poor; and their destruction is foretold, which will set them a mourning, ver. 4—10. III. A famine of the word of God is here made the punishment of a people that go a whoring after other gods (ver. 11—14); yet for this, which is the most mournful judgment of all, they are not here brought in mourning.

THUS hath the Lord God showed unto me: and behold a basket of summer-fruit. 2 And he said, Amos, what seest thou? And I said, A basket of summer-fruit. Then said the LORD unto me, The end is come upon my people of Israel; I will not again pass by them any more. 3 And the songs of the temple shall be howlings in that day, saith the Lord God: *there shall be* many dead bodies in every place; they shall cast *them* forth with silence.

The great reason why sinners defer their repentance *de die in diem*—*from day to day*, is because they think God thus defers his judgments, and there is no song wherewith they so effectually sing themselves asleep as that, *My Lord delays his coming;* and therefore God, by his prophets, frequently represents to Israel the day of his wrath not only as just and certain, but as very near and hastening on apace; so he does in these verses.

I. The approach of the threatened ruin is represented by *a basket of summer-fruit* which Amos saw in vision; for the *Lord showed it* to him (*v.* 1) and obliged him to take notice of it (*v.* 2): *Amos, what seest thou?* Note, It concerns us to enquire whether we do indeed see that which God has been pleased to show us, and hear what he has been pleased to say to us; for many a thing God speaks, God shows *once, yea twice*, and men *perceive it not.* Are we in the midst of the visions of the Almighty? Let us consider what we see. He saw *a basket of summer-fruit* gathered and ready to be eaten, which signified, 1. That they were ripe for destruction, rotten ripe, and it was time for God to put in the sickle of his judgments and to cut them off; nay, the thing was in effect done already, and they lay ready to be eaten up. 2. That the year of God's patience was drawing towards a conclusion; it was autumn with them, and their year would quickly have its

period in a dismal winter. 3. Those we call *summer-fruits* that will not keep till winter, but must be used immediately, an emblem of this people, that had nothing solid or consistent in them.

II. The intent and meaning of this vision is no more than this: It signifies that *the end has come upon my people Israel.* The word that signifies *the end* is *ketz*, which is of near affinity with *kitz*, the word used for *summer-fruit.* God has long spared them, and borne with them, but now his patience is tired out; they are indeed *his people Israel*, but their end, that *latter end* they have been so often reminded of, but have so long forgotten, has now come. Note, If sinners do not make an end of sin, God will make an end of them, yea though they be *his people Israel.* What was said *ch.* vii. 8 is here repeated as God's determined resolution, *I will not again pass by them any more;* they shall not be connived at as they have been, nor the judgment coming turned away.

III. The consequence of this shall be a universal desolation (*v.* 3): When *the end* shall come sorrow and death shall ride in triumph; they are accustomed to go together, and shall at length go away together, when in heaven *there shall be no more death, nor sorrow*, Rev. xxi. 4. But here in a sinful world, in a sinful nation, 1. Sorrow reigns, reigns to such a degree that *the songs of the temple shall be howlings*—the songs of God's temple at Jerusalem, or rather of their idol-temples, where they used, when, in honour of the golden calves, they had *eaten and drunk*, to *rise up to play.* They were perhaps wanton profane songs; and it is certain that sooner or later those will be turned into howlings. Or, if they had a sound and show of piety and religion, yet, not coming from the heart, nor being sung to the glory of God, he valued them not, but would justly turn them into howlings. Note, Mourning will follow sinful mirth, yea, and sacred mirth too, if it be not sincere. And, when God's judgments are abroad, they will soon turn the greatest joy into the greatest heaviness, the temple-songs, which used to sound so pleasantly, not only into sighs and groans, but into loud howlings, which sound dismally. They shall come to the temple, and, finding that in ruins, there they shall howl most bitterly. 2. Death reigns, reigns to such a degree that there shall be *dead bodies, many* dead bodies *in every place* (Ps. cx. 6), slain by sword or pestilence, so many that the survivors shall not bury them with the usual pomp and solemnity of funerals; they shall not so much as have the bell tolled, but they shall *cast them forth with silence*, shall bury them in the dead of the night, and charge all about them to be silent and to take no notice of it, either because they have not wherewithal to bear the charges of a funeral, or because, the killing disease being infectious, none will come near them, or for fear the enemy should be provoked, if they should be known to lament their slain. Or they shall charge themselves and one another silently to submit to the hand of God in these desolating judgments, and not to repine and quarrel with him. Or it may be taken not for a patient, but a sullen silence; their hearts shall be hardened, and all these judgments shall not extort from them one word of acknowledgment either of God's righteousness or their own unrighteousness.

4 Hear this, O ye that swallow up the needy, even to make the poor of the land to fail, 5 Saying, when will the new moon be gone, that we may sell corn? and the sabbath, that we may set forth wheat, making the ephah small, and the shekel great, and falsifying the balances by deceit? 6 That we may buy the poor for silver, and the needy for a pair of shoes; *yea*, and sell the refuse of the wheat? 7 The LORD hath sworn by the excellency of Jacob, Surely I will never forget any of their works. 8 Shall not the land tremble for this, and every one mourn that dwelleth therein? and it shall rise up wholly as a flood; and it shall be cast out and drowned, as *by* the flood of Egypt. 9 And it shall come to pass in that day, saith the Lord GOD, that I will cause the sun to go down at noon, and I will darken the earth in the clear day: 10 And I will turn your feasts into mourning, and all your songs into lamentation; and I will bring up sackcloth upon all loins, and baldness upon every head; and I will make it as the mourning of an only *son*, and the end thereof as a bitter day.

God is here contending with proud oppressors, and showing them,

I. The heinousness of the sin they were guilty of; in short, they had the character of the unjust judge (Luke xviii. 2) that neither *feared God* nor *regarded man*.

1. Observe them in their devotions, and you will say, "They have no reverence for God." Bad as they are, they do indeed keep up a show and form of godliness; they observe the *sabbath* and the *new moon:* they put some difference between those days and other days, but they were soon weary of them, and had no affection at all to them, for their hearts were wholly set upon the world and the things of it. It is a sad character which this gives of them, that they said, *When will the sabbath be gone, that we may sell corn?* Yet it is still the character

of many that are called Christians. (1.) They were weary of sabbath days. "When will they be *gone?*" They were weary of the restraints of the sabbaths and the new-moons, and wished them over because they might *do no servile work therein.* They were weary of the work or business of the sabbaths and new-moons, snuffed at it (Mal. i. 13), and were, as *Doeg, detained before the Lord* (1 Sam. xxi. 7); they would rather have been any where else than about God's altars. Note, Sabbath days and sabbath work are a burden to carnal hearts, that are always afraid of doing too much for God and eternity. Can we spend our time better than in communion with God? And how much time do we spend pleasantly with the world? Will not the sabbath be gone before we have done the work of it and reaped the gains of it? Why then should we be in such haste to part with it? (2.) They were fond of market-days; they longed to be *selling corn* and *setting forth wheat.* When they were employed in religious services they were thinking of their marketings; their hearts *went after their covetousness* (Ezek. xxxiii. 31), and thus made my Father's house a house of merchandise, nay, a den of thieves. They were weary of holy duties because their worldly business stood still the while; in this they were as in their element, but in God's sanctuary as a fish upon dry ground. Note, Those are strangers to God, and enemies to themselves, that love market days better than sabbath days, that would rather be selling corn than worshipping God.

2. Observe them in their conversations, and you will see they have no regard to man; and this commonly follows upon the former; those that have lost the savour of piety will not long retain the sense of common honesty. They neither *do justly* nor *love mercy.* (1.) They cheat those they deal with. When they *sell their corn* they impose upon the buyer, both in giving out the goods and in receiving the money for them. They measure him the corn by their own measure, and pretend to give him what he agreed for, but they make *the ephah small.* The measure is scanty, and not statute-measure, and so they wrong him that way. When they receive his money they must weigh it in their own scales, by their own weights, and the *shekel* they weigh by is above standard: They *make the shekel great*, so that the money, being found too light, must have more added to it; and so they cheat that way too, and this under colour and pretence of exactness in doing justice. By such wicked practices as these men show such a greediness of the world, such a love of themselves, such a contempt of mankind in general, of the particular persons they deal with, and of the sacred laws of justice, as prove them to have in their hearts neither the fear nor the love of that God who has so plainly said that *false weights and balances are an abomination to him.* An-

other instance of their fraudulent dealing is that they *sell the refuse of the wheat*, and, taking advantage of their neighbour's ignorance or necessity, make them take it at the same price at which they sell the *finest of the wheat.* (2.) They are barbarous and unmerciful to the poor: They *swallow up the needy*, and *make the poor of the land to fail.* [1.] They valued themselves so much on their wealth that they looked upon all that were poor with the highest contempt imaginable; they hated them, could not endure them, but abandoned them, and therefore did what they could to make them cease, not by relieving them to make them cease to be poor, but by banishing and destroying them to make them cease to be, or at least to be in their land. But he who thus *reproaches the poor despises his Maker*, in whose hands *rich and poor meet together.* [2.] They were so eager to increase their wealth, and make it more, that they robbed the poor to enrich themselves; and they fastened upon the poor, to *make a prey* of them, because they were not able to obtain any redress nor to resist or revenge the violence of their oppressors. Those riches that are got by the ruin of the poor will bring ruin on those that get them. They swallowed up the poor by making them hard bargains, and cheating them in those bargains; for *therefore* they *falsify the balances by deceit*, not only that they *may enrich themselves*, may have money at command, and so may have every thing else (as they think) at command too, but that they may impoverish those about them, and bring them so low that they may force them to become slaves to them, and so, having drained them of every thing else, they may have their labour for nothing, or next to nothing. Thus *they buy the poor for silver ;* they bring them and their *children into bondage*, because they have not wherewithal to pay for the corn they have bought; see Neh. v. 2—5. And there were so many that were reduced to this extremity that the price was very low; and the oppressors had beaten it down so that you might buy a poor man to be your slave *for a pair of shoes.* Property was first invaded and then liberty; it is the method of oppressors first to make men beggars and then to make them their vassals. Thus is the dignity of the human nature lost in the misery of those that are trampled on and the tenderness of it in the sin of those that trample on them.

II. The grievousness of the punishment that shall be inflicted on them for this sin. When the poor are injured they will *cry unto God*, and he will hear their cry, and reckon with those that are injurious to them, for, they being his receivers, he takes the wrongs done to them as done to himself, Exod. xxii. 23, 24.

1. God will remember their sin against them: *He has sworn by the excellency of Jacob (v. 7)*, by himself, for he can swear by

no greater; and who but he is the glory and magnificence of Jacob? He has sworn by those tokens of his presence with them, and his favour to them, which they had profaned and abused, and had done what they could to make them detestable to him; for he is said (*ch.* vi. 8) to *abhor the excellency of Jacob.* He swears *in his wrath*, swears by his own name, that name which was so well known and was so great in Israel. He swears, *Surely I will never forget any of their works*, but upon all occasions they shall be remembered against them, for more is implied than is expressed. *I will never forget them* is as much as to say, *I will never forgive them ;* and then it proclaims the case of these unjust unmerciful men to be miserable indeed, eternally miserable; woe, and a thousand woes, to that man that is cut off by an oath of God from all benefit by pardoning mercy; and those have reason to fear judgment without mercy that have *shown no mercy.*

2. He will bring utter ruin and confusion upon them. It is here described largely, and in a great variety of emphatic expressions, that, if possible, they might be frightened into a sincere repentance and reformation. (1.) There shall be a universal terror and consternation: *Shall not the land tremble for this* (v. 8), *this land*, out of which you thought to drive the poor? *Shall not every one mourn that dwells therein?* Certainly he shall. Note, Those that will not tremble and mourn as they ought for national sins shall be made to tremble and mourn for national judgments; those that look without concern upon the sins of the oppressors, which should make them tremble, and upon the miseries of the oppressed, which should them mourn, God will find out a way to make them tremble at the fury of those that oppress them and mourn for their own losses and sufferings by it. (2.) There shall be a universal deluge and desolation. When God comes forth against them the waters of trouble and calamity shall *rise up wholly as a flood*, that swells, when it is dammed up, and soon overflows its banks. Every thing shall make against them. That with which they thought to check the progress of God's judgments shall but make them rise the higher. Judgments shall force their way as the *breaking forth of waters.* The whole land *shall be cast out, and drowned*, and laid under water, as the land of Egypt is every year by the overflowing of its river Nile. Or the expressions may allude to some former judgments of God. Their ruin *shall rise up wholly as a flood*, as Noah's flood, which overwhelmed the whole world, so shall this the whole land; and the land shall be *cast out, and drowned, as by the flood of Egypt*, as Pharaoh and his Egyptians were buried in the Red Sea, which was to them the *flood of Egypt*, both which judgments, as this which is here threatened, were the punishment of violence and oppression, which the Lord is the avenger of.

3. It shall surprise them, and come upon them when they little think of it (*v.* 9): "*I will cause the sun to go down at noon,* when it is in its full strength and lustre, at their noon, when they promise themselves a long afternoon, and think they have at least half a day good before them. The *earth* shall be *darkened in the clear day,* when every thing looks pleasant and hopeful." Thus uncertain are all our creature-comforts and enjoyments, even life itself; the highest degree of health and prosperity often proves the next degree to sickness and adversity; Job's sun *went down at noon;* many are taken away in the midst of their days, and their sun goes down at noon. In the midst of life we are in death. Thus *terrible* are the judgments of God to those that sleep in security; they are to them as the sun's *going down at noon;* the less they are expected the more confounding they are. When they *cry Peace and safety* then *sudden destruction* comes, comes *as a snare,* Luke xxi. 35.

4. It shall change their note, and mar all their mirth (*v.* 10): *I will turn your feasts into mourning,* as (*v.* 3) the *songs of the temple into howlings.* Note, The end of the sinner's mirth and jollity is heaviness. As *to the upright there arises light in the darkness,* which gives them *the oil of joy for mourning,* so on the wicked there falls darkness in the midst of light, which turns their *laughter into mourning,* their *joy into heaviness.* So great, so general, shall the desolation be, that *sackcloth shall be brought upon all loins, and baldness upon every head,* instead of the *well-set hair* and the rich garments they used to wear. The mourning at that day shall be as *mourning for an only son,* which denotes the most bitter and lasting lamentation. But are there are no hopes that when things are at the worst they will mend, and that at evening time it will yet be light? No, even *the end thereof shall be as a bitter day,* a day of bitter mourning; the state of impenitent sinners grows worse and worse, and the last of all will be the worst of all. *This shall you have at my hand, you shall lie down in sorrow.*

11 Behold, the days come, saith the Lord GOD, that I will send a famine in the land, not a famine of bread, nor a thirst for water, but of hearing the words of the LORD: 12 And they shall wander from sea to sea, and from the north even to the east, they shall run to and fro to seek the word of the LORD, and shall not find *it.* 13 In that day shall the fair virgins and young men faint for thirst. 14 They that swear by the sin of Samaria, and say, Thy god, O Dan, liveth; and, The manner of Beer-sheba liveth;

even they shall fall, and never rise up again.

In these verses is threatened,

I. A general judgment of spiritual famine coming upon the whole land, a *famine of the word of God,* the failing of oracles and the scarcity of good preaching. This is spoken of as a thing at some distance: *The days come,* they will come hereafter, when another kind of darkness shall come upon that land of light. When Amos prophesied, and for a considerable time after, they had great plenty of prophets, abundant opportunities of *hearing the word of God,* in season and out of season; they had precept upon precept and line upon line; prophecy was their daily bread; and it is probable that they surfeited upon it, as Israel on the manna, and therefore God threatens that hereafter he will deprive them of this privilege. Probably in the land of Israel there were not so many prophets, about the time that their destruction came upon them, as there were in the land of Judah; and when the ten tribes went into captivity they *saw not their signs,* there were *no more any prophets,* none to *show them how long,* Ps. lxxiv. 9. The Jewish church, after Malachi, had no prophets for many ages; and some think this threatening looks further yet, to the blindness which has in part happened to Israel in the days of the Messiah, and the veil that is on the heart of the unbelieving Jews. They reject the gospel, and the ministers of it that God sends to them, and covet to have prophets of their own, as their fathers had, but they shall have none, *the kingdom of God* being *taken from them* and *given to another people.* Observe here,

1. What the judgment itself is that is threatened. It is a famine, a scarcity, not of bread and water (which are the necessary supports of the body, and the want of which is very grievous), but a much sorer judgment than that, even a *famine of hearing the words of the Lord.* There shall be no congregations for ministers to preach to, nor any ministers to preach, nor any instructions and abilities given to those that do set up for preachers, to fit them for their work. The *word of the Lord* shall be *precious* and scarce; there shall be no *vision,* 1 Sam. iii. 1. They shall have the written word, Bibles to read, but no ministers to explain and apply it to them, the water in the well, but nothing to draw with. It is a gracious promise (Isa. xxx. 20) that though they have a scarcity of bread they shall have plenty of the means of grace. God will *give them the bread of adversity and the water of affliction,* but their eyes shall see their teachers; and it was a common saying among the Puritans that brown bread and the gospel are good fare. But it is here a threatening that on the contrary they should have plenty enough of bread and water, and yet their teachers should

be removed. Now, (1.) This was the departure of a great part of their glory from their land. This made their nation great and high, that *to them were committed the oracles of God;* but, when these were taken from them, their beauty was stained and their honour laid in the dust. (2.) This was a token of God's highest displeasure against them. Surely he was angry indeed with them when he would no more speak to them as he had done, and had abandoned them to ruin when he would no more afford them the means of bringing them to repentance. (3.) This made all the other calamities that were upon them truly melancholy, that they had no prophets to instruct and comfort them from the word of God, nor to give them any hopeful prospect. We should say at any time, and shall say in a time of trouble, that a famine of the word of God is the sorest famine, the heaviest judgment.

2. What will be the effect of this (*v.* 12): *They shall wander from sea to sea,* from the sea of Tiberias to the Great Sea, from one border of the country to another, to see if God will send them prophets, either by sea or land, from other countries; since they have none among themselves, they shall go from the *north to the east;* when they are disappointed in one place they shall try another, and shall *run to and fro,* as men at a loss, and in a hot pursuit to *seek the word of the Lord,* to enquire if there be any prophets, any prophecy, any message from God, but they *shall not find it.* (1.) Though to many this is no affliction at all, yet some will be very sensible of it as a great grievance, and will gladly travel far to hear a good sermon; but they shall sensibly feel the loss of those mercies which others have foolishly sinned away. (2.) Even those that slighted prophets when they had them shall wish for them, as Saul did for Samuel, when they are deprived of them. Many never know the worth of mercies till they feel the want of them. Or it may be meant thus, Though they should thus wander from sea to sea, in quest of the word of God, yet they shall not find it. Note, The means of grace are moveable things; and the candlestick, when we think it stands most firmly, may be removed out of its place (Rev. ii. 5); and those that now slight the *days of the son of man* may wish in vain to see them. And *in the day* of this famine *the fair virgins and the young men shall faint for thirst* (*v.* 13); those who, one would think, could well enough have borne the toil, shall sink under it. The *Jewish churches,* and the *masters of their synagogues,* some take to be meant by the *virgins* and the *young men;* these shall lose the word of the Lord, and the benefit of divine revelation, and shall faint away for want of it, shall lose all their strength and beauty. Those that trust in their own merit and righteousness, and think they have no need of Christ, others take to be meant by the *fair virgins* and the

1264

choice young men; they shall *faint for thirst,* when those that *hunger and thirst after the righteousness* of Christ shall be abundantly satisfied and filled.

II. The particular destruction of those that were ringleaders in idolatry, *v.* 14. Observe, 1. The sin they are charged with: They *swear by the sin of Samaria,* that is, by the god of Samaria, the idol that was worshipped at Bethel, not far off from Samaria. Thus did they glory in their shame, and swear by that as their god which was their iniquity, thinking that could help them which would certainly ruin them, and giving the highest honour to that which they should have looked upon with the utmost abhorrence and detestation. They say, *Thy god, O Dan! liveth;* that was the other golden calf, a dumb dead idol, and yet caressed and complimented as if it had been the living and true God. They say, *The manner,* or way, of *Beer-sheba liveth;* they swore by the *religion* of Beer-sheba, the way and manner of worship used there, which they looked upon as sacred, and therefore swore by and appealed to as a judge of controversy. Thus the papists swear by the mass, as the *manner of Beer-sheba.* 2. The destruction they are threatened with. Those who thus give that honour to idols which is due to God alone will find that the God they affront is thereby made their enemy, so that *they shall fall,* and the gods they serve cannot stand their friends, so that they shall *never rise again.* They will find that God is jealous and will resent the indignity done him, and that he will be victorious and it is to no purpose to contend with him.

CHAP. IX.

In this chapter we have, I. Judgment threatened, which the sinners shall not escape (ver. 1—4), which an almighty power shall inflict (ver. 5, 6), which the people of Israel have deserved as a sinful people (ver. 7, 8); and yet it shall not be the utter ruin of their nation (ver. 8), for a remnant of good people shall escape, ver. 9. But the wicked ones shall perish, ver. 10. II. Mercy promised, which was to be bestowed in the latter days (ver. 11—15), as appears by the application of it to the days of the Messiah, Acts xv. 16. And with those comfortable promises, after all the foregoing rebukes and threatenings, the book concludes.

I SAW the Lord standing upon the altar: and he said, Smite the lintel of the door, that the posts may shake: and cut them in the head, all of them; and I will slay the last of them with the sword: he that fleeth of them shall not flee away, and he that escapeth of them shall not be delivered. 2 Though they dig into hell, thence shall mine hand take them; though they climb up to heaven, thence will I bring them down: 3 And though they hide themselves in the top of Carmel, I will search and take them out thence; and though they be hid from my sight in the bottom of the sea, thence will I command the serpent, and he shall bite them : 4 And though they go into captivity before their enemies, thence will I command the sword, and it shall slay them : and I will set mine eyes upon them for evil, and not for good. 5 And the Lord God of hosts *is* he that toucheth the land, and it shall melt, and all that dwell therein shall mourn: and it shall rise up wholly like a flood; and shall be drowned, as *by* the flood of Egypt. 6 *It is* he that buildeth his stories in the heaven, and hath founded his troop in the earth ; he that calleth for the waters of the sea, and poureth them out upon the face of the earth : The Lord *is* his name. 7 *Are* ye not as children of the Ethiopians unto me, O children of Israel ? saith the Lord. Have not I brought up Israel out of the land of Egypt? and the Philistines from Caphtor, and the Syrians from Kir ? 8 Behold, the eyes of the Lord God *are* upon the sinful kingdom, and I will destroy it from off the face of the earth ; saving that I will not utterly destroy the house of Jacob, saith the Lord. 9 For, lo, I will command, and I will sift the house of Israel among all nations, like as *corn* is sifted in a sieve, yet shall not the least grain fall upon the earth. 10 All the sinners of my people shall die by the sword, which say, The evil shall not overtake nor prevent us.

We have here the justice of God passing sentence upon a provoking people ; and observe,

I. With what solemnity the sentence is passed. The prophet saw in vision *the Lord standing upon the altar* (*v.* 1), the altar of burnt-offerings ; for the *Lord has a sacrifice,* and multitudes must fall as victims to his justice. He is removed from the *mercy-seat* between the *cherubim,* and stands upon *the altar,* the *judgment-seat,* on which the fire of God used to fall, to devour the sacrifices. He stands upon *the altar,* to show that the ground of his controversy with this people was their profanation of his holy things ; here he stands to avenge the quarrel of his altar, as also to signify that the sin of the house of Israel, like that of the house of Eli, shall *not be purged with sacrifice nor offering for ever,* 1 Sam. iii. 14. He stands on the altar, to prohibit sacrifice. Now the order given is, *Smite the lintel of the door* of the temple, the chapter, smite it with such a blow *that the*

posts may shake, and *cut them,* wound them *in the head, all of them ;* break down the door of God's house, or of the courts of his house, in token of this, that he is going out from it, and forsaking it, and then all judgments are breaking in upon it. Or it signifies the destruction of those in the first place that should be as the door-posts to the nation for its defence, so that, they being broken down, it becomes as a *city without gates and bars.* " Smite the king, who is as the lintel of the door, that the princes, who are as *the posts,* may *shake ; cut them in the head,* cleave them down, *all of them,* as wood for the fire ; and *I will slay the last of them,* the posterity of them, them and their families, or the *least* of them, them and all that are employed under them ; or, I will *slay them all,* them and all that remain of them, till it comes to the last man ; the slaughter shall be general." There is no living for those on whom God has said, *I will slay* them, no standing before his sword.

II. What effectual care is taken that none shall escape the execution of this sentence. This is enlarged upon here, and is intended for warning to all that *provoke the Lord to jealousy.* Let sinners read it, and tremble ; as there is no fighting it out with God, so there is no fleeing from him. His judgments, when they come with commission, as they will overpower the strongest that think to outface them, so they will overtake the swiftest that think to out-run them, *v.* 2. Those of them that flee, and take to their heels, shall soon be out of breath, and shall not flee away out of the reach of danger ; for, as sometimes *the wicked flee when none pursues,* so he cannot flee away when God pursues, though *he would fain flee out of his hand.* Nay, *he that escapes of them,* that thinks he has gained his point, *shall not be delivered. Evil pursues sinners,* and will arrest them. This is here enlarged upon by showing that wherever sinners flee for shelter from God's justice, it will overtake them, and the shelter will prove but a *refuge of lies.* What David says of the ubiquity of God's presence (Ps. cxxxix. 7—10) is here said of the extent of God's power and justice. (1.) Hell itself, though it has its name in English from its being *hilled,* or *covered over,* or *hidden,* cannot hide them (*v.* 2) : "Though *they dig into hell,* into the centre of the earth, or the darkest recesses of it, yet *thence shall my hand take them,* and bring them forth to be made public monuments of divine justice." The grave is a hiding-place to the righteous from the malice of the world (Job iii. 17), but it shall be no hiding-place to the wicked from the justice of God ; thence God's hands shall take them, when they shall rise in the great day to *everlasting shame and contempt.* (2.) Heaven, though it has its name from being *heaved,* or lifted up, shall not put them out of the reach of God's judgments ; as hell cannot hide them, so heaven will not.

Though they *climb up to heaven* in their own conceit, yet *thence will I bring them down.* Those whom God brings to heaven by his grace shall never be brought down; but those who climb thither themselves, by their own presumption, and confidence in themselves, will be brought down and filled with shame. (3.) *The top of Carmel,* one of the highest parts of the dust of the world in that country, shall not protect them: " *Though they hide themselves there,* where they imagine nobody will look for them, *I will search, and take them out thence;* neither the thickest bushes, nor the darkest caves, in the *top of Carmel,* will serve to hide them." (4.) The *bottom of the sea* shall not serve to conceal them; though they think to hide themselves there, even there the judgments of God shall find them out, and lay hold on them : *Thence will I command the serpent, and he shall bite them,* the crooked serpent, even *the dragon that is in the sea,* Isa. xxvii. 1. They shall find their plague and death where they hope to find shelter and protection; diving will stand them in no more stead than climbing. (5.) Remote countries will not befriend them, nor shall less judgments excuse them from greater (*v.* 4) : *Though they go into captivity before their enemies,* who carry them to places at a great distance, and mingle them with their own people, among whom they seem to be lost, yet that shall not serve their turn : *Thence will I command the sword, and it shall slay them,* the sword of the enemy, or one another's sword. When God judges he will overcome. That which binds on all this, makes their escape impossible and their ruin inevitable, is that God will *set his eyes upon them for evil, and not for good.* His eyes are in every place, are upon all men and upon all the ways of men, upon some for good, to *show himself strong* on their behalf, but upon others for evil, to take notice of their sins (Job xiii. 27) and take all opportunities of punishing them for their sins. *Their* case is truly miserable who have the providence of God : and all the dispensations of it, against them, working for their hurt.

3. What a great and mighty God he is that passes this sentence upon them, and will take the executing of it into his own hands. Threatenings are more or less formidable according to the power of him that threatens. We laugh at impotent wrath; but the wrath of God is not so; it is omnipotent wrath. *Who knows the power* of it? What he had before said he would do (*ch.* viii. 8) is here repeated, that he would *make the land melt* and tremble, and *all that dwell therein mourn,* that the judgment should *rise up wholly like a flood,* and the country should *be drowned,* and laid under water, *as by the flood of Egypt, v.* 5. But is he able to make his words good? Yes, certainly he is; he does but *touch the land* and *it melts, touch the mountains* and they smoke; he can do it with the greatest ease, for, (1.) He is *the Lord God of hosts,*

who undertakes to do it, the God who has all the power in his hand, and all creatures at his beck and call, who having made them all, and given them their several capacities, makes what use he pleases of them and all their powers. Very miserable is the case of those who have the Lord of hosts against them, for they have hosts against them, the whole creation at war with them. (2.) He is the Creator and governor of the upper world : *It is he that builds his stories in the heavens,* the celestial orbs, or spheres, one over another, as so many stories in a high and stately palace. They are his, for he built them at first, when he said, *Let there be a firmament, and he made the firmament ;* and he builds them still, is continually building them, not that they need repair, but by his providence he still upholds them; his power is the pillars of heaven, by which it is borne up. Now he that has the command of those stories is certainly to be feared, for thence, as from a castle, he can fire upon his enemies, or cast upon them great hailstones, as on the Canaanites, or make the stars in their courses, the furniture of those stories, to fight against them, as against Sisera. (3.) He has the management and command of this lower world too, in which we dwell, the terraqueous globe, both *earth* and *sea,* so that, which way soever his enemies think to make their escape, he will meet them, or to make opposition, he will match them. Do they think to make a land-fight of it? He *has founded his troop in the earth,* his troop of guards, which he has at command, and makes use of for the protection of his subjects and the punishment of his enemies. All the creatures on earth make one bundle (as the margin reads it), one bundle of arrows, out of which he takes what he pleases to discharge against the persecutors, Ps. vii. 13. They are all one *army,* one *body,* so closely are they connected, and so harmoniously and so much in concert do they act for the accomplishing of their Creator's purposes. Do they think to make a sea-fight of it? He will be too hard for them there, for he has the waters of the sea at command; even its waves, the most tumultuous rebellious waters, do obey him. He *calls for the waters of the sea* in the course of his common providence, *causes vapours to ascend* out of it, and *pours them out* in showers, the small rain and the great rain of his strength, *upon the face of the earth;* this was mentioned before as a reason why we should *seek the Lord* (*ch.* v. 8) and make him our friend, as it is here made a reason why we should fear him and dread having him for our enemy.

4. How justly God passes this sentence upon the people of Israel. He does not destroy them by an act of sovereignty, but by an act of righteousness; for (*v.* 8), it is a *sinful kingdom,* and the *eyes of the Lord* are upon it, discovering it to be so; he sees the great sinfulness of it, and therefore he will

destroy it from off the face of the earth. Note, When those kingdoms that in name and profession were holy kingdoms, and kingdoms of priests, as Israel was, become sinful kingdoms, no other can be expected than that they should be cut off and abandoned. Let sinful kingdoms, and sinful families, and sinful persons too, see the eyes of the Lord upon them, observing all their wickedness, and reserving the notice of it for the day of reckoning and recompence. This being a sinful kingdom, see how light God makes of it, *v.* 7.

(1.) Of the relation wherein he stood to it: *Are you not as children of the Ethiopians unto me, O children of Israel?* A sad change! Children of Israel become as children of the Ethiopians! [1.] They were so in themselves; that was their sin. It is a thing to be greatly lamented that the children of Israel often become as children of the Ethiopians; the children of godly parents degenerate, and become the reverse of those that went before them. Those that were well-educated, and trained up in the knowledge and fear of God, and set out well, and promised fair, throw off their profession and become as bad as the worst. *How has the gold become dim!* [2.] They were so in God's account, and that was their punishment. He valued them no more, though they were children of Israel, than if they had been *children of the Ethiopians.* We read of one in the title of Ps. vii. that was *Cush* (an *Ethiopian*, so some understand it) and yet a Benjamite. Those that by birth and profession are children of Israel, if they degenerate, and become wicked and vile, are to God no more than children of the Ethiopians. This is an intimation of the rejection of the unbelieving Jews in the days of the Messiah; because they embraced not the doctrine of Christ, the kingdom of God was taken from them, they were unchurched, and cast out of covenant, became as children of the Ethiopians, and are so to this day. And it is true of those that are called Christians, but do not live up to their name and profession, that rest in the form of piety, but live under the power of reigning iniquity, that they are to God as children of the Ethiopians; he rejects them, and their services.

(2.) See how light he makes of the favours he had conferred upon them; they thought he would not, he could not, cast them off, and put them upon a level with other nations, because he had done that for them which he had not done for other nations, whereby they thought he was bound to them, so as never to leave them. " No," says he, " The favours shown to you are not so distinguishing as you think they are: *Have not I brought up Israel out of the land of Egypt?* It is true I have; but I have also brought the *Philistines from Caphtor,* or *Cappadocia,* where they were natives, or captives, or both;

they are called the *remnant of the country of Caphtor* (Jer. xlvii. 4), and the Philistim are joined with the Caphtorim, Gen. x. 14. In like manner the Syrians were brought up from Kir when they had been carried away thither, 2 Kings xvi. 9. Note, If God's Israel lose the peculiarity of their holiness, they lose the peculiarity of their privileges; and what was designed as a favour of special grace shall be set in another light, shall have its property altered, and shall become an act of *common providence;* if professors liken themselves to the world, God will level them with the world. And, if we live not up to the obligation of God's mercies, we forfeit the honour and comfort of them.

5. How graciously God will separate between the precious and the vile in the day of retribution. Though the wicked Israelites shall be as the wicked Ethiopians, and their being called Israelites shall stand them in no stead, yet the pious Israelites shall not be as the *wicked* ones; no, the *Judge of all the earth will do right,* more right than to *slay the righteous with the wicked,* Gen. xviii. 25. His *eyes are upon the sinful kingdom,* to spy out those in it who preserve their integrity and swim against the stream, who sigh and cry for the abominations of their land, and they shall be marked for preservation, so that the destruction shall not be total: *I will not utterly destroy the house of Jacob,* not ruin them by wholesale and in the gross, good and bad together, but I will distinguish, as becomes a righteous judge. The house of Israel shall be *sifted as corn is sifted;* they shall be greatly hurried, and shaken, and tossed, but still in the hands of God, in both his hands, as the sieve in the hands of him that sifts (*v.* 9): *I will sift the house of Israel among all nations.* Wherever they are shaken and scattered, God will have his eye upon them, and will take care to separate between the corn and chaff, which was the thing he designed in sifting them. (1.) The righteous ones among them, that are as the solid wheat, shall none of them perish; they shall be delivered either from or through the common calamities of the kingdom; *not the least grain shall fall on the earth,* so as to be lost and forgotten—not the least *stone* (so the word is), for the good corn is weighty as a stone in comparison with that which we call *light corn.* Note, Whatever shakings there may be in the world, God does and will effectually provide that none who are truly his shall be truly miserable. (2.) The wicked ones among them who are hardened in their sins shall all of them perish, *v.* 10. See what a height of impiety they have come to: *They say, The evil shall not overtake nor prevent us.* They think they are innocent, and do not deserve punishment, or that the profession they make of relation to God will be their exemption and security from punishment, or that they shall be able to make their part good against the judgments of

God, that they shall flee so swiftly from them that they shall not overtake them, or guard so carefully against them that they shall not prevent or surprise them. Note, Hope of impunity is the deceitful refuge of the impenitent. But see what it will come to at last: *All the sinners* that thus flatter themselves, and affront God, shall *die by the sword,* the sword of war, which to them shall be the sword of divine vengeance; yea, though they be the *sinners of my people,* for their profession shall not be their protection. Note, Evil is often nearest those that put it at the greatest distance from them.

11 In that day will I raise up the tabernacle of David that is fallen, and close up the breaches thereof; and I will raise up his ruins, and I will build it as in the days of old: 12 That they may possess the remnant of Edom, and of all the heathen, which are called by my name, saith the LORD that doeth this. 13 Behold, the days come, saith the LORD, that the ploughman shall overtake the reaper, and the treader of grapes him that soweth seed; and the mountains shall drop sweet wine, and all the hills shall melt. 14 And I will bring again the captivity of my people of Israel, and they shall build the waste cities, and inhabit *them;* and they shall plant vineyards, and drink the wine thereof; they shall also make gardens, and eat the fruit of them. 15 And I will plant them upon their land, and they shall no more be pulled up out of their land which I have given them, saith the LORD thy God.

To him to whom all the prophets bear witness this prophet, here in the close, bears his testimony, and speaks of *that day,* those days that shall come, in which God will do great things for his church, by the setting up of the kingdom of the Messiah, for the rejecting of which the rejection of the Jews was foretold in the foregoing verses. The promise here is said to agree to the planting of the Christian church, and in that to be fulfilled, Acts xv. 15—17. It is promised,

I, That in the Messiah the kingdom of David shall be restored (*v.* 11); the *tabernacle of David* it is called, that is, his house and family, which, though great and fixed, yet, in comparison with the kingdom of heaven, was mean and movable as a tabernacle. The church militant, in its present state, dwelling as in shepherds' tents to feed, as in soldiers' tents to fight, is the *tabernacle of David.* God's tabernacle is called the tabernacle of David because David de-

sired and chose to *dwell in God's tabernacle for ever,* Ps. lxi. 4. Now, 1. These tabernacles had fallen and gone to decay, the royal family was so impoverished, its power abridged, its honour stained, and laid in the dust; for many of that race degenerated, and in the captivity it lost the imperial dignity. Sore breaches were made upon it, and at length it was laid in ruins. So it was with the church of the Jews; in the latter days of it its glory departed; it was like a tabernacle broken down and brought to ruin, in respect both of purity and of prosperity. 2. By Jesus Christ these tabernacles were raised and rebuilt. In him God's covenant with David had its accomplishment; and the glory of that house, which was not only sullied, but quite sunk, revived again; the *breaches* of it were *closed* and its *ruins raised up, as in the days of old;* nay, the spiritual glory of the family of Christ far exceeded the temporal glory of the family of David when it was at its height. In him also God's covenant with Israel had its accomplishment, and in the gospel-church the tabernacle of God was set up among men again, and raised up out of the ruins of the Jewish state. This is quoted in the first council at Jerusalem as referring to the calling in of the Gentiles and God's *taking out of them a people for his name.* Note, While the world stands God will have a church in it, and, if it be fallen down in one place and among one people, it shall be raised up elsewhere.

II. That that kingdom shall be enlarged, and the territories of it shall extend far, by the accession of many countries to it (*v.* 12), that the house of David may possess the *remnant of Edom, and of all the heathen,* that is, that Christ may have them given him for his *inheritance,* even *the uttermost parts of the earth for his possession,* Ps. ii. 8. Those that had been strangers and enemies shall become willing faithful subjects to the Son of David, shall be *added to the church,* or those of them that are *called by my name, saith the Lord,* that is, that belong to the election of grace and are ordained to eternal life (Acts xiii. 48), for it is true of the Gentiles as well as of the Jews that *the election hath obtained* and *the rest were blinded,* Rom. xi. 7. Christ died to *gather together in one the children of God that were scattered abroad,* here said to be those that were *called by his name.* The promise is to all that are *afar off,* even as *many* of them as *the Lord our God shall call,* Acts ii. 39. St. James expounds this as a promise *that the residue of men should seek after the Lord, even all the Gentiles upon whom my name is called.* But may the promise be depended upon? Yes, the Lord says this, who does this, who can do it, who has determined to do it, the power of whose grace is engaged for the doing of it, and with whom saying and doing are not two things, as they are with us.

III That in the kingdom of the Messiah

there shall be great plenty, an abundance of all good things that the country produces (*v.* 13): *The ploughman shall overtake the reaper,* that is, there shall be such a plentiful harvest every year, and so much corn to be gathered in, that it shall last all summer, even till autumn, when it is time to begin to plough again; and in like manner the vintage shall continue till seed-time, and there shall be such abundance of grapes that even the *mountains shall drop new wine* into the vessels of the grape-gatherers, and the hills that were dry and barren shall be moistened and shall melt with the *fatness* or *mellowness* (as we call it) of *the soil.* Compare this with Joel ii. 24, and iii. 18. This must certainly be understood of the abundance of spiritual blessings in heavenly things, which all those are, and shall be, blessed with, who are in sincerity added to Christ and his church; they shall be abundantly replenished with the goodness of God's house, with the graces and comforts of his Spirit; they shall have bread, the bread of life, to *strengthen their hearts,* and the wine of divine consolations to *make them glad*—*meat indeed* and *drink indeed* —all the benefit that comes to the souls of men from the word and Spirit of God. These had been long confined to the vineyard of the Jewish church; divine revelation, and the power that attended it, were to be found only within that enclosure; but in gospel-times the mountains and hills of the Gentile world shall be enriched with these privileges by the gospel of Christ preached, and professed, and received in the power of it. When great multitudes were converted to the faith of Christ, and nations were born at once, when the preachers of the gospel were *always caused to triumph in* the success of their preaching, then the *ploughman overtook the reaper;* and, when the Gentile churches were *enriched in all utterance, and in all knowledge,* and all manner of *spiritual gifts* (1 Cor. i. 5), then the *mountains dropped sweet wine.*

IV. That the kingdom of the Messiah shall be well peopled; as the country shall be replenished, so shall the cities be; there shall be mouths for this meat, *v.* 14. Those that were carried captives shall be brought back out of their captivity; their enemies shall not be able to detain them in the land of their captivity, nor shall they themselves incline to settle in it, but the remnant shall return, and shall *build the waste cities and inhabit them,* shall form themselves into Christian churches and set up pure doctrine, worship, and discipline among them, according to the gospel charter, by which Christ's cities are incorporated; and they shall enjoy the benefit and comfort thereof; they shall *plant vineyards,* and *make gardens.* Though the mountains and hills drop wine, and the privileges of the gospel-church are laid in common, yet they shall enclose for themselves, not to monopolize these privileges, to the exclusion of others, but to appropriate and improve these privileges, in communion with others, and they shall *drink the wine,* and *eat the fruit,* of their own *vineyards and gardens;* for those that take pains in religion, as men must do about their vineyards and gardens, shall have both the pleasure and the profit of it. The *bringing again* of the *captivity* of God's Israel, which is here promised, may refer to the cancelling of the ceremonial law, which had been long to God's Israel as a *yoke of bondage,* and the investing of them in the liberty wherewith Christ came to make his church free, Gal. v. 1.

V. That the kingdom of the Messiah shall take such deep rooting in the world as never to be rooted out of it (*v.* 15): *I will plant them upon their land.* God's spiritual Israel shall be planted by the right hand of God himself upon the land assigned them, and *they shall no more be pulled up out of it,* as the old Jewish church was. God will preserve them from throwing themselves out of it by a total apostasy, and will preserve them from being thrown out of it by the malice of their enemies; the church may be corrupted, but shall not quite forsake God, may be persecuted, but shall not quite be forsaken of God, so that the gates of hell, neither with their temptations nor with their terrors, shall prevail against it. Two things secure the perpetuity of the church:—1. God's grants to it: It is *the land which I have given them;* and God will confirm and maintain his own grants. The part he has given to his people is that good part which shall never be taken from them; he will not revoke his grant, and all the powers of earth and hell shall not invalidate it. 2. Its interest in him: He is *the Lord thy God,* who has said it, and will make it good, *thine, O Israel!* who shall *reign for ever* as thine *unto all generations.* And because he lives the church shall live also.

AN

EXPOSITION,

WITH PRACTICAL OBSERVATIONS,

OF THE PROPHECY OF

OBADIAH.

THIS is the shortest of all the books of the Old Testament, the least of those tribes, and yet is not to be passed by, or thought meanly of, for this penny has Cæsar's image and superscription upon it; it is stamped with a divine authority. There may appear much of God in a short sermon, in a little book; and much good may be done by it, *multum in parvo—much in a little.* Mr. Norris says, "If angels were to write books, we should have few folios." That may be very precious which is not voluminous. This book is entitled, *The Vision of Obadiah.* Who this Obadiah was does not appear from any other scripture. Some of the ancients imagined him to be the same with that Obadiah that was steward to Ahab's household (1 Kings xviii. 3); and, if so, he that hid and fed the prophets had indeed a prophet's reward, when he was himself made a prophet. But that is a conjecture which has no ground. This Obadiah, it is probable, was of a later date, some think contemporary with Hosea, Joel, and Amos; others think he lived about the time of the destruction of Jerusalem, when the children of Edom so barbarously triumphed in that destruction. However, what he wrote was what he saw; it is his *vision.* Probably there was much more which he was divinely inspired to speak, but this is all he was inspired to write; and all he writes is concerning Edom. It is a foolish fancy of some of the Jews that because he prophesies only concerning Edom he was himself an Edomite by birth, but a proselyte to the Jewish religion. Other prophets prophesied against Edom, and some of them seem to have borrowed from him in their predictions against Edom, as Jer. xlix. 7, &c.; Ezek. xxv. 12, &c. Out of the mouth of these two or three witnesses every word will be established.

This book is wholly concerning Edom, a nation nearly allied and near adjoining to Israel, and yet an enemy to the seed of Jacob, inheriting the enmity of their father Esau to Jacob. Now here we have, after the preface, ver. 1, I. Threatenings against Edom, 1. That their pride should be humbled, ver. 2—4. 2. That their wealth should be plundered, ver. 5—7. 3. That their wisdom should be infatuated, ver. 8, 9. 4. That their spiteful behaviour towards God's Israel should be avenged, ver. 10—16. II. Gracious promises to Israel; that they shall be restored and reformed, and shall be victorious over the Edomites, and become masters of their land and the lands of others of their neighbours (ver. 17—20), and that the kingdom of the Messiah shall be set up by the bringing in of the great salvation, ver. 21.

THE vision of Obadiah. Thus saith the Lord GOD concerning Edom; We have heard a rumour from the LORD, and an ambassador is sent among the heathen, Arise ye, and let us rise up against her in battle. 2 Behold, I have made thee small among the heathen: thou art greatly despised. 3 The pride of thine heart hath deceived thee, thou that dwellest in the clefts of the rock, whose habitation *is* high; that saith in his heart, Who shall bring me down to the ground?

4 Though thou exalt *thyself* as the eagle, and though thou set thy nest among the stars, thence will I bring thee down, saith the LORD. 5 If thieves came to thee, if robbers by night, (how art thou cut off!) would they not have stolen till they had enough? if the grape-gatherers came to thee, would they not leave *some* grapes? 6 How are *the things* of Esau searched out! *how* are his hidden things sought up! 7 All the men of thy confederacy have brought thee *even* to the border: the men that were at peace with thee have deceived thee, *and* prevailed against thee; *they that eat* thy bread have laid a wound under thee: *there is* none understanding in him. 8 Shall I not in that day, saith the LORD, even destroy the wise *men* out of Edom, and under-

standing out of the mount of Esau?
9 And thy mighty *men,* O Teman,
shall be dismayed, to the end that
every one of the mount of Esau may
be cut off by slaughter.

Edom is the nation against which this
prophecy is levelled, and which, some think,
is put for all the enemies of Israel, that
shall be brought down first or last. The
rabbin by Edom understand Rome. Rome
Christian they understand it of, and have
an implacable enmity to it as such; but, if
we understand it of Rome antichristian, we
shall find the passages of it applicable
enough. And though Edom was mortified
in the times of the Maccabees, as it had
been before by Jehoshaphat, yet its destruction seems to have been typical, as their father
Esau's rejection, and to have had further
reference to the destruction of the enemies
of the gospel-church; for so shall all God's
enemies perish; and we find (Isa. xxxiv. 5)
the *sword of the Lord* coming down *upon
Idumea,* to signify the general day of God's
recompences for the controversy of Zion, *v.*
8. Some have well observed that it could
not but be a great temptation to the people
of Israel, when they saw themselves, who
were the children of beloved Jacob, in trouble, and the Edomites, the seed of hated
Esau, not only prospering, but triumphing
over them in their troubles; and therefore
God gives them a prospect of the destruction
of Edom, which should be total and final,
and of a happy issue of their own correction.
Now we may observe here,

I. A declaration of war against Edom,
(*v.* 1): " *We have heard a rumour,* or rather
an order, from the Lord, the God of hosts;
he has given the word of command; it is his
counsel and decree, which can neither be
reversed nor resisted, that all who do mischief to his people shall certainly bring mischief upon themselves. We have heard a
report that God is raised up out of his holy
habitation, and is preparing his throne for
judgment; and *an ambassador is sent among
the heathen,"* a herald rather, some minister
or messenger of Providence, to alarm the
nations, or the Lord's prophets, who gave
each nation its burden. Those whom God
employs cry to each other, *Arise ye,* stir up
yourselves and one another, and let *us rise
up against Edom in battle.* The confederate
forces under Nebuchadnezzar thus animate
themselves and one another to make a descent upon that country: *Gather yourselves
together, and come against her;* so it is in
the parallel place, Jei. xlix. 14. Note, When
God has bloody work to do among the enemies of his church he will find out and fit
up both hands and hearts to do it.

II. A prediction of the success of that war.
Edom shall certainly be subdued, and spoiled, and brought down; for all her confidences shall fail her and stand her in no

stead, and in like manner shall all the enemies of God's church be disappointed in those
things which they stayed themselves upon.

1. Do they depend upon their grandeur,
the figure they make among the nations,
their influence upon them, and interest
in them? That shalt dwindle (*v.* 2): *" Behold, I have made thee small among the
heathen,* so that none of thy neighbours
will court thy friendship, or court an alliance with thee; *thou art greatly despised*
among them, and looked upon with contempt, as an infatuated and unfaithful nation." And thus (*v.* 3) *the pride of thy
heart has deceived thee.* Note, (1.) Those
that think well of themselves are apt to fancy
that others think well of them too; but,
when they come to make trial of them, they
will find themselves mistaken, and thus
their pride deceives them and by it slays
them. (2.) God can easily lay those low
that have magnified and exalted themselves,
and will find out a way to do it, for he *resists the proud;* and we often see those small
and greatly despised who once looked very
big and were greatly caressed and admired.

2. Do they depend upon the fortifications
of their country, both by nature and art,
and glory in the advantages they have thereby? Those also shall deceive them. They
dwelt in the clefts of the rock, as an eagle in
her nest, and their *habitation was high,* not
only exalted above their neighbours, which
was the matter of their pride, but fortified
against their enemies, which was the matter
of their security, so high as to be out of the
reach of danger. Now observe, (1.) What
Edom says in the pride of his heart: *Who
shall bring me down to the ground?* He
speaks with a confidence of his own strength,
and a contempt of God's judgments, as if
almighty power itself could not overpower
him. As for *all his enemies,* even God himself, he *puffs at them* (Ps. x. 5), sets them
all at defiance. Their father Esau had *sold
his birthright,* and yet they lifted up themselves, as if to them had still pertained the
excellency of dignity and power. Many forfeit their privileges, and yet boast of them.
Because Edom is high and lifted up, he
imagines none can bring him down. Note,
Carnal security is a sin that most easily besets
men in the day of their pomp, power, and
prosperity, and does, as much as any thing,
both ripen men for ruin and aggravate it
when it comes. (2.) What God says to this,
v. 4. If men will dare to challenge Omnipotence, their challenge shall be taken up:
Who shall bring me down? says Edom. *" I
will,"* says God, *" Though thou exalt thyself
as the eagle* that soars high and builds high,
nay, *though thou set thy nest among the stars,*
higher than ever any eagle flew, it is but in
thy own imagination, and *thence will I bring
thee down."* This we had Jer. xlix. 15, 16.
Note, Sinners will certainly be made ashamed
of their pride and security of their pride

when it has a fall and of their security when their confidences fail their expectation.

3. Do they depend upon their wealth and treasure, the abundance of which is looked upon as the sinews of war? Is their money their defence? Is that their strong city? It is so only in their own conceit, for it shall rather expose them than protect them; it shall be made a prey to the enemy, and they for the sake of it, *v.* 5, 6. Much to this purport we had Jer. xlix. 9, 10. Only here comes in, in a parenthesis, *How art thou cut off!* thou and all thy stores. The prophet foretels it, but laments it, that the thread of their prosperity was cut off. How art thou fallen, and how great is thy fall! *How art thou stupified!* so the Chaldee words it. How senseless art thou under these desolating judgments, as if they were but common strokes! But he shows that it should be an utter ruin, not a usual calamity; for, (1.) It is indeed a usual calamity for those that have wealth to have it stolen, and to lose a little out of their great deal. *Thieves come to them* (for where the carcase is, there will the birds of prey be gathered together), *robbers come by night,* and they *steal till they have enough,* what they have occasion for, what they have a mind for; they steal no more than they think they can carry away, and out of a great stock it is scarcely missed. Those that rob orchards, or vineyards, carry off what they think fit; but they *leave some grapes,* some fruit for the owner, who easily bears his loss perhaps and soon recruits it. But, (2.) It shall not be so with Edom; his wealth shall all be taken away, and nothing shall escape the hands of the destroying army, not that which is most precious and valuable, *v.* 6. *How are the things of Esau,* the things he sets his heart upon and places his happiness in, his good things, his best things, how are these things, which were so carefully treasured up and concealed, now *searched out* by the enemy and seized! *How are his hidden things,* his hidden treasures, plundered, rifled, and *sought up!* His hoards, that had not seen the light for many years, are now a spoil to the enemy. Note, Treasures on earth, though ever so fast locked up and ever so artfully hidden, cannot be so safely laid up but that thieves may break through and steal; it is therefore our wisdom to *lay up for ourselves treasures in heaven.*

4. Do they depend upon their alliances with neighbouring states and potentates? Those also shall fail them (*v.* 7): "The *men of thy confederacy,* all of them, the Ammonites and Moabites, and other thy high allies that were at *peace with thee,* that entered into a league offensive and defensive with thee, that solemnly engaged not only to do thee no hurt, but to do thee all the service they could, *did eat thy bread,* were magnificently treated and entertained by thee, lived upon thee; their soldiers had free quarter in thy country, and took pay as thy auxiliaries; they
1272

brought thee even to the border of thy land, were very respectful to thy ambassadors, and brought them on their way home, even to the utmost limits of their country; they seemed forward to serve thee with their forces when thou hadst occasion for them, and came along with thee *to the border,* till thou wast just ready to engage the invading enemy; but then," (1.) "They have *deceived thee;* they flew back and retreated when thou wast in extremity, and proved as a broken reed to the traveller that is weary, and as the brooks in summer to the traveller that is thirsty; they bear no weight, yield no relief." Nay, (2.) They have *prevailed against thee;* they were too hard for thee in the treaty imposed upon thee, and by cheating thee ruined thee, brought thee into danger, and there left thee an easy prey to thy enemy." Note, Those that make flesh their arm arm it against them. Yet this was not the worst. (3.) "They have *laid a wound under thee;* that is, they have laid that under thee for a stay and support, for a foundation to rely on, for a pillow to repose on, which will prove a wound; not as thorns only, but as swords." If God lay under us the arms of his power and love, these will be firm and easy under us; the God of our covenant will never deceive us. But if we trust to *the men of our confederacy,* and what they will lay under us, it may prove to us a *wound* and *dishonour.* And observe the just censure here passed upon Edom for trusting to those who thus played tricks with him: " *There is no understanding in him,* or else he would never have put it into their power to betray him by putting such a confidence in them. Note, Those show they have no understanding in them who, when they are encouraged to trust in the Creator, put a cheat upon themselves by reposing a confidence in the creature.

5. Do they depend upon the politics of their counsellors? These shall fail them, *v.* 8. Edom had been famous for great statesmen, men of learning and experience, that sat at the helm of government, and were masters of all the arts of management, that in all treaties used to outwit their neighbours; but now the *counsellors* have become *fools,* and the wise God makes them so: *Shall I not in that day destroy the wise men out of Edom?* As men they shall fall by the sword in common with others (Ps. xlix. 10), and their wisdom shall not secure them; as wise men they shall be infatuated in all their counsels; their best-laid designs shall be baffled, their measures broken, and those very projects by which they thought to establish themselves and the public interests shall be the ruin of both. Thus *wisdom perishes from Teman,* as it is in the parallel place, Jer. xlix. 7. This was, (1.) The just punishment of their folly in trusting to an arm of flesh: *There is no understanding in them, v.* 7. They have not sense to trust in

a living God, and a God of truth, but put confidence in men that are frail, fickle, and false; and therefore God will *destroy their understanding.* Note, God will justly deny those understanding to keep out of the way of danger that will not use their understanding to keep out of the way of sin. He that will be foolish, let him be foolish still. (2.) It was the forerunner of their destruction. A nation is certainly marked for ruin when God hides the things that belong to its peace from the eyes of those that are entrusted with its counsels. *Quos Deus vult perdere, eos dementat—God infatuates those whom he designs to destroy.* Job xii. 17.

6. Do they depend upon the strength and courage of their soldiers? They are not only able-bodied, but men of spirit and courage, that can face an enemy and stand their ground; but now (*v.* 9), *Thy mighty men, O Teman! shall be dismayed; their courage shall fail them, to the end that every one of the mount of Esau may be cut off by slaughter,* and none escape. The weak, and feeble, and unarmed must fall of course into the hand of the destroyer when the *mighty men are dismayed,* and not only lose the day, but lose their lives, because they have lost their spirit. *Howl, fir-trees, if the cedars be shaken.* Note, The death or disuniting of the mighty often proves the death and destruction of the many; and it is in vain to depend upon mighty men for our protection if we have not an almighty God for us, much less if we have an almighty God against us.

10 For *thy* violence against thy brother Jacob shame shall cover thee, and thou shalt be cut off for ever. 11 In the day that thou stoodest on the other side, in the day that the strangers carried away captive his forces, and foreigners entered into his gates, and cast lots upon Jerusalem, even thou *wast* as one of them. 12 But thou shouldest not have looked on the day of thy brother in the day that he became a stranger; neither shouldest thou have rejoiced over the children of Judah in the day of their destruction; neither shouldest thou have spoken proudly in the day of distress. 13 Thou shouldest not have entered into the gate of my people in the day of their calamity; yea, thou shouldest not have looked on their affliction in the day of their calamity, nor have laid *hands* on their substance in the day of their calamity; 14 Neither shouldest thou have stood in the cross-way, to cut off those of his that did escape; neither shouldest

thou have delivered up those of his that did remain in the day of distress. 15 For the day of the LORD *is* near upon all the heathen: as thou hast done, it shall be done unto thee: thy reward shall return upon thine own head. 16 For as ye have drunk upon my holy mountain, *so* shall all the heathen drink continually, yea, they shall drink, and they shall swallow down, and they shall be as though they had not been.

When we have read Edom's doom, no less than utter ruin, it is natural to ask, *Why, what evil has he done?* What is the ground of God's controversy with him? Many things, no doubt, were amiss in Edom; they were a sinful people, and *a people laden with iniquity.* But that one single crime which is laid to their charge, as filling their measure and bringing this ruin upon them, that for which they here stand indicted, of which they are convicted, and for which they are condemned, is the injury they had done to the people of God (*v.* 10): "It is *for thy violence against thy brother Jacob,* that ancient and hereditary grudge which thou hast borne to the people of Israel, that all this *shame shall cover thee* and *thou shalt be cut off for ever."* Note, Injuries to men are affronts to God, the righteous God, that loveth righteousness and hateth wickedness; and, as the Judge of all the earth, he will give redress to those that suffer wrong and take vengeance on those that do wrong. All violence, all *unrighteousness, is sin;* but it is a great aggravation of the violence if it be done either, 1. Against any of our own people; it is violence *against thy brother,* thy near relation, to whom thou shouldst be a *goël—a redeemer,* whom it is thy duty to right if others wronged him; how wicked is it then for thee thyself to wrong him! Thou *slanderest* and abusest *thy own mother's son;* this makes the sin *exceedingly sinful,* Ps. l. 20. Or, 2. Much more if it be done against any of God's people; "it is thy brother Jacob that is in covenant with God, and dear to him. Thou hatest him whom God has loved, and because God has loved him, him whose cause God espouses and will plead with jealousy, and in whose interests God is pleased so far to interest himself that he takes the violence done to him as done to himself. *Whoso touches Jacob touches the apple of the eye of Jacob's God."* So that it is *crimen læsæ majestatis—high treason,* for which, as for high treason, let Edom expect an ignominious punishment: *Shame shall cover thee,* and a ruining one; *thou shalt be cut off for ever.*

In the following verses we are told more particularly,

I. What the violence was which Edom

did against his brother Jacob, and what are the proofs of this charge. It does not appear that the Edomites did themselves invade Israel, but that was more for want of power than will; they had malice enough to do it, but were not a match for them. But that which is laid to their charge is their barbarous conduct towards Judah and Jerusalem when they were in distress, and ready to be destroyed, probably by the Chaldeans, or upon occasion of some other of the calamities of the Jews; for this seems to have been always their temper towards them. See this charged upon the Edomites (Ps. cxxxvii. 7), that *in the day of Jerusalem they said, Rase it, rase it,* and Ezek. xxv. 12. They are here told particularly what they did, by being told what they should not have done (*v.* 12—14): "Thou *shouldst not have looked,* thou *shouldst not have entered;* but thou didst do so." Note, In reflecting upon ourselves it is good to compare what we have done with what we should have done, our practice with the rule, that we may discover wherein we have done amiss, have *done those things which we ought not to have done.* We should not have been where we were at such a time, should not have been in such and such company, should not have said what we said, nor have taken the liberty that we took. Sin thus looked upon, in the glass of the commandment, will appear exceedingly sinful. Let us see,

1. What was the case of Judah and Jerusalem when the Edomites behaved themselves thus basely and insulted over them. (1.) It was a day of distress with them (*v.* 12): It was the *day of their calamity,* so it is called three times, *v.* 13. With the Edomites it was a day of prosperity and peace when with the Israelites it was a day of distress and calamity, for judgment commonly *begins at the house of God.* Children are corrected when strangers are let alone. (2.) It was the day *of their destruction* (*v.* 12), when both city and country were laid waste, were laid *in ruins.* (3.) It was a day when *foreigners entered into the gates of Jerusalem,* when the city, after a long siege, was broken up, and the great officers of the king of Babylon's army came, and sat in the gates, as judges of the land; when they cast lots upon the spoils of Jerusalem, as the soldiers on Christ's garments, what shares each of the conquerors shall have, what share of the lands, what share of the goods; or they cast lots to determine when and where they should attack it. (4.) It was a day when the *strangers carried away captive his forces* (*v.* 11), took the men of war prisoners of war, and carried them off, in poverty and shame, to their own country, or such a multitude of captives that they were as an army. (5.) "It was a day when thy brother himself, that had long been at home, at rest in his own land, *became a stranger,* an exile in a strange land." Now, when this was

the woeful case of the Jews, the Edomites, their neighbours and brethren, should have pitied them and helped them, condoled with them and comforted them, and should have trembled to think that their own turn would come next; for, *if this was done in the green tree, what shall be done in the dry?* But,

2. See what was the conduct of the Edomites towards them when they were in this distress, for which they are here condemned. (1.) They looked with pleasure upon the affliction of God's people; they *stood on the other side* (*v.* 11), afar off, when they should have come in to the relief of their distressed neighbours, and *looked upon them,* and *their day, looked on their affliction* (*v.* 12, 13), with a careless unconcerned eye, as the priest and Levite looked upon the wounded man, and *passed by on the other side.* Those have a great deal to answer for that are idle spectators of the troubles and afflictions of their neighbours, when they are capable of being their active helpers. But this was not all; they looked upon it with a scornful eye, with an eye of complacency and satisfaction; they looked and laughed to see Israel in distress, saying, *Aha! so would we have it.* They fed their eyes with the rueful spectacle of Jerusalem's ruin, and looked at it as those that had long looked for it and often wished to see it. Note, We must take heed with what eye we look upon the afflictions of our brethren; and, if we cannot look upon them with a gracious eye of sympathy and tenderness, it is better not to look upon them at all : *Thou shouldst not have looked* as thou didst *upon the day of thy brother.* (2.) They triumphed and insulted over them, upbraided their brethren with their sorrows, and made themselves and their companions merry with them. They *rejoiced over the children of Judah in the day of their destruction.* They had not the good manners to conceal the pleasure they took in Judah's destruction and to dissemble it, but openly declared it, and rudely and insolently declared it *to them;* they *rejoiced over them,* crowed, and hectored, and trampled upon them. Those have the spirit of Edomites that can rejoice over any, especially over Israelites, in the day of their calamity. (3.) They *spoke proudly—magnified the mouth* (so the word is), against Israel, talked with a great disdain of the suffering Israelites, and with an air of haughtiness of the present safety and prosperity of Edom, as if it might be inferred from their present different state that the tables were turned, and now Esau was beloved, and the favourite of heaven, and Jacob hated and rejected. Note, Those must expect to be in some way or other effectually humbled and mortified themselves that are puffed up and made proud by the humiliations and mortifications of others. (4.) They went further yet, for they *entered into the gate* of God's people in the

day of their calamity, and *laid hands on their substance.* Though they did not help to conquer them, they helped to plunder them, and put in for a share in the prey, v. 13. Jerusalem was thrown open, and then they entered in; its wealth was thrown about, and they seized it for themselves, excusing it with this, that they might as well take it as let it be lost; whereas it was taking what was not their own. Babylon lays Jerusalem waste, but Edom, by meddling with the spoil, becomes *particeps criminis—partaker of the crime,* and shall be reckoned with as an accessary *ex post facto—after the fact.* Note, Those do but impoverish themselves that think to enrich themselves by the ruins of the people of God; and those deceive themselves who think they may call all that substance their own which they can lay their hands on in a day of calamity. (5.) They did yet worse things; they not only robbed their brethren, but murdered them, in the day of' their calamity; laid hands not only on their substance, but on their persons, v. 14. When the victorious sword of the Chaldeans was making bloody work among the Jews many made their escape, and were in a fair way to save themselves by flight; but the Edomites basely intercepted them, *stood in the cross-way* where several roads met, by each of which the trembling Israelites were making the best of their way from the fury of the pursuers, and there they stopped them: some they barbarously and cowardlike cut off themselves; others they took prisoners, and delivered up to the pursuers, only to ingratiate themselves with them, because they were now the conquerors. They *should not have been* thus *cruel* to those that lay at their mercy, and never had done, nor were ever likely to do, them any hurt; they should not have betrayed those whom they had such a fair opportunity to protect; but such are the *tender mercies of the wicked.* One cannot read this without a high degree of compassion towards those who were thus basely abused, who when they fled from the sword of an open enemy, and thought they had got out of the reach of it, fell upon and fell by the sword of a treacherous neighbour, whom they were not apprehensive of any danger from. Nor can one read this without a high degree of indignation towards those who were so perfectly lost to all humanity as to exercise such cruelty upon such proper objects of compassion. (6.) In all this they joined with the open enemies and persecutors of Israel: *Even thou wast as one of them,* an accessary equally guilty with the principals. He that joins in with evil doers, and is aiding and abetting in their evil deeds, shall be reckoned, and shall be reckoned with, as one of them.

II. What the shame is that shall cover them for this violence of theirs. 1. They shall soon find that the cup is going round, even the cup of trembling; and, when they

come to be in the same calamitous condition that the Israel of God is now in, they will be ashamed to remember how they triumphed over them (v. 15): *The day of the Lord is near upon all the heathen,* when God will recompense tribulation to the troublers of his church. Though judgment begin at the house of God, it shall not end there. This should effectually restrain us from triumphing over others in their misery, that we know not how soon it may be our own case. 2. Their enmity to the people of God, and the injuries they have done them, shall be recompensed into their own bosoms: *As thou hast done, it shall be done unto thee.* The righteous God will render both to nations and to particular persons *according to their works;* and the punishment is often made exactly to answer to the sin, and those that have abused others come to be themselves abused in like manner. The just and jealous God will find out a time and way to avenge the wrongs done to his people on those that have been injurious to them. *As you have drunk upon my holy mountain* (v. 16), that is, as God's professing people, who inhabit his holy mountain, have drunk deeply of the cup of affliction (and their being of the holy mountain would not excuse them), *so shall all the heathen drink,* in their turn, of the same bitter cup; for, if God *bring evil on the city that is called by his name, shall those be unpunished* that never knew his name? See Jer. xxv. 29. And it is part of the burden of Edom (Jer. xlix. 12), *Those whose judgment was not to drink of the cup* (who had reason to promise themselves an exemption from it) have assuredly drunken, and *shall Edom* that is the generation of God's wrath *go unpunished?* No, *thou shalt surely drink of it ;* the *cup of trembling shall be taken out of the hand* of God's people, and put *into the hand of those that afflict them,* Isa. li. 22, 23. Nay, they may expect their case to be worse in the day of their distress than that of Israel was in their day; for, (1.) The afflictions of God's people were but for a moment, and soon had an end, but their enemies shall *drink continually* the *wine of God's wrath,* Rev. xiv. 10. (2.) The dregs of the cup are reserved for the *wicked of the earth* (Ps. lxxv. 8); they shall *drink and swallow down,* or *sup up* (as the margin reads it), shall drink it to the bottom. (3.) The people of God, though they may be made to drink of the wine of astonishment for a while (Ps. lx. 3), shall yet recover, and come to themselves again; but the heathen shall drink and be *as though they had not been;* there shall be neither any remains nor any remembrance of them, but they shall be wholly extirpated and rooted out. *So let all thy enemies perish, O Lord!* so they shall perish, if they turn not.

17 But upon mount Zion shall be deliverance, and there shall be holi-

ness; and the house of Jacob shall possess their possessions. 18 And the house of Jacob shall be a fire, and the house of Joseph a flame, and the house of Esau for stubble, and they shall kindle in them, and devour them; and there shall not be *any* remaining of the house of Esau; for the LORD hath spoken *it*. 19 And *they of* the south shall possess the mount of Esau; and *they of* the plain the Philistines: and they shall possess the fields of Ephraim, and the fields of Samaria: and Benjamin *shall possess* Gilead. 20 And the captivity of this host of the children of Israel *shall possess* that of the Canaanites, *even* unto Zarephath; and the captivity of Jerusalem, which *is* in Sepharad, shall possess the cities of the south. 21 And saviours shall come up on mount Zion to judge the mount of Esau; and the kingdom shall be the LORD's.

After the destruction of the church's enemies is threatened, which will be completely accomplished in the great day of recompence, and that judgment for which Christ came once, and will come again, into this world, here follow precious promises of the salvation of the church, with which this prophecy concludes, as those of Joel and Amos did, which, however they might be in part fulfilled in the return of the Jews out of Babylon notwithstanding the triumphs of Edom in their captivity, as if it were perpetual, are yet, doubtless, to have their full accomplishment in that great salvation wrought out by Jesus Christ, to which all the prophets bore witness. It is promised here,

I. That there shall be salvation upon Mount Zion, that holy hill where God sets his anointed King (Ps. ii. 6): *Upon Mount Zion shall be deliverance, v.* 17. There shall be *those that escape;* so the margin. A remnant of Israel, *upon the holy mountain,* shall be saved, *v.* 16. Christ said, *Salvation is of the Jews,* John iv. 22. God wrought deliverances for the Jews, typical of our redemption by Christ. But Mount Zion is the gospel-church, from which the New-Testament law *went forth,* Isa. ii. 3. There salvation shall be preached and prayed for; to the gospel-church those are added who *shall be saved;* and for those who come in faith and hope to this Mount Zion deliverance shall be wrought from wrath and the curse, from sin, and death, and hell, while those who continue afar off shall be left to perish.

II. That, where there is salvation, there shall be sanctification in order to it: *And there shall be holiness,* to prepare and qualify the children of Zion for this deliverance; for wherever God designs glory he gives grace. Temporal deliverances are indeed wrought for us in mercy when with them there is holiness, when there is wrought in us a disposition to receive them with love and gratitude to God; when we are sanctified, they are sanctified to us. Holiness is itself a great deliverance, and an earnest of that eternal salvation which we look for. *There,* upon Mount Zion, in the gospel-church, *shall be holiness;* for that is it which *becomes God's house for ever,* and the great design of the gospel, and its grace, is to plant and promote holiness. There shall be the Holy Spirit, the holy ordinances, the holy Jesus, and a select remnant of holy souls, in whom, and among whom, the holy God will delight to dwell. Note, Where there is holiness there shall be deliverance.

III. That this salvation and sanctification shall spread, and prevail, and get ground in the world: The *house of Jacob,* even this *Mount Zion,* with the deliverance and the holiness there wrought, shall *possess their possessions;* that is, the gospel-church shall be set up among the heathen, and shall replenish the earth; the apostles of Christ by their preaching shall gain possession of the hearts of men for him whose messengers and ministers they are, and when they possess their hearts they shall *possess their possessions,* for those who have given up themselves to the Lord give up all they have to him. When Lydia's heart was opened to Christ her house was opened to his ministers. When the Gentile nations became *nations of those that were saved,* were discipled, *walked in the light* of the Lord, *and brought their glory and honour into the new Jerusalem* (Rev. xxi. 24), then the *house of Jacob possessed their possessions.* This is in part fulfilled by the planting of the Christian religion in the world, and shall be fulfilled yet more and more by the setting up of Christ's throne where Satan's seat is, and the erecting of the trophies of his victory upon the ruins of the devil's kingdom. Now here is foretold,

1. How this possession shall be *gained,* and the opposition given to it got over (*v.* 18): *The house of Jacob shall be a fire, and the house of Joseph a flame,* for their God is, and will be, a *consuming fire;* and the house of Esau shall be for *stubble,* easily devoured and consumed by this fire. This is fulfilled, (1.) In the conversion of multitudes by the grace of Christ; the gospel, preached in the house of Jacob and Joseph, and there owned and professed, shall be as a fire and a flame to melt and to soften hard hearts, to burn up the dross of sin and corruption, that they may be purified and refined with the *spirit of judgment and* the *spirit of burning.* Christ, when he comes, shall be *as a refiner's fire,* Mal. iii. 1, 2. (2.) In the confusion of all the impenitent implacable enemies of the gospel of

Christ, that oppose it and do all they can to hinder the setting up of the kingdom of the Messiah by it. The gospel day is a day that *burns like an oven,* in which *all the proud, and all that do wickedly, shall be as stubble,* Mal. iv. 1. Jacob and Joseph shall be as a fire and a flame; for those that meddle with them, to do them hurt, will find that they do so at their peril; they shall be to them as *a torch of fire in a sheaf,* Zech. xii. 6. The word of God in the mouth of his ministers is said to be like fire, and the people as wood to be devoured by it, Jer. v. 14. And the *man of sin* is to be *consumed by the breath of Christ's mouth,* 2 Thess. ii. 8. Those that are not refined as gold by the fire of the gospel shall be consumed as dross by it; for it will be a savour either of life or of death. When idols and idolatry were abolished, and the wealth and power of the nations were brought into the service of Christ and his gospel, and the spoils of the *strong man armed* were divided by him that was *stronger than he,* then the house of Jacob and Joseph devoured *the house of Esau,* so that there was none of them left remaining. This the *Lord spoke* by his prophets, and this he did by his apostles.

2. How far this possession shall extend, *v.* 19, 20. This is described in Jewish language, which speaks the accession made to the land of Israel, after the return out of captivity in Babylon. The *captivity of this host of Israel,* that is, this host of Israel that have been so long in captivity and now they have come back are still called the *children of the captivity,* these shall not only recover their own land, but shall gain ground upon their neighbours adjoining to them, some of whom shall become proselytes and shall incorporate with the Jews, who, by possessing them in a holy communion, possess their land. We must reckon ourselves truly enriched by the conversion of our neighbours to the fear of God and the faith of Christ, and their coming to join with us in the worship of God. Such an accession to our Christian communion we must reckon to be more our wealth and strength than an accession to our estates. Or, The ancient inhabitants of those lands that were carried away into captivity being lost, and never returning to their estates, the children of Israel shall take possession of that which lies next them; for their numbers shall so increase that their own land shall be too strait for them, and their neighbours' estates shall escheat to them *ob defectum sanguinis—through default of heirs.* They shall enter upon that which is adjoining to them. The country of Esau shall be possessed by those *of the south* parts of Canaan, for to them it lies contiguous. Those *of the plain,* on the *west* of Canaan, which was a champaign country, shall enter upon *the land of the Philistines,* their neighbours. Those of Judah, which was the chief of the two returning tribes shall possess *the field of Ephraim and*

Samaria, which before belonged to the ten tribes; and Benjamin, the other tribe, shall possess Gilead on the other side Jordan, which had belonged to the two tribes and a half. The kingdom of Israel shall join with that of Judah both in civil and sacred interests, and, as friends and brethren, shall mutually possess and enjoy one another; and both together shall *possess the Canaanites,* even to Zarephath, which *belongeth to Zidon;* and Jerusalem shall possess the *cities of the south,* even to Sepharad. Thus did the Jews enlarge their borders on all sides. The modern rabbin teach their scholars by Zarephath and Sepharad to understand France and Spain, grounding upon this a foolish groundless expectation that some time or other the Jews shall be masters of those countries; and they call and count the Christians *Edomites,* over whom they are to have dominion. But the promise here, no doubt, has a spiritual signification, and had its accomplishment in the setting up of the Christian church, the gospel-Israel, in the world, and shall have its accomplishment more and more in the enlargement of it and the additions made to it, till the mystical body is completed. When ministers and Christians prevail with their neighbours to come to Christ, to yield themselves to the Lord, they possess them. The converts that Abraham made are said to be the *souls that he had gotten,* Gen. xii. 5. The possession is gained, not *vi et armis—by force and arms;* for the *weapons of our warfare are not carnal,* but *spiritual;* it is by the preaching of the gospel, and the power of divine grace going along with it, that this possession is got and kept.

IV. That the kingdom of the Redeemer shall be erected and maintained, to the comfort of his loyal subjects and the terror and shame of all his enemies (*v.* 21): *The kingdom shall be the Lord's,* the Lord Christ's. God shall give it to him, by putting all things into his hand, all power both in heaven and in earth; men shall give it to him, by resigning themselves to him as his willing people, and appointing him their head. Now the work of kings is to protect their subjects and suppress their enemies; and this Christ will do; he will both reward and punish. 1. The mountain of Zion shall be saved; on it *saviours* shall *come,* the preachers of the gospel, who are called saviours, because their business is to save themselves and those that hear them; and in this they are *workers together with Christ,* but to little purpose if he by his grace did not *work together with them.* 2. The mountain of Esau shall be judged; and the same that come as saviours on Mount Zion shall *judge the mountain of Esau;* for the word of the gospel in their mouth, that saves believers, judges unbelievers, convinces and condemns them. Christ's ministers are *saviours on Mount Zion* when they preach that he *that believes shall be saved;* but they judge the mount of Esau when they preach that he *that believeth not shall be damned,* which they are not only commissioned, but commanded to do, Mark xvi. 16. And in the course of God's providence his scripture is fulfilled; when God raises up friends to the church in her distress (as he *raised up judges* to deliver Israel of old, Judg. ii. 16), then *saviours come on Mount Zion,* to save it from being sunk and ruined; and when the enemies of the church are brought down, and their power broken, then is the *mount of Esau judged;* and this shall be done in every age in such a way as God thinks best; we may depend upon it that the gates of hell shall not prevail against the church, but the church shall prevail against them; *for the kingdom shall be the Lord's;* the kingdoms of the world shall become his, and he has taken, and will take, to himself his great power and reign.

EXPOSITION,

WITH PRACTICAL OBSERVATIONS,

OF THE BOOK OF

JONAH.

THIS book of Jonah, though it be placed here in the midst of the prophetical books of scripture, is yet rather a history than a prophecy; one line of prediction there is in it, *Yet forty days, and Nineveh shall be overthrown;* the rest of the book is a narrative of the preface and the conse-quences of that prediction. In the midst of the obscure prophecies before and after this book, wherein are many things dark and hard to be understood, which are puzzling to the learned, and are *strong meat for strong men,* comes in this plain and pleasant story, which is entertaining to the weakest, and *milk for babes.* Probably Jonah was himself the penman of this book, and he, as Moses and other inspired penmen, records his own faults, which is an evidence that in these writings they designed God's glory and not their own. We read of this same Jonah 2 Kings xiv. 25, where we find that he was of Gath-hepher in Galilee, a city that belonged to the tribe of Zebulun, in a remote corner of the land of Israel; for the Spirit, which, like the wind, *blows where it listeth,* will as easily find out Jonah in Galilee as Isaiah at Jerusalem. We find also that he was a messenger of mercy to Israel in the reign of Jeroboam the second; for the success of his arms, in the *restoring of the coast of Israel,* is said to be *according to the word of the Lord which he spoke by the hand of his servant Jonah the prophet.* Those prophecies were not committed to writing, but this against Nineveh, chiefly for the sake of the story that depends upon it, and that is recorded chiefly for the sake of Christ, of whom Jonah was a type; it con-tains also very remarkable instances of human infirmity in Jonah, and of God's mercy both in pardoning repenting sinners, witness Nineveh, and in bearing with repining saints, witness Jonah.

CHAP. I.

In this chapter we have, I. A command given to Jonah to preach at Nineveh, ver. 1, 2. II. Jonah's disobedience to that command, ver. 3. III. The pursuit and arrest of him for that disobedience by a storm, in which he was asleep, ver. 4—6. IV. The discovery of him, and his disobedience, to be the cause of the storm, ver. 7—10. V. The casting of him into the sea, for the stilling of the storm, ver. 11—16. VI. The miraculous preservation of his life there in the belly of a fish (ver. 17), which was his reservation for further services.

NOW the word of the Lord came unto Jonah the son of Amittai, saying, 2 Arise, go to Nineveh, that great city, and cry against it; for their wickedness is come up before me.

3 But Jonah rose up to flee unto Tarshish from the presence of the Lord, and went down to Joppa; and he found a ship going to Tarshish: so he paid the fare thereof, and went down into it, to go with them unto Tarshish from the presence of the Lord.

Observe, 1. The honour God put upon Jonah, in giving him a commission to go and prophesy against Nineveh. *Jonah signifies a dove,* a proper name for all God's prophets, all his people, who ought to be *harmless as doves,* and to *mourn as doves* for the sins and calamities of the land. His father's name was *Amittai—My truth;* for God's prophets should be sons of truth. To him *the word of the Lord came—to him it was* (so the word signifies), for God's word is a real thing; men's words are but wind, but God's words are substance. He had been before acquainted with the *word of the Lord,* and knew his voice from that of a stranger; the orders now given him were, *Arise, go to Nineveh, that great city, v.* 2. Nineveh was at this time the metropolis of the Assyrian monarchy, an eminent city (Gen. x. 11), *a great city, that great city,* forty-eight miles in compass (some make it much more), great in the number of the inhabitants, as appears by the multitude of infants in it *(ch.* iv. 11), great in wealth (there was no end of its store, Nah. ii. 9), great in power and dominion; it was the city that for some time *ruled over the kings of the earth.* But great cities, as well as great men, are under God's government and judgment. Nineveh was a great city, and yet a heathen city, without the knowledge and worship of the true God. How many great cities and great nations are there that *sit in darkness* and *in the valley of the shadow of death!* This great city was a wicked city: *Their wickedness has come up before me* (their *malice,* so some read it); *their wickedness was presumptuous,* and they sinned with *a high hand.* It is sad to think what a great deal of sin is committed in great cities, where there are many sinners, who are not only all sinners, but making one another sin. *Their wickedness has come up,* that is, it has come to a high degree, to the highest pitch; the *measure of it* is *full* to the brim; *their wickedness has come up,* and then it is time for vengeance to come down. Or, The *cry of their wickedness has come up,* as that of Sodom, Gen. xviii. 20, 21. It has come up *before me—to my face* (so the word is); it is a bold and open affront to God; it is sinning against him, *in his sight;* therefore Jonah must *cry against it;* he must witness against their great wickedness, and must warn them of the destruction that was coming upon them for it. God is coming forth against it, and he sends Jonah before, to proclaim war, and to sound an alarm. *Cry aloud, spare not.* He must not whisper his message in a corner, but publish it in the streets of Nineveh; *he that has ears to hear let him hear* what God has to say by his prophet against that wicked city. When the cry of sin comes up to God the cry of vengeance comes out against the sinner. He must *go to Nineveh,* and cry there upon the spot against the wickedness of it. Other prophets were ordered to send messages to the neighbouring nations, and the prophecy of Nahum is particularly *the burden of Nineveh;* but Jonah must go and carry the message himself:

"Arise quickly; apply thyself to the business with speed and courage, and the resolution that becomes a prophet; *arise, and go to Nineveh."* Those that go on God's errands must rise and go, must stir up themselves to the work cut out for them. The prophets were sent first to the *lost sheep of the house of Israel,* yet not to them only; they had the children's bread, but Nineveh eats of the crumbs. 2. The dishonour Jonah did to God in refusing to obey his orders, and to go on the errand on which he was sent *(v.* 3): *But Jonah,* instead of rising to go to Nineveh, *rose up to flee to Tarshish, to the sea,* not bound for any port, but desirous to get away *from the presence of the Lord;* and, if he might but do that, he cared not whither he went, not as if he thought he could go any where from under the eye of God's inspection, but from his special presence, from the spirit of prophecy, which, when it put him upon this work, he thought himself haunted with, and coveted to get out of the hearing of. Some think Jonah went upon the opinion of some of the Jews that the spirit of prophecy was confined to the land of Israel (which in Ezekiel and Daniel was effectually proved to be a mistake), and therefore he hoped he should get clear of it if he could but get out of the borders of that land. (1.) Jonah would not go to Nineveh to cry against it either because it was a long and dangerous journey thither, and in a road he knew not, or because he was afraid it would be as much as his life was worth to deliver such an ungrateful message to that great and potent city. He *consulted with flesh and blood,* and declined the embassy because he could not go with safety, or because he was jealous for the prerogatives of his country, and not willing that any other nation should share in the honour of divine revelation; he feared it would be the beginning of the removal of the kingdom of God from the Jews to another nation, that would bring forth more of the fruits of it. He owns himself *(ch.* iv. 2) that the reason of his aversion to this journey was because he foresaw that the Ninevites would repent, and God would forgive them and take them into favour, which would be a slur upon the people of Israel, who had been so long a peculiar people to God. (2.) He therefore went to Tarshish, to Tarsus in Cilicia (so some), probably because he had friends and relations there, with whom he hoped for some time to sojourn. He went to Joppa, a famous seaport in the land of Israel, in quest of a ship bound for Tarshish, and there he found one. Providence seemed to favour his design, and give him an opportunity to escape. We may be out of the way of duty and yet may meet with a favourable gale. The ready way is not always the right way. He found the ship just ready to weigh anchor perhaps, and to set sail for Tarshish, and so he lost no time. Or, perhaps, he went to Tarshish because he found the ship

going thither; otherwise all places were alike to him. He did not think himself out of his way, the way he would go, provided he was not in his way, the way he should go. So he *paid the fare thereof;* for he did not regard the charge, so he could but gain his point, and get to a distance *from the presence of the Lord.* He went *with them,* with the mariners, with the passengers, with the merchants, whoever they were that were going to Tarshish. Jonah, forgetting his dignity as well as duty, herded with them, and *went down* into the ship to go *with them to Tarshish.* See what the best of men are when God leaves them to themselves, and what need we have, when the *word of the Lord* comes to us, to have the *Spirit of the Lord* come along with the word, to bring every thought within us into obedience to it. The prophet Isaiah owns that *therefore* he was not *rebellious,* neither *turned away back,* because God not only spoke to him, but *opened his ear,* Isa. l. 5. Let us learn hence to *cease from man,* and not to be too confident either of ourselves or others in a time of trial; but *let him that thinks he stands take heed lest he fall.*

4 But the Lord sent out a great wind into the sea, and there was a mighty tempest in the sea, so that the ship was like to be broken. 5 Then the mariners were afraid, and cried every man unto his god, and cast forth the wares that *were* in the ship into the sea, to lighten *it* of them. But Jonah was gone down into the sides of the ship; and he lay, and was fast asleep. 6 So the ship-master came to him, and said unto him, What meanest thou, O sleeper? arise, call upon thy God, if so be that God will think upon us, that we perish not. 7 And they said every one to his fellow, Come, and let us cast lots, that we may know for whose cause this evil *is* upon us. So they cast lots, and the lot fell upon Jonah. 8 Then said they unto him, Tell us, we pray thee, for whose cause this evil *is* upon us; What *is* thine occupation? and whence comest thou? what *is* thy country? and of what people *art* thou? 9 And he said unto them, I *am* a Hebrew; and I fear the Lord, the God of heaven, which hath made the sea and the dry *land.* 10 Then were the men exceedingly afraid, and said unto him, Why hast thou done this? For the men knew that

1280

he fled from the presence of the Lord, because he had told them.

When Jonah was set on ship-board, and under sail for Tarshish, he thought himself safe enough; but here we find him pursued and overtaken, discovered and convicted as a deserter from God, as one that had *run his colours.*

I. God sends a pursuer after him, *a mighty tempest in the sea, v.* 4. God has the *winds in his treasure* (Ps. cxxxv. 7), and out of these treasures God *sent forth,* he *cast forth* (so the word is), with force and violence, a *great wind into the sea;* even *stormy winds fulfil his word,* and are often the messengers of his wrath; he *gathers the winds in his fist* (Prov. xxx. 4), where he holds them, and whence he squeezes them when he pleases; for though, as to us, the *wind blows where it listeth,* yet not as to God, but where he directs. The effect of this wind was *a mighty tempest;* for when the winds rise the waves rise. Note, Sin brings storms and tempests into the soul, into the family, into churches and nations; it is a disquieting disturbing thing. The tempest prevailed to such a degree that *the ship was likely to be broken;* the mariners expected no other; *that ship* (so some read it), that and no other. Other ships were upon the same sea at the same time, yet, it should seem, that ship in which Jonah was was tossed more than any other and was more in danger. This wind was sent after Jonah, to fetch him back again to God and to his duty; and it is a great mercy to be reclaimed and called home when we go astray, though it be by a tempest.

II. The ship's crew were alarmed by this mighty tempest, but Jonah only, the person concerned, was unconcerned, *v.* 5. The mariners were affected with their danger, though it was not with them that God had this controversy. 1. They were *afraid;* though, their business leading them to be very much conversant with dangers of this kind, they used to make light of them, yet now the oldest and stoutest of them began to tremble, being apprehensive that there was something more than ordinary in this tempest, so suddenly did it rise, so strongly did it rage. Note, God can strike a terror upon the most daring, and make even *great men and chief captains* call for shelter from rocks and mountains. 2. They *cried every man unto his god;* this was the effect of their fear. Many will not be brought to prayer till they are frightened to it; he that would learn to pray, let him go to sea. *Lord, in trouble have they visited thee. Every man* of them prayed; they were not some praying and others reviling, but every man engaged; as the danger was general, so was the address to heaven; there was not one praying for them all, but every one for himself. They cried *every man to his god,* the god of his country or city, or his own tutelar deity; it is a testimony against atheism that every man had a god, and had the belief of a God; but it is an instance of the folly of paganism that they had gods many, every man the god he had a fancy for, whereas there can be but one God, there needs be no more. But, though they had lost that dictate of the light of nature that there is but *one God*, they still were governed by that direction of the law of nature that God is to be prayed to *(Should not a people seek unto their God?* Isa. viii. 19), and that he is especially to be prayed to when we are in distress and danger. *Call upon me in the time of trouble. Is any afflicted?* Is any frightened? *Let him pray.* 3. Their prayers for deliverance were seconded with endeavours, and, having called upon their gods to help them, they did what they could to help themselves; for that is the rule, *Help thyself and God will help thee.* They *cast forth the wares that were in the ship into the sea, to lighten it of them,* as Paul's mariners in a like case cast forth even the *tackling of the ship,* and *the wheat,* Acts xxvii. 18, 19, 38. They were making a trading voyage, as it should seem, and were laden with many goods and much merchandise, by which they hoped to get gain; but now they are content to suffer loss by throwing them all overboard, to save their lives. See how powerful the natural love of life is. *Skin for skin,* and *all that a man has, will he give for it.* And shall we not put a like value upon the spiritual life, the life of the soul, reckoning that the gain of all the world cannot countervail the loss of the soul? See the vanity of worldly wealth, and the uncertainty of its continuance with us. Riches make themselves wings and fly away; nay, and the case may be such that we may be under a necessity of making wings for them, and driving them away, as here, when they could not be *kept for the owners thereof* but to their hurt, so that they themselves are glad to be rid of them, and sink that which otherwise would sink them, though they have no prospect of ever recovering it. Oh that men would be thus wise for their souls, and would be willing to part with that wealth, pleasure, and honour which they cannot keep without *making shipwreck of faith and a good conscience* and ruining their souls for ever! Those that thus quit their temporal interests for the securing of their spiritual welfare will be unspeakable gainers at last; for what they lose upon those terms they shall find again to life eternal. But where is Jonah all this while? One would have expected him busier than any there, but we find him gone down into his cabin, nay, into *the hold, between the sides of the ship,* and there he lies, and is *fast asleep;* neither the noise without, nor the sense of guilt within, awoke him. Perhaps for some time before he had avoided sleeping, for fear of God's speaking to him again in a dream; and now that he imagined himself out of the reach of that

danger he slept so much the more soundly. Note, Sin is of a stupifying nature, and we are concerned to *take heed lest at any time our hearts be hardened by the deceitfulness of it.* It is the policy of Satan, when by his temptations he has drawn men from God and their duty, to rock them asleep in carnal security, that they may not be sensible of their misery and danger. It concerns us all to *watch therefore.*

III. The master of the ship called Jonah up to his prayers, *v.* 6. The *ship-master came to him,* and bade him for shame get up, both to *pray for life* and to *prepare for death;* he gave him, 1. A just and necessary chiding: *What meanest thou, O sleeper?* Here we commend the ship-master, who gave him this reproof; for, though he was a stranger to him, he was, for the present, as one of his family; and whoever has a precious soul we must help, as we can, to *save it from death.* We pity Jonah, who needed this reproof; as a prophet of the Lord, if he had been in his place, he might have been reproving the king of Nineveh, but, being out of the way of his duty, he does himself lie open to the reproofs of a sorry ship-master. See how men by their sin and folly diminish themselves and make themselves mean. Yet we must admire God's goodness in sending him this seasonable reproof, for it was the first step towards his recovery, as the crowing of the cock was to Peter. Note, Those that sleep in a storm may well be asked what they mean. 2. A pertinent word of advice: *"Arise, call upon thy God;* we are here crying every man to his god, why dost not thou get up and cry to thine? Art not thou equally concerned with the rest both in the danger dreaded and in the deliverance desired?"* Note, The devotions of others should quicken ours; and those who hope to share in a common mercy ought in all reason to contribute their quota towards the prayers and supplications that are made for it. In times of public distress, if we have any interest at the throne of grace, we ought to improve it for the public good. And the servants of God themselves have sometimes need to be called and stirred up to this part of their duty. 3. A good reason for this advice: *If so be that God will think upon us, that we perish not.* It should seem, the many gods they called upon were considered by them only as mediators between them and the supreme God, and intercessors for them with him; for the ship-master speaks of one God still, from whom he expected relief. To engage prayer, he suggested that the danger was very great and imminent: "We are all likely to *perish;* there is but a step between us and death, and that just ready to be stepped." Yet he suggested that there was some hope remaining that their destruction might be prevented and they might *not perish.* While there is life there is hope, and while there is hope there is room for prayer.

He suggested also that it was God only that could effect their deliverance, and it must come from his power and his pity. "If he *think upon us*, and act for us, we may yet be saved." And therefore to him we must look, and in him we must put our trust, when the danger is ever so imminent.

IV. Jonah is found out to be the cause of the storm.

1. The mariners observed so much peculiar and uncommon either in the storm itself or in their own distress by it that they concluded it was a messenger of divine justice sent to arrest some one of those that were in that ship, as having been guilty of some enormous crime, judging as the barbarous people (Acts xxviii. 4), "*no doubt one of us is a murderer*, or guilty of sacrilege, or perjury, or the like, who is thus *pursued* by the *vengeance of the sea*, and it is for his sake that we all suffer." Even the light of nature teaches that in extraordinary judgments the wrath of God is revealed from heaven against some extraordinary sins and sinners. Whatever evil is upon us at any time we must conclude *there is a cause* for it; there is evil done by us, or else this evil would not be upon us; there is a ground for God's controversy.

2. They determined to refer it to the lot which of them was the criminal that had occasioned this storm: *Let us cast lots, that we may know for whose cause this evil is upon us.* None of them suspected himself, or said, *Is it I*, Lord; *is it I?* But they suspected one another, and would find out the man. Note, It is a desirable thing, when any evil is upon us, to know for what cause it is upon us, that what is amiss may be amended, and, the grievance being redressed, the grief may be removed. In order to this we must look up to heaven, and pray, Lord, *show me wherefore thou contendest with me ; that which I see not teach thou me.* These mariners desired to know the person that was the dead weight in their ship, the accursed thing, that that one man might *die for the people* and that the whole ship *might not be lost;* this was not only expedient, but highly just. In order to this they cast lots, by which they appealed to the judgment of God, to whom *all hearts are open, and from whom no secret is hid,* agreeing to acquiesce in his discovery and determination, and to take that for true which the lot spoke; for they knew by the light of nature, what the scripture tells us, that *the lot is cast into the lap, but the whole disposal thereof is of the Lord.* Even the heathen looked upon the casting of lots to be a sacred thing, to be done with seriousness and solemnity, and not to be made a sport of. It is a shame for Christians if they have not a like reverence for an appeal to Providence.

3. The *lot fell upon Jonah*, who could have saved them this trouble if he would but have told them what his own conscience told him, *Thou art the man;* but as is usual with criminals, he never confesses till he finds he cannot help it, till *the lot falls upon him.* We may suppose there were those in the ship who, upon other accounts, were greater sinners than Jonah, and yet he is the man that the tempest pursues and that the lot pitches upon; for it is his own child, his own servant, that the parent, that the master, corrects, if they do amiss; others that offend he leaves to the law. The storm is sent after Jonah, because God has work for him to do, and it is sent to fetch him back to it. Note, God has many ways of bringing to light concealed sins and sinners, and making manifest that folly which was thought to be hidden from the eyes of all living. God's right hand will find out all his servants that desert him, as well as all his enemies that have designs against him; yea, though they flee to the uttermost parts of the sea, or go down to the sides of the ship.

4. Jonah is hereupon brought under examination before the master and mariners. He was a stranger; none of them could say that they knew the prisoner, or had any thing to lay to his charge, and therefore they must extort a confession from him and judge him *out of his own mouth ;* and for this there needed no rack, the shipwreck they were in danger of was sufficient to frighten him, so as to make him tell the truth. Though it was discovered by the lot that he was the person for whose sake they were thus damaged and exposed, yet they did not fly outrageously upon him, as one would fear they might have done, but calmly and mildly enquired into his case. There is a compassion due to offenders when they are discovered and convicted. They give him no hard words, but, "*Tell us, we pray thee,* what is the matter?" Two things they enquire of him:—(1.) Whether he would himself own that he was the person for whose sake the storm was sent, as the lot had intimated: "*Tell us for whose cause this evil is upon us ;* is it indeed for thy cause, and, if so, *for what cause?* What is the offence for which thou art thus prosecuted?" Perhaps the gravity and decency of Jonah's aspect and behaviour made them suspect that the lot had missed its man, had missed its mark, and therefore they would not trust it, unless he would himself own his guilt; they therefore begged of him that he would satisfy them in this matter. Note, Those that would find out the cause of their troubles must not only begin, but pursue the enquiry, must descend to particulars and *accomplish a diligent search.* (2.) What his character was, both as to his calling and as to his country. [1.] They enquire concerning his calling: *What is thy occupation?* This was a proper question to be put to a vagrant. Perhaps they suspected his calling to be such as might bring this trouble upon them: "Art thou a diviner, a sorcerer, a student in the black art? Hast thou been conjuring for this wind? Or what business

art thou now going on? Is it like Balaam's, to curse any of God's people, and is this wind sent to stop thee?" [2.] They enquire concerning his country. One asked, *Whence comest thou?* Another, not having patience to stay for an answer to that, asked, *What is thy country?* A third to the same purport, " *Of what people art thou?* Art thou of the Chaldeans," that were noted for divination, "or of the Arabians," that were noted for stealing? They wished to know of what country he was, that, knowing who was the god of his country, they might guess whether he was one that could do them any kindness in this storm.

5. In answer to these interrogatories Jonah makes a full discovery. (1.) Did they enquire concerning his country? He tells them he is *a Hebrew* (*v.* 9), not only of the nation of Israel, but of their religion, which they received from their fathers. He is a Hebrew, and therefore is the more ashamed to own that he is a criminal; for the sins of Hebrews, that make such a profession of religion and enjoy such privileges, are greater than the sins of others, and more exceedingly sinful. (2.) Did they enquire concerning his calling —*What is thy occupation?* In answer to that he gives an account of his religion, for that was his calling, that was his occupation, that was it that he made a business of: " *I fear the Lord Jehovah;* that is the God I worship, the God I pray to, even *the God of heaven,* the sovereign Lord of all, that has *made the sea and the dry land* and has the command of both." Not the god of one particular country, which they enquired after, and such as the gods were that they had been every man calling upon, but *the God of the whole earth,* who, having made both the sea and the dry land, makes what work he pleases in both and makes what use he pleases of both. This he mentions, not only as condemning himself for his folly, in fleeing from the presence of this God, but as designing to bring these mariners from the worship and service of their many gods to the knowledge and obedience of the one only living and true God. When we are among those that are strangers to us we should do what we can to bring them acquainted with God, by being ready upon all occasions to own our relation to him and our reverence for him. (3.) Did they enquire concerning his crime, for which he is now prosecuted? He owns that he *fled from the presence of the Lord,* that he was here running away from his duty, and the storm was sent to fetch him back. We have reason to think that he told them this with sorrow and shame, justifying God and condemning himself and intimating to the mariners what a great God Jehovah is, who could send such a messenger as this tempest was after a runagate servant.

6. We are told what impression this made upon the mariners: *The men were exceedingly afraid,* and justly, for they perceived, (1.) That God was angry, even that God that made *the sea and the dry land.* This tempest comes from the hand of an offended justice, and therefore they have reason to fear it will go hard with them. Judgments inflicted for some particular sin have a peculiar weight and terror in them. (2.) That God was angry with one that feared and worshipped him, only for once running from his work in a particular instance; this made them afraid for themselves. " If a prophet of the Lord be thus severely punished for one offence, what will become of us that have been guilty of so many, and great, and heinous offences?" *If the righteous be* thus *scarcely saved,* and for a single act of disobedience thus closely pursued, *where shall the ungodly and the sinner appear?* 1 Pet. iv. 17, 18. They said to him, " *Why hast thou done this?* If thou fearest the God that *made the sea and the dry land,* why wast thou such a fool as to think thou couldst flee from his presence? What an absurd unaccountable thing is it!" *Thus he was reproved,* as Abraham by Abimelech (Gen. xx. 16); for if the professors of religion do a wrong thing they must expect to hear of it from those that make no such profession. " *Why hast thou done this to us?*" (so it may be taken) " Why hast thou involved us in the prosecution?" Note, Those that commit a wilful sin know not how far the mischievous consequences of it may reach, nor what mischief may be done by it.

11 Then said they unto him, What shall we do unto thee, that the sea may be calm unto us? for the sea wrought, and was tempestuous. 12 And he said unto them, Take me up, and cast me forth into the sea; so shall the sea be calm unto you: for I know that for my sake this great tempest *is* upon you. 13 Nevertheless the men rowed hard to bring *it* to the land; but they could not: for the sea wrought, and was tempestuous against them. 14 Wherefore they cried unto the LORD, and said, We beseech thee, O LORD, we beseech thee, let us not perish for this man's life, and lay not upon us innocent blood: for thou, O LORD, hast done as it pleased thee. 15 So they took up Jonah, and cast him forth into the sea: and the sea ceased from her raging. 16 Then the men feared the LORD exceedingly, and offered a sacrifice unto the LORD, and made vows. 17 Now the LORD had prepared a great fish to swallow up Jonah. And Jonah was in the

belly of the fish three days and three nights.

It is plain that Jonah is the man for whose sake this evil is upon them, but the discovery of him to be so was not sufficient to answer the demands of this tempest; they had found him out, but something more was to be done, for still *the sea wrought and was tempestuous* (v. 11), and again (v. 13), it *grew more and more tempestuous* (so the margin reads it); for if we discover sin to be the cause of our troubles, and do not forsake it, we do but make bad worse. Therefore they went on with the prosecution.

I. They enquired of Jonah himself what he thought they must do with him (v. 11): *What shall we do unto thee, that the sea may be calm to us?* They perceive that Jonah is a prophet of the Lord, and therefore will not do any thing, no, not in his own case, without consulting him. He appears to be a delinquent, but he appears also to be a penitent, and therefore they will not insult over him, nor offer him any rudeness. Note, We ought to act with great tenderness towards those that are overtaken in a fault and are brought into distress by it. They would not *cast him into the sea* if he could think of any other expedient by which to *save the ship.* Or, perhaps, thus they would show how plain the case was, that there was no remedy but he must be thrown overboard; let him be his own judge as he had been his own accuser, and he himself will say so. Note, When sin has raised a storm, and laid us under the tokens of God's displeasure, we are concerned to enquire what we shall do that the sea may be calm; and what shall we do? We must pray and believe, when we are in a storm, and study to answer the end for which it was sent, and then the storm shall become a calm. But especially we must consider what is to be done to the sin that raised the storm; that must be discovered, and penitently confessed; that must be detested, disclaimed, and utterly forsaken. What have I to do any more with it? Crucify it, crucify it, for this evil it has done.

II. Jonah reads his own doom (v. 12): *Take me up, and cast me forth into the sea.* He would not himself leap into the sea, but he put himself into their hands, to cast him into the sea, and assured them that then the *sea would be calm,* and not otherwise. He proposed this, in tenderness to the mariners, that they might not suffer for his sake. " Let thy hand be upon me" (says David, 1 Chron. xxi. 17), "who am guilty; let me die for my own sin, but let not the innocent suffer for it." This is the language of true penitents, who earnestly desire that none but themselves may ever smart, or fare the worse, for their sins and follies. He proposed it likewise in submission to the will of God, who sent this tempest in pursuit of him; and *therefore* judged himself to be cast into the

1284

sea, because to that he plainly saw God judging him, that he might not be *judged of the Lord* to eternal misery. Note, Those who are truly humbled for sin will cheerfully submit to the will of God, even in a sentence of death itself. If Jonah sees this to be the punishment of his iniquity, he accepts it, he subjects himself to it, and justifies God in it. No matter though the *flesh* be *destroyed,* no matter how it is destroyed, so that the *spirit may* but *be saved in the day of the Lord Jesus,* 1 Cor. v. 5. The reason he gives is, *For I know that for my sake this great tempest is upon you.* See how ready Jonah is to take all the guilt upon himself, and to look upon all the trouble as theirs: " It is purely for my sake, who have sinned, that this tempest is upon you; therefore cast me forth into the sea; for," 1. " I deserve it. I have wickedly departed from my God, and it is upon my account that he is angry with you. Surely I am unworthy to breathe in that air which for my sake has been hurried with winds, to live in that ship which for my sake has been thus tossed. Cast me into the sea after the wares which for my sake you have thrown into it. Drowning is too good for me; a single death is punishment too little for such a complicated offence." 2. " Therefore there is no other way of having the sea calm. If it is I that have raised the storm, it is not casting the wares into the sea that will lay it again; no, you must cast me thither." When conscience is awakened, and a storm raised there, nothing will turn it into a calm but parting with the sin that occasioned the disturbance, and abandoning that. It is not parting with our money that will pacify conscience; no, it is the Jonah that must be thrown overboard. Jonah is herein a type of Christ, that he *gives his life a ransom for many;* but with this material difference, that the storm Jonah gave himself up to still was of his own raising, but that storm which Christ gave himself up to still was of our raising. Yet, as Jonah delivered himself up to be cast into a raging sea that it might be calm, so did our Lord Jesus, when he died that we might live.

III. The poor mariners did what they could to save themselves from the necessity of throwing Jonah into the sea, but all in vain (v. 13): *They rowed hard to bring the ship to the land,* that, if they must part with Jonah, they might set him safely on shore; *but they could not.* All their pains were to no purpose; *for the sea wrought* harder than they could, and *was tempestuous against them,* so that they could by no means *make the land.* If they thought sometimes that they had gained their point, they were quickly thrown off to sea again. Still their ship was overladen; their lightening it of the wares made it never the lighter as long as Jonah was in it. And, besides, they rowed against wind and tide, the wind of God's vengeance, the tide of his counsels; and it is in vain to contend with God, in vain to think of saving ourselves any other way than by destroying our sins. By this it appears that these mariners were very loth to execute Jonah's sentence upon himself, though they knew it was for his sake that this tempest was upon them. They were thus very backward to it partly from a dread of bringing upon themselves the guilt of blood, and partly from a compassion they could not but have for poor Jonah, as a good man, as a man in distress, and as a man of sincerity. Note, The more sinners humble and abase themselves, judge and condemn themselves, the more likely they are to find pity both with God and man. The more forward Jonah was to say, *Cast me into the sea,* the more backward they were to do it.

IV. When they found it necessary to cast Jonah into the sea they first prayed to God that the guilt of his blood might not lie upon them, nor be laid to their charge, *v.* 14. When they found it in vain to row hard they quitted their oars and went to their prayers: *Wherefore they cried unto the Lord,* unto Jehovah, the true and living God, and no more to the *gods many,* and *lords many,* that they had *cried to, v.* 5. They prayed to the *God of Israel,* being now convinced, by the providences of God concerning Jonah and the information he had given them, that he is God *alone.* Having determined to cast Jonah into the sea, they first enter a protestation in the court of heaven that they do not do it willingly, much less maliciously, or with any design to be revenged upon him because it was for his sake that this tempest was upon them. No; *his God forgive him,* as *they do!* But they are forced to do it *se defendendo—in self-defence,* having no other way to save their own lives; and they do it as ministers of justice, both God and himself having sentenced him to *so great a death.* They *therefore* present a humble petition to the God whom Jonah feared, that they might not *perish for his life.* See, 1. What a fear they had of contracting the guilt of blood, especially the blood of one that feared God, and worshipped him, and had fellowship with him, as they perceived Jonah had, though in a single instance he had been faulty. Natural conscience cannot but have a dread of blood-guiltiness, and make men very earnest in prayer, as David was, to be delivered from it, Ps. li. 14. So they were here: *We beseech thee, O Lord! we beseech thee, lay not upon us innocent blood.* They are now as earnest in praying to be saved from the peril of the sin as they were before in praying to be saved from the peril of the sea, especially because Jonah appeared to them to be no ordinary person, but a very good man, a man of God, a worshipper of the great Creator of heaven and earth, upon which account even these rude mariners conceived a veneration for him, and trembled at the thought of taking away his life. Inno-

cent blood is precious, but saints' blood, prophets' blood, is much more precious, and so those will find to their cost that any way bring themselves under the guilt of it. The mariners saw Jonah pursued by divine vengeance, and yet could not without horror think of being his executioners. Though his God has a controversy with him, yet, think they, *Let not our hand be upon him.* The Israelites were at this time killing the prophets for doing their duty (witness Jezebel's late persecution), and were prodigal of their lives, which is aggravated by the tenderness these heathens had for one whom they perceived to be a prophet, though he was now out of the way of his duty. 2. What a fear they had of incurring the wrath of God; they were jealous lest he should be angry if they should be the death of Jonah, for he had said, *Touch not my anointed, and do my prophets no harm;* it is at your peril if you do. " Lord," say they, " *let us not perish for this man's life.* Let it not be such a fatal dilemma to us. We see we must perish if we spare his life; Oh let us not perish for taking away his life." And their plea is good: " *For thou, O Lord! hast done as it pleased thee;* thou hast laid us under a necessity of doing it; the wind that pursued him, the lot that discovered him, were both under thy direction, which we are herein governed by; we are but the instruments of Providence, and it is sorely against our will that we do it; but we must say, *The will of the Lord be done.*" Note, When we are manifestly led by Providence to do things contrary to our own inclinations, and quite beyond our own intentions, it will be some satisfaction to us to be able to say, *Thou, O Lord! hast done as it pleased thee.* And, if God please himself, we ought to be satisfied though he do not please us.

V. Having deprecated the guilt they dreaded, they proceeded to execution (*v.* 15): *They took up Jonah,* and *cast him forth into the sea.* They cast him out of their ship, out of their company, and cast him into the sea, a raging stormy sea, that cried, " Give, give; surrender the traitor, or expect no peace." We may well think what confusion and amazement poor Jonah was in when he saw himself ready to be hurried into the presence of that God as a Judge whose presence as a Master he was now fleeing from. Note, Those know not what ruin they run upon that run away from God. *Woe unto them! for they have fled from me.* When sin is the Jonah that raises the storm, that must thus be cast forth into the sea; we must abandon it, and be the death of it, must drown that which otherwise will *drown us in destruction and perdition.* And if we thus by a thorough repentance and reformation cast our sins forth into the sea, never to recal them or return to them again, God will by pardoning mercy subdue our iniquities, and *cast them into the depths of the sea* too, Mic. vii. 19.

VI. The throwing of Jonah into the sea immediately put an end to the storm. The sea has what she came for, and therefore rests contented; she *ceases from her raging.* It is an instance of the sovereign power of God that he can soon turn the storm into a calm, and of the equity of his government that when the end of an affliction is answered and attained the affliction shall immediately be removed. He will not contend for ever, will not contend any longer than till we submit ourselves and give up the cause. If we turn from our sins, he will soon turn from his anger.

VII. The mariners were hereby more confirmed in their belief that Jonah's God was the only true God (*v.* 16): *Then the men feared the Lord with a great fear,* were possessed with a deep veneration for the God of Israel, and came to a resolution that they would worship him only for the future; for *there is no other God that can* destroy, that *can deliver, after this sort.* When they saw the power of God in raising and laying the tempest, when they saw his justice upon Jonah his own servant, and when they saw his goodness to them in saving them from the brink of ruin, *then they feared the Lord,* Jer. v. 22. As an evidence of their fear of him, they *offered sacrifice* to him when they came ashore again in the land of Israel, and for the present made vows that they would do so, in thankfulness for their deliverance, and to make atonement for their souls. Or, perhaps, they had something yet on board which might be for a sacrifice to God immediately. Or it may be meant of the spiritual sacrifices of prayer and praise, with which God is better pleased than with that of an ox or bullock that has horns and hoofs. See Ps. cvii. 22, &c. We must make vows, not only when we are in the pursuit of mercy, but, which is much more generous, when we have received mercy, as those that are still studying what we shall render.

VIII. Jonah's life, after all, is saved by a miracle, and we shall hear of him again for all this. In the midst of judgment God *remembers mercy.* Jonah shall be worse frightened than hurt, not so much punished for his sin as reduced to his duty. Though he flees from the presence of the Lord, and seems to fall into his avenging hands, yet God has more work for him to do, and therefore has *prepared a great fish* to swallow up Jonah (*v.* 17), *a whale* our Saviour calls it (Matt. xii. 40), one of the largest sorts of whales, that have wider throats than others, in the belly of which has sometimes been found the dead body of a man in armour. Particular notice is taken, in the history of the creation, of God's *creating great whales* (Gen. i. 21) and the *leviathan* in the waters *made to play therein,* Ps. civ. 26. But God finds work for this leviathan, has *prepared* him, has *numbered* him (so the word is), has appointed him to be Jonah's receiver and

1286

deliverer. Note, God has command of all the creatures, and can make any of them serve his designs of mercy to his people, even the fishes of the sea, that are most from under man's cognizance, even the great whales, that are altogether from under man's government. This fish was prepared, lay ready under water close by the ship, that he might keep Jonah from sinking to the bottom, and save him alive, though he deserved to die. Let us *stand still and see this salvation of the Lord,* and admire his power, that he could thus save a drowning man, and his pity, that he would thus save one that was running from him and had offended him. It was of the Lord's mercies that Jonah was not now consumed. The fish swallowed up Jonah, not to devour him, but to protect him. *Out of the eater comes forth meat;* for Jonah was alive and well *in the belly of the fish three days and three nights,* not consumed by the heat of the animal, nor suffocated for want of air. It is granted that to nature this was impossible, but not to the God of nature, with whom all things are possible. Jonah by this miraculous preservation was designed to be made, 1. A monument of divine mercy, for the encouragement of those that have sinned, and gone away from God, to return and repent. 2. A successful preacher to Nineveh; and this miracle wrought for his deliverance, if the tidings of it reached Nineveh, would contribute to his success. 3. An illustrious type of Christ, who was buried and rose again according to the scriptures (1 Cor. xv. 4), according to this scripture, for, *as Jonah was three days and three nights in the whale's belly, so was the Son of man three days and three nights in the heart of the earth,* Matt. xii. 40. Jonah's burial was a figure of Christ's. God prepared Jonah's grave, so he did Christ's, when it was long before ordained that he should *make his grave with the rich,* Isa. liii. 9. Was Jonah's grave a strange one, a new one? So was Christ's, one in which never man before was laid. Was Jonah there the best part of three days and three nights? So was Christ; but both in order to their rising again for the bringing of the doctrine of repentance to the Gentile world. *Come, see the place where the Lord lay.*

CHAP. II.

We left Jonah in the belly of the fish, and had reason to think we should hear no more of him, that if he were not destroyed by the waters of the sea he would be consumed in the bowels of that leviathan, " out of whose mouth go burning lamps, and sparks of fire, and whose breath kindles coals," Job xli. 19, 21. But God brings his people through fire, and through water (Ps. lxvi. 12); and by his power, behold, Jonah the prophet is yet alive, and is heard of again. In this chapter God hears from him, for we find him praying; in the next Nineveh hears from him, for we find him preaching. In his prayer we have, I. The great distress and danger he was in, ver. 2, 3, 5, 6. II. The despair he was thereby almost reduced to, ver. 4. III. The encouragement he took to himself, in this deplorable condition, ver. 4, 7. IV. The assurance he had of God's favour to him, ver. 6, 7. V. The warning and instruction he gives to others, ver. 8. VI. The praise and glory of all given to God, ver. 9. In the last verse we have Jonah's deliverance out of the belly of the fish, and his coming safe and sound upon dry land again.

THEN Jonah prayed unto the Lord his God out of the fish's

belly, 2 And said, I cried by reason of mine affliction unto the LORD, and he heard me; out of the belly of hell cried I, *and* thou heardest my voice. 3 For thou hadst cast me into the deep, in the midst of the seas; and the floods compassed me about: all thy billows and thy waves passed over me. 4 Then I said, I am cast out of thy sight; yet I will look again toward thy holy temple. 5 The waters compassed me about, *even* to the soul: the depth closed me round about, the weeds were wrapped about my head. 6 I went down to the bottoms of the mountains; the earth with her bars *was* about me for ever: yet hast thou brought up my life from corruption, O LORD my God. 7 When my soul fainted within me I remembered the LORD: and my prayer came in unto thee, into thine holy temple. 8 They that observe lying vanities forsake their own mercy. 9 But I will sacrifice unto thee with the voice of thanksgiving; I will pay *that* that I have vowed. Salvation *is* of the LORD.

God and his servant Jonah had parted in anger, and the quarrel began on Jonah's side; he fled from his country that he might outrun his work; but we hope to see them both together again, and the reconciliation begins on God's side. In the close of the foregoing chapter we found God returning to Jonah in a way of mercy, *delivering him from going down to the pit,* having *found a ransom;* in this chapter we find Jonah returning to God in a way of duty; he was called up in the former chapter to pray to his God, but we are not told that he did so; however, now at length he is brought to it. Now observe here,

I. When he prayed (v. 1): *Then Jonah prayed;* then when he was in trouble, under the sense of sin and the tokens of God's displeasure against him for sin, then he prayed. Note, When we are in affliction we must pray; then we have occasion to pray, then we have errands at the throne of grace and business there; then, if ever, we shall have a disposition to pray, when the heart is humbled, and softened, and made serious; then God expects it *(in their affliction they will seek me early,* seek me earnestly) ; and, though we bring our afflictions upon ourselves by our sins, yet, if we pray in humility and godly sincerity, we shall be welcome to the throne of grace, as Jonah was. Then when he was in a hopeful way of deliverance, being preserved alive by miracle, a plain indication that he was reserved for further

mercy, then he prayed. An apprehension of God's good-will to us, notwithstanding our offences, gives us boldness of access to him, and opens the lips in prayer which were closed with the sense of guilt and dread of wrath.

II. Where he prayed—in *the fish's belly.* No place is amiss for prayer. *I will that men pray every where.* Wherever God casts us we may find a way open heaven-ward, if it be not our own fault. *Undique ad cœlos tantundem est viæ—The heavens are equally accessible from every part of the earth.* He that has Christ dwelling in his heart by faith, wherever he goes carries his altar along with him, that *sanctifies the gift,* and is himself a *living temple.* Jonah was here in confinement; the belly of the fish was his prison, was a close and dark dungeon to him; yet there he had freedom of access to God, and walked at liberty in communion with him. Men may shut us out from communion with one another, but not from communion with God. Jonah was now in the bottom of the sea, yet *out of the depths he cries to God;* as Paul and Silas prayed in the prison, in the stocks.

III. To whom he prayed—*to the Lord his God.* He had been fleeing from God, but now he sees the folly of it, and returns to him; by prayer he draws near to that God whom he had gone aside from, and *engages his heart to approach him.* In prayer he has an eye to him, not only as *the Lord,* but as *his God,* a God in covenant with him; for, thanks be to God, every transgression in the covenant does not throw us out of covenant. This encourages even backsliding children to return. Jer. iii. 22, *Behold, we come unto thee, for thou art the Lord our God.*

IV. What his prayer was. He afterwards recollected the substance of it, and left it upon record. He reflects upon the workings of his heart towards God when he was in his distress and danger, and the conflict that was then in his breast between faith and sense, between hope and fear.

1. He reflects upon the earnestness of his prayer, and God's readiness to hear and answer (v. 2): He said, *I cried, by reason of my affliction, unto the Lord.* Note, Many that prayed not at all, or did but whisper prayer, when they were in prosperity, are brought to pray, nay, are brought to cry, *by reason of their affliction;* and it is for this end that afflictions are sent, and they are in vain if this end be not answered. Those *heap up wrath* who *cry not when God binds them,* Job xxxvi. 13. " *Out of the belly of hell* and the grave *cried I.*" The fish might well be called a grave, and, as it was a prison to which Jonah was condemned for his disobedience and in which he lay under the wrath of God, it might well be called the belly of hell. Thither this good man was cast, and yet thence he cried to God, and it was not in vain; God *heard him,* heard the

voice of his affliction, the voice of his supplication. There is a hell in the other world, out of which there is no crying to God with any hope of being heard; but, whatever hell we may be *in the belly of* in this world, we may thence *cry to God.* When Christ lay, as Jonah, three days and three nights in the grave, though he prayed not, as Jonah did, yet his very lying there cried to God for poor sinners, and the cry was heard.

2. He reflects upon the very deplorable condition that he was in when he was in the belly of hell, which, when he lay there, he was very sensible of and made particular remarks upon. Note, If we would get good by our troubles, we must take notice of our troubles, and of the hand of God in them. Jonah observes here, (1.) How low he was thrown (*v.* 3): *Thou hadst cast me into the deep.* The mariners cast him there; but he looked above them, and saw the hand of God casting him there. Whatever deeps we are cast into, it is God that casts us into them, and he it is who, *after he has killed, has power to cast into hell.* He was cast *into the midst of the seas—the heart of the seas* (so the word is), and thence Christ borrows that Hebrew phrase, when he applies it to his own lying so long in the *heart of the earth.* For he that is laid dead in the grave, though it be ever so shallow, is cut off as effectually from the land of the living as if he were laid in the *heart of the earth.* (2.) How terribly he was beset: *The floods compassed me about.* The channels and springs of the waters of the sea surrounded him on every side; it was always high-water with him. God's dear saints and servants are sometimes encompassed with the floods of affliction, with troubles that are very forcible and violent, that bear down all before them, and that run constantly upon them, as the waters of a river in a continual succession, one trouble upon the neck of another, as Job's messengers of evil tidings; they are enclosed by them on all sides, as the church complains, Lam. iii. 7. *He has hedged me about, that I cannot get out,* nor see which way I may flee for safety. *All thy billows and thy waves passed over me.* Observe, He calls them God's billows and his waves, not only because he made them *(the sea is his, and he made it),* and because he *rules* them (for *even the winds and the seas obey him),* but because he had now commissioned them against Jonah, and limited them, and ordered them to afflict and terrify him, but not to destroy him. These words are plainly quoted by Jonah from Ps. xlii. 7, where, though the translations differ a little, in the original David's complaint is the same *verbatim—word for word,* with this of Jonah's: *All thy billows and thy waves passed over me.* What David spoke figuratively and metaphorically Jonah applies to himself as literally fulfilled. For the reconciling of ourselves to our afflictions, it is good to search precedents, that we may

1288

find *there has no temptation taken us but such as is common to men.* If ever any man's case was singular, and not to be paralleled, surely Jonah's was, and yet, to his great satisfaction, he finds even the man after God's own heart making the same complaint of God's *waves and billows going over him* that he has now occasion to make. When God *performs the thing that is appointed for us* we shall find that *many such things are with him,* that even our path of trouble is no untrodden path, and that God deals with us no otherwise than as he *uses to deal with those that love his name.* And therefore for our assistance in our addresses to God, when we are in trouble, it is good to make use of the complaints and prayers which the saints that have been before us made use of in the like case. See how good it is to be ready in the scriptures; Jonah, when he could make no use of his Bible, by the help of his memory furnished himself from the scripture with a very proper representation of his case: *All thy billows and thy waves passed over me.* To the same purport, *v.* 5, *The waters compassed me about even to the soul;* they threatened his life, which was hereby brought into imminent danger; or they made an impression upon his spirit; he saw them to be tokens of God's displeasure, and in them the *terrors of the Almighty set themselves in array against him;* this reached to his soul, and put that into confusion. And this also is borrowed from David's complaint, Ps. lxix. 1, The *waters have come in unto my soul.* When *without are fightings* it is no marvel that *within are fears.* Jonah, in the fish's belly, finds the *depths enclosing him round about,* so that if he would get out of his prison, yet he must unavoidably perish in the waters. He feels the *sea-weed* (which the fish sucked in with the water) *wrapped about his head,* so that he has no way left him to help himself, nor hope that any one else can help him. Thus are the people of God sometimes perplexed and entangled, that they may learn not to *trust in themselves, but in God that raises the dead,* 2 Cor. i. 8, 9. (3.) How fast he was held (*v.* 6): He *went down to the bottom of the mountains,* to the rocks in the sea, upon which the hills and promontories by the seaside seem to be bottomed; he lay among them, nay, he lay under them; the *earth with her bars was about him,* so close about him that it was likely to be about him for ever. The earth was so shut and locked, so barred and bolted, against him, that he was quite cut off from any hope of ever returning to it. Thus helpless, thus hopeless, did Jonah's case seem to be. Those whom God contends with the whole creation is at war with.

3. He reflects upon the very black and melancholy conclusion he was then ready to make concerning himself, and the relief he obtained against it, *v.* 4, 7. (1.) He began to sink into despair, and to give up himself for gone and undone to all intents and

purposes. When the *waters compassed him about even to the soul* no marvel that *his soul fainted within him,* fainted away, so that he had not any comfortable enjoyments or expectations; his spirits quite failed, and he looked upon himself as a dead man. *Then I said, I am cast out of thy sight,* and the apprehension of that was the thing that made his spirit faint within him. He thought God had quite forsaken him, would never return in mercy to him, nor show him any token for good again. He had no example before him of any that were brought alive out of a fish's belly; if he thought of Job upon the dunghill, Joseph in the pit, David in the cave, yet these did not come up to his case. Nor was there any visible way of escape open for him but by miracle; and what reason had he to expect that a miracle of mercy should be wrought for him who was now made a monument of justice? His own conscience told him that he had wickedly *fled from the presence of the Lord,* and therefore he might justly *cast him away from his presence,* and, in token of that, *take away his Holy Spirit from him,* never to visit him more. What hopes could he have of deliverance out of a trouble which his *own ways and doings* had *procured to himself?* Observe, When Jonah would say the worst he could of his case he says this, *I am cast out of thy sight;* those, and those only, are miserable, whom God has cast out of his sight, whom he will no longer own and favour. What is the misery of the damned in hell but this, that they are cast out of God's sight? For what is the happiness of heaven but the vision and fruition of God? Sometimes the condition of God's people may be such in this world that they may think themselves quite excluded from God's presence, so as no more to see him, or to be regarded by him. Jacob and Israel said, *My way is hidden from the Lord, and my judgment is passed over from my God,* Isa. xl. 27. *Zion said, The Lord has forsaken me, my God has forgotten me,* Isa. xlix. 14. But it is only the surmise of unbelief, for God has not *cast away his people whom he has chosen.* (2.) Yet he recovered himself from sinking into despair, with some comfortable prospects of deliverance. Faith corrected and controlled the surmises of fear and distrust. Here was a fierce struggle between sense and faith, but faith had the last word and came off a conqueror. In trying times, the issue will be good at last, provided our faith do not fail; it was therefore the continuance of that in its vigour that Christ secured to Peter. *I have prayed for thee, that thy faith fail not,* Luke xxii. 32. David would have fainted if he had not *believed,* Ps. xxvii. 13. Jonah's faith said, *Yet I will look again towards thy holy temple.* Thus, though he was *perplexed,* yet *not in despair;* in the depth of the sea he had this hope in him, as an *anchor of the*

soul, *sure and steadfast.* That which he supports himself with the hope of is that he shall yet *look again towards God's holy temple.* [1.] That he shall live; he shall look again heaven-ward, shall again see the light of the sun, though now he seems to be cast into utter darkness. Thus *against hope he believed in hope.* [2.] That he shall *live, and praise God;* and a good man does not desire to live for any other purpose, Ps. cxix. 175. That he shall enjoy communion with God again in holy ordinances, shall *look towards,* and go up to, *the holy temple,* there to enquire, there to *behold the beauty of the Lord.* When Hezekiah desired that he might be assured of his recovery, he asked, *What is the sign that I shall go up to the house of the Lord?* (Isa. xxxviii. 22), as if that were the only thing for the sake of which he wished for health; so Jonah here hopes he shall *look again towards the temple;* that way he had looked many a time with pleasure, rejoicing when he was called *to go up to the house of the Lord;* and the remembrance of it was his comfort, that, when he had opportunity, he was no stranger to the holy temple. But now he could not so much as look towards it; in the fish's belly he could not tell which way it lay, but he hopes he shall be again able to look towards it, to look on it, to look into it. Observe, How modestly Jonah expresses himself; as one conscious to himself of guilt and unworthiness, he dares not speak of dwelling in God's house, as David, knowing that he is *no more worthy to be called a son,* but he hopes he may be admitted to look towards it. He calls it the *holy temple,* for the holiness of it was, in his eye, the beauty of it, and that for the sake of which he loved and looked towards it. The temple was a type of heaven; and he promises himself that though being now a *captive exile,* he should never be *loosed,* but *die in the pit,* yet he should look towards the heavenly temple, and be brought safely thither. Though he die in the fish's belly, in the bottom of the sea, yet thence he hopes his soul shall be carried by angels into Abraham's bosom. Or these words may be taken as Jonah's vow when he was in distress, and he speaks (v. 9) of paying what he vowed; his vow is that if God deliver him he will praise him *in the gates of the daughter of Zion,* Ps. ix. 13, 14. His sin for which God pursued him was *fleeing from the presence of the Lord,* the folly of which he is now convinced of, and promises not only that he will never again look towards Tarshish, but that he will again look towards the temple, and will go *from strength to strength* till he appear before God there. And thus we see how faith and hope were his relief in his desponding condition. To these he added prayer to God (v. 7): "*When my soul fainted within me,* then *I remembered* the Lord, I betook myself to that cordial." He remembered what he is, how

1289

nigh to those that seem to be thrown at the greatest distance by trouble, how merciful to those that seem to have thrown themselves at a distance from him by sin. He remembered what he had done for him, what he had done for others, what he could do, what he had promised to do; and this kept him from fainting. Remembering God, he made his addresses to him: " *My prayer came in unto thee;* I sent it in, and expected to receive an answer to it." Note, Our afflictions should put us in mind of God, and thereby put us upon prayer to him. When our souls faint we must remember God; and, when we remember God, we must send up a prayer to him, a pious ejaculation at least; when we think on his name we should call on his name.

4. He reflects upon the favour of God to him when thus in his distress he sought to God and trusted in him. (1.) He graciously accepted his prayer, and gave admission and audience to it (*v.* 7): *My prayer,* being sent to him, *came in unto him,* even *into his holy temple;* it was heard in the highest heavens, though it was prayed in the lowest deeps. (2.) He wonderfully wrought deliverance for him, and, when he was in the depth of his misery, gave him the earnest and assurance of it (*v.* 6): *Yet hast thou brought up my life from corruption, O Lord my God!* Some think he said this when he was vomited up on dry ground; and then it is the language of his thankfulness, and he sets it over-against the great difficulty of his case, that the power of God might be the more magnified in his deliverance: *The earth with her bars was about me for ever,* and yet *thou hast brought up my life from the pit,* from the *bars of the pit.* Or, rather, we may suppose it spoken while he was yet in the fish's belly, and then it is the language of his faith: " Thou hast kept me alive here, in the pit, and therefore thou canst, thou wilt, *bring up my life from the pit;*" and he speaks of it with as much assurance as if it were done already: *Thou hast brought up my life.* Though he has not an express promise of deliverance, he has an earnest of it, and on that he depends; he has life, and therefore believes his life shall be *brought up from corruption;* and this assurance he addresses to God: *Thou hast done it, O Lord my God!* Thou art the Lord, and therefore *canst* do it for me, my God, and therefore wilt do it. Note, If the Lord be our God, he will be to us the *resurrection and the life,* will redeem our lives from destruction, from the power of the grave.

5. He gives warning to others, and instructs them to keep close to God (*v.* 8): *Those that observe lying vanities forsake their own mercy,* that is, (1.) Those that worship other gods, as the heathen mariners did, and call upon them, and expect relief and comfort from them, *forsake their own mercy;* they stand in their own light; they turn their back upon their own happiness, and go quite out of the way of all good. Note, Idols are *lying vanities,* and those that pay that homage to them which is due to God only act as contrarily to their interests as to their duty. Or, (2.) Those that follow their own inventions, as Jonah himself had done when he *fled from the presence of the Lord* to go to Tarshish, *forsake their own mercy,* that mercy which they might find in God, and might have such a covenant-right and title to it as to be able to call it their own, if they would but keep close to God and their duty. Those that think to go any where to be from under the eye of God, as Jonah did—that think to better themselves by deserting his service, as Jonah did—and that grudge his mercy to any poor sinners, and pretend to be wiser than he in judging who are fit to have prophets sent them and who not, as Jonah did—they *observe lying vanities,* are led away by foolish groundless fancies, and, like him, they *forsake their own mercy,* and no good can come of it. Note, Those that forsake their own duty forsake their own mercy; those that run away from the work of their place and day run away from the comfort of it.

6. He solemnly binds his soul with a bond that, if God work deliverance for him, the God of his mercies shall be the God of his praises, *v.* 9. He covenants with God, (1.) That he will honour him in his devotions with the *sacrifice of thanksgiving;* and God has said, for the encouragement of those that do so, that those that *offer praise glorify him.* He will, according to the law of Moses, bring a *sacrifice of thanksgiving,* and will offer that according to the law of nature, with the *voice of thanksgiving.* The love and thankfulness of the heart to God are the life and soul of this duty; without these neither the sacrifice of thanksgiving nor the voice of thanksgiving will avail any thing. But gratitude was then, by a divine appointment, to be expressed by a sacrifice, in which the offerer presented the beast slain to God, not in lieu of himself, but in token of himself; and it is now to be expressed by the *voice of thanksgiving,* the *calves of our lips* (Hos. xiv. 2), the *fruit of our lips* (Heb. xiii. 15), speaking forth, singing forth, the high praises of our God. This Jonah here promises, that with the sacrifice of thanksgiving he will *mention the lovingkindness of the Lord,* to his glory, and the encouragement of others. (2.) That he will honour him in his conversation by a punctual performance of his vows, which he made in the fish's belly. Some think it was some work of charity that he vowed, or such a vow as Jacob's was, *Of all that thou hast given me I will give the tenth unto thee.* More probably his vow was that if God would deliver him he would readily go wherever he should please to send him, though it were to Nineveh. When we smart for deserting our duty it is time to promise that we will adhere to it, and abound in it. Or, perhaps,

the sacrifice of thanksgiving is the thing he vowed, and that is it which he will pay, as David, Ps. cxvi. 17—19.

7. He concludes with an acknowledgment of God as the Saviour of his people : *Salvation is of the Lord; it belongs to the Lord,* Ps. iii. 8. He is the *God of salvation,* Ps. lxviii. 19, 20. He only can work salvation, and he can do it be the danger and distress ever so great; he has promised salvation to his people that trust in him. All the salvations of his church in general, and of particular saints, were wrought by him; he is the *Saviour of those that believe,* 1 Tim. iv. 10. Salvation is still of him, as it has always been; from him alone it is to be expected, and on him we are to depend for it. Jonah's experience shall encourage others, in all ages, to trust in God as the God of their salvation; all that read this story shall say with assurance, say with admiration, that *salvation is of the Lord,* and is sure to all that belongs to him.

10 And the LORD spake unto the fish, and it vomited out Jonah upon the dry *land.*

We have here Jonah's discharge from his imprisonment, and his deliverance from that death which there he was threatened with—his return, though not to life, for he lived in the fish's belly, yet to the *land of the living,* for from that he seemed to be quite cut off—his resurrection, though not from death, yet from the grave, for surely never man was so buried alive as Jonah was in the fish's belly. His enlargement may be considered, 1. As an instance of God's power over all the creatures. God *spoke to the fish,* gave him orders to return him, as before he had given him orders to receive him. God speaks to other creatures, and *it is done;* they are all his ready obedient servants. But to man he *speaks once, yea, twice, and he perceives it not,* regards it not, but turns a deaf ear to what he says. Note, God has all creatures at his command, makes what use he pleases of them, and serves his own purposes by them. 2. As an instance of God's mercy to a poor penitent, that in his distress prays to him. Jonah had sinned, had done foolishly, very foolishly; his own backslidings did not correct him, and it appears by his after-conduct that his foolishness was not quite driven from him, no, not by the rod of this correction; and yet, upon his praying, and humbling himself before God, here is a miracle in nature wrought for his deliverance, to intimate what a miracle of grace, free grace, God's reception and entertainment of returning sinners are. When God had him at his mercy he showed him mercy, and did not *contend for ever.* 3. As a type and figure of Christ's resurrection. He died and was buried, to lay the storm which our sin had raised, and lay in the grave, as Jonah did, three days and three nights, a prisoner for

our debt; but the third day he came forth, as Jonah did, by his messengers to preach repentance, and remission of sins, even to the Gentiles. And thus was another scripture fulfilled, *After two days he will receive us, and the third day he will raise us up,* Hos. vi. 2. The earth trembled as if full of her burden, as the fish was of Jonah.

CHAP. III.

In this chapter we have, I. Jonah's mission renewed, and the command a second time given him to go preach at Nineveh, ver. 1, 2. II. Jonah's message to Nineveh faithfully delivered, by which its speedy overthrow was threatened, ver. 3, 4. III. The repentance, humiliation, and reformation of the Ninevites hereupon, ver. 5—9. IV. God's gracious revocation of the sentence passed upon them, and the preventing of the ruin threatened, ver. 10.

AND the word of the LORD came unto Jonah the second time, saying, 2 Arise, go unto Nineveh, that great city, and preach unto it the preaching that I bid thee. 3 So Jonah arose, and went unto Nineveh, according to the word of the LORD. Now Nineveh was an exceeding great city of three days' journey. 4 And Jonah began to enter into the city a day's journey, and he cried, and said, Yet forty days, and Nineveh shall be overthrown.

We have here a further evidence of the reconciliation between God and Jonah, and that it was a thorough reconciliation, though the controversy between them had run high.

I. Jonah's commission is renewed and readily obeyed.

1. By this it appears that God was perfectly reconciled to Jonah, that he employed him again in his service; and the commission anew given him was an evidence of the remission of his former disobedience. Among men, it has been justly pleaded that the giving of a commission to a criminal convicted is equivalent to a pardon, so it was to Jonah. *The word of the Lord came unto Jonah the second time* (v. 1); for, 1. Jonah must be tried, whether he do indeed repent of his former disobedience or no, and whether he have gotten the good designed him both by his strange punishment and by his strange deliverance. He had deserted his work and duty, and had been under an arrest for it, had received a *sentence of death within himself;* but, upon his submission, God had released him, had given him his life, had given him his liberty; but it is upon his good behaviour that he is released, and he must again be put upon the trial whether he will follow the will of God or his own will. After he has been thrown into the sea, and thrown out of it again, God comes and asks him, " Jonah, wilt thou go to Nineveh now?" For *when God judges he will overcome,* he will gain his point; he will bring the disobedient stubborn child to his foot at last. Note, When God has afflicted us, and delivered us out of affliction, we must hear

his voice, saying to us, Now return to the duties which before you neglected, and which by these providences you are called to. God now said, in effect, to Jonah, as Christ said to the impotent man, when he had healed him, " Now go and sin no more, *lest a worse thing come unto thee* (John v. 14), a worse thing than lying three days and three nights in the whale's belly." God looks upon men, when he has afflicted them and has delivered them out of their affliction, to see whether they will mend of that fault, particularly, for which they were corrected ; and therefore in that thing we are concerned to see to it that we receive not the grace of God in vain, neither in the correction nor in the deliverance, for both are designed to be means of grace. (2.) Jonah shall be trusted, in token of God's favour to him. God might justly have said concerning Jonah, as we should concerning one that had cheated us and dealt treacherously with us, that though we would not proceed to the rigour of the law against him, nor ruin him, yet we would never again repose a confidence in him; justly might the Spirit of prophecy, which Jonah had resisted and rebelled against, depart from him, with a resolution never to return to him any more. One would have expected that though his life was spared, yet he would be laid under a disability and incapacity ever to serve the government again in the character of a prophet. But, behold ! the word of the Lord comes to him again, to show that when God forgives he forgets, and whom he forgives he gives a new heart and a new spirit to ; he receives those into his family again, and restores them to their former estate, that had been prodigal children and disobedient servants. Note, God's making use of us is the best evidence of his being at peace with us. Hereby it will appear that our sins are pardoned, and we have the good-will of God towards us ; does his good word come unto us, and do we experience his good work in us ! if so, we have reason to admire the riches of free grace and to own our obligations to the Lord Jesus, who received gifts for men, *yea, even for the rebellious also, that the Lord God might dwell* even among them, and employ them in his word, Ps. lxviii. 18.

2. By this it appears that Jonah was well reconciled to God, that he was not now, as he had been before, *disobedient to the heavenly vision,* did not *flee from the presence of the Lord,* as he had done. He neither endeavoured to avoid hearing the command, nor did he decline obeying it; he made no objections, as he had done, that the journey was *long,* the errand invidious, the delivery of it perilous, and, if the threatened judgment did not come, he should be reproached as a false prophet, and the impenitence of his own nation would be upbraided, which he had objected, *ch.* iv. 2. But now, without murmuring and disputing, *Jonah arose,*

1292

and went unto Nineveh, according to the word of the Lord, v. 3. See here, (1.) The nature of repentance ; it is the change of our mind and way, and a return to our work and duty, from which we had turned aside ; it is doing that good which we had left undone. (2.) The benefit of affliction ; it reduces those to their place that had deserted it. Jonah might truly say with David, " *Before I was afflicted I went astray, but now have I kept thy word ;* and therefore, though it was dreadful, though it was painful to me, and for the present *not joyous, but grievous,* yet *it was good,* very good, *for me, that I was afflicted.*" (3.) See the power of divine grace working with affliction, for otherwise affliction of itself would rather drive men from God than bring them to him; but God by his grace can *turn the disobedient to the wisdom of the just,* and make those *willing in the day of his power,* freely willing to come under his yoke, whose *neck* had been *as an iron sinew.* (4.) See the duty of all those to whom the word of the Lord comes ; they must in all points conform themselves to it, and yield a cheerful faithful obedience to the orders God gives them. *Jonah arose,* and did not sit still in sloth or sullenness ; he went directly to Nineveh, though it was a great way off, and a place where, it is likely, he never was before ; yet thither he took his journey, *according to the word of the Lord.* God's servants must go where he sends them, come when he calls them, and do what he bids them ; whatever appears to be the word of the Lord we must conscientiously do according to it.

II. Let us now see what was the command or commission given him, and what he did in prosecution of it.

1. He was sent as a herald at arms, in the name of the God of heaven, to proclaim war with Nineveh (*v.* 2) : " *Arise, go to Nineveh, that great city,*" that metropolis, and *preach unto it,* preach *against it,* so the Chaldee. What is against us is preached to us, that we may hear it and take warning ; and what is preached to us, if we do not give ear to it, and mix faith with it, will prove to be against us. Jonah is sent to Nineveh, which was at this time the chief city of the Gentile world, as an indication of God's gracious intentions in process of time to make the light of divine revelation to shine in those dark regions. God knew that if Sodom and Gomorrah, Tyre and Sidon, had had the means of grace, they would have repented, and yet he denied them those means, Matt. xi. 21, 23. He knew that if Nineveh had now the means of grace they would repent, and he gave them those means, sent Jonah, though not to preach repentance to them expressly (for we find not that he had that in his commission), yet to preach them to repentance, for that was the happy effect of what he had in commission. If God thus in dispensing his favours, in giving the means of

grace to some places and not to others, and the spirit of grace to some persons and not to others, acts by prerogative and in a way of sovereignty, who may say unto him, What doest thou? *May he not do what he will with his own?* He is debtor to no man. Go, and preach (says God) *the preaching that I bid thee.* That is, (1.) "The preaching that I did bid thee when I first ordered thee to go thither (*ch.* i. 2); go, *and cry against it;* denounce divine judgments against it; tell the men of Nineveh that their wickedness has come up to God, and God's vengeance is coming down upon them." This was the message Jonah was then very loth to deliver, and therefore flew off and went to Tarshish; but, when he is brought to it the second time, God does not at all alter the message, to gratify him, or make it the more passable with him; no, he must now preach the very same that he was then ordered to preach and would not. Note, The word of God is an unalterable thing, and will not be made to bend to the humours either of its preachers or of its hearers; it shall never comply with their humours and fancies, but they must comply with its truths and laws. See Jer. xv. 19. *Let them return unto thee, but return not thou unto them.* Or, (2.) "The preaching that I shall bid thee when thou comest thither." This was an encouragement to him in his undertaking, that God would go along with him, that the Spirit of prophecy should abide upon him, and be ready to him, when he was at Nineveh, to give him all the further instructions that were needful for him. This intimated that he should hear from him again, which would be his great support in this hazardous expedition; as, when God sent Abraham to offer up Isaac, he gave him a similar intimation, by telling him he must do it upon *one of the mountains which he would* afterwards direct *him to. The steps of a good man are ordered by the Lord;* he leads his people step by step, and so he expects they should follow him. Jonah must go with an implicit faith. Though he knows whither he goes, he shall not know, till he come thither, what message he must deliver, but, whatever it is, he must deliver it, be it pleasing or displeasing. Thus God will keep us in a continual dependence upon himself, and the directions of his word and providence. What he does, and what he will have us to do, we *know not now,* but we *shall know hereafter.* Admirals, sometimes, when they are sent abroad, are not to open their commission till they have got so many leagues off at sea; so Jonah must go to Nineveh, and, when he comes there, shall be told what to say.

III. He faithfully and boldly delivered his errand. When he came to Nineveh he found his diocese large; it was an *exceedingly great city of three days' journey* (v. 3); a city *great to God,* so the Hebrew phrase is, meaning no more than as we render it, *exceedingly*

great; this honour that language does to the great God that great things derive their denomination from him. The greatness of Nineveh consisted chiefly in the extent of it; it was much larger than Babylon, such a city, says Diodorus Siculus, as no man ever after built. It was 150 furlongs long and 90 broad, and 480 in compass; the walls 100 feet high, and so thick that three chariots might go a-breast upon them; on them were 1500 towers, each of them 200 feet high. It is here said to be of *three days' journey;* for the compass of the walls, as some relate, was 480 furlongs, which, allowing eight furlongs to a mile, makes sixty miles, which may well be reckoned *three days' journey* for a footman, twenty miles a day. Or, walking slowly and gravely as Jonah must when he went about preaching, it would take him up at least *three days* to go through all the principal streets and lanes of the city, to proclaim his message, that all might have notice of it. When he came thither he lost no time; he did not come to look about him, but applied closely to his work; and, when he began to enter into the city, he did not retire into an inn, to refresh himself after his journey, but opened his commission immediately, according to his instructions, and he *cried, and said, Yet forty days, and Nineveh shall be overthrown.* This, no doubt, he had particular warrant and direction to say; whether he enlarged upon this text, as is most probable, showing them the controversy God had with them, and how provoking their wickedness was, and what reason they had to expect destruction and to give credit to this warning, or whether he only repeated those words again and again, is not certain, but this was the purport of his message. 1. He must tell them that this great city shall be overthrown; he meant, and they understood him, that it should be overthrown, not by war, but by some immediate stroke from heaven, either by an earthquake or by fire and brimstone as Sodom was. The wickedness of cities ripens them for destruction, and their wealth and greatness cannot protect them from destruction when the measure of their iniquity is full and the measure of their vengeance has come. Great cities are easily overthrown when the great God comes to reckon with them. 2. He must tell them that it shall shortly be overthrown, at the end of forty days. It has a reprieve granted. So long God will wait to see if, upon this alarm given, they will humble themselves and amend their doings, and so prevent the ruin threatened. See how slow God is to wrath; though Nineveh's wickedness cried for vengeance, yet it shall be spared for forty days, that it may have space to repent and meet God in the way of his judgments. But he will wait no longer; if in that time they turn not, they shall know that he has *whet his sword, and made it ready.* Forty days is a long time for a righteous God to defer his judgments, yet it is but a little time for an unrighteous people to repent and reform in, and so turn away the judgments coming. The fixing of the day thus, with all possible assurance, would help to convince them that it was a message from God, for no man durst be so positive in fixing a time, however he might prognosticate the thing itself; it would also startle them into preparation for it. It may justly awaken secure sinners by a sincere conversion to prevent their own ruin when they see they have but a little time to turn in. And should it not awaken us to get ready for death, to consider that the thing itself is certain, and the time fixed in the counsel of God, but that we are kept in the dark and uncertainty about it in order that we may be always ready? We cannot be so sure that we shall live forty days as Nineveh now was that it should stand forty days; nay, I think it is more probable that we shall die within thirty or forty days than that we should live thirty or forty years; and so many years in the day of our security we are apt to promise ourselves.

Fleres, si scires unum tua tempora mensem ;
Rides, cum non sit forsitan una dies.

We should be alarmed if we were sure not to live a month, and yet we are careless, though we are not sure to live a day.

5 So the people of Nineveh believed God, and proclaimed a fast, and put on sackcloth, from the greatest of them even to the least of them. 6 For word came unto the king of Nineveh, and he arose from his throne, and he laid his robe from him, and covered *him* with sackcloth, and sat in ashes. 7 And he caused *it* to be proclaimed and published through Nineveh by the decree of the king and his nobles, saying, Let neither man nor beast, herd nor flock, taste any thing : let them not feed, nor drink water : 8 But let man and beast be covered with sackcloth, and cry mightily unto God : yea, let them turn every one from his evil way, and from the violence that *is* in their hands. 9 Who can tell *if* God will turn and repent, and turn away from his fierce anger, that we perish not ? 10 And God saw their works, that they turned from their evil way; and God repented of the evil, that he had said that he would do unto them; and he did *it* not.

Here is, I. A wonder of divine grace in

the repentance and reformation of Nineveh, upon the warning given them of their destruction approaching. *Verily I say unto you*, we have not found so great an instance of it, no, not in Israel; and it will *rise up in judgment against the men of* the gospel-*generation, and condemn them ; for the Ninevites repented at the preaching of Jonas, but behold, a greater than Jonas is here*, Matt. xii. 41. Nay, it did condemn the impenitence and obstinacy of Israel at that time. God sent many prophets to Israel, and those well known among them to be *mighty in word and deed ;* but to Nineveh he sent only one, and him a stranger, whose aspect was mean, we may suppose, and his *bodily presence weak*, especially after the fatigue of so long a journey; and yet they repented, but Israel repented not. Jonah preached but one sermon, and we do not find that he gave them any sign or wonder by the accomplishment of which his word might be confirmed; and yet they were wrought upon, while Israel continued obstinate, whose prophets chose out words wherewith to reason with them, and confirmed them by signs following. Jonah only threatened wrath and ruin ; we do not find that he gave them any calls to repentance or directions how to repent, much less any encouragements to hope that they should find mercy if they did repent, and yet they repented ; but Israel persisted in impenitence, though the prophets sent to them drew them *with cords of a man, and with bands of love*, and assured them of great things which God would do for them if they did repent and reform. Now let us see what was the method of Nineveh's repentance, what were the steps and particular instances of it.

1. They *believed God ;* they gave credit to the word which Jonah spoke to them in the name of God : they believed that though they had many that they called gods, yet there was but *one living and true God*, the sovereign Lord of all,—that to him they were accountable,—that they had sinned against him and had become obnoxious to his justice,—that this notice sent them of ruin approaching came from him, and consequently that the ruin itself would come from him at the time prefixed if it were not prevented by a timely repentance,—that he is a merciful God, and there might be some hopes of the turning away of the wrath threatened, if they did turn away from the sins for which it was threatened. Note, Those that *come to God*, that come back to him after they have revolted from him, must believe, must believe that he is, that he is reconcilable, that he will be theirs if they take the right course. And observe what great faith God can work by very small, weak, and unlikely means ; he can bring even Ninevites by a few threatening words to be *obedient to the faith.* Some think the Ninevites heard, from the mariners or others, or from Jonah himself, of his being cast into

the sea and delivered thence by miracle, and that this served for a confirmation of his mission, and brought them the more readily to believe God speaking by him. But of this we have no certainty. However, Christ's resurrection, typified by that of Jonah's, served for the confirmation of his gospel, and contributed abundantly to their great success who in his name *preached repentance and remission of sins to all nations, beginning at Jerusalem.*

2. They brought word to the king of Nineveh, who, some think, was at this time Sardanapalus, others Pul, king of Assyria. Jonah was not directed to go to him first, in respect to his royal dignity; crowned heads, when guilty heads, are before God upon a level with common heads, and therefore Jonah is not sent to the court, but to the streets of Nineveh, to make his proclamation. However, an account of his errand is brought to the king of Nineveh, not by way of information against Jonah, as a disturber of the public peace, that he might be silenced and punished, which perhaps would have been done if he had cried thus in the streets of Jerusalem, who *killed God's prophets and stoned those that were sent unto her.* No; the account was brought him of it, not as of a crime, but as a message from heaven, by some that were concerned for the public welfare, and whose hearts trembled for it. Note, Those kings are happy who have such about them as will give them notice of the things that belong to the kingdom's peace, of the warnings both of the word and of the providence of God, and of the tokens of God's displeasure which they are under; and those people are happy who have such kings over them as will take notice of those things.

3. The king set them a good example of humiliation, *v.* 6. When he heard of the *word of God* sent to him he *rose from his throne,* as Eglon king of Moab, who, when Ehud told him he had a message to him from God, *rose up out of his seat.* The king of Nineveh *rose from his throne,* not only in reverence to a word from God in general, but in fear of a word of wrath in particular, and in sorrow and shame for sin, by which he and his people had become obnoxious to his wrath. He rose from his royal throne, and laid aside his royal robe, the badge of his imperial dignity, as an acknowledgment that, having not used his power as he ought to have done for the restraining of violence and wrong, and the maintaining of right, he had forfeited his throne and robe to the justice of God, had rendered himself unworthy of the honour put upon him and the trust reposed in him as a king, and that it was just with God to take his kingdom from him. Even the king himself disdained not to put on the garb of a penitent, for he *covered himself with sackcloth, and sat in ashes,* in token of his humiliation for sin and his dread of divine vengeance. It well becomes the great-

est of men to abase themselves before the great God.

4. The people conformed to the example of the king, nay, it should seem, they led the way, for they first began to *put on sackcloth, from the greatest of them even to the least of them, v.* 5. The least of them, that had least to lose in the overthrow of the city, did not think themselves unconcerned in the alarm; and the greatest of them, that were accustomed to lie at ease and live in state, did not think it below them to put on the marks of humiliation. The wearing of sackcloth, especially to those who were used to fine linen, was a very uneasy thing, and they would not have done it if they had not had a deep sense of their sin and their danger by reason of sin, which hereby they designed to express. Note, Those that would not be ruined must be humbled, those that would not destroy their souls must afflict their souls; when God's judgments threaten us we are concerned to *humble ourselves under his mighty hand;* and though bodily exercise alone profits nothing, and a man's *spreading sackcloth and ashes under him,* if that be all, is but a jest (it is the heart that God looks at, Isa. lviii. 5), yet on solemn days of humiliation, when God in his providence *calls to mourning and girding with sackcloth,* we must by the outward expressions of inward sorrow *glorify God with our bodies,* at least by laying aside their ornaments.

5. A general fast was proclaimed and observed throughout that great city, *v.* 7—9. It was ordered *by the decree of the king and his nobles;* the whole legislative power concurred in appointing it, and the whole body of the people concurred in observing it, and in both these ways it became a national act, and it was necessary that it should be so when it was to prevent a national ruin. We have here the contents of this proclamation, and it is very observable. See here,

(1.) What it is that is required by it. [1.] That the fast (properly so called) be very strictly observed. On the day appointed for this solemnity, *let neither man nor beast taste any thing;* let them not take the least refreshment, no, not so much as *drink water;* let them not plead that they cannot fast so long without prejudice to their health, or that they cannot bear it; let them try for once. What if they do feel it an uneasiness, and feel from it for some time after? It is better to submit to that than be wanting in any act or instance of that repentance which is necessary to save a sinking city. Let them make themselves uneasy in body by *putting on sackcloth,* as well as by fasting, to show how uneasy they are in mind, through sorrow for sin and the fear of divine wrath. Even the *beasts* must do penance as well as man, because they had been made *subject to vanity* as instruments of man's sin, and that, either by their complaints or their silent pining for want of meat, they might stir up their owners, and those that attended them, to the expressions of sorrow and humiliation. Those cattle that were kept within doors must not be fed and watered as usual, because no meat must be stirring on that day. Things of that kind must be forgotten, and not minded. As when the psalmist was intent upon the praises of God he called upon the inferior creatures to join with him therein, so when the Ninevites were full of sorrow for sin, and dread of God's judgments, they would have the inferior creatures concur with them in the expressions of penitence. The beasts that used to be covered with rich and fine trappings, which were the pride of their masters, and theirs too, must now be *covered with sackcloth;* for the great men will (as becomes them) lay aside their equipage. [2.] With their fasting and mourning they must join prayer and supplication to God; for the fasting is designed to fit the body for the service of the soul in the duty of prayer, which is the main matter, and to which the other is but preparatory or subservient. *Let them cry mightily to God;* let even the brute creatures do it according to their capacity; let their cries and moans for want of food be graciously construed as cries to God, as the cries of the *young ravens* are (Job xxxviii. 41), and of the *young lions,* Ps. civ. 21. But especially let the men, women, and children, *cry to God;* let them *cry mightily* for the pardon of the sins which cry against them and the preventing of the judgments which were by Jonah cried against them. It was time to cry to God when there was but a step between them and ruin—high time to seek the Lord. In prayer we must cry mightily, with a fixedness of thought, firmness of faith, and fervour of pious and devout affections. By crying mightily we wrestle with God; we take hold of him; and we are concerned to do so when he is not only departing from us as a friend, but coming forth against us as an enemy. It therefore concerns us in prayer to stir up all that is within us. Yet this is not all; [3.] They must to their fasting and praying add reformation and amendment of life: *Let them turn every one from his evil way,* the evil way he has chosen, the evil way he is addicted to, and walks in, the evil way of his heart, and the evil way of his conversation, and particularly *from the violence that is in their hands;* let them restore what they have unjustly taken, and make reparation for what wrong they have done, and let them not any more oppress those they have power over nor defraud those they have dealings with; let the men in authority, at the court-end of the town, turn *from the violence that is in their hands,* and not *decree unrighteous decrees,* nor give wrong judgment upon appeals made to them. Let the men of business, at the trading-end of the town, turn *from the violence in their hands,* and use no unjust weights or measures, nor impose upon the ignorance or necessity of

those they trade with. Note, It is not enough to fast for sin, but we must fast from sin, and, in order to the success of our prayers, must no more *regard iniquity in our hearts,* Ps. lxvi. 18. This is *the only fast that God has chosen* and will accept, Isa. lviii. 6; Zech. vii. 5, 9. The work of a fast-day is not done with the day; no, then the hardest and most needful part of the work begins, which is to turn from sin, and to live a new life, and not return with the dog to his vomit.

(2.) Upon what inducement this fast is proclaimed and religiously observed (*v.* 9) *Who can tell if God will turn and repent?* Observe, [1.] What it is that they hope for —that God will, upon their repenting and turning, change his way towards them and revoke his sentence against them, that he will *turn from his fierce anger,* which they own they deserve and yet humbly and earnestly deprecate, and that thus their ruin will be prevented, and they perish not. They cannot object against the equity of the judgment, they pretend not to set it aside by appealing to a higher court, but hope in God himself, that he will repent, and that his own mercy (to which they fly) *shall rejoice against judgment.* They believe that God is justly angry with them, that, their sin being very heinous, his anger is very fierce, and that, if he proceed against them, there is no remedy, but they die, they perish, they all perish, and are undone; for who knows the power of his anger? It is not therefore the threatened overthrow that they pray for the prevention of, but the anger of God that they pray for the turning away of. As when we pray for the favour of God we pray for all good, so when we pray against the wrath of God we pray against all evil. [2.] What degree of hope they had of it: *Who can tell if God will turn to us?* Jonah had not told them; they had not among them any other prophets to tell them, so that they could not be so confident of finding mercy upon their repentance as we may be, who have the promise and oath of God to depend upon, and especially the merit and mediation of Christ to trust to, for pardon upon repentance. Yet they had a general notion of the goodness of God's nature, his mercy to man, and his being pleased with the repentance and conversion of sinners; and from this they raised some hopes that he would spare them; they dare not presume, but they will not despair. Note, Hope of mercy is the great encouragement to repentance and reformation; and though there be but some glimmerings of hope mixed with great fears arising from a sense of our own sinfulness, and unworthiness, and long abuse of divine patience, yet they may serve to quicken and engage our serious repentance and reformation. Let us boldly cast ourselves at the footstool of free grace, resolving that if we perish, we will perish there; yet who knows but God will look upon us with compassion?

II. Here is a wonder of divine mercy in the sparing of these Ninevites upon their repentance (*v.* 10) : *God saw their works;* he not only heard their good words, by which they professed repentance, but saw their good works, by which they brought forth *fruits meet for repentance;* he saw that they *turned from their evil way,* and that was the thing he looked for and required. If he had not seen that, their fasting and sackcloth would have been as nothing in his account. He saw there was among them a general conviction of their sins and a general resolution not to return to them, and that for some days they lived better, and there was a new face of things upon the city; and this he was well pleased with. Note, God takes notice of every instance of the reformation of sinners, even those instances that fall not under the cognizance and observation of the world. He sees who turn from their evil way and who do not, and meets those with favour that meet him in a sincere conversion. When they repent of the evil of sin committed by them he repents of the evil of judgment pronounced against them. Thus he spared Nineveh, and *did not the evil which he said he would do against it.* Here were no sacrifices offered to God, that we read of, to make atonement for sin, but the *sacrifice of God is a broken spirit; a broken and contrite heart,* such as the Ninevites now had, is what he *will not despise;* it is what he will give countenance to and put honour upon.

CHAP. IV.

We read, with a great deal of pleasure, in the close of the foregoing chapter, concerning the repentance of Nineveh; but in this chapter we read, with a great deal of uneasiness, concerning the sin of Jonah; and, as there is joy in heaven and earth for the conversion of sinners, so there is grief for the follies and infirmities of saints. In all the book of God we scarcely find a "servant of the Lord" (and such a one we are sure Jonah was, for the scripture calls him so) so very much out of temper as he is here, so very peevish and provoking to God himself. In the first chapter we had him fleeing from the face of God; but here we have him, in effect, flying in the face of God; and, which is more grieving to us, there we had an account of his repentance and return to God; but here, though no doubt he did repent, yet, as in Solomon's case, no account is left us of his recovering himself; but, while we read with wonder of his perverseness, we read with no less wonder of God's tenderness towards him, by which it appeared that he had not cast him off. Here is, I. Jonah's repining at God's mercy to Nineveh, and the fret he was in about it, ver. 1—3. II. The gentle reproof God gave him for it, ver. 4. III. Jonah's discontent at the withering of the gourd, and his justifying himself in that discontent, ver. 5—9. IV. God's improving it for his conviction, that he ought not to be angry at the sparing of Nineveh, ver. 10, 11. Man's badness and God's goodness serve here for a foil to each other, that the former may appear the more exceedingly sinful and the latter the more exceedingly gracious.

BUT it displeased Jonah exceedingly, and he was very angry. 2 And he prayed unto the LORD, and said, I pray thee, O LORD, *was* not this my saying, when I was yet in my country? therefore I fled before unto Tarshish: for I knew that thou *art* a gracious God, and merciful, slow to anger, and of great kindness, and repentest thee of the evil. 3 Therefore now, O LORD, take, I beseech thee, my life from me; for *it is* better for me to die than to live. 4 Then saith the LORD, Doest thou well to be angry?

See here, I. How unjustly Jonah quarrelled with God for his mercy to Nineveh, upon their repentance. This gives us occasion to suspect that Jonah had only delivered the message of wrath against the Ninevites, and had not at all assisted or encouraged them in their repentance, as one would think he should have done; for when they did repent, and found mercy,

1. Jonah grudged them the mercy they found (*v.* 1): *It displeased Jonah exceedingly;* and (would you think it?) *he was very angry,* was in a great heat about it. It was very wrong, (1.) That he had so little government of himself as to be displeased and very angry; he had *no rule over his own spirit,* and therefore, as a city broken down, lay exposed to temptations and snares. (2.) That he had so little reverence of God as to be displeased and angry at what he did, as David was when the Lord had made a breach upon Uzza; whatever pleases God should please us, and, though we cannot account for it, yet we must acquiesce in it. (3.) That he had so little affection to men as to be displeased and very angry at the conversion of the Ninevites and their reception into the divine favour. This was the sin of the scribes and Pharisees, who murmured at our Saviour because he entertained publicans and sinners; but *is our eye evil because his is good?* But why was Jonah so uneasy at it, that the Ninevites repented and were spared? It cannot be expected that we should give any good reason for a thing so very absurd and unreasonable; no, nor any thing that has the face or colour of a reason; but we may conjecture what the provocation was. Hot spirits are usually high spirits. *Only by pride comes contention* both with God and man. It was a point of honour that Jonah stood upon and that made him angry. [1.] He was jealous for the honour of his country; the repentance and reformation of Nineveh shamed the obstinacy of Israel that repented not, but *hated to be reformed;* and the favour God had shown to these Gentiles, upon their repentance, was an ill omen to the Jewish nation, as if they should be (as at length they were) rejected and cast out of the church and the Gentiles substituted in their room. When it was intimated to St. Peter himself that he should make no difference between Jews and Gentiles he startled at the thing, and said, *Not so, Lord;* no marvel then that Jonah looked upon it with regret that Nineveh should become a favourite. Jonah herein had *a zeal for God* as the God of Israel in a particular manner, *but not according to knowledge.* Note, Many are displeased with God under pretence of concern for his glory. [2.] He was jealous for his own honour, fearing lest, if Nineveh was not destroyed

within forty days, he should be accounted a false prophet, and stigmatized accordingly; whereas he needed not be under any discontent about that, for in the threatening of ruin it was implied that, for the preventing of it, they should repent, and, if they did, it should be prevented. And no one will complain of being deceived by him that is better than his word; and he would rather gain honour among them, by being instrumental to save them, than fall under any disgrace. But melancholy men (and such a one Jonah seems to have been) are apt to make themselves uneasy by fancying evils to themselves that are not, nor are ever likely to be. Most of our frets, as well as our frights, are owing to the power of imagination; and those are to be pitied as perfect bond-slaves that are under the power of such a tyrant.

2. He quarrelled with God about it. When his heart was hot within him, he *spoke unadvisedly with his lips;* and here he tells us what he said (v. 2, 3): He *prayed unto the Lord,* but it is a very awkward prayer, not like that which he prayed in the fish's belly; for affliction teaches us to pray submissively, which Jonah now forgot to do. Being in discontent, he applied to the duty of prayer, as he used to do in his troubles, but his corruptions got head of his graces, and, when he should have been praying for benefit by the mercy of God himself, he was complaining of the benefit others had by that mercy. Nothing could be spoken more unbecomingly. (1.) He now begins to justify himself in fleeing *from the presence of the Lord* when he was first ordered to go to Nineveh, for which he had before, with good reason, condemned himself: " *Lord,*" said he, " *was not this my saying when I was in my own country?* Did I not foresee that if I went to preach to Nineveh they would repent, and thou wouldst forgive them, and then thy word would be reflected upon and reproached as yea and nay?" What a strange sort of man was Jonah, to dread the success of his ministry! Many have been tempted to withdraw from their work because they have despaired of doing good by it, but Jonah declined preaching because he was afraid of doing good by it; and still he persists in the same corrupt notion, for, it seems, the whale's belly itself could not cure him of it. It was his saying when he was *in his own country,* but it was a bad saying; yet here he stands to it, and, very unlike the other prophets, *desires the woeful day* which he had foretold and grieves because it does not come. Even Christ's disciples *know not what manner of spirit they are of;* those did not who wished for fire from heaven upon the city that did not receive them, much less did Jonah, who wished for fire from heaven upon the city that did receive him, Luke ix. 55. Jonah thinks he has reason to complain of that, when it is done, which he was before afraid of; so hard is it to get a root

of bitterness plucked out of the mind, when once it is fastened there. And why did Jonah expect that God would spare Nineveh? *Because I knew that thou wast a gracious God,* indulgent and easily pleased, that *thou wast slow to anger and of great kindness, and repentest thee of the evil.* All this is very true; and Jonah could not but know it by God's proclamation of his name and the experiences of all ages; but it is strange and very unaccountable that that which all the saints had made the matter of their joy and praise Jonah should make the matter of reflection upon God, as if that were an imperfection of the divine nature which is indeed the greatest glory of it—that God is *gracious and merciful.* The servant that said, *I knew thee to be a hard man,* said that which was false, and yet, had it been true, it was not the proper matter of a complaint; but Jonah, though he says what is true, yet, speaking it by way of reproach, speaks very absurdly. Those have a spirit of contention and contradiction indeed that can find in their hearts to quarrel with the goodness of God, and his sparing pardoning mercy, to which we all owe it that we are out of hell. This is making that to be to us *a savour of death unto death* which ought to be *a savour of life unto life.* (2.) In a passion, he wishes for death (v. 3), a strange expression of his causeless passion! " *Now, O Lord! take, I beseech thee, my life from me.* If Nineveh must live, let me die, rather than see thy word and mine disproved, rather than see the glory of Israel transferred to the Gentiles," as if there were not grace enough in God both for Jews and Gentiles, or as if his countrymen were the further off from mercy for the Ninevites being taken into favour. When the prophet Elijah had laboured in vain, he wished he might die, and it was his infirmity, 1 Kings xix. 4. But Jonah labours to good purpose, saves a great city from ruin, and yet wishes he may die, as if, having done much good, he were afraid of living to do more; he *sees of the travail of his soul, and is dissatisfied.* What a perverse spirit is mingled with every word he says! When Jonah was brought alive out of the whale's belly, he thought life a very valuable mercy, and was thankful to that God who brought up *his life from corruption,* (ch. ii. 6), and a great blessing his life had been to Nineveh; yet now, for that very reason, it became a burden to himself and he begs to be eased of it, pleading, *It is better for me to die than to live.* Such a word as this may be the language of grace, as it was in Paul, who desired to depart and be with Christ, *which is far better;* but here it was the language of folly, and passion, and strong corruption; and so much the worse, [1.] Jonah being now in the midst of his usefulness, and therefore fit to live. He was one whose ministry God wonderfully owned and prospered. The conversion of Nineveh might give him hopes of being instrumental to convert the whole kingdom of Assyria; it was therefore very absurd for him to wish he might die when he had a prospect of living to so good a purpose and could be so ill spared. [2.] Jonah being now so much out of temper and therefore unfit to die How durst he think of dying, and going to appear before God's judgment-seat, when he was actually quarrelling with him? Was this a frame of spirit proper for a man to go out of the world in? But those who passionately desire death commonly have least reason to do it, as being very much unprepared for it. Our business is to get ready to die by doing the work of life, and then to refer ourselves to God to take away our life when and how he pleases.

II. See how justly God reproved Jonah for this heat that he was in (*v.* 4): The Lord said, *Doest thou well to be angry? Is doing well a displeasure to thee?* so some read it. What! dost thou repent of thy good deeds? God might justly have rejected him for this impious heat which he was in, might justly have taken him at his word, and have struck him dead when he wished to die; but he vouchsafes to reason with him for his conviction and to bring him to a better temper, as the father of the prodigal reasoned with his elder son, when, as Jonah here, he murmured at the remission and reception of his brother. *Doest thou well to be angry?* See how mildly the great God speaks to this foolish man, to teach us to restore those that have fallen with a *spirit of meekness,* and with *soft answers* to *turn away wrath.* God appeals to himself and to his own conscience: " *Doest thou well?* Thou knowest thou dost not." We should often put this question to ourselves, Is it well to say thus, to do thus? Can I justify it? Must I not unsay it and undo it again by repentance, or be undone for ever? Ask, 1. Do I well to be angry? When passion is up, let it meet with this check, " Do I well to be so soon angry, so often angry, so long angry, to put myself into such a heat, and to give others such ill language in my anger? Is this well, that I suffer these headstrong passions to get dominion over me?" 2. " Do I well to be angry at the mercy of God to repenting sinners?" That was Jonah's crime. Do we well to be angry at that which is so much for the glory of God and the advancement of his kingdom among men—to be angry at that which angels rejoice in and for which abundant thanksgivings will be rendered to God? We do ill to be angry at that grace which we ourselves need and are undone without; if room were not left for repentance, and hope given of pardon upon repentance, what would become of us? Let the conversion of sinners, which is the joy of heaven, be our joy, and never our grief.

5 So Jonah went out of the city, and sat on the east side of the city,

and there made him a booth, and sat under it in the shadow, till he might see what would become of the city. 6 And the LORD God prepared a gourd, and made *it* to come up over Jonah, that it might be a shadow over his head, to deliver him from his grief. So Jonah was exceeding glad of the gourd. 7 But God prepared a worm when the morning rose the next day, and it smote the gourd that it withered. 8 And it came to pass, when the sun did arise, that God prepared a vehement east wind; and the sun beat upon the head of Jonah, that he fainted, and wished in himself to die, and said, *It is* better for me to die than to live. 9 And God said to Jonah, Doest thou well to be angry for the gourd? And he said, I do well to be angry, *even* unto death. 10 Then said the LORD, Thou hast had pity on the gourd, for the which thou hast not laboured, neither madest it grow; which came up in a night, and perished in a night: 11 And should not I spare Nineveh, that great city, wherein are more than sixscore thousand persons that cannot discern between their right hand and their left hand; and *also* much cattle?

Jonah persists here in his discontent; for the *beginning of strife* both with God and man *is as the letting forth of waters,* the breach grows wider and wider, and, when passion gets head, bad is made worse; it should therefore be silenced and suppressed at first. We have here,

I. Jonah's sullen expectation of the fate of Nineveh. We may suppose that the Ninevites, giving credit to the message he brought, were ready to give entertainment to the messenger that brought it, and to show him respect, that they would have made him welcome to the best of their houses and tables. But Jonah was out of humour, would not accept their kindness, nor behave towards them with common civility, which one might have feared would have prejudiced them against him and his word; but when there is not only the *treasure* put into *earthen vessels,* but the trust lodged with men *subject to like passions as we are,* and yet the point gained, it must be owned that the *excellency of the power* appears so much the more to be of *God and not of man.* Jonah retires, *goes out of the city,* sits alone, and keeps silence, because he sees the Ninevites repent and reform, *v.* 5. Perhaps he told those about him that he went out of the city for fear of perishing in the ruins of it; but he went to *see what would become of the city*, as Abraham went up to see what would become of Sodom, Gen. xix. 27. The forty days were now expiring, or had expired, and Jonah hoped that, if Nineveh was not overthrown, yet some judgment or other would come upon it, sufficient to save his credit; however, it was with great uneasiness that he waited the issue. He would not sojourn in a house, expecting it would fall upon his head, but he *made himself a booth* of the boughs of trees, and sat in that, though there he would lie exposed to wind and weather. Note, It is common for those that have fretful uneasy spirits industriously to create inconveniences themselves, that, resolving to complain, they may still have something to complain of.

II. God's gracious provision for his shelter and refreshment when he thus foolishly afflicted himself and was still adding yet more and more to his own affliction, *v.* 6. Jonah was sitting in his booth, fretting at the cold of the night and the heat of the day, which were both grievous to him, and God might have said, It is his own choice, his own doing, a house of his own building, let him make the best of it; but he looked on him with compassion, as the tender mother does on the froward child, and relieved him against the grievances which he by his own wilfulness created to himself. He *prepared a gourd*, a plant with broad leaves, and full of them, that suddenly grew up, and covered his hut or booth, so as to keep off much of the injury of the cold and heat. It was *a shadow over his head, to deliver him from his grief*, that, being refreshed in body, he might the better guard against the uneasiness of his mind, which outward crosses and troubles are often the occasion and increase of. See how tender God is of his people in their afflictions, yea, though they are foolish and froward, nor is he *extreme to mark what they do amiss*. God had before *prepared a great fish* to secure Jonah from the injuries of the water, and here a great gourd to secure him from the injuries of the air; for he is the protector of his people against evils of every kind, has the command of plants as well as animals, and can soon prepare them, to make them serve his purposes, can make their growth sudden, which, in a course of nature, is slow and gradual. A gourd, one would think, was but a slender fortification at the best, yet Jonah *was exceedingly glad of the gourd;* for, 1. It was really at that time a great comfort to him. A thing in itself small and inconsiderable, yet, coming seasonably, may be to us a very valuable blessing. A gourd in the right place may do us more service than a cedar. The least creatures may be great plagues (as flies and lice were to Pharaoh) or great comforts (as the gourd to Jonah), according as God is pleased to make them. 2. He being now much

1300

under the power of imagination took a greater complacency in it than there was cause for. He was exceedingly glad of it, was proud of it, and triumphed in it. Note, Persons of strong passions, as they are apt to be cast down with a trifle that crosses them, so they are apt to be lifted up with a trifle that pleases them. A small toy will serve sometimes to pacify a cross child, as the gourd did Jonah. But wisdom and grace would teach us both to *weep* for our troubles *as though we wept not,* and to *rejoice* in our comforts *as though we rejoiced not.* Creature-comforts we ought to enjoy and be thankful for, but we need not be exceedingly glad of them; it is God only that must be our *exceeding joy,* Ps. xliii. 4.

III. The sudden loss of this provision which God had made for his refreshment, and the return of his trouble, *v.* 7, 8. God that had provided comfort for him provided also an affliction for him in that very thing which was his comfort; the affliction did not come by chance, but by divine direction and appointment. 1. God *prepared a worm* to destroy the gourd. He that gave took away, and Jonah ought to have *blessed his name* in both; but because, when he took the comfort of the gourd, he did not give God the praise of it, God deprived him of the benefit of it, and justly. See what all our creature-comforts are, and what we may expect them to be; they are gourds, have their root in the earth, are but a thin and slender defence compared with the *rock of ages;* they are withering things; they perish in the using, and we are soon deprived of the comfort of them. The gourd withered the next day after it sprang up; our comforts *come forth like flowers and are soon cut down.* When we please ourselves most with them, and promise ourselves most from them, we are disappointed. A little thing withers them; a small worm at the root destroys a large gourd. Something unseen and undiscerned does it. Our gourds wither, and we know not what to attribute it to. And perhaps those wither first that we have been more exceedingly glad of; that proves least safe that is most dear. God did not send an angel to pluck up Jonah's gourd, but sent a worm to smite it; there it grew still, but it stood him in no stead. Perhaps our creature-comforts are continued to us, but they are embittered; the creature is continued, but the comfort is gone; and the remains, or ruins of it rather, do but upbraid us with our folly in being exceedingly glad of it. 2. He *prepared a wind* to make Jonah feel the want of the gourd, *v.* 8. It was a *vehement east wind*, which drove the heat of the rising sun violently upon the head of Jonah. This wind was not as a fan to abate the heat, but as bellows to make it more intense. Thus poor Jonah lay open to sun and wind.

IV. The further fret that this put Jonah

into (v. 8): He *fainted*, and *wished in himself that he might die.* "If the gourd be killed, if the gourd be dead, kill me too, *let me die with the gourd.*" Foolish man, that thinks his life bound up in the life of a weed! Note, It is just that those who love to complain should never be left without something to complain of, that their folly may be manifested and corrected, and, if possible, cured. And see here how the passions that run into an extreme one way commonly run into an extreme the other way. Jonah, who was in transports of joy when the gourd flourished, is in pangs of grief when the gourd has withered. Inordinate affection lays a foundation for inordinate affliction; what we are over-fond of when we have it we are apt to over-grieve for when we lose it, and we may see our folly in both.

V. The rebuke God gave him for this; he again reasoned with him: *Dost thou well to be angry for the gourd? v.* 9. Note, The withering of a gourd is a thing which it does not become us to be angry at. When afflicting providences deprive us of our relations, possessions, and enjoyments, we must bear it patiently, must not be angry at God, must not be angry *for the gourd.* It is comparatively but a small loss, the loss of a shadow; that is the most we can make of it. It was a gourd, a withering thing; we could expect no other than that it should wither. Our being angry for the withering of it will not recover it; we ourselves shall shortly wither like it. If one gourd be withered, another gourd may spring up in the room of it; but that which should especially silence our discontent is that though our gourd be gone our God is not gone, and there is enough in him to make up all our losses.

Let us therefore own that we do ill, that we do very ill, to be angry for the gourd; and let us under such events quiet ourselves *as a child that is weaned from his mother.*

VI. His justification of his passion and discontent; and it is very strange, *v.* 9. He said, *I do well to be angry, even unto death.* It is bad to speak amiss, yet if it be in haste, if what is said amiss be speedily recalled and unsaid again, it is the more excusable; but to speak amiss and stand to it is bad indeed. So Jonah did here, though God himself rebuked him, and by appealing to his conscience expected he would rebuke himself. See what brutish things ungoverned passions are, and how much it is our interest, and ought to be our endeavour, to chain up these roaring lions and ranging bears. *Sin* and *death* are two very dreadful things, yet Jonah, in his heat, makes light of them both. 1. He has so little regard for God as to fly in the face of his authority, and to say that he did well in that which God said was ill done. Passion often over-rules conscience, and forces it, when it is appealed to, to give a false judgment, as Jonah here did. 2. He has so little regard to himself as to abandon

his own life, and to think it no harm to indulge his passion even to death, to kill himself with fretting. We read of *wrath* that *kills the foolish man,* and *envy* that *slays the silly one* (Job v. 2), and foolish silly ones indeed those are that cut their own throats with their own passions, that fret themselves into consumptions and other weaknesses, and put themselves into fevers with their own intemperate heats.

VII. The improvement of it against him for his conviction that he did ill to murmur at the sparing of Nineveh. Out of his own mouth God will judge him; and we have reason to think it overcame him; for he made no reply, but, we hope, returned to his right mind and recovered his temper, though he could not keep it, and all was well. Now,

1. Let us see how God argued with him (v. 10, 11): "*Thou hast had pity on the gourd,* hast *spared* it" (so the word is), "didst what thou couldst, and wouldst have done more, to keep it alive, and saidst, *What a pity it is* that this gourd should ever wither! and *should not I then spare Nineveh?* Should not I have as much compassion upon that as thou hadst upon the gourd, and forbid the earthquake which would ruin that, as thou wouldst have forbidden the worm that smote the gourd? Consider," (1.) "The gourd thou hadst pity on was but one; but the inhabitants of Nineveh, whom I have pity on, are numerous." It is a great city and very populous, as appears by the number of the infants, suppose from two years old and under; there are 120,000 such in Nineveh, that have not come to so much use of understanding as to know *their right hand from their left,* for they are yet but babes. These are taken notice of because the age of infants is commonly looked upon as the age of innocence. So many there were in Nineveh that had not been guilty of any actual transgression, and consequently had not themselves contributed to the common guilt, and yet, if Nineveh had been overthrown, they would all have been involved in the common calamity; "and *shall not I spare* Nineveh then, with an eye to them?" God has a tender regard to little children, and is ready to pity and succour them, nay, here a whole city is spared for their sakes, which may encourage parents to present their children to God by faith and prayer, that though they are not capable of doing him any service (for they cannot discern *between their right hand and their left,* between good and evil, sin and duty), yet they are capable of participating in his favours and of obtaining salvation. The great Saviour discovered a particular kindness for the children that were brought to him, when he *took them up in his arms, put his hands upon them, and blessed them.* Nay, God took notice of the abundance of cattle too that were in Nineveh, which he had more reason to pity and spare than Jonah had to pity and to spare the gourd,

inasmuch as the animal life is more excellent than the vegetable. (2.) The gourd which Jonah was concerned for was none of his own; it was that for which he did not labour and which he made not to grow; but the persons in Nineveh whom God had compassion on were all the *work of his own hands,* whose being he was the author of, whose lives he was the preserver of, whom he planted and made to grow; he made them, and his they were, and therefore he had much more reason to have compassion on them, for he cannot *despise the work of his own hands* (Job x. 3); and thus Job there argues with him (v. 8, 9), *Thy hands have made me, and fashioned me,* have *made me as the clay;* and *wilt thou destroy* me, *wilt thou bring me into dust again?* And thus he here argues with himself. 3. The gourd which Jonah had pity on was of a sudden growth, and therefore of less value; it *came up in a night, it was the son of a night* (so the word is); but Nineveh is an ancient city, of many ages standing, and therefore cannot be so easily given up; "the persons I spare have been many years in growing up, not so soon reared as the gourd; and shall not I then have pity on those that have been so many years the care of my providence, so many years my tenants?" (4.) The gourd which Jonah had pity on *perished in a night;* it withered, and there was an end of it. But the precious souls in Nineveh that God had pity on are not so short-lived; they are immortal, and therefore to be carefully and tenderly considered. One soul is of more value than the whole world, and the gain of the world will not countervail the loss of it; surely then one soul is of more value than many gourds, of more value than many sparrows; so God accounts, and so should we, and therefore have a greater concern for the children of men than for any of the inferior creatures, and for our own and others'

precious souls than for any of the riches and enjoyments of this world.

2. From all this we may learn, (1.) That though God may suffer his people to fall into sin, yet he will not suffer them to lie still in it, but will take a course effectually to show them their error, and to bring them to themselves and to their right mind again. We have reason to hope that Jonah, after this, was well reconciled to the sparing of Nineveh, and was as well pleased with it as ever he had been displeased. (2.) That God will justify himself in the methods of his grace towards repenting returning sinners as well as in the course his justice takes with those that persist in their rebellion; though there be those that murmur at the mercy of God, because they do not understand it (for his thoughts and ways therein are as far above ours as heaven above the earth), yet he will make it evident that therein he acts like himself, and will be *justified when he speaks.* See what pains he takes with Jonah to convince him that it is very fit that Nineveh should be spared. Jonah had said, *I do well to be angry,* but he could not prove it. God says and proves it, *I do well to be merciful;* and it is a great encouragement to poor sinners to hope that they shall find mercy with him, that he is so ready to justify himself in showing mercy and to triumph in those whom he makes the monuments of it, against those whose eye is evil because his is good. Such murmurers shall be made to understand this doctrine, that, how narrow soever their souls, their principles, are, and how willing soever they are to engross divine grace to themselves and those of their own way, there is one *Lord over all, that is rich in mercy to all that call upon him,* and in *every nation,* in Nineveh as well as in Israel, *he that fears God and works righteousness is accepted of him;* he that repents, and turns from his evil way, shall find mercy with him.

AN

EXPOSITION,

WITH PRACTICAL OBSERVATIONS

OF THE PROPHECY OF

MICAH.

WE shall have some account of this prophet in the first verse of the book of his prophecy; and therefore shall here only observe that, being contemporary with the prophet Isaiah (only that he began to prophesy a little after him), there is a near resemblance between that prophet's prophecy and this; and there is a prediction of the advancement and establishment of the gospel-church, which both of them have, almost in the same words, that out of the mouth of two such witnesses so great a word might be established. Compare Isa. ii. 2, 3, with Mic. iv. 1, 2. Isaiah's prophecy is said to be concerning *Judah and Jerusalem,* but Micah's concerning *Samaria and Jerusalem;* for, though this prophecy be dated only by the reigns of the kings of Judah, yet it refers to the kingdom of Israel, the approaching ruin of which, in the captivity of the ten tribes, he plainly foretels and sadly laments. What we find here in writing was but an abstract of the sermons he preached during the reigns of three kings. The scope of the whole is, I. To convince sinners of their sins, by setting them in order before them, charging both Israel and Judah with idolatry, covetousness, oppression, contempt of the word of God, and their rulers especially, both in church and state, with the abuse of their power; and also by showing them the judgments of God ready to break in upon them for their sins. II. To comfort God's people with promises of mercy and deliverance, especially with an assurance of the coming of the Messiah and of the grace of the gospel through him. It is remarkable concerning this prophecy, and confirms its authority, that we find two quotations out of it made publicly upon very solemn occasions, and both referring to very great events. 1. One is a prediction of the destruction of Jerusalem (*ch.* iii. 12), which we find quoted in the Old Testament, by *the elders of the land* (Jer. xxvi. 17, 18), in justification of Jeremiah, when he foretold the judgments of God coming upon Jerusalem, and to stay the proceedings of the court against him. "Micah (say they) foretold that *Zion should be ploughed as a field,* and Hezekiah did not put him to death; why then should we punish Jeremiah for saying the same?" 2. Another is a prediction of the birth of Christ (*ch.* v. 2) which we find quoted in the New Testament, by the *chief priests and scribes of the people,* in answer to Herod's enquiry, *where Christ should be born* (Matt. ii. 5, 6); for still we find that to him bear all the prophets witness.

CHAP. I.

In this chapter we have, I. The title of the book (ver. 1) and a preface demanding attention, ver. 2. II. Warning given of desolating judgments hastening upon the kingdoms of Israel and Judah (ver. 3, 4), and all for sin, ver. 5. III. The particulars of the destruction specified, ver. 6, 7. IV. The greatness of the destruction illustrated, 1. By the prophet's sorrow for it, ver. 8, 9. 2. By the general sorrow that should be for it, in the several places that must expect to share in it, ver. 10—16. These prophecies of Micah might well be called his lamentations.

THE word of the LORD that came to Micah the Morasthite in the days of Jotham, Ahaz, *and* Hezekiah, kings of Judah, which he saw concerning Samaria and Jerusalem. 2 Hear, all ye people; hearken, O earth, and all that therein is: and let the Lord GOD be witness against you, the Lord from his holy temple. 3 For, behold, the LORD cometh forth out of his place, and will come down, and tread upon the high places of the earth. 4 And the mountains shall be molten under him, and the valleys shall be cleft, as wax before the fire, *and* as the waters *that are* poured down a steep place. 5 For the transgression of Jacob *is* all this, and for the sins of the house of Israel. What *is* the transgression of Jacob? *is it* not Samaria? and what *are* the high places of Judah? *are they* not Jerusalem? 6 Therefore I will make Samaria as a heap of the field, *and* as plantings of a vineyard: and I will pour down the stones thereof into the valley, and I will discover the foundations thereof. 7 And all the graven images thereof shall be beaten to pieces, and all the hires thereof shall be burned with the fire, and all the idols thereof will I lay desolate: for she gathered *it* of the hire of a harlot, and they shall return to the hire of a harlot.

Here is, I. A general account of this prophet and his prophecy, *v.* 1. This is prefixed for the satisfaction of all that read and hear the prophecy of this book, who will give the more credit to it when they know the author and his authority. 1. The prophecy is the *word of the Lord;* it is a divine revelation. Note, What is written in the Bible, and what is preached by the ministers of Christ according to what is written there, must be heard and received, not as the word of dying men, which we may be judges of, but as the word of the living God, which we must be judged by, for so it is. This word of the Lord came to the prophet, came plainly, came powerfully, came in a preventing way, and he saw it, saw the vision in which it was conveyed to him, saw the things themselves which he foretold, with as much clearness and certainty as if they had been already accomplished. 2. The prophet is Micah the Morasthite; his name *Micah* is a contraction of *Micaiah,* the name of a prophet some ages before (in Ahab's time, 1 Kings xxii. 8); his surname, the *Morasthite,* signifies that he was born, or lived, at Moresheth, which is mentioned here (*v.* 14), or Mareshah, which is mentioned *v.* 15, and Josh. xv. 44. The place of his abode is mentioned, that any one might enquire in that place, at that time, and might find there was, or had been, such a one there, who was generally reputed to be a prophet. 3. The date of his prophecy is in the reigns of three kings of Judah —Jotham, Ahaz, and Hezekiah. Ahaz was one of the worst of Judah's kings, and Hezekiah one of the best; such variety of times pass over God's ministers, times that frown and times that smile, to each of which they must study to accommodate themselves, and to arm themselves against the temptations of both. The promises and threatenings of this book are interwoven, by which it appears that even in the wicked reign he preached comfort, and said *to the righteous* then that it should be *well with them;* and that in the pious reign he preached conviction, and said to the wicked then that it should be *ill with them;* for, however the times change, the word of the Lord is still the same. 4. The parties concerned in this prophecy; it is *concerning Samaria and Jerusalem,* the head cities of the two kingdoms of Israel and Judah, under the influence of which the kingdoms themselves were. Though the ten tribes have deserted the houses both of David and Aaron, yet God is pleased to send prophets to them.

II. A very solemn introduction to the following prophecy (*v.* 2), in which, 1. The people are summoned to draw near and give their attendance, as upon a court of judicature: *Hear, all you people.* Note, Where God has a mouth to speak we must have an ear to hear; we all must, for we are all concerned in what is delivered. " *Hear, you people" (all of them,* so the margin reads it), " all you that are now within hearing, and all others that hear it at second hand." It is an unusual construction; but those words with which Micah begins his prophecy are the very same in the original with those wherewith Micaiah ended his, 1 Kings xxii. 28. 2. The earth is called upon, with *all that therein is,* to hear what the prophet has to say: *Hearken, O earth!* The earth shall be made to shake under the stroke and weight of the judgments coming; sooner will the earth hear than this stupid senseless people; but God will be heard when he pleads. If the church, and those in it, will not hear, the earth, and those in it, shall, and shame them. 3. God himself is appealed to, and his omniscience, power, and justice, are vouched in testimony against this people: " *Let the Lord God be witness against you,* a witness that you had fair warning given you, that your prophets did their duty faithfully as watchmen, but you would not take the warning; let the accomplishment of the prophecy be a witness against your contempt and disbelief of it, and prove, to your conviction and confusion, that it was the word of God, and no word of his shall fall to the ground." Note, God himself will be a witness, by the judgments of his hand, against those that would not receive his testimony in the judgments of his mouth. He will be a witness *from his holy temple* in heaven, when he comes down to execute judgment

(*v.* 3) against those that turned a deaf ear to his oracles, wherein he witnessed to them, out of his holy temple at Jerusalem.

III. A terrible prediction of destroying judgments which should come upon Judah and Israel, which had its accomplishment soon after in Israel, and at length in Judah; for it is foretold, 1. That God himself will appear against them, *v.* 3. They boasted of themselves and their relation to God, as if that would secure them; but, though God never deceives the faith of the upright, he will disappoint the presumption of the hypocrites, for, *behold, the Lord comes forth out of his place,* quits his mercy-seat, where they thought they had him fast, and prepares his throne for judgment; his glory departs, for they drive it from them. God's way towards this people had long been a way of mercy, but now he changes his way, he *comes out of his place,* and will come down. He had seemed to retire, as one regardless of what was done, but now he will show himself, he will *rend the heavens* and will *come down,* not as sometimes, in surprising mercies, but in surprising judgments, to do things not for them, but against them, which they *looked not for,* Isa. lxiv. 1; xxvi. 21. 2. That when the Creator appears against them it shall be in vain for any creature to appear for them. He will *tread* with contempt and disdain *upon the high places of the* earth, upon all the powers that are advanced in competition with him or in opposition to him; and he will so tread upon them as to tread them down and level them. High places, set up for the worship of idols or for military fortifications, shall all be trodden down and trampled into the dust. Do men trust to the height and strength of the mountains and rocks, as if they were sufficient to bear up their hopes and bear off their fears? They shall be *molten under him,* melted down *as wax before the fire,* Ps. lxviii. 2. Do they trust to the fruitfulness of the valleys, and their products? They *shall be cleft,* or rent, with those *fiery streams* that shall come pouring down from the mountains when they are melted. They shall be ploughed and washed away as the ground is by *the waters that are poured down a steep place.* God is said to *cleave the earth with rivers,* Hab. iii. 9. Neither men of *high degree,* as the mountains, nor *men of low degree,* as the valleys, shall be able to secure either themselves or the land from the judgments of God, when they are sent with commission to lay all waste, and, like *a sweeping rain,* to *leave no food,* Prov. xxviii. 3. This is applied particularly to the head city of Israel, which they hoped would be a protection to the kingdom (*v.* 6): I *will make Samaria,* that is now a rich and populous city, as *a heap of the field,* as a heap of dung laid there to be spread, or as a heap of stones gathered together to be carried away, and *as plantings of a vineyard,* as hillocks of earth raised to plant vines in.

God will make of that *city a heap*, of that *defenced city a ruin*, Isa. xxv. 2. Their *altars* had been as *heaps in the furrows of the fields* (Hos. xii. 11) and now their houses shall be so, as ruinous heaps. The *stones of the city* are *poured down into the valley* by the fury of the conqueror, who will thus be revenged on those walls that so long held out against him They shall be quite pulled down, so that the very *foundations* shall be *discovered*, that had been covered by the superstructure; and not one stone shall be left upon another.

IV. A charge of sin upon them, as the procuring cause of these desolating judgments (*v.* 5): *For the transgression of Jacob is all this.* If it be asked, " Why is God so angry, and why are Jacob and Israel thus brought to ruin by his anger?" the answer is ready: Sin has done all the mischief; sin has laid all waste; all the calamities of Jacob and Israel are owing to their transgressions; if they had not gone away from God, he would never have appeared thus against them. Note, External privileges and professions will not secure a sinful people from the judgments of God. If sin be found in the *house of Israel*, if Jacob be guilty of transgression and rebellion, God will not spare them; no, he will punish them first, for their sins are of all others most provoking to him, for they are most reproaching. But it is asked, *What is the transgression of Jacob?* Note, When we feel the smart of sin it concerns us to enquire what the sin is which we smart for, that we may particularly war against that which wars against us. And what is it? 1. It is idolatry; it is the *high places;* that is the transgression, the great transgression, which reigns in Israel; that is spiritual whoredom, the violation of the marriage-covenant, which merits a divorce. Even the *high places of Judah*, though not so bad as the transgression of Jacob, were yet offensive enough to God, and a remaining blemish upon some of the good reigns. *Howbeit the high places were not taken away.* 2. It is the idolatry of Samaria and Jerusalem, the royal cities of those two kingdoms. These were the most populous places, and where there were most people there was most wickedness, and they made one another worse. These were the most pompous places; there men lived most in wealth and pleasure, and they forgot God. These were the places that had the greatest influence upon the country, by authority and example; so that from them idolatry and *profaneness went forth throughout all the land*, Jer. xxiii. 15. Note, Spiritual distempers are most contagious in persons and places that are most conspicuous If the head city of a kingdom, or the chief family in a parish, be vicious and profane, *many will follow their pernicious ways*, and write after a bad copy when great ones set it for them. The vices of leaders and rulers are leading ruling vices, and therefore shall be surely and sorely punished. Those have

a great deal to answer for indeed that not only sin, but *make Israel to sin.* Those must expect to be made examples that have been examples of wickedness. If the transgression of Jacob is Samaria, therefore shall *Samaria become a heap.* Let the ringleaders in sin hear this and fear.

V. The punishment made to answer the sin, in the particular destruction of the idols, *v.* 7. 1. The gods they worshipped shall be destroyed: *The graven images shall be beaten to pieces* by the army of the Assyrians, *and all the idols shall be laid desolate.* Samaria *and her idols* were ruined together by Sennacherib (Isa. x. 11), and *their gods cast into the fire*, for *they were no gods* (Isa. xxxvii. 19); and this was the Lord's doing: *I will lay the idols desolate.* Note, If the law of God prevail not to make men in authority destroy idols, God will take the work into his own hands, and will do it himself. 2. The gifts that passed between them and their gods shall be destroyed; for *all the hires thereof shall be burnt with fire*, which may be meant either of the presents they made to their idols for the replenishing of their altars, and the adorning of their statues and temples (these shall become a prey to the victorious army, which shall rifle not only private houses, but the houses of their gods), or of the corn, and wine, and oil, which they called the *rewards*, or *hires*, which *their idols*, their *lovers*, gave them (Hos. ii. 12); these shall be taken from them by him whom (by ascribing them to their dear idols) they had defrauded of the honour due to him. Note, That cannot prosper by which men either are hired to sin or hire others to sin; for *the wages of sin* will be *death. She gathered it of the hire of the harlot*, and *it shall return to the hire of a harlot.* They enriched themselves by their leagues with the idolatrous nations, who gave them advantages, to court them into the service of their idols, and their idols' temples were enriched with gifts by those who went a whoring after them. And all this wealth shall become a prey to the idolatrous nations, and so be the *hire of a harlot* again, wages to an army of idolaters, who shall take it as a reward given them by their gods. *It shall be a present to king Jareb*, Hos. x. 6. What they gave to their idols, and what they thought they got by them, shall be as the hire of a harlot; the curse of God shall be upon it, and it shall never prosper, nor do them any good. It is common that what is squeezed out by one lust is squandered away upon another.

8 Therefore I will wail and howl, I will go stripped and naked: I will make a wailing like the dragons, and mourning as the owls. 9 For her wound *is* incurable; for it is come unto Judah; he is come unto the gate of my people, *even* to Jerusalem.

10 Declare ye *it* not at Gath, weep ye not at all : in the house of Aphrah roll thyself in the dust. 11 Pass ye away, thou inhabitant of Saphir, having thy shame naked : the inhabitant of Zaanan came not forth in the mourning of Beth-ezel; he shall receive of you his standing. 12 For the inhabitant of Maroth waited carefully for good : but evil came down from the LORD unto the gate of Jerusalem. 13 O thou inhabitant of Lachish, bind the chariot to the swift beast : she *is* the beginning of the sin to the daughter of Zion : for the transgressions of Israel were found in thee. 14 Therefore shalt thou give presents to Moresheth-gath : the houses of Achzib *shall be* a lie to the kings of Israel. 15 Yet will I bring an heir unto thee, O inhabitant of Mareshah : he shall come unto Adullam the glory of Israel. 16 Make thee bald, and poll thee for thy delicate children ; enlarge thy baldness as the eagle ; for they are gone into captivity from thee.

We have here a long train of mourners attending the funeral of a ruined kingdom.

I. The prophet is himself chief mourner (v. 8, 9) : *I will wail and howl : I will go stripped and naked,* as a man distracted with grief. The prophets usually expressed their own grief for the public grievances, partly to mollify the predictions of them, and to make it appear that it was not out of ill-will that they denounced the judgments of God (so far were they from desiring the woeful day that they dreaded it more than any thing), partly to show how very dreadful and mournful the calamities would be, and to stir up in the people a holy fear of them, that by repentance they might turn away the wrath of God. Note, We ought to lament the punishments of sinners as well as the sufferings of saints in this world ; the weeping prophet did so (Jer. ix. 1) ; so did this prophet. He *makes a wailing like the dragons,* or rather the *jackalls,* ravenous beasts that in those countries used to meet in the night, and *howl,* and make *hideous noises ;* he mourns *as the owls,* the *screech-owls,* or *ostriches,* as some read it. Two things the prophet here thus dolefully laments :—1. That Israel's case is desperate : *Her wound is incurable ;* it is ruin without remedy ; man cannot help her ; God will not, because she will not by repentance and reformation help herself. There is indeed balm in Gilead and a physician there ; but they will not apply to the physician, nor

1306

apply the balm to themselves, and therefore *the wound is incurable.* 2. That Judah likewise is in danger. The cup is going round, and is now put into Judah's hand : *The enemy has come to the gate of Jerusalem.* Soon after the destruction of Samaria and the ten tribes, the Assyrian army, under Sennacherib, laid siege to Jerusalem, came to the gate, but could not force their way any further ; however, it was with great concern and trouble that the prophet foresaw the fright, so dearly did he love the peace of Jerusalem.

II. Several places are here brought in mourning, and are called upon to mourn ; but with this proviso, that they should not let the Philistines hear them (v. 10) : *Declare it not in Gath ;* this is borrowed from David's lamentation for Saul and Jonathan (2 Sam. i. 20), *Tell it not in Gath,* for the uncircumcised will triumph in Israel's tears. Note, One would not, if it could be helped, gratify those that make themselves and their companions merry with the sins or with the sorrows of God's Israel. David was silent, and stifled his griefs, when *the wicked were before him,* Ps. xxxix. 1. But, though it may be prudent not to give way to a noisy sorrow, yet it is duty to admit a silent one when the church of God is in distress. "*Roll thyself in the dust*" (as great mourners used to do) "and so let the house of Judah and every house in Jerusalem become a *house of Aphrah,* a *house of dust,* covered with dust, crumbled into dust." When God makes the house dust it becomes us to humble ourselves under his mighty hand, and to put our mouths in the dust, thus accommodating ourselves to the providences that concern us. Dust we are ; God brings us to the dust, that we may know it, and own it. Divers other places are here named that should be sharers in this universal mourning, the names of some of which we do not find elsewhere, whence it is conjectured that they are names put upon them by the prophet, the signification of which might either indicate or aggravate the miseries coming upon them, thereby to awaken this secure and stupid people to a holy fear of divine wrath. We find Sennacherib's invasion thus described, in the prediction of it, by the impressions of terror it should make upon the several cities that fell in his way, Isa. x. 28, 29, &c. Let us observe the particulars here, 1. *The inhabitants of Saphir,* which signifies *neat* and *beautiful (thou that dwellest fairly,* so the margin reads it), shall *pass away* into captivity, or be forced to flee, stripped of all their ornaments *and having their shame naked.* Note, Those who appear ever so fine and delicate know not what contempt they may be exposed to ; and the more grievous will the shame be to those who have been inhabitants of Saphir. 2. *The inhabitants of Zaanan,* which signifies the *country of flocks,* a populous country, where the people are as numerous and thick as flocks of sheep, shall yet be so taken up with their own calamities, felt or feared, that they shall *not come forth in the mourning of Bethezel,* which signifies a *place near,* shall not condole with, nor bring any succour to, their next neighbours in distress; for *he shall receive of you his standing;* the enemy shall encamp among you, O inhabitants of Zaanan! shall take up a station there, shall find footing among you. Those may well think themselves excused from helping their neighbours who find they have enough to do to help themselves and to hold their own. 3. As for *the inhabitants of Maroth* (which, some think, is put for Ramoth, others that it signifies the *rough places),* they *waited carefully for good,* and were grieved for the want of it, but were disappointed; for *evil came from the Lord unto the gate of Jerusalem,* when the Assyrian army besieged it, *v.* 12. The inhabitants of Maroth might well overlook their own particular grievances when they saw the holy city itself in danger, and might well overlook the Assyrian, that was the instrument, when they saw the evil coming *from the Lord.* 4. Lachish was a city of Judah, which Sennacherib laid siege to, Isa. xxxvi. 1, 2. The inhabitants of that city are called to *bind the chariot to the swift beast,* to prepare for a speedy flight, as having no other way left to secure themselves and their families; or it is spoken ironically: " You have had your chariots and your swift beasts, but where are they now?" God's quarrel with Lachish is that she is *the beginning of sin,* probably the sin of idolatry, *to the daughter of Zion* (*v.* 13); they had learned it from the ten tribes, their near neighbours, and so infected the two tribes with it. Note, Those that help to bring sin into a country do but thereby prepare for the throwing of themselves out of it. Those must expect to be first in the punishment who have been ringleaders in sin. *The transgressions of Israel were found in thee;* when they came to be traced up to their original they were found to take rise very much from that city. God knows at whose door to lay the blame of the transgressions of Israel, and whom to find guilty. Lachish, having been so much accessory to the sin of Israel, shall certainly be reckoned with: *Thou shalt give presents to Moresheth-gath,* a city of the Philistines, which perhaps had a dependence upon Gath, that famous Philistine city; thou shalt send to court those of that city to assist thee, but it shall be in vain, for (*v.* 14) *the houses of Achzib* (a city which joined to Mareshah, or Moresheth, and is mentioned with it, Josh. xv. 44) *shall be a lie to the kings of Israel;* though they depend upon their strength, yet they shall fail them. Here there is an allusion to the name. *Achzib* signifies *a lie,* and so it shall prove to those that trust in it. 5. Mareshah, that could not, or would not, help Israel, shall herself be made a prey

(*v.* 15): *" I will bring a heir* (that is, an enemy) that shall take possession of thy lands, with as much assurance as if he were heir at law to them, and *he shall come to Adullam,* and *to the glory of Israel,* that is, to Jerusalem the head city;" or, *" The glory of Israel* shall come to be as Adullam, a poor despicable place;" or, " The king of Assyria, whom Israel had gloried in, shall come to Adullam, in laying the country waste." 6. The whole land of Judah seems to be spoken to (*v.* 16) and called to weeping and mourning : *" Make thee bald,* by tearing thy hair and shaving thy head; *poll thee for thy delicate children,* that had been tenderly and nicely brought up; *enlarge thy baldness as the eagle* when she casts her feathers and is all over bald; *for they have gone into captivity from thee,* and are not likely to return; and their captivity will be the more grievous to them because they have been brought up delicately and have not been inured to hardship." Or this is directed particularly to the inhabitants of *Mareshah,* as *v.* 15. That was the prophet's own city, and yet he denounces the judgments of God against it; for it shall be an aggravation of its sin that it had such a prophet, and knew not the day of its visitation. Its being thus privileged, since it improved not the privilege, shall not procure favour for it either with God or with his prophet.

CHAP. II.

In this chapter we have, **I.** The sins with which the people of Israel are charged—covetousness and oppression, fraudulent and violent practices (ver. 1, 2), dealing barbarously, even with women and children, and other harmless people, ver. 8, 9. Opposition of God's prophets and silencing them (ver. 6, 7), and delighting in false prophets, ver. 11. **II.** The judgments with which they are threatened for those sins, that they should be humbled, and impoverished (ver. 3—5), and banished, ver. 10. **III.** Gracious promises of comfort, reserved for the good people among them, in the Messiah, ver. 12, 13. And this is the sum and scope of most of the chapters of this and other prophecies.

WOE to them that devise iniquity, and work evil upon their beds ! when the morning is light, they practise it, because it is in the power of their hand. 2 And they covet fields, and take *them* by violence; and houses, and take *them* away : so they oppress a man and his house, even a man and his heritage. 3 Therefore thus saith the LORD; Behold, against this family do I devise an evil, from which ye shall not remove your necks; neither shall ye go haughtily : for this time *is* evil. 4 In that day shall *one* take up a parable against you, and lament with a doleful lamentation, *and* say, We be utterly spoiled : he hath changed the portion of my people : how hath he removed *it* from me ! turning away he hath divided our fields. 5 Therefore thou shalt have none that shall cast a cord by lot in the congregation of the LORD.

Here is, I. The injustice of man contriving the evil of sin, *v.* 1, 2. God was coming forth against this people to destroy them, and here he shows what was the ground of his controversy with them; it is that which is often mentioned as a sin that hastens the ruin of nations and families as much as any, the sin of oppression. Let us see the steps of it. 1. They eagerly desire that which is not their own—that is the *root of bitterness*, the root of all evil, *v.* 2. They *covet fields and houses*, as Ahab did Naboth's vineyard. " Oh that such a one's field and house were mine! It lies convenient for me, and I would manage it better than he does; it is fitter for me than for him." 2. They set their wits on work to invent ways of accomplishing their desire (*v.* 4); they devise iniquity with a great deal of cursed art and policy; they plot how to do it effectually, and yet so as not to expose themselves, or bring themselves into danger, or under reproach, by it. This is called *working evil !* they are working it in their heads, in their families, and are as intent upon it, and with as much pleasure, as if they were doing it, and are as confident of their success (so wisely do they think they have laid the scheme) as if it were assuredly done. Note, It is bad to do mischief upon a sudden thought, but much worse to devise it, to do it with design and deliberation; when the craft and subtlety of the old serpent appear with his poison and venom, it is wickedness in perfection. They devised it *upon their beds*, when they should have been asleep; care to compass a mischievous design held their eyes waking. *Upon their beds*, where they should have been remembering God, and meditating upon him, where they should have been *communing with their own hearts* and examining them, they were *devising iniquity*. It is of great consequence to improve and employ the hours of our retirement and solitude in a proper manner. 3. They employ their power in executing what they have designed and contrived; they practise the iniquity they have devised, *because it is in the power of their hand :* they find that they can compass it by the help of their wealth, and the authority and interest they have, and that none dare control them, or call them to an account for it; and this, they think, will justify them and bear them out in it. Note, It is the mistake of many to think that as they can do they may do; whereas no power is given for destruction, but all for edification. 4. They are industrious and very expeditious in accomplishing the iniquity they have devised; when they have settled the matter in their thoughts, in their beds, they lose no time, but as soon as the *morning is light* they practise it; they are up early in the prosecution of their de-
1308

signs, and what ill their hand finds to do they do it *with all their might*, which shames our slothfulness and dilatoriness in doing good, and should shame us out of them. In the service of God, and our generation, let it never be said that we left that to be done to-morrow which we could do to-day. 5. They stick at nothing to compass their designs ; what they *covet* they *take away*, if they can, and, (1.) They care not what wrong they do, though it be ever so gross and open; they take away men's fields by violence, not only by fraud, and underhand practices, and colour of law, but by force and with a high hand. (2.) They care not to whom they do wrong nor how far the iniquity extends which they devise : They *oppress a man and his house ;* they rob and ruin those that have numerous families to maintain, and are not concerned though they send them and their wives and children a begging. They *oppress a man and his heritage ;* they take away from men that which they have an unquestionable title to, having received it from their ancestors, and which they have but in trust, to transmit it to their posterity ; but those oppressors care not how many they impoverish, so they may but enrich themselves. Note, If covetousness reigns in the heart, commonly all compassion is banished from it; and if any man *love this world*, as the *love of the Father*, so the love of his neighbour *is not in him*.

II. The justice of God contriving the evil of punishment for this sin (*v.* 3) : *Therefore thus saith the Lord*, the righteous God, that judges between man and man, and is an avenger on those that do wrong, *Behold, against this family do I devise an evil*, that is, against the whole kingdom, the *house of Israel*, and particularly those families in it that were cruel and oppressive. They unjustly devise evil against their brethren, and God will justly devise evil against them. Infinite Wisdom will so contrive the punishment of their sin that it shall be very sure, and such as cannot be avoided, very severe, and such as they cannot bear, very signal and remarkable, and such as shall be universally observed to answer to the sin. The more there appears of a wicked wit in the sin the more there shall appear of a holy wisdom and fitness in the punishment; for the Lord will be *known by the judgments he executes ;* he will be owned by them. 1. He finds them very secure, and confident that they shall in some way or other escape the judgment, or, though they fall under it, shall soon throw it off and get clear of it, and therefore he tells them, It is *an evil from which they shall not remove their neck*. They were children of *Belial*, that would not endure the easy yoke of God's righteous commands, but *broke those bonds* asunder, and *cast away those cords from them ;* and therefore God will lay upon them the heavy yoke of his righteous judgments, and they shall not be able to withdraw their necks from that; those that will not be overruled shall be overcome. 2. He finds them very proud and stately, and therefore he tells them that they shall not go haughtily, with *stretched-forth necks and wanton eyes, walking and mincing as they go* (Isa. iii. 16) ; for *this time is evil,* and the events of it are very humbling and mortifying, and such as will bring down the stoutest spirit. 3. He finds them very merry and jovial, and therefore tells them their note shall be changed, their laughter shall be turned into mourning and their joy into heaviness (*v.* 4): *In that day,* when God comes to punish you for your oppression, *shall one take up a parable against you,* and *lament with a doleful lamentation,* with *a lamentation of lamentations* (so the word is), a most lament-able lamentation, as a song of songs is a most pleasing song. Their enemies shall insult over them, and make a jest of their griefs, for they shall *take up a parable against them.* Their friends shall mourn over them, and lay to heart their calamities, and this shall be the general cry, " *We are utterly spoiled ; we are all undone.*" Note, Those that were most haughty and secure in their prosperity are commonly most dejected and most ready to despair in their adversity. 4. He finds them very rich in houses and lands, which they have gained by oppression, and there-fore tells them that they shall be stripped of all. (1.) They shall, in their despair, give it all up; they shall say, *We are utterly spoiled ; he has changed the portion of my people,* so that it is now no longer theirs, but it is in the possession and occupation of their enemies: *How has he removed it from me !* How suddenly, how powerfully ! What is unjustly got by us will not long con-tinue with us; the righteous God will re-move it. *Turning away* from us in wrath, he *has divided our fields,* and given them into the hands of strangers. Woe to those from whom God turns away. The margin reads it, " *Instead of restoring, he has divided our fields ;* instead of putting us again in the possession of our estates, he has con-firmed those in the possession of them that have taken them from us." Note, It is just with God that those who have dealt fraudu-lently and violently with others should them-selves be dealt fraudulently and violently with. (2.) God shall ratify what they say in their despair (*v.* 5); so it shall be : *Thou shalt have none to cast a cord by lot in the congregation of the Lord,* none to divide in-heritances, because there shall be no inheri-tances to divide, no courts to try titles to lands, or determine controversies about them, or cast lots upon them, as in Joshua's time, for all shall be in the enemies' hand. This land, which should be taken from them, they had not only an unquestionable title to, but a very comfortable enjoyment of, for it was *in the congregation of the Lord,* or rather the congregation of the Lord was in

it; it was God's land; it was a holy land, and therefore it was the more grievous to them to be turned out of it. Note, Those are to be considered the sorest calamities which cut us off from the congregation of the Lord, or cut us short in the enjoyment of the privileges of it.

6 Prophesy ye not, *say they to them that* prophesy : they shall not prophesy to them, *that* they shall not take shame. 7 O *thou that art* named the house of Jacob, is the Spirit of the LORD straitened? *are* these his doings? do not my words do good to him that walketh up-rightly? 8 Even of late my people is risen up as an enemy : ye pull off the robe with the garment from them that pass by securely as men averse from war. 9 The women of my peo-ple have ye cast out from their plea-sant houses ; from their children have ye taken away my glory for ever. 10 Arise ye, and depart ; for this *is* not *your* rest : because it is polluted, it shall destroy *you,* even with a sore destruction. 11 If a man walking in the spirit and falsehood do lie, *saying,* I will prophesy unto thee of wine and of strong drink ; he shall even be the prophet of this people.

Here are two sins charged upon the peo-ple of Israel, and judgments denounced against them for each, such judgments as exactly answer the sin—persecuting God's prophets and oppressing God's poor.

I. Persecuting God's prophets, suppress-ing and silencing them, is a sin that pro-vokes God as much as any thing, for it not only spits in the face of his authority over us, but spurns at the bowels of his mercy to us; for his sending prophets to us is a sure and valuable token of his goodwill. Now observe here,

1. What the obstruction and opposition were which this people gave to God's pro-phets : They *said to those that prophesy, Prophesy ye not,* as Isa. xxx. 10. They *said to the seers,* " *See not ;* do not trouble us with accounts of what you have seen, nor bring us any such frightful messages." They must either not prophesy at all or prophesy only what is pleasing. The word for *pro-phesying* here signifies *dropping,* for the words of the prophets dropped from heaven as the dew. Note, Those that hate to be reformed hate to be reproved, and do all they can to silence faithful ministers. Amos was forbidden to prophesy, Amos vii. 10, &c. *Therefore* persecutors stop their breath, because they have no other way to stop their

mouths; for, if they live, they will preach and torment those that dwell on the earth, as the *two witnesses* did, Rev. xi. 10. Some read it, *Prophesy not ; let these prophesy.* Let not those prophesy that tell us of our faults, and threaten us, but *let those prophesy* that will flatter us in our sins, and cry peace to us. They will not say that they will have no ministers at all, but they will have such as will say just what they would have them and go their way. This they are charged with (*v.* 11), that when they silenced and frowned upon the true prophets they countenanced and encouraged pretenders, and set them up, and made an interest for them, to confront God's faithful prophets : *If a man walk in the spirit of falsehood*, pretend to have the Spirit of God, while really it is a spirit of error, a spirit of delusion, and he himself knows that he has no commission, no instruction, from God, yet, if he says, *I will prophesy unto thee of wine and strong drink*, if he will but assure them that they shall have wine and strong drink enough, that they need not fear the judgments of war and famine which the other prophets threatened them with, that they shall always have plenty of the delights of sense and never know the want of them, and if he will but tell them that it is lawful for them to drink as much as they please of their wine and strong drink, and they need not scruple being drunk, that they *shall have peace though they go on and add drunkenness to thirst*, such a prophet as this is a man after their own heart, who will tell them that there is neither sin nor danger in the wicked course of life they lead : *He shall even be the prophet of this people ;* such a man they would have to be their prophet, that will not only associate with them in their rioting and revellings, but will pretend to consecrate their sensualities by his prophecies and so harden them in their security and sensuality. Note, It is not strange if people that are vicious and debauched covet to have ministers that are altogether such as themselves, for they are willing to believe God is so too, Ps. l. 21. But how are sacred things profaned when they are prostituted to such base purposes, when prophecy itself shall be pressed into the services of a lewd and profane crew ! But thus that servant who said, *My Lord delays his coming*, by the spirit of falsehood, *smote his fellow servants* and *ate and drank with the drunken.*

2. How they are here expostulated with upon this matter (*v.* 7): "*O thou that art named the house of Jacob*, does it become thee to say and do thus? Wilt thou silence those that prophesy, and forbid them to speak in God's name?" Note, It is an honour and privilege to be *named of the house of Jacob.* Thou art *called a Jew*, Rom. ii. 17. But, when those who are called by that worthy name degenerate, they commonly prove the worst of men themselves and the worst enemies to God's prophets. The Jews

who were *named of the house of Jacob* were the most violent persecutors of the first preachers of the gospel. Upon this the prophet here argues with these opposers of the word of God, and shows them, (1.) What an affront they hereby put upon God, the God of the holy prophets : "*Is the Lord's Spirit straitened?* In silencing the Lord's prophets you do what you can to silence his Spirit too ; but do you think you can do it? Can you make the Spirit of God your prisoner and your servant? Will you prescribe to him what he shall say, and forbid him to say what is displeasing to you? If you silence the prophets, yet cannot the Spirit of the Lord find out other ways to reach your consciences? Can your unbelief frustrate the divine counsels?" (2.) What a scandal it was to their profession as Jews : " You are *named the house of Jacob*, and this is your honour ; but *are these his doings?* Are these the doings of your father Jacob? Do you herein tread in his steps? No; if you were indeed his children you would do his works; but now you seek to kill and silence *a man that tells you the truth*, in God's name ; *this did not Abraham* (John viii. 39, 40) ; this did not Jacob. Or, " *Are these God's doings?* Are these the doings that will please him? Are these the doings of his people? No, you know they are not, however some may be so strangely blinded and bigoted as to kill God's ministers and think that therein they *do him service*," John xvi. 2. (3.) Let them consider how unreasonable and absurd the thing was in itself : *Do not my words do good to those that walk uprightly?* Yes; certainly they do; it is an appeal to the experiences of the *generation of the upright*: " *Call now if there be any of them that will answer you, and to which of the saints will you turn?* Turn to which you will, and you will find they all agree in this, that the word of God *does good to those that walk uprightly ;* and will you then oppose that which does good, so much good as good preaching does? Herein you wrong God, who owns the words of the prophets to be his words (they are *my words*) and who by them aims and designs to do good to mankind (Ps. cxix. 68); and will you hinder the great benefactor from doing good? Will you put the light of the world under a bushel? You might as well say to the sun, Shine not, as *say to the seers, See not.* Herein you wrong the souls of men, and deprive them of the benefit designed them by the word of God." Note, Those are enemies not only to God, but to the world, they are enemies to their country, that silence good ministers, and obstruct the means of knowledge and grace ; for it is certainly for the public common good of states and kingdoms that religion should be encouraged. God's words do good to those *that walk uprightly.* It is the character of good people that they *walk uprightly* (Ps. xv. 2); and it is their comfort that the words of God are good and do good to them; they find comfort in them. God's words are good words to good people, and speak comfortably to them. But those that opposed the words of God, and silenced the prophets, pleaded, in justification of themselves, that God's words were unprofitable and unpleasant to them, and did them no good, nor prophesied any good concerning them, but evil, as Ahab complained of Micaiah, in answer to which the prophet here tells them that it was their own fault; they might thank themselves. They might find it of good use to them if they were but disposed to make a good use of it; if they would but walk uprightly, as they should, and so qualify themselves for comfort, the word of God would speak comfortably to them. *Do that which is good, and thou shalt have praise for the same.*

3. What they are threatened with for this sin; God also will choose their delusions, and, (1.) They shall be deprived of the benefit of a faithful ministry. Since they say, *Prophesy not,* God will take them at their word, and *they shall not prophesy to them;* their sin shall be their punishment. If men will silence God's ministers, it is just with God to silence them, as he did Ezekiel, and to say, They shall *no more be reprovers* and monitors to them. Let the physician no longer attend the patient that will not be healed, for he will not be ruled. They *shall not prophesy to them,* and then they will not take shame. As it is the work of magistrates, so is it also of ministers, to put men to shame when they do amiss (Judg. xviii. 7), that, being made ashamed of their folly, they may not return again to it; but, when God gives men up to be impudent and shameless in sin, he says to his prophets, *They are joined to idols; let them alone.* (2.) They shall be given up to the blind guidance of an unfaithful ministry. We may understand *v.* 11 as a threatening: *If a man be found walking in the spirit of falsehood,* having such a lying spirit as was in the mouth of Ahab's prophets, that will strengthen their hands in their wicked ways, he *shall be the prophet of this people,* that is, God will leave them to themselves to hearken to such; since they will be deceived, let them be deceived; since they will not admit the *truth in the love of it,* God will send them *strong delusions to believe a lie,* 2 Thess. ii. 10, 11. They shall have prophets that will prophesy to them for *wine and strong drink* (so some read it), that will give you a cast of their office to your mind for a bottle of wine or a flagon of ale, will soothe sinners in their sins if they will but feed them with the gratifications of their lusts; to have such prophets, and to be ridden by them, is as sad a judgment as any people can be under and as bad a preface of ruin approaching as it is to a particular person to be under the influence of a debauched conscience.

II. Oppressing God's poor is another sin they are charged with, as before (*v.* 1, 2), for it is a sin doubly hateful and provoking to God. Observe,

1. How the sin is described, *v.* 8, 9. When they contemned God's prophets and opposed them they broke out into all other wickedness; what bonds will hold those that have no reverence for God's word? Those who formerly rose up against the enemies of the nation, in defence of their country, and therein behaved themselves bravely, now of late *rose up as enemies of the nation,* and, instead of defending it, destroyed it, and did it more mischief (as usually such vipers in the bowels of a state do) than a foreign enemy could do. They made a prey of men, women, and children, (1.) Of men, that were travelling on the way, that *pass by securely as men averse from war,* that were far from any bad designs, but went peaceably about their lawful occasions; those they set upon, as if they had been dangerous obnoxious people, and *pulled off the robe with the garment from them,* that is, they stripped them both of the upper and the inner garment, took away *their cloak,* and would have *their coat also;* thus barbarously did they use those that were *quiet in the land,* who, being harmless, were fearless, and so the more easily made a prey of. (2.) Of women, whose sex should have been their protection (*v.* 9): *The women of my people have you cast out from their pleasant houses.* They devoured *widows' houses* (Matt. xxiii. 14), and so turned them out of the possession of them, because they were pleasant houses, and such as they had a mind for. It was inhuman to deal thus barbarously with women; but that which especially aggravated it was that they were the women of God's *people,* whom they knew to be under his protection. (3.) Of children, whose age entitles them to a tender usage: *From their children have you taken away my glory for ever.* It was the glory of the Israelites' children that they were free, but they enslaved them—that they were born in God's house, and had a right to the privileges of it, but they sold them to strangers, sent them into idolatrous countries, where they were deprived for ever of that glory; at least the oppressors designed their captivity should be perpetual. Note, The righteous God will certainly reckon for injuries done to the widows and fatherless, who, being helpless and friendless, cannot otherwise expect to be righted.

2. What the sentence is that is passed upon them for it (*v.* 10): "*Arise ye, and depart;* prepare to quit this land, for you shall be forced out of it, as you have forced the women and children of my people out of their possessions; it is not, it shall not, be your rest, as it was intended that Canaan should be, Ps. xcv. 11. You shall have neither contentment nor continuance in it, *because it is polluted* by your wickedness." Sin is defiling

1311

to a land, and sinners cannot expect to rest in a land which they have polluted, but it will spew them out, as this land spewed out the Canaanites of old when they had polluted it with their abominations, Lev. xviii. 27, 28. "Nay, you shall not only be obliged to depart out of this land, but *it shall destroy you even with a sore destruction;* you shall either be turned out of it or (which is all one) you shall be ruined in it." We may apply this to our state in this present world; it is polluted; there is a great deal of *corruption in the world, through lust,* and therefore we should *arise, and depart out of it,* keep at a distance from the corruption that is in it, and *keep ourselves unspotted* from it. It *is not our rest;* it was never intended to be so; it was designed for our passage, but not for our portion—our inn, but not our home. Here *we have no continuing city;* let us therefore *arise and depart;* let us sit loose to it and live above it, and think of leaving it and seek a continuing city above.

12 I will surely assemble, O Jacob, all of thee; I will surely gather the remnant of Israel; I will put them together as the sheep of Bozrah, as the flock in the midst of their fold: they shall make great noise by reason of *the multitude of* men. 13 The breaker is come up before them: they have broken up, and have passed through the gate, and are gone out by it: and their king shall pass before them, and the LORD on the head of them.

After threatenings of wrath, the chapter here concludes, as is usual in the prophets, with promises of mercy, which were in part fulfilled when the Jews returned out of Babylon, and had their full accomplishment in the kingdom of the Messiah. Their grievances shall be all redressed. 1. Whereas they were dispersed, they shall be brought together again, and shall jointly receive the tokens of God's favour to them, and shall have communion with each other and comfort in each other (*v.* 12): " *I will surely assemble, O Jacob! all of thee,* all that belong to thee, all that are *named of the house of Jacob* (*v.* 7) that are now expelled your country, *v.* 10. I will bring you together again, and not one of you shall be lost, not one of you shall be missing. *I will surely gather the remnant of Israel,* that remnant that is designed and reserved for salvation; they shall be brought to incorporate in one body. *I will put them together as the sheep of Bozrah.*" Sheep are inoffensive and sociable creatures; they shall be *as the flock in the midst of their fold,* their own fold, where they are safe under the shepherd's eye and

care; and *they shall make great noise* (as numerous flocks and herds do, with their bleating and lowing) *by reason of the multitude of men* (for the sheep are *men,* as the prophet explains this comparison, Ezek. xxxiv. 31), not by reason of their strifes and contentions, but by reason of their great numbers. This was accomplished when Christ by his gospel gathered together in one *all the children of God that were scattered abroad,* and united both Jews and Gentiles in one fold, and under one Shepherd, when all the complaint was that the *place was too strait* for them—that was *the noise, by reason of their multitude* (Isa. xlix. 19, 20), when there were some added to the church from all parts of the world, and all men were drawn to Christ by the attractive power of his cross, which shall be done yet more and more, and perfectly done, when he shall send forth his angels to *gather in his elect from the four winds.* 2. Whereas God had seemed to desert them, and cast them off, now he will own them, and head them, and help them through all the difficulties that are in the way of their return and deliverance (*v.* 13): *The breaker has come up before them,* to break down all opposition, and clear the road for them; and under his guidance *they have broken up, and have passed through the gate,* the door of escape out of their captivity, and have *gone out by it* with courage and resolution, having Omnipotence for their van-guard. *Their King shall pass before them,* to head them in the way, even Jehovah (he is their king) *on the head of them,* as he was on the head of the armies of Israel when they followed the pillar of cloud and fire through the wilderness and when he appeared to Joshua as *captain of the Lord's host.* Christ is the church's King; he is Jehovah; he heads them, passes before them, brings them out of the land of their captivity, brings them into the land of their rest. He is the *breaker,* that broke in upon the powers of darkness and broke through them, that rent the veil, and opened the kingdom of heaven to all believers. The learned bishop Pearson applies it to the resurrection of Christ, by which he obtained the power and became the pattern of our resurrection. *The breaker has gone up before us* out of the grave, and has carried away its gates, as Samson did Gaza's, bar and all, and by that breach we go out. The learned Dr. Pocock mentions, as the sense which some of the ancient Jews give of it, that the breaker is Elias, and their *King* the *Messiah,* the Son of David; and he thinks we may apply it to Christ and his forerunner *John the Baptist.* John was the breaker; he broke the ice, prepared the way of the Lord by the baptism of repentance; in him the gospel began; from his time *the kingdom of heaven suffered violence;* and so the Christian church is introduced, with *Messiah the Prince* before it, on the head of it, going forth *conquering and to conquer.*

CHAP. III.

What the apostle says of another of the prophets is true of this, who was also his contemporary—" Esaias is very bold," Rom. x. 20. So, in this chapter, Micah is very bold in reproving and threatening the great men that were the ringleaders in sin ; and he gives the reason (ver. 8) why he was so bold, because he had commission and instruction from God to say what he said, and was carried out in it by a higher spirit and power than his own. Magistracy and ministry are two great ordinances of God, for good to his church, but these were both corrupted and the intentions of them perverted ; and upon those that abused them, and so abused the church with them, the prophet is very severe, and justly so. I. He gives them their lesson severally, reproving and threatening princes (ver. 1—4) and false and flattering prophets, ver. 5—7. II. He gives them their lesson jointly, putting them together, as acting in conjunction for the ruin of the kingdom, which they should see the ruins of, ver. 9—12.

AND I said, Hear, I pray you, O heads of Jacob, and ye princes of the house of Israel ; *Is it* not for you to know judgment ? 2 Who hate the good, and love the evil ; who pluck off their skin from off them, and their flesh from off their bones ; 3 Who also eat the flesh of my people, and flay their skin from off them ; and they break their bones, and chop them in pieces, as for the pot, and as flesh within the caldron. 4 Then shall they cry unto the Lord, but he will not hear them : he will even hide his face from them at that time, as they have behaved themselves ill in their doings. 5 Thus saith the Lord concerning the prophets that make my people err, that bite with their teeth, and cry, Peace ; and he that putteth not into their mouths, they even prepare war against him : 6 Therefore night *shall be* unto you, that ye shall not have a vision ; and it shall be dark unto you, that ye shall not divine ; and the sun shall go down over the prophets, and the day shall be dark over them. 7 Then shall the seers be ashamed, and the diviners confounded : yea, they shall all cover their lips ; for *there is* no answer of God.

Princes and prophets, when they faithfully discharge the duty of their office, are to be highly honoured above other men ; but when they betray their trust, and act contrary to it, they should hear of their faults as well as others, and shall be made to know that there is a God above them, to whom they are accountable ; at his bar the prophet here, in his name, arraigns them.

I. Let the princes hear their charge and their doom. The *heads of Jacob, and the princes of the house of Israel,* are called upon to *hear* what the prophet has to say to them, *v.* 1. The word of God has reproofs for the greatest of men, which the ministers of that

word ought to apply as there is occasion. The prophet here has comfort in the reflection upon it, that, whatever the success was, he had faithfully discharged his trust : *And I said, Hear, O princes!* He had the testimony of his conscience for him that he had not shrunk from his duty for fear of the face of men. He tells them,

1. What was expected from them : *Is it not for you to know judgment?* He means to *do* judgment, for otherwise the knowledge of it is of no avail. " Is it not your business to administer justice impartially, and not to *know faces*" (as the Hebrew phrase for partiality and respect of persons is), " but to *know judgment,* and the merits of every cause?" Or it may be taken for granted that the heads and rulers are well acquainted with the rules of justice, whatever others are ; for they have those means of knowledge, and have not those excuses for ignorance, which some others have, that are poor and foolish (Jer. v. 4) ; and, if so, their transgression of the laws of justice is the more provoking to God, for they sin against knowledge. " Is it not for you to know judgment? Yes, it is ; therefore stand still, and hear your own judgment, and judge if it be not right, whether any thing can be objected against it."

2. How wretchedly they had transgressed the rules of judgment, though they knew what they were. Their principle and disposition are bad : They *hate the good and love the evil :* they hate good in others, and hate it should have any influence on themselves ; they hate to do good, hate to have any good done, and hate those that are good and do good ; and they *love the evil,* delight in mischief and in those that do mischief. This being their principle, their practice is according to it ; they are very cruel and severe towards those that are under their power, and whoever lies at their mercy will find that they have none. They barbarously devour those whom they should protect, and, as unfaithful shepherds, fleece the flock they should feed ; nay, instead of feeding it, they feed upon it, Ezek. xxxiv. 2. It is fit indeed that he who feeds a flock should *eat of the milk of the flock* (1 Cor. ix. 7), but that will not content them : They *eat the flesh of my people.* It is fit that they should be clothed with the wool, and that will not serve : They *flay the skin from off them, v.* 3. By imposing heavier taxes upon them than they can bear, and exacting them with rigour, by mulcts, and fines, and corporal punishments, for pretended crimes, they ruined the estates and families of their subjects, took away from some their lives, from others their livelihoods, and were to their subjects as beasts of prey, rather than shepherds. " They *break their bones* to come at the marrow, and *chop* the flesh *in pieces as for the pot.*" This intimates that they were, (1.) Very ravenous and greedy for

themselves, indulging themselves in luxury and sensuality. (2.) Very barbarous and cruel to those that were under them, not caring whom they beggared, so they could but enrich themselves; such evil is the love of money the root of

3. How they might expect that God should deal with them, since they had been thus cruel to his subjects. The rule is fixed, Those shall have judgment without mercy that have shown no mercy (*v.* 4): "*They shall cry to the Lord, but he will not hear them,* in the day of their distress, as the poor cried to them in the day of their prosperity and they would not hear them." There will come a time when the most proud and scornful sinners will *cry to the Lord,* and sue for that mercy which they once neither valued nor copied out. But it will then be in vain; God will even hide his face from them at that time, that time when they need his favour, and see themselves undone without it. At another time they would have turned their back upon him; but at that time he will turn his back upon them, *as they have behaved themselves ill in their doings.* Note, Men cannot expect to do ill and fare well, but may expect to find, as Adoni-bezek did, that done to them which they did to others; for *he is righteous who takes vengeance. With the froward God will show himself froward,* and he often gives up cruel and unmerciful men into the hands of those who are cruel and unmerciful to them, as they themselves have formerly been to others. This agrees with Prov. xxi. 13, *Whoso stoppeth his ears at the cry of the poor, he shall cry himself and shall not be heard;* but the merciful have reason to hope that they shall obtain mercy.

II. Let the prophets hear their charge too, and their doom; they were such as prophesied falsely, and the princes bore rule by their means. Observe,

1. What was their sin. (1.) They made it all their business to flatter and deceive the people: *They make my people err,* lead them into mistakes, both concerning what they should do and concerning what God would do with them. It is ill with a people when their leaders cause them to err, and those draw them out of the way that should guide them and go before them in it. "They make them to err by crying peace, by telling them that they do well, and that all shall be well with them; whereas they are in the paths of sin, and within a step of ruin. They *cry peace,* but they *bite with their teeth,*" which perhaps is meant of their biting their own lips, as we are apt to do when we would suppress something which we are ready to speak. When they cried *peace* their own hearts gave them the lie, and they were just ready to eat their own words and to contradict themselves, but they bit with their teeth, and kept it in. They were not blind leaders of the blind, for they saw the ditch

before them, and yet led their followers into it. (2.) They made it all their aim to glut themselves, and serve their own belly, as the seducers in St. Paul's time (Rom. xvi. 18), for *their god is their belly,* Phil. iii. 19. They *bite with their teeth, and cry peace;* that is, they will flatter and compliment those that will feed them with good bits, will give them something to eat; but as for those that *put not into their mouths,* that are not continually cramming them, they look upon them as their enemies; to them they do not *cry peace,* as they do to those whom they look upon as their benefactors, but they *even prepare war against them;* against them they denounce the judgments of God; they preach either comfort or terror to men, not according as they are to God, but as they are to them, as the crafty priests of the church of Rome, in some places, make their image either to smile or frown upon the offerer according as his offering is. Justly is it insisted on as a necessary qualification of a minister (1 Tim. iii. 3, and again Tit. i. 7) that he be not *greedy of filthy lucre.*

2. What is the sentence passed upon them for this sin, *v.* 6, 7. It is threatened, (1.) That they shall be involved in troubles and miseries with those to whom they had cried peace: *Night shall be upon them,* a dark cold night of calamity, such as they, in their flattery, led the people to hope would never come. *It shall be dark unto you,* darker to you than to others; *the sun shall go down over the prophets,* shall go down at noon; all comfort shall depart from them, and they shall be deprived of all hope of it. The *day shall be dark over them,* in which they promised themselves light. Nor shall they be surrounded with outward troubles only, but their mind shall be full of confusion, and they shall be brought to their wits' end; their heads shall be clouded, and their own thoughts shall trouble them; and that is trouble enough. They kept others in the dark, and now God will bring them into the dark. (2.) That thereby they shall be silenced, and all their pretensions to prophecy for ever shamed. They never had any true vision; and now, the event disproving their predictions of peace, it shall be made to appear that they never had any, that there never was an answer of God to them, but it was all a sham, and they were cheats and impostors. Their reputation being thus quite sunk, their confidence would of course fail them. And, their spirits being ruffled and confused, their invention would fail them too; and by reason of this darkness, both without and within too, *they shall not divine,* they shall not have so much as a counterfeit vision to produce, they shall be *ashamed,* and *confounded,* and *cover their lips,* as men that are quite baffled and have nothing to say for themselves. Note, Those who deceive others are but preparing confusion for their own faces.

8 But truly I am full of power by the Spirit of the LORD, and of judgment, and of might, to declare unto Jacob his transgression, and to Israel his sin. 9 Hear this, I pray you, ye heads of the house of Jacob, and princes of the house of Israel, that abhor judgment, and pervert all equity. 10 They build up Zion with blood, and Jerusalem with iniquity. 11 The heads thereof judge for reward, and the priests thereof teach for hire, and the prophets thereof divine for money: yet will they lean upon the LORD, and say, *Is* not the LORD among us? none evil can come upon us. 12 Therefore shall Zion for your sake be ploughed *as* a field, and Jerusalem shall become heaps, and the mountain of the house as the high places of the forest.

Here, I. The prophet experiences a divine power going along with him in his work, and he makes a solemn profession and protestation of it, as that which would justify him, and bear him out, in his plain dealing with the princes and rulers. He would not, he durst not, make thus bold with the great men, but that he was carried out to do it by a prophetical impulse and impression. It was not he that said it, but God by him, and he could not but speak the word that God put into his mouth. It comes in likewise by way of opposition to the false prophets, who were full of shame when they lived to see themselves proved liars, and who never had courage to deal faithfully with the people, but flattered them in their sins; they were *sensual, not having the Spirit,* but truly (says Micah) *I am full of power by the Spirit of the Lord, v.* 8. Having in himself an assurance of the truth of what he said, he said it with assurance. Compare him with those false prophets, and you will say, There is no comparison between them. *What is the chaff to the wheat?* Jer. xxiii. 28. What is painted fire to real fire? Observe here, 1. What the qualifications were with which this prophet was endued: He was *full of power, and of judgment, and of might;* he had an ardent love to God and to the souls of men, a deep concern for his glory and their salvation, and a flaming zeal against sin. He had likewise courage to reprove it and witness against it, not fearing the wrath either of great men or of great multitudes; whatever difficulties or discouragements he met with, they did not deter him nor drive him from his work; *none of these things moved him.* And all this was guided by judgment and discretion; he was a man of wisdom as well as courage; in all his preaching there

was light as well as heat, and a spirit of wisdom as well as of zeal. Thus was this man of God *thoroughly furnished* for every good word he had to say, and every good work he had to do. Those he preached to could not but perceive him to be full both of *power* and *judgment,* for they found both their *understandings opened* and their *hearts* made *to burn within them,* with such evidence and demonstration, and with such power, did the word come from him. 2. Whence he had these qualifications, not from and of himself, but he was *full of power by the Spirit of the Lord.* Knowing it was indeed the *Spirit of the Lord* that was in him, and spoke by him, that it was a divine revelation that he delivered, he spoke it boldly, and as one having authority, *set his face as a flint,* knowing he should be justified and borne out in what he said, Isa. l. 7, 8. Note, Those who act honestly may act boldly; and those who are sure that they have a commission from God need not be afraid of opposition from men. Nay, he had not only a Spirit of prophecy, which was the ground of his boldness, but the Spirit of sanctification endued him with the boldness and wisdom which were requisite for him. It was not in any strength of his own that he was strong; *for who is sufficient for these things?* but in *the Lord, and in the power of his might; for from him* all *our sufficiency* is. Are we full of power at any time, for that which is good? It is purely by *the Spirit of the Lord,* for of ourselves we are weak as water; it is the God of Israel that gives strength and power both to his people and to his ministers. 3. What use he made of these qualifications— this judgment and this power; he *declared to Jacob his transgression and to Israel his sin.* If transgression be found in Jacob and Israel, they must be told of it, and it is the business of God's prophets to tell them of it, to *cry aloud* and *not to spare,* Isa. lviii. 1. Those who come to hear the word of God must be willing to be told of their faults, and must not only give their ministers leave to deal plainly and faithfully with them, but take it kindly, and be thankful; but, since few have meekness enough to receive reproof, those have need of a great deal of boldness who are to give reproofs, and must pray for a spirit both of wisdom and might.

II. The prophet exerts this power in dealing with the *heads of the house of Jacob,* both the princes and the prophets, whom he had drawn up a high charge against in the former part of the chapter. He repeats the summons of their attendance and attention (n. 9), the same that we had *v.* 1, directing himself to *the princes of the house of Israel,* yet he means those of *Judah;* for it appears (Jer. xxvi. 18, 19, where *v.* 12 is quoted) that this was spoken in Hezekiah's kingdom; but, the ten tribes being gone into captivity, Judah is all that is now left of Jacob and Israel. The prophet speaks respectfully to them (*hear, I pray you*) and gives them their titles of *heads* and *princes*. Ministers must be faithful to great men in reproving them for their sins, but they must not be rude and uncivil to them. Now observe here,

1. The great wickedness that these heads of the house of Jacob were guilty of, *princes, priests,* and *prophets;* in short, they were covetous, and prostituted their offices to their love of money. (1.) The *princes abhorred all judgment;* they would not be governed by any of its laws, either in their own practice or in passing sentence upon appeals made to them; they *perverted all equity,* and scorned to be under the direction or correction of justice, when it could not be made pliable to their secular interests. When, under pretence of doing right, they did the most palpable wrongs, then they perverted equity, and made it serve a purpose contrary to the intention of the founder of magistracy and fountain of power. It is laid to their charge (*v.* 10) that *they build up Zion with blood.* "They pretend, in justification of their extortion and oppressions, that they build up Zion and Jerusalem; they add new streets and squares to the holy cities, and adorn them; they establish and advance the public interests both in church and state, and think that therein they do God and Israel good service. But it is *with blood* and *with iniquity,* and therefore it cannot prosper; nor will their intentions of good to the city of God justify their contradictions to the law of God." Those mistake who think that a burning flaming zeal for holy church, and the propagating of the faith, will serve to consecrate robberies and murders, massacres and depredations; no, Zion's walls owe those no thanks that build them up with blood and iniquity. The sin of man works not the righteousness of God. "The office of the princes is to judge upon appeals made to them; but *they judge for reward* (*v.* 11); they give judgment on the side of those that give the bribe; the most righteous cause shall not be carried without a fee, and for a fee the most unrighteous cause shall be carried." Miserable is the people's case when the judge's enquiry upon a cause is not, "What is to be done in it?" but, "What is to be got by it?" (2.) The priests' work was to teach the people, and for that the law had provided them a very honourable comfortable maintenance; but that will not content them, they *teach for hire* over and above, and will be hired to teach any thing, as an oracle of God, which they know will please and gain them an interest. (3.) The prophets, it should seem, had honorary fees given them by way of gratuity (1 Sam. ix. 7, 8); but these prophets governed themselves in their prophesying by the prospect of temporal advantage and that was the main thing they had in their eye: They *divine for money.* Their tongues were mercenary; they would either prophesy or

1316

let it alone, according as they found it most for their advantage; and a man might have what oracle he would from them if he would but pay them for it. Thus they were fit successors of Balaam, who *loved the wages of unrighteousness.* Note, Though that which is wicked can never be consecrated by a zeal for the church, yet that which is sacred may be, and often is, desecrated, by the love of the world. When men do that which in itself is good, but do it for filthy lucre, it loses its excellency, and becomes an abomination both to God and man.

2. Their vain presumption and carnal confidence, notwithstanding: They *lean upon the Lord,* and because they are, in profession, his people, they think there is neither harm nor danger in these their wicked practices. Faith builds upon the Lord, rests in him, and relies upon him, as the soul's foundation; presumption only *leans upon the Lord* as a prop, makes use of him to serve a turn, while still the world is the foundation that is built upon. They speak with a great deal of confidence, (1.) Of their honour: "*Is not the Lord among us?* Have we not the tokens of his presence with us, his temple, his ark, his lively oracles?" They are *haughty because of the holy mountain* and its dignities (Zeph. iii. 11), as if their church-privileges would palliate the worst of practices, or as if God's presence with them were intended to make the priests and people rich with the sale of their performances. It was true that the Lord was among them by his ordinances, and this puffed them up with pride; but, if they imagined that he was among them by his favour and love, they were mistaken: but it is a cheat the children of men often put upon themselves to think they have God with them, when they have by their sin provoked him to depart from them. (2.) They are confident of their own safety: *No evil can come upon us.* Many are rocked asleep in a fatal security by their church-privileges, as if those would protect them in sin, and shelter them from punishment, which are really, and will be, the greatest aggravations both of their sin and of their punishment. If men's having the Lord among them will not restrain them from doing evil, it can never secure them from suffering evil for so doing; and it is very absurd for sinners to think that their impudence will be their impunity.

3. The doom passed upon them for their real wickedness, notwithstanding their imaginary protection (*v.* 12): *Therefore shall Zion for your sake be ploughed as a field.* This is that passage which is quoted as a bold word spoken by Micah (Jer. xxvi. 18), which yet Hezekiah and his princes took well, though in another reign it might have gone near to cost him his head; nay, they repented and reformed, and so the execution of this threatening was prevented, and did not come in those days. (1.) It is the ruin of holy places that is here foretold, places that had

been highly honoured with the tokens of God's presence and the performances of his worship; it is Zion that shall be ploughed as a field, the building burnt to the ground and levelled with it. Some observe that this was literally fulfilled in the destruction of Jerusalem by the Romans, when the ground on which the city stood was ploughed up in token of its utter desolation, and that no city should be built upon that ground without the emperor's leave. Even *Jerusalem,* the holy city, shall *become heaps* of ruins, and the *mountain of the house,* on which the temple is built, shall be overgrown with briars and thorns, *as the high places of the forest.* If sacred places be polluted by sin, they must expect to be wasted and ruined by the judgments of God. (2.) It is the wickedness of those who preside in them that brings the ruin: "It is *for your sake* that *Zion shall be ploughed as a field;* you pretend to build up Zion, but, doing it by blood and iniquity, you pull it down." Note, The sin of priests and princes is often the ruin of states and churches. *Delirant reges, plectuntur Achivi—The kings act foolishly and the people suffer for it.*

CHAP. IV.

Comparing this chapter with the close of the foregoing chapter, the comfortable promises here with the terrible threatenings there, we may, with the apostle, "behold the goodness and severity of God," (Rom. xi. 22), towards the Jewish church which fell, severity when Zion was ploughed as a field, but towards the Christian church, which was built upon the ruins of it, goodness, great goodness; for it is here promised, I. That it shall be advanced and enlarged by the accession of the nations to it, ver. 1, 2. II. That it shall be protected in tranquillity and peace, ver. 3, 4. III. That it shall be kept close, and constant, and faithful to God, ver. 5. IV. That, under Christ's government, all its grievances shall be redressed, ver. 6, 7. V. That it shall have an ample and flourishing dominion, ver. 8. VI. That its troubles shall be brought to a happy issue at length, ver. 9, 10. VII. That its enemies shall be disquieted, nay, that they shall be destroyed in and by their attempts against it, ver. 11—13.

BUT in the last days it shall come to pass, *that* the mountain of the house of the LORD shall be established in the top of the mountains, and it shall be exalted above the hills; and people shall flow unto it. 2 And many nations shall come, and say, Come, and let us go up to the mountain of the LORD, and to the house of the God of Jacob; and he will teach us of his ways, and we will walk in his paths: for the law shall go forth of Zion, and the word of the LORD from Jerusalem. 3 And he shall judge among many people, and rebuke strong nations afar off; and they shall beat their swords into ploughshares, and their spears into pruninghooks: nation shall not lift up a sword against nation, neither shall they learn war any more. 4 But they shall sit every man under his vine and under his fig-tree; and none

shall make *them* afraid : for the mouth of the LORD of hosts hath spoken *it.* 5 For all people will walk every one in the name of his god, and we will walk in the name of the LORD our God for ever and ever. 6 In that day, saith the LORD, will I assemble her that halteth, and I will gather her that is driven out, and her that I have afflicted; 7 And I will make her that halted a remnant, and her that was cast far off a strong nation: and the LORD shall reign over them in mount Zion from henceforth, even for ever.

It is a very comfortable *but* with which this chapter begins, and very reviving to those who lay the interests of God's church near their heart and are concerned for the welfare of it. When we sometimes see the corruptions of the church, especially of church-rulers, princes, priests, and prophets, seeking their own things and not the things of God, and when we soon after see the desolations of the church, *Zion* for their sakes *ploughed as a field,* we are ready to fear that it will one day perish between both, that the name of Israel shall be no more in remembrance; we are ready to give up all for gone, and to conclude the church will have neither root nor branch upon earth. But let not our faith fail in this matter; out of the ashes of the church another phœnix shall arise. In the last words of the foregoing chapter we left *the mountain of the house* as desolate and waste as the *high places of the forest;* and is it possible that such a wilderness should ever become a fruitful field again? Yes, the first words of this chapter bring in *the mountain of the Lord's house* as much dignified by being frequented as ever it had been disgraced by being deserted. Though Zion be ploughed as a field, yet God has not *cast off his people,* but by the fall of the Jews salvation has come to the Gentiles, so that it proves to be the riches of the world, Rom. xi. 11, 12. This is the mystery which God by the prophet here shows us, and he says the very same in the first three verses of this chapter which another prophet said by the word of the Lord at the same time (Isa. ii. 2—4), that *out of the mouth of these two witnesses* these promises might be established; and very precious promises they are, relating to the gospel-church, which have been in part accomplished, and will be yet more and more, for he is faithful that has promised.

I. That there shall be a church for God set up in the world, after the defection and destruction of the Jewish church, and this in the last days; that is, as some of the rabbin themselves acknowledge, *in the days of the Messiah.* The people of God shall be incorporated by a new charter, a new spiritual way of worship shall be enacted, and a new institution of offices to attend it; better privileges shall be granted by this new charter, and better provision made for enlarging and establishing the kingdom of God among men than had been made by the Old-Testament constitution: *The mountain of the house of the Lord* shall again appear firm ground for God's faithful worshippers to stand, and go, and build upon, in their attendance on him, *v.* 1. And it shall be a centre of unity to them; a church shall be set up in the world, to which the Lord will be daily *adding such as shall be saved.*

II. That this church shall be firmly founded and well built: It *shall be established in the top of the mountains;* Christ himself will build it upon a rock; it shall be an impregnable fort upon an immovable foundation, so that the gates of hell shall neither overthrow the one nor undermine the other (Matt. xvi. 18); its foundations are still in the *holy mountains* (Ps. lxxxvii. 1), the *everlasting mountains,* which cannot, which shall not, be removed. It shall be established, not as the temple, upon one mountain, but upon many; for the foundations of the church, as they are sure, so they are large.

III. That it shall be highly advanced, and become eminent and conspicuous: It *shall be exalted above the hills,* observed with wonder for its growing greatness from small beginnings. The kingdom of Christ shall shine with greater lustre than ever any of the kingdoms of the earth did. It shall be as a *city on a hill, which cannot be hid,* Matt. v. 14. The glory of this latter house is greater than that of the former, Hag. ii. 9. See 2 Cor. iii. 7, 8, &c.

IV. That there shall be a great accession of converts to it and succession of converts in it. *People shall flow unto it* as the waters of a river are continually flowing; there shall be a constant stream of believers flowing in from all parts into the church, as the people of the Jews flowed into the temple, while it was standing, to worship there. Then many tribes came to the mountain of the house, to enquire of God's temple; but in gospel-times many nations shall flow into the church, shall *fly like a cloud and as the doves to their windows.* Ministers shall be sent forth to *disciple all nations,* and they shall not *labour in vain;* for, multitudes being wrought upon to believe the gospel and embrace the Christian religion, they shall excite and encourage one another, and shall say, " *Come, and let us go up to the mountain of the Lord* now raised among us, even *to the house of the God of Jacob,* the spiritual temple which we need not travel far to, for it is brought to our doors and set up in the midst of us." Thus shall people be *made willing in the day of his power* (Ps. cx. 3), and shall do what they can to make others willing, as Andrew invited Peter, and Philip Nathanael, to be acquainted

with Christ. They shall *call the people to the mountain* (Deut. xxxiii. 19), for there is in Christ enough for all, enough for each. Now observe what it is, 1. Which these converts expect to find in *the house of the God of Jacob.* They come thither for instruction : " *He will teach us of his ways,* what is the way in which he would have us to walk with him and in which we may depend upon him to meet us graciously." Note, Where we come to worship God we come to be taught of him. 2. Which they engage to do when they are thus taught of God : *We will walk in his paths.* Note, Those may comfortably expect that God will teach them who are firmly resolved by his grace to do as they are taught.

V. That, in order to this, a new revelation shall be published to the world, on which the church shall be founded, and by which multitudes shall be brought into it : *For the law shall go forth of Zion, and the word of the Lord from Jerusalem.* The gospel is here called *the word of the Lord,* for *the Lord gave the word, and great was the company of those that published it,* Ps. lxviii. 11. It was of a divine original, a divine authority ; it began to be spoken by the Lord Christ himself, Heb. ii. 3. And it is *a law,* a law of faith ; we are *under the law to Christ.* This was to go *forth from Jerusalem, from Zion,* the metropolis of the Old-Testament dispensation, where the temple, and altars, and oracles were, and whither the Jews went to worship from all parts ; thence the gospel must take rise, to show the connexion between the Old Testament and the New, that the gospel is not set up in opposition to the law, but is an explication and illustration of it, and a *branch growing out of its roots.* It was in Jerusalem that Christ preached and wrought miracles ; there he died, rose again, and ascended ; there the Spirit was poured out ; and those that were to preach repentance and remission of sins to all nations were ordered to *begin at Jerusalem,* so that thence flowed the streams that were to water the desert world.

VI. That a convincing power should go along with the gospel of Christ, in all places where it should be preached (*v.* 3) : *He shall judge among many people.* Messiah, the lawgiver (*v.* 2), is here *the judge,* for to him the Father *committed all judgment,* and *for judgment he came into this world;* his word, the *word of his gospel,* that was to go forth from Jerusalem, was the golden sceptre by which he shall rule and judge when he sits as *king on the holy hill of Zion,* Ps. ii. 6. By it he shall *rebuke strong nations afar off;* for the Spirit working with the word shall *reprove the world,* John xvi. 8. It is promised to the Son of David that he shall *judge among the heathen* (Ps. cx. 6), which he does when in the chariot of his everlasting gospel he goes forth, and goes on, *conquering and to conquer.*

VII. That a disposition to mutual peace and love shall be the happy effect of the setting up of the kingdom of the Messiah: *They shall beat their swords into plough-shares;* that is, angry passionate men, that have been fierce and furious, shall be wonderfully sweetened, and made mild and meek, Tit. iii. 2, 3. Those who, before their conversion, did injuries, and would bear none, after their conversion can bear injuries, but will do none. As far as the gospel prevails it makes men peaceable, for such is *the wisdom from above;* it is *gentle and easy to be entreated;* and, if nations were but leavened by it, there would be universal peace. When Christ was born there was universal peace in the Roman empire; those that were first brought into the gospel church were all of *one heart and of one soul* (Acts iv. 32); and it was observed of the primitive Christians how well *they loved one another.* In heaven this will have its full accomplishment. It is promised, 1. That none shall be quarrelsome. The art of war, instead of being improved (which some reckon the glory of a kingdom), shall be forgotten and laid aside as useless. They *shall not learn war any more* as they have done, for they shall have no need to defend themselves nor any inclination to offend their neighbours. *Nation shall no longer lift up sword against nation;* not that the gospel will make men cowards, but it will make men peaceable. 2. That all shall be quiet, both from evil and from the fear of evil (*v.* 4): *They shall sit safely,* and none shall disturb them; they shall sit securely, and shall not disturb themselves, every man *under his vine and under his fig-tree,* enjoying the fruit of them, and needing no other shelter than the leaves of them. *None shall make them afraid;* not only there shall be nothing that is likely to frighten them, but they shall not be disposed to fear. Under the dominion of Christ, as that of Solomon, there shall be *abundance of peace.* Though his followers have trouble in the world, in him they enjoy great tranquillity. If this seems unlikely, yet we may depend upon it, *for the mouth of the Lord has spoken it,* and no word of his shall fall to the ground; what he has spoken by his word he will do by his providence and grace. He that is the *Lord of hosts* will be the *God of peace;* and those may well be easy whom *the Lord of hosts,* of all hosts, undertakes the protection of.

VIII. That the churches shall be constant in their duty, and so shall make a good use of their tranquillity and shall not provoke the Lord to deprive them of it, *v.* 5. When *the churches have rest* they shall be edified, and confirmed, and comforted, and shall resolve to be as firm to their God as other nations are to theirs, though they be no gods. Where we find the foregoing promises, Isa. ii. 2, &c. it follows (*v.* 5), *O house of Jacob! come ye, and let us walk in the light of the Lord;* and here, *We will walk in the name of the Lord our God.* Note, Peace is a blessing indeed when it strengthens our resolutions to

cleave to the Lord. Observe, 1. How constant other nations were to their gods: *All people will walk every one in the name of his god,* will own their god and cleave to him, will worship their god and serve him, will depend upon him and put confidence in him. Whatever men make a god of they will make use of, and take his name along with them in all their actions and affairs. The mariners, in a storm, *cried every man to his god,* Jonah i. 5. And no instance could be found of a nation's changing its gods, Jer. ii. 11 : If the hosts of heaven were their gods, they loved them, and served them, and *walked after them,* Jer. viii. 2. 2. How constant God's people now resolve to be to him : " *We will walk in the name of the Lord our God,* will acknowledge him in all our ways, and govern ourselves by a continual regard to him, doing nothing but what we have warrant from him for, and openly professing our relation to him." Observe, Their resolution is peremptory; it is not a thing that needs be disputed: " *We will walk in the name of the Lord our God.*" It is just and reasonable : He is *our God.* And it is a resolution for a perpetuity : " We will do it *for ever and ever,* and will never leave him. He will be ours for ever, and therefore so we will be his, and never repent our choice."

IX. That notwithstanding the dispersions, distress, and infirmities of the church, it shall be formed and established, and made very considerable, *v.* 6, 7. 1. The state of the church had been low, and weak, and very helpless, in the latter times of the Old Testament, partly through the corruptions of the Jewish nation, and partly through the oppressions under which they groaned. They were like a *flock of sheep* that were *maimed, worried,* and *scattered,* Ezek. xxxiv. 16; Jer. l. 6. 17. The good people among them, and in other places, that were well inclined, were dispersed, were very infirm, and in a manner lost and cast far off. 2. It is promised that all these grievances shall be redressed and the distemper healed. Christ will come himself (Matt. xv. 24), and send his apostles to *the lost sheep of the house of Israel,* Matt. x. 6. From among the Jews that halted, or that, for want of strength, could not go upright, God gathered a remnant (*v.* 7), that *remnant according to the election of grace* which is spoken of in Rom. xi. 7, which embraced the gospel of Christ. And from among the Gentiles that were cast far off (so the Gentiles are described to be, Eph. ii. 13, Acts ii. 39) he raised a strong nation; greater numbers of them were brought into the church than of the Jews, Gal. iv. 27. And such a strong nation the gospel-church is that the gates of hell shall never be able to prevail against it. The church of Christ is more numerous than any other nation, and *strong in the Lord and in the power of his might.*

X. That the *Messiah* shall be the king of

this kingdom, shall protect and govern it, and order all the affairs of it for the best, and this to the end of time. The Lord Jesus *shall reign over them in Mount Zion* by his word and Spirit in his ordinances, and this *henceforth and for ever*, for *of the increase of his government and peace there shall be no end.*

8 And thou, O tower of the flock, the strong hold of the daughter of Zion, unto thee shall it come, even the first dominion ; the kingdom shall come to the daughter of Jerusalem. 9 Now why dost thou cry out aloud ? *is there* no king in thee ? is thy counsellor perished ? for pangs have taken thee as a woman in travail. 10 Be in pain, and labour to bring forth, O daughter of Zion, like a woman in travail : for now shalt thou go forth out of the city, and thou shalt dwell in the field, and thou shalt go *even* to Babylon ; there shalt thou be delivered ; there the LORD shall redeem thee from the hand of thine enemies. 11 Now also many nations are gathered against thee, that say, Let her be defiled, and let our eye look upon Zion. 12 But they know not the thoughts of the LORD, neither understand they his counsel : for he shall gather them as the sheaves into the floor. 13 Arise and thresh, O daughter of Zion : for I will make thine horn iron, and I will make thy hoofs brass : and thou shalt beat in pieces many people : and I will consecrate their gain unto the LORD and their substance unto the Lord of the whole earth.

These verses relate to Zion and Jerusalem, here called the *tower of the flock*, or the *tower of Edor ;* we read of such a place (Gen. xxxv. 21) near Bethlehem ; and some conjecture it is the same place where the shepherds were keeping their flocks when the angels brought them tidings of the birth of Christ, and some think Bethlehem itself is here spoken of, as *ch.* v. 2. Some think it is a tower at that gate of Jerusalem which is called the *sheep-gate* (Neh. iii. 32), and conjecture that through that gate Christ rode in triumph into Jerusalem. However, it seems to be put for Jerusalem itself, or for Zion the *tower of David.* All the sheep of Israel flocked thither three times a year ; it was the *stronghold (Ophel,* which is also a name of a place in Jerusalem, Neh. iii. 27), or castle, of the *daughter of Zion.* Now here,

I. We have a promise of the glories of the spiritual Jerusalem, the gospel-church, which

is the tower of the flock, that one fold in which all the sheep of Christ are protected under one Shepherd : "*Unto thee shall it come ;* that which thou hast long wanted and wished for, *even the first dominion,* a dignity and power equal to that of David and Solomon, by whom Jerusalem was first raised, that *kingdom* shall again *come to the daughter of Jerusalem,* which it was deprived of at the captivity. It shall make as great a figure and shine with as much lustre among the nations, and have as much influence upon them, as ever it had ; this is the *first* or *chief* dominion." Now this had by no means its accomplishment in Zerubbabel ; his was nothing like the first dominion either in respect of splendour and sovereignty at home or the extent of power abroad ; and therefore it must refer to the kingdom of the *Messiah* (and to that the Chaldee-paraphrase refers it) and had its accomplishment when God gave to our Lord Jesus *the throne of his father David* (Luke i. 32), set him king *upon the holy hill of Zion,* and *gave him the heathen for his inheritance* (Ps. ii. 6), *made him, his first-born, higher than the kings of the earth,* Ps. lxxxix. 27 ; Dan. vii. 14. *David, in spirit, called him Lord,* and (as Dr. Pocock observes) he witnessed of himself, and his witness was true, that he was greater than Solomon, none of their dominions being like his for extent and duration. The common people welcomed Christ into Jerusalem with *hosannas to the son of David,* to show that it was the *first dominion* that came *to the daughter of Zion ;* and the evangelist applies it to the promise of Zion's king coming to her, Matt. xxi. 5 ; Zech. ix. 9. Some give this sense of the words : To Zion, and Jerusalem that tower of the flock, to the nation of the Jews, *came the first dominion ;* that is, there the kingdom of Christ was first set up, the *gospel of the kingdom* was first *preached* (Luke xxiv. 47), there Christ was first called *king of the Jews.*

II. This is illustrated by a prediction of the calamities of the literal Jerusalem, to which some favour and relief should be granted, as a type and figure of what God would do for the gospel-Jerusalem in the last days, notwithstanding its distresses. We have here,

1. Jerusalem put in pain by the providences of God. "She *cries out aloud,* that all her neighbours may take notice of her griefs, because there is *no king in her,* none of that honour and power she used ‘to have. Instead of ruling the nations, as she did when she *sat a queen,* she is ruled by them, and has become a captive. Her *counsellors* have *perished ;* she is no longer at her own disposal, but is given up to the will of her enemies, and is governed by their counsellors. *Pangs have taken her.*" (1.) She is carried captive to Babylon, and there is in pangs of grief. "She *goes forth out of the city,* and is constrained to *dwell in the field,* exposed to all

manner of inconveniences; she *goes even to Babylon,* and there wears out *seventy tedious* years in a miserable captivity, all that while *in pain, as a woman in travail,* waiting to be delivered, and thinking the time very long." (2.) When she is delivered out of Babylon, and redeemed from the hand of her enemies there, yet still she is in pangs of fear; the end of one trouble is but the beginning of another; for *now also,* when Jerusalem is in the rebuilding, *many nations are gathered against her, v.* 11. They were so in Ezra's and Nehemiah's time, and did all they could to obstruct the building of the temple and the wall. They were so in the time of the Maccabees; they said, *Let her be defiled;* let her be looked upon as a place polluted with sin, and be forsaken and abandoned both of God and man; let her holy places be profaned and all her honours laid in the dust; *let our eye look upon Zion,* and please itself with the sight of its ruins, as it is said of Edom (Obad. 12, *Thou shouldst not have looked upon the day of thy brother)* ; let our eyes see our desire upon Zion, the day we have long wished for. When they hear the enemies thus combine against them, and insult over them, no wonder that they are in pain, and cry aloud. *Without are fightings, within are fears.*

2 Jerusalem made easy by the promises of God: " *Why dost thou cry out aloud?* Let thy griefs and fears be silenced; indulge not thyself in them, for, though things are bad with thee, they shall end well; thy pangs are great, but they are like those of a *woman in travail* (*v.* 9). that *labours to bring forth* (*v.* 10), the issue of which will be good at last." Jerusalem's pangs are not as dying agonies, but as travailing throes, which after a while will be forgotten, for joy that a child is born into the world. Let the literal Jerusalem comfort herself with this, that, whatever straits she may be reduced to, she shall continue until the coming of the Messiah, for there his kingdom must be first set up, and she shall not be destroyed while that blessing is in her; and when at length she is ploughed as a field, and become heaps (as is threatened, *ch.* iii. 12), yet her privileges shall be resigned to the spiritual Jerusalem, and in that the promises made to her shall be fulfilled. Let Jerusalem be easy then, for, (1.) Her captivity in Babylon shall have an end, a happy end (*v.* 10): *There shalt thou be delivered, and the Lord shall redeem thee from the hand of thy enemies there.* This was done by Cyrus, who acted therein as God's servant; and that deliverance was typical of our redemption by Jesus Christ, and the release from our spiritual bondage which is proclaimed in the everlasting gospel, that *acceptable year of the Lord,* in which Christ himself preached *liberty to the captives, and the opening of the prison to those that were bound,* Luke iv. 18, 19. (2.) The designs of her enemies against her afterwards shall be

baffled, nay, they shall turn upon themselves, *v.* 12, 13. They promise themselves a day of it, but it shall prove *God's day.* They are *gathered against Zion,* to destroy it, but it shall prove to their own destruction, which Israel and Israel's God shall have the glory of. [1.] Their coming together against Zion shall be the occasion of their ruin. They *associate themselves, and gird themselves,* that they may break Jerusalem in pieces, but it will prove that they shall be *broken in pieces,* Isa. viii. 9. *They know not the thoughts of the Lord.* When they are gathering together, and Providence favours them in it, they little think what God is designing by it, nor do they understand his counsel; they know what they aim at in coming together, but they know not what God aims at in bringing them together; they aim at Zion's ruin, but God aims at theirs. Note, When men are made use of as instruments of Providence in accomplishing its purposes it is very common for them to intend one thing and for God to intend quite the contrary. The king of Assyria is to be a rod in God's hand for the correction of his people, in order to their reformation; *howbeit he means not so, nor does his heart think so,* Isa. x. 7. And thus it is here; the nations are gathered against Zion, as soldiers into the field, but God gathers them *as sheaves into the floor,* to be beaten to pieces; and they could not have been so easily, so effectually, destroyed, if they had not *gathered together against Zion.* Note, The designs of enemies for the ruin of the church often prove ruining to themselves; and thereby they prepare themselves for destruction and put themselves in the way of it; they are *snared in the work of their own hands.* [2.] Zion shall have the honour of being victorious over them, *v.* 13. When they are *gathered as sheaves into the floor,* to be trodden down, as the corn then was by the oxen, then, " *Arise, and thresh, O daughter of Zion!* instead of fearing them, and fleeing from them, boldly set upon them, and take the opportunity Providence favours thee with of trampling upon them. Plead not thy own weakness, and that thou art not a match for so many confederated enemies; God will make *thy horn iron,* to push them down, and *thy hoofs brass,* to tread upon them when they are down; and thus thou shalt *beat in pieces many people,* that have long been beating thee in pieces." Thus, when God pleases, the *daughter of Babylon is made a threshing floor (it is time to thresh her,* Jer. li. 33), and the *worm Jacob* is made *a threshing instrument,* with which God will *thresh the mountains, and make them as chaff,* Isa. xli. 14, 15. How strangely, how happily, are the tables turned, since Jacob was the threshing-floor and Babylon the threshing instrument! Isa. xxi. 10. Note, When God has conquering work for his people to do he will furnish them with strength and ability for it, will make the horn iron and the hoofs brass; and, when he does so, they must exert the power he gives them, and execute the commission; even the daughter of Zion must arise, and thresh. [3.] The glory of the victory shall redound to God. Zion shall thresh these sheaves in the floor, but the corn threshed out shall be a meat-offering at God's altar: *I will consecrate their gain unto the Lord* (that is, I will have it consecrated) and *their substance unto the Lord of the whole earth.* The spoils gained by Zion's victory shall be brought into the sanctuary, and devoted to God, either in part, as those of Midian (Num. xxxi. 28), or in whole, as those of Jericho, Josh. vi. 17. God is Jehovah, the fountain of being; he is the *Lord of the whole earth,* the fountain of power; and therefore he needs not any of our gain or substance, but may challenge and demand it all if he please; and with ourselves we must devote all we have to his honour, to be employed as he directs. Thus far all we have must have *holiness to the Lord* written upon it, all our gain and substance must be *consecrated to the Lord of the whole earth,* Isa. xxiii. 18. And extraordinary successes call for extraordinary acknowledgments, whether they be of spoils in war or gains in trade. It is God that *gives us power to get wealth,* which way soever it is honestly got, and therefore he must be honoured with what we get. Some make all this to point at the defeat of Sennacherib when he besieged Jerusalem, others to the destruction of Babylon, others to the successes of the Maccabees; but the learned Dr. Pocock and others think it had its full accomplishment in the spiritual victories obtained by the gospel of Christ over the powers of darkness that fought against it. The nations thought to ruin Christianity in its infancy, but it was victorious over them; those that persisted in their enmity were *broken to pieces* (Matt. xxi. 44), particularly the Jewish nation; but multitudes by divine grace were gained to the church, and they and their substance were consecrated to the Lord Jesus, *the Lord of the whole earth.*

CHAP. V.

In this chapter we have, I. A prediction of the troubles and distresses of the Jewish nation, ver. 1. II. A promise of the Messiah, and of his kingdom, to support the people of God in the day of these troubles. 1. Of the birth of the Messiah, ver. 2, 3. 2. Of his advancement, ver. 4. 3. Of his protection of his people, and his victory over his and their enemies, ver. 5, 6. 4. Of the great increase of the church, and the blessings that shall come to the world by it, ver. 7. 5. Of the destruction of the enemies of the church, both those without, that attack it, and those within, that expose it, ver. 8—15.

NOW gather thyself in troops, O daughter of troops: he hath laid siege against us: they shall smite the judge of Israel with a rod upon the cheek. 2 But thou, Beth-lehem Ephratah, *though* thou be little among the thousands of Judah, *yet* out of thee shall he come forth unto me *that*

is to be ruler in Israel; whose doings forth *have been* from of old, from everlasting. 3 Therefore will he give them up, until the time *that* she which travaileth hath brought forth: then the remnant of his brethren shall return unto the children of Israel. 4 And he shall stand and feed in the strength of the LORD, in the majesty of the name of the LORD his God; and they shall abide: for now shall he be great unto the ends of the earth. 5 And this *man* shall be the peace, when the Assyrian shall come into our land: and when he shall tread in our palaces, then shall we raise against him seven shepherds, and eight principal men. 6 And they shall waste the land of Assyria with the sword, and the land of Nimrod in the entrances thereof: thus shall he deliver *us* from the Assyrian, when he cometh into our land, and when he treadeth within our borders.

Here, as before, we have,

I. The abasement and distress of Zion, *v.* 1. The Jewish nation, for many years before the captivity, dwindled, and fell into disgrace: *Now gather thyself in troops, O daughter of troops!* It is either a summons to Zion's enemies, that had troops at their service, to come and do their worst against her (God will suffer them to do it), or a challenge to Zion's friends, that had troops too at command, to come and do their best for her; let them *gather in troops,* yet it shall be to no purpose; for, says the prophet, in the name of the inhabitants of Jerusalem, *He has laid siege against us;* the king of Assyria has, the king of Babylon has, and we know not which way to defend ourselves; so that the enemies shall gain their point, and prevail so far as *to smite the judge of Israel*—the king, the chief justice, and the other inferior judges—*with a rod upon the cheek,* in contempt of them and their dignity; having made them prisoners, they shall use them as shamefully as any of the common captives. Complaint had been made of the judges of Israel (*ch.* iii. 11) that they were corrupt and took bribes, and this disgrace came justly upon them for abusing their power; yet it was a great calamity to Israel to have their judges treated thus ignominiously. Some make this the reason why the troops (that is, the Roman army) shall lay siege to Jerusalem, because the Jews *shall smite the judge of Israel upon the cheek,* because of the indignities they shall do to the Messiah, the Judge of Israel, whom they smote on the cheek, saying, *Prophesy, who smote thee.* But the former sense seems more probable, and that it is meant of the besieging of Jerusalem, not by the Romans, but the Chaldeans, and was fulfilled in the indignities done to king Zedekiah and the princes of the house of David.

II. The advancement of Zion's King. Having shown how low the house of David should be brought, and how vilely the shield of that mighty family should be cast away, as though it had not been anointed with oil, to encourage the faith of God's people, who might be tempted now to think that his covenant with David and his house was abrogated (according to the psalmist's complaint, Ps. lxxxix. 38, 39), he adds an illustrious prediction of the Messiah and his kingdom, in whom that covenant should be established, and the honours of that house should be revived, advanced, and perpetuated. Now let us see,

1. How the Messiah is here described. It is he that is to be *ruler in Israel, whose goings forth have been from of old, from everlasting,* from the *days of eternity,* as the word is. Here we have, (1.) His existence from eternity, as God: *His goings forth,* or *emanations,* as the going forth of the beams from the sun, were, or have been, *of old, from everlasting,* which (says Dr. Pocock) is so signal a description of Christ's eternal generation, or his going forth as the Son of God, begotten of his Father before all worlds, that this prophecy must belong only to him, and could never be verified of any other. It certainly speaks of a going forth that was now past, when the prophet spoke, and cannot but be read, as we read it, his *outgoings have been;* and the putting of both these words together, which severally are used to denote eternity, plainly shows that they must here be taken in the strictest sense (the same with Ps. xc. 2, *From everlasting to everlasting thou art God*), and can be applied to no other than to him who was able to say, *Before Abraham was, I am,* John viii. 58. Dr. Pocock observes that the *going forth* is used (Deut. viii. 3) for a *word* which *proceeds out of the mouth,* and is therefore very fitly used to signify the eternal generation of him who is called the *Word of God,* that was *in the beginning with God,* John i. 1, 2. (2.) His office as Mediator; he was to be *ruler in Israel,* king of his church; he was to *reign over the house of Jacob for ever,* Luke i. 32, 33. The Jews object that our Lord Jesus could not be the Messiah, for he was so far from being ruler in Israel that Israel ruled over him, and put him to death, and would not have him to reign over them; but he answered that himself when he said, *My kingdom is not of this world,* John xviii. 36. And it is a spiritual Israel that he reigns over, the children of promise, all the followers of believing Abraham and praying Jacob. In the hearts of these he reigns by his Spirit and grace, and in the society of

these by his word and ordinances. And was not he *ruler in Israel* whom winds and seas obeyed, to whom legions of devils were forced to submit, and who commanded away diseases from the sick and called the dead out of their graves? None but he whose *goings forth were from of old, from everlasting,* was fit to be *ruler in Israel,* to be head of the church, and *head over all things to the church.*

2. What is here foretold concerning him.

(1.) That Bethlehem should be the place of his nativity, *v.* 2. This was the scripture which the scribes went upon when with the greatest assurance they told Herod *where Christ should be born* (Matt. ii. 6), and hence it was universally known among the Jews that *Christ should come out of the town of Bethlehem where David was,* John vii. 42. *Beth-lehem* signifies *the house of bread,* the fittest place for him to be born in who is *the bread of life.* And, because it was the city of David, by a special providence it was ordered that he should be born there who was to be the *Son of David,* and his heir and successor for ever. It is called *Bethlehem-Ephratah,* both names of the same city, as appears Gen. xxxv. 19. It was *little among the thousands of Judah,* not considerable either for the number of the inhabitants or the figure they made; it had nothing in it worthy to have this honour put upon it; but God in that, as in other instances, chose to *exalt those of low degree,* Luke i. 52. Christ would give honour to the place of his birth, and not derive honour from it: *Though thou be little,* yet this shall make thee great, and, as St. Matthew reads it, Thou *art not the least among the princes of Judah,* but upon this account art really honourable above any of them. A relation to Christ will magnify those that are little in the world.

(2.) That in the fulness of time he should be born of a woman (*v.* 3): *Therefore will he give them up;* he will give up his people Israel to distress and trouble, and will defer their salvation, which has been so long promised and expected, *until the time,* the set time, *that she who travails has brought forth,* or (as it should be read) *that she who shall bring forth shall have brought forth,* that the blessed virgin, who was to be the mother of the Messiah, shall have brought him forth at Bethlehem, the place appointed. This Dr. Pocock thinks to be the most genuine sense of the words. Though the out-goings of the Messiah were *from everlasting,* yet the *redemption in Jerusalem,* the *consolation of Israel,* must be *waited for* (Luke ii. 25—38) until the time that *she who should bring forth* (so the virgin Mary is called, as Christ is himself called, *He that shall come*) shall *bring forth;* and in the mean time *he will give them up.* Divine salvations must be waited for until the time fixed for the bringing of them forth.

(3.) That *the remnant of his brethren shall*

then return to the children of Israel. The remnant of the Jewish nation shall return to the spirit of the true genuine children of Israel, a people in covenant with God; the hearts of the children shall be turned to the fathers, Mal. iv. 6. Some understand it of all believers, Gentiles as well as Jews; they shall all be incorporated into the commonwealth of Israel; and, as they are all brethren to one another, so *he is not ashamed to call them brethren,* Heb. ii. 11.

(4.) That he shall be a glorious prince, and his subjects shall be happy under his government (*v.* 4): *He shall stand and feed,* that is, he shall both teach and rule, and continue to do so, as a good shepherd, with wisdom, and care, and love. So it was foretold. *He shall feed his flock like a shepherd,* shall provide green pastures for them, and under-shepherds to lead them into these pastures. He is the *good shepherd* that *goes before the sheep,* and presides among them. He shall do this, not as an ordinary man, but *in the strength of the Lord,* as one clothed with a divine power to go through his work, and break through the difficulties in his way, so as not to *fail,* or be *discouraged;* he shall do it *in the majesty of the name of the Lord his God,* so as plainly to evidence that *God's name was in him* (Exod. xxiii. 21) the majesty of his name, for *he taught as one having authority and not as the scribes.* The prophets prefaced their messages with, *Thus saith the Lord;* but Christ spoke, not as a servant, but as a Son—*Verily, verily, I say unto you.* This was feeding *in the majesty of the name of the Lord his God. All power was given him in heaven and in earth,* a *power over all flesh,* by virtue of which he still rules *in the majesty of the name of the Lord his God,* a name above every name. Christ's government shall be, [1.] Very happy for his subjects, for *they shall abide;* they shall be safe and easy, and continue so for ever. *Because he lives, they shall live also.* They shall lie down in the green pastures to which he shall lead them, *shall abide in God's tabernacle for ever,* Ps. lxi. 4. His church shall abide, and he in it, and with it, always, even to the end of the world. [2.] It shall be very glorious to himself: *Now shall he be great to the ends of the earth.* Now that he stands and feeds his flock, *now shall he be great.* For Christ reckons it his greatness to do good. Now he shall be *great to the ends of the earth,* for the uttermost parts of the earth shall be given him for his possession, and the ends of the world shall see his salvation.

(5) That he shall secure the peace and welfare of his church and people against all the attempts of his and their enemies (*v.* 5, 6): *This man,* as king and ruler, *shall be the peace when the Assyrians shall come into our land.* This refers to the deliverance of Hezekiah and his kingdom from the power of Sennacherib, who invaded them, in the

1324

type; but, under the shadow of that, it is a promise of the safety of the gospel-church and of all believers from the designs and attempts of the powers of darkness, Satan and all his instruments, the dragon and his angels, that seek to devour the church of the first-born and all that belong to it. Observe, [1.] The peril and danger which Christ's subjects are supposed to be in. The Assyrian, a potent enemy, *comes into their land* (*v.* 5, 6), *treads within their borders,* nay, prevails so far as to *tread in their palaces;* it was a time of *treading down and of perplexity* when Sennacherib made a descent upon Judah, took all the defenced cities, and laid siege to Jerusalem, Isa. xxxvi. 1; xxxvii. 3. This represented the gates of hell fighting against the kingdom of Christ, *encompassing the camp of the saints and of the holy city,* and threatening to bear down all before them. When the terrors of the law set themselves in array against a convinced soul, when the temptations of Satan assault the people of God, and the troubles of the world threaten to rob them of all their comforts, then the *Assyrian comes into their land* and treads in their palaces. *Without are fightings, within are fears.* [2.] The protection and defence which his subjects are then sure to be under. *First,* Christ will himself be *their peace.* When the Assyrian comes with such a force into a land, can there be any other peace than a tame submission and an unresisted desolation? Yes, even then the church's King will be the conservator of the church's peace, will be *for a hiding-place,* Isa. xxxii. 1, 2. Christ is our peace as a priest, making atonement for sin, and reconciling us to God; and he is our peace as a king, conquering our enemies and commanding down disquieting fears and passions; he *creates the fruit of the lips, peace.* Even when the Assyrian comes into the land, when we are in the greatest distress and danger and have received a sentence of death within ourselves, yet *this man may be the peace. In me,* says Christ, *you shall have peace,* when *in the world you have tribulation;* at such a time our souls may dwell at ease in him. *Secondly,* He will find out proper instruments to be employed for their protection and deliverance, and the defeat of their enemies: *Then shall we raise against him seven shepherds and eight principal men,* that is, a competent number of persons, proper to oppose the enemy, and make head against him, and protect the church of God in peace, men that shall have the care and tenderness of shepherds and the courage and authority of *principal men,* or *princes of men. Seven* and *eight* are a certain number for an uncertain. Note, When God has work to do he will not want fitting instruments to do it with; and when he pleases he can do it by a few; he needs not raise thousands, but seven or eight principal men may serve the turn if God be with them. Magistrates and ministers are shepherds and principal men, raised in defence of religion's righteous cause against the powers of sin and Satan in the world. *Thirdly,* The opposition given to the church shall be got over, and the opposers brought down. This is represented by the laying of Assyria and Chaldea waste, which two nations were the most formidable enemies to the Israel of God of any, and the destruction of them signified the making of Christ's enemies his footstool: *They shall waste the land of Assyria with the sword, and the land of Nimrod in the entrances thereof;* they shall make inroads upon the land, and put to the sword all that they find in arms. Note, Those that threaten ruin to the church of God hasten ruin to themselves; and their destruction is the church's salvation: *Thus shall he deliver us from the Assyrian.* When *Satan fell as lightning from heaven* before the preaching of the gospel, and Christ's enemies, that would not have him to reign over them, were *slain before him,* then this was fulfilled.

7 And the remnant of Jacob shall be in the midst of many people as a dew from the LORD, as the showers upon the grass, that tarrieth not for man, nor waiteth for the sons of men. 8 And the remnant of Jacob shall be among the Gentiles in the midst of many people as a lion among the beasts of the forest, as a young lion among the flocks of sheep : who, if he go through, both treadeth down, and teareth in pieces, and none can deliver. 9 Thine hand shall be lifted up upon thine adversaries, and all thine enemies shall be cut off. 10 And it shall come to pass in that day, saith the LORD, that I will cut off thy horses out of the midst of thee, and I will destroy thy chariots : 11 And I will cut off the cities of thy land, and throw down all thy strong holds : 12 And I will cut off witchcrafts out of thine hand; and thou shalt have no *more* soothsayers : 13 Thy graven images also will I cut off, and thy standing images out of the midst of thee; and thou shalt no more worship the work of thine hands. 14 And I will pluck up thy groves out of the midst of thee: so will I destroy thy cities. 15 And I will execute vengeance in anger and fury upon the heathen, such as they have not heard.

Glorious things are here spoken of *the*

remnant of Jacob, that remnant which was raised of *her that halted* (*ch.* iv. 7), and it seems to be that *remnant which the Lord our God shall call* (Joel ii. 32), on whom the Spirit shall be poured out, the remnant that shall be saved, Rom. ix. 27. Note, God's people are but a remnant, a small number in comparison with the many that are left to perish, a *little flock;* but they are *the remnant of Jacob,* a people in covenant with God, and in his favour. Now concerning this remnant it is here promised,

I. That they shall be *as a dew* in the midst of the nations, *v.* 7. God's church is dispersed all the world over; it is *in the midst of many people,* as gold in the ore, wheat in the heap. Israel according to the flesh dwelt alone, and was not numbered among the nations ; but the spiritual Israel lies scattered *in the midst of many people,* as the *salt of the earth,* or as seed sown in the ground, here a grain and there a grain, Hos. ii 23. Now this remnant shall be *as dew from the Lord.* 1. They shall be of a heavenly extraction; as *dew from the Lord,* who is the *Father of the rain,* and has *begotten the drops of the dew,* Job xxxviii. 28. They are *born from above,* and are not of the earth, savouring the things of the earth. 2. They shall be numerous as the drops of dew in a summer's morning. Ps. cx. 3, *Thou hast the dew of thy youth.* 3. They shall be pure and clear, not muddy and corrupt, but crystal drops, as the *water of life.* 4. They shall be produced silently and without noise, as the dew that distils insensibly, we know not how; such is the way of the Spirit. 5. They shall live in a continual dependence upon God, and be still deriving from him, as the dew, which *tarries not for man,* nor *waits for the sons of men;* they shall not rely upon human aids and powers, but on divine grace, for they are, and own that they are, no more than what the free grace of God makes them every day. 6. They shall be great blessings to those among whom they live, as the dew and the showers are to the grass, to make it grow without the help of man, or the sons of men. Their doctrine, example, and prayers, shall make them as dew, to soften and moisten others, and make them fruitful. Their speech shall *distil as the dew* (Deut. xxxii. 2), and all about them shall *wait for them as for the rain,* Job xxix. 23. The people among whom they live shall be as the grass, which flourishes only by the blessing of God, and not by the art and care of man; they shall be beneficial to those about them by drawing down God's blessings on them, as Jacob on Laban's house, and by cooling and mitigating God's wrath, which otherwise would burn them up, as the dew preserves the grass from being scorched by the sun; so Dr. Pocock; they shall be mild and gentle in their behaviour, like their Master, who comes down *like rain upon the new-mown grass,* Ps. lxxii. 6.

II. That they shall be *as a lion among the beasts of the forest,* that *treads down and tears in pieces, v.* 8. As they shall be silent, and gentle, and communicative of all good, to those that receive the truth in the love of it, so they shall be bold as a lion in witnessing against the corruptions of the times and places they live in, and strong as a lion, in the strength of God, to resist and overcome their spiritual enemies. The *weapons of their warfare are mighty, through God, to the pulling down of strongholds,* 2 Cor. x. 4, 5. They shall have *courage which all their adversaries shall not be able to resist* (Luke xxi. 15), as when the lion tears none can deliver. When infidelity is silenced, and all iniquity made *to stop her mouth,* when sinners are convinced and converted by the power of the gospel, in the doctrine of its ministers and the conversation of its professors, then the remnant of Jacob is like a lion. This is explained, *v.* 9, *Thy hand shall be lifted up upon thy adversaries;* the church shall have the upper hand at last of all that oppose her. Her *enemies shall be cut off;* they shall cease to be enemies; their enmity shall be cut off. Christ's arrows of conviction shall be sharp in their hearts, so that they shall fall under him; they shall yield themselves subjects to him (Ps. xlv. 5) and be happily conquered and subdued, Ps. cx. 2.

III. That they shall be brought off from all carnal confidences, which they have relied on, that by the providence of God they shall enjoy such a security that they shall not need them, and by the grace of God they shall be brought to see the folly of them and come off from them. It was the sin of Israel that they furnished themselves extravagantly with *horses and chariots,* and were *soothsayers* and *idolaters;* see Isa. ii. 6—8. But here it is promised that they shall not regard them any more. The tranquillity of the kingdom of Christ is intended in that promise, which explains this, Zech. ix. 10, *I will cut off the chariot from Ephraim and the horse from Jerusalem.* Note,. It is a great mercy to be deprived of those things in which we have reposed a confidence in competition with God, which we have made our arm, and after which we have gone a whoring from God. Let us observe the particulars: —1. They had trusted in chariots and horses, and multiplied them (Ps. xx. 7); but now God will *cut off their horses,* and *destroy their chariots* (*v.* 10), as *David houghed the chariot-horses,* 2 Sam. viii. 4. They shall not have them, lest they should be tempted to trust in them. 2. They depended upon their strongholds, and fortified cities, for their security; but God will take care that they be demolished (*v.* 11): *I will cut off the cities of thy land;* I will *throw down thy strongholds.* They shall have them for habitations, but not for garrisons, for God will be their only place of defence, their *high tower,* and *their deliverer.* 3. Many of them

depended much upon the conduct and advice of their conjurors, diviners, and fortune-tellers; and those God will cut off, not only as weak things, and insufficient to relieve them, but as wicked things, and sufficient to ruin them (*v.* 12): "*I will cut off witchcrafts out of thy hand,* that thou shalt no more take hold of them, and stay thyself upon them, and *thou shalt have no more soothsayers,* for thou shalt be convinced that all their pretensions are a cheat." The justice of the nation shall cut them off according to law, Lev. xx. 27. The preaching of the gospel brought men off from using curious arts, Acts xix. 19. 4. Many of them had said to the work of their hands, *You are our gods:* but now idolatry shall be abolished and abandoned (*v.* 13): "*Thy graven images will I cut off, and thy standing images,* both those that were movable and those that were fixed; they shall be destroyed by the power of the law of Moses and deserted by the power of the gospel of Christ, so that *thou shalt no more worship the work of thy hands,* but be ashamed that ever thou hast been so deluded. Among other monuments of idolatry, *I will pluck up thy groves out of the midst of thee," v.* 14. These were planted and preserved in honour of their idols, and used in the worship of them; these they were ordered to burn (Deut. xii. 2, 3), and, if they do not, God will, so that they shall not have them to trust to. And so *will I destroy their cities,* meaning the cities that were dedicated to the idols, to some dunghill-deity or other, which they confided in for their protection.

IV. That those who stand it out against the gospel of Christ, and continue in league with their idolatries and witchcrafts, shall fall under the wrath of God, and be consumed by it (*v.* 15): *I will execute vengeance in anger and fury upon the heathen* (that is, upon heathenism), *such as they have not heard;* idolatries shall be done away, and idolaters put to shame. I will execute vengeance upon the heathen *who have not heard* (so some read it), or who would not hear and receive the doctrine of Christ. God will give his Son either the hearts or the necks of his enemies, and make them either his friends or his footstool.

CHAP. VI.

After the precious promises in the two foregoing chapters, relating to the Messiah's kingdom, the prophet is here directed to set the sins of Israel in order before them, for their conviction and humiliation, as necessary to make way for the comfort of gospel-grace. Christ's forerunner was a reprover, and preached repentance, and so prepared his way. Here, I. God enters an action against his people for their base ingratitude, and the bad returns they had made him for his favours, ver. 1—5. II. He shows the wrong course they took when they were under conviction, and the frivolous proposals they made, in answer to his charge, and what course they should have taken, ver. 6—8. III. He calls upon them to hear the voice of his judgments, and sets the sins in order before them for which he still proceeded in his controversy with them (ver. 9), their injustice (ver. 10—15), and their idolatry (ver. 16), for both which ruin was coming upon them.

HEAR ye now what the LORD saith; Arise, contend thou before the mountains, and let the hills hear thy voice. 2 Hear ye, O mountains, the LORD's controversy, and ye strong foundations of the earth: for the LORD hath a controversy with his people, and he will plead with Israel. 3 O my people, what have I done unto thee? and wherein have I wearied thee? testify against me. 4 For I brought thee up out of the land of Egypt, and redeemed thee out of the house of servants; and I sent before thee Moses, Aaron, and Miriam. 5 O my people, remember now what Balak king of Moab consulted, and what Balaam the son of Beor answered him from Shittim unto Gilgal; that ye may know the righteousness of the LORD.

Here, I. The prefaces to the message are very solemn and such as may engage our most serious attention. 1. The people are commanded to give audience: *Hear you now what the Lord says.* What the prophet speaks he speaks from God, and in his name; they are therefore bound to hear it, not as the word of a sinful dying man, but of the holy living God. *Hear now* what he saith, for, first or last, he will be heard. 2. The prophet is commanded to speak in earnest, and to put an emphasis upon what he said: *Arise, contend thou before the mountains,* or *with the mountains, and let the hills hear thy voice,* if it were possible; contend with the mountains and hills of Judea, that is, with the inhabitants of those mountains and hills; and, some think, reference is had to those mountains and hills on which they worshipped idols and which were thus polluted. But it is rather to be taken more generally, as appears by his call, not only to the mountains, but to the *strong foundations of the earth,* pursuant to the instructions given him. This is designed, (1.) To excite the earnestness of the prophet; he must speak as vehemently as if he designed to make even the hills and mountains hear him, must *cry aloud, and not spare;* what he had to say in God's name he must proclaim publicly before the mountains, as one that was neither ashamed nor afraid to own his message; he must speak as one concerned, as one that desired to speak to the heart, and therefore appeared to speak from the heart. (2.) To expose the stupidity of the people; "*Let the hills hear thy voice,* for this senseless careless people will not hear it, will not heed it. Let the rocks, the *foundations of the earth,* that have no ears, hear, since Israel, that has ears, will not hear." It is an appeal to the mountains and hills; let them bear witness that Israel has fair warning given them, and good counsel, if they would but take it. Thus Isaiah begins with, *Hear, O heavens! and give ear, O earth!* Let them *judge between God and his vineyard.*

II. The message itself is very affecting. He is to let all the world know that God has a quarrel with his people, good ground for an action against them. Their offences are public, and therefore so are the articles of impeachment exhibited against them. Take notice *the Lord has a controversy with his people and he will plead with Israel,* will plead by his prophets, plead by his providences, to make good his charge. Note, 1. Sin begets a controversy between God and man. The righteous God has an action against every sinner, an action of debt, an action of trespass, an action of slander. 2. If Israel, God's own professing people, provoke him by sin, he will let them know that he has a controversy with them; he sees sin in them, and is displeased with it, nay, their sins are more displeasing to him than the sins of others, as they are a greater grief to his Spirit and dishonour to his name. 3. God will plead with those whom he has a controversy with, will plead with his people Israel, that they may be convinced and that he may be justified. In the close of the foregoing chapter he pleaded with the heathen in anger and fury, to bring them to ruin; but here he pleads with Israel in compassion and tenderness, to bring them to repentance, *Come now, and let us reason together.* God reasons with us, to teach us to reason with ourselves. See the equity of God's cause, it will bear to be pleaded, and sinners themselves will be forced to confess judgment, and to own that *God's ways are equal,* but their *ways are unequal,* Ezek. xviii. 25. Now, (1.) God here challenges them to show what he had done against them which might give them occasion to desert him. They had revolted from God and rebelled against him; but had they any cause to do so? (*v.* 3): "*O my people! what have I done unto thee? Wherein have I wearied thee?* If subjects quit their allegiance to their prince, they will pretend, as the ten tribes did when they revolted from Rehoboam) that his yoke is too heavy for them; but can you pretend any such thing? *What have I done to you* that is unjust or unkind? *Wherein have I wearied you* with the impositions of service or the exactions of tribute? *Have I made you to serve with an offering?* Isa. xliii. 23. *What iniquity have your fathers found in me?* Jer. ii. 5. He never deceived us, nor disappointed our expectations from him, never did us wrong, nor put disgrace upon us; why then do we wrong and dishonour him, and frustrate his expectations from us? Here is a challenge to all that ever were in God's service to testify against him if they have found him, in any thing, a hard Master, or if they have found his demands unreasonable. (2.) Since they could not show any thing that he had done against them, he will show them a great deal that he has done for them, which should have engaged them for ever to his service, v. 4, 5. They are here directed, and we in them, to look a great way back in their reviews of the divine favour; let them remember their former days, their first days, when they were formed into a people, and the great things God did for them, [1.] When he brought them out of Egypt, the land of their bondage, v. 4. They were content with their slavery, and almost in love with their chains, for the sake of the garlic and onions they had plenty of; but God *brought them up*, inspired them with an ambition of liberty and animated them with a resolution by a bold effort to shake off their fetters. The Egyptians held them fast, and would not let the people go; but God *redeemed them*, not by price, but by force, *out of the house of servants*, or, rather, *the house of bondage*, for it is the same word that is used in the preface to the ten commandments, which insinuates that the considerations which are arguments for duty, if they be not improved by us, will be improved against us as aggravations of sin. When he brought them out of Egypt into a vast howling wilderness, as he left not himself without witness, so he left not them without guides, for he sent before them *Moses, Aaron, and Miriam, three prophets* (says the Chaldee paraphrase), Moses the great prophet of the Old Testament, Aaron his prophet (Exod. vii. 1), and Miriam a prophetess, Exod. xv. 20. Note, When we are calling to mind God's former mercies to us we must not forget the mercy of good teachers and governors when we were young; let those be made mention of, to tne glory of God, who went before us, saying, *This is the way, walk in it;* it was God that sent them before us, to prepare the way of the Lord and to prepare a people for him. [2.] When he brought them into Canaan. God no less glorified himself, and honoured them, in what he did for them when he brought them into the land of their rest than in what he did for them when he brought them out of the land of their servitude. When Moses, Aaron, and Miriam, were dead, yet they found God the same. Let them remember now what God did for them, *First*, In baffling and defeating the designs of Balak and Balaam against them, which he did by the power he has over the hearts and tongues of men, v. 5. Let them remember *what Balak the king of Moab consulted*, what mischief he devised and designed to do to Israel, when they encamped in the plains of Moab; that which he consulted was to *curse Israel*, to divide between them and their God, and to disengage him from the protection of them. Among the heathen, when they made war upon any people, they endeavoured by magic charms or otherwise to get from them their tutelar gods, as to rob Troy of its Palladium. Macrobius has a chapter *de ritu*

1328

evocandi Deos—concerning the solemnity of calling out the gods. Balak would try this against Israel; but remember *what Balaam the son of Beor answered him*, how contrary to his own intention and inclination; instead of cursing Israel, he blessed them, to the extreme confusion and vexation of Balak. Let them remember the malice of the heathen against them, and for that reason never *learn the way of the heathen,* nor associate with them. Let them remember the kindness of their God to them, how he *turned the curse into a blessing (because the Lord thy God loved thee,* as it is, Deut. xxiii. 5), and for that reason never forsake him. Note, The disappointing of the devices of the church's enemies ought always to be remembered to the glory of the church's protector, who can make *the answer of the tongue* directly to contradict the preparation and consultation of the heart, Prov. xvi. 1. *Secondly,* In bringing them *from Shittim,* their last lodgment out of Canaan, *unto Gilgal,* their first lodgment in Canaan. There it was, between Shittim and Gilgal, that, upon the death of Moses, Joshua, a type of Christ, was raised up to put Israel in possession of the land of promise and to fight their battles; there it was that they passed over Jordan through the divided waters, and renewed the covenant of circumcision; these mercies of God to their fathers they must now remember, that they may *know the righteousness of the Lord, his righteousness* (so the word is), his justice in destroying the Canaanites, his goodness in giving rest to his people Israel, and his faithfulness to his promise made unto the fathers. The remembrance of what God had done to them might convince them of all this, and engage them for ever to his service. Or they may refer to the controversy now pleaded between God and Israel; let them remember God's many favours to them and their fathers, and compare with them their unworthy ungrateful conduct towards him, *that they may know the righteousness of the Lord* in contending with them, and it may appear that in this controversy he has right on his side; his ways are equal, for he will be *justified when he speaks,* and *clear when he judges.*

6 Wherewith shall I come before the LORD, *and* bow myself before the high God? shall I come before him with burnt-offerings, with calves of a year old? 7 Will the LORD be pleased with thousands of rams, *or* with ten thousands of rivers of oil? shall I give my first-born *for* my transgression, the fruit of my body *for* the sin of my soul? 8 He hath showed thee, O man, what *is* good; and what doth the LORD require of thee, but to do justly, and to love

mercy, and to walk humbly with thy God?

Here is the proposal for accommodation between God and Israel, the parties that were at variance in the beginning of the chapter. Upon the trial, judgment is given against Israel; they are convicted of injustice and ingratitude towards God, the crimes with which they stood charged. Their guilt is too plain to be denied, too great to be excused, and therefore,

I. They express their desires to be at peace with God upon any terms (*v.* 6, 7): *Wherewith shall I come before the Lord?* Being made sensible of the justice of God's controversy with them, and dreading the consequences of it, they were inquisitive what they might do to be reconciled to God and to make him their friend. They apply to a proper person, with this enquiry, to the prophet, the Lord's messenger, by whose ministry they had been convinced. Who so fit to show them their way as he that had made them sensible of their having missed it? And it is observable that each one speaks for himself: *Wherewith shall I come?* Knowing every one the plague of his own heart, they ask, not, *What shall this man do?* But, *What shall I do?* Note, Deep convictions of guilt and wrath will put men upon careful enquiries after peace and pardon, and then, and not till then, there begins to be some hope of them. They enquire *wherewith they may come before the Lord, and bow themselves before the high God.* They believe there is a God, that he is Jehovah, and that he is the *high God,* the *Most High.* Those whose consciences are convinced learn to speak very honourably of God, whom before they spoke slightly of. Now, 1. We know we must *come before God;* he is the God with whom *we have to do;* we must come as subjects, to pay our homage to him, as beggars, to ask alms from him, nay, we must *come before him,* as criminals, to receive our doom from him, must come before him as our Judge. 2. When we come before him we must *bow before him;* it is our duty to be very humble and reverent in our approaches to him; and, when we come before him, there is no remedy but we must submit; it is to no purpose to contend with him. 3. When we come and bow before him it is our great concern to find favour with him, and to be accepted of him; their enquiry is, *What will the Lord be pleased with?* Note, All that rightly understand their own interest cannot but be solicitous what they must do to please God, to avoid his displeasure and to obtain his good-will. 4. In order to God's being pleased with us, our care must be that the sin by which we have displeased him may be taken away, and an atonement made for it. The enquiry here is, *What shall I give for my transgression, for the sin of my soul?* Note, The transgression we are

guilty of is the sin of our soul, for the soul acts it (without the soul's act it is not sin) and the soul suffers by it; it is the disorder, disease, and defilement of the soul, and threatens to be the death of it: *What shall I give for my transgressions?* What will be accepted as a satisfaction to his justice, a reparation of his honour? And what will avail to shelter me from his wrath? 5. We must therefore ask, *Wherewith may we come before him?* We must not appear before the Lord empty. What shall we bring with us? In what manner must we come? In whose name must we come? We have not that in ourselves which will recommend us to him, but must have it from another. What righteousness then shall we appear before him in?

II. They make proposals, such as they are, in order to it. Their enquiry was very good and right, and what we are all concerned to make, but their proposals betray their ignorance, though they show their zeal; let us examine them:—

1. They bid high. They offer, (1.) That which is very rich and costly—*thousands of rams.* God required one ram for a sin-offering; they proffer flocks of them, their whole stock, will be content to make themselves beggars, so that they may but be at peace with God. They will bring the best they have, the rams, and the most of them, till it comes to thousands. (2.) That which is very dear to them, and which they would be most loth to part with. They could be content to part with *their first-born for their transgressions,* if that would be accepted as an atonement, and the *fruit of their body for the sin of their soul.* To those that had become *vain in their imaginations* this seemed a probable expedient of making satisfaction for sin, because our children are pieces of ourselves; and therefore the heathen sacrificed their children, to appease their offended deities. Note, Those that are thoroughly convinced of sin, of the malignity of it, and of their misery and danger by reason of it, would give all the world, if they had it, for peace and pardon.

2. Yet they do not bid right. It is true some of these things were instituted by the ceremonial law, as the bringing of burnt-offerings to God's altar, and calves of a year old, rams for sin-offerings, and oil for the meat-offerings; but these alone would not recommend them to God. God had often declared that *to obey is better than sacrifice,* and to *hearken than the fat of rams,* that *sacrifice* and *offering he would not;* the legal sacrifices had their virtue and value from the institution, and the reference they had to Christ the great propitiation; but otherwise, of themselves, it was *impossible that the blood of bulls and goats should take away sin.* And as to the other things here mentioned, (1.) Some of them are impracticable things, as *rivers of oil,* which nature has not provided to feed men's luxury, but rivers of water to

supply men's necessity. All the proposals of peace but those that are according to the gospel are absurd. One stream of the blood of Christ is worth ten thousand rivers of oil. (2.) Some of them are wicked things, as to give our *first-born* and the *fruit of our body* to death, which would but add to the transgression and the *sin of the soul*. He that hates robbery for burnt-offerings much more hates murder, such murder. What right have we to our *first-born* and the *fruit of our body?* Do they not belong to God? Are they not his already, and born to him? Are they not sinners by nature, and their lives forfeited upon their own account? How then can they be a ransom for ours? (3.) They are all external things, parts of that bodily exercise which profiteth little, and which could not *make the comers thereunto perfect*. (4.) They are all insignificant, and insufficient to attain the end proposed; they could not answer the demands of divine justice, nor satisfy the wrong done to God in his honour by sin, nor would they serve in lieu of the sanctification of the heart and the reformation of the life. Men will part with any thing rather than their sins, but they part with nothing to God's acceptance unless they part with them.

III. God tells them plainly what he demands, and insists upon, from those that would be accepted of him, *v.* 8. Let their money perish with them that think the pardon of sin and the favour of God may be so purchased; no, *God has shown thee, O man! what is good.* Here we are told,

1. That God has made a discovery of his mind and will to us, for the rectifying of our mistakes and the directing of our practice. (1.) It is God himself that has shown us what we must do. We need not trouble ourselves to make proposals, the terms are already settled and laid down. He whom we have offended, and to whom we are accountable, has told us upon what conditions he will be reconciled to us. (2.) It is to man that he has shown it, not only to thee, *O Israel!* but *to thee, O man!* Gentiles as well as Jews—to men, who are rational creatures, and capable of receiving the discovery, and not to brutes,—to men, for whom a remedy is provided, not to devils, whose case is desperate. What is spoken to *all men every where* in general, must by faith be applied to ourselves in particular, as if it were spoken *to thee, O man!* by name, and to no other. (3.) It is a discovery of *that which is good,* and which *the Lord requires of us.* He has shown us our end, which we should aim at, in showing us what is good, wherein our true happiness does consist; he has shown us our way in which we must walk towards that end in showing us what he requires of us. There is something which God requires we should do for him and devote to him; and it is good. It is good in itself; there is an innate goodness in moral duties, antecedent

1330

to the command; they are not, as ceremonial observances, good because they are commanded, but commanded because they are good, consonant to the eternal rule and reason of good and evil, which are unalterable. It has likewise a direct tendency to our good; our conformity to it is not only the condition of our future happiness, but is a great expedient of our present happiness; *in keeping* God's *commandments there is a great reward,* as well as after keeping them. (4.) It is shown us. God has not only made it known, but made it plain; he has discovered it to us with such convincing evidence as amounts to a demonstration. *Lo this, we have searched it, so it is.*

2. What that discovery is. The good which God requires of us is not the paying of a price for the pardon of sin and acceptance with God, but doing the duty which is the condition of our interest in the pardon purchased. (1.) We must *do justly,* must *render to all their due,* according as our relation and obligation to them are; we must do wrong to none, but do right to all, in their bodies, goods, and good name. (2.) We must *love mercy,* not only be just to all we deal with, but kind to all that need us, and that we are in a capacity of doing good to. Nor must we only show mercy, but we must *love mercy ;* we must delight in it, as our God does, must be glad of an opportunity to do good, and do it cheerfully. Justice is put before mercy, for we must not give that in alms which is wrongfully got, or with which our debts should be paid. *God hates robbery for a burnt-offering.* (3) We must *walk humbly with our God.* This includes all the duties of the first table, as the two former include all the duties of the second table. We must take the Lord for our God in covenant, must attend on him and adhere to him as ours, and must make it our constant care and business to please him Enoch's walking with God is interpreted (Heb. xi. 5) his *pleasing God.* We must, in the whole course of our conversation, conform ourselves to the will of God, keep up our communion with God, and study to approve ourselves to him in our integrity; and this we must do humbly (submitting our understandings to the truths of God and our will to his precepts and providences); we must *humble ourselves to walk with God* (so the margin reads it); every thought within us must be brought down, to be brought into obedience to God, if we would walk comfortably with him. This is that which God requires, and without which the most costly services are *vain oblations ;* this is more than *all burnt-offerings and sacrifices.*

9 The Lord's voice crieth unto the city, and *the man of* wisdom shall see thy name: hear ye the rod, and who hath appointed it. 10 Are there yet the treasures of wickedness in the

house of the wicked, and the scant measure *that is* abominable? 11 Shall I count *them* pure with the wicked balances, and with the bag of deceitful weights? 12 For the rich men thereof are full of violence, and the inhabitants thereof have spoken lies, and their tongue *is* deceitful in their mouth. 13 Therefore also will I make *thee* sick in smiting thee, in making *thee* desolate because of thy sins. 14 Thou shalt eat, but not be satisfied; and thy casting down *shall be* in the midst of thee; and thou shalt take hold, but shalt not deliver; and *that* which thou deliverest will I give up to the sword. 15 Thou shalt sow, but thou shalt not reap; thou shalt tread the olives, but thou shalt not anoint thee with oil; and sweet wine, but shalt not drink wine. 16 For the statutes of Omri are kept, and all the works of the house of Ahab, and ye walk in their counsels; that I should make thee a desolation, and the inhabitants thereof a hissing: therefore ye shall bear the reproach of my people.

God, having shown them how necessary it was that they should do justly, here shows them how plain it was that they had done unjustly; and since they submitted not to his controversy, nor went the right way to have it taken up, here he proceeds in it. Observe,

I. How the action is entered against them, *v.* 9. God speaks to *the city,* to Jerusalem, to Samaria. His *voice cries* to it by his servants the prophets who were to *cry aloud and not spare.* Note, The voice of the prophets is *the Lord's voice,* and that *cries to the city,* cries to the country. *Doth not wisdom cry?* Prov. viii. 1. When the sin of a city cries to God his voice cries against the city; and, when the judgments of God are coming upon a city, his voice first *cries unto it.* He warns before he wounds, because he is *not willing that any should perish.* Now observe, 1. How the voice of God is discerned by some: *The man of wisdom will see thy name.* When the voice of God cries to us we may by it see his name, may discern and perceive that by which he makes himself known. Yet many see it not, are not aware of it, because they do not regard it. God *speaks once, yea, twice, and they perceive it not* (Job xxxiii. 14); but those that are men of wisdom will see it, and perceive it, and make a good use of it. Note, It is a point of true wisdom to discover the name of God in the voice of God, and to

learn what he is from what he says. *Wisdom shall see thy name,* for *the knowledge of the holy is understanding.* 2. What this voice of God says to all: " *Hear you the rod, and who hath appointed it.* Hear the rod when it is coming; hear it at a distance, before you see it and feel it; and be awakened to go forth to meet the Lord in the way of his judgments. Hear the rod when it has come, and is actually upon you, and you are sensible of the smart of it; hear what it says to you, what convictions, what counsels, what cautions, it speaks to you." Note, Every rod has a voice, and it is the voice of God that is to be heard in the rod of God, and it is well for those that understand the language of it, which if we would do we must have an eye to *him that appointed it.* Note, Every rod is appointed, of what kind it shall be, where it shall light, and how long it shall lie. God in every affliction *performs the thing that is appointed for us* (Job xxiii. 14), and to him therefore we must have an eye, to him we must have an ear; we must hear what he says to us by the affliction. *Hear it, and know it for thy good,* Job v. 6. The work of ministers is to explain the providences of God and to quicken and direct men to learn the lessons that are taught by them.

II. What is the ground of the action, and what are the things that are laid to their charge.

1. They are charged with injustice, a sin against the second table. Are there yet to be found among them the marks and means of fraudulent dealing? What! after all the methods that God has taken to teach them to do justly, will they yet deal unjustly? It seems, they will, *v.* 10. And *shall I count them pure?* *v.* 11. No; this is a sin which will by no means consist with a profession of purity. Those that are dishonest in their dealings have not the spots of God's children, and shall never be reckoned pure, whatever shows of devotion they may make. *Be not deceived, God is not mocked.* When a man is suspected of theft, or fraud, the justice of peace will send a warrant to search his house. God here does, as it were, search the houses of these citizens, and there he finds, (1.) *Treasures of wickedness,* abundance of wealth, but it is ill-got, and not likely to prosper; for *treasures of wickedness profit nothing.* (2.) A *scant measure,* by which they sold to the poor, and so exacted upon them and cheated them. (3.) They had *wicked balances and a bag of false weights,* by which, under a pretence of weighing what they sold, and giving the buyer what was right, they did him the greatest wrong, *v.* 11. (4.) Those that had wealth and power in their hands abused it to oppression and extortion: *The rich men thereof are full of violence;* for those that have much would have more, and are in a capacity of making it more by the power which their abundance of wealth gives them.

They are *full of violence*, that is, they have their houses full of that which is got by violence. (5.) Those that had not the advantage of doing wrong by their wealth yet found means of defrauding those they dealt with : *The inhabitants thereof have spoken lies;* if they are not able to use force and violence, they use fraud and deceit; the *inhabitants* have *spoken lies, and their tongue is deceitful in their mouth;* they do not stick at a deliberate lie, to make a good bargain. Some understand it of their speaking falsely concerning God, saying, *The Lord seeth not; he hath forsaken the earth,* Ezek. viii. 12.

2. They are charged with idolatry (*v.* 6): *The statutes of Omri are kept, and all the work of the house of Ahab.* Both these kings were wicked, and *did evil in the sight of the Lord;* but the wickedness which they established by a law, concerning which they made statutes, and which was the peculiar work of that house, was idolatry. Omri walked in the way of Jeroboam, and *in his sin of provoking God to anger with their vanities,* 1 Kings xvi. 26, 31. Ahab introduced the worship of Baal. These reigns were some ages before the time when this prophet lived, and yet the wickedness which they established by their laws and examples remained to this day; those statutes were still kept, and that work was still done; and the princes and people still *walked in their counsels,* took the same measures, and governed themselves and the people by the same politics. Observe, (1.) The same wickedness continued from one generation to another. Sin is a *root of bitterness,* soon planted, but not so soon plucked up again. The iniquity of former ages is often transmitted to, and entailed upon, the succeeding ones. Those that make corrupt laws, and bring in corrupt usages, are doing that which perhaps may prove the ruin of the child unborn. (2.) It was not the less evil in itself, provoking to God, and dangerous to the sinners, for its having been established and confirmed by the laws of princes, the examples of great men, and a long prescription. Though the worship of idols is enacted by the statutes of Omri, recommended by the practice of the house of Ahab, and pleads that it has been the usage of many generations, yet it is still displeasing to God and destructive to Israel; for no laws nor customs are of force against the divine command.

III. What is the judgment given upon this. Being found guilty of these crimes, the sentence is that that which God had given them warning of (*v.* 9) shall be brought upon them (*v.* 13): *Therefore also will I make thee sick, in smiting thee.* As they had smitten the poor with the rod of their oppressions, so would God in like manner smite them, so as to make them sick, sick of the gains they had unjustly gotten, so that though they had *swallowed down riches* they should *vomit them up again,* Job xx. 15. Their doom is,

1. That what they have they shall not have any comfortable enjoyment of; it shall do them no good. They grasped at more than enough, but, when they have it, it shall not be enough to make them easy and happy. What is got by fraud and oppression cannot be kept or enjoyed with any satisfaction. (1.) Their food shall not nourish them : *Thou shalt eat, but not be satisfied,* either because the food shall not digest, for want of God's blessing going along with it, or because the appetite shall by disease be made insatiable and still craving, the just punishment of those that were greedy of gain and enlarged their desires as hell. Men may be surfeited with the good things of this world and yet not satisfied, Eccl. v. 10 ; Isa. lv. 2. (2.) Their country shall not harbour and protect them : " *Thy casting down shall be in the midst of thee,* that is, thou shalt be broken and ruined by intestine troubles, mischiefs at home enough to cast thee down, though thou shouldst not be invaded by a foreign force." God can cast a nation down by that which is in the midst of them, can consume them by a fire in their own bowels. (3.) They shall not be able to preserve what they have from a foreign force, nor to recover what they have lost : " *Thou shalt take hold* of what is about to be taken from thee, but thou shalt not hold it fast, shalt catch at it, but *shalt not deliver it,* shalt not retrieve it." It is meant of their wives and children, that were very dear to them, which they took hold of, as resolved not to part with them, but there is no remedy, they must go into captivity. Note, What we hold closest we commonly lose soonest, and that proves least safe which is most dear. (4.) What they save for a time shall be reserved for a future and sorer stroke : *That which thou deliverest* out of the hand of one enemy *will I give up to the sword* of another enemy; for God has many arrows in his quiver; if one miss the sinner, the next shall not. (5.) What they have laboured for they shall not enjoy (*v.* 15): " *Thou shalt sow, but thou shalt not reap;* it shall be blasted and withered, and there shall be nothing to reap, or an enemy shall come and reap it for himself, or thou shalt be carried into captivity, and leave it to be reaped by thou knowest not whom. Thou shalt *tread the olives,* but *thou shalt not anoint thyself with oil,* having no heart to make use of ornaments and refreshments when all is going to ruin. Thou shalt tread out *the sweet wine,* but *shalt not drink wine,* for many things may fall between the cup and the lip." Note, It is very grievous to be disappointed of our expectations, and not to have the pleasure of that which we have taken pains for; and this will be the just punishment of those that frustrate God's expectations from them, and answer not the cost he has been at upon them. See this threatened in the law, Lev. xxvi. 16 ; Deut. xxviii. 30, 38, &c.; and compare Isa. lxii. 8, 9.

2. That all they have shall at length be taken from them (*v.* 13) : *Thou shalt be made desolate because of thy sins;* and *v.* 16, *a desolation and a hissing.* Sin makes a nation desolate ; and when a people that have been famous and flourishing are made desolate it is the astonishment of some and the triumph of others ; some lament it, and others hiss at it. Thus *you shall bear the reproach of my people.* Their being the people of God, in name and profession, while they kept close to their duty and kept themselves in his love, was an honour to them, and all their neighbours thought it so ; but now that they have corrupted and ruined themselves, now that their sins and God's judgments have made their land desolate, their having been once the people of God does but turn so much the more to their reproach ; their enemies will say, *These are the people of the Lord,* Ezek. xxxvi. 20. Note, If professors of religion ruin themselves, their ruin will be the most reproachful of any ; and they in a special manner will rise at the last day to everlasting shame and contempt

CHAP. VII.

In this chapter, I. The prophet, in the name of the church, sadly laments the woeful decay of religion in the age wherein he lived, and the deluge of impiety and immorality which overwhelmed the nation, which levelled the differences, and bore down the fences, of all that is just and sacred, ver. 1—6. II. The prophet, for the sake of the church, prescribes comforts, which may be of use at such a time, and gives counsel what to do. 1. They must have an eye to God, ver. 7. 2. They must courageously bear up against the insolences of the enemy, ver. 8—10. 3. They must patiently lie down under the rebukes of their God, ver. 9. 4. They must expect no other than that the trouble would continue long, and must endeavour to make the best of it, ver. 11—13. 5. They must encourage themselves with God's promises, in answer to the prophet's prayers. ver. 14, 15. 6. They must foresee the fall of their enemies, that now triumphed over them, ver. 16, 17. 7. They must themselves triumph in the mercy and grace of God, and his faithfulness to his covenant (ver. 18—20), and with that comfortable word the prophecy concludes.

WOE is me ! for I am as when they have gathered the summer-fruits, as the grape-gleanings of the vintage : *there is* no cluster to eat : my soul desired the first-ripe fruit. 2 The good *man* is perished out of the earth : and *there is* none upright among men : they all lie in wait for blood ; they hunt every man his brother with a net. 3 That they may do evil with both hands earnestly, the prince asketh, and the judge *asketh* for a reward ; and the great *man*, he uttereth his mischievous desire : so they wrapt it up. 4 The best of them *is* a brier : the most upright *is sharper* than a thorn hedge : the day of thy watchmen *and* thy visitation cometh ; now shall be their perplexity. 5 Trust ye not in a friend, put ye not confidence in a guide : keep the doors of thy mouth from her that lieth in thy bosom. 6 For the son

dishonoureth the father, the daughter riseth up against her mother, the daughter-in-law against her mother-in-law ; a man's enemies *are* the men of his own house.

This is such a description of bad times as, some think, could scarcely agree to the times of Hezekiah, when this prophet prophesied ; and therefore they rather take it as a prediction of what should be in the reign of Manasseh. But we may rather suppose it to be in the reign of Ahaz (and in that reign he prophesied, *ch.* i. 1) or in the beginning of Hezekiah's time, before the reformation he was instrumental in ; nay, in the best of his days, and when he had done his best to purge out corruptions, still there was much amiss. The prophet cries out, *Woe is me !* He bemoans himself that his lot was cast in such a degenerate age, and thinks it his great unhappiness that he lived among a people that were ripening apace for a ruin which many a good man would unavoidably be involved in. Thus David cries out, *Woe is me that I sojourn in Mesech !* He laments, 1. That there were so few good people to be found, even among those that were God's people ; and this was their reproach : *The good man has perished out of the earth,* or out of the land, the land of Canaan ; it was a good land, and a *land of uprightness* (Isa. xxvi. 10), but there were few good men in it, none upright among them, *v.* 2. The *good man* is a *godly man* and a *merciful man :* the word signifies both. Those are completely good men that are devout towards God and compassionate and beneficent towards men, that love mercy and walk with God. "These have perished ; those few honest men that some time ago enriched and adorned our country are now dead and gone, and there are none risen up *in their* stead that tread in their steps ; honesty is banished, and there is no such thing as a good man to be met with. Those that were of religious education have degenerated, and become as bad as the worst ; *the godly man ceases,*" Ps. xii. 1. This is illustrated by a comparison (*v.* 1) : They were *as when they have gathered the summer fruits ;* it was as hard a thing to find a good man as to find any of the summer-fruits (which were the choicest and best, and therefore must carefully be gathered in) when the harvest is over. The prophet is ready to say, as Elijah in his time (1 Kings xix. 10), *I, even I only, am left.* Good men, who used to hang in clusters, are now as the *grape-gleanings of the vintage,* here and there a berry, Isa. xvii. 6. You can find no societies of them as bunches of grapes, but those that are single persons : *There is no cluster to eat :* and the best and fullest grapes are those that grow in large clusters. Some think that this intimates not only that good people were few, but that those few who remained, who went for good people, were good for little, like the small withered grapes, the refuse that were left behind, not only by the gatherer, but by the gleaner. When the prophet observed this universal degeneracy it made him *desire the first-ripe fruit:* he wished to see such worthy good men as were in the former ages, were the ornaments of the primitive times, and as far excelled the best of all the present age as the first and full-ripe fruits do those of the latter growth, that never come to maturity. When we read and hear of the wisdom and zeal, the strictness and conscientiousness, the devotion and charity, of the professors of religion in former ages, and see the reverse of this in those of the present age, we cannot but sit down, and wish, with a sigh, *O for primitive Christianity again!* Where are the plainness and integrity of those that went before us? Where are the Israelites indeed, without guile? Our souls desire them, but in vain. The golden age is gone, and past recal; we must make the best of what is, for we are not likely to see such times as have been. 2. That there were so many wicked mischievous people among them, not only none that did any good, but multitudes that did all the hurt they could: *"They all lie in wait for blood,* and *hunt every man his brother.* To get wealth to themselves, they care not what wrong, what hurt, they do to their neighbours and nearest relations. They act as if mankind were in a state of war, and force were the only right. They are as beasts of prey to their neighbours, for *they all lie in wait for blood* as lions for their prey; they thirst after it, make nothing of taking away any man's life or livelihood to serve a turn for themselves, and lie in wait for an opportunity to do it. Their neighbours are as beasts of prey to them, for they *hunt every man his brother with a net:* they persecute them as noxious creatures, fit to be taken and destroyed, though they are innocent excellent ones." We say of him that is outlawed, *Caput gerit lupinum—He is to be hunted as a wolf.* "Or they hunt them as men do the game, to feast upon it; they have a thousand cursed arts of ensnaring men to their ruin, so that they may but get by it. Thus *they do mischief with both hands earnestly;* their hearts desire it, their heads contrive it, and then *both hands* are ready to put it in execution." Note, The more eager and intent men are upon any sinful pursuit, and the more pains they take in it, the more provoking it is. 3. That the magistrates, who by their office ought to have been the patrons and protectors of right, were the practisers and promoters of wrong: *That they may do evil with both hands earnestly,* to excite and animate themselves in it, *the prince asketh, and the judge asketh, for a reward,* for a bribe, with which they will be hired to exert all their power for the supporting and carrying on of any wicked design *with*

both hands. *They do evil with both hands well* (so some read it); they do evil with a great deal of art and dexterity; they praise themselves for doing it so well. Others read it thus: *To do evil they have both hands* (they catch at an opportunity of doing mischief), *but to do good the prince and the judge ask for a reward;* if they do any good offices they are mercenary in them, and must be paid for them. The great man, who has wealth and power to do good, is not ashamed to utter his mischievous desire in conjunction with the prince and the judge, who are ready to support him and stand by him in it. *So they wrap it up;* they perplex the matter, involve it, and make it intricate (so some understand it), that they may lose equity in a mist, and so make the cause turn which way they please. It is ill with a people when their princes, and judges, and great men are in a confederacy to pervert justice. And it is a sad character that is given of them (v. 4), that *the best of them is as a brier, and the most upright is sharper than a thorn-hedge;* it is a dangerous thing to have any thing to do with them; *he that touches them must be fenced with iron* (2 Sam. xxiii. 6, 7), he shall be sure to be scratched, to have his clothes torn, and his eyes almost pulled out. And, if this be the character of the best and most upright, what are the worst? And, when things have come to this pass, *the day of thy watchmen comes,* that is, as it follows, *the day of thy visitation,* when God will reckon with thee for all this wickedness, which is called *the day of the watchmen,* because their prophets, whom God set as watchmen over them, had often warned them of that day. When all flesh have corrupted their way, even the best and the most upright, what can be expected but a day of visitation, a deluge of judgments, as that which drowned the old world when *the earth was filled with violence?* 4. That there was no faith in man; people had grown so universally treacherous that one knew not whom to repose any confidence in, v. 5. "Those that have any sense of honour, or spark of virtue, remaining in them, have a firm regard to the laws of friendship; they would not discover what passed in private conversation, nor divulge secrets, to the prejudice of a friend. But those things are now made a jest of; you will not meet with a friend that you dare trust, whose word you dare take, or who will have any tenderness or concern for you; so that wise men shall give it and take it for a rule, *Trust you not in a friend,* for you will find him false, you can trust him no further than you can see him; and even him that passes for an honest man you will find to be so only with good looking to. Nay, as for him that undertakes to be *your guide,* to lead you into any business which he professes to understand better than you, you cannot *put a confidence* in him, for he will be sure to mislead you if he can get any thing by it."

Some by a guide understand a husband, who is called *the guide of thy youth;* and that agrees well enough with what follows, "*Keep the doors of thy lips from her that lieth in thy bosom,* from thy own wife; take heed what thou sayest before her, lest she betray thee, as Delilah did Samson, lest she be the *bird of the air* that *carries the voice* of that which thou sayest *in thy bed-chamber,*" Eccl. x. 20. It is an evil time indeed when the prudent are obliged even thus far to keep silence. 5. That children were abusive to their parents, and men had no comfort, no satisfaction, in their own families and their nearest relations, *v.* 6. The times are bad indeed when *the son dishonours his father,* gives him bad language, exposes him, threatens him, and studies to do him a mischief, *when the daughter rises up* in rebellion against her own mother, having no sense of duty, or natural affection; and no marvel that then the *daughter-in-law* quarrels with her *mother-in-law,* and is vexatious to her. Either they cannot agree about their property and interest, or their humours and passions clash, or, from a spirit of bigotry and persecution, *the brother shall deliver up the brother to death, and the father the child,* Matt. x. 4; Luke xxi. 16. It is sad when a man's betrayers and worst enemies are the men of his own house, his own children and servants, that should be his guard and his best friends. Note, The contempt and violation of the laws of domestic duties are a sad symptom of a universal corruption of manners. Those are never likely to come to good that are undutiful to their parents, and study to be provoking to them and cross them.

7 Therefore I will look unto the Lord; I will wait for the God of my salvation: my God will hear me. 8 Rejoice not against me, O mine enemy: when I fall, I shall arise; when I sit in darkness, the Lord *shall be* a light unto me. 9 I will bear the indignation of the Lord, because I have sinned against him, until he plead my cause, and execute judgment for me: he will bring me forth to the light, *and* I shall behold his righteousness. 10 Then *she that is* mine enemy shall see *it,* and shame shall cover her which said unto me, Where is the Lord thy God? mine eyes shall behold her: now shall she be trodden down as the mire of the streets. 11 *In* the day that thy walls are to be built, *in* that day shall the decree be far removed. 12 *In* that day *also* he shall come even to thee from Assyria, and *from* the fortified

cities, and from the fortress even to the river, and from sea to sea, and *from* mountain to mountain. 13 Notwithstanding the land shall be desolate because of them that dwell therein, for the fruit of their doings.

The prophet, having sadly complained of the wickedness of the times he lived in, here fastens upon some considerations for the comfort of himself and his friends, in reference thereunto. The case is bad, but it is not desperate. *Yet now there is hope in Israel concerning this thing.*

I. "Though God be now displeased he shall be reconciled to us, and then all will be well, *v.* 7, 9. We are now under *the indignation of the Lord;* God is angry with us, and justly, because *we have sinned against him.*" Note, It is our sin against God that provokes his indignation against us; and we must see it, and own it, whenever we are under divine rebukes, that we may justify God, and may study to answer his end in afflicting us, by repenting of sin and breaking off from it. Now, at such a time, 1. We must have recourse to God under our troubles (*v.* 7): *Therefore I will look unto the Lord.* When a child of God has ever so much occasion to cry, *Woe is me* (as the prophet here, *v.* 1), yet it may be a comfort to him that he has a God to look to, a God to come to, to fly to, in whom he may rejoice and have satisfaction. All may look bright above him when all looks black and dark about him. The prophet had been complaining that there was no comfort to be had, no confidence to be put, in friends and relations on earth, and this drives him to his God: *Therefore I will look unto the Lord.* The less reason we have to delight in any creature the more reason we have to delight in God. If princes are not to be trusted, we may say, *Happy is the man that has* the God of Jacob for his help, and *happy am I,* even in the midst of my present woes, if he be my help. If men be false, this is our comfort, that God is faithful; if relations be unkind, he is and will be gracious. Let us therefore look above and beyond them, and overlook our disappointment in them, and look unto the Lord. 2. We must submit to the will of God in our troubles: "*I will bear the indignation of the Lord,* will bear it patiently, without murmuring and repining, *because I have sinned against him.*" Note, Those that are truly penitent for sin will see a great deal of reason to be patient under affliction. *Wherefore should a man complain for the punishment of his sin?* When we complain to God of the badness of the times we ought to complain against ourselves for the badness of our own hearts. 3. We must depend upon God to work deliverance for us, and put a good issue to our troubles in due time; we must not only look to him, but look for him : " I will *wait for the God of my salvation,* and for his gracious returns to me." In our greatest distresses we shall see no reason to despair of salvation if by faith we eye God as the *God of our salvation,* who is able to save the weakest upon their humble petition, and willing to save the worst upon their true repentance. And, if we depend on God as the God of our salvation, we must wait for him, and for his salvation, in his own way and his own time. Let us now see what the church is here taught to expect and promise herself from God, even when things are brought to the last extremity. (1.) *My God will hear me;* if the Lord be our God, he will hear our prayers, and grant an answer of peace to them. (2.) " *When I fall,* and am in danger of being dashed in pieces by the fall, yet *I shall arise,* and recover myself again. *I fall,* but am not *utterly cast down,*" Ps. xxxvii. 24. (3.) " *When I sit in darkness,* desolate and disconsolate, melancholy and perplexed, and not knowing what to do, nor which way to look for relief, yet then *the Lord shall be a light to me,* to comfort and revive me, to instruct and teach me, to direct and guide me, as a light to my eyes, a light to my feet, a light *in a dark place.*" (4.) *He will. plead my cause, and execute judgment for me,* v. 9. If we heartily espouse the cause of God, the just but injured cause of religion and virtue, and make it our cause, we may hope he will own our cause, and plead it. The church's cause, though it seem for a time to go against her, will at length be pleaded with jealousy, and judgment not only given against, but executed upon, the enemies of it. (5.) "He *will bring me forth to the light,* make me shine eminently out of obscurity, and become conspicuous, will make my righteousness shine evidently from under the dark cloud of calumny, Ps. xxxvii. 6; Isa. lviii. 10. The morning of comfort shall shine forth out of the long and dark night of trouble." (6.) " *I shall behold his righteousness;* I shall see the equity of his proceedings concerning me and the performance of his promises to me."

II. Though enemies triumph and insult, they shall be silenced and put to shame, *v.* 8, 10. Observe here,

1. How proudly the enemies of God's people trample upon them in their distress. They said, *Where is the Lord their God?* As if because they were afflicted God had forsaken them, and they knew not where to find him with their prayers, and he knew not how to help them with his favours. This David's enemies said to him, and it was a sword in his bones, Ps. xlii. 10, and see Ps. cxv. 2. Thus, in reproaching Israel as an abandoned people, they reflected on the God of Israel as an unkind unfaithful God.

2. How comfortably the people of God by faith bear up themselves under these insults (*v.* 8): " *Rejoice not against me, O my enemy!*

I am now down, but shall not be always so, and when my God appears for me then *she that is my enemy shall see it, and be ashamed*" (not only being disappointed in her expectations of the church's utter ruin, but having the same cup of trembling put into her hand), " then *my eyes shall behold her* in the same deplorable condition that I am now in; *now shall she be trodden down.*" Note, The deliverance of the church will be the confusion of her enemies; and their shame shall be double, when, as they have trampled upon God's people, so they shall themselves be trampled upon.

III. Though the land continue a great while desolate, yet it shall at length be replenished again, when the time, even the set time, of its deliverance comes. 1. Its salvation shall not come *till after it has been desolate;* so the margin reads it, *v.* 13. God has a controversy with the land, and it must lie long under his rebukes, *because of those that dwell therein;* it is their iniquity that makes their land desolate (Ps. cvii. 34); it is *for the fruit of their doings,* their evil doings which they have been themselves guilty of, and the evil fruit of them, the sins of others, which they have been accessory to by their bad influence and example. For this they must expect to smart a great while; for the world shall know that God hates sin even in his own people. 2. When it does come it shall be a complete salvation; and it seems to refer to their deliverance out of Babylon by Cyrus, which Isaiah about this time prophesied of, as a type of our redemption by Christ. (1.) *The decree shall be far removed.* God's decree concerning their captivity, and Nebuchadnezzar's decree concerning the perpetuity of it, his resolution never to release them, "these shall be set aside and revoked, and you shall hear no more of them; they shall no more lie as a yoke upon thy neck." (2.) Jerusalem and the cities of Judah shall be again reared : Then *thy walls shall be built,* walls for habitation, walls for defence, house-walls, town-walls, temple-walls; it is in order to these that the decree is repealed, Isa. xliv. 28. Though Zion's walls may lie long in ruins, there will come a day when they shall be repaired. (3.) All that belong to the land of Israel, whithersoever dispersed, and howsoever distressed, far and wide over the face of the whole earth, shall come flocking to it again (*v.* 12) : *He shall come even to thee,* having liberty to return and a heart to return, from Assyria, whither the ten tribes were carried away, though it lay remote, and *from the fortified cities,* and *from the fortress,* those strongholds in which they thought they had them fast; for when God's time comes, though Pharaoh will not *let the people go,* God will fetch them out with a high hand. They shall come from all the remote parts, *from sea to sea* and *from mountain to mountain,* not turning back for fear of your discouragements, but they shall go from strength to strength till they come to Zion. Thus in the great day of redemption *God will gather his elect from the four winds.*

14 Feed thy people with thy rod, the flock of thine heritage, which dwell solitarily *in* the wood, in the midst of Carmel: let them feed *in* Bashan and Gilead, as in the days of old. 15 According to the days of thy coming out of the land of Egypt will I show unto him marvellous *things.* 16 The nations shall see and be confounded at all their might: they shall lay *their* hand upon *their* mouth, their ears shall be deaf. 17 They shall lick the dust like a serpent, they shall move out of their holes like worms of the earth: they shall be afraid of the LORD our God, and shall fear because of thee. 18 Who *is* a God like unto thee, that pardoneth iniquity, and passeth by the transgression of the remnant of his heritage? he retaineth not his anger for ever, because he delighteth *in* mercy. 19 He will turn again, he will have compassion upon us; he will subdue our iniquities; and thou wilt cast all their sins into the depths of the sea. 20 Thou wilt perform the truth to Jacob, *and* the mercy to Abraham, which thou hast sworn unto our fathers from the days of old.

Here is, I. The prophet's prayer to God to take care of his own people, and of their cause and interest, *v.* 14. When God is about to deliver his people he stirs up their friends to pray for them, and pours out *a spirit of grace and supplication,* Zech. xii. 10. And, when we see God coming towards us in ways of mercy, we must go forth to meet him by prayer. It is a prophetic prayer, which amounts to a promise of the good prayed for; what God directed his prophet to ask no doubt he designed to give. Now, 1. The people of Israel are here called the *flock of God's heritage,* for they are the sheep of his hand, the sheep of his pasture, his little flock in the world; and they are his heritage, his portion in the world. *Jacob is the lot of his inheritance.* 2. This flock *dwells solitarily in the wood,* or *forest, in the midst of Carmel,* a high mountain. Israel was a peculiar people, *that dwelt alone, and was not reckoned among the nations,* like a flock of sheep in a wood. They were now a desolate people (*v.* 13), were in the land of their captivity as sheep in a forest, in danger of being lost and made a prey of to the beasts of the forest.

They are *scattered upon the mountains as sheep having no shepherd.* 3. He prays that God would *feed them there with his rod,* that is, that he would take care of them in their captivity, would protect them, and provide for them, and do the part of a good shepherd to them: "Let *thy rod and staff comfort* them, even in that darksome valley; and even there let them want nothing that is good for them. Let them be governed by thy rod, not the rod of their enemies, for they are thy people." 4. He prays that God would in due time bring them back to feed in the plains of Bashan and Gilead, and no longer to be fed in the woods and mountains. *Let them feed in their own country again, as in the days of old.* Some apply this spiritually, and make it either the prophet's prayer to Christ or his Father's charge to him, to take care of his church, as the great Shepherd of the sheep, and to go in and out before them while they are here in this world as in a wood, that they may find pasture as in Carmel, as in Bashan and Gilead.

II. God's promise, in answer to this prayer; and we may well take God's promises as real answers to the prayers of faith, and embrace them accordingly, for with him saying and doing are not two things. The prophet prayed that God would feed them, and do kind things for them; but God answers that he *will show them marvellous things* (*v.* 15), will do for them more than they are able to ask or think, will out-do their hopes and expectations; he will *show them his marvellous lovingkindness,* Ps. xvii. 7. 1. He will do that for them which shall be the repetition of the wonders and miracles of former ages—*according to the days of thy coming out of the land of Egypt.* Their deliverance out of Babylon shall be a work of wonder and grace not inferior to their deliverance out of Egypt, nay, it shall eclipse the lustre of that (Jer. xvi. 14, 15), much more shall the work of redemption by Christ. Note, God's former favours to his church are patterns of future favours, and shall again be copied out as there is occasion. 2. He will do that for them which shall be matter of wonder and amazement to the present age, *v.* 16, 17. The *nations about* shall take notice of it, and it shall be said *among the heathen, The Lord has done great things for them,* Ps. cxxvi. 2. The impression which the deliverance of the Jews out of Babylon shall make upon the neighbouring nations shall be very much for the honour both of God and his church. (1.) Those that had insulted over the people of God in their distress, and gloried that when they had them down they would keep them down, *shall be confounded, when* they see them thus surprisingly rising up; they shall be *confounded at all the might* with which the captives shall now exert themselves, whom they thought for ever disabled. They shall now *lay their hands upon their mouths,* as being ashamed of what they have said, and not able to say any more, by way of triumph over Israel. Nay, *their ears shall be deaf* too, so much shall they be ashamed at the wonderful deliverance; they shall stop their ears, as being not willing to hear any more of God's wonders wrought for that people, whom they had so despised and insulted over. (2.) Those that had impudently confronted God himself shall now be struck with a fear of him, and thereby brought, in profession at least, to submit to him (*v.* 17): *They shall lick the dust like a serpent,* they shall be so mortified, as if they were sentenced to the same curse the serpent was laid under (Gen. iii. 14), *Upon thy belly shalt thou go, and dust shalt thou eat.* They shall be brought to the lowest abasements imaginable, and shall be so dispirited that they shall tamely submit to them. *His enemies shall lick the dust,* Ps. lxxii. 9. Nay, they shall *lick the dust* of the church's feet, Isa. xlix. 23. Proud oppressors shall now be made sensible how mean, how little, they are, before the great God, and they shall with trembling and the lowest submission *move out of the holes* into which they had crept (Isa. ii. 21), *like worms of the earth* as they are, being ashamed and afraid to *show their heads;* so low shall they be brought, and such abjects shall they be, when they are abased. When God did wonders for his church *many of the people of the land became Jews,* because *the fear of the Jews,* and of their God, *fell upon them,* Esth. viii. 17. So it is promised here: *They shall be afraid of the Lord our God, and shall fear because of thee, O Israel!* Forced submissions are often but feigned submissions; yet they redound to the glory of God and the church, though not to the benefit of the dissemblers themselves.

III. The prophet's thankful acknowledgment of God's mercy, in the name of the church, with a believing dependence upon his promise, *v.* 18—20. We are here taught,

1. To give to God the glory of his pardoning mercy, *v.* 18. God having promised to bring back the captivity of his people, the prophet, on that occasion, admires pardoning mercy, as that which was at the bottom of it. As it was their sin that brought them into bondage, so it was God's pardoning their sin that brought them out of it; Ps. lxxxv. 1, 2, and Isa. xxxiii. 24; xxxviii. 17; xl. 1, 2. The pardon of sin is the foundation of all other covenant-mercies, Heb. viii. 12. This the prophet stands amazed at, while the surrounding nations stood amazed only at those deliverances which were but the fruits of this. Note, (1.) God's people, who are the *remnant of his heritage,* stand charged with many transgressions; being but a remnant, a very few, one would hope they should all be very good, but they are not so; God's children have their spots, and often offend their Father. (2.) The gracious God is ready to pass by and pardon the iniquity and transgression of his people, upon their repentance and return to him. God's people are a pardoned people, and to this they owe their all. When God pardons sin, he passes it by, does not punish it as justly he might, nor deal with the sinner according to the desert of it. (3.) Though God may for a time lay his own people under the tokens of his displeasure, yet he will not *retain his anger for ever,* but *though he cause grief he will have compassion;* he is not implacable; yet against those that are not of the remnant of his heritage, that are unpardoned, he will keep his anger for ever. (4.) The reasons why God pardons sin, and keeps not his anger for ever, are all taken from within himself; it is *because he delights in mercy,* and the salvation of sinners is what he has pleasure in, not their death and damnation. (5.) The glory of God in forgiving sin is, as in other things, matchless, and without compare. There is *no God like unto him* for this; no magistrate, no common person, forgives as God does. In this his thoughts and ways are infinitely above ours; in this he is *God, and not man.* (6.) All those that have experienced pardoning mercy cannot but admire that mercy; it is what we have reason to stand amazed at, if we know what it is. Has God forgiven us our transgressions? We may well say, *Who is a God like unto thee?* Our holy wonder at pardoning mercy will be a good evidence of our interest in it.

2. To take to ourselves the comfort of that mercy and all the grace and truth that go along with it. God's people here, as they look back with thankfulness upon God's pardoning their sins, so they look forward with assurance upon what he would yet further do for them. His mercy *endures for ever,* and therefore as he has *shown mercy* so he will, *v.* 19, 20. (1.) He will renew his favours to us: *He will turn again; he will have compassion;* that is, he will again have compassion upon us as formerly he had; his compassions shall be *new every morning;* he seemed to be departing from us in anger, but he will turn again and pity us. He will turn us to himself, and then will *turn to us, and have mercy upon us.* (2.) He will renew us, to prepare and qualify us for his favour: *He will subdue our iniquities;* when he takes away the guilt of sin, that it may not damn us, he will break the power of sin, that it may not have dominion over us, that we may not fear sin, nor be led captive by it. Sin is an enemy that fights against us, a tyrant that oppresses us; nothing less than almighty grace can subdue it, so great is its power in fallen man and so long has it kept possession. But, if God forgive the sin that has been committed by us, he will subdue the sin that dwells in us, and in that there is none like him in forgiving; and all those whose sins are pardoned earnestly desire and hope to have their corruptions mortified and their iniquities subdued, and please themselves

with the hopes of it. If we be left to ourselves, our iniquities will be too hard for us; but God's grace, we trust, shall be sufficient for us to subdue them, so that they shall not rule us, and then they shall not ruin us. (3.) He will confirm this good work, and effectually provide that his act of grace shall never be repealed : *Thou wilt cast all their sins into the depth of the sea,* as when he brought them out of Egypt (to which he has an eye in the promises here, *v.* 15) he subdued Pharaoh and the Egyptians, and cast them into the depth of the sea. It intimates that when God forgives sin he *remembers it no more,* and takes care that it shall never be remembered more against the sinner. Ezek. xviii. 22, *His transgressions shall not be mentioned unto him;* they are *blotted out as a cloud* which never appears more. He casts them into the sea, not near the shore-side, where they may appear again next low water, but into *the depth of the sea,* never to rise again. *All their sins* shall be cast there without exception, for when God forgives sin he forgives all. (4.) He will perfect that which concerns us, and with this good work will do all that for us which our case requires and which he has promised (*v.* 20) : *Then wilt thou perform thy truth to Jacob and thy mercy to Abraham.* It is in pursuance of the covenant that our sins are pardoned and our lusts mortified ; from that spring all these streams flow, and with these he shall *freely give us all things.* The promise is said to be *mercy to Abraham,* because, as made to him first, it was mere mercy, preventing mercy, considering what state it found him in. But it was *truth to Jacob,* because the faithfulness of God was engaged to make good to him and his seed, as heirs to Abraham, all that was graciously promised to Abraham. See here, [1.] With what solemnity the covenant of grace is ratified to us ; it was not only spoken, written, and sealed, but, which is the highest confirmation, it was *sworn to our fathers;* nor is it a modern project, but is confirmed by antiquity too ; it was sworn *from the days of old;* it is an ancient charter. [2.] With what satisfaction it may be applied and relied upon by us ; we may say with the highest assurance, *Thou wilt perform the truth and mercy;* not one iota or tittle of it shall fall to the ground. Faithful is he that has promised, who also will do it.

AN

EXPOSITION,

WITH PRACTICAL OBSERVATIONS,

OF THE PROPHECY OF

N A H U M.

THE name of this prophet signifies a *comforter;* for it was a charge given to all the prophets, *Comfort you, comfort you, my people:* and even this prophet, though wholly taken up in foretelling the destruction of Nineveh, which speaks terror to the Assyrians, is, even in that, comforter to the ten tribes of Israel, who, it is probable, were now lately carried captives into Assyria. It is very uncertain at what time he lived and prophesied, but it is most probable that he lived in the time of Hezekiah, and prophesied against Nineveh, after the captivity of Israel by the king of Assyria, which was in the ninth year of Hezekiah, and before Sennacherib's invading Judah, which was in the fourteenth year of Hezekiah, for to that attempt, and the defeat of it, it is supposed, the first chapter has reference ; and it is probable that it was delivered a little before it, for the encouragement of God's people in that day of treading down and perplexity. It is the conjecture of the learned Huetius that the two other chapters of this book were delivered by Nahum some years after, perhaps in the reign of Manasseh, and in that reign the Jewish chronologies generally place him, somewhat nearer to the time when Nineveh was conquered, and the Assyrian monarchy reduced, by Cyaxares and Nebuchadnezzar, some time before the first captivity of Judah. It is probable that Nahum did by word of mouth prophesy many things concerning Israel and Judah, as it is certain that Jonah did (2 Kings xiv. 25), though we have nothing of either of them in writing, but what related to Nineveh, of which, though a great and ancient city, yet probably we should never have heard in sacred writ if the Israel of God had not had some concern in it.

CHAP. I.

In this chapter we have, I. The inscription of the book, ver. 1. II. A magnificent display of the glory of God, in a mixture of wrath and justice against the wicked, and mercy and grace towards his people, and the discovery of his majesty and power in both, ver. 2—8. III. A particular application of this (as most interpreters think) to the destruction of Sennacherib and the Assyrian army, when they besieged Jerusalem, which was a very memorable and illustrious instance of the power both of God's justice and of his mercy, and spoke abundance of terror to his enemies and encouragement to his faithful servants, ver. 9—16.

THE burden of Nineveh. The book of the vision of Nahum the Elkoshite.

This title directs us to consider, 1. The great city against which the word of the Lord is here delivered; it is the *burden of Nineveh*, not only a prophecy and a weighty one, but a burdensome prophecy, a dead weight to Nineveh, a mill-stone hanged about its neck. Nineveh was the place concerned, and the Assyrian monarchy, which that was the royal seat of. About 100 years before this Jonah had, in God's name, foretold the speedy overthrow of this great city; but then the Ninevites repented and were spared, and that decree did not *bring forth*. The Ninevites then saw clearly how much it was to their advantage to turn from their evil way; it was the saving of their city; and yet, soon after, they returned to it again; it became worse than ever, *a bloody city*, and *full of lies* and *robbery*. They repented of their repentance, returned with the dog to his vomit, and at length grew worse than ever they had been. Then God sent them not this prophet, as Jonah, but this prophecy, to read them their doom, which was now irreversible. Note, The reprieve will not be continued if the repentance be not continued in. If men turn from the good they began to do, they can expect no other than that God should turn from the favour he began to show, Jer. xviii. 10. 2. The poor prophet by whom the word of the Lord is here delivered: It is *the book of the vision of Nahum the Elkoshite.* The burden of Nineveh was what the prophet plainly foresaw, for it was his vision, and what he left upon record (it is the *book of the vision),* that, when he was gone, the event might be compared with the prediction and might confirm it. All the account we have of the prophet himself is that he was an *Elkoshite*, of the town called *Elkes*, or *Elcos*, which, Jerome says, was in Galilee. Some observe that the scripture ordinarily says little of the prophets themselves, that our faith might not stand upon their authority, but upon that of the blessed Spirit by whom their prophecies were indited.

2 God *is* jealous, and the Lord revengeth; the Lord revengeth, and *is* furious; the Lord will take vengeance on his adversaries, and he reserveth *wrath* for his enemies. 3 The Lord *is* slow to anger, and great in power, and will not at all acquit the

1340

wicked: the Lord *hath* his way in the whirlwind and in the storm, and the clouds *are* the dust of his feet. 4 He rebuketh the sea, and maketh it dry, and drieth up all the rivers: Bashan languisheth, and Carmel, and the flower of Lebanon languisheth. 5 The mountains quake at him, and the hills melt, and the earth is burned at his presence, yea, the world, and all that dwell therein. 6 Who can stand before his indignation? and who can abide in the fierceness of his anger? his fury is poured out like fire, and the rocks are thrown down by him. 7 The Lord *is* good, a strong hold in the day of trouble; and he knoweth them that trust in him. 8 But with an over-running flood he will make an utter end of the place thereof, and darkness shall pursue his enemies.

Nineveh knows not God, that God that contends with her, and therefore is here told what a God he is; and it is good for us all to mix faith with that which is here said concerning him, which speaks a great deal of terror to the wicked and comfort to good people; for this glorious description of the Sovereign of the world, like the pillar of cloud and fire, has a bright side towards Israel and a dark side towards the Egyptians. Let each take his portion from it; let sinners read it and tremble; let saints read it and triumph. The wrath of God is here revealed from heaven against his enemies, his favour and mercy are here assured to his faithful loyal subjects, and his almighty power in both, making his wrath very terrible and his favour very desirable.

I. He is a God of inflexible justice, a jealous God, and will take vengeance on his enemies; let Nineveh know this, and tremble before him. Their idols are insignificant things; there is nothing formidable in them. But the God of Israel is greatly to be feared; for, 1. He resents the affronts and indignities done him by those that deny his being or any of his perfections, that set up other gods in competition with him, that destroy his laws, arraign his proceedings, ridicule his word, or are abusive to his people. Let such know that Jehovah, the one only living and true God, is a *jealous God, and a revenger:* he is jealous for his own honour in the matters of his worship, and will not endure a rival; he is jealous for the comfort of his worshippers, *jealous for his land* (Joel ii. 18), and will not have that injured. He is a revenger, *and he is furious:* he *has fury* (so the word is), not as man has it, in whom it is an ungoverned passion (so he has said,

Fury is not in me, Isa. xxvii. 4), but he has it in such a way as becomes the righteous God, to put an edge upon his justice, and to make it appear more terrible to those who otherwise would stand in no awe of it. He is *Lord of anger* (so the Hebrew phrase is for that which we read, *he is furious)* ; he has anger, but he has it at command and under government. Our anger is often lord over us, as theirs that have *no rule over their own spirits,* but God is always *Lord of his anger* and *weighs a path to it,* Ps. lxxviii. 50. 2. He resolves to reckon with those that put those affronts upon him. We are told here, not only that he is a revenger, but that he *will take vengeance ;* he has said he will, he has sworn it, Deut. xxxii. 40, 41. Whoever are his adversaries and enemies among men, he will make them feel his resentments ; and, though the sentence against his enemies is not executed speedily, yet he reserves wrath for them and reserves them for it in the day of wrath. Against his own people, who repent and humble themselves before him, he keeps *not his anger for ever,* but against his enemies he will for ever let out his anger. *He will not at all acquit the wicked* that sin, and stand to it, and do not repent, *v.* 3. Those *wickedly depart from their God* that depart, and never return (Ps. xviii. 21), and these he will not acquit. Humble supplicants will find him gracious, but scornful beggars will not find him easy, or that the door of mercy will be opened to a loud, but late, Lord, Lord. This revelation of the wrath of God against his enemies is applied to Nineveh (*v.* 8), and should be applied by all those to themselves who go on still in their trespasses : *With an over-running flood he will make an utter end of the place thereof.* The army of the Chaldeans shall overrun the country of the Assyrians, and lay it all waste. God's judgments, when they come with commission, are like a deluge to any people, which they cannot keep off nor make head against. *Darkness shall pursue his enemies ;* terror and trouble shall follow them, whithersoever they go, shall pursue them to utter darkness ; if they think to flee from the darkness which pursues them they will but fall into that which is before them.

II. He is a God of irresistible power, and is able to deal with his enemies, be they ever so many, ever so mighty, ever so hardy. He is *great in power* (*v.* 3), and therefore it is good having him our friend and bad having him our enemy. Now here,

1. The power of God is asserted and proved by divers instances of it in the kingdom of nature, where we always find its visible effects in the ordinary course of nature, and sometimes in the surprising alterations of that course. (1.) If we look up into the regions of the air, there we shall find proofs of his power, for *he has his ways in the whirlwind and the storm.* Which way soever God goes he carries a whirlwind and a storm along with him, for the terror of his enemies, Ps. xviii. 9, &c. And, wherever there is a whirlwind and a storm, God has the command of it, the control of it, makes his way through it, goes on his way in it, and serves his own purposes by it. He spoke to Job out of the whirlwind, and even *stormy winds fulfil his word.* He has *his way in the whirlwind,* that is, he goes on undiscerned, and the methods of his providence are to us unaccountable ; as it is said, *His way is in the sea. The clouds are the dust of his feet ;* he treads on them, walks on them, raises them when he pleases, as a man with his feet raises a cloud of dust. It is but by permission, or usurpation rather, that the devil is the prince of the power of the air, for that power is in God's hand. (2.) If we cast our eye upon the great deeps, we find that the sea is his, for he made it ; for, when he pleases, *he rebukes the sea and makes it dry, by drying up all the rivers* with which it is continually supplied. He gave those proofs of his power when he divided the Red Sea and Jordan,, and can do the same again whenever he pleases. (3.) If we look round us on this earth, we find proofs of his power, when, either by the extreme heat and drought of summer or the cold and frost of winter, *Bashan languishes, and Carmel, and the flower of Lebanon languishes,* the choicest and strongest flower languishes. His power is often seen in earthquakes, which shake the mountains (*v.* 5), melt the hills, and melt them down, and level them with the plains. When he pleases *the earth is burnt at his presence* by the scorching heat of the sun, and he could burn it with fire from heaven, as he did Sodom, and at the end of time he will burn the world *and all that dwell therein.* The earth, and all the works that are therein, shall be burnt up. Thus *great is the Lord* and *of great power.*

2. This is particularly applied to his anger. If God be an almighty God, we may thence infer (*v.* 6), *Who can stand before his indignation?* The Ninevites had once found God *slow to anger* (as he says *v.* 3), and perhaps presumed upon the mercy they had then had experience of, and thought they might make bold with him ; but they will find he is just and jealous as well as merciful and gracious, and, having shown the justice of his wrath, in the next he shows the power of it, and the utter insufficiency of his enemies to contend with him. It is in vain for the stoutest and strongest of sinners to think to make their part good against the power of God's anger. (1.) See God here as *a consuming fire,* terrible and mighty. Here is his indignation against sin, and the *fierceness of his anger,* his fury *poured out,* not like water, but *like fire,* like the fire and brimstone rained on Sodom, Ps. xi. 6. Hell is the fierceness of God's anger, Rev. xvi. 19. God's anger is so fierce that it beats down all before it : *The rocks are thrown*

down by him, which seemed immovable. Rocks have sometimes been rent by the eruption of subterraneous fires, which is a faint resemblance of the fierceness of God's anger against sinners whose hearts are rocky, for none ever hardened their hearts against him, and prospered. (2.) See sinners here as stubble before the fire, weak and impotent, and a very unequal match for the wrath of God. [1.] They are utterly unable to bear up against it, so as to resist it, and put by the strokes of it : *Who can stand before his indignation?* Not the proudest and most daring sinner ; not the world of the ungodly ; no, not the angels that sinned. [2.] They are utterly unable to bear up under it so as to keep up their spirits, and preserve any enjoyment of themselves : *Who can abide in the fierceness of his anger?* As it is irresistible, so it is intolerable. Some of the effects of God's displeasure in this world a man may bear up under, but the *fierceness of his anger,* when it fastens immediately upon the soul, who can bear? Let us therefore *fear before him ;* let us *stand in awe, and not sin.*

III. He is a God of infinite mercy ; and in the midst of all this wrath mercy is remembered. *Let the sinners in Zion be afraid,* that go on still in their transgressions, but let not those that trust in God tremble before him. For, 1. He *is slow to anger* (*v.* 3), not easily provoked, but ready to show mercy to those who have offended him and to receive them into favour upon their repentance. 2. When the tokens of his rage against the wicked are abroad he takes care for the safety and comfort of his own people (*v.* 7): *The Lord is good* to those that are *good,* and to them he will be *a stronghold in the day of trouble.* Note, The same almighty power that is exerted for the terror and destruction of the wicked is engaged, and shall be employed, for the protection and satisfaction of his own people ; he is able both to save and to destroy. In the day of public trouble, when God's judgments are in the earth, laying all waste, he will be a place of defence to those that by faith put themselves under his protection, those that trust in him in the way of their duty, that live a life of dependence upon him and devotedness to him ; he knows them, he owns them for his, he takes cognizance of their case, knows what is best for them, and what course to take most effectually for their relief. They are perhaps obscure and little regarded in the world, but the Lord knows them, Ps. i. 6.

9 What do ye imagine against the LORD? he will make an utter end : affliction shall not rise up the second time. 10 For while *they be* folden together *as* thorns, and while they are drunken *as* drunkards, they shall be devoured as stubble fully dry. 11 There is *one* come out of thee, that

imagineth evil against the LORD, a wicked counsellor. 12 Thus saith the LORD ; Though *they be* quiet, and likewise many, yet thus shall they be cut down, when he shall pass through. Though I have afflicted thee, I will afflict thee no more. 13 For now will I break his yoke from off thee, and will burst thy bonds in sunder. 14 And the LORD hath given a commandment concerning thee, *that* no more of thy name be sown : out of the house of thy gods will I cut off the graven image and the molten image : I will make thy grave ; for thou art vile. 15 Behold upon the mountains the feet of him that bringeth good tidings, that publisheth peace ! O Judah, keep thy solemn feasts, perform thy vows : for the wicked shall no more pass through thee ; he is utterly cut off.

These verses seem to point at the destruction of the army of the Assyrians under Sennacherib, which may well be reckoned a part of the burden of Nineveh, the head city of the Assyrian empire, and a pledge of the destruction of Nineveh itself about 100 years after ; and this was an event which Isaiah, with whom probably this prophet was contemporary, spoke much of. Now observe here,

I. The great provocation which the Assyrians gave to God, the just and jealous God, for which, though *slow to anger,* he would take vengeance (*v.* 11): *There is one come out of thee, that imagines evil against the Lord*—Sennacherib, and his spokesman Rabshakeh. They framed an evil letter and an evil speech, not only against Hezekiah and his people, but against God himself, reflecting upon him as level with the gods of the heathen, and unable to protect his worshippers, dissuading his people from putting confidence in him, and urging them rather to put themselves under the protection of the *great king, the king of Assyria.* They contrived to alter the property of Jerusalem, that it should be no longer the city of the Lord, the holy city. This one, this mighty one, so he thinks himself, that comes out of Nineveh, *imagining evil against the Lord,* brings upon Nineveh this burden. Never was the glorious Majesty of heaven and earth more daringly, more blasphemously affronted than by Sennacherib at that time. He was *a wicked counsellor* who counselled them to despair of God's protection, and surrender themselves to the king of Assyria, and endeavour to put them out of conceit with Hezekiah's reformation (Isa. xxxvi. 7) ; with this wicked counsellor he here expostulates (*v.* 9): "*What do you imagine against the Lord?* What a foolish wicked thing it is for you to plot against God, as if you could outwit divine wisdom and overpower omnipotence itself!" Note, There is a great deal imagined against the Lord by the gates of hell, and against the interests of his kingdom in the world; but it will prove a *vain thing,* Ps. ii. 1, 2. *He that sits in heaven laughs* at the imaginations of the pretenders to politics against him, and will turn their counsels headlong.

II. The great destruction which God would bring upon them for it, not immediately upon the whole monarchy (the ruin of that was deferred till the measure of their iniquity was full), but,

1. Upon the army; God will *make an utter end* of that; it shall be totally cut off and ruined at one blow; one fatal stroke of the destroying angel shall lay them dead upon the spot; *affliction shall not rise up the second time,* for it shall not need. With some sinners God makes a quick despatch, does their business at once. Divine vengeance goes not by one certain rule, nor in one constant track, but one way or other, by acute diseases or chronical ones, by slow deaths or lingering ones, he will *make an utter end* of all his enemies, who persist in their imaginations against him. We have reason to think that the Assyrian army were mostly of the same spirit, and spoke the same language, with their general, and now God would take them to task, though they did but say as they were taught; and it shall appear that they have laid themselves open to divine wrath by their own act and deed, *v.* 10. (1.) They are *as thorns* that entangle one another, and are *folded together.* They make one another worse, and more inveterate against God and his Israel, harden one another's hearts, and strengthen one another's hands, in their impiety; and therefore God will do with them as the husbandman does with a bush of thorns when he cannot part them: he puts them all into the fire together. (2.) They are *as drunken men,* intoxicated with pride and rage; and such as they shall be irrecoverably overthrown and destroyed. They shall be as drunkards, besotted to their own ruin, and shall stumble and fall, and make themselves a reproach, and be justly laughed at. (3.) They shall be *devoured as stubble fully dry,* which is irresistibly and irrecoverably consumed by the flame. The judgments of God are as devouring fire to those that make themselves as stubble to them. It is again threatened concerning this great army (*v.* 12) that *though they be quiet and likewise many,* very secure, not fearing the sallies out of the besieged upon them, because *they are numerous,* yet *thus shall they be cut down,* or certainly shall they be cut down, as grass and corn are cut down, with as little ado, when *he shall pass through,* even the destroying angel

that is commissioned to cut them down. Note, The security of sinners, and their confidence in their own strength, are often presages of ruin approaching.

2. Upon the king. He *imagined evil against the Lord,* and shall he escape? No (*v.* 14): "*The Lord has given a commandment concerning thee;* the decree has gone forth, *that thy name be no more sown,* that thy memory perish, that thou be no more talked of as thou hast been, and that the report of thy mighty actions be dispersed upon the wings of fame and celebrated with her trumpet." Because Sennacherib's son reigned in his stead, some make this to point at the overthrow of the Assyrian empire not long after. Note, Those that *imagine evil against the Lord* hasten evil upon themselves and their own families and interests, and ruin their own names by dishonouring his name. It is further threatened, (1.) That the images he worshipped should be cut off from their temple, the *graven image* and the *molten image out of the house of his gods,* which, some think, was fulfilled when Sennacherib was slain by his *two sons, as he was worshipping in the house of Nisroch his god,* by which barbarous parricide we may suppose the temple was looked upon as defiled, and was therefore disused, and the images were cut off from it, the worshippers of those images no longer attending there. Or it may be taken more generally to denote the utter ruin of Assyria; the army of the enemy shall lay all waste, and not spare even the images of their gods, by which God would intimate to them that one of the grounds of his controversy with them was their idolatry. (2.) That Sennacherib's grave shall be made there, some think in the house of his god; there he is slain, and there he shall be buried, for *he is vile;* he lies under this perpetual mark of disgrace, that he had so far lost his interest in the natural affection of his own children that two of them murdered him. Or it may be meant of the ignominious fall of the Assyrian monarchy itself, upon the ruins of which that of Babylon was raised. What a noise was made about the grave of that once formidable state, but now despicable, is largely described, Ezek. xxxi. 3, 11, 15, 16. Note, Those that make themselves vile by scandalous sins God will make vile by shameful punishments.

III. The great deliverance which God would hereby work for his own people and the city that was called by his name. The ruin of the church's enemies is the salvation of the church, and a very great salvation it was that was wrought for Jerusalem by the overthrow of Sennacherib's army.

1. The siege shall hereby be raised: "*Now will I break his yoke from off thee,* by which thou art kept in servitude, and *will burst thy bonds asunder,* by which thou seemest bound over to the Assyrian's wrath." That vast victorious army, when it forced

free quarters for itself throughout all the land of Judah, and lived at discretion there, was as yokes and bonds upon them. Jerusalem, when it was besieged, was, as it were, bound and fettered by it; but, when the destroying angel had done his work, Jerusalem's bonds were burst asunder, and it was set at liberty again. This was a figure of the great salvation, by which the Jerusalem that is above is made free, is made free indeed.

2. The enemy shall be so weakened and dispirited that they shall never make any such attempt again, and the end of this trouble shall be so well gained by the grace of God that there shall be no more occasion for such a severe correction. (1.) God will not again afflict Jerusalem; his anger is *turned away,* and he says, *It is enough;* for he has by this fright *accomplished his whole work upon Mount Zion* (Isa. x. 12), and therefore "*though I have afflicted thee, I will afflict thee no more;*" the bitter portion shall not be repeated unless there be need and the patient's case call for it; for God *doth not afflict willingly.* (2.) The enemy shall not dare again to attack Jerusalem (*v.* 15): *The wicked shall no more pass through thee* as they have done, to lay all waste, *for he is utterly cut off* and disabled to do it. His army is cut off, his spirit cut off, and at length he himself is cut off.

3. The tidings of this great deliverance shall be published and welcomed with abundance of joy throughout the kingdom, *v.* 15. While Sennacherib prevailed, and carried all before him, every day brought bad news; but now, *behold, upon the mountains, the feet of him that bringeth good tidings,* the *feet of the evangelist;* he is seen coming at a distance upon the mountains, as fast as his feet will carry him; and how pleasant a sight is it once more to see a messenger of peace, after we have received so many of Job's messengers! We find these words made use of by another prophet to illustrate the mercy of the deliverance of the people of God out of Babylon (Isa. lii. 7), not that the prophets stole the word one from another (as those did, Jer. xxiii. 30), but, speaking by the same Spirit, they often used the same expressions; and it may be of good use for ministers to testify their consent to wholesome truths (1 Tim. vi. 3) by concurring in the same forms of sound words, 2 Tim. i. 13. These words are also quoted by the apostle, both from Isaiah and Nahum, and applied to the great redemption wrought out for us by our Lord Jesus, and the publishing of it to the world by the everlasting gospel, Rom. x. 15. Christ's ministers are those messengers of good tidings, that preach *peace by Jesus Christ. How beautiful are the feet of* those *messengers!* How welcome their message to those that see their misery and danger by reason of sin! And observe, He that brings these good tidings brings with them a

call to Judah to *keep her solemn feasts* and *perform her vows.* During the trouble, (1.) The ordinary feasts had been intermitted. *Inter arma silent leges—The voice of law cannot be heard amidst the shouts of battle.* While Jerusalem was *encompassed with armies* they could not go thither to worship; but now that the embargo is taken off they must return to the observance of their feasts; and the feasts of the Lord will be doubly sweet to the people of God when they have been for some time deprived of the benefit of them and God graciously restores them their opportunities again, for we are taught the worth of such mercies by the want of them. (2.) They had made vows to God, that, if he would deliver them out of this distress, they would do something extraordinary in his service, to his honour; and now that the deliverance is wrought they are called upon to perform their vows; the promise they had then made must now be made good, for *better it is not to vow than to vow and not to pay.* And those words, *The wicked shall no more pass through thee,* may be taken as a promise of the perfecting of the good work of reformation which Hezekiah had begun; the wicked shall not, as they have done, walk on every side, but they shall be cut off, and the baffling of the attempts from the wicked enemies abroad is a mercy indeed to a nation when it is accompanied with the restraint and reformation of the wicked at home, who are its more dangerous enemies.

CHAP. II.

We now come closer to Nineveh, that great city; she took not warning by the destruction of her armies and the fall of her king, and therefore may expect, since she persists in her enmity to God, that he will proceed in his controversy with her. Here is foretold, I. The approach of the enemy that should destroy Nineveh, and the terror of his military preparations, ver. 1—5. II. The taking of the city, ver. 6. III. The captivity of the queen, the flight of the inhabitants, the seizing of all its wealth, and the great consternation it should be in, ver. 7—10. IV. All this is traced up to its true causes—their sinning against God and God's appearing against them, ver. 11—13. All this was fulfilled when Nebuchadnezzar, in the first year of his reign, in conjunction with Cyaxares, (or Ahasuerus, king of the Medes,) conquered Nineveh, and made himself master of the Assyrian monarchy.

HE that dasheth in pieces is come up before thy face: keep the munition, watch the way, make *thy* loins strong, fortify *thy* power mightily. 2 For the LORD hath turned away the excellency of Jacob, as the excellency of Israel: for the emptiers have emptied them out, and marred their vine-branches. 3 The shield of his mighty men is made red, the valiant men *are* in scarlet: the chariots *shall be* with flaming torches in the day of his preparation, and the firtrees shall be terribly shaken. 4 The chariots shall rage in the streets, they shall justle one against another in the broad ways: they shall seem like torches, they shall run like the lightnings. 5 He shall recount his worthies: they shall stumble in their walk; they shall make haste to the wall thereof, and the defence shall be prepared. 6 The gates of the rivers shall be opened, and the palace shall be dissolved. 7 And Huzzab shall be led away captive, she shall be brought up, and her maids shall lead *her* as with the voice of doves, tabering upon their breasts. 8 But Nineveh *is* of old like a pool of water: yet they shall flee away. Stand, stand, *shall they cry;* but none shall look back. 9 Take ye the spoil of silver, take the spoil of gold: for *there is* none end of the store *and* glory out of all the pleasant furniture. 10 She is empty, and void, and waste: and the heart melteth, and the knees smite together, and much pain *is* in all loins, and the faces of them all gather blackness.

Here is, I. An alarm of war sent to Nineveh, *v.* 1. The prophet speaks of it as just at hand, for it is neither doubtful nor far distant: "Look about thee, an' see, *he that dashes in pieces has come up before thy face.* Nebuchadnezzar, who is noted, and will be yet more so, for dashing nations in pieces, begins with thee, and will dissipate and disperse thee;" so some render the word. Babylon is called the *hammer of the whole earth,* Jer. l. 23. The attempt of Nebuchadnezzar upon Nineveh is public, bold, and daring: "He *has come up before thy face,* avowing his design to ruin thee; and therefore stand to thy arms, O *Nineveh! keep the munition;* secure thy towers and magazines: *watch the way;* set guards upon all the avenues to the city; *make thy loins strong;* encourage thy soldiers; animate thyself and them; *fortify thy power mightily,* as cities do when an enemy is advancing against them" (this is spoken ironically); "*do the utmost thou canst, yet thou shalt not be able to put by the stroke of this judgment, for there is no counsel or strength against the Lord.*"

II. A manifesto published, showing the causes of the war (*v.* 2): *The Lord has turned away the excellency of Jacob, as the excellency of Israel,* that is, 1. The Assyrians have been abusive to Jacob, the two tribes (have humbled and mortified them), as well as to Israel, the ten tribes, *have emptied them, and marred their vine-branches.* For this God will reckon with them; though done long since, it shall come into the account now against that kingdom, and Nineveh the head-city of it. God's quarrel with them is *for the violence done to Jacob.* Or, (2.) God is now by Nebuchadnezzar about *to turn away the pride of Jacob* by the captivity of the two tribes, as he did the pride of Israel by their captivity; he has done it; he has determined to do it, to bring *emptiers* upon them, and the enemy that is to do it must begin with Nineveh, and reduce that first, and humble the pride of that. God is looking upon proud cities, and abasing them, even those that are nearest to him. Samaria is humbled, and Jerusalem is to be humbled, and their pride brought low; and shall not Nineveh, that proud city, be brought down too? *Emptiers have emptied* the cities, *and marred the vine-branches* in the country of Jacob and Israel; and must not the excellency of Nineveh, that is so much her pride, be turned away too?

III. A particular account given in of the terrors wherein the invading enemy shall appear against Nineveh; every thing shall contribute to make him formidable. 1. *The shields of his mighty men are made red,* and probably their other arms and array, as if they were already tinctured with the blood they had shed, or intended hereby to signify they would put all to the sword; they hung out a red flag, in token that they would give no quarter. 2. *The valiant men are in scarlet;* not only red clothes, to intimate what bloody work they designed to make, but rich clothes, to intimate the wealth of the army, and that is the sinews of war. 3. *The chariots shall be with flaming torches in the day of his preparation;* when they are making their approaches, they shall fly as swiftly as lightning; the wheels shall strike fire upon the stones, and those that drive them shall drive furiously with a flaming indignation, as Jehu drove. Or they carried flaming torches with them in the open chariots, when they made their approach in the night, as Gideon's soldiers carried lamps in their pitchers, to be both a guide to themselves and a terror to their enemies, and with them to set all on fire wherever they went. 4. *The fir-trees shall be terribly shaken;* the great men of Nineveh, that overtop their neighbours, as the stately firs do the shrubs; or the very standing trees shall be made to shake by the violent concussions of the earth, which that great army shall cause. 5. The chariots of war shall be very terrible (*v.* 4): *They shall rage in the streets,* that is, those that drive them shall rage; you would think the chariots themselves raged; they shall be so numerous, and drive with so much fury, that even *in the broad ways,* where, one would think, there should be room enough, they shall *jostle one another;* and these iron chariots shall be made so bright that in the beams of the sun *they shall seem like torches* in the night; they shall *run like the lightnings,* so swiftly, so furiously. Nebuchadnezzar's commanders are here called his *worthies,* his *gallants* (so the margin reads it), his *heroes;* those *he shall recount,* and order them immediately and without fail to render themselves at their respective posts, for he is entering upon action, is resolved to take the field immediately, and to open the campaign with the siege of Nineveh. *His worthies shall remember* (so some read it); they shall be mindful of the duty of their place, and the charge they have received, and shall thereby be made so intent upon their business that they *shall stumble in their walks*, shall make more haste than good speed; they stumble, but shall not fall; for *they shall make haste to the wall thereof*, shall open the trenches; and the defence, or the covered way, shall be prepared (something to shelter them from the darts of the besieged), and they shall so closely carry on the siege, and with so much vigour, that at length the *gates of the rivers shall be opened* (*v.* 6); those gates of Nineveh which open upon the river Tigris (on which Nineveh was built) shall be first forced by, or betrayed to, the enemy, and by those gates they shall enter. And then the *palace shall be dissolved*, either the king's house or the house of Nisroch his god; the same word signifies both a palace and a temple. When the God of heaven goes forth to contend with a people, neither the palaces nor their kings, neither the temples nor their gods, can protect and shelter them, but must all inevitably fall with them.

IV. A prediction of the consequences of this; and it is easy to guess how dismal those will be. 1. The queen shall fall into the hands of the enemy (*v.* 7): *Huzzab shall be led away captive;* she that was *established* (so some read it), thought herself safe because she was concealed and shut up in secret, shall be *discovered* (so the margin reads it) and shall be led *away captive*, in greater disgrace than that of common prisoners; she shall be *brought up* in a mock state, *and her maids* of honour *shall lead her*, because she is weak and faint, not able to bear such frights and hardships, which are doubly hard and frightful to those that have not been used to them; they shall attend her, not to speak cheerfully to her and to encourage her, but murmuring and moaning themselves, as *with the voice of doves*, the *doves of the valleys* (Ezek. vii. 16), noted for their *mourning*, Isa. xxxviii. 14; lix. 11. They shall be *tabering upon their breasts*, beating their own breasts in grief and vexation, as if they were *drumming* upon them, for so the word signifies. 2. The inhabitants, though numerous, shall none of them be able to make head against the invaders, or stand their ground (*v.* 8): *Nineveh is of old like a pool of water*, replenished with people as a pool with water (and *waters* signify *multitudes*, Rev. xvii. 15), or as those waters with fish; it was long ago a populous city; in Jonah's time there were 120,000 little children in it (Jonah iv. 11), and, ordinarily, cities and countries are increasing in their number every year; but, though they have so many hands to be employed in the public

service, yet they shall not be able to inspire one another with courage, but *they shall flee away like cowards.* Their commanders shall do what they can to animate them; they shall cry, " *Stand, stand*, have a good heart on it, and we shall do well enough;" *but none shall* so much as *look back;* they shall not have the least spark of courage remaining, but every one shall think it his wisest course to make his best of the opportunity to escape; they shall not so much as look back to see who calls for them. Note, God can dispirit the strongest and boldest, in the day of distress, so that they shall not be what one would expect from them, but *like a pool of water*, the water whereof is dried up and gone. 3. The wealth of the city shall become a prey, and all its rich furniture shall fall into the hands of the victorious enemy (*v.* 9); they shall thus animate and excite one another to plunder: *Take the spoil of silver; take the spoil of gold;* thus the officers shall stir up the soldiers to improve their opportunity; here are silver and gold enough for them, for *there is no end of the store of money and plate*. Nineveh, having been *of old like a pool of water*, has gathered a vast deal of mud; and abundance of glory it has *out of all the pleasant furniture*, all the *vessels of desire*, which they have gloried in and which shall now be a prey and a pride to the conquerors. Note, Those who prepare raiment as the clay, and heap up silver as the dust, know not who may put on the raiment and divide the silver, Job xxvii. 16, 17. Thus this rich city is empty, and void, and waste, *v.* 10. See the vanity of worldly wealth; instead of defending its owners, it does but expose them, and enable their enemies to do them so much the more mischief. 4. The soldiers and people shall have no heart to appear for the defence of the city. Their spirits shall *melt* away like wax before the fire; their *knees shall smite together* (as Belshazzar's did, in his agony, Dan. v. 6), so that they shall not be able to stand their ground, no, nor to make their escape; *much pain* shall be *in all loins*, as is the case in extreme frights, so that they shall not be able to hold up their backs. And the *faces of them all shall gather blackness*, like that of a pot that is every day over the fire; so the word signifies. Note, Guilt in the conscience will fill men with terror in an evil day, and those who place their happiness in the wealth of this world and set their hearts upon it think themselves undone when their silver, and their gold, and their pleasant furniture are taken from them.

11 Where *is* the dwelling of the lions, and the feeding-place of the young lions, where the lion, *even* the old lion, walked, *and* the lion's whelp, and none made *them* afraid? 12 The lion did tear in pieces enough for his

whelps, and strangled for his lionesses, and filled his holes with prey, and his dens with ravin. 13 Behold, I *am* against thee, saith the LORD of hosts, and I will burn her chariots in the smoke, and the sword shall devour thy young lions : and I will cut off thy prey from the earth, and the voice of thy messengers shall no more be heard.

Here we have Nineveh's ruin, 1. Triumphed in by its neighbours, who now remember against it all the oppressions and abuse of power it had been guilty of in its pomp and prosperity (*v.* 11, 12) : *Where is the dwelling of the lions?* It is gone ; there appear no remnants, no footsteps, of it. *Where is the feeding place of the young lions,* where they glutted themselves with prey? The princes of Nineveh had been as lions, as beasts of prey ; cruel tyrants are no better, nay, in this respect much worse—that, being men, humanity is expected from them ; nay, if they were indeed lions, they would not prey upon those of their own kind. *Sævis inter se convenit ursæ—Fierce bears agree together.* But in the shape of men they had the cruelty of lions : they walked in Nineveh as a lion in the woods, and *none made them afraid;* every one stood in awe of them, and they were under no apprehensions of danger from any ; though nobody loved them, every body feared them, and that was all they desired. *Oderint, dum metuant—Let them hate, so that they do but fear.* The king himself, as well as every prince, made it his business, by all the arts of violence and extortion, to enrich himself and raise his family ; he did *tear in pieces enough for his whelps* (and no little would be enough for them) and he *strangled for his lionesses,* killed all that came near him, and seized what they had for his children, for his wives and concubines, and *filled his holes with prey and his dens with ravin,* as lions are wont to do. Note, Many make it an excuse for their rapine and injustice that they have wives and children to provide for, whereas what is so got will never do them any good ; those that *fear the Lord,* and get what they have honestly, shall not want a competency for themselves and theirs ; *verily they shall be fed,* when *the young lions,* though dens and holes were *filled with prey and ravin* for them, *shall lack, and suffer hunger,* Ps. xxxiv. 10. 2. It is avowed by the righteous Judge of heaven and earth ; it is his doing, and let all the world take notice that it is so (*v.* 13). *Behold, I am against thee, saith the Lord of hosts.* And what good can hosts do for her in her defence, when *the Lord of hosts* is against her for her destruction ? The oppressors in Nineveh thought they only set their neighbours against them, who were not a match for them, and whom they could easily overpower ;

but it proved they set God against them, who is, and will be, the asserter of right and the avenger of wrong. God is against the princes of Nineveh, and then, (1.) These military preparations will stand them in no stead : *I will burn their chariots in the smoke;* he does not say *in the fire,* but, in contempt of them, the very *smoke* of God's indignation shall serve to burn their chariots ; they shall be consumed as soon as the fire of his indignation is kindled, while as yet it does but smoke, and not flame out. Or, The drivers of the chariots shall be smothered and stifled with the smoke ; then the *chariots of their glory* shall be the shame of their families, Isa. xxii. 18. (2.) Their children, the hopes of their families, shall be cut off : *The sword shall devour the young lions,* whom they were so solicitous to provide for by oppression and extortion. Note, It is just with God to deprive those of their children, or (which is all one) of comfort in them, that take sinful courses to enrich them, and (as has been said of some) damn their souls to make their sons gentlemen. (3.) The wealth they have heaped up by fraud and violence shall neither be enjoyed by them nor employed for them : *I will cut off thy prey from the earth;* not only thou shalt not be the better for it, but no one else shall. Some understand it of the disabling of them for the future to prey upon their neighbours. (4.) Their agents abroad shall not have that respect from their neighbours and that influence upon them which sometimes they had had : *The voice of thy messengers shall no more be heard,* no more be heeded, which some think refers to Rabshakeh, one of Nineveh's messengers, that had blasphemed the living God, an iniquity which was remembered against Nineveh long after. Those are not worthy to be heard again that have once spoken reproachfully of God.

CHAP. III.

This chapter goes on with the burden of Nineveh, and concludes it. I. The sins of that great city are charged upon it, murder (ver. 1), whoredom and witchcraft (ver. 4), and a general extent of wickedness, ver. 19. II. Judgments are here threatened against it, blood for blood (ver. 2, 3), and shame for shameful sins, ver. 5–7. III. Instances are given of the like desolations brought upon other places for the like sins, ver. 8–11. IV. The overthrow of all those things which they depended upon, and put confidence in, is foretold, ver. 12–19.

WOE to the bloody city ! it *is* all full of lies *and* robbery ; the prey departeth not ; 2 The noise of a whip, and the noise of the rattling of the wheels, and of the prancing horses, and of the jumping chariots. 3 The horseman lifteth up both the bright sword and the glittering spear : and *there is* a multitude of slain, and a great number of carcases ; and *there is* none end of *their* corpses ; they stumble upon their corpses : 4 Because of the multitude of the whoredoms of the well-favoured harlot, the mistress of witchcrafts, that selleth nations through her whoredoms, and families through her witchcrafts. 5 Behold, I *am* against thee, saith the LORD of hosts; and I will discover thy skirts upon thy face, and I will show the nations thy nakedness, and the kingdoms thy shame. 6 And I will cast abominable filth upon thee, and make thee vile, and will set thee as a gazing-stock. 7 And it shall come to pass, *that* all they that look upon thee shall flee from thee, and say, Nineveh is laid waste : who will bemoan her? whence shall I seek comforters for thee?

Here is, I. Nineveh arraigned and indicted. It is a high charge that is here drawn up against that great city, and neither her numbers nor her grandeur shall secure her from prosecution. 1. It is a *city of blood,* in which a great deal of innocent blood is shed by unrighteous war, or under colour and pretence of public justice, or by suffering barbarous murders to go unpunished ; for this the righteous God will make inquisition. 2. *It is all full of lies :* truth is banished from among them ; there is no such thing as honesty ; one knows not whom to believe nor whom to trust. 3. It is all full of *robbery* and rapine ; no man cares what mischief he does, nor to whom he does it : *The prey departs not,* that is, they never know when they have got enough by spoil and oppression. They shed blood, and told lies, in pursuit of the prey, that they might enrich themselves. 4. There is a *multitude of whoredoms* in it, that is, idolatries, spiritual whoredoms, by which she defiled herself, and to which she seduced the neighbouring nations, as a well-favoured harlot, and sold and ruined *nations through her whoredoms.* 5. She is a *mistress of witchcrafts,* and by them she *sells families, v.* 4. That which Nineveh aimed at was a universal monarchy, to be the metropolis of the world, and to have all her neighbours under her feet; to compass this, she used not only arms, but arts, compelling some, deluding others, into subjection to her, and wheedling them as a harlot by her charms to lay their necks under her yoke, suggesting to them that it would be for their advantage. She courted them to join with her in her idolatrous rites, to tie them the faster to her interests, and made use of her wealth, power, and greatness, to draw people into alliances with her, by which she gained advantages over them, and made a hand of them. These were her whoredoms, like those of Tyre, Isa. xxiii. 15, 17. These were her witchcrafts, with which she unaccountably gained dominion. And for this that God has a quarrel with her who, having

made of one blood all nations of men, never designed one to be a nation of tyrants and another of slaves, and who claims it as his own prerogative to be universal Monarch.

II. Nineveh condemned to ruin upon this indictment. Woe to this bloody city! *v.* 1. See what this woe is.

1. Nineveh had with her cruelties been a terror and destruction to others, and therefore destruction and terror shall be brought upon her. Those that are for overthrowing all that come in their way will, sooner or later, meet with their match. (1.) Hear the alarm with which Nineveh shall be terrified, *v.* 2. It is a formidable army that advances against it ; you may hear them at a distance, the *noise of the whip,* driving the chariot-horses with fury ; you may hear the noise of the *rattling of the wheels, the prancing horses, and the jumping chariots ;* the very noise is frightful, but much more so when they know that all this force is coming with all this speed against them, and they are not able to make head against it. (2.) See the slaughter with which Nineveh shall be laid waste (*v.* 3), the sword drawn with which execution shall be done, *the bright sword lifted up and the glittering spear,* the dazzling brightness of which is very terrible to those whom they are lifted up against. See what havoc these make when they are commissioned to slay : *There is a great number of carcases,* for the slain of the land shall be many ; *there is no end of their corpses ;* there is such *a multitude of slain* that it is in vain to go about to take the number of them ; they lie so thick that passengers are ready to stumble *upon their corpses* at every step. The destruction of Sennacherib's army, which, in the morning, were *all dead corpses,* is perhaps looked upon here as a figure of the like destruction that should afterwards be in Nineveh ; for those that will not take warning by judgments at a distance shall have them come nearer.

2. Nineveh had with her whoredoms and witchcrafts drawn others to shameful wickedness, and therefore God will load her with shame and contempt (*v.* 5—7) : *The Lord of hosts* is *against her,* and then she shall be exposed to the highest degree of disgrace and ignominy, shall not only lose all her charms, but shall be made to appear very odious. When it shall be seen that while she courted her neighbours it was with design to ruin their liberty and property, when all her wicked artifices shall be brought to light, then her *shame is discovered to the nations.* When her proud pretensions are baffled, and her vain towering hopes of an absolute and universal dominion brought to nought, and she appears not to have been so strong and considerable as she would have been thought to be, then *to see the nakedness of the land do they come,* and it appears ridiculous. Then do they *cast abominable filth upon her,* as upon a carted strumpet, and

make her vile as the offscouring of all things; that great city, which all the nations had made court to and coveted an alliance with, has become a gazing-stock, a laughing-stock. Those that formerly looked upon her, and fled to her, in hopes of protection from her, now *look upon her and flee from her*, for fear of being ruined with her. Note, Those that abuse their honour and interest will justly be disgraced and abandoned, and, because miserable, will be made contemptible, and thereby be made more miserable. When Nineveh is laid waste *who will bemoan her?* Her trouble will be so great, and her sense of it so deep, as not to admit relief from sympathy, or any comforting considerations; or, if it would, none shall do any such good office: *When shall I seek comforters for thee?* Note, Those that showed no pity in the day of their power can expect to find no pity in the day of their fall. When those about Nineveh, that had been deceived by her wiles, come to be undeceived in her ruin, every one shall insult over her, and none bemoan her. This was Nineveh's fate, when she was made a spectacle, or gazing-stock. Note, The greater men's show was in the day of their abused prosperity the greater will their shame be in the day of their deserved destruction. *I will make thee an example;* so Drusus reads it. Note, When proud sinners are humbled and brought down it is designed that others should take example by them not to lift up themselves in security and insolence when they prosper in the world.

8 Art thou better than populous No, that was situate among the rivers, *that had* the waters round about it, whose rampart *was* the sea, *and* her wall *was* from the sea? 9 Ethiopia and Egypt *were* her strength, and *it was* infinite; Put and Lubim were thy helpers. 10 Yet *was* she carried away, she went into captivity: her young children also were dashed in pieces at the top of all the streets: and they cast lots for her honourable men, and all her great men were bound in chains. 11 Thou also shalt be drunken: thou shalt be hid, thou also shalt seek strength because of the enemy. 12 All thy strong holds *shall be like* fig-trees with the first-ripe figs: if they be shaken, they shall even fall into the mouth of the eater. 13 Behold, thy people in the midst of thee *are* women: the gates of thy land shall be set wide open unto thine enemies: the fire shall devour thy bars. 14 Draw thee waters for the siege, fortify thy

strong holds: go into clay, and tread the mortar, make strong the brick-kiln. 15 There shall the fire devour thee; the sword shall cut thee off, it shall eat thee up like the canker-worm: make thyself many as the cankerworm, make thyself many as the locusts. 16 Thou hast multiplied thy merchants above the stars of heaven: the canker-worm spoileth, and fleeth away. 17 Thy crowned *are* as the locusts, and thy captains as the great grasshoppers, which camp in the hedges in the cold day, *but* when the sun ariseth they flee away, and their place is not known where they *are.* 18 Thy shepherds slumber, O king of Assyria: thy nobles shall dwell *in the dust:* thy people is scattered upon the mountains, and no man gathereth *them.* 19 *There is* no healing of thy bruise; thy wound is grievous: all that hear the bruit of thee shall clap the hands over thee: for upon whom hath not thy wickedness passed continually?

Nineveh has been told that God is against her, and then none can be for her, to stand her in any stead; yet she sets God himself at defiance, and his power and justice, and says, *I shall have peace.* Threatened folks live long; therefore here the prophet largely shows how vain her confidences would prove and insufficient to ward off the judgment of God. To convince them of this,

I. He shows them that other places, which had been as strong and as secure as they, could not keep their ground against the judgments of God. Nineveh shall fall unpitied and uncomforted (for miserable comforters will those prove who speak peace to those on whom God will fasten trouble), and she shall not be able to help herself: *Art thou better than populous No? v.* 8. He takes them off from their vain confidences by quoting precedents. The city mentioned is *No,* a great city in the land of Egypt (Jer. xlvi. 25), *No-Ammon,* so some read it both there and here. We read of it, Ezek. xxx. 14—16. Some think it was *Diospolis,* others *Alexandria.* As God said to Jerusalem, *Go, see what I did to Shiloh* (Jer. vii. 12), so to Nineveh that great city, *Go, see what I did to populous No.* Note, It will help to keep us in a holy fear of the judgments of God to consider that we are not better than those that have fallen under those judgments before us. We deserve them as much, and are as little able to grapple with them. This also should help to reconcile us to afflictions. Are we better than such and such, who were in like manner exercised? Nay, were not they better than we, and less likely to be afflicted? Now, concerning No, observe, 1. How firm her standing seemed to be, *v.* 8. She was fortified both by nature and art, was *situate among the rivers.* Nile, in several branches, not only watered her fields, but guarded her wall. *Her rampart was the sea,* the *lake of Mareotis,* an Egyptian sea, like the sea of Tiberias. Her *wall was from the sea;* it was fenced with a wall which was thought to make the place impregnable. It was also supported by its interests and alliances abroad, *v.* 9. *Ethiopia,* or Arabia, *was her strength,* either by the wealth brought to her in a way of trade or by the auxiliary forces furnished for military service. The whole country of Egypt also contributed to the strength of this populous city; so that it was *infinite, and there was no end of it* (so it might be rendered); she set no bounds to her ambition and knew no end of her wealth and strength; people flocked to her endlessly, and she thought there never would be any end of it; but it is God's prerogative to be infinite. *Put and Lubim were thy helpers,* two neighbouring countries of Africa, Mauritania and Libya, that is, Libya Cyrenica, a country that Egypt had much dependence upon. No, thus helped, seemed to sit as a queen, and was not likely to see any sorrow. But, 2. See how fatal her fall proved to be (*v.* 10): *Yet was she carried away,* and her strength failed her; even she that was so strong, so secure, yet *went into captivity.* This refers to some destruction of that city which was then well-known, and probably fresh in memory, though not recorded in history; for the destruction of it by Nebuchadnezzar (if we should understand this prophetically) could not be made an example to Nineveh; for the reducing of Nineveh was one of the first of his victories and that of Egypt one of the last. The strength and grandeur of that great city could not be its protection from military execution. (1.) Not from that which was most barbarous; for *her young children* had no compassion shown them, but were *dashed in pieces at the top of all the streets* by the merciless conquerors. (2.) Not from that which was most inglorious and disgraceful: *They cast lots for her honourable men* that were made prisoners of war, who should have them for their slaves. So many had they of them that they knew not what to do with them, but they made sport with throwing dice for them; *all her great men,* that used to be adorned on state-days with chains of gold, *were* now *bound in chains of iron;* they were *pinioned* or *handcuffed* (so the word properly signifies), not only as slaves, but as condemned malefactors. What a mortification was this to *populous No,* to have her honourable men and great men, that were her pride and confidence, thus abused! Now hence he infers against Nineveh (*v.* 11), " Thou also shalt be intoxicated, infatuated;

thou also shalt reel and stagger, as drunk with the cup of the Lord's fury, that shall be put into thy hand" (see Jer. xxv. 17, 27); " *Thou shalt fall and rise no more.* The cup shall go round, and come to thy turn, O Nineveh! to drink off at last, and shall be to thee as the waters of jealousy."

II. He shows them that all those things which they reposed a confidence in should fail them. 1. Did the men of Nineveh trust to their own magnanimity and bravery? Their hearts should sink and fail them. *They shall be hid,* shall abscond for shame, being in disgrace, abscond for fear, being in distress and danger, and not able to face the enemies, because of whose strength and terror, having no strength of their own, they shall *seek strength,* shall come sneaking to their neighbours to beg their assistance in a time of need. Thus God can *cut off the spirit* of princes, and *take away their heart.* 2. Did they depend upon their barrier, the garrisons and strongholds they had, which were regularly fortified and bravely manned? Those shall prove but paper-walls, and *like the first-ripe figs,* which, if you give the tree but a little shake, will *fall into the mouth of the eater* that gapes for them; so easily will all their strongholds be made to surrender to the advancing enemy, upon the first summons, *v.* 12. Note, Strongholds, even the strongest, are no fence against the judgments of God, when they come with commission. *The rich man's wealth is his strong city, and a high wall,* but only *in his own conceit,* Prov xviii. 10. They are supposed to make their strongholds as strong as possible, and are challenged to do their utmost to make them tenable, and serviceable to them against the invader (*v.* 14): *Draw thee water for the siege;* lay in great quantities of water, that that which is so necessary to the support of human life may not be wanting; it is put here for all manner of provision, with which Nineveh is ironically told to furnish herself, in expectation of a siege. " Take ever so much care that thou mayest not be starved out, and forced by famine to surrender, yet that shall not avail. *Fortify the strongholds,* by adding out-works to them, or putting men and arms into them," as with us by planting cannon upon them. " *Go into clay, and tread the mortar,* and *make strong the brick-kiln;* take all the pains thou canst in erecting new fortifications; but it shall be all in vain, for (*v.* 15) there shall even *the fire devour thee* if the stronghold be burnt, or *the sword cut thee off* if it be taken by storm." It is by fire and sword that in time of war the great devastations are made. 3. Did they put confidence in the multitude of their inhabitants? Were they, from their number and valour, reckoned their strongest walls and fortifications? Alas! these shall stand them in no stead; they shall but sink the sooner under the weight of their own numbers (*v.* 13): *Thy people in the midst of thee are women;* they have no wisdom, no courage; they shall be fickle, feeble, and faint-hearted, as women commonly are in such times of danger and distress; they shall be at their wits' end, adding to their griefs and fears by the power of their own imagination, and utterly unable to do any thing for themselves; the valiant men shall become cowards. *O verè Phrygiæ, neque enim Phryges—Phrygian dames, not Phrygian men.* Though they *make themselves many (v. 15),* as the *canker-worm* and *as the locust,* that come in vast swarms, *though thou hast multiplied thy merchants above the stars of heaven,* though thy exchange be thronged with wealthy traders, who, having so much money to stand up in defence of and so much to lay out in the means of their defence, should, one would think, give the enemy a warm reception, yet their hearts shall fail them too; though they be numerous as caterpillars, yet the fire and sword shall eat them up easily and irresistibly as the canker-worm, *v.* 15. They are as numerous as those wasting insects, but their enemies shall be mischievous like them. He adds (*v.* 16), *The canker-worm spoils,* or *spreads herself, and flies away.* Both the merchants and the enemies were compared to canker-worms. The enemies shall spoil Nineveh, and carry away the spoil, without opposition, or any hope of recovering it. Or the rich merchants, who have come from abroad to settle in Nineveh, and have raised vast estates there, out of which it was hoped they would contribute largely for the defence of the city, when they see the country invaded and the city likely to be besieged, will send away their effects, and remove to some other place, will *spread their wings* and *fly away* where they may be safe, and Nineveh shall be never the better for them. Note, It is rare to find even those that have shared with us in our joys willing to share with us in our griefs too. The canker-worms will continue upon the field while there is any thing to be had, but they are gone when all is gone. Those that men have got by they do not care to lose by. Nineveh's merchants bid her farewell in her distress. Riches themselves are as the canker-worms, which on a sudden *fly away as the eagle towards heaven,* Prov. xxiii. 5. 4. Did they put a confidence in the strength of their gates and bars? What fence will those be against the force of the judgments of God? *v.* 13. *The gates of thy land shall be set wide open unto thy enemies,* the gates of thy rivers (*ch.* ii. 6), the flood-gates, or the passes and avenues, by which the enemy would make his entrance into the country, or the gates of the cities; these, though ever so strong and well-guarded, shall not answer their end: *The fire shall devour thy bars,* the bars of thy gates, and then they shall fly

open. 5. Did they put a confidence in their king and princes? They should do them no service (*v.* 17): *Thy crowned heads are as the locusts;* those that had pomp and power, as crowned heads, were enfeebled, and had no power to make resistance, when the enemy came in like a flood. " *Thy captains,* that should lead thy forces into the field, are great indeed, and look great, but they are as the great *grasshoppers,* the *maximum quod sic—the largest specimens* of that *species;* still they are but grasshoppers, worthless things, that can do no service. *They encamp in the hedges, in the cold day,* the cold weather, *but, when the sun arises, they flee away,* and are gone, nobody knows whither. So these mercenary soldiers that lay slumbering about Nineveh, when any trouble arises, flee away, and shift for their own safety. *The hireling flees, because he is a hireling.*" The *king of Assyria* is told, and it is a shame he needs to be told it (who might observe it himself), that *his shepherds slumber;* they have no life or spirit to appear for the flock, and are very remiss in the discharge of the duty of their place and the trust reposed in them : Thy *nobles shall dwell in the dust,* and be buried in silence. 6. Did they hope that they should yet recover themselves and rally again? In this also they should be disappointed; for, when the shepherds are smitten, the *sheep are scattered;* the people are dispersed *upon the mountains* and *no man gathers them,* nor will they ever come together of themselves, but will wander endlessly, as scattered sheep do. The judgment they are under is as a wound, and it is incurable; there is no relief for it, "*no healing of thy bruise,* no possibility that the wound, which is so grievous and painful to thee, should be so much as skinned over; thy case is desperate (*v.* 19) and thy neighbours, instead of lending a hand to help thee, shall *clap their hands over thee,* and triumph in thy fall; and the reason is, because thou hast been one way or other injurious to them all : *Upon whom has not thy wickedness passed continually?* Thou hast been always doing mischief to those about thee; there is none of them but what thou hast abused and insulted; and therefore they shall be so far from pitying thee that they shall be glad to see thee reckoned with." Note, Those that have been abusive to their neighbours will, one time or another, find it come home to them; they are but preparing enemies to themselves against their day comes to fall : and those that dare not lay hands on them themselves will *clap their hands over them,* and upbraid them with their former wickedness, for which they are now well enough served and paid in their own coin. *The troublers shall be troubled* will be the burden of many, as it is here *the burden of Nineveh.*

AN

EXPOSITION,

WITH PRACTICAL OBSERVATIONS,

OF THE PROPHECY OF

HABAKKUK.

It is a very foolish fancy of some of the Jewish rabbin that this prophet was the son of the Shunamite woman that was at first miraculously given, and afterwards raised to life, by Elisha (2 Kings iv.), as they say also that the prophet Jonah was the son of the widow of Zarephath, which Elijah raised to life. It is a more probable conjecture of their modern chronologers that he lived and prophesied in the reign of king Manasseh, when wickedness abounded, and destruction was hastening on, destruction by the Chaldeans, whom this prophet mentions as the instruments of God's judgments; and Manasseh was himself carried to Babylon, as an earnest of what should come afterwards. In the apocryphal story of Bel and the Dragon mention is made of Habakkuk the prophet in the land of Judah, who was carried thence by an angel to Babylon, to feed Daniel in the den; those who give credit to that story take pains to reconcile our prophet's living before the captivity, and foretelling it, with that. Huetius thinks that that was another of the same name, a prophet, this of the tribe of Simeon, that of Levi; others that he lived so long as to the end of the captivity, though he prophesied of it before it came. And some have imagined that Habakkuk's feeding Daniel in the den is to be understood mystically, that Daniel then *lived by faith*, as Habakkuk had said *the just should do ;* he was *fed* by that word, Hab. ii. 4. The prophecy of this book is a mixture of the prophet's addresses to God in the people's name and to the people in God's name; for it is the office of the prophet to carry messages both ways. We have in it a lively representation of the intercourse and communion between a gracious God and a gracious soul. The whole refers particularly to the invasion of the land of Judah by the Chaldeans, which brought spoil upon the people of God, a just punishment of the spoil they had been guilty of among themselves; but it is of general use, especially to help us through that great temptation with which good men have in all ages been exercised, arising from the power and prosperity of the wicked and the sufferings of the righteous by it.

CHAP. I.

In this chapter, I. The prophet complains to God of the violence done by the abuse of the sword of justice among his own people and the hardships thereby put upon many good people, ver. 1—4. II. God by him foretels the punishment of that abuse of power by the sword of war, and the desolations which the army of the Chaldeans should make upon them, ver. 5–11. III. Then the prophet complains of that too, and is grieved that the Chaldeans prevail so far (ver. 12—17), so that he scarcely knows which is more to be lamented, the sin or the punishment of it, for in both many harmless good people are very great sufferers. It is well that there is a day of judgment, and a future state, before us, in which it shall be eternally well with all the righteous, and with them only, and ill with all the wicked, and them only; so the present seeming disorders of Providence shall be set to rights, and there will remain no matter of complaint whatsoever.

THE burden which Habakkuk the prophet did see. 2 O Lord, how long shall I cry, and thou wilt not hear! *even* cry out unto thee *of* violence, and thou wilt not save! 3 Why dost thou show me iniquity, and cause *me* to behold grievance? for spoiling and violence *are* before me: and there are *that* raise up strife and contention.

4 Therefore the law is slacked, and judgment doth never go forth : for the wicked doth compass about the righteous ; therefore wrong judgment proceedeth.

We are told no more in the title of this book (which we have, *v.* 1) than that the penman was *a prophet*, a man divinely inspired and commissioned, which is enough (if that be so, we need not ask concerning his tribe or family, or the place of his birth), and that the book itself is *the burden which* he *saw ;* he was as sure of the truth of it as if he had seen it with his bodily eyes already accomplished. Here, in these verses, the prophet sadly laments the iniquity of the times, as one sensibly touched with grief for the lamentable decay of religion and righteousness. It is a very melancholy complaint which he here makes to God, 1. That no man could call what he had his own; but, in defiance of the most sacred laws of property and equity, he that had power on his side had what he had a mind to, though he had no right on his side: the land was *full of violence*, as the old world was, Gen. vi. 11. The prophet *cries out of violence* (v. 2), *iniquity* and *grievance*, *spoil* and *violence*. In families and among relations, in neighbourhoods and among friends, in commerce and in courts of law, every thing was carried with a high hand, and no man made any scruple of doing wrong to his neighbour, so that he could but make a good hand of it for himself. It does not appear that the prophet himself had any great wrong done him (in losing times it fared best with those that had nothing to lose), but it grieved him to see other people wronged, and he could not but mingle his tears with those of the oppressed. Note, Doing wrong to harmless people, as it is an iniquity in itself, so it is a great grievance to all that are concerned for God's Jerusalem, who *sigh and cry for abominations* of this kind. He complains (v. 4) that *the wicked doth compass about the righteous*. One honest man, one honest cause, shall have enemies besetting it on every side; many wicked men, in confederacy against it, run it down; nay, one wicked man (for it is singular) with so many various arts of mischief sets upon a righteous man, that he perfectly besets him. 2. That the kingdom was broken into parties and factions that were continually biting and devouring one another. This is a lamentation to all the sons of peace: *There are that raise up strife and contention* (v. 3), that foment divisions, widen breaches, incense men against one another, and sow discord among brethren, by doing the work of him that is the accuser of the brethren. Strifes and contentions that have been laid asleep, and begun to be forgotten, they awake, and industriously raise up again, and blow up the sparks that were hidden under the embers. And, if *blessed are the peace-makers*, cursed are such peace-breakers, that make parties, and so make mischief that spreads further, and lasts longer, than they can imagine. It is sad to see bad men warming their hands at those flames which are devouring all that is good in a nation, and stirring up the fire too. 3. That the torrent of violence and strife ran so strongly as to bid defiance to the restraints and regulations of laws and the administration of justice, v. 4. Because God did not appear against them, nobody else would; *therefore the law is slacked*, is silent; it breathes not; *its pulse beats not* (so, it is said, the word signifies); it intermits, *and judgment does not go forth* as it should; no cognizance is taken of those crimes, no justice done upon the criminals; nay, *wrong judgment proceeds*: if appeals be made to the courts of equity, the righteous shall be condemned and the wicked justified, so that the remedy

proves the worst disease. The legislative power takes no care to supply the deficiencies of the law for the obviating of those growing threatening mischiefs; the executive power takes no care to answer the good intentions of the laws that are made; the stream of justice is dried up by violence, and has not its free course. 4. That all this was open and public, and impudently avowed; it was barefaced. The prophet complains that this iniquity was shown him; he *beheld it* which way soever he turned his eyes, nor could he look off it: *Spoiling and violence are before me.* Note, The abounding of wickedness in a nation is a very great eye-sore to good people, and, if they did not see it, they could not believe it to be so bad as it is. Solomon often complains of the vexation of this kind which he *saw under the sun;* and the prophet would therefore gladly turn hermit, that he might not see it, Jer. ix. 2. But *then we must needs go out of the world*, which *therefore* we should long to do, that we may remove to that world where holiness and love reign eternally, and no spoiling and violence shall be before us. 5. That he complained of this to God, but could not obtain a redress of those grievances: " *Lord,*" says he, " *why dost thou show me iniquity?* Why hast thou cast my lot in a time and place when and where it is to be seen, and why do I continue to *sojourn in Mesech* and *Kedar? I cry to thee* of this violence; I cry aloud; I have cried long; but *thou wilt not hear, thou wilt not save;* thou dost not take vengeance on the oppressors, nor do justice to the oppressed, as if thy arm were shortened or thy ear heavy." When God seems to connive at the wickedness of the wicked, nay, and to countenance it, by suffering them to prosper in their wickedness, it shocks the faith of good men, and proves a sore temptation to them to say, *We have cleansed our hearts in vain* (Ps. lxxiii. 13), and hardens those in their impiety who say, *God has forsaken the earth.* We must not think it strange if wickedness be suffered to prevail far and prosper long. God has reasons, and we are sure they are good reasons, both for the reprieves of bad men and the rebukes of good men; and therefore, though we plead with him, and humbly expostulate concerning his judgments, yet we must say, " He is wise, and righteous, and good, in all," and must believe the day will come, though it may be long deferred, when the cry of sin will be heard against those that do wrong and the cry of prayer for those that suffer it.

5 Behold ye among the heathen, and regard, and wonder marvellously: for *I* will work a work in your days, *which* ye will not believe, though it be told *you.* 6 For, lo, I raise up the Chaldeans, *that* bitter and hasty

nation, which shall march through the breadth of the land, to possess the dwelling-places *that are* not their's. 7 They *are* terrible and dreadful: their judgment and their dignity shall proceed of themselves. 8 Their horses also are swifter than the leopards, and are more fierce than the evening wolves: and their horsemen shall spread themselves, and their horsemen shall come from far; they shall fly as the eagle *that* hasteth to eat. 9 They shall come all for violence: their faces shall sup up *as* the east wind, and they shall gather the captivity as the sand. 10 And they shall scoff at the kings, and the princes shall be a scorn unto them: they shall deride every strong hold; for they shall heap dust, and take it. 11 Then shall *his* mind change, and he shall pass over, and offend, *imputing* this his power unto his god.

We have here an answer to the prophet's complaint, giving him assurance that, though God bore long, he would not bear always with this provoking people; for the day of vengeance was in his heart, and he must tell them so, that they might by repentance and reformation turn away the judgment they were threatened with.

I. The preamble to the sentence is very awful (*v.* 5): *Behold, you among the heathen, and regard.* Since they will not be brought to repentance by the long-suffering of God, he will take another course with them. No resentments are so keen, so deep, as those of abused patience. The Lord will inflict upon them, 1. A public punishment, which shall be beheld and regarded among the heathen, which the neighbouring nations shall take notice of and stand amazed at; see Deut. xxix. 24, 25. This will aggravate the desolations of Israel, that they will thereby be made a spectacle to the world. 2. An amazing punishment, so strange and surprising, and so much out of the common road of Providence, that it shall not be paralleled among the heathen, shall be sorer and heavier than what God has usually inflicted upon the nations that know him not; nay, it shall not be credited even by those that had the prediction of it from God before it comes, or the report of it from those that were eye-witnesses of it when it comes: *You will not believe it, though it be told you;* it will be thought incredible that so many judgments should combine in one, and every circumstance so strangely concur to enforce and aggravate it, that so great and potent a nation should be so reduced and broken, 1354

and that God should deal so severely with a people that had been taken into the bond of the covenant and that he had done so much for. The punishment of God's professing people cannot but be the astonishment of all about them. 3. A speedy punishment: " *I will work a work in your days,* now quickly; this generation shall not pass till the judgment threatened be accomplished. The sins of former days shall be reckoned for in your days; for now the measure of the iniquity is full," Matt. xxiii. 36. 4. It shall be a punishment in which much of the hand of God shall appear; it shall be a work of his own working, so that all who see it shall say, *This is the Lord's doing;* and it will be found a fearful thing to fall into his hands; woe to those whom he takes to task! 5. It shall be such a punishment as will typify the destruction to be brought upon the despisers of Christ and his gospel, for to that these words are applied Acts xiii. 41, *Behold, you despisers, and wonder, and perish.* The ruin of Jerusalem by the Chaldeans for their idolatry was a figure of their ruin by the Romans for rejecting Christ and his gospel, and it is a very marvellous thing, and almost incredible. *Is there not a strange punishment to the workers of iniquity?*

II. The sentence itself is very dreadful and particular (*v.* 6): *Lo, I raise up the Chaldeans.* There were those that raised up a great deal of strife and contention among them, which was their sin; and now God will raise up the Chaldeans against them, who shall strive and contend with them, which shall be their punishment. Note, When God's professing people quarrel among themselves, snarl at, and devour one another, it is just with God to bring the common enemy upon them, that shall make peace by making a universal devastation. The contending parties in Jerusalem were inveterate one against another, when the Romans came and *took away their place and nation.* The Chaldeans shall be the instruments of the destruction threatened, and, though themselves acting unrighteously, they shall *execute the righteousness of the Lord* and punish the unrighteousness of Israel. Now here we have,

1. A description of the people that shall be raised up against Israel, to be a scourge to them. (1.) They are *a bitter and hasty nation,* cruel and fierce, and what they do is done with violence and fury; they are precipitate in their counsels, vehement in their passions, and push on with resolution in their enterprises; they show no mercy and they spare no pains. Miserable is the case of those that are given up into the hand of these cruel ones. (2.) They are strong, and therefore formidable, and such as there is no standing before, and yet no fleeing from (*v.* 7): *They are terrible and dreadful,* famed for the gallant troops they bring into the field (*v.* 8); *their horses are swifter than leopards*

to charge and pursue, and *more fierce than the evening wolves ;* and wolves are observed to be the most ravenous towards the evening, after they have been kept hungry all day, waiting for that darkness under the protection of which *all the beasts of the forest creep forth,* Ps. civ. 20. Their squadrons of horse shall be very numerous : "*Their horsemen shall spread themselves* a great way, for they shall *come from far,* from all parts of their own country, and shall be dispersed into all parts of the country they invade, to plunder it, and enrich themselves with the spoil of it. And, *in making speed to spoil, they shall hasten to the prey* (as those, Isa. viii. 1, *margin),* for they shall *fly as the eagle* towards the earth when she *hastens to eat,* and strikes at the prey she has an eye upon." (3.) Their own will is a law to them, and, in the fierceness of their pursuits, they will not be governed by any laws of humanity, equity, or honour : *Their judgment and their dignity shall proceed of themselves, v.* 7. Appetite and passion rule them, and not reason nor conscience. Their principle is, *Quicquid libet, licet—My will is my law.* And, *Sic volo, sic jubeo ; stat pro ratione voluntas— This is my wish, this is my command ; it shall be done because I choose it.* What favour can be hoped for from such an enemy ? Note, Those who have been unjust and unmerciful, among whom *the law is slacked, and judgment doth not go forth,* will justly be paid in their own coin and fall into the hands of those who will deal unjustly and unmercifully with them.

2. A prophecy of the terrible execution that shall be made by this terrible nation : *They shall march through the breadth of the earth* (so it may be read) ; for in a little time the Chaldean forces subdued all the nations in those parts, so that they seemed to have conquered the world ; they overran Asia and part of Africa. Or, through the breadth of *the land* of Israel, which was wholly laid waste by them. It is here foretold, (1.) That they shall seize all as their own that they can lay their hands on. They shall come to *possess the dwelling-places that are not theirs,* which they have no right to, but that which their sword gives them. (2.) That they shall push on the war with all possible vigour : *They shall all come for violence (v.* 9), not to determine any disputed right by the sword, but, right or wrong, to enrich themselves with the spoil. *Their faces shall sup up as the east wind ;* their very countenances shall be so fierce and frightful that a look will serve to make them masters of all they have a mind to ; so that they shall *swallow up* all, as the east wind nips and blasts the buds and flowers. *Their faces shall look towards the east* (so some read it) ; they shall still have an eye to their own country, which lay eastward from Judea, and all the spoil they seize they shall remit thither. (3.) That they shall take a vast number of prisoners, and send them into Babylon : *They shall gather the captivity as the sand* for multitude, and shall never know when they have enough, as long as there are any more to be had. (4.) That they shall make nothing of the opposition that is given to them, *v.* 10. Do the distressed Jews depend upon their great men to make a stand, and with their wisdom and courage to give check to the victorious arms of the Chaldeans? Alas ! they will make nothing of them. *They shall scoff* (he shall, so it is in the original, meaning Nebuchadnezzar, who, being puffed up with his successes, shall scoff) *at the kings* and commanders of the forces that think to make head against him ; and *the princes shall be a scorn to them,* so unequal a match shall they appear to be. Do they depend upon their garrisons and fortified towns ? *He shall deride every stronghold,* for to him it shall be weak, and *he shall heap dust, and take it ;* a little soil, thrown up for ramparts, shall serve to give him all the advantage against them that he can desire ; he shall make but a jest of them, and a sport of taking them. (5.) By all this he shall be puffed up with an intolerable pride, which shall be his destruction (*v.* 11): *Then shall his mind change* for the worse. The spirit both of the people and of the king shall grow more haughty and insolent. Those that will not be content with their own rights will not be content when they have made themselves masters of other people's rights too ; but as the condition rises the mind rises too. This victorious king shall *pass over* all the bounds of reason, equity, and modesty, and break through all their bonds, and thereby *he shall offend,* shall make God his enemy, and so prepare ruin for himself by *imputing this his power to his god,* whereas he had it from the God of Israel. *Bel* and *Nebo* were the gods of the Chaldeans, and to them they gave the glory of their successes ; they were hardened in their idolatry, and blasphemously argued that because they had conquered Israel their gods were too strong for the God of Israel. Note, It is a great offence (and the common offence of proud people) to take that glory to ourselves, or to give it to gods of our own making, which is due to the living and true God only. These closing words of the sentence give a glimpse of comfort to the afflicted people of God ; it is to be hoped that they will change their minds, and grow better, and ripen for deliverance ; and they did so. However, their enemies will change their minds, and grow worse, and ripen for destruction, which will inevitably come in God's due time ; for a haughty spirit, lifted up against God, *goes before a fall.*

12 *Art* thou not from everlasting, O LORD my God, mine Holy One ? we shall not die. O LORD, thou hast ordained them for judgment ; and, O

mighty God, thou hast established them for correction. 13 *Thou art* of purer eyes than to behold evil, and canst not look on iniquity : wherefore lookest thou upon them that deal treacherously, *and* holdest thy tongue when the wicked devoureth *the man that is* more righteous than he ? 14 And makest men as the fishes of the sea, as the creeping things, *that have* no ruler over them ? 15 They take up all of them with the angle, they catch them in their net, and gather them in their drag : therefore they rejoice and are glad. 16 Therefore they sacrifice unto their net, and burn incense unto their drag ; because by them their portion *is* fat, and their meat plenteous. 17 Shall they therefore empty their net, and not spare continually to slay the nations ?

The prophet, having received of the Lord that which he was to deliver to the people, now turns to God, and again addresses himself to him for the ease of his own mind under the burden which he saw. And still he is full of complaints. If he look about him, he sees nothing but violence done by Israel; if he look before him, he sees nothing but violence done against Israel ; and it is hard to say which is the more melancholy sight. His thoughts of both he pours out before the Lord. It is our duty to be affected both with the iniquities and with the calamities of the church of God and of the times and places wherein we live; but we must take heed lest we grow peevish in our resentments, and carry them too far, so as to entertain any hard thoughts of God, or lose the comfort of our communion with him. The world is bad, and always was so, and will be so ; it is out of our power to mend it; but we are sure that God governs the world, and will bring glory to himself out of all, and therefore we must resolve to make the best of it, must be ourselves better, and long for the better world. The prospect of the prevalence of the Chaldeans drives the prophet to his knees, and he takes the liberty to plead with God concerning it. In his plea we may observe,

I. The truths which he lays down, which he resolves to abide by, and with which he endeavours to comfort himself and his friends, under the growing threatening power of the Chaldeans ; and they will furnish us with pleasing considerations for our support in the like case.

1. However it be, yet God is *the Lord our God,* and *our Holy One.* The victorious Chaldeans impute their power to their idols, but we are taught to tell them that the God

1356

of Israel is the true God, the living God, Jer. x. 10, 11. (1.) He is *Jehovah,* the fountain of all being, power, and perfection. *Our rock is not as theirs.* (2.) " He is *my God.*" He speaks in the people's name ; every Israelite may say, " He is *mine.* Though we are thus sore broken, and *all this has come upon us, yet have we not forgotten the name of our God,* nor quitted our relation to him, yet have we not disowned him, nor hath he disowned us, Ps. xliv. 17. We are an offending people; he is an offended God ; yet he is ours, and we will not entertain any hard thoughts of him, nor of his service, for all this." (3.) " He is *my Holy One.*" This intimates that the prophet loved God as a holy God, loved him for the sake of his holiness. " He is *mine* because he is a *Holy One;* and *therefore* he will be my sanctifier and my Saviour, because he is *my Holy One.* Men are unholy, but *my God is holy.*"

2. Our God is from everlasting. This he pleads with him : *Art thou not from everlasting, O Lord my God?* It is matter of great and continual comfort to God's people, under the troubles of this present life, that their God is from everlasting. This intimates, (1.) The eternity of his nature ; if he is from everlasting, he will be to everlasting, and we must have recourse to this first principle, when things seen, which are temporal, are discouraging, that we have hope and help sufficient in a God that is not seen, that is eternal. " Art thou not from everlasting, and then wilt thou not make bare thy everlasting arm, in pursuance of thy everlasting counsels, to make unto thyself an everlasting name ?" (2.) The antiquity of his covenant : " Art thou not *from of old,* a God in covenant with thy people" (so some understand it), " and hast thou not done great things for them *in the days of old,* which we have heard with our ears, and which our fathers have told us of ; and art thou not the same God still that thou ever wast ? Thou art *God, and changest not.*"

3. While the world stands God will have a church in it. Thou art from everlasting, and then *we shall not die.* The Israel of God shall not be extirpated, nor the name of Israel blotted out, though it may sometimes seem to be very near it ; like the apostles (2 Cor. vi. 9), *chastened, and not killed ; chastened sorely, but not delivered over to death,* Ps. cxviii. 18. See how the prophet infers the perpetuity of the church from the eternity of God ; for Christ has said, *Because I live,* and therefore as long as I live, *you shall live also,* John xiv. 19. He is the rock on which the church is so firmly built that the *gates of hell shall not, cannot, prevail against it. We shall not die.*

4. Whatever the enemies of the church may do against her, it is according to the counsel of God, and is designed and directed for wise and holy ends : *Thou hast ordained them ; thou hast established them.* It was

God that gave the Chaldeans their power, made them a formidable people, and in his counsel determined what they should do, nor had they any power against his Israel but what was *given them from above.* He gave them their commission *to take the spoil and to take the prey,* Isa. x. 6. Herein God appears a mighty God, that the power of mighty men is derived from him, depends upon him, and is under his cheek; he says concerning it, *Hitherto shall it come, and no further.* Those whom God ordains shall do no more than what God has ordained, which is a great comfort to God's suffering people. Men are God's hand, the rod in his hand, Ps. xvii. 14. And he has *ordained them for judgment,* and *for correction.* God's people need correction, and deserve it; they must expect it; they shall have it; when wicked men are let loose against them, it is not for their destruction, that they may be ruined, but for their correction, that they may be reformed; they are not intended for a sword, to cut them off, but for a rod, to drive out the foolishness that is found in their hearts, though they *mean not so, neither does their heart think so,* Isa. x. 7. Note, It is matter of great comfort to us, in reference to the troubles and afflictions of the church, that, whatever mischief men design to them, God designs to bring good out of them, and we are sure that *his counsel shall stand.*

5. Though the wickedness of the wicked may prosper for a while, yet God is a holy God, and does not approve of that wickedness (*v.* 13): *Thou art of purer eyes than to behold evil.* The prophet, observing how very vicious and impious the Chaldeans were, and yet what great success they had against God's Israel, found a temptation arising from it to say that it was vain to serve God, and that it was indifferent to him what men were. But he soon suppresses the thought, by having recourse to his first principle, That God is not, that he cannot be, the author or patron of sin; as he cannot do iniquity himself, so he is *of purer eyes than to behold it* with any allowance or approbation; no, it is that *abominable thing which the Lord hates.* He sees all the sin that is committed in the world, and it is an offence to him, it is odious in his eyes, and those that commit it are thereby made obnoxious to his justice. There is in the nature of God an antipathy to those dispositions and practices that are contrary to his holy law; and, though an expedient is happily found out for his being reconciled to sinners, yet he never will, nor can, be reconciled to sin. And this principle we must resolve to abide by, though the dispensations of his providence may for a time, and in some instances, seem to be inconsistent with it. Note, God's connivance at sin must never be interpreted into a giving countenance to it; for *he is not a God that has pleasure in wickedness,* Ps. v. 4, 5. The iniquity which, it is here said, God does not look upon, may be

meant especially of the mischief done to God's people by their persecutors; though God sees cause to permit it, yet he does not approve of it; so it agrees with that of Balaam (Num. xxiii. 21), *He has not beheld iniquity against Jacob,* nor *seen,* with allowance, *perverseness against Israel,* which is very comfortable to the people of God, in their afflictions by the rage of men, that they cannot infer God's anger from it; though the instruments of their trouble hate them, it does not therefore follow that God does; nay, he loves them, and it is in love that he corrects them.

II. The grievances he complains of, and finds hard to reconcile with these truths: " Since we are sure that thou art a holy God, why have atheists temptation given them to question whether thou art so or no? *Wherefore lookest thou upon the Chaldeans* that *deal treacherously* with thy people, and givest them success in their attempts upon us? Why dost thou suffer thy sworn enemies, who blaspheme thy name, to deal thus cruelly, thus perfidiously, with thy sworn subjects, who desire to fear thy name? What shall we say to this?" This was a temptation to Job (*ch.* xxi. 7 ; xxiv. 1), to David (Ps. lxxiii. 2, 3), to Jeremiah, *ch.* xii. 1, 2. 1. That God permitted sin, and was patient with the sinners. He *looked upon them ;* he saw all their wicked doings and designs, and did not restrain nor punish them, but suffered them to speed in their purposes, to go on and prosper, and to carry all before them. Nay, his looking upon them intimates that he not only gave them no check or rebuke, but that he gave them encouragement and assistance, as if he smiled upon them and favoured them. He *held his tongue* when they went on in their wicked courses, said nothing against them, gave no orders to stop them. *These things thou hast done, and I kept silence.* 2. That his patience was abused, and, *because sentence* against these evil works and workers *was not executed speedily,* therefore *their hearts* were the more *fully set in them to do evil.* (1.) They were false and deceitful, and there was no credit to be given them, nor any confidence to be put in them. They deal *treacherously ;* under colour of peace and friendship, they prosecute and execute the most mischievous designs, and make no conscience of their word in any thing. (2.) They hated and persecuted men because they were better than themselves, as Cain hated Abel because *his own works were evil and his brother's righteous. The wicked devours the man that is more righteous than he,* for that very reason, because he shames him; they have an ill will to the image of God, and *therefore* devour good men, because they bear that image. Though many of the Jews were as bad as the Chaldeans themselves, and worse, yet there were those among them that were much more righteous, and yet were devoured by them. (3.) They made no

1357

more of killing men than of catching fish. The prophet complains that, Providence having delivered up the weaker to be a prey to the stronger, they were, in effect, made as *the fishes of the sea, v.* 14. So they had been among themselves, preying upon one another as the greater fishes do upon the less (*v.* 3), and they were made so to the common enemy. They were *as the creeping things,* or *swimming* things (for the word is used for *fish,* Gen. i. 20), *that have no ruler* over them, either to restrain them from devouring one another or to protect them from being devoured by their enemies. They are given up to the Chaldeans as fish to the fishermen. Those proud oppressors make no conscience of killing them, any more than men do of pulling fish out of the water, so small account do they make of human lives. They make no difficulty of killing them, but do it with as much ease as men catch fish, that make no resistance, but are unguarded and unarmed, and it is rather a pastime than any pains to take them. They make no distinction among them, but all is fish that comes to their net; and they reckon every thing their own that they can lay their hands on. They have various ways of spoiling and destroying, as men have of taking fish. Some they *take up with the angle* (*v.* 15), one by one; others *they catch* in shoals, and by wholesale, *in their net,* and *gather them in their drag,* their enclosing net. Such variety of methods have they to destroy those by whom they hope to enrich themselves. (4.) They gloried in what they got, and pleased themselves with it, though it was got dishonestly: *Their portion is fat, and their meat plenteous;* they prosper in their oppression and fraud; they have a great deal, and it is of the best; their land is good, and they have abundance of it. And therefore, [1.] They have great complacency in themselves, and are very pleasant; they live merrily (*v.* 15): *Therefore they rejoice and are glad,* because their wealth is great, and their projects succeed for the increase of it, Job xxxi. 25. *Soul, take thy ease,* Luke xii. 19. [2.] They have a great conceit of themselves, are very much in love with themselves, and are great admirers of their own ingenuity and management: They *sacrifice to their own net, and burn incense to their own drag;* they applaud themselves for having got so much money, though ever so dishonestly. Note, There is a proneness in us to take the glory of our outward prosperity to ourselves, and to say, *My might, and the power of my hands, have gotten me this wealth,* Deut. viii. 17. This is idolizing ourselves, sacrificing to the dragnet, because it is our own, which is as absurd a piece of idolatry as sacrificing to Neptune or Dagon. That which makes them adore their net thus is because by it *their portion is fat.* Those that make a god of their money will make a god of their drag-net, if they can but get money by it.

III. The prophet, in the close, humbly expresses his hope that God will not suffer these destroyers of mankind always to go on and prosper thus, and expostulates with God concerning it (*v.* 17): " *Shall they therefore empty their net?* Shall they enrich themselves, and fill their own vessels, with that which they have by violence and oppression taken away from their neighbours? Shall they empty their net of what they have caught, that they may cast it into the sea again, to catch more? And wilt thou suffer them to proceed in this wicked course? Shall they not *spare continually to slay the nations?* Must the numbers and wealth of nations be sacrificed to their net? As if it were a small thing to rob men of their estates, shall they rob God of his glory? Is not God the king of nations, and will he not assert their injured rights? Is he not jealous for his own honour, and will he not maintain that?" The prophet lodges the matter in God's hand, and leaves it with him, as the psalmist does. Ps. lxxiv. 22, *Arise, O God! plead thy own cause.*

CHAP. II.

In this chapter we have an answer expected by the prophet (ver. 1), and returned by the Spirit of God, to the complaints which the prophet made of the violences and victories of the Chaldeans in the close of the foregoing chapter. The answer is, I. That after God has served his own purposes by the prevailing power of the Chaldeans, has tried the faith and patience of his people, and distinguished between the hypocrites and the sincere among them, he will reckon with the Chaldeans, will humble and bring down, not only that proud monarch Nebuchadnezzar, but that proud monarchy, for their boundless and insatiable thirst after dominion and wealth, for which they themselves should at length be made a prey, ver. 2—8. II. That not they only, but all other sinners like them, should perish under a divine woe. 1. Those that are covetous, are greedy of wealth and honours, ver. 9, 11. 2. Those that are injurious and oppressive, and raise estates by wrong and rapine, ver. 12—14. 3. Those that promote drunkenness that they may expose their neighbours to shame, ver. 15—17. 4. Those that worship idols, ver. 18—20.

I WILL stand upon my watch, and set me upon the tower, and will watch to see what he will say unto me, and what I shall answer when I am reproved. 2 And the LORD answered me, and said, Write the vision, and make *it* plain upon tables, that he may run that readeth it. 3 For the vision *is* yet for an appointed time, but at the end it shall speak, and not lie: though it tarry, wait for it; because it will surely come, it will not tarry. 4 Behold, his soul *which* is lifted up is not upright in him: but the just shall live by his faith.

Here, I. The prophet humbly gives his attendance upon God (*v.* 1): " *I will stand upon my watch,* as a sentinel on the walls of a besieged city, or on the borders of an invaded country, that is very solicitous to gain intelligence. I will look up, will look round, will look within, *and watch to see what he will say unto me,* will listen attentively to the words of his mouth and carefully observe the steps of his providence, that I may not lose the least hint of instruction or direction. *I will watch to see what he will say in me"* (so it may be read), " what the Spirit of prophecy in me will dictate to me, by way of answer to my complaints." Even in an ordinary way, God not only speaks to us by his word, but speaks in us by our own consciences, whispering to us, *This is the way, walk in it ;* and we must attend to the voice of God in both. The prophet's standing upon his *tower,* or high place, intimates his prudence, in making use of the helps and means he had within his reach to know the mind of God, and to be instructed concerning it. Those that expect to hear from God must withdraw from the world, and get above it, must raise their attention, fix their thought, study the scriptures, consult experiences and the experienced, continue instant in prayer, and thus set themselves *upon the tower.* His standing upon his watch intimates his patience, his constancy and resolution ; he will wait the time, and weather the point, as a watchman does, but he will have an answer ; he will know what God will *say to him,* not only for his own satisfaction, but to enable him as a prophet to give satisfaction to others, and answer their exceptions, when he is reproved or argued with. Herein the prophet is an example to us. 1. When we are tossed and perplexed with doubts concerning the methods of Providence, are tempted to think that it is fate, or fortune, and not a wise God, that governs the world, or that the church is abandoned, and God's covenant with his people cancelled and laid aside, then we must take pains to furnish ourselves with considerations proper to clear this matter ; we must stand upon our watch against the temptation, that it may not get ground upon us, must set ourselves upon the tower, to see if we can discover that which will silence the temptation and solve the objected difficulties, must do as the psalmist, *consider the days of old* and make *a diligent search* (Ps. lxxvii. 6), must go into the sanctuary of God, and there labour to understand the end of these things (Ps. lxxiii. 17) ; we must not give way to our doubts, but struggle to make the best of our way out of them. 2. When we have been at prayer, pouring out our complaints and requests before God, we must carefully observe what answers God gives by his word, his Spirit, and his providences, to our humble representations ; when David says, *I will direct my prayer unto thee,* as an arrow to the mark, he adds, *I will look up,* will look after my prayer, as a man does after the arrow he has shot, Ps. v. 3. We must *hear what God the Lord will speak,* Ps. lxxxv. 8. 3. When we go to read and hear the word of God, and so to consult the lively oracles, we must set ourselves to observe what God will thereby *say unto us,* to suit our case, what word of conviction, caution, counsel, and comfort, he

will bring to our souls, that we may receive it, and submit to the power of it, and may consider what we shall answer, what returns we shall make to the word of God, when we are reproved by it. 4. When we are attacked by such as quarrel with God and his providence as the prophet here seems to have been—beset, besieged, as in a tower, by hosts of objectors—we should consider how to answer them, fetch our instructions from God, hear what he says to us for our satisfaction, and have that ready to say to others, *when we are reproved,* to satisfy them, as a *reason of the hope that is in us* (1 Pet. iii. 15), and beg of God *a mouth and wisdom,* and that it may be *given us in that same hour what we shall speak.*

II. God graciously gives him the meeting ; for he will not disappint the believing expectations of his people hat wait to hear what he will say unto them, but will *speak peace,* will *answer them with good words and comfortable words,* Zech. i. 13. The prophet had complained of the prevalence of the Chaldeans, which God had given him a prospect of ; now, to pacify him concerning it, he here gives him a further prospect of their fall and ruin, as Isaiah, before this, when he had foretold the captivity in Babylon, foretold also the destruction of Babylon. Now, this great and important event being made known to him by a vision, care is taken to publish the vision, and transmit it to the generations to come, who should see the accomplishment of it.

1. The prophet must *write the vision, v.* 2. Thus, when St. John had a vision of the New Jerusalem, he was ordered to *write,* Rev. xxi. 5. He must write it, that he might imprint it on his own mind, and make it more clear to himself, but especially that it might be notified to those in distant places, and transmitted to those in future ages. What is handed down by tradition is easily mistaken and liable to corruption ; but what is written is reduced to a certainty, and preserved safe and pure. We have reason to bless God for written visions, that God has written to us the great things of his prophets as well as of his law. He must *write the vision,* and *make it plain upon tables,* must write it legibly, in large characters, so that *he who runs may read it,* that those who will not allow themselves leisure to read it deliberately may not avoid a *cursory* view of it. Probably, the prophets were wont to write some of the most remarkable of their predictions in tables, and to hang them up in the temple, Isa. viii. 1. Now the prophet is told to *write this* very *plain.* Note, Those who are employed in preaching the word of God should study plainness as much as may be, so as to make themselves intelligible to the meanest capacities. The things of our everlasting peace, which God has written to us, are made plain, *they are all plain to him that understands* (Prov. viii. 9), and they are pub-

lished with authority; God himself has pre-fixed his *imprimatur* to them; he has said, *Make them plain.*

2. The people must wait for the accomplishment of the *vision* (v. 3): " *The vision is yet for an appointed time* to come. You shall now be told of your deliverance by the breaking of the Chaldeans' power, and that the time of it is fixed in the counsel and decree of God. *There is an appointed time,* but it is not near; it is yet to be deferred a great while;" and that comes in here as a reason why it must be written, that it may be reviewed afterwards and the event compared with it. Note, God has an appointed time for his appointed work, and will be sure to do the work when the time comes; it is not for us to anticipate his appointments, but to wait his time. And it is a great encouragement to wait with patience, that, though the promised favour be deferred long, it will come at last, and be an abundant recompence to us for our waiting: *At the end it shall speak and not lie.* We shall not be disappointed of it, for it will come at the time appointed; nor shall we be disappointed in it, for it will fully answer our believing expectations. The promise may seem silent a great while, but at the end it shall speak; and therefore, *though it tarry* longer than we expected, yet we must continue *waiting for it*, being assured it will come, and willing to tarry until it does come. The day that God has set for the deliverance of his people, and the destruction of his and their enemies, is a day, (1.) That will surely come at last; it is never adjourned *sine die—without fixing another day*, but it will without fail come at the fixed time and the fittest time. (2.) It *will not tarry*, for God *is not slack, as some count slackness* (2 Pet. iii. 9); *though it tarry* past our time, yet *it does not tarry* past God's time, which is always the best time.

3. This vision, the accomplishment of which is so long waited for, will be such an exercise of faith and patience as will try and discover men what they are, *v.* 4. (1.) There are some who will proudly disdain this vision, whose hearts are so lifted up that they scorn to take notice of it; if God will work for them immediately, they will thank him, but they will not give him credit; their hearts are lifted up towards vanity, and, since God puts them off, they will shift for themselves and not be beholden to him; they think *their own hands sufficient for them,* and God's promise is to them an insignificant thing. That man's soul that is thus *lifted up is not upright in him;* it is not right with God, is not as it should be. Those that either distrust or despise God's all-sufficiency will not walk uprightly with him, Gen. xvii. 1. But, (2.) Those who are truly good, and whose hearts are upright with God, will value the promise, and venture their all upon it; and, in confidence of the truth of it, will keep close to God and duty in the most difficult trying

1360

times, and will then live comfortably in communion with God, dependence on him, and expectation of him. *The just shall live by faith;* during the captivity good people shall support themselves, and live comfortably, by faith in these precious promises, while the performance of them is deferred. *The just shall live by his faith,* by that faith which he acts upon the word of God. This is quoted in the New Testament (Rom. i. 17, Gal. iii. 11. Heb. x. 38), for the proof of the great doctrine of justification by faith only and of the influence which the grace of faith has upon the Christian life. Those that are made *just by faith shall live,* shall be happy here and for ever; while they are here, they live by it; when they come to heaven faith shall be swallowed up in vision.

5 Yea also, because he transgresseth by wine, *he is* a proud man, neither keepeth at home, who enlargeth his desire as hell, and *is* as death, and cannot be satisfied, but gathereth unto him all nations, and heapeth unto him all people: 6 Shall not all these take up a parable against him, and a taunting proverb against him, and say, Woe to him that increaseth *that which is* not his! how long? and to him that ladeth himself with thick clay! 7 Shall they not rise up suddenly that shall bite thee, and awake that shall vex thee, and thou shalt be for booties unto them? 8 Because thou hast spoiled many nations, all the remnant of the people shall spoil thee; because of men's blood, and *for* the violence of the land, of the city, and of all that dwell therein. 9 Woe to him that coveteth an evil covetousness to his house, that he may set his nest on high, that he may be delivered from the power of evil! 10 Thou hast consulted shame to thy house by cutting off many people, and hast sinned *against* thy soul. 11 For the stone shall cry out of the wall, and the beam out of the timber shall answer it. 12 Woe to him that buildeth a town with blood, and stablisheth a city by iniquity! 13 Behold, *is it* not of the LORD of hosts that the people shall labour in the very fire, and the people shall weary themselves for very vanity? 14 For the earth shall be filled with the knowledge of the glory of the LORD, as the waters cover the sea.

The prophet having had orders to *write the vision*, and the people to wait for the accomplishment of it, the vision itself follows; and it is, as divers other prophecies we have met with, the burden of Babylon and Babylon's king, the same that was said to *pass over* and *offend, ch.* i. 11. It reads the doom, some think, of Nebuchadnezzar, who was principally active in the destruction of Jerusalem, or of that monarchy, or of the whole kingdom of the Chaldeans, or of all such proud and oppressive powers as bear hard upon any people, especially upon God's people. Observe,

I. The charge laid down against this enemy, upon which the sentence is grounded, *v.* 5. The *lusts of the flesh, the lusts of the eye*, and *the pride of life*, are the entangling snares of men, and great men especially; and we find him that led Israel captive himself led captive by each of these. For, 1. He is sensual and voluptuous, and given to his pleasures : *He transgresses by wine.* Drunkenness is itself a transgression, and is the cause of abundance of transgression. We read of those that *err through wine*, Isa. xxviii. 7. Belshazzar (in whom particularly this prophecy had its accomplishment) was in the height of his transgression by wine when the hand-writing upon the wall signed the warrant for his immediate execution, pursuant to this sentence, Dan. v. 1.　2. He is haughty and imperious : *He is a proud man*, and his pride is a certain presage of his fall coming on. If great men be proud men, the great God will make them know he is above them. His transgressing by wine is made the cause of his arrogance and insolence : therefore *he is a proud man.* When a man is drunk, though he makes himself as mean as a beast, yet he thinks himself as great as a king, and prides himself in that by which he shames himself. We find the *crown of pride* upon the head of the *drunkards of Ephraim*, and a *woe* to both, Isa. xxviii. 1. 3. He is covetous and greedy of wealth, and this is the effect of his pride ; he thinks himself worthy to enjoy all, and therefore makes it his business to engross all. The Chaldean monarchy aimed to be a universal one. He *keeps not at home*, is not content with his own, which he has an incontestable title to, but thinks it too little, and so enjoys it not, nor takes the comfort he might in his own palace, in his own dominion. His sin is his punishment, his ambition is his perpetual uneasiness. Though the home be a palace, yet to a discontented mind it is a prison. He *enlarges his desire as hell*, or *the grave*, which daily receives the body of the dead, and yet still cries, *Give, give :* he is *as death*, which continues to devour, and *cannot be satisfied.* Note, It is the sin and folly of many who have a great deal of the wealth of this world that they do not know when they have enough, but the more they have the more they would have, and the more eager they

are for it. And it is just with God that the desires which are insatiable should still be unsatisfied ; it is the doom passed on those that *love silver* that they shall never be *satisfied with it*, Eccl. v. 10. Those that will not be content with their allotments shall not have the comfort of their achievements. This proud prince is still *gathering to him all nations, and heaping to him all people*, invading their rights, seizing their properties, and they must not be unless they will be his, and under his command. One nation will not satisfy him unless he has another, and then another, and all at last ; as those in a lower sphere, to gratify the same inordinate desire, lay *house to house, and field to field, that they may be placed alone in the earth*, Isa. v. 8. And it is hard to say which is more to be pitied, the folly of such ambitious princes as place their honour in enlarging their dominions, and not in ruling them well, or the misery of those nations that are harassed and pulled to pieces by them.

II. The sentence passed upon him (*v.* 6) : *Shall not all these take up a parable against him?* His doom is,

1. That, since pride has been his sin, disgrace and dishonour shall be his punishment, and he shall be loaded with contempt, shall be laughed at and despised by all about him, as those that look big, and aim high, deserve to be, and commonly are, when they are brought down and baffled.

2. That, since he has been abusive to his neighbours, those very persons whom he has abused shall be the instruments of his disgrace : *All those shall take up a taunting proverb against him.* They shall have the pleasure of insulting over him and he the shame of being trampled upon by them. Those that shall triumph in the fall of this great tyrant are here furnished with a *parable*, and a *taunting proverb*, to take up against him. *He shall say* (he that draws up the insulting ditty shall say thus), Ho, *he that increases that which is not his! Aha!* what has become of him now? So it may be read in a taunting way. Or, *He shall say*, that is, *the just*, who *lives by his faith*, he to whom the vision is written and made plain, with the help of that shall say this, shall foretel the enemy's fall, even when he sees him flourishing, and *suddenly curse his habitation*, even when he is *taking root*, Job v. 3. He shall indeed denounce woes against him.

(1.) Here is a woe against him for increasing his own possessions by invading his neighbour's rights, *v.* 6—8. He *increases that which is not his*, but other people's. Note, No more of what we have is to be reckoned ours than what we came honestly by ; nor will it long be ours, for *wealth gotten by vanity will be diminished.* Let not those that thrive in the world be too forward to bless themselves in it, for, if they do not thrive lawfully, they are under a woe. See here, [1.] What this prosperous prince is

doing; he is *lading himself with thick clay.*
Riches are but clay, thick clay; what are
gold and silver but white and yellow earth?
Those that travel through thick clay are
both retarded and dirtied in their journey;
so are those that go through the world in
the midst of an abundance of the wealth of
it; but, as if that were not enough, what
fools are those that *load themselves with it*, as
if this trash would be their treasure! They
burden themselves with continual care about
it, with a great deal of guilt in getting, saving, and spending it, and with a heavy account which they must give of it another
day. They overload their ship with this
thick clay, and so sink it and themselves
into destruction and perdition. [2.] See what
people say of him, while he is thus increasing
his wealth; they cry, "*How long?* How
long will it be ere he has enough?" They
cry to God, "How long wilt thou suffer this
proud oppressor to trouble the nations?"
Or they say to one another, "See how long
it will last, how long he will be able to keep
what he gets thus dishonestly." They dare
not speak out, but we know what they mean
when they say, *How long?* [3.] See what
will be in the end hereof. What he has got
by violence from others, others shall take
by violence from him. The Medes and Persians shall make a prey of the Chaldeans, as
they have done of other nations, *v. 7, 8.*
"There shall be those that will *bite thee* and
vex thee; those from whom thou didst not
fear any danger, that seemed *asleep*, shall
rise up and *awake* to be a plague to thee.
They shall rise up *suddenly* when thou art
most secure, and least prepared to receive
the shock and ward off the blow. *Shall they
not rise up suddenly?* No doubt they shall,
and thou thyself hast reason to expect it, to
be dealt with as thou hast dealt with others,
that *thou shalt be for booties unto them,* as
others have been unto thee, that, according
to the law of retaliation, as *thou hast spoiled
many nations* so thou shalt thyself be *spoiled*
(*v. 8*); *all the remnant of the people shall
spoil thee.*" The king of Babylon thought
he had brought all the nations round about
him so low that none of them would be able
to make reprisals upon him; but though
they were but a remnant of people, a very
few left, yet these shall be sufficient to spoil
him, when God has such a controversy with
him, *First,* For *men's blood,* and the thousands of lives that have been sacrificed to his
ambition and revenge, especially for the blood
of Israelites, which is in a special manner
precious to God. *Secondly,* For *the violence
of the land,* his laying waste so many countries, and destroying the fruits of the earth,
especially in the land of Israel. *Thirdly,* For
the violence *of the city,* the many cities that
he had turned into ruinous heaps, especially
Jerusalem the holy city, and of *all that dwelt
therein,* who were ruined by him. Note,
The violence done by proud men to advance

1362

and enrich themselves will be called over
again (and must be accounted for) another
day, by him *to whom vengeance belongs.*

(2.) Here is a woe against him for coveting
still more, and aiming to be still higher, *v.*
9—11. The crime for which this woe is
denounced is much the same with that in the
foregoing article—an insatiable desire of
wealth and honour; it is *coveting an evil covetousness to his house,* that is, grasping at
an abundance for his family. Note, Covetousness is a very evil thing in a family;
it brings disquiet and uneasiness into it (*he
that is greedy of gain troubles his own house*),
and, which is worse, it brings the curse of
God upon it and upon all the affairs of it.
Woe to him that gains an evil gain; so the
margin reads it. There is a lawful gain,
which by the blessing of God may be a comfort to a house (*a good man leaves an inheritance to his children's children*), but what is
got by fraud and injustice is ill-got, and will
be poor gain, will not only do no good to a
family, but will bring poverty and ruin upon
it. Now observe, [1.] What this covetous
wretch aims at; it is *to set his nest on high,*
to raise his family to some greater dignity
than it had before arrived at, or to set it, as
he apprehends, out of the reach of danger,
that he may be *delivered from the power of
evil,* that it may not be in the power of the
worst of his enemies to do him a mischief
nor so much as to disturb his repose. Note,
It is common for men to pretend it as an
excuse for their covetousness and ambition
that they only consult their own safety, and
aim to secure themselves; and yet they do
but deceive themselves when they think
their wealth will be a *strong city* to them, *and
a high wall,* for it is so only *in their own conceit,* Prov. xviii. 11. [2.] What he will get
by it: *Thou hast consulted,* not safety, but
*shame, to thy house, by cutting off many peo-
ple, v.* 10. Note, An estate raised by iniquity is a scandal to a family. Those that
cut off, or undermine, others, to make room
for themselves, that impoverish others to
enrich themselves, do but consult shame to
their houses, and fasten upon them a mark
of infamy. Yet that is not the worst of it:
"*Thou hast sinned against thy own soul,* hast
brought that under guilt and wrath, and
endangered that." Note, Those that do
wrong to their neighbour do a much greater
wrong to their own souls. But if the sinner
pleads, Not guilty, and thinks he has managed his frauds and violence with so much
art and contrivance that they cannot be proved
upon him, let him know that if there be no
other witnesses against him *the stone shall
cry out of the wall* against him, and *the beam
out of the timber* in the roof *shall answer it,*
shall second it, shall witness it, that the
money and materials wherewith he built the
house were unjustly gotten, *v.* 11. The
stones and timber cry to heaven for vengeance, as *the whole creation groans under*

the sin of man and waits to be delivered from that *bondage of corruption.*

(3.) Here is a woe against him for building a town and a city by blood and extortion (*v.* 12): He *builds a town,* and is himself lord of it; he *establishes a city,* and makes it his royal seat. So Nebuchadnezzar did (Dan. iv. 30): *Is not this great Babylon that I have built for the house of the kingdom?* But it is built with the blood of his own subjects, whom he has oppressed, and the blood of his neighbours, whom he has unjustly invaded; it is *established by iniquity,* by the unrighteous laws that are made for the security of it. *Woe* to him that does so; for the towns and cities thus built can never be established; they will fall, and their founders be buried in the ruins of them. Babylon, which was built by blood and iniquity, did not continue long; its day soon came to fall; and then this woe took effect, when that prophecy, which is expressed as a history (Isa. xxi. 9), proved a history indeed: *Babylon has fallen, has fallen!* And the destruction of that city was, [1.] The shame of the Chaldeans, who had taken so much pains, and were at such a vast expense, to fortify it (*v.* 13): *Is it not of the Lord of hosts that the people* who have laboured so hard to defend that city shall *labour in the very fire,* shall see the out-works which they confided in the strength of set on fire, and shall labour in vain to save them? Or they, in their pursuits of worldly wealth and honour, put themselves to great fatigue, and ran a great hazard, as those that *labour in the fire* do. The worst that can be said of the labourers in God's vineyards is that they *have borne the burden and heat of the day* (Matt. xx. 12); but those that are eager in their worldly pursuits *labour in the very fire,* make themselves perfect slaves to their lusts. There is not a greater drudge in the world than he that is under the power of reigning covetousness. And what comes of it? Though they take a world of pains they are but poorly paid for it; for, after all, *they weary themselves for very vanity;* they were told it was vanity, and when they find themselves disappointed of it, and disappointed in it, they will own it is worse than vanity, it is *vexation of spirit.* [2.] It was the honour of God, as a God of impartial justice and irresistible power; for by the ruin of the Chaldean monarchy (which all the world could not but take notice of) *the earth was filled with the knowledge of the glory of the Lord, v.* 14. *The Lord is known by* these *judgments which he executes,* especially when he is pleased to *look upon proud men and abase them,* for he thereby proves himself to be *God alone,* Job xl. 11, 12. See what good God brings out of the staining and sinking of earthly glory; he thereby manifests and magnifies his own glory, and *fills the earth* with the knowledge of it as plentifully as the *waters cover the sea,* which lie deep, spread far, and shall not be

dried up until time shall be no more. Such is the *knowledge of the glory of God in the face of Jesus Christ* given by the gospel (2 Cor. iv. 6), and such was the knowledge of his glory by the miraculous ruin of Babylon. Note, Such as will not be taught the knowledge of God's glory by the judgments of his mouth shall be made to know and acknowledge it by the judgments of his hand.

15 Woe unto him that giveth his neighbour drink, that puttest thy bottle to *him,* and makest *him* drunken also, that thou mayest look on their nakedness! 16 Thou art filled with shame for glory: drink thou also, and let thy foreskin be uncovered: the cup of the LORD's right hand shall be turned unto thee, and shameful spewing *shall be* on thy glory. 17 For the violence of Lebanon shall cover thee, and the spoil of beasts, *which* made them afraid, because of men's blood, and for the violence of the land, of the city, and of all that dwell therein. 18 What profiteth the graven image that the maker thereof hath graven it; the molten image, and a teacher of lies, that the maker of his work trusteth therein, to make dumb idols? 19 Woe unto him that saith to the wood, Awake; to the dumb stone, Arise, it shall teach! Behold, it *is* laid over with gold and silver, and *there is* no breath at all in the midst of it. 20 But the LORD *is* in his holy temple: let all the earth keep silence before him.

The three foregoing articles, upon which the woes here are grounded, are very near akin to each other. The criminals charged by them are oppressors and extortioners, that raise estates by rapine and injustice; and it is mentioned here again (*v.* 17), the very same that was said *v.* 8, for that is the crime upon which the greatest stress is laid; it is *because of men's blood,* innocent blood, barbarously and unjustly shed, which is a provoking crying thing; it is *for the violence of the land, of the city, and of all that dwell therein,* which God will certainly reckon for, sooner or later, as the asserter of right and the avenger of wrong.

But here are two articles more, of a different nature, which carry a *woe* to all those in general to whom they belong, and particularly to the Babylonian monarchs, by whom the people of God were taken and held captives.

I. The promoters of drunkenness stand here impeached and condemned. Belshazzar was one of those; he was so, remarkably that very night that the prophecy of this chapter was fulfilled in the period of his life and kingdom, when he *drank wine before a thousand* of his lords (Dan. v. 1), began the healths, and forced them to pledge him. And perhaps it was one reason why the succeeding monarchs of Persia made it a law of their kingdom that *in drinking none should compel*, but *they should do according to every man's pleasure* (as we find, Esth. i. 8), because they had seen in the kings of Babylon the mischievous consequences of forcing healths and making people drunk. But the woe here stands firm and very fearful against all those, whoever they are, who are guilty of this sin at any time, and in any place, from the stately palace (where that was) to the paltry ale-house. Observe,

1. Who the sinner is that is here articled against; it is he that *makes his neighbour drunk*, v. 15. To give a neighbour drink who is in want, who is thirsty and poor, though it be but a cup of cold water to a disciple, in the name of a disciple, to give drink to weary traveller, nay, and to give strong drink to him that is ready to perish, and wine to those that are heavy of heart, is a piece of charity which is required of us, and shall be recompensed to us. *I was thirsty, and you gave me drink.* But to give a neighbour drink who has enough already, and more than enough, with design to intoxicate him, that he may expose himself, may talk foolishly, and make himself ridiculous, may disclose his own secret concerns, or be drawn in to agree to a bad bargain for himself—this is abominable wickedness; and those who are guilty of it, who make a practice of it, and take a pride and pleasure in it, are rebels against God in heaven, and his sacred laws, factors for the devil in hell, and his cursed interests, and enemies to men on earth, and their honour and welfare; they are like the son of Nebat, who *sinned and made Israel to sin*. To entice others to drunkenness, to *put the bottle to them*, that they may be allured to it by its charms, by *looking on the wine when it is red and gives its colour in the cup*, or to force them to it, obliging them by the rules of the club (and club-laws indeed they are) to drink so many glasses, and so filled, is to do what we can, and perhaps more than we know of, towards the murder both of soul and body; and those that do so have a great deal to answer for.

2. What the sentence is that is here passed upon him. There is a woe to him (*v*. 15), and a punishment (*v*. 16) that shall answer to the sin. (1.) Does he put the cup of drunkenness into the hand of his neighbour? The cup of fury, the cup of trembling, the *cup of the Lord's right hand*, shall be *turned unto him;* the power of God shall be armed against him. That cup which had gone round among the nations, to make them *a desolation, an astonishment, and a hissing,*

which had made them stumble and *fall,* so that they could *rise no more,* shall at length be put into the hand of the king of Babylon, as was foretold, Jer. xxv. 15, 16, 18, 26, 27. Thus the New-Testament Babylon, which had made the nations drunk with the cup of her fornications, shall *have blood given her to drink, for she is worthy*, Rev. xviii. 3, 6. (2.) Does he take a pleasure in putting his neighbour to shame? He shall himself be loaded with contempt: "*Thou art filled with shame for glory, with shame instead of glory*, or art filled now with shame more than ever thou wast with glory; and the glory thou hast been filled with shall but serve to make thy shame the more grievous to thyself, and the more ignominious in the eyes of others. Thou *also shalt drink* of the cup of trembling, and shalt expose thyself by thy fear and cowardice, which shall be as the *uncovering of thy nakedness*, to thy shame; and all about thee shall load thee with disgrace, for *shameful spewing shall be on thy glory*, on that which thou hast most prided thyself in, thy dignity, wealth, and dominion; those whom thou hast made drunk shall themselves spew upon it. For *the violence of Lebanon shall cover thee, and the spoil of beasts* (v. 17); thou shalt be hunted and run down with as much violence as ever any wild beasts in Lebanon were, shall be spoiled as they are, and thy fall made a sport of; for thou art as one of the beasts that made them afraid, and therefore they triumph when they have got the mastery of thee." Or, "It is because of the violence thou hast done to Lebanon, that is, the land of Israel (Deut. iii. 25) and the temple (Zech. xi. 1), that God now reckons with thee; that is the sin that now covers thee."

II. The promoters of idolatry stand here impeached and condemned; and this also was a sin that Babylon was notoriously guilty of; it was the *mother of harlots*. Belshazzar, in his revels, *praised his idols*. And, for this, here is a woe against them, and in them against all others that do likewise, particularly the New-Testament Babylon. Now see here,

1. What they do to promote idolatry; they are *mad upon their idols;* so the Chaldeans are said to be, Jer. l. 38. For, (1.) They have a great variety of idols, their *graven images* and *molten images*, that people may take their choice, which they like best. (2.) They are very nice and curious in the framing of them: The *maker of the work* has performed his part admirably well, the *fashioner of his fashion* (so it is in the margin), that contrived the model in the most significant manner. (3.) They are at great expense in beautifying and adorning them: *They lay them over with gold and silver;* because these are things people love and dote upon wherever they meet with them, they dress up their idols in them, the more effectually to court the adoration of the children of

this world. (4.) They have great expectations from them: *The maker of the work trusts therein* as his god, puts a confidence in it, and gives honour to it as his god. The worshippers of God give honour to him, by offering up their prayers to him, and waiting to receive instructions and directions from him; and these honours they give to their idols. [1.] They pray to them: *They say to the wood, Awake* for our relief, " awake to hear our prayers;" and to the dumb stone, " *Arise, and save us,*" as the church prays to her God, *Awake, O Lord! arise,* Ps. xliv. 23. They own their image to be a god by praying to it. *Deliver me, for thou art my God,* Isa. xliv. 17. *Deos qui rogat ille facit—That to which a man addresses petitions is to him a god.* [2.] They consult them as oracles, and expect to be directed and dictated to by them: *They say to the dumb stone,* though it cannot speak, *yet it shall teach.* What the wicked demon, or no less wicked priest, speaks to them from the image, they receive with the utmost veneration, as of divine authority, and are ready to be governed by it. Thus is idolatry planted and propagated under the specious show of religion and devotion.

2. How the extreme folly of this is exposed. God, by Isaiah, when he foretold the deliverance of his people out of Babylon, largely showed the shameful stupidity and sottishness of idolaters, and so he does here by the prophet, on the like occasion. (1.) Their images, when they have made them, are but mere matter, which is the meanest lowest rank of being; and all the expense they are at upon them cannot advance them one step above that. They are wholly void both of sense and reason, lifeless and speechless (the idol is a *dumb idol,* a *dumb stone,* and there is *no breath at all in the midst of it*), so that the most minute animal, that has but breath and motion, is more excellent than they. They have not so much as the spirit of a beast. (2.) It is not in their power to do their worshippers any good (*v.* 18): *What profits the graven image?* Though it be mere matter, if it were cast into some other form it might be serviceable to some purpose or other of human life; but, as it is made a god of, it is of no profit at all, nor can do its worshippers the least kindness. Nay, (3.) It is so far from profiting them that it puts a cheat upon them, and keeps them under the power of a strong delusion; they say, It *shall teach,* but it is a *teacher of lies;* for it represents God as having a body, as being finite, visible, and dependent, whereas he is a Spirit, infinite, invisible, and independent, and it confirms those that become vain in their imaginations in the false notions they have of God, and makes the idea of God to be a precarious thing, and what every man pleases. If we may say to the *works of our hands, You are our gods,* we may say so to any of the creatures of our own fancy, though the chimera be ever so extravagant. An image is a

doctrine of vanities; it is *falsehood,* and a *work of errors,* Jer. x. 8, 14, 15. It is therefore easy to see what the religion of those is, and what they aim at, who recommend those teachers of lies as laymen's books, which they are to study and govern themselves by, when they have locked up from them the book of the scriptures in an unknown tongue.

3. How the people of God triumph in him, and therewith support themselves, when the idolaters thus shame themselves (*v.* 20): *But the Lord is in his holy temple.* (1.) *Our rock is not as their rock,* Deut. xxxii. 31. Theirs are dumb idols; ours is Jehovah, a living God, who is what he is, and not, as theirs, what men please to make him. He is in his holy temple in heaven, the residence of his glory, where we have access to him in the way, not which we have invented, but which he himself has instituted. Compare Ps. cxv. 3, *But our God is in the heavens,* and Ps. xi. 4. (2.) The multitude of their gods which they set up, and take so much pains to support, cannot thrust out our God; he is, and will be, in his holy temple still, and glorious in holiness. They have laid waste his temple at Jerusalem; but he has a temple above that is out of the reach of their rage and malice, but within the reach of his people's faith and prayers. (3.) Our God will make all the world silent before him, will strike the idolaters as dumb as their idols, convincing them of their folly, and covering them with shame. He will silence the fury of the oppressors, and check their rage against his people. (4.) It is the duty of his people to attend him with silent adorings (Ps. lxv. 1), and patiently to wait for his appearing to save them in his own way and time. *Be still, and know that he is God,* Zech. ii. 13.

CHAP. III.

Still the correspondence is kept up between God and his prophet. In the first chapter he spoke to God, then God to him, and then he to God again; in the second chapter God spoke wholly to him by the Spirit of prophecy; now, in this chapter, he speaks wholly to God by the Spirit of prayer, for he would not let the intercourse drop on his side, like a genuine son of Abraham, who "returned not to his place until God had left communing with him." Gen. xviii. 33. The prophet's prayer, in this chapter, is in imitation of David's psalms, for it is directed "to the chief musician," and is set to musical instruments. The prayer is left upon record for the use of the church, and particularly of the Jews in their captivity, while they were waiting for their deliverance, promised by the vision in the foregoing chapter. I. He earnestly begs of God to relieve and succour his people in affliction, to hasten their deliverance, and to comfort them in the mean time, ver. 2. II. He calls to mind the experiences which the church formerly had of God's glorious and gracious appearances on her behalf, when he brought Israel out of Egypt through the wilderness to Canaan, and there many a time wrought wonderful deliverances for them, ver. 3—15. III. He affects himself with a holy concern for the present troubles of the church, but encourages himself and others to hope that the issue will be comfortable and glorious at last, though all visible means fail, ver. 16—19.

A PRAYER of Habakkuk the prophet upon Shigionoth. 2 O LORD, I have heard thy speech, *and* was afraid: O LORD, revive thy work in the midst of the years, in the midst of the years make known; in wrath remember mercy.

This chapter is entitled *a prayer of Habakkuk*. It is a meditation with himself, an intercession for the church. Prophets were praying men; this prophet was so *(He is a prophet, and he shall pray for thee*, Gen. xx. 7); and sometimes they prayed for even those whom they prophesied against. Those that were intimately acquainted with the mind of God concerning future events knew better than others how to order their prayers, and what to pray for, and, in the foresight of troublous times, could lay up a stock of prayers that might then receive a gracious answer, and so be serving the church by their prayers when their prophesying was over. This prophet had found God ready to answer his requests and complaints before, and therefore now repeats his applications to him. Because *God has inclined his ear to us*, we must resolve that *therefore we* will *call upon him as long as we live*. 1. The prophet owns the receipt of God's answer to his former representation, and the impression it made upon him (v. 2): "*O Lord! I have heard thy speech, thy hearing*" (so some read it), "that which thou wouldst have us hear, the decree that has gone forth for the afflicting of thy people. *I received thine, and it is before me.*" Note, Those that would rightly order their speech to God must carefully observe, and lay before them, his speech to them. He had said (*ch.* ii. 1), *I will watch to see what he will say;* and now he owns, Lord, *I have heard thy speech;* for, if we turn a deaf ear to God's word, we can expect no other than that he should turn a deaf ear to our prayers, Prov. xxviii. 9. I heard it, *and was afraid.* Messages immediately from heaven commonly struck even the best and boldest men into a consternation; Moses, Isaiah, and Daniel, did *exceedingly fear and quake.* But, besides that, the matter of this message made the prophet afraid, when he heard how low the people of God should be brought, under the oppressing power of the Chaldeans, and how long they should continue under it; he was afraid lest their spirits should quite fail, and lest the church should be utterly rooted out and run down, and, being kept low so long, should be lost at length. 2. He earnestly prays that *for the elect's sake* these *days of trouble* might be *shortened*, or the trouble of these days mitigated and moderated, or the people of God supported and comforted under it. He thinks it very long to wait till the *end of the years;* perhaps he refers to the seventy years fixed for the continuance of the captivity, and therefore, "Lord," says he, "do something on our behalf *in the midst of the years,* those years of our distress; though we be not delivered, and our oppressors destroyed, yet let us not be abandoned and cast off." (1.) "Do something for thy own cause: *Revive thy work,* thy church" (that is the *work of God's own hand,* formed by him, formed for

him); "*revive* that, even when it *walks in the midst of trouble,* Ps. cxxxviii. 7, 8. Grant thy people *a little reviving in their bondage,* Ezra ix. 8; Ps. lxxxv. 6. *Preserve alive thy work*" (so some read it); "though thy church be chastened, let it not be killed; though it have not its liberty, yet continue its life, save a remnant alive, to be a seed of another generation. *Revive the work of thy grace* in us, by sanctifying the trouble to us and supporting us under it, though the time be not yet come, *even the set time,* for our deliverance out of it. Whatever becomes of us, though we be as dead and dry bones, Lord, let *thy work be revived,* let not that sink, and go back, and come to nothing." (2.) "Do something for thy own honour: *In the midst of the years make known,* make thyself known, for now *verily thou art a God that hidest thyself* (Isa. xlv. 15), make known thy power, thy pity, thy promise, thy providence, in the government of the world, for the safety and welfare of thy church. Though we be buried in obscurity, yet, Lord, make thyself known; whatever becomes of Israel, let not the God of Israel be forgotten in the world, but discover himself even in the midst of the dark years, before thou art expected to appear." When *in the midst of the years* of the captivity God miraculously owned the three children in the fiery furnace, and humbled Nebuchadnezzar, this prayer was answered, *In the midst of the years make known.* (3.) "Do something for thy people's comfort: *In wrath remember mercy,* and *make that known.* Show us thy mercy, O Lord!*" Ps. lxxxv. 7. They see God's displeasure against them in their troubles, and that makes them grievous indeed. There is wrath in the bitter cup; that therefore they deprecate, and are earnest in begging that *in the midst of wrath* God would *remember mercy* to them, would make it appear that he is a merciful God and they are vessels of his mercy. Note, Even those that are under the tokens of God's wrath must not despair of his mercy; and mercy, mere mercy, is that which we must flee to for refuge, and rely upon as our only plea. He does not say, Remember our merit, but, Lord, *remember thy own mercy.*

3 God came from Teman, and the Holy One from Mount Paran. Selah. His glory covered the heavens, and the earth was full of his praise. 4 And *his* brightness was as the light; he had horns *coming* out of his hand: and there *was* the hiding of his power. 5 Before him went the pestilence, and burning coals went forth at his feet. 6 He stood, and measured the earth: he beheld, and drove asunder the nations; and the everlasting mountains were scattered,

the perpetual hills did bow: his ways *are* everlasting. 7 I saw the tents of Cushan in affliction: *and* the curtains of the land of Midian did tremble. 8 Was the LORD displeased against the rivers? *was* thine anger against the rivers? *was* thy wrath against the sea, that thou didst ride upon thine horses *and* thy chariots of salvation? 9 Thy bow was made quite naked, *according* to the oaths of the tribes, *even thy* word. Selah. Thou didst cleave the earth with rivers. 10 The mountains saw thee, *and* they trembled: the overflowing of the water passed by: the deep uttered his voice, *and* lifted up his hands on high. 11 The sun *and* moon stood still in their habitation: at the light of thine arrows they went, *and* at the shining of thy glittering spear. 12 Thou didst march through the land in indignation, thou didst thresh the heathen in anger. 13 Thou wentest forth for the salvation of thy people, *even* for salvation with thine anointed; thou woundedst the head out of the house of the wicked, by discovering the foundation unto the neck. Selah. 14 Thou didst strike through with his staves the head of his villages: they came out as a whirlwind to scatter me: their rejoicing *was* as to devour the poor secretly. 15 Thou didst walk through the sea with thine horses, *through* the heap of great waters.

It has been the usual practice of God's people, when they have been in distress and ready to fall into despair, to help themselves by recollecting their experiences, and reviving them, *considering the days of old*, and *the years of ancient times* (Ps. lxxvii. 5), and pleading them with God in prayer, as he is pleased sometimes to plead them with himself. Isa. lxiii. 11, *Then he remembered the days of old*. This is that which the prophet does here, and he looks as far back as the first forming of them into a people, when they were brought by miracles out of Egypt, *a house of bondage*, through the wilderness, *a land of drought*, into Canaan, then possessed by *mighty nations*. He that thus brought them at first into Canaan, through so much difficulty, can now bring them thither again out of Babylon, how great soever the difficulties are that lie in the way. Those works of wonder, wrought of old, are here

most magnificently described, for the greater encouragement to the faith of God's people in their present straits.

I. God appeared in his glory, so as he never did before or since (v. 3, 4): *He came from Teman, even the Holy One from Mount Paran*. This refers to the visible display of the glory of God when he gave the law upon Mount Sinai, as appears by Deut. xxxiii. 2, whence these expressions are borrowed. Then *the Lord came down* upon Mount Sinai in a cloud (Exod. xix. 20) and his glory was *as the devouring fire*, not only to enforce the law he then gave them, but to avow the deliverance he had wrought for them and to magnify it; for the first word he said there was, "*I am the Lord thy God, that brought thee out of the land of Egypt*. I that appear in this glory am the author of that work." Then *his glory covered the heavens*, which shone with the reflection of that glorious appearance of his; the *earth also* was *full of his praise*, or of his *splendour*, as some read it. People at a distance saw the cloud and fire on the top of Mount Sinai, and praised the God of Israel. Or the earth was full of those works of God which were to be praised. *His brightness was as the light*, as the light of the sun when he goes forth in his strength; *he had horns*, or *bright beams* (so it should be rendered), *coming out of his side* or *hand*. Rays of glory were darted forth around him; and with some rays borrowed thence it was that Moses's face shone when he *came down from* that *mount* of glory. Some by the horns, the *two horns* (for the word is dual), *coming out of his hand*, understand the *two tables of the law*, which perhaps, when God delivered them to Moses, though they were tables of stone, had a glory round them; those books were gilt with beams, and so it agrees with Deut. xxxiii. 2, *From his right hand went a fiery law for them*. It is added, *And there was the hiding of his power;* there was his hidden power, in the rays that came out of his hand. The operations of his power, compared with what he could have done, were rather the hiding of it than the discovery of it; the secrets of his power, as well as of his wisdom, are *double to that which is*, Job xi. 6.

II. God sent plagues on Egypt, for the humbling of proud Pharaoh, and the obliging of him to let the people go (v. 5): *Before him went the pestilence*, which slew all the first-born of Egypt in one night; and *burning coals went forth at his feet*, when, in the plague of hail, there was *fire mingled with hail—burning diseases* (so the margin reads it), some think those that wasted Egypt, others those with which the number of the Canaanites was diminished before Israel was brought in upon them. These were *at his feet*, that is, at his coming, for they are at his command; he says to them, Go, and they go, Come, and they come, Do this, and they do it.

III. He divided the land of Canaan to

his people Israel, and expelled the heathen from before them (*v.* 6) : *He stood, and measured the earth,* measured that land, to assign it for an inheritance to Israel his people, Deut. xxxii. 8, 9. *He beheld, and drove asunder the nations* that were in possession of it; though they combined together against Israel, God dispersed and discomfited them before Israel. Or he exerted such a mighty power as was enough to shake in pieces all the nations of the earth. Then *the everlasting mountains were scattered, and the perpetual hills did bow ;* the mighty princes and potentates of Canaan, that seemed as high, as strong, and as firmly fixed, as the mountains and hills, were broken to pieces; they and their kingdoms were totally subdued. Or the power of God was so exerted as to shake the mountains and hills; nay, and Sinai did tremble, and the adjacent hills; see Ps. lxviii. 7, 8. To this he adds, *His ways are everlasting,* that is, all the motions of his providence are according to his eternal counsels; and he is the same for ever, that which he was yesterday and to-day. His covenant is unchangeable, and *his mercy endures for ever.* When he *drove asunder the nations of Canaan* one might have seen the *tents of Cushan in affliction, the curtains of the land of Midian trembling,* and all the inhabitants of the neighbouring countries taking the alarm; and though they were not in the commission given to Israel to destroy, nor their land within the warrant given to Israel to possess, yet they thought their own house in danger when their neighbour's house was on fire, and therefore they were in a great fright, *v.* 7. Balak the king of Moab was so, Num. xxii. 3, 4. Some make the tents of Cushan to be in affliction when, in the days of judge Othniel, God delivered Cushan-rishathaim into his hand (Judg. iii. 8), and the *curtains of the land of Midian* to *tremble* when, in the days of judge Gideon, a barley cake, in a dream, overthrew the tent of Midian, Judg. vii. 13.

IV. He divided the Red Sea and Jordan, when they stood in the way of Israel's progress, and yet fetched a river out of a rock when Israel wanted it, *v.* 8. One would have thought that God was *displeased with the rivers,* and that *his wrath was against the sea,* for he made them give way and flee before him when he *rode upon his horses and chariots of salvation,* as a general at the head of his forces, mighty to save. Note, God's chariots are not so much chariots of state to himself as chariots of salvation to his people; it is his glory to be Israel's Saviour. This seems to be referred to again (*v.* 15) : "*Thou didst walk th*rough the sea, through the Red Sea, *with thy h*orses, in the pillar of cloud and fire (that was his chariot drawn by angels); thus thou didst walk secure, and so as to accommodate thyself to the slow pace that Israel could go, as Jacob tenderly drove, in consideration of his children and cattle :

Thou didst walk through the heap, or mud, *of great waters ;* and Israel likewise was led *through the deep as a horse through the wilderness,*" Isa. lxiii. 13, 14. When they came to enter Canaan the *overflowing of the water passed by,* that is, Jordan, which at that time overflowed all his banks, was divided, Josh. iii. 15. Note, When the difficulties in the way of perfecting the salvation of Israel seem most insuperable, when they rise to the height, and overflow, yet then God can put them by, break through them, and get over them. Then *the deep uttered his voice,* when, the Red Sea and Jordan being divided, the waters roared and made a noise, as if they were sensible of the restraint they were under from proceeding in their natural course, and complained of it. They *lifted up their hands,* or sides, *on high* (for the waters *stood up on a heap,* Josh. iii. 16), as if they would have made opposition to the orders given them. They *lifted up their voice, lifted up their waves ;* but in vain. *The Lord on high was mightier than they,* Ps. xciii. 3, 4. With the dividing of the sea and Jordan, notice is again taken of the trembling of the mountains, as if the stop given to the waters gave a shock to the adjacent hills; they are put together, Ps. cxiv. 3, 4. When *the sea saw it and fled,* and *Jordan was driven back, the mountains skipped like rams and the little hills like lambs.* The whole creation yielded; earth and waters trembled *at the presence of the Lord, at the presence of the mighty God of Jacob.* But (as Mr. Cowley paraphrases it)

Fly where thou wilt, thou sea ; and, Jordan's current, cease.
　　Jordan, there is no need of thee ;
　　For at God's word, whene'er he please,
The rocks shall weep new waters forth instead of
　　these.

So here, *Thou didst cleave the earth with rivers ;* channels were made in the wilderness, such as seemed to cleave the earth, for the waters to run in, which issued out of the rock, to supply the camp of Israel, and which followed them in all their removes. Note, The God of nature can alter and control the powers of nature, which way he pleases, can turn waters into crystal rocks and rocks into crystal streams.

V. He arrested the motion of the sun and moon, to befriend and complete Israel's victories (*v.* 11): *The sun and moon stood still* at the prayer of Joshua, that the Canaanites might not have the benefit of the night to favour their escape; they *stood still in their habitation* in the heaven (Ps. xix. 4), but with an eye to Gibeon and the *valley of Ajalon,* where God's work was in the doing, and of which they, though at so vast a distance, attended the motions. *At the light,* at the direction, *of thy arrows, they went,* and at the *shining of thy glittering spear ;* they followed Israel's arms, to favour them; according to the intimation of the arrows God shot (as Jonathan's arrows, 1 Sam. xx. 20), and which way soever his spear pointed (the glittering light of which they acknowledged to outshine theirs) that way they directed their influences, benign to Israel and malignant against their enemies, as when *the stars in their courses fought against Sisera.* Note, The heavenly bodies, as well as earth and seas, are at God's command, and, when he pleases, at Israel's service too.

VI. He carried on and completed Israel's victories over the nations of Canaan and their kings; he *slew great kings* and *famous,* Ps. cxxxvi. 17, 18. This is largely insisted upon here, as a proper plea with God to enforce the present petition, that he would restore them again to that land which they were, at the expense of so many lives, so many miracles, first put in possession of.

1. Many expressions are here used to set forth the conquest of Canaan. (1.) God's *bow was made quite naked,* taken out of the case, to be employed for Israel; we should say, his *sword was quite unsheathed,* not drawn out a little way, to frighten the enemy, and then put up again, but quite drawn out, not to be returned till they are all cut off. (2.) He *marched through the land* from end to end, *in indignation,* as scorning to let that wicked generation of Canaanites any longer possess so good a land. He marched *cum fastidio*—*with disdain* (so some), despising their confederacies. (3.) He *threshed the heathen in anger,* trod them down, nay, he trod them out, as corn in the floor, to give them, and what they had, to be meat to his people Israel, Mic. iv. 13. (4.) He *wounded the heads out of the house of the wicked;* he destroyed the families of the Canaanites, and wounded their princes, the heads of their families; nay, he cut off the heads, and so *discovered the foundations of them,* even to the neck. Are they a building? They are razed even to the foundation. Are they a body? They are plunged into deep mire even to the neck, so that they cannot get out, or help themselves. He *broke the heads of leviathan in pieces,* Ps. lxxiv. 14. Some apply this to Christ's victories over Satan and the powers of darkness, in which he *wounded the heads over many countries,* Ps. cx. 6. (5.) He *struck through with his staves the head of the villages* (v. 14); with Israel's staves God *struck through the head of the villages* of the enemies, whether Egypt or Canaan. Staves shall do the same execution as swords when God pleases to make use of them. The enemy came out with the utmost force and fury, *as a whirlwind to scatter me* (says Israel); *for many a time have they thus afflicted me,* thus attacked me, *from my youth,* Ps. cxxix. 1. Pharaoh, when he pursued Israel to the Red Sea, *came out as a whirlwind;* so did the kings of Canaan in their confederacies against Israel. *Their rejoicing was as to devour the poor secretly;* they were as confident of success in their enterprise as ever any great man was of devouring a poor man, that was no way a match for

him; and his design against him was carried on with secresy. But God disappointed them, and their pride did but make their fall the more shameful and God's care of his poor the more illustrious. (6.) He *walked to the sea with his horses* (so some read it, v. 15), that is, he carried Israel's victories to the Great Sea, which was opposite to that side of Canaan at which they entered, so that they went quite through it, and made themselves masters of it all, or rather God made them so, for they *got it not by their own sword,* Ps. xliv. 3. Now,

2. There were three things that God had an eye to, in giving Israel so many bloody victories over the Canaanites:—(1.) He would hereby make good his promise to the fathers; it was *according to the oaths of the tribes, even his word, v.* 9. He had sworn to give this land to the *tribes of Israel;* it was his oath *to Isaac confirmed to Jacob,* and repeated many a time to *the tribes of Israel, Unto thee will I give the land of Canaan.* This word God will accomplish, though Israel be ever so unworthy (Deut. ix. 5) and their enemies ever so many and mighty. Note, What God does for his tribes is according to the oaths of the tribes, according to what he has said and sworn to them; *for he is faithful that has promised.* (2.) He would hereby show his kindness to *his people,* because of their relation to him, and his interest in them: *Thou wentest forth for the salvation of thy people, v.* 13. All the powers of nature are shaken, and the course of nature changed, and every thing seems to be thrown into disorder, and all is *for the salvation of God's people.* There are a people in the world who are God's people, and their salvation is that which he has in his eye in all the operations of his providence. Heaven and earth shall sooner come together than any of the links in the golden chain of their salvation shall be broken; and even that which seems most unlikely shall by an overruling hand be made to work for their salvation, Phil. i. 19. (3.) He would hereby give a type and figure of the redemption of the world by Jesus Christ. It is *for salvation with thy anointed,* with Joshua, who led the armies of Israel and was a figure of him whose name he bore, even Jesus our Joshua. What God did for his Israel of old was done with an eye to his anointed, for the sake of the Mediator, who was both the founder and foundation of the covenant made with them. It was salvation *with him,* for in all the salvations wrought for them, God looked upon the face of the anointed, and did them by him.

16 When I heard, my belly trembled; my lips quivered at the voice: rottenness entered into my bones, and I trembled in myself, that I might rest in the day of trouble: when he cometh up unto the people, he will invade them with his troops. 17 Al-

though the fig-tree shall not blossom, neither *shall* fruit *be* in the vines ; the labour of the olive shall fail, and the fields shall yield no meat ; the flock shall be cut off from the fold, and *there shall be* no herd in the stalls : 18 Yet I will rejoice in the LORD, I will joy in the God of my salvation. 19 The LORD God *is* my strength, and he will make my feet like hinds' *feet,* and he will make me to walk upon mine high places. To the chief singer on my stringed instruments.

Within the compass of these few lines we have the prophet in the highest degree both of trembling and triumphing, such are the varieties both of the state and of the spirit of God's people in this world. In heaven there shall be no more trembling, but everlasting triumphs.

I. The prophet had foreseen the prevalence of the church's enemies and the long continuance of the church's troubles ; and the sight made him tremble, *v.* 16. Here he goes on with what he had said *v.* 2, " *I have heard thy speech and was afraid.* When I *heard* what sad times were coming upon the church *my belly trembled, my lips quivered at the voice ;* the news made such an impression that it put me into a perfect ague fit." The blood retiring to the heart, to succour that when it was ready to faint, the extreme parts were left destitute of spirits, so that *his lips quivered.* Nay, he was so weak, and so unable to help himself, that he was as if *rottenness had entered into his bones ;* he had no strength left in him, could neither stand nor go ; he *trembled in himself,* trembled all over him, trembled within him ; he yielded to his trembling, and *troubled himself,* as our Saviour did ; his *flesh trembled for fear of God* and *he was afraid of his judgments,* Ps. cxix. 120. He was touched with a tender concern for the calamities of the church, and trembled for fear lest they should end at length in its ruin, and the *name of Israel be blotted out.* Nor did he think it any disparagement to him, nor any reproach to his courage, but freely owned he was one of those that *trembled at God's word,* for to them he will look with favour : *I tremble in myself, that I might rest in the day of trouble.* Note, When we see a day of trouble approaching it concerns us to provide accordingly, and to lay up something in store, by the help of which we may rest in that day ; and the best way to make sure rest for ourselves in the day of trouble is to tremble within ourselves at the word of God and the threatenings of that word. He that has joy in store for those that *sow in tears* has rest in store for those that tremble before him. *Good hope through grace* is founded in a *holy fear.* Noah, who was *moved with*

1370

fear, and trembled within himself at the warning given him of the deluge coming, had the ark for his resting place in the day of that trouble. The prophet tells us what he said in his trembling. His fear is that, *when he comes up to the people,* when the *Chaldean comes up to the people* of Israel, *he will invade them,* will surround them, will break in upon them, nay (as it is in the margin), he will *cut them in pieces with his troops ;* he cried out, We are all undone ; the whole nation of the Jews is lost and gone. Note, When things look bad we are too apt to aggravate them, and make the worst of them.

II. He had looked back upon the experiences of the church in former ages, and had observed what great things God had done for them, and so he recovered himself out of his fright, and not only retrieved his temper, but fell into a transport of holy joy, with an express *non obstante*—*notwithstanding* to the calamities he foresaw coming, and this not for himself only, but in the name of every faithful Israelite.

1. He supposes the ruin of all his creature comforts and enjoyments, not only of the delights of this life, but even of the necessary supports of it, *v.* 17. Famine is one of the ordinary effects of war, and those commonly feel it first and most that sit still and are quiet ; the prophet and his pious friends, when the Chaldean army comes, will be plundered and stripped of all they have. Or he supposes himself deprived of all by blasting and unseasonable weather, or some other immediate hand of God. Or though the captives in Babylon have not that plenty of all good things in their own land. (1.) He supposes the fruit-tree to be withered and become barren ; the *fig-tree* (which used to furnish them with much of their food ; hence we often read of *cakes of figs)* shall not so much as *blossom, nor shall fruit be in the vine,* from which they had their drink, that made glad the heart : he supposes *the labour of the olive* to *fail,* their oil, which was to them as butter is to us ; the *labour of the olive shall lie* (so it is in the margin) ; their expectations from it shall be disappointed. (2.) He supposes the bread-corn to fail ; *the fields shall yield no meat :* and, since the king himself is served of the field,* if the productions of that be withdrawn, every one will feel the want of them. (3.) He supposes the cattle to perish for want of the food which the field should yield and does not, or by disease, or being destroyed and carried away by the enemy : *The flock is cut off from the fold, and there is no herd in the stall.* Note, When we are in the full enjoyment of our creature comforts we should consider that there may come a time when we shall be stripped of them all, and use them accordingly, as not abusing them, 1 Cor. vii. 29, 30.

2. He resolves to delight and triumph in

God notwithstanding; when all is gone his God is not gone (*v.* 18): "*Yet will I rejoice in the Lord:* I shall have him to rejoice in, and will rejoice in him." *Destroy the vines and the fig-trees,* and you make all the mirth of a carnal heart to cease, Hos. ii. 11, 12. But those who, when they were full, enjoyed God in all, when they are emptied and impoverished can *enjoy all in God,* and can sit down upon a melancholy heap of the ruins of all their creature comforts and even then can sing to the praise and glory of God, as the God of their salvation. This is the principal ground of our joy in God, that he is the God of our salvation, our eternal salvation, the salvation of the soul; and, if he be so, we may rejoice in him as such in our greatest distresses, since by them our salvation cannot be hindered, but may be furthered. Note, Joy in God is never out of season, nay, it is in a special manner seasonable when we meet with losses and crosses in the world, that it may then appear that our hearts are not set upon these things, nor our happiness bound up in them. See how the prophet triumphs in God: *The Lord God is my strength, v.* 19. He that is the *God of our salvation* in another world will be our strength in this world, to carry us on in our journey thither, and help us over the difficulties and oppositions we meet with in our way. Even when provisions are cut off, to make it appear that *man lives not by bread alone,* we may have the want of bread supplied by the graces and comforts of God's Spirit and with the supplies of them. (1.) We shall be strong for our spiritual warfare and work: *The Lord God is my strength,* the strength of my heart. (2.) We shall be swift for our spiritual race: "*He will make my feet like hinds' feet,* that with enlargement of heart I may run the way of his commands and outrun my troubles." (3.) We shall be successful in our spiritual enterprises: "*He will make me to walk upon my high places;* that is, I shall gain my point, shall be restored unto my own land, and tread upon the high places of the enemy," Deut. xxxii. 13; xxxiii. 29. Thus the prophet, who began his prayer with fear and trembling, concludes it with joy and triumph, for prayer is heart's ease to a gracious soul. When Hannah had prayed she *went her way, and did eat, and her countenance was no more sad.* This prophet, finding it so, publishes his experience of it, and puts it into the hand of the *chief singer* for the use of the church, especially in the day of our captivity. And, though then the harps were hung upon the willow-trees, yet in the hope that they would be resumed, and their right hand retrieve its cunning, which it had forgotten, he set his song upon *Shigionoth* (*v.* 1), wandering tunes, *according to the variable songs,* and upon *Neginoth* (*v.* 19), *the stringed instruments.* He that is afflicted, and has prayed aright, may then be so easy, may then be so merry, as to sing psalms.

AN

EXPOSITION,

WITH PRACTICAL OBSERVATIONS,

OF THE PROPHECY OF

ZEPHANIAH.

THIS prophet is placed last, as he was last in time, of all the minor prophets before the captivity, and not long before Jeremiah, who lived at the time of the captivity. He foretels the general destruction of Judah and Jerusalem by the Chaldeans, and sets their sins in order before them, which had provoked God to bring their ruin upon them, calls them to repentance, threatens the neighbouring nations with the like destructions, and gives encouraging promises of their joyful return out of captivity in due time, which have a reference to the grace of the gospel. We have, in the first verse, an account of the prophet and the date of his prophecy, which supersedes our enquiry concerning them here.

CHAP. I.

After the title of the book (ver. 1) here is, I. A threatening of the destruction of Judah and Jerusalem, an utter destruction, by the Chaldeans, ver. 2—4. II. A charge against them for their gross sin, which provoked God to bring that destruction upon them (ver. 5, 6); and so he goes on in the rest of the chapter, setting both the judgments before them, that they might prevent them or prepare for them, and the sins that destroy them, that they might judge themselves, and justify God in what was brought upon them.

1. They must hold their peace because they had greatly sinned,

ver. 7—9. But, 2, They shall howl because the trouble will be great. The day of the Lord is near, and it will be a terrible day, ver. 10—18. Such fair and timely warning as this did God give to the Jews of the approaching captivity; but they hardened their neck, which made their destruction remediless.

THE word of the LORD which came unto Zephaniah the son of Cushi, the son of Gedaliah, the son of Amariah, the son of Hizkiah, in the days of Josiah the son of Amon, king of Judah. 2 I will utterly consume all *things* from off the land, saith the LORD. 3 I will consume man and beast; I will consume the fowls of the heaven, and the fishes of the sea, and the stumbling-blocks with the wicked; and I will cut off man from off the land, saith the LORD. 4 I will also stretch out mine hand upon Judah, and upon all the inhabitants of Jerusalem; and I will cut off the remnant of Baal from this place, *and* the name of the Chemarims with the priests; 5 And them that worship the host of heaven upon the housetops; and them that worship *and* that swear by the LORD, and that swear by Malcham; 6 And them that are turned back from the LORD; and *those* that have not sought the LORD, nor enquired for him.

Here is, I. The title-page of this book (*v.* 1), in which we observe, 1. What authority it has, and who gave it that authority; it is from heaven, and not of men: It is *the word of the Lord.* 2. Who was the instrument of conveying it to the church. His name was *Zephaniah*, which signifies the *servant of the Lord*, for God *revealed his secrets to his servants the prophets*. The pedigree of other prophets, whose extraction we have an account of, goes no further back than their father, except Zecharias, whose grandfather also is named. But this of Zephaniah goes back four generations, and the highest mentioned is *Hizkiah;* it is the very same name in the original with that of Hezekiah king of Judah (2 Kings xviii. 1), and refers probably to him; if so, our prophet, being lineally descended from that pious prince, and being of the royal family, could with the better grace reprove the folly of the king's children as he does, *v.* 8. 3. When this prophet prophesied—*in the days of Josiah king of Judah,* who reigned well, and in the twelfth year of his reign began vigorously, and carried on a work of reformation, in which he destroyed idols and idolatry. Now it does not appear whether Zephaniah prophesied in the beginning of his reign; if so, we may suppose his prophesying had a great and good influence on that reformation. When he, as God's messenger, reproved the idolatries of Jerusalem, Josiah, as God's vicegerent, removed them; and reformation is likely to go on and prosper when both magistrates and ministers do their part towards it. If it were towards the latter end of his reign that he prophesied, we sadly see how

a corrupt people relapse into their former distempers. The idolatries Josiah had abolished, it should seem, returned in his own time, when the heat of the reformation began a little to abate and wear off. What good can the best reformers do with a people that hate to be reformed, as if they longed to be ruined?

II. The summary, or contents, of this book. The general proposition contained in it is, That utter destruction is coming apace upon Judah and Jerusalem for sin. Without preamble, or apology, he begins abruptly (*v.* 2): *By taking away I will make an end of all things from off the face of the land, saith the Lord.* Ruin is coming, utter ruin, destruction from the Almighty. He has said it who can, and will, make good what he has said: "*I will utterly consume all things.* I will *gather* all things" (so some); "I will recal all the blessings I have bestowed, because they have abused them and so forfeited them." The consumption determined shall take away, 1. The inferior creatures: *I will consume the beasts, the fowls of the heaven, and the fishes of the sea* (*v.* 3), as, in the deluge, *every living substance was destroyed that was upon the face of the ground,* Gen. vii. 23. The creatures were made for man's use, and therefore when he has perverted the use of them, and made them *subject to vanity*, God, to show the greatness of his displeasure against the sin of man, involves them in his punishment. The expressions are figurative, denoting universal desolation. Those that fly ever so high, as the fowls of heaven, and think themselves out of the reach of the enemies' hand—those that hide ever so close, as the fishes of the sea, and think themselves out of the reach of the enemies' eye—shall yet become a prey to them, and be utterly consumed. 2. The children of men: "*I will consume man; I will cut off man from the land.* The land shall be dispeopled and left uninhabited; I will destroy, not only Israel, but *man.* The land shall enjoy her sabbaths. I will cut off, not only the wicked men, but all men; even the few among them that are good shall be involved in this common calamity. Though they shall not be cut off from the Lord, yet they shall be *cut off from the land.*" It is with Judah and Jerusalem that God has this quarrel, both city and country, and upon them he will *stretch out his hand*, the hand of his power, the hand of his wrath; and *who knows the power of his anger? v.* 4. Those that will not humble themselves under God's mighty hand shall be humbled and brought down by it. Note, Even Judah, where God is known, and Jerusalem, where his dwelling-place is, if they revolt from him and rebel against him, shall have his hand stretched out against them. 3. All wicked people, and all those things that are the matter of their wickedness (*v.* 3): "*I will consume the stumbling-blocks with the wicked,* the idols with the idolaters, the offences with the offenders." Josiah had taken away the stumbling-blocks, and, as far as he could, had purged the land of the monuments of idolatry, hoping that there would be no more idolatry; but *the wicked will do wickedly,* the dog will return to his vomit, and therefore, since the sin will not otherwise be cured, the sinners must themselves be consumed, even the *wicked with the stumbling-blocks* of their iniquity, Ezek. xiv. 3. Since it was not done by the sword of justice, it shall be done by the sword of war. See who the sinners are that shall be consumed. (1.) The professed idolaters, who avowed idolatry, and were wedded to it. The *remnant of Baal* shall be *cut off,* the images of Baal, and the worshippers of those images. Josiah cut off a great deal of Baal; but that which was so close as to escape the eye, or so bold as to escape the hand, of his justice, God will cut off, even all the remains of it. The Chaldeans would spare none of the images of Baal, or the worshippers of those images. The *Chemarim* shall be *cut off;* we read of them in the history of Josiah's reformation. 2 Kings xxiii. 5, *He put down the idolatrous priests:* the word is the *Chemarim.* The word signifies *black men,* some think because they wore black clothes, affecting to appear grave, others because their faces were black with attending the altars, or the fires in which they burnt their children to Moloch. They seem to have been immediate attendants upon the service of Baal. They shall be *cut off with the priests,* the regulars with the seculars. The very name of them shall be cut off; the order shall be quite abolished, so as to be forgotten, or remembered with detestation. And, among other idolaters, the *worshippers of the host of heaven upon the house-tops* shall be cut off (*v.* 5), who justified themselves in their idolatry with those that did not worship images, the work of their own hands, but offered their sacrifices and burnt their incense to the sun, moon, and stars, immediately upon the tops of their houses. But God will let them know that he is a jealous God, and will not endure any rival; and, though some have thought that the most specious and plausible idolatry, yet it will appear as great an offence to God to give divine honours to a star as to give them to a stone or a stock. Even the worshippers of the host of heaven shall be consumed as well as the worshippers of the beasts of the earth or the fiends of hell. The sin of the adulteress is not the less sinful for the gaiety of the adulterer. (2.) Those also shall be consumed that think to compound the matter between God and idols, and keep an even balance between them, that halt between God and Baal, and worship between Jehovah and Moloch, and *swear by both;* or, as it might better be read, swear *to the Lord and to Malcham.* They bind themselves by oath and covenant to the service both of

God and idols. They have a good opinion of the worship of the God of Israel; it is the religion of their country, and has been long so, and therefore they will by no means quit it; but they think it will be very much improved and beautified if they join with it the worship of Moloch, for that also is much used in other countries, and travellers admire it; there is a great deal of good fancy and strong flame in it. They cannot keep always to the worship of a God whom they have no visible representation of, and therefore they must have an image; and what better than the image of *Moloch—a king?* They think they shall effectually atone for their sin if they *swear to Moloch,* and, pursuant to that oath, burn their children in sacrifice to that idol; and yet, if they do amiss in that, they hope to atone for it in worshipping the God of Israel too. Note, Those that think to divide their affections and adorations between God and idols will not only come short of acceptance with God, but will have their doom with the worst of idolaters; for what communion can there be between light and darkness, Christ and Belial, God and mammon? She whose own the child is not pleads for the dividing of it, for, if Satan have half, he will have all; but the true mother says, *Divide it not,* for, if God have but half, he will have none. Such waters will not be long sweet, if they come from a fountain that sends forth bitter water too; what have those to do to swear by the Lord that swear by Malcham? (3.) Those also shall be consumed that have apostatized from God, together with those that never gave up their names to him, *v.* 6. I will cut off, [1.] Those *that are turned back from the Lord,* that were well taught, and began well, that had given up their names to him, and set out at first in the worship of him, but have flown off, and turned aside, and fallen in with idolaters, and deserted those good ways of God which they were brought up in, and despised them. Those God will be sure to reckon with who are renegadoes from his service, who began in the Spirit and ended in the flesh; they shall be treated as deserters, to whom no mercy is shown. [2.] Those that *have not sought the Lord,* nor ever *enquired for him,* never made any profession of religion, and think to excuse themselves with that, shall find that this will not excuse them; nay, this is the thing laid to their charge; they are atheistical careless people, that *live without God in the world;* and those that do so are certainly unworthy to live upon God in the world.

7 Hold thy peace at the presence of the Lord GOD: for the day of the LORD *is* at hand: for the LORD hath prepared a sacrifice, he hath bid his guests. 8 And it shall come to pass in the day of the LORD's sacrifice,

that I will punish the princes, and the king's children, and all such as are clothed with strange apparel. 9 In the same day also will I punish all those that leap on the threshold, which fill their masters' houses with violence and deceit. 10 And it shall come to pass in that day, saith the Lord, *that there shall be* the noise of a cry from the fish-gate, and a howling from the second, and a great crashing from the hills. 11 Howl, ye inhabitants of Maktesh, for all the merchant-people are cut down; all they that bear silver are cut off. 12 And it shall come to pass at that time, *that* I will search Jerusalem with candles, and punish the men that are settled on their lees: that say in their heart, The Lord will not do good, neither will he do evil. 13 Therefore their goods shall become a booty, and their houses a desolation: they shall also build houses, but not inhabit *them;* and they shall plant vineyards, but not drink the wine thereof.

Notice is here given to Judah and Jerusalem that God is coming forth against them, and will be with them shortly; his *presence,* as a just avenger, *his day,* the day of his judgment and his wrath, are not far off, *v.* 7. Those that improve not the presence of God with them as a Father, but sin away that presence, may expect his presence with them as a Judge, to call them to an account for the contempt put upon his grace. The *day of the Lord* will come. Men have their day now, when they take a liberty to do what they please; but *God's day is at hand;* it is here called his *sacrifice,* a sacrifice of his preparing, for the punishing of presumptuous sinners is a sacrifice to the justice of God, some reparation to his injured honour. Those that brought their offerings to other gods were themselves justly made victims to the true God. On a day of sacrifice great slaughter was made; so shall there be in Jerusalem; men shall be killed up as fast as lambs for the altar, with as little regret, with as much pleasure: *The slain of the Lord shall be many.* On a day of sacrifice great feasts were made upon the sacrifices; so the inhabitants of Judah and Jerusalem shall be feasted upon by their enemies the Chaldeans; these are the guests God has prepared and invited to come and glut themselves—their revenge with slaughter and their covetousness with plunder. Now observe,

I. Who those are that are marked to be sacrificed, that shall be visited and punished

1374

in this day of reckoning, and what it is they shall be called to an account for. 1. The royal family, because of the dignity of their place, shall be first reckoned with for their pride, and vanity, and affectation (*v.* 8): *I will punish the princes, and the king's children,* who think themselves exempt from punishment; they shall find themselves accountable to God, and that, high as they are, he is above them. They shall be punished, and all such as, like them, are clothed *with strange apparel,* such as, in contempt of their own country (where, probably, it was the custom to go in a very plain dress, as became the seed of Jacob that *plain man),* affected to appear in the fashion of other nations and introduced their modes in apparel, studying to resemble those from whom God had appointed them, even in their clothes, industriously to distinguish themselves. *The princes and the king's children* scorned to wear any home-made stuffs, though God had provided them *fine linen* and *silks* (Ezek. xvi. 10), but they must send abroad to strange countries for their clothes, which would not please unless they were far-fetched and dear-bought; and even those of inferior rank affected to imitate the princes and the king's children. Pride in apparel is displeasing to God, and a symptom of the degeneracy of a people. 2. The noblemen, and their stewards and servants, come next to be reckoned with (*v.* 9): *In the same day will I punish those that leap on the threshold,* a phrase, no doubt, well understood then, and which probably signified the invading of their neighbour's rights. Entering their houses by force and violence, and seizing their possessions, they *leap on the threshold,* as much as to say that the house is their own and they will keep their hold of it; and, accordingly, they make all in it their own that they can lay their hands on, and so *fill their masters' houses* with goods gotten *by violence and deceit* and with all the guilt thereby contracted. Nor shall it suffice them to say that the ill-gotten gains were not for themselves but for their masters, and that what they did was by their order; for the obligations we lie under to keep God's commandments are prior and superior to the obligations we lie under to serve the interests of any master on earth. 3. The trading people, and the rich merchants, are next called to account. Iniquity is found in their end of the town, among *the inhabitants of Maktesh,* a low part of Jerusalem, deep like a mortar (for so the word signifies); the *goldsmiths* lived there (Neh. iii. 32) and the merchants; and they are now *cut down* (they are broken, and have shut up their shops, and become bankrupts); nay, *All those that bear silver are cut off,* in the first place, by the invaders, for the sake of the silver they carry, which is so far from being a protection to them that it will expose and betray them. The conquerors aimed at the wealthy men, and carried them off first, while *the poor of the land* escaped. Or it may be meant of a general decay of trade, which was a preface and introduction to the general destruction of the land. It is the token of a declining state when great dealers are cut down, and great bankers are cut off and become bankrupts, who cannot fall alone, but with themselves ruin many. 4. All the secure and careless people, the sons of pleasure, that live a loose idle life, are next reckoned with (*v.* 12); they come from all parts of the country, to take up their quarters in the head-quarters of the kingdom, where they take private lodgings, and indulge themselves in ease and luxury; but God will find them out, and punish them: *At that time I will search Jerusalem with candles*, to discover them, that they may be brought out to condign punishment. This intimates that they conceal themselves, as being either ashamed of the sin or afraid of the punishment of it; when the judgments of God are abroad they hope to escape by absconding and getting out of the way, but God will *search Jerusalem*, as search is made for a malefactor in disguise, that is harboured by his accomplices. God's hand will *find out all his enemies*, wherever they lie hid, and will punish not only the secret idolaters, but the secret epicures and profane; and those are the persons that are here described, and marks are given by which they will be discovered when strict search is made for them. (1.) Their dispositions are sensual: They *are settled on their lees*, intoxicated with their pleasures, strengthening themselves in their wealth and wickedness; they are secure and easy, and, because they have had no changes, they fear none, as Moab, Jer. xlviii. 11. They *have not been emptied from vessel to vessel*. They *fill themselves with wine and strong drink*, and banish all thought, saying, *To-morrow shall be as this day*, Isa. lvi. 12. Their being *settled on their lees* signifies the same with being *enclosed in their own fat*, Ps. xvii. 10. (2.) Their notions are atheistical. They could not live such loose lives but that they say *in their heart, The Lord will not do good, neither will he do evil;* that is, *He will do nothing.* They deny his providential government of the world: "What good and evil there is in the world comes by the wheel of fortune, and not by the disposal of a wise and supreme director." They deny his moral government, and his dispensing rewards and punishments: "*The Lord will not do good* to those that serve him, nor *do evil* to those that rebel against him; and therefore there is nothing got by religion, nor lost by sin." This was the effect of their sensuality; if they were not drowned in sense, they could not be thus senseless, nor could they be so stupid if they had not stupified themselves with the love of pleasure. It was also the cause of their sensuality; men would not make a god of their belly if they had not at first become so vain, so vile, in their imagi-

nations, as to think the God that made them *altogether such a one as themselves.* But God will *punish them; their end is destruction*, Phil. iii. 19.

II. What the destruction will be with which God will punish these sinners, and what course he will take with them. 1. He will silence them (*v.* 7): *Hold thy peace at the presence of the Lord.* He will force them to hold their peace, will strike them dumb with horror and amazement. They shall be speechless. All the excuses of their sin, and exceptions against the sentence, will be over-ruled, and they shall not have a word to say for themselves. 2. He will *sacrifice* them, for it is *the day of the Lord's sacrifice* (*v.* 8); he will give them into the hands of their enemies, and glorify himself thereby. 3. He will fill both city and country with lamentation (*v.* 10): *In that day there shall be a noise of a cry from the fish-gate*, so called because near either to the fish-ponds or to the fish-market. It belonged to the city of David (2 Chron. xxxiii. 14; Neh. iii. 3); perhaps the same with that which is called the *first gate* (Zech. xiv. 10), and, if so, it will explain what follows here, *And a howling from the second*, that is, the second gate, which was next to that *fish-gate*. The alarm shall go round the walls of Jerusalem from gate to gate; and there shall be *a great crashing from the hills*, a mighty noise from the mountains round about Jerusalem, from the acclamations of the victorious invaders, or from the lamentations of the timorous invaded, or from both. The inhabitants of the city, even of the closest safest part of the city, shall *howl* (*v.* 11), so clamorous shall the grief be. 4. They shall be stripped of all they have; it shall be a prey to the enemy (*v.* 13): *Their household goods*, and *shop-goods*, shall *become a booty*, and a rich booty they shall be; *their houses shall be* levelled with the ground and be *a desolation;* those of them that have *built* new houses *shall not inherit them*, but the invaders shall get and keep possession of them. And the *vineyards* they have planted they shall not *drink the wine of*, but, instead of having it for the relief of their friends that faint among them, they shall part with it for the animating of their foes that fight against them, Deut. xxviii. 30.

14 The great day of the LORD *is* near, *it is* near, and hasteth greatly, *even* the voice of the day of the LORD: the mighty man shall cry there bitterly. 15 That day *is* a day of wrath, a day of trouble and distress, a day of wasteness and desolation, a day of darkness and gloominess, a day of clouds and thick darkness, 16 A day of the trumpet and alarm against the fenced cities, and against the high

towers. 17 And I will bring distress upon men, that they shall walk like blind men, because they have sinned against the LORD: and their blood shall be poured out as dust, and their flesh as the dung. 18 Neither their silver nor their gold shall be able to deliver them in the day of the LORD's wrath; but the whole land shall be devoured by the fire of his jealousy: for he shall make even a speedy riddance of all them that dwell in the land.

Nothing could be expressed with more spirit and life, nor in words more proper to startle and awaken a secure and careless people, than the warning here given to Judah and Jerusalem of the approaching destruction by the Chaldeans. That is enough to make the sinners in Zion tremble—that it is *the day of the Lord*, the day in which he will manifest himself by taking vengeance on them. It is *the great day of the Lord*, a specimen of the day of judgment, a kind of doom's-day, as the last destruction of Jerusalem by the Romans is represented to be in our Saviour's prediction concerning it, Matt. xxiv. 27.

I. This *day of the Lord* is here spoken of as very near. The vision is not *for a great while to come*, as those imagine who *put the evil day far from them*. Those deceive themselves who look upon it as a thing at a distance, for *it is near—it is near—it hastens greatly*. The prophet gives the alarm like one that is in earnest, like one that awakens a family with the cry of *Fire! fire!* when it is at the next door that the danger is: "*It is near! it is near!* and therefore it is high time to bestir yourselves, and do what you can for your own safety before it be too late." It is madness for those to slumber whose *damnation slumbers not*, and to linger when it hastens.

II. It is spoken of as a very dreadful day. The very *voice* of this *day of the Lord*, the noise of it, when it is coming, shall be so terrible as to make *the mighty men cry there bitterly*, cry for fear as children do. *It shall be a vexation to hear the report* of it. In the last great day of the Lord the mighty men shall cry bitterly to rocks and mountains to shelter them; but in vain. Observe how emphatically the prophet speaks of this day approaching (*v.* 15): It is *a day of wrath*, God's wrath, wrath in perfection, wrath to the utmost. It will be a day of *trouble and distress* to the sinners; they shall be in pain, and shall see no ways of easing or helping themselves. The miseries of the damned are summed up (perhaps with reference to this) in the *indignation and wrath of God*, which are the cause, and the *tribulation and anguish* of the sinner's *soul*, which are the

1376

effect, Rom, ii. 8, 9. It will be a day of *trouble and distress* to the inhabitants, and a day of *wasteness and desolation* to the whole land; that fruitful land shall be turned into a wilderness. It shall be *a day of darkness and gloominess;* every thing shall look dismal, and there shall not be the least gleam of comfort, or glimpse of hope; look round, and it is all black. It is *a day of clouds and thick darkness;* there is not only nothing encouraging, but every thing threatening; the thick clouds are big with storms and tempests.

III. It is spoken of as a destroying day, *v.* 16, 17. It shall be destroying, 1. To places, even the strongest and best fortified: *A day of the trumpet and alarm against the fenced cities*, to break into them, and against the *high towers*, to bring them down; for what forts, what fences, can hold out against the wrath of God? 2. To persons (*v.* 17): "*I will bring distress upon men*, the strongest and stoutest of men; their hearts and hands shall fail them; they shall *walk like blind men*, wandering endlessly, *because they have sinned against the Lord.*" Note, Those that walk as bad men will justly be left to walk as blind men, always in the dark, in doubt and danger, without any guide or comfort, and falling at length into the ditch. Because they have *sinned against the Lord* he will deliver them into the hands of cruel enemies, that shall *pour out their blood as dust*, so profusely, and with as little regret, and *their flesh* shall be thrown *as dung* upon the dunghill.

IV. The destruction of that day will be unavoidable and universal, *v.* 18. 1. There shall be no escaping it by ransom: *Neither their silver nor their gold*, which they have hoarded up so covetously against the evil day, or which they have spent so prodigally to make friends for such a time, *shall be able to deliver them in the day of the Lord's wrath*. Another prophet borrowed these words from this, with reference to the same event, Ezek. vii. 19. Note, Riches profit not in the day of wrath, Prov. xi. 4. Nay, riches expose to the wrath of men (Eccl. v. 13), and riches abused to the wrath of God. 2. There shall be no escaping it by flight or concealment; for the *whole land shall be devoured by the fire of his jealousy*, and where then can a hiding-place be found? See what the fire of God's jealousy is, and what the force of it; it will devour whole lands; how then can particular persons stand before it? He shall make riddance, *a speedy riddance, of all those that dwell in the land*, as the husbandman, when he rids his ground, cuts up all the briers and thorns for the fire. Note, Sometimes the judgments of God make riddance, even utter riddance, with sinful nations, a speedy riddance; their destruction is effected, is completed, in a little time. Let not sinners be laid asleep by the patience of God, for when the measure of their iniquity is full his justice will both overtake and overcome, will make quick work and thorough work.

CHAP. II.

In this chapter we have, I. An earnest exhortation to the nation of the Jews to repent and make their peace with God, and so to prevent the judgments threatened before it was too late (ver. 1—3), and this inferred from the revelation of God's wrath against them in the foregoing chapter. II. A denunciation of the judgments of God against several of the neighbouring nations that had assisted, or rejoiced in, the calamity of Israel. 1. The Philistines, ver. 4—7. 2. The Moabites and Ammonites, ver. 8—11. 3. The Ethiopians and Assyrians, ver. 12—15. All these shall drink of the same cup of trembling that is put into the hands of God's people, as was also foretold by other prophets before and after.

GATHER yourselves together, yea, gather together, O nation not desired; 2 Before the decree bring forth, *before* the day pass as the chaff, before the fierce anger of the LORD come upon you, before the day of the LORD's anger come upon you. 3 Seek ye the LORD, all ye meek of the earth, which have wrought his judgment; seek righteousness, seek meekness: it may be ye shall be hid in the day of the LORD's anger.

Here we see what the prophet meant in that terrible description of the approaching judgments which we had in the foregoing chapter. From first to last his design was, not to drive the people to despair, but to drive them to God and to their duty—not to frighten them out of their wits, but to frighten them out of their sins. In pursuance of that he here calls them to repentance, national repentance, as the only way to prevent national ruin. Observe,

I. The summons given them to a national assembly (v. 1): *Gather yourselves together.* He had told them, in the last words of the foregoing chapter, that God would make a *speedy riddance of all that dwelt in the land,* upon which, one would think, it should follow, " Disperse yourselves, and flee for shelter where you can find a place." When the decree had absolutely gone forth for the last destruction of Jerusalem by the Romans, that was the advice given (Matt. xxiv. 16), *Then let those who are in Judea flee into the mountains;* but here it is otherwise. God warns, that he may not wound, threatens, that he may not strike, and therefore calls to the people to use means for the turning away of his wrath. The summons is given to a *nation not desired.* The word signifies either, 1. Not desiring, that has not any desires towards God or the remembrance of his name, is not desirous of his favour or grace, but very indifferent to it, has no mind to repent and reform. " Yet *come together,* and see if you can stir up desires in one another." Thus God is often *found of those that sought him not,* nor *asked for him,* Isa. lxv. 1. Or, 2. Not desirable, no ways lovely, nor having any thing in them amiable, or which might recommend them to God. The land of Is-

rael had been a *pleasant land, a land of delight* (Dan. xi. 41); but now it is unlovely, it is a *nation not desired,* to which God might justly say, *Depart from me;* but he says, " *Gather together to me,* and let us see if any expedient can be found out for the preventing of the ruin. *Gather together,* that you may in a body humble yourselves before God, may fast, and pray, and seek his face. *Gather together,* to consult among yourselves what is to be done in this critical juncture, that every one may consider of it, may give and take advice, and speak his mind, and that what is done may be done by consent and so may be a national act." Some read it, " *Enquire into yourselves;* yea, *enquire into yourselves;* examine your consciences; look into your hearts; search and try your ways; *enquire into yourselves,* that you may find out the sin by which God has been provoked to this displeasure against you, and may find out the way of returning to him." Note, When God is contending with us it concerns us to enquire into ourselves.

II. Arguments urged to press them to the utmost seriousness and expedition herein (v. 2): " Do it in earnest; do it with all speed before it is too late, *before the decree bring forth, before the day pass.*" The manner of speaking here is very lively and awakening, designed to make them apprehensive, as all sinners are concerned to be, 1. That their danger is very great, that their all lies at stake, that it is a matter of life and death, which therefore well requires and well deserves the closest application of mind that can be. It is not a trifle, and therefore is not a thing to be trifled about. It is the *fierce anger of the Lord* that is kindled against them, and is just ready to kindle upon them, that *devouring fire* which none can *dwell with,* which none can make head against or hold up their head under. " It is the *day of the Lord's anger,* the day set for the pouring out of the full vials of it, that you are threatened with, that *great day of the Lord*" spoken of, *ch.* i. 14. " Are you not concerned to prepare for that day?" 2. That it is very imminent: " Bestir yourselves now quickly, *before the decree bring forth,* and then it will be too late, the opportunity will be lost and never retrieved. The decree is as it were big with child, and it will *bring forth the day,* the terrible day, which shall *pass as chaff,* which shall hurry you away into captivity as chaff before the wind." *We know not what a day may bring forth* (Prov. xxvii. 1), but we do know what the decree will bring forth against impenitent sinners, whom therefore it highly concerns to repent in time, in *the accepted time.* Note, It is the wisdom of those whom God has a controversy with to agree with him quickly, while they are in the way, before his fierce anger comes upon them, not to be turned away. In a case of this nature delays are highly dangerous and may be fatal; they will be so if by them the heart is hardened. How solicitous should we all be to make our peace with God before the Spirit withdraw from us, or cease to strive with us, before the day of grace be over or the day of life, before our everlasting state shall be determined on the other side of the great gulf fixed!

III. Directions prescribed for the doing of this effectually. It is not enough to gather together in a consternation, but they must seriously and calmly apply to the duty of the day (*v.* 3): *Seek you the Lord.* That they might find mercy with God, they are here put upon seeking; for so is the rule—*Seek, and you shall find.* A general call was given to the whole nation to *gather together*, but little good is to be expected from the far greater part of them; if the land be saved, it must be by the interest and intercession of the pious few, and therefore to them the exhortation here is particularly directed. And observe, 1. How they are described—they are *the meek of the earth*, or of *the land*. It is the distinguishing character of the people of God that they are the *meek ones of the earth*; this is their badge; it is their livery. They are modest, and humble, and low in their own eyes; they are mild, and gentle, and yielding to others, not soon angry, not very angry, not long angry; they are the *quiet in the land*, Ps. xxxv. 20. And they are subject and submissive to their God, to all his precepts and all his providences. Actuated by this principle and disposition, they have *wrought his judgments*, that is, have obeyed his laws, observed his institutions, have made conscience of their duty to him, and have laid out themselves for the advancement of his honour and interest in the world. 2. What they are required to do; they must *seek*, which denotes both a careful enquiry and a constant endeavour, that they may know and do their duty. (1.) They must *seek the Lord*, seek his favour and grace, address him upon all occasions, ask of him what they need, seek him early, seek him diligently, and continue seeking him. (2.) They must *seek righteousness*. "Seek to God for the performance of his promises to you, and see to it that you abound yet more in duty to him; seek for the righteousness of Christ to be imputed to you, for the graces of God's Spirit to be implanted in you; hunger and thirst after them." (3.) They must *seek meekness*. This is a grace they were so eminent for that they were denominated *the meek of the land*, and yet this they must *seek*. Note, Those that are ever so good must still strive to be better, those that have ever so much grace must be still praying and labouring for more. Nay, those that excel in any particular grace must still seek to excel yet more in that, because in that most assaults will be made upon them by their enemies, in that most is expected from them by their friends, and in that they are most apt to be themselves secure. *Si dixisti,*

Sufficit, periisti—Say but, I am all that I ought to be, and you are undone. In the difficult trying times approaching, the meek will find exercise for all the meekness they have, and all little enough, and therefore should seek it earnestly, and pray that when God in his providence gives them occasion for it he would by his grace enable them to exercise it, *to show all meekness to all men*, in all instances, that, *as the day is, so may the strength be.*

IV. Encouragements given to take these directions: *It may be, you shall be hid in the day of the Lord's anger.* 1. "You particularly that are the *meek of the earth.* Though the day of the Lord's anger do come upon the land, yet you shall be safe, you shall be taken under special protection. *Verily it shall be well with thy remnant*, Jer. xv. 11. *Thy life will I give unto thee for a prey*, Jer. xlv. 5. *I will deliver thee in that day*, Jer. xxxix. 17. *It may be, you shall be hid;* if any be hid, you shall." Good men cannot be sure of temporal preservation, for *all things come alike to all*, but they are most likely to be hid, and stand fairest for a distinguishing care of Providence. It is expressed thus doubtfully to try if they will trust the goodness of God's nature, though they have but the *it may be* of a promise, and to keep up in them a holy fear and watchfulness lest they should seem to come short, and should do any thing to throw themselves out of the divine protection. Note, Those that hold fast their integrity, in times of common iniquity, have reason to hope that God will find out a hiding-place for them, where they shall be safe and easy, in times of common calamity. They shall be hid (as Luther says) *aut in cælo, aut sub cælo—either in heaven or under heaven*, either in the possession of heaven or under the protection of heaven. Or, 2. "You of this nation, though it be a *nation not desired*, yet, in the day of the Lord's anger with the neighbouring nations, when his judgments are abroad, *you shall be hid;* your land shall be preserved for the sake of those few meek ones that stand in the gap to *turn away the wrath of God.*" It concerns us all to make it sure to ourselves that we shall be hid in the great day of God's wrath; and, if we hide ourselves in chambers of duty, God will hide us in chambers of safety, Isa. xxvi. 20. If we prepare an ark, that shall be our hiding-place, Gen. vii. 1.

4 For Gaza shall be forsaken, and Ashkelon a desolation: they shall drive out Ashdod at the noon day, and Ekron shall be rooted up. 5 Woe unto the inhabitants of the seacoasts, the nation of the Cherethites! the word of the LORD *is* against you; O Canaan, the land of the Philistines, I will even destroy thee, that there

shall be no inhabitant. 6 And the sea-coast shall be dwellings *and* cottages for shepherds, and folds for flocks. 7 And the coast shall be for the remnant of the house of Judah; they shall feed thereupon : in the houses of Ashkelon shall they lie down in the evening : for the Lord their God shall visit them, and turn away their captivity.

The prophet here comes to foretel what share the neighbouring nations should have in the destruction made upon those parts of the world by Nebuchadnezzar and his victorious Chaldees, as others of the prophets did at that time, which is designed, 1. To awaken the people of the Jews, by making them sensible how strong, how deep, how large, the inundation of calamities should be, that the *day of the Lord*, which was near, might appear the more dreadful, and they might thereby be quickened to prepare for it as for a general deluge. 2. To comfort them with this thought, that their case, though sad, should not be singular *(Solamen miseris socios habuisse doloris—The wretched find it consolatory to have companions of their woe)*, and much more with this, that though God had seemed to be their enemy, and to fight against them, yet he was still so far their friend, and an enemy to their enemies, that he resented, and would revenge, the indignities done them.

In these verses we have the doom of the Philistines, who were near neighbours, and old enemies, to the people of Israel. Five lordships there were in that country; only four are here named—*Gaza* and *Ashkelon, Ashdod* and *Ekron;* Gath, the fifth, is not named, some think because it was now subject to Judah. They were the *inhabitants of the sea-coasts (v. 5)*, for their country lay upon the Great Sea. The *nation of the Cherethites* is here joined with them, which bordered upon them (1 Sam. xxx. 14) and fell with them, as is foretold also, Ezek. xxv. 16. The Philistines' land is here called *Canaan,* for it belonged to that country which God gave to his people Israel, and was inserted in the grant made to them, Josh. xiii. 3. This land is yet to be possessed *(five lords of the Philistines)*, so that they wrongfully kept Israel out of the possession of it (Judg. iii. 3), which is now remembered against them. For, though the rights of others may be long detained unjustly, the righteous God will at length avenge the wrong.

I. It is here foretold that the Philistines, the usurpers, shall be dispossessed and quite extirpated. In general, here is a woe to them *(v. 5)*, which, coming from God, denotes all misery : *The word of the Lord is against them*—the word of the former prophets, which, though not yet accomplished, will be

in its season, Isa. xiv. 31. This word, now by this prophet, is against them. Note, Those are really in a woeful condition that have the word of the Lord against them, for no word of his shall fall to the ground. Those that rebel against the precepts of God's word shall have the *threatenings* of the word against them. The effect will be no less than their destruction, 1. God himself will be the author of it : *" I will even destroy thee,* who can make good what I say and will." 2. It shall be a universal destruction ; it shall extend itself to all parts of the land, both city and country : *Gaza shall be forsaken,* though now a populous city. It was foretold (Jer. xlvii. 6) that *baldness* should come upon Gaza; Alexander the Great razed that city, and we find (Acts viii. 26) that Gaza was a desert. *Ashkelon* shall be *a desolation,* a pattern of desolation. *Ashdod shall be driven out at noon-day;* in the extremity of the scorching heat they shall have no shade, no shelter to protect them ; but then, when most incommoded by the weather, they shall be forced away into captivity, which will be an aggravating circumstance of it. *Ekron likewise* shall be *rooted up,* that had been long taking root. The land of the Philistines shall be dispeopled; there *shall be no inhabitant, v.* 5. God made the earth *to be inhabited* (Isa. xlv. 18), otherwise he would have made it in vain; but, if men do not answer the end of their creation in serving God, it is just with God that the earth should not answer the end of its creation in serving them for a habitation ; man's sin has sometimes subjected it to this vanity. 3. It shall be an utter destruction. The sea-coast, which used to be a harbour for ships and a habitation for merchants, shall now be deserted, and be only *cottages for shepherds* and *folds for flocks (v. 6)*, and then perhaps put to better use than when it was possessed by the lords of the Philistines.

II. It is here foretold that the house of Judah, the rightful owners, shall recover the possession of it, *v.* 7. The remnant of those that shall *return out of captivity*, when God visits them, shall be made to *lie down* in safety *in the houses of Ashkelon,* to lie down *in the evening,* when they are weary and sleepy. There *they shall feed* themselves and their flocks. Note, God will at length restore his people to their rights, though they may be long kept out from them.

8 I have heard the reproach of Moab, and the revilings of the children of Ammon, whereby they have reproached my people, and magnified *themselves* against their border. 9 Therefore *as* I live, saith the Lord of hosts, the God of Israel, Surely Moab shall be as Sodom, and the children of Ammon as Gomorrah,

even the breeding of nettles, and salt-pits, and a perpetual desolation: the residue of my people shall spoil them, and the remnant of my people shall possess them. 10 This shall they have for their pride, because they have reproached and magnified *themselves* against the people of the LORD of hosts. 11 The LORD *will be* terrible unto them: for he will famish all the gods of the earth; and *men* shall worship him, every one from his place, *even* all the isles of the heathen.

The Moabites and Ammonites were both of the posterity of Lot; their countries joined, and, both adjoining to Israel, they are here put together in the prophecy against them.

I. They are both charged with the same crime, and that was reproaching and reviling the people of God and triumphing in their calamities (*v.* 8): *They have reproached my people;* while God's people kept close to their duty it is probable that they reproached them for the singularities of their religion; and now that they had revolted from God, and fallen under his displeasure, they reproached them for that too. It has been the common lot of God's people in all ages to be reproached and reviled upon one account or other. Thus the old serpent spits his venom; and pride is at the bottom of it; it is in their pride that they have *magnified themselves against the people of the Lord of hosts,* thinking themselves as good as they, as great, and every way as happy. It is the *contempt of the proud* that God's people are filled with, Ps. cxxiii. 4. They have *spoken big* (so some read it, *magna locuti sunt—they have spoken great things) against their border* (*v.* 8), against those of them that bordered upon their country, whom upon all occasions they insulted, or against the property they claimed, which they disputed, or the protection they boasted of, which they ridiculed; they *spoke big against the people of the Lord of hosts* as a deserted abandoned people. *Great swelling words of vanity* are the genuine language of the church's enemies. "But *I have heard them*" (says God), "and will let you know that I have heard them. I have heard, and I will reckon for them," Jude 15. And, if God hears the reproaches and revilings we are under, it is a good reason why we should be as a *deaf man that hears not,* Ps. xxxviii. 14, 15. Nay, God not only takes notice of, but interests himself in the reproaches cast on his people, because they are his; and it is certain that those who look with disdain upon the people of the Lord of hosts thereby dishonour the Lord of hosts himself. See this very thing charged on Moab and Ammon, Ezek. xxv. 3, 8.

II. They are both laid under the same doom. Associates in iniquity may expect

1380

to be such in desolation. See with what solemnity sentence is pronounced upon them, *v.* 9. It is *the Lord of hosts,* the sovereign Lord of all, who has authority to pass this sentence and ability to execute it; it is *the God of Israel,* who is jealous for their honour; it is he that has said it, nay, he has sworn it, *As I live, saith the Lord.* The sentence is, 1. That the Moabites and Ammonites shall be quite destroyed; they *shall be as Sodom and Gomorrah,* the marks of whose ruins in the Dead Sea lay near adjoining to the countries of Moab and Ammon; they shall, though not by the same means (even fire from heaven), yet almost in the same manner, be laid waste; not again to be inhabited, or not of a long time. The country shall produce nothing but *nettles,* instead of corn; and there shall be *brine-pits,* instead of the pleasant fountains of water with which the country had abounded. 2. That Israel shall be too hard for them, shall *spoil them* of their goods and *possess* their country by lawful war. Note, Proud men sometimes, by the just judgment of God, fall under the mortification of being trampled upon themselves by those whom once they haughtily trampled upon. And *this shall they have for their pride.*

III. Other nations shall in like manner be humbled, that the Lord alone may be exalted (*v.* 11): *The Lord will be terrible* unto the Moabites and Ammonites in particular, who have made themselves a terror to his Israel. For, 1. Heathen gods must be abolished. They have long had possession, and their worshippers have both glorified them and gloried in them. But *the Lord* will *famish all the gods of the earth,* will starve them out of their strong-holds. The Pagans had a fond conceit that their idols were regaled by their offerings, and did *eat the fat of their sacrifices,* Deut. xxxii. 38. *Omnia comesta à Belo—Bel has eaten all.* But it is here promised that when the Christian religion is set up in the world men shall be turned from the service of these dumb idols, shall forsake their altars, and bring no more sacrifices to them, and thus they shall be famished, or *made lean* (as the word is), their priests shall. This intimates the vanity of those idols; it lies in the power of their worshippers to famish them; whereas the true God says, *If I were hungry, I would not tell thee.* It intimates also the victory of the God of Israel over them. *Now know we that he is greater than all gods.* 2. Heathen nations must be converted; when the gospel gets ground, by it men shall be brought to worship him who lives for ever (for that is the command of the everlasting gospel, Rev. xiv. 7), *every one from his place;* they shall not need to go up to Jerusalem to worship the God of Israel, but, wherever they are, they may have access to him. *I will that men pray every where.* God shall be worshipped, not only by all the tribes of Israel and the strangers who join themselves to them, but by all *the isles of the heathen.* This is a promise which looks favourably upon our native country, for it is one of the most considerable of the isles of the Gentiles, by which God will be glorified.

12 Ye Ethiopians also, ye *shall be* slain by my sword. 13 And he will stretch out his hand against the north, and destroy Assyria; and will make Nineveh a desolation, *and* dry like a wilderness. 14 And flocks shall lie down in the midst of her, all the beasts of the nations : both the cormorant and the bittern shall lodge in the upper lintels of it; *their* voice shall sing in the windows; desolation *shall be* in the thresholds: for he shall uncover the cedar-work. 15 This *is* the rejoicing city that dwelt carelessly, that said in her heart, I *am,* and *there is* none beside me : how is she become a desolation, a place for beasts to lie down in ! every one that passeth by her shall hiss, *and* wag his hand.

The cup is *going round,* when Nebuchadnezzar is going on conquering and to conquer ; and not only Israel's near neighbours, but those that lay more remote, must be reckoned with for the wrongs they have done to God's people ; the Ethiopians and the Assyrians are here taken to task. 1. The Ethiopians, or Arabians, that had sometimes been a terror to Israel (as in Asa's time, 2 Chron. xiv. 9), must now be reckoned with : They *shall be slain by my sword, v.* 12. Nebuchadnezzar was God's sword, the instrument in his hand with which these and other enemies were subdued and punished, Ps. xvii. 14. 2. The Assyrians, and Nineveh the head city of their monarchy, are next set to the bar, to receive their doom : *He* that is God's sword *will stretch out his hand against the north, and destroy Assyria,* and make himself master of it. Assyria had been the rod of God's anger against Israel, and now Babylon is the rod of God's anger against Assyria, Isa. x. 5. He *will make Nineveh a desolation,* as was lately and largely foretold by the prophet Nahum. Observe, (1.) How flourishing Nineveh's state had formerly been (*v.* 15): *This is the rejoicing city that dwelt carelessly.* Nineveh was so strong that she feared no evil, and therefore dwelt carelessly and set danger at defiance; she was so rich that she thought herself sure of all good, and therefore was a rejoicing city, full of mirth and gaiety ; and she had such a dominion that she admitted no rival, but said in her heart, " *I am, and there is none besides me* that can compare with me, no city in the

world that can pretend to be equal with me." God can with his judgments frighten the most secure, humble the most haughty, and mar the mirth of those that most laugh now. (2.) How complete Nineveh's ruin shall now be ; it shall be made *a desolation, v.* 13. Such a heap of ruins shall this once pompous city be that it shall be, [1.] A receptacle for beasts, such a wilderness that *flocks shall lie down in it ;* nay, such a waste, desolate, frightful place, that wild beasts, the *beasts of the nations,* all kinds of beasts, shall take up their abode there ; the melancholy birds, as the *cormorant and bittern,* shall make their nests in what remains of the houses, as they sometimes do in old ruinous buildings that are uninhabited and unfrequented. The *lintels,* or chapiters of the pillars, the *windows* and *threshoids,* and all the fine *cedar-work* curiously engraven, shall lie exposed ; and on them these rueful ominous birds shall perch, and their *voice shall sing.* How are the songs of mirth turned into hideous horrid noises ! What little reason have men to be proud of stately buildings, and rich furniture, when they know not what all the pomp of them may come to at last ! [2.] A derision to travellers. Those that had come from far, to gratify their curiosity with the sight of Nineveh's splendour, shall now look on her with as much contempt as ever they looked upon her with admiration (*v.* 15) : *Every one that passes by shall hiss* at her, and *wag his hand,* making light of her desolations, nay, and making sport with them—"There is an end of proud Nineveh." They shall not weep, and wring their hands (the adversities of those are unpitied and unlamented who were insolent and haughty in their prosperity), but they shall *hiss and wag their hands,* forgetting that perhaps their own ruin is not far off.

CHAP. III.

We now return to Jerusalem, and must again hear what God has to say to her, I. By way of reproof and threatening, for the abundance of wickedness that was found in her, of which divers instances are given, with the aggravations of them, ver. 1–7. II. By way of promise of mercy and grace, which God had yet in reserve for them. Two general heads of promises here are :—1. That God would bring in a glorious work of reformation among them, cleanse them from their sins, and bring them home to himself; many promises of this kind here are, ver. 8–13. 2. That he would bring about a glorious work of salvation for them, when he had thus prepared them for it, ver. 14–20. Thus the " Redeemer shall come to Zion," and, to clear his own way, shall " turn away ungodliness from Jacob." These promises were to have their full accomplishment in gospel-times and gospel-graces.

WOE to her that is filthy and polluted, to the oppressing city ! 2 She obeyed not the voice ; she received not correction ; she trusted not in the LORD ; she drew not near to her God. 3 Her princes within her *are* roaring lions ; her judges *are* evening wolves ; they gnaw not the bones till the morrow. 4 Her prophets *are* light *and* treacherous persons : her priests have polluted the sanctuary, they have done violence to the law. 5 The just LORD *is* in the midst thereof; he will not do iniquity: every morning doth he bring his judgment to light, he faileth not; but the unjust knoweth no shame. 6 I have cut off the nations: their towers are desolate; I made their streets waste, that none passeth by: their cities are destroyed, so that there is no man, that there is none inhabitant. 7 I said, Surely thou wilt fear me, thou wilt receive instruction; so their dwelling should not be cut off, howsoever I punished them: but they rose early, *and* corrupted all their doings.

One would wonder that Jerusalem, the holy city, where God was known, and his name was great, should be the city of which this black character is here given, that a place which enjoyed such abundance of the means of grace should become so very corrupt and vicious, and that God should permit it to be so; yet so it is, to show that *the law made nothing perfect;* but if this be the true character of Jerusalem, as no doubt it is (for God's judgments will make none worse than they are), it is no wonder that the prophet begins with *woe to her.* For the holy God hates sin in those that are nearest to him, nay, in them he hates it most. A sinful state is, and will be, a woeful state.

I. Here is a very bad character given of the city in general. How has the faithful city become a harlot! 1. She shames herself; she is *filthy and polluted* (v. 1), has made herself *infamous* (so some read it), the *gluttonous* city (so the margin), always cramming, and making provision for the flesh, to fulfil the lusts of it. Sin is the filthiness and pollution of persons and places, and makes them odious in the sight of the holy God. 2. She wrongs her neighbours and inhabitants; she is *the oppressing city.* Never any place had *statutes and judgments so righteous* as this city had, and yet, in the administration of the government, never was more unrighteousness. 3. She is very provoking to her God, and in every respect walks contrary to him, v. 2. He had given his law, and spoken to her by his servants the prophets, telling her what was the good she should do and what the evil she should avoid; but *she obeyed not his voice,* nor made conscience of doing as he commanded her, in any thing. He had taken her under an excellent discipline, both of the word and of the rod; but she did not receive the instruction of the one nor the correction of the other, did not submit to God's will nor answer his end in either. He encouraged her to depend upon him, and his power and

promise, for deliverance from evil and supply with good; but she *trusted not in the Lord;* her confidence was placed in her alliances with the nations more than in her covenant with God. He gave her tokens of his presence, and instituted ordinances of communion for her with himself; but she *drew not near to her God,* did not meet him where he appointed and where he promised to meet her. She stood at a distance, and *said to the Almighty, Depart.*

II. Here is a very bad character of the leading men in it; those that should by their influence suppress vice and profaneness there are the great patterns and patrons of wickedness, and those that should be her physicians are really her worst disease. 1. *Her princes are* ravenous and barbarous as *roaring lions* that make a prey of all about them, and they are universally feared and hated; they use their power for destruction, and not for edification. 2. *Her judges,* who should be the protectors of injured innocence, *are evening wolves,* rapacious and greedy, and their cruelty and covetousness both insatiable: *They gnaw not the bones till the morrow;* they take so much delight and pleasure in cruelty and oppression that when they have devoured a good man they reserve the bones, as it were, for a sweet morsel, to be gnawed the next morning, Job xxxi. 31. 3. *Her prophets,* who pretend to be special messengers from heaven to them, *are light and treacherous persons,* fanciful, and of a vain imagination, frothy and airy, and of a loose conversation, men of no consistency with themselves, in whom one can put no confidence. They were so given to bantering that it was hard to say when they were serious. Their pretended prophecies were all a sham, and they secretly laughed at those that were deluded by them. 4. *Her priests,* who are teachers by office and have the charge of the holy things, are false to their trust and betray it. They were to preserve the purity of the *sanctuary,* but they did themselves *pollute* it, and the sacred offices of it, which they were to attend upon—such priests as Hophni and Phinehas, who by their wicked lives *made the sacrifices of the Lord to be abhorred.* They were to expound and apply *the law,* and to judge according to it; but, in their explications and applications of it, they *did violence to the law;* they corrupted the sense of it, and perverted it to the patronising of that which was directly contrary to it. By forced constructions, they made the law to speak what they pleased, to serve a turn, and so, in effect, *made void the law.*

III. We have here the aggravations of this general corruption of all orders and degrees of men in Jerusalem.

1. They had the tokens of God's presence among them, and all the advantages that could be of knowing his will, with the strongest inducements possible to do it, and

yet they persisted in their disobedience, *v.* 5. (1.) They had the honour and privilege of the Shechinah, God's dwelling in their land, so as he dwelt not with any other people : "*The just Lord is in the midst of thee,* to take cognizance of all thou doest amiss and give countenance to all thou doest well ; he is in the midst of thee as a holy God, and therefore thy pollutions are the more offensive, Deut. xxiii. 14. He is in the midst of you as a just God, and therefore will punish the affronts you put upon him, and the wrongs and injuries you do to one another." (2.) They had God's own example set before them, in the discovery he made of himself to them, that they might conform to it : "*He will not do iniquity,* and therefore you should not ;" for this was the great rule of their institution, "*Be you holy, for I am holy.*" God will be true to you ; be not you then false to him." (3.) He sent to them his prophets, rising up early and sending them : *Every morning he brings his judgment to light,* as duly as the morning comes ; *he fails not.* He shows them plainly what the good is which he requires of them, and puts them in mind of it ; he *wakens morning by morning* (Isa. l. 4), wakens his prophets with the rising sun, to bring to light the things which belong to their peace. So that, upon the whole matter, what more could have been done to his vineyard, to make it fruitful ? Isa. v. 4. And yet, after all, *the unjust know no shame ;* those that have been unjust are unjust still, and are not ashamed of their unrighteousness, *neither can they blush.* If they had any sense of honour, any shame left in them, they would not go so directly contrary to their profession and to the instructions given them. But those that are past shame are past cure.

2. God had set before their eyes some remarkable monuments of his justice, which were designed for warning to them (*v.* 6) : *I have cut off the nations,* the seven nations of Canaan, which the land spewed out for their wickedness, upon which they had this caution given them, to take heed lest it *spew them out also,* Lev. xviii. 28. Or it may refer to some of the neighbouring nations that were made desolate for their wickedness, especially to the nations of Israel, the ten tribes. *Their towers were desolate,* their high towers, their strong towers, their pride and power broken ; their *streets were wasted,* so that none passed along through them ; *their cities* were *destroyed* and laid in ruins ; *no man* was to be found in them, *no inhabitant,* all were slain or carried into captivity. The enemies did it, but God avows it ; *I cut them off,* says he. And God designed this for an admonition to Jerusalem (Ezek. xxiii. 9, 11) : " *I said, Surely thou wilt fear me ;* surely these judgments upon others will deter thee from the wicked practices ; *surely thou wilt receive instruction* by these providences ; it ought reasonably to be ex-

pected that thou wouldst not continue to sin like the nations when thou seest the ruin which their sin brought upon them." They could not but see their own house in danger when their neighbour's was on fire ; and, when we are frightened, God should be feared.

3. He had set before them life and death, good and evil, both in his word and in his providence. (1.) He had assured them of the continuance of their prosperity if they would fear him and receive instruction, for so *their dwelling would not be cut off* as their neighbour's was ; if they took the warning given them, and reformed, what was past should be pardoned, and their tranquillity lengthened out. (2.) He had made them feel the smart of the rod, though he reprieved them from the sword : *Howsoever I punished them,* that, being chastened, they might not be condemned. Such various methods did God take with them, to reclaim them, but all in vain ; they were not won upon by gentle methods, nor had severe ones any effect, for *they rose early, and corrupted all their doings ;* they were more resolute and eager in their wicked courses than ever, more studious and solicitous in making provision for their lusts, and let slip no opportunity for the gratification of them. God *rose up early,* to send them his *prophets,* to reduce and reclaim them, but they were *up before him,* to shut and bolt the door against them. Their wickedness was universal : *All their doings* were corrupted ; and it was all owing to themselves ; they could not lay the blame upon the tempter, but they alone must bear it ; they themselves wilfully and designedly *corrupted all their doings ;* for *every man is tempted when he is drawn aside of his own lust and enticed.*

8 Therefore wait ye upon me, saith the LORD, until the day that I rise up to the prey : for my determination *is* to gather the nations, that I may assemble the kingdoms, to pour upon them mine indignation, *even* all my fierce anger : for all the earth shall be devoured with the fire of my jealousy. 9 For then will I turn to the people a pure language, that they may all call upon the name of the LORD, to serve him with one consent. 10 From beyond the rivers of Ethiopia my suppliants, *even* the daughter of my dispersed, shall bring mine offering. 11 In that day shalt thou not be ashamed for all thy doings, wherein thou hast transgressed against me : for then I will take away out of the midst of thee them that rejoice in thy pride, and thou shalt no more be

haughty because of my holy mountain. 12 I will also leave in the midst of thee an afflicted and poor people, and they shall trust in the name of the LORD. 13 The remnant of Israel shall not do iniquity, nor speak lies; neither shall a deceitful tongue be found in their mouth: for they shall feed and lie down, and none shall make *them* afraid.

Things looked very bad with Jerusalem in the foregoing verses; she has got into a very bad name, and seems to be incorrigible, incurable, mercy-proof and judgment-proof. Now one would think it should follow, Therefore expect no other but that she should be utterly abandoned and rejected as *reprobate silver;* since they will not be wrought upon by prophets or providences, let them be made a desolation as their neighbours have been. But behold and wonder at the riches of divine grace, which takes occasion from man's badness to appear so much the more illustrious. They still grew worse and worse, *therefore wait you upon me, saith the Lord, v.* 8. "Since the *law,* it seems, will *make nothing perfect,* the *bringing in of a better hope shall.* Let those that lament the corruptions of the church *wait upon God,* till he send his Son into the world, to *save his people from their sins,* till he send his gospel to reform and refine his church, and to purify to himself a peculiar people both of Jews and Gentiles." And there were those who, according to this direction and encouragement, *waited for redemption,* for this redemption in Jerusalem; and long-looked-for came at last, Luke ii. 38. *For judgment* Christ will *come into this world,* John ix. 39.

I. To avenge what has been done amiss against his church, to bring down and destroy the enemies of it, its spiritual enemies, of which the destruction of Babylon, and other oppressors of God's people, in the Old-Testament times, was a type, and would be a happy presage. He will *rise up to the prey,* to *lead captivity captive* (Ps. lxviii. 18), to conquer and spoil the powers of darkness, and the powers on earth that set themselves *against the Lord and his anointed;* he will *break them with a rod of iron* (Ps. ii. 5, 9; xi. 5, 6); his *determination is to gather the nations* and to *assemble the kingdoms.* By the gospel of Christ preached to every creature all nations are summoned, as it were, to appear in a body before the Lord Jesus, who is about to set up his kingdom in the world. But, since the greatest part of mankind will not obey the summons, he will *pour upon them his indignation,* for he that *believes not is condemned already.* At the time of the setting up of the kingdom of the Messiah, there shall be on earth *distress of nations with perplexity* (Luke xxi. 25), *great*

tribulation, such as *never was, nor ever shall be,* Matt. xxiv. 21. Then God pours upon the nations his indignation, even *all his fierce anger,* for their indignation and fierce anger against the Messiah and his kingdom, Ps. ii. 1, 2. Then *all the earth shall be devoured with the fire of his jealousy;* both Jews and Gentiles shall be reckoned with for their enmity to the gospel. Principalities and powers shall be spoiled, and *made a show of openly,* and the victorious Redeemer shall triumph over them. The end of those that continue to be of the earth, and to *mind earthly things,* after God has set up the *kingdom of heaven* among men, *shall be destruction* (Phil. iii. 19); they shall be *devoured with the fire of God's jealousy.*

II. To amend what he finds amiss in his church. When God intends the restoration of Israel, and the revival of their peace and prosperity, he makes way for the accomplishment of his purpose by their reformation and the revival of their virtue and piety; for this is God's method, both with particular persons and with communities, first to make them holy and then to make them happy. These promises were in part accomplished after the return of the Jews out of Babylon, when by their captivity they were thoroughly cured of their idolatry; and this was all the fruit, even the taking away of sin. But they look further, to the blessed effects of the gospel and the grace of it, to those *times of reformation* in which we live, Heb. ix. 10.

1. It is promised that there shall be a reformation in men's discourse, which had been generally corrupt, but should now be with grace seasoned with salt (*v.* 9): "*Then will I turn to the people a pure language;* I will turn the people to such a language from that *evil communication* which has almost ruined all *good manners* among them." Note, Converting grace refines the language, not by making the phrases witty, but the substance wise. Among the Jews, after the captivity, there needed a reformation of the dialect, for they had mingled the language of Canaan with that of Ashdod (Neh. xiii. 24), and that grievance shall be redressed. But that is not all: their language shall be purified from all profaneness, filthiness, and falsehood. I will turn them to a *choice language* (so some read it); they shall not speak rashly, but with caution and deliberation; they shall *choose out their words.* Note, An air of purity and piety in common conversation is a very happy omen to any people; other graces, other blessings, shall be given where God gives a pure language to those who have been a *people of unclean lips.*

2. That the worship of God, according to his will, shall be more closely applied to, and more unanimously concurred in. Instead of sacrifice and incense, they shall *call upon the name of the Lord.* Prayer is the spiritual offering with which God must be honoured;

and, to prepare and fit us for that duty, it is necessary that we have a *pure language.* We are utterly unfit to take God's name into our lips, unless they be pure lips. The purifying of the language in common conversation is necessary to the acceptableness of the words of our mouth and the meditation of our heart in our devotion; for how can *sweet waters and bitter* come *out of the same fountain?* James iii. 9—12. It is likewise promised that their language being thus purified they shall serve God *with one consent,* with *one shoulder* (so the word is), alluding to oxen in the yoke, that draw even. When Christians are unanimous in the service of God the work goes on cheerfully. This is the effect of the pure language, purified from passion, envy, and censoriousness. Note, Purity is the way to unity; the reformation of manners is the way to a comprehension. *The wisdom from above is first pure, then peaceable.*

3. That those that were driven from God shall return to him and be accepted of him (*v.* 10): *From beyond the rivers of Ethiopia,* that is, from Egypt (so described, Isa. xviii. 1) or from some other very remote country—*my suppliants, even the daughter of my dispersed, shall bring my offering.* Those that by reason of their distance had almost forgotten God, and their obligations to him, shall be put in mind of him, as the prodigal son was of his father's house, in the far country. Those that by reason of their dispersion, under the tokens of his displeasure, might be afraid of coming to him, yet even they shall be gathered under his wings; the *daughter of his dispersed,* that is *afar off,* will be found among those whom *the Lord our God shall call;* and, though they are dispersed, he will own them for his; his calling them *my dispersed* puts honour upon them, sufficient to counterbalance all the disgrace of their dispersion. These shall come, (1.) With their humble petitions: They are *my suppliants.* Note, True converts are suppliants to God; they do not plead, but *make supplication to their Judge* (Job ix. 15); and wherever they are, though *beyond the rivers of Ethiopia,* a great way off from his house of prayer, he has his eye upon them and his ear open to them; they are his suppliants. (2.) With their spiritual sacrifices: *They shall bring my offering,* shall bring themselves as spiritual sacrifices to God (Rom. xii. 1); the conversion of the Gentiles is called *the offering up of the Gentiles* (Rom. xv. 16); and with themselves they shall bring the gospel-sacrifices of prayer, and praise, and alms, with which God is well pleased.

4. That sin and sinners shall be purged out from among them, *v.* 11. God will take away, (1.) Their just reproach: *In that day shalt thou not be ashamed for all thy doings.* They shall be ashamed as penitents, and shall continue to be so (see Ezek. xvi. 63), but they shall not be ashamed as sinners that

return to folly again. *"Thou shalt not be ashamed,* that is, thou shalt no more do a shameful thing, as thou hast done." The guilt of sin being taken away by pardoning mercy, the reproach of it shall be rolled away from the sinner's own conscience, that being *purified,* and *pacified,* and *cleansed from dead works.* When wickedness and wicked people abound in a nation those few in it that are good are ashamed of them and of their land; but when sinners are converted, and the land reformed, that shame and the cause of it are removed. (2.) Their unjust glorying: *"I will take away out of the midst of thee,* not only the profane, who are a shame to thy land, but the hypocrites, who appear beautiful outwardly, and *rejoice in thy pride,* in the holy city, the holy house." These were indeed Israel's glory, but they made them their pride, and rejoiced in them, as if they were an invincible bulwark to secure them in their sinful ways; they relied on them as their righteousness and strength, boasting of *the temple of the Lord, the temple of the Lord* (Jer. vii. 4); they were *haughty because of the holy mountain,* were conceited of themselves, scornful of others, and set even the judgments of God at defiance. Note, Church-privileges, when they are not duly improved as they ought to be, are often made the matter of men's pride and the ground of their security. But that haughtiness is the most offensive to God which is supported and fed by the pretensions of holiness. This God will silence and take away.

5. That God will have a remnant of holy, humble, serious people among them, that shall have the comfort of their relation to him and interest in him (*v.* 12): *I will leave in the midst of thee an afflicted and poor people.* When the Chaldeans carried away the Jews into captivity they *left of the poor of the land for vine-dressers and husbandmen,* a type and figure of God's distinguished remnant, whom he sets apart for himself. They are *afflicted* and *poor,* low in the world; such *God has chosen,* James ii. 5. The poor are evangelized, low in their own eyes, afflicted for sin, poor in spirit. They are God's leaving, for it is a *remnant according to the election of grace. I have reserved them to myself,* says God (Rom. xi. 4, 5), *and they shall trust in the name of the Lord.* Note, Those whom God designs for the glory of his name he enables to trust in his name; and the greater their affliction and poverty in the world are the more reason they see to trust in God, having nothing else to trust to, 1 Tim. v. 5.

6. That this select remnant shall be blessed with purity and peace, *v.* 13. (1.) They shall be blessed with purity, both in words and actions: They *shall neither do iniquity nor speak lies.* Justice and veracity shall command them and govern them, though they be ever so much against their secular interest. They shall not only not speak a direct

deliberate lie, but *there shall not be a deceitful tongue found in their mouth*, not in the mouth of any of them ; not the least equivocation shall come from them. (2.) They shall be blessed with peace. They shall, as the sheep of God's pasture, *feed* and *lie down, and none shall make them afraid.* They shall not be fearful themselves, nor shall any about them be frightful to them. Note, Those that are careful not to do iniquity need not be afraid of any calamity, for it cannot hurt them, and therefore should not terrify them.

14 Sing, O daughter of Zion ; shout, O Israel ; be glad and rejoice with all the heart, O daughter of Jerusalem. 15 The Lord hath taken away thy judgments, he hath cast out thine enemy : the king of Israel, *even* the Lord, *is* in the midst of thee : thou shalt not see evil any more. 16 In that day it shall be said to Jerusalem, Fear thou not : *and to* Zion, Let not thine hands be slack. 17 The Lord thy God in the midst of thee *is* mighty ; he will save, he will rejoice over thee with joy ; he will rest in his love, he will joy over thee with singing. 18 I will gather *them that are* sorrowful for the solemn assembly, *who* are of thee, *to whom* the reproach of it *was* a burden. 19 Behold, at that time I will undo all that afflict thee : and I will save her that halteth, and gather her that was driven out ; and I will get them praise and fame in every land where they have been put to shame. 20 At that time will I bring you *again*, even in the time that I gather you : for I will make you a name and a praise among all people of the earth, when I turn back your captivity before your eyes, saith the Lord.

After the promises of the taking away of sin, here follow promises of the taking away of trouble ; for when the cause is removed the effect will cease. What makes a people holy will make them happy of course. The precious promises here made to the purified people were to have their full accomplishment in the comforts of the gospel, in the hope, and much more in the enjoyment, of which, they are here called upon, 1. To rejoice and sing (*v.* 14) : *Sing, O daughter of Zion !* sing for joy ; *shout, O Israel !* in a holy transport and exultation ; *be glad and rejoice with all the heart ;* let the joy be inward, let it be great. Those that love God
1386

with all their heart have occasion with all their heart to rejoice in him. It was promised (*v.* 13) that their sins should be mortified and their fears silenced, and then follows, *Sing* and *rejoice*. Note, Those that reform have cause to rejoice, whereas Israel cannot rejoice for joy as other people, while she goes a whoring from her God. God's promises, applied by faith, furnish the saints with constant and abundant matter for joy ; they are filled with joy and peace in believing them. 2. To throw off all their discouragements (*v.* 16) : *In that day it shall be said to Jerusalem* (God will say it by his prophets, by his providences, their neighbours shall say it, they shall say it to one another), " *Fear thou not*, be not disposed to fear, do not easily admit the impressions of it ; when things are bad, fear not their being worse, but hope they will mend ; frighten not thyself upon every occasion. *Let not thy hands be slack* or *faint ;* wring not thy hands in despair ; drop not thy hands in despondency ; disfit not thyself for thy work and warfare by giving way to doubts and fears. Pluck up thy spirits, and, in token of that, lift up thy hands, the *hands that hung down*, Heb. xii. 12 ; Isa. xxxv. 3. Lift up thy hands in prayer to God ; lift up thy hands to help thyself." Fear makes the hands slack, but faith and hope make them vigorous, and the joy of the Lord will be our strength both for doing and suffering.

Let us now see what these precious promises are which are here made to the people of God, for the banishing of their griefs and fears and the encouraging of their hopes and joys ; and to us are these promises made as well as to them.

I. An end shall be put to all their troubles and distresses (*v.* 15) : " *The Lord has taken away thy judgments*, has removed all the calamities thou hast been groaning under, which were the punishments of thy sin ; the noise of war shall be silenced, the reproach of famine done away, and the captivity brought back. Though some grievances remain, they shall be only afflictions, and not judgments, for sin shall be pardoned. *He has cast out thy enemy*, that has thrust himself into thy land, and triumphed over thee. He has *swept out thy enemy*" (so some read it), " as dirt is swept out of the house to the dunghill." When they sweep out their sins with the besom of reformation God will sweep out their enemies with the besom of destruction. If they should need correction, they shall fall into the hands of the Lord, whose mercies are great, and shall not again fall into the hands of man, whose tender mercies are cruel : " *Thou shalt not see evil any more*, not such evil days as thou hast seen." Note, The way to get clear of the evil of trouble is to keep clear from the evil of sin ; and to those that do so trouble has no real evil in it.

II. God will give them the tokens of his

presence with them; though he has long seemed to stand at a distance (they having provoked him to withdraw), he will make it to appear that he is *with them of a truth :* " *The Lord is in the midst of thee, O Zion!* of thee, *O Jerusalem!* as the sun in the centre of the universe, to diffuse his light and influence upon every part. He is *in the midst of thee,* to preside in all thy affairs and to take care of all thy interests." And, 1. " He is the *King of Israel* (*v.* 15) and is in the midst of thee as a king in the midst of his people." With an eye to this, our Lord Jesus is called the *King of Israel* (John i. 49); and he is, and will be, in the midst of his church always, even to the end of the world, to receive the homage of his subjects, and to give out his favours to them, even *where* but *two or three are gathered together in his name.* 2. " He is the Lord thy God, thine in covenant, and he is in the midst of thee as thy God, whom thou hast an interest in and whose own thou art. He has put himself into dear relations to thee, laid himself by promise under obligations to thee, and, that thou mayest have abundant comfort in both, he *is in the midst of thee,* nigh at hand to answer both." 3. " He that is in the midst of thee as thy God and King is *mighty,* is almighty, is able to do all that for thee that thou needest and canst desire." 4. " He has engaged his power for thy succour : *He will save. He will be Jesus,* will answer the name, for he will save his people from their sins."

III. God will take delight in them, and in doing them good. The expressions of this are very lively and affecting (*v.* 17): *He will rejoice over thee with joy,* will not only be well pleased with thee, upon thy repentance and reformation, and take thee into favour, but will take a complacency in thee, as the bridegroom does in his bride, or the bride in her ornaments, Isa. lxii. 3—5. The conversion of sinners and the consolation of saints are the joy of angels, for they are the joy of God himself. The church should be the *joy of the whole earth* (Ps. xlviii. 2), for it is the joy of the whole heaven. He will *rest in his love,* will be *silent in his love,* so the word is. " I will not rebuke thee as I have done, for thy sins; I will acquiesce in thee, and in my relation to thee." I know not where there is the like expression of Christ's love to his church, unless in that song of songs, Cant. iv. 9, *Thou hast ravished my heart, my sister, my spouse, with one of thy eyes.* O the condescensions of divine grace ! The great God not only loves his saints, but he loves to love them, is pleased that he has pitched upon these objects of his love. He *will joy over them with singing.* He that is grieved for the sin of sinners rejoices in the graces and services of the saints, and is ready to express that joy by singing over them. *The Lord takes pleasure in those that fear him,* and in them Jesus Christ will shortly be glorified and admired.

IV. God will comfort Zion's mourners, who sympathize with her in her griefs, and will wipe away their tears (*v.* 18): *I will gather those who are sorrowful for the solemn assemblies, to whom the reproach of it was a burden.* See, 1. Who those are whom God will rejoice in and make to rejoice. They are such as are sorrowful. Those only must expect to reap in joy that sow in tears. The sorrowful now shall be for ever joyful. 2. What is the great matter of sorrow to Zion's mourners, when Zion is in mourning. Many are her calamities. The city is ruined, and the palaces are demolished ; trade is at an end, and the administration of public justice ; but all these are nothing to them in comparison with the desolations of the sanctuary, the destruction of the temple and the altar, to attend on which, in solemn feasts, all Israel used to come together three times a year. It is for those sacred solemn assemblies that they are sorrowful, ·(1.) Because they are dispersed ; there is no temple to come up to, or, if there were, no people to come up to it; so that the *solemn feasts and sabbaths are forgotten in Zion,* Lam. ii. 6. Note, The restraining of public assemblies for religious worship, the scattering of them by their enemies, or the forsaking of them by their friends, so that either there are no assemblies or not solemn ones, is a very sorrowful thing to all good people. If *the ways of Zion mourn,* the sons of Zion mourn too. And hereby they make it to appear that they are indeed of Zion, living members of that body with the grievances of which they are so sensibly affected. (2.) Because they are despised ; the reproach of the solemn assemblies is a burden to them. It had been the lot of the solemn assemblies to lie under a great deal of reproach, Satan and his instruments having a particular spite at them, as the great support of the interest of God's kingdom among men. Black and odious characters have been put upon those assemblies ; and this is a burden to all those that have a cordial concern for the glory of God and the welfare of the souls of men. They reckon that the reproaches of those who reproach the solemn assemblies fall upon them, fall foul upon them.

V. God will recover the captives out of the hands of their oppressors, and bring home the banished that seemed to be expelled, *v.* 19, 20. 1. Their enemies shall be disabled to detain them in bondage : " *At that time I will undo all that afflict thee,* will break their power, and blast their counsels, so that they shall be forced to surrender the prey they have taken." *Conficiam*—*I will take them to task ;* " I will be doing with them shortly, and so as to make an end of them." Note, Those that abuse and oppress God's people take the ready way to undo themselves. 2. They shall be enabled to assert and recover their liberty, and all the difficulties in the way of it shall be surmounted.

Is the church weak and wounded? *I will save her that halts*, as was promised, Mic. iv. 7. He will help her when she cannot help herself; even *the lame shall take the prey*, Isa. xxxiii. 23. Is she dispersed, and not likely to incorporate for her common benefit? I will *gather her that was driven out*, and *bring her again at the time that I gather her*. One act of mercy and grace shall serve both to collect them out of their dispersions and to conduct them to their own land. When the *people's hearts are prepared*, the work will be done suddenly; and who can hinder it if God undertake to effect it? " *I will turn back your captivity before your eyes, saith the Lord ;* you shall plainly discern the hand of God in it, and say, *This is the Lord's doing*."

VI. God will by all this put honour upon them and gain them respect from all about them. Israel was at first *made high above all nations in praise and fame*, Deut. xxvi. 19. The reproach brought upon them was therefore one of the sorest of their grievances (nothing cuts deeper to those that are in honour than disgrace does); and therefore when God returns, in mercy, to his church, it is here promised that she shall regain her credit; all the reproach shall be for ever rolled way, as Israel's at Gilgal, Josh. v. 9. The church shall be as honourable as ever she has been despicable. 1. Even those that reproached her shall be made to respect her : " *I will get them praise and fame in every land, where they have been put to shame*, that the same who were the witnesses of their disgrace may see cause to change their mind concerning them." Those that said, "This is Zion whom no man looks after," shall say, " This is Zion whom the great God looks after." And she that was looked upon to be the *offscouring of the earth* now appears to be the darling of heaven. 2. Even those that never knew her shall be brought to honour her (*v.* 20): *I will make you a name and a praise among all people of the earth*. So the Jewish church was when *the fear of the Jews* fell upon their neighbours (Esth. viii. 17), and some of all nations said, *We will go with you, for we have heard that God is with you*, Zech. viii. 23. So the Christian church was when it was made to flourish in the world, for there is that in it which may justly recommend it to the value and esteem of all the people of the earth. And so the universal church of the first-born will be in the great day, when the saints shall be brought together to Christ, that he may be admired and glorified in them, and they admired and glorified in him before angels and men. Then will God's Israel be *made a name and a praise* to eternity.

AN

EXPOSITION,

WITH PRACTICAL OBSERVATIONS,

OF THE PROPHECY OF

HAGGAI.

The captivity in Babylon gave a very remarkable turn to the affairs of the Jewish church both in history and prophecy. It is made a signal epocha in our Saviour's genealogy, Matt. i. 17. Nine of the twelve minor prophets, whose oracles we have been hitherto consulting, lived and preached before that captivity, and most of them had an eye to it in their prophecies, foretelling it as the just punishment of Jerusalem's wickedness. But the last three (in whom the Spirit of prophecy took its period, until it revived in Christ's forerunner) lived and preached after the return out of captivity, not immediately upon it, but some time after. Haggai and Zechariah appeared much about the same time, eighteen years after the return, when the building of the temple was both retarded by its enemies and neglected by its friends. *Then the prophets, Haggai the prophet and Zechariah the son of Iddo, prophesied unto the Jews that were in Jerusalem, in the name of the God of Israel, even unto them* (so we read Ezra v. 1), to reprove them for their remissness, and to encourage them to revive that good work when it had stood still for some time, and to go on with it vigorously, notwithstanding the opposition they met with in it. Haggai began two months before Zechariah, who was raised up to second him, that out of the mouth of two witnesses the word might be established. But Zechariah continued longer at the work; for all Haggai's pro phecies that are recorded were delivered within four months, in the second year of Darius, between the beginning of the sixth month and the end of the ninth. But we have Zechariah's prophecies dated above two years after, Zech. vii. 1. Some have the honour to lead, others to last, in the work of God. The Jews ascribe to these two prophets the honour of being members of the great synagogue (as they call it), which was formed after the return out of captivity; we think it more certain, and it was their honour, and a much greater honour, that they prophesied of Christ. Haggai spoke of him as the *glory of the latter house,* and Zechariah as *the man, the branch.* In them the light of that morning star shone more brightly than in the foregoing prophecies, as they lived nearer the time of the rising of the Sun of righteousness, and now began to see his day approaching. The LXX. make Haggai and Zechariah to be the penmen of Ps. cxxxviii. and of Ps. cxlvi., cxlvii., and cxlviii.

CHAP. I.

In this chapter, after the preamble of the prophecy, we have, I. A reproof of the people of the Jews for their dilatoriness and slothfulness in building the temple, which had provoked God to contend with them by the judgment of famine and scarcity, with an exhortation to them to resume that good work and to prosecute it in good earnest, ver. 1—11. II. The good success of this sermon, appearing in the people's return and close application to that work, wherein the prophet, in God's name, animated and encouraged them, assuring them that God was with them, ver. 12—15.

IN the second year of Darius the king, in the sixth month, in the first day of the month, came the word of the LORD by Haggai the prophet unto Zerubbabel the son of Shealtiel, governor of Judah, and to Joshua the son of Josedech, the high priest, saying, 2 Thus speaketh the LORD of hosts, saying, This people say, The time is not come, the time that the LORD's house should be built. 3 Then came the word of the LORD by Haggai the prophet, saying, 4 *Is it* time for you, O ye, to dwell in your ceiled houses, and this house *lie* waste? 5 Now therefore thus saith the LORD of hosts; Consider your ways. 6 Ye have sown much, and bring in little; ye eat, but ye have not enough; ye drink, but ye are not filled with drink; ye clothe you, but there is none warm; and he that earneth wages earneth wages *to put it* into a bag with holes. 7 Thus saith the LORD of hosts; Consider your ways. 8 Go up to the mountain, and bring wood, and build the house; and I will take pleasure in it, and I will be glorified, saith the LORD. 9 Ye looked for much, and, lo, *it came* to little; and when ye brought *it* home, I did blow upon it. Why? saith the LORD of hosts. Because of mine house that *is* waste, and ye run every man unto his own house. 10 Therefore the heaven over you is stayed from dew, and the earth is stayed *from* her fruit. 11 And I called for

a drought upon the land, and upon the mountains, and upon the corn, and upon the new wine, and upon the oil, and upon *that* which the ground bringeth forth, and upon men, and upon cattle, and upon all the labour of the hands.

It was the complaint of the Jews in Babylon that they *saw not their signs,* and there was *no more any prophet* (Ps. lxxiv. 9), which was a just judgment upon them for mocking and misusing the prophets. We read of no prophets they had in their return, as they had in their coming out of Egypt, Hos. xii. 13. God stirred them up immediately by his Spirit to exert themselves in that escape (Ezra i. 5); for, though God makes use of prophets, he needs them not, he can do his work without them. But the lamp of Old-Testament prophecy shall yet make some bright and glorious efforts before it expire; and Haggai is the first that appears under the character of a special messenger from heaven, when the *word of the Lord* had been long *precious* (as when prophecy began, 1 Sam. iii. 1) and *there had been no open vision.* In the reign of Darius Hystaspes, the third of the Persian kings, in the second year of his reign, this prophet was sent; and the word of the Lord came to him, and came by him to the leading men among the Jews, who are here named, v. 1. The chief governor, 1. In the state; that was *Zerubbabel, the son of Shealtiel,* of the house of David, who was commander-in-chief of the Jews, in their return out of captivity. 2. In the church; and that was *Joshua the son of Josedech,* who was now *high priest.* They were great men and good men, and yet were to be stirred up to their duty when they grew remiss. What the people also were faulty in they must be told of, that they might use their power and interest for the mending of it. The prophets, who were extraordinary messengers, did not go about to set aside the ordinary institutions of magistracy and ministry, but endeavoured to render both more effectual for the ends to which they were appointed, for both ought to be supported. Now observe,

I. What the sin of the Jews was at this time, v. 2. As soon as they came up out of captivity they set up an altar for sacrifice, and within a year after laid the foundations of a temple, Ezra iii. 10. They then seemed very forward in it, and it was likely enough that the work would be done suddenly; but, being served with a prohibition some time after from the Persian court, and charged not to go on with it, they not only yielded to the force, when they were actually under it, which might be excused, but afterwards, when the violence of the opposition had abated, they continued very indifferent to it, had no spirit nor courage to set about it again, but seemed glad that they had a pretence to let it stand still. Though those who are employed for God may be driven off from their work by a storm, yet they must return to it as soon as the storm is over. These Jews did not do so, but continued loitering until they were afresh reminded of their duty. And that which they suggested one to another was, *The time has not come, the time that the Lord's house should be built;* that is, 1. " Our time has not come for the doing of it, because we have not yet recovered, after our captivity; our losses are not repaired, nor have we yet got before-hand in the world. It is too great an undertaking for new beginners in the world, as we are; let us first get our own houses up, before we talk of building churches, and in the mean time let a bare altar serve us, as it did our father Abraham." They did not say that they would not build a temple at all, but, " Not yet; it is all in good time." Note, Many a good work is put by by being put off, as Felix put off the prosecution of his convictions to a more convenient season. They do not say that they will never repent, and reform, and be religious, but, " Not yet." And so the great business we were sent into the world to do is not done, under pretence that it is all in good time to go about it. 2. God's time has not come for the doing of it; for (say they) the restraint laid upon us by authority in a legal way is not broken off, and therefore we ought not to proceed, though there be a present connivance of authority." Note, There is an aptness in us to misinterpret providential discouragements in our duty, as if they amounted to a discharge from our duty, when they are only intended for the trial and exercise of our courage and faith. It is bad to neglect our duty, but it is worse to vouch Providence for the patronising of our neglects.

II. What the judgments of God were by which they were punished for this neglect, *v.* 6, 9—11. They neglected the building of God's house, and put that off, that they might have time and money for their secular affairs. They desired to be excused from such an expensive piece of work under this pretence, that they must provide for their families; their children must have meat and portions too, and, until they have got beforehand in the world, they cannot think of re-

building the temple. Now, that the punishment might answer to the sin, God by his providence kept them still behind-hand, and that poverty which they thought to prevent by not building the temple God brought upon them for not building it. They were sensible of the smart of the judgment, and every one complained of the unseasonable weather, the great losses they sustained in their corn and cattle, and the decay of trade; but they were not sensible of the cause of the judgment, and the ground of God's controversy with them. They did not, or would not, see and own that it was for their putting off the building of the temple that they lay under these manifest tokens of God's displeasure; and therefore God here gives them notice that this is that for which he contended with them. Note, We need the help of God's prophets and ministers to expound to us, not only the judgments of God's mouth, but the judgments of his hands, that we may understand his mind and meaning in his rod as well as in his word, to discover to us not only wherein we have offended God, but wherein God shows himself offended at us. Let us observe,

1. How God contended with them. He did not send them into captivity again, nor bring a foreign enemy upon them, as they deserved, but took the correcting of them into his own hands; for his mercies are great. (1.) He that *gives seed to the sower* denied his blessing upon the *seed sown*, and then it never prospered; they had nothing, or next to nothing, from it. *They sowed much* (v. 6), kept a great deal of ground in tillage, which they might expect, would turn to a better advantage than usual, because their land had long *lain fallow* and had *enjoyed its sabbaths.* Having sown much, they looked for much from it, enough to spend and enough to spare too; but they were disappointed: *They bring in little*, very little (v. 6); when they have made the utmost of it, *it comes to little* (v. 9); it did not yield as they expected. Isa. v. 10, *The seed of a homer shall yield an ephah*, a bushel's sowing shall yield a peck. Note, Our expectations from the creature are often most frustrated when they are most raised; and then, when we look for much, it comes to little, that our expectation may be from God only, in whom it will be outdone. We are here told how they came to be disappointed (v. 10): *The heaven over you is stayed from dew;* he that has the key of the clouds in his hands shut them up, and withheld the rain when the ground called for it, the former or the latter rain, and then of course *the earth is stayed from her fruit;* for, if the heaven be as brass, the earth is as iron. The corn perhaps came up very well, and promised a very plentiful crop, but, for want of the dews at earing-time, it never filled, but was parched with the heat of the sun and withered away. The restored captives, who had long been kept bare in Babylon,

thought they should never want when they had got their own land in possession again and had that at command. But what the better are they for it, unless they had the clouds at command too? God will make us sensible of our necessary and constant dependence upon him, throughout all the links in the chain of second causes, from first to last; so that we can at no time say, " Now we have no further occasion for God and his providence." See Hos. ii. 21. But God not only withheld the cooling rains, but he appointed the scorching heats (*v.* 11): *I called for a drought upon the land,* ordered the weather to be extremely hot, and then the fruits of the earth were burnt up. See how every creature is that to us which God makes it to be, either comfortable or afflictive, serving us or incommoding us. Nothing among the inferior creatures is so necessary and beneficial to the world as the heat of the sun; it is that which puts life into the plants and *renews the face of the earth at* spring. And yet, if that go into an extreme, it undoes all again. Our Creator is our best friend; but, if we make him our enemy, we make the best friends we have among the creatures our enemies too. This drought God called for, and it came at the call; as the winds and the waves, so the rays of the sun, obey him. It was universal, and the ill effects of it were general; it was a drought *upon the mountains,* which, lying high, were first affected with it. The mountains were their pasture-grounds, and used to be *covered over with flocks,* but now there was no grass for them. It was *upon the corn, the new wine, and the oil;* all failed through the extremity of the hot weather, even *all that the ground brought forth;* it all withered. Nay, it had a bad influence upon men; the hot weather enfeebled some, and made them weary and faint, and spent their spirits; it inflamed others, and put them into fevers. It should seem, it brought diseases upon cattle too. In short, it spoiled *all the labour of their hands,* which they hoped to eat of and maintain their families by. Note, Meat for the belly is meat that perishes, and, if we labour for that only, we are in danger of losing our labour; but we are sure *our labour shall not be in vain in the Lord* if we labour for *the meat which endures to eternal life.* For the *hand of the diligent,* in the business of religion, will infallibly *make rich,* whereas, in the business of this life, the most solicitous and the most industrious often lose the labour of their hands. *The race is not to the swift, nor the battle to the strong.* (2.) He that gives *bread to the eater* denied his blessing upon the bread they ate, and then that did not nourish them. The cause of the withering and failing of the corn in the field was visible—it was for want of rain; but, besides that, there was a secret blast and curse attending that which they brought home. [1.] When they had it in the barn

they were not sure of it: *I did blow upon it, saith the Lord of hosts* (*v.* 9), and that withered it, as buds are sometimes blasted in the spring by a nipping frost, which we see the effects of, but know not the way of. *I did blow it away;* so the margin reads it. When men have heaped wealth together God can scatter it with the breath of his mouth as easily as we can blow away a feather. Note, We can never be sure of any thing in this world; it is exposed, not only when it is in the field, but when it is housed; for there *moth and rust corrupt,* Matt. vi. 19. And, if we would have the comfort and continuance of our temporal enjoyments, we must make God our friend; for, if he bless them to us, they are blessings indeed, but if he blow upon them we can expect no good from them: they *make themselves wings and fly away.* [2.] When they had it upon the board it was not that to them that they expected: " *You eat, but you have not enough,* either because the meat is washy, and not satisfying, or because the stomach is greedy, and not satisfied. You eat, but you have no good digestion, and so are not nourished by it, nor does it answer the end, or you have not enough because you are not content, nor think it enough. *You drink,* but are not cooled and refreshed by it; *you are not filled with drink;* you are stinted, and have not enough to quench your thirst. The *new wine is cut off from your mouth* (Joel i. 5), nay, and you *drink your water* too by *measure and with astonishment;* you have no comfort of it, because you have no plenty of it, but are still in fear of falling short." [3.] That which they had upon their backs did them no good there: " *You clothe yourselves, but there is none warm;* your clothes soon wear out, and wax old, and grow thin, because God blows upon them," contrary to what Israel's did in the wilderness when God blessed them. It is God that *makes our garments warm upon* us, when he *quiets the earth,* Job xxxvii. 17. [4.] That which they had in their bags, which was not laid out, but laid up, they were not sure of: " *He that earns wages* by hard labour, and has it paid him in ready current money, *puts it into a bag with holes;* it drops through, and wastes away insensibly. Every thing is so scarce and dear that they spend their money as fast as they get it." Those that lay up their treasure on earth put it into a bag with holes; they lose it as they go along, and those that come after them pick it up. But, if we lay up our treasure in heaven, we provide for ourselves *bags that wax not old,* Luke xii. 33.

2. Observe wherefore God thus contended with them, and stopped the current of the favours promised them at their return (Joel ii. 24); they provoked him to do it: *It is because of my house that is waste.* This is the quarrel God has with them. The foundation of the temple is laid, but the building does not go on. " Every man *runs to his*

own house, to finish that, and to make that convenient and fine, and no care is taken about the Lord's house; and therefore it is that God crosses you thus in all your affairs, to testify his displeasure against you for that neglect, and to bring you to a sense of your sin and folly." Note, As those who seek first the kingdom of God and the righteousness thereof shall not only find them, but are most likely to have other things added to them, so those who neglect and postpone those things will not only lose them, but will justly have other things taken away from them. And if God cross us in our temporal affairs, and we meet with trouble and disappointment, we shall find this is the cause of it, the work we have to do for God and our own souls is left undone, and we *seek our own things more than the things of Jesus Christ,* Phil. ii. 21.

III. The reproof which the prophet gives them for their neglect of the temple-work (*v.* 4): "*Is it time for you, O you! to dwell in your ceiled houses,* to have them beautified and adorned, and your families settled in them?" They were not content with walls and roofs for necessity, but they must have for gaiety and fancy. "It is high time," says one, "that my house were wainscoted." "It is high time," says another, "that mine were painted." And God's house, all this time, *lies waste,* and nothing is done at it. "What!" says the prophet, "is it time that you should have your humour pleased, and not time you should have your God pleased?" How much was their disposition the reverse of David's, who could not be easy in his *house of cedar* while the *ark of God* was *in curtains* (2 Sam. vii. 2), and of Solomon's, who built the temple of God before he built a palace for himself. Note, Those are very much strangers to their own interest who prefer the conveniences and ornaments of the temporal life before the absolute necessities of the spiritual life, who are full of care to enrich their own houses, while God's temple in their hearts lies waste, and nothing is done for it or in it.

IV. The good counsel which the prophet gives to those who thus despised God, and whom God was therefore justly displeased with. 1. He would have them reflect: *Now therefore consider your ways, v.* 5 and again *v.* 7. "Be sensible of the hand of God gone out against you, and enquire into the reason; think what you have done that has provoked God thus to break in upon your comforts; and think what you will do to testify your repentance, that God may return in mercy to you." Note, It is the great concern of every one of us to consider our ways, to *set our hearts to our ways* (so the word is), to *think on our ways* (Ps. cxix. 59), to *search* and *try* them (Lam. iii. 40), to *ponder the path of our feet* (Prov. iv. 26), to apply our minds with all seriousness to the great and necessary duty of self-examination, and com-

1392

muning with our own hearts concerning our spiritual state, our sins that are past, and our duty for the future; for sin is what we must answer for, duty is what we must do; about these therefore we must be inquisitive, rather than about events, which we must leave to God. Many are quick-sighted to pry into other people's ways who are very careless of their own; whereas our concern is to *prove every one his own work,* Gal. vi. 4. 2. He would have them reform (*v.* 8): "*Go up to the mountain,* to Lebanon, *and bring wood,* and other materials that are wanting, *and build the house* with all speed; put it off no longer, but set to it in good earnest." Note, Our considering our ways must issue in the amending of whatever we find amiss in them. If any duty has been long neglected, that is not a reason why it should still be so, but why now at length it should be revived; better late than never. For their encouragement to apply in good earnest to this work, he assures them, (1.) That they should be accepted of him in it: *Build the house, and I will take pleasure in it;* and that was encouragement enough for them to apply to it with alacrity and resolution, and to go through with it, whatever it cost them. Note, Whatever God will take pleasure in, when it is done, we ought to take pleasure in the doing of, and to reckon that inducement enough to set about it, and go on with it in good earnest; for what greater satisfaction can we have in our own bosoms than in contributing any thing towards that which God will take pleasure in? It ought to be the top of our ambition to be *accepted of the Lord,* 2 Cor. v. 9. Though they had foolishly neglected the house of God, yet, if at length they will resume the care of it, God will not remember against them their former neglects, but will take pleasure in the work of their hands. Those who have long deferred their return to God, if at length they return with all their heart, must not despair of his favour. (2.) That he would be honoured by them in it: *I will be glorified, saith the Lord.* He will be served and worshipped in the temple when it is built, and sanctified in those that come nigh to him. It is worth while to bestow all possible care, and pains, and cost, upon that by which God may be glorified.

12 Then Zerubbabel the son of Shealtiel, and Joshua the son of Josedech, the high priest, with all the remnant of the people, obeyed the voice of the LORD their God, and the words of Haggai the prophet, as the LORD their God had sent him, and the people did fear before the LORD. 13 Then spake Haggai the LORD's messenger in the LORD's message unto the people, saying, I *am* with

you, saith the LORD. 14 And the LORD stirred up the spirit of Zerubbabel the son of Shealtiel, governor of Judah, and the spirit of Joshua the son of Josedech, the high priest, and the spirit of all the remnant of the people; and they came and did work in the house of the LORD of hosts, their God, 15 In the four and twentieth day of the sixth month, in the second year of Darius the king.

As an ear-ring of gold (says Solomon), and *an ornament of fine gold, so* amiable, so acceptable, in the sight of God and man, *is a wise reprover upon an obedient ear,* Prov. xxv. 12. The prophet here was a wise but faithful reprover, in God's name, and he met with an obedient ear. The foregoing sermon met with the desired success among the people, and their obedience met with due encouragement from God. Observe,

I. How the people returned to God in a way of duty. All those to whom that sermon was preached received the word in the love of it, and were wrought upon by it. Zerubbabel, the chief governor, did not think himself above the check and command of God's word. He was a man that had been eminently useful in his day, and serviceable to the interest of the church, yet did not plead his former merits in answer to this reproof for his present remissness, but submitted to it. Joshua's business, as high priest, was to teach, and yet he was willing himself to be taught, and willingly received admonition and instruction. *The remnant of the people* (and the whole body of them was but a remnant, a very few of the many thousands of Israel) also were very pliable; they all *obeyed the voice of the Lord their God,* and bowed their neck to the yoke of his commands, and it is here recorded to their honour that they did so, *v.* 12. Their father said, *Sons, go work to-day in my vineyard,* in my temple; and they not only said, *We go, sir,* but they went immediately. 1. They looked upon the prophet to be the Lord's messenger, and the word he delivered to be the Lord's message to them; and therefore received it *not as the word of man, but as the word of* Almighty God; they obeyed his words, *as the Lord their God had sent him, v.* 12. Note, In attending to God's ministers we must have an eye to him that sent them, and receive them for his sake, while they act according to their commission. 2. They *did fear before the Lord.* Prophecy was a new thing with them; they had had no special messenger from heaven for a great while, and therefore now that they had one, and but one, they paid an extraordinary regard to him; whereas their fathers, who had many prophets, mocked and misused them. It is

sometimes so; when good preaching is most scarce it does most good, whereas the manna that is rained in plenty is loathed as *light bread.* And, because they so readily received this prophet, God, within a month or two after, raised them up another, Zech. i. 1. They *feared before the Lord;* they had a great regard to the divine authority and a great dread of the divine wrath, and were of those that *trembled at God's word.* The judgments of God which they had been under, though very severe, had not prevailed to make them fear before the Lord, until the word of God was sent to expound his providences, and then they feared; then, when they saw their own sin to be the cause of those judgments, then they feared. Note, A holy fear of God will have a great influence upon our obedience to him. *Serve the Lord with fear;* if we fear him not, we shall not serve him. 3. *The Lord stirred up* their spirits, *v.* 14. (1.) He excited them to their duty, and put it into their hearts to go about it. Note, Then the word of God has its success when God by his grace stirs up our spirits to comply with it; and without that grace we should remain stupid and utterly averse to every thing that is good. It is in the day of a divine power that we are made willing. (2.) He encouraged them in their duty, and with those encouragements enlarged their hearts, Ps. cxix. 32. When they heard the word they feared; but, lest they should sink under the weight of that fear, God stirred them up, and made them cheerful and bold to encounter the difficulties they might meet with. Note, When God has work to do, he will either find or make men fit to do it, and stir them up to it. 4. They applied to their work with all possible vigour: *They came and did work in the house of the Lord of hosts their God.* Every one, according as his capacity or ability was, lent a hand, some way or other, to further that good work; and this they did with an eye to God as the *Lord of hosts,* and as their God, the God of Israel. The consideration of God's sovereign dominion in the world by his providence, and his covenant-relation to his people by his grace, should stir up our spirits to act for him, and for the advancement of the interest of his kingdom among men, to the utmost of our power. 5. They did this speedily; it was but on the first day of the sixth month that Haggai preached them this sermon, and by the twenty-fourth of the same month, little more than three weeks after, they were all busy working in the house of the Lord their God, *v.* 15. To show that they were ashamed of their delays hitherto, now that they were convinced and called they were resolved to delay no longer, but to strike while the iron was hot, and to set about the work while they were under convictions. Note, Those that have lost time have need to redeem time; and the longer we have loitered in that which is good the more haste we should make when we are convinced of our folly.

II. How God met them in a way of mercy. The same prophet that brought them the reproof brought them a very comforting encouraging word (*v.* 13) : *Then spoke Haggai, the Lord's messenger, in the Lord's message, in his name, and as from him, saying, I am with you, saith the Lord.* That is all he has to say, and that is enough; as that word of Christ to his disciples is (Matt. xxviii. 20), *" Lo, I am with you always, even to the end of the world. I am with you,* that is, I will forgive your neglects hitherto, and they shall not be remembered against you; I will remove the judgments you have been under for those neglects, and will appear for you, as I have in them appeared against you. *I am with you* to protect you against your enemies that bear ill-will to your work, and to prosper you, and to give you success in it—with you to strengthen your hands, and bless the work of them, without which blessing those labour in vain that build." Note, Those that work for God have God with them; and, if he be for us, who can be against us? If he be with us, what difficulty can stand before us?

CHAP. II.

In this chapter we have three sermons preached by the prophet Haggai for the encouragement of those that are forward to build the temple. In the first he assures the builders that the glory of the house they were now building should, in spiritual respects, though not in outward, exceed that of Solomon's temple, in which he has an eye to the coming of Christ, ver. 1—9. In the second he assures them that though their sin, in delaying to build the temple, had retarded the prosperous progress of all their other affairs, yet now that they had set about it in good earnest he would bless them, and give them success, ver. 10—19. In the third he assures Zerubbabel that, as a reward of his pious zeal and activity herein, he should be a favourite of Heaven, and one of the ancestors of Messiah the Prince, whose kingdom should be set up on the ruins of all opposing powers, ver. 20—23.

I N the seventh *month*, in the one and twentieth *day* of the month, came the word of the Lord by the prophet Haggai, saying, 2 Speak now to Zerubbabel the son of Shealtiel, governor of Judah, and to Joshua the son of Josedech, the high priest, and to the residue of the people, saying, 3 Who *is* left among you that saw this house in her first glory? and how do ye see it now? *is it* not in your eyes in comparison of it as nothing? 4 Yet now be strong, O Zerubbabel, saith the Lord; and be strong, O Joshua, son of Josedech, the high priest; and be strong, all ye people of the land, saith the Lord, and work: for I *am* with you, saith the Lord of hosts: 5 *According to* the word that I covenanted with you when ye came out of Egypt, so my spirit remaineth among you: fear ye not. 6 For thus saith the Lord of

1394

hosts; Yet once, it *is* a little while, and I will shake the heavens, and the earth, and the sea, and the dry *land;* 7 And I will shake all nations, and the desire of all nations shall come: and I will fill this house with glory, saith the Lord of hosts. 8 The silver *is* mine, and the gold *is* mine, saith the Lord of hosts. 9 The glory of this latter house shall be greater than of the former, saith the Lord of hosts: and in this place will I give peace, saith the Lord of hosts.

Here is, I. The date of this message, *v.* 1. It was sent on the twenty-first day of the seventh month, when the builders had been about a month at work (since the twenty-fourth day of the sixth month), and had got it in some forwardness. Note, Those that are hearty in the service of God shall receive fresh encouragements from him to proceed in it, as their case calls for them. Set the wheels a going, and God will oil them.

II. The direction of this message, *v.* 2. The encouragements here are sent to the same persons to whom the reproofs in the foregoing chapter are directed; for those that are wounded by the convictions of the word shall be healed and bound up by its consolations. *Speak to Zerubbabel, and Joshua, and the residue of the people,* the very same that *obeyed the voice of the Lord* (*ch.* i. 12) and whose spirits God stirred up to do so (*ch.* i. 14); to them are sent these words of comfort.

III. The message itself, in which observe,

1. The discouragements which those laboured under who were employed in this work. That which was such a damp upon them, and an alloy to their joy, when the foundation of the temple was laid, was still a clog upon them—that they could not build such a temple now as Solomon built, not so large, so stately, so sumptuous, a one as that was. This fetched tears from the eyes of many, when the dimensions of it were first laid (Ezra iii. 12), and still it made the work go on heavily—that the glory of this house, *in comparison* with that of the former, was *as nothing, v.* 3. It was now about seventy years since Solomon's temple was destroyed (for that was in the nineteenth year of the captivity, and this about the nineteenth after the captivity), so that there might be some yet alive who could remember to have seen it, and still they would be upbraiding themselves and their brethren with the great disparity between this house and that. One could remember the gold with which it was overlaid, another the precious stones with which it was garnished; one could describe the magnificence of the porch, another of the pillars—and where are these now? This weakened the hands of the builders; for, though our gracious God is pleased with us

if we do in sincerity as well as we can in his service, yet our proud hearts will scarcely let us be pleased with ourselves unless we do as well as others whose abilities far exceed ours. And it is sometimes the fault of old people to discourage the services of the present age by crying up too much the performances and attainments of the former age, with which others should be provoked to emulation, but not exposed to contempt. *Say not thou that the former days were better than these* (Eccl. vii. 10), but thank God that there is any good in these, bad as they are.

2. The encouragement that is given them to go on in the work, notwithstanding (*v.* 4): *Yet now*, though this house is likely to be much inferior to the former, *be strong, O Zerubbabel! and be strong, O Joshua!* Let not these leading men give way to this suggestion, nor be disheartened by it, but do as well as they can, when they cannot do so well as they would; and let *all the people of the land be strong* too, *and work;* and, if the leaders have but a good heart on it, it is hoped that the followers will have the better heart. Note, Those that work for God ought to exert themselves with vigour, and then to encourage themselves with hope that it will end well.

3. The grounds of these encouragements. God himself says to them, *Fear you not* (*v.* 5), and he gives good reasons for it.

(1.) They have God with them, his Spirit and his special presence: *Be strong, for I am with you, saith the Lord of hosts, v.* 4. This he had said before (*ch.* i. 13), *I am with you.* But we need to have these assurances repeated, that we may have strong consolation. The presence of God with us, as the *Lord of hosts*, is enough to silence all our fears and to help us over all the discouragements we may meet with in the way of our duty. The Jews had hosts against them, but they had the Lord of hosts with them, to take their part and plead their cause. He is with them; for, [1.] He adheres to his promise. His covenant is inviolable, and he will be always theirs, and will appear and act for them, *according to the word that he covenanted with them when they came out of Egypt.* Though *he chastens them for their transgressions with the rod,* yet he will not make his faithfulness to fail. [2.] He dwells among them by his Spirit, the Spirit of prophecy. When he first formed them into a people *he gave his good Spirit to instruct them* (Neh. ix. 20); and still the Spirit, though often grieved and provoked to withdraw, remained among them. It was the Spirit of God that stirred up their spirits to come out of Babylon (Ezra i. 5), and now to build the temple, Hag. i. 14. Note, We have reason to be encouraged as long as we have the Spirit of God remaining among us to work upon us, for so long we have God with us to work for us.

(2.) They shall have the Messiah among them shortly—*him that should come.* To him bore all the prophets witness and this prophet particularly here, *v.* 6, 7. Here is an intimation of the time of his coming, that it should not be long ere he came: "*Yet once, it is a little while,* and he shall come. The Old-Testament church has but one stage more (if we may say so) to travel; five stages were now past, from Adam to Noah, thence to Abraham, thence to Moses, thence to Solomon's temple, thence to the captivity, and now yet one stage more, its sixth day's journey, and then comes the sabbatism of the Messiah's kingdom. Let the Son of man, when he comes, find faith on the earth, and let the children of promise continue still looking for him, for now it is but *a little while* and he will come; *hold out, faith and patience*, yet awhile, for *he that shall come will come, and will not tarry.*" And, as he then said of his first appearance, so now ot his second, *Surely I come quickly.* Now concerning his coming it is here foretold, [1.] That it shall be introduced by a general shaking (*v.* 6): *I will shake the heavens, and the earth, and the sea, and the dry land.* This is applied to the setting up of Christ's kingdom in the world, to make way for which he will *judge among the heathen*, Ps. cx. 6. God will once again do for his church as he did when he brought them out of Egypt; he shook the heavens and earth at Mount Sinai, with thunder, and lightnings, and earthquakes; he shook the sea and the dry land when lanes were made through the sea and streams fetched out of the rock. This shall be done again, when, at the sufferings of Christ, the sun shall be darkened, the earth shake, the rocks rend—when, at the birth ot Christ, Herod and all *Jerusalem are troubled* (Matt. ii. 3), and he is *set for the fall and rising again of many.* When his kingdom was set up it was with a shock to the nations; the oracles were silenced, idols were destroyed, and the powers of the kingdoms were moved and removed, Heb. xii. 27. It denotes *the removing of the things that are shaken.* Note, The shaking of the nations is often in order to the settling of the church and the establishing of the things that cannot be shaken. [2.] That it shall issue in a general satisfaction. He shall come as *the desire of all nations*—desirable to all nations, for *in him shall all the families of the earth be blessed* with the best of blessings—long expected and desired by the good people in all nations, that had any intelligence from the Old-Testament predictions concerning him. Balaam in the land of Moab had spoken of a star that should arise out of Jacob, and Job in the land of Uz of his living Redeemer; the concourse of devout men from all parts at Jerusalem (Acts ii. 5) was in expectation of the setting up of the Messiah's kingdom about that time. All the nations that are brought in to Christ, and discipled in his name, have called him, and will call him, *all their salvation and all their desire.* This glorious title of Christ seems to refer to Jacob's prophecy (Gen. xlix. 10), that *to him shall the gathering of the people be.*

(3.) The house they are now building shall be filled with glory to such a degree that its glory shall exceed that of Solomon's temple. The enemies of the Jews followed them with reproach, and cast contempt upon the house they were building; but they might very well endure that when God undertook to fill it with glory. It is God's prerogative to fill with glory; the glory that comes from him is satisfying, and not vain glory. Moses's tabernacle and Solomon's temple were filled with glory when God in a cloud took possession of them; but this house shall be filled with glory of another nature. [1.] Let them not be concerned because this house will not have so much silver and gold about it as Solomon's temple had, *v.* 8. God needs not the silver and gold to adorn his temple, for (says he), *The silver is mine, and the gold is mine.* All the silver and gold in the world are his; all that is hid in the bowels of the earth (for *the earth is the Lord's and the fulness thereof*), all that is laid up in the exchequers, banks, and treasuries of the children of men, and all that circulates for the maintaining of trade and commerce; it is all *the Lord's.* Every penny bears his image as well as Cæsar's; and therefore when gold and silver are dedicated to his honour, and employed in his service, no addition is made to him, for it was his before. When David and his princes offered vast sums for the service of the house of God, they acknowledged, *It is all thy own, and of thy own, Lord, have we given thee,* 1 Chron. xxix. 14, 16. Therefore God needs not sacrifice, for *every beast of the forest is his,* Ps. l. 10. Note, If we have silver and gold, we must serve and honour God with them, for they are all his own, we have but the use of them, the property remains in him; but, if we have not silver and gold to honour him with, we must honour him with such as we have, and he will accept us, for he needs them not; all the *silver and gold* in the world are his already. *The earth is full of his riches,* so is *the great and wide sea also.* [2.] Let them be comforted with this, that, though this temple have less gold in it, it shall have more glory than Solomon's (*v.* 9): *The glory of this latter house shall be greater than of the former.* This was never true in respect of outward glory. This latter house was indeed in its latter times very much beautified and enriched by Herod, and we find the disciples admiring the stones and buildings of the temple, how fine they were (Mark xiii. 1); but it was nothing in comparison with Solomon's temple; and, besides, the Jews own that several of the divine glories of the first temple were wanting in this—the *ark,* the *urim* and *thummim,* the *fire from heaven,* and the *Schechinah;* so that we cannot conceive how the glory of this

latter house should in any thing exceed that of the former, but in that which would indeed excel all the glories of the first house—the presence of the Messiah in it, the Son of God, his being presented there *the glory of his people Israel,* his attending there at twelve years old, and afterwards his preaching and working miracles there, and his driving the buyers and sellers out of it. It was necessary, then, that the Messiah should come while the second temple stood; but, that being long since destroyed, we must conclude that our Lord Jesus is the Christ, is *he that should come,* and we are to *look for no other.* It was also the *glory of this latter house, First,* That, before the coming of Christ, it was always kept free from idols and idolatries, and was never polluted with those abominable things, as the first temple often was (2 Kings xxiii. 11, 12), and in this its glory excelled all the glory of that. Note, The purity of the church, and the strict adherence to divine institutions, are much more its glory than external pomp and splendour. *Secondly,* That, after Christ, the gospel was preached in it by the apostles, even all the words of this life, Acts v. 20. In the temple Jesus Christ was daily preached, Acts v. 42. Now the ministration of righteousness and life by the gospel was unspeakably more glorious than the law, which was a *ministration of death and condemnation,* 2 Cor. iii. 9, 10. Note, That is the most valuable glory which arises from our relation to Christ and our interest in him. As, where Christ is, *behold a greater than Solomon is there,* so the heart in which he dwells, and makes a living temple, behold it is more glorious than Solomon's temple, and will be so to eternity.

(4.) They should see a comfortable end of their present troubles, and enjoy the pleasure of a happy settlement: *In this place will I give peace, saith the Lord of hosts.* Note, God's presence with his people in his ordinances secures to them all good. If God be with us, peace is with us. But the Jews under the latter temple had so much trouble that we must conclude this promise to have its accomplishment in that spiritual peace which Jesus Christ has by his blood purchased for, and by his last will and testament bequeathed to, all believers (John xiv. 27), that peace which Christ himself preached as the prophet of peace, and gives as the prince of peace. God will *give peace in this place;* he will give his Son to be the peace, Eph. ii. 14.

10 In the four and twentieth *day* of the ninth *month,* in the second year of Darius, came the word of the Lord by Haggai the prophet, saying, 11 Thus saith the Lord of hosts; Ask now the priests *concerning* the law, saying, 12 If one bear holy flesh in the skirt of his garment, and with his skirt do touch bread, or pottage, or

wine, or oil, or any meat, shall it be holy? And the priests answered and said, No. 13 Then said Haggai, If *one that is* unclean by a dead body touch any of these, shall it be unclean? And the priests answered and said, It shall be unclean. 14 Then answered Haggai, and said, So *is* this people, and so *is* this nation before me, saith the LORD; and so *is* every work of their hands; and that which they offer there *is* unclean. 15 And now, I pray you, consider from this day and upward, from before a stone was laid upon a stone in the temple of the LORD: 16 Since those *days* were, when *one* came to a heap of twenty *measures*, there were *but* ten: when *one* came to the press-fat for to draw out fifty *vessels* out of the press, there were *but* twenty. 17 I smote you with blasting and with mildew and with hail in all the labours of your hands; yet ye *turned* not to me, saith the LORD. 18 Consider now from this day and upward, from the four and twentieth day of the ninth *month, even* from the day that the foundation of the LORD's temple was laid, consider *it.* 19 Is the seed yet in the barn? yea, as yet the vine, and the fig-tree, and the pomegranate, and the olive-tree, hath not brought forth: from this day will I bless *you.*

This sermon was preached two months after that in the former part of the chapter. The priests and Levites preached constantly, but the prophets preached occasionally; both were good and needful. We have need to be taught our duty *in season and out of season.* The people were now going on vigorously with the building of the temple, and in hopes shortly to have it ready for their use and to be employed in the services of it; and now God sends them a message by his prophet, which would be of use to them,

I. By way of conviction and caution. They were now engaged in a very good work, but they were concerned to see to it, not only that it was good for the matter of it, but that it was done in a right manner, for otherwise it would not be accepted of God. God sees there are many among them that spoil this good work, by going about it with unsanctified hearts and hands, and are likely to gain no advantage to themselves by it; these are here convicted, and all are warned thereby to purify the hands they employ in this work, for *to the pure* only *all things are pure,* and

from the pure only that comes which is pure. This matter is here illustrated by the established rules of the ceremonial law, in putting *a difference between the clean and the unclean,* about which many of the appointments of the law were conversant. Hereby it appears that a spiritual use is to be made of the ceremonial law, and that it was intended, not only as a divine ritual to the Jews, but for *instruction in righteousness* to all, even to us upon whom the ends of the world have come, to discover to us both sin and Christ, both our disease and our remedy. Now observe here,

1. What the rule of the law was. The prophet is ordered to enquire of the priests concerning it (*v.* 11); for their *lips* should *keep this knowledge,* and the people should *enquire the law at their mouth,* Mal. ii. 7. Haggai himself, though a prophet, must *ask the priests concerning the law.* His business, as an extraordinary messenger, was to expound the providences of God, and to give directions concerning particular duties, as he had done, *ch.* i. 8, 9. But he would not take the priests' work out of the hands of those who were the ordinary ministers, and whose business it was to expound the ordinances of God, to teach the people the meaning of them, and to give the general rules for the observance of them. In a case of that nature, Haggai must himself consult them. Note, God has given to his ministers diversities of gifts, and calls them out to do diversities of services, so that they have need one of another, should make use one of another, and be helpful one to another. The prophet, though divinely inspired, cannot say to the priest, *I have no need of thee,* nor can the priest say so to the prophet. Perhaps Haggai was *therefore* ordered to consult the priests, that out of their own mouths he might judge both them and the people committed to their charge, and convict them of worse than ceremonial pollution. See Lev. x. 10, 11. Now the rules of the law, in the cases propounded, are, (1.) That he that has holy flesh in his clothes cannot by the touch of his clothes communicate holiness (*v.* 12): *If one bear holy flesh in the skirt of his garment,* though the garment is thereby so far made a devoted thing as that it is not to be put to common use till it has first been washed in the holy place (Lev. vi. 27), yet it shall by no means transmit a holiness to either meat or drink, so as to make it ever the better to those that use it. (2.) That he that is ceremonially unclean by the touch of a dead body does by his touch communicate that uncleanness. The law is express (Num, xix, 22), *Whatsoever the unclean person touches shall be unclean;* yet this Haggai will have from the priests' own mouth, for concerning those things that we find very plain in our Bibles yet it is good to have the advice of our ministers. The sum of these two rules is that pollution is more easily communicated than sanctifica-

tion; that is (says Grotius), There are many ways of vice, but only one of virtue, and that a difficult one. *Bonum oritur ex integris; malum ex quolibet defectu—Good implies perfection; evil commences with the slightest defect.* Let not men think that living among good people will recommend them to God if they are not good themselves, but let them fear that touching the unclean thing will defile them, and therefore let them keep at a distance from it.

2. How it is here applied (*v.* 14): *So is this people, and so is this nation, before me.* He does not call 'hem his people and his nation (they are unworthy to be owned by him), but *this people*, and *this nation.* They have been thus before God; they thought their offering sacrifices on the altar would sanctify them, and excuse their neglect to build the temple, and remove the curse which by that neglect they had brought upon their common enjoyments: "No," says God, "your holy flesh and your altar will be so far from sanctifying your meat and drink, your wine and oil, to you, that your contempt of God's temple will bring a pollution, not only on your common enjoyments, but even on your sacrifices too; so that while you continued in that neglect all was unclean to you, nay, and *so is this people* still; and so they will be; on these terms they will still stand with me, and on no other—that if they be profane, and sensual, and morally impure, if they have wicked hearts, and live wicked lives, though they work ever so hard at the temple while it is building, and though they offer ever so many and costly sacrifices there when it is built, yet that shall not serve to sanctify their meat and drink to them, and to give them a comfortable use of them; nay, the impurity of their hearts and lives shall make even that work of their hands, and all their offerings, unclean, and an abomination to God." And the case is the same with us. Those whose devotions are plausible, but whose conversation is wicked, will find their devotions unable to sanctify their enjoyments, but their wickedness prevailing to pollute them. Note, When we are employed in any good work we should be jealous over ourselves, lest we render it unclean by our corruptions and mismanagements.

II. By way of comfort and encouragement. If their hearts be right with God, and their eye single in his service, they shall have the benefit of their devotion. God will take away the judgment of famine wherewith they have been corrected for their remissness, and will restore them great plenty. This they are called to consider, and to observe whether God would not be to the utmost as good as his word, and by his providence remarkably countenance and recompense their reformation in this matter. To make this the more signal, let them set down the day when they began to work at the building of the temple, to raise the structure

upon the foundations that had been laid some time before. On the twenty-fourth day of the sixth month they began to prepare materials (*ch.* i. 15), and now on the twenty-fourth day of the ninth month they began to *lay a stone upon a stone in the temple of the Lord;* let them take notice of this day, and observe, 1. How they had gone behind-hand in their estates before this day. Let them remember the time when there was a sensible waste and decay in all they had, *v.* 16. A man went to his garner, expecting to find *a heap of twenty measures* of corn, so much he used to have from such a piece of ground, or so much used to be left at that time of the year, or so much he took it for granted there was when he fetched the last from it, but he found it unaccountably diminished, and, when he came to measure it, *there were but ten* measures; it had run in and dried away in the keeping, or vermin had eaten it, or it was stolen. In like manner he went to *the wine-press,* expecting to draw *fifty vessels* of wine, for so much he used to have from such a quantity of grapes, but they did not yield as usual, for he could get *but twenty.* This agrees with what we had, *ch.* i. 9, *You looked for much, and it came to little.* Note, It is our folly that we are apt to raise our expectation from the creature, and to think tomorrow must needs be as this day and much more abundant, but we are commonly disappointed, and the more we expect the more grievous the disappointment is. In the stores and treasures of the new covenant we need not fear being disappointed when we come by faith to draw from them. But this was not all. God did visibly contend with them in the weather (*v.* 17): *I smote you with blastings,* winds and frosts, which made every green thing to wither, *and with mildew,* which choked the corn when it was knitting, *and with hail,* which battered it down and broke it when it had grown to some maturity; thus they were disappointed *in all the labour of their hands,* while they neglected to lay their hand to the work of God and to labour in that. Note, While we take no care of God's interest we cannot expect he should take care of ours. And, when he thus walks contrary to us, he expects that we should return to him and to our duty. But this people either saw not the hand of God in it (imputing it to chance) or saw not their own sin as the provoking cause of it, and therefore turned not to him. They were a long time incorrigible and unhumbled under these rebukes, so that God's hand was *stretched out still,* for *the people turned not to him that smote them,* Isa. ix. 12, 13. They might easily observe that as long as they continued in neglect of the temple work all their affairs went backward. But, 2. Let them now observe, and they should find that from this day forward God would bless them (*v.* 18, 19): "*Consider now* whether when you begin to change your way towards God you do not find God changing his way towards you; from *this day*, when you fall to work about the temple, *consider it*, I say, and you shall find a remarkable turn given for the better to all your affairs. *Is the seed yet in the barn?* Yes it is, and not yet thrown into the ground. The fruit-trees do not as yet bud, *the vine, and the fig-tree, and the olive-tree*, have not as *yet brought forth*, so that nothing appears to promise a good harvest or vintage next year. Nature does not promise it; but, now that you begin to apply in good earnest to your duty, the God of nature promises it; he has said, *From this day I will bless you.* It is the best day's work you ever did in your lives, for hence you may date the return of your prosperity." He does not say what they shall be, but, in general, *I will bless you;* and those that know what are the fruits flowing from God's blessing know they can desire no more to make them happy. " *I will bless you*, and then you shall soon recover all your losses, shall thrive as fast as before you went backward; for *the blessing of the Lord, that maketh rich*, and those *whom he blesses are blessed indeed.*" Note, When we begin to make conscience of our duty to God we may expect his blessing; and this tree of life is so known by its fruits that one may discern almost to a day a remarkable turn of Providence in favour of those that return in a way of duty; so that they and others may say that *from this day they are blessed.* See Mal. iii. 10. And *whoso is wise will observe these things, and understand* by them *the lovingkindness of the Lord.*

20 And again the word of the Lord came unto Haggai in the four and twentieth *day* of the month, saying, 21 Speak to Zerubbabel, governor of Judah, saying, I will shake the heavens and the earth; 22 And I will overthrow the throne of kingdoms, and I will destroy the strength of the kingdoms of the heathen; and I will overthrow the chariots, and those that ride in them; and the horses and their riders shall come down, every one by the sword of his brother. 23 In that day, saith the Lord of hosts, will I take thee, O Zerubbabel, my servant, the son of Shealtiel, saith the Lord, and will make thee as a signet: for I have chosen thee, saith the Lord of hosts.

After Haggai's sermon *ad populum—to the people*, here follows one, the same day, *ad magistratum—to the magistrates*, a word directed particularly to Zerubbabel, *the governor of Judah*, who was a leading active man

in this good work which the people now set about, and therefore he shall have some particular marks put upon him (*v.* 21): *Speak to Zerubbabel, governor of Judah*, speak to him by himself. He has thoughts in his head far above those of the common people, as wise princes are wont to have, who move in a higher and larger sphere than others. The people of the land are in care about their corn-fields and vineyards; God has assured them that they shall prosper, and we hope that will make them easy; but Zerubbabel is concerned about the community and its interests, about the neighbouring nations, and the revolutions of their governments, and what will become of the few and feeble Jews in those changes and convulsions, and how such a poor prince as he is should be able to keep his ground and serve his country. "Go to him," says God, "and tell him it shall be well with him and his remnant, and let that make him easy."

I. Let him expect to hear of great commotions in the nations of the earth, and let them not be a surprise to him; behold, he is told of them before (*v.* 21, 22): *I will shake the heavens and the earth.* This he had said before (*v.* 6, 7), and now says it again to Zerubbabel; let him expect shaking times, universal concussions. The world is like the sea, like the wheel, always in motion, but sometimes in a special manner turbulent. But, blessed be God, if the earth be shaken, it is to *shake the wicked out of it*, Job xxxviii. 13. In the apocalyptic visions earthquakes bode no ill to the church. Here the heavens and the earth are shaken, that proud oppressors may be broken and brought down: *I will overthrow the throne of kingdoms.* The Chaldean monarchy, which had been the throne of kingdoms a great while, was already overthrown; and the powers that are, and are yet to come, shall in like manner be overthrown; their day will come to fall. 1. Though they be ever so powerful, yet the *strength of their kingdoms* shall be destroyed. They *trust in chariots and horses* (Ps. xx. 7), but their *chariots* shall be *overthrown*, and *those that ride in them*, so that they shall not be able to attack the people of God, whom they persecute, nor to escape the judgments of God, which persecute them. 2. Though there appear none likely to be the instruments of their destruction, yet God will bring it about, for they shall be brought down *every one by the sword of his brother.* This reads the doom of all the enemies of God's church, that will not repent to give him glory; it seems likewise designed as a promise of Christ's victory over the powers of darkness, his overthrow of Satan's throne, that *throne of kingdoms*, the throne of the god of this world, the taking from him all the armour wherein he trusted and *dividing the spoil.* And all opposing *rule, principality, and power*, shall be put down, that the *kingdom* may be *delivered up to God, even the Father.*

II. Let him depend upon it that he shall be safe under the divine protection in the midst of all these commotions, *v.* 23. Zerubbabel was active to build God a house, and therefore God makes the same promise to him as he did to David on the like occasion—that he would *build him a house,* and establish it, even *in that day* when heaven and earth are shaken. This promise refers to this good man himself and to his family. He honoured God, and God would honour him. His successors likewise in the government of Judah might take encouragement from it; though their authority was very precarious as to men, yet God would confirm it, and this would contribute to the stability of the people over whom God had set them. But this promise has special reference to Christ, who lineally descended from Zerubbabel, and is the sole builder of the gospel-temple. 1. Zerubbabel is here owned as *God's servant,* and it is an honourable mention that is hereby made of him, as Moses and David *my servants.* When God destroys his enemies he will prefer his servants. Our Lord Jesus is his Father's servant in the work of redemption, but faithful as a Son, Isa. xlii. 1. 2. He is owned as God's elect: *I have chosen thee*

to this office; and whom God makes choice of he will make use of. Our Lord Jesus is chosen of God, 1 Pet. ii. 4. And he is the head of the chosen remnant; in him they are chosen. 3. It is promised that, being chosen, God will make him *as a signet.* Jeconiah had been as the *signet on God's right hand,* but was *plucked thence* (Jer. xxii. 24); and now Zerubbabel is substituted in the room of him. He shall be near and dear to God, precious in his sight, and honourable, and his family shall continue till the Messiah spring out of it, who is *the signet on God's right hand.* This intimates, (1.) The delight the Father has in him. In him he once and again declared himself to be *well pleased.* He is set as a *seal upon his heart, a seal upon his arm,* is brought near unto him (Dan. vii. 13), is *hidden in the shadow of his hand,* Isa. xlix. 2. (2.) The dominion the Father has entrusted him with. Princes sign their edicts, grants, and commissions, with their signet-rings, Esth. iii. 10. Our Lord Jesus is the signet on God's right hand, for all power is given to him and derived from him. By him the great charter of the gospel is signed and ratified, and it is in him that all the promises of God are yea and amen.

AN

EXPOSITION,

WITH PRACTICAL OBSERVATIONS,

OF THE PROPHECY OF

ZECHARIAH.

THIS prophet was colleague with the prophet Haggai, and a worker together with him in forwarding the building of the second temple (Ezra v. 1); for two are better than one. Christ sent forth his disciples two and two. Zechariah began to prophesy some time after Haggai. But he continued longer, soared higher in visions and revelations, wrote more, and prophesied more particularly concerning Christ, than Haggai had done; so *the last shall be first :* the last in time sometimes proves first in dignity. He begins with a plain practical sermon, expressive of that which was the scope of his prophesying, in the first five verses; but afterwards, to the end of *ch.* vi., he relates the visions he saw, and the ,instructions he received immediately from heaven by them. At *ch.* vii., from an enquiry made by the Jews concerning fasting, he takes occasion to show them the duty of their present day, and to encourage them to hope for God's favour, to the end of *ch.* viii., after which there are two sermons, which are both called *burdens of the word of the Lord* (one begins with *ch.* ix., the other with *ch.* xii.), which probably were preached some time after ; the scope of them is to reprove for sin, and threaten God's judgments against the impenitent, and to encourage those that feared God with assurances of the mercy God had in store for his church, and especially of the coming of the Messiah and the setting up of his kingdom in the world.

CHAP. I.

In this chapter, after the introduction (ver. 1), we have, I. An awakening call to a sinful people to repent of their sins and return to God, ver. 2—6. II. Great encouragement given to hope for mercy. 1. By the vision of the horses, ver. 7—11. 2. By the prayer of the angel for Jerusalem, and the answer to that prayer, ver. 12—17.

3. By the vision of the four carpenters that were employed to cut off the four horns with which Judah and Jerusalem were scattered, ver. 18—21.

IN the eighth month, in the second year of Darius, came the word of the LORD unto Zechariah, the son of Berechiah, the son of Iddo the prophet, saying, 2 The LORD hath been sore displeased with your fathers. 3 Therefore say thou unto them, Thus saith the LORD of hosts; Turn ye unto me, saith the LORD of hosts, and I will turn unto you, saith the LORD of hosts. 4 Be ye not as your fathers, unto whom the former prophets have cried, saying, Thus saith the LORD of hosts; Turn ye now from your evil ways, and *from* your evil doings: but they did not hear, nor hearken unto me, saith the LORD. 5 Your fathers, where *are* they? and the prophets, do they live for ever? 6 But my words and my statutes, which I commanded my servants the prophets, did they not take hold of your fathers? and they returned and said, Like as the LORD of hosts thought to do unto us, according to our ways, and according to our doings, so hath he dealt with us.

Here is, I. The foundation of Zechariah's ministry; it is laid in a divine authority: *The word of the Lord came to him.* He received a divine commission to be God's mouth to the people and with it instructions what to say. He received of the Lord that which also he delivered unto them. *The word of the Lord was to him;* it came in the evidence and demonstration of the Spirit, as a real thing, and not a fancy. For the ascertaining of this, we have here, 1. The time when the word of the Lord came first to him, or when the word that next follows came to him: it was *in the second year of Darius.* Before the captivity the prophets dated their writings by the reigns of the kings of Judah and Israel; but now by the reigns of the kings of Persia, to whom they were subjects. Such a melancholy change had sin made of their circumstances. Zerubbabel took not so much state upon him as to have public acts dated by the years of his government, and in things of this nature the prophets, as is fit, complied with the usage of the time, and scrupled not to reckon by the years of the heathen kings, as Dan. vii. 1; viii. 1. Zechariah preached his first sermon in the *eighth month* of this *second year* of Darius; Haggai preached his in the sixth month of the same year, Hag. i. 1. The people being readily obedient to the word of the Lord in the mouth of Haggai, God blessed them with another prophet; for to him that has, and uses well what he has, more shall be given. 2. The name and family of the prophet to whom the word of the Lord came: He was *Zechariah,*

the son of Barachiah, the son of Iddo, and he was *the prophet,* as Haggai is called *the prophet,* Hag. i. 1. For, though in former ages there was one Iddo a prophet (2 Chron. xii. 15), yet we have no reason to think that Zechariah was of his progeny, or should be denominated from him. The learned Mr. Pemble is decidedly of opinion that this Zechariah, the son of Barachiah, is the same that our Saviour says was *slain between the temple and the altar,* perhaps many years after the rebuilding of the temple (Matt. xxiii. 35), and that our Saviour does not mean (as is commonly thought) Zechariah the son of Jehoiada, for why should Jehoiada be called Barachiah? And he thinks the manner of Christ's account persuades us to think so; for, reckoning up the innocent blood shed by the Jews, he begins at Abel, and ends even in the last of the holy prophets. Whereas, after Zechariah the son of Jehoiada, many prophets and righteous men were put to death by them. It is true there is no mention made in any history of their slaying this Zechariah, but Josephus might industriously conceal that shame of his nation. Perhaps what Zechariah spoke in his prophesying concerning Christ of his being sold, his being wounded in the house of his friends, and the shepherd being smitten, was verified in the prophet himself, and so he became a type of Christ. Probably, being assaulted by his persecutors, he took sanctuary in the court of the priests (and some think he was himself a priest), and so was slain between the porch and the altar.

II. The first-fruits of Zechariah's ministry. Before he came to visions and revelations, and delivered his prophetic discourses, he preached that which was plain and practical; for it is best to begin with that. Before he published the promises of mercy, he published calls to repentance, for thus *the way of the Lord* must be *prepared.* Law must be first preached, and then gospel. Now,

1. The prophet here puts them in mind of the controversy God had had with their fathers (v. 2): *"The Lord has been sorely displeased with your fathers,* and has laid them under the tokens of his displeasure. You have heard with your ears, and your fathers have told you of it; you have seen with your eyes the woeful remains of it. God's quarrel with you has been of long standing, and therefore it is time for you to think of taking it up."* Note, The judgments of God, which those that went before us were under, should be taken as warnings to us not to tread in their steps, and calls to repentance, that we may cut off the entail of the curse and get it turned into a blessing.

2. He calls them, in God's name, to return to him, and make their peace with him, v. 3. God by him says that to this backsliding people which he had often said by his servants the prophets: *" Turn you to me* in a way of faith and repentance, duty and obe-

dience, and *I will turn to you* in a way of favour and mercy, peace and reconciliation." Let the rebels return to their allegiance, and they shall be taken under the protection of the government and enjoy all the privileges of good subjects. Let them change their way, and God will change his. See Mal. iii. 7. But that which is most observable here is that God is called here the *Lord of hosts* three times : *Thus saith the Lord of hosts.* It is he that speaks, and therefore you are bound to regard what he says." *Turn you to me, saith the Lord of hosts* (this intimates the authority and obligation of the command), *and I will turn to you, saith the Lord of hosts* —this intimates the validity and value of the promise ; so that it is no vain repetition. Note, The consideration of God's almighty power and sovereign dominion should both engage and encourage sinners to repent and turn to him. It is very desirable to have the Lord of hosts our friend and very dreadful to have him our enemy.

3. He warns them not to persist in their impenitence, as their fathers had done (*v.* 4) : *Be you not as your fathers.* Instead of being hardened in their evil courses by the example of their fathers' sins, let them rather be deterred from them by the example of their fathers' punishment. We are apt to be governed very much by precedent, and we are well or ill governed according to the use we make of the precedents before us. The same examples to some are a savour of life unto life, to others a savour of death unto death. Some argued, " Shall we be wiser than our fathers ? They never minded the prophets, and why then should we mind them ? They made laws against them, and why should we tolerate them ?" But they are here taught how they should argue : " Our fathers slighted the prophets, and God was sorely displeased with them for it ; therefore let us the more carefully regard what God says to us by his prophets." " Review what is past, and observe,"

(1.) " What was the message that God sent by his servants the prophets to your fathers : *The former prophets cried to your fathers,* cried aloud, and did not spare, not spare themselves, not spare your fathers ; they cried as men in earnest, as men that would be heard ; they spoke not as from themselves, but in the name of *the Lord of hosts ;* and this was the substance of what they said, the burden of every song, the application of every sermon—*Turn you now from your evil ways, and from your evil doings ;* the very same that we now preach to you. Be persuaded to leave your sins ; resolve to have no more to do with them. A speedy reformation is the only way to prevent an approaching ruin : *Turn you now from sin to God without delay."*

(2.) " How little this message was regarded by your fathers : *But they did not hear,* they did not heed. They turned a deaf ear to

1402

these calls : *They would not hearken unto me, saith the Lord.* They would not be reclaimed, would not be ruled, by the word I sent them ; say not then that you will do as your fathers did, for they did amiss ;" see Jer. xliv. 17. Note, We must not follow the examples of our dear fathers unless they were God's dear children, nor any further than they were dutiful and obedient to him.

(3.) " What has become both of your fathers and of the prophets that preached to them ? They are all dead and gone," *v.* 5. [1.] *Your fathers, where are they ?* The whole generation of them is swept away, and their place knows them no more. Note, When we think of our ancestors, that have gone through the world and gone out of it before us, we should think, *Where are they ?* Here they were, in the towns and countries where we live, passing and repassing in the same streets, dwelling in the same houses, trading in the same shops and exchanges, worshipping God in the same churches. But where are they ? They are somewhere still ; when they died there was not an end of them. They are in eternity, in the world of spirits, the unchangeable world, to which we are hastening apace. Where are they ? Those of them that lived and died in sin are in torment, and we are warned by Moses and the prophets, Christ and his apostles, to look to it that we *come not to that place of torment,* Luke xvi. 28, 29. Those of them that lived and died in Christ are in paradise ; and, if we live and die as they did, we shall be with them shortly, with them eternally. [2.] *The prophets* also, *did they live for ever ?* No, they are gone too. The treasure is put into earthen vessels, the water of life into earthen pitchers, often cracked, and brought home broken at last. Christ is a prophet that lives for ever, but all other prophets have a period put to their office. Note, Ministers are dying men, and live not for ever in this world. They are to look upon themselves as such, and to preach accordingly, as those that must be silenced shortly, and know not which sermon may be the last. People are to look upon them as such, and to hear accordingly, as those that yet a little while have the *light with them,* that they may walk and work *while they have the light.* Oh that this weighty consideration had its due weight given it, that we are dying ministers dealing with dying people about the concerns of immortal souls and an awful eternity, which both they and we are standing upon the brink of ! It concerns us to think of the prophets that are gone, that were *before us of old,* Jer. xxviii. 8. Those that were the glory of men withered and fell ; but the *word of the Lord endures for ever,* 1 Pet. i. 24, 25. The prophets that are now, do *we live for ever ?* (so some read it) ; no, Haggai and Zechariah will not be long with you, and prophecy itself shall shortly cease. In another world both we and our prophets shall live for ever; and to prepare for that world ought to be our great care and business in this.

(4.) " What were the effects of the word which God spoke to them by his prophets, *v.* 6. The preachers died, and the hearers died, but the word of God died not; that took effect, and not one iota or tittle of it fell to the ground." As the *rain* and *snow* from heaven, *it shall not return void,* Isa. lv. 11. He appealed to themselves; they knew very well, [1.] That the judgments God had threatened were executed upon their fathers, and they were made to feel what they would not believe and fear : *" My statutes which I commanded my servants the prophets,* the precepts with the penalties annexed, which I charged them with the delivery of, *did they not take hold of your fathers ?"* Though God's prophets could not fasten convictions upon them, the calamities threatened overtook them, and they could not escape them, nor get out of the reach of them. God's words took hold of them as the bailiff arrests the debtor, and takes him in execution for contempt. Note, The unbelief of man cannot make the threatenings of God's word of no effect, but, sooner or later, they will take place, if the prescribed course be not taken to prevent the execution of them. God's anger will certainly take hold of those that will not be taken hold of by his authority; for when he judges he will overcome. [2.] That they themselves could not but own the accomplishment of the word of God in the judgments of God that were upon them, and that therein he was righteous, and had done them no wrong: *They returned, and said* (they changed their mind, and when it was too late to prevent the ruin of their nation they acknowledged), *Like as the Lord of hosts thought to do unto us according to our ways and doings,* to reckon with us for them, *so has he dealt with us,* and we must acknowledge both his truth and his justice, must blame ourselves only, and have no blame to lay to him. *Sero sapiunt Phryges—It is late before the Phrygians become wise.* This after-wit, as it is a proof of the truth of God, so it is a proof of the folly of men, who will look no further than they can see. They would never be persuaded to say in time, " God will be as good as his word, for he is faithful; he will deal with us according to our deserts, for he is righteous." But now they see both plainly enough when the sentence is executed; now he that runs may read, and publish the exact agreement that appears between the present providences and the former predictions which then were slighted, between the present punishments and the former sins which then were persisted in. Now they cannot but say, *The Lord is righteous,* Dan. ix. 11—13.

7 Upon the four and twentieth day

of the eleventh month, which *is* the month Sebat, in the second year of Darius, came the word of the LORD unto Zechariah, the son of Berechiah, the son of Iddo the prophet, saying, 8 I saw by night, and behold a man riding upon a red horse, and he stood among the myrtle-trees that *were* in the bottom ; and behind him *were there* red horses, speckled, and white. 9 Then said I, O my lord, what *are* these? And the angel that talked with me said unto me, I will show thee what these *be*. 10 And the man that stood among the myrtle-trees answered and said, These *are they* whom the LORD hath sent to walk to and fro through the earth. 11 And they answered the angel of the LORD that stood among the myrtle-trees, and said, We have walked to and fro through the earth, and, behold, all the earth sitteth still, and is at rest. 12 Then the angel of the LORD answered and said, O LORD of hosts, how long wilt thou not have mercy on Jerusalem and on the cities of Judah, against which thou hast had indignation these threescore and ten years? 13 And the LORD answered the angel that talked with me *with* good words *and* comfortable words. 14 So the angel that communed with me said unto me, Cry thou, saying, Thus saith the LORD of hosts ; I am jealous for Jerusalem and for Zion with a great jealousy. 15 And I am very sore displeased with the heathen *that are* at ease: for I was but a little displeased, and they helped forward the affliction. 16 Therefore thus saith the LORD; I am returned to Jerusalem with mercies : my house shall be built in it, saith the LORD of hosts, and a line shall be stretched forth upon Jerusalem. 17 Cry yet, saying, Thus saith the LORD of hosts; My cities through prosperity shall yet be spread abroad; and the LORD shall yet comfort Zion, and shall yet choose Jerusalem.

We now come to visions and revelations of the Lord; for in that way God chose to speak by Zechariah, to awaken the people's attention, and to engage their humble reverence of the word and their humble enquiries into it, and to fix it the more in their minds and memories. Most of the following visions seem designed for the comfort of the Jews, now newly returned out of captivity, and their encouragement to go on with the building of the temple. The scope of this vision (which is as an introduction to the rest) is to assure the Jews of the care God took of them, and the eye of his providence that was upon them for good, now in their present state, when they seem to be deserted, and their case deplorable. The vision is dated (*v.* 7) *the twenty-fourth day of the eleventh month*, three months after he preached that sermon (*v.* 1), in which he calls them to repentance from the consideration of God's judgments. Finding that that sermon had a good effect, and that they returned to God in a way of duty, the assurances he had given them are confirmed, that God would return to them in a way of mercy. Now observe here,

I. What the prophet saw, and the explication of that. 1. He saw a grove of *myrtle-trees*, a dark shady grove, down *in a bottom*, hidden by the adjacent hills, so that you were not aware of it till you were just upon it. This represented the low, dark, solitary, melancholy condition of the Jewish church at this time. They were over-topped by all their neighbours, buried in obscurity; what friends they had were hidden, and there appeared no way of relief and succour for them. Note, The church has not been always visible, but sometimes hidden, as the *woman in the wilderness*, Rev. xii. 6. 2. He saw *a man* mounted upon *a red horse*, standing in the midst of this shady myrtle-grove. This man is no other than the *man Christ Jesus*, the same that appeared to Joshua with *his sword drawn in his hand* as *captain of the host of the Lord* (Josh. v. 13, 14) and to John with his *bow* and his *crown*, Rev. vi. 2. Though the church was in a low condition, yet Christ was present in the midst of it. Was it hidden by the hills? He was much more hidden in the myrtle-grove, yet hidden as in an ambush, ready to appear for the seasonable relief of his people, to their happy surprise. Compare Isa. xlv. 15, *Verily thou art a God that hidest thyself*, and yet *Israel's God and Saviour* at the same time, their *Holy One in the midst of them*. He was *riding*, as a man of war, as a man in haste, *riding on the heavens for the help* of his people, Deut. xxxiii. 26. He rode on a *red horse*, either naturally so or dyed red with the blood of war, as this same victorious prince appeared *red in his apparel*, Isa. lxiii. 1, 2. Red is a fiery colour, denoting that he is *jealous for Jerusalem* (*v.* 14) and very angry at her enemies. Christ, under the law, appeared on a red horse, denoting the terror of that dispensation, and that he had yet his conflict before him, when he was to *resist unto blood*. But, under the gospel, he appears on a *white horse* (Rev. vi. 2, and again *ch.* xix. 11), denoting that he has now gained

the victory, and rides in triumph, and hangs out the white, not the bloody flag. 3. He saw a troop of horse attending him, ready to receive and obey his orders: *Behind him there were some red horses, and* some *speckled, and* some *white*, angels attending the Lord Jesus, ready to be employed by him for the service of his church, some in acts of judgment, others of mercy, others in mixed events. Note, The King of the church has angels at command, not only to do him honour, but to minister for the good of those that are his. 4. He enquired into the signification of this vision. He had an angel talking with him, as his instructor, besides those he saw in the vision; so had Ezekiel (*ch.* xl. 3), and Daniel, *ch.* viii. 16. Zechariah asked him (*v.* 9), *O my Lord! what are these?* And, it should seem, this *angel that talked with him* was Christ himself, the *man on the red horse*, whom the rest were attendants on; to him immediately Zechariah addresses himself. Would we be acquainted with the mysteries of the kingdom of heaven, we must make our application, not to angels (they are themselves learners), but to Christ himself, who is alone *able to take the book, and open the seals*, Rev. v. 7. The prophet's question implies a humble acknowledgment of his own ignorance and an earnest desire to be informed. O let me know what these are! This he desired, not for the satisfying of his curiosity, but that he might be furnished with something proper for the comfort and encouragement of the people of God, in their present distress. 5. He received from the *angel that talked with him* (*v.* 9), and from *the man that stood among the myrtle-trees* (*v.* 10), the interpretation of this vision. Note, Jesus Christ is ready to instruct those that are humbly desirous to be taught the things of God. He immediately said, *I will show thee what these are*. What knowledge we have, or may have, concerning the world of spirits, we are indebted to Christ for. The account given him was, *These are those whom the Lord has sent;* they are his messengers, his envoys, appointed (as his eyes are said to do, 2 Chron. xvi. 9) to *walk*, to *run*, to fly swiftly *through the earth*, to observe what is done in it and to execute the divine commands. God needs them not, but he is pleased to employ them, and we need the comfort arising from the doctrine of their administration.

II. What the prophet heard, and what instructions were thereby given him. Faith comes by hearing, and, generally, in visions there was something said.

1. He heard the report or representation which the angels made to Christ of the present state of the world, *v.* 11. They had been out abroad, as flying posts (*being hastened by the King of kings' commandment*, Esth. iii. 15), and, having returned, they give this account to the *Angel that stood among the myrtle-trees* (for to the Lord Jesus angels

themselves are accountable): *We have walked to and fro through the earth, and, behold, all the earth sits still and is at rest.* We are taught to pray that the will of God may be done by men on earth as it is done by the angels in heaven; and here we see what need we have to pray so, for it is far from being so. For, (1.) We find the world of angels here very busy. Those that are employed in the court above rest not day nor night from praising God, which is their business there; and those that are employed in the camp below are never idle, nor lose time; they are still *ascending and descending* upon *the Son of man* (John i. 51, as on Jacob's ladder, Gen. xxviii. 12); they are still *walking to and fro through the earth.* Thus active, thus industrious, *Satan* owns himself to be in doing mischief, Job i. 7. It is well for us that good angels bestir themselves as much to do good, and that here in this earth we have guardians going about continually seeking to do us a kindness, as we have adversaries which, as roaring lions, go about continually, seeking to devour us. Though holy angels in this earth meet with a great deal that is disagreeable, yet, while they are going on God's errands, they hesitate not to *walk to and fro through it.* Their own habitation, which those that fell liked not, they will like the better when they return. (2.) We find the world of mankind here very careless: *All the earth sits still, and is at rest,* while all the church is made uneasy, *tossed with tempests and not comforted.* Those that are strangers to the church are secure; those that are enemies to it are successful. The Chaldeans and Persians dwell at ease, while the poor Jews are continually alarmed; as when *the king and Haman sat down to drink, but the city Shushan was perplexed.* The children of men are merry and jovial, but *none grieve for the affliction* of God's children. Note, It is sad to think what a deep sleep the world is cast into, what a spirit of slumber has seized the generality of mankind, that are under God's wrath and Satan's power, and yet secure and unconcerned! They sit still and are at rest, Luke xvii. 26, &c.

2. He heard Christ's intercession with the Father for his afflicted church, *v.* 12. The angels related the posture of affairs in this lower world, but we read not of any prayers they made for the redress of the grievances they had made a remonstrance of. No; it is *the Angel among the myrtle-trees* that is the great intercessor. Upon the report of the angels he immediately turned heavenward, and said, *Lord, wilt thou not have mercy* on thy church? (1.) The thing he intercedes for is *mercy;* as Ps. lxxxv. 7, *Show us thy mercy, O Lord!* Note, God's mercy is all in all to the church's comfort; and all his mercy must be hoped for through Christ's mediation. (2.) The thing he complains of is the delay of this mercy: *How long wilt*

thou *not have mercy!* He knows that *mercies* through him *shall be built up for ever* (Ps. lxxxix. 2), but thinks it long that the building is deferred. (3.) The objects of compassion recommended to the divine mercies are, Jerusalem, the holy city, and the other cities of Judah that were now in ruins; for God had had *indignation against them* now *threescore and ten years.* He mentions seventy years because that was the time fixed in the divine councils for the continuance of the captivity; so long the indignation lasted, and though *now for a little space grace* had been *shown them from the Lord their God,* to *give them some reviving* (Ezra ix. 8), yet the scars of those seventy years' captivity still remained so deep, so painful, that this is the melancholy string they still harp upon—the divine indignation during those seventy years. Dr. Lightfoot thinks that whereas the seventy years of the captivity were reckoned from Jehoiakim's fourth year, and ended in the first of Cyrus, these seventy years are to þe computed from the eleventh of Zedekiah, when Jerusalem and the temple were burnt, about nineteen years after the first captivity, and which ended in this second year of Darius Hystaspes, about seventeen years after Cyrus's proclamation, as that seventy years mentioned *ch.* vii. 5 was about nineteen years after; the captivity went off, as it came on, gradually. "Lord, we are still under the burden of the seventy years' wrath, *and wilt thou be angry with us for ever?*"

3. He heard a gracious reply given to this intercession of Christ's for his church; for it is a prevailing intercession, always acceptable, *and him the Father heareth always* (v. 13): *The Lord answered the angel,* this angel of the covenant, *with good words and comfortable words,* with promises of mercy and deliverance, and the perfecting of what he had begun in favour to them. These were comfortable words to Christ, who is grieved in the grievances of his church, and comfortable to all that mourn with Zion. God often answers prayer with good words, when he does not immediately appear in great works; and those good words are real answers to prayer. Men's good words will not feed the body (Jam. ii. 16), but God's good words will feed the faith, for saying and doing with him are not two things, though they are with us.

4. He heard that reply which was given to the angel repeated to himself, with a commission to publish it to the children of his people, for their comfort. *The revelation of Jesus Christ which God gave to him* he *signified to his servant John,* and by him *to the churches,* Rev. i. 1, 4. Thus all the good words and comfortable words of the gospel we receive from Jesus Christ, as he received them from the Father, in answer to the prayer of his blood, and his ministers are appointed to preach them *to all the world.*

Now that God would *speak comfortably to Jerusalem*, Zechariah is *the voice of one crying in the wilderness, Prepare you the way of the Lord. The voice said, Cry. Cry then.* The prophets must now cry as loudly to show God's people their comforts as ever they did formerly to show them *their transgressions*, Isa. xl. 2, 3, 6. And if he ask, *What shall I cry?* he is here instructed. (1.) He must proclaim the wrath God has in store for the enemies of Jerusalem. He is *jealous for Zion with great jealousy, v.* 14. He takes himself to be highly affronted by the injuries and indignities that are done to his church, as he had been formerly by the iniquities found in his church. The earth *sat still and was at rest* (v. 11), not relenting at all, nor showing the least remorse, for all the mischief they had done to Jerusalem, as Joseph's brethren, who, when they had sold him, sat down to eat bread; and this God took very ill (v. 15): *I am very sorely displeased with the heathen, that are at ease,* and have no concern for the afflicted church. Much more will he be displeased with those that are *at ease in Zion* (Amos vi. 1), with Zion's own sons, that sympathize not with her in her sorrows. But this was not all; they were not only not concerned for her, but they were concerned against her : *I was but a little displeased* with my people, and designed to correct them moderately, but those that were employed as instruments of the correction cast off all pity, and with the greatest rage and malice *helped forward the affliction* and added to it, *persecuting those whom God had smitten* (Ps. lxix. 26) and insulting over those whom he had troubled. See Isa. xlvii. 6; x. 5; Ezek. xxv. 12, 15. Note, God is displeased with those who help forward the affliction even of such as suffer justly ; for true humanity, in such a case, is good divinity. (2.) He must proclaim the mercy God has in store for Jerusalem and the *cities of Judah, v.* 16. He must cry, "*Thus saith the Lord, I have returned to Jerusalem with mercies.* I was going away in wrath, but I am now returning in love. *Cry yet* to the same purport, v. 17. There must now be line upon line for consolation, as formerly there had been for conviction. *The Lord,* even the Lord of hosts, assures them, [1.] That the temple shall be built that is now but in the building. This good work which they are now about, though it meet with much discouragement, shall be perfected, and they shall have the tokens of God's presence, and opportunities of conversing with him, and worshipping him, as formerly. Note, It is good news indeed to any place to hear that God will build his house in it. [2.] That Jerusalem shall again be *built as a city compact together,* which had formerly been its glory, Ps. cxxii. 3. *A line shall be stretched forth upon Jerusalem,* in order to the rebuilding of it with great exactness and uniformity. [3.] That the na-

tion shall again become populous and rich, though now diminished and impoverished. Not only Jerusalem, but other cities that are reduced and lie in a little compass, shall yet *spread abroad,* or be diffused ; their suburbs shall extend far, and colonies shall be transplanted from them ; and this *through prosperity :* they shall be so numerous, and so wealthy, that there shall not be room for them ; they shall complain that *the place is too strait,* Isa. xlix. 20. As they had been scattered and spread abroad, through their calamities, so they should now be through their prosperity. *Let thy fountains be dispersed,* Prov. v. 16. The cities that should thus increase God calls his cities ; they are *blessed* by him, and they are *fruitful and multiply, and replenish the land.* [4.] That all their present sorrows should not only be balanced, but for ever silenced, by divine consolations : *The Lord shall yet comfort Zion.* Yet at length, though her griefs and grievances may continue long, God has comforts in reserve for Zion and all her mourners. [5.] That all this will be the fruit of God's preventing distinguishing favour : He shall yet *choose Jerusalem,* shall renew his choice, renew his covenant, shall make it appear that he has chosen Jerusalem. As he first built them up into a people when he brought them out of Egypt, so he will now rebuild them, when he brings them out of Babylon, not for any worthiness of theirs, but in pursuance of his own choice, Deut. vii. 7, 8. Jerusalem is the city he has chosen, and he will not cast it off.

18 Then lifted I up mine eyes, and saw, and behold four horns. 19 And I said unto the angel that talked with me, What *be* these? And he answered me, These *are* the horns which have scattered Judah, Israel, and Jerusalem. 20 And the LORD showed me four carpenters. 21 Then said I, What come these to do? And he spake, saying, These *are* the horns which have scattered Judah, so that no man did lift up his head: but these are come to fray them, to cast out the horns of the Gentiles, which lifted up *their* horn over the land of Judah to scatter it.

It is the comfort and triumph of the church (Isa. lix. 19) that *when the enemy shall come in like a flood,* with mighty force and fury, then the *Spirit of the Lord shall lift up a standard against him.* Now, in this vision (the second which this prophet had), we have an illustration of that, God's Spirit making a stand, and making head, against the formidable power of the church's adversaries.

I. We have here the enemies of the church bold and daring, and threatening to be its death, to *cut off the name of Israel;* such the people of God had lately been insulted by: *I looked and behold four horns* (v. 18), which are explained v. 19. They *are the horns which have scattered Judah, Israel, and Jerusalem,* that is, the Jews both in the country and in the city, because they were the Israel of God. They have *tossed them* (so some read it), as furious bulls with their horns toss that which they are enraged at. They have scattered them, *so that no man did lift up his head,* v. 21. No man durst show his face for fear of them, much less give them any opposition, or make head against them. They are *horns,* denoting their dignity and dominion,—*horns exalted,* denoting also their strength, and power, and violence. They are *four horns,* for the Jews are surrounded with them on every side; when they avoid one horn that pushes at them they run upon another. The men of Judah and the inhabitants of Jerusalem, and many of Israel that joined themselves to them, set about the building of the temple; but the enemies of that work from all sides pushed at them, and drove them from it. Rehum, and Shimshai, and the other Samaritans that opposed the building of the temple, were these horns, Ezra iv. 8. So were Sanballat and Tobiah, and the Ammonites and Arabians, that opposed the building of the wall, Neh. iv. 7. Note, The church's enemies have horns, and use them to the hindrance of every good work. The great enemy of the New-Testament church has *seven heads and ten horns* (Rev. xvii. 3), so that those who endeavour to do the church any service must expect to be pushed at.

II. We have here the friends of the church active and prevailing. The prophet did himself lift up his eyes and see the four horns, and saw them so formidable that he began to despair of the safety of every good man, and the success of every good work; but *the Lord* then *showed him four carpenters,* or *smiths,* who were empowered to cut off these horns, v. 20, 21. With an eye of sense we see the power of the enemies of the church; look which way we will, the world shows us that. But it is with an eye of faith that we see it safe, notwithstanding; it is the Lord that shows us that, as he opened the eyes of the prophet's servant to see the angelic guards round about his master, 2 Kings vi. 17. Observe, Those that were to fray or break the horns of the Gentiles, and to cast them out, were, 1. *Carpenters* or *smiths* (for they are supposed by some to have been horns of iron), men who had skill and ability to do it, whose proper business it was, and who understood their business and had tools at hand to do it with. Note, God calls those to serve the interests of his church whom he either finds, or makes, fit for it. If there be horns (which denote the force and fury of beasts) against the church, there are carpenters (which denote the wisdom and fore-

cast of men) for the church, by which they find ways to master the strongest beasts, for *every kind of beasts is tamed, and has been tamed, of mankind,* Jam. iii. 7. 2. They were *four carpenters,* as many horns so many hands to saw them off. Note, Which way soever the church is threatened with mischief, and opposition given to its interests, God can find out ways and means to check the force, to restrain the wrath, and make it turn to his praise. Some by these four carpenters understand Zerubbabel and Joshua, Ezra and Nehemiah, who carried on the work of God in spite of the opposition given to it. Those horned beasts broke into God's vineyard to tread it down; but the good magistrates and the good ministers whom God raised up, though they had not power to *cut off the horns of the wicked* (as David did, Ps. lxxv. 5, 10), yet frightened them and cast them out. Note, When God has work to do he will raise up some to do it and others to defend it and protect those that are employed in the doing of it.

CHAP. II.

In this chapter we have, I. Another vision which the prophet saw, not for his own entertainment, but for his satisfaction and the edification of those to whom he was sent, ver. 1, 2. II. A sermon upon it, in the rest of the chapter, 1. By way of explication of the vision, showing it to be a prediction of the replenishing of Jerusalem and of its safety and honour, ver. 3—5. 2. By way of application. Here is, (1.) A use of exhortation to the Jews that were yet in Babylon, pressing them to hasten their return to their own land, ver. 6—9. (2.) A use of consolation to those that were returned, in reference to the many difficulties they had to struggle with, ver. 10—12. (3.) A use of caution to all not to prescribe to God, or limit him, but patiently to wait for him, ver. 13.

I LIFTED up mine eyes again, and looked, and behold a man with a measuring-line in his hand. 2 Then said I, Whither goest thou? And he said unto me, To measure Jerusalem, to see what *is* the breadth thereof, and what *is* the length thereof. 3 And, behold, the angel that talked with me went forth, and another angel went out to meet him, 4 And said unto him, Run, speak to this young man, saying, Jerusalem shall be inhabited *as* towns without walls for the multitude of men and cattle therein: 5 For I, saith the LORD, will be unto her a wall of fire round about, and will be the glory in the midst of her.

This prophet was ordered, in God's name, to assure the people (*ch.* i. 16) that a *line should be stretched forth upon Jerusalem.* Now here we have that promise illustrated and confirmed, that the prophet might deliver that part of his message to the people with the more clearness and assurance.

I. He sees, in a vision, a man going to measure Jerusalem (*v.* 1, 2): *He lifted up his eyes again, and looked.* God had shown him that which was very encouraging to him, (*ch.* i. 20), and therefore now he *lifted up his eyes again and looked.* Note, The comfortable sights which by faith we have had of God's goodness made to pass before us should engage us to lift up our eyes again, and to search further into the discoveries made to us of the divine grace; for there is still more to be seen. In the close of the foregoing chapter he had seen Jerusalem's enemies baffled and broken, so that now he begins to hope she shall not be ruined. But that is not enough to make her happy, and therefore that is not all that is promised. Here is more carpenter's work to be done. When David had resolved to *cut off the horns of the wicked* he engaged likewise that the *horns of the righteous* should be *exalted*, Ps. lxxv. 10. And so does the *Son of David* here; for he is *the man,* even *the man Christ Jesus,* whom the prophet sees *with a measuring line in his hand;* for he is the master builder of his church (Heb. iii. 3), and he builds exactly by line and level. Zechariah took the boldness to ask him *whither he was going* and what he designed to do with that measuring line. And he readily told him that he was going to *measure Jerusalem,* to take a particular account of the dimensions of it each way, that it might be computed what was necessary for the making of a wall about it, and that it might appear, by comparing its dimensions with the vast numbers that should inhabit it, what additions were necessary to be made for the receiving and containing of them; when multitudes flock to Jerusalem (Isa. lx. 4) it is time for her to *enlarge the place of her tent,* Isa. liv. 2. Note, God takes notice of the extent of his church, and will take care that, when ever so many guests are brought in to the wedding supper, still there *shall be room,* Luke xiv. 22. *In* the New Jerusalem, *my Father's house* above, *there are many mansions.*

II. He is informed that this vision means well to Jerusalem, that the measuring line he saw was not a *line of confusion* (as that Isa. xxxiv. 11), not a line to mete out for destruction, as when God *purposed to destroy the wall of the daughter of Zion he stretched out a line* (Lam. ii. 8); but it is as when he *divided the inheritance by line,* Ps. lxxviii. 55. The *angel that talked with* the prophet *went forth,* as he designed, *to measure Jerusalem,* but *another angel went out to meet him,* to desire that he would first explain this vision to the prophet, that it might not occasion him any uneasy speculations: *Run, and speak to this young man* (for, it seems, the prophet entered upon his prophecy when he was young, yet no man ought to despise his youth when God thus highly honoured it); he is a young man, not experienced, and may be ready to fear the worst; therefore bid him hope the best; tell him that Jerusalem shall be both safe and great, 1. As safe and great as numbers of men can make it (*v.* 4): *Jerusalem shall be inhabited as towns without walls;* the inhabitants of it shall increase,
1408

and multiply, and replenish it to admiration, so that it shall extend itself far beyond the present dimensions which now there is an account taken of. The walls of a city, as they defend it, so they straiten and confine it, and keep its inhabitants from multiplying beyond such a pitch; but Jerusalem, even when it is walled, to keep off the enemy, shall be inhabited *as towns without walls.* The city shall be in a manner lost in the suburbs, as London is, where the out-parishes are more populous than those within the walls. So shall it be with Jerusalem; it shall be extended as freely as if it had no walls at all, and yet shall be as safe as if it had the strongest walls, such a *multitude of men* (which are the best walls of a city) *shall there be therein,* and of *cattle too,* to be not only food, but wealth too, for those men. Note, The increase of the numbers of a people is a great blessing, is a fruit of God's blessing on them and an earnest of further blessings, Ps. cvii. 38. *They are multiplied, for he blesses them.* 2. As safe and great as the presence of God can make it, *v.* 5. (1.) It shall be safe, for God himself will be a *wall of fire round about it.* Jerusalem had no walls about it at this time, but lay naked and exposed; formerly, when it had walls, the enemies not only broke through them, but broke them down; but now God will be unto her a wall of fire. Some think it alludes to shepherds that made fires about their flocks, or travellers that made fires about their tents in desert places, to frighten wild beasts from them. God will not only *make a hedge* about them as he did about Job (*ch.* i. 10), not only make walls and bulwarks about them, Isa. xxvi. 1 (those may be battered down), not only be as the mountains round about them, Ps. cxxv. 2 (mountains may be got over), but he will be a wall of fire round them, which cannot be broken through, nor scaled, nor undermined, nor the foundations of it sapped, nor can it be attempted, or approached, without danger to the assailants. God will not only make a wall of fire about her, but he will himself be such a wall; for *our God is a consuming fire* to his and his church's enemies. He is a wall of fire, not on one side only, but round about on every side. (2.) It shall be great, for God himself *will be the glory in the midst of it.* His temple, his altar, shall be set up and attended there, and his institutions observed, and there then shall the tokens of his special presence and favour be, which will be the glory in the midst of them, will make them truly admirable in the eyes of all about them. God will have honour from them, and put honour upon them. Note, Those that have God for their God have him for their glory; those that have him in the midst of them have glory in the midst of them, and thence the church is said to be *all glorious within.* And those persons and places that have God to be the glory in the midst of them have him for a wall of fire round about them, for *upon all that glory there is, and shall be, a defence,* Isa. iv. 5. Now all this was fulfilled in part in Jerusalem, which in process of time became a very flourishing city, and made a very great figure in those parts of the world, much beyond what could have been expected, considering how low it was brought and how long it was ere it recovered itself; but it was to have its full accomplishment in the gospel-church, which is extended far, as towns without walls, by the admission of the Gentiles into it, and which has God, the Son of God, for its prince and protector.

6 Ho, ho, *come forth*, and flee from the land of the north, saith the LORD: for I have spread you abroad as the four winds of the heaven, saith the LORD. 7 Deliver thyself, O Zion, that dwellest *with* the daughter of Babylon. 8 For thus saith the LORD of hosts; After the glory hath he sent me unto the nations which spoiled you: for he that toucheth you toucheth the apple of his eye. 9 For, behold, I will shake mine hand upon them, and they shall be a spoil to their servants : and ye shall know that the LORD of hosts hath sent me.

One would have thought that Cyrus's proclamation, which gave liberty to the captive Jews to return to their own land, would suffice to bring them all back, and that, as when Pharaoh gave them leave to quit Egypt and their house of bondage there, they would not leave a hoof behind ; but it seems it had not that effect. There were about 40,000 whose spirits God stirred up to go, and they went; but many, perhaps the greater part, staid behind. The land of their captivity was to most of them the land of their nativity ; they had taken root there, had gained a settlement, and many of them a very comfortable one ; some perhaps had got estates and preferments there, and they did not think they could better themselves by returning to their own land. *Patria est ubicunque bene est—My country is every spot where I feel myself happy.* They had no great affection to their own land, and apprehended the difficulties in their way to it insuperable. This proceeded from a bad cause—a distrust of the power and promise of God, a love of ease and worldly wealth, and an indifference to the religion of their country and to the God of Israel himself ; and it had a bad effect, for it was a tacit censure of those as foolish, rash, and given to change, that did return, and a weakening of their hands in the work of God. Such as these could not sing (Ps. cxxxvii.) in their captivity, for they had *forgotten thee, O Jerusalem!* and were so far

from preferring thee before their chief joy that they preferred any joy before thee. Here is therefore another proclamation issued out by the God of Israel, strictly charging and commanding all his free-born subjects, wherever they were dispersed, speedily to return into their own land and render themselves at their respective posts there. They are loudly summoned (*v.* 6) : *Ho! ho! come forth, and flee from the land of the north, saith the Lord.* This fitly follows upon the promise of the rebuilding and enlarging of Jerusalem. If God will build it for them and their comfort, they must come and inhabit it for him and his glory, and not continue sneaking in Babylon. Note, The promises and privileges with which God's people are blessed should engage us, whatever it cost us, to join ourselves to them and *cast in our lot among them.* When Zion is enlarged, to make room for all God's Israel, it is the greatest madness imaginable for any of them to stay in Babylon. The captivity of a sinful state is by no means to be continued in, though a man be ever so easy upon temporal accounts. No : *Come forth and flee* with all speed, and lose no time. *Escape for thy life : look not behind thee.* To induce them to hasten their return, let them consider, 1. They are now dispersed, and are concerned to incorporate themselves for their mutual common defence (*v.* 6) : "*I have spread you abroad as the four winds of heaven,* sent some into one corner of the world and some into another; this has been your condition a long time, and therefore you should now think of coming together again, to help one another." God owns that his scattering them was in wrath, and therefore they must take this invitation as a token of God's being willing to be reconciled to them again, so that they kicked at his kindness in refusing to accept the call. 2. They are now in bondage, and are concerned to assert their own liberty ; and therefore, "*Deliver thyself, O Zion!* flee from the oppressor, and make the best of thy way. Let us see some such bold efforts and struggles to help thyself as become the generous gracious seed of Abraham," *v.* 7. Note, When Christ has proclaimed that deliverance to the captives which he has himself wrought out it then concerns each of us to *deliver ourselves,* to *loose ourselves from the bands of our necks* (Isa. lii. 2), and, since we are under grace, to resolve that *sin shall not have dominion over us.* Zion herself is here said to *dwell with the daughter of Babylon,* because many of the *precious sons of Zion* dwelt there, and where the people of God are there the church of God is, for it is not tied to places. Now it is not fit that Zion should dwell with the daughter of Babylon; what communion can light have with darkness? Zion will be in danger of partaking with the daughter of Babylon both *in her sins* and *in her plagues ;* and therefore, "*Come out of her, my people,* Rev. xviii. 4.

Deliver thyself, O Zion! by a speedy return to thy own land, and do not destroy thyself by continuing in that polluted devoted land." Those that would be found among the generation of God's children must *save themselves from* the *untoward generation* of this world; it was St. Peter's charge to his new converts, Acts ii. 40. 3. They have seemed to be forsaken and forgotten of God, but God will now make it to appear that he espouses their cause and will plead it with jealousy, *v.* 8, 9. It was a discouragement to those who remained in Babylon to hear of the difficulties and oppositions which their brethren met with that had returned, by which they were still in danger of being crushed and overpowered. "And we might as well sit still" (think they) "as rise up and fall." In answer to this objection, the *angel that talked with* the prophet (that is, Jesus Christ) tells him what he had commission to do for their protection and the perfecting of their salvation, and herein he has an eye to the great redemption which, in the fulness of time, he was to be the author of. Christ, who is Jehovah, and the *Lord of hosts,* of all the hosts of heaven and earth, in both which he has a sovereign power, *says,* He (that is, the Father) *has sent me.* Note, What Jesus has done, and does, for his church against his enemies, he was sent and commissioned by the Father to do. With great satisfaction he often speaks of *the Father that sent him.* (1.) He is sent *after the glory.* After the glorious beginning of their deliverance he is sent to perfect it, for he is the finisher of that work which he is the author of. Christ is sent, in the first place, to the nation and people of the Jews, *to whom pertained the glory,* Rom. ix. 4. And he was himself the *glory of his people Israel.* But *after the glory,* after his care of them, he is *sent to the nations, to be a light to lighten the Gentiles,* by the power of his gospel to captivate them, and bring them, and every high thought among them, into obedience to himself. (2.) He is *sent to the nations that spoiled them,* to take vengeance on them for the wrongs done to Zion, when the year of his redeemed comes and the *year of recompences for the controversy of Zion,* Isa. xxxiv. 8. He is sent to *shake his hand upon them,* to lift up his mighty hand against them and to lay upon them his heavy hand, to *bruise them with a rod of iron* and *dash them in pieces like a potter's vessel,* Ps. ii. 9. Some think it intimates how easily God can subdue and humble them with the turn of his hand; it is but shaking his hand over them and the work is done. *They shall be a spoil to their servants,* shall be enslaved to those whom they had enslaved, and be plundered by those whom they had plundered. In Esther's time this was fulfilled, when the *Jews had rule over those that hated them* (Esth. ix. 1), and often in the time of the Maccabees. The promise is further fulfilled in Christ's victory over our spiritual enemies, his *spoiling principa-*
1410

lities and powers and making a show of them openly, Col. ii. 15. And it is still in force to the gospel-church. Christ will reckon with all that are enemies to it, and sooner or later will make them *his footstool,* Ps. cx. 1; Rev. iii. 9. (3.) What he will do for his church shall be an evident proof of God's tender care of it and affection to it: *He that touches you touches the apple of his eye.* This is a high expression of God's love to his church. By his resentment of the injuries done to her it appears how dear she is to him, how he interests himself in all her interests, and takes what is done against her, not only as done against himself, but as done against the very apple of his eye, the tenderest part, which nature has made very fine, has put a double guard upon, and taught us to be in a special manner careful of, and which the least touch is a great offence to. This encourages the people of God to pray with David (Ps. xvii. 8), *Keep me as the apple of thy eye;* and engages them to do as Solomon directs (Prov. vii. 2), to *keep his law as the apple of their eye.* Some understand it thus: *" He that touches you touches the apple of his own eye;* whoever do you any injury will prove, in the issue, to have done the greatest injury to themselves." (4.) It shall be an evident proof of Christ's mission: *You shall know that the Lord of hosts has sent me* to be the protector of his church, that the promises made to the church are yea and amen in him. Christ's victory over our spiritual enemies proves that the Father sent him and was with him.

10 Sing and rejoice, O daughter of Zion: for, lo, I come, and I will dwell in the midst of thee, saith the LORD. 11 And many nations shall be joined to the LORD in that day, and shall be my people; and I will dwell in the midst of thee, and thou shalt know that the LORD of hosts hath sent me unto thee. 12 And the LORD shall inherit Judah his portion in the holy land, and shall choose Jerusalem again. 13 Be silent, O all flesh, before the LORD: for he is raised up out of his holy habitation.

Here is, I. Joy proclaimed to the church of God, to the *daughter of Zion,* that had separated herself from the *daughter of Babylon.* The Jews that had returned were in distress and danger, their enemies in the neighbourhood were spiteful against them, their friends that remained in Babylon were cool towards them, shy of them, and declined coming in to their assistance; and yet they are directed to *sing,* and to *rejoice* even in tribulation. Note, Those that have recovered their purity, and integrity, and spiritual liberty, though they have not yet recovered their outward prosperity, have reason to sing and rejoice, to give glory to God and take comfort to themselves.

I. God will have a people among them. If their brethren in Babylon will not come to them, those of other nations shall, and shall replenish Jerusalem and the cities of Judah: *Many nations shall be joined to the Lord in that day* that are now at a distance from him and strangers to him. The Jewish nation, after the captivity, multiplied very much, by the accession of proselytes to it, that were naturalized, and were entitled to all the privileges of native Israelites, and perhaps they were equal in number; and therefore Paul mentions it as an honour to him which many Jews had not, that he was of *the tribe of Benjamin, a Hebrew of the Hebrews*, Phil. iii. 5. And this was an earnest of the bringing in of the Gentiles into the Christian church, and in that this and other similar promises were to have their full accomplishment. It was therefore strange that that should be so great an offence to the Jews, as we find it was in the apostles' times, which was promised them as a blessing in the prophets' times—that *many nations* should be *joined to the Lord.* And, as there had been one law, so should there be one gospel *for the stranger and for those born in the land;* whatever nation they come from, when they *join themselves to the Lord, they shall be my people,* as dear to God as ever Israel had been. Note, God will own those for his people who with purpose of heart join themselves to him; and, when many do so, we ought to look upon them, not with a jealous eye, but with a joyful one. Angels rejoice, and therefore so should the daughter of Zion, when many nations are joined to the Lord.

II. They shall have his presence among them: *Sing and rejoice, for I come.* Those to whom God comes have reason to rejoice, for he will be to them their chief joy. God will come, not to make them a visit only, but to reside with them and preside over them: *I will dwell in the midst of thee* (v. 10), and it is repeated (v. 11), because it was to have a double accomplishment, 1. In the dedication of the temple, in their regularly observing all God's institutions there and God's owning them therein. Those have God *dwelling in the midst of them* that have his ordinances administered in their purity, and a divine power going along with them; with these tokens of God's presence the Jewish church was blessed, after this, as much as ever. 2. In the incarnation of Christ. He that here promises to dwell among them is that *Lord whom the Lord of hosts has sent* (v. 11), and therefore must be the *Lord Jesus*, who came and dwelt in the midst of the Jewish nation, the eternal *Word,* that was *made flesh, and dwelt among us.* This was the great honour reserved for that nation in its last days; the promise of it effectually secured their continuance till it was accomplished. They could not be de-

stroyed while that blessing was in them; and the prospect of it, according to the promise, was the great support and comfort of those who *looked for redemption in Jerusalem.* It is promised that when Christ comes and dwells among them *they shall know that the Lord of hosts has sent him;* all that were Israelites indeed were made to know it; sufficient proofs were given of it by the miracles Christ wrought, so that they might have known it, and yet there were those that perished in ignorance and unbelief, that would not know it, for, *if they had known it, they would not have crucified the Lord of glory.*

III. They shall have all their ancient dignities and privileges restored to them again, v. 12. 1. Canaan shall be a holy land again, not polluted by sin as it had been formerly, not profaned by the enemies as it had been of late; it shall be an enclosure again, and not laid in common. 2. Judah shall be in this holy land, shall inhabit it, and enjoy the comfort of it, and no longer be lost and scattered in Babylon. 3. Judah shall be God's portion, which he will delight in, which shall be dear to him, by which he will be served, and in which he will be glorified. *The Lord's portion is his people.* 4. God will *inherit Judah* again as *his portion,* will claim his interest, and recover the possession out of the hands of those that had invaded his right. He will protect his people and govern them as a man does his inheritance, and will be at home among them. 5. He will *choose Jerusalem again,* as he had chosen it formerly, to *put his name there;* he will renew and confirm the choice, and continue it a chosen place, till it must resign its honours to the Jerusalem that is from above. Though the election seemed to be set aside for a while, yet it *shall obtain.*

II. Here is silence proclaimed to all the world besides, v. 13. The daughter of Zion must sing, but *all flesh* must *be silent.* Observe here, 1. A very awful description of God's appearances for the relief of his people. He is *raised up out of his holy habitation;* as a man out of sleep (Ps. xliv. 23; lxxviii. 65), or as a man entering with resolution upon a business that he will go through with. Heaven is his holy habitation above; thence we must expect him to appear, Isa. lxiv. 1. His temple is so in this lower world; thence from *between the cherubim* he will *shine forth,* Ps. lxxx. 1. He is about to do something unusual, unexpected, and very surprising, and to plead his people's cause, which had long seemed neglected. 2. A seasonable caution and direction at such a time: *Be silent, O all flesh! before the Lord* before Christ and his grace (let not flesh object against the methods he takes)—before God and his providence; the enemies of the church shall be silenced; all iniquity shall stop her mouth. The friends of the church also must be silent. Leave it to God to take his own way, and neither prescribe to him what he should do nor quarrel with him whatever he does. *Be still, and know that he is God. Stand still, and see his salvation.* See Hab. ii. 20; Zeph. i. 7. Silently acquiesce in his holy will, and patiently wait the issue, as those who are assured that when God is *raised up out of his holy habitation* he will not retreat, nor sit down again, till he has accomplished his whole work.

CHAP. III.

The vision in the foregoing chapter gave assurances of the re-establishing of the civil interests of the Jewish nation, the promises of which terminated in Christ. Now the vision in this chapter concerns their church-state, and their ecclesiastical interests, and assures them that they shall be put into a good posture again; and the promises of this also have an eye to Christ, who is not only our prince, but the high priest of our profession, of whom Joshua was a type. Here is, I. A vision relating to Joshua, as the representative of the church in his time, representing the disadvantages he laboured under, and the people in him, with the redress of the grievances of both. 1. He is accused by Satan, but is brought off by Christ, ver. 1, 2. 2. He appears in filthy garments, but has them changed, ver. 3—5. 3. He is assured of being established in his office if he conduct himself well, ver. 6, 7. II. A sermon relating to Christ, who is here called " The branch," who should be endued with all perfections for his undertaking, should be carried triumphantly through it, and by whom we should have pardon and peace, ver. 8—10.

AND he showed me Joshua the high priest standing before the angel of the LORD, and Satan standing at his right hand to resist him. 2 And the LORD said unto Satan, The LORD rebuke thee, O Satan; even the LORD that hath chosen Jerusalem rebuke thee: *is* not this a brand plucked out of the fire? 3 Now Joshua was clothed with filthy garments, and stood before the angel. 4 And he answered and spake unto those that stood before him, saying, Take away the filthy garments from him. And unto him he said, Behold, I have caused thine iniquity to pass from thee, and I will clothe thee with change of raiment. 5 And I said, Let them set a fair mitre upon his head. So they set a fair mitre upon his head, and clothed him with garments. And the angel of the LORD stood by. 6 And the angel of the LORD protested unto Joshua, saying, 7 Thus saith the LORD of hosts; If thou wilt walk in my ways, and if thou wilt keep my charge, then thou shalt also judge my house, and shalt also keep my courts, and I will give thee places to walk among these that stand by.

There was a Joshua that was a principal agent in the first settling of Israel in Canaan; here is another of the same name very active in their second settlement there after the captivity; Jesus is the same name, and it signifies *Saviour;* and they were both figures of him that was to come, our chief

1412

captain and our chief priest. The angel that talked with *Zechariah showed him Joshua the high priest;* it is probable that the prophet saw him frequently, that he spoke to him, and that there was a great intimacy between them; but, in his common views, he only saw how he appeared before men; if he must know how he stands before the Lord, it must be shown him in vision; and so it is shown him. And men are really as they are with God, not as they appear in the eye of the world. He stood *before the angel of the Lord,* that is, before Christ, the Lord of the angels, to whom even the high priests themselves, of Aaron's order, were accountable. He *stood before the angel of the Lord,* to execute his office, to minister to God under the inspection of the angels. He stood to consult the oracle on the behalf of Israel, for whom, as high priest, he was agent. Guilt and corruption are our two great discouragements when we stand before God. By the guilt of the sins committed by us we have become obnoxious to the justice of God; by the power of the sin that dwells in us we have become odious to the holiness of God. All God's Israel are in danger upon these two accounts. Joshua was so here, for *the law made men priests that had infirmity,* Heb. vii. 28. And, as to both, we have relief from Jesus Christ, who is made of God to us both *righteousness and sanctification.*

I. Joshua is accused as a criminal, but is justified. 1. A violent opposition is made to him. *Satan stands at his right hand to resist him,* to be a Satan to him, a law-adversary. He stands at his right hand, as the prosecutor, or witness, at the right hand of the prisoner. Note, The devil is the accuser of the brethren, that *accuses them before God day and night,* Rev. xii. 10. Some think the chief priest was accused for the sin of many of the inferior priests, in marrying strange wives, which they were much guilty of after their return out of captivity, Ezra ix. 1, 2; Neh. xiii. 28. When God is about to re-establish the priesthood Satan objects the sins that were found among the priests, as rendering them unworthy the honour designed them. It is by our own folly that we give Satan advantage against us and furnish him with matter for reproach and accusation; and if any thing be amiss, especially with the priests, Satan will be sure to aggravate it and make the worst of it. He *stood to resist him,* that is, to oppose the service he was doing for the public good. He stood *at his right hand,* the hand of action, to discourage him, and raise difficulties in his way. Note, When we stand before God to minister to him, or stand up for God to serve his interests, we must expect to meet with all the resistance that Satan's subtlety and malice can give us. Let us then resist him that resists us and he shall flee from us. 2. A victorious defence is made for him (*v.* 2): *The Lord* (that is, the Lord Christ) *said unto Satan, The Lord rebuke thee.* Note, It is the happiness of the saints that the Judge is their friend; the same that they are accused to is their patron and protector, and an advocate for them, and he will be sure to bring them off. (1.) Satan is here checked by one that has authority, that has conquered him, and many a time silenced him. *The accuser of the brethren,* of the ministers and the ministry, *is cast out;* his indictments are quashed, and his suggestions against them, as well as his suggestions to them, are shown to be malicious, frivolous, and vexatious. *The Lord rebuke thee, O Satan! The Lord said* (that is, the Lord our Redeemer), *The Lord rebuke thee,* that is, the Lord the Creator. The power of God is engaged for the making of the grace of Christ effectual. "*The Lord* restrain thy malicious rage, reject thy malicious charge, and revenge upon thee thy enmity to a servant of his." Note, those that belong to Christ have him ready to appear vigorously for them when Satan appears most vehement against them. He does not parley with him, but stops his mouth immediately with this sharp reprimand: *The Lord rebuke thee, O Satan!* This is the best way of dealing with that furious enemy. *Get thee behind me, Satan.* (2.) Satan is here argued with. He resists the priest, but let him know that his resistance, [1.] Will be fruitless; it will be to no purpose to attempt any thing against Jerusalem, for *the Lord has chosen* it, and he will abide by his choice. Whatever is objected against God's people, God saw it; he foresaw it when he chose them and yet he chose them, and therefore that can be no inducement to him now to reject them; he knew the worst of them when he chose them; and his election shall obtain. [2.] It is unreasonable; for *is not this a brand plucked out of the fire?* Joshua is so, and the priesthood, and the people, whose representative he is. Christ has not that to say for them for which they are to be praised, but that for which they are to be pitied. Note, Christ is ready to make the best of his people, and takes notice of every thing that is pleadable in excuse of their infirmities, so far is he from being extreme to mark what they do amiss. They have been lately in the fire; no wonder that they are black and smoked, and have the smell of fire upon them, but they are therefore to be excused, not to be accused. One can expect no other than that those who but the other day were captives in Babylon should appear very mean and despicable. They have been lately brought out of great affliction; and is Satan so barbarous as to desire to have them thrown into affliction again? They have been wonderfully delivered out of the fire, that God might be glorified in them; and will he then cast them off and abandon them? No, he

will not quench the smoking flax, the smoking fire-brand; for he snatched it out of the fire because he intended to make use of it. Note, Narrow escapes from imminent danger are happy presages and powerful pleas for more eminent favours. A converted soul is a *brand plucked out of the fire* by a miracle of free grace, and therefore shall not be left to be a prey to Satan.

II. Joshua appears as one polluted, but is purified; for he represents the Israel of God, who are all *as an unclean thing,* till they are washed and sanctified *in the name of the Lord Jesus* and *by the Spirit of our God.* Now observe here, 1. The impurity wherein Joshua appeared (*v.* 3): *He was clothed,* not only in coarse, but in *filthy garments,* such as did very ill become the dignity of his office and the sanctity of his work. By the law of Moses the garments of the high priest were to be *for glory and for beauty,* Exod. xxviii. 2. But Joshua's garments were a shame and reproach to him; yet in them *he stood before the angel of the Lord;* he had no clean linen wherein to minister and to do the duty of his place. Now this intimates, not only that the priesthood was poor and despised, and loaded with contempt, but that there was a great deal of iniquity cleaving to the holy things. The returned Jews were so taken up with their troubles that they thought they needed not complain of their sins, and were not aware that those were the great hindrances of the progress of God's work among them; because they were free from idolatry they thought themselves chargeable with no iniquity. But God showed them there were many things amiss in them, which retarded the advances of God's favours towards them. There were spiritual enemies warring against them, more dangerous than any of the neighbouring nations. The Chaldee paraphrase says, *Joshua had sons who took unto them wives which were not lawful for the priests to take;* and we find it was so, Ezra x. 18. And, no doubt, there were other things amiss in the priesthood, Mal. ii. 1. Yet Joshua was permitted to *stand before the angel of the Lord.* Though his children did not as they should, yet the covenant of priesthood was not broken. Note, Christ bears with his people, whose hearts are upright with him, and admits them into communion with himself, notwithstanding their manifold infirmities. 2. The provision that was made for his cleansing. Christ gave orders to the angels that attended him, and were ready to do his pleasure, to put Joshua into a better state. Joshua presented himself before the Lord in his filthy garments, as an object of his pity; and Christ graciously looked upon him with compassion, and not, as justly he might have done, with indignation. Christ loathed the filthiness of Joshua's garments, yet did not put him away, but put them away. Thus God by his grace does with those whom he chooses to be priests to himself; he parts between them and their sins, and so prevents their sins parting between them and their God; he reconciles himself to the sinner, but not to the sin. Two things are here done for Joshua, representing a double work of divine grace wrought in and for believers:—(1.) His filthy garments are taken from him, *v.* 4. The meaning of this is given us in what Christ said, and he said it as one having authority, *Behold, I have caused thy iniquity to pass from thee.* The guilt of it is taken away by pardoning mercy, the stench and stain of it by peace spoken to the conscience, and the power of it broken by renewing grace. When God forgives our sins he *causes our iniquity to pass from us,* that it may not appear against us, to condemn us; it passes from us *as far as the east is from the west.* When he sanctifies the nature he enables us to *put off the old man,* to cast away from us the filthy rags of our corrupt affections and lusts, as things we will never have any thing more to do with, will never gird to us or appear in. Thus Christ *washes those from their sins in his own blood* whom he *makes to our God kings and priests,* Rev. i. 5, 6. Either we must be cleansed from the pollutions of sin or we shall, *as polluted, be put from* that *priesthood,* Ezra ii. 62. (2.) He is clothed anew, has not only the shame of his filthiness removed, but the shame of his nakedness covered: *I will clothe thee with change of raiment.* Joshua had no clean linen of his own, but Christ will provide for him, for he will not let a priesthood of his own instituting be lost, be either contemptible before men or unacceptable before God. The change of raiment here is rich costly raiment, such as is worn on high days. Joshua shall appear as lovely as ever he appeared loathsome. Those that minister in holy things shall not only cease to do evil, but learn to do well; God will make them wise, and humble, and diligent, and faithful, and examples of every thing that is good; and then Joshua is clothed with change of raiment. Thus those whom Christ makes spiritual priests are clothed with the spotless robe of his righteousness and appear before God in that, and with the graces of his Spirit, which are ornaments to them. *The righteousness of saints,* both imputed and implanted, is the fine linen, clean and white, with which *the bride, the Lamb's wife,* is arrayed, Rev. xix. 8.

III. Joshua is in danger of being turned out of office; but, instead of that, he is reinstalled and established in his office. He not only has his sins pardoned, and is furnished with grace sufficient for himself, but, as *rectus in curia—acquitted in court,* he is restored to his former honours and trusts. 1. The crown of the priesthood is put upon him, *v.* 5. This was done at the special instance and request of the prophet: I said,

" Let them set a fair mitre upon his head, as a badge of his office. Now that he looks clean, let him also look great; let him be dressed up in all the garments of the high priest."* Note, When God designs the restoring or reviving of religion he stirs up his prophets and people to pray for it, and does it in answer to their prayers. Zechariah prayed that the angels might be ordered to set the mitre on Joshua's head, and they did it immediately, and *clothed him with* the priestly *garments;* for no man took this honour to himself, *but he that was called of God* to it. *The angel of the Lord stood by,* as having the oversight of the work which the created angels were employed in. He stood by, as one well pleased with it, and resolved to stand by the orders he had given for the doing of it and to continue his presence with that priesthood. 2. The covenant of the priesthood is renewed with him, which is called God's *covenant of peace,* Num. xxv. 12. Mr. Pemble calls it *the patent of his office,* which is here declared and delivered to him before witnesses, *v.* 6, 7. The angel of the Lord, having taken care to make him fit for his office (and all that God calls to any office he either finds fit or makes so), invests him in it. And though he is not *made a priest with an oath* (that honour is reserved for him who is a priest after the order of Melchisedek, Heb. vii. 21), yet, being a type of him, he is inaugurated with a solemn declaration of the terms upon which he held his office. The angel of the Lord protested to Joshua that, if he would be sure to do the duty of his place, he should enjoy the dignity and reward of it. Now see, (1.) What the conditions are upon which he enters into his office. Let him know that he is upon his good behaviour; he must *walk in God's ways,* that is, he must live a good life and be holy in all manner of conversation; he must go before the people in the paths of God's commandments, and walk circumspectly. He must also *keep God's charge,* must carefully do all the services of the priesthood, and must see to it that the inferior priests performed the duties of their place decently and in order. He must *take heed to himself, and to all the flock,* Acts xx. 28. Note, Good ministers must be good Christians; yet that is not enough: they have a trust committed to them, they are charged with it, and they must keep it with all possible care, that they may give up their account of it with joy, 1 Tim. vi. 14. (2.) What the privileges are which we may expect, and be assured of, in the due discharge of his office. His patent runs, *Quamdiu se bene gesserit—During good behaviour.* Let him be sure to do his part, and God will own him. [1.] *" Thou shalt judge my house;* thou shalt preside in the affairs of the temple, and the inferior priests shall be under thy direction." Note, The power of the church, and of church

rulers, is not a legislative, but only a judicial power. The high priest might not make any new laws for God's house, nor ordain any other rites of worship than what God had ordained; but he must judge God's house, that is, he must see to it that God's laws and ordinances were punctually observed, must protect and encourage those that did observe them, and enquire into and punish the violation of them. [2.] *" Thou shalt also keep my courts ;* thou shalt have oversight of what is done in all the courts of the temple, and shalt keep them pure and in good order for the worship to be performed in them."* Note, Ministers are God's stewards, and they are to keep his courts, in honour of him who is the chief Lord and for the preserving of equity and good order among his tenants. [3.] *" I will give thee places to walk among those that stand by,* among these angels that are inspectors and assistants in this instalment." They shall stand by while Joshua is at work for God, and shall be as a guard to him, or he shall be highly honoured and respected as an *angel of God,* Gal. iv. 14. Ministers are called *angels,* Rev. i. 20. Those that *walk in God's ways* may be said to *walk among the angels* themselves, for they do the will of God as the angels do it that are in heaven, and are their *fellow-servants,* Rev. xix. 10. Some make it a promise of eternal life, and of a reward of his fidelity in the future state. Heaven is not only a palace, a place to repose in, but a paradise, a garden, a place to walk in; and there are walks among the angels, in society with that holy and glorious company. See Ezek. xxviii. 14.

8 Hear now, O Joshua the high priest, thou, and thy fellows that sit before thee: for they *are* men wondered at: for, behold, I will bring forth my servant, The BRANCH. 9 For behold the stone that I have laid before Joshua; upon one stone *shall be* seven eyes: behold, I will engrave the graving thereof, saith the LORD of hosts, and I will remove the iniquity of that land in one day. 10 In that day, saith the LORD of hosts, shall ye call every man his neighbour under the vine and under the fig-tree.

As the promises made to David often slide insensibly into promises of the Messiah, whose kingdom David's was a type of, so the promises here made to Joshua immediately rise as far upward, and look as far forward, as to Christ, whose priesthood Joshua's was now a shadow of, not only in general, as it kept up the line of Aaron's priesthood, but especially as it was the reviving of that happy method of correspondence between heaven and earth, to which a great interruption had been given by the iniquity and captivity of Israel. Christ is a high priest, as Joshua was, for sinners and sufferers, to mediate for those that have been under guilt and wrath. And it was fit that Joshua should understand the priesthood of Christ, because all the virtue of his priesthood, its value and usefulness to the church, depended upon and was derived from the priesthood of Christ. See,

I. To whom this promise of Christ is directed (*v.* 8): *" Hear now, O Joshua !* Thou hast heard with pleasure what belongs to thyself; but, behold, a greater than Joshua is at hand. *Hear now* concerning him, *thou* and the rest of the priests, *thy fellows, who sit before thee,* at thy feet, as learners, but whom thou art to look upon as *thy fellows,* for all you are brethren; let the high priest, and all the inferior priests, take notice of this, for they are *men wondered at."* They are set *for signs,* for types and figures of Christ's priesthood. What God now did for Joshua and his fellows was a happy omen of the coming of the Messiah promised, and would be so interpreted, with a pleasing wonder, by all that had understanding of the times. Or they are men *wondered at* for their singularity, hooted at as strange sort of people, because they *run not with others to the same excess of riot* (1 Pet. iv. 4), or for their strange afflictions and surprising deliverance out of them, as Ps. lxxi. 7, *I am as a wonder unto many.* They are *men of wonder ;* they are a wonder to themselves, are amazed to think how happily their condition is altered. God's people and ministers are, upon many accounts, men wondered at. The high priest and his fellows here (as the prophet and his children, Isa. viii. 18) are for signs and for wonders. But men's wonder at them will cease when the Messiah comes, as the stars are eclipsed by the light of the sun; for *his name shall be called Wonderful.*

II. The promise itself, which consists of several parts, all designed for the comfort and encouragement of Joshua and his friends in that great good work of building the temple, which they were now engaged in. An eye to Christ, and a believing dependence upon the promises relating to him and his kingdom, would carry them through the difficulties they met with in that and their other services. 1. The Messiah shall come : *Behold, I will bring forth my servant the branch.* He has been long hid, but the fulness of time is now at hand, when he shall be brought forth into the world, brought forth among his people Israel. God himself undertakes to bring him forth, and therefore, no doubt, he will own him and stand by him. He is God's servant, employed in his work, obedient to his will, and entirely devoted to his honour and glory. He is the branch ; so he was called Isa. iv. 2, *The branch of the Lord.* Isa. xi. 1, *A branch out of the roots*

of Jesse. Jer. xxiii. 5, *A righteous branch;* and Jer. xxiii. 15, *The branch of righteousness.* His beginning was small, as a tender branch, but in time he should become a great tree and fill the earth, Isa. liii 2. He is the branch from which all our fruit must be gathered. 2. Many eyes shall be upon him. He is *the stone laid before Joshua,* alluding to the foundation, or chief corner-stone, of the temple, which probably was laid, with great solemnity, in the presence of Joshua. Christ is not only the branch, which is the beginning of a tree, but the foundation, which is the beginning of a building; and, when he shall be brought forth, *seven eyes shall be upon him.* The eye of his Father was upon him, to take care of him, and protect him, especially in his sufferings; when he was buried in the grave, as the foundation-stones are under ground, the eyes of Heaven were still upon him, buried out of men's sight, but not out of God's. The eyes of all the prophets and Old-Testament saints were upon this one stone; Abraham rejoiced to see Christ's day, and he *saw it and was glad.* The eyes of all believers are upon him; they look unto him and are saved, as the eyes of the stung Israelites were upon the brazen serpent. Some understand this *one stone* to have the seven eyes in it as the wheels had in Ezekiel's vision, and think it denotes that perfection of wisdom and knowledge which Jesus Christ was endued with, for the good of his church. *His eyes run to and fro through the earth.* 3. God himself will beautify him, and put honour upon him: *I will engrave the graving thereof, saith the Lord of hosts.* This stone the builders refused, as rough and unsightly; but God undertakes to smooth and polish it, nay, and to carve it so that it shall be the *head stone of the corner,* the most beautiful in all the building. Christ was God's workmanship; and abundance of his wisdom appears in the contrivance of our redemption, which will appear when the engraving is perfected. This stone is a *precious stone,* though laid for a *foundation;* and the *graving* of it seems to allude to the precious stones in the breast-plate of the high priest, which had the names of the tribes *graven* upon them, as the *engraving of a signet,* Exod. xxviii. 21, 22. In that breast-plate there were twelve stones laid before Aaron, and for aught that appears those were lost; but there shall be one worth them all laid before Joshua, and that is Christ himself. This precious stone shall sparkle as if it had seven eyes; there shall appear a perfection of wisdom and prudence in the oracles that proceed from the breast-plate of judgment. And God will *engrave the engraving thereof;* he will entrust Christ with all his elect, and he shall appear as their representative, and agent for them, as the high priest did when he went in before the Lord with the names of all Israel engraven in the precious stones of his breast-plate.
1416

When God gave a remnant to Christ, to be brought through grace to glory, then he *engraved the graving* of this *precious stone.* 4. By him sin shall be taken away, both the guilt and the dominion of it: *I will remove the iniquity of that land in one day.* When the high priest had the names of Israel engraven on the precious stones he was adorned with he is said to *bear the iniquity of the holy things* (Exod. xxviii. 38); but the law *made nothing perfect,* Heb. x. 1. He bore the iniquity of the land, as a type of Christ; but he could not remove it; the doing of that was reserved for Christ, that blessed *Lamb of God, that takes away the sin of the world;* and he did it *in one day,* that day in which he suffered and died; that was done by the sacrifice offered that day which could not be done by the sacrifices of ages before, no, nor by all the days of atonement which from Moses to Christ returned every year. This agrees with the angel's prediction (Dan. ix. 24): He shall *finish transgression and make an end of sin.* And some make the engravings wherewith God engraved him to signify the wounds and stripes which were given to his blessed body, which he underwent for our *transgression,* for our *iniquity,* and *by which we are healed.* 5. The effect of all this shall be the sweet enjoyment which all believers shall have of themselves, and the sweet communion they shall have with one another (*v.* 10): *In that day you shall call every man his neighbour under the vine and the fig-tree,* which yield most pleasant fruit, and whose leaves also afford a refreshing shade for arbours. When iniquity is taken away, (1.) We reap precious benefits and privileges from our justification, more precious than the products of the vine or the fig-tree, Rom. v. 1. (2.) We repose in a sweet tranquillity and are quiet from the fear of evil. What should terrify us when iniquity is taken away, when nothing can hurt us? We sit down under Christ's shadow with delight, and by it are sheltered from the scorching heat of the curse of the law. We live as Israel in the peaceable reign of Solomon (1 Kings iv. 24, 25); for he is the prince of peace. (3.) We ought to invite others to come to partake with us in the enjoyment of these privileges, to *call every man his neighbour* to come and sit with him, for mutual converse, under the vine and fig-tree, and to share with him in the fruits he is surrounded with. Gospel-grace, as far as it comes with power, makes men neighbourly; and those that have the comfort of acquaintance with Christ themselves, and communion with God through him, will be forward to court others to it. *Let us go unto the house of the Lord.*

CHAP. IV.

In this chapter we have another comfortable vision, which, as it was explained to the prophet, had much in it for the encouragement of the people of God in their present straits, which were so great that they thought their case helpless, that their temple could never be rebuilt nor their city replenished; and therefore the scope of the vision is to show that God would, by his own power, perfect the work, though the assistance given to it by its friends were ever so weak, and the resistance given to it by its enemies were ever so strong.　Here is, I. The awakening of the prophet to observe the vision, ver. 1. II. The vision itself, of a candlestick with seven lamps, which were supplied with oil, and kept burning, immediately from two olive-trees that grew by it, one on either side, ver. 2, 3. III. The general encouragement hereby intended to be given to the builders of the temple to go on in that good work, assuring them that it should be brought to perfection at last, ver. 4—10. IV. The particular explication of the vision, for the illustration of these assurances, ver. 11—14.

AND the angel that talked with me came again, and waked me, as a man that is wakened out of his sleep, 2 And said unto me, What seest thou? And I said, I have looked, and behold a candlestick all *of* gold, with a bowl upon the top of it, and his seven lamps thereon, and seven pipes to the seven lamps, which *are* upon the top thereof: 3 And two olive-trees by it, one upon the right *side* of the bowl, and the other upon the left *side* thereof. 4 So I answered and spake to the angel that talked with me, saying, What *are* these, my lord? 5 Then the angel that talked with me answered and said unto me, Knowest thou not what these be? And I said, No, my lord. 6 Then he answered and spake unto me, saying, This *is* the word of the LORD unto Zerubbabel, saying, Not by might, nor by power, but by my Spirit, saith the LORD of hosts. 7 Who *art* thou, O great mountain? before Zerubbabel *thou shalt become* a plain: and he shall bring forth the head stone *thereof with* shoutings, *crying,* Grace, grace unto it. 8 Moreover the word of the LORD came unto me, saying, 9 The hands of Zerubbabel have laid the foundation of this house; his hands shall also finish it; and thou shalt know that the LORD of hosts hath sent me unto you. 10 For who hath despised the day of small things? for they shall rejoice, and shall see the plummet in the hand of Zerubbabel *with* those seven; they *are* the eyes of the LORD, which run to and fro through the whole earth.

Here is, I. The prophet prepared to receive the discovery that was to be made to him: *The angel that talked with him came and waked him, v.* 1. It seems, though he was in conference with an angel, and about matters of great and public concern, yet he grew dull and fell asleep, as it should seem, while the angel was yet talking with him. Thus the

disciples, when they saw Christ transfigured, *were heavy with sleep,* Luke ix. 32. The prophet's spirit, no doubt, was willing to attend to that which was to be seen and heard, but the flesh was weak; his body could not keep pace with his soul in divine contemplations; the strangeness of the visions perhaps stupified him, and so he was overcome with sleep, or perhaps the sweetness of the visions composed him and even sung him asleep. Daniel was in a *deep sleep when he heard the voice of the angel's words,* Dan. x. 9. We shall never be fit for converse with spirits till we have got clear of these bodies of flesh. It should seem, the angel let him lose himself a little, that he might be fresh to receive new discoveries, but then *waked him,* to his surprise, *as a man that is wakened out of his sleep.* Note, We need the Spirit of God, not only to make known to us divine things, but to make us take notice of them. *He wakens morning by morning, he wakens my ear,* Isa. l. 4. We should beg of God that, whenever he speaks to us, he would awaken us, and we should then *stir up ourselves.*

II. The discovery that was made to him when he was thus prepared. The angel asked him, *What seest thou? v.* 2. When he was awake perhaps he would not have taken notice of what was presented to his view if he had not thus been excited to look about him. When he observed he saw a *golden candlestick,* such a one as was in the temple formerly, and with the like this temple should in due time be furnished. The church is a candlestick, set up for the enlightening of this dark world and the holding forth of the light of divine revelation to it. The candle is God's; the church is but the candlestick, but all of gold, denoting the great worth and excellence of the church of God. This golden candlestick had *seven lamps* branching out from it, so many sockets, in each of which was a burning and shining light. The Jewish church was but one, and though the Jews that were dispersed, it is probable, had synagogues in other countries, yet they were but as so many lamps belonging to one candlestick; but now, under the gospel, Christ is the centre of unity, and not Jerusalem, or any one place; and therefore seven particular churches are represented, not as *seven lamps,* but as seven several *golden candlesticks,* Rev. i. 20. This candlestick had one *bowl,* or common receiver, on the top, into which oil was continually dropping, and from it, by seven secret pipes, or passages, it was diffused to the seven lamps, so that, without any further care, they received oil as fast as they wasted it (as in those which we call *fountain-ink-horns,* or *fountain-pens) ;* they never wanted, nor were ever glutted, and so kept always burning clear. And the bowl too was continually supplied, without any care or attendance of man; for (*v.* 3) he saw *two*

1417

olive-trees, one on each side the candlestick, that were so fat and fruitful that of their own accord they poured plenty of oil continually into the bowl, which by two larger pipes (*v.* 12) dispersed the oil to smaller ones and so to the lamps; so that nobody needed to attend this candlestick, to furnish it with oil (it tarried not for man, nor waited for the sons of men), the scope of which is to show that God easily can, and often does, accomplish his gracious purposes concerning his church by his own wisdom and power, without any art or labour of man, and that though sometimes he makes use of instruments, yet he neither needs them nor is tied to them, but can do his work without them, and will rather than it shall be undone.

III. The enquiry which the prophet made concerning the meaning of this, and the gentle reproof given him for his dulness (*v.* 4): *I answered and spoke to the angel*, saying, *What are these, my lord?* Observe how respectfully he speaks to the angel; he calls him *my lord*. Those that would be taught must give honour to their teachers. He saw what these *were*, but asked what these *signified*. Note, It is very desirable to know the meaning of God's manifestations of himself and his mind both in his word and by his ordinances and providences. *What mean you by these* services, by these signs? And those that would understand the mind of God must be inquisitive. *Then shall we know if we follow on to know*, if we not only *hear*, but, as Christ, *ask questions* upon what we hear, Luke ii. 46. The angel answered him with a question, *Knowest thou not what these be?* intimating that if he had considered, and compared spiritual things with spiritual, he might have guessed at the meaning of these things; for he knew that there was a golden candlestick in the tabernacle, which it was the priests' constant business to supply with oil and to keep burning, for the use of the tabernacle; when therefore he saw, in vision, such a candlestick, with lamps always kept burning, and yet no priests to attend it, nor any occasion for them, he might discern the meaning of this to be that though God had set up the priesthood again, yet he could carry on his own work for and in his people without them. Note, We have reason to be ashamed of ourselves that we do not more readily apprehend the meaning of divine discoveries. The angel asked the prophet this question, to draw from him an acknowledgment of his own dulness, and darkness, and slowness to understand, and he had it immediately: "*I said, No, my lord;* I know not what these are." Visions had their significance, but often dark and hard to be understood, and the prophets themselves were not always aware of it at first. But those that would be taught of God must see and acknowledge their own ignorance, and their need to be taught, and must apply to God for instruction. To him that gave us

the cabinet we must apply for the key wherewith to unlock it. God will teach the meek and humble, not those that are conceited of themselves and lean on the broken reed of their own understanding.

IV. The general intention of this vision. Without a critical descant upon every circumstance of the vision, the design of it is to assure the prophet, and by him the people, that this good work of building the temple should, by the special care of divine Providence, and the immediate influence of divine grace, be brought to a happy issue, though the enemies of it were many and mighty and the friends and furtherers of it few and feeble. Note, In the explication of visions and parables, we must look at the principal scope of them, and be satisfied with that, if that be clear, though we may not be able to account for every circumstance, or accommodate it to our purpose. The angel lets the prophet know, in general, that this vision was designed to illustrate a word which the Lord had to say to Zerubbabel, to encourage him to go on with the building of the temple. Let him know that he is a worker together with God in it, and that it is a work which God will own and crown.

1. God will carry on and complete this work, as he had begun their deliverance from Babylon, not by external force, but by secret operations and internal influences upon the minds of men. *He* says this who is the *Lord of hosts*, and could do it *vi et armis—by force*, has legions at command; but he will do it, *not by* human *might or power*, but *by his own Spirit*. What is done by his Spirit is done by might and power, but it stands in opposition to visible force. Israel was brought out of Egypt, and into Canaan, by might and power; in both these works of wonder great slaughter was made. But they were brought out of Babylon, and into Canaan the second time, *by the Spirit of the Lord of hosts* working upon the spirit of Cyrus, and inclining him to proclaim liberty to them, and working upon the spirits of the captives, and inclining them to accept the liberty offered them. It was by the *Spirit of the Lord of hosts* that the people were excited and animated to build the temple; and *therefore* they are said to be *helped by the prophets of God*, because they, as the Spirit's mouth, spoke to their hearts, Ezra v. 2. It was by the same Spirit that the heart of Darius was inclined to favour and further that good work and that the sworn enemies of it were infatuated in their councils, so that they could not hinder it as they designed. Note, The work of God is often carried on very successfully when yet it is carried on very silently, and without the assistance of human force; the gospel-temple is built, not by might or power (for *the weapons of our warfare are not carnal*), but by the *Spirit of the Lord of hosts*, whose work on men's consciences is mighty to the pulling down of

strong holds; thus the excellency of the power is of God, and not of man. When instruments fail, let us therefore leave it to God to do his work himself by his own Spirit.

2. All the difficulties and oppositions that lie in the way shall be got over and removed, even those that seem insuperable (*v.* 7) : *Who art thou, O great mountain? Before Zerubbabel thou shalt become a plain.* See here, (1.) How the difficulty is represented ; it is a *great mountain,* impassable and immovable, a heap of rubbish, like a great mountain, which must be got away, or the work cannot go on. The enemies of the Jews are proud and hard as great mountains ; but, when God has work to do, the mountains that stand in the way of it shall dwindle into mole-hills ; for see here, (2.) How these difficulties are despised : " *Who art thou, O great mountain!* that thou shouldst stand in God's way and think to stop the progress of his work? Who art thou that lookest so big, that thus threatenest, and art thus feared? *Before Zerubbabel,* when he is God's agent, *thou shalt become a plain.* All the difficulties shall vanish, and all the objections be got over. *Every mountain and hill* shall be *brought low* when the *way of the Lord* is to be *prepared,*" Isa. xl. 4. Faith will remove mountains and make them plains. Christ is our Zerubbabel ; mountains of difficulty were in the way of his undertaking, but before him they were all levelled ; nothing is too hard for his grace to do.

3. The same hand that has begun this good work will perform it : *He shall bring forth the head-stone* (*v.* 7) ; and again (*v.* 9), *The hands of Zerubbabel have laid the foundation of this house,* be it spoken to his honour (perhaps with his own hands he laid the first stone), and though it has been long retarded, and is still much opposed, yet it shall be finished at last ; he shall live to see it finished, nay, and *his hands shall also finish it ;* herein he is a type of Christ, who is both the *author* and the *finisher of our faith ;* and his being the *author* of it is an assurance to us that he will be the *finisher,* for, *as for God, his work is perfect ;* has he begun and shall he not make an end? Zerubbabel shall himself *bring forth the head-stone with shoutings,* and loud acclamations of joy, among the spectators. The acclamations are not *huzzas,* but *Grace, grace ;* that is the burden of the triumphant songs which the church sings. It may be taken, (1.) As magnifying free grace, and giving to that all the glory of what is done. When the work is finished it must be thankfully acknowledged that it was not by any policy or power of our own that it was brought to perfection, but that it was grace that did it—God's good-will towards us and his good work in us and for us. *Grace, grace,* must be cried, not only to the head-stone, but to the foundation-stone, the corner-stone, and indeed to every stone in God's building ; from first to last it is no-

thing of works, but all of grace, and all our crowns must be cast at the feet of free grace. *Not unto us, O Lord! not unto us.* (2.) As depending upon free grace, and desiring the continuance of it, for what is yet to be done. *Grace, grace,* is the language of prayer as well as of praise ; now that this building is finished, all happiness attend it ! Peace be within its walls, and, in order to that, *grace.* Let the beauty of the Lord our God be upon it ! Note, What comes from the grace of God may, in faith, and upon good grounds, be committed to the grace of God, for God will not forsake the work of his own hands.

4. This shall be a full ratification of the prophecies which went before concerning the Jews' return, and their settlement again. When the temple is finished then *thou shalt know that the Lord of hosts has sent me unto you.* Note, The exact accomplishment of scripture prophecies is a convincing proof of their divine original. Thus God *confirms the word of his servant,* by *saying to Jerusalem, Thou shalt be built,* Isa. xliv. 26. No word of God shall fall to the ground, nor shall there fail one iota or tittle of it. Zechariah's prophecies of the approaching day of deliverance to the church would soon appear, by the accomplishment of them, to be of God.

5. This shall effectually silence those that looked with contempt upon the beginning of this work, *v.* 10. Who, where, is he now that despised the day of small things, and thought this work would never come to any thing? The Jews themselves despised the foundation of the second temple, because it was likely to be so far inferior to the first, Ezra iii. 12. Their enemies despised the wall when it was in the building, Neh. ii. 19 ; iv. 2, 3. But let them not do it. Note, In God's work the day of small things is not to be despised. Though the instruments be weak and unlikely, God often chooses such, by them to bring about great things. As a great mountain becomes a plain before him when he pleases, so a little stone, cut out of a mountain without hands, comes to fill the earth, Dan. ii. 35. Though the beginnings be small, God can make the latter end greatly to increase ; a grain of mustard-seed may become a great tree. Let not the dawning light be despised, for it will shine more and more to the perfect day. The day of small things is the day of precious things, and will be the day of great things.

6. This shall abundantly satisfy all the hearty well-wishers to God's interest, who will be glad to see themselves mistaken in *despising the day of small things.* Those that despaired of the finishing of the work shall rejoice when they *see the plummet in the hand of Zerubbabel,* when they see him busy among the builders, giving orders and directions what to do, and taking care that the work be done with great exactness, that it may be both fine and firm. Note, It is matter of great rejoicing to all good people

to see magistrates careful and active for the edifying of the house of God, to see the plummet in the hand of those who have power to do much, if they have but a heart according to it; we see not Zerubbabel with the trowel in his hand (that is left to the workmen, the ministers), but we see him with the plummet in his hand, and it is no disparagement, but an honour to him. Magistrates are to inspect ministers' work, and to speak comfortably to the Levites that do their duty.

7. This shall highly magnify the wisdom and care of God's providence, which is always employed for the good of his church. Zerubbabel does his part, does as much as man can do to forward the work, but it is *with those seven, those seven eyes of the Lord* which we read of *ch.* iii. 9. He could do nothing if the watchful, powerful, gracious providence of God did not go before him and go along with him in it. Except the Lord had built this house, Zerubbabel and the rest would have *laboured in vain*, Ps. cxxvii. 1. These *eyes of the Lord* are those that *run to and fro through the whole earth*, that take cognizance of all the creatures and all their actions (2 Chron. xvi. 9), and inspire and direct all, according to the divine counsels. Note, We must not think that God is so taken up with the affairs of his church as to neglect the world; but it is a comfort to us that the same all-wise almighty Providence that governs the nations of the earth is in a particular manner conversant about the church. Those *seven eyes* that *run through the earth* are all *upon the stone* that Zerubbabel is laying straight with his plummet, to see that it be well laid. And those that have the plummet in their hand must look up to *those eyes of the Lord*, must have a constant regard to divine Providence, and act in dependence upon its guidance and submission to its disposals.

11 Then answered I, and said unto him, What *are* these two olive-trees upon the right *side* of the candlestick and upon the left *side* thereof? 12 And I answered again, and said unto him, What *be these* two olive-branches which through the two golden pipes empty the golden *oil* out of themselves? 13 And he answered me and said, Knowest thou not what these *be*? And I said, No, my lord. 14 Then said he, These *are* the two anointed ones, that stand by the Lord of the whole earth.

Enough is said to Zechariah to encourage him, and to enable him to encourage others, with reference to the good work of building the temple which they were now about, and that was the principal intention of the vision

he saw; but still he is inquisitive about the particulars, which we will ascribe, not to any vain curiosity, but to the value he had for divine discoveries and the pleasure he took in acquainting himself with them. Those that know much of the things of God cannot but have a humble desire to know more. Now observe,

I. What his enquiry was. He understood the meaning of the candlestick with its lamps: It is Jerusalem, it is the temple, and their salvation that is to *go forth as a lamp that burns;* but he wants to know what are these *two olive-trees* (*v.* 11), these *two olive-branches?* v. 12. Observe here, 1. He asked. Note, Those that would be acquainted with the things of God must be inquisitive concerning those things. Ask, and you shall be told. 2. He asked twice, his first question having no reply given to it. Note, If satisfactory answers be not given to our enquiries and requests quickly, we must renew them, and repeat them, and continue instant and importunate in them, and the vision shall at length *speak, and not lie*. 3. His second query varied somewhat from the former. He first asked, What are *these two olive-trees*, but afterwards, *What are these two olive-branches?* that is, those boughs of the tree that hung over the bowl and distilled oil into it. When we enquire concerning the grace of God, it must be rather as it is communicated to us by the fruitful boughs of the word and ordinances (for that is one of the *things revealed*, which *belong to us and to our children*) than as it is resident in the good olive where all our springs are, for that is one of the *secret things*, which *belong not to us*. 4. In his enquiry he mentioned the observations he had made upon the vision; he took notice not only of what was obvious at first sight, that the two olive-trees grew, one *on the right side and the other on the left side of the candlestick* (so nigh, so ready, is divine grace to the church), but he observed further, upon a more narrow inspection, that the *two olive-branches*, from which in particular the candlestick did receive of *the root and fatness of the olive* (as the apostle says of the church, Rom. xi. 17), did empty the *golden oil* (that is, the clear bright oil, the best in its kind, and of great value, as if it were *aurum potabile—liquid gold*) *out of themselves through the two golden pipes*, or (as the margin reads it) which *by the hand of the two golden pipes empty out of themselves oil into the gold*, that is, into the *golden bowl* on the head of the candlestick. Our Lord Jesus emptied himself, to fill us; his precious blood is the golden oil in which we are supplied with all we need.

II. What answer was given to his enquiry. Now again the angel obliged him expressly to own his ignorance, before he informed him (*v.* 13): "*Knowest thou not what these are?* If thou knowest the church to be the candlestick, canst thou think the olive-trees, that supply it with oil, to be any other than the grace of God?" But he owned he either did not fully understand it or was afraid he did not rightly understand it: *I said, No, my Lord, how should I, except some one guide me?* And then he told him (*v.* 14): *These are the two sons of oil* (so it is in the original), *the two anointed ones* (so we read it), rather, *the two oily ones.* That which we read (Isa. v. 1) a *very fruitful hill* is in the original *the horn of the son of oil,* a fat and fattening soil. 1. If by the candlestick we understand the visible church, particularly that of the Jews at that time, for whose comfort it was primarily intended, these *sons of oil,* that *stand before the Lord of the whole earth,* are the two great ordinances and offices of the magistracy and ministry, at that time lodged in the hands of those two great and good men Zerubbabel and Joshua. Kings and priests were anointed; this prince, this priest, were *oily ones,* endued with the gifts and graces of God's Spirit, to qualify them for the work to which they were called. They *stood before the Lord of the whole earth,* to minister to him, and to receive direction from him; and a great influence they had upon the affairs of the church at that time. Their wisdom, courage, and zeal, were continually emptying themselves into the golden bowl, to keep the lamps burning; and, when they are gone, others shall be raised up to carry on the same work; Israel shall no longer be without prince and priest. Good magistrates and good ministers that are themselves anointed with the grace of God and *stand by the Lord of the whole earth,* as faithful adherents to his cause, contribute very much to the maintaining and advancing of religion and the shining forth of the word of life. 2. If by the candlestick we understand the church of the first-born, of true believers, these sons of oil may be meant of Christ and the Spirit, the Redeemer and the Comforter. Christ is not only the Messiah, the *Anointed One* himself, but he is the *good olive* to his church; and *from his fulness we receive,* John i. 16. And the Holy Spirit is the *unction* or *anointing* which we have received, 1 John ii. 20, 27. From Christ, the *olive tree,* by the *Spirit, the olive branch,* all the golden oil of grace is communicated to believers, which keeps their lamps burning, and without a constant supply of which they would soon go out. They *stand by the Lord of the whole earth,* who is in a special manner the church's Lord; for the Son was to be sent by the Father, and so was the Holy Ghost, in the time appointed, and they stand by him ready to go.

CHAP. V.

Hitherto we have seen visions of peace only, and all the words we have heard have been good words and comfortable words. But the pillar of cloud and fire has a black and dark side towards the Egyptians, as well as a bright and pleasant side towards Israel; so have Zechariah's visions; for God's prophets are not only his ambassadors, to treat of peace with the sons of peace, but heralds, to proclaim war against those that delight in war, and persist in their rebellion. In this chapter we have two visions, by which "the wrath of God is revealed from heaven against all ungodliness and unrighteousness of men." God will do great and kind things for his people, which the faithful sons of Zion shall rejoice in; but " let the sinners in Zion be afraid;" for, I. God will reckon severely with those particular persons among them that are wicked and profane, and that hated to be reformed in these times of reformation; while God is showing kindness to the body of the nation, and loading that with his blessings, they and their families shall, notwithstanding that, lie under the curse, which the prophet sees in a flying roll, ver. 1—4. II. If the body of the nation hereafter degenerate, and wickedness prevail among them, it shall be carried off and hurried away with a swift destruction, under the pressing weight of divine wrath, represented by a talent of lead upon the mouth of an ephah, carried upon the wing I know not where, ver. 5—11.

THEN I turned, and lifted up mine eyes, and looked, and behold a flying roll. 2 And he said unto me, What seest thou? And I answered, I see a flying roll; the length thereof *is* twenty cubits, and the breadth thereof ten cubits. 3 Then said he unto me, This *is* the curse that goeth forth over the face of the whole earth: for every one that stealeth shall be cut off *as* on this side according to it; and every one that sweareth shall be cut off *as* on that side according to it. 4 I will bring it forth, saith the Lord of hosts, and it shall enter into the house of the thief, and into the house of him that sweareth falsely by my name: and it shall remain in the midst of his house, and shall consume it with the timber thereof and the stones thereof.

We do not find that the prophet now needed to be awakened, as he did *ch.* iv. 1. Being awakened then, he kept wakeful after; nay, now he needs not be so much as called to look about him, for of his own accord he *turns and lifts up his eyes.* This good men sometimes get by their infirmities, they make them the more careful and circumspect afterwards. Now observe,

I. What it was that the prophet saw; he looked up into the air, and *behold a flying roll.* A vast large scroll of parchment which had been rolled up, and is therefore called a *roll,* was now unrolled and expanded; this roll was flying upon the wings of the wind, carried swiftly through the air in open view, as an eagle that shoots down upon her prey; it was a *roll,* like Ezekiel's that was *written within and without* with *lamentations, and mourning, and woe,* Ezek. ii. 9, 10. As the command of the law is in writing, for certainty and perpetuity, so is the *curse of the law;* it *writes bitter things* against the sinner. "What I have written I have written and what is written remains." The angel, to engage the prophet's attention, and to raise in him a desire to have it explained, asks him *what he sees?* And he gives him this account of it: *I see a flying roll,* and as near as he can guess by his eye it is *twenty cubits long* (that is, ten yards) and *ten cubits broad,* that is, five yards. The scriptures of the Old Testament and the New are *rolls*, in which God has *written to us the great things of his law* and gospel. Christ is the Master of the rolls. They are large rolls, have much in them. They are *flying* rolls; the angel that had *the everlasting gospel to preach flew in the midst of heaven*, Rev. xiv. 6. God's word *runs very swiftly*, Ps. cxlvii. 15. Those that would be let into the meaning of these rolls must first tell what they see, must go as far as they can themselves. *"What is written in the law? how readest thou?* Tell me that, and then thou shalt be made to *understand what thou readest."*

II. How it was expounded to him, *v.* 3, 4. This flying roll is a *curse:* it contains a declaration of the righteous wrath of God against those sinners especially who by swearing affront God's majesty or by stealing invade their neighbour's property. Let every Israelite rejoice in the blessings of his country with trembling; for if he swear, if he steal, if he live in any course of sin, he shall see them with his eyes, but shall not have the comfort of them, for against him the curse has gone forth. *If I be wicked, woe to me* for all this. Now observe here,

1. The extent of this curse; the prophet sees it flying, but which way does it steer its course? It *goes forth over the face of the whole earth*, not only of the land of Israel, but the *whole world:* for those that have sinned against the *law written in their hearts* only shall by that law be judged, though they have not the book of the law. Note, All mankind are liable to the judgment of God; and, wherever sinners are, any where upon the face of the whole earth, the curse of God can and will find them out and seize them. Oh that we could with an eye of faith see the flying roll of God's curse hanging over the guilty world as a thick cloud, not only keeping off the sun-beams of God's favour from them, but big with thunders, lightnings, and storms, ready to destroy them! How welcome then would the tidings of a Saviour be, who came to *redeem us from the curse of the law* by being himself *made a curse for us,* and, like the prophet, *eating this roll!* The vast length and breadth of this roll intimate what a multitude of curses sinners lie exposed to. God will make their plagues wonderful, if *they turn not.*

2. The criminals against whom particularly this curse is levelled. The world is full of sin in great variety: so was the Jewish church at this time. But two sorts of sinners are here specified as the objects of this curse:—(1.) Thieves; it is *for every one that steals*, that by fraud or force takes that which is not his own, especially that robs God and converts to his own use what was devoted to God and his honour, which was a sin much complained of among the Jews at this time, Mal. iii. 8; Neh. xiii. 10. Sacrilege is, without doubt,

the worst kind of thievery. He also that *robs his father or mother, and saith, It is no transgression* (Prov. xxviii. 24), let him know that against him this curse is directed, for it is against *every one that steals.* The letter of the eighth commandment has no penalty annexed to it; but the curse here is a sanction to that command. (2.) Swearers. Sinners of the former class offend against the second table, these against the first; for the curse meets those that break either table. He that swears rashly and profanely shall not be held guiltless, much less he that swears falsely (*v.* 4); he imprecates the curse upon himself by his perjury, and so shall his doom be; God will say *Amen* to his imprecation, and turn it upon his own head. He has appealed to God's judgment, which is always according to truth, for the confirming of a lie, and to that judgment he shall go which he has so impiously affronted.

3. The enforcing of this curse, and the equity of it: *I will bring it forth, saith the Lord of hosts, v.* 4. He that pronounces the sentence will take care to see it executed. His bringing it forth denotes, (1.) His giving it commission. It is a righteous curse, for he is a righteous God that warrants it. (2.) His giving it the setting on. He brings it forth with power, and orders what execution it shall do; and who can put by or resist the curse which a God of almighty power brings forth?

4. The effect of this curse; it is very dreadful, (1.) Upon the sinner himself: *Every one that steals shall be cut off*, not corrected, but destroyed, cut off from the land of the living. The curse of God is a cutting thing, a killing thing. He shall be cut off *as on this side* (cut off from this place, that is, from Jerusalem), and so he that swears from *this side* (it is the same word), from this place. God will not spare the sinners he finds among his own people, nor shall the holy city be a protection to the unholy. Or they shall be cut off *from hence*, that is, from the face of the whole earth, over which the curse flies. Or he that steals shall be cut off *on this side*, and he that swears *on that side:* they shall all be cut off, one as well as another, and both according to the curse, for the judgments of God's hand are exactly agreeable with the judgments of his mouth. (2.) Upon his family: *It shall enter into the house of the thief and of him that swears.* God's curse comes with a warrant to break open doors, and cannot be kept out by bars or locks. There where the sinner is most secure, and thinks himself out of danger,—there where he promises himself refreshment by food and sleep,—there, in his own house, shall the curse of God seize him; nay, it shall fall not upon him only, but upon all about him for his sake. *Cursed shall be his basket and his store, and cursed the fruit of his body,* Deut. xxviii. 17, 18. The *curse of the Lord is in the house of the wicked*, Prov. iii. 33.

It shall not only beset his house, or he at the door, but *it shall remain in the midst of his house,* and diffuse its malignant influences to all the parts of it. *It shall dwell in his tabernacle because it is none of his,* Job xviii. 15. It shall dwell where he dwells, and be his constant companion at bed and board, to make both miserable to him. Having got possession, it shall keep it, and, unless he repent and reform, there is no way to throw it out or cut off the entail of it. Nay, it shall so remain in it as to *consume it with the timber thereof, and the stones thereof,* which, though ever so strong, though the timber be heart of oak and the stones hewn out of the rocks of adamant, yet they shall not be able to stand before the curse of God. We heard the stone and the timber complaining of the owner's extortion and oppression, and groaning under the burden of them, Hab. ii. 11. Now here we have them delivered *from that bondage of corruption.* While they were in their strength and beauty they supported, sorely against their will, the sinner's pride and security; but, when they are consumed, their ruins will, to their satisfaction, be standing monuments of God's justice and lasting witnesses of the sinner's injustice. Note, Sin is the ruin of houses and families, especially the sins of injury and perjury. *Who knows the power of God's anger,* and the operations of his curse? Even timber and stones have been consumed by them; let us therefore stand in awe and not sin.

5 Then the angel that talked with me went forth, and said unto me, Lift up now thine eyes, and see what *is* this that goeth forth. 6 And I said, What *is* it? And he said, This *is* an ephah that goeth forth. He said moreover, This *is* their resemblance through all the earth. 7 And, behold, there was lifted up a talent of lead: and this *is* a woman that sitteth in the midst of the ephah. 8 And he said, This *is* wickedness. And he cast it into the midst of the ephah; and he cast the weight of lead upon the mouth thereof. 9 Then lifted I up mine eyes, and looked, and, behold, there came out two women, and the wind *was* in their wings; for they had wings like the wings of a stork: and they lifted up the ephah between the earth and the heaven. 10 Then said I to the angel that talked with me, Whither do these bear the ephah? 11 And he said unto me, To build it a house in the land of Shinar: and it shall be esta-blished, and set there upon her own base.

The foregoing vision was very plain and easy, but in this are things *dark and hard to be understood;* and some think that the scope of it is to foretel the final destruction of the Jewish church and nation and the dispersion of the Jews, when, by crucifying Christ and persecuting his gospel, they should have filled up the measure of their iniquities; therefore it is industriously set out in obscure figures and expressions, " lest the plain denunciation of the second overthrow of temple and state might discourage them too much from going forward in the present restoration of both." So Mr. Pemble.

The prophet was contemplating the power and terror of the curse which consumes the houses of thieves and swearers, when he was told to turn and he should see greater desolations than these made by the curse of God for the sin of man: *Lift up thy eyes now,* and see what is here, v. 5. *What is this that goeth forth?* Whether over the face of the whole earth, as the flying roll (v. 3), or only over Jerusalem, is not certain. But, it seems, the prophet now, through either distance or the dimness of his sight, could not well tell what it was, but asked, *What is it?* v. 6. And the angel tells him both what it is and what it means.

I. He sees an *ephah,* a measure wherewith they measured corn; it contained *ten omers* (Exod. xvi. 36) and was the tenth part of a *homer* (Ezek. xlv. 11); it is put for any measure used in commerce, Deut. xxv. 14. And *this is their resemblance,* the resemblance of the Jewish nation *over all the earth,* wherever they are now dispersed, or at least **it** will be so when their ruin draws near. They are filling up the measure of their iniquity, which God has set them; and when it is full, as the ephah of corn, they shall be delivered into the hands of those to whom God has sold them for their sins; they are *meted* to destruction, as an ephah of corn measured to the market or to the mill. And some think that the mentioning of an ephah, which is used in buying and selling, intimates that fraud, and deceit, and extortion in commerce, were sins abounding much among them, as that people are known to be notoriously guilty of them at this day. This **is** a proper representation of them *through all the earth.* There is a measure set them, and they are filling it up apace. See Matt. xxiii. 32; 1 Thess. ii. 16.

II. He sees a *woman sitting in the midst of the ephah,* representing the sinful church and nation of the Jews in their latter and degenerate age, when *the faithful city became a harlot.* He that weighs the mountains in scales and the hills in a balance measures nations and churches as in an ephah; so exact is he in his judicial dealings with them. God's people are called *the corn of his floor*, Isa. xxi. 10. And here he puts this corn into the bushel, in order to his parting with it. The angel says of the woman in the *ephah, This is wickedness ;* it is a wicked nation, else God would not have rejected it thus ; it is as wicked as *wickedness* itself, it is abominably wicked. *How has the gold become dim ! Israel was holiness to the Lord* (Jer. ii. 3) ; but now *this is wickedness*, and wickedness is nowhere so scandalous, so odious, and, in many instances, so outrageous, as when it is found among professors of religion.

III. He sees the woman thrust down into the ephah, and a *talent*, or large weight, *of lead*, cast upon the *mouth* of it, by which she is secured, and made a close prisoner in the *ephah*, and utterly disabled to get out of it. This is designed to show that the wrath of God against impenitent sinners is, 1. Unavoidable, and what they cannot escape ; they are bound over to it, concluded under sin, and shut up under the curse, as this woman in the ephah ; *he would fain flee out of his hand* (Job xxvii. 22), but he cannot. 2. It is insupportable, and what they cannot bear up under. Guilt is upon the sinner as a talent of lead, to sink him to the lowest hell. When Christ said of the things of Jerusalem's peace, *Now they are hidden from thy eyes*, that threw a talent of lead upon them.

IV. He sees the ephah, with the woman thus pressed to death in it, carried away into some far country. 1. The instruments employed to do it were *two women*, who had *wings like* those *of a stork*, large and strong, and, to make them fly the more swiftly, they had the *wind in their wings*, denoting the great violence and expedition with which the Romans destroyed the Jewish nation. God has not only winged messengers in heaven, but he can, when he pleases, give wings to those also whom he employs in this lower world ; and, when he does so, he forwards them with the wind in their wings ; his providence carries them on with a favourable gale. 2. They bore it up in the air, denoting the terrors which pursued the wicked Jews, and their being a public example of God's vengeance to the world. They *lifted it up between the earth and the heaven*, as unworthy of either and abandoned by both ; for the Jews, when this was fulfilled, *pleased not God and* were *contrary to all men*, 1 Thess. ii. 15. *This is wickedness*, and this comes of it ; heaven thrust out wicked angels, and earth spewed out wicked Canaanites. 3. When the prophet enquired whither they carried their prisoner whom they had now in execution (*v.* 10) he was told that they designed *to build it a house in the land of Shinar*. This intimates that the punishment of the Jews should be a final dispersion ; they should be hurried out of their own country, *as the chaff which the wind drives away*, and should be forced to dwell in far countries, particularly in the country of Babylon,

whither many of the scattered Jews went, after the destruction of their country by the Romans, as they did also to other countries, especially in the Levant parts, not to sojourn, as in their former captivity, for seventy years, but to be nailed down for perpetuity. There the *ephah* shall *be established, and set upon her own base.* This intimates, (1.) That their calamity shall continue from generation to generation, and that they shall be so dispersed that they shall never unite or incorporate again ; they shall settle in a perpetual unsettlement, and Cain's doom shall be theirs, to dwell in the land of shaking. (2.) That their iniquity shall continue too, and their hearts shall be hardened in it. *Blindness* has *happened* unto Israel, and they are settled upon the lees of their own unbelief ; their wickedness is established upon its *own basis*. God has given them a *spirit of slumber* (Rom. xi. 8), *lest at any time they should convert, and be healed.*

CHAP. VI.

The two kingdoms of providence and grace are what we are all very nearly interested in, and therefore are concerned to acquaint ourselves with, all our temporal affairs being in a necessary subjection to divine Providence, and all our spiritual and eternal concerns in a necessary dependence upon divine grace ; and these two are represented to us in this chapter—the former by a vision, the latter by a type. Here is, I. God, as King of nations, ruling the world by the ministry of angels, in the vision of the four chariots, ver. 1—8. II. God, as King of saints, ruling the church by the mediation of Christ, in the figure of Joshua the high priest crowned, the ceremony performed, and then explained concerning Christ, ver. 9—15.

AND I turned, and lifted up mine eyes, and looked, and, behold, there came four chariots out from between two mountains ; and the mountains *were* mountains of brass. 2 In the first chariot *were* red horses ; and in the second chariot black horses ; 3 And in the third chariot white horses ; and in the fourth chariot grisled and bay horses. 4 Then I answered and said unto the angel that talked with me, What *are* these, my lord ? 5 And the angel answered and said unto me, These *are* the four spirits of the heavens, which go forth from standing before the Lord of all the earth. 6 The black horses which *are* therein go forth into the north country ; and the white go forth after them ; and the grisled go forth toward the south country. 7 And the bay went forth, and sought to go that they might walk to and fro through the earth : and he said, Get you hence, walk to and fro through the earth. So they walked to and fro through the earth. 8 Then cried he upon me, and spake unto me, saying, Behold, these that go toward the north country have quieted my spirit in the north country.

The prophet is forward to receive this vision, and, as if he expected it, he *turned and lifted up his eyes and looked.* Though this was the seventh vision he had had, yet he did not think he had had enough; for the more we know of God and his will, if we know it aright, the more desirous we shall be to get a further acquaintance with God. Now observe here the sight that the prophet had of *four chariots* drawn by horses of divers colours, together with the explication of the sight, *v.* 1—5. He did not look long before he discovered that which was worth seeing, and which would serve very much for the encouraging of himself and his friends in this dark day. We are very much in the dark concerning the meaning of this vision. Some by the *four chariots* understand the four monarchies; and then they read (*v.* 5), *These are the four winds of the heavens,* and suppose that therein reference is had to Dan. vii. 2, where Daniel saw, in vision, the *four winds of the heavens striving upon the great sea,* representing the four monarchies. The Babylonian monarchy, they think, is here represented by the *red horses,* which are not afterwards mentioned, because that monarchy was now extinct. The second chariot with the *black horses* is the Persian monarchy, which went forth north-ward against the Babylonians, and *quieted God's Spirit in the north country,* by executing his judgments on Babylon and freeing the Jews from their captivity. The *white,* the Grecians, go *forth after them* in the north, for they overthrow the Persians. The *grizzled,* the Romans, who conquered the Grecian empire, are said to *go forth towards the south country,* because Egypt, which lay southward, was the last branch of the Grecian empire that was subdued by the Romans. The *bay horses* had been with the *grizzled,* but afterwards went forth by themselves; and by these they understand the Goths and Vandals, who with their victorious arms walked to and fro through the earth, or the Seleucidæ and Lagidæ, the two branches of the Grecian empire. Thus Grotius and others.

But I incline rather to understand this vision more generally, as designing to represent the administration of the kingdom of Providence in the government of this lower world. The *angels* are often called the *chariots of God,* as Ps. lxviii. 17; xviii. 10. The various providences of God concerning nations and churches are represented by the different colours of horses, Rev. vi. 2, 4, 5, 8. And so we may observe here, 1. That the counsels and decrees of God are the spring and original of all events, and they are immovable, as *mountains of brass.* The chariots came *from between the two mountains;* for God *performs the thing that is ap-*

pointed *for us:* his appointments are the originals, and his performances are but copies from them; he does all *according to the counsel of his will.* We could as soon grasp the mountains in our arms as comprehend the divine counsels in our finite understandings, and as soon remove *mountains of brass* as alter any of God's purposes; for *he is in one mind, and who can turn him?* Whatever the providences of God are concerning us, as to public or private affairs, we should see them all coming from *between the mountains of brass,* and therefore see it as much our folly to quarrel with them as it is our duty to acquiesce in them. Who may say to God, *What doest thou, or why doest thou so?* Acts ii. 23; iv. 28. 2. That God executes his decrees in the works of Providence, which are as chariots, in which he rides as a prince in an open chariot, to show his glory to the world, in which, as in chariots of war, he rides forth *conquering and to conquer,* and triumphing over all the enemies of his glory and government. God is great and terrible in his doings (Ps. lxvi. 3), and in them we *see the goings of our God, our King,* Ps. lxviii. 24. His providences move swiftly and strongly as chariots, but all directed and governed by his infinite wisdom and sovereign will, as chariots by their drivers. 3. That the holy angels are the ministers of God's providence, and are employed by him, as *the armies of heaven,* for the executing of his counsels among *the inhabitants of the earth;* they are the *chariots,* or, which comes all to one, they are the horses that draw the chariots, great in power and might, and who, like the horse that God himself describes (Job xxxix. 19, &c.), are clothed with thunder, are terrible, but cannot be *terrified* nor *made afraid;* they are *chariots of fire, and horses of fire,* to carry one prophet to heaven and guard another on earth. They are as observant of and obsequious to the will of God as well-managed horses are to their rider or driver. Not that God needs them or their services, but he is pleased to make use of them, that he may put honour upon them, and encourage our trust in his providence. 4. That the events of Providence have different aspects and the face of the times often changes. The *horses in the first chariot* were *red,* signifying war and bloodshed, *blood to the horse-bridles,* Rev. xiv. 20. Those in the *second chariot* were *black,* signifying the dismal melancholy consequences of war; it puts all into mourning, lays all waste, introduces famines, and pestilences, and desolations, and makes whole lands to languish. Those in the *third chariot* were *white,* signifying the return of comfort, and peace, and prosperity, after these dark and dismal times: though God cause grief to the children of men, yet will he have compassion. Those in the *fourth chariot* were of a mixed colour, *grizzled* and *bay:* some *speckled* and *spotted,* and *ash-coloured,* signifying events of *differ-*

ent complexions interwoven and counter-changed, a day of prosperity and a day of adversity set *the one over-against the other.* The cup of Providence in the hand of the Lord is *full of mixture,* Ps. lxxv. 8. 5. That all the instruments of Providence, and all the events of it, come from God, and from him they receive their commissions and instructions (*v.* 5): *These are the four spirits of heaven, the four winds* (so some), which seem to blow as they list, from the various points of the compass; but God has them *in his fists* and brings them out of *his treasuries.* Or, rather, These are *the angels* that *go forth from standing before the Lord of all the earth,* to attend upon him and minister to him, to behold his glory in the upper world, which is their blessedness, and to serve his glory in this lower world, which is their business. They *stand before him* as the *Lord of the whole earth,* to receive orders from him and give up their accounts to him concerning their services on this earth, for it is all within his jurisdiction. But, when he appoints, they *go forth* as messengers of his counsels and ministers of his justice and mercy. Those secret motions and impulses upon the spirits of men by which the designs of Providence are carried on, some think, are these *four spirits of the heavens,* which *go forth from God* and fulfil what he appoints, who is *the God of the spirits of all flesh.* 6. That there is an admirable beauty in Providence, and one event serves for a balance to another (*v.* 6): *The black horses went forth,* carrying with them very dark and melancholy events, such as made every person and every thing look black; but presently *the white went forth after them,* carrying joy to those that mourned, and, by a new turn given to affairs, making them to look pleasant again. Such are God's dealings with his church and people: if the black horses go forth, the white ones presently go after them; for *as affliction abounds consolation much more abounds.* 7. That the common general aspect of providence is mixed and compounded. The *grizzled* and *bay horses* were both in the *fourth chariot* (*v.* 3), and though they went forth, at first, towards the *south country,* yet afterwards they *sought to walk to and fro through the earth* and were directed to do so, *v.* 7. If we go to and fro through the earth, we shall find the events of Providence neither all black nor all white, but ash-coloured, or gray, mixed of black and white. Such is the world we live in; that before us is unmixed. Here we are singing, at the same time, of *mercy and judgment,* and we must *sing unto God* of both (Ps. ci. 1) and labour to accommodate ourselves to God's will and design in the mixtures of Providence, rejoicing in our comforts as though we rejoiced not, because they have their allays, and weeping for our afflictions as though we wept not, because there is so much mercy mixed with them. 8. That God is well-pleased with all

the operations of his own providence (*v.* 8): *These have quieted my spirit,* these *black horses* which denote extraordinary judgments, and the *white* ones which denote extraordinary deliverances, both which *went towards the north country,* while the common mixed providences went all the world over. These have *quieted my spirit in the north-country,* which had of late been the most remarkable scene of action with reference to the church; that is, by these uncommon appearances and actings of providence God's wrath is executed upon the enemies of the church, and his favours are conferred upon the church, both which had long been deferred, and in both God had fulfilled his will, accomplished his word, and so *quieted his Spirit. The Lord is well-pleased for his righteousness' sake;* and, as he speaks, Isa. i. 24, made himself easy.

9 And the word of the LORD came unto me, saying, 10 Take of *them of* the captivity, *even* of Heldai, of Tobijah, and of Jedaiah, which are come from Babylon, and come thou the same day, and go into the house of Josiah the son of Zephaniah; 11 Then take silver and gold, and make crowns, and set *them* upon the head of Joshua the son of Josedech, the high priest; 12 And speak unto him, saying, Thus speaketh the LORD of hosts, saying, Behold the man whose name *is* The BRANCH; and he shall grow up out of his place, and he shall build the temple of the LORD: 13 Even he shall build the temple of the LORD; and he shall bear the glory, and shall sit and rule upon his throne; and he shall be a priest upon his throne: and the counsel of peace shall be between them both. 14 And the crowns shall be to Helem, and to Tobijah, and to Jedaiah, and to Hen the son of Zephaniah, for a memorial in the temple of the LORD. 15 And they *that are* far off shall come and build in the temple of the LORD, and ye shall know that the LORD of hosts hath sent me unto you. And *this* shall come to pass, if ye will diligently obey the voice of the LORD your God.

God did not only at *sundry times,* but *in divers manners,* speak in time past by the prophets to his church. In the former part of this chapter he spoke by a vision, which only the prophet himself saw; here, in this latter part, he speaks by a sign, or type, which many saw, and which, as it was explained, was an illustrious prediction of the Messiah as the priest and king of his church. Here is,

1426

I. The significant ceremony which God appointed, and that was the *coronation of Joshua* the high priest, *v.* 10, 11. It is observable that there should be two eminent types of Christ in the Old Testament that were both named *Joshua* (the same name with *Jesus*, and by the LXX., and in the New Testament, rendered *Jesus*, Acts vii. 45)—Joshua the chief captain, a type of Christ the captain of our salvation, and Joshua the chief priest, a type of Christ the high priest of our profession, and both in their day saviours and leaders into Canaan. And this is peculiar to Joshua the high priest, that here was something done to him by the divine appointment on purpose that he might be a type of Christ, a priest after the order of Melchizedek, who was both a king and a priest. Joshua was far from being ambitious of a crown, and the people of having a crowned head over them; but the prophet, to the great surprise of both, is ordered to crown Joshua as if he had been a king. And, as Zerubbabel's prudence and piety kept this from being any affront to him (as the setting up of a rival with him), so God's providence kept the kings of Persia from taking umbrage at it, as raising a rebellion against them. In doing what we are sure is God's pleasure, as this was, we may well venture men's displeasure. 1. Here were some Jews come from Babylon that brought an offering to the house of God, *some of the captivity*, here named to their honour, that *came from Babylon* on a visit to Jerusalem. They ought to have bidden a final farewell to Babylon, and to have come and settled with their brethren in their own land, and for their remissness and indifference in not doing so they thought to atone by this visit. Perhaps they came as ambassadors from the body of the Jews that were in Babylon, who lived there in ease and fulness; and, hearing that the building of the temple went on slowly for want of money, they sent them with an offering of gold and silver for the service of the house of God. Note, Those that by reason of distance, or otherwise, cannot forward a good work by their persons, must, as they are able, forward it by their purses; if some find hands, let others fill them. 2. Time and place are appointed for the prophet to meet them. They thought to bring their present to the priest, God's ordinary minister; but God has a prophet, an extraordinary one, ready to receive them and it, which would be an encouragement to them, who, in their captivity, had so often complained, *We see not our signs, there is no more any prophet*, and would invite them and others to re-settle in their own land, which then began to look like itself, like a holy land, when the Spirit of prophecy was revived in it. Zechariah was ordered to give them the meeting *the same day* they came (for when they had arrived they would *lose no time*, but present their offering immedi-

ately), and to bid them welcome, assuring them that God now accepted their gifts. He was to meet them in the house of Josiah, the son of Zephaniah, who probably was receiver-general for the temple, and kept the treasures of it. They brought their gold and silver, to be employed about the temple, but God ordered it to be used in honour of One *greater than the temple*, Matt. xii. 6. 3. Crowns are to be *made*, and *put upon the head of Joshua, v.* 11. It is supposed that there were two crowns provided, one of silver and the other of gold; the former (as some think) denoting his priestly dignity, the latter his kingly dignity. Or, rather, he being a priest already, and having a crown of gold, of pure gold, already, to signify his honour and power as a priest, these crowns of silver and gold both signify the *royal dignity*, the crown of silver being perhaps designed to typify the kingdom of the Messiah when he was here on earth, for then he was the *King of Israel* (John i. 49), but the crown of gold his kingdom in his exalted state, the glory of which as far exceeded that of the former as gold does silver. The sun shines as gold, when he *goes forth in his strength;* and the beams of the moon, when she *walks in brightness*, we call *silver beams*. Those that had worshipped the sun and moon shall now fall down before the golden and silver crowns of the exalted Redeemer, before whom the sun shall be ashamed and the moon confounded, being both out-shone.

II. The signification which God gave of this ceremony. Every one would be ready to ask, "What is the meaning of Joshua's being crowned thus?" And the prophet is as ready to tell them the meaning of it. Upon this speaking sign is grafted a prediction, and the sign was used to make it the more taken notice of and the better remembered. Now the promise is,

1. That God will, in the fulness of time, raise up a great high priest, like Joshua. Tell Joshua that he is but the figure of one that is to come, a faint shadow of him (*v.* 12): *Speak unto him* in the name of *the Lord of hosts*, that *the man whose name is The BRANCH* shall *grow up out of his place*, out of Bethlehem the city of David, the place appointed for his birth; though the family be a root in a dry ground, yet this branch shall spring out of it, as in the spring, when the sun returns, the flowers spring out of the roots, in which they lay buried out of sight and out of mind. He shall *grow up for himself* (so some read it) *propriâ virtute —by his own vital energy*, shall be exalted *in his own strength*.

2. That, as Joshua was an active useful instrument in building the temple, so *the man, the branch*, shall be the master-builder, the sole builder of the spiritual temple, the gospel-church. He *shall build the temple of the Lord;* and it is repeated (*v.* 13), *Even*

he shall build the temple of the Lord. He shall grow up to do good, to be an instrument of God's glory and a great blessing to mankind. Note, The gospel-church is the *temple of the Lord,* a *spiritual house* (1 Pet. ii. 5), a *holy temple,* Eph. ii. 21. In the temple God made discoveries of himself to his people, and there he received the service and homage of his people; so, in the gospel-church, the light of divine revelation shines by the word, and the spiritual sacrifices of prayer and praise are offered. Now Christ is not only the foundation, but the founder, of this temple, by his Spirit and grace.

3. That *Christ shall bear the glory.* Glory is a burden, but not too heavy for him to bear who upholds all things. The cross was his glory, and he bore that; so was the crown *an exceeding weight of glory,* and he bears that. The *government* is *upon his shoulders,* and in it *he bears the glory,* Isa. ix. 6. *They shall hang upon him all the glory of his Father's house,* Isa. xxii. 24. It becomes him, and he is *par negotio—well able to bear it.* The glory of the priesthood and royalty had been divided between the house of Aaron and that of David; but now he alone shall bear all the glory of both. That which he shall bear, which he shall undertake, shall be indeed the *glory of Israel;* and they must wait for that, and, in prospect of it, must be content in the want of that external glory which they formerly had. He shall bear such a glory as shall make the glory of this latter house greater than that of the former. He shall *lift up the glory* (so it may be read); the glory of Israel had been thrown down and depressed, but he shall raise it out of the dust.

4. That he shall have a throne, and be both priest and king upon his throne. A throne denotes both dignity and dominion, an exalted honour with an extensive power. (1.) This priest shall be a king, and his office as a priest shall be no diminution to his dignity as a king: *He shall sit and rule upon his throne.* Christ, as a priest, ever lives to make intercession for us; but he does it sitting at his Father's right hand, as one having authority, Heb. viii. 1. We have *such a high priest* as Israel never had, for he is *set on the right hand of the throne of the Majesty in the heavens,* which puts a prevailing virtue into his mediation; he that appears for us within the veil is one that sits and rules there. Christ, who is ordained to offer sacrifices for us, is authorized to give law to us. He will not save us unless we be willing that he should govern us. God has prepared him a throne *in the heavens;* and, if we would have any benefit by that, we must prepare him a throne in our hearts, and be willing and glad that he should *sit and rule upon that throne;* and to him every thought within us must be brought into obedience. (2.) This king shall be a priest, a *priest upon his throne.* With the majesty and

1428

power of a king, he shall have the tenderness and simplicity of a priest, who, being *taken from among men,* is *ordained for men,* and *can have compassion on the ignorant,* Heb. v. 1, 2. In all the acts of his government as a king he prosecutes the intentions of his grace as a priest. Let not therefore those that are his look upon his throne, though a throne of glory and a throne of judgment, with terror and amazement; for, as there is a *rainbow about the throne,* so he is a *priest upon the throne.*

5. That *the counsel of peace shall be between them both.* That is, (1.) Between *Jehovah* and the *man the branch,* between the Father and the Son; the counsels concerning the peace to be made between God and man, by the mediation of Christ, shall be concerted (that is, shall *appear to have been* concerted) by Infinite Wisdom in the covenant of redemption; the Father and the Son understood one another perfectly well in that matter. Or, rather, (2.) Between the priest and the throne, between the priestly and kingly office of Jesus Christ. *The man the branch* must grow up to carry on a *counsel of peace,* peace on earth, and, in order to that, peace with heaven. God's thoughts towards us were *thoughts of peace,* and, in prosecution of them, he exalted his Son Christ Jesus to be *both a prince* and a *Saviour;* he gave him a throne, but with this proviso, that he should be a priest upon his throne, and by executing the two offices of a priest and king should bring about that great undertaking of man's reconciliation to God and happiness in God. Some think it alludes to the former government of the Jews' state, wherein the king and priest, separate officers, did take counsel one with another, for the maintenance of peace and prosperity in church and state, as did Zerubbabel and Joshua now. I may add, the *prophets of God helping them.* So shall the peace and welfare of the gospel-church, and of all believers, be wrought, though not by two separate persons, yet by virtue of two separate offices meeting in one—Christ purchasing all peace by his priesthood and maintaining and defending it by his kingdom; so Mr. Pemble. And his prophetic office is serviceable to both in this great design.

6. That there shall be a happy coalition between Jews and Gentiles in the gospel-church, and they shall both meet in Christ, the priest upon his throne, as the centre of their unity (v. 15): *Those that are far off shall come and build in the temple of the Lord.* Some understand it of the Jews that were now afar off in Babylon, that staid behind in captivity, to the great discouragement of their brethren that had returned, who wanted their help in building the temple. Now God promises that many of them, and some of other nations too, proselyted to the Jewish religion, should come in, and lend a helping hand to the building of the temple, and many hands would make light work. The

kings of Persia contributed to the building of the temple (Ezra vi. 8) and the furnishing of it, Ezra vii. 19, 20. And, in after-times, Herod the Great, and others that were strangers, helped to beautify and enrich the temple. But it has a further reference to that *temple of the Lord* which *the man the branch* was to build. The Gentiles, *strangers afar off,* shall help to build it, for from among them God will raise up ministers that shall be workers together with Christ about that building; and all the Gentile converts shall be stones added to this building, so that it shall *grow up to a holy temple,* Eph. ii. 20—22. When God's temple is to be built he can fetch in those that are afar off and employ them in the building of it.

7. That the accomplishment of this will be a strong confirmation of the truth of God's word : *You shall know that the Lord of hosts has sent me unto you.* That promise, that those that were afar off should come and assist them in *building the temple of the Lord,* was as it were the *giving of them a sign ;* by this they might be assured that the other promises should be fulfilled in due time. This should be fulfilled now very speedily ; it was so, for those that had been their enemies and accusers, in obedience to the king's edict, became their helpers and did speedily what they were ordered to do for the furtherance of the work, and by that means the work went on and was finished ; see Ezra vi. 13, 14. Now, by this surprising assistance which they had from afar off in building the temple, they might know that Zechariah, who told them of it before, was sent of God, and that therefore his word concerning the man the branch should be fulfilled.

8. That these promises were strong obligations to obedience : " *For this shall come to pass* (you shall have help in building the temple) *if you will diligently obey the voice of the Lord your God.* You shall have the help of foreigners in building the temple, if you will but set about it in good earnest yourselves." The assistance of others, instead of being an excuse for our slothfulness, should be a spur to our industry. " You shall have the benefit and comfort of all those promises if you make conscience of your duty." They must know that they are upon their good behaviour ; and, though their God is coming towards them in a way of mercy, they cannot expect him to proceed in it unless they conform to his laws. Note, That which God requires of us, to qualify us for his favour, is obedience to his revealed will ; and it must be a diligent obedience. We cannot *obey the voice of God* without a great deal of care and pains, nor will our obedience be accepted of God unless it be laboured by us.

III. The provision that was made to preserve the remembrance of this. *The crowns* that were used in this solemnity were not given to Joshua, but must be *kept for a memorial in the temple of the Lord, v.* 14. Either they were laid up in the temple treasury or (as the Jews' tradition is) they were hung up in the windows of the temple, in the view of all, *in perpetuam rei memoriam—for a perpetual memorial,* for a traditional evidence of the promise of the Messiah and this typical transaction used for the confirmation of that promise. The crowns were delivered to those who found the materials (and some think their names were engraven on the crowns), to be preserved as a public testimony of their pious liberality and an encouragement to others in like manner to bring presents to the house of God. Note, Various means were used for the support of the faith of the Old-Testament saints, who waited for the consolation of Israel, till the time, the set time, for it came.

CHAP. VII.

We have done with the visions, but not with the revelations of this book ; the prophet sees no more such signs as he had seen, but still " the word of the Lord came to him." In this chapter we have, I. A case of conscience proposed to the prophet by the children of the captivity concerning fasting, whether they should continue their solemn fasts which they had religiously observed during the seventy years of their captivity, ver. 1—3. II. The answer to this question, which is given in this and the next chapter ; and this answer was given, not all at once, but by piece-meal, and, it should seem, at several times, for here are four distinct discourses which have all of them reference to this case, each of them prefaced with " the word of the Lord came," in this chapter, ver. 4—8, and ch. viii. 1, 18. The method of them is very observable. In this chapter, 1. The prophet sharply reproves them for the mismanagements of their fasts, ver. 4—7. 2. He exhorts them to reform their lives, which would be the best way of fasting, and to take heed of those sins which brought those judgments upon them which they kept these fasts in memory of, ver. 8—14. And then in the next chapter, having searched the wound, he binds it up, and heals it, with gracious assurances of great mercy God had yet in store for them, by which he would turn their fasts into feasts.

A ND it came to pass in the fourth year of king Darius, *that* the word of the LORD came unto Zechariah in the fourth *day* of the ninth month, *even* in Chisleu ; 2 When they had sent unto the house of God Sherezer and Regem-melech, and their men, to pray before the LORD, 3 *And* to speak unto the priests which *were* in the house of the LORD of hosts, and to the prophets, saying, Should I weep in the fifth month, separating myself, as I have done these so many years ? 4 Then came the word of the LORD of hosts unto me, saying, 5 Speak unto all the people of the land, and to the priests, saying, When ye fasted and mourned in the fifth and seventh *month,* even those seventy years, did ye at all fast unto me, *even* to me ? 6 And when ye did eat, and when ye did drink, did not ye eat *for yourselves,* and drink *for yourselves?* 7 *Should ye* not *hear* the words which the LORD hath cried by the former prophets, when Jerusalem was inhabited and in prosperity, and the cities thereof round about her, when *men* inhabited the south and the plain?

This occasional sermon, which the prophet preached, and which is recorded in this and the next chapter, was above two years after the former, in which he gave them an account of his visions, as appears by comparing the date of this (*v.* 1), in the *ninth month* of the *fourth year* of Darius, with the date of that (*ch.* i. 1), in the eighth month of the second year of Darius; not that Zechariah was idle all that while (it is expressly said that he and Haggai continued *prophesying* till the temple was finished in the sixth year of Darius; Ezra vi. 14, 15), but during that time he did not preach any sermon that was afterwards published, and left upon record, as this is. God may be honoured, his work done, and his interest served, by word of mouth as well as by writing; and by inculcating and pressing what has been taught, as well as by advancing something new. Now here we have,

I. A case proposed concerning fasting. Some persons were sent to enquire of the priests and prophets whether they should continue to observe their yearly fasts, particularly that in the fifth month, as they had done. It is uncertain whether the case was put by those that yet remained in Babylon, who, being deprived of the benefit of the solemn feasts which God's ordinance appointed them, made up the want by the solemn fasts which God's providences called them to; or by those that had returned, but lived in the country, as some rather incline to think, because they are called the *people of the land*, *v.* 5. But, as to that, the answer given to the messengers of the captive Jews might be directed, not to them only, but to *all the people*. Observe,

1. Who they were that came with this enquiry—*Sherezer* and *Regem-melech*, persons of some rank and figure, for they came *with their men*, and did not think it below them, or any disparagement to them, to be sent on this errand, but rather an addition to their honour to be, (1.) Attendants in God's house, there to do duty and receive orders. The greatest of men are less than the least of the ordinances of Jesus Christ. (2.) Agents for God's people, to negociate their affairs. Men of estates, having more leisure than men of business, ought to employ their time in the service of the public, and by doing good they make themselves truly great; the *messengers of the churches* were the *glory of Christ*, 2 Cor. viii. 23.

2. What the errand was upon which they came. They were sent perhaps not with *gold and silver* (as those, *ch.* vi. 10, 11), or, if they were, that is not mentioned, but upon the two great errands which should bring us all to the house of God, (1.) to intercede

with God for his mercy. They were sent to *pray before the Lord*, and, some think (according to the usage then), to *offer sacrifice*, with which they offered up their prayers. The Jews, in captivity, prayed towards the temple (as appears Dan. vi. 10); but now that it was in a fair way to be rebuilt they sent their representatives to pray in it, remembering that God had said that his house should be called *a house of prayer for all people*, Isa. lvi. 7. In prayer we must set ourselves as *before the Lord*, must see his eye upon us and have our eye up to him. (2.) To enquire of God concerning his mind. Note, When we offer up our requests to God it must be with a readiness to receive instructions from him; for, if we turn away our ear from hearing his law, we cannot expect that our prayers should be acceptable to him. We must therefore desire to dwell in the house of the Lord all the days of our life *that we may enquire* there (Ps. xxvii. 4), asking, not only, Lord, what wilt thou do for me? but, Lord, *what wilt thou have me to do?*

3. Whom they consulted. They spoke *to the priests that were in the house of the Lord and to the prophets;* the former were an oracle for ordinary cases, the latter for extraordinary; they were blessed with both, and would try if either could acquaint them with the mind of God in this case. Note, God having given diversities of gifts to men, and all to profit with, we should make use of all as there is occasion. They were not so wedded to the priests, their stated ministers, as to distrust the prophets, who appeared, by the gifts given them, well qualified to serve the church; nor yet were they so much enamoured with the prophets as to despise the priests, but they spoke both to the priests and to the prophets, and, in consulting both, gave glory to the God of Israel, and that one Spirit who *works all in all*. God might speak to them either by *urim* or *by prophets* (1 Sam. xxviii. 6), and therefore they would not neglect either. The priests and the prophets were not jealous one of another, nor had any difference among themselves; let not the people then make differences between them, but thank God they had both. The prophets did indeed reprove what was amiss in the priests, but at the same time told the people that the *priest's lips* should *keep knowledge*, and they must *enquire the law at his mouth, for he is the messenger of the Lord of hosts*, Mal. ii. 7. Note, Those that would know God's mind should consult God's ministers, and in doubtful cases ask advice of those whose special business it is to *search the scriptures*.

4. What the case was which they desired satisfaction in (*v.* 3): *Should I weep in the fifth month, separating myself, as I have done these so many years*. Observe, (1.) What had been their past practice, not only during the seventy years of the captivity, but to this

time, which was twenty years after the liberty proclaimed them; they kept up solemn stated fasts for humiliation and prayer, which they religiously observed, according as their opportunities were, in their closets, families, or such assemblies for worship as they had. In the case here, they mention only one, that of the fifth month; but it appears, by *ch.* viii. 19, that they observed four anniversary fasts, one in the fourth month *(June* 17), in remembrance of the breaking up of the wall of Jerusalem (Jer. lii. 6), another in the fifth month *(July* 4), in remembrance of the burning of the temple (Jer. lii. 12, 13), another in the seventh month *(September* 3), in remembrance of the killing of Gedaliah, which completed their dispersion, and another in the tenth month *(December* 10), in remembrance of the beginning of the siege of Jerusalem, 2 Kings xxv. 1. Now it was very commendable in them to keep those fasts, thus to humble themselves under those humbling providences, by which God called them to weeping and mourning, thus to accommodate themselves to their troubles, and prepare themselves for deliverance. It would likewise be a means of possessing their children betimes with a due sense of the hand of the Lord gone out against them. (2.) What was their present doubt—whether they should continue these fasts or no. The case is put as by a single person: *Should I weep?* But it was the case of many, and the satisfaction of one would be a satisfaction to the rest. Or perhaps many had left it off, but the querist will not be determined by the practice of others; if God will have him continue it, he will, whatever others do. His fasting is described by his *weeping, separating himself.* A religious fast must be solemnized, not only by abstinence, here called a separating ourselves from the ordinary lawful comforts of life, but by a godly sorrow for sin, here expressed by weeping. " Should I still keep such *days to afflict the soul* as *I have done these so many years?*" It is said (*v.* 5) to be seventy years, computed from the last captivity, as before, *ch.* i. 12. The enquiry intimates a readiness to continue it, if God so appoint, though it be a mortification to the flesh. [1.] Something is to be said for the continuance of these fasts. Fasting and praying are good work at any time, and do good; we have always both cause enough and need enough to humble ourselves before God. To throw off these fasts would be an evidence of their being too secure, and a cause of their being more so, They were still in distress, and under the tokens of God's displeasure; and it is unwise for the patient to break off his course of physic while he is sensible of such remains of his distemper. But, [2.] There is something to be said for the letting fall of these fasts. God had changed the method of his providences con-

cerning them, and returned in ways of mercy to them; and ought not they then to change the method of their duties? Now that the bridegroom has returned, why should the *children of the bride-chamber fast?* Every thing is beautiful in its season. And as to the fast of the fifth month (which is that they particularly enquire about), that, being kept in remembrance of the burning of the temple, might seem to be superseded rather than any of the other, because the temple was now in a fair way to be rebuilt. But, having long kept up this fast, they would not leave it off without advice, and without asking and knowing God's mind in the case. Note, A good method of religious services, which we have found beneficial to ourselves and others, ought not to be altered without good reason, and therefore not without mature deliberation.

II. An answer given to this case. It should seem that, though the question looked plausible enough, those who proposed it were not conscientious in it, for they were more concerned about the ceremony than about the substance; they seemed to boast of their fasting, and to upbraid God Almighty with it, that he had not sooner returned in mercy to them; " for we have done it *these so many years.*" As those, Isa. lviii. 3, *Wherefore have we fasted, and thou seest not?* And some think that unbelief, and distrust of the promises of God, were at the bottom of their enquiry; for, if they had given them the credit that was due to them, they needed not to doubt but that their fasts ought to be laid aside, now that the occasion of them was over. And therefore the first answer to their enquiry is a very sharp reproof of their hypocrisy, directed, not only to the *people of the land,* but to *the priests,* who had set up these fasts, and perhaps some of them were for keeping them up, to serve some purpose of their own. Let them all take notice that, whereas they thought they had made God very much their debtor by these fasts, they were much mistaken, for they were not acceptable to him, unless they had been observed in a better manner and to better purpose.

1. What they did that was good was not done aright (*v.* 5): *You fasted and mourned.* They were not chargeable with the omission or neglect of the duty, though it was displeasing to the body (thy fasts were *continually before me,* Ps. l. 8), but they had not managed them aright. Note, Those that come to enquire of their duty must be willing first to be told of their faults. And those that seem zealous for the outside of a duty ought to examine themselves faithfully whether they have the regard they ought to have to the inside of it. (1.) They had not an eye to God in their fasting: *Did you at all fast unto me, even to me?* He appeals to their own consciences; they will witness against them that they had not been sincere

in it, much more will God, who is greater than the heart and knows all things. You know very well that *you did not at all fast to me; in fasting did you fast to me?* There was the carcase and form of the duty, but none of the life, and soul, and power of it. Was it *to me, even to me?* The repetition intimates what a great deal of stress is laid upon this as the main matter, in that and other holy exercises, that they be done to God, even to him, with an eye to his word as our rule, and his glory as our end, in them, seeking to please him and to obtain his favour, and studious by the sincerity of our intention to approve ourselves to him. When this was wanting every fast was but a jest. To fast, and not fast to God, was to mock him and provoke him, and could not be pleasing to him. Those that make fasting a cloak for sin, as Jezebel's fast, or by it make their court to men for their applause, as the Pharisees, or that rest in outward expressions of humiliation while their hearts are unhumbled, as Ahab, do they *fast to God, even to him? Is this the fast that God has chosen?* Isa. lviii. 5. If the solemnities of our fasting, though frequent, long, and severe, do not serve to put an edge upon devout affections, to quicken prayer, to increase godly sorrow, and to alter the temper of our minds and the course of our lives for the better, they do not at all answer the intention, and God will not accept them as performed to him, even to him. (2.) They had the same eye to themselves in their fasting that they had in their eating and drinking (v. 6): "*When you did eat, and when you did drink,* on other days (nay, perhaps on your fast-days, in the observation of which you could, when you saw cause, dispense with yourselves, and take a liberty to eat and drink), did you not *eat for yourselves and drink for yourselves?* Have you not always done as you had a mind yourselves? Why then do you now pretend a desire to know the mind of God? In your religious feasts and thanksgivings you have had no more an eye to God than in your fasts." Or, rather, it refers to their common meals; they did no more design the honour of God in their fasting and praying than they did in their eating and drinking; but self was still the centre in which the lines of all their actions, natural, civil, and religious, met. They needed not be in such care about the continuance of their fasts, unless they had kept them better. Note, We miss our end in eating and drinking when we eat to ourselves and drink to ourselves, whereas we should *eat and drink to the glory of God* (1 Cor. x. 31), that our bodies may be fit to serve our souls in his service.

2. The principal good thing they should have done was left undone (v. 7): "*Should you not hear the words which the Lord has cried by the former prophets?* Yes, that you should have done on your fast-days; it was

not enough to *weep* and *separate yourselves* on your fast-days, in token of your sorrow for the judgments you were under, but you should have *searched the scriptures* of the prophets, that you might have seen what was the ground of God's controversy with your fathers, and might have taken warning by their miseries not to tread in the steps of their iniquities. You ask, Shall we do as we have done, in fasting? No, you must do that which you have not yet done; you must repent of your sins and reform your lives. This is what we now call you to, and it is the same that the former prophets called your fathers to." To affect them the more with the mischief that sin had done them, that they might be brought to repent of it, he puts them in mind of the former flourishing state of their country: Jerusalem *was* then *inhabited and in prosperity*, that is now desolate and in distress. The *cities round about*, that are now in ruins, were then inhabited too and *in peace*. The country likewise was very populous: *Men inhabited the south of the plain*, which was not at all fortified, and yet they lived safely, and which was fruitful, and so they lived plentifully. But then God *by the prophets cried* to them, as one in earnest, and importunate with them, to amend their ways and doings, or else their prosperity would soon be at an end. "Now," says the prophet, "you should have taken notice of that, and have inferred that what was required of them for the preventing of the judgments, and which they did not, is required of you for the removal of the judgments; and, if you do it not, all your fasting and weeping signify nothing." Note, The words of the later prophets agree with those of the former; and, whether people are in prosperity or adversity, they must be called upon to leave their sins and do their duty; this must still be the burden of every song.

8 And the word of the LORD came unto Zechariah, saying, 9 Thus speaketh the LORD of hosts, saying, Execute true judgment, and show mercy and compassions every man to his brother: 10 And oppress not the widow, nor the fatherless, the stranger, nor the poor; and let none of you imagine evil against his brother in your heart. 11 But they refused to hearken, and pulled away the shoulder, and stopped their ears, that they should not hear. 12 Yea, they made their hearts *as* an adamant stone, lest they should hear the law, and the words which the LORD of hosts hath sent in his spirit by the former prophets: therefore came a great wrath from the LORD of hosts. 13 There-

fore it is come to pass, *that* as he cried, and they would not hear; so they cried, and I would not hear, saith the LORD of hosts: 14 But I scattered them with a whirlwind among all the nations whom they knew not. Thus the land was desolate after them, that no man passed through nor returned: for they laid the pleasant land desolate.

What was said *v. 7,* that they *should have heard the words of the former prophets,* is here enlarged upon, for warning to these hypocritical enquirers, who continued their sins when they asked with great preciseness whether they should continue their fasts. This prophet had before put them in mind of their fathers' disobedience to the calls of the prophets, and what was the consequence of it (*ch.* i. 4—6), and now here again; for others' harms should be our warnings. God's judgments upon Israel of old for their sins were written for admonition to us Christians (1 Cor. x. 11), and the same use we should make of similar providences in our own day. I. This prophet here repeats the heads of the sermons which the former prophets preached to their fathers (*v.* 9, 10), because the very same things were required of them now. " Thus does the *Lord of hosts speak* to you now, and thus he did speak to your fathers, saying, *Execute true judgment.*" The duties here required of them, which would have been the lengthening of the tranquillity of their fathers and must be the restoring of their tranquillity, are not keeping fasts and offering sacrifices, but *doing justly* and *loving mercy,* duties which they were bound to by the light and law of nature, though there had been no prophets sent to insist upon them, duties which had a direct tendency to the public welfare and peace, and which they themselves would be the gainers by, and not God. 1. Magistrates must administer justice impartially, according to the maxims of the law and the merits of the cause, without respect of persons: " *Judge judgment of truth,* and execute it when you have judged it." 2. Neighbours must have a tender concern for one another, and must not only do one another no wrong, but must be ready to do one another all the good offices that lie in their power. They must *show mercy and compassion every man to his brother,* as the case called for it. The infirmities of others, as well as their calamities, are to be looked upon with compassion. *Hanc veniam petimusque damusque vicissim—This kindness we ask and exercise.* 3. They must not bear hard upon those whom they they have advantage against, and who, they know, are not able to help themselves. They must not, either in commerce or in course of law, oppress *the widow, the fatherless, the stranger,*

and the poor, *v.* 10. The weakest must not be thrust to the wall because they are weakest. No thanks to men not to deny right to those who are in a capacity to demand it and recover it; but we must, not only for wrath, but also for conscience' sake, give those their own who have not power to force it from us. Or it intimates that that which is but exactness with others is exaction upon the widows and the fatherless; nay, that not relieving and helping them as we ought is, in effect, oppressing them. 4. They must not only not do wrong to any, but they must not so much as desire it nor think of it: " *Let none of you imagine evil against his brother in your heart.* Do not project it; do not wish it; nay, do not so much as please yourself with the fancy of it." The law of God lays a restraint upon the heart, and forbids the entertaining, forbids the admitting, of a malicious, spiteful, ill-natured thought. Deut. xv. 9, *Beware that there be not a thought in thy Belial heart against thy brother.*

II. He describes the wilfulness and disobedience of their fathers, who persisted in all manner of wickedness and injustice, notwithstanding these exhortations and admonitions frequently given them in God's name; various expressions to this purport are here heaped up (*v.* 11, 12), setting forth the stubbornness of that carnal mind which is *enmity against God, and is not in subjection to the law of God, neither indeed can be.* They were obstinate and refractory, and persisted in their transgressions of the law purely from a spirit of contradiction to the law. 1. They would not, if they could help it, come within hearing of the prophets, but kept at a distance; or, if they could not avoid hearing what they said, yet they resolved they would not heed it: *They refused to hearken,* and looked another way as if they had not been spoken to. 2. If they did hear what was said to them, and, as it seemed, inclined at first to comply with it, yet they flew off when it came to the setting to, and, like a bullock unaccustomed to the yoke, *they pulled away the shoulder,* and would not submit to the *easy yoke and light burden* of God's commandments. *They gave a withdrawing shoulder* (so the word is); they seemed to lay their shoulder to the work, but they presently withdrew it again, as those Jer. xxxiv. 10, 11. They were like a deceitful bow, as that son that said, *I go, sir, but went not.* 3. They filled their own minds with prejudices against the word of God, and had some objection or other ready wherewith to fortify themselves against every sermon they heard. *They stopped their ears, that they should not hear,* as the deaf adder (Ps. lviii. 4), and none are so deaf as those that will not hear, that *make their own ear heavy,* as the word is. 4. They resolved that nothing which was said to them, for the enforcing of these injunctions, should make any impression upon them: *They made their hearts as an* adamant-stone, as a *diamond,* the hardest of stones to be wrought upon, or as a *flint,* which the mason cannot hew into shape as he can other stone out of the quarry. Nothing is so hard, so unmalleable, so inflexible, as the heart of a presumptuous sinner; and those whose hearts are hard may thank themselves; they are of their own hardening, and it is just with God to give them over to a reprobate sense, to the hardness and impenitence of their own hearts. These stubborn sinners hardened their hearts on purpose *lest they should hear* what God said to them by the written word, *by the law of Moses,* and by the *words of the prophets* that preached to them; they had *Moses and the prophets,* but resolved they would hear neither, nor would they have been persuaded though one had been sent to them from the dead. The *words of the prophet* were not regarded by them, though they were words which the Lord of hosts sent and directed to them, though he sent them immediately *by his Spirit* in the prophets; so that in despising them they affronted God himself and *resisted the Holy Ghost.* Note, The reason why men are not good is because they will not be so; they will not consider, will not comply; and therefore, *if thou scornest, thou alone shalt bear it.*

III. He shows the fatal consequences of it to their fathers: *Therefore came great wrath from the Lord of hosts.* God was highly displeased with them, and justly; he required nothing of them but what was reasonable in itself and beneficial to them; and yet they refused, and in a most insolent manner too. What master could bear to be so abused by his own servant? Such an implacable enmity to the gospel as this was to the law and the prophets was that which brought *wrath to the uttermost* upon the last generation of the Jewish church, 1 Thess. ii. 16. Great sins against *the Lord of hosts,* whose authority is incontestable, bring *great wrath from the Lord of hosts,* whose power is irresistible. And the effect was, 1. As they had turned a deaf ear to God's word, so God turned a deaf ear to their prayers, *v. 13. As he cried* to them in their prosperity to leave their sins, *and they would not hear,* but persisted in their iniquities, so *they cried to him* in the day of their trouble to remove his judgments, and he would not hear, but lengthened out their calamities. Those that set God at defiance, in the height of their pride, when pangs came upon them cried unto him. *Lord, in trouble have they visited thee.* But God has said it, and will abide by it, *He that turns away his ear from hearing the law, even his prayer shall be an abomination,* Prov. xxviii. 9; i. 24, &c. Iniquity, regarded in the heart, will certainly spoil the success of prayer, Ps. lxvi. 18. 2. As they flew off from their duty and allegiance to God, and were of desultory and unsettled spirits, so God dissipated them and threw

1434

them about as chaff before a whirlwind: *He scattered them among all the nations whom they knew not,* and whom therefore they could not expect to receive any kindness from, *v.* 14. 3. As they violated all the laws of their land, so God took away all the glories of it: *Their land was desolate after them, and no man passed through or returned.* All that country that was the kingdom of the two tribes, after the dispersion of the remaining Jews, upon the slaughter of Gedaliah, was left utterly uninhabited; there was not man, woman, or child, in it, till the Jews returned at the end of seventy years' captivity; nay, it should seem, the very roads that lay through the country were deserted (none passed or repassed), which, as it had an intimation of mercy in it (though they were cast out of it, yet it was kept empty for their return), so for the present it made the judgment appear much the more dismal; for what a horrid wilderness must a land be that had been so many years uninhabited! And they might thank themselves; it was they that by their own wickedness laid *the pleasant land desolate.* It was not so much the Chaldeans that did it. No; they did it themselves. The desolations of a land are owing to the wickedness of its inhabitants, Ps. cvii. 34. This came of their wilful disobedience to the law of God. And the present generation saw how desolate sin had made that pleasant land, and yet would not take warning.

CHAP. VIII.

The work of ministers is rightly to divide the word of truth and to give every one his portion. So the prophet is here instructed to do, in the further answer he gives to the case of conscience proposed about continuing the public fasts. His answer, in the foregoing chapter, is by way of reproof to those that were disobedient and would not obey the truth. But here he is ordered to change his voice, and to speak by way of encouragement to the willing and obedient. Here are two words from the Lord of hosts, and they are both good words and comfortable words. In the former of these messages (ver. 1) God promises that Jerusalem shall be restored, reformed, replenished (ver. 2—8), that the country shall be rich, and the affairs of the nation shall be successful, their reputation retrieved, and their state in all respects the reverse of what it had been for many years past (ver. 9—15); he then exhorts them to reform what was amiss among them, that they might be ready for these favours designed them, ver. 16, 17. In the latter of these messages (ver. 18) he promises that their fasts should be superseded by the return of mercy (ver. 19), and that thereupon they should be replenished, enriched, and strengthened, by the accession of foreigners to them, ver. 20—23.

AGAIN the word of the LORD of hosts came *to me,* saying, 2 Thus saith the LORD of hosts; I was jealous for Zion with great jealousy, and I was jealous for her with great fury. 3 Thus saith the LORD; I am returned unto Zion, and will dwell in the midst of Jerusalem: and Jerusalem shall be called a city of truth; and the mountain of the LORD of hosts the holy mountain. 4 Thus saith the LORD of hosts; There shall yet old men and old women dwell in the streets of Jerusalem, and every man with his staff in his hand for very age. 5 And the streets of the city shall be full of boys and girls playing in the streets thereof. 6 Thus saith the LORD of hosts; If it be marvellous in the eyes of the remnant of this people in these days, should it also be marvellous in mine eyes? saith the LORD of hosts. 7 Thus saith the LORD of hosts; Behold, I will save my people from the east country, and from the west country; 8 And I will bring them, and they shall dwell in the midst of Jerusalem: and they shall be my people, and I will be their God, in truth and in righteousness.

The prophet, in his foregoing discourses, had left his hearers under a high charge of guilt and a deep sense of wrath; he had left them in a melancholy view of the desolations of their pleasant land, which was the effect of their fathers' disobedience; but because he designed to bring them to repentance, not to drive them to despair, he here sets before them the great things God had in store for them, encouraging them hereby to hope that their case of conscience would shortly determine itself and that God's providence would as loudly call them to *joy and gladness* as ever it called them to *fasting and mourning.* It is here promised,

I. That God will appear for Jerusalem, and will espouse and plead her cause. 1. He will be revenged on Zion's enemies (*v.* 2): *I was jealous for Zion, or of* Zion; that is, " I have of late been heartily concerned for her honour and interests, *with great jealousy.* The great wrath that was against her (*ch.* vii. 12) now turns against her adversaries. I am now *jealous for her with great fury*, and can no more bear to have her abused in her afflictions than I could bear to be abused by her provocations." This he had said before (*ch.* i. 14, 15), that they might promise themselves as much from the power of his anger, when it was turned for them, as they had felt from it when it was against them. The sins of Zion were her worst enemies, and had done her the most mischief; and therefore God, in his jealousy for her honour and comfort, will *take away her sins*, and then, whatever other enemies injured her, it was at their peril. 2. He will be resident in Zion's palaces (*v.* 3): " *I have returned to Zion*, after I had seemed so long to stand at a distance, and I will again *dwell in the midst of Jerusalem* as formerly." This secures to them the tokens of his presence in his ordinances and the instances of his favour in his providences.

II. That there shall be a wonderful reformation in Jerusalem, and religion, in the power of it, shall prevail and flourish there.

"*Jerusalem*, that has dealt treacherously both with God and man, shall become so famous for fidelity and honesty that it *shall be called* and known by the name of *a city of truth*, and the inhabitants of it shall be called *children that will not lie.* The *faithful city* has become a *harlot* (Isa. i. 21), but shall now become a *faithful city* again, faithful to the *God of Israel* and to the worship of him only." This was fulfilled; for the Jews after the captivity, though there was much amiss among them, were never guilty of idolatry. Jerusalem shall be called *the mountain of the Lord of hosts*, owning him and owned by him, and therefore *the holy mountain*, cleared from idols and consecrated to God, and not, as it had been, the *mount of corruption*, 2 Kings xxiii. 13. Note, The city of God ought to be *a city of truth* and the *mountain of the Lord of hosts a holy mountain.* Those that profess religion, and relation to God, must study to adorn their profession by all instances of godliness and honesty.

III. That there shall be in Jerusalem a great increase of people, and all the marks and tokens of a profound tranquillity. When it has become a *city of truth* and a *mountain of holiness*, it is then peaceable and prosperous, and every thing in it looks bright and pleasant. 1. You may look with pleasure upon the generation that is going off the stage, and see them fairly quitting it in the ordinary course of nature, and not driven off from it by war, famine, or pestilence (*v.* 4): *In the streets of Jerusalem*, that had been filled with the bodies of the slain, or deserted and left desolate, shall now dwell *old men* and *old women*, who have not been cut off by untimely deaths (either through their own intemperance or God's vengeance), but have the even thread of their days spun out to a full length; they shall feel no distemper but the decay of nature, and go to their grave in a full age, as a *shock of corn in his season.* They shall have *every one his staff in his hand, for very age*, to support him, as Jacob, who *worshipped, leaning upon the top of his staff*, Heb. xi. 21. Old age needs a support, and should not be ashamed to use it, but should furnish itself with divine graces, which will be the strength of the heart and a better support than a staff in the hand. Note, The hoary head, as it is a crown of glory to those that wear it, so it is to the places where they live. It is a graceful thing to a city to see abundance of old people in it; it is a sign, not only of the healthfulness of the air, but of the prevalence of virtue and the suppression and banishment of those many vices which cut off the number of men's months in the midst; it is a sign, not only that the climate is temperate, but that the people are so. 2. You may look with as much pleasure upon the generation that is rising up in their room (*v.* 5): *The streets of the city shall be full of boys and girls playing in the streets.* This intimates, (1.) That they shall be blessed with a multitude of children; their families shall increase and multiply, and replenish the city, which was an early product of the divine blessing, Gen. i. 28. Happy the man, happy the nation, whose quiver is full of these arrows! They shall have of both sexes, *boys and girls,* in whom their families shall afterwards be joined, and another generation raised up. (2.) That their children shall be healthful, and strong, and active; their boys and girls shall not lie sick in bed, or sit pining in the corner, but (which is a pleasant sight to parents) shall be hearty and cheerful, and play in the streets. It is their pleasant playing age; let us not grudge it to them; much good may it do them and no harm. *Evil days* will come time enough, and *years* of which they will *say* that they have *no pleasure in them,* in consideration of which they are concerned not to spend all their time in play, but to remember their Creator. (3.) That they shall have great plenty, meat enough for all their mouths. In time of famine we find the children *swooning as the wounded, in the streets of the city,* Lam. ii. 11, 12. If they are playing in the streets, it is a good sign that they want for nothing. (4.) That they shall not be terrified with the alarms of war, but enjoy a perfect security. There shall be *no breaking* in of invaders, *no going out* of deserters, *no complaining in the streets* (Ps. cxliv. 14); for, when there is playing in the streets, it is a sign that there is little care or fear there. Time was when the enemy hunted their steps so closely that they could not go in their streets (Lam. iv. 18), but now they shall *play in the streets* and fear no evil. (5.) That they shall have love and peace among themselves. The boys and girls shall not be fighting in the streets, as sometimes in cities that are divided into factions and parties the children soon imbibe and express the mutual resentments of the parents; but they shall be innocently and lovingly *playing in the streets,* not devouring, but diverting, one another. (6.) That the sports and diversions used shall be all harmless and inoffensive; the boys and girls shall have no other play than what they are willing that persons should see *in the streets,* no play that seeks corners, no playing the fool, or playing the wanton, for it is the mountain of the Lord, the *holy mountain,* but honest and modest recreations, which they have no reason to be ashamed of. (7.) That childish youthful sports shall be confined to the age of childhood and youth. It is pleasing to see the *boys and girls playing in the streets,* but it is ill-favoured to see men and women playing there, who should fill up their time with work and business. It is well enough for *children* to be *sitting in the market-place,* crossing questions (Matt. xi. 16, 17), but it is no way fit that men, who are able to *work in the vineyard,* should *stand all the day idle* there, Matt. xx. 3.

IV. That the scattered Israelites shall be brought together again from all parts whither they were dispersed (*v.* 7): "*I will save my people from the east country, and from the west;* I will save them from being lost, or losing themselves, in Babylon, or in Egypt, or in any other country whither they were driven." They shall neither be detained by the nations among whom they sojourn nor shall they incorporate with them; but I will *save them,* will separate them, and will bring them to their own land again; by the prosperity of their land I will invite them back, and at the same time incline them to return; and *they shall dwell in the midst of Jerusalem,* shall choose to dwell there, because it is the holy city, though, upon many other accounts, it was more eligible to dwell in the country; and therefore we find (Neh. xi. 2) that *the people blessed all the men who willingly offered themselves to dwell at Jerusalem.* V. That God would renew his covenant with them, would be faithful to them and make them so to him: *They shall be my people and I will be their God.* That is the foundation and crown of all these promises, and is inclusive of all happiness. They shall obey God's laws, and God will secure and advance all their interests. This contract shall be made, shall be new-made, *in truth* and *in righteousness.* Some think that the former denotes God's part of the covenant (he will be *their God in truth,* he will make good all his promises of favour to them) and the latter man's part of the covenant—they shall be his people in *righteousness,* they shall be a righteous people and shall abound in the *fruits of righteousness,* and shall not, as they have done, deal treacherously and unjustly with their God. See Hos. ii. 19, 20. God will never leave nor forsake them in a way of mercy, as he has promised them; and they shall never leave nor forsake him in a way of duty, as they have promised him. These promises were fulfilled in the flourishing state of the Jewish church, for some ages, between the captivity and Christ's time; they were to have a further and a fuller accomplishment in the gospel-church, that *heavenly Jerusalem,* which is from above, is free, and is the *mother of us all;* but the fullest accomplishment of all will be in the future state.

All these precious promises are here ratified, and the doubts of God's people silenced, with that question (*v.* 6): "*If it be marvellous in the eyes of this people, should it be marvellous in my eyes?* If it seem unlikely to you that ever Jerusalem should be thus repaired, should be thus replenished, is it therefore impossible with God?" The *remnant of this people* (and God's people in this world are but a remnant), being few and feeble, thought all this was too good news to be true, especially *in these days,* these difficult days, these cloudy and dark days. Considering how bad the times are, it is highly improbable, it is morally impossible, they should ever come to be so good as the prophet speaks. How can these things be? How can dry bones live? But should it therefore appear so in the eyes of God? Note, We do both God and ourselves a deal of wrong if we think that, when we are *non-plussed,* he is so, and that he cannot get over the difficulties which to us seem insuperable. *With men this is impossible; but with God all things are possible;* so far are God's thoughts and ways above ours.

9 Thus saith the LORD of hosts; Let your hands be strong, ye that hear in these days these words by the mouth of the prophets, which *were* in the day *that* the foundation of the house of the LORD of hosts was laid, that the temple might be built. 10 For before these days there was no hire for man, nor any hire for beast; neither *was there any* peace to him that went out or came in because of the affliction : for I set all men every one against his neighbour. 11 But now I *will* not *be* unto the residue of this people as in the former days, saith the LORD of hosts. 12 For the seed *shall be* prosperous; the vine shall give her fruit, and the ground shall give her increase, and the heavens shall give their dew; and I will cause the remnant of this people to possess all these *things.* 13 And it shall come to pass, *that* as ye were a curse among the heathen, O house of Judah, and house of Israel; so will I save you, and ye shall be a blessing : fear not, *but* let your hands be strong. 14 For thus saith the LORD of hosts; As I thought to punish you, when your fathers provoked me to wrath, saith the LORD of hosts, and I repented not : 15 So again have I thought in these days to do well unto Jerusalem and to the house of Judah : fear ye not. 16 These *are* the things that ye shall do; Speak ye every man the truth to his neighbour; execute the judgment of truth and peace in your gates : 17 And let none of you imagine evil in your hearts against his neighbour; and love no false oath : for all these *are things* that I hate, saith the LORD.

God, by the prophet, here gives further assurances of the mercy he had in store for

Judah and Jerusalem. Here is line upon line for their comfort, as before there was for their conviction. These verses contain strong encouragements with reference to the difficulties they now laboured under. And we may observe,

I. Who they were to whom these encouragements did belong—to those who, in obedience to the call of God by his prophets, applied in good earnest to the building of the temple (*v.* 9) : " *Let your hands be strong, that are busy at work for God, you that hear in these days these words by the mouth of the prophets,* and are not disobedient to them *as your fathers were,* in the former days, to the words of those prophets that were sent to them. You may take the comfort of the promises, and shall have the benefit of them, who have obeyed the precepts given you *in the day that the foundation of the house of the Lord was laid,* when you were told that, having begun with it, you must go on, *that the temple might be built;* God told you that you must go on with it, and you have laboured hard at it for some time, in obedience to the heavenly vision. Now you are those whose hands must be strengthened and whose hearts must be comforted, with these precious promises; to you is the word of this consolation sent." Note, Those, and those only, that are employed for God, may expect to be encouraged by him; those who lay their hands to the plough of duty shall have them strengthened with the promises of mercy; and those who avoid their fathers' faults, not only cut off the entail of the curse, but have it turned into a blessing.

II. What the discouragements were which they had hitherto laboured under, *v.* 10. These are mentioned as a foil to the blessings God was now about to bestow upon them, to make them appear the more strange, to the glory of God, and the more sweet, to their comfort. The truth was the times had long been very bad, and the calamities and difficulties of them were many and great. 1. Trade was dead; there was nothing to be done and therefore nothing to be got. *Before these days* of reformation began *there was no hire for man, nor any hire for beasts.* The fruits of the earth (though it had long lain fallow, and therefore, one would think, should have been the more fertile) were thin and poor, so that the husbandman had no occasion to hire harvest people to reap his corn, nor teams to carry it home, for he could be scarcely said to have any. Merchants had no goods to import or export, so that they needed not to hire either men or beasts; hence the poor people, who lived by their labour, had no way of getting bread for themselves and their families. 2. Travelling was dangerous, so that all commerce both by sea and land was cut off; nay, none durst stir abroad so much as to visit their friends, for *there was no peace to him that went out, or came in, because of the affliction.* The Samaritans, and Ammonites, and their other evil neighbours, made inroads upon them in small parties, and seized all they could lay their hands on; the roads were infested with highwaymen, and both city and country with housebreakers; so that neither men's persons nor their goods were safe at home or abroad. 3. There was no such thing as friendship or good neighbourship among them: *I set all men every one against his neighbour.* In this there was a great deal of sin, for these wars and fightings came from men's lust, and this God was not the author of; but there was in it a great deal of misery also, and so God was in it a just avenger of their disobedience to him; because they were of an *evil spirit* towards him, a spirit of contradiction to his laws, God sent among them an evil spirit, to make them vexatious one to another. Those that throw off the love of God forfeit the comfort of brotherly love.

III. What encouragement they shall now have to proceed in the good work they are about, and to hope that it shall yet be well with them: "Thus and thus you have been harassed and afflicted, but now God will change his way towards you, *v.* 11. Now that you return to your duty God will comfort you according to the time that he has afflicted you; the ebbing tide shall flow again." 1. God will not proceed in his controversy with them: *I will not be to them as in the former days.* Note, It is with us well or ill according as God is to us; for every creature is that to us which he makes it to be. And, if we walk not contrary to God as in the former days, he will not walk contrary to us as in the former days; for it is only *with the froward* that he will *wrestle.* 2. They shall have great plenty and abundance of all good things (*v.* 12): *The seed sown shall be prosperous,* and yield a great increase; *the vine shall give her fruit,* which makes glad the heart, and *the ground* its products, which strengthen the heart; they shall have all they can desire, not only for necessity, but for ornament and delight. The *heavens shall give their dew,* without which the earth would not yield her increase, which is a constant intimation to us of the beneficence of the God of heaven to men on earth and of their dependence on him. It is said of a *sweeping rain* that it *leaves no food* (Prov. xxviii. 3); but here the *gentle dew* waters the earth, that it may give *seed to the sower and bread to the eater.* And thus God will *cause the remnant of this people to possess all these things.* They are but a *remnant,* a *residue,* very few, one would think scarcely worth looking after; but, now that they are at work for God, he will take care that they shall want nothing which is fit for them. This confirms what the prophet's colleague had said, a little before (Hag. ii. 16, 19), *From this day will I bless you.* Note, God's people, that serve him faithfully, have

1438

great possessions. "*All* is yours, for you are Christ's." 3. They shall recover their credit among their neighbours (*v.* 13): *You were a curse among the heathen.* Every one censured and condemned them, spoke ill of them, and wished ill to them, upon the account of the great disgrace that they were under; some think that they were made a form of execration, so that if a man would load his enemy with the heaviest curse he would say, *God make thee like a Jew!* "But now, *I will save you, and you shall be a blessing.* Your restoration shall be as much taken notice of to your honour as ever your desolation and dispersion were to your reproach; you shall be applauded and admired as much as ever you were vilified and run down, shall be courted and caressed as much as ever you were slighted and abandoned." Most men smile or frown upon their neighbours according as Providence smiles or frowns upon them; but those whom God plainly blesses as his own, shows favour to and puts honour upon, we ought also to respect and be kind to. The blessed of the Lord are the blessing of the land, and should be so accounted by us. This is here promised to the house both of Israel and Judah; for many of the ten tribes returned out of captivity with the two tribes, and shared with them in those blessings; and, it is probable, besides what came at first, many, very many, flocked to them afterwards, when they saw their affairs take this turn. 4. God himself will determine to do them good, *v.* 14, 15. All their comforts take rise from the thoughts of the love that God had towards them, Jer. xxix. 11. Compare these promises with the former threatenings. (1.) When they *provoked him* to anger with *their sins,* he said that he would *punish them,* and so he did; it was his declared purpose to bring destroying judgments upon them, and, because they repented not of their rebellions against him, he repented not of his threatenings against them, but let the sentence of the law take its course. Note, God's punishing sinners is never a sudden and hasty resolve, but is always the product of thought, and there is a counsel in that part of the will of God. If the sinner turn not, God will not turn. (2.) Now that they pleased him with their services; he said that he would *do them good;* and will he not be as true to his promises as he was to his threatenings? No doubt he will: "*So again have I thought to do well to Jerusalem in those days,* when you begin to hearken to the voice of God speaking to you by his prophets; and these thoughts also shall be performed."

IV. The use they are to make of these encouragements.

1. Let them take the comfort which these promises give to them: *Fear you not* (*v.* 15); *let your hands be strong* (*v.* 9); and both together (*v.* 13), *Fear not, but let your hands be strong.* (1.) The difficulties they met with in their work must not drive them from it,

nor make them go on heavily in it, for the issue would be good and the reward great. Let this therefore animate them to proceed with vigour and cheerfulness. (2.) The dangers they were exposed to from their enemies must not terrify them; those that have God for them, engaged to do them good, need not fear *what man can do against them.*

2. Let them do the duty which those promises call for from them, *v.* 16, 17. The very same duties which the former prophets pressed upon their fathers from the consideration of the wrath threatened (*ch.* vii. 9, 10) this prophet presses upon them from the consideration of the mercy promised: " Leave it to God to perform for you what he has promised, in his own way and time, but upon condition that you make conscience of your duty. *These are the things then that you shall do;* this is your part of the covenant; these are the articles which you are to perform, fulfil, and keep, that you may not put a bar in your own door and stop the current of God's favours." (1.) " You must never tell a lie, but always speak as you think, and as the matter is, to the best of your knowledge: *Speak you every man the truth to his neighbour,* both in bargains and in common converse; dread every word that looks like a lie." This precept the apostle quotes (Eph. iv. 25), and backs it with this reason, *We are members one of another.* (2.) Those that are entrusted with the administration of public justice must see to it, not only that none be wronged by it, but that those who are wronged be righted by it: *Execute the judgment of truth and peace in your gates.* Let the judges that sit in the gates in all their judicial proceedings have regard both to truth and to peace; let them take care to do justice, to accommodate differences, and to prevent vexatious suits. It must be a judgment of truth in order to peace, and making those friends that were at variance, and a judgment of peace as far as is consistent with truth, and no further. (3.) No man must bear malice against his neighbour upon any account; this is the same with what we had *ch.* vii. 10. We must not only keep our hands from doing evil, but we must watch over our hearts, that they *imagine not any evil* against our neighbour, Prov. iii. 29. Injury and mischief must be crushed in the thought, in the embryo. (4.) Great reverence must be had for an oath, and conscience made of it: " Never take a false oath, nay, *love no false oath;* that is, hate it, dread it, keep at a distance from it. Love not to impose oaths upon others, lest they swear falsely; love not that any should take a false oath for your benefit, and forswear themselves to do you a kindness." A very good reason is annexed against all these corrupt and wicked practices: " For *all these are things that I hate,* and therefore you must hate them if you expect to have God your friend." These things

here forbidden are all of them found among the *seven things which the Lord hates,* Prov. vi. 16—19. Note, We must forbear sin, not only because God is angry at it, and therefore it is dangerous to us, but because he hates it, and therefore it ill becomes us and is a very ungrateful thing.

18 And the word of the LORD of hosts came unto me, saying, 19 Thus saith the LORD of hosts; The fast of the fourth *month,* and the fast of the fifth, and the fast of the seventh, and the fast of the tenth, shall be to the house of Judah joy and gladness, and cheerful feasts; therefore love the truth and peace. 20 Thus saith the LORD of hosts; *It shall* yet *come to pass,* that there shall come people, and the inhabitants of many cities: 21 And the inhabitants of one *city* shall go to another, saying, Let us go speedily to pray before the LORD, and to seek the LORD of hosts: I will go also. 22 Yea, many people and strong nations shall come to seek the LORD of hosts in Jerusalem, and to pray before the LORD. 23 Thus saith the LORD of hosts; In those days *it shall come to pass,* that ten men shall take hold out of all languages of the nations, even shall take hold of the skirt of him that is a Jew, saying, We will go with you: for we have heard *that* God *is* with you.

These verses contain two precious promises, for the further encouragement of those pious Jews that were hearty in building the temple.

I. That a happy period should be put to their fasts, and there should be no more occasion for them, but they should be converted into thanksgiving days, *v.* 19. This is a direct answer to the enquiry concerning their fasts, *ch.* vii. 3. Those of them that fasted in hypocrisy had their doom in the foregoing chapter, but those that in sincerity humbled themselves before God, and sought his face, have here a comfortable assurance given them of a large share in the happy times approaching. The four *yearly fasts* which they had religiously observed should be *to the house of Judah joy and gladness, and solemn feasts,* and those cheerful ones. Note. Joyous times will come to the church after troublous times; if weeping endure for more than a night, and joy come not next morning, yet the morning will come that will introduce it at length. And, when God comes towards us in ways of mercy, we must meet him with joy and thankfulness; when God turns judgments into mercies we must turn fasts into festivals, and thus *walk after the Lord*. And those who *sow in tears* with Zion shall *reap in joy* with her ; those who submit to the restraints of her solemn fasts while they continue shall share in the triumphs of her cheerful feasts when they come, Isa. lxvi. 10. The inference from this promise is, " *Therefore love the truth and peace;* be faithful and honest in all your dealings, and let it be a pleasure to you to be so, though thereby you cut yourselves short of those gains which you see others get dishonestly ; and, as much as in you lies, live peaceably with all men, and be in your element when you are in charity. Let the truths of God rule in your heads, and let the peace of God rule in your hearts."

II. That a great accession should be made to the church by the conversion of many foreigners, *v.* 20—23. This was fulfilled but in part when, in the latter times of the Jewish church, there were abundance of proselytes from all the countries about, and some that lay very remote, who came yearly to worship at Jerusalem, which added very much both to the grandeur and wealth of that city, and contributed greatly to the making of it so considerable as it came to be before our Saviour's time, though now it was but just peeping out of its ruins. But it would be acccomplished much more fully in the conversion of the Gentiles to the faith of Christ, and the incorporating of them with the believing Jews in one great body, under Christ the head, a *mystery* which is *made manifest* by the *scriptures of the prophets* (Rom. xvi. 26), and by this among the rest, which makes it strange that when it was accomplished it was so great a surprise and stumbling-block to the Jews. Observe,

1. Who they are that shall be added to the church—*people, and the inhabitants of many cities* (*v.* 20); not only a few ignorant country people that may be easily imposed upon, or some idle people that have nothing else to do, but intelligent inquisitive citizens, men of business and acquaintance with the world, shall embrace the gospel of Christ ; *yea, many people and strong nations* (*v.* 22), some of *all languages, v.* 23. By this it appears that they are brought into the church, not by human persuasion, for they are of different languages, not by external force, for they are strong nations, able to have kept their ground if they had been so attacked, but purely by the effectual working of divine truth and grace. Note, God has his remnant in all parts ; and in the general assembly of the church of the first-born some will be found *out of all nations and kindreds*, Rev. vii. 9.

2. How their accession to the church is described : They shall come *to pray before the Lord and to seek the Lord of hosts* (*v.* 21); and, to show that this is the main matter in which their conversion consists,

it is repeated (*v.* 22) : They *shall come to seek the Lord of hosts in Jerusalem, and to pray before the Lord*. No mention is made of their offering sacrifices, not only because these were not expected from the proselytes of the gate, but because, when the Gentiles should be brought in, sacrifice and offering should be quite abolished. See who are to be accounted converts to God and members of the church : and all that are converts to God are members of the church. (1.) They are such as *seek the Lord of hosts*, such as enquire for *God their Maker*, covet and court his favour, and are truly desirous to know his mind and will and sincerely devoted to his honour and glory. *This is the generation of those that seek him.* (2.) They are such as *pray before the Lord*,—such as make conscience, and make a business, of the duty of prayer,—such as dare not, would not, for all the world, live without it,—such as by prayer pay their homage to God, own their dependence upon him, maintain their communion with him, and fetch in mercy and grace from him. (3.) They are such as herein have an eye to the divine revelation and institution, which is signified by their doing this *in Jerusalem*, the place which God had chosen, where his word was, where his temple was, which was a type of Christ and his mediation, which all faithful worshippers will have a believing regard to.

3. How unanimous they shall be in their accession to the church, and how zealous in exciting one another to it (*v.* 21) : *The inhabitants of one city shall go to another*, as formerly when they went up from all parts of the country to worship at the yearly feasts ; and they shall say, *Let us go speedily to pray before the Lord ; I will go also.* This intimates, (1.) That those who are brought into an acquaintance with Christ themselves should do all they can to bring others acquainted with him ; thus Andrew invited Peter to Christ and Philip invited Nathanael. True grace hates monopolies. (2.) That those who are duly sensible of their need of Christ, and of the favour of God through him, will stir up themselves and others without delay to hasten to him : " *Let us go speedily to pray ;* it is for our lives, and the lives of our souls, that we are to petition, and therefore it concerns us to lose no time ; in a matter of such moment delays are dangerous." (3.) That our communion with God is very much assisted and furthered by the communion of saints. It is pleasant to go *to the house of God in company* (Ps. lv. 14), *with the multitude* (Ps. xlii. 4), and it is of good use to those that do so to excite one another to go speedily and lose no time ; we should be glad when it is said to us, *Let us go*, Ps. cxxii. 1. As iron sharpens iron, so may good men sharpen the countenances and spirits one of another in that which is good. (4.) That those who stir up others to that which is good must take heed that they do

not turn off, or tire, or draw back themselves; he that says, *Let us go*, says, *I will go also.* What good we put others upon doing we must see to it that we do ourselves, else we shall be judged out of our own mouths. Not, " Do you go, and I will stay at home ;" but, " Do you go, and I will go with you." " A singular pattern (says Mr. Pemble) of zealous charity, that neither leaves others behind nor turns others before it."

4. Upon what inducement they shall join themselves to the church, not for the church's sake, but for his sake who dwells in it (*v.* 23): *Ten men* of different nations and languages *shall take hold of the skirt of him that is a Jew*, begging of him not to outgo them, but to take them along with him. This intimates the great honour they have for a Jew, as one of the chosen people of God, and therefore well worthy their acquaintance; they cannot all come to take him by the hand, or embrace him in their arms, but are ambitious to take hold of the skirt of his robe, to touch the hem of his garment, saying, *We will go with you, for we have heard that God is with you.* The gospel was preached to the Jews first (for of that nation the apostles were) and by them it was carried to the Gentiles. St. Paul was a Jew whose skirt many took hold of when they welcomed him as *an angel of God*, and begged him to take them along with him to Christ ; thus the Greeks took hold of Philip's skirt, saying, *Sir, we would see Jesus*, John xii. 21. Note, It is the privilege of the saints that they have God with them, have him among them —the knowledge, and fear, and worship of him ; they have his favour and gracious presence, and this should invite us into communion with them. It is good being with those who have God with them, and those who *join themselves to the Lord* must *join themselves to his disciples ;* if we take God for our God, we must take his people for our people, cast in our lot among them, and be willing to take our lot with them.

CHAP. IX.

At this chapter begins another sermon, which is continued to the end of ch. xi. It is called, " The burden of the word of the Lord," for every word of God has weight in it to those who regard it, and will be a heavy weight upon those who do not, a dead weight. Here is, I. A prophecy against the Jews' unrighteous neighbours —the Syrians, Tyrians, Philistines, and others (ver. 1—6), with an intimation of mercy to some of them, in their conversion (ver. 7), and a promise of mercy to God's people, in their protection, ver. 8. II. A prophecy of their righteous King, the Messiah, and his coming, with a description of him (ver. 9) and of his kingdom, the nature and extent of it, ver. 10. III. An account of the obligation the Jews lay under to Christ for their deliverance out of their captivity in Babylon, ver. 11, 12. IV. A prophecy of the victories and successes God would grant to the Jews over their enemies, as typical of our great deliverance by Christ, ver. 13—15. V. A promise of great plenty, and joy, and honour, which God had in reserve for his people (ver. 16, 17), which was written for their encouragement.

THE burden of tho word of thc Lord in the land of Hadrach, and Damascus *shall be* the rest thereof: when the eyes of man, as of all the tribes of Israel, *shall be* toward the Lord. 2 And Hamath also shall

border thereby ; Tyrus, and Zidon, though it be very wise. 3 And Tyrus did build herself a strong hold, and heaped up silver as the dust, and fine gold as the mire of the streets. 4 Behold, the Lord will cast her out, and he will smite her power in the sea ; and she shall be devoured with fire. 5 Ashkelon shall see *it*, and fear ; Gaza also *shall see it*, and be very sorrowful, and Ekron ; for her expectation shall be ashamed; and the king shall perish from Gaza, and Ashkelon shall not be inhabited. 6 And a bastard shall dwell in Ashdod, and I will cut off the pride of the Philistines. 7 And I will take away his blood out of his mouth, and his abominations from between his teeth : but he that remaineth, even he, *shall be* for our God, and he shall be as a governor in Judah, and Ekron as a Jebusite. 8 And I will encamp about mine house because of the army, because of him that passeth by, and because of him that returneth: and no oppressor shall pass through them any more : for now have I seen with mine eyes.

After the precious promises we had in the foregoing chapter of favour to God's people, their persecutors, who hated them, come to be reckoned with, those particularly that bordered close upon them.

I. The Syrians had been bad neighbours to Israel, and God had a controversy with them. The word of the Lord shall be a *burden in the land of Hadrach*, that is, of *Syria*, but it does not appear why it was so called. That that kingdom is meant is plain, because Damascus, the metropolis of that kingdom, is said to be the *rest* of this burden ; that is, the judgments here threatened shall light and lie upon that city. Those are miserable upon whom the burden of the word of the Lord rests, upon whom *the wrath of God abides* (John iii. 36) ; for it is a weight that they can neither shake off nor bear up under. There are those whom God *causes his fury to rest* upon. Those whom the wrath of God makes its mark it will be sure to hit ; those whom it makes its rest it will be sure to sink. And the reason of this burden's resting on Damascus is because *the eyes of man, as of all the tribes of Israel* (or rather, *even of all the tribes of Israel*), are *towards the Lord*, because the people of God by faith and prayer look up to him for succour and relief and depend upon him to take their part against their enemies. Note, It is a sign that God is about to appear remarkably for his people when he raises their believing expectations from him and dependence upon him, and when by his grace he turns them from idols to himself. Isa. xvii. 7, 8, *At that day shall a man look to his Maker.* It may be read thus, *for the Lord has an eye upon man, and upon all the tribes of Israel;* he is King of nations as well as King of saints; he governs the world as well as the church, and therefore will punish the sins of other people as well as those of his own people. God is *Judge of all,* and therefore all must give account of themselves to him. When St. Paul was converted at Damascus, and preached there, and disputed with the Jews, then the word of the Lord might be said to rest there, and then *the eyes of men,* of other men besides *the tribes of Israel,* began to be *towards the Lord;* see Acts ix. 22. Hamath, a country which lay north of Damascus, and which we often read of, *shall border thereby* (v. 2) ; it joins to Syria, and shall share in the *burden of the word of the Lord* that rests upon Damascus. The Jews have a proverb, *Woe to the wicked man, and woe to his neighbour,* who is in danger of partaking in his sins and in his plagues. Woe to *the land of Hadrach,* and woe to *Hamath that borders thereby.*

II. Tyre and Zidon come next to be called to an account here, as in other prophecies, v. 2—4. Observe here,

1. Tyrus flourishing, thinking herself very safe, and ready to set God's judgments, not only at a distance, but at defiance; for, (1.) She is *very wise.* It is spoken ironically; she thinks herself very wise, and able to outwit even the wisdom of God. It is granted that her king is a great politician, and that her statesmen are so, Ezek. xxviii. 3. But with all their wit and policy they shall not be able to evade the judgments of God when they come with commission; there is no *wisdom* nor *counsel against the Lord;* nay, it is his honour to take the wise in their own craftiness. (2.) She is very strong, and well fortified both by nature and art : *Tyrus did build herself a strong-hold,* which she thought could never be brought down nor got over. (3.) She is very rich; and *money is a defence;* it is the sinews of war, Eccl. vii. 12. By her vast trade she has *heaped up silver as the dust, and fine gold as the mire of the streets,* that is, she has an abundance of them, heaps of silver as common as heaps of sand, Job xxvii. 16. Solomon made silver to be in Jerusalem as the *stones of the streets;* but Tyre went further, and made *fine gold* to be as *the mire of the streets.* It were well if we could all learn so to look upon it, in comparison with the merchandise of wisdom and grace and the gains thereof.

2. Tyrus falling, after all. Her wisdom, and wealth, and strength, shall not be able to secure her (v. 4) : *The Lord will cast her out* of that strong-hold wherein she has for-

tified herself, will *make her poor* (so some read it); there have been instances of those that have fallen from the height of plenty to the depth of poverty, and great riches have come to nothing. God will *smite her power in the sea:* her being surrounded by the water shall not secure her, but *she shall be devoured with fire,* and burnt down to the ground. Tyrus, being seated in the midst of the water, was, one would have thought, in danger of being some time or other overflowed or washed away by that; yet God chooses to destroy it by the contrary element. Sometimes he brings ruin upon his enemies by those means which they least suspect. Water enough was nigh at hand to quench the flames of Tyre, and yet by them she shall be devoured; for who can put out the fire which the breath of the Almighty blows up?

III. God next contends with the Philistines, with their great cities and great lords, that bordered southward upon Israel.

1. They shall be alarmed and affrighted by the word of the Lord lighting and resting upon Damascus (v. 5); the disgraces of Israel had many a time been *published in the streets of Ashkelon,* and they had triumphed in them; but now *Ashkelon shall see* the ruin of her friends and allies, and shall *fear; Gaza also shall see it, and be very sorrowful, and Ekron,* concluding that their own turns come next, now that the cup of trembling goes round. What will become of their house when their neighbour's is on fire? They had looked upon Tyre and Zidon as a barrier to their country; but, when those strong cities were ruined, their *expectations* from them *were ashamed,* as our expectation from all creatures will be in the issue.

2. They shall themselves be ruined and wasted. (1.) The government shall be dissolved : *The king shall perish from Gaza,* not only the present king shall be cut off, but there shall be no succession, no successor. (2.) The cities shall be dispeopled : *Ashkelon shall not be inhabited;* the rightful owners shall be expelled, either slain or carried into captivity. (3.) Foreigners shall take possession of their land and become masters of all its wealth (v. 6) : *A bastard shall dwell in Ashdod;* a spurious brood of strangers shall enter upon the inheritances of the natives, which they have no more right to than a bastard has to the estates of the legitimate children. And thus God will *cut off the pride of the Philistines,* all the strength and wealth which they prided themselves in, and which were the ground of their confidence in themselves and their contempt of the Israel of God. This prophecy of the destruction of the Philistines, and of Damascus, and Tyre, was accomplished, not long after this, by Alexander the Great, who ravaged all these countries with his victorious army, took the cities, and planted colonies in them, which Quintus Curtius gives a particular account of in the history of his conquests. And some

1442

think he is meant by the bastard that shall dwell in Ashdod, for his mother Olympia owned him begotten in adultery, but pretended it was by Jupiter. The Jews afterwards got ground of the Philistines, Syrians, and others of their neighbours, took some of their cities from them and possessed their countries, as appears by the histories of Josephus and the Maccabees, and this was foretold before, Zeph. ii. 4, &c. ; Obad. 20.

3. Some among them shall be converted, and brought home to God, by his gospel and grace; so some understand *v.* 7, as a promise, (1.) That God would take away the sins of these nations—*their blood* and *their abominations*, their cruelties and their idolatries. God will part between them and these sins which they have rolled under their tongue as a sweet morsel, and are as loth to part with as men are to part with the meat out of their mouths, and which they hold fast between their teeth. Nothing is too hard for the grace of God to do. (2.) That he would accept of a remnant of them for his own: *He that remains shall be for our God.* God would preserve a remnant even of these nations, that should be the monuments of his mercy and grace and be set apart for him; and the disadvantages of their birth shall be no bar to their acceptance with God, but a Philistine shall be as acceptable to God, upon gospel-terms, as one of Judah, nay, as a governor, or chief one, in Judah, and a man of Ekron shall be as a Jebusite, or a man of Jerusalem, as a proselyted Jebusite, as Araunah the Jebusite, 2 Sam. xxiv. 16. In Christ Jesus there is no distinction of nations, but all are one in him, all alike welcome to him.

IV. In all this God intends mercy for Israel, and it is in kindness to them that God will deal thus with the neighbouring nations, to avenge their quarrel for what is past and to secure them for the future.

1. Thus some understand the seventh verse, as intimating, (1.) That thus God would deliver his people from their bloody adversaries, who hated them, and to whom they were an abomination, when they were just ready to devour them and make a prey of them: I will *take away his blood* (that is, the blood of Israel) out of the mouth of the Philistines and *from between their teeth* (Amos iii. 12), when, in their hatred of them and enmity to them, they were greedily devouring them. (2.) That he would thus give them victory and dominion over them: And *he that remains* (that is, the remnant of Israel) *shall be for our God,* shall be taken into his favour, shall own him and be owned by him, and *he shall be as a governor in Judah;* though the Jews have been long in servitude, they shall recover their ancient dignity, and be victorious, as David and other governors in Judah formerly were; and Ekron (that is, the Philistines) shall be as the Jebusites, and the rest of the devoted nations, who were brought into subjection under them.

2. However, this is plainly the sense of *v.* 8, that God will take his people under his special protection, and *therefore* will weaken their neighbours, that it may not be in their power to do them a mischief: *I will encamp about my house because of the army.* Note, God's house lies in the midst of an enemy's country, and his church is as a lily among thorns; and therefore God's power and goodness are to be observed in the special preservation of it. The *camp of the saints,* being a little flock in comparison with the numerous armies of the powers of darkness that are set against it round about, would certainly be swallowed up if the angels of God did not encamp about it, as they did about Elisha, to deliver it, Rev. xx. 9; Ps. xxxiv. 7. When the times are unusually perilous, when armies are marching and counter-marching, and all bearing ill-will to Zion, then Providence will as it were double its guards upon the church of God, *because of him that passes by and because of him that returns,* that whether he return a conqueror or conquered he may do it no harm. And, as none that pass by shall hurt them, so *no oppressor shall pass through them any more;* they shall have no enemy within themselves to rule them with rigour, and *to make their lives bitter* to them *with sore bondage,* as of old in Egypt. This was fulfilled when, for some time after the struggles of the Maccabees, Judea was a free and flourishing state, or perhaps when Alexander the Great, struck with an awe of Jaddus the high priest, favoured the Jews, and took them under his protection, at the same time when he wasted the neighbouring countries. And the reason given for all this is, "*For now have I seen with my eyes,* now have I carefully distinguished between my people and other people, with whom before they seemed to have their lot in common, and have made it to appear that I know those that are mine." This agrees with Ps. xxxiv. 15, *The eyes of the Lord are upon the righteous;* now his eyes, which *run to and fro through the earth,* shall fix upon them, that he may show himself tender of them, and *strong on their behalf,* 2 Chron. xvi. 9.

9 Rejoice greatly, O daughter of Zion; shout, O daughter of Jerusalem : behold, thy King cometh unto thee : he *is* just, and having salvation ; lowly, and riding upon an ass, and upon a colt the foal of an ass. 10 And I will cut off the chariot from Ephraim, and the horse from Jerusalem, and the battle bow shall be cut off : and he shall speak peace unto the heathen : and his dominion *shall be* from sea *even* to sea, and from the river *even* to the ends of the earth. 11 As for thee also, by the blood of

thy covenant I have sent forth thy prisoners out of the pit wherein *is* no water.

That here begins a prophecy of the Messiah and his kingdom is plain from the literal accomplishment of the ninth verse in, and its express application to, Christ's riding in triumph into *Jerusalem*, Matt. xxi. 5; John xii. 15.

I. Here is notice given of the approach of the Messiah promised, as matter of great joy to the Old-Testament church: *Behold, thy king cometh unto thee.* Christ is a king, invested with regal powers and prerogatives, a sovereign prince, an absolute monarch, having all power both in heaven and on earth. He is Zion's king. God has *set him upon his holy hill of Zion,* Ps. ii. 6. In Zion his glory as a king shines; thence *his law went forth,* even the *word of the Lord.* In the gospel-church his spiritual kingdom is administered; it is by him that the ordinances of the church are instituted, and its officers commissioned; and it is taken under his protection; he fights the church's battles and secures its interests, as its king. "This King has been long in coming, but now, *behold, he cometh;* he is at the door. There are but a few ages more to run out, and he that shall come will come. He *cometh unto thee;* the Word will shortly be made flesh, and dwell within thy borders; he will *come to his own.* And therefore *rejoice,* rejoice *greatly,* and *shout for joy;* look upon it as *good news,* and be assured it is true; please thyself to think that he is coming, that he is on his way towards thee; and be ready to go forth to meet him with acclamations of joy, as one not able to conceal it, it is so great, nor ashamed to own it, it is so just; cry *Hosanna* to him." Christ's approaches ought to be the church's applauses.

II. Here is such a description of him as renders him very amiable in the eyes of all his loving subjects, and his coming to them very acceptable. 1. He is a righteous ruler; all his acts of government will be exactly according to the rules of equity, for *he is just.* 2. He is a powerful protector to all those that bear faith and true allegiance to him, for he *has salvation;* he has it in his power; he has it to bestow upon all his subjects. He is the *God of salvation;* treasures of salvation are in him. He is *servatus—saving himself* (so some read it), rising out of the grave by his own power and so qualifying himself to be our Saviour. (3.) He is a *meek, humble, tender Father* to all his subjects as his children; he is *lowly;* he is *poor* and *afflicted* (so the word signifies), so it denotes the meanness of his condition; having *emptied himself,* he was *despised and rejected of men.* But the evangelist translates it so as to express the temper of his spirit: he is *meek,* not taking state upon him, nor resenting injuries, but *humbling himself* from first 1444

to last, condescending to the mean, compassionate to the miserable; this was a bright and excellent character of him as a prophet (Matt. xi. 29, *Learn of me, for I am meek and lowly in heart*), and no less so *as a king.* It was a proof of this that, when he made his public entry into his own city (and it was the only passage of his life that had any thing in it magnificent in the eye of the world), he chose to ride, not upon a stately horse, or in a chariot, as great men used to ride, but *upon an ass,* a beast of service indeed, but a poor silly and contemptible one, low and slow, and in those days ridden only by the meaner sort of people; nor was it an ass fitted for use, but an *ass's colt,* a little foolish unmanageable thing, that would be more likely to disgrace his rider than be any credit to him; and that not his own neither, nor helped off, as sometimes a sorry horse is, by good furniture, for he had no saddle, no housings, no trappings, no equipage, but his disciples' clothes thrown upon the colt; for he *made himself of no reputation* when he visited us in great humility.

III. His kingdom is here set forth in the glory of it. This king has, and will have, a kingdom, not of this world, but a spiritual kingdom, a *kingdom of heaven.* 1. It shall not be set up and advanced by external force, by an arm of flesh or carnal weapons of warfare. No; he *will cut off the chariot from Ephraim and the horses from Jerusalem* (v. 10), for he shall have no occasion for them while he himself rides upon an ass. He will, in kindness to his people, cut off their horses and chariots, that they may not cut themselves off from God by putting that confidence in them which they should put in the power of God only. He will himself undertake their protection, will himself be *a wall of fire about Jerusalem* and give his angels charge concerning it (those *chariots of fire and horses of fire*), and then the chariots and horses they had in their service shall be discarded and cut off as altogether needless. 2. It shall be propagated and established by the preaching of the gospel, the *speaking of peace to the heathen;* for Christ *came and preached peace to those that were afar off and to those that were nigh;* and so established his kingdom by proclaiming *on earth peace,* and *good-will towards men.* 3. His kingdom, as far as it prevails in the minds of men and has the ascendant over them, will make them peaceable, and slay all enmities; it will cut off the battle-bow, and *beat swords into plough-shares.* It will not only command the peace, but will *create the fruit of the lips,* peace. 4. It shall extend itself to all parts of the world, in defiance of the opposition given to it. "The chariot and horse that come against Ephraim and Jerusalem, to oppose the progress of Zion's King, shall be cut off; his gospel shall be preached to the world, and be received among the heathen, so that *his dominion shall be from sea to sea, and from the river even to the ends of the earth,* as was foretold by David," Ps. lxxii. 8. The preachers of the gospel shall carry it from one country, one island, to another, till some of the remotest corners of the world are enlightened and reduced by it.

IV. Here is an account of the great benefit procured for mankind by the Messiah, which is redemption from extreme misery, typified by the deliverance of the Jews out of their captivity in Babylon (*v.* 11): *As for thee also* (thee, O daughter of Jerusalem! or thee, O Messiah the Prince!) *by the blood of thy covenant,* by force and virtue of the covenant made with Abraham, sealed with the blood of circumcision, and the covenant made with Israel at Mount Sinai, sealed with the blood of sacrifices, in pursuance and performance of that covenant, *I have* now of late *sent forth thy prisoners,* thy captives out of Babylon, which was to them a most uncomfortable place, as *a pit* in which was *no-water.*" It was part of the covenant that, if in the land of their captivity, they sought the Lord, he would be found of them, Lev. xxvi. 42, 44, 45; Deut. xxx. 4. It was *by the blood of that covenant,* typifying the blood of Christ, in whom all God's covenants with man are yea and amen, that they were released out of captivity; and this was but a shadow of the great salvation wrought out by *thy King, O daughter of Zion!* Note, A sinful state is a state of bondage; it is a spiritual prison; it is a pit, or a dungeon, in which *there is no water,* no comfort at all to be had. We are all by nature prisoners in this pit; the *scripture has concluded* us all *under sin,* and bound us over to the justice of God. God is pleased to deal upon new terms with these prisoners, to enter into another covenant with them; the blood of Christ is the blood of that covenant, purchased it for us and all the benefits of it; by that blood of the covenant effectual provision is made for the sending forth of these prisoners upon easy and honourable terms, and proclamation made of *liberty to the captives and the opening of the prison to those that were bound,* like Cyrus's proclamation to the Jews in Babylon, which all those whose spirits God stirs up will come and take the benefit of.

12 Turn you to the strong hold, ye prisoners of hope: even to-day do I declare *that* I will render double unto thee; 13 When I have bent Judah for me, filled the bow with Ephraim, and raised up thy sons, O Zion, against thy sons, O Greece, and made thee as the sword of a mighty man. 14 And the LORD shall be seen over them, and his arrow shall go forth as the lightning:

and the LORD GOD shall blow the trumpet, and shall go with whirlwinds of the south. 15 The LORD of hosts shall defend them; and they shall devour, and subdue with sling-stones; and they shall drink, *and* make a noise as through wine; and they shall be filled like bowls, *and* as the corners of the altar. 16 And the LORD their God shall save them in that day as the flock of his people: for *they shall be as* the stones of a crown, lifted up as an ensign upon his land. 17 For how great *is* his goodness, and how great *is* his beauty! corn shall make the young men cheerful, and new wine the maids.

The prophet, having taught those that had returned out of captivity to attribute their deliverance to the *blood of the covenant* and to the promise of the Messiah (for they were so wonderfully helped because that blessing was in them, was yet in the womb of their nation), now comes to encourage them with the prospect of a joyful and happy settlement, and of glorious times before them; and such a happiness they did enjoy, in a great measure, for some time; but these promises have their full accomplishment in the spiritual blessings of the gospel which we enjoy by Jesus Christ.

I. They are invited to look unto Christ, and flee unto him as their city of refuge (*v.* 12): *Turn you to the strong-hold, you prisoners of hope.* The Jews that had returned out of captivity into their own land were yet, in effect, but *prisoners (We are servants this day,* Neh. ix. 36), yet *prisoners of hope,* or *expectation,* for God had given them a *little reviving in their bondage,* Ezra ix. 8, 9. Those that yet continued in Babylon, detained by their affairs there, yet lived in hope some time or other to see their own land again. Now both these are directed to turn their eyes upon the Messiah, set before them in the promise as their strong-hold, to shelter themselves in him, and stay themselves upon him, for the perfecting of the mercy which by his grace, and for his sake, was so gloriously begun. *Look unto him, and be you saved,* Isa. xlv. 22. The promise of the Messiah was the strong-hold of the faithful long before his coming; they saw his day at a distance and were glad, and the believing expectation of this *redemption in Jerusalem* was long the support and *consolation of Israel,* Luke ii. 25, 38. They, in their dangers and distresses, were ready to turn towards this and the other creature for relief; but the prophets directed them still to turn to Christ, and to comfort themselves with the joy of their king coming to them with salvation. But, as their deliverance was typical of our redemption by Christ (*v.* 11), so this invitation to the strong-hold speaks the language of the gospel-call. Sinners are prisoners, but they are prisoners of hope ; their case is sad, but it is not desperate ; yet now there is hope in Israel concerning them. Christ is a strong-hold for them, a strong tower, in whom they may be safe and quiet from the fear of the wrath of God, the curse of the law, and the assaults of their spiritual enemies. To him they must turn by a lively faith ; to him they must flee, and trust in his name.

II. They are assured of God's favour to them : "*Even to day do I declare,* when things are at the worst, and you think your case deplorable to the last degree, yet I solemnly promise that *I will render double unto thee,* to thee, O Jerusalem! to every one of you prisoners of hope. I will give you comforts double to the sorrows you have experienced, or blessings double to what I ever bestowed upon your fathers, when their condition was at the best ; the glory of your latter state, as well as of your latter house, shall be greater, shall be twice as great as that of your former." And so it was no otherwise than by the coming of the Messiah, the preaching of his gospel, and the setting up of his kingdom ; these spiritual blessings in heavenly things were double to what they had ever enjoyed in their most prosperous state. As a pledge of this, in the fulness of time God here promises to the Jews victory, plenty, and joy, in their own land, which yet should be but a type and shadow of more glorious victories, riches, and joys, in the kingdom of Christ.

1. They shall triumph over their enemies. The Jews, after their return, were surrounded with enemies on all sides. They were *as a speckled bird ;* all the birds of the field were against them. Their land lay between the two potent kingdoms of Syria and Egypt, branches of the Grecian monarchy, and what frequent dangers they should be in between them was foretold, Dan. xi. But it is here promised that out of them all the Lord would deliver them ; and this promise had its primary accomplishment in the times of the Maccabees, when the Jews made head against their enemies, kept their head above water, and, after many struggles and difficulties, came to be head over them. It is promised, (1.) That they shall be instruments in God's hand for the defeating and baffling of their persecutors : " I *have bent Judah for me,* as my bow of steel ; that *bow I have filled with Ephraim* as my arrows, have drawn it up to its full bent, till the arrow be at the head ;" for some think that this is signified by the phrase of *filling the bow.* The expressions here are very fine, and the figures lively. Judah had been *taught the use of the bow* (2 Sam. i. 18), and Ephraim had been famous for it, Ps. lxxviii. 9. But let them not think that they gain

their successes by their own bow, for they themselves are no more than God's bow and his arrows, tools in his hands, which he makes use of and manages as he pleases, which he holds as his bow and directs to the mark as his arrows. The best and bravest of men are but what God makes them, and do no more service than he enables them to do. The preachers of the gospel were the bow in Christ's hand, with which he went forth, he went on, *conquering and to conquer,* Rev. vi. 2. The following words explain this : *I have raised up* and animated *thy sons, O Zion ! against thy sons, O Greece!* This was fulfilled when *against Antiochus,* one of the kings of the Grecian monarchy, the people that knew their God were *strong* and *did exploits,* Dan. xi. 32. And they in the hand of an almighty God were made *as the sword of a mighty man,* which none can stand before. Wicked men are said to be God's sword (Ps. xvii. 13), and sometimes good men are made so ; for he employs both as he pleases. (2.) That God will be captain, and commander-in-chief, over them, in every expedition and engagement (*v.* 14) : *The Lord shall be seen over them ;* he shall make it appear that he presides in their affairs, and that in all their motions they are under his direction, as apparently, though not as sensibly, as he was *seen over Israel* in the pillar of cloud and fire when he led them through the wilderness. [1.] Is their army to be raised, or mustered, and brought into the field ? *The Lord shall blow the trumpet,* to gather the forces together, to proclaim the war, to sound the alarm, and to give directions which way to march, which way to move ; for, if God blow the trumpet, it shall not give an uncertain sound, nor a feeble ineffectual one. [2.] Is the army taking the field, and entering upon action ? Whatever enterprise the campaign is opened with, God shall go forth at the head of their forces, *with whirlwinds of the south,* which were of incredible swiftness and fierceness ; and before these whirlwinds thy sons, O Greece! shall be as chaff. [3.] Is the army actually engaged ? God's *arrows shall go forth as lightning,* so strongly, so suddenly, so irresistibly ; his *lightnings* shall go forth *as arrows ;* see Ps. xviii. 14. He *sent out his arrows* and *scattered them,* that is, he *shot out his lightnings and discomfited them.* This alludes to that which God had done for Israel of old when he brought them out of Egypt, and into Canaan, and had its accomplishment partly in the wonderful successes which the Jews had against their neighbours that attacked them in the time of the Maccabees, by the special appearances of the divine Providence for them, and perfectly in the glorious victories gained by the cross of Christ and the preaching of the cross over Satan and all the powers of darkness, whereby we are made more than conquerors. [4.] Are they in danger of being overpowered by the enemy ? *The Lord of hosts shall defend them* (v. 15); *The Lord their God shall save them* (v. 16); so that their enemies shall not prevail over them, nor prey upon them. God shall be unto them for defence as well as offence, *the shield of their help* as well as *the sword of their excellency*, and this as *the Lord of hosts*, who has power to defend them, and as *their God*, who is engaged by promise to defend them, and by the property he has in them. He shall save them in *that day*, that critical dangerous day, *as the flock of his people*, with the same care and tenderness that the shepherd protects his sheep with. Those are safe whom God saves. [5.] Did their enemies hope to swallow them up? It shall be turned upon them, and they shall *devour* their enemies, and shall *subdue with sling-stones*, for want of better weapons, those that come forth against them. The *stones of the brook*, when God pleases, shall do as great execution as the best train of artillery; for the *stars in their courses* shall fight on the same side. Goliath was subdued with a sling-stone. Having subdued, they shall *devour, shall drink* the blood of their enemies, as it were, and, as conquerors are wont to do, they shall *make a noise as through wine*. It is usual for conquerors with loud huzzas and acclamations to glory in their victories and proclaim them. We read of those that *shout for mastery*, and of the *shout of a king* among God's people. They shall be filled with blood and spoil, as the bowls and basins of the temple, or the *corners of the altar*, were wont to be filled with the blood of the sacrifices; for their enemies shall fall as victims to divine justice.

2. They shall triumph in their God. They shall take the comfort and give God the glory of their successes. So some read *v.* 15. *They shall eat* (that is, they shall quietly enjoy) what they have got; God will give them power to eat it *after they have subdued the sling-stones* (that is, their enemies that slung stones at them), and *they shall drink and make a noise*, a joyful noise, before the Lord their maker and protector, *as through wine*, as men are merry at a banquet of wine. *Being not drunk with wine, wherein is excess*, but *filled with the Spirit*, they shall *speak* to themselves and one another *in psalms, and hymns, and spiritual songs*, as those that are drunk do with vain and foolish songs, Eph. v. 18, 19. And, in the fulness of their joy, they shall offer abundance of sacrifices to the honour of God, so that *they shall fill both the bowls and the corners of the altar* with the fat and blood of their sacrifices. And, when they thus triumph in their successes, their joy shall terminate in God as their God, the God of their salvation. They shall triumph, (1.) In the love he has for them, and the relation wherein they stand to him, that they are *the flock of his people* and he is their Shepherd, and that they are to him *as the stones of a crown*, which are very precious and of great value, and which are kept under

a strong guard. Never was any king so pleased with the jewels of his crown as God is, and will be, with his people, who are near and dear unto him, and in whom he glories. They are a *crown of glory* and a *royal diadem* in his hand, Isa. lxii. 2, 3. And *they shall be mine, saith the Lord, in that day when I make up my jewels*, Mal. iii. 17. And *they shall be lifted up as an ensign upon his land*, as the royal standard is displayed in token of triumph and joy. God's people are his glory; so he is pleased to make them, so he is pleased to reckon them. He sets them up as a banner upon his own land, waging war against those who hate him, to whom it is a flag of defiance, while it is a centre of unity to all that love him, to all the children of God, that are scattered abroad, who are invited to come and enlist themselves under this banner, Isa. xi. 10, 12. (2.) In the provision he makes for them, *v.* 17. This is the matter of their triumph (*v.* 17): *For how great is his goodness and how great is his beauty!* This is the substance, this the burden, of the songs wherewith they shall *make a noise* before the Lord. We are here taught, [1.] To admire and praise the amiableness of God's being: *How great is his beauty!* All the perfections of God's nature conspire to make him infinitely lovely in the eyes of all that know him. They are to him as the *stones of a crown*; but what is he to them? Our business in the temple is to *behold the beauty of the Lord* (Ps. xxvii. 4), and *how great is that beauty!* How far does it transcend all other beauties, particularly the *beauty of his holiness*. This may refer to the Messiah, to Zion's *King* that *cometh*. See *that king in his beauty* (Isa. xxxiii. 17), who is *fairer than the children of men*, the *fairest of ten thousand*, and *altogether lovely*. Though, in the eye of the world, he had no form or comeliness, in the eye of faith how great is his beauty! [2.] To admire and give thanks for the gifts of God's favour and grace, his bounty as well as his beauty; for *how great is his goodness!* How rich in mercy is he! How deep, how full, are its springs! How various, how plenteous, how precious, are its streams! What a great deal of good does God do! How rich in mercy is he! Here is an instance of his goodness to his people: *Corn shall make the young men cheerful and new wine the maids;* that is, God will bless his people with an abundance of the fruits of the earth. Whereas they had been afflicted with scarcity to such a degree that the *young men* and the *maidens* were ready to swoon and faint away for hunger and thirst (Lam. ii. 12, 21; iv. 7, 8; v. 10), now they shall have bread enough and to spare, not water only, but *wine, new wine*, which shall make the young people grow and be cheerful, and (which some have observed to be the effect of plenty and the cheapness of corn) the poor will be encouraged to marry, and re-people the land, when they shall have wherewithal to maintain their families. Note, What good gifts God bestows upon us we must serve him cheerfully with, and must race the streams up to the fountain, and, when we are refreshed with corn and wine, must say, *How great is his goodness!*

CHAP. X.

The scope of this chapter is much the same with that of the foregoing chapter—to encourage the Jews that had returned with hopes that though they had been under divine rebukes for their negligence in rebuilding the temple, and were now surrounded with enemies and dangers, yet God would do them good, and make them prosperous at home and victorious abroad. Now, I. They are here directed to eye the great God in all events that concerned them, and, both in the evils they suffered and in the comforts they desired, to acknowledge his hand, ver. 1—4. II. They are encouraged to expect strength and success from him in all their struggles with the enemies of their church and state, and to hope that the issue would be glorious at last, ver. 5—12.

A SK ye of the LORD rain in the time of the latter rain; *so* the LORD shall make bright clouds, and give them showers of rain, to every one grass in the field. 2 For the idols have spoken vanity, and the diviners have seen a lie, and have told false dreams; they comfort in vain: therefore they went their way as a flock, they were troubled, because *there was* no shepherd. 3 Mine anger was kindled against the shepherds, and I punished the goats: for the LORD of hosts hath visited his flock the house of Judah, and hath made them as his goodly horse in the battle. 4 Out of him came forth the corner, out of him the nail, out of him the battle-bow, out of him every oppressor together.

Gracious things and glorious ones, very glorious and very gracious, were promised to this poor afflicted people in the foregoing chapter; now here God intimates to them that he will *for these things be enquired of* by them, and that he expects they should acknowledge him in all their ways and in all his ways towards them—and not idols that were rivals with him for their respects.

I. The prophet directs them to apply to God by prayer for rain in the season thereof. He had promised, in the close of the foregoing chapter, that there should be great plenty of corn and wine, whereas for several years, by reason of unseasonable weather, there had been great scarcity of both; but the earth will not yield its fruits unless the heavens water it, and therefore they must look up to God for the *dew of heaven*, in order to the fatness and fruitfulness of the earth (*v.* 1): " *Ask you of the Lord rain*. Do not pray to the clouds, nor to the stars, for rain, but *to the Lord*; for he it is that *hears the heavens*, when they *hear the earth*," Hos. ii. 21. Seasonable rain is a great mercy, which we must *ask of God, rain in the time of the lat-*
1448

ter rain, when there is most need of it. The former rain fell at the seed-time, in autumn, the latter fell in the spring, between March and May, which brought the corn to an ear and filled it. If either of these rains failed, it was very bad with that land; for from the end of May to September they never had any rain at all. Jerome, who lived in Judea, says that he never saw any rain there in June or July. They are directed to ask for it *in the time* when it used to come. Note, We must, in our prayers, dutifully attend the course of Providence; we must ask for mercies in their proper time, and not expect that God should go out of his usual way and method for us. But, since sometimes God denied rain in the usual time as a token of his displeasure, they must pray for it then as a token of his favour, and they shall not pray in vain. *Ask and it shall be given you. So the Lord shall make bright clouds* (which, though they are without rain themselves, are yet presages of rain)—*lightnings* (so the margin reads it), for *he maketh lightnings for the rain.* He will *give them showers of rain* in great abundance, and so give *to every one grass in the field*; for God is universally good, and *makes his rain to fall upon the just and the unjust.*

II. He shows them the folly of making their addresses to idols as their fathers had done (*v.* 2): *The idols have spoken vanity;* the teraphim, which they courted and consulted in their distress, were so far from being able to command rain for them that they could not so much as tell them when they should have rain. They pretended to promise them rain at such a time, but it did not come. *The diviners*, who were the prophets of those idols, *have seen a lie* (their visions were all a cheat and a sham); and *they have told false dreams*, such as the event did not answer, which proved that they were not from God. Thus they *comforted in vain* those that consulted the lying oracles; all the *vanities of the heathen* put together could not *give rain*, Jer. xiv. 22. Yet this was not the worst of it; they not only got nothing by the false gods, but they lost the favour of the true God, for *therefore they went their way* into captivity *as a flock* driven into the fold, and *they were troubled* with one vexation after another, as scattered sheep are, *because there was no shepherd*, no prince to rule them, no priest to intercede for them, none to take care of them and keep them together. Those that wandered after strange gods were made to wander into strange nations.

III. He shows them the hand of God in all the events that concerned them, both those that made against them and those that made for them, *v.* 3. Let them consider, 1. When every thing went cross it was God that walked contrary to them (*v.* 3): " *My anger was kindled against the shepherds* that should have fed the flock, but neglected it, and starved it. I was displeased at the wicked magistrates and ministers, the idol-shepherds." The captivity in Babylon was a token of God's anger against them ; in it likewise he *punished the goats,* those of the flock that were filthy and mischievous ; they were set on the left hand, to go away into punishment. Though the body of the nation suffered in the captivity, yet it was only the goats and the shepherds that God was angry with, and that he punished ; the same affliction to others came from the love of God, and was but a fatherly chastisement, which to them came from his wrath, and was a judicial punishment. 2. When things began to change for the better it was God that gave them the happy turn. " He has now *visited his flock* with favour, to enquire after them, and provides what he finds proper for them, and he has made them *as his goodly horse in the battle,* has beautified them, taken care of them, managed and made use of them, as a man does the horse he rides on, has made them valuable in themselves and formidable to those about them, *as his goodly horse.*" It is God that makes us what we are, and it is with us as he appoints.

IV. He shows them that every creature is to them what God makes it to be (*v.* 4): *Out of him came forth the corner, out of him the nails.* 1. All the power that was engaged against them was from God. *Out of him* came all the combined force of their enemies ; every *oppressor together* (and the oppressors of Israel were not a few) did but what his hand and his counsel determined before to be done ; nor could they have had such power against them unless it had been given them from above. 2. All the power likewise that was engaged for them was derived from him and depended on him. Out of him came forth *the corner-stone* of the building, the power of magistrates, which keeps the several parts of the state together. Princes are often called the *corners of the people,* as 1 Sam. xiv. 38, marg. Out of him came forth *the nail* that fixed the state, the *nail in the sure place* (Isa. xxii. 23), the *nail in his holy place,* Ezra ix. 8. Out of him came forth *the battle-bow,* the military power, and out of him *every oppressor,* or exactor, that had the civil power in his hand ; and therefore to God, the fountain of power, we must always have an eye, and see every man's judgment proceeding from him.

5 And they shall be as mighty *men,* which tread down *their enemies* in the mire of the streets in the battle: and they shall fight, because the LORD *is* with them, and the riders on horses shall be confounded. 6 And I will strengthen the house of Judah, and I will save the house of Joseph, and I will bring them again to place them ; for I have mercy upon them :

and they shall be as though I had not cast them off : for I *am* the LORD their God, and will hear them. 7 And *they of* Ephraim shall be like a mighty *man,* and their heart shall rejoice as through wine : yea, their children shall see *it,* and be glad ; their heart shall rejoice in the LORD. 8 I will hiss for them, and gather them : for I have redeemed them : and they shall increase as they have increased. 9 And I will sow them among the people : and they shall remember me in far countries ; and they shall live with their children, and turn again. 10 I will bring them again also out of the land of Egypt, and gather them out of Assyria ; and I will bring them into the land of Gilead and Lebanon ; and *place* shall not be found for them. 11 And he shall pass through the sea with affliction, and shall smite the waves in the sea, and all the deeps of the river shall dry up : and the pride of Assyria shall be brought down, and the sceptre of Egypt shall depart away. 12 And I will strengthen them in the LORD ; and they shall walk up and down in his name, saith the LORD.

Here are divers precious promises made to the people of God, which look further than to the state of the Jews in the latter days of their church, and have certain reference to the spiritual Israel of God, the gospel-church, and all true believers.

I. They shall have God's favour and presence, and shall be owned and accepted of him. This is the foundation of all the rest : *The Lord is with them, v.* 5. He espouses their cause, takes their part, is on their side ; and, if he be for them, who can be against them ? Again (*v.* 6), *I have mercy upon them.* All their dignity and joy are owing purely to God's mercy ; and mercy, as it supposes misery, so it excludes merit. They had been cast off, the effect of which could not but be misery ; they had been justly cast off, and therefore could pretend to merit nothing at God's hand but wrath and the curse ; yet it is promised, *They shall be as though I had not cast them off.* The transgressions of their fathers, for which they had been rejected, shall not only not be visited upon them, but shall not be so much as remembered against them. God will be as perfectly reconciled to them as if he had never contended with them, and the falling out of these lovers shall rather be the renewing than the weakening of love. They shall have such a full assurance of God's being reconciled to them, and upon that shall be so well reconciled to themselves, that they shall be as easy as if they had never been cast off; and their condition, after their restoration to the divine favour, shall be so very happy that there shall not remain the least scar from the wounds which were given them by their being cast off. Such favour does God show to returning repenting sinners, who were by nature at a distance, and children of wrath; such fellowship are they admitted into, and such freedom does he use with them, that they are *as though they had never been cast off*. 1. The covenant they are admitted into is the same that ever it was: *I am the Lord their God*, according to the original contract, the covenant made with their fathers. 2. The communion they are admitted into is the same that ever it was: *I will hear them*. They shall be as welcome as ever to speak to him, and as sure as ever to receive from him an answer of peace; for, as he never did, so he never will, say to Jacob's seed, *Seek you me in vain*.

II. They shall be victorious over their enemies, that would draw them from either their duty to God or their comfort in God (v. 5): *They shall be as mighty men*, that are both strong in body and bold in spirit, men of vigour, men of valour, effective men. *Those of Ephraim*, as well as those of Judah, shall be *like a mighty man* (v. 7), that dares to go about a difficult enterprise and is able to go through with it. They shall, as mighty men, *tread down their enemies in the battle*, as the dirt that is thrown out of the houses is trodden with other dirt *in the mire of the streets*. And *they shall* therefore *fight, because the Lord is with them*. Some would argue that they may *therefore* sit still, and do nothing, because the Lord is with them, who can and will do all. No; God's gracious presence with us to help us must not supersede, but quicken and animate, our endeavours to help ourselves; and we must therefore *work out our salvation with fear and trembling*, because *it is God that works in us both to will and to do*. They shall fight with readiness and resolution because, if God be with them, they are sure to be conquerors, more than conquerors. For then *the riders on horses shall be confounded*. The cavalry of the enemies shall be routed, and put into disorder, by the infantry of the Jews. The preachers of the gospel of Christ went forth to war a good warfare; they charged bravely, because God was with them; and the *riders on horses* that opposed them *were confounded*, for God chose the *weak* and *foolish things of the world to confound the wise and mighty*. But whence have they all this might? How come they to be so able, so active? It is in the Lord, and in the power of his might, that they are so (v. 6): *I will strengthen the house of Judah*, and
1450

so I will save the house of Joseph. Note, God saves us by strengthening us, and works out our happiness by working in us to do our duty. And thus we are engaged to the utmost diligence in using the strength God gives us; and yet, when all is done, God must have the glory of all. God is our strength, and so becomes both our song and our salvation.

III. Those of them that are dispersed shall be gathered together into one body (v. 6): *I will bring them again to place them*, bring them from other lands to place them in their own land. This was a token of their being perfectly restored to all their other ancient privileges—they shall be restored to the possession of their own land. This was fulfilled when the *children of God that were scattered abroad* were by faith in Christ incorporated in the gospel-church, and Jews and Gentiles became *one fold*, John x. 16. In order to this (v. 8) *I will hiss for them*, or, rather, *whistle* for them, as the shepherd with his pipe calls his sheep together, that *know his voice;* and so *I will gather them*. The preaching of the gospel was, as it were, God's hissing for souls to come to Jesus Christ, his calling in his scattered sheep to the green pastures. *I will gather them, for I have redeemed them*. Note, Those whom Christ has redeemed by his blood God will gather by his grace, as a *hen gathers her brood under her wings*. This promise is enlarged upon v. 10, *I will bring them again also out of the land of Egypt*. Some think this was literally fulfilled when Ptolemæus Philadelphus king of Egypt sent 120,000 Jews out of his country into their own land, as was the promise of gathering them out of Assyria by Alexander the son of Antiochus Epiphanes. But it has its spiritual accomplishment in the gathering in of precious souls out of a bondage worse than that in Egypt or Assyria, and the bringing of them into the glorious liberties of the children of God and their enjoyments, which are as the beautiful fruitful pastures in *the land of Gilead and Lebanon*. All the land of promise is theirs, even Gilead, the utmost border of it eastward, and Lebanon, the utmost border northward. But how shall this be? How shall a people so dispersed be got together? How shall those that are set at such a distance from their own country be brought to it again? It is true the difficulties seem insuperable, but they shall be got over as easily, as effectually as those that lay in the way of their deliverance out of Egypt and their entrance into Canaan: *He shall pass through the sea with affliction*, as of old through the Red Sea, to the sore affliction of Pharaoh and his hosts, or to the sore affliction of the sea, the waves whereof *he shall smite*, so that it shall be *driven back*, as when *the sea saw and fled*, Ps. cxiv. 3. And *all the deeps of the river* (all the rivers, though ever so deep) *shall dry up*, as Jordan did, to make way for Israel's passage into that good land which God had given them. Does *the pride of Assyria* stand in the way of their deliverance? He shall give check to it who sets bounds to the *proud waves of the sea*, and it *shall be brought down.* Does the sceptre of Egypt oppose it? That shall *depart away*, so that it shall not be able to obstruct the gathering in of God's Israel when his time shall come for the doing of it. When the gospel-church was to be gathered out of all nations by the preaching of the gospel great opposition was given to it by the enraged combined powers of earth and hell. Insuperable difficulties seemed to be in the way of it. But, by a divine power going along with the doctrine of Christ, it became *mighty to the pulling down of strong holds*, and the conversion and salvation of thousands. Then the sea fled, and Jordan was *driven back at the presence of the Lord.*

IV. They shall greatly multiply, and the church, that new world, shall be replenished (*v.* 8): *They shall increase as they have increased* formerly in Egypt, and great additions shall be made to their numbers, as in the days of David and Solomon. When God gathers his redeemed ones to himself they shall help to gather in others with them, and their motion homeward shall be like that of a snow-ball. *Crescit eundo—The further it goes the larger it grows by accretion. I will gather them, and they shall increase.* Note, The church of Christ is a growing body, as long as it is in the present state of minority, till it comes *to the measure of the stature of the fulness of Christ.* There are added to it *daily such as shall be saved.* 1. It shall spread to distant places. It shall fill Canaan, even to the lands of Gilead and Lebanon, so that no more place, no more room, shall be found for it there, *v.* 10. *In Judah* only God had been *known*, and his *name was great in Israel* only; here only he revealed his *statutes* and *judgments.* But in gospel-times that place shall be much too strait; the church's tent must be enlarged, and its *cords lengthened:* Then *I will sow them among the people, v.* 9. Their scattering shall be like the scattering of seed in the ground, not to bury it, but to increase it, that it may bring forth much fruit. The Jews are said to be dispersed *into every nation under heaven* (Acts ii. 5); and, as it was their troubles that dispersed some of them, so perhaps others transplanted themselves into colonies because the land of Israel was too strait for them; and many were natives of other nations, but proselyted to the Jewish religion. Now these were *sown among the people*, Hos. ii. 23. And this contributed very much to the spreading of the gospel. The Jews that came from all parts to worship at Jerusalem fetched thence the gospel light and fire to their own countries, as those Acts ii., and the eunuch, Acts viii. And their own synagogues in the several cities of the Gentiles were the first receptacles of the apostles and their preaching, wherever they came. Thus when God *sowed them among the people*, that they might not get hurt by the Gentiles, but do good to them, he took care that they should *remember him*, and make mention of his name *in far countries;* and, by keeping up the knowledge of God among them as he had revealed himself in the Old Testament, they would be the more ready to admit the knowledge of Christ as he has revealed himself in the New Testament. 2. It shall last to future *ages.* The church shall not be *res unius ætatis—a temporary thing*, but a seed in it shall *serve the Lord, v.* 7. *Yea, their children shall see it and be glad;* and *they shall live with their children, and turn again, v.* 9. Converts to Christ shall have their children about them, whom they shall teach the knowledge of the Lord, and bring with them when they turn again to the holy land and the way of holiness. It was said to those to whom the gospel was first preached, *The promise is to you and to your children*, Acts ii. 39. They shall be *so sown among the people* as never to be extirpated. Christ's family upon earth shall never be extinct, nor his purchased possession lost for want of heirs.

V. God himself will be both their strength and their song. 1. In him they shall be comforted, and shall have abundant satisfaction (*v.* 7): *Their heart shall rejoice as through wine;* for Christ's *love*, which is their joy, is *better than wine.* They shall be *like a mighty man*, and *their heart shall rejoice.* When we resolutely resist, and so overcome, our spiritual enemies, then our hearts shall rejoice. But we ruin our own joy if our resistance be feeble and we yield to the temptations of Satan. Their *heart shall rejoice*, and then they shall be as a *mighty man;* for the *joy of the Lord* will be *our strength.* And with their graces their joys shall be propagated: *Their children shall see it and be glad, and their hearts* also *shall rejoice in the Lord.* It is good to acquaint children betimes with the delights of religion, and to make the services of it as pleasant as may be to them, that, learning betimes to rejoice in the Lord, they may with purpose of heart cleave to him. 2. By him they shall be carried on with vigour, and enlargement of heart, in his service (*v.* 12): *I will strengthen them in the Lord*, strengthen them for their walk and work, as well as for their warfare. It is the God of Israel that *gives strength and power unto his people*, that strengthens all their powers and faculties for spiritual performances, above what they are by nature and against what they are by the corruption of nature. Now observe, (1.) How they are thus enabled and invigorated for their duty: *I the Lord will strengthen them in the Lord*, in the *Messiah*, who is *Jehovah our strength*, as well as *Jehovah our righteousness.* Strength is treasured up for us in Christ, and from him it is communicated to us. It is *through Christ strengthening* us that we can *do all things,* and *without him we can do nothing.* His *strength is commanded* him *for this* purpose, Ps. lxviii. 28. (2.) What good use they shall make of this strength given unto them: *They shall walk up and down in his name.* If God strengthen us, we must bestir ourselves, must *walk up and down* in all the duties of the Christian life, must be active and busy in the work of God, must walk up and down as industrious men do, losing no time, and letting slip no opportunity. But still we must *walk up and down in the name of Christ,* must do all by warrant from him and in dependence on him, with an eye to his word as our rule and his glory as our end. To us to live must be Christ; and, *whatever we do in word or deed,* we must *do all in the name of the Lord Jesus,* that we receive not the strengthening grace of God in vain. See Ps. lxxx. 17, 18.

CHAP. XI.

God's prophet, who, in the chapters before, was an ambassador sent to promise peace, is here a herald sent to declare war. The Jewish nation shall recover its prosperity, and shall flourish for some time and become considerable; it shall be very happy, at length, in the coming of the long-expected Messiah, in the preaching of his gospel, and in the setting up of his standard there. But, when thereby the chosen remnant among them are effectually called in and united to Christ, the body of the nation, persisting in unbelief, shall be utterly abandoned and given up to ruin, for rejecting Christ; and it is this that is foretold here in this chapter—the Jews rejecting Christ, which was their measure-filling sin, and the wrath which for that sin came upon them to the uttermost. Here is, I. A prediction of the destruction itself that should come upon the Jewish nation, ver. 1—3. II. The putting of it into the hands of the Messiah. 1. He is charged with the custody of that flock, ver. 4—6. 2. He undertakes it, and bears rule in it, ver. 7, 8. 3. Finding it perverse, he gives it up (ver. 9), breaks his shepherd's staff (ver. 10, 11), resents the indignities done him and the contempt put upon him (ver. 12, 13), and then breaks his other staff, ver. 14. 4. He turns them over into the hands of foolish shepherds, who, instead of preventing, shall complete their ruin, and both the blind leaders and the blind followers shall fall together into the ditch, ver. 15—17. This is foretold to the poor of the flock before it comes to pass, that, when it does come to pass, they may not be offended.

OPEN thy doors, O Lebanon, that the fire may devour thy cedars. 2 Howl, fir-tree; for the cedar is fallen; because the mighty is spoiled: howl, O ye oaks of Bashan; for the forest of the vintage is come down. 3 *There is* a voice of the howling of the shepherds; for their glory is spoiled: a voice of the roaring of young lions; for the pride of Jordan is spoiled.

In dark and figurative expressions, as is usual in the scripture predictions of things at a great distance, that destruction of Jerusalem and of the Jewish church and nation is here foretold which our Lord Jesus, when the time was at hand, prophesied of very plainly and expressly. We have here, 1. Preparation made for that destruction (*v.* 1): "*Open thy doors, O Lebanon!* Thou wouldst not open them to let thy king in—he came *to his own and his own received him not;* now thou must open them to let thy ruin in.

Let the gates of the forest, and all the avenues to it, be thrown open, and let the fire come in and devour its glory." Some by Lebanon here understand the temple, which was built of cedars from Lebanon, and the stones of it white as the snow of Lebanon. It was burnt with fire by the Romans, and its gates were forced open by the fury of the soldiers. To confirm this, they tell a story, that forty years before the destruction of the second temple the gates of it opened of their own accord, upon which prodigy Rabbi Johanan made this remark (as it is found in one of the Jewish authors), "Now I know," said he, "that the destruction of the temple is at hand, according to the prophecy of Zechariah, *Open thy doors, O Lebanon! that the fire may devour thy cedars.*" Others understand it of Jerusalem, or rather of the whole land of Canaan, to which Lebanon was an inlet on the north. All shall lie open to the invader, and the cedars, the mighty and eminent men, shall be devoured, which cannot but alarm those of an inferior rank, *v.* 2. If *the cedars* have *fallen* (if *all the mighty are spoiled,* and brought to ruin), let the *fir-tree howl.* How can the slender fir-trees stand if stately cedars fall? If cedars are devoured by fire, it is time for the fir-trees to howl; for no wood is so combustible as that of the fir. And let the *oaks of Bashan,* that lie exposed to every injury, *howl, for the forest of the vintage* (or the *flourishing vineyard,* that used to be guarded with a particular care) has come down, or (as some read it) when the *defenced forests,* such as Lebanon was, have come down. Note, The falls of the wise and good into sin, and the falls of the rich and great into trouble, are loud alarms to those that are every way their inferiors not to be secure. 2. Lamentation made for the destruction (*v.* 3): *There is a voice of howling.* Those who have fallen howl for grief and shame, and those who see their own turn coming howl for fear. But the great men especially receive the alarm with the utmost confusion. Those who were roaring in the day of their revels and triumphs are howling in the day of their terrors; *for now they are tormented* more than others. Those great men were by office shepherds, and such should have protected God's flock committed to their charge; it is the duty both of princes and priests. But they were as *young lions,* that made themselves a terror to the flock with their roaring and the flock a prey to themselves with their tearing. Note, It is sad with a people when those who should be as shepherds to them are as young lions to them. But what is the issue? The shepherds *howl,* for *their glory is spoiled.* Their pastures, and the flocks which covered them, which were the glory of the swains, are laid waste. The *young lions howl,* for *the pride of Jordan is spoiled.* The pride of Jordan was the thickets on the banks, in which the lions reposed themselves; and therefore, when the river overflowed and spoiled them, the lions came up from them (as we read Jer. xlix. 19), and they came up roaring. Note, When those who have power proudly abuse their power, and, instead of being shepherds, are as young lions, they may expect that the righteous God will humble their pride and break their power.

4 Thus saith the LORD my God; Feed the flock of the slaughter; 5 Whose possessors slay them, and hold themselves not guilty: and they that sell them say, Blessed *be* the LORD; for I am rich: and their own shepherds pity them not. 6 For I will no more pity the inhabitants of the land, saith the LORD: but, lo, I will deliver the men every one into his neighbour's hand, and into the hand of his king: and they shall smite the land, and out of their hand I will not deliver *them.* 7 And I will feed the flock of slaughter, *even* you, O poor of the flock. And I took unto me two staves; the one I called Beauty, and the other I called Bands; and I fed the flock. 8 Three shepherds also I cut off in one month; and my soul loathed them, and their soul also abhorred me. 9 Then said I, I will not feed you: that that dieth, let it die; and that that is to be cut off, let it be cut off; and let the rest eat every one the flesh of another. 10 And I took my staff, *even* Beauty, and cut it asunder, that I might break my covenant which I had made with all the people. 11 And it was broken in that day: and so the poor of the flock that waited upon me knew that it *was* the word of the LORD. 12 And I said unto them, If ye think good, give *me* my price; and if not, forbear. So they weighed for my price thirty *pieces* of silver. 13 And the LORD said unto me, Cast it unto the potter: a goodly price that I was prised at of them. And I took the thirty *pieces* of silver, and cast them to the potter in the house of the LORD. 14 Then I cut asunder mine other staff, *even* Bands, that I might break the brotherhood between Judah and Israel.

The prophet here is made a type of Christ,

as the prophet Isaiah sometimes was; and the scope of these verses is to show that *for judgment Christ came into this world* (John ix. 39), for judgment to the Jewish church and nation, which were, about the time of his coming, wretchedly corrupted and degenerated by the worldliness and hypocrisy of their rulers. Christ would have healed them, but they would not be healed; they are therefore left desolate, and abandoned to ruin. Observe here,

I. The desperate case of the Jewish church, under the tyranny of their own governors. Their slavery in their own country made them as miserable as their captivity in strange countries had done: *Their possessors slay them and sell them, v.* 5. In Zechariah's time we find the rulers and the nobles justly rebuked for *exacting usury of their brethren;* and the governors, even by their servants, oppressive to the people, Neh. v. 7, 15. In Christ's time the *chief priests* and the *elders*, who were the possessors of the flock, by their traditions, the commandments of men, and their impositions on the consciences of the people, became perfect tyrants, devoured their houses, engrossed their wealth, and fleeced the flock instead of feeding it. The Sadducees, who were deists, corrupted their judgments. The Pharisees, who were bigots for superstition, corrupted their morals, by making void the commandments of God, Matt. xv. 16. Thus they slew the sheep of the flock, thus they sold them. They cared not what became of them so they could but gain their own ends and serve their own interests. And, 1. In this they justified themselves: They *slay them* and *hold themselves not guilty.* They think that there is no harm in it, and that they shall never be called to an account for it by the chief Shepherd; as if their power were given them for destruction, which was designed only for edification, and as if, because they sat in Moses's seat, they were not under the obligation of Moses's law, but might dispense with it, and with themselves in the breach of it, at their pleasure. Note, Those have their minds woefully blinded indeed who do ill and justify themselves in doing it; but God will not hold those guiltless who hold themselves so. 2. In this they affronted God, by giving him thanks for the gain of their oppression: They said, *Blessed be the Lord, for I am rich,* as if, because they prospered in their wickedness, got money by it, and raised estates, God had made himself patron of their unjust practices, and Providence had become *particeps criminis—the associate of their guilt.* What is got honestly we ought to give God thanks for, and to bless him whose blessing *makes rich and adds no sorrow with it.* But with what face can we go to God either to beg a blessing upon the unlawful methods of getting wealth or to return him thanks for success in them? They should rather have gone to God to confess the sin, to take shame to themselves for it, and to vow restitution, than thus to mock him by making the gains of sin the gift of God, who *hates robbery for burnt-offerings,* and reckons not himself praised by the thanksgiving if he be dishonoured either in the getting or the using of that which we give him thanks for. 3. In this they put contempt upon the people of God, as unworthy their regard or compassionate consideration : *Their own shepherds pity them not ;* they make them miserable, and then do not commiserate them. Christ had *compassion on the multitude because they fainted and were scattered abroad, as if they had no shepherd* (as really they had worse than none); but *their own shepherds pitied them not,* nor showed any concern for them. Note, It is ill for a church when its pastors have no tenderness, no compassion for precious souls, when they can look upon the ignorant, the foolish, the wicked, the weak, without pity.

II. The sentence of God's wrath passed upon them for their senselessness and stupidity in this condition. There was a general decay, nay, a destruction, of religion among them, and it was all one to them; they regarded it not. *My people love to have it so,* Jer. v. 31. Though they were *oppressed and broken in judgment,* yet they *willingly walked after the commandment,* Hos. v. 11. And, as their shepherds pitied them not, so they did not bemoan themselves ; therefore God says (*v.* 6), " *I will no more pity the inhabitants of the land.* They have courted their own destruction, and so let their doom be." But those are truly miserable whom the God of mercy himself will no more have compassion upon. Those who are willing to have their consciences oppressed by those who *teach for doctrines the commandments of men* (as the Jews were, who called those *Rabbi, Rabbi,* that did so, Matt. xv. 9 ; xxiii. 7), are often punished by oppression in their civil interests, and justly, for those forfeit their own rights who tamely give up God's rights. The Jews did so; the Papists do so; and who can pity them if they be ruled with rigour? God here threatens them, 1. That he will deliver them into the hand of oppressors, *every one into his neighbour's hand,* so that they shall use one another barbarously. The several parties in Jerusalem did so; the *zealots,* the *seditious,* as they were called, committed greater outrages than the common enemy did, as Josephus relates in his history of the wars of the Jews. They shall be delivered every one *into the hand of his king,* that is, the Roman emperor, whom they chose to submit to rather than to Christ, saying, *We have no king but Cæsar.* Thus they thought to ingratiate themselves with their lords and masters. But for this God brought the Romans upon them, who *took away their place and nation.* 2. That he will not deliver them out of their hands : *They shall smite the land,* the whole land,

1454

and *out of their hand I will not deliver them ;* and, if the Lord do not help them, none else can, nor can they help themselves.

III. A trial yet made whether their ruin might be prevented by sending Christ among them as a shepherd ; God had sent his servants to them in vain, *but last of all he sent unto them his Son, saying, They will reverence my Son,* Matt. xxi. 37. Divers of the prophets had spoken of him as the *Shepherd of Israel,* Isa. xl. 11 ; Ezek. xxxiv. 23. He himself told the Pharisees that he was the *Shepherd of the sheep,* and that those who pretended to be shepherds were *thieves and robbers* (John x. 1, 2, 11), apparently referring to this passage, where we have, 1. The charge he received from his Father to try what might be done with this flock (*v.* 4) : *Thus saith the Lord my God* (Christ called his Father *his God* because he acted in compliance with his will and with an eye to his glory in his whole undertaking), *Feed the flock of the slaughter.* The Jews were God's flock, but they were *the flock of slaughter,* for their enemies had killed them all the day long and *accounted them as sheep for the slaughter ;* their own *possessors slew them,* and God himself had doomed them to the slaughter. Yet " *feed them* by reproof, instruction, and comfort ; provide wholesome food for those who have so long been soured with the leaven of the scribes and Pharisees." *Other sheep he had, which were not of this fold,* and which afterwards must be *brought ;* but he is first *sent to the lost sheep of the house of Israel,* Matt. xv. 24. 2. His acceptance of this charge, and his undertaking pursuant to it, *v.* 7. He does as it were say, *Lo, I come to do thy will, O my God !* and, since this is thy will, it is mine : *I will feed the flock of slaughter.* Christ will care for these lost sheep; he will go about among them, *teaching* and *healing even you, O poor of the flock !* Christ did not neglect the meanest, nor overlook them for their meanness. The shepherds that made a prey of them regarded not the poor ; they were conversant with those only that they could get by; but Christ preached his gospel *to the poor,* Matt. xi. 5. It was an instance of his humiliation that his converse was mostly with the inferior sort of people ; his disciples, who were his constant attendants, were of the poor of the flock. 3. His furnishing himself with tools proper for the charge he had undertaken : *I took unto me two staves,* pastoral staves ; other shepherds have but one crook, but Christ had two, denoting the double care he took of his flock, and what he did both for the souls and for the bodies of men. David speaks of God's *rod* and his *staff* (Ps. xxiii. 4), a correcting rod and a supporting staff. One of these staves was called *Beauty,* denoting the temple, which is called *the beauty of holiness* and one of its gates *beautiful,* which Christ called his Father's house, and for which he showed a great zeal when he cleared it of the *buyers and sellers;* the other he called *Bands,* denoting their civil state, and the incorporate society of that nation, which Christ also took care of by preaching love and peace among them. Christ, in his gospel, and in all he did among them, consulted the advancement both of their civil and of their sacred interests. 4. His execution of his office, as the chief Shepherd. *He fed the flock* (*v.* 7), and he displaced those under-shepherds that were false to their trust (*v.* 8): *Three shepherds I cut off in one month.* Through the deficiency and uncertainty of the history of the Jewish church, in its latter ages, we know not what particular event this had its accomplishment in; in general, it seems to be an act of power and justice for the punishment of the sinful shepherds and the redress of the grievances of the abused flock. Some understand it of the three orders of princes, priests, and scribes or prophets, who, when Christ had finished his work, were laid aside for their unfaithfulness. Others understand it of the three sects among the Jews, of Pharisees, Sadducees, and Herodians, all whom Christ silenced in dispute (Matt. xxii.) and soon after *cut off,* all in a little time.

IV. Their enmity to Christ, and making themselves odious to him. He came to his own, the sheep of his own pasture; it might have been expected that between them and him there would be an entire affection, as between the shepherd and his sheep; but they conducted themselves so ill that *his soul loathed them,* was *straitened* towards them (so it may be read); he intended them kindness, but could not do them the kindness he intended them, *because of their unbelief,* Matt. xiii. 58. He was disappointed in them, discouraged concerning them, *grieved* for them, not only for the shepherds, whom he cut off, but for the people, whom Christ often looked upon with grief in his heart and tears in his eyes. Their provocations even wore out his patience, and he was weary of that *faithless and perverse generation. Their soul also it abhorred me;* and therefore it was that his soul loathed them; for, whatever estrangement there is between God and man, it begins on man's side. The Jewish shepherds rejected this chief Shepherd, as the Jewish builders rejected this chief corner stone. They *had indignation* at Christ's doctrine and miracles, and his interest in the people, to whom they did all they could to render him odious, as they had made themselves odious to him. Note, There is a mutual enmity between God and wicked people; they are hateful to God and haters of God. Nothing speaks more the sinfulness and misery of an unregenerate state than this does. The carnal mind, the friendship of the world, are enmity to God, and God hates all the workers of iniquity; and it is easy to foresee what this will end in, if

the quarrel be not taken up in time, Isa. xxvii. 4, 5.

V. Christ's rejecting them as incurable, and leaving them their house desolate, Matt. xxiii. 38. The things of their peace are now hidden from their eyes, because they knew not the day of their visitation. Here we have,

1. The sentence of their rejection passed (*v.* 9): "*Then said I, I will not feed you.* I will take no further care of you; *you shall not see me again;* take your own course. As I will not feed you, so I will not cure you; *that that dieth, let it die* (the Shepherd will do nothing to save its forfeited life); *that that is to be cut off, let it be cut off;* that which will make itself a prey to the wolf, let it be a prey, and let the rest so far forget their own mild and gentle nature as to *eat the flesh of one another;* let these sheep fight like dogs." Those that reject Christ will be certainly and justly rejected by him, and then are miserable of course.

2. A sign of it given (*v.* 10): *I took my staff, even Beauty, and cut it asunder,* in token of this, that he would be no longer a shepherd to them, as the lord high steward determines his commission by breaking his white staff, and as Moses's breaking the tables of the law put a stop, for the present, to the treaty between God and Israel. The breaking of this staff signified the breaking of God's covenant which he had *made with all the people,* the covenant of peculiarity made with all the tribes of *Israel,* and all other people who, by being proselyted to their religion, were incorporated into their nation. The Jewish church was now stripped of all its glory; its crown was profaned and cast to the ground, and all its honour laid in the dust; for God departed from it, and would no more own it for his. When Christ told them plainly that the *kingdom of God* should be *taken from them,* and *given to another people,* then he broke the *staff of Beauty,* Matt. xxi. 43. And *it was broken in that day,* though Jerusalem and the Jewish nation held up forty years longer, yet from that day we may reckon the staff of Beauty broken, *v.* 11. And though the great men did not, or would not, understand it as a divine sentence, but thought to put it by with a cold *God forbid* (Luke xx. 16), yet the *poor of the flock,* the disciples of Christ, that *waited on him,* and understood with what authority he spoke, and could distinguish the voice of their Shepherd from that of a stranger, *knew that it was the word of the Lord,* and trembled at it, and were confident that it should not fall to the ground. Note, Christ is waited on by the poor of the flock; he chose them to be with him, to be his pupils, to be his witnesses; the poor received him and his gospel, when those that had great possessions turned their backs upon him. And those that wait upon Christ, that sit at his feet, to hear and receive his words,

shall *know of the doctrine whether it be of God,* John vii. 17.

3. A further reason given for their rejection. It was said before, *Their souls abhorred him;* and here we have an instance of it, their buying and selling him for thirty pieces of silver, either thirty Roman pence, or rather thirty Jewish shekels; this is here foretold in somewhat obscure expressions, as it is fit that such particular prophecies should be delivered, lest otherwise the plainness of the prophecy might prevent the accomplishment of it. Here, (1.) The Shepherd comes to them for his wages (*v.* 12): "*If you think good, give me my price;* you are weary of me, pay me off and discharge me; *and, if not, forbear;* if you be willing to continue me longer in your service, I will continue, or, if to turn me off without wages, I am content." Christ was no hireling, and yet the labourer is worthy of his hire. Compare with this what Christ said to Judas when he was going to sell him, "*What thou doest do quickly;* be at a word with the chief priests; let them either take the bargain or leave it," John xiii. 27. Those that betray Christ are not forced to it; they might have chosen. (2.) They value him at *thirty pieces of silver.* Many years' service he had done them as a Shepherd, yet this is all they will now turn him off with—"*A goodly price that I* with all my care and pains *was valued at by them.*" If Judas fixed this sum in his demand, it is observable that his name was *Judah,* the same name with that of the body of the people, for it was a national act; or, if (as it rather seems) the chief priests pitched upon this sum in their proffers, they were the representatives of the people; it was part of the priest's office to *put a value* upon the *devoted things* (Lev. xxvii. 8), and thus they valued the Lord Jesus. It was the ordinary price of a slave, Exod. xxi. 32. Making light of Christ, and undervaluing the love of that great and good Shepherd, are the ruin of multitudes, and justly so. (3.) The silver being no way proportionable to his worth, it is *thrown to the potter* with disdain: "Let him take it to buy clay with, or for any use that a little money will serve to, for it is not worth hoarding; it may be enough for a potter's stock, but not for the pay of such a shepherd, much less for his purchase." So the prophet *cast the thirty pieces of silver to the potter in the house of the Lord:* "Let him take them, and do what he will with them." Now we find a particular accomplishment of this in the history of Christ's sufferings, and reference is had to this prophecy, Matt. xxvii. 9, 10. *Thirty pieces of silver* was the very sum for which Christ was sold to the chief priests; the money, when Judas would not keep it, and the chief priests would not take it back, was laid out in the purchase of *the potter's field.* Even that sudden resolve of the chief priests was according to an ancient prophecy and the more ancient counsel and foreknowledge of God.

4. The completing of their rejection in the cutting asunder of the other staff, *v.* 14. The former denoted the ruin of their church, by breaking the covenant between God and them —that defaced their *beauty;* this denotes the ruin of their state, by breaking the brotherhood between Judah and Israel, by reviving animosities and contention among them, such as were of old between Judah and Israel, the writing of whom as *one stick in the hand of the Lord* was one of the blessings promised after their return out of captivity, Ezek. xxxvii. 19. But that union shall now be dissolved; they shall be crumbled into parties and factions, exasperated one against another; and their kingdom, being thus divided, shall be *brought to desolation.* (1.) Nothing ruins a people so certainly, so inevitably, as the breaking of *the staff of Bands,* and the weakening of the brotherhood among them; for hereby they become an easy prey to the common enemy. (2.) This follows upon the dissolving of the covenant between God and them, and the decay of religion among them. When iniquity abounds love waxes cold. No wonder if those fall out among themselves that have provoked God to fall out with them. When the staff of Beauty is broken the staff of Bands will not hold long. An unchurched people will soon be an undone people.

15 And the LORD said unto me, Take unto thee yet the instruments of a foolish shepherd. 16 For, lo, I will raise up a shepherd in the land, *which* shall not visit those that be cut off, neither shall seek the young one, nor heal that that is broken, nor feed that that standeth still: but he shall eat the flesh of the fat, and tear their claws in pieces. 17 Woe to the idol shepherd that leaveth the flock! the sword *shall be* upon his arm, and upon his right eye: his arm shall be clean dried up, and his right eye shall be utterly darkened.

God, having shown the misery of this people in their being justly abandoned by the good Shepherd, here shows their further misery in being shamefully abused by a foolish shepherd. The prophet is himself to personate and represent this pretended shepherd (*v.* 15): *Take unto thee the instruments* or accoutrements *of a foolish shepherd,* that are no way fit for the business, such a shepherd's coat, and bag, and staff, as a foolish shepherd would appear in; for such a shepherd shall be set over them (*v.* 16), who, instead of protecting them, shall oppress them and do them mischief. 1. They shall be under the inspection of unfaithful ministers. Their scribes, and priests, and doctors of their law, shall bind heavy burdens upon them, and grievous to be borne, and, with their traditions imposed, shall make the ceremonial law much more a yoke than God had made it. The description here given of the foolish shepherd suits very well with the character Christ gives of the scribes and Pharisees, Matt. xxiii. 2. They shall be under the tyranny of unmerciful princes, that shall rule them with rigour, and make their own land as much a house of bondage to them as ever Egypt or Babylon was. When they had rejected him *by whom princes decree justice* it was just that they should be turned over to those who *decree unrighteous decrees.* 3. They shall be imposed upon and deluded by false Christs and false prophets, as our Saviour foretold, Matt. xxiv. 5. Many such there were, who by their seditious practices provoked the Romans, and hastened the ruin of the Jewish nation; but it is observable that they were never cheated by a counterfeit Messiah till they had refused and rejected the true Messiah. Now observe,

I. What a curse this foolish shepherd should be to the people, *v.* 16. God will, for their punishment, *raise up a* foolish *shepherd,* who will not do the duty of a shepherd; he will not *visit those that are cut off,* nor go after those that go astray, nor seek those that are missing, to find them out and bring them home, as the good shepherd does, Matt. xviii. 12, 13. Their shepherds take no care of the *young ones,* that need their care and are well worthy of it, as Christ does, Isa. xl. 11. They do not *heal that* which was *broken,* which was worried and torn, but let it die of its bruises, when a little thing, in time, would have saved it. They do not *feed* those who, through weakness, *stand still,* and are ready to faint, and cannot get forward, but leave them behind, let who will take them up; they do not *carry* that which *stands still* (so some read it); they never do any thing to *support the weak* and comfort the *feeble-minded;* but, on the contrary, 1. They are luxurious themselves: They *eat of the flesh of the fat;* they will have of the best for themselves; and, like that *wicked servant* that said, *My lord delays his coming,* they *eat and drink with the drunken,* and *serve their own bellies.* 2. They are barbarous to the flock. Their passions are as ill-governed as their appetites, for, when they are in a rage against any of the flock, they *tear their* very *claws in pieces* by over-driving them; they beat their hoofs; they *smite their fellow servants. Woe unto thee, O land! when thy king is* such *a child!*

II. What a curse this foolish shepherd should bring upon himself (*v.* 17): *Woe to the idol-shepherd,* who, like an idol, has eyes and sees not, who, like an idol, receives abundance of respect and homage from the people and the chief of their offerings, but neither can nor will do them any kindness. He *leaves the flock* when they most need his care, leaves them destitute, and flees, *because he is a hireling;* his doom is that *the sword* of God's justice shall be *upon his arm* and *his right eye,* so that he shall quite lose the use of both. *His arm shall* wither and *be dried up,* so that he who would not help his friends when it was required shall not know how to help himself; *his right eye shall be utterly darkened,* that he shall not discern the danger that his flock is in, nor know which way to look for relief. This was fulfilled when Christ said to the Pharisees, *I have come that those who see may be made blind,* John ix. 39. Those that have gifts which qualify them to do good, if they do not do good with them, shall be deprived of them; those that should have been workmen, but were slothful and would do nothing, will justly have their arm dried up; and those that should have been watchmen, but were sleepy and would never look about them, will justly have their eye blinded.

CHAP. XII.

The apostle (Gal. iv. 25, 26) distinguishes between " Jerusalem which now is, and is in bondage with her children"—the remaining carcase of the Jewish church that rejected Christ, and " Jerusalem that is from above, that is free, and is the mother of us all"—the Christian church, the spiritual Jerusalem, which God has chosen to put his name there; in the foregoing chapter we read the doom of the former, and left that carcase to be a prey to the eagles that should be gathered to it. Now, in this chapter, we have the blessings of the latter, many precious promises made to the gospel-Jerusalem by him who (ver. 1) declares his power to make them good It is promised, I. That the attempts of the church's enemies against her shall be to their own ruin, and they shall find that it is at their peril if they do her any hurt, ver. 2—4, 6. II. That the endeavours of the church's friends and patrons for her good shall be pious, regular, and successful, ver. 5. III. That God will protect and strengthen the meanest and weakest that belong to his church, and work salvation for them, ver. 7, 8. IV. That as a preparative for all this mercy, and a pledge of it, he will pour upon them a spirit of prayer and repentance, the effect of which shall be universal and very particular, ver. 9—14. These promises were of use then to the pious Jews that lived in the troublous times under Antiochus, and other persecutors and oppressors; and they are still to be improved in every age for the directing of our prayers and the encouraging of our hopes with reference to the gospel-church.

THE burden of the word of the LORD for Israel, saith the LORD, which stretcheth forth the heavens, and layeth the foundation of the earth, and formeth the spirit of man within him. 2 Behold, I will make Jerusalem a cup of trembling unto all the people round about, when they shall be in·the siege both against Judah *and* against Jerusalem. 3 And in that day will I make Jerusalem a burdensome stone for all people: all that burden themselves with it shall be cut in pieces, though all the people of the earth be gathered together against it. 4 In that day, saith the LORD, I will smite every horse with astonishment, and his rider with madness: and I will open mine eyes upon the house of Judah, and will smite every horse of the people with blindness. 5 And the governors of Judah shall say in their heart, The inhabitants of Jerusalem *shall be* my strength in the LORD of hosts their God. 6 In that day will I make the governors of Judah like a hearth of fire among the wood, and like a torch of fire in a sheaf; and they shall devour all the people round about, on the right hand and on the left: and Jerusalem shall be inhabited again in her own place, *even* in Jerusalem. 7 The LORD also shall save the tents of Judah first, that the glory of the house of David and the glory of the inhabitants of Jerusalem do not magnify *themselves* against Judah. 8 In that day shall the LORD defend the inhabitants of Jerusalem; and he that is feeble among them at that day shall be as David; and the house of David *shall be* as God, as the angel of the LORD before them.

Here is, I. The title of this charter of promises made to God's Israel; it is the *burden of the word of the Lord*, a divine prediction; it is of weight in the delivery of it; it is to be pressed upon people, and will be very pressing in the accomplishment of it; it is a *burden*, a heavy burden, to all the church's enemies, like that *talent of lead, ch.* v. 7, 8. But it is *for Israel;* it is for their comfort and benefit. As even the *fiery law* (Deut. xxxiii. 2), so the fiery prophecies and fiery providences that come from God's right hand, come for them; the word that speaks terror to their enemies speaks peace to them, as the pillar of cloud and fire, which turned a bright side towards the Israelites, to direct and encourage them, but a black side towards the Egyptians, to terrify and dispirit them. Happy are those that have even the burdens of God's word for them, as well as the blessings of it.

II. The title of him that grants this charter, which is prefixed to it to show that he has both authority to make these promises and ability to make them good, for he is the Creator of the world and our Creator, and therefore has an incontestable irresistible dominion. 1. He *stretches out the heavens;* not only he did so at the first, when he said, *Let there be a firmament*, and he *made the firmament*, but he does so still; he keeps them stretched out *like a curtain*, keeps them from running in, and will do so till the end come, when *the heavens shall be rolled together as a scroll*. No bounds can be set to his power who stretches out the heavens, nor can any thing be too hard for him. 2. He *lays the foundation of the earth*, and keeps it firm and

fixed on its own basis, or rather on its own axis, though it is *founded on the seas* (Ps. xxiv. 1, 2), nay, though it is *hung upon nothing*, Job xxvi. 7. The founder of this earth is no doubt the ruler of it, and judges in it, and those deceive themselves who say, *The Lord has forsaken the earth*, for, if he had, it would have sunk, since it is he that not only did lay its foundations at first, but does still lay them, still uphold them. 3. He *forms the spirit of man within him.* He *made us these souls*, Jer. xxxviii. 16. He not only breathed into the first man, but still breathes into every man the breath of life; the body is derived from the *fathers of our flesh*, but the soul is infused by the *Father of spirits*, Heb. xii. 9. He *fashions men's hearts;* they are *in his hand*, and he turns them *as the rivers of water*, and casts them into what mould he pleases, so as to serve his own purposes with them; and he can therefore save his church by inspiriting his friends and dispiriting his enemies, and will eternally save all his chosen by forming their spirits anew.

III. The promises themselves that are here made them, by which the church shall be secured, and in which all its friends may enjoy a holy security.

1. It is promised that, whatever attacks the enemies of the church may make upon her purity or peace, they will certainly issue in their own confusion. The enemies of God and of his kingdom bear a great deal of malice and ill-will to Jerusalem, and form designs for its destruction; but it will prove, at last, that they are but preparing ruin for themselves; Jerusalem is in safety, and those are in all the danger who fight against it. This is here illustrated by three comparisons:—

(1.) *Jerusalem* shall be *a cup of trembling* to all that lay siege to it, *v*. 2. They promise themselves that it shall be to them a cup of wine, which they shall easily and with pleasure drink off, and they thirst for its spoils, nay, they thirst for its blood, as for such a cup; but it shall prove a *cup of slumber*, nay, a *cup of poison*, to them, which, when they take it into their hands, and think it is all their own, they shall not be able to drink off: the fumes of it shall give them enough. When *the kings were assembled* against her, and saw how *God was known in her palaces for a refuge*, they *trembled and hasted away; fear took hold upon them*, as we find, Ps. xlviii. 3—6. Thus Alexander the Great was struck with amazement when he met Jaddus the high priest, and was deterred thereby from offering any violence to Jerusalem. When Sennacherib laid siege *against Judah* and *Jerusalem* he found them such a cup of stupifying wine as laid all his mighty men asleep, Ps. lxxvi. 5, 6. Some read it, *I will make Jerusalem a post of contrition* or *breaking.* Those that make any attempts upon Jerusalem do but run their heads against a post, which they cannot move, but are sure to hurt themselves. The *blast of the terrible ones* is *as a storm against the wall* (Isa. xxv. 4), broken by it, but not shaking it. God's church is a cup of consolation to all her friends (Isa. lxvi. 11), but a cup of trembling to all that would either debauch her by errors and corruptions or destroy her by wars and persecutions. See Isa. li. 22, 23.

(2.) *Jerusalem* shall be *a burdensome stone* to all that attempt to remove it or carry it away, *v.* 3. All *the people of the earth* are here supposed to be *gathered together against it,* some one time and some another; there has been a succession of enemies, from age to age, making war upon the church. But though they were all at once in a confederacy against it, and had formed a resolution to *cut off the name of Israel, that it should be no more in remembrance* (Ps. lxxxiii. 4), they will find it a task too hard for them. Those that are for keeping up and advancing the kingdom of sin in the world look upon Jerusalem, even the church of God, as the great obstacle to their designs, and they must have it out of the way; but they will find it heavier than they think it is; so that, [1.] They cannot remove it. God will have a church in the world, in spite of them; it is *built upon a rock,* and is as *Mount Zion, that abides for ever,* Ps. cxxv. 1. This *stone, cut out of the mountain without hands,* will not only keep its ground, but, fill the earth, Dan. ii. 35. Nay, [2.] It will *break in pieces all that burden themselves* with it, as that stone *smote the image,* Dan. ii. 45. All that think themselves a match for it shall be *cut in pieces* by it. Some think it is an allusion to a sport which Jerome, upon this place, says was in use among the Jews, as among us: young men tried their strength, and strove for mastery, by heaving up great stones, which, if they proved too heavy for them, fell upon them, and bruised them. Those that make a jest of religion, and banter sacred things, will find them a burdensome stone, that it is ill-jesting with edged-tools, and though they make light of it (saying, *Am not I in sport?*) they bring upon themselves an insupportable sinking load of guilt. Our Saviour seems to allude to these words when he speaks of himself as a burdensome stone to those that will not have him for their foundation-stone, which shall *fall upon them and grind them to powder,* Matt. xxi. 44.

(3.) The governors of Judah shall be among their enemies like *a hearth of fire among the wood, and a torch of fire in a sheaf, v.* 6. Not that their own passions shall make them incendiaries and firebrands to all about them; no; Zion's King is *meek and lowly,* and all subordinate governors must be like him; but God's justice will make them avengers of his cause, and theirs, upon their enemies. Those that contend with them will find it is like an opposition given by briers and

thorns to a consuming fire, Isa. xxvii. 4. It will go through them, and burn them together. It is God's wrath, and not theirs, that is the fire which devours the adversaries. God's fire is said to be *in Zion,* and *his furnace in Jerusalem,* Isa. xxxi. 9. The enemies thought to be as water to this fire, to extinguish it and put it quite out; but God will make them as wood, nay, as a sheaf of corn (which is more combustible), to this fire, not only to be consumed by it, but to be made thereby to burn the more strongly. When God would make Abimelech and the men of Shechem one another's destroyers fire is said to *come out from the one to devour the other,* Judg. ix. 20. So here, Fire shall come out from the *governors of Judah* to *devour all the people round about,* as from the mouth of God's witnesses to consume those who offer to hurt them, Rev. xi. 5. The persecutors of the primitive church found this fulfilled in it, witness Lactantius's history of God's judgments upon the primitive persecutors, and the confession of Julian the apostate at last, *Thou hast overcome me, O thou Galilean!* The church's motto may be, *Nemo me impune lacesset—He that assails me does it at his peril. If you are weary of your life,* persecute the Christians, was once a proverb.

2. It is promised that God will infatuate the counsels and enfeeble the courage of the church's enemies (*v.* 4): " *In that day,* when the people of the earth are gathered together against Jerusalem, *I will smite every horse with astonishment, and his rider with madness;*" and again, " *I will smite every horse of the people with blindness,* so that they shall be no way serviceable to them; blinding the horses will be as bad as houghing them." The horses and their horsemen shall both forget the military exercise to which they were trained, and, instead of keeping ranks and observing the rules of their discipline, they shall both grow mad, and ruin themselves. The church's infantry shall be too hard for the enemy's cavalry; and those who were upbraided with trusting in horses shall be baffled by those who were forbidden to multiply horses.

3. It is promised that Jerusalem shall be re-peopled and replenished (*v.* 6): *Jerusalem shall be inhabited again in her own place, even in Jerusalem.* The natives of Jerusalem shall not incorporate in a colony in some other country, and build a city there, and call that *Jerusalem,* and see the promises fulfilled in that, as those in New England called their towns by the names of towns in Old England. No; they shall have a new Jerusalem upon the same foundation, the same spot of ground, with the old one. They had so after their return out of captivity, but this was to have its full accomplishment in the gospel-church, which is a Jerusalem inhabited *in its own place;* for, the gospel being to be preached to all the world, it may call every place its own.

4. It is promised that the inhabitants of Jerusalem shall be enabled to defend themselves, and yet shall be taken under the divine protection, *v.* 8. See here in what method God preserves his church, and those that are his, from the gates of hell to and through the gates of heaven. (1.) He does himself secure them: *In that day shall the Lord defend the inhabitants of Jerusalem,* not only Jerusalem itself from being taken and destroyed, but every inhabitant of it from being any way damaged. God will not only be a *wall of fire* about the city, to fortify that, but he will encompass particular persons with his favour *as with a shield,* so that no dart of the besiegers shall touch them. (2.) He does it by giving them strength and courage to help themselves. What God works in his people by his grace contributes more to their preservation and defence than what he works for them by his providence. *The God of Israel gives strength and power to his people,* that they may do their part, and then he will not be wanting to do his. It is the glory of God to strengthen the weak, that most need his help, that see and own their need of it, and will be the most thankful for it. [1.] In that day the feeblest of the inhabitants of Jerusalem *shall be as David,* shall be men of war, as bold and brave, as skilful and strong, as David himself, shall attempt and accomplish great things, as David did, and become as serviceable to Jerusalem in guarding it as David himself was in founding it, and as formidable as he was to the enemies of it. See what divine grace does; it makes children not only men, but champions, makes weak saints to be not only good soldiers, but great soldiers, like David. And see how God often does his own work as easily and effectually, and more to his own glory, by weak and obscure instruments than by the most illustrious. [2.] *The house of David shall be as God,* that is, *as the angel of the Lord, before them.* Zerubbabel was now the top-branch of the house of David; he shall be endued with wisdom and grace for the service to which he is called, and shall go before the people as an angel, as that angel (so some think) which went before the people of Israel through the wilderness, which was God himself, Exod. xxiii. 20. God will increase the gifts and abilities both of the people and princes, in proportion to the respective services for which they are designed. It was said of David that he was *as an angel of God, to discern good and bad,* 2 Sam. xiv. 17. Such shall the house of David now be. The inhabitants of Jerusalem shall be as strong and fit for action as nature made David, and their magistrates as wise and fit for counsel as grace made him. But this was to have its full accomplishment in Christ; now the house of David looked little and mean, and its glory was eclipsed, but in Christ the house of

David shone more brightly than ever, and its countenance was as that of an angel; in him it became more blessed, and more a blessing, than ever it had been.

5. It is promised that there shall be a very good understanding between the city and the country, and that the balance shall be kept even between them; there shall be no mutual envies or jealousies between them; they shall not keep up any separate interests, but shall heartily unite in their counsels, and act in concert for the common good; and this happy agreement between the city and the country, the head and the body, is very necessary to the health, welfare, and safety of any nation. (1.) *The governors of Judah,* the magistrates and gentry of the country, shall think honourably of the citizens, *the inhabitants of Jerusalem,* the merchants and tradesmen; they shall not run them down, and contrive how to keep them under, but they *shall say in their hearts,* not in compliment, but in sincerity, *The inhabitants of Jerusalem shall be my strength,* the strength of my country, of my family, *in the Lord of hosts their God, v.* 5. They will therefore, upon all occasions, pay respect and deference to Jerusalem, as the mother-city, the ruling-city, and the city that is to be first served, because they look upon it to be the bulwark of the nation and its strongest fortification in times of public danger and distress, which therefore they would all come in to the assistance of and come under the protection of, and this not so much because it was a rich city, and money is the sinews of war, nor because it was a populous city and could bring the greatest numbers into the field, nor because its inhabitants were generally the most ingenious active men, the best soldiers and the best commanders *(of Zion it shall be said,* This and that brave *man were born there),* but because it was a *holy city,* where God's house and household, the temple and the priests, were, where his worship was kept up and his feasts were observed, and because it should now be more than ever a praying city, for *upon the inhabitants of Jerusalem* God will *pour a spirit of supplication (v.* 10); therefore the governors of Judah shall say, *These are my strength;* they are so upon the account of their relation to, their interest in, and their communion with, *the Lord of hosts, their God.* Because *the Lord of hosts* is in a particular manner *their God* (for *in Salem is his tabernacle and his dwelling-place in Zion),* therefore *they shall be my strength.* Note, It is well with a kingdom when its great men know how to value its good men, when its governors look upon religion and religious people to be their strength, and consider it their interest to support them, and learn to call godly praying people, and skilful faithful ministers, *the chariots and horsemen of Israel,* as Joash called Elisha, and not the troublers of the land, as Ahab called Elijah. (2.) The court

and the city shall not despise, nor look with contempt upon, the inhabitants of the country; no, not the meanest of them, much less upon the governors of Judah; for God will put signal honour upon Judah, and so save them from the contempt of their brethren. As Jerusalem was dignified by special ordinances, so Judah shall be dignified with special providences. God says (v. 4), *I will open my eyes upon the house of Judah,* upon the poor country people. Proud men scornfully overlook them, but the great God will graciously look upon them and look after them. Nay (v. 7), *the Lord shall save the tents of Judah first.* Those that dwell in tents lie most exposed; but God will remarkably protect and deliver them before those that dwell in Jerusalem. He will appear glorious in what he does for the *inhabitants of his villages in Israel,* Judg. v. 11. Thus, in the mystical body, God *gives more abundant honour to that part which lacked, that there may be no schism in the body* (see 1 Cor. xii. 22—25), which is the reason here given why *the glory of the house of David,* which has great power, and *the glory of the inhabitants of Jerusalem,* who have great wealth, and both which live in great pomp and pleasure, *may not magnify themselves against Judah* and the *tents of Judah,* the dwellers in which work hard, and fare hard, and perhaps are not so well bred. Note, Courtiers and citizens ought not to despise country people, nor look with disdain upon those whom God *opens his eyes upon* and who are *first saved,* while it is so hard for the rich and great to *enter the kingdom of God.* If God by his grace has magnified the dwellers in the tents of Judah, having chosen the weak and foolish things of the world and chosen to employ them, we affront him if we vilify them, or magnify ourselves against them, Jam. ii. 5, 6. This promise has a further reference to the gospel-church, in which no difference shall be made between high and low, rich and poor, bond and free, circumcision and uncircumcision, but all shall be alike welcome to Christ, and partake of his benefits, Col. iii. 11. Jerusalem shall not then be thought, as it had been, more holy than other parts of the land of Israel.

9 And it shall come to pass in that day, *that* I will seek to destroy all the nations that come against Jerusalem. 10 And I will pour upon the house of David, and upon the inhabitants of Jerusalem, the spirit of grace and of supplications: and they shall look upon me whom they have pierced, and they shall mourn for him, as one mourneth for *his* only *son,* and shall be in bitterness for him, as one that is in bitterness for *his* first-born. 11

In that day shall there be a great mourning in Jerusalem, as the mourning of Hadadrimmon in the valley of Megiddon. 12 And the land shall mourn, every family apart; the family of the house of David apart, and their wives apart; the family of the house of Nathan apart, and their wives apart; 13 The family of the house of Levi apart, and their wives apart; the family of Shimei apart, and their wives apart; 14 All the families that remain, every family apart, and their wives apart.

The *day* here spoken of is the day of Jerusalem's defence and deliverance, that glorious day when God will appear for the salvation of his people, which, if it do refer to the successes which the Jews had against their enemies in the time of the Maccabees, yet certainly looks further, to the *gospel-day,* to Christ's victories over the powers of darkness and the great salvation he has wrought for his chosen. Now we have here an account of two remarkable works designed *in that day.*

I. A glorious work of God to be wrought for his people: "*I will seek to destroy all the nations that come against Jerusalem, v. 9.* Nations come against Jerusalem, many and mighty nations; but they shall all be destroyed, their power shall be broken, and their attempts baffled; the mischief they intend shall return upon their own head." God will seek to destroy them, not as if he were at a loss for ways and means to bring it about (Infinite Wisdom was never nonplussed), but his seeking to do it intimates that he is very earnest and intent upon it (he is jealous for Zion with great jealousy, and has the *day of vengeance* in his heart) and that he overrules means and instruments, and all the motions and operations of second causes, in order to it. He is *framing evil* against them; when he seems to be setting them up he is seeking to destroy them. In Christ's first coming, he *sought to destroy him that had the power of death,* and did destroy him, bruised the serpent's head, and broke all the *powers of darkness* that fought against God's kingdom among men and against the faithful friends and subjects of that kingdom; he *spoiled* them, and *made a show of them openly.* In his second coming, he will complete their destruction, when he shall *put down all* opposing *rule, principality, and power,* and *death* itself shall be *swallowed up in* that *victory. The last enemy shall be destroyed* of all that *fought against Jerusalem.*

II. A gracious work of God to be wrought in his people, in order to the work that is to be wrought for them. When he seeks to destroy their enemies he will *pour upon them the Spirit of grace and supplication.* Note,

When God intends great mercy for his people the first thing he does is to set them a praying; thus he seeks to destroy their enemies by stirring them up to seek to him that he would do it for them; because, though he has proposed it and promised it, and it is for his own glory to do it, yet he will *for this be enquired of by the house of Israel*, Ezek. xxxvi. 37. *Ask, and it shall be given.* This honour will he have to himself, and this honour will he put upon prayer and upon praying people. And it is a happy presage to the distressed church of deliverance approaching, and is, as it were, the dawning of its day, when his people are stirred up to cry mightily to him for it. But this promise has reference to, and is performed in, the graces of the Spirit given to all believers, as that Isa. xliv. 3, *I will pour my Spirit upon thy seed*, which was fulfilled when *Jesus was glorified*, John vii. 39. It is a promise of the Spirit, and with him of all *spiritual blessings in heavenly things by Christ*. Now observe here,

1. On whom these blessings are poured out. (1.) *On the house of David*, on the great men; for they are no more, and no better, than the grace of God makes them. It was promised (*v.* 8) that *the house of David* should be *as the angel of the Lord.* Now, in order to that, the Spirit of grace is poured upon them; for the more the saints have of the Spirit of grace the more like they are to the holy angels. When God was about to appear for the land, he poured his Spirit of grace upon the house of David, the leading men of the land. It bodes well to a people when princes and great men go before the rest in that which is good, as 2 Chron. xx. 5. The house of David is all summed up in Jesus Christ, *the Son of David;* and upon him, as the head, the Spirit of grace is poured out, from him to be diffused to all his members; *from his fulness we receive, and grace for grace.* (2.) *On the inhabitants of Jerusalem*, the common people; for the operations of the Spirit are the same upon the mean and weak Christians that they are upon the strong and more grown. The inhabitants of Jerusalem cannot influence public affairs by their powers and policies, as the great men of the house of David may, yet they may do good service by their prayers, and therefore upon them the Spirit shall be poured out. The church is Jerusalem, the heavenly Jerusalem; all true believers, that have their conversation in heaven, are inhabitants of this Jerusalem, and to them this promise belongs. God will *pour his Spirit upon them.* This is the earnest which all that *believe in Christ shall receive;* thus they are sanctified; thus they are sealed.

2. What these blessings are: *I will pour upon them the Spirit.* That includes all good things, as it qualifies us for the favour of God, and all his other gifts. He will pour

1462

out the Spirit, (1.) As a *Spirit of grace*, to sanctify us and to make us gracious. (2.) As a *Spirit of supplications*, inclining us to, instructing and assisting us in, the duty of prayer. Note, Wherever the Spirit is given as a Spirit of grace, he is given as a Spirit of sanctification. Wherever he is a Spirit of adoption, he *teaches to cry, Abba, Father.* As soon as ever Paul was converted, *Behold, he prays*, Acts ix. 11. You may as soon find a living man without breath as a living saint without prayer. There is a more plentiful effusion of the Spirit of prayer now under the gospel than was under the law; and the further the work of sanctification is carried in us the better is the work of supplication carried on by us.

3. What the effect of them will be: *I will pour upon them the Spirit of grace.* One would think that it should follow, " And they shall look on him whom they have believed, and shall rejoice" (and it is true that that is one of the fruits of the pouring out of the Spirit, whence we read of *the joy of the Holy Ghost*), but it follows, *They shall mourn:* for there is a holy mourning, that is the effect of the pouring out of the Spirit, a mourning for sin, which is of use to quicken faith in Christ and qualify for joy in God. It is here made the matter of a promise that they shall mourn, for there is a mourning that will end in rejoicing and has a blessing entailed upon it. This mourning is a fruit of the Spirit of grace, an evidence of a work of grace in the soul, and a companion of the Spirit of supplication, as it expresses lively affections working in prayer; hence prayers and tears are often put together, 2 Kings xx. 5. Jacob, that wrestler with God, *wept and made supplication.* But here it is a mourning for sin that is the effect of the pouring out of the Spirit.

(1.) It is a mourning grounded upon a sight of Christ: *They shall look on me whom they have pierced, and shall mourn for him.* Here, [1.] It is foretold that Christ should be pierced, and this scripture is quoted as that which was fulfilled when Christ's side was pierced upon the cross; see John xix. 37. [2.] He is spoken of as one whom we have pierced; it is spoken primarily of the Jews, who persecuted him to death (and we find that *those who pierced him* are distinguished from the other *kindreds of the earth* that shall *wail because of him*, Rev. i. 7); yet it is true of us all as sinners, we have pierced Christ, inasmuch as our sins were the cause of his death, for he was *wounded for our transgressions*, and they are the *grief of his soul;* he is *broken with the whorish heart* of sinners, who *therefore* are said to *crucify him afresh* and put him to open shame. [3.] Those that truly repent of sin look upon Christ as one whom they have pierced, who was pierced for their sins and is pierced by them; and this engages them to *look unto him*, as those that are deeply concerned for him. [4.] This is the effect of their looking to Christ; it makes them mourn. This was particularly fulfilled in those to whom Peter preached Christ crucified; when they heard it those who had had a hand in piercing him were *pricked to the heart*, and cried out, *What shall we do?* It is fulfilled in all those who sorrow for sin after a godly sort; they look to Christ, and *mourn for him*, not so much for his sufferings as for their own sins that procured them. Note, The genuine sorrows of a penitent soul flow from the believing sight of a pierced Saviour. Looking by faith upon the cross of Christ will set us a mourning for sin after a godly sort.

(2.) It is a great mourning. [1.] It is like the mourning of a parent for the death of a beloved child. They shall mourn for sin *as one mourns for an only son*, in whose grave the hopes of his family are buried, and shall be inwardly *in bitterness as one that is in bitterness for his first-born*, as the Egyptians were when there was a cry throughout all their land for the death of their first-born. The sorrow of children for the death of their parents is sometimes counterfeited, is often small, and soon wears off and is forgotten; but the sorrow of parents for a child, for a son, for an only son, for a first-born, is natural, sincere, unforced, and unaffected, it is secret and lasting; such are the sorrows of a true penitent, flowing purely from love to Christ above any other. [2.] It is like the mourning of a people for the death of a wise and good prince. It shall be *like the mourning of Hadadrimmon in the valley of Megiddon*, where good king Josiah was slain, for whom there was a general lamentation (*v.* 11), and perhaps the greater because they were told that it was their sin that provoked God to deprive them of so great a blessing; therefore they cried out, *The crown has fallen from our head. Woe unto us, for we have sinned!* Lam. v. 16. Christ is our King; our sins were his death, and, for that reason, ought to be our grief.

(3.) It is a general universal mourning (*v.* 12): *The land shall mourn.* The land itself put on mourning at the death of Christ, for there was then *darkness over all the land*, and the earth trembled; but this is a promise that, in consideration of the death of Christ, multitudes shall be effectually brought to sorrow for sin and turn to God; it shall be such a universal gracious mourning as was when *all the house of Israel lamented after the Lord*, 1 Sam. vii. 2. Some think this is yet to have its complete accomplishment in the general conversion of the Jewish nation.

(4.) It is also a private particular mourning. There shall be not only a mourning of *the land*, by its representatives in a general assembly (as Judg. ii. 5, when the place was called *Bochim—A place of weepers*), but it shall spread itself into all corners of the land: *Every family apart* shall mourn (*v.*

12), *all the families that remain, v.* 14. All have contributed to the guilt, and therefore all shall share in the grief. Note, The exercises of devotion should be performed by private families among themselves, besides their joining in public assemblies for religious worship. National fasts must be observed, not only in our synagogues, but in our houses. In the mourning here foretold the wives mourn apart by themselves, in their own apartment, as Esther and her maids. And some think it intimates their denying themselves the use even of lawful delights in a time of general humiliation, 1 Cor. vii. 5. Four several families are here specified as examples to others in this mourning :—[1.] Two of them are royal families; the *house of David*, in Solomon, and the *house of Nathan*, another son of David, brother to Solomon, from whom Zerubbabel descended, as appears by Christ's genealogy, Luke iii. 27—31. The house of David, particularly that of Nathan, which is now the chief branch of that house, shall go before in this good work. The greatest princes must not think themselves exempted from the law of repentance, but rather obliged most solemnly to express it, for the exciting of others, as Hezekiah humbled himself (2 Chron. xxxii. 26), the princes and the king (2 Chron. xii. 6), and the king of Nineveh, Jonah iii. 6. [2.] Two of them are sacred families (*v.* 13), *the family of the house of Levi*, which was God's tribe, and in it particularly the family of Shimei, which was a branch of the tribe of Levi (1 Chron. vi. 17), and probably some of the descendants of that family were now of note for preachers to the people or ministers to the altar. As the princes must mourn for the sins of the magistracy, so must the priests for the *iniquity of the holy things*. In times of general tribulation and humiliation the Lord's ministers are concerned to *weep between the porch and the altar* (Joel ii. 17), and not only there, but in their houses apart; for in what families should godliness, both in the form and in the power of it, be found, if not in ministers' families?

CHAP. XIII.

In this chapter we have, I. Some further promises relating to gospel-times. Here is a promise of the remission of sins (ver. 1), of the reformation of manners (ver. 2), and particularly of the convicting and silencing of false prophets, ver. 2—6. II. A clear prediction of the sufferings of Christ and the dispersion of his disciples thereupon (ver. 7), of the destruction of the greater part of the Jewish nation not long after (ver. 8), and of the purifying of a remnant of them, a peculiar people to God, ver. 9.

IN that day there shall be a fountain opened to the house of David and to the inhabitants of Jerusalem for sin and for uncleanness. 2 And it shall come to pass in that day, saith the LORD of hosts, *that* I will cut off the names of the idols out of the land, and they shall no more be remembered: and also I will cause the prophets and the unclean spirit to pass out of the land. 3 And it shall come to pass, *that* when any shall yet prophesy, then his father and his mother that begat him shall say unto him, Thou shalt not live; for thou speakest lies in the name of the LORD: and his father and his mother that begat him shall thrust him through when he prophesieth. 4 And it shall come to pass in that day, *that* the prophets shall be ashamed every one of his vision, when he hath prophesied; neither shall they wear a rough garment to deceive: 5 But he shall say, I *am* no prophet, I *am* a husbandman; for man taught me to keep cattle from my youth. 6 And *one* shall say unto him, What *are* these wounds in thine hands? Then he shall answer, *Those* with which I was wounded *in* the house of my friends.

Behold the Lamb of God *taking away the sin of the world*, the sin of the church; for *therefore* was the Son of God manifested, to *take away our sin*, 1 John iii. 5.

I. He takes away the guilt of sin by the blood of his cross (*v.* 1): *In that day*, in the gospel-day, *there shall be a fountain opened*, that is, provision made for the cleansing of all those from the pollutions of sin who truly repent and are sorry for them. *In that day*, when the Spirit of grace is poured out to set them a mourning for their sins, they shall not mourn as those who have no hope, but they shall have their sins pardoned, and the comfort of their pardon in their bosoms. Their consciences shall be purified and pacified by the *blood of Christ, which cleanses from all sin*, 1 John i. 7. For Christ is exalted to give both repentance and remission of sins; and where he gives the one no doubt he gives the other. This *fountain opened* is the pierced side of Jesus Christ, spoken of just before (*ch.* xii. 10), for thence came there out *blood and water*, and both for cleansing. And those who *look upon Christ pierced*, and mourn for their sins that pierced him, and are therefore in bitterness for him, may look again upon Christ pierced and rejoice in him, because it pleased the Lord thus to smite this rock, that it might be to us a *fountain of living waters*. See here, 1. How we are polluted; we are all so; we have sinned, and sin is uncleanness; it defiles the mind and conscience, renders us odious to God and uneasy in ourselves, unfit to be employed in the service of God and admitted into communion with him, as those who were ceremonially unclean were shut out of the sanctuary. The *house of David* and the *inhabitants of Jerusalem* are under *sin*, which is uncleanness. The truth is, we are all *as an unclean*

thing, and deserve to have our portion with the unclean. 2. How we may be purged. Behold, there is a fountain opened for us to wash in, and there are streams flowing to us from that fountain, so that, if we be not made clean, it is our own fault. The blood of Christ, and God's pardoning mercy in that blood, revealed in the new covenant, are, (1.) A fountain; for there is in them an inexhaustible fulness. There is mercy enough in God, and merit enough in Christ, for the forgiving of the greatest sins and sinners, upon gospel-terms. *Such were some of you, but you are washed*, 1 Cor. vi. 11. Under the law there were a brazen laver and a brazen sea to wash in; those were but vessels, but we have a fountain to ourselves, overflowing, ever-flowing. (2.) *A fountain opened;* for, whoever will, may come and take the benefit of it; it is opened, not only to *the house of David*, but to *the inhabitants of Jerusalem*, to the poor and mean as well as to the rich and great; or it is opened for all believers, who, as the spiritual seed of Christ, are of the house of David, and, as living members of the church, are inhabitants of Jerusalem. Through Christ all that believe are justified, are *washed from their sins in his blood*, that they may be *made to our God kings and priests*, Rev. i. 5, 6.

II. He takes away the dominion of sin by the power of his grace, even of beloved sins. This evermore accompanies the former; those that are washed in the fountain opened, as they are justified, so they are sanctified; the water came with the blood out of the pierced side of Christ. It is here promised that in that day, 1. Idolatry shall be quite abolished and the people of the Jews shall be effectually cured of their inclination to it (*v.* 2): *I will cut off the names of the idols out of the land.* The worship of the idols of their fathers shall be so perfectly rooted out that in one generation or two it shall be forgotten that ever there were such idols among them; they shall either not be named at all or not with any respect; *they shall no more be remembered*, as was promised, Hos. ii. 17. This was fulfilled in the rooted aversion which the Jews had, after the captivity, to idols and idolatry, and still retain to this day; it was fulfilled also in the ready conversion of many to the faith of Christ, by which they were taken off from making an idol of the ceremonial law, as the unbelieving Jews did; and it is still in the fulfilling when souls are brought off from the world and the flesh, those two great idols, that they may cleave to God only. 2. False prophecy shall also be brought to an end: *I will cause the prophets and the unclean spirit*, the prophets that are under the influence of the unclean spirit, *to pass out of the land.* The devil is an *unclean spirit*; sin and uncleanness are from him; he has his prophets, that serve his interests and receive their instructions from him. Take away the unclean spirit, and the prophets would not deceive as they do; take away the false prophets that produce sham commissions, and the unclean spirit could not do the mischief he does. When God designs the silencing of the false prophets he banishes the unclean spirit out of the land, that wrought in them, and was a rival with him for the throne in the heart. The church of the Jews, when they were addicted to idols, did also dote much upon false prophets, who flattered them in their sins with promises of impunity and peace; but here it is promised, as a blessed effect of the promised reformation, that they should be very much set against false prophets, and zealous to clear the land of them; they were so after the captivity, till, through the blindness of their zeal against false prophets, they had put Christ to death under that character, and, after that, there arose many *false Christs and false prophets, and deceived many,* Matt. xxiv. 11. It is here foretold, (1.) That false prophets, instead of being indulged and favoured, should be brought to condign punishment even by their nearest relations, which would be as great an instance as any of flagrant zeal against those deceivers (*v.* 3): *When any shall* set up for a prophet, and shall *speak lies in the name of the Lord,* shall preach that which tends to draw people from God and to confirm them in sin, his own parents shall be the first and most forward to prosecute him for it, according to the law. Deut. xiii. 6—11, *"If thy son entice thee secretly* from God, *thou shalt surely kill him.* Show thy indignation against him, and prevent any further temptation from him." His *father and his mother shall thrust him through when he prophesies.* Note, We ought to conceive, and always to retain, a very great detestation and dread of every thing that would draw us out of the way of our duty into by-paths, as those who cannot *bear that which is evil,* Rev. ii. 2. And holy zeal for God and godliness will make us hate sin, and dread temptation, most in those whom naturally we love best, and who are nearest to us; there our danger is greatest, as Adam's from Eve, Job's from his wife; and there it will be the most praiseworthy to show our zeal, as Levi, who, in the cause of God, did not *acknowledge his brethren,* nor *know his own children,* Deut. xxxiii. 9. Thus we must hate and forsake our nearest relations when they come in competition with our duty to God, Luke xiv. 26. Natural affections, even the strongest, must be overruled by gracious affections. (2.) That false prophets should be themselves convinced of their sin and folly, and let fall their pretensions (*v.* 4): *" The prophets shall be ashamed every one of his vision;* they shall not repeat it, or insist upon it, but desire that it may be forgotten and no more said of it, being ready themselves to own it was a sham, because God has by his grace awakened their consciences and shown them their error, or

because the event disproves their predictions, and gives them the lie, or because their prophecies do not meet with such a favourable reception as they used to meet with, but are generally despised and distasted; they perceive the people ashamed of them, which makes them begin to be ashamed of themselves. And therefore they shall no longer *wear a rough garment,* or *garment of hair,* as the true prophets used to do, in imitation of Elijah, and in token of their being mortified to the pleasures and delights of sense." The pretenders had appeared in the habit of true prophets; but, their folly being now made manifest, they shall lay it aside, no more to deceive and impose upon unthinking unwary people by it. A modest dress is a very good thing, if it be the genuine indication of a humble heart, and is to instruct; but it is a bad thing if it be the hypocritical disguise of a proud ambitious heart, and is to deceive. Let men be really as good as they seem to be, but not seem to be better than really they are. This pretender, as a true penitent, [1.] Shall undeceive those whom he had imposed upon: *He shall say,* " I am no prophet, as I have pretended to be, was never designed nor set apart to the office, never educated nor brought up for it, never conversant among the sons of the prophets. *I am a husbandman,* and was bred to that business; I was never taught of God to prophesy, but *taught of man to keep cattle."* Amos was originally such a one too, and yet was afterwards called to be a prophet, Amos vii. 14, 15. But this deceiver never had any such call. Note, Those who sorrow after a godly sort for their having deceived others will be forward to confess their sin, and will be so just as to rectify the mistakes which they have been the cause of. Thus those who had *used curious arts,* when they were converted *showed their deeds,* and by what fallacies they had cheated the people, Acts xix. 18. [2.] He shall return to his own proper employment, which is the fittest for him: *I will be a husbandman* (so it may be read); " I will apply myself to my calling again, and meddle no more with things that belong not to me; for *man taught me to keep cattle from my youth,* and cattle I will again keep, and never set up for a preacher any more." Note, When we are convinced that we have gone out of the way of our duty we must evince the truth of our repentance by returning to it again, though it be the severest mortification to us. [3.] He shall acknowledge those to be his friends who by a severe discipline were instrumental to bring him to a sight of his error, *v.* 6. When he who with the greatest assurance had asserted himself so lately to be a prophet suddenly drops his claims, and says, I am no prophet, every body will be surprised at it, and some will ask, " *What are these wounds,* or marks of stripes, *in thy hands?* How camest thou by them? Hast thou not been *examined by scourging?* And is not that it that has brought thee to thyself?" *(Vexatio dat intellectum—Vexation sharpens the intellect.)* " Hast thou not been beaten into this acknowledgment? Was it not the rod and reproof that gave thee this wisdom?" And he shall own, "Yes, it was; these are the *wounds with which I was wounded in the house of my friends,* who bound me, and used me hardly and severely, as a distracted man, and so brought me to my senses." By this it appears that those parents of the false prophet that *thrust him through* (v. 3) did not do it till they had first tried to reclaim him by correction, and he would not be reclaimed; for so was the law concerning a disobedient son—his parents must first have chastened him in vain before they were allowed to bring him forth to be stoned, Deut. xxi. 18, 19. But here is another who was reduced by stripes, and so prevented the capital punishment; and he had the sense and honesty to own that they were his friends, his real friends, who thus wounded him, that they might reclaim him; for *faithful are the wounds of a friend,* Prov. xxvii. 6. Some good interpreters, observing how soon this comes after the mention of Christ's being pierced, think that these are the words of that great prophet, not of the false prophet spoken of before. Christ was wounded in his hands, when they were nailed to the cross, and, after his resurrection, he had the marks of these wounds; and here he tells how he came by them; he received them as a false prophet, for the chief priests called him a deceiver, and upon that account would have him crucified; but he received them in the house of his friends—the Jews, who should have been his friends; for *he came to his own,* and, though they were his bitter enemies, yet he was pleased to call them his *friends,* as he did Judas *(Friend, wherefore hast thou come?)* because they forwarded his sufferings for him; as he called Peter *Satan—an adversary,* because he dissuaded him from them.

7 Awake, O sword, against my shepherd, and against the man *that is* my fellow, saith the LORD of hosts: smite the shepherd, and the sheep shall be scattered: and I will turn mine hand upon the little ones. 8 And it shall come to pass, *that* in all the land, saith the LORD, two parts therein shall be cut off *and* die; but the third shall be left therein. 9 And I will bring the third part through the fire, and will refine them as silver is refined, and will try them as gold is tried: they shall call on my name, and I will hear them: I will say, It *is* my people: and they shall say, The LORD *is* my God.

Here is a prophecy,

I. Of the sufferings of Christ, of him who was to be pierced, and was to be the fountain opened. *Awake, O sword! against my Shepherd,* v. 7. These are the words of God the Father, giving order and commission to the sword of his justice to awake against his Son, when he had voluntarily made his soul an offering for sin; for *it pleased the Lord to bruise him* and *put him to grief;* and *he was stricken, smitten of God, and afflicted,* Isa. liii. 4, 10. Observe, 1. How he calls him. "As God, he is *my fellow;*" for he thought it *no robbery to be equal with God.* He and *the Father* are one. He was from eternity by him, as one brought up with him, and, in the work of man's redemption, he was his elect, in whom his soul delighted, and the counsel of peace was between them both. "As Mediator, he is *my Shepherd,* that great and good Shepherd that undertook to feed the flock," *ch.* xi. 7. He is the Shepherd that was to lay down his life for the sheep. 2. How he uses him: *Awake, O sword! against him.* If he will be a sacrifice, he must be slain, for without the shedding of blood, the life-blood, there was no remission. Men thrust him through as a foolish shepherd; God thrust him through as the good Shepherd (compare *v.* 3), that he might *purchase the flock of God* with *his own blood,* Acts xx. 28. It is not a charge given to a rod to correct him, but to a sword to slay him; for *Messiah the prince must be cut off, but not for himself,* Dan. ix. 26. It is not the sword of war that receives this charge, that he may die in the bed of honour, but the sword of justice, that he may die as a criminal, upon an ignominious tree. This sword must awake against him; he having no sin of his own to answer for, the sword of justice had nothing to say to him of itself, till, by particular order from the Judge of all, it was warranted to brandish itself against him. He was the Lamb *slain from the foundation of the world,* in the decree and counsel of God; but the sword designed against him had long slumbered, till now at length it is called upon to awake, not, "Awake, and frighten him," but, "Awake, and smite him; strike home; not with a drowsy blow, but an awakened one;" for God *spared not his own Son.*

II. Of the dispersion of the disciples thereupon: *Smite the Shepherd, and the sheep shall be scattered.* This our Lord Jesus himself declares to have been fulfilled when *all his disciples were offended because of him* in the night wherein he was betrayed, Matt. xxvi. 31; Mark xiv. 27. They all *forsook him and fled.* The smiting of the Shepherd is the scattering of the sheep. They were *scattered every one to his own, and left him alone,* John xvi. 32. Herein they were like timorous sheep; yet the Shepherd thus provided for their safety, for he said, *If you seek me, let these go their way.* Some make another application of this; Christ was the *Shepherd* of the Jewish nation; he was smitten; they themselves smote him, and therefore they were justly scattered abroad, and dispersed among the nations, and remain so at this day. These words, *I will turn my hand upon the little ones,* may be understood either as a threatening (as Christ suffered, so shall his disciples, they shall *drink of the cup that he drank of* and be *baptized with the baptism that he was baptized* with) or as a promise that God would gather Christ's scattered disciples together again, and he should give them the meeting in Galilee. Though the little ones among Christ's soldiers may be dispersed, they shall rally again; the lambs of his flock, though frightened by the beasts of prey, shall recover themselves, shall be gathered in his arms and laid in his bosom. Sometimes, when the sheep are scattered and lost in the wilderness, yet the little ones, which, it was feared, would be a prey (Num. xiv. 31), are brought in, are brought home, and God turns his hand upon them.

III. Of the rejection and ruin of the unbelieving Jews (*v.* 8); and this word has, and shall have, its accomplishment, in the destruction of the corrupt and hypocritical part of the church. *It shall come to pass that in all the land of Israel two parts shall be cut off and die.* The Roman army laid the country waste, and slew at least two-thirds of the Jews. Some understand by the *cutting off,* and *dying,* of *two parts* in all *the earth,* the abolishing of heathenism and Judaism, that Christianity, the third part, might be left to reign alone. The Jewish worship was quite taken away by the destruction of Jerusalem and the temple. And, some time after, Pagan idolatry was in a manner extirpated, when the empire became Christian.

IV. Of the reformation and preservation of the chosen remnant, those of them that believed, and the Christian church in general (*v.* 9): *The third part shall be left.* When Jerusalem and Judea were destroyed, all the Christians in that country, having among them the warning Christ gave them to *flee to the mountains,* shifted for their own safety, and were sheltered in a city called *Pella,* on the other side Jordan. We have here first the trials and then the triumphs of the Christian church, and of all the faithful members of it. 1. Their trials: *I will bring that third part through the fire* of affliction, *and will refine* and try *them* as *silver and gold are refined and tried.* This was fulfilled in the persecutions of the primitive church, the *fiery trial* which tried the people of God then, 1 Pet. iv. 12. Those whom God sets apart for himself must pass through a probation and purification in this world; they must be *tried* that *their faith* may he *found to praise and honour* (1 Pet. i. 6, 7), as Abraham's faith was when it was tried by the command given him to offer up Isaac, *Now know I that thou fearest me.* They must be tried, that both those that are perfect and

those that are not may be *made manifest.* They must be refined from their dross; their corruption must be purged out; they must be brightened and bettered. 2. Their triumphs. (1) Their communion with God is their triumph: *They shall call on my name, and I will hear them.* They write to God by prayer, and receive from him answers of peace, and thus keep up a comfortable communion with him. *This honour have all his saints.* (2.) Their covenant with God is their triumph: "*I will say, It is my people,* whom I have chosen and loved, and will own; *and they shall say, The Lord is my God,* and a God all-sufficient to me; and in me they shall boast every day and all the day long. *This God is our God for ever and ever.*"

CHAP. XIV.

Divers things were foretold, in the two foregoing chapters, which should come to pass "in that day;" this chapter speaks of a "day of the Lord that cometh," a day of his judgment, and ten times in the foregoing chapters, and seven times in this, it is repeated, "in that day;" but what that day is that is here meant is uncertain, and perhaps will be so (as the Jews speak) till Elias comes; whether it refer to the whole period of time from the prophet's days to the days of the Messiah, or to some particular events in that time, or to Christ's coming, and the setting up of his kingdom upon the ruins of the Jewish polity, we cannot determine, but divers passages here seem to look as far forward as gospel-times. Now the "day of the Lord" brings with it both judgment and mercy, mercy to his church, judgment to her enemies and persecutors. I. The gates of hell are here threatening the church (ver. 1, 2) and yet not prevailing. II. The power of Heaven appears here for the church and against the enemies of it, ver. 3, 5. III. The events concerning the church are here represented as mixed (ver. 6, 7), but issuing well at last. IV. The spreading of the means of knowledge is here foretold, and the setting up of the gospel-kingdom in the world (ver. 8, 9), which shall be the enlargement and establishment of another Jerusalem, ver. 10, 11. V. Those shall be reckoned with that fought against Jerusalem (ver. 12—15) and those that neglect his worship there, ver. 17—19. VI. It is promised that there shall be great resort to the church, and great purity and piety in it, ver. 16, 20, 21.

BEHOLD, the day of the LORD cometh, and thy spoil shall be divided in the midst of thee. 2 For I will gather all nations against Jerusalem to battle: and the city shall be taken, and the houses rifled, and the women ravished; and half of the city shall go forth into captivity, and the residue of the people shall not be cut off from the city. 3 Then shall the LORD go forth, and fight against those nations, as when he fought in the day of battle. 4 And his feet shall stand in that day upon the mount of Olives, which *is* before Jerusalem on the east, and the mount of Olives shall cleave in the midst thereof toward the east and toward the west, *and there shall be* a very great valley; and half of the mountain shall remove toward the north, and half of it toward the south. 5 And ye shall flee *to* the valley of the mountains; for the valley of the mountains shall reach unto Azal : yea, ye shall flee, like as ye fled from before the earthquake in the days of Uzziah king of Judah : and the LORD my God shall come, *and* all the saints with thee. 6 And it shall come to pass in that day, *that* the light shall not be clear, *nor* dark : 7 But it shall be one day which shall be known to the LORD, not day, nor night : but it shall come to pass, *that* at evening time it shall be light.

God's providences concerning his church are here represented as strangely changing and strangely mixed.

I. As strangely changing. Sometimes the tide runs high and strong against them, but presently it turns, and comes to be in favour of them ; and God has, for wise and holy ends, set the one over against the other.

1. God here appears against Jerusalem ; judgment begins at the house of God. When the *day of the Lord comes* (*v.* 1) Jerusalem must pass through the fire to be refined. God himself *gathers all nations against Jerusalem to battle* (*v.* 2) ; he gives them a charge, as he did Sennacherib, to *take the spoil* and to *take the prey* (Isa. x. 6), for the people of Jerusalem have now become the *people of his wrath.* And who can stand before him or before nations gathered by him? Where he gives commission he will give success. The *city shall be taken by the* Romans, who have *nations* at command ; the houses shall be rifled, and all the riches of them taken away, by the enemy ; and, to gratify an insatiable lust of uncleanness as well as avarice, *the women* shall *be ravished,* as if victory were a license to the worst of villanies, *jusque datum sceleri—and crimes were sanctioned by law. One-half of the city* shall then be carried *into captivity,* to be sold or enslaved, and shall not be able to help itself, such is the destruction that shall be made in the great and terrible *day of the Lord.*

2. He presently changes his way, and appears for Jerusalem ; for, though judgment begin at the house of God, yet, as it shall not end there, so it shall not make a full end there, Jer. iv. 27 ; xxx. 11.

(1.) A remnant shall be spared, the same with that *third part* spoken of, *ch.* xiii. 8. *One-half shall go into captivity,* whence they may hereafter be fetched back, *and the residue of the people shall not* be cut off, as one would have feared, *from the city.* Many of the Jews shall receive the gospel, and so shall prevent their being cut off from the city of God, his church upon earth. *In it shall be a tenth,* Isa. vi. 13 ; See Ezek. v. 3.

(2.) Their cause shall be pleaded against their enemies (*v.* 3) : *Then,* when God has made use of these nations as a scourge to his people, he shall *go forth* and *fight against them* by his judgments, *as when he fought*

against the enemies of his church formerly *in the day of battle,* with the Egyptians, Canaanites, and others. Note, The instruments of God's wrath will themselves be made the objects of it ; for it will come to their turn to drink of the cup of trembling ; and whom God fights against he will be sure to overcome and be too hard for. And every former *day of battle,* which God has made to his people a *day of triumph,* as it is an engagement to God to appear for his people, because he is the same, so it is an encouragement to them to trust in him. It is observable that the Roman empire never flourished after the destruction of Jerusalem as it had done before, but in many instances God fought against it.

(3.) Though Jerusalem and the temple be destroyed, yet God will have a church in the world, into which Gentiles shall be admitted, and with whom the believing Jews shall be incorporated, *v.* 4, 5. These verses are dark and hard to be understood ; but divers good expositors take this to be the meaning of them. [1.] God will carefully inspect Jerusalem, even then when the enemies of it are laying it waste : *His feet shall stand in that day upon the mount of Olives,* whence he may take a full view of the city and temple, Mark xiii. 3. When the refiner puts his gold into the furnace he stands by it, and has his eye upon it, to see that it receive no damage ; so when Jerusalem, God's gold, is to be refined, he will have the oversight of it. He will stand by *upon the mount of Olives ;* this was literally fulfilled when our Lord Jesus was often upon this mountain, especially when thence he *ascended up into heaven,* Acts i. 12. It was the last place on which his feet stood on this earth, the place from which he took rise. [2.] The partition-wall between Jews and Gentiles shall be taken away. The *mountains about Jerusalem,* and particularly this, signified it to be an enclosure, and that it stood in the way of those who would approach to it. Between the Gentiles and Jerusalem this *mountain of Bether, of division,* stood, Cant. ii. 17. But by the destruction of Jerusalem this mountain shall be made to *cleave in the midst,* and so the Jewish pale shall be taken down, and the church laid in common with the Gentiles, who were made one with the Jews by the breaking down of this *middle wall of partition,* Eph. ii. 14. *Who art thou, O great mountain?* And a great mountain the ceremonial law was in the way of the Jews' conversion, which, one would think, could never have been got over ; yet before Christ and his gospel it was made plain. This *mountain departs,* this *hill removes,* but the *covenant of peace cannot be broken ;* for peace is still *preached to him that is afar off* and *to those that are nigh.* [3.] A new and living way shall be opened to the new Jerusalem, both to see it and to come into it. The mountain being divided, one-half *towards the north* and the other half *towards the south,* there shall be *a very great valley,* that is, a broad way of communication opened between Jerusalem and the Gentile world, by which the Gentiles shall have free admission into the gospel-Jerusalem, and the word of the Lord, that *goes forth from Jerusalem,* shall have a *free course* into the Gentile world. Thus the *way of the Lord* is prepared, for *every mountain and hill shall be brought low,* and plain and pleasant valleys shall come in the room of them, Isa. xl. 4. [4.] Those of the Jews that believe shall come in, and join themselves to the Gentiles, and incorporate with them in the gospel-church : *You shall flee to the valley of the mountains,* that valley that is opened between the divided halves of the mount of Olives ; they shall hasten into the church with the Gentiles, as formerly the Gentiles with them, *ch.* viii. 23. The *valley of the mountains* is the gospel-church, to which there were added of the Jews daily *such as should be saved,* who fled to that valley as to their refuge. This *valley of the mountains* is said to *reach unto Azal,* or *to the separate place,* that is, to all those whom God has *set apart for himself.* When God *makes his mountains a way* (Isa. xlix. 11), by making them a valley, the way shall be opened to all the *way-faring men* (Isa. xxxv. 8), and, *though fools,* they *shall not err therein.* Or, to those that are now separated from God this valley shall reach ; for the Gentiles, who are afar off, shall be made nigh, with the Jews, who are a *people near unto him,* and both have *an access,* a mutual access to each other and a joint access to God as a Father by one Spirit, Eph. ii. 18. [5.] They shall flee to *the valley of the mountains,* to the gospel-church, under dreadful apprehensions of their danger from the curse of the law. They shall *flee from the wrath to come,* from the avenger of blood, who is in pursuit of them, to the church as to a *city of refuge,* or *as doves to their windows,* as they *fled from before the earthquake in the days of Uzziah,* Amos. i. 1. Therefore the gospel reveals the wrath of God from heaven (Rom. i. 18) that we might be awakened to *escape for our lives,* to flee as from an earthquake, for we feel the earth ready to sink under us, and we can find no firm footing in it, and therefore must flee to Christ, in whom alone we can stand fast and be easy.

(4.) God shall appear in his glory for the accomplishing of all this : *The Lord my God shall come, and all the saints with thee,* which may refer to his coming to destroy Jerusalem, or to destroy the enemies of Jerusalem, or his coming to set up his kingdom in the world, which is called the *coming of the Son of man* (Matt. xxiv. 37), or to his last coming, at the end of time ; however, it teaches us, [1.] That the Lord will come ; it has been the faith of all the saints, *Behold, the Lord comes* to fulfil every word that he has spoken

in its season. [2.] When he comes all his saints come with him ; they attend his motions and are ready to serve his interests. Christ will come at the end of time with *ten thousands of his saints,* as when he came to give the law upon Mount Sinai. [3.] Every particular believer, being related to God as his God, may triumph in the expectation of his coming and speak of it with pleasure, *The Lord my God shall come,* shall come to the comfort of all that are his ; for, "Blessed Lord, *all the saints shall be with thee,* and it shall be their everlasting happiness to dwell in thy presence ; and therefore *come, Lord Jesus.*" And some think that this may be read as a prayer, *Yet, O Lord my God! come, and bring all the saints with thee.*

II. God's providences appear here strangely mixed (*v.* 6, 7) : *In that day of the Lord the light shall not be clear nor dark, not day nor night ; but at evening time it shall be light.* Some refer this to all the time from hence to the coming of the Messiah ; the Jewish church had neither perfect peace nor constant trouble, but a cloudy day, neither rain nor sunshine. But it may be taken more generally, as designed to represent the method God usually takes in the administration of the kingdom both of providence and grace. Here is, 1. An idea of the usual course and tenour of God's dispensations ; the day of his grace and the day of his providence are *neither clear nor dark, not day nor night.* It is so with the church of God in this world ; where the Sun of righteousness has risen it cannot be dark night, and yet short of heaven it will not be clear day. It is so with particular saints ; they are not darkness, but *light in the Lord,* and yet, while there is so much error and corruption remaining in them, it is not perfect day. So it is as to the providences of God that relate to his church ; in general the affairs of the church are neither good nor bad in any extremity, but there is a mixture of both ; we are singing both of mercy and judgment, and are uncertain which will prevail, whether it be an evening or a morning twilight. We are between hope and fear, not knowing what to make of things. 2. An intimation of comfort with reference hereunto : *It shall be one day which shall be known to the Lord.* This intimates, (1.) The beauty and harmony of such mixed events ; there is one and the same design and tendency in all ; all the wheels make but one wheel, all the revolutions but one day. (2.) The brevity of them ; it is, as it were, but for one day, for a little moment ; the cloud that darkens the light will soon blow over. (3.) The eye God has upon all these events, and the hand he has in them all ; they are *known to the Lord ;* he takes notice of them, and orders and disposes of all for the best, according to the counsel of his will. 3. An issue very joyful secured at last : *At evening-time it shall be light :* it shall be clear light, and no longer dark ;

we are sure of it in the other world, and we hope for it in this world—at *evening-time*, when our hopes are quite spent with waiting all day to no purpose, nay, when we fear it will be quite dark, when things are at the worst and the case of the church is most deplorable. As to the church's enemies *the sun goes down at noon*, so to the church it rises at night; unto the upright springs *light out of darkness* (Ps. cxii. 4); deliverance comes when the tale of bricks is doubled, and when God's people have done looking for it, and so it comes with a pleasing surprise.

8 And it shall be in that day, *that* living waters shall go out from Jerusalem; half of them toward the former sea, and half of them toward the hinder sea: in summer and in winter shall it be. 9 And the LORD shall be king over all the earth: in that day shall there be one LORD, and his name one. 10 All the land shall be turned as a plain from Geba to Rimmon south of Jerusalem: and it shall be lifted up, and inhabited in her place, from Benjamin's gate unto the place of the first gate, unto the corner gate, and *from* the tower of Hananeel unto the king's wine-presses. 11 And *men* shall dwell in it, and there shall be no more utter destruction; but Jerusalem shall be safely inhabited. 12 And this shall be the plague wherewith the LORD will smite all the people that have fought against Jerusalem; their flesh shall consume away while they stand upon their feet, and their eyes shall consume away in their holes, and their tongue shall consume away in their mouth. 13 And it shall come to pass in that day, *that* a great tumult from the LORD shall be among them; and they shall lay hold every one on the hand of his neighbour, and his hand shall rise up against the hand of his neighbour. 14 And Judah also shall fight at Jerusalem; and the wealth of all the heathen round about shall be gathered together, gold, and silver, and apparel, in great abundance. 15 And so shall be the plague of the horse, of the mule, of the camel, and of the ass, and of all the beasts that shall be in these tents, as this plague.

Here are, I. Blessings promised to Jeru-

salem, the gospel-Jerusalem, in the day of the Messiah, and to all the earth, by virtue of the blessings poured out on Jerusalem, especially to the land of Israel.

1. Jerusalem shall be a spring of living waters to the world; it was made so when there the Spirit was poured out upon the apostles, and thence the word of the Lord diffused itself to the nations about (*v.* 8): *Living waters shall go out from Jerusalem;* for there they began, and thence those set out who were to preach *repentance* and *remission* of sins *unto all nations,* Luke xxiv. 47. Note, Where the gospel goes, and the graces of God's Spirit go along with it, there living waters go; those streams that *make glad the city of our God* make glad the country also, and make it like paradise, like the *garden of the Lord,* which was *well watered.* It was the honour of Jerusalem that *thence the word of the Lord went forth* (Isa. ii. 3); and thus far, even in its worst and most degenerate age, for old acquaintance-sake, it was made a blessing, and to be so is to be blessed. Half of these waters shall go *towards the former sea* and *half towards the hinder sea,* as all rivers bend their course towards some sea or other, some eastward, others westward. The gospel shall spread into all parts of the world, into some that lie remote from Jerusalem one way and others that lie as far off another way; for the dominion of the Redeemer, which was thereby to be set up, must be *from sea to sea* (Ps. lxxii. 8), and the earth must be *full of the knowledge of the Lord, as the waters cover the sea,* and as the waters that in various channels run to the sea. The knowledge of God shall diffuse itself, (1.) Every way. These living waters shall produce both eastern churches and western churches, that shall each of them in its turn be illustrious. (2.) Every day: In *summer and in winter it shall be.* Note, Those who are employed in spreading the gospel may find themselves work both *winter* and *summer,* and are to serve the Lord therein at all seasons, Acts xx. 18. And such a divine power goes along with these living waters that they shall not be dried up, nor the course of them be obstructed, either by the droughts in summer or by the frosts in winter.

2. The kingdom of God among men shall be a universal and united kingdom, *v.* 9. (1.) It shall be a universal kingdom: *The Lord shall be King over all the earth.* He is, and ever was, so of right, and in the sovereign disposals of his providence his kingdom does *rule over all* and none are exempt from his jurisdiction; but it is here promised that he shall be so by actual possession of the hearts of his subjects; he shall be acknowledged King by all in all places; his authority shall be owned and submitted to, and allegiance sworn to him. This will have its accomplishment with that word (Rev. xi. 15), *The kingdoms of this world have become*

the kingdoms of our Lord and of his Christ.
(2.) It shall be a united kingdom : *There shall be one Lord, and his name one.* All shall worship one God only, and not idols, and shall be unanimous in the worship of him. All false gods shall be abandoned, and all false ways of worship abolished ; and as God shall be the centre of their unity, in whom they shall all meet, so the scripture shall be the rule of their unity, by which they shall all walk.

3. The land of Judea, and Jerusalem, its mother-city, shall be repaired and replenished, and taken under the special protection of Heaven, *v.* 10, 11. Some think this denotes particular favour to the people of the Jews, and points at their conversion and restoration in the latter days ; but it is rather to be understood figuratively of the gospel-church, typified by Judah and Jerusalem, and it signifies the abundant graces with which the church shall be crowned, and the fruitfulness of its members, and the vast numbers of them. (1.) The church shall be like a fruitful country, abounding in all the rich products of the soil. The whole land of Judea, which is naturally uneven and hilly, shall be *turned as a plain ;* it shall become a smooth level valley, from Geba, or Gibeah, its utmost border north, to Rimmon, which lay *south of Jerusalem* and was the utmost southern limit of Judea. The gospel of Christ, where it comes in its power, levels the ground ; mountains and hills are brought low by it, that the Lord alone may be exalted. (2.) It shall be like a populous city. As the holy land shall be levelled, so the holy city shall be peopled, shall be rebuilt and replenished. *Jerusalem shall be lifted* up out of its low estate, shall be raised out of its ruins ; when *the land is turned as a plain,* and not only the *mount of Olives* removed (*v.* 4), but other mountains too, then Jerusalem shall be *lifted up,* that is, shall appear the more conspicuous ; she *shall be inhabited in her place,* even *in Jerusalem, ch.* xii. 6. The whole city shall be inhabited in the utmost extent of it, and no part of it left to lie waste. The utmost limits of it are here mentioned, between which there shall be no ground lost, but all built upon, from *Benjamin's-gate* north-east to the *corner-gate* north-west, and *from the tower of Hananeel* in the south to the *king's wine-presses* in the north ; when the churches of Christ in all places are replenished with great numbers of holy, humble, serious Christians, and many such are daily added to it, then this promise is fulfilled. (3.) This country and this city shall both be safe, both the meat in the country and the mouths in the city : *Those that dwell in it* shall dwell securely, and there shall be none to make them afraid ; there shall be no more of that utter destruction that has laid both town and country waste, no more anathema (as some read it), no more cutting off, no more curse, or separation from God to evil,

no more such desolating judgments as you have been groaning under, but Jerusalem *shall be safely inhabited ;* there shall be no danger, nor any apprehension of it ; neither shall its friends be fearful to disquiet themselves nor its enemies formidable to disquiet them. That promise of Christ explains this—that *the gates of hell shall not prevail against the church ;* and so do the holy security and serenity of mind which believers enjoy in relying on the divine protection.

II. Here are judgments threatened against the enemies of the church, that *have fought,* or do fight, against Jerusalem ; and the *threatening of these* judgments is in order to the preservation of the church in safety. Men that read and hear of these plagues will be afraid of fighting against Jerusalem, much more when these threatenings are fulfilled in some will others hear and fear. Those that fight against the city of God, and his people, will be found fighting against God, against whom none ever hardened his heart and prospered (*v.* 12) : *This shall be the plague wherewith the Lord will smite all the people that have fought against Jerusalem ;* whoever they are, God will punish them for the affront done to him, and avenge Jerusalem upon them. 1. They shall waste away under grievous and languishing diseases : *Their flesh shall consume away,* and they shall be miserably emaciated, even *while they stand on their feet,* so that they shall be walking skeletons ; nothing shall remain but skin and bones. The flesh which they pampered and indulged, and made provision for, when they were fed to the full with the spoils of God's people, shall now *consume away, that it cannot be seen, and the bones that were not seen shall stick out,* Job xxxiii. 21. They *keep their feet,* and hope to *keep their ground,* crawling about as long as they can ; but they must yield at last. The organs of sight, the outlets of sin, *their eyes, shall consume away in their holes,* shall sink into their heads or perhaps start out of them ; their envious, malicious, adulterous eyes, the eyes they had so often fed with spectacles of misery, these shall consume, which shall make not only their countenances ghastly, but their lives wretched. The organs of speech, the outlets of sin, *their tongue, shall consume away in their mouth,* whereby God will reckon with them for all their blasphemies against himself and invectives against his people. Thus *their own tongues shall fall upon them,* and their punishment shall be legible in their sin, as his was whose tongue was tormented in hell-flames. Thus Antiochus and Herod consumed away. 2. They shall be dashed in pieces one against another (*v.* 13) : *A great tumult from the Lord shall be among them.* But are tumults from the Lord, who is the *God of order, and not of confusion ?* As they are the sin of those that raise them they are not from the Lord, but from the wicked one, and from men's own lusts ; but, as they are the punishment of those that suffer by them, they are from the Lord, who serves his own purposes, and carries on his intentions, by the sins, and follies, and restless spirits, of men. It is of themselves that they *bite and devour one another*, but it is of the Lord, the righteous Judge, that thus they are *consumed one of another* (Gal. v. 15); as Ahab was deceived by a lying spirit from the Lord, so Abimelech and the men of Shechem were *divided*, and so *destroyed*, by an *evil spirit from the Lord*, Judg. ix. 23. Note, Those that are confederate and combined against the church will justly be separated, and set against one another; and their tumults raised against God will be avenged in tumults among themselves. And they shall *lay hold every one on the hand of his neighbour*, to hold him from striking, or to bind him as his prisoner; nay, *his hand shall rise up against the hand of his neighbour*, to strike and wound him. Note, Those that aim to destroy the church are often made to destroy one another; and every man's sword is sometimes set against his fellow, by him whose sword they all are. Some think this was fulfilled in the factions and dissensions that were among the Jews, when the Romans were destroying them all; for they had fought against the spiritual Jerusalem, the gospel-church; and to that well enough agrees *v.* 14, *Thou also, O Judah! shalt fight against Jerusalem ;* the Jewish nation shall be ruined by itself, shall die by its own hands; the city and country shall be at war with each other, and so both shall be destroyed. *Suis et ipsa Roma viribus ruit—Rome was urged into ruin by its very strength.* 3. The plunder of their camp shall greatly enrich the people of God, or the spoils of their country (*v.* 14): *Judah also shall eat at Jerusalem* (so one learned interpreter reads it); people shall come from all parts to share in the prey; as when Sennacherib's army was routed before Jerusalem there was *the prey of a great spoil divided* (Isa. xxxiii. 23), so it shall be now; the *wealth of all the heathen round about*, that had spoiled *Jerusalem, shall be gathered together, gold, and silver, and apparel, in great abundance*, that an equal dividend may be made among all the parties entitled to a share of the prize. Note, The *wealth of the sinner is* often *laid up for the just*, and the Israel of God enriched with the spoil of the Egyptians. 4. The very cattle shall share in the plague with which the enemies of God's church shall be cut off, as they did in divers of the plagues of Egypt (*v.* 15): All *the beasts that shall be in the tents* of these wicked men, when God comes to contend with them, shall perish with them, not only beasts used in war, as the horse, but those used for travel, or in the plough, as the *mule*, the *camel*, and the *ass*. Note, The inferior creatures often suffer for the sin of man and in his plagues. Thus God will show his indignation against sin, and will make the creature that is thus

subject to vanity groan to be *delivered* into the glorious liberty of the children of God, Rom. viii. 21, 22.

16 And it shall come to pass, *that* every one that is left of all the nations which came against Jerusalem shall even go up from year to year to worship the King, the LORD of hosts, and to keep the feast of tabernacles. 17 And it shall be, *that* whoso will not come up of *all* the families of the earth unto Jerusalem to worship the King, the LORD of hosts, even upon them shall be no rain. 18 And if the family of Egypt go not up, and come not, that *have* no *rain ;* there shall be the plague, wherewith the LORD will smite the heathen that come not up to keep the feast of tabernacles. 19 This shall be the punishment of Egypt, and the punishment of all nations that come not up to keep the feast of tabernacles. 20 In that day shall there be upon the bells of the horses, HOLINESS UNTO THE LORD; and the pots in the LORD's house shall be like the bowls before the altar. 21 Yea, every pot in Jerusalem and in Judah shall be holiness unto the LORD of hosts: and all they that sacrifice shall come and take of them, and seethe therein: and in that day there shall be no more the Canaanite in the house of the LORD of hosts.

Three things are here foretold :—
I. That a gospel-way of worship being set up in the church there shall be a great resort to it and a general attendance upon it. Those that were left of the enemies of religion shall be so sensible of the mercy of God to them in their narrow escape that they shall apply themselves to the worship of the God of Israel, and pay their homage to him, *v.* 16. Those that were not consumed shall be converted, and this makes their deliverance a mercy indeed, a double mercy. It is a great change that the grace of God makes upon them; those that had *come against Jerusalem*, finding their attempts vain and fruitless, shall become as much her admirers as ever they had been her adversaries, and shall *come to Jerusalem* to worship there, and go in concurrence with those whom they had gone contrary to. Note, As some of Christ's foes shall be made his footstool, so others of them shall be made his friends; and, when the principle of enmity is slain in them, their former acts of hosti-

lity are pardoned to them, and their services are admitted and accepted, as though they had never *fought against Jerusalem.* They shall *go up to worship* at Jerusalem, because that was the place which God had chosen, and there the temple was, which was a type of Christ and his mediation. Converting grace sets us right, 1. In the object of our worship. *They shall* no longer *worship* the Molochs and Baals, the *kings* and *lords*, that the Gentiles worship, the creatures of their own imagination, but *the King*, the *Lord of hosts*, the everlasting King, the King of kings, the sovereign Lord of all. 2. In the ordinances of worship, those which God himself has appointed. Gospel-worship is here represented by the *keeping of the feast of tabernacles*, for the sake of those two great graces which were in a special manner *acted* and *signified* in that feast—contempt of the world, and joy in God, Neh. viii. 17. The life of a good Christian is a constant *feast of tabernacles*, and, in all acts of devotion, we must retire from the world and rejoice in the Lord, must worship as in that feast. 3. In the *Mediator* of our worship; we must go to Christ our temple with all our offerings, for in him only our *spiritual sacrifices* are acceptable to God, 1 Pet. ii. 5. If we rest in ourselves, we come short of pleasing God; we must go up to him, and mention his righteousness only. 4. In the time of it; we must be constant. They shall go up *from year to year*, at the times appointed for this solemn feast. Every day of a Christian's life is a day of the *feast of tabernacles*, and every Lord's day especially (that is the *great day of the feast);* and therefore every day we must worship the Lord of hosts and every Lord's day with a peculiar solemnity.

II. That those who neglect the duties of gospel-worship shall be reckoned with for their neglect. God will compel them to come and worship before him, by suspending his favours from those that keep not his ordinances: *Upon them there shall be no rain, v.* 17. Some understand it figuratively; the rain of heavenly doctrine shall be withheld, and of the heavenly grace, which should accompany that doctrine. God will *command the clouds that they rain no rain upon them.* Note, It is a righteous thing with God to withhold the blessings of grace from those that do not attend the means of grace, to deny the *green pastures* to those that attend not the *shepherd's tents.* Or we may take it literally: *On them there shall be no rain*, to make their ground fruitful. Note, The gifts of common providence are justly denied to those that neglect and despise instituted ordinances. Those that neglected to build the temple were punished with the want of rain (Hag. ii. 17), and so were those that neglected to attend there when it was built. If we be barren and unfruitful towards God, justly is the earth made so to us. Many are crossed, and go

backward, in their affairs, and this is at the bottom of it—they do not keep close to the worship of God as they should; they go off from God, and then he walks contrary to them. If we omit or postpone the duties he expects from us, it is just with him to deny the favours we expect from him. But what shall be done to the defaulters of the land of Egypt, to whom the threatening of the want of rain is no threatening, for they have no rain at any time; they need none; they desire none; the river Nilus is to them instead of the clouds of heaven, waters their land, and makes it fruitful, so that what is a punishment to others is none to them? *v.* 18, 19. It is threatened that *if the family of Egypt go not up, that have no rain,* yet God will find out a way to meet with them, for there shall be, in effect, the same plague wherewith other nations are smitten for their neglect. God can, and often did, restrain the overflowing of the river, which was equivalent to the shutting up of the clouds; or if the river did its part, and rose as high as it used to do, God had other ways of bringing famine upon them, and destroying the fruits of their ground, as he did by several of the ten plagues of Egypt, so that *this* (that is, the same) shall be *the punishment of Egypt* that is the punishment of other *nations* who come not up to *keep the feast of tabernacles.* Note, Those who think themselves least indebted to, and depending on, the mercy of heaven, cannot *therefore* think themselves guarded against the justice of Heaven. It does not follow that those who can live without rain can therefore live without God; for not the heavens only, but all other creatures, are that to us that God makes them to be, and no more; nor can any man's way of living enable him to set light by the judgments of God. This shall be the *punishment*—margin, *This shall be the sin of Egypt, and the sin of all nations, that come not up to keep the feast of tabernacles.* The same word signifies both *sin* and the *punishment* of sin, so close and inseparable is the connexion between them (as Gen. iv. 7), and sin is often its own punishment. Note, Omissions are sins, and we must come into judgment for them; those contract guilt that *go not up to worship* at the times appointed, as they have opportunity; and it is a sin that is its own *punishment*, for those who forsake the duty forfeit the privilege of communion with God.

III. That those who perform the duties of gospel-worship shall have grace to adorn their profession by the duties of a gospel-conversation too. This is promised (*n.* 20, 21), and it is necessary to the completing of the beauty and happiness of the church. In general, all shall be *holiness to the Lord.*

1. The name and character of holiness shall not be so confined as formerly. *Holiness to the Lord* had been written only upon the high priest's forehead, but now it shall not

be so appropriated. All Christians shall be *living temples*, and *spiritual priests*, dedicated to the honour of God and employed in his service.

2. Real holiness shall be more diffused than it had been, because there shall be more powerful means of sanctification, more excellent rules, more cogent arguments, and brighter patterns of holiness, and because there shall be a more plentiful effusion of the Spirit of holiness and sanctification, after Christ's ascension than ever before.

(1.) There shall be holiness introduced into common things; and those things shall be devoted to God that seemed very foreign. [1.] The furniture of their horses shall be consecrated to God. *"Upon the bells of the horses* shall be engraven *Holiness to the Lord,* or upon the *bridles* of the horses (so the margin) or the *trappings.* The horses used in war shall no longer be used against God and his people, as they have been, but for him and them. Even their wars shall be holy wars, their troopers serving under God's banner. Their great men, who ride in state with a pompous retinue, shall reckon it their greatest ornament to honour God with their honours. *Holiness to the Lord* shall be written on the harness of their chariot-horses, as great men have sometimes their coat of arms with their motto painted on their coaches; every gentleman shall take the high priest's motto for his, and glory in it, and make it a memento to himself not to do any thing unworthy of it. Travellers shall have it upon their bridles, with which they guide their horses, as those who desire always to be put in mind of it, by having it continually before them, and to guide themselves in all their motions by this rule. The *bells of the horses,* which are designed to quicken them in their journey and to give notice of their approach, shall have *Holiness to the Lord* upon them," to signify that this is that which we ought to be influenced by ourselves, and make profession of to others, wherever we go. [2.] The furniture of their houses too shall be consecrated to God, to be employed in his service. *First,* The furniture of the priests' houses, or apartments adjoining to the house of the Lord. The common drinking cups they used shall be *like the bowls before the altar,* that were used either to receive the blood of the sacrifices or to present the wine and oil in, which were for the *drink-offerings.* The vessels which they used for their own tables shall be used in such a religious manner, with such sobriety and temperance, such devotedness to the glory of God, and such a mixture of pious thoughts and expressions, that their meals shall look like sacrifices; they shall eat and drink, not to themselves, but to him that spreads their tables and fills their cups. And thus, in ministers' families especially, should common actions be done after a godly sort, however they are done in other families.

Secondly, The furniture of other houses, those of the common people : *" Every pot in Jerusalem and in Judah shall be holiness to the Lord.* The pots in which they boil their meat, the cups out of which they drink their wine (Jer. xxxv. 5), in these God's good creatures shall never be abused to excess, nor that made the food and fuel of lust which should be oil to the wheels of obedience," as had formerly been, when *all tables were full of vomit and filthiness,* Isa. xxviii. 8. " What they eat and drink out of these shall nourish their bodies for the service of God; and out of these they shall give liberally for the relief of the poor ;" then are they *Holiness to the Lord,* as the merchandise and the hire of the converted Tyrians are said to be (Isa. xxiii. 18); for both in our gettings and in our spendings we must have an eye to the will of God as our rule and the glory of God as our end. *Thirdly,* When there shall be such an abundance of real holiness people shall not be nice and curious about ceremonial holiness : *"Those that sacrifice shall come and take* of these common vessels, *and seethe* their sacrifices *therein,* making no distinction between them and the *bowls before the altar."* In gospeltimes the true worshippers shall worship God *in spirit and in truth,* and *neither in this mountain nor yet at Jerusalem,* John iv. 21. One place shall be as acceptable to God as another *(I will that men pray every where):* and one vessel shall be as acceptable as another. Little regard shall be had to the circumstance, provided there be nothing indecent or disorderly, while the substance is religiously preserved and adhered to. Some think it intimates that there should be greater numbers of sacrifices offered than the vessels of the sanctuary would serve for; but, rather than any should be turned back or deferred, they shall make no difficulty at all of using common vessels, as the Levites in a case of necessity helped the priests to kill the sacrifices, 2 Chron. xxix. 34.

(2.) There shall be no unholiness introduced into their sacred things, to corrupt them : *In that day there shall be no more the Canaanite in the house of the Lord of hosts.* Some read it, There sh ll be no more *the merchant,* for so a Canaanite sometimes signifies; and they think it was fulfilled when Christ once and again drove the buyers and sellers out of the temple. Or though those that were Canaanites, strangers and foreigners, shall be brought into the house of the Lord, yet they shall cease to be Canaanites; they shall have nothing of the spirit or disposition of Canaanites in them. Or it intimates that though in gospel-times people should grow indifferent as to holy vessels, yet they should be very strict in churchdiscipline, and careful not to admit the profane to special ordinances, but to separate between the precious and the vile, between Israelites and Canaanites. Yet this will not have its full accomplishment short of the heavenly Jerusalem, that *house of the Lord of hosts*, into which *no unclean thing shall enter ;* for at the end of time, and not be-fore, Christ shall gather out of his king-dom every thing that offends, and the tares and wheat shall be perfectly and eternally separated.

AN

EXPOSITION,

WITH PRACTICAL OBSERVATIONS,

OF THE PROPHECY OF

MALACHI.

GOD's prophets were his witnesses to his church, each in his day, for several ages, witnesses for him and his authority, witnesses against sin and sinners, attesting the true intents of God's pro-vidences in his dealings with his people then and the kind intentions of his grace concerning his church in the days of the Messiah, to whom all the prophets bore witness, for they all agreed in their testimony ; and now we have only one witness more to call, and we have done with our evidence ; and though he be the last, and in him prophecy ceased, yet the Spirit of prophecy shines as clearly, as strongly, as brightly in him as in any that went before, and his testimony challenges an equal regard. The Jews say, Prophecy continued forty years under the second temple, and this prophet they call the *seal of prophecy*, because in him the series or succession of prophets broke off and came to a period. God wisely ordered it so that divine inspiration should cease for some ages before the coming of the Messiah, that that great prophet might appear the more conspicuous and distinguishable and be the more welcome. Let us consider, I. The person of the prophet. We have only his name, *Malachi*, and no account of his country or parentage. *Malachi* signifies *my angel*, which has given occasion for a conjecture that this prophet was indeed an angel from heaven and not a man, as that Judges ii. 1. But there is no just ground for the conjecture. Prophets were messengers, God's messengers ; this prophet was so ; his name is the very same with that which we find in the original (*ch.* iii. 1) for *my messenger ;* and perhaps from that word he might (though, probably, he had another name) be called *Malachi*. The Chaldee paraphrase, and some of the Jews, suggest that Malachi was the same with Ezra ; but that also is groundless. Ezra was a scribe, but we never read that he was a prophet. Others, yet further from probability, make him to be Mordecai. But we have reason to conclude he was a person whose proper name was that by which he is here called ; the tradition of some of the ancients is that he was of the tribe of Zebulun, and that he died young. II. The scope of the pro-phecy. Haggai and Zechariah were sent to reprove the people for delaying to build the temple ; Malachi was sent to reprove them for the neglect of it when it was built, and for their profanation of the temple-service (for from idolatry and superstition they ran into the other ex-treme of impiety and irreligion), and the sins he witnesses against are the same that we find com-plained of in Nehemiah's time, with whom, it is probable, he was contemporary. And now that prophecy was to cease he speaks more clearly of the Messiah, as nigh at hand, than any other of the prophets had done, and concludes with a direction to the people of God to keep in remem-brance the law of Moses, while they were in expectation of the gospel of Christ.

CHAP. I.

This prophet is sent first to convince and then to comfort, first to discover sin and to reprove for that and then to promise the com-ing of him who shall take away sin. And this method the blessed Spirit takes in dealing with souls, John xvi. 8. He first opens the wound and then applies the healing balm. God had provided (and one would think effectually) for the engaging of Israel to him-self by providences and ordinances ; but it seems, by the com-plaints here made of them, that they received the grace of God in both these in vain. I. They were very ungrateful to God for his favours to them, and rendered not again according to the benefit they received, ver. 1—5. II. They were very careless and remiss

in the observance of his institutions ; the priests especially were so, who were in a particular manner charged with them, ver. 6—14. And what shall we say of those whom neither providences nor ordinances work upon, and who affront God in those very things wherein they should honour him ?

T HE burden of the word of the Lord to Israel by Malachi. 2 I have loved you, saith the Lord. Yet ye say, Wherein hast thou loved us? *Was* not Esau Jacob's brother? saith the LORD: yet I loved Jacob, 3 And I hated Esau, and laid his mountains and his heritage waste for the dragons of the wilderness. 4 Whereas Edom saith, We are impoverished, but we will return and build the desolate places; thus saith the LORD of hosts, They shall build, but I will throw down; and they shall call them, The border of wickedness, and, The people against whom the LORD hath indignation for ever. 5 And your eyes shall see, and ye shall say, The LORD will be magnified from the border of Israel.

The prophecy of this book is entitled, *The burden of the word of the Lord* (*v.* 1), which intimates, 1. That it was of great weight and importance; what the false prophets said was light as the chaff, what the true prophets said was ponderous as the wheat, Jer. xxiii. 28. 2. That it ought to be often repeated to them and by them, as the burden of a song. 3. That there were those to whom it was a burden and a reproach; they were weary of it, and found themselves so aggrieved by it that they were not able to bear it. 4. That to them it would prove a burden indeed, to sink them to the lowest hell, unless they repented. 5. That to those who loved it and embraced it, and bade it welcome, though it was a light burden, as our Saviour calls it (Matt. xi. 30), yet it was a burden.

This *burden of the word of the Lord* was sent, 1. To Israel, for to them pertained the lively oracles of prophecy as well as those of the written word. Many prophets God had sent to Israel, and now he will try them with one more. 2. *By Malachi, by the hand of Malachi,* as if it were not a message by word of mouth, but a letter put into his hand, for the greater certainty.

In these verses, they are charged with ingratitude, in that they were not duly sensible of God's distinguishing goodness to them; and such a charge as this may well be called a burden, for it is a heavy one.

I. God asserts the great kindness he had, and had often expressed, for them (*v.* 2): *I have loved you, saith the Lord.* Thus abruptly does the sermon begin, as if God intended, whatever reproofs should be given them, to reconcile them to his love, and to take care that they should still have good thoughts of him. *As many as I love I rebuke and chasten.* Thus kindly does the sermon begin. God will have his people satisfied that he loves them and is ever mindful of his love. This is the same with what he said of old to the virgin of Israel, that he might engage her affections to himself (Jer. xxxi. 3, 4): *Yea,*

1476

I have loved thee with an everlasting love. In this one word God sums up all his gracious dealings with them; love was the spring of all; he loved them because he would *love them* (Deut. vii. 7, 8), loved them in their childhood, Hos. xi. 1. His delight was in them, Isa. lxii. 4. " *I have loved you,* but you have not loved me, nor made any suitable returns for my love." Note, God's people need to be often reminded of his love to them.

II. They question his love, and diminish the instances of it, and seem to quarrel with him for telling them of it: *Yet you say, Wherein hast thou loved us?* As God traces up all his favours to them to the fountain, which was his love, so he traces up all their sins against him to the fountain, which was their contempt of his love. Instead of acknowledging his kindness, and studying what they shall render, they scorn to own that they have been beholden to him, challenge him to produce proofs of his love that are material, and think and speak very slightly of the instances they have had of his kindness, as if they were so few, so small, as not to be worth taking notice of, and no more than what they had sufficiently made returns for, or at least than he had sufficiently balanced with instances of his wrath. " Have we not been wasted, impoverished, and carried captive; and wherein then *hast thou loved us?*" Note, God justly takes it very ill to have his favours slighted, as not worth speaking of; and it is very absurd for us to ask wherein he has loved us, when, which way soever we look, we meet with the proofs and instances of his love to us.

III. He makes it out, beyond contradiction, that he has loved them, loved them in a distinguishing way, which was in a special manner obliging. For proof of this he shows the difference he had made, and would still make, between Jacob and Esau, between Israelites and Edomites. Some read their question, *Wherefore hast thou loved us?* as if they did indeed own that he had loved them, but withal insinuate that there was a reason for it—that he loved them because their father Abraham had loved him, so that it was not a free love, but a love of debt, to which he replies, " *Was not Esau* as near akin to Abraham as you are? Was he not *Jacob's own brother,* his elder brother? And therefore, if there were any right to a recompence for Abraham's love, Esau had it, and yet *I hated Esau* and *loved Jacob.*"

1. Let them see what a difference God had made between Jacob and Esau. Esau was Jacob's brother, his twin-brother: " *Yet I loved Jacob* and *I hated Esau,* that is, took Jacob into covenant, and entailed the blessing on him and his, but refused and rejected Esau." Note, Those that are taken into covenant with God, that have the lively oracles and the means of grace committed to them, have reason to look upon these as

tokens of his love. Jacob is loved, for he has these, Esau hated, for he has not. The apostle quotes this (Rom ix. 13), and compares it with what the oracle said to Rebecca concerning her twins (Gen. xxv. 23), *The elder shall serve the younger,* to illustrate the doctrine of God's sovereignty in dispensing his favours; for *may he not do what he will with his own?* Esau was justly hated, but Jacob freely loved; even so, Father, *because it seemed good in thy eyes,* and it is not for us to ask why or wherefore.

2. Let them see what he was now doing and would do with them, pursuant to this original difference.

(1.) The Edomites shall be made the monuments of God's justice, and he will be glorified in their utter destruction: For *Esau have I hated; I laid his mountains waste,* the mountains of Seir, which were *his heritage.* When all that part of the world was ravaged by the Chaldean army the country of Edom was, among the rest, laid in ruins, and became a habitation *for the dragons of the wilderness,* so perfectly desolate was it; as was foretold, Isa. xxxiv. 6, 11. The Edomites had triumphed in Jerusalem's overthrow (Ps. cxxxvii. 7), and therefore it was just with God to put the same cup of trembling into their hands. And, though Edom's ruins were last, yet they were lasting, and the desolation perpetual; and in this the difference was made between Jacob and Esau, and is made between the righteous and the wicked, to whom otherwise all things come alike, and there seems to be one event. Jacob's cities are laid waste, but they are rebuilt; Edom's are laid waste, and never rebuilt. The sufferings of the righteous will have an end and will end well; all their grievances will be redressed, and their sorrow turned into joy; but the sufferings of the wicked will be endless and remediless, as Edom's desolations, *v.* 4. Observe here, [1.] The vain hopes of the Edomites, that they shall have their ruins repaired as well as Israel, though they had no promise to build their hope upon. They say, " It is true, *we are impoverished;* it is the common chance, and there is no remedy; but *we will return and build the desolate places;* we are resolved we will" (not so much as asking God leave); " *we will* whether he will or no; nay, we will do it in defiance of God's curse, and that sentence pronounced upon Edom (Isa. xxxiv. 10), *From generation to generation it shall lie waste.*" They build presumptuously, as Hiel built Jericho in direct contradiction to the word of God (1 Kings xvi. 31), and it shall speed accordingly. Note, It is common for those whose hearts are unhumbled under humbling providences to think to make their part good against God himself, and to build, and plant, and flourish again as much as ever, though God has said that they shall be impoverished. But see, [2.] The dashing of these hopes

and the disappointment of them. They say, *We will build;* but what says *the Lord of hosts?* For we are sure his word shall stand, and not theirs; and he says, First, Their attempts shall be baffled: *They shall build, but I will throw down.* Note, Those that walk contrary to God will find that he wil walk contrary to them; for *who ever hardened his heart against God and prospered?* When the Jews had rejected Christ and his gospel they became Edomites, and this word was fulfilled in them; for when, in the time of the emperor Adrian, they attempted to rebuild Jerusalem, God by earthquakes and eruptions of fire threw down what they built, so that they were forced to quit the enterprise. *Secondly,* They shall be looked upon by all as abandoned to utter ruin. All that see them shall call them *the border of wickedness,* a sinful nation, incurably so, and therefore *the people against whom the Lord has indignation for ever.* Since their wickedness is such as will never be reformed, their desolations shall be such as are never to be repaired. Against Israel God was a *little displeased* (Zech. i. 15), but against Edom he has indignation, and will have for ever, for they are *the people of his curse,* Isa. xxxiv. 5.

(2.) The Israelites shall be made the monuments of his mercy, and he will be glorified in their salvation, *v.* 5. "The Edomites shall be stigmatized as a people hated of God, *but your eyes shall see* your doubts concerning his love to you for ever silenced; for you shall say, and have cause to say, *The Lord is and will be magnified from the border of Israel,* from every part and border of the land of Israel." The border of Edom is a *border of wickedness,* and therefore the Lord will have *indignation against it for ever;* but the *border of Israel* is a *border of holiness,* the *border of the sanctuary* (Ps. lxxviii. 54), and therefore God will make it to appear (though it may for a time lie desolate) that he has mercy in store for it, and thence *he will be magnified;* he will give his people Israel both cause, and hearts, to praise him. When the border of Edom still remains desolate, and the border of Israel is repaired and replenished, then it will appear that God has loved Jacob. Note, [1.] Those who doubt of God's love to his people shall, sooner or later, have convincing and undeniable proofs given them of it: " *Your own eyes shall see* what you will not believe." [2.] Deliverances out of trouble are to be reckoned proofs of God's good-will to his people, though they may be suffered to fall into trouble, Ps. xxxiv. 19. [3.] Distinguishing favours are very obliging. If God rear up again the border of Israel, but leave the border of Edom in ruins, let no Israelite ask, for shame, *Wherein hast thou loved us?* [4.] The dignifying of Israel is the magnifying of the God of Israel, and, one way or other, God will have honour from his professing people. [5.] God's goodness being his glory, when he does us good we must proclaim him great, for that is magnifying him. It is an instance of his goodness that he has *pleasure in the prosperity of his servants,* and for this those that love his salvation say, *The Lord be magnified,* Ps. xxxv. 27.

6 A son honoureth *his* father, and a servant his master : if then I *be* a father, where *is* mine honour ? and if I *be* a master, where *is* my fear ? saith the LORD of hosts unto you, O priests, that despise my name. And ye say, Wherein have we despised thy name ? 7 Ye offer polluted bread upon mine altar ; and ye say, Wherein have we polluted thee ? In that ye say, The table of the LORD *is* contemptible. 8 And if ye offer the blind for sacrifice, *is it* not evil ? and if ye offer the lame and sick, *is it* not evil ? offer it now unto thy governor ; will he be pleased with thee, or accept thy person ? saith the LORD of hosts. 9 And now, I pray you, beseech God that he will be gracious unto us : this hath been by your means : will he regard your persons ? saith the LORD of hosts. 10 Who *is there* even among you that would shut the doors *for nought ?* neither do ye kindle *fire* on mine altar for nought. I have no pleasure in you, saith the LORD of hosts, neither will I accept an offering at your hand. 11 For from the rising of the sun even unto the going down of the same my name *shall be* great among the Gentiles ; and in every place incense *shall be* offered unto my name, and a pure offering : for my name *shall be* great among the heathen, saith the LORD of hosts. 12 But ye have profaned it, in that ye say, The table of the LORD *is* polluted ; and the fruit thereof, *even* his meat, *is* contemptible. 13 Ye said also, Behold, what a weariness *is it !* and ye have snuffed at it, saith the LORD of hosts ; and ye brought *that which was* torn, and the lame, and the sick ; thus ye brought an offering : should I accept this of your hand ? saith the LORD. 14 But cursed *be* the deceiver, which hath in his flock a male, and voweth, and

sacrificeth unto the LORD a corrupt thing : for I *am* a great King, saith the LORD of hosts, and my name *is* dreadful among the heathen.

The prophet is here, by a special commission, calling the priests to account, though they were themselves appointed judges, to call the people to an account. Let the rulers in the house of God know that there is one above them, who will reckon with them for their mal-administrations. Thus *saith the Lord of hosts to you, O priests ! v.* 6. God will have a saying to unfaithful ministers ; and it concerns those who speak from God to his people to hear and heed what he says to them, that they may *save themselves* in the first place, otherwise how should they help to *save those that hear them ?* It is a severe, and no doubt a just reproof, that is here given to the *priests,* for the profanation of the holy things of God, with which they were entrusted ; and, if this was the crime of the priests, we have reason to fear the people also were guilty of it : so that what is said to *the priests* is *said to all,* nay, it is *said to us,* who, as Christians, profess ourselves, not only the people of God, but priests to him. Observe here,

I. What it was that God expected from them, and with what good reason he expected it (*v.* 6) : *A son honours his father,* because he is his father ; nature has written this law in the hearts of children, before God wrote it at Mount Sinai ; nay, *a servant,* though his obligation to his master is not natural, but by voluntary compact, yet thinks it his duty to honour him, to be observant of his orders, and true to his interests. Children and servants pay respect to their parents and masters ; every one cries out shame on them if they do not, and their own hearts cannot but reproach them too ; the order of families is thus kept up, and it is their beauty and advantage. But the priests, who are God's children and his servants, do not fear and honour him. They were *fathers* and *masters* to the people, and expected to be called so (Judges xviii. 19, Matt. xxii. 7, 10) and to be reverenced and obeyed as such ; but they forgot their Father and Master in heaven, and the duty they owed to him. We may each of us charge upon ourselves what is here charged upon the priests. Note, 1. We are every one of us to look upon God as our Father and Master, and upon ourselves as his children and servants. 2. Our relation to God as our Father and Master strongly obliges us to fear and honour him. If we honour and fear the fathers of our flesh, much more the Father and Master of our spirits, Heb. xii. 9. 3. It is a thing to be justly complained of, and lamented, that God is so little feared and honoured even by those that own him for their Father and Master. *Where is his honour ? Where is his fear ?*

II. What the contempt was which the priests put upon God.

1. This is that, in general, which is charged upon them :—(1.) They despised God's name; their familiarity with it, as priests, bred contempt of it, and served them only to gain a veneration by it for themselves and their own name, while God's name was of small account with them. God's name is all that whereby he has made himself known—his word and ordinances; these they had low thoughts of, and vilified that which it was their business to magnify; and no wonder that when they despised it themselves they did that which made it despicable to others, causing even the *sacrifices of the Lord to be abhorred,* as Eli's sons did. (2.) They *profaned* God's name, *v.* 12. They *polluted* it, *v.* 7. They not only made no account of sacred things, but they made an ill use of them, and perverted them to the service of the worst and vilest purposes— their own pride, covetousness, and luxury. There cannot be a greater provocation to God than the profanation of his name; for it is holy and reverend. His purity cannot be polluted by us, for he is unspotted, but his name may be profaned; and nothing profanes it more than the misconduct of priests, whose business it is to do honour to it. This is the general charge exhibited against them. To this they plead *Not guilty,* and challenge God to prove it upon them, and to make good the charge, which added daring impudence to their daring impiety: *You say, Wherein have we despised thy name?* (*v.* 6), and *wherein have we polluted thee? v.* 7. It is common with proud sinners, when they are reproved, to stand thus upon their own justification. These priests had most horridly profaned sacred things, and yet, like the *adulterous woman,* they said that they had *done no wickedness;* they were so inobservant of themselves that they remembered not or reflected not upon their own acts, or they were so ignorant of the divine law that they thought there was no harm in them, and that what they did could not be construed into despising God's name, or they were so atheistical as to imagine that though they knew their own guilt yet God did not, or they were so scornful in their conduct towards God and his prophets that they took a pride in bantering a serious and just reproof, and turning it off with a jest. They either laugh at the reproof, as those that despise it, and harden their hearts against it, or they laugh it off, as those that resolve they will not be touched by it, or will not seem to be so. Which way soever we take it, their defence was their offence, and, in justifying themselves, their own tongues condemned them, and their saying, *Wherein have we despised thy name?* proved them proud and perverse. Had they asked this question with a humble desire to be told more particularly wherein they had offended,

it would have been an evidence of their repentance, and would have given hopes of their reformation; but to ask it thus in disdain and defiance of the word of God argues their hearts *fully set in them to do evil.* Note, Sinners ruin themselves by studying to baffle their own convictions; but they will find it *hard to kick against the pricks.*

2. Justly might they have been convicted and condemned upon the general charge, and their plea thrown out as frivolous; but God will not only overcome, but will be clear, will be justified when he judges, and therefore he shows them very particularly wherein they had despised his name, and what the contempt was that they cast upon him. As formerly, when he charged them with idolatry, so now, when he charges them with profaneness, he bids them *see their way in the valley* and *know what they have done,* Jer. ii. 23.

(1.) They despised God's name in what they said, in the low opinion they had of his institutions : " *You say* in your hearts, and perhaps speak it out when you priests get together over your cups, out of the hearing of the people, *The table of the Lord is contemptible* " (*v.* 7), and again (*v.* 12), " You say, *The table of the Lord is polluted;* it is to be no more regarded than any other table." Either the table in the temple, on which the show-bread was placed, is that which they reflect upon (not understanding the mystery of it, they despised it as an insignificant thing), or rather the altar of burnt-offerings is here called the table, for there God, and his priests, and his people, did, as it were, feast together upon the sacrifices, in token of friendship. This they thought was contemptible. Formerly, in the days of superstition, it was thought contemptible in comparison with the idolatrous altars that the heathen had, and was set aside to make room for a new-fashioned one (2 Kings xvi. 14, 15); now it is thought contemptible in comparison with their own tables, and those of their great men : *The fruit thereof, even his meat, is contemptible.* Those who served at the altar were to live upon the altar; but they complained that they lived poorly and meanly, and that it was not worth while to attend the service of the altar for the fruit and meat of it, for it was very ordinary and always the same again; they had no dainties, no varieties, no nice dishes. Nay, that part of the sacrifices which was given to God, the blood and the fat, they looked upon with contempt, as not worthy the multitude of laws God had made about it; they asked, " What need is there of so much ado about burning the fat and pouring out the blood ?" Note, Those greatly profane and pollute God's name who despise the business of religion, though it is very honourable, as not worth taking pains in, and the advantages of religion, though highly valuable, as not worth taking pains for. Those who live in a careless neglect of holy ordinances, who come to them and attend on them irreverently, and go away from them never the better and under no concern, do in effect say, " *The table of the Lord is contemptible;* there is neither virtue nor value in it, neither credit nor comfort from it."

(2.) They despised God's name in what they did, which was of a piece with what they said, and flowed from it; corrupt principles and notions are roots of bitterness, which bear the gall and wormwood of corrupt practices. They looked upon the table and altar of the Lord as contemptible, and then, [1,] They thought any thing would serve for a sacrifice, though ever so coarse and mean, and were so far from bringing the best, as they ought to have done, that they picked out the worst they had, which was fit neither for the market nor for their own tables, and offered that at God's altar. With every sacrifice they were to bring a meat-offering of *fine flour mingled with oil;* but they brought *polluted bread* (*v.* 7), coarse bread, servants' bread, perhaps it was dry and mouldy, or made of the refuse of the wheat, which they thought good enough to be burnt upon the altar; for had it been better they would have said, *To what purpose is this waste?* And as to the beasts they offered, though the law was express that what was offered in sacrifice should not have a blemish, yet they brought *the blind, and the lame, and the sick* (*v.* 8), and again (*v.* 13), *the torn, and the lame, and the sick,* that was ready to die of itself. They looked no further than the burning of the sacrifice, and they pleaded that it was a pity to burn it if it was good for any thing else. The people were so far convinced of their duty that they would bring sacrifices; they durst not wholly omit the duty, but they brought vain oblations, mocked God, and deceived themselves, by bringing the worst they had; and the priests, who should have taught them better, accepted the gifts brought to the altar and offered them up there, because, if they should refuse them, the people would bring none at all, and then they would lose their perquisites; and therefore, having more regard to their own profit than to God's honour, they accepted that which they knew he would not accept. Some make *v.* 8 to be a continuation of what the priests profanely said *v.* 7, *You say* to the people, *If you offer the blind for sacrifice, it is not evil; or the lame and the sick, it is not evil.* Note, It is a very evil thing, whether men think so or no, to offer the blind and the lame, the torn and the sick, in sacrifice to God. If we worship God ignorantly, and without understanding, we bring the blind for sacrifice; if we do it carelessly, and without consideration, if we are cold, and dull, and dead, in it, we bring the sick; if we rest in the bodily exercise, and do not make heart-work of it, we bring the *lame;* and, if we suffer vain
1480

thoughts and distractions to lodge within us, we bring the torn. And *is not this evil?* Is it not a great affront to God and a great wrong and injury to our own souls? Do not our books tell us, nay, do not our own hearts tell us, that *this is evil?* for God, who is the best, ought to be served with the best we have. [2.] They would do no more of their work than what they were paid for. The priests would offer the sacrifices that were brought to the altar, because they had their share of them; but as for any other service of the temple, that had not a particular fee belonging to it, they would not stir a step, nor lend a hand, to it; and this was the general temper of them, *v.* 10. There is not a man among the priests that would *shut the doors,* or *kindle a fire, for nought.* If he were required to do the smallest piece of service, he would ask, how shall I be paid for it? They would do nothing *gratis,* but were all for what they could get, *every one for his gain, from his quarter,* Isa. lvi. 11. Note, Though God has given order that his servants be well paid in this world, yet those are no acceptable servants to him who are mercenary, and would never do the work but for the wages. [3.] Their work was a perfect drudgery to them (*v.* 13): *You said also, Behold, what a weariness is it!* Both priests and people were of this mind, that they thought God imposed too hard a task upon them; the people grudged the charge of providing the sacrifice and the priests grudged the pains of offering it; they thought the feasts of the Lord came too thick, and they were forced to attend too often, and too long, in the courts of the Lord; the priests thought it a severe penance imposed upon them to purify themselves as was required when they attended the altar and ate of the holy things; they thought the duty of their office toilsome and troublesome, and *snuffed at it* as unreasonable, and bearing hard upon them; they did it, but it was grudgingly and with reluctance. God speaks of it, in justification of his law, that he had not *made them to serve with an offering, nor wearied them with incense,* Isa. xliii. 23. *Wherein have I wearied thee?* Mic. vi. 3. But their own wicked hearts made it a weariness; and they were, as Doeg, *detained before the Lord;* they would rather have been any where else. Note, Those are highly injurious, both to God and themselves, who are weary of his service and worship, and snuff at it.

III. Observe how God expostulates and reasons the case with them, for their conviction and humiliation. 1. Would they, durst they, affront an earthly prince thus? You offer to God *the lame and the sick; offer it now unto thy governor* (*v.* 8), either as tribute or as a present, when thou art entreating his favour, or in gratitude for some favour received; *will he be pleased with thee?* Or, rather, will he not take himself to be affronted by it?" Note, Those who are careless and irreverent in the duties of religious worship should consider what a shame it is to offer that to their God which they would scorn to offer to their governor, to be more observant of the laws of breeding and good manners than of the laws of religion, and more afraid of being rude than of being profane. 2. Could they imagine that such sacrifices as these would be pleasing to God, or answer the end of sacrifices? *" Should I accept this at your hand, saith the Lord? v.* 13. Have you any reason to think I should either not discern or not resent the affront, that I should connive at the violation of my own laws? No (*v.* 10); *I have no pleasure in you,* and therefore *I will not accept an offering,* such an offering, *at your hand."* If God has no pleasure in the person, if the person be not in a justified state, if he be not sanctified, God will not accept the offering. God had respect to Abel first and then to his sacrifice. Note, In order to our acceptance with God it is not enough to do that which, for the matter of it, is good, but we must do it from a right principle, in a right manner, and for a right end. It was the ancient rule laid down (Gen. iv. 7), *If thou doest well, shalt thou not be accepted?* Now, if we be not accepted of God, in vain do we worship him; it is all lost labour; nay, we are all undone, for ever undone, if we come short of God's acceptance. Those therefore make a bad bargain for themselves who, to save charges in their religion, miss all the ends of it, and, by thinking to go the nearest way to work, bring nothing to pass. Those who make it the top of their ambition, as we all ought to do, *whether present or absent, to be accepted of the Lord,* will not dare to bring the *torn, and the lame, and the sick, for sacrifice.* 3. How could they expect to prevail with God in their intercessions for the people when they thus affronted God in their sacrifices? So some understand *v.* 9, as spoken ironically, *" And now if you will do the duty of priests, and stand in the gap to turn away the judgments of God that you see ready to pour in upon us, I pray you, beseech God that he will be gracious to us,* and to our land which is almost eaten up with locusts and caterpillars," as appears *ch.* iii. 11. " Try now what interest you have at the throne of grace; improve it for the removing of this plague, for *it has been by your means;* you have provoked God to send it. But as you go on thus to profane his sacred things *will he regard your persons* or your prayers? No, you cannot prevail with him to command it away." For, *if we regard iniquity in our hearts, God will not hear us,* either for ourselves or for others. 4. Had God deserved this at their hands? No, he had provided comfortably for them, and had given them such encouragement in their work as might have engaged them to do it cheerfully and well; so some understand *v.* 10, " *Who is there among you that shall shut*

a door, or kindle a fire, for nought? No, God does not expect you should serve him for nothing; you are well paid for it, and shall be so; not a cup of cold water, given for the honour of God, shall *lose its reward."* Note, The consideration of our constant receivings from God, and the present rewards of obedience in obedience, very much aggravates our slothfulness and niggardliness in our returns of duty to God.

IV. He calls them to repentance for their profanations of his holy name. So we may understand *v.* 9, " *Now, I pray you, beseech God that he will be gracious to us.* Humble yourselves for your sin, cry mightily to God for pardon, and make up in the faith and fervency of your prayers what has been wanting in the worth and value of your sacrifices; for all the rebukes of Providence we are under *are by your means."* Note, Those who have by their sins helped to kindle a fire are highly concerned by their repentance, prayers, and personal reformation, to help to quench it. We must see how much God's judgments are by our means, and be awakened thereby to be earnest with him to return in mercy; and, if we take not this course, how can we think he should regard our persons?

V. He declares his resolution both to secure the glory of his own name and to reckon with those who profane it. Those who put contempt upon God and religion, and think to run down sacred things, let them know,

1. That they shall not gain their point. God will magnify his law and make it honourable, though they vilify it and make it contemptible; for (*v.* 11) *from the rising of the sun to the going down of the same my name shall be great among the Gentiles.* It might be said, "If these are not the worshippers whom God will accept, then he has no worshippers." As if he must make the best of their service, or else he would have no service done him; and then *what will he do for his great name?* But let him alone for that; *though Israel* be not faithful, *be not gathered,* yet God will be *glorious.* Though these priests provoke him to take down the ceremonial economy, and to abolish that *law of commandments,* which *could not make the comers thereunto perfect,* yet he will be no loser by that, at the long run; for, (1.) Instead of those carnal ordinances, which they profaned, a spiritual way of worship shall be introduced and established : *Incense shall be offered to God's name* (which signifies prayer and praise, Ps. cxli. 2; Rev. viii. 3), instead of the blood and fat of bulls and goats. And it shall be a *pure offering,* refined, not only from the corruptions that were in the priests' practice, but from the mere bodily exercise that was in the institutions themselves, which are called *carnal ordinances, imposed till the time of reformation,* Heb. ix. 10. When the hour came in which *the true worshippers worshipped the Father in spirit and in truth,* then

this *incense* was *offered,* even this *pure offering.* (2.) Instead of his being worshipped and served among the Jews only, a small people in a corner of the world, he will be served and worshipped in all places, *from the rising of the sun to the going down of the same ; in every place,* in every part of the world, *incense shall be offered to his name ; nations* shall be discipled, and shall speak of the wonderful works of God, and have them spoken to them in their own language. This is a plain prediction of that great revolution in the kingdom of grace by which the Gentiles, who had been *strangers and foreigners,* came to be *fellow-citizens with the saints and of the household of God,* and as welcome to the throne of grace as ever the Jews had been. It is twice said (for the thing was certain), *My name shall be great among the Gentiles,* whereas hitherto in Judah only he was *known,* and *his name was great,* Ps. lxxvi. 1. God's name shall be declared to them, the declaration of it shall be received and believed, and there shall be those among the Gentiles who shall magnify and glorify the name of God better than ever the Jews had done, even the priests themselves.

2. That they shall not go unpunished, *v.* 14. Here is the doom of those who do like these priests, for the sentence on them is a sentence on all such. Observe, (1.) The description of profane and careless worshippers. They are such as *vow and sacrifice to the Lord a corrupt thing* when they have in their flock a male. They have of the best, wherewith to serve and honour him, so bountiful has he been in his gifts to them, but they put him off with the worst, and think that good enough for him, so ungrateful are they in their returns to him. This was the fault of the people, but the priests connived at it, and indulged them in it. We find a distinction in the law which allowed *that* to be *offered for a free-will offering* which would *not be accepted for a vow,* Lev. xxii. 23. But the priests would accept it though God would not, pretending to be more indulgent than he was, for which he will give them no thanks another day. (2.) The character given of such worshippers. They are *deceivers ;* they deal falsely and fraudulently with God ; they play the hypocrite with him ; they pretend to honour him, in making the vow, but, when it comes to be performed, they put an affront upon him, to such a degree that it would have been *better not to have vowed than to vow* and *thus to pay ;* but let not such be themselves deceived, for *God is not mocked.* Those who think to put a cheat upon God will prove, in the end, to have put a damning cheat upon their own souls. Hypocrites are deceivers, and they will prove self-deceivers, and so self-destroyers. (3.) The doom passed upon them : They are *cursed ;* they expect a blessing, but will meet with a curse, the tokens of God's wrath, according to the judgment written.
1482

(4.) The reason of this doom : " *For I am a great King, saith the Lord of hosts,* and therefore will reckon with those who deal with me but as a man like themselves ; *my name is dreadful among the heathen,* and therefore I will not bear that it should be contemptible among my own people." The heathen paid more respect to their gods, though idols, than the Jews did to theirs, though the only true and living God. Note, The consideration of God's universal dominion, and the universal acknowledgment of it, should restrain us from all irreverence in his service.

CHAP. II.

There are two great ordinances which divine wisdom has instituted, the wretched profanation of both of which is complained of and sharply reproved in this chapter. I. The ordinance of the ministry, which is peculiar to the church, and is designed for the maintaining and keeping up of that ; this was profaned by those who were themselves dignified with the honour of it and entrusted with the business of it. The priests profaned the holy things of God ; this they are here charged with ; their sin is aggravated, and they are severely threatened for it, ver. 1—9. II. The ordinance of marriage, which is common to the world of mankind, and was instituted for the maintaining and keeping up of that ; this was profaned both by the priests and by the people, in marrying strangers (ver. 11, 12), treating their wives unkindly (ver. 13), putting them away (ver. 16), and herein dealing treacherously, ver. 10, 14, 15. And that which was at the bottom of this and other instances of profaneness was downright atheism, thinking God altogether such a one as themselves, which was, in effect, to say, There is no God, ver. 17. And these reproofs to them are warnings to us.

A ND now, O ye priests, this commandment *is* for you. 2 If ye will not hear, and if ye will not lay *it* to heart, to give glory unto my name, saith the Lord of hosts, I will even send a curse upon you, and I will curse your blessings : yea, I have cursed them already, because ye do not lay *it* to heart. 3 Behold, I will corrupt your seed, and spread dung upon your faces, *even* the dung of your solemn feasts ; and *one* shall take you away with it. 4 And ye shall know that I have sent this commandment unto you, that my covenant might be with Levi, saith the Lord of hosts. 5 My covenant was with him of life and peace ; and I gave them to him, *for* the fear wherewith he feared me, and was afraid before my name. 6 The law of truth was in his mouth, and iniquity was not found in his lips : he walked with me in peace and equity, and did turn many away from iniquity. 7 For the priest's lips should keep knowledge, and they should seek the law at his mouth : for he *is* the messenger of the Lord of hosts. 8 But ye are departed out of the way ; ye have caused many to stumble at the law ; ye have corrupted the covenant of Levi, saith the Lord of hosts. 9

Therefore have I also made you contemptible and base before all the people, according as ye have not kept my ways, but have been partial in the law.

What was said in the foregoing chapter was directed to the priests (*ch.* i. 6) : *Thus saith the Lord of hosts to you, O priests! that despise my name.* But the crimes there charged upon them they were guilty of as sacrificers, and for those they might think it some excuse that they offered what the people brought, and therefore that, if they were not so good as they should be, it was not their fault, but the people's; and therefore here the corruptions there complained of are traced to the source and spring of them—the faults the priests were guilty of as teachers of the people, as expositors of the law and the lively oracles ; and this is a part of their office which still remains in the hands of gospel-ministers (who are appointed to be pastors and teachers, like the priests under the law, though not sacrificers, like them), and therefore by them the admonition here is to be particularly regarded. If the priests had given the people better instructions, the people would have brought better offerings ; and therefore the blame returns upon the priests: "*And now, O you priests! this commandment is* purely *for you* (*v.* 1), who should have taught the people the good knowledge of the Lord, and how to worship him aright." Note, The governors of the churches are under God's government, and to him they are accountable. Even for those who command God has commandments. Nay (*v.* 4), *you shall know that I have sent these commandments for you.* They should know it either, 1. By the power of the Spirit working with the word for their conviction and reformation : "You shall know its original by its efficacy, whence it comes by what it does." When the word of God to us brings about, and carries on, the work of God in us, then we cannot but know that he sent it to us, that it is not the word of *Malachi—God's messenger,* but it is indeed the word of God, and is sent, not only in general to all, but in particular to us. Or, 2. By the accomplishment of the threatenings denounced against them: "*You shall know,* to your cost, *that I have sent this commandment to you,* and it shall not return void."

Let us now see what this commandment is which is for the priests, which, they must know, was sent to them ; and let us put into method the particulars of the charge.

I. Here is a recital of the covenant God made with that sacred tribe, which was their commission for their work and the patent of their honour : The *Lord of hosts sent a commandment* to them, for the establishing of this covenant (*v.* 4), for his covenant is said to be the *word which he commanded* (Ps.

cv. 8); and he sent *this commandment* by the prophet at this time for the re-establishing of it, that it might not be cut off for their persisting in the violation of it. Let the sons of Levi know then (and particularly the sons of Aaron) what honour God put upon their family, and what a trust he reposed in them (*v.* 5) : *My covenant was with him of life and peace.* Besides the covenant of peculiarity made with all the house of Israel, there was a covenant of priesthood made with one family, that they should do the services, and, upon condition of that, should enjoy all the privileges, of the priest's office—that, as Israel was a peculiar nation, a *kingdom of priests,* so the house of Aaron should be a family of priests, set apart for the service and honour of God, to bear up his name in that nation, as they were to bear up his name among the nations ; both the one and the other, in different degrees, were to *give glory unto God's name, v.* 2. God covenanted with them as his menial servants, obliged them to do his work and promised to own and accept them in it. This is called *his covenant of life and peace,* because it was intended for the support of religion, which brings life and peace to the souls of men—life to the dead, peace to the distressed, or because life and peace were by this covenant promised to those priests that faithfully and conscientiously discharged their duty; they shall have peace, which implies security from all evil, and life, which comprises the summary of all good. What is here said of the covenant of priesthood is true of the covenant of grace made with all believers, as spiritual priests ; it is a covenant of life and peace ; it assures all believers of life and peace, everlasting peace, everlasting life, all happiness both in this world and in that to come. This covenant was made with the whole tribe of Levi when they were distinguished from the rest of the tribes, were not numbered with them, but were *taken from among* them and *appointed over the tabernacle of testimony* (Num. i. 49, 50), by virtue of which appointment God says (Num. iii. 12), *The Levites shall be mine.* It was made with Aaron when he and his sons were taken to *minister unto the Lord in the priest's office,* Exod. xxviii. 1. Aaron is therefore called *the saint of the Lord,* Ps. cvi. 16. It was made with Phinehas and his family, a branch of Aaron's, upon a particular occasion, Num. xxv. 12, 13. And there the covenant of priesthood is called, as here, the *covenant of peace,* because by it peace was made and kept between God and Israel. These great blessings of life and peace, contained in that covenant, God *gave to him,* to Levi, to Aaron, to Phinehas ; he promised life and peace to them and their posterity, entrusted them with these benefits for the use and behoof of God's Israel; they received that they might give, as Christ himself did, Ps. lxviii. 18. Now, for the further opening of this covenant, observe,

1. The considerations upon which it was grounded: It was *for the fear wherewith he feared me, and was afraid before my name.* The tribe of Levi gave a signal proof of their holy fear of God, and their reverence for his name, when they appeared so bravely against the worshippers of the golden calf (Exod. xxxii. 26); and for their zeal in that matter God bestowed this blessing upon them and invited them to consecrate themselves unto him. Phinehas also showed himself zealous in the fear of God and his judgments when, to stay the plague, he stabbed *Zimri and Cozbi,* Ps. cvi. 30, 31. Note, Those, and those only, who fear God's name, can expect the benefit of the *covenant of life and peace;* and those who give proofs of their zeal for God shall without fail be recompensed in the glorious privileges of the Christian priesthood. Some read this, not as the consideration of the grant, but as the condition of it: *I gave them to him, provided* that he should *fear before me.* If God grant us life and peace, he expects we should fear before him. 2. The trust that was lodged in the priests by this covenant, *v.* 7. They were hereby made *the messengers of the Lord of hosts,* messengers of that covenant of life and peace, not mediators of it, but only messengers, or ambassadors, employed to treat of the terms of peace between God and Israel. The priests were *God's mouth* to his people, from whom they must receive instructions according to the lively oracles. This was the office to which Levi was advanced; because, in his zeal for God, he *did not acknowledge his brethren, nor know his own children,* therefore *they shall teach Jacob God's judgments,* Deut. xxxiii. 9, 10. Note, It is an honour to God's servants to be employed as his messengers and to be sent on his errands. Angels have their name thence. Haggai was called *the Lord's messenger.* This being their office, observe, (1.) What is the duty of ministers: *The priests' lips should keep knowledge,* not keep it from the people, but keep it for them. Ministers must be men of knowledge; for how are those able to teach others the things of God who are themselves unacquainted with those things or unready in them? They must keep knowledge, must furnish themselves with it and retain what they have got, that they may be like the *good householder,* who *brings out of his treasury things new and old.* Not only their heads, but their lips, must keep knowledge; they must not only have it, but they must have it ready, must have it at hand, must have it (as we say) at their tongue's end, to be communicated to others as there is occasion. Thus we read of *wisdom in the lips of him that has understanding,* with which they *feed many,* Prov. x. 13, 21. (2.) What is the duty of the people: *They should seek the law at his mouth;* they should consult the priests as God's messengers, and not only hear the message, but ask questions upon it,

1484

that they may the better understand it and that mistakes concerning it may be prevented and rectified. We are all concerned fully to know *what the will of the Lord is,* to know it distinctly and certainly; we should be desirous to know it and therefore inquisitive concerning it. *Lord, what wilt thou have me to do?* We must not only consult the written word *(to the law and to the testimony),* but must have recourse to God's messengers, and desire instruction and advice from them in the affairs of our souls as we do from physicians and lawyers concerning our bodies and estates. Not but that ministers ought to lay down the law of God to those who do not enquire concerning it, or desire the knowledge of it (they must *instruct those that oppose themselves,* 2 Tim. ii. 25, as well as those that offer themselves), but it is people's duty to apply to them for instruction, not only to hear, but to ask questions. *Watchman, what of the night?* Thus *if you will enquire, enquire you;* see Isa. xxi. 8, 11, 12. People should not only seek comfort at the mouth of their ministers, but should seek the law there; for, if we be found in the way of duty, we shall find it the way of comfort.

II. Here is a memorial of the fidelity and zeal of many of their predecessors in the priest's office, which are mentioned as an aggravation of their sin in degenerating from such honourable ancestors and deserting such illustrious examples, and as a justification of God in withdrawing from them those tokens of his presence which he had granted to those that kept close to him. See here (v. 6) how good the godly priest was, whose steps they should have trod in, and what good he did, God's grace working with him. 1. See how good he was. He was ready and mighty in the scriptures: *The law of truth was in his mouth,* for the use of those that *asked the law at his mouth;* and in all his discourses there appeared more or less of the law of truth. Every thing he said was under the government of that law, and with it he governed others. He spoke as one having authority (every word was *a law),* and as one that had both wisdom and integrity—it was a *law of truth,* and truth is a law, it has a commanding power. It is by truth that Christ rules. *The law of truth was in his mouth,* for his resolutions of cases of conscience proposed to him were such as might be depended upon; his opinion was good law. *Iniquity was not found in his lips;* he did not *handle the word of God deceitfully,* to please men, to serve a turn, or to make an interest for himself, but told all that consulted him what the law was, whether it were pleasing or displeasing. He did not pronounce that unclean which was clean, nor that clean which was unclean, as one of the rabbin expounds it. And his conversation was of a piece with his doctrine. God himself gives him this honourable testimony: *He walked with me in peace and equity.* He did not think it enough to talk of God, but he walked with him. The temper of his mind, and the tenour of his life, were of a piece with his doctrine and profession; he lived a life of communion with God, and made it his constant care and business to please him; he lived like a priest that was chosen to *walk before God*, 1 Sam. ii. 30. His conversation was quiet; he was meek and *gentle towards all men*, was a pattern and promoter of love; he walked with God in peace, was himself peaceable and a great peace-maker. His conversation was also honest; he did no wrong to any, but made conscience of rendering to all their due: *He walked with me in equity*, or rectitude. We must not, for peace-sake, transgress the rules of equity, but must keep the peace as far as is consistent with justice. *The wisdom from above is first pure, then peaceable*. Ministers, of all men, are concerned to *walk with God in peace and equity*, that they may be *examples to the flock*. 2. See what good he did; he answered the ends of his advancement to that office: *He did turn many away from iniquity;* he made it his business to do good, and God crowned his endeavours with wonderful success; he helped to save many a soul from death, and there are multitudes now in heaven blessing God that ever they knew him. Ministers must lay out themselves to the utmost for the conversion of sinners, and even among those that have the name of Israelites there is need of conversion-work, there are many to be turned from iniquity; and they must reckon it an honour, and a rich reward of their labour, if they may but be instrumental herein. It is God only that by his grace can turn men from iniquity, and yet it is here said of a pious laborious minister that he turned men from iniquity, as a worker together with God, and an instrument in his hand; and *those that turn many to righteousness shall shine as the stars*, Dan. xii. 3. Note, Those ministers, and those only, are likely to turn men from iniquity, that preach sound doctrine and live good lives, and both according to the scripture; for, as one of the rabbin observes here, *When the priest is upright many will be upright*.

III. Here is a high charge drawn up against the priests of the present age, who violated the covenant of the priesthood and went directly contrary both to the rules and to the examples that were set before them. Many particulars of their sins we had in the foregoing chapter, and we find (Neh. xiii.) that many corruptions had crept into the church of the Jews at this time, mixed marriages, admitting strangers into the house of God, profanation of the sabbath-day, which were all owing to the carelessness and unfaithfulness of the priests; here it is charged upon them in general, 1. That they transgressed the rule: *You have departed out of the way* (v. 8), out of the good way which

God has prescribed to you, and which your godly ancestors walked before you in. It is ill with a people when those whose office it is to guide them in the way do themselves depart out of it: " *You have not kept my ways*, not kept in them yourselves, nor done your part to keep others in them," *v.* 9. 2. That they betrayed their trust: " *You have corrupted the covenant of Levi*, have violated it, have contradicted the great intentions of it, and have done what in you lay to frustrate and defeat them; you have managed your office as if it were designed only to feed you fat and make you great, and not for the glory of God and the good of the souls of men." This was a corrupting of the covenant of Levi; it was perverting the ends of the office, and making it subservient to those sensual secular things over which it ought always to have dominion. And thus they forfeited the benefit of that covenant, and corrupted it to themselves; they *made it void*, and lost the life and peace which were by it settled upon them. We have no reason to expect God should perform his part of the covenant if we do not make conscience of performing ours. Another instance of their betraying their trust was that they were *partial in the law, v.* 9. In the law given to them they would pick and choose their duty; this they would do and that they would not do, just as they pleased; this is the fashion of hypocrites, while those whose hearts are upright with God have a *respect to all his commandments*. Or, rather, in the law they were to lay down to the people; in this they *knew faces* (so the word is); they *accepted persons;* they wilfully misinterpreted and misapplied the law, either to cross those they had a spleen against or to countenance those they had a kindness for; they would wink at those sins in some which in others they would be sharp upon, according as their interest or inclination led them. God is *no respecter of persons* in making his law, nor will he in reckoning for the breach of it; he *regards not the rich more than the poor*, and therefore his priests, his ministers, misrepresent him, and do him a great deal of dishonour, if, in doctrine or discipline, they be respecters of persons. See 1 Tim. v. 21. 3. That they did a great deal of mischief to the souls of men, which they should have helped to save: *You have caused many to stumble at the law*, not only to *fall in the law* (as the margin reads it) by transgressing it, taught and encouraged to do so by the examples of the priests, but to *stumble at the law*, by contracting prejudices against it, as if the law were the minister of sin and gave countenance to it. Thus Hophni and Phinehas by their wickedness *made the sacrifices of the Lord to be abhorred*, 1 Sam. ii. 17. There are many to whom the law of God is a *stumbling-block*, the gospel of Christ *a savour of death unto death*, and Christ himself *a* rock *of offence;* and nothing contributes more to this than the vicious lives of those that make a profession of religion, by which men are tempted to say, " It is all a jest." This is properly a *scandal, a stone of stumbling;* there is no good reason why it should be so to any, but *woe to those by whom this offence comes.* 4. That, when they were under the rebukes both of the word and of the providence of God for it, they *would not hear,* that is, they would not heed, they *would not lay it to heart;* they were not at all grieved or shamed for their sin, nor affected with the tokens of God's displeasure which they were under. What we hear does us no good unless we lay it to heart and admit the impressions of it : *You will not lay it to heart, to give glory unto my name,* by repentance and reformation. *Therefore* we should lay to heart the things of God, that we may give glory to the name of God, may praise him in and for all that whereby he has made himself known. It is bad in any to rob God of his honour, but worst in ministers, whose office and business it is to bear up his name and to give him the glory due to it.

IV. Here is a record of the judgments God had brought upon these priests for their profaneness, and their profanation of holy things. 1. They had lost their comfort (*v.* 2): *I have already cursed your blessings.* They had not the comfort of their work, which is the satisfaction of doing good; for the blessings with which they, as priests, blessed the people, God was so far from saying *Amen* to that he turned them into curses, as he did Balaam's curses into blessings. That profane people should not have the favour of receiving God's blessings, nor those profane priests the honour of conferring and conveying them, but both should lie under the tokens of his wrath. Nor had they the comfort of their wages, for the blessings with which God blessed them were turned into a curse to them by their abuse of them; they could not receive them as the gifts of his favour when they had made themselves so obnoxious to his displeasure by not laying to heart the reproofs given them. 2. They had lost their credit (*v.* 9): *Therefore have I also made you contemptible and base before all the people.* While they glorified God he dignified them and supported their reputation, and a great interest they had in the love and esteem of the people while they did their duty and *walked with God in peace and equity;* every one had a value and veneration for them ; they were truly styled *the reverend, the priests;* but when they forsook the ways of God, and corrupted the covenant of Levi, they thereby made themselves not only mean, but vile, in the eyes even of the common people, who, the more they honoured the order, the more they hated the men that were a dishonour to it. Their conduct, their misconduct, had a direct tendency to this, and God owns his hand

in it, and will have it looked upon as a just judgment of his upon them, and not only produced by their sin but answering to it ; they put dishonour upon God, and made *his table and the fruit thereof contemptible* (*ch.* i. 12), and therefore God justly put dishonour upon them and made them contemptible ; they exposed themselves, and therefore God exposed them. Note, As sin is a reproach to any people, so especially to priests ; there is not a more despicable animal upon the face of the earth than a profane, wicked, scandalous minister.

V. Here is a sentence of wrath passed upon them ; and this the prophet begins with, *v.* 2, 3. But it is conditional : *If you will not lay it to heart,* implying, " If you will, God's anger shall be turned away, and all shall be well ; but, if you persist in these wicked courses, hear your doom—Your sin will be your ruin." 1. They shall fall and lie under the curse of God : *I will send a curse upon you.* The wrath of God shall be revealed against them, according to the threatenings of the written word. Note, Those who violate the commands of the law lay themselves under the curses of the law. 2. Neither their employments nor their enjoyments, as priests, shall be clean to them : " I *will curse your blessings,* so that you shall neither be blessed yourselves nor blessings to the people, but even your plenty shall be a plague to you and you shall be plagues to your generation." 3. The fruits of the earth, which they had the tithe of, should be no comfort to them : " *Behold, I will corrupt your seed;* the corn you sow shall rot under ground and never come up again, the consequence of which must needs be famine and scarcity of provisions ; so that no meat-offerings shall be brought to the altar, which the priests will soon have a loss of." Or it may be understood of the seed of the word which they preached ; God threatens to deny his blessing to the instructions they gave the people, so that their labour shall be lost, as that of the husbandman is when the seed is corrupt ; and so it agrees with that threatening (Jer. xxiii. 32), *They shall not profit this people at all.* 4. They and their services shall be rejected of God ; he will be so far from taking any pleasure in them that he will loathe and detest them : I *will spread dung in your faces, even the dung of your solemn feasts.* He refers to the sacrifices that were offered at those feasts. Instead of being himself pleased with the fat of their sacrifices, he will show himself displeased by throwing the dung of them in their faces, which he does, in effect, when he says, *Bring no more vain oblations; your incense is an abomination* to me. Note, Those who rest in their external performances of religion, which they should count but *dung, that they may win Christ,* shall not only come short of acceptance with God in them, but shall be filled with sh?ve and confusion for their folly. 5. All will end, at last, in their utter ruin : *One shall take you away with it.* They shall be so overspread with the dung of their sacrifices that they shall be carried away with it to the dunghill, as a part of it. Any one shall serve to take you away, the common scavenger. *Reprobate silver shall men call them,* and treat them accordingly, *because the Lord has rejected them.*

10 Have we not all one father? hath not one God created us? why do we deal treacherously every man against his brother, by profaning the covenant of our fathers? 11 Judah hath dealt treacherously, and an abomination is committed in Israel and in Jerusalem; for Judah hath profaned the holiness of the LORD which he loved, and hath married the daughter of a strange god. 12 The LORD will cut off the man that doeth this, the master and the scholar, out of the tabernacles of Jacob, and him that offereth an offering unto the LORD of hosts. 13 And this have ye done again, covering the altar of the LORD with tears, with weeping, and with crying out, insomuch that he regardeth not the offering any more, or receiveth *it* with good will at your hand. 14 Yet ye say, Wherefore? Because the LORD hath been witness between thee and the wife of thy youth, against whom thou hast dealt treacherously : yet *is* she thy companion, and the wife of thy covenant. 15 And did not he make one? yet had he the residue of the spirit. And wherefore one? That he might seek a godly seed. Therefore take heed to your spirit, and let none deal treacherously against the wife of his youth. 16 For the LORD, the God of Israel, saith that he hateth putting away : for *one* covereth violence with his garment, saith the LORD of hosts : therefore take heed to your spirit, that ye deal not treacherously. 17 Ye have wearied the LORD with your words. Yet ye say, Wherein have we wearied *him?* When ye say, Every one that doeth evil *is* good in the sight of the LORD, and he delighteth in them; or, Where *is* the God of judgment?

Corrupt practices are the genuine fruit

and product of corrupt principles; and the badness of men's hearts and lives is owing to some loose atheistical notions which they have got and which they govern themselves by. Now, in these verses, we have an instance of this; we here find men dealing falsely with one another, and it is because they think falsely of their God. Observe,

I. How corrupt their practices were. In general, they *dealt treacherously every man against his brother, v.* 10. It cannot be expected that he who is false to his God should be true to his friend. They had dealt treacherously with God in his tithes and offerings, and had defrauded him, and thus conscience was debauched, its bonds and cords were broken, a door was opened to all manner of injustice and dishonesty, and the bonds of relation and natural affection are broken through likewise and no difficulty made of it. Some think that the treacherous dealings here reproved are the same with those instances of oppression and extortion which we find complained of to Nehemiah about this time, Neh. v. 3—7. Therein they forgot the God of their fathers, and the covenant of their fathers, and rendered their offerings unacceptable, Isa. i. 11. But it seems rather to refer to what was amiss in their marriages, which was likewise complained of, Neh. xiii. 23. Two things they are here charged with, as very provoking to God in this matter—taking strange wives of heathen nations, and abusing and putting away the wives they had of their own nation; in both these they dealt treacherously and violated a sacred covenant; the former was in contempt of the covenant of peculiarity, the latter of the marriage-covenant.

1. In contempt of the covenant God made with Israel, as a peculiar people to himself, they married strange wives, which was expressly prohibited, and provided against, in that covenant, Deut. vii. 3. Observe here,

(1.) What good reason they had to deal faithfully with God and one another in this covenant, and not to make marriages with the heathen. [1.] They were expressly bound out from such marriages by covenant. God engaged to do them good upon this condition, that they should not mingle with the heathen; this was the *covenant of their fathers,* the covenant made with their fathers, denoting the antiquity and the authority of it, and its being the great charter by which that nation was incorporated. They lay under all possible obligations to observe it strictly, yet they profaned it, as if they were not bound by it. Those profane the covenant of their fathers who live in disobedience to the command of the God of their fathers. [2.] They were a peculiar people, united in one body, and therefore ought to have united for the preserving of the honour of their peculiarity : *Have we not all one Father?* Yes, we have, for *has not one God created us?* Are we not all *his offspring?* And are we no *made of one blood?* Yes, certainly we are. God is a common Father to all mankind, and, upon that account, *all we are brethren*, members one of another, and therefore ought to *put away lying* (Eph. iv. 25), and not to *deal treacherously*, no, not *any man against his brother.* But here it seems to refer to the Jewish nation: *Have we not all one father*, Abraham, or Jacob? This they prided themselves in, *We have Abraham to our father;* but here it is turned upon them as an aggravation of their sin in betraying the honour of their nation by intermarrying with heathens: "*Has not one God created us*, that is, formed us into a people, made us a nation by ourselves, and put a life into us, distinct from that of other nations? And should not this oblige us to maintain the dignity of our character?" Note, The consideration of the unity of the church in Christ, its founder and Father, should engage us carefully to preserve the purity of the church and to guard against all corruptions. [3.] They were dedicated to God, as well as distinguished from the neighbouring nations. *Israel was holiness to the Lord* (Jer. ii. 3), taken into covenant with him, set apart by him for himself, to be to him for a name and a praise, and upon this account he *loved them* and delighted in them; the sanctuary set up among them was the *holiness of the Lord, which he loved*, of which he said, It is *my rest for ever, here will I dwell, for I have desired it;* but by marrying strange wives they profaned this holiness, and laid the honour of it in the dust. Note, Those who are devoted to God, and beloved of him, are concerned to preserve their integrity, that they may not throw themselves out of his love, nor lose the honour, or defeat the end, of their dedication to him.

(2.) How treacherously they dealt, notwithstanding, They profaned themselves in that very thing which was prescribed to them for the preserving of the honour of their singularity: *Judah has married the daughter of a strange god.* The harm was not so much that she was the daughter of a strange nation (God has made *all nations of men*, and is himself *King of nations)*, but that she was the daughter of a strange god, trained up in the service and worship of false gods, at their disposal, as a daughter at her father's disposal, and having a dependence upon them; hence some of the rabbin (quoted by Dr. Pocock) say, *He that marries a heathen woman is as if he made himself son-in-law to an idol.* The corruption of the old world began with the intermarriages of the *sons of God* with the *daughters of men*, Gen. vi. 2. It is the same thing that is here complained of, but as it is expressed it sounds worse: The *sons of God married the daughters of a strange god.* Herein Judah is said to have *dealt treacherously*, for they basely betrayed their own honour and *profaned* that *holiness of the Lord* which they *should have*

1488

loved (so some read it); and it is said to be *an abomination committed in Israel and in Jerusalem;* it was hateful to God, and very unbecoming those that were called by his name. Note, It is an abominable thing for those who profess the holiness of the Lord to profane it, particularly by yoking themselves unequally with unbelievers.

(3.) How severely God would reckon with them for it (*v.* 12): *The Lord will cut off the man that doeth this*, that marries the daughter of a strange god. He has, in effect, cut himself off from the holy nation, and joined in with foreigners and *aliens to the commonwealth of Israel*, and so shall his doom be; *God will cut him off, him and all that belongs to him;* so the original intimates. He shall be cut off from Israel and from Jerusalem, and not be *written among the living* there. The Lord will cut off both *the master and the scholar*, that are guilty of this sin, both the teachers and the taught. The blind leaders and the blind followers shall fall together into the ditch, both *him that wakeneth* and *him that answereth* (so it is in the margin), for the master calls up his scholar to his business, and stirs him up in it. They shall be cut off together *out of the tabernacles of Jacob.* God will no more own them as belonging to his nation; nay, and the priest that *offers an offering to the Lord*, if he marry a strange wife (as we find many of the priests did, Ezra x. 18), shall not escape; the offering he offers shall not atone for him, but he shall be cut off from the temple of the Lord, as others from the tabernacles of Jacob. *Nehemiah chased away from him*, and from the priesthood, one of the sons of the high priest, whom he found guilty of this sin, Neh. xiii. 28.

2. In contempt of the marriage-covenant, which God instituted for the common benefit of mankind, they abused and put away the wives they had of their own nation, probably to make room for those strange wives, when it was all the fashion to marry such (*v.* 13): *This also have you done;* this is the second article of the charge. For the way of sin is down-hill, and one violation of the covenant is an inlet to another.

(1) Let us see what it is that is here complained of. They did not behave as they ought to have done towards their wives. [1.] They were cross with them, froward and peevish, and made their lives bitter to them, so that when they came with their wives and families to worship God at the solemn feasts, which they should have done with rejoicing, they were all out of humour; the poor wives were ready to break their hearts, and, not daring to make their case known to any other, they complained to God, and *covered the altar of the Lord with tears, with weeping, and with crying.* This is illustrated by the instance of Hannah, who, upon the account of her husband's having another wife (though otherwise a kind husband), and the discon-

tent thence arising, whenever they went up to the house of the Lord to worship *fretted and wept*, and was in *bitterness of soul*, and *would not eat*, 1 Sam. i. 6, 7, 10. So it was with these wives here; and this was so contrary to the cheerfulness which God requires in his worshippers that it spoiled the acceptableness of their devotions: God *regards not their offering any more*. See here what a good Master we serve, who will not have his altar covered with tears, but compassed with songs. This condemns those who left his worship for that of idols, among the rites of which we find *women weeping for Tammuz* (Ezek. viii. 14), and the blood of the worshippers gushing out upon the altar, 1 Kings xviii. 28. See also what a wicked thing it is to put others out of frame for the cheerful worship of God; though it is their fault by their fretfulness to indispose themselves for their duty, yet it is much more the fault of those who *provoked them to make them to fret*. It is a reason given why yoke-fellows should live in holy love and joy—*that their prayers may not be hindered*, 1 Pet. iii. 7. [2.] They dealt treacherously with them, *v.* 14—16. They did not perform their promises to them, but defrauded them of their maintenance or dower, or took in concubines, to share in the affection that was due to their wives only. [3.] They *put them away*, gave them a bill of divorce, and turned them off, nay, perhaps they did it without the ceremony that the law of Moses prescribed, *v.* 16. [4.] In all this *they covered violence with their garment;* they abused their wives, and were vexatious to them, and yet, in the sight of others, they pretended to be very loving to them and tender of them, and to cast a skirt over them. It is common for those who do violence to advance some specious pretence or other wherewith to cover it as with a garment.

(2.) Let us see the proof and aggravations of the charge. [1.] It is sufficiently proved by the testimony of God himself: " *The Lord has been witness between thee and the wife of thy youth* (*v.* 14), has been witness to the marriage-covenant between thee and her, for to him you appealed concerning your sincerity in it and fidelity to it; he has been a witness to all the violations of it, and all thy treacherous dealings in contempt of it, and is ready to judge between thee and her." Note, This should engage us to be faithful both to God and to all with whom we have to do, that God himself is a witness both to all our covenants and to all our covenant-breaches; and he is a witness against whom there lies no exception. [2.] It is highly aggravated by the consideration of the person wronged and abused. *First*, " She is *thy wife;* thy own, bone of thy bone and flesh of thy flesh, the nearest to thee of all the relations thou hast in the world, and to cleave to whom thou must quit the rest." *Secondly*, " She is *the wife of thy youth, who*

had thy affections when they were at the strongest, was thy first choice, and with whom thou hast lived long. Let not the darling of thy youth be the scorn and loathing of thy age." *Thirdly*, " She is *thy companion;* she has long been an equal sharer with thee in thy cares, and griefs, and joys." The wife is to be looked upon, not as a servant, but as a companion to the husband, with whom he should freely converse and *take sweet counsel*, as with a friend, and in whose company he should take delight more than in any other's; for *is she not* appointed to be *thy companion?* *Fourthly*, " She is *the wife of thy covenant*, to whom thou art so firmly bound that, while she continues faithful, thou canst not be loosed from her, for it was a covenant for life. It is the wife with whom thou hast covenanted, and who has covenanted with thee; there is an oath of God between you, which is not to be trifled with, is not to be played fast and loose with." Married people should often call to mind their marriage-vows, and review them with all seriousness, as those that make conscience of performing what they promised.

(3.) Let us see the reasons given why man and wife should continue together, to their lives' end, in holy love and peace, and neither quarrel with each other nor separate from each other. [1.] Because God has joined them together (*v.* 15): *Did not he make one*, one Eve for one Adam, that Adam might never *take another to her to vex her* (Lev. xviii. 18), nor put her away to make room for another? It is great wickedness to complain of the law of marriage as a confinement, when Adam in innocency, in honour, in Eden, in the garden of pleasure, was confined to one. Yet *God had the residue of the Spirit;* he could have made another Eve, as amiable as that he did make, but, designing *Adam a help meet for him*, he made him *one wife:* had he made him more, he would not have had a *meet help*. And wherefore did he make but one woman for one man? It was *that he might seek a godly seed—a seed of God* (so the word is), a seed that should bear the image of God, be employed in the service of God, and be devoted to his glory and honour,—that *every man having his own wife*, and *but one*, according to the law, (1 Cor. vii. 2), they might live in chaste and holy love, under the directions and restraints of the divine law, and not, as brute beasts, under the dominion of lust, and thus might propagate the nature of man in such a way as might make it most likely to participate of a divine nature,—that the children, being born in holy matrimony, which is an ordinance of God, and by which the inclinations of nature are kept under the regulations of God's command, might thus be made a *seed to serve him*, and be bred, as they are born, under his direction and dominion. Note, The raising up of a godly seed, which shall *be accounted to the Lord for a generation*, is one great end of the institution of marriage; but that is a good reason why the marriage-bed should be kept undefiled and the marriage bond inviolable. Husbands and wives must *therefore* live in the fear of God, that their seed may be a godly seed, else were they *unclean*, but *now they are holy, as children of the covenant*, the marriage-covenant, which was a type of the covenant of grace, and the conjugal union, when thus preserved entire, of the mystical union between Christ and his church, in which he seeks and secures to himself a godly seed; see Eph. v. 25, 32. [2.] Because he is much displeased with those who go about to put asunder *what he has joined together* (v. 16): *The God of Israel saith that he hateth putting away.* He hath indeed permitted it to the Jews, *for the hardness of their hearts*, or, rather, limited and clogged it (Matt. xix. 8); but *he hated* it, especially as those practised it who *put away their wives for every cause*, Matt. xix. 3. Let those wives that elope from their husbands and put themselves away, those husbands that are cruel to their wives and turn them away, or take their affections off from their wives and place them upon others, yea, and those husbands and wives that live asunder by consent, for want of love to each other, let such as these know that the God of Israel hates such practices, however vain men may make a jest of them.

(4.) Let us see the caution inferred from all this. We have it twice (v. 15): *Therefore take heed to your spirit, and let none deal treacherously against the wife of his youth;* and again, v. 16. Note, Those that would be kept from sin must *take heed to their spirits*, for there all sin begins; they must keep their hearts with all diligence, must keep a jealous eye upon them and a strict hand, and must watch against the first risings of sin there. We shall act as we are spirited; and therefore, that we may regulate our actions, we must consider *what manner of spirit we are of;* we must *take heed to our spirits* with reference to our particular relations, and see that we stand rightly affected to them and be of a good temper, for otherwise we shall be in danger of dealing treacherously. If our own hearts deal treacherously with us, whom will they not deal treacherously with?

II. Observe how corrupt their principles were, to which were owing all these corrupt practices. Let us trace up the streams to the fountain (v. 17): *You have wearied the Lord with your words.* They thought to evade the convictions of the word, and to justify themselves by cavilling with God's proceedings; but their defence was their offence, and their vindication of themselves was the aggravation of their crime; they affronted the Lord with their words, and repeated them so often, and persisted so long in their contradictions, that they even *wearied him;* see

1490

Isa. vii. 13. They made him weary of doing them good as he had done, and stopped the current of his favours; or they represented him as weary of governing the world, and willing to quit it and lay aside the care of it. Note, It is a wearisome thing, even to God himself, to hear people insist upon their own justification in their corrupt and wicked practices, and plead their atheistical principles in vindication of them. But, as if God by his prophet had done them wrong, see how impudently they ask, *Wherein have we wearied him?* What are those vexatious words whereby we have wearied him? Note, Sinful words are more offensive to the God of heaven than they are commonly thought to be. But God has his proofs ready; two things they had said, at least in their hearts (and thoughts are words to God), with which they had wearied him:—1. They had denied him to be a holy God, and had asserted that concerning him which is directly contrary to the doctrine of his holiness. As he is a holy God, he hates sin, *is of purer eyes than to behold it*, and *cannot endure to look upon it*, Hab. i. 13. He *is not a God that has pleasure in wickedness*, Ps. v. 4. And yet they had the impudence to say, in direct contradiction to this, *Every one that does evil is good in the sight of the Lord, and he delights in them.* This wicked inference they drew, without any reason, from the prosperity of sinners in their sinful courses (see ch. iii. 15), as if God's love or hatred were to be known by that which is before us, and those must be concluded *good in the sight of the Lord* who are rich in the world. Or this they said because they wished it might be so; they were resolved to *do evil*, and yet to think themselves *good in the sight of the Lord*, and to believe that *he delighted in them*, notwithstanding; and therefore, under pretence of making God not so severe as he was commonly represented, they said as they would have it, and thought he was *altogether such a one as themselves.* Note, Those who think God a friend to sin affront him and deceive themselves. 2. They had denied him to be the righteous governor of the world. If he did not delight in sin and sinners, yet it would serve their turn to believe that he would never punish it or them. They said, "*Where is the God of judgment?*" That God who, we have been so often told, would call us to an account, and reckon with us for what we have said and done—where is he? He has forsaken the earth, and takes no notice of what is said and done there; he has said that he will *come to judgment;* but *where is the promise of his coming?* We may do what we please; he sees us not, nor will regard us." It is such a challenge to the Judge of the whole earth as bids defiance to his justice, and, in effect, dares him to *do his worst.* Such scoffers as these there were in the latter days of the Jewish church, and such there shall be in the latter days of the

Christian church; but their unbelief shall not make the promise of God of no effect; for the day of the Lord will come. *Behold, the Judge stands before the door ;* the God of judgment *is at hand.*

CHAP. III.

In this chapter we have, I. A promise of the coming of the Messiah, and of his forerunner; and the errand he comes upon is here particularly described, both the comfort which his coming brings to his church and people and the terror which it will bring to the wicked, ver. 1—6. II. A reproof of the Jews for their corrupting God's ordinances and sacrilegiously robbing him of his dues, with a charge to them to amend this matter, and a promise that, if they did, God would return in mercy to them, ver. 7—12. III. A description of the wickedness of the wicked that speak against God (ver. 13—15), and of the righteousness of the righteous that speak for him, with the precious promises made to them, ver. 16—18.

BEHOLD, I will send my messenger, and he shall prepare the way before me: and the LORD, whom ye seek, shall suddenly come to his temple, even the messenger of the covenant, whom ye delight in: behold, he shall come, saith the LORD of hosts. 2 But who may abide the day of his coming? and who shall stand when he appeareth? for he *is* like a refiner's fire, and like fullers' soap: 3 And he shall sit *as* a refiner and purifier of silver: and he shall purify the sons of Levi, and purge them as gold and silver, that they may offer unto the LORD an offering in righteousness. 4 Then shall the offering of Judah and Jerusalem be pleasant unto the LORD, as in the days of old, and as in former years. 5 And I will come near to you to judgment; and I will be a swift witness against the sorcerers, and against the adulterers, and against false swearers, and against those that oppress the hireling in *his* wages, the widow, and the fatherless, and that turn aside the stranger *from his right,* and fear not me, saith the LORD of hosts. 6 For I *am* the LORD, I change not; therefore ye sons of Jacob are not consumed.

The first words of this chapter seem a direct answer to the profane atheistical demand of the scoffers of those days which closed the foregoing chapter: *Where is the God of judgment?* To which it is readily answered, " Here he is; he is just at the door; the long-expected Messiah is ready to appear; and he says, *For judgment have I come into this world,* for that judgment which you have so impudently bid defiance to." One of the rabbin says that the meaning of this is, That God will raise up a righteous King, to set things in order, even *the king Messiah.* And the *beginning of the gospel of*

Christ is expressly said to be the accomplishment of this promise, with which the Old Testament concludes, Mark i. 1, 2. So that by this the two Testaments are, as it were, tacked together, and made to answer one another. Now here we have,

I. A prophecy of the appearing of his forerunner John the Baptist, which the prophet Isaiah had foretold (*ch.* xl. 3), as the *preparing* of the *way of the Lord,* to which this seems to have a reference, for the words of the latter prophets confirmed those of the former: *Behold, I will send my messenger,* or *I do send him,* or *I am sending* him. " I am determined to send him; he will now shortly come, and will not come unsent, though to a careless generation he comes unsent for." Observe, 1. He is *God's messenger ;* that is his office; he is *Malachi* (so the word is), the same with the name of this prophet; he is *my angel,* my *ambassador.* John Baptist had his commission *from heaven, and not of men.* All held John Baptist for a prophet, for he was God's messenger, as the prophets were, and came on the same errand to the world that they were sent upon—to call men to repentance and reformation. 2. He is Christ's harbinger: He *shall prepare the way before me,* by calling men to those duties which qualify them to receive the comforts of the Messiah and his coming, and by taking them off from a confidence in their relation to Abraham *as their father* (which, they thought, would serve their turn without a saviour), and by giving notice that the Messiah was now at hand, and so raising men's expectations of him, and making them readily to go into the measures he would take for the setting up of his kingdom in the world. Note, God observes a method in his work, and, before he comes, takes care to have his way prepared. This is like the giving of a sign. The church was told, long before, that the Messiah would come; and here it is added that, a little before he appears, there shall be a signal given; a great prophet shall arise, that shall give notice of his approach, and call to the everlasting gates and doors to *lift up their heads* and give him admission. The accomplishment of this is a proof that *Jesus is the Christ,* is he that *should come,* and we are to *look for no other ;* for there was such a messenger sent before him, who *made ready a people prepared for the Lord,* Luke i. 17. The Jewish writers run into gross absurdities to evade the conviction of this evidence ; some of them say that this messenger is the *angel of death,* who shall take the wicked out of this life, to be sent into hell torments; others of them say that it is Messiah the son of Joseph, who shall appear before Messiah the son of David; others, this prophet himself; others, an angel from heaven: such mistakes do those run into that will not receive the truth.

II. A prophecy of the appearing of the

Messiah himself: "*The Lord, whom you seek, shall suddenly come to his temple,* even *the God of judgment,* who, you think, has forsaken the earth, and you *wot not what has become of him.* The Messiah has been long called *he that should come,* and you may assure yourselves that now shortly he will come." 1. He is *the Lord—Adonai,* the basis and foundation on which the world is founded and fastened, the ruler and governor of all, that one *Lord over all* (Acts x. 36) that has all power committed to him (Matt. xxviii. 18) and is to *reign over the house of Jacob for ever,* Luke i. 33. 2. He is the *Messenger of the covenant,* or the *angel of the covenant,* that *blessed one* that was *sent* from heaven to negociate a peace, and settle a correspondence, between God and man. He is the *angel,* the *archangel,* the Lord of the angels, who received commission from the Father to bring man home to God by a covenant of grace, who had revolted from him by the violation of the covenant of innocency. Christ is the *angel of this covenant,* by whose mediation it is brought about and established, as God's covenant with Israel was made by the *disposition of angels,* Acts vii. 53; Gal. iii. 19. Christ, as a prophet, is the *messenger* and *mediator* of the covenant; nay, he is *given for a covenant,* Isa. xlix. 8. That covenant which is all our *salvation began to be spoken by the Lord,* Heb. ii. 3. Though he is the *prince of the covenant* (as some read this) yet he condescended to be the *messenger of it,* that we might have full assurance of God's good-will towards man, upon his word. 3. He it is *whom you seek, whom you delight in,* whom the pious Jews expect and desire, and whose coming they think of with a great deal of pleasure. In looking and waiting for him, they *looked for redemption in Jerusalem* and *waited for the consolation of Israel,* Luke ii. 25, 38. Christ was to be the *desire of all nations,* desirable to all (Hag. ii. 7); but he was *the desire* of the Jewish nation actually, because they had the promise of his coming made to them. Note, Those that seek Jesus shall find pleasure in him. If he be our heart's desire he will be our heart's delight; and we have reason to delight in him who is the *messenger of the covenant,* and to bid him welcome who came to us on so kind an errand. 4. He *shall suddenly come:* his coming draws nigh, and we see it not at so great a distance as the patriarchs saw it at. Or, He shall come immediately after the appearing of John Baptist, shall even tread on the heels of his forerunner; when that *morning-star* appears, believe that the *Sun of righteousness* is not far off. Or, He *shall come suddenly,* that is, he shall come when by many he is not looked for; as his second coming will be, so his first coming was, *at midnight,* when some had done looking for him, for *shall he find faith on the earth?* Luke xviii. 8. The Jews reckon

the Messiah among the things that come *unawares;* so Dr. Pocock. And the coming of the Son of man in his day is said to be *as the lightning,* which is very surprising, Luke xvii. 24. 5. He *shall come to his temple,* this temple at Jerusalem, which was lately built, that *latter house* which he was to be the glory of. It is his temple, for it is *his Father's house,* John ii. 16. Christ, at forty days old, was presented in the temple, and thither Simeon went *by the Spirit,* according to the direction of this prophecy, to see him, Luke ii. 27. At twelve years old he was in the temple *about his Father's business,* Luke ii. 49. When he rode in triumph into Jerusalem, it should seem that he went directly *to the temple* (Matt. xxi. 12), and (*v.* 14) thither the *blind and the lame came to him to be healed;* there he often preached, and often disputed, and often wrought miracles. By this it appears that the Messiah was to come while *that temple* was standing; that, therefore, being long since destroyed, we must conclude that he has come, and we are to look for no other. Note, Those that would be acquainted with Christ and obtain his favour must meet him in his temple, for there he *records his name* and there he will bless his people. There we must receive his oracles and there we must pay our homage. 6. The promise of his coming is repeated and ratified: *Behold, he shall come, saith the Lord of hosts;* you may depend upon his word, who cannot lie, he *shall come,* he *will come,* he *will not tarry.*

III. An account given of the great ends and intentions of his coming, *v.* 2. He is one whom they seek, and one whom they delight in; and yet *who may abide the day of his coming?* It is a thing to be thought of with great seriousness, and with a holy awe and reverence; for who *shall stand when he appears,* though he comes not to condemn the world, but that the world through him might have life? This may refer,

1. To the terrors of his appearance. Even in the days of his flesh there were some emanations of his glory and power, such as none could stand before, witness his transfiguration, and the prodigies that attended his death; and we read of some that trembled before him, as Mark v. 33.

2 To the troublous times that should follow soon after. The Jewish doctors speak of the *pangs* or *griefs* of the Messiah, meaning (they say) the great afflictions that should be to Israel at the time of his coming; he himself speaks of great tribulation then approaching, *such as was not since the beginning of the world, nor ever shall be,* Matt. xxiv. 21.

3. To the trial which his coming would make of the children of men. *He shall be like a refiner's fire,* which separates between the gold and the dross by melting the ore, or like *fuller's soap,* which with much rubbing fetches the spots out of the cloth. Christ came to discover men, *that the thoughts of many hearts*

might be revealed (Luke ii. 35), to distinguish men, to separate between the precious and the vile, for *his fan in his hand* (Matt. iii. 12), to *send fire on the earth, not peace, but rather division* (Luke xii. 49, 51), to *shake heaven and earth,* that the *wicked might be shaken out* (Job xxxviii. 13) and *that the things which cannot be shaken might remain,* Heb. xii. 27. See what the effect of the trial will be that shall be made by the gospel.

(1.) The gospel shall work good upon those that are disposed to be good, to them it shall be a savour of life unto life (*v.* 3): *He shall sit as a refiner.* Christ by his gospel shall purify and reform his church, and by his Spirit working with it shall regenerate and cleanse particular souls; for to this end he gave himself for the church, *that he might sanctify and cleanse it with the washing of water by the word* (Eph. v. 26) and *purify to himself a peculiar people,* Tit. ii. 14. Christ is the great refiner. Observe, [1.] Who they are that he will purify—*the sons of Levi,* all those that are devoted to his praise and employed in his service, as the tribe of Levi was, and whom he designs to make unto our God spiritual priests (Rev. i. 6), a *holy priesthood,* 1 Pet. ii. 5. Note, All true Christians are sons of Levi, set apart for God, to do the service of his sanctuary, and to *war the good warfare.* [2.] How he will purify them; he will *purge them as gold and silver,* that is, he will sanctify them inwardly; he will not only wash away the spots they have contracted from without, but will take away the dross that is found in them; he will separate from them their indwelling corruptions, which rendered their faculties worthless and useless, and so make them like gold refined, both valuable and serviceable. *He will purge them* with fire, *as gold and silver are purged,* for *he baptizes with the Holy Ghost and with fire* (Matt. iii. 11), with the Holy Ghost working like fire. He will purge them by *afflictions and manifold temptations,* that the *trial of their faith* may be *found to praise and honour,* 1 Pet. i. 6, 7. He will purge them so as to make them a precious people to himself. [3.] What will be the effect of it: *That they may offer unto the Lord an offering in righteousness,* that is, that they may be in sincerity converted to God and consecrated to his praise (hence we read of the *offering up,* or *sacrificing, of the Gentiles* to God, when they were *sanctified by the holy Ghost,* Rom. xv. 16), and that they may in a spiritual manner worship God according to his will, may *offer the sacrifices of righteousness* (Ps. iv. 5), the offering of prayer, and praise, and holy love, that they may be the *true worshippers,* who *worship the Father in spirit and in truth,* John iv. 23, 24. Note, We cannot offer unto the Lord any right performances in religion unless our persons be justified and sanctified. Till we ourselves be refined and purified by the grace of God, we cannot do any thing that will redound to the glory of God. God had respect to Abel first, and then to his offering; and *therefore* God purges his people, that they may offer their offerings to him in righteousness, Zeph. iii. 9. He makes the tree good that the fruit may be good. And then it follows (*v.* 4), *The offering of Judah and Jerusalem shall be pleasant unto the Lord.* It shall no longer be offensive, as it has been, when, in the former days, they worshipped other gods with the God of Israel, or when, in the present days, they brought the torn, and the lame, and the sick, for sacrifice; but it shall be *acceptable;* he will be pleased with the offerers, and their offerings, *as in the days of old and as in former years,* as in the primitive times of the church, as when God had respect to Abel's sacrifice and smelled a savour of rest from Noah's, and when he kindled Aaron's sacrifice with fire from heaven. When the Messiah comes, *First,* He will, by his grace in them, make them acceptable; when he has purified and refined them, then they shall offer such sacrifices as God requires and will accept. *Secondly,* He will, by his intercession for them, make them accepted; he will recommend them and their performances to God, so that their prayers, being perfumed with the incense of his intercession, shall be pleasant unto the Lord; for he has *made us accepted in the Beloved,* and in him is well pleased with those that are in him (Matt. iii. 17) and bring forth fruit in him.

(2.) It shall turn for a testimony against those that are resolved to go on in their wickedness, *v.* 5. This is the direct answer to their challenge, "*Where is the God of judgment?* You shall know where he is, and shall know it to your terror and confusion, for *I will come near to you to judgment;* to you that set divine justice at defiance." To them the gospel of Christ will be a *savour of death unto death;* it will bind them over to condemnation and will judge them in the great day, John xii. 48. Let us see here, [1.] Who the sinners are that must appear to be judged by the gospel of Christ. They are the *sorcerers,* who deal in spiritual wickedness, that forsake the oracles of the God of truth to consult the father of lies; and the *adulterers,* who wallow in the lusts of the flesh, those adulterers who were charged with *dealing treacherously* (*ch.* ii. 15); and the *false swearers,* who profane God's name and affront his justice, by calling him to witness to a lie; and the oppressors, who barbarously injure and trample upon those who lie at their mercy, and are not able to help themselves: they *defraud the hireling in his wages* and will not give him what he agreed for; they crush *the widow and fatherless,* and will not pay them their just debts, because they cannot prove them, or have not wherewithal to sue for them; the poor *stranger* too, who has no friend to stand by him and is ignorant of the laws of the country, they *turn aside from his right*, so that he cannot keep or cannot recover his own. That which is at the bottom of all this is, *They fear not me, saith the Lord of hosts.* The *transgression of the wicked* plainly declares *that there is no fear of God before his eyes.* Where no fear of God is no good is to be expected. [2.] Who will appear against them : *I will come near*, says God, *and will be a swift witness against* them. They justify themselves, and, their sins having been artfully concealed, hope to escape punishment for want of proof ; but God, who sees and knows all things, will himself be witness against them, and his omniscience is instead of a thousand witnesses, for to it the sinner's own conscience shall be made to subscribe, and so *every mouth shall be stopped.* He will be a swift witness ; though they reflect upon him as slow and dilatory, and ask, *Where is the God of judgment*, and where the promise of his coming ? they will find that *he is not slack* concerning his threatenings any more than he is concerning his promises. Judgment against those sinners shall not be put off for want of evidence, for he will be a swift witness. His judgment shall overtake them, and it shall be impossible for them to outrun it. *Evil pursues sinners.*

IV. The ratification of all this (*v.* 6) : *For I am the Lord ; I change not ; therefore you sons of Jacob are not consumed.* Here we have, 1. God's immutability asserted by himself, and glorified in : "*I am the Lord ; I change not ;* and therefore no word that I have spoken shall fall to the ground." Is God a just revenger of those that rebel against him ? Is he the bountiful rewarder of those that diligently seek him ? In both these he is unchangeable. Though the sentence passed against evil works (*v.* 5) be not executed speedily, yet it will be executed, for he is *the Lord ;* he *changes not ;* he is as much an enemy to sin as ever he was, and impenitent sinners will find him so. There needs no *scire facias—a writ calling one to show cause*, to revive God's judgment, for it is never antiquated, or out of date, but against those that go on still in their trespasses the curse of his law still remains *in full force, power, and virtue.* 2. A particular proof of it, from the comfortable experience which the people of Israel had had of it. They had reason to say that he was an unchangeable God, for he had been faithful to his covenant with them and their fathers ; if he had not adhered to that, they would have been consumed long ago and cut off from being a people ; they had been false and fickle in their conduct to him, and he might justly have abandoned them, and then they would soon have been consumed and ruined ; but because he *remembered his covenant*, and would not violate that, nor alter the thing that had gone forth out of his lips, they were preserved from ruin and recovered from the brink of it. It was purely because he would

1494

be as good as his word, Deut. vii. 8 ; Lev. xxvi. 42. Now as God had kept them from ruin, while the covenant of peculiarity remained in force, purely because he would be faithful to that covenant, and would show that *he is not a man that he should lie* (Num. xxiii. 19), so, when that covenant should be superseded and set aside by the New Testament, and they, by rejecting the blessings of it, lay themselves open to the curses, he will show that in the determinations of his wrath, as well as in those of his mercy, *he is not a man, that he should repent*, but will then be as true to his threatenings as hitherto he had been to his promises ; see 1 Sam. xv. 29. We may all apply this very sensibly to ourselves ; because we have to do with a God that *changes not*, therefore it is that *we are not consumed*, even *because his compassions fail not ; they are new every morning ; great is his faithfulness*, Lam. iii. 22, 23.

7 Even from the days of your fathers ye are gone away from mine ordinances, and have not kept *them*. Return unto me, and I will return unto you, saith the LORD of hosts. But ye said, Wherein shall we return ? 8 Will a man rob God ? yet ye have robbed me. But ye say, Wherein have we robbed thee ? in tithes and offerings. 9 Ye *are* cursed with a curse : for ye have robbed me, *even* this whole nation. 10 Bring ye all the tithes into the store-house, that there may be meat in mine house, and prove me now herewith, saith the LORD of hosts, if I will not open you the windows of heaven, and pour you out a blessing, that *there shall* not *be room* enough *to receive it.* 11 And I will rebuke the devourer for your sakes, and he shall not destroy the fruits of your ground ; neither shall your vine cast her fruit before the time in the field, saith the LORD of hosts. 12 And all nations shall call you blessed : for ye shall be a delightsome land, saith the LORD of hosts.

We have here God's controversy with the men of that generation, for deserting his service and robbing him—wicked servants indeed, that not only run away from their Master, but run away with their Master's goods.

I. They had run away from their Master, and quitted the work he gave them to do (*v.* 7) : *You have gone away from my ordinances and have not kept them.* The ordinances of God's worship were the business which as servants they must mind, the talents which they must trade with, and the trust which was committed to them to keep; but they went away from them, grew weary of them, and withdrew their neck from that yoke; they deviated from the rule that God had prescribed to them, and betrayed the trust lodged with them. They had revolted from God, not only in worship, but in conversation; they had not *kept his ordinances.* This disobedience they were chargeable with, and had been guilty of, even *from the days of their fathers;* either as in the days of their fathers of old, who were sent into captivity for their disobedience, or, "Now, for some generations past, you have fallen off from what you were, when first you came back out of captivity." Ezra owns it in one particular instance: *Since the days of our fathers have we been in a great trespass unto this day,* Ezra ix. 7. Now observe, 1. What a gracious invitation God gives them to return and repent: ' *Return unto me,* and to your duty, return to your service, return to your allegiance, return as a traveller that has missed his way, as a soldier that has run his colours, as a treacherous wife that has gone away from her husband; return, thou backsliding Israel, return to me; and then *I will return unto you* and be reconciled, will remove the judgments you are under and prevent those you fear." This had been of old the burden of the song (Zech. i. 3), and is still. 2. What a peevish answer they return to this gracious invitation: "*But you said* with disdain, said it to the prophets that called you, said it to one another, said it to your own hearts, to stifle the convictions you were under; you said, *Wherein shall we return?*" Note, God takes notice what returns our hearts make to the calls of his word, what we say and what we think when we have heard a sermon, what answer we give to the message sent us. When God calls us to *return,* we should answer as those did Jer. iii. 22, *Behold, we come.* But not as these here, *Wherein shall we return?* (1.) They take it as an affront to be *told of their faults,* and called upon to amend them; they are ready to say, "What ado do these prophets make about returning and repenting; why are we disgraced and disturbed thus, our own consciences and our neighbours stirred up against us?" It is ill with those who thus count reproofs reproaches, and *kick against the pricks.* (2.) They are so ignorant of themselves, and of the strictness, extent, and spiritual nature, of the divine law, that they see nothing in themselves to be repented of, or reformed; they are pure in their own eyes, and think they need no repentance. (3.) They are so firmly resolved to go on in sin that they will find a thousand foolish frivolous excuses to shift off their repentance, and turn away the calls that are given them to repent. They seem to speak only as those that wanted something to say; it is a mere evasion, a banter upon the pro-

phet, and a challenge to him to descend to particulars. Note, Many ruin their own souls by baffling the calls that are given them to repent of their sins.

II. They had robbed their Master, and embezzled his goods. They had asked, "*Wherein shall we return?* What have we done amiss?" And he soon tells them. Observe, 1. The prophet's high charge exhibited, in God's name, against the people. They stand indicted for robbery, for sacrilege, the worst of robberies: *You have robbed me.* He expostulates with them upon it: *Will a man* be so daringly impudent as to *rob God?* Man, who is a weak creature, and cannot contend with God's power, will he think to rob him *vi et armis—forcibly?* Man, who lies open to God's knowledge, and cannot conceal himself from that, will he think to rob him *clam et secreto—privily?* Man, who depends upon God, and derives his all from him, will he rob him that is his benefactor? This is ungrateful, unjust, and unkind, indeed; and it is very unwise thus to provoke him from whom our judgment proceeds. *Will a man do violence to God?* so some read it. *Will a man stint or straiten him?* so others read it. Robbing God is a heinous crime. 2. The people's high challenge in answer to that charge: *But you say, Wherein have we robbed thee?* They plead *Not guilty,* and put God upon the proof of it. Note, Robbing God is such a heinous crime that those who are guilty of it are not willing to own themselves guilty. They rob God, and know not what they do. They rob him of his honour, rob him of that which is devoted to him, to be employed in his service, rob him of themselves, rob him of sabbath-time, rob him of that which is given for the support of religion, and give him not his dues out of their estates; and yet they ask, *Wherein have we robbed thee?* 3. The plain proof of the charge, in answer to this challenge; it is *in tithes and offerings.* Out of these the priests and Levites had maintenance for themselves and their families; but they detained them, defrauded the priests of them, would not pay their tithes, or not in full, or not of the best; they brought not the offerings which God required, or brought the torn, and lame, and sick, which were not fit for use. They were all guilty of this sin, even *the whole nation,* as if they were in confederacy against God, and all combined to rob him of his dues and to stand by one another in it when they had done. For this they were *cursed with a curse. v. 9.* God punished them with famine and scarcity, through unseasonable weather, or insects that ate up the fruits of the earth. God had thus punished them for neglecting to build the temple (Hag. i. 10, 11), and now for not maintaining the temple-service. Note, Those that deny God his part of their estates may justly expect a curse upon their own part of them: "*You are cursed with a curse* for robbing me, and yet you go on to do it." Note, It is a great aggravation of sin when men persist in it notwithstanding the rebukes of Providence which they are under for it. Nay, it should seem, because God had punished them with scarcity of bread, they made that a pretence for robbing him —that now, being impoverished, they could not afford to bring their tithes and offerings, but must save them, that they might have bread for their families. Note, It argues great perverseness in sin when men make those afflictions excuses for sin which are sent to part between them and their sins. When they had but little they should have done the more good with that little, and that would have been the way to make it more; but it is ill with the patient when that which should cure the disease serves only to palliate it, and prevent its being searched into. 4. An earnest exhortation to reform in this matter, with a promise that if they did the judgments they were under should be quickly removed. (1.) Let them take care to do their duty (v. 10): *Bring you all the tithes into the storehouse.* They had brought some; but, like Ananias and Sapphira, had *kept back part of the price,* pretending they could not spare so much as was required, and *necessity has no law;* but even necessity must have this law, and it would redress the grievance of their necessity: " Bring in the full tithes to the utmost that the law requires, *that there may be meat in God's house* for those that serve at the altar, whether there be meat in your houses or no." Note, God must be served in the first place, and our quota must be contributed for the support of religion in the place where we live, that God's name may be sanctified, and his kingdom may come, and his will be done, even before we provide our daily bread; for the interests of our souls ought to be preferred before those of our bodies. (2.) Let them then trust God to provide for them and their comfort: " Let God be first served, and then *prove me herewith, saith the Lord of hosts, whether I will not open the windows of heaven.*" They said, " Let God give us our plenty again, as formerly, and try us whether we will not then bring him his tithes and offerings, as we did formerly." " No," says God, " do you first bring in all your tithes as they become due, and all the arrears of what is past, and try me, whether I will not then restore you your plenty." Note, Those that will deal with God must deal upon trust; and we may all venture to do so, for, though many have been losers for him, never any were losers by him in the end. It is fit that we should venture first, for *his reward* is *with him,* but *his work is before him;* we must first do the work which is our part, and then try him and trust him for the reward. Elijah put the widow of Zarephath into this method when he said (1 Kings xvii. 13), " *Make me a little cake first,* and then prove me whether

there shall not be enough afterwards *for thee and thy son.*" That which discourages people from the expenses of charity is the weakness of their faith concerning the gains and advantages of charity; they cannot think that they shall get by it. But it is a reasonable demand that God here makes: " *Prove me now;* is any thing to be got by charity? *Come and see;* Nothing venture, nothing win. Trust upon honour, " And you shall find," [1.] " That, whereas the heavens have been shut up, and there has been no rain, now God will *open* to you *the windows of heaven,* for in his hand the key of the clouds is, and you shall have seasonable rain." Or the expression is figurative; every good gift coming from above, thence God will plentifully pour out upon them the bounties of his providence. Very sudden plenty is expressed by *opening the windows of heaven,* 2 Kings vii. 2. We find the *windows of heaven opened,* to pour down a deluge of wrath, in Noah's flood, Gen. vii. 11. But here they are opened to *pour down blessings,* to such a degree that there should not be *room enough to receive* them. So plentifully shall their ground bring forth that they shall be tempted to *pull down their barns and build greater,* for want of room, Luke xii. 18. Or, as Dr. Pocock explains it, " I will pour out on you such a blessing as shall be not *enough only,* and such as shall be sufficient, but *more and more than enough;*" that is, a great addition. The oil that is multiplied shall not be stayed as long as there are vessels to receive it, 2 Kings iv. 6. Note, God will not only be reconciled to sinners that repent and reform, but he will be a benefactor, a bountiful benefactor, to them. We are never straitened in him, but often straitened in our own bosoms. God has blessings ready to bestow upon us, but, through the weakness of our faith and narrowness of our desires, we have not room to receive them. [2.] That, whereas the fruits of their ground had been eaten up by locusts and caterpillars God would now remove that judgment (v 11): " *I will rebuke the devourer for your sakes,* and will check the progress of those destroying animals, that they shall no more destroy the products of the earth and the fruits of the trees." God has all creatures at his beck, can command them and remand them at his pleasure. *Neither shall the vine cast her fruit before the time;* it shall not be blasted or blown off. Or, as some read it, *Neither shall the devourer make your vine barren,* as the locusts did, Joel i. 7. [3.] That, whereas their neighbours had upbraided them with their scarcity, and they had lain under the *reproach of famine,* which was the more grievous because their country used to be boasted of for its plenty, now *all nations shall call them blessed,* shall speak honourably of them, and own them to be a happy people. [4.] That whereas their sin had made their land unpleasing to God (even their temple, and altars, and offerings were so, *ch.* ii. 13), and whereas his judgments had made their land unpleasant to them, and very melancholy, " Now *you shall be a delightsome land,* your country shall be acceptable to God and comfortable to yourselves." Note, The reviving of religion in a land will make it indeed a delightsome land both to God and to all good people; he will say, It is *my rest for ever ; here will I dwell ;* and they will say the same, Isa. lxii. 4; Deut. xi 12. It should seem that this charge to bring in the tithes had its good effect, for we find (Neh. xiii. 12) that *all Judah did bring in their tithe into the treasuries,* and, no doubt, they had the benefit of these promises, in the return of their plenty, immediately upon their return to their duty, that they might plainly discern for what cause the evil had been upon them (for when the cause was removed the evil was removed), and that they might see how perfectly reconciled God was to them upon their repentance, and how their transgression was remembered no more, for the curse was not only taken away, but turned into an abundant blessing.

13 Your words have been stout against me, saith the LORD. Yet ye say, What have we spoken *so much* against thee? 14 Ye have said, It *is* vain to serve God: and what profit *is it* that we have kept his ordinance, and that we have walked móurnfully before the LORD of hosts? 15 And now we call the proud happy; yea, they that work wickedness are set up; yea, *they that* tempt God are even delivered. 16 Then they that feared the LORD spake often one to another: and the LORD hearkened, and heard *it,* and a book of remembrance was written before him for them that feared the LORD, and that thought upon his name. 17 And they shall be mine, saith the LORD of hosts, in that day when I make up my jewels; and I will spare them, as a man spareth his own son that serveth him. 18 Then shall ye return, and discern between the righteous and the wicked, between him that serveth God and him that serveth him not.

Among the people of the Jews at this time, though they all enjoyed the same privileges and advantages, there were men of very different characters (as ever were, and ever will be, in the world and in the church), like Jeremiah's figs, some very good and others very bad, some that plainly appeared to be the children of God and others that as plainly discovered themselves to be the children of the wicked one. There are tares and wheat in the same field, chaff and corn in the same floor; and here we have an account of both.

I. Here is the angry notice God takes of the impudent blasphemous talk of the sinners in Zion and his just resentments of it. Probably there was a club of them that were in league against religion, that set up for wits, and set their wits on work to run it down and ridicule it, and herein strengthened one another's hands. Here is,

1. An indictment found against them, for treasonable words spoken against the King of kings: *Your words have been stout against me, saith the Lord.* They spoke *against* God, in reflection upon him, in contradiction to him, as their fathers *in the wilderness* (Ps. lxx. 19); *yea, they spoke against* God. What he said, and what he designed, they opposed, as if they had been retained of counsel against him and his cause. Their words against God were *stout ;* they came from their pride, and haughtiness, and contempt of God. What they said against God they spoke loudly, as if they cared not who heard them; they were not themselves ashamed to say it, and they desired to propagate their atheistical notions and to infect the minds of others with them. They spoke it boldly, as those that were resolved to stand to it, and were in no fear of being called to an account. They spoke it proudly, and with insolence and disdain, scorning to be under the divine check and government. They *strengthened themselves ;* they would be valiant *against the Almighty,* Job xv. 25.

2. Their plea to this indictment. They said, *What have we spoken so much against thee?* They deny the words, and put the prophet to prove them; or, if they spoke the words, they did not design them against God, and therefore will not own there was any harm in them; at least they extenuate the matter: *What have we spoken so much against thee,* so much that there needs all this ado about it? They cannot deny that they have spoken against God, but they make a light matter of it, and wonder it should be taken notice of: " *Words*" (say they) " *are but wind ;* others have said more and done worse; if we are not so good as we should be, yet we hope we are not so bad as we are represented to be." Note, It is common for sinners that are unconvinced and unhumbled to deny or extenuate the faults they are justly charged with, and to insist upon their own justification, against the reproofs of the word and of their own consciences. But it will be to no purpose.

3. The words themselves which they are charged with. God keeps an account of what men say, as well as of what they do, and will let them know that he does so. We quickly forget what we have said, and are ready to deny what we have said amiss; but

God can say, *You have said* so and so. They had said it as their deliberate judgment.

(1.) That there is nothing to be got in the service of God, though it is a service that subjects men to labour and sorrow. They said, *It is vain to serve God,* or, " *He is vain that serves God,* that is, he labours in vain and to no purpose ; he has his labour for his pains, and therefore is a fool for his labour. *What profit is it that we have kept his ordinance,* or *his observation,* that we have observed what he has appointed us to observe ?" *What mammon,* or *wealth,* have we gained, says the Chaldee, intimating (says Dr. Pocock) that it was for mammon's sake only that they served God, and so indeed not God at all, but mammon. " We have walked *mournfully,* or *in black,* with great gravity and great grief, *before the Lord of hosts,* have afflicted our souls at the times appointed for that purpose, and yet we are never the better." Perhaps this comes in as a reason why they would not trust God to prosper them upon their *bringing in the tithes* (*v.* 10); " For," say they, " we have tried him in other things, and have lost by him." This is a very unjust and unreasonable reflection upon the service of God, and we can call witnesses enough to confront the slander. [1.] They would have it thought that they had served God and had kept his ordinances, whereas it was only the external observance of them that they had kept up, while they were perfect strangers to the inward part of the duty, and therefore might say, It is *in vain.* God says so (Matt. xv. 9), *In vain do those worship me* whose *hearts are far from me* while they *draw near with their mouth ;* but whose fault is that ? Not God's, who is the rewarder of those that seek him diligently, but theirs who seek him carelessly. [2.] They insisted much upon it that they had *walked mournfully* before God, whereas God had required them to serve him with gladness, and to walk cheerfully before him. They by their own superstitions made the service of God a task and drudgery to themselves, and then complained of it as a hard service. The yoke of Christ is easy ; it is the yoke of antichrist that is heavy. [3.] They complained that they had got nothing by their religion ; they were still in poverty and affliction, and behindhand in the world. This is an old piece of impiety. Job xxi. 14, 15, *What profit shall we have if we pray unto him ?* Elihu charges Job with saying something like like this. Job xxxiv. 9, *It profits a man nothing that he should delight himself with God.* The enemies of religion do but set up against it the old cavils that have been long since answered and exploded. Perhaps this refers to the errors of the sect of the Sadducees, which was the scandal of the Jewish church in its latter days ; they denied a future state, and then said, It is *vain to serve God,* which has indeed some colour in

it, for, *if in this life only we had hope in Christ, we were of all men most miserable,* 1 Cor. xv. 19. Note, Those do a great deal of wrong to God's honour who say that religion is either an unprofitable or an unpleasant thing ; for the matter is not so : wisdom's *ways are pleasantness,* and wisdom's gains better than that of *fine gold.*

(2.) They maintained that wickedness was the way to prosperity, for they had observed that the *workers of wickedness* were set up in the world, and those that *tempted God* were *delivered, v.* 15. The outward prosperity of sinners in their sins, as it has weakened the hands of the godly in their godliness (Ps. lxxiii. 13), so it has strengthened the hands of the wicked in their wickedness. Note, [1.] Those that work wickedness tempt God by presumptuous sins ; they do, as it were, try God, whether he can and will punish them as he has said in his word, and, in effect, challenge him to do his worst, by provoking him in the highest degree. [2.] Those that tempt God by their wicked works are many times both delivered out of the adversity into which they were justly brought and advanced to the prosperity which they were utterly unworthy of. They are not only set up once, but when we thought their day had come to fall, and they were in trouble, they were delivered and set up again ; so strangely did Providence seem to smile upon them. [3.] Though it be thus, yet it will not warrant us to *call the proud happy.* For they may be delivered and set up for a while, but it will appear that God resists them, and that their pride is a preface to their fall ; and, if so, they are truly miserable, and it is folly to call them happy, and to bless those whom the Lord abhors. Wait awhile, and you shall see *those that work wickedness set up* as a mark to the arrows of God's vengeance, and *those that tempt God delivered* to the tormentors. Judge of things as they will appear shortly, when the doom of these proud sinners (which follows here, *ch.* iv. 1) comes to be executed to the utmost.

II. Here is the gracious notice God takes of the pious talk of the saints in Zion, and the gracious recompence of it. Even in this corrupt and degenerate age, when there was so great a decay, nay, so great a contempt, of serious godliness, there were yet some that retained their integrity and zeal for God ; and let us see,

1. How they distinguished themselves, and what their character was ; it was the reverse of theirs that spoke so much against God ; for, (1.) They *feared the Lord*—that is the beginning of wisdom and the root of all religion ; they reverenced the majesty of God, submitted to his authority, and had a dread of his wrath in all they thought and said ; they humbly complied with God, and never spoke any stout words against him. In every age there has been a remnant that feared the Lord, though sometimes but a

little remnant. (2.) They *thought upon his name;* they seriously considered and frequently meditated upon the discoveries God has made of himself in his word and by his providences, and their *meditation of him* was *sweet* to them and influenced them. They *thought on his name;* they consulted the honour of God and aimed at that as their ultimate end in all they did. Note, Those that know the name of God should often think of it and dwell upon it in their thoughts; it is a copious curious subject, and frequent thoughts of it will contribute very much to our communion with God and the stirring up of our devout affections to him. (3.) They *spoke often one to another* concerning the God they feared, and that name of his which they thought so much of; for out of the abundance of the heart the mouth will speak, and a good man, out of a *good treasure* there, will *bring forth good things.* *Those that feared the Lord* kept together as those that were company for each other; they spoke kindly and endearingly one to another, for the preserving and promoting of mutual love, that that might not *wax cold* when *iniquity* did thus *abound.* They spoke intelligently and edifyingly to one another, for the increasing and improving of faith and holiness; they *spoke one to another* in the language of those that fear the Lord and think on his name—the language of Canaan. When profaneness had come to so great a height as to trample upon all that is sacred, *then* those that feared the Lord *spoke often one to another.* [1.] Then, when iniquity was bold and barefaced, the people of God took courage, and stirred up themselves, *the innocent against the hypocrite,* Job xvii. 8. The worse others are the better we should be; when vice is daring, let not virtue be sneaking. [2.] Then, when religion was reproached and misrepresented, its friends did all they could to support the credit of it and to keep it in countenance. It had been suggested that the ways of God are melancholy unpleasant ways, solitary and sorrowful; and therefore then those that feared God studied to evince the contrary by their cheerfulness in mutual love and converse, that they might *put to silence the ignorance of foolish men.* [3.] Then, when seducers were busy to deceive and to possess unwary souls with prejudices against religion, those that feared God were industrious to arm themselves and one another against the contagion by mutual instructions, excitements, and encouragements, and to strengthen one another's hands. As evil communication corrupts good minds and manners, so good communication confirms them.

2. How God dignified them, and what further honour and favour he intended for them. Those who spoke stoutly against God, no doubt looked with disdain and displeasure upon those that feared him, hectored and bantered them; but they had little reason

to regard that, or be disturbed at it, when God countenanced them.

(1.) He took notice of their pious discourses, and was graciously present at their conferences: *The Lord hearkened and heard it,* and was well pleased with it. God says (Jer. viii. 6) that he *hearkened and heard* what bad men would say, and they *spoke not aright;* here he hearkened and heard what good men did say, for they spoke aright. Note, The gracious God observes all the gracious words that proceed out of the mouths of his people; they need not desire that men may hear them, and commend them; let them not seek praise from men by them, nor affect to be taken notice of by them; but let it satisfy them that, be the conference ever so private, God sees and hears in secret and will *reward openly.* When the two disciples, going to Emmaus, were discoursing concerning Christ, he hearkened and heard, and joined himself to them, and made a third, Luke xxiv. 15.

(2.) He kept an account of them: *A book of remembrance was written before him.* Not that the Eternal Mind needs to be reminded of things by books and writings, but it is an expression after the manner of men, intimating that their pious affections and performances are kept in remembrance as punctually and particularly as if they were written in a book, as if journals were kept of all their conferences. Great kings had books of remembrance written, and read before them, in which were entered all the services done them, when, and by whom, as Esther ii. 23. God, in like manner, remembers the services of his people, that, in the review of them, he may say, *Well done; enter thou into the joy of thy Lord.* God has a book for the sighs and tears of his mourners (Ps. lvi. 8), much more for the pleadings of his advocates. Never was any good word spoken of God, or for God, from an honest heart, but it was registered, that it might be recompensed in the resurrection of the just, and in no wise lose its reward.

(3.) He promises them a share in his glory hereafter (v. 17): *They shall be mine, saith the Lord of hosts, in that day when I make up my jewels.* When God utterly cuts off the Jewish church and nation for their infidelity, the remnant among them, that believed his word, and, having waited for the consolation of Israel, welcome him when he comes, shall be admitted into the Christian church, and shall become a peculiar people to God; God will take care of them, that they *perish not with those that believe not;* but that they be *hidden in the day of the Lord's anger* against that nation. *They shall be my segullah—my peculiar treasure* (it is the word used, Exod. xix. 5), *in the day when I make* or *do* what I have said and designed to do; so some read it. These pious ones shall have all the glorious privileges of God's Israel appropriated to them and centering in them; they shall now be his peculiar treasure, when the rest are rejected; they shall now be the vessels of mercy and honour, when the rest are made vessels of wrath and dishonour, vessels in which is no pleasure. This may be applied to all the faithful people of God, and the distinction he will put between them and others in the great day. Note, [1.] The saints are God's jewels; they are highly esteemed by him and are dear to him; they are comely with the comeliness that he puts upon them, and he is pleased to glory in them; they are a *royal diadem* in his hand, Isa. lxii. 3. He looks upon them as his own proper goods, his choice goods, his treasure, laid up in his cabinet, and the furniture of his closet, Ps. cxxxv. 4. The rest of the world is but lumber, in comparison with them. [2.] There is a day coming when God will *make up his jewels*. They shall be gathered up out of the dirt into which they are now thrown, and gathered together from all places to which they are now scattered; he shall *send forth his angels* to *gather his elect*, who are his jewels, *from the four winds of heaven* (Matt. xxiv. 31), to gather his jewels into his jewel-house, as the wheat from several fields into the barn. All the saints will then be gathered to Christ, and none but saints, and saints made perfect; then God's jewels will be made up, as stones into a crown, as stars into a constellation. [3.] Those who now own God for theirs, he will then own for his, will publicly confess them before angels and men: " *They shall be mine;* their sanctification shall be completed, and so they shall be perfectly and entirely mine, without any remaining interests of the world and the flesh." Their relation to God shall be acknowledged, and his property in them. He will separate them from those that are not his, and give them their portion with those that are his; for to them it shall be said, *Come, you blessed of my Father, inherit the kingdom prepared for you.* They were in doubt, sometimes, whether they were belonging to God or no; but the matter shall then be put out of doubt. God himself will say unto them, *You are mine.* Now their relation to God is what they are reproached with, but it will then be gloried in; God himself will glory in it.

(4.) He promises them a share in his grace now: *I will spare them as a man spares his own son that serves him.* God had promised to own them as his and take them to be with him; but it might be a discouragement to them to think that they had offended God, and that he might justly disown them, and cast them off; but, as to that, he says, "*I will spare them;* I will not deal with them as they deserve. *I will rejoice over them*" (so some expound it) "as the bridegroom over his bride," Isa. lxii. 5; Zeph. iii. 17. But the word usually signifies to spare with commiseration and compassion, *as a father pities his children,* Ps. ciii. 13.

Note, [1.] It is our duty to serve God with the disposition of children. We must be his sons, must by a new birth partake of a divine nature, must consent to the covenant of adoption and partake of the spirit of adoption. And we must be his servants; God will not have his children trained up in idleness; they must do him service, and they must do it from a principle of love, with cheerfulness and delight, and as those that are therein serving their own true interest, and this is serving as *a son with the father,* Phil. ii. 22. [2.] If we serve God with the disposition of children, he will spare us with the tenderness and compassion of a Father. Even God's children that serve him stand in need of sparing mercy, that mercy to which we owe it that we are not consumed, that mercy which keeps us out of hell. Nehemiah, when he had done much good, yet, knowing there is not a *just man on earth,* that *does good and sins not,* and that every sin deserves God's wrath, prays, *Lord, spare me according to the greatness of thy mercy;* see Neh. xiii. 22. And God, as a Father, will show them this mercy. He will not be extreme to mark what we do amiss, but will make the best of us and our poor performances; he will mitigate the afflictions his children are exercised with, and save them from the ruin they deserve. The father continues to spare the son, and does it with complacency, because he is his own; thus God will spare humble penitents and petitioners, *as a man spares his son that serves him,* though we do him so little service, nay, though we do him so much disservice.

3. How they will thus be distinguished from the children of this world (*v.* 18): " *Then shall you return, and discern between the righteous and the wicked,* between sinners and saints, between those that *serve God* and make conscience of their duty to him and those that *serve him not,* but put contempt upon his service. You that now speak against God as making no difference between good and bad, and therefore say, *It is in vain to serve him* (v. 14), you shall be made to see your error; you that would speak for God, but know not what to say as to this, that there seems to be *one event to the righteous and to the wicked,* and *all things come alike to all,* will then have the matter set in a true light, and will see, to your everlasting satisfaction, the difference between the righteous and the wicked. Then *you shall return,* that is, you shall *change your mind,* and come to a right understanding of the thing." This primarily respects the manifest difference that was made by the divine Providence between the believing Jews and those that persisted in their infidelity, at the time of the destruction of Jerusalem, and of the Jewish church and nation, by the Romans. But it is to have its full accomplishment at the second coming of Jesus Christ, and on that great discriminating day when it shall be

easy enough to *discern between the righteous* and *the wicked.* Note, (1.) All the children of men are either righteous or wicked, either such as serve God or such as serve him not. This is that division of the children of men which will last for ever, and by which their eternal state will be determined; all are going either to heaven or to hell. (2.) In this world it is often hard to *discern between the righteous and the wicked.* They are mingled together, good fish and bad in the same net. The righteous are so distempered, and the wicked so disguised, that we are often deceived in our opinions concerning both the one and the other. There are many who, we think, serve God, who, having not their hearts right with him, will be found none of his servants; and, on the other hand, many will be found his faithful servants, who, because they followed not with us, did not, as we thought, serve him. But that which especially raised the difficulty here was that the divine Providence seemed to make no difference between the righteous and the wicked; you could not know wicked men by God's frowning upon them, for they commonly prospered in the world, nor righteous men by his smiling upon them, for they were involved with others in the same common calamity. None now knows God's *love or hatred* by *all that is before him,* Eccl. ix. 1. (3.) At the bar of Christ, in the last judgment, it will be easy to *discern between the righteous and the wicked;* for then every man's character will be both perfected and perfectly discovered, every man will then appear in his true colours, and his disguises will be taken off. Some men's sins indeed go beforehand, and you may now tell who is wicked, but others follow after; however, in the great day, we shall see who was righteous and who wicked. Every man's condition likewise will be both perfected and everlastingly determined; the righteous will then be perfectly happy and the wicked perfectly miserable, without mixture or allay. When the righteous are all set on the right hand of Christ, and invited to come for a blessing, and all the wicked on his left hand, and are told to depart with a curse, then it will be easy to discern between them. As to ourselves, therefore, we are concerned to think among which we shall have our lot, and, as to others, we must *judge nothing before the time.*

CHAP. IV.

We have here proper instructions given us (very proper to close the canon of the Old Testament with), I. Concerning the state of recompense and retribution that is before us, the misery of the wicked and the happiness of the righteous in that state, ver. 1—3. And this is represented to us under a prophecy of the destruction of Jerusalem, and the unbelieving Jews with it, and of the comforts and triumphs of those among them that received the gospel. II. Concerning the state of trial and preparation we are now in, in which we are directed to have an eye to divine revelation, and to follow that; they then must keep to the law of Moses (ver. 4) and expect a further discovery of God's will by Elijah the prophet, that is, by John Baptist, the harbinger of the Messiah, ver. 5, 6. The last chapter of the New Testament is much to the same purport, setting before us heaven and hell in the other world, and obliging us to adhere to the word of God in this world.

FOR, behold, the day cometh, that shall burn as an oven; and all the proud, yea, and all that do wickedly, shall be stubble: and the day that cometh shall burn them up, saith the LORD of hosts, that it shall leave them neither root nor branch. 2 But unto you that fear my name shall the Sun of righteousness arise with healing in his wings; and ye shall go forth, and grow up as calves of the stall. 3 And ye shall tread down the wicked; for they shall be ashes under the soles of your feet in the day that I shall do *this,* saith the LORD of hosts.

The great and terrible day of the Lord is here prophesied of. This, like the pillar of cloud and fire, shall have a dark side turned towards the Egyptians that fight against God, and a bright side towards the faithful Israelites that follow him: *The day cometh,* that is, the Lord cometh, the day of the Lord; and it has reference both to the first and to the second coming of Jesus Christ; the day of both was fixed, and should answer the character here given of it.

I. In both Christ is a consuming fire to those that rebel against him. The day of his coming *shall burn as an oven;* it shall be a day of wrath, of *fiery indignation.* This was foretold concerning the Messiah, Ps. xxi. 9, *Thy hand shall find out all thy enemies,* and *shall make them as a fiery oven in the time of thy anger.* It will be a day of terror and destruction like the burning of a city, or rather of a wood, the trees whereof are withered and dried, for to that the allusion seems to be, as Isa. x. 17, 18, *The light of Israel shall be for a fire, and his Holy One for a flame, and it shall consume the glory of his forest and of his fruitful field.* Now observe here, 1. Who shall be fuel to this fire —all *the proud* in heart, whose words have been stout against God, and their necks stiff and unapt to yield to the yoke of his commandments (all those that *in the pride of their countenances will not seek after God,* nor submit to the grace and government of Jesus Christ—all that proudly say they *will not have Christ to reign over them),* and all those that *do wickedly* in their affections and conversations, that wilfully persist in sin, in contempt of and contradiction to the law of God, they are such as *do wickedly against the covenant,* as another prophet had lately expressed it, Dan. xi. 32. God, that has perfect knowledge of every one's character, knows who are *the proud,* and of every one's actions, knows who they are that *do wickedly;* and they shall be as *stubble* to this fire; they shall be consumed by it, easily consumed, utterly consumed, and it is wholly owing to themselves that they shall be so, for they make themselves stubble, that is, combustible matter, to this fire. If they were not stubble, it would not burn them; for the fire will be to every man according as he and his works are found; if they be *wood, hay,* and *stubble,* they will be *consumed;* but if they be *gold, silver, and precious stones,* they will *abide the fire* and be purified by it, 1 Cor. iii. 13—15. Those that by their unbelief oppose Christ thereby set themselves as *briers and thorns* before a *devouring fire,* Isa. xxvii. 4, 5. 2. What shall be the force and what the fruit of this fire: *The day that cometh shall burn them up,* shall both terrify and ruin them, and shall *leave them neither root nor branch,* neither *son* nor *nephew* (so the Chaldee paraphrase): neither they nor their posterity shall be spared; they shall be wholly extirpated and cut off. *Who knows the power of God's anger? The proud and those that do wickedly* will not fear it, but they shall be made to feel it. Where are those now that *called the proud happy,* when thus they are made completely miserable, when there remains no branch of their happiness to be enjoyed for the present, nor any root of it out of which it might again spring up? Now this was fulfilled, (1.) When Christ, in his doctrine, spoke terror and condemnation to the proud Pharisees and the other Jews that did wickedly, when he sent that fire on the earth which burnt up the chaff of the traditions of the elders and the corrupt glosses they had put upon the law of God. (2.) When Jerusalem was destroyed by the Romans, and the nation of the Jews, as a nation, quite blotted out from under heaven, and neither root nor branch left them. This seems to be principally intended here; our Saviour says that those should be the *days of vengeance,* when all the things that were written to that purport should be fulfilled, Luke xxi. 22. Then the unbelieving Jews were as stubble to the devouring fire of God's judgments, which gathered together to them as the eagles to the carcase. (3.) It is certainly applicable, and is to be applied, to the day of judgment, to the particular judgment at death (some of the Jewish doctors refer it the *punishment that seizes on the souls of the wicked immediately after they go out of the body*), but especially to the general judgment, at the end of time, when Christ shall be *revealed in flaming fire,* to execute judgment on *the proud, and all that do wickedly.* The whole world shall then *burn as an oven,* and all the children of this world, that set their hearts upon it and choose their portion in it, shall take their ruin with it, and the fire then kindled shall never be quenched.

II. In both Christ is a rejoicing light to those who serve him faithfully, to those who fear his name and give him the glory due to it (*v.* 2), who stand in awe of that name of his which the wicked profane and trample upon.

Here are mercy and comfort kept in store for all those who fear the Lord and think on his name. Observe,

1. Whence this mercy and comfort shall flow to them: *To you that fear my name shall the Sun of righteousness arise, with healing in his wings.* The day that comes, as it will be a stormy day to the wicked, a day in which God will rain upon them *fire and brimstone, and a horrible tempest,* as he did on Sodom (Ps. xi. 6), a *day of clouds and thick darkness* (Amos v. 18, 20), so it will be a fair and bright day to those who fear God, and reviving as the rising sun is to the earth; and particular notice is taken of the rising of the sun upon Zoar when that was mercifully distinguished from the cities of the plain, which the fire *consumed;* see Gen. xix. 23. So to those that fear God is comfort spoken. When the hearts of others *fail for fear* let them *lift up their heads for joy,* for *their redemption draws nigh,* Luke xxi. 28. But by the *Sun of righteousness* here we are certainly to understand Jesus Christ, who would undertake to secure the believing remnant, in the day of the general destruction of the Jews, from falling with the rest, and to comfort them in that day of distress and perplexity with his consolations; he directed those that were in Judea to *flee to the mountains* (Matt. xxiv. 16), and they did so, and were all safe and easy in Pella. But it is to be applied more generally, (1.) To the coming of Christ in the flesh to seek and save those that were lost; then the *Sun of righteousness* arose upon this dark world. Christ is the *light of the world,* the true light, the great light that makes day and rules the day (John viii. 12), as the sun. He is the *light of men* (John i. 4), is to men's souls as the sun is to the visible world, which without the sun would be a dungeon; so would mankind be darkness itself without the *light of the glory of God* shining *in the face of Christ.* Christ is the Sun that has light in himself, and is the fountain of light (Ps. xix. 4—6); he is the *Sun of righteousness,* for he is himself a righteous Saviour. Righteousness is both the light and the heat of this Sun; the word of his righteousness is so; it guides, instructs, and quickens; so is the *everlasting righteousness* he has brought in. He is *made of God to us righteousness;* he is the *Lord our righteousness,* and therefore is fitly called *the Sun of righteousness.* Through him we are justified and sanctified, and so are brought to see light. This Sun of righteousness, in the fulness of time, arose upon the world, and with him *light came into the world* (John iii. 19), a *great light,* Matt. iv. 16. In him the *day-spring from on high visited us, to give light to those that sit in darkness,* Luke i. 78, 79. Righteousness sometimes signifies mercy or benignity, and it was in Christ that the *tender mercy of our God* visited us. (2.) It is applicable to the

graces and comforts of the Holy Spirit, brought into the souls of men. Grotius understands it of Christ's giving the Spirit to those that are his, to shine in their hearts, and to be a *comforter* to them, a *sun and a shield*. Those that are possessed and governed by a holy fear of God and a dread of his majesty shall have his *love* also *shed abroad in their hearts by the Holy Ghost;* and then the sun may be said to arise there, and to bring both a delightful day and a fruitful spring along with it. (3.) Christ's second coming will be a glorious and welcome sun-rising to all that *fear his name;* it will be that morning of the resurrection in which *the upright shall have dominion*, Ps. xlix. 14. That day which to the wicked will *burn as an oven* will to the righteous be bright as the morning; and it is what they wait for, *more than those that wait for the morning.*

2. What this mercy and comfort shall bring to them: He *shall arise with healing under his wings*, or in his *rays* or *beams*, which are as the wings of the sun. Christ came, as *the sun*, to bring not only light to a dark world, but health to a diseased distempered world. The Jews (says Dr. Pocock) have a proverbial saying, *As the sun riseth, infirmities decrease;* the flowers which drooped and languished all night revive in the morning. Christ came into the world to be the great physician, yea, and the great medicine too, both the balm in Gilead and the physician there. When he was upon earth, he went about as the sun in his circuit, doing this good; he *healed all manner of sicknesses and diseases among the people;* he healed by wholesale, as the sun does. He shall arise *with healing in his skirts;* so some read it, and they apply it to the story of the woman's touching *the hem of his garment*, and being thereby *made whole*, and his finding that *virtue went out of him*, Mark v. 28—30. But his healing bodily diseases was a specimen of his great design in coming into the world to heal the diseases of men's souls, and to put them into a good state of health, that they may serve and enjoy both God and themselves.

3. What good effect it shall have upon them. (1.) It shall make them vigorous in themselves: " *You shall go forth*, as those that are healed go abroad and return to their business." The souls shall go forth out of their bodies at death, and the bodies out of their graves at the resurrection, as prisoners out of their dungeons, and both to see the light and be set at liberty. " *You shall go forth* as plants out of the earth, when in the spring the sun returns." Some make it to mean the going forth of the Christians from Jerusalem, and the escape they thereby made from its destruction. And thus the souls on whom the Sun of righteousness arises go forth out of the world, go forth out of Babylon, as those that are made *free indeed.*

" You shall likewise *grow up;* being restored to health and liberty, you shall increase in knowledge, and grace, and spiritual strength." The souls on which the Sun of righteousness arises are growing up towards *the perfect man;* those that by the grace of God are made wise and good are by the same grace made wiser and better; and their path, like that of the rising sun, *shines more and more to the perfect day*, Prov. iv. 18. Their growth is compared to that of *the calves of the stall*, which is a quick, strong, and useful growth. " You shall grow up, not as the *flower of the field*, which is slender, and weak, and of little use, and withers soon after it has grown up, but as the *calves of the stall*," that, as one of the rabbin expounds it, *grow great in flesh and fatness*, with which both God's altars and men's tables are replenished; so the growth of the saints, on whom the Sun of righteousness arises, honours both God and man. Some read it, instead of *You shall grow up*, You shall *move yourselves*, or *leap for joy*, shall be as frolicsome as calves of the stall, when they are let loose in the open field; it denotes the joy of the saints, who rejoice in Christ Jesus; they shall even leap for joy; they are *always caused to triumph.*

(2.) It shall make them victorious over their enemies (v. 3): *You shall tread down the wicked*. Time was when the wicked trod them down, and said to their souls, *Bow down, that we may go over;* but the day will come when they shall *tread down the wicked*. The wicked, being made Christ's footstool, are made theirs also (Ps. cx. 1), and come and *worship before the feet* of the church, Rev. iii. 9. *The elder shall serve the younger*. When believers by faith *overcome the world*, when they suppress their own corrupt appetites and passions, when the God of peace bruises Satan under their feet, then they *tread down the wicked*. When it came to the turn of the Christians to triumph over the Jews that had insulted over them, then this promise was fulfilled: *They shall be ashes under the soles of your feet;* they shall not only be *trodden down*, but trodden *to dirt*. When the day that comes shall have *burnt them up*, they shall trample upon them as ashes. When the righteous shall rise to *everlasting life*, the wicked shall rise to *everlasting contempt;* and, though they shall not triumph over them, they shall triumph in that God whose justice is glorified in their destruction. The saints in glory are said to have power given them over the nations, to *rule them with a rod of iron*, Rev. ii. 26, 27. This *you shall do, in the day that I shall do this*. Note, The saints' triumphs are all owing to God's victories; it is not they that do this, but God that does it for them, that says, *Come set your feet on the necks of these kings*. Some read it, " *In the day that I make*, or shall make, the *great day* that I shall make remarkable, of which you will say with joy, *This is the day which the Lord has made."* The day of the destruction of Jerusalem is called the *great and notable day of the Lord* (Acts ii. 20), and our Saviour in foretelling that destruction made use of such expressions as, like these, might be applied likewise to the *end of the world* and the *last judgment;* for it was such a terrible revelation of the wrath of God from heaven, and caused such a scene of horror upon this earth, that it might fitly serve for a type of that glorious transaction which will be an outlet to the days of time and an inlet to the days of eternity. By the accomplishment of these prophecies in the ruin of the Jewish nation, we should have our faith confirmed in the assurances Christ has given us concerning the dissolution of all things. *Surely I come quickly;* so says Christ, *the Lord of hosts,* to whom all power in heaven and earth is committed.

4 Remember ye the law of Moses my servant, which I commanded unto him in Horeb for all Israel, *with* the statutes and judgments. 5 Behold, I will send you Elijah the prophet before the coming of the great and dreadful day of the LORD: 6 And he shall turn the heart of the fathers to the children, and the heart of the children to their fathers, lest I come and smite the earth with a curse.

This is doubtless intended for a solemn conclusion, not only of this prophecy, but of the canon of the Old Testament, and is a plain information that they were not to expect any more sayings nor writings by divine inspiration, any more of the dictates of the Spirit of prophecy, till the beginning of the gospel of the Messiah, which sets aside the Apocrypha as no part of holy writ, and which therefore the Jews never received.

Now that prophecy ceases, and is about to be sealed up, there are two things required of the people of God, that lived then:—

I. They must keep up an obedient veneration for the law of Moses (*v.* 4): *Remember the law of Moses my servant,* and observe to do according to it, even that law which *I commanded unto him in Horeb,* that fiery law which was intended *for all Israel, with the statutes and judgments,* not only the law of the ten commandments, but all the other appointments, ceremonial and judicial, then and there given. Observe here, 1. The honourable mention that is made of *Moses,* the first writer of the Old Testament, in *Malachi,* the last writer. God by him calls him *Moses my servant;* for the righteous shall be had in everlasting remembrance. See how the penmen of scripture, though they lived in several ages at a great distance from each other (it was above 1200 years from Moses to Malachi), all concurred in the same thing,

and supported one another, being all actuated and guided by one and the same Spirit. 2. The honourable mention that is made of the *law of Moses;* it was what God himself *commanded;* he owns it for his law, and he commanded it *for all Israel,* as the municipal law of their kingdom. Thus will God *magnify his law and make it honourable.* Note, We are concerned to keep the law because God has commanded it and commanded it for us, for we are the spiritual Israel; and, if we expect the benefit of the covenant with Israel (Heb. viii. 10), we must observe the commands given to Israel, those of them that were intended to be of perpetual obligation. 3. The summary of our duty, with reference to the law. We must remember it. Forgetfulness of the law is at the bottom of all our transgressions of it; if we would rightly remember it, we could not but conform to it. We should remember it when we have occasion to use it, remember both the commands themselves and the sanctions wherewith they are enforced. The office of conscience is to bid us *remember the law.* But how does this charge to remember the law of Moses come in here? (1.) This prophet had reproved them for many gross corruptions and irregularities both in worsh'p and conversation, and now, for the reforming and amending of what was amiss, he only charges them to *remember the law of Moses:* "Keep to that rule, and you will do all you should do." He will *lay upon them no other burden* than what they *have received; hold that fast,* Rev. ii. 24, 25. Note, Corrupt churches are to be reformed by the written word, and reduced into order by being reduced to the standard of *the law and the testimony,* see 1 Cor. xi. 23. (2.) The church had long enjoyed the benefit of prophets, extraordinary messengers from God, and now they had a whole book of their prophecies put together, and it was a finished piece; but they must not think that hereby the *law of Moses* was superseded, and had become as an almanac out of date, as if now they were advanced to a higher form and might forget that. No; the prophets do but confirm and apply the law, and press the observance of that; and therefore still *Remember the law.* Note, Even when we have made considerable advances in knowledge we must still retain the first principles of practical religion and resolve to abide by them. Those that study the writings of the prophets, and the apocalypse, must still remember the law of Moses and the four gospels. (3.) Prophecy was now to cease in the church for some ages, and the Spirit of prophecy not to return till the *beginning of the gospel,* and now they are told to *remember the law of Moses;* let them live by the rules of that, and live upon the promises of that. Note, We need not complain for want of visions and revelations as long as we have the written word, and the canon of scripture complete, to be our guide; for that is the most *sure word of prophecy*, and the touchstone by which we are to *try the spirits*. Though we have not prophets, yet, as long as we have Bibles, we may keep our communion with God, and keep ourselves in his way. (4.) They were to expect the coming of the Messiah, the preaching of his gospel, and the setting up of his kingdom, and in that expectation they must *remember the law of Moses*, and live in obedience to that, and then they might expect the comforts that the Messiah would bring to *the willing and obedient*. Let them observe the law of Moses, and live up to the light which that gave them, and then they might expect the benefit of the gospel of Christ, for *to him that has*, and uses what he has well, *more shall be given, and he shall have abundance*.

II. They must keep up a believing expectation of the gospel of Christ, and must look for the beginning of it in the appearing of Elijah the prophet (v. 5, 6): *Behold, I send you Elijah the prophet*. Though the Spirit of prophecy cease for a time, and you will have only the law to consult, yet it shall revive again in one that shall be sent *in the spirit and power of Elias*," Luke i. 17. The *law and the prophets were until John* (Luke xvi. 16); they continued to be the only lights of the church till that morning-star appeared. Note, As God never *left himself without witness* in the world, so neither in the church, but, as there was occasion, carried the light of divine revelation further and further to the perfect day. They had now Moses and the prophets, and might hear them; but God will go further: he will send them Elijah. Observe,

I. Who this prophet is that shall be sent; it is *Elijah*. The Jewish doctors will have it to be the same Elijah that prophesied in Israel in the days of Ahab—that he shall come again to be the forerunner of the Messiah; yet others of them say not the same person, but another of the same spirit. It should seem, those different sentiments they had when they asked John, "*Art thou Elias, or that prophet* that should bear his name?" John i. 19—21. But we Christians know very well that John Baptist was the Elias that was to come, Matt. xvii. 10—13; and very expressly, Matt. xi. 14, *This is Elias that was to come;* and v. 10, the same of whom it is written, *Behold, I send my messenger, ch.* iii. 1. Elijah was a man of great austerity and mortification, zealous for God, bold in reproving sin, and active to reduce an apostate people to God and their duty; John Baptist was animated by the same spirit and power, and preached repentance and reformation, as Elias had done; and all held him for a prophet, as they did Elijah in his day, and that his baptism was *from heaven*, and not *of men*. Note, When God has such work to do as was formerly to be done he can raise up such men to do it as he formerly

raised up, and can put into a John Baptist the spirit of an Elias.

2. When he shall be sent—before the appearing of the Messiah, which, because it was the judgment of this world, and introduced the ruin of the Jewish church and nation, is here called the *coming of the great and dreadful day of the Lord*. John Baptist gave them fair warning of this when he told them of the *wrath to come* (that *wrath to the uttermost* which was hastening upon them) and put them into a way of escape from it, and when he told them of the *fan in Christ's hand*, with which Christ would thoroughly purge his floor; see Matt. iii. 7, 10, 12. That day of Christ, when he came first, was as that day will be when he comes again—though a great and joyful day to those that embrace him, yet a *great and dreadful day* to those that oppose him. John Baptist was sent before the coming of this day, to give people notice of it, that they might get ready for it, and go forth to meet it.

3. On what errand he shall be sent: *He shall turn the heart of the fathers to their children, and the heart of the children to their fathers;* that is, "he shall be employed in this work; he shall attempt it; his doctrine and baptism shall have a direct tendency to it, and with many shall be successful: he shall be an instrument in God's hand of *turning* many *to righteousness*, to *the Lord their God*, and so *making ready a people prepared for him*," Luke i. 16, 17. Note, The turning of souls to God and their duty is the best preparation of them for the great and dreadful day of the Lord. It is promised concerning John, (1.) That he shall give a turn to things, shall make a bold stand against the strong torrent of sin and impiety which he found in full force among the children of his people, and beating down all before it. This is called his *coming to restore all things* (Matt. xvii. 11), to set them to rights, that they may again go in the right channel. (2.) That he shall preach a doctrine that shall reach men's hearts, and have an influence upon them, and work a change in them. God's word, in his mouth, shall be *quick* and *powerful*, and a *discerner of the thoughts and intents of the heart*. Many had their consciences awakened by his ministry who yet were not thoroughly wrought upon, such a spirit and power was there in it. (3.) That he shall turn the hearts of the fathers with the children, and of the children with the fathers (for so some read it), to God and to their duty. He shall call upon young and old to repent, and shall not labour in vain, for many of the fathers that are going off, and many of the children that are growing up, shall be wrought upon by his ministry. (4.) That thus he shall be an instrument to revive and confirm love and unity among relations, and shall bring them closer and bind them faster to each other, by bringing and binding them all to their God. He shall

prepare the way for that kingdom of heaven which will make all its faithful subjects of *one heart* and *one soul* (Acts iv. 32), which will be a kingdom of love, and will slay all enmities.

4. With what view he shall be sent on this errand: *Lest I come and smite the earth,* that is, the land of Israel, the body of the Jewish nation (that were of the earth earthy), *with a curse.* They by their impiety and impenitence in it had laid themselves open to the curse of God, which is a separation to all evil. God was ready to smite them with that curse, to bring utter ruin upon them, to strike home, to strike dead, with the curse; but he will yet once more try them, whether they will repent and return, and so prevent it; and therefore he sends John Baptist to preach repentance to them, that their conversion might prevent their confusion; so unwilling is God that any should perish, so willing to have his anger turned away. Had they universally repented and reformed, their repentance would have had this desired effect; but, they generally rejecting the counsel of God in John's baptism, it proved against themselves (Luke vii. 30) and their land was smitten with the curse which both it and they lie under to this day. Note, Those must expect to be smitten with a sword, with a curse, who *turn not to him that smites them* with a rod, with a cross, Isa. ix. 13. Now the *axe is laid to the root of the tree,* says John Baptist, and it is ready to be smitten, to be cut down, *with a curse;* therefore *bring forth fruit meet for repentance.* Some observe that the last word of the Old Testament is a curse, which threatens the earth (Zech. v. 3), our desert of which we must be made sensible of, that we may bid Christ welcome, who comes with a blessing; and it is with a blessing, with the choicest of blessings, that the New Testament ends, and with it let us arm ourselves, or rather let God arm us, against this curse. *The grace of our Lord Jesus Christ be with us all. Amen.*

Thoms, Printer Warwick Square.

stress, perhaps the greatest casualty of the
of the established values of a social order, of
, extending back to the French Revolution.
ived the conflagrations of 1830, 1848, and 1870,
s unequal to the struggle posed by the Great War.
to this struggle not because the struggle was no
red necessary or right but because civilization was
the radical nature of a time when history was being
of its past. The Great War degraded the civilizing reti-
cences, whether in the methods and weapons of modern warfare
or in the cause and manner of death. What the survivors often decry
in their writings is the obscenity of the war and, in turn, the obscenity of the "modern mind." On the front lines, as well as at the home,
among statesmen, priests, generals, among soldiers, their parents,
their wives—allies and enemies alike—everyone had submitted to
the obscene process of the war, to that "modern mind" that, out-
distancing itself in its inventions and capacity for invention, had
depraved itself. A war that for many started somehow with a vague
dream of a better world gradually brought the realization that civilization was reverting to the obscenities of life at its most primitive
level. That this shock was overpowering and even impossible to
fathom becomes the burden of the message of the literature of the
Great War and the source of its prophecy.

Many writers depict the Great War as a tragedy in the history of
European civilization. Certainly when the period of this "war-
disease" is examined; when the war's barbarism, both "scientific"
and "systematic," is seen in all its pain and horror; when European
society was reduced to a collective state of destruction or one of
awaiting destruction; when the spirit of the time was no more than
a "hymn to hate," with the voices of reason and compassion giving
way to those of violence—"Have no fear, our force will slay theirs,"
the French philosopher Henri Bergson asserted,[47] and his words
summed up the sentiments on both sides, as even intellectuals and
academicians affirmed that force contains the only solutions—it is
not difficult to detect the tragic ramifications of this war: the calamity, the anguish, the despair, the oppressiveness, the pathos, the
fatefulness which are the constants of all tragedy, classical and

---

47 *The Meaning of the War* (London, 1915) , p. 47.

as tragedy
beauty, without the wisdom, with
that redeem tragedy and man. In the
puniness was laid bare with devastating co
ing, degraded as he was to instrumentality by a
process. In a word, the tragedy of the Great
tragedy of obscenity, when neither man's und
virtues could resemble or equal those endemic
rhythm of ancient tragedy. Such a tragedy could i
except on the humiliating note of insult and sneer, as t
of the postwar period, right up to 1939, iterated with m
examples.

By no means should these remarks imply that the generation of
1914–18 was unequal to or incapable of tragedy. Their writings on
the war show only too clearly a grasp of the tragic elements that no
survivor of World War II has yet to disclose. From every standpoint
the generation that fought in the Great War was a generation made
for suffering and heroism in a "war against war." That they were
an unsuspicious generation with a passion for idealism and justice
and freedom; that they were responsive to "cause" and "principle"
and "duty"; that they were as proud and self-confident as they were
romantic and naïve; that they were a generation that believed in
creative reason, in progress, in civilization, and hence in man's
destiny are qualities that the men of 1914 reveal without conscious
effort. But if this generation was worthy of heroic attitudes and
gestures that still looked back to early times, they were not ready
for the changes that affected tragic experience in the modern world.
For millions of men the experience of the war was tragic in its
physical and mental suffering; in its exposure of the inchoate evil
and the chaos existent in the visible world; in its desperation and
dilemma, as well as in its hopelessness. But although the phenome-
nal experience of the war was for many men tragic, the vision implicit in tragedy was not. The mechanical nature of modern warfare
had neutralized not only men, but also values. Life had been terribly
cheapened; suffering itself had been devalued. The ultimate meaning of the war had been translated into something soulless, into a
state that gravitated not to a higher recognition of human value but
to meaninglessness.

The war finally constituted an unelevated tragedy, lifted to no
noble scale or design, and thus holding no visionary, no revivifying,
meaning for man and his world. In place of magnanimity, which is
intrinsic to the experience of tragedy with its "divine worth of tones
and tears," the war ordained a squalid human destiny, one of

bondage to distortions and perverseness. If, therefore, the historical situation was conducive to tragic experience, with the warning to man not to boast in his strength as applicable to European man in 1914–18 as it was to the ancient Greek heroes, the unnatural and immoral conditions of the war failed, necessarily, to produce vision. A war that violated and scorned the dignity of and a reverence for life precluded tragic vision—precluded, that is, the possibility of a deep, redeeming awareness of man's place in the modern world. A sense of nothingness, of futility, of cynicism, of alienation from the past (now there would be "no more parades!" "No more Hope, no more Glory, no more parades for you and me any more," wrote Ford Madox Ford[48]), which the conflict resulted in, signified not the attainment of vision, and thus of truth and value, but the impasse of despair and the death of hope in the midst of the obscene. The Great War became tragedy without vision, the experience of evil and suffering without value, without the culminating affirmation and decisiveness that bring with them even a fleeting comprehension of victory over the seal of man's betrayal and condemnation.

"The war," wrote Benedetto Croce, "which had been announced to the peoples with the promise of a general catharsis, in its course and its end was completely untrue to this promise."[49] Not a transfiguring nobility but a sense of disgust beyond despair marked the temper of Europe by November 11, 1918. The very sordidness of the war, the whole demeaning process of its rapacity, had cheated man of any positiveness of a tragic vision, of something valuable and lasting in life and in the universe, some conception of wisdom and regeneration. In short, war, once again, but on a more monstrous scale, had not enlarged the meaning of life, had not, in an integrally tragic sense, revealed either humility or enlightenment, or shown man, trapped by conflict, a different shape of his destiny. No longer was it even a matter of optimism or pessimism. At the end of the war, man's apathy, his smallness, and, indeed, his loathsomeness informed the prevailing view of events and consequences. More than life itself had died in the conflict. Max Ernst, the German painter who had fought at the front and had been wounded, said that the question that the war finally posed for him was: "How to overcome the disgust and fatal boredom that military life and the horrors of war create. Howl? Blaspheme? Vomit?"[50] His words epitomize the feelings of men who, recognizing the fact that with

[48] *No More Parades*, in *Parade's End* (New York, 1961 [1925]), p. 307.

[49] *History of Europe in the Nineteenth Century*, trans. by Henry Furst (New York, 1933), p. 350.

[50] *Max Ernst*, William S. Lieberman, ed. (New York, 1961), p. 11.

this war, senselessness had made its appearance in society, wanted to spit in the eye of the world, as well as the mood that swept over postwar Europe, when, as Aldous Huxley was to write, "To-morrow . . . will be as awful as to-day."[51]

That the Great War could go beyond a tragedy of phenomena to become a tragedy of vision and knowledge, that tragedy which Karl Jaspers defines as "the measure of man's greatness in breakdown and failure"[52] and which transcends man's "limit-situation," was a promise that never materialized. The promise of greatness with which the war was identified at the outset when, as a poet rhapsodized, the time was ripe "To win Eternity/ And claim God's kiss,"[53] was dead by 1918. As undoubtedly an experience of failure dramatizing the precariousness of human meaning and truth, the war had in the end hardly affirmed "the measure of man's greatness." History since 1914 has reinforced man's view of a world adying and of an existence more deeply despised, even as new cataclysms appear. More than at any other time in the history of civilization, what happened in 1914–18 imparted the force of the truth that "Every truth we may think complete will prove itself untruth at the moment of shipwreck."[54] The Great War, marking the triumph of such a "moment"—a moment that now spans more than fifty years as a chronicle of an age and a condition of a civilization—negated not alone the human possibility, as war must always negate it, but also man's expedition toward the goal which Jaspers sees as carrying the only promise of greatness which can overcome the fear and the expiration of hope itself: "This is the vision of a great and noble life: to endure ambiguity in the movement of truth and to make light shine through it; to stand fast in uncertainty; to prove capable of unlimited love and hope."[55]

GEORGE ANDREW PANICHAS

,

Winter-Spring, 1967–1968

---

51 *Antic Hay* (New York, 1965 [1923]) , p. 283.

52 *Tragedy Is Not Enough*, trans. by Harald A. T. Reiche, Harry T. Moore, and Karl W. Deutsch (Boston, 1952) , p. 45.

53 "The Dead Heroes," in *The Collected Poems of Isaac Rosenberg*, Gordon Bottomley and Denys Harding, ed. (New York, 1949) , p. 42.

54 *Tragedy Is Not Enough, op. cit.,* p. 104.

55 *Ibid.,* p. 105.

A Total View

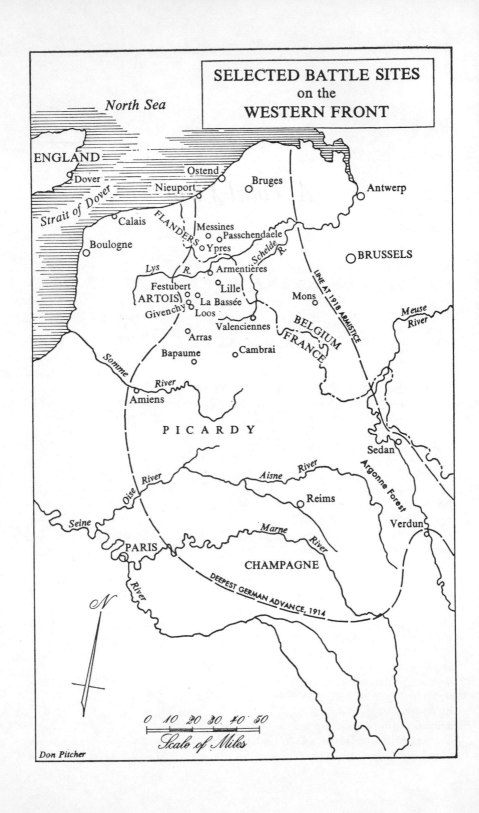

SELECTED BATTLE SITES
on the
WESTERN FRONT

North Sea

ENGLAND

Dover

Ostend

Nieuport

Bruges

Antwerp

Strait of Dover

Calais

FLANDERS

Messines

Passchendaele

Ypres

BRUSSELS

Boulogne

Schelde R.

Armentières

Lys R.

Festubert

Lille

ARTOIS

La Bassée

Mons

Meuse River

Givenchy

Loos

BELGIUM

Valenciennes

FRANCE

LINE AT 1918 ARMISTICE

Arras

Somme

Bapaume

Cambrai

River

Amiens

PICARDY

Sedan

Argonne Forest

Oise River

Aisne River

Reims

Seine

Marne River

Verdun

PARIS

CHAMPAGNE

DEEPEST GERMAN ADVANCE, 1914

River

N

0 10 20 30 40 50
Scale of Miles

Don Pitcher

Robert Graves

ROBERT GRAVES' *autobiography* Good-bye to All That (1927) *has been termed "a permanently valuable work of literary art, and indispensable for the historian either of the First World War or of modern English poetry." What Mr. Graves speaks of in this book as his "conditioning in the Protestant morality of the English governing classes, though qualified by mixed blood, a rebellious nature, and an overriding poetic obsession, . . . not easily outgrown" can be seen in his contributions to literature. His books of mythology and collected essays are admired by scholars and used in college courses, and he has composed many distinguished translations from Latin, Greek, German, French, and Spanish texts. He is frequently invited to the United States to lecture and read from his work, especially from his famous poetry. In 1963 he was poet in residence at the Massachusetts Institute of Technology, where he enjoyed teasing the "scientific mind."*

Born in London in 1895, Mr. Graves fought with the Royal Welch Fusiliers in France during World War I and then earned a degree at Oxford. In 1926 he was professor of English literature at Cairo University in Egypt. He has lived in Majorca since 1929, except for a period which he describes in the Epilogue to Good-bye to All That: *"The one serious set-back to my quiet life [in Majorca] came with the Spanish Civil War in 1936, when all British subjects were advised to leave, by warship. I wandered around Europe and the United States for three years; and spent the Second World War in England, because three of my children had joined the Armed Forces—the fourth, Sam, being prevented by deafness from doing the same." His oldest son, David, having joined the First Royal Welch in World War II, was shot and killed on the Arakan peninsula, Burma, in March, 1943, while rushing a Japanese strongpoint single-handed.*

Mr. Graves, his second wife, and the youngest of his eight children now live in Deyá, Majorca, a section where tourists are seldom seen. Long hours at his desk are interrupted by swimming in the Mediterranean and leisurely conversations with his family and friends. Majorca Observed *eloquently expresses his love of that island. As for the rest of his work, however, Mr. Graves affirms, "I think it has nothing in it that is not fundamentally English. There is perhaps one olive tree in my poems; otherwise, they are from my native island—not my adopted one."*

THE KAISER'S WAR:
A BRITISH POINT OF VIEW

WHEN THE NEWSPAPER PLACARDS on August 4, 1914, read: ENGLAND DECLARES WAR ON GERMANY—"Britain" being a word not yet in current use—there was no prouder nation in the world than ours. Though possessing the greatest Empire ever known and ruling it, on the whole, humanely, we nevertheless supplemented the national anthem with "Land of Hope and Glory":

> Wider still and wider
> Shall thy bounds be set!
> God who made thee mighty
> Make thee mightier yet!

As successors of the Romans, it suited our governing classes to continue their imperial tradition. The nobility and landed gentry sent their sons to public schools and the major universities for the discipline of Latin, Greek, and the birch rod. The unassuming and ultrarespectable "middle class" enjoyed a shorter but more practical education. Our profane laboring classes struggled against ignorance and dire poverty, spent a large part of their wages on drink, and nursed a stubborn pride in being English. Socialism seemed on the decline: Labour had lost ten seats in the general election of 1910 and now held a mere 41 out of 670. Women could not vote; neither, for that matter, could millions of men who lacked substantial property—such as the lower ranks in the Army and Navy.

Motorcars had not yet seriously challenged horse traffic; filthy street crossings were still swept by ragged, barefoot boys for button-booted ladies to negotiate with raised skirts. Electric light was a rare domestic luxury, the telephone rarer; laborsaving devices were limited to carpet sweeper, meat grinder, knife-cleaning machine; and the racks worked by a pulley for drying wet clothes over the kitchen range. Airplanes in their infancy; jerky, silent, moving pictures enlivened by piano music; no broadcasting. Untarred main roads; slums of appalling horror in every big city. A powerful Liberal Party. Eire not yet a republic. Free trade; no check on immigration; a minimal income tax. The civil service about a fiftieth of its present size, working short hours and still using quill pens and red tape. Divorces unusual and disgraceful. . . .

We were the envy of the world, especially of our "German cousins" who, because of their preeminence in music, philosophy, and social sciences, believed themselves chosen by God to succeed us. Their temperamental Kaiser, a grandson of Queen Victoria, had declared that Germany's future lay on the sea and undertaken never to rest until her fleet was as strong as her army—already the most powerful in the world. In 1900 he told German troops whom he sent to defend the Peking foreign legations against Boxer rebels that they must emulate the terrible Huns of old: hence the newspaper use of "Huns" for Germans. His frequent "saber rattling," from the time of the Boer War until the Agadir incident in 1912, his attempt to break the Anglo-French Entente Cordiale, and the covetous eye he threw at our colonies annoyed us almost beyond endurance. His excuse for Germany's invasion of Belgium—the murder of an Austrian archduke in the Balkans—seemed cynically irrelevant. We felt relieved when *Der Tag*, solemnly toasted by German naval officers, dawned at last.

Most historians present the war as a sort of chess game between rival supreme commands: the united British, French, Belgian, Russian, and Serbian commands on one hand, and the united German, Austrian, Turkish, and Bulgarian on the other. But what a game! Each group of players in persistent disunity, everyone new to the game, fresh pieces continually introduced, and fresh rules extemporized. . . .

None of us had the least presentiment of coming catastrophe. The Fleet had taken up its battle station at Scapa Flow; the British Expeditionary Force had landed in France. Our French and Russian allies were mobilizing twice as many divisions as the Germans; the Austrian Army seemed a liability rather than an asset to the Kaiser's forces; Italy had declared herself neutral and later joined us. "War will be over by Christmas." "Business as Usual!" Which was like saying: "The best cure for a cold is hot rum and a couple of days in bed."

Memories of the Boer War—only twelve years behind us—came flooding back. The heroic departure of the City Imperial Volunteers:

> Duke's son, cook's son, son of a hundred kings:
> Fifty-thousand horse and foot going to Table Bay—
> Each of them doing their country's work. . . .

The glorious bonfires of Mafeking night:

> We're the soldiers of the King, my lad;
> The King, my lad; the King, my lad:
> We shall fight for England's glorious name
> Like the soldiers of the King. . . .

All our generals were cavalrymen, for in this respect alone the English did not imitate the Romans, who had treated infantry as their most honorable arm, with cavalry as mere flank protection supplied by subject allies. Not until A.D. 378, when Gothic heavy cavalry broke the legions at Adrianople, did European horsemen count themselves superior beings. Then arose the code of chivalry, borrowed from Islam by our Norman ancestors. In medieval times, King Arthur and his Knights of the Round Table—commemorated in the Order of the Garter—meant more to our chivalrous governing classes than all the saints in the calendar except their patron, St. George. Every duke led out his mounted vassals; every lesser peer his knights; every knight his rabble of footmen armed with bows, bills, and long knives, whom he called "my dear children," or "infantry." And, blind to change, Generals French, Haig, Plumer, Cavan, and the rest still thought of war as a succession of heroic cavalry charges: their territorial gains consolidated by slow-marching infantry.

They made a point of opposing every mechanical innovation that might disturb this dream. They loved horses; they excelled in polo; they hated motorcars and lorries—nasty-smelling things at which horses shied. Apart from a few traction engines for pulling heavy siege guns, the B.E.F. was completely unmechanized until, at the last moment, a couple of Royal Engineer officers were sent to commandeer a few score brewery lorries. No provision had, of course, been made for a supply of magnetos, and the disgraceful story of how the War Office obtained them by secret trading with the Bosch Company of Stuttgart has never yet, I believe, been told! The German Army was equipped with 500 lorries, each towing a trailer: Mercedes-Benz, Dürkopp, and others. Their plan of attack had been prepared down to the last detail.

In late August the British Expeditionary Force—which the Kaiser described as "that contemptible small army" (hence the "Old Contemptibles") —were forced by French defeat on their flank to a headlong retreat from Mons. Small, yes: six divisions, compared with the Germans' eighty-seven. Yet when in October the Germans —now held at the Aisne—decided to smother the B.E.F. by a mass attack at Ypres and seize the Channel ports, they suffered fantastic casualties from musketry so rapid and accurate that they mistook it for machine-gun fire. There were no British reserves, however. On November 14, our 1st and 7th Divisions had been practically annihilated, and Prussian troops poured through a gap. They were met by the Royal Field Artillery firing over open sights, and then counterattacked by a scratch force: cooks, tailors, transportmen, headquarter clerks—being the thirty survivors from the 2d Queens and forty from the 1st Royal Welch Fusiliers, commanded by a second lieutenant named Orme (just arrived from Sandhurst) whose death left the battalion officerless. The Prussians hesitated and dug in. Heavy rain fell; the line held.

More then half our Army had become casualties at Ypres. The ranks were refilled with Special Reservists who could at least form fours and use their rifles. Comfortable West End clubmen argued that although the Germans had overrun all Belgium and a great part of northern France and beaten the Russians decisively at Tannenberg, they had now shot their bolt. Our French and Russian allies would soon grind them to powder.

What began as an ordinary old-fashioned campaign took on, by the spring of 1915, the nightmare quality of total war. The period of fluid fighting—enjoyed by Uhlans, Hussars, and Lancers—had ended in the previous September, and every month of stalemate now made it more difficult for the Germans to break our front, which ran from the North Sea to Switzerland. Formed accidentally by the useless attempts of both sides to outflank one another, it consisted of a front line protected by barbed-wire entanglements, machine-gun nests, and listening posts, and behind it support lines, rear lines, and tactical reserves. Soon all the higher commands caught the same obsessional madness: a conviction that the enemy line could be breached by intense bombardment, with cavalry held in readiness to gallop through, fan out, and pave the way for an infantry advance. But the German General Staff, still set on capturing the Channel ports, decided to fortify their artillery fire with a surprise weapon banned by the Hague Convention: poison gas.

They tried it on April 22 at the Ypres Salient. The 1st Canadian Division, its principal victims, did not panic—as their French-Algerian neighbors had done—and the line, though flattened, remained unbroken. This shocking event, and the later German use of flame throwers, made us so credulous of German atrocity stories served up by official war correspondents that any compromise peace became unthinkable.

Our declared policy was now "attrition," meaning the daily and nightly bombardment of trenches to weaken enemy morale. That needed an unlimited supply of shells (but David Lloyd George, our new Minister of Munitions, saw to it) and, since the Germans might imitate our strategy, an unlimited supply of cannon fodder: namely, conscripts. We had suffered 500,000 casualties by the summer of 1915, and at the Battle of the Somme—Sir Douglas Haig's first attempt at a breakthrough—another 500,000. Yet he claimed (untruly) that our losses were inconsiderable compared with the Germans', and the Military Service Act soon swelled his command to a generous 1,500,000. Haig grudged the divisions sent away to "sideshows"—facing the Austrians in Italy, the Turks in Egypt, the Bulgarians in Greece—believed that the war could be won only on the western front, and wrote in his diary that Almighty God Himself seemed to guide whatever decisions he made.

The British despised Continental armies on the grounds that one volunteer was a match for four conscripts. But in a war of attrition, the volunteer's prowess was not often put to the test by hand-to-hand fighting. Besides, conscripts soon acquired the appearance of volunteers by wearing the same uniforms and sharing the same discomforts.

Each army in turn attempted the knockout punch: that glorious swing from hip to jaw. Each failed. The most unspeakably horrible, pointless, and costly campaign ever fought by British troops was Haig's 1917 offensive. He told the Cabinet that he had "no intention of entering into a tremendous offensive involving heavy loss," and told his Army commanders that "opportunities for the employment of cavalry in masses are likely to occur." Although warned by Engineer experts that prolonged shelling of the Ypres area would inevitably destroy the drainage system and return the land to swamp, he subjected the enemy trenches to a fortnight's bombardment: 4,500,000 shells. Even this failed to silence the German machine guns ensconced in concrete pillboxes on higher ground. We made gains of a few hundred yards, but the Engineers' prediction was fulfilled. The Passchendaele battlefield became a quagmire in which not only hundreds of men, but even mules, were drowned, guns disappeared, and to dig a trench was merely to create a canal. . . . Another 400,000 casualties; yet Haig was not superseded.

He had ridiculed tanks—a British invention—as impracticable toys, and lost their surprise effect on the Somme, in September, 1916, by wasting the first small consignment on a purely local gain. It was not until November 20, 1917, that he permitted a mass attack by 380 tanks across hard ground near Cambrai, without preliminary bombardment. They made an advance of 5 miles, breaking through to open country; but our cavalry were not alerted, and Haig, with no reserves left after Passchendaele, had proudly refused Foch's offer of a French Army corps to exploit the breach, which the Germans did not close for several hours.

This was the month of the Bolshevik Revolution, when Russia's armies ceased fighting. The Germans would soon be able to transfer 2,000,000 men from their eastern front to the west. Meanwhile, they further alienated themselves from the rest of the world by a more serious defiance of international law. Their submarines were ordered to torpedo merchant vessels on the high seas, including neutrals, without examining their cargoes or allowing the crews time to escape in lifeboats. They even sank hospital ships and justified this on the ground that our blockade had been starving children and noncombatants. Thus the United States was eventually brought into the war; but by April, 1917, the Allies lost nearly 1,000,000 tons of shipping each month, despite the 3,000 destroyers and other light craft allotted to submarine chasing. Fortunately, by autumn, the convoy system and American naval help had reduced these losses to 200,000 a month.

England was transformed. Rationing, for the first time in history: unbuttered muffins, wedding cakes without sugar. Golf links commandeered as drill grounds. Country houses turned into hospitals. Servant girls deserting ducal kitchens for the munitions factory. Class distinctions disappearing, as when wounded officers promoted from the ranks fell in love with aristocratic V.A.D. (Voluntary Aid Detachment) nurses. Zeppelin raids, and boy scouts blowing the all clear on bugles. Women enrolled as Army cooks, typists, *chauffeuses*: saluting like men, instead of curtsying. The universities taken over by cadet battalions. Expansion of the Royal Flying Corps and the Royal Naval Air Services into the world's largest air force, though suffering immensely high training losses, and without parachutes. War babies; hated war profiteers; despised conscientious objectors. An alarming increase in venereal disease. A sudden boom in poetry. . . .

We were now shouldering the heaviest burden of the war, America's new armies being still untrained and short of weapons; the French Army having mutinously refused any more offensives; and the Italians not having recovered from their fearful defeat at Caporetto. Attrition, attrition, attrition! One thousand men killed daily, and a daily 7,000,000 pounds of war debt. Trench life was as obsessive as alcohol. Only in the trenches did we feel free—from generals, staff officers, military police, drill sergeants, lead-swingers, journalists, civilian bores, patriots, or religious fanatics. . . . But continuous shell fire and the lesser nuisances of machine guns, trench mortars, rifle grenades so stimulated our adrenal glands that, after three months, we became mentally off-center; after six, certifiably insane. We welcomed an occasional ten days' leave but, if lightly wounded, soon grew bored with hospital and depot and schemed to get back again, our wounds half-healed. The trenches made us feel larger than life: only there was death a joke rather than a threat.

The better divisions, which could take up to 90 percent casualties without breaking, were thrown into every important attack. A soldier who had the honor to serve with one of them could count on no more than three months' trench service before being wounded or killed; a junior officer, on a mere six weeks. This difference was largely caused by the officer's being condemned, as an honorary horseman, to wear riding breeches and a swordless leather sword belt and thus to provide a tempting target for German marksmen.

We held two irreconcilable beliefs: that the war would never end and that we would win it. Eventually it was won, not by us infantrymen so much as by the naval blockade—which starved the Germans into surrender while still occupying Belgium and a great part of France. Their troops on the western front were withdrawing to the Rhine, but in excellent order, as even Haig admitted. They accepted an Armistice on November 11th, 1918, and peace was proclaimed in the following July.

At the Peace Conference attended by President Wilson, God, who made us mighty, made us mightier yet: on paper. The seizure of German colonies added immense new tracts to our Empire; but we had lost 1,000,000 dead, and as many permanently disabled, besides incurring some 5,000,000,000 pounds' worth of war debts. The Americans, who had sent 2,000,000 men to our rescue and lost 800,000, now led the world and were in a position to take over our lost foreign markets and turn their backs on Europe. Why not? The original quarrel had not been theirs. In May, 1920, the Senate refused to ratify the peace treaty signed by the President and, in 1921, withdrew their representative from the Council of Ambassadors at Paris, thus opting out of the Supreme Council at the League of Nations. The policing and rehabilitation of Germany were left to the French and us.

A generation later the Germans, driven to despair by the wreck of their sacred ambitions, made a second bid for world mastery. Although in Hitler's war our armies were commanded by prudent and capable infantry generals, the subsequent peace reduced us from a second-class power to a third-. We were forced at last to stop thinking like Romans and jettison all but a few fragments of our Empire. Thanks to the nuclear bomb, however, we have been spared a third world war and, in our quiet way, are sane again: prosperous, lively, inventive, and unresentful. Class distinctions have all but vanished; so has real poverty; we are seldom deceived by political handouts; religion is a matter of choice, not social pressure; and though oppressed by hordes of faceless bureaucrats, we have preserved our national liberty, our Crown, and our sense of humor. Nor have we yet forgotten our debt to the United States for having saved us, in Hitler's war, from an infinitely worse fate than the Kaiser ever threatened.

Myself, I value the Kaiser's war as having given me not only an unsurpassable standard of danger, discomfort, and horror by which to judge more recent troubles, but a confidence in the golden-heartedness and iron endurance of my fellow countrymen (proved again during Hitler's war), which even the laxity of this new plastic age cannot disturb.

Roland Dorgelès

In the eyes of World War I veterans, Roland Dorgelès is the writer who has best described their common memories, their courage, their misery, and fifty years after the war, his books have become pages of history. He may be said to symbolize a generation.

Born at Amiens in the Somme on June 15, 1885, prior to 1914 he led a happy, though often difficult, life in Montmartre which was later to inspire absorbing writings. But his destiny was cast, and suddenly, at the mobilization.

Classified as unfit to serve because of pulmonary illness by the draft board in 1906, and thus exempted from all military duty, he nonetheless enlisted in the infantry in August, 1914. Assigned to the 74th Infantry (Rouen), he asked to leave for the front immediately; and with neither the instruction nor the training that would have followed, he reached the combat zone at the beginning of September and was assigned to the 39th Infantry.

In the Artois attacks of June, 1915, he received the Croix de guerre with this first citation: "Remarkable asset to morale. Under heavy bombardment and though all his machine gunners were disabled, alone assured the functioning of his piece. Himself wounded, refused to be evacuated and continued to fire."

At the end of 1915, he was called into the Air Force. After a serious crash, he was assigned to the auxiliary forces and classified as definitively unfit, then appointed to be an instructor.

When he was discharged, in April, 1919, he published Les Croix de bois, a work that brought him immediate fame. Two years later, having brought out a second war book, Le Cabaret de la Belle Femme, he was made a chevalier of the Legion of Honor.

Since then, Dorgelès has published twenty volumes—novels, travel books, memoirs—all of which have proved to be resounding successes: Partir, La Caravane san chameaux, Vive la liberté, Sous le casque blanc, Bouquet de Bohème, Portraits sans retouche, Tout est à vendre, A Bas l'argent, and others.

Early during the Occupation several of his books were banned. The author was officially notified that the Germans would authorize the reprinting of these war books, provided certain cuts were made. He refused emphatically. Soon after the liberation, moreover, Dorgelès wrote Carte d'identité, describing how he was tracked by the Gestapo to the Haute-Garonne village where he had taken refuge and from which he had to flee after an inquiry.

Dorgelès was elected to the Académie Goncourt in 1929, to fill the seat left vacant by Georges Courteline, and succeeded Colette in the presidency of that body. He was made a grand officer of the Legion of Honor in 1962.*

---

* The Legion of Honor, the order of merit instituted by Napoleon in 1802, consists of the ranks (in ascending order) of chevalier (or knight), officer, commander, grand officer, and grand cross.—Tr.

AFTER FIFTY YEARS*

———◆———

FIFTY YEARS!

It has already been fifty years since the thunder of the shells fell silent, more than half a century since the war exploded upon a frightened world.

For us who lived those exalting hours, this past is very close. In the bat of an eyelid it rises again; the events are revived; faces that have disappeared are resurrected. This is a page of history we are unresigned to turning. Our musing leads us back to August, 1914. A terrible date in the young century.

For a week Paris had been living in a fever. We swung from anguish to hope in the wake of telegrams coming from the four corners of Europe:ultimatum to Serbia . . . the English intercede . . . Berlin refuses . . . appeal to The Hague . . . mobilization in Russia . . . state of war in Germany—then Saturday, August 1, in the afternoon, the suffocating time of storms, the terrible news broke like a lightning bolt.

"It's come! It's posted at the district mayor's office," a passerby shouted to me as he ran.

I reached the Rue Drouot in one leap and shouldered through the mob that already filled the courtyard to approach the fascinating white sheet pasted to the door. I read the message at a glance,

---

* Translated from the French by Sally Abeles.

then reread it slowly, word for word, to convince myself that it was true:

THE FIRST DAY OF
MOBILIZATION WILL BE
SUNDAY, AUGUST 2

Only three lines, written hastily by a hand that trembled. It was an announcement to a million and a half Frenchmen.

The people who had read it moved away, stunned, while others crowded in, but this silent numbness did not last. Suddenly a heroic wind lifted their heads. What? War, was it? Well, then, let's go! Without any signal, the "Marseillaise" poured from thousands of throats, sheafs of flags appeared at windows, and howling processions rolled out on the boulevards. Each column brandished a placard: ALSACE VOLUNTEERS, JEWISH VOLUNTEERS, POLISH VOLUNTEERS. They hailed one another above the bravos of the crowd, and this human torrent, swelling at every corner, moved on to circle around the Place de la Concorde, before the statue of Strasbourg banked with flowers, then flowed toward the Place de la République, where mobs from Belleville and the Faubourg St. Antoine yelled themselves hoarse on the refrain from the great days, *"Aux armes, citoyens!"* (To arms, citizens!) But this time it was better than a song.

To gather the news for my paper, I ran around the city in every direction. At the Cours la Reine I saw the fabled cuirassiers in their horsetail plumes march by, and at the Rue La Fayette footsoldiers in battle garb with women throwing flowers and kisses to them. In a marshaling yard I saw guns being loaded, their long, thin barrels twined around with branches and laurel leaves, while troops in red breeches piled gaily into delivery vans they were scrawling with challenges and caricatures. Young and old, civilians and military men burned with the same excitement. It was like a Brotherhood Day.

Dead tired but still exhilarated, I got back to *L'Homme libre* and burst into the office of Georges Clemenceau, our chief.[1]

"What is Paris saying?" he asked me.

"It's singing, sir!"

"Then everything will be all right. . . ."

His old patriot's heart was not wrong; no cloud marred that fabulous day. Yet anything could have happened. The workers,

---

1 *L'Homme libre* (The Free Man) was but one of several periodicals Clemenceau founded and directed during his long political career.—Tr.

overwhelmed by Jean Jaurès' death,[2] might demand revenge. The day before, a few minutes after the attack, I had leaned over the eloquent leader's body, stretched out on two marble-top tables at the Croissant Bar; I had read the anger in the faces of the workers who had surged out of the neighboring printshops. A word, a gesture and there would have been a riot; but an associate of Jaurès', standing in the vehicle where they were laying the tall body, exhorted the men, many of whom were weeping, to contain their rage, and heads lowered, teeth clenched, they watched in silence as the first death of the war was carried away in the night.

Less than twenty-four hours later, seeing their old dreams of peace crumble, they would stream out into the boulevards to demonstrate. But this time they would break into the "Marseillaise," not the "Internationale"; they would cry, "To Berlin!," not "Down with war!"

What did they have to defend, these black-nailed patriots? Not even a shack, an acre to till, indeed hardly a patch of ground reserved at the Pantin Cemetery; yet they would depart, like their rivals of yesterday, a heroic song on their lips and a flower in their guns. No more poor or rich, proletarians or bourgeois, right-wingers or militant leftists; there were only Frenchmen.

Beginning the next day, thousands of men eager to fight would jostle one another outside recruiting offices, waiting to join up. Men who could have stayed home, with their wives and children or an imploring mama. But no. The word "duty" had a meaning for them, and the word "country" had regained its splendor.

I close my eyes, and they appear to me, those volunteers on the great day; then I see them again in the old kepi or blue helmet, shouting, "Here!" when somebody called for men for a raid, or hurling themselves into an attack with fixed bayonets, and I wonder, and I question their bloody shades.

Tell me, comrades in eternal silence, would you have besieged the enlistment offices with the same enthusiasm, would you have fought such a courageous fight had you known that fifty years later those men in gray knit caps or steel helmets you were ordered to kill would no longer be enemies and that we would have to open our arms to them? Wouldn't the heroic "Let's go!" you shouted as you cleared the parapets have stuck in your throats? Deep in the grave where you dwell, don't you regret your sacrifice? "Why did we fight? Why did we let ourselves get killed?" This is the murmur of a million and a half voices rising from the bowels of the earth, and we, the survivors, do not know what to answer.

---

2 French Socialist, politician, and labor figure.—Tr.

Were they dupes, then, the men who valiantly offered themselves to the massacre? Were they being gulled when they were taught from childhood that dying for their country was the noblest of fates? Must we trample down the frontiers for which they were killed? Does duty continuously change meaning, depending on how the whimsical wind blows? So many questions we don't dare ask those heads with empty sockets. I would like to cry out to them, "No, your sacrifice was not in vain! Your valiance saved not only your country but the entire universe, which Germany would have crushed under her iron heel; the final victory is only an offspring of yours, and the great men of our time remain in your debt." But what would be the use? You don't console the dead with speeches. . . .

Taught by the events, we know today that we must forget. France and Germany are penned up in Europe like animals in a cage; if they do not come to terms, they will eat into each other till the end of time. Even if the heart is mute, reason gives us the word: We must cross out the years of war and occupation. Yes, I want to forget.

But the others, whose young mouths are sealed forever, who gave their lives to take a scrap of French soil back from the enemy, would they also be forgiving?

I feel no hatred for the hardy fighters whom I saw with my own eyes fire a shot or throw a grenade at me—they were tending to their terrible trade, as I to mine—but are all our dead equally at peace? I ask this question of my cousin, whom I went to dig up with my hands near Château-Thierry. He had a black hole in the back of his neck: the mark of the bullet fired from behind, coward fashion, when he had just been taken prisoner. Would you hold out your hand, your skeleton of a hand, to your murderer?

And you, gentle René Blum, you, proud François de Tessan, my closest friends, dead in Nazi camps, would you have the funereal courage to murmur, "Enough, let's be friends"?

All of us, of course, have had men before us who were not brutes. To allay my bitterness, I will evoke that bloodless wounded man our stretcher-bearers put down in front of the colonel's quarters late one night. His raiding party had slipped noiselessly up to our barbed wire, a handkerchief tied around their arms so as not to kill each other in the dark, and when they reached our zigzag trench they leaped at it shouting. This one had slumped over our parapet, wounded in the belly, and now, motionless under the brown blanket, he had stopped groaning. As the stretcher-bearers waited for his last breath, he made an effort and opened his eyes once more and begged in a hollow voice, "I want to die looking toward my country." A liaison officer who understood German translated, and lifting the dying man by the shoulders, my comrades, holding back their tears, propped him up facing his lines. The last flares were fading in the gray sky. He looked at that pale frontier a long moment, and then, murmuring perhaps a good-bye, he fell back heavily. We did not have to close his eyes. . . .

Along with him, I recall another. Not dying, this one; not even wounded. Quite sound, in fact, and almost provocative. Captured between the lines when he was on patrol, he had been taken to the colonel to be interrogated. He had been brought up in a school in Neuilly and spoke our language perfectly, but he refused to answer. He was asked what regiments were in his sector: "I don't know." Whether reinforcements were coming in: "I don't know." Whether they were digging attack trenches, whether the Brimont artillery was changing its emplacements: "I don't know." The colonel finally got angry: "If you don't speak, I'll have you shot!" The threat did not shake the prisoner. Then, shifting his tactics, our chief broke off a chunk of the still warm bread the orderly had just brought from the neighboring village and held it out to him: "It's good, huh, the bread of France. It makes your mouth water. Here, eat!"

The hungry soldier stood at attention. "Thank you, Colonel, I like black bread better. . . ."

Can we despise such men? Can we impute the crimes of the swastikaed butchers to them? I ask myself this uneasily; I ask it of my comrades of *Les Croix de bois,* the wooden crosses,[3] who fought at my side. Of my gunner pal, a Norman kid, I remember, who when the mist suddenly dissipated on the Loire plain spotted some men on fatigue duty in the German lines. Thinking they were invisible, they had come out of the communication trench to go faster and were moving toward their own trench across open ground.

"Fire! Mow them down!" our lieutenant ordered.

The gunner hesitated a second, then said resolutely, "No, Lieutenant. They aren't armed. You don't fire at sitting ducks."

The officer insisted, threatened, spoke of refusing to obey orders. Nothing worked. Our stubborn gunner had his concept of war and would not fire on defenseless men. The Germans, seeing they had been discovered, took to their heels and leaped into a sap. Do you know, poor Prussian or Bavarian devils, that if you are still alive, you owe it to this obstinate *Franzose* who risked a court-martial for you?

I could give other examples like these. Christmas night when Frenchmen and Germans on patrol came together between the

---

[3] Roland Dorgelès, *Les Croix de bois,* Paris, A. Michel, 1919; *Wooden Crosses,* G. P. Putnam's Sons, New York, 1921.—Ed.

lines, rifles slung on shoulders, and shook one another's hands and exchanged greetings they did not understand. Headquarters denounced these attempts to fraternize and threatened severe reprisals. On the German side the repressive measures were undoubtedly worse. Yet these soldiers were not mutineers who refused to fight. They proved it six weeks later in a savage attack which left hundreds of corpses on the ground. Perhaps the very ones who had shaken one another's hands Christmas night. . . .

To gird my loins, I appeal to the dead. To Edmond Adam, a clerk in the bridges and roads department, an infantry enlistee, a simple engineer they had made into a lieutenant, killed in Champagne at the end of the war. Between hard drives he scribbled poems in his shelter, and if they are unknown, I have not forgotten them. This one especially, which he dedicated to a combatant across from him:

> I bear you little ill will, you know,
> It's four years you've done your bit
> Behind your lookout slit. . . .
> Well, us, too, it's four years we've worked
> To knit these great meshes of nets
> And cut them the eve of attacks,
> To get through and chase you
> From your trenches.
> You see, we are neighbors,
> Almost buddies, in our labors.
> We sweat for rival houses.
> Agh! Maybe they deserve each other,
> Nobody knows. . . .

"Buddies," he wrote the word. . . . This one, I'm sure, would be forgiving.

Doubtless I haven't his greatness of soul: I still hesitate. The hand I would like to extend stays in a fist in my pocket. Not from the memory of my own wrath but from the thought of those who cursed them in agony. "You do not have the right," they could say in reproach.

This idea tormented me when I found myself in Berlin shortly before the last war. I had been invited to the final meeting of a veterans' conference presided over by the Duke of Saxe-Coburg-Gotha, and after a speaker had sounded my praises, I was pushed to the rostrum. Not wanting, not able, to talk of reconciliation to them, I said:

"As you have just been told, I belong to a generation which left its fields, its factories, its desks, its schools in August of 1914 to run for the frontier shouting, 'To Berlin!' " Here I paused a moment. Then: "Excuse me for getting to the appointment twenty-two years late."

They could have taken this as braggadocio and booed me, but General von Armin, seated in the first row, gave the signal for applause, and everyone followed.

I looked down on those aging men from the dais and thought I recognized them. Weren't they the same men, with their scars and campaign ribbons, whom I found each spring in the Invalides chapel attending the mass for my regiment? Yes, "neighbors, almost buddies, in our labors," the poet wrote.

Like us, they ran in frenzy through the flag-decked avenues of Munich and Hamburg in August, 1914, waving banners, brandishing placards. Their "Marseillaise" was the "Deutschland über Alles," and instead of shouting, "À Berlin!" they yelled, "Nach Paris!" The two roads led to the same slaughterhouse. . . .

They, too, fifty years later, must be questioning themselves about their reasons for fighting, and weighing the wasteful horror of those massacres. They, too, must be wondering at this moment whether our two countries are condemned to hate each other eternally and repay their ruins with the ruin of the neighbor. So I make an effort; I try to tender this resisting hand. I force myself to believe that men of my age have understood the last wars, that tomorrow's nations, reconciled at last, will form only a single great bloc, united for peaceful pursuits. I repeat to myself: "Brothers all!" I write it to convince myself of it.

But I love my country too much to accept the notion that it can lose its identity and become merely a district in a flat-faced Europe. I want it always to be as it was in the geography book of my boyhood, a pretty rose color, scored with blue rivers, protected by dark mountains, and wearing a mourning band along the border showing the lost provinces we were to liberate. Nothing can obliterate this map etched in me. So too do I remain loyal to the history of glorious events we marveled at, and so am I proud that men of my age added to it a chapter worthy of the past.

And if all peoples must dissolve one day in a uniform mold where they will blend together, I cling to the hope that centuries and centuries from now teachers will still read to children, like a fairy tale, "Once upon a time, between the Rhine and the Atlantic, there was a valiant little country which was called France."

The Fighting Fronts

Edmund Blunden

EDMUND BLUNDEN, the son of Charles Edmund Blunden, schoolmaster, and Georgina Margaret Blunden, née Tyler, was born in London on November 1, 1896. He was educated at Christ's Hospital School and Queen's College, Oxford. Serving in the Royal Sussex (infantry) Regiment in World War I from 1915 to 1919, he was awarded the Military Cross in 1916.

He was professor of English from 1924 to 1927 in the University of Tokyo, and returned to Japan to be cultural adviser with the British Liaison Mission, in Tokyo, from 1947 to 1950. The Order of the Rising Sun, Third Class, was conferred on him in Japan. From 1930 to 1943 he was a fellow of Merton College, Oxford, and from 1953 to 1964 he was professor of English in the University of Hong Kong. For his distinguished accomplishments he was made a C.B.E. (Commander of the British Empire).

His first publications were small collections of verse, Poems 1913–1914, The Harbingers (1916), and Pastorals (1916). The Waggoner (1920) and The Shepherd (1922) made his name known; for The Shepherd he was given the Hawthornden Prize. Of many other volumes the latest is A Hong Kong House (1962).

The best known of his prose books is Undertones of War (1928). He assisted his former wife, Sylvia Norman, in an experiment called We'll Shift Our Ground: Almost a Novel (1933). His many literary biographies include those of Charles Lamb, Shelley, Leigh Hunt, Keats' publisher (John Taylor), and Thomas Hardy. Miscellaneous essays were collected in The Mind's Eye and Votive Tablets. He published many works chiefly for Japanese readers in Japan.

In 1945 Mr. Blunden married Claire Margaret Poynting; they have four daughters, and live in Long Melford, Suffolk. He has written a short guide to its much admired ancient church.

INFANTRYMAN PASSES BY

I

In the early months of 1941 I was very little concerned with world affairs, except that my mother used sometimes to caution us under the rubric "when you go out into the world" which we told her meant at the moment the small market town 2 or 3 miles off. The scene of her repeated admonition was the schoolhouse in a very small village in Sussex, in the south of England, within comfortable reach—by bicycle—of the seacoast and above all the enchantments of "London by the Sea," Brighton. Heroic expeditions to that city with all its huge hotels and piers and fashion parades along the seafront were sometimes managed, but my leadership could only be infrequent and while I was on holiday from my school.

The school was in the same county of Sussex and also inland, about as far away from the sea as our village, and that geographical detail used to matter in one's feelings. It is strange now to think what a distance lay between the schoolhouse and the English Channel in a sense of security (Napoleon having gone away) and equally between Christ's Hospital, Horsham, and those waters. That noble foundation had been removed from its ancient premises near St. Paul's Cathedral, in London, to the former estate of the poet Shelley's family near sleepy Horsham in Sussex. It was (and is) a magnificent, mighty school, but the scholars were by charter boys whose parents were poor, though not all of the same social degrees. In 1914 I had been at this school, which is known for such literary representatives as S. T. Coleridge and Charles Lamb and for all sorts of others in all walks of life, for six years and was on the staircase to the university. Lucky boys could look to Oxford or Cambridge in particular as they rose in classes in the school and could count on school exhibitions so long as at the finish they carried off university scholarships. Those would usually be concerned with classics or mathematics. They were worth about seventy or eighty pounds a year—amazing opulence!—or "just enough."

All at school went happily, occasionally hungrily, in most pastoral alluring surroundings and in an air well blending ancient and modern. There was a clear division between two tracks of education—classical and modern. A boy had to be placed, on his entering the school, in one of these two sides. My father firmly replied, "Classical," to the headmaster's question on my first appearing, and probably that decision affected the unexpected experiences which were to follow. I missed, for instance, except for a few terms, the German classes, though French somehow was a stylish study abundantly available. That perhaps was due to an eager enthusiasm on the part of some masters for French literature and particularly French poetry. "Modern" boys seemed rather to be involved in a commercial language.

Our acceptance of anything in classrooms can be imagined, and equally of our daily life altogether, well occupied from the early waking bell to the evening prayers called duty, and I must here note the description of our school, "The religious, royal and ancient foundation of Christ's Hospital"—the temper of the place was distinctive. After nearly 400 years it could hardly be otherwise, even though we had been transplanted from town to country, wisely no doubt. The peace of the boys' lives would have been the same in the buildings of the old Greyfriars in London. These "echoing cloisters pale," which are celebrated in a poem by Coleridge, remained, and they still do, as the calm pathway of the learned youths at the head of the school.

I have spoken of the peace which quite simply ruled our lives in our very orderly school, with its centuries of family spirit and useful duty continuing, and our Tudor uniform, the blue coats and yellow stockings, seeming to express a particular unity and concord among us; but there was one matter which did not harmonize, or so I used to feel in 1914. It looked to me as an influence directing the world, in its limited way, out of the paths of peace. All the boys—this was a recent ordinance—at quite an early age were required to become members of an officers training corps. This "fine body of men" regularly paraded in accurate khaki uniform and often went afield for sham fights, charging over fields and up hillsides and letting off some noisy blank ammunition and generally trying to imagine what war itself would be like. From time to time these young warriors were paraded on the playing fields and inspected by a real general, who perhaps made a speech at the conclusion and might utter a view which I confess seemed to me a gloomy, even horrible view: We were not just playing soldiers; we should be "wanted." At school camp, in the holidays, with its diversions and realistic excitements, that note could be heard even without speeches. "You'll be a man, my son."

As the year 1914 wore on, the newspapers in the dayroom made us aware of troubles in Ireland which were regarded as capable of bringing on a fighting war, but for most of the busy little readers the political side of that crisis was too difficult. Presently, far away it was and seemed, a brutal assassination in some strange capital came into the news. To interpret its consequences was beyond us, but the occurrence was not to be forgotten in a moment or two even while our beautiful peace and our almost untiring industry and great events like cricket cup ties and swimming sports went on. The summer holidays came into the prospect, and sunshine seemed likely to abound. Our military carbines would soon be stacked away in the armory, and our blue clothes, which made us rather conspicuous, except I suppose in London, could be exchanged for less antique and ornamental clothes at home.

We had our meals in the great dining hall, and at the midday meal the housemasters would take their places at the top of the long tables. One day my own senior housemaster came in, and as he sat down, with a curious ambiguous look, he said in a quiet way, "Well, boys, it looks as though within a month the whole of Europe will be at war." This from him was something to be taken seriously, and it was. But I do not remember that any of us had any spoken comment to make. We were not prophets. In a way not all of us were surprised. But perhaps things would take another turn, and we had plenty on our hands—the immediate trouble was probably how to borrow a bicycle for the next enchanting Sunday afternoon ride through the rich byways of Sussex.

> Beat! beat! drums!—blow! bugles! blow!
> Through the windows—through doors—burst like a ruthless force,
> Into the solemn church, and scatter the congregation,
> Into the school where the scholar is studying:
> Leave not the bridegroom quiet—no happiness must he have now
>   with his bride,
> Nor the peaceful farmer any peace, ploughing his field or gathering
>   his grain,
> So fierce you whirr and pound you drums—so shrill you bugles blow.

When World War I was declared, Walt Whitman's poems of 1861 did not obviously correspond to all that happened within my own observation in England in 1914, but they describe the effect of all as the new age established itself on our old world. When the diplomats gave up their riddle, and the word "ultimatum" had become like the last trumpet or nearly, I was at home in our gentle village, and for a time—it would have been "invasion country" if any were—there was excitement. My father even declared his intention of confronting any invaders at his front door, not the back door. The cleverest of all rumors was widely believed—the Russian Army, having dealt with Germany, would shortly be over the Channel and dealing with the United Kingdom. Meanwhile, some of our untalkative farm laborers and tradespeople quietly disappeared from the scene, having "jowned up" in one of the services or another. And some young men who had come home from business desks for summer holidays, masters of the great world, suddenly looked quite as brilliant in well-fitting uniforms.

Weeks were soon drifting by, and I could do much as I liked, discovering other villages, catching carp, reading and writing—and always listening to some wiseacre announcing that the war would be over by Christmas. The war somehow dodged our observation very annoyingly. Summer holidays passed, and great victories went to sleep again, and wearisome new songs drew attention to sewing socks for soldiers or the long way to Tipperary. I was now writing verses with great eagerness, but not often on the war; what was near at hand usually started me off, and a friendly bookseller in Shelley's old town was so kind as to print a little volume or two for me, which at least kept me from thinking too long about the prospect for those of my age. The poems by the older generation in periodicals which I came upon were mostly admonitions to us to join the forces at once and be killed with all cheerfulness. The penalties invented for not doing these things were severe:

> What will you lack, sonny, what will you lack
>   When the girls line up the street,
> Shouting their love to the lads come back
>   From the foe they rushed to beat?
> Will you send a strangled cheer to the sky
>   And grin till your cheeks are red?
> But what will you lack when your mates go by
>   With a girl who cuts you dead?

However, it was decided that the boys at our school who were working for places in the universities should complete their courses, which meant staying with one's books until the summer of 1915. The girls whom I knew did not punish me for that or present me with white feathers, as was a reported fashion of those days.

On a glorious day that August I got out my bicycle for a longish ride across our county to Chichester, where the renowned Royal Sussex Regiment had its headquarters. I was equipped with papers which were to support my application for His Majesty's commission, and however dusty I was on arrival, the guard received me in the dignified way of an ancient regiment. A less bellicose place could hardly be imagined, and there seemed hardly any soldiers in it, but one was deputed to lead me to the major in charge of the barracks that day. He, too, put me at my ease at once, and I began to think the war was remarkably friendly after all. He told me to go over to the sergeant major and get him to run a tape measure round my chest and then come back for a drink and lunch. What promotion! The sequel perhaps a fortnight after was my receiving a commission and the outfit allowance—fifty pounds in that period was liberal. It easily covered the price—incidentally—of a sword.

Wearing this embarrassing romantic weapon, before many days I was traveling with other new subalterns to a training outfit at Weymouth, and still it was a pleasant war. We rose early for physical training on the beach, which exercise was broken off one morning by news that the British Army on the western front had made a successful attack at a place called Loos. It might be true; anyway it ended boredom, and following days gave the skeptics their opportunity. Altogether we were enjoying Weymouth without the holiday multitude when our orders arrived for doing something somewhere else, and I was one of those consigned to a large camp on the Sussex coast. We were so many that there were not enough "other ranks" for us to play at officering, and the medical officer was exceedingly sympathetic in excusing us from duty, which let us disappear into joyous Brighton—or I would sometimes walk home, 20 miles, in those days.

Some of the second lieutenants in my hut had seen a bit of active service and had their curious experiences to tell, but not much about the small battles which I heard of as making life miserable on the western front. The idea of everybody seemed to be to recite more outrageous limericks and ballads than anybody else. Lectures and exercises there were indeed, but it was argued that nothing in training was in the least like the actual war, so why worry? I was permitted without interference to collect around my bed a library of books, some even of the eighteenth century, the spoils of Brighton bystreets. These, however, could not go with me on the next stage of this odd indolent training—toward the end of 1915 the young officers found themselves crossing a very angry midnight Irish Sea. The destination was not many miles from Cork, a park with a large ruined mansion and plenty of huts, a rifle range, and very nice surrounding scenery.

Other arrangements had not been completed, and for some days the most enterprising officers were searching the country for supplies; I remember one of the plumpest of them driving some fat pigs into camp; it was surprising how soon the amateur organization for food and drink was working. We were in this place, we gathered, partly because of the state of Ireland and partly so as to be trained in earnest by some powerful Guardsmen, one of whom was soon nicknamed the Human Machine Gun. It came out that we were to take at an early date an examination: To fail would be, perhaps, not to be shot at dawn; to succeed would mean to be sent promptly to that almost forgotten place, the western front. So (and there were other reasons) night schemes were better attended now than in the region of Brighton, England.

In this camp, it is curious but pleasant to recall, I had quite an allowance of talk about the English poets, ancient and modern. The bed next to mine was occupied by one of the descendants of Keats' friend Richards, a learned reader indeed. Then one evening I was surprised and just a shade frightened by a message from the adjutant, desiring me to go see him. The reason was that he had heard something of my scribbling verses at the expense of some prominent personalities in the camp, which he even applauded, and soon we fell into serious discourse on poetry. He could quote very choicely, and his taste then was for the sadder tones:

O to recall—
What to recall?

or "Through the dark postern of time long elapsed. . . ." I never saw Gordon Reah after this Irish episode, though once in the ramparts of Ypres in Belgium I had an affectionate note from him, and I did my utmost to get along the chaos and see him—but the attempt failed. It was an event, by the way, when I bought an edition of some of Tom Moore's Irish songs in Fermoy for one penny, "as new."

Early spring over southern Ireland and our songs as we ventured on the River Blackwater were disputing poetic rights in my mind when, having passed the threatened examination, I was with many friends on the way back to England, and once again the destination was that vast camp at Shoreham. This time I was given a daily job, marching a company of convalescent soldiers anywhere out of the way. They would not talk, though they were most amiable and humble, of their war. So I was still in the dark about it, more or less, when I found my name on the notice board in the mess among those of subalterns who would "proceed" to the British Expeditionary Force in two or three days. I should have been noisily glad, of course, but—some other time!

II

The scene has changed indeed, and the month is May (1916).
With two other young officers who have been on training with me, I
am finding my way about in a quiet sector of the western front (but
it has seen its bitter fighting) with one of our county battalions. A
few miles east of these trenches (most of them are more or less
passages between low embankments of sandbags) there is the big
city of Lille, but except for hearing the city-hall clock strike
midnight (or so we believe), it does not enter into our thoughts.
Our landscape is flat, mostly, agricultural, and after nearly two
years of war something of a wilderness. Here and there as we near
the firing line we find a permanent-looking machine-gun emplacement built largely of brick, and the company headquarters look
solid enough; but we also see a few ruins to suggest that artillery
can swiftly obliterate such shelters.

The cheerfulness and attention to detail of those already experienced infantrymen with whom I now was have sounded on through
my life as a simple music of an excellent old England. Even allusions to the Germans facing us over shattered fruit trees, deserted
farm roads, hedges of crowded barbed wire, were quiet in tone and
in thought. The ordinary references were to the Alleymans, Jerry,
or Fritz. Even the two machine guns which were the greatest
nuisance, at night, from the German strongpoints had nicknames.
As for firing, at that time and place the artillery took only a share
now and then; but there was a strange and unforgettable performance from the rifles of both sides as day broke. Every man who
had ammunition, on both sides, seemed to join in a great wave of
shooting across no-man's-land, which swelled up and traveled along
the line for ten minutes or a quarter of an hour and died down.
This meant that about a mile behind the trenches the oddest noises
of bullets swishing over or spinning from anything they hit surrounded us, walking from keep to dump, and the puzzle was, so far
as we could observe, how seldom they caused casualties.

Danger there was in less obvious forms or methods. The firing
lines twisted about so that often the enemy was able to look into a
stretch of the other trenches, and from the snipers' posts a deadly
shot might find its mark at any time. This uncertainty led to a
superstitious quality in otherwise steady enough coming and going.
The sun might glow long hours on a peaceful, even drowsy scene,
but something was always lurking besides those frogs with their
nightlong croaking and the more detested myriads of mosquitoes

also claiming their ancient rights to the swampy pools. So, when it began to be remarked that the battalion was due to be relieved, and actually some officers and men had been named as an advance party to go back and arrange the company's billets, there was a slightly anxious thankfulness among us all, not simply owing to a need of rest. Nor was monotony quite the cause.

At that date, long-range firing was not much tried, and billets in small towns or villages were pleasant places, with the luxury of *estaminets* almost able to vie with the locals in England as scenes of mild refreshment and many anecdotes. But the war was not to be kept away even from rest areas, and often within a few hours of arrival in a more or less comfortable barn its requirements changed the outlook. Finding guards, for example, and drill and training almost caused revolutions, but no: Much worse things could happen. There was "something in the air." Raids were perhaps being thought out, and indeed one of those operations on a grimly large scale was staged by the whole brigade with a great display of grenades, guns, trench mortars—and all to no purpose.

This attack was of the kind sometimes called Chinese attacks, or feints, and occurred on the day before the French and British armies began the Battle of the Somme, many miles south; its object was thought to have been the deceiving of the Germans into keeping some of their artillery away from that huge challenge, awaiting a new stroke in the north of the long line. Our battlefield adjoined the remains of the village Neuve-Chapelle, then famous as the objective of a greater assault a year and more earlier. But what was more conspicuous to our eyes, looking over the top of our breastwork front line for some days, was a gloomy wood, the Bois du Biez, with a few innocent-looking cottages along its hitherward edge, and in some way a legend emanated and circulated that this solid deep-green wood had been entered by British troops before in a "censured" attack and not a man had come out of it.

Still, the new assault. . . . A beautiful darkness ended, a sweet morning began, and there were some of us in a recognizable brewery ruin, waiting for the wonders. Right on the moment the flashes and thunders of our (then not too frightful) artillery began, and instantly from eastward quite an equivalent amazed us; where had been silence there seemed endless supplies of death, flame, and noise. We were saved at the moment in a small tunnel which the enemy himself had dug long ago. Then the slow day began; the poor chaps who were crossing no-man's-land and some of them carrying wooden bridges to defeat the deep drains dividing fields of rye or even tobacco, apart from "the wire," were stopped. Some hobbled and crawled home at last, as horrified by what they had seen happen to men (of whatever nation) as had almost happened to them. Their clothing and equipment told that part of the story. "And I live."

The June day grew quieter, and the sinister wood kept its secret. It seemed as though the Germans had forgotten the episode, but perhaps they had merely taken away the batteries that were to have been detained. Our front line had been, in spite of knocks, kept scrupulously neat, almost domesticated; now it was punched shapeless, scarcely passable, but in those days the farmlands which it traversed had their harmless look still, apart from some ancient deserted trenches with a reputation for horrors, mysteries.

All this may be termed in its context elementary education. So too other passages in that summer of siege warfare slightly revised. Hamlet commented some time earlier that:

> . . . 'tis the sport to have the engineer
> Hoist with his own petard

and I believe he was alluding to the kind of war fought by the tunnelers with the cooperation of us footsoldiers, probably never again to achieve its vast, infernal perfections. Our chief observation of that kind of fighting came when we were sent into the line one side or another of the canal from Béthune to La Bassée (unprovocative little towns with Marlborough's wars of two centuries before haunting them quite without ghostly representatives in 1916). Here the landscape was fierce in a glaring sunlight, and industrial buildings in ruin hovered through the haze. When we took over a section of the parching front line, I talked with a philosophical engineer officer who remarked on the number of German mines known or suspected to be in construction underneath these trenches. And we, it was presumed, would have to occupy the place for a fortnight! In the end we emerged from that region and the one on the far side of the canal with mere examples of what might happen; we had had one small mine blown by the Germans underneath us, but a little short of a length, and had taken part in a loud bombing dispute following our own sappers' exploding a "small mine" again, defensively, toward the enemy position. The first incident on a night streaming with rain and resounding and lanterning with scores of shellbursts was a bad one. "It might have been worse," but even Germans miscalculated. I remember that I had to make my way from our headquarters in a shaky brick cellar along glistening, soaked trenches I had never seen, and to find the real way after so many shells, until I was trying to say a word to a dying man, whose quiet manner by the dark canal bank was beyond any words then or now.

We grew, you may say cynically, accustomed to having things of this kind befall us, until we had seen many miles of the northward front line of the British Expeditionary Force and knew the unnatural history of numbers of death-dealing "aerial torpedoes"—the word may serve for a whole genus of larger and smaller monsters—better than that of the rats who shared our trenches and equipment and evaded revolver shots in miraculous fashion. We had spells of emancipation, and out of the trenches an officer had a right to an actual bedroom and a humpy but exquisitely clean bed in a cottage or perhaps a mansion. The summer of 1916 almost made it a throne. The real throne was perhaps the incomparable loving-kindness of all, officers and all, who lived and worked so much together, grumbling away at times, seeing past the war yet never judging their own fate. "The British Army will all go home in one boat." . . . "When this war ends, we shall see four blue lights go up." "No, mate, four black lights." . . . "Here they come again, throwing gun and all at us." . . . "They were shooting at our post with iron foundries." . . . "Wind favorable for whizbangs, Jim?" The last was a mild joke on the gas warnings, "wind favorable" and the rest, which had become an ordinary part of the soldier's reading hereabouts.

To the next phase of our campaigning I shall not devote so much detail; the bewildering Battle of the Somme has been so often copiously described. We marched south toward it in golden weather and through what might have been described as France at peace. The roads were all cobblestone roads, and after our months in the mud of trenches the feet of many high-spirited soldiers were low-spirited; we passed the Guards marching equally, and indeed in the splendid heat and along those stone roads even they also seemed to be weary. We reached our attack area after an interval of rehearsals in a woodland and plowland place west of Arras, said to be a facsimile of our assigned "over the top." If it was, it was no help in the frantic realities of the day when it came, then called Z day. The village which gave us a home during our exercises was perfect eighteenth century, a peasant picturesque dream, in Corot's country. But soon, onward into a solitude; there the inhabitants had been withdrawn, and our position in a dusky wood was not only gas-scented but ghost-ridden—the sense of some intolerable presences had nothing to do with us, presumably, but that wood was deadly in gunfire fact and in some other way. Mailly Wood.

From here or near it the first of our three main ordeals in the Somme battles was begun. Begun, but the misery of being ordered up to the line and sent back for postponement was repeated a time or two. The first actual attack on a glowing autumn day—it opened before daylight and hardly a man had any chance of knowing the ups and downs of the hollow to be crossed on the way to the enemy's line—was an obliteration. It was completely mysterious; the troops just disappeared. Perhaps the Germans' deep dugouts, especially those under a railway embankment on our right, were too many for the bombers especially. No message came from those merry boys, no acknowledgment of new supplies of hand grenades. Further, as we were on the little hills sloping toward the Ancre River's north side, the German guns on the hills opposite, their destruction of the unlucky British infantry attacking there having been easy for them, had no trouble in switching to us, and the network camouflage over our little slit trenches soon vanished, and our headquarters were simple targets.

So we were "a complete failure," and there were miles of that; but southward the armies made some progress over the most terrifying devastated area perhaps ever yet seen on our planet. I remember coming in sight of it for the first time; gunnery had extinguished every sign of life every step to the horizon and left a specimen of a world without a God. But the battle went on. We were used as a holding battalion, securing miles of front, as the autumn also went on. Late in October our function changed, and we again attacked. "We" now meant almost a new battalion, so many reinforcements had been called for, poor fellows, many of whom made their short acquaintance with modern war in the moment of mad battle itself. They largely fell in the next two days. The battle took place in white frost and began in full daylight. Underfoot was mud or corpses. We somehow gained Stuff Trench, and such was its desolation that the battalion relieving us (they had to be led in almost individually) hated it and us, too (a rare thing).

November brought clammy fogs and deeper mud, besides war itself, and a third attack was required of us. It was successful! The Germans were betrayed by their enormous deep dugouts. But nothing much came of that. The *Sommeschlacht* (Battle of the Somme) was somehow wearing out. It had introduced the tanks to the fighting man's world. We saw some examples, heard of their wonders, and dragged ourselves along. Then one night our grand colonel for once spoke out and said that we were to be taken out of the Somme battle, immediately. And we were—those who then made up "we"—and again were men marching, with even our band playing us into unspoiled Doullens (the stretcher-bearers formed the band) . Where were we going?

North this time, to a city with a glory about it but also an air of mortality—Ypres in Belgium. Of course, in incurable ruins, but serviceable as the stronghold of the Ypres Salient, a pattern of trenches of all sorts defying any advance of the German powers that way to the Channel ports. It had been tolerably quiet during 1916 but was constantly under observation and frequently under heavy fire. It was managed by the British garrison in a businesslike way, thanks especially to the ancient ramparts which guarded the gray, lifeless city on the east side. They are still standing over the lovely moat, which even in war was beautiful with swans. They conceal many spacious excavations, usually safe protections, in our time—at any time since perhaps the Romans held outposts here.

But we had no leisure or inspiration to think of other legions in Flanders. A dismal and painful winter was seizing the Ypres Salient when we rather amazedly arrived. Going out of the place to the area of Hill 60 on reconnaissance, my dear Sergeant Wally Ashford, walking with me through a grove of skeleton trees, remarked, with his ambiguous grin, "Looks just like the Somme . . . well, rather worse." It bore the strange title Sanctuary Wood. It had been no sanctuary to generations of doomed young soldiers of several nationalities.

Intense winter ended the year 1916 in those parts and went on without mercy until sudden kind spring poured sunshine over the snow and ice. Fighting and digging had gone on, but now that mercy seemed to descend, it was apparent that the year 1917 was to produce war of a new ferocity and, as many ordinary soldiers thought, futility. The name Passchendaele is inscribed on that page of war history. It was intended at first that, from Ypres, the low ridge of Passchendaele and other uninteresting farmland round it should be captured in the spring. The ridge was said to overlook the English Channel, and if it did, it could not worry the British Navy. But it had a good view, and so did other low uplands, of everything in or around mutilated Ypres. A further intention of the battle was to advance as far as Ostend.

"That agony returns." On July 31 the worst and most hated of the British offensives was begun, against all reason, all around or nearly all around Ypres. Reason had had no luck for weeks before; the preparations, including new roads and railways everywhere into the forward area, had been fantastically shown off, as though the Germans would be scared by the exhibition. The farmlands over which we were to advance had been drained in former times with minute care, and now that honest, wise labor was all lost with the increasing bombardments—and the weather. It was well known that at the end of July Flanders weather almost inevitably became foul.

On July 31 then, as the darkness was dying, the Passchendaele battle began with an orgy of gunfire and of machine-gun barrages which I thought noisier than all the artillery, and on our share of the line we were surprised to get across entanglements and tattered trenches without extraordinary difficulty. We soon found the concrete blockhouses which the Germans had been building for their defense system, often within barns and farmhouses, great and small, but the principle of the opening of the defense was mainly to withdraw the majority of the troops. At any rate we moved forward and, when we had reached the positions to be seized were even bewildered by having done so—at a price. But we for a moment felt that success had beamed on us. The other side's guns were not doing much just then. Another enemy came into action. Almost silently the rain began. It went on, grew heavier, and the vision of victory dissolved in the grayness.

To try to chronicle the miseries and destructions of the days thus begun would be to invite sleepless nights or insane dreams, which have been exorcised, in any event, during the half century, and the battle with its variations of place and problem had my attention until summer had become winter, and however I was released from it (the authorities had not been altogether monsters, but had laid on a scheme of schools behind the line which were perhaps rest stations, as well as places of instruction), I was still back among the captured concrete pillboxes. The natural history of these was that their entrances, once we had possession, faced the German guns, and so always a direct hit from them was especially murderous. It was so on the celebrated Menin Road, in royal autumn sunshine, at the end of September, 1917. We could not avoid these concrete shelters, but the German gunners had them before them whenever they cared to bump them. Sunshine and irony united then. But late in the year a brilliant surprise far to the south, a tank battle toward Cambrai, diverted the war proper for a few days. "Think we shall win?" It was almost a possibility.

What ideas were now going around among the fighting men? Not many more than usual, but that America's armies were in the business was knowingly mentioned by some not loquacious sergeants. Our performances became a little less urgent, I thought, though hardly less deathly. At the end of that year of pain, 1917, it was strange for me to be in freezing starshine, staring east over the death-strewn miles, waiting for the rival guns to say something. They did, but as though bored. "How long, O Lord, how long?"

Before long we had moved far south to the Cambrai battlefield and been happy to find comparatively dry green ground and firm roads around our front line. The remains of the recent contest, which was a wonderful performance on both sides, offered no early end to the war. My expectation of being on the scene, God willing, through the new year, 1918, was simple; old friends were still there; the comforts were tolerable, and it was said we should soon have leave to visit Amiens even. But a system of transferring some who had a certain front-line length of experience had begun, and it included me. It happened so while we were digging miles of trenches and putting out entanglements of barbed wire apparently against a German offensive of considerable depth. It was assigned to me to prepare defense orders for our front. That done, and even approved by our commanding officer, I was—away!

The hope of returning to the line may seem to have been a symptom of madness, but such a hope stirred in me in a camp in England, and I nearly got back, when the German attack antici- pated had roared itself along far beyond our trace trenches. The half-starved German soldiery and civilians could not now quite win, and my next contribution to the declining battle was in November, 1918, when the war was slackening from several causes into its mortification. A godforsaken winter followed the Armistice, but at any rate the guns were silent; the starvation state of affairs went on but could not go on forever; the last booby trap of the German retreat had at length compelled amazement if it had failed to kill.

What out of all this miscellany abides after so long? The war cemeteries. But somebody was saying lately, when viewing one of them with 20,000 graves in it (near Passchendaele), such a total was only chick feed in comparison with other displays of inhumanity. Then, perhaps what goes on is the memory of anonymous heroes, who personally had nothing to hope for and who had nothing "patriotic" to say and went on day after day with a countenance of invincibility, not notably referring to any known enemy, just facing whatever gods may be.

Gerald Brenan

"I was born in Malta in 1894 of an English father and a Scottish-Irish mother from Ulster and spent my early childhood in South Africa, India, and Ireland. Then in 1902 my parents settled in a remote village in Gloucestershire. From there I went to the usual private and public schools, but not to a university because I was intended for the family career of the Army. However, I had come under the spell of poetry and travel books, so in 1912, having just passed into Sandhurst, I ran away from home with the idea of traveling by land to China. I got as far as Bosnia, where I was forced to turn back, and then was put by my parents to cram for the Indian police. I was awaiting the result of my exam when the war broke out.

"After the war I settled with several thousand books in a mountain village in Spain, which I have described in South from Granada. Later I lived in London, where I got to know the literary group known as Bloomsbury. Then in 1930, having come into a little money, I married an American poetess from South Carolina and three years later bought the house near Málaga where we still live. I have written four books on Spanish subjects: The Spanish Labyrinth (1943); The Literature of the Spanish People (1951); The Face of Spain (1950); and South from Granada (1957). I have also written under my own name two novels, A Holiday by the Sea (1961) and The Lighthouse Always Says Yes (1960), and an autobiography up to 1919, entitled A Life of One's Own (1962). This last contains a fuller account of my war experiences than is given here."

A SURVIVOR'S STORY

IN AUGUST, 1914, I was staying at my parents' house in the Cotswolds. The weather was fine and warm, the wheat stood ready for cutting in the fields, and a deep peace hung over everything. Then the German Army invaded Belgium, and a shock of dismay and horror ran through the country as the first reports of the fighting came through. It seemed incredible that in our orderly, civilized world such things could happen.

Since I was going through a period of adolescent revolt against school and parents, I was not in a very patriotic frame of mind, but I wished to be in the war because I felt it would be a great experience. I was therefore delighted when my father returned from Gloucester with a commission for me in the local Territorials. As soon as my uniform was ready I joined my battalion, the 5th Gloucesters, at Chelmsford. Except that I had done a little drill at my public school, I knew nothing of soldiering, but in those days the division between officers and men was one of class. Almost at once I was put to a sharp test. On my third day after arriving I had to take my company onto battalion parade because the other officers were absent on courses. I had to shout the correct orders, drill and maneuver my company, and salute with my sword. Somehow I got through it, but nothing in the whole course of the war was to frighten me so much.

We now settled down to training. On three mornings a week we marched our companies about on the parade ground in massed formations as though we were preparing to fight in the Marlborough wars. On other mornings we practiced in open formations for the Boer War. But we were not taught how to fight in trenches. These, we were told, were merely a temporary phase. In the spring, when our new armies were ready, we would break out of the trench line and chase the Germans back to the Rhine, while the Russian steamroller advanced slowly but surely on the other side. Our chief fear was that the war might be over before we got out to it.

Our adjutant rightly took a poor view of my efficiency so that in December I found myself seconded to a cyclist company which our division, the 48th, was forming. These companies were intended to serve the same purpose as the mounted infantry had done in the Boer War. With their superior mobility they could be rushed to any point of danger or else used as advance guards. I now found myself messing with eight young officers, all of them except our company commander under twenty-one, who for various reasons had made themselves disliked in their battalions. We got on well, so that for the first time I began to feel confidence in myself and to enjoy training my platoon. Then one day in March, 1915 we embarked for France.

A week later we found ourselves in billets in a farmhouse just behind Armentières on the Belgian frontier. Spring had already come. The trees were bursting into leaf; the grass was scattered with flowers; the fruit blossoms coming out. The country around was green and lush, with more civilians to be seen than soldiers. In contrast with this was the continual roll of the guns. When on my first night I walked down the lane, I could see the sky lit up for miles on either side by flashes and the Very lights floating like water lilies above them. At that moment the war seemed beautiful.

The 4th Division was holding the line in front of us. They had been in these trenches all winter, and the 48th was to relieve them. As it happened, I had a great friend called Taylor in that division, and I got leave to go look for him. I found him only 3 miles away at Le Bizet. He was the brigade machine-gun officer with six machine guns in his charge, and he offered to take me down at once to the front line.

The approach lay through a long row of red brick workmen's houses, in which a hole had been knocked in every partition wall. From this one emerged into the front trenches, which were not trenches at all, because the ground was waterlogged, but a narrow parapeted lane built of sandbags. It had a few strands of barbed wire in front of it and ended suddenly in a field. One had to talk in whispers because the Germans were only 30 yards away, and if they heard voices they would send over a rifle grenade or a jam jarful of shrapnel. In fact, as we stood there, a trench mortar shell burst above us, and a piece of metal tore my breeches and drew a few drops of blood. It was my twenty-first birthday, and I was delighted to feel I had been initiated.

Taylor had a long tale to tell of the sufferings of the troops during the previous winter. The trenches had been deep in water, the shelters had not kept out the rain, and casualties had been heavy. But now that spring had come, he was feeling more cheerful. I myself was in the highest spirits. In small doses danger is a great stimulant, and as I watched the shells exploding close by or heard the bullets whistling overhead, that old feeling of the romance of war took hold of me. Besides, the whole scene was so fantastic. All around me there were shattered houses with new pieces being knocked out of them as I watched, and this appealed to a repressed destructive instinct. As in a Chaplin film, the continual breaches of the ordinary usages of civilized life released a flood of excitement—almost of gaiety. To make it stranger, civilians were still living in many of these houses. For example, just behind our front trench there was a cottage that might have come out of a painting by Brueghel which was occupied by an old woman who could not go out by day without being sniped. Her cows lay around her dead on their sides; but she would not leave, and the Army had no authority to move her. Then it seemed incredible that those tall buildings one saw only a few hundred yards away were as inaccessible as the summit of Everest because they lay behind the German lines. The absolute impossibility of reaching them fascinated me, all the more as one never saw a German.

A few days after this my company had a short spell in the trenches opposite Messines. As at Le Bizet, they did not form a continuous line, but a string of unconnected positions. There was hardly any wire, so that the only things that prevented us from going forward and occupying the village on the hill above us were a few rifles and machine guns. In other days troops had had shields and armor, and it did not seem to me beyond the wit of man to devise some mechanical means of advancing under shelter. As I stood there considering this, the sentry next to me was shot in the head and fell back dead. But I was too excited by the novelty of everything to be affected by this, my first sight of death. I was young and full of life—it could not happen to me.

I saw a good deal of my friend Taylor during the next two weeks. Either I went down to the trenches with him or he rode over on his horse to my farm, where we drank coffee with fresh cream and ate cakes and talked poetry. I read him my favorite pieces from Rimbaud and Laforgue or spouted from *Also sprach Zarathustra,* which he admired in English but could not read in German. Then one night, as I lay sleeping in the orchard, where I had spread my sleeping bag under a pear tree in blossom, I was awakened by the trampling of boots and the rumble of vehicles along the great cobbled road. It was, I guessed, the 4th Division marching north to fill the gap left by the German gas attack at Ypres. Taylor must be there riding on his horse among them.

Meanwhile, we were given little to do, and I had most of my afternoons to myself. Armentières, a large ugly manufacturing town, was only a couple of miles away. The German lines ran through its farther suburbs, and shells fell on it all the time; but in spite of that, it was full of civilians. Close to the station there was a restaurant patronized by officers which became very gay in the evenings. The lovely spring weather put everyone in good spirits, and as in previous wars, there was a pervasive feeling of sex in the air which quickened the senses. The girls seemed to feel it, too. When a party of men bathed—naked, of course—in the Lys, they would gather around and make their comments. Then at the delousing baths that had been set up in a brewery we would see the eyes of the laundry girls who worked next door peering at us through the gaps in the wooden partition and hear their excited giggles. In the yard of the restaurant the men queued up to have the waitresses, who charged nothing.

But this pleasant lazy life did not last for long. Soon we were put to digging a redoubt on a hill opposite Messines. Since it was not far from the German lines, we worked by night, and every time a flare went up, we had to freeze. The nightingales, excited by the whistle of the machine-gun bullets, sang loudly, and we had a few casualties. Then sometimes, instead of returning to our billets, we would bivouac in the grounds of a chateau nearby. The front of the building had been ripped off by a shell, which had also destroyed the staircase, and looking up, we could see the brass bedsteads still heaped with sheets and a mirrored wardrobe disgorging female garments. In the garden below, the peonies, irises, and tulips were in full flower, along with rhododendrons and lilacs. The men wandered about like children on a school feast, picking bunches of them and green gooseberries to cook.

Toward the middle of May I had word that Taylor had been killed in the fighting near Ypres, and I got leave to ride up with my batman and learn how it had happened. I had already visited Ypres a few days before the gas attack. Then it had been crowded with people and little damaged, but now it was completely deserted and out-of-bounds to troops. Whole streets were burning, and packs of dogs roamed around, feeding on the corpses that one could smell everywhere. In the great market square the shattered cathedral and Cloth Hall stood up out of a pile of rubble, while in the bars and cafés half-filled glasses still stood on the tables, for with the first rumor of gas the population had fled in panic. We found Taylor's battalion holding the line near St.-Julien and came back.

A few weeks later I rode up to Ypres again to look for the grave of a cousin of mine who had been killed at Hill 60. This time I found the city more shattered than ever, its towers jagged and broken and its walls gleaming in the damp air like marble. The notorious Hill 60 turned out to be an inconspicuous lump rising a few feet above the pockmarked plain and containing an immense mine crater on its summit. It had been continuously fought over, both above- and belowground, so that its surface had taken on that pitted, tormented look which was later to characterize the whole of the Ypres Salient. Shell craters, mounds, rotting sandbags, coils of wire, latrines, graves with rats and flies, and the faint, inescapable smell of putrefaction mingling with that of chloride of lime and, where a shell had burst, the fumes of picric acid.

During the last days of June we moved south to Picardy, where a new British army was taking over the sector that stretched from Arras to the Somme. We established ourselves in the ruins of Hébuterne, a village that stood just behind the front line, and were assigned the task of repairing the communication trenches. Later we were given a piece of the line to hold, and I got a certain pleasure from going out on night patrols. The front was very quiet, and the trenches were more comfortable than those at Armentières, as well as drier.

The Somme region consists of long rolling valleys sown with wheat, with every few miles a village surrounded by apple orchards. It is a monotonous country, and our lives became monotonous to match it, for in the autumn we were moved back to billets 6 miles behind the line and put onto repairing roads. The romance of the war had now departed, and boredom set in. To relieve it, I and my friend Partridge would ride into Amiens on Sunday afternoons, have a good dinner, and look for girls. *La chasse aux filles* became our only serious activity; but the villages around had filled up with troops, and success was difficult. Then in the spring we returned to Hébuterne, and I was put in charge of an observation post just outside it.

Soon after this the divisional cyclist companies were broken up to form the 8th Corps Cyclist Battalion. Some of my fellow officers, among them Partridge, went back to the infantry, but when I applied to do this, I was told that I must stay with my O.P. (observation post) . Meanwhile, the preparations had begun for the great push that was to roll the Germans back 100 miles. Every day new batteries would arrive and begin registering, new light railways would spring up, new shell dumps and notice boards, while the whole countryside began to teem with khaki figures till it looked like an overstocked rabbit warren. Through my telescope I could see mounds of white chalk appearing in the German support trenches. Evidently they were building deep shellproof dugouts in preparation for our expected attack.

The 8th Corps, which was commanded by a spit-and-polish ma-

niac called General Hunter-Weston, was to form the left hinge of
our advance, and its first objective was the hamlet of Serre, which
stood on the skyline some 900 yards from our front trenches. My
O.P. was immediately opposite it and about a mile away. The battle
opened a little after sunrise on July 1, 1916, with a bombardment
that shook the air with its roar and sent up the earth on the German
trenches in gigantic fountains. It seemed as if no human being
could live through that. Then our men climbed by short ladders
onto the parapet and began to move forward, shoulder to shoulder,
one line behind the other, across the rough ground. They went
slowly because each of them carried a weight of 66 pounds. A
moment later the German barrage fell on our trenches, and their
machine guns began to rattle furiously. Clouds of blue and gray
smoke from the bursting shells, mingling with a light ground mist,
hid the general view, but through the gaps I could see the little
antlike figures, some of them keeping on, others falling, creeping,
writhing, lying still. Each of them carried on his back a tin triangle
to assist in his identification by our artillery, and the early morning
sun shone on these triangles and made them glitter. But as the
hours passed, I could not see that any of them had reached the
German support line, and later I knew why: The Boche machine
gunners had come out of their deep dugouts and were mowing
them down.

All this time the barrage that had fallen on our shallow assault
trenches had continued and was churning up the earth all around.
As I learned later, they were still packed with troops because they
had been manned in the wrong order, and two of the waves had
been caught by the barrage and had never got off. Slowly the sun
rose higher and higher in the sky, and the heat of that scorching day
grew and grew; but I could detect no movement on the slope in
front of me except that here and there a wounded man could be
seen creeping toward a shell hole. It became clear that our attack
had failed. Then, when darkness fell, terrible stories began to come
in. They told of appalling casualties, of whole battalions reduced to
thirty or forty men, and I have since read that no British Army
corps had ever before suffered such losses in a single day. The pick
of our young men, the first to volunteer for the war, were dead, and
on our corps front not a yard had been gained.

Ten days later I was brought face to face and in the most repellent way with the consequences of this battle. My platoon was detailed for a burying party. The bodies of our men who had been
mashed to pieces in the assault trenches had been brought up by
night on a trench railway and bundled out onto the ground. Legs

had broken off from trunks, heads came off at a touch, and nauseous liquids oozed out of the cavities. The stench was overpowering. Our job was to cut off the identity disks and bury these decomposing corpses in shallow trenches. After a few hours of this the fear of death had so entered into me that if I had been ordered to go over the top next morning I should not have been able to.

Meanwhile, as there was no more observing to be done, I had some time off. I decided to use it by looking up my friend Partridge, who was with his battalion in the new ground that had been won to the east of Albert. As, accompanied by my batman, I crossed the old front line, I seemed to be leaving a gale-swept, yet solid shore for a treacherous, chaotic region recently abandoned by the tide. The farther we went, the more desperate and confused the landscape became—shattered woods and villages, shattered trenches, abandoned equipment, and then unburied bodies. But it was also thickly populated: There was a heavy traffic of mule-drawn limbers and wagons choking the roads, and around us batteries were firing and soldiers camping by companies and battalions around their stacked rifles in open bivouacs. Then the numbers thinned out, and after a little we came to Mametz Wood, which had been the scene of heavy fighting. Its trees were torn and shattered, its leaves had turned brown, and there was a shell hole every 3 yards. This was a place where something unheard of in this war had taken place—hand-to-hand fighting in the open with bombs and bayonets. What seemed extraordinary was that all the dead bodies there lay just as they had fallen, as though they were being kept as exhibits for a war museum. Germans in their field gray uniforms, British in their khaki, lying side by side, their faces and their hands a pale waxy green, the color of a rare marble. Some of these figures still sat with their backs against a tree, and two of them stood locked together by their bayonets, which had pierced each other's bodies; they were sustained in that position by the tree trunk against which they had fallen. I felt that I was visiting a room in Madame Tussaud's Chamber of Horrors, for I could not imagine any of those corpses having ever been alive.

We kept on across the battlefield—dead bodies of men, dead mules and horses, rifles, hand grenades, German spiked helmets, gas masks, haversacks, scattered like the debris on a beach after a winter storm—till we came to Trones Wood, which, though greatly battered, had kept its green leaves. Here we were close to the front line, and since the machine-gun bullets began to whistle round us and I could hear no word of my friend's battalion, we turned back. After this we ran into a nasty patch of shelling and were glad to find ourselves in Albert again and to recover our cycles. Although I had failed to find Partridge, I had now learned where he was.

A few days later therefore—it was around July 21—I went back and, after crossing again the old front line, turned left toward Ovillers. Everything here was in a terrible state, the ground torn up by shells and littered with dead bodies from the attack on July 1. The wounded, who could not be brought in, had crawled into shell holes, wrapped their waterproof sheets round them, taken out their Bibles, and died like that. The stench from all these corpses was unbearable. I found Partridge commanding a company. The farther end of the trench he was occupying was held by the Germans. What was needed, he said, was to bomb up it so as to reach a machine gun that was holding up our advance, but his men were tired and not out to take risks. As usual, he said, the staff was execrable. It took hours to get a message back to brigade H.Q., and the orders they received from them were usually impossible to carry out because they came too late. I had lunch, washed down by a bottle of German champagne, with him in his deep German dugout and came away.

The letter I wrote home two days later is, in a way that amazes me today, a eulogy of battle. War was, of course, horrible, yet I could not help liking it because it was a great challenge. Only exceptional people were capable of rising to its worst moments, for the majority had no heart for it. These were Partridge's views, and since I admired his soldierly qualities, I was temporarily inclined to share them. Yet although I envied him for being in the thick of things, I wondered how I would come out of the supreme test of battle. I knew that I could take shellfire, for I was doing it all the time, but how should I stand going over the top and facing machine guns? That was a question which every infantryman in this war asked himself.

A few days after this my battalion got its marching orders. We were to move to Poperinge, behind the Ypres Salient. After a few weeks there, spent in reading Gibbon's *Decline and Fall*, I was again put onto observation work. My new O.P. was on the bank of the Ypres Canal, a little to the north of the city and not far from where the German lines came down to it and the Belgian sector began. This canal was a decidedly unprepossessing place. Enclosed by high banks and frequently shelled, it had taken on the baleful aspect of the front region and grew more sinister and tainted as it approached the point where it became the boundary between the lines. With the destruction of the locks most of the water had run out, leaving only a few feet of oily liquid resting on a bed of black and even oilier mud. Rotting branches and nameless objects of twisted metal rose out of its surface, and the rats had made their tunnels in the banks and swarmed in their thousands. I and my observers were given two dugouts which were dry and comfortable, as well as reasonably safe. Since our O.P. commanded only a small sector of the German trenches, I took to moving about with a small telescope and periscope and in this way got to know the whole northern half of the salient. It was a dismal region of mud and shell holes with only an occasional tree stump to relieve the monotony.

I was also expected to report on British and German raids. As soon, therefore, as I heard a German barrage come down, I would pull on my clothes and hurry to the front line. These occasions were apt to be unpleasant. The shattered trenches, the reek of powder, the black darkness fitfully lit up by a flare, the dead or dying that one stumbled over were unnerving, as was the possibility that the raiders might not yet have gone back. Then one saw by torchlight the shattered looks of the men who had survived and perhaps heard the moaning and sobbing of a poor fellow who had broken down. On one occasion I was caught in the German barrage. I do not think that anyone who has not lived through one of these can form a conception of what they were like. The earth appears to rock and tremble. The air is filled by a persistent rushing sound, broken by the crash of explosions. The mind cannot think, the arms and legs tremble automatically, and the tough man is the one who recovers quickest. I have read that concentrations of artillery fire such as these were never attained in the Second World War.

After spending the whole winter like an anchorite in my canal dugout, I was given another O.P. a couple of miles away. This was in a disused brickyard known as La Brique, standing on a low hill just beyond the Menin Gate. To get a better view, we hammered horseshoes into a thin elm tree and installed our telescope 30 feet above the ground. As the summer drew on, we learned that our big attack of the year was going to be on this sector. The Germans evidently knew it, too. Most of the traffic that supplied the salient had to pass through Ypres, and so morning, noon, and night the heavy shells fell on it, scattering clouds of white and rose-colored dust from the great shapeless mounds of the cathedral and Cloth Hall. I had watched this beautiful city crumble slowly away through the past two years, and now nothing but rubble was left.

The attack was to take place at dawn on July 31. I was to go over the top with the second wave and send reports back. But on the twenty-ninth I was wounded in the arm and side by a piece of shell. When I walked over to the dressing station to get myself bandaged, the major in charge sent me off, in spite of my strong protests, to a base hospital. It was not exactly that I was looking forward to the battle, for I had not forgotten the Somme, but no one likes to have his plans upset.

I found the atmosphere in England intensely unpleasant. The women were all agog for atrocity stories, while the hatred of the Germans that had been worked up by the Northcliffe press boded ill for the eventual peace. I soon got tired of peacetime soldiering and asked my C.O. in Belgium to apply for my return.

By February I was back in Poperinge. A long-distance shell burst at the railway station as I arrived, but though I ducked like a staff officer, I was not sorry to be back in the old haunts again. War was hateful, but if it had to be, the best place for a young unmarried man was in the front line. And there I went—to another O.P.

The five months' battle that was to have sent the Germans scurrying back to Antwerp had carried us less than 6 miles forward over an expanse of mud to what had once been the village of Passchendaele. This place with the beautiful name crowned a low ridge which provided cover from view until one was almost in the front line. My O.P. was a tiny ramshackle affair 50 yards behind it, but our living quarters were some way back in a large white pillbox built by the Germans. It was completely shellproof, but unfortunately it was sinking in the mud, so that one had to stoop low to enter it. A few weeks later it had sunk so far that we left it and went back to La Brique.

The country around was as strange to look at as anything I had ever seen. All about us stretched a broad, slightly undulating plain of brown sodden earth and shell craters filled to the brim with water. These craters touched and intersected so frequently that it sometimes seemed as if there were more water than mud. The valleys were completely flooded, and there was no sign of houses or trees and no grass or vegetation. The only objects that stood out from the morass were the white German pillboxes, massive and rounded as elephants, and now and then in the back regions a half-buried tank. It goes without saying that there were no support or communication trenches. The way up to the front line was by 4-mile-long footways made of duckboards and raised on piles above the mud. If one fell off, one would sink to one's waist or deeper, which made them unhealthy places on which to be caught by shellfire. The villages marked on the map had completely vanished: not a stone of them remained.

I had not been here long when we learned that the Germans had attacked and broken through our line opposite Amiens and then, which was more dangerous, between Armentières and Messines. To shorten our front, we gave up all we had gained in the last battle and withdrew to the outskirts of Ypres. The 8th Corps handed over its divisions to another corps, and I went back to Cassel.

How was it, every soldier asked himself, that while we had been attacking on the largest scale, at enormous cost, without obtaining any significant results, the Germans had in a few days smashed through our front in two places? Obviously our generals were bad, and the morale of the troops fell accordingly. Living in comfort far behind the lines and rarely seen where shells were falling, these haughty brass hats had always been unpopular. But I had no time to dwell on these matters, for I was sent out with a small patrol to keep in touch with the situation around Mount Kemmel.

After two and a half years of being penned up in the trenches it was strange to see fighting taking place in the open country—men lying behind hedges or advancing by sections across fields, signal-men semaphoring, field guns cantering along and then unlimbering and firing. French cavalry uniforms alternated with British ones, but the only shelling was from 18-pounders because the Germans had not yet brought up their heavy artillery. Instead one heard the sharp *rat-tat-tat* of machine guns and the crack of rifle fire. No one seemed to know where the front line was—indeed it was changing all the time.

My memory of these days is very hazy. I find that I have a tendency to forget unpleasant experiences unless I record them soon afterward. What I chiefly remember is the green leafy country with its old brick farmhouse, its tangled lanes, and its English flowers—and then the dead and wounded in their blue or khaki uniforms, sprinkled with blood. I got mixed up in a German attack and then in a French one, and two of the three men with me were killed. The reports I sent back must have been quite useless.

I had been a captain for some time, and when, as now happened, I returned to my battalion, I was given the command of a company. A week later we entrained for a place far to the south—Châlons-sur-Marne in the Champagne. Here we were attached to the French, and so we settled down to learn how to fire their machine guns. Then suddenly the news of a fresh German advance came through. They had attacked on the Chemin des Dames and within three days had reached the Marne. We rode off and a few hours later were digging in between Vandières and Châtillon with our left flank on that river. At dawn on the following day I sent out a patrol of five men to watch a farmhouse that stood halfway between the lines and that I suspected was occupied by the enemy. The lance corporal, after keeping it under observation for a time, surprised the seven Germans who were holding it while they were eating their lunch and brought them back. They belonged to a *corps d'élite*, the Prussian Guard, and the French were very pleased.

I wanted to take some offensive action with my company, and my C.O. gave me a free hand. The first attempt was a fiasco, for at the last moment I realized that we were attempting too much and, after an agony of indecision, canceled the attack. But two nights later I led out a patrol of three men from the French lines opposite a hamlet called Trotte, and after crawling painfully on our bellies across a stubble field, we struck a gap in the German lines and got right through.

This was for me the most exhilarating moment of the war. Here we were, after staring at that impassable frontier for three years, walking about in safety behind it. An almost mystical feeling of release and liberation came over me. Moving down the slope, I could see the broad valley lit up by the dim moonlight and hear the sound of heavy motor traffic at the bottom. What should we do with our discovery? Wild schemes rushed through my head, but then I saw that our best plan would be to capture the hamlet of Trotte from behind. It offered a much better defensive position than the wood held by the French because it overlooked the main German communications with the rear and could only be approached up a long open slope. We therefore made a careful reconnaissance of it, creeping up in the shadow of the barns to locate two machine-gun posts and then returning by the way we had come.

On the following night I went back with a sergeant and two men to reconnoiter the further end of the place. We located a third machine gun and what seemed to be a company headquarters; we were just about to leave when a sentry came down the sunk road which served as their front line toward us. We were crouching one behind the other in the shadow of a wall, and he did not see us until he was within a few yards. I covered him with my revolver, but instead of putting up his hands, he slowly and deliberately unslung his rifle from his shoulder and aimed at me. I watched him do this in a sort of trance, for, seeing his young face with its blue saucer eyes in the moonlight, I felt unable to pull the trigger. I could no doubt kill a German in hot blood or at a distance, but I was not a homicide. Then his shot rang out, I felt a blow in my side, and said, "I'm hit." But I was not hit, for the bullet had only torn my tunic. My men finished him off, and we ran out over the stubble field toward the French lines. About 50 yards on we came to the carcass of a cow and, just as a machine gun opened fire, threw ourselves down behind it. As we did so, a dozen rats leaped out of its belly and scurried away over our backs. There we lay for a long time, pressed into the earth, with the bullets, each time the gun traversed, passing just over us, almost shaving us. But at last they ceased, and very slowly we crept off to the wood, where we narrowly escaped being shot by the French sentry.

The prospects for capturing Trotte were no longer so good because the Germans had been alerted, yet I reckoned that they could not know that we had passed behind their lines. I decided, therefore, to go through with the attack that night. I would lead the first patrol—with only a couple of men in case they set an ambush. Two larger patrols would follow, and the rest of the company would stand by to await the signal to rush forward. As soon as it was dark then, our faces and hands blackened with charcoal, we left the wood for the haystack that marked the gap. We had got within 20 or 30 yards of it, crawling on our bellies over the prickly stubble, when I saw a German raise his head over the bank and heard the clink of metal. They were waiting for us, and there was nothing to be done but fade out. Since we were plainly visible as dark blotches on the pale background, this meant that we must wriggle backward, waiting to move till a passing shell would deaden our sound. It took us two hours to do the couple of hundred yards, and then I found that the officer in charge of the second patrol had returned to the village with all the men and reported that we had been either killed or captured.

So I had failed twice. Disgusted at this and ashamed at my failure over the German sentry, I took out a fighting patrol on the following night in a new sector where the lines were a mile apart, in the hope of getting a German alive or dead for identification. But it was blowing and raining hard, and though we thought we saw an enemy patrol on the skyline, we failed to intercept it. Then, on the next night, my battalion was asked by the French to raid two machine-gun posts that were annoying them. My company was detailed to take on one of them, and my C.O. told me to put a junior officer in charge. But after my last night's experience I did not trust the only one I had, so though I was very tired, I persuaded him to let me lead it. Just as we were starting, the Germans began to shell our village, and a whizbang hit a man just outside company headquarters. We carried him in on a stretcher and found that the whole of the lower part of his face had been carried away, leaving a red palpitating hole. But he was still alive, and his eyes were moving about in a serious, inquiring way as if he did not understand what had happened to him. He was very young, perhaps not more than nineteen, and as I trudged up the road with my men, I kept seeing those eyes, and they gave me a bad feeling.

We got to the French front line, which was along the edge of a wood, and saw the poilus sitting around in easy attitudes. But the sergeant in charge said that he had strict orders not to let any patrol go out. We must wait for the company commander. So we squatted down in the ditch, and then, from the gray open country beyond, a machine gun began to fire from close range. The bullets swished by overhead, bringing down small twigs and leaves, and I knew that they came from the post that we had orders to raid and which I had reconnoitered that afternoon. As I sat there in the moist, warm trench with the dark trees clustering thickly around, listening to that ear-shattering stutter, a very unpleasant feeling came over me. I had never had quite that sensation in the pit of my stomach before.

We sat there for some time, and then the French captain arrived. He said he could not possibly allow us to do our raid that night because he had a working party out. I asked him to sign a paper to that effect and with unspeakable relief led my men back.

I had now been out on patrols for six nights in succession and had been far too busy to lie down by day. I was therefore very tired and slept for twelve hours without waking. When I did wake, I learned that the other company's raid had been a failure and that an officer and several men had been killed trying to rush a machine gun. But we were being relieved next day, so that I should not have to go out on patrol again. Within a week we were in billets on the Somme. Here I went down with the Spanish flu that was sweeping through the Army and was invalided back to England. I was still there when the Armistice came.

Jacques Meyer

Born in 1895 at Valenciennes, to a modest family of Alsatian origin, Jacques Meyer got his secondary schooling first at the Lycée de Valenciennes and then in Paris at the Lycée Charlemagne and, to prepare for the École Normale Supérieure, the Lycée Louis-le-Grand. He applied to the École Normale and was accepted in 1914, eight days before the war.

All the members of Jacques Meyer's class, including himself, enlisted immediately, and after a short training program he was commissioned as an officer in the infantry and went to the front, where he spent a number of months in a first-line unit. Badly wounded in the Somme attack, he was mentioned in dispatches several times and was named a chevalier of the Legion of Honor.

After the war he finished his studies, earned a doctorate in law, and passed the examination in philosophy. Then he went into journalism. General manager of Paris' biggest evening paper, L'Intransigeant, in 1931, he became the president of a privately owned broadcasting station, Radio-Cité.

The Second World War found him a captain at general headquarters. After the fall of France, he was able to reach Gibraltar and join the Free French government in Algiers. He participated in the Provence landing as the chief of intelligence services of General Jean de Lattre de Tassigny's army, and reorganized the press and broadcasting facilities in the southern zone of liberated France. His military activities led to his being named a commander of the Legion of Honor.[1]

In September, 1944, he became general manager of Radio Française. He was appointed a government adviser in 1949, a post he retained until 1963.

His intellectual activity has found expression in a number of books. One treats French politics—Question de confiance (1948)—but most of his works concern the war of 1914–18 and have earned him a reputation as an expert in this field. In 1928 he wrote La Biffe (The Infantry) and in 1931 La Guerre, mon vieux. . . . His Vie et mort des Français, 1914–1918 was written jointly with two former classmates from the École Normale Supérieure and carried an introduction by Maurice Genevoix, the permanent secretary of the Académie Française. Meyer's Le 11 Novembre came out in 1964 and La Vie quotidienne des soldats pendant le Grande Guerre in 1966.

---

[1] He had been named an officer of the Legion of Honor in 1935, in his capacity as a writer.

VERDUN, 1916*

Verdun was a whole war, inserted into the Great War. . . . It was also a kind of duel before the universe, a singular and almost symbolic tourney.   —PAUL VALÉRY

I. THE THEATER OF OPERATIONS

THE GREAT German sweep on Verdun in February, 1916, first checked through the strength of sheer despair and then arrested after months of superhuman resistance and pushed back to its point of departure at the end of the year, cannot be separated from the great French-English attack on the Somme of July 1. The latter, initially undertaken for another purpose—to break through on a larger scale than in the unsuccessful offensives of 1915—had the effect above all of relieving Verdun. The Germans, who had had grounds for believing the war finished in 1914, made an enormous effort in 1916, which they hoped would be decisive, to bring it to an end. In their view, Britain's staying power depended entirely on the French Army. It was thus the French Army's men and matériel they had to exhaust, so as to deprive England of its "best sword,"[1] in bullfighting parlance. Moreover, Russia's strength had already been considerably reduced by its reverses, aggravated by the check at the Dardanelles, the closing of the Black Sea by the Turks, and the crushing of Serbia.

On their side, the French government and General Staff had to take into account in their planning the delay of the English conscription and consequently the slow dispatch of British divisions. Nonetheless, after General Sir Douglas Haig took command in December, 1915, they replaced our troops in the north of France little by little. And it was primarily the offensive which Major General Erich von Falkenhayn expected from the Anglo-French forces in the spring or summer that prompted him to launch a preventive attack against Verdun on February 21.

Why was Verdun chosen by the German high command? It was not simply to heighten the glory of his dynasty that the Kaiser detailed the army led by his son, the Crown Prince, for the "victory

---

* Translated from the French by Sally Abeles.
1 Major General von Falkenhayn's phrase.—Tr.

offensive." The main reasons were of a strategic and psychological order. The front, as it had been defined by the battles of the Marne and the fighting in the winter of 1914–15, followed a large salient between Argonne and Lorraine which embraced the fortified region at Verdun and continued southward along advance posts in the Woëvre plain. The position, almost closed in on three sides, was all the more vulnerable because it straddled a river, which could make communications from one bank to the other tricky.

A system of fourteen major railway lines served the German front; Verdun, on the contrary, could no longer use its two lines when it was attacked; the one from the south had been cut at St.-Mihiel since the end of 1914, and the other, from the west, would be severed by the bombardments of the left bank of the Meuse. Only the winder,[2] a narrow-gauge line from Bar-le-Duc to Verdun by way of Souilly, the Army's headquarters, remained to ensure the food supply (800 tons a day). Fortunately, the parallel road, which had been widened to seven meters by March, 1915, was immediately activated by Captain Doumenc's vehicle transport service, alerted on February 18. It became the Sacred Road, and its special width is today marked out for the attention of indifferent motorists. As of the twentieth, Captain Doumenc committed himself to transporting munitions and men, the foodstuff of battle, provided that he remained absolute master of the road. It was set up like a two-track railway line, divided into sections, each with its own organization. At noon on February 20, the 20th Army Corps debarked at the Bar-le-Duc station, the 1st Army Corps being already en route to Verdun. Beginning on February 29, eight days after the German attack was launched, 3,000 trucks—the count rose to 3,500 shortly—divided into 51 groups carried 50,000 tons of munitions and 90,000 men toward the front each week. If we add the light vans, ambulances, touring cars, tractors, and the like to the trucks, 11,500 vehicles were using the road in June—one every fourteen seconds, sometimes even one every five seconds. This endless chain, this "bucket conveyor," ran along the 75 miles of the artery that brought to Verdun the generous blood of the reinforcements and carried back the exhausted troops and the pitiable wounded. The 8,500 men and 300 officers of the 2d Army Transport Service could claim full credit for this success. Their chief, Captain-become-Major Doumenc, had decided that:

We will totally exclude horse or foot convoys, by shuttling them off onto parallel routes; finally, we will in no case interrupt traffic to make

---

[2] The popular name given to trains serving a local line and stopping at every station.

systematic repairs of the roadway. . . . Nonmotor convoys will cross it, but without being allowed to turn onto it. . . . Any vehicle that cannot be towed off must be pushed into the ditch. No one has the right to stop, except for a serious breakdown; no truck may pass another.

If Von Falkenhayn decided to launch his attack—which he hoped to be conclusive—on Verdun, it was because he adjudged it so important from the standpoint of morale that the French command would be forced to engage every last man in its defense. "Verdun is the heart of France," the Crown Prince had said. In addition to these considerations, the Verdun region, with its numerous woods where artillery and infantry could hide from sight, even from the air, lent itself admirably to the camouflaging of preparations for attack. Thus was the German 5th Army able to keep its deployment utterly invisible. Not a single parallel takeoff trench had been dug. The assault troops lay covered in deep shelters. The average distance between the two lines, 800 to 1,000 meters, was such that the French command, though on the alert, could only believe that the preparations were incomplete, judging by precedent. Bombardment without range setting, directed against individual objectives corresponding to each artillery cluster, was made possible thanks to the German supremacy in aerial observation by planes and balloons (*Drachen*). This had the purpose of crushing everything that might oppose the advance of the assault troops. German reconnaissance was to make sure that nothing was left before three waves— each more dense than the preceding—moved forward to occupy the position, equipped with matériel to overthrow it and munitions to defend it. If the objective had not been totally destroyed, the guns were to go to work again.

On the French side, the obtuseness of the general headquarters (G.H.Q.) intelligence service, despite an abundance of warning signs, allowed an attack known about throughout the Crown Prince's army and signaled by numerous deserters to be turned into a surprise. At a time when all the defenders of Verdun sensed a gigantic attack on Verdun coming, the high command proceeded with the disarmament of the forts, because they had been shown up as worthless in the early days of the war, at Liège and Maubeuge. It was thought that their artillery would be put to better use in preparing new offensives. The surroundings of the town brought to mind an abandoned construction yard, rather than a stronghold on the alert. General Henri Pétain, who was to take command of the Army at Verdun, later described the disorganization of the sector in these words:

The fortified region had not been the object of any undertaking on the adversary's part since 1914; military activity there seemed less in 1914 than it had been in peacetime. The forts rose silent and as if abandoned. Between the forts and beyond, there was only ruin: trenches largely caved in; barbed wire cut to pieces, its inextricable tangles covering the Côtes de Meuse woods and the muddy Woëvre plains; roads and tracks turned into quagmires; equipment scattered about, wood rotting and metal rusting in the rain.

Yet there had been no lack of warnings. General Herr, who commanded the fortified region of Verdun, had issued them repeatedly. Much movement of German troops and great activity on the rail lines in the area had been reported by aerial observers. Letters taken from prisoners and the prisoners themselves referred to a review the Kaiser was going to hold at Verdun the end of February and to the peace that would follow. Reinforcements were requested, to work on strengthening the positions, as well as to hold the lines. Feverishly, at the front as in the rear, positions were blocked out again and again without any being settled on and without a fixed idea of what line of resistance to choose. The line of the forts should stand in good stead, though no attempt had been made to put their solid concrete masses to full use. We know that their artillery, though well aimed and protected, had had most of its guns withdrawn. The infantry garrisons, reduced in number, now included only Territorial troops. Behind an unsubstantial first line poorly defended by intermittent wire fencing, the support and redoubt lines comprised only widely separated and inadequately manned trenches. The second-position works were embryonic; they had not been begun until fourteen days before the attack. There were no communication trenches between the positions or linking them with the forts.

Yet Deputy Émile Driant, an infantry lieutenant colonel who would die in glory early in the day, had notified his fellow members of the Chamber of Deputies' Commission of the Army of these conditions on December 1. On December 12, General Joseph Simon Galliéni, the Minister of War, had written Field Marshal Joseph Joffre to tell him what he had learned about the lack of organization at Verdun. Joffre had replied, "Nothing justifies the fears expressed," and he made it clear that he would resign if "the complete confidence of the government" was not vested in him and if it tolerated practices which would diminish his moral authority. He admitted only that the barbed-wire fencing was inadequate. Joffre's chief of staff, General Édouard de Curières de Castelnau, was sent to inspect the area on January 25, and he found: "The organization of the first position *on the right bank* of the Meuse corresponds exactly with the directives given by the commanding general in his instructions." He nonetheless ordered the construction of shelters for the Reserves and the reinforcement of the flanks and the second position. On his return, he began to send reinforcements, but the work could not be carried out owing to lack of time. Leaves were, of course, canceled on February 9. But G.H.Q., misled by a series of diversionary actions that took place January 9– February 21 from Artois to the upper Alsace and through the Somme region and Champagne, and showered with calls for reinforcements from all these points, continued to think that German activity would boil up again primarily on the eastern front instead, "even if the Allies do not retain the initiative on operations until next summer."

Two days after the opening of the attack, Joffre again declared, with his unshakable optimism, "All precautions have been taken." Fortunately, Castelnau was able to get himself sent to Verdun immediately with full powers. Surveying the situation at firsthand, he decided to put the fortified region of Verdun under the command of the head of the 2d Army, General Pétain, who was then available, arranging a meeting at Souilly. Pétain had already received the order to send his General Staff toward Bar-le-Duc and made contact with Joffre at Chantilly. The conversation ended with this comment by Joffre: "So, my friend, now you're at ease." But it was already too late for this; the enemy had cut the standard-gauge rail lines to Verdun, and the drama was ended—the Crown Prince's troops, outnumbering the defenders five to two, bowled over the first lines of the French defense. Driant was killed in the midst of his infantrymen, and Fort Douaumont was taken (February 21–25).

The reorganized high command made the necessary decisions. But what could the soldier, even the subordinate officer, know of what was happening in that other world? From February 21 at least until the Somme attack—that is, for more than four months—the fighters at Verdun were almost constantly cut off, by German fire, from their own command, which began at the battalion level, and even more so from the artillery and the air units. The Battle of Verdun, for those who fought it in the flesh, was a battle of very small units, each directing its own fate, to the degree that the enemy fire did not totally destroy them. The actions of the head men, taken very late and often by default, were in any case remote, incapable of reaching the fighting men. The combatants were most often left to their own devices, and thus was the soldier of Verdun molded.

II. THE SOLDIER OF VERDUN

THE NARROWNESS of the terrain, the jumbling of the lines, the pounding of enemy, and, alas, friendly artillery which the sketchily dug trenches could not withstand made the war at Verdun something it rarely was elsewhere, even during the big attacks: a war fought by small isolated groups, living—and dying—in shell holes. If the positions were no more than precarious slopes of sandbags, and the communicating trenches furrows barely begun before they were stopped, they still gave an illusion of psychological protection, for they could save one from bullets and shrapnel. It was in the craters hollowed by the shells that "groups piled in the bottom . . . invisible to each other . . . form the first line. Crisscrossing of gray craters (the German *Feldgrau*) and blue craters (the French *bleu-horizon*), indistinguishable one from another. . . . Farther on, other groups, other regiment numbers."[3] There they waited; there they slept and defended themselves with tossed grenades. There they took shelter in the vague belief that two shells never fall in the same hole, a belief that often proved false.

Verdun was most often a war of abandoned men, a few men around a chief, a junior officer, a noncom, even a simple soldier whom circumstances had shown capable of leadership. Sometimes it was a single man reduced to leading himself. Handfuls of men or individuals forced to act, to take the initiative of defense—or withdrawal. Failures of nerve—there were some—generally occurred in bigger units, which were not always the most hardened but were the most shocked by the unexpectedness of the disaster. Decisive and courageous acts were mainly individual, leaving most of them unknown.

By day, impossible to make a move without emerging waist-high and being pitilessly popped off. On the left bank of the Meuse, around Hill 304, no food came in; no wounded could be taken out for two days. Nightfall hardly freed the soldiers: "Flares burst out of the darkness every minute to make sure that not a shovelful of earth was shifted by the victims designated for crushing shellfire."[4] Farther to the rear, reinforcements wandered about for hours because of the darkness before finding their positions:

The guide who was leading us was making his last turn of duty with this trip, and he quickened his pace, spurred by the anticipation of being

---

[3] Joseph Jolinon, *Le Valet de gloire* (Paris, F. Rieder) .

[4] Charles L. Delvert, *Histoire d'une compagnie* (Paris-Nancy, Berger-Levrault, 1918) .

relieved. He was our only safeguard; without him we would have been a herd of blind men. Our fate hung on his memory and his cool nerve. . . . It wasn't rare for units to wander all night among the shell holes, unable to find their place. It even happened that roving companies ran into Boche lines in the morning, where they were surrounded and slaughtered.[5]

What could have brought a measure of order into the infantry movements, active *command,* no longer existed, as we have seen. When bombardment reached the dimensions it had for months at Verdun, telephone communications were completely cut off; liaison personnel, wounded or dead, could no longer do their job. Regimental and battalion leaders, sometimes even company commanders no longer knew where their men were, nor did the men know where their lines were. Day, as well as night, in the fog of gas and the smoke of explosions, on torn-up ground where advances and partial retreats made it impossible to fix a continual line, who could tell whether the flames of firing and the whistling bullets were French or German? And the same was true on the other side.

The battered earth bore nothing but groaning wounded who couldn't be helped, distended bodies that your foot sank into, among broken guns, punctured helmets, scattered equipment. You advanced by leaping from shell hole to shell hole, their bottoms covered with muddy water and often dead men, half-buried by an explosion. Sometimes no one was in them, sometimes there were men, who welcomed you with muttered curses because you would get their precious shelter spotted. A spectral, semiconscious life, interrupted only by the eruption of danger: sudden attacks, periodic bombardments, the insidious accumulation of gas in gullies and hollows, machine guns discovered by surprise—everything overwhelmed the footsoldier. All this explains the eternal fame of Verdun—as hell, created as much by misery as by danger.

Yet the bucket conveyor, also called the pulley, of trucks from the Sacred Road continued to provide Verdun with men for devouring, whose divisions were relieved after some days. All they needed to do for this was to lose at least a third, if not half, of their strength; then their blood-sucked regiments again took their places on the too-roomy benches of the trucks that had brought them. All the *bonhommes*[6] knew this, and yet the system was less demoralizing than that of the Germans: most of their units assigned at the outset were kept at Verdun all during 1916. So those who had escaped

---

[5] Pierre Chaîne, *Les Mémoires d'un rat* (Paris, Payot, 1930) .

[6] The popular name generally given to soldiers at the front; the term "hairy" poilu was used mainly in the rear.

death and capture or had not been evacuated had to endure a like hell for months on end.

Doubtless it came about that both sides exaggerated the losses. The figure of 1,000,000 men was given. Actually, despite the heat of the fighting at Verdun and the Somme, the year 1916 took less of a toll than 1915, the year of nibbling actions and insane attempts at breakthroughs. At Verdun, the trenches were reduced to such inconsequence that the enemy did not know our exact positions, which were in the balance very thin and irregular. "He was therefore forced to shower a whole sector with shells instead of concentrating his fire on target areas."[7] The probable figure of losses at Verdun for both sides nonetheless reached some 700,000, with 300,000 killed or definitely missing, and the French share a little higher. All this ending with the two adversaries only a few kilometers from their original positions, after ten months of savage fighting. But the same axiom ruled on both sides: *Every position lost must be retaken.* Thus, the town of Fleury changed hands sixteen times between June 23 and July 17. Thousands of deaths for a few hundred yards of ground: On February 28, after two days of attack, 98 of Driant's men remained out of 1,200; and 64 men were standing out of eight companies of the 362d Infantry Regiment. Counterattacking Le Mort-Homme on May 24, 6th Company of the 60th Infantry was reduced from 143 men to 11. The losses among junior officers were proportionally higher, for their role was enlarged by the isolation of the battlefield. From July 13 to 28, the 115th Infantry lost 24 officers:

Lieutenant V——, who arrived for support a few days ago, has just been killed . . . two minutes after shaking my hand; a shell fragment hit his haversack full of grenades and reduced him to pulp. Cadet S——, 19, has been killed. Likewise Cadet M——, the same age, and Sergeant Major C——. They are stretched out here side by side, all three of them, my poor buddies, in front of my aid station.[8]

The superior officers who were close by their men, like Driant, did not escape death. Captain Imhaus, who had joined up again at the age of sixty, was killed in a 163d Infantry counterattack on March 30. Three of his sons were already dead at the front; the fourth was to be killed in August, 1918.

For the rest, the usual miseries of men at the front—the cold, the smell of corpses, too little and often no food when the men on field

7 Chaîne, *op. cit.*
8 Delvert, *op. cit.*

kitchen duty were killed before they returned—were heightened at Verdun. The mud following the rain, which fell until the summer, had tragic consequences. Wounded men drowned in shell holes filled to the brim with water. More often, the living sank into the mud near the planks that lined the pathways or the bottom of communication trenches in a very few places.

For the injured, there was no such thing as a "good wound." Even those who could try to get away from the battlefield on their own were not necessarily saved. Their trip down was as risky as their trip up to the line: How many of them were killed en route! If they had the luck to be stretcher-borne, the danger multiplied with the number of men grouped together, making a target for the machine guns or a "bundle" for a shell falling on the heap. Getting killed on a stretcher and surviving alongside a smashed stretcher and dead bearers came to the same thing. Worst of all, many wounded could not be picked up and died of gangrene or exhaustion, either where they fell or as they dragged themselves from hole to hole. This explains why the figures on Verdun include twice as many missing—that is, unidentified dead—as certain dead. Moreover, the daily inoculation of horror inevitably bred insensitivity.

In June, which was the peak of the battle, the men were not so much hungry as tired and, above all, thirsty, a thirst that the poisoned dust made a torture. Hunger would have been easier to satisfy, if only because the dead could be relieved of their reserve rations; but when a man had a few biscuits and a can of monkey meat[9] in hand, he might hesitate to eat them for fear of getting thirsty. The loss of sleep at night, spent in relief work, duty, anxious watches, was not made up by catnaps during the day, subject to the fracas of bombardments and to sudden alerts. Of course, the intensity of the bombardment could itself cause a semiconscious torpor which might let a man slip into sleep, his head between his knees or on a comrade's shoulder—or on a corpse that hadn't been discovered when the dead were being picked up. This torpor often became a kind of apathy or insensitivity in the face of death.

No distinction between the shells that blew you up. All the witnesses have said the same thing: One out of five times—some claimed one out of four or three—it was fragments from our 75 shells that shredded our *bonhommes*, the blast of our 155's that crushed the shelters. Nor were the Germans spared shells falling short. So the infantrymen in the two camps could have joined in

---

9 Popular name for canned processed beef.

muttering the same imprecations against the artillery. Ours especially, blinded by the haze and smoke and almost totally deprived of observation posts, most often could not reply either to the red flares summoning a barrage or to the green calling for a lengthening of range. The German gas shells in particular hounded the artillery gun crews, although starting with the first days of attack the Germans did not neglect also to shoot tear gas and asphyxiating gas into all the ditches and woods, where the branches held the fumes in suspension.

Another agony, almost exclusively visited on the footsoldiers, for it required close quarters: the flamethrower. Its use was not initiated at Verdun. But it was there that the Germans applied it whole scale, and the more effectively in that its dreadful operation generally followed a heavy bombardment. It contributed to the German success in the February attack. After that, the footsoldiers learned how to defend themselves; they tried to explode the fuel tanks with a grenade, which transformed the carriers into living torches, or if they could fell the sapper who held the flamethrower, the jet of flame, no longer aimed, would then wash over its immediate surroundings.

The solidarity among the men—old and young, soldiers and the officers near them—was never more important than at Verdun. This moral force, said Pétain, consisted "less of ardor than of hardy determination, and lay mainly in an inflexible will to defend their families and their goods against the invader." And this was true, for at Verdun, the simplest fellow felt obscurely that he had a *mission* to protect what was for him, quite unpretentiously, "the sacred soil of our country," a mission which, at the worst moments, the chiefs did not hesitate to call sacrificial. But unlike what devolved after the unsuccessful 1915 offensives, the men at Verdun were no longer haunted by the feeling that they were dying for nothing. For the first and only time, in fact, between the Germans' invasion arrested at the Marne in September, 1914, and their do-or-die onslaught stopped at the same river in May, 1918, the Germans were attempting a widescale attack, with the aim of "bleeding the French Army," in Von Falkenhayn's phrase. And once again, as the first time, the soldiers knew they had to dam the mounting tide, by raising a wall of their own bodies against it, "so that they will not pass." They will not pass became the motto of Verdun.

In the mutual exhaustion of a mercilessly prolonged struggle, this time it was the Germans' turn to weigh the vanity of war. The Germans, who in the early days had thought they would break our resistance without a fight, crushing us with their *Trommelfeuer*, their "drum-roll" fire, began to suffer the same miseries as deeply as our soldiers, with the added mortification of not having finished the war upon penetrating Verdun. They crumbled as we regained our feet. As the loss of Douaumont, through confusion and surprise, had long demoralized the French, its recapture in the autumn of 1916 sealed the reverse of the Germans and definitively destroyed their hopes. "That hill of Douaumont has become our destiny," said the German writer and military man Werner Beumelburg. They would not take Verdun; they would not yet finish a war which might never end. Thus was Verdun, which was a French victory only in the sense of an invincible resistance, a defeat of Germany before the final defeat, the only one after the Marne.[10]

But in exhausting itself, the German Army had almost succeeded in "bleeding the French Army," and the land was so crammed with corpses that Henry de Montherlant could write: "You walk on the ground of Verdun as though on the face of the Country." For the rest, the living themselves were only dead men reprieved, living an epic—the epic of suffering.

Verdun was martyrdom for its men, its footsoldiers especially, in an almost unmitigated hell, where the hours of so-called respite, in the Tavanne tunnel, for instance, were at best a purgatory. The men of the field kitchens very often could not satisfy the hunger and especially the thirst of their comrades, for, humble unsung heroes, they were struck down on the unsafe terrain among their scanty cooking pots. The calvary of the liaison men, Verdun's runners, and the litter-bearers was even worse, because it went on all night for the stretcher men and recurred at least once a day for the liaison personnel.

As for those who had to go to earth, immobile and passive and awaiting the worst under the infernal pounding, it seemed impossible to expect them to rise, exhausted, from the debris of their departure points or shell holes when the enemy attack finally rolled in, following the flamethrowers, and fire on an attacker who thought our positions were deserted, their occupants crushed. And yet almost every time, despite the lack of possible help, with their distress signals unseen, their guns plugged up, the machine guns jammed, the survivors pulled themselves up to try to check the flood. For aside from a rare and understandable panic, these men seemed still to prefer death or capture to the safety of flight.

The image that formed of this "war within the war" came to

10 The final relief of Verdun was accomplished on September 12, 1918, by the American 1st Army.

create a sort of myth of Verdun. That special aura was the basis of a state of mind among the soldiers which can be divided into three successive stages. When a man went up there, he felt a dim fear. When he left, he no longer was afraid of being afraid. When he left for good, he carried a sense of pride away in his memory. An officer recounts that once he was reading his men the day's communiqué, and it told about a German reverse near the Thiaumont farm where his regiment had stayed. "Don't say nothing about our losses," growled a *bonhomme*. But he was the only one to grumble. The others had a little flame of pride in their eyes: "That's us, it is!" Human beings draw their pride from their worst sufferings.

Vivian de Sola Pinto

VIVIAN DE SOLA PINTO *was born in Hampstead, England, in 1895, and was educated at University College School, London, and Christ Church, Oxford. In World War I he served as an officer in the Royal Welch Fusiliers in Gallipoli, Egypt, France, and Belgium, and was wounded twice on the western front. In the summer of 1918 he was second-in-command to Captain Siegfried Sassoon, the late poet, in the 25th Royal Welch. In 1921 he graduated with first-class honors from Oxford University and in 1926 was awarded the degree of Doctor of Philosophy. He was professor of English at University College, Southampton, from 1926 till 1938 and at the University of Nottingham from 1938 till 1961. He was elected a fellow of the Royal Society of Literature in 1929. In World War II he served as a captain in the British Intelligence Corps and the Royal Engineers. He has lectured in Belgium, Holland, India, Italy, the United States, and Yugoslavia, and he spent the academic year 1965–66 as visiting professor at the University of California, Davis. He married Irène Adeline Pittet in 1922 and has two sons. His publications include* Sir Charles Sedley (1927), Peter Sterry, Puritan and Platonist (1934), The English Renaissance (1938), Crisis in English Poetry (1951), Restoration Carnival (1954), Enthusiast in Wit (1962), The Restoration Court Poets (1965), William Blake (1965), *as well as two volumes of verse,* The Invisible Sun (1934) *and* This Is My England (1941). *He has also edited* The Poetical and Dramatic Works of Sir Charles Sedley, The Poems of John Wilmot, Earl of Rochester, *and* (with Warren Roberts) The Complete Poems of D. H. Lawrence.

MY FIRST WAR: MEMOIRS OF A
SPECTACLED SUBALTERN

IN THE SUMMER of 1914 I was a tall, lanky, spectacled youth of eighteen; I had just left school and was to go up to Oxford in October. At the end of July, I went with my father and sister to spend our usual summer holiday on the Scottish coast. When we left London, we had just heard of the assassination of the Austrian archduke at Sarajevo. By the end of the month the news was becoming not merely exciting but alarming. At first it seemed as if the conflict might be confined to the Balkans, but the refusal of the German government to cooperate with Sir Edward Grey's strenuous efforts to damp down the flames and the successive mobilizations of the Austrian, Russian, German, and French armies soon made it clear that a major European war was inevitable.

In the last days of July, however, and even in the first two of August, it was by no means certain that Britain would be drawn into the conflict. On Monday the third we read Grey's speech in the Commons in which he declared that the British Fleet would oppose any attempt of the German Navy to sail down the Channel and attack the French ports and indignantly rejected the German attempt to buy British neutrality by promising to restore French territorial integrity after the war. Then came in quick succession the German violations of France, Luxembourg, and, finally, Belgium, the country whose neutrality Britain was pledged to defend, the ultimatum and declaration of war on August 4.

A comparison at once suggests itself between the way in which the news of these world-shaking events was received by our little party at Dunbar in 1914 and the impact of the declaration of World War II twenty-five years later. Then, too, I was holiday making. I was with my wife and two young sons at a farmhouse in north Wales when we heard on a primitive radio set Mr. Chamberlain's announcement that we were at war with Hitler's Germany. In 1939 our reaction, like that, I believe, of most English people, was one of grim acceptance of a terrible necessity. Our mood in August, 1914, was very different. It was a mixture of relief, enthusiasm, and, I must admit, something like exultation.

Of course, we had no idea of the horrors of modern warfare. What we felt was relief from an intolerable tension, a sense of liberation from the deadly stuffiness of a commercialized civilization and of participation in a heroic adventure. Here, it seemed, was a chance for a wonderful renovation of human life, almost an apocalypse. At last we were being asked to fight and suffer not for imperial aggrandizement or material gain but for justice and liberty. Not only would we save the French and the Belgians, but we would rebuild our own society on a basis of social justice. This confused, nebulous, but fundamentally generous and humane enthusiasm was certainly the mood of millions of young Britons in the first weeks of the war. Rupert Brooke gave it a rather strained and melodramatic expression in his sonnet beginning "Now, God be thanked, Who has matched us with His Hour." Thomas Hardy, a much greater poet, alone found the right words for it in his "Song of the Soldiers":

> What of the faith and fire within us
> Men who march away
> Ere the barn-cocks say
> Night is growing grey,
> Leaving all that here can win us;
> What of the faith and fire within us
> Men who march away?

I find it hard to understand how people whom I respect, like Bertrand Russell, can still argue that we could and should have stood aside from the European conflict in 1914. If the pacifist minority in the Liberal government had had its way and we had failed to fulfill our legal obligation to Belgium and our moral obligation to France, the nation would certainly have been split from top to bottom. The Germans would, doubtless, have overrun western Europe as they did in 1940; but in the meantime, I have no doubt that thousands of British volunteers without adequate arms or organization would have streamed across the Channel to help the resistance, and the tragedy of the International Brigade in Spain in 1936–37 would have been anticipated on a much larger scale in France and Flanders. In the meantime, the German militarists controlling the resources of the whole Continent would have dictated their own terms to a divided and isolated Britain without a friend in the world, and the next victim would certainly have been the wealthy and, at that time, almost defenseless American democracy.

The feelings that I have tried to describe were certainly shared by many older English people, but in their minds they were often mixed, doubtless half-consciously, with less idealistic motives. Here was a unique opportunity to militarize the whole nation, to put a stop to all democratic progress and to use the naïve idealism of the young to buttress the domination of the privileged classes and enlarge and strengthen the British Empire. At the beginning of the war perhaps only a few crusted old colonels and the like would have explicitly accepted this view of the situation, but very soon such ideas began to gain ground especially among the "hard-faced men" who, as usual in times of national crisis, soon occupied key positions. More and more the war became *their* war, and not that of the young enthusiasts of August, 1914, and the results were tragic for Britain and the world. The betrayal of "the faith and fire within us" of August, 1914, is surely one of the great disasters of history and was to lead inevitably to the miserable reversion to the old game of power politics in the postwar period and the terrible results that followed.

We cut short our holiday at Dunbar and returned to London immediately after the declaration of war. I remember the next few weeks in our suburban home as a strange, feverish time. As there was no radio or television in those days, our only source of information about the war was the newspapers. I spent much of my time buying and reading the numerous editions of the morning and evening papers which appeared at all sorts of odd times. The smooth routine of middle-class suburban life seemed quite unreal. I felt that this world was now dead, a sort of ghastly simulacrum from which I must escape as soon as possible. Soon we heard of the landing of the B.E.F. in France, the retreat from Mons, the "miracle of the Marne," and the "race to the sea." Kitchener became War Minister, and his heavily moustached face appeared on all the hoardings, making his famous appeal for 1,000,000 recruits (conscription was still politically impossible under a Liberal government) . I waited in a long queue at a local recruiting office; when my turn came to be medically examined, I was told to remove my glasses for the eyesight test, and it was found that I could only with difficulty decipher the top letter on the card at the prescribed distance. So, like other myopic enthusiasts, at the time I was promptly rejected. I tried again at other recruiting offices with the same result, and I learned that only men who could read the first four lines without glasses were accepted. The British Army had no use for spectacled soldiers in 1914.

I went up to Oxford in October and joined the senior division of the O.T.C. to prepare myself for the time when the rigid rule debarring myopics from the fighting forces should be relaxed, as I was sure it would be if the war continued for any length of time.

Life at Oxford was pleasant but, like everything else in England at that time, seemed unreal. By the autumn the great line stretching from the North Sea to Switzerland had been established, Antwerp had been lost; but the old British Regular Army had withstood the German onslaught at Ypres, and the Channel ports had been saved. We heard now for the first time of the strange new phenomenon of trench warfare, and Bruce Bairnsfather's drawings helped us visualize its humors and miseries. I loved Oxford, but my demon kept telling me that I must get away from it and take my place among the men who were fighting and suffering. Paradoxically, at that moment it seemed that the only real life was to be found where there was the greatest chance of meeting a violent death.

When I came home for the Christmas vacation, London seemed to wear its usual appearance except for the recruiting posters and the number of men in uniform in the streets. It was the period of "business as usual," and so far there had been no air raids and no rationing. In fact, for a great part of the population it was a lovely war. Wages were high, unemployment had disappeared, profiteers were making huge profits, and money was flowing freely. Conscription was still far off, and numerous recruiting meetings were addressed by all sorts of people ranging from Cabinet ministers to music hall stars. Hysterical young women persecuted men of military age seen in the street in "civvies," and to protect myself from their attentions, I used to wear my O.T.C. uniform.

At the end of my second term I felt that it was impossible to live any longer in the Oxford dreamworld. In March I made several more assaults on recruiting offices with the same result as before. Then I heard that I might have a chance of being accepted by a unit called the Inns of Court O.T.C., which was a sort of offshoot of the famous Artists' Rifles. At this time officer cadet schools had not yet been organized, and the Inns of Court Battalion was being used to help with the supply of junior officers for the rapidly expanding Army. When I was medically examined at their headquarters, I was confronted by a kindly doctor who tactfully left me alone for a few minutes with the eyesight testing card before he asked me to remove my glasses. In these few minutes I memorized the first four lines of letters on the card and was able to recite them glibly when the doctor returned and my glasses were removed. So I became a private or rather rifleman in the Inns of Court Battalion and remained with them for a few weeks. My memory of those weeks is of strenuous drilling mostly at the double and being shouted at by a foulmouthed Cockney corporal who initiated us into the mysteries of the drill of the rifle regiments, which differed from the ordinary infantry drill which I had learned in my school and university O.T.C.'s. We also had bayonet practice which consisted of charging with rifle and fixed bayonet at a sack stuffed with straw suspended from a wooden frame and shouting imprecations at this imaginary enemy. Later, I believe, red paint was used to simulate blood on these sacks, but this charming refinement had not been introduced in the spring of 1915.

My fellow riflemen-cadets were constantly leaving to take up commissions, and soon my turn came. I was summoned to the orderly room and asked by the C.O. if I would accept a commission in a Territorial battalion of the Royal Welch Fusiliers. I suspected that this invitation may have been due to a Major M——, an officer in that battalion who had some acquaintance with my father. I knew nothing of the Royal Welch except that their officers wore a bunch of black ribbons on the backs of their tunics; but Major M—— was a kind, fatherly sort of person, and I thought I might as well enter this new and somewhat alarming world under his wing.

It is October, 1915. The scene is the rocky coast of the Gallipoli Peninsula in Turkey. The shy young undergraduate has been transformed into a second lieutenant in the Royal Welch Fusiliers dressed in dirty khaki drill uniform. He has recently arrived with a draft of junior officers to replace those killed or wounded at the August landings. His battalion is at present in a so-called rest camp consisting (I quote a diary kept at the time) "of numerous holes dug in the side of a hill called Ghazi Baba overlooking the sea. The holes are for the most part about 6×3 feet covered with a single ground sheet. Senior officers have somewhat larger ones with walls of sandbags or stones covered with several ground sheets stitched together. The place has the appearance of a huge antheap swarming with greyshirted, khaki-trousered tommies, mostly wearing woollen 'cap-comforters' on their heads (as yet there are no steel helmets). Looking southward, there is a magnificent view across Suvla Bay and Anzac Cove with the promontory called Lala Baba jutting out between them and behind it the sheet of water called the Salt Lake. On the right across the Aegean we can see the islands of Imbros and Samothrace and on the left, across a sandy plain dotted with a few stunted trees and ruined farmhouses, are the heights held by the Turks with the village of Anafarta Sagir (this name is naturally the subject of many lewd jests). The sea is full of allied warships, including a queer-looking Russian cruiser with four funnels called by our men 'the packet of woodbines,' which constantly shell the Turkish positions. Just out of range of the Turkish guns are a number of hospital ships painted green and white with large red crosses which are illuminated at night."

I am talking to a friendly Irish subaltern called Close, one of the survivors of the August landings, who tells me how the incompetent corps commander, General Stopford, kept our division, the 53d

Welch, and the Scottish 51st on the beach for nearly forty-eight hours after landing, during which time the Turks and Germans brought up heavy reinforcements. Even then our men reached Anafarta Sagir and could have pressed on across the peninsula to the straits if they had received adequate support and supplies.

Our food, mainly tinned stuff, is always full of sand and grit and infested with swarms of flies. Practically the whole Army is suffering from diarrhea and dysentery. The latrines are poles stretched across open trenches. On these poles rows of scarecrows, many of them dying of dysentery, sit continuously. It is a sight to which Goya at his most macabre might have done justice.

On the night of October 19 the Turkish field guns (which included many of the deadly French 75's) get the range of our camp and shell it with shrapnel, killing four men in the dugouts, including one of the subalterns who has come with me from England. The wounds are mostly in the head and could have been avoided if we had had steel helmets. The next night our battalion goes up to the front line, which is less than 100 yards from the Turkish trenches. Now for the first time I become acquainted with the routine of trench warfare: daylight hours of enforced idleness in trenches or dugouts, alternating with nights of activity with working parties and patrols and subalterns taking their turns as officers of the watch between the two important rituals of standing to arms at an hour before sunset and an hour before sunrise. The Turks are well supplied with ammunition and keep up a pretty incessant rifle and machine-gun fire during the hours of darkness. By daylight their very competent snipers were active, and we were warned not to expose any part of our anatomies above the parapet of the front-line trenches by day.

A jolly red-haired boy in my platoon called "Ginger" Jenkins disregarded this injunction on our first morning in the front line. I was in the next bay when I heard the crack of a rifleshot and found poor Ginger lying in a pool of blood on the fire step. As the body was being carried away by the stretcher bearers the platoon sergeant said, "Strong as a little 'orse 'e was. 'E never got no dysentery." I thought of Rupert Brooke: "If I should die, think only this of me. . . ." and Sergeant Cooper's epitaph seemed to me far more to the point than Brooke's highfalutin fancy. On November 18 I was sent with a working party in the early morning to a place some way behind the front line near the Salt Lake. We found there on the brown grass and buried a number of corpses of men of the Worcesters which had been there since the landings in August. The stench was horrible; I describe them in my diary as "gruesome black masses of decomposition with pitiful, loose arms and legs, their white sunhelmets lying beside them adding to the nightmare quality of the scene." This sight haunted my memory, and henceforward I was proof against all the clichés about "sacrifice," "glory," and "never sheathing the sword." All such expressions were for me now permanently tainted by the thought of those vigorous young bodies turned into objects of horror.

Toward the end of November the weather broke. On the twenty-seventh rain fell in torrents, and it turned very cold. It was the beginning of the worst winter known in the Aegean for many years, a grimly appropriate conclusion to the ill-starred Gallipoli campaign. We were flooded out of our trenches, which were knee-deep in water. The Turks probably suffered as much as we did, and their rifle and machine-gun fire ceased. We had no dry clothes or hot rations, our tobacco and matches were soaked so that we could not smoke, and we spent the night shivering in the fields behind the trenches. The next day some hot food was brought to us and that night we were relieved by a Scottish battalion of the 51st Division.

We marched in single file in pitch-darkness down endless water-logged communication trenches. When we emerged into open country, the word was passed down that we were to halt and bivouac for the night. "Bivouac" was a grim joke as, with wonderful foresight, our waterproof sheets and blankets had been collected before we left the trenches. An icy wind was now blowing, and the rain had turned to sleet. Soon it was freezing and snowing, and our clothes were caked with mud and frozen stiff. In the early morning I helped another subaltern, my friend Vernon Anson, and his batman, John Evans, enlarge a shell hole over which we stretched an old blanket and secured the edges with stones. The three of us huddled together in this improvised dugout. Anson had a tin of condensed milk, and I had a flask with a little brandy, and we shared these scanty supplies for the rest of the day while a blizzard swept over us. This was November 30, the day long remembered by survivors of the Gallipoli army as "frozen foot day," when more than 200 British soldiers are said to have died of exposure on that storm-swept Gallipoli coast.

In the evening Anson, Evans, and I were picked up by a party of R.A.M.C. (Royal Army Medical Corps) men who took us to the 1st Welch Field Ambulance on the beach. "What a wretched crowd of scarecrows we were," I wrote in my diary some days later, "all ranks huddled together, livid with cold and dressed in filthy, ragged uniforms, one man writhing and wailing on the ground." The R.A.M.C. men did their best to make us comfortable with blankets and mugs of hot tea; but the blizzard was still raging, and the cold was intense. On the following night we were put on stretchers and carried onto a lighter, which took us to one of those beautiful hospital ships we had looked at so often with longing eyes from our trenches. Our dirty clothes were removed; we were washed by tender, skillful hands, dressed in clean pajamas, and put to bed in white cots. For the first time I knew the wonderful joy of getting out of the fighting line into the peace and cleanliness of a hospital.

In the spring of 1917, after being invalided home from Egypt, I was sent with a draft from our 4th Reserve Battalion to the 19th Royal Welch Fusiliers (a newly formed "Kitchener Battalion") in France. I reached them in April, when their division (the 40th) was just moving forward in pursuit of the Germans, who were carrying out their famous strategic withdrawal from their old positions on the Somme after the bloody battles of 1916. I was lucky enough to be posted to C Company commanded by Captain "Pip" Powell, a burly, dark-haired Cambridge man who had been a schoolteacher in civilian life. The second-in-command, Hal Parry, a lean, bronzed little Welshman, had been a skipper in the merchant marine and always carried a telescope slung over his shoulder. I struck up a warm friendship with these two admirable men, who were amused by my exotic name and promptly nicknamed me Gondola. Pip was a natural leader of men, generous, humane and intelligent, and Hal had a fine, dry, salty humor that no amount of physical hardship could quench.

It was very cold and constantly raining as we advanced along the Péronne-Cambrai road. We bivouacked at night in old German trenches and dugouts but had to exercise caution because the enemy had left behind numerous booby traps. One of our men picked up an object that looked like a fountain pen. It contained a detonator which blew off several of his fingers. Our advance continued up to the ridge in front of the village of Gouzeaucourt and into the neighboring villages of Gonnelieu and La Vacquerie. Here the retreating Germans fought a rearguard action before retreating to their famous Hindenburg Line in front of Cambrai and St.-Quentin.

The official *History of the Royal Welch Fusiliers* calls this "a small affair," but an action which seems small to the military historian is often quite formidable to the troops who take part in it. By the time we reached Gouzeaucourt, we were, as I wrote in a letter to my father, "a horrible sight, unwashed, unshaven with our clothes, which we had not been able to take off for a week, sticking to us." At any rate, however, we now had "battle bowlers," or steel helmets, and also leather jerkins, which would have been a godsend in that November blizzard at Suvla Bay.

We dug ourselves in, using partly an old German trench line on the ridge in front of Gouzeaucourt, and there, one early morning, our divisional artillery and that of the Guards Division put down a tremendous barrage, which was suitably accompanied by a terrific thunderstorm. Behind this wall of flame we went into La Vacquerie where our sappers blew up a number of gun emplacements and dugouts. However, it was decided not to hold the village, and we went back to our ridge in front of Gouzeaucourt, now named in honor of our regiment "Fusilier Ridge." Three of our company commanders (fortunately not Pip) and a good many "other ranks" were killed in this "small affair." In the following weeks our division organized an elaborate trench system in front of Gouzeaucourt. Through our field glasses (and Hal's telescope) we could see the sun glinting on the huge bands of wire entanglements in front of the much talked-of Hindenburg Line. Our front line was separated from that of the enemy by a wide no-man's-land of 800 to 1,000 yards.

After the action at La Vacquerie our sector became fairly quiet. "Quiet" on the western front was, of course, a relative term. There was constant desultory shelling, bursts of machine-gun fire, snipers on the lookout for unwary enemies who exposed themselves above parapets by daylight, and trench mortars lobbing their murderous missiles periodically over no-man's-land. Our brigade now spent three weeks in the line without being relieved. Very soon we were all lousy, and our webbing equipment was nibbled by the large rats which abounded in the trenches. Nevertheless, in spite of all the hardships and discomforts, I remember that spring of 1917 as a time of warmhearted comradeship both with the men of my platoon and the other company officers, and although I naturally missed my books and the amenities of civilized life, I was a good deal happier than in the comfort and security of my "nice" prewar bourgeois suburban home.

After a period of divisional rest in the devastated country near Péronne, we were back in our old sector in front of Gouzeaucourt. The bright boys on the staff were always thinking of new ways of keeping the men in the line occupied. The idea that was dominant in our division in those summer months of 1917 was the "fighting patrol." When we first established our new line in April, we used to send out small parties, consisting of two or three men with an officer or N.C.O., into no-man's-land after dark to patrol the area in front of our wire. The fighting patrol was a much more ambitious affair, consisting of fifteen to twenty men commanded by a subaltern or, sometimes, a captain. Its orders were to patrol the whole of no-man's-land up to the enemy wire and engage any enemy patrols that it might meet. The members of these patrols had their faces blackened, wore woolen cap comforters instead of battle bowlers, and had the buttons of their tunics covered or tarnished. I rather enjoyed going out on patrol. I liked the thrill of danger, the sense of escaping from the troglodyte existence of the trenches and being out in the open under the night sky. We used to creep through the long grass in no-man's-land up to the German line, and when one of the numerous German flares went up, we would stay in frozen immobility till the light faded. There was a sunken road which provided excellent cover for our return.

On the night of July 8, after completing our usual tour of no-man's-land, I led my patrol over the bank into the sunken road. It was bright moonlight, and as we dropped into the road, we found ourselves in the middle of a number of men in flat caps, obviously a German patrol. For a moment the English and the Germans stared at each other in amazement. I had my loaded revolver hung around my neck on a lanyard, and in my excitement, I raised it and fired into the mass of strangers. I certainly hit a man near me and saw him fall. Then there was a blinding flash, and I heard a tremendous roar. The next thing I remember was regaining consciousness on a stretcher in our front line with a bandage round the lower part of my face and my mouth full of blood, feeling as though my lower jaw had been blown off.

Later I learned that after I fired my revolver, a German threw one of their stick bombs, which exploded above my head and knocked me senseless. My excellent sergeant and others of our patrol then threw some Mills bombs at the Germans, who promptly scattered, and I was carried back to our front line with a field dressing tied around my bleeding mouth. I remember Pip leaning over my stretcher and saying, "Poor old Gondola. You've certainly got a Blighty one this time."[1] Actually, he was wrong. When my wound was dressed, it was found that my jaw was intact; but some teeth had been knocked out, and various pieces of bomb had been lodged in my tongue and cheek.

I was taken to a hospital run by a Harvard medical team at Étretat in Normandy, where a skillful American surgeon extracted the pieces of bomb and sewed up my perforated cheek. My healthy young body soon recovered from the injury, the hole in my cheek healed, and my swollen tongue went down to its normal size. Instead of going home, I was sent to Lady Michelham's convalescent home at Dieppe. This wealthy and generous woman had taken the two best hotels in this Norman seaside resort as a con-

[1] A "Blighty one" was a wound which would send you back to "Blighty," the soldier slang word for England.

valescent home for wounded British officers. One day, while I was enjoying a delectable fortnight in these pleasant surroundings, I picked up a glossy magazine which contained a poem by an author of whom I had never heard before with the resonant name of Siegfried Sassoon. It was an attractive piece of verse expressing the longing for beautiful things felt by many sensitive spirits amid the drabness of trench warfare:

> Return to me, colours that were my joy,
> Not in the woeful crimson of men slain
> But shining as a garden; come with streaming
> Colours of dawn, and sundown after rain.

It seemed to me that this was a poet who was to be watched. Shortly afterward, when I was at the base camp at Rouen, waiting to be sent back to my unit, I read a review of a recently published book of verse by Sassoon called *The Old Huntsman*; the reviewer quoted in full a poem of a very different kind from the mellifluous lines quoted above. It was called "Blighters," and its quality of burning sincerity made every other war poem that I had seen fade into insignificance:

> The House is crammed: tier upon tier they grin
> And cackle at the Show, while prancing ranks
> Of harlots shrill the chorus, drunk with din;
> "We're sure the Kaiser loves the dear old Tanks!"
>
> I'd like to see a Tank come down the stalls,
> Lurching to rag-time tunes, or "Home, sweet Home,"
> And there'd be no jokes in Music-halls
> To mock the riddled corpses round Bapaume.[2]

Here was a man who had found the supremely right words for the growing indignation of the men of the front line at the heartless vulgarity of the people at home who were enjoying "a lovely war." I cut the poem out and learned it by heart: It seemed to crystallize feelings which had been growing up obscurely in my mind ever since I saw those pathetic corpses at Suvla Bay.

When I returned to my battalion in September, they were still in the Gouzeaucourt sector, which had become much livelier. Large trench mortars were active on both sides, and Jerry (as we called the Germans)[3] had developed an unpleasant habit of bringing up captured French 75's to his front line and sniping at us at point-blank range with formidable field guns. In 1917 it was exceptional

---

[2] Bapaume is a town on the Somme near Péronne where many thousands of British and German troops were slaughtered in the battles of 1916.

[3] The words "Hun" and "Boche" were mainly used by armchair patriots at home.

for infantry subalterns in the line to escape wounds or death for any length of time. I was lucky. On October 27 I was hit in the right forearm by a German machine-gun bullet when I was in no-man's-land. This time my wound was a perfect "Blighty one." I was given one of the horrible anesthetics of those days at an advanced dressing station while the bullet was extracted, and it was found that the bone was splintered and the wound was septic. Very soon I found myself gliding in a hospital train into Victoria Station in London, where a lady in black offered me some cake, which I accepted, and a religious tract, which I refused. That night, lying in bed in a hospital in Camberwell, I heard the bark of antiaircraft guns and the thud of bombs. It was my first experience of an air raid on London.

My arm took longer to heal than I expected, and I was at home on sick leave at Christmas. I was now the perfect exhibit for an English middle-class family in the winter of 1917 with my conspicuous wound, my full lieutenant's uniform (I had now had my second pip) with the divisional flash on my shoulders showing that I had come from "overseas," the ribbon of the 1914–15 star and two golden wound stripes. My proud father took me on a round of visits to various friends, and I was lavishly dined and wined. These were people of the sort who always referred to the enemy as the "Hun," looked forward with glee to hanging the poor old Kaiser, and were now vociferous in denouncing the wicked Bolshevists who had "let us down" on the eastern front.

As I gulped down their champagne with a fatuous smile on my face, I felt horribly unreal, a sort of ghost from another world, the real world of the brotherhood of the front line, and, when we went to the theater to see *Chu Chin Chow* and *The Bing Boys,* as I looked at the crowded auditorium and the glittering lights, I could not help wondering whether it would not, perhaps, be a good thing if a tank should come lurching through the stalls to jolt out of their complacency all these well-fed people who were enjoying "a lovely war." Actually, the war was not quite so lovely now even for these sheltered London suburbans. There were occasional air raids, tiny affairs, indeed, compared with the blitzes of the forties, yet sufficient to cause some alarm and despondency, and the German U-boat campaign was causing a shortage of various foodstuffs, notably butter and sugar, though the better-class restaurants still continued to serve succulent meals. As soon as I was well enough to go out, I bought a copy of *The Old Huntsman,* in which, besides the poems I had already seen, I found much that was congenial to my present mood.

When I returned to the Reserve Battalion in Wales, in view of my wounds and service on two fronts, I was placed on the strength as second-in-command of a company, which meant that I should not be sent overseas again for six months unless there was an urgent need for officers in the line. Such a need arose in the spring of 1918 after the devastating offensives of Ludendorff on the Somme and at Armentières. So, on June 17, I found myself crossing the Channel once more on a crowded troopship; this time it was full of American officers, one of whom, seeing my 1914–15 ribbon, came up to me and said, "Say, Lootenant, were you at Mons?"

At the base camp at Rouen, I found that I was posted to the 25th Royal Welch Fusiliers, a battalion formed originally from an amalgamation of two dismounted Welsh yeomanry regiments, belonging to the 74th Division, which had recently come to the western front from Palestine. When I arrived at the battalion headquarters in a partly ruined chateau near Arras, I sensed an entirely different atmosphere from that of the other fighting battalions in which I had served. These men had taken part in Allenby's advance to Jerusalem. They were, for the most part, big bronzed fellows with something of the panache of victorious troops and something of the swagger of cavalrymen. Many of them had their puttees wound in the reverse way from that of infantrymen and carried their haversacks hitched up, cavalry fashion, under their arms. The divisional sign was a broken spur, and the very smart flash was a green diamond with a vertical white stripe, which I had sewn onto the shoulders of my tunic as soon as possible. The adjutant, a stout, dark man with a row of decorations, ushered me into the presence of the colonel, who said, "You're to go to A Company as second-in-command to Captain Sassoon." I pricked up my ears at these words. Could it really be that I should have the incredible luck of serving under the author of *The Old Huntsman?*

The rest of the day had an apocalyptic quality for me. A guide led me down a muddy path to A Company headquarters, a hut in front of a mass of trees silhouetted against a sky in which a fine June sunset was flaring through broken clouds. A tall figure came out of the hut to meet me. Ignoring my smart salute, he shook me by the hand.

"I suppose you're my new second-in-command. I've never had one before—"

"Yes, sir, er, are you the poet Siegfried Sassoon?"

As I blurted out these words I knew what the answer was. That splendid, erect form with the noble head, mane of dark hair, piercing black eyes, and strongly sculptured features could belong only to a poet. He took me into the hut and made me talk about myself. I tried to describe very inadequately the effect "Blighters" and Siegfried's other trench poems had had on me. In his book *Sherston's Progress,* where he calls me Velmore, he describes his new second-in-command as he appeared to him on that June evening in 1918: "a tall, dark young man who had been up at Oxford for an academic year when the outbreak of war interrupted his studies. More scholastic than soldier-like in appearance (mainly because he wore spectacles) he had the look of one who might some day occupy a professorial chair."[4]

Pip Powell had been an excellent company commander, but Siegfried was something quite different. He was what, in modern jargon, is called a charismatic personality who radiated heroic energy and generosity. He is good enough to write that when I was his second-in-command, I gave him "an extra head and a duplicate pair of eyes." The fact was that like every man in A Company, I at once became his devoted servant and, seeing that he was bored by the immense quantities of paper that descended on every company commander in 1918 from "higher up" "for necessary attention," I tried to relieve him as far as possible of this part of the work and deal with the innumerable instructions, directions, requests for returns, etc. as punctually and expeditiously as I could.

Soon after my arrival our division began to move "up North." On July 12 our battalion took over part of the line in front of St.-Floris near Armentières in the sector where the Portuguese had been pushed back in the German offensive in April. Here we found something very different from the well-organized trench systems to which I had been accustomed in 1917. The "line" here was a series of breast-high posts strung out over a wide area and connected by a shallow ditch. A little way behind the posts was an enlarged shell hole dignified by the name of company headquarters and, close by, two similar excavations occupied respectively by the company sergeant major and the signalers. No-man's-land varied from 100 to 200 yards and consisted of beautiful fields of nearly ripe wheat and barley.

There were two other subalterns besides me in A Company; but one of them soon went off to be battalion Lewis gun officer, and the other, an attractive youth called Jowitt, was sent on a short course. In these circumstances Siegfried and I decided to divide the night into two watches, during which one of us would stay at company headquarters to deal with messages while the other patrolled the posts. I found it a curious paradox that the author of *Counter Attack,* which had just been published, that volume full of bitter indignation at the hideous cruelty of modern warfare, should also

---

4 *Sherston's Progress* (London, 1936), p. 230.

be a first-rate soldier and a most aggressive company commander. He was determined that A Company should demonstrate its superiority to the enemy as soon as possible, and he spent a large part of his nocturnal watches crawling through the deep corn in no-man's-land with a couple of bombs in his pocket and a knobkerric in his hand. On the first night after our arrival he crawled up to a German post and brought back one of their stick bombs. I implored him to be careful and told him his life was too valuable to be risked in this way.

By the middle of July the German artillery had got our range, and we were heavily shelled with their big 5.9's or crumps. After breakfast on the seventeenth, Siegfried and I were squatting together in our cubbyhole when a series of heavy thuds warned us that the crumps were getting uncomfortably near. Finally, a tremendous impact sent us flying across the mouth of the dugout, but there was no explosion; a dud had landed just behind us, and a great crack opened in the earth at the back of our hole. It looked like a huge, grinning, diabolical mouth, and we christened it "the grin of death." Most of the German shells at this time contained phosgene gas, and some of them the recently introduced and even more horrific mustard variety, so that we had to spend much of our time very uncomfortably wearing our respirators. On the night of the eighteenth, Siegfried took the second watch from midnight onward, and as usual, I begged him to be careful and do nothing foolhardy. When we stood to an hour before dawn, he had not returned. At about five thirty I began to get anxious and, leaving Company Sergeant Major Evans to hold the fort, I went up to the posts with my batman and a runner.

The first three platoons that I visited had seen nothing of Siegfried, and when I reached No. 4 Post, it was broad daylight. The corporal in charge of the section on our extreme right told me that the captain had gone into no-man's-land sometime ago. Taking this corporal with me, I was just getting through our wire when I saw Siegfried's head bobbing up in the pale yellow corn about twenty yards away. As he raised his arm to wave to me, I heard the sharp crack of a rifleshot from No. 3 Post. It came from one of our overzealous sergeants who mistook his company commander for a German. When I reached Siegfried, his face was covered with blood, and I thought for a moment that he was badly wounded; but he assured me that the bullet had only grazed his temple, and leaning on my shoulder, he was able to limp back to the post, where he fainted. He regained consciousness lying on a stretcher on which he was carried down to the dressing station. As I walked beside him I could not help saying, "O dear, Siegfried, I was afraid something like this would happen. Now you've left the ruddy company on my hands."

I was now, at the age of twenty-two, commanding a company in a rather sticky sector of the line with no officers. My second-in-command was, therefore, Sergeant Major Evans, who, I must say, was worth a half a dozen average subalterns. I decided to divide the nights with him as I had formerly divided them with Siegfried. The next morning the divisional general came to see me and asked if I thought I could carry on for another week, and I told him I would do my best. The following days were the most unpleasant and exhausting that I spent in the line. I had hardly any sleep, gas shells rained down on us continually, and we had numerous casualties. An additional pleasantry was supplied by our own artillery. They started shelling the German front line with projectiles which emitted a horrible gas that blew back onto our own posts. The staff gave me almost as much trouble as the enemy. Runners were constantly appearing with messages from "higher up" claiming "immediate attention." One of these gave me some grim amusement. It was an urgent request from divisional headquarters to let them know at once how many men in my company wanted divisional Christmas cards! I scrawled across it, "Probably none if present conditions continue."

It was a great relief to see Jowitt's cheerful face when he returned three days after Siegfried's departure. He and I promptly got to work on preparations for a daylight raid on an enemy post which Siegfried had planned before he was wounded. The raid was a complete success. We took five prisoners—a corporal and four privates. Sitting on the fire step in one of our posts, these Saxons looked very young, thin, and pale in their dirty field gray uniforms as they drank mugs of tea and smoked cigarettes that our men gave them. It seemed incredible that these young English and German soldiers who were now on such excellent terms should have been trying a short time before to slaughter each other with all sorts of diabolical instruments.

Soon after we came out of the line, a gas shell fell on my company headquarters in a ruined farmhouse and filled my lungs with phosgene. I was sent to a hospital at Étaples in a very uncomfortable condition diagnosed as "phosgene poisoning and bronchitis." After a period of light duty at Rouen, I was lucky enough to be able to rejoin my battalion just in time for the great advance in the beginning of October.

In the light of a gray, misty dawn near La Bassée we scrambled through our wire in fighting equipment with iron rations (canned meat) for three days. In front of us was a smoke barrage through which we could dimly see the shapes of tanks, and when we reached the enemy wire, we found that it had been effectively flattened by these monsters. Going gingerly for fear of booby traps, we managed to get clear of the German trench system by the late afternoon, and I shall never forget the thrill of breaking through the barrier which had resisted Allied attacks for four years and reaching the first inhabited building, a farmhouse with a light in the window, where an elderly Frenchwoman and her daughter, looking pale and ghostly in their black clothes, made us some coffee. Very early the next morning we entered Lille. As we marched through this great city, the first important town to be liberated by the Allies, with fixed bayonets and drums beating, the whole population seemed to be in the streets, on the balconies or at the windows of the houses, from which tricolors and an occasional Union Jack were flying.

There followed a period of several days during which the dream of all the generals on the western front was at last realized and we were able to take part in "open warfare." In a letter dated October 18 I wrote, "I have been walking or riding for thirty-six hours without a wash, change, sleep or anything to eat except army biscuits and an occasional cup of *ersatz* coffee supplied by the inhabitants who turn out to greet us." During the advance we had to drink quantities of this curious liquid made chiefly, I believe, from acorns and chicory. We soon crossed the Belgian frontier and reached the line of the Scheldt at Tournai, where the Germans made a stand for a few days.

On November 1, a bright autumn morning, we crossed the Scheldt on a temporary bridge erected by our sappers in place of the one that had been blown up by the retreating Germans. On entering the ancient city of Tournai, we found it almost completely intact and were surprised to notice that the provisions shops were well stocked with such luxuries as creamcakes and pastries which it would have been impossible to obtain at that time in most English and French towns. When we left Tournai, A Company, which I was now commanding again, with a detachment of cyclists, was sent forward as an advance guard.

Covering 15 to 20 miles a day, we soon left the main body of the brigade far behind. Walkie-talkies were still in the future; but my signalers had some carrier pigeons, and we sent back one of these birds every evening with the map reading of our position. Each village that we entered was adorned with Allied flags, and a malicious and probably apocryphal story was circulating that these flags had been sold to the peasants by an enterprising German business-man before the enemy left. The Belgian villagers seemed in much better shape than the inhabitants of the French liberated territory;

and we were now regaled not only with *ersatz* coffee but also with stronger liquids and cigars. I have a Brueghel-like memory picture of a kermess organized in our honor at a little inn, where we danced with strapping Flemish girls to the music of a bagpipe into the small hours.

When we halted for the night at a village on November 6, I received a visit from my brigadier. It was a dark, rainy evening, and as we squatted in a shed looking at a map by the light of my electric torch, I said, "Can I push on and take Brussels, sir?" Considering that my advance guard consisted of about 100 infantry and a few cyclists, I always regard this question as the highlight of my military career. The brigadier, however, told me to stop where I was and await the arrival of the rest of the brigade as he had information that there was a mutiny among the German troops in Brussels and we had better not get involved.

The next day the rest of the battalion caught me up, and we now continued our advance along the main road, passing hastily over the mined crossroads. The great stream of British troops moving eastward was now met by another stream going in the opposite direction. It consisted of ragged, footsore German deserters and Allied prisoners who had walked out of German prison camps, now deserted by their mutinous guards. We all knew now that German envoys were at G.H.Q. and that an armistice was imminent. On the morning of November 11 we were still being shelled and machinegunned occasionally by German rear guards, and one of our captains was killed by a direct hit on a latrine. Our objective that day was Perquise, a village on the Tournai-Brussels road, and we were probably farther east than any other unit in the British Army.

That morning our staff captain galloped along the line of march shouting, "No firing after eleven o'clock!" We halted just outside Perquise, and at midday some German officers came and showed us where the road was mined. As we approached the village, we were met by a crowd of peasants headed by a little hunchback with an accordion who led us in triumph into Perquise playing the "Marseillaise." That evening copies of the Armistice terms roughly printed on broadsheets by the famous secret press of the *Indépendance belge* at Brussels were distributed among the troops. The weather was cold and rainy. No wine was available in the village; but I managed to obtain a chicken for the evening meal of A Company mess, and we washed it down with some rum and water. After dark, as I strolled around some farm buildings where our men were billeted, I heard a voice complaining of "the bleeding weather" and another replying, "Put a sock in it. After what we've heard today, I could sleep like a bird in a tree."

Georges Gaudy

GEORGES GAUDY *was born at St.-Junien, in the department of Haute-Vienne, on February 18, 1895. He developed a taste for studying for a religious vocation, and conceived the desire to enter the seminary, but this inclination did not withstand the sound of arms in 1914.*

He tried to enlist, but was turned down because he was underweight. He then set himself to eating great quantities of sugar to gain the pounds he needed. Whether the regimen worked or not, he was finally accepted, and ably participated in almost all 57th Infantry Regiment actions from January 10, 1916, through September 2, 1918.

In 1920 Gaudy published his first account of the war, L'Agonie du Mont-Renaud. *"If I had to classify the war books, rank them," Albert Thibaudet has written, "I am quite sure that this is the one I would put first."*

Trous d'obus de Verdun *and* Chemin-des-Dames en feu *appeared in 1922 and 1923. In 1926, Gaudy published a social study,* La Ville rouge.

Having belonged to the nationalist movement Action Française, Gaudy became editor of the daily paper of that name and began to give numerous lectures. His books continued to appear: a war novel, Les Galons noirs, *a fourth volume of memoirs,* Le Drame à Saconin et l'épopée sur l'Ingon *in 1930, and* La France cherche un homme *in 1934.*

Called up again as a captain in 1939 for service, in the rear, he volunteered and left for the front on December 31, and participated in rearguard actions. After the fall of France, Gaudy published Combats sans gloire *at Lyons, in the free zone. In more than 310 copies given him to autograph, he reinserted—by hand—passages cut by the censors.*

From July 27, 1945, to August 16, 1950, following service in Africa and Italy under General Alphonse-Pierre Juin, Gaudy was involved in the occupation of Austria, and during that period—in 1946—he published Combats libérateurs. *On his return to France, he took up his profession of journalism and lecturing.*

OUR OLD FRONT*

Man, in all he does in every age, will blend
Measures of music and song. That is why, my friend,
The war that moves our passions—
Noble goddess, who dwelled in our childhood dreaming regions—
Calls out the voice, before the somber marching legions,
Of the brass-throated clarions.

—VICTOR HUGO, *"Les Voix intérieures"*

IT WAS January 20, 1916, when I arrived at the front to join the
57th Infantry Regiment as a private.

By then, if you went through the communication trenches, you
heard very different songs coming out of the hollows from those
that shook the depots in August, 1914, like the "Marseillaise," the
"Sambre-et-Meuse," the "Chant du départ."

The trench slaves found expression for their feelings in the
repertory of wretchedness and various ballads and verses from the
most deprived proletariat.

Yet they were always ready for heavy work and combat.

What struck you was the physical vigor of these poilus, washing
up half-nude in the snow. Their gaze was calm, their smiles a little
mocking, their faces tanned.

A strength capable of taking on the roughest battle of all time,
the Battle of Verdun, had been forged in suffering—which is,
mysteriously, the condition of all perfection.

This maturing of the French man of war can also be predicated
of the English and the German. Like Ernst Jünger, author of
Stahlgewitter,[1] I have observed that it took two years of trials for
the front to carve the fighter's countenance. Its intensely virile expression was lit with a look broadened by the flash of shells, deepened by an inner struggle. His soul appeared in its light.

When peace returned, the survivors needed no ribbons on their
jackets to recognize and greet one another with a grave smile in a
crowd. Today their number is very reduced. The youngest are

---

* Translated from the French by Sally Abeles.

1 *Storm of Steel: From the Diary of a German Storm-Troop Officer on the Western
Front,* tr. by Basil Creighton (Garden City, 1929) .—Tr.

seventy years of age. But from time to time I meet an eighty-two-year-old veteran in Montmartre—Berthieu, who was a lieutenant in the 57th. He goes shopping there, walking with a military step as if he were leaving for the Marne or Marengo.[2] I see another, named Éveille, who still wears a moustache, and who was the quartermaster corporal of the 11th Company in the same corps. An artist could paint him in either the busby of Napoleonic days or the helmet of 1915. It would look as though the man had deceived time and had simply changed uniform.

If February 21, 1916, had ended the conflict, instead of opening the inferno of Verdun, history would still have gathered a rich enough harvest to call this war the Great War.

The battle of the frontiers, the battles of the Marne, of the Yser, Éparges, Vieil-Armand;[3] of Artois, where Vimy, Souchez, Carency, Notre-Dame-de-Lorette, Ablain-St.-Nazaire stand out in memory; the offensive in Champagne on September 25, 1915, the matrix of the incessant struggles for Tahure, Souain, Massiges, Mesnil-les-Hurlus; and corresponding with these constantly rekindled fires, the conflagrations in the Argonne in the ever-smoking sectors of Fille Morte, La Harazée, Haute-Chevauchée, Four de Paris, Vauquois—ample scenes for illustrating dramatic pages.

The single image of Verdun presently eclipses the battles which flamed before it and which it would be unjust to veil. No Verdun would have been possible without the savage apprenticeship imposed during the preceding eighteen months.

But after World War II, a confusion of claims arose, contrasting the incomparable Battle of Verdun with the justly famous Stalingrad and Cassino campaigns.

There are degrees of hell, abysses below abysses. Even a tempest on the Ushant cliffs is not the maelstrom described by Edgar Allan Poe.

In the Stalingrad tragedy the Wehrmacht had from 220,000 to 230,000 men. The German losses at Verdun, of 325,000 killed and wounded for a similar period, were far larger than General Friedrich Paulus' total force.

I watched Cassino flame for weeks, like Vieil-Armand in the Vosges fifty years ago.

I cannot repeat here accounts from *Choses vues et vécues* at

---

[2] An Italian village where the French, under Napoleon, defeated the Austrians in June, 1800.—Tr.

[3] The name the French troops gave to the Hartmannswillerkopf spur, in the Vosges Mountains.—Tr.

Verdun,[4] but here are some typical happenings that are not spoken of there.

The first day of the German onslaught, as all our field pieces were destroyed behind the Caures Wood where Colonel Émile Driant's men hung on, only one 75 field gun remained. Dr. Voivenel heard it firing all night long, alone against the whole horde of German heavy artillery.

To the last gun and to the last man—that was characteristic of Verdun.

There were days, particularly in late June and early July, when the shadows that covered the ground, the artificial night created by the dust and smoke, made it impossible to maintain any contact or exercise any command, even at the company level. This was due to the dreadful intensity of the shelling. Germans and French found themselves mingling at several points, with the General Staffs incapable of knowing their positions and fixing their limits. Then the battle was reduced to one-to-one combat, each man fighting for his shell hole. A shell hole where one tenacious man, in a fever of anguish, his throat burning with thirst, drank the water from a hollow containing a decaying corpse, surer of fetching himself dysentery than glory. The final victory, certainly, was due to the high command, but it belonged as well to the terrified soldiers, who transformed their fear into fighting fury when the enemy rose before them.

This phenomenon can only be explained as the result of intensive training.

The Battle of the Somme, launched by British and French forces on July 1 of the same year, became particularly arduous when the Picardy plain turned into a sea of mud that sucked at men and animals.

We were arriving from rest camps when we met the Foreign Legion returning from the lines. Plastered to the ears with the sticky clay of the Santerre district, the legionnaires, like the other soldiers, had cut off the tails of their overcoats, which would have got coated with earth and would have weighed them down. As they caught sight of us, they shouted, "Hey, reinforcements for the cemetery!"

When the frost came, the guns shot slivers of clay as trenchant as steel, and we gathered up the bodies of men on watch in the front positions who had frozen to death.

In 1917 on the Chemin des Dames ridge, General Robert

---

4 *Verdun et le Chemin-des-Dames: Choses vues et vécues* (Paris, 1966).

Georges Nivelle's staff, which had replaced General J. J. C. Joffre's, believed the French forces could win and communicated this conviction to the troops.

On the eve of an offensive claimed to be the last one, the drive which was to have carried us into Belgium in four days, all the men with leave from our regiment, except one who left and didn't return, wanted to stand by so they wouldn't miss the victory blow they thought was so close, alas.

We were behind the colonials, who were to launch the breakthrough. Half an hour after the attack was launched—this was April 16, at six in the morning—we learned that the attempt had failed.

The next night we slept in a drizzle and in the snow on the Paissy plateau.

The following May 5, our Army corps, the 18th, snatched the Craonne and Vauclerc plateaus from the Prussian Guard. This terrain drank the blood of 10 of our regiment's officers and 404 men of the ranks killed and 11 officers and 461 men wounded. Though exhausted, the regiment kept its morale up.

Great was the universal disappointment caused by the collapse of excessive hopes. Agitators took advantage of this. At the end of May, I saw men at a control depot who were wearing uniforms but without any collar tabs, collecting soldiers on leave and trying to make them sing the "Internationale" and march on Paris. A people till now united could end in crisis like this. General Henri Philippe Pétain restored balance to the troops.

Two or three years before World War II the Germans were asking themselves how they could have missed the chance of profiting by this serious unrest. Ettighofer asked this question in his book *Eine Armee meutert.*

In the same period, they were examining why they had taken Verdun as an objective, a choice that strategic reasons alone could not justify.

When these publications appeared, I was scheduled to make a speech at a conference in Nîmes, which was presided over by General de Bourgon, former Chief of Staff to Verdun's military governor, General Coutanceau. De Bourgon told me that General Erich von Falkenhayn had succeeded in imposing his views at the Charleville meeting called by William II in September, 1915. His goal was to break the defense of Verdun with a blow so massive and so stunning that, he thought, French morale would collapse, the Cabinet would fall, and a separate peace could be concluded with a new government.

Then: 1918! In the spring, the sky opened, and divisions that had fought so hard for a few acres of ground were on the move again.

The storm broke on our British allies, as it would beat down on us equally effectively the following May 27.

During the night of March 20–21, Lieutenant Jünger of the Hannoverian 73d and his comrades, dizzy from the din of the explosions, whistled and struck the table in their shelter with their fists, imitating the fall and boom of the shells.

Asked to say a poem that would express the surroundings, Jünger recited the Frenchman Arthur Rimbaud's "Le Bateau ivre."

When all the figures of the war in the trenches have disappeared, there will be no one left who understands this choice. I tried to explain it in an article in the May 17, 1936, *Revue de Paris.*

The lines that seem the clearest are not the least obscure:

> In the tempestuous swell of the tidal sea
> I in that past winter, deafer than children's brains,
> Ran, and the peninsulas unmoored and land-free
> Have not known more sovereign brouhaha unconstrained.

The first, third, and fourth lines pose no problem. But the second?

The notion of time in life at the front, so intense, so laden with events and emotions, was not the same as derives from customary pace of life in peace.

For we would say "in the past" about episodes that had occurred the previous year.

If children's thought processes seem simple, it is because they have not yet experienced the multitude of sensations that generate images and ideas. Now, on the subject of life and death, the combatant got such a powerful initiation that he felt as though he had been born on the battlefield, especially if he were one of the younger men.

Four days after the German offensive, our battalions moved toward the enemy. And certainly no one saw any of those melancholy faces, those funereal expressions so dear to the post-1930 film makers, who thought they were representing the soldiers as they were that last springtime.

Later, in 1923, I decided to return to Ourscamp in Chiry (Oise), which was our reserve position from March 26 to May 15, 1918, during the bitter defense of Mont-Renaud.

"I hadn't left the village," a civilian told me, "when the Fifty-seventh came through. You wouldn't have thought these were fellows who'd just spent two nights in trucks and were going to their deaths. What spirit! And how they sang!"

The songs were certainly joyful, but they weren't very proper.

In September, 1936, I chanced to be in Nuremberg in the Hofbraühaus, sitting at the table of a Mr. Schultz, a pleasant Berliner who had commanded a light artillery battery in 1918.

"The first French troops we encountered, at the Crozat Canal, had on new outfits and fought like tigers," he said.

"They were General Brecard's cuirassiers," I explained.

"Then," Mr. Schultz continued, "we wanted to blast Mont-Renaud, which barred the way to Paris. We could have flattened the objective under a massive shelling and so won a quick victory. Nothing of the kind. You'll see on a map that a chateau tops that elevation. I was the one who fired the first shots to hit that chateau."

"And I was the one who got them," I said.

He didn't believe me. I asked for some blank paper and drew him sketches and described the timing in such detail that he was convinced.

"So there you are!" he said to the two brown-shirted storm troopers who were with him. "In 1918 we faced each other as enemies. Today we're sitting together as comrades at the Nuremberg *Parteitag*."[5]

I refrained from revealing to him that the German ambassador in Paris had refused me admission to this *Parteitag*. Mr. Schultz decided that a *Frontkamerad,* a comrade at the front, as he called me, should have one of the best places. The next day he gave me a card meant for the editor of a Berlin paper, who had been prevented from attending at the last minute.

I have often taken pleasure in meeting German soldiers. If hatred sometimes fired our words during the hostilities, it did not live in our hearts. The most dreadful violence subsided as soon as it was no longer necessary. If we felt a hearty friendship for our own, the brave conquered enemy soon inspired nothing more than pity. The most human of the combatants was the infantryman who saw the pathetic face of the man he might have killed, but the gunner and the pilot would have been even more distraught had they known the suffering of those souls. "If the artillerymen over there felt our pain," we would think at Verdun, "they would stop this cruel pounding."

The same was true for us at Mont-Renaud when we were targets for Mr. Schultz and his compatriots.

Since 1920, the date when my book *L'Agonie du Mont-Renaud*[6]

---

5 Party Day, one of a series of Nazi Party conventions at Nuremberg; the first was held in August, 1927.—Tr.

6 *L'Agonie du Mont-Renaud,* reissued (Paris, 1957).

appeared, reverent visitors, coming alone, in groups, and sometimes even in masses, have continued to crowd that promontory closing the valley two miles to the south of Noyon. I have spoken there to 12, to 100, to 30,000 people.

There our regiment broke twenty-two attacks.

The bevel-cornered post was taken, lost, retaken twenty-six times in one hour.

More than 100 lightly wounded in this regiment alone refused to be evacuated. I was among them. I say this to counter those who know neither suffering nor death and who deny indisputable facts.

Over the duration of the hostilities, 25 officers and 545 men refused to be sent to the dressing station.

The merit of a troop complement lies more with its elite than with its body of men.

On May 27, 1918, the awesome bastions of Chemin des Dames fell before the German onslaught. The enemy's advance was rapid. Second Lieutenants Turbet-Delof and Drouault heard the news in Paris, where they were on convalescence leave, and took the train for Compiègne. But our regiment was no longer in the vicinity of that city where it had regrouped its forces. Now walking, now hitching rides on trucks, Turbet-Delof and Drouault rejoined the 57th on the Saconin plateau, southwest of Soissons.

In that battle, as Louis Madelin has put it well, the divisions thrown in to fill the breach melted like wax on white-hot metal. Turbet-Delof and Drouault, still wearing parade dress, with elegant tunics and thin-soled shoes, hurled themselves into the movement. Our battalions, cut to ribbons, quivered under the bursts of gunfire.

Jünger's observation is accurate. Yes, these were very young and inexperienced soldiers, but under leaders seasoned in combat they formed redoubtable assault troops.

The beardless young men in *feldgrau* fighting on the Saconin plateau, May 31–June 2, camouflaged their helmets with stalks of grain and rushed the French machine guns. Sergeant Major Richard and Sergeant Havard shot down seven with the Lebel rifle. Automatic guns mowed them down in clusters, point-blank. Without knowing it, they were imitating our soldiers of the Year II.[7]

After the spring losses, we in turn had companies almost entirely re-formed out of 1918 blues,[8] who had never been under fire and

---

7 Year II according to the Republican calendar, initiated by the National Convention on September 22, 1792. The reference is to the high spirit and aggressive daring of the otherwise ill-prepared French troops, which brought them their victories of 1793–94 against Prussian and Austrian units.—Tr.

8 Recruits.—Tr.

for whom we felt real tenderness. On August 28 in the Somme, I commanded two light infantry sections and a machine-gun group. There were two veterans among us: the poilu Larrieu, who had seen action everywhere since the Marne, and I. The eyes of our conscripts were big as saucers. They watched our smallest gestures with absolute trust; they took in every word as devoted and obedient young footsoldiers, intent on victory. They saw us as old hands at battle, accustomed to its surprises, conditioned to act in combat as are colliers in a mine, sailors in a storm. The flame of 1914, in this last season of the war, quickened an army which had both a willing heart and fighting experience.

We had to advance eastward under 150-millimeter percussion shells over a vast grass-grown plain north of Nesle, for a distance of about 800 yards. In 1914, half our forces would have been lost in a dangerous move like this; it cost us only 4 wounded.

But a tributary of the Somme, the Ingon, bordered with marshes, posed an obstacle to us, which we nonetheless overcame. Two bold maneuvers, one of them carried off by Second Lieutenants Fischer and Drouault, delivered the entire enemy bank into our hands. Later Drouault fell, forever, a bullet through his belly.

Initiative and daring caught fire and grew with the flush of success. Two months later, at Mennevret, two battalions of the 112th Infantry under Colonel de France formed a single column and penetrated the German position after sundown; they advanced five miles without firing a shot, and took 1,200 prisoners.

It was harder for us to take Hill 77, peppered with Prussian machine-gun nests, on September 2 and 3; we wrested it from them piece by piece. Eleven officers and 318 men killed, 17 officers and 715 men wounded—such was the price of victory.

Prouder than ever of our regiment, repeatedly celebrated through the centuries, the survivors went to sleep among the dead. The regiment, based on mutual respect and brotherhood, was a family every member wanted to honor. Where *esprit de corps* flags, there remains only a collection of individuals, without a unifying soul.

The Great War, as we have seen, was not at all uniform and homogeneous, but so varied that it was impossible for someone entering the scene for the last half of 1918 to imagine its previous seasons.

The songs, when they can be unearthed, express these differences. Napoleon's swashbuckling marchers in 1796, on the road to Milan, swelled the echoes with Fanchon's lively refrain, which the Italians would hear once again in 1944.

But the troops going up to the Verdun sectors were mute, like the men at the Moscow.[9] It was useless, Marshal Pétain observed, to question those returning. They did not answer and looked at the interlocutor without seeing him. In that hellish sector, where shot and shell had left not a leaf on the ruined trees or a scrap of green on the ground, where all the natural smells except that of the Meuse had been destroyed, the Frenchman, who laughs in adversity, joked no more. The poilus exchanged only wan smiles. If there were songs in that time, my comrades and I know nothing about them.

But during the heavy action of May 31–June 2, 1918, reinforcements swung along the base of the Soissons plateaus with a step that spoke of confidence and gallantry. A half league away, Maxims and Hotchkisses sputtered, and 105's burst in the clear sky.

Peasants who had stayed placed buckets of water at the side of the road. It was very hot. Sweat ran under the unbuttoned coats. A soldier would gulp down a good mugful and then rejoin his unit in a couple of bounds and take up the singing again:

> When the leaves appear in the spring,
> A balmy breeze comes soft as a dove,
> And lifting its crooning voice to sing,
> It tells the heart it's time to love.
>
> If Cupid knocks upon your door,
> Lovely Liz, don't hide your charms.
> For he brings joy you can't ignore.
> So then, Liz, open your arms.
>
> Here come the poilus, here come the poilus,
> Back from Verdun, from the Yser,
> Back from Hurlus.
> Choose the one for whom you care.
> Choose him, and if you love him true,
> He'll love you fair.

And the men from beyond the Rhine went to battle singing sad and melodious airs.

Minds change in our ebullient race like the wind. But combat tactics and form were modified just as often.

My account *"Les Postes de l'Armée Gouraud"*[10] reveals a scene

---

9 The Moscow River, which Napoleon's multinational and unenthusiastic forces reached but then retreated from in the unsuccessful campaign of 1812.—Tr.

10 ["The Gouraud Army Posts,"] *Revue des deux mondes* (July 15, 1929). General Henri J. E. Gouraud was commander of the French 4th Army, which attacked on the Verdun and Champagne fronts on September 26, 1918, with General Pershing's American forces, in the final Allied offensive of the war.—Tr.

that was unlike any other moment of the fighting. We seemed to be immersed in a fantastic setting, a universe devastated by some earlier cataclysm, where our units lived in the wild grass in a solitude and silence deep as death.

I commanded two of these units. Only the post commander knew that, on watch in that abandoned zone by General Pétain's orders, we would have to hold out to the last man without the slightest hope of relief. Like the fighting men of Carthage, we had no other roof but the sky. Wire entanglements barred the entrance to the shelters so that no one would give way to the very strong temptation to take refuge in them when the aggressor appeared. We lived like wild animals in old Argonne. If one of its frequent storms soaked us, we could hope only to be dried by the sun.

That was one of the happiest periods of my life. The realization that there was no one in front of us, that we were covering an opposition line running two and one-half miles, that we were the country's living shield, that an imperative mission of sacrifice, which set us apart from the others, ennobled us, filled my soul with a holy joy.

But on July 14 I went on leave. I was in a depot at Châlons-sur-Marne when the front erupted at midnight. Paris heard that nocturnal rumbling of guns.

Our train arrived. There was a high-level debate over whether we should go our way or had to be returned to the lines.

Neither I nor my fellow travelers, so willing the day before to bear the brunt of an attack as stoic soldiers, wanted to return to the lines. Finally, the locomotive whistled, and the train began to move. We felt a selfish joy.

To break the enemy's offensive, attack, counterattack—this is killing work. Far from the war in space and time, we no longer recall any but the spectacular battles, and we forget that life in the open demanded more patience than valor. Our *Grande Armée* veterans had endured forced marches like Marius' "mules," especially in 1805.[11] And like them, we slept as we marched.

There were also times of crucifying immobility. On May 8–9 we stood packed together in a passageway in Fort Vaux at Verdun for thirty-six hours, crammed in a human mass. Hardly was one of us able to squat down from time to time.

I was already familiar with these things, the evening I arrived to join the 57th. From the camp at Souge to the trench, reached two days later, we moved into a different hemisphere. I had been

---

11 The Grande Armée was Napoleon's army. Caius Marius (155–86 B.C.) was a gifted and popular Roman general.—Tr.

ordered on duty at that point. Instead of sleeping, we worked in pairs carrying logs soaked by the snow; they slipped through our frozen hands and bruised our shoulders.

Then I slept the sleep of an animal crushed with fatigue, in the shelter swarming with rats, and soon I in turn was being eaten alive by the vermin.

For two-thirds of the year in that northern land we were regularly drenched by rain, which seemed to penetrate to our bones.

We lived Goethe's description of the night of the Battle of Valmy—September 20, 1792—on October 5, 1917. Leaving Suippes in a twilight night, we advanced to the Souain ridge. A squall rode the barren wastes of Champagne in a raging downpour. We had to march the flooded road in water to our ankles. Coat, tunic, sweater, pants, skin dripping, we stayed that way for two weeks, unable to dry off or change clothes, seeing nothing but barbed-wire fencing on the clay soil potted with holes filled with a liquid gray mud.

But the worst thing was the lack of sleep. In the sector where I first served, we came down from the first line like drunks zigzagging on the road. So Foch's battles in 1918 were fought by poilus who were drunk on the need for sleep as if on wine.

Happy is he who knows that man is on earth not to enjoy life, but to find his salvation.

A military vocation grows stronger in a man who never sounds a complaint.

Sir Basil Liddell Hart

CAPTAIN SIR BASIL LIDDELL HART was born on October 31, 1895, in Paris. After his parents' return to England, he went to St. Paul's School and then to Corpus Christi College, Cambridge, where he took the honors course in history. In 1914 he became an officer in the King's Own Yorkshire Light Infantry. After two periods of service on the western front, where he was wounded and gassed, he first made a mark in the field of military theory by evolving the battle drill system in 1917 and other new tactical ideas subsequently adopted, particularly the "expanding torrent" method of attack that became the basis of the blitzkrieg technique. In 1920, when only twenty-four, he was given the opportunity of writing the first postwar official manual on infantry training and subsequently edited the weapons manual Small Arms Training.

Invalided to the half-pay list in 1924 (and to the retired list in 1927), he was appointed military correspondent of the Daily Telegraph in 1925 as successor to the renowned Colonel Repington. Ten years later he moved to the Times in the same role and as its adviser on defense as a whole. Meanwhile, he had also been military editor of the Encyclopaedia Britannica.

In 1927 he became personal adviser to the new War Minister, Mr. Hore-Belisha, and helped initiate a far-reaching program for the modernization of the Army. Many of the proposed reforms were achieved, but opposition continued to delay the development of the tank and antiaircraft forces. Feeling that progress was too slow compared with the imminent danger of war, Liddell Hart gave up his advisory role in the summer of 1938 in order to press the needs publicly.

Throughout the years since the First World War, he had been a leading advocate of airpower, armored forces, and amphibious strategy. Many of the foremost commanders of the Second World War called themselves his disciples and pupils—including General Guderian, the creator and leader of the panzer forces. The German encyclopedia Der Grosse Brockhaus quotes Guderian as saying that Liddell Hart was "the creator of the theory of the conduct of mechanized war," and General Chassin of France described him as "the greatest military thinker of the twentieth century, whose ideas have revolutionized the art of war." The late President Kennedy more recently paid tribute to his revolutionary influence on "two generations."

In all he has written some thirty books, and his writings have been trans lated into more than thirty languages. He was knighted in 1966.

FORCED TO THINK

LOOKING BACK on my experiences in what is now generally called World War I, my chief impression in retrospect is of its *amateurishness,* especially in the first year, or even two.

When Britain entered that war, in August, 1914, I was a student at Corpus Christi College, Cambridge, working for the history tripos—the honors course in history—and spending the summer vacation in Cornwall, the family part on my mother's side, where it had been since migrating there from the Scottish border in the eighteenth century. A few weeks later I received a summons to a medical board in London and there passed the still stringent eyesight test with the aid of a medical officer who was more than willing to prompt me in reading the smaller letters on the chart.

After passing the medical board, I waited more than two months for further word from the War Office, where a very inadequate staff was trying to cope with the immense flood of volunteers that Kitchener's call had produced. Meanwhile, I joined the special commissions class formed in the Cambridge O.T.C. and soon qualified as a musketry instructor—all the sooner by reconciling myself to the nonsensical fact that the veteran experts provided by the school of musketry favored a parrotlike quotation of passages in the official manual rather than any simpler explanation of their meaning.

At the beginning of December I received my commission, as second lieutenant, in the King's Own Yorkshire Light Infantry (K.O.Y.L.I.), and was sent to an officers' course of instruction at Tunbridge Wells, the headquarters of the 2d Army. Among my experiences there was one that provided an illuminating sidelight on the crustier kind of old-style general. While on weekend leave I was recalled by telegram, and on returning found myself under what the Army calls open arrest. For on the Saturday night some officers attending the course had staged a rag in the local theater, and when this was reported to the Army commander, General Stopford, he had ordered that the whole course was to be placed under arrest without discrimination. This rigid martinet was the man who, eight months later, bungled the Suvla Bay landing on Gallipoli by the rigidity of his inertia, with fatal effect to the Dardanelles expedition.

Although Stopfords were plentiful in the old Army, there were also many refreshing exceptions—and at that time there was a junior member of his staff, Captain J. F. C. Fuller, who after the war took a lead in the effort to broaden the outlook of the Army and modernize its structure. Although our friendship and cooperation in that effort did not develop until 1920, it was in a way fateful that our first link should have been the experience of serving under Stopford.

In January, after passing out of the course with good marks, I was sent to a recently formed service battalion of my regiment. By that time it was being provided with khaki uniforms to replace the makeshift blue that had been originally issued—and had made them look more like a gang of convicts than a military body—but it had still only 100 rifles for nearly 1,000 men, and these were of out-of-date pattern.

The commanding officer, a Regular, was a martinet of the better kind and was quickly producing good results—although his severity in dealing out punishments was such that it might well have caused complaint from men less enthusiastic, or less ignorant, than these eager volunteers. The two senior majors, however, were far from being as competent. One of them greatly impressed us on arrival with his three rows of medal ribbons—an array that could then only be rivaled by the Commander in Chief of the British armies in France. But comic relief was provided when he attempted to drill a company and, having ordered it to "advance in echelon," kept on ordering it to turn right, turn left, and turn about in the vain hope that he would find that it had somehow got back into line. He then began feverishly turning over the pages of a little drill guide in search of the solution, until at last he was driven, ignominiously, to call on the senior subaltern to straighten out the now breathless company. We discovered later that he had never been in action but had gathered his medals by hurrying to visit base areas, as an Intelligence officer, wherever minor campaigns took place.

Many of the dugout warrant and noncommissioned officers were no better, except as tutors in the ways of military wangling. Our company sergeant major had a habit of remembering some urgent office duty when a route march had gone as far as his feet and fatness would comfortably permit and would then hail any passing civilian motorcar with the impressive shout, "On His Majesty's service," and demand to be driven back to camp, regardless of where the driver might be going.

Further evidence of amateurishness, and in higher quarters, came after I went to France, shortly before the abortive September offensive there—the British Army's first large-scale offensive— wherein both the British and the much larger French Army suffered losses that were out of all proportion to the slight gains. During the British offensive in the Loos sector, the 21st and 24th divisions, composed of splendid human material, were thrown into the battle in a shockingly bungled way. A sequel to it was the replacement of Sir John French, as Commander in Chief of the British, by Sir Douglas Haig—whose 1st Army had actually carried out the attack.

Not only at the front but in the rear the war was conducted in a very easygoing way during 1915, whereas by the next year not only the troops but military bureaucracy were entrenched; the exhilarating "fun" of active service, brightened by a moderate spice of danger, passed away with that change to machinelike organization. In 1915 one often came across officers who, disliking conditions or superiors in their particular area, had moved themselves to another and been taken on there with little difficulty in getting their self-transfers authorized.

I had a personal experience of the prevailing casualness when sent to conduct a large draft from the Somme to the other end of the British front at Ypres, where casualties had been heavy. Marching to the railhead, Méricourt-Ribemont, the draft embarked in the usual string of boxcars, labeled CHEVAUX 8, HOMMES 40, that were used for transporting troops, and the train then meandered through the countryside at the usual pace, so slow that those who felt cramped could jump off and stretch their legs by a run without risk of getting left behind. About 11 P.M. we reached Abbeville, which had been developed into a large military rail center, and were shunted into a siding, where I was told at the R.T.O.'s (railway transport officer) office that there was no possibility of going on until the following night and advised to get a room in the town meanwhile. So after seeing the draft fed and bedded down, I followed this advice. At daybreak I went back to the station but found no sign of them on the siding where I had last seen them, and a search of the many other sidings was equally fruitless. Then I went to the R.T.O.'s office and was blandly told that the cars had been hooked on about 3 A.M. to a train that was shorter than expected. I then had to wait a further twenty-four hours until there was a train which could carry me on in the wake of the draft.

On reaching Calais, about 7 A.M. on the third day, the R.T.O. there told all on board that the train could not be sent on northward until the next morning, "so leave your kit on the train, where

I'll look after it, and spend the day in the town." When we made our way back to the station at the specified time that evening, the train had disappeared, and the R.T.O. quite cheerfully explained: "I found that I could send the train on, after all, but there will be another one this evening which you can take." Thus, I had now lost my kit as well as my draft! I recovered the former late that night from a siding at Hazebrouck, and, after spending the night in that town, went on by train to Poperinge, the railhead for Ypres, and there got a lift on a horsed limber to the battalion—where I found, to my relief, that the draft had safely arrived the day before. The commanding officer was evidently so familiar with the happy-go-lucky ways of the Railway Transport Service that he took the miscarriage as a matter of course. After a drink and a chat I started on my way back to the Somme, which turned out to be another interrupted journey. On returning, I put in a claim for four nights' "detention allowance" to cover my hotel expenses. The base paymaster returned it with a puzzled query but, on hearing the story, was so amused that he promptly approved the claim.

A little later, stricken by sudden sickness and a high fever, caused either by the fumes of a bursting shell or by something bad I had eaten, I was carted off on a stretcher to the nearest field ambulance and then to the casualty clearing station at Corbie. Next day I felt better, and my temperature was down, so I wanted to go back to the battalion—which merely convinced the doctors that I must be ill, so I was sent off, still on a stretcher, by hospital train to the base hospital at Rouen. There the same thing happened, and I had trouble in persuading the doctors to let me off being put on a hospital ship for England.

That ironical experience would seem to suggest that a would-be malingerer's best chance might lie not in feigning illness but in clamoring to be allowed to stay at the front! The tedium of a fortnight in the hospital was relieved by a visit from the King, George V, who came around the wards—a few days before the bad fall he suffered when riding Haig's horse. The King, poor man, looked more embarrassed in trying to make conversation and ask suitable questions than we were in responding.

Eventually, when allowed out on afternoon leave, I slipped down to the base headquarters at Rouen and induced a friendly staff officer there to post me to a battalion of the regiment stationed in the Ypres Salient that, after suffering heavy losses, was very short of officers. In retrospect it seems a strange choice and desire on my part—as Ypres was notoriously the worst sector of the front—but many of us at that time of inexperience had a similar desire to test ourselves by experience of the worst.

The conditions of trench warfare at Ypres have been depicted by so many pens that an addition would be superfluous. But it may be worth mentioning another illustration of the same widespread impulsion that was characteristic of that relatively early period of the war. It came when I was sent up with two weak platoons to hold a stretch of trench line which had been abandoned three months earlier after a flattening bombardment and had since fallen in more fully during the autumn rains. Two companies previously having held it, its reoccupation to cover a gap was ordered because of an expected German attack on the sector. After a reconnaissance by our senior major and a brigade staff officer, they reported that it was a "death trap" and that it would be "murder" to send anyone there, but their protests were overruled by the divisional staff, *who* had not seen it. Paradoxically, it gave me a thrill of pride to be entrusted with such a mission.

During the night I kept the men hard at work in bailing out the water and digging themselves in as far as possible, while getting news that the enemy were clearing away the barbed wire in front of their trenches in preparation for an assault and that Prussian troops were taking over from the Saxons who had been there. But the next day passed without more than frequent shelling, and it became evident that the Germans had canceled the attack. We were then withdrawn to the canal line.

I was less fortunate soon after when concussed by sandbags brought down by a shell exploding in a trench and can acutely remember how, when I was sick and vomiting, every successive shell was a shock and strain—showing how much reaction depends on physical state. This time, when carried back on a stretcher, I made no protest, but felt only relief when the doctors sent me back successively to a forward hospital at Hazebrouck, a base hospital at Le Touquet, and then by hospital ship to England.

In my memoirs I have dealt with a number of my impressions of the front, and Ypres in particular, at that time, so here am mentioning only experiences and aspects that I did not touch on there. One is that under such tiring and chilling conditions, sexual desire was not very strongly felt by most men—contrary to the picture painted in some of the war novels—and only a small minority sought the local brothels when out of the line. But many more of us missed, and felt a longing for, the sight of some attractively feminine women. That was not so much an actively sexual desire as an esthetic desire for the beauty and grace of womanhood. It was evidently realized in choosing the junior nursing staff, the V.A.D.'s, for the Duchess of Westminster's hospital at Le Touquet. The duchess herself, the quintessence of elegance, glided around the wards in a dark dress, with a faint suggestion of nursing uniform, superbly cut and molded to her figure, while adorned with a string of lovely pearls. The sight of her was a tonic in itself, and as I was there again the following year, it became stamped on my memory.

I also felt an intense desire to see plays again—more intense than ever before or since. So when I had recovered sufficiently to be allowed out of the hospital, in London, I went twice a day to the theater.

Soon afterward I renewed contact with Charles Grey, the editor of *The Aeroplane*, who told me in confidence about a new armored fighting vehicle capable of moving across shell-torn ground and breaching the enemy's trench front, which a friend of his, Lieutenant R. F. Macfie, was developing along with others in the Armoured Car Force of the Royal Naval Air Service. This was my first news of what was subsequently called the tank, to keep its nature secret, which made its battlefield debut on September 15, 1916, during the Battle of the Somme—a new instrument with which I was to be closely associated in later years.

After two months' convalescent leave, I was posted to the 3d K.O.Y.L.I., the draft-finding unit for the Regular battalions. It was then stationed at Hull. The battalion sent a detachment nightly to guard the large cluster of oil tanks on the bank of the Humber estuary near the city. It was difficult to imagine what value this guard could be, and when zeppelins were overhead it was not a comfortable thought that if one of their bombs dropped onto an oil tank, little would be left of the infantry guard. Even more uncomfortable, however, was that the only accommodation for the guard was a laundry building filled with corrugated iron sheets—the most uncomfortable form of bed that I have ever known.

Another trial followed in the form of being sent to what the subalterns called the penal settlement of Aldbrough, where a detachment was stationed to guard the coast road. It involved a long and lone walk every night to visit each of the posts along the road, which was closed to traffic. Pitch-darkness and current spy scares made the round rather eerie. The adjutant, an old-style soldier, considered that young officers who had served at the front needed "to be taken down a peg" and shown that this experience had not earned them any special consideration by prewar standards. But once I passed the kinds of tests which he deemed necessary, his attitude completely changed. Now welcomed as a suitable officer of the regiment in postwar years, I was recommended for a Regular commission with retention of my full seniority and the step in rank which I had recently been given.

Unfortunately, battalion headquarters had not received a new

Army form produced for such purpose, and the recommendation was returned by northern command headquarters with instructions that it must be submitted in triplicate on the correct form. By the time a supply was obtained, I was out in France again. Thus, the commanding officer's good intentions were temporarily frustrated, while the delay impaired my situation in the long run, since injuries suffered in the summer fighting led to a further postponement.

While I was at Aldbrough, the whole battalion had been moved out to the Yorkshire coast as a precaution against a feared invasion, and anxiety about this possibility became so marked that for three weeks we had to sleep fully dressed and equipped, standing to arms at 2 A.M., and sometimes marching from our camp to the beaches to occupy trenches dug along the seafront at Withernsea. This period of tension ended when the Irish Rising came, at Easter, and it became clear that the Germans were not going to exploit it by an invasion of England.

Meanwhile, I had gone before a medical board at Hull, where the president opened by asking me if I wished to return to France. On replying yes, I was promptly passed as fit—with a commendation that was in sharp contrast with the treatment this notorious medical board dealt out to anyone who was hesitant in giving such an answer—a senior officer in the regiment, who had amply proved his courage, was virtually accused of cowardice when he said that his wounds were still troublesome. The different attitudes of medical boards were very strange.

In my case the medical board's verdict of fit was confirmed in a better way when a week or two later, after only a few practice runs, I led the regimental team in the north of England cross-country championships—a 10-mile race over the rough ground outside the famous St. Leger course at Doncaster, which we lapped four times. After the first round I felt ghastly but by the end felt relatively fresh—a wonderful feeling. That turned out to be the last race of my brief running career—which was cut short by German gas a few months later. But in consolation the doctors told me that my lung development had helped save my life.

On returning to France in the spring of 1916, I traveled by an embarkation train to Folkestone that started from the same platform at Charing Cross as in 1915—and to which I also returned each time in the hospital train. On this occasion I was in charge of eight junior officers—five of whom were killed on July 1, the opening day of the Somme offensive, while all the remainder, including myself, were casualties by the end of that month.

Before leaving England, I had been told at the War Office that as

I was now on the list of the Regular battalions, I should go to the 2d K.O.Y.L.I.; but on reaching the base camp at Étaples, I was disappointed to hear that under a new policy of blending old and new, officers with previous experience at the front were being posted to service battalions. I was all the less happy to hear that under this ruling I would go to the 9th K.O.Y.L.I., which was in the 21st Division—one of the two that had been blamed for the autumn failure at Loos.

It was now on the Somme sector, and events were soon to show that apart from being unjustly blamed for the way it had been used when inexperienced, it had become one of the best in the field. That was due not only to the quality of the material but to the way it had been developed during the winter by Major General Claud Jacob, the future field marshal, who took over the badly shaken division after Loos. In the spring he was promoted to command a corps and succeeded by Major General David Campbell, who commanded the division in the Somme offensive and until the end of the war. I came to know him much more closely in the immediate postwar years as he took up many of my tactical ideas and became one of my best friends. It was thus an interesting coincidence that he came to the division at the same time as I did—a fact of which I, as a very junior member, was naturally more aware than he was at the time!

By another coincidence the initial task I had been given on reaching Étaples was to conduct a draft to the 18th Division, commanded by Major General Ivor Maxse, who became my other principal backer after the war and to whom I owed even more for encouragement and help. These two men were my military foster parents, and I am deeply indebted to them for the early opportunity they did so much to create.

"Amateurishness" Continues—on the Higher Levels

On returning to the Somme, I found the staggering difference between the tranquil conditions of the autumn and those now existing. Formerly quiet roads and villages behind the front were now under frequent shellfire, while the formerly shallow and weak German lines had become a web of strong trenches, with deep and well-built dugouts. By the constant raids and harassing during the winter and spring that the British high command had ordained, it had virtually driven the Germans to develop and fortify the front against which it was planning to launch its next offensive. Moreover, the chances of surprise were diminished by the all too manifest preparations for such an offensive, especially in the spread of light railways near the front, to carry up supplies as close as possible. From the amount of shelling they received, it became obvious to some of us that their portent was obvious to the Germans.

In sum, the growing experience of the troops and their still undimmed spirit were offset by continued amateurishness on the higher levels of command.

Extraordinary optimism predominated there, and even where there were doubts, these were suppressed from a misguided loyalty or desire to retain the confidence of superiors. Although Sir Harry Rawlinson, the commander of the 4th Army, which was entrusted with the main part of the offensive, seems to have felt considerable doubts, he kept them private and assured his executants that there would be no resistance after the prolonged bombardment of the enemy position, so that the infantry would only have to walk over and take possession. So infectious was such optimism, or so blinding the loyalty to superiors, that when assaulting battalions "reported that the enemy machine guns had not been silenced" and were mowing down their men, they were told by some divisional staffs, unwilling to believe the truth, that "they were scared." It does not seem to have occurred to the commanders and staffs in general that if the trenches were made untenable, the enemy machine gunners were likely to move out and occupy the shell holes, created by the bombardment, from which they could resume and maintain their fire.

The rigidity of the plan, with its insistence on strict conformity in alignment, was itself a severe handicap to success by surprise. The handicap was increased by the slow pace ordained, in order to conform with the barrage, and that in turn was enforced by the heavy load of equipment that the infantryman carried—66 pounds, which was more than half his own average body weight. Even an Army mule, the proverbial beast of burden, is not expected to carry more than a third of his own weight.

In the final preattack stage, three cavalry divisions were brought up close to the front, and Haig's instructions were that they should ride through on the first morning to Bapaume, 10 miles beyond the front. In the event, Haig's troops were still several miles short of Bapaume after nearly five months' struggle—and by then had lost more than 400,000 men.

My only sight of the cavalry was when, a couple of days before the attack, I rode back to the railhead village to visit the town major, an elderly soldier whom I had known in 1915. On reaching his office, I found a swarm of angry cavalry officers around it, seeking promised accommodation. Pushing inside, I found him too drunk to deal with anything and then found his sergeant major and his clerk similarly disabled in a bedroom and a latrine respectively. In retrospect, this comic episode of intoxication seemed a portent of the cavalry's frustration.

In the preattack period, we had a visit from Colonel "Ronnie" Campbell's bayonet fighting team, sent by G.H.Q. to instill the troops with what was called the spirit of the bayonet. Its frenzied performance may have had some effect in increasing the number of Germans who were bayoneted after surrendering, but its worse effect was in multiplying our own men's loss of life by teaching them to push on and "close with the bayonet," without firing, while the more cool-headed enemy, who did not fix their bayonets, went on shooting them down as they approached, realizing that a bullet outranges a bayonet until the bayonet-fighting attacker is within 2 yards' reach of him.

A more effective spur was produced by David Campbell, our new divisional commander, when he addressed the battalions. Known to us as the man who had won the Grand National—in 1896, when riding the Soarer—he applied a touch of whip and spur by telling them that they had to wipe out "the shame" of the division's performance at Loos. Resented at the moment, this sharp criticism impelled the troops to strive all the harder to prove that it was unjust. Although the fences were found to be much worse than anyone expected, the 21st Division penetrated half a mile deep into the German position, whereas all the divisions on its left and immediate right flank failed to make even a dent in the enemy's front and were mostly back in their own trenches that night.

The offensive was launched on the morning of July 1 at 7:30—long after dawn—by which time there was not even a morning haze to obscure the view of the German machine gunners, who were thus able to scythe down the close-packed lines of our slow-moving infantry with deadly ease. Most of our troops were dead or wounded before the parapet of the enemy's front line was even reached. The survivors on our sector, discarding their imposed formalism, soon broke up into little groups that used their initiative and worked their way from shell hole to shell hole, taking advantage of this and any other cover they could find, so that they then succeeded in penetrating more than half a mile into the lines, with relatively small loss.

Most of the men and almost all the officers had been knocked out in crossing the short distance of no-man's-land—the commanding officer and all four company commanders had been killed. I and other seconds-in-command of companies had been kept in immediate reserve, as well as a few other officers, but a call came for us as soon as the extent of the losses became known at brigade headquarters. We found the survivors in a sunken trench and took over charge. That night the leading battalions of the division's reserve brigade came up to strengthen the wedge but did not push on farther. If fresh divisions had been brought up, they might have pushed through with little opposition before the Germans had recovered their balance. But nothing was done on the second day.

On July 3, about midday, our reserve brigade mounted an attack against a small wood lying a quarter of a mile beyond our left flank and captured it after an early check, repulsing two strong counterattacks. As ammunition was running short and a further counterattack expected from reinforcements coming up from Bapaume, a lot of the prisoners were pressed into service at bayonet point as ammunition carriers—with entire disregard of the Geneva Convention!

At nightfall the division was withdrawn to rest. When we reached "Happy Valley," a sheltered hollow behind our original front line, we were revived with panniers of tea laced with rum. Of our battalion of about 800 strong, fewer than 70 men, with 4 officers, came back. On reaching the road, this remnant formed into columns of fours and moved along singing, "Pack up your troubles in your old kit bag"—just as the full battalion had done six days earlier when setting out for "the great adventure." This now ever-unforgettable marching song raised a lump in the throat at the thought of the many friends who would never sing it again. We continued on our way to entrain at "Edge Hill," a forward railhead recently built to support the advance and about 5 miles behind the front line. Here we were rejoined by a number of strays, who had missed their way during these confused days.

We soon heard that our own losses were far from being exceptional. From our own regiment, six battalions had been engaged, and hardly any had come out of action 100 strong. The total losses of the 4th Army on the first day alone were almost 60,000—the heaviest day's loss in the history of the British Army.

The burden of the attack had been borne mainly by Kitchener's New Armies, and these quondam civilians carried on the fight after suffering a percentage of loss such as no professional army in recent centuries had been deemed able to bear without breaking. Yet most of the divisions engaged in the opening assault were in action again within a fortnight.

On July 4 a train carried us back to Ailly-sur-Somme. The news of our destination filled me with keen anticipation of a good meal and bed at the chateau overlooking the village, which was the country place of my father's close friend, M. Carmichael, who had generously played a godfatherly part in my life. Both before the battle and the previous year I had seized opportunities for brief but refreshing visits to Ailly. But when we disentrained there, we were told that we had to move on to Picquigny, and by a circuitous march, as another cavalry division was moving up to the front along the main road.

That march, although only about 5 miles, was the most agonizing I ever experienced—we were so dead beat that every step became more aching, while hunger pains became acute, after living for several days mainly on biscuits and bits of chocolate. But at the end of that trek I had what is engraved on my memory as the best meal of my life, followed by the longest sleep. For after seeing the men billeted and given a hot meal, I went into a little village café and ordered for myself an *omelette pour deux*. It proved to be the size of a normal omelet for four, while accompanied by a yard-long loaf of French bread and a bowl of *café au lait*. Having finished the meal, I ordered a repeat, except for the loaf, and then two quarts of beer. After all that I had a different kind of pain in my stomach, but tumbled into bed in my billet and slept around the clock.

I managed to ride over to M. Carmichael's for dinner twice that week—and am amused to see that in a letter to my parents, which they preserved, he described how "Lt. acting as Captain arrived on His charger with his suite" and went on to say of me "Spirits excellent, even avowing a military career would be very satisfactory." I am surprised to find that I felt so fond of soldiering at that moment, after the experience of the previous weekend! A more jocular comment in his letter was: "Upon my word a Hart on horseback seems the most extraordinary thing in this war." But that obviously applied to his recollection of my father in the pulpit, for my mother had ridden a lot when young, and even bareback. My seat on a horse was far from being as firm, and having a very thin bottom, I often found it painful after a long ride.

After six days of so-called rest—which was occupied mostly in writing letters of sympathy to widows or bereaved parents and in absorbing fresh drafts from the base—we moved up to the front again, for the assault on the Germans' second line. After the repulse suffered at the start all along the northerly half of the 14-mile attack frontage, Haig had decided to abandon the attack there and concentrate his further efforts on the southerly part, where wedges had been driven into the German front and where the French, on the adjoining sector astride the Somme, had made bigger progress at much less cost. The Germans' second line position was buttressed by Bazentin-le-Petit Wood, High Wood, and Delville Wood.

The leading British troops, nibbling their way forward during the past week, were still some distance—varying from 300 to 1,000 yards—from that position. So Rawlinson decided to cross the space by a night approach and assault it at dawn on July 14, after a brief hurricane bombardment—another new feature. Haig had at first objected to this apparently hazardous experiment but eventually agreed to it.

The outcome was the capture of the German second line with comparatively light casualties. Whereas on the battlefield of July 1 the khaki-clad corpses were far more numerous than German ones, the latter outnumbered the former on the battlefield of July 14. Unfortunately, the experiment was not repeated in the months that followed or in the following year. But the sight and contrast of the two battlefields made and left a deep impression on my mind—and subsequent military thinking.

Our brigade was in close support on this occasion, the assault of the 21st Division being delivered by a newly transferred brigade. But on the third day my company was detached and sent forward as an immediate brigade reserve and then moved forward again to fill a gap in the new front line, which was now on the far side of Bazentin-le-Petit Wood. On the way I had got a puncture in my hand, but after getting the wound bandaged, I carried on, as only one other officer was left. Moreover, he was so inexperienced and jumpy that the N.C.O.'s who were commanding the platoons came to me, together, to complain that he was upsetting the men. Shortly afterward he came to show me an almost invisible prick in his skin, so I seized the chance of sending him back for medical treatment, with a note asking that he should not be returned as I could manage better without his assistance.

At midnight on the seventeenth-eighteenth my company was relieved, when reinforcements arrived, and we moved back to rejoin our battalion. Passing through Mametz Wood, we suddenly heard a lot of shells landing around us, but as they did not explode with a bang, we imagined that they must be duds—until there was a strong smell of gas. It was our first notice and warning that the enemy had begun to use a lethal gas shell, filled with phosgene and more deadly, though less painful, than the former chlorine gas that had been projected from cylinders. Coughing violently, I stayed to warn and divert the platoons that were following and then led the company back to the battalion bivouac. In the morning I went to the nearest field ambulance to get my earlier wound freshly dressed —feeling bad, but still unaware how bad. There the doctors examined my chest and promptly put me on a stretcher. From there, by stages, I was sent to King Edward VII's Hospital for Officers in London, founded and run by that dynamic and unconventional personality known as Sister Agnes, a friend of the late King.

Close to twenty years later, when visiting General Dill there, I saw how her intervention saved the life of that outstanding soldier after mistaken treatment by the Army's medical service had brought him to the verge of death. I did not myself return there as a patient until forty years later, for a major operation, when I was happy to find that her successor as matron, Miss Alice Saxby, was quite as dynamic while more knowledgeable.

Six months in the hospital or convalescent leave gave me opportunity to think over the lessons of experience.

"To Reason Why. . . ."

IN REFLECTION it gradually became clear that while the troops were growing in experience, there was something seriously wrong in the doctrines inculcated by the higher command. Among the troops the "amateurishness" of 1915 had developed into the blind but trusting obedience of 1916. By 1917 this became habitual obedience but was no longer so trusting.

"Theirs not to reason why; theirs but to do and die" had become a habit, as in the Army of the Crimean War—and to a large extent it persisted until the end of the war. But I wanted to know "the reason why" in order to teach and train the men under me. And the more I studied the question, the clearer it became that there was little or no reason in the methods we were pursuing or in the doctrines we were taught. Indeed, they were flouting the lessons of history. So I sought to think out and improve our tactics.

In January, 1917, I was returned to "light duty in an office—the Record Office at York," and then obtained an appointment as adjutant to an Australian squadron of the Royal Flying Corps— which proved to be a valuable experience in the difference between intelligent working discipline and the formal discipline that prevailed in our Army. Then in the spring I was offered the post of Regular adjutant to a battalion of the recently constituted Volunteer Force. Here the main responsibility for its training was thrown on me—a responsibility and opportunity that were very welcome. It was a challenge to think out and a chance to try out new methods.

The commanding officer, a former Regular cavalryman, often talked of how during the London season he and his brother officers only visited their regiment when it came to their turn as the officer on duty. He was a man distinguished by natural ability and charm, and his use of these gifts had been restricted by having an ample private income—which is far more often stultifying to talent than the opposite condition. On the few occasions when he came to see tactical exercises he used to ask my views privately and then repeated them verbatim as his own comment. But his absence and deficiency of professional knowledge provided me with all the fuller opportunity.

One of the early products was a battle drill that enabled any unit of infantry—platoon, company, or battalion—to be opened out or closed in varying degrees by signal, so as to avoid loss from enemy fire during the approach. The use of a simple code of signals was better than vocal and complex orders, often inaudible under fire, or slowly transmitted messages, while it also made possible quicker and more flexible control. Even when fully opened out, a commander could maneuver the whole instantaneously, like a naval flotilla. It could be used not only in the approach but subsequently whenever and wherever suitable. By trying out the system with a whole battalion on the training areas, I was able to see how and where it could be improved.

Another development of it was a progressive series of attack drills that brought out the various kinds of maneuver that could be used, which were in essence few, and could be carried out with or without live ammunition—this being used to simulate battle conditions better.

I incorporated all these forms of battle drill, along with other developments in new tactics, in a little book, *New Methods in Infantry Training*, I produced in 1918 through the Cambridge University Press. It was widely used in other units, particularly officer cadet battalions, during the last part of the war, and in 1920, when called in to rewrite the official *Infantry Training* manual, I got the battle drill accepted by the War Office and included in the manual. By that time I had also worked out a completely new form of parade ground drill based on battle drill, but this was rejected by conservative influences, particularly in the Brigade of Guards, as incompatible with ceremonial. They did not realize that the existing close-order drill was an obsolete survival of what in the eighteenth century had been designed as a tactical drill suitable for battle. It was not until the eve of the next war that the War Office sanctioned the introduction of a new drill based on modern tactics, and even then it was an unsatisfactory compromise—as all official developments tend to be.

Battle drill itself, in its two forms, was accepted and incorporated in the official manual. But as the years of peace passed, it fell gradually into disuse—until it was revived in 1940, and then largely by the efforts of younger men, many of whom were not even aware that it had been introduced and adopted a generation earlier.

The opportunity of rewriting the official manual after World

War I also enabled me to get the value of night approaches and attacks emphasized, as well as the use of other kinds of "obscurity." But these likewise became neglected in peacetime training until again strongly urged in the report of a War Office committee, of eight generals, constituted in 1932 to examine the "Lessons of the War"—a report to which I was asked to contribute. Even then its application soon lapsed, while little was done to develop my supplementary proposals for the development of artificial fog and of artificial light to aid movement and exploitation in the dark. It was only when Montgomery took command in the field in 1942 that real progress was made in these respects—he used night attacks in most of his battles from Alamein onward and used what was called artificial moonlight increasingly from 1944 on.

In the course of recasting the *Infantry Training* manual in 1920, I had evolved a method of attack that I christened the expanding torrent. It was a development of the infiltration tactics of 1918, based on the ideas of deep penetration and of maintaining the momentum by sustained pressure along the line of least resistance— through the continuous and habitual use of reserves, on each higher level successively, to back up such forward troops as were making progress, instead of reinforcing those who were held up.

In further reflection I realized that armored forces were the ideal instrument of such an attack technique, and far better than infantry for the purpose because of their capacity for faster and more prolonged movement. So from then on I became the advocate of armored forces and of their employment in this exploitation and deep penetration role.

Mobile armored and mechanized forces were likewise far superior to infantry or horsed cavalry for applying the "indirect approach"— the name I gave to the fuller development of it into a general theory of doing the "unexpected" and pursuing "the line of least expectation," strategically and tactically, that I worked out in the later 1920's and set forth in a book that has run through a series of editions and translations.

The compound idea was enthusiastically taken up by our armored forces, but unfortunately resisted by the preponderant elements in the British Army, so that the Hitlerite German Army, taking up the idea with greater energy, as well as being given ampler resources, became the one that applied it and proved its decisive value in their *blitzkriegs* of World War II. It was some consolation that the Israelis subsequently became its best exponents and have proved its continued value in three successive tests—1948, 1956, and 1967.

Paolo Monelli

PAOLO MONELLI *was born on July 15, 1894, into an old family of Crema* (*Lombardy*), *who later moved to the neighborhood of Modena, in Fiorano di Modena, at the foot of the Apennines. At the lyceum in Ancona he became a good friend of the now-famous architect Pier Luigi Nervi, and since Nervi wanted to become an artillery officer, Monelli decided to do the same, not having any definite plans for the future. But he flunked the entry exam to the Accademia Militare. Then, crying, "Down with the Army!" he registered at the law school of the University of Bologna, considering law the least difficult field of study.*

At the beginning of World War I Monelli was completing his fourth year at the university and was glad that the war gave him the opportunity to defer the choice of a profession to a later time. Drafted in 1915, he was assigned to the Alpine Corps, destined, on the whole, for mountain warfare. Captured and held as a prisoner of war 1917 to 1918, he became a member of military missions from 1919 to 1921. He was a Vienna correspondent for the Gazetta del Popolo *from 1921 to 1922 and Berlin correspondent for* La Stampa *from 1922 to 1926, being sent on special missions to, among other places, the Near East and Spitsbergen. He was a special correspondent for* Corriere della Sera *from 1926 to 1929 and with* La Stampa *from 1929 to 1935. In 1935 and 1936 he was a war correspondent in Ethiopia and was director of the Paris offiice of* Corriere della Sera *from 1936 to 1939. During World War II he served as a war correspondent until he was imprisoned by the Fascist government in 1943. In 1944 and 1945 he was a lieutenant colonel in the Corpo Italiano di Liberazione. After the war, he was a special correspondent for* La Stampa *from 1946 to 1967 and for* Corriere della Sera *from 1967 on.*

His books Toes Up *and* Mussolini: Intimate Life of a Dictator, *translated into English, French, and Dutch are among his best known, and Italian readers are especially familiar with such works as* Io e i tedeschi (1929), Barbaro dominio (1933), Roma (1943), Naia parla (1947), Nessuna nuvola in cielo (1957), Avventura nel primo secolo (1958), Il vero bevitore (1963), *and* Ombre Cinesi (1965). *He has won many prizes for his outstanding contributions as a journalist, including the Saint Vincent Great Prize for Journalism (1960), the Great Prize for Journalism of the Accademia della Crusca, Florence (1965). He has also received four Medaglie al valore, and the Croix de guerre Belge.*

ALPINE WARFARE*

"THIS WAR is not a gentleman's war," I was told one day in Marmarica, in 1942, by Paolo Caccia Dominioni, a lieutenant colonel in the Reserves, who later toiled for years in order to recover the bodies of the soldiers who had fallen in that campaign and gathered them mercifully in an ossuary.

That day we had eluded the solitary hunt by a lone enemy bomber of our camouflaged car, the only one crossing the desert that afternoon on the track leading to the front lines of El Alamein. The lone car must have had on the pilot the effect of a speck in the eye. He overtook us, returned at once, and zeroed in on us. Realizing his intentions, we just about had time to throw ourselves under the car when it was hit by a volley of machine-gun fire. The bomber passed over us again and again until it tired of its little game, and we were relieved to hear it rise and get away.

Both of us, stretched out flat on our faces, couldn't help thinking of the destruction brought upon cities of all nations involved in the war by such attacks from the sky, the torment inflicted on the peaceful citizens, the destruction of irreplaceable historical monuments. And naturally this led us both to compare the present war with World War I, cleansed in our minds from all horrors twenty-five years later.

Twenty more years have gone by since World War II. Other wars have followed—skirmishes and destruction in Korea, in the Near and Far East—and more and more the war of 1914–18 appears to us who have taken part in it incredible and fabulous.

Having by now come to the end of our day, looking back on our past, our youth devoured without our having had any awareness of it, the rest of our life used up in the practice of our profession, in caring for one's family, in the monotony of everyday occurrences, in the plot here and there somewhat confused in our reminiscences, the years from 1914 to 1918 stand out immutably clear, precisely outlined, never blending with the few that preceded and the many that followed them like a long, unforgettable dream beyond time.

This feeling was immediate. Two years after having returned to civilian life, upon publishing my war diary, I felt compelled to

---

* Translated from the Italian by Lucille Carasso.

advise my readers in a short introduction of how much of that past
had already died in me—"that past whose ineffaceable furrows are
carved in my memory like the abandoned trenches on the peaks of
the mountains once again alone." Then, already looking back on
my carefree and serene adolescence, I felt as if it were on the other
side of an abyss that it hardly seemed possible for me to have physically crossed.

Then another phenomenon intervened, I wouldn't say to mar,
but to blur the awareness of that crystal-clear intact recollection of
the experience that lifted us into a new dimension, and that, when
concluded, made us feel dissatisfied and dazed upon getting back to
earth, as if we had returned from an interplanetary flight.

I beg the reader to forgive me if I once again talk about myself,
but the editor of this volume has prevailed on me once again to take
a stark look at that past. During the last months of the war, while
still in uniform and vegetating in a prison camp, I mentioned, as
follows, the sudden revelation of having landed in a superhuman
adventure: "Dreamer, the good times are over . . . Finished are
the bloom of youth, the dangers always negotiated, our humble
pride, at that time still devoid of sin, that snowlike freshness
capping our thoughts when life was so light, without yesterdays or
tomorrows, hung on one second as on a cobweb thread shining in
the dawn, appearing over the mountain."

Another phenomenon, as I say, came in time to perturb our
awareness of that youthful experience. Stormy events in all parts of
the globe, another war—not bloodier, but in some ways more
terrible than the first one. The upset brought to our lives by impetuous technical progress, swifter than any social advancement and
often in contrast with it, and new meanings in the relationships
among peoples made us doubt the fairness of the motives that sustained and comforted us then. And the charge made against us by
writers, politicians, thinkers of the generations that followed of
complicity with the governments of those days, while unfair, provoked in us, nevertheless, a feeling of guilt.

(Alberto Moravia, who was still a child when World War I broke
out, gives a concise and spiteful opinion of it. He calls it "an outbreak of collective madness, the reasons of which should be studied
by the psychoanalyst rather than by the historian." He speaks of the
retrospective disgust inspired in us nowadays by that ignoble
slaughter. He affirms that war lacked the contrast between reason
and madness, between truth and falsehood, between civilization and

barbarity, which in World War II managed somehow to light up the darkness of the massacre.)

My generation, whose destiny it was to take part in World War I and World War II, tends to upset that opinion. In World War I, the contrast Moravia spoke about between truth and falsehood, between reason and madness, was obvious, whereas World War II was all barbarity—what with genocide, the concentration camps, the extermination of war prisoners and of the civilian populations. (In Italy, the civilian dead killed by aerial bombardments equaled in number the soldiers killed in battle.)

And if not exactly a sense of guilt, we feel the bitterness brought on by a useless experience—worse, by a deadly one. We Italians, those who were found good for another massacre, fought in World War II as dutiful citizens and well-disciplined soldiers, but with the anguish of an abjurer, as if we were forswearing the motives of the first war by participating in a second one from the opposite camp, while feeling that this was wrong.

Not only to us veterans is World War I that crystalline abstraction that I have tried to define. It stands as well in the fabric of history as a unique phenomenon. It was a crisis that upset humanity, forswearing century-old principles, without establishing new and valid ones for the centuries to come; it was the end of an era, without being the heartening beginning of a better one; it was an abrupt crossing from the gullible and smug Middle Ages to an iconoclastic and faithless era. None of the myths and values that made us—the very young—accept that war and the sad duty of having to take part in it is still valid today. I believe this may be said of the youth of all nations that took part in the conflict—the French were animated by a spirit of revenge, the English by the pride of their Empire, the Germans by a mystic folly of being the master race. We Italians had the certainty of fighting for a generous cause—the completion of the movement for political unity in Italy in the nineteenth century with the annexation of the two noble cities that had remained outside the country's boundaries, Trent and Trieste. Civilians, students, young professional men felt that it was good and dignified, as in the times of Horace *pro patria mori* (to die for one's country) ; we considered ourselves a select group, as opposed to those civilians who, in spite of the fact that an aviation still in its infancy would occasionally kill a few with little 50-kilogram bombs, continued to live a peaceful and well-sheltered existence. In one camp as in the other of all participating nations, everyone thought that this was going to be the last war ("a war to end all wars") and that it was, therefore, right to sacrifice oneself in order to give one's children and all humanity an everlasting peace. (It has been our bitter experience later to see how many more wars have come from that first one.) We still live today with a nightmare of a third world war's breaking out at almost any time, in which atomic weapons shall be used—weapons we do not dare use at present, so frightening is the thought of the consequences. In the meanwhile, we perfect the so-called conventional weapons to such an extent that they become only a little less terrifying. Humanity is perhaps the victim of an inexorable biological law sentenced by an obscure necessity of the species to a bloodletting of many millions of lives, almost with every generation.

I do not know in what manner other countries that took part in World War I honor their survivors. In our skeptical, practical, intolerant Italy, they have been excluded with no consideration from the mainstream of the nation. They have been reproached first for having taken part in World War I with patience and a strong sense of duty and now for not dying soon enough. About a dozen years ago they were promised a life annuity as evidence of their country's gratitude, and many proposed bills all became shelved in the offices of the Chamber of Deputies and of the Senate until this year a pension of 5,000 lire each month was at last awarded to the neediest—less than $8.50—and each man was knighted; this order was created especially for them and will end with the last survivors.

When I was drafted in the year 1915, I had the good fortune of being assigned to the Alpine Corps destined on the whole to mountain warfare. It was a war very different from the one being fought on all other fronts, and it especially deserves to be described because I don't believe one will ever again see the like of it. It could be that in wars to come—should they be inevitable—some aspects of the preceding wars may still be seen, such as pitched battles swiftly fought with armored vehicles and Commando engagements. Mountain warfare immediately appeared to be obsolete after the invention of the helicopter and the creation of the paratroopers. For example, today, when entire divisions can be transported by air and dropped into enemy territory over the most arduous natural obstacles, it appears to be absurd that in the year 1916 one thought it both necessary and convenient to mine entire mountains garrisoned by the enemy, as did the Italians and the Austrians.

But in the years from 1914 to 1918 some of the categorical imperatives dating back to the Napoleonic Wars, when a war was won only by crossing the borders and physically occupying the enemy territory, were still valid. Italy found herself having a common border with her enemies—a border about 13,000 feet high, bristling with plateaus, glaciers, snowy mountain peaks, and the ramparts of the Dolomites—and there was no alternative than to leave from there on our way to a battlefield or from there to resist the enemy onslaught.

The Alpines and, for that matter, also the Austrian and the German mountain-based troops (Kaiserjäger, Landesschützen, Alpenkorps) had a regional recruiting system that gave these soldiers, of whom exceptional performance beyond the call of duty was demanded, a strangely homey mentality. The draftees of the older classes would return to the battalion in which they had served as enlisted men only to find sons and nephews there and would live together under conditions that often were inhuman and certainly much more uncomfortable than those of other specialties; boys of twenty and men over forty would run the same risks.

The English translator of my war diary, *Le Scarpe al Sole* (*Toes Up,* New York, 1930), Orlo Williams, has described the Alpine soldier in the following terms:

Perhaps the proudest and the toughest corps engaged on any front. They labored and fought amid the grandeur of the Dolomites, their homeland, fragrant with wet rocks and pinewood; by day a sparkling world of sun and snow, by night cold starlight. In their lonely positions at the forepart of the desperate battle against superior Austrian and German artillery, their success depended on individual prowess and courage, not on machines. Hard drinkers, swearers, and champion scroungers with an immeasurable pride in themselves and their corps, they lived brutally and died heroically.

It is a rather accurate and concise judgment. I must add, however, that the Alpine battlefields were not limited to the harsh and romantic Dolomites, the desolate glaciers of the Adamello, the Ortles, the Monte Cristallo, the inhospitable plateaus on which winters were just as hard as on the mountaintops. And with regard to the definition of "hard drinkers," it was mostly wine—even the wine that on the plains below would have been considered vinegar. And it didn't take long to find out that above the 5,000-feet mark all wine is always good and has to be drunk in much larger quantities than usual before going to one's head. But *graspa,* too, the strong liquor of the mountaineer, a brandy made with the stalk that remains of the cluster of grapes after the grapes have been removed; it really is *aqua vitae* (water of life) in its most perfect essence.

More than once did I see a fatally wounded soldier on a stretcher, who having been given a glass of *graspa* in order to ease his passing, recover his senses durably after having drunk it. Anyone who does not believe me should ask Captain Somaggio of the 7th Alpine, who under Mount Tomatico, while leading the Val Cismon Battalion, was hit by a bullet that everyone, especially the doctor, considered to be an immediate send-off to greet the angels. "A sip of *graspa*," murmured the dying soldier. "Let him have it," said the doctor to the stretcher-bearer, "he will not be drinking it much longer." (Somaggio is still repeating these words today.) But as I was saying, in reference to "hard drinkers," it is not true that, according to a slanderous legend, the Alpines are formidable and incorrigible drinkers. Only when forced to live during weeks and months under the most difficult conditions, which often made it impossible for fresh supplies to reach them, did they express their longing for wine in songs—"We are Alpines; we like wine." And if I once wrote that the word "Alpine" doesn't stem from "Alps," but consists of two Greek words for "once more" and "drink," meaning, therefore, "he who is always drinking one more," I am afraid that no philologist will ever accept my etymology.

The Italians and the Germans (with this word I am referring to the Austrians, the Tyroleans, the Bavarians in the Alpenkorps) fought battles during World War I at altitudes never heard of before. Even today, in the Dolomites, anyone who has breath, good legs, and doesn't suffer from vertigo, can reach heights that would be ill suited for a bivouac of only a few hours, yet these soldiers stayed there for weeks and months, winter as well as summer. One can still see the remains of small huts hardly visible on rocky ledges, held up by ropes or dug into the rock itself, that could only be reached through a narrow rim carved out of the mountainside. Do you remember Charlie Chaplin's film *The Gold Rush,* in which a small hut was poised half on the snow and half in the empty space? Some of ours were always like that, yet we lived in them, and the sentry on duty shivering on the outside, in a temperature that could dip to 25 degrees below zero, would call AWOL those of us who stayed inside where a small stove that became red-hot in no time at all would bring the temperature up to 25 degrees above zero. Just by entering or by leaving the hut, one would experience a sudden change in temperature of about 50 degrees. But the tiny hut was often a luxury; the squadrons above us often had to be satisfied with aerial niches lined with planks or tar paper that one could reach by narrow stairs secured to the rock or by clinging to a fixed rope, and the mountain drop was so sheer on all sides that not even the snow could cling to it.

As the war went on, both sides felt more acutely the need to garrison lastingly or to conquer passes and summits always higher, always more difficult to reach, in order to expand the defenses and create a springboard for future encounters. If at first we went on the glaciers and climbed the sheerest walls of the Dolomites with small patrols of specialists, such as Alpine guides—volunteers who in peacetime were experienced mountaineers and skiers—in order to fight a surprise attack, we soon destined to lasting Alpine engagements entire battalions, in which the great majority were far from being champion climbers or skiers; the skiers were still a small minority or came from hasty training courses of one month's duration, and the climbers, too, were inexperienced. All the others were even less brilliant, but better suited to fight at altitudes above the 6,500-feet mark, and in winter at that—men born in the mountains, excellent hikers, resistant to fatigue, exceedingly strong beasts of burden, and good sharpshooters. Above all, they were men with introspective natures, especially the older ones who had matured as shepherds, woodcutters, coal miners, immigrants, laborers through a hard life, similar to life in wartime. Furthermore, thanks to their natural qualities, the self-denial of the officers, the example set by the Alpine guides, the mountaineering technicians, the desire to emulate an enemy who had confronted them with selected and exceedingly strong mountaineers and sharpshooters, they succeeded in ascending the sheerest mountain walls; they fought, spent nights in the bivouac, and securely established themselves on the glaciers. They went into exile in the wintry mountains under conditions that appeared to be prodigious.

In peacetime the Alpines used to poke fun at one another, for being by birth and tradition in such an uncomfortable (to say the least) service, for having to march during long hours over snow or stones, for carrying in their knapsacks (large as wardrobes) loads double those of the rest of the soldiers, and for going so rarely to the city. "Did you sell the cow? . . . Did you bring the butter to the mayor?" they would ask one another—because legend has it that with the proceeds from the sale of the cow, or by lavishing rustic gifts on the highest authority in the town, the young draftee could buy the coveted assignment in the Alpine battalion in which the older men in the family had served before him and in which it would have been disgraceful not to be admitted. While climbing in single file along the steep paths or going up the softened glaciers, where at each step the foot sank in the snow up to the ankle, they would often say, *"Passa parola che la monta."* These words would reach the men below still trudging along, and those who already had reached the top would bend down scoffing at them, while offering their mountain poles for them to hold onto.

In the Alpine warfare of the years 1915–18 *Passa parola che la monta* was again repeated. It started in the Alps, the high plateaus, the mountains 6,500 feet high. And there were the conquest of Monte Nero, 7,400 feet high up the precipitous rocks of a lean slope, the engagements on the Alpi Carniche (Carnic Alps), Pal Piccolo, Pal Grande, Canin, Rombó—mountains more difficult to negotiate than their heights would indicate. Battles were fought at heights of 8,000 feet and more for the conquest of the Fiemme Alps, at more than 10,000 feet in Le Tofane, which has walls that reach for the sky, *E passaggi di quarto grado* and at 11,000 feet on the Marmolada. Always higher up, closer to the stars, by paths that constantly became more precipitous. Here were the engagements on the Loccia Alta, on the Dosson di Genova (10,800 feet), the Crozzon di Lares (11,000 feet), and the Adamello (11,650 feet), occupied in the dead of winter. Then came the Corno di Cavento (11,150 feet), taken, lost, and taken again. Last, the San Matteo (11,900 feet), or let's say 12,000 in round figures). This one was, I believe, the highest battle—or I should say battles, since it was taken from the enemy with tremendous difficulty on September 1, 1917, then lost again to the enemy in spite of our desperate resistance on September 3. (Beautiful soldiers theirs, too—tenacious and reckless, Kaiserjäger and Landesschützen.) I omit mentioning the patrol engagements; the war bulletin of August 14, 1918, cites an attack by the Austrians to our advance posts in the high valley of Zebrù at 12,680 feet.

Someone defined those aerial fighters as the madmen of the mountain, probably believing this would please them. The expression was wrong and hyperbolic; these were not mad, but very wise, men. (Less wise, perhaps, were the orders emanating from the supreme command which they were forced to execute.) Never were plans studied in greater detail or carried out with more wisdom than those on the glaciers or up the breathtaking paths amid showers of falling stones. Such adventures were not made in a spirit of bravado or for the fun of it all. One who can take the staircase will not enter someone else's house through the wall, but on the staircase the enemy was on the lookout. That's why we would send decoys on one side exposing them as targets, while the rest of us would go up the other side cautiously and unsuspected. In this manner we took the Corno di Cavento (11,150 feet above sea level, a large, tangled rock springing up from the glacier), while the skiers on it exposed themselves to machine-gun fire, and the Austrians laughed at those idiots who expected to reach the top from such a low altitude in spite of their well-equipped positions. The climbers of the Val Baltea Battalion, climbing over a rock so sheer that it would have been sufficient for a sentry to look down and release a stone in order to make them all tumble into the valley below, set foot on the summit. Most of the time an engagement was preceded by weeks of careful and minute preparation: escalades by specialists testing ropes fastened to the most precipitous spots or chiseling steps in the rock. The chronicle of that war doesn't limit itself to aerial battles fought over snowcapped mountaintops, to escalades over impervious granite ramparts, or to surprise attacks in a storm—the storm being protector and enemy at the same time. (That is how San Matteo was conquered, during an unexpected blizzard; many were killed by lightning.) That war was, above all, a matter of great patience. "When these mountains shall turn to plains, I will go home," written—in the guest book of the Milan hut in one of those moments of dejection not too rare among good soldiers, when one no longer believes the war will ever end—by the corporal commanding the patrol that occupied it.

During the winter months the engagements were few, almost as if only in order to stretch oneself out a bit, to surprise an outpost, or to mock the opponent. The most frightening enemy was nature itself; stormy and icy days were followed by periods of rain, winds from the southeast triggered the fall of avalanches, other avalanches of softened snow came cascading down the mountain, and powdery snow was whipped around the mountain slopes by hurricane winds that often blew the men away like twigs even before knocking them down. Mountain batteries with mules and cannons, huts, entire platoons were hit, smothered, buried without a trace, without a cry, with no other sound than the one made by that gigantic white mass itself. The first winter, 1915–16, was especially horrible because we hadn't as yet mastered the art of living at such supreme heights in places, until then precluded from all human experience. More men died under avalanches and by freezing than by gunfire in the summer.

Each and every one of nature's obstacles or the defenses prepared by the enemy would have appeared to be a sufficient deterrent to any action; all around us the enemy was almost always above us. Because of the mania of our commanding officers in keeping the front-line defenders in contact with the adversary, instead of placing them on an equal footing on the opposite mountaintop, the difficulty of finding shelter and of keeping our supply lines open compounded the problem. It was extremely hard to tow up to the summits Da 149 cannons to counter the 305 of the Austrians. Long lines of men tugging at the ropes would drag up with difficulty the cannon placed on a sled, while others armed with poles would keep it from sliding to the right or the left of the track and fall to the valley below. It took seventy-seven days to carry up to the Venerócolo Pass a venerable piece, "Da 149G" (the G stands for *ghisa*, or cast iron). One day we succeeded in hoisting with enormous difficulty a small mountain cannon on the Tofána di Roces (10,590 feet). The first shot had just been fired, and we were observing with great interest the damage it had done, when the cannon quietly began sliding backward and tumbled 3,000 feet below, where it remained until the end of the war. And we had also to contend with the shifty and treacherous snow that could in any season start falling precisely where the mountain experts would swear this could never happen and where avalanches were considered an impossibility, as were the stone and rock landslides held together only by overnight freezing, but very dangerous if walked on when the sun was shining.

The battle was always the fulfillment, possibly with a feeling of relief at that, of many months of waiting, of monotonous excavation and other careful preparations. The real battle would start the moment the peace-loving Alpine removed the knapsack from his shoulders and began to enjoy the spot he had reached. In order to get there, he had traveled during endless hours over stony or icy paths, climbing during the night, carrying the load of a mule (machine guns, bombs, and provisions), pausing occasionally while waiting for the advance patrol to prepare the way with fixed ropes or nails driven into the mountain wall. And when at last he had arrived just below the top's rim, the mortal combat would begin.

Naturally intelligent, when tired of such a life, the good soldier often hoped to get hit—but not on a path barely traced on a perpendicular mountain wall where the first dizzy spell would have landed him in the chasm below. However, when all went well and one was picked up by the stretcher-bearer, it could happen that, as in the dizzy Tofane, one would be placed in a sack, gaping wound and all, and thus lowered on a rope along the side of the mountain, often banging against it, to the snowy field below. Upon arrival the stretcher-bearer had to take a good look to make sure no entrails had escaped from the wound and gotten lost at the bottom of the sack.

I said earlier that in possible wars of the future we shall never again see that medieval kind of warfare so often waged with mines with equal stubbornness on the part of both the Italians and the Austrians during the years from 1916 to 1918, whose first innocent victims were the mountains themselves, savagely hit and mutilated for all eternity.

A harsh peak in the Dolomites (9,160 feet high), the Piccolo Legazuoi, was hit four times by three successive Austrian and one Italian mines; the second explosion caused a bold side of that mountain to come crashing down. Even now, the tourist climbing from Cortina d'Ampezzo to the Falzárego Pass, looking up to the mountain at his right, can identify the new texture of the lighter rock next to the century-old folds of the Punta Berrino, and can see, over a narrow plateau—the Cengia Martini—where the Alpines of the Val Chisone Battalion and the ones from a company of the Belluno lived together, holding onto a narrow ledge.

The ledge and the plateau were considered the hardest positions on the entire Dolomite front. They were bare, inhospitable rocks exposed to direct gunfire and to showers of bombs from above, the highest peaks being in enemy hands. Plagued in the winter by terrible blizzards, they could be reached only by ropes stretched out across ravines and crevasses.

Although aware of the fact that the enemy was excavating a tunnel under their positions in order to blow them up, the Alpines wore themselves out for months in those horrible outposts, so irksome to the enemy, since it was from there that the accesses to their own outposts could be hit directly.

During several weeks, the unmarried officers of that battalion took hourly turns inspecting a certain cave where a Geophone was placed in order to determine whether the enemy's drilling apparatus preparing the detonation chamber was still at work.

It was an uneasy time, with the constant prospect of being trapped like a mouse, since there was always a possibility that the Austrians would keep their machine going once the job had been done in order to delude the Italians into believing that it still had to be completed. At the end of every man's tour of duty, even the dizzy plateau on which one emerged, so exposed to cannon and gunfire, looked like paradise.

News that the explosion was imminent finally came from our garrison in the nearby Col di Lana—it, too, the victim of a ruinous explosion that exposed the reverse of the enemy lines. Our men informed us that the rubble had been cleared away, which meant that the detonation chamber was ready. We, therefore, stopped spying and waited with bated breath for the explosion to take place.

Now can the reader imagine the dismay of the enemy, near and far, when during the night of May 23, 1917, the mine exploded, and when, no sooner had the roar and the echoes died down, he heard the never-dreamed-of and extraordinarily out-of-place sound of a fanfare of bugles, cornets, and basses coming from the exact spot which was to have been blown off the map? This is what had, instead, taken place. In the imminence of the detonation, the company at the rear had leaped to the counterattack while the sparks, the rocks, and the stones were still cascading down to the Falzárego Valley, repelling the enemy who was advancing in order to take possession of that ruin.

Adding insult to injury, the battalion's commanding officer had summoned the fanfare and kept it in readiness; it now broke out in a stirring march, indicating the immediate return of the Alpines to what had remained of the plateau.

During those three years, similar engagements took place frequently in several parts of the Alpine front. The job of digging a tunnel often proceeded simultaneously on both sides, as a sort of competition that would determine who was going to be the first one to detonate the mine.

One of the first and most powerful ones exploded on the Castelletto (8,700 feet high) and called by the Germans *Schreckenstein* or Rock of Terror. It was a formidable rock with almost vertical walls, crowned by fantastic pinnacles barring any attempt of advance in the Dolomites, separated by narrow crevasses from the walls of other mountains dominating it on all sides.

Those passes were equally well policed by experienced German and Austrian mountain troops of the Kaiserjäger and of the Alpenkorps. Since the winter of 1915, the Italian command had proposed eliminating that natural barrier and to that effect had mined some of its higher spires. At the beginning of February, 1916, those Alpines patiently started to dig a tunnel more than 1,600 feet in length, in the heart of the mountain; work in the detonation chamber proper got under way at the end of March with two gasoline-powered drills. The enemy soon got wind of the menace and started at once to dig a countermine. Ten weeks went by, during which both sides worked feverishly, each one trying to spy on the enemy and annoy him in every possible way; selected sharpshooters were lowered on a rope, and from that precarious position they shot at enemy outposts 1,300 and even 2,000 feet away. It was agonizingly difficult for both sides to get supplies and machinery through under the frequent fire of the enemy's artillery.

The detonation was later described as follows by the major of the Kaiserjäger, Carl von Raschin, in his *Skizze über die Tofána-Kämpfe, im Jahre 1916:*

On July 11, 1916, at 3:20 A.M., the long explosion of the Castelletto took place. In a huge blaze the entire south side of the mountain came crashing down with an ominous and sinister sound. The earth shook, as if hit by a cataclysm, tremendous boulders were hurled into space— as high up as two and one-half miles. Rocky walls crumbled amid dense clouds of gas and a thick rain of debris. The center of the explosion was exactly where we had expected, and therefore destroyed a hut in which, in spite of the prohibition, twenty men had just then sought refuge. They, plus two sentries and two more men, were killed while trying to escape the boulders cascading all around them. They were the immediate victims of that explosion. The rest of the garrison (about 100 men) had been felled by gas, but they were soon revived by their comrades and by the medics summoned for this purpose.

Everything had been prepared for a struggle, though no longer in the pre-established positions; they, too, were upset by the frightening earthquake. Everyone was possessed by a belligerent ardor and eagerness to fight. The explosion was accompanied by an unbelievably intense artillery fire from the Italians, and the entire region shook under it during the next five hours.

On our side, however, the situation was even worse. Fumes from the explosion frustrated all attempts of the 77th Alpine Company to get over the gap it had created in just a few short leaps. Men were falling one on top of the other, hit by the mephitic gas that found no outlet. It became imperative to save the men that were being asphyxiated before doing anything else. The soldiers that found themselves at the entrance to the tunnel were ordered to reenter it, holding their breath (on that front we still had no gas masks) , get the inanimate bodies of their buddies, and quickly carry them out into the open.

During the next two days the tunnel remained an insurmountable obstacle. The definitive conquest of that wounded mountain cost the Alpines three days of incredibly hard battles against an enemy determined not to let them reap the fruits of that explosion. Only on July 14, at noon, did the defenders give up, and the officer in charge of that campaign could finally inform his superiors that he had placed two cannons on the top of Castelletto.

I have always spoken of the Alpines, in this reminiscence of mountain warfare, meaning, of course, also the soldiers in charge of the Alpine artillery. But I must add that they were often joined by courageous and efficient infantry brigades not always composed of people from the north of Italy or from the region of the Apennines. Yet these men adapted readily and good-naturedly to surroundings that were especially hostile to them.

I remember Alpine battalions that were often destined to fight in places other than the high mountains—on the last hilly bulwarks of the Po Valley against which the 1916 Strafe expedition was crushed; on the Isonzo front where they vigorously resisted the overpowering German offensive, eventually retreating to new positions; in the valleys; and up the sides of the Montello; and over the Grappa massif—in their victorious counterattack.

Thus, on one hand, we celebrate Alpine patrol and squadron engagements in which each individual stands out in sharp contrast with his comrades, each with his primitive virtues, his dignity, and his pride; on the other, pitched battles, the most tragic being the one fought on the Ortigara, in June, 1917.

It was a barren rampart with three peaks on the edge of the Asiago Plateau, at the point where it drops perpendicularly to the Val Sugana, similar to a gigantic Carso (Karst)—parched, lonely, desolate, with not a single river, road, or house to cross or dot the landscape, where, at certain points, the mountain reached heights of 6,500 feet.

This battle lasted twenty hellish days and cost the Austrians their selected battalions of the celebrated 3d Army Corps, the "Iron Corps." (In a report from the Austrian headquarters one can read, "The battalions who have returned from the Ortigara Inferno are dross.")

We lost two infantry brigades, a regiment of sharpshooters, twenty-six Alpine battalions, some which had been hastily regrouped after having been destroyed a first time and driven back up to be annihilated a second time. Mountain batteries rushed to the front lines to shoot with cannons as if they had been guns.

The mountain itself was also hit, turned upside down, destroyed, as were the most severely hit points on the Carso front. In an incredibly narrow space, men by the tens of thousands were nailed to the rock under artillery fire hitting them from every inch on the horizon, and under avalanches of fire, clouds of gas, and torrents of *liquidi infiammati,* the three peaks were won, lost, retaken, and finally abandoned when we no longer had a single battalion with which to continue the struggle.

I returned, after long years had gone by, to the field of the 10,000 dead. It was somber, forbidding, doomed to barrenness for eternity, still looking as it had appeared during a battle when a sudden lull took place—those deceitful lulls, during which we would find ourselves emerging from the tumult bewildered in the silence that surrounded us and pervaded by a feeling of loneliness and abandonment, in view of the serene, faraway mountains, looming under an endless sky without light and with God.

Visions of my beloved comrades still alive, wrecks burned by deadly fumes, wary and bent during an assault, flashed through my mind. I heard the awkward echoing of metal against the rock, messtins, sword sheaths, gas mask containers. I saw the crushed battalions bearing the good old names of home, the men I had known and whose deaths I had witnessed, and the countless others that had been for me nothing more than a gray veil over the mountain—men with the hard and absent look of combat on their faces; only the eyes appeared somewhat dazed because they were dead, all the dead reenacting for my hallucination the deadly game of half a century ago.

But these facts are not relevant to the story I am relating. In conclusion, as an example of those engagements in which individual men appeared to be waging an assault on the sky itself (as H. G. Wells wrote when he was war correspondent on the Dolomite front), I will cite an episode of July, 1915, in which Sepp Innerkofler, the most famous guide in the Dolomites and a volunteer in the Landesschützen, lost his life.

The Alpines had occupied the forks on both sides of Mount Paterno (9,000 feet high), a tremendously bold pinnacle near the Tre Cime di Lavaredo, where they were holding a small outpost at the top, which could be reached only by steps in the rock and fixed ropes. The Austrian headquarters ordered that important position retaken. The episode is related as follows in a book written by a medical officer in the Alpine Corps, who from the Lavaredo fork witnessed it through his binoculars:

There are six, all volunteers, of which three are over fifty years of age, renowned guides in the Val di Sesto (Sepp Innerkofler, Hans Forcher, Andreas Piller). They have received the order to climb the Paterno and occupy its top. Armed with rifles and hand grenades, they leave a hut near the Dreizinnenhütte. With them is a patrol consisting of thirty Kaisersschützen and a few military engineers led by Christl, who is Sepp's brother. They set out on a gravel path descending from the Forcella del Camoscio, and proceed slowly and stealthily, being careful not to displace any stone that might arouse the enemy's suspicion. Christl and his platoon stop at the top of the path, waiting for things to start happening. The six put on their hiking boots and start up the wall of the Paterno. With complete assurance they climb under cover of darkness; the way is known as the northwest passage, the same one Sepp was the first man to ascend in 1896, and had climbed countless times since. One hour later they reach the top in the dim light of dawn. From Monte Rudo the Austrians start to shoot at once. Then twice again the roar and the hiss of the cannons are heard from a lower altitude; a fourth roar brings down a hail of shattered rocks—then a silence. The six men keep on climbing in single file along the edge of the peak. From Forcella di Pian di Cengia, the Alpines can clearly see them looming against the red sky. That is the awaited signal, and while the six climb toward the west, the Italians open fire from Lavaredo. Immediately the Austrians respond, bringing their own machine guns into action. Over the din one can hear the cannons on Monte Rudo, a mortar from Sasso di Sesto, a 105 Howitzer shooting without let up toward the Forcella di Pian di Cengia from the Torre degli Scarperi. And the six are still climbing, cautiously, in spurts, hiding in every hollow. A fragment of grenade hits Sepp on his forehead. Blood comes streaking down his face and covers his eyeglasses; yet he continues to climb. A rock hits Forcher, also on the forehead; he bleeds, but he, too, continues to climb —they have almost reached the top. Suddenly, as if by a pre-arranged signal, an eerie quiet succeeds the racket. A silence of death spreads through the valley, over the mountaintops, on all sides of the trenches. At this precise moment, slowly, and clearly visible, one man alone begins to ascend. Ten steps below the top he crosses himself and with a sweeping motion hurls a grenade over the wall of the outpost above—then a second, and a third one.

Suddenly, his face still bleeding from the effects of the first bomb, his figure sharply etched against the incredibly terse sky, an Alpine soldier appears, standing over the wall; he holds a rock high over his head. He throws it, and Sepp is fatally hit. Raising his arms toward the sky, he falls on his back and drops into a crevasse. On the mountaintop, the Alpine who saved the Paterno is still standing upright; he is Piero de Luca of the Val Piave Battalion.

I later read in an Austrian report that the Italian Alpines had lowered themselves to the bottom of the crevasse, in spite of untold difficulties, returning Sepp's body to the top. There they buried him, inscribing a reverent epitaph on the grave of their valiant opponent.

The Men of 1914

R. C. Sherriff

R. C. SHERRIFF joined the Army on leaving school in 1914 and served as an infantry officer on the western front until wounded at Passchendaele in 1917.

On demobilization as a captain he joined the staff of a London insurance office and wrote plays as a hobby for a local amateur dramatic club. After the professional production of Journey's End *(1929), about which Stark Young wrote, "The most striking thing about this English play is this underlying poetic feeling, not a poetry of the imagination so much, but rather a poetry of human concern," he went to Oxford to read history at New College and subsequently made writing his career. There were 594 performances of* Journey's End *at the Savoy Theater in London and 485 at the Henry Miller Theater on Broadway. It was produced in all parts of the world in twenty-seven different foreign translations.*

Mr. Sherriff's novels, including The Fortnight in September, Greengates, *and* The Hopkins Manuscript, *have been widely translated and published abroad, and several of his plays had long runs in West End theaters. He has done much work in Hollywood, writing the scripts for numerous films, including* Goodbye Mr. Chips, The Invisible Man, *and* Lady Hamilton.

Now living in the country, he is interested in farming, archeology, and rowing. He was captain for some years of the Kingston Rowing Club, for whose members he wrote several plays in his amateur days.

He is a Fellow of the Royal Society of Literature and a member of the Athenaeum.

THE ENGLISH PUBLIC SCHOOLS
IN THE WAR

————◆————

WHEN MY WAR PLAY *Journey's End* was first performed, some people said there was too much of the English public schools about it. Some thought it glorified them without good reason; others that it discredited them unfairly. It depended on the way they thought about these schools.

For my own part I had no ax to grind one way or the other. I didn't go to a public school myself. I was at my small hometown grammar school, and in those days the gulf between a local school and a public school was so wide that the boys lived practically in different worlds. I hardly ever met a public school boy until I joined the Army. As a junior officer, I lived among them. Almost every young officer was a public school boy, and if I had cut them out of *Journey's End,* there wouldn't have been a play at all.

As they have no counterpart in any other country, it is worth saying something here about the way they came into existence and how they attained their unique prestige and influence.

It must first be said that an English public school isn't public. On the contrary, it is private and exclusive. Nobody seems to know how it got the misleading name. It is a mystery buried in the past.

No two of them are alike. All have their own distinct character and traditions. All are quite independent of one another, and all grew up in a casual, haphazard way, without a thought of the glamorous future in store for them.

They began in a small way: mostly town schools for the sons of local tradesmen. Some were founded by charitable men as "free schools" for destitute boys. A lot of them never got any further. They remain to this day the schools for local boys. The ones that broke loose from their local anchorage and achieved wide recognition did so mainly by luck and chance.

Sometimes an outstanding headmaster would build up a reputation for scholarship among his boys. The news would get around among well-to-do men living at a distance from the school. They would send their sons to the school as boarders, and once the school had secured a wealthy clientele, it was on its way to fame and fortune. Old boys, proud of the school, would send their sons to it. In due time the sons would send their sons, and generations of a family would become associated. It would be taken for granted that their boys would go there, even if by then the parents were living in the farthest corners of England. Most boys would remain loyal to their old schools all their lives. Handsome legacies were made by will. Treasuring old traditions, the governors of these schools would never pull down their ancient buildings, but as money came in, they would renovate them, enlarge them, and add wide playing fields. Some of the best medieval and Tudor architecture in England survives in these old school buildings.

It was difficult for a man to get his sons into these successful schools unless his family had past associations with them. There would be a waiting list, and the headmaster could pick and choose. There were no open scholarships for boys from the lower classes. Intellectual ability was less important than that the boy should be the "right sort." A good family background meant more than good brains, but by and large these two distinctions went together. The schools in a position to demand them would charge high fees. This enabled them to employ good masters, and good masters produced good scholars.

Until about 1860 no formal link existed between these schools. They plowed their own furrows and went their own ways. They developed independently along the lines that suited them.

Then one day about half a dozen headmasters of the leading schools got together and decided that it would be a good thing to establish some sort of organization through which they could meet on regular occasions to exchange views on education—to discuss their problems and debate various ways and means for expanding the scope of their teaching to embrace new aspects of scientific knowledge. It was an excellent idea, and they all stood to gain from it.

And so the Headmasters' Conference was established.

At first it was like a small, exclusive club consisting only of the founder members. But to make the enterprise more effective, it was decided to bring in other schools that had the prestige to qualify them for membership.

There were no defined rules. It didn't depend on the age or the size of the school. The founder members were a law unto themselves and invited only the schools they liked the look of. That meant, of course, the elite: the schools with firmly established reputations that only took the best type of boy and aimed at the highest standards of scholarship and behavior.

And so it grew up. Headmasters were proud to be invited. It gave their schools an uplift and placed them among the best in the land. They became known as the public schools.

It was a valued, exclusive trademark that schools outside the Headmasters' Conference would not presume to use. It was a scholastic aristocracy, and the pupils of these schools were proud to call themselves public school boys.

There was more to it than pride and snobbery. Professional and business firms would always prefer a boy from a public school. It opened the gates to many fields denied the boys from lesser schools.

I knew nothing about all this when I was a boy myself. I had never heard of the Headmasters' Conference, and it would have mattered little if I had.

We were happy enough in our small local grammar school. It was an ugly old place in the main street of the town. We had no playing fields of our own and had to play our games on the public recreation ground, but we had our own little built-in pride. Our parents had to pay ten pounds a term for our education, and the boys with parents who couldn't or wouldn't pay went to what were known as board schools. We at the grammar school wore scarlet caps, with the crest of the school sewn on them, and gray flannel jackets with scarlet trimmings. The board school boys wore any old clothes, which made us feel superior. It gave us "class," and that was everything. It gave us self-respect and a pride in our school, and I was grateful to my father for sending me to it. He had very little money and had to pinch to pay the fees, but he was as happy as I was that his son should be a grammar school boy with such a good start in life.

The shock came when the war began in the summer of 1914.

I had just left school and started work in a London office.

It was announced that a volunteer army was to be enlisted to reinforce the hard-pressed Regular Army in France: Kitchener's Army it was called, and they wanted 100,000 men.

It was also announced that suitable young men were required for training as officers.

I was excited, enthusiastic. It would be far more interesting to be an officer than a man in the ranks. An officer, I realized, had to be a bit above the others, but I had had a sound education at the grammar school and could speak good English. I had had some experience of responsibility. I had been captain of games at school. I was fit and strong. I was surely one of the "suitable young men" they were calling for.

I put on my best suit and went to the headquarters of our county regiment.

I was sent to a room where about a dozen young men like myself were waiting to be interviewed.

The adjutant came in. He sorted out some papers on his table and called for the first applicant to come forward.

"School?" inquired the adjutant.

"Winchester," replied the boy.

"Good," said the adjutant. There was no more to say. Winchester was one of the most renowned schools in England. He filled in a few details on a form and told the boy to report to the medical officer for routine examination. He was practically an officer. In a few days his appointment would come through.

The next applicant was from another famous public school. He too sailed through triumphantly.

My turn came.

"School?" inquired the adjutant. I told him, and his face fell. He took up a printed list from his desk and searched through it.

"I'm sorry," he said, "but I'm afraid it isn't a public school."

I was mystified. Until that moment I knew nothing about these strange distinctions. I told him that my school, though small, was a very old and good one—founded, I said, by Queen Elizabeth in 1567.

The adjutant was not impressed. He had lost all interest in me. "I'm sorry," he repeated. "But our instructions are that all applicants for commissions must be selected from the recognized public schools, and yours is not among them."

And that was that. I was told to go to another room where a sergeant major was enlisting recruits for the ranks, and it was a long, hard pull before I was at last accepted as an officer. Only then because the prodigious loss of officers in France had forced the authorities to lower their sights and accept young men outside the exclusive circle of the public schools.

It seemed to me at the time a silly way to go about things. To say that no young man was suitable to be an officer unless he was public school was humiliating and unfair, but looking back on those confused and difficult days, I can see the common sense and reason in it.

Britain was not a military nation. Napoleon called it a nation of shopkeepers, and the Kaiser described its armed forces as a contemptible little army. Both were no doubt right. An island nation with no frontiers to defend had small need for soldiers. All it wanted was a strong navy to guard its shores and a small, highly trained and disciplined army to protect its empire.

It numbered about 250,000 men, and it had an elite officer class.

Sandhurst was the chief military academy for infantry officers, and in those days the infantry predominated.

When a young man entered Sandhurst, it was almost like entering a monastery. He would never be in touch again with the civilians outside the Army. His life would be spent principally on service with his regiment abroad. When on duty at home, he would live in Army camps. His friends, apart from his own family, would nearly all be from his regiment. Even when he retired, he tended to live in select little communities of old officers with interests and memories of the only sort of life they knew about.

He was devoted to his profession. He was proud of it and had good reason to be. An officer was expected to live up to the highest standards of personal and professional integrity. If he fell short, if he discredited his regiment in any way, he was quickly hounded out by his fellow officers, even if he wasn't told officially to go. "An officer and a gentleman" were bywords.

Until the Great War the Regular Army had always been able to look after itself. In the comparatively small campaigns of the past the losses were easily made good from its own resources. There were plenty of good men willing to take the King's shilling and join the ranks, plenty of eager young officers coming out of the military academies, well prepared and fully trained. The officer class remained elite, remote, inviolate.

Now suddenly the Army command was up against a problem it had never had to face before.

In the first few months in France the Army lost more officers than in all the wars of the previous 100 years put together.

It was a shock to the people, a humiliating shock to the Army itself that it could no longer defend the nation as it had done in the past and had to call in the civilians to help them.

There was no problem about recruits for the ranks. They were lining up in crowds at every recruiting station in the land. The first 100,000 were enlisted in a few days.

But officers were the problem. That first Volunteer Army would need at least 5,000 officers, but where were they to come from?

The men at the top—the generals at the War Office from Lord Kitchener downward—were bred in the old traditions. It was difficult for them to envisage an officer who had not qualified through the long and arduous training at a military academy. But Sandhurst could barely supply replacements for the losses in the Regular Army. It would need a dozen Sandhursts to train the officers now required.

Naturally the authorities wanted the new officers to be men with the same background and character as those of the Regular Army, with a dedication to their duty that was ingrained in a Sandhurst cadet long before he was considered fit to join a regiment.

Undoubtedly there were men of the officer type among those unwieldy crowds who were pouring into the recruiting offices, but there was no time to sort them out, no existing tribunals to examine them individually and separate the wheat from the chaff.

But the need was pressing. Officers had to be made quickly, with the least possible trouble. The Army command had to find some sort of yardstick, and naturally they turned to the public schools.

Most of the generals had been public school boys before they went to military academies. They knew from firsthand experience that a public school gave something to its boys that had the ingredients of leadership. They had a good background. They came from good homes. At school they gained self-confidence, the beginnings of responsibility through being prefects over younger boys. Pride in their schools would easily translate into pride for a regiment. Above all, without conceit or snobbery, they were conscious of a personal superiority that placed on their shoulders an obligation toward those less privileged than themselves. All this, together with the ability to speak good English, carried the public school boy a considerable way toward the ideals that the generals aimed at for good officers. And so the edict went out that all young men selected for training as officers in the New Army must come from the public schools.

It was a rough method of selection, a demarcation line hewn out with a blunt ax; but it was the only way in the face of a desperate emergency, and as things turned out, it worked.

It worked in a way that could scarcely have been envisaged at the time. The generals naturally assumed that under their experienced leadership the public schools boys would mature into officers of the old traditional type and lead their men to victory in the old traditional way that the generals had learned so thoroughly from their textbooks.

But these young men never turned into officers of the old traditional type. By hard experience they became leaders in a totally different way and, through their patience and courage and endurance, carried the Army to victory after the generals had brought it within a hairsbreadth of defeat.

These hapless generals have received such torrents of condemnation from young historians in recent years that they at least deserve a few extenuating words of sympathy.

For the most part they were men in their middle fifties, some around sixty, all near retirement age, and they had spent their best years in an army that had mainly been at peace. Their whole training had been for a type of open warfare that served well in years gone by: the Boer War and the Afghan War, campaigns against hostile tribes around the frontiers of the Empire. Many of these campaigns had needed skill and courage, and they had acquitted themselves well.

Now suddenly, as elderly men, they were confronted with a totally different sort of war. The Army had fought valiantly at Mons and in the retreating engagements that followed. It played a decisive part in stemming the German hordes and to its honor well nigh destroyed itself in the process.

To that point the generals had fought a war of tactics and maneuver that they understood. In a bigger way it was like the wars they had fought in the past and were competent to manage.

But when the stalemate came, when the armies entrenched themselves in a line of impenetrable fortifications from the sea to Switzerland, the old sort of war was over, and a new and totally different one began. It needed men with resilient, imaginative minds who could discard all the old outdated methods and adapt themselves to new ones.

But you can't teach an old dog new tricks, and that went for the generals.

It is reasonable to say that when the initial assault of the Germans was defeated, when they failed to take Paris and were forced back to a line of defensive trenches, the Allies had them beaten.

The Germans had been bent on quick victory by attack. The Allies' main purpose was defense. They had won the first and vital round. If they had then thrown all their resources into building a line of fortifications and had garrisoned it with their ample supplies of men, they could obviously have denied the enemy all hope of victory, and the end would eventually have come, as it did in fact come, through the starvation of the German homeland through blockade. By that means victory would have come with a negligible loss of men instead of through the slaughter and maiming of a generation.

But the generals saw things in a different way. It wasn't war to dig oneself in behind a line of impregnable fortifications. It was demoralizing, humiliating, a confession that you had sacrificed the initiative and lost your fighting spirit.

Most of them had won medals for open warfare in campaigns gone by, and they wanted to get back to the sort of fighting they were good at. Trench warfare, in fact, gave them nothing to do, no opportunity to display their prowess. The trenches, they admitted, were a tiresome necessity until they had mobilized enough men to break through into the open country behind the enemy lines. Once that was achieved, they could show their mettle. By bold maneuver, brilliant strategy and tactics they could soon have the Germans beaten. In that they were probably right. They all had experience of active warfare abroad, and the German generals had none. They hadn't fought a war since 1870, nearly fifty years before.

The British generals had every justification in believing that once they had broken through those German trenches, a brilliant and decisive victory lay ahead.

And so began the long and ghastly sequence of offensives.

The first was an attack that became known as the Battle of Loos. It was a historic occasion in the sense that for the first time the civilian Army fought beside the Regulars. The first contingent of Kitchener's Army went into the assault together with battalions of the Territorials, who were voluntary "weekend" soldiers in peacetime.

By then a good supply of ammunition had arrived from the new munitions factories in England. The generals began by plastering the German positions with shells. It was, of course, an obvious advertisement to the enemy that an attack was pending and gave them valuable time to make their preparations.

At zero hour the infantry advanced, and the carnage began. They were caught in the wire entanglements and mowed down by German machine guns. In the end a small dent had been made in the enemy lines—a few miles wide and a few miles deep. The territory gained had no strategic value.

The Germans fortified the edges of the gap, and the thing was over. For the gain of a few square miles of useless land the generals had sacrificed thousands of men.

For this they could be forgiven. It was the first trial of strength against a new sort of military barrier, and the only way to test its effectiveness was to attack it. The attack might have succeeded. The German line might have collapsed and left the way clear for the open warfare that the British generals yearned for.

The reasons for the failure were clear enough to every soldier who came out of it alive.

The first was that you can't destroy barbed-wire entanglements with shellfire. The more you shell them, the worse they get. The generals apparently hoped that the shells would blow the wire away and leave a clear passage for the advancing infantry. But I saw barbed-wire entanglements after days of intensive shellfire. The stakes supporting them were blown out of the ground, but the wire was still there—all twisted and distorted and more difficult to get through than when it was taut and straight.

The second lesson taught by that abortive attack was that land churned up by a massive bombardment of shells was impossible for the rapid advance of infantry. They had to pick a slow and arduous way around the craters, at the mercy of enemy machine guns.

The third and final lesson was that the Germans had built deep dugouts impervious to shellfire. Most of them were more than 20 feet deep, strutted with stout pit props. The defenders could remain down there in safety while the enemy artillery churned the ground above them. When the barrage lifted for the attackers to advance, the Germans would come out with their machine guns and mow them down.

If these obvious lessons had been taken to heart the terrible losses in the Battle of Loos could almost have been justified.

But they made no impression on the generals. They decided that all they needed was another and more copious supply of men and a larger quantity of ammunition.

They planned the Battle of the Somme upon an epic scale, but with no new weapons, no new ideas. It was the same old scheme that had failed at Loos—horribly magnified.

Massive reinforcements had poured in from England. Mainly hastily trained volunteers. The P.B.I. they called themselves: the poor bloody infantry. The more cynical label was cannon fodder.

There was a tremendous bombardment. The attack was launched, and by the end of the first day the Army had lost 60,000 men. They were lost for the reasons that had made themselves plain a year before at Loos: unbroken wire, ground made impassable by shell craters, enemy machine gunners protected by deep shelters until the barrage had been lifted for the infantry to advance as easy targets.

The generals were undeterred, and the slaughter went on for weeks. The final result was another dent in the German lines, a few miles wide and a few miles deep. Nothing had been gained. The captured ground had no strategic value, and the total British casualties amounted to 250,000 men.

Passchendaele, 1917, was the final, crowning misery. I was in it myself and can speak from personal, unforgettable experience.

One of the difficulties of a junior officer was that nobody ever told him what these attacks were intended to achieve.

In the Second World War the generals would brief their officers before an attack. They would get them together and give them a clear preview. The officers would go back and explain things to their men, and every soldier would go into the attack as well informed as the generals in command.

Nothing like that happened in the First World War. The Army commander briefed his division and brigade commanders, who in turn passed on the information to the colonels of battalions. But it never got to the junior officers, who were to lead the men. Secrecy appeared to be the watchword, and you just waited and did what you were told when the time arrived.

I never knew a thing about the Battle of Passchendaele except that I was in it. I only discovered what it was about years later when I read a history of the war.

The Ypres Salient had always been a thorn in the side of the Germany Army. It was a narrow wedge jutting into the German lines around the town of Ypres. For them it was the gateway to the Channel ports. For the British it was the gateway back to Belgium. The British had held on desperately and beaten off every German attack, but the salient was hell on earth for British battalions that held the trenches there. Our own battalion had done its spell of duty. We had held the trenches at Zillebeke for several weeks. The Germans held the high ground all around the salient, and you were shot at from three sides.

The idea of this new offensive was to burst open the German lines around the salient with a massive blow that would open the way to the Belgian coast and turn the northern flank of the German line. Among the plums that were to fall into our hands were some of the ports from which the Germans operated their U-boats, and the British Navy would cooperate.

It was an excellent idea on paper. Planning it all at Army headquarters down to the last detail, the generals must have believed that the war was practically won. All that they didn't take into account were the tiresome realities.

Our battalion was holding some trenches at the southern end of the British line when one night, without warning, we were replaced by another battalion and marched back to a village a few miles behind. This in itself was ominous. If they took you out for a rest, it usually meant that you were for it in the near future.

After a few days, during which the battalion was brought up to strength with drafts from England, we were ordered to parade and set out for an unknown destination. The way of our march was to the north, and that meant back to the Ypres Salient. Rumors were already drifting around that something big was brewing up there, but we junior officers were told nothing officially. We had to depend on cookhouse rumors, which usually turned out to be right.

We marched about 20 miles a day in the sweltering summer heat, and it took three days to reach the assembly area behind Ypres. One of the factors overlooked by the Army command was the condition of the men they were sending into battle. Most of ours had been serving in the trenches for the past few months and were quite unfit to face those long forced marches. In the trenches they got no physical exercise. They lived crouched up in sentry posts and slept beneath flimsy shelters roofed with corrugated iron. They slept in their uniforms and were not allowed to take their boots off. Most of their food came out of tins with no fresh vegetables or fruit. If they got bound up inside, the doctor would give them a pill, called a number nine, that purged them, then left them bound up again. They suffered from skin eruptures through ill-balanced food, and foot blisters would frequently turn septic.

As a lieutenant, I was in charge of about thirty men. Some were old friends, who had served with me since I joined the battalion a year before, but most of the newcomers were conscripts, often around forty years of age.

At the end of each day's march there would be a "foot parade." The men would take off their boots and socks and sit in a row in the barn where they were to sleep the night on straw.

Some of the feet were horrible to look at: raw skin and bleeding blisters and big, angry sores. Their Army boots rarely fitted comfortably. They were made in a few standard sizes, and a man was lucky if he got a pair that were neither too big nor too small. To march all day in them with blistered feet must have been a torment. The Army socks were hard and filthy through wearing them night and day. There was nothing you could do for these poor men but get the medical orderly to give them some ointment to rub in. Most of them needed at least a week of careful attention, but we had passed the point of no return. The medical officer could send a man down only if he had completely collapsed and could no longer stand.

There was no mechanical transport in those days. A few mule-drawn wagons carried the cooking utensils and spare equipment, but the men marched like beasts of burden with heavy packs on their backs, rifles and bandoliers of ammunition slung across their shoulders.

Sometimes they would break into a marching song to ease the misery, but now and then, as I marched at the head of my platoon, I would hear a clatter behind me and turn to see a man lying prostrate in the road.

The sergeants were instructed to prod them and order them to get up. There was always the possibility that the man had decided that he had taken as much as he could bear and had staged his collapse to get out of it. But most of them were genuine—down-and-out.

We arrived at last at a cluster of tin huts that was to be our camp until we went into the attack.

The great preliminary bombardment had begun. We were surrounded by batteries of artillery, and for three nights it was bedlam. It had now begun to rain. Some people said that the artillery fire brought down the rain, but it was probably just bad luck. The generals had planned the attack for August and naturally reckoned that the weather would be good. But for three nights and days it rained incessantly, and the ground became a quagmire.

Living conditions in our camp were sordid beyond belief. The cookhouse was flooded, and most of the food was uneatable. There was nothing but sodden biscuits and cold stew. The cooks tried to supply bacon for breakfast, but the men complained that it "smelled like dead men."

The latrines consisted of buckets with wet planks for the men to sit on, but there weren't enough of them. Something had given the men diarrhea. They would grope out of their shelters, flounder helplessly in the mud, and relieve themselves anywhere. Some of the older men, worn out by the long marching and wretched food, were sick. They would come groping out of their shelters, lean their heads against the corrugated iron walls, and stand there retching and vomiting and groaning. Then they would go back to their huts and lie on the damp straw with their canvas packs for pillows.

These were the men who were to break through the German lines, advance into Belgium, and win the war.

In contrast with this human misery, there was something grand and awe-inspiring in that tremendous cannonade of guns. If you stood out there at night, you would see the whole surrounding country lit with thousands of red stabs of flame as salvo after salvo went screaming overhead.

By the end of the third day of ceaseless rain everything in reason and humanity called for the attack to be postponed. It was an effort to walk around among our huts. At every step you went up to your ankles in mud. What it would be like in the forward battle area we dared not think.

Our one hope, until the last, was that the attack would be called off. But the generals went on.

At dawn on the morning of the attack the battalion assembled in the mud outside the huts. I lined up my platoon and went through the necessary inspection. Some of the men looked terribly ill: gray, worn faces in the dawn, unshaved and dirty because there was no clean water. I saw that characteristic shrugging of their shoulders that I knew so well. They hadn't had their clothes off for weeks, and their shirts were full of lice.

Our battalion was to be in the second wave of the attack. The first wave, we understood, was to go over soon after dawn and advance to certain defined positions. We were to follow, move through their positions, and capture the next objective about a half mile farther on. A third wave was to follow us and so on.

It must have looked fine in the planning room at Army headquarters, but unfortunately, we had been told nothing at all. The officers had been served out with maps that covered a wide area of Belgian towns and villages miles behind the German lines, but as things turned out, we got only about 500 yards.

Our progress to the battle area was slow and difficult. We had to move forward in single file along duckboard tracks that were loose and slimy. If you slipped off, you went up to your knees in mud.

During that walk the great bombardment from the British guns fell silent. For days it had wracked our nerves and destroyed our sleep. The sudden silence was uncanny. A sort of stagnant emptiness surrounded us. Your ears still sang from the incessant uproar, but now your mouth went dry. As an orchestral overture dies away in a theater as the curtain rises, so the great bombardment faded into silence as the infantry went into the attack. We knew now that the first wave had left the British front-line trenches, that we were soon to follow.

When we reached the old, deserted front line, the battalion was deployed along it.

Ahead of us was what had been the no-man's-land between the two contending armies: a horrible desert of twisted wire and churned-up mud.

The newspapers, to keep up morale at home, would describe the moment of attack in dramatic, inspiring words: a line of stalwart, resolute soldiers, burning to go like greyhounds on the leash, impatient for the word to leap out of the trenches and charge forward with a cheer.

It wasn't quite like that with our exhausted, dejected men. All of us, I knew, had one despairing hope in mind: that we should be lucky enough to be wounded, not fatally, but severely enough to take us out of this loathsome ordeal and get us home. But when we looked out across that awful slough ahead of us, even the thought of a wound was best forgotten. If you were badly hit, unable to move, what hope was there of being carried out of it? The stretcher-bearers were valiant men; but there were far too few of them, and no stretcher-bearers could carry wounded men across that shell-churned mud.

The order came to advance. There was no dramatic leap out of the trenches. The sandbags on the parapet were so slimy with rain and rotten with age that they fell apart when you tried to grip them. You had to crawl out through a slough of mud. Some of the older men, less athletic than the others, had to be heaved out bodily.

From then the whole thing became a drawn-out nightmare. There were no tree stumps or ruined buildings ahead to help you keep direction. The shelling had destroyed everything. As far as you could see, it was like an ocean of thick brown porridge. The wire entanglements had sunk into the mud, and frequently, when you went in up to the knees, your legs would come out with strands of barbed wire clinging to them, and your hands were torn and bleeding through the struggle to drag them off.

The enemy began to send over heavy shells called coalboxes. Fired from away behind the German lines, they came down almost perpendicularly and exploded with a thunderous crash and a huge cloud of thick black smoke.

All this area had been desperately fought over in the earlier battles of Ypres. Many of the dead had been buried where they fell, and the shells were unearthing and tossing up the decayed bodies. You would see them flying through the air and disintegrating. It was a warm, humid day, and the stench was horrible.

We began to see the relics of the first wave of the attack. It had apparently been caught in machine-gun fire. Most of the dead men had rolled down into the waterlogged shell holes and lay grotesquely sprawled like broken wax dolls, drained of blood by the stagnant water.

We came to the shattered trenches of the German front line. According to plan, the first attacking wave should by now have reached its objective about half a mile ahead, but it was soon clear that barely a remnant of that doomed first wave had got there.

In the old German trench we came upon a long line of men, some lolling on the fire step, some sprawled on the ground, some standing upright, leaning against the trench wall. They were British soldiers—all dead or dying. Their medical officer had set up a first-aid station here, and these wounded men had crawled to the trench for his help. But the doctor and his orderlies had been killed by a shell that had wrecked his station, and the wounded men could only sit or lie there and die. There was no conceivable hope of carrying them away.

We came at last to some of the survivors of the first wave. They had reached what had once been the German support line, still short of their objective. An officer said, "I've got about fifteen men here. I started with a hundred. I don't know where the Germans are." . . . He pointed vaguely out across the land ahead. "They're somewhere out there. They've got machine guns, and you can see those masses of unbroken wire. It's useless to go on. The best you can do is to bring your men in and hold this line with us."

The plans laid down for the attack had apparently made no allowance for a setback or emergency. They were based on the assumption that when a general pressed a button, the whole thing would go like clockwork. The first men who land on the moon will undoubtedly be in better touch with the men on earth than we were with the generals who had sent us into this catastrophe. In theory the engineers were to lay telegraph wires through which Morse signals could be transmitted, but the engineers had got bogged down or killed. We were completely isolated. The only communication with the rear was to scribble messages in notebooks and give them to orderlies to take back. But the orderlies wouldn't have the faintest idea where the nearest command post was, even if they survived.

We found an old German shelter and brought into it all our wounded that we could find. We carried pocket first-aid dressings, but the small pads and bandages were useless on great gaping wounds. You did what you could, but it was mainly a matter of watching them slowly bleed to death. Even if there had been stretcher-bearers, it would have been impossible to carry them to safety.

It came to an end for me sometime that afternoon. For an hour or more we waited in that old German trench. Sometimes a burst of machine-gun bullets whistled overhead, as if the Germans were saying, "Come on if you dare."

Our company commander had made his headquarters under a few sheets of twisted corrugated iron.

"I want you to explore along this trench," he said to me, "and see whether you can find B Company. They started off on our right flank, but I haven't seen anything of them since. If you can find them, we can link up together and get some sort of order into things."

So I set off with my runner. It was like exploring the mountains of the moon. We followed the old trench as best we could but had to crawl across the blown in gaps. There were small concrete blockhouses here and there called pillboxes that the Germans built when the swampy country prevented dugouts.

The Germans were now shelling us with whizbangs—light shells fired at comparatively short range with a low trajectory. It was a soldier's legend that you never heard the shell coming that was going to hit you, but I know from firsthand experience that you did. We heard the report of it being fired, and we heard the thin whistle of its approach, rising to a shriek. It landed on top of a concrete pillbox that we were passing, barely five yards away. A few yards farther, and it would have been the end of us. The crash was deafening. My runner let out a yell of pain. I didn't yell so far as I know because I was half-stunned. I remember putting my hand to the right side of my face and feeling nothing; to my horror I thought that the whole side had been blown away.

Afterward, with time to think in the hospital, I pieced the thing together. The light shell, hitting the solid concrete top of the pillbox had sent its splinters upward, mercifully above our heads; but it had sent a ferocious spattering of pulverized concrete in all directions, and that was what we got.

How badly we were wounded we didn't know. We were covered with blood and mud. All that mattered was that we were still on our feet, with our wits about us, and we stumbled back the way we had come. The company commander took one look at us and said, "Get back as best you can, and find a dressing station."

We began the long trek back, floundering through the mud, through the stench and black smoke of the coalboxes that were still coming over. Here and there were other walking wounded, mainly in pairs, supporting themselves pitifully with arms around each other's shoulders. Many were so badly wounded that they could barely drag themselves along, but to save themselves was their only hope. There was no one else to save them. How many survived I didn't know. We saw some fall and lie prostrate in the mud. We could only hope that they went on again when they had rested.

It seemed hours before we reached a dressing station, then only by a lucky chance. It was a ramshackle tin shelter amid a dump of sandbags that once had been a gun emplacement.

The doctor was treating anybody who managed to find his way there. A lot of men were lying around, and some stretcher-bearers were sorting out the living from the dead. The doctor swabbed the wounds on our hands and faces and tried to see through the holes in our uniforms where pieces had gone in. "You don't seem to have got anything very deep," he said. "Can you go on?"

We were practically down-and-out, from exhaustion as much as from the wounds. But anything was better than staying in that dump of carnage. We said we could, and he told us the way to the nearest field hospital—another mile or more beyond. It was nearly dark when we saw at last the subdued glimmer of lights in the tents where the wounded were receiving their first proper attention. It must have been six hours since we were hit. We had come on our feet at least 5 miles, but we were among the lucky ones.

Back at the base hospital, with the aid of probes and tweezers, a doctor took fifty-two pieces of concrete out of me—all about the size of beans or peas. "Fifty-two pieces," he said, "one for every week of the year!" He wrapped them in a piece of lint and gave them to me as a souvenir.

I needed no souvenir to remind me of the monstrous disgrace of Passchendaele. It was proof, if proof were needed, that the generals had lost all touch with reality.

Passchendaele was the fruit of more than two years of experience that had shown beyond all doubt that you couldn't break through the German defenses with the weapons available or with the tactics employed.

But even after that dreadful start the generals went on with it for weeks, losing about 10,000 men a day. And all they had to show for it was another dent in the German line that didn't get them anywhere.

But I have to tell about the public school boy officers and the part they played.

The offensives staged by the generals were like the spasmodic eruptions of a volcano that smoldered on in the long months between.

It smoldered in the trenches, and it was there that the foundations were laid for the final victory.

The trenches were the bulwark. Even when the big attacks were on, the whole line had to be garrisoned and held, and the British Army was responsible for more than 100 miles of it.

The winters were merciless, but trench life in summer and good weather was tolerable if the generals left us alone. All you needed in this garrison work was endurance, patience, and a ceaseless watchfulness, protecting the men from unnecessary risk and exposure.

But the generals couldn't see it that way. They were obsessed with the idea that we should keep up the "offensive spirit." We always had to be firing mortar shells or rifle grenades at the German trenches that were usually not more than 100 yards away across no-man's-land. The Germans were prepared to live and let live and kept quiet if we kept quiet, but naturally, if we fired at them, they fired back. They had a more destructive mortar shell than ours—a huge missile called a *Minenwerfer*. It was shot high into the air and came down with sparks spluttering out the back. If it fell in the trench, it would blow a crater about 10 yards wide, and hours would be spent in repairing it. If it hit a shelter where men were sleeping, it would blow them to pieces, and we rarely came out of our spell in the front line without the loss of several good men.

This business of keeping up the offensive spirit in static trench garrison work was senseless and wasteful. In those four years along 100 miles of trenches we must have lost thousands of men for no purpose at all.

We lost, I am sure, far more men than the Germans did. The German command had organized the structure of deep dugouts in which the men off duty could rest in peace and safety. But the British command had no use for deep dugouts. They considered them contrary to the offensive spirit, that the men would grow soft and enervated and think too much of safety, rather than attack.

So we had to spend our time off duty in shelters dug out of the sides of the trenches—nothing but a few corrugated iron sheets above us, with a single covering of sandbags. The only times we could rest with any assurance of safety was when we held trenches that had been captured from the Germans and could benefit from their fine, deep dugouts.

The trouble was that trench warfare bored the British high command. It wasn't warfare as they had been trained to understand it. It gave them no opportunity to exercise their skill in tactics and maneuver, from which they had gained distinction in African and Indian campaigns gone by. Trench warfare was a tiresome, but unavoidable, necessity when they were planning their next big offensive, and they took as little personal interest in it as possible.

I was in and out of the front-line trenches for a year and saw a general only once. That was on a day when the divisional commander came around. It happened that we had been through a bad night of continuous shell and mortar fire. We were very tired and dirty, and there was something incongruous, almost ludicrous, in the sight of that extraordinary old man, beautifully spruced up in his well-cut tunic, riding breeches, and immaculately polished boots. He had rows of medal ribbons from past campaigns, a light blue armlet, and the emblem of his rank emblazoned upon his polished tin hat. He looked like a man on his way to a fancy dress party.

He stopped and glared fiercely at me. I remember he had a lot of hairs bristling in his nostrils. He fixed me with his eyes as if to instill a bit more offensive spirit in me and went on without a word. He complained to our colonel that some of the men looked dirty and unshaved and went on his way, never to be seen by us again.

Such episodes like this built up in the minds of the fighting soldiers a conviction that the generals cared nothing about the war that the rank and file were fighting and were running their own exclusive war of fantasy, dragging in the fighting men as pawns and cannon fodder.

There had been widespread mutinies in the French Army that suffered, it seemed, from generals no better than ours, and it may be wondered why there was never a murmur of revolt among the British infantry in the face of such indifference and disregard for their well-being and their lives.

Without raising the public school boy officers onto a pedestal it can be said with certainty that it was they who played the vital part in keeping the men good-humored and obedient in the face of their interminable ill treatment and well-nigh insufferable ordeals.

The colonels of battalions were mainly professional soldiers, survivors of the old Regular Army. They were good men who shared the hardships of the fighting soldier. But the junior officers— the commanders of companies and lieutenants in charge of platoons —were predominantly from the public schools, and it was they who lived in close personal touch with the soldiers in the ranks. They led them, not through military skill, for no military skill was needed. They led them from personal example, from their reserves of patience and good humor and endurance. They won the trust and respect of their men, not merely through their willingness to share the physical privations, but through an understanding of their spiritual loneliness. Many of the younger ones had never been away from home before. Their lives had been spent in a simple and secluded way with their parents, young brothers and sisters, a few intimate friends from the neighborhood who shared their interests and recreations, including perhaps the girl they were courting. They knew little or nothing of the world beyond, and they found no true comradeship with the strange men that the war had chosen for them to serve with. They were desperately homesick, with a pathetic yearning for their own people in the towns and villages of England.

These boys were only happy, perhaps, when they were on sentry duty alone, with the moon and the stars for their companions. It was the duty of the officer on watch to visit these sentry posts. If you could break through their shyness, they would sometimes talk to you of their homes, and you could lead them on to tell you of their work and small achievements, their hopes and ambitions if, one day, they returned. You might be able to help them see a glimmer of light at the end of the dark tunnel that enclosed them.

It was on such quiet nights of communion between man and officer that the foundations of final victory were laid, not in the planning rooms at Army headquarters. And it was in this way that the public school boy officer could play so true a part.

When a man surrendered himself to the Army machine, his individuality was exchanged for a number. When he put on his uniform and wrapped up his civilian clothes, he wrapped up with them his personal initiative and the right to think. "Think!" shouted a sergeant to a recruit who had had the effrontery to use the word. "For a common soldier it's mutiny to think!"

But the common soldier naturally expected something in return for all that he surrendered. He expected leadership, an officer who thought for him—better still, an officer who thought with him.

The general had lost all personal touch with the common soldier. He lived in a remote French chateau miles behind the line. The soldiers never saw him, never even knew his name. If some of them had come around the trenches, talked to the men in their dugouts, made the men realize that they all were in it together, then they might have become legendary heroes, as men like Montgomery and Alexander became to the soldiers of the Second World War. As it was, the generals gave nothing to the common soldier to gain his respect or affection. They were a menace lurking in the background, always concocting a new devil's brew with the same old poisonous ingredients.

And so the common soldier turned instinctively to his own company officers for the leadership that he required, to the young officers who lived with him and talked to him as a human being like themselves and helped him hold onto a shred of pride and self-respect.

Fortunately, the great majority of these young officers were worthy of the trust imposed on them. If they had behaved, in miniature, as the generals behaved, then God knows what would have happened in the end.

In those days, in England, there were class distinctions that everyone recognized and accepted without resentment so long as they were not abused. In civilian life the humble workman was content to obey a foreman who had risen from his own class so long as the boss was socially a cut above the foreman.

By the same token, a common soldier would obey the sergeants and the sergeants major who had risen from the ranks, but when it came to his officer, commissioned by the King, he expected something more. What it was he could never have defined in words. But if the officer had it, then the soldier instinctively recognized it, and that indefinable something was what was instilled into a boy at the public school.

It had nothing to do with wealth or privilege. Very few of the public school boys came from the landed gentry or distinguished families. For the most part they came from modest homes, the sons of local lawyers, doctors, or schoolmasters—hardworking professional men. Some were the sons of country clergymen who lived on the verge of poverty and sold their precious family heirlooms for the money to send their boy to a public school.

Too often the sacrifice was in vain. The Army ordained that officers should wear distinctive tunics, cut differently from the private soldier. When they led an attack, this made it easy for the Germans to pick them out and shoot them down before they turned their attention to the men. At the Battle of the Somme, thirty young officers went in with our battalion, and only four survived.

These public school boy officers were not soldiers in the ordinary meaning of the word. Very few of them would have wanted to stay on in the Army when the war was done. They only wanted to get the thing over and return to the jobs they had planned to do. But while the thing was on, they did their best, not realizing at the time what a vital part they were playing. The common soldier liked them because they were "young swells," and with few exceptions the young swells delivered the goods.

Charles Edmund Carrington

CHARLES EDMUND CARRINGTON, *born in England but brought up in New Zealand, ran away from school and joined Kitchener's army. He was a volunteer from the first month to the last in both world wars. After graduating from Oxford, he was for some years a schoolmaster; then, removing to Cambridge, he spent his professional career as a publisher, on the staff of the University Press. His first book,* A Subaltern's War *(1929), appeared under the pen name of Charles Edmonds. A reaction against the modish pacifism of that time, it was more extensively reviewed than sold. Thirty years later, using his own name, he rewrote and enlarged it with the title* Soldier from the Wars Returning.

He traveled widely, for business and pleasure, especially in the countries of the British Commonwealth, on which he has written much. His British Overseas *came out in 1950. He contributed to Lord Hailey's African Survey, to the* Cambridge History of the British Empire, *to the Chatham House Surveys of International Affairs, and to other such works. He wrote the authorized biography of Kipling, reviewed for the* Times Literary Supplement, *and lectured in many countries for the British Council. For seven years he was a research professor at Chatham House, the Royal Institute of International Affairs, and he has also been a visiting professor in America. His only indisputable best seller is a school history of England.*

Describing himself as the "unpropagandable" man, he is frequently found on the unfashionable side in public controversies. Happily married, he lives, retired, in London.

SOME SOLDIERS

A YEAR OR TWO AGO, my wife and I fell into a motoring mis-
adventure when driving through Sicily. It was no great matter, and
it was a relief to find that the gesticulating crowd of Italians who
surrounded us were on our side, taking the view that the other
driver had been at fault. While I was trying to justify myself in
tourist phrases, I heard someone who seemed to be saying, "Send for
Giuseppe. He speaks English." There came out of a shop a man of
my own age, with square shoulders and a look in his eye that I
understood. "You're an old soldier, I think," said I; and then, in a
louder voice, *"Sono combattente della prima guerra, io, sull' Altipi-
ano di Asiago."* It may not have been good Italian, but it was
enough. The name of the Asiago Plateau worked like a charm,
softening his face into smiles, and I knew that I had made a friend.
He took my affairs in hand, settled with the other driver, placated
the police, and would not let us go until he had regaled us in a
wineshop.

Why do the battles of the First World War evoke such sentiments? Why did this common memory form so immediate a bond
between me and this elderly Italian, in a society that has—very
reasonably—forgotten the battles of Asiago? Of course, this is not a
new factor in history, which abounds with evidence of old bores
talking about old fights. In this instance it is a universal phenomenon to be observed in the whole generation of Western men
who were young between 1914 and 1918, so widespread that to this
day some of my contemporaries are a little ashamed to admit that
they were not in the trenches, even if they had an adequate excuse.
There is no tradition like this from the Second World War, when
no one knew who was on active service. In 1944 the man in uniform
might be a clerk, living in comfort and safety, while the man, or
woman, in civilian clothes might be a hero of the Resistance or the
Blitz. But among survivors of the earlier war, you were either in it
or out of it, and the password—Asiago, for example—will quickly
reveal your genuine status.

We may bore you with our anecdotage, but we don't bore one
another. If an outsider should crash one of our reunions, his

imposture is revealed as soon as the conversation moves into the jargon of names and half-hints and allusions which cannot be counterfeited, which defy the interpretations given by young historians when they write about the First World War today. We are still an initiate generation, possessing a secret that can never be communicated.

We have not suffered more than other men; we have not been struck harder blows by fate; we have not been more self-sacrificing; and are not more bloodthirsty. Our characteristic is that we were all put to the same test; all exposed our strength and weakness to the same public gaze; all, when young, rejected the illusions about life and death that some men nourish in old age. Twenty million of us, of whom perhaps 2,000,000 are still alive, shared the experience with one another but with no one else, and are what we are because, in that war, we were soldiers. There are many such dedicated societies in the world, but no other, so far as I know, which comprises a whole age group of the able-bodied men, while excluding other age groups and the other sex. Why else, after fifty years, have we written this book?

I never meet an "old sweat," as we liked to describe ourselves, who accepts or enjoys the figure in which we are now presented, though it is useless—undignified—to protest. Just smile and make an old soldier's wry joke when you see yourself on the television screen, agonized and woebegone, trudging from disaster to disaster, knee-deep in moral as well as physical mud, hesitant about your purpose, submissive to a harsh, irrelevant discipline, mistrustful of your commanders. Is it any use to assert that I was not like that, and my dead friends were not like that, and the old cronies that I meet at reunions are not like that? But as for what they were and are, I'm sorry, I can't explain. Is it worthwhile to write once more about a subject on which a later generation has made up its mind? Let me try to reconstruct some portraits of soldiers, in the figure they cut, fifty years ago, when I was young and impressionable, and let me begin at the top.

Kitchener meant as much to the British in 1914 as Churchill meant in 1940, and his direct achievement was greater. No account has yet been written of the complete revolution in the national life which he carried out almost single-handed. In his first month of office, with no precedents, no staff, no political machine behind him, no authority over organized labor, no national registration, no tradition of compulsory service, but, on the other hand, a deep-rooted suspicion of militarism to overcome, Kitchener envisaged and planned the recruiting, officering, arming, equipping, and training, of a new army of thirty divisions. At the same time, he doubled the strength of the Regular Army in France, doubled the Territorial Army so that half of it could be released for service abroad, and mustered the armies from the Dominions. After a year of war he had forty British divisions in action, most of them new formations. The Americans, with all the British experience to improve upon, had only managed to get one Regular Army division into battle at the end of their first year of war.

Kitchener has been ill served by his biographers, who concentrate on the political intrigues in which he became enmeshed at the end of his life and say little of this creative task which has no parallel in British history, perhaps none in any history. Inevitably, he made mistakes, but as he used to say, "No one has ever made war who has not made mistakes." All Kitchener's men were volunteers and had been warned by him at the beginning that the war would be long and hard—three years at least. Neither he nor they nourished illusions about what they were in for. No doubt, when we were young, we indulged in fantasies about this father figure, nor need we be surprised when a maturer knowledge reveals that, like you or me, he had weaknesses and inconsistencies. When he died, and the whole Army went into mourning, we felt the loss. Has any general accomplished greater things? But no legend can make him a lovable figure, as Churchill was. We never supposed that it could.

Kitchener's army was our university; never again have I experienced such enthusiasm, so firm an impulse to overcome obstacles and improvise substitutes when every military requirement was lacking, to persevere with our training for the crusade, having no desire so strong as that of forcing our way overseas and into it. Meanwhile, leave all else to Kitchener, who would provide everything in due course—as Kitchener did.

No great knowledge of the world was needed to appreciate that his 3,000,000 volunteers included as high a proportion of pretentious, corrupt, and silly rogues and fools as any other random group of 3,000,000 human beings or that some of the least deserving would quickly ensconce themselves in places where they could exploit their talent for imposing upon simpler and better men. But I never came across a glorification of war; I heard no bloodthirsty sermons by militant clergy; I remember no invocations of the joys of battle; I was never in the company of Regular soldiers who talked, as French soldiers did, of *la Gloire* and *la Patrie*. All that would have been called "damned bad form" in the British Army. We were deadly serious about our assignment, without finding a necessity of often saying so, and there seemed no reason why we should not have fun when off duty, since we expected to die tomorrow.

If I had studied military matters I should have known, in 1914, that Sir Douglas Haig had been already selected by Haldane, the most able War Minister Britain has ever known, as the general with a future, our most thoughtful and proficient soldier. His chronicler has done his reputation no good by publishing extracts from his private diaries which reveal a grudging, critical, streak in his nature. A self-effacing man, he never supposed that the course of action to which he stubbornly devoted himself would be advanced by a display of exhibitionism. Perhaps his cold logistic theory of command needed the corrective that was applied in the next war, by such flamboyant generals as Patton and Montgomery. So confident was Haig, so assured of his professional mastery, that his mind, once made up, moved slowly. He lacked that brilliant, imaginative coup d'oeil which distinguishes genius from mere talent, and the plain fact that he was no Napoleon obscures what should be equally plain, that his tactics, appalling as they seem, won the war. In the dreadful campaigns of attrition, Haig at last achieved his object, whereas the German generals, who planned similar battles, could never reach a decisive victory, even when they had all the material advantages. Battles are won by margins, and there was a marginal quantum lacking in the German high command. Haig's superiority was the moral factor which always prevails in war.

It is hard to forgive him for not going to examine the battlefield of Passchendaele for himself, but it was his stated policy to leave tactical decisions to the man on the spot. I myself saw Haig in a front-line village on the Somme and was mightily impressed to know that he had made my sector his personal concern; it was not his custom. We all knew that at Ypres in 1914 he had ridden forward through the Menin Gate to take command at the crisis of the battle, but he was then a corps commander, and we knew other corps commanders who had lamentably failed at such crises.

Civilians misunderstand the ribaldry of soldiers, who commonly rail against their commanders, as the Continental Army did against Washington, and make scurrilous songs about them as the legions did about Caesar. Since all war is a chaotic improvisation, a continuous process of trial and error, in which the forfeits are paid with blood, generals must speculate with men's lives and cannot expect to be thanked for their lost wagers. Wellington once said (though he never lost a battle) that a victory is the greatest tragedy in the world except a defeat.

As I remember, the corps commander, whom we sometimes saw at a safe distance, and the divisional commander, whom we often saw, lived in a cold shower of critical comment, blamed for everything that went wrong. Haig's name, somehow, was not vilified, and if it had been, his army would not have survived to win the hard-fought Battle of the Hindenburg Line, the tactical blow that brought Germany to its knees, in September, 1918.

I saw Haig lead the victory procession in London, through cheering crowds who left no doubt that he was still their hero. The anti-Haig reaction sprang up at a later date, mostly among the postwar generation.

Bless my soul! I could tell you some tales about bad generals, while trying to allow for the fact that neither you nor I have any experience of the strains to which generals are exposed. It will make a change to write about a good general—good, that is, as generals go.

Sir Robert Fanshawe commanded the 48th Division throughout the three campaigns that I served in it. He was about as unlike as one could be to that bloated figure, so dear to the funny men, the stereotype of a British general. A thin sandy-haired little fellow in his fifties, with a quiet pleasant voice, he often reminded me of Chaucer's Knight. We called him Fanny, "and in his port he meek was as a maid"; but a soldier from an Army family, he had fought in Africa and India, and his recreations were given in the books of reference as fox hunting and pigsticking. He always "gave tongue" at staff conferences, he once told me, and was no sooner allotted a command than he pestered G.H.Q. to allow him to attack. His plan was duly pigeonholed by the staff as "Fanny's First Play," since they knew their man. He spent more days in the front line than any man in his command and always followed up the attack behind the leading troops, assuring questioners that it was the safest place in battle. He would drift unobtrusively into a trench, wearing an old raincoat over his decorations, would ply the sentry with chocolate or beef cubes, and would listen to complaints before making his comment. "You say you are uncomfortable here. The Germans over there have very good dugouts. You can go and take them as soon as you like." But he never set his men impossible tasks, never fell into the classic error of generals in all armies of those days, the tendency to press on with an attack long after the opportunity of victory had slipped away. He and his brother, also a general, were knighted by the King on the field of battle, side by side, something that hadn't happened since the Middle Ages.

Colonel Sladen was a big-game hunter from East Africa, the best-dressed man in the regiment, and my hero. Once, in Kenya, he came on three lions over a kill; bagged two of them with a right and left; dropped his rifle; and photographed the third as it ran away. I thought well of that. I was with him twice in situations of real combat, learning to rely on his instant decisions. One cold night I came in late to report at his headquarters, with a fighting patrol, wet through and exhausted.

"See that your men get their rum ration," said the colonel.

"Sorry, sir, there's no rum ration."

He thought for a moment, then called his servant, who brought out a case of whisky, obtained with no little bother for his own mess. It was precious as molten gold.

"How many men? Fifty? Share six bottles among them."

Soldiers never forget a thing like that.

But, then, I have to think of Jim Aldridge, a quiet sensible efficient man. "Higher Authority," that formidable phantom, had decreed that neglect of rifles and rifle shooting was the bane of the Army and must be rigorously punished, a doctrine that no one held more firmly than the colonel.

I was young and knew no better, not even that Jim Aldridge was an exemplary soldier. I "crimed" him for having a dirty rifle on sentry duty and, though the sergeant swore it was an unheard-of event, the colonel was liverish, that morning, and inflicted a savage sentence of field punishment. The horror of this was that Jim, who had already been a year in France, lost his turn for home leave. His name went down to the bottom of the list and did not come up again for nine months, when he joined the last batch of men who for one reason or another had been held back. As they left the trenches, on their way home after so long a delay, Jim Aldridge was killed by a chance shot. I still feel bad about this, though he never seemed to bear me any malice.

For about nine months, Captain Edward Hawke (or that is what I shall call him) commanded the company, and I was his second-in-command. One or the other of us would be detached for special duty sometimes or allowed on leave for a spell, but mainly, we lived together, eating at the same rough board and sleeping in a hut or cave, smaller than a convict's cell, with two or three others who came and went, after a short trench life. We were jolly, as a rule, smoked too much, played cards, drank a little—if there was anything to drink—and often quarreled furiously. Though, by the laws of probability, one or both of us should have been killed, we're very much alive today. He was a year or two older than I, perhaps twenty-one, and—as I now see—was a great deal less silly. (What children we were! I don't set much store by the wisdom of the teen-agers.) I learned how to keep him sweet, chiefly by finding in the canteen the brand of marmalade he liked for breakfast. And what I remember best of that long winter in the trenches is snuggling round a charcoal stove in the dugout, singing. We had a large repertoire of drawing-room ballads, "nigger minstrel" songs, musical numbers from the revues then playing in London, folk songs, and the bawdy old soldier's catches that run right back to the eighteenth-century wars. Then a noise would break out or a sweating runner would arrive in the trench with a message from headquarters, and the fun would stop. "Sorry, it's your turn, Carrie," Hawke would say—this was long before the day of easy Christian naming. "You've got to take a patrol out from the Z Hedge, and find out if there are any Boches in the Sixteen Poplars."

What a jab at the solar plexus, but neither he nor I must show the strain we were under, by a twitch of the lip or flicker of the eye. To release the slightest sign of emotion was to lose a point in the game we played, all day and all night. He was a better player than I was. Once, I remember—dare I say it even now—I quite broke down under shellfire, yammered and shook, till Hawke, just as frightened as I was, but a shade tougher, quieted my hysterics with one sharp word.

I first took note of him in a trench raid at Gommecourt Wood, shortly before the Somme, my first action. I had volunteered for the storming party and enjoyed the experience, though the raid was a bloody failure. Why else remember it or write about it now? In front of us, the demolition party blew a hole through the first belt of barbed wire with explosives, then tried to clip their way through the second belt of barbed wire with wire cutters. Behind them, Hawke and I lay, side by side in the gap, ready to rush in and kill as many Germans as we could find in the trench, before bringing back one or two live prisoners—not too many—as specimens to be examined by Intelligence. We never got through. After twenty minutes the wire was still impassable, while their guns were pounding the trench from which we had started, and a line of Germans was firing at us from 30 or 40 yards away. On one side of me a man, shot through the groin, was lugged away screaming, while his sergeant shouted at him to be quiet. As we were getting ready to retire, I saw a bullet strike Hawke's helmet with a shower of sparks, not 2 feet away from me. "Dead!" I thought, but he jumped up and ran back to our lines, bleeding and blaspheming. "They've shot my bloody ear off!" They had indeed. Somehow this seemed more like comedy than tragedy, and we treated it as a joke when he came back to duty with no lobe to his ear. War was a rough game to be relished, if one was young enough, in those days, and as the man shot through the groin never came back, we soon forgot him.

Little Tich Bashford was the smallest man in the regiment, and one of the most willing. How he got past the recruiting sergeant at 2 inches below the minimum height was as much a puzzle as how some of us got past at two years below the minimum age. He didn't say much, and he rarely smiled, but regarded me with a cold suspicious eye and silently did the same amount of work as men twice his size. On one dark wet summer night, when we were digging a communication trench up to the Thiepval Skyline, on the Somme, we noticed that he was making slow progress. It was not the 8-inch shells, falling at regular intervals that deterred him; it was the tough, murky, malodorous task. Then someone showed a hooded light that revealed his obstacle. He had dug his way resolutely through a buried corpse, decapitating it with his spade. Even then he had no words for his discovery.

I killed Tich Bashford, the only man I'm sure I've killed. Of course, I've tried hard; I've charged with the bayonet and been the first man in the trench, used a revolver once or twice, point-blank, thrown half a dozen bombs in action, fired a machine gun, now and then, at a distant target; but I was never a good shot. With Tich it was different. When we attacked at Passchendaele, I chose four good orderlies to stand by me and lost them all. One simply vanished and was heard of no more; then there were three. We were stopped by a group of Germans, shooting coolly from a shell hole, and when I looked back for comfort, I saw another of my band lying gray-faced and dead; only two left now, Tich Bashford and my servant, Bradley, who was brandishing his bayonet and urging me, "Come on, sir, let's go for the buggers." "No," say I, "get down and open fire." Too late. Bashford is shot through the chest and staggers about, roaring like a bull. (Little men often have big voices.) Then Bradley falls, shot through the head. What can I do now? I can think of nothing but relieving—and silencing—Bashford. I had a tube of morphine tablets, bought from some shabby chemist in Amiens, and, holding Bashford down, I gave him—one—two—three —until, suddenly, he died under my hand. Then a supporting platoon came up, and we got on with the battle.

We were searching the dugouts in a captured trench when the first bomb landed in the fire bay above me. Did I run up from the rabbit hole? I put my skates on. Away and back. "Get out of my road, bayonet man, and let them run that can run." Back to the bomb stop, where grim old Corporal Patterson sat behind a barricade, firm as the Rock of Gibraltar, with his hand clenched upon a bomb. Plainly, my platoon could advance no farther, and here we were at the appointed spot, our final objective. I distributed my men in pits and holes, choosing for myself the one with the best view, although there was already someone in possession.

He is the only German soldier I can now clearly visualize, among some dozens of whom I caught a scared glimpse in battle, and the only remembered corpse, among hundreds from which I turned disdainfully away. After spending three or four tense hours in his company, I had got to know him well, a tall, pale, plump, blond, young Teuton of my own age or a little more. He lay as he had fallen, in an attitude of running, struck by three shrapnel bullets in the back—not running away but carrying a message, for in his hand was a dirty scrap of paper on which three words were scribbled: "*die Engländer kommen.*" His gray eyes were open, and his mouth showed strong white teeth. I looked on him and loved him. There was no hostility between us, as there had been no malice when he was alive. When the time came for us to withdraw, it was as if I had lost a friend. I covered his face and—which seems hard to explain—I brought away his Iron Cross ribbon for a memento. Robert Graves had not yet introduced me to the notion of combat as a love-hate relation.

From these sentiments I was distracted by Corporal Patterson, who was in some physical trouble, which he unwillingly revealed. All afternoon he had been gripping the safety lever of his bomb, since he had pulled out the pin and couldn't get it back. White-knuckled and with shaking fingers, he could hold no longer and dared not throw the bomb which would "give away our position" to the enemy. "Throw and be damned," I said. "We're off."

The return journey in the dusk was down 2 miles of battered trench, under enemy observation and gunfire. Shellburst after shellburst followed us along the valley, till something struck me a blow on the shoulder and knocked me down. "I've got one," I said. But Patterson felt me all over and pronounced me unhurt; it was no more than a clod of earth that had numbed my right arm. We staggered at last into what we thought a safe trench, where I had time to total up the day's account.

"Why, it's Sunday," I said. "What a way to spend a Sunday!"

"Only lost one man from my section," said Corporal Patterson. "It's enough to mak a mon believe in releegion."

The only live enemy I ever loved was an Austrian journalist, Richard Bermann, who wrote novels under the name of Arnold

Höllriegel. He was through the war from beginning to end, on the eastern and western fronts, mostly as a reporter for the *Berliner Tageblatt*. When we met in later times, we never disagreed on politics or on the anomalies of a soldier's life, and his sardonic tales about staff officers were just like mine. Whatever was the nature of the trap we had been caught in, it was the same trap, and the Germans had endured it with the same rough humor. (Not at all like that unreal civilian's fantasy of the back areas, *All Quiet on the Western Front*.)

A young soldier friend of Bermann's was lying wounded in hospital when the sergeant came round with a clerk to complete the records. "Name? Regimental number? Profession in civil life?" What was he to say, having left school, like me, to join the Army?

"Philosopher," he suggested.

"What's that?"

"Philosopher."

The sergeant looked fiercely at the hesitant clerk. "Yes. Philosopher. There is such a thing. Write it down."

My philosophy, and the young German's, which did not probe deeper than an Epicurean acceptance of our world as it was, generated no self-pity.

Richard Bermann was a little older than us and much more worldly. He told me many tales of the trenches from the other side, which he regarded with a sophisticated eye, having known the upper world as well as our underworld. He had seen the funeral of the Emperor Franz Joseph; and had suffered the indignities heaped on the delegates of the defeated powers at Versailles; and had watched two regiments of Polish patriots, one fighting on the Austrian, the other on the Russian side, march into action against each other, both singing the same Polish national song. His romantic tales of cavalry skirmishes by moonlight in the Rumanian snows and his cynical account of Austrian archdukes served to round out my picture of a world that was dying. I had no doubts, in those days, that to wrench Central Europe into the twentieth century by force was a justifiable war aim. But this picturesque absurdity was to give way to something worse. I cannot bear to let my mind rest on Richard Bermann, that tubby, comical, little man, who looked more Jewish than he was. He died in Auschwitz, by tortures that I would rather not imagine.

On the old war memorials one sometimes read the words *"dulce et decorum est pro patria mori."* Once in the war, when I had nothing better to do, I thought of brushing up an interrupted education, even to the extent of trying to read Latin, since Horace, the old poser, had interested me at fifteen years old. What did he mean by this famous tag? How far was his tongue stuck in his cheek? "To die for one's country brings delight as well as honor." Well! Rupert Brooke had said much the same to my own generation. I read on:

> *dulce et decorum est pro patria mori*
> *mors et fugacem persequitur virum,*
> *nec parcit imebllis iuventae*
> *poplitibus timidove tergo.*

I have been trying to translate these verses for nearly sixty years. That second line can hardly come into less than two of English:

> He who fights and runs away
> Lives to die another day.

How feeble a rendering of *fugacem virum*, for the blond German, struck dead while running. Horace had a word for him, and having disposed of the brave soldiers and the cowards with a right- and left-hander, he dismissed the pacifists with a kick on the arse, the "trembling backside." Let me put it more politely.

> In the cause of your country you die with delight,
> But Death's still at your heels if you run from the fight;
> Even pacifist youngsters no mercy will find,
> When shamefully stricken by Death from behind.

Read on again. We have not yet come to the end.

> *est et fideli tuta silentio*
> *merces. . . .*

Heroes and cowards die the same death, and the literary men who agonize about one or the other sort die after them. Perhaps silence is best. "And," says Horace (who ran away from the Battle of Philippi) , "and, honest silence brings a sure reward." "Blab," says Horace, "and you shan't step into the same boat as me. Tell no more about the blood-soaked earth. Reveal its secrets and you expose only your own folly."

René Naegelen

RENÉ NAEGELEN, *who is married and has three children, was born at Belfort in eastern France, on August 27, 1894. His father and mother were natives of Alsace, but they left their village in order to escape the German occupation. The youngest in a family of seven, René Naegelen was compelled to leave school at the age of fourteen. His parents then decided that he should be apprenticed as a pastry cook. When he was still a sensitive boy, he saw in his father's bakery housewives buying their daily bread on credit. He also saw workmen in wooden shoes going to the local mills before daybreak and not leaving work until night. He saw families reduced to misery by disease, and he was aware of the harshness of working conditions in France at the turn of the century. From his early adolescence his observation of social inequalities prompted him to join labor unions and the Socialist movement. His whole life has been devoted to the cause of the underdog. As early as 1913 he was already recognized as the leader of the Belfort branch of the Socialists.*

In August, 1914, when the Kaiser's Germany triggered off the First World War, France called on all her sons. Twice wounded and seven times mentioned in dispatches, Sergeant Naegelen, who had been awarded the Médaille militaire (Military Cross), came back from the bloodbath more of a pacifist than ever, with the strong determination to defend his ideals. He founded a printing house, a newspaper, and a literary magazine and fought passionately against the abuses of capitalism. His revolutionary mystique led him to a four months' stay in Soviet Russia. There he met Lenin and Trotsky, interviewed the famous writer Maxim Gorky, and came into close contact with the Russian people.

He was bitterly disappointed when he came back from Moscow; the police dictatorship of the Soviets appeared to him a betrayal of Socialism, a form of bondage for the working classes, not the intended emancipation. From then on, René Naegelen was to oppose Communist despotism, as well as social conservatism.

He received as he gave. Being at once the owner of a pastry shop, a journalist, a writer, and a militant left-winger, René Naegelen meant to remain free in a free world. Therefore, he did not accept the fall of France in 1940; he joined the anti-Nazi underground, playing a dangerous and important role, miraculously avoiding the clutches of the Gestapo. Made an officer of the Legion of Honor, he received the following statement of recognition from General Eisenhower: "The name of René Naegelen has been placed on record at the Supreme Headquarters of the Allied Expeditionary Force as being commended for brave conduct while acting under my orders in the liberation of his country, 1944–45."

In 1946 he was elected to the French parliament on a Socialist ticket in the Belfort constituency. He resigned, however, to devote himself exclusively to journalism. From 1948 until 1965 he was the managing editor of Populaire de Paris, *the Socialist Party daily paper. He considered the trust and affection placed in him by the prestigious President Léon Blum as the greatest honor in his life.*

René Naegelen has written Les Suppliciés, *an account of his own experiences in World War I, which was a best seller in 1927,* Les Vacances du courage, *and* Cette Vie que j'aime *(in three volumes), all of which attracted notice for their racy style and frankness. He was awarded the Louis Pergaud Prize and a prize from the Académie Française.*

RECOLLECTIONS*

November 11, 1918. O God, fifty years have passed, half a century! On November 11, 1918, at 11 A.M. after five years of uninterrupted fighting, the last shell was fired, the last man was shot. Then our church bells chimed in unison, for peace was restored.

The First World War, which was to be the last of all wars, had been won! 1,400,000 of our men had perished. How many of our allies? And of the enemy?

Twenty years later, Poland, after Austria and Czechoslovakia, fell under the claws of demented Hitlerism; the sons of those who had fought in 1914–18, the sons of those who survived and of those who died, set out on a new war—five years again, and an even more frightful slaughter.

Having fallen in 1940, France was unfortunately to give up the fight, shrouded in her own defeat. If the free world overcame at all a form of barbarity incredible in our age, it was thanks to the almost desperate doggedness of Great Britain; thanks to the United

---

* Translated from the French by Hélène and François Marchessou.

States of America, whose colossal industry provided the "weapons for democracy" before she sailed across the Atlantic infested with enemy submarines and laid the lives of her boys down for our country; thanks also to the courage of the indomitable soldiers of Soviet Russia.

Since I have the honor of contributing to this commemoration of the first worldwide tragedy, I consider it my duty to call up the infantrymen, those outcasts in every war, laboring under exhaustion and affliction, and I feel the urge to spin the yarn of their ever disappointed hopes, of their fits of dejection and despair. Eager never to swerve from the realities through which I have lived, I feel bound to use the hated "I," so that I may retrace, stage by stage, the long Calvary.

September 24, 1915. On the eve of the great Champagne offensive, my regiment in parade order listened to the intoxicating words delivered to the troops on that day by the commander in chief. The brass instruments and the cymbals gave the tone. The colonel's voice carried well: "Soldiers of the Republic: The hour has come to attack and to win. In the wake of a hurricane of iron and fire, you will storm forward together! Your onslaught won't be resisted. Its first wave will carry you to the enemy's batteries, behind the fortified area from which they are opposing us. You will fight them relentlessly until victory is yours. Fight wholeheartedly for the liberation of your country, for the triumph of Justice and Liberty!"

On that day—however incredible it may seem—I would not have changed places with anyone, not even for an empire!

We advanced only 4 miles, sustaining heavy losses, then digging trenches into the chalky soil of Champagne, burrowing our way into the ground during the long months of a dismally trying war.

February, 1916. Verdun! The Kaiser's Germany also hoped for the end of the conflict. Verdun! The famous battle was to last six months, without achieving any other result than the deaths of 370,000 men, Germans and French together.

"Stand your ground!" was General Pétain's order. "No retreat! Meet death on the field! Let survivors launch counterattacks!"

Having been lost, recaptured, and lost again—sixteen times in the case of a village called Fleury—our positions ultimately remained in the enemy's hands; the breakthrough did not take place.

In June, 1916, my regiment went up to Verdun.

The front line lay ahead of us, concentric and incandescent, its thousands of artillery batteries belching out fire.

That night believers and unbelievers alike prayed to God, "Lord, let me come back. I am not guilty. Protect me!"

Were they already marked, the men who were to lie in that charnel house? Would I ever say, "I was at Verdun," or would others say of me, "He was killed at Verdun"?

All loaded up and harnessed like pack mules, we set out at dusk in order to reach the front line before daybreak, stumbling in the shell holes, panting, running, stamping, harassedly ducking under the blasts of explosions. The night seemed to proceed toward some monstrous collective crime.

May I tell you my most horrible experience? We were facing the famous Fort de Vaux. Dawn laid bare the harrowed ground. The stench of half-putrescent corpses in the process of being shredded by shells made the air fouler still. Overcoat sleeves flapped in the air. A mass of flaccid flesh fell on me; I used my entrenching tool to throw away this remnant of a soldier which stained my uniform.

Three of us were crouching in a hole under the barrage of artillery fire. Then a flame, a blast; then darkness and smoke, the acrid smell of gunpowder. Was I killed or wounded? I cautiously moved my arms and legs. Nothing. My two friends, however, lying one upon the other, were bleeding. The bowels of one were oozing out. The other had a broken leg; there was a red spot spreading on his breast, and he was rolling his panic-stricken eyes. He looked at me silently, imploringly; then unconsciously he unbuttoned his trousers and died urinating upon the gaping wound of his comrade.

Horrified, I fled from their unbearable presence. I looked for shelter, any shelter from the gunfire. But the dead filled all the available craters and drove me away: yesterday's corpses with their features contorted in painful agony or composed after a merciful end, swollen, gray corpses, corpses almost liquefied and alive with worms and flies.

Ten days of deadly thirst in the blazing June sunshine.

Such was the battlefield at Verdun.

November, 1916. Our fall offensive, which had been launched on September 25, was breathing its last on the plains of the Somme. It had not stopped raining for days: a fine, cold, penetrating rain. The enemy line was 200 yards away from ours, but our makeshift trenches, dug with small portable tools, had become inhospitable ditches filled with ice-cold yellowish water. On each side the men would lie down on the bare ground or walk to and fro in the open. There were no more horizon-blue or *feldgrau* (field gray) great-coats: The wheatland, whose acres had cost so many lives, had

become our common uniform. We could and ought to have frater-
nized since not a single shot was fired, but French and Germans
alike seemed to be in a daze, knowing they were no longer foes and
yet failing to realize they were brothers in misfortune.

After so many days, so many sleepless nights, drenched to the
skin, bespattered with mud from head to foot, shivering and shaking with cold, stiff all over, the gallant infantrymen—the heroes—
were worn out.

My friend Sergeant Anguenot, formerly so brave, so full of life
and humor, came to me, his arms dangling.

"Look at me! I wish you could have a look at yourself. Jesus
Christ, just look at me! Mud on my neck, mud on my shoulders,
and the water dripping down my ass. On my hands, and yours, just
look! What the hell are we doing? Can you tell me?"

"The relief party should arrive tonight or tomorrow."

"The relief party!" he jeered at me. "The relief party, you bet,
will save us for cannon fodder." He shook me like a madman. "Let's
die as soon as possible."

He dropped to the ground dejectedly. I squatted down beside
him. "Come on, boy, the men are watching us. Get up for their
sake."

"The men, the men . . . there are no more men!"

He shrieked again: "Bullshit! Fuck them all! If only I could get a
shell in the belly!"

"Come on, come on."

He wiped his hands on the short grass, nodding. "You get all
covered with mud with these damn paws."

He saw the tears in my eyes; to hold back his own, he overdid it
and said, "Now listen, I'll walk straight across toward those on the
other side, and I'll bawl, 'Now shoot at me, you bastards!' "

We walked for quite a long time under the overcast sky, but
there was nothing I could do for a man who was broken and defeated.

The same night we were relieved by riflemen who were already
bespattered and dispirited.

Sergeant Anguenot was a long way from the front line when a
shell seeking out a convoy hit him directly, fulfilling his desperate
wish.

April, 1917. We thought we were immune from brainwashing.
We were wrong! Once more without any previous flourish we fell
prey to the subtle game of so-called indiscretions whispered around;
besides, we had been eyewitnesses. Once again, we thought, victory

lay near at hand after a mighty assault. Consequently, we acquiesced in the "ultimate" effort. We accepted death.

During the severe winter of 1916–17, we had been sent to a quiet sector in the Aisne: so quiet as to remain undisturbed by shells, bullets, or alarms. The war was fast asleep, and yet in that very district, on a front line of about 60 miles, a tragedy was to be enacted in the spring.

I knew it, for there was every indication that it was going to take place. On the clear January nights, under a magnificent sky, I would take the watch. It was beastly cold—15 degrees below zero. The steel of the gun was biting my bare hand, the frozen mud had cemented the loose duckboards together, the north wind kept sighing softly in the barbed-wire entanglements, and the whole universe seemed to be deserted.

While the man on lookout stood on the fire steps, I walked the whole length of the company frontage, leaning back at times against the parapet, staring and listening. At first I was overwhelmed by a gravelike stillness, but my ears were attuned to the least perceptible sounds: the muffled rumbling of the trunks; rails squeaking on the narrow-gauge line that carried ammunition; the occasional calls of the supply men. In the propitious night a whole body of men were busily carrying out their tasks.

A machine gunner who stood motionless by his weapon, concentrating as much as I did upon the faraway hum, whispered to me, "Life'll be no picnic out here this spring!"

When we came off duty for a short while or went back to the trenches, we saw the pyramid-shaped stacks of shells, the engineers who were installing side tracks on the railway lines for the heavy pieces of ordnance, territorial soldiers carrying huge torpedoes on their backs, others paving the roads and lanes, and huts being erected with gigantic red crosses on their roofs.

In February and March false stories were being spread:

"Nivelle said to Poincaré [then President of the French Republic] that he would break through the lines of the Huns, that his troops would spend their first night at Laon. I am positive. I have it on good authority. And then, old sport, it'll be open warfare, and everyone'll be home for Christmas."

"As for artillery, there'll be no lack of that. Almost as many guns as men on the front line, not only the regular 75's but heavy ones: 155's, 240's, 360's, and even 400's. Have you seen our torpedoes?"

"Renault is turning out hundreds of tanks, and armored tanks at that, complete with heavy guns and machine guns and all! I know a lot about it, I tell you. My brother works on the assembly line at the Renault plant."

"The English will launch an attack on the same day somewhere in the north. The Huns won't know which way to turn."

March 16. In the very sector where we planned to attack, the enemy fell back about 20 miles.

"You see, they're making off before we fired a single shot."

In fact, Ludendorff had foreseen the offensive and ordered his army to withdraw to the heavily fortified Siegfried Line. He was setting a trap, and we fell into it blindly.

April 10. My captain entrusted me with the first platoon of the assault wave. Most of my men were young recruits who had been drafted in 1916 and 1917. Those boys of twenty, who had lived neither through the disaster in Champagne nor through the excruciating days at Verdun nor through the mud and cold on the Somme, would fight better than their seniors. The seductions of danger, the pride arising from the risks incurred, acted as a venomous magic. We had been elected. So many thousands of factory hands had toiled for us. So many engineers, gunners, and airmen were working for us, the infantrymen, forgetful of our sore feet and vulnerable flesh. Tomorrow the eyes of the nation will be upon us!

April 16. Six o'clock. We went over the parapet. Our captain shouted, "For France, forward! For France!"

A surprising lull had replaced the roar of artillery, now lengthening its range. A blue haze hovered over the enemy trenches. A smell of chemicals rose from the plowed soil.

To the right and to the left, the assault waves unfolded, rifles raised; all of a sudden I caught a fleeting glimpse of the whole French Army spread out over miles and miles.

Had we covered 100 yards, or was it more? Unexpectedly, grenades started bursting all about us; at short range a howling machine gun discharged its rounds and forced us all to the ground. The captain lay a few yards away, cruelly hit, mortally wounded. Above the deafening din I could hear screams of pain and calls for help. My thigh was smarting; I had been hit. I felt apprehensively into my trousers; my fingers reached a superficial wound and emerged red: a splinter from a grenade, a mere trifle. If I had attempted, even on all fours, to reach a dressing station, I would certainly have been shot.

Secure in a strong pillbox, the bastards fired at everything that moved. Two of our men, somehow sheltered by a collapsing trench, were firing with an automatic rifle; others hurled their grenades. At last, one after the other, the Germans stealthily crept out of their positions. How many men in my platoon, how many in my company, escaped unhurt?

I found out later that several units and regiments had managed to overrun the front lines of the enemy but had failed at the second.

Sixty French divisions brought into action from Soissons to Rheims, over a distance of 20 miles, lost 45,000 men in no time at all. They captured 22,000 prisoners, seized 180 cannon, and advanced a few miles. So what? The battle for the breakthrough, for the deliverance, was to be lost within its first hour.

If only the General Staff had stopped there! Nivelle must have been insane when he hoped for a success and issued orders for further attacks on April 16–20 and on May 5, 6, and 10, throwing the Reserve Army, without adequate shelling experience, into an assault on the Chemin des Dames. General Hirschauer, however, refused to send his men to this absurd death: "I would rather give up my sword than sacrifice the blood of my soldiers!"

If one general had this exceptional courage, there were many others who kept at a safe distance from the front lines while they sent their troops to the slaughter. The figure of 110,000 men killed or disabled was often mentioned. It caused a stir in official circles. France was to go through a dreadful tragedy.

The first rebellious acts took place on May 4, 1917. On the tenth my regiment, among others, agreed to return to the front, provided that it should remain on the defensive. A company refused to attack the mill at Laffaux. Insubordination spread and became open rebellion. Upon returning from the battle of April 16, the survivors argued in the barns, while rumors were abroad, concerning a new onset. Voices rose in excitement. There would not be enough gendarmes, those hated gendarmes, to compel the soldiers to return to the slaughterhouse. Gatherings took place in the billets. Regimental officers secretly sympathized with their men. At Coeuvres a whole battalion found shelter in a wood, disarmed its officers without violence, and set up defensive positions.

The April mutinies affected whole divisions, including 113 infantry regiments, colonial units, riflemen, and 17 batteries. Was the French Army about to crack, the French nation about to collapse? The answer was no. On the very front line, at the Chemin des Dames, not a single body of soldiers, not a single man, failed to perform what national defense required, because General Pétain, who had succeeded Nivelle, gave orders to stop the offensives.

But before the appointment of the man who thus managed to quell the mutiny, a sly and dark repressive force, all of whose crimes will never be known, sent to the firing squad "as an example" many innocent, brave, and experienced soldiers.

As for me, I heard of the death of my brother Joseph, who was killed at Craonne on April 17, 1917. Joseph had been entrusted with my father's bakery; he was my senior and had two very young children. My parents had four sons and a son-in-law serving in the infantry. I was conscious of their heartrending sorrow and of their apprehensions concerning my brothers and myself. We were "in for it, all of us." That's what my friend Sergeant Anguenot told me, just before he died.

I was perfectly aware, however, that the United States, fortunately enough, had just declared war on the Central Powers. The *Army Bulletin* and the newspapers printed President Wilson's address to Congress under huge headlines. I still have the text, but in order to call up the past, I would rather trust my memory. Phrases flared up inside me, lofty phrases: "We shall draw the sword and fight for Justice, Civilization, Freedom, and Peace, giving our lives, our fortunes, everything we have. . . ."

I knew that victory was a certainty, although not in the near future. And yet I was also aware that the United States had little more than sporting guns and that it would take them months and months of training before they would be able to come and help us. Friends from over there, all our hopes rested with you, just as twenty-five years later, in the dark night of the Nazi occupation, we expected you, we implored you silently, even humbly, from the recesses of our wounded hearts.

Victory! And yet we had to hold on. If we did so, it was thanks to the authority of a chief who was no military genius, but a great man.

Entrusted with the supreme command, Philippe Pétain, the Victor of Verdun—let us not cavil at the title, for his glory lies elsewhere—was at the head of a seriously ill army. He knew the origin of the disease and behaved as a good physician, not as a venturesome captain. His first step was to put an end to the repression and let bygones be bygones. He reintroduced leave periods, made them more frequent, ordered the demoralized divisions to be assigned to quiet sectors, being hard only on officers and N.C.O.'s and kind toward privates. He multiplied his instructions that the soldiers be treated humanely and respectfully, that their food be improved. We felt confident that he would put an end to large-scale offensives—futile battles and slaughters.

Within a few weeks he worked a miracle, breathing new life into the French Army.

We acknowledged him as an authoritative father, wise and kind, concerned about the physical and moral health of his men and unwilling to shed their blood in vain. It never occurred to a soldier to make fun of him. The earnest look on his face encouraged us to trust him. This is why in 1940, 1941, and 1942, the veterans, nonplussed and astounded by an amazing defeat, and the French population as a whole, welcomed back Philippe Pétain, a marshal of France, as the head of the French state. It was the return of the father in the days of distress. I do not mean to recall the inconsistencies, the weaknesses, the errors that were his in 1943 and 1944, when he was eighty-seven.

We held our ground despite the defection of Soviet Russia in October, 1917, despite the Italian rout at Caporetto and the furious onslaughts of the enemy eager to bring things to an end before the arrival of the American divisions.

In the north, in the vulnerable sector of our front, where the French and British armies met, Ludendorff, who had secretly gathered sixty divisions supported by 7,000 pieces of ordnance, launched them on March 21. They hustled the English out of their positions, ran after them, and headed for Amiens.

The road to the sea, the road to Paris, lay open.

We hastily managed to consolidate the breach. The Germans' progress was stopped in view of Amiens and Noyon. Thus, they failed to carry out the expected breakthrough.

On April 9 the enemy had another try at it farther north but went no farther than pushing forward a new bulge.

Things reached such a critical stage that the British finally accepted the idea of a unified command entrusted to General Foch.

Now on French soil, 400,000 American soldiers, fresh from the boat, were undergoing indispensable training. Ludendorff had no more time to lose.

He finally decided on the Chemin des Dames.

On May 27, after a lightninglike shelling, his troops rushed upon reputedly impregnable positions. Thanks to bold, hitherto unheard-of tactics, their success was crushing; they crossed the Vesle the very same night, entered Soissons on the following day, and reached the Marne a few days later. They would soon be no farther than 40 miles from Paris.

They captured 65,000 men and their headquarters, along with aviation and artillery depots, as well as vast quantities of equipment and supplies.

Germany thought that victory was at hand, but France, her leaders and her soldiers, refused to accept defeat.

Our last remaining reserves, the very last, were thrown into the heat of battle, reconstituting the front and paralyzing an enemy weakened by long marches. It should be said that in the quiet sectors American units relieved ours and made the transfer possible.

Georges Clemenceau made an appeal to the whole nation: "I am waging war." France summoned all her strength. So did Germany.

In Champagne, Ludendorff attempted what he had not been able to do on March 21 and 27. It was meant as the final battle, the Kaiser's battle! William II himself was going to the front in order to encourage his troops; such was his intention at least. The Germans believed they were clever when they chose the evening of our national day for their attack. They thought our soldiers would be sleeping off their wine. They were mistaken. On such occasions our lady bountiful, the Army Service Corps, did triple the rations of wine and brandy, with a liberal allowance of champagne. In war, men often get tight while in billets. It is something of a ritual among the soldiers of all nations, but on the front line, everyone, believe me, remains clearheaded.

On July 13 a French patrol chanced to capture a *Feldwebel* (sergeant) who knew the exact time of the attack. The French command proved more farsighted than usual as it ordered the front trenches to be evacuated after adjusting the range of the artillery on the second line, which had also been cleared for the occasion.

The astounded Germans ran across empty trenches, got their feet caught in barbed-wire entanglements, under the heavy pounding of our 75's. Those of their units who had been entrusted with the exploitation of success became mixed with the first assault waves. It was complete chaos, a failure.

At noon, the order to move forward reached my division, hitherto placed on the reserve line, for a possible counterattack.

All danger had vanished from the Champagne front. Germany had played her last stake in a few hours.

Trucks drove us westward and dropped us somewhere in the vicinity of Meaux.

On July 18 General Mangin's army launched an attack in the Aisne Valley. Without any preparatory shelling but with the support of 300 tanks, they obliterated the bulge at Château-Thierry, quite by surprise.

From then on we kept the initiative of joint operations involving the French, the British, and the Americans, under the respective commands of Generals Pétain, Haig, and Pershing.

Foch dealt out sporadic blows, repeatedly ramming a wedge in one sector, then in another, luring the enemy reinforcements, then striking elsewhere, confusing the opponents, dislocating their defenses, compelling them to withdraw irremediably.

My division was brought into action on August 2. One of the great events concerning me took place on August 27, my twenty-fourth birthday. After twenty-five days of fighting—brief skirmishes, advances, and retreats—of sleepless nights with our bowels torn by epidemic dysentery, we were about to die of thirst. Nobody cared, since we were moving forward. The Germans deftly fell back at nightfall. They withdrew so as to give us a warm welcome in their new positions. The German infantrymen fought desperately, courageously, commanding both our anger and our admiration. The prisoners we picked up were underfed and even more exhausted than we were.

On August 8 a heavy shell fell flat on our group. My captain, Louis, a Reservist, fell never to rise again. Two of my dearest friends never rose again either. With shaking hands I collected each of their wretched legacies: a wallet, a watch, a few coins, some letters and photographs—trifles I would send to their parents. Then leaving their mangled bodies on the field, I joined my company, which had dwindled to a mere eighty. I gave vent to my sorrow in tears.

Where did we stand on August 27? In front of the Vesle. Our miserable company occupied an unassuming crest on the counterslope. Experience had taught us how to choose the counterslope and remain motionless in the daytime. For lack of breath, the battle had come to a halt. We wondered whether the Germans would come out of their hiding places to recover the ground we had conquered.

Our front stretched roughly over 300 yards. The men, therefore, were crouching at a distance from each other in their dugouts. Everything was still, but all of a sudden heads and shoulders briefly popped out: "Pass it on: We'll be relieved tonight, pass it on. . . ." The magic whisper ran along the whole line.

We would be relieved that night. The war, my war, would be over that night. For a couple of weeks my ailing stomach could no longer stand canned food or wine. I had survived on a hunk of bread and water—when I happened to find some.

The lieutenant broke the news that Americans were going to replace us. Americans! He was to pass on the orders to their officers. Concerning my own platoon, he left it to me to do the same with the N.C.O.'s.

I saw you at dusk, as you came to us, brothers from beyond the sea. You were dauntless boys who ignored the shelters of our dug-outs. From one end of the sector to the other, you fell into line, as if on parade, exposing yourselves to the vigilant eye of German balloons. You stood erect and undismayed at the very moment when a battery of 150's caught us under its fortunately misdirected fire.

We shook hands and waved good-bye and good luck. An American unit had taken the place of a French one.

While we waited for the crippled, the battalion gathered in a small clump of trees. Then we watched ambulances speeding up to the front: "Gee! They've got guts, those Americans! They're big guys. Never saw one of our cars venturing to the front line to pick up the wounded."

In a nondescript village a military surgeon called to my "bed-side" found me lying hiccuping on the rotten straw of a country barn with a high fever and pinned the red clearance slip on my greatcoat.

A whole month in a lousy place of a hospital; then a two months' sick leave; then at last my dear old bed in my father's house—and my mother's cooking!

Pampered and relaxed, I ate ravenously and picked up again. It could be seen every day, according to my mother. The war was going on for my buddies. How I followed on the map the progress of operations, the march of the armies toward victory and peace! Years later on one of my many pilgrimages to the battlefields I once climbed the 225 steps of the monument erected on the hill at Montfaucon in commemoration of a major victory of the U.S. 1st Army. On September 12, 1918, you alone stormed the St.-Mihiel salient and captured 18,000 prisoners. I also made a point of visiting your huge cemetery at Romagne-sous-Montfaucon, where 14,000 of your boys lie buried beneath 14,000 white marble crosses. With a heavy heart, unable to hold back my tears—but who could have?—I walked slowly along the shady lanes of the soul-stirring city of the dead over which flies the Stars and Stripes.

November 11, 1918. "Why don't you put on your Military Cross?" my mother asked. "You really should pin it on today."

All the houses were decked with flags; everybody—women, men, and children—was in the street. My parents were not a little proud to walk beside me, and I did not object to displaying my military uniform and medals on such a day.

There was a crowd on the central square at Belfort, where the local brass band played appropriate tunes. At 11 A.M. the bells of St. Christopher's rang out to peace, the sole venerable cannon of the citadel fired the twenty-one-gun salute, and the national anthem was heard.

The war was over!

My father and mother kissed me, hugged me, and sobbed. The women, young and old alike, clapped their hands at this touching sight and kissed me in their turn. How many kisses were exchanged! There was much kissing going around; indeed people no longer knew how else to give vent to their emotions. The boys put their arms around the girls' waists, and the girls did not object. I was carried away by the popular rejoicing as by a heady wine. I fancied myself bearing on my shoulders the awesome glory of the victors, the triumphant glory of those who survived.

At the same time, however, an inner voice made itself heard: "I wish you could see what a fool you look. You are walking with such martial strides—chin up, chest thrown out—that your parents can hardly keep up with you. If you dared, you'd hold up that hand of yours which once wielded a rifle and launched grenades. A murderous hand perhaps. . . . And you would shout, 'I was at Verdun!' Of course you are a hero, the hero of the day. Revel in the fulsome flattery, dear fool! It does not stop war from being a filthy trick. You can't help it!"

Finally, we had to return home. In the family dining room everybody resumed his accustomed seat, weary in soul and body. A fourth guest sneaked in. On the mantelpiece, in his gilded frame, Joseph, the most vulnerable of my parents' five sons, stared at us with a frozen smile. He lay out there beneath his wooden cross. His comrades dug a bed for him and, to prevent the earth from hurting his eyes, put over his face the battered tin plate which was in his haversack. That's how they found him. We all turned our eyes toward the photograph that time would turn yellow.

How sad my mother looked! She painfully tore herself away from her armchair and broke the silence: "I don't feel up to anything, but still I have to prepare your dinner."

From the street rose the strains of "La Madelon," that stupid refrain, a blatant lie which the infantrymen never sang.

"We've won the war."

"Look! we fixed them!"

"They're drunk," I said.

My mother stopped her ears: "I can't take it anymore."

I closed the shutters and shut out the world, its cruel joys, and light.

On November 11, 1918, in so many bereaved homes. . . .

To those who asked, "What was the worst trial?" I would answer,

"Lice, the invincible lice, thirst, the fear of being atrociously maimed, of losing an arm or a leg, of being emasculated. . . ." And the memory of the few minutes before the attack at Grivesne, in April, 1918, when I rested under a budding apple tree, the promise of blossoms and fruit, which was no longer meant for me. I was twenty, and I had never embraced a woman; I had never felt her warm, naked skin against my eager body; I thought I would die on the very threshold of my wretched life with an empty heart and empty hands.

As men of the free world, twice, and each time for five years, we risked our young lives for the sake of justice and civilization.

I wish I knew where civilization lies. Certainly not in scientific progress and technical improvements: cars, television, and the rest—junk and gadgets.

Civilization lies in spiritual achievements, in culture, in the arts, in harmony and justice.

The celebrated writer Georges Duhamel, the author of *Vie des Martyrs* has written: "Civilization lies in the hearts of men. If it is not to be found there, it is nowhere."

That's where it lies—the promise of greatness.

Sir Geoffrey Keynes

"I was born in Cambridge on March 25, 1887, the younger son of Dr. John Neville Keynes, later registrary of the university, and Florence Ada Brown, afterward mayor of Cambridge and chairman of the National Council of Women. My brother, four years older, was John Maynard, later Lord Keynes of Tilton, the economist, who married the Russian ballerina, Lydia Lopokova, in 1925. My sister, born in 1885, is Mrs. Margaret Hill, C.B.E. (Commander of the British Empire), wife of A. V. Hill, C.H. (Companion of Honor), F.R.S. (Fellow of the Royal Society), physiologist, and Nobel prizewinner.

"I was educated at a private school in Cambridge, at Rugby School and at Pembroke College, Cambridge, where I was a foundation scholar. In 1910 I went to St. Bartholomew's Hospital, London, as a medical student, qualified in 1913, and was then appointed house surgeon at my hospital. I served in Flanders and France in the Royal Army Medical Corps throughout the First World War, becoming a surgical specialist with the rank of major. While on leave in 1917, I married Margaret Darwin, younger daughter of Professor Sir George Darwin, K.C.B. (Knight Commander of the Bath), F.R.S., and we have four sons. After being demobilized in 1919, I became chief assistant to Professor George Gask at St. Bartholomew's and was elected surgeon to the hospital in 1929. In 1939 I was appointed senior consulting surgeon to the Royal Air Force, in which I served for six years, reaching the rank of air vice marshal. I received a knighthood as a surgeon in 1955 and in 1956 was appointed Sir Arthur Sims Commonwealth Professor, in this capacity visiting all the medical schools in Africa and Canada. I hold the degree of Doctor of Medicine of Cambridge University and am a fellow of the three Royal Colleges: Physicians, Surgeons, and Gynecologists and Obstetricians. In 1922 I published the first English textbook on Blood Transfusion and have made numerous contributions to medical journals and books, relating chiefly to blood transfusion, hernia, cancer of the breast, the thyroid gland, and the thymus gland.

"While an undergraduate at Cambridge, I developed an interest in literature and bibliography, publishing my first book on John Donne in 1914. I have subsequently published many other bibliographies and have edited the works of William Blake, Sir Thomas Browne, Rupert Brooke, and others. I have received honorary doctorates in literature from the universities of Oxford, Cambridge, Edinburgh, Sheffield, Birmingham, and Reading. I served as trustee of the National Portrait Gallery from 1942 to 1966, being chairman of the board from 1958. I retired from active surgery in 1957, but have continued working as a writer, publishing a full-length Life of William Harvey in 1966 and a catalogue of my library in 1964.

"I have visited the United States of America several times and am an honorary fellow of the American Association of Surgeons, an honorary member of the Grolier Club of New York, and an honorary member of the Modern Language Association of America."

A DOCTOR'S WAR

In August, 1914, I was halfway through my twenty-seventh year. Young people of my age had lived through the late Victorian and Edwardian times with a sense of complete physical security, and most of us had never given a thought to the possibility of our being involved in a European war. On August 4 I was enjoying a holiday from my work as a senior house surgeon at St. Bartholomew's Hospital, London, camping with a group of friends on the Cornish coast at Manaccan, a village on the south side of Falmouth Bay. We received the news of the declaration of war with Germany with astonishment almost amounting to incredulity but soon had to face the fact, and everyone arranged to return at once to his home. I went back to St. Bartholomew's and decided without hesitation to offer myself to the War Office for enrollment as a junior officer in the Royal Army Medical Corps. The decision was influenced partly by my not being happy with my chief, but more by a conviction that Great Britain would win the war, that it would not last long, and that the experience must not be missed. Since medical officers were noncombatants, there was no element of heroism in volunteering for the Army. "War" did not suggest unnamed horrors but to a young surgeon meant useful employment in his own profession while doing his bounden duty for his country.

Formalities at the War Office were soon completed, and on August 16 I reported with the rank of lieutenant R.A.M.C. to my unit, a base hospital at Woolwich. Some equipment still had to be bought in London, and on August 18 I chanced to meet my friend Rupert Brooke near my rooms in Bloomsbury. He gazed at my uniform with envy and almost with despair. Like many other young men, he was having great difficulty in deciding in what capacity he ought to serve. For me the decision had been quick and easy. My military inexperience was almost total—a week in camp at Aldershot in the Rugby School cadet corps a few years earlier had not encouraged a military outlook, yet it was not difficult to fit into the framework of an Army medical unit, where everyone but a few senior officers was as innocent as myself. My brief diary tells me that on August 20 the Germans occupied Brussels and that I (fortunately) failed to buy a sword in London. Active service was held to have automatically abolished most ceremony, and even details of uniform could be decided by each individual. In common with my close friend Maurice Perrin from St. Bartholomew's I decided to have a tunic of khaki drill, corduroy riding breeches, and skiing boots reaching to just below the knee, thus getting rid of the constant nuisance of winding on and unwinding puttees, though these were the regulation wear.

On August 22 the unit left Woolwich, by train, for Southampton Docks and embarked the next day on a dirty cargo boat bound for Le Havre and Rouen. The ship's progress up the Seine was enlivened from the banks by cheering crowds composed entirely of women, children, and old men, to whom our troops responded with songs and countercheers. The ship docked at Rouen on the evening of August 24, twenty days after the declaration of war, and our equipment was unloaded with a view to the hospital's being established in tents near the town. Casualties were arriving by train in large numbers by August 28 but were taken to other units. On the following day I was detailed to superintend the digging of latrines, a foretaste of the realities of war, but next morning it was reported that the Germans were marching on Paris. We were instructed to reload everything onto the ship as quickly as possible and to return down the Seine to Le Havre. We knew little of what was happening at the front, so could live only for the moment and obey orders. One of the Regular officers tried to frighten us by assuring us that the ship would be "peppered with bullets" on our way down the river, but our eventual retreat was very much like our arrival, though there was noticeably less enthusiasm on the riverbanks. The ship did not, in fact, leave Rouen until early on September 2, when the Germans were (erroneously) reported to have reached Amiens. We spent the next day steaming round Cape Finistère out of sight of land, while many of the officers and troops became patients with violent gastroenteritis. On September 4 we found ourselves near St.-Nazaire in the estuary of the Loire, and it was several days before we knew where we were to go. Meanwhile, our equipment had been unloaded onto the quay, and time was occupied by taking parties of men down to the sea for bathing, where they surprisingly attempted to observe the conventions with underpants, handkerchiefs, or even puttees. For several nights I slept under the stars or, when it rained, under a small groundsheet. On September 10 our equipment was hopefully loaded onto a train, and next day definite orders were received to proceed to Versailles. This sounded improbable after the rumors that had reached us in the previous week; but it turned out to be true, and by the evening of September 13 we knew that we were to establish our hospital at Versailles in the Hotel Trianon Palace. After so many nights spent on the iron decks of a ship, on the ground, or in luggage wagons, the news seemed improbably good; but it proved true, and so ended the prelude to a doctor's war.

The hotel, situated just outside the gates of the Palace of Versailles, could easily be adapted for use as a hospital, the large *salons* forming admirable wards. For two days I was busy planning and fitting up an operating theater (room), until on September 16 two patients were admitted. One of them, under my care with a compound fracture of the leg, died the next day, the first indication of the lethal nature of wounds received on the richly manured ground of northern France and Flanders. We had been instructed not to interfere with apparently clean bullet wounds, experience of the South African War at the turn of the century being the only evidence available to the senior R.A.M.C. officers of how to deal with penetrating wounds. We soon learned, however, of the difference between wounds sustained on the clean South African veldt and those contaminated by European mud. Anaerobic bacteria lurking in the soil were responsible for the gas gangrene which proved to be one of the chief causes of death among those men who reached a base hospital alive. By September 17, patients were arriving in hundreds, many of them having spent several days on the way from the battlefield of Mons. Hospital trains had been improvised from French *fourgons,* or cattle trucks, and the condition of the men posed many problems to our inexperienced judgment. Common sense was the best guide, but "doing our best" was often distressingly inadequate while we learned the lessons of war surgery by trial and error.

For the next four months I worked at Versailles, steadily gaining experience of how to deal with the wounds of modern warfare. The question of amputating limbs raised the most perplexing and frequent of all problems. Reluctance to perform a mutilating operation, when nonperformance might cost the patient's life, created a difficult situation for a young surgeon. His seniors could give little help. The officers' ward was put in my charge, though the responsibility was no greater than if the patients had been private soldiers. The conditions were the same for all. The work was uneven in intensity, the arrival of ambulance trains from the front naturally increasing the pressure for a time. Always a large proportion of the patients could be sent on to England after a short stay in hospital or returned to duty. Consequently there were leisured periods when we could visit Paris, explore the beauties of the palace and the Petit Trianon, go riding in the park, or, best of all, make friends with the French pilots at the neighboring airfields of Buc and St.-Cyr. All my early experience of flying was gained in this way, my first flight being in a Blériot monoplane. Later flights were in the primitive Farman biplane, where one sat exposed in a sort of open-sided basket, and in the more advanced Caudrons and Moranes. I even enjoyed coming down from 5,000 meters in a spiral descent on edge, followed by an almost vertical dive. It all seemed safe enough, even in the aeronautical dawn of 1914. One of these visits provided the additional satisfaction of taking a salute from Georges Carpentier, the greatest pugilist of his day, though his face was the flattened image of his profession rather than the handsome hero of popular legend. More than once I met my brother Maynard in Paris, where he was investigating French finances.

The proximity of the hospital to Paris naturally brought many interesting visitors. Not only were there official visits from the surgical consultants such as Sir George Makins and Sir Anthony Bowlby—the latter from the staff of my hospital and so particularly welcome—but also from unofficial visitors such as Lord Robert Cecil, Sir Frederick Treves, Prince Arthur of Connaught, and, of most interest to me, the great Élie Metchnikoff, pioneer in the study of rejuvenation by surgical operation and of the prevention of aging by the ingestion of the Bulgarian bacillus in clotted milk.

There were thus many amenities, and life was far too comfortable to constitute real experience of war. It was, therefore, not too unpleasant to learn on February 6, 1915 that I had been detailed by the C.O. for duty on an ambulance train. I accordingly left next day for Boulogne, having enjoyed a last evening in Paris at a revue, *Paris quand même,* at the Folies Bergères. For nearly six months I was to endure the peculiar conditions of life with two other officers on a constantly moving hospital. My bed-sitting room was an ordinary first-class compartment in a train composed mainly of second- and third-class carriages for sitting patients and of *fourgons* adapted for stretchers to carry those more seriously ill or wounded. Headquarters were at Boulogne, but we had to be ready to move at a moment's notice to any part of the front in France or Flanders. Often orders came during the night, and the first question to ask on waking in the morning was: "Where are we?" So I became familiar with many railway stations—there was seldom time to investigate the towns or countryside around them. The number of patients carried on each journey varied between 100 and 400. During my turn of duty in the train we carried nearly 19,000 patients. Medical duties were usually restricted to ensuring that the wounded men, who had already been attended in a field ambulance or casualty clearing station, traveled as comfortably as possible with the help of sedative and analgesic drugs. Frequently they had to suffer violent jolts during shunting operations, occasionally so violent that couplings were smashed. Sometimes the engine driver was placed under arrest when he seemed to have been guilty of extremes of negligence or incompetence. We feared that men with fractured limbs would be subjected to unjustifiable pain or risks by the antics of callous drivers.

Usually the patients had been fully cared for before being sent on by train to the base hospitals, but on one occasion (March 12, 1915), during the Battle of Neuve-Chapelle, the train was ordered to go close to the front line near Armentières and take on casualties who had barely received first aid. The journey to Boulogne was spent working under great difficulties, even the coaches meant for lightly wounded men having to be filled with patients who had to lie down, many of them desperately ill. Several died during the journey or even before the train started to move. This was a distressing introduction to dealing with casualties coming straight from the battlefield. Yet on the whole, life on an ambulance train was fairly easy once we were used to the extreme irregularity of our existence. More than ever we lived in the moment and were largely unaware of what was happening beyond our limited horizon. On April 27, I had news of the death of Rupert Brooke three days earlier in the Aegean, and I began to be more aware of the fate which was to kill the majority of the friends of my generation at Rugby School and Cambridge University.

On July 24, having worked all night with a complement of 364 patients, I received the news at Boulogne that I was ordered to join the 7th Field Ambulance in the 3d Division. After a day spent at

Boulogne with my future brother-in-law, Lieutenant Charles Darwin, I left for Bailleul in a supply train. The next morning a London bus helped me on the road in a search for divisional headquarters, and I finally found my new unit in a field near Poperinge. The town was under intermittent bombardment, though on July 29 ten of fourteen shells failed to explode. I was now more definitely at the front than hitherto and found myself going about my duties on horseback, though I had seldom ridden before. My posting to the 7th Field Ambulance proved, however, to be only a brief interlude, my real destination being the 23d Brigade of the Royal Field Artillery, which I joined on August 5. A year had passed since the declaration of war, but it was only now, while engaged at close quarters with the enemy, that I realized how gently I had been let down into the caldron of war. The 23d Brigade, R.F.A., was stationed in the Ypres Salient, the gun emplacements being in front of the walls of the town beyond the Lille Gate. The area was under constant shellfire from three directions. The brigade H.Q. was in small dugouts in a field near Kruisstraat on the south side of Ypres, about half a mile from the walls. Every hedge was occupied by guns, large and small. The ground was pitted with shell holes, and several shells exploded in the field close behind us during the first evening; but the situation was regarded as fairly peaceful by my four companions, the colonel, the adjutant, the orderly officer, and the interpreter, a son of the governor of Calais. As medical officer, I found to my astonishment that I was attended by a batman, a medical orderly, a groom, and three horses. The animals lived in the wagon lines, some distance farther back, but were brought up to headquarters whenever I had to go anywhere other than the three batteries. At other times, when we were out in a rest area or moving to a fresh station, they were essential, and I found that my life was spent largely on horseback, a totally unexpected experience and most enjoyable. Though quite uninstructed in riding, I fell off only once, when my horse fell in attempting to jump a wide ditch from a slippery takeoff, giving me a severe concussion. When we were in action, I took sick parades at H.Q. and at each of the batteries, doing my rounds on foot along the walls of Ypres. I often rode off to the wagon lines and the ammunition column, where I saw sick parades in my consulting room (a converted pigsty) and ensured that general sanitation was adequate.

Ten days after my joining the brigade, my posting was confirmed, so it seemed that I would do, and this gave me immense satisfaction. Not only were my nerves unruffled by the exceedingly dangerous position in which we lived, but also I was becoming closely attached

to my companions, who received me as their equal in spite of my
utterly unmilitary outlook—so obviously that of a civilian in uniform and a noncombatant. On one of my visits to a battery I sat in a
dugout on the edge of a railway embankment with the major in
command, while shells were thudding into the other side of the
embankment. I noticed to my surprise that the major was trembling and dripping with sweat. Shellbursts were my daily lot, but
none of the shells seemed to be meant for me. Frequently they
would burst 100 yards beyond our dugouts among some empty gun
emplacements, and occasionally it seemed sensible to dodge behind
a tree when we heard them coming; but usually we took no notice.
If the enemy chose to bombard an adandoned gun position, it was
none of our business. One of my favorite entertainments was going
to watch the 17-inch shells roaring into Ypres with a noise like an
express train and making huge craters among the ruins. This
nonchalance was natural but was not to be confused with courage.
It was plain inexperience. My friend, the sweating major, knew
more about it than I did, as I subsequently discovered.

Occasionally there was a quiet day, and on one of these (August
24, 1915) I walked into Ypres and straight through to the central
square. Every house was in ruins, but the streets had been swept
clear of debris. At the time, in midmorning, it was completely
deserted except for an occasional messenger on a bicycle hurrying
through as though pursued by a ghost. The lovely medieval Cloth
Hall was fearfully battered, but the walls remained with one brave
little pinnacle of the central tower still standing. Frescoes on the
walls of the upper floors were hanging in space. The neighboring
cathedral was even more devastated, though the tower was still
erect, surrounded by huge shell craters. The bones of the last ten
centuries were sticking out of the ground and a charnel house odor
filled the air. I took two blue Flemish tiles from a fireplace in one of
the houses in the square as a memento. A few days later, when the
mail had just arrived, I was enjoying the perusal of a new *Bibliography of Dr. Samuel Johnson*, sent from Oxford by a kind friend
(Sir William Osler), when I heard a shell coming. I looked up to
see the last turret of the Cloth Hall actually falling after a direct
hit. Even this did not suggest to my mind the idea of a personal
missile with my name on it. That came on the next day, September
12. German airplanes had been active overhead for two days, and
we had certainly been very careless about getting under cover when
they were around. About 10 A.M. several shells came over as usual to
the end of the next field, and we took no notice, though the last two
did come nearer. At lunchtime we were thinking of our usual

alfresco meal, when we heard another shell coming and realized from the different sound that it was going to land among us. It was too late to move, and I turned to watch it hit the ground 10 yards away. It was an 8-inch shell, and by all the rules I was instantly killed. Instead, I saw a fountain of mud and debris shooting up into the air and attempted to hide under a wooden ledge fixed to a tree as a sort of sideboard, hoping to escape the mud as it came raining down again. No one was hurt, for the ground was so soft that the whole force of the explosion was dissipated upward while the fragments were buried in the soil. The enemy had, in fact, ranged accurately on our headquarters, and it was time to run to some neighboring dugouts, where we crouched until the shelling stopped. Orders had been given to all ranks to evacuate the site, but soon I was summoned to the telephonists' dugout, where three men had chosen to remain. A direct hit had been the price of disobedience, and every trace of the bodies of the men above their waists had vanished. It seemed in a way foolish to worry about what remained; but it was felt that their legs had to be given decent burial, and so I carefully extracted as much as I could and summoned the padre to perform his part. In those few minutes I had learned my lesson. I was no longer a civilian in uniform but was suddenly almost a soldier, though very much afraid.

On August 23 a German airplane dropped a typewritten message near us in a bag weighted with sand:

An das 16 Flying-Corps (Poperinge)
Nachdem wie aus der von Ihnen abgeworfenen Meldung zu ersehen ist, unsere erste Meldung leider nicht in ihren Besitz gelangt ist, versuchen wir nun zum zweiten Mal Sie über Kapitän Pike zu benachrichtigen.
Pike wurde am 9.8 von einem unserer Flügzeuge im Luftkampf heruntergeschossen, und ist kurz nach der Landung seiner Verwundung erlegen. Er hat also einen schönen Fliegertod gefunden und wurde mit allen militärischen Ehren auf einem Kirchhof hinter unserer Linie beigesetzt.*

At this date the courtesies of civilized warfare were still being observed, though we usually referred to the enemy as the Huns,

---

* After we had seen the message dropped by you, our first message unfortunately failed to reach you; we now try for the second time to inform you about Captain Pike.

Pike was shot down in air battle by one of our aircraft on August 9 and, soon after reaching the ground, died of his wounds. So he met with a fine airman's death and was buried with full military honors in a churchyard behind our lines.

without much feeling of personal enmity in spite of experiencing narrow escapes from death many times each day.

Near the end of September, 1915, I was given fourteen days' leave in England, returning to the daily round in the salient on October 6. A fortnight later the brigade moved back to a rest area. The casualties in our brigade had not been serious during my three months in the front line, but there could be no question of the wisdom of giving the troops a prolonged rest from the continual tension of static warfare in an extremely hot corner of the front. On November 30, I was provided with a new medical orderly in the person of an ex-cotton master who had worked with 800 men under him in Russia. He was able to help greatly in the organization of my medical inspections and sick parades, and I began to take lessons in Russian. Meanwhile, there was more free time, and I rode widely around the country, visiting friends in other units and learning something of what was happening on other fronts beyond our own. Our rest was to last until just after Christmas, and on December 16 I rode to Dickebush Lake, only 2 miles from Ypres, which was to be the next station for our brigade.

Three days later, after the sound of very heavy firing at the front line, we became conscious of a strong smell of chlorine. The Germans had made their first gas attack north of Ypres, the discharge lasting one and a half hours, but it had failed, even though followed up by a heavy bombardment with gas shells. We were under orders to stand by, but as few Germans were able to leave their own trenches, no reinforcement had been necessary. We were provided with ludicrously inadequate gas masks—just a pad of cotton wool wrapped in muslin—so it was fortunate that the concentration of gas proved to be so light.

On December 20, while still on my rounds, I found that my horse was being followed by a magnificent deerhound, which appeared to think I was his owner. Indeed, I proudly assumed the part and astonished the officers at the next battery headquarters by appearing with this retinue. The battery major possessed a small terrier bitch, and my magnificent gentleman immediately did the honors by lifting his immense hind leg and saluting the top of the officers' mess table with a generous flow of urine. This was taken in good part, and my deerhound followed me home, sharing my bed for that night. This glory could not last, and next day a messenger came from the mayor of Poperinge to collect the Earl of Feversham's dog.

Christmas was celebrated with the customary dinner, for which a remarkable collection of bottles had been assembled, yet no one was noticeably drunk, perhaps because no one had forgotten that we were to move into our new action stations at Dickebush next day. Two days later the relief of the 40th Brigade, R.F.A., had been completed, and I was able to take stock of my new surroundings in the *brasserie* (brewery), a large building close to the lake, around whose banks the gun emplacements had been fixed. The building was so large that it must have been visible from the German lines and could have been easily destroyed by gunfire. We were convinced that its survival was due to the fact that the owner was in communication with the enemy, though there was never any proof of the truth of this uncharitable belief. Nevertheless, we were thankful that our winter quarters provided a sound roof overhead, and we chose to forget that it might have been at any moment destroyed with ourselves inside.

Though more than fifty years have passed, the name Dickebush still stirs memories of events as vivid and moving as anything that has ever happened to me. After four months I was beginning to realize how deeply my life was bound up with the welfare of the officers and men of the brigade. It had been difficult to feel much personal devotion to a hospital temporarily situated in a French hotel or to an ambulance train with its perpetually changing load of patients. The relation of a medical officer to an artillery brigade in the front line was intensely personal—a noncombatant sharing all the dangers and interests of an Army unit which on active service knew nothing of spit and polish, but was rich in the qualities of courage, friendship and determination. I could not really enjoy the music hall songs they perpetually played on the gramophone in the officers' mess; after my long academic training at the university and hospital I had innumerable interests which none of them could share, but their fine humanity under the conditions we all had to endure was irresistible.

The position of our gun emplacements and headquarters at Dickebush were much nearer the trenches than they had been in the Ypres Salient. We were overlooked by captive balloons and airplanes and might even be seen from lookout posts on the ground. Except that the enemy refrained from destroying our great *brasserie,* life was made more frightening by the frequency of shellbursts. I had to give up Russian lessons with my medical corporal; it was impossible to concentrate on the unaccustomed alphabet and syllables with constant speculation at the back of my mind: "Where will the next one fall?" For six and a half months the tension was unbroken for me except for a brief spell of leave in England. Occasionally a small shell, or whizzbang, hit the *brasserie,* one falling while some troops were in the divisonal baths established in one end of the capacious building. All the men ran out naked but soon preferred to risk the arrival of another shell inside—it was March 25, 1916. There were many other excitements. Mines were sprung under neighboring trenches, local battles swayed to and fro, and it was sometimes satisfactory to see a few hundred prisoners being escorted to our rear. There were frequent dogfights in the air over our heads, fifteen or twenty machines sometimes taking part. Antiaircraft fire was usually ineffectual, the technique of ranging on moving targets being undeveloped. Occasionally a machine was seen to crash, with cheers from the ground if it was thought to be German. Falling fragments of antiaircraft shells were another frequent hazard, though it was seldom that any injury resulted. Although the individual batteries were often shelled, the German gunners were inaccurate, and our casualties were not very heavy. Often I would notice that the enemy was ranging on one of our batteries and would watch from behind a tree to see if my help was likely to be needed.

On one occasion, when I happened to be in my dressing station near the *brasserie,* a message came that a gunner had been wounded and was lying beside his gun at the edge of the lake. Would I, please, come at once? I then experienced a feeling which it is hard to describe. It was my duty to walk immediately with stretcher-bearers from a position of comparative safety to a gun pit, which was being accurately shelled every few minutes. I ordered my legs to take me there, but at first they refused to move. My mind was equal to the ordeal, but another part of my brain declined to pass on the necessary instructions. I soon succeeded in reaching the position, having fallen flat several times on the way when shells were heard approaching. It was only about 200 yards to go, but the cerebral conflict involved in doing anything so contrary to nature caused a most strange sensation. Was this "cowardice"? When I reached the gun pit, the gunner was almost dead, and nothing could have been done to save him.

Earlier in the year I had recorded January 25 as "a bright but terrible day." A German airplane came over about ten o'clock to range a gun firing at one of our batteries with 8-inch shells. Eleven times it came over, dropped a starlight signal, and returned to report, always keeping about 500 yards beyond the range of the nearest antiaircraft gun. About two o'clock the shells were falling faster around the battery, and finally one landed in the middle of a group of officers standing outside the billet where they lived. This shell killed five men altogether, including the major in command

and the French interpreter, whose father, the governor of Calais, had visited the unit only an hour earlier. I attended as best I could to each of them, but all were terribly mutilated and were dead or dying. I felt it my duty to report at once to the colonel. I found him walking in the garden of the *brasserie* and went through the motions of a clumsy salute—I was never able to achieve the smartness of a proper military salute. Though hardly able to speak, I told him that he had lost five men, including the finest soldier in the brigade, the battery commander. He said nothing. We were both on the point of tears, and it was hard to maintain the stiff upper lip proper to the occasion. Far greater tragedies were happening elsewhere all the time. The long, drawn-out horrors of Passchendaele were to take place not far away; but the pattern of war is shaped in the individual mind by small individual experiences, and I can see these things as clearly today as if they had just happened, down to the body of the major's terrier bitch (the same that had been saluted by the deerhound) lying near her master.

During the second week in February, 1916, the brigade was to move back to a rest area 20 miles from Boulogne, and I was given a few days' leave. Less than a month later the brigade returned to Dickebush to find various buildings in the neighborhood had been destroyed, though the *brasserie* was still only slightly damaged. Life at Dickebush continued on an ascending scale of terror. We suffered many casualties, and it was a great relief to be allowed to go again to a rest area on April 15 for a fortnight. Soon afterward rearrangements in the divisional artillery deprived our brigade of all three batteries, so that for a short time I was almost unemployed. It seemed to me to be an appropriate moment to apply for a posting to a casualty clearing station—that is, a tented hospital, at a suitable distance from the front line, able to give full surgical and medical treatment to men brought in by the field ambulances. Patients could sometimes be landed safely in hospital within an hour of being wounded. The brigade, as I had known it for so many months, was disintegrating owing to reorganization, half the officers with whom I had been most friendly had been killed, and I longed to be doing a more professionally useful job. First aid and sick parades were all that a medical officer in the front line could expect to find ready to his hand, and this could not satisfy for very long a young man who knew that his vocation lay in some branch of major surgery.

The reorganized artillery remained in Flanders for another two months, but toward the end of June rumors ran strongly that we were soon to move south into France to take part in the great Battle of the Somme. Our move began on July 1, and six days later we had reached the Ancre, a tributary of the Somme. On the way I had seized the opportunity of visiting a C.C.S. (casualty clearing station) at Heilly, where a surgeon from St. Bartholomew's was working, and had arranged with him that Sir Anthony Bowlby should be asked to have me posted to this unit. As so often happens in real life, it is knowing the right people that counts, and it was this that now provided the key to the actual beginning of my career in surgery. This could not, however, happen at once, and early on July 7 I was watching from the ridge near Carnoy one of the many attempts to capture the notorious Mametz Wood. I can still see the little black figures advancing toward the blasted trees. Later in the day I watched similar figures, this time running in the other direction while shells fell among them. These were probably prisoners being rounded up after the capture of Contalmaison, but, as usual, we, being on the spot, knew little of what was actually happening. While eating breakfast that day, I was hit on the shoulder by the only missile that actually found me throughout the war, but it was a spent shrapnel bullet, which failed even to penetrate my raincoat.

We were now living under very different conditions from those we had endured for so long in Flanders. We were in the middle of one of the great battles of the war, and armies were in movement. We found ourselves on the crest of a ridge in a line of what had been German trenches with very little food and no shelter. Deep dugouts were there in plenty; but they were occupied by German corpses, and we had to do the best we could on the surface of the ground. It was a good vantage point for watching the line of battle, but the noise of guns of every kind firing over our heads and from all sides was distracting; premature bursts caused some casualties. Three divisions of cavalry were at hand, ready to go through the anticipated breach in the enemy line. On July 12 a German prisoner told us that they were beginning to realize that the game was lost but thought that they would still put up a good fight—as indeed they did. Gradually our artillery moved forward, and on July 17 we were in Montauban Alley, a trench just in front of the village of Montauban with a view from Mametz to Delville Wood of evil memory. At nine thirty that evening we had just finished our supper of bully beef, when suddenly small shells began whistling over our heads at the rate of thirty or forty a minute, making no detonation as they hit the ground. Our gunners were at first completely mystified; but presently a shell fell near us, and it became apparent that these were a new form of gas shell. We were in a shallow trench, and while the other officers were putting on their gas masks, I thought it better to climb up into the open air, where the concentration of gas was much lighter, and so escaped with only a mouthful of gas. One man was badly gassed, and I had to carry him half a mile to a collecting post. By then I was so exhausted that I had to rest there for two hours. When I returned to my unit, it was getting light and raining, but the shelling continued until after four thirty. We reckoned that at least 30,000 shells had been used and began to look around to see what effect they had had. My first unpleasant impression was that only by a miracle had I escaped stepping during the night on one of the many German dead bodies, which lay about in the long grass where they had been for several days, their faces pitch-black and decomposing. It appeared that the bombardment had been aimed at a neighboring crossroad, where we found the way blocked by dead mules and horses, some disemboweled by direct hits. I noticed one of our men sitting at the roadside; he was bolt upright but had no head, again the result of a direct hit. As a gas attack, however, it had been a failure in spite of the enormous expenditure of material. Larger shells now began to fall very close, and I rigged up a tiny shelter in a trench with a roof of corrugated iron and sandbags. The protection was mainly of psychological value, for I was only 200 yards from the crossroad. One shell fell within 10 yards of my flimsy hiding place. There were more and larger gas shells, so that I became thoroughly gassed and almost incapacitated, though there was little I could do in any case. Meanwhile, battles in the air were occurring at frequent intervals and provided exciting interludes. On July 22 we moved forward again, our headquarters being situated between two 6-inch howitzer batteries, with another close behind. It would be difficult to imagine a more unpleasant situation or a more likely target for the German guns. I spent the afternoon preparing some sort of dugout which would provide a pretense of safety. Then at last came the message that I was to join a C.C.S. forthwith at Heilly, and it was with profound relief that I made my way to Carnoy and so by stages during the night to Heilly.

I had been in the front line for a year all but a few days, for most of the time in one of the hottest sections of the trench warfare in Flanders. I was spiritually and physically exhausted and felt that I had earned at least a spell of more creative work away from the front line. I learned later that the colonel of my artillery unit had recommended me for a Military Cross, at that time the most coveted decoration a young officer could be given. I did not get it—no doubt there were many others who deserved it more—but the recommendation was enough by itself to assure me that nothing had been shirked, so that I could concentrate for the future with a good conscience on my professional work, while living in comparative safety and fair comfort.

For the remainder of the war I was able to practice surgery on a huge scale in casualty clearing stations in France. From my first day at Heilly I was allowed to perform abdominal operations under the supervision of my future chief, George Gask, who, after the war, initiated at St. Bartholomew's the first professorial surgical unit in London. I began to feel that I had achieved my life's ambition, though I had not anticipated that it would be under the abnormal conditions of a world war.

After a month at Heilly I was instructed to rejoin the artillery in the front line and actually left for Amiens and Doullens, but fortunately my surgery had made a sufficiently good impression to earn a reversal of the order, and I was now told to join a C.C.S. at Edgehill, near Dernancourt, a ridge overlooking the town of Albert with the well-known "hanging Virgin"; the effigy on the cathedral had been damaged by a shell and left projecting horizontally from the roof, where it remained, a bizarre landmark, for two years or more. The operating theaters were in tents where a vast amount of lifesaving surgery was performed on those men too severely wounded for immediate dispatch to the base hospitals. Those who remained in the C.C.S. were kept only as long as was needed to make them capable of transfer to the base. Many died and got no further. The survivors formed a constantly changing population in our wards, surgical success being measured not only by survival but also by the shortness of their necessary stay under our care. Work was continuous, but naturally varied in intensity according to the sequence of events at the front line. The hospital was too far from the front line to be in danger from enemy shells, but the sound of the guns was the incessant background of our lives, and we could often anticipate the arrival of casualties by noting the increased intensity of the bombardment; this sometimes reached a level that had to be heard to be believed. While there were days of comparative inactivity, at other times the surgical teams had to work for an indefinite stretch of time, limited only by the number of patients to be attended. I have vivid memories of one occasion during a major battle when I was working. After three hours' sleep I had to operate continuously for another twenty-one hours. That night I happened to be orderly officer and was called up after only three more hours' sleep. My physical state was such that I was at first unable to stand, and it took some little time before I could collect my faculties in order to carry out my immediate duties.

Meanwhile, the newly developed technique of blood transfusion was being increasingly used. I learned more than one method during a visit to an American C.C.S. from Harvard University and thereafter applied these, using chiefly the technique based on the use of sodium citrate to prevent coagulation of the donor's blood. The donors were chosen by preliminary blood grouping of both patient and prospective donor, a procedure which was still a novelty. Official encouragement took the form of allowing a fortnight's extra leave in "Blighty" (England) to the donors chosen from among the lightly wounded men. Potential donors lined up eagerly for the test—rejection was regarded almost as a slur on their integrity, the scientific aspect being incomprehensible to the average soldier. Transfusion provided an incomparable extension of the possibilities of lifesaving surgery. Trained anesthetists were scarce, and often I dispensed with their services. A preliminary transfusion followed by a spinal analgesic enabled me to do a major amputation single-handed. A second transfusion then established the patient so firmly on the road to recovery that he could be dismissed to the ward without further anxiety. At other times I was greatly distressed by the state of affairs in one large tent known as the moribund ward. This contained all the patients regarded by a responsible officer as being probably past surgical aid, since it was our duty to operate where there was reasonable hope of recovery, rather than to waste effort where there seemed to be none. The possibility of blood transfusion now raised hopes where formerly there had not been any, and I made it my business during any lull in the work to steal into the moribund ward, choose a patient who was still breathing and had a perceptible pulse, transfuse him, and carry out the necessary operation. Most of them were suffering primarily from shock and loss of blood, and in this way I had the satisfaction of pulling many men back from the jaws of death.

The necessity for this rather surreptitious work on my part and the intermittent activity of such intensity that the standard of treatment would obviously be lowered argued that there was some lack of organization. The whole medical service had inevitably been improvised at the start of the war on a scale previously unknown, and it took some time to adjust the available skill to suit the circumstances. During the year 1917 this adjustment was taking shape, and presently the medical higher command was warned of impending battles, and surgical teams, consisting of operating surgeon, unqualified assistant, and anesthetist, were assembled at the clearing stations likely to be most heavily involved. Eight-hour shifts of duty could then be instituted by day and night, thus avoiding the extremes of exhaustion previously experienced. I was sent on many of these expeditions, taking with me the transfusion apparatus which I had evolved. This worked so well that it became the standard apparatus in Great Britain for twenty years after the war—though it is now to be seen only in medical museums.

For eighteen months I was engaged in this exciting and often rewarding work, gaining extraordinary surgical experience from thousands of operations of all types from minor injuries and fractures to abdominal, thoracic, cranial, and even cardiac emergencies. The training was in a way unsatisfactory, since it was easy to slip into bad technical habits through the urgency demanded by the work. Sheer physical and mental tiredness must have taken its toll, though it was hard to admit this form of shortcoming. Novel problems constantly presented themselves, mostly surgical, but sometimes of quite a different kind. One of these was the admission to the ward under my care of Prince Friedrich Karl of Prussia, a second cousin of the Kaiser Wilhelm and a nephew of the Kaiserin. He had been shot down in an airplane, a bullet passing through his abdomen and out through his back, perforating the intestine and injuring lumbar arteries and nerves on its way. The intestinal injury was operated on by a consulting surgeon, and the prince seemed to be making a good recovery for several days. He was an embarrassment to the authorities, being related to the English royal family. His cousin, Prince Arthur of Connaught, was sent to visit him, though he came with obvious reluctance. The Intelligence Department thought this might be an opportunity to extract important information from the German prince. Accordingly, a bilingual British officer was disguised as a wounded German and placed in the bed next to the prince so that he could engage him in conversation. It thus became my duty to carry out each day behind a screen an imaginary dressing of the bogus German officer. I resented this attempted deception being practiced on my patient. He was a fine-looking young man with the brilliant blue eyes peculiar to the royal families of Great Britain and Germany. It was impossible not to admire him and to regret that he should be treated so dishonestly, and I have to admit that I was pleased to learn that nothing whatever of military value had been extracted from him by our spy. He was sent on to the base, after about ten days, apparently well, but died soon after from a secondary hemorrhage from the injured lumbar vessels.

The area behind Albert was, as I have said, relatively quiet, but there were alarms at night from enemy activity in the air. Almost every evening soon after dark several German Goliaths would become audible. These were large bombers immediately recognizable by the peculiar beat heard in the roar of their two engines. They dropped their bombs with impunity, since night flying by our fighters was impracticable, until one memorable night when we at last heard a fighter coming to our defense. We saw his tracer bullets ripping into one of the Goliaths, which fell in flames. All the other Goliaths within sight or hearing immediately fled back to their bases, and we heard no more of them for some time.

Our minds and hands were so fully occupied with our work that we hardly ever thought about the end of the war. War, more or less static, had become a normal state of affairs until on March 21, 1918, rumors came to us that the enemy had effected a wide breach in the Allied lines to the south and that our forces were swinging around in retreat. To me, at any rate, the idea that the Allies might be defeated had never presented itself. Ultimate victory was certain, even though the conflict might continue well into a fifth year. Now suddenly the air was full of doubts. On the next day two German fighters, Messerschmitts, appeared out of the clouds and sprayed our camp with bullets from only 200 or 300 feet over our heads. No one was hurt, but it was clear that the incredible had happened.

For many months I had been receiving antiquarian booksellers' catalogues from England and had often had books sent over to me in France. I still have a copy of Sir Thomas Browne's *Pseudodoxia Epidemica,* 1669, containing the note: "Sent off from Edgehill, Dernancourt, near Albert 21 March 1918, the day of the great German offensive. It passed through Albert on 22 March, the last day on which the post could be sent that way." We were instructed the same day to evacuate all our patients immediately by ambulance train to the base and to make ready for our own departure. We left our camp on foot on the evening of March 25, and I spent the night of my thirtieth birthday tramping across country toward Doullens. Another officer and I were detailed to make sure that none of our hospital staff dropped by the wayside. Many of the men were in the C-3 category—that is, unfit for active service—and so enlisted as hospital orderlies. It was with great difficulty that we persuaded some of them not to sit down in their tracks, though somehow all of them did reach their destination. It was galling to be sternly rebuked in the middle of the night by a red-tabbed staff officer on horseback for not keeping our men in proper ranks. He did not understand that many of them could barely walk, and I did not attempt to enlighten him. So we trailed into the citadel at Doullens next morning. I was utterly exhausted and collapsed onto a stretcher to sleep for nearly eighteen hours.

Fortunately the German offensive proved to be the final effort of despair. It reached its natural term with a large salient denting our lines, but with the Allied defenses not seriously broken. Our hospital on the Dernancourt ridge became the front line soon after we left, but we were already getting to work again, with such material as we had managed to salvage, in the citadel at Doullens, a fortress of such strength that no bomb could penetrate into the dungeons where we labored. Casualties poured in, and there was no time to wonder what was happening elsewhere. One day I was operating on a man whose genitals had been mangled by a fragment of shell when I became aware that I was being watched intently by a visitor. I looked up and saw it was King George V; I tactfully gave no sign of recognition and concentrated again on what I was doing.

The succeeding months saw the closing phases of the war with the Allies advancing relentlessly to victory. Soon after the episode at Doullens I was transferred to another C.C.S. as a fully fledged surgical specialist with the rank of major. In these days pneumonic influenza was killing thousands of men who had come safely through the hazards of war; I can never forget the sight of our mortuary tents with the pathetic rows of bodies of the men killed by one of the most lethal epidemics ever known.

On Armistice Day, November 11, 1918, I was with a surgical team at a C.C.S. near Cambrai. A close friend and former rock-climbing companion, George Leigh Mallory, then in charge of a railway gun, was visiting me and shared my tent for the night. Together we witnessed that extraordinary scene, when the whole front in France seemed to be occupied by maniacs, letting off flares, Very lights, and every other form of demonstration they could lay their hands on. Engines whistled and hooted. Discipline had temporarily vanished. We all thought we had seen the last of war. I could not foresee that twenty-one years later I should again put on uniform, this time blue instead of khaki, and spend six years as consulting surgeon to the Royal Air Force.

R. H. Mottram

RALPH HALE MOTTRAM *was born on October 30, 1883, in Norwich, in the house in which Gurney's Bank was founded in 1786. The ground floor formed the offices, in which previous generations of Mottrams had lived, as chief clerks, since the Quaker Gurneys, becoming wealthy, moved out into the country.*

He joined the staff of the bank in 1900, just after their amalgamation with the intermarried Barclay cousins, of Lombard Street and elsewhere, all of Quaker origin. But he himself wished to become an author and was much encouraged by the friendship of the late John Galsworthy, which continued until the death of the latter in 1933.

The outbreak of war in 1914 cut across all such interests. His essay shows how he enlisted, was commissioned, and sent to Flanders in 1915. By a series of coincidences, all connected with the sudden and never anticipated expansion of the armed forces to embrace the whole manhood of the nation, Mottram served in many minor capacities, ending up, sidetracked, in administration. He was thus forced to see, not strategy or adventure, but the daily life men must live to fight. On demobilization he wrote The Spanish Farm *about this existence. Galsworthy liked it and wrote a preface. It was chosen by the committee which governs the Hawthornden Prize for the award of 1924. Encouraged by this, he gave up the bank and became a professional writer.*

"STAND TO!"

—◆—

"STAND TO!"

That command, in a voice hoarse from damp, compelling from urgency, was repeated a few fire bays to the left. It could not be heard much farther off; it was drowned in a rising clamor made up of the earsplitting whiplash crack of rifle fire, the continuous mechanical stuttering of machine guns, sporadic, unpredictable, less staccato explosions of grenades and mines flung through the air. On many a daybreak, during three and a half years, from the first time I heard it, until November, 1918, it was not often punctured by artillery fire, unless some active operation across the trench line was in progress, or contemplated. The order "Stand to!" may have sounded in such daily circumstances, some 1,200 times, in French or English, Flemish or Portuguese, anywhere between La Panne, just east of Dunkirk, and the Swiss border, say, 400 miles. Fortunately, on that autumn morning when I first heard it, we were spared any calculation of that kind. I was busy, thankful to be in bodily activity, that gradually dispelled the wet chill unavoidable when one has slept in a ditch in a Flemish beet field, on wet sandbags, more or less propped over one by a desultory framework of wood. This was what became known as a dugout, a term that had more reality farther south, in France proper, where such shelters could be dug deeper. My business was to see that the men of my platoon were alert, if huddled, on the fire steps, but with their heads below the ragged and sodden parapet, through which they peered at the enemy, a few yards away, across two belts of barbed-wire entanglements, ours (dilapidated), theirs (much better), rifles at the ready, bayonets fixed. Gradually, the noise subsided. On most mornings, movement became possible, with care. The company commander came wading back from making contact with our "next on the left," to ensure the strung-out defense was intact. He paused and removed his rubber waders (four per company), emptied them, and handed them over:

"I hope you'll be so busy you'll make the water in them boil!"

"Here's the brigadier."

He came, bending cautiously, his red-banded cap crumpled in his pocket, visiting his (nominally) 4,000 men who defended his sector, in turns of duty. He glanced around at us and our plight, but spoke in a voice firm as could be expected:

"You understand, Mottram, this line must be held at all costs!" To less enthusiastic volunteers, it might sound like a death warrant.

"Yes, sir!" one responded.

He did his best to encourage: "You can ask for artillery support, if necessary!"

I try to make this record, in as few words as I hope may be vivid, to recall that scene of fifty years ago. I seek to relive the impact on the senses it made, the deafening noise of two immense armies in static collision, the odor of beet field, liberal disinfectant, and odd whiffs of flowerlike fragrance, a last reminder that poison gas had been used on that site six months before. The daylight gradually strengthened. There was nothing to see but wet fields, at which one squinted between sandbags. To expose one's head or even hand was to court wounds. I hope I have shown how lucky a few of us are to have survived. I have already used terms which mean nothing to those who did not witness what I have tried to describe.

The emergency passed. My company skipper said, as the fusillade diminished: "Stand down, now. See they get breakfast!"

I hurried along to find that in their several holes (they were nothing more) the men of my platoon were already trying to boil water, from their bottles, if they had had forethought to bring with them, next to their skin, the only "dry" place, inflammable wood, paper, and matches to ignite the coke they had lugged through the mud. A week earlier, when we had been in support (as I shall show), one of them said to me: "There's lovely taters in the garden of that blown-down cottage. Can we have them?"

"Yes," I told him. "How will you boil them?"

He gave a sheepish grin: "We found a pot. What mother keeps under the bed!"

Let me try to explain words I have used in this strange recital.

Stand-to happened also at dusk, but with less emphasis. Dawn was the dangerous moment at which some attack might be expected, though surprise became rare in that continuous battle. As it grew dark, both sides would be waiting for their rations, food, ammunition, supplies to be brought up, by horse-drawn limbers, to the dump some hundreds of yards to the rear, from which they were distributed by hand. It was just folly, committed only at the height of "great offensives" (always futile) to goad the enemy (or he, us) by shooting up his (or he, our) supper or other "meals." Stand-to is now an evocative paragraph heading in any eyewitness account of what I have tried to describe. It happened twice a day, for all those years, along all those miles, in half a dozen languages. Why? Let me offer a brief reminder to at least half the readers of these words, who were not participants in these scenes but to whom they constitute history, if only unofficial.

In 1914 Germany was the foremost nation in the world, an empire created in seventy years from some scores of principalities and dukedoms. She justified it by her lead in philosophy and education, manufacturing for export, music, and, above all, her rigid military discipline. Inherited from Frederick the Great, it was based in the twentieth century on the threat: "The French will use their black troops; the Russians will unleash their Asiatic hordes." For, in 1870, Germany, newly united, had defeated France and taken from her the title Empire. She had no less taken from her Austrian partner, the mantle of Charlemagne and Hapsburg under its aging, frequently bereaved hereditary head, the old Emperor. Austria, also an amalgamation of duchies, had a core of German language and habit surrounded by non- and even anti-German races and was competing with Russia for the leadership of those largely Slavic elements in southeastern Europe that had, before 1914, thrown off the centuries-old Turkish regime. A German railway had reached Istanbul.

Germany might well have continued to lead the twentieth century, had there not been the detonating fuse of ill-will between William of Hohenzollern, third Kaiser of the German Reich, and his uncle Edward VII, pleasure-loving, easygoing, who preferred French life and outlook to German. The actual explosion, as anyone can read, came through the assassination of an Austrian imperial heir, while he was visiting what was then Serbia. It was all so remote from Britain, in 1914. Edward VII is credited with having created an *entente*, after years of mistrust, with France. Queen Victoria, the aged little German grandma, was dead. A vaguely progressive political upheaval had given us a so-called liberal government, committed, as various factions that composed it thought, to Home Rule for Ireland, advances in education, housing, wage earning: Even theology blinked an eye. What possible interest had we in the rivalry of Russia and Austria? We were alone, and regarded by both opposing groups as being treacherously alone, in our island. To France we were dubiously, not allied, but in *entente*, whatever that was. Did it extend to her ally Russia, so long a threat to our hold on India? None knew, least of all ourselves, preoccupied with home politics. *"Ils vont nous lâcher,"* M. Cambon lamented. It looked so. To Germany we were the century-old naval obstacle to her aspiration for overseas colonies. To America, socially attractive, but, as it now seems, even then incredibly remote, if no longer antagonistic. Of that August, one quality has outlasted half a century: sheer astonishment. While, in a week or two, immense armies mobilized, we were debating other, nearer matters.

But there was, occasionally remembered, the crowning "treachery" of all. We were parties to "guaranteeing Belgium." The cynical amusement this caused leaped to murderous hatred. "Of course," said the Germans, "if we don't outflank France there, France will outflank us! It is obvious. Will Britain fight?" "Great Britain guarantees only that no other European power shall hold Flushing." "It is obvious!" said the French. "Will Britain fight?" To us, only a signature, years before, on a treaty, was obvious. By the narrowest margin, members of our Cabinet dissenting, the rest of us, as if walking in our sleep, stood by the hardly known treaty, and fell into, rather than made, war.

We didn't nationally mobilize. We couldn't. The idea was anathema. We had the Navy, forbidden to disperse as it concluded its annual maneuvers. We had our professional Army, so accurately described by the Kaiser, from his point of view, as "contemptible." It was 120,000 strong, located in India and Ireland. We got it home in record time, without interference, and sent five divisions to join the French. We had our Territorial Army, "Saturday afternoon soldiers" for "Home Service only." They went to the coast, unless asked (politely) if they would mind serving abroad. (A few did so, at once.)

"Not so long as I can get home at nights," one replied. I heard him.

We had Kitchener, who had defended Egypt from the Mahdi's conquest and subdued the South African republics. He called for 100,000 men to enlist, above those already engaged, for three years or "Duration of the War." No one knew when that would be. He got them and asked for another 100,000. While Russia and Austria, France and Germany were locked in some of the greatest battles of history, these "Kitchener's men" and scores who otherwise couldn't push into the recruiting offices and went to the Territorial battalions were gradually sworn in, given one silver shilling to "serve the King." Our pay was one (shilling) and twopence a day (twopence for Brasso to shine buttons). By Christmas, when the Continental armies were fought to a standstill, we were clothed, billeted, armed, some with rifles from Japan, light as toys, drilled, and organized.

How did I fit into this unique, rabidly individualistic lack of preparation? I was then thirty-one, with aging parents to care for and a job one couldn't just abandon. I managed to "enlist," with difficulty on account of the crowd. Barclay's Bank, in which I was employed, promised to give us back our places in it, when "Duration" permitted. I was no soldier. Under the influence of my friend Galsworthy, I wanted to write poetry. But by the early weeks of 1915 the old regular ex-sergeant major who drilled us at Lowestoft was saying: "You young men with education ought to take commissions."

I applied, was gazetted on April 1 (ominous date), little knowing that this alacrity to make me an officer was caused by the casualties we had suffered. Even so I had months of trying to train even less trained enlistments. I heard about various expeditions to Antwerp, the eastern Mediterranean, and Asia. By September, Kitchener's first 100,000 and his second, some Territorials, and the Regular Army were launched on their first major offensive in Flanders, the Battle of Loos. Magnificently gallant, it just failed. The Germans, startled, were preparing to evacuate Lille.

I now have to record a series of strokes of good fortune so personal that I cannot claim I deserved them. They must be what are called coincidences. They are these:

I was given my embarkation orders to join the 9th Battalion of the Norfolk Regiment. I found these troops outside the Belgian horse-coping town of Poperinge, railhead of the Ypres sector of the British-held line of defense. Shattered and hastily re-formed, they were billeted in farmhouses as the bombardment of Loos died down. I found a "mess" of what were the unwounded survivors. There were only 8 out of 32 officers. I was hardly surprised, having threaded my way through the evening hate, long-distance bombardment at stand-to. We were relics of K 3, Kitchener's third 100,000. It did not take me long to discover what this extemporization lacked. There were just no more trained experienced officers. Had the confusion been less, I myself might have been dragged into Loos and killed out of hand. Instead, I was sent in the morning to interview the brigadier, an ex-professional soldier.

"Can you ride a horse?"

"Yes, sir!" (I could sit on one without falling off.)

"Can you use a motorcycle?" from the staff captain.

"Yes, sir!" (I had had one of an early type.)

"Can you speak foreign languages?" (He was thinking of Indian dialects probably.)

"Yes, sir!" (French fluent, some German, Flemish seldom written.)

"You'll have to do Intelligence!" He did not say that the real Intelligence officer had been killed.

"We take over the line tomorrow. Report at the Furnes Canal Bank at stand-down."

I was given a lift. From ancient picturesque Ypres, already largely rubble, within 100 yards of the line, the canal to the North Sea soon ran into inundations that preserved that tip of our defenses on to the beach, for four years. The spoil bank had already been thoroughly honeycombed with more elaborate dugouts than were possible behind the fire steps. I was bidden to sit down with the brigadier (a great privilege), his brigade major (deputy, for Operations), and staff captain (administration), all professional soldiers.

What was this line of defense into which the earlier combats of 1915 had stagnated?

I have said it ran continuously for 400 miles. It was triple. Facing the enemy were the fire steps from which we watched. Some hundred yards west (i.e., on our side) was the support line the various units exchanged for the fire steps at intervals of (we hoped) a week. That was about as much as men could stand of being wet and missing sleep. More hundred yards farther back at the reserve line, where the dump for rations lay, one could walk about, at that distance, just out of bullet range. Thence stretched back toward Poperinge and the railway, some 11 kilometers, a view of ruined Ypres, abandoned farms, tracks in the mud, avoiding roads which the enemy was liable to snipe. I tried walking along one and was pursued by field gun shells. The troops in this situation were formed (in all armies of that period) into infantry divisions. Ours consisted of three brigades of infantry, of four battalions of approximately 1,000 bayonets each, three brigades of artillery called gunners (18-pounder field guns, 4-inch field howitzers), three companies of Engineers (called sappers), four field ambulances (called all sorts of names, but gladly resorted to), and supply and transport details, perhaps, in theory, some 20,000 men commanded by a major general. Owing to some reorganization after Loos, we had been shunted into the 6th Division, largely of Regular professional troops, which had joined the first five divisions of the British Expeditionary Force after Mons. The 7th and 8th divisions accounted for the rest of what had been the old prewar Army. Those numbered 9th to 14th were Kitchener's first 100,000, Scottish, Irish, northern, and so on according to their districts of enlistment. The 15th to the 20th were the second 100,000. K 3 was never so clearly identifiable; there were just no more volunteers, and units were raised where they could be. The divisions numbered 30th onward were formed of the Territorial Army and eventually ran up to the 70th. Cavalry were seldom seen except as individuals. The air was the element left to the Royal Flying Corps, newly formed.

Divisions held the line for varying periods of weeks, brigades alternating and then (until active operations occurred) went back some miles to rest (reinforcements and renewals). This rough description begs at once the question: This town of English-speaking near soldiers, strung out for all those miles, had to be housed (a whole fringe in the open), clothed, fed, sanitated, cared for in wounds and sickness, transported, and kept in fighting trim. For years. How? One element at least, was our divisional "Follies," an amateur music hall entertainment held in a concert hall at Poperinge. If the enemy bombarded, the actor next to sing would say, "The town major wishes to evacuate the theater." This was greeted by howls of derision by members of the audience who had been under much closer bombardment for weeks. This entertainment was unofficial, but it played its part, in the morale of volunteer conscripts. In 1918 they were more homogeneous, less restive than any other army. All the others, save the Americans of 1918, collapsed and disintegrated; even the French Army had critical moments of disruption. The British, for only a few days. I saw their final parade at Lille in 1918. Tired, battered, disillusioned, the slow-tempered, compromising British lasted best. But mark one element of this dryasdust paper view. Men were being killed all the time. Miraculously, I wasn't.

But to resume my account of my reception at brigade headquarters. I was given a wire netting mattress under the telephone. The others disappeared. I was rather pleased to feel I was, apparently, of some use. That didn't last long. Shortly, there was a crescendo in the continual firing just ahead. Field guns joined in. Then our 9-inch.

What on earth was I supposed to do? Wake the brigadier? Ring the artillery? I had just no guidance. Fortunately I did nothing. Gradually the noise died down. I suppose I drowsed. Months later I heard an explanation. The first enlisted Canadian troops wrote home describing the conditions on troopships (cattle boats strewn with straw). This adversely affected recruiting. The authorities (can they have been so intelligent?) said: "Very well. Plutocratic young Canadians can book their own passages and enlist at Liverpool."

When this news (Canadian pay was a dollar, not one shilling

twopence) reached Reservists who had not been called up, they discovered relatives in Canada and went to Liverpool to enlist. The authorities were delighted. No longer would a Canadian colonel have to greet his parade: "See here boys. An English general is coming around. Stand up straight in line, and quit spitting, and for Christ's sake don't call me Alf."

The Canadian formation we were relieving had thus become sprinkled with old soldiers. Told, that night, that they were going to march back to camps near Poperinge, they knew better than to carry 120 rounds they had been issued and emptied their pouches into the enemy. The Germans, still very nervous, responded, but not for long. They wanted to be relieved, too. Luckily I didn't wake the brigadier. Did he guess? But Intelligence was a farce. Then and for years after there was little information you couldn't gather from air scouting. I did odd clerical jobs for the staff captain and rode his horse. He was busy. In about a week the brigadier said: "Your company commander is short of officers. He wants you back." I was rather pleased to go. I was wrong.

Trench warfare, someone said, consisted of boredom relieved by moments of terror. I took part in the endless round of fire step, support, reserve, company reserve, brigade reserve (that meant going up at night to dig). The days of the week meant nothing. There was nothing to do but prop up our dissolving piles of wet sandbags, which might be useless any moment when we got the order to go forward, and clear the enemy out of Belgium. We were getting more guns, even more shells. Rations did come up. We were not seriously attacked. The enemy was busy with the Russians. But there were always fewer men, never enough or better ones.

With one's feet in the snow and one's head and shoulders meagerly sheltered, one wrote to relatives of casualties: "Dear——, I regret to say your son is posted missing. I cannot say what happened, but will let you have any news of him I can gather. He was liked by his comrades and did his duty courageously." Sometimes we were able to mumble, crouching over dead bodies, as much of the burial service as we could recall. There was sickness, of course. There were "schools" to attend when one could be spared for riding, bombing, machine gun, the Mills grenade, and the Lewis gun as they eventually appeared. To what purpose, we wondered. Then amid such routine, among so many wartime lives, something did happen. Apparently irrelevant, it happened to me.

In the darkness of those nights, wading through a spatter of bullets, a runner brought a pink message form: "Officers having knowledge of foreign languages are to report to divisional headquarters."

By the light of a flickering candle, crouching in the company commander's shelter, we read it over. He said:

"This is IT. We are going to break through at last. We shall see what your French and German are worth. You'd better report." He kindly added: "We shall miss you!"

I dodged along to the dump and got a lift. It was an instructive ride. Behind me was the flicker of star shells fired by nervous foes. All around, in gun positions and hideouts, revealed by cracks of light or snatches of talk and song, was that vast "town" of an army in position, waiting for (we hoped) a spring offensive, the dream of successive years. I was decanted at POP (Poperinge) and found divisional headquarters in the *Salle des Mariages* of the town hall. An elderly, tired, disgusted ex-Indian officer grasped, at length, why I had appeared.

"Look at this," he demanded. "Can you deal with it?"

"This" was a pile of blue forms, printed in French, filled up by people more used to hoes than pens. The title was *Réclamations pour les dégâts occasionés par les troupes britanniques*. There was voluminous detail.

"You'd better have a look in the morning." He wanted to get away. I didn't want to stop him, dumped my pack in a corner, and proceeded to loosen my belts.

"Get someone to find you a billet," interposed he, horrified at the idea of my trying to sleep in his "office." It was, in fact, drier, safer, and quieter than I had been for some weeks. A night-duty signaler found me a mattress. At stand-to, the junior staff captain put me right.

What had happened was this: At the Second Battle of Ypres, in April, 1915, the Germans had endeavored, by the first use of poison gas, to reach the Channel ports. Canadian troops, directed by "Old Plum" (General Plumer, the only Army commander with any understanding of the use of infantry in an essentially static infantry battle; the others were of cavalry training), had narrowly fought off the attack. The line had been pushed back to the walls of Ypres; the inhabitants fled, leaving half-cooked meals and beds unmade. British cavalry, coming up to restore the situation, found theselves in (wartime) clover. They ate the food, slept in beds (beds!), used chairs, or shelves, any dry wood, to light fires. In that hop-growing district, in which vines are trained on great poles, we were said subsequently to have burned a million of these. All this didn't matter, until, in a few days, the Germans were obliged to fall back. The inhabitants returned and found what use had been made of the houses they had so prematurely abandoned. Now the French are used to nationwide army maneuvers and their national interruption of civil life. Householders, farmers, and tradesmen, under French law, were entitled to claim for such depredations, hedges gapped, broken windows, endless disagreeable demands of soldiers practicing their trade.

When the inhabitants of the Flemish border found what had been done (with all the exaggerations of real war conditions by *British* troops), they made a first-class row in the Chamber of Deputies. To appease French opinion and keep them in active participation, these special forms were printed and circulated to the British armies concerned. South of Plumer's 2d Army at Ypres, Horne's 1st Army extended, then, or shortly, to Arras, and the 3d and 4th eventually took over, later down to St.-Quentin. But the most continuous occupation was in the Département du Nord, and that was what the H.Q. of the 6th Division wanted me to deal with. It was the sort of job no real soldier liked and, in fact, resented. It was interference of the "natives" (that was how staff colonels and majors thought of the inhabitants) in the business of war. It was no glorious project of a breakthrough. It was a tedious, repulsive business they were determined to shift onto other shoulders. Mine were apparently appropriate. It was all part, little realized at times, of a war that went on too long, in closely populated, civilized country, not the wastes of Indian frontier or African veldt, where there was nothing to destroy. I was given a desk in the corner of the office of the deputy assistant adjutant and quartermaster general, the Q or "Admin." office, out of the way of the real staff officers "busy fighting the war," and told to get on with it. To me, it was not only safer than anything I had known for months. It was something TO DO, other than the futile business of propping up an ever-demolished parapet and enduring extreme discomfort, if not actual wounds.

The real staff officers were very cordial, once I was installed. I saved them trouble. They willingly lent me their horses they had no time to ride, gave me a brief booklet edited by the War Office, and put me in G Mess with the vet., the medical officers, and to my great pleasure, Comte Sanche de Gramont (junior branch of the family) and Baron de Wynck. These were the French and Belgian liaison officers. Often with them, by any transport available, I set to work. De Gramont was a handsome, educated fellow, speaking excellent English his Scots nanny had taught him in infancy. Like most Frenchmen of his kind, he expected adequate catering from life, war or no war. When our messing was not good enough for him, he just said, often effectively, "Change the cook." When his young woman of the moment disappointed him (they had many counter-attractions with the British Army), he changed her for another. I am not criticizing him. He left his comfortable, easy job to join the French Flying Corps and was soon killed. De Wynck was less spectacular. But as the ominous news leaked out that the Germans were taking advantage of the Russian winter to mount a massive onslaught on Verdun, De Gramont was likely to say: "When are your people going to do something, Mottram?"

About that time, in fact, we were coming to the end of our volunteers. Various national service expedients were tried. The 6th Division, after months, was moved out, reinforced, and prepared for what we dimly heard of as a great offensive, in the Somme district, miles to the south. I was so busy it meant little to me. I was getting about to the various farms and hamlets to which the blue forms *"Réclamations pour les dégâts"* related. Some I satisfied with a small payment in lieu of rent they had been deprived of. Sometimes it was a question of persuading the unit billeted not to tether their horses to the destruction of enclosures. Sometimes it was a new road through a pasture. At others, an airdrome, then demanding 80 yards' runway, absorbed a whole field. If the old farmer (all the men of military age were gone) spoke only Flemish, he usually had a daughter or wife who had learned French and, as time went on, some English. The glad news that something was being done about damage in billets ensured that there were always more fresh claims to be dealt with. The news of the Irish Rebellion hardly stirred our consciousness, occupied by more immediate risks.

I recall queer incidents. The Guards Division relieved us. I was bidden (I had become general utility man) to hand over various trench stores, tents, latrine buckets, I forget what else. I was left in our camp, my horse tied up, until a nice-looking young officer in a raincoat (no badges) appeared.

"You're dashed late," I told him. "My division has been gone for hours. Sign for this stuff. I want to get off!"

To my surprise he beckoned a senior near him, who signed for him. Outside, as I mounted, I noticed an unusual number of military police about. I then realized I had been addressing someone who is now known as the Duke of Windsor. I caught up with the division, but there was no rest for me. "Tell Mottram to do it" was applied to all sorts of odd jobs. Eventually I got a lift in De Gramont's car. We went south, by ever more crowded roads. We overtook a marching unit. I recognized the cap badges and waved. It was the last I saw of my own battalion, the men I had commanded, or indeed of the division in which I had served. I suppose it was something to do with the Somme battle. Apparently someone had felt the need for an overall direction that constantly shifting infantry divisions couldn't provide. All I know is that I was (at some length necessary to any official organization) removed from the division and placed under a commission presided over by a general. I found later that the same sort of thing happened to the officer in charge of laundries (imagine organizing the washing of a million shirts a week! If they became lousy, that meant typhus, as in many another army before or since). It might be trench tramways (another specialist job). It might be fire fighting (billets were always liable to be carelessly handled). It might be water supply (great canvas tanks drenched with chlorine). Roads (the French second-class roads were quite inadequate, though Napoleon's granite-paved military main roads were excellent, so far as they went—*i.e.*, from one center to another). I was allotted to an area. It happened to be not the Somme, but Ypres-Messines. I had to ease the installation of all the troops that, after months of mining and countermining, blew up the whole ridge shielding Lille. Was it a diversion to succeed the Somme? Lloyd George thought it had shortened the war! But not by much. It may have caused the great retreat of the enemy, who drew back some miles. That was far more impressive to us than the dim rumor of a revolution in Russia:

"Good thing, too," someone said; "perhaps that'll shake them up."

We hardly listened. I was out all day and every day, by whatever means I could secure, trying to fit more and more troops into my area, from which was to be launched what is now known to history as the Battle of Passchendaele. I forget what number of guns was employed. I do not forget (there are photographs now to show) the effect. It turned a wide belt of wet Flemish farmland into a sea of over-knee-deep mud.

When, at length, this failure, like all the other failures of those years, was abandoned, people as preoccupied as I had been had leisure to read the papers. We learned that the much discussed Russian armies had made peace. This had set free an extra sixty German divisions to forestall the American armies that the conduct of total war had called into being. But when would they be ready?

The outlook was so bleak that I obtained eight days' leave and had just time to be married. It was January 1, 1918. Not a very auspicious day.

The Germans did their best to prevent me. It is all history, now, that on March 21 they attacked and shattered the southernmost sectors of the British-held line. They just failed to break through. Their second stroke fell on April 11, on the edge of my area in the

Lys Valley. The salient of Armentières was pinched off. My last view of the rich farmlands in which I had helped to find some respite, I hope, for thousands of tired, dispirited, decimated troops, was taken from an automobile I commandeered. I had been as far as Bailleul, shelled to the ground. I had seen a whole civil population walking, with what they could carry on their backs, to what they hoped was safety. As it grew dark, star shells hung over Estaires and Merville, Locre and Kemmel Hill, familiar places where I had so often smoothed over the *"occupation par troupes britanniques"* with small doles from an imprest account. *"Mais vous êtes si riches!"* was the hopeful protest. On that night a whole countryside was in flight. I met no one. Shuttered houses were empty and silent.

That was forty-nine years ago, almost to a week, as I record it. There is something in tenacity, Galsworthy's favorite virtue. "Old Plum" never relinquished Ypres. The magnificent American armies of General Pershing were in France. Ominous enough at the moment, that exhausting day proved to be the peak of the enemy effort. After weeks of hasty readjustment, the old 2d Army front sagged but held fast. A few weeks later, calling on French troops that had been brought up to support us, I saw the weary old liaison officer in their divisional headquarters, moving the little flags on the Operations office wall map FORWARD. I nearly corrected him. But a few days later, a British brigadier asked me to arrange a maneuver area for him, as he took over.

"You can't have it there, sir," I pointed out; "that's in enemy occupation now."

"No, it isn't. He's gone. My patrols can't find him!"

It was true. The victorious German Army had overreached itself. It melted away. My next orders were to arrange for the return of civilians to the area that had been fought over. They had sown their potatoes and wanted to harvest them, so brief had been the recoil of the 2d Army. The magnificent American Army was in France. Even so, it was almost too late. When the Armistice came it was nearly an anticlimax. The war of those days (they call it conventional warfare now) had gone on too long, demanded too much. Demobilization, so eagerly looked for, became a hardly bearable strain. It was haunted by the same astonishment as in 1914. No one had ever demobilized 1,000,000 British men from overseas or knew how. It was five years, when I returned to my desk in Barclay's Bank, since I quit it to enlist. It was occupied by girls. However, I was reinstated. I felt numb but thankful. Many a man had had worse luck than I.

Recovering gradually, I tried to make amends. I, at least, knew what I was fighting for, and how that old frontier, from Dunkirk

down to Cambrai, had been fought over again and again, down the
centuries. By the series of coincidences, I saw and handled the
British who fought and the civilians on the spot who made summary room for them. Many a man must have been marched up to
some half-destroyed village and killed there not knowing where it
was or why. The most striking features of that landscape were great
solid old farmhouses, we knew as billets, many of them called *Ferme
l'espagnole*, the Spanish farm, because they had been built as blockhouses, in the sixteenth century, to accommodate Spanish troops of
the medieval Austro-Spanish Empire to keep back the French. We
were facing the other way, but the ghost of half-forgotten conflicts
haunted that area, and the anxieties of the women who braved life,
the courage of men like De Gramont, gave me a theme and I wrote
of it all as *The Spanish Farm*.

It is, of course, the wrong sort of book of the war. It is not about
military triumphs or political results. It is about the uneasy alliance
or *entente* that barely outlasted five years of British or French
history. Galsworthy liked it, and wrote a preface to say why. That,
perhaps, persuaded the committee who choose the award of the
Hawthornden Prize to bestow it on me in 1924. Galsworthy is now
enjoying a posthumous boom, and that may be why I am asked to
recall my "experiences in or understanding of the Great War." The
letters we exchanged while we served encouraged me to do as I am
now asked.

If my book gives an intimate picture of the daily course of the
war, fought between English-speaking men, scattered among
French and Flemish borderers, it must be in the last scene, in which
a "stranger" goes back to survey one of the 2,000 graveyards in
which British dead are marked by memorial crosses. He finds the
names of those he had commanded "properly at ease," beneath their
little crosses.

Edwin Erich Dwinger

"I was born in Kiel on April 23, 1898. My father was an Imperial Marine officer from Holstein, and my mother, Russian by birth, was from the Tula district. I went to school in Kiel, but spent every free hour on horseback. My father's home, an estate in Holstein, bred splendid riding horses.

"In the spring of 1920, after my return home from Russia, I was found to be highly tubercular. Staying first in an Alpine sanatorium, I soon managed to become the owner of a small estate, dividing my time between the breeding of horses and the writing of novels. My first book, Korsakoff, *appeared the very next year, and I wrote usually a novel a year. Army Behind Barbed Wire (1929) and Between White and Red (1930) were translated into twelve languages.*

"I spent World War II with the 10th Tank Division, whose staff officers Klammroth and Hargan procured the bombs for the intended assassination of Hitler. They were my friends; thus, in the summer of 1943 Himmler confined me under heavy guard on my estate.

"Since World War II, I have written five books, and I have traveled all over the world."

THE FIRST CIVIL WAR
OF THE WEST*

I SHALL NEVER forget the first of August, 1914, a Saturday. Suddenly, up from the street, came drumbeats and the shrill signals of two trumpeters. I ran down, and saw two drummers, an officer behind them, and back of him the trumpeters. The officer read in a

---

* Translated from the German by Herbert Schaumann.

far-carrying voice: "His Majesty has ordered a general mobilization. Starting the first of August. . . ."

The small group marched down the street. At the next intersection they assumed the identical formation. Again the drums rattled, the trumpets brayed, and the officer's sharp voice proclaimed: "His Majesty has ordered. . . ."

The days immediately following were charged with a turbulence of which I would not miss an hour. From dawn to night I roamed the streets, happy that our summer vacation from school was still in force. Every soldier in his new gray field uniform was heartily being cheered, troops on their way to the station were pelted with flowers, and the liveliest hubbub rocked taverns and cafés, where, with hardly a pause, bands kept up the playing of patriotic tunes. Till their voices gave out in utter hoarseness, all rose to share in the singing of *"Deutschland über Alles," "Die Wacht am Rhein"* and *"O Deutschland, hoch in Ehren."*

It is impossible to convey to anyone nowadays the genuine enthusiasm that animated us and our absolute conviction of a real danger. Perhaps I might now falter in my description of this "rise of a nation," but I have as a co-witness the report of Carl Zuckmayer in his splendid book *Als wär's ein Stück von mir (A Piece of Me)*. No one, surely, will charge Zuckmayer with nationalism, and with him I reassert unequivocally: The German people felt that they had been unjustly attacked; they genuinely believed that they had to beat off an encircling aggression. They fought not to conquer, but to save their very lives.

I had just turned sixteen, but I knew, of course, I would enlist. Getting hold of a picture atlas of regiments of cavalry, I wrote that same day to a dozen garrisons. Naturally, I chose regiments by their uniform: Cuirassiers, Uhlans, and Hussars—in that order. I did not bother about Dragoons. Were their uniforms at all fit to ride in?

Never will I forget the painful morning that brought the first batch of replies. The very envelopes enthralled me. "The 3d Pomeranian Cuirassiers," "The 2d Uhlans of Brandenburg," "The 1st Silesian Hussars." At last I had opened them all, and my proud head was bowed. Every one of the regiments was packed to bursting. They no longer accepted volunteers.

At once I became more modest, choosing less illustrious outfits. In place of the Cuirassiers, for instance, I tried the Hunters on Horseback, whose uniform, if not their fame, resembled the Cuirassiers'. Of late His Majesty had authorized them as the alternative to the Cuirassiers, to accommodate the sons of rich industrialists. This creation of the regiment explained its derogatory epithet: "Shopkeepers' Cavalry."

My second try yielded three affirmative replies. They were terse. I was to report for an examination in the business offices of the regiments. I traveled from regiment to regiment. The verdict, in each case, after a glance, was: much too young, admissible perhaps in a year. . . . I was to come back in a year? But then the war would be over.

My modesty now had sunk to the point where on my way home I made the rounds of all cavalry garrisons, even the Dragoons, "the Black Parchimer" and the "Red Ludwigsluster." I begged, I implored them, and they laughed in my face, the heartless sergeants. They were only Dragoons, I consoled myself, a common outfit. But they kept up their song: As yet we have enough seventeen-year-olds. There is not a chance for anyone born in ninety-eight.

Again I was back in the Hamburg railway station, when I chanced to hear of a regiment of Dragoons lately shifted to Wadsbeck owing to the evacuation of Alsace-Lorraine. Instantly I rode out to Wadsbeck, my last chance. I completely disregarded the old saying,

> Dragoons, part man and partly cattle,
> Are infantry thrown on a saddle.

Bold-faced, I set all on one card, answering the decisive question: "I'm seventeen. . . ."

This, at least, got me as far as the examination. I was declared fit. Proudly, I again presented myself at the business office of the regiment, and I was admitted into the presence of a benevolent major. He once more asked me my age. I could not lie to so fatherly a gentleman, and shyly, like a young girl, I whispered, "Sixteen." He was about to dismiss me, when I was seized with the courage of a steeplechase rider facing his topmost hurdle. "Is it then," I piped up in my most manly manner, "a question purely of age, without regard to suitability?"

With a laugh, he grasped both my shoulders. "All right, you're in."

The very next day we got our uniforms. They were fifth-hand, of course, each item being too large by at least three sizes. The dark blue trousers, stiff with patches, could stand up by themselves, the sky blue tunics were the merest threadbare semblance of the original fabric, and the white cuffs and white trim appeared never to have been white at all.

Our first days passed in emptying with our hands the stables of horse manure. Polishing of gear, luckily, soon was added, though for a long time not a word was breathed about any of us mounting a horse. That day, too, arrived, and each of us got his very own "critter." They were easily the worst. We called them bargains. They were conscripted nags, in all stages of the life of the animal, newly come from pulling a milk cart, or beer barrels, or a plow, or a gypsy caravan. Mine, a veritable elephant, was called Valkyrie. I could scarcely see across its withers. In time I managed the beast, but only by drilling her for hours in the stable during every one of my night watches.

There followed, a few weeks later, the first exercises in the open. How wildly our hearts beat whenever the staff trumpeter galloped past our platoon. He held the trumpet flush with his horse's neck, and the braying metal screamed as though the sound were torn from the throat of the animal. And how handsome the signals were: staccato for trot and a melodiously rocking interval to start the gallop. At other moments, if the sergeant caught us crampedly seating our mount, we had to walk the next evolution, pacing at a long-legged gallop alongside our horse, while the hoofbeats of the next row of riders all but drummed up the length of our spine. Still, no one, though it is now fashionable, should speak here of military chicanery. We were young, and the hard training, far from hurting us, later saved our lives. How else could we learn to mount with lungs heaving from exhaustion, the mouth fighting for breath, and the heart about to burst?

After another four weeks we were handed what we had been waiting for uneasily, yet with a secret pride: the lance. It sounds like the Middle Ages. Yet I actually wielded a lance, and this very moment I could perform its manual: "Thrust to the ground." "Thrust backward." And the chief command: "Lances lowered for the attack."

The lance not only necessitated our managing the horse with one hand, but at the thrust one had to bend deep down to the earth. We had to learn to shift the lance and, finally, to twirl it at a gallop above our heads. The lance taught us to ride.

I never will forget the spring evening we passed through Hamburg in our gray field uniforms, headed for the freight terminal and our shipment to Russia. At the head of our horses nodded flowers, and flowers were stuck in our carbines and tied to the tips of our lances. The reins lay knotted at the horses' necks, for our hands were held by girls walking on either side of our mounts. Eternally in force, despite all wars, continues the ancient saying: horses—riders—girls.

We arrived directly in Kurland (a former Russian province on the Baltic Sea, now a part of the Latvian S.S.R.), and we were fed into the great advance, the last victorious ride of divisions of cavalry. And we faced cavalry, Dragoons from Petersburg, royal Hussars from Moscow, and Cossacks, countless like the hordes of Genghis Khan. We had to ride—ride—ride.

The pine forests churned with heat, the rosin heavy with a fragrance as of burning. The sand stirred dustily, and the fens sucking our horses' hooves made a smacking sound. We passed the spot where our regiment had ridden an attack in the grand style, a ride that was history. Learning of it and knowing that half the men of my outfit had died in that charge, a Mars-la-Tour of our times, reconciled me completely to being a Dragoon. I no longer felt sorry for myself. Rather, I considered myself lucky in having hit on a regiment whose fame, outlasting that of all others, shall remain.

One fact dawned on me even then: This was to be the last war using cavalry. Technology was about to obviate the horse; machines would take its place. With the passing of the horse, all noblesse of warfare would die. The laws would cease to be honored that so far had cast wars in a knightly mold. I was a part of the last military engagements embodying a higher tradition.

And another fact not only reconciled me to my place with the Dragoons, but filled me with a heady pride: My commander was Count Holck, the greatest steeplechase rider of the century. I recalled his having worn our regimental uniform over the hurdles in Kiel. Rarely did he enter a race without winning it. Light blue and white were his colors. What could exceed the thrill of riding under such a man?

The attack I finally rode was not in the grand historical manner or under Count Holck. I was simply another young ensign in a small patrol. It was premature, this last attack of mine, and the occasion of my being shot down, off my horse, and of my dear comrade, little Nil, being shot, and of my capture by the Cossacks.

I was hit the very instant I was waving my naked sword to flash to my platoon the signal for the attack. "Attack. . . . Lances lowered," I was about to call, and "At—" was all I could get out. My sector sprang apart like a puddle hit by a fist. Little Nil straightened in the saddle, stiff as a candle, wavered, and fell over backward. This was the end of our rocking rides with lances hip-high. This ended the war of noble knights.

Of course, I should have cried, "Mother," but instead I called, "My God, why have You forsaken me?" Professor Schwartz in Biblical studies had singled out this cry as "strikingly indicative of the humanity of the Son of God," and at this moment it spontaneously rose to my lips. I was, after all, only seventeen.

I awoke with a sense of someone sawing off my legs. My mouth was full of earthy crumbs, for in my pain I had bitten into a plowed field. My hand blindly fingered for my sword, but I had been robbed clean. My telescope, my watch, my revolver, the small bag I carried on a string around my neck—all were gone. "I'm a prisoner," a small voice kept screeching, and the realization hit me worse than a bullet, dead center inside my skull.

Can I possibly save myself? My legs are lamed, my back is rigid, and I can't even shift my weight. A fire rages between my thighs as though they clasped burning coals. I open the trouser fly and insert a hand. To the right, along the inside, four of my fingers slip into a gaping hole. To the left, farther down, close above the knee, only one finger finds room in a wound.

"I shall bleed to death." The recognition scarcely pains me. Already I have lost too much blood to be strongly affected. Death, after all, might be preferable to captivity. Gazing up into the blue sky, I strain my head toward a wind-whipped flapping. It is one of our lances. Its wimple, black and white, tugs at the staff in a call for help.

Some Cossacks eventually ride by. They have tied our subaltern to a stirrup. His face is white as chalk, and he is limping. Being hurried past breathlessly at a distance of about five steps, he sees that I am still alive, and he points my way. Two Cossacks jump from their horses and come strutting toward me, bow-legged. One of them looks at my bloody belly and motions as if to say, it's no use. . . .

But they do not prevent Schmidt II from stripping down my pants to bandage me. Tensely I watch my right thigh. If it now gushes, then I've had it; but if it merely wells, gently. . . . "It merely wells," says Schmidt II, reading my thoughts. About me lie a few of the dead of my troop, and passing among them, Schmidt appropriates their small packets of bandages. With a groan he lowers himself to his knees and starts bandaging and bandaging. "What a stinking mess," he says darkly; "it keeps oozing through."

At last they button my tunic, and supporting my back, they lift me. With my right arm around Schmidt's shoulder and my left hugging a Cossack's neck, my legs dangle jointless like a puppet's filled with excelsior. "Get going," the Cossacks call, swinging themselves into their saddles with a metallic clatter.

At the next field station I am being properly bandaged. With other wounded in a small Cossack cart I am driven to Mitau, then to Riga, and finally to Moscow. Here in the quarters of the Gruditzki Regiment, transformed into a military hospital, I look down from my window on all the Kremlin.

After about four weeks I am told that my once chance for

survival lies in amputation. My right leg will have to go. "But," I groan, "then I couldn't ride. What's the use of living if I can't ride?"

At the very last moment, Bruno von Brehm, the Austrian writer who later will gain fame with his book *Apis and Este,* chances to pass my bed. At the time he is a young cavalry officer with the Artillery. He does not cease his efforts until he locates a professor who saves my leg. I owe him not only my life, but all my hours on horseback that were yet to come.

That autumn suddenly we were chucked from our beds, and in a march on crutches through all Moscow we were led to the Ugrieschkaja Station for the transport to Totskoye. This prison camp turned out to be the worst in Russia, though it lay in the European part of the empire. Typhoid here in one winter killed 17,000 out of 20,000 men.

In justice it must be said that the disaster of Totskoye genuinely moved the Russian people. At the time of the highest daily losses, Delegate Gladisch delivered in the Duma an unpitying accusation that made the other delegates blush with shame.

"These horrors," he said, "are perhaps the worst of all time, because this senseless destruction of thousands of young people was caused not by primitive men, but by beings on a higher stage of their development. Only last year a sanitary commission categorically declared these barracks unsuitable, being infested with typhoid. The interdict did not keep us from piling into them twenty thousand men, and the epidemic, of course, followed. But since this billeting had been carried through against the express order of the sanitary commission, the disaster assiduously was kept from the authorities. Hence its uncontrollable proportions: no one dared request medicines for a camp that had never been listed." The representative closed his speech with a reminder of the pyramids of human skulls raised by Genghis Khan. He called these less degrading than the pyramids of human corpses achieved by the twentieth century at Totskoye.

So great a panic seized the guards at the height of our dying that they and their horses were about to take flight, leaving the camp to its fate in the steppes. But then appeared the governor of Orenburg, General von Sacharow. "I have heard," he said, addressing the officers of Totskoye, "that this camp is to be left to its fate since its inmates apparently are past help. Yet since five thousand are still alive, I order all men and officers back to their posts. As for my issuing this order from a safe distance, I shall take quarters here for the duration."

True to his word, General von Sacharow moved into the barracks. He caught typhoid. In a few weeks he died on his voluntary post.

Some statistics may be in order here. Of 170,000 German prisoners of war in Russia, only 90,000 returned home. This means that nearly every second man perished. In combat only every eighth soldier was a casualty. The probability of losing one's life was four times larger in captivity than in the field. And more would have perished except for the good offices of Elsa Brändström, the daughter of the Swedish ambassador in Petersburg. She with other women of the Red Cross brought trainloads of help to almost every prison camp in Siberia.

In spring, Siberia was our destination. The survivors were shipped a month's journey by boxcar, to Camp Dauria in the Transbaikal. This camp lay in the midst of a frontier garrison of Cossacks near the Chinese border. The Cossacks here wore the same yellow stripes down their trouser seams as those who had taken me prisoner in Kurland. This, in a sense, made them old acquaintances. For two years I lived here near the Gobi Desert. The next station on our railway line was Manchuria. We built a camp theater, where I performed as an "actress." Epidemics now claimed only a few victims.

During the Kerenski revolt in February and in the six months following, all went well, for we had befriended many Kerenski officers. But the regime was toppled in October, and Red Guards entered the Transbaikal. At the time we cheered them, for they embodied, or so we thought, a national upheaval engaging our deepest sympathies. We turned from them after their atrocities committed on our friends, the Kerenski officers. These horrors inwardly enlisted us on the side of the counterrevolution, which was about to reconquer all Siberia. We hardly resisted Admiral Kolchak's call to join his White Army. We were promised our instant return home after the conquest of Moscow, and we joined the Whites with easy hearts. At the time they were on a victorious sweep westward.

With a few officer comrades I was part of the Cossack Corps of General Kappel, the best general in Kolchak's service. The last chief-in-command of our army was a Lieutenant General von Sacharow. Having to report to him, I expected to meet Governor von Sacharow from Orenburg. "That," he said with a smile, "was my father." This was the second Sacharow I met in Russia. A third one was to follow, and I would like to mention him briefly, though my dealings with him relate to World War II. I met this Sacharow while I, with General Wlassow of the Soviet Union, was in process of forming an army of liberation, to fight on our side in the over-throw of Bolshevism. The Sacharow I met on this occasion was a fine captain of infantry, the son of my former chief-in-command. Like his father, he became my friend. The general, until he died, had been a frequent guest in my home. The third Sacharow is every inch worthy of his grandfather who, as a White Russian, perished under the Soviets.

Our victorious advance on Moscow faltered in the late summer of 1919. It turned into the riotous flight east, which really had been expected. The nearer Moscow, the more our troops melted away. Our reinforcements had to negotiate 12,000 kilometers and Red partisans who, having been left behind, infested the forests every-where. The congested Red Army of Trotsky, ebbing backward at last, instantly and in many places pushed through our thinned ranks.

Our renewed trek all the way back to the Transbaikal—the *Anabasis* of modern history—left 1,000,000 dead in the snows of Siberia. In Atschinsk alone died in one night 40,000 horses, and a whole row of towns perished of epidemics in the wake of our passing. General Kappel, who had been wounded, froze to death in crossing the frozen Baikal, but General von Sacharow, with the last of his faithful followers, managed to reach Chita.

The Red Guard caught up with us, the remnant of Kappel's corps, in the center of the blue ice of the enormous Baikal Lake. I succeeded in dressing in the uniform of a dead Red Guard, and I appropriated his papers. Later I identified myself as a certain Trossmann, a German prisoner of war forcibly abducted by White Russians.

For the third time I entered a prisoner-of-war camp, this time near Irkutsk, but I soon escaped its barbed wire. Pretending to be a Red Guard out of service, I traveled west, chiefly in trains, which once again were running. For the fourth time I managed the distance of 10,000 kilometers, posing as a Red Guard in districts run by Reds and presenting papers provided by a Swedish delegate in the few dispersed sectors still held by White Russians. With the help of Swedish delegates I also saved nearly all my notes which underlie my books *Army Behind Barbed Wire* and *Between White and Red*.

In 1920, long after the war, I finally made it back to Germany. I bought a small estate, and again I was on horseback. The breeding of noble strains of horses is still my passion. Looking back from this height of life to World War I, I repeatedly reach the conclusion that it was the first civil war of the West.

Cyril Falls

"*I was born on March 2, 1888, at a nursing home in Dublin, my parents then living in County Longford. I have no memory of this phase because, before I was a year old, we moved to County Fermanagh, where we took a handsome late Georgian house, Killyreagh, some 3 miles from Enniskillen. My schooling began at a dame school in the London suburb of Norwood, chosen because it was near my maternal grandfather's house, continued at Bradfield College, Berkshire, and concluded at Portora Royal School, Enniskillen. I was a somewhat unsatisfactory pupil, except in history.*

"*My first book of any importance was a study of Rudyard Kipling, the proofs being corrected in a tent early in the First World War.*

"*Having published a history of the 36th (Ulster) Division, in which I had finally served as general staff officer (G.S.O.) 3 (my material coming from the office in which the official histories were compiled), the director liked it well enough to appoint me to write several of the volumes. This made me sufficiently known for the London* Times *to take me as military correspondent to succeed Liddell Hart at the beginning of the Second World War.*

"*Soon after this war I was appointed Chichele Professor of the History of War and Fellow of All Souls College, Oxford, both appointments coming to an end in 1953. Since then I have been a free-lance writer and have published a number of books, one a best seller, entitled* The First World War *in England and* The Great War *in the United States.*

"*I was married on leave in 1915 and we have two daughters with large families, one married to a lieutenant colonel in the Royal Marines, the other to a former lieutenant in the Coldstream Guards and now representing in London a big firm of New York brokers.*"

THE BEST OF MY WAR

I. LIAISON WITH THE FRENCH

MY EARLY SERVICE in the First World War was with my regiment as what is known as G.S.O. 3, a junior officer on the Operations staff of my division. I shall begin recounting my experiences with 1918, when I was appointed a liaison officer with a French division. I owed this great pleasure to one of our staff who had been appointed to G.H.Q. and, when more liaison officers were needed because a British corps was serving under French command on the Chemin des Dames, mentioned that I spoke good French.

I was, of course, delighted because this would be an interesting job and would give me an opportunity to see what the French had left in them after the terrible defeats they had undergone. The journey, in three successive cars, was somewhat farcical because no one had heard about my appointment—not even the French Mission at the headquarters of our 4th Army, or even the French corps to which my division belonged.

When I arrived at corps headquarters, the laison officer, Romer Williams, well known as a hard rider to hounds, told me I must stay for dinner and for the night. Then I was initiated into the game of keeping one's end up. The next day the corps commander was entertaining the *commandant d'armes* of Amiens, now nearly deserted, and the Chief of Staff said I must lunch with the junior staff officers. Williams said that if so, he would do the like, a good riposte because he was a favorite with the corps commander. So it came about that we all sat elbow to elbow and had an excellent luncheon.

That afternoon Colonel Lister, the liaison officer with the French 1st Army, came over and we three drove to the headquarters of the 37th Division. On the way he improved the occasion by giving fatherly advice. My chief task would be to "create an atmosphere" and keep the French and the Australians on their left on good terms. There would be little office work. I would have a car and a British driver, a very rare amenity for one of my status in those days.

When I was left amid a babble of French, my own seemed rusty. The divisional commander, Garnier Duplessis, patted my shoulder and said he hoped I would be happy and must complain to him if I were not. The headquarters, in a chalk quarry, consisted of two big huts, one for the staff, the other for the artillery headquarters, and everyone slept in saps cut into the chalk. It looked comfortless, but that night's dinner was far better than in our messes. Only the general had even a minute room to himself, and the rest slept in bunks—calling up memories of decent trenches in a warm spring or summer. The next day I looked into a little cottage across the road and found it empty, but undamaged. On asking why, I heard that the general had forbidden anyone to sleep outside after there had been some bombing at night. Later on I ventured to move in with all my possessions, including canvas bath and bed. I believe he was the only one unaware of my disobedience.

I saw a very different background when I visited the 3d Australian Division soon afterward. There they had comfortable huts in a valley and kept their dugouts for emergency. A day or two later I paid my first visit to the front line, accompanied by my opposite number with the Australian right division. Villers-Bretonneaux, in the front line, had been captured by the Germans and retaken by the British. We found officers of both nationalities playing poker, and the Australians complained jocularly that a fat French company commander, known as Captain "Pinard" for his pleasure in the ration wine, was cleaning them out.

This sounds as though it were an extremely quiet front, which it was not. The Germans fired quite heavy bombardments from time to time and made some raids. The Australians were first-class raiders, but the French division, the infantry being half Zouaves—now largely made up of Parisians, the capital city having no regiments of its own because most revolutions had started there—and two Algerian Tirailleurs did not gain much success.

The enemy also made great use of mustard gas. It has been said that this was a disgusting weapon, but in fact, even those fairly close to the explosions suffered no pain and indeed often remained with their units. The horror came when the burst was so close that the victim was splashed. Then, indeed, he suffered agony, was sometimes returned to civil life, and occasionally died.

I got a shock when I discovered that Garnier-Duplessis *never* visited the front line. Had he been a British divisional commander and had this been discovered, he would have been sent home immediately and at best given some job such as a civilian could have undertaken. Yet the Frenchman was one of the ablest soldiers of his grade in his country's army. From first to last he treated me with great kindness. The staff officers did visit the line, but much less often than ours.

It may seem absurd that, though it was obviously desirable for Australian and French staff officers to do so together, it was not easy to arrange this, though I occasionally managed to do so and acted as interpreter. The Frenchman stood at a table, sometimes as early as 6:30, drank coffee or chocolate, and perhaps ate a piece of toast. The Australian breakfasted a good deal later, and heavily. He did not care what time he got back, whereas the Frenchman felt he had to do so by 11:30 for *déjeuner,* his main meal of the day. It may be a slight exaggeration to say that he was almost as liable to reproof as a British officer on a guest-night in time of peace, but that was how it struck me.

However, there was eventually a change. Garnier-Duplessis was promoted to the command of a corps, to be succeeded by Simon, till now commanding one of the brigades. Intellectually he was not the equal of his predecessor; but he went up often, and I, of course, always accompanied him if he was visiting the junction with the Australians. One occasion sticks in my mind. Though there was some shelling, occasionally nearer than I liked, he insisted on entering an unpleasant advance post, where he fell and cut his hand badly on broken glass. To our shame, neither of us had the bandage or the disinfectant everyone was supposed to carry. An Australian private insisted on using his and tied up the wound. What grand men they were! In the line their discipline was first-class, but it was sometimes free and easy when they were not.

One serious offense, very amusing in its way, was related to me by a medical officer. An Australian private had reported to him that he had been peppered in the back by shrapnel. On examining the wounds, he realized that they had been inflicted by something much smaller and, when the man refused to come clean, gave him a jag that hurt. The Australian then confessed that he had entered a farmyard far behind the front and stolen a sucking pig. As he reached the gate, an old farmer in nightshirt and nightcap had fired at him with a shotgun from his bedroom window.

There had been some speculation on whether the enemy would launch yet another offensive and that it would cover our front; but this soon passed, and Lister said there was nothing to stop my going on leave. My wife and I had a pleasant time, first in London, then at the seaside. About ten days after my return, when I was visiting the Australian corps headquarters, the brigadier general, Thomas Blamey—famous in the next great war and dying a field marshal— kept me to luncheon and told me that my division was to be relieved by Canadians and that I would move to the next French division. This suggested to me that it was not the enemy who were going to take the offensive. Thenceforward I had a series of visits to make and interpreter's jobs to do.

There were some comic incidents. For instance, when I returned from escorting several officers from G.H.Q. and army headquarters "to see the strength of our defenses," I told Simon that they had examined the crossings of the Luce River, almost in the front line. He grinned and said this seemed unnecessarily far forward. I gathered that he knew by now what was really brewing, a major Allied offensive, before which his division would be relieved by a Canadian—though Blamey had said I must not tell him so—leaving a few Australians in the front line in case of a raid.

Champagne was served in my honor, and the general made a delightful farewell speech, ending with a toast. When I rose to reply, I stammered—I do not think my French failed me, but a lump in my throat made me pause and stutter. "If the French do not like you," Lister had said soon after my arrival, "they can be poisonous; if they do like you, there's no limit to their kindness." I decided, I hope with gratitude and no conceit, that these Frenchmen must like me.

On August 2 I drove to the headquarters of the 42d Division, humble beside what I had left. General Deville sat at the head of the table in a shabby tunic and served the soup himself. At first sight he seemed to me a mass of nerves. Then I recalled having heard that the division, in which he had served in the Battle of the Marne as a brigadier and never left, had a high reputation. Two days later Simon arrived with Beauregard, both very smart now that their division was temporarily out of the line, for a conference. Before departing, he asked Deville if he could spare me for luncheon the next day, at which he smiled and said he would try.

What a morning! Everyone was busy, but after about half an hour the general appeared. *"Mon cher Falls, on vous à fait attendre. Vous aller mourir de faim. Mais avant de nous mettre à table j'ai un mot à vous dire."* He got out a piece of paper and read the following: *"Chargé d'assurer un service de liaison, s'est porté a maintes reprises, pour l'accomplissement de cette mission, jusqu'aux postes les plus avancées et les plus exposées. N'a cessé de faire preuve d'entrain, de bonne humeur, de sang-froid, et de bravoure."* Then: *"Je vous remets votre Croix de guerre,"* and it was pinned on. After that we sat down to the happiest of luncheons.

On the fifth I took the French orders to my fellow Ulsterman, Major General Lipsett, commanding the 3d Canadian Division, and got a copy of his, after which he kept me for dinner. Not long afterward I was sad to hear that this good soldier and charming man had been killed when commanding a British division.

During the afternoon before the assault we moved to an advanced post. I had to face various crises, inevitable on such occasions. It seemed that I had hardly got to sleep when an orderly shook my arm, and I got up to find it still dark and very foggy. After our *petit déjeuner* we were handed sandwiches, and our water bottles were filled with wine. We soon moved up to a dugout in the old front line, where I found the general talking in quite good German to a group of officer prisoners, who addressed him as *Eure Exzellenz.*

He began to fidget about the lack of news from the left, but all I could get from the Canadians was that things were going very well. However, the visit was made worthwhile by what I saw on the main Roye-Amiens road. A long column of prisoners was approaching, those at the head carrying wounded of both sides on stretchers. In front of all was a magnificent young Canadian, carried shoulder high by four Germans, lying on his stomach with his chin propped on his forearms, obviously enjoying his position and making me think of a victorious Roman general in a triumph.

I now said I would try to cross the trenches in my car, memories of former offensives having prevented our horses, just what we now wanted, from being brought up. The trenches were being filled in by troops of the oldest classes, and the car lurched over easily enough. The German proved worse, and we should not have got over had not the *pépères,* as these men were called, heaved the car across. I got a fair amount of news and witnessed the rout of a German counterattack by a French column which formed line as if on parade and swept the enemy away with light machine-gun and rifle fire. On my return I found Deville, who had also been out, in the highest spirits. *"Nous avons indiqué à nos troupes leurs objectifs avec notre canne, avec cette canne là,"* he cried. A change after sitting at a telephone and perhaps finding that the troops were back in their old front line!

The next day I transferred to the 126th Division, commanded by General Mathieu. I was driving through our new headquarters when I heard a voice shouting: *"Monsieur le capitaine Falls!"* It was General Deville. He said he had cited me in his divisional orders, which meant that I had got the *Croix de guerre* twice in four days and was entitled to wear two stars on the ribbon. A great day, and my joy kept me going, though I had had only seven hours' sleep in the last two nights.

Now came an unhappy affair. The 126th Division was to make a dawn attack, but the British 32d, rushed up from reserve to the Canadian Corps, would be unable to do so until 7 A.M. Romer Williams telephoned that he had been unable to get either the French or the Canadian corps to see reason. I stayed up till I learned that orders had been changed for the better. At 4:30 A.M. Aublin, my French opposite number, arrived in a fury with new orders: The 32d would not attack until 9:30. Mathieu picked up the telephone to stop our assault but had hardly begun to speak when we heard the roar of our artillery. The French, thus starting alone, made fine progress but were driven back by a counterattack on their open flank, and the British division was later repulsed with heavy loss.

On August 12 a crack division of Chasseurs, the 47th relieved the 126th, and I finally discovered why the British did not want to push on. Haig was determined to break off the attack and set his 3d and 1st armies, reinforced by the Canadian Corps, going, while Foch wanted to continue on our front. The generalissimo finally gave way and agreed that it should be released for the new offensive.

I pass over some of my worst days of the war until the early hours of the eighteenth, when the telephone woke me and I learned that General Rawlinson, who commanded the 4th Army, had issued orders that all liaison officers were to be replaced and that I was to report at G.H.Q. The speaker, Lister's successor, said that everyone in the liaison knew I had done my best and had said so, but Rawlinson would listen to no explanation. Lister had left a note mentioning my *Croix de guerre* and added that he had meant to put my name forward for a further honor, which could only have been the Military Cross.

Dillemain said he would gladly give me a good-conduct mark, and Mathieu, who had somehow got my news, offered to write to our G.H.Q. to say that I was in no way to blame for the misfortune of his division. I was deeply touched, though I did not feel that their kindly intervention would do much good.

After about a week at corps headquarters, helping Lister's busy successor, I drove to G.H.Q. at Montreuil. There I was told that I was not to return to regimental duty because there was a shortage of trained staff officers. The officer concerned asked if I would like to visit the United States to talk about Intelligence staff duties. This was a fascinating opportunity, but I said I would rather see things through. He then told me that until a vacancy occurred, I was to go to 6th Corps headquarters for attachment, and he then sent me off by car. There I picked up useful lessons but became bored by having no responsibility. I had to wait with what patience I could muster until October 8, when I joined the 62d Division, commanded by General Sir Robert Whigham—and lived happily ever after.

II. WHIGHAM AND THE 62D DIVISION

WHIGHAM was by far the best of the three British divisional commanders whom I served. He had recently returned to France after a long spell at the War Office and refused the command of a corps because during his absence the type of warfare had so greatly changed. He demanded a great deal of his staff, but the only time I saw him lose his temper was when our capable signals officer was for once remiss.

Soon after my arrival we ran into trouble. The G.S.O. 1, a gunner officer with an excellent record, had no previous staff experience and proved unsatisfactory. On a vacancy occurring in one of our artillery brigades, he was sent to fill it and did so well. His successor, a very senior officer for the grade, also proved indifferent, but it was impossible to swap horses again. The consequence was embarrassing because the general virtually always dealt with our brilliant G.S.O. 2, "Mouse" Bissett, who took charge with such aid as I could give him.

On the day I arrived, a great attack was launched by the 3d and 2d Divisions, and the Guards made ready to go through. It will be seen that we were in excellent company, but the 62d deserved to be in it. It had come out late, as all second-line Territorials did, and gone too soon into the horrible Bullecourt affair, to suffer crippling casualties. Its commander, Major General Braithwaite, had pulled the survivors together, and it had been joined by three crack battalions from Palestine, one to each brigade, to replace Yorkshire battalions broken up. Everyone was delighted that he had been promoted to the command of a corps because this expunged the blot on his scutcheon created by the fact that he was considered to have been a failure as Chief of Staff at Gallipoli.

The attack was generally a great success, but at the junction between our corps and that on our left the enemy made a damaging counterattack with five captured British tanks. I wrote in my diary: "Our infantry cannot face them any more than can the Germans. How would the war have ended had Germany been first in the field with tanks? I am afraid there is only one answer, even though she probably has not had, anyhow since 1917, the industrial resources to develop them as we have."

On the morning of October 9 we moved up to the neighborhood

of Flesquières, of evil memory because of the repulse suffered there on the first day of the Battle of Cambrai. The next morning it appeared certain that the Germans would make their next stand on the Selle River, running northward to the Sensée at Denain, and that our turn had come.

When we were given our objective, we realized that our task would be difficult because the enemy had dammed that river by blowing up the railway bridge at Solesmes, so that we could not cross it on our own front but would have to do so on the fronts of the flanking divisions and then turn inward. There was another complication: The corps orders said that though many civilians were known to be in the town, there should be a heavy bombardment. Whigham showed himself at his best here. We knew that even though there were plenty of strong cellars, many of them would be smashed by high explosive, whereas those taking refuge in them would be safe if only shrapnel were used. On the other hand, if the enemy launched counterattacks against our flanks, he would not be stopped by shrapnel. Yet Whigham decided to take the risk and proved right, since there was no flanking counterattack.

Our assault was launched at 2 A.M. on the twentieth and was so successful that nothing more need be said of it. I went forward after daylight and met a lightly wounded private coming up from Solesmes, who called to me: "There's kissing going on down there, and a bit more than kissing, with Jerry shelling like hell all the time." I questioned civilians regarding any signs of a new line of defense, but they knew of none, though they said the country became close a little farther on. I gave the children the biscuits in my pocket, to their great delight. In all, I was about for twenty-four hours without feeling very tired. The wine of victory is stimulating.

Shelling continued to be very heavy the next day; but there was good shelter, and the 3d Division was about to pass through us. I rode into a village ahead hoping to acquire information about the Ecaillon. The villagers did not think it formidable, though they said there was now a good flow of water. They insisted on my drinking a cup of their very small store of coffee, and I had to wipe away a tear or two created by their plight. This time I had filled my pockets with biscuits and earned popularity by kissing a golden-haired beauty of six on a comparatively clean spot.

On October 30 we learned that we were to relieve part of the 2d Division and found good billets and a good house for headquarters in Solesmes. November opened with grinding work, but I found some relief in riding to get information about the enemy, especially his battery positions. I was given remarkable aid by an extremely intelligent priest about the little towns of Gommagies and Fresnoy, as likely to be obstacles. Then I returned to give such aid as I could to Bissett. He now excelled his best hitherto, remaining as cool as a cucumber, however hot the pace. I never heard a grumble from the brigade commanders from the time I joined the division. The next day I compiled a list headed "What to Look For," giving such information as I had picked up about fences and hedges, with map coordinates of all known German batteries, many of which had escaped in this open warfare simply because the troops had not known where they were. I had fifty copies sent out.

On the night of the third I drove up to synchronize the watches of the brigade concerned in the first phase, leaving the car outside the village because it was pretty close to the front line. It was pitch-dark, and I had hard work finding the headquarters. Suddenly there was a series of crashes, and a salvo—heavy stuff—fell unpleasantly near. The whole business did not last more than a minute, but it was a very unpleasant one. Not given to prayer, I found myself repeating a school mnemonic for Latin adverbs, beginning: *"Ante, apud, ad, adversus."* The shooting over, I eventually found the headquarters, had a chat, and set watches for the morrow's "zero."

November 4 was a great day, that of the launch of an offensive on the front of three British armies, everywhere successful. Our brigade crossed the Rhonelle, a tributary of the Ecaillon, and captured Fresnoy. We took more than 700 prisoners for some 500 casualties, a high proportion wounded because the German artillery was either quickly silenced or pulled out. The next day saw another big advance but few prisoners. We could not realize that this would be the pattern until the end of hostilities, the enemy never making a strong stand but handling machine guns and a few batteries very cleverly. To our delight we kept neck and neck with the Guards Division, which took some doing. Whigman jumped into open warfare as though he had experienced it for the last four years, and Mathieson, commanding the Guards, was equally good. On the whole front the British took about 400 guns, but the Germans did well as regards the number they got away. On November 5 we reached the outskirts of the famous Forest of Mormal side by side with the New Zealand Division on our right.

The next day we found that every captured or evacuated position had a little mound of empty cartridge cases, as Whigham rubbed into corps headquarters when it suggested we might get on a little faster. Some of our supply column lorries were on the roads from sixteen to twenty hours of the twenty-four. Another handicap was that the Germans had left a number of hidden delayed-action explosives on the railway, which went off days or even a week after being laid. However, we reached our objective, neck and neck with the Guards.

On we went again on the seventh, but advanced only 3,000 yards, good in the old days but not now up to expectations. Whigham and my seniors pushed on to establish a new headquarters, leaving me in a fairly responsible position for some two hours. When I moved on in the dark with the clerks who had remained with me, the car stuck in a ditch in pitch-darkness, and I had to tell the driver he must wait for a lorry to pull it out. By road it was nearly 2 miles to the new headquarters; but on studying my map with a torch I found that directly through the Forest of Mormal, it was only about 600 yards, so I bade the doubting clerks follow me and set off down a ride. That soon ended, and we plunged into the forest at its thickest—the clerks angry because they thought we were lost. Next, we heard a car running its engine, which meant a road ahead. On we went, to find it was the engine of the headquarters electric light set, running in its lorry. Honor was saved.

Great news came in that night. German *parlementaires* came through the lines near Guise, with a pioneer company to repair the road. We picked up a plaintive message on the wireless beseeching the French to stop shelling in order to let them through and later learned that they were to meet Foch on the morrow.

The next day I ran into a horrible incident. An old man, one of a party helping us fill in a crater, mumbled that a girl had been murdered by a German. I went with him to a cottage, and the parents told me the story. When our foremost troops drew near, the girl, aged sixteen, called exultantly to a German who was making off: *Courés vite! Voici les anglais!"* The brute swung around and shot her dead. I sent in a formal report, knowing that it was useless because the family did not know the man's name.

November 10 was quiet, so that I could ride round Maubeuge and its splendid Vauban fortress. November 11 was one of the most famous days in history, when the Armistice began and hostilities ceased at 11 A.M. I give the opening of an article I wrote in the *Times* for the fortieth anniversary:

Just before 11 A.M. on November 11, 1918, many British batteries fired defiant last salvos, carefully ranged as ever. Then silence fell. The gunners' gesture was not a sign of excitement. There was little of that. Many doubtless thought of lost kinsmen and friends, but the prevailing mood seemed to be a groping effort to realize that all was over. At night, however, some bonfires were lit. Very lights and coloured rockets streamed into skies illuminated by a sickle moon entering her first quarter. This was 40 years ago to-morrow. Many thousands of the youngest soldiers in this Armistice scene are now grandfathers.

I myself felt that vile as the war had been, it had been so vast, such a mad upheaval of the greater part of Europe, that survivors would always feel they had played a part in one of the most curious events in world history. That night came exciting news: We were to form part of the Army of Occupation. This was a tremendous honor for a second-line Territorial division, and we were the only ones to enjoy it. Many men, including the dead, had contributed to our standard, but it would not have reached this without Whigham's leadership. This was still tested because the Territorial officers, who had become excellent leaders in battle, could not induce the rank and file to think of anything but demobilization, as Regulars would have contrived to do.

From now on I had to do a great deal of riding, because in picking up knowledge of the country ahead, I had to take short cuts along lanes so muddy and churned up by the Germans that they might have put a car out of action. The Germans had supplied location lists of unexploded delayed-action mines on the railways, but these had been so well hidden that they could not always be found even with this information. The officers responsible were sent for to find them and, as might be expected from engineers, showed as much courage in extracting them as they had in laying them.

For brigade and divisional headquarters the slow march through the Ardennes was fun. The latter stayed at several chateaus of great antiquity and beauty, but the longest stop was at a modern one. We gave a big dance there, fetching most of the ladies in warm and comfortable ambulance wagons. When the guests departed I pushed the French liaison officer, Polignac, member of a famous family, into one unlit inside. He was good-looking and said to be a terror to the opposite sex, but they faced the terror unflinchingly.

I pass on to our arrival at the little town of Schleiden, in the pleasant but primitive Eifel, inhabited by primitive people. In some villages they had not seen a car for years and did not know whether we were German, English, or French. There we had a happy Christmas dinner.

Some of the troops not having behaved quite like little gentle-men, I was hardly surprised when a man was charged with rape. The officer defending him asked the girl three questions. "Where and when did this take place?" Answer: "Outside the stables about seven P.M." "How long had you been talking to this man when it happened?" Answer: "Not more than half an hour." "Now [loudly and impressively] tell me whether the same thing happened the previous night." Answer (with tears) : "Yes." The court: "The case is dismissed."

We ended the year with a great binge in B Mess. After dinner there were tugs-of-war, cockfights, juggling, and songs. Just before midnight there was banging on the street door. We ran out to find A Mess, headed by Whigham, standing in the snow. In they came, and he was saluted with "For He's a Jolly Good Fellow," to which he replied that we all were jolly good fellows. Soon afterward the headquarters moved to Düren, where there was an excellent theater and a good permanent company, equally at home with plays and opera. There was a ban on fraternization, but this did not affect me because, as G.S.O. 3, I was responsible for arranging these affairs and concerts. The German players and singers might almost have been described as neutrals, devoted only to their art. The prima donna was something more. A big military car often called for her after the show and took her to Cologne to spend the night in presumably fairly senior British company. Those of us who enjoyed opera also went there from time to time, and I have seldom attended one more delightful.

Before I returned to England, I witnessed Germany's sufferings at their worst. I came on a big party of boys seated at the roadside lunching off leeks and thick slices of dry bread. I mustered enough German to ask the supervisor who they were. He told me they came from an orphanage—90 percent war orphans—and were working on the repair of the road. They were chatting as boys do, but distressingly emaciated. It took days to get the memory out of my mind. These poor youths were not criminals; they were paying for what the country's leaders had done in starting the war.

By May I had to think seriously about my future. I knew I should enjoy the Army in peace but would almost certainly be reduced to the rank of lieutenant, a prospect I did not relish as a married man. I am sure I took the right course when I decided to return to civil life.

Sir Compton Mackenzie

SIR EDWARD MONTAGUE COMPTON MACKENZIE *was born on January 17, 1883. His father was Edward Compton (Mackenzie), who for more than thirty years kept old English comedy alive in Great Britain and in Ireland. His mother was Virginia Bateman, the third daughter of H. L. Bateman, the first American impresario to invade England. He discovered the genius of Henry Irving.*

Compton Mackenzie was educated at St. Paul's School and at Magdalen College, Oxford. He started and edited a paper called The Oxford Point of View *and was a leading figure in the Oxford University Dramatic Society. He took a second class in history.*

His first book was a volume of Poems *published in 1907. His first play was* The Gentleman in Grey, *produced in that year. His first novel,* The Passionate Elopement, *was published by Martin Secker in 1911 after having been refused by many publishers. This was the first of more than forty novels and fifty works of autobiography, history, memories, belles lettres, etc.*

During World War I he served with the Royal Naval Division at Gallipoli and, after being invalided out, was military control officer in Athens and director of the Aegean Intelligence Service in Syra. He received the O.B.E. (Order of the British Empire) and was a Chevalier of the Legion of Honor and of the Redeemer (Greece). In 1923 he founded and edited The Gramophone. *He first broadcast in 1923 and is still broadcasting. He made his first appearance on television in 1938. In 1931 he was elected Lord Rector of Glasgow University as the candidate of the Scottish Nationalists.*

In 1946 he was commissioned by the Indian government to write the history of the Indian Army's achievement in the Second World War and spent more than eighteen months traveling all over the East. He is LL.D. (Glasgow and St. Francis Xavier, Antigonish), Hon. R.S.A., F.R.S.L., and a Knight Commander of the Royal Order of the Phoenix (Greece). He was knighted by Queen Elizabeth II in 1952.

FROM NAPLES TO CALAIS

ON NOVEMBER 11, 1968, the end of the First World War will have happened fifty years ago. Am I being extravagant when I surmise that if television had existed then in its condition today the First World War would not have happened? When I look back to 1914, I am hardly able to believe that the outbreak of that war came as it did.

In June, 1914, I was in Capri working hard at the second volume of my novel *Sinister Street*, the first volume of which had been published the previous autumn. It was growing very hot, and I felt that a little holiday would help my progress with the book. Three days but not a minute more could be spared: three full days of sun and seawater and laziness. Vincenzo, my boatman, had relatives in Nerano, a village on the far side of the Sorrentine Peninsula, and he knew of a house, right on the beach of Cantone below, a tumble-down old *palazzo* where we could spend as many nights as we liked. On the third evening Vincenzo had gone up to Nerano to get the evening's provisions and newspapers. I see him now coming down with them through the dusky olive grove above the beach.

"What news?" I asked.

"No news," he said; "some Austrian duke has been killed somewhere. *Ecco il giornale!*"

It was too dark by now to read even the headlines, but in the candlelight of that tumbledown *palazzo* by the sea's edge I read how the Archduke Francis Ferdinand had been assassinated at Sarajevo. I must have had a moment's illumination of the future, for I declared that this murder would mean a European war.

Vincenzo smiled. *"O signor scherza,"* he said politely. All believed that I was joking.

Four months later, when we met again, he would be reproaching himself for being such a fool as to think I was joking on that fateful June evening.

I decided that my wife and I must get back to England as soon as possible. That journey from Naples to Calais has remained in my memory as the end of an epoch. As the train runs northward through France, the names of the stations we passed—like Verdun—seem printed in blood. Yet the head steward of the restaurant car, a German with a fair Kaiserish moustache, was so courteous and attentive that on our way north I began to think we might have been premature in hurrying home so quickly. Michael Arlen came along and made himself known to us. When I told him we were hurrying home in case war was on its way, he smiled indulgently at my overheated fancy.

It was in the middle of July when we got back to London, and I went off to Lords to see Oxford beat Cambridge at the university match.

Various friends I met asked what had suddenly brought me back from Capri.

"I'm worried about this war," I told them.

"This Irish business? Oh, that'll be all over presently."

"I don't mean civil war in Ireland. I mean a European war."

"Of course, you would have to work out for yourself something improbable."

That state of mind could not exist today in similar circumstances, thanks to television.

Nobody I met would consider a European war even a remote possibility. On the posters advertising that infernal paper, *John Bull*, at the tail end of the omnibuses was TO HELL WITH SERVIA.

Convinced as I was of the imminence of war, I was in a fever to finish *Sinister Street*. My wife and I went to stay in the country where I would often be writing and revising all night and going to bed at seven o'clock in the morning. The book was being set up as I wrote it, so that revision had to be meticulous.

For the rest of that July I was obsessed with the fear that we were going to let France down if things came to the worst. In the air race from London to Paris and back, two out of the six starters finished, taking about three and a half hours each way. The Home Rule Conference failed, and the Ulster Volunteers had obtained from Germany 35,000 rifles and 3,000,000 cartridges in the spring without any attempt being made to stop them. No wonder the Germans supposed that we were too preoccupied with Irish affairs to pay any attention to Europe.

When Austria-Hungary declared war on what we were told should be called Serbia, not Servia, Russia began to mobilize. Desperate last-minute efforts were made to prevent the conflict's extending (that pompous neologism "escalating" was not found necessary in 1914) into a European war. It was too late. Next day Germany declared war on France and Russia. We still abstained. I believe that if Germany had not violated Belgium's neutrality, we should not have entered the war.

I was writing away through that Tuesday evening of August 3, the countryside hushed. When midnight struck, that hushed countryside was filled with the rumble of trains running southward. All night, while I was writing, that rumble continued, and when I leaned out of the window to drink in the morning air before going to bed, the rumble of the trains bearing equipment and munitions and stores to the south coast could still be heard.

I went up to London that afternoon to consult a soldier friend at the War Office about a commission.

He smiled indulgently.

"We don't want married subalterns of thirty-one."

"But I did hold a commission in the Volunteers fourteen years ago."

"I daresay, and if you were still eighteen, I would do all I could to put you in the way of a commission today. But you are thirty-one. Your job is to keep us amused by writing books. You'll be much more use to your country that way than as a subaltern on active service."

I decided to finish *Sinister Street* somehow and after that somehow to get into the war. The manuscript of that second volume is now in the Bodleian at Oxford, and from time to time on the opposite sheet are the names of the cities and towns falling before the German advance—Namur, Liège, Valenciennes, and the rest of them. I do not know how I managed to concentrate on *Sinister Street,* so much was I longing to be in the war. This longing was not inspired by any lofty sentiments of patriotism or even by sympathy with "plucky little Belgium." It was inspired by the realization that this was the greatest moment in the history of my time and that somehow I must be sharing in the excitement of it.

Most people in that autumn of 1914 were still incapable of appreciating how utterly this war was going to change their world; it is difficult to believe now that in the shop windows of London there were placards with BUSINESS AS USUAL, to which some shopkeepers added THOUGH THERE'S A WAR ON. At the same time too many Londoners were wondering why others had not enlisted, and too many idiotic young women were handing white feathers to boyfriends they were tired of.

All that autumn I tried hard to get into the war, but without success. I hear now Henry Newbolt consoling me for my failure:

"From what I hear the whole business will be over by February at latest. That's the general feeling among those who know."

"Kitchener doesn't seem to think that. He asks for three-year volunteers for his army."

"Ah, well, Kitchener's a cautious chap," Newbolt said with a smile.

"I don't believe Winston thinks the war will be over by February," I argued.

Newbolt smiled again.

"Winston is enjoying himself too much to think that."

"I wanted to get into his naval division, but I wouldn't have a chance to get through a medical. I'll have to go somewhere with a fairly decent winter climate."

By the end of October, still with no prospect of getting into the war, I decided to return to Italy. The desperate Battle of Ypres was at its height when my wife and I crossed the Channel. On the boat I saw my War Office friend in khaki and told him I was going to Capri to write a book.

"The best thing you could do," he assured me.

"I was hoping for some kind of obscure staff job in Egypt."

"My dear man, the last people we want on the staff are charming amateurs like yourself. And anyway, this business of diverting to Egypt troops we require in France will have to stop. The only place where anybody is any use at all just now is over there."

He pointed to the misty outline of the French coast beyond that ashen autumnal sea. I felt apologetically superfluous among that crowd of mixed uniforms on the quay at Boulogne. Even that little fellow with the face of a provincial comedian, in a uniform between the Salvation Army and the Church Lads' Brigade, who was going to hand out tracts and toffee somehow or other behind the lines, was living life as it ought to be lived, not as I proposed to live it presently in Capri, writing one more unnecessary novel. I waved my War Office friend good-bye in the blusterous chill of late October and enviously watched him like a senior schoolboy greeting other and important seniors at the beginning of a new term.

The peace of Capri in that cloudless November made me feel even more guilty about inaction when things were so desperate in France and Flanders. I was thankful when I was asked to write an article on behalf of the Commission for Relief in Belgium.

I felt a little less guilty about my inaction when Mr. Hoover, who was doing such a superb job for the Belgian refugees and was to become President of the United States one day, wrote to tell me I had described the work of the commission "in a manner which reaches an absolute ideal."

Nevertheless, I was still set on getting into the war. When I sat down to write my novel *Guy and Pauline* (called *Plasher's Mead* in the United States) , I had debated with myself for a long time whether I had a right to draw on the emotion of my own experience over a broken engagement. Finally I decided that if I were destined to be killed in the war in which I believed I should somehow succeed in playing an active part, it was my duty to put into what might be the last book I should ever write the most poignant experience of my life, while at the same time changing all the externals of the real story into a work of imagination.

My belief that I should manage to get into the war was justified. When I was three-quarters of the way through my novel, a letter came from an old friend written on board the R.M.S. *Franconia*:

"I am writing to you by order of Sir Ian Hamilton, Commander-in-Chief of the Mediterranean Expeditionary Force. I'm cipher-officer on his staff. . . . I noticed a day or two ago that he had bought Vol. II of *Sinister Street* to read. . . . I told him I knew you, etc., and that you had tried for a commission in Egypt without success. He said at once, 'Write to him and tell him to get into communication with Eddie Marsh [the late Sir Edward Marsh was Winston Churchill's private secretary] and get sent out to me as a Marine, and I'll find him a job of some kind. . . .' The possibilities of this show are romantic to a degree."

So that is how I reached the Dardanelles and was to play my part in what would officially be known as the Great War for Civilization.

That last remark in my friend's letter may suggest that we all thought of ourselves as romantic figures. When Rupert Brooke wrote his sonnet, he was not romanticizing himself consciously. He did not join the Royal Naval Division as a patriotic duty but because it was likely to provide the most familiar companionship in the exciting days ahead.

In the 1920's it became the fashion to sneer at Rupert Brooke's poetry. When in 1928 a fountain memorial in memory of the dead of the Royal Naval Division was unveiled by Winston Churchill, there were sneers at the sonnet by Rupert Brooke engraved upon it. I wrote in *G. K's Weekly*:

Mr. Winston Churchill's noble words will probably strike as mere rhetoric in the ears of the devitalized young intellectuals by whom Rupert Brooke's sonnet is no longer regarded as poetry. The war was not many months old before the humanitarian press was inveighing against the romantics who were to arise after it was over and glorify the beastly thing. They have not yet appeared. They lie in Flanders— those romantics. Their dust is mingled with the tawny soil of Hellas.

The mighty cone of Athos observes their tombs. They went early to the fight, those romantics; conscription does not breed martial apologists.

The real lesson to be gained from the last war, as it seems to me, is that never again shall we wage war as we waged it in Flanders and France. Yet, the bitterest supporter of the Western school of tactics was the humanitarian *Nation*, which shed as many crocodile tears as would have set the Nile in flood over the waste of the world's youth, rather than forget its vendetta against Mr. Lloyd George and admit that the Eastern school of strategy was right. Better the bloody mess of Passchendaele than the romantic side-show; better that thousands of conscripts should be slain than that those romantic volunteers should have taken Constantinople.

In reading through once again the sonnet of Rupert Brooke that is carved upon the mermaid fountain, we may find it untouched by time. ... To pretend that Rupert Brooke is not a figure on which the imaginative mind may dwell with greater exaltation than on some pale and trembling junket of a creature in a book or a play is mere wantonness.

When my friend wrote about the romantic possibilities before the Mediterranean Expeditionary Force in 1915, he was thinking of the fall of Constantinople and of the British and the French marching on across the plains of Hungary to attack Germany from the northeast, which had only one great fortress, Breslau. If the British and French high command on the western front had not been so fearful of the war's being decided on an eastern front and therefore had not done all that was possible to make Gallipoli a failure, if Kitchener and Fisher had stood firmly behind Winston Churchill, if the Conservatives out of office had not concentrated on forming a coalition government with the excuse of getting on with the war, Constantinople would have fallen and the war would have been over by the autumn of 1916 at latest, possibly even by the end of 1915.

I recall sitting from midnight until 4 A.M. waiting for news of the Suvla landing on that August night. When without the news we had hoped for at G.H.Q. I was on the way to my tent, the thin slip of the waning moon was rising over Asia. I remember as if it were last night, not fifty-three years ago, my sudden realization that if we were going to win the war, we should have to become as ungentlemanly as Germans to do so.

If the war had ended in that autumn of 1915, the sacrifice which so many contemporaries of mine had made would hardly have been appreciated. It was not until the material discomfort of the war began to affect the civilian population that there was induced a state of mind which was to respond to the obscene horrors of postwar books written with a self-pity that expressed the self-pity of their readers. Those who volunteered to give their lives and gave them without complaint were not praised in such books, lest a hint of admiration should render to war one tattered shred of the glory that was once believed to enfold it. There may have been nothing heroic in the readiness of those young men of 1914 and 1915 to volunteer. There may have been nothing behind that impulse except a desire to do the right thing. However, since none of them considered himself a hero and none of them made a book about his sufferings, those still alive in the "twittering twenties" might have spared them at least as much respect as they gave to writers by whose sufferings some of us might have felt more pitifully moved if they did not seem to have lavished all the pity in the world on themselves.

I must quickly add that I was lucky enough to escape the protracted misery of the western front and, therefore, was never tempted to be sorry for myself. Instead, I was employed in Intelligence and so discovered paradoxically how low the level of human intelligence can sink. If I were asked what I considered the most injurious legacy of what was officially called the Great War for Civilization, I might vote first for the habit of inhaling the smoke of cigarettes. It is difficult to believe now that by 1917 one was offered a cigarette with an apology because it was a "gasper." The gasper of 1917 is the cigarette inhaled all over the world today, and when one is offered any other kind of cigarette, it is with an apology. However, the damage done by swallowing cigarette smoke is a personal risk. A far more injurious legacy of the First World War is the mania for what is called security. The millions of pounds and dollars and rubles being wasted on this idol fifty years after the First World War came to an end makes one wonder why humanity is set on reaching the moon when lunacy is so widely spread on earth.

Espionage in time of war may be inevitable, but in the world today such espionage has nothing like the importance it had in Old Testament days or in ancient Rome or even as late as in the American Civil War. Nevertheless, espionage is still inevitable. It was to counter espionage that the passport system under which we suffer today was invented. I reflect with sorrow that I was much involved in the creation of that passport system. I did not realize that something necessary in time of war would become a lucrative profession after the war. In my third volume of war memories, published in 1932, I related how the Passport Department of the British Legation was the center of our Intelligence work. For revealing this, I was prosecuted under the Official Secrets Act, although by 1932 every embassy, legation, and consulate all over the world used information about passports as the cover for Intelligence.

When the case was over, I wrote a skit on the Secret Service called *Water on the Brain* to contribute something to what the case had cost me. After the Second World War, *Water on the Brain* was reissued as a paperback. I received a letter from a doctor in San Francisco telling me that during the war the O.S.S. in Cairo had found a copy of the original edition, of which they had made more than a hundred photostat copies. These were given to young American Intelligence officers to teach them their job. I thought my correspondent was pulling my leg, but the next day I had a letter from Cleveland, Ohio, telling me the same story. So I told the story in print both in the U.S.A. and in England. It was not contradicted. I think I may be forgiven for wondering whether the millions of pounds, dollars, and rubles spent on "security" is money well spent or wasted.

I wish that President Roosevelt had included freedom of travel among his freedoms. I do not waste emotion on regrets for the past, but I still sigh sometimes for the time before the Great War for Civilization when one could decide to go anywhere in Europe at a moment's notice, though one was advised that it would be prudent to carry a passport in Russia, Turkey, or Spain.

It can be argued that the First World War hastened material progress. That may be true, but material progress without corresponding mental progress is like giving children elaborate toys they are not yet capable of appreciating. Undoubtedly the development of the airplane was due to the First War, and the infernal triumph of air warfare in the Second War made the prospect of a third war as appalling as once upon a time was doomsday.

Thankfully I reflect that to plunge into a third world war as we plunged into that First War without the faintest conception of how it was going to affect the world is no longer imaginable. We drifted into the Second World War because owing to the loss of the flower of our youth, there were too many second-rate careerists in politics. When I look back on so many contemporaries of mine who were killed, I know that their loss was one of the causes of the Second World War. We were lucky, of course, in not having any apprehension of the First World War, because we enjoyed our youth to the full. To the young people of today the Edwardian decade appears the way the Regency appeared to those of us who were feeling oppressed by the tail end of Victorianism.

It could be argued that her country might have benefited if Queen Victoria had left it not long after her golden jubilee, because the Prince of Wales would not have had to spend what were thirteen years of frustration before he ascended the throne.

If Edward VII had begun his reign in 1888, changes that the First World War brought about might already have begun. Women would have had the vote. The lot of the poorer classes would have been ameliorated. Ireland would have had Home Rule. Friendship with France might have led to a triple alliance with France and Russia. At the time of the Entente Cordiale in 1904 I pleaded for that alliance in the paper I edited at Oxford and used to speak in favor of it at college debates, always in a small minority. Such a triple alliance would have made a European war at least unlikely.

Naturally the war affected me as much as it affected other writers about my age. There had been bother with the circulating libraries over the first volume of *Sinister Street*. That was in September, 1913. When the second volume was published in November, 1914, the libraries circulated it without a blush. When I sat down to write *Sylvia Scarlett* while on sick leave in Capri, I found it impossible to recapture the leisurely and decorated style of my first novels. During the two years when I was working in Athens and afterward in the Cyclades in Intelligence, I must have written not less than 5,000 telegrams, many of them of great length. At more than a shilling a word I could not afford to indulge in adjectives, and I had to say what I had to say as briefly as possible. In Athens I had read for the first time Stendhal's *Chartreuse de Parme*. I had tried to read it when I was an undergraduate, but without success. Now with the experience of life in a small country with a court that resembled the small Italian courts of the eighteenth century and the very early nineteenth century, I was able to realize what a master of his art Stendhal was. He spoke of the Code Napoleon as a model for style. I found the writing of telegrams an equally good model for telling a tale as directly as possible.

My experience in Greece had been so wide and exciting that later I felt I should be wise to withdraw from the center of things in order to escape from the prevailing belief of some of my juniors that art and literature had not begun to exist until the twenties. So I withdrew to a small island in the Channel and deliberately wrote against the mood of the moment.

I recall Logan Pearsall Smith's saying after the Great War for Civilization that the continuity of culture had been broken. That is even more evident after the Second World War. I find in my old age that I am becoming less and less hopeful of that break's ever being mended. The past is increasingly despised and ignored; the present is being acclaimed by too many as of almost religious significance, probably because young people today have always at the back of their minds the dark shape of a third world war.

One advantage they enjoy over the young people of 1914: They will not be plunged into war as abruptly as their predecessors. Television and international sport, particularly football, are pacifying influences. Of course, there is always the chance that some lunatic affected by the rays of the moon will drop the bomb. We can only pray that this will not happen.

Pax Britannica! There is something to be said for it when we look at the state of Africa and Asia today. But *Pax Britannica* vanished after the Great War for Civilization.

L. P. Hartley

"I was born in Whittlesey, a small town in the Cambridgeshire fens, whose church has the loveliest spire in England. My father was a solicitor there; he also practiced in the cathedral city of Peterborough, a few miles away, to which we moved in 1900, when I was four. My father did not believe in sending his children (I have two sisters, one older and one younger than myself, and both unmarried, as I am) to boarding school, early; he was a man of culture, and at least half of my education was due to him.

"Eventually, in 1910, I went to Harrow School, and after an interval in the Army, during which I did not see service abroad, I returned to Balliol College, Oxford, where I held an exhibition. I stayed there until 1922 and then got a job as fiction reviewer for The Spectator. A book of short stories (Night Fears) and a nouvelle (Simonetta Perkins) brought me only twelve pounds each, so I concentrated on reviewing until about 1942, when I finished a novel I had begun about twenty years before—The Shrimp and the Anemone. This was a success, and I gave up reviewing and have written fiction more or less successfully (The Go-Between was my best effort) ever since.

"I now live chiefly in London, but I have a house in Bath on the River Avon, where I have a boat and find much relaxation in rowing it."

THREE WARS

——◆——

PEOPLE sometimes ask me—people much younger than I—what it felt like to be living in England before the First World War. Was the "atmosphere," the spirit of the age, the Zeitgeist, different from what it is now?

It was different, but I find it hard to define the difference. To say it was the difference between feeling that life was then a boon, but is now a menace, does partly describe it; in those days hope took for granted what in these days fear takes for granted. The idea of a general catastrophe, which may annihilate us all and which is somehow more terrifying and life-destroying than the thought of one's own death, didn't exist: Indeed it didn't come into being until after the Second World War. The First World War shook one's belief in the essential goodness of humanity—the belief that all's for the best in the best of all possible worlds that, with many conspicuous exceptions, had dominated Victorian thought. But one felt that it was a "war to end war," that experience teaches, and that humanity had learned its lesson. The period between the wars was one of uneasy hope, compared with now, when we all are, consciously or not, in dread of some nuclear catastrophe which will nullify whatever aims we have.

Such a state of mind was unthinkable before 1914, for although philosophers like Schopenhauer and novelists like Thomas Hardy had taken a gloomy view of the human lot, they were pessimists and not misanthropes: they put the blame on fate, not on man. The old saying *homo homini lupus* did not occur to them and might, indeed, have shocked them.

Boarding school was such an arduous experience that I, for one, was often unaware of what was taking place outside the microcosm. But at that time, and indeed for many years, I had been learning to play the piano, and in 1912, or thereabouts, I was suddenly confronted by the new phenomenon of jazz music, "Hitchy-Koo," and so on. I disliked it very much, and all the more because, as a pianist, I couldn't manage the syncopation.

"Never mind," I thought, "it is one of these new crazes, those songs that catch the public ear, like 'A Grasshopper Sat on a Railroad Track,' and it will soon be forgotten," but it wasn't, and hasn't been. Somebody said that "the rot started with Beethoven"; I think it started with jazz and the indifference to sense, and morality, and genuine emotion that goes with jazz, which in any case has to be sung slightly out of tune. Perhaps the world has been slightly out of tune ever since.

In the summer of 1914 I was still at school, at Harrow-on-the-Hill, and there was an epidemic of mumps. At Harrow nearly all the boys had rooms to themselves, and if any of them fell ill, not so seriously ill as to be taken to the sanatorium, but seriously enough to keep other boys out, the matron would fix on the door a card labeled NO ADMITTANCE which allowed the invalid to rest in peace. I did not expect to catch mumps, nor had I caught them when the school broke up for the summer holidays. But the incubation period of mumps is longer than that of any other of the ordinary infectious illnesses—twenty-six days, I think. On the night of August 3, while I was at home, I realized that I had the symptoms. I got out of bed and pinned a notice on the door, NO ADMITTANCE, MUMPS IN HERE!

I don't know if I imagined that no one, my mother or anyone else, would take the risk of visiting me, but I felt that, medically speaking, I was a pariah. The next day it was announced that we were at war with Germany.

The old dispensation had come to an end. I was not aware of this; I was aware only of high fever and a pain in my neck. By comparison, the political situation meant nothing to me. Fever always brings a kind of schizophrenia, and it did then. NO ADMITTANCE, MUMPS IN HERE!

But, of course, the world is not to be kept out by a warning on one's door. When mumps had subsided, I went back to school. I was at an age to have joined up. I didn't, because I didn't want to. I was utterly unbelligerent and hated the thought of fighting, in however good a cause. But I was obliged to join the school corps.

In prewar days I had always held out against joining the corps, preferring lessons to field days, although I quite enjoyed practicing at the rifle range—an exercise which was compulsory, though I never excelled at it. Before 1914 I think that in England warfare was envisaged in terms of the Boer War, a gallant enterprise in which none but self-chosen heroes, with a vocation for arms, took part. It didn't affect the majority of the population, whose role was to look on and admire. And admire I did, at the age of four or five, in spite of the fact that my father, who was a Volunteer, and must to some extent have enjoyed military training, was also by conviction a pro-Boer, an unpopular thing to be. I enjoyed singing, or hearing sung (for I doubt if, at that tender age, I could have sung a tune), such martial ditties as "The soldiers of the Queen, my lad, have been, my lad, have seen, my lad, have fought for England's glory, lad," etc. and, more poignant:

> Goodbye Dolly, I must leave you
> Though it breaks my heart to go;
> Something tells me I am needed
> At the front to fight the foe.

And one of my earliest and most recurrent memories is of the night of the relief of Ladysmith, when the whole of the little town in which we lived (Sir Harry Smith's birthplace) went mad with excitement. The noise in the streets still lingers in my mind like a great red blur. It terrified me, and I remember that my mother told me afterward that I cried, "I don't like the jum-jums," meaning the drums which reverberated under our windows.

But I also thrilled to the excitement and the patriotic fervor, and even my father would recite Kipling's "Absent-minded Beggar," with its refrain:

> So pass your hat for your credit's sake,
> And pay, pay, pay!

I was never sure, and still am not, whether the "beggar" was just any man, a "bloke" as people would say now, or someone who was actively soliciting alms for the war effort, as in 1914 it came to be called.

But in those days I was only an infant spectator of that national, very limited conflict and never dreamed that anything of the sort could ever affect me. I laughed heartily at the answer to the riddle "Why does Kruger wear thick boots?" "To Keep De Wet from defeat." South Africa was so far away, and what happened there was only, for me, a stimulus for emotion and romantic excitement, with heroism, not death, as its leading motif.

In a way, my wartime attack of mumps was symbolical. I had to accept it, just as I had to accept the war; but I couldn't and wouldn't regard the war as belonging to the natural course of events, any more than I could regard a state of fever as life advanced to a higher power, although some might argue that it is.

Unfortunately for me, the war lasted much longer than my attack of mumps. For many in England and the United States and other countries its duration was all too short. We bow the head but do not understand.

The rifle regiment to which we were affiliated at school had differences in drill from other infantry regiments—e.g., such words of command as "carry arms" and "trail arms." These nuances of training in weapon warfare meant nothing to me, nor did I mind being cursed by the sergeant major or the drill sergeant, for my clumsy efforts to comply. Neither of them treated us anything as severely as recruits in the Regular Army were treated. We were not subjected to a fusillade of four-letter words, nor were doubts cast on our paternity or maternity.

In any case, public school life in those days had inured us to a good deal of verbal and physical unpleasantness. I remember how, in the Second World War, a friend of mine who was too old to fight

joined the local fire brigade. The other firemen complained bitterly
of their lot, their hardships of one sort and another, and they said to
him, "Why don't *you* complain?" He replied, "Because I was at
school at Eton, a much tougher upbringing than any of you have
had." Which was true, for the children of the well-to-do, in those
days, had a harder time than the children of the underprivileged.
They had to eat what was put before them, however nauseating,
whereas the children of the less fortunate members of the community were allowed to refuse any dish they didn't like, just as
animals do.

In the autumn of 1915 I went to Balliol College, Oxford, where I
had been given an exhibition. I expected, as I believe many of my
fellow countrymen did, a recrudescence of the Boer War spirit in
1914, and for a while—a little while—it did come back, with the
poems of Rupert Brooke and the famous poster of Kitchener, one of
the heroes of the Boer War, pointing an accusing finger above the
slogan, "Your King and your Country Need YOU!" In those early
days, the romance of war did stage a comeback. The whole country
was electrified. But not for long. When the casualty lists began to
pile up and it was gradually realized that the war was not for a few
professional soldiers—a football team fighting on our behalf—but a
catastrophe that might go on for years and involve millions of
people, including myself, the climate of opinion began to change,
and mine changed with it. War was not a kind of play to be enacted
before an enthusiastic but detached audience: It was something that
affected everyone and would change their lives. Wartime was a
different kind of life from peacetime, nor have we in England ever
recovered the pre-1914 feeling. At least that is my opinion.

It is not only that crime has grown steadily with the growth of
material prosperity, so that the English, instead of being one of the
most honest people in the world, are now not noted for honesty; it
is the loss of confidence in human nature, the general feeling that
the other fellow will do you down if he can—and, doing so, will
have the sympathy of the community at large, implicit if not
expressed. This moral deterioration can be laid at the door of the
state, which, in 1914, so grossly increased its powers. Power corrupts, as we have often been told, and absolute power corrupts
absolutely.

I was brought up on the theories of John Stuart Mill to believe
that the state is the great enemy because it takes man's moral responsibility out of his own hands and imposes its decisions on him,
which have come to be accepted as fatalistically as if they were laws
of God—more so, indeed, for they have thrived on the decline of the

belief in God as the supreme lawgiver, to whom man is responsible for his acts and who is the only keeper of his conscience. The laws of God depend on faith; the laws of the state depend on fact: In the material and to some extent in the moral sphere, the state can make you do what it likes, whereas God cannot; the state has usurped the kingdom, the power, and the glory. The individual has been devalued: He takes his orders from the state.

Herbert Spencer wrote a book called *The Man Versus the State,* whose very title thrilled me, but when I went to Oxford in 1915, before I joined the Army, I had to listen to the then master of Balliol, A. L. Smith, giving his famous series of lectures, "From Hobbes to Maine," in which he argued that the state, as an embodiment of the community, could make the individual dance to its tune, however unjust, in the eyes of the individuals who composed it, its commands and demands were.

While I listened, my blood boiled, for had not these doctrines of Hobbes, Locke, Rousseau, Bosanquet, etc., with their insistence on the omnipotence of the state, made the Four Years' War possible? Not quite in the same way as it made possible the Six Years' War, for the Four Years' War was for King and Country and inspired to some extent by the patriotism that was a legacy from the Boer War. The country, remembering those glamorous days, went into it with songs on their lips. Whereas the Six Years' War was a war against Hitler; it was a war of resistance, and though it ended in victory, it produced no poetry.

I stayed at Balliol for two terms and then joined the Army as a gunner in a regiment called the Royal Garrison Artillery. I doubt if it exists now, but they thought I should be suitable for it, because of my academic leanings. Actually I was not, because such gifts as I had inclined to the humanities, whereas the Royal Garrison Artillery demanded a certain mathematical aptitude for the use of the slide rule, for calculating trajectories, and the whole mystique of gunfire, which I simply didn't possess. When inspecting officers came around, I was sometimes pointed out to them, almost with awe, as a man from Balliol, but when the time for examinations came, I did not live up to my legendary reputation.

Being medically unfit for active service, I was then transferred to an infantry regiment where ballistics was not required, and I served as camp postman in an enormous camp called Catterick Bridge in Yorkshire. So large was it that it had a railway of its own, with two stops between each end, and was facetiously called the Catterick Bridge Express.

On my way to Catterick I remember seeing a poster from *John*

Bull, Horatio Bottomley's popular paper, saying, "Why so many suicides at Catterick?"

The November of 1916 was bitterly cold. Our hut had a central stove, which sometimes got red-hot, so that one could hardly get near it, while beyond the radius of its influence the temperature was almost freezing.

But apart from the cold, I wasn't altogether unhappy at Catterick (a beautiful place, seen from a tourist's eye). I read Montaigne's *Essays* and the *Apology* of Raymonde Sebonde, and I delivered the letters. As Christmas drew near, a great many parcels were added to the letters, and although the "Catterick Express" was a help, I had to do most of my rounds on foot, carrying a sack on my back, which grew heavier every day. But the job had its compensations, for never have I been made so welcome as I was then. Whenever I approached the lighted door of a hut (it always seemed to be dark outside, whatever the time of day), I was greeted with frantic cheers from the inmates, whether I had a missive for them or not.

At last, and most unexpectedly, I received a summons to attend an O.T.C. (Officers Training Corps). No one was more surprised than I, for I had shown so little military ability! But some high-up from my old school had tracked me down and wangled (as we used to say) this promotion for me.

I remember the corporal in charge of our hut saying to me—it touched me then and still does—"We always knew you were a gentleman," and I remember a fellow gunner (Redfern his name was) advising me, "If you talked more, you'd get on better."

The O.T.C. was housed in Sidney Sussex College, Cambridge. There we slept 4 in a room—instead of 30, as at Catterick, and 250, as in my first camp. I studied the infantry regulations and learned, more or less, how to behave as an officer. But owing to some physical disability, I could never, marching, quite keep in step, and I remember our sergeant major walking alongside of me and pointing out this defect. But unlike what sergeants major are supposed to be, and often are, he was a kindhearted man, and I owe it to him (I'm nearly sure) that I was never called on to drill the battalion, a feat of which, from nerves and other reasons (*e.g.,* lack of a resonant voice), I should never have been capable of, although the test was part of our schedule.

So having passed or avoided these various pitfalls, I became Second Lieutenant Hartley, fit only for Home Service, which in my case meant defending the coast of East Anglia from possible German invasion.

My life then became, materially and in all ways, much easier. At

Colchester, where I was stationed in the Meeanee Barracks (Meeanee must have been the scene of some British victory in India), the officers were given V.I.P. treatment, and my greatest hardship was being sent, as a contact, to an isolation hospital for infectious diseases. It was so cold (March, 1917) that my hands swelled up to double their size with chilblains, and I remember my batman saying to a doctor who came to inspect us, "I have three officers here, frozen to dead."

However, we weren't dead, and the war went on peacefully for me until I had an attack of bronchopneumonia, after which I spent two months at the Third London General Hospital. Neither my heart nor my lungs were thought to be in good order. Eventually I went before a medical board. While I was waiting for my turn to come, an orderly said to me, "You ought to drink some black coffee." "Why?" I asked. "Because it plays your heart up," he said.

Perhaps there wasn't time for me to take his advice; at any rate I didn't. The president of the board was a benign old gentleman called Sir Frederick Treves, who many years before had had the honor and responsibility of taking out King Edward VII's appendix. Throughout my war service I had felt that authority was, or would be, against me. Even as an officer, I envisaged, Kafka-like, officers above me who would call me to account. Suddenly all this was changed. The orderly was right when he told me that this medical board was "a good crowd." No doubt I stood to attention and saluted; but after that all the multiple obligations of discipline faded away, and I was an equal, except insofar as I was an object of pity. "My poor boy," Sir Frederick said, "you have done your utmost for your King and Country."

It wasn't true, but after the harshness of Army life, underlying or apparent, it was a soothing and gratifying thing to hear.

In August, 1918, I was discharged and could wear "civvy" clothes if I wanted to. I was advised to go to a health resort to recuperate. My mother took me to Mundesley on the Norfolk coast, where there was a hospital for tuberculous patients nearby. No sooner had we settled down in lodgings than we heard that the little town was stricken with Spanish influenza: More coffins were being carried out than there were visitors coming in. In these plague-ridden conditions I hardly noticed the Armistice on November 11, any more than, thanks to mumps, I had noticed the outbreak of war more than four years before.

The Second World War came, and we, who could remember the First, had no illusions as to what it would be like—it was a grim task that we set ourselves. There was resolution and determination in it, but in spite of Churchill's inspiring speeches, there was little of the enthusiasm and almost joyful acquiescence in self-sacrifice which gave a romantic panache to the First War, which had been the war of Rupert Brooke—something to glory in—until it became the war of Siegfried Sassoon and Wilfrid Owen—something to shudder at.

"Thou hast multiplied the nations and not increased the joy." How true are those words of Isaiah, and nothing has been more of a killjoy than the two world wars. The first did indeed leave behind the reaction of a brittle, evanescent gaiety: The "bright young people" made merry, as far as they could, now that the threat of extinction had been (as they thought) permanently banished. Sentiment and emotion lived on, as witness the hold that Armistice Day, November 11, 1918, still keeps on the public mind. Whereas the conclusions, or inconclusions, of the Second World War brought no such elation, only a dreary sense of relief, for who but a few can recall the dates of V day and VJ day?

It will be many years, if ever, before we recover the pre-1914 *joie de vivre* and confidence in life.

Sir Charles Petrie

SIR CHARLES PETRIE *was born in Liverpool, Lancashire, in 1895 of an Irish father and a Scottish mother. He was thus eighteen years of age at the beginning of the First World War. At its conclusion he returned to Corpus Christi College, Oxford, where he had been studying when it began, and took his degree in modern history in 1920.*

Since then he has devoted himself to authorship and journalism and more recently to the radio and television. Between the wars he traveled widely on the continent of Europe, and for his historical work he has been decorated by the governments of Greece, Italy, and Spain. During the Second World War he was an official lecturer to the British forces. In 1957 he was made a Commander of the Order of the British Empire, and in 1965 he was the recipient of an honorary degree at the University of Valladolid.

Sir Charles has so far paid only one visit to the United States, and that was in 1953, when he was in New York, Boston, and Princeton. Recently his activities have been confined to Ireland and Spain, for he is both the president of the Military History Society of Ireland and a corresponding member of the Royal Academy of the History of Spain.

For some years Sir Charles was in publishing, and he is a regular contributor to the Illustrated London News, *as well as editor of the* Household Brigade Magazine. *His latest book is* Don John of Austria.

FIGHTING THE FIRST WORLD WAR IN LONDON

THE OUTBREAK of the First World War found me at the age of eighteen residing with my parents in Liverpool and about to go up to Oxford. After vainly trying to get into the Army and being rejected on account of my eyesight, I went into residence at Corpus Christi College and remained there for twelve months. By the autumn of 1915 the military authorities were not so particular, and as I had had a year's training in the Oxford University Officers Training Corps, I was given a commission in the Royal Garrison Artillery.

I was posted to Tynemouth, and a very bleak spot it was. My quarters were in the castle, which had been built in the reign of Henry VIII and which appeared to have remained unchanged ever since. The first night I was there, my bedroom window blew in. Sometimes the wind was so strong that a rope had to be put across the barracks square to enable the men to get from one side to the other, and on more than one occasion a parade had to be dismissed because it was impossible to preserve any sort of formation. Such discomforts, however, were amply compensated for by the unfailing kindness of the people of Northumberland, and by the beauty of the scenery on the upper Tyne. After I had been some months at Tynemouth, the medical authorities decided that my sight was not good enough to allow me to be sent overseas, so the military powers-that-be somewhat paradoxically decided that I should go to anti-aircraft. Accordingly, I was sent for a course to Shoeburyness, where I remained for a month, and at the end of this period I was sent to gun stations at, successively, Halifax, Rugby, and Banbury. While I was at Shoeburyness, the Easter Rising took place in Dublin, but those of us who had relatives in Ireland were allowed to opt out of service there so far as possible against the republicans.

My men were mostly Reservists from Cork and Kerry, and my feelings on first taking command were somewhat akin to those of Parnesius, in Kipling's *Puck of Pook's Hill,* when he led his detachment out of Anderida. However, my own Irish background soon enabled us to understand one another, and all went well. In a typical English countryside there were, all the same, some awkward moments. At Christmas, 1916, we were outside Rugby, and the local inhabitants got up a concert for us. The day before it was due to take place the sergeant major asked me whether the national anthem was going to be sung. On my replying that this would certainly be the case, he told me that the men would refuse to sing it. No ordinary argument would have been of the least avail, so I decided to appeal to the innate courtesy of the Irish. When I had all the men collected in the barracks room, I asked them if they would join in "God Save the King" out of compliment to their English hosts if "The Wearing of the Green" were also sung. To a man they said they would, and so it was settled, after I had assured those who were arranging the concert that far from having a political significance, "The Wearing of the Green" was just a sentimental tune which would remind the men of home.

In those days antiaircraft was still very much in its infancy, and the enemy was the zeppelin rather than the airplane. At Shoeburyness we were trained on a variety of guns, both fixed and mobile, and there were not a few accidents owing to the different lengths of the recoil, which varied from 45 inches in the case of the 13-pounder to 11 inches in that of the 3-inch naval gun. All these guns were converted, and many of them left a good deal to be desired. For nearly a year I had a 6-pounder Nordenfelt, which I am glad to say I never had a chance to fire. The only time a zeppelin came within range we had no ammunition and were constrained to admire her beauty in the moonlight. Perhaps, however, the lack of shells did not matter so much as we imagined at the time, for when they did arrive, they were filled with only salt. Indeed, the position of many gun stations seemed to be dictated by political, rather than by military, considerations. Lack of ammunition was the rule rather than the exception, but all the same, officers and men had to pretend that the guns were ready for action, presumably to impress the civilian population, and each night we were compelled to stand by as if we were in a position to open fire. It was a sorry and somewhat demoralizing piece of make-believe.

What made antiaircraft so onerous was not the amount of work there was to do but the necessity of being at call on short notice, as they say in the City. For twelve months I had no other officer with me and no leave at all: Once a week I was allowed to be away from the gun station for three hours, but the rest of the time I had to be within ten minutes' reach by day, while by night it was forbidden to leave the compound. The men were in no better plight: They got one late pass every ten days or fortnight, though in defiance of the regulations, I used to allow those on duty to go one at a time to the village pub for a "quick one."

To those of us at home the war seemed a distant affair. From time to time there were scares of invasion, but outside the War Office no one took them seriously, and we had our daily routine. The men had little to do off parade, and they were often profoundly bored. The war seemed to have always been going on, and there appeared to be no likelihood that it would ever cease. We were mere pieces in a game, and we moved about the board for no apparent reason. No initiative of any sort was required of us, and the result was that the most important event made little impression on minds which were half-atrophied. Had it not been for the unfailing kindness of the local inhabitants at all levels, life would have been intolerable.

In the spring of 1917 an event occurred which made me a Hispanophile for life. The Conde de Romanones, the Prime Minister of Spain, was strongly pro-Ally, and the British government came to the conclusion that he was going to follow the example of President Wilson and bring his country into the war. Accordingly, one day at Banbury we received orders to send in a list of all officers who could speak Spanish. I knew a few words, so I sent in my name and then rushed off to Oxford for a phrase book, from which I proceeded to acquire some sentences of "the-pen-of-my-aunt-is-in-the-garden" variety. In due course orders came for me to report to a certain room at the War Office for an interview. When I got there, not a word was said to me about Spain or Spanish, but I was asked if I could ride a horse and told to translate aloud the opening lines of the second book of the *Iliad*. I then went back to Banbury and a week or two afterward was told to report at King's College, Strand, for a three months' course of Spanish.

I had always been interested in foreign affairs, and Spain had a special attraction for me, but my selection for this course definitely decided my vocation. There were about twenty-five of us, drawn from all arms of the service, and no instruction could have been more thorough than that which we received: We were taught not only the language, but also the literature, history, and customs of the country, presumably with the idea of fitting us to become liaison officers should Spain join the Allies. I write "presumably," because neither then nor at any other time were we told why we had been sent for the course. Those were the days of the daylight air raids on London. So novel were they that during the one on July 7, I was riding in Hyde Park and somewhat optimistically pulled up under a tree until the enemy had passed. As soon as the course was over, we all were returned to duty, and not a word did any of us ever hear on the subject of it again. It is true that Spain did not enter the war, but one would have thought that somewhere in the government service, use might have been made of men who had been trained with so much care and at such expense.

Autumn found me back at antiaircraft on the outer defenses of London at Much Hadham in Hertfordshire. The raids during the summer had galvanized the authorities into action, and the whole of the A.A. (antiaircraft) services were on a much more business-like footing than had been the case earlier in the year. The zeppelin was being defeated with comparative ease, though its real Waterloo did not come until this same autumn, when of eleven airships that came over on one raid, only four returned safely to Germany. It was clear that no country could stand losses at that rate. The airplane was another matter. At Much Hadham we had two of the then new 3-inch guns, and during moonlight raids at the end of September, 1917, we were in action nearly every evening. It was a curious change to be having tea at Rumpelmeyers at five in a relatively carefree London and to be in the middle of a battle only 25 miles away three hours later.

It was rarely that we could see our target, and mostly we were employed on barrage work, when we used to fire something like 30 rounds a minute from each gun. Anything up to 200 rounds a gun an evening was the normal procedure. Of course, height and direction were in those days largely a matter of guesswork, but we managed to keep the enemy up to over 10,000 feet, and in the First World War accurate bombing at that height was impossible. One night a German plane shut off its engines, glided under the barrage, and machine-gunned us: At first we thought the patter of bullets on the fallen leaves betokened a thunderstorm, but we were soon undeceived. We had no tin hats; but fortunately the enemy did not persist in his attack, and our only casualty was one man slightly wounded in the arm.

As will have been gathered, while I was on antiaircraft I moved about England a good deal. The countryside during the First World War was very much more like what it must have been in the eighties or nineties than what it was to be during the next conflict. The private motorcar was never seen, but that was no great hardship since the horse had not been driven from the roads by August, 1914. For instance, I remember once having to go to Chelmsford in a hurry from a camp near Chipping Ongar, and the only method of doing so was to hire a dogcart: I did this without difficulty and drove myself over, though it now seems in passing strange to be living in this space age, and yet to have driven into the yard of the Saracen's Head at Chelmsford, and to have called for the ostler to take one's horse. Official cars there were in plenty for the staff, but the ordinary regimental officer had to get across country as best he could, using horses, bicycles, the slowest of trains, and his own feet in the process. It was often a nuisance at the time, but one realizes now that one was seeing the last of Victorian England, the England of Trollope and Whyte-Melville.

The autumn of 1917 saw me away at last from antiaircraft, for which the badness of my sight had never really fitted me, and at a desk in the R.G.A. (Royal Garrison Artillery) Record Office at Dover. The office was on the seafront, and as I lived in the castle, I got plenty of exercise walking to or from my work four times a day. The mess was a pleasant enough place, though this was in no way due to the C.R.A. (Commander of the Royal Artillery), who was a typical field officer of an earlier day. On one occasion he came to the conclusion that too much whisky was being consumed, which, as far as some half dozen officers were concerned, was true. Accordingly he gave orders that no officer was to have more than two doubles a day. The only result, however, was that the consumers of whisky drank more than ever, for they "borrowed" the two doubles from those— the vast majority—who did not drink whisky, and settled up when the mess bill came in. Such is often the fate of ill-conceived sumptuary legislation. From time to time, I may add, the scene was enlivened by bombs from the air or shells from the sea, though not to anything like the extent that was to be the case in the next war.

My experience in a long mess like that at Dover led me to the conclusion that, at any rate at home, there was less camaraderie in the First World War than there was to be in its successor, nor is this surprising in view of the fact that English society as a whole was much more formal in 1914 than it became as a result of the struggle against Hohenzollern Germany. The senior officers in the main were very stiff toward their juniors, who were given the impression that try as they might they would never become soldiers in any real sense. The "spit and polish" brigade was firmly entrenched in the seat of the mighty, and those who had not been in the Army before the war were too often regarded as "temporary gentlemen," irrespective of their personal character and social background. This has always been my impression, and it was confirmed in the autumn of 1940, when I was lecturing to the Australians on Salisbury Plain, for those who had fought in the First World War all commented on the increased friendliness among both soldiers and civilians. A good many of the pre-1914 regular officers had never seen a shot fired in anger, as the saying goes, and they were inclined to regard the Army as their own special preserve from which intruders should be barred or, if this was impossible, admitted only on sufferance. The dividing line between Regulars, Special Reservists, Territorials, and New Army also strengthened the centrifugal influences in military circles.

In the spring of 1918 I was, to my great satisfaction, attached to the Historical Section of the War Cabinet, of which the offices, long since pulled down, were in Whitehall Gardens. They constituted a veritable rabbit warren, for they spread over several large houses, and during the whole twelve months I was there, the only part of the labyrinth with which I was thoroughly acquainted was the way from the entrance to the room in which I worked. The staff was small—half a dozen of us in all—and we were generally regarded by politicians and soldiers alike as an encyclopedia on all that had hitherto happened in the war, our main job being to keep such information up-to-date. A great many people of note came in and out of the office, not least Austen Chamberlain, whose official biography I was to write in later years.

The latest joined member of the Historical Section was made responsible for what were known in the office as the three beasts— black, pink, and red. The black beast contained the minutes of earlier Cabinet meetings, while the pink and red beasts were fortnightly publications giving the disposition of troops at home and abroad respectively. All three were highly confidential. They were kept in a most imposing safe, whose key was locked in a smaller safe; the key of the second safe was kept in a drawer, whose key, in its turn, was placed each evening in an ornament on the mantelpiece, because, as the custodian was brightly informed, "The Hun will never think of looking for it there. He'll think you've got it on you, so that he may cut your throat when you're in bed, but he won't find the key." There were also secret papers, respectively termed P. and W.C., for which the same luckless officer was responsible: they were private and War Cabinet papers.

Once during my time at Whitehall Gardens I saw the "Purple Emperor" himself, namely Lord Curzon, then Lord President of the Council. I had to take some document to the Persia Committee, over which he was presiding, but all I remember of the incident was that although I had to remain in the room for an hour, he never had the courtesy to offer me a chair. It is to be feared that such treatment of those whom he considered to be his inferiors was typical, not exceptional, and it explains his widespread unpopularity.

A good deal has been written about the number of incompetent people who, owing to social or political influence, were in high places in those days. All I can say is that during the time I was at the War Cabinet Office, I did not come across them, though whether they had been weeded out earlier or whether they never existed I do not profess to know. There were a few obvious misfits, but that was all. The incompetents were numerous enough lower down at depots, training centers, and the like, but certainly by 1918 they were not in Whitehall.

This was my second experience of wartime London, and there can be no doubt that the lot of the capital in the First World War was far happier than it was to be in its successor. There were, it is true, air raids, but they were relatively insignificant. Then the difficulty was to find accommodation of any sort, and money flowed into London from all over the kingdom: Civil servants, far from being evacuated to Blackpool, were recruited from the provinces to staff the new government departments which came into being owing to the needs of the war or the whims of the politicians. Indeed, the period of the First World War is one of the most important in the recent history of the capital, for the pressure lasted not only throughout the conflict, but after its conclusion, partly owing to the short-lived boom, but chiefly owing to the continued presence of large numbers of demobilized officers and men who regarded London as the best center from which to reenter civil life. The capital, too, largely escaped the subsequent slump, and it did not begin visibly to be affected by the international situation until the Munich crisis. In the period of which I am writing the chief centers of attraction for the officer off duty or on leave were the Berkeley, Hatchett's, and the Piccadilly Grill. That was the heyday of the revues, and of those that stick in the memory the best known were *The Bing Boys* (with George Robey and Violet Loraine), *Theodore and Co.,* and *Cheep.* Also, there was always *Chu Chin Chow.* To London flocked in the thousands the relatives and friends of men on leave, and never can any city have been so thronged with men and women solely intent on enjoying themselves as was the capital during the First World War.

What is often forgotten about that war is how unexpectedly it ended. In the middle of July, 1918, the Central Powers were spread all over the map, Russia and Rumania were out of the fight, and the Allies were everywhere on the defensive; yet by the middle of November the Allied troops were in Cologne, and Austria-Hungary had ceased to exist. We know now that Ludendorff had prophesied disaster at the beginning of the year, but all we saw then were the apparently invincible German armies, flushed with the series of offensives which had begun in March. When a secret report came into the office to the effect that the apparent might of Germany was a mere façade, behind which was a growing chaos and despair, we dismissed it as what a later generation would have called wishful thinking, for the wish seemed not merely father to the thought, but its whole ancestry.

Even when Turkey and Bulgaria had collapsed, the belief of those best qualified to express an opinion was that the war would last well into 1919, and men talked gloomily of the Germans desperately defending every hill, river, and town all the way back to Berlin. There had been so many disappointments and disillusionments that we no longer dared to hope, and it was not until the middle of October that we became convinced that the great military machine, which had been the wonder and terror of Europe for nearly fifty years, was really on the verge of collapse.

Such being the case, I settled down at the War Cabinet Office in the expectation of remaining there for a year or two. One of my jobs was to keep in touch with the Italian and Serbian military missions and with the Russian exiles, whose headquarters were at Whitehall Court, at the back of the War Office. There was a speciousness about the Russians which the Italians and Serbs lacked, but they were much more difficult to deal with, for they themselves did not know what they wanted, whereas the others knew only too well. Much undeserved ridicule has been poured on these Russian exiles trying to earn a living as taxi drivers or by selling their bodies and their jewelry, but the real tragedy of Imperial Russia was that by the time the breaking point came, she had lost her best. Admittedly, the attitude of her government on the eve of war was disingenuous in the extreme, and the Czar could hardly have been weaker, but what is not always remembered is that those who might have saved the situation at the time of the revolution were killed in the early days of hostilities during that invasion of East Prussia which was made very largely for the purpose of easing the pressure on the Allies in the West: So I felt that we owed their surviving friends and relatives something more than the sneer which was only too often their lot. Furthermore, I had been in Russia as a boy, and one year when we were spending a holiday at Samaden, in Switzerland, my father used to play golf with the Grand Duke Nicholas, the future Russian commander in chief, and Guchkov, the Octobrist leader, was more than once a guest at our house. So I had seen something of Russians elsewhere than in exile at Whitehall Court, and I did not get on with them too badly; anyhow I much preferred being sent to interview the Russians than the Serbs or the Italians.

There were many disillusionments to be experienced by a young man at the War Cabinet Office in those days, and not the least was contained in a box file labeled THE WAR AIMS OF THE ALLIES. One evening when we were on late duty with nothing much to do, a colleague and I got this file out, took a few blank maps, and set about tracing on them these war aims. We had not, however, gone very far before we discovered that vast areas, particularly in the Near East, had been promised to at least two separate powers, so we put the cards back in their box, tore up the maps, and returned to our normal work sadder, if wiser, men.

As September passed into October and it became clear that the collapse of Germany was imminent, the one subject of conversation in Whitehall was what sort of peace we were likely to have. Although those of us who worked at the War Cabinet Office had naturally more idea of the real situation than had the general public, even we imagined that the government had some plan for a final settlement other than the above-mentioned contradictory promises which had been made to various allies: In these circumstances it is hardly surprising that we should have been wildly out in our forecasts. Also, until a few days before the Armistice, it was never anticipated that there would be an internal revolution of any magnitude in Germany. What was expected was that the Kaiser would be forced to agree to a much more democratic constitution which would bring the Army under the control of the Reichstag and that the influence of Prussia in the Reich would be greatly weakened. Perhaps had these somewhat modest expectations been fulfilled, the future of Europe might have been happier.

What none of us anticipated was that the Allies, in opposition to their own interests, would carry the work of Bismarck to its logical conclusion and complete the unification of Germany, thereby paving the way for Hitler and the Third Reich. The strongest centrifugal force lay in the dynasties which ruled the various kingdoms and duchies, and which were always restive under the tutelage of Berlin; yet the German people were deliberately encouraged to overthrow their ruling houses, to many of which they were deeply attached, as the price of peace, and so the last obstacle to a unified Reich was removed by those concerned in its retention. Once the dynasties had gone, there was no reason for the continued existence of their former dominions as separate units, and so the path was cleared for that complete Prussianization of Germany which was to be the outstanding accomplishment of the Nazi regime.

Few voices were raised at the time against this mistaken policy, but now that fifty years have elapsed, it is difficult to disagree with the late Jacques Bainville that the war was lost in the first clause of the peace treaty, in that the settlement should not have been made with Germany as a whole, but rather that there should have been separate treaties with Prussia, Bavaria, Saxony, and the other states which had composed the Hohenzollern empire. Unhappily, the French were so determined to reverse the verdict of 1870 that they forgot that this in its turn had been rendered possible only by the victory of Prussia over Austria four years before, while the British government does not appear to have thought about the matter at all, having drifted into peace almost as inconsequently as it had drifted into war.

With the arrival of November events began to move so fast that their effect was numbing. The Kaiser's flight into Holland was the only incident of itself to strike the imagination, for it seemed inconceivable until it had happened, since at that time we knew nothing of the drama that had been enacted at Spa: For the rest one heard, almost without grasping its significance, the daily list of places captured by the advancing Allies—places that only a week or two before seemed outside the scope of any offensive possible until the following year at the earliest. Then the rumor began to go round that if the Germans delayed signing the Armistice, preparations had been made for the bombing of Berlin, for that city had hitherto been too remote a target for the airplanes of those days, and such was the prevailing climate of public opinion that most people hoped this would take place.

The actual events of November 11, 1918, must always remain fresh in the memory of any who were in London at the time. The day began in the normal way, and people went to their work as usual. As eleven o'clock approached, it was as if the population of the capital were coming out of a trance—a trance that had lasted for more than four years. The war was nearly over: In a few moments the last shot would have been fired. The moment for which millions had been waiting and which had been so long delayed that they had almost ceased to hope for it had arrived. Soon all pretense at work was abandoned, and in the West End a great crowd surged into Downing Street to salute the architect of the victory. Mr. Lloyd George duly appeared and said a few words, chiefly to the effect that the time had come to relax, after which there was a stampede to Buckingham Palace, where a very remarkable demonstration of loyalty took place toward the monarch who had played his part so well in the conflict that was now at an end. As the crowd cheered itself hoarse, it was impossible not to reflect on that other monarch, the Hohenzollern, fleeing from the people to whom he had so recently been little less than a god. Thus ended what we now know to have been the Peloponnesian War of modern Europe.

Few Londoners, however, were in a mood that morning for abstract questions of national psychology or political science, and the scene was soon transformed into something reminiscent of the Roman Saturnalia. In the main streets wheeled traffic eventually became impossible, but before this was the case, taxis by the dozen carried excited patriots on their roofs up and down Piccadilly and the Strand, while east of Temple Bar the magnates of the City were dancing on the tables in the restaurants. By one o'clock it was only with the greatest difficulty that one could get a drink anywhere. As the afternoon progressed, the disorder grew worse, but the King and Queen received an ovation as they drove through the packed streets. Older people recalled Mafeking night. The lights were on again, and that in itself was an inducement to come into the streets. In Trafalgar Square a huge bonfire was started at the foot of the Nelson Column and was fed with the notice boards from the buses. An old gentleman asked a policeman the quickest way to Charing Cross Hospital. "Call for three cheers for the Kaiser," was the immediate reply. I went to the Savoy that evening, and the first thing I saw was a girl in evening dress being sick in the gutter in Savoy Court. Nobody minded or appeared to think it odd. Inside the hotel a number of young officers were trying to burn a German flag in spite of the protests of the management. As I was going home on the District Railway, a rather drunken workman got into the carriage and kept on repeating, "We've won the bloody war, but we'll lose the bloody peace: You see if we don't." *In vino veritas?*

For two or three nights the authorities very wisely tolerated a good deal of rowdyism, and then it was stopped; after that there was a reaction, and people began to wonder just what the victory really meant. There were some major excitements, such as the surrender of the German Fleet, which I should have witnessed but for an inopportune attack of measles, the visit to London of Foch and Clemenceau, and one or two minor events, such as a general election, in which, however, no one took much interest. The war was over, and the one desire of officers and men alike was to get back to civil life. Few stopped to realize that there was no magician's wand to put everything back where it had been in July, 1914, and the government, with slogans such as "A land fit for heroes to live in," did nothing to dispel the illusion that the golden age was at hand. No hint was ever dropped that the period of adjustment after the war was likely to be at least as difficult to win through as had been the war itself. People were definitely encouraged to believe that without any effort on their part all would soon be for the best in the best of all possible worlds.

The fact was that the government, both at home and abroad, was, as I have already suggested, as unprepared for peace in 1918 as it had been for war in 1914, and it was heartrending to see the rapid dissipation of all those centrifugal forces that had contributed so much to the winning of the war. In their place grew up a spirit of envy and malice, an attitude of every man for himself, which boded ill for the future and which characterized every class of the community. . . . But that is another story, and the spring of 1919 saw me back at my studies at Corpus Christi College, Oxford.

Awakening

Henri Massis

HENRI MASSIS *has written some of the most significant works of our time and received many honors, including the* Grand Prix de Littérature *of the* Académie Française *in 1929 and the* Grand Prix Osiris *in 1966. Born in Paris on March 21, 1886, he entered the Condorcet Lyceum where, in 1903, he studied philosophy for a year in the class of Alain-Fournier, who, like André Maurois, inspired him. Later he prepared for his degree at the Sorbonne.*

During the years 1905–7 Massis frequented the home of Anatole France, to whom he dedicated Le Puits de Pyrrhon. *Then he fell under the influence of Maurice Barrès, who "properly engendered spirit into life." He was also influenced by Henri Bergson, under whom he studied at the Collège de France. The grandson of Renan, Ernest Psichari (1883–1914), who was killed in World War I, was for Massis a companion and a guide in spiritual growth.*

Having gone through a period of religious doubt and searching, Massis returned to the Roman Catholic faith in May, 1913, striving through his writing to illuminate the mind by faith. He had already begun to publish his critical essays on Renan, on France, on Gide, when World War I broke out. He joined the 152 Infantry Regiment.

In May, 1923, Massis published the first volume of his Jugements *(on Renan, France, Barrès), dedicated to Jacques Maritain "in testimony of their common hope in the metaphysical restoration." In January, 1924, he brought out the second series of* Jugements *(on André Gide, Romain Rolland, Georges Duhamel, Julien Benda, etc.)*

Massis published in 1941 at Lyon Les Idées restent, *wherein he reassembled his ideas on art, literature, morals, politics, and history, not as an anthology, but as a summary of the essential realities of which his work is a defense and an illustration.*

In 1948 a definitive edition of his essays was published: D'André Gide à Marcel Proust. *The following year he wrote* L'Allemagne d'hier et d'après-demain. *In 1951 he published* Charles Maurras et notre temps, *wherein an epoch is relived around a great figure. His whole life, he felt, was a preparation for* De l'Homme à Dieu *(1959). In the period between these two he wrote* L'Occident et son destin, Visages des Idées, *and* L'Europe en question.

Elected to the Académie Française on May 19, 1960, Massis published in

1962 Barrès et nous, *followed by an edited correspondence. In 1967 he wrote* Au long d'une vie, *in which he traces the various stages of his spiritual journey.*

THE WAR WE FOUGHT*

—◆—

I COULD NOT give a historic opinion on the war of 1914–18 in the evening of my life. For me, the whole war is contained in a corner of land and a few hours, hours and land like all the others where the living and the dead stand together, and nothing seems to me more suited to evoking that war than the notes I scribbled in the trenches. Better than general observations, they seem to my mind to give an image of the event as a lived truth and, by their power of applying generally, to show the thoughts that moved us then. I transcribe them without any changes.

January 8, 1915. It will be six days tomorrow that the 3d Battalion has quartered at Noeux-les-Mines. A short breather, a bit of rest when in the movement of an almost ordinary life the will relaxes, yields to former habits, when the mind lingers on what we have just suffered and lived through. . . .

All the men drift into similar thoughts. I know just what they are saying in those letters the post orderly will carry off this evening; these long letters written in camp are less strained than the cards written in pencil the other week in the front lines; the courage they show will be no less steadfast, but there is a break, and perhaps a few weary words will slip out, the weariness that makes us seek distractions and pleasure in the moment. . . .

How dismal the last days of the year were! Yes, for weeks, though death is always on the prowl, invisible, permanent, wandering in all directions, though it never gives us respite, we have had a kind of tranquillity. Anyhow, what action could we attempt in this mud that coats our burdened troops with clay, that makes the ground treacherous, this ground churned by shells, sown with blood, and

---

* Translated from the French by Sally Abeles.

that increases the anguish of the nights in which we move toward our lairs like blind shadows?

Oh, those cold December nights, when we huddled in our disgusting ditches, phantoms with cheeks as dark as bark, in the great black silence, deeper yet from being pierced with solitary spaced shots. . . .

. . . Well, there is the secret of our weariness: we are not yet up to this war which makes a man disown himself in going to ground, which makes courage useless, which makes heroism seem to be nothing anymore, unless it has changed from an exalted state into a steady and humble attitude.

But the war seems to us to be first a dreadful resignation, a renunciation, a humiliation; there is no place for pleasurable sensation in it, and you don't understand immediately the grandeur of the beauty of the asceticism it forces on us, of the punishment it lays on the fighting man. . . .

If for a few days, shaking off the coat of mud our last retreat to the trenches has covered us with, we want gentler human pleasures, it is because after four months we have not yet relinquished our will to act. You feel the same impatience among the men, among our officers; this is the source of their melancholy and weariness. We had to be put in our soil to defend it, but the hour is still far away when our feet will sound on the ground, when it will become hard like a road again. . . .

In this village, where our troops are staying to rest, we are learning to live again.

Tranquillity for a few hours; momentary, but in war never total numbness. You drink, you read, you sing; everybody seeks out his pleasure, takes refuge in what consoles him for the moment, but with a weird sense of discomfiture and as if it were forbidden! The soul does not demobilize at all, and in this instant of abandon, it always has this sober vision present, this tragic vision of the reality which tomorrow will perhaps lead it back to. . . . A presence you expect a sign from. . . .

Also, in this diversion, it keeps alive a murmur of the talk passing around: "It looks as if we'll attack around the fifteenth. . . ." "No, we'll be in the second line, and we won't do anything before spring."

Alternating fears, hopes, with everyone trying to find out what is going to happen. . . .

January 9. By what mysterious signal are all our men crowding into this exact church in Bouvigny where a mass was said for our battalion? . . . Do they know that for many of us this will be the last Sunday and the last blessing?

Their fervor in praying, a virile, military fervor, has something about it that grips the heart. In this meditative silence, they feel that the coming week will not be a waste, that things will come out, and they are thinking about it already: The priest and the soldier bow before the sacrifice. They have regained confidence and gravity, which you feel in the fever of the preparations; you eat hastily, you get ready, the companies assemble, and the dark column of footsoldiers advances through the villages, collected and cheerful.

January 10. Our company has laid up at Marles; the others have left for the rear area. We will go on up day after tomorrow; two days there, in the Bouvigny woods; two days, here again, quartered on alert, at Ditch 3; then two more days in the trenches, and we return to Hersin-Coupigny, which draws us with the memory of peaceful hours.

Those are the orders: So this week, too, will pass without incident, dreary, muddy, indifferent, just like the others. Come now, let's learn to endure these rough winter quarters! . . .

By the light of a candle this evening in the devastated trench, Ducollet[1] read to several of us comrades from a comedy by Musset. And we didn't get back to our barn until midnight. How lovely the night is, and how sweet life! . . . We carry back *Fantasio*'s dreams, and they are killing each other 800 meters away, behind the black hill. . . .

January 12. A day of waiting. This morning an inspection of the men, equipment, and arms. Barracks work. At noon a liaison officer comes bringing orders. All companies fall in; we are shifting sectors. We are going to relieve the 21st Infantry at Ablain-St.-Nazaire, where our battalion fought before, in November. So sudden a decision, the puzzlement over such a decision and the memory among the veterans of recent engagements suddenly bring down a slightly weary quiet, in which we slide away.

Five o'clock. . . . In column by twos, we leave. . . . Our whole being is mobilized within, and the sober file, silent, enters the dark, damp communication trenches. Stray bullets whistle over our heads: orders are passed *sotto voce* that everyone repeats to himself. We step in one another's footprints, so acute is our fear of getting lost. Then, jumping a mud-filled ditch, where many fall and sink in

---

[1] A young Comédie Française actor. (The play was Alfred de Musset's *Fantasio*. —Tr.)

up to the neck, we are in the open, on the flank of a hill. A sergeant from the 21st serves as our guide: movements and muffled voices. . . . We go into the unknown, lurching, anxious. Over there, impatient with another impatience, those we will relieve are waiting. . . .

Finally, here is the trench we are to occupy: a commonplace hummock, but its intertwined pattern of communicating trenches and paths make it a secret thing, a labyrinth full of mystery and danger. It must be reconnoitered, men must be placed. . . . Several times before dawn, we move through this black and sticky path inhabited by shadows. . . .

The sentries have taken their places in the lookout posts; behind them their comrades, crouching and curled up, sink into the embankment like vines and blend with it. And around us, the ghastly night: The shots pace the anguished hours; there is the poignant melancholy of those nights in which death lives; the heart stays suspended in terror; dreams grow feverish when overtired limbs do not bring sleep to these stiff, heaped bodies. . . .

But day breaks, reviving all these phantoms, and restores confidence. You can see before you. . . . *They* are there, 15 meters away, behind that fringe of roiled land. And for two days the eyes will be riveted, hypnotized, on that knoll, that fold of ground, that curve of landscape, that ridge, that clump of trees, that short stretch of horizon which will be the last view of the earth for some. . . .

All day there is clumsy stirring about in this scruffy ditch; the air is wet and cold. They are firing, on this side and the other. . . . Some bombs loosen the dirt of the parapet. They pack it back. . . . Soldiers without pleasure in warring, they wait. For what? Nothing and everything, for death can bury them here during this desolate assignment, without their testing their strength against it; death is as if oblivious, mindless. It does not even want their courage, at least what used to be meant by courage, for in this war it demands a harder virtue: It wants to be waited for, at every hour, with patience. It is not at all the adventure of a heroic moment, the exalted passage of the hero into eternity, the sublime vocation of the warrior. It is less solemn: It takes whom it will, when it will, in the most humble posture, always imposing its ceaseless presence, requiring us to be always ready. . . .

This is how it went after you at the front, innocent child whom we laid in a corner of our mud prison at the end of this sad and useless day. You hadn't ever seen the enemy yet: You made your bloody sacrifice in ignorance, and it is not less beautiful. . . .

Grieved by this death, which made our inactivity lie heavy, we saw night fall again. . . . Yet another day just like this one; then others will replace us here, and we will lay down, for a few hours, this anguish that cleaves the soul like a sword.

January 13. This evening we will be relieved. . . . Everybody is waiting for this as for a deliverance. We are dogged by fatigue, insomnia; it is cold. . . . The hours pass, and always that fold of earth, that curve of landscape, that ridge, motionless but concealing such tragic, invisible life.

We will never again be able to contemplate the French country-side without peopling it with these bloody realities. Behind its vistas, so delightful, so similar, we will put the abundant tombs of our actions, which will give it a deeper beauty from dawn to dark, and the stack of perishable sheafs, which will rise where we have bled, will produce the imperishable bread of memory. . . .

More firing. . . . Nothing happens. It is four o'clock. More than two hours. In our command post, Knoertzer, Meunier, and I are reading Stendhal's *Rouge*[2] to one another. . . . The liaison officer brings letters and an order for Lieutenant Knoertzer.

"The company commander wants me," he tells us. "I'll be back for the relief."

A half hour later he returns, his face set, and the seriousness of our young chief makes us shiver before he has said a word. We are alone. . . .

"Well, here it is," he tells us. "We attack tomorrow evening at six o'clock. Our mission is to take the two lines of German trenches in front of us—the first one fifteen meters away; the second twenty meters behind it. Two platoons will charge the trench facing ours with bayonets; a platoon of First Company will rake the second line, while the platoon now at the far end of our trench will give us fire cover on the left.

"We will be supported by seventy-fives and nineties, which will prevent the formation of reinforcements in the village of Ablain. So that's it; I'm telling you, but I won't notify the men till tomorrow, a couple of hours before the attack. . . ."

Deep silence in the narrow hut, lighted by a meager candle set on the cross section of a bayonet. We looked at one another worriedly, saying nothing, but we saw into the depths of one another's breath-less souls; you could have heard our heartbeats, and if we did not speak, it was so they would not make our voices tremble.

---

2 The nineteenth-century novel *Le Rouge et le noir* (*The Red and the Black*).
—Tr.

"God doesn't give courage, he only lends it," said D'Aubigné,[3] and after this admission by the great captain, who would hesitate to say that he shook before danger for a moment? It is true: For several minutes my body was shaken by a violent trembling in spite of me. What did my two companions feel? I do not know, but I know that all three of us judged this attack so perilous that we were certain it would bring us death. The Germans 15 meters away—we would be slaughtered as we left the trench. . . .

This certainty agitated in us during the long night as side by side we tried to sleep—a savage night like a hallucination, when our willpower flagged with our fatigue and we did not know whether it was the cold or horror that shook us—and this delay the action gave us aggravated the instinctive agitation of our being.

As we get up, as we escape from these nightmares that roll out all our past life, we say to one another almost joyfully, "It's eight o'clock; it'll all be over in ten hours! We've got to get ready, study this attack a little." We sketch out the positions on a piece of paper and comment on the order given the day before. The same certainty still possesses us, is even augmented by the study we are making. But it is no longer a question of us, and this necessity we have to get out of ourselves frees us of anguish.

We summon the platoon leaders to our command post right away; we explain the maneuver, the orders to them. Quietly we assure them of success—"We've got to succeed"—and now our whole being inspires confidence. . . . In a while, when they leave, we will destroy our private papers and make our final arrangements with the same interior peacefulness. Each of us draws up letters for his people that seem written from the same dictation:

"We are going into attack this evening at six o'clock; it'll be a particularly rough business. If these words come to you, it will be because I will have fallen. . . ."

"Still, it's hard," says Knoertzer in a low voice. . . .

A final moment of weakness, a final look cast behind, regrets suppressed that already have a note of resolution about them. . . .

We eat; you have to eat. . . .

Noon. Let's go notify our men. . . . We move out into the trench. The men, dazed with fatigue and hoping to hear the order to fall back for rest, accept the one to attack without flinching; a light glimmers in the eyes of these groups in clay, living sculptures carved from the narrow trench. We comment on the coming attack

---

3 Théodore Agrippa d'Aubigné, 1552–1630, a writer and companion in arms of Henri IV.—Tr.

to almost every one of them, for our men like to know what they are doing; they ask for details; we give them to them. . . .

Now they know; they get to work. With their shovels they make grooves in the outer wall, prepare steps to use for leaping out of the furrow. . . . A single will drives them; then they exchange hasty confidences, similar promises. Some embrace. . . .

A magnificent moment when man puts his trust in man, gives himself simply; incomparable human friendship, communion whose memory will light our souls until death. And in this warmth they work, clean their guns, load them, adjust their bayonets. . . . We tend to the final preparations.

Some who know that Lieutenant Meunier is a priest go to confession to him; hastily he gives absolution. Besides, it will be given to the whole company before it moves to the assault, and the great divine mystery of war passes over us, the superhuman reality for which our feeble explanations fail, the inconceivable sacrament that we will receive in a while in the frenzy of battle. . . .

Five o'clock. Night is coming. A feverish muffled murmur runs through the whole trench. Here comes Sergeant Vanier's platoon. Explanations exchanged in low voices; then the stretcher-bearers, who are put in the rear communication trench. . . . Deep silence over the countryside, where a thick, cold fog is falling; occasional gunshots. . . . Our men are no longer firing. . . .

A few minutes to go. . . . We wait for the signal from the chief. . . . Your whole being is miraculously calm; nothing except a hot forehead. . . . Lieutenant Knoertzer is to our left; I am beside him with the liaison officer. A smothered voice: "Ask Lieutenant Meunier if he is ready. . . . Pass it on. . . ."

And you hear the question pass from mouth to mouth, then fade away. . . . But before the reply comes back to us, the black cyclone of the artillery soughs overhead. . . . An instant of hesitation, during which it seems to us that a battle is already raging beyond the impenetrable horizon.

Spurred suddenly by a mad force, we leap into the night. . . . All of a sudden a flare bursts in an ashen green glare, weird, fantastic, and we jerk about in it like outsize shadows. . . . Around us the heavy boom of the 90's sounding like a bass to the inexorable song of the 75's, and distinct from them the stuttering of the machine guns; over there, the night crisscrossed with flashes. . . . Is it this sight that holds us poised, immobile, a step away from the German trench, or astonishment at being there alive?

"Advance, advance, damn it!" Knoertzer howls. "Jump, we've got 'em. . . ."

Is it possible? We *have* their first line: A few shots, and they've run. . . . We fling ourselves into the communication trench leading to the second line, which Sergeant Gérard's platoon has already occupied. We shout wildly, *"Victory! Victory!"* It's the rallying cry.

Exhausted, Knoertzer shouts his orders. We call out to one another; we run in all directions; we find them in their huts, hands up, pale, trembling, crying, *"Kamerad! Kamerad! . . ."* More than 20,000 prisoners are evacuated to the rear. . . . Salvos in the air: It's over! . . . We have possession of the area.

On the opposite ridge the infantrymen have come out of their trench, and under the livid glow of the sky we see their shadows hailing us. "Joy, joy, tears of joy." This is the same kind of mystical illumination. . . . To have been able to live to taste such a joy is enough to make you faint with happiness. . . . How magnificent it is! How magnificent! . . . Our group leads a strange saraband in the night. Mighty shouts resound with the rhythm of a chant: "Bravo! Victory!" . . .

A beautiful night, with the beauty of a festival. . . . The last shots cast their red light. . . . The din of the artillery stops suddenly; the sky turns black again.

Midnight. We expect the enemy to counterattack at daybreak. Can 2d Company, exhausted from lack of sleep and hunger, shattered by the emotions of this fight, make this new effort? The company commander doesn't think so: he will have it relieved in an hour. Only the platoon leaders will stay. . . . More than a few minutes. . . . Muffled steps, much stirring of shadows returning to our old line. Crossing it, my foot is fractured. . . .

Hardly have we left the area taken the evening before than the enemy crosses the way in the sooty dawn, then deploys suddenly, reoccupies his original position, throws back into their trench those of our men who haven't yet got there. . . . A platoon from 4th Company has already replaced the 2d and is there. . . .

At only eight in the morning, Lieutenant Knoertzer receives the order to report to Commander Mademin's H.Q. "For the honor of the 3d Battalion," they've decided to launch a new attack. . . . It will begin at noon. . . .

Our men have barely got a leg over the parapet before a machine-gun fusillade drops them in a line on the lip of the trench. . . . Knoertzer, who is leading them, falls, hit in the hand. I hoist myself to him, drag him by his overcoat to get him back to our lines. . . . Then I'm conscious of nothing anymore. . . . The attack is broken. . . . It's over. . . .

Knoertzer and I make it to the rear, through the lateral connecting trench filled with dredging mud, in which we push along flat on our bellies. . . . The two of us are alone, groping our way, our straining bodies sinking into the oozing ground. . . . The sheer effort of pulling ourselves free of its suction. . . . I claw the slippery sides of the ditch we are submerged in. . . . My coat has turned to clay. . . . I can no longer lift my feet, a chunk of muck imbedded in the viscous slime. . . .

Evening is falling already. . . . Solitary spaced shots ricochet through the copse we are trying to reach, cutting branches. . . . An exploding shell wounds me in my left hand, and I fall again, my head in the mud, to drag along again on my belly. . . . Knoertzer is still in front of me; I grab his arm, which stiffens and sags with an exhausted movement. . . . Where do all these detours lead? Which is the way out? What is in front of us? To the right, the left? It seems as though there is nothing anymore. . . .

The farther we get from danger, the more we are overtaken by an unutterable dread. . . . Night is falling. . . . Are we making any headway? We feel as though we haven't gained an inch. . . . Ah, there, behind that knoll covered with a clump of trees, we glimpse something. . . . Yes, we're approaching the H.Q. . . . But here's the battalion ambulance looking for us. They take us out and lift us into a transport, on stretchers. . . . And suddenly I hear, "Are you there, fellow? Are you there?" A fraternal voice has come through the dimness. . . . Drouot, my dear Drouot! Before I can take the hand he is holding out to me, the ambulance has departed into the night. . . . Will I ever see him again?[4]

January 17. Here I am in the hospital in Tours on the Rue Descartes, with the Sisters of Perpetual Adoration; I was evacuated from the front and brought here. . . .

I spend part of my days rereading the notes I wrote up there, and what strikes me is the nature of this war, which is asking a man for

---

4 Paul Drouot, who would have been one of the great poets of his generation, was killed on June 9, 1915. Before leaving on August 2, 1914, Drouot wrote this will: "I do not want to leave a trace. Everything is useless here below, you see, everything except the soul. . . . I leave nothing that is worthy of publication. I ask that all my papers, notes, drafts, beginnings of poems or isolated verses be destroyed—which will hardly change them. A work must be finished. I thank those who have so indulgently given me credit on the appearances. I would have liked to prove them right sometime. A thousand concerns have prevented me till now, and at the present hour, nothing is important anymore except great issues, the country's, the soul's. We have to go off on crusade, the mind free of vanity and the heart wholly devoted to its business of being a heart. I wouldn't want to mouth phrases. I embrace my two masters, Élémir Bourges, the great poet of *"La Nef,"* and Henri de Régnier. I pray my friends, if I do not see them again in this world, to lift their minds to God when the memory of me touches them. My trust is henceforth in Him."

virtues that no army in any period has required. No tangible satisfaction: Everything about it is done within, in the ground, in a man. The whole of a man is involved in it, not only the conqueror or the businessman, the man fighting for domination or gain; it is a man in his entirety who is taking up his country's cause, it goes without saying, since it is with all his soul and all that has formed it for him. But in return a man expects the renewal of his soul from it, a means to an inner perfecting. This is the unexpected thing. Never had these spiritual elements been incorporated into war to the point of dominating it. Never had men heard a like call to moral notions to live this event. Never had the fighter's feelings reached such a depth. . . .

I remember something one of my men said in my hearing as we went to the trenches: "We are all here for misery." A sublime acceptance, a recognition of a necessity deeper than any other. This man gave misery the right to exist; he experienced it in his exact understanding of what it demands and consented to everything. A dedicated victim, he knew that the hour had come to carry the whole weight of human suffering, without tiring, without giving way. Whether he chooses the pick that digs up the soil or the shovel that throws it aside, everyone hollows out his grave. Then what can be the hope that lifts the eyes above the furrow choked with human wreckage? If he assents, it is because he feels obscurely that when the end comes, all suffering is fulfilled in glory and salvation, and that "All suffering which serves a purpose, all suffering which can serve a purpose, is the daughter of the suffering of God." This is a kind of grace, the outpouring of a faithful heart that suffers in silence.

But out of the depths of its silence a voice rises from this Army dripping with its native earth. And it is the voice of its eternal vocation, which Paul Claudel makes us hear in his *"Nuit de Noël de 1914"* (Christmas Night, 1914) ; I read this page of it yesterday to my comrades in the hospital:

What we are defending with our wealth, with the acre in which our right and our destiny vest, what we are defending is God Himself who has put Himself in our keeping, is that decent place in our heart where He is, is the infinitely weak all-powerful, is that lowly breath in our heart that has made us all upright!

It is God we are defending, even those who do not know His name. For each people is born for itself, but France has been born for the whole universe, in order to bring it joy!

It is not only her body she is defending, it is her soul, which belongs to the whole universe; it is not only her life she is defending, it is the word of God to the whole universe, which is eternal joy, in eternal freedom.

This is what we believed.

Even now, in the evening of our life, how deep is the echo of the cry that Georges Bernanos flung us from the heart of that past, ten years after the war of 1914–18: "Old friends of the heights battered by the wind, companions of raging nights, solid band, inflexible band . . . who one day took the burning spurt of the enemy's artery and all his heart's blood full in the face, oh, boys! November 11 we drank the last cup from our vines. November 11 we broke the black bread baked for us."

Yes, the war was the home of our youth. We were born of the war, the war was immediately upon us, and in truth we have never done anything else. . . . After an armistice of some years, war led us back up there, to those regions we never departed, which guard our deepest secrets, where we have left our souls with the bodies of our friends. Twenty years it had not stopped holding us under its law, for the most serious, the most decisive of wars is perhaps the one fought when we are no longer battling one another. It has left us with "such a wrinkle of hurt at the corners of the mouth" that death alone can relax that line marking our faces. But it has also given us Hope, a Hope that has consumed us ever since, a Hope that itself is invincible, even in death. Yes, "the divine gaze rested on us," that gaze "so steady, so tender" which still stirred Bernanos when, in 1919, returning from the war, that war we withstood, were really able to withstand, he said: "In that sheath of instincts, of acquired or hereditary habits, in the flesh and the blood, something has awakened, has moved once and for all, irreversibly. It is done. We can no longer be mistaken about ourselves now. We must make ourselves free or die!"

The war would never cease to mark our work and our days.

L. Wyn Griffith

"I was born in 1890, the eldest son of a village schoolmaster in Wales. Some years later, married and with three children, my father scraped his way through University college, Bangor, took an honors degree, and for many years was headmaster of Dolgellau Grammar School. There, after years in village schools, I was educated until I was nineteen, when I entered the civil service as an assistant surveyor of taxes. In 1914 I enlisted in the Royal Welch Fusiliers and went to France in 1915 as an infantry captain, became a staff officer, and was demobilized in 1919. I was married in 1915, and my eldest son was killed in action in 1942.

"For me, writing has always been a spare-time activity, shared with serving on committees concerned with Wales and with the arts. Most of my books deal with Wales, two of them novels, one a war book, Up to Mametz, one an account of my childhood called Spring of Youth, the others being various attempts to interpret the life of my country to those who cannot speak its language. I was privileged to spend eleven years as vice-chairman of the Arts Council of Great Britain, after being chairman of its Welsh Committee. I have been broadcasting regularly, in Welsh and in English, for more than thirty years, and I am a vice-president of the London Center of P.E.N., chairman of the Council of the Honourable Society of Cymmrodorion, a Welsh society now in its third century. I have never been at a loss for something to do and have enjoyed doing it."

THE PATTERN OF
ONE MAN'S REMEMBERING

Reach back to years I spent, to men I knew,
to days I drank each minute dry,
give tongue to want: I must not die
mere wisdom-bound because the hurt
grew great and this my loss is loss of men.

Reach hand to touch rough-coated arm,
let none dismiss with pity grief
this company of ghosts about my heart,
they were my youth, the sorrow mine.
I bought this peace but paid no price
so great as theirs.

I HAVE QUOTED the beginning of a long poem about the war that I
wrote twenty years after it ended, for several reasons, none of which
is concerned with its merits or demerits as verse. It would have
extended the powers of a great poet to measure up to the greatness
of the occasion and the intention, and such powers were never
mine. Nevertheless, it expresses something I had never succeeded in
putting into prose, although I had written a book about the war
that was well received by the generation involved in it.

The processes, emotional and intellectual, attached to a concern
about reliving and rethinking so tremendous an event in the life of
an individual are not without interest, and if I recall them, it is
because they may not be familiar to many and because, fifty years
later, it is possible to do so with detachment.

When war broke out in 1914, I was twenty-four years old,
employed in the service of the government, and forbidden to join
the armed forces because the work on which I was engaged was
considered important. Flattering, you might think. But no: I was a
Welshman, and my contemporaries were enlisting in the Royal
Welch Fusiliers. They were escaping from offices, shops, farms, and
factories, from the humdrum duties of civilian life to which I was
condemned. I cannot remember that I ever thought of soldiering as
anything but a better way of life than sitting at a desk: Killing or

being killed was something that might happen to someone else. None of my contemporaries thought that there was anything "noble" about joining the armed forces. It was what your friends were doing, and it was only natural that you should do the same, if you could. By devious ways, I succeeded in joining them and became a mere "number" clad in uniform—became in fact, uniform, undistinguishable, responsible for nothing more than obeying orders and keeping clean and tidy myself and an obsolete weapon.

This is what happened to many millions of men in many countries. But if, as I do, you belong to a small nation, with its own language, Welsh, surrounded by a large nation speaking English, you enter into a double life. English is the language of the Army, Welsh the language of friendship and companionship, "ours" against "theirs." There is, inside you, a citadel which cannot be stormed by force, but which can be entered with the key of language. And when you find yourself in the company of your fellow countrymen, private soldiers with a private language with which to escape from this new world of drill and parade and discipline, a language belonging exclusively to a way of life in which you were nurtured and from which you are now exiled, companionship brings a new kind of intimacy. A new bond is created, a sense of being a community within a community, which intensifies the very meaning of comradeship.

I was in the Army for four and a half years, three of them on active service in France as an infantry officer, a company commander, and finally as a general staff officer on what was called Operations (to distinguish it from Intelligence!), so that I had to undergo a number of transformations of body and mind. This involved a series of apprenticeships, and now, fifty years later, I can recognize a succession of events that remain in my memory and bring with them a resurgence of emotions, pleasant and unpleasant, associated with learning the various trades.

Associated also with another kind of adjustment, I have referred to the dichotomy brought about by this matter of language, of living in Welsh and in English. My regiment, the Royal Welch Fusiliers, consisted mostly of Welsh-speaking Welshmen whose background was similar to my own. In Welsh, we could talk freely, officers and men alike and with each other, without impinging in any way on matters of military protocol that seemed to belong exclusively to the world of English. This created a bond of unity, that sense of being an enclave within a community. This was the regiment in which Robert Graves, Siegfried Sassoon, David Jones, and Frank Richards served, authors of the best of the war books. But they did not speak Welsh, and so there was a world into which they could not enter. This does not detract from the value of their books, but it impoverished them at the time. And now, for me, it complicates this matter of "remembering," bringing in a range of emotions that do not depend on the hazards of war for their potency. Though I write in English, I have only to think or speak in Welsh, and they spring to life. These "men I knew" were of my own kin because we spoke the same language, the one we had inherited, not the one we used as we learned our trade of soldiering.

Let me give an instance of what I mean. The scene is the canal bank near Ypres, on a dark winter night in 1916: some desultory shelling, an occasional rattle of machine-gun fire, a Very light shooting up into the blackness and falling to make it even darker. A company waiting to go up into the trenches on relief, waiting, "always bloody well waiting," for the order to move up the communication trenches to the front line. They start singing, in harmony, being Welsh, a fine old Welsh hymn tune in a minor key. The brigadier general asks me, "Why do they always sing these mournful hymns? Most depressing—bad for morale. Why can't they sing something cheerful, like the other battalions?"

I try to explain to him that what they are singing now is what they sang as children, as I did, in chapel, in the world to which they really belong. They are being themselves, not men in uniform. They are back at home, with their families, in their villages. But he does not understand. Nor can he, with his background. I do not think I "understand" it myself; but the facts were there, and they still are. While they sang, they, and I, were in another country.

There have been, and there will be, other wars, and men will sit down to remember them and to write about them. It would be foolish to try to generalize about the way in which they will do so, but it is at least possible and permissible for one writer to recount the various processes of remembering that time brought with it and the different impulses which he experienced at successive periods and how all this took shape in the written word.

Back, then, to 1919 when I was demobilized and went back to my wife and my job and to an orgy of reading, making up for lost time. The cares and the pleasures of living drove away all thoughts of war. I did not dream about it. It was something that had happened to someone else. I had a house and a garden, and the business of life was to grow children and to succeed in my work. My colleagues in the office had not been allowed to join the forces, and I rarely met any fellow soldiers. I was living in England, away from my countrymen, out of contact with men who spoke my own language. This was a new life, unrelated to the past.

Some two or three years later, I made a brief record of my share of the war, a mere account of events, some 1,500 words in all, because I thought it might interest my sons when they grew up. I put it in a drawer and forgot all about it. It was quite impersonal, and as I had not kept a proper diary, it all came from what I can only call the top layer of my memory: a mere chronology, and incomplete at that. It has now disappeared, and no one is any the poorer for its loss.

However, some three years later, in one of those domestic upheavals called spring cleaning, it came out of a pile of papers, and I sat down to read it. I can still remember the shock I received, saying to myself, "Well, if this is all you can say about the biggest experience of your life, of years of hazardous living, it would be better to say nothing than to be proved incapable of writing an account of it." So I tore it up. However, the matter would not rest there, for there was an implied challenge, and inside me there seemed to be an upsurge of remembering that brought back the war that I thought I had overlaid with the day-to-day business of living.

I accepted the challenge, and set out to put on paper all I felt and saw and did on one day in February, 1916, when I was in the trenches opposite Givenchy in Flanders. It was an unpleasant occasion, and I began to relive the days and nights that followed, in all their terror and discomfort, with the stench of mud and chloride of lime and the smell of bacon frying on a mess-tin lid in the early morning. I can only call it a kind of emotional explosion inside me, and under its impetus I wrote on and on until I came toward a kind of climax, the Battle of Mametz Wood in July, 1916, where so many of my countrymen, including my own brother, were killed. There I stopped, because I was afraid of my own memories and dreaded their coming to life. So I turned back and wrote about the way from Winchester to Givenchy, so as to give some shape to the account. I found that I had given some kind of picture of the war as I had seen it, and in doing so, I had become accustomed, even reconciled, to remembering. My sons might even learn something about me, as well as about the war. I had no thought that anyone else would share this knowledge.

But the challenge was still there, in Mametz Wood, and I found that there was no peace within me until I had faced and recorded this high point of the war where for me and so many other Welshmen the tragedy reached its culmination. The words had to be torn out of me, hurt as it must. The events are mere history, to be found in many books, but my own reactions, as I recorded them, turned remembering into a surgical operation. And, as happens with the body, there came afterward a kind of peace within. I had spent my emotional capital, in this detailed recovery of what I thought to have been buried beneath years of happiness, and I was left in what I can only call a neutral state. This kind of remembering had done its work, and I was purged of the pain of war, untroubled, confident that I had nothing more to fear from its recurrence in the years ahead.

But the mind has its own timetable in these matters, and later on, looking back on what I had written, I found that though I had had some measure of success in recording what I felt and did and saw during a period of six months in the trenches, it had become a minor fragment of written history. The thoughts and emotions that went into the making of it were now no longer those of the living author. There was a change in the nature of day-to-day remembering, a fusion between the event and wisdom-after-the-event, an impulse to achieve something more general in character. Something that might, perhaps, if it succeeded, reflect what was universal in an experience that was personal. And here, I now can see, I became once more the inheritor of generations of Welsh peasants who had been conditioned by years of long sermons, of Sunday school, of moralizing, of life in a community where there was a "lesson to be learnt" from even the most insignificant of daily happenings. This belongs to a world that has now vanished, but it was relevant at the time, and certainly potent in 1914, so that it was not irrelevant in the 1930's when one was thinking about the war.

And so it came about that the next phase of remembering was harnessed to a search for something I had failed to say in prose. If I could find it, it could be true of others besides myself. The upshot took the form of a long poem in blank verse. It was not a good poem, because I was not a good poet, but the discipline of writing it compelled a sharpening of the mind, a concentration of thought, a paring down of vague emotions, and a sharpening of their expression, as well as an attempt to expand the particular into the general. In one sense, it was an effort at greater objectivity: Memories of sheer delight, of undiluted pleasure, forced themselves into it. Long days of marching in the autumn through all the colors of the woodlands in the Vale of Severn as well as long nights of standing in the mud of the trenches, a feather bed in a billet, as well as a duckboard on the fire step in the front line.

This was a move toward a greater honesty, but it was only partly successful. There was more self-pity in it than pity, and overelaboration of the obvious emotional response. Its importance to me lay in the fact that this indulgence in remembering began a process that continued over the years, a kind of dehydration of sentiment, bringing about at the same time a growth of anger, as well as a tendency to dwell on the happier memories. War has its joys and its agonies, and to think of it otherwise, in retrospect is to be dishonest. And anger, while it lasts, neutralizes sorrow.

The long poem—it was called "The Fading Years," and for its motto I wrote out the words and music of the old Welsh hymn tune sung on the canal bank at Ypres—had done its work for me, and that was the end of it. Some years later it was reborn, in a different shape, harsher in form, truer to its time and to the ears of a new generation; under the title " 'Tis Not the Song They Wish to Hear," it had a measure of currency, and it marked the end of all I wished to say about the war. Or so I thought. But in 1945 I was asked to write a program in verse to be broadcast to celebrate the end of another war, some of it to be spoken, some set to music, and I found that in it I was still remembering the 1914–18 war, the only war I knew. I can recall nothing of it except one line—"Great companies of men who answer not their names"—and two lines of a chorus sung by women:

> The world is waiting for the grace of love,
> And in our pity lies our power.

If these have stayed in my memory, it can only be because they epitomize two ways of responding to the phenomenon of war: of saying farewell to the sorrow that had lived with me for so long, for thirty years.

Since then the memories that come unbidden to the mind are of incidents that have not been recorded in any of the many books and histories, and they are pleasant ones. The others have evaporated and are no longer troublesome: They were part of the burden of another man, younger and perhaps better able to bear them.

We reached Mons the day after the Armistice and began to learn what the years of enemy occupation had meant to the ordinary men, women, and children of Belgium. As it drew toward Christmastime, General Godley (who went on to command the Army of the Rhine) called together his staff one morning and said, "We must do something for the children of this town. Some of them have never known a proper Christmas. How much money is there in the canteen fund?" Plenty, he was told. "We'll throw a children's party. Ask the mayor for the use of the town hall." Someone pointed out that you couldn't get all the children into it. "The party will last three days then. That ought to be enough. Send some lorries to Paris to get oranges and apples and toys, if there are any, and plenty of buns. We'll fill them up with buns and biscuits."

I do not know how many thousands of children of all ages and sizes came to the party or how often they came. Some of the smaller ones had never seen an orange before. They ate their buns at the party—they could not wait—and they took buns home with them. Nobody cried; they all looked starry-eyed in wonder at this profusion. And towering above them stood General Godley, six feet six inches in height, as happy as any child at the party.

Another unrecorded incident is still vivid in memory. It was April, 1918, at the height of the battle which was to determine the fate of the Channel ports, with the German thrust forward at its peak. General Godley was in command of some eight or nine divisions hurriedly sent to fill the gap and block the way. As a rule corps headquarters was some distance away from the scene of battle, for obvious reasons, the chief of which was the necessity of maintaining communication forward and back. There was no radio in those days. Godley said, "I can't fight a battle from here. Find me a signal office as far forward as you can." Eventually I found a signalers' dugout, well forward, but in contact with divisions and with the army headquarters so long as shelling did not cut the lines. Godley and his chief of staff, General Gwynn, came there with their maps and operation orders. There were two telephones, and my job was to listen to everything and keep a record. I was privileged to watch a general fighting a battle. It might have been the Napoleonic Wars. He moved brigades and battalions and batteries to meet the varying hazards and opportunities. And when it became apparent that the defense was assured and a signal came to say that the 2d French Cavalry Corps was coming to our aid, he said to me, "Go to meet them and tell them to stay where they are. There's no room for them."

I set off and met General Robillot, who commanded the corps. In my best French I tried to explain that the roads forward were so congested that it would be impossible for him to advance. He bridled and said they were cavalry and did not depend on roads. "But your transport and artillery do," I replied. He was forced to agree. I then asked him whether it was true that his corps had traveled all these miles in two days, that we could not believe it possible, that no one but the French could have done it. The butter did its work, I was asked to lunch, and the French corps stayed where it was.

An empty house in Bailleul in June, 1917, just before the Battle of Messines. I had been sent to the 2d Anzac Corps, as what was called a learner, an infantry captain who had been allowed to absorb some of the wisdom and experience of the staff at the headquarters of a brigade of infantry and who was more aware of his shortcomings than of his knowledge. The day after I got there, the general staff officer, third grade, was wounded on a visit to the front line. Contrary to general belief, junior staff officers were often in the front line. As I was on the spot, I was appointed to succeed him. I can think of no better reason. I put on my red tabs, very proudly, as soon as I could get them. When I went to that house in Bailleul where I was to join the mess, I heard a gramophone: The record was *En Bâteau*, by Debussy, the orchestral version. Suddenly I seemed to have come home; I was in my own country. And when David Liddell put on the next record, of the first two movements of Bach's *Concerto for Two Violins*, the war seemed to have ended. I was back in 1914. The third movement has always come as a surprise to me ever since. And as I listen to the concerto nowadays, I am back in 1917, in a small town in Flanders, with lorries and guns thundering over the *pavé* toward the opening stages of the Battle of Messines. But only for a moment. The music conquers the memory and lives on in its own right, as it should.

The flow of the years has eroded the power of response to the stimuli of fear, anger, sorrow that were once so potent. Events in retrospect have died into words on the printed page, incapable of producing anything but a "Yes, that was how it was" by way of reaction. No more dreams of being involved. And as it all recedes, almost beyond recall, it has become something impersonal, as remote as the Trojan War. The sorrow of losing comrades who did not survive the war has turned into the sorrow of losing those who did survive it and whom I have outlived.

This, then, is a record of the impact of the war upon my life after the Armistice, so far as it has been made manifest to me. I cannot say what the unrevealed effects are, what unnoticed modulations have taken place, and it may well be that these have proved more powerful than my attempted rational explanations of matters that are, after all, a blend of thought and feeling, difficult to bring within the net of words. The knowledge that the Somme and Passchendaele had more than decimated the youth of Wales, had almost destroyed a generation of my countrymen, may have brought me closer to my own country and helped to make me devote myself to playing a part in some kind of reconstruction of what we regarded as our national culture. But, on the other hand, it may only have been the pull of generations of my forebears. The strands are too closely knit for me to unravel, and all that matters is that it happened, and that it continues, with some measure of achievement.

I have reason to be grateful. I escaped physical hurt and financial loss, I emerged capable of dealing with daily life, fortified by the steadfast love of a wife who suffered torments of suspense for four years of war. My reward is that when I think of the war, the elements of fear, of real and imagined danger, of discomfort and of deprivation, of filth and of repulsiveness, of anger and hate, of contempt for the ignorance above which insisted on the continuance of Passchendaele have lost their strength. They have been overlaid by the memory of men I can no longer speak to, by the incidents of escape into short spells of life in a cottage overlooking the River Dee:

> Noon is a silence, dusk a candlelight
> On rough walls slanting.
> Heap wood upon the fire: no evil in this flame.
> Would I were done with all but love
> And in the morning grey smoke curling.

It must be one of the few rewards of growing old that fifty years have proved long enough to turn hate into acceptance. And that is the pattern of one man's remembering.

Montgomery Belgion

MONTGOMERY BELGION *was born in Paris of English parents in 1892. Thus, at the age of twenty-one, he had to exercise an option to be either French or British. He chose British. Paris is where he went to school, and he was still there when Europe went to war in August, 1914. During the early stages of World War I he was ill, but on being passed by the doctor, he went to London as a volunteer and in January, 1916, was elected to the Honourable Artillery Company, in which he became an infantryman and saw service in France in that same year. Invalided home, he was commissioned in the Dorsetshire Regiment and went to France again for the closing battles. He was at the front on Armistice Day. In World War II he again volunteered and became a captain in the Royal Engineers, Movement Control, part of the railways branch of the British Army. He was in France till June 1940. He was taken prisoner in Greece in 1941 and exchanged in 1944.*

For some years Mr. Belgion was a newspaperman. He has twice lived in New York. In 1921 and 1922 he was successively on the New York Daily News *and on the now extinct New York* World. *He has contributed to the* Sewanee Review, Southern Review, Hound and Horn, *the* Saturday Review, *etc. From 1925 to 1929 he was with Harcourt, Brace, publishers.*

His books cover a wide range: Our Present Philosophy of Life, The Human Parrot, News of the French, Reading for Profit, *and* Victors' Justice. *Awaiting publication is his* Megalopolitics, *and he is completing a book of memoirs. His* Reading for Profit *sold 100,000 copies and has been translated into French.*

In 1945 he married Gladys Helen Mattock, and they live in the country in England.

A REMINISCENCE AND
A MEDITATION

---◆---

I. THE REMINISCENCE

AT THE TIME THE SHOOTING, shelling, and bombing stopped in France in November, 1918, I commanded an infantry platoon in the 3d British Army (General Byng). We did not in that army march forward into Germany. The moment the Armistice was in force we were on our way to the neighborhood of the Channel coast. We were then far from being a battalion 1,000 strong. Some companies were commanded by subalterns, some platoons by sergeants. The sections were about half their proper number, the men barely adult and under the height of the peacetime regular footslogger. But before we set out to cross what were called the devastated regions, we were richly reinforced. Other ranks poured out from England—sleek, well-fed officers from the north of Ireland. With insufficient appreciation of the rot wrought in Germany by the blockade, the high-ups in London expected the war to go on into the spring of 1919, and they were husbanding their personnel so that it might last out that long despite front-line casualties. Our company commander, a Canadian lieutenant five feet high, handed us over to an upstanding, bridge-playing captain of distinctly higher social status.

The latter described to us Armistice Day in London. From Piccadilly Circus and the adjoining streets anything on wheels had been banished by the size of the delirious crowd. The beer and spirits merchants did a feverish trade. The verb "to maffick" came into its own again. Girls gave kisses to any man in khaki within sight. It was a great time. Out in France it had been different.

On the day before, Sunday, the tenth of November, in a village southeast of Maubeuge and almost in Belgium, I awoke to an unwonted quiet. We were in support. The front, if front there was still as the retreating enemy seemed to dissolve, was some distance ahead. The sun was shining. The day contrasted with the rain, noise, and confusion of the night before. We had been marching we did not know whither. In the rain the muddy *pavé* had to be disputed step by step with the vehicles and men coming the other way. Ahead of us was an occasional gun flash, but it hardly lit up the dead horses and mules that lined our road. A Gustave Doré would have been needed to do pictorial justice to the scene. Abruptly we were brought to a halt. The men were glad to fall out in the right-hand ditch and to slip off their equipment. The pause was just long enough for us to look forward to relaxing. We were fallen in facing the other way. We retraced our steps. We asked ourselves the idiotic question: Had we been brought forward by mistake? Soon we saw that we were being taken back only a short distance. We had taken the wrong turning, and now we had to go straight on, to the right instead of, as we had done, to the left. The rain stopped. We shambled on, and at last, still in the dark, we reached the village where I was to awake next morning. We were put into billets, the men in a barn and I on the tiled floor of a house. After our nightmarish march it was Eden.

That Sunday morning was still no respecter of persons. The senior subaltern of C Company was walking up the road that led forward out of the village when he was hit in the thigh by a shell splinter. Very likely he would lose his leg. I, too, went up that road, I forget why, but undisturbed. I came upon a solitary private half-sitting, half-crouching in his equipment on the verge close to the hedge. He seemed to be waiting and looked as lifelike as any figure in the waxworks. But, of course, he was dead. Later I passed him a second time, and now he was in his socks. His ammunition boots had vanished—no doubt into the thrifty possession of a French peasant. In his socks he figured death more strikingly than would a grinning skull.

We had no newspapers. Wireless was reserved for ships. Yet we knew that events were impending. I was in too great a suspense to keep still. The Canadian company commander I have already mentioned agreed that I might go off in the afternoon in search of news. I borrowed his horse and reached the outskirts of Berlaimont, aware of my unhappy seat. I failed to synchronize my own rise and fall with that of the animal that bore me. My good humor was unaffected. I felt that the news I wanted was only waiting to be learned. But when outside Berlaimont I sought out the divisional D.A.A.G., he was circumspect. All he would say was: "Tomorrow you will hear something of interest. Till then you'll have to wait." Such was the message I took back to my company commander. It was enough to fill me with a secret glee.

The little man suggested we should go to the movies. The marquee which exhibited them was in an adjoining field. When we came out, it was dark. We heard the unmistakable drone of an airplane. A couple of distant explosions followed. After our peaceful day the sound was intrusive. How appalling to be killed or wounded by a stray bomb splinter at this stage, I thought. But already the dark sky had regained its silence.

Next morning, sure enough, the D.A.A.G.'s promise was fulfilled. It was Monday, the eleventh of November, an unforgettable day in my life. Across the wide village street from my billet was the inn. It had an external balcony that ran the length of its front one floor above the ground. About nine o'clock we were fallen in by platoons and companies facing this balcony, and the colonel appeared on it and told us what I had been waiting to hear. At eleven—in under two hours—the Great War would be over. At last!

Compared with the relief and joy in my heart, our cheers sounded perfunctory. Our feelings were too deep for expression.

That day we did not march back any farther than Berlaimont. We were there by midday. On account of my familiarity with French, I was detached to find billets. How wonderful it was! No precautions need be taken against enemy hostility. For my own shelter I went to the *juge de paix*. He was elderly and dignified. He said he had had a German officer quartered upon him, who had behaved well. I could have his room. I said, "I expect you have a few bottles of wine buried in your garden. Perhaps you'll let me have one on such a day as this?" He agreed.

I brought the bottle to the company mess for dinner. I thought I should have to share it with three other officers. I found the company commander and a subaltern had excused themselves. I was left alone with a young man, who, when I offered him a glass of the wine, remarked, "I'd rather have a glass of sherbet." As soon as he had finished his meal, he left me with the bottle. It was a pleasant wine, not meant to be savored in solitude.

II. The Meditation

SUCH WAS my last day of World War I. Looking over its events across an interval of nearly half a century, I wonder how far it may be made to sum up the whole war—particularly for those to whom that war was, in the words of D. H. Lawrence, "tawdry and vain." I had never believed in the war. I did not believe that Germans were wicked. I did not believe that Germany had plotted the destruction of the West. I did not see why any Frenchman or Englishman should die or be irretrievably damaged so that a moribund Russia might a little longer simulate life and lay a palsied grip upon Constantinople. Above all, I was sure that Germans (who were nearly all strangers to me) were not really any different from Frenchmen (whom I knew well). Perhaps I was too young to realize the vital importance for Europe and Western civilization of a compromise peace, a negotiated peace, but I was already predisposed to such a solution. All that matters in a war is not victory, but escaping defeat.

I did not believe in the war, but nevertheless, I was a volunteer. I need never have donned uniform. I was living in Paris. For much of the early part of the war I was unfit. In about November, 1915, the doctor having now passed me, I went over to London and tried to persuade a Captain Douglas at the War Office to get me commissioned in the Army Service Corps, Mechanical Transport. He suggested I should content myself with driving an ambulance for either the American or the British Hospital in Paris. But this did not satisfy me. The time had come when I felt I could no longer stand aside while most young and fit Englishmen were offering up their lives and facing fear, dirt, and danger for the sake of country or for some cause such as the extermination of Prussian militarism, which, so it was alleged, the war was being waged in order to accomplish.

I admit that in principle I did not feel bound to join the P.B.I. (poor bloody infantry). Normally a volunteer chooses his arm of the service. The siege artillery would have been attractive, and in 1917 I knocked in vain at the door of the Intelligence Corps, in 1918 at the door of the room in which personnel was being selected for the Murmansk expedition. I should not have minded beginning as an officer. I vaguely thought of some specialist job in which I could be of real use. When I came over to London a second time, at the beginning of 1916, Arnold Bennett gave me a note to Ian Malcolm, the Undersecretary for War, but Malcolm advised me to follow the example of a cousin of his and begin in the ranks. I had given up my livelihood in Paris, with which, anyhow, I was dissatisfied. I could not turn back. So I offered myself for election to the Honourable Artillery Company, which had vacancies only in its infantry section.

It was hardly a passport to longevity. I made three friends in the H.A.C.: Crosby was killed on the Somme while still a private; Handyside, who had come from Brazil to volunteer, did not long survive obtaining a commission; and if Hammond, like myself, was unscathed at the armistice, it was, I feel, thanks to getting commissioned early in his military career in the Army Service Corps, Mechanical Transport. I was a private in the 2d Battalion of the

H.A.C. when at the beginning of October, 1916, it marched from the Tower of London to Waterloo Station with fixed bayonets, as it was entitled to do. We went first into the trenches at a reputedly quiet spot, just beyond the woods at Ploegsteert ("Plugstreet") , and when we pulled out of these after a week or so, it was to march to the Somme. On the way I had influenza and was sent to hospital, No. 10 General at St.-Omer. There it was noticed that I had a rupture, and the rupture took me back to England in a hospital ship. Nearly a year's light duty followed my operation, and then I was eight months at cadet school. I graduated at the end of July, 1918. By then I had been away from the front in France for twenty-two months. I had entirely missed Passchendaele and the like.

Moreover, the cadet school was providing officers for the Tank Corps, and had I, as thus designed, gone into the tanks, I should have seen no more warfare in France. Newly commissioned tank officers were sent to some place in the center of that country. But when I graduated, the Tank Corps was full, and I and my contemporaries were advised to apply for infantry commissions. That is how I came to be in the Dorsets. It seems I could have persisted and got into the tanks after all. But I and two cronies gave up our striving. At the end of September, 1918, we were, all three, sent out to reinforce the Dorsets in France, and two of us were posted to the same battalion of the New Army. The war was to go on for only another six weeks. It was long enough for me to be in two major battles. I came out of both without a scratch. I was lucky.

I do not mean I did not have some narrow escapes, and not every one of them from the evil intent of the enemy. We had begun the battle for the Forest of Mormal early in the morning. By the afternoon we had made much headway when we were ordered to lie prone. I can still remember spent German bullets hitting the pebbles just ahead of me as I lay in that position. Before the Second Battle of Neuvilly—my first experience of open warfare—we had done a turn and were relieved in the dark. I had brought my platoon almost to the road that would take us back to rest in Caudry as, just ahead of us, three whizbangs burst incandescently in a row on the road itself. We took to the grassy hillside and so ran into our guns, so numerous as to be side by side. In the actual battle, two nights later, my platoon reached its allotted objective, and men of another battalion passed through us. A panicky lad in this second wave suddenly pushed his bayonet against the gas mask across my chest and cried, "Hands up, you German bastard!" Instead of obeying, I snatched the rifle barrel away. "Don't be a damned little fool," I said in some indignation. "Can't you see I've got on an English tin hat?"

After the battle a subaltern in the same battalion as myself told our fire-eating brigadier that he had killed no fewer than five Germans. The brigadier put him in for the M.C. (Military Cross), and he was duly awarded this decoration. He neglected to tell the brigadier that the Germans he said he had shot were disarmed prisoners being led to the rear by a corporal from another battalion. The same man, whom I shall call Kerr, took a dislike to me; he warned the company commander that if I stayed in the same company with him, he would bump me off from behind next time we went over the top. So I was transferred to D Company, and at first I was puzzled to understand why. About Christmastime we were in billets near the coast of Artois, and one night Kerr further tried to push me into a village pond, again from behind. Altogether a choice specimen—a farmer's boy, it was said.

It is only fair to add that the officers of my battalion were told before that particular battle not to take prisoners. Evidently that was not the order given to the battalion which took the prisoners that Kerr shot. It should also be noted that in World War I, as I found out when, after the Armistice, I joined divisional staff, decorations came up with the rations, and it only remained to dish them out. For instance, the divisional French interpreter received the M.C. although he had not unduly exposed himself.

To return to my lot as an infantryman, I had been let off lightly. I was never in a raid when, usually with blackened faces, a small party went out at night into no-man's-land and, keeping stock-still whenever a Very light went up, tried to get through the barbed wire, invade a German trench, and bring back one or two prisoners. A raid was held to give adventure to trench life. It was not an exercise in which I should have excelled. Again, I never had to take part in withstanding a counterattack, which meant, according to the book, that the defenders were to wait till they saw the whites of the attackers' eyes before firing at them. Many times in England I had rehearsed the final assault course; never while in France did I meet an armed German face to face and have to plunge my bayonet into him as I had into the swaying sack back at home.

Had I not missed all that kind of thing, the chances of losing my life or of being crippled and handicapped (so that I should have been left with only half a life) would have been very much greater. It needed but to stay out at the front long enough, it seems to me in retrospect, and, as I have already indicated, death or mutilation was assured. In my last battles I took the precaution of carrying the blade of my entrenching tool across my private parts. In attacking the Passchendaele ridge in 1917 and in keeping communication across the intervening sea of mud, British casualties mounted to

400,000. Haig attacked at Passchendaele in the vain expectation of a breakthrough. His persistence in shelling for days before each attack broke up the ground and made movement on foot difficult.

> (They called it Passchendaele); my wound was slight,
> And I was hobbling back, and then a shell
> Burst slick upon the duck-boards; so I fell
> Into the bottomless mud, and lost the light.

Thousands shared the grave of mud. In defending Verdun the year before the casualties numbered 362,000. And Verdun, as the late General Fuller once explained to me, had to be denied to the Germans for political and not tactical reasons. If it had fallen, the line would have been improved for the French. But with the fall of Verdun the French government of the day would have fallen too. By the end of 1915 the French had suffered 1,001,271 killed or missing. In December, 1917, the French forces were wasting at the rate of 40,000 a month. The offensives of General Nivelle in the previous April had brought the French Army to a state of collapse. It was only a matter of time, and nobody could fail to have been wounded or killed. The subaltern in the Dorsets who had a shell splinter in his thigh on November 10, 1918, had been through Passchendaele and survived only to be hit, as I have told, on the Armistice eve.

Moreover, a soldier could deliberately take risks and be unhurt. More often than not, one would be struck down by chance, not only in an attack or opposing a counterattack, but either going up to the front from rest or coming away from it, while on the way to the latrine or in it. We had a Sergeant Potter at Plugstreet who was killed while lying in his dugout in the woods while we were in support. He was sorting the contents of his pack. The danger was constantly lurking, and the blow, when it fell, came unheralded, unseen. If you heard a shell coming, it was not for you; the one with your name on it you never heard. You might not duck low enough as you passed the spot on which the enemy sniper had trained his sights. You might be done in (from behind) by one of your own comrades-in-arms.

These conditions of the war affected the nature of martial valor. If you took an enemy trench single-handed, you certainly risked your life. Siegfried Sassoon was awarded the M.C. for doing this. In the 1st H.A.C. we had a Captain Pritchard who received the V.C. (Victoria Cross) for a similar feat. Both survived, but some soldiers might be killed on leave; some civilians, while doing no more than cross the street in the blackout. A soldier in France was equally exposed while engaged in a deed of derring-do as he was in coming simply within range. To crawl out into no-man's-land and bring in a wounded comrade, or to go out there and bury a dead one, might not be as spectacular as taking a trench single-handed, and yet it was indisputably as heroic—perhaps more so, for the capture of a trench would very likely be done in a mood of exaltation; crawling out to retrieve the wounded or the dead had to be in cold blood.

A soldier in World War I, however brave or foolhardy, could not deliberately die as a hero; he could only live as one. He could give dignity to enduring an ever-present but, most often, hidden menace. Some men and women have been carried kicking and screaming to the scaffold, and yet it is only the man who knows he is under sentence of death who can die violently, if he is equal to it, in the grand manner. Other violent deaths are fortuitous. But the condemned can be heroic to the last. There have been the Christian martyrs. Take a man who accepted execution rather than deny the ecclesiastical supremacy of the Pope in 1535—St. Thomas More. How dignified his end! What a model! But what did More really die for? He was beatified in 1935 as one who preferred to lose life itself rather than recognize his secular King as entitled to proclaim himself head of the Church of England and therefore independent of Rome. In fact, of course, he was simply insisting that he was right and that his King and the King's advisers were wrong. That is what all martyrs do. They die for the sake of maintaining that they themselves cannot be mistaken.

To find an instance of execution nobly suffered when it is not on account of present belief, but owing to previous acts, we have to go to the French reprisals in World War II upon men of Vichy. The victims of such reprisals could, if they had the necessary self-possession, die nobly, while aware, of course, that their demeanor would be described to posterity. Such a death was that of the Frenchman Pierre Pucheu at Algiers in 1944.

The son of a suburban tailor and a woman bookkeeper, Pucheu was trained as a secondary schoolmaster, but he swiftly turned into a financial wizard, such as a bank puts at the head of affairs in a firm whose overdraft seems to be rising too high. Born in 1899, he never engaged in politics till the Vichy government, set up in France when the Germans had overrun the country, was six months old. Then, in February, 1941, he was appointed Vichy Secretary of State for Industrial Production, and from July, 1941, to April, 1942, he was Minister of the Interior. With Laval's return to power in the spring of 1942, Pucheu grew disappointed with the Vichy government and wished to join the new military forces being employed against the Germans in North Africa. He had met General Giraud when the latter returned to France after making a sensational escape from a prisoner-of-war camp in Germany. Now the general was in Algiers, and Pucheu wrote to him, proposing to come to Algeria, and asking for modest military employment. He was ready to serve, if need be, in the ranks. Giraud replied that in North Africa Pucheu would meet with much hostility, owing to his Vichy past, but that if nevertheless he came over under an alias, he would be found a job with the troops. Three days after he had reported to a unit in Morocco, he read in the newspaper that he was being put under house arrest farther south. He wrote several protests to General Giraud against this treatment, and one to General de Gaulle, once the latter was in Algeria also. In August, 1943, Pucheu was imprisoned at Meknès, and in March, 1944, he was tried in Algiers and sentenced to death.

If I am to make my point about the manner in which Pucheu died, so much had first to be set out. I need hardly say that he felt he had been poorly done by, and he was, and is, not alone in this respect. He was convinced that he was the victim of a judicial murder. As M. Robert Aron shows,* Pucheu was merely the first to suffer in a series of reprisals which the men who had declared a provisional French government at Algiers, and in particular General de Gaulle, were determined to inflict on men of Vichy so as to brand them as usurpers and hence to reinforce their own claim to office and power.

On March 20, 1944, Pucheu was awakened in his cell at four thirty in the morning. He would understand at once why he was being called so early. He heard mass. Next, he declared that he intended to command the firing squad himself. Consulted by telephone, a well-known French politician, Le Troquer, who was then Minister of Defense in the Algiers provisional administration, agreed. Pucheu was told that three generals proposed to attend his execution. He insisted that they must go away. General Cochet, who had been one of his three military judges, persisted in staying. Pucheu, on catching sight of him, said, "Out with you, sir. Go away. I don't want to see you. You might have remembered that it was I who had you freed from prison, and that but for me God knows where you would be now. Get out!" A little before six o'clock he reached the execution ground. He asked for the colonel in charge. He wanted the warrant officer introduced. He shook hands with him. "What regiment?" "The guards." "Sir, I'm taking your place.

---

* *Histoire de l'épuration*, I (Paris, 1967), pp. 202–36.

I shall give the words of command. What is usual?" "Ready! Aim! Fire!" "You will present your men to me. I want to shake hands with them." He went up to the squad. "Gentlemen, I pardon you in advance. You are obeying orders. You are not involved in this political murder; I have nothing against you." One by one the soldiers were presented, and with each he shook hands.

He then took off his overcoat. The chaplain held out a crucifix. He kissed it. He embraced the chaplain. He turned to one of his two counsels and embraced him. He then embraced the other.

He stood erect in front of the stake and faced the squad. The soldiers stepped forward to within seven yards. He folded his arms across his chest. "Gentlemen, are you ready?" He raised his right arm. "Aim!" He dropped his right arm. "Fire!" The rifles spoke together. He was dead. Several of the soldiers wept.

We owe the account of how Pierre Pucheu died to his senior counsel, Maître Buttin. It makes my point that no soldier in action, and indeed no soldier exposed to shell or bomb or aircraft machine gun in the immediate theater of operations, can die in that way by his own decision. In World War I there were, of course, not only brave Frenchmen, not only brave Englishmen, not only brave Americans. There were also brave Germans. Ernst Jünger has contended that the flower of German youth answered the call to the colors in August, 1914, as though going to a bridal union with Death.

> If I must die,
> I will encounter darkness as a bride,
> And hug it in mine arms.

But, in fact, that was impossible. Pucheu died a victim of war, but not while soldiering. Of course, he knew that the world would be told how he died, as the world was told of the sacrifice at Thermopylae. He was showing what he could do. I am sure it was beyond the reach of most men. Few would have been equal to his self-possession and his ready ascendancy over his executioners. By his display of self-possession he showed that only the condemned can die with nobility. A soldier in action may be fatally wounded, and then he may be granted time to muster human dignity before his end. But for most soldiers in World War I to be wounded was to be knocked insensible without warning or to be thrown into so much pain and anguish as to be lost to directing one's actions. So the modern soldier cannot in action strike an attitude. He can no more die like Antony or Cleopatra than he can die like Socrates.

A soldier goes to help another under fire. He surprises a whole party of the enemy and takes them prisoner, single-handed. By his cool daring he exposes himself and yet succeeds in bringing a number through danger to comparative safety. The order comes to climb out of the trenches and advance in the attack: the soldier, officer or man, who has the self-mastery to keep cool and to steady his fellows will perhaps steer clear of the most obvious perils. All decorations are awarded in theory for that kind of action. But in World War I death or mutilation had less and less relation to bravery. You were as likely to be hit if you cowered as if you moved resolutely and openly.

Hence, in World War I the real heroism, the true greatness of the soldier, was shown, I submit, not in his daring, not in his bravery on occasion, but in his steady endurance. From his first moment in the firing line he was in danger, and nearly always it was a danger he could not ward off. He might duck to escape snipers; he might take cover from shrapnel. He could not counter the chance shot, the chance shell splinter, the bursting whizbang, and it was usually the chance blow that was going to get him. So long as he was unhit, he was in peril, and he might pose as indifferent; but he knew it, day after day, week after week, till he was actually hit or he went on leave.

No wonder the endurance sometimes broke. That was how in 1917, after Verdun and after Nivelle, the mutinies broke out in the French Army, and France was saved by Marshal Pétain. I have never read a full account of those mutinies. We know that French privates simply walked away from the front line. But when on leave in Paris in 1918, I heard from a French colonial soldier of at least one battalion also having to be surrounded by loyal troops as it was marched to the station from barracks in Lyons. In 1918 the 1st H.A.C. had to restore discipline among a rebellious unit in Étaples. The war strained endurance to the breaking point.

Therefore, when the Dorsets marched back on November 11, 1918, not only were we assured that our lives once again lay before us; we were released from that steady, nagging compulsion to stick it. Since 1914 masses of men, many of them humble, simple men, had shown what they could endure and for how long they could endure. By comparison, what mattered a preference for sherbet over a beaker full of the warm south, full of the true, the blushful Hippocrene? The need for endurance was over.

Francis Foster

Successively ordinand, soldier, author and literary critic, and priest, Major the Reverend Reginald Francis Foster (pen name, Francis Foster) was born in 1896, a scion of a long line of Sussex landowners. He was trained for Anglican holy orders but enlisted in the British Army in early 1915 and, later commissioned, served in France till he was wounded, when he was granted a permanent commission in the Indian Army, spending the rest of the war on the Palestine front. He was with his regiment in Egypt for two years thereafter and later served in the Waziristan campaigns of 1919–21 and 1921–24.

He resigned his commission in order to enter the literary world, in which he had already gained a footing. Deeply interested in esoteric religion, he was ordained priest by a Syro-Chaldean Church bishop in 1933 and acted as a missionary in England, though he continued to earn his living by writing. When, in 1940, a German invasion of England seemed inevitable, he volunteered and was accepted for combatant service in the British Army.

Since the end of the 1939–45 war he has devoted himself exclusively to writing. Some thirty books (novels, an autobiography, belles lettres, and technical works on fiction writing and punctuation) and several hundred short stories, essays, etc. of his have been published, and his two plays have been broadcast by the B.B.C. He has just completed what he regards as his magnum opus, entitled The Perennial Religion.

He is married to Joan Elizabeth, daughter of Sir A. Harold Bibby, Bart., D.S.O. (Distinguished Service Order), the ship owner, and Lady Bibby, and has three sons and three daughters.

HOLY GROUND

DURING what in Britain was officially termed the Great War, full conscription did not come into force till 1917, though a modified form of it was authorized by Parliament during the previous year, before which the armed forces had had to rely on voluntary enlistment for recruits. It may be assumed that most of those who joined the Army or Navy during the first few months following the declaration of war in August, 1914, were motivated less by recognition of the country's peril (for the general belief was that Germany would be defeated by the end of that first year) than by fervent patriotism or the spirit of adventure. I was not one of them, though, having reached the age of eighteen in April, 1914, I was old enough to enlist.

By the beginning of 1915, however, most people were forced by stark facts to realize that Lord Kitchener's forecast that hostilities would last at least three years was justified. Yet still I remained a civilian, though I was perfectly healthy. The plain truth is that a recent experience had convinced me that I was a coward. It occurred during the late summer of 1914. I was returning home from a convivial evening spent with artist friends in Chelsea when I heard an uproar outside a tavern whose doors had just been closed for the night. A small crowd of cheering people surrounded a man who held a woman's head in chancery (a stranglehold) and was vigorously punching her face. I stopped, horrified, and shouted indignantly, "Let her go, you brute!" whereat, to my surprise, the man released the woman. She stumbled toward me, waving her arms and crying, "Go away, mister! 'E'll murder you if 'e gits 'old of you!"

The man, a hulking fellow of less than middle age, was obviously fighting drunk. Rubbing sweat from his eyes, he lurched toward me, the spectators enthusiastically urging him on. For a few seconds I stood my ground; then I turned and fled incontinently. To say that I was deeply ashamed of my cowardice is a wholly inadequate description, for indeed I felt utterly despicable. I did not reason to myself that what I had witnessed was common outside many public houses on Saturday nights and that anyone who tried to intervene was a fool.

When at length I sought my bed, I lay awake reflecting unhappily on what had occurred and imagining various different endings of the episode, and at last falling asleep, I dreamed continuously on similar lines. Next morning, full of self-contempt—though I did not recognize my feeling as that—my one desire was to avoid other people, even though my own company was so disturbing.

About a month later recruiting sergeants began to appear on the streets of London, and invariably when I saw one in the distance, I would cross the road to avoid his solicitations. Though nobody reproached me for still being a civilian, I gradually became sure that I was an object of other people's scorn. It was precisely this that caused me, in May, 1915—nine months after the beginning of the war—to enlist in the Artists' Rifles, which is to say that I became a soldier only because I feared to be deemed the coward that I believed I was.

Later I discovered that the 2d Battalion that I had joined had recently become an Officers Training Corps and that conditions in it were considerably more unpleasant than those prevailing in ordinary infantry units: We had to sleep on bare ground or hard floors; our rations were of poor quality and badly cooked by amateurs; leave was rarely granted; training was rigorous and intensive. But once my body became inured to these hardships, I welcomed the long hours of work and the general discomfort because they staved off the dreadful anticipation of eventually going into the firing line.

I must have managed to impress my superiors, for the following November, with five other private soldiers, I was paraded before a visiting lieutenant colonel whose purpose was to choose two of us to be granted commissions and posted to his battalion. I was one of the men selected. A fortnight or so later my name was listed in the London *Gazette* as a second lieutenant, and later I received an order to join a battalion of the East Lancashire Regiment.

During the year of intensive training that followed, I gained two first-class certificates at courses on musketry and bombing, the effect being that I became somewhat more self-confident. Nevertheless, the prospect of eventually going on active service continued to fill me with apprehension. When, therefore, the division in which my battalion was included received orders to join the Expeditionary Force in France, my only happiness derived from the fact that at last the monotonous training was at an end. When I returned from embarkation leave, I was informed that I and my platoon sergeant, together with one officer and one sergeant from each of the other three companies, were to form an advance party and proceed to

France, with similar parties from other units in the division, our purpose being to learn the ropes in the part of the line that the division would eventually take over.

Four days later the advance party was in Boulogne, and thence, after some delay, we entrained for an unspecified destination. After many hours of excruciatingly slow travel we reached Béthune. Thence the contingents of the brigade that included my battalion marched along the towpath of the La Bassée Canal, halting at length to consume a brief meal. As the winter dusk was beginning to fall, we resumed our journey, and soon the thudding of big guns and the occasional stutter of a machine gun could be heard. Eventually my battalion party was detached from the rest of the column and allotted one of a number of soldier guides, who had apparently been waiting for us at this point. He would, he told us, conduct us to our destination.

I was ready to drop from extreme fatigue when at length the guide announced that we had reached "Windy Corner." He responded to a sentry's challenge and then, turning, remarked to me, "The N.C.O.'s are to remain here, sir, and you are to report to battalion H.Q. It's down here, sir."

I went gingerly forward in the intense darkness and found that the man was holding back something that had been apparently covering the entrance to what seemed to be a hole in the ground but proved to be a cellar—next morning I found it was all that was left, apart from rubble, of a sizable house. We officers descended a flight of steps, at the bottom of which, in an underground room, we were greeted by a young captain, who told us he was the adjutant. He had been seated at an improvised table on which stood a field telephone set. A couple of wax candles stuck in beer bottles provided illumination.

"You chaps are to be detailed one per each of our companies, so you'd better toss up to decide who goes to which," the adjutant informed us.

We decided the issue accordingly, and I was told that C Company, to which I was to proceed, was in the close support line, "just along the road." Another guide was summoned from a neighboring cellar, and following in his wake, I climbed up the steps into the darkness again. My destination was not far away, and it, too, proved to be a cellar, which was occupied by a single subaltern, huddled in a greatcoat.

"Been waiting for you," he greeted me, grinning in a friendly manner. "You're late. Expect you'd like some grub. My name's Bunch, by the way. You won't see the O.C. [officer commanding] till the morning. He's gone to bed. So have the others."

I was provided with bully beef (corned beef) and bread for supper and invited to make free with a bottle of whisky. I began my meal while Bunch produced a brier pipe, which he filled from an oilskin pouch. When the tobacco was burning to his satisfaction, he remarked, "This is a very quiet part of the line nowadays. We were sent here two months back for a rest—we'd had a rather hot time on the Somme earlier. Captain Bill—that's the O.C., and Bill's his surname, by the way—is the only surviving original officer in this company. I'm the next oldest, for the other subalterns haven't been with us more than a few months."

"Why is it so quiet here?" I ventured.

"Because in the winter the front in this section is just a quagmire—the water in the trenches is knee-deep mostly. Apart from an occasional gun battle, there's very little doing."

The "bedroom" allotted to me proved to be a corner of the neighboring cellar that had been partitioned off by means of blankets suspended from the ceiling. The bed was a wooden frame across which wire netting had been stretched and nailed. I was so weary by the time I lay down that I fell asleep instantly and did not awake till I was roused next morning by an orderly who brought me a mug of "gunfire" (early morning tea). My watch told me that the hour was half past five o'clock.

While, a little later, I was shaving, a heavy thud caused the candle flame to be suddenly extinguished. The orderly produced an electric torch and switched it on. "No good relighting the candle," he explained. "The usual morning hate [bombardment] has begun and—" He paused as another heavy thud sounded. "That's one of our six-inch howitzers back at Gorre. Jerry'll start up shortly, you'll find."

His ears were so experienced that he was able to differentiate between British and German gunfire, for after about a dozen rounds had been fired by the battery he had referred to, he assured me when the next thud occurred that it was from Jerry cannon; since he had no reason to lie about the matter, I accepted his words. I was gratified to find that the bombardment caused me no undue alarm, though I was glad when it ended.

When I later went for breakfast in the neighboring cellar, a tall captain was seated at an improvised table, eating, and Bunch presented me to him. He was Bill. I liked him on sight; later I was to find that he was a very prince among men. After the meal he took me sightseeing. I had already learned that the village was Festubert, the scene of very heavy fighting earlier in the war. The support line ran through it, and the front-line trenches were only about half a mile distant. Houses and church in the single street were mere heaps of rubble, and every tree had been reduced to a pathetic stump. In the churchyard, coffins, some of them gaping open, were exposed as a result of gunfire. What astonished me was the fact that though at certain phases of our stroll streams of machine-gun bullets whined unpleasantly nearby, Bill did not take cover; I myself was horribly scared, but fear of revealing what I felt prevented my taking any action. At length I ventured a request for an explanation, and his answer was a laconic, "You don't hear the bullet that hits you!"

That evening, while dusk was falling, the company was mustered and afterward proceeded, platoon by platoon, to a store from which thigh boots were issued to each man. Having donned them and left our ammunition [regular Army] boots behind, we went forward to relieve the company in the front line, proceeding thither by way of communication trenches, through which we waded knee-deep and more in filthy water. The O.C. had directed me to join Bunch's platoon, and when we arrived at our destination, I watched interestedly the routine of taking over from the outgoing garrison. The Germans seemed to be aware that something was afoot in our trench, for they constantly put up flares till just after the take-over was completed. At length Bunch showed me the officer's funk hole that had been dug out of the side of the parapet—the front wall of the trench—and which I was to share with him. He explained that it was not possible to excavate proper dugouts in this sector because of the waterlogged condition of the trenches. The German line, I learned, was 250 yards distant across no-man's-land.

The month was December, and the night cold was intense. At about half past eleven Bunch suggested my going to bed till an hour before dawn, when everyone would have to stand to on the fire step because it was during that period (and also during the evening hour before full darkness) that an attack was most likely to be made. I crawled into the funk hole, therefore, and, huddled in my greatcoat, lay down, my head pillowed on my haversack. For some minutes I listened to distant gunfire; then, falling asleep, I did not wake up till Bunch summoned me for the dawn stand-to. When the hour's vigil ended, breakfast was brought to the men from the support line, and they were each given an issue of rum. Bunch told me that he and I would feed at company H.Q. and that though he would conduct me there on this first occasion, in the future I should have to go alone and relieve him on my return.

To reach company headquarters involved our wading along a communication trench to the close support line. Captain Bill was in high spirits when we arrived. "Enjoying life?" he asked me, and trying to match his gaiety, I replied, "It's endurable, anyhow."

The day passed quietly, though a constant rumble of distant gunfire came from the east, where, Bunch told me, a "bit of a battle" was in progress. A little before sunset Captain Bill appeared in the front trench with his sergeant major. Bunch was absent, being asleep in the funk hole. "Lovely evening," Bill commented cheerfully when he joined me alongside a sentry who, standing on the duckboards on the trench bottom, was peering through a periscope at no-man's-land in order to be able to spot any sign of enemy activity. Then, to my astonishment, Bill mounted the fire step (which, I knew, was contrary to routine orders regarding daytime procedure) and, his head above the top of the parapet, began to survey the wasteland beyond. Half a minute later he beckoned me to mount beside him. After a little hesitation, wondering whether he was daring me, I climbed up fearfully beside him.

I could see through the British wire fronting our trench and approximately halfway between us and the German wire the pathetic stumps of several trees. Feeling sure that our exposed heads must be clearly visible to the enemy, for we were silhouetted against the sunset behind us, I was expecting a rain of bullets, but no shot was fired.

"Let's go stretch our legs for a bit," Bill suggested, and without waiting for a reply, he put the palms of his hands on the parapet and heaved himself over the top. I wondered whether he had become insane. He stood there grinning down at me. I glanced back at the sergeant major. His face was enigmatic. What had I expected of him, in any case? I asked myself, feeling quite desperate because of the position in which I was placed. Then, deeply reluctant, I slowly clambered up beside Bill, who now turned to the wire and began to search for one of the usual gaps that was left to make access to no-man's-land beyond possible. Meanwhile, I waited motionless, my pulses racing and bile in my throat.

Finding at length what he sought, Bill turned to me again and beckoned. His expression was now semiserious. It invited confidence. The sickness in my throat subsided, and I went to him, following him afterward through the gap in the first belt of wire and zigzagging behind him through gaps in later belts. Finally, we emerged into open ground. Bill now headed as straight for the clump of blasted trees as the many waterlogged shell holes would allow, I close behind him and feeling that I was dreaming. He neither paused nor hesitated till he reached the remains of what (I could see now) must once have been willows, and arriving there at length, I at his heels, he seated himself on one of the stumps and calmly lighted a cigarette. I could see the German wire defenses quite clearly, for they were now little more than 100 yards distant. From somewhere close and to the left came the detonation of mortar bombs or artillery shells; my insufficiently experienced ears were not yet able to differentiate between the two.

We did not speak. At length Bill threw his cigarette end away. "Ah, well," he said laconically, "I suppose we'd better be getting back." He rose to his feet.

The sunset glow was beginning to fade from the western sky. Side by side now, we began to saunter back. Because I was now no longer fearful, elation filled me. But I could not understand what had caused the transformation. It was as though I had become another person altogether or, rather, as though I had entered another life. When at length I clambered after Bill into our familiar trench, I was even regretting that the expedition had ended.

Waving a hand to me, Bill set off back to his headquarters. Before following in his wake, the sergeant major saluted me smartly, giving me a prodigious wink the while. And when I was alone with the sentry again, I knew that during the last half hour I had undergone the most momentous experience of my life.

Some five weeks later I was again in the line, but this time with men of my own battalion, which had meanwhile arrived in France and taken over this sector of the front from the battalion of the Warwickshire Regiment in which I had been initiated into trench warfare. I, with my platoon, was ordered to occupy "Death or Glory" sap, alongside the La Bassée Canal. As the name implies, this was a trench that had been dug forward of the rest of the front line, the distance between its head and that of a similar sap in the German line being less than 150 yards. Earlier in the war this had been the scene of particularly violent fighting, but now conditions were very quiet.

Ever since my expedition with Captain Bill into no-man's-land, I had been aware of a profound mental change in myself. Now it seemed to me essential that both to prove its realness and to complete the metamorphosis, I must venture into the wasteland again, and this time alone. But I knew that here there was no dead ground between the lines, so to go out in daylight would be altogether indefensible. After stand-down on the second evening, therefore, I told my sergeant that I was going over the top to examine our wire entanglements. He expostulated, but bidding him warn the platoon that I should be out in front, I clambered onto the parapet and crossed to the wire. The moonlight being bright, I found the first gap without difficulty, and passing through it, I made my way forward till I was in open ground. Now I could see the German wire vaguely in the moonlight, and realizing that I might be visible to sentries in the enemy line, I got down on my hands and knees and began to crawl toward it.

It must have been more than half an hour later when I returned to the sap, feeling extraordinarily exhilarated. My sergeant helped me down from the parapet and then began to protest vehemently on account of what I had done. "All right," I told him; "next time you and I shall go out together," to which he returned, "Even so, there'd probably be a stink if the O.C. learned about it, so I'll have to warn the men not to talk about it—even among themselves." The following night, therefore, he accompanied me on my next exploratory tour, and thereafter we were constantly out in front at night. Sometimes, however, I would receive an order to take out an armed patrol of several men to investigate the state of the German wire following a bombardment or to discover whether pumps were clearing waterlogged enemy trenches or to effect liaison with a similar patrol operating on our left—our right was, of course, flanked by the canal.

On one such occasion of the last kind my patrol was near the German wire when one of the men, stumbling into a shell hole, accidentally discharged his rifle. At once flares rose from the enemy line. All but one of us dropped to the ground to avoid being detected, the exception being a man whose tunic had become caught up on the German wire. Then a machine gun began to chatter, and bullets whined about us, the man who was still standing being hit in the forearm. A corporal and I tore him from the wire, and making him lie down, I roughly bandaged his wound with my khaki handkerchief. Then I passed word to the others that they were to crawl in my wake, and I set off, heading for a derelict trench that I had discovered several nights earlier. Luckily I found it soon, for there was now continuous firing from the enemy line.

In a short while the stutter of machine guns began to subside, and only an occasional flare was put up. Presently, as I was rounding a traverse, I bumped into something that yielded and let out a grunt. The man behind me collided with me as I halted, for here in the old trench it was difficult to see clearly. I had already taken my pistol from its holster and was crouching when, looking up and forward, I discerned the unmistakable shape of a German helmet. I guessed that we had run into an enemy patrol that was sheltering from gunfire in the trench. Aiming just under the helmet, I fired. I heard the bullet strike metal; then followed a veritable shriek, and several forms heaved themselves out of the trench and began to run toward the German line. Since dawn was now not far off, I decided that we should get back to "Death or Glory" sap without delay, so I ordered my men out of the old trench, and we set off at a run for "home."

Because I am intent not on recording all or even the outstanding episodes in which I played a part during the Great War but on achieving a special purpose that may already have become evident, I shall now pass to what happened some months later when, in early May, 1917, just after my twenty-first birthday, I became a casualty and my service in France ended. On an occasion when the lieutenant colonel commanding the battalion paid a routine visit to the front line, he invited me to volunteer to lead my platoon on a night raid on the enemy trench opposite. I had not the least inclination to do so, for it was commonly believed that the officer in command of such an operation was invariably killed, but refusal, of course, being impossible, when the battalion returned in due course to rest billets, I was directed to take my platoon to a chateau near Gorre, where we should undergo a week's special training.

The raid was planned by the divisional staff. Zero hour would be at 2300 on the night of May 14. At zero minus thirty minutes an artillery barrage would be put on the trench we were to raid; at zero minus fifteen my platoon would go over the top, and meanwhile the barrage would gradually creep back to the German support line to prevent reinforcements from going forward. Two sappers of the Royal Engineers would accompany the raiding party, carrying a Bangalore torpedo to blow a gap in the enemy wire. This device consisted of a number of lengths of tubing filled with high explosive. The first section being pushed under the wire; another would be screwed to it; this was thrust forward; then a third was attached; and so on till the wire was fully penetrated. The torpedo was operated by turning a cock on the end section that ignited a fuse which, five seconds later, would detonate the charge. The cock was to be turned precisely at zero hour, and the gap being made, my men would pass through it, enter the enemy trench, killing all its occupants except two, who were to be brought back to our own line for interrogation. At zero plus twenty minutes a bugler stationed in the middle of no-man's-land would sound the familiar cookhouse call to signal the withdrawal.

On the night of the raid everything went according to plan—except that while we lay waiting alongside the wire, one of the sappers crawled to me and reported that the cock on the torpedo was apparently jammed. Scrambling to my feet, I ran forward, intending to try to operate the thing myself. No sooner did I touch it, however, than the torpedo detonated; the other sapper must himself have succeeded in turning it in his mate's absence. The ensuing blast rocked me back on my feet, but I seemed not to have been injured except that, despite the illumination from many flares in the air above, I could see nothing whatever. My men were already running through the new-made gap, and the press of their bodies carried me some distance with them. Then they all were past me. By now I had realized that I was blind. I could do nothing but stand where I was and hope that my officerless men would be able to carry on. Meanwhile, hand grenades thrown by enemy survivors were falling all about me. One at length fell on my foot. I kicked lustily. It exploded in the air before me, and my right arm suddenly jerked back as a fragment had hit it. There was no immediate pain, but I could feel blood soaking into my right trouser leg. Able, I found, to raise the injured arm, I put it across my body, pushing the hand into my tunic.

The piercing call of a bugle signaling the withdrawal sounded above the clamor of the gunfire. A few seconds later my men were returning through the gap. I shouted to attract attention and tried to grasp at one of them. Then they all were past me. By now enemy guns were also in action, but the detonations of shells fired by our own enabled me to distinguish between them. I turned, and keeping my back to the sound of the explosions and my good hand out-stretched to encounter possible obstacles, I contrived to get clear of the wire. Then followed a seemingly endless nightmare journey back across the wasteland, feeling forward with each foot before every step. Four times I fell into shell holes, and soon my clothing reeked of foul water.

Despite continuous machine-gun and rifle fire, I was miraculously not hit. At last my left hand outstretched before me touched wire— our own, I knew, for the barbs were not so long as those on German wire. Knowing that it was impossible to find my way through the echeloned gaps in the various belts, I shouted, "Help! Wounded British officer!" repeatedly. Fortunately the gunfire was already subsiding, and flares were now comparatively few. I heard a noise nearby at length; then a voice called clearly, "Here he is, Tom," and a hand touched me. I explained my condition, and one of my two rescuers told me he would lead if I kept hold of his shoulder and his companion would follow me. A little while later I was lifted over the parapet into the trench. Thence I was carried on a stretcher for a considerable distance, and when it was finally set down, I heard the voice of our battalion's medical officer.

He examined and bandaged my wounded forearm, telling me that a fragment of bomb was imbedded deeply in it and that an operation would be needed for its extraction. He was greatly concerned about my blindness, which, however, later proved not to be permanent, for when at length I was put to bed in a field hospital, I found that I could see dimly with one eye, which eventually became nearly normal, whereas I regained only partial sight in the other.

When, some months later, I was discharged from the hospital in England I was posted to the reserve battalion in Yorkshire. Several weeks afterward volunteers for permanent commissions in the Indian Army were called for to replace heavy British officer casualties in Mesopotamia, and because I had discovered that I enjoyed soldiering, I responded, was accepted, and in due course was dispatched to India. Three weeks after I joined my new regiment there, it was ordered to proceed to Palestine to join General Allenby's army. Now a captain, I did not become a casualty again till, in August, 1918, I succumbed to amoebic dysentery. It was not till just after the Armistice, three months later, that I was discharged from the hospital in Alexandria, Egypt.

The fact that the transformation that I have recorded must have been experienced, though not, of course, in exactly similar circumstances, by very many civilian soldiers in the new armies during the major wars of this century should suffice to acquit me of egoism in writing autobiographically on the subject. The problem that I now have to solve concerns the precise cause of the change.

The genesis of the affair obviously occurred on that memorable occasion when Captain Bill invited me to go for a stroll with him in no-man's-land. Since he was a veteran soldier and well acquainted with the Festubert sector, he must have been well aware that, some of the area between the opposed lines being in "dead" ground, to venture out there even in daylight was reasonably safe. But I myself knew nothing of local conditions, so it is just possible that in inviting me to share his seemingly dangerous project, he was testing my courage or even daring me; nevertheless, I am convinced that he merely wanted a congenial companion to accompany him while he stretched his legs out of the waterlogged trenches.

While I stood trembling in apprehension on the parapet, watching him search for the first gap in the wire, I recalled that I had had to force myself to climb out of the trench—that I had acted as though I were two persons, I and also *myself*. And in a flash the memory came to me of the incident outside a London tavern in the late summer of 1914 when I was menaced by a drunken man, and I realized simultaneously that on that occasion I had similarly visualized myself objectively and, moreover, not as I was at that moment but as I imagined I should be shortly, and as a consequence I had fled in panic. Then Bill found the gap and, turning, beckoned to me. Inevitably I was now regarding him, not the Germans, as my enemy, for he was virtually forcing me to do something that I dreaded. But I liked and admired him enormously and wanted to emulate him and win his esteem, so to regard him as an enemy was irrational. Very reluctantly I followed as he zigzagged through the gaps in successive belts of barbed wire. Then, as I emerged from the last into the open and saw him calmly surveying the clearly visible German wire defenses, it was as though a veil had been lifted from my eyes. If I was in peril, so was he; we were sharing a common danger. For the first time in my life I stopped visualizing myself and was suddenly tranquil. When Bill began to stroll forward, I followed in complete confidence.

Not till more than six months later in a military hospital in England, when one night I lay sleepless because of pain in my wounded arm, did I gain full comprehension of what had happened to me. I realized that originally, while I had been in the habit of visualizing what I feared would shortly occur, I was irrationally splitting myself in two so that I was both the subject (the thinking *I*) and the object (the *me*) of my contemplation and, moreover, that I was projecting myself into an imaginary future. The habit had been conquered on the occasion that I forced myself to accompany Captain Bill on that excursion into no-man's-land, the genesis of the change in myself occurring when I became aware that he and I were sharing a common peril and that though I had met him only thirty-six hours earlier, I already esteemed him and regarded him as my friend. It was this thought that put an end to anxiety on my own behalf and hence began the process of extinguishing the love I bore my objectified self.

While we proceeded toward the clump of stricken trees, I became sure that if I could abandon forever the old and evil habit of visualizing myself in danger and anticipating an imaginary future—if I could destroy completely my objectified self with whom I had become so familiar and so much loved—I should become an effective fighting soldier. When we reached our objective and Bill nonchalantly lighted a cigarette, I was as calm as he was, and I became certain that the transformation was already complete.

Five weeks later, when I ventured out alone from "Death or Glory" sap into no-man's-land to test my courage and at length lay alongside the enemy wire, listening to Germans talking among themselves, I knew that the reason why I was completely unafraid was that as a result of having destroyed my imaginary objective self, I had become fully integrated, which is to say that I had gained integrity, and that in future I should invariably live—and live fully—in the present time, leaving the future to take care of itself.

In view of the circumstances in which I discovered the cause of my believed cravenheartedness—when, that is, the fear of seeming to be fearful forced me to accompany Captain Bill on a stroll toward the German trenches—I have always since then regarded the no-man's-land of the Great War, blood-soaked, ravished and ravaged by shellfire, strewn with the debris of earlier battles, and stinking of unburied corpses though it was, as holy ground. Indeed, to me it resembles the Gethsemane in which Christ prayed that He might be relieved of the necessity for immolating Himself and then, in communion with God, discovered the peace that is the fruit of negating the objective self.

The truth is that to think of, and thus objectify, oneself is the root cause of all the evil that mankind commits.

Basil Willey

BASIL WILLEY, *the only child of William Herbert Willey and Alice Ann Le Gros (of Jersey), was born in London on July 25, 1897. He was educated at University College School, London, and Peterhouse, Cambridge. During World War I he was a lieutenant in the West Yorkshire Regiment in France (1917–18).*

In 1915 he was awarded a history scholarship at Peterhouse, where he was graduated with first class honors in history (1920) and first class honors in English (1921). He was a Hugo de Balsham Student at Peterhouse and won the university Le Bas Prize (1922) with the essay "Tendencies in Renaissance Literary Theory." In 1923 he became a lecturer in English at Cambridge, and in 1935 he was made a fellow of Pembroke College. From 1946 to 1964 he was King Edward VII Professor of English at Cambridge, succeeding Sir Arthur Quiller-Couch. He was a visiting professor at Columbia University from 1948 to 1949 and at Cornell in 1953. From 1958 to 1964 he was president of Pembroke College, and in 1964 he was made an honorary fellow of Pembroke. In 1959 he was a Hibbert lecturer and in 1964 a Ballard Matthews lecturer (Bangor, North Wales). He was made a Fellow of the Royal Society of Literature in 1950 and an Ho.Litt.D. (Manchester) in 1948. He is also a Fellow of the British Academy.

His published works include The Seventeenth Century Background *(1934),* The Eighteenth Century Background *(1940),* Nineteenth Century Studies *(1949),* Christianity Past and Present *(1952),* More Nineteenth Century Studies *(1956),* The English Moralists *(1964), and* Spots of Time, A Retrospect *[1897–1920] (1965). His literary approach is summarized in the Foreword to* The Seventeenth Century Background: *"When speaking of philosophical matters I have supposed myself to be addressing, not professional philosophers, but students of literature, and not professed students merely, but all to whom poetry, and religion, and their relation to the business of living, are matters of importance."*

In 1923 he married Zélie Murlis Ricks. They have two sons and two daughters.

A SCHOOLBOY IN THE WAR

I SIT DOWN to begin this chapter in the garden of my Lakeland cottage, once the home of Wordsworth's daughter Dora Quillinan. The April sun shines warmly, the wind roars through the bare trees on Loughrigg Fell, and a beck from the hilltop tinkles at my side. The Great War of 1914–18 seems remote and unreal indeed. And yet just now I read in my *Times* that yesterday in France the Canadians were celebrating the fiftieth anniversary of the Battle of Vimy Ridge. The correspondent who described the occasion spoke of "the immense and melancholy plain between Arras and Lens, dominated by Vimy Ridge," and this phrase caused a lost pulse of feeling to stir in me again, for it was on that plain, soon after the Vimy battle, that I had my first experience of trench warfare. And in that sector I was in and out of the line with my battalion (the 18th West Yorkshire Regiment, and later the 15th) for about a twelvemonth. Now, in my seventieth year, as I look back across that half century to myself at twenty, "some inward agitations thence are brought," and do they "impregnate and elevate the mind"? Yes, in spite of the brutality and filth and fear, they do in a way. And this is because I was then living at a pitch of physical and imaginative excitement never since equaled, so that to recall that time sets the spirit working again among the embers.

The *Times* correspondent goes on to say that "nature has clothed the sea of mud and shell-holes in a decent mantle of green; but the trees have not had time to age, and the villages of sad, unmellowed brick have not recaptured their shattered personalities. . . . Time," he adds, "has moved more slowly here than on the Normandy battlefields" of the Second Great War. It had certainly moved but slowly on the only occasion that I revisited Vimy (just before the Second War), and if the same is still true, it can surely be allowed some symbolic meaning. Symbolic, for Englishmen of my generation at least (and perhaps for history, too), of the prepotency of the First War over the Second. It may be that this does not apply to some other nations—nations which in the Second War suffered disasters from which they have never recovered. But for Western Europe, and above all for us Britons in our island sanctuary, 1914 fell like a thunderbolt from a blue sky, and no subsequent event could ever appall and shake us as that did. Here, as always, I speak for my own generation—for those of us who were born under Queen Victoria and began to grow up under Edward VII and George V. Elder statesmen even then had premonitions of things to come, but for the young (and well-to-do) it was bliss to be alive. Those were the halcyon days when birds of calm sat brooding on the charmèd wave (waves which, to the world's great benefit, were ruled by Britannia), and when anyone who, like the young Churchill, longed for military honors, had to seek them at the ends of the earth: the North-West Frontier, Cuba, the Sudan, or South Africa. Throughout the nineteenth century after Waterloo, it was possible for Englishmen, despite the Crimea and other people's wars, to feel that the *Pax Britannica* had come to stay, and liberal optimism looked forward to ever-widening international friendship based on commerce and reason. Had there not been the Great Exhibition? Had not the laureate prophesied the Parliament of Man, the Federation of the world?

It was from this deep security—if you like, this fools' paradise— that we who were too young to know better were suddenly pitch- forked into the holocaust. We, the heirs of all the ages in the foremost files of time, had to behold and take part in the collapse of the most imposing and seemingly permanent structure of civiliza- tion ever known, and watch it melt into blood and mud. It was not like this in 1939. Terrible as the Second War was, it lacked this contrasting background, since for the preceding decade there had been a hardening of hearts, a rattling of sabers, and an ever-growing spirit of violence and unreason.

I do not want to repeat overmuch what I wrote in *Spots of Time*, but I should like to say that I tried there to convey the feeling of this irruption of evil into our paradise under the symbol of the bugle call I heard in childhood, sounding across the tranquil Brent Valley (still virgin countryside then) from the Mill Hill barracks. At an upper window of our house, which overlooked open country on the northern fringe of London, I used (for I was an only child) to spend blissful hours, especially on June evenings, gazing out upon the quiet scene and identifying myself with the afterglow in the northern sky, the ivy-covered Seller's Hall with its cedar silhou- etted against yellow, and the unseen owls tu-whitting in the twi- light. And from time to time, breaking the hush and trance, the pert, brassy bugle would insult the ear, fit emblem of the military mind—too insensitive to move outside its narrow diatonic groove or to be aware of its own limitations. I instinctively loathed this alien sound, long before I knew that it meant the loss of my Eden. And not only *my* Eden, but everybody else's too, including the Rupert Brookes who went gaily "forth into God."

In 1914 I was only seventeen and did not think I should ever be in the war. I was, therefore, not involved in that wave of patriotic idealism which sent the flower of our young manhood, with a song in the heart, to its destruction. But as the years went by, and Marne was succeeded by Givenchy, Ypres, and Somme, it became obvious that I should be called up. So I joined my school O.T.C. and went straight from that, in July, 1916, to an officer cadet battalion to be trained for a commission. Although war and soldiering were so remote from my real life and inner world that I could never feel I had anything to do with them, it did not occur to me to take the pacifist line. I simply faced the inevitable, perhaps not with a very good grace, and certainly without any flourish, but without question. I knew that I could not object for conscience's sake because I had no firm convictions, religious or other, and had not examined the theoretic grounds for such a position. Moreover, in my own way I was, as I still am, intensely patriotic. I loved England with all my heart and soul, but abominated the British Army. For me, there was absolutely nothing—no pride, pomp and circumstance of glorious war, no desire to excel in smartness or efficiency, no eagerness for promotion, honorable mention, or medals—just nothing whatever to mitigate the loathsomeness of military training with its routines of drill, the foulmouthed sergeants, the chlorinated gas masks, the bayonet practice where we were incited to blood lust, the musketry, and perhaps worst of all the insolence of the officers, with their "brows villainous low."

I am trying to describe how it all felt to live through, not to justify my own attitude on abstract grounds. Naturally I now see certain merits in military discipline to which I was then blind, and even before I had done with soldiering I had outgrown my callow reluctances and distastes and come to think most other men better fellows than myself. But it was harder for me to learn this lesson, I think I may truly and humbly say, than it was for many—perhaps most—others, because I was the only child of a very sheltered, pure, and religious home and had never been to a boarding school. More fearful to me than bullets or shells or sudden death was the experience of being snatched away from what I now know to have been a way of life exceptional in its Christian innocence and unworldliness and plunged straight into what then seemed to me a sink of all iniquities. In the cadet battalion I was one of only a very few who had come straight from school; nearly all the others had seen active service as privates or N.C.O.'s in France or elsewhere and had done well enough to be recommended for commissions. Never having had the normal boarding-school contacts with vice, prurience, snobbery, brutality, and worldliness, I was aghast at the sort of men these seemed and at the things they said and thought and did. Music had always shared, with the beauty of landscape, my heart's allegiance, but the songs these men sang on the march (in George Fox's phrase) "struck at my life." All this nauseated me so much that my "psyche" revolted, and I actually succumbed to a bad attack of jaundice during the training period.

I soon began to see that my horror of these men would not do, that, in fact, I was wrong in judging them to be merely immoral, brutal, and bloody-minded. They *were* all those things, but then they were also kind, brave, self-forgetful, heroic, and gay to a degree far beyond my reach. To be a good soldier, I thought and continued to think throughout, meant to have many qualities the reverse of those recommended by the Christian religion. But then I found that most of these men excelled me not only in soldierly qualities, but in the best human virtues, too. In my puritan priggishness, I was like the man who thought his whole platoon out of step but himself; it was I who was the oddity, the exception, the odd man out. My comrades were simply average specimens of a species I had never before met: *l'homme moyen sensuel.* All I could claim were the negative, the pharisaic virtues of not smoking and not drinking, not swearing and not whoring. It also came to me that perhaps even the hated bugle had been the appointed summons (it might have come in some other form, but it came in this) to bid me emerge from the womblike insulation in which I had tarried too long. Life inflicts this trauma upon us all in due season, but what a price my generation had to pay for such "deliverance"!

In France the lessons continued in a new guise. In the cadet battalion, which was in Cambridge, I had had a billet almost to myself; it was, in fact, by what may or may not have been pure chance, a room in my own college. But in France, as a second lieutenant, I was perforce a member of an officers' mess, sometimes in rest billets and sometimes in the line. Privacy ceased to exist, and my fellow officers, as well as the men of my platoon (nearly all of them Yorkshiremen), were at first as strange to me as foreigners. They spoke an alien dialect, and when I could understand what they said, it was generally bawdry. Long winter evenings spent huddled with them in billets or dugouts, they smoking and drinking and playing cards and telling dirty stories, and I trying to read a serious book as though I were at home—these things at first nearly broke me down. However, a certain native adaptability and (thank God) a sense of humor kept me going, and though I stuck to my guns and remained myself, I learned tolerance and humility. I was, of course, mercilessly mocked and derided for my puritanism by everyone from the colonel downward, but as I very soon found, they were fine and magnanimous fellows and managed to put up with me as a harmless oddity. But it did amaze me that they should think my sort so very queer and exceptional.

To me these were the real issues; machine guns and whizbangs and 5.9's almost irrelevant sideshows. As I look back, I seem to see myself trying to live my own sort of life as if there were no war on and as if I expected to survive it (a very unlikely thing for a subaltern in those days). My letters home and my diaries were filled with descriptions, in the distilled language of literary youth, of places and buildings, of sunsets and scenery, and occasionally of people, and with "great thoughts" about life and destiny. The letters must have been highly unsatisfactory to my parents (to whom nearly all were addressed), and they did once plead for something more down-to-earth, something more human, about everyday doings. But they understood, what some reviewers of *Spots of Time* missed, that I was deliberately playing down the horrors of war for their benefit, and giving them a *couleur de rose* view to allay their gnawing anxiety about their (unworthy but sole) offspring. Even when I was in the trenches, I would try to interest them in the amenities of our dugout or the humors of a front-line dinner with the C.O. and make no mention of the time when the Germans pinpointed the dugout with 5.9 shells and blew to smithereens an observer who had just gone out after reporting to us.

Some of my experiences were of a kind new and valuable to me, not because I was a soldier but because I had lived most of my life on the outskirts of London. For instance, I had never before lived in a country house in midwinter. When I joined my battalion in January, 1917, Europe was in the grip of one of this century's most arctic winters. My unit had just come out of the line for a month's rest, and the officers of my company were billeted for a time in the *mairie* of a village called Le Meillard. That lovely eighteenth-century mansion, with its farmhouse smells of woodsmoke and stored fodder, its pigeons, and especially its kind and cultivated inhabitants (who cannot fail to have thought the English barbarians, though they did not show it), remains associated forever with the searing cold of that January and mitigates the memory of it. Nor, again, had I ever before spent the month of May in a nightingale-haunted village beside a turreted castle—as I did later that same year. This was when I was sent on a course to be trained as a signal officer, and never before or since have I seen the glories of that loveliest of months more lavishly displayed. No doubt the beauty of it was heightened and made more poignant by the sound of the distant guns—the guns of the battle at Gavrelle in which half my battalion was wiped out. Another such experience was the week's route march (for there was little mechanized transport in those days) from the Somme to Béthume in early spring. Each day's march, though exhausting on account of the weight of equipment, was enjoyable because it took us through an undevastated rolling countryside not unlike Buckinghamshire and ended each night with a feast of new-laid eggs in a picturesque, if stercoraceous, farmhouse. The change in the scenery, as we came down from the uplands into the northern plains and saw coal mines far away on the horizon, was exciting.

It is on scenes like these that I prefer now, as I did then, to dwell; they permanently enrich the memory and remain as vivid as ever, while the images of shell holes, trenches, barbed wire, corpses, and tragic ruins have worn thin and spectral. I could have said more about such things—about lice and mud and stench and the spasms of fear—but I see no reason for it. Battlefields and the stark facts of the actual fighting have been described with incomparable power, in prose and verse, by writers, some of whom are contributors to the present volume. Moreover, I saw much less of these things than men like Blunden, Sassoon, or Graves, who were in the thick of them and have given us classic accounts of them. Twice when my battalion went over the top, I was away on courses of training, and later in 1917 our parts of the line (in front of Vimy Ridge and Arras) were, shelling apart, relatively quiet. It is almost true to say that the first German soldier I saw was the one who took me prisoner on March 27, 1918, at Moyenneville near Albert. It is literally true that I never set eyes on a single German until, in March, 1918, our division was rushed to the Somme to try to stop the enemy breakthrough of that month. At that critical time and in that sector, the trench system had been left far behind and the fighting was more of the traditional kind, in open country. I remember well the incredulity with which I first saw, swarming toward us over a hill about half a mile away, a lot of men in gray, accompanied by others on horseback. Hitherto I had thought of the territory behind the German barbed wire as a tabooed and malignant region in which danger lurked and out of which death, impersonally, might at any moment spring on us. It was a new realization, though not new knowledge, to find that it contained real men.

Every night for about a week in that month of March, we retired before the German advance, presumably with a view to consolidating a defensible position farther back. Nobody seemed to know quite what was going on or what to do; the staff may have known, but our colonel certainly didn't. (When later I read Tolstoy's *War and Peace* I recognized in his big battle scene the authentic notes of vagueness and confusion.) It was my duty as signal officer to walk back each night under cover of dark to find a new battalion headquarters. The sleeplessness and bewilderment of that week and the final battle in which many of us were taken prisoner have left an ineffaceable memory, with a dark emotional coloring peculiar to itself. On the day of that battle, March 27, I saw more horrific sights than in all the rest of my military days put together. For years afterward I was never safe from the recurring vision (one of several) of a young officer I had known and liked, stumbling toward the dressing station with a gaping wound in his abdomen and whispering, "Oh, Doctor, is there any hope?" Or the sound made by the prone figure beside me, the private soldier with a bullet through his head, whose body went on breathing stertorously, it seemed forever, after the death of his mind.

I myself had a bullet wound, but it was only through the thigh, and I was a walking case for the first few days behind the German lines. Later, in a lazaret at Mons, the wound began to suppurate, and at Antwerp (where I had become a stretcher case) blood poisoning caused fever and semidelirium. However, a sudden improvement began on the hospital train to Hamburg, when the suppuration discharged of its own accord. But I was in the hospital in Hamburg for nearly three months. At last, on my twenty-first birthday, July 25, 1918, I was sent under military guard, but by a civilian train, to the distributing camp at Rastatt in Baden. I was there for more than a month, and then, just as the German regime began to crack, I was with the party which was sent right across to Kamstigall-bei-Pillau, a remote East Prussian seaport on the Baltic Frisches Haff. The three-day train journey from Rastatt to Kamstigall was the second worst I have known; it was in fourth-class carriages with bare wooden seats and no corridor amenities. We were detrained from time to time at the bigger railway stations (Halle, Berlin, etc.) to receive our ration of soup—generally ersatz macaroni and dried pears with sour rye bread. We passed through some fine mountain scenery at one point, but here I learned something new (new to me then, though I found it later in one of Coleridge's letters from the Harz country) about the landscape emotion. I found to my surprise that it depended on associations and memories. These German mountains were of the sort which, had they been in England, would have made my heart leap up. But here, they were only protuberances in an alien and hostile land: faceless, expressionless, and blank. I called this my second worst train journey; the worst of all was between Cambrai and Mons, when, as a walking-wounded case, I was put with others like me into a truck lined with straw, of the *Hommes 40 Chevaux 8* type so familiar to the troops in France.

I have given a full account in *Spots of Time* of my eight months as a *Kriegsgefangener,* and perhaps in any case it would be out of place to enlarge upon them here. During those last months in East Prussia it was obvious that Germany was on the point of collapse, and the German troops in charge of the camp became openly friendly. In fact I came across very little hostile feeling or arrogance toward our side during my whole time in Germany; from the day of capture onward the usual approach to "Tommee" was a cigarette and a handshake. But now it was all brotherliness and to hell with the Kaiser. On Armistice Day, November 11, 1918, the red flag was hoisted over the camp, and the private soldier who had been the interpreter announced himself as president of the local soviet ("Workers' and Soldiers' Council") and commandant of the camp in place of the (deposed) Prussian general. He courteously threw open the camp gates and invited us to walk wherever we liked. However, this was wisely vetoed by our own senior officer (a brigadier), and in due time (it seemed endless to our impatience) we sailed from Danzig to Leith in a Danish ship.

Those final weeks, when the smell of victory and liberation was in the air, set flowing in our veins a current of expectancy and exultation which would have been still more eager if we all had not been laid low, for weeks, by the grippe or influenza which swept the Continent that autumn. If we arrived home, as most of us did, looking like skeletons, that was due to the virus, not to starvation. The wretched Germans were, indeed, starving and used to beg us to spare them things from the food parcels which kept us going at a higher standard than their own and which nevertheless were never looted in transit. The streets of Danzig were placarded with FRIEDE UND BROT, and crowds (mostly of pale and ragged children) shouted, "Englishman!" to us as our ship prepared to sail, holding up their hands for the crusts we threw to them.

A heroes' welcome awaited us at Leith, and there was cheering and waving along the line southward. But the shouting and the jubilation died down, as such things must, and my return to my old home in north London, late on a December evening, was outwardly an anticlimax. My parents awaited me with hearts too full for much speaking, and I could see that the years of anxiety—so much more corrosive for them than for me—had worn and weakened them, my mother especially.

Within a month I was back at my Cambridge college, where but for the war I should by now at twenty-two have been a third-year man. I was still in uniform for a while, but a real undergraduate at last reading history. In those immediate postwar days the students fell into three fairly self-contained groups: the freshmen straight from school, who to us seemed little boys; the small group of men who through unfitness or other cause had been up at college all the time; and last—by far the largest—the returned warriors. We of the veteran group felt that the place belonged to us and that the university curricula must be adapted to our needs. The founding of the Cambridge English School was symbolical of this. It is perhaps not generally known that the first tripos (*i.e.*, honors) examination in English, as an independent subject, was held in 1919. The founding fathers, H. M. Chadwick, Sir Arthur Quiller-Couch, and the Reverend H. F. Stewart, who during the war years had been making the blueprints, knew that as soon as peace came, there would be an influx of mature and experienced men who would stand for no nonsense and who would demand something more modern and more relevant than the classics, yet something which would mediate the same humane values as classics had done. It was to meet this expected demand that Cambridge English was started. Sure enough, the demand came, and English got off to a spectacular start. True, it was viewed with grave suspicion by the academic old guard, and it long remained a Cinderella subject. When in 1920 I switched over from history to English, my college shook its head sadly and sent me to a tutor of the old school who prophesied disaster for the new subject and unemployment for me or anyone else deluded enough to take it. Yet it was in those years, and for many to come, that "Q," the main propagandist for English, was drawing audiences unexampled in Cambridge history, and soon I. A. Richards was to begin those lectures which revolutionized the approach to literature and founded the New Criticism.

But it would be quite wrong to give the impression that winds of change began to blow immediately after the war. It is true that we of the new English school felt that the future was on our side, and we were glad and proud to be in at the start of so promising an experiment. But the feeling which overrode all others was a deep longing to pick up the old threads again and return to the *status quo ante bellum*. And here I am speaking not only of the university, but of the whole nation. It was a good world into which the monstrous horror had broken, and we must build it up again, into something better, if possible, than we had before, but on the old principles and the old assumptions. Above all, never, never again could there be, never must there be, another war.

It was in that sort of spirit that we resumed our normal lives in the early twenties, those years which are so often said to have been disillusioned, but which in reality were innocent and auroral—the years when liberalism and romanticism seemed still unchallenged, the years before the east winds really did begin to rise. The nineteenth century might have been the biggest casualty of the war, but the fact was not yet generally known.

Alec Waugh

ALEC WAUGH *was born in London in July, 1898, the son of Arthur Waugh, a distinguished man of letters who directed for many years the fortunes of Chapman & Hall, the house that first published Dickens. He was educated at Sherborne School and at the Royal Military College, Sandhurst. Gazetted to the Dorsetshire Regiment, he served in France as a machine-gun officer from July, 1917, until he was taken prisoner in the big retreat in March, 1918. In July, 1917, he published his first novel, written when he was seventeen,* The Loom of Youth—*a realistic story of public school life that was sufficiently realistic to cause Sherborne to remove not only his name but his father's from the old boys' society.*

The first number of the United States Celebrity Register says of him: "His first book was too localized to enjoy success in America. It was not until eight years later, in 1925, that with the publication of Kept, a story of London Post-War Society, he reached an American public. Its success enabled him to begin his extensive travels. The South Seas, the Far East and the West Indies have provided material for many of his novels as well as his later histories. Since 1927 he has been a frequent visitor to the United States and for over thirty years New York's Hotel Algonquin has been his second home. . . . Not so humorous in his writings as his brother Evelyn, he has a keen wit in person. . . . He has friends all over the world."

He has written more than forty books, of which his West Indian novel, Island in the Sun, *an international best seller, is both the best and the most successful.*

His brother, Evelyn, was by five and a quarter years his junior.

A LIGHT RAIN FALLING

MY SIXTEENTH BIRTHDAY fell in July, 1914. I was then in the sixth form at Sherborne School. That summer I had, as a cricketer, got into the first eleven. The previous term I had earned my house colors at football. Literature was opening its wide doors for me. My father, Arthur Waugh, the managing director of Chapman & Hall, the publishing house that had launched Charles Dickens, was a prominent man of letters; he had won the Newdigate Prize Poem at Oxford; he had contributed to the first number of *The Yellow Book*; he had published several books of criticism. He and I were very close. In the holidays he read me poetry every evening; my essays were peppered with quotations. My love of literature was being fostered as warmly and as wisely at school as it was at home. I was singularly lucky in my schoolmasters. My headmaster was Nowell Charles Smith, a distinguished Wordsworthian; the sixth-form tutor was H. T. Wade-Gery, to whom many references are made in C. M. Bowra's *Memories*. My special tutor was S. P. B. Mais, the erratic rebel whose entry in *Who's Who* is probably as long as any in the volume. I was pouring out reams of Byronic verse. Life was roseate with promise.

To nearly everyone the outbreak of war was utterly unexpected. School broke up on the last Tuesday in July. The headmaster in his farewell speech on the previous evening had referred to the bad news in the morning papers. I thought he was referring to the threat of civil war in Ulster. Myself, I was concerned with the cricket championship. My county, Middlesex, was lying close behind the leaders, Kent and Surrey, which were playing each other at Blackheath at the end of the week. The result of that match would improve Middlesex's chances against one or other of its adversaries. I had spent half a morning working out in terms of percentages which result would best suit Middlesex. It appeared that a draw, with Surrey getting points for a first innings lead, would be the most satisfactory. My father had promised to take me out to watch the game on the last day—Saturday, August 1.

When that Saturday came, war had become inevitable. Yet we went out to the Rectory Field all the same. So did several thousand others. It was a warm, sunny morning. We sat with Philip Trevor, the *Daily Telegraph* cricket correspondent. "I'll write a report of this," he said, "but it will never be printed. Monday's paper won't have room for anything but war news." During the morning telegrams were brought out to two of the fieldsmen. "Calling up orders, I suppose," said Trevor.

The game followed its course; it was fairly exciting, up till teatime, with a chance of Surrey winning, but the Kent tail held firm. The sky clouded over; rain began to fall, and soon after five o'clock, play was abandoned. It was the conclusion I had hoped for, five days earlier—a draw, with Surrey taking points for a first innings lead. Now I could not have cared less. In retrospect, that game petering out into a draw, with a light rain falling, became symbolic of the extinction of a way of life.

On the next day, Sunday, I went down in the evening to my old preparatory school at Haslemere, where my former headmaster had arranged a cricket match for the August bank holiday. We found a small crowd of some thirty people gathered round the entrance to the station. "Any news?" they asked. There was no radio then; there were no evening papers on a Sunday. They had gathered by ones and twos independently to meet the trains in the hope that someone from London could tell them something.

How different was the start of the Second War. In September, 1939, there was that gray, tired voice announcing over the air the failure of his policy of appeasement, and next morning the billboards were covered with security posters—"Careless talk costs lives" —a symbol of the period of gray repression on which the country was entering. In contrast, in August, 1914, there had been a stirring call to arms, with the posters of Kitchener's pointing finger, "Your King and your Country Need YOU!"

There was no conscription till 1916, and there was a gallantry to "the taking of the King's shilling." The recruit was treated as a hero. The spirit of the hour was caught by Rupert Brooke's sonnet "Now, God be thanked, who has matched us with his hour." All my friends were hurrying to enlist or were applying for commissions, and I was furious at being under age. Boys who had failed to get their house colors the term before were now in khaki. Had I not proved that I was physically fitter than they were? Was I not higher placed in form? Why should I have to return to school to mark time for another year at least?

That, I think, was how everyone of my age who had my kind of public school upbringing felt. We were all impatient to be in it. We were afraid that the war would be over before we could "get across." When I read in August, 1915, of the fall of Warsaw, I could not resist thinking with part of my mind, "That's bound to mean another year of war. For certain I'll be in it." I question if any teen-ager had that feeling in the Second War. We went where we were sent. We were resolved to do our utmost. But with the end of the voluntary system of enlistment, there was no longer the challenge to oneself to take one's place beside one's friends in battle.

It is inevitable that a young man of vitality and ambition should be in his early years self-absorbed. No one of my age could have failed to see the First War other than as a background to himself. Whatever happened to me, the fifty-two months following my sixteenth birthday could not have failed to be crowded, colored, and dramatic. They were no less so because they were set within the framework of a war. When as a schoolboy I had looked ahead during the long summer evenings of 1914, I had pictured myself in the autumn of 1918 as starting my second year at Oxford; actually I was to find myself in an officers' prisoner-of-war camp on the Rhine; but I was not only a lieutenant in confinement, I was the author of a realistic story of school life that, published in July, 1917, was the center of violent controversy and that is still in print. I was also engaged to be married.

I have heard people say, "I would not be eighteen again," or, "I wouldn't be twenty-two again," as though each age had its special intrinsic disability. That has not been my experience. I have had my share of bad years, but they have not been bad because I happened to be eighteen, twenty-one, thirty-four, or fifty-four, but because the conditions of my life irrespective of my age happened at that moment to be unsatisfactory. My eighteenth year did happen to be such a year, because as a private in the Inns of Court Officers Training Corps, I found myself with a group of men much older than myself, from backgrounds that were unfamiliar to me, whom I found uncongenial. Yet it was during that year that I wrote the novel that "made my name," and I should be grateful to it.

I had a lucky war. I was unwounded; my health was not impaired by gas. Most men, if they have enjoyed good health, if they have been reasonably successful in their undertakings, can look back gratefully on their years between sixteen and twenty. Certainly I can.

Those years were marked out for me in a series of defined sec-tions, separate and distinct: I had another year at school. I left in the summer of 1915 to join the Inns of Court O.T.C., in the belief that I should be gazetted shortly to the Dorsets, but the age limit for a commission was raised from seventeen to eighteen and a half; so to fill in the time I went to Sandhurst, to the Royal Military College, and I was not gazetted until April, 1917. I did not, however, join the Dorsets. At Sandhurst my rough and cumbersome tactics on the football field had earned me the nickname Tank, so that when a notice was put on the company board asking for applications to join the heavy-machine-gun corps (Tanks), my friends insisted on entering my name on it. I found, however, the training for it longer than I had expected, and being anxious to get to France as soon as possible, I broke it off halfway, settling for the Machine Gun Corps *tout simple*, so that it was as a machine-gun officer that I sailed for France in July, to be attached to the 3d Division, to fight in the battles of Passchendaele and Cambrai, and to be taken prisoner in the big retreat south of Arras on March 28, 1918.

"The Lost Generation" is a cliché: it has been claimed that Gertrude Stein used it first in reference to Hemingway and Scott Fitzgerald, but it was in general currency earlier than that. I met it myself for the first time in 1920, when Douglas Jerrold, for many years a prominent London journalist and the author of several substantial books, in particular his autobiography, *Georgian Adventure*, offered Chapman & Hall a novel with that title. There was a very small market then for war books. Jerrold's novel was not particularly good, and we declined it. As far as I know, it never found a publisher. All that I can remember about it is the title.

There were, in fact, a number of lost generations, each being lost in a different way. I belonged to the generation that had had no adult life before the war, that grew up during the war and, if it was lost at all, was lost in this, that it never became a generation. A generation is formed when a group of young contemporaries, on the brink of their careers, meet and exchange ideas either on a college campus or in a sidewalk café. Myself, I never had that. By the time the war was over, I was launched on a literary career. I was also engaged to be married. For me to go up to Oxford seemed a putting back of the clock. But only a portion of my generation found itself in that position. Sir Maurice Bowra, for instance, who is my exact contemporary and who in March, 1918, was engaged in the same campaign around Arras that I was, but who was a scholar, whereas I was not, went up to Oxford and became one of the most significant figures in a significant generation. I am sure that he would not think of himself as belonging to a lost generation, nor for that matter do I.

Apart from my one year in the Inns of Court, I enjoyed Army life—its comradeship, its open-air routine, the buoyant consciousness of being supremely fit. I should be well content to relive my nine months at Sandhurst. My fellow cadets were in a high degree congenial. The training was interesting. There was a day-to-day eventfulness about the progress that one made; there was an urgency about everything one did—a need to get one's commission quickly, to get out to France as soon as possible. There was the excitement of the last exams with one's marks coming through. Then there was the "passing out" parade, mercifully on a warm late April morning, with the adjutant riding up the steps of the Old Building on his horse; the final handing in of one's equipment; the prospect of two weeks' leave and the opening of one's first bank account; having money that one had earned oneself. And it was exciting at that to become an officer, to wear a Sam Browne belt, to be saluted in the streets.

I think that the First War was more exciting than the Second; or am I only thinking that it is more exciting to be eighteen than forty-two? The First War was a grimmer one. The casualties were much higher. Of the forty-four boys who went to Sherborne on the same day that I did in September, 1911, only half lived to see their fortieth birthday. About as many Shirburnians fell during the Second War as in the First, but the numbers of the school were twice as big in 1939 as they had been in 1914. The western desert was not squalid in the way that the western front was, and the First War did not offer the opportunities that the Second did, for the "Renaissance man" of enterprise and courage who performed spectacular raids in the Commandos. But the Second War was dreary, because it was a total war, because the periods of training were so lengthy, because for so long nothing happened or appeared likely to happen. Recruits of 1939 did not, many of them, see fighting until the D-day landings in 1944. My brother has given in *Brideshead Revisited* a vivid account of the boredom that descended on a unit that had been kept in training long after it was fully trained. There was none of that waiting around in the First War. But the real difference lay in this: Civilian life was drab during the Second War. I myself was posted to the Middle East in September, 1941, so that I was spared the most depressing period. But when I returned to England in the summer of 1945, I could appreciate what had happened in the intervening forty months. There had been the blackout; there had been the bombing; there had been rationing of food and gasoline; there had been restrictions of every kind: The country had become a dormitory for our allies' troops. Everyone was overworked; everyone was slightly undernourished: My friends were either drawn, lined, and thin or unhealthily obese through an excess of starchy foods—bread, potatoes, and macaroni. Nobody had much fun.

But in the First War private life went on, in large part undisturbed. If you read Arnold Bennett's journals, you will see that he and his friends were living very much as they had been four years before; only their day-to-day living was given a sense of added urgency by the war across the water. England was never in any danger, but after June, 1940, for the next fifteen months England was in very actual danger. There was a definite threat of invasion. In the First War there was some kind of defense organization, of men in fancy uniform who drilled on Hampstead Heath. My father at the age of fifty never considered enrolling in it, but I am quite certain that if he had been fifty in 1940, he would have enrolled in the Home Guard. In the summer of 1940 it was difficult for a civilian to continue his private business with any enthusiasm, unless through that business he was making a contribution to what was called the war effort. Personal ambition, the demands of a personal career were meaningless. It was not like that in the First War. The men who were not eligible for military service went on with their private lives.

London was very gay during the First War. Such bombing as there was was negligible; so was the blackout: The tops of the streetlamps were blackened, so that cones of light were thrown on the pavement. The streets were romantic with short-skirted women on the arms of khaki escorts emerging from and vanishing into the darkness.

Until 1944 the actual fighting took place far away, in the Far East and the Middle East; there was no such thing as a fortnight's leave. When a man sailed for Suez and beyond, he went for keeps. In the first War, soldiers were constantly coming back on leave, expecting to be amused and with money in their pockets, anxious to spend it on their friends. London was, in fact, a sustained, continuous party, even when the war news was at its worst. I have few more thrilling memories than that of the February morning in 1918 when I was sitting in my dugout checking the figures of a machine-gun barrage and expecting the day ahead to be an exact replica of its predecessor and of its successors, but a runner arrived from details with the news that I was to report immediately at company headquarters and proceed that night on two weeks' U.K. leave.

There was nothing exceptional about my war record—except that I had the good luck to come through unscathed, and I felt about the war very much as my contemporaries did: My feelings toward it changed with the recognition of what modern war—or, rather, what that kind of modern war—involved.

In every country in Europe, war was welcomed not only with enthusiasm but with exultation, particularly so in Britain, which had not been involved in a major war for a hundred years. The country felt restored, rejuvenated: "like a swimmer into cleanness leaping" was Rupert Brooke's phrase for it. We saw war in terms of

Agincourt and Crécy, of battles won in a day, "of bannered broidery." But within three years that first heady excitement had been replaced by Siegfried Sassoon's savage satires:

> To-day he's in the pink, but soon he'll die
> And still the war goes on, he don't know why.

In part this change of temper was due to the deadlock that lasted on the western front for three and a half years. There it stretched between Switzerland and the sea, that long line of shell holes and barbed-wire entanglements, week after week, month after month, with the flags on the maps scarcely moving. Every few months there would be an offensive that would be hailed as a titanic victory. A few weeks later it would be recognized that only a few yards of swamp had been acquired at the cost of many thousands of lives and at a great expenditure of bullion. Loos, Verdun, the Somme, the Chemin des Dames, Passchendaele, Cambrai—one by one they came and went with the same result, the same absence of result. In the late autumn of 1917 Lord Lansdowne wrote a long letter to the *Times*, arguing that the war was ceasing to serve any purpose, that the time had come to call a halt. Many were in agreement with him. The thing had gone on too long.

At the beginning an attempt had been made to whip up hatred of the Germans, as in Germany there were slogans of *Gott Straffe England*. There was a recital of atrocities, but that spirit of hatred did not last for long. It was hard for soldiers in the line to feel any hatred for the poor devils who a few yards away were in the same mess as they. It was impossible not to regard them as fellow victims in a shared calamity.

The apparent pointlessness of the war on the western front bred a feeling of resentment against the governments who were responsible for it and for the generals who carried out or failed to carry out their orders. There was talk of bad faith and of mismanagement in high places. Sassoon's poem "The General" was read with chuckles. A general was described as greeting heartily a regiment on its way to battle:

> "He's a cheery old card," grunted Harry to Jack
> As they slogged up to Arras with rifle and pack. . . .
> But he did for them both by his plan of attack.

In no other war—unless the current campaign in Vietnam provides a parallel—was there such a prolonged period of stagnation where nothing seemed to be done, where nothing seemed to be achieved. Because of the immobility of the line, the higher commands were completely cut off from the men they led. The staff at divisional headquarters lived in comfort and in safety behind the lines. They were immune from attack; bombing had not been highly developed; they were very rarely shelled. Though their troops might be only a few miles away, they were virtually out of reach. During the eight months that I was in the line, I did not see a single senior officer over the rank of lieutenant colonel. A machine gunner's position was to a certain extent exceptional, in that he occupied a series of isolated posts and was not, when he was out of the line, involved in divisional or corps maneuvers, where he would have been exposed to exhortations from "brass hats," but the fact remains that I did not see "red flannel" for eight months.

Much has been written for and against the strategy of Passchendaele. The attack was launched in 1917 at the end of July at a time of year when there was more likely to be rain than not in an area where the low-lying ground with a water system only a few feet below the surface was certain to be churned into mud very quickly. By the end of the first week it was clear that the primary objectives had not been reached, that sustained bombardment would reduce the mud into a quagmire. There was no longer any possibility of the planned-for breakthrough; yet the attack was continued into November.

The defense of Haig's strategy has been that the continued assault aided a general campaign of attrition and also relieved pressure on the French. Such arguments could no doubt be maintained effectively in a debate, and we do not know what would have happened had Haig not continued his attack. He might have given the Germans the breathing space they needed, and the attack that they launched in March, 1918, might have proved irresistible. That is as it may be; of one thing we can be certain: The fighting man was convinced that Haig had no idea what he was doing, that he had not seen with his own eyes—how could he have?—the terrain over which he was ordering his men to advance, that he had to rely on second- and third-hand reports, often from interested parties who were anxious to report smooth things. He was operating in the dark. There was no equivalent for this situation in the Second War, which was a war of movement, and it should not be forgotten that the generals of the Second War had been the subalterns of the First. They had learned a lesson. On both sides of the line they shared the dangers and discomforts of the men they led, and they retained their trust and confidence.

The First War generals forfeited that trust. Before the Battle of the Somme the troops had been assured that the artillery would put down a barrage that no living object could survive; yet the moment the barrage had lifted, the Germans came up from their deep dug-outs, mounted their machine guns on the parapets, and mowed down the advancing troops.

The fighting man in the First War felt that he was being lied to; he also felt that he was being lied about. He felt that the "people at home" had no idea of the ordeal he was enduring.

If the static conditions of fighting on the western front bred a resentment against and distrust of the staff officers at the rear, far more did it create a resentment against civilians. Civilians were very little affected by the war; there was rationing during the last months, but housekeeping was far less difficult than it was to be during the austerity years after the Second War; the blackout was mild; there were no unemployed; a great deal of money was being made. It used to be said, "This war is not likely to end; too many people are doing well out of it." There was special animosity against the politicians whose positions depended on the continu-ance of the war, who could not afford to admit that they had made mistakes, who had to maintain the public's enthusiasm for "the sacred cause." It infuriated the soldier. In the autumn of 1916, after the slaughter of the Somme, the men in public life were mouthing the same platitudes that they had on recruiting drives two years before. It had been all right to call war the great game when regiments had gone over the top dribbling a football and colonels had led their men brandishing a hunting crop. But it was not like that any longer.

It was in the Battle of the Somme that the majority of Kitchener's 1914 recruits first saw real fighting, and that autumn constituted a watershed for the soldier's attitude toward the war. He fully real-ized then for the first time the squalor and horror of a modern battlefield.

In a novel, *The Balliols,* that I published in 1934, I tried to explain what it was that he discovered. I described the hero of the story:

. . . leaning against the parapet of a narrow trench while the shells crashed round him. . . . He tried to find, in a desperate attempt to occupy his mind, a simile that would explain the contrast between this war and war as he had seen it during the trench routine of the winter months.

He found a simile.

He thought of sickness as the ordinary healthy man pictures it. There are headaches, there are bilious attacks, there are colds, there are epidemics of influenza, with ricocheting temperatures and a night or two of anxiety. . . . It was in such terms that the average healthy man saw sickness. And then one day he is taken round a hospital. He sees what sickness is for those who are really ill. The operating tables, the rubber gloves, the knives, the chloroform, the antiseptic bandages, the suppurating wounds, the injections of morphia and strychnine. He thinks "Is this what sickness really is?"

The simile held true. Trench routine bore the same routine to the warfare of the battlefield that the casual sickness of the healthy man bore to the illness of the mortally stricken invalid; that headaches and feverish colds bore to organic ailment. In trench routine there were the discomforts of cold, exposure, lack of sleep; there was the unending friction of exhausted nerves; there was at night the sharp ping of bullets, the occasional direct hit with a shell, when a dugout would be blown to pieces and casualties rushed to a field dressing station. It was this that the eminent visitors to the line were shown; the publicists, politicians and priests who went home imagining that they had been shown war.

But *this:* the desolate carnage of the battlefield: this was an altogether other thing—the long unending plain of mudholes, waterfilled, precariously lined by duckboard tracks; the bombardments during which it was impossible to make one's voice carry beyond a traverse; when the shells hailed down so fast that you could not distinguish individual trajectories when there would be a roar at one side or another; and a fountain of earth and iron tossed in a high cascade; when the stretcher bearers were fewer than their tasks, when not only No Man's land but the long stretch of reclaimed land over which the tide of field grey uniforms had receded slowly, was littered with the bodies of distorted and unburied men.

A new note now entered into the writing about the war. There was a resolve on the part of the soldier to present war as the ugly thing it was, to do with words what painters like C. R. W. Nevinson had done on canvas. From France came Henri Barbusse's novel *Under Fire* (*Le feu*), and in England there was Siegfried Sassoon's satires. The refrain line "Mustn't the dear old Kaiser love the tanks" was followed by the quatrain:

> I'd like to see a tank come down the stalls
> Lurching to ragtime ditties and "home sweet home"
> And there'd be no more jokes in music halls,
> To mock the riddled corpses in Bapaume.

Simultaneously for many young soldiers, certainly for me, there came a newly awakened social consciousness. Up till now the average public school boy had been automatically a Conservative. His father had voted Tory, and he was resolved to do the same when he was old enough. He was trained to think of himself as a leader. He was a privileged person, and privilege entailed its own responsibilities. He might have sponsored a program of government for the people, but government by the people was quite another thing.

The young officer began to feel differently about the men he led in action. What voice had they had in determining their present fate? They had been taken from their homes and jobs; a gun had been put into their hands, and they had been told to kill Germans with it. What were they getting out of it? Had any government the right to do this to them? Many young officers carried back with them to civilian life a number of unanswered questions.

Many of us returned, too, in a spirit of crusade, resolved to ensure that the crime of war would never be reenacted. The world must be convinced of the horror and the waste of war; power must be taken from those in whose interests, in the defense of whose property and privileges, in the acquisition of whose wealth and powers, wars were begun and waged. Wars never brought anything but misery and deprivation to the proletariat. We reminded ourselves that the I.L.P. (Independent Labour Party) alone had protested against the continuation of the fighting long after it had ceased to be a war of self-defense. There was a big swing to the left, and within a year or two Oxford University had elected as the president of its Union a member of the Labour Party, Kenneth Lindsay, later to be a member of Ramsay MacDonald's Ministry.

What happened to that spirit of crusade? Most of us too soon were caught up by the problems of civilian life: There were livings to be earned; there was the relief that the war was over; there was the exhaustion that follows the completion of a sustained effort, as runners collapse when the tape is breasted. The old men were firmly in their saddles. By the time we had recovered our breath, it was too late, and we realized that far from learning the lessons that the war should have taught, the world was busily repeating its mistakes and that "the war that will end war" (H. G. Wells' phrase) was being followed by "the peace that will end peace." We shrugged. There did not seem a thing to do about it. Anyhow it was a long way off. We had the present, and we had our youth. Our health was unimpaired. Let us enjoy ourselves while we could, so we embarked on the frivolities and excesses of the period of "the bright young people" whose spirit was expressed in Scott Fitzgerald's stories and my brother's *Vile Bodies* and *A Handful of Dust*. It was in the main an outburst of high spirits, but it had an undercurrent of despair: the making the most of the sunlight while it lasted. 1939 was still a long way off.

Amos Wilder

AMOS NIVEN WILDER *was born in Madison, Wisconsin, on September 18, 1895, the son of Amos Parker Wilder, then editor of the* Wisconsin State Journal *and later Consul General in Hong Kong and Shanghai. He prepared for college at the Thacher School, Ojai, California, spent two years at Oberlin College, transferred to Yale, and after his junior year there went to France in the fall of 1916. After a winter with the Paris section he joined Section 2 of the American Field Service in February, 1917, and then Section 3 in Serbia in July. When the United States Army took over the ambulance sections, he enlisted in Paris in the United States Field Artillery in November, 1917. He served as a corporal in the 17th Field Artillery of the 2d Division and was discharged in France in June, 1919.*

He took his B.A. at Yale in 1920, his B.D. in 1924 (after three years' study at Brussels and Oxford), and his Ph.D. in 1933, also at Yale. He was ordained to the ministry of the Congregational Churches (now the United Church of Christ) in 1926 and served as minister of the Congregational Church in North Conway, New Hampshire for three years. He taught first at Hamilton College (1930–33) and then as professor of the New Testament at Andover Newton Theological School (1933–43), the Chicago Theological Seminary and the Federated Theological Faculty of the University of Chicago (1943–54), and the Harvard Divinity School, from which he retired in 1963 as Hollis Professor of Divinity, Emeritus.

Amos Wilder has been a Fellow of the Belgian-American and the Guggenheim foundations, a visiting professor at the University of Frankfort, editor of the Journal of Religion, *a member of the editorial board of* Christianity and Crisis, *a member of the Yale Corporation, and president of the Society of Biblical Literature. He has received honorary degrees from Hamilton, Oberlin, and the universities of Chicago, Yale, and Basel. His publications include works on the New Testament and on contemporary literature. His first volume of poetry was entitled* Battle-Retrospect and Other Poems, *published in 1923 in the Yale Series of Younger Poets.*

AT THE NETHERMOST PIERS
OF HISTORY
World War I, A View from the Ranks
For Jules Deschamps

THE FIGURE of the old soldier reminiscing about his battles has often been disparaged in life and letters. New generations have other interests, and the grandchildren are restive, as guests are when they are confronted with a travelogue even though enlivened by homemade movies. When veterans forgather, of course, the situation is different. Old cronies will evoke common memories and even get out their maps and souvenirs. But outside the guild all such rehearsals carry the suspicion of parade. There have been too many examples of those who have traded on their exploits like the old rascal in O'Neill's *Touch of the Poet* who had gone so far as to fictionalize his martial disgraces into honors. There is also, of course, the impulse of the combatant to draw the veil upon the atrocious and to say good-bye to all that. In our period, moreover, the taboo on sentiment, rhetoric, and, worst of all, idealization works as a final check on any annals save the most austere.

It is at this last point, however, that I make bold to demur and to take all the risks, with the further excuse, indeed, of the editor's invitation. However it be with World War II and more recently, one cannot properly evoke service in World War I without according a place to sentiment and ideals, and not only as a recognition of regrettable illusions. So far as concerns America's part in that war, I write as an unreconstructed Wilsonian. One thing that specially engages my interest in these annals after so many years is precisely the ambiguity of those ideals as they animated so many of us, the rights and wrongs of our crusading impulse and rhetoric, the fine distinction between truth and propaganda, between historical mission and manufactured inducements, between authentic hopes and deceptive, apocalyptic anticipations.

A related matter that impels my fascinated scrutiny, also in its ambiguous character, is that of the war experience in its dramatic aspect, in its dimension of myth, the resonances of the sensibility and imagination of youth in its confrontation with the prodigious, and the strange postwar sense of anticlimax and disillusionment that accompanied the return to civilian life defined as normalcy.

Many college men of my generation volunteered in the American Field Service before America entered the war. Our motives were varied. The main idea, as with the Lafayette Escadrille, was to be where things were going on, and with this was mixed the romance of adventure. The urge of the Francophile played no small part. An early appeal of the Field Service for volunteers began with the words of Joffre: "The United States of America have not forgotten that the first page of the history of their independence was written with a little of the blood of France." There was an increasing sentiment, moreover, that America should be in the war. I had been on a Y.M.C.A. staff at a boys' Plattsburg (or training) Camp at Fort Terry (Plum Island, off New London, Connecticut) in the summer of 1916 and had heard Theodore Roosevelt fulminate to the ranks of teen-agers on the disgrace of our delay.

More significant to me as one concerned with the issues of pacifism and the moral aspects of the war was my experience as a student at Oberlin College in 1914–15. President Henry Churchill King in his large Sunday Bible class dealt for many months with the origins of the war, with an analysis of Prussianism, traditional Christian views of church and state, and the Christian attitude to war. The upshot was in effect a justification of American participation with the Allies. No doubt King did not know some of the things that were brought out later by men like Sidney Fay about the origins of the war. In any case the lurid tales of German atrocities were not part of the argument. King, like myself, was a Congregationalist and with Oberlin as a whole represented the tradition of the abolitionists and of the New England theocrats, according to which the church associates itself with the moral responsibility of the state. It was the same Calvinist tradition which led Woodrow Wilson later to select the term "covenant" used by John Calvin for the ordering of Geneva (not to mention the Scotch and English Covenanters) for the instrument of the League of Nations. In the spring of 1919 when the Army of Occupation in Germany released many college men to attend French and British universities, I was in the Army School Detachment at the University of Toulouse. Several of us interested in the Christian ministry were assigned to the old French Huguenot seminary at Montauban. The dean, Émile Doumergue (close relative of the later President of France, Paul Doumergue), was the greatest Calvin scholar of the time. He took immense delight in recognizing this link between the Geneva of John Calvin and the political and international idealism of Woodrow Wilson, son of a Presbyterian manse.

Americans who were in Europe before our declaration of war encountered bitterness over our delay. Passing through London on my way to the Continent in October, 1916, I heard the following *réplique* on the stage of a music hall. One comedian observed that George Washington "never let a lie slip through his teeth." "Yes," was the answer, "because like all Americans he spoke through his nose." But the disparagement, at least of American civilians, continued after the war in France, and sometimes for good reasons. In his *Chant funèbre pour les morts de Verdun*[1] Henry de Montherlant exclaims at the sacrilege of the first American tourists of the Verdun battlefields who carried off skulls in the trunks of their cars. "Peoples without a past need souvenirs. Already Washington used to exhibit piously one of the supposed keys to the Bastille, which actually were fabricated at Paris by the dozen."[2] But the American vanguard in France was honored, often in embarrassing ways. Arriving from the front with soiled uniform and, no doubt, marks of fatigue, I was offered a seat by a Frenchwoman in the crowded *métro*. The irritations that are perennial between the Americans and the French at the superficial levels of politics and tourism do not touch the deep confraternity in arms of the anonymous combatants in the ranks.

On the fourth of July, 1917, I was in Paris on the way from the French front to join an ambulance section with the French in Serbia. Thus, it came about that I was present at the Picpus cemetery where Pershing went that day to visit the grave of Lafayette. It has often served me as warning to the historian that though I was an eyewitness within hearing, I long told the story of hearing Pershing say, "Lafayette, we are here." I learned later that the words were spoken by a Colonel Stanton. One sometimes hears it said that the whole episode was a myth. This is going too far, but such are the perils of firsthand reminiscence. In any case I can remember accurately the day in April of that year when we saw the official French *affiche* at Ste.-Menehould announcing the American declaration of war and the emotion it aroused in the army zone among the French poilus and the few Americans already in service.

For the purposes of this chronicle I have disinterred from old trunks and cartons the letters I wrote home from France and Serbia, not looked at for fifty years. Most of them were written on the

---

1 Paris, 1924.
2 *Ibid.,* p. 38.

cheap lined sheets picked up in a village *papeterie*. Correspondence from the Field Service includes the official French postcard designated *Correspondence militaire* and sometimes carries the surcharge *Contrôle postal militaire*. One envelope was stamped RECEIVED WITHOUT CONTENTS. N.Y.P.O., PENN. TERM. STA. One illegible letter received in France had the written annotation *accident de mer*. After I transferred to the U.S. Army the letterhead of the Y.M.C.A. often appears with its red triangle and ON SERVICE WITH THE AMERICAN EXPEDITIONARY FORCES or that of the Knights of Columbus with its emblem and the American flag in color. From this time on each letter was censored: thus, "John Smith, Lt. 17th F.A." The envelopes carry the seals U.S. ARMY POSTAL SERVICE and A.E.F. PASSED AS CENSORED, again with the signature, which after all these years reminds me of the names of the several officers of my battery.

Army letters were often written in a dugout at night by the light of the little lamps which like our briquettes the French had taught us to improvise. With a small can and gasoline parleyed from a camion driver, supplemented by a strip of cloth for a wick and a sawed-off cartridge, one had a flare that would burn for hours. Books could not be sent through Army mail to the front, but my family tore the covers off them and sent them rolled up like magazines. My letters carry a running comment on classics thus available.

Besides the letters other survivals came to light: a receipt for $25 from a New Haven garage for a "Course in automobile repair and driving"; a Paris driving license, November 28, 1916 (my driving test was on the Champs Élysées); every kind of identity card, *permis de séjour, ordre de mouvement*—including the tour de force of red tape overcome for permission to spend a week's leave in the Lake District, wangled from both civil and military authorities, French and British, as well as the American Embassy in Paris. Here is a receipt from "Lloyd & Co., High Class English Tailors," Place de la Madeleine, for my ambulance uniform, "tunic, breeches and insignia"; an inventory of equipment received when enlisting in the Field Artillery; a penciled plan of a small French village indicating billeting arrangements for A Battery: officers, men, picket lines, infirmary, pumps for drinking water. A printed set of rules handed to men on leave in Paris included as No. 7: "The Military Police have been ordered to take the names and report all ranks, including Militarized Civilians, who permit themselves to be solicited on the streets."

Even the most trifling of such items gratify by their concreteness.

The past swims less in the vague. So the historian cherishes his papyri fragments, coins, and graffiti. Sometimes such archives have more importance. I found the original of a traced firing mission for batteries of our regiment indicating the successive advances of a creeping barrage, by minutes, in the area of Belleau Wood (duly deposited with the historical section of the 2d Division).

More of the order of minor graffiti is my on-the-spot notation of the humor and profanity of doughboys loading terrified horses by a ramp into a French boxcar (eight *chevaux*—twenty *hommes*). The first horses driven in plunge, kick out, and fall down.

"Bang! Bang! They're making a noise like a dozen batteries. There won't be anything left of this sawed-off freight car."

"Whoa! Whoa! Tie the S.O.B.'s in here before they trample me to death."

"Put a little straw up to 'em. A horse will come out of delirium tremens for a wisp of hay."

"As soon as they get done with it, though, they begin to see things."

Two men come out of the menagerie, pale and limping. "That's the way it goes. I was drunk as a cuckoo when I joined this man's army."

Singing: "Why didn't we wait to be drafted?" "Whoa there, you——brutes! Shut the door on them. They'll all be dead when we open it again, anyhow."

"There gotta be three men stay in there with 'em, too."

The Field Service had had its origins in the activities already initiated by Americans in 1914 under the auspices of the antebellum American Hospital in Neuilly. Before going to Section 2 in the Argonne, I served three months in the Paris section, our cars being stationed at the large new Lycée Pasteur, which had been converted to a hospital. We met the long hospital trains that came from the front into the Gare de la Chapelle. From Neuilly we would go across Paris to this station behind the Gare du Nord in a convoy of twenty or thirty heavy Buick ambulances. The Paris taxi drivers were already at this date a legend and were looked on as our only rivals in the skills of the road. They were not supposed to cut through our convoys, and if they so presumed, they were fair game for reprisal. Some of our soldier-of-fortune drivers boasted of neatly taking a wheel off one or more of these intruders. We took our loads of stretcher cases to hospitals in and around Paris often in the small hours of the night and made it a point of honor to know our way without the aid of the gendarme-guides provided.

I have lately been reminded that it is precisely to this Paris of 1916 that Proust brings back his narrator in the last part of his great work. Marcel observes the city in wartime. Referring to the duels in the sky, the searchlights, and the sirens, he invokes the Walküre of Wagner and the *Götterdämmerung*. He plays with the analogy of Pompeii and Herculaneum and, with his own scrutiny in mind, thinks of how "the frivolity of an epoch, when ten centuries have passed over it, becomes the matter of a grave erudition." He evokes the "august" or "supernatural" aspect of the combatants on leave from the front who in a few hours have exchanged the fabulous world of the lines for the world of the boulevards. He speaks of the touching charm of the young poilus: *"le petit Parigot . . . avec son air dessalé, sa mine éveillée et drôle—quelle finesse, quel bon sens!"* And *"les gars de province, comme ils sont amusants et gentils avec leur roulement d'r et leur jargon patoiseur!"*[3]

Speaking of the slang phrases of the war, *"passeront pas," "poilus," "on les aura,"* Proust finds his teeth set on edge by the vulgarisms, but then finds them sanctified. His sentiment about the warriors in faded blue brings back something of the mood and piety of the time:

> But if you saw all this world, especially those of humble lot, the workmen, the small tradesmen, who had no idea of their hidden capacities for heroism and who would have died in bed without ever suspecting it, if you had seen them run through the fire to assist a comrade, to carry off a wounded officer, and when themselves hit smile at the moment of death when the army surgeon says that the trench has been recaptured from the enemy, I assure you . . . that one gets a worthy idea of the French and one can appreciate better the epochs of the past which in our school days struck us as somewhat overdrawn.[4]

The French combatant writers of the time—Duhamel, Dorgelès, Montherlant—all disparage the city and the civilian in contrast with the tenor of the front. In the novel, by Philippe Barrès, *La Guerre a vingt ans*,[5] Alain, the soldier on leave, attends a dance hall with a companion and is made aware of the abyss between. One could lend oneself, he reflects, to the fiction of a dance on the edge of the volcano. But the affair was flat and gross. The joy with which he had begun his leave from the front, "as one who had escaped from

3 *À la recherche du temps perdu*, III (Paris, 1954), pp. 806–7.
4 *Ibid.*, pp. 752–53.
5 Paris, 1924.

among the dead," is suddenly deflated. "We alone, in our Gehenna, know the value of the world's marvels." Looking about him at these men and women who do not love what he loves or hate what he hates, he would like to "blow up the ceiling of the hall and let them see suddenly, as they lay trembling on the floor, the sky where the sooty cloud of the shell expands like a tragic poem."[6]

During the spring of 1917 I was with Section 2 of the Field Service in the Argonne. This sector was relatively quiet at this time, though at night we witnessed the appalling flashes, star shells, rockets, and glare and heard the interminable hammering of the inferno of the Champagne attacks on our left. Driving to and from the dressing stations in the lines without lights, the ditches on either side of the road masked by the snow in the darkness of the forest; evacuating besides the usual cases now and then a wounded prisoner, and once shut in for the trip with a distracted poilu; running the gauntlet of shelled roads—all this was the common experience of the service. I have lately noted that Dos Passos refers to one of these same posts and shelling at its approaches in his account of ambulance driving, *First Encounter*,[7] the post at the monastery-church of La Chalade, reached, as he notes, from Les Islettes on the east-west road through the Argonne.

The terrain, topography, place-names associated with the incommensurable drama of war took on, especially for the fresh sensibility of youth, a mythic character. Moving up to the front was like entering a preternatural landscape. The soldier in the twentieth century felt himself enveloped as it were by archaic spells. Especially as one moved into the calcined desolation of the forward trenches, a kind of electric alertness metamorphosed all perception. The peculiar feature of so much of World War I, with its relatively stable lines and no-man's-land, meant that the advanced trenches were like the frontier of chaos, charged with the passion of the world.

When this area was convulsed by barrages, mortars, attacks, while the hinterland teemed with supporting units, and laboring gun crews and harassed convoys of supplies, batteries, tanks, cars, ambulances, the whole experience took on a legendary character. Montherlant's war novel *Le Songe*[8] operates with a continuous counterpointing of the experiences of 1917–18 with motifs drawn from the *Iliad*, Plutarch, and other ancient fables like the *Song of Roland*. The drama is caught up into a timeless epic. "The ancient realm

---

6 *Ibid.*, p. 257.
7 New York, 1945. Republication of *One Man's Initiation*, 1919.
8 Paris, 1922.

and the modern, the realm of phantasms and the realm of things, were confounded in a fantastic universe which no longer threatened him."[9] The night-shrouded camion carrying the casqued men to battle is *Argo*. The eve of battle with its omens and hallucinations is described in a chapter entitled "Noctium Phantasmata." Strains of music are heard in the heavens, and Plutarch is recalled and his account of the strange harmonies of instruments and voices that were heard overhead by the armies in the middle of the night that preceded the decisive battle between Antony and Octavius. "Once again at the right moment the great life of antiquity imparted to its exiled child what little was required . . . ; the great tomb opened and a swallow or an eagle flew to him bearing its omens." And noting that this tormented night ushered in the decisive victories of July, 1918, the narrator hails the "fabulous concordance" with the eve of that battle in which the Roman order and the world's weal were born in the victory of Octavius.[10]

I recognize that readers today may be puzzled, if not scandalized, by this theme of the prestige of the war experience and its imaginative overtones. I can only quote again from Montherlant, in this case from his *Chant funèbre pour les morts de Verdun:* "One would prefer that nothing resulted from war except evil. Many problems would thus be simplified. But this violin bow, spotted with blood, draws profound accents from man which it alone can evoke from him."[11] One can illustrate further from the related mystique of the fraternity of the combatants over against the civilian world and their disenchantment with and alienation from the postwar world. The then young French writers, Joseph Kessel, Philippe Barrès, Montherlant, focus their early war novels (*L'Équipage, La Guerre a vingt ans,* and *Le Songe,* respectively) on the gulf between the solidarity of combatants on the one hand and the relative insipidity of all civilian relationships. These first testimonies reflected the shared experience of an incommensurable action and passion and the bonds of fealty to the dead, as also in the greater works of Georges Duhamel. Montherlant cites[12] three similar passages from the novels in question:

[The war] altogether a somber and sublime universe in which the spirit drew near to the depth of things.

P. Barrès

---

9 *Ibid.,* p. 183.
10 *Ibid.,* p. 182.
11 *Op. cit.,* p. 109.
12 *Ibid.,* pp. 21–22.

Now that he emerged from the kingdom of shades and of naked souls, he knew.

J. Kessel

Now he knew what counted and what did not count.

H. de Montherlant

From July to October, 1917, I was with one of the two ambulance sections in the Balkans. Evacuating French casualties and victims of malaria from Monastir most of the time, we were also confronted in this colorful theater of the war with Serbian, British, Annamite, Greek, and even Russian troops—the latter vituperated as they lay down their arms in consequence of the revolution. Returning to France and enlisting in Paris in the U.S. Field Artillery as a private in November, 1917, I was assigned to a battery in the 17th F.A. and so served in the ranks through the rest of the war in the 2d, or Indian Head, Division.

I cite passages from two letters written in this period which, naïve as they are, may be taken as firsthand documentation of the men in the ranks, the American doughboy: "One hundred years—five hundred years from now, what idea will the historian or the average American have of the men who fought his second War of Independence[13] for him? They have the soldier's vices—wine, women and dice. What are their virtues? The men are so young. Their qualities are all condensed in the one great quality of zest for life. That overflowing consciousness of being alive is the basis of any amount of generosity and lavishness of power which makes the French love us so much. And add to this something which the 'bossy' American is not accustomed to in his imperial days of peace—the pause that comes before a revelation of the *épouvantable*, the appalling, in life, as I have seen it show in eye and cheek after the first experiences of shelling—and you get a malleability, a disposable enthusiasm, that overrides all the vices. The shock of war tempers the bravado, recklessness and insubordination of this human type which are nevertheless admirable traits. They have such surpluses of vigor that they take their zest as a witness against the possibility of their doing or taking harm. That's exactly what I mean to say: they feel like kings and the king can do no wrong."

Again, in a letter from a replacement camp in September, 1918, I describe the ethnic variety and savor and unexpected talents that abounded in the ranks. Here was a corporal among these casuals

---

13 No doubt what I had in mind by this curious designation was that America was now again finding its identity in the world of nations, as was not the case in the Civil War.

who had mined in Kentucky and in the Andes and who, though like most he had never been to college, had his own curiosities: He was an expert on the Cherokee Indians and on the habits of spiders. Here was a Swede who had run away from home in Sweden to go to sea, been shipwrecked on his own coast, and had eventually become a foreman in Colorado. He was a gifted narrator and talked among other things about Socialism among the workers in Denver. Here was a Galveston longshoreman who told a kind of Eugene O'Neill story about proving himself on the docks against his father's veto. "What an amount of fine raw-material is going into the war in the ranks. Unschooled, coarse often, disrespectful, but variously disciplined by home memories—a stern but just father, a worn-down but unflinching mother—or by a long pull in the first years of bread-winning, or by some schoolboy romance, or by some unknown grade-school teacher, or childhood imagination captured by some forgotten Decoration Day ceremony. Most of this is pretty well submerged by the recklessness that they like to put on. And there is a tendency to assume a crowd spirit with much grumbling and sometimes worse. But getting at each man alone, or getting the crowd in good spirits, you have a promise for America that is immeasurable."

The deeper currents of history and its meaning are better sensed among the anonymous many or the common soldiers than in loftier quarters. By the same token the professional historian writes at two removes from the dense reality of events and from those who carry the burden of time and who are exposed to its hidden intentions and secret omens. Even the writer or artist is disqualified to the extent that his vocation separates him from the mass or makes him a nonpolitical being. It was unfortunate that our best-known World War I American writers as a rule (in contrast with such French writers as I have named) were not fully immersed in the war and in the ranks.[14] We had no Duhamel, and none with the human-politi-

---

14 E. E. Cummings served in an ambulance unit, not the Field Service, until his unpardonable arrest and mistreatment by French authorities. After his release and return to the States the war ended before his enlistment in the Army could return him to France. John Dos Passos notes in data supplied to a reference work that he served in several ambulance units, again not the Field Service, and the U.S. Medical Corps. Hemingway, who sought active service but was rejected because of his eyes, served in Italy in ambulance and canteen service briefly before he was wounded in the summer of 1918 and then returned to the same service for a few weeks before the Armistice. He did not serve in the elite corps of the Italian *arditi*, as is sometimes stated, but with them. Nothing could be further from my thought here than to question their courage or motives or to lack appreciation for their talent. It is simply a question of the narrow base of experience in this war which lay behind their writings.

cal commitment of a Charles Péguy. The soldier characters of our American writers go A.W.O.L. like Dos Passos' artist-hero, John Andrews; or are affronted by the unwonted austerity of discipline, sometimes indeed excessive as in E. E. Cummings' *Enormous Room*; or make an esthetic separate peace, as in Hemingway. The prestige of such writers has done much to encourage a foreshortened view of the American role in the war, something less than honor to its dead, and misjudgment as to the instincts of the nation in that juncture as they came to expression and to temporary frustration in the tragic drama of Woodrow Wilson and our relapse into normalcy.

As one who served in the ranks in a Regular Army division that was among the first in the field, I take this occasion to testify that our indeed inarticulate common soldiers so far from their native ground had, nevertheless, a sense of being willing actors in a necessary drama and one inseparably linked with the meaning of the American story. The core of the matter was not some engineered hatred of the "Hun," or sentiment for France, or the jeopardy of Britain, or unlimited submarine warfare and the honor of the flag, but an instinct for civil order and due political authority among the peoples. Though the United States had had a short history, its Roman and Calvinist heritages from the founders, together with its experience with lawlessness on the frontier, had conferred on us a sense of the life-and-death urgency of public authority, the a priori necessity of law and its sanctions over against human veracities, and dikes against anarchy and mania. This issue explains the stubbornness with which Wilson linked the peace treaties with the League of Nations. This issue, more general than that of who started the war and deeper than that of democracy and self-determination, was obscurely recognized by the American soldier. And it was in this context that we construed the apocalyptic overtones of the war and of such actions as the attack at dawn on July 18, 1918, in the forest of Villers-Cotterêts or that of November 1 in the Argonne.

Three days afterward I described the bombardment which preceded the latter attack in a letter which for all its ingenuousness suggests the sensitivities in question: "I went outside when it started, and as far as one could see either way there were the continuous flashes and roar, which went on hour after hour until light and then on until midday. When one lay down indoors the guns sounded like the sucking and ebbing and swirling of a great whirlpool. At such times one feels with uncomfortable clearness that sense of awe towards the future. History making itself now,

now, at this ordinary night and day and in this ordinary gray landscape. One comes close to the Plan and sees Castor and Pollux fighting over the Romans palpably."

At another angle, as of any war, the aspect of this war was loathsome and atrocious. It is not surprising that any inducements to Americans to participate in it would appear fraudulent. I choose one example among many and cite a discussion of the war by soldiers in various of the Allied armies as presented in John Dos Passos' *First Encounter*.[15] Here, in Chapter IX, there is a long diatribe against "the lies, the phrases, the press" that brought America into the war, seen as "a tragedy," and as "goin' back on our only excuse for existin'! Who shall ever know what dark forces bought and bought until we should be ready to go blinded and gagged to war? . . . People seem to so love to be fooled. . . . We are slaves of bought intellect, willing slaves."[16] In the context the speakers identify themselves as "merely intellectuals" over against "the stupid average working-people who have the power." The Americans, it is explained to the Europeans, "are like children. They believe everything they are told, you see; they have no experience in international affairs, like you Europeans."[17]

This reaction to the enormity of war on the part of the more emancipated artists and intellectuals in the Army was understandable. But it was superficial. The artists have their own admirable personal codes—for example, the heroic code of Hemingway—or their iconoclastic enthusiasms: Dos Passos' group in the passage in question unite in the hope of an eventual revolutionary Socialism. It is relevant to cite here as representative for many of the artists and writers of the period André Gide's statement that he "regretted that under Mallarmé's influence he had long been unpolitical."[18] Dos Passos himself, writing an introduction to the 1945 reprinting of his book (*First Encounter* was first published as *One Man's Initiation* in 1919) , calls attention to the impact of the war of 1914–18 on Americans as "a horrible monstrosity, outside of the normal order of things," as compared with World War II.[19] And he has presented a radically different picture of the earlier war and its issues in his recent work *Mr. Wilson's War* (1962) .

The Americans in the ranks were certainly less sophisticated and articulate, but they had an obscure sense of the meaning or inevita-

---

15 *Op. cit.*
16 *Ibid.*, p. 144.
17 *Ibid.*, p. 141.
18 Van Meter Ames, *André Gide* (New York, 1947) , p. 162.
19 *Op. cit.*, p. 8.

bility of the war. Woodrow Wilson expressed it after an imperfect fashion, and his personal tragedy was an index of the same impasse and resistances that determined the ordeal of the soldier. No doubt there was sentimentality and utopianism in the idea that this was the war to end war. But such intensity of hope when all is at stake is not unfamiliar, nor was it silly in analogous periods, like those of the English Puritans or the founders of New England, not to mention the beginnings of Christianity. Certainly the goals of Wilson were less sentimental than those of the contemporary Marxists, and he was more realistic than those who sought a vindictive peace and the several forms of national aggrandizement or those Americans who failed to recognize that the time had come for committing the nation to responsible international structures.

At the conclusion of his massive work on this war the French historian Pierre Renouvin notes that though Wilson was only the final compiler-editor of the many elements that went into the Covenant of the League of Nations, yet "it remains true that without him, his tenacity, his faith, the new conception of international relations would not have been made the foundation of the peace treaties of 1919–20."[20]

Yet if at this remove in time one still defends America's participation in the war and insists on the core of truth in the high-flown rhetoric of promise, one can do so only in full recognition of the abomination of the slaughter: the ghastly and protracted carnage which understandably motivated the revulsion and even the cynicism of many interpreters. This consideration excludes any rational justification of the war. What we are pointed to is the kind of historical fate or linkage of events which Lincoln dealt with in the categories of offense and judgment with respect to the Civil War. We are pointed to the human condition itself whose cure exacts these kinds of fates which transpire over our heads and which are wiser than any of those who either protest or serve them.

---

[20] *La Crise européenne et la première guerre mondiale* (Paris, 1962) , p. 663.

Frederick A. Pottle

"I was born in 1897, grew up on a farm in Maine, attended the local schools, and graduated from Colby College in 1917. My major was in chemistry, but in my senior year I came upon Shelley, suffered a violent conversion, and proclaimed myself a poet. After teaching a few months at Hebron Academy, I enlisted in the Medical Corps, was assigned to Evacuation Hospital No. 8, and went overseas in the spring of 1918. Our outfit was established first at Juilly, near Meaux, during Belleau Wood and the summer offensives, and then at Petit Maujouy, near Verdun, during the St.-Mihiel and Meuse-Argonne actions. I worked in the operating room as private first class with the rating of surgical assistant. In the spring of 1919 I left my outfit, then functioning as a post hospital in Mayen, near Coblenz, to teach chemistry at the A.E.F. University at Beaune, in Burgundy. I came home as a casual and was discharged in July, 1919.

"After teaching high school for a year in Portland, Maine, I entered the Yale Graduate School and happily embraced a career of scholarship and teaching. Except for two years at the University of New Hampshire (1921–23), I have been at Yale ever since, retiring in June, 1966, as Sterling Professor of English, emeritus.

"My book Stretchers, the Story of a Hospital Unit on the Western Front, was published in 1929. I gave the Messenger lectures at Cornell in 1941, publishing them that same year as The Idiom of Poetry (revised and enlarged edition, 1946). My teaching at Yale was principally in the Romantics, but my research has mainly centered on Boswell, of whose private papers I have edited many volumes, both alone and in collaboration. My magnum opus, James Boswell, The Earlier Years, 1740–1769, was published in 1966."

CREED NOT ANNULLED

SOME WEEKS AGO, as I was sitting in a college dining room filled with undergraduates—it was about the time of the march on Washington to protest the war in Vietnam—I said to a faculty friend considerably younger than myself, "It makes me sad to think that so many of those boys are unknowingly depriving themselves of a valuable experience. What would they say if I told them that I seriously considered my Army service the best-invested years of my life?" His reply was probably not unlike what theirs would have been: "All that blood and suffering so that you could think better of yourself!" The reproof waked old echoes. It brought back powerfully the feelings I had when I first got to France in 1918, not feelings that war was essentially and always evil; oh, no. Feelings rather of shame and regret that I had not got more deeply immersed in the war. "What right," I then kept saying to myself, "what right have I to be safe and enjoying these memorable experiences while other men are being maimed and killed?"

What memorable experiences? Such as being for the first time in a foreign country, of strolling greedily through sun-drenched old villages in the Seine-et-Marne, its enchanting landscapes impressing themselves on my memory by a heightening of consciousness such as I had never felt before and have not felt since. The joy of frank, unreserved male friendship found at last by me, who all through college never had a real chum. The French soldier of my own age, four years a veteran, who gave me his *croix de guerre.* The woman at Domrémy who said, "*Vous américains, vous êtes la Jeanne d'Arc des alliés.*" That moment on July 4, 1918, as the band was playing "*La Marseillaise,*" when the wind swirled our flag completely around the French flag. Such as the wounded boys lying patiently in the old courtyard waiting their turn in the operating room. In a sunset thrilling with larks, the row of raw mounds and open graves under the wall of the old cemetery. Me, light-headed with tonsillitis, embracing the trunk of an oak tree and cursing feebly as the bomb goes off 100 yards away. Me, working hours and hours and hours on wounded men, till my knees won't bend and thigh cramps bring me up moaning when at last I can stretch out on a litter.

And other gains as regards what I hope it will not be thought priggish to call my character and morals. It was in the Army, not in college, that I acquired such a modicum of manliness as I have been able to attain to. It was the Army that taught me my limitations. I am ambitious, and I wanted promotion—not, of course, a commission, for to be an officer in the Medical Corps one must be a Doctor of Medicine, but a mere sergeancy. Time after time after time, in company formation, I heard the names of the chosen read out with keen disappointment and then, at the very end, the fighting over for months, was awarded a ridiculous corporalcy, the last promotion, I fancy, made in the outfit. But by that time I had sincerely come to prefer my status as private because promotion would have cost me my best friends, and I was no longer disposed to think myself unjustly treated. In World War I there were no technical ratings conferring rank, and corporalcies and sergeancies implied a power of command. The Army taught me that I did not possess powers of command and that the only areas in which I could certainly excel were scholarship and writing. It was a painful lesson, but it was useful to learn it at the age of twenty-one and in an interim employment.

And another lesson only slightly less useful. What I have been saying may seem like a eulogy of the Army system as such, but it isn't. I still subscribe to all the expressed and implied criticism of the Army I put my name to almost forty years ago. I deplore and resent the Army's ingrained anti-intellectualism, its distrust and dislike of book learning. I despise martinet discipline, the theory that you must break a man's will before he is any good as a soldier. I repudiate indignantly the practical assumption, so contrary to the facts and to all American political theory, that officers are a social elite and enlisted men canaille. I loathe the pervasive dishonest "soldiering" practice of the Army, the elaborate pretense of keeping men usefully employed when in fact they and their noncoms are hiding under the barracks. But out of the official inefficiency, stupidity, injustice, brutality, and (worst of all) boredom of the Army, no less than from its terrors, pains, degradations, and exhaustions, I learned that anything, literally anything, can be endured. The cries of hysteria and despair that have rung in my ears for close on to forty years now have seldom come from men who saw service in either world war. We don't believe that the human race is going to kill itself off. We know that man is tough and resourceful. The prospect of the future is bleak, but we shall squeak through.

But to return to what I was saying earlier. I felt guilty about being safe in a countryside where the guns only muttered; when I looked at those mangled young bodies, I didn't feel so much that war was evil as that in decency I ought to lose a hand or a leg. I'm afraid that to this day I'd rather have a Purple Heart (that decoration wasn't conferred in 1917–18) than any other honor or decoration whatever. But gradually the feeling of unworthiness wore off as I found that the wounded men themselves, the men who had unarguable proof that they had really been at the real front, had no scorn for any soldier who was doing his job anywhere, even if it happened to be behind the lines. They were skeptical and cynical like young men now—when do you think the word "profiteer" was invented?—and they would have returned you a ribald answer if you had asked them if they were fighting to make the world safe for democracy. But they sincerely thought they were, all the same, and they counted us their partners in the task. We thought so, too, and I think that most of us now, in spite of the disillusionment of fifty violent years, in spite of our shyness at even thinking such old-fashioned language, believe that our cause was just and, well, heroic. It is because of that that I feel no shame in saying that the war was for me personally a most valuable experience. Life is not fulfilled without intimations of the heroic; nothing else brings a man fully alive. I do not say that one must go to war to receive intimations of the heroic; I do report that the only memories I have that reflect even a gleam of the heroic are of my war years.

I was not engaged in any way in World War II, but I taught a great many veterans of that war, and I found that they went far beyond my generation in their inability to speak the unqualified language of martial valor. They would not tolerate Churchill's patriotic rhetoric, and they would not tolerate any patriotic poetry as quickly as possible. Yet there was something very positive in their whatever. Unlike us, they would not even let themselves *think* that they had fought to make the world safe for democracy. To them the war was a dirty, hateful, incomprehensible job that had to be done attitude: dirty and distasteful as the job seemed to them, and impatient as they were at any attempt to glorify it, they never doubted that it was a *necessary* job. And this unvoiced, unacknowledged acknowledgment of the call of duty (again those naked, embarrassing, old-fashioned words) substituted to a considerable extent for the glimpses of glory we experienced. Though my veterans of World War II spent three, four, even five years in service as compared with my scant nineteen months, I am sure that many of them would agree with me that no years of their life had been better invested.

As regards Korea and especially Vietnam, I would wish to speak very tentatively and uncertainly, for the situation rouses passionate feelings and I have access to no special source of wisdom. Certainly, many of our people now are denying both the heroism of the present conflict and the duty of any man to engage in it, and they would as certainly be very impatient with anyone who said he thought a man who went to Vietnam as a soldier would be making a good investment of his time. That angry impatience, that sense of intolerable frustration ready to flash into violence, makes one suspect something less than clear conviction, makes one wonder whether most of the people who feel themselves opposed to the war in Vietnam really know the fundamental cause of their opposition. The war in Vietnam, I would suggest, is mainly unpopular because it is a war with limited aims, a police action, and Americans do not identify with the police. Yet it is precisely in having achieved these unpopular limited wars—police actions—that many men of my age feel that the world has taken its first tottering steps out of an inveterate anarchy. Few of us were so saintly or so silly as to suppose that our war would end wars all by itself: it would end world wars as it caused the nations to scale down their armaments radically and combine to set up an effective international police force. If looting and arson start instantly in the cities of the United States when police power is withdrawn, it is fairly obvious that the international equivalent of looting and arson is going to occur in the absence of an international police force. And it is equally clear that the presently fumbling but incalculably precious idea of responsible international police action can be kept alive in our time only if the United States assumes the responsibility of furnishing most of the soldiers required for the next fifty years or so. The young in the United States today respond readily enough to a call to serve humanity which they recognize as such—witness the Peace Corps— but it is going to take a powerful surge of the will to make service in Vietnam seem to them service to humanity. The young men of World War II were spared this painful exertion; their dirty mess was dumped on them in the bombs at Pearl Harbor. Our young men of today must force themselves against instinct to take up this dangerous and distasteful job for the benefit of humanity, and they must do it unexalted by glimpses of the heroic and unconfirmed by the sense of responding to duty. But they can without shame expect that the years they spend at the job will be deeply rewarding.

Vera Brittain

"I was born when the nineteenth century was passing into the twentieth, and can just remember the war songs which the slouch-hatted soldiers sang as they marched to their deaths at Spion Kop or Magersfontein. Never, I suppose, has a generation of children been so heavily shrouded by the shadow of future events or so serenely unaware of its impending fate.

"I came from a typically unambitious Staffordshire family, the only daughter of a Midland small-town manufacturer with no interest in literature or learning. The ambition to go to college, which I developed while still at school, appeared to my family and neighbors to be extremely revolutionary. My provincial contemporaries wanted only to have a good time and marry early; their demands on their parents did not include the expenses of higher education. Eventually I was largely self-educated, went in for and passed the necessary examinations, and even landed an exhibition at Somerville College, then, as now, the most learned and intimidating of the Oxford women's colleges.

"Marriage in 1925 took me even further from my background, for when we met, my husband, Professor George Catlin, was assistant professor of politics at Cornell University and himself an exhibitioner of New College, Oxford. He was an early instance of the brain drain, for his subject was not then taught at his own university. His teaching at Cornell meant that our lives have been divided between England and the United States.

"Our son, John, has followed the family tradition by going in for business, but our daughter, Shirley, broke new ground by becoming a politician. Like myself, she took the Somerville College scholarship examination and became a history scholar. In 1948 she won a Smith-Mundt Fellowship at Columbia University and, on returning to England, immediately began to stand for Parliament. After fighting one by-election and two general elections, she became Labour M.P. in 1964 for the Hitchin Division of Hertfordshire. In 1966 she won the seat again with a 10,000 majority.

"That long step ahead of me was characteristic of our relationship, for—as my essay reveals—I belong to the 'breakthrough generation' of women who have transformed a track to the future into a highway for our successors to tread. My writings, especially the Testaments of Youth, Friendship, and Experience, describe this great creative adventure."

WAR SERVICE IN PERSPECTIVE

SINCE THE FIFTIETH ANNIVERSARY of the outbreak of the First World War, I have kept a pile of newspaper clippings beside me in a big folder. What do these clippings, collected from a large number of papers and magazines, emphasize from the impressions of numerous contributors?

First, I find a long section on the weapons of war, showing many varieties of protective device, from the gas masks developed out of the primitive protection of a wet handkerchief to elaborate helmets resembling a Martian face mask dreamed of in a science-fiction story by H. G. Wells. The clippings go on to give pictures of different types of shells, designs for experimental airplanes, and plans for the vulnerable zeppelins. Then come photographs of the terrifying tanks, which at first overwhelmed Britain's enemies by their strange monstrosity. Finally, by way of an anticlimax, we see pictures of London's terra-cotta-colored B type buses which proved ideal for the transport of troops in France.

Another bundle of clippings is devoted to the assorted war posters by means of which truth—"the first casualty in war-time"—gradually lost its integrity. This was achieved through the undermining of mental independence by emotional appeals which varied from representations of the Kaiser as an inventor of ingenious atrocities to the sentimental pictures of white-haired mothers urging their sons to fight. There followed a series of grotesque legends, which began with the story of the corpse factory in which the bodies of dead soldiers were said to be converted into explosives and went on to the tale of the entirely fictitious *Lusitania* Medal reported to have been struck at the Kaiser's suggestion and bestowed on the crew of the submarine which sank the *Lusitania* in 1915.

I still recall the contemporary reactions, including my own, to these crude but graphic appeals. Even in the eyes of an ingenuous girl recently out of school, most of them seemed just plain silly. Kitchener's finger pointing from numerous hoardings left me quite unmoved by its hysterical monotony. Though I was about to become a college highbrow, my responses to pressure, so untypical in most ways of the society in which I was brought up, were, I think, characteristic of the nation as a whole. Before the Second World War the patient work of such political research workers as Arthur Ponsonby—a founder of the Union of Democratic Control and Foreign Secretary in Britain's first Labour government, whose classic *Falsehood in Wartime* was published in 1928—had unmasked the most extravagant stories. These investigations left the British people imbued with a healthy skepticism which even the newer forms of propaganda, such as radio and television, failed to undermine. A comment made to me by a London workingwoman on the consequences of an air raid in 1944 must have been typical of many others: "I heard it on the B.B.C., so it can't be true."

From graphic examples of propaganda, my collection moves on to the numerous portraits of British war leaders—Haig, Plumer, Herbert Lawrence, William Robertson, all of whom looked well fed, substantial, and complacent. They make a gruesome contrast to the fragile wraith of bedridden Private George Oakley of the Middlesex Regiment, who enlisted at the age of eighteen and, when his picture was published, had spent forty-eight years in the Star and Garter Home for ex-servicemen at Richmond, Surrey. He was one of 28,000,000 men, wounded on both sides of the struggle, many of whom are still living a hidden death-in-life existence in servicemen's hospitals.

Other pictures show the gruesome litter of war amid the forests of black crosses in a German cemetery. One newspaper sent a special correspondent to travel round the former battlefronts and photograph whatever items of surviving debris seemed most worthy of record after fifty years. He came back with pictures, among many other things, of bent bayonets protruding from the earth at Verdun—a reminder of the men buried alive by bombardment as they waited to go over the top.

On the slope of what was once Hill 60 the breech of a machine gun lies slowly rusting away. In a private wood near Albert in Picardy, the ground is still thick with remnants of war: helmets and old boots, barbed wire and beer bottles, which lie undisturbed amid branches and brambles where they were left by departing British soldiers half a century ago.

From the nature study of war's somber remains, we move on to the special supplement of a historically minded editor who chose to commemorate the fiftieth anniversary of the war by pictures of the Archduke Franz Ferdinand and his family—a mild and well-intentioned man who did not deserve his fate of identification with the tragedy that sparked off four years of atrocity and mutilation. One cracked picture shows him with a brisk handlebar moustache in a bright blue uniform which seems to reflect the limpid color of the unferocious, philosophical Hapsburg eyes.

A "family portrait" brings back to life the plain, Teutonic Duchess Sophie and the three morganatic children—the handsome Maximilian, their elder son, who was mayor of Artstetten until his death in 1962; the second son, Ernst, who was sent to Dachau for five years by the Nazis and who died after his release; and Sophie, Franz Ferdinand's only daughter, an amiable-looking *Hausfrau* who is now the Countess von Nostitz-Rieneck and lives with her husband in a small villa at Salzburg.

As though by intentional contrast, the same magazine shows a grimacing art student in Munich listening to the proclamation of war from the midst of the crowd. It is Adolf Hitler, whose words from *Mein Kampf* are quoted:

My own attitude towards the conflict was both simple and clear. In my eyes it was not Austria fighting to get a little satisfaction out of Serbia but Germany fighting for her life, the German nation for its "to be or not to be," its freedom and future. It would have to follow in Bismarck's footsteps; young Germany must again defend what the fathers had heroically fought for from Weissenburg to Sedan and Paris. But if the struggle was to be a victorious one, our people would by their own force take their place again among the great nations, and then the German Reich could stand as a mighty guardian of peace, without the necessity to curtail its children's daily bread for the sake of this peace.

On the Third of August I addressed a petition to His Majesty King Ludwig III to be allowed to serve in a Bavarian regiment. The Cabinet Office during those days certainly had its hands pretty full, and my joy was all the greater when my petition was granted the same day.

Now began for me, as for every German, the greatest and most unforgettable period of my life on earth. Compared with the events of that mighty struggle, all the past fell into empty oblivion. I think with pride and sorrow of those days and back to the weeks of the beginning of our nation's heroic fight, in which kind fortune allowed me to take part.

Finally, I turned amid my press clippings to the reviews of some of the war books which recorded those years and were published between thirty and forty years ago. They bring back the names of some still-living authors whose work seems likely to endure, such as Edmund Blunden and Robert Graves. Among them I find an anniversary article in the London *Times* by no less a personality than its former editor, Sir William Haley.

Writing as Oliver Edwards, the pseudonym that he adopted for the literary articles that he contributed to the columns of his paper, he included an assessment of the books which were, in his view, the most memorable to come out of the First World War. In this article he described *Testament of Youth,* published by Victor Gollancz in London in August, 1933, and by the Macmillan companies of New York and Toronto shortly afterward, as "the war book of the Women of England."

This was not, perhaps, quite the tribute that it might have appeared, for relatively few women played an active part in the First World War. They were, on the whole, merely aides operating behind the various fronts. Such roles as they did fulfill were modest, subsidiary, and insignificant. War was a man's business. In 1914 the women who volunteered to serve as nurses with the Scottish Women's Hospitals in areas where qualified women of any description were extremely scarce were told by the Establishment to "go home and keep quiet." This was, it seemed, in masculine opinion the only useful thing that women could do.

Even after the war was over, women of relevant age were not regarded as having had any real contact with its realities. Some years after my own direct experience had ended, I came to know a cultured and critical young man named Roy Randall who wrote for several highbrow weeklies. His literary ambitions were unlimited, and he liked to discuss them with me. Occasionally, out of politeness, he referred to the modest free-lance journalism by which I was struggling to find a foothold in the writing world.

One day, much to my embarrassment, he asked me what work I hoped to undertake in the near future. I had then published two short novels and three unimportant little volumes of nonfiction and was living largely on the meager proceeds of my free-lance articles and book reviews. After three or four years of intimidated and spasmodic endeavor, I was also trying to draft the outline of *Testament of Youth* and did not want to disclose the ambitious character of this effort, which I knew that my companion would regard as extremely presumptuous. So when Roy pressed me for an answer, I replied vaguely that I was trying to do "a kind of autobiography."

His contemptuous reply was even more devastating than I had foreseen:

"An autobiography! But I shouldn't have thought that anything in *your* life was worth recording!"

This shattering judgment, though it shook my equilibrium, did not put me off my project. At that time I had served for four grueling years in London, France, and the Mediterranean and had seen my nearest and dearest contemporaries—lover, brother, and two much-loved friends—hounded to death in the holocaust of a male generation. But knowing that my appearance still suggested that of a half-fledged university student I did not protest but merely resolved with the more determination to record while light lasted the events that I remembered.

When I related this conversation at a dinner with my near contemporary Rebecca West and her husband, Henry Andrews, Henry seemed disposed to agree with the skeptical Roy, but Rebecca, echoing my private thoughts, turned on him and said: "You mean she's not a field marshal? But it's the psychological kind of autobiography that succeeds nowadays, not the old dull kind."

The idea of a war book had come with the publication of memoirs by some of the few male literary contemporaries who had survived the war. It was also provoked by sheer perversity. I knew well that no one expected a woman to understand anything about war, much less to try to record it. But it must have come into my mind soon after the first performance of R. C. Sherriff's *Journey's End*—that famous swallow that was to make a summer—which I saw with Winifred Holtby, the author of *South Riding,* when we realized that an electric atmosphere of reminiscent emotion had replaced the mere *succès d'estime* which we had both expected.

Soon after seeing the play and reading the too poignant published memoirs, I began to ask myself: "Why should these young men have the war to themselves? Didn't women have their war as well? They weren't all, as these men make them out to be, only suffering wives and mothers, or callous parasites, or mercenary prostitutes. Does no one remember the women who began their war service with such high ideals or how grimly they carried on when that flaming faith had crumbled into the gray ashes of disillusion? Who will write the epic of the women who went to the war, and came back leaving the bones of their men in the trampled fields of France and amid the gray rocks of the Asiago Plateau?"

Could I, who had done nothing important yet, carry through such a massive undertaking? With scientific precision, I studied the memoirs of Blunden, Sassoon, and Graves. Surely, I thought, my story is as interesting as theirs. Besides, I see things other than they have seen, and some of the things they perceived, I see differently.

The kind of memoir that could be written only by a prime minister or an ambassador, I believed with Rebecca West, was ceasing to have much appeal. A new type of autobiography was coming into fashion, which would represent the ordinary people of the world upon whom wars were imposed. I wanted to make my own story as truthful as history but as readable as fiction, and in it I intended to speak, not for those in high places, but for my own generation of obscure young women.

Inspired by blind faith and the urgent need for reconciliation with the past, I began to collect and reread letters and memoirs and to try to assess the significance of my own adventures which Roy Randall had thought so trivial. I soon realized how typical they were—not so much in terms of women's experience, as of that of an entire generation. The details of our lives had naturally differed; there was clearly a great contrast at that date between the stories of men and women. But we all had experienced the tremendous revolution—one of the greatest in history—which carried the nineteenth century into the twentieth. It became my intention to attempt to estimate the apocalyptic quality of these changes which transformed forever the world into which my contemporaries and I were born.

A woman could perceive the picture as clearly as a man—perhaps more clearly, owing to the inevitably greater detachment which a woman's wartime insignificance gave her. Gradually now I began to perceive my "war book" as a vehicle for the picture of a vast age of transition, slowly becoming evident through the illuminating details which changed as each disastrous, tragic, and dramatic epoch merged into another.

Midway between the beginning and end of the war I had written to my brother in the trenches about the quality of our age. He was then on the Italian front and, though only twenty-one, was the kind of correspondent who understands everything. Such individuals are so rare that I have missed him all my life and still wish that I could refer to him some of the problems that I now have to face.

About the summer of 1917 I wrote to him: "I think that 'Before' and 'After' this war will make the same kind of division in human history as 'B.C.' and 'A.D.'" At the time this seemed an extravagant and even absurd assessment, but after half a century it does not seem to me that I was so far wrong in my estimate of that tremendous perspective.

The quality of the two titanic revolutions was, of course, quite different. The transition from the pagan to the Christian world meant a vast spiritual change affecting all human lives from the first century onward; it challenged existing values irrespective of whether those challenged understood the issues involved.

The changes created by the events of 1914 and the years immediately afterward were social and political, but they, too, were apocalyptic and fundamental. Mankind was never the same again after 1914, any more than it was ever the same again after the Crucifixion. Only those who recall, however dimly, the vanishing sunset splendor of the final Victorian years can estimate in their personal histories the quality of the transformation which the events of 1914 created for the much battered human race.

The normal experience of mortal life has been one of war and catastrophe. This was a fact very difficult to realize by the young of my generation. In spite of the tragedies and errors of the South African War—which are only now fully reaching realization in the spiritual bankruptcy of *apartheid*—our earliest memories, especially if we came from the ever-growing middle classes, are of prosperity and security. These ultimately proved as ephemeral as most varieties of good fortune, giving rise to such cynical obiter dicta as "Life is the predicament that precedes death." But at the time they seemed permanent—a fact that explains the contrast between the poets of the two war generations. The work of Sassoon and his near contemporaries was one long cry of protest precisely because they were the products of an exceptionally fortunate social era. When their Second War successors reached adulthood, the world had reverted to the normal human experience of frustration and disappointment, and the horrors of war casualties offered a less emphatic contrast with preceding events.

In the verses entitled "The War Generation: Ave," with which I opened Chapter 1 of *Testament of Youth*, I endeavored to put into words the innocent contentment of late Victorian childhood, especially among those born far from the influence of formative political events.

> In cities and in hamlets we were born,
> And little towns behind the van of time;
> A closing era mocked our guileless dawn
> With jingles of a military rhyme.
> But in that song we heard no warning chime,
> Nor visualized in hours benign and sweet
> The threatening woe that our adventurous feet
> Would starkly meet.
>
> Thus we began, amid the echoes blown
> Across our childhood from an earlier war,
> Too dim, too soon forgotten, to dethrone
> Those dreams of happiness we thought secure;
> While, imminent and fierce outside the door,
> Watching a generation grow to flower,
> The fate that held our youth within its power
> Waited its hour.

The belief that individuals were entitled to expect peace and happiness as their normal fate took so long to die that remnants of it still came to life even when the First War had been over for years. In 1939, when I took my son, then a boy of twelve, to his preparatory school for his first term, I happened to make a conventional comment to his headmaster about the misfortune for a child of having to begin his schooldays in a year when the unhappy history of my own generation was about to repeat itself in a series of dire events. The headmaster, a grave Quaker, mildly reprimanded me for the lack of historical perspective of which I seemed to him to be guilty.

"Think what it must have meant to start your education at the beginning of the Thirty Years' War!"

But for all its problems which affected our children as those of the First War did not, I have never been able to feel that September 3, 1939, presented a comparable cataclysm to that of August 4, 1914. The second date had been long foreseen, and though it heralded more and worse disasters which were to come closer to the comfortable British people than the cross-Channel terrors of the First World War, it lacked the same quality of shock. It was that sense of shock which, as it came into perspective, eclipsed all the other and more recent memories.

What does that date, August 4, 1914, immediately bring back to me? Not, certainly, the recollection of gunrunning in Ulster which so oddly preceded much greater anxieties, or yet the assassination of the Archduke Franz Ferdinand, though it was soon associated with macabre rumors that blood had been seen on the sun and moon. The immediate memories are purely personal and do not concern the statistics of world transformation, though I was to give so much attention to them later. The huge figures of the war casualties and the cost of war expenditure vanish in a phantasmagoria of human scenes and sounds. I think, instead, of names, places, and individuals and hear, above all, the echo of a boy's laughing voice on a school playing field in that golden summer.

And gradually the voice becomes one of many; the sound of the Uppingham School choir marching up the chapel for the Speech Day service in July, 1914, and singing the Commemoration hymn:

> O Merciful and Holy
> Who once by ways unknown
> In simple hearts and lowly
> Dost build Thy loftiest throne,
> As Thou of old wast near us

> To bless our Founder's care,
> Bow down Thine ear and hear us
> In this, Thy house of prayer.

There was a thrilling, a poignant quality in those boys' voices, as though they were singing their own requiem—as indeed many of them were. Among these were my brother, Edward, and his best friend, the prizewinning Roland Leighton, who had hoped to marry me and become a *Times* leader (editorial) writer, but instead found a lowly grave amid the white crosses which marked the Somme even before the great battles of 1916 were fought. But when the personal memories are, with difficulty, banished, it is the suddenness and shock of the whole event which remains with me longest.

Many years before the Great War, George Eliot, though she lived in one of history's calmest centuries, had prophetically visualized the situation of the war generation in her novel *Daniel Deronda:*

There comes a terrible moment to many souls when the great movements of the world, the larger destinies of mankind, which have lain aloof in newspapers and other neglected reading, enter like an earthquake into their own lives—when the slow urgency of growing generations turns into the tread of an invading army or the dire clash of civil war. Then it is that the submission of the soul to the Highest is tested and . . . life looks out from the scene of human struggle with the awful face of duty.

That "awful face of duty" sent the generation which had known no major war since their grandparents had fought in the Crimea into the interminable miles of trenches which stretched from the Ardennes to the North Sea or took them in the ships, great and small, which when they were sunk carried hundreds of young men—many of them midshipmen barely in their teens—into a cold anonymous grave without hope of rescue or the least understanding of the issue for which they had sacrificed their lives. They belonged to a sheltered human vintage for which occasional disasters, such as the sinking of the *Titanic* in 1912, were isolated reminders that tragedy existed. But no one, before 1914, expected it to come nearer, for smooth events had established the conviction that human happiness was normal and disaster exceptional; those to whom it happened were thought to be particularly unlucky.

To us, with our cheerful confidence in the benignity of fate, war was something remote, unimaginable, its monstrous destructions and distresses safely shut up, like the Black Death and the Great Fire, between the covers of history books. In spite of the efforts of a few percipient teachers who taught a generation of schoolchildren unaccustomed to read the newspapers to take an interest in at least the headlines, "current events" had remained unimportant just because they were national; they represented "subjects" that were habitually taught in classrooms but would never, conceivably, have to be lived.

What really mattered were not these public issues, but the absorbing incidents of our private lives—our careers, ambitions, friendships, and love affairs. And now, with the suddenness that George Eliot had described, the one had impinged on the other, and public issues and private lives had become bewilderingly inseparable. The significance of these events did not become clear until those who had suffered them began to write about them— which meant that they had to think about them. In some cases, as in my own, the thinking process lasted for years before it was decanted into words. And part of the process showed that *anyone* whom those years concerned was entitled to assess them—young or old, men or women. War was a human event, not a happening which affected one age or sex rather than another.

Yet if the whole comfortable generation had felt sheltered and secure, its women seemed to be especially cut off from reality. Their subservience was not a matter for discussion except by a handful of wild fanatics who had begun to make extravagant claims to equality and opportunity. The inferiority of women was accepted as part of the natural order of creation. The suffragettes, to the amusement of the unthinking public, began to make their vehement demands, less than a decade before the world changed forever.

As I was to realize many years later when, at long last, the war insisted on being put into words, the very detachment of women from the most direct forms of active service impressed on me once and for all the domination by war between 1914 and 1919 of even the most trivial aspects of everyday life. The war could not be escaped even by the most skillfully devised plays, books, and concerts. It permeated the arts; in my first year at Oxford the Bath Choir, which I had joined, gave a moving performance of the Verdi *Requiem* which haunts me to this day, and I still remember listening at Southwark Cathedral in July, 1916, to the Brahms *Requiem* which so poignantly coincided with the first day of the tremendous Somme battle. Even today the First War atmosphere is immediately brought back to me by the plaintive notes of Cowper's hymn "God moves in a mysterious way," so often sung at church services by congregations growing ever more anxious to be consoled and reassured.

The wearing anxiety of waiting for letters probably made all noncombatants feel more distracted than anything else in that sustained nightmare. Even when the letters came, they were at least four days old; the writers after sending them would have had time to die many times. This particular form of painful suspense, which had to be ignored on duty with as much resolution as the individual could muster, began for me when Roland Leighton went to the front as a boy barely twenty in March, 1915, and ended for me only in June, 1918, when my brother's death after that of Roland and our two dearest friends left me with no one else for whom to feel anxiety.

During the periods of waiting, especially when the newspapers, with inevitable vagueness, reported the imminence of a "great push," ordinary household sounds became a torment. The striking of a clock, marking off each hour of dread, broke into the immobility of tension with the shattering effect of a thunderclap. Every ring at the bell suggested a telegram, the only method of conveying urgent news before the days of radio and television; every telephone call implied a long-distance message giving bad news.

The extent of this torment naturally varied with both the quality of individual imagination and the measure of personal involvement. Probably I should never have been the only woman to contribute to this symposium had not my own involvement been so deep and so continuous. Even today, after fifty years, it still seems to me almost incredible that during those four years there actually were women who had no friends or relatives in the trenches or on the perilous seas, who were not perpetually waiting for messages of disaster. It is not surprising that many women developed an anxiety neurosis which lasted until the end of their lives.

To this constant dread was added, as the end of the fighting moved ever onward into an incalculable future, a new fear that the war would come between the men at the front and the women who loved them. Between 1914 and 1919 the war always did, putting a barrier of indescribable experience between the two sexes, thrusting horror deeper and deeper inward, linking the dread of spiritual death to the apprehension of physical disaster. When one of two dear friends was blinded at Arras in 1917 and sent to England to die in a London military hospital, I went to his funeral in Sussex, where his family lived. More bitter even than the sorrow of his death was my acute consciousness of England's uncomprehending remoteness from the tragic, profound freemasonry which united the men and, very rarely, the women who accepted death together overseas.

The women who served or only waited in the Second World

War, though they experienced fresh horrors and many other dangers, such as the V-1's and V-2's with their incalculable descents on undefended targets, were at least spared this fear of estrangement due to ignorance, for in this second onslaught of fate men and women alike shared the perils that threatened both sexes. In some countries, such as Germany, which endured the terror of saturation raids by British and American bombers, women faced greater risks than their men, who had at least better protection in the forces than in the barely defended small towns and villages in or near the major target areas, such as Kiel and Hamburg, and the vulnerable closely packed cities of the Ruhr.

I recall reading in a German newspaper quoted in England about 1944 of the distress experienced by a group of servicemen traveling on leave from the Russian front to their homes in Hamburg, then virtually extinguished by the merciless raids on civilian areas of 1942–44. Standing in the corridor of their train, these soldiers, who had been out of Germany for two or three years, were rendered almost speechless by seeing the ruins of their homes and "bowing before the sacrifice."

This meant that the experiences of the women of the First World War were, in fact, unique and probably could not now be duplicated by any woman in any war—irrespective of the certainty that no woman and no man would be likely to survive a major conflict at all. In such a conflict, as Shakespeare wrote in *The Tempest:*

> The cloud-capp'd towers, the gorgeous palaces,
> The solemn temples, the great globe itself,
> Yea, all which it inherit, shall dissolve;
> And, like this insubstantial pageant faded,
> Leave not a rack behind.

Assuming, meanwhile, that the menaced human race can count on a few more years of life on its insecure planet, the two wars, surprisingly, went far to solve the problems involved by women's social and political status, a matter with which I have always been deeply concerned. The myth of female inferiority has always been rooted in the contention that men die for their country but women do not. Now neither sex, except in very primitive societies, can do this with any expectation that their efforts will be effective against the colossal amoralities of dominant science. If any of us is to have a future on this earth, it must depend on man's ability to reconquer his power over the machine, which he yielded in the First World War.

When I finally went down in 1921 from the Oxford that, in spite of parental skepticism, I had first tried to enter in 1914 (winning an exhibition to everybody's astonishment, including my own), I was just in time to take part in the struggle for degrees for women, which Oxford granted twenty-seven years before Cambridge.

The war was often said to be responsible for the immediate postwar feminist reforms in Britain, and indeed it helped, in the sense that it did give women the opportunity to show that they could do what they had long claimed. These results would not, however, have achieved their purpose without the preliminary years of feminist spadework, ending in the spectacular protests of the suffragettes, who put the women's cause on the map.

But in a much deeper sense the two wars made the sexes equal, not merely because women proved that they could do the work of men (as they did), but because they could, and did, die the deaths of men. Thus, they shared the "supreme sacrifice," which made them equals in death as in life.

The implications of this immense social fact have still to be worked out in this second half of the twentieth century, which has sent so many women into key positions in public life and given them an equal share of such human experience as any of us alive today can hope to achieve.

Social-Historical Perspectives

Esmé Wingfield-Stratford

"I was born on September 20, 1882. My father was Brigadier General C. V. Wingfield-Stratford, C.B. [Companion of the Bath]. I was educated at Eton and King's College, Cambridge, where I studied history under Oscar Browning, and in 1904 I took a research scholarship at the London School of Economics. In 1907 I was elected to a fellowship of King's, which I held till 1913. in which year I became a D.Sc. (Econ.) of London University. In September, 1914, I received a commission in the Q.O. Royal West Kent Regiment—which in the following month was sent out to India and in which I became a captain.

"In December, 1915, Miss Barbara Errington, daughter of Colonel and the Honorable Mrs. Errington, came out and married me in Bombay. We had one daughter, Roshnard, now Mrs. Norman Johnstone. When at the holy city of Multra, I was fortunate enough to be able to study the inner side of Hindu philosophy and religion under the auspices of Pundit Rai Bahadur Radhakrishna, not only one of the greatest of Brahmans but also a leading authority in archeology and all things Indian. I returned to England in 1919 and have ever since resided at Berkhampsted, pursuing my calling of author and historian.

"Between 1908 and 1964 I wrote thirty-six books—ten of history, including The History of British Civilization and my Victorian trilogy; five of biography, including my Charles I trilogy; one of autobiography; three on psychology; twelve on various aspects of political and social philosophy; two of poetry; and three novels. I am a believer in liberty raised to that highest plane on which it is identified with God's service; I am allergic to every sort and kind of ism from existential to Marx; I am a humble patriot of the Anglo-American Commonwealth of Free Nations; in theory I am a skeptic, and in practice I aspire to be a Christian."

WHAT REALLY HAPPENED

THE HIGH SUMMER of 1914 was to all outward appearance a time of unprecedented and mounting prosperity for the nations of Europe. The replacement of animal by mechanized power was paying fatter and fatter dividends to its human beneficiaries on the sole, and what might have seemed the obvious, condition that it should be directed to their common benefit and not to their mutual destruction; in other words, that the peace that had been kept for forty-three years to the advantage of everyone concerned should continue to be kept.

And yet, as they can testify who are old enough to remember that glorious July, there brooded over Europe the same sort of almost intolerable tension on the mental, as one gets on the physical plane in the East before the monsoon clouds that have been packing the sky more and more thickly from day to day discharge themselves in deluge and thunder on the parched earth. It was no longer a question of *whether* but of *when*. Those best qualified to judge were surest that the unspeakable event was ripe, like a time bomb, to detonate—old Admiral Fisher had even fixed the date for September, and his calculation might well have proved correct had not a couple of shots fired in a remote Balkan town had the effect of short-circuiting the mechanism.

But though the newspaper-reading public had been properly shocked on hearing that the heir to the rickety Austrian throne had got what he had been asking for, in the course of what appeared to be a deliberately provocative visit to a notorious Balkan trouble center,* he was not the sort of person likely to be missed by anyone, least of all his senile and imperial uncle. It was a nine days' wonder soon forgotten by those not actually in the know. None of the ostensible danger signals was up. As in the days before the Flood, ordinary folk went about their peaceful avocations until, without warning, the thing happened, and these same people, with no quarrel against each other or conceivable interest in the fate of the ill-starred archduke, were rushing to arms in their millions as

---

* Though, as a matter of fact, it was with no more sinister object than that of giving his poor morganatic wife a treat by allowing her to function as a real royalty.

if bitten by a common impulse of mutual extermination. And one asks why—need it have happened?

To answer that, we shall need to go back to another August just forty-four years previously, when the shabby adventurer who had jockeyed himself into the quasi-dictatorship of France was himself jockeyed by his Spanish wife and the Paris mob into picking a reckless quarrel with the new power that was in process of amalgamation in the center of Europe, under the iron rule of the Prussian Hohenzollerns, directed with consummate skill and economy of means by their Chancellor Bismarck.

Reckless most of all because it presented the Prussian commander Moltke, who had recently disposed of the Imperial Army of Austria in a matter of seven weeks, the opportunity to repeat the performance by a sort of fool's mate. For the French armies, hopelessly inferior in every respect, were strung out in what was in effect a fatal salient, which enabled Moltke to attack not from east to west but from north to south and, having overwhelmed the French force nearest the Rhine, to execute a gigantic right wheel, pivoting round the great fortress of Metz and presenting the main French Army with the choice of being shut up in it or getting out in time, which latter it attempted to do just too late. There was then nothing that the unhappy emperor, with his throne at stake, could do but march to its relief with the scratch force that was all that was left to him, and this Moltke, completing his wheel, duly rounded up against the Belgian frontier at Sedan. Thus, practically the whole French Regular Army had been effectually accounted for, and there was nothing that the new republican government could—or indeed wanted to—do but sue for peace on terms that would have put paid to any chance of outside interference with the formation and stability of the new Prussianized Reich. Had these been granted, this second Seven Weeks' War would have set the seal on a consummate triumph of military and diplomatic genius, a European peace that might well have lasted to this day.

Had the master diplomat only retained the artistry in dealing with fallen France that he had shown in dealing with Austria four years previously, when he had gone to the verge of resignation and even suicide to prevent the King and generals from turning a defeated opponent into a permanent enemy! Had he known then, as he did on every other occasion, when to stop! But whether he lacked the strength to stand out a second time or whether for this once he succumbed to the incurable Prussian itch for grabbing everything in reach regardless of consequences, he stooped to what his only comparable rival in the same field would have described as not only a crime but a blunder, in refusing to grant peace at any lesser price than that of tearing from the body of France the very two provinces that had constituted the fatal salient, thus not only prolonging the war by months of accumulating expense and hatred and planting a malignant tumor of irredentism in the body of his new Reich, but depriving Germany, in the now eventually inevitable second war, of the winning advantage she had enjoyed in the first.

It seems incredible that Moltke, of all people, who, backed by the rest of the military chiefs, had been the prime agent in insisting on this, should not have realized what a blunder—and a military blunder—they were perpetrating. But the inheritor of his post and tradition at the turn of the century, Count von Schlieffen, to whom war was as purely a matter of inhuman calculation as chess, rightly appreciated that France, no longer out on a limb as she had been in the last war, could now stand on a comparatively straight and heavily fortified defensive line that an invader would have to force by direct frontal attack, which was clearly contrary to the Moltkean strategy of envelopment. The problem was, therefore, to find a way around, and there being no such way *through* French territory, the count drew the logical conclusion that it would have to be through that of Belgium, an unoffending neutral whose neutrality had been explicitly guaranteed by Prussia. But in working out chess problems, one does not concern oneself with the sanctity of bishops or the honor of knights. The plan was accordingly docketed in the pigeonholes of the General Staff, which was incapable of thinking up any alternative, so that Germany was irrevocably, though secretly, committed to it in the event of war on one or more probably two fronts. Whether these purely technical calculations would ever have to be translated into action was a matter with which the count and the staff were in no way concerned—that would be for the supreme war lord and his ministers to decide.

But it was just about the time of Schlieffen's retirement that a gradual and fatal change began from the conditional to the imperative mood. As long as there had been a firm civilian hand on the controls of state, there had been no danger of their passing into those of the military. Bismarck had been no warmonger. It had been his object, once he had established his new Reich, to maintain it as a center of European gravity, a power, though inviolate, yet, as he put it, "saturated" and capable of imposing its peace on the whole system.

But after the neuropathic William II had gratified his power or inferiority complex by getting rid of him, his place was filled by a succession of mediocrities and charlatans, who were incapable of maintaining his policy or indeed of pursuing any consistent line of policy whatever. First, the liaison with Russia was allowed to lapse, and not content with France's having thus been presented with this incongruous ally, the Kaiser, backed by an easily inflamed Anglophobiac chauvinism, must needs be drawn into the suicidal folly of challenging the sea power of a Britain that desired nothing better than to cooperate with him in maintaining the Bismarckian peace. And thus, between bombast and jitters, Germany began to believe the self-created legend of her own encirclement, and the staff to base its plans on the assumption of not a hypothetical but an inevitable war, whose date it was, therefore, essential to fix at the moment of maximum relative strength, which, for a variety of reasons, would be not far from the late summer of 1914.

The archduke's murder, therefore, provided an ideal excuse for precipitating the desired event at the desired moment, and the royalty-obsessed Kaiser, by going into one of his periodical brain-storms and firing off hysterical messages that were taken only too seriously by a fribble of a Foreign Minister and a fire-eating Chief of Staff (in collusion with his own) at Vienna, had set in motion a European avalanche that it was beyond his, or any other ruler's, power to control. The plans for the mobilization and launching of the vast conscript armies began to function automatically, and even the staffs themselves, though capable of overriding their own governments, were powerless to modify or even to apply the brake to them. Too late did the supreme war lord, in a state of dithering despair at the prospect of the catastrophe he himself had precipitated, exchange frantic telegrams with the equally helpless autocrat of all the Russians. The Czar's order, and promise to Germany, to limit the extent of his mobilization was simply disregarded, and when the Kaiser pleaded with his own commander in chief at least to delay the transition from mobilization to actual hostilities, he was brusquely notified that the Schlieffen plan had got to run to its predetermined timetable, because the staff, having spent years in working it out to the last detail, could do no other.

That this included the rape of Belgium and thus a direct challenge to Britain on the plainest moral and political grounds formed no deterrent. Her military power, by German calculations, could be ruled out as negligible, and her sea power, as far as the land-minded staff planners appreciated it at all, they believed could be circumvented by the slight inconvenience of refraining from marching across Dutch, as well as Belgian, soil, thus leaving open a passage for German trade, impervious to British blockade. As for the moral aspect of this wrong that in the words of their own Chancellor they were doing, such considerations no more troubled them than they had their much belauded sage Nietzsche, who had proclaimed in one of his more lucid ebullitions that it is the good war—and not vice versa—that sanctifies every cause. But to Britain this aspect made the decisive difference. No one who remembers that time will forget the surge of horror and wrath that swept the country to the support of what was then spoken of as "Little Belgium," and an otherwise almost invincibly pacific majority in Cabinet and Parliament along with it, into a conflict in which there was never, for all its unforeseen length and agonies, to be the least question of letting up till that wrong at least had been righted.

It had been assumed by the experts who planned it, and was taken for granted by the propaganda-drunken masses, that this was going to be a war of battles and decisions in the old style, over, like the European ones of the mid-nineteenth century, in a matter of weeks or months. The military mind, whose nature it is always to think of the present in terms of the past, had utterly failed to appreciate the revolutionary change in the nature of warfare that a Polish banker called Bloch, at the *fin de siècle*, had accurately foretold, whether or not he had fully diagnosed its underlying causes.

War was, in fact, like industry, advancing at an accelerating pace toward a goal of total mechanization. Up to the present century it had been waged on a two-dimensional surface, and on land the mobile and, therefore, potentially decisive arm had been, as at Cannae and Blenheim, the mounted one, counterbalanced in various degrees by the mass and missile power of the footslogging infantryman. But in the new European conditions the horse had become a useless encumbrance, maintained at enormous expense of manpower and resources by commanders brought up in the cavalry tradition, always hoping for the chance that never came for it to resume its decisive function of mobility. But this, until a mechanized substitute could be created, was to reduce war to a tactical stalemate and a long drawn-out agony of attrition, since the man on two legs, if a smaller target than the beast on four, was another unmechanized anachronism, capable of being mowed down in such disproportionate quantities by the mechanized firepower of a properly entrenched enemy as to put any attacking force at a murderous disadvantage.

Had the military chiefs been capable of perceiving what had been so plainly set forth by a civilian financier, it is probable that the hordes of Germans, with their unmechanized transport and cavalry screen trudging the dusty August roads, could have been held up, and the Schlieffen plan stalemated, sufficiently near the frontier to make it possible for both sides, without loss of face, to cry quits and come to the conference table. But the French command, obsessed with notions dating from the third or even the first Napoleon, had thought up its own recipe for a quick victory, out-Schlieffening Schlieffen's, of a counteroffensive in Lorraine, in which hundreds of thousands of recently mobilized conscripts were driven forward to be as easily and cheaply exterminated as the Dervish masses had recently been in front of Kitchener's lines before Omdurman. This at least enabled a German supreme commander, whose only qualification for the post was that his name happened to be Moltke, to carry out the plan, which he was so little capable of understanding as fatally to compromise by depleting (in the teeth of its author's dying entreaty) its vital right wing, until it came up against the obstacle of fortified Paris. Here the Army commander on that flank, finding himself too weak to sweep round, according to program, swerved inward, throwing the whole vast enveloping movement out of gear. It was in vain that a motorized staff colonel went careening about behind the lines in the attempt to infuse some sort of order into this chaos of milling armies.

It was now the turn for the stolid French generalissimo, who had at least kept his nerve, to hurl all the remaining Allied forces he had been able to rally or rush up on the now exhausted and bewildered invaders, in a confused counteroffensive that caused them to recoil from the line of the Marne to that of the Aisne, on which they had the sense to dig themselves in and present their pursuer with the *ne plus ultra* of a mechanized defensive. It now only remained, in a mutual outflanking competition, to prolong the double line of entrenchments to a point on the seacoast as far forward as possible from each combatant's point of view, in the course of which the British Regular Army, in a heroic and successful attempt to keep this to the east of the Channel ports, came not far short of annihilation.

Such was the upshot of the so-called Battle of the Marne, hailed at the time, as it has been ever since, as a great and decisive Allied victory, which it may have been in the sense of averting the complete knockout of France envisaged by Schlieffen and actually brought off under Hitler's auspices in 1940. But the plan had all the same scored a win on points that might easily have meant a decisive balance of advantage, in the long run, for the invaders. For the double trench line from Switzerland to the sea had been so drawn as to leave behind it on the German side practically the whole of Belgium and the most highly industrialized region of France.

So the fatal but foreseen competition was set of bleeding to death behind the lines for as many years as it would take for the first of the multinational leviathans to reach the point of total collapse. In the west the Germans had only to sit tight on their gains to compel the Allies to waste their manpower and resources in a series of disproportionately bloody attempts to dislodge them, while in the east they were free to match their incomparably superior mechanical weapons against the vast superiority of Russian manpower, backed by the invasion-swallowing spaces into which the still unbroken lines were pushed back in an agony of expansive, instead of comparatively static, attrition. This war of the trench line was plainly developing into the most prolonged and massive exercise in collective suicide on human record up to that date.

And yet what might have seemed the obvious idea of saving millions of lives, by desisting from a course so plainly fraught with loss and misery beyond computation to all parties concerned and concluding a peace on the basis of the *status quo ante* with perhaps a few commonsense mutual adjustments of outstanding grievances, was hardly broached. Even the suggestion would have been accounted treasonable. The Germans were more even than in 1870 obsessed by the doctrine of "what I grab I hold"—or do not let go without a multiple *quid pro quo*. The French, after a slight initial penetration, were almost equally obsessed with the desire to recover their lost provinces, while with England the righting of the wrong done to "Little Belgium" had become more of a moral imperative than ever.

So by common consent this agony of the trench lines and of the populations behind them was to go on as interminably as the hell it was. A vast literature has been produced in the attempt to bring it into line with other wars by highlighting its so-called battles by such impressive names as Loos, Verdun, the Somme, and Passchendaele, and a fashion has been set of blaming it all on the Allied commanders—the catchphrase being one attributed to Ludendorff of "lions led by donkeys"—though hardly, on the same reckoning, such colossal superdonkeys as its author. But granted that imaginative genius is not—and certainly was not then—a quality fostered by military training, it is hard to suggest what genius itself could have done to break the deadlock on the western front, while for the Allies just to have given up trying and sat pretty in their trenches would have left the Germans free to concentrate all their resources on a Russia that, even before the war, had been so ripe for revolution that it has been plausibly asserted that only the war could have postponed it as long as it did.

The inexorable fact of the situation, as it was in 1914, was that until a mechanized substitute could be evolved for the obsolete cavalry and the obsolescent infantry, the defensive, under such conditions as those on the western front, could take a disproportionate and murderous toll of any direct attack—and on that front no other sort of attack was possible.

It was a facile lead to urge that the alternative to forcing a way through was to find a way around, by striking a dislocating blow at some point away from the main European fronts. What seemed the most promising of several attempts to find such a short cut to victory was sponsored by the First Lord of the Admiralty, Winston Churchill, a man conspicuously endowed with the creative energy that is the essential of genius, but less so with that coolness of judgment that Napoleon desiderated as the first quality in a commander.

His idea was to knock out of the war Germany's latest ally, Turkey, which might never have come into it had not the Admiralty in the first instance allowed one of the most up-to-date enemy warships to slip through its fingers and get to Constantinople. To force the maritime approach to that city through the Dardanelles by a combined naval and military coup, while the Turk was off his guard and his main forces otherwise engaged, would have been almost certainly feasible, though that this would have led to the fall of Constantinople, or even to the collapse of Turkey, or have enabled the Allies to have averted that of Russia by supplying her armies with the munitions of which they themselves were notoriously short for their own armies, is mere wishful assumption. But it would doubtless have been a point in the game worth scoring.

But it is one thing to think up an idea in the abstract, and another to apply the necessary means of realizing it, and an operation that, if undertaken at all, demanded the utmost speed, secrecy, and all-out concentration stands on record as a supreme example of their exact opposite. It was made the subject of prolonged debate between civilian ministers, of dispute between rival commanders, and friction between allies, ending in that most fatal of all martial solutions—a compromise, and the almost insane one at that, of trying to force a collection of obsolete warships through the bottleneck of the strait, without breaking the neck of the bottle with the comparatively small number of troops that would then have been required to occupy their enclosing shores. Under these circumstances it was perhaps fortunate that an unswept minefield sent four of these expendible crocks to the bottom, thus preventing the rest from achieving the success of the lobster in thrusting himself into the pot.

It was then that the British command bethought itself of saving face by the use of troops, and a scratch force of such units as could be spared was got together in Egypt, and this, even when it at last got to sea, had to put back to port because the improvised staff had so bungled the loading of the equipment that the whole job had to be done again. By this time even the tardy Turk had turned the Gallipoli Peninsula into an almost impregnable fortress, and it was only by a miracle of heroism that such as survived of the attackers managed to obtain a precarious lodgment on the beaches, leaving the Turks ensconced on the heights above them, and themselves, instead of bypassing the agony of the trenches, stuck fast in another and worse one.

The culminating act in this tragedy of blunders was that when, at long last, fresh forces were sent out to surprise the unoccupied heights behind the Turkish position and had made an unopposed landing, the men were turned loose to disport themselves in the waters of the blue Aegean, while their amiable, but unblooded, commander remained on board for his afternoon siesta, and the future dictator, Kemal, was rushing up every man he could lay hands on to secure the heights that might have been had that afternoon for the British asking. Next morning it was too late, and another force was added to those stuck fast on the beaches. The only success achieved in the whole miserable business, which brought down the last Liberal government and seemed likely to end the career of its still undiscouraged promoter, was the unexpectedly bloodless evacuation that wound it up, though only after it had cost some half a million futile casualties.

The war was now fixed inexorably in its predicted deadlock of attrition, and to that of bloodletting was added starvation, as the stranglehold of sea power came cumulatively into play. Britain's rule of the waves, or rather the surface of them, was confirmed only after a major fleet action in which the German Fleet, having scored most of the ostensible points and having got back to port unintercepted by an overwhelmingly superior British one, remained there as effectively immobilized as if it had been sent to the bottom or worse, as the idle crews became ripe for the mutiny that precipitated the final collapse.

But in the old two-dimensional war, and even after such a decision as Trafalgar, blockade had been a two-way process, and now the idea had dawned on the Germans of conducting it in three dimensions, by the employment of submarines. This was the most deadly threat that Britain had ever experienced, as with her ruined agriculture and disproportionately urbanized population, she was utterly dependent for her daily bread on supplies from overseas.

And the German submarines, continuously reinforced, had taken to haunting the trade routes and coming up to the surface to torpedo the ships that were bringing it. This presented at the same time a dazzling prospect of Germany's starving Britain out of the war and a temptation for her suicidally to overplay her hand by bringing an even mightier antagonist into it.

It was only the pachydermatous obtuseness of her Prussianized power complex that could have led Germany into the colossal blunder of forcing on Britain a conflict that could hardly fail, eventually, to involve all those white communities who shared her heritage of language and tradition, irrespective of membership in her grotesquely misnamed Empire. It needed such a shock to put into reverse—even for the "duration"—the indurated habit of the two chief of these regarding one another as alien and potentially hostile powers, instead of partners in defense of a common and evolving tradition of liberty which transcended all national differences and upon whose maintenance, in face of the total sublimation of the will to power that threatened to engulf it, the future and even the survival of human civilization depended.

It was all a question of whether, at this hour of supreme crisis, Britain and the United States would sink their differences in the realization of this overmastering unity and common trusteeship. The idea that Britain could have remained in even formal association with her transatlantic colonies during the conquest, development, and repeopling of their vast hinterland is fantastic. One service, even if the war of mutual independence had never been fought, could she have been capable of rendering, and that she did when, in the early 1820's, she called—in the words of the greatest of her Foreign Ministers (Canning) —"the new world into existence to redress the balance of the old" by interposing the veto of her then unchallenged sea power between the two hemispheres, thus denying the Western to imperialist exploitation, and giving the basis of permanency to the doctrine that would otherwise have passed for no more than a gesture of rhetorical bravado by a somewhat dim American President.

This effect of a sea power, which America would in due course be able to provide for herself, was what it had been on Britain in the critical phase of *her* development: It made her for all practical purposes an invasion-proof island, free to shape her destinies in her own way of constitutional freedom. Not all the accompaniments of that process were the most edifying, but they did not include the tyranny of autocratic or imperial discipline which is the lot of those who are conditioned to a struggle for existence over open land frontiers. America's isolationism was not only a product but a sublimation of British insularity, and it was but natural that her almost unanimous belief should have been that it was incumbent on her to hold aloof from, and make such profit as she could out of, a war between the contending military and imperial powers of the Old World, among whom owing to an agelong accumulation of bitter memories and misunderstandings, she did not hesitate to include Britain.

For a time it worked. Neutrality not only satisfied her moral consciousness, but rewarded virtue by even more satisfactory dividends. So long as British overseas assets lasted, they were mopped up by American industry in a spending orgy, and when these ran out and the creditor became the debtor nation, the process was continued by dint of ever-mounting loans that it was plain to see gave the lender a vital stake in the solvency and, therefore, the survival of the debtor, whom defeat would plainly turn into a total defaulter. Thus, the effect of Britain's control of the sea routes was to harness the gigantic resources of American industry to her own war effort, which in a war of attrition had all the effect of an alliance short of actual belligerency. Not that American industry would have been loath to double its profits by supplying both combatants impartially with the means to destroy each other, but this, in spite of the bottleneck, so conveniently left open, of neutral Holland, the British blockade, applying America's own Civil War doctrine of the continuous voyage, was geared up to prevent. And to her inevitable and formidably worded protests, Britain continued to react, as tactfully as might be, to the principle that "sticks and stones may break my bones, but words can never hurt me." For indeed the deep heart of American public opinion was already being penetrated by the certainty that, however desirable it might be to keep out of the war, to throw her weight into it *against* Britain would spell moral even more than material suicide. And they judged but superficially who imagined her to be solely swayed by the cult of the dollar, and ignored the deeper impulse of moral idealism that was embodied in no one more representatively than her own President, Woodrow Wilson, though he, like that other idealist avatar Mahatma Gandhi was a more mixed human product than either his fans or debunkers have given him credit for, his idealism being tempered by unpredictable infusions of professorial donnishness and party gamesmanship.

But the genuine and not ignoble desire to keep the United States in proud and peaceful detachment from the jarring imperialisms and power politics of the Old World was frustrated by an irresistible propaganda applied with Teutonic thoroughness by Germany.

From the first, she lost no opportunity of rubbing it in that she stood for everything that the American nature most hated. The stopping and searching of American cargoes bound for neutral ports might be irritating to the last degree, but not shocking and horrifying like the rape of Belgium and the shooting of a British nurse—consoled in her last moments by an American chaplain. Such imponderables could not fail to build up a highly unflattering image of the Kaiser-christened Hun—but when it came to what was regarded as the cold-blooded murder of American citizens on the high seas and the deliberate restaging of the tragedy of the *Titanic* in that of the *Lusitania,* with the loss of 112 American lives, the patience of Wilson himself became strained to the verge of breaking point, and despite some hardly plausible verbiage about being too proud to fight, he did put his foot down with sufficient firmness to extract an undertaking that the sinking of unarmed ships by submarines should be stopped from now on.

But for *how* long in face of the perennial Prussian practice of grab all and concede nothing and the virtually uninhibited sway that the military command had acquired over the civil power? The agony of the trench lines had risen to a climax to which there seemed to be no prospect of a denouement. Bigger and bloodier offensives continued to be mounted in which the flower of European youth suffered itself to be immolated in the exchange of a few acres of churned mud. Behind the lines the hundreds of thousands of war-horses continued to munch their fodder, and only a mild sensation was caused by the appearance of a few British units of mechanized cavalry, inappropriately called tanks, in such scanty numbers and to so little effect as to excite the easily aroused contempt of the hard-bitten German commanders. But behind the lines the strain of not only bloodshed but privation was beginning to tell even upon the patient populace of the fatherland. The stranglehold of sea power was gradual, but cumulative, in its effects. And patience was not the strong suit of the Hindenburg-Ludendorff combination that had now come, in an aura of fanatical hero worship, to embody the German will to victory. Though landsmen, they had convinced themselves that their submarine blockade was capable of throttling Britain in a matter of weeks if applied with out-and-out rigor and that the unmilitary Americans, in the doubtful event of their ever getting from words to deeds, could be brushed aside with as much contempt as the tanks. They, therefore, decided to take the plunge of causing Germany to announce in effect that she would repudiate her promise to Wilson and send every American ship and citizen that her submarines could come by to Davy Jones.

This would have seemed the limit of provocation, but it would have taken nothing short of the Prussianized mentality to think up the colossal *gaffe* of sending a message, which the British Intelligence duly intercepted and publicized, to the Mexican, of all governments, offering German backing for grabbing back those portions of her territory that had been embodied in the United States in the middle of the previous century. A ludicrously impracticable suggestion in itself, but the plainest possible intimation that in the event of a German victory and the consequent annihilation of British sea power, the Monroe Doctrine would go up in hot air, and German ambition, having triumphed in Europe, would extend its talons westward to make nonsense of any dream of a New World safer for democracy than the Old.

For indeed the German war lords had done, just in time for their enemies, what they were incapable of doing for themselves. They had gambled, and gambled against an eventual certainty. They had torpedoed not the last British food ship, but the last hesitation even of President Wilson about putting the full force of American belligerency behind the Allied war effort. And in so doing, they had exchanged what, if they had only had the self-restraint to bank on it, was not far short of a winning advantage in a European war for the almost certainty of defeat in a world war.

For in the war of attrition it was becoming more and more of a probability that it was Britain's European allies who would come to the breaking point before Germany. The series of holocaust offensives that they were practically compelled to launch as long as the enemy remained entrenched on their soil, though the comparative figures are to this day widely disputed, must, by their very nature and pending the advent of a mechanized mobile army, be more prodigal of blood to the attacking party. All were feeling the strain to the verge of the mortal limit, but the first to break under it was not Germany, though the gamble of her neutral-drowning blockade had failed, by the narrowest of margins, to come off. For not only did Lloyd George, a far more capable war leader—though of very different moral caliber from Wilson—who had jockeyed himself into the premiership, force the winning card of the convoy system on the British admirals, as he had previously forced a sufficiency of machine guns on the generals; but with America no longer too proud to fight, there was no more nonsense about the freedom of the seas. The blockade was applied with a ruthlessness that made strange reading of her previous notes of protest. Not only was her grip tightening mortally on Germany's throat—or rather stomach—but her aid and comfort were now extended to the full relief of Britain's necessity, both naval and economic.

It was high time. For hardly had America come into the war than the event happened that ought, by all previous reckonings, to have tipped the scales decisively in Germany's favor. The revolutionary forces that had been gathering beneath the surface of Russian life now erupted with spontaneous violence and swallowed up the bedlam autocracy of the unhappy Nicholas II. The event was hailed at first with joy by her allies as a sort of democratic rebirth—but the removal even of the craziest keystone from its supporting arch was fatal to the structure of imperial authority on which the Russian war effort depended. The patient Ivan Ivanovich, deprived of his Little Father, was no longer content to be driven, in his millions, to the slaughter. Authority had departed from the administration, and fighting spirit from the Army. And the Germans, little realizing the nemesis they were invoking on themselves, clinched the matter by smuggling into Russia an agitator of genius, who in due course, under a smokescreen of ideological verbiage, set up in his own person a Red czardom more ruthless than the White had been since the days of Ivan the Terrible and who had not the least idea of honoring Russia's pledges to either allies or creditors. Thus, her seemingly inexhaustible resources of manpower, which, on a count of heads, had made up more than half the Allied war potential, were wiped off the slate.

Nor was this all, for in this same year, 1917, the French Army missed by the narrowest of margins going the way of the Russian. A new offensive by a new general, who had an infallible recipe for effecting the long deferred breakthrough, was launched with every circumstance of suicidal publicity and petered out in the usual bloody fiasco. The French Army, paralyzed by mutiny, was on the point of going the same way as the Russian. But it was Hindenburg and Ludendorff, of all people, who let slip their supreme opportunity, and a French commander, who was subsequently to die in confinement as a traitor to France, stopped the rot, thereby rendering her no less a service than Joan of Arc. And as if that were not enough, the Italian Army, which having come into the alliance as the result of Italy's having put up her services to auction and launched the usual series of fruitless offensives on the Austrians, turned tail on the appearance among them of a few German divisions and was only rallied on the Piave by the rushing up of Anglo-French supports that could be ill spared from their own front.

By the beginning of 1918 the military forces of the original alliance seemed plainly incapable of driving the Germans off their soil or of getting them to discuss any terms of less abject surrender than those that they had already demanded from Russia and that

the wily Lenin had not hesitated to concede in all their preposterous totality, leaving the Prussian Gargantua to expand to
bursting point in the effort to digest his vast meal of annexed
territory—a process that used up the greater part of the forces that
would have been otherwise available to be switched over to his now
only remaining militant front.

Even so a sufficiently formidable addition was expected in the
spring to convince Ludendorff that he had only to go over to an all-
out offensive to make the Allied western front go the way of the
eastern, before the half-baked American forces could arrive—if they
did at all—in sufficient numbers to intervene. The French morale
was, to say the least of it, doubtful, and though, to the eternal honor
of the British soldier, his had shown no signs of wilting after the
cruelest of all the offensive holocausts in Flanders mud, which
would have broken the spirit of any other army. But the murder-
ously thinned British lines were stretched still thinner by the need
for taking over yet another sector of the joint front from their
almost exhausted allies.

It was here that Ludendorff struck with all the gathered might of
his reinforced armies, using the element of surprise that had been so
strangely neglected in previous offensives. Germany, her internal
economy strained nearer and nearer to collapse by the blockade,
was out for the kill, and as blow followed blow, the Allied lines
went reeling backward in what by all previous standards would
have counted for a shattering series of defeats. At one point, when
the objective was a hill supposed to be of vital strategic importance,
Field Marshal Haig made his historic appeal to the defenders to put
their backs against the wall and fight to the last, which even so did
not prevent the enemy from accomplishing the feat ascribed to the
Grand Old Duke of York of marching up the hill.

All through the spring and into the height of the summer the
devastating process continued, and what Ludendorff had accomplished was precisely this—he had caused his victorious hordes to
quit their almost impregnable lines, and get themselves killed at
last on a scale proper to the offensive, in a gigantic battle of the
bulge that never bulged quite far enough to cover any objective of
strategic significance but caused them to extend their new lines like
stretched elastic nearer and nearer to snapping, while behind, their
communications ran over a conquered wilderness of mud and ruins.
And still Ludendorff went on, confident that every new blow would
be the last, or the last but one.

And then, as he drove his weary infantry on to punch a fresh dent
into the bulge, he was struck in the flank by a charge of the new

mechanized cavalry that the French Army had at last acquired. And—what was of even more ominous significance—American troops, the first of millions to follow, took an active and enthusiastic part in the proceedings. Ludendorff, sent reeling back, re-formed his front, confident that he had a winning card up his sleeve in a knockout offensive on the already sorely tried British. But the British got in first with the new arm, to such effect that Ludendorff himself spoke of the "black day of the German Army" and felt in his heart that its game was up. So from the opposite point of view did Haig, who, alone among the Allied high commanders, believed that the way was open to victory before the end of the year. A way not of massed breakthroughs, but of swift concentrated attacks on one part of the enemy line after the other, each pressed just far enough to gain the full advantage of the initiative, and no farther. As one black day for the German Army followed another, and as the new army out of the west swept in ever-mounting strength into the Allied counteroffensive, the subconscious foundations of German morale became impalpably undermined. Their armies fought on with a desperation that was no longer quickened by hope. And Haig, who had sustained such bloody frustration in previous offensives, but now seemed to have found the inspired touch, judged that the moment had come for an all-out frontal assault on the enemy's strongest position, the famous Hindenburg Line, and, with his new mechanized arm employed to the limit, succeeded in forcing it.

That was the decision. There was even now no breakthrough, no pursuit in the old pattern. It could be argued that the Germans were capable of standing indefinitely on a shorter line and holding up the now exhausted Allies *sine die*. But, in boxing parlance, this latest blow had knocked the stuffing out of them. It had already been knocked out of their allies, who anticipated them by collapsing one after another—even the poor old horse had his last martial gallop in pursuit of the once unbudgeable Turk. Under these circumstances even Ludendorff lost his nerve and began to talk of seeking terms, and though he wanted to return to his former intransigence, the spell—like the spellbinder—was broken.

The ordinary German, whatever else he was, was no fool. He could read the writing on the wall as plainly as any man. Even if he could hold out till next spring, his family would be sinking to deeper and deeper extremes of misery, and next year he would be invaded from all sides, and with the American Army swollen to millions his collapse would be certain. Whereas, as matters stood, the soil of the fatherland was, unlike that of the countries he had ravaged, intact, and the permanent damage it had sustained was proportionately less. And now terms were offered him, not such as he had, and would have, imposed on a defeated enemy or even such as his European enemies would have imposed on him, but based on principles of philosophic impartiality formulated by the American President, who spoke with a voice of sufficient authority to obtain at least the formal subscription of his cobelligerents. What it plainly amounted to was that Germany had only to lay down the arms that rendered her a universal menace, set free the peoples she had enslaved, make good as much as possible of the damage she had wantonly perpetrated, and retire within her natural frontiers to cultivate her garden in peace. This was better than the whipped, but unrepentant, German had dared to hope for. Nothing could stop him now—first his fleet mutinied; then all his extravagantly belauded ruling caste of emperor, kings, princes, and panjandrums of all sorts of fantastic designations were consigned, by one sweep of the revolutionary broom, to the rubbish bin. The terms of surrender that Marshal Foch demanded and that even Haig had feared would prove too tough a morsel were greedily swallowed, and the German Army quietly dissolved, in the proud conviction that it had never been beaten, but only, somehow, betrayed—it would in due course be apprised by whom.

That this almost unhoped-for victory should have been greeted by the civilian populations of the winning side with orgies of hysterical jubilation was no more than human; but how much of a victory it would prove to be, and for how long, would depend on whether the victors could show a wisdom in framing a peace proportionate to their valor in winning the power to frame it.

The principles on which that peace was to be framed, and to which the honor of the victors was explicitly committed, Wilson had defined with an explicitness befitting the most outstanding example of a philosopher-statesman since Marcus Aurelius, and its objective he had sufficiently indicated as that of "a world safe for democracy," coupled, perhaps, with the phrase coined by the English Premier of "a war to end war." And had they and their peoples been capable of rising to the height of their all too fleeting opportunity, who can say that even this might not have been attained and safeguarded for as long as could have been humanly foreseen?

But Lloyd George, at that moment, had other fish to fry and was stumping the country whipping up the basest passions of the victory-drunken mob in order to secure his triumph at the general election he had lost no time in precipitating, and Wilson had already fatally compromised the hero's part for which he had cast himself in the tragic drama of world peacemaking by doubling it with that of political gamester, thereby alienating, instead of draw-ing into the common effort, the bosses of the rival faction in a contest that was itself a product and symbol of American isolation-ism and had hardly more basis of intelligible principle than that of the blues and greens in the circus of Byzantium.

He came to Europe—the first reigning President to do so—amid the thunder of a hero's ovation of record-eclipsing expectancy. After which preliminary flourish the delegates of the victor powers settled down to the practical task of formulating the terms to be imposed on the vanquished, and the tragedy moved with Sophoclean in-evitability to its denouement.

The visionary idealist was, by the very integrity of his pursuit of a reformed world order, no match at their own game for the hard-bitten realists of nationalist diplomacy; but he clung with invincible persistence to his vital point of a supernational League, though at the price of abandoning one after another of the points and princi-ples which he had so meticulously formulated and on the strength of which the enemy had laid down his arms. But he had at least obtained the consent of the French to drop Marshal Foch's demand for the permanent occupation of the Rhine line as a *sine qua non* of national security by pledging America and England to guarantee the now restored French frontier of 1870. He clung with a pathetic faith to the belief not only that he had averted the danger of a second world conflict but that, when the passions inflamed by the first had had time to cool, the League, enlarged by degrees to world-wide dimensions, would be capable of smoothing out the dispro-portions and injustices of the only peace that, *faute de mieux,* he could get agreed to by the Allies and imposed on an enemy now hardly less ready to sign the most outrageous demands on the dotted line. Thus, the steadfast President had got his way on his main point of an American-imposed, and what no one doubted to be an American-guaranteed, United States of the World, with the power to perpetuate its own peace.

There had been a textbook of comparative politics prescribed in at least one English university at the beginning of the century and designated by the name of its author, Woodrow Wilson, from which it might have been gathered—what its author seems to have for-gotten—that an American President has power only to conclude a treaty, subject to its endorsement by two-thirds of the Senate. And now that body, swayed by the faction that Wilson had gone out of his way to alienate and subordinating all other considerations to the party game, lost no time in jettisoning the whole treaty, League and all, and returning to its vomit of prewar "normalcy." Wilson, holding fast to his own integrity and with tragic confidence in his power to carry the people over the heads of the politicians, broke under the strain and lingered on as a paralyzed and slowly dying invalid—even so fated to survive the bewildered nonentity who, as his successor, was to serve as figurehead and victim of a saturnalia of graft and corruption eclipsing all previous records.

In the atmosphere of victory-drunken intoxication which was the equivalent of normalcy among America's now deserted allies, no one was specially bothered by this latest ebullition of transatlantic cussedness or appreciated its real and fatal significance of another and worse war in the next generation, renewed under circumstances incomparably less favorable than those of 1914. Germany, though down and out for the moment, was still substantially intact, and nothing had been done to get Prussia off her back—or perhaps could have been, short of wiping Prussia off the map, by exterminating and expelling part of her population and enslaving the rest, an idea that would have excited incredulous horror *then*, but might not always.

The American action had, in fact, not only prepared the way for the next war, but ensured the worst of all possible peaces. The French rightly felt themselves double-crossed, now that the guarantee of their frontier, which they had purchased at so great a price, had gone up in smoke, and were determined to stick at nothing to recoup themselves. The Germans had been no less defrauded in the terms of a peace bearing no relation to the terms on which they had been induced to surrender. Even Britain, bilked of the vast sums she had advanced to her European allies, was held by her American ex-ally to the uttermost farthing that in the hour of her need had been advanced to her. "They hired the money, didn't they?"

Those whom God wishes to destroy He first makes mad, and this is not the place to describe the utter blindness to reality that was to render the story of the interwar years, with its alternation of blind hopes and paralyzed impotence, a case history of collective lunacy. Those who had just emerged from the war were too much in a state resembling shell shock to bother about the future.

Typical, it might have been thought, of these was one humble member of the German Army who had ended up a half-blinded casualty. A good soldier, but a modest and singularly unambitious one, to judge from his having gained the highest distinctions for valor without ever rising above the rank of corporal. A model soldier, indeed, of incorruptible austerity and a freedom from the common human weaknesses that have characterized not a few budding saints. His father had been called Schicklgruber but had changed his name for that of Hitler.

George E. G. Catlin

One of the most influential political theorists of the modern age, George E. G. Catlin was born on July 29, 1896, the son of the late Reverend George E. G. Catlin, sometime Vicar of St. Luke's, Kew Gardens, Surrey, and of the late Mrs. Catlin, née Orton. He was educated at St. Paul's School and at New College, Oxford, where he was an exhibitioner in modern history in 1914. Graduating from the Oxford Modern History School cum laude, he received the Lothian Prize in 1920 and went on to be a Gladstone Prizeman and a Matthew Arnold Memorial Prizeman at Oxford in 1921. In 1925 he married Vera Brittain. From 1924 to 1936 he was professor of politics at Cornell University, and became acting head of the department in 1928. He was Bronman Professor of Political Science at McGill University from 1956 to 1960.

A lecturer at universities on three continents, Mr. Catlin has been a Goethe Bicentenary lecturer at Heidelberg University; lecturer in the Peking, Cologne, and Bologna universities; Weil lecturer (University of North Carolina); and Walker Ames lecturer (University of Washington). He is also vice-president of the World Academy of Art and Science (Israel). Among his honors bestowed by many countries are Commander, Grand Cross Order of Merit (Germany); Miembre de Honor, Instituto de Estudios Politicos (Spain); medalist, Societé à l'Encouragement au Progrès (France). His publications include The Science and Methods of Politics, The Principles of Politics, The Story of Political Philosophers, and Systematic Politics. Of his autobiography, Campaign, C. A. Ralph has written that the author can "lay his hand on his heart and say that he has done as much as any man writing to try to bring the English and American peoples together."

"MONSTROUSLY UNNECESSARY"?

THIS TERRESTRIAL GLOBE has endured many millions of years, indeed above 10 billion, and man, in some recognizable form, for more than 1,000,000. There is, hence, no intrinsic reason why the world and man should not endure for many million more years. There are wide-open reaches of time for slow social improvement. Why hurry? Why rage? Indeed few thoughts are more startling and yet more sobering than the reflections upon the hundreds of thousands of years that men have been around in this globe, compared with the mere decades or few centuries of high civilization as yet, with—if all goes well—millions of years of that civilization still to go, during which time civilized man does—what?

We may feverishly challenge this notion of continuity by saying, with Lewis Mumford, that man used to attempt the conquest of nature with his muscles, whereas now, in an utterly new era, we have the "megamachine." This is inaccurate. The sail and the windmill and the horse and wheel are not extensions of human muscle. And however much efficiency fanatics may seek to turn men into ant machines, the computer is controlled by the same human intelligence as before.

There is one dark cloud that spreads over the face of this reasonable optimism. What if the change, the technical change, the scientific invention, brought no such human improvement as was hoped and the wrong priorities were chosen? It is the historian A. J. P. Taylor who suggests that the probable future of mankind will be "to blow itself up." If not Aristotle, then Darwin and Freud have surely taught us enough of the malice or original sin in man for us to realize that this is fully possible. Moreover, this does not require a million or so years to bring it to pass. If mankind has no decent respect for its own future, if it remains obsessed with power and with the rhetoric of freedom (which is the reverse side of the coin of power), it can bring this apocalypse about within a few years. This general incineration is fully technically possible, and so many physical scientists and men ambitious for reputation are waiting in the wings and ready to help forward the destruction. The feckless or greedy exhaustion of irreplaceable natural resources and the fall of the water level; that gross overpopulation to which almost all animal species are occasionally liable; and indiscriminatory atomic war—these are the prime threats to mankind, having clear priority before all considerations of forms of government, liberty, and welfare, considerations often subjective in character. Even democracy we have to make safe for all the world, and to make justice compatible with survival.

The globe itself, then, and the primitive human race have been around for a long time. What, however, is quite pathethically recent, in the time scale, is recorded history and all that we call civilization, a fleeting matter of a few seconds in geological time. One can visit Neolithic temples in Malta, as I have done, and marvel both how "recent" they are and how frighteningly blood-stained and primitive. But a brief jet-plane flight, and we can also discover the primitive beside us today. We need not even go as far as Haiti. In *Palinurus* Cyril Connolly writes: "Civilization is maintained by a very few people in a small number of places. . . . The civilized are those who get more out of life than the uncivilized; and for this we are not likely to be forgiven." Here the second clause may be guilty of too much *aristocratisme,* even if it has not a Sybarite touch. What finally matters is not "getting more out of life" for the individual, but physically maintaining and over all improving the human species. But Connolly's first clause is valid enough. So is the story of the Tower of Babel. Civilization is a very fragile thing and newborn. In the words of André Malraux, it has a concern for "the images which creativity has opposed to time." It is opposed by anarchism, by fashionable "trendism," and what Lionel Trilling classes "the anti-culture." Power is morally neutral, but high civilization demands power for its protection. It demands protection against its enemies, among whom I count our uncontrolled and amoral scientists, technologists, and production-obsessed profit grubbers, who corrupt our democracies for gain, demolish our aristocracies, and pervert our education. The Great War was allegedly—or so we were told at the time—fought "for the defense of civilization." Was it?

The Great War, which was the First World War and another of those civil wars which has destroyed European power, a power which developed since Marathon and has declined since Port Arthur, began on August 4, 1914. A few days before its outbreak I recall seeing in London the placard of a popular journal of those days, *John Bull.* It read: TO HELL WITH SERVIA. It voiced the unwillingness of the mass of Englishmen to spill blood on behalf of a little, remote country—it is a liberal error that little countries are always more moral than big—ruled by a contemptible and murderous dynasty and infested by Pan-Slav conspirators, who had only recently organized the assassination of the Archduke Franz Ferdinand. The only fault of this worthy man was that he wanted such reform as would benefit the political condition of the Slav subjects of that Austro-Hungarian Empire which advantageously held the Danubian area together. In the eyes of the Pan-Slavs the fault was unforgivable, the hope something to be extinguished. It was intolerable that the typecast villain should behave like a reformer.

At the same time, in France, Jean Jaurès, patriot but pacifist, was protesting against the plunge of France into war. "The workers of the world" in fact did not unite—or strike. In practice the theory of the general strike for peace collapsed. The majority of the French Assembly, in 1914, were in fact anxious for a pacific policy in foreign relations. They were, however, much more obsessed with a secularist program of anticlericalism. But for the very purposes of getting that program through, they had reached compromises. They got their priorities wrong. They left the shaping of foreign policy to that section of the assembly which was by no means so peace-minded, which found its voice in Delcassé and its most acute memories in recollections of Sedan. As a result, the Germans crossed the Belgian border, and as M. Mitterun has recently pointed out, the French crossed the German border.

In 1935, traveling in a train to Moscow which was carrying Sir Anthony Eden, I remarked to Lord Cranborne (now Lord Salisbury) that I hoped that Hitler and his associates would be given such a clear declaration of our policy as the Kaiser should have received before 1914. The trouble, however, here was that no unambiguous declaration of support for France could have been given in 1914 in the British Parliament since the Liberal majority in Parliament and country alike would have denounced it. That majority was pacific but escapist. Pledges, "in the spirit of the *Entente Cordiale*," had indeed been given, and Anglo-French staff talks had taken place—and, even more secret, an Anglo-Russian naval agreement—but only the Prime Minister and his Foreign Secretary, Grey, knew the full extent of the commitments which French Ambassador Cambon was to recall. No wonder the Union for Democratic Control—democratic control of foreign policy—received later some measure of support. Lord Morley of Blackburn —"Honest John Morley"—insisted that although a member of the Cabinet, he had never been informed of these commitments. A Cabinet memorandum was produced with his own signature on it.

It seems as if "Honest John" had not attended quite closely enough to his homework. As for Lloyd George, he switched after the Germans crossed the Belgian frontier. Of the original Anglo-French Entente for amity, progress, and peace the ex-Liberal Premier Lord Rosebery had prophetically remarked that it was "much more likely to lead to complications than to peace." It was a policy pushed over on an unsuspecting nation, innocent of the implications.

The common people and even keen party politicians knew little of these things. It might too late emerge that not only the good Hamburg merchants but the Kaiser himself had neither wanted nor expected war. They merely wanted to support Austrian "pressure" in the Austro-Russian balance of power in the wild Balkans. Leon Trotsky places the prime blame for the war on the Russian government—and this may indeed have had its own motives for distracting attention from domestic affairs to foreign. But here, too, "Nicky"—Czar Nicholas II—was of two minds, wanting peace but going through the motions that led to war. What the people did hear was that German foreign policy was expansive and aggressive, like the Germany economy, seeking "a place in the sun"; that the German Navy and Army chiefs were noisily demanding the fulfillment of this policy, with sinister plans (even if in pigeonholes) for a strategic sweep; and that the German military was capable of infinite psychological blunders as at Zabern. The result was a condition of suspicion and even of public alarm. Lord Roberts of Kandahar, "Bobs," roused the complacent people.

A bright schoolboy, like the young Denis Brogan, might note the movement of naval craft on the Clyde, and others might remark the excessively large orders in Oxford for Cooper's Marmalade. A few, in the know, might be aware of detailed train schedules France-ward and even just where the troops would take coffee. These were yet plans and not decisions. It remained true that the vast mass of Liberals, not least the intelligent, and the mass of the country, after a century since Napoleon and the admirable Conference of Vienna, so long a summer of peace, could not believe that enlightenment could be followed by a major war. After all, the Franco-German War had been localized, and the Crimean War (not to speak of innumerable bush wars) had been in remote theaters. Similarly Voltaire had persuaded himself, just before the French Revolutionary Wars and Napoleon, that enlightenment had reached a point where no great wars would take place. He did not allow for Danton and for the people's capacity for impassioned folly.

Hence, when the war was about to come, there was a profound trauma for the Liberal consciousness. Was it not truly a great illusion? Could there not be "peaceful change"? The very trauma issued, as immediate consequence, in a hysteria of righteous rage. The "Huns" (the overweening Kaiser's own term) must be veritable devils, unspeakable in their antiliberal wickedness. People who had never read Nietzsche heard all about Nietzsche, whose volumes it was assumed that every German schoolchild read. When a solitary zeppelin, in 1916, appeared over Paris, there were shrieks of press protest against these "sky murderers," who indiscriminately killed even women and children. Since those days, of course, not only are soldiers burned by napalm in Jordan and Sinai, but women and children (many of them refugees) have been burned wholesale in Guernica, Lidice, Hamburg, and Dresden. So, aided by moral popular passion, civilization degenerates. ("Popular"? What majority supported Hitler and Stalin? About 90 percent.)

Was, then, the war of 1914–18 "that monstrously unnecessary war," as Leonard Woolf says in his autobiography, *Downhill All the Way*?[1] (Was that of 1939–45 the same?) It is relevant here to quote the words of two men who knew perhaps more about it than anybody else, the two major statesmen most deeply involved—Lloyd George and Winston Churchill. In his *War Memoirs*,[2] Lloyd George wrote:

> In looking back upon the incidents of those few eventful days one feels like recalling a nightmare; and, after reading most of the literature explaining why the nations went to war, and who was responsible, the impression left in my mind is one of utter chaos, confusion, feebleness and futility, especially of a stubborn refusal to look at the rapidly approaching cataclysm. The nations backed their machinery over the precipice. . . . The elder statesmen did their feckless best to prevent war, whilst the youth of the rival countries were howling impatiently at their doors for immediate war.

(So much for the beneficial effects of giving youth, Komsomols, Hitlerjunge, Red Guards, the vote. In Sparta they prudently gave the vote at thirty and remained a great military people.)

Winston Churchill, in 1929, in *The World Crisis*,[3] wrote: "One rises from the study of the causes of the Great War with a prevailing sense of the defective control of individuals upon war fortunes." In a later volume, *Aftermath*, he added that "the prevention of another great war" should be "the main preoccupation of mankind." So it was. Pacifists and collective security men battled over the issue,

---

1 London, 1967, p. 225.
2 London, 1930, vol. 1, pp. 52, 60.
3 London, 1929, vol. I, p. 13.

"Appeasement" for a while was an honorable word. But the Second World War came.

When the Great War broke in 1914, there were journalists, soldiers, and politicians confident that the war would be won by the Entente in six weeks. However, there were Germans equally confident of a German victory in the same time. Anyone who chooses to read the New York *Herald Tribune* reports of the war communiqués of the time, with never a suggestion of other than Entente advance—even the Russian Revolution, it was stated, would "prove helpful"—can only be surprised that the Entente troops were not in Berlin within six months. (Some war communiqués from Saigon show here a family resemblance.) The military realities were, for others, the realities of the Somme and Passchendaele. By 1916 the French troops were mutinous and had to be stiffened, Pétain's great achievement. In my recollection the black day which produced gloom among the general British public came, in 1917, with the death of Kitchener of Khartoum, drowned with the sinking of H.M.S. *Hampshire*. Ironically, it was yet almost a good fortune since, once a totem, his military skill had declined and his power of direction was impaired. Few, however, knew this. It is important not to be misled about public opinion by the currents in the small world of letters. It is quite true that the lyric romanticism of Rupert Brooke, and the ambiguous revival of William Blake, gave way to the melancholy gloom of the work (still then unpublished) of Wilfred Owen and Siegfried Sassoon. At the highest levels the suggestions for peace of Lansdowne, ex-Foreign Secretary, Sixte Bourbon, and Pope Benedict XV might come to the surface in 1916–17. But they were finally to be checked by Haig—and by, of all people, our old Boer enemy, Field Marshal Jan Smuts, member of the Empire War Cabinet.

The great mass of the people did not hesitate until the unexpected success of the German offensive of the spring of 1918. There were indeed British military mutinies—but not until the war was won and troops, new and old, insisted (unwisely) on massive and instant demobilization. There were indeed local demands—*e.g.*, by Welsh miners for better conditions—met by troop *démarches en force*, route marches through the areas, in which I myself took part. But it was not until the spring of 1918, the March offensive, that there was a public sense that "it was all touch-and-go." Young men registered as "totally rejected"—I was one—were suddenly called up.

I heard of the abdication of the Kaiser in Rouen. At 11 A.M. on the eleventh day of November, the eleventh month, the Armistice was declared, although it was not certain for the troops that this also meant the immediate end of the war. In Britain, on the heels of victory, Lloyd George called for the delayed general election—the first since 1911—the Khaki Election, which turned on the vote of the troops. In the canteens and *estaminets* of Flanders and Hainaut we discussed it. The Fourteen Points of Woodrow Wilson, regarded by many as almost a messiah, were discussed by the troops with skepticism but with benevolence.

In 1945 many people at the highest levels expected a result similar to that gained by Lloyd George in 1918. Winston Churchill, despite test polls by his own party, was among them. Max Beaverbrook persuaded him that he would win massively. They forgot that, in 1940–45, the opposition was itself an active member of the coalition. Indeed Churchill had himself written his own epitaph: The best statesman for war is not, therefore, he wrote, the best statesman for peace. In the 1914–18 war the opposition was not in coalition but a small, noncooperating, pacifist minority, led by Ramsay MacDonald. I did not myself so much vote for MacDonald as for Woodrow Wilson. I did not myself so much vote against Lloyd George, the tricky Welsh attorney, as against Clemenceau and against his British supporters, not least of them the Harmsworth press, "the wicked uncles," with their announced policy of a victory of revenge.

In winter quarters near Mons, in that hard winter of 1918–19, awaiting demobilization, I spent my time writing notes and, not least, upon the basic causes of war and the conditions of stable peace. It is a work which actually has steadily engaged me from that time for the rest of my life. Much turns upon whether despite the comfortable skeptics and the temperamental obstructionists and defeatists, the dogmatic "no men," we can produce a genuine political science and an authentic scientific analysis of these causes. At that time there was nothing of the kind. The philosophers changed with the wind of fashion, and the historians floundered as usual in the morass of irrelevant detail, forever believing that a fact about how offered an explanation of why.

René Descartes, in winter quarters with the French Army in Bavaria, had written his *Discours de la méthode*. Descartes' quarters in Bavaria, we are told, were "warm"; mine were not. As a schoolboy, I had become acquainted with his work. (The sociologist Durkheim also wrote on method, and I got his work translated.) I, too, was concerned with method, with finding analytically the real causes of war, knowledge of which could avert their recurrence, and with the human uses of history. Marx indeed offered fundamental explanations, and Spengler and Toynbee later were to do so. None of them seemed to me satisfactory. I had indeed written a school prize essay on "Cosmopolitanism" and a university entrance examination paper on "The Causes of War." I was not ignorant of history; I was indeed perhaps too erudite in it. But was study of the superficies of historical facts enough? My preoccupation absorbed my later days at Oxford, at Sheffield, and my first days at Cornell. The fruit of the meditations was my Cornell doctoral thesis of 1924, later published in 1927 as *The Science and Method of Politics.* Forty years later it has just been republished.

I had noted in my reading that Aristotle, "the Master of Them That Know," was not only a political philosopher but also a political scientist. In discussing revolutions, he was not concerned to ask whether they were good or bad, but what factors brought them about and what means were adjusted to what ends. Also, his concern was with the web of society and not with any sovereign states. The great work of Machiavelli was based on Livy's *History* and on the conviction that the fundamental motivations of human nature do not change. Hence, where the circumstances were pragmatically equivalent, the same causes would produce, *mutatis mutandis,* the same results. And, finally, in the same mood as Spinoza, Thomas Hobbes had maintained that politics was a science with clear patterns to be observed in human behavior. Also, Hobbes had basically concerned himself, as I was concerned, with the issue of peace, civil peace, himself writing against the experience of two wars, English and French civil wars. My concern was with international peace against the experience of world war. Nevertheless, although Hobbes significantly based himself on a psychology, that psychology was so crassly egoistic and materialist that it could no longer be maintained to hold water. Hobbes was among the earliest psychologists, but his psychology was crude. My own interest was in following the clue of power—of being the student of power as means.

The twenties was the period when psychoanalysis, developed earlier in Vienna, became fashionable, although the major universities regarded even orthodox psychology with a disinterest verging on contempt and the connected philosophy of William James as fallacious. However, amid the more pretentious systems of Freud and Jung, the clinical work of Alfred Adler provided interesting confirmation of Hobbes' thesis of human preoccupation with power, illuminating the political arena, and gave a new precision and correctness to terms. Even the conservative Bryce had indicated the study of psychology as basic in political analysis, while such men as Rivers made their own contribution and Graham Wallas illustrated, almost anecdotally, the story of local government by psychological comment on the "human nature" of those involved. The systematic work of such an Austrian sociologist as Ratzenhofer should not be overlooked, or the more dubious and biased themes of Pareto.

Economics rests on a psychological hypothesis concerning the pursuit of wealth and of the control of property, so massively discussed by Marx. It deliberately avails itself, in this hypothesis, of abstractions and working models. The question was whether politics could do the same. At last, with the concurrent work of Bentley, Merriam, and Lasswell, a systematic conceptual scheme was worked out, which gave a new dimension to political studies. Owing much to Aristotle, Machiavelli, and Hobbes, my scheme was not merely a regurgitation of, or scholarly gloss upon, these ideas. However, the system, articulating experimentally the lines of control of political power, also returns to its own origins. The study began, for me, in observation of practice in war and ended in conclusions in practice about war. And unlike Marxism, it was competent to cope with insurgent problems such as those of nationalism. It comes to grips with Immanuel Kant's old problem of lasting peace.

At the Rome Conference, in 1965, of the Einstein-inspired World Academy of Art and Science, I put forward specific proposals for a study of conflict, peace, and war, not only economic, anthropological, and biological—and the study of animal behavior is of extreme relevance—but psychological and political. There are various local institutes already engaged in these studies, and it has been my suggestion that one in India might appropriately take the form of a memorial to Gandhi. Anyhow we have work in progress.

It was an observation of my revered sometime colleague Carl L. Becker that "all politics is power politics." It was a remark which, properly understood—and it must be borne in mind that cooperative political control can be as effective as, and even more effective realistically than, dominative control—remains true, even if it confuses or dismays many.

The problem of war and the control of power become intolerably immediate as well-intentioned attempts at securing the non-dissemination of nuclear weapons fail and as not only the United States and the U.S.S.R., not only Britain, France, and China, not only Israel and the U.A.R., have or develop nuclear weapons, but they can be expected to fall into the hands of the fanatic fringe of humanity. It is an issue not theoretical and academic, but intensely urgent and most practical.

It has to be faced that fed on slogans and doped with emotion, some peoples prefer suicide to accommodation, called surrender. In their own eyes, they are heroes. After a rebellious and stiff-necked Jerusalem was literally demolished by the massive might of the 10th Legion under Vespasian and Titus, the Zealots made their suicidal choice at Masada. Likewise, in recent years, Islamic fanaticism inspired the followers of the megalomaniac Mahdi to pursue through to their final destruction in the Sudan. The Hobbesian thesis here applies. Sympathy is wasted on such ill-proportioned fanaticism, and as Hobbes says, they have to be persuaded to peace by terror. Wrong, "objectively" evil, potentially enemies of the whole human race, if hydrogen bombs are to fall, the proper target for bombs is themselves. In the alternative, world war resumes—this time, atomic war.

Incidentally, there is an interesting rider to this argument. If the major powers, with nuclear arms, hold the use of these arms to be unthinkable, then the balance of power reverts to being the role of conventional armies and navies, with air power or, alternatively, to the highly unconventional and in the last resort anarchist power of guerrilla groups, operating outside the so-called laws of war.

It may be thought that, in the interest of peace, I am here advocating the restoration of the Roman Empire. The idea is as old as Dante and indeed demands consideration. If, as Tacitus said, the Romans "made a desolation" in rebel areas, at least they provided the imperial peace, maintained, in the words of the Code of Justinian, *armis et legibus*. Nor would I regard any consideration of forms of government or chatter about some anticivilized "liberty" as of equal importance. Liberty is that freedom which a civil society thinks it right to confer. Humanity has to confront the plain issue of whether armed and enforced peace, as stated here, an objective and not a subjective theory, is a first political priority or whether it is not. The goal agreed, the means can be assessed. How many men we should be prepared to kill for the sake of our subjective or ideological or fanatical notions about subjective freedom or justice or national glory is another story. My own answer is: very few.

Despite the judgment, which demands respect, of one of the greatest of the world's historians, Edward Gibbon, to the effect that in no other time would he have preferred to live, the government of the Roman Empire even under the Antonines was by no means perfect, and during long periods, even if primarily government by the civil service, it was markedly imperfect. Today we tend, if anything, to underestimate the role of reason. Nevertheless, rational men cling to the hope that the twentieth century can improve upon the rule of the Caesars—not to speak of Kaiser, Czar, Kaisar-i-Hind, and Turkish Kaisar-i-Rum which, being merely local, do not answer our problem. All one can say is that to base the structure of peace on the proposition that most men are rational and would seek peace is a fairly reckless optimism, contradicted by most of history, and that the record of democracy since the days of Athens and Syracuse is no better than other systems. Indeed, precisely clinging to local community loyalties broke the Hellenic power to resist Macedon. A democracy is resistant to going into a war but, when at war, is no less resistant to forgetting emotion and discussing a peace. Likewise, clinging to our pleasant local habits and freedoms and what some psychologists may call (and others would not) our natural rights—better, "natural claims"—may, in fact, prove obstacles to the rule of law.

The conclusion of Hobbes on this problem is unambiguous: strong government. Actually the settlement reached in England was not entirely his prescription. It was a firm Hanoverian Establishment compromise. It is too facile to say that the conclusion in today's international field must be a strong international authority prepared and willing to pressure and even bomb the rebels. We may logically want a world gendarme. We cannot so readily get one.

It can be suggested that a quite other policy is possible, far more humanitarian, pleasant and sweet. It is that outlined by the pacifists. It also appeals to the anarchists and "flower people." The theme is well known: that, if everybody abjured war, there would be no war. Those who do not abjure are to be met by sit-down resistance. It is, of course, entirely true that moods and fashions of violence (as in Sicily and Corsica) have to be educationally replaced by moods of valuation of civil peace as such. It is further true and commonplace that the civil peace is actually maintained, in daily life, not by a quite limited, if skilled and sometimes armed, police force but by the law-abiding sentiment of the great mass of the citizen population. The same position may be expected to be true in the international world. However, to accept this is assuredly not to say that criminals and aggressors will, therefore, go out of business or that a universal masochism is to be approved. As for the civil peace, it used for a while to come near to being the case in the city of Chicago that the underworld ruled. Too many "peaceful citizens" displayed timidity, cynicism, disinterestedness, sheer lack of civic spirit, so that the forces of order were losing their fight to those of anarchy. Recent sociological studies have shown that most of the public is pretty "disinterested" i.e., cowardly. "Aren't the police paid to do the job?" By vigor and imagination at the top, this situation has been so far redressed that Chicago has become here a model studied by others throughout the world. The same comment applies in the international world. "Patriotism is not enough or pacifism either."

If the recognition of a world authority, holding the scales and the bomb and willing to use the latter against all rebels against its sole sovereign authority, is unfortunately not practicable for the present, what feasible alternatives have we? It is seldom indeed that I find myself in agreement with Mr. V. M. Molotov, but here I hold that his judgment expressed at the San Franciso Conference of 1945 is correct. The politics of the future must necessarily be the politics of the major powers—the two (or maybe three) major powers. This system is called duopoly. Its chief opponent is traditional tribalism, such as flourishes today in Africa—but not there alone—and which flourishes in what G. Lowes Dickinson used to call "the International Anarchy." The major exponent today of this atavism is M. de Gaulle.

To clarify matters, let us turn for a moment to a slightly different issue, although one most directly relevant to this essay. Leonard Woolf, in his autobiography *Downhill All the Way,* speaks (as I have said) of the Great War as "monstrously unnecessary." In view of the blood and treasure spent, the millions of lives lost, these are—and it is an understatement—challenging words.

Without discounting the ill-considered (although no unprovoked) character of the Austro-Hungarian ultimatum to a deplorable little Balkan country or the aggressive militancy of a Prussian-dominated Germany, it can be argued that even Edward Grey, the most high-minded, liberal, and "noble" of the statesmen involved, was like a locomotive driver who is more concerned to observe the strict rule of the railroad and to be "correct" than actually to avert a collision. He was a liberal Francophile at a time when France was not guiltless of nursing an egoistic spirit of revenge.

Again, it is arguable that Lloyd George, who at least considered it, should have actually pushed through in 1916 negotiations—something Winston Churchill also considered in 1940—despite the Army under Haig, the King, and Smuts. It is true that this would have spelled negotiation with the Kaiser, still in possession of almost all Belgium and much of France. That Germany would have retained German-speaking Alsace, earlier stolen by Louis XIV, would not have been so serious as a "nonchange." In retrospect it may yet seem that "change," even if not "peaceful," and a redistribution of power would have been veritable paradise compared with the problems which in fact eventuated from "victory." Twice Russia was brought in and placated in order to "wage war for democracy," and twice Russia dominated the historical scene, under Lenin by uproar and under Stalin by sheer power.

In the issue five empires fell—unfortunately, in the case of the Austrian and Turkish, and including the British. England, as a direct consequence of the two wars, was so far economically weakened that it is busy at this moment, with ignominy, in abandoning its world role and in endeavoring to placate the arrogance of "the Constable of France." Only a neutral and neuterized Sweden and a Switzerland, of which John Foster Dulles said that it was "neutral between good and evil," were left happy. Perhaps Leonard Woolf is right. A small, perhaps united, but protectionist so-called Europe (*i.e.*, Northwestern Europe), divisive of the West, is not likely to be of much weight. The sole thing that emerges from the record that is encouraging is the rise of American power. Whether, granted this power, the United States will be able to enter into such pragmatic agreement with the Soviet Union (which, under the present archaic system of voting by tribal patches called sovereign states, may yet make a take-over bid for the United Nations) as can enforce peace on the ambitious and insurgent has yet to be proved.

What, however, emerged also from the Great War was the theory of self-determination and the actual encouragement of nationalism. They connect with the rise of America because both were made by Woodrow Wilson the almost sacred bases of his liberal policy. What President Wilson failed to recognize was the double incompatibility (a) between self-determination, as any absolute principle, and nationalism itself, and (b) the even more patent hostility between nationalism, as an absolute, and the rule of international law which he affirmed. Strategic considerations of security apart, majority Canadian nationalism and self-determination in Quebec do not necessarily run in harness; or nationalism and self-determination in Czechoslovakia, as the Czechs found to their cost; or in drawing the frontiers in Palestine; or in Nigeria; or in the counties of Ulster. What *is* the community unit?

The problem of nationalism (which, in much of Africa, is a thinly disguised ancestral tribalism) is far more grave. Since the days of Cleisthenes the clash between the smaller community and the larger has been recognized as a menace. After the centuries of the Roman Empire in some form or other, even if only acknowledged as a principle of government—from the eighteenth century and the French Revolution on—the epidemic of nationalism spread over Europe. Abating in Europe in the twentieth century, it rages in Asia and Africa, as a disease of social adolescence. Today in Europe itself the optimistic see a distinction being drawn between local patriotism, cooperative and capable of stressing interdependence, and a chauvinism of which the slogan is strict "independence," except where, successful, it takes side-glances at empire. Nationalism in the early sense, it may be thought, is passing away in the West, to yield to enthusiasm for some political union of Europe. However, I speak of this as being optimistic, since it seems to underestimate the contemporary force of the phenomenon of Gaullism.

I have said elsewhere, in my autobiography, *Campaign*,[4] that I regard General de Gaulle as a greater threat to the future of peace than Nikita Khrushchev ever was. By this I mean that Khrushchev was able, as in Cuba and elsewhere, to make a correct estimate of the realities of power. De Gaulle lives in a world not so much of power as of hitherto successful bluff. Khrushchev as a Marxist, even if on narrow nineteenth-century lines of antagonism of class, is yet an internationalist in spirit. De Gaulle is not. He is obsessed by an archaic and atavistic mood which looks back to the epoch of Louis XIV, and he stirs the embers of chauvinist nationalism. He is dedicated to an anti-American policy. I am not saying that he is not *un grand homme*. I can think of some countries that could benefit by a De Gaulle. But success can produce its own nemesis. I tremble at the thought of some proximate German De Gaulle. We shall be back in 1914 again. The crime of General de Gaulle is that he sits back and seeks to reverse that tide of authentic internationalism which was one of the few entirely good consequences of the Great War. A revenant from another age, he is a danger to the present one.

The fear of M. de Gaulle is of a great power, and specifically of an American, hegemony. The message, however, of 1914–18 is that of the danger of uncontrolled, competitive ramifications, Balkan or otherwise. Insofar as the pragmatic mutual understanding and executive cooperation of the two great powers is the best guarantee, short of any world authority, for the maintenance of peace against anarchy, his fear is misplaced. However, it also rests on a misunderstanding. Rational Western policy does not involve, and it is historically preposterous to suppose that it involves, some political or military or even technical dictatorship from Washington, which rather aspires to interdependence and consensus. On the contrary, what is a more grave matter for consideration is the withdrawal of

---

4 New York, 1968.

some European countries from contributing their full cooperative measure of responsibility for world problems and from taking any world role. The correct picture of the future is of an Atlantic community, not dominated exclusively by one power, but, while led by the stronger, yet consisting of a group of powers, each able to share the common burden.

It may be argued that this is today impossible owing to economic weaknesses. The victories of 1918 and 1945 were more "Dead Sea fruit." It is indeed one of the merits of M. de Gaulle's policy that he has consistently and successfully put political considerations (however wrongheaded) before economic considerations. "The politics of France is not decided on the Bourse." It is he who lands in North America from the *Colbert*, as the destroyer of France and as, in her own person, deliberate demonstration of power and influence.

The reply may be that it is the needs of the welfare state which require the running down of defense to a level dangerously comparable to the weaknesses of 1936–39, with consequences we all recall. It is represented as an economic necessity. It has yet been suggested by Professor Kenneth Galbraith that it is a misfortune of our Western civilization that we spend our time thrusting goods on the consumer, often unwanted until the advertiser gets to work, stuffing the unhappy citizen like a Strasbourg goose, all in homage to the fetish of more and more production, for home market or export. A nation, such as Britain, dependent on exports to pay for food for a swollen population may be excused, although in the long run it must find its cure in a new species of larger integrated or "home" market—which need not be exclusively European and could be an Atlantic free trade area.

Everywhere this feverish stress on competitive production, while increasing present profits (and future complications), does yet provide employment for labor. However, a smaller labor market and a reduced population could be assured of full employment and high wages. Here is an alternative. One of the most startling changes in the whole eventful twentieth century has just been initiated in India, although its revolutionary importance has not yet been adequately grasped. It is far more radical than any legislation for semipermissive abortion or proposals for indiscriminate and nonselective (and hence dysgenic) birth control. For the moment it also is indiscriminate and nonselective as between genius and the recidivist criminal, but this can be changed. It is the proposed Indian legislation for the compulsory sterilization— presumably not compulsory but voluntary for the moral citizen who volunteers—of all males, who are fathers of three children or

more. Once started and the initial shock overcome, it will become a
world program. It cuts far deeper than present schemes for the
building of larger schools and hospitals and for welfare work for
the alleviation of poverty and unemployment. It is outside the
scope of this essay to pursue further these speculations here. But the
program would leave money available, not in terms just of use for
massive untrained manpower as in China, for that defense which,
whether we like it or not, is the prime concern of any political
society pending world organization. It would also end the dis-
appearance of sound economies, aid, and seed corn into the sands of
unlimited fecundity.

To revert to the position of the United Kingdom, it cannot be
supposed that a country, with such a history as Britain's, will
continue supinely and ignominiously to abdicate from all effectiveness in power. This will be true whatever may be the temporary
position of some political party leaders. Edward Heath, indeed like
Richard Nixon, may have tried, but failed, to reach success in a
policy—in Mr. Heath's case a policy of entry into Europe by
accommodation with M. de Gaulle. Thanks to views of the general
which were amply on the record, in *e.g., Le Fils de l'épée*, but
which few people chose to study, this attempt reached an impasse.
Much of the contemporary trouble arises from an unwillingness to
admit that effective peace must rest in the hands of the great powers
and, hence, that support for great power diplomacy, as against over-
swollen nationalist ambitions and rhetoric, is the route of progress
and peace. One may talk of hegemony if one chooses, but an
integrated Atlantic community, such as N.A.T.O. somewhat narrowly sought to provide, has the character of a great power in a
fashion to which even a United Europe cannot aspire—and should
not aspire.

We may not choose to say that the core of power is to be found
in the Anglo-Saxon world—*les pouvoirs anglo-saxens.* But that core
can be found, as Senator Jacob Javits and David Rockefeller have
said, in a special relationship (including Canada) and in an Atlantic free trade area, which yet can, in due course, include Western
Europe. It can be found in a policy, not defeatist, which turns away
from the memories of 1914–18 with distaste, but affirmative. The
object of an effective peace policy should be, if experience counts
for anything, the concentration of massive power and a pragmatic
understanding between Washington and the Kremlin.

In this essay I have sought to draw upon the traumatic experience
of two wars to reach some comment on the politically and humanly

prime problem of peace. It is both usual and polite to pursue, for the answers, liberal, pacifist, even Quaker recommendations. Indeed some young people, without any claims to special study, have appropriated to themselves the sole right to give the answers. The answers given here are in terms of the study of power and of support of great power controls, against national divisiveness and "the International Anarchy." Rather than this last I would prefer the restoration of the Roman Empire and the Code of Justinian.

My own thought on the subject, as I have said, began in the practical and, after moving through the arch of theory, has ended in the practical. It began in December, 1918. One of the most forceful of all political theorists, Hobbes, built his work, which was primarily concerned with the establishment of civil peace, even if by terror, on his personal experience of two civil wars—the Puritan Revolution and the Fronde. Our experience, in confronting without evasion the problem of international peace, is based on two world wars, culminating in the terror of the hydrogen bomb. We shall be unimaginative in experience and dull of wit, indeed, if we can draw no conclusions.

Trevor Wilson

TREVOR GORDON WILSON *was born in December, 1928, in Auckland, New Zealand. He was educated at Auckland University, where he received an M.A. with first-class honors. He won a New Zealand traveling scholarship in 1955 and went to Oxford, where he received the degree of Doctor of Philosophy. He held a research post at Manchester University 1957–59, then in 1960 took up a history lectureship at the University of Adelaide, South Australia.*

In 1965 he was awarded the Higby Prize by the American Historical Association for an article on the British general election of 1918. In 1966 he published The Downfall of the Liberal Party, 1914–1935. *He is at present engaged in editing the diaries of C. P. Scott, newspaper editor and friend of Lloyd George and Winston Churchill.*

In January, 1968, he succeeded George Rudé as professor of history at Adelaide University.

He is married and has two daughters.

BRITISH LIBERALISM AND THE
FIRST WORLD WAR

ON AUGUST 1, 1914, the radical British weekly *The Nation* wrote:

It is safe to say that there has been no crisis in which the public opinion of the English people has been so definitely opposed to war as it is at this moment. . . . [It] is everywhere recognised that a Minister who led this country into war would be responsible for a war as causeless and unpopular as any war in history, and that he would cease to lead the Liberal Party.

A week later the same journal stated: "the feeling is unanimous that the struggle must now be carried on with the utmost energy . . . until a German aggression is defeated and German militarism broken."

The oscillations of *The Nation* did not end here. By 1917 it had become disenchanted with the prospects of the conflict and was demanding a negotiated peace. Indeed, the Prime Minister, Lloyd George—admittedly no stickler for accuracy—accused the journal of being run by a "pacifist directorate" and said that its foreign circulation had been banned because some of its articles were "an encouragement to the enemy." Yet when the Germans launched their massive offensive against the British lines in March, 1918, *The Nation* rallied unflinchingly to the national cause. "In the full brunt of the German assault on France, the true character of the war stands revealed . . . not as a war of adventure but morally and physically as a war of defence. . . . The war was not for colonies, Imperial ambitions, or a balance of power. It was to teach militarism a lesson of restraint."

This ambivalence toward the conflict was not confined to *The Nation*. The Liberal editor C. P. Scott warned a Cabinet minister on July 27, 1914, that if the government led Britain into the war, "there would be an end of the existing Liberal combination." And a week later he related to a friend: "I was working desperately all Saturday & Sunday to work up opposition to the War . . . but events moved too fast for us & it was all in vain. It reminded me terribly of all that went before the Boer War." Yet the following May he told an antiwar Liberal that "the aggressive imperialism of Germany had to be resisted," and his newspaper declared that it could imagine no event more disastrous to civilization than a definite victory for Germany.[1]

These sharply alternating opinions point to the cruel dilemma in which Liberals were placed by the war. It would be easy to say, as did a small but important section of the party, that a Liberal government ought never to have become involved in the struggle and that by doing so it had violated Liberal ideals. The classic Liberal foreign policy was aloofness from affairs on the Continent

---

[1] Quotations are from C. P. Scott's diary, July 27, 1914; Scott to L. T. Hobhouse, August 4, 1914; and Scott to Francis Hirst, May 24, 1915.

and abstention from entangling relations with foreign powers. Had not Gladstone said that in foreign affairs all nations must be treated as equals? It seemed that the Asquith government had abandoned this principle in the years before the war, by becoming involved in an arms race, secret diplomacy, and international crises. Hence Britain found itself in August, 1914, caught up in the destinies of other countries—including the hated Czarist regime in Russia.

This was one side of the Liberals' dilemma: that by going to war they seemed to be violating Liberal principles. The other side was that, had they refused to go to war, they would have equally betrayed Liberal ideals. The party was a victim of the classic tragic conflict. Britain was the greatest of European democracies. Germany was the most potent—because the most efficient, ruthless, and successful—menace to democracy. If Britain stood aside, German militarism would sweep across Western Europe. Democracy there would never recover. The invasion of Belgium crystallized this issue. The right of small countries to survive unmolested, the right of separate nationalities to self-government, the sanctity of treaties, the rule of law in relations between states—all were great Liberal principles, and all were being trampled underfoot by the German military machine. The duty of Liberals to defend them was clear. Yet, as has been said, to do so meant violating other sacred principles: international conciliation, disarmament, equal treatment for all nations. It is little wonder that Liberals became distracted as they saw one set of beliefs being submerged so that the other might survive.

Nor was this all. Whichever course they followed would involve them in further dilemmas of principle. As they decided on war, the dilemma was how to reconcile its successful conduct with the ideals of a free, democratic society. To begin with, they hoped to evade this issue. The war would be "over by Christmas," and meanwhile, the nation would conduct "business as usual"—which, in addition, meant a free press, freedom of movement, free recruiting, and freedom for aliens, all as usual. But the nature of the war, with its fearful rate of casualties and its Europe-wide stalemate, ended all this. It became impossible for the nation to continue along Liberal paths while a small section of freely enlisted fighting men attended to the business of war. Free trade had to give way to the exigencies of blockading the enemy and producing goods once supplied by Germany. When the *Times* and *Daily Mail* printed information about French troop movements valuable to the enemy, even a Liberal editor like Scott admitted that censorship was necessary. (Within a few months, however, he was recording with dismay that the censor was also trying to suppress information about the Vatican's appeal for peace.) When the public became obsessed about spies roaming the land and took reprisal for the sinking of passenger ships by wrecking shops owned by people of German origin, it became necessary to restrict movement in the country and to intern aliens. When the production of shells and the recruitment of soldiers fell short of the pace at which both were being consumed, further inroads into freedom became necessary. The country could not afford to wait on private enterprise and personal decision for its munitions and soldiers. Industry had to be organized, trade-union restrictions curtailed, men fetched for the Army. The Liberal doctrines of free trade, free expression, and free service retreated before the demands of a central authority.

Once more, Liberals were caught. If it was necessary to withstand Germany, ought they to quibble about the methods employed? Were trade-union liberties more important than the production of munitions? When men were called on to risk their lives in the national cause, why should some (offering no ground of conscience) be allowed to refuse? Fiscal policy was also called in question. If free trade must be submerged for the duration, what about afterward? In the event of the Kaiser's regime's surviving the war, were Liberals—knowing what they now knew about it—prepared to throw wide the doors of trade to it? Even that eminent Liberal fundamentalist J. M. Robertson admitted: "I hae ma doots."

There was a broader issue involved. What was the Liberal attitude to the state? Once Liberals had sought to restrict its action at every turn. But in recent years they had extended the sphere of government against a particular evil. That evil was poverty. To combat it, the prewar Liberal government had introduced anti-sweating legislation, old-age pensions, and state insurance against sickness and unemployment. Liberals—notwithstanding the presence of charming relics in their midst—were no longer people who resisted government direction in all circumstances.

This was all very well. But a nation in which the government could censor what people read, could punish aliens, not for any offenses committed, but on account of their national origin, could maintain a large Army and drive individuals into it, and could use trade discrimination as an instrument of national policy was not a Liberal state any longer. It was a Conservative state. Tariffs, conscription, restrictions on free expression, discrimination against minorities, were seen by Liberals as fundamental to the conservative outlook. And once they had been admitted, where would they end? The Conservatives, in Liberal eyes, had on the very eve of war been using the Army to suborn the supremacy of Parliament, much as James II had tried to do in the seventeenth century. Their object had been to sabotage the Liberals' proposals for Irish Home Rule, and the consequence had been that the British Army would probably have refused to obey orders to suppress an Ulster revolt against the measure. With a much larger Army, drilled into subservience like other conscript forces, what use would the Conservatives make of it after the war? One Liberal thought he knew: Its purpose was "to discipline & enslave the working classes & to keep down Ireland."[2]

So at every turn Liberals felt themselves trapped. Their leaders did not help. Nearly all of them became involved, to some extent, in deviations from liberalism during the war—sometimes, as in their treatment of Ireland, quite wanton deviations. Asquith, the party leader (and Prime Minister until 1916), committed these breaches of principle with many signs of reluctance, but often with the appearance of surrendering to political expediency. Lloyd George, the party's most brilliant wartime figure, seemed by contrast positively zestful in throwing off many Liberal trammels. Neither attitude brought comfort to the harassed Liberal rank and file.

This conflict of principle and uncertainty of mind destroyed the party as an organized political force. Some of its members abandoned Liberal principles and turned to the Conservatives, whose devotion to nationalism as an ideal and to state compulsion as the means of applying it seemed more appropriate in wartime. Others retained the principles but defected to Labour, where they believed the ideals of Liberalism were being upheld in a purer, unsullied form. Their defection was made easier by the enhanced status of the Labour Party and the trade unions in wartime and by the readier acceptance in war conditions of state intervention in the economy—a practice which Labour adherents had generally been prepared to carry further than Liberals. Those who remained in the Liberal ranks were torn between opposing leaders and fatally unsure of their position or their party's destiny. Loss of faith in itself became the party's distinguishing feature by 1918. In 1914 it had governed the country. Four years later it was not even offering itself as a potential government—or for that matter as a potential opposition. The role of governing party had passed to the Conservatives (though with a group of secessionist Liberals under Lloyd George as their allies). The role of opposition had passed to Labour. The Liberal Party had no role. At a general election a month after the war ended the Liberal leader—so recently leader of the nation—suffered political annihilation.

---

[2] Francis Hirst to Scott, May 28, 1915.

Many Liberal principles went with him. Liberties which had been surrendered "for the duration" never returned. The passport and all the restrictions on movement which it implied had come to stay. Legislation controlling aliens persisted even after Englishmen stopped wanting to ill-treat Germans. Laws against espionage and sedition and the panoply of interference in the privacy of individuals needed to enforce them continued into peacetime. Only today (*i.e.*, July, 1967) are Englishmen becoming aware of some of these legacies of World War I: that all cables passing in and out of the country, though theoretically private, are subject to government scrutiny and that press censorship continues in the form of D notices—warnings to newspapers against revealing information on defense matters whose publication is deemed "not in the public interest."[3]

Yet clearly this is an incomplete picture. For one thing, many intrusions into personal liberty have persisted, not because of the war, but because of one of its most potent consequences: the triumph of Bolshevism in Russia and its presumed challenge to stability in Britain. For another, although liberty has suffered considerable inroads since 1914, these have not gone so far as to destroy confidence in the existence of liberty. Englishmen still believe themselves to be free to say pretty much what they please, free above all to criticize the government of the day and to advocate its overthrow by constitutional means.

Further, although the Liberal Party ceased to be an effective force after 1918, many of its leading principles were adopted by one or both of the other major parties. Wartime innovations which Liberals had feared would never be discarded disappeared promptly with the coming of peace, even under Conservative-dominated governments. The most striking case was conscription. No standing Army was maintained in Britain to "enslave the working classes" or even (after a brief but deplorable period) to "keep down Ireland." Instead the antimilitarist traditions of England rapidly reasserted themselves.

Other Liberal causes prospered after 1918. Ireland ultimately received a measure of self-government wider than any proposed before the war (except for the exclusion of Ulster, itself something of a triumph for self-determination). India also progressed toward self-government. At home the franchise was made more democratic, and the supremacy of the House of Commons over both monarchy

---

3 See David Williams, *Not in the Public Interest* (London, 1965). I am grateful to Mr. Williams for drawing my attention to many intrusions into liberty which are legacies of the First World War and for letting me see the manuscript of the relevant parts of his forthcoming book *Keeping the Peace*.

and House of Lords was preserved. Moreover, the decade after the war, far from being an era of tariffs, was the Indian summer of free trade. The Conservatives held office, but only on the understanding that they did not introduce tariffs. When they tried to, at the end of 1923, they were rudely voted out of power. The first Labour government to hold office in Britain, in 1924, had a clear mandate for only one thing: the preservation of free trade. Its Chancellor of the Exchequer, Philip Snowden, wanted nothing more.

Admittedly, after 1930 the situation changed. Free trade (along with the gold standard) disappeared. But this was not primarily because Englishmen willed it. Rather, it was their desperate response to economic collapse abroad and Britain's decline as a world economic power—a decline which itself may have been in part caused by the war, but only in part. Even so, it is generally true that as long as Englishmen felt they had any real choice in the matter, they clung to Liberal economic principles.

The same applies to another great Liberal doctrine which had fallen in the dust in 1914: international conciliation. From about 1924 Conservative and Labour governments vied with each other in the quest for peace and disarmament. Indeed, the Conservative regimes of the 1930's were so anxious to avoid war that they suffered rebuffs and humiliations at the hands of Germany which the prewar Liberal government would never have tolerated. One needs only to contrast Neville Chamberlain's performance at Munich in 1938 with Lloyd George's Mansion House speech in 1911 to recognize that the Conservatives, far from rejecting Liberal principles, had embraced some of them not wisely but too well.

This argument can be carried too far. The Conservatives, it is true, put up with free trade in the 1920's and shunned rearmament in the 1930's. Yet this hardly proves that they were imbued with the spirit of prewar Liberalism. Rather, it suggests that they had been seared by the experiences of the First World War. They lacked the vigor to apply their own principles in face of criticism and fell easily into well-tried Liberal grooves. To change the fiscal basis of the economy, to enforce British rule on Ireland and India, to withstand a renascent and aggressive Germany—all required great effort. Governments after 1918 proved incapable of great effort. Hence they acquiesced in traditional economic customs. Hence, at least in some measure, they capitulated to the justifiable demands of Ireland and the wanton demands of the European dictators. Their actions reflected less the positive spirit of Liberalism than a negative spirit of inertia and failure of grip. The First World War appeared to have made the difference.

Yet this is too strong a note on which to end. There seems to have been a sharp break in British history between the great exertions of 1905–18 and the ineffectualness of 1919–39, with the war as its most obvious cause. Yet in a longer perspective there is also continuity. The Liberal government before 1914 had sought to attain certain objectives: to assuage the misery caused by sickness and unemployment; to assert the primacy of a democratically elected House of Commons; to foster self-government and self-determination overseas. In the fifty years since that government fell, there has been a steady, if irregular, advance toward these goals. The First World War may have affected the tempo of advance. It scarcely affected their attainment.

The twists and turns of the foregoing argument suggest that there can be no final assessment of the effects of the war on Liberalism. They also show why: because one is trying to measure intangibles. Nevertheless, two points of importance have emerged clearly enough: First, the war dealt heavy and irreparable blows to the party calling itself Liberal and made permanent inroads into the liberties of the individual. But, second, it did not overthrow the Liberal state, if by this we mean a state in which free speech and free elections are accepted as a matter of course, in which the direst effects of poverty are in the course of being mitigated and in which the urge to dominate and intimidate other peoples is held in check. We may even wonder at how many of these features of British life survived the war, as they have since survived Britain's steady decline as an international force and the rejection of these values through a growing part of the world.

C. A. W. Manning

Except for wartime occupations (1939–43), C. A. W. Manning has been in university teaching since 1923, when he was elected into a fellowship at New College. His ensuing Oxford period included an absence, as Rockefeller fellow, at Harvard, where he extended his reading and encountered Roscoe Pound. Roman law, jurisprudence, and international law—in which at times he deputized for J. L. Brierly—were among his teaching subjects. His international interests derived from a Geneva interlude, first with the International Labor Office, then as personal assistant to the Secretary-General of the League. Frequently, in the summers between 1925 and 1937, he lectured, and tutored the law group, in Sir Alfred Zimmern's famous Geneva School. In 1930 he moved, as professor of international relations, to London, where, though emeritus since 1962, he continues to lecture on the philosophical aspects of the subject. His contribution is epitomized in The Nature of International Society *(1962), an inquiry into the texture of the "social cosmos," the context, comprehensively conceived, of the life of political man.*

Born in 1894 of English, Scotch, and French Huguenot stock, Manning was educated in South Africa and at Brasenose College, Oxford, where (1919–22) he took degrees in philosophy and in law.

His reexamination of John Austin appeared in Modern Theories of Law *(ed. W. Ivor Jennings, 1933). Each year from 1932 to 1938 he participated in the International Studies Conference. His report, for UNESCO, on the university teaching of international relations in six representative countries was published in 1954. In 1963 and in 1964, lecturing on South Africa, he toured Canada and the United States. In 1965 he testified on the self-determination of peoples in the South-West Africa case at The Hague.*

"EMPIRE" INTO "COMMONWEALTH"

WHEN, on August 4, 1914, Britain's Foreign Secretary spoke in the House of Commons on the probability of war, he ended on a note of confidence in the sources, popular and parliamentary, from which his government would be looking for support. However, he made no mention of British colonies—such as Canada and Australia —beyond the seas. There was, of course, no question of their formal noninvolvement. That for them in those days would, in British eyes, have been constitutionally inconceivable. But what in practice was he assuming they would do? It is perhaps reasonable to suppose that he found it best to wait and see. He can hardly have been wholly unmindful of the Empire.

For a British Empire then indeed there was, on whose long road into dissolution the war years would mark a stage. The United States, thirteen of them, had formerly been in it. And in it, still, was the country, South Africa, which is mine.

The tale of British decolonization has yet to be told. But the plot and its principles are familiar. In well-known instances subject peoples contributed toward their emancipation with their blood, waging war against their British "oppressors." But others, more propitiously, won freedom by making war at Britain's side. The transition to sovereign statehood of Canada, Australia, South Africa, and New Zealand would surely in any case have come, but it was expedited by the war.

For—as present-day Americans are in so good a position to know— there is nothing like having its loved ones fighting on a faraway front, for feeding a people's consciousness of its involvement in international affairs and its need to bring them within the purview of its constant concern. And an England so dependent on and sensible of the sacrifices in men and money that the Dominions were so resolutely accepting, in a conflict not immediately their own, would not have been very well situated, even had she wanted to, for resisting any suggestions that their wartime leaders might choose to offer on the subject of constitutional reform. Nor would she in any case be very likely to have wanted to.

Years ago I heard one Sunday a sermon in celebration of American independence. My companion, as we left the church, asked if I, as a Britisher, had felt *de trop*. This was, I may say, in one of the Carolinas, on the one hundred and fiftieth anniversary of the famous Declaration. "Not at all," I replied; "I was thinking of what people like you had accomplished for people like me." Freedom had been ours virtually for the asking.

Elsewhere the pattern was somewhat other. In at least three ways the process in Britain's Asian and African possessions has differed from that in "her" Dominions a generation before. Her acquiescence in the coming-of-age was not, in our earlier case, much influenced by third-party, notably American, opinion; there was not in 1917, in the shape of a world assembly, a floodlit platform to excite the narcissistic ambitions of the newly fledged, and our advance, if impressive at the time, was not yet a leap into full independence. All we had aspired to was a hand on the tiller of the family boat. And theretofore we had wanted hardly even that. Self-determination? I, for one, had never heard of it.

My father, a civil servant, had taught me no politics. But he had admonished me not to underestimate the Boers—"a fine people, an indomitable little nation," which had held at bay the mighty British Empire for two and a half years. He insisted that I study their Dutch language, not as yet then locally an "official" language, to the neglect of my tenuous French.

With my parent's occupational displacement, after Union in 1910, from Cape Town to Pretoria, I came to experience the neighborly kindness, at his Irene home, of General Jan Christiaan Smuts. I thus early became Smuts-conscious and was pleased, when subsequently enrolled in "his" new defense force in 1913, to be serving, in a sense, under him. Years later, in July, 1919, I was to find myself his fellow passenger when sailing from Southampton for home. And so at Cape Town I witnessed, on the quay, his reunion with General Botha, on whose death, within the month, he was to inherit the premiership of the Union. Two outstanding characters and great South Africans.

From London in May, 1917, Smuts had written to his wife: "A big movement to take me into the Cabinet, but I shall prefer to return to my little country and nation, otherwise people will entirely forget me and I shall perhaps be regarded as English."[1]

Many saw in Botha the greater of the two, as he was certainly the better loved. Of him, when he died, the *Round Table* wrote:

---

[1] *Smuts Papers*, Vol. III, p. 498.

A modern Plutarch would write for us the Parallel Lives of General Washington and General Botha. He would find the link between them less in the outward circumstances of their lives—though there it is sufficiently striking; both, though men of peace at heart, first won distinction and influence in the field, both were called from military to political leadership—than in an inward harmony of character. A strong sense of duty, the love of all that was honorable, and a certain serene wisdom were the distinguishing qualities of General Botha as of Washington.[2]

South Africa's is a checkered story. From Europe in the early 1600's there had migrated to North America people who made no attempt to form there, along with the indigenous communities, a single, hybrid society. Instead, they established a replica of Europe. Almost contemporaneously, Dutchmen settled at what is now the Cape. There were thenceforth two societies—we, the "Europeans," they, the "Natives." The British, gaining control in the Napoleonic upheaval, thought to impose other, equalitarian standards. Many of the Dutch, *alias* Boers, *alias* Afrikaners, trekked away, to found new little Europes in the north. At the turn of the century Britain subdued the Boer republics, and in 1910 she combined them, with the Cape and Natal, into the Union of South Africa, under a system of white oligarchical rule. ("Under certain conditions," writes Robert MacIver, "the only possible form of government is some kind of oligarchy."[3])

Though not all of Britain's constitutional creations have endured, this one most definitely did. For lads like me had understood that our "first step towards being a citizen of the Empire" was "to be a citizen of South Africa" and that "the only condition" on which South Africa could remain a member of the Empire was that "British and Dutch South Africans must be able to work out a common basis of citizenship."[4] And this we tried, and still are trying, to do.

Of the ruling minority, the Boers form some 60 percent, and under the Westminster type of constitution a party representing Afrikaner nationalism has since 1948 been in control. In 1914 this party, then small, stood, as in 1939 it would again, for neutrality. "We are not pro-German, but anti-British."[5] "I see," wrote Smuts in May, 1917, "Hertzog has just made another embittered attack on the Government because we have not stayed out of the European complications! He is really quite mad, although there are many

---

2 *Round Table,* X, p. 98.
3 Robert M. MacIver, *The Web of Government,* New York, 1947, p. 191.
4 *Round Table,* IX, p. 626.
5 *Ibid.,* p. 626.

who are mad with him. Wilson also wanted, oh so much, to stay out of it, and what has happened? In the end almost no nation in the world will stay out of it."[6]

Hertzog, who had left the Botha Ministry in 1912 and was in 1924 to replace Smuts in the premiership, was already becoming a power in the land. I, as a youngster, had met him, too, and been told of how, having first thought to study, as did Smuts, at Cambridge, he had, on a disagreeable first impression there of undergraduate deportment, switched instead to Holland. On what trifles does man's history turn!

The part played in the war and at the peace table by Botha and Smuts, so recently Britain's adversaries in the field, was often to be cited as vindication for the methods of British Liberalism in the years between. But not by everybody. When in 1922 Irish leaders were being cast in Whitehall for a comparable role, it befell me at a luncheon table to hear the views of him whose style, in negotiation with Kruger in 1899 and as ruler of the ex-republics on the morrow of their defeat, had left scars on the susceptibilities of the Boers. He, Lord Milner, and Smuts and Botha had twice been peacemakers together, in 1902 on opposite sides, in 1919 on the same side, of the table. Britain's experience, he now advised us, with those two men, was in his opinion "a most *im*moral lesson." Not necessarily always would trustful policies elicit from erstwhile enemies such loyalty and magnanimity as from these.

And, he might have added, such cooperation. When in 1914 Britain conceived as a first wartime objective the elimination from South-West Africa of German power and proposed to Botha that he assume the task, this was not, of course, with any pretension to dictate. It was simply a matter of moral suasion. While South Africans, myself included, might indeed have grown up seeing South-West as the possible source of future attacks on the Union, the thought of becoming the attackers there was something different and had little local appeal. Even so, Botha deferred to Asquith's urging and, to commend his policy to the public, decided personally to command South Africa's forces in the campaign. But for the Rhodes scholarship which was now heading me for Oxford, I might well have been there with him.

As it was, that August had found me in Switzerland, where my grandmother then resided. For three weeks, during French mobilization, trains for returning British tourists could not run. But eventually the ways were cleared, and we, *les anglais,* encumbered

---

[6] *Smuts Papers,* Vol. III, p. 498.

with too much hand luggage, *plus* magnums of Montreux water, bade farewell to the pleasant, neutral lakeside scene. We were to be fifty-nine hours on the journey and to cross over not, as planned, from Boulogne, now on the point of being abandoned, but Dieppe.

At Geneva we changed trains, with crashings of dropped bottles by the way. Soon we were once more on the move. Someone scribbled copies of a supposed verse of *"La Marseillaise,"* and in France, at the larger stops, we would line up and sing it, to the apparent consolation of the harassed townsfolk. *"Vive la France! Vive l'Angleterre!"* It was all very pre-De Gaulle.

It was in late June that the Sarajevo killings had occurred. To the South African schoolboy—for I was scarcely more—the news meant little. But the Paris *Daily Mail* saw something in it, as did the *Feuille d'Avis* of Montreux, before whose windows one stood for postings of the latest information.

My granny, whose memories included the accession of Queen Victoria, was confident, from her experience, that "the Powers" would "find a way." And even should they fail and England be involved, Lord Kitchener would be sent for, so all would be well. And when he duly was, there appeared, in tiny print in the usual window, an item on his calling for 100,000 men.

There was nothing particularly theatrical about my motivations, on reaching London, in joining up. His Majesty was at war, and I was his faithful subject.

Sometimes I have wondered what proportion of those phlegmatic volunteers, representing England's cream, along with whom I queued to be recruited, will have seen a thirtieth birthday. Physically, they might have come from California!

We paraded, our first fortnight, in the park. There one morning we were reviewed, nonofficially, by a horseman in a trilby hat, with a cigar. First Lord, not for the only time, of the Admiralty Mr. Churchill was returning, when our officer intercepted him, from a canter in the Row.

No one, then or ever, saw anything out of the ordinary in the presence of a boy from Cape Town in a British unit. Even when, in autumn, 1918, I was for six unforgettable days to be a guest with the British Fleet, it was always as "soldier" that they addressed me, never as "you from overseas."

It was indeed unforgettable, the spectacle of those immense ships, more than fifty of them, with a Yankee squadron—*Arkansas, Wyoming,* and a couple more—steaming magnificently, yet modestly behind. Had the Hun then put to sea, as was thought at that stage not unlikely, it was Beatty's considered policy this time to brave, not evade, the torpedoes—so there could soon have been gaps, in the fighting formation, for Britain's associates to fill.

I had not anticipated seeing there those naval Americans. True, I had, during a convalescence in London a year before, applauded the marching, past the palace and afterward the War Office—where from a balcony the Cabinet looked pensively on—of the first portentous contingent, technicians I gathered, of the burgeoning new armies of the United States. These men were mostly from homes not more remote from the war than mine, but it was, I knew, as natural that their advent should be thus belated as that mine should have been the earlier, in the operational zone.

How welcome they were, at that stressful juncture, with their promise of victory by and by! With what relish did I not appreciate the Bruce Bairnsfather cartoon: "Another two million men just arrived from the base, Colonel." "All right, give 'em tea, Sergeant." I would gladly have given 'em more than tea.

As natural, I said, for me. It is perhaps worth further considering what it was that had brought the quick response of colonial Britishers in England's day of need. Reasoned explanations are offered. Recently I suggested one. With what feelings had the young men made themselves available "in what was for them their own cause only in so far as it was Britain's cause"? What would surely have counted for something, I wrote, "in the minds at least of many, was the confidence that should they themselves or their country be at some future time in trouble the mighty hand of Britain would be there to see them through. . . . If tomorrow it could be for others to render help, it happened to be their turn now."

But since then, in paging the *Round Table,* I have come upon a phrase, "the instinct of Imperial solidarity," and on reflection I believe that with those of us who were bred as little colonials, conditioned to reverence a queen and then a king and to think in idealistic imagery of the old country, the impulse to rally round rose from something deeper within us than any rational judgment. That something—brought up in England, I might possibly not have had it. Whereas, albeit an alien now in Britain, I have traces of it still. Hence the sharpness of my latter-day disenchantment. Hence the false bravado of lines I indited, that bleak, sunny morning of May 31, 1961,[7] in my determination not to care. "The break with Britain—what is that to me? The England of my dreams so far has died. So much my early vision is belied by what in practice she has proved to be." Sour grapes?

---

[7] The day South Africa's loss of Commonwealth membership became effective.

But then, with that amiable sentiment off my chest, I went on more authentically: "The Commonwealth, by contrast, that indeed it is for me a tragedy to quit: so much my life was all bound up in it, its values so embedded in my creed." However, here, too, there had been change. "Those values, with their lessons for the wise in how extremes in peace may coexist, outmoded are: the Afro-Asianist shatters the air with shouts of 'Ostracize!' "

It was partly, I suspect, in appreciation of the seemingly instinctual nature of the Empire's wartime cohesion that its assembled leaders, challenged in those anxious days to visualize the future of their association and urged by the proponents of federation to seize what they saw as the psychological moment for a decisive advance, found refuge in an agreed postponement of the issue. Call it an act of official faith, call it a cynical subterfuge, a sophisticated maneuver, call it a confidence trick, an exercise in diplomatic stalling—in retrospect, that resolution of 1917 stands out as a feat of collective statecraft, a blessed alternative to the untimely admission that, in academic logic, the federation-mongers were only too unanswerably right. Sooner or later, they were showing, it must be either federation or else separation into independent sovereign states. This, for the *Round Table*, was the essential question—"are we determined that come what may the Empire shall endure?"[8]

Granted, however, that the conditions of 1914 must never be suffered to recur, that there must be some change, what hope was there at that untranquil moment of easy agreement on its nature? Let the matter therefore be examined by a conference after the war, and first, let the war be won. Thus, in unity of spirit and in singleness of belligerent purpose, but with the constitutional issue unresolved, the Commonwealth soldiered on.

Federation. Who was it that had obliterated that particular cock robin? To a meeting in late 1919 at Victoria West, Smuts explained: "When I went to England I found that there was a totally wrong movement afoot, a movement to establish an Imperial Federation. . . . I made it perfectly clear to the English that the system was absolutely impossible. . . . Largely as a result of my attitude in England, that view of Empire . . . has been given up. . . ."[9]

While throughout the war South Africa thus partnered Canada in the leadership for Dominion equality and freedom, their preoccupations in the matter were not, therefore, necessarily the same.

---

8 *Round Table*, Vol. VI, p. 706.
9 *Ibid.*, Vol. X, 199–200.

Smuts' paramount interest was in promoting fuller acceptance in his country of its status and future in the Commonwealth. "I want very much," he wrote to Mrs. Smuts, "to see that in future our position in the Dominions is improved. I cannot and never shall forget that we were free republics." He believed he could influence his colleagues of the other Dominions "in the right direction."[10]

Looking back, one now may wonder, though I certainly did not do so at the time, with how much confidence those Empire statesmen can have reckoned on an eventual solving of their problem, after the war. Smuts, it is true, with a facility all too typical of his tongue, declared in Edinburgh: "The spirit of comradeship which is the only basis of union is there, and on that basis I am sure we shall find a solution of our constitutional relations in future."[11]

The supposition that when two or more nations, differently situated, their leaders responsible to electorates differing in traditions and outlook, are gathered together in unity's name, a spirit of comradeship will suffice to bridge the divergences and dissolve the conflicts between them is attractive, but irrational. The affecting of such a belief may serve a public purpose. But if, in fact, those Robert Bordens, Lloyd Georges, and the rest did indeed have so much faith in what one may call the myth of the diplomatic indivisibility of the Commonwealth as a formula for the strategic future, this will surely have been the classic instance of the triumph of courage over dubiety, if not of hope over experience.

But that resolution did indeed serve their turn. Innocents like myself were content to believe in that spirit of comradeship and its sufficiency to the Commonwealth's need. *Our* Empire was basically a single system, with a single situation and, at moments of crisis, a single interest, to be reflected, after discussion, in a single stance. Professor Mazrui, of Makerere, has remarked dryly on the proneness of the late Lord Lugard to posit as axiomatic a community of interest between the Empire and its several parts.[12] I own that when young, I, too, took this for granted. And so indeed, one might have inferred, did Smuts: "If your foreign policy is going to rest, not only on the basis of your Cabinet here, but finally on the whole of the British Empire, it will have to be a simpler and more intelligible policy, which will, I am sure, lead in the end to less friction, and the greater safety of the Empire."[13] "And why not?" I might have commented. Yet it all turned on that enormous "if." Brave

10 *Smuts Papers*, Vol. III, p. 474.
11 *Ibid.*, p. 506.
12 Ali A. Mazrui, *Towards a Pax Africana.* Chicago, 1967, p. 149.
13 H. Duncan Hall, *The British Commonwealth of Nations*, p. 320.

words, but how breezily unrealistic. Could anyone seriously imagine that, merely because it might be more convenient, it would, therefore, be easier in the future than in the past for Britain's policy to be made simple and intelligible? Not a hint here of how exactly that policy was to be caused to rest "on the whole of the British Empire." As well might the decisions of the United States be required to rest on the whole of the North Atlantic alliance.

And as for that postulated spirit of comradeship. Were the Commonwealth leaders not the spokesmen of dynamic democracies, all with opponents eager to supersede them in the seats of power—possibly with different views? Current between the wars and nourished further by the events of 1939 were suggestions of a theory that whereas in the League of Nations the members, though having sworn solidarity, found excuses when put to the test, in the Commonwealth, by contrast, the members, pledging nothing in advance, were as one when any of their number was in trouble. When the late Leo Amery once developed this idea to me, I was uncouth enough to retort that it was, on the contrary, rather as in a horse race, where the starter's special concern was to give the signal only when all were just ready to go. Why no war in 1938? Partly because Britain must play for time, till the Commonwealth, too, would be likely to come in. At this, Mr. Amery fell silent, then chose another topic.

As Duncan Hall had put it, "The core of the problem of Dominion status" was "how to reconcile the *'absolute* equality of nationhood,' and the constitutional independence demanded by the Dominions, with the maintenance of the formal unity of the Empire, which is equally desired by them."[14] In his own remarkable view, the British Commonwealth would "in the last resort . . . rely upon the force of public opinion throughout the group to bring a recalcitrant state into line with the others."[15] So, too, Lord Milner: "Anything like dissension between different British States in the Councils of the League would be so overwhelmingly condemned by public opinion in all of them that it should be an easy task for statesmanship to avoid it."[16] Easy? Whose pliability was here being presupposed? Some problems are not to be solved by simply dismissing them, in words. Had Smuts not written, in 1917: "The British Empire must be based on freedom or go down?"[17] One is reminded of the *Round Table,* June, 1916: "The British

---

14 *Ibid.,* p. 3.
15 *Ibid.,* p. 314.
16 *Ibid.,* p. 344.
17 *Smuts Papers,* Vol. III, 498.

Commonwealth is often misunderstood by shallow minds. . . ."[18]
And also, it would seem, by minds by no means shallow!

How about this one, for a misunderstanding? It concerns the historical dating of Dominion independence. In current controversy over Rhodesia, South Africa is not infrequently referred to as a warning of what may happen if a colony is given its independence before the introduction of majority rule. This, in a way, is doubtless fair enough. But when did the alleged procedural blunder occur? Early, it is implied. By the Colin Legums, South Africa's independence is antedated to 1910![19] Yet in 1915 the *Round Table* was still at most foreseeing that Canada would "clearly be content hereafter, like Scotland [*sic*], with making a distinctive national contribution to a broader Commonwealth."[20] Like Scotland— goodness me! And even Smuts, expatiating in 1919 on the improved position of the Dominions, on how their "status of complete nationhood" had now received international recognition, and on how "as members of the Britannic League" they would "henceforth go forward on terms of equal brotherhood with the other nations on the great paths of the world,"[21] forbore to say "with other sovereign states." No Dominion, in 1919, had thought as yet to provide itself with a department of external affairs.

But the image that its members had of the Commonwealth and of themselves would never cease to change. "We are not," Smuts had said, "an Empire, but a system of nations . . . not only a static system, a stationary system, but a dynamic system, growing, evolving all the time towards new destinies."[22] And this, after all, was not anything very new. "What was really happening," Duncan Hall was to write, of a somewhat earlier period, "was that the colonists were in fact ceasing to be citizens of England and were becoming citizens of Massachusetts or Virginia."[23] "In 1914," the same writer pointed out, "the term 'British Empire' signified a central government surrounded by a number of more or less dependent states: in 1919 it signified a new type of political association, namely a group of autonomous states organized on a basis of complete constitutional equality under a common Crown."[24]

At what precise point in their evolution do nations become just

---

[18] *Round Table,* Vol. VI, 117.

[19] Colin and Margaret Legum, *South Africa: Crisis for the West.* New York, 1964, pp. 7, 146.

[20] *Round Table,* Vol. VI, p. 156.

[21] Hall, *op. cit.,* p. 338.

[22] *Smuts Papers,* Vol. III, p. 510.

[23] Hall, *op. cit.,* p. 9.

[24] *Ibid.,* p. 195.

that? It seems wisest to reply that this is first and foremost a question of a specific mode of emerging collective self-awareness. It seems agreed, for instance, that in 1867, when Canada was constituted, there existed as yet no Canadian nation, whereas in 1900 it was an Australian nation already in being which created for itself a national government. "It may be," reflected the *Round Table,* December, 1915, "that the Canadian nation was born on the battlefield of St. Julien. . . . On the morning of Monday, April 26th . . . the general sorrow was more than neutralized by pride in the heroism of the dead."[25]

And what then of my own South Africa? Of her must, I fear, be conceded rather what Prime Minister Ileo, in 1961, said of his likewise complex country: "The Congo is not a people. It is a collection of large ethnic groups and each of them is a people."[26] Nevertheless the personified South Africa, the "country" of my mystic, sentimental attachment, was for me a reality even before the South Africa of my present-day citizenship left the runway. For had "she" not shown herself a worthy match for England—at cricket in 1905, at rugby football in 1906? With a small *n,* I was already a South African nationalist, sportswise, when the Union was at most but a project in the mind. Who knows? Had Canada long since, like Australia and South Africa, sent her cricketers to Lord's, it might not have required a costly battle to imbue her scattered citizenry with a common pride, in the performance of their "boys over there."

In the war years all the Empire had its boys over there. And already in early 1915 the British Colonial Secretary was announcing his government's intention to consult the Dominions on the framing of the eventual peace. Moreover, "since 1916," it was subsequently said, "every Dominion has been fully informed both by cable and despatch on all aspects of the foreign policy of the Empire."[27] Yet when Mr. Churchill in 1940 was asked about this sharing of cabled information, he minuted: "While . . . there is no change in principle, there should be considerable soft-pedalling in practice."[28] One may wonder if there will ever, in practice, have been a total nonemployment of the pedal.

Meanwhile, when at last the war had ended, it was no longer just a question of shared information or consultation. On the insistence more especially of Canada, with Lloyd George's backing, and in

---

[25] *Round Table,* Vol. VI, 156.
[26] New York *Times,* February 12, 1961.
[27] *Round Table,* Vol. XIII, p. 19.
[28] Winston S. Churchill, *The Second World War.* Boston, 1949, Vol. II, p. 631.

face of stiff, but not unlimited, resistance from puzzled friendly powers, the Dominions, albeit anomalously, were present, if not as parties, then at least as signatories, to the treaty.

The truth seems to be that the changes wrought in the imperial structure by the pressures of the war should be measured, as it were, on more levels than one. Sociologically speaking, the progress was considerable. Constitutionally, there was at most an irreversible shift of emphasis as between legal and conventional points of view. And at the level of formal recognition there was the demonstration, quiet but unequivocal, of a type of participating personality new to the council rooms and corridors of diplomacy. The arrangement here in question was said to be designed not to give the British Empire any undue recognition, but "to recognize the position of the Dominions in the Empire and assure to the overseas British countries equal authority with the smaller nations many of whom had made no sacrifices in the long struggle for freedom and civilisation. . . ."29

Nevertheless, as though by necessary consequence of their mere presence at the table, the Dominions got included, as members individually, in Woodrow Wilson's League. Individually, as members, but not yet, therefore, as sovereign states. Was not India, too, a member, being not even a Dominion?

Even so, once members of the League, the Dominions were, as persons in their own right, performers, as never previously, in the international drama. It could be only a matter of time and circumstances—we now may feel—before they would stand forth on their unchallengeable own as sovereign states. Was all this then foreseen? Not explicitly, at the time. Sensible men, if asked, would doubtless have endorsed Sir Robert Borden: "It is unwise, having regard to the lessons of the past, for any of us to predict absolutely the developments of the future."30

29 Hall, *op cit.*, p. 154.
30 *Ibid.*, p. 167.

Pierre Renouvin

PIERRE RENOUVIN, *historian and president of the Fondation Nationale des Sciences Politiques (National Foundation of Political Science), was born on January 9, 1893, at Paris. His father was a manufacturer; his mother belonged to an academic family. Having finished his secondary education at the Lycée Louis-le-Grand, he began to study for a degree at the Faculté de Droit (Law School) and concurrently for a degree in history at the Sorbonne. At nineteen and a half, Renouvin passed the examination in history, and the following year he won his degree in law.*

The First World War intervened, and it marked him deeply. Wounded twice, he had to have his left arm amputated in April, 1917. He received the Croix de guerre *of the Legion of Honor for military service.*

Professor at the Sorbonne (since 1933) and at the Institut d'Études Politiques (Institute of Political Studies), he has taught generations of students, focusing in his courses on the problem of nationhood, relations among the great powers in the nineteenth and twentieth centuries, methods of European expansion, and the question of the Far East.

As a historian, he has written vast syntheses in L'Histoire des relations internationales *(The History of International Relations), which he edited. He was also the editor of the* Revue d'histoire de la Guerre Mondiale *(Journal of the History of the World War) until 1939, and has directed the* Revue historique *since 1942. He is the author of more than sixty articles published in various magazines and newspapers. Among his published books are* Les Formes du gouvernement de guerre *(1924),* Les Origines immédiates de la guerre *(1925), and* La Crise européenne et la Grande Guerre *(1934). In this third book Renouvin discussed not only the military and political events of the war, but entered into the study of the economic and moral forces behind the conflict, an approach for which he has since become famous.*

Along with his research and writing, Renouvin has performed official duties; he has been a member of the Institut d'Études Politiques since 1946, president of the Fondation Nationale des Sciences Politiques, dean of the Faculté des Lettres (School of Humanities) in Paris from 1955 to 1958, and a member of the University Council from 1952 to 1958.

Renouvin holds the grand cross of the Legion of Honor.

THE ROLE OF PUBLIC OPINION,
1914–18*

IN A "TOTAL" WAR, to which the belligerent states commit all their might without limitation, not only is victory the outcome of the collision of arms, but it also depends on the state's capacity for organization and endurance in the realm of economic resources and, above all, on the moral cohesion of its populace. For governments to be able to devote all their efforts to conducting the war, they must feel they are supported by public opinion. Knowing the state of the public mind in their own country is thus one of their major concerns, and it is no less important for them to know what the adversary's is; each watches for signs of weakening.

But how can one get a real knowledge of public opinion? The government is aware of currents of opinion in the legislature, if not from the floor (for in time of war speakers hesitate to express their thoughts publicly), then from conversations held in the corridors and in committee meetings. It knows what opinions are being expressed in the press and, more significantly, those that would have been expressed but could not break through the wall of censorship. But it fully realizes that journalists' appraisals of events never give an exact idea of their readers' state of mind; it realizes also that some opinion trends develop independently of any written coverage. Hence, it seeks to learn through its agents about the exchanges that occur in the midst of opinion groups or professional associations, particularly in trade unions. It often has soundings taken in letters—civilians' as well as soldiers'—and has attitude reports drawn up by the inspectors. Finally, it inquires of local administrative chiefs and police departments, who are in a position to give an overall impression without reference to specific documentation and who can indicate the diffuse trends expressed in conversations, particularly among the peasants.

When these records are preserved, the materials at the disposal of historical investigators are abundant. The history of public opinion has hardly begun to be studied. At present, it is possible to draw

* Translated from the French by Sally Abeles.

only a simple sketch of it, which nonetheless allows us to point up some essential lines and to answer the question that demands attention: What part did public opinion trends play in the confrontation of the forces which contended from 1914 to 1918? At what points were these trends determining?

What share in the immediate origins of the conflict should be accorded to opinion trends? In Serbia, directly threatened by the Austro-Hungarian Army, and in Belgium, whose neutrality was violated by the German invasion, the people were obviously almost unanimous in their protest against the aggression. But these positions were consequent on the event; they were in no wise causative. Was it otherwise in the major states that took up arms in August, 1914?

In large measure, public opinion seems to have accepted government policies, which were dominated by a concern for security and prestige. At Berlin on July 29, 1914, the Social Democratic Party promised the government not to interfere with its decisions, and the French Socialist Party was then led to take the same stance. The International Socialist Bureau, which at the beginning of the diplomatic crisis had asked all Socialist parties to demonstrate against war, quickly abandoned this attempt. In France, as in Germany, after a few brief demonstrations on the evening of July 28, in Paris and in Berlin, the masses of workers discarded the notion of proletarian solidarity that the International Socialist congresses had continuously expressed over the previous ten years and brought national interests to the fore.

The governments proclaimed the *union sacrée*. In England, the left wing of the Labour Party with Ramsay MacDonald and a few scattered members of the Liberal Party refused to vote war allocations, but these independents found no support in the trade-union movement. In Austria-Hungary, the Socialist newspapers clearly expressed the wish to safeguard the peace but made not the slightest gesture of resistance. Only in Russia did an antiwar movement appear among the Socialists, through a strike of the metalworkers. Minister of the Interior Maklakov expressed anguish when he was summoned to put his signature on the order for general mobilization on July 30; it seemed to him that the Russian masses were readier to hear a call to revolution than a call to national defense. Yet at no time did the Socialist opposition present a serious obstacle to government decisions. Basically, public opinion in the belligerent states was very largely resigned, doubtless because it had grown accustomed to the idea of war over ten years of repeated diplomatic crises. And this assent confirmed the governments in the path of resoluteness.

But it seems that nowhere did this state of the public mind act as a *stimulus*. In Austria-Hungary, where opposition between national groups excluded the possibility of a broad current of opinion, the newspapers which endorsed a policy of force were expressing the views of only the high officials, the diplomatic corps, or the military General Staffs. In Russia, some liberal bourgeois circles and intellectuals joined in a nationalistic trend, but in July, 1914, according to all the evidence, the spokesmen of this nationalism had no influence over political action. In Great Britain, public opinion was slow to awaken; it remained hesitant and divided until the news of the German ultimatum to Belgium, whereas the Prime Minister and the majority of the Cabinet had already decided twenty-four hours earlier to intervene in the war. In France and Germany, it is true, expressions of opinion in favor of the war were more vigorous; but these were not very widespread, and they were late. In Paris, street processions (three columns of demonstrators, numbering no more than 7,000 people in all) formed only on August 2, *after* the publication of the general mobilization order. Local officials in the provinces reported the populace calm and unexcited and confident, the draftees spirited; but only in the Midi, at Nice and Toulon, where the people are more exuberant, did they record "enthusiasm."

In sum—and this is the essential point—at no time did currents of opinion *determine* the decisions of the governments, but they did show officialdom that it could envisage the eventuality of war without danger to the country's internal stability; once the decisions were taken, public opinion approved them.

These peoples who gave their consent to war in August, 1914, following a long period of peace, were only vaguely aware of the trials and sufferings they would have to face. On the contrary, those who entered the conflict later knew through the press the nature of the conflict and the magnitude of the losses in human life, and yet they too were willing to take part in it. Were they resigned, or cooperative, or enthusiastic?

In the Balkan states, the mass of the people, who were rural, had no political education and had hardly any opportunity to exercise seriously the right to vote; political decisions were the affair of a few men, leaders of cliques rather than parties; the legislative institutions were at the mercy of the powers-that-were. The restricted circles which shared in the decision making were divided on the question of launching the country into the venture of war. At

Constantinople, Enver Pasha's policy, leading Turkey to enter the conflict on the side of Germany, was fought by Talaat Bey. At Sofia in September–October, 1915, parliamentary opposition to the policy of King Ferdinand and his Prime Minister, Vasil Radoslavov, was vehement; the leaders of this opposition warned the King they would make him personally responsible for the consequences of his policy, but their efforts were in vain. At Bucharest on August 27, 1916, when the Royal Council was presented with the decision made by the King and the President of the Council, the policy of intervention ran afoul of some criticism, in one case vehement. But it would be quite excessive to think that these displays expressed an opinion trend; these were the reactions of some political "professionals" whose concepts of the national interest were divergent but who were not concerned with the behavior of the masses.

In the case of Italy's intervention, the situation is entirely different. After conducting negotiations with the two groups of belligerents simultaneously, the Italian government ended by signing the Pact of London with the Entente states on April 26, 1915. While this government was seeking its course, the public openly discussed the possible solutions; it divided into two currents, which split open the ranks of the political parties: On the one hand were the proponents of intervention—a few Socialists, grouped around Benito Mussolini, and some trade unionists joined together with Christian Democrats and a segment of the liberal bourgeoisie and on the other, neutrality—but a "paying" neutrality—was preached by the leader of the Liberal Party, Giovanni Giolitti, and was wanted by almost all the Socialists and most of the Catholics. Here, then, were real currents of opinion.

Now, when the government was preparing to sign the Pact of London and to ask the Parliament to vote war appropriations, the majority of the deputies (320 out of 508) showed themselves adherents to Giolitti's policy. On May 13 the government resigned. But the proponents of intervention raised a violent protest against the parliamentary majority; part of the press led a heated campaign against the neutralists, for only participation in the war would enable Italy fully to achieve its national aspirations. This current of opinion displayed itself "in the street": at Rome, Gabriele D'Annunzio's appeal to the people; at Milan, Florence, Turin, processions of people forming to the cry of "We want war!" The demonstrations were effective: The King rejected the government's resignation, and the Parliament submitted to voting the war allocations, by a large majority, on May 20. Yet only a minority of the population actually wanted intervention, for the mass of the peasants remained passive. But it was enough for the partisans of intervention to demonstrate their resolution and their strength in numbers in the big cities for their will to be imposed. It was this current of opinion that furnished the decisive stimulus.

The role of public opinion was equally important in the decision of the United States, but it was defined in different terms. The question of what posture to adopt toward the European conflict had, of course, given rise to broad discussions in 1915 and 1916, particularly since the considerable increase in American exports had been somewhat checked by the blockade and submarine warfare; but the Presidential elections in November, 1916, clearly demonstrated that the great majority of citizens, while evincing moral disapproval of Germany, wanted neutrality maintained—to keep the United States "out of the war" had been the slogan adopted by both the Democrats and the Republicans.

In early February, 1917, when Germany had decided on submarine warfare "to the death," President Wilson was well aware that neutrality was no longer possible; he was convinced that the United States had to enter the war. However, he temporized for two months longer because he wanted to be able to count on the support of public opinion. In fact, opinion was very largely favorable to intervention in the Eastern states after Germany repudiated the promises it had made in May, 1916; but in the Central and Western states it was quite reserved. The economic congestion created in American ports by the submarine warfare shook loose the neutralism of the Midwestern farmers and Southern cotton planters; the publication of the Zimmermann telegram aroused indignation in the West, echoed in the sense of national honor expressed throughout the press.

Yet the President was still uneasy, because he feared that public opinion was not yet ripe. He was reassured only when he saw the vibrant welcome the vast majority of the public gave his message to Congress announcing America's entrance into the war on April 2. In this case, the opinion trends did not act as a *stimulus,* they did not provoke the government's decisions, but they provided the President's policy with an indispensable buttress. Without them, could Wilson have made his final decisions?

In 1915 and 1916 the public in France and Great Britain, as in Germany, persisted in the main in vigorously supporting the war effort; pacifist ideas, which had almost completely disappeared from view at the outset of the hostilities, nonetheless reappeared in the early months of 1915, though they found only timid expression.

The Zimmerwald movement, which aimed to end international conflict, but in order to substitute civil war for it, had few adherents as yet. Only in Russia was national unity badly shaken and a broad segment of public opinion agitated. Yet this agitation was not pacifist; it carried a reproach to the government for its inability to give a vigorous stimulus to national defense.

But in 1917, signs of lassitude were appearing. The duration of a war whose end no one could perceive, the mental suffering, the economic difficulties led a large part of the population in all the belligerent states to hope for a compromise peace. At the moment when the general conditions of the struggle were being transformed by the threat of Russian defection and the intervention of the United States, this idea of peace was being openly envisaged.

It is important to compare the forms, the characteristics, and the practical implications of this crisis in morale in the major belligerent nations.

This decline in morale was least serious in Great Britain. The big metalworkers' strike in April–May, 1917, which hampered the manufacture of armaments, had the unique purpose of protecting the interests of "qualified" workers against the invasion of "unqualified" manpower; it was decided on contrary to the views of the trade-union chiefs; it was condemned by the great majority of the newspapers and does not seem to have been a sign of a pacifist trend in the thinking of the mass of the population. On August 10, it is true, the Trades Union Congress declared its approval of sending a delegation to the Stockholm conference, but it abandoned the project three weeks later. In November the public letter of a political liberal of great authority, Lord Lansdowne, recommending the conclusion of a peace with "no annexations," was at first favorably received by a goodly segment of the public, but the Labour Party and the trade unions disavowed this vein of thought on December 28 and declared that the peace should allow France to recover Alsace-Lorraine and Italy to satisfy its irredentist claims. Thus, on every major occasion, the ranks of the union movement provided backing for the policy of Lloyd George's Cabinet.

In Germany, war weariness reached critical proportions in April and July, 1917. The immediate cause of the strike movements, which were as serious in mid-April as in Great Britain, was the shortage in the food supply, but they rapidly took on a political cast: The Socialist press stressed the desire for peace. In July, economic difficulties were again at the bottom of protests and disturbances in several country towns. This time the question of peace was at the forefront. The Social Democratic Party declared itself in favor of a peace of "conciliation" and rejected any notion of annexation; it got support from the Progressives and Catholic Centrists. The peace resolution voted for by the majority of the Reichstag on July 19 was intended to impose a political orientation on the government, and the vote gave rise to vehement protests from the rightist parties in the press. Public opinion thus seemed capable of providing a stimulus, but it quickly weakened; six weeks later, when the Social Democrats mounted an attack against nationalist propaganda at a Reichstag session, they were not supported by the Progressives and Catholics. This decline of the movement for a peace of conciliation was connected with the signs of distintegration of which Russia was the prime example and with the hope of concluding a separate peace with that country.

From January, 1917, onward, lassitude quickly overran "all parts of the country" in Austria-Hungary, as the president of the Austrian Council observed at a session of the Council of Ministers. The Minister of Foreign Affairs told the German Chancellor in March that the Dual Monarchy was at the end of its strength and that it wanted an early peace; he renounced any annexation and wished to induce the German government to abandon Alsace-Lorraine. The press, which gave considerable space to the question of "war aims" during the summer, rarely referred to eventual territorial annexations. It printed much discussion on the nationalities issue and the right of peoples to self-determination, and it envisaged the "renovation" of the Dual Monarchy—that is, its transformation into a federal state. The leaders of the national groups nonetheless affirmed their loyalty with regard to the dynasty and envisaged, they said, only a reform of the institutions. This was doubtless a necessary precaution to sidestep the exactions of the censors and the police. But these opinion trends had an undeniably broad base, at least among the bourgeois and trade unionists. Yet at no point did they take on a revolutionary character in 1917; the workers' protest was indeed much less active than in the other belligerent states in the same period.

In France and Italy, the opinion trends at certain moments during that critical year had features with more serious implications for national solidarity and the war effort.

In June and October–November, 1917, all the reports from the administrative officials, police, and postal inspectors in France signaled a crisis in morale. In June, the causes of this were the concern aroused by Russia's situation, economic difficulties, and, above all, the failure of the April 16 offensive. The loss of morale was serious in the Army, where 68 out of 112 infantry divisions were hit by mutinous uprisings, though actually most of these were short-lived flare-ups. It was also serious among the civilian populace; only ten department prefects stated that morale remained "satisfactory," all the others reporting a decline—"weakening," "edginess," "uneasiness," "sharp change in the public spirit." Several departments recorded "confusion" among a majority of the populace, and four of them spoke of an opinion trend which demanded peace "at any price."

In the course of the summer, this restlessness died down; the people again adopted an attitude of weary resignation. But in the autumn, the Italian defeat at Caporetto and especially the Bolshevik Revolution, which opened up the possibility of a separate peace with Russia, reawakened pessimism. Mid-November saw new and vehement expressions of pacifist feeling. The postal inspection services picked up allusions in letters to an imminent revolutionary movement. Only five or six weeks later, when the impetus furnished by Clemenceau began to be felt, did observers report a recovery of public spirit.

Public opinion was even more sensitive in Italy, where economic deprivation was severer than in France and neutralist propaganda more active, since only a minority of the population had wanted the country to enter into war. This climate of doubt was already noticeable in the spring of 1917. In August and September, the crisis showed itself simultaneously in renewed neutralist activity (the public's reception of Pope Benedict XV's peace note and of Giolitti's address at Cuneo), popular disorders (the serious disturbances at Turin, which led the government to declare a "state of siege" in three provinces), and demonstrations by Socialist municipalities, which did not want to participate in the war effort. The government did not submit to these opinion pressures, but its opposition to them was rather weak. In fact, it was the military defeat, the Battle of Caporetto, which ended the internal crisis; the Austro-German invasion of Venetia provoked a tide of patriotism in the labor associations as in Catholic groups. The great majority of the public agreed that it was no longer possible to hope for peace, for the conditions would now be disastrous.

In sum, no more in Italy than in France did the opinion trends and the increasing pacifist feeling succeed in influencing government policy in 1917.

But in Russia, public opinion played an important role in the development of the revolution. Does it alone explain the revolution's course? Surely not. Economic difficulties must be taken into account; the shortage in the bread and coal supplies was the immediate cause of the revolutionary disorders at Petrograd which were to end in the fall of the czarist regime, and the stagnation of industry, aggravated by the transportation crisis, markedly weakened the authority of the provisional government. Consideration must also and particularly be given to the undertakings of the militants, who exploited the trends of public thinking, and the activities of Lenin personally, who at an opportune moment proposed a program of immediate action to the "anonymous revolutionary masses."

Yet on at least two occasions, public opinion furnished a decisive stimulus.

The first instance was the rise of the February Revolution. Well before finding itself at grips with the workers' protests, the government had lost the confidence of a good number of the businessmen, who would no longer put up with the inefficiencies of the bureaucracy; it was this revolution of attitude among the bourgeoisie that opened the way to the political revolution. But this segment of opinion was not pacifist. The workers' protest, on the contrary, was, not so much from ideological choice as from the desire to escape the hardships the war imposed on the mass of the people in their daily life. During the first two days of the revolutionary uprising, this protest was spontaneous; it surprised even the revolutionary leaders, who thought it premature. Thus, the trend of public opinion here did play a determining role.

It still retained that role in the days following the fall of the Czar, when the provisional government and the Soviet received petitions, manifestos, proposals by the thousands from every quarter, expressing the aspirations of the peasants, workers, soldiers, but also the middle classes, artists, intellectuals, without prior suggestion from the revolutionary organizations. It was a great spontaneous flood, remarkable for the vigor of the convictions and the ardor of the feelings expressed. Public opinion "outran" the public powers.[1]

But it was not public opinion which laid the way for the October Revolution, whose plan had been drawn up and whose timing had been set by Lenin. The central committee of the Bolshevik Party decided on an armed coup, because it thought that the Constituent Assembly elections would not be favorable to it. It anticipated only that a large part of public opinion would remain passive and that the promise of immediate agrarian reform and peace would ensure

[1] On this point, see Marc Ferro, *La Révolution de 1917: La Chute du tsarisme et les origines d'Octobre* [The Revolution of 1917: The Fall of Czarism and the Origins of the October Uprising] (Paris, 1967) , with a preface by Roger Portal.

it the sympathies or at least the neutrality of the rural population. The events proved this prediction correct.

In the final analysis, is it possible to weigh the role of public opinion trends in the outcome of the conflict? After the sharp turn in the military situation on July 18, 1918, the Allied and Associated armies marched toward victory. Doubtless that victory did not seem very close until the early days of October, but it was assured, thanks to the influx of American troops. The prospect of a fifth winter of war was, therefore, fairly easy for the combatants and the civilian population to accept. When the German petition for an armistice in early October made it possible to believe that the end would perhaps arrive before the end of the year, public opinion expressed deep satisfaction, of course, but exhibited no impatience.

In the United States, what was most often read in the papers and heard in Congressional debates was the intention to impose "unconditional" surrender on the Central Powers; only gradually was President Wilson able to rally a segment of opinion to his policy of a negotiated armistice. The press in Great Britain, except for the labor papers, was distrustful of the German initiative. In France, at the heart of the radical groups, as well as on the extreme right, a portion of the opinion wanted Germany's petition to be rejected and the Allied armies to enter Germany, so as to give the enemy a direct and painful taste of the horrors and devastations of the war; but the majority wanted an immediate armistice, provided that the conditions were severe, while only a small minority wanted peace at any price. These currents of opinion effectively allowed the governments rather broad freedom of action. When all was said and done, the Armistice of November 11, 1918, was cordially received, even by those who a month earlier had protested against undertaking negotiations with Germany.

But the opinion trends whose influence it is important to assess were those in Austria-Hungary and Germany.

Public opinion had a considerable share in the breakup of Austria-Hungary, where the Slavic nationalities found themselves under a political regime structured to benefit the Germans and Magyars. The right of peoples to self-determination had already been invoked, in 1917, to demand statutory autonomy within the framework of the Empire.[2] Since the defeat of the Central Powers had become a certainty, the national groups were no longer content with that demand: They sought independence. It was the threat of

---

2 See above, p. 445.

separatist movements in Czech lands and among the southern Slavs that led the Emperor Charles to make a peace offer on September 14, which was immediately rejected. As soon as Bulgaria's defection on September 28 was a *fait accompli*, the Austro-Hungarian government expected to see these opinion trends develop speedily; the signs of disintegration worsened during the first two weeks of October.

On October 21, 1918, when President Wilson declared that autonomy could no longer be considered an adequate solution, his note fell "like a bomb" that blew up the framework of the state. The Austro-Hungarian Empire was dead. The news from the interior, spread by the papers and the Italian propaganda services, ruined the discipline and sense of duty in the Army. Why should the contingents recruited from the national minorities agree to fight to defend a state which they had no patriotic attachment for? On October 23, in two sectors of the front, small units made up of Hungarians, Czechs, and southern Slavs refused to obey orders; these mutinous troops declared that they would no longer fight in the ranks of the Imperial Army, but were prepared to defend the territory of the new national state to which they would henceforth belong. The next day the Archduke Joseph informed the Emperor that it was necessary to conclude an armistice with little delay if he wanted to prevent the disintegration of the Army.

It was this very unsound Army which took the first shock of the Italian offensive that day. The Austro-Hungarian defeat at Vittorio Veneto on October 30 was a direct result of the national movements working for the dissolution of the Dual Monarchy. The Villa Giusti armistice was negotiated by a moribund government which no longer possessed even the semblance of power. Thus public opinion was the determining force in this dislocation of the state and the Army.

The same was not true in Germany. It was not prior to the great battle but in keeping with the pace of the fighting that the decline in morale developed. Of course, a major strike of the metalworkers in January, 1918, in which the demands were predominantly political, had shown that a portion of the workers wanted peace. But during the following months, when the Treaty of Brest-Litovsk had established the victory in the east and the German offensive on the French front had met with great success, these demonstrations of war weariness and inclinations toward pacifism had disappeared. Only in mid-August, a month after the shift in the military situation, did public opinion begin to show signs of uneasiness and edginess. At the beginning of September, the press was reporting on the progress of a "tide of skepticism" which was overtaking even the Army. The political parties began to revive their disputes, and the criticisms addressed to the government were bitter: Why had it maintained false hopes so long? The conviction thus began to take hold that Germany should seek an occasion to make peace. Yet even the pessimists did not believe that this move toward peace was urgent; they thought they had several weeks' time ahead of them.

Then, at the end of September, Ludendorff suddenly decided to present President Wilson with not just a peace offer but a petition for an armistice; he imposed his decision, not without trouble, on the new Chancellor, Prince Max of Baden. This was an admission of defeat; it staggered public opinion. Reports from provincial government officials were almost unanimous in signaling profound lassitude; those from industrial regions noted signs of agitation. It was at this point that the far-left Spartacus League sent out a call to revolution through secret channels. After President Wilson issued his notes inviting the German people to free itself from "its masters," the government soon realized that it was losing control over public opinion. The mutiny of the ships' crews at Kiel and the pacifist demonstrations at Munich in early November were followed by the revolutionary actions which took place on November 8 and 9, at the same time that Marshal Foch was presenting the German delegation at Rethondes with the conditions for armistice set by the Allied and Associated governments.

These currents of German public opinion thus had an incontestable breadth and influence. It is certain that when the government and the military leaders learned the conditions for an armistice, they were no longer in a position to discuss them; the revolutionary threat at that point eclipsed all other preoccupations. But this decline of morale, these violent reactions of the public mind were not the cause of the military collapse; they were the result. The public resolve showed itself to be weakening when it became evident that the Army was pursuing a hopeless struggle.

Do these very hasty notes allow us to sketch out a general interpretation? They do at least suggest two observations.

1. Aside from Italy, public opinion trends did not have a *determining* influence on government decisions at the time the belligerent states entered into conflict. The government of each state indubitably took the set of public thinking into account; if a broad current of opinion had showed itself hostile to the war, the government obviously would have weighed the risks of the undertaking and would in all likelihood have given it up. But wherever the

public expressed an opinion, it was positive. Yet it did not provide a stimulus. It was not tides of feeling, waves of passion that directed governmental actions; it was political interests.

2. These public opinion trends had far greater influence when war weariness and the burden of long suffering led the peoples to contemplate peace. In two instances—Russia in February–March, 1917, and Austria-Hungary in October, 1918—these trends opened the way to revolutionary disturbances, in which the desire to put an end to the war played an active role. Yet these two cases were quite different. In Russia, all segments of opinion wanted or were willing to see a transformation of the social condition; in Austria-Hungary, the appeal to the right of peoples to self-determination provided the impetus. Everywhere else, the crises of low morale were not sharp or enduring enough to seriously threaten public order or impel the government to reorient its policy. They were most often directly related to the disappointments caused by war operations, and they abated as soon as the news from the front lines of combat improved. Actually, the signs of weariness and discouragement did not hinder the war effort in cases where the administrative and societal structures remained steady. But here again, Italy was the exception; the crisis in morale, which was serious in the summer of 1917 at a time when the situation on the Italian front was satisfactory, lightened in November at the moment when the defeat at Caporetto confronted the nation with grave peril.

These provisory conclusions must indeed be re-examined and modified when the study of public opinion trends has given rise to further research. But they may at present suggest reflections which studies of social psychology will perhaps be called on to evaluate.

Bishop John W. C. Wand

BISHOP WAND was born in Grantham, England, in 1885; he was educated at the King's School in that town and later at St. Edmund Hall, Oxford, and at Bishop Jacob Hostel, Newcastle-on-Tyne.

He was ordained in 1908, and after serving two curacies, he became a minor canon of Salisbury Cathedral and tutor at the Salisbury Theological College. During World War I he served as chaplain in the Dardanelles, France, and Germany. On his return he became vicar of St. Mark's, Salisbury, but in 1925 was appointed fellow, dean, and tutor of Oriel College, Oxford, later being made lecturer on church history at the same university.

In 1934 he was consecrated as Archbishop of Brisbane, Australia, but after nine years he was recalled to England to become Bishop of Bath and Wells. Less than two years later, in 1945, he was translated to the see of London. There he had the heavy task of restoring the leading diocese of the Anglican Communion after the ravages of war. He retired from the bishopric of London at the age of seventy and was made canon and treasurer of St. Paul's in 1955, a double post which he still holds.

He has been a member of Her Majesty's Privy Council since 1945 and was made K.C.V.O. (Knight Commander of the Royal Victorian Order) ten years later. He is an honorary D.D. of Oxford, Toronto, and West Ontario, an S.T.P. (Professor of Divinity) of Columbia, and a D.Litt. of Ripon; Honorary Fellow of Oriel College and St. Edmund Hall, Oxford, and also of King's College, London. He is the author of forty volumes, including histories of the early church and the modern church, the Westminster Commentary on I and II Peter and Jude, Anglicanism in History and Today, *and* Changeful Page *(autobiography). For ten years he was an editor of the* Church Quarterly Review.

THE EFFECT OF WORLD WAR I
ON RELIGION

THE PERIOD just before the war saw the heyday of religious observance in the West. In Rome there was a pronounced move to greater paternalism on the part of Pius X, which led to a closer centralization through the codification of canon law in 1917 and the reorganization of the Curia. In England the beginning of the twentieth century had marked the peak of the Anglo-Catholic movement. There was also a great emphasis on churchgoing. It is true that England had never caught up in the provision of churches with the needs provoked by the Industrial Revolution and that members of the new proletariat had seldom acquired religious habits. But among the middle classes, to absent oneself from church was to become *déclassé*. At weekend house parties in the country, Sunday morning church formed a regular part of the hospitality.

In the United States the upward movement became really marked a little later. But when it came, it was prolonged and raised the figures of church affiliation to the highest point (more than 60,000,000) they had reached since the union.

In Greece, Christian activity had received especially vital expression in the Zoë movement (1907). This had done much to bring the Orthodox Church up-to-date. Its struggle to free Christian social influence from the dead hand of unthinking traditionalism had spread to Orthodox churches far beyond the limits of Greece. But the only Orthodox Church doing missionary work outside its own borders at the beginning of the twentieth century was that of Russia.

"From the date of Waterloo to the beginning of the First World War Christianity had enjoyed the greatest century of its expansion and the largest influence it had ever exerted." If we are to estimate the extent of the decline that came about as the result of the war and investigate its cause or causes, we may be well advised to begin with external features and try to penetrate later to the underlying causes. For this purpose we might start with habits, pass on to morals, and end with theology.

I

Perhaps the greatest blow to the Christian religion, regarded as a habit, was the abdication of the Czar of Russia in 1917 and the subsequent establishment of an atheistic regime. That the greatest Christian country in the world, which had been Christian for nearly 1,000 years, should repudiate its connection with religion was bound to loosen the hold of the Christian faith everywhere.

On the whole the Treaty of Versailles (1919) improved the position of Protestants as against Roman Catholics. Communism met Protestantism first in East Germany, where four-fifths of the population were Protestant. A by-product of these relations was seen in Czechoslovakia, where 1,000,000 people broke away from the Roman obedience and formed the Czech National Church (1920). In Russia the declension was from Orthodoxy; in Mexico, as in Czechoslovakia, it was from Roman Catholicism. The new constitution, accepted in 1917, nationalized church property and restricted the power of the clergy. The church's constitutional demotion in these instances weakened the influence of religion in millions of lives.

There was one comparatively small instance where the opposite has been noticed. The Anglican Church in the principality of Wales was disestablished in 1920. The result has been to increase, rather than diminish, the efficiency and zeal of its members. It is now estimated that the standing of the church in that country and its influence in the community are greater than at any time since the Reformation.

In England the war brought a definitive end to what is known as the Victorian period. The few intervening years of Edwardian license had affected only the more dubious strata of the aristocracy and their hangers-on, but the loosening of the bonds between church and society that had been then begun was carried a great deal further as a result of the war.

The war effort itself assisted the decline. The dislocation of families and the long hours spent in Sunday labor tended to break up the churchgoing habit among the elderly, and the discomfort of unheated churches did not encourage it among the young. On the Continent women were employed as members of the fighting services and, being divorced from their homes, were divorced also from the habits of family religion. The men, resting at some base town before going up to the front, saw for the first time in their lives queues forming outside the brothels as for a cinema. Violence, which the vast majority of all classes repudiated with horror during times of peace, had become a virtue under conditions of war. The theft on behalf of one's mess of anything that might add to the amenities of life under the appalling conditions of trench warfare was regarded as commendable and even necessary.

All this administered a decided shock to conventional religion. When the war was over, many failed to pick up again the old religious habits. Families were no longer so closely united. Family prayers were resumed by only a few old-fashioned people. The churches as a whole, with the notable exception of the Roman Catholics, never recovered their old swelling congregations. Nor were parents able to recover family discipline, which had perforce been intermitted during the separation caused by the war.

The intention to develop peaceful relations on international lines was seen in the creation of the League of Nations. This attempt at a new world order was not originally inspired by President Wilson of the United States, but it was his idealism which insisted, rightly or wrongly, on its incorporation into the peace treaty of 1919. He was, in the long run, unable to carry his countrymen with him, and the ultimate failure of the League was one of the severest blows that Christian utopianism has received in modern times.

In the ecclesiastical sphere a parallel effort to effect some kind of world organization was seen in the tentative approaches to the reunion of the churches. Of these the most notable example was the statement issued by the bishops of the Anglican Communion meeting at Lambeth Palace (the Archbishop of Canterbury's residence) in 1920. They announced that if other terms of union could be suitably arranged, they would be prepared to offer themselves for an interchange of rites of ordination with other Christian bodies. The effect of this would be to create a ministry mutually acceptable to all the denominations concerned. It would thus be the most valuable step toward complete unity. For the time being the appeal was not seriously regarded. But it sowed a seed which was to germinate later.

Certainly, as far as statistics and other external tests go, this was a period of very serious decline in religious habits. A significant clue to the narrowing limits of practicing churchmanship may be seen in the difficulty experienced in compiling the parochial rolls which had become the basis of the English electoral system leading to the new Church Assembly. Out of an estimated total of 30,000,000 nominal members of the Church of England not much more than a tenth could be induced to register themselves as qualified electors (3,601,782 in 1925).

In general, we may say that the most important religious effect of the war was to produce throughout mankind a new habit of mind. Whereas hitherto the majority had looked at least nominally beyond space and time for its incentives and rewards, now the outlook became frankly this-worldly. Man himself, rather than his gods, became the measure of all things. The example of Russia and later also of China seemed to show that this theory actually worked.

Inevitably such a mental attitude first expressed itself in an upsurge of nationalism. The individual was taught to merge his personality in that of the local community, and the community was determined to exercise its right to run itself. The self-determination that had been accepted as a governing principle in the Treaty of Versailles soon showed itself a dangerous expedient, but it was too late for the great powers to recall it. Soon it was working like leaven among the tribes and races of Africa and Asia. As the great powers began to lose their grip on their colonies, the peoples hastened to take advantage of the situation prematurely to free themselves from outside tutelage. Having no adequately trained civil service to run their affairs, they began to fall upon each other in an effort to gain by a ruthless display of power the wealth that they could not gain by good management.

In such a situation religion for the time being was the loser. In many countries where education and health were departments of especial missionary concern, schools and hospitals fell under government suspicion, which was not lightened by the fact that most of the trained personnel were Christian. In many instances the resultant tension between government and missions has not yet been resolved.

The effect of this kind of reasoning was seen most clearly in Japan, which even now has "a smaller proportion of Christians than any major country" and has deliberately rejected Christianity as a possible national religion. In other parts of what used to be known as the mission field, however, in spite of the rude shocks received, Christians have increased their numbers at a surprising rate. In Africa south of the Sahara between 1912 and 1956 the numbers rose from something over 1,000,000 to 21,000,000. In India, in spite of the rapid increase in population, the proportion has more than trebled, while, what is perhaps more significant, 3 out of every 4 trained nurses are Christians. In China the number of Christians had trebled before the revolution came and the missionaries were excluded.

Another feature in the postwar religious situation, of which due account must be taken, is the resurgence of other religions. No doubt this movement is partly to be accounted for by the rise of a perfervid nationalism. It was natural that emphasis should be placed on what were believed to be national characteristics in language, art, and religion. The movement grew as fresh efforts were made to reduce the large rate of illiteracy in the respective countries. In many instances there is a good deal of imitation of Christianity. Nevertheless, it does obviously mean that the lasting effect of the war was not universally detrimental to religion.

II

Habits are in large measure a reflection of moral attitudes. It is natural, therefore, in an effort to reach to the deeper consequences of the war to ask how far changing habits revealed a change in the moral standards of the nations engaged in it. Here we are helped by the fact that rapidly growing ease of communication began to make the whole world kin in a measure that had never been true before. Radio and telegraph, to say nothing of the gramophone and the cinema, made great cities aware of one another's life and thought the world over, and news penetrated with unprecedented rapidity even to the jungle and the desert. The latest women's fashions began to appear in the streets of Hong Kong and Achimota while they were still in the shop windows of Oxford Street and Fifth Avenue.

Sport, like fashion, began to give nations a common interest. The war had spread the knowledge of English team games to almost every part of the globe. Association football achieved a popularity never before reached by any national pastime. Compared with this extraordinary development, even the Olympic Games must probably take second place. Their modern history begins from 1896. They were canceled in 1916, when the four-year meeting should have been held in Berlin, but they were resumed when the war was over, the sixth Olympiad being convened at Antwerp in 1920.

If the optimists, who saw in common sport a panacea for the ills of the world, were disappointed, the pessimists, who thought that every kind of encounter between nations was bound to lead to internecine strife, were compelled to take shelter in a little mild cynicism. But inasmuch as the more important games everywhere are governed by a set of rules internationally enforced, sport may serve its part in the slow education of the nations in the acceptance of a commonly agreed supranational law. Its moral potentiality is, therefore, very great.

Something must be said about morals in the narrow and limited sense of the term. The traditional view of sexuality, at least in Anglo-Saxon countries, may have sufficed to keep the majority within the bounds of conventional respectability before the war. But when the soldier has lived several years in an atmosphere quite alien to the puritan spirit, during which every time he went on leave, he was offered prophylactics under the apparent assumption that that spirit no longer had any meaning for him, it is likely that after he has returned to civilian life, whatever may be his personal conduct, his mental attitude to moral questions will have suffered some considerable change.

It may be said that every change in moral attitude comes about through the questioning of hitherto accepted authority. The present instance was no exception to the rule. A common view is that the Victorian era was the last age in which tradition was accepted without question. There are, of course, some world-famous examples to the contrary, but by and large the judgment may be allowed to pass. In the intellectual sphere it had been only the favored few in the universities who were trained to accept nothing on authority and to think things out for themselves. The refusal to accept tradition at its own valuation now began to spread throughout the nations and all classes within the nations. This was to be the main element in the process which was a generation later to be described by Bonhoeffer as "the world's coming of age." It meant that man had begun to take a hand in his own evolution: He was at last an adult, grown up.

We have already remembered the violence with which the revolution broke down all existing authorities in Russia. In the United States change was not so marked, perhaps because it was not so necessary. The American way of life spelled the utmost possible freedom for the individual, and where poverty and want still existed, they were generally considered to be due to the individual's own fault. Further, on its religious side the American way of life was generally identified with the Protestant form of Christianity, and it has been pointed out that Protestantism, although there is no established religion in America, is generally regarded as the "national" religion. Before the outbreak of war the prevailing tendency in American religion had been clearly marked as activist. Great stress was laid on social service: Unkindly critics were wont to say that for the American the Kingdom of Heaven was deemed to have arrived as soon as the plumbing was right. The movement had already produced one important book in Rauschenbusch's *Christianity and the Social Crisis* (1907).

The social gospel was one of the chief casualties of the war so far as the United States was concerned. Its facile optimism seemed too superficial to stand up to the devastating calamities of the period. Presently the influence of Karl Barth and "Biblical theology" began to seep in from the Continent and ran parallel with the fundamentalism that took its place among the unlearned. The progress of both was helped by the combined psychological and economic depression of the middle of the century. As a result, religion reported a steady rate of progress during the first half century or so; as against 36 percent of the population in 1900 no less than 63 percent admitted affiliation to some religious body in 1959.

In other countries the revolution was more thorough, even where it came short of the horrors of violence. By a process of gradually increasing taxation the old aristocratic landlords of England were either forced out of their properties or compelled to turn themselves into limited liability companies. Mounting death duties broke up the great estates. Increasing government grants changed the character of the universities. Instead of being the finishing schools of a hereditary governing class, they became the training ground for the professional and managerial classes. With characteristic differences the same movement went on in various parts of the Commonwealth. But it was in the British Isles that the changeover was most complete. That so great a revolution could have taken place without bloodshed is perhaps the clearest evidence of Christian forbearance that civilization has achieved in the course of the century.

Nor is it to be thought that in other respects the effect of the war on the moral fiber of the people was wholly bad. So much heroism and self-sacrifice could not go wholly for nothing. The sense of comradeship engendered among troops on campaign was not completely lost. Not only did veterans' associations continue to encourage the spirit of mutual aid long after the war was over, but more definitely religious organizations such as Toc H (soldiers' club founded by P. B. Clayton and Neville Talbot, 1915) tried to preserve the memory of spiritual dedication that had been first aroused or quickened on active service.

In addition to all this, we must not fail to remember the effect of the war in making even the most careless face the issues of life and death. The fundamental questions of religion and philosophy had to be tackled afresh by each thinking individual according to his ability.

To this issue we must now turn and ask what was the effect of the war on theological thinking.

III

Of course, the first and most relevant question was one of theodicy: Why did God allow the war? The question grew more insistent as the horrors of trench warfare became more fully known and as the appalling lists of the dead piled up to millions. If God was good and omnipotent, as Christianity had always claimed, why did He allow such misery to affect His children?

For the professional theologian this situation was only a particular instance, though a specially poignant one, of the problem of evil, which is always his bugbear. Simple people who made much of the epithet "Almighty" were apt to think of God as a kind of policeman on point duty, who had only to hold up his hand to stop the traffic. Many did not get beyond this idea and allowed the dilemma to ruin their faith. Others by slow and painful steps learned to see God's governance of his universe exercised within the consciences of men, showing them the bitter consequences of man's inhumanity to man and teaching them to avoid war as a child learns to avoid the fire. It was in this atmosphere that some of the future theological leaders such as Barth, Brunner, and Tillich were nurtured.

In spite of such difficulties, many national leaders felt that so devastating an experience as worldwide war in its most horrible form ought to lead to a revival of religion. In England an effort to reassure the doubters and to strengthen the faithful was made in the National Mission of Repentance and Hope (1916). Either the people were too preoccupied or too many of the spiritual guides were away at the war. In any case, whatever the reason, the effort, made at the cost of considerable time and energy, was not voted a success.

Perhaps the most noteworthy result of the stresses of the period was a marked increase in spiritualism. Some inquirers were led to take an interest in it on what might be termed a scientific basis, hoping to establish beyond reasonable doubt the presence or absence of living beings on the other side of the grave. As usual, however, these inquiries proved indecisive. It was not by such mechanical means that the uncertainties stirred up by the war would be put to rest. A way must be found to the deeper springs of religion and reason. But it was just here that conditions were most difficult.

The latter part of the nineteenth century had been taken up largely with discussions of the theory of evolution. Although theologians had called in aid the Logos doctrine from the early apologists and had shown that evolution was more at home with that doctrine than was any theory of instantaneous creation, the faith of many never recovered from the shock of initial discovery.

When the evolutionary method was applied to the Bible itself and the Scriptures were read as a library of books with a complicated history of composition, the blow to the old unitary conception of inspiration and revelation was equally severe. Although the theologians themselves were responsible for this development and although they were able to adjust it to a more adequate and likely theory of revelation, the general effect was to make recovery from the intellectual malaise of the war still more difficult.

To this one must add the corrosive effect of the new theory of relativity (Einstein, c. 1919), which, beginning with physics, presently invaded philosophy and many other regions of thought. Even when it did not achieve precise formulation, the theory produced an attitude of mind in which there was no recognition of an absolute or an ultimate. However illogical the transition, there was produced in the minds of many a feeling that not only standards of taste but also rules of morals were merely relative and could, therefore, be adjusted to suit the ideas of each individual and occasion. For many, there remained no sound basis on which to rest, no solid rock on which to build.

A despairing effort to weld the new attitude of mind with Christian apologetics was made by the modernists. Of these there were two schools: the later in England and the earlier in France, the one Protestant and the other Catholic. The former was prepared to accept the "assured results" of current natural science and Biblical criticism as fundamental truth with which Christian dogma, whether to be found in the Bible or not, must be made to square. By the same token the doctrine of the Incarnation must be approached from the side of the humanity rather than the divinity of Christ. The certain fact was the high quality of His humanity: How and to what extent He was divine was a matter of debate.

French modernism seems to have begun in much the same way. Certainly Loisy struggled long and learnedly to find a reliable substratum in the Gospels upon which to erect an authentic image of Jesus which would square with traditional portraits, only in the end to abandon the unequal struggle. The philosophers of the movement, such as Blondin, took the more characteristic line of dissociating the practical importance of Christian dogmas from their allegedly doubtful historical origins. Relying on Ritschl's philosophy of values, they taught that one could dispense with the whole historical foundation of dogma so long as one could see that the doctrines themselves were useful for the salvation of souls.

As far as Roman Catholics were concerned, the modernist movement had been driven underground by the papal decree *Lamentabili* (1907), only to reappear in a modified form at the middle of the century in the *Aggiornamento* of Pope John XXIII. In England the storm burst after the notorious Girton Conference of Modern Churchmen in 1921. This meeting may be regarded as the peak of the movement. Characteristically no official action was taken to subdue it; it gradually died down, but not without imbuing nearly all other church movements with some, more or less liberal, elements of its spirit.

Among the members of most churches there remained a group of conservatives, for the most part of an evangelical persuasion, who clung to the literal interpretation of the Bible. Those who went so far as to retain the view of precise verbal inspiration were known as fundamentalists, from their emphasis on the "fundamental" truths of Christianity at the Niagara Bible Conference of 1895.

Others, who were not prepared to take quite so rigid a line, preferred to be described as conservative evangelicals. As such they have shown remarkable devotion and have produced a large and growing proportion of candidates for the ministry.

On the whole it can be said that "science" and theology reached an agreement to differ in their respective methods. It was admitted that whereas exact measurement was of the very essence of science, it was not applicable to religion any more than to morals or art. A generation was to elapse before it was widely realized that such a view necessarily involved that there could be no scientific proof of religious truth—or disproof either. No doubt there were those who had already reached this conclusion. "Nothing worth proving can be proven, nor yet disproven," was the way in which Tennyson had settled the question. But this was regarded as a piece of poetic hyperbole, and the majority still stuck to the view that somewhere and somehow there must be a logical and indisputable proof of the correctness of Christian teaching.

The attitude of mind that demands proof was further developed under the influence of the amazing advance in technology. The tendency of war is always to speed up research and inventiveness in those areas where advance is likely to be most favorable to its successful prosecution. The impetus will carry on into the peace; and in this case did carry on until a Second War came to rejuvenate it and multiply its energy. Radar and sound ranging led to the splitting of the atom and the lunar sputnik. As at the Renaissance five centuries before, man seemed again to become master of his environment. While everything else was in disarray, he could congratulate himself on the concrete successes achieved in his understanding and control of the material universe in which he lived. This temperament was not conducive to religion—"Glory to Man in the highest! for Man is the master of things."

What made matters worse was the spread of doubt into a fresh intellectual sphere. Christianity had always been regarded as a historical religion, and it had often boasted against its rivals that whereas they belonged to myth and legend, it had its roots firmly planted in historic fact. But now the philosophers of history—not the historians themselves (they have always rested confident in the value of their own technique), but the historical philosophers—began to question whether anyone can ever arrive at historical fact. Ranke's dictum that the historian's first duty is to establish the facts as they really happened gave way before the recognition that in every piece of reporting there must always be an element of interpretation.

Croce in Italy had put this big question mark beside history at the very beginning of the war, but England, because of its preoccupations, was slow in receiving the message. It was not until 1941 that *La Storia* was translated into *History as the Story of Liberty* and made a somewhat astonished public aware of the axiom that "all history is contemporary philosophy." This was soon followed by R. G. Collingwood's *Idea of History* (1946), which naturalized the point of view in Oxford lecture rooms.

As far as theology was concerned, the soil was already prepared for the new seed by the steady progress of Biblical criticism. Documentary analysis had given way to "form criticism" (Dibelius' *Fresh Approach to the New Testament*, 1936), and the endeavor to reach the *ipsissima verba* of oral tradition had made even the general reader realize how difficult it was to be sure that one had got back to the original word or act. History thus appeared to provide no safer "proof" for a Biblical religion than did science.

In this impasse the religious man is thrown back on his faith. This faith is not, as many suggest, an unreasoning credulity, but a reasoned acceptance of the tradition of his church combined with a consciousness of his personal contact with the unseen. Of such a faith the Bible remains a corroboration and an explanation. This is the point, succinctly expressed, to which he has been brought as the result of influences stemming from the First World War.

Sir Richard Rees

"A few years ago I published my autobiography. It contained so few facts about myself and such a lot of preaching that I subtitled it An Essay in Didactic Reminiscence. In order to preach, it is, of course, not necessary to have a doctrine, but it does help, and in 1924, when I joined the Labour Party in the fatuous belief that I was escaping from my upper-class background and education, I had thought I agreed with people like Bernard Shaw and H. G. Wells. After discovering my mistake, I met an author whose didacticism was much more congenial, J. Middleton Murry, and through him, D. H. Lawrence. (Not that I met Lawrence personally, though after his death I knew and greatly admired Frieda.) From 1930 to 1936 I edited Murry's magazine, The Adelphi. Murry's thought was anything but static, and he was prone to intellectual lapses, but he possessed critical genius (compare, for example, Bertrand Russell's puerile gibes against Rousseau in his History of Western Philosophy with Murry's luminous essay on him in Selected Criticism, 1916–1957). The Adelphi's course was erratic, but it fostered, and in many cases virtually discovered, a number of remarkable talents, among them George Orwell and Dylan Thomas. The contemporary intellectuals who chiefly influenced me, however, were T. S. Eliot and Lawrence, with Murry—in some ways the most intelligent of the three—as a sort of mediator between them.

"Between 1937 and 1945, in the Spanish Civil War and the Second World War, I was successively an ambulance driver, a gunnery rating, an obscure secretary in the same department of the Admiralty as Ian (James Bond) Fleming, and interpreter afloat, sometimes in more than one sense, in a French cruiser. After all this I was still prepared to be didactic, though still a little short on doctrine.

"Not long after the war I began to read Simone Weil's books, in which I found a synthesis of much of the best that I had learned from the others. And I continued to be as didactic as ever."

NEMESIS

———◆———

THE FIRST WORLD WAR was the background of my schooldays. On leaving school, a boy went straight into the Army, and his chance of being alive and unwounded by the end of the war was not much better than 50-50. Of the boys who left during my time at school, which was exactly from 1914 to 1918, the number killed was 157.[1]

But the mind of youth is conformist, as we see today in the conformism of "protest," and to us this 50 percent tax on youth in the form of death and wounds seemed in the nature of things. I think indeed that when the tax was lifted in 1918, there were even some who felt vaguely cheated. A very junior boy in the school at that time called Blair, later to be known as George Orwell, was almost certainly one of these. And yet I doubt if there were many who felt any particular animus against the Germans. They were the baddies, of course, and we were the goodies, and we had been brought up to think of them as the opposing team. But there was hardly more to it than that.

> Cuff the Kaiser!
> The Kaiser cuff'd the cat.
> King George never never did a thing like that.

From our point of view, this version of "Rule Britannia" said just about all that needed saying.

Maybe I underestimate my schoolfellows' interest in public affairs, but what brought the situation home to me personally, perhaps more than anything else was the number of soldiers on leave to be seen in London restaurants and theaters and the fact that so many music hall songs and sketches were about the war. However, since it is the main theme of this essay that the war was, above all, symptomatic of a cultural decadence which had been in process for at least two centuries and which has accelerated since 1918, it would be dishonest to omit one other recollection which may appear to contradict this thesis. In the early days of the war I

---

[1] Total figures for the school (Eton), including those who had already left before 1914: out of 5,688 who served in the war, 1,159 killed and 1,469 wounded.

saw a regiment of soldiers in training pass along the road outside our house. They were workingmen from the north of England, and I suppose I had never before seen such a large number of working-men all at once. I was astonished at how small most of them were.

I do not know the average height of contemporary Englishmen, but there is no class of the population today which strikes me as conspicuously shorter than any other class, and even if I should be wrong about this, there is still no doubt that standards of health and well-being have enormously improved during the last fifty years, while many inequalities have been greatly reduced. But whether the soldiers I saw in 1914, so stunted in growth and many of them from slum homes, were less happy than those of 1939, or than the Englishmen of today, is perhaps a question. They were certainly not less brave and humorous and friendly.

In any case, however, the theme of this essay is unaffected, because a civilization whose culture is in decay is not necessarily for that reason technologically incompetent. In spite of decadence, it may continue for a long time to improve its standards of health and physical comfort, and both the world wars of this century seem to have actually stimulated progress of this kind in all the partici-pating nations. But they also intensified the process of cultural decay, and by the end of the First World War many of the civilized, as well as many of the barbarous, aspects of the world I knew as a child had been swept away forever.

In reality, of course, although as a child one could not know it, for at least fifty years the world had been changing more rapidly and more spectacularly than ever before. But that only takes us back to the 1860's, and the process had begun much earlier still. It was the French Revolution and then the first great expansion, in Britain, of modern industry that politically and economically dis-rupted the old world. (I shall argue in this essay that the psycho-logical disruption began long before.) But it was not until after 1860 that the snowball began to turn into an avalanche.

In the 1860's, after the Civil War, it began to be possible for North America to develop its full industrial potential. At the same time the victories of Prussia began to upset the balance of power in Europe. The new plague of jingo nationalism, or idolatry of the nation-state, was growing more virulent throughout the West, and the population explosion was spreading from Britain to the other industrial countries. But Asia, except for those parts of it that were being modernized under European control, was static or decadent. It had become clear during the eighteenth century that the Turk-ish, Persian, and Mogul empires could no longer compete against the rising European power, which had already achieved world maritime supremacy two centuries earlier. And in Far Eastern Asia the West had begun to penetrate Japan in the 1850's, at about the same time as the shameful Opium War against China, which had still been a great power in the eighteenth century.

Between the 1860's and the outbreak of the Great War in 1914 there seems to have been little awareness in the West of the revolution in world economics and politics that was implicit in the gigantic strides being made by applied science and machine industry. There were very few who perceived that the world empires of the European powers and the mentality that went with them were doomed or that the privileged status in the world of both Europeans and Americans was soon to be challenged. I believe few people were any more aware of all this than I myself was aware, as a schoolboy, that the world of my childhood had gone forever.

Today, fifty years after 1918, the world is so different that the mind can hardly grasp the extent of the change. North America, Europe, Japan, and several other parts of the world are urbanized and industrialized to a degree that would have been unimaginable in the 1860's. Russia hopes to catch up with them, and China has thrown off its lethargy and become at least potentially a great world power again. Imperialism in the old sense of the word is dead, having been replaced by new forms of nationalistic, racial, economic, and ideological—or quasi-religious—power politics. And there is a population explosion almost everywhere.

Looking back, from our viewpoint in the 1960's, one can see that it was the First World War which was the great catalytic agent. And one of the most striking effects of the transformation is that the world has become much smaller. Journeys that still took months in 1914 take a few days in 1968. Long-distance verbal and visual communications are instantaneous, and the great powers are in continual nerve-racking and unneighborly proximity to one another.

In the days of the later Han dynasty and of the Antonine dynasty, the Chinese and the Roman empires were not absolutely isolated from each other. Both were affected by wars and migrations in the countries that separated them, and their tenuous trade relations fluctuated accordingly. A Chinese victory over the Mongols could lead to displacements of population which had repercussions on the Roman frontiers. A Hun or Turkic invasion of Bactria or Persia could cut the silk route. But for nearly all practical purposes the two empires could ignore each other's existence. And through all the succeeding centuries, until our own, war has been a more or less local and limited phenomenon, and every war has been waged for more or less definite and intelligible aims. Not even the wars of Napoleon were total war in the sense of the great wars of the twentieth century.

But in addition to being worldwide in its political repercussions, the war of 1914–18 was the first large-scale demonstration of what modern science and industry can contribute to man's powers of destruction.

For all these reasons, then, and many others, no one is likely to deny that the war of 1914–18 was a major event in world history. It was also one of the most frightful events in all history. Nevertheless, those who feel on the whole optimistic about the new world that has developed since 1918 can perhaps contrive to see that war as one of the sanguinary crises through which mankind progresses toward new and better ways of life. But those who feel otherwise will see it rather as a sinister warning that our civilization has gone astray. And that is how the most perceptive thinkers saw it at the time: Paul Valéry in France, for example, and D. H. Lawrence, Middleton Murry, and T. S. Eliot in England. When Eliot and Valéry agreed after the war that it was "the end of Europe," they meant, of course, the end of European culture. A glimpse into the future, revealing a Second World War followed by the booming, swinging Europe of the 1960's would only have confirmed their judgment. By comparison, those who scolded and tried to belittle the war as an irrelevant interruption and intrusion into a tidy Fabian evolutionary progress toward world Socialism—I am thinking of Bernard Shaw and H. G. Wells, for example—appear shrill and shallow today.

Thirty years after the First World War Eliot published a small book with the title *Notes Towards the Definition of Culture.* In one short passage of this book[2] he suggests a theory of religion and culture which is extremely relevant to the study of cultural declines. It is put forward with characteristically cautious reservations, and it looks very modest alongside the grandiose historicist theses of a Spengler or a Toynbee, and yet it touches on a profound and luminous truth. It could be developed into a theory of culture which sets the two great wars of the century in their true perspective.

Culture, says Eliot, never exists except in connection with a religion, although the culture may outlive the associated religion

2 London, 1948, pp. 28–31.

and even achieve some of its most brilliant successes long after the religion has been more or less abandoned. But it cannot do this indefinitely, because the association is even closer than interdependence. Rather, it is as if they were two aspects of the same thing: the culture being, as it were, the incarnation of the religion. It is the religion as it is actually lived by the people who profess it or who formerly used to do so.

But what does Eliot mean by "religion"? Obviously he does not confine it to the rather prim Anglo-Catholicism which he himself professed, and one can probably assume that he intended to define the essential common factor in everything that can be called a religion when he wrote the following passage in his essay "Second Thoughts About Humanism": "Man is man because he can recognise supernatural realities, not because he can invent them. Either everything in man can be traced as a development from below, or something must come from above. There is no avoiding that dilemma: you must be either a naturalist or a supernaturalist."[3] When certain realities are recognized as supernatural, there is religion; when everything is assumed to be traceable as a development from below, there is not. But since the word "supernatural" has come to be associated with ghosts, miracles, and superstitions, it is perhaps better to use instead the word "transcendent," in its simple meaning of "existing apart from the material universe." In the terms of Eliot's theory we can then say that every culture ultimately derives from a belief in some reality apart from that of the material universe and that when a culture becomes completely saturated with antitranscendental thought, such as Marxism, positivism, and the contemporary form of humanism, it is a proof that the culture is in decline, even though it may still be achieving brilliant successes.

The belief that the good is a human invention or that the universal human hunger for goodness and justice is a product of the material universe implies the belief that the less good can produce something better than itself. An even more remarkable thinker and moralist than Eliot, the French Jewish philosopher Simone Weil, reduced this belief *ad absurdum* by describing it as the theory that "matter is a machine for manufacturing good."

It would no doubt be impossible to fix an exact date in European history when the belief that matter is a machine for manufacturing good, that evolution is a moral process, and that a corrupt tree can bring forth good fruit began to prevail over the Christian (and

---

[3] *Selected Essays* (London, 1932), p. 447.

Judaic, Platonic, Islamic, Indian, Egyptian, and Persian) belief in a supernatural or transcendental source of morality. But if such a date could be fixed, it would mark the point where, in European culture, decline began to prevail over growth. But both tendencies were no doubt always present, or at least ever since the religious faith began to weaken, and the declining period has been so brilliant that the decline was for a long time unperceived.

Before attempting to show the relevance of these thoughts to the war of 1914–18, it may be desirable to emphasize more clearly the sense in which the word "religion" is being used, and this, unfortunately, involves a brief recapitulation of arguments which have been bandied to and fro ever since the human mind began to meddle with the problem of good and evil. First, then, religion as here understood is entirely distinct and independent from a number of ideas and phenomena which are often associated with it: emotional satisfactions, consolations for the ego, personal rewards in the sky, providential interferences with the course of nature, and so on. Second, religion is perfectly compatible with materialism, so long as the materialism is pure and not adulterated with a surreptitiously introduced morality, as both Marxism and naturalistic humanism are.

It is only the supernaturalist in Eliot's sense of the word who has no difficulty in admitting that the whole of the universe as known to or knowable by a human mind is purely material. And this, of course, includes the human mind itself, since all its thoughts and imaginings are to be regarded as psychic matter, which contains no mysterious material factor capable of generating *ex nihilo* an evolving and progressive morality. (In this résumé I am relying largely on terms borrowed from Simone Weil, but many others are available. Bergson, for example, whose *élan vital* is a concept almost antipodal to those of Eliot and Weil, nevertheless establishes clearly that what he calls an "open morality" is incompatible with any kind of naturalism or positivism. "We can never proceed," he says, "by a method of expansion from the closed society to the open, from the city to humanity. They are not of the same essence."[4])

The existence of a universal human aspiration toward an unknown good is totally anomalous in the material universe, but the existence of evil is less so, because what we call evil is simply matter, insofar as matter (including psychic matter) can obstruct, oppose, or confuse the aspiration toward the good. Apart from that, and in itself, matter is not evil, but amoral. But the good itself remains

---

[4] *Les Deux Sources de la morale et de la réligion* (Paris, 1933) , p. 288.

always inconceivable. We can define it only by negatives, by the degree to which everything in which we think to find it always in the end falls short of our desire.

To be a supernaturalist or transcendentalist in the sense here used means recognizing this state of affairs, recognizing that the good is unattainable in the universe as we know it, except in degraded and ultimately unsatisfying forms. The essential act of religious faith is the recognition that goodness and justice and our aspiration toward them belong to a different order of reality from the only one we know; and that, nevertheless, every human being in the world is connected, in a totally mysterious way, with that reality; and, further, that it is only through this connection that any approximation to goodness and justice is ever effectively realized within the material universe.

The implications of this belief are all-embracing, and they can and should be indefinitely explored; but all that is necessary here is to establish that this belief is the essential religious belief and is, therefore, according to Eliot's theory, a prerequisite for the development of culture.

There is no need to labor the point that Christianity, the religion which inspired the development of Western culture out of the remains of Roman civilization as inherited by the Germanic invaders of Europe, was a transcendentalism according to our definition of the term, and the great cultural achievements of the twelfth, thirteenth, and fourteenth centuries—the cathedrals, Franciscanism, the *Divine Comedy*—are of quintessentially Christian inspiration. But just as every religion is indebted to earlier religion, so every culture includes elements from earlier culture, and medieval civilization, of course, included elements from Judaism, Islam, Hellenism, and, mainly through the latter, from Egyptian, pre-Islamic Persian and Babylonian culture as well. At the Renaissance it received a fresh infusion of Hellenism. But already in the fifteenth and sixteenth centuries the religious faith was beginning to weaken, and from the seventeeth century onward the cultural sphere of the profane, including science, and the sphere of religion became separated in two distinct compartments in the human mind.

This was an entirely new historical phenomenon. European science was derived from Greek science, and the Greeks would have been astonished at the post-Renaissance dichotomy between scientific and religious thought. The subsequent history of Europe, with the growth of the hitherto unknown idea of "progress," conceived not merely as technological development, but also as ethical improvement, would have struck them as a sinister example of what they called hubris. But there was worse to come. In the nineteenth century the belief in progress was thought to be confirmed by the biological theory of evolution, with the result that fantasies of Communist or anarchist millennia and other earthly paradises began to dizzy the minds of many educated people and even the heads of the uneducated as well, who are usually saner and more tough-minded, and, finally, in the twentieth century it has been believed by progressive thinkers in all classes that mankind, by the sole use of scientific know-how and by lifting itself up morally like an Indian juggler performing the rope trick, might create in the future a superstate inhabited by "men like gods," as H. G. Wells put it in 1923.

This essay is not concerned with prophecy but with history, so the future is outside its scope. But we may note parenthetically that if the obvious dangers of world famine and atomic war are averted, it does now seem to be conceivably within the bounds of technological possibility that a sort of Marxian or Wellsian utopia might in the end be established on a worldwide scale. And since, by our hypothesis, this irreligious earthly paradise could possess no culture of any kind, it would be something almost too horrible to contemplate, but of which one's everyday experience in technologically sophisticated countries and, still more, almost every issue of almost every newspaper already provide horrifying intimations: It would be a worldwide barbarism de luxe.

In case I seem to exaggerate, here is an example of the inroads already made by barbarism in the field of higher education. I have heard references in the highest academic circles to the "producers" and the "consumers" of culture—these words being used seriously and not as a joke. Culture is seen as a sort of prestige commodity, which ought to be available for every citizen of the democratic status state. Thus, if a citizen feels a lack of culture one morning, he can acquire some by visiting a culturama after lunch and consuming a few hundredweights of solid-culture producer Henry Moore or some decibels of the famous eighteenth-century producer of aural culture, W. A. Mozart, or if he is more serious-minded, he can visit a swami and join a group of pop singers and top models in a brief bout of deep meditation. But to speak seriously, it is the dismal truth that there are learned academics today who think of culture as a commodity or product, produced by producers for consumption by consumers, and who are incapable of grasping that culture is a way of life created collectively by a whole community, both in its work and in its play.

As a complement to their word "hubris" (approximately, insolence) the Greeks had another word: "nemesis" (approximately, vengeance) . The nemesis for creating an earthly paradise without religion or culture is not difficult to foresee: It would be boredom, frustration, and finally desperation—with the consequences that can be imagined.

Of the wars known to historians, some appear to have been in the nature of things while others appear to have been unnecessary. That upland tribes like the Elamites, Medes, and Persians should have invaded the rich kingdoms of Mesopotamia seems natural. But the wars of the Greek city-states seem more like the result of political incompetence. We have described the war of 1914–18 as the precipitating agent of worldwide changes which appear to have been the inevitable result of the progress of Western technology. But the form taken by the precipitating agent seems to have been quite unnecessary. It was fratricidal strife between kindred peoples and attributable, like the wars of the Greek city-states, very largely to political and diplomatic incompetence.

"The war was a lie. . . . It never happened," says a character in D. H. Lawrence's *Aaron's Rod*[5] (1922) , and when he is pressed to explain himself, he insists that none of the millions who took part in the war really experienced it. They lived through it or died in it somnambulistically, in a nightmare. And this was Lawrence's own view. He saw the war as a form of mass hypnosis by which millions of brave, kindhearted, and decent men were turned into flocks of sheep and driven to slaughter.

The theory of culture which I am trying to state can make this view intelligible. It gives a more precise and definite meaning to the old familiar commonplace that man's physical power has broken free from his spiritual, mental, and psychological control. In the course of the twentieth century religion and science have become completely divorced in the minds of civilized men. And alongside the spectacular triumphs of applied science and technology, religion has appeared increasingly irrelevant. It has, therefore, been on science, guided by the promptings of a supposedly natural and evolutionary morality, that man has come to rely for the fulfillment of his millennial hopes. But in minds that were not sophisticated, intellectual, or corrupt enough to accept the belief in evolutionary moral progress as an ersatz religion, the waning of real religious belief left a void. It is difficult to turn science into a satisfactory idol

---

[5] London, Penguin Books, 1950, p. 144.

for focusing the human need of self-dedication and devotion, but there was another candidate for the role, an idol which had become popular in the nineteenth century and had grown very powerful long before the year 1900—namely, the nation-state.

The worshipers of the nation-state disguise their idolatry as patriotism, which is itself a humane and beautiful emotion, akin to the love of family and of one's home and traditions. But the modern nation-state has almost no connection with such things. It consists of a bureaucratic administrative machine and of the population and territory administered by it, which need not have any cultural, traditional, historical, or even geographical coherence, and the bureaucracy, like all bureaucracies, is self-centered, self-perpetuating, imperialistically expansive, and amoral. But for lack of anything better in an age of waning religious faith and materialistic culture, the nation-state became idealized and personified in millions of minds as the focus of patriotic and quasi-religious devotion.

Or is all this too cynical? It may be objected that the young volunteers who joined the British Army in 1914 were not fighting for the British state machine; they were fighting for the British way of life against Prussian militarism; they were defending democracy and the rights of small nations. And the objection is true. That is precisely what the British thought they were fighting for, and just as sincerely the young Germans opposing them believed they were fighting for Germany's "place in the sun." But one can see today, fifty years later, that insofar as the war can be regarded as an intra-European struggle the real issue was a shift in the European balance of power—which might, at least in theory, have been effected by diplomatic, instead of military, action—and from this point of view the illusion of the young German soldiers was less remote from twentieth-century reality than that of the young Englishmen. The causes for which the English fought—antimilitarism and the rights of small nations—have scarcely prospered in Eastern Europe since 1918, whereas Germany, in spite of her disasters in two world wars, seems almost certain to obtain sooner or later a more important place in the European sun. In a sense, therefore, it appears that Britain, whose efforts in the two wars were no less heroic than Germany's and whose suffering was hardly less, has been in the long run the chief loser in the two world wars. Certainly, by her complacent isolationist lethargy, to give it no worse a name, since the Second War, she has lost weight as a factor in the European balance of power, and she has done less than nothing to counteract the nation-state idolatry which is what De Gaulle means by a *Europe des patries*—though it must be admitted that in the world as it is today the only alternative to De Gaulle's stuffy obsession is the equally squalid totalitarian progressive myth.

In spite of the great "War to End War" of 1914–18, this century has seen the bellicose European nation-state idolatry imitated in every continent of the world—most recently and most dismally in black Africa. In its most powerful and highly developed form this ersatz religion becomes an ideological imperialism; in its elementary form it is little more than a rationalized xenophobia. But in all its forms it is a sterile substitute for religion, and if sufficiently highly developed, it would lead to humanity's self-annihilation. But in the twentieth-century world, what is the alternative? There is nothing but the progressivist dream of a materialistic utopian world-state inhabited by Socialized world citizens, each of them fitted with a built-in, self-perfecting mechanism, and this, according to our thesis, could be, at best, only a deluxe barbarism incapable of developing any culture. It would end by inducing frenzies of frustration and desperation which might culminate in a paroxysm even more frightful than a war of ideological imperialisms.

The 1914–18 war brought two facts to light: first, that technological development had reached a point where it could continue without disaster only in a unified world and, second, that the existing political and social organizations in the world made its unification impossible. It will certainly continue to be impossible for a very long time, but it will never be possible at all so long as we continue to believe that morality is independent of religion in the transcendental sense defined in this essay. To repeat Bergson's point: You cannot proceed by any method of expansion from the closed morality to the open, from the city to humanity. "They are not of the same essence." (If space allowed, how many examples one could give from the contemporary scene of the difficulty of promoting goodwill, harmony, or even tolerance, among dissimilar national, racial, or social groups, when the only dynamic is a well-intentioned humanistic rationalism, to say nothing of the so frequently toxic effects of similar good intentions in private life.)

But how can any two things be in the last resort "not of the same essence"? For some 200 years educated people have been finding it more and more difficult to conceive the possibility of any essence apart from the one we fancy we know something about, probing it with our minds and our scientific instruments. It is now the official doctrine of the world's two largest states, China and Russia, that there *is* no other essence, and this is also the opinion of, probably, the great majority of what we call educated people in the West. Not only have they been conditioned to disbelieve in superstition and in wishful fantasies about "the next world"—which would be all to the good—but they have been educated into a mixture of skepticism and hubristic complacency which makes them see what Eliot called "supernatural realities" either as unreal or else as natural. And this is precisely the sign of a culture whose religious roots have withered. To believe that goodness and justice are natural products is to believe that matter is a machine for manufacturing good and that a corrupt tree can bear good fruit. Whatever its technological virtuosity, a culture which harbors such a belief is sterile, and that is why Western culture has been a poison, where it might have been a stimulus, to the cultures of the surviving older civilizations.

If Eliot's theory of the relation between culture and religion is true, there can be no future either for Western culture or for any of the others, unless there is a revival of religious inspiration. It is far beyond the scope of this essay to speculate whether and in what way such a revival might occur. Eliot himself believed or hoped that, for the West, a revived inspiration might come sooner or later from the existing Christian churches. Or so I deduce from his sketch *The Idea of a Christian Society*. Simone Weil was much more critical of the churches, and of the two thinkers mentioned earlier, Middleton Murry and D. H. Lawrence, whose reaction to the war of 1914–18 was comparable to Eliot's, the attitude of Murry was very similar to Simone Weil's. His continual debate with Eliot concerning heresy and orthodoxy was the most serious intellectual controversy in England between the two wars, and it is regrettable, though not at all surprising, that it attracted much less interest than Marxism, psychoanalysis, surrealism, and the other talking points of the post–1918 decadence.

As for Lawrence, it is difficult to imagine, in spite of his passionately religious spirit, that he could ever have entertained the idea of a Christian revival. But nobody recognized more clearly or exposed with more perceptiveness, and vehemence, the sterility of modern Western culture. And nobody suffered more excruciatingly at the prospect of the barbarous utopia which is the worldwide political objective of our age. He would certainly have agreed that the war of 1914–18 was the first installment of the nemesis which awaits a civilization dedicated to such an ideal.

Literature of War

Maurice Genevoix

MAURICE GENEVOIX was born on November 29, 1890, at Decize (Nièvre) of a father from Paris and a mother from Orléans. He spent his childhood in a borough of Loiret, Châteauneuf-sur-Loire, then studied at the lycées of Orléans and Lakanal and at the École Normale Supérieure (Lettres), which he left for the combat zone in August, 1914.

Commissioned on August 2, 1914, as a second lieutenant in the 106th Infantry Regiment, he took part in the combat and the retreat at the end of August, at the battles of the Marne, of Hauts-de-Meuse, of Éparges, of the trenches of Calonne. Promoted to lieutenant and later to major of the 15th Company, he was wounded on April 25, 1915, and discharged after spending seven months in the hospital.

The next several years he spent in Paris. Then he returned to Châteauneuf-sur-Loire and, after 1930, to St.-Denis-de-l'Hôtel, where he still resides during the summer months. He has traveled extensively across Europe and also in Tunisia, Algeria, and Morocco. Before the last war he visited the United States and Canada. Since that war he has traveled in Senegal, Guinea, the Ivory Coast, Sudan, British Nigeria, Mexico, etc.

Maurice Genevoix has been publishing literary works for more than fifty years, beginning with Sous Verdun (1916). He has written more than twenty novels and was awarded the Prix Goncourt in 1925 for his novel Raboliot. On October 24, 1946, he was elected to the Académie Française, and in 1958 he became its secrétaire perpétuel (permanent secretary).

COMMENTARIES ON THE WAR:
SOME MEANINGS*

———◆———

TODAY more than ever, after celebrating the fifty-second anniversary of the Battle of Verdun, how could we, the veterans, not feel drawn by the magnet of memory? For most of us, the return in time is at once bitter and sweet, a paradoxically nostalgic pilgrimage back to the years of our great suffering. But how, too, in the actual time when we relive these battles, these trials, can we push away the thought that soon there will be no more witnesses left of that drama which was simultaneously individual and worldwide in scale and whose dimensions, therefore, cannot be encompassed either by personal recall or by collective remembrance?

Quite naturally, then, in the reawakened sense of truly brotherly companionship—that of my comrades whom I joined in this recent celebration—have I found myself led to question myself anew. As the crowd of witnesses thins out from year to year, as the moment approaches when they all will have disappeared, what can have been the real meaning and the import, ephemeral or lasting, of the testimony they will have left?

The final years of the war, I remember, were peppered with an extraordinary superabundance of the writings called war literature—private diaries, field notes, narratives, essays, books written "in the heat of battle," so to speak, in actual touch with the happening and as if dictated by the events. Even so, this superabundance was only the residue of an enormous mass of written accounts. Rare in fact were the men of arms who, gripped from the outset by the feeling that they were participating in an unparalleled experience, did not bow to the need to record its sights and vicissitudes. However assorted it may have been, the war literature, it is appropriate to stress, thus stands witness—and this is its reason for being, as well as its justification—for all the fighting men.

Responding to this very keen need, to a kind of internal obligation, these testimonials would constitute a mine of firsthand infor-

* Translated from the French by Sally Abeles.

mation which would give the reader, knowledgeable or not, the chance of seeing the war not as a military staff problem or a historic account, but as a human event, through the life of a soldier or line officer, in its most concrete or I should say its most carnal aspects.

Some of these reports are still in our minds: Jean-Marie Carré's *L'Histoire d'une division de couverture,* Jacques Meyer's *La Biffe,* Galtier-Boissière's *En Rase Campagne;* similar books by René Naegelen, Georges Gaudy, Pierre Paraf; Jean Pottecher's *Les Lettres d'un fils;* or, more fictionalized, Henri Barbusse's *Le Feu,* Roland Dorgelès' *Les Croix de bois,* Georges Duhamel's *Vie des martyrs,* Henri Massis' *Les Impressions de guerre 1914–1915,* Henry Malherbe's *La Flamme au poing.*

The very variety of these records is such that even today it is hard to list a few without immediately wondering whether they or the hundreds of other titles that could have been cited fulfilled their purpose, whether they or the others are up to the level of the experience they were concerned with transmitting.

From this a basic dispute arose among the witnesses—some holding that literary creation allowed them to reach a deeper truth, a verisimilitude which was less slavish and which stepped back only in order to go further, beyond the specific; others considering, on the contrary, that in this case a truth was involved whose very nature and compelling dimensions constrained the witness to subjugate himself entirely to the subject. To put it another way, after 1919 wasn't there a risk of confusion, and weren't many of these records already highly unreliable from the viewpoint of the future historian?

This is quite likely; the best and the worst stood side by side. From which it follows that in order to test their genuineness, one would have to have known the realities of the war through personal experience. This was not always the case. Yet one man wanted to make the attempt, without waiting any longer for the requisite discrimination. His name was Jean Norton Cru. A serviceman and hence a witness himself, this French-born American professor, who returned to fight in the army of his native country, devoted fifteen years of his life to this task of discriminating. He read all the books by soldiers, testing their veracity in the light of his own recollections and little by little, from comparison to comparison, in the illumination of his readings themselves.

His large work *Témoins,* which appeared in 1929, had the primary purpose of addressing itself to future historians of the war. He intended above all to make their task easier, to clear the ground, to pave the way for them, to furnish them with an Ariadne's thread which would allow them at least to direct and assure their progress. He was inspired and sustained by that horror of falsification, of the fabricated tale, that thirst for truth blended with the need for fairness which were common to all the veterans.

It was high time. Already "histories of the war" were beginning to appear which themselves in turn mixed the best and the worst, too often taking up suspect reports and, for want of guidelines grounded in experience, combining them with others more trust-worthy. Norton Cru remarked on this bluntly in his introduction: "Military history up to the present has been written solely on the basis of documents issuing from people who could not have seen or heard or had the direct experience of combat, but who are familiar with orders that together, along with those of the enemy, only partly influenced the combat areas." In thus stressing the impor-tance and enormous value of eyewitness accounts, classifying them by degree of truthfulness, Norton Cru intended primarily to serve history.

Very quickly, we can say in fact beginning in 1920, war literature was lost and buried in the sand drift of indifference. The success of Erich Maria Remarque's book [*All Quiet on the Western Front*], a war novel, is thoroughly exceptional, for example. Public interest found new objectives and demands. Having exhausted feeling in a way, it now called to reason, to understanding. What awaited the reader in the future were cool-headed works, reflective and analyti-cal, works by moralists, sociologists, philosophers, historians.

It seems to be only just today—that is, after fifty years of docu-mentation and reflection—that the propitious time has finally come for the vast syntheses. We are in sum close enough to the event for its reality not yet to have escaped our memory, but far enough from it to be able to think about it tranquilly.

On the basis of these comments, I would like now to consider two works among others, both books of quality which seem to me to coincide well with the two viewpoints I have posited. They come to my hand by chance and not by predetermined choice. The parallels I find in them seem all the more significant, and more so still because they suggest points of agreement and even lines of con-vergence that we may henceforth no longer merely wish for but hope for.

One is a *Histoire de la guerre 1914–1918,* which will appear very shortly and whose editors are General Valluy and the historian Pierre Dufourcq. The other, *Vie et mort des Français, 1914–1918,* is the work of three infantrymen, Jacques Meyer, André Ducasse, and

Gabriel Perreux, all three former students at the École Normale Supérieure, certified through qualification in different specialties—philosophy, literature, and history—but all three molded according to the highest cultural traditions.

What particularly struck me on reading the first work is a kind of universality, not so unusual in itself as new in this sort of undertaking. In terms first of nationalism, or rather internationalism, the contributors observe war operations not by taking position in only one of the hostile camps, as it were, but from the viewpoint—actually indivisible—of both. This leads rather naturally to parallel analyses of the psychology of peoples (and hence of the fighting men, since the subject is a war and national armies) and of the ethnic characteristics through which the dominant notes of their collective behavior are revealed. These create something like illuminating cipher keys which help, almost always considerably, to decode paradoxical or at least baffling facts.

Here are some examples, intentionally taken at random: What were the determining causes of the evolution that led the United States to enter a war whose principal battlefields were in Europe? What were the reasons for the subsequent American delay which—I remember well—kept us on the boil a long time? Again, how was the Russian Revolution, a huge occurrence with enormous repercussions, prompted, made possible, triggered? Finally, how did the differences (and what sorts of differences) that intervened among the Central Powers themselves come into play, from interference to interference, from reaction to reaction, sometimes to frustrate an event and sometimes, contrary to apparently reasonable expectations, to hasten its ripening and picking, as of a ripe fruit?

Who could really have answered all these questions in the year 1919?

It would be easy to cite many other examples of these cipher keys that would have remained hidden had not enough time elapsed. Who would have thought, under the still painful shock of the event and the grip of the early-born stories, even to recall the military regulations, French and German, in force in 1914? If both affirmed the primacy of the infantry, they parted ways on the role of the artillery. While the first, holding that the artillery "does not prepare the way for attacks" and carrying the logic of the system to its worst conclusions, described the movement of the infantry, the assault, and hand-to-hand combat as continuing "until the last enemy combatant is disabled, has laid down his arms, or has fled," the second, more realistic, wrote about the infantry's role that it should stand to battle "together with the artillery" and even with heavy field artillery, which was to be used both against the opposing batteries and to prepare the way for an infantry attack supported by light cannon. Another fundamental difference that likewise only today explains many things about yesterday: the concept of discipline. Contrary to prevailing notions, it was the regulations of the "sheeplike" Germans that gave credit to the individual, to the initiative of the individual as circumstances demanded. On the contrary, what did the French regulations say? "Discipline constituting the primary strength of armies, it is essential that each superior officer obtain from his subordinates total obedience and submission at all times." Fortunately, the French Army and its chiefs were on the whole more intelligent than were their regulations.

It has thus become possible, without appearing hereafter to resort to paradox or Procrustean solutions, to show how unforeseen factors, and which ones, eluded the planners and seized the most perfect and formidable war machine there was, though all the conditions were present which, according to the notions of modern warfare, should logically and almost inevitably have asserted victory to the Central Powers. Given this, moreover, the nature of the check is all the more dramatic, and psychologically the more charged with meaning and moral.

Thus, by a detour which has become possible and from now on almost inevitable, we have necessarily come back to the man, the fighter, the footsoldier, the poilu. And that is why, in counterpoint to the commentaries of today's historian—and this for the first time—something in me, an old warrior, is stirring, agreeing, and echoing. Even if, like everyone who harks back, I have all my life deplored the impossibility of transcribing our harsh experience, it is nonetheless true (and I have proof of it now) that there are meeting grounds where the most visceral experience and the most rigorous objectivity become one.

At this point, it would perhaps be appropriate to evoke some of the accounts that might be called intermediate, written not "in the heat of battle" like those I was speaking of a moment ago, but, while objectively, with fellow feeling. I am thinking of certain novels, Jules Romains' *Verdun* being the most striking example to me. It is perhaps thanks to books of this kind, where talent never overrides honesty and concern with reality, that the surviving witnesses of battles have not surrendered to the temptation to give up, that they have preserved any feeling that they have not been thoroughly and definitively disregarded and thus betrayed. How often, indeed, have they been disillusioned and even, in their innermost selves, disgusted! How often have they felt as though dispossessed, reading certain accounts, hearing certain words! Not that they saw traces of any ill will in them, but that the kind of objectivity these accounts laid claim to *sounded false* to their ears, that they sinned by levity, by coldness, and, therefore, by the omission of what the survivors knew to be essential.

This exigency in them has not weakened. On the contrary. As their vitality declines, as they see the shadow of evening advancing to meet them, their thoughts return increasingly to their martyred youth, take them back with all the strength of their being to what they know to be, beyond *their* truth, *the* truth. It is stronger than they. They would like not to leave this world with such sadness in their hearts.

This leads me directly back to the books by my professorial comrades. For their work responds to this need that haunts the surviving soldiers. In this connection, we have seen a sort of new war literature come to life during the last several years. It constitutes a new testimony, which is really testamentary. Raymond [Marcel Edmond] Naegelen, brother of the author of *Les Suppliciés,* has turned again toward the well-traveled path, and he, too, has found, *Avant que meure le dernier,* the truth that is an integral part of us. Pierre Jolly wanted to retrace his steps on the battlefields of the Somme once more, for *Les Survivants vont mourir.* There have been others, many others. How could we not be struck by this anxiety, this poignant, haunting memory, and this unanimity? All these essays, otherwise and likewise concerned with the generalities and generalizations of history, strain almost desperately to bring back that sort of visceral tremor they remembered in their bodies.

There is something here, obviously, that transcends conscious will. I have said it. It is an internal obligation that is involved. And all the more so because the preestablished ideas, the prejudices, the legends have shown themselves hard to kill. Almost always dangerous, baneful, and having demonstrated this too well, they can exercise their harmfulness tomorrow still. If they indeed offend intellectual rectitude and a certain honesty of feeling, less than ever do the men who fought the war consent to pardon them the extra sufferings they sustained because of these works, or the useless deaths which they are responsible for in their eyes, or the distorted images which are given out as truthful but in which they do not recognize themselves.

In this regard the book by Meyer, Ducasse, and Perreux is a summation. Its subtitle alone is significant: *Simple Histoire de la grande guerre.* A "simple" history in the sense that while it does not aspire to making systematic and authoritative syntheses, it nonetheless presents an objective and complete overview—that is, one which attempts to communicate what by nature was little or not at all communicable. Rather than a history of the war, what we who fought it have always hoped for and what these three writers have tried to give us is a history of men at war.

What does this mean? It is neither desirable nor good that the professional historian prevail over the veteran; it is also not good that the veteran prevail over the historian. This is why the history of the 1914–18 war remains so hard to write. When, in fact, one aspect is isolated—for instance, the study of military events—a given episode will seem to have been sacrificed or omitted for the sake of closely related events whose importance will thus tend to appear disproportionate. Where was the mud the stickiest, the heaviest? Where were there the most frozen feet? Which sector had the heaviest bombardments, the most savage counterattacks, the most monstrous mines? What sector did not have its "Death Gully" or "Plague Ravine"? This is a veteran's approach, not a historian's. But the historian who was blind to it would be a poor historian.

On the other hand, if the veteran came to write a history of the war, he would also be a poor historian if he did not forget his sector loyalty and determine his choices for reasons better detached from his personal memories. For some the Battle of Verdun is the capital battle, for instance; hasn't it become a symbol, and rightly so? For General Erich Ludendorff, it was the Somme. According to the fighters in the hottest sectors, it was the Yser, Artois, Argonne, Éparges, the hills of Champagne, the Vardar, or the Dardanelles. But it is well for the historian who relates the Battle of Verdun and describes the calvary of the infantryman there to know that this calvary did not last only a few months, but four years and more, and that its stations spread along a front extending hundreds of miles.

Everyone agrees in recognizing that in the whole history of mankind, few dates have had the importance of August 2, 1914. First Europe and soon after almost all humanity found themselves plunged into a dreadful event. Conventions, agreements, moral laws, all the foundations shook; from one day to the next, everything was called into question. The event was to exceed both instinctive forebodings and reasonable anticipations. Enormous, chaotic, monstrous, it still drags us in its wake.

Consequently we concur, so important is it not only to us, men of this time, but to the generations to come, that the historian must broach this event with a deep, unwavering sense of his responsibility. Mild or minor errors, distortions, levities, flights of imagination on lesser events would seem here to have no excuse. Jean de Pierrefeu, writing somewhere of an obviously inspired and tendentious staff document, added sadly: "Here is how history will be written in fifty years, when, with the witnesses dead, conscientious historians, wanting to go back to sound sources, will read the staff records."

Forty years have passed since he wrote these lines. We now have reason to believe that "conscientious historians" will no longer write the history of the Great War as Pierrefeu feared they would. To this end, and with the selectivity they now have the means to apply, they will need to take account of the experience of the witnesses thrown into the core of the event and matured in its pain.

"Those who say," wrote Maurice Donnay fifty years ago, "that there will always be wars, that war is a necessary evil, perhaps do not understand exactly what this war is. . . . We are not out of the moving sand of events, we do not have the necessary perspective. But when the frightful drama can be judged as a whole. . . ." So did Donnay understand in advance the demands on us today.

These demands are not contradictory. They must in actuality complement each other. I would like simply to compare Maurice Donnay's reflections with a few lines taken from a letter written by one of Captain Jean Vigier's* sergeants shortly after his chief's death: "We were glorying in combat. . . . Two months of war showed us the inanity of this way of looking at things. When we were in disarray, our captain told us: 'The duty of a true soldier is not where you've put it. The present war has nothing glorious about it; we are monks of nomadic monasteries, whose rule is honor, and our rule is to suffer. . . .' "

Perhaps this is what they called the spirit of the front. For myself, I would rather speak of a kind of collective soul, elementary but admirably lucid, courageous, fraternal under every circumstance. Suffering, yes, involved in painful flesh, but this is its stirring beauty and its greatness, measuring up to our human condition.

No, emphatically no: Because of this soul, it will no longer be possible to write the history of the Great War like the histories of bygone wars. Pierrefeu has to have been wrong.

---

* Jean Vigier, who had also been studying to teach, first in his class, a resident student at the Fondation Thiers, was already a master whose profound and enduring influence as a professor, as a writer, could be foreseen. A light infantry officer, he was killed in 1916.

G. Wilson Knight

Described by one critic as an "interpreter of genius . . . concerned with bringing to consciousness the experience of literature," George Wilson Knight has enhanced students' understanding of Shakespeare in such volumes as The Wheel of Fire *(1930),* The Imperial Theme *(1931),* The Shakespearian Tempest *(1932),* Principles of Shakespearian Production *(1936; as* Shakespearian Production, *1964),* The Crown of Life *(1947),* The Mutual Flame *(1955),* The Sovereign Flower *(1958), and* Shakespeare and Religion *(1967). Moreover, Knight has not restricted himself to Shakespeare. He has gone on to analyze Milton, Swift and Byron in* The Burning Oracle *(1939; as* Poets of Action, *1968); Wordsworth, Coleridge, Shelley, and Keats in* The Starlit Dome *(1941); Byron in* Lord Byron: Christian Virtues *(1952),* Lord Byron's Marriage *(1957), and* Byron and Shakespeare *(1966); Pope in* Laureate of Peace *(1954); and John Cowper Powys in* The Saturnian Quest *(1964). He has also produced and acted in dramatic productions at Hart House Theater, Toronto, from 1932 to 1940, and at the University of Leeds from 1946 to 1960.*

Born in Sutton, Surrey, England, on September 19, 1897, he was educated at Dulwich College, London, and at St. Edmund Hall, Oxford. From 1916 to 1920 he served with the British forces in Mesopotamia, Persia, and India as a motorcyclist dispatch rider. After the war he became English master at Dean Close School, Cheltenham (1925–31); Chancellors' Professor of English, Trinity College, University of Toronto (1931–40); master at Stowe School, Buckingham (1941–46); reader and later professor of English literature, University of Leeds (1946–62), and subsequently emeritus professor at Leeds. He is an honorary fellow of St. Edmund Hall.

Apart from his work as a literary critic, Knight has written Atlantic Crossing *(1936),* The Dynasty of Stowe *(1945), the play* The Last of the Incas *(1954), and the poems* Gold-Dust *(1968). He is a C.B.E., an F.I.A.L., and an F.R.S.L., and has received honorary doctorates of letters from the universities of Sheffield (1966) and Exeter (1968).*

RUPERT BROOKE

ON THE MENTION of Brooke's name we think first either of his five war sonnets or of the famous bare-shouldered photograph by S. Schell, used for the 1914 collection of his *Poems* and the original of the plaque in Rugby Chapel by Harvard Thomas, whose version is in the National Portrait Gallery, where copies are sold. I shall indicate a relation between Brooke's poetry and this portrait, called by Christopher Hassall in his biography *Rupert Brooke*[1] "A visual image that met the needs of a nation at a time of crisis" (390; my numerals refer to Hassall's volume).

Brooke was not obviously fitted for the role of patriot. He had, it is true, certain social advantages. He struck a figure at Rugby and Cambridge, his poetic powers rapidly won attention, and he mixed with leading personalities in literature and politics. He had brilliance and wit. But the general tone of his conversation and writing was iconoclastic and unorthodox; he was a Socialist in politics and a pagan if not atheist in religion. His poetry was often of a kind to shock. He links the estheticism of the nineties to the realisms of postwar writing; he has affinities with both Wilde and Eliot.

Like Byron and Wilde, he had a strong personal impact. His appearance was striking; men such as Henry James, Walter de la Mare, and Sir Ian Hamilton were conquered by it. The many records are extraordinary: "astounding apparition" with eyes "like the sky" (221) ; "so beautiful that he's scarcely human" (258) ; "a young man more beautiful than he I had never seen" (399) ; one who summed "the youth of all the world" (441). But the accounts vary. Though he had the "rosy" skin of a "girl" (240), of "girlish" smoothness (442), his appearance was all male, "there was nothing effeminate" (441), and we hear also of a deeply tanned face and sturdy form, large feet and hands, and clumsy movements (241–42). It seems that he could appear variously male and female, clumsy and ethereal, according to mood. His complexion was rich, as though the blood "was near the surface" (242). An inward power radiated out through the blood to the complexion, the eyes,

---

[1] London, 1964.

and red-gold waves of hair, and it was some inner, spiritual, reality that gave him "a shining impression" as of one "from another planet" (524), so that he entered a room "like a prince" (527). According to Henry James, much of Brooke's importance as both poet and person could not be conveyed to posterity, since it depended on "the simple act of presence and communication" (523).

He was an *embodiment* of poetry: "There are only three good things," he once said, "in the world. One is to read poetry, another is to write poetry, and the best of all is to *live* poetry"; it "kept one young" (143). Siegfried Sassoon felt poetry in his presence, as of a "being singled out for some transplendent performance, some enshrined achievement" (451). He had the baffling bisexuality of such persons. Though he could oppose bisexual doctrines, he also admitted that "the soul of persons who write verse is said to be hermaphroditic" (442, 446; and see 440). He was well aware of his endowments—"I looked at myself, drying, in the glass, and I thought my body was very beautiful and strong, and that I was keeping it and making it splendid for you" (304)—but also, perhaps more, for himself, since there was in him an element of Whitman-esque narcissism. He was bodily conscious: "While the Samoans," he once wrote, "are not so foolish as to 'think,' their intelligence is incredibly lively and subtle"; even a European living among them "soon learns to *be* his body (and so his true mind) instead of using it as a stupid convenience for his personality, a moment's umbrella against the world" (460).

He preserved a child's bodily self-interest and a child's integrity; as "both man and boy" he was "the child he had grown from" (231); he was "a symbol of youth for all time," doing up his shoes with "the absorbed seriousness of a child" (277). Brooke remembered as a child often touching a "higher level" of existence and recognizing that we are normally "asleep," and the experience could be repeated in maturity, when he could say "I more than exist" (257). In the South Seas he came near to a full recapture of this childhood magic (421).

He was obsessed with nakedness, usually in relation to bathing, at Grantchester and the South Seas or by a Canadian lake, "lying quite naked on a beach of golden sand" (409). In the South Seas he wrote of himself "in a loin-cloth, brown and wild" by a "sun-saturated sea," among "naked people of incredible loveliness" (419). Here men were strong and beautiful in their unclothed bodies, and with finer sensibilities than Europeans (427-28), so that "one's European literary soul begins to be haunted by strange doubts" (421). When war came, Brooke expected to "find incredible beauty in the washing place, with rows of naked, superb men," either by sun or moon (463). If the many revulsions in his poetry point on to Eliot, his body obsession points to Lawrence. It is less likely that this obsession (other relevant references occur in Hassall's biography at pp. 255, 265, 266, 280, 282, 304, 390, 410, 413, 418, 424, 427, 429, 443, 523, 526) came from knowledge of his own beauty than that that beauty flowered from the inward obsession. He was, in fact, an integrated, or near integrated, man.

His sex life was difficult. Living within the presexual or super-sexual, Nietzschean, and lonely, integration at an age of physical maturity may be hard. His experience in the South Seas was not, he said, that of a love paradise; it was the opposite to alcohol according to the Porter's definition in *Macbeth*, "for it promotes performance but takes away desire" (422). That is, sex functioned without a partner. Brooke knew intense love in England, but his artistic and political interests combined with "some obscure emotional distemper" (521) to make him unable to love. His biographer leaves the "root of his unsureness" undefined (445). Here is Brooke's own account:

Oh, I've loved you a long time, child: but not in the complete way of love. I mean, there was something rooted out of my heart by things that went before. I thought I couldn't love wholly, again. I couldn't worship—I could see intellectually that some women were worshipful, perhaps. But I couldn't find the flame of worship in me. I was unhappy. Oh, God, I *knew* how glorious and noble your heart was. But I couldn't burn to it. I mean, I loved you with all there was of me. But I was a cripple, incomplete. [462]

In some moods he was an antifeminist (445), rating friendship above love (425). But he does not appear to have experienced male romantic friendships: imagination was turned inward, narcissistically, on himself.

We pass now to the poetry. It strongly attacks romantic love. The two sonnets "Menelaus and Helen" show knightly romance giving place to blear-eyed impotence and nagging. "The Beginning," "Sonnet Reversed," "Beauty and Beauty" tell the same story. In "Kindliness" youth's infinite hunger has to make terms with a "second-best." In "Mutability" our "melting flesh" aims at impossible absolutes. "Jealousy" contrasts young love with the slobbering age which follows, and in "A Channel Passage" there is little difference between "a sea-sick body or a you-sick soul." In "Dead Men's Love" love is reduced to "dust and a filthy smell." There appears to be some achievement in "Lust," but the only real gleams are, as we shall see, in some new dimension beyond earth.

Brooke's sense of physical perfection led to a corresponding reaction. Man's body could so easily be repellent: In "Wagner" and "Dawn" physical nausea is emphatic. Brooke questions the human form itself: In "Heaven" the fishes must see God as a great fish, and "On the Death of Smet-Smet" shows savages worshiping a hippopotamus goddess. Our human valuations are arbitrary. "Thoughts on the Shape of the Human Body" is a critique of sexual intercourse:

> . . . We love, and gape,
> Fantastic shape to mazed fantastic shapes,
> Straggling, irregular, perplexed, embossed,
> Grotesquely twined, extravagantly lost
> By crescive paths and strange protuberant ways
> From sanity and from wholeness and from grace.

What is wanted is a more harmonious love "disentangled from humanity," "whole," a "simplicity" like a "perfect sphere," loving "moon to moon"—the kind of love so often found in Platonic-homosexual engagements, though there are none recorded of Brooke. The moon's radiance is white, and whiteness is Brooke's color for beyond-earthly intimations.

Brooke was thrown back on himself. In "Success" his love's "white godhead," "holy and far," is entangled with "foul you," "shame" and a "black word," leaving the poet "alone." In "I said I splendidly loved you" he admits the lie, conscious that he has been following "phantoms" or "his own face." "Waikiki" shows him correspondingly "perplexed." In "The Voice" a love assignation horribly interrupts his lonely meditations in the night-darkened woods: "By God! I wish—I wish that you were dead!" Elsewhere, in the dark woods of "Flight," he has left daytime loves for the night's scents, weeping and stroking his own face. "Paralysis" shows him in his "white neat bed" laughing in his "great loneliness." In "Town and Country" two lovers may be "drunk with solitude" in the city, but in the woods by night love dissolves away into a vaster, cosmic, loneliness. "The Chilterns" tells us that:

> . . . a better friend than love have they,
> For none to mar or mend,
> That have themselves to friend.

He will have freedom enjoying the roads and winds and hedgerows. He is with Wordsworth and John Cowper Powys, for whom the natural partner of the human soul is, not a sexual partner, but the objective universe (*In Spite Of*, IV, 116; in my study of Powys, *The Saturnian Quest*,[2] 90). "The Great Lover" is a key poem, listing a fine assortment of loves ranging through all the senses from wet roofs, the smell of burning wood, "the rough male kiss of blankets" and "furs to touch," to the miracles of earth nature. This Powysian mystique is expanded in a remarkable letter to Ben Keeling, quoted in Hassall's biography (236–39).

Perfection is attainable in young beauty or in sense enjoyment of external objects. But what of the future? In "The Great Lover" he knows that life beyond death must be very different. He is ready to distinguish body from soul or spirit. In sleep the "soul" leaves the body like a "dress" laid by, and yet why then can the countenance appear troubled? Or smile? Surely, too, the sensuous is itself spirit-born, as in the mysterious sleep of "Doubts":

> And if the spirit be not there,
> Why is fragrance in her hair?

This was Powys' concern. On its bodiless excursions the soul still, even at a great distance, uses the senses of the body it has left behind. (*In Spite Of*, IV, 109; VII, 215; *The Saturnian Quest*, 88, and see 75).

This thought-teasing paradox of soul and body is brilliantly handled in a poem from Fiji, on the old cannibal practice of letting the victim see parts of himself eaten. Will this be his own fate? In brilliant if almost unreadable couplets, composed as for a past lover, he traces the horrors:

> Of the two eyes that were your ruin,
> One now observes the other stewing. [Hassall 426]

The verses are simultaneously a critique of physical glamor and an assertion of the mind, or soul's, independence. Perhaps nowhere else, apart from Byron, are crucial metaphysics so lightly handled.

Brooke was as strongly obsessed with the spiritual as with the physical. Though love fails on earth, there is hope for it beyond. "The Goddess in the Wood" sets, in mythological terms, a type. In "The Call" lovers may be "one" *above* the "Night," and in "Victory" "beyond all love or hate," "perfect from the ultimate

---

2 London, 1964.

height of living," they challenge "supernal" hosts. Wounded on earth, love may win success at the "eventual limit of our light," in "The Wayfarers." "Choriambics II" balances solitude in dark woods and some "face of my dreams" gleaming down through the forest "in vision white." White is for Brooke, as for Powys (*The Saturnian Quest,* 24, 26, 48), a mystical color. In "Blue Evening," after "agony" and "hatred" the poet's love is felt within the moon's "white ways of glamour," blessing him with "white brows." "Finding" shows him after love's failure "lone and frightened" in the "white" moonlight's "silver way," with around him trees "mysteriously crying," "dead voices" and "dead soft fingers," and "little gods" whispering, and he sees his love radiant beyond "the tides of darkness," so that nothing was true

> But the white fire of moonlight
> And a white dream of you.

Such love is not sexually limited. "Sleeping Out: Full Moon" shows him alone under the lonely Moon-Queen, and he feels the whole world pressing toward "the white one flame" of a "heatless fire" and "flameless ecstasy"; "earth fades"; "radiant bands" and "friendly" presences help the stumbler to the "infinite height" and *maternal* eyes. We remember Brooke's desire for a perfect, unentangled, love, loving "moon to moon" in "Thoughts on the Shape of the Human Body." The visions are beyond sexuality in line with the contrast in "Success" of "white godhead" with "that foul you"—a contrast, in some vital way, of spirit with personality. We are all, already, part of some other, spiritual dimension. "In Examination" develops a vision of ordinary life transfigured, revealing "scribbling fools" as with flaming hair, God-like, "white-robed" in the "white undying Fire" among archangels and angels—beings in a dimension of which our normal seeing refracts only a miserable simulacrum. "Desertion," on the death of a loved friend, asks pathetically *why* he has gone? Had he known something that made him distrust earth's "splendid dream"? Is perhaps earth's seeming splendor—and often to Brooke it seemed sordid enough—a mere nothing in comparison?

Such intuitions touch spiritualism. Though "The True Beatitude" asserts "an earthly garden hidden from any cleric" Brooke's poetry can be intensely spiritualistic, as when in "Oh, Death will find me. . . ." he imagines his love's arrival in Hades tossing her hair "among the ancient Dead." "Dust" vividly exploits the freedoms of an afterlife. Though the "white flame" of love's earthly visions has gone and we "stiffen" in darkness, yet, in the manner of Byron's *Childe Harold* (III, 74):

> Not dead, not undesirous yet,
>   Still sentient, still unsatisfied,
> We'll ride the air, and shine, and flit,
>   Around the places where we died . . .

Beyond "thinking" and "out of view" (*i.e.*, in an existence impossible to define) :

> One mote of all the dust that's I
> Shall meet one atom that was you.

The old love reflames in the "garden"; all senses are mixed—is it "fire," "dew," of "earth" or the "height," "singing, or flame, or sense, or hue"? All that can be said is that it is "light" passing on to "light."

Brooke had extrasensory experience. "Home" recounts how, returning by night to his room, he was aware of

> The form of one I did not know
> Sitting in my chair.

Then it goes. All night he "could not sleep."

He wonders variously about the afterlife. "The Life Beyond" imagines it as hideous. "Mutability" asks if indeed there is "a high windless world and strange" beyond time? "Our melting flesh" fixes Beauty there and "imperishable Love," but all we actually know is earth experience, where kisses do not last. "Clouds" ponders the belief that "the Dead" remain close to those on earth but suggests rather that they pass above like clouds, reflecting "the white moon's" beauty, and "break and wave and flow" like a silent sea. But shall we remember the past? "Hauntings" imagines a "poor ghost" "haunted" by vague recollections of earth life—as earth beings are "haunted" by spirit life—which are unintelligible:

> And light on waving grass, he knows not when,
> And feet that ran, but where, he cannot tell.

Official spiritualism is given the fine "Sonnet (Suggested by some of the Proceedings of the Society for Psychical Research.) " After death we shall

> Spend in pure converse our eternal day;
>   Think each in each, immediately wise;
> Learn all we lacked before; hear, know, and say
>   What this tumultuous body now denies;
> And feel, who have laid our groping hands away;
>   And see, no longer blinded by our eyes.

The lines report what spiritualism tells us: speech by telepathic immediacy, halls of learning and progress; the earth body as a limiting factor which narrows and constricts, so that we feel more keenly and see more clearly without it, as in Marvell's *Dialogue Between the Soul and Body*. The next plane, where sound and color are one, is richer, not poorer, in sense experience, depending not on a mentalized summation derived from separate sense inlets. We shall respond directly to the totality of which these allow parts only to trickle through and which we can on earth only approach by attempts at some total dramatic art blending intellectual awareness with sound and color.[3]

Brooke came near such a total experience in the South Sea Islands. "Tiare Tahiti," rejecting the "broken things" of earth, introduces us to a world of Platonic archetypes, to "the Face, whose ghosts we are" and to "Dance" without "the limbs that move," all lovely things meeting in "Loveliness." All colors, white especially, but also coral, pearl, green, gold, red, are there; all earth beauty recaptured and eternalized. And yet—must "feet" become "Ambulation," and what of kisses? Meanwhile, let us enjoy the "flowered way" and "whiteness of the sand," "well this side of Paradise." We may be nearer the spirit reality at choice, sense-summing moments of earthly life than with *mental* accounts, however accurate, of that reality, which is all, and more, of what we experience on earth. Such is the truth flowering from this cleverly balanced poem.

Brooke lived and wrote on the border between earth and paradise, life and death. The transition, as with Powys, involves what may be called the elemental. In nature Brooke loved night woods and the moon, and also his own, and others', nakedness, swimming, and water. These are as transition mediums between modes of existence.

Herein lies the importance of the poem "The Old Vicarage, Grantchester." It contrasts the regulated officialdom of Berlin, where the lines were composed, with the luxuriant freedoms and "unofficial rose" of Grantchester—more widely, civilized constrictions and elemental freedom. At Grantchester one runs on "bare feet" to the river "deep as death":

> In Grantchester their skins are white,
> They bathe by day, they bathe by night. . . .

Spirits are here: "His ghostly Lordship swims his pool," and among the trees flits "the sly shade of a Rural Dean." It is a place of "lithe

---

[3] See my discussions in *The Starlit Dome* (London, 1959), 318–20 and *The Christian Renaissance* (London, 1962) 328–29.

children lovelier than a dream" and "youth," where suicide is preferable to "feeling old."

The phrase "deep as death" is important. In the Hades of Byron's *Cain* and in Ibsen's *Lady from the Sea* and *Little Eyolf* water naturally blends with the dimension of death. Brooke once, in imaginative vein, described his Grantchester night bathing:

I stood naked at the edge of the black water in a perfect silence. I plunged. The water stunned me as it came upwards with its cold, life-giving embrace. . . . [Hassall, 208]

Then a figure appeared, some "local deity" or "naiad of the stream," who urged him as Powys often urged us, not to search beyond present existence. But with the elements, especially by night, we are already on the border line, living life and death. Diving into blue waters at Fiji was perhaps more ultimate than poetry (Hassall, 421). Water is death and life. The dead of "Clouds" "break and wave and flow" like a silent sea. The visionary figure of "Blue Evening" comes "rippling" down the moon's "glamour." "Day That I Have Loved" imagines the day as a dead loved one, gone out to sea, and darkness. "Finding" tells of "the words of night" and "dead" spirit-voices and "the dark, beyond the ocean." Brooke's lines in "Seaside":

> In the deep heart of me
> The sullen waters swell towards the moon,
> And all my tides set sea-ward

correspond exactly to the conclusion to Powys' *Rodmoor*. In both Powys and Brooke we meet a mystique of water, darkness, and a great *white* peace (*The Saturnian Quest*, 26). In "The Jolly Company" the stars are "a white companionship" of "lonely light."

Sea life is as a new dimension. "The Fish" blends life and death:

> The strange soft-handed depth subdues
> Drowned colour there, but black to hues,
> As death to living, decomposes—
> Red darkness of the heart of roses,
> Blue brilliant from dead starless skies,
> And gold that lies behind the eyes,
> The unknown unnameable sightless white
> That is the essential flame of night. . . .

As elsewhere, *darkness* is one with the *white* vision. "Behind the eye" corresponds to Eliot's "More distant than stars and nearer than the eye" in "Marina." A fish's life contrasts with love's unrest; it is a lonely self-enjoyment of the blood rhythms. In Powysian vein, for these cool, atavistic depths are exactly Powysian, "His bliss is older than the sun."

Brooke's progress through love agony and love failure to a lonely delight in his solitary, narcissistic, childlike, integrated self, body and soul, to a superb culmination of swimming naked among the glorious nakednesses of the South Sea Islanders, was not all easy and innocent. It had its violent, nonmoral aspect: "I had to have a bath and dance many obscene dances, in lonely nakedness, up and down my room, to get sober" (Hassall, 443). In the early "Song of the Beasts" we leave the house by night when "shameful" desires awake, going

> Down the dim stairs, through the creaking door,
> Naked, crawling on hands and feet. . . .

We are "Beast and God," serving "blind desire," past "evil faces" and "mad whispers," out of the "city," "beyond lust," to level moon-lit waters, and the "calling sea." An embarrassment, half-shame, half-pride, is written into "Mary and Gabriel," wherein Mary feels both "her limbs' sweet treachery" and her "high estate," to be used for some high purpose. She feels "alone," her "womb"—or Brooke's own beauty—"not" exactly hers, and yet it *will* be; some half-glimpsed purpose will be fulfilled and known.

Death is, and yet is not, the end. In the early (1908) "Second Best" the poet is "alone with the enduring Earth, and Night." Death, he thinks, is the end. If so:

> Proud, then, clear-eyed and laughing, go to greet
> Death as a friend!

The poem advances to sense of death as containing all that was life:

> Exile of immortality, strongly wise,
> Strain through the dark with undesirous eyes
> To what may lie beyond it. Sets your star,
> O heart, for ever! Yet, behind the night,
> Waits for the great unborn, somewhere afar,
> Some white tremendous daybreak. And the light,
> Returning, shall give back the golden hours,
> Ocean a windless level, Earth a lawn
> Spacious and full of sunlit dancing-places,

> And laughter, and music, and, among the flowers,
> The gay child-hearts of men, and the child-faces,
> O heart, in the great dawn!

Brooke's earthly poetry is mostly a nighttime poetry. The gold, the sun, the white dawn—like that in the penultimate chapter of Powys' *Weymouth Sands* (*The Saturnian Quest*, 48) —all lie, except for his experiences in the South Seas, beyond.

"The Little Dog's Day" is an early forecast of his death. After these supreme experiences in the South Seas, he had had his day: on his chosen line, there was little more. He had realized himself on the border where supreme self-enjoyment touches a new dimension, and he knew himself ripe for death. There was, he said, "point in my not getting shot," but "also there's point in my getting shot"; "death might be an admirable solution" (Hassall, 491). The famous war sonnets are less like patriotic trumpetings than paeans in praise of death. As in Sherriff's *Journey's End*, war is simply an elemental power, or death force: the sonnets could be applied, *mutatis mutandis*, to a young German.

The first, "Peace," contrasts the inadequacies of poetry and love with "swimmers into cleanness leaping" and a consequent "release." Only the body will be broken, and Death is both "enemy" and "friend."

In the second, "Safety," war, or death, "knows no power." One will be "safe" whatever happens: "And if these poor limbs die, safest of all." "Poor" registers both Brooke's emotional self-involvement and a recognition of the body's inadequacy.

"The Dead" celebrates "honour" but remains typical in "the rich Dead" who "poured out the red sweet wine of youth." Youth's sacrifice is more than patriotism: Called "holiness," it is a thing in itself, youth's perfect hour.

The fourth, also called "The Dead," remembers how they, as in "The Great Lover," had known the varied sense impressions of earth. "All this is ended." Instead, the glittering wavelets are now frosted to

> a white
> Unbroken glory, a gathered radiance,
> A width, a shining peace, under the night.

Moonlight is assumed, or stars.

In "The Soldier" Brooke concentrates on his body, made by England, after dying. The "heart," now "a pulse in the eternal mind," preserves the sounds and scents of its earthly experience; it is a "rich dust." The impressions are both physical and eternal.

These sonnets necessarily avoid explicit statements on spirit life. The problem of war sacrifice is one mainly of *body* sacrifice, as in Masefield's remarkable quatrain, printed in the *Times*, September 16, 1938, on the occasion of Neville Chamberlain's meeting with Hitler in 1938:

> As Priam to Achilles for his Son,
>   So you into the night, divinely led,
>   To ask that young men's bodies, not yet dead,
> Be given from the battle not begun.

Those lines and Brooke's five sonnets preserve necessary limits.

We now return to the Schell portrait. The mockery it at first received at Cambridge as "obscene" or as "your favourite actress" (Hassall, 390) signals the nature of its importance. It was used as a frontispiece to the 1914 collection of his poems and copied for the Rugby Chapel plaque. It became symbolic: "bare-shouldered, long-haired, Greek god-like, mystic, wonderful," it was "on the retina of the public eye, the soldier poet, the nation's sacrifice" (Richard Usborne, "The Lost Heroes," *Sunday Times Magazine*, pictorial supplement, January 29, 1967) .

What is its secret? The head rising from bare shoulders suggests a totality unconstricted by the mufflings of civilization. The profile of lips and nose, the waves of hair, the upward tilt of the head and eager eyes, are riveting. Its deliberated pose may have seemed "a travesty" of one whose attractions were normally "unconscious," lacking the "candour" of glance his friends knew (Hassall, 390–91) ; but though critics thought the Rugby plaque "sentimental-ized," his mother saw it as the living image of the youth she had loved, and liked its appearance of "pressing forward" (Hassall, 525) .

The upward challenge of its meaning corresponds to Brooke's desire in the early "Second Best" to "meet Death as a friend," "clear-eyed and laughing," and to the use of "lift" in the 1913 poem "The Night Journey," wherein a rushing train symbolizes human destiny:

> Hands and lit faces eddy to a line;
>   The dazed last minutes click; the clamour dies.
> Beyond the great-swung arc o' the roof, divine,
>   Night, smoky-scarv'd, with a thousand coloured eyes

Glares the imperious mystery of the way.
  Thirsty for dark, you feel the long-limbed train
Throb, stretch, thrill motion, slide, pull out and sway,
  Strain for the far, pause, draw to strength again . . .

As a man, caught by some great hour, will rise,
  Slow-limbed, to meet the light or find his love;
And breathing long, with staring sightless eyes,
  Hands out, head back, agape and silent, move

Sure as a flood, smooth as a vast wind blowing;
  And, gathering power and purpose as he goes,
Unstumbling, unreluctant, strong, unknowing,
  Borne by a will not his, that lifts, that grows,

Sweep out to darkness, triumphing in his goal,
  Out of the fire, out of the little room . . .
—There is an end appointed, O my soul!
  Crimson and green the signals burn; the gloom

Is hung with steam's far-blowing livid streamers.
  Lost into God, lights in light, we fly,
Grown one with will, end-drunken huddled dreamers.
  The white lights roar. The sounds of the world die.

And lips and laughter are forgotten things.
  Speed sharpens; grows. Into the night, and on,
The strength and splendour of our purpose swings,
  The lamps fade; and the stars. We are alone.

Compulsion that "lifts"; the darkness; the white lights roaring, sound and sight one in the new dimension; the intoxicating purpose and the conclusion on "alone"—here is Brooke's total metaphysic, nobly stated.

The Schell portrait is, in its quiet way, a statement of this empowered message. It shows, necessarily, nothing of the blood radiance or red-gold hair which Brooke's friends knew. The definition is faint, a shadow kills the head's outline at the nape, and the far shoulder is lost in light. The dominating effect is of whiteness, as of a spirit body, its nakedness that of the "naked seraph" of Shelley's additional lines to "Epipsychidion" or the "immortal nakedness" of the young Caponsacchi's ecstatic sacrifice in Browning's *The Ring and the Book* (VI, 971). Some lines of Brooke's 1908 "Choriambics II" were prophetic:

Somewhere lay, as a child sleeping, a child suddenly reft from
  mirth,

White and wonderful yet, white in your youth, stretched upon
    foreign earth,
God, immortal and dead!

The child, or youth, may seem to sleep, but the seraph awakes,
eager, as in the portrait. "Immortal" yet "dead": death in youth,
and youth in death.

The bare-shouldered portrait was Brooke's own idea. Of it he
wrote:

Nothing's happened: except that my American photographer has sent
me a photograph of me—very shadowy and ethereal and poetic, of me in
profile, and naked—shouldered. Eddie says it's very good. I think it's
rather silly. But anyhow, I don't look like an amateur popular preacher
—as in those others.

And no one will ever be able to put it into an interview, with the words
"We want great serious drama" underneath. [Hassall, 390]

His self-exploitation might, he knew, incur mockery, but at least it
distinguished him from conventional religion and the literary intel-
ligentsia.

Brooke's death was in attunement with his life and thought. It
came as an inevitable, half-willed, instinctive flowering. This does
not detract from the sacrifice but rather raises it to artistic and
universal status. It was not by chance but rather, to quote *Coriola-
nus,* by a certain "sovereignty of nature" that his dying became,
like Byron's, symbolic, and his memorial at Skyros (Hassall, 528)
was well devised by the sculptor Tombros as a nude statue not so
much of Brooke himself as of "a young man symbolizing Youth."

Walter Allen

WALTER ALLEN, *English novelist and critic, professor of English studies in the New University of Ulster, was born in Birmingham, England, in 1911. He is a graduate in English of the University of Birmingham. For most of his adult life he has been a free-lance writer. His novels include* Innocence Is Drowned, Blind Man's Ditch, Rogue Elephant, Dead Man over All [Square Peg *in the United States*], *and* All in a Lifetime (Three Score and Ten *in the United States*). *His critical books,* The English Novel: A Short Critical History *and* Tradition and Dream (The Modern Novel *in the United States*) *are familiar to students of English and American literature throughout the world. He has also written critical biographies of Arnold Bennett and George Eliot. As a literary journalist and a book reviewer, he has contributed to most of the leading British literary periodicals. For many years he was closely associated with the* New Statesman *and for a time was its literary editor. He now reviews books for the London* Daily Telegraph *and is a frequent contributor to the* New York Times Book Review. *He says that he has lost count of the number of times he has broadcast on literary subjects on the BBC's internal and external services.*

He has visited the United States on several occasions and has been a visiting Professor of English at, among others, Vassar College, the University of Kansas, and the University of Washington. His main interest now is in American literature.

Married, with four children, he now divides his time between Northern Ireland and London, the only place in the world in which he would wish to live permanently, though, failing London, he would put up with New York.

A LITERARY AFTERMATH

IT CANNOT be merely the persistence of habit that prompts us, after fifty years and the experience of another war more widely ranging, more devastating, and more terrifying in its cruelty and barbarity, still to think of the war of 1914–18 as the Great War. Initially, perhaps, the phrase records the sense of awe with which the British, at any rate, contemplated what for them was the sudden and almost incredible end of a hundred years of peace. It had not, of course, been a century of total peace, but the wars the British had known at firsthand during the period, in the Crimea, in India, in South Africa, had been peripheral to the lives of most Englishmen, conflicts fought thousands of miles away from Britain by small professional armies. Yet the continued use of the phrase "Great War" must denote something beyond this—the recognition that the war destroyed a relatively stable world and substituted for probable evolutionary development violently revolutionary change, and as we know, the Second World War itself, though not a continuation of the First, was one of its consequences.

For us, it is difficult not to think of the war as one of the catastrophic turning points in history; like the fall of Constantinople, it seems to mark the end of one cycle of history and the beginning of another. Because of this, it appears at first sight strange that the literature it inspired, at least in English, should prove, when the wheat is sifted from the chaff, so small in bulk. Still, there are things to be remembered. It was not until more than fifty years after the French invasion of Russia that *War and Peace* appeared and almost a hundred years after the end of the Napoleonic threat to England that *The Dynasts* was published. It may be significant that Tolstoy and Hardy were born years after the events they describe.

Then, too, most of the best writers in English of our time did not fight in the war. "The lives of us all," Eliot remarks in his introduction to David Jones' *In Parenthesis*—the "all" meaning himself, Joyce, and Pound, but he might have added Yeats, Lawrence, and Forster as well—"were altered by that war, but David Jones is the only one to have fought in it." In a general sense this must be true, as it was true for everyone who lived through the period, whether as soldier or civilian. It is possible to doubt whether *Ulysses* and *Finnegans Wake* would have been much different from what they are had there been no war, but the effect on Pound is plain for all to see in the *Mauberley* poems, while *The Waste Land* is a typical product of the bitter disillusionment that was the immediate aftermath of the war, though it is also much more. To discover how the war impinged on Lawrence, for whom it was the final degrading triumph of industrialism, one has only to read *Kangaroo*.

So, it is tempting to say, the best writers of the time were not there. But that, as David Jones' title *In Parenthesis* reminds us, is too easy. One meaning of the title Jones explains in his preface: ". . . for us amateur soldiers (and especially for the author, who was not only amateur, but grotesquely incompetent, a knocker-over of piles, a parade's despair) the war itself was a parenthesis—how glad we thought we were to step outside its brackets at the end of '18. . . ." This must have been true for hundreds of thousands, no doubt the majority, of soldiers. J. B. Priestley confirms it. He joined the Army in September, 1914, aged nineteen, and spent the next four and a half years in it, mostly in the front line or not far from it. More than forty years later, we find him saying in his reminiscences, *Margin Released:*

There are those—and Hemingway may stand for many writers—who found in war, however much they hated it, the deeper reality we all look for. . . . And almost all these men . . . seemed to feel more confused and unhappy as the war receded, as if they felt they were drifting away from reality, as if a world with its guns silenced was an uneasy dream. To this class, neither inferior nor superior but different, I never belonged. The dream for me began when the guns roared. Except at certain rare moments, and these were far outnumbered by their peacetime counterparts, I did not discover any deeper reality in war. . . . Its obvious one-sidedness soon made it seem to me a vast piece of imbecility.

For Priestley the war was essentially an affair in parenthesis, a boring, though nightmarish, interruption of real life.

But there were also those for whom the war was not an affair in parenthesis but a dead stop. Writing on the literature of the Great War, inevitably today one thinks first of Wilfred Owen, killed on the eve of the Armistice at the age of twenty-five, of Isaac Rosenberg, killed at twenty-eight, of Charles Hamilton Sorley, killed at twenty. Speculation about what they might have done had they survived is futile; they were the best of the poets who wrote, as it were, straight from the front. For them no recollection of emotion in tranquillity was possible; they wrote, it still seems as one reads them, in the white heat of the experience itself; and Owen especially has conditioned the thinking on war of all who read him at an impressionable age. As for Sorley, he was given scarcely time enough before he died to do anything at all, but the handful of poems he did write, together with his letters, reveals an astonishingly tough and mature mind that must, one feels, have been capable of enduring work.

But these were not the only deaths. It has become a cliché to say that the best of a generation of Englishmen were wiped out in the years 1914–18. It is a little too easy and emotional. Excellent men in all walks of life survived. Nevertheless, the country lost thousands of talented young men, and among them there must have been many who would have become good writers and some who might have been great. The slaughter itself is one reason why the writing that came out of the war is less in quality and in quantity than, on the surface, might have been expected.

It was not until the last years of the twenties, ten years after the war's ending, that war books—novels, autobiographies, reminiscences—suddenly appeared in spate, more or less simultaneously from all the major combatant countries except Russia. It was as though a dam had burst, a dam of repression, imposed by common consent, on all memories of the war. The first breach in the dam was made by Arnold Zweig's *Case of Sergeant Grischa* in 1927. It was followed in the next year by Remarque's *All Quiet on the Western Front,* Edmund Blunden's *Undertones of War,* and Robert Graves' *Goodbye to All That.* Richard Aldington's *Death of a Hero* and Hemingway's *A Farewell to Arms* appeared in 1929, and Siegfried Sassoon's *Memoirs of an Infantry Officer* a year later. The spate became a trickle in the years that followed but even now has not yet quite died away. War books, products of personal experience of the Great War, still appear. There is Henry Williamson's *roman fleuve, A Chronicle of Ancient Sunlight,* of which five volumes, the last being published in 1960, are devoted to the hero's experience of war. Inadequate as novels as these books seem to me, they are still impressive as what appears to be an act of total recall of one man's life as a soldier. Even as recently as 1962 yet another important book, Gerald Brenan's autobiography, *A Life of One's Own,* appeared; the last two chapters can be compared only with the war chapters of *Goodbye to All That.*

From Zweig's onward, these books I have mentioned were works of prose: Time had to pass before the perspective necessary for prose, whether in fiction or autobiography, could be gained. The only work of value that has lasted from the war years themselves is lyric poetry. Here the great names are Owen, Rosenberg, and Sassoon. I have listed them in what seems to me the order of their poetic achievement, but Sassoon was the first of them to appear and, immediately, the most effective. He was also the only one of the three to survive the war, and its effect on him seems typical of that of many other writers who survived, for example, Graves, Blunden, Herbert Read, Wyndham Lewis, and perhaps Hemingway in the United States, all writers of distinction in their various fields whose achievements still seem conditioned by their war experience, which for them had the quality of a trauma to be lived through again and again before release was possible. And perhaps it has proved wholly possible for only one of them, Robert Graves, who has found something like salvation in his worship of the White Goddess.

In a sense, Sassoon remains the standard of reference by which one judges the other British writers of the war and their achievements. He was the first British soldier-poet to capture public attention as the opponent of the war. He was the first to expose its miseries, and the attitude he expressed toward it in his verse he translated into actuality, so that for a time, until he was persuaded otherwise by Graves and W. H. R. Rivers, the medical psychologist who was so great an influence on both poets, he even opted out of the war, committing an act of private rebellion that might have been construed as mutiny. The record, in fact, is anything but crystal clear. There can be no doubt that the Sherston trilogy, which consists of *Memoirs of a Fox-Hunting Man, Memoirs of an Infantry Officer*, and *Sherston's Progress*, is artistically much superior to the three volumes of straight autobiography that followed a decade later as more or less a gloss on the earlier books. *The Memoirs of George Sherston* is already an English classic, containing, as it does, some of the best accounts of fox hunting, steeplechasing, village cricket, and trench warfare that we have. But it does at crucial points fall, at times disastrously, between autobiography and fiction. Sherston is only one side of Sassoon; he is, so to say, Sassoon minus the poet, and it is that which makes his behavior in the later pages of *Memoirs of an Infantry Officer* incomprehensible.

Sassoon joined the Army as a private soldier in September, 1914, at the age of twenty-eight, several years older than Owen, Graves, Blunden, and Herbert Read, who joined as little more than schoolboys, and, indeed, a year older than Rupert Brooke. Though he had nothing like Brooke's reputation, he had published one book of verse by the time he joined up, and he was the friend of such figures of the Literary Establishment as Edmund Gosse and Eddie Marsh.

He was, in other words, much more than the amiable young fox-hunting cricketer that is George Sherston as we first meet him. As his early war poems, some of which were published in the London *Times,* show, he went to the war in much the same spirit of idealistic patriotism as Brooke. He was commissioned as an officer and proved himself an extraordinarily brave man; he won the highest honor but one for courage in action and, as Graves tells us in *Goodbye to All That,* was known as "Mad Jack." Then, already famous as the protesting war poet, he signed, under the influence of Bertrand Russell, a separate peace. He publicly denounced the war. Later—the British Establishment has never exhibited its qualities of tact and skill, its capacity for assimilating alien bodies, more strikingly than in its treatment of Sassoon—he returned to the war and the trenches. His gesture was at once noble and futile—and the logical consequence of his poems.

They are not, the poems of *The Old Huntsman* and *Counter Attack,* great poems. They are crude and immediate, and it is here that their power, which seems to me still great, resides:

> I'd like to see a Tank come down the stalls,
> Lurching to rag-time tunes, or "Home, sweet home,"
> And there'd be no more jokes in Music-halls
> To mock the riddled corpses round Bapaume.

What we have, immediately transcribed, almost without pause for reflection, is the impact of the war on lacerated nerves. Sassoon's response to trench warfare and its horrors, though not conceived in intellectual terms, is generous and disinterested. These are not egotistical poems; they are the poems of a man responsible for the lives of others, who has made himself the spokesman of the inarticulate. Chesterton has a line: "We are the people of England, who have not spoken yet." Through Sassoon, part of that silent England, the part that served in the trenches in the P.B.I.—the Poor Bloody Infantry—spoke.

In Sassoon's verse, the poetry, to adapt Owen's famous phrase, is the indignation, and it survives. Better, no doubt, that the poetry should be the pity, as it was with Owen. Owen's poetry, which is rooted in trench warfare as fully as Sassoon's, is the more universal because compassion is there as well as indignation. Lines such as:

> Move him into the sun—
> Gently its touch awoke him once,
> At home, whispering of fields unsown,
> Always it woke him, even in France,

Until this morning and this snow.
If anything might rouse him now
The kind old sun will know.

Think how it wakes the seeds,—
Woke, once, the clays of a cold star.
Are limbs, so dear-achieved, are sides,
Full-nerved—still warm—too hard to stir?
Was it for this the clay grew tall?
—O what made fatuous sunbeams toil
To break earth's sleep at all?

have a quality beyond Sassoon, a quality that comes from Owen's ability to stand back from his subject and see it *sub specie aeternitatis*. And this is associated with, perhaps is even in part the product of, a much greater command of poetic techniques than Sassoon ever had. Owen was the greater poet partly because he devised the medium—conspicuously, the use of assonance and half rhyme—fitting to his subject matter, though this should still not tempt us to minimize the achievement of Sassoon.

It seems clear now that one important factor that influenced writers' attitudes toward the war was the age at which they entered it, and age implies experience of life. Isaac Rosenberg is a case in point. Younger than Sassoon, older than Owen, his experience had been very different from theirs. He was from the working class, had left school at fourteen and become a painter. He was a Jew who had, one feels, not become assimilated into traditional English life as Sassoon had. As Bernard Bergonzi has noted in his valuable study of the English literature of the war, *Heroes' Twilight*, Rosenberg's working-class background, which was mainly Cockney, meant that he had "no English pastoral nostalgia to set against front-line experience." Moreover, when he returned from South Africa to join the Army in 1915, he was inspired by no such patriotic impulses as fired Brooke and Sassoon. He strikes a down-to-earth, working-class note in a letter in which he writes, "I thought if I'd join there would be the separation allowance for my mother." Killed in 1918, he remained throughout his service a private soldier, in contradistinction to Sassoon, Owen, Graves, Blunden, and Herbert Read. To that extent, he had it "cushy," to use the slang word of the P.B.I. that reechoes through the writings of the war, meaning something like not too bad or bearable and a notable example of what is called Anglo-Saxon understatement.

This is not to say that the private soldier's lot was a comfortable one; once behind the lines his material condition was much worse than the junior officer's. But at any rate he was spared the burden of responsibility for men under him that was the junior officer's. As we know it from its literature, from Sassoon, Owen, Graves, the Great War was largely a junior officer's war. But if only because he who is down need fear no fall, the private soldier could be his own man as the officer could not be, as Frederic Manning's *Her Privates We* seems to suggest. So that Rosenberg in his poems is detached from his material, as the officer-poets, who were mostly younger than he, were not. He was helped here, perhaps, by his training as a painter; his attitude toward the scenes of war is partly esthetic; they exist in a sharp and sure perspective that is impersonal. It would be both futile and small-minded to attempt to set off Rosenberg's achievement against Owen's; but it is very difficult to imagine the kind of poetry Owen would have gone on to write if he had lived, since so much of what we have is the lyrical response to immediate experience, whereas Rosenberg's verse, one feels, was the response to war of a man who was already mature, formed and set, as it were, before he went to the war.

In this he resembles a much older writer, Ford Madox Ford, who volunteered for the Army when he was forty-two. He was, of course, already very well known as a novelist, poet, and editor, the intimate, for longer or shorter periods, of men such as James, Conrad, Stephen Crane, and Wells. He recorded what one assumes to be his own war experience through the character of Tietjens in his *Parade's End* sequence of novels. He cannot be said to have had a "good war," to use the phrase of a later one. He was not long in the trenches, but long enough to be gassed and shell-shocked, and he did not hit it off with his superior officers. His military career, indeed, reflected remarkably the pattern of his civilian life; rightly or wrongly, he was a man toward whom the usual English reaction was suspicion and distrust, so much so that even now his reputation as a novelist is smaller in Britain than in the United States. There is irony here, for whatever else Ford may have been, he was certainly a patriotic Englishman. It is in *Parade's End* that both his patriotism and his notion of Englishness, which I must admit seems to me largely a sentimental dream, come together.

Parade's End is only incidentally a war novel. Primarily, it is Ford's dramatization of the breakup of the Edwardian era, of the degeneration of a ruling class. Seen from this point of view, the war, one cannot help feeling, came as a godsend to Ford: it proved his point. His hero, Tietjens, is done down by those who control the running of the war exactly as he is done down by their counterparts in civil life. There is a critical problem here. Tietjens was the final and most complete version of what may be called the Ford man. Whatever his name, whether Moffatt in *The Benefactor*, Ashburnham in *The Good Soldier*, Tietjens in *Parade's End*, he is the English gentleman, sometimes called the Tory, who does his duty regardless of consequences and who is done down precisely because of this. The problem is one that can be solved only by reference to Ford's own life; it seems plain that Ford saw himself as just such a man. The character, in other words, is a projection of his own paranoia. But this, though it may raise questions about *Parade's End* as a whole, does not invalidate the treatment of the war in the novel. In his impressionistically vivid style Ford renders the scene of Flanders brilliantly, and the picture is the more impressive because it is the work of a man who in a sense was an incurable civilian, already middle-aged, able to compare and contrast the war with the years of peace, the "summer afternoon" of Edwardian England, and to see the war as the consequence of those years of peace.

In Ford's sequence there is no nostalgia for the past, for the years of peace. The war is necessary almost to the conception of Tietjens; it is part of the "lasting tribulation"—Ford's words—that he must endure. In this absence of nostalgia Ford differs sharply from most of the poets, who were men in many instances more than twenty years younger. In Owen and Sassoon alike, nostalgia alternates with indignation; *Memoirs of a Fox-Hunting Man* in particular is a loving celebration of the "summer afternoon" of Edwardian England. In Edmund Blunden's poetry, as in his prose work *Undertones of War*, the horrors of the trenches are counterpointed against memories, almost visions, of a pastoral England. The title of one of Graves' wartime volumes, *Fairies and Fusiliers*, indicates the conflict in the poet's mind at the time. He was, as we know from *The Memoirs of George Sherston*, in which he appears as David Cromlech, a singularly tough, efficient, almost arrogantly self-confident and courageous officer; but the verse he was writing, based on nursery rhymes and ballads and with obvious affinities to the poetry of Walter de la Mare, seems now a wistful dream of childish innocence and arcadian simplicity. In the years immediately after the war, when he was much preoccupied with theories of depth psychology and was using the writing of verse as a kind of self-therapy, his poetry deepened and became darker. The simple wish-fulfillment dreams turn into nightmare. This period ended with the writing of his autobiography, *Goodbye to All That*, one of the great autobiographies, the most complete account we have of a young poet at war, a poet whose complexities include a pride in the soldierly virtues and in the traditions of his regiment. It is the self-portrait of a remarkable man characterized by what one is tempted to call a crotchety integrity and an independence that have allowed him to go his own way regardless of praise, neglect, and changes in literary fashion and to write probably more good poems than any other living poet writing in English, poems that, however traditional they may seem at first glance, are wholly original.

So far the writing we have looked at, with the partial exception of Rosenberg's, is the literature of personal response, almost of the private agony. Its value largely consists in this, but all the same one asks for something else as well, for the synoptic view as we find it in Tolstoy's and Hardy's renderings of the Napoleonic campaigns. Owen seems to have been working toward something like this in the months before he was killed, especially in his poem "Strange Meeting," in which, as Bergonzi has said, a "double vision" is imposed on the reader. Two works there are, possibly three, that attempt a synoptic vision, that attempt to speak not for one man, a single individual, but generically. They are Frederic Manning's novel *Her Privates We,* David Jones' *In Parenthesis*, a work that defies categories but may best be read as a long poem in a form related to *The Waste Land* and Pound's *Cantos*, and, more dubiously, Herbert Read's poem "The End of the War." I say "more dubiously" because I find it lacking in a certain quality of sensuousness, magic, unexpectedness, that for me is essential to poetry. Having said this, I must also say that it is greatly admired by better critics than I, critics who are themselves fine poets. Allen Tate has called it "a great poem on a great subject: the impact on the contemplative mind of universal violence, whether the violence be natural or man-made." I find the poem cold and abstract; even so, I recognize the nobility of Read's intention and the high seriousness of the work. His prose piece "In Retreat" is certainly one of the best descriptions of one aspect of the war that we have, the more moving because of its objectivity.

I think there can be no such reservations about *Her Privates We* and *In Parenthesis*. Manning's novel was published in 1930. Manning himself died five years later, a somewhat mysterious figure who had been writing since 1910, a more or less wealthy Australian who, as his early verse shows, had come under the influence of Pound. *Her Privates We* seems to me the best of the English war novels and to possess enduring merit. The central character is named Bourne; we are not told his Christian name or anything about his antecedents. He is wealthy: he is a connoisseur of wine and gets food parcels from Fortnum & Mason. He is not—and this is important—an officer, but a private soldier, though at the end of the novel he has submitted to the pressure brought upon him to take a commission. He is a very accomplished private soldier; he can scrounge—the Second War's word for it was "liberate"—with the best. His position as a rich man in the ranks is ambiguous, but he becomes the leader of a small group of very tough privates with whom in peacetime he could have had almost no conceivable contact. One of the themes of the novel is comradeship, which, Manning makes clear, is not the same as friendship, but something more impersonal and in some ways closer. *Her Privates We* is not an antiwar novel; rather, war is seen as life heightened, intensified; as Bourne reflects: "Life was a hazard enveloped in a mystery, and war quickened the sense of both in men: the soldier also, as well as the saint, might write his tractate *de contemptu mundi*, and differ from him only in the angle and spirit from which he surveyed the same bleak reality."

Her Privates We, then, is not a personal cry of anguish, indignation, or pity. It is a very impersonal novel, and the impersonality seems stressed by the fact that we never know the hero's Christian name; whether there is symbolic intention in his surname I do not pretend to know. The impersonality, which is bound up with a striving for universality, is reinforced by the references implicit in the structure of the book. The title is from *Hamlet*, and the mottoes affixed to the chapters are also from Shakespeare. As one reads, one feels more and more that the novel is rooted in Shakespeare, though I think one would search in vain for any correspondence between Manning's characters and those in the plays. The closest parallel is with *Henry V*. One chapter seems quite certainly based on Act IV, Scene 1, in which the King, incognito, talks to the private soldiers Bates, Court, and Williams on the eve of Agincourt, though there is one essential difference between Manning and Shakespeare: in Manning the King, or any equivalent of him, is missing.

Nevertheless, the Shakespearean echoes provide a frame of reference that compels us to look at the Great War in a long perspective of time, to see the war in the context of English history, and this Manning succeeds in doing, while at the same time rendering the very feel of trench life as experienced by the private soldier, the man without privileges on whom, ultimately, everything depends. And he does this in part through the extreme vividness of his realization of individual private soldiers, of, for example, the half-Caliban figure of "Weeper" Smart, one of the most memorable and challenging minor figures in modern fiction.

In Parenthesis, as I have suggested, is probably best approached as a work with a general affinity to both *The Waste Land* and *Cantos*. It is not presented formally as a poem, though punctuation and typography are used, as Jones says, "to indicate some change of tone, inflexion, or emphasis." Its initial difficulty, like that of Eliot's and Pound's poems, is that it demands of the reader knowledge, in the way of allusion and mythology, that he cannot be expected automatically to have. The matter of ancient Welsh poetry is one of Jones' constant references. Jones is liberal with his notes, and the poem is much less difficult than it might otherwise have been because of the author's view of the British, whom he sees as at once Celtic and Anglo-Saxon. In his preface he tells us that his companions in the war were mostly Londoners, together with some Welshmen. "Together they bore in their bodies the genuine tradition of the Island of Britain, from Bendigeid Vran to Jingle and Marie Lloyd. These were the children of Doll Tearsheet. Those are before Caractacus was. . . . It was curious to know them harnessed together, and together caught in the toils of 'good order and military discipline.' "

The Cockney elements in the poem, along with the recurring echoes of *Henry V*, seem to me an essential factor in the success of *In Parenthesis*. They peg down and give immediate actuality to the older, more esoteric matter on which the work is based, the world of Welsh legend and Malory's *Le Morte d'Arthur*. And in Jones these juxtapositions between past and present, between medieval myth and grimy reality, work toward a quite different end from the comparable juxtapositions in *The Waste Land*. Neither intent nor effect is satirical. Past and present are fused into one, as is suggested by the name, John Ball, that Jones gives to the private soldier who is at the center of the action.

The result is a poem that may be taken as an expression of a whole people throughout their history, but focused in one specific episode of that history, the Great War. Nothing is burked; there is no palliation of the horrors of war; yet the poem exists in a strange beauty, even in a serenity, which comes in part, it is difficult not to think, from Jones' Catholicism, his habit of seeing his immediate subject, the Great War, *sub specie aeternitatis*. There is a simple instance of this in the preface, in which Jones notes: " . . . the 'Bugger! Bugger!' of a man detailed, had often about it the 'Fiat! Fiat!' of the Saints." Perhaps the last lines of the poem, the final sentence of which is from the *Chanson de Roland*, may be quoted as an instance of its serenity and acceptance as well as of its method:

Lie still under the oak
next to the Jerry
and Sergeant Jerry Coke.
   The feet of the reserves going up tread level
with your forehead; and no word for you; they
                  whisper one with another;

pass on, inward;
these latest succours:
green Kimmerii to bear up the war.

Oeth and Annoeth's hosts they were
who in that night grew
younger men
younger striplings.

The geste says this and the man who was on the field . . .
and who wrote the book . . . the man who does not know
this has not understood anything.

There seems to be an obvious contrast between the English literature of the Great War and the American. The war brought the United States into the world, but its effect on American writers was slight, and different in kind from that on the English. So far as one can tell, Fitzgerald's few months of service in the United States Army was the merest parenthesis in his life. He saw no action, and it seems significant that the Americans we think of as war writers were volunteers in other armies: Faulkner in the Royal Canadian Air Force, Cummings and Dos Passos as ambulance drivers with the French, Hemingway with the Italians. They were fighting somebody else's war, which makes it possible for Hemingway's Frederic Henry in *A Farewell to Arms* to desert and make his separate peace. There is, in other words, an absence of the sense of commitment and obligation. This is strikingly apparent in Dos Passos' *Three Soldiers;* at times while reading it, it is difficult not to think that the author conceives the major tragedy of the war to be the loss of John Andrews' symphony. There is, of course, hatred of the war in Dos Passos' novel, but the deeper hatred is for Army life itself and the restrictions it imposes on individual rights. All of which is merely to say that for Americans the Great War was not the traumatic experience it was for the British. For anything comparable America had to wait for the economic depression of the thirties.

Frederick J. Hoffman

FREDERICK J. HOFFMAN, who died suddenly on December 24, 1967, was born in Port Washington, Wisconsin, on September 21, 1909, and was educated at Stanford, Minnesota, and Ohio State universities. He taught at the universities of Ohio State, Oklahoma, Wisconsin (at Madison), California (at Riverside), Harvard, Stanford, Washington, and Duke before joining the University of Wisconsin (at Milwaukee) faculty in September, 1965, as distinguished professor of English.

He was the author of more than 300 articles and reviews and more than 20 books, some of which were translated into other languages. His most well-known volume, The Mortal No (1964), attempts, in the words of one critic, "a redefinition of modern literature in terms of a new set of metaphors, concerned with the intruding presence of the secular in the midst of the religious, of the spatial in the midst of the temporal, of the decorous in the midst of the violent." The theme of violence in modern literature, as well as the theme of death, is seen in The Mortal No as being significantly affected by the events of World War I and the postwar temper.

In works like Freudianism and the Literary Mind (1945), The Modern Novel in America (1951), The Twenties (1955), and Samuel Beckett: The Language of Self (1962), he was to elaborate on his belief that literature "helps us to see the reality of any idea in a full, clear, and meaningful form; the form is the matter, the matter is in the form, and the reality which is thus formally given is a moral and aesthetic anecdote of one or another aspect of the time."

THE NOVEL OF WORLD WAR I:
A DOCUMENT IN THE
HISTORY OF SURPRISE

IF THERE is a major fact of the war novel of World War I, it has to do with the rude contrast between expectations and reality. Any number of adjustments had to be made to the immense acceleration of violence since the Franco-Prussian War of the 1870's and to the shock of discovering that this was no longer either a "gentleman's war" or a war in which the assailant and the victim had a clear view of each other.[1] The sense of outrage which followed upon a too naïve set of determinations and propaganda enterprises that were much more successful than their agents dreamed was interpreted in many ways. Of course, there were novels which preached the Great Crusade (Edith Wharton's, Dorothy Canfield Fisher's, Arthur Train's), but these are rather crude efforts to retain a tradition that had already been running down in the late nineteenth century.

It is possible to measure the energy of the postwar novel in terms of a calculus of violence and of its relation to rhetoric.[2] At its simplest, we can only say that the propaganda preceding the entrance of the United States into the war was very erratic and that the consequences for literature were quite explicit. It was not just a matter of disillusion; as a number of novelists asserted (Thomas Boyd, E. E. Cummings, and Ernest Hemingway among them), there was a violent disruption of the conventional and traditional ways of defining man and his moral responsibilities. In one of my attempts to describe this situation, I suggested following the lead of Kenneth Burke, in *Counter-Statement* (1931), in his definitions of violence and the mitigating effects of "eloquence":

. . . The purpose of eloquence is to direct the reader's attention away from fact, or to link fact with one or several of the systems of larger

---

[1] A recent book by Stanley Cooperman, *World War I and the American Novel* (Baltimore, 1967), is perhaps the best book on its subject. Especially relevant to the war's backgrounds are Parts I and II, pp. 3–125.

[2] This I have tried to do in several parts of *The Mortal No: Death and the Modern Imagination* (Princeton, 1964), and I depend much upon that book for this essay. The two are, however, quite separate from each other.

meaning which in any period circumscribe fact. Eloquence also acts to slow the rhythm of factual succession. . . . The more intensely violent fact becomes, the more solicitous is eloquence to mitigate its intensity.

A related problem is that of the pace of experience. Eloquence funcions to moderate the pace, by interjecting matters that are only relatively pertinent to fact. This function is most successful in circumstances that are not in themselves shocking, though they may be profoundly disturbing. . . . [*The Mortal No,* pp. 158–62.]

As Stanley Cooperman has so accurately pointed out, there was a vast difference between local heroics and the "filth of no man's land." (*World War I and the American Novel,* p. 33.) The rhetoric of prowar propagandists sounded a refrain that must have sickened the air; it had little or no recognizable relation to the war's reality. The shock of discovery led to a form of postwar nominalism, signalized by Lieutenant Frederic Henry's thoughts, after his return to the front from the hospital in Milan. These famous remarks deserve at least one more repetition because they are so representative of the postwar decade:

I was always embarrassed by the words sacred, glorious, and sacrifice and the expression in vain. We had heard them, sometimes standing in the rain almost out of earshot, so that only the shouted words came through, and had read them, on proclamations that were slapped up by billposters over other proclamations, now for a long time, and I had seen nothing sacred, and the things that were glorious had no glory and the sacrifices were like the stockyards at Chicago if nothing was done with the meat except to bury it. . . . Abstract words were obscene beside the concrete names of villages, the numbers of roads, the names of rivers, the numbers of regiments and the dates. [*A Farewell to Arms,* p. 196.]

These reflections fit so well into a pattern that it is as though they had been machine-tooled. Henry begins his participation in the war on the Italian front equipped with the usual illusions and expectations. He is not sure just why he is at the front at all. And he almost passively lets the war experience happen to him. He obeys orders, to the point when they no longer make any sense to him. Having submitted to a depersonalized machine, whose closest approximation to reality is its frequent accesses to confusion, he has gradually to disembarrass himself of the war world and to reassert himself, as individual man, lover, husband, father. All these last roles are apparently out of place in a condition of war, so Henry has to remove himself via a "separate peace," to a world in which the sound of the war is remote. We must note that Hemingway's novel was published in 1929, after a full decade of looking back at the events which are its setting. Hemingway deliberately set up his soldier as the man open to influences, not yet educated or firmly convinced regarding the justice of any acts or rhetorics. Henry is, nevertheless, of a group of American heroes (his immediate predecessor was probably Huckleberry Finn) who seem to have an instinctive sense of justice, a cautionary view of imbalances, and a proper view of what is wrong and right. So that he acts as a gauge of morality and has a basic moral sense.

There are two facts of the war that disturb him: The violence of it overwhelms all attempts to understand it rationally, and, of course, there is a point at which people behave irrationally in it. Henry's wound is perhaps symbolic of all the meretricious violence of the war. He is eating cheese and drinking wine when it happens, and it is least expected when it does: "There was a flash, as when a blast-furnace door is swung open, and a roar that started white and went red and on and on in a rushing wind. . . . I went out swiftly, all of myself, and I knew I was dead and that it had all been a mistake to think you just died. Then I floated, and instead of going on I felt myself slide back." (*Arms*, p. 58.) The unexpected, sudden violence and the fact that Henry was not "face to face" with his assailant are facts of the modern violent situation. As for the irrationality of the war scene, he encounters that later, during and at the end of the retreat from Caporetto, when the behavior of men toward one another could not be explained on any rational level. At the inquisition before the Tagliamento River the Italian military police "had the beautiful detachment and devotion to stern justice of men dealing in death without being in any danger of it." (Pp. 240–241.)

To these irrationalities, Henry opposes the love of Catherine Barkley, an English nurse who has already lost one lover in the war. The love begins in the sullen and tawdry world of the house of prostitution: Catherine, at least, is better than the girls in the brothel. Both of them accept it at first as "a rotten game we play." (P. 32.) But it becomes much more than that—in fact, a genuine assertion of his humanity and his manhood, in an inhuman situation. There are times when he even considers the affair close to being religious, in the presence of Count Greffi and of the priest. Mainly, the love for Catherine Barkley becomes a romantic affirmation in the midst of impersonal calamity. As such, it is doomed. It is true that the affair superficially turns out to be a biological "trap" and that success or failure in the maternity hospital represents the margin of loss. Yet the affair and the pregnancy are in themselves assertions of the humane in defiance of war. The margin is great between the girls in the house provided as an accommodation for the officers (they are, in the movements about the war scene, parts of the "baggage") and the figure of Catherine, dedicated wholly to her man ("There isn't any me any more." P. 113). In the end, however, the affair has turned out to be a gamble, and a losing one. Henry walks out of the Swiss hospital in the rain back to his hotel. His physical and sexual assertions have not prevailed. In the true economy of Hemingway's work, as Malcolm Cowley has said, the Lieutenant Henry of *Arms* walks away from the hospital to become the Jake Barnes of *The Sun Also Rises*. The affair has from the beginning been disturbed by its setting. Both Henry and Catherine have had trouble avoiding the atmosphere of casual prostitution, simply because *all* evidence of permanence is out of order in the war scene. On the evening of his departure from Milan, they rent a hotel room which has all the appearance and the trappings of a lavish and expensive whorehouse.

I went to the window and looked out, then pulled a cord that shut the thick plush curtains. Catherine was sitting on the bed, looking at the cut glass chandelier. She had taken her hat off and her hair shone under the light. She saw herself in one of the mirrors, and put her hands to her hair. I saw her in three other mirrors. She did not look happy. She let her cape fall on the bed.
"What's the matter, darling?"
"I never felt like a whore before," she said. I went over to the window and pulled the curtain aside and looked out. I had not thought it would be like this.
"You're not a whore."
"I know it, darling. But it isn't nice to feel like one." Her voice was dry and flat.

The real meaning of this and several other scenes is that the war scene, as Henry once put it, is not for virgins. It is not, in brief, the place for responsible behavior. The violence, the suddenness and unseemliness of death, the furtive nature of catch-as-catch-can pleasures—all militate against anything that may remotely be called normal. Hemingway's favorite image for this idea is that of the confusion of the retreat, when all semblance of normal human relationships are thrown into imbalance: "In the night many peasants had joined the columns from the roads of the country and in the column there were carts loaded with household goods; there were mirrors projecting up between mattresses, and chickens and ducks tied to carts. There was a sewing machine on the cart ahead of us in the rain." (P. 211.) The most familiar objects are piled in a helter-skelter, absurd arrangement, suggesting a hasty retreat before the threat of violence.

The violent upheaval had different meanings for the nationalities engaged in the hostilities. The Americans were likely to be the more shocked, because the less emotionally prepared. As Stanley Cooperman has said, "After the revolution-in-morals of the 1920's, it is not always easy to remember that the soldiers setting out in 1917 were leaving what was an essentially puritan, Victorian society, modified by frontier-developed emphasis on the virtues of righteous struggle, for a world in which every standard seemed torn apart." (P. 43.) There was variety, of course, in the war fiction, but the best of it usually represented a slide down into the experiencing of mud, filth, and surprise. As a result, the hero of our postwar fiction thought of the war as a devastating criticism of the society that preceded it. The two landscapes, those of war and of peace, continue to amaze, as the following lines from a recent poem by Philip Larkin suggest. The poem is cryptically called "MCMXIV":

> Never such innocence,
> Never before or since
> As changed itself to past
> Without a word—the men
> Leaving the gardens tidy,
> The thousands of marriages
> Lasting a little while longer:
> Never such innocence again. [*Poetry 1967*, p. 19.]

This is by way of retrospect of some fifty or so years. The immediate reaction was often more vivid, as in this portion of Ezra Pound's "Hugh Selwyn Mauberley" (1920) :

> There died a myriad,
> And of the best, among them,
> For an old bitch gone in the teeth,
> For a botched civilization,
>
> Charm, smiling at the good mouth,
> Quick eyes gone under earth's lid,
>
> For two gross of broken statues,
> For a few thousand battered books. [*Selected Poems*, p. 176.]

"It was the entire concept of the proving ground," says Cooperman, "that was broken in World War I; and it was broken violently enough to affect permanently the literature of a generation." (P. 48.)

War as a "proving ground" of heroism, of manliness, and of maturity had apparently disappeared forever. Perhaps the major reason is that force and energy were gradually being put to maximum utility. The American soldiers often found themselves in a war for which they had not prepared themselves, or they were commanded by officers who had learned to fight another kind of war. Friedrich Juenger speaks of the man-made transformation of entire landscapes; at Flanders, for example, "The artillery barrages which had hailed down for weeks had turned this theater of war into a sort of moonscape covered with craters." (*The Failure of Technology,* p. 117.)

In many cases there was an almost absolute loss of decorum, caused by indiscriminate saturation bombing. Pound speaks with bitterness and irony, in another part of his "Hugh Selwyn Mauberley":

> Died some, pro patria,
> 　　　　　　non "dulce" non "et decor" . . .
> walked eye-deep in hell
> believing in old men's lies, then unbelieving
> came home, home to a lie,
> home to many deceits,
> home to old lies and new infamy.

His shock here is obviously the direct result of a disappointment in expectations. But the effect is not only this; it comes from the fact of what Pound calls "wastage as never before." World War I was a war of attrition, on a scale never before seen; men were used (deliberately or aberrantly) as so much matériel against the enemy's force.

It was a violent experience, but there were cases in which it was not unwelcome. Willa Cather's *One of Ours* (1922) portrayed what Cooperman calls the "war drive seething beneath the peaceful surface of American life during these years." (P. 51.) Its hero, Claude Wheeler, is an example of what he calls "the midwesterner reaching for war as a means of achieving what his society simply ruled out as unthinkable (unless for missionary work) : adventure, daring, 'the bright face of danger.' " (P. 52.) In a number of cases the war came, or seemed to have come, as an opportunity to escape tedium; in others, it appeared to be a chance for a quick rise in society, through whatever dynamics it offered. Almost universally, it proved a shock and a disillusionment. Louis-Ferdinand Céline speaks of the war in *Journey to the End of Night* (1934) as follows:

It was an occasion when "everyone queued up to go and get killed."
(P. 26.) This phrase suggests a degree of impersonality almost
unheard of before. The tactics of attrition led to about 10,000,000
casualties. Men were killed without being able to face, even to
identify, their assailants. As Cooperman says, "The man was separated from the act; the potential hero could be—and often was—
splattered by a stray shell under circumstances that had nothing
whatever to do with soldiering." (P. 63.)

The psychology of war literature correspondingly changed, to
adjust to the alterations made in the machinery of war. One of the
most important protective reactions was the abandonment of personal attachment to causes, ideals, principles. The adjustment to
violence almost invariably meant the denial of the self; the pressure
of force was too great for the individual to perform matching
stratagems. The soldier, after having been saturated by abstractions
concerning a heroism that was passé, had almost no genuine recourse when he became involved with reality. Cooperman says that
only 23 percent of the casualties "earned their red badges of
courage in any sort of direct encounter with the Hun." (Pp.
63–64.) The American soldiers did learn about the harsh realities of
mass war, but they were also introduced to the disillusioning truths
of a depersonalized and despiritualized war world. Nothing is more
appalling than the total collapse of cause and reason. The soldier
must readjust quickly and totally to radically new circumstances. In
the trench warfare of World War I especially, he had to imagine
himself in several dangerous positions and to improvise defenses for
them. The consequences are several forms of dislocation, both
physical and psychological. Sequences of events and the interpretations of them change radically. Since death is so frequent, it becomes less a climax of events as a small event itself, as in this case,
the death of Aymo in *Arms*: ". . . We went down the north side of
the embankment. I looked back. Aymo lay in the mud with the
angle of the embankment. He was quite small and his arms were by
his side, his puttee-wrapped legs and muddy boots together, his cap
over his face. He looked very dead. It was raining. I had liked him
as well as any one I ever knew. . . ." (P. 229.)

The full flush of naturalistic stench and filth was recorded in
many of these novels, whose authors for the most part had suddenly
come upon the facts of indiscriminate killing. "Things were getting
all mixed up in his mind," says Humphrey Cobb in *Paths of Glory*
(1935), one of the most popular of World War I novels. "It seemed
to be filled with flesh, cloyed with the sweetish smell of flesh that is
torn open and over which blood is pouring." (P. 31.) In another

place, Cobb describes the scene of death: ". . . a rat climbed noiselessly up the jamb of the gallery entrance and watched Paolacci for a while, then it stepped onto the lieutenant's chest and squatted there. It looked to the right and to the left, two or three times, then lowered its head and began to eat Paolacci's under lip." (P. 48.) In some such way as this, the phenomenon of what Erich Kahler has called the *neue Sachlichkeit* (new factuality) can be illustrated:

. . . Factuality is handled so pointedly that it becomes symbolic; abruptness produces compression. Indeed, this peculiar factuality radiates an atmosphere which reflects the overstrained neutrality of the author—a neutrality that appears like an inversion of all the bitter experiences and disillusionments of the generation. The detachment and self-restraint of the author weighs upon the story like a tense aura, like a ghostly presence of fate. [*The Tower and the Abyss*, p. 99.]

It is obvious that the situation of modern violence required a full measure of *Sachlichkeit*. The central ambiguities of the postwar situation were rhetorical equivalents of the fragments of body and machine strewn about the landscape. Hemingway developed his famous style with close attention to the scene. The scene was itself disjunct, and its design was a ghastly and deadly, but calculated, disarray, directly related to the expenditure of mechanized force within an area. Cooperman speaks of the impact of twentieth-century fire power on the American troops first opposed to it: It "helped produce the combination of absurdity, protest, and numbness which were to become characteristics of the antihero in the post–World War I novel." (P. 73.) The circumstances were almost altogether antiheroic: soldiers being ordered mistakenly into a trap; the errantry of flying objects and parts of bodies; coffins exploding into midair, in effect celebrating the ritual of the funeral a second time; the trench itself taking on the appearances of an open grave. Cooperman quotes with some effectiveness a passage from Theodore Fredenburgh's novel *Soldiers March* (1930):

. . . On all sides lay great holes, half-filled with water. The chalky soil had been churned and rechurned until its vitals were spewed to the surface. Fragments of stained and rotten uniforms projected from the ground. The dirty bones of corpses reached despairingly from the soil that gave them no rest. . . .
On the floor of the valley a sickly stream flowed. Its banks of yellow mud looked slimy and unclean in the sun. As far as the valley continued —a yellow, pestilent muck-heap. [P. 112.]

From this bewildering mass and mess of thoughtless, aimless, aberrant carnage, what conceivable types of hero, or antihero, could emerge? There were the "quiet types" of English gentlemen who seemed at least to die willingly to save their England. But in the best of these there is no denial of the confusion and the desperate world of fighting to no immediately clear purpose. Edmund Blunden's war world is "punctured" a bit, but he is alert to its dangers:

. . . [We] enter Mailly, and turn at the church, still neatly jacketed with straw, but with a new hole or two in it, along a leafy side-road; another turn, and we are between excellent meadow-grounds, which lack only a few fat sheep, an old mole-catcher, and some crows. Groups of shell-holes, however, restrain the fancy from useless excursions, and, sitting under some tall slender elms on a convenient bank for a few minutes' rest, we keep our ears eastwardly attentive. [*Undertones of War*, 1928, pp. 124–25.]

But in American equivalents, the surprise of the soldier was neither contained within gentility nor discounted by illusion. As in *Paths of Glory*, the protest was often leveled against the leadership, which was frequently unprepared and stupid. In a real sense, the "separate peace" of Lieutenant Henry was based on the assumption, as Cooperman puts it, that "the war has deserted him"—that is, that its absurdity and its meaningless violence had in effect deserted any principle or basis according to which he can serve in it any longer. In the American image of him, the soldier "suffers, and is broken and coarsened by a military environment which he never expected and which, in many ways, never expected him." (P. 83.)

Cooperman has a number of ingenious classes of war heroes: the war lover (Willa Cather's *One of Ours;* the phrase is taken from John Hersey's novel about World War II) ; the surprised innocent (Zorn of Fredenburgh's *Soldiers March*) ; the depraved opportunist (Richard Savage of John Dos Passos' *1919*) ; the "Babbitt in Khaki" (James Stevens' *Mattock*) ; the lost souls (Elliot Paul's Irwin and Fuselli of John Dos Passos' *Three Soldiers*) ; the residents of hell (Donald Mahon of Faulkner's *Soldiers' Pay* and William Hicks of Thomas Boyd's *Through the Wheat*) . But for reasons that ought to be obvious, he saves his major analysis for what he calls the anti-heroes of World War I: the narrator of E. E. Cummings' *The Enormous Room,* John Andrews of *Three Soldiers,* and Lieutenant Henry. It is not hard to accept the preference. The last three represent the cry of agonized protest against the irrationalities of an

impossible circumstance. Each of them has, or temporarily enter-
tains, an alternative: Cummings, the quaint, erratic version of the
American underground, called by him the "Delectable Mountains"; Dos Passos' Andrews, art, in a strangely pseudoromantic
antiwar gesture; and Lieutenant Henry, the assertion of virility,
love, and the prospect of fatherhood—in short, a normal "life" as
opposed to the dark night and the shrapnel bursts of the northern
Italian front.

There are many gestures like this, many attempts to rescue the
ego from an incredible landscape destroyed by violence. The major
facts (at least for American authors) have to do with the elements
of surprise in the war scene. Perhaps there is some naïveté in these
demonstrations of shock, as well as in the resulting reactions. But
the shock was genuine, and however naïve the response, it, too, was
genuine. Cummings' love of the little man, the special and unique
"antimostarian" (as he called him in another place), has a special
role in the literature of the 1920's. In the last paragraph of his book,
he describes his sense of a newly found New York City, seen in the
perspective of the small unknown men and women of La Ferté
Macé prison camp:

The tall, impossibly tall, incomparably tall, city shoulderingly upward into hard sunlight leaned a little through the octaves of its parallel
edges, leaningly strode upward into firm hard snowy sunlight; the noises
of America nearingly throbbed with smokes and hurrying dots which are
men and which are women and which are things and curious and hard
and strange and vibrant and immense, lifting with a great ondulous stride
firmly into the immortal sunlight. [*The Enormous Room*, p. 271.]

The fact is that the best American writers prepared for the
twentieth century by rejecting the nineteenth and resenting their
nineteenth-century education into "realities" that were no longer
true or viable. There were fragments of romanticism left: John
Andrews of *Soldiers Three* just isn't quite real to any audience
observing his protest against the world he was thrown into. In
Lieutenant Henry's choice of values, there is a sense of the lavishly
romantic, a pseudometaphysical interpretation of the conjunction
of souls and bodies. But in these and in other interpretations of the
war, there are both realism and wisdom. We have the view of a man
shortly out of a prewar, post-Victorian, still largely puritan world
thrust into a world antithetically opposed to it. More important, he
has been assured that: (1) his cause is just; and (2) Germans cut
off the hands of Belgian infants. The explosion of mistrust, surprise,

and rebellion is comparably strong and violent. These men are antiheroes only in the sense that they cannot conceive of heroism in the altered circumstances. The political and military history of World War I is only on the periphery of the personal history of engagement and disengagement, which is the literary history of this segment of the 1920's. The difference from World War II is enormous. The mechanics of violence are sometimes similar. But in World War II men were sure (almost always) that there was an enemy; they believed, and justly so, their propaganda. In World War I the soldier suffered many surprises, mainly because he had not been sophisticated or aware of the historical circumstances of the war. The major element was surprise. Surprise is in itself the result of a lack of being briefed or it is a consequence of being briefed erroneously. The American soldier withdraws from the primary engagement, declares a separate peace, finds himself in the wrong company, and eventually describes the horrendous results of impersonal warfare in a realistic splurge of shocked acknowledgment. This act appears to be temporary, though it probably has a permanence not initially seen. The reaction to Vietnam in 1967 owes something to Lieutenant Henry's amazement over the sheer absurdity of Caporetto.

J. K. Johnstone

J. K. JOHNSTONE *was born on February 12, 1923, at Ferintosh, Alberta, Canada, where he lived on a farm until 1945. He attended the University of Alberta from 1945 to 1950, receiving his B.A. in 1948 and an M.A. in English literature in 1950. He then studied at the University of Leeds, England, where he received the degree of Ph.D. in English literature in 1952.*

His book The Bloomsbury Group: A Study of E. M. Forster, Lytton Strachey, Virginia Woolf, and Their Circle *was published in London and New York in 1954. He was elected a Fellow of the Royal Society of Literature, London, in 1955.*

He has taught at Mirfield Grammar School, Yorkshire; the College of General Education, Boston University; and the University of New Brunswick. He is now a professor of English at the University of Saskatchewan, Saskatoon.

He is married and has three children. He and his wife led a Boston University summer course in Europe in 1955 and a Nasson College semester abroad in Vienna in 1965. In 1966 he was awarded Canada Council and Nuffield Foundation grants for study in London of the contemporary English novel.

WORLD WAR I AND THE NOVELS OF VIRGINIA WOOLF

IT IS, of course, impossible to measure accurately the effect of World War I on Virginia Woolf's fiction. Yet the effect was stronger than might be expected in the work of a feminine novelist whose main concern was the inner life. The ultimate effect of the war on the individuals who survived it was, however, on the inner life, and Virginia Woolf, to a much greater extent than has been generally recognized, is a chronicler, if not of contemporary events themselves, of what is at least as significant, the effect of contemporary events on individuals.

"Virginia was the least political animal that has lived since Aristotle invented the definition," says her husband, Leonard Woolf, "though," he goes on with cranky, but understandable, hyperbole, "she was not a bit like the Virginia Woolf who appears in many books written by literary critics or autobiographers who did not know her, a frail invalidish lady living in an ivory tower in Bloomsbury and worshipped by a little clique of aesthetes. She was intensely interested in things, people, and events, and, as her new books [after the war] show, highly sensitive to the atmosphere which surrounded her, whether it was personal, social, or historical. She was therefore the last person who could ignore the political menaces under which we all lived."[1]

Virginia Woolf apparently did not anticipate war. "Suddenly, like a chasm in a smooth road," she said, "the war came."[2] Most of her friends, successors to a liberal optimism of the Victorians, though rebels to some other aspects of Victorianism, had buoyant hopes for the future.[3] Maynard Keynes speaks of a belief among his friends of "the Society" at Cambridge, who became Virginia Woolf's friends in Bloomsbury, in "the beginning of a renaissance, the opening of a new heaven on a new earth."[4] Leonard Woolf says, "We found ourselves living in the springtime of a conscious revolt against the social, political, religious, moral, intellectual, and artistic institutions, beliefs, and standards of our fathers and grandfathers. . . . We were out to construct something new; we were in the van of the builders of a new society which should be free, rational, civilized, pursuing truth and beauty. It was tremendously exhilarating."[5] Clive Bell, Virginia Woolf's brother-in-law, planned a book to be entitled *The New Renaissance.* Roger Fry introduced Post-Impressionist paintings to Britain in 1910 and 1912 in two of the liveliest and most significant exhibitions in London's

---

[1] *Downhill All the Way* (London, 1967), p. 27.

[2] "The Leaning Tower," *The Moment and Other Essays* (London, 1947), p. 111.

[3] E. M. Forster, as *Howards End* (London, 1910) makes clear, with its concern about certain aspects of life in contemporary Britain and Germany and its suggestion that force can be "kept in its box" for only brief periods of civilization, was an exception.

[4] *Two Memoirs* (London, 1949), p. 82.

[5] *Sowing* (London, 1960), pp. 160–61.

history and established in 1913 the Omega Workshops to provide employment for young artists and to improve British design. "At last, he felt," Virginia Woolf tells us in her biography of him, "after the hypocrisy of the Victorian age, of which he had many anecdotes drawn from his own past, a time was at hand when a real society was possible. It was to be a society of people of moderate means, a society based upon the old Cambridge ideal of truth and free speaking, but alive, as Cambridge had never been, to the importance of the arts. . . . 'We are at last,' he summed it up, 'becoming a little civilised.' And then of course the war came."[6]

Virginia Woolf and her friends of the Bloomsbury group regarded the war as an unmitigated disaster. It was unsoftened for them by a belief in the popular shibboleths that helped men into battle or by the hope that the catastrophe might accelerate desirable social change.[7] "It destroyed, I think, the bases of European civilization," says Leonard Woolf, looking back on the war in the recently published volume of his autobiography.[8] The mood and tense of the verb have changed; otherwise, the statement might have been made by Leonard Woolf in 1914, expressing, as it does, the disappointed hopes of a Fabian who had looked forward to peaceful, rational social evolution and of an artist, or rather, of a man in close association with artists, who valued art of the past. "I hoped never to see this mad destruction of all that really counts in life," said Roger Fry in that first year of the war. "We were just beginning to be a little civilised and now it's all to begin over again."[9] Though to superficial contemporary observers the social attitudes of the Bloomsbury group and the works of art of its members sometimes seemed revolutionary, its background was Victorian liberalism,[10] and unlike T. E. Hulme, who found the war less unpalatable, it saw no need for a break between twentieth-century and nineteenth-century European art.[11]

The few references that Virginia Woolf makes in her published writings to life in England during the war are consistent in their emphasis on dreariness. The person who goes out to buy a newspaper at the end of "The Mark on the Wall" curses the war and,

---

6 *Roger Fry* (London, 1940), pp. 184, 199.

7 For two quite different expressions of this hope, see Edward Carpenter, *My Days and Dreams* (London, 1916), pp. 311–15, and D. H. Lawrence's letter of May 29, 1915, to Bertrand Russell, *The Collected Letters of D. H. Lawrence*, Harry T. Moore, ed. (New York, 1962), Vol. I, p. 346.

8 *Downhill All the Way, op. cit.,* p. 9.

9 Quoted by Virginia Woolf, *Roger Fry, op. cit.,* p. 200.

10 Noel Annan, *Leslie Stephen* (London, 1951). "We were not part of a negative movement of destruction against the past," says Leonard Woolf, *Sowing, op. cit.,* p. 161.

11 T. E. Hulme, *Speculations,* Herbert Read, ed. (London, 1924).

apparently, the stalemate on the western front.[12] Because of the personal tone of the story, or reverie, one is inclined to associate this speaker with Leonard Woolf, whose comments about civilian life as he experienced it during the war, about the sound of the guns in Flanders as they were heard near the Woolfs' country house, Asham, in Sussex, and the report of the death of his brother in France, are of interest not only in this context, but also in relation to imagery in *Jacob's Room* and *To the Lighthouse* that will be considered later:

The horror of the years 1914 to 1918 was that nothing seemed to happen, month after month and year after year, except the pitiless, useless slaughter in France. Often if one went for a walk on the downs above Asham one could hear the incessant pounding of the guns on the Flanders front. And even when one did not hear them it was as though the war itself was perpetually pounding dully on one's brain, while in Richmond and Sussex one was enmeshed in a cloud of boredom, and when one looked into the future, there was nothing there but an unending vista of the same boredom. When the telephone rang on December 2, 1917, and they told me that Cecil had been killed in France, in the dull, static greyness of one's days it was as if one had suddenly received a violent blow on the head.[13]

Cold and mist outside, squalor inside, characterize the wartime scenes in Virginia Woolf's novel *The Years*. In 1917 Eleanor Pargiter dines with her cousins in an untidy house. They begin their meal in the basement, since there are no servants to bring it up from the kitchen, and are forced, because of an air raid, to complete it in the cellar. On November 11, 1918, the old servant, Crosby, drags herself across Richmond Green to shop, complaining to herself, shortly before sirens and guns announce the Armistice, about "the Belgian who called himself a Count," whose spittle she has had to clean from a bathtub. In *To the Lighthouse* Mrs. McNab struggles, successfully at last, against the decay which nearly destroys the Ramsays' summer house during a vacancy of ten years, brought about in part by the war. In *Roger Fry* Virginia Woolf describes, in biography as she had in fiction, the cold drabness of the war years. Fry's charwoman, Mrs. Filmer, whose name is given to Septimus Warren Smith's landlady in *Mrs. Dalloway*, less heroic than Mrs. McNab, left untouched more than the arrangement for a still life that Fry was painting. "Rows of dusty medicine bottles stood on the mantelpiece; frying pans were mixed with palettes; some plates

---

[12] *A Haunted House and Other Stories* (London, 1944), p. 48.
[13] *Beginning Again* (London, 1964), p. 197.

held salad, others scrapings of congealed paint. The floor was strewn with papers." Amid the squalor of the studio, however, it was the still life that was important: "those symbols of detachment, those tokens of a spiritual reality immune from destruction, the immortal apples, the eternal eggs." Virginia Woolf conjectures that it was the application of esthetic theory both to art and to "the problems of private life" which gave Fry the detachment necessary to enable him to survive the war, "and not with his intellect merely."[14]

Statements such as that about the miseries of life at home during the war, trivial miseries when compared to the misery of the trenches and of battle, may seem histrionic. Yet Virginia Woolf, if not Roger Fry, did struggle for survival as a person and an artist during the war, and her struggle, though not caused by the war, was intensified by it. At the beginning of the war she was suffering from an attack, which had begun in 1913, of the mental illness that recurred four times in her life and led, finally, to her suicide. "Her mental breakdown lasted in an acute form from the summer of 1913 to the autumn of 1915, but it was not absolutely continuous," Leonard Woolf says. "There were two insane stages, one lasting from the summer of 1913 to the summer of 1914 and the other from January, 1915, to the winter of 1915; there was an interlude of sanity between the summer of 1914 and January, 1915."[15] After her recovery she began her second and perhaps her dullest novel, *Night and Day,* which she completed in March, 1919.

She had so far written nothing which would have caused her to be remembered for long, but she had begun, in 1917 in "The Mark on the Wall," to experiment and to find the discursive, but disciplined, method which was to be characteristic of her future work. Other significant experimental short stories followed from 1919 to 1921: "Kew Gardens," "Monday or Tuesday," "A Haunted House," "The String Quartet," and "An Unwritten Novel." An essay, "Modern Fiction," if it did not explain the method very clearly, expressed, in 1919, the excitement of its discovery.

Since all these stories deal with immediate experience, attempting to catch it, one might say, at the moment of its creation, as sensation, memory, intellect, and emotion interact in the psyche, it is inevitable that there should be references in them to the war and its aftermath: to spiritualism, the influenza epidemic, the peace treaty. In Virginia Woolf's next three novels, *Jacob's Room, Mrs. Dalloway,* and *To the Lighthouse,* published, respectively, in 1922, 1925, and 1927, the war is more central.

---

14 *Roger Fry, op. cit.,* pp. 214–15.
15 *Beginning Again, op. cit.,* p. 160.

In *Jacob's Room* Jacob Flanders, whose name suggests his fate, grows from childhood to maturity or near maturity and is then killed in the war. In *Mrs. Dalloway* Septimus Warren Smith is the victim of the war and of arbitrary authority. Suffering from hallucinations and a feeling of guilt as a result of his war experiences, he leaps to his death, in a moment of clarity, to escape the doctors who would confine him. In *To the Lighthouse*, as has already been mentioned, the war contributes to the vacant period, in the Ramsays' summer home and in the novel, when nonhuman forces are dominant and human things disintegrate. During this period, Andrew Ramsay, like Jacob Flanders, is killed in battle.

The aural imagery of the sound of guns is heard in *Jacob's Room*, as the sound itself was heard on the downs near Asham. In an early page of the novel Mrs. Cranch, Mrs. Flanders' neighbor, beats a mat against a garden wall, as she watches Mrs. Flanders feeding chickens. Mrs. Jarvis, another neighbor, is aware, a few pages later, of "distant concussions in the air" as she walks on the moor. On the night, apparently, of Jacob's death, Mrs. Flanders is awakened by what she at first, though she lives in Scarborough, takes to be the guns:

"The guns?" said Betty Flanders, half asleep, getting out of bed and going to the window, which was decorated with a fringe of dark leaves.
"Not at this distance," she thought. "It is the sea."
Again, far away, she heard the dull sound, as if nocturnal women were beating great carpets. There was Morty lost, and Seabrook dead; her sons fighting for their country. But were the chickens safe? Was that some one moving downstairs? Rebecca with the toothache? No. The nocturnal women were beating great carpets. Her hens shifted slightly on their perches.[16]

Clearer, more vivid sounds are heard by Jacob. In his childhood a tree fell near him at night as he sought specimens in a forest for his collection of butterflies and moths. He recalls the incident twice (we see it only in his memory) , and each time, in the description of it, it is associated with pistol shots and with death, as indeed it was already associated with death through the moth that he had collected that night:

The tree had fallen the night he caught it. There had been a volley of pistol-shots suddenly in the depths of the wood. And his mother had taken him for a burglar when he came home late. . . .
The tree had fallen, though it was a windless night, and the lantern,

---

16 *Jacob's Room*, pp. 14, 25, 175. All references to Virginia Woolf's novels are to the Hogarth Press uniform edition.

stood upon the ground, had lit up the still green leaves and the dead beech leaves.[17]

A terrifying volley of pistol-shots rings out—cracks sharply; ripples spread—silence laps smooth over sound. A tree—a tree has fallen, a sort of death in the forest.[18]

The first recollection occurs as Jacob examines the moth in his collection; the second, in the present tense, as he attends a service at King's College Chapel and is reminded of a lantern by the light coming through the stained-glass windows. Memory, it may be observed, extends the metaphorical pistol shots and their association with death into a kind of continuous present. Meanwhile, other, more common sounds contribute more quietly to the aural pattern of the novel and to the ominous suggestion, linked with it, of death. Doors slam as Jacob goes out of his lodgings in London; swing doors open and shut "with a soft thud" as the diners go in and out from the hall at Cambridge; after dinner, objects fall in the college rooms with a thud.[19]

In *Mrs. Dalloway*, which is set in London on a June day in 1923, the pattern of sound is based on the striking of clocks and other sounds of the postwar city, in place of the sharp report of a pistol, the pounding of guns, and, one is tempted to conjecture, the thud of a falling body, which echo in *Jacob's Room*. It is worth noting, however, that Clarissa Dalloway saw, in her youth, her sister killed by a falling tree; that she is startled in the morning in a Bond Street flower shop by an explosion from a car in the street, which she at first takes to be a pistol shot; and that the explosion provides a means of transition to the street, where Septimus Warren Smith is encountered for the first time. The incident brings traffic to a standstill, and "the throb of the motor engines sounded like a pulse irregularly drumming through an entire body."[20] That night, when Clarissa hears at her party of Septimus' suicide, she vividly imagines his fall onto Mrs. Filmer's area railings: "Up had flashed the ground; through him, blundering, bruising, went the rusty spikes. There he lay with a thud, thud, thud in his brain, and then a suffocation of blackness."[21] In the "thud, thud, thud," with its suggestion of both a pulse and Septimus' fall, life and death are inextricably mixed, as they are mixed also in the thudding of the

---

17 *Ibid.*, p. 21.
18 *Ibid.*, p. 30.
19 *Ibid.*, pp. 37, 41, 88.
20 *Mrs. Dalloway*, p. 17.
21 *Ibid.*, p. 202.

waves on the beach, measuring time and suggesting eternity, in *To the Lighthouse* and in the novel that followed it, *The Waves* (1931).

From one point of view, the war is in the distant background in *To the Lighthouse*; from another, it is at the heart of the novel as the most violent of those blind forces described in the middle part of the book, "Time Passes," which destroy the order, the significant form, which humans impose on life. Time and decay are Mrs. Ramsay's chief antagonists as she guards her home and her family and attempts to give significance to their lives. The war, which coincides with her death, hastens and intensifies the destructiveness of time.[22]

War is foreshadowed and depicted in *To the Lighthouse*, as in *Jacob's Room*, chiefly through the aural imagery. Early in the book Mrs. Ramsay hears the waves on the beach and finds in their sound suggestions of life and death. Within the passage the sounds of drums and guns are heard:

. . . the monotonous fall of the waves on the beach, which for the most part beat a measured and soothing tattoo to her thoughts and seemed consolingly to repeat over and over again as she sat with the children the words of some old cradle song, murmured by nature, "I am guarding you—I am your support," but at other times suddenly and unexpectedly, especially when her mind raised itself slightly from the task actually in hand, had no such kindly meaning, but like a ghostly roll of drums remorselessly beat the measure of life, made one think of the destruction of the island and its engulfment in the sea, and warned her whose day had slipped past in one quick doing after another that it was all ephemeral as a rainbow—this sound which had been obscured and concealed under the other sounds suddenly thundered hollow in her ears and made her look up with an impulse of terror.[23]

In "Time Passes" there are further premonitions of war. The shawl that Mrs. Ramsay had wrapped around the boar's skull that her son, James, had collected and that frightened his sister, Cam, loosens and begins to unwind.[24] "As summer neared . . . there came to the wakeful . . . imaginations of the strangest kind—of flesh turned to atoms which drove before the wind."[25] Then the distant sounds of the war itself are heard:

22 Leonard Woolf's and Roger Fry's comments about the destructiveness of the war and Virginia Woolf's conjectures about the way in which Fry survived the war, cited above, are relevant here.

23 *To the Lighthouse*, pp. 29–30.

24 *Ibid.*, pp. 202, 206.

25 *Ibid.*, p. 204.

. . . there came later in the summer ominous sounds like the measured blows of hammers dulled on felt, which, with their repeated shocks still further loosened the shawl and cracked the tea-cups. Now and again some glass tinkled in the cupboard as if a giant voice had shrieked so loud in its agony that tumblers stood inside a cupboard vibrated too. Then again silence fell; and then, night after night, and sometimes in plain mid-day when the roses were bright and light turned on the wall its shape clearly there seemed to drop into this silence this indifference, this integrity, the thud of something falling.

[A shell exploded. Twenty or thirty young men were blown up in France, among them Andrew Ramsay, whose death, mercifully, was instantaneous.][26]

Death is emblemized in *To the Lighthouse* by James's boar's skull, which is nailed to the nursery wall.[27] In *Jacob's Room*, Jacob is associated with death from the first scene, in which, as a toddler, he picks up a jawbone from a sheep's skull and insists on taking it with him, in spite of his mother's protests. On the last page of the book, as Jacob's mother and his friend gather up his belongings after his death, carvings over the doorways of his lodgings of "a rose or a ram's skull" are mentioned. The two images, the one intensifying the other, remind us of what is now fully evident: the beauty and brevity of Jacob's life. This double truth has been stated throughout the novel by other images. By the account of the fad for "little paper flowers which opened on touching water" and then sank in finger bowls.[28] By the comments on real flowers: "But real flowers can never be dispensed with. If they could, human life would be a different affair altogether. For flowers fade. . . ."[29] By the sadness perceived by Jacob and his friend in the "sunny peace" of the Cornish countryside: "But imperceptibly the cottage smoke droops, has the look of a mourning emblem, a flag floating its caress over a grave."[30] By the moonlight, chalk, and bones that Mrs. Jarvis and Betty Flanders see on the moor.[31] Above all, by the frequently recurring images of butterflies, consistently associated, as in Jacob's collection, with death: "The pale clouded yellows had pelted over the moor; they had zigzagged across the purple clover. The fritillaries flaunted along the hedgerows. The blues settled on little bones lying on the turf with the sun beating on them, and the painted ladies and the peacocks feasted upon bloody entrails

---

26 *Ibid.*, pp. 206–7.
27 See the images of stoats nailed to a stable door and jays nailed to a wall in *The Waves*, p. 12.
28 *Jacob's Room*, pp. 81–82.
29 *Ibid.*, p. 82.
30 *Ibid.*, p. 47.
31 *Ibid.*, p. 131.

dropped by a hawk."[32] "The chestnuts have flirted their fans. And the butterflies are flaunting across the rides in the Forest. Perhaps the Purple Emperor is feasting, as Morris [an authority on butterflies] says, upon a mass of putrid carrion at the base of an oak tree."[33] Like the lives of the butterflies, Jacob's life is ephemeral, beautiful, doomed.

His life is, of course, the more significant for the reader because of its brevity, as it would be for Jacob himself, could he catch the hints of his early death that the reader is given in the novel. Similarly, the experiences of the Ramsays in the first part of *To the Lighthouse* are made more significant by the realization, given to the reader of this novel, as we have seen, by Mrs. Ramsay herself, that "it was all ephemeral as a rainbow." "There was no treachery too base for the world to commit; she knew that. No happiness lasted; she knew that."[34] She may wrap a shawl around the boar's skull to make it less frightening for Cam, she may say, as Lily Briscoe, a painter, thinks of her as saying, "Life stand still here,"[35] but older and more aware than Jacob, she knows that her creative powers can resist destruction and death only briefly.

It is this mood of a happy present made more vivid and valuable by the knowledge that it cannot endure that dominates *Mrs. Dalloway*. In the near past is the war and in the present some of its aftereffects: Miss Kilman's bitterness at having been dismissed from her job for suspected German sympathies; Septimus Warren Smith's insanity and suicide. A keen awareness of death is present in Septimus' and in Clarissa Dalloway's minds, and for Clarissa, at least, it intensifies the awareness of life. Septimus has seen his officer and friend killed in battle; Clarissa is pale and fifty-one, she has recovered from influenza, but her heart has been affected; "year by year her share was sliced," she thinks; "narrower and narrower would her bed be."[36] Septimus' suicide is a dark fact in the novel, and Clarissa learns of it at her party. Yet it is the beauty of the June day and Clarissa's enjoyment of it and of other ephemeral things, flowers, her party, which are most apparent. "In people's eyes, in the swing, tramp, and trudge; in the bellow and the uproar . . . was what she loved; life; London; this moment of June."[37] "What she liked was simply life."[38]

Clarissa's outlook is like the state of mind that Siegfried Sassoon

---

32 *Ibid.*, p. 22.
33 *Ibid.*, p. 123.
34 *To the Lighthouse*, p. 102.
35 *Ibid.*, pp. 249–50.
36 *Mrs. Dalloway*, pp. 34–35.
37 *Ibid.*, p. 6.
38 *Ibid.*, p. 134.

describes as his during a convalescent leave in 1916: "The war had taught me one useful lesson—that on the whole it was very nice to be alive at all; and I had also acquired the habit of observing things with more receptiveness and accuracy than I had ever attempted to do in my undisciplined past."[39] Richard Dalloway has similar thoughts as he goes home with roses for Clarissa: "Really it was a miracle thinking of the war, and thousands of poor chaps, with all their lives before them, shovelled together, already half forgotten; it was a miracle. Here he was walking across London to say to Clarissa in so many words that he loved her."[40]

Clarissa's happy alertness as she sets out at the beginning of the novel to buy flowers for her party is composed partly of the fine June morning, partly of anticipation of her party, but chiefly of the realization that the war and the influenza epidemic are over and that she is still alive:

For it was the middle of June. The War was over, except for some one like Mrs. Foxcroft at the Embassy last night eating her heart out because that nice boy was killed and now the old Manor House must go to a cousin; or Lady Bexborough who opened a bazaar, they said, with the telegram in her hand, John, her favourite, killed; but it was over; thank Heaven—over. It was June.[41]

One may conjecture that the happiness and vivid beauty that Clarissa experiences, set against the dark experience of Septimus, is ultimately derived from the relief, transformed by art, that Virginia Woolf herself felt that the war was over and that she had survived it, sane, and with increased powers as a writer. Certainly her ability to portray Septimus so well was derived from her own experience of insanity and attempted suicide.[42]

Moreover, Virginia Woolf was more optimistic than her husband about postwar society, if his attitude in this respect is reflected accurately in his autobiography, written after World War II. Peter

---

[39] *Siegfried's Journey, 1916–1920* (London, 1945), p. 16.

[40] *Mrs. Dalloway*, p. 127.

[41] *Ibid.*, pp. 6–7. Why, with this emphasis, Virginia Woolf set *Mrs. Dalloway* in 1923, instead of 1919 or 1920, is unexplained. Perhaps the dates of the writing (1922–1924) and the publication (1925) of the novel affected the year of its setting, and Peter Walsh, who has returned to England after five years in India, can observe more changes in postwar London in 1923 than he might have done in 1919 or 1920.

[42] Like Septimus, but less successfully than he, she attempted to commit suicide after seeing a consultant who recommended that she have a few weeks' rest in a nursing home. Her own hallucination of sparrows singing Greek words is given to Septimus rather inappropriately, since he is scarcely well enough educated to have studied Greek. See Leonard Woolf, *Beginning Again, op. cit.*, pp. 148–65.

Walsh, back from India, observes with approval, in *Mrs. Dalloway*, changes that have taken place in London since the war, "more than suspecting from the words of a girl, from a housemaid's laughter—intangible things you couldn't lay your hands on—that shift in the whole pyramidal accumulation which in his youth had seemed immovable. On top of them all it had pressed; weighed them down, the women especially. . . ."[43] In *The Years*, published in 1937, Eleanor Pargiter, at the wartime dinner already referred to, reflects that the war removes barriers and discusses with Nicholas, a Polish homosexual, how a better society and freer individuals might be created.

In a paper read to the Workers' Educational Association at Brighton in 1940, Virginia Woolf differentiates the writers of the generation of Auden and Isherwood from those who were educated and began to write before August, 1914. The latter writers, she says, "when the crash came in 1914 . . ., had their past, their education, safe behind them, safe within them. They had known security; they had the memory of a peaceful boyhood, the knowledge of a settled civilization."[44] Virginia Woolf herself belonged to that fortunate generation, and undoubtedly she owes much to the calm development which Victorian and Edwardian civilization made possible for her. She had learned in that quieter time the value of art and of personal relations and, as she believed, of the application of esthetic theory and of detached observation and reflection to the problems both of art and of the private life, lessons which, in her opinion, had enabled Roger Fry to survive the war as an individual and an artist.

Yet her sensibility, if one may generalize for a moment about something so individual, is not Edwardian, much less Victorian. She is intensely aware of flux and of the impermanence of individual human experience, an awareness which the war sharpened and which caused her, like Mrs. Ramsay and Mrs. Dalloway, to value the significant moment the more and to attempt to make it, as Lily Briscoe did, permanent in art. Death, violent or natural, is usually sudden in her novels, not the conclusion of a long decline. When she attempts a novel in what may broadly be called the Edwardian manner, as she did in *Night and Day* and in *The Years*, which has affinities with both *The Forsyte Saga* and *The Old Wives' Tale*, she fails.

Her own style as a novelist, which she set aside briefly as she

---

43 *Mrs. Dalloway*, p. 178.
44 "The Leaning Tower," *op. cit.*, pp. 110–16.

wrote *The Years*, was not developed until after the war. It is associated always with a concentration on the inner life, which, fluid and impermanent as it is, she finds not only more valuable, but also more reliable, in a changing world, than the outer life. This style and subject are found in *Jacob's Room, Mrs. Dalloway,* and *To the Lighthouse*, in which, as we have seen, the war has a significant place; in *The Waves*, in which her concentration on the inner life and on personal relations is most singleminded and profound and the war plays no part (though the central, silent figure, Percival, dies violently in India, as Jacob Flanders and Andrew Ramsay died in the war) ; and finally, in *Between the Acts* (1941), in which Isa Oliver anticipates personal annihilation and her husband foresees bombs shattering the English countryside as another war threatens.

The evidence in *Jacob's Room, Mrs. Dalloway,* and *To the Lighthouse*, Virginia Woolf's first novels of major significance, suggest that her sensibility as a novelist, though not formed by the war, was strongly affected by it and by her experience, coincidental with war, of insanity and that war and mental illness gave her materials which she used to express her vision of life. The war heightened her awareness of flux, impermanence, and death, causing her to value personal experience the more and to examine the more closely the experience of the present moment, seeking what permanence she could find in it and in its representation in fiction. It increased her astonishment at the miracle, which it made plainer, of being alive, and it intensified her presentation of the beauty of that miracle, as the bloody entrails, the putrid carrion, and the bones on the turf intensify the beauty of the butterflies in *Jacob's Room*.

Melvin J. Friedman

MELVIN J. FRIEDMAN *was born in Brooklyn, New York, in 1928, and was educated at Bard College, Columbia University, and Yale University. He served in the Army from 1954 to 1956. He has taught at the University of Maryland and the University of Wisconsin and is presently a professor of comparative literature at the University of Wisconsin at Milwaukee. He has held fellowships from Yale University and the American Council of Learned Societies and was a Fulbright predoctoral fellow in Lyon, France, in 1950–51.*

His published writings—in English, French, German, and Italian—are mainly concerned with twentieth-century fiction and drama. He has contributed essays and reviews to The New Republic, Modern Age, Comparative Literature, Modern Drama, La Revue des lettres modernes, Symposium, The French Review, Yale French Studies, Commonweal, Books Abroad, Journal of Popular Culture, *and* Umanesimo, *among others. He has written and edited books on the twentieth-century experimental novel, Samuel Beckett, Flannery O'Connor, and William Styron.*

He has served as editor or associate editor of three learned journals and now is assistant managing editor for comparative literature of The Modern Language Journal. *He has served as secretary and chairman of the Franco-American group of the Modern Language Association of America and is presently chairman of the nominating committee of the group.*

He is preparing a book on Samuel Beckett and editing a book on the Roman Catholic novel of the twentieth century, as well as a collection of Beckett criticism.

THREE EXPERIENCES OF THE WAR:
A TRIPTYCH

This book is Art—War—Art, in three panels. War is the centre panel.—
Blasting and Bombardiering, Part II

WHEN WE THINK of the First World War, we are reminded dramati-
cally of the way so many younger writers, in midcareer, lost their
lives: Rupert Brooke, Wilfred Owen, and Isaac Rosenberg among
the English; Alain-Fournier, Charles Péguy, and Guillaume Apollinaire among the French; Ernst Stadler, Reinhard Sorge, and Walter
Flex among the Germans. Péguy's death in the first year of the war
at the Battle of the Marne is perhaps the most heroic; Apollinaire's
death probably from influenza, some six months after being
wounded at the front, is perhaps the most ironical. Literary historians have concentrated valuable attention on the mythos of the
Kriegstod but have tended, unfortunately, to romanticize its conditions and circumstances. The following inscription which appears
on a memorial to Spain's war dead is not untypical of these
sentiments: *"Corona de la vida es morir por la patria pero esa
corona brilla más si la acompãna el Heroísmo."* The Romans,
through Horace, expressed this somewhat differently, but with
much the same feeling: *"Dulce et decorum est pro patria mori."*
The compassionate response is probably even stronger when a
writer was killed in the war, especially in the Great War—as World
War I historians still fondly refer to it.

The case of Alain-Fournier is fairly typical. His life has been
turned into legend, and his single novel, *Le Grand Meaulnes*
(translated as *The Wanderer*), has been treated as a delicate case
apart—almost as if it deserved a special place by itself, not part of
any tradition, in the history of the French novel. Havelock Ellis'
description of Fournier's death (in his introduction to the standard
American translation of *Le Grand Meaulnes*) has this quality of the
legendary:

When the Great War broke out in the summer of 1914 Fournier
happened to be in the south of France. Like others he was hurried

among many hardships to the front, and found himself eventually in the Meuse, near Vaux-les-Palameix. Fournier, "timid but fearless," for whom life was a "great game," never drew back. The inevitable end swiftly ensued. On the 22d of September at Saint-Rémy a vague figure was seen in the enemy's lines. The captain rushed forward, revolver in hand, followed by Fournier, but only by a small number of men. They were being led into an ambush on the edge of the wood. Most of them were shot down. Fournier fell struck in the forehead, according to the only report that could be obtained, but his body was not recovered.

Fournier the romantic, the figure of myth, and Fournier the author of perhaps the finest "adventure" novel written by a Frenchman in the twentieth century are often hopelessly confused. Our image of him is further distorted because of our tendency to connect him with that other writer-hero, Charles Péguy, whose literary spell and warm friendship Fournier succumbed to in the years preceding the war in which they both lost their lives.

I

There is certainly a quite different literary reaction to the war which Leonard Woolf soberly described as ending "19th-century civilization." The title he gave the third installment of his autobiography, *Beginning Again* (New York, 1964), gives us fair warning that for him and for others connected with the Bloomsbury group the world of Victorian values was officially over and a new one had to be negotiated. This is a far less romantic view than the one usually associated with the English war poets—a *Weltanschauung* which spoke in terms of *ends* rather than of *beginnings*.

It is the more sober, less spectacular concern with the war which we shall concentrate on here. The three writers whose experiences we shall examine are Wyndham Lewis, Virginia Woolf, and James Joyce. It is interesting to note that in his "Chronology of Publications," found at the end of his fine book on the literature of the First World War, *Heroes' Twilight* (New York, 1966), Bernard Bergonzi lists only one book by any of the three , Lewis' *Blasting and Bombardiering*. And this autobiography of the years 1914–26 is given only two pages in Bergonzi's study. *Blasting and Bombardiering* is clearly not a book about twilight; it is a book about beginnings rather than ends.

The grouping of the three now seems particularly timely. Within the past year we have seen the appearance of the second and third volumes of Joyce's letters, which completes the image of the Irish writer which Richard Ellmann has been painstakingly giving us since the publication of his monumental biography in 1959; the appearance of the collected essays of Virginia Woolf in four volumes, as well as the fourth installment of her husband Leonard's autobiography, *Downhill All the Way;* the appearance of the second, revised edition (Berkeley, 1967), of Lewis' *Blasting and Bombardiering* (long out of print). It is interesting that these writers who reached early primes during or just after the First World War have now reached enviable maturities posthumously as we approach the fiftieth anniversary of the end of the Great War. None, I am afraid, would have much cared about celebrating the golden anniversary if he were still alive.

One of England's most talented novelists, Anthony Burgess, has recently brought the three together in his *The Novel Now* (New York, 1967). In a chapter entitled "Giants in Those Days" he says:

The humour of Lewis's books is usually too clotted with detail to hit home, but, because of the highly individual manifesto they exemplify— "I am for the Great Without, for the method of *external* approach," said Lewis—the books have to be read. They are the best possible foil to Virginia Woolf and Joyce. [P. 28.]

Burgess has already written a loving study of Joyce, called *Re Joyce* in its American edition, and is perhaps himself the happiest blending we have today of Lewis' "Great Without" and Joyce's and Virginia Woolf's *"tellers-from-the-inside"* (Lewis' own special vocabulary found in his chapter on himself in *Men Without Art*). Burgess can calmly assess this literary problem, writing as he does about an earlier generation at a comfortable remove from it.

The Woolf-Joyce-Lewis confrontations were in their own time stormy and often unsettling. Yet they bring to the fore certain essential issues concerned with the development of twentieth-century literature. Lewis is at his most polemical when he attacks the effeteness of Bloomsbury. He speaks of E. M. Forster, in *Blasting and Bombardiering*, as "a quiet little chap, of whom no one could be jealous, so he hit it off with the 'Bloomsburies,' and was appointed male opposite number to Virgina Woolfe [*sic*]."[1] (Pp. 235–36.) He gets at Virginia Woolf more directly in his chapter on her in *Men Without Art*; here her work is dismissed as the "feminine" expression of the " 'Bloomsbury' technique" (which is in

---

[1] It is likely that Lewis intentionally misspelled Virginia Woolf's last name. We have this other striking example of it: "We were all in the post-war, but that period produced nothing but a lot of sub-Sitwells and sheep in Woolfe's clothing. . . ." (P. 249.)

itself, according to Lewis, singularly lacking in masculinity). We know how much this attack disturbed the always sensitive Virginia Woolf when we open her *A Writer's Diary* dated "Thursday, October 11th," "Sunday, October 14th," "Tuesday, October 16th," and "Friday, November 2nd" (all 1934). It takes her from Thursday, when she first discovers *Men Without Art* advertised in the *"Lit. Sup."* until the following Tuesday to recover: Thus we have the entry for Tuesday, October 16, beginning: "Quite cured today. So the W.L. illness lasted. . . ."

Virginia Woolf mildly disapproved of Joyce's *Ulysses* but had fond words for his experiments with consciousness in her most influential essay, "Modern Fiction" (see Volume II, *Collected Essays*, New York, 1967). In this essay, which features the suggestive metaphor of "a semi-transparent envelope surrounding us from the beginning of consciousness to the end," she speaks of *Ulysses:*

. . . there can be no question but that it is of the utmost sincerity and that the result, difficult or unpleasant as we may judge it, is undeniably important. In contrast with those whom we have called materialists, Mr. Joyce is spiritual; he is concerned at all costs to reveal the flickerings of that innermost flame which flashes its messages through the brain, and in order to preserve it he disregards with complete courage whatever seems to him adventitious, whether it be probability, or coherence, or any other of these signposts which for generations have served to support the imagination of a reader when called upon to imagine what he can neither touch nor see. [P. 107.]

Her response is more qualified in the entry of Wednesday, September 6, 1922, of *A Writer's Diary:*

I finished *Ulysses* and think it a mis-fire. Genius it has, I think; but of the inferior water. The book is diffuse. It is brackish. It is pretentious. It is underbred, not only in the obvious sense, but in the literary sense. A first rate writer, I mean, respects writing too much to be tricky; startling; doing stunts.

Leonard Woolf, in *Beginning Again*, reports on the ambiguous circumstances leading to the Hogarth Press' final inability to publish "this remarkable piece of dynamite," *Ulysses.*

Joyce did not answer Virginia Woolf; his silence was rather like Virginia Woolf's confiding her "hurt," received at the hands of Wyndham Lewis, to the muted pages of her *Writer's Diary.* There is no mention of her anywhere in *The Critical Writings of James*

Joyce (edited by Ellsworth Mason and Richard Ellmann) and only a single passing reference—Joyce mentions that he had received a copy of *The Voyage Out* from Mrs. Woolf—in the three volumes of Joyce letters.

The Joyce-Lewis relationship is quite different from the others we have spoken of. It is a case study in literary polemic. Lewis attacked Joyce in a variety of places: in the chapter entitled "An Analysis of the Mind of James Joyce" in *Time and Western Man;* in an essay entitled "The Diabolical Principle," which first appeared in *The Enemy*[2]; more obliquely in *The Apes of God* and *The Childermass.* Lewis is not consistently harsh with Joyce as we observe from the fond, if at times foolish, portrait he gives of him in *Blasting and Bombardiering* ("First Meeting with James Joyce"). Joyce retaliated with the fable of the Ondt and the Gracehoper in *Finnegans Wake*—putting the Joyce-Lewis conflict in superb poetic relief.[3]

We have given only a few details of these various literary confrontations involving Virginia Woolf, James Joyce, and Wyndham Lewis. The essential point to be made is that Lewis distrusted the post-Bergsonian "time-books" which Joyce and Mrs. Woolf were writing; he was especially hard on Virginia Woolf, probably because of her Bloomsbury affiliations. Virginia Woolf could not quite stomach a book of the physical dimensions and erotic leanings of *Ulysses;* she would have preferred something more classically lean and morally reticent. Joyce used the elaborate pastiches of *Finnegans Wake* to have his say against Lewis.

II

I have spent so much time on matters which seem to have little to do with the First World War because of a basic irony involving these three writers. Each was more involved in the proverbial war of words than in the war contested on the battlefields of Europe. None could agree with Wilfred Owen: "My subject is War, and the

---

[2] Sylvia Beach tells us in her *Shakespeare and Company* (New York, 1959) how Wyndham Lewis had asked Joyce for a section of *Finnegans Wake* (then known as "Work in Progress") for the literary review he was then launching. The first issue of *The Enemy* appeared, we are told: "Joyce's text was not in it. All the space was taken up by a violent attack on Joyce's new work by Wyndham Lewis." (Pp. 168–69.)

[3] See Geoffrey Wagner's chapter "Master Joys and Windy Nous" in his brilliant book *Wyndham Lewis: A Portrait of the Artist as the Enemy* (New Haven, 1957) for the most complete and convincing discussion of the Joyce-Lewis relationship. My discussion here is indebted to it. Wagner concludes, "In his lampoon of Lewis Joyce was as fair as Lewis was unfair to him." (P. 174.) See also Richard Ellmann's *James Joyce* (New York, 1959) for revealing details on the same subject.

pity of War./ The poetry is in the pity." Wyndham Lewis, the only one of the three who actively participated in the war, puts the case for all three when he says at the beginning of Part II of *Blasting and Bombardiering:*

I show, too, going from the particular to the general, how War and Art in those days mingled, the features of the latter as stern as—if not sterner than—the former. This book is Art—War—Art, in three panels. War is the centre panel. But for me it was only a part of Art: my sort of life— the life of the "intellect"—come to life. A disappointing imitation. I preferred the real thing: namely Art. [P. 63.]

Neither Joyce nor Virginia Woolf was capable of this glibness or this Wilde-inspired paradox, yet the sentiment is one they doubtless would have approved. *Blasting and Bombardiering* is filled with the notion that all experience, even fighting in the war, must be turned into art; for Lewis that meant painting and literature. Lewis left for the war in 1916 after neatly and meticulously bringing his "early period" to a close; by this time he had finished the first version of *Tarr* (not published as a book till 1918), brought out two numbers of his Vorticist review *Blast,* and had successfully exhibited some of his drawings.[4] Lewis made the transition from peacetime blaster to wartime artilleryman with exemplary ease. He could say in *Blasting and Bombardiering,* with a trace of a smile, "All Europe was at war and a bigger *Blast* than mine had rather taken the wind out of my sails." (P. 85.) He went to the front, appropriately enough, with a copy of *La Chartreuse de Parme* in his baggage; he delighted in the ineptitude of Fabrice del Dongo at Waterloo. Mixing Stendhal with the battlefields of World War I was Lewis' way of showing "how War and Art in those days mingled."

Lewis' brief period as editor of *Blast* was considerably more unsettling than his experience in the war. His *engagement* was always a matter of art, never of causes. He was more interested in blasting "ROUSSEAUISMS" (he capitalized all its letters in *Blast*) than Germans. He was, as Geoffrey Wagner has told us, an outspoken enemy of Romanticism; he joined, intellectually, those who gathered around the *Action française* in their hatred of the flabbiness of the nineteenth century (summarily dismissed by Léon Daudet as *"le stupide dix-neuvième siècle").* War was a kind of interlude for him, a time for catching up with himself and regroup-

---

4 See Geoffrey Wagner's introductory section of his book on Lewis for more details. See also *The Art of Wyndham Lewis,* Charles Handley-Read, ed. (London, 1951), and Hugh Kenner's excellent little book *Wyndham Lewis* (New York, 1954).

ing his moral and intellectual forces. Yet some of his descriptions of battle scenes in *Blasting and Bombardiering* are as vivid and compelling as any we have:

> Going through the lines of "the Field" the shelling was heavy—though on the whole there was every evidence that the enemy were not replying with their customary aggressiveness. Their artillery was being moved back.
>
> A Field Battery beside which we were making our way was having a rough time, however. There were several casualties while we were passing its guns, but my little O.C. [officer commanding] might have been taking a walk with his dog for all the notice he took. [P. 13.]

A kind of romanticism creeps into descriptions of this sort, but it is always a romanticism tempered by irony. Despite his uneasiness with this kind of sentiment, he is forced reluctantly to admit:

> Need I say that there is nothing so romantic as war? If you are "a romantic," you have not lived if you have not been present at a battle, of that I can assure you. I am very sorry to have to say this. Only a care for truth compels me to avow it. I am not a romantic—though I perfectly understand romance. And I do not like war. It is under compulsion that I stress the exceedingly romantic character of all the scenes I am about to describe. [P. 114.]

(Later on, in quite a different context, Lewis admits: "Perhaps I am *half* a romantic." [P .195.])

The most eloquent and compelling chapters in *Blasting and Bombardiering* are probably the two which deal with T. E. Hulme and Gaudier-Brzeska—both admired by Lewis and killed in the war. Hulme, who was in a neighboring battery, was killed, "within a quarter of a mile of where [Lewis] was standing." (P. 99.) The death of Gaudier-Brzeska seemed at the time more remote because Lewis learned of it indirectly from Ezra Pound. Yet later in *Blasting and Bombardiering* there is a courageously forthright statement, quite worthy of Voltaire's famous suggestion that the Lisbon earthquake should have occurred in a less populated area if indeed there were a Providence: "When I had first attested, I was talking to Ford Madox Hueffer about Gaudier's death. I'd said it was too bad. Why should Gaudier die, and a 'Bloomsbury' live? I meant that *fate* ought to have seen to it that that didn't happen. It was absurd." This gives Lewis his occasion to describe the "military" activities of his favorite literary group:

The "Bloomsburies" were all doing war-work of "National importance," down in some downy English county, under the wings of powerful pacifist friends; pruning trees, planting gooseberry bushes, and haymaking, doubtless in large sunbonnets. One at least of them, I will not name him, was disgustingly robust. All were of military age. All would have looked well in uniform. [P. 184.]

Lewis then mockingly singles out Lytton Strachey and supplies us with the terms of his "exemption" from military service. Strachey, one of the Bloomsbury "faithful," had written Virginia Woolf on March 19, 1918 (see *Virginia Woolf and Lytton Strachey Letters*, New York, 1956, p. 95) about his eagerness for things military: "My 'medical board' yesterday pronounced me 'permanently & totally unfit for any form of Military Service'—which is a great relief. The whole thing was infinitely more civilised than I've ever known it before. The doctors, and even the clerks, were positively polite."

Lewis wants very much to be identified with the "Men of 1914," as he calls them. Among this group, which curiously enough includes Joyce and Eliot (the "pseudoist," as Lewis once called him), he shows the most profound attachment for Ezra Pound. We might even say that the "mask" he chose as a point-of-view character for certain sections of *Blasting and Bombardiering*, Cantleman, bears a likeness in certain ways to Pound's Hugh Selwyn Mauberley. When Lewis insists, "Need I repeat that this hero of mine is not to be identified with me?" (p. 84), we are reminded of the complex relationship which exists between Pound and his persona. The war sections of Pound's poem "Hugh Selwyn Mauberley" are more to the point here than the esthetic forays (like the famous lines, "His true Penelope was Flaubert,/ He fished by obstinate isles;"). Lewis, through Cantleman, would be capable of the sentiment, if not the poetic splicing, of Pound's well-known reworking of Horace: "Died some, pro patria,/ non 'dulce' non 'et decor'. . . ." When Lewis bemoans the death of Hulme, "in one of England's stupidest wars," one is surprised he didn't quote the first stanza of Part V of "Mauberley":

> There died a myriad,
> And of the best, among them,
> For an old bitch gone in the teeth,
> For a botched civilization.[5]

---

[5] For the best discussion of "Mauberley" and its relationship to the ambience of World War I, see Frederick J. Hoffman, "The Temper of the 1920s," in *The Twenties* (New York, 1962), pp. 21–66.

The language should be sufficiently un-Bloomsbury to attract Lewis.

The war, for Lewis, was more a matter of persons than of causes. He can be unconcerned and even disdainful when faced with the rhetoric of war; the idea of losing his life in combat did not seem especially frightening to him. He could make very light of the possibility, as in a letter to Pound: "If I get my head blown off when I am pottering about Flanders. . . ." (*The Letters of Wyndham Lewis,* W. K. Rose, ed., New York, 1963, p. 67.) He is much more serious about the whole thing when confronted with the deaths of Hulme and Gaudier-Brzeska or with the "war-work" of the "Bloomsburies." He seems to ask for an imaginary court of military justice to intercede in favor of Hulme and Gaudier-Brzeska against the "effete" Lytton Strachey, E. M. Forster, Virginia and Leonard Woolf, and the others associated with Bloomsbury. While Lewis again and again reveals unconcern for his own safety, both in *Blasting and Bombardiering* and in his letters of the war years, he still can express a metaphysical hurt in the name of the "Men of 1914." He could write to Herbert Read just after the war ended: "What a nightmare this wicked war has been! . . ."

Lewis saw very active combat for a sustained six-month period in 1917. He was hospitalized following a siege of "trench-fever." He ended the war by serving as what he called "a painter-soldier, attached to the Corps-headquarter Staff of the Canadian Army." (P. 191). W. K. Rose mentions, in his excellent edition of Lewis' letters, how Pound had tried for more than a year to get him to leave the trenches for a cushier position and quotes Pound's splendid remark from one of his letters to Lewis: ". . . you should not be allowed to spill your gore in heathen and furrin places."

The year 1917 found Lewis vigorously publishing again, especially in *The Little Review.* Pound led off the May issue with his famous editorial about what he planned to do with Margaret Anderson's magazine: "I wished a place where the current prose writings of James Joyce, Wyndham Lewis, T. S. Eliot, and myself might appear regularly, promptly, and together, rather than irregularly, sporadically, and after useless delays." Lewis published "Imaginary Letters" in five issues between May, 1917, and April, 1918. He also placed in the pages of *The Little Review,* during this period, "Cantleman's Spring-Mate" (included in the 1967 edition of *Blasting and Bombardiering*), "A Soldier of Humour," the essay "Inferior Religions," an abstract drawing called "The Starry Sky," and the three-scene playlet "The Ideal Giant." He missed appearing in only two issues during the year from May, 1917, to May, 1918—a remarkable record for anyone, especially for an artilleryman recently turned "painter-soldier." (His "Imaginary Letters, VIII," by the way, appeared in the same issue as the first installment of Joyce's *Ulysses*—March, 1918.) [6]

Lewis emerged from the war, then, as active creatively as when he entered it. (We are fortunate to have this new edition of Lewis' brilliant book of 1937, *Blasting and Bombardiering*, for what it tells of this transitional period; it is, along with Leonard Wolf's, clearly one of the finest literary autobiographies of the century.) The lines were perhaps more firmly drawn between the "Men of 1914" and the "Bloomsburies"—which was entirely to Lewis' liking. *The Little Review* took the place of the defunct *Blast*, at least until Lewis could start another review of his own.

III

Virginia Woolf's experience during the war was quite different from the one which Lewis ascribed to her "group": ". . . the 'Bloomsburies' all exempted themselves, in one way or another." (P. 185.) We know from Part III of *Beginning Again* some of the details of Virginia Woolf's nervous breakdown, "neurasthenia" as her doctors called it, which corresponded roughly with the first two years of the war. Leonard Woolf remarked about them: "In many ways 1914 and 1915 were years which we simply lost out of our lives, for we lived them in the atmosphere of catastrophe or impending catastrophe." (*Beginning Again*, p. 166.) Leonard himself was "exempted" (he uses the very word which Lewis was fond of directing against the "Bloomsburies") from military service because of Virginia's illness and because of a "nervous disease" he himself had. He spent the middle years of the war admirably investigating the causes of it and working on solutions for its curtailment in the future; he did this under the auspices of the Fabian Society. Although he was very far away from the trenches, Leonard Woolf could experience the same sense of irony about the war as Wyndham Lewis. When he speaks about his brothers at the front, he could be borrowing a page from *Blasting and Bombardiering:* "Cecil was killed and Philip severely wounded and it was appropriate that the death of the one and the wounds of the other were caused by the same shell. The episode was characteristic of the 1914 war." (P. 181.)

---

6 Geoffrey Wagner's "Checklist of the Writings of Wyndham Lewis," placed at the end of his *Wyndham Lewis*, has proved very helpful here. I have also had occasion to examine *The Little Review* papers in the special collection at the library of the University of Wisconsin at Milwaukee.

It is unfortunate that Leonard Woolf's edition of his wife's *A Writer's Diary* offers as its first entry August 4, 1918. Virginia makes no mention of the war, which was to end in three months. However, if we turn to her entries for 1939 and 1940, we find a person profoundly distressed with the horror and meaninglessness of war. There is nothing feminine or Bloomsbury (in Wyndham Lewis' sense) about her responses. Leonard, in *Beginning Again,* made the crucial distinction between the First and Second World Wars; the 1914 war, he felt, was characterized by a dullness and boredom ("Nothing seemed to happen"), while in the 1939 war "things moved and happened and one was kept keenly alive by the danger of death continually hanging just above one's head." (P. 197.) It was this sense of danger—perhaps psychologically anticipating Virginia Woolf's suicide in 1941—which seems to get into the texture of her prose in the later entries of her *A Writer's Diary;* thus, we have reactions like: "The war is like a desperate illness. For a day it entirely obsesses: then the feeling faculty gives out; next day one is disembodied, in the air. Then the battery is recharged and again—what? Well, the bomb terror. Going to London to be bombed." (May 20, 1940.) Unlike the years of World War I, when Virginia Woolf was relatively unproductive, she was able during this later period to advance her brilliant novel *Between the Acts* (always referred to in *A Writer's Diary* as *P.H.*). She seems to echo Lewis' sentiments about the convergence of war and art. There are many passages in which only a delicate thread divides the two. Virginia Woolf's imagination moves along wearily, often without the benefit of transition: "The Press [Hogarth Press]—what remains—is to be moved to Letchworth. A grim morning. How can one settle into Michelet and Coleridge? As I say, we have need of courage. A very bad raid last night on London—waiting for the wireless. But I did forge ahead with *P.H.* all the same." (September 18, 1940.)

There is an essay to be written, certainly, on Virginia Woolf's great courage and her reaction to World War II, but that is not our intention here. Still *A Writer's Diary* is a valuable document for the study of a "neurasthenic" in civilian war conditions. One should look also at several of her later essays, especially "Thoughts on Peace in an Air Raid" (contained in Volume IV of her *Collected Essays*), which was written in 1940 and contains much of the ambience of war. We can begin to see the desperation building up and perhaps understand James Southall Wilson's remark that her suicide was, in the end, a choice between death and insanity.

Perhaps Viriginia Woolf's most revealing statement about the effects of war on the writer is found in her late essay "The Leaning Tower" (included in Volume II of her *Collected Essays*). She wrote this essay during World War II, but something of what she had to say pertained to the war of 1914. She makes an important distinction between the nineteenth and twentieth centuries: "War then we can say, speaking roughly, did not affect either the writer or his vision of human life in the nineteenth century." (P. 164.) She points out, for example, how little the Napoleonic Wars affected the novels of Jane Austen and Scott. The change seems to come with the 1914 war, which for her, as for Leonard, ended "19th-century civilization." She clearly takes the Bloomsbury position and insists on the enviable priority of the "educated class" over the "working class" in shaping modern British literature. She notices a change in the generation which began to write in 1925 and uses the metaphor of the leaning tower to express their displacement. This generation wrote "under the influence of change, under the threat of war." (P. 170.) Almost all the writers Virginia Woolf uses to illustrate her theories in "The Leaning Tower," by the way, have Oxford or Cambridge backgrounds. The embarrassing exception is D. H. Lawrence, whom she manages to dismiss with her accustomed delicacy.

While Wyndham Lewis is for persons and "things," the Woolfs are for causes. Virginia Woolf is haunted by the very notion of war while Lewis can calmly dodge every variety of enemy fire at the front. There is no possible meeting except in the matter of art, which for both is the "real thing." It does not matter that Virginia Woolf's *A Writer's Diary* has nothing to say about World War I; the fact that it comments so poignantly about World War II is quite enough. Lewis, on the other hand, if he had written in such depth about his experiences in World War II, would probably have written a very different book from *Blasting and Bombardiering*.

IV

In "The Leaning Tower," Virginia Woolf speaks of Jane Austen's and Walter Scott's literary careers during the Napoleonic Wars: "each wrote through them." We can say this also about James Joyce, that he "wrote through" the First World War. He divided the war years between Trieste and Zurich, quite out of touch with events at the front. Joyce had considerably less involvement with the Great War than even Virginia Woolf had. We know how much, for example, Virginia Woolf's novels of the twenties were crucially involved with the 1914 war and its aftermath; we need only recall Jacob Flanders' death (*Jacob's Room*) ; the shell-shocked condition leading to the suicide of Septimus Warren Smith (*Mrs. Dalloway*) ; the report, in brackets, of the death of Andrew Ramsay (the "Time Passes" section of *To the Lighthouse*) . There is nothing quite like this in Joyce's work.

These were the years when he was writing *Ulysses* and suffering publishing and financial indignities. The war rarely finds a place in his creative work, and it is singularly absent from his letters. It does enter through the back door of *Finnegans Wake*, but as an almost indistinguishable part of war from the beginning of time. There is the brief lyric in *Chamber Music* (1907) , number XXXVI, which starts in this way:

> I hear an army charging upon the land,
> 　　And the thunder of horses plunging, foam about
> 　　　　their knees:
> Arrogant, in black armour, behind them stand,
> Disdaining the reins, with fluttering whips,
> 　　　　the charioteers.

This was written many years before the war, and W. B. Yeats, for one, who placed it highest among Joyce's lyric poems, spoke of it in a letter to Joyce as "a poem of yours about the sea." We remember the presence of Private Carr and Private Compton in the Nighttown section of *Ulysses*, but there is little about them and their behavior to remind us of the Great War. Nor is Major Tweedy, who also turns up briefly in Nighttown, of much help.

The letters are scarcely more revealing. Joyce's private epistolary war with his publishers dominates the years when others were at the front. He even blithely disregards his brother Stanislaus' internment during a significant part of the war. In Richard Ellmann's edition of the Joyce correspondence we find a letter from Stanislaus, dated May 25, 1919, expressing contempt for Joyce's methods: "I have just emerged from four years of hunger and squalor, and am trying to get on my feet again. Do you think you can give me a rest?" A later letter, dated February 26, 1922, reinforces Stanislaus' sense of outrage: "In fact this seems to me only part and parcel of the careless indifference with which you have always acted in affairs that concerned me."

The only compelling statement about the war, in the three volumes of Joyce letters we have, is in a letter to Joyce from his sister May:

Have you heard from Stannie [Stanislaus] lately? I was expecting a letter from him. I sent him shoes about six weeks ago. I dont know whether he got them or not. He is wonderful to keep up so well during all this time, it must be dreadful for him being a prisoner and idle all this time, but he says he has nothing to complain of in his treatment, which is some consolation. Will all this never end? When the war started it was said it could not last more than six months, but now there seems as much prospect of a finish as then. [Ellmann edition, September 1, 1916.]

Joyce's remoteness from the war perhaps explains a sentence from a letter he wrote to Harriet Shaw Weaver on December 1, 1918 (Stuart Gilbert's edition) : "I hope you are well in these dangerous days." Could Joyce not have realized that the Great War ended on November 11?[7]

V

It might perhaps seem arbitrary to bring these three writers together under the same umbrella. Yet they will always be connected through literary history, whether one refers to them obliquely as social reactionaries as C. P. Snow has done[8] or whether one confronts the "Great Without" position of Lewis with Joyce's and Virginia Woolf's *"tellers-from-the-inside"* position. But most interesting, for our purposes, are the extremes in respect to the war: Lewis the ironical combatant, Virginia Woolf the psychologically disrupted observer, Joyce the detached nonobserver. All three are very far from the literature of *Kriegstod* celebrated in books like Bernard Bergonzi's *Heroes' Twilight*.

---

[7] Joyce does mention in a letter to Ezra Pound of about July 15, 1915 (Ellmann edition), that he read about an Italian raid of the Trieste shipyard, which was located a few minutes from his house there. In an "open letter" of April 28, 1919, Joyce offers this interesting autobiographical information: "I am a prisoner of war liberated on parole to Switzerland in July 1915 by the Austrian Government in consideration of my health. Three months after the occurrences narrated, Mr. Consul Bennett summoned me for combatant military service in the United Kingdom and threatened that if I did not comply with his proposal within 48 hours he would blacklist me. I declined to accept service of this monstrous document and sent it back to him by return of post with two lines of courteous refusal."

[8] See Rubin Rabinovitz, "C. P. Snow vs. The Experimental Novel," *Columbia University Forum*, X (Fall, 1967) , pp. 37–41.

The Guilt

Correlli Barnett

CORRELLI BARNETT *was born in Norbury, Surrey, on June 28, 1927. He was educated at Whitgift Middle School, Croydon (now the Trinity School of John Whitgift), and at Exeter College, Oxford, where he read modern history with, as a special subject, military history and the theory of war. He graduated in 1951 with second-class honors. He also won a college naval history prize with an essay on the development of aircraft carriers.*

From 1945 to 1948 he served with the British Army, mostly in Palestine, and held the rank of sergeant.

His first work of military history, The Desert Generals, *published in 1960, excited both praise and heavy attack. It has been translated into four languages. His second work of military history,* The Swordbearers: Studies in Supreme Command in the First World War *(critical portraits of the younger Moltke, Jellicoe, Pétain, and Ludendorff), was also widely praised.*

In 1963 Correlli Barnett was one of the historical consultants for the BBC television series The Great War, *and wrote a third of the programs. In 1964–65 he was a historical consultant for the television sequel,* The Lost Peace. 1918–1933, *and wrote nearly all the programs.*

Currently he is finishing a short history of the British Army, considered as a national institution. He also teaches part time at the University of East Anglia and lectures elsewhere by invitation of such institutions as the Staff College, Camberley. He is a Fellow of the Royal Society of Literature, a member of the Royal United States Institution, and a member of the Institute for Strategic Studies. He is married, has two daughters, and lives in Norfolk.

THE ILLOGICAL PROMISE

THERE IS, successive generations have discovered, a persuasive force about a victory that is lacking in even the most cogently argued diplomatic note. War is, therefore, a continuation of policy by other means. History bears Clausewitz out: Where negotiation and nonviolent pressure have failed to secure an object, the armies have marched. Such is the diversity of human interests that armies have marched to decide the candidature of vacant thrones, to determine how much of Europe should believe in transubstantiation and accept papal authority, to define the English constitution, and conclude whether or not the United States of America should be dissolved. The armies have marched in pursuit of provinces and of markets. War, or threat of war, has been one of the essential tools of statecraft.

The immediate and fundamental difficulty with the Great War is that it, biggest of all wars, does not fit Clausewitz's definition. It was not consciously embarked on by any power (except Austria) in pursuit of positive objectives of policy. The greatest war in history was a meaningless accident: It went on to a finish of exhaustion because no one could see how to stop it.

Austria alone went into war deliberately to achieve a limited and perfectly rational objective: the crushing of Serbia and the ending of the unrest Serbia had encouraged among Austria's south Slav peoples. Every other nation in 1914 entered the war for negative reasons—not in pursuit of aims, but because of obligations and fear of others. Russia did not go to war to win Constantinople or destroy Austrian influence in the Balkans, but defensively, in support of her Serbian clients. France did not go to war to reverse the verdict of 1870 and make France the dominant great power of Europe again in place of Germany; she did not even go to war, as Déroulède would have wished, to regain Alsace-Lorraine; she went to war in fulfillment of her treaty obligations to Russia. Germany did not go to war to conquer Russian territory in the East or industrial areas and Channel ports in France and Belgium, or even to speed up her commercial defeat of British industry by naval and military victory over Britain: She went to war because her ally Austria was going to war. All the nations went to war defensively, believing themselves threatened, believing they must support their allies and fight now if they were not to be left fatally exposed to attack alone later. The Schlieffen plan, often wrongly thought to be a miscarried master-piece of long-matured and arrogant aggression, was, in fact, stra-tegically defensive. It was a gamble, a desperate gamble, to save Germany from overwhelming onslaught from east and west. Ger-many's weakness, not her strength, was the leitmotiv in the thinking of her prewar chiefs of the General Staff, from the elder Moltke, through Waldersee and Schlieffen, to the younger Moltke in 1914. And Britain did not declare war in order to crush the German Navy or destroy the growing German threat to British world markets and industrial supremacy; she declared war reluctantly, and in troubled mind, because of informal obligations to come to the aid of France.

Whatever the underlying rivalries between the nations and the social tensions within each state, war itself had thus come about by accident, by nobody's design, out of a chain of defensive obligations. No statesman of any nation (except the Austrians) had any idea of what sort of settlement might follow the swift military victories so confidently expected. The great battles of 1914 therefore took place in a vacuum so far as grand strategy, or national policy, was concerned. They were what Clausewitz had believed impossible: meaningless acts of violence, irrelevant contests of strength, the instrument of nothing.

The chains of treaty obligations that had pulled the nations into this meaningless war had been the work of the narrow prewar ruling classes. Their peoples had been spectators, crowds at the back of the stage, although their own racial and nationalist hatreds had been felt by the governments, and had helped create the prewar atmosphere of mutual fear in Europe. But once war was declared, the peoples began to take it over. The exquisite courtesies between ambassador and foreign minister when a declaration of war was delivered—the common memories even in such a moment of the single international world of the upper classes—were one thing. The hatreds being bayed and screeched in the streets of European capitals were another. The masses had been let out of their cage— the cage of a colorless and shabby, highly disciplined life in the dreary rats' nests of modern industrial cities. The existence of the masses was boring, monotonous, and insecure, their leisure short and lacking in outlet, their emotional and sexual life deprived and repressed. Even before the war, contemplation of their own coun-try's strength and glory had served to give vicarious color and ful-fillment to the narrow lives of the lower-middle and working classes. These urban masses were people without the peasant's understanding of life and of his own familiar world, without his hard, if limited, realism and sagacity. These people—like Hitler and H. G. Wells' early heroes—had no roots, no secure emotional foundations, no personal independence, no education but the ability haltingly to read and write. They had not the ability to analyze and reason or the information by which such an ability could form sound judgments. Instead, they were ruled by emotion and romance. Men like Pearson and Harmsworth had grown rich by providing them with reading matter: nothing boringly factual or closely argued, of course, but highly colored and exciting stuff to flatter prejudice and bring artificial excitement and action to the lives of people like pet mice on a wheel in a cage.

On this aimless conflict in fulfillment of prewar defensive treaties there thus impinged the quenchless hate of the common man for any person who was different. The ever-responsive popular press gave its readers what it wanted: atrocity stories by the columnful. The dreariness of urban life was reflected in the torrent of volunteers to British recruiting offices seeking escape, a bit of foreign travel and adventure, the opportunity legitimately to clobber other human beings, the splendor of uniform instead of the baggy shabbiness of shiny hand-me-downs.

The consequence of letting the little man and his wife out of their cage of obscurity might yet not have been disastrous if only one of the combatants had won a clear victory in the field in August and September, 1914, and ended the war before it really got started. There was no such decision. Instead, there was stalemate in the worst possible circumstances. Had the stalemate come about with both sides having enjoyed roughly equal success in the 1914 battles, a peace on the basis of the *status quo ante* might just have been possible. Instead, when the armies came to rest, Germany occupied eleven departments of northern France and most of Belgium. In the east, although the Serbs had chucked the Austrians back over the Danube, the Germans had also won great successes against the Russians. Stalemate it might be, but the visible balance of the war was wholly and greatly in Germany's favor. Peace by negotiation was thus impossible, for Germany could legitimately make claims that would be utterly unacceptable to the Allies. The Allies would have been bound at least to demand the evacuation of the German armies from their conquests as a preliminary to negotiation, an evident impossibility. There were therefore not the faintest beginnings of hope that the stalemate would lead to early peace negotiations; the Allies were bound to fight on in the faith that victories would give them a better platform for negotiation. Just as the nature of the stalemate on a line of German success meant the war must go on, so in terms of strategy it meant that the Allies must attack and keep on attacking. The course of the war from November, 1914, till March, 1918, was thus determined by the initial German partial success.

It gradually dawned on the nations that this was going to be a long war, that all conceptions of a large-scale, but quick and purely military, effort had been misguided. A long war, either side of a trench system well wired and fortified and densely held by troops, meant the total mobilization of the human and material resources of the combatants. In British and French industry the years 1915 and 1916 saw the replacement of Victorian small-scale organization and handicraft attitudes with modern (German and American) conceptions of huge-scale and mass production. In Germany the transition to the needs of total war implied no such revolution: Her mercantilist tradition, the large-scale organization of her industries, and the cooperative attitude of her trade unions all favored massive coordinated effort, in a way that the British tradition of small-scale enterprise and the British trade-union system, with its endless proliferation of specialist craft unions and elaborate and rigid demarcation of jobs, did not.

However, in all the combatant countries industrial mobilization meant that the ardent participation of the masses in the war had to be enlisted. It could not be a "Cabinet" war, a relatively precise instrument of realistic policy firmly under the control of the cool judgment of statesmen. Governments therefore had to meet the uncaged little man halfway: the little man had to be flattered, encouraged, filled with a sense of his importance, of the glory and righteousness of the cause, and of the criminal depravity of the enemy. Primitive government propaganda machines were created. They disseminated lies and hatred with the willing cooperation of privately owned newspapers and journals. It cannot be said that they created or "fanned" the hatred of the little man, which existed spontaneously and which seized eagerly on the gratifications offered by the press. From the end of 1914 till the end of 1916 the nations sought "victory." "Victory"—whatever that really meant in hard terms of a settlement or a prior military achievement—was the only outcome of the conflict that now would satisfy the little man's hatred of the enemy or compensate for his heroic exertions.

The state of mind of Europe at this juncture hardly boded well for any kind of ultimate, constructive peacemaking. The phlegmatic British broke out into anti-German riots, with plenty of looting of shops with German names, on account of the Germans having sunk the liner *Lusitania*, which carried a consignment of arms and which sailed from New York in defiance of a public German warning that it would be in danger. In every country, men like Horatio Bottomley thrived by publishing what the little man wanted to read. Bottomley referred constantly to "Germ-huns" in his journal *John Bull*, whose contents so appealed that its circulation became the largest in the country.

There was little to choose between the ignorance and the violence of the opinions expressed by the peoples of the different belligerents. A German, for example, made this penetrating diagnosis of the causes of the war:

"What is the war itself but the outcome only of British cunning, British lying, British hypocrisy and cant and treachery? No means can be too unholy to combat this hideous octopus, whose tentacles have too long encircled the peoples of the world."

A Briton outlined a long-term policy for the war:

"The huns—vicious in victory, cowardly in defeat—deserve no more consideration than a mad dog or a venomous snake and it is our duty to humanity to carry death and devastation into the heart of their country. We're out for War—let it be War to the death!"

Then there was another important question, with evident bearing on the peace settlement: Was the enemy human? On the one hand a Briton pointed out that "There are only two divisions in the world today—human beings and Germans," while on the other a German no less closely reasoned that "The Englishman, indeed, is not to be classed among human beings."

Above all, there was the question of why everybody was going on fighting, other than that it was a meaningless predicament from which nobody knew how to escape. The common man would not fight for anything so prosaic as coal and iron fields or to weaken a trade competitor. His mind was above such things. His purpose was as Christian as his sentiments. A war begun without aims had now been allotted an aim—total victory over evil. As a British bishop put it from the fire step of his cathedral pulpit: "Such a war is a heavy price to pay for our progress towards the realization of the Christianity of Christ, but duty calls."

However, there was a German claim as well to godliness: "One thing is clear. God must stand on Germany's side. We fight for truth, culture and civilization and human progress and true Christianity." A picture was thus conveyed by the religious ecstasies of the combatants that the soldiers were beating each other's heads in with crucifixes.

In fact, of course, at the front, where the reality was instead of the fantasy, the emotional transports that filled the silly heads of the masses had no place. The soldiers of all the combatant nations were unfortunately placed between the enemy barbed wire and machine guns in front, and their relatives behind demanding total victory at all costs.

What is especially depressing is the degree to which men who ought to have known better—politicians, diplomats, soldiers, writers —were unable to preserve their good sense and detachment, but themselves caught the popular mood. The only people bucking the tide—pacifists of one kind or another—were just as emotionally in the fidgets as the war winners. Virtually nowhere was to be found the political realism, the practical good sense, the sagacity of judgment of a Talleyrand, a Metternich, a Castlereagh, a Bismarck. In its combination of boy scout idealism and romanticized aggression, Europe seemed to have regressed to a mental age of thirteen.

However, not only were there journals like *John Bull* to read; but there were casualty lists. Although evey patriotic German, Frenchman, or Briton knew that one of his soldiers was worth three of the enemy and that every offensive had been a brilliant demonstration of military superiority over a cowardly and despicable enemy, the fact remained that the front stayed much where it was. By the end of 1916, when both sides had made a supreme effort to win and failed, even the British people, last to commit a great army to battle, began to notice that a lot of their sons, husbands, fathers, nephews, cousins, uncles, and friends had been killed or wounded.

The autumn of 1916 and the winter of 1916–17 (cold and long) mark the point at which some dawning sense of reality about the war came to the bemused mind of the common man of Europe, rather like sobriety returning to drunks who have just unloaded a vast cargo of inhibited lusts and aggressions by wrecking a pub and fighting everybody in reach. Or perhaps like a man falling out of love. The war was no longer so glorious and colorful and exciting. How long would it go on for? Could anybody win? Would it be worth winning?

In the absence of public opinion polls it is impossible to judge to what extent a shift of opinion (so to dignify the varying moods of the common man) had taken place among the warring peoples. It was certainly enough to create a climate where it seemed worthwhile to various diverse individuals—Lord Lansdowne, Bethmann-Hollweg, Henry Ford, the Pope, and the new Austrian Emperor Karl—to try for a compromise peace, not all at the same time. However, opinion in favor of carrying on the war until total victory apparently remained the stronger, among both governments and peoples. The mood of the war winners was now grim and dour, more of obstinacy than of wild passion. New leaders like Lloyd George and Ludendorff brought a promise of new ideas and talent, a sense of a second wind. The war went on to the final, sterile conclusion of the total victory demanded by the masses.

The common man did not so much enjoy the latter half of the war; it ceased to be like an exciting serial story in his paper. People he was related to or knew socially kept getting killed or wounded. The war came right home when the Germans bombed Paris and London, and the Allies bombed the Rhineland. The indignation, uproar, and damage to war production owing to absenteeism caused by these trivial attacks indicated that the common man's appetite for battle was strictly vicarious. Then there was rationing and substitute foods: Who could enjoy a Christian, patriotic war against subhuman monsters on cod steak and unsweetened tea?

The "aim" of victory over evil was no longer quite enough in itself. Something more was now needed to keep up flagging spirits and interest—to provide some kind of justification for the unending waste and killing. The idea of war aims gradually emerged. Nobody noted that the time to decide on war aims is before you get into a war. The course and character of the war now molded the evolution of these war aims; the peoples demanded compensation for their enormous efforts, sacrifices, and losses since the beginning of the war. The French looked beyond the recovery of Alsace-Lorraine to a French puppet state in the Rhineland and the breakup of united Germany. The Germans looked to a protectorate of some kind over Belgium and the Channel ports and a colonial empire in Poland and the Baltic. Both the French and the German aims were concrete enough, despite their ambition, given that total victory could first be achieved. It was the Anglo-Americans who produced a new fantasy, a new focus for the simple emotional reactions of the common man, that partly replaced the earlier fantasy of a crusade against evil. This fantasy was a Better World, to be created by a Postwar Reconstruction. It was just the stuff for people who were thinking more about peace, now they had got bored with war. Within national society, a Better World was to take the form of social reform, industrial reorganization, greater equality and political democracy, an attack on poverty and misery. In terms of a European and world peace settlement it was to take the form of a League of Nations. The genuine and spontaneous idealism of the Better-Worlders was never better expressed than in the disastrous figure of Woodrow Wilson.

With the advent of Wilson and those who passionately believed with him in Better Worlds and Leagues of Nations, there evolved the ultimate in war aims. It was proclaimed that this was a War to End War. Thus, after four years of hapless slaughter, a war that had begun unintentionally, because of treaty obligations intended to *preserve* the existing European political system, ended with such vaulting and visionary aims as had no previous war in history.

However, the mood of Wilson and the victorious Allies in November, 1918, was not all passionate idealism; there was a good deal still of earlier sentiment that the enemy was a wild beast to be castrated, hobbled, and caged forever. Some people managed to blend relentless hatred of the Germans with Christian hopes for future international amity; others specialized in one or the other. The climate of the peacemaking was thus determined by the evolving psychology of the common man and his prophets in the course of war. Unlike their happier predecessors at the Congress of Vienna, the statesmen gathered in Paris in 1919 were acutely conscious of, and had to be responsive to, public opinions that had not really existed in so powerful and vociferous a form even in 1914. Promises both to squeeze Germany till the pips squeaked and to usher in a millennium of peace and love had in some way to be simultaneously redeemed by the ingenuity of statesmen. At the same time, some hard and practical questions of the old, sordid kind familiar to the realistic past had also to be arranged.

There was thus at the base of the peacemaking the same irrationality that had determined the people's attitudes to the war. It made sense only in terms of psychological explanation to say that *because* this had been the most hideous and pointless war in history, the peace by compensation must be the most beautiful, just, idealistic, and long-lasting. It can be understood how people who think with their guts instead of their heads came to believe that such unspeakable hatred, cruelty, and horror must naturally lead to a world of love, kindness, and international understanding, came to believe that people who had wrestled with each other to the last gasp would now abjure force. It is also understandable that ignorant people of weak understanding should see social justice and unprecedented prosperity as the consequence of all the destruction and waste of the war. The logic of the urban common man, like that of all primitives, was emotional and symbolical, not reasonable or analytical. What is less comprehensible is that intelligent and educated men with a knowledge of history, as well as of affairs, from Wilson himself down to young idealists like Harold Nicolson of the British delegation to the Peace Conference, could believe that the

Great War provided a wonderful springboard to a better world. The gulf between the real state of the world and the blueprint of the idealists was absolutely unbridgeable. The gulf within the personalities of the idealists themselves—between Wilson the toughened politician and Wilson the prophet, for example—was no less wide.

Thus a war of irrationality paved the way for a peace of irrationality: The emotional fantasies of the emancipated masses were the key to the making of both.

The core of the postwar European problem, as it had been of the war and of the prewar problem, was a united Germany. Germany occupied the center of Europe, the largest single nation-state (excepting Russia) and the most powerful and enterprising industrial nation in Europe, bar none. Despite her defeat in the Great War, the conflict only proved Germany's dominating strength: She had beaten Russia, had held off France and Britain, and had succumbed only to the fresh and overwhelming weight of America. The verdict of victory could be only temporary; German relative weakness would last only as long as the Allied wartime coalition stayed in being. There were two answers to this problem of German power. First, the peacemakers could accept that, willy-nilly, Germany would always dominate Europe and therefore make a very lenient peace so that Germany would harbor the least resentment. Unfortunately the war had come to be fought just to deny this German domination, and the common man had been taught to expect that Germany would be heavily "punished." In any case, Wilson had already broken up the German monarchy and reduced the country to political chaos. So the kind of peace that had been granted France in 1814 was impossible.

There was the second alternative: Weaken Germany so that she no longer dominated Europe; in other words, so that she was no stronger than another single great power, i.e., France. This meant either breaking up the united Germany made by Bismarck into small states (which the French in fact wanted to do) or reducing the German population and industrial resources to the level of France by cession of territory to the victors. However, such a solution would be too brutal for Wilsonian idealism, for the new world of justice being created in Paris. Instead, a compromise was finally evolved that tried to take in punishment, reconciliation, self-determination (even for Germans), and the weakening of German power. It was a compromise that reflected the conflicting pressures of political reality and idealistic fantasy. It did not solve the central problem of power. Postwar Germany matched 60,000,000 of population against 40,000,000 in France. The Ruhr and Silesian industrial areas made her still the most powerful industrial country in Europe. Cessions of territory to Poland and Belgium, reparations, French occupation of the Rhineland, and German disarmament eroded only the edges of German strength: The core remained intact. At the same time the Allies had ensured that this potentially still-powerful Germany would have a weak and unpopular republican regime and would harbor strong resentments. Owing also to the collapse of the Austrians in the last days of the war enforced by Wilson, there was no great power to balance Germany in the center of Europe, as Austria had balanced Prussia until the 1880's. The new Germany, though itself weakened, was bordered by second-class states like Poland, Czechoslovakia, and Austria (the German-speaking rump). The prewar balance of power in Europe (how good a balance it was is proved by the stalemate of the war) had in fact been replaced by arrangements that left Germany relatively stronger in potential, not weaker.

More irrationality is found in the painstaking drawing of borders for the new states so as to get people speaking one language all on one side of a frontier. Harold Nicolson in his diary of the Peace Conference portrays the conscientious agonizing of the peacemakers as they tried to apply the principles of self-determination to areas where the populations were hopelessly jumbled up. The state lines drawn according to this doctrinaire ideal divided up the balanced economic system of the Austrian Empire into peasant agricultural states without access to their old urban markets or industrial supplies, and cities and industrial areas with no agriculture to feed them and no markets for their products. To, therefore, the ruin of industry, trade, and agriculture throughout central and eastern Europe caused by the war was gratuitously added further dislocation instead of a settlement realistically based on economics. A further irrationality was found in the colossal reparation demands on Germany made by the Allies, which were based on the proposition that Germany *ought* to pay for all damage incurred by the Allies in the course of the war. How much Germany *could* pay was a question dealt with only in the Dawes and Young plans later in the 1920's.

It is not merely hindsight to perceive how unrealistic and incoherent a peace had emerged; there were those who were aghast even before the draft was rammed down the German throat without negotiation.

To recapitulate: The war began without purposes; it became a meaningless dilemma; it entailed the participation of the common man to a novel extent; the common man's demand for total victory over "evil" helped lead to the war's immense destruction and Europe's final exhaustion; and increasingly statesmen were trapped (or at least hindered) by their own tributes to the common man's sentimentality, whether sugary-idealistic or romantically aggressive and indignant. By 1918, therefore, a powerful element of sentimentality had been injected into the conduct of international affairs, where, instead, sober and materialistic calculation is required for businesslike and workable settlements. The anatomy of the urban little man's unreason and sentimentality has never been better laid out than in *Mein Kampf* by Adolf Hitler, himself a prime example of what he was dissecting.

Henceforward, the machinery of mass communications grew more sophisticated and placed leaders and led in closer intimacy: radio, cinema, mass-circulation press. The spread of parliamentary government and universal suffrage demolished autocracy and oligarchy everywhere, sometimes replacing them with plebiscitary dictatorships. It was impossible to place complicated political issues factually before the masses, impossible to appeal to their reason, which did not exist. The trend of the war and the peacemaking continued: Advertising and statesmanship went forward together in appealing to the irrational in the mind of the masses, to their primitive emotional drives. The new statesmanship of the mass age was a matter of slogans evoking or exploiting sentimental moods. A double standard evolved: what a politician wrote and said in private and what he said to his gormless electors. No longer could statesmen come to arrangements in private according to the merits of the case and the reality of the balance of bargaining power, for there were always the sentimental expectations of their own masses to cumber their freedom of maneuver.

Since these sentimental expectations were subject to all the violent swings of emotion and mood, and not to the consistent guidance of reason and information, they were often untimely and disastrous. At the end of the 1920's a deep and irrational refusal to think about the true nature of the Great War and its causation led to a blind faith in the League of Nations and in unilateral disarmament as preservatives of peace. Those who had been filled with bloody desires for vengeance and victory in 1914–18 now espoused the cause of peace at all costs, and funk replaced vicarious enjoyment of violence. The masses ducked their own responsibility for the xenophobic tension of the prewar period, and they ducked their responsibility for the length and violence of the war. They refused to see that the demand for total victory plus a trench system (without flanks) inevitably equaled stalemated slaughter. Instead, the masses eagerly swallowed fables that blamed the origins of the war on armament manufacturers, that blamed the long duration and unspeakable horror of the fighting on the generals. As a result of this escapist mood of the masses, Baldwin was unable to swing British public opinion behind timely rearmament and opposition to Hitler. By their escapism in the 1930's the masses ensured that they would catch the full consequences of the muddled peace that their irrational hopes and inconsistent attitudes had done so much to make: another war.

"The Promise of Greatness," therefore, so fruitily expounded by such men as Wilson (and Lloyd George in public utterances to the masses), was surely in the short term a baseless self-delusion. The physical destruction and dislocation of the war, the human loss, pointed toward exhaustion and poverty, not toward a bounding prosperity more fairly shared. Four years of unleashed hatred and violence and the destruction of social ties and habits pointed logically to a future of neurotic restlessness, suspicion, and more violence, not to a new social order of self-discipline, calm mutual understanding, and brotherly love. However, the Promise of Greatness itself made worse the universal and insidious disintegrating effects of war by raising hopes incapable of fulfillment and demanding of statesmen what they could not possibly deliver, by making a peace which was fundamentally ill-adapted to the practical requirements of Europe in 1919.

Thus, to recapitulate, the nature of the Great War after 1914 and the nature of the peace from 1919 to 1939 are the immediate consequences of the uncaging of the little man, the eruption of mass opinion as a force of which statesmen must take continuous account. This eruption marks the advent of the irrational, of fantasy and ignorance, into the higher conduct of human affairs to a degree never before seen in modern times. The short-term consequences were disastrous in 1914–19. The long-term consequences are still manifesting themselves. The pattern established during the Great War is still with us: Great international questions are seen in simple moralistic and idealistic terms, as emotional crusades; statesmen still find their freedom to strike realistic bargains hampered by the ingenuous expectations of electorates at home. In an attempt to manipulate the fantasies of the masses in support of their real, but rarely publicly expounded policies, statesmen have developed the double personality: the actor-statesman, all ideals and generalized goodness for the television, and the real statesman behind the TV makeup. The influence of the masses has introduced falsity, as well as rigidity, into international affairs.

In so many ways the Great War began or quickened the transi-

tion of Western society from one of privilege to one of mass participation. Optimists can therefore point to all the contemporary
phenomena of mass enjoyment and prosperity ("Greatness"?) that
have their origins in aspirations awakened during the Great War.
However, the influence of ignorance and unreason in the higher
conduct of affairs, national and international, is a less agreeable and
more dangerous product of the Great War. It never has carried—
and it does not carry now—any Promise of Greatness. It carries
rather the promise that in questions vitally affecting national well-
being or international relations, the measures demanded by the
reality of a problem are precisely those which are most difficult to
carry out because of public opinion.